Hoover's Handbook of

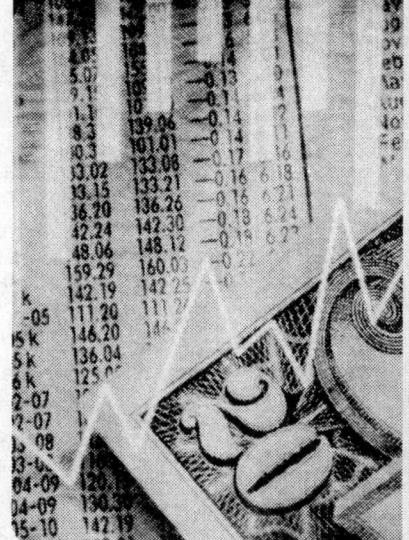

American Business

2019

Austin, Texas

Hoover's Handbook of American Business 2019 is intended to provide readers with accurate and authoritative information about the enterprises covered in it. Hoover's researched all companies and organizations profiled, and in many cases contacted them directly so that companies represented could provide information. The information contained herein is as accurate as we could reasonably make it. In many cases we have relied on third-party material that we believe to be trustworthy, but were unable to independently verify. We do not warrant that the book is absolutely accurate or without error. Readers should not rely on any information contained herein in instances where such reliance might cause financial loss. The publisher, the editors, and their data suppliers specifically disclaim all warranties, including the implied warranties of merchantability and fitness for a specific purpose. This book is sold with the understanding that neither the publisher, the editors, nor any content contributors are engaged in providing investment, financial, accounting, legal, or other professional advice.

The financial data (Historical Financials sections) in this book are from a variety of sources. Mergent Inc., provided selected data for the Historical Financials sections of publicly traded companies. For private companies and for historical information on public companies prior to their becoming public, we obtained information directly from the companies or from trade sources deemed to be reliable. Hoover's, Inc., is solely responsible for the presentation of all data.

Many of the names of products and services mentioned in this book are the trademarks or service marks of the companies manufacturing or selling them and are subject to protection under US law. Space has not permitted us to indicate which names are subject to such protection, and readers are advised to consult with the owners of such marks regarding their use. Hoover's is a trademark of Hoover's, Inc.

A D&B COMPANY

10 9 8 7 6 5 4 3 2 1

Publishers Cataloging-in-Publication Data

Hoover's Handbook of American Business 2019

    Includes indexes.

    ISBN: 978-1-64141-141-7

    ISSN 1055-7202

    1. Business enterprises — Directories. 2. Corporations — Directories.

HF3010 338.7

U.S. AND WORLD BOOK SALES

Mergent Inc.

580 Kingsley Park Drive
Fort Mill, SC
29715
Phone: 800-342-5647
e-mail: orders@mergent.com
Web: www.mergentbusinesspress.com

Mergent Inc.

Executive Managing Director: John Pedernales

Publisher and Managing Director of Print Products : Thomas Wecera

Director of Print Products: Charlot Volny

Quality Assurance Editor: Wayne Arnold

Production Research Assistant: Davie Christna

Data Manager: Jason Horvat

MERGENT CUSTOMER SERVICE
Support and Fulfillment Manager: Melanie Horvat

ABOUT MERGENT INC.

For over 100 years, Mergent, Inc. has been a leading provider of business and financial information on public and private companies globally. Mergent is known to be a trusted partner to corporate and financial institutions, as well as to academic and public libraries. Today we continue to build on a century of experience by transforming data into knowledge and combining our expertise with the latest technology to create new global data and analytical solutions for our clients. With advanced data collection services, cloud-based applications, desktop analytics and print products, Mergent and its subsidiaries provide solutions from top down economic and demographic information, to detailed equity and debt fundamental analysis. We incorporate value added tools such as quantitative Smart Beta equity research and tools for portfolio building and measurement. Based in the U.S., Mergent maintains a strong global presence, with offices in New York, Charlotte, San Diego, London, Tokyo, Kuching and Melbourne. Mergent, Inc. is a member of the London Stock Exchange plc group of companies. The Mergent business forms part of LSEG's Information Services Division, which includes FTSE Russell, a global leader in indexes.

MERGENT
BUSINESS PRESS
by FTSE Russell

Abbreviations

AFL-CIO – American Federation of Labor and Congress of Industrial Organizations

AMA – American Medical Association

AMEX – American Stock Exchange

ARM – adjustable-rate mortgage

ASP – application services provider

ATM – asynchronous transfer mode

ATM – automated teller machine

CAD/CAM – computer-aided design/computer-aided manufacturing

CD-ROM – compact disc – read-only memory

CD-R – CD-recordable

CEO – chief executive officer

CFO – chief financial officer

CMOS – complementary metal oxide silicon

COO – chief operating officer

DAT – digital audiotape

DOD – Department of Defense

DOE – Department of Energy

DOS – disk operating system

DOT – Department of Transportation

DRAM – dynamic random-access memory

DSL – digital subscriber line

DVD – digital versatile disc/digital video disc

DVD-R – DVD-recordable

EPA – Environmental Protection Agency

EPROM – erasable programmable read-only memory

EPS – earnings per share

ESOP – employee stock ownership plan

EU – European Union

EVP – executive vice president

FCC – Federal Communications Commission

FDA – Food and Drug Administration

FDIC – Federal Deposit Insurance Corporation

FTC – Federal Trade Commission

FTP – file transfer protocol

GATT – General Agreement on Tariffs and Trade

GDP – gross domestic product

HMO – health maintenance organization

HR – human resources

HTML – hypertext markup language

ICC – Interstate Commerce Commission

IPO – initial public offering

IRS – Internal Revenue Service

ISP – Internet service provider

kWh – kilowatt-hour

LAN – local-area network

LBO – leveraged buyout

LCD – liquid crystal display

LNG – liquefied natural gas

LP – limited partnership

Ltd. – limited

mips – millions of instructions per second

MW – megawatt

NAFTA – North American Free Trade Agreement

NASA – National Aeronautics and Space Administration

NASDAQ – National Association of Securities Dealers Automated Quotations

NATO – North Atlantic Treaty Organization

NYSE – New York Stock Exchange

OCR – optical character recognition

OECD – Organization for Economic Cooperation and Development

OEM – original equipment manufacturer

OPEC – Organization of Petroleum Exporting Countries

OS – operating system

OSHA – Occupational Safety and Health Administration

OTC – over-the-counter

PBX – private branch exchange

PCMCIA – Personal Computer Memory Card International Association

P/E – price to earnings ratio

RAID – redundant array of independent disks

RAM – random-access memory

R&D – research and development

RBOC – regional Bell operating company

RISC – reduced instruction set computer

REIT – real estate investment trust

ROA – return on assets

ROE – return on equity

ROI – return on investment

ROM – read-only memory

S&L – savings and loan

SCSI – Small Computer System Interface

SEC – Securities and Exchange Commission

SEVP – senior executive vice president

SIC – Standard Industrial Classification

SOC – system on a chip

SVP – senior vice president

USB – universal serial bus

VAR – value-added reseller

VAT – value-added tax

VC – venture capitalist

VoIP – Voice over Internet Protocol

VP – vice president

WAN – wide-area network

WWW – World Wide Web

Contents

List of Lists

HOOVER'S RANKINGS

Companies Profiled

Companies Profiled (continued)

Companies Profiled (continued)

Companies Profiled (continued)

Companies Profiled (continued)

About Hoover's Handbook of American Business 2019

In these tough economic times, it pays to have all the facts, whether you're making business, financial, or employment decisions. When you need information about companies, *Hoover's Handbook of American Business* is the place to turn for answers. Throughout its history, it has stood as one of America's respected sources of business information, packed with the information you need.

We at Hoover's Business Press pledge we will continue our work to add more value to this already valuable resource. So search away for the business information you need to make the important decisions facing you. Leave the fact-finding and digging and the sorting and sifting to the editors at Hoover's.

Hoover's Handbook of American Business is the first of our four-title series of handbooks that covers, literally, the world of business. The series is available as an indexed set, and also includes *Hoover's Handbook of World Business, Hoover's Handbook of Private Companies,* and *Hoover's Handbook of Emerging Companies*. This series brings you information on the biggest, fastest-growing, and most influential enterprises in the world.

HOOVER'S ONLINE FOR BUSINESS NEEDS

In addition to the 2,550 companies featured in our handbooks, comprehensive coverage of more than 40,000 business enterprises is available in electronic format on the Mergent website. Our goal is to provide one site that offers authoritative, updated intelligence on US and global companies, industries, and the people who shape them. Hoover's has partnered with other prestigious business information and service providers to bring you all the right business information, services, and links in one place.

We welcome the recognition we have received as a provider of high-quality company information — online, electronically, and in print — and continue to look for ways to make our products more available and more useful to you.

We believe that anyone who buys from, sells to, invests in, lends to, competes with, interviews with, or works for a company should know all there is to know about that enterprise. Taken together, this book and the other Hoover's products and resources represent the most complete source of basic corporate information readily available to the general public.

This latest version of *Hoover's Handbook of American Business* contains, as always, profiles of the largest and most influential companies in the United States. Each of the companies profiled here was chosen because of its important role in American business. For more details on how these companies were selected, see the section titled "Using Hoover's Handbooks."

HOW TO USE THIS BOOK

This book has four sections:

1. "Using Hoover's Handbooks" describes the contents of our profiles and explains the ways in which we gather and compile our data.

2. "A List-Lover's Compendium" contains lists of the largest, smallest, best, most, and other superlatives related to companies involved in American business.

3. The company profiles section makes up the largest and most important part of the book — 750 profiles of major US enterprises.

4. Three indexes complete the book. The first sorts companies by industry groups, the second by headquarters location. The third index is a list of all the executives found in the Executives section of each company profile.

Using Hoover's Handbooks

SELECTION OF THE COMPANIES PROFILED

The 750 enterprises profiled in this book include the largest and most influential companies in America. Among them are:

- more than 710 publicly held companies, from 3M to Zions Bancorporation
- more than 30 large private enterprises (such as Cargill and Mars)
- several mutual and cooperative organizations (such as State Farm and Ace Hardware)
- a selection of other enterprises (such as Kaiser Foundation Health Plan, the US Postal Service, and the Tennessee Valley Authority) that we believe are sufficiently large and influential enough to warrant inclusion.

In selecting these companies, our foremost question was "What companies will our readers be most interested in?" Our goal was to answer as many questions as we could in one book — in effect, trying to anticipate your curiosity. This approach resulted in four general selection criteria for including companies in the book:

1. Size. The 500 or so largest American companies, measured by sales and by number of employees, are included in the book. In general, these companies have sales in excess of $2 billion, and they are the ones you will have heard of and the ones you will want to know about. These are the companies at the top of the *FORTUNE*, *Forbes*, and *Business Week* lists. We have made sure to include the top private companies in this number.

2. Growth. We believe that relatively few readers will be going to work for, or investing in, the railroad industry. Therefore, only a few railroads are in the book. On the other hand, we have included a number of technology firms, as well as companies that provide medical products and services — pharmaceutical and biotech companies, health care insurers, and medical device makers.

3. Visibility. Most readers will have heard of the Hilton Worldwide and Harley-Davidson companies. Their service or consumer natures make them household names, even though they are not among the corporate giants in terms of sales and employment.

4. Breadth of coverage. To show the diversity of economic activity, we've included, among others, a professional sports team, one ranch, the Big Four accounting firms, and one of the largest law firms in the US. We feel that these businesses are important enough to enjoy at least "token" representation. While we might not emphasize certain industries, the industry leaders are present.

ORGANIZATION

The profiles are presented in alphabetical order. This alphabetization is generally word by word, which means that Legg Mason precedes Leggett & Platt. You will find the commonly used name of the enterprise at the beginning of the profile; the full, legal name is found in the Locations section. If a company name is also a person's name, like Walt Disney, it will be alphabetized under the first name; if the company name starts with initials, like J. C. Penney or H.J. Heinz, look for it under the combined initials (in the above examples, JC and HJ, respectively). Basic financial data is listed under the heading Historical Financials; also included is the exchange on which the company's stock is traded if it is public, the ticker symbol used by the stock exchange, and the company's fiscal year-end.

The annual financial information contained in the profiles is current through fiscal year-ends occurring as late as May 2014. We have included certain nonfinancial developments, such as officer changes, through September 2014.

OVERVIEW

In the first section of the profile, we have tried to give a thumbnail description of the company and what it does. The description will usually include information on the company's strategy, reputation, and ownership. We recommend that you read this section first.

HISTORY

This extended section, included for almost all companies in the book, reflects our belief that every enterprise is the sum of its history and that you have to know where you came from in order to know where you are going. While some companies have limited historical awareness, we think the vast majority of the enterprises in this book have colorful backgrounds. We have tried to focus on the people who made the enterprises what they are today. We have found these histories to be full of twists and ironies; they make fascinating reading.

EXECUTIVES

Here we list the names of the people who run the company, insofar as space allows. In the case of public companies, we have shown the ages and total compensation of key officers. In some cases the published data is for the previous year although the company has announced promotions or retirements since year-end. Total compensation is the sum of salary, bonus, and the value of any other benefits, such as stock options or deferred compensation.

Although companies are free to structure their management titles any way they please, most modern corporations follow standard practices. The ultimate power in any corporation lies with the shareholders, who elect a board of directors, usually including officers or "insiders" as well as individuals from outside the company. The chief officer, the person on whose desk the buck stops, is usually called the chief executive officer (CEO). Often, he or she is also the chairman of the board.

As corporate management has become more complex, it is common for the CEO to have a "right-hand person" who oversees the day-to-day operations of the company, allowing the CEO plenty of time to focus on strategy and long-term issues. This right-hand person is usually designated the chief operating officer (COO) and is often the president of the company. In other cases one person is both chairman and president.

A multitude of other titles exists, including chief financial officer (CFO), chief administrative officer, and vice chairman. We have always tried to include the CFO, the chief legal officer, and the chief human resources or personnel officer. Our best advice is that officers' pay levels are clear indicators of who the board of directors thinks are the most important members of the management team.

The people named in the Executives section are indexed at the back of the book.

The Executives section also includes the name of the company's auditing (accounting) firm, where available.

LOCATIONS

Here we include the company's full legal name and its headquarters, street address, telephone and fax numbers, and Web site, as available. The back of the book includes an index of companies by headquarters locations.

In some cases we have also included information on the geographic distribution of the company's business, including sales and profit data. Note that these profit numbers, like those in the Products/Operations section below, are usually operating or pretax profits rather than net profits. Operating profits are generally those before financing costs (interest income and payments) and before taxes, which are considered costs attributable to the whole company rather than to one division or part of the world. For this reason the net income figures (in the Historical Financials section) are usually much lower, since they are after interest and taxes. Pretax profits are after interest but before taxes.

Headquarters for companies that are incorporated in Bermuda, but whose operational headquarters are in the US, are listed under their US address.

PRODUCTS/OPERATIONS

This section lists as many of the company's products, services, brand names, divisions, subsidiaries, and joint ventures as we could fit. We have tried to include all its major lines and all familiar brand names. The nature of this section varies by company and the amount of information available. If the company publishes sales and profit information by type of business, we have included it.

COMPETITORS

In this section we have listed companies that compete with the profiled company. This feature is included as a quick way to locate similar companies and compare them. The universe of competitors includes all public companies and all private companies with sales in excess of $500 million. In a few instances we have identified smaller private companies as key competitors.

HISTORICAL FINANCIALS

Here we have tried to present as much data about each enterprise's financial performance as we could compile in the allocated space. The information varies somewhat from industry to industry and is less complete in the case of private companies that do not release data (although we have always tried to provide annual sales and employment). There are a few industries, venture capital and investment banking, for example, for which revenue numbers are unavailable as a rule.

The following information is generally present.

A 5-year table, with relevant annualized compound growth rates, covers:
- Sales — fiscal year sales (year-end assets for most financial companies)
- Net income — fiscal year net income (before accounting changes)
- Net profit margin — fiscal year net income as a percent of sales (as a percent of assets for most financial firms)
- Employees — fiscal year-end or average number of employees
- Stock price — the fiscal year close
- P/E — high and low price/earnings ratio
- Earnings per share — fiscal year earnings per share (EPS)
- Dividends per share — fiscal year dividends per share
- Book value per share — fiscal year-end book value (common shareholders' equity per share)

The information on the number of employees is intended to aid the reader interested in knowing whether a company has a long-term trend of increasing or decreasing employment. As far as we know, we are the only company that publishes this information in print format.

The numbers on the left in each row of the Historical Financials section give the month and the year in which the company's fiscal year actually ends. Thus, a company with a March 31, 2018, year-end is shown as 3/18.

In addition, we have provided in graph form a stock price history for most public companies. The graphs, covering up to five years, show the range of trading between the high and the low price, as well as the closing price for each fiscal year. Generally, for private companies, we have graphed net income, or, if that is unavailable, sales.

Key year-end statistics in this section generally show the financial strength of the enterprise, including:

- Debt ratio (long-term debt as a percent of shareholders' equity)
- Return on equity (net income divided by the average of beginning and ending common shareholders' equity)
- Cash and cash equivalents
- Current ratio (ratio of current assets to current liabilities)
- Total long-term debt (including capital lease obligations)

- Number of shares of common stock outstanding
- Dividend yield (fiscal year dividends per share divided by the fiscal year-end closing stock price)
- Dividend payout (fiscal year dividends divided by fiscal year EPS)
- Market value at fiscal year-end (fiscal year-end closing stock price multiplied by fiscal year-end number of shares outstanding)

Per share data has been adjusted for stock splits. The data for public companies has been provided to us by Mergent Inc. Other public company information was compiled by Hoover's, which takes full responsibility for the content of this section.

In the case of private companies that do not publicly disclose financial information, we usually did not have access to such standardized data. We have gathered estimates of sales and other statistics from numerous sources.

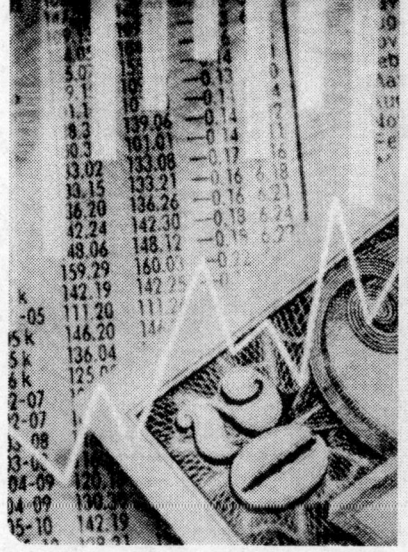

Hoover's Handbook of

American Business

A List-Lover's Compendium

The 300 Largest Companies by Sales in
Hoover's Handbook of American Business 2019

Rank	Company	Sales ($ mil.)
1	Walmart Inc	$500,343
2	Apple Inc	$265,595
3	Exxon Mobil Corp	$244,363
4	Berkshire Hathaway Inc	$242,137
5	Amazon.com Inc	$232,887
6	McKesson Corp	$208,357
7	UnitedHealth Group Inc	$201,159
8	CVS Health Corp	$184,765
9	AmerisourceBergen Corp.	$167,940
10	AT&T Inc	$160,546
11	Ford Motor Co. (DE)	$156,776
12	General Motors Co	$147,049
13	Chevron Corporation	$141,722
14	Costco Wholesale Corp	$141,576
15	Alphabet Inc	$136,819
16	Cardinal Health, Inc.	$136,809
17	Walgreens Boots Alliance Inc	$131,537
18	Verizon Communications Inc	$126,034
19	Kroger Co (The)	$122,662
20	General Electric Co	$122,092
21	Federal Reserve System	$116,764
22	JPMorgan Chase & Co	$113,899
23	Fannie Mae	$112,394
24	Microsoft Corporation	$110,360
25	Phillips 66	$104,622
26	Boeing Co.	$101,127
27	Home Depot Inc	$100,904
28	Bank of America Corp	$100,264
29	Wells Fargo & Co (New)	$97,741
30	Comcast Corp	$94,507
31	Valero Energy Corp	$93,980
32	Anthem Inc	$90,039
33	Citigroup Inc	$87,966
34	DowDuPont Inc	$85,977
35	International Business Machi	$79,139
36	Dell Technologies Inc	$78,660
37	Johnson & Johnson	$76,450
38	Marathon Petroleum Corp.	$75,369
39	Freddie Mac	$74,676
40	Target Corp	$71,879
41	Intel Corp	$70,848
42	Lowe's Companies Inc	$68,619
43	Procter & Gamble Co (The)	$66,832
44	United Technologies Corp	$66,501
45	United Parcel Service Inc	$65,872
46	FedEx Corp	$65,450
47	Federal Reserve Bank Of New Y	$65,090
48	PepsiCo Inc	$63,525
49	MetLife Inc	$62,308
50	Archer Daniels Midland Co.	$60,828
51	Albertsons Companies Inc	$59,925
52	Prudential Financial Inc	$59,689
53	Disney (Walt) Co. (The)	$59,434
54	Sysco Corp	$58,727
55	HP Inc	$58,472
56	Facebook Inc	$55,838
57	Humana, Inc.	$53,767
58	Lockheed Martin Corp	$53,762
59	Pfizer Inc	$52,546
60	American International Group	$49,520
61	Cisco Systems Inc	$49,330
62	Centene Corp	$48,382
63	Caterpillar Inc.	$45,462
64	Morgan Stanley	$43,642
65	Charter Communications Inc (	$43,634
66	HCA Healthcare Inc	$43,614
67	T-Mobile US Inc	$43,310
68	Goldman Sachs Group Inc	$42,254
69	American Airlines Group Inc	$42,207
70	Best Buy Inc	$42,151
71	Honeywell International Inc	$41,802
72	Cigna Holding Co	$41,616
73	Delta Air Lines Inc (DE)	$41,244
74	Energy Transfer LP	$40,523
75	Merck & Co Inc	$40,122
76	Tyson Foods Inc	$40,052
77	Oracle Corp	$39,831
78	Allstate Corp	$38,524
79	United Continental Holdings	$37,736
80	Deere & Co.	$37,358
81	Tech Data Corp.	$36,775
82	NIKE Inc	$36,397
83	Exelon Corp	$35,985
84	TJX Companies, Inc.	$35,865
85	American Express Co.	$35,583
86	Coca-Cola Co (The)	$35,410
87	Publix Super Markets, Inc.	$34,837
88	World Fuel Services Corp.	$33,696
89	3M Co	$32,765
90	CHS Inc	$32,683
91	ConocoPhillips	$32,584
92	Sprint Corp (New)	$32,406
93	General Dynamics Corp	$30,973
94	Hewlett Packard Enterprise C	$30,852
95	21st Century Fox Inc	$30,400
96	Micron Technology Inc.	$30,391
97	Northrop Grumman Corp	$30,095
98	Capital One Financial Corp	$29,999
99	Arrow Electronics, Inc.	$29,677
100	Philip Morris International	$29,625
101	Enterprise Products Partners	$29,242
102	Energy Transfer Operating LP	$29,054
103	Travelers Companies Inc (The	$28,902
104	AbbVie Inc	$28,216
105	INTL FCStone Inc.	$27,542
106	Abbott Laboratories	$27,390
107	Progressive Corp. (OH)	$26,839
108	Kraft Heinz Co (The)	$26,232
109	Plains GP Holdings LP	$26,223
110	Plains All American Pipeline	$26,223
111	Gilead Sciences Inc	$26,107
112	Mondelez International Inc	$25,938
113	Altria Group Inc	$25,576
114	Raytheon Co.	$25,348
115	Jabil Inc	$22,095
116	Southwest Airlines Co	$21,965
117	PBF Energy Inc	$21,787
118	Macy's Inc	$24,837
119	Starbucks Corp.	$24,720
120	US Foods Holding Corp	$24,147
121	U.S. Bancorp (DE)	$23,996
122	Duke Energy Corp	$23,565
123	Dollar General Corp	$23,471
124	Southern Co.	$23,031
125	Marriott International, Inc.	$22,894
126	Eli Lilly & Co	$22,871
127	Amgen Inc	$22,849
128	Union Pacific Corp	$22,832
129	McDonald's Corp	$22,820
130	Qualcomm Inc	$22,732
131	Dollar Tree Inc	$22,246
132	Icahn Enterprises LP	$21,744
133	International Paper Co	$21,743
134	AFLAC Inc.	$21,667
135	AutoNation, Inc.	$21,535
136	Rite Aid Corp.	$21,529
137	Penske Automotive Group Inc	$21,387
138	Whirlpool Corp	$21,253
139	Lear Corp.	$21,149
140	ManpowerGroup	$21,034
141	Thermo Fisher Scientific Inc	$20,918
142	Bristol-Myers Squibb Co.	$20,776
143	Burlington Northern & Santa F	$20,747
144	Western Digital Corp	$20,647
145	Halliburton Company	$20,620
146	Visa Inc	$20,609
147	Lennar Corp	$20,572
148	Cummins, Inc.	$20,428
149	Nucor Corp.	$20,252
150	AECOM	$20,156
151	Synnex Corp	$20,054
152	Molina Healthcare Inc	$19,883
153	Fluor Corp.	$19,521
154	Paccar Inc.	$19,456
155	Tenet Healthcare Corp.	$19,179
156	Kohl's Corp.	$19,095
157	Avnet Inc	$19,037
158	Kimberly-Clark Corp.	$18,486
159	Exelon Generation Co LLC	$18,466
160	Danaher Corp	$18,330
161	PNC Financial Services Group	$18,035
162	CenturyLink Inc	$17,656
163	Performance Food Group Co	$17,620
164	Emerson Electric Co.	$17,408
165	NGL Energy Partners LP	$17,283
166	Baker Hughes A GE Co	$17,259
167	Applied Materials, Inc.	$17,253
168	NextEra Energy Inc	$17,195
169	PG&E Corp (Holding Co)	$17,135
170	Carmax Inc.	$17,120
171	WellCare Health Plans Inc	$17,007
172	Hartford Financial Services	$16,974
173	Sears Holdings Corp	$16,702
174	Synchrony Financial	$16,695
175	Bank of New York Mellon Corp	$16,617
176	Freeport-McMoRan Inc	$16,403
177	Genuine Parts Co.	$16,309

SOURCE: MERGENT INC., DATABASE, FEBRUARY 2019

The 300 Largest Companies by Sales in
Hoover's Handbook of American Business 2019 (continued)

Rank	Company	Sales ($ mil.)	Rank	Company	Sales ($ mil.)	Rank	Company	Sales ($ mil.)
178	WestRock Co	$16,285	219	FlrstEnergy Corp	$14,017	260	Tesla Inc	$11,759
179	DR Horton Inc	$16,068	220	Devon Energy Corp.	$13,949	261	Sunoco LP	$11,723
180	Becton Dickinson And Co	$15,983	221	Ecolab Inc	$13,838	262	Alcoa Corporation	$11,652
181	Gap Inc	$15,855	222	Loews Corp.	$13,735	263	Discover Financial Services	$11,545
182	Netflix Inc	$15,794	223	CBS Corp	$13,692	264	Norfolk Southern Corp.	$11,458
183	Aramark	$15,790	224	Lauder (Estee) Cos., Inc. (T	$13,683	265	Linde plc	$11,437
184	General Mills Inc	$15,740	225	Stryker Corp	$13,601	266	Xcel Energy Inc	$11,404
185	Core Mark Holding Co Inc	$15,688	226	Biogen Inc	$13,453	267	Unum Group	$11,287
186	Nordstrom, Inc.	$15,478	227	Automatic Data Processing In	$13,326	268	Tennessee Valley Authority	$11,233
187	Goodyear Tire & Rubber Co.	$15,475	228	Occidental Petroleum Corp	$13,274	269	Expedia Group Inc	$11,223
188	Colgate–Palmolive Co.	$15,454	229	Celgene Corp	$13,003	270	AutoZone, Inc.	$11,221
189	PayPal Holdings Inc	$15,451	230	Arconic Inc	$12,960	271	EOG Resources, Inc.	$11,208
190	American Electric Power Co I	$15,425	231	Viacom Inc	$12,943	272	Sempra Energy	$11,207
191	XPO Logistics, Inc.	$15,381	232	Kellogg Co	$12,923	273	Group 1 Automotive, Inc.	$11,124
192	Community Health Systems, In	$15,353	233	Las Vegas Sands Corp	$12,882	274	Lam Research Corp	$11,077
193	Omnicom Group, Inc.	$15,274	234	Murphy USA Inc	$12,827	275	Entergy Corp. (New)	$11,074
194	CDW Corp	$15,192	235	BJs Wholesale Club Holdings	$12,755	276	Molson Coors Brewing Co.	$11,003
195	Jacobs Engineering Group, In	$14,985	236	Stanley Black & Decker Inc	$12,747	277	Ball Corp	$10,983
196	Sherwin–Williams Co (The)	$14,984	237	Booking Holdings Inc	$12,681	278	DaVita Inc	$10,877
197	Texas Instruments, Inc.	$14,961	238	L Brands, Inc	$12,632	279	MGM Resorts International	$10,774
198	Robinson (C.H.) Worldwide, I	$14,869	239	Dominion Energy Inc (New)	$12,586	280	Pilgrims Pride Corp.	$10,768
199	Cognizant Technology Solutio	$14,810	240	Reinsurance Group of America	$12,516	281	eBay Inc.	$10,746
200	PPG Industries Inc	$14,750	241	AXA Equitable Holdings Inc	$12,514	282	Santander Holdings USA Inc.	$10,716
201	Newell Brands Inc	$14,742	242	Penney (J.C.) Co.,Inc. (Hold	$12,506	283	NRG Energy Inc	$10,629
202	Federal Reserve Bank of San F	$14,660	243	Mastercard Inc	$12,497	284	Baxter International Inc	$10,561
203	Waste Management, Inc. (DE)	$14,485	244	BlackRock Inc	$12,491	285	AES Corp.	$10,530
204	Dish Network Corp	$14,391	245	Henry Schein Inc	$12,462	286	Salesforce.Com Inc	$10,480
205	Illinois Tool Works, Inc.	$14,314	246	Bed, Bath & Beyond, Inc.	$12,349	287	Consolidated Edison Co. of N	$10,468
206	Parker–Hannifin Corp	$14,302	247	Edison International	$12,320	288	LabCorp	$10,441
207	Lincoln National Corp.	$14,257	248	Southern California Edison C	$12,254	289	Grainger (W.W.), Inc.	$10,425
208	HollyFrontier Corp	$14,251	249	CSX Corp	$12,250	290	Universal Health Services, I	$10,410
209	DTE Energy Co	$14,212	250	United States Steel Corp.	$12,250	291	Qurate Retail Inc	$10,404
210	CBRE Group Inc	$14,210	251	ONEOK Inc	$12,174	292	Autoliv Inc	$10,383
211	Textron Inc	$14,198	252	BB&T Corp.	$12,156	293	Qurate Retail Inc – Com Ser	$10,381
212	Kinder Morgan Inc.	$14,144	253	First Data Corp (New)	$12,052	294	Live Nation Entertainment In	$10,337
213	Ross Stores, Inc.	$14,135	254	Consolidated Edison Inc	$12,033	295	Liberty Expedia Holdings Inc	$10,286
214	Voya Financial Inc	$8,618	255	Ameriprise Financial Inc	$12,027	296	Xerox Corp	$10,265
215	Dick's Sporting Goods, Inc	$8,590	256	Florida Power & Light Co.	$11,972	297	Navistar International Corp.	$10,250
216	Qwest Corp	$8,550	257	Anadarko Petroleum Corp	$11,908	298	Office Depot, Inc.	$10,240
217	Principal Financial Group In	$14,093	258	Toyota Motor Credit Corp.	$11,856	299	United Natural Foods Inc.	$10,227
218	Marsh & McLennan Companies I	$14,024	259	State Street Corp.	$11,774	300	PulteGroup Inc	$10,188

The 300 Most Profitable Companies in
Hoover's Handbook of American Business 2019

Rank	Company	Net Income ($ mil.)	Rank	Company	Net Income ($ mil.)	Rank	Company	Net Income ($ mil.)
1	Apple Inc	$59,531	60	Bank of New York Mellon Corp	$4,090	119	HCA Healthcare Inc	$2,216
2	Berkshire Hathaway Inc	$44,940	61	Valero Energy Corp	$4,065	120	Emerson Electric Co.	$2,203
3	Alphabet Inc	$30,736	62	CME Group Inc	$4,063	121	Fifth Third Bancorp (Cincinn	$2,194
4	Verizon Communications Inc	$30,101	63	MetLife Inc	$4,010	122	State Street Corp.	$2,177
5	AT&T Inc	$29,450	64	Mastercard Inc	$3,915	123	Williams Cos Inc (The)	$2,174
6	JPMorgan Chase & Co	$24,441	65	DowDuPont Inc	$3,844	124	International Paper Co	$2,144
7	Wells Fargo & Co (New)	$22,183	66	Anthem Inc	$3,843	125	United Continental Holdings	$2,131
8	Facebook Inc	$22,112	67	Oracle Corp	$3,825	126	General Mills Inc	$2,131
9	Pfizer Inc	$21,308	68	Texas Instruments, Inc.	$3,682	127	Discover Financial Services	$2,099
10	Intel Corp	$21,053	69	Delta Air Lines Inc (DE)	$3,577	128	Dish Network Corp	$2,099
11	Exxon Mobil Corp	$19,710	70	Stryker Corp	$3,553	129	Energy Transfer Operating LP	$2,081
12	Bank of America Corp	$18,232	71	Lowe's Companies Inc	$3,447	130	Lincoln National Corp.	$2,079
13	Microsoft Corporation	$16,571	72	Marathon Petroleum Corp.	$3,432	131	PayPal Holdings Inc	$2,057
14	Micron Technology Inc.	$14,135	73	Toyota Motor Credit Corp.	$3,410	132	Travelers Companies Inc (The	$2,056
15	Disney (Walt) Co. (The)	$12,598	74	Mondelez International Inc	$3,381	133	Liberty Broadband Corp	$2,034
16	Burlington Northern & Santa F	$12,119	75	Applied Materials, Inc.	$3,313	134	Raytheon Co.	$2,024
17	Comcast Corp	$11,731	76	CSX Corp	$3,309	135	Colgate–Palmolive Co.	$2,024
18	Kraft Heinz Co (The)	$10,999	77	Northrop Grumman Corp	$3,229	136	Exelon Corp	$2,010
19	UnitedHealth Group Inc	$10,558	78	Allstate Corp	$3,189	137	Intercontinental Exchange In	$1,988
20	Boeing Co.	$10,460	79	Costco Wholesale Corp	$3,134	138	Capital One Financial Corp	$1,982
21	Visa Inc	$10,301	80	Duke Energy Corp	$3,059	139	Amgen Inc	$1,979
22	Altria Group Inc	$10,222	81	NVIDIA Corp	$3,047	140	MGM Resorts International	$1,960
23	Amazon.com Inc	$10,073	82	Tyson Foods Inc	$3,024	141	Waste Management, Inc. (DE)	$1,949
24	Walmart Inc	$9,862	83	Ford Motor Credit Company LL	$3,007	142	Simon Property Group, Inc.	$1,948
25	Procter & Gamble Co (The)	$9,750	84	Dominion Energy Inc (New)	$2,999	143	Synchrony Financial	$1,935
26	Chevron Corporation	$9,195	85	Celgene Corp	$2,940	144	NIKE Inc	$1,933
27	Home Depot Inc	$8,630	86	Target Corp	$2,934	145	American Airlines Group Inc	$1,919
28	General Motors Co	$8,014	87	General Dynamics Corp	$2,912	146	American Electric Power Co I	$1,913
29	Philip Morris International	$7,911	88	T–Mobile US Inc	$2,888	147	Hewlett Packard Enterprise C	$1,908
30	Prudential Financial Inc	$7,863	89	Las Vegas Sands Corp	$2,806	148	Kroger Co (The)	$1,907
31	Ford Motor Co. (DE)	$7,602	90	Enterprise Products Partners	$2,799	149	WestRock Co	$1,906
32	Sprint Corp (New)	$7,389	91	Newell Brands Inc	$2,749	150	Florida Power & Light Co.	$1,880
33	Honeywell International Inc	$6,765	92	American Express Co.	$2,736	151	Reinsurance Group of America	$1,822
34	CVS Health Corp	$6,622	93	Exelon Generation Co LLC	$2,694	152	Freeport–McMoRan Inc	$1,817
35	U.S. Bancorp (DE)	$6,218	94	Norfolk Southern Corp.	$2,666	153	Zimmer Biomet Holdings Inc	$1,814
36	Morgan Stanley	$6,111	95	Park Hotels & Resorts Inc	$2,625	154	CenterPoint Energy, Inc	$1,792
37	Union Pacific Corp	$5,966	96	TJX Companies, Inc.	$2,608	155	Sherwin–Williams Co (The)	$1,772
38	International Business Machi	$5,753	97	Adobe Inc	$2,591	156	Viacom Inc	$1,719
39	Freddie Mac	$5,625	98	EOG Resources, Inc.	$2,583	157	Dollar Tree Inc	$1,714
40	NextEra Energy Inc	$5,378	99	eBay Inc.	$2,530	158	Prologis LP	$1,697
41	3M Co	$5,349	100	Danaher Corp	$2,492	159	Lennar Corp	$1,696
42	PNC Financial Services Group	$5,338	101	Southwest Airlines Co	$2,465	160	Illinois Tool Works, Inc.	$1,687
43	HP Inc	$5,327	102	Fannie Mae	$2,463	161	Paccar Inc.	$1,675
44	AbbVie Inc	$5,309	103	Humana, Inc.	$2,448	162	PG&E Corp (Holding Co)	$1,660
45	United Technologies Corp	$5,269	104	Regeneron Pharmaceuticals, I	$2,444	163	AmerisourceBergen Corp.	$1,658
46	McDonald's Corp	$5,192	105	Qurate Retail Inc	$2,441	164	Qwest Corp	$1,657
47	Phillips 66	$5,106	106	Icahn Enterprises LP	$2,430	165	Prologis Inc	$1,652
48	Lockheed Martin Corp	$5,046	107	Merck & Co Inc	$2,394	166	Citizens Financial Group Inc	$1,652
49	Walgreens Boots Alliance Inc	$5,024	108	BB&T Corp.	$2,394	167	Duke Realty L.P.	$1,650
50	BlackRock Inc	$4,970	109	Lam Research Corp	$2,381	168	Duke Realty Corp	$1,634
51	United Parcel Service Inc	$4,910	110	Deere & Co.	$2,368	169	Automatic Data Processing In	$1,621
52	PepsiCo Inc	$4,857	111	Charles Schwab Corp	$2,354	170	Kinder Morgan Inc.	$1,609
53	Gilead Sciences Inc	$4,628	112	Booking Holdings Inc	$2,341	171	Archer Daniels Midland Co.	$1,595
54	AFLAC Inc.	$4,604	113	Constellation Brands Inc	$2,319	172	Progressive Corp. (OH)	$1,592
55	FedEx Corp	$4,572	114	Principal Financial Group In	$2,310	173	PPG Industries Inc	$1,591
56	Starbucks Corp.	$4,518	115	Publix Super Markets, Inc.	$2,292	174	Public Service Enterprise Gr	$1,574
57	21st Century Fox Inc.	$4,464	116	SunTrust Banks Inc	$2,273	175	Annaly Capital Management In	$1,570
58	Biogen Inc	$4,431	117	Cigna Holding Co	$2,237	176	Macy's Inc	$1,547
59	Goldman Sachs Group Inc	$4,286	118	Thermo Fisher Scientific Inc	$2,225	177	Virginia Electric & Power Co	$1,540

SOURCE: MERGENT INC., DATABASE, FEBRUARY 2019

Rank	Company	Net Income ($ mil.)	Rank	Company	Net Income ($ mil.)	Rank	Company	Net Income ($ mil.)
178	Dollar General Corp	$1,539	219	Regions Financial Corp	$1,263	260	Southwestern Energy Co	$1,046
179	Consolidated Edison Inc	$1,525	220	Hilton Worldwide Holdings In	$1,259	261	Cincinnati Financial Corp.	$1,045
180	Altice USA Inc	$1,520	221	Coca-Cola Co (The)	$1,248	262	Fortive Corp	$1,045
181	EQT Corp	$1,509	222	Linde plc	$1,247	263	Electronic Arts	$1,043
182	Ecolab Inc	$1,508	223	Fiserv Inc	$1,246	264	Republic Services Inc	$1,037
183	Cognizant Technology Solutio	$1,504	224	American Tower Corp (New)	$1,239	265	Alaska Air Group, Inc.	$1,034
184	Air Products & Chemicals Inc	$1,498	225	GCI Liberty Inc	$1,233	266	Jefferies Financial Group In	$1,027
185	T Rowe Price Group, Inc.	$1,498	226	Charter Communications Inc (	$1,230	267	PulteGroup Inc	$1,022
186	S&P Global Inc	$1,496	227	Stanley Black & Decker Inc	$1,226	268	KKR & Co Inc	$1,018
187	Analog Devices Inc	$1,495	228	Wells Fargo Real Estate Inve	$1,219	269	Hormel Foods Corp.	$1,012
188	Marsh & McLennan Companies I	$1,492	229	Duke Energy Carolinas LLC	$1,214	270	Bristol-Myers Squibb Co.	$1,007
189	Ameriprise Financial Inc	$1,480	230	Netflix Inc	$1,211	271	Moody's Corp.	$1,001
190	TD Ameritrade Holding Corp	$1,473	231	Intuit Inc	$1,211	272	Best Buy Inc	$1,000
191	Blackstone Group LP	$1,471	232	Qurate Retail Inc – Com Ser	$1,208	273	Cummins, Inc.	$999
192	First Data Corp (New)	$1,465	233	Celanese Corp (DE)	$1,207	274	Unum Group	$994
193	DR Horton Inc	$1,460	234	WEC Energy Group Inc	$1,205	275	Eversource Energy	$988
194	Torchmark Corp	$1,454	235	Northern Trust Corp	$1,199	276	L Brands, Inc	$983
195	Public Storage	$1,442	236	Santander Consumer USA Holdi	$1,188	277	Roper Technologies Inc	$972
196	Sysco Corp	$1,431	237	Huntington Bancshares Inc	$1,186	278	Mohawk Industries, Inc.	$972
197	Georgia Power Co	$1,428	238	Protective Life Insurance Co	$1,182	279	HD Supply Holdings Inc	$970
198	Molson Coors Brewing Co.	$1,414	239	Sirius XM Holdings Inc	$1,176	280	New Residential Investment C	$958
199	Kimberly-Clark Corp.	$1,410	240	Loews Corp.	$1,164	281	TransDigm Group Inc	$957
200	M & T Bank Corp	$1,408	241	Lear Corp.	$1,150	282	Concho Resources Inc	$956
201	CenturyLink Inc	$1,389	242	Xcel Energy Inc	$1,148	283	Energy Transfer LP	$954
202	Eastman Chemical Co	$1,384	243	JetBlue Airways Corp	$1,147	284	Chesapeake Energy Corp.	$949
203	Marriott International, Inc.	$1,372	244	Symantec Corp	$1,138	285	Rite Aid Corp.	$943
204	Ross Stores, Inc.	$1,363	245	Southern California Edison C	$1,136	286	Paychex Inc	$934
205	Liberty Media Corp (DE)	$1,354	246	O'Reilly Automotive, Inc.	$1,134	287	McCormick & Co Inc	$933
206	Yum! Brands Inc	$1,340	247	PPL Corp	$1,128	288	Ally Financial Inc	$929
207	Smucker (J.M.) Co.	$1,339	248	Intuitive Surgical Inc	$1,128	289	Skyworks Solutions, Inc.	$918
208	AutoZone, Inc.	$1,338	249	CoBank, ACB	$1,125	290	CNA Financial Corp	$899
209	Fidelity National Informatio	$1,319	250	Liberty Com SiriusXM Group	$1,124	291	Devon Energy Corp.	$898
210	Nucor Corp.	$1,319	251	DTE Energy Co	$1,120	292	Southern Co.	$880
211	Occidental Petroleum Corp	$1,311	252	Tennessee Valley Authority	$1,119	293	AvalonBay Communities, Inc.	$877
212	IQVIA Holdings Inc	$1,309	253	Lauder (Estee) Cos., Inc. (T	$1,108	294	Jones Financial Companies LL	$872
213	Westlake Chemical Corp	$1,304	254	Consolidated Edison Co. of N	$1,104	295	Wyndham Destinations Inc	$871
214	Apache Corp	$1,304	255	United Rentals Inc	$1,096	296	Magellan Midstream Partners	$870
215	Johnson & Johnson	$1,300	256	Omnicom Group, Inc.	$1,088	297	Alabama Power Co	$866
216	KeyCorp	$1,296	257	Keurig Dr Pepper Inc	$1,076	298	Zoetis Inc	$864
217	Kellogg Co	$1,269	258	Southern Power Co	$1,071	299	Kohl's Corp.	$859
218	LabCorp	$1,268	259	Parker-Hannifin Corp	$1,061	300	Raymond James Financial, Inc	$857

The 300 Largest Employers in
Hoover's Handbook of American Business 2019

Rank	Company	Employees	Rank	Company	Employees	Rank	Company	Employees
1	Walmart Inc	2,300,000	60	Barrett Business Services, I	124,212	119	HanesBrands Inc	68,000
2	Amazon.com Inc	647,500	61	Tyson Foods Inc	121,000	120	Sysco Corp	67,000
3	Kelly Services, Inc.	507,800	62	Honeywell International Inc	114,000	121	Danaher Corp	67,000
4	Energy Transfer Operating LP	506,829	63	Intel Corp	107,400	122	GameStop Corp	67,000
5	Yum China Holdings Inc	450,000	64	Lockheed Martin Corp	105,000	123	Marsh & McLennan Companies I	65,000
6	Kroger Co (The)	449,000	65	Abbott Laboratories	99,000	124	Bed, Bath & Beyond, Inc.	65,000
7	Home Depot Inc	413,000	66	Alphabet Inc	98,771	125	Caesars Entertainment Corp	65,000
8	Berkshire Hathaway Inc	377,000	67	General Dynamics Corp	98,600	126	Laureate Education Inc	65,000
9	International Business Machi	366,600	68	Caterpillar Inc.	98,400	127	Raytheon Co.	64,000
10	Walgreens Boots Alliance Inc	354,000	69	DowDuPont Inc	98,000	128	Baker Hughes A GE Co	64,000
11	Target Corp	345,000	70	Charter Communications Inc (	98,000	129	Goodyear Tire & Rubber Co.	64,000
12	General Electric Co	313,000	71	Penney (J.C.) Co.,Inc. (Hold	98,000	130	Ascena Retail Group Inc	63,000
13	Lowe's Companies Inc	310,000	72	Microsoft Corporation	97,535	131	Brinks Co (The)	62,300
14	Starbucks Corp.	291,000	73	XPO Logistics, Inc.	95,000	132	Coca-Cola Co (The)	61,800
15	United Parcel Service Inc	280,000	74	Community Health Systems, In	95,000	133	Hewlett Packard Enterprise C	60,000
16	Albertsons Companies Inc	275,000	75	Bloomin' Brands Inc	94,000	134	LabCorp	60,000
17	Aramark	274,400	76	3M Co	93,516	135	Yum! Brands Inc	60,000
18	PepsiCo Inc	263,000	77	L Brands, Inc	93,200	136	ASGN Inc	59,200
19	Wells Fargo & Co (New)	262,700	78	Procter & Gamble Co (The)	92,000	137	Rite Aid Corp.	59,000
20	UnitedHealth Group Inc	260,800	79	Whirlpool Corp	92,000	138	Southwest Airlines Co	58,800
21	Cognizant Technology Solutio	260,000	80	Pfizer Inc	90,200	139	Cummins, Inc.	58,600
22	HCA Healthcare Inc	253,000	81	AutoZone, Inc.	90,000	140	Brinker International, Inc.	58,478
23	JPMorgan Chase & Co	252,539	82	Conduent Inc	90,000	141	Stanley Black & Decker Inc	57,765
24	AT&T Inc	252,000	83	United Continental Holdings	89,800	142	Morgan Stanley	57,633
25	TJX Companies, Inc.	249,000	84	Icahn Enterprises LP	89,034	143	Parker-Hannifin Corp	57,170
26	CVS Health Corp	246,000	85	Sears Holdings Corp	89,000	144	Automatic Data Processing In	57,000
27	Costco Wholesale Corp	245,000	86	Emerson Electric Co.	87,500	145	Fluor Corp.	56,706
28	United Technologies Corp	240,200	87	Delta Air Lines Inc (DE)	87,000	146	Texas Roadhouse Inc	56,300
29	McDonald's Corp	235,000	88	AECOM	87,000	147	Anthem Inc	56,000
30	Synnex Corp	231,600	89	Northrop Grumman Corp	85,000	148	International Paper Co	56,000
31	Half Robert International In	228,600	90	Ross Stores, Inc.	82,700	149	TTEC Holdings Inc	56,000
32	FedEx Corp	227,000	91	Jones Lang LaSalle Inc	81,900	150	HP Inc	55,000
33	Bank of America Corp	209,000	92	Jacobs Engineering Group, In	80,800	151	American Express Co.	55,000
34	Citigroup Inc	209,000	93	Mondelez International Inc	80,000	152	Halliburton Company	55,000
35	Ford Motor Co. (DE)	202,000	94	CBRE Group Inc	80,000	153	IQVIA Holdings Inc	55,000
36	Disney (Walt) Co. (The)	201,000	95	McKesson Corp	78,000	154	Healthcare Services Group In	55,000
37	Jabil Inc	199,000	96	Philip Morris International	77,400	155	Sykes Enterprises, Inc.	55,000
38	Publix Super Markets, Inc.	193,000	97	Omnicom Group, Inc.	77,300	156	Freeport-McMoRan Inc	53,200
39	Comcast Corp	184,000	98	Universal Health Services, I	76,600	157	Fidelity National Informatio	53,000
40	Darden Restaurants, Inc. (Un	180,656	99	Becton Dickinson And Co	76,032	158	PNC Financial Services Group	52,906
41	Marriott International, Inc.	177,000	100	Brookdale Senior Living Inc	75,600	159	Sherwin-Williams Co (The)	52,695
42	Dollar Tree Inc	176,100	101	O'Reilly Automotive, Inc.	75,289	160	RMR Group Inc (The)	52,600
43	General Motors Co	173,000	102	DaVita Inc	74,500	161	Bank of New York Mellon Corp	52,500
44	Lear Corp.	169,000	103	Deere & Co.	74,413	162	T-Mobile US Inc	52,000
45	Hilton Worldwide Holdings In	163,000	104	Cisco Systems Inc	74,200	163	Chevron Corporation	51,900
46	Verizon Communications Inc	155,400	105	NIKE Inc	73,100	164	Pilgrims Pride Corp.	51,300
47	Boeing Co.	153,000	106	Chipotle Mexican Grill Inc	73,000	165	CenturyLink Inc	51,000
48	Dell Technologies Inc	145,000	107	Cracker Barrel Old Country S	73,000	166	Las Vegas Sands Corp	50,500
49	ABM Industries, Inc.	140,000	108	Nordstrom, Inc.	72,500	167	Cardinal Health, Inc.	50,200
50	Oracle Corp	137,000	109	U.S. Bancorp (DE)	72,402	168	Interpublic Group of Compani	50,200
51	Kohl's Corp.	137,000	110	Autoliv Inc	72,000	169	Illinois Tool Works, Inc.	50,000
52	Gap Inc	135,000	111	Western Digital Corp	71,600	170	American International Group	49,800
53	Johnson & Johnson	134,000	112	Advance Auto Parts Inc	71,000	171	Prudential Financial Inc	49,705
54	Apple Inc	132,000	113	Thermo Fisher Scientific Inc	70,000	172	Capital One Financial Corp	49,300
55	Macy's Inc	130,000	114	Amphenol Corp.	70,000	173	Foot Locker, Inc.	49,209
56	Dollar General Corp	129,000	115	Exxon Mobil Corp	69,600	174	MetLife Inc	49,000
57	American Airlines Group Inc	126,600	116	Merck & Co Inc	69,000	175	Newell Brands Inc	49,000
58	Tenet Healthcare Corp.	125,820	117	Genesis Healthcare Inc	68,700	176	Michaels Companies Inc	49,000
59	Best Buy Inc	125,000	118	MGM Resorts International	68,000	177	Ecolab Inc	48,400

SOURCE: MERGENT INC., DATABASE, FEBRUARY 2019

Rank	Company	Employees	Rank	Company	Employees	Rank	Company	Employees
178	Genuine Parts Co.	48,000	219	Casey's General Stores, Inc.	37,205	260	Sprint Corp (New)	30,000
179	Six Flags Entertainment Corp	48,000	220	Textron Inc	37,000	261	Avery Dennison Corp	30,000
180	Humana, Inc.	47,900	221	Hertz Global Holdings Inc (N	37,000	262	Sally Beauty Holdings Inc	29,970
181	PPG Industries Inc	47,200	222	State Street Corp.	36,643	263	Texas Instruments, Inc.	29,714
182	Baxter International Inc	47,000	223	Goldman Sachs Group Inc	36,600	264	Energy Transfer LP	29,486
183	Sanmina Corp	47,000	224	PVH Corp	36,500	265	Encompass Health Corp	29,370
184	Cedar Fair LP	46,900	225	BB&T Corp.	36,484	266	Red Robin Gourmet Burgers In	29,349
185	Corning Inc	46,200	226	Ryder System, Inc.	36,100	267	BG Staffing Inc	29,349
186	Cigna Holding Co	46,000	227	Micron Technology Inc.	36,000	268	Amkor Technology Inc.	29,300
187	Lauder (Estee) Cos., Inc. (T	46,000	228	Stryker Corp	36,000	269	United States Steel Corp.	29,200
188	Dick's Sporting Goods, Inc	45,200	229	Republic Services Inc	36,000	270	Cerner Corp.	29,200
189	WestRock Co	45,100	230	Colgate-Palmolive Co.	35,900	271	Duke Energy Corp	29,060
190	Office Depot, Inc.	45,000	231	Facebook Inc	35,587	272	AbbVie Inc	29,000
191	Quest Diagnostics, Inc.	45,000	232	Qualcomm Inc	35,400	273	ManpowerGroup	29,000
192	Jones Financial Companies LL	45,000	233	Xerox Corp	35,300	274	Salesforce.Com Inc	29,000
193	Hyatt Hotels Corp	45,000	234	Big Lots, Inc.	34,800	275	BorgWarner Inc	29,000
194	Marathon Petroleum Corp.	43,800	235	Ulta Beauty Inc	34,700	276	Boston Scientific Corp.	29,000
195	LKQ Corp	43,000	236	NCR Corp.	34,000	277	Dover Corp	29,000
196	Allstate Corp	42,900	237	ON Semiconductor Corp	34,000	278	AMERCO	29,000
197	RR Donnelley & Sons Company	42,700	238	Centene Corp	33,700	279	TTM Technologies Inc	29,000
198	Waste Management, Inc. (DE)	42,300	239	Progressive Corp. (OH)	33,656	280	Qurate Retail Inc	28,255
199	Select Medical Holdings Corp	42,200	240	Exelon Corp	33,383	281	Qurate Retail Inc – Com Ser	28,255
200	Union Pacific Corp	41,967	241	Vail Resorts Inc	33,300	282	Cinemark USA Inc	28,100
201	Arconic Inc	41,500	242	Command Center Inc	33,220	283	Cinemark Holdings Inc	28,100
202	Burlington Northern & Santa F	41,000	243	Kellogg Co	33,000	284	News Corp (New)	28,000
203	Kimberly-Clark Corp.	41,000	244	Quanta Services, Inc.	32,800	285	Tractor Supply Co.	28,000
204	Cintas Corp	41,000	245	Tenneco Inc	32,000	286	Mattel Inc	28,000
205	American Eagle Outfitters, I	40,700	246	EMCOR Group, Inc.	32,000	287	Williams Sonoma Inc	27,800
206	Eli Lilly & Co	40,655	247	YRC Worldwide Inc	32,000	288	ExlService Holdings Inc	27,800
207	Acadia Healthcare Company In	40,600	248	Cooper-Standard Holdings Inc	32,000	289	Cannae Holdings Inc	27,385
208	General Mills Inc	40,000	249	National Oilwell Varco Inc	31,889	290	Civitas Solutions Inc	27,100
209	Dillard's Inc.	40,000	250	Bright Horizons Family Solut	31,600	291	Sprouts Farmers Market Inc	27,000
210	Burlington Stores Inc	40,000	251	Southern Co.	31,344	292	Regis Corp.	27,000
211	AMC Entertainment Holdings I	39,843	252	Archer Daniels Midland Co.	31,300	293	Norfolk Southern Corp.	26,662
212	Wyndham Destinations Inc	39,200	253	Leidos Holdings Inc	31,000	294	BJs Wholesale Club Holdings	26,520
213	Cheesecake Factory Inc. (The	39,100	254	L3 Technologies Inc	31,000	295	Owens-Illinois, Inc.	26,500
214	Kraft Heinz Co (The)	39,000	255	Avis Budget Group Inc	31,000	296	Linde plc	26,461
215	Mohawk Industries, Inc.	38,800	256	Travelers Companies Inc (The	30,800	297	SPAR Group, Inc.	26,100
216	Huntington Ingalls Industrie	38,000	257	Genesco Inc.	30,500	298	Addus HomeCare Corp	26,097
217	Abercrombie & Fitch Co	38,000	258	Gallagher (Arthur J.) & Co.	30,362	299	AutoNation, Inc.	26,000
218	Tesla Inc	37,543	259	Dana Inc	30,100	300	Penske Automotive Group Inc	26,000

The Mergent 500 Largest Global Corporations (By Revenues)

Rank	Company	Sales ($ mil.)	Rank	Company	Sales ($ mil))	Rank	Company	Sales ($ mil.)
1	Walmart Inc	$500,343	68	Valero Energy Corp	$93,980	135	Archer Daniels Midland Co.	$60,828
2	China Petroleum & Chemical C	$362,692	69	Bosch (Robert) GmbH (Germany	$93,582	136	AEGON NV	$60,542
3	Royal Dutch Shell Plc	$311,870	70	Banco Santander SA	$93,330	137	Albertsons Companies Inc	$59,925
4	PetroChina Co Ltd	$309,783	71	Nestle SA	$92,340	138	Prudential Financial Inc	$59,689
5	Toyota Motor Corp	$276,677	72	Credit Agricole SA	$90,447	139	Disney (Walt) Co. (The)	$59,434
6	Volkswagen AG	$276,531	73	Hyundai Motor Co., Ltd.	$90,400	140	Rewe-Zentral AG (Germany, Fed	$59,300
7	Cementos Bio-Bio S.A. (Chile)	$266,557	74	Anthem Inc	$90,039	141	Sysco Corp	$58,727
8	Apple Inc	$265,595	75	Deutsche Telekom AG	$89,843	142	HP Inc	$58,472
9	Exxon Mobil Corp	$244,363	76	Enel SpA	$89,474	143	LG Electronics Inc	$57,589
10	BP PLC	$243,372	77	Petroleo Brasileiro SA	$88,827	144	Vodafone Group Plc	$57,410
11	Berkshire Hathaway Inc	$242,137	78	Hitachi, Ltd.	$88,228	145	Roche Holding AG	$57,119
12	Amazon.com Inc	$232,887	79	Citigroup Inc	$87,966	146	POSCO (South Korea)	$56,894
13	Samsung Electronics Co Ltd	$224,719	80	SoftBank Group Corp	$86,251	147	Anheuser Busch InBev SA/NV	$56,444
14	McKesson Corp	$208,357	81	DowDuPont Inc	$85,977	148	Seven & i Holdings Co. Ltd.	$56,373
15	Glencore PLC	$205,476	82	ENI S.p.A.	$85,084	149	Korea Electric Power Corp KE	$56,106
16	UnitedHealth Group Inc	$201,159	83	EDF Trading Ltd	$83,472	150	Facebook Inc	$55,838
17	Daimler AG	$196,991	84	Electricite de France	$83,472	151	JD.com, Inc.	$55,680
18	CVS Health Corp	$184,765	85	HSBC Holdings Plc	$82,012	152	Tokyo Electric Power Company	$55,100
19	AmerisourceBergen Corp.	$167,940	86	Sony Corp	$80,462	153	ING Groep NV	$55,059
20	Industrial and Commercial Ba	$165,301	87	Tesco PLC	$80,368	154	Lloyds Banking Group Plc	$54,991
21	AT&T Inc	$160,546	88	Airbus SE	$80,037	155	Legal & General Group PLC (U	$54,691
22	Hon Hai Precision Industry C	$158,733	89	International Business Machi	$79,139	156	Deutsche Bahn AG	$54,655
23	Ford Motor Co. (DE)	$156,776	90	Dell Technologies Inc	$78,660	157	CNP Assurances S.A.	$53,966
24	AXA SA	$153,665	91	Engie SA	$78,478	158	Humana, Inc.	$53,767
25	Total SA	$149,099	92	Aeon Co. Ltd. (Japan)	$78,335	159	Lockheed Martin Corp	$53,762
26	General Motors Co	$147,049	93	Peugeot SA	$78,171	160	Nippon Steel & Sumitomo Meta	$53,384
27	Honda Motor Co., Ltd.	$144,661	94	BASF SE	$77,290	161	Continental AG (Germany, Fed	$52,757
28	China Construction Bank Corp	$143,968	95	Johnson & Johnson	$76,450	162	Pfizer Inc	$52,546
29	Chevron Corporation	$141,722	96	CITIC Ltd	$76,208	163	Christian Dior SE	$52,345
30	Costco Wholesale Corp	$141,576	97	Koninklijke Ahold Delhaize N	$75,390	164	Banco Bilbao Vizcaya Argenta	$52,273
31	Alphabet Inc	$136,819	98	Marathon Petroleum Corp.	$75,369	165	ITOCHU Corp (Japan)	$51,890
32	Cardinal Health, Inc.	$136,809	99	Panasonic Corp	$75,171	166	America Movil SAB de CV	$51,859
33	SAIC Motor Corp Ltd	$133,792	100	Societe Generale	$74,831	167	Alimentation Couche-Tard Inc	$51,394
34	Fiat Chrysler Automobiles NV	$132,983	101	Deutscher Sparkassen-und Giro	$74,762	168	LVMH Moet Hennessy Louis Vui	$51,106
35	Walgreens Boots Alliance Inc	$131,537	102	Freddie Mac	$74,676	169	RWE AG	$50,868
36	Agricultural Bank of China	$127,091	103	China Communications Constru	$74,193	170	Banco Bradesco SA	$50,864
37	BNP Paribas (France)	$126,264	104	Japan Post Insurance Co Ltd	$73,897	171	Kia Motors Corp. (South Kore	$50,216
38	Verizon Communications Inc	$126,034	105	Deutsche Post AG	$72,458	172	Repsol S.A.	$50,197
39	Kroger Co (The)	$122,662	106	AUDI AG	$72,079	173	Tokio Marine Holdings Inc	$50,175
40	General Electric Co	$122,092	107	Target Corp	$71,879	174	Novartis AG Basel	$50,135
41	Allianz SE	$121,960	108	Mitsubishi Corp	$71,265	175	Sberbank Russia	$49,886
42	Japan Post Holdings Co Ltd	$121,676	109	Marubeni Corp.	$71,010	176	American International Group	$49,520
43	Bayerische Motoren Werke AG	$118,291	110	Mexican Petroleum	$70,915	177	Vinci SA	$49,416
44	Prudential Plc	$117,326	111	Intel Corp	$70,848	178	Wesfarmers Ltd.	$49,386
45	Federal Reserve System	$116,764	112	Indian Oil Corp., Ltd. (Indi	$70,561	179	Cisco Systems Inc	$49,330
46	JPMorgan Chase & Co	$113,899	113	Renault S.A. (France)	$70,451	180	Orange	$49,271
47	China Mobile Limited	$113,795	114	ArcelorMittal SA	$68,679	181	JBS S.A.	$49,255
48	PJSC Gazprom	$112,945	115	Lowe's Companies Inc	$68,619	182	ThyssenKrupp AG	$48,969
49	Nissan Motor Co., Ltd.	$112,548	116	Aviva Plc (United Kingdom)	$67,066	183	Compagnie de Saint-Gobain	$48,961
50	Fannie Mae	$112,394	117	Procter & Gamble Co (The)	$66,832	184	Tianjin Tianhai Investment C	$48,477
51	Nippon Telegraph & Telephone	$111,121	118	United Technologies Corp	$66,501	185	Centene Corp	$48,382
52	Microsoft Corporation	$110,360	119	United Parcel Service Inc	$65,872	186	Denso Corp. (Japan)	$48,107
53	China Railway Group Ltd	$106,550	120	Nippon Life Insurance Co.	$65,664	187	China Evergrande Group	$47,795
54	Assicurazioni Generali S.p.A	$105,297	121	FedEx Corp	$65,450	188	MS&AD Insurance Group Holdin	$47,601
55	China Railway Construction C	$104,647	122	Itau Unibanco Holding S.A.	$65,142	189	KDDI Corp	$47,482
56	Phillips 66	$104,622	123	Federal Reserve Bank Of New Y	$65,090	190	Hanwha Corp	$47,279
57	Rosneft Oil Co OJSC (Moscow)	$104,023	124	Unilever Plc (United Kingdom	$64,391	191	State Bank Of India	$47,181
58	PJSC Lukoil	$102,687	125	Unilever N.V.	$64,391	192	Manufacturers Life Insurance	$46,621
59	Boeing Co.	$101,127	126	Reliance Industries Ltd	$64,281	193	Manulife Financial Corp	$46,523
60	Home Depot Inc	$100,904	127	Zurich Insurance Group AG	$63,961	194	Aedas Homes SAU	$46,385
61	Bank of America Corp	$100,264	128	PepsiCo Inc	$63,525	195	Rallye S.A. Neuilly-Sur-Sein	$46,313
62	Hyundai Pharmaceutical Co Ltd	$98,741	129	Telefonica SA	$62,345	196	E.ON SE	$46,144
63	Wells Fargo & Co (New)	$97,741	130	MetLife Inc	$62,308	197	Mitsui & Co., Ltd.	$46,071
64	Carrefour S.A.	$97,069	131	PTT Public Co Ltd	$61,259	198	Bunge Ltd.	$45,794
65	JXTG Holdings Inc	$97,009	132	Dai-ichi Life Holdings Inc	$61,242	199	Deutsche Bank AG	$45,746
66	Siemens AG (Germany)	$96,187	133	Equinor ASA	$61,187	200	Caterpillar Inc.	$45,462
67	Comcast Corp	$94,507	134	Toyota Tsusho Corp	$61,128			

The Mergent 500 Largest Global Corporations (By Revenues)

Rank	Company	Sales ($ mil.)	Rank	Company	Sales ($ mil.)	Rank	Company	Sales ($ mil.)
201	Sumitomo Corp.	$45,461	268	United Continental Holdings	$37,736	335	Samsung Life Insurance Co Lt	$30,145
202	Lenovo Group Ltd	$45,350	269	Metallurgical Corp China Ltd	$37,496	336	Veolia Environnement	$30,118
203	Casino Guichard Perrachon S.	$45,339	270	Iberdrola SA	$37,477	337	Northrop Grumman Corp	$30,095
204	Mitsubishi UFJ Financial Gro	$45,069	271	Deere & Co.	$37,358	338	Capital One Financial Corp	$29,999
205	Sumitomo Mitsui Financial Gr	$44,963	272	China Vanke Co Ltd	$37,326	339	Medtronic PLC	$29,953
206	NTT DoCoMo Inc	$44,915	273	Loblaw Companies Ltd	$37,254	340	Compass Group PLC (United Ki	$29,950
207	Shanghai Jinfeng Investment C	$44,629	274	Meiji Yasuda Life Insurance	$36,930	341	Compal Electronics Inc	$29,936
208	Baoshan Iron & Steel Co Ltd	$44,487	275	Aisin Seiki Co Ltd	$36,812	342	Arrow Electronics, Inc.	$29,677
209	Tata Motors Ltd	$44,312	276	Hongkong And Shanghai Bankin	$36,787	343	Schneider Electric SE	$29,661
210	SSE PLC	$43,879	277	Tech Data Corp.	$36,775	344	Medipal Holdings Corp	$29,630
211	Royal Bank of Canada (Montre	$43,719	278	Barclays PLC	$36,544	345	Philip Morris International	$29,625
212	ZF Friedrichshafen AG (Germa	$43,687	279	Tencent Holdings Ltd.	$36,537	346	Danone	$29,582
213	Morgan Stanley	$43,642	280	Barclays Bank Plc	$36,435	347	Lloyds Bank plc	$29,533
214	BHP Group Plc	$43,638	281	NIKE Inc	$36,397	348	Kansai Electric Power Co., I	$29,511
215	BHP Group Ltd	$43,638	282	Canon, Inc.	$36,261	349	Enterprise Products Partners	$29,242
216	Charter Communications Inc (	$43,634	283	Exelon Corp	$35,985	350	Wal-Mart de Mexico S.A.B. de	$29,100
217	HCA Healthcare Inc	$43,614	284	TJX Companies, Inc.	$35,865	351	Energy Transfer Operating LP	$29,054
218	Sanofi	$43,400	285	Daiwa House Industry Co Ltd	$35,748	352	Sumitomo Electric Industries	$29,027
219	SK Innovation Co Ltd	$43,392	286	American Express Co.	$35,583	353	Travelers Companies Inc (The	$28,902
220	T-Mobile US Inc	$43,310	287	Coca-Cola Co (The)	$35,410	354	Suning Appliance Co., Ltd.	$28,879
221	Lufthansa AG (Germany, Fed.	$42,778	288	Enbridge Inc	$35,400	355	Cnooc Ltd.	$28,643
222	Zhejiang Material Industrial	$42,508	289	Suzuki Motor Corp.	$35,383	356	Adecco Group AG	$28,363
223	Woolworths Group Ltd	$42,307	290	Sompo Holdings Inc	$35,228	357	SK Hynix Inc	$28,242
224	Goldman Sachs Group Inc	$42,254	291	Idemitsu Kosan Co Ltd	$35,133	358	AbbVie Inc	$28,216
225	China Unicom (Hong Kong) Ltd	$42,233	292	Mitsubishi Chemical Holdings	$35,074	359	Wistron Corp	$28,196
226	China United Network Communi	$42,233	293	Country Garden Holdings Co L	$34,868	360	SAP SE	$28,124
227	American Airlines Group Inc	$42,207	294	Publix Super Markets, Inc.	$34,837	361	Naturgy Energy Group SA	$27,938
228	ACS Actividades de Construcc	$42,202	295	JFE Holdings Inc	$34,643	362	Randstad NV	$27,808
229	Best Buy Inc	$42,151	296	LyondellBasell Industries NV	$34,484	363	East Japan Railway Co.	$27,783
230	Bayer AG	$41,974	297	Quanta Computer Inc	$34,439	364	Nokia Corp	$27,748
231	Honeywell International Inc	$41,802	298	ABB Ltd	$34,312	365	Aluminum Corp of China Ltd.	$27,673
232	Mitsubishi Electric Corp	$41,730	299	Vale SA	$33,967	366	Westpac Banking Corp	$27,550
233	Cigna Holding Co	$41,616	300	Sumitomo Life Insurance Co.	$33,801	367	INTL FCStone Inc.	$27,542
234	Accenture plc	$41,603	301	World Fuel Services Corp.	$33,696	368	International Consolidated A	$27,538
235	Delta Air Lines Inc (DE)	$41,244	302	Xiamen C & D Inc	$33,593	369	Samsung C&T Corp (New)	$27,463
236	Power Corp. of Canada	$41,055	303	BT Group Plc	$33,335	370	British American Tobacco Plc	$27,408
237	Toronto Dominion Bank	$40,943	304	Schlumberger Ltd	$33,179	371	Abbott Laboratories	$27,390
238	Brookfield Asset Management	$40,786	305	Hyundai Mobis Co Ltd (South	$32,965	372	PKN Orlen SA	$27,381
239	GlaxoSmithKline Plc	$40,772	306	Taiwan Semiconductor Manufac	$32,964	373	CNH Industrial NV	$27,361
240	Fresenius SE & Co KGaA	$40,621	307	3M Co	$32,765	374	Hochtief AG	$27,065
241	Energy Transfer LP	$40,523	308	Mazda Motor Corp. (Japan)	$32,716	375	Orix Corp	$26,956
242	China Pacific Insurance (Gro	$40,500	309	CHS Inc	$32,683	376	Chubu Electric Power Co., In	$26,871
243	Pegatron Corp	$40,261	310	ConocoPhillips	$32,584	377	Progressive Corp. (OH)	$26,839
244	Merck & Co Inc	$40,122	311	Sprint Corp (New)	$32,406	378	NEC Corp	$26,787
245	Tyson Foods Inc	$40,052	312	Bridgestone Corp. (Japan)	$32,381	379	LafargeHolcim	$26,772
246	Rio Tinto Ltd	$40,030	313	Great-West Lifeco Inc	$32,334	380	HSBC Bank Plc (United Kingdo	$26,718
247	Rio Tinto Plc (United Kingdo	$40,030	314	Chubb Ltd	$32,243	381	Banco Santander Brasil SA	$26,630
248	Power Financial Corp	$39,947	315	Gazprom Neft PJSC	$32,136	382	ENBW Energie Baden-Wuerttem	$26,530
249	Saudi Basic Industries Corp -	$39,938	316	Subaru Corp	$32,068	383	Cie Generale des Etablisseme	$26,325
250	Alibaba Group Holding Ltd	$39,866	317	CK Hutchison Holdings Ltd	$31,799	384	Anglo American Plc (United K	$26,243
251	Oracle Corp	$39,831	318	NATIXIS SA	$31,634	385	Heineken NV (Netherlands)	$26,238
252	Imperial Brands PLC	$39,810	319	Jardine Strategic Holdings L	$31,556	386	Heineken Holding NV (Netherl	$26,238
253	Bouygues S.A.	$39,624	320	Industria De Diseno Textil I	$31,554	387	Kraft Heinz Co (The)	$26,232
254	Intesa Sanpaolo S.P.A.	$39,476	321	Jiangxi Copper Co., Ltd.	$31,510	388	Plains GP Holdings LP	$26,223
255	Jardine Matheson Holdings Lt	$39,456	322	Johnson Controls Internation	$31,400	389	Plains All American Pipeline	$26,223
256	J.Sainsbury PLC	$39,330	323	Commonwealth Bank of Austral	$31,259	390	Ceconomy AG	$26,176
257	Toshiba Corp	$39,084	324	Xiamen Xiangyu Co Ltd	$31,240	391	Gilead Sciences Inc	$26,107
258	Magna International Inc	$38,946	325	L'Oreal S.A.	$31,196	392	LG Display Co Ltd	$26,067
259	Mitsubishi Heavy Industries	$38,713	326	General Dynamics Corp	$30,973	393	McKesson Europe AG	$25,999
260	Fujitsu Ltd	$38,596	327	Bank Nova Scotia Halifax	$30,959	394	Mondelez International Inc	$25,938
261	Allstate Corp	$38,524	328	A.P. Moller - Maersk A/S	$30,945	395	Australia & New Zealand Bank	$25,708
262	George Weston Ltd	$38,522	329	Air France-KLM	$30,909	396	Volvo Car Corp. (Sweden)	$25,707
263	Talanx AG	$38,387	330	Hewlett Packard Enterprise C	$30,852	397	Suncor Energy Inc	$25,666
264	AIA Group Ltd.	$38,330	331	Unicredit SpA	$30,557	398	Altria Group Inc	$25,576
265	China Shenhua Energy Co., Lt	$38,225	332	21st Century Fox Inc	$30,400	399	Flex Ltd	$25,441
266	Centrica Plc	$37,850	333	Micron Technology Inc.	$30,391	400	Adidas AG	$25,435
267	UBS Group AG	$37,768	334	CRH Plc	$30,233			

Rank	Company	Sales ($ mil.)	Rank	Company	Sales ($ mil.)	Rank	Company	Sales ($ mil.)
401	Raytheon Co.	$25,348	435	Imperial Oil Ltd	$23,471	469	KT Corp (Korea)	$21,937
402	Xiamen International Trade Gr	$25,302	436	Dollar General Corp	$23,471	470	Shanghai Construction Group	$21,834
403	National Australia Bank Ltd.	$25,274	437	Huaneng Power International	$23,429	471	PBF Energy Inc	$21,787
404	China Taiping Insurance Hold	$25,160	438	Sun Life Financial Inc	$23,399	472	Oversea-Chinese Banking Corp	$21,766
405	Telecom Italia SpA	$25,146	439	Fomento Economico Mexicano,	$23,373	473	Icahn Enterprises LP	$21,744
406	Macy's Inc	$24,837	440	Weichai Power Co Ltd	$23,292	474	International Paper Co	$21,743
407	BAE Systems Plc	$24,747	441	Yanzhou Coal Mining Co Ltd	$23,239	475	Safran	$21,697
408	Starbucks Corp.	$24,720	442	Gree Electric Appliances Inc	$23,054	476	Royal Bank of Scotland Group	$21,696
409	China Grand Automotive Servi	$24,697	443	Southern Co.	$23,031	477	AFLAC Inc.	$21,667
410	L'Air Liquide S.A.	$24,659	444	Standard Life Aberdeen PLC	$22,935	478	Huayu Automotive Systems Com	$21,589
411	Morrison (Wm.) Supermarkets	$24,546	445	FUJIFILM Holdings Corp	$22,916	479	Daikin Industries Ltd	$21,571
412	Telefonaktiebolaget LM Erics	$24,536	446	Marriott International, Inc.	$22,894	480	AutoNation, Inc.	$21,535
413	Ericsson	$24,536	447	Eli Lilly & Co	$22,871	481	Rite Aid Corp.	$21,529
414	Alfresa Holdings Corp Tokyo	$24,513	448	Sharp Corp.	$22,858	482	National Grid plc	$21,429
415	Bank of Montreal (Quebec)	$24,504	449	Amgen Inc	$22,849	483	Credit Suisse Group AG	$21,415
416	ONEX Corp (Canada)	$24,497	450	Union Pacific Corp	$22,832	484	Penske Automotive Group Inc	$21,387
417	Qingdao Haier Co Ltd	$24,473	451	Brookfield Business Partners	$22,823	485	Standard Chartered Plc	$21,377
418	OMV AG (Austria)	$24,241	452	McDonald's Corp	$22,820	486	Fresenius Medical Care AG &	$21,318
419	Faurecia	$24,193	453	Qualcomm Inc	$22,732	487	Royal Philips NV	$21,314
420	Ultrapar Participacoes SA	$24,151	454	TUI AG	$22,614	488	Whirlpool Corp	$21,253
421	US Foods Holding Corp	$24,147	455	Poly Real Estate Group Co.,	$22,488	489	China Overseas Land & Invest	$21,246
422	LG Chem Ltd (New)	$24,104	456	AstraZeneca Plc	$22,465	490	POSCO Daewoo Corp	$21,172
423	Endesa S.A.	$24,043	457	X5 Retail Group NV	$22,400	491	Lear Corp.	$21,149
424	Ping An Insurance (Group) Co	$24,015	458	Teva Pharmaceutical Industri	$22,385	492	Formosa Petrochemical Corp	$21,048
425	Henkel AG & Co KGAA	$24,010	459	WH Group Ltd	$22,379	493	ManpowerGroup	$21,034
426	U.S. Bancorp (DE)	$23,996	460	Dollar Tree Inc	$22,246	494	Thermo Fisher Scientific Inc	$20,918
427	Great-West Life Assurance Co	$23,955	461	Valeo	$22,237	495	Hannover Rueck SE	$20,866
428	Hennes & Mauritz AB	$23,878	462	NN Group NV (Netherlands)	$22,160	496	Broadcom Inc (DE)	$20,848
429	Sodexo	$23,771	463	Bollore SA	$22,148	497	Korea Gas Corp. (South Korea	$20,797
430	Cosmo Energy Holdings Co Ltd	$23,761	464	Financiere De L Odet SA (Fra	$22,148	498	Bristol-Myers Squibb Co.	$20,776
431	Mitsubishi Shokuhin Co., Ltd	$23,670	465	Jabil Inc	$22,095	499	Toray Industries, Inc.	$20,764
432	KB Financial Group, Inc.	$23,606	466	Rolls Royce Holdings Plc	$22,026	500	China Life Insurance Co Ltd	$20,760
433	Duke Energy Corp	$23,565	467	Southwest Airlines Co	$21,965			
434	Komatsu Ltd	$23,554	468	JSC VTB Bank	$21,951			

Hoover's Handbook of

American Business

The Companies

1st Source Corp

Need a bank? Don't give it a 2nd thought. Contact 1st Source Corporation parent of 1st Source Bank which provides commercial and consumer banking services through some 80 branches in northern Indiana and southwestern Michigan. The bank offers deposit accounts; business agricultural and consumer loans; residential and commercial mortgages; credit cards; and trust services. Its specialty finance group provides financing for aircraft automobile fleets trucks and construction and environmental equipment through about two-dozen offices nationwide; such loans account for nearly half of 1st Source's portfolio.

Operations

1st Source Bank subsidiary Specialty Finance Group offers specialized financing for new and used private and cargo aircraft automobiles and light trucks for leasing and rental agencies medium and heavy duty trucks and construction and environmental equipment. Another subsidiary 1st Source Insurance provides commercial and retail property/casualty coverage and life and health coverage. 1st Source Corporation Investment Advisors serves trust and investment clients of 1st Source Bank as well as the investment advisor of Wasatch Mutual Funds.

Geographic Reach

Indiana-based 1st Source serves customers across around 20 counties in Michigan and its home state.

Sales and Marketing

1st Source offers commercial and agricultural loans and leases to the transportation construction and real estate sectors. It offers retail loans to individuals.

Financial Performance

1st Source Corporation's revenues have been climbing for the past five years. Similarly net income has been on an upward trajectory.

In 2017 revenue increased 10% to a record $284.3 million as both interest and non-interest income rose. Net interest income grew 9% while non-interest income (including equipment rentals trust and wealth advisory fees and gains on investment securities) grew 11%.

Thanks to the higher revenue net income rose 18% to $68.1 million in 2017.

The company ended 2017 with $78 million in cash and cash equivalents a 28% decline from what it had at the end of 2016. Operating activities provided some $113 million and financing activities provided another $315 million but investment activities used $462 million that year.

Strategy

1st Source has been investing in its technology to better serve its customers. It invested $1.3 million on a new customer relationship management system during 2017 and it expects to continue development and implementation of that project. It also spent $2.2 million on cyber security initiatives that year. Additionally the company is increasing the bandwidth at its branches.

When it believes it can serve a new customer base the bank adds new branches to its network. In 2018 it opened a location on the campus of Indiana University South Bend. However like all banking companies 1st Source has seen a decline in transactions at its branches as customers embrace mobile banking. During 2017 the company consolidated three locations.

To improve its mobile experience 1st Source offers live customer support via Facebook Messenger.

EXECUTIVES

Chairman And Ceo, Christopher J. (Chris) Murphy, age 71, $726,923 total compensation
Evp Administration Secretary And General Counsel, John B. Griffith, age 60, $328,429 total compensation
Evp Cfo And Treasurer, Andrea G. Short, age 55, $275,769 total compensation
President 1st Source Bank, James R. Seitz, age 65, $325,010 total compensation
Svp And Chief Credit Officer 1st Source Bank, Jeffrey L. Buhr, $226,565 total compensation
President 1st Source Insurance, John Ball
Vice President, John Lutz
Vice President Marketing, Melissa Collins
Assistant Vice President Lease Accounting Manager, Joe Malinowski
Vice President Business Banking, Cecile A Weir
Auditors: BKD, LLP

LOCATIONS

HQ: 1st Source Corp
  100 North Michigan Street, South Bend, IN 46601
Phone: 574 235-2000
Web: www.1stsource.com

PRODUCTS/OPERATIONS

2017 Sales

	$ mil.	% of total
Interest		
Loans & leases	194	62
Taxable investment securities	13	4
Tax-exempt investment securities	2	1
Other	1	-
Interest expenses		
Non-interest		
Equipment rentals	30	10
Trust fees	21	7
Debit card income	11	4
Service charges on deposit accounts	9	3
Insurance commissions	5	2
Mortgage banking	4	2
Gains on investment securities available-for-sale	4	1
Other	10	4
Total	**284**	**100**

Selected Subsidiaries

1st Source Bank
  1st Source Capitol Corporation
  1st Source Corporation Investment Advisors Inc.
  1st Source Insurance Inc.
  1st Source Solar 1 LLC
  1st Source Specialty Finance Inc.
  Michigan Transportation Finance Corporation
  SFG Aircraft Inc.
  SFG Commercial Aircraft Leasing
  SFG Equipment Leasing Corporation I
  Washington and Michigan Insurance Inc.
1st Source Funding LLC
1st Source Intermediate Holding LLC
1st Source Master Trust
Trustcorp Mortgage Company

COMPETITORS

Bank of America	Old National Bancorp
Fifth Third	PNC Financial
Huntington Bancshares	U.S. Bancorp
JPMorgan Chase	Wells Fargo
KeyCorp	

HISTORICAL FINANCIALS

Company Type: Public

Income Statement

FYE: December 31

	ASSETS ($ mil.)	NET INCOME ($ mil.)	INCOME AS % OF ASSETS	EMPLOYEES
12/17	5,887	68	1.2%	1,125
12/16	5,486	57	1.1%	1,150
12/15	5,187	57	1.1%	1,150
12/14	4,829	58	1.2%	1,100
12/13	4,722	54	1.2%	1,100
Annual Growth	5.7%	5.5%	—	0.6%

2017 Year-End Financials

Debt ratio: 1.39%
Return on equity: 9.78%
Cash ($ mil.): 78
Current ratio: —
Long-term debt ($ mil.): —
No. of shares (mil.): 25
Dividends
  Yield: 0.0%
  Payout: 29.2%
Market value ($ mil.): 1,283

	STOCK PRICE ($) FY Close	P/E High/Low		PER SHARE ($) Earnings	Dividends	Book Value
12/17	49.45	20	16	2.60	0.76	27.70
12/16	44.66	20	12	2.22	0.72	26.00
12/15	30.87	16	13	2.17	0.67	24.75
12/14	34.31	16	13	2.17	0.65	23.41
12/13	31.94	16	11	2.03	0.62	21.88
Annual Growth	11.5%	—	—	6.4%	5.3%	6.1%

3M Co

Loath to be stuck on one thing 3M makes everything from tape to high-tech security gear. The diversified company makes products through five operating segments: Industrial; Safety and Graphics; Electronics and Energy; Health Care; and Consumer. Well-known brands include Post-it notes Scotch tapes Scotchgard fabric protectors Scotch-Brite scouring pads and Filtrete home air filters. 3M sells products directly to users and through numerous wholesalers retailers distributors and dealers worldwide.

Operations

The company operates five business segments: Industrial; Safety and Graphics; Electronics and Energy; Health Care; and Consumer.

The Industrial segment brings in around 35% of revenue and serves a broad range of markets such as automotive original equipment manufacturing and aftermarket electronics appliance paper and printing packaging food and beverage and construction. Products include vinyl polyester foil and specialty industrial tapes and adhesives.

The Safety and Graphics segment (around 20% of revenue) includes architectural building and commercial services commercial graphics industrial minerals personal safety and traffic safety and security (including border and civil security). Major products offerings include architectural surface and lighting solutions; personal protection products; traffic safety and security products; commercial graphics sheeting and systems.

The Health Care segment (around 20%) serves medical clinics and hospitals pharmaceuticals dental and orthodontic practitioners health information systems food manufacturing and testing and others. Its products and services include medical and surgical supplies skin health and infection prevention products inhalation and transdermal drug delivery systems and oral care products and food safety products.

The Electronics and Energy segment (more than 15%) includes communication electrical electronics materials electronics infrastructure protection optical systems renewable energy and 3M Touch Systems. Its products include electrical telecommunications renewable energy and infrastructure protection goods and services.

The Consumer segment (around 15%) includes consumer retail office retail home improvement drug and pharmacy retail building maintenance and other markets. Major consumer products include ScotchA® brand products; construction and home improvement products include surface-preparation and wood-finishing materials and filters for furnaces and air conditioners; home care products include Scotch-Brite pads and sponges.

Geographic Reach

3M has more than 80 manufacturing plants in about 30 US states and operates +120 manufacturing and converting facilities in about 35 other countries across the Asia/Pacific region; Europe Middle East and Africa (EMEA); Latin America; and elsewhere in North America. Overall 3M has operations in more than 70 countries.

3M generates around 40% of its revenue from the US; 30% from the Asia/Pacific region; some 20% from EMEA; and 10% from other Americas (Latin America and Canada).

Sales and Marketing

3M sells its products globally though a wide range of distribution channels including directly to users and through numerous wholesalers retailers jobbers distributors sales reps and dealers.

Industries served include automotive commercial solutions communications consumer design & construction electronics energy health care manufacturing mining oil & gas safety and transportation.

The company spends around $400 million on average in advertising each year.

Financial Performance

3M's revenue has been on solid footing for a decade with somewhat lackluster growth. Earnings grew from $25.2 billion in 2008 to over $30 billion by 2016. In the same timeframe company profits trended upwards increasing from $3.5 billion in 2008 to $4.9 billion in 2017.

In 2017 3M posted $31.6 billion in revenue the highest ten years. The $1.5 billion increase since last year came from all the major segments. Three in particular? Industrial; Safety and Graphics; and Health Care? grew close to 5% year-over-year while revenues from Electronics and Energy sector shot up above 10%. Higher organic sales of 3M various tech products boosted earnings.

Net income in 2017 was $4.8 billion a slight decrease from the $5 billion profit reported for 2016. A combination of two factors explain the dip. First operating expenses increased by some $950 million an increase the company attributed to strategic investment as well as higher pension benefit expenses. A $680 million increase in income tax provisions also reduced the 2017 coffers.

Cash holdings increased from $2.3 billion to $3 billion. Operating activities provided $6.2 billion in cash. Cash flow from investing activities used up more than $3 billion mostly in acquisition costs as well as purchase of securities and investments. Financing activities which saw a flurry of activity utilized a further $2.6 billion.

Strategy

3M's growth strategy is based on acquisitions divestitures and significant R&D efforts.

The company conducts acquisitions and divestitures at what can be described as a frenzied rate. The approach is intended to get 3M's revenue moving at a faster pace. To focus on high-growth operations 3M has reduced its exposure to the consumer and electronics markets over the last several years selling off around 15 businesses.

Meanwhile the company has also pursued strategic but costly acquisitions. The company has pumped up its presence in firefighter breathing apparatus heath care product disinfectant and protection and filtration membranes. It is also working jointly with ON Semiconductor to improve communication between vehicles and roadway infrastructure by building new capabilities for image sensing technology. 3M is likely to spend $20 billion on acquisitions by 2020.

3M has been equally busy on the divestitures front offloading any company that performs poorly in its ever-evolving portfolio. In February 2018 3M sold several personal safety product offerings primarily focused on noise environmental and heat stress monitoring for $20 million.

The year before 3M sold most of its Communications Markets Division to Corning Inc. for about $900 million. Earlier that year it also sold its safety prescription eyewear business to HOYA Vision Care for $45 million.

As a technology-driven company 3M continues to make research and development a top priority investing heavily in new product development efforts which explains its top rank among the most innovative companies in the world. In 2017 the company invested almost $420 million in future growth opportunities. It also continues to see emerging markets like China and other developing countries as promising avenues for growth.

Mergers and Acquisitions

In 2017 3M announced a $2 billion acquisition of Scott Safety from Johnson Controls. The US based company manufactures safety and protection devices like self-contained breathing apparatus systems gas and flame detection instruments.

3M also purchased Elution Technologies a Vermont-based manufacturer of allergen test kits to boost its Health Care business segment. The announcement came in September 2017

In September of the year before the company acquired Semfinder a leading developer of precision software that enables efficient coding of medical procedures in multiple languages. The Swiss acquisition enables the company to accelerate the availability of its 3M 360 encompass system in countries adopting electronic medical records.

HISTORY

Five businessmen in Two Harbors Minnesota founded Minnesota Mining and Manufacturing (3M) in 1902 to sell corundum to grinding-wheel manufacturers. The company soon needed to raise working capital. Co-founder John Dwan offered his friend Edgar Ober 60% of 3M's stock. Ober persuaded Lucius Ordway VP of a plumbing business to help underwrite 3M. In 1905 the two took over the company and moved it to Duluth.

In 1907 future CEO William McKnight joined 3M as a bookkeeper. Three years later the plant moved to St. Paul. The board of directors declared a dividend to shareholders in the last quarter of 1916 and 3M hasn't missed a dividend since. The next two products 3M developed — Scotch-brand masking tape (1925) and Scotch-brand cellophane tape (1930) — assured its future.

McKnight introduced one of the first employee pension plans in 1931 and in the late 1940s he implemented a vertical management structure. 3M introduced the first commercially viable magnetic recording tape in 1947.

In 1950 after a decade of work and $1 million in development costs 3M employee Carl Miller completed the Thermo-Fax copying machine which was the foundation of 3M's duplicating division.

Products in the 1960s included 3M's dry-silver microfilm photographic products carbonless papers overhead projection systems and medical and dental products. The company moved into pharmaceuticals radiology energy control and office markets in the 1970s and 1980s.

Interestingly one of 3M's highlight products is one of its scientist's invention of Post-it Notes (1980) because the employee wanted to attach page markers to his church hymnal. Recalling that a colleague had developed an adhesive that wasn't very sticky he brushed some on paper and began a product line that now generates hundreds of millions of dollars each year for the company.

Testing historical change log update type (annual or interval)

EXECUTIVES

Vice President West Europe, Paul Rosso

Evp Safety And Graphics, Frank R. Little, age 57

Chairman President And Ceo, Inge G. Thulin, age 65, $1,483,929 total compensation

Research And Development Corporate Technology (industrial Markets), Joaquin Delgado, age 58, $629,074 total compensation

Vice Chair And Evp, Hak Cheol (H.C.) Shin, age 61, $765,496 total compensation

Evp International Operations, Julie L. Bushman, age 56, $599,029 total compensation

Evp Industrial Business Group, James L. (Jim) Bauman, age 58

Evp And Coo, Michael F. Roman, age 58, $747,022 total compensation

Svp And Cfo, Nicholas C. Gangestad, age 53, $681,551 total compensation

Evp Health Care, Michael G. Vale, age 52, $633,302 total compensation

Evp Electronics And Energy Business Group, Ashish K. Khandpur, age 50

Svp Business Development And Marketing And Sales, Jon T. Lindekugel, age 54

Svp Business Transformation And Information Technology, Eric Hammes

Vice President Investor Relations And Treasurer, Matt Ginter

Vice President, Judith Galiana

Vice President Medical Key Accounts, Nancy Dyslin

National Sales Manager, Jim Stevens

Senior Vice President Marketing Sales And Communications, Ian Hardgrove

National Sales Manager, Daryl Charton

Vice President New Market Development, Patrick Hiner

Vice President Finance And Treasurer, Sarah Grauze

Vp Corporate Development And New Ventures, Jerry Will

National Sales Manager, Jay Reese

Vice President Of Finance, Mary Cannon

Vice President Of Business Development, Richard Nimer

National Account Manager, Rick Bennett

Vice President, Paul Acito

Vice President Electronic Markets, Edward Suchman

Vice President, David Schwedler

National Account Manager, Brad Logsdon

Executive Vice President Life Insurance, Lesli Johnson

Executive Vice President Corporate Marketing, Michael Macdonald

Vice President And Associate General Counsel, Ann M Hanrahan

Vice President, Mary Rada

National Account Manager, Christian Rudeen

Vice President, Charles M Byrne

Vice President Engineering, Hector Dalton

Vice President Mobile Interactive Solutions Division, Mark Colin

Vice President International, Jim Walsh
Vice President, John Simon
International Vice President, Simon Hearne
Vice President Investor Relations And Corporate
 Communications, Dan Mcintyre
Vice President Of Marketing, Sharon Cohen
Vice President And Gm 3m Espe, Jeffrey Lavers
Vice President Of Operations, Martin Barila
Vice President And General Manager Corrosion
 Protection Products, Paiul Acito
Market Vice President For Automotive, Steve Deb
 Schreiner
Vice President, Jamie Meilahn
Vice President Of Research Devt, Gary Silvers
Vice President Of Technology, Witold Witwicki
Vice President And Chief Sustainability Officer
 3m Research And Development, Gayle Schueller
Vice President Of Finance, Gerardo Pereyra
National Account Manager, Bart Rasmussen
Vice President, Christina Kim
Senior Management (senior Vice President
 General Manager Director), Mark Sutton
Division Vice President, Martyn Tiplady
Vice President Latin America, Rosa M Miller
Vice President 3m Transportation Safety Division,
 John Riccardi
National Sales Manager, Michael Kidd
Vice President, Brian Spiewak
Finance Vice President, Tom Pepinski
Vice President Quality And Safety, Molly Wallace
National Sales Manager, Chris Decolli
Vice President Environmental Health And Safety
 Operations, Jean Sweeney
National Sales Manager, Scott McConnell
Vice President, Patrick Parks
Vice President Global Marketing 3m Unitek
 Orthodontic Products, Marcello Napol
Vice President And General Manager Security
 Systems Division, Mike Delkoski
Vice President Sales And Marketing, Eric Dornak
Senior Vice President Human Resources, Marlene
 McGrath
Vice President Cio, Ernie Park
Senior Vice President, Ivan Fong
National Account Manager, Brian Abernethy
National Account Manager, Ryan Carl
Vice President Research And Development,
 Michael Cameron
Vice President, Bill Myers
Vice President And General Manager Automotive
 Afte, Laino Richard
National Account Manager, Andrew Zimmerman
Vice President Of Business Development, Jack
 Driessen
National Account Manager, MIKE ZIELINSKI
Vice President Home Care Division, Andrew Naber
Vice President Biometrics Solutions, Ramsey
 Billups
Vice President And General Manager, Erik Aunan
National Sales Manager, Andrew Petrone
Vp And Associate General Counsel, Ann Marie
 Hanrahan
National Account Manager, Brooke Golwas
National Sales Manager, Kuehn Gina
Vice Chair And Evp, Hak Cheol (H.C.) Shin, age 61
Treasurer, Jan Angell
Board Director, Herbert Henkel
Board Member, Vance Coffman
Board Member, Sondra Barbour
Board Member, David Dillon
Board Member, Gregory Page
Board Member, Muhtar Kent
Auditors: PricewaterhouseCoopers LLP

LOCATIONS

HQ: 3M Co
 3M Center, St. Paul, MN 55144
Phone: 651 733-1110 **Fax:** 651 733-9973
Web: www.3M.com

2016 Sales

	$ mil.	% of total
United States	12,188	41
Asia Pacific	8,847	29
Europe Middle East and Africa	6,163	20
Latin America and Canada	2,901	10
Other Unallocated	10	-
Total	**30,109**	**100**

PRODUCTS/OPERATIONS

2016 Sales

	$ mil.	% of total
Industrial	10,313	33
Safety and Graphics	5,660	18
Health Care	5,527	18
Electronics and Energy	4,826	16
Consumer	4,482	15
Corporate and unallocated	9	-
Eliminations	(708)	-
Total	**30,109**	**100**

Selected Segments and Products

Industrial and Transportation
 Automotive aftermarket products
 Automotive products
 Closures for disposable diapers
 Coated and nonwoven abrasives
 Films
 Filtration products
 Specialty adhesives
 Tapes
Health Care
 Dental products
 Drug delivery systems
 Health information systems
 Infection prevention
 Medical and surgical supplies
 Microbiology products
 Skin health products
Safety Security and Protection
 Commercial cleaning products
 Consumer safety products
 Corrosion protection products
 Floor matting
 Occupational health and safety products
 Safety and security products
 Track and trace products
Consumer and Office
 Carpet and fabric protectors
 Commercial cleaning products
 Fabric protectors (Scotchgard)
 High-performance cloth (Scotch-Brite)
 Home-improvement products
 Repositionable notes (Post-it)
 Scour pads (Scotch-Brite)
 Sponges (O-Cel-O)
 Tape (Scotch)
Display and Graphics
 Commercial graphics systems
 Optical films for electronic display
 Specialty film and media products
 Traffic control materials
Electro and Communications
 Insulating and splicing products for electronics
 telecommunications and electrical industries
 Packaging and interconnection devices

Selected Mergers and Acquisitions

COMPETITORS

ACCO Brands	Henkel
BASF SE	Honeywell
Bayer AG	International
Beiersdorf	Illinois Tool Works
Bostik	Johnson & Johnson
Bridgestone	Kimberly-Clark
Carlisle Companies	RPM International
Corning	Ricoh Company
Danaher	S.C. Johnson

DuPont	Sealed Air Corp.
GE	Sika
H.B. Fuller	

HISTORICAL FINANCIALS
Company Type: Public

Income Statement
FYE: December 31

	REVENUE ($ mil.)	NET INCOME ($ mil.)	NET PROFIT MARGIN	EMPLOYEES
12/18	32,765	5,349	16.3%	93,516
12/17	31,657	4,858	15.3%	91,536
12/16	30,109	5,050	16.8%	91,584
12/15	30,274	4,833	16.0%	89,446
12/14	31,821	4,956	15.6%	89,800
Annual Growth	0.7%	1.9%	—	1.0%

2018 Year-End Financials

Debt ratio: 40.27% — No. of shares (mil.): 594
Return on equity: 50.09% — Dividends
Cash ($ mil.): 2,853 — Yield: 2.8%
Current ratio: 1.89 — Payout: 72.7%
Long-term debt ($ mil.): 13,486 — Market value ($ mil.): 113,349

	STOCK PRICE ($) FY Close	P/E High/Low	PER SHARE ($) Earnings	Dividends	Book Value
12/18	190.54	28 20	8.89	5.44	16.47
12/17	235.37	30 21	7.93	4.70	19.44
12/16	178.57	22 16	8.16	4.44	17.26
12/15	150.64	22 18	7.58	4.10	19.21
12/14	164.32	22 16	7.49	3.42	20.64
Annual Growth	3.8%	— —	4.4%	12.3%	(5.5%)

A-Mark Precious Metals, Inc

Auditors: Grant Thornton LLP

LOCATIONS

HQ: A-Mark Precious Metals, Inc
 2121 Rosecrans Ave., Suite 6300, El Segundo, CA
 90245
Phone: 310 587-1477
Web: www.amark.com

HISTORICAL FINANCIALS
Company Type: Public

Income Statement
FYE: June 30

	REVENUE ($ mil.)	NET INCOME ($ mil.)	NET PROFIT MARGIN	EMPLOYEES
06/18	7,606	(3)	—	188
06/17	6,989	7	0.1%	127
06/16	6,784	9	0.1%	83
06/15	6,070	7	0.1%	52
06/14	5,979	8	0.1%	55
Annual Growth	6.2%	—	—	36.0%

2018 Year-End Financials

Debt ratio: 27.89% — No. of shares (mil.): 7
Return on equity: (-5.02%) — Dividends
Cash ($ mil.): 6 — Yield: 0.0%
Current ratio: 1.06 — Payout: —
Long-term debt ($ mil.): 7 — Market value ($ mil.): 93

STOCK PRICE ($) FY Close	P/E High/Low	PER SHARE ($) Earnings	Dividends	Book Value
06/18	13.28	— —	(0.48)	0.24	9.34
06/17	16.39	21 15	1.00	0.30	9.90
06/16	16.18	17 8	1.30	0.24	9.02
06/15	10.47	12 9	1.00	0.10	8.02
06/14	11.16	13 10	1.09	0.00	7.10
Annual Growth	4.4%	— —	—	—	7.1%

Abbott Laboratories

With activities ranging from filling baby bottles to making generic medications and cardiovascular devices Abbott Laboratories is a diverse health care products manufacturer. Its newly established cardiovascular and neuromodulation segment formed after the 2017 acquisition of St. Jude Medical develops products for cardiac rhythm management electrophysiology vascular and other areas of cardiovascular care. Abbott's nutritional products division makes such well-known brands as Similac infant formula and the Ensure line of nutrition supplements while its drug division sells branded generic medicines (including gastroenterology and women's health products) in emerging markets. The company also makes diagnostic instruments (including tests and assays) and the FreeStyle diabetes care line.

Operations

Abbott operates in four reportable segments: Cardiovascular and Neuromodulation Nutritional Products Diagnostic Products and Established Pharmaceutical Products.

The Cardiovascular and Neuromodulation segment is Abbott's largest bringing in about one-third of total sales. It conducts R&D programs in the areas of cardiac rhythm management electrophysiology heart failure and vascular and structural heart devices as well as neuromodulation devices to treat chronic pain and movement disorders.

The Nutritional Products segment brings in 25% of Abbott's revenue. It sells pediatric and adult formulations around the world. Brands include Similac Ensure Isomil Glucerna PediaSure Zone Perfect and Myoplex. The segment also provides nutritional products used for enteral feeding in health care facilities.

The Diagnostics segment (about 20% of total sales) makes laboratory systems that screen and/or diagnose for cancer cardiovascular disease fertility and infectious diseases among others.

Abbott's Established Pharmaceutical Products (some 15% of sales) are branded generics marketed in emerging markets. These include gastroenterology products (such as Creon Duspatel and Heptral) women's health products (Duphaston and Femoston) cardiovascular and metabolic products (Lipanthyl Teveten and Synthroid among others) pain and central nervous system products (Serc Brufen and Sevedol) and respiratory drugs and vaccines (Influvac Biaxin Klacid and Klacirid).

The group's Other segment which brings in around 5% of revenue includes Abbott's Diabetes Care operations.

Geographic Reach

Abbott has plants in Brazil China Canada Germany India Ireland the Netherlands Pakistan Russia Spain Singapore the UK and the US.

The company's products are sold in more than 150 countries. Abbott earns more than 35% of its revenues in the domestic market. Europe the Middle East and Africa sales account for another 20% of revenues. The Asia/Pacific also brings in 20% of sales and Latin America brings in 5%.

Sales and Marketing

Abbott conducts distribution operations both from its own distribution centers and through third-party partners. Established pharmaceutical and nutritional customers include health care organizations wholesalers pharmacies retailers government agencies and third-party distribution entities. Diagnostic and cardiovascular and neuromodulation products are sold to blood banks hospitals and other health care facilities physicians plasma protein therapeutic companies government agencies alternative testing sites and commercial laboratories.

Financial Performance

Abbott's annual revenues hovered around $20 billion after its 2013 spinoff of AbbVie until 2017 when revenue increased 31% to $27.4 billion. This gain was largely due to the acquisition of St. Jude Medical which greatly expanded the company's cardiovascular business. The Diagnostics segment grew 17% that year with the acquisition of Alere while the Nutritionals and Established Pharmaceuticals segments had modest organic growth. Sales in emerging markets rose 14% in 2017. These gains were partially offset by foreign currency exchange rates.

However higher operating expenses including research and development costs (primarily driven by the purchase of St. Jude Medical) and amortization of intangible assets drove net income down 66% to $477 million. Cash flow from operations increased 74% to $5.6 billion due to factors including positive adjustments to amortization inventory and income taxes.

Strategy

Abbott has a diverse set of operations and it has lined up strategies specific to its different segments.

The Cardiovascular and Neuromodulation segment has several new products on the market including its Assurity MRI pacemaker its MitraClip valve repair device and its Xience Sierra coronary stent. After the 2017 acquisition of St. Jude Medical Abbott is a leader in the field of non-opioid pain relief a market with great potential as health care providers seek safer methods to treat chronic pain.

The Diagnostic segment is focused on commercializing its blood screening immunoassay clinical chemistry and hematology systems as well as various assays and management solutions. It also has molecular in vitro diagnostic products and systems under development. Recent developments include the roll-out of its suite of next-generation Alinity diagnostic systems which the company sees as laboratory game-changers. To boost its point-of-care diagnostics offerings Abbott acquired Alere for $5.8 billion in 2017. Alere makes tests for cancers cardiovascular disease and infections such as HIV and malaria among others.

In the Nutritionals segment the company is focused on R&D activities in the pediatric adult and performance nutrition fields. It has a number of products in development which it expects to launch over the next few years.

In the Established Pharmaceuticals segment Abbott is working to build portfolios of branded generic medicines for emerging markets. It focuses on building country-specific portfolios to best meet the needs of each nation. The company has more than 400 projects under development and it hopes to acquire more products through licensing activities. Among its key brands are Creon Duphaston and Influvac.

In the Other segment diabetes care remains an area of focus. Its FreeStyle Libre Flash (approved in Europe in 2014 and in the US in mid-2017) is the first continuous glucose monitoring system that doesn't require a fingerstick.

Furthering its focus on cardiovascular and diagnostic operations Abbott sold its Abbott Medical Optics subsidiary to Johnson & Johnson for $4.3 billion in early 2017.Also that year the company divested certain assets as a condition for its acquisition of Alere. It sold its Triage MeterPro cardiovascular and toxicology business to Quidel Corporation and its Epocal subsidiary to Siemens Diagnostics.

After the 2017 acquisitions of St. Jude Medical and Alere Abbott's debt levels increased to some $28 billion. That level of indebtedness leaves the group somewhat strapped for cash which could create problems if market or business conditions arise that require capital investment.

Furthermore with its global operations the company is vulnerable to changing regulatory conditions. For example its baby formula business in China had a setback in 2016 as that country's government required infant formula manufacturers to re-register their products. (Sales of these products began recovering in 2017.)

Mergers and Acquisitions

In 2017 Abbott completed a major deal to further grow its line of heart-related devices. It bought St. Jude Medical a maker of such products as heart catheters and defibrillators in a deal valued at $23.6 billion. The combination of the two firms created one of the world's largest makers of cardiovascular devices.

Also in 2017 Abbott acquired Alere a provider of diagnostic health tests. That transaction was valued at $5.3 billion.

HISTORY

Dr. Wallace Abbott started making his dosimetric granule (a pill that supplied uniform quantities of drugs) at his home outside Chicago in 1888. Aggressive marketing earned Abbott the American Medical Association's criticism though much of the medical profession supported him.

During WWI Abbott scientists synthesized anesthetics previously available only from Germany. Abbott improved its research capacity in 1922 by buying Dermatological Research Laboratories; in 1928 it bought John T. Milliken and its well-trained sales force. Abbott went public in 1929.

International operations began in the mid-1930s with branches in Argentina Brazil Cuba Mexico and the UK.

Abbott was integral to the WWII effort; the US made only 28 pounds of penicillin in 1943 before the company began to ratchet up production. Consumer infant and nutritional products (such as Selsun Blue shampoo Murine eye drops and Similac formula) joined the roster in the 1960s. The FDA banned Abbott's artificial sweetener Sucaryl in 1970 saying it might be carcinogenic and in 1971 millions of intravenous solutions were recalled following contamination deaths.

EXECUTIVES

Svp And Chief Marketing And External Affairs Officer, Elaine R. Leavenworth, age 60

Vice President Diagnostic Commercial Operations Europe Africa And Middle East, Jaime Contreras

Chairman And Ceo, Miles D. White, age 62, $1,900,000 total compensation

Evp Human Resources, Stephen R. (Steve) Fussell, age 61, $454,689 total compensation

Evp Ventures, John M. Capek, age 56, $675,000 total compensation

Evp Nutritional Products, Heather L. Mason, age 58

Svp And Group President Cardiovascular And Neuromodulation, Eric S. Fain, age 57

Evp Medical Devices, Robert B. Ford, age 44

Evp Diagnostic Products, Brian J. Blaser, age 53, $692,057 total compensation

Evp General Counsel And Secretary, Hubert L. Allen, age 52, $650,000 total compensation

Svp Finance And Cfo, Brian B. Yoor, age 48, $584,231 total compensation

Svp U.s. Nutrition, Roger M. Bird, age 61

Svp Abbott Vascular, Deepak Nath, age 45

Svp Established Pharmaceuticals Latin America, Daniel Salvadori, age 39

Svp Diabetes Care, Jared L. Watkin, age 50

Evp Established Pharmaceuticals Emerging Markets, Andrew H. Lane, age 47

President Cardiovascular And Neuromodulation, Michael T. (Mike) Rousseau, age 62

Svp International Nutrition, Joseph (Joe) Manning, age 49

Senior Non It Management Chief Executive Officer Chief Financial Officer Vice President Directo, Randi Pickens

Senior Vice President, Ann Long

Divisional Vice President, Andy Brookes

Medical Director, Thomas Podsadecki

Senior Vice President Central Region, Pamela Switalski

Evp Corporate Development, Richard W Ashley, age 76

Divisional Vice President, Brian Wentworth

Senior Vice President, Maureen Snider

Vice President Sales Training And Development, Randee Stelman

Group Vice President, Tiffany Cincotta

Division Vice President Pediatric Commercial Operations, Rich Schaefer

Vice President Marketing And Human Resources, Jennifer Pestikas

Medical Director, Roger Trinh

Medical Director, Gwendolyn Janssen

Evp General Counsel And Secretary, Hubert L. Allen, age 52

Area Treasurer, Quintin Noble

Auditors: Ernst & Young LLP

LOCATIONS

HQ: Abbott Laboratories
100 Abbott Park Road, Abbott Park, IL 60064-6400
Phone: 224 667-6100
Web: www.abbott.com

2017 Sales

	$ mil.	% of total
US	9,673	35
China	2,146	8
Germany	1,366	5
Japan	1,255	5
India	1,237	4
Netherlands	929	3
Switzerland	841	3
Russia	664	2
France	628	2
Brazil	541	2
Italy	507	2
UK	498	2
Colombia	494	2
Canada	443	2
Vietnam	427	2
Other countries	5,741	21
Total	**27,390**	**100**

PRODUCTS/OPERATIONS

2017 Sales by Segment

	$ mil.	% of total
Cardiovascular and Neuromodulation	8,911	33
Nutritionals	6,925	25
Diagnostics	5,616	20
Established Pharmaceuticals	4,287	16
Other	1,651	6
Total	**27,390**	**100**

Selected Products

Nutritional

Alimentum (infant formula)
EAS nutritional brands
AdvantEdge (nutritional supplements)
Myoplex (nutritional supplements)
Ensure (adult nutrition)
Freego (enteral pump)
Glucerna (nutritional beverage for diabetics)
Isomil (soy-based infant formula)
Jevity (liquid food for enteral feeding)
NeoSure (infant formula)
Osmolite
Pedialyte (pediatric electrolyte solution)
PediaSure (children's nutrition)
Similac (infant formula)
Zone Perfect (nutritional bars)
Established Pharmaceuticals (branded generics)
Creon (pancreatic enzyme replacement therapy)
Duphaston (progesterone deficiency)
Klacid (macrolide antibiotic)
Diagnostic
Abbott PRISM (high-volume blood-screening system)
ARCHITECT (clinical chemistry system)
Cell-Dyn (hematology systems and reagents)
Diagnostic and screening assays
Informatics and automation solutions for lab use
i-STAT (blood analyzer)
m2000 (instrument that detects and measures infectious agents)
Vysis (genomic-based tests)
Medical Devices
Acculink/Accunet (carotid stent)
Hi-Torque Balance Middleweight (coronary guidewire licensed from Asahi Intecc)
MitraClip (valve repair)
Multi-Link 8 Multi-Link Mini Vision and Multi-Link Vision (coronary metallic stents)
Perclose (vessel closure)
StarClose (vessel closure)
Trek (balloon dilation)
Xience V Xience nano and Xience Prime (drug-eluting stents)

Selected Acquisitions

COMPETITORS

Allergan plc	Mannatech
Bard	Mead Johnson
Baxter International	Mylan
Becton Dickinson	Nestlé
Boston Scientific	Perrigo
Cordis	Roche Holding
Danone	Sandoz International
Dr. Reddy's	GmbH
GNC	Schiff Nutrition
Heinz	International
Herbalife Ltd.	Sun Pharmaceutical
Johnson & Johnson	Teva
LifeScan	

HISTORICAL FINANCIALS

Company Type: Public

Income Statement   FYE: December 31

	REVENUE ($ mil.)	NET INCOME ($ mil.)	NET PROFIT MARGIN	EMPLOYEES
12/17	27,390	477	1.7%	99,000
12/16	20,853	1,400	6.7%	75,000
12/15	20,405	4,423	21.7%	74,000
12/14	20,247	2,284	11.3%	77,000
12/13	21,848	2,576	11.8%	69,000
Annual Growth	**5.8%**	**(34.4%)**	**—**	**9.4%**

2017 Year-End Financials

Debt ratio: 36.62%
Return on equity: 1.85%
Cash ($ mil.): 9,407
Current ratio: 2.26
Long-term debt ($ mil.): 27,210
No. of shares (mil.): 1,743
Dividends
  Yield: 0.0%
  Payout: 392.5%
Market value ($ mil.): 99,507

	STOCK PRICE ($) FY Close	P/E High/Low	PER SHARE ($) Earnings	Dividends	Book Value
12/17	57.07	213 145	0.27	1.06	17.72
12/16	38.41	48 39	0.94	1.04	13.94
12/15	44.91	17 13	2.92	0.96	14.40
12/14	45.02	31 24	1.49	0.88	14.27
12/13	38.33	40 20	1.62	0.56	16.26
Annual Growth	**10.5%**	**— —**	**(36.1%)**	**17.3%**	**2.2%**

AbbVie Inc

AbbVie is vying for dominance in the world of medications. The firm discovers develops and commercializes both biopharmaceutical and small molecule drugs with a focus on autoimmune diseases hepatitis C HIV and other ailments. Its primary product is Humira best known as a rheumatoid arthritis drug; it accounts for some 65% of AbbVie's sales and is the world's top-selling prescription drug. Other key products include cancer treatment Imbruvica and hepatitis C drug Viekira. The firm has 11 facilities making products that are available globally. After the expiration of Humira's compound patent protection in late 2016 the R&D firm is looking for the next big thing.

Operations

AbbVie's products focus on treating conditions such as chronic autoimmune diseases (including rheumatoid arthritis psoriasis and Crohn's disease) hepatitis C HIV endometriosis thyroid disease Parkinson's disease low testosterone and complications from chronic kidney disease and cystic fibrosis. The company has a pipeline of promising new medications in clinical development that covers such areas as oncology neurology and women's health.

The company has a number of partnerships with other pharmaceuticals to develop new treatments. Partners include C2N Diagnostics (Alzheimer's disease) Calico Life Sciences (age-related diseases) and Infinity Pharmaceuticals (cancer).

In addition to its portfolio of existing and developmental drugs AbbVie's operations include its global R&D apparatus focused on small molecule drugs and biologics and its sales marketing and distribution network.

Geographic Reach

AbbVie collects 65% of its sales from the US. Key foreign markets include Brazil Canada France Germany Italy Japan the Netherlands Spain and the UK. The company also has R&D facilities in Germany and has a goal of expanding in emerging markets.

The company has seven R&D facilities in the US (located in Abbott Park Illinois; Chicago; Redwood City San Francisco and Sunnyvale California; and Cambridge and Worcester Massachusetts).

Sales and Marketing

AbbVie markets its products to managed care providers including health maintenance organizations (HMOs) and pharmacy benefit managers (PBMs) hospitals and government agencies (including the US Department of Veterans Affairs and the Department of Defense). Its pharmaceutical products are primarily distributed in the US through independent wholesalers; to a lesser extent it also sells them directly to pharmacies and patients. Internationally AbbVie principally markets to payors physicians and state regulatory bodies.

In 2017 three wholesale distributors — McKesson Cardinal Health and AmerisourceBergen— accounted for practically all the company's sales in the US. This reliance on those firms could leave AbbVie vulnerable to distribution issues should any of them face financial difficulties.

AbbVie spent $846 million on advertising in 2017 versus $764 million in 2016 and $704 million in 2015.

Financial Performance

Despite facing a number of patent expirations AbbView has seen steady growth since its 2013 spin-off from Abbott. In 2017 net revenue grew 10% to $28.2 billion as sales of Humira continued to grow both in the US and abroad (thanks largely to its approval for new indications). Two drugs cancer treatment Imbruvica and leukemia treatment Viekira also bring in more than $1 billion in sales each; sales of Imbruvica have more than tripled since 2015. Other products that have performed well include Lupron and Creon.

Net income nearly doubled to $5.1 billion in 2015 after a couple of years of declines. It rose another 16% in 2016 but then fell 11% to $5.3 million in 2017. Despite the higher revenue AbbVie's operating expenses increased and cut into its bottom line.

Cash flow from operations (which has been erratic) rose 41% to $10 billion in 2017 thanks to positive adjustments to reconcile net earnings to net cash from operating activities. These adjustments ranged from a $1.2 billion tax benefit related to the 2017 Tax Act and changes in fair value of contingent consideration liabilities.

Strategy

As AbbVie faced the patent expirations of many of its top sellers between 2011 and 2016 (Aluvia TriCor Niaspan Humira) having a strong R&D focus was key to AbbVie's continued success. The company has more than 60 compounds or indications in the pipeline including treatments in immunology oncology neuroscience hepatitis C chronic kidney disease and women's health. If any one of those reaches the market the risky development process will pay off for the research pharmaceuticals company. The company plans to keep adding to its pipeline through strategic licensing deals and partnerships.

The company also pursues strategic acquisitions to boost its drug development stockpile and lighten its dependence on Humira and other key treatments. In 2016 it acquired Stemcentrx and its potential blockbuster Rova-T for small cell lung cancer for $5.8 billion. However Rova-T has had poor results in clinical trials and in early 2019 AbbVie posted a $4 billion impairment charge on the acquisition.

In a move that speaks to AbbVie's need to get blockbusters on the market soon the company has a priority review voucher (PRV) which it intends to use for an existing product in development. It purchased the rare pediatric disease PRV giving it the option to speed up the FDA's review process for $350 million from United Therapeutics in 2015.

In mid-2017 the FDA approved AbbVie's hepatitis C treatment Mavyret which should challenge such pricier drugs as Gilead Science's Epclusa and Vosevi. Mavyret performed well in its first year on the market helping boost AbbVie's net revenue that year. The company then gained US approval for myeloid leukemia drug Venclexta in 2018 (some two years earlier than initially predicted).

AbbVie is also concentrating on boosting sales of Humira — the world's biggest-selling prescription medicine — by expanding its share of the market and its presence in underserved markets. In 2017 global Humira sales increased 14% and the company continues to seek additional indications for the blockbuster drug. However Humira now faces competition in Europe where its basic patent expired in October 2018. At the time of the patent expiration five biosimilars from companies including Amgen and Mylan had gained approval in Europe.

Thanks to years of revenue growth the company plans to invest some $2.5 billion in capital projects in the US; it is also exploring the expansion of certain domestic facilities.

Mergers and Acquisitions

To pump up its oncology pipeline AbbVie in 2016 paid $5.8 billion for Stemcentrx which has four early-stage cancer treatments and the late-stage Rova-T treatment for small-cell lung cancer in clinical testing.

Company Background

Biopharmaceutical research company AbbVie was spun off from its former parent Abbott Labs in 2013.

EXECUTIVES

Chairman And Ceo, Richard A. (Rick) Gonzalez, age 64, $1,600,000 total compensation
Evp External Affairs General Counsel And Corporate Secretary, Laura J. Schumacher, age 55, $979,369 total compensation
Evp Commercial Operations, Carlos Alban, age 55, $888,461 total compensation
Evp And Cfo, William J. Chase, age 50, $979,369 total compensation
President Pharmacyclics, Wulff-Erik von Borcke
Svp Operations, Azita Saleki-Gerhardt, age 55
Evp Research And Development And Chief Scientific Officer, Michael E. Severino, age 52, $960,969 total compensation
Evp And Chief Strategy Officer, Henry O. Gosebruch, $894,523 total compensation
Vp And Chief Ethics And Compliance Officer, Karen Hale
Vice President Human Resources And Operations, Leanna Walther
Vice President Pharmacy Immunology And Neurology Supply Chain, Chris Mlynek
Vice President, Tiffany Cincotta
Dvp Immunology Research, Lisa Olson
Vice President Immunology Global Commercial Development, Nisha Burns
Vice President Quality Assurance, Marilyn Frontz
Vice President And General Manager Abbvie Germany, Patrick Horber
Vice President Business Human Resources Global Commercial Operations, Heather Lowe
Vice President Legal, Lara Levitan
Vice President Regional Manufacturing Operations Europe, Thomas Scheidmeir
Vice President Licensing And Aqcuisitions Immunology, Suzanne Lebold
Medical Director, Kevin Douglas
Vice President And Assistant Corporate Controller, Ross Berman
Vice President And Treasurer, Amarendra Duvvur
Medical Director, Anjla Sood
Medical Director Neuroscience Development, Maurizio Facheris
Vice President Corporate Strategy Group, Leah Bloom
Vp Clinical Field Operations, Gregory Larson
Evp External Affairs General Counsel And Corporate Secretary, Laura J. Schumacher, age 55
Auditors: Ernst & Young LLP

LOCATIONS

HQ: AbbVie Inc
1 North Waukegan Road, North Chicago, IL 60064-6400
Phone: 847 932-7900
Web: www.abbvie.com

2017 Sales

	$ mil.	% of total
US	18,251	65
Germany	1,157	4
UK	807	3
Japan	764	3
France	730	3
Canada	659	2
Spain	521	2
Italy	475	2
Brazil	410	1
The Netherlands	362	1
Other	4,080	14
Total	**28,216**	**100**

PRODUCTS/OPERATIONS

2017 Sales

	$ mil.	% of total
Humira	18,427	65
Imbruvica	2,573	9
Hepatitis C products	1,274	5
Creon	831	3
Lupron	829	3
Synthroid	781	3
Synagis	738	3
AndroGel	577	2
Kaletra	423	1
Sevoflurane	410	1
Duodopa	355	1
Other	998	4
Total	**28,216**	**100**

COMPETITORS

Amgen	Merck
AstraZeneca	Novartis
Bayer AG	Pfizer
Bristol-Myers Squibb	Roche Holding
Eli Lilly	Sanofi
GlaxoSmithKline	Teva
Johnson & Johnson	

HISTORICAL FINANCIALS

Company Type: Public

Income Statement
FYE: December 31

	REVENUE ($ mil.)	NET INCOME ($ mil.)	NET PROFIT MARGIN	EMPLOYEES
12/17	28,216	5,309	18.8%	29,000
12/16	25,638	5,953	23.2%	30,000
12/15	22,859	5,144	22.5%	28,000
12/14	19,960	1,774	8.9%	26,000
12/13	18,790	4,128	22.0%	25,000
Annual Growth	10.7%	6.5%	—	3.8%

2017 Year-End Financials

Debt ratio: 52.79%
Return on equity: 109.09%
Cash ($ mil.): 9,303
Current ratio: 1.28
Long-term debt ($ mil.): 30,953

No. of shares (mil.): 1,592
Dividends
  Yield: 0.0%
  Payout: 77.5%
Market value ($ mil.): 153,975

	STOCK PRICE ($) FY Close	P/E High/Low		Earnings	Dividends	Book Value
12/17	96.71	30	18	3.30	2.56	3.20
12/16	62.62	18	14	3.63	2.28	2.91
12/15	59.24	23	15	3.13	2.02	2.45
12/14	65.44	63	42	1.10	1.66	1.09
12/13	52.81	21	13	2.56	1.60	2.83
Annual Growth	16.3%	—	—	6.6%	12.5%	3.1%

ABM Industries, Inc.

Many businesses hope to clean up but diversified facilities services contractor ABM counts on it. The company primarily offers janitorial services to owners and operators of office buildings hospitals manufacturing plants schools shopping centers and transportation facilities throughout the US UK Canada Puerto Rico the UAE and Saudi Arabia. Through other units ABM maintains mechanical electrical and plumbing systems. Its Ampco System Parking operates more than 2000 parking lots and garages mainly at airports across 41 states while ABM Security Services provides security officers and security systems monitoring services.

Operations

ABM's reportable segments consist of Business & Industry (?B&I?) Aviation Emerging Industries Group Technical Solutions and the newly acquired GCA Services. Following the full integration of GCA into ABM's industry group model in 2018 the company anticipates its Education industry group will become a reportable segment.

Geographic Reach

ABM has 350 locations throughout the US UK Puerto Rico Canada the UAE and Saudi Arabia. The US accounts for about 95% of revenue.

Sales and Marketing

ABM sells its services directly in client locations which enable to provide full range of solutions through intra-company sales referrals multi-service sales and national account sales. Its sales and marketing efforts are conducted by corporate subsidiary regional branch and district offices.The company serves some 20000 clients.

ABM spent $2.2 million on advertising expenses in fiscal 2017 up from $2.1 million in fiscal 2016.

Financial Performance

ABM's revenue has been trending up across the past several fiscal years. Acquisitions have largely driven the growth while increased demand for the company's services has also led to organic growth.

ABM reported revenue of $5.4 billion for fiscal 2017 up from $5.14 billion in fiscal 2016. The company's revenues increased by $308.9 million or 6.0% during 2017 as compared to 2016. The increase in revenues was partly the result of $208.1 million in revenue associated with acquisitions including $169.7 million related to the 2017 acquisition of GCA Services Group. The revenue spike was also the result of organic growth of $121.0 million in Aviation and $38.5 million in Business & Industry (?B&I?).

Aviation revenues increased by $136.3 million or 16.0% during 2017 as compared to 2016. The increase was primarily attributable to organic growth in parking transportation passenger services cabin cleaning and facility services. B&I revenues increased by $43.4 million or 1.5% during fiscal 2017 as compared to the previous fiscal year. The increase was primarily attributable to new janitorial business including new contract wins in the UK.

The company's Emerging Industries Group revenues decreased by $24.8 million or 3.1% during fiscal 2017 as compared to fiscal 2016. The decrease was caused by the losses of certain High Tech and Education facility services accounts.

ABM's Technical Solutions revenues increased by $14.3 million or 3.4% during 2017 as compared to the prior fiscal period. The increase was primarily attributable to incremental revenues from acquisitions of $18.1 million and higher project revenues partially offset by the completion of a large ESPC project.

ABM's net income was a little more than $3 million in fiscal 2017 down from $57 million in fiscal 2016. The company's operating expenses increased by $277.8 million or 6.0% during 2017 as compared to 2016.

ABM's net cash provided by operating activities of continuing operations was $101.7 million during 2017 after ending fiscal 2016 with $83 million.

Strategy

Like other conglomerates in the business services sector ABM has grown mainly by acquiring local and regional operating companies and their client rosters. ABM generates cost savings by centralizing many business functions such as marketing sales and accounting.

The company's 2020 Vision strategic transformation initiative is intended to differentiate ABM in the marketplace. ABM's transformation initiative includes plans to accelerate revenue growth for certain industry groups and beneficial cost savings through the realignment of ABM's business operations to better support specific industries. ABM hopes the 2020 Vision plan will improve the effectiveness of its risk management and safety programs solidify the strategic direction of its government services business and improve its overall operating and financial performance.

Mergers and Acquisitions

In a sweeping move to expand ABM agreed to acquire rival GCA Services Group (GCA) for $1.25 billion in cash and stock in mid-2017. The purchase will fortify ABM's own core facility services offerings and enhance its presence in the education market and commercial sector. ABM also expects to achieve a significant revenue surge of $1.1 billion; of this amount about $600 million will reside within the education industry group and the remaining $500 million will be allocated to other key industry groups.

In 2016 ABM acquired Mechanical Solutions Inc. a provider of specialized HVAC chiller and plumbing services and OFJ Connections Ltd a provider of transportation services in the UK for $12 million and $6.3 million respectively. Also in 2016 the company acquired BRBIBR Limited for $16.1 million.

HISTORY

Morris Rosenberg invested $4.50 in a bucket and cleaning tools and began cleaning San Francisco storefront windows in 1909. Later that year he purchased Chicago Window Cleaning for $300 and armed with new supplies and a Ford Model T began offering annual cleaning contracts. He changed the company's name to American Building Maintenance in 1913 to emphasize its broadening services. By 1920 the company had established three west coast offices and it became the first contractor to clean a major college campus when it signed an agreement with Stanford University in 1921.

The company added cleaning supplies to its offerings in 1927 with the acquisition of Easterday Janitorial Supply Company and continued to grow even during the Great Depression by providing cleaning services cheaper than its clients could provide for themselves. ABM expanded to the East Coast in 1932. Morris Rosenberg died in 1935 leaving the company to his oldest son Theodore who bought electrical services company Alta Electric the following year. During WWII ABM cleaned Navy ships and wired amphibious vehicles called Water Buffaloes. By the end of the war it operated 17 offices in the US and Canada.

Now called American Building Maintenance Industries the company went public in 1962 with Theodore serving as chairman and younger brother Sydney as CEO. To diversify its services ABM Industries stepped up its acquisition pace in the late 1960s buying Ampco Auto Parks (1967 parking facilities) Commercial Air Conditioning (1968 equipment maintenance) and General Elevator Corporation (1969 elevator maintenance and repair).

ABM Industries continued to expand its business into diverse services and regions through a three-decade buying spree. In 1981 the company combined its air-conditioning elevator lighting and energy services into American Technical Services Company (Amtech) to better focus on the high-growth tech and energy businesses. A management-led buyout of the company failed in 1990 on opposition from the Rosenberg brothers. Although ABM Industries' president stepped down and several lawsuits were filed following the aborted LBO the company continued to post impressive sales and profit numbers.

The company shortened its name to ABM Industries in 1994 the same year William Steele was named CEO. Sydney Rosenberg retired as chairman in 1997 marking the end of family control. The following year the company formed a Facility Services division to provide one-stop shopping for all of its services. It moved into landscaping services in 1999 with the purchase of Commercial Landscape Systems. The following year Steele stepped down as CEO and Henrik Slipsager a former executive of Dutch services giant ISS was tapped as the company's new chief.

In 2001 ABM sold off its Easterday Janitorial Supply subsidiary to AmSan West. ABM acquired six companies in 2001 and 2002 including Lakeside Building Maintenance a large Midwestern janitorial contractor. In 2003 the company sold its Amtech Elevator Services to Otis Elevator Company for $112 million. Two years later the company sold its CommAir Mechanical Services unit to Carrier Corp.

In 2005 ABM sold the last of its mechanical operations divesting its water treatment business to San Joaquin Chemicals. ABM made one of the biggest deals in its history in 2007 when it obtained rival facility services company OneSource Services paying about $390 million. The operations of OneSource including more than 10000 commercial accounts in the US Canada and Puerto Rico were integrated into those of ABM Janitorial throughout 2008.

In order to focus on its core operations in late 2008 the company sold the operating assets of its Amtech Lighting Services business to a unit of OSRAM SYLVANIA for about $34 million. ABM acquired several companies in 2009 and 2010 including Diversco and The Linc Group. It also snatched up several cleaning and engineering businesses — Control Building Services Control Engineering Services and TTF Assets — located primarily in New Jersey and New York. Collectively these businesses generate annual revenues of about $50 million and cater to the commercial institutional and pharmaceutical industries.

EXECUTIVES

President And Ceo, Scott Salmirs, age 56, $793,333 total compensation

Evp And Cfo, D. Anthony Scaglione, age 45, $466,666 total compensation

Evp And President Business And Industry, Rene Jacobsen

Evp And Coo, Scott Giacobbe, age 55

Vice President Safety, Duong HO

Vice President Operations And Strategic Accounts Abm Healthcare, Michael Tolliver

Executive Vice President And President Aviation Group, Tom Marano

Chairman, Sudhakar Kesavan, age 64

Auditors: KPMG LLP

LOCATIONS

HQ: ABM Industries, Inc.
One Liberty Plaza, 7th Floor, New York, NY 10006
Phone: 212 297-0200
Web: www.abm.com

2016 Sales

	$ mil.	% of total
United States	4,845	94
All other countries	299	6
Total	**5,144**	**100**

PRODUCTS/OPERATIONS

2016 Sales

	$ mil.	% of total
Janitorial	2,768	54
Parking	666	13
Facility Services	597	12
Building & Energy Solutions	643	12
Other	469	9
Total	**5,144**	**100**

Selected Services

Electrical & lighting
Energy
Engineering
Facility services
HVAC & mechanical
Janitorial
Landscape & golf
Maintenance & repair
Parking & transportation
Security

COMPETITORS

ARAMARK	Menzies Aviation
AlliedBarton Security	Mercury Air Group
Comfort Systems USA	PrimeFlight
EMCOR	SP Plus
Guardsmark	ServiceMaster
Healthcare Services	Siemens AG
IAP Worldwide Services	Sodexo USA
ICTS International	Temco Service
ISS A/S	Industries
Impark	

HISTORICAL FINANCIALS

Company Type: Public

Income Statement

FYE: October 31

	REVENUE ($ mil.)	NET INCOME ($ mil.)	NET PROFIT MARGIN	EMPLOYEES
10/18	6,442	97	1.5%	140,000
10/17	5,453	3	0.1%	140,000
10/16	5,144	57	1.1%	110,000
10/15	4,897	76	1.6%	120,000
10/14	5,032	75	1.5%	118,000
Annual Growth	**6.4%**	**6.6%**	**—**	**4.4%**

2018 Year-End Financials

Debt ratio: 25.89%
Return on equity: 6.91%
Cash ($ mil.): 39
Current ratio: 1.48
Long-term debt ($ mil.): 902

No. of shares (mil.): 66
Dividends
  Yield: 2.2%
  Payout: 47.6%
Market value ($ mil.): 2,030

	STOCK PRICE ($) FY Close	P/E High/Low	PER SHARE ($) Earnings	Dividends	Book Value
10/18	30.75	30 19	1.47	0.70	22.04
10/17	41.97	640 546	0.07	0.68	21.00
10/16	39.08	40 26	1.01	0.66	17.52
10/15	28.40	25 20	1.33	0.64	17.96
10/14	27.64	22 18	1.32	0.62	17.40
Annual Growth	**2.7%**	**—**	**2.7%**	**3.1%**	**6.1%**

ACCESSLEX INSTITUTE

EXECUTIVES

Ceo, Christopher P Chapman
Chb, Hannah R Arterian
Coo, Charles Albano
Human Resources Manager, Tanya Papahristos
Marketing Staff, Krysten Levin
Vice President of Legal Affair, Debbie Swartz
Auditors: GRANT THORNTON LLP PHILADELPH

LOCATIONS

HQ: ACCESSLEX INSTITUTE
10 N HIGH ST STE 400, WEST CHESTER, PA
193803014
Phone: 484 653-3300
Web: WWW.ACCESSGROUP.ORG

COMPETITORS

Bank of America	First Marblehead
College Loan	JPMorgan Chase
Corporation	Nelnet
Discover	Sallie Mae

HISTORICAL FINANCIALS

Company Type: Private

Income Statement

FYE: March 31

	ASSETS ($ mil.)	NET INCOME ($ mil.)	INCOME AS % OF ASSETS	EMPLOYEES
03/17	4,584	91	2.0%	60
03/16	5,056	16	0.3%	—
03/11	8,767	58	0.7%	—
03/10	10,316	(0)	—	—
Annual Growth	**(10.9%)**	**—**	**—**	**—**

2017 Year-End Financials

Debt ratio: —
Return on equity: 150.00%
Cash ($ mil.): 5
Current ratio: —
Long-term debt ($ mil.): —

Dividends
  Yield: —
  Payout: —
Market value ($ mil.): —

ACE HARDWARE CORPORATION

In an age of big-box home improvement centers (Home Depot Lowes) wholesaler Ace makes the case for the local hardware store. By sales it is the #1 hardware cooperative in the US ahead of Do It Best. Ace dealer-owners operate more than 95% of the 4800 Ace Hardware-branded stores home centers and lumber and building materials locations selling more than 75000 products across all 50 US states and about 70 other countries. Stores range in size from small urban shops to large rural locations. From about 15 warehouses Ace distributes such products as electrical and plumbing supplies garden equipment hand tools housewares and power tools. Ace was founded in 1924 by a group of Chicago hardware store owners.

HISTORY

A group of Chicago-area hardware dealers — William Stauber Richard Hesse Gern Lindquist and Oscar Fisher — decided in 1924 to pool their hardware buying and promotional costs. In 1928 the group incorporated as Ace Stores named in honor of the superior WWI fliers dubbed aces. Hesse became president the following year retaining that position for the next 44 years. The company also opened its first warehouse in 1929 and by 1933 it had 38 dealers.

The organization had 133 dealers in seven states by 1949. In 1953 Ace began to allow dealers to buy stock in the company through the Ace Perpetuation Plan. During the 1960s Ace expanded into the South and West and by 1969 it had opened distribution centers in Georgia and California — its first such facilities outside Chicago. In 1968 it opened its first international store in Guam.

By the early 1970s the do-it-yourself market began to surge as inflation pushed up plumber and electrician fees. As the market grew large home center chains gobbled up market share from independent dealers such as those franchised through Ace. In response Ace and its dealers became a part of a growing trend in the hardware industry — cooperatives.

Hesse sold the company to its dealers in 1973 for $6 million (less than half its book value) and the following year Ace began operating as a cooperative. Hesse stepped down in 1973. In 1976 the dealers took full control when the company's first Board of Dealer-Directors was elected.

After signing up a number of dealers in the eastern US Ace had dealers in all 50 states by 1979. The co-op opened a plant to make paint in Matteson Illinois in 1984. By 1985 Ace had reached $1 billion in sales and had initiated its Store of the Future Program allowing dealers to borrow up to $200000 to upgrade their stores and conduct market analyses. Former head coach John Madden of the National Football League's Oakland Raiders signed on as Ace's mouthpiece in 1988.

A year later the co-op began to test ACENET a computer network that allowed Ace dealers to check inventory send and receive e-mail make special purchase requests and keep up with prices on commodity items such as lumber. In 1990 Ace established an International Division to handle its overseas stores. (It had been exporting products since 1975.) EVP and COO David Hodnik became president in 1995. That year the co-op added a net of 67 stores including a three-store chain in Russia. Expanding further internationally Ace signed a five-year joint-supply agreement in 1996 with Canadian lumber and hardware retailer Beaver Lumber. Hodnik added CEO to his title in 1996.

Ace fell further behind its old rival True Value in 1997 when ServiStar Coast to Coast and True Value merged to form TruServ (renamed True Value in 2005) a hardware giant that operated more than 10000 outlets at the completion of the merger.

Late in 1997 Ace launched an expansion program in Canada. (The co-op already operated distribution centers in Ontario and Calgary.) In 1999 Ace merged its lumber and building materials division with Builder Marts of America to form a dealer-owned buying group to supply about 2700 retailers. Ace gained 208 member outlet stores in 2000 but saw 279 member outlets terminated. The next year it gained 220 but lost 255.

Sodisco-Howden bought all the shares of Ace Hardware Canada in February 2003. To better serve international members Ace opened its first international buying office in Hong Kong in April 2004.

In all the company added 131 new stores in 2005. That year after 33 years with the company David F. Hodnik retired as president and CEO of Ace Hardware. He was succeeded by COO Ray A. Griffith.

In 2007 Griffith sent a letter to Ace's retailers saying the company was considering changing from a cooperative to a traditional corporation to become more competitive and to better fuel growth. Shortly after the company announced an accounting shortfall of about $150 million or nearly half of its equity which was uncovered while Ace prepared to convert formats. The error turned out to be an accident by a mid-level employee.

In 2009 Ace launched Aisle411 a free product-location service that can be accessed via phone similar to dialing for information. The company launched the service after learning that shoppers who were unable to find a product either left (about 20% of the time) or asked store associates for assistance (about 60%) which created a high demand for staff attention. Dedicated to pleasing its shoppers Ace was ranked "Highest in Customer Satisfaction among Home Improvement Stores" by J.D. Power and Associates in 2007 2008 and 2009.

In mid-2010 the hardware store chain became the first retailer — outside of Sears and Kmart stores — to sell Craftsman brand tools.

In January 2011 the company reorganized its international division into a stand-alone entity: Ace Hardware International Holdings. Ace Hardware owns about 78% of the newly-created entity.

In December 2012 Ace exited the paint manufacturing business with the sale of its paint manufacturing division including two paint manufacturing plants near Chicago to Valspar Corp. for about $45 million. Under the terms of the sale Valspar will continue to make and supply Ace-branded paint under a long-term supply agreement. Also it will supply a comprehensive line of Valspar-branded paints to Ace retail stores.

EXECUTIVES

President And Ceo, John S. Venhuizen, age 48
Vp Information Technology And Cio, Karen Fedyszyn
Evp Cfo And Chief Risk Officer, Bill Guzik
Chairman, Jim Ackroyd
Auditors: ERNST & YOUNG LLP CHICAGO IL

LOCATIONS

HQ: ACE HARDWARE CORPORATION
2200 KENSINGTON CT, OAK BROOK, IL 605232100
Phone: 866 681-1836
Web: WWW.ACEHARDWAREINTL.COM

PRODUCTS/OPERATIONS

2014 Sales

	$ mil.	% of total
Wholesale Revenues	4,466	95
Retail Revenues	233	5
Total	**4,700**	**100**

Selected Services

Assembly
Automotive chip key cutting
Blade sharpening
Glass & Acrylic sheet cutting
Glass Repair
Hunting/Fishing license
In-store lock servicing
Selected Brands
ACCO BRANDS
ACE
ACME
ADANAC
BIG BEN

BILCO
EUREKA
EVEREADY
Selected ProductsAdhesives

COMPETITORS

84 Lumber	McCoy Corp.
Akzo Nobel	Menard
BMC Stock	Northern Tool
Costco Wholesale	Orgill
Do it Best	Sears
Fastenal	Sutherland Lumber
Grossman's	True Value
Home Depot	United Hardware
Kmart	Distributing
Lowe's	Wal-Mart

HISTORICAL FINANCIALS
Company Type: Private

Income Statement
FYE: December 30

	REVENUE ($ mil.)	NET INCOME ($ mil.)	NET PROFIT MARGIN	EMPLOYEES
12/17	5,388	147	2.7%	4,500
12/16*	5,125	161	3.1%	—
01/16	5,045	156	3.1%	—
01/15	4,700	141	3.0%	—
Annual Growth	**4.7%**	**1.4%**		**—**

*Fiscal year change

2017 Year-End Financials

Debt ratio: —
Return on equity: 2.70%
Cash ($ mil.): 23
Current ratio: 0.50
Long-term debt ($ mil.): —

Dividends
Yield: —
Payout: —
Market value ($ mil.): —

ACNB Corp

EXECUTIVES

Assistant Vice President Adams County National Bank, Kim Elmo
Vice President, Dennis Hollinger
Executive Vice President And Chief Lending And Revenue Officer Of Acnb Bank, Douglas Seibel
Board Member, Thomas Ritter
Chief Governance Officer Secretary And Executive Vice President Of The Corporation And The Bank, Lynda Glass
Auditors: RSM US LLP

LOCATIONS

HQ: ACNB Corp
16 Lincoln Square, Gettysburg, PA 17325
Phone: 717 334-3161
Web: www.acnb.com

COMPETITORS

First Commonwealth Financial	PNC Financial
	Univest
Fulton Financial	Wells Fargo
M&T Bank	

HISTORICAL FINANCIALS
Company Type: Public

Income Statement
FYE: December 31

	ASSETS ($ mil.)	NET INCOME ($ mil.)	INCOME AS % OF ASSETS	EMPLOYEES
12/17	1,595	9	0.6%	358
12/16	1,206	10	0.9%	303
12/15	1,147	11	1.0%	296
12/14	1,089	10	0.9%	297
12/13	1,046	9	0.9%	290
Annual Growth	**11.1%**	**1.2%**	**—**	**5.4%**

2017 Year-End Financials

Debt ratio: 0.60%
Return on equity: 7.14%
Cash ($ mil.): 34
Current ratio: —
Long-term debt ($ mil.): —

No. of shares (mil.): 7
Dividends
Yield: 0.0%
Payout: 53.3%
Market value ($ mil.): 208

	STOCK PRICE ($) FY Close	P/E High/Low		PER SHARE ($) Earnings	Dividends	Book Value
12/17	29.55	21	17	1.50	0.80	21.92
12/16	31.25	18	12	1.80	0.80	19.80
12/15	21.30	12	11	1.83	0.80	18.99
12/14	21.75	13	11	1.71	0.77	18.29
12/13	18.06	12	10	1.56	0.76	17.83
Annual Growth	**13.1%**	**—**	**—**	**(1.0%)**	**1.3%**	**5.3%**

Activision Blizzard, Inc.

Activision Blizzard answers the Call of Duty to make video games that millions of users play for billions of hours. The company is the biggest producer of video games including some of the most durable franchises: World of Warcraft Guitar Hero Candy Crush and of course Call of Duty. Newer blockbuster titles are Overwatch and Skylanders. Users play Activision Blizzard?s games on PCs game consoles and mobile devices. The company also creates games based on licensed properties from Marvel DreamWorks Animation and EON Production. Activision Blizzard is expanding its theater of operations to games products and service for TV movies toys and a professional esports league.

Operations

Activision Blizzard operates in three segments: Activision Blizzard and King.

Activision which accounts for about a third of revenue produces the company?s signature Call of Duty franchise a first-person shooter game for console and PCs; Destiny an online shared-world shooter game for console; and Skylanders a children?s-oriented game primarily for consoles. The segment has more than 55 million monthly active users.

Blizzard about 40% of revenue produces another high-profile game World of Warcraft a subscription-based massive multi-player online role-playing game (MMORPG) for the PC as well as StarCraft a real-time strategy game for the PC and Overwatch a team-based first-person shooter game PC and console platforms. Blizzard?s monthly active user count is about 40 million

King more than a quarter of revenue develops PC and mobile games that include Candy Crush Farm Heroes Pet Rescue and Bubble Witch. The segment rules the company?s roost for monthly active users with 300 million.

Activision Blizzard is showing decreasing dependence on it top franchise games. The top four games Call of Duty Candy Crush World of Warcraft and Overwatch account for two-thirds of revenue down from about three-quarters of revenue a couple of years ago.

The company?s other operations are Major League Gaming the company?s esports business; Activision Blizzard Studios which develops film and TV programming based on the company?s games; Activision Blizzard Distribution which are operations in Europe that provide warehousing logistics and sales distribution services.

Geographic Reach

Activision Blizzard gets more than half of its revenue from the Americas about a third from Europe and the rest from the Asia/Pacific region. The company has about 100 offices in some 20 countries around the world. Overall the company has players in about every country and it notes that Candy Crush is played on all continents including Antarctica.

Sales and Marketing

Activision Blizzard markets its games on multiple platforms including social media such as Facebook Twitter and YouTube online advertising print and broadcast advertising direct response and product sampling. The company delivers content through retail channels or digital downloads including subscriptions full-game sales and in-game purchases as well as licenses of software to third-party or related-party companies that distribute Blizzard products.

The company?s major customers are Apple more than 15% if revenue Sony about 15% and Google about 10%.

Financial Performance

Activision Blizzard?s revenue has risen for the past three years with help from the King Digital Media acquisition. Sales jumped more than 40% in 2016 immediately following the deal and increased another 7% to $7 billion in 2017 from 2016.

The King assets continued to fuel growth in 2017 which included higher revenue from the Candy Crush franchise due to in-game events and features. Activision Blizzard also scored with the continued strength of Call of Duty: Black Ops III the downloadable content pack Zombies Chronicles released in 2017 and the continued strength of microtransactions. Sales of Call of Duty: WWII added revenue toward the end of the year following its November release. The Asia/Pacific region?s sales slowed in 2017 because of lower revenue from Overwatch and Hearthstone that weren?t quite offset by higher revenue from King titles and Crash Bandicoot N. Sane Trilogy.

The company?s 2017 profit nosedived about 70% to $273 million from $966 million in 2016. The US tax reform law enacted late in 2017 grabbed about $880 million due to fund brought back to the US from foreign sales.

Activision Blizzard held about $4.7 billion in cash at the end of 2017 up from about $3.2 billion the year before.

Strategy

Part of Activision Blizzard's strategy is the same as it ever was: Develop blockbuster games and issue sequels that people play for hours and hours. The Call of Duty and World of Warcraft franchises have produced steady streams of income for the company. The acquisition of King Digital has already proved lucrative with the King games providing billions of dollars of in-game sales to Activision Blizzard. The acquisition also significantly increased the company's presence on mobile devices and social media platforms. The added revenue also put Activision Blizzard on the Fortune 500 at No. 406.

Games produce a lot of revenue but Activision Blizzard sees opportunities for more sales in game-related ventures. The company's biggest move comes in esports where users play each other while spectators watch. Activision Blizzard organizes and broadcasts tournaments for players of Call of Duty Hearthstone StarCraft and Heroes of the Storm. In order to show these games the company bought Major League Gaming (MLG) a team-based esports venture in 2015.

Activision Blizzard is going a step further and organizing a league for its Overwatch game one of the company?s fastest growing properties. It reached 30 million players and $1 billion in revenue within a year of its release. The league is one of several emerging organizations based on video games as a spectator sport. The Overwatch league has attracted high-profile investors such as Robert Kraft owner of the New England Patriots who has put money into the Boston franchise. Activision Blizzard has ambitions to create professional a esports league that rivals the NFL and professional sports leagues.

In other beyond-game activity a movie based on Call of Duty is due out by 2018. On the small screen ABC viewers could watch live-action Candy Crush competition in the summer of 2017 and Skylandershas spawned an animated series on Netflix and a line of toys.

In another revenue-producing initiative Activision Blizzard is proceeding with selling advertising within the King digital games. After testing the concept in 2016 the company reported that users play more rounds of a game spend more time in the game and report a better game experience with advertising. Early advertisers have included Nestle Visa and Fox Entertainment.

Mergers and Acquisitions

With its $5.9 billion purchase of King Digital Entertainment Activision Blizzard is putting its money where people play games: on mobile devices. King developed the popular Candy Crush game but other efforts such as Farm Heroes and Pet Rescue haven't been as successful. Mobile games are growing faster than console or PC-based games and some such as Candy Crush reach a female demographic. Competitors in the mobile game arena include Zynga maker of Farmville and Rovio the creator of Angry Birds.

EXECUTIVES

Ceo, Robert A. (Bobby) Kotick, age 55, $2,375,858 total compensation
Cfo, Spencer Neumann, age 48
Ceo Activision, Eric Hirshberg, age 50, $961,677 total compensation
President And Ceo Blizzard Entertainment, Michael (Mike) Morhaime, age 50, $957,378 total compensation
President And Ceo Consumer Products Division, Timothy J. (Tim) Kilpin, age 58
Chief Customer Officer, Brian Hodous, age 54, $533,365 total compensation
Chief Corporate Officer, Dennis Durkin, age 47, $787,185 total compensation
Ceo King Digital Entertainment, Riccardo Zacconi, age 49, $415,928 total compensation
President And Ceo Major League Gaming (mlg), Pete Vlastelica
President And Coo, Collister (Coddy) Johnson, age 41
Vice President, Linda Howard
Vp Infrastructure And Operations, Todd Szalla
Vice President Global Facilities And Real Estate, Mark Fuller
Vice President Infrastructure And Operations, Pmp Archer
Vice President Corporate Financial Planning And Analysis, Marcus Sanford

Vice President Of Marketing, Laura Lombardi
Vice President Of Marketing, Byron Beede
Svp Global Communications, Mary Osako
Vice President Global Consumer Marketing, Ian Trombetta
Executive Vice President And Managing Director As, Phillip Earl
Vice President Of International Consumer Products, Philippe Bost
Chairman, Brian G. Kelly, age 55
Vice Chairman, Thomas Tippl, age 52
Board Member, Barry Meyer
Board Member, Elaine Wynn
Board Member, Hendrik Hartong
Auditors: PricewaterhouseCoopers LLP

LOCATIONS

HQ: Activision Blizzard, Inc.
  3100 Ocean Park Boulevard, Santa Monica, CA 90405
Phone: 310 255-2000
Web: www.activisionblizzard.com

2017 Sales

	$ mil.	% of total
Americas	3,607	51
Europe Middle East and Africa	2,464	35
Asia Pacific	964	14
Total	**7,017**	**100**

PRODUCTS/OPERATIONS

2017 Sales

	$ mil.	% of total
Blizzard	2,628	37
Activision	2,139	30
King	1,998	28
Other segments	410	5
Net effect from recognition (deferral) of deferred net revenues and related cost of revenues	(139)	-
Elimination	(19)	-
Total	**7,017**	**100**

2017 Sales

	$ mil.	% of total
Console	2,389	34
Mobile and ancillary	2,081	30
PC	2,042	29
Other	505	7
Total	**7,017**	**100**

2017 Sales

	$ mil.	% of total
Subscription licensing and other revenues	4,907	70
Product sales	21,110	30
Total	**7,017**	**100**

COMPETITORS

Capcom	SEGA
Disney Interactive Studios	Sony
Electronic Arts	Square Enix
Konami	Take-Two
Lucasfilm Entertainment	Tencent Holdings
Microsoft	Turbine Inc.
Namco Limited	Ubisoft
Nintendo	Valve Corporation
Rovio Entertainment	ZeniMax Media
	Zynga

HISTORICAL FINANCIALS

Company Type: Public

Income Statement
FYE: December 31

	REVENUE ($ mil.)	NET INCOME ($ mil.)	NET PROFIT MARGIN	EMPLOYEES
12/17	7,017	273	3.9%	9,800
12/16	6,608	966	14.6%	9,600
12/15	4,664	892	19.1%	7,300
12/14	4,408	835	18.9%	6,800
12/13	4,583	1,010	22.0%	6,900
Annual Growth	11.2%	(27.9%)	—	9.2%

2017 Year-End Financials

Debt ratio: 23.52%
Return on equity: 2.94%
Cash ($ mil.): 4,713
Current ratio: 1.78
Long-term debt ($ mil.): 4,390

No. of shares (mil.): 757
Dividends
Yield: 0.0%
Payout: 83.3%
Market value ($ mil.): 47,965

	STOCK PRICE ($) FY Close	P/E High/Low	PER SHARE ($) Earnings	Dividends	Book Value
12/17	63.32	185 102	0.36	0.30	12.49
12/16	36.11	35 22	1.28	0.26	12.23
12/15	38.71	33 15	1.19	0.23	10.98
12/14	20.15	21 15	1.13	0.20	10.02
12/13	17.83	19 11	0.95	0.19	9.41
Annual Growth	37.3%	— —	(21.5%)	12.1%	7.3%

Adobe Inc

Adobe Systems is the house that desktop publishing software built and now it helps customers create distribute and manage digital content from the cloud. One of the top publishing software providers it has been known for brands such as Acrobat Photoshop Flash and Dreamweaver. Adobe serves customers such as content creators and web application developers with its digital media products and marketers advertisers publishers and others with its digital marketing business. A long-time publisher of traditional software packages Adobe is moving its products to cloud-based versions. Subscriptions account for about 80% of revenue. In 2018 Adobe bought Marketo a marketing-automation company for $4.75 billion.

Operations

Adobe's Digital Media segment (about 70% of revenue) includes products such as Flash Photoshop and Illustrator. Its Digital Marketing segment (30% of revenue) includes a host of tools for creating managing and measuring digital advertising and marketing initiatives. Digital Marketing became Digital Experience in 2018. The Print and Publishing unit (less than 5% of revenue) includes authoring and publishing software and tools.

Geographic Reach

The US is Adobe's largest market representing more than 50% of revenue; other North American countries contribute about 5%. The EMEA (Europe Middle East and Africa) region generates nearly 30% of revenue and the Asia-Pacific region led by Japan contributes about 15%.

Headquartered in San Jose California Adobe has field offices in about 35 countries across the Americas Asia and Europe.

Sales and Marketing

Adobe sells directly and through distributors resellers systems integrators and retailers. In addition it licenses its technology to hardware manufacturers for integration into their products.

Financial Performance

Adobe Systems has posted steadily increasing revenue and profit in recent years propelled by the digital offerings.

Revenue jumped 25% to $7.3 billion in 2017 on higher sales in Digital Media driven by demand for its creative offerings (up about 30%) and in Digital Experience fueled by a 25% increase in Adobe Marketing Cloud revenue from rising adoption of Adobe Experience Manager.

An 33% increase in subscription revenue across Adobe?s offerings lifted net income to about $1.7 billion in 2017 a 45% rise from 2016.

Cash on hand rose to $2.3 billion in 2017 from about $1 billion in 2016 .

Strategy

Adobe Systems? charge into the cloud and a subscription-based business model has paid off for the company. It has reported rising revenue and net income for the past three years and driven its profit margin to about 23% in 2017 from about 6% in 2014.

Just about every product in Adobe?s stock has the word cloud in it. The company has added digital marketing applications and services to its digital media offerings which has raised subscriptions to account for about 85% of revenue from about 75% of revenue in 2016. Its applications also are made to use and view on mobile devices.

The Adobe Experience Manager (AEM) product which helps customers organize create and manage the delivery of creative assets and other content across digital marketing channels has been a hit with customers according to the company. Increasing adoption of AEM was one of the drivers of the company?s 2017 revenue increase.

Mergers and Acquisitions

In 2019 Adobe Systems bought Allegorithmic the maker of Substance a tool for creating 3D textures and materials in game and video post-production. Adobe intends to combine Allegorithmic's Substance 3D design tools with Creative Cloud's imaging video and motion graphics tools for video game creators visual effects artists in film and television designers and marketers.

Adobe Systems acquired Marketo for $4.75 billion in 2018 in Adobe's biggest acquisition. The deal bolstered Adobe's marketing offerings with Marketo's business-to-business marketing platform combining Adobe's Experience Cloud analytics content personalization advertising and commerce capabilities with Marketo's lead management and account-based marketing technology. Marketo had been bought out by Vista Equity Partners in 2016 for $1.8 billion after about three years as a public company.

Earlier in 2018 Adobe Systems agreed to buy Magento Commerce for $1.7 billion in an attempt to move into ecommerce. Magento's customers use its technology to operate their online stores. Adobe intends to cross-sell its digital marketing products to Magento customers. The companies have some customers in common such as Coca-Cola Warner Music Group Nestlé and Cathay Pacific. Customers that Magento brings to the table include Canon Helly Hansen Paul Smith and Rosetta Stone. The deal is expected to close in the 2018 third quarter.

In 2017 Adobe Systems bought the SkyBox technology assets from Mettle a developer 360-degree and virtual reality software. The Skybox tools are designed for post-production in Adobe Premiere Pro CC and Adobe After Effects CC and complement Adobe Creative Cloud's 360/VR cinematic production technology. Adobe integrated SkyBox plugin functionality into subsequent releases of Premiere Pro and After Effects.

In 2016 Adobe bought TubeMogul for $540 million. With TubeMogul on board Adobe could offer more video marketing options to its customers.

In May 2016 Adobe acquired Livefyre a privately-held content curation and audience engagement company. Livefyre will be part of Adobe Experience Manager and integrated across Adobe Marketing Cloud to make user-generated content available across all digital marketing solutions.

To further expand its product offerings in 2014 Adobe purchased the privately-held stock-photography website company Fotolia for roughly $800 million. The acquisition will allow Adobe to obtain a market exchange with over 34 million stock images and videos and sell them to its Creative Cloud customers on one cloud-based software platform.

HISTORY

When Charles Geschke hired John Warnock as chief scientist for Xerox's new graphics and imaging lab he set the stage for one of the world's largest software makers. While at the Xerox lab the pair developed the PostScript computer language which tells printers how to reproduce digitized images on paper. When Xerox refused to market it the duo left that company and started Adobe (named after a creek near their homes in San Jose California) in 1982.

EXECUTIVES

Evp And General Manager Digital Media, Bryan Lamkin, age 57, $568,590 total compensation
Evp And Chief Marketing Officer, Ann Lewnes, age 56
Evp General Counsel And Corporate Secretary, Michael A. (Mike) Dillon, age 59
Evp And Cfo, Mark S. Garrett, age 60, $698,977 total compensation
Chairman President And Ceo, Shantanu Narayen, age 54, $1,010,260 total compensation
Evp Customer And Employee Experience, Donna Morris, age 50
Evp Worldwide Field Operations, Matthew A. (Matt) Thompson, age 60, $673,720 total compensation
Evp And General Manager Digital Marketing, Bradley (Brad) Rencher, age 44, $573,514 total compensation
Evp And Cto, Abhay Parasnis, age 43, $183,583 total compensation
Vice President Licensing And Associate General Counsel, Joe Ramirez
Senior Vice President Worldwide Sales And Field Operations, Matt Thompson
Vice President Customer Care, Lambert Walsh
Vice President Product Management, Bill Ingram
Auditors: KPMG LLP

LOCATIONS

HQ: Adobe Inc
345 Park Avenue, San Jose, CA 95110-2704
Phone: 408 536-6000
Web: www.adobe.com

2016 Sales

	$ mil.	% of total
Americas:		
United States	3,087	53
Other	312	5
Europe Middle East & Africa	1,619	28
APAC:		
Japan	401	7
Other	433	7
Total	**5,854**	**100**

PRODUCTS/OPERATIONS

2017 Sales

By Segment	$ mil.	% of total
Digital Media	5,010	69
Digital Marketing	2,120	29
Print and Publishing	170	2
Total	**7,301**	**100**

2017 Sales

	$ mil.	% of total
Subscription	6,133	84
Product	706	10
Services and support	460	6
Total	**7,301**	**100**

ProductsCreativity and Design
Creative Cloud
Photoshop
Lightroom
Dreamweaver
InDesign
Illustrator (graphic artwork creation)
Adobe XD
Adobe Premiere Pro
After Effects
Dimension
Acrobat Pro
Adobe Muse
Animate
Adobe Audition
Bridge
Media Encoder
InCopy
Prelude
Fuse
Marketing and Analytics
Analytics
Audience Manager
Campaign
Experience Manager
Media Optimizer
Target
PDF and E-Signature
Acrobat DC
Acrobat Standard DC
Adobe DC for teams
Adobe DC for enterprise

COMPETITORS

ACD Systems	Microsoft
Apple Inc.	Monotype
ArcSoft	Nexaweb
Autodesk	Nikon
Avid Technology	Nuance Communications
Bare Bones Software	Oracle
Box Inc.	Pegasystems
Canon	Quark
Citrix Systems	RealNetworks
Corel	Rovi
Coremetrics	SAS Institute
Dell	Shutterstock
Eastman Kodak	Sony
Eloqua	TIBCO Software
Facebook	Teradata
Getty Images	Ultimus
Google	Webtrends
HP	Xara
IBM	Yahoo!
Marketo	Zinio Systems

HISTORICAL FINANCIALS

Company Type: Public

Income Statement   FYE: November 30

	REVENUE ($ mil.)	NET INCOME ($ mil.)	NET PROFIT MARGIN	EMPLOYEES
11/18*	9,030	2,590	28.7%	21,357
12/17	7,301	1,693	23.2%	17,973
12/16	5,854	1,168	20.0%	15,706
11/15	4,795	629	13.1%	13,893
11/14	4,147	268	6.5%	12,499
Annual Growth	**21.5%**	**76.3%**	—	**14.3%**

*Fiscal year change

2018 Year-End Financials

Debt ratio: 21.98%
Return on equity: 29.15%
Cash ($ mil.): 1,642
Current ratio: 1.13
Long-term debt ($ mil.): 4,124

No. of shares (mil.): 487
Dividends
Yield: —
Payout: —
Market value ($ mil.): 122,350

	STOCK PRICE ($) FY Close	P/E High/Low	PER SHARE ($) Earnings	Dividends	Book Value
11/18*	250.89	52 32	5.20	0.00	19.20
12/17	179.52	54 30	3.38	0.00	17.22
12/16	99.73	47 31	2.32	0.00	15.02
11/15	92.17	73 55	1.24	0.00	14.06
11/14	73.68	— —	0.53	0.00	13.62
Annual Growth	**35.8%**	— —	**77.0%**	—	**9.0%**

*Fiscal year change

Advance Auto Parts Inc

Advance Auto Parts (AAP) has taken the lead in the race to become the #1 provider of automotive aftermarket parts in North America. Serving both the do-it-yourself (DIY) and professional installer markets AAP operates nearly 5200 stores under the Advance Auto Parts Autopart International (AI) Carquest and Worldpac banners in the US and Canada. Its stores carry brand-name and private-label replacement parts batteries maintenance items and automotive chemicals for individual car and truck owners. AAP's Carquest AI and Worldpac stores cater to commercial customers including garages service stations and auto dealers.

Operations

Parts and batteries account for about 65% of Advance Auto Parts' total product sales; the rest comes from accessories and chemicals (about 20%) engine maintenance (nearly 15%) and other products. It carries a wide range of national and private label brands including Bosch Castrol Moog and Prestone as well as Autocraft Tough One Wearever and Carquest.

The company's namesake banner is the largest and includes about 4400 stores that serve both the professional and DIY markets with some 22000 aftermarket auto parts. Carquest which has nearly 450 locations focuses more heavily on the professional market and also serves about 1200 independently owned stores that operate under the Carquest name. The Autopart International and Worldpac banners (with nearly 190 stores and about 130 stores respectively) target the professional market offering imported aftermarket and OEM products and private-label parts.

Geographic Reach

Roanoke Virginia-based Advance Auto Parts has stores across the US as well as Puerto Rico the US Virgin Islands and Canada. Florida is the company's largest market with nearly 540 stores. North Carolina New York Ohio Texas Pennsylvania and Georgia are also major markets for Advance Auto Parts each home to more than 250 stores.

The company has store support centers in Newark California; Raleigh North Carolina; and Roanoke Virginia. It has distribution centers in some 35 US states and about 5 Canadian provinces.

Sales and Marketing

Advance Auto Parts serves professional customers (garages service stations auto dealers) as well as DIY consumers. The professional market accounts for about 60% of total sales.

The company builds its marketing and advertising campaigns around radio television direct marketing mobile and social media and local in-store marketing. It is focused on creating an omnichannel experience where customers can buy online and pick up in stores. In addition its "Speed Perks" customer loyalty campaign targets core DIY customers and emphasizes service. Advance Auto Parts spends about $100 million on advertising.

Financial Performance

Since hitting nearly $10 billion in 2014 following the purchase of General Parts International Advance Auto Parts' revenue has declined slowly but steadily. Net income has been a little more sporadic see-sawing between $400 million and $500 million over the past five years.

In 2017 the company reported revenue of $9.4 billion down 5% from the prior year. It operated fewer stores in 2017 and also saw same-store sales decline by 2% driven by a decrease in overall transactions.

Net income however rose to $476 million that year up 3% from 2016. The result is primarily because of a much smaller provision for income taxes in 2017 as a result of the new US Tax Cuts and Jobs Act.

Cash at the end of 2017 was nearly $550 million an increase of $410 million from the prior year. Cash from operations contributed $600 million to the coffers while investing activities used nearly $180 million mainly for capital expenditures. Financing activities used another $15 million for dividends to stockholders and a stock repurchase program.

Strategy

In 2017 Advance Auto Parts announced a five-year plan to improve the customer experience and drive consistent results in both the professional and DIY spaces. A significant part of this initiative involves investing in technology.

The company is focused on creating a common product catalog visible to customers and team members across all its brands and using data from that catalog (lookups purchase history) to evolve from a supply-driven to a demand-driven inventory. A related project is the optimization and streamlining of Advance Auto Parts' end-to-end supply chain.

With Amazon encroaching on many industries including auto parts retail enhancing its omnichannel capabilities is also a major component of the company's strategy. It launched a faster website in mid-2017 that also offers an expanded product portfolio for online shoppers. In addition Advance Auto Parts introduced AdvancePro an e-commerce platform for professional customers that provides full access to the common product catalog and announced plans for a mobile app.

Other recent moves include expanded use of telematics for fleet management and tracking and a partnership with Interstate Batteries through which Advance Auto Parts and Carquest stores will be the only US locations to carry a complete range of Interstate Batteries in store and online.

Company Background

Founded as Advance Stores Company in 1929 AAP was a general merchandise retailer until the '80s. From there the company shifted its focus to automotive parts retailing targeting DIY customers.

In 2014 AAP acquired General Parts International (GPI) for about $2.1 billion — creating the largest automotive aftermarket parts provider in North America with $9 billion-plus in annual sales. GPI a privately-held distributor and supplier of original equipment and aftermarket replacement parts to commercial markets owned the CARQUEST and WORLDPAC brands. The deal added

1233 Carquest stores 103 Worldpac branches in 45 states and Canada and the business of nearly 1400 independently-owned Carquest stores to AAP's network.

EXECUTIVES

President And Ceo, Thomas R. (Tom) Greco, age 59, $803,852 total compensation

Svp E-commerce, Scott Bauhofer

President Â– Northern Division, Maria Ayres

President Southern Division, David McCartney

President Western Division, Mike Pack

President Autopart International, Michael Creedon

President Worldpac, Robert B. (Bob) Cushing, age 64, $453,910 total compensation

President Carquest Canada, Steve Gushie

Evp General Counsel And Secretary, Tammy M. Finley, age 51, $400,005 total compensation

Svp And Cio, James A. (Andy) Paisley

Svp And Chief Marketing Officer, Walter Scott

Evp And Cfo, Thomas B. (Tom) Okray, age 55, $86,540 total compensation

Svp Supply Chain, Todd Greener

Evp Supply Chain Strategy And Transformation, Leslie Keating

Svp Professional Business, Al Wheeler

Assistant Vice President Strategic Store Systems, Craig Anderman

Senior Vice President Sales, Troy Downing

Vp Retail Human Resources, Brian Leavens

Regional Vice President, Scott Kear

National Sales Manager, Chad Schnitz

Regional Vice President, Ernesto Valderrama

Vice President, Warren Shatzer

Vice President Professional And Product Marketing, Lauren Beaulieu

Vice President Of Human Resources, Kathy Gillis

Vice President Store Development, Jim Germann

Senior Vice President General Counsel And Corporate Secretary, Sarah Powell

Senior Vice President Finance, James Doran

Vice President Finance, Charles Phillips

Vice President Of Purchasing, Dave Viele

Vice President, Joey Blackburn

Vice President Commercial Marketing, John Hanighen

Vice President Professional Central Region, Mark Zuanich

Vice President Commercial Sales And New Customer Development, Lawrence Nelson

Vice President, Matt Sapere

Vice President Strategic Accounts, Todd Sanders

Vice President Total Rewards, Melissa Lesley

Vice President Infrastructure Engineering Operations And Support, Ken Moore

Vice President Chief Inclusion And Diversity Officer, Heather Lawley

Vice President Contract And Real Estate Counsel, Brian Dan

Vice President Professional Sales, Kevin DeLillo

Senior Vice President Sales, Michael Cooper

Vice President Logistics, Greg Kovach

Executive Vice President Human Resources, Natalie Rothman Schechtman

Vp Communications, Kevin Nash

Vice President Human Resources, Lisa Tyree

Evp General Counsel And Secretary, Tammy M. Finley, age 51

Chairman, Jeffrey C. Smith

Auditors: Deloitte & Touche LLP

LOCATIONS

HQ: Advance Auto Parts Inc
5008 Airport Road, Roanoke, VA 24012
Phone: 540 362-4911
Web: www.AdvanceAutoParts.com

PRODUCTS/OPERATIONS

2017 Sales

	% of total
Parts & Batteries	65
Accessories & Chemicals	20
Engine Maintenance	14
Other	1
Total	**100**

Selected Products

Parts & Batteries
Batteries and battery accessories
Belts and hoses
Brakes and brake pads
Chassis parts
Climate control parts
Clutches and drive shafts
Engines and engine parts
Exhaust systems and parts
Hub assemblies
Ignition components and wire
Radiators and cooling parts
Starters and alternators
Steering and alignment parts
Accessories & Chemicals
AC chemicals and accessories
Air fresheners
Antifreeze and washer fluid
Electrical wire and fuses
Electronics
Floor mats seat covers and interior accessories
Hand and specialty tools
Lighting
Performance parts
Sealants adhesives and compounds
Tire repair accessories
Vent shades mirrors and exterior accessories
Washes waxes and cleaning supplies
Wiper blades
Engine Maintenance
Air filters
Fuel and oil additives
Fuel filters
Grease and lubricants
Motor Oil
Oil filters
Part cleaners and treatments
Transmission fluid

Selected Brands

Bosch
Castrol
Dayco
Denso
Gates
Monroe
Moog
Prestone
Purolator
Trico
Wagner

COMPETITORS

Amazon.com	Replacement Parts
AutoZone	Sears
Fisher Auto Parts	Somerset Tire Service
Genuine Parts	TBC Retail
Keystone Automotive Operations	U.S. Auto Parts
	Uni-Select
O'Reilly Automotive	VIP
Pep Boys	Wal-Mart

HISTORICAL FINANCIALS

Company Type: Public

Income Statement

FYE: December 30

	REVENUE ($ mil.)	NET INCOME ($ mil.)	NET PROFIT MARGIN	EMPLOYEES
12/17	9,373	475	5.1%	71,000
12/16*	9,567	459	4.8%	74,000
01/16	9,737	473	4.9%	73,000
01/15	9,843	493	5.0%	73,000
12/13	6,493	391	6.0%	71,867
Annual Growth	**9.6%**	**5.0%**	—	**(0.3%)**

*Fiscal year change

2017 Year-End Financials

Debt ratio: 12.31%	No. of shares (mil.): 73
Return on equity: 15.06%	Dividends
Cash ($ mil.): 546	Yield: 0.0%
Current ratio: 1.56	Payout: 3.7%
Long-term debt ($ mil.): 1,044	Market value ($ mil.): 7,371

	STOCK PRICE ($) FY Close	P/E High/Low		PER SHARE ($) Earnings	Dividends	Book Value
12/17	99.69	27	12	6.42	0.24	46.19
12/16*	169.12	28	22	6.20	0.24	39.54
01/16	150.51	31	22	6.40	0.24	33.56
01/15	158.56	24	16	6.71	0.24	27.41
12/13	109.92	21	13	5.32	0.24	20.82
Annual Growth	**(2.4%)**	—	—	**4.8%**	**(0.0%)**	**22.1%**

*Fiscal year change

Advanced Micro Devices Inc

Advanced Micro Devices (AMD) makes a wide range of processors that power a wide range of devices. The company produces processors that power PCs servers and game consoles as well as embedded processors that control functions in machines used in industrial control and automation machinery and for medical imaging telecommunications and avionic applications. Besides processors AMD makes graphics cards and systems-on-a-chip. In recent years the company has armed itself with new product families: Radeon for graphics and Ryzen for computing to compete against longtime rival and market leader Intel.

Operations

AMD operates through two segments: computing and graphics and enterprise embedded and semi-custom. Computing and graphics products accounting for more than 55% of sales include AMD's Ryzen chips for PCs and Radeon graphic processors game systems and other devices. The products from the enterprise embedded and semi-custom segment more than 40% of sales are used in data centers kiosks machine-to-machine applications and security and storage systems.

AMD outsources manufacturing of its products to third-party foundries including GLOBAL-FOUNDRIES and Taiwan Semiconductor Manufacturing Company. AMD performs assembly test and packaging of its microprocessor and embedded processors at its own facilities in China Malaysia and Taiwan.

Geographic Reach

Accounting for about a third of sales China is the AMD?s largest geographic market. The US and

China each generate about 25% of AMD?s sales while Singapore accounts for about 10%.

AMD?s corporate headquarters is in Sunnyvale California but most of its US operations are handled at its Austin Texas facilities. Overall the company has more than 50 locations worldwide with about two dozen in the Asia/Pacific region.

Sales and Marketing

AMD markets its products through a direct sales force as well as through a network of independent distributors and sales representatives. Microsoft HP Inc. and Sony are the company?s largest customers each accounting for more than 10% of sales and a total of 45% of sales.

Other customers include Acer Apple Asus Cisco Dell Technologies GE Lenovo Nintendo Samsung Toshiba Vizio and XFX.

Financial Performance

AMD?s revenue and profit have fluctuated in recent years as its products have fallen in and out of favor with makers of computers game consoles datacenter servers and other electronics.

In the 2017 the company?s finances strengthened as it released a bevy of new products. Revenue rose 25% to $5.3 billion in 2017 from 2016 driven by a 54% sales increase in its Computing and Graphics business. The average selling price of the segment?s products jumped nearly 50% from the introduction of the Radeon GPU and Ryzen desktop processors while shipments were up 2%. Revenue was flat year-to-year in the Enterprise Embedded and Semi-Custom segment though it had higher sales of the EPYC datacenter processors. Sales to US customers rose about 4% in 2017 on domestic purchases of desktop processors graphics processors and semi-custom SoC products.

AMD posted a $43 million profit in 2017 an improvement from a loss of nearly $500 million in 2016 fueled by higher revenue and the lack of charges for restructuring costs and one-time charges in 2016.

The company?s cash dropped to $1.2 billion in 2017 from $1.3 billion in 2016. The company had more capital spending and reduced debt in 2017.

Strategy

AMD has plotted a comeback over the past several years after it lost ground to Intel in microprocessors and to Nvidia in graphics processors. The 25% sales increase in 2017 from 2016 indicates that AMD is back.

PC makers and other electronics firms snapped up the Ryzen family of processors which includes the Threadripper a high-end chip for desktop computers and Mobile a fast processor for ultrathin notebooks. The Ryzen PRO processor was adopted by major PC manufacturers.

The Radeon graphics chips played a significant role in the revenue increase finding datacenter customers in Baidu and Amazon Web Services.

AMD has shown off its gaming expertise in becoming the sole supplier of semi-custom graphics cards for Microsoft?s Xbox and Sony?s Playstation consoles. (Those companies account for about 20% of AMD?s sales.)

Over the years AMD has competed with Intel by providing electronics makers with lower-priced chips. But the price differential might disappear as AMD strengthened pricing in 2017. Most of the revenue increase in the Computing and Graphics segment came from higher average selling prices.

AMD and Intel found a way to work together. AMD in 2017 began making a semi-custom chip that integrates into an Intel multi-chip processor for graphics. AMD sees the deal as a way to get its graphics capabilities into more products.

Beyond the PC AMD looks to provide processors for virtual reality devices and other technologies that have the potential to become big markets. The company's acquisition of Nitero was made to further its ambitions in virtual reality and augmented reality.

Mergers and Acquisitions

In 2017 AMD acquired Nitero a developer of technologies for making wireless headsets for virtual reality and augmented reality applications. User would get a more immersive virtual reality experience without being tethered to a device by wired headsets. The acquisition provides AMD with a broader portfolio of intellectual property capable for Wi-Fi headsets.

AMD acquired HiAlgo Inc. a developer of unique PC gaming software in 2016. AMD planned to deploy HiAlgo's technologies to increase the efficiency and performance of its Radeon RX Series GPUs tto improve the consistency of gaming experiences.

EXECUTIVES

Svp And Cfo, Devinder Kumar, age 63, $530,005 total compensation
President And Ceo, Lisa Su, age 49, $886,340 total compensation
Svp Global Operations, Chekib Akrout, age 60
Svp And Cto, Mark D. Papermaster, age 57, $549,994 total compensation
Svp And General Manager Enterprise Embedded And Semi-custom Business Group, Forrest E. Norrod, age 52, $530,005 total compensation
Svp And General Manager Computing And Graphics Business Group, James R. (Jim) Anderson, age 46, $499,990 total compensation
Vice President Information Technology And Chief Information Officer, Frederick Mapp
Corporate Vice President Finance, Gary Lloyd
Chairman, John E. Caldwell, age 68
Auditors: Ernst & Young LLP

LOCATIONS

HQ: Advanced Micro Devices Inc
2485 Augustine Drive, Santa Clara, CA 95054
Phone: 408 749-4000
Web: www.amd.com

2017 Sales

	$ mil.	% of total
China	1,747	33
US	1,364	26
Japan	1,242	23
Singapore	551	10
Europe	263	5
Other regions	162	3
Total	**5,329**	**100**

PRODUCTS/OPERATIONS

2017 Sales

	$ mil.	% of total
Computing and Graphics	3,029	57
Enterprise Embedded and Semi-Custom	2,300	43
Total	**5,329**	**100**

Selected Products

Computing
  Accelerated processing units (APUs; Fusion combines central processing and graphics processing units on a single chip)
  Microprocessors (Ryzen Athlon Opteron Phenom Sempron and Turion lines)
  Motherboard reference design kits and chipsets
Graphics
  Embedded graphics processing units
  Macintosh notebook and desktop PC graphics processors (Radeon)
  Motherboard chipsets (for AMD and Intel processors)
  Server and workstation graphics processing units
Personal connectivity
  Embedded processors
  Networking chips

COMPETITORS

ARM Holdings	NVIDIA
Analog Devices	NXP Semiconductors
Atmel	SANYO Semiconductor
Centaur Technology	STMicroelectronics
Hitachi	Samsung Electronics
Imagination	Sigma Designs
Technologies	Silicon Image
Infineon Technologies	Silicon Integrated
Intel	Systems
Marvell Technology	Silicon Motion
Matrox Electronic	Texas Instruments
Systems	VIA Technologies
MediaTek	

HISTORICAL FINANCIALS

Company Type: Public

Income Statement

FYE: December 29

	REVENUE ($ mil.)	NET INCOME ($ mil.)	NET PROFIT MARGIN	EMPLOYEES
12/18	6,475	337	5.2%	10,100
12/17	5,329	43	0.8%	8,900
12/16	4,272	(497)	—	8,200
12/15	3,991	(660)	—	9,100
12/14	5,506	(403)	—	9,700
Annual Growth	**4.1%**			**1.0%**

2018 Year-End Financials

Debt ratio: 27.44%	No. of shares (mil.): 1,005
Return on equity: 36.01%	Dividends
Cash ($ mil.): 1,156	Yield: —
Current ratio: 1.78	Payout: —
Long-term debt ($ mil.): 1,114	Market value ($ mil.): 17,909

	STOCK PRICE ($) FY Close	P/E High/Low	PER SHARE ($) Earnings	Dividends	Book Value
12/18	17.82	96 28	0.32	0.00	1.26
12/17	10.28	380244	0.04	0.00	0.63
12/16	11.34	— —	(0.60)	0.00	0.44
12/15	2.92	— —	(0.84)	0.00	(0.52)
12/14	2.65	— —	(0.53)	0.00	0.24
Annual Growth	**61.0%**	**— —**	**—**	**—**	**51.2%**

ADVENTIST HEALTH SYSTEM SUNBELT HEALTHCARE CORPORATION

EXECUTIVES

Pres, Donald Jernigan
V Pres, Robert Henderschedt
Coordinator, Pennie Moore

LOCATIONS

HQ: ADVENTIST HEALTH SYSTEM SUNBELT HEALTHCARE CORPORATION
900 HOPE WAY, ALTAMONTE SPRINGS, FL 327141502
Phone: 407 357-1000
Web: WWW.ADVENTISTHEALTHSYSTEM.COM

HISTORICAL FINANCIALS

Company Type: Private

Income Statement

	REVENUE ($ mil.)	NET INCOME ($ mil.)	NET PROFIT MARGIN	EMPLOYEES
12/17	10,083	1,167	11.6%	78,000
12/16	9,651	806	8.4%	—
12/14	519	26	5.1%	—
12/13	530	73	13.9%	—
Annual Growth	108.8%	99.6%	—	—

2017 Year-End Financials

Debt ratio: ——
Return on equity: 11.60%
Cash ($ mil.): 338
Current ratio: 0.30
Long-term debt ($ mil.): —

Dividends
Yield: —
Payout: —
Market value ($ mil.): —

ADVOCATE HEALTH CARE NETWORK

Advocating wellness in the Midwest Advocate Aurora Health is a not-for-profit integrated health care network with some 500 care sites serving Illinois and Wisconsin. Formerly named Advocate Health Care Advocate operates about nearly 30 acute and specialty care hospitals (including Advocate BroMenn Medical Center Aurora BayCare Medical Center Aurora Lakeland Medical Center and Lutheran General Hospital) with more than 7150 beds as well as community health clinics and home health care and hospice services. Illinois-based Advocate Health merged with Wisconsin-based Aurora Health Care in 2018; the merger created one of the nation's largest not-for-profit health systems in the US.

Operations

With more than 70000 associates Advocate Aurora Health is one of the largest employers in the region. Its staff also includes more than 8100 affiliated physicians.

The system has teaching affiliations with area medical schools such as the University of Illinois at Chicago and the University of Chicago Pritzker School of Medicine. Its three major teaching hospitals — Christ Medical Center Illinois Masonic Medical Center and Lutheran General Hospital — train 600 residents and fellows per year and provide more than 1600 medical student rotations annually

Geographic Reach

Advocate Aurora Health operates more than 500 care sites serving eastern Wisconsin and northeast Illinois.

Strategy

Even prior to merging with Aurora Health Care Advocate Health had grown through a series of acquisitions. Recent purchases include central Illinois health network BroMenn Healthcare System the 280-bed Condell Medical Center the Midwest Physician Group (now part of the Advocate Medical Group division) and Sherman Health Systems.

In 2017 Advocate Health dropped its plans to merge with NorthShore University Health System another Illinois hospital operator. The combination would have created a 16-hospital market leader in Chicago's North Shore area. The merger was blocked by the FTC which claimed that it would harm consumers by raising prices and lowering health care quality.

Later that year Advocate Health and Wisconsin-based Aurora Health Care agreed to combined forces. The merged company now named Advocate Aurora Health Care operates 27 hospitals and more than 500 care sites; it has the capacity to serve nearly 3 million patients annually. The two companies already had a working relationship through their ACL Laboratories joint venture.

Company Background

Advocate Health was formed in 1995 by the United Church of Christ and the Evangelical Lutheran Church in America.

EXECUTIVES

Evp And Chief Medical Officer; President Advocate Physician Partners, Lee B. Sacks
Svp Cfo Treasurer, Dominic J. Nakis
President Advocate Condell Medical Center, Ann Errichetti
President, Karen A. Lambert
President Advocate Home Health Services, Denise M. Keefe
President Advocate Physician Partners, Martin F. (Marty) Manning, age 63
President Advocate Medical Group, James R. Dan
President Recognized Associates, John Bruss
Svp And Chief Marketing Officer, Kelly Jo Golson
President Dreyer Clinic, Donna Copper
President Acl Laboratories, Barbara Bigler
Coo, Dana Gilbert
Vice President Talent Management And Staffing, Anne Callen
Vice President Physician And Ambulatory Services, Lois Elia
Vice President Corporate Is Physician Services, John Norenberg
Vice President Of Clinical Effectiveness, Debra Oconnor
Vice President App Advisors, Charlyn Slade
Medical Director, Martin Doot
Vice President Public Affairs, Lisa Lesniak
Vice President Of Finance And Ambulatory Division, Neil Beck
Vice President Development, Doug Hutchings
Pharmacy Manager, Paul Miller
Vice President Operations, Karen Moore
Vice President Professional Arrangements Professional Arrangements, Peg Stone
Assistant To Vice President Network Sales Vice President Govt And Community Relations Vice President Marketing, Judy Zumpano
Secretary, Olga Wegehaupt
Auditors: ERNST & YOUNG LLP CHICAGO IL

LOCATIONS

HQ: ADVOCATE HEALTH CARE NETWORK
3075 HIGHLAND PKWY FL 6, DOWNERS GROVE, IL 605155563
Phone: 630 572-9393
Web: WWW.ADVOCATEHEALTH.COM

PRODUCTS/OPERATIONS

Selected Locations

Advocate BroMenn Medical Center (Normal Illinois) - 221 beds
Advocate Christ Medical Center (Oak Lawn Illinois) - 695 beds
Advocate Condell Medical Center (Libertyville Illinois) - 281 beds
Advocate Good Samaritan Hospital (Downers Grove Illinois) -340 beds
Advocate Eureka Hospital (Eureka Illinois)- 25 beds
Advocate Good Shepherd Hospital (Barrington Illinois) - 183 beds
AdvoAdvocate Hope Children's Hospital (Oak Lawn Illinois)

Advocate Illinois Masonic Medical Center (Chicago Illinois) -408 beds
Advocate Lutheran General Hospital (Park Ridge Illinois) - 639 beds
Advocate Sherman Hospital (ElginIllinois)- 225 beds
Advocate South Suburban Hospital (Hazel Crest Illinois) - 284 beds
Advocate Trinity Hospital (Chicago Illinois) - 250 beds

COMPETITORS

Alexian Brothers Health System
Central DuPage Hospital
Children's Hopsital of Chicago
Covenant Ministries
Elmhurst Memorial Healthcare
Gottleib Memorial Hospital
HCA
Hospital Sisters Health System
KishHealth
Loyola University Health System

Mercy Hospital and Medical Center
NorthShore University HealthSystem
Northwest Community Healthcare
Northwestern Lake Forest Hospital
Northwestern Memorial HealthCare
Pronger Smith
Rush System for Health
SSM Health Care
Silver Cross Hospital
Sinai Health System
University of Chicago Medical Center

HISTORICAL FINANCIALS

Company Type: Private

Income Statement

	REVENUE ($ mil.)	NET INCOME ($ mil.)	NET PROFIT MARGIN	EMPLOYEES
12/15	5,392	60	1.1%	25,000
12/06	3,268	286	8.8%	—
12/05	2,973	140	4.7%	—
12/04	2,779	143	5.2%	—
Annual Growth	6.2%	(7.6%)	—	—

2015 Year-End Financials

Debt ratio: ——
Return on equity: 1.10%
Cash ($ mil.): 203
Current ratio: 0.60
Long-term debt ($ mil.): —

Dividends
Yield: —
Payout: —
Market value ($ mil.): —

AECOM

AECOM is one of the world's top engineering and design groups. The company provides planning consulting architectural and engineering design services for civil and infrastructure construction to public and private clients in more than 150 countries. The company also offers other services including logistics and consulting in a range of end markets that include energy and environmental construction. Some of AECOM's major projects include the USTA Billie Jean King National Tennis Center Taizhou Bridge in China Crossrail London (the largest construction in Europe) and New York City's Second Avenue Subway. AECOM generates more than a quarter of its sales outside the US.

Operations

AECOM operates through four business segments: Design and Consulting Services (DCS) Construction Services (CS) Management Services (MS) and AECOM Capital.DCS generates about 40% of the company's total revenue and consists of planning consulting architectural and engineering design services. CS includes construction of buildings energy infrastructure and industrial facilities and accounts for around 40% of sales. MS at about 20% of revenue includes AECOM's facilities management and maintenance training logistics consulting technical assistance and systems integration and IT services. The company invests in real estate infrastructure projects and public/private partnerships through AECOM Capital.

Geographic Reach

Based in Los Angeles AECOM serves clients in more than 150 countries. The company generates more than 70% of its revenue from the US about 10% from Europe and less than 20% from the Asia-Pacific region Canada and other areas.

It has primary office locations in the US as well as in Australia Hong Kong Russia the United Arab Emirates and the UK.

Sales and Marketing

AECOM serves several sectors such as transportation facilities environmental energy water and government.

AECOM's revenue is split about evenly between private sector clients and government entities. Roughly 45% of its revenue derived from governments is from direct contracts with US federal government agencies (Departments of Defense Energy Justice and Homeland Security); the remainder comes from state and local governments as well as foreign governments.

Financial Performance

After a breakout year in fiscal 2015 which saw revenue more than double due to its acquisition of URS AECOM reported a small drop in revenue in 2016 but rebounded in 2017 and 2018 on strong performance from its three main segments particularly Construction Services. The company's net income fell 40% between 2014 and 2018 due to massive losses in 2014 and 2015 partially offset by gains of more than 250% in 2017 when its acquisition and integration expenses dropped significantly.

AECOM added 11% to its revenue in 2018 compared with 2017. The company saw sales in its Design and Consulting Services (DCS) Construction Services (CS) and Management Services (MS) segments increase by 8.7% 12.9% and 10.6% respectively. Residential housing storm disaster relief in the Americas and increases in the Asia-Pacific and Europe Middle East and Africa (EMEA) regions drove up DCS income. Gains in its CS segment owed to construction of residential high-rise buildings in New York City and the inclusion of revenue from acquisitions in 2018 and 4Q17. US government projects — including US Army projects in the Middle East and US Air Force contracts — bolstered MS revenue.

The company's net income fell 60% to $136.5 million in 2018 due mostly to an impairment of assets held for sale including goodwill related to the anticipated selloff of the company's non-core oil and gas businesses (which AECOM announced in Q2 of 2018).

AECOM added $84.4 million to its cash stores in 2018. Operations provided $774.6 million; Investments used $59 million and financings used $624.9 million. Investment spend decreased compared to the previous year thanks to the company abstaining from acquisitions and greater return on investment from unconsolidated joint ventures. Financing activity increased due to common stock repurchases net distributions to noncontrolling interests and net debt repayments.

Strategy

AECOM believes that its diversification is key to growth. It has cultivated diversified end markets funding (50:50 private:public) and capabilities during its transition from solely engineering design to construction and then ultimately operations and maintenance.

Infrastructure is a major target for the company which is boosting its expertise in that area through internal investment (including the creation of a federal contracting division) and acquisitions (including the 2017 purchase of Shimmick). In January 2019 the company released its second annual report on the future of infrastructure which surveyed more than 10000 residents of 10 major global cities on their infrastructure concerns. In addition in mid-2017 the company announced plans to hire some 3000 workers to support its infrastructure operations in the US and the rest of the North America.

The company is already a leader in "mega projects" worth more than $1 billion; current projects that fit that description include West Gate Tunnel in Melbourne Australia and the San Roque Multipurpose Dam in Luzon Philippines.

Although AECOM's acquisition spending in its last three fiscal years has been miniscule compared to the billions it paid for USR in late 2014 growth by acquisition remains a large part of the company's strategy as it works to cement its leadership position in existing markets and enter new ones.

Mergers and Acquisitions

In 2017 AECOM agreed to pay $175 million to acquire heavy civil construction company Shimmick which operates primarily in California and the western US. The purchase complements AECOM's North American offerings and better positions it to take advantage of upcoming infrastructure projects particularly in the western US.

Company Background

AECOM formed in 1990 through the merger of five subsidiaries of Ashland Inc. Since then more than 50 companies have joined AECOM. The company completed its initial public offering in 2007.

EXECUTIVES

Associate Vice President Network Architect, Michael Bradvica
Vice President Leasing, David B Kilpatrick
Chief Executive Aecom Capital, John T. Livingston
President Major Pursuits, Frederick W. (Fred) Werner, age 65, $661,540 total compensation
Svp And Chief Marketing And Communications Officer, Heather Rim
Chairman And Ceo, Michael S. (Mike) Burke, age 54, $1,276,928 total compensation
Group President Construction Services, Daniel P. McQuade, age 58
Evp And General Counsel, Carla J. Christofferson, age 50
Chief Executive Europe The Middle East India And Africa (emia), Steve Morriss
Coo, Randall A. (Randy) Wotring, age 61, $705,389 total compensation
Evp And Cfo, W. Troy Rudd, age 54, $528,851 total compensation
Evp And Chief Human Resources Officer, Mary E. Finch, age 48
Chief Executive Australia-new Zealand, Lara Poloni
Vice President, Herbert Higginbotham
Vice President, Jeff Khouri
Vice President And Laccd Program Director, Terri Mestas
Svp Mergers And Acquisitions, Matt Clark
Vice President, Will Wright
Vice President, Juli Binaco
Group Associate Vice President Contracts Compliance And Internal Audit, Edward Condoleo
Senior Vice President, Stephen Engblom
First Vice President, Ryan Mahoney
Vice President Legal, Bob Foran
Vice President, Christopher McDermott
Senior Vice President Corporate Finance, Roger Willard
Vice President Technical Services, Jeff Brier
Vice President Chief Ethics And Compliance Officer, Michael Kostiw
Senior Vice President Assistant General Counsel Head Of Litigation, Laura Abrahamson
Senior Vice President Operations, David Geller
Associate Vice President Project Management, Jeff Endersby
Senior Vice President Operations, D Linford
Vice President Corporate Shande Management Solutions, Cece Weldon
Senior Vice President Operations Finance, Charles Thuss
Vice President Federal Programs, Mark Handley
Vice President Operations And, Brad White
Vice President, Dan Shumaker
First Vice President, Amy Chase
Vice President Marketing And Business Development, Carol Papillo
Vice President Strategic Captures Managementservices Group, Matt Einseln
Vice President Georgia Alabama Carolinas Tennessee Building+places Business Unit Leader, Joe Riddle
Senior Vice President, Jim Kunz
Vice President, Darren Caswell
Vice President, James Karl
Senior Vice President Power, Greg Brown
Vice President Director Of Healthcare Facilities Business Line Infrastructure Environment, Joe Greenan
Corporate Vice President Strategy, Jennifer Whiting
Vice President Alternative Delivery Group, K Gunalan
Vice President, Garry Lay
Associate Vice President, Jerry Farhat
Vice President, Joseph West
Vice President, Daryl Taavola
Vice President, Ivan Kuncheff
Vice President Project Executive, Robert Sullivan
Senior Vice President Civil And Infrastructure Apac, Patrick Chao
Vice President Principal Geologist, Robert Macwilliams
Vice Chairman, Daniel R. (Dan) Tishman, age 63
Board Member, Ken Brown
Auditors: Ernst & Young LLP

LOCATIONS

HQ: AECOM
1999 Avenue of the Stars, Suite 2600, Los Angeles, CA 90067
Phone: 213 593-8000
Web: www.aecom.com

2018 Sales

	$ mil.	% of total
US	14,753	73
Europe	1,984	10
Asia/Pacific	1,440	7
Canada	1,212	6
Other foreign countries	765	4
Total	**20,155**	**100**

PRODUCTS/OPERATIONS

Selected Services
Architecture & Design
Construction
Decommissioning & Closure
Engineering
Environmental Services
International Development
IT & Cybersecurity
Operations & Maintenance
Planning & Consulting
Program Management/Construction Management
Risk Management & Resilience
Specialized Services
  Cities Solutions
  Equity Investment
  Fabrication
  Process Technologies
  Public/Private Partnerships
Technical Services

2018 Sales

	$ mil	% total
Design and Consulting Services	8,223	41
Construction Services	8,238	41
Management Services	3,693	18
Total	**20,155**	**100**

COMPETITORS

Amec Foster Wheeler	MWH Global
Bechtel	Parsons Brinckerhoff
Black & Veatch	Parsons Corporation
CH2M HILL	STV
EMCOR	Skidmore Owings
Fluor	Stantec
Henkels & McCoy	Terracon
Jacobs Engineering	Tetra Tech
KBR	Tutor Perini
Louis Berger	

HISTORICAL FINANCIALS

Company Type: Public

Income Statement   FYE: September 30

	REVENUE ($ mil.)	NET INCOME ($ mil.)	NET PROFIT MARGIN	EMPLOYEES
09/18	20,155	136	0.7%	87,000
09/17	18,203	339	1.9%	87,000
09/16	17,410	96	0.6%	87,000
09/15	17,989	(154)	—	92,000
09/14	8,356	229	2.8%	43,300
Annual Growth	**24.6%**	**(12.2%)**	**—**	**19.1%**

2018 Year-End Financials

Debt ratio: 24.70%	No. of shares (mil.): 156
Return on equity: 3.37%	Dividends
Cash ($ mil.): 886	Yield: —
Current ratio: 1.16	Payout: —
Long-term debt ($ mil.): 3,483	Market value ($ mil.): 5,127

	STOCK PRICE ($) FY Close	P/E High/Low	PER SHARE ($) Earnings	Dividends	Book Value
09/18	32.66	46 37	0.84	0.00	26.07
09/17	36.81	18 12	2.13	0.00	25.37
09/16	29.73	58 37	0.62	0.00	21.88
09/15	27.51	— —	(1.04)	0.00	22.53
09/14	33.75	16 12	2.33	0.00	22.61
Annual Growth	**(0.8%)**	**— —**	**(22.5%)**	**—**	**3.6%**

AEROTEK, INC.

Aerotek a unit of staffing powerhouse Allegis Group offers commercial and technical staffing services throughout North America. Through several divisions Aerotek staffs workers such as engineers mechanics scientists and technical professionals as well as administrative staff members general laborers and tradespeople. The company also provides training and support services. Along with aerospace auto and engineering companies Aerotek's clients include companies from the construction energy manufacturing health care and finance industries.

Geographic Reach

Aerotek is headquartered in Hanover Maryland. The company has office locations in Asia Australia Europe and North America. Aerotek also operates a network of more than 250 non-franchised offices.

Sales and Marketing

Aerotek serves a wide variety of industries including the accounting construction engineering financial services government and public administration health care manufacturing and pharmaceutical industries among others. The company serves more than 18000 clients and 300000 contract employees every year.

Strategy

Aerotek has expanded its operations over the years through organic growth and acquisitions especially in niche markets such as the biotechnology health care clinical research chemical and plastics sectors. Despite the economic downturn demand within these industries has been consistent along with engineering giving Aerotek some continuity during the recession. Aerotek has also widened its client focus to include the niche market of minority and woman-owned companies.

EXECUTIVES

Vp Technical And Professional Services, Mark Cooper
President, Todd M. Mohr
Cfo, Thomas B. (Tom) Kelly
Svp Operations, John Flanigan
Regional Vp Northeast, John Rudy
Regional Vp Midwest, Marty Schager
Regional Vp Central, Mike Hansen
Regional Vp West, Tony Bartolucci
Regional Vp Northwest, Brooks Wells
Vp Canada, Bryan Toffey
Regional Vp Southwest, Brad Kennedy
Regional Vp Mid-atlantic, Jeff Colvin
Regional Vp Southeast, Greg Jones
Vice President Client Delivery, Vinayak Nayak
Vice President Of Finance, James Mann
Auditors: PRICEWATERHOUSECOOPERS LLP B

LOCATIONS

HQ: AEROTEK, INC.
  7301 PARKWAY DR, HANOVER, MD 210761159
Phone: 410 694-5100
Web: WWW.AEROTEK.COM

PRODUCTS/OPERATIONS

INDUSTRIES SERVED

Accounting
Administrative & Support Services
Aerospace Aviation & Defense
Architecture & Design
Automotive
Construction
Customer Service
Energy & Utilities
Engineering
Environmental
Financial Services
Government & Public Administration
Healthcare
Manufacturing
Pharmaceutical
Sciences
Warehouse & Distribution

COMPETITORS

AMN Healthcare	MSX International
Adecco	ManpowerGroup
Bryant Bureau	On Assignment
CDI	Pinnacle Staffing
COMFORCE	Randstad Holding
Kelly Services	Robert Half
Kforce	

HISTORICAL FINANCIALS

Company Type: Private

Income Statement   FYE: December 31

	REVENUE ($ mil.)	NET INCOME ($ mil.)	NET PROFIT MARGIN	EMPLOYEES
12/17	6,070	0	—	4,200
12/16	5,565	0	—	—
12/15	5,492	0	—	—
12/14	5,353	0	—	—
Annual Growth	**4.3%**	**—**	**—**	**—**

2017 Year-End Financials

Debt ratio: ——	
Return on equity: —	Dividends
Cash ($ mil.): 8	Yield: —
Current ratio: 3.50	Payout: —
Long-term debt ($ mil.): —	Market value ($ mil.): —

AES Corp.

EXECUTIVES

Pres-Ceo, Andres R Gluski
Non Exec Chb, John B Morse Jr
Exec V Pres-Coo, Bernerd Da Santos
Exec V Pres-Cfo, Thomas M O'Flynn
Sr V Pres-Chief Hr Officer, Tish Mendoza
Sr V Pres-General Counsel, Paul L Freedman
Financial Analyst, Adrienne Austin
Accounting Coordinator Cac, Americo Bejaran
Director, Anitha Chalasani
Data Analyst, Bill Beecher
Project Manager, Bill Edwards
Auditors: Ernst & Young LLP

LOCATIONS

HQ: AES Corp.
  4300 Wilson Boulevard, Arlington, VA 22203
Phone: 703 522-1315   **Fax:** 703 528-4510
Web: www.aes.com

COMPETITORS

Alliant Energy	Exelon
Bonneville Power	GenOnEnergy
CMS Energy	Huadian Power
CPFL Energia	IBERDROLA
Calpine	Indeck Energy
CenterPoint Energy	International Power
Duke Energy	MidAmerican Energy
Dynegy	NRG Energy
E.ON UK	NextEra Energy
Edison International	Nicor Gas
El Paso Corporation	PG&E Corporation
Endesa S.A.	Public Service
Energias de Portugal	Enterprise Group
Energy Future	Sempra Energy
Enersis	Siemens AG
Entergy	Tractebel Engineering
Enterprise Products	Xcel Energy

HISTORICAL FINANCIALS

Company Type: Public

Income Statement
FYE: December 31

	REVENUE ($ mil.)	NET INCOME ($ mil.)	NET PROFIT MARGIN	EMPLOYEES
12/17	10,530	(1,161)	—	—
12/16	13,586	(1,130)	—	—
12/15	14,963	306	2.0%	21,000
12/14	17,146	769	4.5%	18,500
12/13	15,891	114	0.7%	22,000
Annual Growth	(9.8%)	—	—	—

2017 Year-End Financials

Debt ratio: 60.30%
Return on equity: (-33.76%)
Cash ($ mil.): 949
Current ratio: 1.06
Long-term debt ($ mil.): 17,801

No. of shares (mil.): 660
Dividends
Yield: 0.0%
Payout: —
Market value ($ mil.): 7,152

	STOCK PRICE ($) FY Close	P/E High/Low	PER SHARE ($) Earnings	Dividends	Book Value
12/17	10.83	— —	(1.76)	0.48	5.00
12/16	11.62	— —	(1.71)	0.44	5.42
12/15	9.57	31 20	0.44	0.40	5.53
12/14	13.77	15 12	1.06	0.20	6.18
12/13	14.51	102 71	0.15	0.16	6.10
Annual Growth	(7.1%)	— —	—	31.6%	(4.9%)

AFLAC Inc

To soften the financial stresses during periods of disability or illness Aflac sells supplemental health and life insurance policies including coverage for accidents intensive care dental vision and disability as well as for specific conditions (primarily cancer) and general life policies. It is a leading supplier of supplemental insurance in the US and is an industry leader in Japan's life and cancer insurance markets. Aflac which is marketed through — and is an acronym for — American Family Life Assurance Company sells policies that pay cash benefits for hospital confinement emergency treatment and medical appliances.

Operations

Aflac operates through two reportable segments — Aflac Japan and Aflac U.S. The Japan segment accounts for about 70% of total revenue while the US accounts for the remainder.

The firm acts as a management company overseeing the operations of its subsidiaries by providing funding and management services. Its primary line of business is voluntary supplemental and life insurance which is offered in both the US and Japan. Aflac U.S. markets and administers group products through Continental American Insurance Company (dba Aflac Group Insurance).

In addition to accident intensive care life and cancer coverage Aflac offers general medical indemnity plans medical and sickness riders living benefit life plans short-term disability and annuities. Aflac individual and group insurance products help provide protection to more than 50 million people.

Geographic Reach

Despite its US roots Aflac makes about 70% of its insurance sales in Japan where its policies fill in gaps not covered by the national health insurance system. Aflac has a presence in all 50 US states (the US accounts for nearly 30% of revenue) and in Puerto Rico and the Virgin Islands.

Sales and Marketing

In Japan Aflac primarily sells through an independent corporate agency system in which corporations form subsidiaries to sell Aflac insurance to their employees. The company also sells through banks and post offices and it has opened retail shops where consumers can purchase directly from sales associates.

By the end of 2017 the company had agreements to sell its products with 374 banks approximately 90% of banks in Japan. Banks contributed 5% of Aflac Japan's new annualized premium sales that year.

In the US Aflac sells mainly at the workplace with employers deducting premiums from paychecks through sales associates of Aflac Group Insurance. Building on its strong brand recognition — due largely to the company's popular TV ads featuring a valiant spokes-duck — Aflac has invested in its US business by adding more sales associates and expanding its distribution to include independent insurance brokers.

Aflac's extensive distribution network includes about 10900 sales agencies with some 109200 licensed sales associates. In 2017 the company recruited approximately 175 new sales agencies. Independent corporate and individual agencies contribute nearly half of new annualized premium sales each year.

The company's advertising costs in 2017 were $210 million compared to $224 million in 2016 and $211 million in 2015.

Financial Performance

Aflac saw steady revenue declines from 2012 until 2016 when revenue rose 8% to $22.6 billion. However sales dipped again the following year falling 4% to $21.7 billion. This was primarily due to a drop in sales for Aflac Japan where cancer medical and other health and life insurance premiums fell. US premiums across all categories saw gains in 2017.

Despite the lower revenue Aflac enjoyed declines in benefits and claims payouts and other expenses. This helped drive net earnings up 73% to $4.6 billion. Cash flow from operations which has generally fallen for the past few years fell another 10% to $1.9 billion. Negative adjustments in equity in earnings of subsidiaries and other operating activities led to the decrease.

Strategy

Aflac is focusing on improving and expanding its distribution network and product development processes and on improving its customer service activities.

In Japan where Aflac already covers about 25% of all households the company has created new health and life insurance products to attract even more customers. In addition to standard life insurance it has child endowment products that pay out part of the benefit when the child enters high school and then functions like an annuity for four years during college. In 2016 the company launched a new income support insurance product which provides support when a sickness keeps customers from working long-term. That product targets younger customers which the company hopes to keep with different products as they age. And to boost distribution Aflac Japan and Japan Post Holdings have an alliance which has boosted the number of postal outlets offering Aflac's cancer products from 1000 to more than 20000.

Aflac U.S.'s primary focus is on offering voluntary coverage at the worksite. As part of its US strategy the company aims to grow and enhance the effectiveness of its sales team.

HISTORY

American Family Life Assurance Company (AFLAC) was founded in Columbus Georgia in 1955 by brothers John Paul and William Amos to sell life health and accident insurance. Competition was fierce and the little company did poorly. With AFLAC nearing bankruptcy the brothers looked for a niche.

The polio scares of the 1940s and 1950s had spawned insurance coverage written especially against that disease; the Amos brothers (whose father was a cancer victim) took a cue from that concept and decided to sell cancer insurance. In 1958 they introduced the world's first cancer-expense policy. It was a hit and by 1959 the company had written nearly a million dollars in premiums and expanded across state lines.

The enterprise grew quickly during the 1960s especially after developing its cluster-selling approach in the workplace where employers were usually willing to make payroll deductions for premiums. By 1971 the company was operating in 42 states.

While visiting the World's Fair in Osaka in 1970 John Amos decided to market supplemental cancer coverage to the Japanese whose national health care plan left them exposed to considerable expense from cancer treatment. After four years the company finally won approval to sell in Japan since the policies did not threaten existing markets and because the Amoses found notable backers in the insurance and medical industries. AFLAC became one of the first US insurance companies to enter the Japanese market and it enjoyed an eight-year monopoly on the cancer market. Back in the US in 1973 AFLAC organized a holding company and began buying television stations in the South and Midwest.

The 1980s were marked by US and state government inquiries into dread disease insurance. Critics said such policies were a poor value because they were relatively expensive and covered only one disease. However the inquiries led nowhere and demand for such insurance increased bringing new competition. In the 1980s AFLAC's scales tilted: US growth slowed while business grew in Japan which soon accounted for most of the company's sales.

EXECUTIVES

Evp Treasurer And Head Of Corporate Finance And Development, Kenneth S. (Ken) Janke, age 60
President, Kriss Cloninger, age 70, $975,000 total compensation
Chairman And Ceo, Daniel P. (Dan) Amos, age 66, $1,441,100 total compensation
Senior Vice President, Thomas Giddens
Evp And Cfo, Frederick J. (Fred) Crawford, age 54, $700,000 total compensation
President Aflac International; Chairman Aflac Japan, Charles D. Lake, age 57, $333,333 total compensation
Evp And General Counsel, Audrey Boone Tillman, age 53
President Aflac, Paul S. Amos, age 43, $700,000 total compensation
President Aflac U.s., Teresa L. White, age 52
Svp And Chief Marketing Officer, Gail A. Galuppo, age 54
Svp Business Services; President And Ceo Communicorp, Eric B. Seldon
Evp And Global Chief Investment Officer, Eric M. Kirsch, age 57, $593,800 total compensation
Managing Director And Global Head Of Credit Global Investments, Bradley E. Dyslin
Svp And Cio, Julia K. Davis
Managing Director And Head Of Global Investments And Corporate It, J. Pete Kelso

PRODUCTS/OPERATIONS

2017 Sales

	$ mil.	% of total
Aflac Japan	15,028	69
Aflac U.S.	6,289	29
Corporate	210	1
Other	140	1
Total	**21,667**	**100**

2017 Sales

	$ mil.	% of total
Net premiums	18,531	85
Net investment income	3,220	15
Other	67	-
Adjustments	(151)	-
Total	**21,667**	**100**

COMPETITORS

American Fidelity Assurance Company
American National Insurance
Asahi Mutual Life
CNO Financial
Colonial Life & Accident

Meiji Yasuda Life
MetLife
Nippon Life Insurance
Taiyo Life
Torchmark
Unum Group

HISTORICAL FINANCIALS

Company Type: Public

Income Statement
FYE: December 31

	ASSETS ($ mil.)	NET INCOME ($ mil.)	INCOME AS % OF ASSETS	EMPLOYEES
12/17	137,217	4,604	3.4%	11,318
12/16	129,819	2,659	2.0%	10,212
12/15	118,296	2,533	2.1%	9,915
12/14	119,767	2,951	2.5%	9,525
12/13	121,307	3,158	2.6%	9,141
Annual Growth	**3.1%**	**9.9%**	**—**	**5.5%**

2017 Year-End Financials

Debt ratio: 3.85%
Return on equity: 20.43%
Cash ($ mil.): 3,491
Current ratio: —
Long-term debt ($ mil.): —

No. of shares (mil.): 780
Dividends
Yield: 0.0%
Payout: 15.0%
Market value ($ mil.): 68,548

	STOCK PRICE ($) FY Close	P/E High/Low		Earnings	Dividends	Book Value
12/17	87.78	15	12	5.77	0.87	31.50
12/16	69.60	23	17	3.21	0.83	25.24
12/15	59.90	22	19	2.93	0.79	20.86
12/14	61.09	20	17	3.25	0.75	20.73
12/13	66.80	20	14	3.38	0.71	15.91
Annual Growth	**7.1%**	**—**	**—**	**14.3%**	**5.2%**	**18.6%**

AGCO Corp.

This company has been plowing the furrow of premium agricultural equipment since 1990. AGCO makes tractors combines hay and forage tools sprayers grain storage and protein production systems seeding and tillage implements and replacement parts for agricultural end uses. It sells through a global network of some 4200 dealers and distributors spanning more than 150 countries. It also builds diesel engines gears and generators through its power engines unit. Core brands include Massey Ferguson GSI Challenger Valtra (Finland-based) and Fendt (Germany).

AGCO Finance offers financing services to retail customers and dealers via a venture with Rabobank a Dutch bank specializing in agricultural loans.

Operations

Tractors account for more than 55% of its total sales and replacement parts more than 15%.

Geographic Reach

AGCO has manufacturing locations in the US France Italy Finland Germany Austria Hungary Denmark Brazil and China. It manufactures and assembles its products in more than 50 locations worldwide including seven locations where the company operates joint ventures. Europe is its largest market representing about 55% of net sales followed by North America at around a quarter of sales.

Sales and Marketing

AGCO distributes its products primarily through a network of 4200 independent dealers and distributors who are responsible for retail sales to the equipment's end user in addition to after-sales service and support of the equipment. Distributors also sell its products through a network of dealers supported by the distributor. Sales are not dependent on any specific dealer distributor or group of dealers.It also sources machinery and parts from third parties to control costs inventory and supply partly in response to the high seasonality of agricultural machinery demand.

Financial Performance

AGCO's revenue is closely linked to shifts in the agricultural industry. In recent years AGCO has been stung by crop oversupply reducing farmers' revenue and expenditure on machinery and equipment. AGCO's revenue dipped more than 30% from 2013-16 as a result.

In 2017 the agricultural machinery industry began to recover as harvests and crop production fell from record highs and pushed up commodity prices restoring farmers' buying power once more. The recovery helped AGCO's grow its revenue for the first time since 2013 reaching $8.3 billion up 12% on 2016. Contributions from acquisitions and favorable currency exchange effects accounted for $295.1 million of the approximately $900 million top-line growth.

Net income also grew up 18% to $189.3 million on the back of higher net sales and increased productivity levels in Europe and North America; North America also benefited from cost reduction methods. On the downside margins shrank in Latin America due to lower production levels material cost inflation and a transition to higher horsepower tier 3 emission technology.

Cash inflow from operations increased 51% to $577.6 million thanks to higher net income and an increase in accounts payable and accrued expenses partially offset by an increase in inventories.

Strategy

AGCO continued to invest through the market downturn. The squeeze forced the company into seeking solutions to product development that marry innovation with cost reduction. AGCO developed its global platform and module strategy which leverages common product architectures and standardizes components across AGCO's sites and brands lowering costs and improving its products. The company is increasing the technological sophistication of its products; in 2017 it launched the Fendt 1000 tractor equipped with auto steering a connectivity module and Tractor Management System. It also made a number of acquisitions in the downturn to diversify its products and geographic spread.

The market downturn had the additional effect of forcing AGCO to improve its operational efficiency in search of margin growth amid low revenue. It targeted purchasing factory productivity and product development. It balanced reductions in sales and administrative and fixed manufacturing costs with focused spending.

Emerging economies present an opportunity for AGCO to introduce its high-tech machinery. Inefficiencies in the crop handling sector in Brazil and Eastern Europe offer the company with long-term opportunities for its grain storage and handling products. In China to grow its presence in the animal rearing industry AGCO established a joint venture with CP Foods to manufacture protein production equipment which will support sales and margin growth in the region.

Adhering to this strategy AGCO in 2017 announced plans to further develop its Challenger farm machinery business in Africa by integrating it with Fendt AGCO?s partner brand that manufactures agriculture tractors and machines. Challenger is AGCO?s core brand in Africa the Asia-Pacific region and North and South America.

Mergers and Acquisitions

Strategic acquisitions have supported AGCO's international growth.

In 2017 AGCO completed the $940 million of GSI Holdings Corp from Centerbridge Partners. GSI's primary business lines are grain-storage equipment and equipment used in raising hogs and poultry such as ventilation fans for barns and watering systems. The company markets its equipment under half a dozen brand names.

Also in 2017 the company also acquired Precision Planting LLC for $198.1 million. Precision Planting headquartered in Tremont Illinois manufactures high-tech planting equipment. The acquisition provides AGCO with an opportunity to expand its precision farming technology offerings globally.

HISTORY

In 1861 American Edward Allis purchased the bankrupt Reliance Works a leading Milwaukee-based manufacturer of sawmills and flour-milling equipment. Under shrewd management The Reliance Works of Edward P. Allis & Co. weathered financial troubles — bankruptcy in the Panic of 1873 — but managed to renegotiate its debt and recover. By the time Allis died in 1889 Reliance Works employed some 1500 workers.

The company branched into different areas of manufacturing in the late 19th century and by the 20th century the Edward P. Allis Co. (as it was then known) was the world leader in steam engines. In 1901 the company merged with another manufacturing giant Fraser & Chalmers to form the Allis-Chalmers Company. In the 1920s and 1930s Allis-Chalmers entered the farm equipment market.

Although overshadowed by John Deere and International Harvester (IH) Allis-Chalmers made key contributions to the industry — the first rubber-tired tractor (1932) and the All-Crop harvester. Allis-Chalmers spun off its farm equipment business in the 1950s and phased out several unrelated products. The company with its orange-colored tractors expanded and prospered from the 1940s through the early 1970s. Then the chafing farm economy of the late 1970s and early 1980s hurt Allis-Chalmers' sales.

After layoffs and a plant shutdown in 1984 the company was purchased in 1985 by German machinery maker Klockner-Humbolt-Deutz (KHD) who moved the company (renamed Deutz-Allis) to Georgia. In the mid-1980s low food prices hurt farmers and low demand hurt the equipment market. KHD was never able to bring profits up to a satisfactory level and in 1990 the German firm sold the unit to the US management in a buyout led by Robert Ratliff. Ratliff believed the company

could succeed by acquiring belly-up equipment makers turning them around and competing on price. It was renamed AGCO in 1991.

EXECUTIVES

Svp And Cfo, Andrew H. (Andy) Beck, age 54, $530,000 total compensation
Svp; General Manager Asia/pacific And Africa, Gary L. Collar, age 61, $480,000 total compensation
Chairman President And Ceo, Martin H. Richenhagen, age 65, $1,345,575 total compensation
Svp; General Manager Americas, Robert B. Crain, age 58, $306,667 total compensation
Svp And Chief Supply Chain Officer, Hans-Bernd Veltmaat, age 63, $575,000 total compensation
Svp; General Manager Europe And Middle East, Rob Smith, age 52, $566,512 total compensation
Vice President General Counsel, Debra Kuper
National Sales Manager, Martin Mills
Vice President Global Purchasing And Materials, Josip Tomasevic
Vice President Finance, Brian Zydel
Vice President Purchasing, Torsten Dehner
Vice President Finance, Frederic Devienne
Senior Vice President, Norman Boyd
Senior Vice President Human Resources, Lucinda Smith
Vice President, Steve White
Vice President Finance, Frederic Devienne
Vice President And General Manager Harvesting Eame Chief Executive Officer Laverda S.p.a., Francesco Quaranta
National Sales Manager, Martin Mills
Senior Vice President Global Business Services, Lucinda Smith
Vice President Distribution Development, Alistair Mclelland
Senior Vice President Engineering, Helmut Endres
Vice President And Managing Director Gsi Sa, Piero Abbondi
Vice President Global Purchasing Materials Logistics And 3rd Party, Mike Clem
Assistant Secretary, Lynnette Schoenfeld
Auditors: KPMG LLP

LOCATIONS

HQ: AGCO Corp.
4205 River Green Parkway, Duluth, GA 30096
Phone: 770 813-9200
Web: www.agcocorp.com

2017 Sales

	$ mil.	% of total
Europe/Africa/Middle East	4,614	57
North America	1,876	24
South America	1,063	12
Asia/Pacific	752	7
Total	**8,306**	**100**

2016 Sales

	% of total
United States	19
Other Europe	15
Germany	12
South America	12
France	10
Finland and Scandinavia	9
United Kingdom and Ireland	6
Canada	4
Middle East and Algeria	4
Asia	4
Australia and New Zealand	3
Mexico Central America and Caribbean	2
Africa	2
Total	**100**

PRODUCTS/OPERATIONS

2017 Sales

	$ mil.	% of total
Tractors	4,785	57
Replacement parts	1,305	16
Grain storage and protein production systems	1,049	13
Other machinery	582	7
Combines	349	4
Application equipment	235	3
Total	**8,306**	**100**

Selected Products

Application equipment
Combine Harvesters
Grounds care
Hay and forage
Implements attachments and material handling
Power generation
Seeding and tillage
Tractors

COMPETITORS

Buhler Industries	Komatsu
CNH Industrial	Kubota
Caterpillar	Mahindra
Deere	Toro Company

HISTORICAL FINANCIALS

Company Type: Public

Income Statement

FYE: December 31

	REVENUE ($ mil.)	NET INCOME ($ mil.)	NET PROFIT MARGIN	EMPLOYEES
12/17	8,306	186	2.2%	20,500
12/16	7,410	160	2.2%	19,800
12/15	7,467	266	3.6%	19,600
12/14	9,723	410	4.2%	20,800
12/13	10,786	597	5.5%	22,100
Annual Growth	**(6.3%)**	**(25.3%)**	**—**	**(1.9%)**

2017 Year-End Financials

Debt ratio: 21.49%	No. of shares (mil.): 79
Return on equity: 6.42%	Dividends
Cash ($ mil.): 367	Yield: 0.0%
Current ratio: 1.37	Payout: 24.1%
Long-term debt ($ mil.): 1,618	Market value ($ mil.): 5,683

	STOCK PRICE ($) FY Close	P/E High/Low		PER SHARE ($) Earnings	Dividends	Book Value
12/17	71.43	32	25	2.32	0.56	38.08
12/16	57.86	31	22	1.96	0.52	34.93
12/15	45.39	19	14	3.06	0.48	33.86
12/14	45.20	13	10	4.36	0.44	38.68
12/13	59.19	10	8	6.01	0.40	41.19
Annual Growth	**4.8%**	—	—	**(21.2%)**	**8.8%**	**(1.9%)**

AGFIRST FARM CREDIT BANK

The expenses involved in equipping and operating a farm add up quickly which is where AgFirst Farm Credit Bank comes in. AgFirst is one of a half-dozen members of the Farm Credit System a federally chartered network of agricultural and rural lending cooperatives. Boasting $30 billion in assets the bank provides financing to 19 farmer-owned agricultural credit associations. The associations in turn offer mortgages and loans to some

80000 farmers agribusinesses and rural homeowners through 280 branches in 15 eastern states and Puerto Rico. They also offer crop insurance credit-related life insurance and financial planning services. Instead of accepting deposits AgFirst raises money by selling bonds and notes on the capital markets.

Operations

AgFirst's capital markets arm arranges participates in and sells loan syndications for agribusinesses. Its correspondent lending unit buys sells and services agricultural and rural home loans throughout the US. About 68% of the bank's loan portfolio consisted of direct notes in 2014 while purchased participations/syndications made up another 19% of loan assets. The rest of the portfolio consisted of correspondent lending (12%) and loans to OFIs (less than 1%).

The bank makes almost all of its money from interest income. About 79% of its total revenue came from loan interest in 2014 with another 18% of revenue coming from interest on investment securities and other assets. The remainder of its revenue mostly came from loan fees.

Geographic Reach

Columbia South Carolina-based AgFirst serves 15 eastern US states and Puerto Rico. Its largest markets are in Florida North Carolina Georgia Virginia and Pennsylvania. The bank is also active in Alabama Delaware the District of Columbia Kentucky Louisiana Maryland Mississippi Ohio South Carolina Tennessee West Virginia and Puerto Rico.

Financial Performance

AgFirst Farm Credit Bank has struggled to grow its annual revenues and profits over the past several years as its loan assets have not increased and as interest margins continue to be squeezed in the low-interest environment.

The bank's revenue fell 7% to $703.8 million during 2014 as its loan assets barely grew to $20.9 billion or about the same levels as they've been since 2010.

Revenue declines in 2014 coupled with a rise in insurance fund premiums and salaries caused AgFirst's net income to shrink 17% to $380.3 million for the year. The bank's operating cash levels fell sharply to $370.9 million on lower cash earnings and unfavorable working capital changes mostly related to changes in accounts receivables balances.

Strategy

AgFirst has focused on maintaining strong personal relationships with its local customer base. It's also been investing more in security-based IT investments to protect its customers from security breaches. In 2015 it built a modern Data Center to accommodate the bank's growth with 1 Petabyte of data.

Company Background

The Farm Credit System was established by Congress in 1916 to provide a reliable source of credit for US farmers and ranchers.

EXECUTIVES

Ceo, Leon T. (Timmy) Amerson
Svp And Cfo, Charl L. Butler
Svp And Cio, Benjamin F. Blakewood
Vice President, Felicia Morant
Vice President Capital Mkts, John Burnside
Vice President Correspondent Lending, Eric Wilkowski
Vice Chairman, Dale R. Hershey
Chairman, Robert H. Spiers
Auditors: PRICEWATERHOUSECOOPERS LLP MI

LOCATIONS

HQ: AGFIRST FARM CREDIT BANK
1901 MAIN ST, COLUMBIA, SC 292012443
Phone: 803 799-5000
Web: WWW.AGFIRST.COM

PRODUCTS/OPERATIONS

2014 Sales

	$ mil.	% of total
Interest		
Loans	566	79
Investment securities & other	127	18
Non-interest		
Loan fees	8	2
Building lease income	3	-
Net other-than-temporary impairment losses	(1.4)	-
Gains (losses) on called debt	(7.7)	-
Gains (losses) on investments net	0	-
Gains (losses) on other transactions	0	-
Other	7	1
Total	**703**	**100**

COMPETITORS

AgriBank	Farm Family Holdings
Bank of America	First National of
COUNTRY Financial	Nebraska
Cat Financial	Rabo AgriFinance

HISTORICAL FINANCIALS

Company Type: Private

Income Statement — FYE: December 31

	ASSETS ($ mil.)	NET INCOME ($ mil.)	INCOME AS % OF ASSETS	EMPLOYEES
12/17	32,487	344	1.1%	530
12/15	30,620	336	1.1%	—
Annual Growth	3.0%	1.2%	—	—

2017 Year-End Financials

Debt ratio: —
Return on equity: 39.00%
Cash ($ mil.): 713
Current ratio: —
Long-term debt ($ mil.): —

Dividends
Yield: —
Payout: —
Market value ($ mil.): —

Agilent Technologies, Inc.

Products from Agilent Technologies have a measurable effect on the scientific world. A leading maker of scientific testing equipment Agilent supplies a slew of analytical and measurement instruments including gas and liquid chromatographs mass spectrometers vacuum pumps anatomic pathology workflows and genetic and diagnostic instruments and tools. Its operations include products used in life sciences chemical analysis energy and food forensics and environment. Agilent's customers include Bristol-Myers Squib Co. Dow Chemical Merck and the University of California Davis.

Operations

Agilent operates through three business segments: life sciences and applied markets diagnostics and genomics and Agilent CrossLab.

The life sciences and applied markets business bring in about half of Agilent's revenue by providing instruments and software that customers use to identify quantify and analyze the physical and biological properties of substances and products.

Agilent CrossLab accounts for about a third of the company's revenue with its portfolio of consumables and services.

Diagnostics and genomics generates more than 15% of Agilent's revenue from reagents instruments microarrays and synthetic RNA.

Geographic Reach

The US is Agilent's largest single geographic market accounting for 40% of sales. China the only other country Agilent reports separately accounts for a fifth of sales. Other international operations provide the remainder of revenue. Agilent has manufacturing plants in Australia China Denmark Germany India Italy Japan Malaysia The Netherlands Poland Singapore the UK and the US.

Sales and Marketing

Agilent sells most of its products directly although it also sells through resellers distributors e-commerce and other channels. It also has a diverse customer base — some 26000 customers in the life sciences and applied markets business about 49000 Agilent CrossLab customers and about 11000 diagnostics and genomics customers. The company spends nearly $40 million a year on advertising.

Financial Performance

Agilent maintained its steady growth over several years with a 6% increase to about $4.5 billion in 2017 (ended October) from 2016 driven by stronger sales in each of the company's three segments.

The company said life sciences had solid growth in biotechnology while the applied side of the segment had growth in the chemical and energy food and environmental markets. The diagnostics and pathology businesses drove revenue higher in diagnostics and genomics. In Agilent CrossLab the biotechnology and pharmaceutical chemical and energy and food markets boosted sales. Foreign currency exchange rates reduced its overall earnings by a percentage point in 2017 from 2016.

Agilent posted about a 50% gain in net income to about $684 million in 2017 from 2016. The company kept expenses to a lower percentage of sales in 2017 compared to 2016 producing the profit leap.

Agilent has about $2.8 billion cash on hand at the end of 2017 compared to about $2.3 billion the year before.

Strategy

Agilent has identified product and geographic markets primed for growth while it relies on the slower-growing chemical and energy and environment and forensics markets where it's the market leader for sustaining revenue. The company sees growth opportunities in food pharmaceuticals academic and government and clinical diagnostics areas where its market share lags the competition.

The company has invested about $1 billion on research and development in the past three years which has resulted in several new product that have caught customers' attention. An example is the Agilent Ultivo LC/MS triple quadrupole mass spectromter introduced in 2017. The instrument is 70% smaller than the previous model while performing as well or better than bigger devices. The company said it would maintain a similar level of research investment in the next three years.

The company also looks outside for technologies. Acquisitions in 2016 2017 and 2018 have helped Agilent expand its product lines for diagnostics therapeutics and genomics research. The purchases of Cobalt and Multiplicom have revved up Agilent's revenue in those areas.

Agilent continues to pursue opportunities in China and India where combined revenue surpassed $1 billion for the first time. The company intends to leverage its high position in instrumentation to gain share in services and consumables in those markets. Overall the Asia/Pacific region accounts for more than 35% of Agilent's revenue surpassing the Americas and Europe.

The company has maintained control of costs which it says should be aided by consolidating its company-wide financial reporting on one platform.

Mergers and Acquisitions

Agilent Technologies has been active in acquisitions in the past two or three years to add technologies to its portfolio.

In 2018 Agilent closed its acquisition of ProZyme a provider of glycan reagents kits and standards. The deal fortifies Agilent in glycobiology a fast-growing part of biopharma. Agilent also bought Ultra Scientific a provider of chemical standards and certified reference materials. Taken together the deals are part of Agilent's effort to provide customers with more workflow-specific consumables and tools.

Also in 2018 Agilent Technologies acquired Luxcel Biosciences developer of real-time fluorescence plate-reader–based in vitro cell-assay kits. The deal expands Agilent's cell-analysis portfolio with Luxcel assay kits designed for ease-of-use and compatible with industry-standard plate readers.

In 2017 Agilent purchased Cobalt Light Systems a provider of differentiated raman spectroscopic instruments for more than $50 million in cash. The acquisition of puts immediately slots Agilent into the fast-growing spectroscopy segment.

Another 2017 acquisition of Multiplicom N.V. added to Agilent's genomics portfolio with sequencing workflow capabilities from Multiplicom's molecular-diagnostics kits.

Agilent bought iLab Solutions a provider of cloud-based services for core laboratory management for $26 million in 2016. The deal gave Agilent an offering for managing laboratory time and work.

In 2016 Agilent bought a 48% stake in Lasergen Inc. a biotechnology company that develops sequencing technology to collaborate on sequencing workflow for clinical applications based on Lasergen's Lightning Terminators sequencing chemistry.

HISTORY

Agilent Technologies was formed in 1999 when Hewlett-Packard (HP) split off its measurement business. But Agilent's roots run as deep as HP's — Agilent's core products served as the original business of Stanford-trained electrical engineers William Hewlett and David Packard. The friends started HP in 1939 as a test and measurement equipment maker.In 1999 HP formed Agilent as a separate company for its test and measurement and other non-computer operations which by then accounted for 16% of sales. Edward Barnholt a 30-year HP veteran was named CEO of the new company.

EXECUTIVES

Svp And Cto, Darlene J. S. Solomon
Svp And Cfo, Didier Hirsch, age 66, $600,000 total compensation
President And Ceo, Michael R. (Mike) McMullen, age 57, $1,041,667 total compensation
Svp Global Infrastructure Services, Rick Burdsall, age 55
Svp; President Order Fulfillment And Supply Chain, Henrik Ancher-Jensen, $398,867 total compensation
Svp; President Agilent Crosslab Group, Mark Doak, $470,833 total compensation

Svp; President Life Sciences And Applied Markets Group, Patrick Kaltenbach, $487,976 total compensation
Svp; President Diagnostics And Genomics Group, Jacob Thaysen, $436,667 total compensation
Svp General Counsel And Secretary, Michael Tang
Svp Human Resources, Dominique Grau
Vp And Treasurer, Guillermo Gualino
Vice President Assistant General Counsel And Assistant Secretary, Diana Chiu
Vp Business Development And Strategy, Dave Tambling
Avp Finance Operations, Sanjay Abichandani
Vice President And General Manager Global Customer Service Operations Service And Support Division, Douglas Mcdougall
Chairman, Koh Boon Hwee, age 68
Treasurer, Barbara Nowaczyk
Auditors: PricewaterhouseCoopers LLP

LOCATIONS

HQ: Agilent Technologies, Inc.
5301 Stevens Creek Blvd., Santa Clara, CA 95051
Phone: 408 345-8886
Web: www.investor.agilent.com

2017 Sales

	$ mil.	% of total
US	1,314	30
China	900	20
Other countries	2,258	51
Total	**4,472**	**100**

PRODUCTS/OPERATIONS

2017 Sales

	$ mil.	% of total
Products	3,410	76
Services & other	1,062	24
Total	**4,202**	**100**

2017 Sales

	$ mil.	% of total
Life Sciences and Applied Markets	2,169	49
Agilent CrossLab	1,531	34
Diagnostics and Genomics	772	17
Total	**4,472**	**100**

Selected Products

Life Sciences and Chemical Analysis
  Clinical diagnostics
  Allergy testing
  Autoimmune testing
  Infectious disease
  Urinalysis
  Columns and supplies
  Informatics and software
  Instruments and systems
  Automation solutions
  DNA microarrays
  Electrophoresis
  Gas chromatography
  ICP-MS
  Lab-on-a-chip
  Liquid chromatography
  Mass spectrometry
  PCR and QPCR
  Spectroscopy
  Reagents standards and kits
  Cloning and competent cells
  DNA microarrays
  DNA target enrichment
  Instrument standards and kits
  Mutagenesis
  Nucleic acid purification and analysis
  PCR and reverse transcription
  Protein expression and analysis
  Protein preparation
  Real-time/quantitative PCR
  Total RNA and cDNA libraries

COMPETITORS

Abbott Labs	National Instruments
Advantest	PerkinElmer
Affymetrix	Rohde & Schwarz
Anritsu	Shimadzu
Applied Materials	Spirent
Beckman Coulter	Tektronix
Bio-Rad Labs	Teledyne LeCroy
Bruker	Thermo Fisher
Danaher	Scientific
Fluke Corporation	Ventana Medical
Illumina	Waters Corp.
Life Technologies	Zygo
Corporation	

HISTORICAL FINANCIALS

Company Type: Public

Income Statement

FYE: October 31

	REVENUE ($ mil.)	NET INCOME ($ mil.)	NET PROFIT MARGIN	EMPLOYEES
10/18	4,914	316	6.4%	5,100
10/17	4,472	684	15.3%	13,500
10/16	4,202	462	11.0%	12,500
10/15	4,038	401	9.9%	11,800
10/14	6,981	504	7.2%	21,400
Annual Growth	**(8.4%)**	**(11.0%)**	**—**	**(30.1%)**

2018 Year-End Financials

Debt ratio: 21.06%	No. of shares (mil.): 317
Return on equity: 6.72%	Dividends
Cash ($ mil.): 2,247	Yield: 0.9%
Current ratio: 3.29	Payout: 61.4%
Long-term debt ($ mil.): 1,799	Market value ($ mil.): 20,585

	STOCK PRICE ($) FY Close	P/E High/Low		PER SHARE ($) Earnings	Dividends	Book Value
10/18	64.79	76	62	0.97	0.60	14.37
10/17	68.03	32	20	2.10	0.53	15.00
10/16	43.57	34	25	1.40	0.46	13.12
10/15	37.76	46	28	1.20	0.40	12.57
10/14	55.28	40	33	1.49	0.53	15.82
Annual Growth	**4.0%**	—	—**(10.2%)**		**3.1%**	**(2.4%)**

AGSOUTH FARM CREDIT ACA

EXECUTIVES

Ceo-Pres, J Pat Calhoun
Director, Arthur Q Black
Director, James C Carter Jr
Director, Thomas H Coward
Director, Jimmy B Metts
Director, Jerome G Parker
Director, Charles C Rucks
Director, Hugh E Weathers
Director, Phillip E Love
Director, David H Womack
Director, Loy D Cowart
Auditors: PRICEWATERHOUSECOOPERS LLP FO

LOCATIONS

HQ: AGSOUTH FARM CREDIT ACA
26 S MAIN ST, STATESBORO, GA 304585256
Phone: 912 764-9091
Web: WWW.AGSOUTHFC.COM

HISTORICAL FINANCIALS

Company Type: Private

Income Statement

FYE: December 31

	ASSETS ($ mil.)	NET INCOME ($ mil.)	INCOME AS % OF ASSETS	EMPLOYEES
12/17	1,800	55	3.1%	226
12/16	1,722	40	2.3%	—
12/15	1,651	39	2.4%	—
12/14	1,594	49	3.1%	—
Annual Growth	4.1%	3.8%	—	—

2017 Year-End Financials

Debt ratio: ——
Return on equity: 42.40%
Cash ($ mil.): 4
Current ratio: —
Long-term debt ($ mil.): —

Dividends
Yield: —
Payout: —
Market value ($ mil.): —

Air Products & Chemicals Inc

Air Products and Chemicals has built a solid business out of gasses and liquids. The company produces and distributes atmospheric process and specialty gases in the US and across the world. It is a leading hydrogen supplier and also provides helium nitrogen argon and carbon dioxide among other gases. Air Products and Chemicals which generates more than half its revenue outside the Americas also provides related equipment and services (air separation hydrocarbon recovery natural gas liquefaction etc.) to customers in the energy electronics chemicals metals and manufacturing industries.

Operations

Air Products and Chemicals operates through four primary segments: Americas EMEA (Europe Middle East and Africa) Asia and Global.

The Americas is the company?s largest segment accounting for some 40% of sales and encompasses some 400 production and distribution facilities.

The Asia segment with its 170 facilities accounts for more than 30% of company sales while EMEA consisting of some 150 production and distribution facilities brings in more than 20%.

The Global segment (10%) includes R&D facilities in the US UK and Spain as well as Helium processing facilities in the US.

Geographic Reach

Air Products and Chemicals has major offices in the US (Pennsylvania) as well as in the UK (Hersham England) China (Shanghai) and Chile (Santiago).

It also has majority or wholly owned subsidiaries in the US and Canada as well as some 25 countries across Europe and Asia and about 15 countries in Latin America Africa and the Middle East.

The US generates about 35% of the company's revenue.

Sales and Marketing

Air Products and Chemicals sells its products to customers in many industries including metals glass chemical processing electronics energy production and refining food processing medical and general manufacturing. It distributes its products in liquid bulk (supplied by tanker or tube trailer) as packaged gases for smaller quantities (by cylinders and dewars) and at on-site facilities for large quantities to serve long-term contracts.

Financial Performance

Air Products and Chemicals has only seen modest revenue growth in the last five years growing from $8.3 billion in 2014 to $8.9 billion in 2018. Revenue jumped nearly 10% from $8.1 billion reported in 2017 with underlying sales growth driven by higher volumes across all regional industrial gases segments partially offset by lower sale of equipment activity in the global industrial gases segment. Some growth also stemmed from favorable currency impacts.

Despite the jump in revenue net income fell to $1.4 billion in 2018 (from $3 billion the year before) mostly due to the absence of $1.8 billion from discontinued operations posted in 2017. Ignoring that operating income actually climbed by $525 million in 2018 thanks to reductions in business separation costs asset impairment charges and other expenses totaling some $415 million.

Cash holdings at the end of 2018 was $2.7 billion a slight decrease from $3.2 billion the company held last year-end. Operations provided $2.5 billion offset by $1.6 billion used in investments (mostly in additions to plants and equipments) and a further $1.3 billion was used in financing activities (mostly in dividends to shareholders).

Strategy

Air Products is focusing on deploying $7 billion into high-return industrial gas projects across the world an area it has aggressively invested in. Despite cost headwinds in 2018 related to supply chain demands the company is focusing on improving cost performance in 2019. One of its biggest advantages may be leveraging newly acquired gasification technologies to drive additional gasification projects.

In 2018 the company completed the formation of a syngas supply joint venture with Lu'An and ramping up its recently concluded international operations including a hydrogen plant in India and air separation facilities in South Korea and China.

Divestitures have also been key to Air Products and Chemicals's funding generation strategy. In the 2016-17 period the company sold off its Performance Materials and Electronic Materials business while also exiting its Energy-from-Waste (EfW) business in the UK.

Mergers and Acquisitions

In 2018 Air Products and Chemicals acquired General Electric?s gasification business for an undisclosed amount. The acquisition helps the company to expand its syngas product offerings and reach. It comes with a 50/50 joint venture with a subsidiary of China Energy Group for gasification projects in China. The GE gasification technology has an extensive track record of processing solid liquid gaseous and blended lower-value feedstock into syngas. Air Products can then provide this syngas to customers to make higher-value products.

In 2018 the company completed eight acquisition in total that were accounted as business combinations. These acquisition had aggregate purchase price net of cash acquired of $355.4 million.

Company Background

Leonard Parker Pool founded Air Products in 1940 in Detroit Michigan on a simple but revolutionary idea: the ?on-site? concept of producing and selling industrial gases. The company started leasing out its oxygen gas generators in 1941. By the mid-60s the company expanded to Belgium West Germany and South Africa. In 1978 Air Products became a Fortune 500 company with $1 billion in sales. Today Air Products serves industrial gases to many industries including the food beverage chemical pharmaceutical oil field services and metals fabrication.

HISTORY

In the early 1900s Leonard Pool the son of a boilermaker began selling oxygen to industrial users. By the time he was 30 he was district manager for Compressed Industrial Gases. In the late 1930s Pool hired engineer Frank Pavlis to help him design a cheaper more efficient oxygen generator. In 1940 they had the design and Pool established Air Products in Detroit (initially sharing space with the cadavers collected by his brother who was starting a mortuary science college). The company was based on a simple breakthrough concept: the provision of on-site gases. Instead of delivering oxygen in cylinders Pool proposed to build oxygen-generating facilities near large-volume gas users and then lease them reducing distribution costs.

Although industrialists encouraged Pool to pursue his ideas few orders were forthcoming and the company faced financial crisis. The outbreak of WWII got the company out of difficulty as the US military became a major customer. During the war the company moved to Chattanooga Tennessee for the available labor.

The end of the war brought with it another downturn as demand dried up. By waiting at the Weirton Steel plant until a contract was signed Pool won a contract for three on-site generators. Weirton was nearly the company's only customer. Pool relocated the company to Allentown Pennsylvania to be closer to the Northeast's industrial market where he could secure more contracts with steel companies.

The Cold War and the launching of the Sputnik satellite in 1957 propelled the company's growth. Convinced that Soviet rockets were powered by liquid hydrogen the US government asked Air Products to supply it with the volatile fuel. The company entered the overseas market that year through a joint venture with Butterley (UK) to which it licensed its cryogenic processes and equipment. The company went public in 1961 and formed a subsidiary in Belgium in 1964.

Air Products diversified into chemicals when it bought Houdry Process (chemicals and chemical-plant maintenance 1962) and Airco's chemicals and plastics operations in the 1970s. The company continued to diversify in the mid-1980s as it built large-scale plants for its environmental- and energy-systems business and added Anchor Chemical and the industrial chemicals unit of Abbott Labs.

In 1995 and 1996 Air Products expanded into China and other countries by winning 20 contracts with semiconductor makers. It bought Carburos MetA?licos Spain's #1 industrial gas supplier in 1996. To focus on its core gas and chemical lines the company shed most of its environmental- and energy-systems business.

Expanding further in Europe Air Products bought the methylamines and derivatives unit of UK-based Imperial Chemical Industries (ICI) in 1997. The company sold its remaining interest in American Ref-Fuel (a waste-to-energy US operation).

In 1998 Air Products bought Solkatronic Chemicals and opened a methylamines plant in Florida to complement its ICI purchase. To further target semiconductor makers it formed Air Products Electronic Chemicals and allied with AlliedSignal Chemical (now part of Honeywell International).

The next year Air Products and France's L'Air Liquide agreed to buy and break up BOC Group. European Union regulators initially approved the deal but in 2000 the companies shelved the plan when other regulatory issues arose. Also in 2000 Air Products sold its polyvinyl alcohol business to Celanese for about $326 million. The company boosted its European presence in 2001 with the acquisition of Messer Griesheim's (Germany) respiratory home-care business and 50% of AGA's Net

EXECUTIVES

Chairman President And Ceo, Seifi Ghasemi, age 72, $1,200,000 total compensation

Evp Industrial Gases, Corning F. Painter, age 57, $573,077 total compensation

President Industrial Gases Europe And Africa, Ivo Bols

President Industrial Gases Asia, Wilbur W. Mok, age 58

President Industrial Gases Middle East India Egypt And Turkey, Richard Boocock

Svp And Cfo, M. Scott Crocco, age 55, $581,923 total compensation

President Industrial Gases Americas, Marie Ffolkes

Evp Materials Technologies, Guillermo Novo, age 57, $465,000 total compensation

President China Industrial Gases, Choon Seong Saw

Vp And Cio, Alyssa A. Budraitis

President Air Products Korea, Kyo Yung (K Y) Kim

President Air Products San Fu, Eugene Y. C. Lu

President Southeast Asia Industrial Gases, Alex Tan

Vice President And General Manager Epoxy Materials, Min Chong

Chairman President And Ceo, Seifi Ghasemi, age 72

Auditors: KPMG LLP

LOCATIONS

HQ: Air Products & Chemicals Inc
7201 Hamilton Boulevard, Allentown, PA 18195-1501
Phone: 610 481-4911   **Fax:** 610 481-5900
Web: www.airproducts.com

2018 Sales

	$ mil.	% of total
US	3,149	35
Europe/Middle East	2,292	26
Asia (Excluding China & India)	904	10
China	1,585	18
Other (Canada Latin America India)	998	11
Total	**8,930**	**100**

PRODUCTS/OPERATIONS

2018 Sales

	% of total
Industrial Gases- Americas	42
Industrial Gases- EMEA	24
Industrial Gases- Asia	28
Industrial Gases- Global	5
Corporate and other	1
Total	**100**

Selected Products and Services

Industrial Gases
  Argon
  Carbon dioxide
  Carbon monoxide
  Helium
  Hydrogen
  Nitrogen
  Oxygen
  Synthesis gas
Equipment and Services
  Air-pollution control systems
  Air-separation equipment
  Hydrogen-purification equipment
  Natural gas-liquefaction equipment

COMPETITORS

Airgas	Messer Group
Iwatani International	Praxair
L'Air Liquide	Taiyo Nippon Sanso
Matheson Tri-Gas	The Linde Group

HISTORICAL FINANCIALS

Company Type: Public

Income Statement

FYE: September 30

	REVENUE ($ mil.)	NET INCOME ($ mil.)	NET PROFIT MARGIN	EMPLOYEES
09/18	8,930	1,497	16.8%	16,300
09/17	8,187	3,000	36.6%	15,300
09/16	9,524	631	6.6%	18,600
09/15	9,894	1,277	12.9%	19,700
09/14	10,439	991	9.5%	21,200
Annual Growth	**(3.8%)**	**10.9%**	**—**	**(6.4%)**

2018 Year-End Financials

Debt ratio: 17.79%
Return on equity: 14.30%
Cash ($ mil.): 2,791
Current ratio: 2.17
Long-term debt ($ mil.): 2,951

No. of shares (mil.): 219
Dividends
  Yield: 0.0%
  Payout: 76.7%
Market value ($ mil.): 36,670

	STOCK PRICE ($) FY Close	P/E High/Low	PER SHARE ($) Earnings	Dividends	Book Value
09/18	167.05	25 22	6.78	5.20	49.46
09/17	151.22	11 10	13.65	3.62	46.19
09/16	150.34	54 40	2.89	3.34	32.57
09/15	127.58	27 20	5.88	3.20	33.66
09/14	130.18	29 22	4.61	3.02	34.49
Annual Growth	**6.4%**	**— —**	**10.1%**	**14.6%**	**9.4%**

AIRGAS, INC.

Airgas hopes its industrial customers walk on its air. The US industrial gas distributor's North American network of more than 1100 locations includes retail stores gas fill plants specialty gas labs production facilities (17 air separation plants) and distribution centers. Airgas distributes argon carbon dioxide hydrogen nitrogen oxygen and a variety of medical and specialty gases as well as dry ice and protective equipment (hard hats goggles). Its gases production unit operates air-separation plants that produce oxygen nitrogen and argon. The company also sells welding machines. The company is owned by Air Liquide SA.

Operations

The industrial manufacturing and repair and maintenance industries account for about a quarter each of the Airgas' sales; customers primarily make fabricated metal products industrial transportation and equipment chemical products and primary metal products. Other industries served include medical and health services agriculture mining repair and maintenance and wholesale trade.

Airgas' distribution business accounts for 88% of the company's 2016 sales. Almost all of its sales come from distributing bulk gases (nitrogen oxygen argon helium) gas cylinders and welding equipment. Airgas also produces gases to supply its regional distribution companies. Its other operations consist of six business units that manufacture and/or distribute carbon dioxide dry ice nitrous oxide ammonia and refrigerant gases. Gas and rent represented 61% of the distribution business segment's sales in fiscal 2016; hard goods 39%.

The distribution business operates a network of multiple use facilities consisting of 900 branches 300 cylinder fill plants 70 regional specialty gas laboratories 11 national specialty gas laboratories one research and development center two specialty gas equipment centers 11 acetylene plants and 16 air separation units as well as six national hard-goods distribution centers and various customer call centers buying centers and administrative offices.

Airgas' All Other Operations business segment consists of six operating segments all of which primarily manufacture and/or distribute single gas product lines (carbon dioxide dry ice nitrous oxide ammonia and refrigerant gases along with a nitrogen services business). It has 90 branch/distribution locations eight liquid carbon dioxide and 14 dry ice production facilities and three nitrous oxide production facilities.

Geographic Reach

Operating in all 50 states Airgas is the largest distributor of packaged gases in the US with a 25% market share. Outside the US it conducts operations mostly in Canada but also operates in the UAE Mexico Russia and in parts of Europe. It got less than 2% of its fiscal 2016 (ending in March) revenues from outside the US.

Sales and Marketing

The company serves customers in a range of industries including Manufacturing and Metal Fabrication Non-Residential (Energy and Infrastructure) Construction Life Sciences and Healthcare Food Beverage and Retail Energy and Chemical Production and Distribution Basic Materials and Services. It also has government clients.

Airgas markets its products and services through multiple sales channels including branch-based representatives retail stores telesales strategic customer account programs catalogs e-Business and other distributors.

Manufacturing & Metal Fabrication customers account for 30% of sales while Non-Residential (Energy & Infrastructure) Construction accounts for 15% and Food Beverage & Retail for 13%. Each bringing in more than 10% of sales are its Energy & Chemical Production & Distribution and Basic Materials & Services customers. Government & Other Life and Sciences & Healthcare customers account for the rest.

Strategy

Prior to its 2016 acquisition by global rival Air Liquide Airgas had grown its operations through acquisitions in its core businesses. It has bought more than 500 companies since its founding in 1986 and focuses on high-growth products with strong cross-selling opportunities. In fiscal 2016 it purchased 18 businesses (22 in fiscal 2015) with historical annual sales of $85 million. Airgas also grew through organic expansion.

HISTORY

In the early 1980s Peter McCausland was a corporate attorney involved in mergers and acquisitions for Messer Griesheim a large German industrial gas producer. When the German firm declined McCausland's recommendation in 1982 to buy Connecticut Oxygen he raised money from private sources and bought it himself. He acquired other distributors and then left Messer Griesheim in 1987 to run Airgas full-time.

Airgas began buying mostly small local and regional gas distributors in the US. By 1994 strategy shifted to purchasing larger "superregional" distributors such as Jimmie Jones Co. and Post Welding Supply of Alabama which added about $70 million combined to the company's revenues.

Airgas then began "rolling up" additional similar businesses. In 1995 it bought more than 25 companies and two years later it added more than 20 gas distributors. Also in 1997 Airgas expanded its manufacturing capabilities by building five plants that could fast-fill whole pallets of gas cylinders (the old manual system rolls cylinders two at a time). By 2000 the company had about 100 cylinder fill plants.

Struggling to integrate acquisitions while dealing with softening markets Airgas began a companywide realignment in 1998. To that end it sold its calcium carbide and carbon products operations to former partner Elkem ASA later that year; the company also consolidated 34 hubs into 16 regional companies and sold its operations in Poland and Thailand to Germany-based Linde in 1999.

In 2000 Airgas acquired distributor Mallinckrodt's Puritan-Bennett division (gas products for medical uses) with 36 locations in the US and Canada. The company also acquired the majority of Air Products' US packaged gas business excluding its electronic gases and magnetic resonance imaging-related helium operations in 2002.

In 2004 and 2005 it bought units from giants like Air Products and Chemicals BOC and LaRoche Industries. In 2006 Airgas continued to build with the purchase of 10 businesses including Union Industrial Gas which supplies Texas and much of the Southwest and then Linde's US bulk gas business for $495 million the next year. Linde in the process of integrating its 2006 acquisition of BOC then sold to Airgas a portion of its US packaged gas business for $310 million.

Rival Air Products had made a major bid to buy Airgas in 2010 but was rebuffed. Air Products extended its tender offer to Airgas stockholders several times and made a "best and final offer" of $70 a share (almost $6 billion) in December 2010. Airgas said it was holding out for $78 a share and rejected that offer too. In early 2011 a Delaware judge ruled for Airgas in a suit brought by Air Products to set aside a "poison pill" defense used by the Airgas board to fend off the takeover try. Following the verdict Air Products dropped its bid.

Airgas acquired six businesses in 2010 including Tri-Tech an independent distributor with 16 locations throughout Florida Georgia and South Carolina and annual sales of $31 million.

In 2011 Airgas reorganized its 12 regional segments into four new business support divisions — North South Central and West — to leverage a new SAP information systems platform in 2011. Each of the units is headed by a division president. The new company structure is designed to accelerate sales growth and pricing management and create operating efficiencies.

In fiscal 2012 the company added eight businesses with total annual sales of about $106 million. The largest of the busines

EXECUTIVES

Coo, Andrew R. (Andy) Cichocki, $296,936 total compensation
Svp Human Resources, Pamela J. (Pam) Claypool
Svp Sales And Marketing, Ronald J. (Ron) Stark
Svp And Cio, Robert A. Dougherty, $263,779 total compensation
President Airgas South, John F. Sheehan
Svp And Cfo, Robert M. (Bob) McLaughlin, $470,453 total compensation
Division President Gases Production, Thomas S. Thoman
Division President West, Douglas L. (Doug) Jones
Svp And General Counsel, Robert H. Young, $397,272 total compensation
Division President Central, Terry L. Lodge
President East Region, Jack Appolonia
Ceo, Pascal Vinet
Area Vice President, Denton Thompson
Vice President Human Resources, Tom Sheridan
Vice President Area Sales, Ross Jones
Vice President Of Information Technology Airgas Mid South, George Turner
Vice President, James Cook
National Sales Manager, Jerry Anderskow

Vice President Sales And Marketing, David Webb
Vice President Of Plant Operations, Roger Weber
Vice President Of Bulk Operations, Steve Scheuring
Vice President, Ted Schulte
Area Vice President, Jake Lucier
Vice President Of Finance, Jennifer Mihaljcic
Vice President Of Finance, Michael Maley
Area Vice President, Jeff Mann
Assistant Vice President Corporate Development, Brian Shammo
Senior Vice President, Ken Beringer
National Account Manager, Ken Ashworth
Division Vice President Of Sales, Mark Johnston
Vice President, Wayne Wilson
National Account Manager, Don Wallenfelsz
Area Vice President, Gene Klein
Vice President Operations, Robbie Cosner
National Account Manager, Victoria Ektarian
Vice President Bulk Gases, David Stockmal
Vice President Strategic Accounts, Jim Meyer
National Account Manager, Earl Dyck
Vice President, Kathryn Shuler
National Account Manager Metal Fabrication Markets, James Doyle
Vice President Gulf Coast Region, Scott Koonce
National Account Manager, Joe Sebastian
Vice President Credit And Collections, Ed Burke
Vice President Bulk Gases, Stephanie Benham
Vice President Bulk Sales And Operations, Richard Cassano
National Account Manager, Danielle Pogue
Vp Safety And Compliance, Curtis Henson
Vice President Safety And Compliance North Division, Benson Scott
Chairman, Pierre Dufour
Vice Chairman, Michael J. (Mike) Graff
Auditors: KPMG LLP PHILADELPHIA PENNSY

LOCATIONS

HQ: AIRGAS, INC.
259 N RADNOR CHESTER RD # 100, RADNOR, PA 190875240
Phone: 610 687-5253
Web: WWW.AIRGAS.COM

PRODUCTS/OPERATIONS

2016 sales

	% of total
Manufacturing & Metal Fabrication	29
Non Residential (Energy & Infrastructure) construction	15
Life Science & Healthcare	14
Food Beverage & Retail	13
Energy & Chemical Production & Distribution	12
Basic Material & Services	11
Government & Others	6
Total	**100**

2016 sales

	$ mil.	% of total
Distribution	4,716	88
Other Operations	635	12
Adjustments	(38.2)	-
Total	**5,313**	**100**

Selected Products and Services

Products
Carbon dioxide
Dry ice
Industrial gases
Argon
Helium
Hydrogen
Liquid oxygen
Nitrogen
Nitrous oxide
Oxygen
Safety equipment
Specialty gases

Services
Container rental
Welding equipment rental

Selected Subsidiaries
Airgas Canada
Airgas Carbonic
Airgas East
Airgas Great Lakes
Airgas Intermountain
Airgas Medical Services
Airgas Mid America
Airgas Mid South
Airgas Nitrous Oxide
Airgas Nor Pac
Airgas North Central
Airgas Northern California & Nevada
Airgas Refrigerant
Airgas Safety
Airgas South
Airgas Southwest
Airgas Specialty Gases
Airgas Specialty Products
Airgas West
National Welders Supply Company dba Airgas National Welders
Nitrous Oxide Corp.
Red-D-Arc
WorldWide Welding LLC

COMPETITORS

Air Products	Praxair Distribution
Lincoln Electric	Valley National Gases
Matheson Tri-Gas	W.W. Grainger

HISTORICAL FINANCIALS

Company Type: Private

Income Statement   FYE: March 31

	REVENUE ($ mil.)	NET INCOME ($ mil.)	NET PROFIT MARGIN	EMPLOYEES
03/15	5,304	368	6.9%	17,070
03/13	4,957	340	6.9%	—
Annual Growth	3.4%	3.9%	—	—

2015 Year-End Financials
Debt ratio: —
Return on equity: 6.90%
Cash ($ mil.): 50
Current ratio: 0.70
Long-term debt ($ mil.): —

Dividends
Yield: —
Payout: —
Market value ($ mil.): —

AK Steel Holding Corp.

Automobile sales help AK Steel's business keep rolling though it also has operations in the infrastructure and manufacturing industries. The company manufactures carbon stainless and electrical steel. It sells hot- and cold-rolled carbon steel to construction companies steel distributors and service centers and automotive and industrial machinery producers. AK Steel also sells cold-rolled and aluminum-coated stainless steel to automakers. The company produces electrical steels (iron-silicon alloys with unique magnetic properties) for makers of power transmission and distribution equipment.

HISTORY

George Verity who was in the roofing business in Cincinnati around the turn of the century often had trouble getting sheet metal so in 1900 he founded his own steel company American Rolling

Mill. His first plant in Middletown Ohio was followed by a second production facility 11 years later in Ashland Kentucky. Plant superintendent John Tytus whose family was in paper milling applied those rolling techniques to make American Rolling Mill's steel more uniform in thickness.

In 1926 Columbia Steel developed a process to overcome several production problems inherent in the Tytus method and in 1930 American Rolling Mill bought Columbia Steel. The company changed its name to Armco Steel in 1948.

Armco began diversifying in the 1950s and continued diversifying until the early 1980s. Subsidiaries were involved in coal oil and gas-drilling equipment and insurance and financial services among other things. In 1978 the company changed its name to Armco Inc.

Armco began shedding subsidiaries in the early 1980s. Sales and market share increased as the company approached the billion-dollar mark at the end of the decade. In 1989 Armco formed Armco Steel Company with Japan's Kawasaki Steel Corporation.

The company's sales reached $1.3 billion in 1991 though the high operating expenses in the steel industry of the 1990s kept profits low. Armco began looking outside the company for help and in 1992 it persuaded retired steel executive Tom Graham to head the company. Graham brought with him another industry veteran Richard Wardrop who would succeed Graham as CEO in 1995. After evaluating the company's holdings the two divested more than 10 subsidiaries and divisions. Armco also worked on improving quality and customer service with special emphasis placed on timely delivery.

In 1994 Armco's limited partnership with Kawasaki was altered and AK Steel Holding Corporation was formed with AK Steel Corporation as its main subsidiary and the Middletown and Ashland plants as its production base. The holding company went public the same year raising more than $650 million enabling the company to pay off its debt.

AK Steel Holding moved its headquarters to Middletown Ohio in 1995. Despite many naysayers Graham then pushed a plan to build a state-of-the-art $1.1 billion steel production facility. Many doubted the wisdom of going into long-term debt so soon after coming out of the hole — especially when a similar facility had produced lackluster results for Inland Steel. Graham stuck by his plant and in 1997 ground was broken on the facility in Spencer County near Rockport Indiana (Rockport Works). Graham retired that year and Wardrop took over as chairman.

In 1998 the company opened its Rockport Works cold-rolling mill and began operating a hot-dip galvanizing and galvannealing line. The next year AK Steel bought former parent Armco for $842 million. AK Steel acquired welded steel tubing maker Alpha Tube Corporation (renamed AK Tube LLC) in 2001. In late 2001 the company took a charge of $194 million for losses in its pension fund which had been battered by a weak stock market and lowered interest rates.

AK Steel sold its Sawhill Tubular Division to John Maneely Company (Collingswood NJ) for roughly $50 million in 2002.

AK Steel offered to purchase National Steel which was operating under Chapter 11 bankruptcy protection. However AK Steel's bid was trumped in 2003 by one from U.S. Steel that included a ratified labor agreement with the United Steelworkers of America. AK Steel also lost out in an effort to acquire Rouge Industries (later Severstal North America).

Chairman and CEO Wardrop and president John Hritz left their posts in September 2003. CFO James Wainscott was named president and CEO

and Robert Jenkins became chairman. (Wainscott succeeded Jenkins as chairman in January 2006.)

In an effort to reduce its debt AK Steel in 2004 sold its Douglas Dynamics unit a maker of snow and ice removal equipment for $260 million and its Greens Port Industrial Park a 600-acre development in Houston for $75 million.

In 2007 the company moved its corporate headquarters to West Chester Ohio.

EXECUTIVES

Vp Finance And Cfo, Jaime Vasquez, age 57
Ceo, Roger K. Newport, age 53, $579,551 total compensation
President And Coo, Kirk W. Reich, age 50, $479,551 total compensation
Vp Engineering Raw Materials And Energy, Maurice A. Reed, age 55
Vp Operations, Keith Howell
Executive Vice President Of Information Technology, Steve Boston
Vp Hr, Stephanie Bisselberg
Senior Vice President Of Human Resources, Larry Zizzo
Director, James A. Thomson, age 74
Auditors: Ernst & Young LLP

LOCATIONS

HQ: AK Steel Holding Corp.
9227 Centre Pointe Drive, West Chester, OH 45069
Phone: 513 425-5000   **Fax:** 513 425-5220
Web: www.aksteel.com

2016 Sales

	$ mil.	% of total
United States	5,226	89
Foreign countries	655	11
Total	**5,882**	**100**

PRODUCTS/OPERATIONS

2016 Sales (by Market)

	% of total
Automotive	66
Distributors & converters	18
Infrastructure & manufacturing	16
Total	**100**

2016 Sales (by product)

	$ mil.	% of total
Carbon steel	4,014	68
Stainless & electrical steel	1,654	29
Tubular steel	193	3
Other	20	0
Total	**5,882**	**100**

Carbon Steels

Carbon Steels
Alumized
Coil coated products
Cold rolled
Electrogalvanized
Enameling products
Hot dip galvanized
Hot dip galvannealed
Hot rolled
Ultalume®;
Stainless Steels
Austentic
Duplex Alloy
Ferritic
Martensitic
Precipitation hardening
Electrical Steels
Nonoriented
Oriented
TRAN-COR®; H
Antimicrobial Coated Steels

COMPETITORS

ArcelorMittal USA	Steel Dynamics
Dofasco	Union Electric Steel
Ferralloy	United States Steel
Kobe Steel USA	Worthington Industries
Nucor	

HISTORICAL FINANCIALS

Company Type: Public

Income Statement

FYE: December 31

	REVENUE ($ mil.)	NET INCOME ($ mil.)	NET PROFIT MARGIN	EMPLOYEES
12/17	6,080	6	0.1%	9,200
12/16	5,882	(7)	—	8,500
12/15	6,692	(509)	—	8,500
12/14	6,505	(96)	—	8,000
12/13	5,570	(46)	—	6,400
Annual Growth	**2.2%**			**9.5%**

2017 Year-End Financials

Debt ratio: 49.12%	No. of shares (mil.): 314
Return on equity: —	Dividends
Cash ($ mil.): 38	Yield: —
Current ratio: 1.83	Payout: —
Long-term debt ($ mil.): 2,110	Market value ($ mil.): 1,782

	STOCK PRICE ($) FY Close	P/E High/Low	Earnings	PER SHARE ($) Dividends	Book Value
12/17	5.66	556207	0.02	0.00	(0.69)
12/16	10.21	— —	(0.03)	0.00	(0.87)
12/15	2.24	— —	(2.86)	0.00	(5.50)
12/14	5.94	— —	(0.65)	0.00	(2.78)
12/13	8.20	— —	(0.34)	0.00	(1.62)
Annual Growth	**(8.9%)**	—	—	—	—

Alabama Power Co

Alabama Power sure powers much of Alabama. In continuous existence since 1906 this wholly-owned subsidiary of the Southern Company is a vertically integrated utility that provides electric service to retail and wholesale customers in Alabama and to wholesale customers in the Southeast region. Owning coal reserves near Plant Gorgas it boasts an annual production capacity of 6.2 million KWs of fossil steam from six generation stations as well as 1.7 million KWs each of nuclear steam and hydroelectric generation capacity. The company also markets and sells electric appliances and outdoor lighting services.

Geographic Reach

Alabama Power sells electricity and services to approximately 400 cities and towns including Anniston Birmingham Gadsden Mobile Montgomery and Tuscaloosa as well as in rural areas. It also sells electricity wholesale to 14 municipally-owned electric distribution systems.

Financial Performance

Revenue of Alabama Power went up by $150 million in 2017 to just over $6 billion. Most of that gain from rates and pricing hikes in retail and affiliate wholesale revenue increases of 40% due to higher natural gas prices. However the company has limited growth potential in the near term due to the lack of scope for customer growth and fluctuating revenue due to weaker demand stemming from warmer winters.

Profits went up just over 3% to $848 million due to an increase in higher rates charged to customers in 2017 in addition to refunds gained from 2016 partially offset by a decrease in retail revenues due to milder weather and slightly lower customer usage.

Cash holdings went up to $544 million. Operations provided $1.8 billion which was more than offset by investments of $1.9 billion mostly in property additions. However financing contributed $163 million keeping cash holdings in the positive.

Company Background

In 2011 Alabama Power completed a six-year $1.7 billion clean air project that called for the installation of scrubbers (air pollution control devices) at all seven of its largest coal fired plants in Alabama. By 2010 six scrubbers were in operation at four power plants in Jefferson Shelby Walker and Mobile counties.

In 2009 Alabama Power began exploring the possibility of generating power by burning wood and other renewable fuels at one of its coal-fired plants in response to government regulations calling for lower carbon emissions. In 2010 the company teamed up with The Westervelt Company agreeing to buy biomass-fuel (waste wood material) from the timber company.

EXECUTIVES

Vice President, William Johnson
Evp Customer Services, Greg Barker
Chairman President And Ceo, Mark Crosswhite
Vice President, Philip Raymond
Vice President, Kathleen King
Vice President, Richard Hutto
Vice President, Michael Saxon
Vice President It, Bob Bailey
Vice President, William Bowers
Vice President Of Marketing, Tony Smoke
Vice President Birmingham Division, Bobbie Knight
Executive Vice President, Steve Spencer
Vice President Employee Relations And Associate General Counsel, Chris Miller
Vice President Sales And Marketing, Barbara J Knight
Vice President Of Corporate Services, Bob Weaver
Vice President And Assistant Treasurer, Ronald Patterson
Vice President, Mark Crews
Vice President, Nicholas Sellers
Chairman President And Ceo, Mark Crosswhite
Auditors: Deloitte & Touche LLP

LOCATIONS

HQ: Alabama Power Co
600 North 18th Street, Birmingham, AL 35203
Phone: 205 257-1000
Web: www.alapower.com

PRODUCTS/OPERATIONS

2016 Sales

	$ mil.	% of total
Retail		
Residential	2,322	39
Commercial	1,627	27
Industrial	1,416	24
Other retail	(43)	-
Wholesale	352	6
Other	215	4
Total	**5,889**	**100**

COMPETITORS

AEP	Entergy
AES	Ferrellgas Partners
Alagasco	NextEra Energy
Duke Energy	Sempra Energy

HISTORICAL FINANCIALS

Company Type: Public

Income Statement
FYE: December 31

	REVENUE ($ mil.)	NET INCOME ($ mil.)	NET PROFIT MARGIN	EMPLOYEES
12/17	6,039	866	14.3%	6,613
12/16	5,889	839	14.2%	6,805
12/15	5,768	811	14.1%	6,986
12/14	5,942	800	13.5%	6,935
12/13	5,618	751	13.4%	6,896
Annual Growth	1.8%	3.6%	—	(1.0%)

2017 Year-End Financials

Debt ratio: 31.96%	No. of shares (mil.): 30
Return on equity: 12.62%	Dividends
Cash ($ mil.): 544	Yield: 0.0%
Current ratio: 1.43	Payout: 84.2%
Long-term debt ($ mil.): 7,628	Market value ($ mil.): 812

	STOCK PRICE ($) FY Close	P/E High/Low	PER SHARE ($) Earnings	Dividends	Book Value
12/17	26.58	— —	(0.00)	0.39	233.16
Annual Growth	—	—	—	—	—

Alaska Air Group, Inc.

Alaska Air Group operates through subsidiaries Alaska Airlines Horizon Air and Virgin America. The fifth-largest airline in the US Alaska flies more than 44 million passengers to more than 120 destinations with an average of 1200 daily flights in the US (mainly western states including Alaska and Hawaii) Canada and Mexico. The group's primary hub is Seattle (accounting for around three-quarters of passengers) but it also flies out of key markets such as Portland Oregon; Los Angeles; and Anchorage Alaska. Alaska Airlines has a fleet of about 155 Boeing 737 jets. Horizon Air operates some 50 Bombardier Q400 turboprops. Alaska Air Group in late 2016 achieved growth through the purchase of Virgin America for $2.6 billion.

Operations

Alaska Air generates 85% of its sales from passenger fares. Its passenger segment comprises Alaska Mainline its longer-haul operation with flight lengths averaging more than 1200 miles; and Alaska Regional offers shorter flights operated by Horizon SkyWest and PenAir. Mainline accounts for some 85% of passenger ticket revenue. The Horizon airline sells all of its capacity to Alaska under a capacity purchase agreement. In a given year Mainline operations carry 35 million paying customers while regional operations which includes Horizon transport around 9 million paying customers mainly in Washington Oregon Idaho and California. The passenger segment also generates non-ticket revenue as reservations fees ticket change fees and charges for baggage service.

Freight and mail account for 2% of revenue. Other activities which together account for around 15% of revenue includes the Mileage Plan on-board food and beverages commissions from car and hotel vendors and travel insurance. The Mileage Plan awards miles for flights on Alaska Horizon and partner airlines and sells miles to third parties.

Geographic Reach

Alaska Air Group serves more than 120 cities through an expansive network in Alaska the con-

tiguous 48 states Hawaii Canada Costa Rica Cuba and Mexico. The company leases operations training and aircraft maintenance facilities in Portland and Spokane as well as line maintenance stations in Boise Bellingham Eugene San Jose Medford Redmond Seattle and Spokane. It also leases call center facilities in Phoenix and Boise.

Sales and Marketing

Alaska Air's airline tickets are distributed through the airline's website and through traditional and online travel agencies. The travel agencies use global distribution systems to obtain fare and inventory data from airlines and reservation call centers located in Phoenix; Kent Washington; and Boise Idaho.

As its name implies Alaska Air Group transports more passengers between Alaska and the US mainland than any other airline. Besides its own flights the passenger segment provides passenger service through contracts with SkyWest Airlines and Peninsula Airways.

Financial Performance

Alaska Air's revenue has achieved lift-off in recent years as it adds new routes and planes and reconfigures seating plans.

In fiscal 2017 the acquisition of Virgin America took revenue to new heights climbing 34% to $7.9 billion. The company also grew organically adding 44 new markets and took delivery of 10 Embraer E175 regional jets. Passenger numbers grew 9.7 million to 44.0 million in 2017.

Net income increased 27% to $1.0 billion as tax benefits bestowed by the US Tax Cuts and Jobs Act lowered the effective tax rate to 14.3%. Tax gains were offset by a notable increase in operating expenses relating to higher wages a 21% rise in fuel costs and integration expenses meaning that despite the significant revenue increase operating profit was down.

Cash inflow from operations increased 14% to $1.6 billion due mostly to higher net income.

Strategy

Alaska Air is primarily focused on the successful integration of Virgin America into its own operations. In 2017 it merged back-office functions kicked off station co-locations and launched an interface that allows front-line employees to bounce between Alaska Air and Virgin America applications. In 2018 after it attained a single operating certificate from the Federal Aviation Administration the company brought Virgin America under the Alaska Air brand although Virgin livery will remain in place for several months while the company undertakes re-painting.

The company continues to find ways to improve the inflight experience. Recent developments have included in-flight WiFi menu upgrades and lounge expansion at JFK and Seattle airports.

Mergers and Acquisitions

In a noteworthy move within the US airline industry Alaska Air Group in late 2016 acquired Virgin America for $2.6 billion. The company expects the deal to boost its annual revenue by 27% and to add to its earnings within the transaction's first year. The combined company replaced JetBlue as the fifth-largest US airline by traffic.

The Virgin America acquisition helped Alaska Air Group to better serve West Coast travelers. Virgin America also provides a platform for Alaska Air's low-fare growth as well as enhanced international partnerships. Additionally the deal provides an opportunity to grow and improve the company's loyalty program while gaining access to constrained gates particularly on the East Coast.

HISTORY

Pilot Mac McGee started McGee Airways in 1932 to fly cargo between Anchorage and Bristol Bay Alaska. He joined other local operators in 1937 to form Star Air Lines which began airmail service between Fairbanks and Bethel in 1938. In 1944 a year after buying three small airlines Star adopted the name Alaska Airlines.

The company expanded to include freight service to Africa and Australia in 1950. This expansion coupled with the seasonal nature of the airline's business caused losses in the early 1970s. Developer Bruce Kennedy gained control of the board turning the firm around by the end of 1973. But the Civil Aeronautics Board forced the carrier to drop service to northwestern Alaska in 1975 and by 1978 it served only 10 Alaskan cities and Seattle.

Kennedy became CEO the next year. The 1978 Airline Deregulation Act allowed Alaska Air to move into new areas as well as regain the routes it had lost. By 1982 it was the largest airline flying between Alaska and the lower 48 states.

In 1985 the airline reorganized forming Alaska Air Group as its holding company. The next year Alaska Air Group bought Jet America Airlines (expanding its routes eastward to Chicago St. Louis and Dallas) and Seattle-based Horizon Air Industries (which served 30 Northwest cities). When competition in the East and Midwest cut profits in 1987 Kennedy shut down Jet America to focus on West Coast operations.

To counterbalance summer traffic to Alaska the airline began service to two Mexican resorts in 1988. Fuel prices and sluggish traffic hurt 1990 earnings but Alaska Air Group stayed in the black unlike many other carriers. Kennedy retired as chairman and CEO in 1991.

That year the airline began service to Canada and seasonal flights to two Russian cities. Neil Bergt's MarkAir airline declared war cutting fares and horning in on Alaska Air Group's territory. Alaska Air Group's profits were slashed and MarkAir went into bankruptcy.

Alaska Air extended Russian flights to year-round in 1994. The airline began service to Vancouver in 1996. That year it became the first major US carrier to use the GPS satellite navigation system. In 1997 it added service to more than a dozen new cities but halted service to Russia because of that country's economic woes in 1998.

Alaska Air Group and Dutch airline KLM agreed to a marketing alliance in 1998 that included reciprocal frequent-flier programs and code-sharing and in 1999 it added code-sharing agreements with several major airlines including American and Continental. Alaska Airlines developed an online check-in system a first among US carriers.

In 2000 an Alaska Airlines MD-83 crashed into the Pacific Ocean near Los Angeles killing all 88 people on board. A federal investigation of Alaska Airlines' maintenance practices found deficiencies but the FAA eventually accepted the airline's plan to tighten safety standards.

Like most carriers in the latter part of 2001 Alaska Airlines cut back its flights as a result of reduced demand after the September 11 terrorist attacks. As demand slowly returned in 2002 Alaska Airlines began to add new destinations and increase the number of flights on some established routes.

In its biggest deal ever Alaska Air Group in late 2016 acquired Virgin America for $2.6 billion.

EXECUTIVES

Vice President Information And Technology Alaska Airlines, Kris Kutchera
Chairman President And Ceo Alaska Air Group Inc. Chairman And Ceo Alaska Airlines Inc. And Chairman Virgin America And Horizon Air Industries Inc., Bradley D. (Brad) Tilden, age 57, $487,600 total compensation
President And Ceo Horizon Air Industries Inc., Gary L. Beck

Svp Communications And External Affairs, Joseph A. (Joe) Sprague, $303,846 total compensation
Staff Vp Finance And Controller; Staff Vp Finance And Controller Alaska Airlines, Brandon S. Pedersen, age 51, $390,769 total compensation
Evp And Chief Commercial Officer Alaska Airlines, Andrew R. Harrison, age 47, $383,077 total compensation
President And Coo Alaska Airlines, Benito (Ben) Minicucci, age 51, $426,923 total compensation
Coo Horizon Air Industries Inc., Constance Von Muehlen
Assistant To The Executive Vice President Finance And Chief Financial Officer, Lorraine Hurt
Vp Strategic Sourcing And Supply Chain Management Alaska Airlines, Ann Ardizzone
Vice President Marketing Alaska Airlines, Sangita Woerner
Vp Legal General Counsel And Corporate Secretary, Kyle Levine
Vice President Revenue Management, Kevin Ger
Vice President Capacity Planning, John Kirby
Chairman President And Ceo Alaska Air Group Inc. Chairman And Ceo Alaska Airlines Inc. And Chairman Virgin America And Horizon Air Industries Inc., Bradley D. (Brad) Tilden, age 57
Vice President Finance And Treasurer Alaska Airlines, Mark Eliasen
Auditors: KPMG LLP

LOCATIONS

HQ: Alaska Air Group, Inc.
19300 International Boulevard, Seattle, WA 98188
Phone: 206 392-5040
Web: www.alaskaair.com

PRODUCTS/OPERATIONS

2017 Sales

	$ mil.	% of total
Passenger Revenue — Mainline	5,858	74
Passenger Revenue — Regional	960	12
Freight & mail	114	1
Other	1,001	13
Total	**7,933**	**100**

2017 Sales

	$ mil.	% of total
Alaska		
Mainline	6,890	83
Regional	1,023	12
Horizon	430	5
Consolidating	(424)	-
Total	**7,933**	**100**

Selected Products and Services

Accessible services
Baggage
Book a Shipment
Children traveling alone
Customer of size
Delayed baggage
Emergency exit row
General Air Freight
GoldStreak®; Package Express
Infants and children
Price a Shipment
Priority Air Freight
Rate charts and surcharges
Ticket receipt
Track a Shipment
Traveling with pets

COMPETITORS

Aeromexico
Air Canada
Allegiant Travel
American Airlines Group
Delta Air Lines
Hawaiian Holdings

JetBlue
Mesa Air
SkyWest
Southwest Airlines
United Continental
WestJet

HISTORICAL FINANCIALS

Company Type: Public

Income Statement

FYE: December 31

	REVENUE ($ mil.)	NET INCOME ($ mil.)	NET PROFIT MARGIN	EMPLOYEES
12/17	7,933	1,034	13.0%	23,156
12/16	5,931	814	13.7%	19,112
12/15	5,598	848	15.1%	15,143
12/14	5,368	605	11.3%	13,952
12/13	5,156	508	9.9%	13,177
Annual Growth	**11.4%**	**19.4%**	**—**	**15.1%**

2017 Year-End Financials

Debt ratio: 23.92%
Return on equity: 31.09%
Cash ($ mil.): 194
Current ratio: 0.79
Long-term debt ($ mil.): 2,262

No. of shares (mil.): 123
Dividends
Yield: 0.0%
Payout: 14.3%
Market value ($ mil.): 9,046

	STOCK PRICE ($) FY Close	P/E High/Low		PER SHARE ($) Earnings	Dividends	Book Value
12/17	73.51	12	7	8.35	1.20	30.24
12/16	88.73	14	8	6.54	1.10	23.77
12/15	80.51	13	9	6.56	0.80	19.26
12/14	59.76	22	9	4.42	0.50	16.18
12/13	73.37	22	12	3.58	0.20	14.76
Annual Growth	**0.0%**	**—**	**—**	**23.6%**	**56.5%**	**19.6%**

ALASKA PERMANENT FUND CORPORATION

EXECUTIVES

Ceo, Angela Rodell
Coo, Marcus Frampton
Chief Financial Officer, Valerie Mertz
Portfolio Manager, Chris Cummins
Information Specialist, Andrew Loney
Principal, Chris Poag
Communications Manager, Paulyn Swanson
Executive Officer, Stephen Moseley
Portfolio Manager, Yup Kim
Information Technology Special, Anthony Shaw
Credit Analyst, Matthew Olmsted
Auditors: KPMG LLP ANCHORAGE AK

LOCATIONS

HQ: ALASKA PERMANENT FUND CORPORATION
801 W 10TH ST STE 302, JUNEAU, AK 998011878
Phone: 907 796-1500
Web: WWW.APFC.ORG

HISTORICAL FINANCIALS

Company Type: Private

Income Statement

FYE: June 30

	ASSETS ($ mil.)	NET INCOME ($ mil.)	INCOME AS % OF ASSETS	EMPLOYEES
06/18	67,671	5,109	7.6%	50
06/17	61,824	6,675	10.8%	—
06/16	55,346	(30)	—	—
06/15	55,900	1,586	2.8%	—
Annual Growth	**6.6%**	**47.7%**		**—**

Albertsons Companies Inc

Auditors: DELOITTE & TOUCHE LLP

LOCATIONS

HQ: Albertsons Companies Inc
250 Parkcenter Blvd., Boise, ID 83706
Phone: 208 395-6200
Web: www.AlbertsonsCompanies.com

HISTORICAL FINANCIALS

Company Type: Public

Income Statement — FYE: February 24

	REVENUE ($ mil.)	NET INCOME ($ mil.)	NET PROFIT MARGIN	EMPLOYEES
02/18	59,924	46	0.1%	275,000
02/17	59,678	(373)	—	—
02/16	58,734	(502)	—	—
Annual Growth	1.0%	—	—	—

2018 Year-End Financials

Debt ratio: 55.80%
Return on equity: 3.35%
Cash ($ mil.): 670
Current ratio: 1.22
Long-term debt ($ mil.): 11,707
No. of shares (mil.): 279
Dividends
Yield: —
Payout: —
Market value ($ mil.): —

	STOCK PRICE ($) FY Close	P/E High/Low	PER SHARE ($) Earnings	Dividends	Book Value
02/18	0.00	— —	(0.00)	0.00	5.00
02/17	0.00	— —	(0.00)	0.00	(0.00)
Annual Growth	—	— —	—	—	—

Alcoa Corporation

Auditors: PricewaterhouseCoopers LLP

LOCATIONS

HQ: Alcoa Corporation
201 Isabella Street, Suite 500, Pittsburgh, PA 15212-5858
Phone: 412 315-2900
Web: www.alcoa.com

HISTORICAL FINANCIALS

Company Type: Public

Income Statement — FYE: December 31

	REVENUE ($ mil.)	NET INCOME ($ mil.)	NET PROFIT MARGIN	EMPLOYEES
12/17	11,652	217	1.9%	14,600
12/16	9,318	(400)	—	14,000
12/15	11,199	(863)	—	16,000
12/14	13,147	(256)	—	—
12/13	12,573	(2,909)	—	—
Annual Growth	(1.9%)	—	—	—

2017 Year-End Financials

Debt ratio: 8.05%
Return on equity: 4.26%
Cash ($ mil.): 1,358
Current ratio: 1.30
Long-term debt ($ mil.): 1,388
No. of shares (mil.): 185
Dividends
Yield: —
Payout: —
Market value ($ mil.): 9,977

	STOCK PRICE ($) FY Close	P/E High/Low	PER SHARE ($) Earnings	Dividends	Book Value
12/17	53.87	46 24	1.16	0.00	24.42
12/16	28.08	— —	(2.19)	0.00	30.91
Annual Growth	17.7%	— —	—	—	(5.7%)

Alerus Financial Corp

EXECUTIVES

Senior Vice President, Mike Winkel
President; Chief Executive Officer Chairman Director, Randy Newman
Vice President Purchasing, Scott Harter
Vice President Commercial Relationship Manager, Robert Hartzell
Auditors: CliftonLarsonAllen LLP

LOCATIONS

HQ: Alerus Financial Corp
401 Demers Avenue, Grand Forks, ND 58021
Phone: 701 795-3200   **Fax:** 701 795-3378
Web: www.alerusfinancial.com

HISTORICAL FINANCIALS

Company Type: Public

Income Statement — FYE: December 31

	ASSETS ($ mil.)	NET INCOME ($ mil.)	INCOME AS % OF ASSETS	EMPLOYEES
12/17	2,137	15	0.7%	—
12/16	2,050	14	0.7%	—
12/15	1,744	16	0.9%	—
12/14	1,488	20	1.4%	—
12/13	1,380	20	1.5%	584
Annual Growth	11.5%	(6.6%)	—	—

2017 Year-End Financials

Debt ratio: 2.75%
Return on equity: 8.84%
Cash ($ mil.): 122
Current ratio: —
Long-term debt ($ mil.): —
No. of shares (mil.): 13
Dividends
Yield: 0.0%
Payout: 43.6%
Market value ($ mil.): 280

	STOCK PRICE ($) FY Close	P/E High/Low	PER SHARE ($) Earnings	Dividends	Book Value
12/17	20.45	18 15	1.10	0.48	13.18
12/16	17.00	19 16	1.00	0.44	12.47
12/15	18.90	17 15	1.17	0.42	13.61
12/14	19.75	42 14	1.44	0.38	(0.00)
12/13	51.00	35 21	1.46	0.34	11.21
Annual Growth	(20.4%)	— —	(6.8%)	9.0%	4.1%

Alleghany Corp.

Alleghany is a holding company with a focus on property/casualty reinsurance and insurance. Its subsidiaries include Transatlantic Holdings (TransRe) which offers property/casualty reinsurance (risk coverage for insurers) globally through Transatlantic Reinsurance Fair American and Trans Re Zurich. The group also issues specialty property/casualty insurance policies through RSUI Group and CapSpecialty. Targeting small and mid-sized US firms CapSpecialty underwrites specialty lines including commercial property fidelity surety and professional lines. Alleghany's offerings are marketed in the US and abroad.

HISTORY

Alleghany was formed in 1929 by Clevelanders Mantis and Oris Van Sweringen as a pyramid railroad holding company. It collapsed in 1934 and after passing through several hands it was bought in 1937 by speculator Robert Young with backing from Woolworth heir Allan Kirby.

Young resurrected the company's Chesapeake and Ohio railroad but another holding Missouri Pacific Railroad (Mo-Pac) failed to thrive and Young embarked on a 40-year struggle to maximize Mo-Pac's value. Young focused on railroads even as the industry declined but he also made other investments including a chunk of IDS (which became the US's largest mutual fund company) and real estate. He also trimmed company holdings from nearly 70 to about 10. By the time Young committed suicide in 1958 Alleghany was in trouble and Kirby who had always kept to the shadows took over.

In his first three years at the helm Kirby fought a takeover attempt by Abraham Sonnabend and a proxy fight with investors John and Clint Murchison. After being ousted briefly in 1961 Kirby re-emerged in control of the company. Allan suffered a stroke in 1965 and his son Fred Morgan "F. M." Kirby II took over.

In 1966 the company sold its interest in the New York Central railroad (bought in 1945) and eight years later finally emerged from the Mo-Pac mess with about $42 million in cash and some stock. Alleghany used the cash to buy metal fabricating company MSL Industries and the rest of IDS.

Fred Kirby's mantra was flexibility and in 1984 he sold IDS to American Express for a then-flabbergasting $800 million including a pile of stock. Kirby used these proceeds to buy Chicago Title & Trust the same year. Two years later he liquidated the old Alleghany and reincorporated Alleghany CT&T's parent as Alleghany Corporation.

Kirby used the cash from the American Express deal to buy and then spin off a construction company. Other purchases followed in the 1990s including more title operations a California thrift and in 1991 Celite which produced filtration materials. This line was expanded the next year with the purchase of Harborlite. After several purchases in direct insurance (quickly flipped for a profit) in 1993 Alleghany bought Underwriters Re.

In 1994 and 1995 the company bought up shares of Burlington Northern Railroad which merged with Santa Fe in 1995.

In the 1990s CT&T lost market share through industry consolidation so in 1998 Alleghany spun off CT&T's title operations (later acquired by Fidelity National Financial). The next year hit by a down market in reinsurance Alleghany agreed to sell Underwriters Re to Swiss Reinsurance keeping its hand in the market via Alleghany Underwriting Holdings Ltd. (AUL).

In 1999 the company bulked up its asset management operations through acquisitions and in 2000 its industrial fastener business Heads & Threads International bought Acktion's Reynold's Fasteners unit. In 2001 Alleghany sold Lloyd's reinsurer Alleghany Underwriting to Bermuda-based Talbot Holdings and Dutch bank ABN Amro bought the company's asset management business.

The company built up its insurance operations with the purchase of Resurgens Specialty Underwriting (RSUI Group) a subsidiary of British insurance powerhouse Royal & Sun Alliance. It also expanded insurance operations with the 2004 acquisitions of Capitol Transamerica and Darwin National Assurance Company (formerly known as U.S. AEGIS Energy Insurance Company) later renamed as Darwin Professional Underwriters. In early 2006 it took Darwin through an initial public offering and used the funds to reduce its equity interest while retaining majority ownership. (Alleghany's 55% stake in Darwin was sold to Allied World Assurance in 2008.)

While Alleghany collected insurance firms it shed other operations. The company sold Heads & Threads to a management-led investors group in 2004. In 2005 it sold its World Minerals subsidiary (diatomite production) to the US branch of Imerys in a deal valued at about $217 million.

Hurricane Katrina took a serious bite out of profits in 2005. In response Alleghany Insurance Holdings created AIHL Re a reinsurance subsidiary to provide reinsurance directly to RSUI while RSUI worked to reduce its exposure and increased its prices on property insurance. Once the reinsurance market settled down AIHL Re was allowed to go dormant in 2008.

During the quieter 2006 and 2007 hurricane seasons Alleghany found it still had an appetite for insurance providers. The company plunked down $120 million in cash to purchase 33% of monoline homeowners insurance provider Homesite Group in 2006 and spent $198 million to acquire Employers Direct in 2007.

Alleghany held 55% of Darwin Professional Underwriters a specialty property/casualty insurance writer but in 2008 sold it to Allied World Assurance for approximately $300 million.

F. M. Kirby retired as chairman at the end of 2006. His brother Allan Kirby retired from the board in 2010 leaving Jefferson Kirby F. M.'s son as the last family member on the board as directors. F. M. died at the age of 91 in early 2011.

Transatlantic Holdings caught Alleghany's eye and in early 2012 the company paid some $3.4 billion for the long-tail reinsurer. The deal's announcement in late 2011 ended a months-long buyout battle for Transatlantic.

EXECUTIVES

Chairman And Ceo Capspecialty Inc. (f/k/a Capitol Transamerica Corporation), Stephen J. Sills, age 69
Chairman Alleghany Capital Corporation, Udi Toledano, age 68
President And Ceo, Weston M. Hicks, age 62, $1,000,000 total compensation
President And Ceo Alleghany Properties, David J. Bugatto, age 53
President And Ceo Transatlantic Holdings Inc., Michael C. (Mike) Sapnar, age 51
Chairman President And Ceo Pacific Compensation Corporation, Janet D. (Jan) Frank, age 67
Svp Head Of Fixed Income And Treasurer, Roger B. Gorham, age 55, $600,000 total compensation
Svp General Counsel And Secretary, Christopher K. Dalrymple, age 50, $650,000 total compensation

Chairman And Ceo Rsui Group Inc., David E. (Dave) Leonard
Svp And Cfo, John L. (Jack) Sennott, age 52, $650,000 total compensation
Evp, Joseph P. Brandon, age 59, $825,000 total compensation
President And Ceo Alleghany Capital Corporation, David Van Geyzel
Vp Finance And Chief Risk Officer, Kerry J. Jacobs
Vice President Controller Assistant Secretary Principal Accoun, Peter R Sismondo
Assistant Vice President Accounting, Natalie Anbinder
Svp Head Of Fixed Income And Treasurer, Roger B. Gorham, age 55
Svp General Counsel And Secretary, Christopher K. Dalrymple, age 50
Chairman, Jefferson W. Kirby, age 56
Auditors: Ernst &Young LLP

LOCATIONS

HQ: Alleghany Corp.
1411 Broadway, 34th Floor, New York, NY 10018
Phone: 212 752-1356
Web: www.alleghany.com

PRODUCTS/OPERATIONS

2017 Sales

	$ mil.	% of total
Reinsurance		
Casualty & other	2,626	41
Property	1,181	18
Insurance		
RSUI Group	721	11
Cap Specialty	260	4
PacificComp	163	3
Net investment income	451	7
Net realized capital gains	107	2
Other	928	14
Adjustments	(16.9)	-
Total	**6,424**	**100**

2017 Sales

	$ mil.	% of total
Net premiums earned	4,955	77
Net investment income	451	7
Net realized capital gains	107	2
Other	928	14
Adjustments	(16.9)	-
Total	**6,424**	**100**

Selected Subsidiaries

Alleghany Capital Corporation
Alleghany Properties LLC
CapSpecialty Inc.
Roundwood Asset Management LLC
RSUI Group Inc.
Transatlantic Holdings Inc.

COMPETITORS

AIG	OdysseyRe
CNA Surety	PartnerRe
California Casualty	Reinsurance Group of
Everest Re	America
General Re	RenaissanceRe
Hannover Re	State Farm
Liberty Mutual Agency	Swiss Re
Munich Re Group	Travelers Companies
Nationwide	

HISTORICAL FINANCIALS
Company Type: Public

Income Statement
FYE: December 31

	ASSETS ($ mil.)	NET INCOME ($ mil.)	INCOME AS % OF ASSETS	EMPLOYEES
12/17	25,384	90	0.4%	4,402
12/16	23,756	456	1.9%	3,420
12/15	22,846	560	2.5%	3,135
12/14	23,489	679	2.9%	2,067
12/13	23,361	628	2.7%	1,985
Annual Growth	2.1%	(38.5%)	—	22.0%

2017 Year-End Financials
Debt ratio: 5.85%
Return on equity: 1.10%
Cash ($ mil.): 838
Current ratio: —
Long-term debt ($ mil.): —
No. of shares (mil.): 15
Dividends
Yield: —
Payout: —
Market value ($ mil.): 9,174

	STOCK PRICE ($) FY Close	P/E High/Low		PER SHARE ($) Earnings	Dividends	Book Value
12/17	596.09	112	89	5.85	0.00	553.20
12/16	608.12	21	15	29.59	0.00	515.24
12/15	477.93	15	13	35.13	0.00	486.02
12/14	463.50	12	9	41.40	0.00	465.51
12/13	399.96	11	9	37.44	0.00	412.96
Annual Growth	10.5%	—	—(37.1%)	—	7.6%	

Allegiance Bancshares Inc

Auditors: Crowe Horwath LLP

LOCATIONS

HQ: Allegiance Bancshares Inc
8847 West Sam Houston Parkway N., Suite 200, Houston, TX 77040
Phone: 281 894-3200
Web: www.alleglancebank.com

HISTORICAL FINANCIALS
Company Type: Public

Income Statement
FYE: December 31

	ASSETS ($ mil.)	NET INCOME ($ mil.)	INCOME AS % OF ASSETS	EMPLOYEES
12/17	2,860	17	0.6%	375
12/16	2,450	22	0.9%	327
12/15	2,084	15	0.8%	310
12/14	1,280	9	0.7%	304
12/13	1,164	6	0.6%	—
Annual Growth	25.2%	26.7%	—	—

2017 Year-End Financials
Debt ratio: 11.58%
Return on equity: 6.01%
Cash ($ mil.): 182
Current ratio: —
Long-term debt ($ mil.): —
No. of shares (mil.): 13
Dividends
Yield: —
Payout: —
Market value ($ mil.): 498

	STOCK PRICE ($) FY Close	P/E High/Low	PER SHARE ($) Earnings	Dividends	Book Value
12/17	37.65	30 23	1.31	0.00	23.20
12/16	36.15	21 9	1.75	0.00	21.59
12/15	23.65	18 15	1.43	0.00	20.17
Annual Growth	12.3%	— —	(2.2%)	—	3.6%

ALLEGIS GROUP, INC.

Allegis Group is one of the world's largest staffing and recruitment firms. Among its group of staffing companies are Aerotek (engineering automotive and scientific professionals) Stephen James Associates (recruitment for accounting financial and cash management positions) and TEKsystems (information technology staffing and consulting). Other Allegis Group units include sales support outsourcer MarketSource. Allegis Group operates through more than 500 offices worldwide. Chairman Jim Davis helped found the company (originally known as Aerotek) in 1983 to provide contract engineering personnel to two clients in the aerospace industry.

Operations
Allegis Group has more than 12000 internal employees including 3000 dedicated recruiters and 130000 contract employees working with customers around the world.

Geographic Reach
Allegis Group's corporate headquarters are located in Hanover Maryland. Outside of the US the company has operations in Canada Europe the Middle East the Pacific Rim Puerto Rico and the UK.

Financial Performance
Allegis Group averages about $11 billion in annual revenue.

Strategy
Allegis Group has expanded its geographical footprint and improved its position in specialist staffing markets through the use of acquisitions. The company's specialized staffing firms cater to various industries.

Mergers and Acquisitions
In 2016 Allegis Group acquired Switzerland-based staffing recruiting and services organization The Stamford Group. The deal increased Allegis Group's global footprint and strengthened its European presence.

EXECUTIVES

Cfo, Paul J. Bowie
President, Andy Hilger
V President-tax, Michael Bison
Chairman, James C. (Jim) Davis
Auditors: PRICEWATERHOUSECOOPERS LLP BA

LOCATIONS

HQ: ALLEGIS GROUP, INC.
7301 PARKWAY DR, HANOVER, MD 210761159
Phone: 410 579-3000
Web: WWW.ALLEGISGROUP.COM

PRODUCTS/OPERATIONS

Selected Subsidiaries
Aerotek
  Aerotek Automotive
  Aerotek Aviation LLC
Aerotek Canada
Aerotek CE
Aerotek Commercial Staffing
Aerotek E&E
Aerotek Energy Services
Aerotek Germany
Aerotek Netherlands
Aerotek Professional Services
Aerotek Scientific LLC
Aerotek United Kingdom
Allegis Group Canada
Allegis Group Europe
Allegis Group India
Allegis Group Services
InSearch Worldwide
Major Lindsey & Africa
MarketSource Inc
Stephen James Associates
TEKsystems
  TEKsystems Canada
  TEKsystems Germany
  TEKsystems Netherlands
  TEKsystems United Kingdom

COMPETITORS

ASG Renaissance	Kelly Services
Adecco	Korn/Ferry
CDI	ManpowerGroup
Curran Partners	RDL Corporation
ExecuNet	Randstad Holding
Heidrick & Struggles	Robert Half
Horton International	Snelling Staffing
Innovative Management Solutions Group	Volt Information

HISTORICAL FINANCIALS
Company Type: Private

Income Statement   FYE: December 31

	REVENUE ($ mil.)	NET INCOME ($ mil.)	NET PROFIT MARGIN	EMPLOYEES
12/17	12,296	0	—	85,000
12/16	11,502	0	—	—
12/15	11,222	0	—	—
12/14	10,827	0	—	—
Annual Growth	4.3%	—	—	—

2017 Year-End Financials

Debt ratio: ——
Return on equity: —
Cash ($ mil.): 414
Current ratio: 2.80
Long-term debt ($ mil.): —

Dividends
Yield: —
Payout: —
Market value ($ mil.): —

Alliance Data Systems Corp.

Alliance Data Systems provides private-label credit card financing and processing and database and direct marketing services to more than 2000 companies. In a given year it holds the credit for more than $15 billion in card balances. Its client base includes retailers like J. Crew Pottery Barn and Victoria's Secret as well as banks (Bank of America) grocery and drugstore chains gas stations and hospitality media and pharmaceutical companies. The company also develops and operates customer loyalty programs such as its Canadian-focused AIR MILES program. Additionally it performs database marketing predictive modeling and strategic consulting.

Operations

Alliance Data Systems operates three main business segments: Card Services Epsilon and LoyaltyOne.

Card Services generates about 55% of the company's revenue by operating private label and co-branded credit card accounts for retailers. The retailers achieve a degree of brand loyalty and Alliance gathers customer information and buying habits with which it helps the retailer more precisely target customers for future sales. Card Services manages more than 160 credit card programs whose consumer membership exceeds 40 million accounts. Alliance provides the credit behind the cards processes sales transactions and helps its clients leverage card branding to drive consumer loyalty.

The Epsilon segment serves roughly 1600 clients in industries such as financial services insurance media and entertainment automotive retail and hospitality. It gathers consumer data largely through its loyalty programs and credit card transactions then analyzes it to design client-customized digital and direct mail marketing programs. The segment generates about 30% of revenue.

LoyaltyOne accounts for about 20% of revenue. The segment gathers customer information through its loyalty programs to help Alliance clients design and implement marketing programs. It operates one of Canada's largest loyalty programs AIR MILES through which consumers earn miles as they shop at more than 150 brand name retailers. The BrandLoyalty program offers similar objectives for grocers primarily in Europe and Asia with a growing presence in North America.

Geographic Reach
The US accounts for more than 80% of Alliance Data Systems' revenue a share that has increased in recent years as Canada's share has decreased. The company is growing in EMEA and Asia Pacific.

Alliance has about a dozen facilities in the US including its corporate headquarters in Plano Texas a large facility in Columbus Ohio and offices in Texas Illinois and Idaho among others. Its LoyaltyOne segment operates in Canada and The Netherlands. The company's only other international facility is an Epsilon office in Bengaluru India.

Sales and Marketing
Although significant revenue is generated by card-carrying consumers Alliance's key customers are name brand retailers. It is through the likes of L Brands (owner of Victoria's Secret and Bath & Body Works) and Ascena Retail Group (Lane Bryant and dressbarn) that Alliance issues new cards increases the number of consumer customers and mines data essential to the Epsilon segment. The company typically enters into multi-year contracts with such retail partners. To manage loan loss risk from its credit card account holders Alliance targets retail brands that appeal to middle and upper-class consumers and intentionally avoids issuing cards to sub-prime borrowers.

Its 10 largest clients account for about 35% of total revenue. The LoyaltyOne business counts Bank of Montreal and Canada-based grocer Sobeys as its largest clients together representing 35% of segment revenue.

The company operates in a highly competitive market contending with marketing services companies credit card issuers and data processing companies as well as with the in-house staffs of current and potential clients.

Financial Performance
Alliance's revenue and profits have more than doubled since 2011 as consumers' use of reward programs and credit and debit cards has ballooned.

Revenue increased 8% to $7.7 billion in 2017 from $7.1 billion in 2016. Services revenue rose 4% driven by double-digit growth in its automotive agency and digital CRM offerings. Finance charges revenue increased 15% from higher average credit card and loan receivables. Redemption revenue slumped 6% from a slowdown in short-term loyalty programs because of fewer campaigns and their timing. Revenue dipped in the second half of 2017 because Alliance suspended payments for customers affected by hurricanes.

Net income jumped 52% to $789 million in 2017 from 2016 with help from higher revenue and a tax benefit from the US Tax Cuts and Jobs Act.

Alliance had $4.2 billion in cash in 2017 compared to $1.8 billion in 2016. In 2017 operations generated $2.6 billion and financing activities provided $4 billion while investing activities used $4.3 billion.

Strategy

Alliance's strategy includes building its Card Services customer base shifting Epsilon's product mix towards targeted direct marketing and shoring up LoyaltyOne following the impact of an Ontario Canada law change.

With credit and debit card use driving Alliance's financial performance the company continues to seek co-branded partnerships with a variety of retailers to increase its borrower base. The company signed a long-term agreement to provide branded credit card programs to Boscov's Department Store (the largest family-owned department chain in the US) clothing retailer Forever 21 and luxury home furnishings shop Restoration Hardware.

Following industry shifts Alliance is trending away from mass marketing (such as direct mailings) and moving towards direct personalized efforts made possible by mining data from its huge consumer base and applying data analytics to design targeted ads. In recent years it experienced time-to-market slowness and cost competition that impeded sales. It is addressing these problems with renewed focus on its less-customized (and less expensive) technology offerings and redirecting some of its focus into the mid-market space and into digital marketing.

The LoyaltyOne business was hit hard in 2016 with a law change in the province of Ontario Canada that rescinded the company's 5-year expiration of loyalty points. Assuming other provinces would follow Alliance took the step to change its valuation model and accepted a more than $200 million hit to revenue. The business stabilized in 2018 fortified by major sponsors and most collectors that stuck with the program. The largest sponsor Bank of Montreal renewed in 2017.

In late 2018 Alliance started shopping its Epsilon business around. The company said that the strategies that would improve Epsilon were different than those for its Card Services business. The decision came out of a strategic review the company conducted. Proceeds from a sale would go to pay down debt and buy back share and pay dividends.

Company Background

Alliance Data Systems was formed by the 1996 acquisition by Welsh Carson Anderson & Stowe of J.C. Penney's transaction services business and L Brands' credit card bank operation Comenity Bank (formerly World Financial Network Bank which is now a subsidiary of the company.

EXECUTIVES

Evp And Cfo, Charles L. Horn, age 57, $627,000 total compensation

President And Ceo, Edward J. (Ed) Heffernan, age 55, $1,114,000 total compensation

Evp; President Loyaltyone, Bryan A. Pearson, age 55, $459,895 total compensation

Evp; President Epsilon, Bryan J. Kennedy, age 49, $602,500 total compensation

Evp; President Retail Credit Services, Melisa A. Miller, age 59, $602,500 total compensation

Svp And Chief Accounting Officer, Laura Santillan

Vice President Corporate Human Resources, Calvin Hilton

Vice President Client Sales, Gwen Mannarino

Senior Vice President Tax, Jeffrey Fair

Regional Vp Care Center Operations, Lance Beck

Senior Vice President And Treasurer, Jeff Chesnut

Svp Corporate Affairs And Chief Of Staff, Karen Wald

Svp Cio And Cto Card Services, Mike Rosello

Svp General Counsel And Secretary, Joseph Motes

Vice President Business Solutions Development, Jen Williamson

Vp Corporate Affairs And Head Strategic Insights, Rodney Davenport

Vp Sales Card Services, Darian Culbertson

Chairman, Robert A. Minicucci, age 65

Auditors: DELOITTE & TOUCHE LLP

LOCATIONS

HQ: Alliance Data Systems Corp.
7500 Dallas Parkway, Suite 700, Plano, TX 75024
Phone: 214 494-3000
Web: www.alliancedata.com

PRODUCTS/OPERATIONS

2017 Sales by Segment

	$ mil.	% of total
Card Services	4,170	55
Epsilon	2,272	29
LoyaltyOne	1,303	16
Corporate & other	0	-
Eliminations	(27.4)	-
Total	**7,719**	**100**

2017 Sales

	$ mil.	% of total
U.S.	6,336	82
Canada	742	10
Europe Middle East & Africa	485	6
Asia Pacific	140	2
Other	15	0
Total	**7,719**	**100**

2017 Sales

	$ mil.	% of total
Finance charges net	4,171	54
Services	2,612	34
Redemption	935	12
Total	**7,719**	**100**

Selected Products and Services

Epsilon
  Marketing Services
  Agency services
  Database design & management
  Data services
  Analytical services
  Traditional & digital communications
LoyaltyOne
  AIR MILES Reward program
  Loyalty services
  Customer analytics
  Creative services
Private Label Services & Credit
  Receivables Financing
  Underwriting & risk management
  Receivables funding
  Processing Services
  New account processing
  Bill processing
  Remittance processing
  Customer care
  Marketing Services

COMPETITORS

ATCO I-Tek	Discover
Affinion Group	Maritz
American Express	PGi
Capital One	Payment Processing
Chockstone	Total System Services

HISTORICAL FINANCIALS

Company Type: Public

Income Statement
FYE: December 31

	REVENUE ($ mil.)	NET INCOME ($ mil.)	NET PROFIT MARGIN	EMPLOYEES
12/17	7,719	788	10.2%	20,000
12/16	7,138	515	7.2%	17,000
12/15	6,439	596	9.3%	16,000
12/14	5,302	506	9.5%	15,000
12/13	4,319	496	11.5%	12,000
Annual Growth	**15.6%**	**12.3%**	**—**	**13.6%**

2017 Year-End Financials

Debt ratio: 48.52%	No. of shares (mil.): 55
Return on equity: 44.90%	Dividends
Cash ($ mil.) 4,190	Yield: 0.0%
Current ratio: 2.43	Payout: 14.7%
Long-term debt ($ mil.): 13,415	Market value ($ mil.): 14,043

	STOCK PRICE ($) FY Close	P/E High/Low		PER SHARE ($) Earnings	Dividends	Book Value
12/17	253.48	19	15	14.10	2.08	33.49
12/16	228.50	38	24	7.34	0.52	28.89
12/15	276.57	35	28	8.85	0.00	33.02
12/14	286.05	34	27	7.87	0.00	37.55
12/13	262.93	26	14	7.42	0.00	16.60
Annual Growth	**(0.9%)**	**—**	**—**	**17.4%**	**—**	**19.2%**

Allstate Corp

Ya gotta hand it to Allstate: The "good hands" company has managed to work its way towards the top of the property/casualty insurance pile. Serving more than 16 million households the company is the second-largest personal lines insurer in the US just behind rival State Farm. Its Allstate Protection segment sells auto homeowners and other property/casualty insurance products in Canada and the US. Allstate Life provides life insurance through subsidiaries including Allstate Life and American Heritage Life. The group also provides voluntary benefits such as short-term disability and critical illness policies. Other units include Allstate Roadside Services and consumer protection plan provider SquareTrade.

Operations

Allstate operates through seven segments: Allstate Protection Service Businesses Allstate Life Allstate Benefits Allstate Annuities Discontinued Lines and Coverages and Corporate and Other.

The Allstate Protection segment's property and liability businesses — which cover about 16 million households — account for more than 90% of Allstate's total premiums. Most of the segment's sales come from traditional auto and homeowners policies. In addition to traditional policies Allstate sells specialty products including coverage for motorcycle and boat owners renters and landlords and mobile home dwellers. The segment includes subsidiaries Esurance (auto insurance) Encompass (package policies) and Answer Financial (agency sales) operate online. Commercial products are geared towards small business owners.

The Service Businesses segment includes consumer protection plan provider SquareTrade telematics unit Arity Allstate Roadside Services and Allstate Dealer Services.

In late 2017 the company restructured its former Allstate Financial segment into three separate segments. Allstate Life offers traditional interest-sensitive and variable life insurance products. Allstate Benefits provides voluntary benefits policies such as life accident short-term disability and critical illness policies. Allstate Annuities comprises the run-off annuity business which the company exited in 2014. While these segments account for approximately 10% of the company's total revenue Allstate primarily considers them to be useful for deepening relationships with Allstate Protection customers.

The Discontinued Lines and Coverages segment includes results from coverage Allstate no longer writes and run-off businesses.

Geographic Reach

Allstate's largest property/casualty markets are California Florida New York and Texas. The company operates throughout the US and in Puerto Rico the US Virgin Islands Guam and Canada. It has some 500 administrative claims handling data processing and other facilities in North America. It also leases properties in Northern Ireland (three) India (two) and London (two).

Sales and Marketing

Allstate maintains a network of about 10400 exclusive agencies which sell its Allstate-branded insurance products through approximately 24000 licensed sales professionals. It also offers these products and Encompass-branded products through some 2500 independent agencies that are primarily located in rural areas of the US.

Allstate Financial products are sold through exclusive agencies (and approximately 100 exclusive specialists) and 6000 workplace enrolling independent agents. Other products are sold through financial representatives online and over the phone.

In 2017 Allstate spend $8.3 million on advertising versus $11.2 million in 2016.

Financial Performance

Allstate's revenue has grown steadily over the past five years; it rose 5% to $38.5 billion in 2017. This gain was largely driven by a 3% or $1 billion increase in property and liability insurance premiums. The acquisition of consumer protection plan firm SquareTrade further helped overall revenue. Additionally the company saw net realized capital gains in 2017 versus net realized capital losses the prior year. These gains were partially offset by higher catastrophe losses related to hurricanes wildfires and wind and hail storms.

The higher revenue boosted net income (which had fallen in 2015 and 2016) by 70% to $3.2 billion. A benefit related to 2017 tax legislation also lifted its bottom line. However net income was negatively impacted by a $59 million net loss in the Service Businesses segment as the company invested in its various units.

Operating cash flow also rose increasing 8% to $4.3 billion.

Strategy

Allstate is focused on growing its number of insurance policies in force increasing premiums maintaining profitability in the auto segment and increasing returns in the homeowners and annuity segments. It is also focused on proactively managing its investments modernizing its operating model and building long-term growth platforms. To grow policy sales the company is enhancing its independent agency network (especially in targeted geographic areas) sales support organization and online sales platforms. It is also working to increase cross-sales of voluntary benefit products through its exclusive agents as well as to form new strategic alliances and develop new product offerings. For example the company has recently launched protection for home-sharing hosts and for Uber rideshare drivers. Allstate Canada introduced products to protect homeowners from sewer backups and water damage in 2018. Subsidiary Esurance

is expanding both by adding new complementary products and by launching its products in new geographical locations. At the same time Allstate is working to reduce its operational costs.

The company is continuing to invest in automotive telematics or wireless device technologies that track drivers' habits through which it can provide more accurate policy pricing.

Catastrophe management is also a key part of the company's stability. To limit its exposure to catastrophic claims in the face of increasing severe weather events in recent years Allstate has quit writing new homeowners policies in some coastal areas including California and Florida that are vulnerable to hurricane wind storms and earthquakes. In 2016 the company began writing a limited number of homeowner policies in certain areas of California. And while it still renews existing homeowners policies in California the company tweaked its underwriting to reduce exposure to claims for fires following earthquakes. Unfortunately 2017 had several major events including hurricanes severe storms and wildfires which caused the company more than $3 billion in catastrophe losses.

Mergers and Acquisitions

In 2018 Allstate bought Arizona-based InfoArmor which provides employee identity protection for $525 million. The acquisition added to Allstate Benefits' voluntary identity protection offerings.

In early 2017 Allstate acquired rapidly growing consumer protection plan provider SquareTrade which specializes in extended warranties for electronics devices. The $1.4 billion deal expanded Allstate's consumer-focused offerings adding some 25 million protection plans.

HISTORY

Allstate traces its origins to a friendly game of bridge played in 1930 on a Chicago-area commuter train by Sears president Robert Wood and a friend insurance broker Carl Odell. The insurance man suggested Sears sell auto insurance through the mail. Wood liked the idea financed the company and in 1931 put Odell in charge (that hand of bridge must have shown Wood that Odell was no dummy). The company was named Allstate after one of Sears' tire brands. Allstate was born just as Sears was beginning its push into retailing and Allstate went with it selling insurance out of all the new Sears stores.

Growth was slow during the Depression and WWII but the postwar boom was a gold mine for both Sears and Allstate. Suburban development made cars a necessity; 1950s prudence necessitated car insurance; and Sears made it easy to buy the insurance at their stores and increasingly at freestanding agencies.

In the late 1950s Allstate added home and other property/casualty insurance lines. It also went into life insurance — in-force policies zoomed from zero to $1 billion in six years the industry's fastest growth ever.

Sears formed Allstate Enterprises in 1960 as an umbrella for all its noninsurance operations. In 1970 that firm bought its first savings and loan (S&L). The insurer continued to acquire other S&Ls and to add subsidiaries throughout the 1970s and 1980s.

This strategy dovetailed with Sears' strategy which was to become a diversified financial services company. In 1985 Sears introduced the Discover Card through Allstate's Greenwood Trust Company. However by the late 1980s it was obvious Sears would never be a financial services giant. Moreover it was losing so much in retailing that by 1987 Allstate was the major contributor to corporate net income. Sears began to dismantle its financial empire in the 1990s.

Allstate also suffered from a backlash against high insurance rates. When Massachusetts instituted no-fault insurance in 1989 Allstate stopped writing new auto insurance there. Later the company had to refund $110 million to customers to settle a suit with California over rate rollbacks required by 1988's Proposition 103.

Allstate went public in 1993 when Sears sold about 20% of its stake. That year it began reducing its operations in Florida to protect itself against high losses from hurricanes. Two years later the retailer sold its remaining interest to its shareholders. Also in 1995 Allstate sold 70% of PMI its mortgage insurance unit to the public.

EXECUTIVES

Senior Vice President Marketing, Robert Apatoff

Executive Vice President, Michael Roche

Chairman President And Ceo The Allstate Corporation And Allstate Insurance Company, Thomas J. Wilson, age 60, $1,200,000 total compensation

Vice President Finance, Norma Gorman

Evp Marketing Innovation And Corporate Relations Allstate Insurance, Sanjay Gupta, age 50

President Allstate Financial, Mary Jane B. Fortin, $632,752 total compensation

President Service Businesses, Don Civgin, age 57, $776,885 total compensation

Evp Product Integration And Management, W. Guy Hill

Evp Product Operations Allstate Insurance, Steven P. Sorenson, age 54

Evp Brand Operations Allstate Insurance, Thomas M. Troy

Evp Technology And Strategic Ventures, Suren Gupta, age 56, $537,404 total compensation

President West Territory Allstate Personal Lines, Thomas F. Clarkson

President East Territory, David Prendergast

President Allstate Personal Lines, Glenn T. Shapiro

Evp Allstate Brand Distribution Allstate Insurance Company (aic), Katherine (Kathy) Mabe

Vice Chairman The Allstate Corporation And Allstate Insurance Company, Steven E. (Steve) Shebik, age 61, $770,673 total compensation

Evp General Counsel And Secretary Allstate Corp And Allstate Insurance Company (aic), Susan L. Lees, age 60

Evp Allstate Personal Lines Business Transformation, Brian R. Bohaty

Evp Human Resources, Harriet K. Harty, age 51

Evp And Chief Investment Officer; President Allstate Investments, John Dugenske

Evp And Cfo The Allstate Corporation And Allstate Insurance Company, Mario Rizzo

Field Vice President Midwest Region, Alice Byrne

Vice President Technology And Operations The Allstate Corpor, Butch Necastro

Department Head, Paul Schutt

Vice President Of Product And Pricing, Keith Green

Assistant Vice President, Steve King

Assistant Vice President, Terrance Ray

Assistant Vice President And Chief Actuary, Errol Cramer

Vice President And Assistant General Counsel, William Vainisi

Senior Vice President Corporate Relations, Stacy Sharpe

Vice President National Accounts, Brian Frank

Assistant Vice President, David Nadig

Senior Vice President And Chief Ethics Compliance And Privacy Officer, Kelly Noll

Associate Vice President Claims, Erik Kiehn

Vice President Human Resources, Joseph Testor

Vice President, Scott Harris

Assistant Vice President, Jeffrey Deigl

Vice President Investor Relations, Robert Block

Assistant Vice President Allstate Insurance Company, Carla Zuniga
Vice President Marketing And Business, Patrick Rogers
Vice President Director Manager, Carl Majeski
Vice President Insurance Reserves, Shantelle Thomas
Assistant Vice President, Kerry Flack
Senior Vice President Digital Transformation, Robert Wasserman
Vice President, Heather Vangrevenhof
Vice President And Senior Key Account Manager, Stephen Lipker
Assistant Vice President Risk Management, Laura Bartlett
Assistant Vice President, Richard Heneberry
Vice President Director Manager, Beth Drinan
Vice President, Robert Transon
Senior Vice President And Group Chief Information Officer, Peter Logothetis
Vice President Business Development, Jerry Lamparski
Senior Vice President, Kellie Rakes
Vice President, Elizabeth Smith
Vice President National Accounts, William Prince
Vice President Internal Audit, Kathy Swain
Vice President, Steve Miller
Assistant Vice President And Assistant General Counsel, Steve Ihm
Vice President Director Manager, Howard Gurvitz
Senior Vice President Human Resources, Joan Crockett
Assistant Vice President Talent Acquisition, Tom Hall
Vice President Talent Acquisition, Cathy Winn
Vice President, Shane O'Brien
Floridian Executive Vice President, George Grawe
Vice President Product Operations Allstate, Guy W Hill
Executive Vice President Human Resources, Liz Oppenhuis
Field Senior Vice President, Alice Byrne
Vice President Of Coiled Tubing And Cementing, Katie R Jones
Vice President Finance, Michael Kasper
Afvp, Brian Walsh
Vice President Finance, Joy Sweet
Vice President, Debbie Parker
Vice President Of Sales Emerging Businesses Affinity Solutions, Rob Gamble Rob Gamble
Senior Vice President, Robert Apatoff
Assistant Vice President Compliance, Diane Ierna
Vice President, Michael Mccabe
Vice President Human Resources, Joan Naughton-Gerdes
Vice President National Accounts, Kim Adler
Vice President, Monika Wirtz
Vice President Marketing, Christian Lopez
Vice President, Shawn Anderson
Vice President Marketing, Lisad Cochrane
Vice President Business Development, Alan Holman
Vice President, Bonnie Lee
Vice President, Patti Lenseth
Vice President Of Private Client Services, Luke Doebele
Vice President, Brandon Richter
Senior Vice President, Donna Morgan
Vice President And Chief Risk Officer (allstate Technology And Strategic Ventures), Kerry Ruhl
Vice President Strategic Alliances, Pamela Reed
Senior Vice President Sales And Strategic Alliances, Neiciee Durrence
Vice President Agency Services, Debbie Shytle
Senior Vice President Global Business Development, Paul Lubbers
Vice President Business Development, David Burgis
Vice President, Daniel Hebel

Vice President Business Development, Mike Weisenberger
Vice President Of Sales, Joe Hallberg
Senior Vice President East Region, Mike Capuzzi
Vice President Allstate Sales Channel, Dennis Adams
Assistant Vice President Information Technology Wo, Mike Escobar
Chairman President And Ceo The Allstate Corporation And Allstate Insurance Company, Thomas J. Wilson, age 60
Vice Chairman The Allstate Corporation And Allstate Insurance Company, Steven E. (Steve) Shebik, age 61
Board Member, Lisa Jennings
Board Member And Mentor, Justin Eggar
Treasurer, Deborah Marcus
Treasurer, Michelle Ackerman
Treasurer, Bill Mann
Board Member, Perry Traquina
Board Member, Jacques Perold
Board Member, Kermit Crawford
Board Member, Michael Eskew
Auditors: DELOITTE & TOUCHE LLP

LOCATIONS

HQ: Allstate Corp
2775 Sanders Road, Northbrook, IL 60062
Phone: 847 402-5000
Web: www.allstate.com

PRODUCTS/OPERATIONS

2017 Sales

	$ mil.	% of total
Property/liability		
Auto	21,878	57
Homeowners	7,310	19
Other personal lines	1,750	5
Commercial lines	495	1
Other business lines	883	2
Others	1,879	5
Allstate Financial	4,294	11
Corporate & other	35	-
Total	**38,524**	**1,010**

Selected Subsidiaries

Allstate Insurance Company of Canada
Allstate Life Insurance Company
Allstate Motor Club
American Heritage Life Insurance Company
Encompass Insurance Company
Esurance Insurance Company
Kennett Capital Inc.
Northbrook Indemnity Company
Pafco Insurance Company (Canada)

COMPETITORS

Farmers Group	Prudential
GEICO	State Farm
Hanover Insurance	The Hartford
Liberty Mutual	Torchmark
MetLife	Travelers Companies
Nationwide	USAA
Progressive Corporation	

HISTORICAL FINANCIALS

Company Type: Public

Income Statement				FYE: December 31
	ASSETS ($ mil.)	NET INCOME ($ mil.)	INCOME AS % OF ASSETS	EMPLOYEES
12/17	112,422	3,189	2.8%	42,900
12/16	108,610	1,877	1.7%	43,500
12/15	104,656	2,171	2.1%	41,600
12/14	108,533	2,850	2.6%	40,200
12/13	123,520	2,280	1.8%	39,400
Annual Growth	(2.3%)	8.8%	—	2.2%

2017 Year-End Financials

Debt ratio: 5.65%
Return on equity: 14.79%
Cash ($ mil.): 617
Current ratio: —
Long-term debt ($ mil.): —
No. of shares (mil.): 355
Dividends
Yield: 0.0%
Payout: 17.7%
Market value ($ mil.): 37,172

	STOCK PRICE ($) FY Close	P/E High/Low		PER SHARE ($)		
				Earnings	Dividends	Book Value
12/17	104.71	12	9	8.36	1.48	63.52
12/16	74.12	16	12	4.67	1.32	56.21
12/15	62.09	14	11	5.05	1.20	52.56
12/14	70.25	11	8	6.27	1.12	53.36
12/13	54.54	11	8	4.81	1.00	47.84
Annual Growth	17.7%	—	—	14.8%	10.3%	7.3%

ALLY BANK

EXECUTIVES

Chb-Pres-Ceo, Diane E Morais
Exec V Pres, Jeffrey J Brown
Cfo, James N Young
Secretary, Cathy L Quenneville
Senior Director of Business De, Craig Nalitt
Portfolio Manager, Janice Waye
Director of Remarketing Sales, Mark Juday
Operations Manager, Michael Snel

LOCATIONS

HQ: ALLY BANK
6985 S UNION PARK CTR # 435, MIDVALE, UT 840474177
Phone: 801 790-5005
Web: WWW.ALLY.COM

COMPETITORS

Bank of America	Citibank
BofI	E*TRADE Bank
Charles Schwab	State Farm

HISTORICAL FINANCIALS

Company Type: Private

Income Statement				FYE: December 31
	ASSETS ($ mil.)	NET INCOME ($ mil.)	INCOME AS % OF ASSETS	EMPLOYEES
12/16	123,547	1,273	1.0%	42
12/07*	28,472	291	1.0%	—
06/06	3,586	0	0.0%	—
Annual Growth	38.0%	114.3%	—	—

*Fiscal year change

2016 Year-End Financials

Debt ratio: ——
Return on equity: 19.80%
Cash ($ mil.): 4,348
Current ratio: —
Long-term debt ($ mil.): —
Dividends
Yield: —
Payout: —
Market value ($ mil.): —

Ally Financial Inc

Ally Financial wants to be your friend in the financing business. Ally operates branchless online-only retail bank Ally Bank which offers deposit mortgage (through Ally Home) and credit card products. Ally also provides auto financing for 18000 auto dealerships (mostly GM and Chrysler) and their customers. Ally Financial offers financing services for large- and mid-market companies through Ally Corporate Finance. Then known as GMAC the company was bailed out by the US government following the global financial crisis after which it took its current name. After several years of majority state ownership it went public in 2014.

Operations

Ally Financial carries more than $167 billion in assets. The company operates four business segments: Automotive Finance Insurance Mortgage and Corporate Finance.

Automotive Finance is Ally?s biggest earner at some 70% of sales. The segment provides auto financing to consumers auto dealers companies and municipalities. Insurance the next biggest at roughly 20% of sales offers consumer finance protection and insurance products through its automotive dealer channel. It also sells commercial insurance directly to dealers.

The Mortgage segment accounting for a few percent of sales manages a held-for-investment consumer mortgage portfolio and bulk purchases high-quality jumbo loans. The segment also offers direct-to-consumer mortgages under Ally Home consisting of a variety of jumbo and conforming fixed- and adjustable-rate mortgage products with the assistance of third-party fulfillment partner LenderLive.

Corporate Finance offers senior secured leveraged cash flow and asset-based loans to US-based middle market companies; it accounts for a few percent of Ally?s total revenue.

Geographic Reach

Ally Financial focuses almost entirely on the US. It has corporate offices in Detroit; New York City; and Charlotte North Carolina. As an online-only bank Ally has no physical branch network. Its services are available in most US states with California and Texas having the highest concentrations of loans (at around 25% combined).

Sales and Marketing

Ally Financial and its subsidiaries serve 5.7 million consumers and 18500 auto dealers. Some of its top clients include General Motors and Chrysler.

Ally sells its consumer financial and insurance products primarily through the automotive dealer channel. It sells commercial insurance products directly to dealers. As a direct bank Ally Bank raises deposit funds via its internet telephone mobile and mail channels.

Financial Performance

Ally Financial?s interest income from its primary businesses has increased by the low double-digits for a few years while revenue from its shrinking legacy GM operating lease portfolio has gone the opposite way to a more-or-less net neutral effect. Total revenue in fiscal 2017 increased an immaterial $31 million to $9.9 billion for that reason.

Net income fell 13% to $929 million as higher operating income was offset by an increase in provision for loan losses an increase in noninterest expense to support the launch of consumer and commercial product offerings and a $111 million increase in income tax paid during the year (relating to US tax reform at the tail end of 2017).

Cash and cash equivalents decreased $1.7 billion to $4.3 billion as cash from operations fell around $500 million; cash used in investing activities decreased $343 million due to lower purchases of available-for-sale securities; and cash from financing activities fell $1.6 billion due to changes in short-term borrowings.

Strategy

Ally is always looking for ways to develop and innovate on its products and services. To enhance its automotive finance offerings relationships and digital capabilities in 2017 Ally Financial expanded on the Blue Yield platform acquired in 2016 by introducing Clearlane an online automotive lender exchange. The product adds to Ally?s direct-to-consumer capabilities and provides an end-to-end digital platform for consumers seeking financing and dealers looking to drive online sales. Clearlane generates revenue by charging fees for successful lead referrals to auto lenders and insurance providers and enhances the bank?s ability to partner with other direct lenders and online auto distributors. The bank also grew its relationship with Carvana an online used car platform by providing $2 billion in purchases of retail installment sales contracts and warehouse financing.

Additionally Ally launched Ally Home a direct-to-consumer mortgage offering in December 2016. The product further fleshed out its online banking service. Unlike Ally Bank?s other products Ally Home?s customers have access to a team of experts in the shape of the Ally Home Team.

Mergers and Acquisitions

In June 2016 Ally expanded into online brokerage after buying digital wealth management and broker-dealer TradeKing Group for $275 million. TradeKing had some $4.5 billion in client assets at the time. It also acquired assets from Blue Yield that Ally rebranded as Clearlane to expand its automotive financing offering.

Company Background

In February 2013 Ally sold its Canadian auto finance business to Royal Bank of Canada. A few months later it sold its Mexican insurance business ABA Seguros to ACE for $865 million. In October it sold its business in Europe and Latin America as well as a joint venture in China to GM Financial for $611 million. Also in 2013 it sold its business lending operations to Walter Investment Management Corp. completed the sales of agency mortgage servicing rights (MSRs) to Ocwen Financial Corp. and Quicken Loans Inc. and exited the correspondent lending channel.

Ally Financial was founded as a subsidiary of General Motors in 1919. It was owned by GM until 2006 when the automaker sold a 51% stake in the company to the Cerberus Capital Management investment group for some $7 billion.

EXECUTIVES

President Auto Finance, Timothy M. (Tim) Russi, age 55, $541,800 total compensation
Cio, Michael Baresich
President And Ceo Dealer Financial Services, Jeffrey J. (JB) Brown, age 44, $1,000,000 total compensation
President And Ceo Ally Commercial Finance Llc, William (Bill) Hall
President Consumer And Commercial Banking Products, Diane Morais, age 52, $550,000 total compensation
Cfo, Christopher A. Halmy, age 49, $600,000 total compensation
President Ally Insurance, Douglas Timmerman
Chief Risk Officer, David Shevsky, age 56, $500,000 total compensation
Executive Vice President Organizational Effectiveness, Renee Otjen
Vice President Alliance Sales, Mark Manzo
President And Ceo Dealer Financial Services, Jeffrey J. (JB) Brown, age 44
Chairman, Franklin W. (Fritz) Hobbs, age 70

Corporate Treasurer, Bradley Brown
Auditors: Deloitte & Touche LLP

LOCATIONS

HQ: Ally Financial Inc
Ally Detroit Center, 500 Woodward Avenue, Floor 10, Detroit, MI 48226
Phone: 866 710-4623
Web: www.ally.com

PRODUCTS/OPERATIONS

2017 sales

	$ mil.	% of total
Financing revenue and other interest income	8,322	84
Insurance premiums and service revenue earned	973	10
Gain on mortgage and automotive loans net	68	1
Other gain on investments net	102	1
Other income	408	4
Loss on extinguishment of debt	(7)	-
Total	**9,866**	**100**

2017 Sales

	% of total
Automotive Finance	71
Insurance	19
Corporate Finance	2
Mortgage Finance	4
Corporate and Other	4
Total	**100**

Selected Products and Services

Bank
Online Savings
Interest Checking
Money Market
Credit Card
Ally CashBack Credit Card
Auto
Personal
Business
RVs
Home Loans
Buy a Home
Refinance
Invest
Self-Directed Trading
Managed Portfolios
Forex & Futures
Research & Tools
Ally Invest API

COMPETITORS

Bank of America
Citigroup
Ford Motor Credit
Mercedes-Benz Credit
Mercedes-Benz Financial Services USA
Mitsubishi Motors Credit of America
Toyota Motor Credit
Volkswagen Financial Services

HISTORICAL FINANCIALS

Company Type: Public

Income Statement

FYE: December 31

	ASSETS ($ mil.)	NET INCOME ($ mil.)	INCOME AS % OF ASSETS	EMPLOYEES
12/17	167,148	929	0.6%	7,900
12/16	163,728	1,067	0.7%	7,600
12/15	158,581	1,289	0.8%	7,100
12/14	151,828	1,150	0.8%	6,900
12/13	151,167	361	0.2%	7,100
Annual Growth	2.5%	26.7%	—	2.7%

2017 Year-End Financials

Debt ratio: 28.36%	No. of shares (mil.): 437
Return on equity: 6.93%	Dividends
Cash ($ mil.): 4,252	Yield: 0.0%
Current ratio: —	Payout: 19.6%
Long-term debt ($ mil.): —	Market value ($ mil.): 12,744

Alphabet Inc

If you don't know what the term Google means there's a leading Internet search engine you can use to find out. Google offers targeted search results from billions of Web pages. Results are based on a proprietary algorithm; its technology for ranking Web pages is called PageRank. The firm generates revenue through ad sales. Advertisers deliver relevant ads targeted to search queries or Web content. The Google Network is a network of third-party customers that use Google's ad programs to deliver relevant ads to their own sites. In October 2015 Google formally became part — and by far the biggest part — of the Alphabet Inc. holding company.

Operations

Because the technology industry demands constant innovation Google has been nothing short of relentless in its efforts to develop or acquire new services and products in order to stay ahead of such rivals as Yahoo! and Microsoft. Since its founding as search engine the company has branched out to provide Web portal services such as Webmail (Gmail) blogging (Blogger) photo sharing (Picasa) interactive maps (Google Maps) and Web browsing (Google Chrome).

In addition its Android operating system is a platform for mobile and tablet products; Google has also released an Android smart phone. The company sells digital content such as apps music and movies through Google Play Store (formerly called Android Market). Google subsidiaries include YouTube and DoubleClick.

Despite this plethora of diverse offerings Google's lead in Internet search is still fueled by its advertising system comprised of its AdWords and AdSense products (90% of its revenue stemmed from advertising in fiscal 2015). Customers of AdWords seek to drive traffic from Google to their sites and generate leads. Advertisers bid on keywords and have their ads appear as links on the right-hand column of Google's search results page under the sponsored links heading.

Through AdSense for Search Google powers the search capabilities of other publishers' websites and search engines product. With AdSense for Content Google delivers ads to a publisher's website that are targeted to the content on the publisher's site and the publisher shares in the revenue generated when readers click on the ads. AdSense customers are publishers of third-party websites that comprise the Google AdSense Network. The AdSense Network includes many small websites but has also attracted several big players in online publishing and e-commerce including AOL Ask.com and NYTimes.com.

Geographic Reach

In order to face its international rivals head on Google operates from more than 70 offices in about 40 countries. International domains include Google.ba Google.dm Google.nr Google.co.jp and Google.ca and the Google interface is available in more than 100 languages. However the US accounted for 46% of the company's revenue during fiscal 2015.

Financial Performance

Google has historically reported year-over-year revenue and net income growth and fiscal 2015 was no different. Its revenues climbed from $66 billion in fiscal 2014 to a record-setting $74.9 billion in fiscal 2015. The company's net income also surged 13% from $14.4 billion in fiscal 2014 to reach a milestone $16.3 billion in fiscal 2015.

The historic growth for 2015 was attributed to the increase in advertising revenues generated by Google websites Google Network Members' websites and hardware product sales. The growth in advertising revenue was fueled by a 16% spike in Google website revenue as a result of increases in mobile search due to ongoing improvements in ad formats as well as growth in YouTube video advertising across TrueView and Google Preferred.

Google's cash flow from operations has also significantly increased year-over-year. Its cash flow in fiscal 2015 increased to $26 billion compared to $22.4 billion in 2014. The spike was mainly due to the company's higher net income and changes in working capital.

Strategy

In order to enter new markets and maintain a portfolio of innovative offerings Google is continuing its strategy of investment in innovation and new product development.

Mergers and Acquisitions

During fiscal 2015 Google paid $380.2 million to acquire bebop Technologies Inc. (bebop) a London-based company with a cloud-based development platform focused on enterprise applications.

HISTORY

Google is the product of two computer science grad students Sergey Brin and Larry Page who met in 1995 at Stanford University where they studied methods of searching and organizing large datasets. They discovered a formula to rank the order of random search results by relevancy and in 1997 they adopted the name Google to their findings. In 1998 the two presented their discovery at the World Wide Web Conference and by 1999 they had raised almost $30 million in funding from private investors venture capital firms and Stanford University. Later that year the Google site was launched.

Brin and Page hired tech industry veteran Eric Schmidt (former CTO at Sun Microsystems and former CEO of Novell) in 2001 as Google's CEO. Brin previously the company's chairman adopted the role of president of technology and Page previously CEO of Google became president of product. Also in 2001 Google launched AdWords its search-based advertising service. The following year the company launched another advertising service the context-based AdSense.

In 2004 the company entered the social networking sphere with the launch of its Orkut product which allows users (by invitation only) to search and connect with one another through online networks of friends. Later that year the once highly secretive company went public in one of the most anticipated IPOs ever raising $1.6 billion.

In October 2015 Google became a subsidiary of Alphabet Inc.

EXECUTIVES

Vice President Engineering Google, Vic Gundotra
Ceo, Sundar Pichai, age 46
Svp And Cfo Alphabet Inc. And Google Inc., Ruth M. Porat, age 61

President Enterprise Sales, Tariq M. Shaukat, age 45
Vp And Ceo Google Israel, Meir Brand
Vice President Google Creative Lab, Robert Wong
Board Member, Ram Shriram
Board Member, Marc Ellenbogen
Auditors: Ernst & Young LLP

LOCATIONS

HQ: Alphabet Inc
1600 Amphitheatre Parkway, Mountain View, CA 94043
Phone: 650 253-0000
Web: www.abc.xyz

PRODUCTS/OPERATIONS

Selected Products & Advertising Platforms
AdWords
DoubleClick Digital Marketing
Google Analytics
Google Consumer Surveys
Google Display Network
Google for Retail
Google+ for Brands
YouTube

COMPETITORS

AOL	MSN
Apple Inc.	Myspace
Ask.com	NetEase
Baidu	SINA
Blucora	Shopping.com
CityGrid Media	Shopzilla
Conversant	Sohu.com
Daum Communications	Spotify
Facebook	Twitter
LiveJournal	Yahoo!
LookSmart	craigslist

HISTORICAL FINANCIALS

Company Type: Public

Income Statement — FYE: December 31

	REVENUE ($ mil.)	NET INCOME ($ mil.)	NET PROFIT MARGIN	EMPLOYEES
12/18	136,819	30,736	22.5%	98,771
12/17	110,855	12,662	11.4%	80,110
12/16	90,272	19,478	21.6%	72,053
12/15	74,989	16,348	21.8%	61,814
12/14	66,001	14,444	21.9%	53,600
Annual Growth	20.0%	20.8%	—	16.5%

2018 Year-End Financials

Debt ratio: 1.72%
Return on equity: 18.62%
Cash ($ mil.): 16,701
Current ratio: 3.92
Long-term debt ($ mil.): 4,012
No. of shares (mil.): 695
Dividends
Yield: —
Payout: —
Market value ($ mil.): 726,828

	STOCK PRICE ($) FY Close	P/E High/Low		PER SHARE ($) Earnings	Dividends	Book Value
12/18	1,044.96	29	22	43.70	0.00	255.38
12/17	1,053.40	59	44	18.00	0.00	219.50
12/16	792.45	30	24	27.85	0.00	201.12
12/15	778.01	33	21	23.59	0.00	175.07
12/14	530.66	57	23	21.02	0.00	153.64
Annual Growth	18.5%	—		20.1%	—	13.5%

Altice USA Inc

Auditors: KPMG LLP

LOCATIONS

HQ: Altice USA Inc
1 CourtSquare West, Long Island City, NY 11101
Phone: 516 803-2300
Web: www.alticeusa.com

HISTORICAL FINANCIALS

Company Type: Public

Income Statement   FYE: December 31

	REVENUE ($ mil.)	NET INCOME ($ mil.)	NET PROFIT MARGIN	EMPLOYEES
12/17	9,326	1,520	16.3%	9,414
12/16	6,017	(832)	—	15,300
Annual Growth	55.0%	—	—	(38.5%)

2017 Year-End Financials

Debt ratio: 63.09%	No. of shares (mil.): 737
Return on equity: 38.86%	Dividends
Cash ($ mil.): 273	Yield: 0.0%
Current ratio: 0.34	Payout: 59.1%
Long-term debt ($ mil.): 21,347	Market value ($ mil.): 15,648

	STOCK PRICE ($) FY Close	P/E High/Low		PER SHARE ($) Earnings	Dividends	Book Value
12/17	21.23	16	8	2.18	1.29	7.77
12/16	0.00	—	—	(8,320.00)	0.00	
20,977.02						
/0.00	—	—	(0.00)	0.00	(0.00)	
/0.00	—	—	(0.00)	0.00	(0.00)	
Annual Growth	—	—	—	—		

ALTICOR INC.

Where there's a will (and an army of independent sales representatives) there's Amway. Operated through holding company Alticor Amway is the world's top direct-selling company with millions of individual ABOs (Amway Business Owners) pitching everything from air filters to vitamins. The company makes some 450 unique products across the categories of nutrition (which generates about half of sales) beauty and personal care and home. It is active in more than 100 countries across the globe with Asia (led by China) its largest market. Alticor is controlled by the families of Rich DeVos and Jay Van Andel who founded Amway in 1959.

Operations

Nutrition products (supplements skin care products weight management programs) account for about 50% of total Amway sales. Beauty and personal care items (makeup shampoo toothpaste) generate about a quarter of sales and home products (water and air filters cookware cleaners) contribute about 20%. The company's top products include Nutrilite supplements Artistry color cosmetics eSpring water treatment systems and XS energy drinks.

Geographic Reach

Based in Ada Michigan Amway operates in more than 100 countries. Its top markets by sales are China the US and South Korea; other leading markets include India Japan Malaysia Russia Taiwan and Thailand.

The company has manufacturing facilities farms and warehouses in Brazil China Hungary India Japan Mexico the Netherlands Poland Russia South Korea Taiwan Thailand Vietnam and the US.

Sales and Marketing

Amway's 450-plus products are marketing worldwide by more than 3 million independent distributors who purchase the products and resell them. The company provides a host of support services including personal mentors brand centers online learning tools and call centers.

Financial Performance

While privately-owned Alticor doesn't report full results Amway reported global sales of $8.6 billion in 2017 down from $8.8 billion in 2016.The company points to a challenging Chinese market for its revenue decline over the past few years

Strategy

Amway's strategy is pretty straight-forward: continue to enhance and expand its line of products to serve more markets and appeal to more customers and create tools that make selling those products easier for the 3+ million ABOs (Amway Business Owners).

In 2017 Amway introduced a new formula for its Nutrilife Double X product one of the best-selling supplements in the world that includes a phytonutrient blend designed to help the body fight free radicals. Other additions to the company's product portfolio that year include a reformulated Essentials by Artistry skincare line and its first in-car air filtration system Atmosphere Drive. Amway also pushed its XS brand of energy drinks into new countries in 2017 including China and India with more launches planned for 2018. The company has more than 800 patents worldwide and another 250 pending applications.

Direct selling of course looks a lot different in the age of Amazon than it did some 60 years ago when Amway was founded. The company has been making significant investment in tools and technologies in recent years to enable its ABOs to better compete. It has spent some $70 million in mobile apps for ABOs including the flagship Amway MyBiz app which provides back office data and analytics. In addition Amway has boosted its own customer service capabilities with instant messaging bots and other technologies to help it handle the more than 12 million annual customer requests. Other recent initiatives include a content sharing app for ABOs in the Philippines a beauty app for customers in South Korea and a one-stop product education and purchase portal in for ABOs in China.

EXECUTIVES

President, Doug DeVos
Vice President, Richard Holwill
Senior Vice President Information Technology, Craig Datema
Vice President Of Purchasing, Judy West
Vice President Supply Chain Planning, Jennifer Williamson
Chairman, Steve Van Andel

LOCATIONS

HQ: ALTICOR INC.
7575 FULTON ST E, ADA, MI 493550001
Phone: 616 787-1000
Web: WWW.ALTICOR.COM

PRODUCTS/OPERATIONS

2017 Sales

	% of total
Nutrition	50
Beauty & personal care	26
Home	21
Other	3
Total	**100**

Selected Brands

Nutrition
  Nutrilite
Beauty & personal care
  Artistry
  G&H
  Glister
  Satinique
Home
  Amway Home
  Atmosphere Sky
  eSpring
  iCook
Other
  XS

COMPETITORS

Avon	Melaleuca
Bath & Body Works	New Avon
Bluestem Brands	Newell Brands
Colgate-Palmolive	Nikken
Estée Lauder	Nu Skin
Forever Living	Procter & Gamble
GNC	Revlon
Herbalife Ltd.	Shaklee
Johnson & Johnson	Tupperware Brands
L'Oréal	Unilever PLC
Mary Kay	

HISTORICAL FINANCIALS

Company Type: Private

Income Statement   FYE: December 31

	REVENUE ($ mil.)	NET INCOME ($ mil.)	NET PROFIT MARGIN	EMPLOYEES
12/16	8,783	0	—	14,000
12/15	9,459	0	—	—
12/14	10,804	0	—	—
12/13	11,754	0	—	—
Annual Growth	(9.3%)	—	—	—

2016 Year-End Financials

Debt ratio: ——	
Return on equity: —	Dividends
Cash ($ mil.): 1,457	Yield: —
Current ratio: 0.80	Payout: —
Long-term debt ($ mil.): —	Market value ($ mil.): —

Altria Group Inc

EXECUTIVES

Chb-Ceo, Howard A Willard III
V Chm-Exec V Pres-Cfo, William F Gifford Jr
Exec V Pres-Gen Counsel, Murray R Garnick
V Pres-Treas, Daniel J Bryant
V Pres-Corp SEC-Assoc Gen Coun, W Hildebrandt Surgner Jr
V Pres-Contrl, Ivan S Feldman
Svp Research Dev't & Science, James E Dillard III
Svp Strategy, Planning & Procu, Salvatore Mancuso
Svp Hr, Compliance & It Svcs, Charles N Whitaker
Manager, Anthony Berrios
Auditors: PricewaterhouseCoopers LLP

LOCATIONS

HQ: Altria Group Inc
6601 West Broad Street, Richmond, VA 23230
Phone: 804 274-2200
Web: www.altria.com

COMPETITORS

Altadis	Lorillard
Anheuser-Busch	Molson Coors
Anheuser-Busch InBev	North Atlantic Trading
British American	Ravenswood Winery
Tobacco	Reynolds American
Constellation Brands	Sebastiani Vineyards
E. & J. Gallo	Swedish Match
Heineken	Treasury Wine Estates
Japan Tobacco	Americas
Loews	Vector Group

HISTORICAL FINANCIALS

Company Type: Public

Income Statement   FYE: December 31

	REVENUE ($ mil.)	NET INCOME ($ mil.)	NET PROFIT MARGIN	EMPLOYEES
12/17	25,576	10,222	40.0%	8,300
12/16	25,744	14,239	55.3%	8,300
12/15	25,434	5,241	20.6%	8,800
12/14	24,522	5,070	20.7%	9,000
12/13	24,466	4,535	18.5%	9,000
Annual Growth	1.1%	22.5%	—	(2.0%)

2017 Year-End Financials

Debt ratio: 32.16%
Return on equity: 72.63%
Cash ($ mil.): 1,253
Current ratio: 0.64
Long-term debt ($ mil.): 13,030

No. of shares (mil.): 1,901
Dividends
  Yield: 0.0%
  Payout: 47.8%
Market value ($ mil.): 135,769

	STOCK PRICE ($) FY Close	P/E High/Low		PER SHARE ($) Earnings	Dividends	Book Value
12/17	71.41	15	12	5.31	2.54	8.09
12/16	67.62	10	8	7.28	2.35	6.57
12/15	58.21	23	18	2.67	2.17	1.47
12/14	49.27	20	13	2.56	2.00	1.53
12/13	38.39	17	14	2.26	1.84	2.07
Annual Growth	16.8%	—	—	23.8%	8.4%	40.7%

Amazon.com Inc

Amazon.com began as Earth's biggest bookstore but has become Earth's biggest everything store. Its website still offers millions of books as well as other media home furnishings clothing pet supplies office products and hundreds of other product categories (with items often ordered and delivered the same day). The company is also the dominant cloud services provider an influential entertainment company through its video operations (it produced 2017 Oscar-nominated Manchester-by-the-Sea) a force to be reckoned with in grocery with its ownership of natural foods chain Whole Foods and a leader in digital personal assistant devices with Alexa and its Echo product line.

HISTORY

Jeff Bezos was researching the Internet in the early 1990s for hedge fund D.E. Shaw. He realized that book sales would be a perfect fit with e-commerce because book distributors already kept meticulous electronic lists. Bezos who as a teen had dreamed of entrepreneurship in outer space took the idea to Shaw. The company passed on the idea but Bezos ran with it trekking cross country to Seattle (close to a facility owned by major

book distributor Ingram) and typing up a business plan along the way.

Bezos founded Amazon.com in 1994. After months of preparation he launched a website in July 1995 (Douglas Hofstadter's Fluid Concepts and Creative Analogies was its first sale); it had sales of $20000 a week by September. Bezos and his team kept working with the site pioneering features that now seem mundane such as one-click shopping customer reviews and e-mail order verification.

Amazon went public in 1997. Moves to cement the Amazon.com brand included becoming the sole book retailer on AOL's website and Netscape's commercial channel.

In 1998 the company launched its online music and video stores and it began to sell toys and electronics. Amazon also expanded its European reach with the purchases of online booksellers in the UK and Germany and it acquired the Internet Movie Database. Bezos also expanded the company's base of online services buying Junglee (comparison shopping) and PlanetAll (address book calendar reminders).

By midyear Amazon.com had attracted so much attention that its market capitalization equaled the combined values of profitable bricks-and-mortar rivals Barnes & Noble and Borders Group even though their combined sales were far greater than the upstart's. Late that year Amazon formed a promotional link with Hoover's publisher of this profile.

After raising $1.25 billion in a bond offering early in 1999 Amazon.com began a spending spree with deals to buy all or part of several dot-coms. However some have since been sold (Home-Grocer.com) and others have gone out of business or bankrupt — Pets.com living.com (furniture). It also bought the catalog businesses of Back to Basics and Tool Crib of the North.

Amazon.com began conducting online auctions in early 1999 and partnered with venerable auction house Sotheby's. Also that year Amazon added distribution facilities including one each in England and Germany.

In 2000 the company inked a 10-year deal with Toysrus.com to set up a co-branded toy and video game store. (The partnership came to a bitter end in 2006 after Toys "R" Us sued Amazon.com when it began selling toys from other companies.) Also that year Amazon.com added foreign-language sites for France and Japan.

In 2001 Amazon cut 15% of its workforce as part of a restructuring plan that also forced a $150 million charge. That year the company also made a deal with Borders to provide inventory fulfillment content and customer service for borders.com. As part of a deal to expand their marketing partnership AOL invested $100 million in Amazon.com in 2001. Later that year Amazon purchased some assets from Egghead.com (which filed for Chapter 11 in August) and relaunched the site.

In 2002 the firm introduced clothing sales featuring hundreds of retailers including names such as The Gap Nordstrom and Lands' End. Amazon.com received accreditation from ICANN (the Internet Corporation for Assigned Names and Numbers) as an Internet domain name registrar becoming one of about 160 entities permitted to register Internet addresses.

The company launched its Search I

EXECUTIVES

Ceo Worldwide Consumer Business, Jeffrey A. (Jeff) Wilke, age 52, $175,000 total compensation

Chairman President And Ceo, Jeffrey P. (Jeff) Bezos, age 55, $81,840 total compensation

Ceo Amazon Web Services, Andrew R. (Andy) Jassy, age 51, $175,000 total compensation

Svp And Cfo, Brian T. Olsavsky, $160,000 total compensation

Vice President Home Improvements, John Witham

Vice President, Seth Dallaire

Vice President, David Criscione

Vice President Worldwide Discovery, Kim Rachmeler

Vice President E Commerce Platform Services, Gene Pope

Vice President Information Technology, Kathryn Giorgianni

Vice President Corporate Sales Development, Robert Saltzman

Vice President Ww Customer Service, Tim Mueller-Hickler

Vice President Logistics, Michael Indresano

Vice President, Ashish Thaker

Vice President, Carmine Arabia

Vice President Global Inventory Platform, Jason Murray

Vice President Finance Softlines, Rebecca Hollingsworth

Vice President, Adrian Cockcroft

Senior Vice President, Steve Kessel

Chairman President And Ceo, Jeffrey P. (Jeff) Bezos, age 55

Auditors: Ernst & Young LLP

LOCATIONS

HQ: Amazon.com Inc
410 Terry Avenue North, Seattle, WA 98109-5210
Phone: 206 266-1000   **Fax:** 206 266-1821
Web: www.amazon.com

2017 Sales

	$ mil.	% of total
North America	106,110	60
International	54,297	30
AWS	17,459	10
Total	**177,866**	**100**

2017 Sales

	$ mil.	% of total
United States	120,486	68
International		
Germany	16,951	9
Japan	11,907	7
United Kingdom	11,372	6
Other countries	17,150	10
Total	**177,866**	**100**

PRODUCTS/OPERATIONS

2017 Sales

	$ mil.	% of total
Online stores	108,354	61
Retail third-party seller services	31,881	18
AWS	17,459	10
Retail subscription services	9,721	5
Physical stores	5,798	3
Other	4,653	3
Total	**177,866**	**100**

2017 Sales

	$ mil.	% of total
Product	118,573	67
Services	59,293	33
Total	**177,866**	**100**

Selected Departments

Apparel shoes and jewelry
Books
  Books
  Kindle e-books
  Textbooks
  Magazines
Computers and office
  Computers and accessories
  Computer components
  Office products and supplies
  PC games

Software
Digital downloads
  Amazon shorts
  Game downloads
  Kindle Store
  MP3 downloads
Electronics
  Audio TV and home theater
  Camera photo and video
  Car electronics and GPS
  Cell phones and service
  Home appliances
  MP3 and media players
  Musical instruments
  Video games
Grocery health and beauty
  Beauty
  Diapers
  Gourmet food
  Grocery
  Health and personal care
  Natural and organic
Home and garden
  Bedding and bath
  Furniture and decor
  Home appliances
  Home improvement
  Kitchen and dining
  Patio lawn and garden
  Pet supplies
  Sewing craft and hobby
  Vacuums and storage
Kindle
  Books
  Blogs
  Magazines
  Newspapers
Movies music and games
  Blu-ray
  Movies and TV
  Music
  Musical instruments
  Video games
  Video On Demand
Sports and outdoors
  Action sports
  Camping and hiking
  Cycling
  Exercise and fitness
  Fan gear
  Golf
  Team sports
Tools auto and industrial
  Automotive
  Home improvement
  Industrial and scientific
  Lighting and electrical
  Motorcycle and ATV
  Outdoor power equipment
  Plumbing fixtures
  Power and hand tools
Toys kids and baby
  Apparel (kids and baby)
  Baby
  Books
  Movies
  Music
  Software
  Toys and games
  Video games

Selected Operations

A9.com (search technology development)
Amazon.ca (Canada)
Amazon.cn (China)
Amazon.de (Germany)
Amazon.fr (France)
Amazon.co.jp (Japan)
Amazon.co.uk (UK)
Audible (audiobooks and other recorded content)
Endless (shoes and handbags)
Internet Movie Database (IMDb)
IVONA Software
Joyo (China)
LOVEFiLM International Ltd.
Whole Foods Market (grocery stores)
Woot.com (US)
Zappos.com (US)

COMPETITORS

Albertsons	Kering
Alibaba Group	Kroger
Apple Inc.	Lowe's
AutoNation	Macy's
AutoZone	Michaels Companies
Barnes & Noble	Microsoft
Bed Bath & Beyond	Netflix
Best Buy	Office Depot
Big Lots	Overstock.com
Buy.com	Peapod LLC
CDW	Safeway
Costco Wholesale	Sears
DSW	Shoe Carnival
Dollar General	Spotify
Dollar Tree	Sprouts
Family Dollar Stores	Staples
Finish Line	TJX Companies
Foot Locker	Target Corporation
GameStop	The Gap
Google	Trader Joe's
HSN	Wal-Mart
Home Depot	Walmart.com
IAC	Wayfair
J. C. Penney	eBay
JD.com	

HISTORICAL FINANCIALS

Company Type: Public

Income Statement   FYE: December 31

	REVENUE ($ mil.)	NET INCOME ($ mil.)	NET PROFIT MARGIN	EMPLOYEES
12/18	232,887	10,073	4.3%	647,500
12/17	177,866	3,033	1.7%	566,000
12/16	135,987	2,371	1.7%	341,400
12/15	107,006	596	0.6%	230,800
12/14	88,988	(241)		154,100
Annual Growth	27.2%	—	—	43.2%

2018 Year-End Financials

Debt ratio: 24.46%
Return on equity: 28.27%
Cash ($ mil.): 41,250
Current ratio: 1.10
Long-term debt ($ mil.): 39,787

No. of shares (mil.): 491
Dividends
  Yield: —
  Payout: —
Market value ($ mil.): 737,467

	STOCK PRICE ($) FY Close	P/E High/Low	PER SHARE ($) Earnings	Dividends	Book Value
12/18	1,501.97	99 57	20.14	0.00	88.69
12/17	1,169.47	189 119	6.15	0.00	57.25
12/16	749.87	169 96	4.90	0.00	40.43
12/15	675.89	542 224	1.25	0.00	28.42
12/14	310.35	— —	(0.52)	0.00	23.10
Annual Growth	48.3%	— —	—	—	40.0%

Ambac Financial Group, Inc.

Ambac has scaled back in a major way. Holding company Ambac Financial operates through subsidiaries including its flagship unit Ambac Assurance Everspan Financial Guarantee and Ambac Assurance UK. The businesses offered financial guarantees and related services to customers around the world. Ambac Assurance guaranteed public finance and structured finance obligations but it has stopped offering new business and placed its existing business in run-off (meaning it still accepts premium payments due on existing policies and pays out claims as it can).

Operations

In addition to its core financial guarantee offerings in better days Ambac also insured infrastructure and utility finance deals internationally. Its Ambac Financial Services unit offered interest rate swaps credit swaps and investment management primarily to states and municipal authorities tied to their bond financing. These operations are also in run-off through means including transaction terminations settlements and scheduled contract amortizations.

How did a once-solid municipal bond insurer fall so hard? Along with other US bond insurers including FGIC and MBIA the US subprime mortgage meltdown knocked the wind out of Ambac. Its financial guarantee business fizzled and the company began to post heavy losses. Meanwhile Ambac's portfolio bulged with collateralized debt obligations (CDOs) of asset-backed securities — the financial equivalent of a sack of rotten potatoes once the credit markets turned sour.

Geographic Reach

Ambac's run-off operations primarily bring in revenues from the US market which accounts for three-fourths of revenues. The company also has international operations (also in runoff) in markets including the UK (some 20% of revenues) Australia Austria Germany and Italy.

Financial Performance

Ambac's run-off (existing account) insurance operations brought in some $644 million in revenues in 2015 nearly doubling that of 2014. Those improved earnings marked a turnaround after a couple of years of declining revenues; they were a result of increased premiums earned lower losses on derivatives and a gain on extinguishment of debt.

Net income has remained relatively flat for the past few years and in 2015 rose a modest 2% to $492 million. That was thanks to the higher revenue but partially offset by goodwill impairment charges incurred in 2014.

After reporting an operating cash outflow of $971 million in 2014 Ambac had an inflow of operating cash totaling $87.5 million in 2015 as it has lower losses and loss expenses.

Strategy

Ambac is hoping to diversify its business and has its sights set on either buying or developing new operations. It is interested in such activities as advisory services asset management and even insurance. In late 2015 the group launched a residential property investment program.

HISTORY

Mortgage Guaranty Insurance Corporation (MGIC) in 1971 founded American Municipal Bond Assurance Corporation (Ambac Indemnity) in Milwaukee. That year Ambac wrote the very first municipal bond insurance policy — for a bond to fund a medical building and a sewage treatment facility in Juneau Alaska. New York City's 1975 moratorium on debt payments helped make the new product more attractive. The company wrote the first insurance policies for mutual funds (1977) and secondary market municipal bonds (1983). In 1981 Ambac moved to New York; four years later it became a Citibank subsidiary. It went public in 1991.

In 1995 Ambac and rival MBIA allied to offer bond insurance overseas. Two years later the company formed a UK subsidiary to serve Europe. In recognition of the growing market the joint venture was amended in 2000 to provide for individual operations by the two partners in Europe though they continued to reinsure each other there and to work jointly in Japan. Ambac went on a buying spree in 1996 and 1997 buying the investment advisory and broker dealer operations of Cadre and Construction Loan Insurance (renamed Connie Lee Holdings) a guarantor of college bonds and hospital infrastructure bonds.

In 1998 as Ambac lost share in the US municipal bond market because it declined to cut premiums the company began concentrating on asset-backed securities and international bonds. Two years later Ambac entered the Japanese market through a joint venture with Yasuda Fire & Marine.

In late 2010 after missing a scheduled interest payment and failing to reach an agreement for a prepackaged bankruptcy proceeding with its creditors the company voluntarily filed for Chapter 11 bankruptcy protection. Through the filing Ambac hoped to restructure more than $1.6 billion in outstanding debt. The company also haggled with the IRS over $700 million in allegedly improper tax refunds received between 2003 and 2008.

The bankruptcy court approved a plan of reorganization for Ambac in 2012 and the plan went into effect the following year.

EXECUTIVES

Senior Managing Director Chief Accounting Officer And Controller, Robert B. Eisman, age 50, $500,000 total compensation
President And Ceo Ambac Financial Group And Ambac Assurance Corporation, Claude L. LeBlanc, age 53
Senior Managing Director Cfo And Treasurer, David Trick, age 47, $770,000 total compensation
President Ceo And Director, Nader Tavakoli, age 59, $1,800,000 total compensation
Senior Managing Director And General Counsel, Stephen M. Ksenak, age 52, $525,000 total compensation
Senior Managing Director Restructuring And Corporate Development, David Barranco, age 47
Senior Managing Director Cio And Chief Administrative Office, Michael Reilly, age 61
Assistant Vice President, John Ng
Assistant Vice President Business Applications And Support, Sarbah Arthur
First Vice President, Patrick Mccormick
Assistant Vice President Financial Control, Shannon Kelly
Vice President, Art Heffner
Assistant Vice President And Closing Coordinator, Yolanda Ortiz
Assistant Vice President, John Osmanzai
First Vice President And Assistant General Counsel, Juan Roman
First Vice President Structured Real Estate, Gregory Mayer
First Vice President, Sunil Rao
Assistant Vice President Application Programming, Aravind Modini
Assistant Vice President Risk Operations, Pranay Nadkarni
Vice President Of Finance, Michael Klaassens
Assistant Vice President, Linda Crocitto
Vice President, Andrew Zuniga
Vice President Senior Vice President Finance Director, Thomas Staskowski
Assistant Vice President Finance, Chris Dudonis
Assistant Vice President In Technology, Venka Korsapati
Assistant Vice President Payroll, Yanira Vergara
First Vice President Housing Group, Kelly Wimmer
First Vice President Credit Risk Management, Robert Bose
First Vice President, Yuliang LI
Vice President Finance, David Harris
Assistant Vice President Payroll, Yanira Vergara
Vice President Technology, Husna Nasser
First Vice President, Sulexan Chery
President Ceo And Director, Nader Tavakoli, age 59

Chairman, Jeffrey S. Stein
Member Board Of Directors, Alexander Greene
Auditors: KPMG LLP

LOCATIONS

HQ: Ambac Financial Group, Inc.
One State Street Plaza, New York, NY 10004
Phone: 212 658-7470   **Fax**: 212 208 3414
Web: www.ambac.com

2015 Permiums by Geographic

	% of total
United States	73
United Kingdom	22
Other international	5
Total	**100**

PRODUCTS/OPERATIONS

2015 Net Premiums

	% of total
Accelerated earnings	44
Public Finance	31
International Finance	14
Structured Finance	11
Total	**100**

2015 Sales

	$ mil
% of total	
Net premiums earned	44
Total	**37**
Net realized investment gains	8
Net change in fair value of credit derivatives	6
Income (loss) on variable interest entities	4
Other income	1
Net other-than-temporary impairment losses recognized in earnings	
Derivative products	-
Total	**100**

Selected Services

Adversely Classified Credit
Amendment Waiver and Consen
Credit Risk Management (CRM)
International Finance Insured Portfolio
U.S. Public Finance Insured Portfolio
U.S. Structured Finance

COMPETITORS

Assured Guaranty   MBIA
FGIC

HISTORICAL FINANCIALS

Company Type: Public

Income Statement

FYE: December 31

	ASSETS ($ mil.)	NET INCOME ($ mil.)	INCOME AS % OF ASSETS	EMPLOYEES
12/17	23,192	(328)	—	124
12/16	22,635	74	0.3%	154
12/15	23,728	493	2.1%	171
12/14	25,159	484	1.9%	188
12/13	27,106	505	1.9%	212
Annual Growth	**(3.8%)**	—	—	**(12.5%)**

2017 Year-End Financials

Debt ratio: 56.71%	No. of shares (mil.): 45
Return on equity: (-21.24%)	Dividends
Cash ($ mil.): 623	Yield: —
Current ratio: —	Payout: —
Long-term debt ($ mil.): —	Market value ($ mil.): 723

STOCK PRICE ($) FY Close	P/E High/Low		Earnings	Dividends	Book Value
12/17	15.98	— —	(7.25)	0.00	30.52
12/16	22.50	16 7	1.64	0.00	37.94
12/15	14.09	3 1	10.72	0.00	37.41
12/14	24.50	3 2	10.31	0.00	31.09
12/13	24.56	2 1	10.91	0.00	15.62
Annual Growth	**(10.2%)**	— —	—	—	**18.2%**

AMC Entertainment Holdings Inc.

AMC Entertainment shines when the lights go down. The company whose initials once stood for American Multi-Cinema is the #1 movie theater chain in the US and the world. It owns partially owns or operates about 660 theaters with 8200 screens most of which are in megaplexes (units with more than 12 screens and stadium seating). It also has a significant presence in Europe through London-based subsidiary Odeon & UCI Cinemas Group. AMC also owns about 25% of MovieTickets.com. Chinese investment firm Wanda Group bought AMC in 2012 and took the company public again in 2013. AMC acquired Odeon and Carmike in 2016 and has agreed to acquire Nordic Cinema Group which will swell its total theater pool to over 1000.

Operations

AMC owns 152 IMAX screens and has a 44% IMAX market share and 2643 3D screens in the US. It has been rolling out plush reclining seats that provide greater comfort and better viewing angles and operates 19 dine-in theaters with seat-side service.

Geographic Reach

AMC Entertainment has 660 theaters with 8200 screens in the US its largest market. It also has 243 theaters with 2236 screens via subsidiary Odeon in the UK Ireland Germany Austria Italy Spain and Portugal. Once the acquisition of Nordic Cinema Group is closed it will have a further 68 theaters across Sweden Norway Finland Lithuania Latvia and Estonia.

Financial Performance

AMC is in good shape. In fiscal 2015 (ended December) AMC recorded revenue growth of 9% to $2.9 billion. Admissions and food and beverage revenue were both up by over $100 million reflecting the success of the company's introduction of dining options. Net income climbed 63% to $103 million. AMC's cash position strengthened with cash from operations climbing 57% to $467 million due to higher earnings and decreases in payments for film.

Strategy

Chinese parent company Dalian Wanda's desire to be global cultural titan has driven AMC into an acquisition frenzy. In the space of four months it made three industry-shaking acquisitions. In November 2016 it acquired Odeon & UCI Cinemas Group a UK-based chain with a presence in Europe for $1.2 billion. At the end of the year it acquired US rival Carmike for $1.1 billion overtaking Regal Entertainment as the US's (and the world's) #1 cinema chain. And in early 2017 it announced an agreement to acquire Nordic Cinema Group which has multiplexes across Scandinavia and the Baltics for $929 million. After the acquisitions are sewn up AMC will own over 1000 multiplexes across the US and Europe.

Higher cinema prices and improved home cinema options have pushed AMC towards ramping up the quality of its multiplexes in order to stay ahead. It has been renovating its theaters including improved sight and sound but efforts have been led by the introduction of plush electric reclining seats that provide greater comfort and improved viewing angles. The reclining seats take up 60% more space than regular seats and thus each theater loses some two-thirds of its seating capacity. However AMC has found counter-intuitively that attendance is up 75% due to the greater appeal of a luxury experience. Mid-week crowds up in particular. AMC freezes prices for the year after renovation in order to drive interest in the new format increasing them thereafter. The company will be rolling out refitted theaters into its acquired Carmike mutiplexes.

AMC is also using enhanced food and beverage options to entice movie lovers. Its dine-in theaters combine the dinner and movie experience with full kitchen facilities seat-side servers and a separate bar and lounge area. The company has converted about a nearly 20 smaller theaters with the new dine-in theatre option. A secondary purpose behind the re-fit is to rejuvenate theaters approaching the end of their useful lives.

Mergers and Acquisitions

AMC acquired UK cinema company Odeon & UCI Cinemas Group for $1.21 billion from private equity firm Terra Firma in November 2016. Odeon & UCI is the UK's largest cinema chain and brings with it 242 theaters with 2236 screens.

In the same year it acquire one of its US rivals Carmike for $1.1 billion. Carmike has 271 locations.

And in January 2017 AMC reached an agreement to acquire Nordic Cinema Group which brings with it 68 screens across Scandinavia and the Baltics. Nordic will be absorbed into Odeon & UCI.

HISTORY

After performing in tent shows around the Midwest Edward Dubinsky settled in Kansas City Missouri and opened his first movie theater in 1920. Dubinsky who later changed his name to Durwood had opened about a dozen theaters and drive-ins by the 1950s. After he died in 1960 his son Stanley took control of the business. Three years later Stanley Durwood ushered in a new age of movie-viewing by opening the first mall-based theater with multiple screens. The company which became American Multi-Cinema in 1968 expanded the multiplex concept throughout the 1970s. In 1983 American Multi-Cinema shortened its name to AMC and went public.

The company opened theaters at a furious rate growing at about 100 screens a year for five years. This left it with a massive debt however and AMC posted little or no profit between 1988 and 1992. The company later restructured laying off employees and reducing its total number of screens to 1600 in 1994. AMC opened a 24-screen theater in Dallas in 1995. A year later a new AMC theater in Ontario California became the first to have 30 screens. In 1997 AMC teamed with Planet Hollywood to develop Planet Movies a restaurant theater and retail concept.

To reduce debt the next year AMC transferred 13 theaters to a real estate investment trust it had created; it then leased the theaters back to AMC. In 1999 the US Justice Department filed a lawsuit against AMC claiming the company's theaters denied handicapped individuals access to better stadium-style seats. The first Planet Movie opened that summer in Columbus Ohio but financial prob-

lems at Planet Hollywood put further projects on hold. Stanley Durwood died later that year after a long battle with cancer. He was replaced by co-chairman Peter Brown.

In 2000 AMC partnered with several entertainment companies to form MovieTickets.com a joint venture created to sell movie tickets over the Web. The company also began experimenting with the digital distribution of movies via satellite. In 2002 AMC acquired Gulf States Theatres (which included five theatres in the New Orleans area) and the bankrupt rival exhibitor GC Companies (which included 66 theatres throughout the US).

The following year a federal court ruled AMC violated regulations regarding accommodations for people in wheelchairs. As a result the company announced plans to spend $21 million over five years to modify 113 stadium-style theaters.

At the end of 2004 AMC ceased to be publicly traded after it was purchased by Marquee Holding an affiliate of J.P. Morgan Partners and Apollo Advisors. Early the next year AMC combined its National Cinema Network movie theater advertising sales business with Regal Entertainment's Regal CineMedia to form the jointly owned National CineMedia. (Cinemark later bought 21% of AMC's interest in National CineMedia.)

The company bought rival Loews Cineplex in 2006 significantly boosting its holdings adding some 2000 screens to AMC's network and expanding its international presence to about 12 countries. The combined company retained the AMC Entertainment name and AMC CEO Peter Brown continued in his position.

AMC filed an IPO in late 2006 hoping to raise $750 million. Investors shunned the $17-a-share asking price. Citing unfavorable market conditions the company withdrew the IPO the following year.

In 2007 AMC Entertainment sold its 9% share in online ticket Fandango to Comcast for some $20 million. Later in 2007 the company announced another IPO. AMC withdrew an IPO in 2008 while the economy was crashing; it had attempted to raise $500 million through the offering after a string of hits at the summer 2007 box office.

Brown retired in 2009 and was replaced by Gerardo Lopez. Also in 2008 AMC exited the Mexican market when it sold its interests in Grupo Cinemex. That chain operated about 45 theaters with nearly 500 screens primarily in the Mexico City metropolitan area.

Hoping the third time's a charm AMC filed another IPO in 2010. However it shelved those plans two years later due to unfavorable market conditions.

The company purchased more than 90 movie houses from Kerasotes ShowPlace Theatres in 2011. In 2012 it announced plans to be acquired by Chinese investment firm Wanda Group.

EXECUTIVES

Evp Global Development, Mark A. McDonald, age 59, $361,490 total compensation
Evp And Cfo, Craig R. Ramsey, age 66, $483,923 total compensation
Evp Us Operations, John D. McDonald, age 60, $467,112 total compensation
President Ceo And Director, Adam M. Aron, age 64
Evp And Chief Marketing Officer, Stephen A. Colanero, age 51
Evp Chief Content And Programming Officer, Elizabeth Frank, age 48, $474,327 total compensation
Senior Vice President Human Resources, Carla Sanders
Vp Food And Beverage Marketing, Tonya Mangels
President Ceo And Director, Adam M. Aron, age 64
Chairman, Lin Zhang, age 46
Auditors: KPMG LLP

LOCATIONS

HQ: AMC Entertainment Holdings Inc.
One AMC Way, 11500 Ash Street, Leawood, KS 66211
Phone: 913 213-2000
Web: www.amctheatres.com

2014 Sales

	$ mil.	% of total
US	2,688	100
Other	7	-
Total	**2,695**	**100**

PRODUCTS/OPERATIONS

2015 Sales

	$ mil.	% of total
Admissions	1,892	64
Food and beverage	910	31
Other	144	5
Total	**2,946**	**100**

2015 Theaters

	No.
California	49
Illinois	43
New York	24
Florida	22
Indiana	20
New Jersey	26
Texas	33
Colorado	12
Georgia	12
Washington	12
Pennsylvania	10
Maryland	10
Missouri	11
Arizona	10
Michigan	9
Ohio	9
Massachusetts	9
Virginia	8
Louisiana	7
Other	51
Total	**387**

COMPETITORS

Brenden Theatre	Laemmle Theatres
Carmike Cinemas	Landmark Theatres
Cinemark	Marcus Corporation
Cineplex	National Amusements
Clearview Cinemas	Pacific Theatres
Hoyts Cinemas	Regal Entertainment
IMAX	

HISTORICAL FINANCIALS

Company Type: Public

Income Statement

FYE: December 31

	REVENUE ($ mil.)	NET INCOME ($ mil.)	NET PROFIT MARGIN	EMPLOYEES
12/17	5,079	(487)	—	39,843
12/16	3,235	111	3.5%	41,373
12/15	2,946	103	3.5%	21,300
12/14	2,695	64	2.4%	19,700
12/13	2,749	364	13.3%	20,600
Annual Growth	**16.6%**	**—**	**—**	**17.9%**

2017 Year-End Financials

Debt ratio: 52.09%	No. of shares (mil.): 127
Return on equity: (-23.63%)	Dividends
Cash ($ mil.): 310	Yield: 0.0%
Current ratio: 0.62	Payout: —
Long-term debt ($ mil.): 5,020	Market value ($ mil.): 1,929

	STOCK PRICE ($) FY Close	P/E High/Low	PER SHARE ($) Earnings	Dividends	Book Value
12/17	15.10	— —	(3.80)	0.80	16.55
12/16	33.65	31 18	1.13	0.80	18.25
12/15	24.00	34 22	1.06	0.80	15.81
12/14	26.18	41 30	0.66	0.60	15.55
12/13	20.55	4 4	4.76	0.00	15.50
Annual Growth	(7.4%)	— —	—	—	1.7%

Ameren Corp

Ameren provides the power that lights much of Illinois and Missouri. The holding company distributes electricity to 2.4 million customers and natural gas to 900000 customers through regulated utility subsidiaries Union Electric (which does business as Ameren Missouri) and Ameren Ilinois. Ameren has generating capacity of about 10000 MW of primarily coal-fired power most of which is owned by Ameren Missouri. Ameren supplements its customers? electricity needs by purchasing additional electricity from third parties.

HISTORY

More than 30 St. Louis companies had built a chaotic grid of generators and power lines throughout the city by 1900. Two years later many of them merged into the Union Company which attracted national notice when it lit the St. Louis World's Fair in the first broad demonstration of electricity's power. In 1913 the company by then named Union Electric (UE) began buying electricity from an Iowa dam 150 miles away — the greatest distance power had ever been transmitted in such quantity.

UE pushed into rural Missouri and began buying and building fossil-fuel plants. Despite a slowdown during the Depression UE built Bagnell Dam on Missouri's Osage River in the early 1930s to gather power for a hydroelectric plant. At the onset of WWII construction began on new plants with larger generators and lower production costs; however demand for electricity lagged. In the late 1940s UE compensated by joining a "power pool" a system of utilities with interconnected transmission lines that shared electricity.

Growth in the 1950s came from acquisitions including Missouri Power & Light (1950) and Missouri Edison (1954). During the 1960s and 1970s UE built five new plants including the Labadie plant (2300 MW) one of the largest coal-fired plants in the US.

UE began producing nuclear energy in 1984 at its Callaway nuke. High costs and the expenses of a scrapped second plant caused UE to battle the Missouri Public Service Commission throughout the 1980s for rate increases.

Charles Mueller became president in 1993 and CEO one year later. He oversaw continued staff reductions and cost cutting through the 1990s in an increasingly competitive market. In 1997 UE expanded into Illinois through its purchase of CIPSCO which owned utility Central Illinois Public Service Company (CIPS).

CIPS began as a Mattoon Illinois streetcar company in the early 1900s. The firm bought Mattoon's electric power plant in 1904 and began growing its power business buying small electric companies in the 1920s and 1930s. CIPS built five generating units in the 1940s and 1950s and became part-owner (along with UE) of Electric Energy Inc. which built a power plant on the Ohio River. The company bought Illinois Electric and Gas Company in the 1960s and the state's Gas Utilities in the 1980s. To prepare for competition under deregulation CIPS created holding company CIPSCO in the 1990s to diversify.

UE's purchase of CIPSCO expanded its geographic scope and the new company was named Ameren in 1997 to reflect its American energy focus. The next year the company committed to adding generating capacity through several natural gas-fired combustion turbines. It joined nine other utilities to form the Midwest Independent System Operator to manage their transmission needs.

In 1999 Ameren bought a 245-mile railroad line between St. Louis and Kansas City to help the area's economic development. Looking for new opportunities in deregulated energy markets the company purchased Data & Metering Specialties.

In 2000 Ameren created subsidiary AmerenEnergy Generating to operate its nonregulated power plants and affiliate AmerenEnergy Marketing to sell the generating facilities' power. When deregulation took effect in Illinois in 2002 the company transferred AmerenCIPS' power plants to AmerenEnergy Generating. In 2003 Ameren acquired CILCORP the holding company for electric and gas utility Central Illinois Light (now operating as AmerenCILCO) from independent power producer AES in a $1.4 billion deal. To further expand its utility operations Ameren acquired power and gas utility Illinois Power from Dynegy in a $2.3 billion deal in 2004.

EXECUTIVES

Senior Vice President Administration, Daniel F Cole
Chairman President And Ceo, Warner L. Baxter, age 57, $1,040,000 total compensation
Evp And Cfo, Martin J. Lyons, age 51, $640,000 total compensation
Chairman And President Ameren Illinois, Richard J. Mark, age 63, $490,000 total compensation
Chairman And President Ameren Missouri, Michael L. Moehn, age 49, $512,000 total compensation
Chairman And President Ameren Transmission Company, Shawn E. Schukar, age 54
Svp And Cio Ameren Services, Mary P. Heger
Vice President Data Analytics And Insights Ameren Services, Lynn Barnes
Senior Vice President Administrator, Brian Detchemendy
Senior Vice President General Counsel And Secretary, Steven R Sullivan
Vice President Power Operations, Chuck Naslund
Vice President External Affairs And Communications Ameren Missouri, Warren Wood
Chairman President And Ceo, Warner L. Baxter, age 57
Assistant Treasurer, Stephen Lux
Board Member, Ellen Fitzsimmons
Board Member, Jennifer Wolfrom
Auditors: PricewaterhouseCoopers LLP

LOCATIONS

HQ: Ameren Corp
1901 Chouteau Avenue, St. Louis, MO 63103
Phone: 314 621-3222
Web: www.ameren.com

PRODUCTS/OPERATIONS

2017 Sales

	$ mil.	% of total
Ameren Missouri	3,490	56
Ameren Illinois Electric Distribution	1,565	25
Ameren Illinois Natural Gas	742	12
Ameren Transmission	382	7
Total	**6,177**	**100**

2017 Sales

	$ mil.	% of total
Electric	5,310	86
Gas	867	14
Total	**6,177**	**100**

COMPETITORS

AES	Exelon
Alliant Energy	Great Plains Energy
Atmos Energy	Midwest Generation
Commonwealth Edison	Nicor Gas
Empire District Electric	Southern Union

HISTORICAL FINANCIALS

Company Type: Public

Income Statement

FYE: December 31

	REVENUE ($ mil.)	NET INCOME ($ mil.)	NET PROFIT MARGIN	EMPLOYEES
12/17	6,177	523	8.5%	8,615
12/16	6,076	653	10.7%	8,629
12/15	6,098	630	10.3%	8,527
12/14	6,053	586	9.7%	8,527
12/13	5,838	289	5.0%	8,527
Annual Growth	1.4%	16.0%	—	0.3%

2017 Year-End Financials

Debt ratio: 32.45%
Return on equity: 7.32%
Cash ($ mil.): 10
Current ratio: 0.55
Long-term debt ($ mil.): 7,094
No. of shares (mil.): 242
Dividends
Yield: 0.0%
Payout: 83.0%
Market value ($ mil.): 14,311

	STOCK PRICE ($) FY Close	P/E High/Low	PER SHARE ($) Earnings	Dividends	Book Value
12/17	58.99	30 24	2.14	1.78	29.61
12/16	52.46	20 16	2.68	1.72	29.28
12/15	43.23	18 14	2.59	1.66	28.63
12/14	46.13	20 15	2.40	1.61	27.67
12/13	36.16	31 26	1.18	1.60	26.97
Annual Growth	13.0%	— —	16.0%	2.7%	2.4%

American Airlines Group Inc

American Airlines Group (AAG) is the largest airline in the US and one of the largest in the world. The company's mainline carriers provide scheduled air transportation along with its group of regional subsidiaries and third-party regional carriers operating as American Eagle. It also offers freight and mail services through its cargo division. In all American operates nearly 6700 flights daily to 350 destinations in more than 50 countries. It operates about 950 mainline aircraft and almost 600 regional aircraft. AAG is also part of the oneworld alliance where member carriers share airport lounge facilities and offer interconnected loyalty programs.

Operations

AAG provides scheduled air transportation through its mainline carrier network as well as through regional carriers. Its mainline segment accounts for more than two thirds of total sales and operates close to 950 aircraft. Regional operations (about 15% of total sales) provide services under the “American Eagle” brand. American Eagle carriers include wholly-owned subsidiaries Envoy PSA and Piedmont. Third-party regional carriers including Republic Mesa Compass ExpressJet SkyWest and Trans States.

The company's Cargo segment (accounts for less than 5% of total sales) also provides a wide range of freight and mail services with facilities and interline connections available across the globe.

Geographic Reach

Headquartered in Fort Worth TX AAG flies to 350-plus destinations in more than 50 countries. Its hubs are located in Charlotte Chicago Dallas/Fort Worth Los Angeles Miami New York Philadelphia Phoenix and Washington DC with international services to Canada Central and South America Asia Europe Australia and New Zealand.

Sales and Marketing

AAG sells its tickets through several distribution channels including its website (www.aa.com) reservations centers and third-party distribution channels. Its loyalty program offers rewards to travelers for their continued patronage. Advertising costs in 2017 were $135 million up $20 million from 2016.

Financial Performance

American Airlines recovered in 2017 after posting two straight years of revenue declines. Net sales increased 5% to $42.2 billion compared with $40.2 billion in 2016. Mainline and regional passenger revenues added up to $36.1 billion a $1.6 billion hike from the previous year.

AAG's net income decreased by 65% from $2.7 billion in 2016 to $1.9 billion in 2017. The drop was mainly due to nearly $1 billion in net interest expense and higher operating costs (primarily increasing fuel prices and employee wages). Since its merger with US Air in 2015 American has been investing more than $5 billion annually in capital expenditures for its fleet products and team members. The company reports that by 2021 it will reduce capex to $2 billion.

Cash at the end of fiscal 2017 was $295 million a decrease of $27 million from the prior year. Cash from operations contributed $4.7 billion to the coffers while investing activities used $3.6 billion mainly for capital expenditures. Financing activities used another $1.1 billion for dividends to stockholders and the company's stock repurchase program.

Strategy

AAG is planning significant investments to expand capacity focusing on its hubs in Dallas/Fort Worth (DFW) and Charlotte and adding new routes to medium- and smaller-sized cities such as South Bend IN Panama City FL and Missoula MT. In 2019 American plans to add 15 gates and 100 departures per day at DFW and in 2020 seven new gates at Charlotte with another 75 daily departures.

The company is targeting increased revenues from continued investments in product and customers. These include a refresh of its Admiral's Club facilities in Boston Charlotte and Pittsburgh TV capabilities for domestic flights and high-speed WiFi. Corporate clients can now book travel through aa.com as a result of the company's integration with SAP Concur TripLink and through a new partnership with Alibaba customers in Asia can make payments using Alipay on aa.com/China. American also cites operational re-

liability as one of its top corporate priorities and is reviewing its planning processes to ensure better service during summer and year-end holiday peak periods.

With a new product segmentation strategy AAG aims to increase passenger sales by close to 10% in 2018. The company introduced Premium Economy an upgrade to its Basic Economy class with plans to further leverage this higher-value product with increased merchandising efforts. It has also removed the carry-on bag restriction in Basic Economy allowing AAG to offer basic economy to more markets.

Mergers and Acquisitions

AAG in mid-2017 made a significant move to expand internationally with the announcement of a $200 million equity investment in China Southern Airlines and a 2018 codesharing agreement with China Southern is giving customers access to additional destinations in China as well as North and South America. AAG customers are able to access nearly 40 destinations beyond Beijing and more than 30 destinations beyond Shanghai.

Company Background

In 2011 American Airlines' parent company AMR Corporation filed for bankruptcy. It emerged from Chapter 11 in late 2013 and at the same time merged with rival US Airways in a mega deal worth $11 billion. The milestone transaction created the world's largest airline. The combined entity formed the American Airlines Group and is led by former US Airways CEO Doug Parker.

HISTORY

In 1929 Sherman Fairchild created a New York City holding company called the Aviation Corporation (AVCO) combining some 85 small airlines in 1930 to create American Airways. In 1934 the company had its first dose of financial trouble after the government suspended private airmail for months. Corporate raider E. L. Cord took over and named the company American Airlines.

EXECUTIVES

Evp Corporate Affairs, Stephen L. (Steve) Johnson, age 61, $600,936 total compensation
Chairman And Ceo, W. Douglas (Doug) Parker, age 56, $1 total compensation
Evp People And Communications, Elise R. Eberwein, age 52
Evp And Cfo, Derek J. Kerr, age 53, $600,936 total compensation
President, Robert D. Isom, age 54, $641,306 total compensation
Evp And Cio, Maya Leibman, age 53, $600,936 total compensation
Evp And Chief Integration Officer, Beverly K. Goulet, age 63
Chairman And Ceo, W. Douglas (Doug) Parker, age 56
Auditors: KPMG LLP

LOCATIONS

HQ: American Airlines Group Inc
4333 Amon Carter Blvd., Fort Worth, TX 76155
Phone: 817 963-1234　　**Fax:** 817 967-9641
Web: www.aa.com

2017 Sales

	$ mil.	% of total
DOT Domestic	29,612	70
DOT Latin America	5,422	13
DOT Atlantic	5,059	12
DOT Pacific	2,114	5
Total	**42,207**	**100**

Selected Hub Locations

Charlotte
Chicago
Dallas/Fort Worth (DFW)
Los Angeles
Miami
New York City
Philadelphia
Phoenix
Washington DC

PRODUCTS/OPERATIONS

2017 Sales

	$ mil.	% of total
Mainline passenger	29,238	69
Regional passenger	6,895	16
Cargo	800	2
Other	5,274	13
Total	**42,207**	**100**

Selected Carriers

Regional Subsidiaries
　Envoy
　PSA
　Piedmont
Regional Third-Party Carriers
　Republic
　Mesa
　Compass
　ExpressJet
　SkyWest
　Trans States

COMPETITORS

Air France-KLM	Hawaiian Holdings
Alaska Air	JetBlue
Delta Air Lines	Lufthansa
Echo Global	Southwest Airlines
FedEx	Spirit Airlines
Frontier Airlines	UPS
Greyhound	United Air Lines

HISTORICAL FINANCIALS

Company Type: Public

Income Statement   FYE: December 31

	REVENUE ($ mil.)	NET INCOME ($ mil.)	NET PROFIT MARGIN	EMPLOYEES
12/17	42,207	1,919	4.5%	126,600
12/16	40,180	2,676	6.7%	122,300
12/15	40,990	7,610	18.6%	118,500
12/14	42,650	2,882	6.8%	113,300
12/13	26,743	(1,834)	—	110,400
Annual Growth	**12.1%**	—	—	**3.5%**

2017 Year-End Financials

Debt ratio: 48.77%	No. of shares (mil.): 475
Return on equity: 49.77%	Dividends
Cash ($ mil.): 613	Yield: 0.0%
Current ratio: 0.61	Payout: 10.2%
Long-term debt ($ mil.): 22,511	Market value ($ mil.): 24,741

	STOCK PRICE ($) FY Close	P/E High/Low	Earnings	PER SHARE ($) Dividends	Book Value
12/17	52.03	14　10	3.90	0.40	8.26
12/16	46.69	10　5	4.81	0.40	7.46
12/15	42.35	5　3	11.07	0.40	9.02
12/14	53.63	13　6	3.93	0.20	2.90
12/13	25.25	—　—	(11.25)	0.00	(10.46)
Annual Growth	**19.8%**	—	—	—	—

AMERICAN ASSETS TRUST, INC.

American Assets Trust is a self-administered real estate investment trust (REIT) that owns develops and operates upscale retail office and residential property mostly in Northern and Southern California but also in Oregon Washington Texas and Hawaii. Its 6 million square foot portfolio includes around 10 shopping centers more than handful of office buildings a 369-room hotel and retail complex and five multi-family residential properties. Its tenants include SalesForce Autodesk the Veterans Benefits Administration and well-known retailers such as Kmart Lowe's Sports Authority Old Navy and Vons. Formed in 1967 as American Assets the firm went public in 2011.

Operations
The REIT leases retail office and multifamily properties as well as hotels. Its retail portfolio which made up 35% of its revenue during 2015 spans 3 million rentable square feet while its office holdings (34% of revenue) measure 2.7 million square feet.

In addition American Assets Trust mixed-use property (19% of revenue) the Embassy Suites at Waikiki Beach Walk in Honolulu is a 369-room all-suite hotel with approximately 97000 square feet of accompanying retail space. The REIT generates the rest of its revenue from its more than 1500 multifamily units in San Diego and Imperial Beach California.

Geographic Reach
San Diego-based American Assets Trust's primary markets include San Diego; the San Francisco Bay area; Portland Oregon; Bellevue Washington; and Oahu Hawaii. More than 50% of its property by square footage was located in Southern and Northern California at the end of 2015 while over 15% of its property space was in Oregon. The rest of its properties were in Hawaii (11% of square footage) Texas (10%) and Washington state (9%).

Sales and Marketing
The REIT's largest five tenants by revenue in 2015 included: Salesforce (8% of annualized base rent) Autodesk (3%) Kmart (3%) Lowe's (3%) the Veterans Benefits Administration (2%) and the Insurance Company of the West (2%). Its properties that year were 98.6% leased.

The company has been increasing its marketing spend in recent years. It spent $2.1 million on marketing during 2015 up from $1.62 million and $1.55 million in 2014 and 2013 respectively.

Financial Performance
America Assets Trusts' annual revenues have risen more than 35% since 2011 as its property valuations have appreciated and have commanded higher rental rates. While more volatile its annual profits have more than doubled over the period on declining interest expenses as the REIT has paid down its long-term debt.

The REIT's revenue climbed 6% to $275.6 million during 2015 thanks to rental income growth mostly from its office properties which benefited from higher occupancy and rental rates. Rental income also grew from its mixed-use property as its hotel occupancy rate jumped by almost 10 percentage points to 89.6% and as its revenue per available room (revPAR) grew 13%. Retail rental revenue grew with higher rental rates while its multifamily rental revenue also rose with the completion of its Hassalo on Eighth property late in the year.

Revenue growth in 2015 combined with a $7.1 million gain from the sale of its Rancho Carmel Plaza property drove the American Asset Trust's net income up 73% to almost $54 million. The REIT's operating cash levels rose 5% to $110.7 million as cash-based rental income increased.

Strategy
American Assets Trust's properties are in located in developed areas where new construction is difficult which helps to keep competition out and rental and occupancy rates stable. The REIT prefers to develop or acquire properties in such high-barrier-to-entry areas in its core markets which include San Diego; the San Francisco Bay area; Portland Oregon; Bellevue Washington; and Oahu Hawaii.

American Asset Trust's other key strategy is redeveloping and improving existing properties to command higher rental rates. It also makes its properties more attractive to potential tenants by signing well-known brands such as Apple Store Banana Republic Pottery Barn and Starbucks as retail tenants.

Company Background
American Assets Trust went public in January 2011 with an offering valued at about $564 million. (About $4 million of that figure went to chairman Ernest Rady who controlled the company prior to its IPO.) The IPO proceeds were used to repay debt and to purchase and renovate property.

EXECUTIVES

Chairman President And Ceo, Ernest S. Rady, $259,616 total compensation
Ceo And President, John W. Chamberlain
Evp And Cfo, Robert F. Barton, $373,846 total compensation
Vp Construction And Development, Jerry Gammieri, $186,923 total compensation
Vp Retail Properties, Chris Sullivan
Vp Office Properties, Jim Durfey
Vp And Regional Manager Portland, Wade Lange
Chairman President And Ceo, Ernest S. Rady
Auditors: ERNST & YOUNG LLP SAN DIEGO

LOCATIONS

HQ: AMERICAN ASSETS TRUST, INC.
11455 EL CAMINO REAL # 200, SAN DIEGO, CA 921302047
Phone: 858 350-2600
Web: WWW.AMERICANASSETSTRUST.COM

2015 Properties

	No.
Southern California	7
Northern California	4
Hawaii	3
Oregon	2
Texas	1
Washington	1
Total	**18**

PRODUCTS/OPERATIONS

2015 Sales

	% of total
Rental Income	
Retail	35
Office	34
Mixed-Use	19
Multifamily	7
Other Property Income	5
Total	**100**

Selected Tenants
Alliant International University
Autodesk Inc.
California Bank & Trust
Caradigm USA LLC
Drug Enforcement Administration
Foodland Super Market
HDR Engineering
Inome Inc.
Insurance Company of the West
Integra Telecom Holdings
Kmart
Lowe's
Marshalls
McDermott Will & Emery
Nordstrom Rack
Officemax
Old Navy
Portland Energy Conservation
Quiksilver
salesforce.com inc.
Sports Authority
Sprouts Farmers Market
Treasury Call Center
Veterans Benefits Administration
Vons

Selected Properties
Retail
  Alamo Quarry
  Carmel County Plaza
  Carmel Mountain Plaza
  Del Monte Shopping Center
  Lomas Sante Fe Plaza
  Rancho Carmel Plaza
  Solana Beach Towne Centre
  South Bay Market Place
  The Shops at Kalakaua
  Waikele Center
Mixed-use
  Waikiki Beach Walk - Hotel
  Waikiki Beach Walk - Retail
Multi-family
  Imperial Beach Gardens
  Loma Palisades
  Mariner's Point
  Santa Fe Park RV Resort
Office
  Fireman's Fund Headquarters
  Solana Beach Corporate Centre
  The Landmark at One Market
  Torrey Reserve Campus
  Valencia Corporate Center

COMPETITORS

CBL & Associates Properties
GGP
Hersha Hospitality
Macerich
Simon Property Group
Taubman Centers

HISTORICAL FINANCIALS
Company Type: Private

Income Statement
FYE: December 31

	ASSETS ($ mil.)	NET INCOME ($ mil.)	INCOME AS % OF ASSETS	EMPLOYEES
12/17	2,259	40	1.8%	113
12/16	1,986	45	2.3%	—
12/15	1,978	53	2.7%	—
12/14	1,941	31	1.6%	—
Annual Growth	5.2%	8.8%	—	—

2017 Year-End Financials

Debt ratio: ——
Return on equity: 12.70%
Cash ($ mil.): 82
Current ratio: ——
Long-term debt ($ mil.): ——

Dividends
  Yield: —
  Payout: —
Market value ($ mil.): —

American Axle & Manufacturing Holdings Inc

American Axle & Manufacturing (AAM) is GM's right-hand man for driveline systems and forged products. AAM manufactures engineers designs axles driveshafts and chassis components mainly for light trucks and SUVs but also for cars and crossover vehicles. The Tier 1 supplier gets nearly half of its business from GM; other customers include Fiat-Chrysler Ford Jaguar Land Rover and Nissan. AAM operates about 90 manufacturing facilities around the world and generates more than half its revenue from North America. In 2017 it completed the acquisition of Metaldyne for around $3.3 billion reducing its dependence on primary customer GM.

Operations

American Axle & Manufacturing operates four business segments: Driveline Metal Forming Powertrain and Casting.

Driveline generates some 65% of sales and designs and manufactures driveshafts power transfer units rear drive modules transfer cases and electric and hybrid driveline products and systems. Its products end up in light trucks SUVs crossover vehicles passenger cars and commercial vehicles.

Metal Forming accounts for nearly 15% of sales and produces axle and transmission shafts ring and pinion gears differentials transmissions and shafts and suspension components. It serves OEMs (original equipment manufacturers) and Tier 1 automotive suppliers.

Powertrain brings in nearly 15% of sales. It produces transmission modules and differential assemblies transmission valve bodies connecting rod forging and assemblies torsional vibration dampers and variable valve timing products.

Lastly Casting produces thin wall castings and high-strength ductile iron castings as well as differential cases steering knuckles control arms brackets and turbo charger housings. It serves the global light vehicle commercial and industrial markets and generates around 10% of sales.

Geographic Reach

American Axle & Manufacturing's more than 90 manufacturing sites are found in the US Midwest (Michigan Indiana Illinois Ohio) as well as 16 other countries including Brazil the UK France Germany India Mexico South Korea and Thailand.

After the US which accounts for more than half of company sales American Axel's second largest market is Mexico at more than 20%. Its other principle geographies — Canada China Other Asia and Europe — generate around 5% each.

Sales and Marketing

GM and Fiat-Chrysler together account for 65% of American Axle & Manufacturing's (AAM) sales. AAM is the principal supplier of light truck and SUV rear-wheel-drive components to GM. It supplies Fiat-Chrysler with driveline systems for heavy-duty Ram full-size pickup trucks the AWD Jeep Cherokee and a passenger car driveshaft program.

Financial Performance

American Axle & Manufacturing (AAM) has achieved consistent and steady revenue growth over the years.

In fiscal 2017 sales jumped 59% to $6.3 billion mostly a result of the Metaldyne acquisition which contributed around $2.0 billion. Organically sales increased 7% or around $296 million due to higher production volumes for the light truck and the SUV programs AAM supports. It also benefited from the launch of programs from its new business backlog and an increase in metal market passthroughs to its customers.

Net income grew 40% to $337.5 million as the significant revenue contribution from Metaldyne was partially offset by lower gross profit in the unit higher general expenses and increased restructuring costs relating to the acquisition.

Cash inflow from operations increased 59% to $607.4 million on the back of higher net income and adjustments to reconcile an increase in depreciation and amortization lower deferred income taxes and changes in inventories and other assets and liabilities.

Strategy

The acquisition of Metaldyne Performance Group in 2017 was a landmark for American Axle & Manufacturing (AAM). In addition to a revenue boost and its ascension to global Tier 1 automotive supplier status the acquisition also represented a major step in AAM's goal to diversify its client base and reduce its dependence on GM in particular. Previously accounting for some 75% of AAM's sales sales to the US auto company fell to just under half of AAM's total sales in the first year after the acquisition.

AAM's product strategy is based on anticipating demand for technologies that reduce emissions increase fuel economy and minimize the environmental impact of vehicles. Recent product developments on those lines have included its EcoTrac Disconnecting AWD system e-AAM hybrid and electric driveline systems Quantum lightweight axle technology high-efficiency axles PowerLite axles and PowerDense gears among other things. The Metaldyne acquisition also brought in new products and technologies.

Mergers and Acquisitions

In one of its largest deals to date AAM in 2017 acquired Metaldyne Performance Group for $3.3 billion. The combination created a global supplier with broad capabilities across the powertrain drivetrain and driveline product lines. More importantly it will also diversify its customer base so it won't be as reliant on GM as a primary customer.

EXECUTIVES

Chairman And Ceo, David C. Dauch, age 54, $1,150,000 total compensation

President, Michael K. Simonte, age 54, $640,000 total compensation

President Powertrain, Gregory S. (Greg) Deveson

President Driveline, Alberto L. Satine, age 61, $510,000 total compensation

President Metal Formed Products, Norman Willemse, age 61, $450,000 total compensation

President Casting, Timothy E. (Tim) Bowes

Vp And Cfo, Christopher J. (Chris) May, age 48, $391,667 total compensation

Vice President Human Resources, Terri M Kemp

Vice President Quality Warr And Customer Satisf American Axle And Manufacturing Holdings Inc, Allan R Monich

Vice President Human Resources, Carla Wesley

Vice President Of Finance, Chaitanya Apte

Chairman And Ceo, David C. Dauch, age 54

Auditors: DELOITTE & TOUCHE LLP

LOCATIONS

HQ: American Axle & Manufacturing Holdings Inc
One Dauch Drive, Detroit, MI 48211-1198
Phone: 313 758-2000
Web: www.aam.com

2017 Sales

	$ mil.	% of total
US	3,319	53
Mexico	1,393	22
Canada	310	5
China	297	5
All Other Asia	291	5
Europe and other	492	8
South America	161	2
Total	**6,266**	**100**

PRODUCTS/OPERATIONS

2017 Sales

	% of total
Driveline	65
Metal Forming	13
Powertrain	13
Casting	9
Total	**100**

Selected Products

Axles
Brackets
Control arms
Connecting rod forging and assemblies
Driveshafts
Differential assemblies and cases
Rear drive modules
Ring and pinion gears
Suspension components
Thin wall castings
high-strength ductile iron castings
Steering knuckles
Torsional vibration dampers
Transfer cases
Transmission modules
Transmission valve bodies
Turbo charger housings
Variable valve timing products

COMPETITORS

AxleTech International	Linamar Corp.
Carraro	Magna International
Dana	Meritor
FCA US	Tower International
Ford Motor	Visteon
GKN	ZF Friedrichshafen

HISTORICAL FINANCIALS

Company Type: Public

Income Statement FYE: December 31

	REVENUE ($ mil.)	NET INCOME ($ mil.)	NET PROFIT MARGIN	EMPLOYEES
12/17	6,266	337	5.4%	25,000
12/16	3,948	240	6.1%	13,100
12/15	3,903	235	6.0%	13,050
12/14	3,696	143	3.9%	12,820
12/13	3,207	94	2.9%	12,650
Annual Growth	18.2%	37.4%	—	18.6%

2017 Year-End Financials

Debt ratio: 50.43%
Return on equity: 32.63%
Cash ($ mil.): 376
Current ratio: 1.60
Long-term debt ($ mil.): 3,969

No. of shares (mil.): 111
Dividends
Yield: —
Payout: —
Market value ($ mil.): 1,895

	STOCK PRICE ($) FY Close	P/E High/Low		PER SHARE ($) Earnings	Dividends	Book Value
12/17	17.03	7	4	3.21	0.00	13.80
12/16	19.30	6	4	3.06	0.00	6.93
12/15	18.94	9	6	3.02	0.00	3.96
12/14	22.59	12	9	1.85	0.00	1.50
12/13	20.45	17	9	1.23	0.00	0.44
Annual Growth	(4.5%)	—		27.1%	—	—136.1%

AMERICAN BALANCED FUND, INC.

EXECUTIVES

Chb-Ceo, Robert G O'Donnell
Pres, Paul G Haaga Jr
V Pres, Hilda L Applbaum
Sr V Pres, Abner Goldstine
Sr V Pres, John H Smet
V Pres, J Dale Harvey
V Pres, Jeffrey T Lager
Asst Treas, R Marcia Gould
SEC, Patrick F Quan
Auditors: DELOITTE & TOUCHE LLP

LOCATIONS

HQ: AMERICAN BALANCED FUND, INC.
1 MARKET, SAN FRANCISCO, CA 941051596
Phone: 707 864-3945

HISTORICAL FINANCIALS

Company Type: Private

Income Statement   FYE: December 31

	ASSETS ($ mil.)	NET INCOME ($ mil.)	INCOME AS % OF ASSETS	EMPLOYEES
12/15	87,394	4,903	5.6%	9
12/00	6,203	832	13.4%	—
12/99	5,996	218	3.6%	—
Annual Growth	18.2%	21.4%	—	—

2015 Year-End Financials

Debt ratio: —
Return on equity: 367.30%
Cash ($ mil.): 0
Current ratio: —
Long-term debt ($ mil.): —

Dividends
Yield: —
Payout: —
Market value ($ mil.): —

American Electric Power Co Inc

American Electric Power (AEP) takes its slice of the US power pie out of Middle America with markets in Ohio Michigan and Indiana. The holding company is one of the largest power generators and distributors in the US. AEP owns the nation's largest electricity transmission system a network of more than 40000 miles. It also has 224000 miles of distribution lines. Its electric utilities have 5.4 million customers in 11 states and have about 26000 MW of largely coal-fired generating capacity although it is adding renewable sources to its generation portfolio. AEP is a top wholesale energy company; it markets electricity in the US.

HISTORY

In 1906 Richard Breed Sidney Mitchell and Henry Doherty set up American Gas & Electric (AG&E) in New York to buy 23 utilities from Philadelphia's Electric Company of America. With properties in seven northeastern US states AG&E began acquiring and merging small electric properties creating the predecessors of Ohio Power

(1911) Kentucky Power (1919) and Appalachian Power (1926). AG&E also bought the predecessor of Indiana Michigan Power (1925).

By 1926 the company was operating in Indiana Kentucky Michigan Ohio Virginia and West Virginia. In 1935 AG&E engineer Philip Sporn later known as the Henry Ford of power introduced his high-voltage high-velocity circuit breaker. AG&E picked up Kingsport Power in 1938.

Becoming president in 1947 Sporn began an ambitious building program that continued through the 1960s. Plants designed by AG&E (renamed American Electric Power in 1958) were among the world's most efficient and electric rates stayed 25%-38% below the national average.

AEP bought Michigan Power in 1967 six years after Donald Cook succeeded Sporn as president. Cook who refused to attach scrubbers to the smokestacks of coal-fired plants was criticized in the early 1970s by environmental protesters. AEP's first nuclear plant named in Cook's honor went on line in Michigan in 1975. He retired in 1976.

The firm moved from New York to Columbus Ohio in 1980 after buying what is now Columbus Southern Power (formed in 1883). It set up AEP Generating in 1982 to provide power to its electric utilities.

AEP began converting its second nuke Zimmer to coal in 1984. In 1992 AEP finally began installing scrubbers at its coal-fired Gavin plant in Ohio after being ordered to comply with the Clean Air Act. It also cleaned up its image by planting millions of trees in 1996.

The company formed AEP Communications after Congress passed the Telecommunications Act of 1996. The next year AEP jumped into the UK's deregulated electric market; AEP and New Century Energies (now Xcel Energy) bought Yorkshire Electricity (later Yorkshire Power Group) for $2.8 billion. However a $109 million UK windfall tax on the transaction — and increased wholesale competition — hurt AEP's bottom line.

As the normally staid electric industry succumbed to merger mania AEP agreed in 1997 to buy Central and South West (CSW) of Texas in a $6.6 billion deal. AEP's sales would nearly double and CSW was to bring its own UK utility SEE-BOARD and other overseas holdings.

In 1998 AEP bought a 20% stake in Pacific Hydro an Australian power producer and CitiPower an Australian electric distribution company. AEP also bought Equitable Resources' Louisiana natural gas midstream operations including an intrastate pipeline. In 1999 China's Pushan Power Plant (70%-owned by AEP) began operations. Environmental concerns resurfaced that year when the EPA sued the utility alleging its old coal-powered plants which had been grandfathered from the Clean Air Act had been quietly upgraded to extend their lives.

Regulators approved the company's acquisition of CSW in 2000 but AEP had to agree to relinquish control of its 22000 miles of transmission lines to an independent operator. The CSW deal closed later that year. (However the SEC's approval of the deal was challenged by a federal appeals court in 2002.)

AEP sold its 50% stake in Yorkshire Power Group to Innogy (now RWE npower) in 2001; it also purchased Houston Pipe Line Co. (which it later sold in early 2005) from Enron for $727 million. AEP became one of the largest US barge operators that year when it bought MEMCO Barge Line from Progress Energy. It also purchased two UK coal-fired power plants (4000 MW) from Edison Mission Energy a subsidiary of Edison International in a $960 million deal.

In 2002 AEP sold its UK utility SEEBOARD to ElectricitA© de France in a $2.2 billion deal; it

also sold its Australian utility CitiPower to a consortium led by Cheung Kong Infrastructure and Hongkong Electric for $855 million. The following year the company sold two of its competitive Texas retail electric providers (WTU Retail Energy and CPL Retail Energy) to UK utility Centrica. It also divested its power plant development subsidiary AEP Pro Serv and its stakes in telecom firms C3 Communications and AFN.

The company sold two UK power plants to Scottish and Southern Energy for $456 million in 2004 and it sold a 50% stake in a third UK plant to Scottish Power in a $210 million deal. AEP also sold four independent power plants in Florida and Colorado to Bear Stearns for $156 million that year.

In 2006 the company sold its Plaquemine cogeneration plant to Dow Chemical for $64 million. Also that year it formed a joint venture company with MidAmerican Energy Holdings to build and own new electric transmission assets within the Electric Reliability Council of Texas.

AEP settled an eight-year lawsuit with the US government in 2007 and agreed to pay more than $4.6 billion to reduce hazardous air pollution from 16 coal-burning power plants.

In 2011 the company reached a $425 million settlement covering all claims with BOA and Enron related to their purchase of Houston Pipeline Company from Enron in 2001.

Growing its retail business in the US in 2012 AEP acquired Chicago-based Blue Star Energy and its independent retail electric supplier BlueStar Energy Solutions. The company has about 23000 customer accounts. The deal also gives AEP the opportunity to hedge the output of its soon-to-be unregulated Ohio power generation.

By the end of 2012 AEP was operating 310 MW of wind power facilities and had about 180 MW of long-term purchase power agreements for wind power.

In 2013 AEP received the regulatory go-ahead to separate its AEP Ohio-owned generation assets from its Ohio distribution and transmission operations and complete transfer of that generation to AEP's competitive generation company (AEP Generation Resources) and regulated affiliates Appalachian Power and Kentucky Power.

To create a more customer friendly service in 2013 AEP launched a new enhanced version of its website at aepenergy.com. optimized for mobile devices.

EXECUTIVES

Evp And Chief Administrative Officer, Lana L. Hillebrand, age 58, $490,680 total compensation
Vice Chairman, Robert P. (Bob) Powers, age 64, $723,773 total compensation
President And Coo Southwestern Electric Power, Venita McCellon-Allen, age 59, $410,919 total compensation
Svp Governmental And Environmental Affairs Aep Service, Dale E. Heydlauff, age 58
Evp External Affairs, Charles R. Patton, age 59
Evp Energy Supply, Charles E. (Chuck) Zebula, age 58, $446,310 total compensation
President And Coo Aep Ohio, Julie Sloat, age 45
Evp And Cfo, Brian X. Tierney, age 51, $730,800 total compensation
President And Coo Public Service Company Of Oklahoma, J. Stuart Solomon, age 56
Chairman President And Ceo, Nicholas K. (Nick) Akins, age 58, $1,325,077 total compensation
Evp General Counsel And Secretary, David M. Feinberg, age 49, $615,354 total compensation
Evp Generation, Mark C. McCullough, age 58
Evp Utilities, Paul Chodak, age 54

Svp Transmission Strategy And Business Development; President Electric Transmission America (eta), Lisa M. Barton, age 52, $532,039 total compensation

President And Coo Kentucky Power, Matthew J. Satterwhite, age 45

President And Coo Indiana Michigan Power, Toby L. Thomas

President And Coo Appalachian Power, Chris T. Beam

President And Coo Aep Texas, Judith Talavera

Vice President Of Human Resources, Lisa Failla

Senior Vice President, Jeffrey Cross

National Account Manager, James B Clark

Vice President Trading, John Sniffen

National Account Manager, James Clark

Vice President, Greg Clark

Vice Chairman, Robert P. (Bob) Powers, age 64

Chairman President And Ceo, Nicholas K. (Nick) Akins, age 58

Evp General Counsel And Secretary, David M. Feinberg, age 49

Auditors: PricewaterhouseCoopers LLP

LOCATIONS

HQ: American Electric Power Co Inc
1 Riverside Plaza, Columbus, OH 43215-2373
Phone: 614 716-1000   **Fax:** 614 223-1823
Web: www.aep.com

PRODUCTS/OPERATIONS

2017 Sales

	$ mil.	% of total
Vertically integrated utilities	9,095	59
Transmission and distribution utilities	4,328	28
Generation and marketing	1,771	12
Other Revenues	229	1
Total	**15,424**	**100**

Selected Subsidiaries

AEP Energy Services Inc. (energy marketing and trading)
AEP Generating Co. (electricity generator marketer)
AEP Retail Energy (retail energy marketing in deregulated territories)
AEP Texas Central Company (formerly Central Power and Light electric utility)
AEP Texas North Company (formerly West Texas Utilities electric utility)
AEP Towers (wireless communications towers)
Appalachian Power Company (electric utility)
Columbus Southern Power Company (electric utility)
Indiana Michigan Power Company (electric utility)
Kentucky Power Company (electric utility)
Kingsport Power Company (electric utility)
Ohio Power Company (electric utility)
Public Service Company of Oklahoma (electric utility)
Southwestern Electric Power Company (electric utility)
Wheeling Power Company (electric utility)
Utility Distribution/Customer Service Divisions
AEP Ohio (handles distribution customer service and external affairs functions for Columbus Southern Power Company Ohio Power Company and Wheeling Power Company)
AEP Texas (handles distribution customer service and external affairs functions for AEP Texas Central Company and AEP Texas North Company)
Appalachian Power (handles distribution customer service and external affairs functions for Appalachian Power Company and Kingsport Power Company)
Indiana Michigan Power (handles distribution customer service and external affairs functions for Indiana Michigan Power Company)
Kentucky Power (handles distribution customer service and external affairs functions for Kentucky Power Company)
Public Service Company of Oklahoma (handles distribution customer service and external affairs functions for Public Service Company of Oklahoma)
Southwestern Electric Power Company (handles distribution customer service and external affairs functions for Southwestern Electric Power Company)

COMPETITORS

BP	Energy Future
CMS Energy	Entergy
Calpine	Exelon
CenterPoint Energy	FirstEnergy
Constellation Energy Group	NiSource
	PG&E Corporation
DTE	Sempra Energy
Delmarva Power	Southern Company
Dominion Energy	TVA
Duke Energy	Xcel Energy

HISTORICAL FINANCIALS

Company Type: Public

Income Statement

FYE: December 31

	REVENUE ($ mil.)	NET INCOME ($ mil.)	NET PROFIT MARGIN	EMPLOYEES
12/17	15,424	1,912	12.4%	17,666
12/16	16,380	610	3.7%	17,634
12/15	16,453	2,047	12.4%	17,405
12/14	17,020	1,634	9.6%	18,529
12/13	15,357	1,480	9.6%	18,521
Annual Growth	**0.1%**	**6.6%**	**—**	**(1.2%)**

2017 Year-End Financials

Debt ratio: 35.24%
Return on equity: 10.72%
Cash ($ mil.): 481
Current ratio: 0.51
Long-term debt ($ mil.): 19,419

No. of shares (mil.): 492
Dividends
  Yield: 0.0%
  Payout: 61.6%
Market value ($ mil.): 36,197

	STOCK PRICE ($) FY Close	P/E High/Low	Earnings	Dividends	Book Value
12/17	73.57	20 16	3.88	2.39	37.19
12/16	62.96	57 46	1.24	2.27	35.38
12/15	58.27	15 13	4.17	2.15	36.44
12/14	60.72	19 14	3.34	2.03	34.37
12/13	46.74	17 14	3.04	1.95	32.98
Annual Growth	**12.0%**	**— —**	**6.3%**	**5.2%**	**3.1%**

American Equity Investment Life Holding Co

American Equity Investment Life Holding (American Equity Life) helps middle-income investors plan for a cushier retirement. The company issues and administers fixed-rate and indexed annuities through subsidiaries American Equity Investment Life Insurance Eagle Life Insurance Company and American Equity Investment Life Insurance Company of New York. Licensed in 50 states and the District of Columbia the company sells its products through various channels including about 23000 independent agents and 32 national marketing associations. American Equity Life targets individuals between the ages of 45 and 75. The company also offers a variety of whole term and universal life insurance products.

Geographic Reach

Though American Equity Life is licensed in all fifty US states five states bring in a large portion of its business. Florida Texas California Pennsylvania and North Carolina together account for nearly 35% of American Equity Life's direct premiums.

Sales and Marketing

American Equity Life sells its products through 32 national marketing associations covering more than 23000 independent agents.

Financial Performance

American Equity Life's revenue declined significantly in 2014 and 2015 but has rebounded (and then some) in the past couple of years. Profits have been up and down for the past five years which reflects the pressures of low interest rates as well as the company's efforts to always operate with efficiency.

In fiscal 2017 revenue increased 75% to $3.9 billion primarily due to changes in fair values of derivatives. A decline in total other than temporary impairment investment losses helped boost revenue too.

Net income more than doubled to $174.6 million in 2017 thanks largely to the higher revenue and despite a steep rise in benefits expenses.

The company had $1.4 billion in cash and cash equivalents at the end of the year — $642.8 million more than it had at the end of 2016.

Strategy

As the company's target demographic — US individuals between the ages of 45 and 75 — continues to expand American Equity Life hopes to take advantage of the resulting demand for fixed index annuity products. It has several strategies in place to encourage growth including expanding and enhancing its distribution network. The firm distributes through several channels including independent agents broker/dealers investment advisors and banks; it intends boost its offerings to these channel partners to ultimately grow its business.

American Equity Life is also working to increase sales by introducing innovative and competitive new products. With its focus on fixed index and fixed rate annuities the company has launched a number of first-of-its-kind policy riders. It uses its expertise as well as technological advances to both improve its investment management activities and operate more efficiently. Exceptional customer experience is another area of focus.

In 2016 the US Department of Labor announced new regulations that tighten standards for the sale of fixed index annuities — core products for the company of course. The conflict of interest fiduciary ruling is intended to minimize advisers selling high-fee products that may not be in customers' best interests; it also favors the sales of fixed-index annuities by broker-dealers and banks over independent agents. American Equity Life's Eagle Life unit operates with a network of broker-dealers banks and investment advisors which benefits the company as it navigates the rule.

EXECUTIVES

Chairman President And Ceo, John M. Matovina, age 63, $727,500 total compensation

President American Equity Life Insurance Co., Ronald J. (Ron) Grensteiner, age 55, $510,000 total compensation

Evp And Chief Investment Officer, Jeffrey D. (Jeff) Lorenzen, age 52, $445,000 total compensation

Cfo And Treasurer, Ted M. Johnson, age 48, $500,000 total compensation

Evp And Coo, Bruce D. Cheek

Evp General Counsel And Corporate Secretary, Renee D. Montz, age 46, $356,250 total compensation

Vice President Information Technology, Ted Hughes

Assistant Vice President Andndash; Technical Services, Kevin Seuferer

Assistant Vice President Commercial Mortgage Administration, Loryssa L Rippey

Assistant Vice President Qa, Dennis Young

Senior Vice President And Chief Human Resources Officer, Jennifer Bryant
Chairman President And Ceo, John M. Matovina, age 63
Evp General Counsel And Corporate Secretary, Renee D. Montz, age 46
Auditors: KPMG LLP

LOCATIONS

HQ: American Equity Investment Life Holding Co
6000 Westown Parkway, West Des Moines, IA 50266
Phone: 515 221-0002
Web: www.american-equity.com

PRODUCTS/OPERATIONS

2017 Sales

	$ mil.	% of total
Net investment income	1,992	51
Change in fair value of derivatives	1,677	43
Annuity product charges	200	5
Premiums	34	1
Net realized gains on investments	10	-
Adjustments	(4.6)	-
Total	**3,891**	**100**

COMPETITORS

Allianz Life	Northwestern Mutual
Aviva	Presidential Life
FBL Financial	Prudential
Great American Life	Sammons Financial
Integrity Life	Security Benefit Group
Midland National Life	The Hartford
National Western	

HISTORICAL FINANCIALS

Company Type: Public

Income Statement

FYE: December 31

	ASSETS ($ mil.)	NET INCOME ($ mil.)	INCOME AS % OF ASSETS	EMPLOYEES
12/17	62,030	174	0.3%	515
12/16	56,053	83	0.1%	530
12/15	49,041	219	0.4%	490
12/14	43,989	126	0.3%	418
12/13	39,621	253	0.6%	416
Annual Growth	**11.9%**	**(8.9%)**	**—**	**5.5%**

2017 Year-End Financials

Debt ratio: 1.19%
Return on equity: 6.79%
Cash ($ mil.): 1,434
Current ratio: —
Long-term debt ($ mil.): —

No. of shares (mil.): 89
Dividends
Yield: 0.0%
Payout: 13.4%
Market value ($ mil.): 2,745

	STOCK PRICE ($) FY Close	P/E High/Low		PER SHARE ($) Earnings	Dividends	Book Value
12/17	30.73	16	11	1.93	0.26	31.91
12/16	22.54	25	13	0.97	0.24	26.04
12/15	24.03	11	8	2.72	0.22	23.90
12/14	29.19	17	12	1.58	0.20	28.13
12/13	26.38	7	3	3.38	0.18	19.63
Annual Growth	**3.9%**	**—**		**(13.1%)**	**9.6%**	**12.9%**

American Express Co.

American Express makes money even if you do leave home without it. Best known for its charge cards and revolving credit cards the company is also one of the world's largest providers of travel services. And yes the company still issues traveler's checks. Its travel agency operations have thousands of locations worldwide and its Travelers Cheque Group is the world's largest issuer of traveler's checks. Still the company's charge and credit cards are its bread and butter; American Express boasts $160 billion in assets and $1 trillion in annual billed business and has about 110 million cards in circulation in 140-plus countries. It?s long-time CEO Kenneth Chenault announced his retirement in late-2017.

HISTORY

In 1850 Henry Wells and his two main competitors combined their delivery services to form American Express. When directors refused to expand to California in 1852 Wells and executive William Fargo formed Wells Fargo while remaining at American Express.

American Express merged with Merchants Union Express in 1868 and developed a money order to compete with the government's postal money order. Fargo's difficulty in cashing letters of credit in Europe led to the offering of Travelers Cheques in 1891.

In WWI the US government nationalized and consolidated all express delivery services compensating the owners. After the war American Express incorporated as an overseas freight and financial services and exchange provider (the freight operation was sold in 1970). In 1958 the company introduced the American Express charge card. It bought Fireman's Fund American Insurance (sold gradually between 1985 and 1989) and Equitable Securities in 1968.

James Robinson CEO from 1977 to 1993 hoped to turn American Express into a financial services supermarket. The company bought brokerage Shearson Loeb Rhoades in 1981 and investment banker Lehman Brothers in 1984 among others. In 1987 it introduced Optima a revolving credit card to compete with MasterCard and Visa. It had no experience in underwriting credit cards though and was badly burned by losses.

Most of the financial units were combined as Shearson Lehman Brothers. But the financial services supermarket never came to fruition and losses in this area brought a steep drop in earnings in the early 1990s. Harvey Golub was brought in as CEO in 1993 to restore stability.

The company sold its brokerage operations as Shearson (to Travelers now Citigroup) and spun off investment banking as Lehman Brothers in 1994. In late 1996 it teamed with Advanta Corp. to allow Advanta Visa and MasterCard holders to earn points in the American Express Membership Rewards program. The move sparked a lawsuit from Visa and MasterCard which prohibit their member banks from doing business with American Express. That set off a spate of lawsuits culminating in the US Justice Department filing an antitrust suit against Visa and MasterCard. A federal judge sided with the Justice Department in 2001 but Visa and MasterCard appealed.

In 1997 Kenneth Chenault became president and COO putting him in line to succeed Golub.

Online banking service Membership B@nking was launched in 1999. That year American Express invested in Ticketmaster (the ticketing giant that merged with Live Nation Entertainment in 2010). In 2000 the company established a headquarters in Beijing to develop business in China. Also that year American Express bought more than 4500 ATMs from Electronic Data Systems (now HP Enterprise Services) making it a leading US operator of ATMs.

In 2001 Chenault replaced Golub as chairman and CEO. American Express was hit hard that year by bad investments in below-investment grade bonds by its money-management unit which shaved about $1 billion from earnings. Adding to its woes the company's employees at its New York City headquarters across the street from the World Trade Center were displaced by the 2001 terrorist attacks; its headquarters reopened in May 2002.

To grow its corporate travel management business Amex acquired Rosenbluth International a leading global travel management company with corporate travel operations in 15 countries in 2003. When Rosenbluth became fully integrated into the organization in mid-2004 American Express announced a relaunch of its corporate travel organization renamed American Express Business Travel.

American Express underwent a mild shakeup in late 2004 when it cut 2.5% of its workforce in a restructuring that included the company's business travel operations. The restructuring also included the sale of the company's banking operations in Bangladesh Egypt Luxembourg and Pakistan and the relocation of some finance operations. On a brighter note the company that year announced a milestone agreement with Industrial and Commercial Bank of China (ICBC) one of the biggest banks in China to issue the first American Express-branded credit cards in that country.

To focus on its travel and credit card operations the company in 2005 spun off Ameriprise Financial (formerly American Express Financial Advisors) a provider of insurance mutual funds investment advice and brokerage and asset management services. Toward that same end American Express sold its Tax and Business Services division to H&R Block and its UK-based American Express Financial Services Europe to TD Waterhouse (now part of TD AMERITRADE). Also in 2005 the company sold its equipment leasing business to Key Equipment Finance.

In 2007 the company's business travel division bought the rest of Farrington American Express Travel Services Limited it didn't already own. The travel management company had been a joint venture with Farrington Travel. The move was part of American Express's global expansion push especially in the Asia-Pacific region.

The company discontinued its Travelers Cheque card that year after determining that customers preferred paper travelers checks over a stored-value card. However sales of the travelers checks continued to decline in 2007 affected by the rising use of ATMs among other factors.

Also in 2007 American Express reached a $2.5 billion settlement with Visa and other defendants including JPMorgan Chase Capital One U.S. Bancorp and Wells Fargo dropping them from the lawsuit that alleged the companies conspired to block American Express from the bank-issued card business in the US. The following year it reached a $1.8 billion settlement with Mastercard the final remaining defendant in the suit.

American Express sold the international operations of American Express Bank to Stanchart in 2008.

American Express became a banking holding company in 2009. As a result it received some $3.4 billion from the Troubled Asset Relief Fund (TARP) early that year; it repaid the debt within months.

EXECUTIVES

Evp And Cio, Marc D. Gordon, age 57
Evp And Cfo, Jeffrey C. (Jeff) Campbell, age 57, $1,000,000 total compensation
Chairman And Ceo, Stephen J. (Steve) Squeri, age 59, $1,350,000 total compensation

Evp And General Counsel, Laureen E. Seeger, age 56, $800,000 total compensation

Group President Global Consumer Services, Douglas E. Buckminster, age 58, $700,000 total compensation

President Global Risk Banking & Compliance And Chief Risk Officer, Denise Pickett

Group President Global Merchant & Network Services, André Williams, age 52

President Global Services Group, Paul D. Fabara, age 52

Chief Corporate Affairs Officer, Michael J. OÂ'Neill, age 64

Chief Strategy Officer, Mohammed Badi

President Global Commercial Services, Anna Marrs

Chief Marketing Officer, Elizabeth Rutledge

Exec V Pres Corp Affairs And Co, Michael J O'neill

Vice President, Anderson Lee

Vp Brand Management, Susan Stashower

Vice President Architecture And Strategy, Howard Johnson

Vice President, Leslie Morris

Senior Vice President Human Resources Relationship Leader And Head Of Talent, Gaby Giglio

Vice President And General Manager Client Solutions, Howard Fulton

Svp Risk Management, Shen Chang

Vice President Data Center 2015 Program, Jason Hall

Senior Vice President Investment Operations, Peter Anderson

Senior Vice President Large Market Global Corporate Payments, Susan Chapman

Svp Global Security Group Global Corporate Services, Mic Chandrani

Vice President Client Management, Larry Restiano

Vice President, David Rabkin

Executive Vice President Human Resources, Manu Narang

Vice President, Ravi Varma

Vice President Finance Manda Controller, Dylan Haverty-Stacke

Vice President Authentication Account Takeover And Enterprise Fraud Capabilities, Chad Gonzales

Vice President And Senior Counsel, Emily Goodman Binick

Vice President Web Engineering Platform Security And Advanced Frameworks, Deepak Arora

Vice President Global Loyalty Solutions, Sarah Sugarman

Evp Enterprise Risk Management, Alex Weldon

Vice President Data Warehouse And Information Management, Grady Wright

Vice President Engineering, Phil Lundrigan

Vice President Operations, John Koslow

Vice President And Chief Advertising Counsel, Ellie Boragine

Vice President, Brady Fife

Vice President And Controller, Lawrence Belmonte

Senior Vice President Of Global Human Resources, Gabriella Giglio

Vice President Enterprise Personalization And Mobile, Wissam Magazachi

Senior Vice President Global Head Of Tax Chief Tax Officer, Joe Gagliano

Vice President Human Resources World Service, Madelyn Marino

Vice President Business Development, Franki Schmidt

Vice President Global Credit And Fraud Risk Management Capabilities, Lynn Almoro

Senior Vice President, Joseph Quagliata

Vice President Global Risk Oversight, Wenbiao Zhao

Vice President State Government Affairs, Steve Lemson

Vice President Strategic Communications, Frank Vaccaro

Vice President Of Finance, Julie Bush

Vice President Global Charge Card Pro, Maryellen Johnsen

Senior Vice President, Sue Rudy

Svp And Head Decision Science, Chao Yuan

Regional Vice President Open Top Client Group, Marty Shugarts

Senior Vice President And General Manager Head Of Service Delivery Emea American Express Business T, Suzan Kereere

Vice President Digital Product Engineering And Data Analytics, Vivek Tripathi

Vice President Technologies Finance, Phil Konort

Vice President Technical Architecture, Jamie Kenas

Vice President, Tom Taris

Vice President Business Development, Lisa L Rankin

Vp Finance, Phyllis Mccormick

Vice President, John Standring

Svp Enterprise Digital Group, Luke Gebb

Senior Vice President Global Brand Integration And Insights, Mary Reilly

Vice President Recruiting Operations, Erin Montgomery

Vice President Digital Partnerships And Development, Andrea Saporito

Assoicate Vice President, Carol Varner

Vice President Of Consumer Lending Products, Jenny Shum

Vice President, Cheryl Daniels

Vice President Service Delivery, Jacinthe Ladouceur

Vice President, Linda Presti

Vice President Uk Small Merchants, John Lemonius

Vice President, Mike Newton

Vice President Consumer Card Customer Strategy, Kelly Stevens

Vice President Executive Compensation, Anil Agarwal

Vice President Mandamp;a Controllership, Cory Vieira

Vice President Open Digital Strategy And Services Development, Scott Belous

Senior Vice President, Pam Codispoti

Vice President And Senior Counsel, Karen Rubin

Vice President Retail Travel Network, Ellen Bettridge

Executive Vice President And General Manager Partnerships And Product Development, Eva Reda

Vice President And Controller Basel, Amit Arora

Senior Vice President And Country Manager France, Nicolas Sireyjol

Vice President International Lending Product Development, Jennifer Hawkins

Vice President Global Card Issuance And World Service Tech Investment Strategy, Deborah Craft

National Account Manager, Emily Gentile

Vice President Advisory Services, Frank Schnur

Vice President Global Business Services Quality And Process Excellence, Alan Daniels

Senior Vice President, Michael Robertson

Senior Vice President Global Product Development A, Wesley Wright

Vice President, Joanna Lambert

Vice President Marketing Technology, Thomas Verutes

Vice President Technologies, Muhammad Khan

Vice President And Regional General Manager Merchant Services Americas, Christopher Lolli

Vice President Marketing, Tracy Hendricks

Vice President Deal Management And New B, Alexandra Martinez

Vice President International Head Of Luxury Products Lifestyle Marketing And Publishing, Lisa Gregg

National Account Manager, Liza Scullin

Vice President Customer Marketing, Alice Colarusso

Senior Vice President, Brett Loper

Vice President Audiences Management And Measurement, Melissa Schwartz Pollock

Vice President Corporate Communications, Rosa Alfonso

Vice President, Pooya Farahvash

Vice President Of Commercial Underwriting, Mira Srinivasan

Vice President, Judy O'connell

Vice President Corporate Charge Cards, Stacey Wilson

Vice President Operational Risk Governance Group Leader, ARTIE AMBROSIO

Vice President Strategic Sourcing And Business Enablement, Donna Donato

Vice President Of Content Collaboration And Enterprise Messaging, Ilene Eng

Senior Vice President Corporate Social Responsibility And President American Express Foundation, Timothy Mcclimon

Vice President Implementation And Technology Solutions, Jennifer Waldron

Vice President Head Of Consumer Product Europe, Rafael Mason

Vp Finance, Caryn Mignemi

Vp Information Technology Operations And Devops, Kai Wang

Vice President Risk And Information Management, Steven Kopleff

Vice President Technologies, Upendra Mardikar

Vice President Operations Enterprise Growth Servicing, Vijay Raghunathan

Vice President Global Data Strategy And Insights Japa, Madelaine Jureta

Vice President Global Corporate Payments, Gia Griffith

Chairman And Ceo, Stephen J. (Steve) Squeri, age 59

Treasurer, Johanne Ghali

Board Member, Theodore J Leonsis

Secretary And Chief Governance Officer, Carol Schwartz

Treasurer, Linda Albornoz

Auditors: PricewaterhouseCoopers LLP

LOCATIONS

HQ: American Express Co.
200 Vesey Street, New York, NY 10285
Phone: 212 640-2000   **Fax:** 212 640-0404
Web: www.americanexpress.com

2016 Sales

	% of total
United States	74
Europe the Middle East and Africa (EMEA)	10
Japan Asia/Pacific and Australia (JAPA)	9
Latin America Canada and the Caribbean (LACC)	7
Total	**100**

PRODUCTS/OPERATIONS

2016 Sales

	$ mil.	% of total
Non-interest		
Discount revenue	18,680	56
Net card fees	2,886	9
Other commissions & fees	2,753	8
Other	2,029	6
Interest		
Loans including fees	7,205	21
Interest & dividends on investment securities	131	-
Deposits with banks & other	139	-
Total	**33,823**	**100**

2016 Sales by Segment

	% of total
U.S. Consumer Services (USCS)	39
Global Commercial Services (GCS)	30
International Consumer and Network Services (ICNS)	17
Global Merchant Services (GMS)	14
Total	**100**

COMPETITORS

BCD Travel	JPMorgan Chase
Bank of America	JTB Corp.
Barclays	MasterCard
Capital One	Ovation Travel Group
Citibank	PayPal
Discover	Visa Inc
Expedia	Western Union
HSBC	

HISTORICAL FINANCIALS

Company Type: Public

Income Statement

FYE: December 31

	ASSETS ($ mil.)	NET INCOME ($ mil.)	INCOME AS % OF ASSETS	EMPLOYEES
12/17	181,159	2,736	1.5%	55,000
12/16	158,893	5,408	3.4%	56,400
12/15	161,184	5,163	3.2%	54,800
12/14	159,103	5,885	3.7%	54,000
12/13	153,375	5,359	3.5%	62,800
Annual Growth	4.3%	(15.5%)	—	(3.3%)

2017 Year-End Financials

Debt ratio: 30.80%	No. of shares (mil.): 859
Return on equity: 14.13%	Dividends
Cash ($ mil.): 32,927	Yield: 0.0%
Current ratio: —	Payout: 44.1%
Long-term debt ($ mil.): —	Market value ($ mil.): 85,307

	STOCK PRICE ($) FY Close	P/E High/Low		PER SHARE ($) Earnings	Dividends	Book Value
12/17	99.31	33	25	2.97	1.31	21.22
12/16	74.08	13	9	5.65	1.19	22.68
12/15	69.55	18	13	5.05	1.10	21.33
12/14	93.04	17	14	5.56	0.98	20.21
12/13	90.73	18	12	4.88	0.86	18.32
Annual Growth	2.3%	—	—	(11.7%)	11.1%	3.7%

American Financial Group Inc

American Financial Group (AFG) insures American businessmen in pursuit of the Great American Dream. Through the Great American Insurance Group of companies and its flagship Great American Insurance Company AFG offers commercial property/casualty insurance with a focus on specialties such as workers' compensation professional liability ocean and inland marine and multiperil crop insurance. The company also provides surety coverage for contractors and risk management services. For individuals and employers AFG provides a wide range of annuity policies through its Great American Financial Resources Inc. (GAFRI) subsidiary.

Operations

AFG operates through two primary segments — Property and Casualty Insurance and Annuity— and two smaller segments — Run-Off Long-Term Care and Life and Other (which includes holding company activities).

The Property and Casualty Insurance segment is the largest accounting for more than 70% of AFG's annual revenues. Its operations are divided into more than 30 businesses including property and transportation (marine crops and commercial auto) specialty casualty (professional excess and surplus workers' compensation and general liabilities) and specialty financial (fidelity and surety lend/lease risk management).

In the Annuities segment (which accounts for about a quarter of total revenue) GAFRI offers fixed rate and indexed annuity products through underwriting companies Great American Life Insurance and Annuity Investors Life Insurance.

Geographic Reach

AFG's largest markets include California Illinois Texas New York and Florida. The company has more than 120 locations throughout North America and Europe.

Sales and Marketing

AFG primarily markets its insurance policies through a nationwide network of independent agents and brokers although a small number are written through employee agents. Annuity products are marketed through a retail network of approximately 65 national marketing organizations managing general agents financial advisors and independent brokers.

The company's customers include Wells Fargo BB&T PNC Financial Services LPL Financial and Regions Financial.

Financial Performance

AFG's revenue which has grown over the past five years increased 6% to $6.9 billion in 2017.Net earned property/causualty premiums rose 6% (largely due to an increase in property and transportation business) and net investment income rose 8% but those gains were partially offset by a very slight decline in net earned life accident and health premiums.

Net income which had been on the decline jumped 84% to a record $649 million in 2016. Leading factors in that jump were decreases in life accident and health benefits paid out and in provisions for income taxes. In 2017 net income normalized somewhat falling to $475 million as property/casualty annuity and other expenses increased. Additionally the company had higher earnings in annuities life and the run-off long-term care segments.

Cash flow from operations increased 57% to $1.8 billion that year due to positive changes in insurance claims and reserves and in managed investment entities' assets and liabilities.

Strategy

Like all property/casualty insurers AFG seeks to balance out calm and catastrophe by operating on long-term income cycles where years of profits balance out years of increased claims. The company sees opportunity in such areas as workers' compensation and commercial auto coverage and it has worked to build its operations both organically and through acquisitions.

In terms of annuities AFG is focused on fixed and indexed products and has steered away from offering variable annuities and other types of offerings where it doesn't have a competitive advantage. The company has invested in these operations and introduced product enhancements recently to take advantage of volatility in the equity markets.

To focus on core operations the company has sold off supplemental benefits and other units. In 2016 it sold its struggling Neon (formerly Marketform) medical malpractice operations which provided coverage in 30 countries (primarily in Australia Italy and the UK).

Mergers and Acquisitions

AFG expands its property/casualty operations through acquisitions in existing and new markets such as medical malpractice and workers' compensation. In 2018 it agreed to buy ABA Insurance Services (ABAIS) from American Bankers Mutual Insurance for $28 million. ABAIS provides directors and officers liability and other insurance products for banks small businesses and not-for-profit organizations. That deal will boost AFG's specialty casualty operations.

In mid-2016 the company acquired the rest of transportation-focused National Interstate Corporation it didn't already own for $320 million.

HISTORY

When his father became ill in the mid-1930s Carl Lindner Jr. dropped out of high school to take over his family's dairy business. He built it into a large ice-cream store chain called United Dairy Farmers. Lindner branched out in 1955 with Henthy Realty and in 1959 he bought three savings and loans. The next year Lindner changed the company's name to American Financial Corp. (AFC). He took it public in 1961 using the proceeds to buy United Liberty Life Insurance (1963) and Provident Bank (1966).

Lindner also formed the American Financial Leasing & Services Company in 1968 to lease airplanes computers and other equipment. In 1969 the company acquired Phoenix developer Rubenstein Construction and renamed it American Continental. AFC bought several life casualty and mortgage insurance firms in the 1970s including National General parent of Great American Insurance Group later the core of AFC's insurance segment. The company also moved into publishing by buying 95% of the Cincinnati Enquirer paperback publisher Bantam Books and hardback publisher Grosset & Dunlap.

But the publishing interests soon went back on the block as Lindner concentrated on insurance which was then suffering from an industry-wide slowdown. In addition to selling the Enquirer AFC spun off American Continental in 1976. American Continental's president was Charles Keating who had joined AFC in 1972 and whose brother published the Enquirer. Keating (who was later jailed released then eventually pleaded guilty in connection with the failure of Lincoln Savings) underwent an SEC investigation during part of his time at AFC for alleged improprieties at Provident Bank. The bank was spun off in 1980.

Lindner took AFC private in 1981. That year following a strategy of bottom-feeding the firm began building its interest in the non-railroad assets of Penn Central the former railroad that had emerged from bankruptcy as an industrial manufacturer. Later that decade AFC increased its ownership in United Brands (later renamed Chiquita Brands International) from 29% to 45%. Lindner installed himself as CEO and reversed that company's losses. In 1987 AFC acquired a TV company Taft Communications (renamed Great American Communications) entailing a heavy debt load. To reduce its debt AFC trimmed its holdings including Circle K Hunter S&L and an interest in Scripps Howard Broadcasting.

Great American Communications went bankrupt in 1992 and emerged the next year as Citicasters Inc. (sold 1996). In 1995 Lindner created American Financial Group to effect the merger of AFC and Premier Underwriters of which he owned 42%. The result was American Financial Group (AFG).

AFG's results in the 1990s were uneven and it typically did not make an underwriting profit. In 2003 the insurer kept operating expenses down (partly by merging two of its holding company subsidiaries into AFG) and swung to a profit even though premium revenue was down.

The company shed some commercial lines to concentrate on its property/casualty and life and annuities businesses. To refine its mix AFG transferred Atlanta Casualty Company Infinity Insurance Company Leader Insurance Company and Windsor Insurance Company into 40%-owned Infinity Property and Casualty which went public in

2003. In 2004 the business exchanged its stake in Provident Financial Group for a holding in National City Corporation.

Founder and chairman Carl Lindner retired as CEO in 2005 and died in 2011. No one was named to replace him as chairman but two of his sons Carl Lindner III and Craig Lindner carried on as

EXECUTIVES

Co-president Co-ceo And Director, S. Craig Lindner, age 63, $1,150,000 total compensation
Co-president Co-ceo And Director, Carl H. Lindner, age 65, $1,150,000 total compensation
Evp And Cfo, Joseph E. (Jeff) Consolino, age 51, $868,269 total compensation
Svp And Chief Administrative Officer, Michelle A. (Shelly) Gillis, age 49, $332,315 total compensation
Svp And General Counsel, Vito C. Peraino, age 62, $565,962 total compensation
Divisional Senior Vice President Product Management Property And Inland Marine Division Gaic, Julie Kadnar
Vice President Strategy Planning And Architecture, Carl Jaekel
Vice President Of Benefits, Spencer Stooksbury
Associate Vice President Infrastructure And Operations, James Niehaus
Vp And Assistant General Counsel, Mark Weiss
Divisional Vice President Development And Reinsurance Crop Insurance Division Gaic, Dean Clarke
Vice President Human Resources, Scott Beeken
Vice President, Howard Baird
Senior Vice President Excess Liability Division Atlanta Gaic, Todd Gambrell
Executive Vice President, Alicia Yoo
Vice President Underwriting Executive Liability Division, Bob Rubin
Vice President Surety Mid Continent Group Gaic, Todd Bazata
Divisional Senior Vice President Bonds North California Office Gaic, Francis Plante
Divisional Vice President Claims Specialty Human Services Division Gaic, Doug Svenkerud
Divisional Vice President Loss Prevention Ocean Marine Division Gaic, Edward Wilmot
Divisional Senior Vice President Gaic, Veronika Willard
Divisional Senior Vice President Specialty Excess And Surplus Division Great American Insurance Group, Brian Sloan
Divisional Vice President Ocean Marine Division West Regional Office Gaic, Thomas Nager
Divisional Assistant Vice President, Helen Lally
Divisional Vice President Chicago Excess Liability Division Gaic, Tom Hart
Divisional Vice President Dallas Excess Liability Division Gaic, Kathleen Zale
Vp Excess Liability Division Great American Insurance Group, Christopher Bright
Vice President Underwriting Environmental Division Gaic, Scott Britt
Divisional Vice President Marketing Trucking Division Gaic, Tim Clinton
Divisional Senior Vice President Ocean Marine East Regional Office Gaic, Forrest Downing
Divisional Svp Occupational Accident Trucking Division Great American Insurance Group, Mary Ford
Vice President Systems American Empire Group Gaic, Leo Haas
Divisional Vice President San Francisco Excess Liability Division Great American Insurance Group, Marcus Lampley
Divisional Vp Claims And Cincinnati Operations Financial Insitution Services Great American Insurance Group, Pat Sinnard
Avp And Actuary Gafri, Richard Sutton

Divisional Vice President Fidelity And Crime Division New York Great American Insurance Group, George Pierce Jr
Divisional Senior Vice President Underwriting And Product Development Trucking, Mark Calkin
Board Member, Gregory Joseph
Board Member, Kenneth Ambrecht
Auditors: Ernst & Young LLP

LOCATIONS

HQ: American Financial Group Inc
301 East Fourth Street, Cincinnati, OH 45202
Phone: 513 579-2121
Web: www.afginc.com

PRODUCTS/OPERATIONS

2017 Sales

	$ mil.	% of total
Net earned insurance premiums	4,601	67
Net investment income	1,831	27
Income of managed investment entities	222	3
Realized gains on securities	5	-
Other	206	3
Total	**6,865**	**100**

COMPETITORS

AIG	MetLife
Allianz	Pacific Life
Arch Capital	RLI
CNA Financial	The Hartford
Chubb Limited	Tokio Marine
Cincinnati Financial	Travelers Companies
HCC Insurance	W. R. Berkley
Jackson National Life	XL Group plc
Liberty Mutual	Zurich Insurance Group
Markel	

HISTORICAL FINANCIALS

Company Type: Public

Income Statement   FYE: December 31

	ASSETS ($ mil.)	NET INCOME ($ mil.)	INCOME AS % OF ASSETS	EMPLOYEES
12/17	60,658	475	0.8%	600
12/16	55,072	649	1.2%	400
12/15	49,859	352	0.7%	400
12/14	47,535	452	1.0%	7,200
12/13	42,087	471	1.1%	6,300
Annual Growth	9.6%	0.2%	—	(44.4%)

2017 Year-End Financials

Debt ratio: 2.14%
Return on equity: 9.27%
Cash ($ mil.): 2,338
Current ratio: —
Long-term debt ($ mil.): —

No. of shares (mil.): 88
Dividends
Yield: 0.0%
Payout: 90.6%
Market value ($ mil.): 9,581

	STOCK PRICE ($) FY Close	P/E High/Low	PER SHARE ($) Earnings	Dividends	Book Value
12/17	108.54	20 16	5.28	4.79	60.38
12/16	88.12	12 9	7.33	2.15	56.55
12/15	72.08	19 14	3.94	2.03	52.50
12/14	60.72	12 10	4.97	1.91	55.63
12/13	57.72	11 7	5.16	1.81	51.38
Annual Growth	17.1%	— —	0.6%	27.6%	4.1%

AMERICAN HONDA FINANCE CORPORATION

If you're fonda the idea of driving a Honda you might want to call on American Honda Finance. Operating as Honda Financial Services the company provides retail financing in the US for Honda and Acura automobiles motorcycles all-terrain vehicles power equipment and outboard motors. Its American Honda Service division administers service contracts while Honda Lease Trust offers leases on new and used vehicles. Honda Financial Services also offers dealer financing and related dealer services. Ancillary services include servicing loans and securitizing and selling loans into the secondary market. A subsidiary of American Honda Motor the company began as a wholesale motorcycle finance provider in 1980.

Operations

American Honda Finance (AHF) acquires retail installment contracts and closed-end vehicle lease contracts from purchasers and lessees and authorized Honda and Acura dealers. It also provides these authorized dealers with wholesale flooring and commercial loans.

AHF also acquires used auto loans of non-Honda and non-Acura vehicles and provides these third-party dealers iwth wholesale loans. Additionally the company offers vehicle service contracts services underwriting and pricing of consumer financing services and incentive financing programs for Honda and Acura products.

Geographic Reach

The company is headquartered in Torrance California and operates nine regional offices that support all authorized Honda and Acura dealers across North America.

Financial Performance

While full financials of the subsidiary were not available American Honda Finance's (AHF) revenue has been on the uptrend as auto sales continue to strengthen along with the US economy. Revenue in fiscal 2014 (ended March 31 2014) grew by 22% to A?5.97 trillion ($58.1 billion) thanks to larger revenues from its parent company's auto business and positive foreign currency exchange rates.

Despite higher selling general and administrative expenses and R&D expenses AHF's operating income also increased 39% to A?290.9 billion ($2.83 billion) in 2014 after the company continued its cost reduction measures.

Strategy

American Honda Finance Corp. (AHFC) exists to provide stability to support sales of new and used Honda and Acura vehicles throughout North America Honda Motor's largest market. To that end AHFC seeks to preserve funding diversity balanced liquidity and maintain a prudent maturity profile. To spur growth of its US business in 2012 the company opened its ninth regional office a 25000-square-foot facility in Charlotte North Carolina to serve Honda buyers in the Carolinas Maryland Tennessee Virginia and West Virginia.

EXECUTIVES

Ceo, Hideo Tamaka
Sr V Pres, Stephan Smith
V Pres-Cfo, John Weisickle
Information Specialist, Hung Le
Recruiter, Breanna Robinson
Assistant Sales Manager, Kevin Dorman
Lead Customer Represen, Rodrigo Mascarenhas
Assistant Manager Administrati, Jennifer Shafer

Manager Mc, Jose Basterrechea
Information Manager, Vern Paylor
Information Technology Directo, Grace Jean
Auditors: KPMG LLP LOS ANGELES CALIFOR

LOCATIONS

HQ: AMERICAN HONDA FINANCE CORPORATION
20800 MADRONA AVE, TORRANCE, CA 905034915
Phone: 310 972-2239
Web: WWW.HONDAFINANCIALSERVICES.COM

Selected Offices
Alpharetta GA
Charlotte NC
Cypress CA
Elgin IL
Holyoke MA
Irving TX
San Ramon CA
Torrance CA
Wilmington DE

COMPETITORS

Ally Financial
Automotive Finance Corporation
Bank of America
Credit Acceptance
Ford Motor Credit
Mercedes-Benz Financial Services USA
Mitsubishi Motors Credit of America
Toyota Motor Credit

HISTORICAL FINANCIALS

Company Type: Private

Income Statement   FYE: March 31

	ASSETS ($ mil.)	NET INCOME ($ mil.)	INCOME AS % OF ASSETS	EMPLOYEES
03/17	69,854	753	1.1%	1,000
03/16	66,653	910	1.4%	—
03/08	50,526	(45)	—	—
03/07	41,431	394	1.0%	—
Annual Growth	5.4%	6.7%	—	—

2017 Year-End Financials

Debt ratio: ——
Return on equity: 36.40%
Cash ($ mil.): 760
Current ratio: —
Long-term debt ($ mil.): —
Dividends
  Yield: —
  Payout: —
Market value ($ mil.): —

American International Group Inc

EXECUTIVES

Pres, Salvatore De Fini
V Pres, David Walsh
Chief of Infrastructure Transf, Al Stuart
Accounting Staff, Ian Galloway
Assistant, Dawn McCauley
Director of Training, Archie Mattis
Auditors: PricewaterhouseCoopers LLP

LOCATIONS

HQ: American International Group Inc
175 Water Street, New York, NY 10038
Phone: 212 770-7000
Web: www.aig.com

HISTORICAL FINANCIALS

Company Type: Public

Income Statement   FYE: December 31

	ASSETS ($ mil.)	NET INCOME ($ mil.)	INCOME AS % OF ASSETS	EMPLOYEES
12/17	498,301	(6,084)	—	49,800
12/16	498,264	(849)	—	56,400
12/15	496,943	2,196	0.4%	66,400
12/14	515,581	7,529	1.5%	65,000
12/13	541,329	9,085	1.7%	64,000
Annual Growth	(2.0%)	—	—	(6.1%)

2017 Year-End Financials

Debt ratio: 6.35%
Return on equity: (-8.60%)
Cash ($ mil.): 2,362
Current ratio: —
Long-term debt ($ mil.): —
No. of shares (mil.): 899
Dividends
  Yield: 0.0%
  Payout: —
Market value ($ mil.): 53,565

	STOCK PRICE ($) FY Close	P/E High/Low		PER SHARE ($) Earnings	Dividends	Book Value
12/17	59.58	—	—	(6.54)	1.28	72.49
12/16	65.31	—	—	(0.78)	1.28	76.66
12/15	61.97	38	29	1.65	0.81	75.10
12/14	56.01	11	9	5.20	0.50	77.69
12/13	51.05	8	6	6.13	0.20	68.62
Annual Growth	3.9%			— 59.1%		1.4%

American National Bankshares, Inc. (Danville, VA)

American National Bankshares with total assets of around $1.5 billion is the holding company for American National Bank and Trust. Founded in 1909 the bank operates some 25 branches that serve southern and central Virginia and north central North Carolina. Operating through two segments — Community Banking and Trust and Investment Services — it offers checking and savings accounts CDs IRAs and insurance. Lending activities primarily consist of real estate loans: Commercial mortgages account for about 40% of its loan portfolio while residential mortgages bring in another 20%. American National Bankshares' trust and investment services division manages nearly $610 million in assets.

Operations

American National Bankshares operates through two segments: Community Banking which accounts for more than 80% of the company's total revenue and offers deposit accounts and loans to individuals and small and middle-market businesses; and Trust and Investment Services which provides estate planning trust account administration investment management and retail brokerage services.

The bank makes more than 80% of its revenue from interest income. About 68% of its total revenue came from loan interest during 2015 while another 13% came from interest income on investment securities. The rest of its revenue came from trust fees (6% of revenue) deposit account service charges (3%) mortgage banking income

(2%) brokerage fees (1%) and other miscellaneous income sources.

Geographic Reach

Danville Virginia-based American National Bankshares has 25 branches mostly in southern Virginia and in North Carolina (including in Alamance and Guilford Counties). It also has two loan production offices in Roanoke Virginia and Raleigh North Carolina.

Sales and Marketing

American National Bankshares has been cutting back on its advertising and marketing spend in recent years. It spent $356000 on advertising and marketing in 2015 up from $453000 and $607000 in 2014 and 2013 respectively.

Financial Performance

The bank group has struggled to consistently grow its revenues and profits over the past several years despite steadily increasing loan business mostly due to shrinking interest margins on loans stemming from the low-interest environment.

American National had a breakthrough year in 2015 however as its revenue jumped 17% to $68.46 million almost entirely thanks to its acquisition of MainStreet BankShares which boosted its loan and other interest-earning assets by double digits and increased its non-interest income by 19% with newly acquired deposit and other fee related income.

Double-digit revenue growth in 2015 drove the group's net income up 18% to $15.04 million. The bank's operating cash levels climbed 16% to $19.26 million for the year thanks to the boost in cash-denominated earnings.

Strategy

American National Bankshares grows its branch reach as well as its loan and deposit business by opening new branch locations or by buying other branches or banks.

The bank continues to have the largest deposit market share in the Dannville Virginia metro area boasting a 32.8% market share in the region as of mid-2015. It also had the second-largest market share in Pittsylvania County Virginia with a 21.1% share.

Mergers and Acquisitions

In January 2015 American National expanded into Roanoke Virginia after purchasing $164 million-asset MainStreet BankShares Inc. for a total purchase price of $24.2 million. The deal added $122 million in new loan assets $137 million in deposits and three Franklin Bank branches in Franklin County and the Smith Mountain Lake area.

Company Background

In 2011 American National acquired bank holding company MidCarolina Financial expanding its presence in North Carolina specifically in both Alamance and Guilford counties.

EXECUTIVES

Evp And Cfo, William W. Traynham, age 61, $211,232 total compensation
President And Ceo, Jeffrey V. Haley, age 57, $240,000 total compensation
Evp; Evp And Chief Administrative Officer American National Bank And Trust, Dabney T. P. (Dexter) Gilliam, age 62, $124,544 total compensation
Svp And Chief Credit Officer American National Bank And Trust, R. Helm Dobbins, age 66, $139,570 total compensation
Executive Vice President President - Alamance Region, Charles T. Canaday, age 57
Evp; Evp And Chief Banking Officer American National Bank And Trust, H. Gregg Strader
Executive Vice President Chief Banking Officer, Gregg Strader
Chairman, Charles H. (Charlie) Majors, age 72
Board Member, Ronda Penn
Auditors: Yount, Hyde & Barbour, P.C.

PRODUCTS/OPERATIONS

2015 Sales

	$ mil.	% of total
Interest and Dividend Income		
Interest and fees on loans	46	69
Taxable	4	6
Tax-exempt	3	5
Other	0	1
Non-interest income		
Trust fees	3	7
Service charges on deposit accounts	2	3
Other fees and commissions	2	3
Other	4	6
Total	**68**	**100**

Selected Subsidiaries

American National Bank and Trust Company
AMNB Statutory Trust I A Delaware Statutory Trust
MidCarolina Trust I A Delaware Statutory Trust
MidCarolina Trust II A Delaware Statutory Trust

Selected Services

Business Banking
  Cash Management
  Checking
  Loans
  Savings
Personal Banking
  Checking
  Loans
  Savings
Insurance
  Business
  Personal

COMPETITORS

BB&T	First Citizens
Bank of America	BancShares
First Century	NewBridge Bancorp
Bankshares	

HISTORICAL FINANCIALS

Company Type: Public

Income Statement — FYE: December 31

	ASSETS ($ mil.)	NET INCOME ($ mil.)	INCOME AS % OF ASSETS	EMPLOYEES
12/17	1,816	15	0.8%	328
12/16	1,678	16	1.0%	320
12/15	1,547	15	1.0%	303
12/14	1,346	12	0.9%	284
12/13	1,307	15	1.2%	290
Annual Growth	8.6%	(0.8%)	—	3.1%

2017 Year-End Financials

Debt ratio: 1.53%	No. of shares (mil.): 8
Return on equity: 7.44%	Dividends
Cash ($ mil.): 52	Yield: 0.0%
Current ratio: —	Payout: 55.1%
Long-term debt ($ mil.): —	Market value ($ mil.): 331

	STOCK PRICE ($) FY Close	P/E High/Low	PER SHARE ($) Earnings	Dividends	Book Value
12/17	38.30	24 20	1.76	0.97	24.13
12/16	34.80	19 12	1.89	0.96	23.37
12/15	25.61	15 12	1.73	0.93	22.95
12/14	24.81	16 13	1.62	0.92	22.07
12/13	26.25	14 10	2.00	0.92	21.23
Annual Growth	9.9%	— —	(3.1%)	1.3%	3.2%

American National Insurance Co. (Galveston, TX)

True to its name American National Insurance Company offers agricultural commercial and personal property/casualty insurance as well as life insurance annuities supplemental health credit and other types of insurance throughout the US Puerto Rico and other territories. Its subsidiaries include Garden State Life Insurance Standard Life and Accident Insurance and Farm Family Holdings. American National markets its products through independent and career agents broker-dealers employee benefit advisors financial representatives and managing general underwriters.

Operations

American National operates in five segments: Life (including whole term universal indexed and variable life insurance) Annuity (fixed indexed and variable annuity products) Health (Medicare Supplement stop-loss credit disability insurance) Property/Casualty (personal and commercial coverage) and Corporate and Other (income from investments not related to the insurance segments as well as non-insurance operations).

While the company considers its Life and Annuity segments its main areas of focus it earns more of its premiums from property/casualty insurance. In fact the Property/Casualty segment brings in some 40% of the company's total revenues. Altogether premiums account for more than 60% of revenues. Investment income accounts for another 30%.

American National has more than $100 billion in life insurance in-force.

Geographic Reach

American National is licensed to conduct business in all 50 states the District of Columbia and Puerto Rico. Business is conducted in New York by American National Life Insurance Company of New York.

The company serves about 6 million customers.

Sales and Marketing

American National markets life insurance and annuities through Independent Marketing Group (IMG) which targets middle-income and wealthy clients. IMG markets policies through financial institutions employee benefits organizations broker-dealers marketing organizations and independent agents and brokers. It also sells life insurance using direct mail internet and telemarketing campaigns. The company's Career Sales and Service Division primarily serves the middle-income market (life annuities and health coverage) though exclusive employee agents.

The group's Health segment serves middle-income seniors self-insured employers and individuals and performs marketing through independent agents and managing general underwriters.

Financial Performance

American National's revenues have hovered around $3 billion for the past five years. In 2017 revenue rose 6% to $3.4 billion. This increase was driven by gains in property/casualty and life premiums (but partially offset by declines in annuity and accident and health premiums). Net investment income also trended upward that year but other policy revenues (including mortality charges and earned policy service fees) fell 19%. Overall the company had a strong performance despite an increase in catastrophe losses — largely as a result of flooding damage to automobiles.

Net income— which had declined for three straight years — rose 173% to $493.7 million in 2017. That was primarily due to higher realized investment earnings and lower policyholder benefits. These gains led to an increase in operating cash flow which rose 23% to $495.9 million.

Strategy

In its quest to be a leading financial products and services company American National aims to maintain the conservative business practices it has upheld for more than a century including controlling risk factors in its growth and investment strategies. The company looks to maintain strong finances through profitable growth primarily by investing in its distribution channels expanding into new geographic markets attracting and training employees and enhancing marketing programs. It also introduces new products it deems promising: For example in 2018 American National began offering flood insurance in California.

As Baby Boomers reach retirement age the company expects that two of its core segments Life and Annuity will continue to see growth. Its size and financial strength provide it with the ability to introduce new products to this demographic to remain competitive.

In the health insurance sector American National is working to expand in the work site market; however it remains cautious as the future of the Affordable Care Act remains in question.

Another key strategy is improving its use of technology to improve its operating efficiencies and the services it offers its customers. The company is committed to providing exemplary customer service and to offering innovative diversified and competitively priced products to meet the needs of its policyholders and agents.

American National occasionally grows by acquiring like-minded businesses. It also divests or shutters businesses after reassessing their value.

Moody National Bank is a trustee agent of various American National shareholders; it has some 49% voting power of American National's common stock which could potentially limit the company's level of flexibility.

Company Background

American National was founded by Galveston businessman W. L. Moody in 1905. The Moody Foundation a charitable trust controlled by W L. Moody descendant Robert Moody and his family and the Moody National Bank together own about 70% of the company.

Based in hurricane-prone Galveston Texas American National knows first-hand the importance of property/casualty insurance and how to evaluate risk. The company withdrew from writing some policies along the Atlantic and Gulf coasts in 2005 and in 2008 it moved its claims processing facilities further inland to San Antonio.

American National launched the American National Life Insurance Company of New York in 2010.

EXECUTIVES

Evp Independent Marketing Group, David A. Behrens, age 55, $532,569 total compensation
Chairman President And Ceo, James E. Pozzi, age 67, $918,847 total compensation
President And Ceo Farm Family Companies, Timothy A. Walsh, age 56, $400,400 total compensation
Evp Career Sales And Service Division, Hoyt J. Strickland, age 61, $375,353 total compensation
Vice President Health Administration, Tracy Milina
Vice President Marketing Operations, Chad Ferrell
Vice President Broker Dealer Marketing, Steven Dobbe
National Sales Manager, Mike Sawdey

Assistant Vice President Life Insurance, Sharon
Garner
Vice President Special Markets, Mark Walker
National Sales Manager, Kendra Kelly
Vice President, Kara Phillips
Vice President, Sabrina Bermudez
**Assistant Vice President Advanced Sales And
Priority Markets,** Walter Rudecki
National Sales Manager, Michael Kresl
National Sales Manager, Cliff McConville
Assistant Vice President, Wayne Cucco
Assistant Vice President And Assistant Actuary,
Michael Shumate
National Sales Manager, J Taylor
Senior Vice President Securities Investments,
Gordon Dixon
Vice President Human Resources, Olivia Smith
Vice President Marketing, Debie Knowles
**Assistant Vice President Data Communications
Messaging (its),** Jimmy Watson
National Sales Manager, Jason Weaver
**Assistant Vice President And Director
Telecommunications,** James McEniry
Vice President Fixed Income, Anne Lemire
Vice President, Bob Schefft
**Assistant Vice President And Associate Medical
Director,** John White
**Assistant Vice President Director Life Marketing
Sales Director,** Clu Jon O'Neal
Svp Independent Marketing Group Operations,
Lee Ferrell
National Sales Manager, Thomas Granata
National Sales Manager, Ronnie Russell
National Sales Manager, Brooke ChFC
Senior Vice President Corporate Digital Officer,
Bernard Svp
Vice President Commercial Services, Iris Gillies
**Avp Financial Marketing Credit Insurance
Division,** Eddie Waters
National Sales Manager, James Tadeo
Chairman President And Ceo, James E. Pozzi, age
67
President And Ceo Farm Family Companies,
Timothy A. Walsh, age 56
Auditors: KPMG LLP

LOCATIONS

HQ: American National Insurance Co. (Galveston, TX)
One Moody Plaza, Galveston, TX 77550-7999
Phone: 409 763-4661   **Fax:** 409 766-6502
Web: www.anico.com

PRODUCTS/OPERATIONS

2017 Sales

	$ mil.	% of total
Premiums		
Property/Casualty	1,360	40
Life	328	10
Annuity	222	6
Accident & Health	156	5
Net investment income	966	28
Other policy revenue	248	7
Realized investment gains	104	3
Other	37	1
Adjustments	(13.3)	-
Total	**3,411**	**100**

Selected Subsidiaries

American National Life Insurance Company of Texas
(ANTEX)
American National Life Insurance Company of New York
American National Property and Casualty Company
(ANPAC)
ANICO Financial Services Inc.
Garden State Life Insurance Company
Pacific Property and Casualty Company
Standard Life and Accident Insurance Company
United Farm Family Insurance Company

COMPETITORS

Allstate	Nationwide
American Financial	New York Life
Group	Penn Mutual
CNO Financial	Prudential
Farmers Group	State Farm
HCI Group	Torchmark
Mutual of Omaha	USAA
National Western	

HISTORICAL FINANCIALS

Company Type: Public

Income Statement

	ASSETS ($ mil.)	NET INCOME ($ mil.)	INCOME AS % OF ASSETS	EMPLOYEES
				FYE: December 31
12/17	26,386	493	1.9%	4,621
12/16	24,533	181	0.7%	4,597
12/15	23,746	242	1.0%	4,736
12/14	23,552	247	1.0%	3,138
12/13	23,324	268	1.2%	3,078
Annual Growth	3.1%	16.5%	—	10.7%

2017 Year-End Financials

Debt ratio: 0.52%
Return on equity: 9.97%
Cash ($ mil.): 375
Current ratio: —
Long-term debt ($ mil.): —
No. of shares (mil.): 26
Dividends
Yield: 0.0%
Payout: 17.9%
Market value ($ mil.): 3,454

	STOCK PRICE ($) FY Close	P/E High/Low		PER SHARE ($) Earnings	Dividends	Book Value
12/17	128.25	7	6	18.31	3.28	194.82
12/16	124.61	19	14	6.71	3.26	172.85
12/15	102.27	13	10	9.02	3.14	165.55
12/14	114.26	13	11	9.18	3.08	164.94
12/13	114.54	12	7	9.97	3.08	155.81
Annual Growth	2.9%	—	—	16.4%	1.6%	5.7%

American Tower Corp (New)

Growth in wireless communications is taking
American Tower to new heights. The company
rents space on towers and rooftop antenna systems to wireless carriers and radio and TV broadcasters who use the infrastructure to enable their
services. It operates about 40000 wireless towers
in the US some 58000 in India and more than
50000 throughout the rest of the world. Its portfolio additionally includes approximately 950 Distributed Antenna System networks used mainly
for indoor communications (malls casinos and arenas). American Tower also offers tower-related
services such as site acquisition structural analysis
to determine support for additional equipment and
zoning and permitting management services.

Operations

American Tower's primary business is the leasing of antenna space on multi-tenant communications sites. It provides the service to wireless
providers radio and television broadcast companies
wireless data providers government agencies and
municipalities and tenants from several other industries.

The company operates five business segments
mostly based in regions where it leases its properties. The US Property segment is its largest and

accounts for nearly 55% of revenue. The three
other geographic segments are Latin America
Property 20% of revenue EMEA Property10% of
revenue and Asia Property 10% of revenue. The
Services segment which generates 1% of revenue
acquires sites and offers zoning and permitting
services and structural analysis to support its site
leasing businesses.

Geographic ReachBoston MA-headquartered
American Tower operates its corporate functions
in the US and runs distributed operations in its
non-US markets. The company produces most of
its revenue in the US. However the company is
pursuing geographic expansion and the percentage of non-US activity is rising. More than 15% of
revenue comes from India about 10% originates
in Brazil and more than 5% comes from Mexico.
The communications firm also operates in a variety
of countries in EMEA (Germany Ghana Nigeria
South Africa and Uganda) and in Latin America
(Argentina Chile Colombia Costa Rica and Peru).

Sales and Marketing American Tower's top
four tenants generate most of its total revenue:
about 20% from AT&T Mobility about 15% from
Verizon Wireless about 10% from Sprint and
about 10% from T-Mobile. Other top tenants include Tata Airtel Idea Cellular Telefonica Nextel
International Telecom Italia MTN Group Limited
and Vodafone.

Financial Performance

American Tower experienced explosive growth
in both revenue and net income over the past several years. Between 2010 and 2016 revenue and
net income averaged a near-20% increase each
year as consumer demand for wireless products
rose around the world.

In 2016 revenue rose 14% year-over-year to
$6.6 billion. Across all geographies American
Tower saw growth in new sites and growth in additional leases on existing sites. More than half of
the year's revenue increase originated in Asia
which saw about $337 million generated by new
sites primarily as the result of the company's 2016
Viom acquisition. Revenue from newly acquired
or constructed sites contributed about $100 million
of growth in 2017.

Net income jumped 25% to $1.2 billion in 2017
compared to 2016's $956 million due to increased
revenue and a multi-point drop in operating expense margin.

Cash grew by about $15 million in 2017 to end
the year with $802 million in the coffers. Uses of
cash included $2.8 billion and $113 million for investing and financing activities respectively. They
were more than offset by contributions from operating activities which included net income.

Strategy

Wireless communication is growing rapidly
throughout the world due to increased demand
for new customers wanting to connect (such as in
emerging markets) and for existing customers
wanting more bandwidth at higher speeds. American Tower wants to capitalize on this trend by expanding its property footprint and making the
most out of the property and towers it already
owns and operates. It intends to achieve this with
geographic expansion opportunistic acquisition of
additional towers and maximizing occupancy of
its existing towers.

As evidenced by the increasing revenue share
coming from non-US sources American Tower is
expanding more rapidly overseas than at home.
Its recent acquisition of Viom Networks more than
tripled its number of towers in India. A follow-on
purchase in late 2017 added 20000 more communication sites to its India portfolio bringing its
total to more than 70000 sites. Its ATC Europe
segment plunged into the French market in 2017
with the acquisition of 2400 wireless towers. Ad-

ditionally the company purchased in 2016 about 900 towers across a variety of countries.

The costs of increasing tenant occupancy on existing sites is less than acquiring a new site and erecting new towers. The company has a global average of approximately 1.9 tenants per tower and hopes to increase that rate through targeted sales and marketing activities. It believes that towers that are at or near capacity can be upgraded or augmented to meet future tenant demand with relatively modest capital investment.

Mergers and Acquisitions

In late 2017 ATC India agreed to purchase some 20000 communication sites in India from two firms Vodafone and Idea Cellular for $1.2 billion.

In early 2017 ATC Europe a 51%-49% joint venture between ATC and Netherlands-based PGGM spent approximately $750 million to acquire FPS Towers an owner and operator of 2400 wireless tower sites in France.

In 2016 American Tower purchased a 51% controlling interest for $1.1 billion in Viom Networks Ltd a telecommunications infrastructure company that owns and operates about 42000 wireless towers and 200 indoor distributed antenna system (DAS) networks in India. Viom was renamed to ATC Telecom Infrastructure Private Ltd and is part of ATC's Asia geographic region.

EXECUTIVES

Evp And Cfo, Thomas A. (Tom) Bartlett, age 59, $750,000 total compensation

Chairman President And Ceo, James D. (Jim) Taiclet, age 57, $1,100,000 total compensation

Evp International Operations; President Latin America And Emea, William H. (Hal) Hess, age 55, $650,000 total compensation

Evp And President Us Tower, Steven C. Marshall, age 57, $650,000 total compensation

Evp; President Asia, Amit Sharma, age 58

Evp Chief Administrative Officer General Counsel And Secretary, Edmund (Ed) DiSanto, age 66, $600,000 total compensation

Ceo Europe Middle East And Africa, Leah C. Stearns

Chairman Atc Europe, Stephen Harris

Chairman President And Ceo, James D. (Jim) Taiclet, age 57

Evp Chief Administrative Officer General Counsel And Secretary, Edmund (Ed) DiSanto, age 66

Auditors: DELOITTE & TOUCHE LLP

LOCATIONS

HQ: American Tower Corp (New)
116 Huntington Avenue, Boston, MA 02116
Phone: 617 375-7500
Web: www.americantower.com

2017 Sales

	$ mil.	% of total
U.S.	3,703	56
India	1,164	17
France	59	1
Germany	63	1
Ghana	122	2
Nigeria	213	3
South Africa	106	2
Uganda	60	1
Argentina	15	-
Brazil	620	10
Chile	40	1
Colombia	89	1
Costa Rica	19	-
Mexico	364	5
Paraguay	2	-
Peru	17	-
Total	**6,663**	**100**

PRODUCTS/OPERATIONS

2017 Sales

	$ mil.	% of total
Property	6,566	99
Services	98	1
Total	**6,664**	**100**

COMPETITORS

Crown Castle International
LCC International
Microwave Transmission Systems
SBA Communications
VelociTel

HISTORICAL FINANCIALS

Company Type: Public

Income Statement

FYE: December 31

	REVENUE ($ mil.)	NET INCOME ($ mil.)	NET PROFIT MARGIN	EMPLOYEES
12/17	6,663	1,238	18.6%	4,752
12/16	5,785	956	16.5%	4,507
12/15	4,771	685	14.4%	3,371
12/14	4,100	824	20.1%	2,974
12/13	3,361	551	16.4%	2,716
Annual Growth	**18.7%**	**22.4%**	**—**	**15.0%**

2017 Year-End Financials

Debt ratio: 60.83%
Return on equity: 19.05%
Cash ($ mil.): 802
Current ratio: 0.81
Long-term debt ($ mil.): 19,430
No. of shares (mil.): 428
Dividends
Yield: 0.0%
Payout: 98.1%
Market value ($ mil.): 61,180

	STOCK PRICE ($) FY Close	P/E High/Low	PER SHARE ($) Earnings	Dividends	Book Value
12/17	142.67	57 38	2.67	2.62	14.56
12/16	105.68	59 42	1.98	2.17	15.84
12/15	96.95	73 61	1.41	1.81	15.69
12/14	98.85	52 39	2.00	1.40	9.97
12/13	79.82	60 49	1.38	1.10	8.95
Annual Growth	**15.6%**	**— —**	**17.9%**	**24.2%**	**12.9%**

Ameriprise Financial Inc

Ameriprise Financial provides a variety of financial products including mutual funds savings plans annuities personal trust services and insurance products. It does so through its various brands and affiliates — which include Ameriprise Financial Services Columbia Management and RiverSource. Ameriprise manages some $900 billion in assets for more than 2 million individual institutional and small business clients primarily in the US with a growing international presence. It markets and administers its products primarily through a network of some 10000 financial advisors. Founded in 1894 Ameriprise Financial was spun off from American Express in 2005.

Operations

Ameriprise operates four main segments: Advice & Wealth Management Asset Management Annuities and Protection.

Its Advice & Wealth Management segment includes 2200 employee advisors and 7700 independent franchises. Together they provide financial planning advice and brokerage services primarily to the firm's US retail clients. The segment generates about 40% of revenue.

Asset Management (25% of revenue) offers investment management and products to retail high-net-worth and institutional clients globally. It does so through Columbia Management in the US and Threadneedle internationally. Columbia manages about 160 140 funds (mutual funds ETFs etc.) and about 70 variable insurance trust funds (VIT Funds) in the US while Threadneedle manages more than 180 funds outside the US.

The Annuities segment provides variable and fixed annuity products to individual clients via Ameriprise's RiverSource subsidiary. The fourth segment Protection offers Ameriprise clients insurance products including life disability income and property casualty. RiverSource accounts for about 20% of net revenue while Protection brings in more than 15%.

Geographic Reach

Ameriprise Financial and its affiliates are headquartered in Minneapolis Minnesota. Other primary offices are in New York City Boston and London. The US is by far its largest market generating more than 95% of the firm's revenue and possessing approximately 90% of its long-lived assets. Ameriprise's non-US presence is mostly through its Columbia Threadneedle brand which has activities in the UK and Europe in addition to an early-stage presence in the other major continents.

Sales and Marketing

Ameriprise's customers are varied ranging from individuals to universities to corporations. It employs a variety of methods to market and sell to this diverse group. The company's primary retail clients come from the 'mass affluent consumer' segment which controls almost half of all investable assets in the US. The firm markets to them through its financial advisor network and its website. Ameriprise tends to the non-retail segment (institutional & high-net-worth individuals) by nurturing direct relationships with entities such as university endowments pension plans sovereign wealth funds and foundations.

Financial Performance

Thanks to appreciating financial markets and a growing investor base Ameriprise Financial's asset-based fees have led it to consistent revenue and profit growth over the past several years. Since the Great Recession of 2008-2009 revenues have steadily climbed from a low of $7 billion to more recent amounts more than $12 billion. Net income followed a similar albeit more varied trend with a loss of $36 million in 2008 followed by years of $1 billion earnings appreciating to $2 billion in 2014 before settling lower in recent years.

In 2017 Ameriprise grew its revenue 3% to just above $12.0 billion reversing two years of revenue decline. The improvement came mostly from the Advice & Wealth management segment which grew due to higher wrap account assets higher earnings on brokerage cash and increased transactional activity. On the downside the Protection segment's revenue fell 9% due to the impact of unlocking and lower premiums.

Net income grew 12% to $1.5 billion roughly par for the course over the last five years. Net income expanded as the company achieved higher net revenue and lower total expenses particularly benefits claims losses and settlement expenses.

Cash on hand declined 5% to $5.1 billion as operating cash was impacted by changes in receivables and and brokerage deposits partially offset by lower purchases of available-for-sale securities.

Strategy

Ameriprise's long-term strategy involves a portfolio shift to pursue high growth areas in Advice & Wealth Management and Asset Management. It also has a near-term tactical strategy to target two key segments: individuals with $100000 or more in investable assets and high-net-worth people and institutional investors.

Between 2010 and 2016 the financial firm orchestrated a shift in assets under management which altered the mix of its pretax operating earnings from one heavily weighted towards Protection & Annuities (55% in 2010) to one weighted towards Advice & Wealth Management (AWM). AWM saw wrap account assets increase $47.1 billion or 23% in 2017

Its advisor network is crucial to growing and maintaining its base of individuals with $100000 or more in assets. The network model is one of a relationship-based direct sales organization in which the company makes considerable investment in technology training and support in addition to a plethora of financial products (mutual funds annuities life insurance). Occasionally Ameriprise adds to its network through acquisition which it did in 2016 with the purchase of Emerging Global Advisors and in 2017 with the purchase of Investment Professionals Inc.

The high-net-worth and institutional client segment is global in scale and therefore requires an approach that is not reliant on the advisor network. Instead Ameriprise offers a broad spectrum of investment advice and products through third parties and its Columbia Threadneedle subsidiary. Global geographic expansion innovations to investment solutions and delivering competitive investment performance are key to growing the fees and commissions received for this segment's fundamental metric assets under management (AUM).

EXECUTIVES

Chairman And Ceo, James M. (Jim) Cracchiolo, age 59, $1,025,000 total compensation
Ceo Global Asset Management, William F. (Ted) Truscott, age 57, $675,000 total compensation
Evp And Cfo, Walter S. Berman, age 76, $675,000 total compensation
Evp Human Resources, Kelli A. Hunter, age 57
President Advice And Wealth Management Products And Service Delivery, Joseph E. (Joe) Sweeney, age 57, $550,000 total compensation
Chief Strategy Officer; President Insurance And Annuities, John R. Woerner, age 49
Evp Marketing Corporate Communications And Community Relations, Deirdre D. McGraw, age 48
Coo; President Advice & Wealth Management Business Development, Neal Maglaque
Evp And Cio, Randy Kupper
Evp And Global Chief Investment Officer, Colin Moore, $475,000 total compensation
Evp Ameriprise Franchise Group, Bill Williams
Evp Ameriprise Advisor Group, Pat O'Connell
Evp And General Counsel, Karen Wilson Thissen
Vp Application Development, Scott Wilgenbusch
Vice President Operations, George Tsafaridis
Vice President, William Emptage
Vice President Of Marketing, Heather Melloh
Vice President Human Resources, Karen Dekker
Vice President Underwriting And Chief Underwriter, Thor Holmgren
Vice President Financial Applications Support Controllership, John Mead
Vice President Appointed Actuary, Stephen Blaske
Vice President External Products Group, Tracy Anderson
Senior Vice President Of Consumer Marketing, Marie O'Neill
Vice President Technical Advisory Group, Michael Mattox
Svp Investor Relations, Alicia Charity
Vice President, Jayme Cleghorn
Vice President Managed Accounts, Eric Paluck
Vice President Marketing, Linda Moriarty

Financial Advisor And Vp Brehm And Murray, Jay Murray
Vice President ??? Field Strategy, Stephen Ehele
Vice President Human Resources Business Partner, Melanie Demont
Vice President Human Resources Services, Jay Rasula
Regional Vice President, Phillip Buckner
Vice President And Group Counsel, Lisa Lewis
Vice President And Group Counsel, David Fogel
Vice President Compliance, Jeff Soderstrom
Vice President, Paul Major
Vice President=clr Project Management Office, Mike Greene
Vice President Underwriting, Tom Botsford
Vice President, Chip Pierron
Vice President General Manager Managed Products, Greg Nordmeyer
Associate Vice President, Aaron Kurasch
Vice President Architecture, Tom Esselman
Vice President And Group Counsel, Christopher Long
Financial Advisor Vice President, Barry Craine
Senior Franchise Field Vice President, Dean Mcgill
Vice President Trading Brokerage Clearin, Gregory Carr
Franchise Field Vice President, Matthew Roesser
Vice President Information Technology, Clarissa C Ramos
Vice President Human Resources Program, Kristi Kooda-Chizek
Vice President Portfolio Manager, Nic Pifer
Senior Vice President Corp Comm And Community Relations Ameriprise Financial Inc., Deirdre Davey
Regional Vice President, Peter Mitchell
Vice President, Erika Perrault
Vp Sox Compliance Re Engineering And Technology Audit, Margo Esson
Vice President, Gerard Smyth
Vice President And Group Counsel, Christopher Petersen
Vice President And Group Counsel, Kurt Johansen
Associate Vice President, Michael King
Region Vice President, Matthew Miller
Vice President Finance, Rob Bardot
Vice President And Head Of Advice And Wealth Management Operations, Manish Ganatra
Vice President Financial Advisor, Paul Hoghaug
Vice President Sales, LeAnn M Thomas
Vice President Training And Development, Lamont Boykins
Vice President Of Technical Department, Jacqueline Glockner
Vice President Field Strategy And Implement, Mark Traut
Vp Technology, Ernie Smith
Vice President Clearing Operations, Michael Pszybylski
Vice President, Nate Pugliese
Vice President, Jason Miller
Senior Regional Vice President Insurance West, Bj Seastone
Vice President And Financial Advisor, Edward Moran
Associate Vice President, Paul Rosenfeld
Vice President Strategic Transformation, Michael Jordan
Vice President Compliance, Surabhi Ahmad
Vice President Information Technology, Rajeev Duggirala
Vice President Communications, Adrienne Nestor
Vice President, Nicolo Manlapaz
Associate Vice President, Michele Kingdeski
Vice President, Russ Zorn
Vice President Derivative And Product Risk, Manuel Balsera
Associate Vice President Financial Advisor, Robert Alexander
Vice President, Gary Farthing

Vice President Financial Advisor, Alan Holt
Vice President, Hoppy Shores
Vice President, Paul Seals
Financial Adviser And Vice President, David Carson
Vice President Investment Advisor, Christine Pall
Vice President Private Wealth Advisor, Daniel Bellino
Vice President Financial Advisor, Jason Wilson
Vice President Cfp Mba, Stan Roberts
Regional Vice President Retirement Wealth Strateg, Joseph Peppe
Evp And General Counsel, Karen Wilson-thissen
Vice President Financial Advisor, Nathan Foret
Vice President Sales, Andrew Wright
Vice President Marketing Strategy Retail Retirement, Abu Arif
Vice President Planning And Administration, Matt Haglund
Divisional Vice President, Michael DeLorenzo
Associate Vice President Of Finance, Brian Mccabe
Associate Vice President, Michael Carboni
Associate Vice President, Karen Hartley
Senior Vice President Senior Portfolio Manager, John Brewster
Regional Vice President, Rob Elstad
Vice President Diversity And Inclusion Ameriprise Financial, Rodolfo Rodriguez
Vice President Quantitative Strategies, Philip Jones
Financial Advisor: Vice President, Amy Boyle
Vice President Treasury, Mike Pollei
Vice President Finance, Dawn Brockman
Franchise Region Vice President, Barry Stockdale
Vice President, James J Obrien
Vice President Of Client Services, Lauren Silva
Vice President Certified Financial Planner, Jennifer Theissing
Vice President Financial Advisor, Brett Dalton
Field Vice President, Ken Franklin
Associate Vice President Financial Advisor, Carl Fazio
Associate Vice President, Paul Donas
Associate Vice President, Paul Liberatore
Senior Regional Vice President, Pj Bonfilio
Vp Big Data Analytics And Corporate Systems Technology, Sachin Mehta
Vice President, Amanda Payne
Franchise Field Vice President Assistant, Deborah Gable
Vice President Financial Advisor, Vincent La Cava
Vice President, Jason Reiling
Vice President Finance, Margulis Michael
Vice President Financial Advisor, Alan Ronald
Associate Vice President, Rick Connett
Evp Hr, Kelli Hunter Petruzillo
Vice President Institutional Marketing, Heather Heald
Chairman And Ceo, James M. (Jim) Cracchiolo, age 59
Auditors: PricewaterhouseCoopers LLP

LOCATIONS

HQ: Ameriprise Financial Inc
1099 Ameriprise Financial Center, Minneapolis, MN 55474
Phone: 612 671-3131
Web: www.ameriprise.com

PRODUCTS/OPERATIONS

2017 Sales

	$ mil.	% of total
Annuities	98,276	67
Protection	18,039	12
Advice & Wealth Management	13,270	9
Corporate & other	9,492	6
Asset Management	8,393	6
Total	**147,470**	**100**

2017 Sales

	$ mil.	% of total
Management & financial advice fees	6,392	53
Distribution fees	1,770	15
Net investment income	1,509	13
Premiums	1,394	12
Other revenues	1,010	7
Banking & deposit interest expense	(48)	-
Total	**12,027**	**100**

PRODUCTS & SERVICES
Cash Cards & Lending
Financial Planning
Insurance & Annuities
Investments
Personal Trust Services

Selected Subsidiaries and Affiliates
American Enterprise Investment Services Inc.
Ameriprise Financial Services Inc.
Ameriprise Certificate Company
Ameriprise Trust Company
Columbia Management Investment Advisers LLC
Columbia Management Investment Distributors Inc.
IDS Property Casualty Insurance Company
J. & W. Seligman & Co. Incorporated
RiverSource Distributors Inc.
RiverSource Life Insurance Co. of New York
Threadneedle Asset Management Holdings

Selected Brands
Ameriprise Financial®;
Columbia Management®;
RiverSource®;

COMPETITORS

AXA Financial	MassMutual
Allstate	Merrill Lynch
Bank of America	MetLife
Bank of New York Mellon	Nationwide Financial
	New York Life
Calamos Asset Management	Northwestern Mutual
	PNC Financial
Capital Group	Primerica
Charles Schwab	Principal Financial
Citigroup	Prudential
FMR	Regions Financial
First Eagle Investment Mangement	State Street
	TIAA
John Hancock Financial Services	U.S. Bancorp
Lincoln Financial Group	

HISTORICAL FINANCIALS
Company Type: Public

Income Statement
FYE: December 31

	REVENUE ($ mil.)	NET INCOME ($ mil.)	NET PROFIT MARGIN	EMPLOYEES
12/17	12,027	1,480	12.3%	13,000
12/16	11,696	1,314	11.2%	13,000
12/15	12,170	1,562	12.8%	13,000
12/14	12,268	1,619	13.2%	12,209
12/13	11,199	1,334	11.9%	12,039
Annual Growth	**1.8%**	**2.6%**	**—**	**1.9%**

2017 Year-End Financials

Debt ratio: 3.59%	No. of shares (mil.): 146
Return on equity: 24.08%	Dividends
Cash ($ mil.): 2,620	Yield: 0.0%
Current ratio: 0.67	Payout: 34.3%
Long-term debt ($ mil.): 5,099	Market value ($ mil.): 24,850

	STOCK PRICE ($) FY Close	P/E High/Low	PER SHARE ($) Earnings	Dividends	Book Value
12/17	169.47	18 12	9.44	3.24	40.90
12/16	110.94	15 10	7.81	2.92	40.66
12/15	106.42	16 12	8.48	2.59	42.20
12/14	132.25	16 12	8.30	2.26	44.37
12/13	115.05	17 10	6.44	2.01	42.64
Annual Growth	**10.2%**	**—**	**10.0%**	**12.7%**	**(1.0%)**

Ameris Bancorp

Ameris Bancorp enjoys the financial climate of the Deep South. It is the holding company of Ameris Bank which holds roughly $3.6 billion in assets and serves retail and consumer customers through more than 75 full-service and mortgage branches in Alabama Georgia South Carolina and northern Florida. In addition to its standard banking products and services the bank also provides treasury services mortgage and refinancing solutions and investment services through an agreement with Raymond James Financial. Loans secured by commercial real estate accounted for approximately 45% of the company's loan portfolio while 1-4 family residential and construction & land development mortgages accounted for nearly a quarter and about 10% respectively.

Operations
Like most banks Ameris earns the vast majority of its recurring revenue (71.5%) from interest income from loans. Nearly 80% of these loans are made up of commercial real estate 1-4 family residential and construction & land development loans. The remaining 20% are from a mix of commercial multi-family residential and consumer loans (home improvement home equity personal lines of credit auto loans and student loans).

Traditional banking products (deposit accounts) and services along with investment products and services (which primarily earn income from fees and commissions) made up about 28% of the bank's annual sales in fiscal 2013.

Sales and Marketing
Through an acquisition-oriented growth strategy Ameris seeks to grow its brand and presence in the markets it currently serves in Georgia Alabama Florida and South Carolina as well as in neighboring communities. In addition the bank expects its community-oriented philosophy will help strengthen existing customer relations and attract new customers.

The company spent $1.62 million on advertising and public relations in Fiscal Year 2013 just under the $1.622 million it spent in 2012 and more than double the $722000 it spent in 2011. The company increased its advertising spending by $900000 during 2012 to support its revenue and growth- strategies during the year.

Financial Performance
Ameris carried $3.67 billion in total assets as of December 31 2013. Loans made up $2.5 billion (approximately 68.9% of total assets). The bank also reported carrying $3 billion in deposits.

Ameris' net revenue dipped in fiscal 2013 declining 5% to $163 million from its high of $172 million in 2012 mostly from an $11.3 million dip in non-interest revenue. But this dip in non-interest revenue is primarily because the bank recorded a large gain of $20 million from acquisitions in 2012. When excluding this acquisition gain from 2012's revenues and thanks to $6.1 million revenue in-

crease in mortgage banking activity management reports that total non-interest income actually increased $8.7 million in 2013 compared to 2012. A decline in interest-earning loan assets from $2.47 billion in 2013 compared to $2.5 billion in 2012 also played a role in the dip in net revenues.

Thanks to aggressive acquisitions and despite revenue decreasing net income jumped a whopping 43% to $20 million in 2013 from $14 million in 2012. This is only slightly below the bank's net income high of $21 million in 2011. It's most notable acquisition of Prosperity Bank increased Ameris' total assets by $744.9 million and added $449.7 million in loans to its interest-earning loan portfolio. Adding to the extra income from new loans Ameris collected higher net interest margins on all of its loans which increased to 4.74% in 2013 from 4.60% in 2012.

Strategy
Ameris plans to continue using its community banking philosophy to lessen its risk and identify prime local lending markets. Management reports that by encouraging a personalized service experience and building deeper customer relationships the bank has already grown a "substantial" base of low-cost core deposits (which pad the bank's reserves and lessen financial risk). And between its bench of experienced decision makers and lenders operating in a "decentralized" structure (which differentiates Ameris from mega banks) and its deep familiarity with local markets management believes the bank can better identify prime growth markets (for lending and bank services) with managed risk in the years ahead.

Mergers and Acquisitions
Integral to the bank's growth strategy Ameris has aggressively acquired banks to broaden its reach into its primary southern markets.

Ameris Bancorp purchased Jacksonville Bancorp and its eight branches more than doubling its branch network in Jacksonville Illinois to 14 branches.

Company Background
In addition to acquiring several troubled and failing banks with help from the FDIC Ameris merged with Prosperity Bank in 2013 which broadened its reach into Florida through Prosperity's branches in St. Augustine Jacksonville Panama City Lynn Haven Palatka and Ormand Beach.

Georgia's economy was one of the hardest hit in the US during the recession and Ameris has taken advantage of the plethora of banks seized by regulators in the state. Since 2009 the company has acquired about 10 failed banks in Georgia though FDIC-assisted transactions adding some 20 branches to its network. Ameris also snagged the failed First Bank of Jacksonville in Florida which had two locations.

EXECUTIVES

Chief Banking Executive Ameris Bancorp And Ameris Bank, Andrew B. (Andy) Cheney, age 68, $400,000 total compensation
Evp And Chief Credit Officer, Jon S. Edwards, age 56, $260,000 total compensation
Svp And Director Of Human Resources, Cindi H. Lewis, age 64, $90,333 total compensation
President And Ceo, Edwin W. (Ed) Hortman, age 64, $625,000 total compensation
Evp And Banking Group President Ameris Bancorp And President Ameris Bank, Lawton E. Bassett
Evp Cfo And Coo, Dennis J. Zember, age 48, $320,000 total compensation
Evp And Chief Risk Officer, Stephen A. Melton, $275,000 total compensation
Evp And Chief Banking Officer, James A. LaHaise
Assistant Vice President, Ann Dunn

Vice President And Business Banker, Charles Hudgens
Senior Vice President, Rob Kowkabany
Vice President Special Assets Division, Leo Story
Vice President Of Residential Mortgage, Greg Seabaugh
Senior Vice President, Karen Cross
Senior Vice President, Jw Dukes
Vice President Mortgage Sales Manager, Jason Fralix
Senior Vice President Special Assets Division, David Aldridge
Vice President Senior Treasury Services Advisor, Lori Putnam
Vice President Accounting Manager P. O. Box 3668, Marsha Dotson
Vice President, Connie Romay
Vice President Regional Area Manager, Candace Adkins
Senior Vice President Commercial Banker, Brian Samson
Senior Vice President, Jayson Griffin
Senior Vice President Branch Manager, Vicki Blanton
Chairman, Daniel B. Jeter, age 66
Auditors: Crowe Horwath LLP

LOCATIONS

HQ: Ameris Bancorp
310 First Street S.E., Moultrie, GA 31768
Phone: 229 890-1111
Web: www.amerisbank.com

PRODUCTS/OPERATIONS

2016 sales chart

	$ mil.	% of total
Interest income:		
Interest and fees on loans	218	64
Interest on taxable securities	17	5
Interest on nontaxable securities	1	-
Interest on deposits in other banks	0	-
Interest on federal funds sold	-	-
Non Interest income:		
Service charges on deposit accounts	42	13
Mortgage banking activity	48	14
Other service charges commissions and fees	3	1
Net gains on sales of securities	-	-
Gain on sale of SBA loans	3	1
Other noninterest income	7	2
Total	**344**	**100**

2016 sales chart

	% of total
Banking Division	91
Retail Mortgage Division	5
Warehouse Lending Division	3
SBA Division	1
Total	**100**

Selected Acquisitions

American United Bank
Central Bank of Georgia
Darby Bank & Trust
First Bank of Jacksonville
High Trust Bank
Montgomery Bank & Trust
One Georgia Bank
Satilla Community Bank
Tifton Banking Company
United Security Bank

COMPETITORS

BBVA Compass Bancshares	First South Bancorp (NC)
Bank of America	Regions Financial
Capital City Bank	Southwest Georgia Financial
Colony Bankcorp	
Community Capital Bancshares	SunTrust
	Thomasville Bancshares

HISTORICAL FINANCIALS

Company Type: Public

Income Statement — FYE: December 31

	ASSETS ($ mil.)	NET INCOME ($ mil.)	INCOME AS % OF ASSETS	EMPLOYEES
12/17	7,856	73	0.9%	1,460
12/16	6,892	72	1.0%	1,298
12/15	5,588	40	0.7%	1,304
12/14	4,037	38	1.0%	1,027
12/13	3,667	20	0.5%	984
Annual Growth	21.0%	38.4%	—	10.4%

2017 Year-End Financials

Debt ratio: 2.05%	No. of shares (mil.): 37
Return on equity: 10.14%	Dividends
Cash ($ mil.): 330	Yield: 0.0%
Current ratio: —	Payout: 20.2%
Long-term debt ($ mil.): —	Market value ($ mil.): 1,796

	STOCK PRICE ($) FY Close	P/E High/Low	PER SHARE ($) Earnings	Dividends	Book Value
12/17	48.20	26 21	1.98	0.40	21.59
12/16	43.60	23 12	2.08	0.30	18.51
12/15	33.99	27 18	1.27	0.20	15.98
12/14	25.64	18 13	1.46	0.15	13.67
12/13	21.11	28 16	0.75	0.00	12.62
Annual Growth	22.9%	— —	27.5%	—	14.4%

Amerisafe Inc

AMERISAFE has what it takes to insure rough-necks and truckers. AMERISAFE specializes in providing workers' compensation insurance for businesses in hazardous industries including agriculture manufacturing construction logging and sawmill oil and gas maritime and trucking. Through its subsidiaries American Interstate Insurance Silver Oak Casualty and American Interstate Insurance of Texas the company writes coverage for more than 7900 employers (mainly small and midsized firms). In addition AMERISAFE offers worksite safety reviews loss prevention and claims management services. AMERISAFE sells its products in more than 30 states and the District of Columbia.

Geographic Reach

AMERISAFE's largest markets are Louisiana Georgia and Pennsylvania with each accounting for roughly 10% of its gross premiums written.

Sales and Marketing

The company sells its products through more than 3100 independent agents as well as through its Amerisafe General Agency.

Financial Performance

Like all workers' compensation providers AMERISAFE saw its revenues drop during the economic recession for the simplest reason: when employers trim their workforces they need less workers' compensation coverage.

However the company's revenue has been increasing year-over-year since 2010. It reported $356.3 million in revenue for fiscal 2013 up from $321.2 million in revenue for fiscal 2012 and $280.7 million in revenue for fiscal 2011.

AMERISAFE's net income has also been trending up across recent fiscal years. The company netted more than $43 million in fiscal 2013 after reporting a net income of about $29 million for fiscal 2012 and $24 million for fiscal 2011.

The company's cash flow remains strong. It had almost $50 million more on hand at the end of fiscal 2013 than it did at the close of fiscal 2012.

Strategy

AMERISAFE's strategy for growth is based on managing its capital and focusing on its underwriting profitability. It hopes to increase its book value and produce favorable returns by maintaining rate levels that are in balance with the risks it underwrites improving its risk selection and pricing and reducing the frequency and severity of claims through workplace safety reviews medical cost containment and rapid closing of claims. Additionally the company is looking to increase market penetration in the states where it operates as well as seek opportunities in the 12 other states and the US Virgin Islands where it licensed.

Another key element of the company's strategy is to capitalize on its information technology tools. These include its GEAUX underwriting and agency management system and ICAMS its customized operational system which together with the analytical data warehouse that ICAMS feeds improve its ability to select risk write profitable business and administer billing claims and audit functions more cost-effectively.

EXECUTIVES

President And Coo, G. Janelle Frost, age 48, $370,833 total compensation
Evp And Chief Risk Officer, Vincent J. Gagliano, age 45, $202,000 total compensation
Vice President Treasurer, Angela Lannen
Vice President Field Safety, Garrett Little
Vice President Sales Northeast Region, Ed Ennis
Senior Vice President Sales Marketing, David Morton
Vice President Sales Midwest Region, Mark Burger
Sales Vice President, Chris Lastoch
Senior Vice President Of Operations, Leon Lagneaux
Vice President Of Sales, Martha Mcleod
Vice President Claims East Region, Jim Leonard
Chairman, Jared A. Morris, age 42
Board Member, Philip Garcia
Board Member, Daniel Phillips
Board Member, Teri Fontenot
Auditors: Ernst & Young LLP

LOCATIONS

HQ: Amerisafe Inc
2301 Highway 190 West, DeRidder, LA 70634
Phone: 337 463-9052
Web: www.amerisafe.com

PRODUCTS/OPERATIONS

2016 Sales

	$ mil.	% of total
Net premiums earned	368	93
Net investment income	28	7
Fee and other income	0	-
Net realized gains (losses) on investments	(0.5)	-
Loss on disposal of assets	(0.001)	-
Total	**396**	**100**

COMPETITORS

ACSTAR	McM Corporation
Baldwin & Lyons	Nationwide
Bituminous Insurance Companies	SeaBright Insurance
	W. R. Berkley
Farm Family Holdings	Zenith National

HISTORICAL FINANCIALS

Company Type: Public

Income Statement

FYE: December 31

	ASSETS ($ mil.)	NET INCOME ($ mil.)	INCOME AS % OF ASSETS	EMPLOYEES
12/17	1,518	46	3.0%	438
12/16	1,518	77	5.1%	439
12/15	1,502	70	4.7%	451
12/14	1,457	53	3.7%	445
12/13	1,329	43	3.3%	437
Annual Growth	3.4%	1.5%	—	0.1%

2017 Year-End Financials

Debt ratio: —	No. of shares (mil.): 19
Return on equity: 10.49%	Dividends
Cash ($ mil.): 55	Yield: 0.0%
Current ratio: —	Payout: 179.1%
Long-term debt ($ mil.): —	Market value ($ mil.): 1,186

	STOCK PRICE ($) FY Close	P/E High/Low	PER SHARE ($) Earnings	Dividends	Book Value
12/17	61.60	28 21	2.40	4.30	22.10
12/16	62.35	16 12	4.05	3.97	23.72
12/15	50.90	15 11	3.69	3.60	23.73
12/14	42.36	15 12	2.84	1.98	23.65
12/13	42.24	19 11	2.32	0.32	22.41
Annual Growth	9.9%	— —	0.9%	91.5%	(0.3%)

AmerisourceBergen Corp.

AmerisourceBergen is the source for many of North America's pharmacies and health care providers. The distribution company serves as a go-between for drug makers and the pharmacies doctors' offices hospitals and other health care providers that dispense drugs. Operating primarily in the US it distributes generic branded and over-the-counter pharmaceuticals as well as some medical supplies and other products using its network of more than two dozen facilities. Its specialty distribution unit focuses on sensitive and complex biopharmaceuticals. Other operations include pharmaceutical packaging commercialization and consulting services and animal health product distribution.

HISTORY

In 1977 Cleveland millionaire and horse racing enthusiast Tinkham Veale went into the drug wholesaling business. His company Alco Standard (now IKON Office Solutions) already owned chemical electrical metallurgical and mining companies but by the late 1970s the company was pursuing a strategy of zeroing in on various types of distribution businesses.

Alco's first drug wholesaler purchase was The Drug House (Delaware and Pennsylvania); the next was Duff Brothers (Tennessee). The company then bought further wholesalers in the South East and Midwest. Its modus operandi was to buy small well-run companies for cash and Alco stock and leave the incumbent management in charge.

By the early 1980s Alco was the US's third-largest wholesale drug distributor and growing quickly (28% between 1983 and 1988) at a time of mass consolidation in the industry (the number of wholesalers dropped by half between 1980 and 1992). In 1985 Alco Standard spun off its drug distribution operations as Alco Health Services retaining 60% ownership.

Alco Health boosted its sales above $1 billion mostly via acquisitions and expanded product lines. The company offered marketing and promotional help to its independent pharmacy customers (which were beleaguered by the growth of national discounters) and also targeted hospitals nursing homes and clinics.

The US was in the midst of its LBO frenzy in 1988 but an Alco management group failed in its attempt. Rival McKesson then tried to acquire Alco Health but that deal fell through for antitrust reasons. Later in 1988 management turned for backing to Citicorp Venture Capital in another buyout attempt. This time the move succeeded and a new holding company Alco Health Distribution was formed.

Alco Health went public as AmeriSource Health in 1995. Throughout the next year AmeriSource made a series of acquisitions to move into related areas including inventory management technology drugstore pharmaceutical supplies and disease-management services for pharmacies.

In 1997 McKesson once again made an offer to buy AmeriSource this time for $2.4 billion while two other major wholesale distributors Cardinal Health and Bergen Brunswig reached a similar pact. The deals were scrapped in 1998 when the Federal Trade Commission voted against both pacts and a federal judge supported that decision.

In 2013 AmerisourceBergen signed a 10-year agreement to supply Walgreen Boots Alliance.

EXECUTIVES

Vice President Corporate And Investor Relations, Barbara Brungess
Chairman President And Ceo, Steven H. Collis, age 57, $1,234,231 total compensation
Evp And Cfo, Tim G. Guttman, age 59, $706,539 total compensation
Evp And Chief Communications & Administration Officer, Gina K. Clark, age 61
Vp Deputy General Counsel And Secretary, John G. Chou, age 62, $621,231 total compensation
Group President Pharmaceutical Distribution And Strategic Global Sourcing, James F. (Jim) Cleary, age 55
Evp And President Health Systems Physician Practices And Strategic Health Solutions, Peyton R. Howell, age 51
Evp And Cio, Dale Danilewitz, age 56
Group President Global Commercialization Services And Animal Health, Robert P. Mauch, age 51, $593,077 total compensation
Evp And Chief Human Resources Officer, Kathy H. Gaddes, age 55
Evp Strategy And Development, Sun Park, age 42
Vice President Government Accounts, Kent Rischar
Vice President Gerneric Rx Product Development, Brian Jones
Vice President Operations, Joe Williamson
Vice President Professional Services, Kathryn Uchida
Vice President Dcm Operations, Frank Dicenso
Senior Vice President Global Generics, Marc T Kikuchi
Vice President Of Strategic Accounts, Matt Johnson
Vice President Financial Planning And Analysis, Jeannine Altrogge
Vice President Sales, David Tingue
Senior Vice President Sales Csp, Lisa Mash
Vice President Supply Chain Solutions, Barbara Miller
Vice President Operations, Terry Forrest
Vice President Of Corporate Development And Strategy, Nate Massari
Vice President Health Systems Sales, Michael Haddad
Vice President Financial Processes, Brian Mangiaracina
Vice President Supply Chain Solutions, Wesley Jones
Senior Vice President Tax, Kevin Conway
Executive Assistant To Senior Vice President Chief Human Resources Officer And Chief Information Officer, Kelly Jakeman
Vice President Tax, Daniel Hirst
Vice President Risk Management, Walter Hope
Vice President Distribution Services, Bernie Hale
Executive Vice President And Chief Ope, Kurt Hilzinger
Senior Vice President Of Marketing, Thomas Connolly
Sales Vice President, Catherine Carminati
Executive Vice President And Chief Fin, Michael Dicandilo
Vice President Of Trpn, Gabriel Weissman
Vp It Global Commercialization And Animal Health, Cory Shouse
Senior Vice President Corporate Controller, Lazarus Krikorian
Vice President Strategy For Provider Solutions, Vicki Albrecht
Vice President Of Sales, Colby Adams
Vice President Specialty Client Strategies, Erin K Rausch
Vice President Business Information Solutions, Eric Besse
Chairman President And Ceo, Steven H. Collis, age 57
Auditors: Ernst & Young LLP

LOCATIONS

HQ: AmerisourceBergen Corp.
1300 Morris Drive, Chesterbrook, PA 19087-5594
Phone: 610 727-7000   **Fax:** 610 647-0141
Web: www.amerisourcebergen.com

PRODUCTS/OPERATIONS

2018 Sales by Segment

	$ mil.	% of total
Pharmaceutical Distribution Services	161,699	96
Other	6,332	4
Adjustments	(92.4)	-
Total	**167,939**	**100**

COMPETITORS

Cardinal Health	Medline Industries
Express Scripts	Owens & Minor
FFF Enterprises	Quality King
Henry Schein	UPS
McKesson	

HISTORICAL FINANCIALS

Company Type: Public

Income Statement

FYE: September 30

	REVENUE ($ mil.)	NET INCOME ($ mil.)	NET PROFIT MARGIN	EMPLOYEES
09/18	167,939	1,658	1.0%	21,000
09/17	153,143	364	0.2%	20,000
09/16	146,849	1,427	1.0%	19,000
09/15	135,961	(134)	—	17,500
09/14	119,569	276	0.2%	14,000
Annual Growth	8.9%	56.5%	—	10.7%

2018 Year-End Financials

Debt ratio: 12.38%	No. of shares (mil.): 213
Return on equity: 66.37%	Dividends
Cash ($ mil.): 2,492	Yield: 0.0%
Current ratio: 0.93	Payout: 20.1%
Long-term debt ($ mil.): 4,510	Market value ($ mil.): 19,663

	STOCK PRICE ($) FY Close	P/E High/Low		PER SHARE ($) Earnings	Dividends	Book Value
09/18	92.22	14	10	7.53	1.52	13.76
09/17	82.75	58	41	1.64	1.46	9.47
09/16	80.78	16	11	6.32	1.36	9.68
09/15	94.99	—	—	(0.62)	1.16	3.06
09/14	77.30	64	50	1.17	0.94	8.82
Annual Growth	**4.5%**	—	—	**59.3%**	**12.8%**	**11.8%**

Amgen Inc

Amgen is among the biggest of the biotechs. The company uses cellular biology and medicinal chemistry to target cancers kidney ailments inflammatory disorders and metabolic diseases. Its top protein-based therapeutic products include Neulasta and Neupogen (both used as anti-infectives in cancer patients) Aranesp and Epogen (used to fight anemia in chronic kidney disease and cancer patients) and Enbrel for rheumatoid arthritis. In addition Amgen has extensive drug research and development programs. Its products are marketed in approximately 100 countries to doctors hospitals pharmacies and other health care providers.

Operations

Amgen's six therapeutic areas of focus are oncology and hematology cardiovascular disease inflammation bone health nephrology and neuroscience.

In addition to Neulasta Neupogen Aranesp Epogen and Enbrel some of the company's marketed drugs include XGEVA and Prolia (for the prevention of skeletal-related events) and Sensipar/Mimpara (for the treatment of secondary hyperparathyroidism in chronic kidney disease patients on dialysis). Amgen also markets Vectibix Nplate Kyprolis BLINCYTO Repatha Corlanor IMLYGIC and Parsabiv.

Like most biotech firms Amgen partners with other companies to get medicines on the market. It has a 50-50 partnership with Japanese brewer and drugmaker Kirin through which it develops and out-licenses certain product rights. (It agreed to buy Kirin out for $780 million in 2017.) Additionally it has a collaboration with AstraZeneca to develop and commercialize some of the monoclonal antibodies from its clinical inflammation portfolio. The company is also working with UCB to develop and commercialize romosozumab which has shown positive results for the treatment of osteoporosis in postmenopausal women. In another collaboration Amgen is working with Bayer HealthCare to develop and commercialize Nexavar around the world. And in 2018 the FDA approved migraine treatment Aimovig which is made by Amgen and Novartis.

Geographic Reach

Amgen operates distribution centers in the US (primarily in California and Kentucky) and the Netherlands. Though its products are marketed in nearly 100 countries (primarily in North America and Europe) the US accounts for some 80% of revenue. Amgen continues to expand into growth markets adding new markets in Latin America Asia and the Middle East.

The company owns about 180 properties including manufacturing facilities in Brazil Ireland the Netherlands Puerto Rico Singapore and Turkey.

Sales and Marketing

Sales of Amgen's top offerings — Neulasta Enbrel Aranesp and Prolia — together account for more than 60% of annual revenues. Most of these sales take place within the US market where they are distributed through wholesalers including AmerisourceBergen McKesson and Cardinal Health. Amgen employs a direct sales force in the US Canadian and European markets to promote its products; it uses partners and independent representatives in other global markets. For instance Kirin sells the Neupogen/Neulasta compounds in Asian markets and Enbrel is marketed internationally by Pfizer.

Amgen also markets certain of its products directly to consumers using print online and television advertising. With partners the company markets products to health care providers including physicians hospitals and pharmacies.

Sales to AmerisourceBergen McKesson and Cardinal Health each account for more than 10% of total revenue.

Financial Performance

Amgen's revenues had been trending up for several years until 2017 when revenue took a slight dip. Net income which had also been rising fell significantly in 2017.

Because product sales and other revenues slipped a bit revenue declined less than 1% to $22.8 billion in 2017. The company's top three products (ENBREL Neulasta and Aranesp) all had lower sales that year. This was partially offset by higher sales of Prolia and Sensipar/Mimpara. Product sales fell in the US largely due to increased competition or reduced demand. Sales outside of the US though rose as a result of higher demand.

Net income on the other hand fell 74% to $2 billion that year. Expenses remained relatively flat but the one-time impact of the 2017 Tax Act cut into the firm's bottom line.

Cash and cash equivalents rose 17% to $3.8 billion during 2017. Although cash used in financing activities (largely paying down debt) more than doubled cash used in investing activities (including investments in properties) declined by more than half.

Strategy

Amgen's strategy for growth covers several key areas including developing innovative medicines transitioning to next-generation biomanufacturing and branching into branded biosimilars. It has made strides in these areas through such efforts as launching products around the world and investing in its manufacturing capabilities (including its new next-generation biomanufacturing plant in Singapore and a similar plant in Rhode Island which broke ground in 2018). However the company faces challenges which it plans to face head on.

To prepare for the pending losses of patent protection on its top products in coming years Amgen is launching new products it hopes will best its bestsellers. The company faces increased competition as the FDA has begun approving biosimilars (generic biotech drugs) in a shorter amount of time. For example in 2018 the FDA approved biosimilar versions of both Epogen and Neulasta. (Neulasta alone brought in some 20% of Amgen's revenue in 2017 so the loss of exclusivity could be very detrimental to the company.) In Europe Amgen faces competition from biologics of products including Aranesp Neupogen and Neulasta.

In fact the company is taking advantage of the increased acceptance of biosimilars by engaging in their development itself. In 2017 its MVASI biosimilar version of Avastin was approved by the FDA and the European Council; MVASI is the first anti-cancer biosimilar. Amgen's AMJEVITA was approved by the FDA as a competitor of Humira.

Looking for other new products Amgen's activities are focused on identifying and validating targets through human genetics. Amgen boasts a bulging pipeline of compounds that target cancer inflammation kidney disease and neurological cardiovascular and bone and blood disorders mostly based on biotech technologies.

HISTORY

Amgen was formed as Applied Molecular Genetics in 1980 by a group of scientists and venture capitalists to develop health care products based on molecular biology. George Rathmann a VP at Abbott Laboratories and researcher at UCLA became the company's CEO and first employee. Rathmann decided to develop a few potentially profitable products rather than conduct research. The company initially raised $19 million.

The company operated close to bankruptcy until 1983 when Amgen scientist Fu-Kuen Lin cloned the human protein erythropoietin (EPO) which stimulates the body's red blood cell production. Amgen went public that year. It formed a joint venture with Kirin Brewery in 1984 to develop and market EPO. The two firms also collaborated on recombinant human granulocyte colony stimulating factor (G-CSF later called Neupogen) a protein that stimulates the immune system.

Amgen joined Johnson & Johnson subsidiary Ortho Pharmaceutical (later Ortho-McNeil Pharmaceutical) in a marketing alliance in 1985 and created a tie with Roche in 1988. Fortunes soared in 1989 when the FDA approved Epogen (the brand name of EPO) for anemia. (It is most commonly used to counter side effects of kidney dialysis.)

In 1991 Amgen received approval to market Neupogen to chemotherapy patients. A federal court ruling also gave it a US monopoly for EPO. The following year Amgen won another dispute forcing a competitor to renounce its US patents for G-CSF.

In 1993 the company became the first American biotech to gain a foothold in China through an agreement with Kirin Pharmaceuticals to sell Neupogen (under the name Gran) and Epogen there. The purchase of Synergen in 1994 added another research facility accelerating the pace of and increasing the number of products in research and clinical trials.

Amgen received the National Medal of Technology which is considered to be on par with the Nobel Prize. The company was recognized for its innovative work in cellular and molecular biology. It was the first biotech to win the award.

The FDA approved Enbrel which became a top seller for the company in late 1998. Three years later Aranesp was also approved. It also became a top-selling product. Neulasta was approved in 2002. Subsequent approvals were given to Sensipar Vectibix Nplate Prolia XGEVA BLINCYTO and Corlanor among others.

In 2011 Amgen partnered with Actavis to develop and commercialize oncology biosimilars which are similar to generic versions of other firms' drugs.

In 2015 the company bought Netherlands-based Dezima Pharma a biotechnology firm working on cardiovascular disease treatments. The $1.55 billion deal added Dezima's AMG 899 and Repatha (cholesterol inhibitors for patients with high lipids in the blood) to Amgen's portfolio.

EXECUTIVES

Senior Vice President Global Value Access And Policy, Joshua Ofman

Svp Us Commercial Operations, Laura Hamill

Evp Full Potential Initiatives, Brian M. McNamee, age 62

Svp Global Marketing And Commercial Development, Suzanne Blaug

Evp Global Commercial Operations, Anthony C. (Tony) Hooper, age 63, $1,031,788 total compensation

Svp General Counsel And Secretary, Jonathan P. Graham, age 57, $916,789 total compensation

Evp And Cfo, David W. Meline, age 60, $946,733 total compensation

Svp Global Business Services, Michael A. Kelly, age 61, $511,757 total compensation

Evp Research And Development, Sean E. Harper, age 55, $946,246 total compensation

Chairman And Ceo, Robert A. (Bob) Bradway, age 56, $1,531,731 total compensation

Svp Global Regulatory Affairs And Safety, Paul R. Eisenberg

Svp And Head European Region, Corinne Le Goff

Evp Operations, Esteban Santos

Vice President, Brian Kotzin

Medical Director, Lucy Yan

Vp Human Resources, John Oakes

First Vice President Wealth Management, Saket Malhotra

Senior Vice President Process Development, Jerry A Murry

Vice President Medical Sciences, David Reese

Vice President Global Regulatory Affairs, Mark Taisey Taisey

Vice President And Chief Financial Officer, Javier Orozco

Vice President And Chief Accounting Officer, George Revelle

Vice President Finance And Treasurer, Mary Lehmann

Vice President General Manager Germany, Roland Wandeler

National Sales Manager, Mike Ellis

Associate Medical Director Medical Affairs, Mark Rutstein

Vice President Corporate Accounts, Aston William

Vice President Of Pre Clinical Research, David Balaban

Vice President General Manager Us Bone Health Bu, Ken Keller

Administrative Coordinate Government Relations, Janice Vasquez

Senior Vice President Global Regulatory Affairs And Safety, Steven Galson

Vice President Operations, Martin Vantrieste

Medical Director, Maria Myagkikh

Senior Vice President Corporate Affairs, Raymond Jordan

Senior Vice President And Regional General Manager Europe, Gilles Marrache

Vp Of Marketing, Dave Marek

Senior Vice President Global Business Services And Finance, Judy Gawlik Brown

Executive Vice President Global Commercial Operations, Tony Hooper

Senior Vice President And Regional General Manager, Ian Thompson

Chairman And Ceo, Robert A. (Bob) Bradway, age 56

Treasurer, Loretta Joseph

Auditors: Ernst & Young LLP

LOCATIONS

HQ: Amgen Inc
One Amgen Center Drive, Thousand Oaks, CA 91320-1799
Phone: 805 447-1000   Fax: 805 447-1010
Web: www.amgen.com

2017 Sales

	$ mil.	% of total
U.S.	18,029	79
Rest of the world	4,820	21
Total	**22,849**	**100**

Selected Locations

Algeria
Australia
Austria
Belgium
Brazil
Bulgaria
Canada
China
Colombia
Croatia
Czech Republic
Denmark
Egypt
Estonia Japan
Finland
France
Germany
Greece
Hong Kong
Hungary
Iceland
India
Ireland
Italy
Latvia
Lithuania
Luxembourg
Mexico
Netherlands
Norway
Poland
Portugal
Romania
Russia
Saudi Arabia
Slovakia
Slovenia
South Africa
Spain
Sweden
Switzerland
Turkey
United Arab Emirates
United Kingdom
United States

PRODUCTS/OPERATIONS

2017 Sales

	$ mil.	% of total
Product sales	21,795	95
Other revenues	1,054	5
Total	**22,849**	**100**

2017 Sales

	$ mil.	% of total
ENBREL	5,433	24
Neulasta	4,534	20
Aranesp	2,053	9
Prolia	1,968	9
Sensipar/Mimpara	1,718	8
XGEVA	1,575	7
EPOGEN	1,096	5
NEUPOGEN	835	4
KYPROLIS	642	3
Vectibix	642	3
Nplate	549	2
Repatha	319	1
BLINCYTO	175	0
Other	256	1
Other revenues	1,054	4
Total	**22,849**	**100**

Top Selling Products
Neupogen/Neulasta (chemotherapy-induced neutropenia - low white blood cells and cancer-related infections)
Enbrel (rheumatoid arthritis psoriasis)
Aranesp (chemotherapy-induced anemia and chronic renal failure anemia sustained duration Epogen)
Epogen (anemia in chronic renal failure)
Sensipar/Mimpara (also known as Mimpara chronic kidney disease)
Xgeva (to prevent bone fractures)
Vectibix (monoclonal antibody for colorectal cancer)
Nplate (romiplostim for autoimmune bleeding disorder ITP or immune thrombocytopenic purpura)
Prolia (postmenopausal osteoporosis)

COMPETITORS

AbbVie	Merck
AstraZeneca	Merck KGaA
Bayer HealthCare Pharmaceuticals Inc.	Millennium: The Takeda Oncology Company
Celgene	Nektar Therapeutics
Chugai	Regeneron
Eli Lilly	Pharmaceuticals
Genentech	Sanofi
GlaxoSmithKline	Teva
Hospira	UCB
Janssen Biotech	

HISTORICAL FINANCIALS

Company Type: Public

Income Statement
FYE: December 31

	REVENUE ($ mil.)	NET INCOME ($ mil.)	NET PROFIT MARGIN	EMPLOYEES
12/17	22,849	1,979	8.7%	20,800
12/16	22,991	7,722	33.6%	19,200
12/15	21,662	6,939	32.0%	17,900
12/14	20,063	5,158	25.7%	17,900
12/13	18,676	5,081	27.2%	20,000
Annual Growth	**5.2%**	**(21.0%)**	**—**	**1.0%**

2017 Year-End Financials

Debt ratio: 44.20%	No. of shares (mil.): 722
Return on equity: 7.18%	Dividends
Cash ($ mil.): 3,800	Yield: 0.0%
Current ratio: 5.49	Payout: 171.0%
Long-term debt ($ mil.): 34,190	Market value ($ mil.): 125,591

	STOCK PRICE ($) FY Close	P/E High/Low	PER SHARE ($) Earnings	Dividends	Book Value
12/17	173.90	70 56	2.69	4.60	34.95
12/16	146.21	17 13	10.24	4.00	40.47
12/15	162.33	19 14	9.06	3.16	37.25
12/14	159.29	25 16	6.70	2.44	33.90
12/13	114.08	18 12	6.64	1.88	29.28
Annual Growth	**11.1%**	**—**	**(20.2%)**	**25.1%**	**4.5%**

Amphenol Corp.

A connected world needs connections at the basic level: from component to component and from device to device. That's where Amphenol Corp. comes in. The company is a leading manufacturer of connector and interconnect products for the communications industrial automotive aerospace and military markets. Amphenol's interconnect products are used to conduct electrical and optical signals in computers wired and wireless communications networking equipment vehicles aircraft and spacecraft and energy applications. Amphenol also makes high-speed and specialized coaxial cable. With customers in about 65 countries more than 70% of its sales come from outside the US.

Operations

Amphenol's Interconnect Products and Assemblies segment accounts for about 95% of sales with Cable Products and Solutions segment accounting for the rest. The cable group makes cables and components for the broadband communications and information technology markets.

In terms of markets information technology and data communications accounts for about 20% of revenue followed by mobile devices about 15%; automotive less than 10%; military and mobile networks about 10% each and broadband communications and commercial aerospace about 5% each.

Geographic Reach

Amphenol has about 420 locations — manufacturing facilities warehouses and offices — in about 30 countries around the world. The company handles its own manufacturing with facilities in low-cost manufacturing areas and near customers. The US and China each account for about 30% of Amphenol's sales with international sales (not counting China) supplying the rest.

Sales and Marketing

Amphenol's products have wide distribution winding up in more than 10000 customer locations worldwide (one customer can have components sent to multiple manufacturing locations). Its products are sold directly to original equipment manufacturers (OEMs) electronics manufacturing services (EMS) firms original design manufacturers (ODMs) cable system operators and IT companies. The company also sells through manufacturers' representatives and distributors which account for about 15% of revenue.

The company?s sales are heavily weighted in the communications industry. The combination of sales to information technology and data communication wireless communications and broadband communications companies adds up to about half of its revenue.

Financial Performance

Amphenol has been on an eight-year run of annual revenue increases averaging about 10%. Net income rose for seven straight years before falling in 2017.

Revenue increased about 12% to $7 billion in 2017 from 2016 led by gains in the automotive industrial and information technology and data communications markets. Only the mobile networks market showed a sales decline for the year as operators moderated network construction. Sales to customers in China and the US (totaling about 60% of company revenue) rose about 10% each.

Amphenol?s streak of rising profit was broken by the US Tax Cuts & Jobs Act enacted in late 2017. It heavily taxed profits repatriated from overseas dropping the company?s profit to $650 million off about 25% year-to-year.

Amphenol holds a good stash of cash with cash on hand rising to $1.7 billion in 2017 up from about $1 billion in 2016. Furthermore the company?s free cash flow also increased in 2017 reaching about $918 million from about $887 million in 2016 and about $860 million in 2015.

Strategy

The 2016 acquisition of FCI is emblematic of Amphenol?s strategy. Amphenol slotted FCI?s products into several of its product areas strengthening the company?s focus on a diverse balanced portfolio. None of the company?s lines of products account for more than about 20% of revenue. FCI was Amphenol?s biggest acquisition at $1.2 billion and contributed about 7% of revenue in its first year. Other recent acquisitions added complementary products to Amphenol?s industrial automotive IT and data communications and broadband markets.

Amphenol has been willing to buy what is doesn't have in-house making more than 20 acquisitions in the past five years.

The company also has embraced geographic diversity. China and the US are its biggest single country markets and international revenue not counting China provides about 40% of the total.

Amphenol places manufacturing facilities globally especially in low-cost areas.

Amphenol has maintained a handle on expenses even as sales have increased. The company has cut the cost of sales as a percentage of revenue for the past three years.

With much of its sales and operations overseas Amphenol could be affected by trade issues that erupted in early 2018. Tariffs set on goods by the US and China the company?s two biggest markets could have an impact of its pricing and its sales. In the Americas changes to the North American Free Trade Agreement (NAFTA) which were being negotiated in early 2018 also could affect Amphenol.

Mergers and Acquisitions

In 2017 Amphenol bought Phitek Systems Limited a New Zealand-based provider of interconnects for in-flight entertainment systems in commercial aircraft for about $60 million. The acquisition adds to Amphenol?s line of products used throughout airplanes a product line that accounts for less than 5% of revenue.

Other acquisitions strengthened Amphenol?s automotive business (about 20% of revenue). In late 2017 the company closed on its acquisition of Sunpool the China-based company that makes antennas for the Chinese automotive market. The company made several other acquisitions in 2017 for a total of about $200 million.

In early 2018 Amphenol acquired CTI Industries based in Canada. Applications for CTI's cable assemblies include automotive embedded computing and industrial.

In 2016 Amphenol made one of its bigger deals spending about $1.2 billion of FCI Electronics a maker of interconnect products. The addition of FCI expands Amphenol range of products as well as its markets. Other 2016 acquisitions included Auxel Custom Cable SGX Sensortech and All Systems Broadband.

Company Background

Amphenol was founded in 1932 to make sockets to plug vacuum tubes into radios. Its first customer was RCA.

EXECUTIVES

Svp And Group General Manager It And Communications Products Division, Richard E. (Rick) Schneider, age 60, $490,000 total compensation

President Ceo And Director, Richard A. (Adam) Norwitt, age 49, $1,061,000 total compensation

Svp And Group General Manager Military And Aerospace Operations Group, Luc Walter, age 59, $560,000 total compensation

Svp And Cfo, Craig A. Lampo, age 48, $450,000 total compensation

Svp And Group General Manager Worldwide Rf And Microwave Products, Zachary W. Raley, age 49, $500,000 total compensation

Vp And Group General Manager Global Interconnect Systems Group, Jean-Luc Gavelle, age 58

Vp And Group General Manager Automotive And Sensor Products Division, John Treanor, age 60

Vp And Group General Manager Industrial Products Group, Martin W. Booker, age 59

Vp And Group General Manager It Communications Products Group, William J. Doherty, age 59

Vp And General Manager Mobile Consumer Products Group, Yaobin (Richard) Gu

Vice President And Corporate Controller, Michael Ivas

Vice President Tax, Tom Meotti

Chairman, Martin H. Loeffler, age 74

President Ceo And Director, Richard A. (Adam) Norwitt, age 49

Auditors: DELOITTE & TOUCHE LLP

LOCATIONS

HQ: Amphenol Corp.
358 Hall Avenue, Wallingford, CT 06492
Phone: 203 265-8900   **Fax:** 203 265-8746
Web: www.amphenol.com

2017 Sales

	$ mil.	% of total
China	2,067	30
US	1,978	28
Other countries	2,965	42
Total	**7,011**	**100**

PRODUCTS/OPERATIONS

2017 Sales

	$ mil.	% of total
Interconnect products & assemblies	6,606	94
Cable products	404	6
Total	**7,011**	**100**

Selected Brands

Amphenol
Kai Jack
Matrix
Pyle-National
Sine
Socapex
Spectra-Strip
Times Fiber
Tuchel

Selected Products

Interconnect products
  Automotive interconnect systems
  CATV interconnects
  Data/telecom connectors
  Fiber-optic connectors and systems
  Filter connectors
  Flexible circuit interconnects
  High-performance connectors
  Industrial power connectors
  Radio-frequency coaxial connectors
  Smart card connectors
Cable products
  Electronic cable
  Engineered cable assemblies
  Times Fiber coaxial cable
  Wireless cable products
Other
  Mobile and portable antennas

COMPETITORS

3M	Methode Electronics
ARRIS	Molex
AVX	Northrop Grumman
Alcatel-Lucent	Panduit
Belden	Radiall
Carlisle Companies	Sensata
CommScope	Smiths Group
Corning	Spirent
Delphi Automotive	Sumitomo Electric
Systems	TE Connectivity
Esterline	TT electronics
FCI	Telect
Hirose Electric	Thomas & Betts
Hon Hai	Tri-Star Electronics
Huber + Suhner Inc.	International
Japan Aviation	Yazaki
Electronics Industry	

Company Type: Public

Income Statement   FYE: December 31

	REVENUE ($ mil.)	NET INCOME ($ mil.)	NET PROFIT MARGIN	EMPLOYEES
12/17	7,011	650	9.3%	70,000
12/16	6,286	822	13.1%	62,000
12/15	5,568	763	13.7%	50,700
12/14	5,345	709	13.3%	50,700
12/13	4,614	635	13.8%	44,500
Annual Growth	11.0%	0.6%	—	12.0%

2017 Year-End Financials

Debt ratio: 35.41%
Return on equity: 16.97%
Cash ($ mil.): 1,719
Current ratio: 2.95
Long-term debt ($ mil.): 3,541

No. of shares (mil.): 305
Dividends
  Yield: 0.0%
  Payout: 33.9%
Market value ($ mil.): 26,840

	STOCK PRICE ($) FY Close	P/E High/Low	PER SHARE ($) Earnings	Dividends	Book Value
12/17	87.80	43 31	2.06	0.70	13.05
12/16	67.20	26 17	2.61	0.58	11.92
12/15	52.23	24 20	2.41	0.53	10.51
12/14	53.81	47 20	2.21	0.45	9.38
12/13	89.18	44 32	1.96	0.31	9.04
Annual Growth	(0.4%)	— —	—	1.3% 23.1%	9.6%

Anadarko Petroleum Corp

Anadarko Petroleum has ventured beyond its original area of operation — the Anadarko Basin — to explore for develop produce and market oil natural gas natural gas liquids and related products worldwide. The company boasts reported proved reserves (90% of which is located in the US) of 1.7 billion barrels of oil equivalent. Additional assets include coal trona (natural soda ash) and other minerals. Anadarko operates a handful of gas-gathering systems in the Mid-Continent. Internationally the company has substantial oil and gas interests in Algeria. It also has holdings in Brazil Mozambique and West Africa.

Operations

Anadarko operates three segments: Oil and Gas Midstream and Marketing.

The Oil and Gas segment explores for and produces oil natural gas and NGLs (natural gas liquids). Its properties in the US consist of some 12700 wells (and 3500 nonoperated wells) across in DJ Basin in Colorado; Delaware Basin Eagleford and Eaglebine in Texas; Greater Natural Buttes in Utah; Greater Green River Basin in Wyoming; and Marcellus in Pennsylvania. It also has operations in Lousiana and Kansas. Internationally in Algeria the company works Blocks 404 and 208 in the Sahara Desert where it has a 24.5% stake; the offshore West Cape Three Points block and Deepwater Tano Block in Ghana; and Offshore Area 1 in Mozambique.

The Marketing segment brings in nearly 45% of sales and actively manages Anadarko's worldwide oil natural gas and NGLs sales minimizing market-related shut-ins maximizing realized prices and managing credit risk exposure.

Accounting for over 5% of sales the Midstream segment aids the oil and gas segment by conducting gas gathering processing transportation and produced-water disposal. It has 34 gathering systems and 72 processing and treating facilities.

Geographic Reach

Texas-based Anadarko's assets include US onshore resource plays in the Rocky Mountains area the southern US and the Appalachian basin. It is one the largest independent producers in the deep-water Gulf of Mexico and has production and exploration activities worldwide including high-potential basins located in Alaska Algeria Brazil CA?te d'Ivoire Ghana Kenya Mozambique New Zealand and other countries.

The US is Anadarko's largest market and accounts for more than 80% of the company's total revenue. Algeria is its primary non-US territory at nearly 15% of sales; other countries account for the remainder.

Sales and Marketing

Anadarko sells crude oil and natural gas via a range of contractual agreements including indexed fixed-price and cost-escalation-based agreements. Most of the company's US oil condensate and NGLs production is sold under contracts.

The company's oil is primarily sold to marketers gatherers and refiners. Natural gas is sold mainly to interstate and intrastate natural gas pipelines direct end-users industrial users local distribution companies and natural gas marketers.

Anadarko is contractually committed to deliver nearly 900 billion cu. ft. of natural gas to various US customers through 2031. It also delivers some 10 million barrels of oil to ports in Algeria and Ghana.

Financial Performance

Weak international oil and natural gas prices have put a huge dent in Anadarko's revenue since 2014.

In fiscal 2016 sales fell a further 10% to $8.4 billion as overall oil production volumes remained steady while prices fell further. Natural gas prices likewise fell as did production. On the upside the company recorded an $88 million improvement in NGLs (natural gas liquids) sales and a $68 million increase in gathering processing and marketing. The latter related to higher gas and NGLs volumes at the DJ Basin and DBM Complex.

Anadarko posted its third consecutive net loss in 2016 as gas prices remained below the break-even point and it suffered hefty write-downs of its producing assets values. In fiscal 2016 the company reduced its net loss to $3.1 billion due to lower impairment charges and layoffs.

Cash from operations was considerably higher in 2016 than 2015 at $3.0 billion versus a cash outflow of $1.9 billion. The improvement relates to the $5.2 billion settlement Anadarko paid in 2015 for environmental damages. Aside from this item operating cash flow benefited from a $881 million tax refund.

Strategy

To cope with revenue falls and heavy losses Anadarko has been selling off $4 billion of assets including in its US Onshore Marcellus and Eagle Ford oil and gas assets as well as its interest in Springfield Pipeline. It also sold shares in Western Gas Equity Partners. Additionally in 2016 Anadarko reduced capital expenditure by 44% laid off 17% of its workforce carried out layoffs and reduced dividends.

The extra liquidity offered by the sales will allow Anadarko to develop its higher margin properties such as Delaware Basin in Texas and DJ Basin in Colorado as well as its deepwater assets in the Gulf of Mexico — it made a major Gulf acquisition in 2016. With gas prices having risen somewhat since 2016 the company has more scope for capital expenditure. It ramped up its capital program to

$4.7 billion 80% of which will be put towards its US onshore upstream and midstream activities and in the Gulf of Mexico.

Mergers and Acquisitions

In 2016 Anadarko acquired the deepwater Gulf of Mexico assets of Freeport McMoRan Oil & Gas for $2 billion.

In 2015 Anadarko made a bid to acquire Apache which was rebuffed.

HISTORY

In 1959 the Panhandle Eastern Pipe Line Company set up Anadarko (named after the Anadarko Basin) to carry out its gas exploration and production activities. The new company was also formed to take advantage of a ruling by the Federal Power Commission (now the Federal Energy Regulatory Commission) to set lower price ceilings for producing properties owned by pipeline companies.

The company grew rapidly during the early 1960s largely because of its gas-rich namesake. It bought Ambassador Oil of Fort Worth Texas in 1965 — adding interests in 19 states in the US and Canada. The firm also relocated from Kansas to Fort Worth.

Anadarko began offshore exploration in the Gulf of Mexico in 1970 and focused there early in the decade. After moving to Houston in 1974 Anadarko increased its oil exploration activities when the energy crisis led to higher gas prices. A deal with Amoco (now part of BP) led to major finds on Matagorda Island off the Texas coast in the early 1980s.

To realize shareholder value Panhandle spun off Anadarko in 1986 — separating transmission from production. At the time more than 90% of Anadarko's reserves were natural gas. The next year Anadarko made new discoveries in Canada.

Low domestic natural gas prices led Anadarko overseas. It signed a production-sharing agreement with Algeria's national oil and gas firm SONATRACH in 1989. The deal covered 5.1 million acres in the Sahara. Two years later Anadarko began operating in the South China Sea and in Alaska's North Slope.

Back home the company spent $190 million in 1992 for properties in West Texas and in 1993 Anadarko began divesting noncore assets. Along with some of its partners the company also discovered oil in the Mahogany Field offshore Louisiana. Production from Mahogany began in 1996.

In 1997 Anadarko added exploration acreage in the North Atlantic and Tunisia.

Anadarko expanded its presence in western Canada in 2001 by buying Berkley Petroleum for more than $1 billion in cash and assumed debt.

Expanding its presence and asset base in the lucrative resource plays in the Rocky Mountains and the deepwater Gulf of Mexico in 2006 Anadarko acquired midstream operator Western Gas and fellow explorer Kerr-McGee for about $26 billion.

In 2013 Anadarko agreed to sell 10% of its property off the shores of Mozambique to Oil and Natural Gas Corp. Ltd. for $2.64 billion.

That year it acquired a number of US oil and gas assets for about $500 million.

EXECUTIVES

Evp Law And Chief Administrative Officer, Robert K. (Bobby) Reeves, age 60, $700,000 total compensation

Chairman President And Ceo, R. A. (Al) Walker, age 60, $1,300,000 total compensation

Evp Operations, Darrell E. Hollek, age 60

Evp Finance And Chief Financial Officer, Robert G. (Bob) Gwin, age 54, $750,000 total compensation

Evp International And Deepwater Exploration, Ernest A. Leyendecker, age 57, $473,654 total compensation

Evp Global Lng, Mitchell W. (Mitch) Ingram, age 55, $625,000 total compensation

Vice President, Philip Peacock

Vice President Tax, Aric Mann

Vice President Africa Operations, Byron McDonald

Finance Vice President, Dustin David

Senior Vice President Finance And Investor Relations, Mike Pearl

Vice President Administration, Frank Patterson

Vice President Advanced Analytics And Emerging Technologies, Sanjay Paranji

Vice President Human Resources, Joe Mongrain

Vice President Dj Basin Development, Carrie Horton

Chairman President And Ceo, R. A. (Al) Walker, age 60

Assistant Treasurer Western Gas Partners Lp, Nick Matovich

Auditors: KPMG LLP

LOCATIONS

HQ: Anadarko Petroleum Corp
1201 Lake Robbins Drive, The Woodlands, TX 77380-1046
Phone: 832 636-1000
Web: www.anadarko.com

Sales by Geography

	% of total
United States	83
Algeria	13
Other International	4
Total	**100**

PRODUCTS/OPERATIONS

Sales by Segment

	% of total
Oil and Gas Exploration & Production	50
Marketing	43
Midstream	7
Total	**100**

Sales by Products

	$ mil.	% of total
Oil sales	4,668	55
Natural-gas sales	1,564	19
Gathering processing and marketing sales	1,294	15
Natural-gas liquids sales	921	11
Gains (losses) on divestitures and other net	(578)	-
Total	**7,869**	**100**

COMPETITORS

Adams Resources	Exxon Mobil
Apache	Hunt Consolidated
BP	Jones Energy
Cabot Oil & Gas	Key Energy
Chesapeake Energy	National Fuel Gas
Chevron	Noble Energy
Cimarex	Pioneer Natural
ConocoPhillips	Resources
Devon Energy	Royal Dutch Shell
EOG	

HISTORICAL FINANCIALS

Company Type: Public

Income Statement   FYE: December 31

	REVENUE ($ mil.)	NET INCOME ($ mil.)	NET PROFIT MARGIN	EMPLOYEES
12/17	11,908	(456)	—	4,400
12/16	7,869	(3,071)	—	4,500
12/15	8,698	(6,692)	—	5,800
12/14	18,470	(1,750)	—	6,100
12/13	14,581	801	5.5%	5,700
Annual Growth	**(4.9%)**	—	—	**(6.3%)**

2017 Year-End Financials

Debt ratio: 37.28%
Return on equity: (-3.98%)
Cash ($ mil.): 4,553
Current ratio: 1.73
Long-term debt ($ mil.): 15,547
No. of shares (mil.): 530
Dividends
  Yield: 0.0%
  Payout: —
Market value ($ mil.): 28,472

	STOCK PRICE ($) FY Close	P/E High/Low		PER SHARE ($) Earnings	Dividends	Book Value
12/17	53.64	—	—	(0.85)	0.20	20.15
12/16	69.73	—	—	(5.90)	0.20	22.16
12/15	48.58	—	—	(13.18)	1.08	25.22
12/14	82.50	—	—	(3.47)	0.99	38.94
12/13	79.32	62	47	1.58	0.54	43.39
Annual Growth **(17.4%)**	**(9.3%)**	—	—	**—**	**(22.0%)**	

Analog Devices Inc

The world is becoming digitized and Analog Devices is paving the way. Its linear integrated circuits (ICs) translate real-world phenomena such as pressure temperature and sound into digital signals. The company is a leading maker of linear ICs as well as mixed-signal analog integrated circuits and digital ICs. Its 22000 devices include converters amplifiers power management products and digital signal processors (DSPs). The company's chips are used in industrial process controls medical and scientific instruments communications gear computers automobiles and consumer electronics. Analog Devices claims more than 125000 customers around the world with most revenue from customers outside the US.

Operations

Analog Devices' industrial segment accounts for about 45% of sales followed by ICs for communications and consumer applications with about 20% of sales each and automotive at about 15%.

The company makes some of its IC products and outsources some 60% of production to third-party manufacturers primarily Taiwan Semiconductor Manufacturing Co. The company follows the same pattern for testing operating some its assembly-and-test facilities as well as using third-party subcontractors.

Geographic Reach

The US is Analog Devices' single biggest market accounting for about 40% of sales followed by China with about 15% and Japan less than 10%. Customers in Europe account for about a quarter of ADI's revenue.

Headquartered in Norwood Massachusetts the company has facilities in the US the Philippines Ireland India and China. Analog Devices has wafer fab facilities in Wilmington Massachusetts and Limerick Ireland.

Sales and Marketing

Although more than 50% of the company's sales are made through distributors Analog Devices also sells through direct sales offices and sales representatives worldwide and via its website. Apple the company's biggest customer accounts for about an eighth of revenue. While Apple has been a strong customer for Analog Devices the phone and computer maker has been moving more of its technology needs in-house. Including Apple the company's 20 largest customers account for about 35% of revenue.

The company has no dominant product with its 10 highest revenue-producing offerings delivering about 15% of revenue.

Financial Performance

Revenue growth interrupted in 2016 resumed in 2017 (ended October) fueled by the acquisition of Linear Technology.

The company's revenue hit $5.1 billion in 2017 an increase of nearly 50% from 2016 with higher sales in the automotive industrial communications and consumer markets. Beyond the impact of the acquisition Analog Devices cited stronger demand for its industrial automotive and communications products. The acquisition also drove higher sales across geographic regions.

Costs associated with the Linear Technology acquisition and those stemming from cost reductions cut Analog Devices' net income 15% to just under $730 million.

The company had about $1 billion in cash on hand at the end of 2017 with about $600 of that amount held overseas.

Strategy

Analog Devices' nearly $15 billion Linear Technology acquisition which closed in 2017 was a major step in the company's expansion of its products and markets. With Linear Analog Devices grabs high-ranking market share across data convertors power management amplifiers interface and high-performance radio frequency and microwave devices. ADI expects the business combination to achieve about $150 million in manufacturing and operating savings. Some of those savings are to come from the closure of a wafer fabrication facility in the US and a test facility in Singapore.

Besides reeling in the big Linear Technology fish Analog Devices has made smaller acquisitions to provide more capabilities that provide additional value to its customers. Transactions have brought board technologies for internet of things applications cloud security and LIDAR.

Mergers and Acquisitions

Analog Devices agreed to buy OneTree Microdevices for an undisclosed amount in March 2017. lone Tree is a fabless semiconductor company with a GaAs and GaN amplifier portfolio for cable TV and fiber-to-the-home applications. The acquisition extends Analog's product lineup to those uses.

ADI concluded its acquisition of Linear Technology also a maker of analog ICs for about $15 billion in 2017. While both companies produce analog devices their product mixes are complementary executives said. The acquisition should expand ADI's possible market from $8 billion to $14 billion. Linear posted profit of about $494 million on $1.4 billion in revenue in 2016 (ended June).

In 2016 ADI acquired SNAP Sensor SA a privately held company that specializes in vision sensing technologies. The acquisition advances ADI's leadership position in sensing and signal processing and build upon platform-level internet of things products such as ADI's Blackfin Low Power Imaging Platform.

ADI also made acquisitions concentrated in autonomous vehicles. ADI acquired Innovasic a developer of Ethernet technology that allows for deterministic real-time communication; the cyber security products of Sypris which can provide customers with sensor-to-cloud security products; and technology from Vescent Photonics that should help ADI develop a solid state scanning LIDAR system that complements its RADAR-based ADAS products.

ADI acquired Hittite Microwave Corporation in 2014 for $2.4 billion. Adding Hittite technologies strengthens ADI's capabilities in RF microwave and millimeter wave applications for developing products for industrial healthcare aerospace and defense automotive safety and communications infrastructure applications.

Vp; General Manager Computer And Networking Products Division, Vincent T. Roche, age 58, $827,692 total compensation

Svp Global Operations And Technology, Joseph (John) Hassett, age 60

Svp And Cto, Peter Real, age 58, $376,008 total compensation

Svp Communications And Automotive Business Group, Rick D. Hess, age 64, $519,231 total compensation

Svp Worldwide Sales And Digital Marketing, Martin Cotter, age 53

Svp Finance And Cfo, Prashanth Mahendra-Rajah, age 48

Vice President Finance And Supply Chain, Jim Mollica

Chairman, Ray Stata, age 84

Auditors: Ernst & Young LLP

LOCATIONS

HQ: Analog Devices Inc
One Technology Way, Norwood, MA 02062-9106
Phone: 781 329-4700
Web: www.analog.com

2017 Sales

	% of total
United States	39
Rest of North and South America	2
Europe	24
Japan	10
China	16
Rest of Asia	9
Total	**100**

PRODUCTS/OPERATIONS

2017 Sales

	% of total
Industrial	46
Automotive	15
Consumer	21
Communications	18
Total	**100**

COMPETITORS

Analogic	Maxim Integrated
Broadcom	Products
Cirrus Logic	Microchip Technology
Conexant Systems	Microsemi
Custom Sensors &	NXP Semiconductors
Technologies	ON Semiconductor
DENSO	Qualcomm CDMA
DSP Group	ROHM
Fairchild	Robert Bosch
Semiconductor	STMicroelectronics
Infineon Technologies	Semtech
Integrated Device	Silicon Image
Technology	Silicon Labs
Intersil	Siliconix
Linear Technology	Skyworks
Marvell Technology	Texas Instruments

HISTORICAL FINANCIALS

Company Type: Public

Income Statement   FYE: November 3

	REVENUE ($ mil.)	NET INCOME ($ mil.)	NET PROFIT MARGIN	EMPLOYEES
11/18*	6,200	1,495	24.1%	15,800
10/17	5,107	727	14.2%	15,300
10/16	3,421	861	25.2%	10,000
10/15	3,435	696	20.3%	9,700
11/14	2,864	629	22.0%	9,600
Annual Growth	**21.3%**	**24.2%**	**—**	**13.3%**

*Fiscal year change

Debt ratio: 30.97%	No. of shares (mil.): 370
Return on equity: 13.91%	Dividends
Cash ($ mil.): 816	Yield: 0.0%
Current ratio: 1.50	Payout: 47.6%
Long-term debt ($ mil.): 6,265	Market value ($ mil.): 32,271

	STOCK PRICE ($) FY Close	P/E High/Low		PER SHARE ($) Earnings	Dividends	Book Value
11/18*	87.18	25	19	3.97	1.89	29.69
10/17	91.21	44	30	2.07	1.77	27.57
10/16	63.53	23	18	2.76	1.66	16.76
10/15	60.12	31	22	2.20	1.57	16.26
11/14	49.62	28	21	1.98	1.45	15.29
Annual Growth	**15.1%**	**—**	**—**	**19.0%**	**6.8%**	**18.0%**

*Fiscal year change

Anixter International Inc

Anixter International is a global distributor of network security and communication components and systems. It sells 600000-plus products — including electrical and electronic wire; copper fiber and coaxial cabling; security system components; and equipment racks and cabinets — to more than 135000 customers across a host of industries. Network and security products account for more than half of sales. Anixter also offers value-added supply chain services such as inventory management logistics sourcing and product enhancement and packaging. The company operates from warehouses and sales centers in some 50 countries although more than 80% of sales are generated in North America.

Operations

Anixter operates through three distinct segments: Network & Security Solutions (NSS) Electrical & Electronic Solutions (EES) and Utility Power Solutions (UPS).

NSS (which accounts for more than 50% of sales) offers a variety of products that run the gamut from copper and fiber optic cable and connectivity products to video surveillance and fire safety products to cabinets and cable management equipment.

EES (nearly 30%) offers several product lines of electrical and electronic wire and cable industrial communication and control products industrial Ethernet switches and voice and data cable.

UPS (about 20%) supplies electrical transmission and distribution products power plant maintenance and repair and operations supplies to the utilities and electrical markets. It also sells smart-grid products conductors transformers and switches.

Geographic Reach

Anixter's distribution network consists of more than 300 locations in about 50 countries with 9 million sq. ft. of space. This total includes around 20 regional distribution centers more than 40 local distribution centers about 180 service centers and some 70 branch locations. It also has roughly 75 sales offices worldwide.

The company is heavily reliant on North America which accounts for more than 80% of revenue; emerging markets (primarily the Asia-Pacific and Latin America regions) contribute about 10% and the EMEA region generates nearly 10%.

Sales and Marketing

More than two dozen industries are represented among Anixter's well-diversified customer base — markets such as education government health care manufacturing retail and transportation. The company also serves contractors and integrators who install and maintain communications networks and data centers. International national regional and local OEMs number among Anixter's customers as well procuring wire cable fasteners and other small components to help finish the manufacturing of their own products typically with short lead times.

Anixter's advertising expenses were $10.6 million in 2017 compared to $12.4 million in 2016 and $13.2 million in 2015.

Financial Performance

Anixter has seen strong top-line growth over the past five years with revenue jumping 50% since 2013 in large part propelled by acquisitions. Net income however has gone in the opposite direction falling about 45% over the same time period.

In 2017 the company reported record revenue of $7.9 billion up 4% from the prior year. It saw growth in all three segments (led by UPS) and all three regions (led by North America). UPS sales were up about 11% as a result of growth among existing customers and a new investor-owned utility customer. EES and NSS sales were up about 6% and 1% respectively.

Anixter's net income declined 10% in 2017 to $109 million primarily because income tax expense jumped nearly 70% as part of the one-time impact from The Tax Cuts and Jobs Act of 2017.

Cash at the end of fiscal 2017 was $116 million about the same as 2016. Cash from operations contributed $184 million to the coffers while investing activities used $41 million mainly for capital expenditures. Financing activities used another $136 million for repayments of borrowings and a Canadian term loan.

Strategy

Through both acquisitions and divestitures over the past few years Anixter has positioned itself as a global leader in three primary areas — network infrastructure and security electrical and electronic wire and cable and utility power services. Going forward it is focused on fully integrating its past acquisitions and growing not only through future acquisitions but organically through cross-selling and new and enhanced products and services.

As it works to eliminate redundancies and deliver cost savings from its recent acquisitions the company has identified a handful of areas ripe for growth: security solutions emerging markets utilities professional audio/visual industrial communications and control and in-building wireless. Anixter has introduced several new products in security (perimeter protection network cameras) and industrial communications and control (ethernet switches).

It is also growing its product and service lines geographically including further expanding its security products into Canada Mexico and the EMEA region and pushing its utility products into Western Canada and Mexico. The company also strengthened its Asia-Pacific operations via acquisition.

Mergers and Acquisitions

In mid-2018 Anixter paid about $150 million for three security products businesses in Australia/New Zealand. The deal strengthens the company's competitive position and adds new products and services to its portfolio.

HISTORY

Anixter International was founded in 1957 by two brothers Alan and Bill Anixter along with a small group of employees in Evanston Illinois. The company was known as Anixter Brothers at the time and it supplied distributors and wholesalers looking for an alternative to buying wire and cable in bulk quantities directly from manufacturers. The company went public on the American Stock Exchange in 1967. Anixter became an international company when Anixter United Kingdom was formed in 1972.

EXECUTIVES

Evp And Cfo, Theodore A. (Ted) Dosch, age 58, $595,000 total compensation

Evp Human Resources, Rodney A. Smith, age 60, $300,000 total compensation

Evp General Counsel And Corporate Secretary, Justin C. Choi, age 52, $455,000 total compensation

Ceo And Director, Robert J. (Bob) Eck, age 59, $980,000 total compensation

President And Coo, William A. (Bill) Galvin, age 55, $525,000 total compensation

Evp Operations, William A. (Bill) Standish, age 63, $455,000 total compensation

Evp Electrical And Electronic Solutions, Robert M. (Bob) Graham, age 50

Evp And Cio, Scott Ramsbottom, age 44

Evp Network And Security Solutions, William C. Geary, age 48

Vice President Marketing, Scott Quinton

Chairman, Samuel Zell, age 76

Evp General Counsel And Corporate Secretary, Justin C. Choi, age 52

Ceo And Director, Robert J. (Bob) Eck, age 59

Auditors: Ernst & Young LLP

LOCATIONS

HQ: Anixter International Inc
  2301 Patriot Blvd., Glenview, IL 60026
Phone: 224 521-8000
Web: www.anixter.com

2017 Sales

	$ mil.	% of total
North America	6,544	82
EMEA	626	8
Emerging Markets	757	10
Total	**7,927**	**100**

PRODUCTS/OPERATIONS

2017 Sales

	$ mil.	% of total
NSS	4,114	52
EES	2,225	28
UPS	1,587	20
Total	**7,927**	**100**

Selected Products

Wire and Cable
  Electrical Wire and Cable
  Electronic Wire and Cable
  Voice and Data Cable
Communications
  Copper Cabling Infrastructure
  Fiber Optic Cabling Infrastructure
  Coaxial Cabling Infrastructure
  Voice Products
  Telecom Power Products
  Software
Security
  Video Surveillance
  Access Control
  Electrified Door Hardware
  Mechanical Door Hardware
  Intrusion Detection
  Fire Alarm Systems
  Professional AV
  Other Security Products
Networking
  Networking
  In-building Wireless
  CATV Video
  Intelligent Lighting
Hardware and Supplies

Racks And Cabinets
Cable Management
Test Equipment
Tools and Supplies
Power Products
Electrical Supplies
Industrial Communication and Control
  Industrial Communication and Control
  Electrical Enclosures

COMPETITORS

Arrow Electronics	Rexel
Avnet	ScanSource
Belden	Tech Data
Fastenal	W.W. Grainger
General Cable	WESCO International
HWC	Watsco
MSC Industrial Direct	

HISTORICAL FINANCIALS

Company Type: Public

Income Statement

FYE: December 29

	REVENUE ($ mil.)	NET INCOME ($ mil.)	NET PROFIT MARGIN	EMPLOYEES
12/17	7,927	109	1.4%	8,900
12/16*	7,622	120	1.6%	8,900
01/16	6,190	127	2.1%	8,700
01/15	6,445	194	3.0%	9,100
01/14	6,226	200	3.2%	8,200
Annual Growth	**6.2%**	**(14.1%)**	—	**2.1%**

*Fiscal year change

2017 Year-End Financials

Debt ratio: 29.35%	No. of shares (mil.): 33
Return on equity: 7.95%	Dividends
Cash ($ mil.): 116	Yield: —
Current ratio: 2.10	Payout: —
Long-term debt ($ mil.): 1,247	Market value ($ mil.): 2,558

	STOCK PRICE ($) FY Close	P/E High/Low	PER SHARE ($) Earnings	Dividends	Book Value
12/17	76.00	27 19	3.21	0.00	43.35
12/16*	81.05	23 11	3.59	0.00	38.64
01/16	60.39	23 15	3.81	0.00	35.44
01/15	88.18	18 13	5.84	0.00	34.19
01/14	89.61	15 11	6.04	5.00	31.27
Annual Growth	**(4.0%)**	—	**—(14.6%)**	—	**8.5%**

*Fiscal year change

Annaly Capital Management Inc

A real estate investment trust (REIT) Annaly Capital Management invests in and finances residential and commercial assets. It primarily manages a portfolio of mortgage-backed securities including mortgage pass-through certificates collateralized mortgage obligations and agency callable debentures. Commencing operations in 1997 the firm typically invests in high-quality securities issued or guaranteed by the likes of Freddie Mac Fannie Mae and Ginnie Mae and backed by single-family residential mortgages. More than 90% of Annaly's assets are agency mortgage-backed securities which carry an implied AAA rating. The firm is externally managed by Annaly Management Company LLC.

Operations

Annaly invests through four primary groups: Agency Residential Credit Commercial Real Estate and Middle Market Lending. The Agency group primarily invests in agency mortgage-backed securities and related derivatives. The Residential Credit group invests in non-agency mortgage-backed assets within securitized products and residential mortgage loan markets. Commercial Real Estate writes and invests in commercial mortgage loans securities and related assets and Middle Market Lending provides customized debt financing to middle-market businesses.

Financial Performance

Annaly's net interest income which comprises the bulk of its annual revenue has been in a slow decline over the last few years. In fiscal 2017 net interest income fell 4% to $1.5 billion as growth in interest earning assets was offset by a higher increase in interest bearing liabilities. Total assets reached a record $99.9 billion a 17% increase.

Net income in 2017 was up 10% to $1.6 billion as lower net interest income was offset by higher realized and unrealized gains higher other income and lower general and administrative expenses.

The company recorded an $833.2 million decrease in cash on hand in 2017 with its coffers standing at $706.6 million at the end of the period.

Strategy

Annaly makes its money based on the interest rate spread: When interest rates go down Annaly's returns tend to go up. It does this by borrowing short-term loans which typically carry lower interest rates and using that money to invest in mortgage-backed securities which typically carry higher rates. As such the troubled economy actually benefited the REIT as lowered short-term interest rates translated into higher interest income.

However in an environment where the Federal Reserve has carried out interest rate hikes Annaly's strategy of earning income from the spread could be threatened. With rate hikes expected to continue the REIT is increasingly focusing on gains from its credit assets investment portfolio which are tied to long-term rates.

In addition to funding purchases of mortgage-backed securities through short-term repurchase agreements Annaly raises investment funds through equity and debt offerings. It seeks to minimize prepayment risk by structuring a diversified portfolio with a variety of prepayment characteristics and through other means; it also increases the size of its balance sheet when opportunities are likely to allow growth in earnings per share.

In mid-2017 Annaly sold Pingora Holdings (acquired the previous year with the purchase of Hatteras Financial) to Bayview Asset Management. Pingora is a specialized asset manager focused on investing in mortgage servicing rights and servicing residential mortgages.

Mergers and Acquisitions

In September 2018 Annaly acquired MTGE Investment Corp. for $900 million. MTGE is an investment trust that invests in and manages a leveraged portfolio of agency mortgage investments non-agency mortgage investments and other real estate-related investments. The acquisition enhances the scale liquidity and access to capital of Annaly's platform.

EXECUTIVES

Cfo, Glenn A. Votek, age 59, $91,346 total compensation

Chairman President And Ceo, Kevin G. Keyes, age 50, $375,000 total compensation

Chief Legal Officer, Anthony C. Green

Chief Investment Officer, David L. Finkelstein, age 45

Chief Credit Officer, Timothy P. Coffey, age 44
Chairman President And Ceo, Kevin G. Keyes, age 50
Auditors: Ernst & Young LLP

LOCATIONS

HQ: Annaly Capital Management Inc
1211 Avenue of the Americas, New York, NY 10036
Phone: 212 696-0100   **Fax:** 212 696-9809
Web: www.annaly.com

COMPETITORS

AG Mortgage Investment Trust	Institutional Financial Markets
Capstead Mortgage	JAVELIN Mortgage
Drive Shack	MFA Financial
Impac Mortgage Holdings	Redwood Trust
	iStar Financial Inc

HISTORICAL FINANCIALS

Company Type: Public

Income Statement

FYE: December 31

	ASSETS ($ mil.)	NET INCOME ($ mil.)	INCOME AS % OF ASSETS	EMPLOYEES
12/17	101,760	1,569	1.5%	152
12/16	87,905	1,433	1.6%	189
12/15	75,190	466	0.6%	149
12/14	88,355	(842)	—	25
12/13	81,922	3,729	4.6%	48
Annual Growth	5.6%	(19.5%)	—	33.4%

2017 Year-End Financials

Debt ratio: 7.00%
Return on equity: 11.44%
Cash ($ mil.): 706
Current ratio: —
Long-term debt ($ mil.): —
No. of shares (mil.): 1,159
Dividends
Yield: 0.2%
Payout: 181.4%
Market value ($ mil.): 13,787

	STOCK PRICE ($) FY Close	P/E High/Low		PER SHARE ($) Earnings	Dividends	Book Value
12/17	11.89	9	7	1.37	2.49	12.82
12/16	9.97	8	6	1.39	3.17	12.33
12/15	9.38	26	22	0.42	1.20	12.71
12/14	10.81	—	—	(0.96)	1.20	14.06
12/13	9.97	4	3	3.74	1.50	13.09
Annual Growth	4.5%	—		(22.2%)	13.5%	(0.5%)

Anthem Inc

Health benefits provider Anthem through a number of subsidiaries provides health coverage to more than 40 million members in the US. One of the nation?s largest health insurers Anthem is a Blue Cross and Blue Shield Association licensee in more than a dozen states (where it operates as Anthem Empire and BCBS) and provides plans under the Unicare Amerigroup CareMore Simply Healthcare HealthSun and HealthLink names in other states. Plans include PPO HMO POS indemnity and hybrid plans offered to employers individuals and Medicare and Medicaid recipients. Anthem also provides administrative services to self-insured groups as well as specialty insurance. In 2017 a federal judge blocked the planned merger between Anthem and rival Cigna.

HISTORY

Anthem's earliest predecessor prepaid hospital plan Blue Cross of Indiana was founded in 1944. Unlike other Blues Blue Cross of Indiana never received tax advantages or mandated discounts so it competed as a private insurer. Within two years it had 100000 members; by 1970 there were nearly 2 million.

Blue Shield of Indiana another Anthem precursor also grew rapidly after its 1946 formation as a mutual insurance company to cover doctors' services. The two organizations shared expenses and jointly managed the state's Medicare and Medicaid programs.

The 1970s and early 1980s were difficult as Indiana's economy stagnated and health insurance competition increased. In 1982 the joint operation restructured adding new management and service policies to improve its performance.

Following the 1982 merger of the national Blue Cross and Blue Shield organizations the Indiana Blues merged in 1985 as Associated Insurance Companies. The next year the company moved outside Indiana began diversifying to help insulate itself from such industry changes as the shift to managed care and renamed itself Associated Group to reflect a broader focus.

By 1990 Associated Group had more than 25 operating units with nationwide offerings including health insurance HMO services life insurance insurance brokerage financial services and software and services for the insurance industry.

The group grew throughout the mid-1990s buying health insurer Southeastern Mutual Insurance (including Kentucky Blue Cross and Blue Shield) in 1992 diversified insurer Federal Kemper (a Kemper Corporation subsidiary) in 1993 and Seattle-based property/casualty brokerage Pettit-Morry in 1994. That year it entered the health care delivery market with the creation of American Health Network.

In 1995 the company merged with Ohio Blues licensee Community Mutual and took the Anthem name. Merger-related charges caused a loss that year.

Anthem bounced back the next year thanks to cost-cutting and customers switching to its more profitable managed care plans. Anthem divested its individual life insurance and annuity business and its Anthem Financial subsidiaries. Its 1996 deal to buy Blue Cross and Blue Shield of New Jersey fell apart in 1997 because of New Jersey Blue's charitable status. Anthem did manage to buy Blue Cross and Blue Shield of Connecticut that year.

Anthem in 1997 sold four property/casualty insurance subsidiaries to Vesta Insurance Group. It bought the remainder of its Acordia property/casualty unit (workers' compensation) then sold Acordia's brokerage operations. That year Anthem was involved in court battles regarding the Blue mergers in Kentucky as well as in Connecticut where litigants feared a rise in their premiums. Expenses related to merging Blues organizations contributed to a loss that year.

Anthem shed the rest of its noncore operations in 1998 selling subsidiary Anthem Health and Life Insurance Company to Canadian insurer Great-West Life Assurance. Its proposed purchase of Blue Cross and Blue Shield of Maine (which it acquired in 2000) and merger with the Blues in Rhode Island were met with outcries similar to those that dogged earlier pairings.

Larry Glasscock was appointed president and CEO of the company in 1999. Under Glasscock's leadership Anthem aggressively expanded through mergers and acquisitions. It bought Blues plans in Colorado Nevada and New Hampshire in 1999

and finalized the acquisition of Maine's Blue plan in 2000.

In 2001 it became a publicly traded company and sold its military insurance business to Humana. In the next couple of years it snapped up Virginia-based Trigon Healthcare and a Wisconsin Blue plan.

And in 2004 Anthem made its biggest leap yet merging with WellPoint Health Networks in a deal that made it the nation's largest health insurer. After the merger — which added Blue plans in California Georgia Missouri and Wisconsin — Anthem changed its name to WellPoint.

EXECUTIVES

Evp And Chief Administrative Officer, Gloria M. McCarthy, age 65, $699,999 total compensation
President Ceo And Director, Gail K. Boudreaux
Evp And Cfo, John E. Gallina, age 58, $623,918 total compensation
Evp And President Government Business, Peter D. Haytaian, age 48, $740,371 total compensation
Evp And General Counsel, Thomas C. Zielinski, age 67
President Commercial Plan, Brian T. Griffin, age 59, $740,368 total compensation
Evp And Chief Clinical Officer, Craig E. Samitt, age 53
President Medicare East Region, Tomas Orozco
President Life And Disability, Greg Poulakos
President Specialty, Nicholas L. Brecker
Senior Vice President; President And Chief Executive Officer Anthem National Accounts, John Langenus
Executive Vice President Chief Human Resources Officer, Jose Tomas
Assistant Vice President Information Technology Project Management Office, Sheri Coyner
Regional Vice President Of Sales And Account Mana, Paul Nobile
Vice President Finance Medicaid, Aimee Dailey
Vice President Provdr Cost Containmnt Sols, Tracey Healey
Vice President Corporate Accounting And Reporting, Ryan Judy
Vice President Financial Aid Processing, John Murphy
Vice President Investor Relations, Doug Simpson
Executive Vice President And President And Chief Executive Officer Commercial And Specialty Busines, Ken Goulet
Medical Director And State, Kimberly L Roop
Vice President National Accounts Underwriting, Andrea Schell
Vice President Marketing, James Jackson
Senior Vice President Public Affairs, Julie Goon
Vice President Strategy Planningandexecution, Manan Shah
Medical Director, Ronald Koenig
Staff Vice President Business Continuation, Steve Labrique
Staff Vice President Systems Migration, Tracy Tutson
Vice President And Counsel, Ronald Odom
Vice President Enterprise Execution, Saurabh Tandon
Vice President And Chief Operating Officer Pharmacy Services, Deepti Jain
Director Of Government Relations, Nick DeJong
Vice President Tax, Christopher LaFollette
Regional Vice President Of Federal Government Relations, Samuel Marchio
Vice President And Counsel, Jason Wagner
Regional Vice President Network Management, Jamie Huether
Assistant Vice President Enterprise Pmo, Vanslyke Carol
Staff Vice President Contracting Admin, Jim Taske

Vice President For Operations Wellpoint Military
  Care, Charlie Abell
Vice President Communications And Beneficiary
  Relations, John Molino
Staff Vice President Strategic Initiatives
  Accountable Care Solutions, Ryan Schoettle
Regional Vice President Senior Clinical Officer,
  Maureen Dempsey
President Ceo And Director, Gail K. Boudreaux
Chairman, Joseph R. Swedish, age 66
Auditors: Ernst & Young LLP

LOCATIONS

HQ: Anthem Inc
  120 Monument Circle, Indianapolis, IN 46204-4903
Phone: 800 331-1476
Web: www.antheminc.com

PRODUCTS/OPERATIONS

2017 Sales

	$ mil.	% of total
Premiums	83,647	93
Administrative fees	5,380	6
Net investment income	866	1
Net realized gains on financial instruments	144	-
Other	33	-
Adjustments	(33.1)	-
Total	**90,039**	**100**

2017 Premiums

	% of total
Government Business	54
Commercial and Specialty Business	46
Other	-
Total	**100**

Selected Operations

Blue-licensed subsidiaries
  Anthem Blue Cross (California)
  Anthem Blue Cross and Blue Shield (Colorado
  Connecticut Kentucky Indiana Maine Missouri Nevada
  New Hampshire Ohio Virginia Wisconsin)
  Blue Cross Blue Shield of Georgia
  Empire Blue Cross Blue Shield (New York)
Non-Blue Cross Subsidiaries and Affiliates
  AIM Specialty Health (benefits management)
  American Imaging Management (Diagnostic imaging)
  Anthem Life Insurance (life and accident)
  Anthem Workers' Compensation
  CareMore (Medicare Advantage and special needs
    plans)
  DeCare Dental (Dental benefit management)
  HealthLink (Administrative services)
  Golden West Dental & Vision (Dental/vision California)
  Meridian Resource Company (Cost containment)
  National Government Services (Administration of
    government contracts)
  Resolution Health (Cost containment)
  TrustSolutions (Fraud prevention)
  UniCare (Health care plans)

COMPETITORS

Aetna	Kaiser Foundation
CIGNA	Health Plan
Centene	Medical Mutual
Delta Dental Plans	Molina Healthcare
EmblemHealth	UnitedHealth Group
Humana	WellCare Health Plans

HISTORICAL FINANCIALS

Company Type: Public

Income Statement				FYE: December 31
	REVENUE ($ mil.)	NET INCOME ($ mil.)	NET PROFIT MARGIN	EMPLOYEES
12/17	90,039	3,842	4.3%	56,000
12/16	84,863	2,469	2.9%	53,000
12/15	79,156	2,560	3.2%	53,000
12/14	73,874	2,569	3.5%	51,500
12/13	71,023	2,489	3.5%	48,200
Annual Growth	**6.1%**	**11.5%**	**—**	**3.8%**

2017 Year-End Financials

Debt ratio: 28.26%
Return on equity: 14.89%
Cash ($ mil.): 3,608
Current ratio: 1.55
Long-term debt ($ mil.): 17,382

No. of shares (mil.): 256
Dividends
  Yield: 0.0%
  Payout: 18.8%
Market value ($ mil.): 57,622

	STOCK PRICE ($) FY Close	P/E High/Low		Earnings	PER SHARE ($) Dividends	Book Value
12/17	225.01	16	10	14.35	2.70	103.49
12/16	143.77	16	12	9.21	2.60	95.17
12/15	139.44	18	13	9.38	2.50	88.21
12/14	125.67	14	9	8.99	1.75	90.45
12/13	92.39	11	7	8.20	1.50	84.44
Annual Growth	**24.9%**	**—**	**—**	**15.0%**	**15.8%**	**5.2%**

Apache Corp

Apache Corporation an oil and gas exploration
and production company has onshore and offshore
operations in major oil patches around the world
including in the US Egypt and the UK's North Sea
oil fields. In the US it is active in the Gulf of Mexico
the Gulf Coast of Texas and Louisiana the Permian
Basin in West Texas the Anadarko Basin in Oklahoma. The company boasts worldwide estimated
proved reserves of 1.2 billion barrels of oil equivalent.

Operations

Apache explores for develops and produces natural gas crude oil and natural gas liquids (NGLs)
in the US Egypt and the UK.

Apache's North America Onshore segment owns
significant liquid hydrocarbon deposits across 6.7
million gross acres onshore in the US of which
around 70% is undeveloped. About 55% of
Apache's worldwide production and 70% of its
proved reserves are onshore in the US. Apache's
major North American holdings are in the Permian
basin in West Texas and New Mexico and the Mid-
continent/Gulf region. It also works offshore in
the Gulf of Mexico.

In Egypt Apache holds 5.6 million acres across
25 concessions in the Western Desert. Leases
range from four to 20 years. Around 70% of its
acreage is undeveloped.

Apache's North Sea operations contribute nearly
15% of total production and consists of around
10% of total proved reserves.

Geographic Reach

Apache has exploration and production assets
in the US Egypt and the UK. The US and Egypt
accounts for about 40% each of total company
revenue. The UK bring in some 20% revenue and
the rest mostly comes from Canada.

Sales and Marketing

Apache sells its natural gas to local distribution
companies utilities end-users and major oil companies.

The company's NGL production is sold under
contracts.

Apache's major customers include China Petro-
leum & Chemical Corporation (20% of sales)
Egyptian General Petrol Corporation and BP and
Royal Dutch Shell.

Financial Performance

Revenue at Apache has fallen by almost half in
the 2008-17 period reducing from a high of $12.4
billion to just over $6 billion. Profits in that decade
fluctuated wildly with the worst hit coming from
the oil price plunge of 2014-16 when the company
lost some $20 billion over three years.

Apache revenue increased 20% from $5.4 billion
in 2016 to $6.4 billion in 2017 thanks to a 25%
spike in crude oil prices leading to a $426 million
increase in revenue over 2016 as well as a $102
million increase in NGL revenue.

Net income fared even better. From losing $1.4
billion in 2016 the company posted profits of $1.3
billion in 2017 breaking a three-year losing streak.
The improvement came mostly due to the reduction of impairment charges in 2017 compared to
the year before (by almost $1 billion) as well as a
$324 million decrease in depreciation and amorti-
zation charges.

Cash holdings increased from $1.4 billion to
$1.7 billion in 2017. Operating activities provided
$2.4 billion in 2017. In contrast investment activ-
ities used some $1.4 billion in cash (mostly in plant
property and equipment purchase) and a further
$720 million in financing activities.

Strategy

The oil price downturn of 2014-16 cost Apache
a massive $20 billion and forced the company to
realign its costs with the new lower commodity
price environment.

The company is pursuing radical portfolio cur-
tailment measures? in 2017 2016 and 2015
Apache divested assets totaling $1.4 billion $134
million and $1.5 billion respectively. In 2017 alone
the company sold off Canadian assets Midale and
House Mountain leases to the Permian and Mid-
continent/Gulf Coast regions and the North Sea
gathering (SAGE) facility.

Some good news came late 2017 as commodity
prices started recovering and benefits from tax reforms kicked in. This will especially be helpful to
Apache?s capital-intensive project to build up the
Alpine High field and infrastructure.

For 2018-20 period Apache plans to invest
around $7.5 billion in its upstream segment and a
further $1.0 billion in the midstream development
of Alpine High. The investments are expected to
increase Apache?s growth rate by more than 10%.

However with global trade war risks rising in
2018 pitting the US against the EU and China
Apache?s dependency on foreign customers including China Petroleum & Chemical Corporation
the Egyptian General Petroleum Company and the
Royal Dutch Shell may become a significant issue.

HISTORY

Originally Raymond Plank wanted to start a
magazine. Then it was an accounting and tax-as-
sistance service. Plank and his co-founding partner
Truman Anderson had no experience in any of
these occupations but their accounting business
succeeded. In the early 1950s Plank and Anderson
branched out again founding APA a partnership
to invest in new ventures including oil and gas exploration. The partnership founded Apache Oil in
Minnesota in 1954. Investors put up the money
and Apache managed the drilling spreading the
risk over several projects.

As problems with government regulations in the oil industry mounted during the 1960s Apache diversified into real estate. The real estate operations were pivotal in driving a wedge between Plank and Anderson. In 1963 Anderson called a board meeting to ask the directors to fire Plank. Instead Anderson resigned and Plank took over.

EXECUTIVES

Vice President Operations, Jon Sauer
Vice President, Lisa Stewart
Evp And General Counsel, P. Anthony Lannie, age 63, $675,000 total compensation
Senior Region Vice President Egypt Mid-continent Gulf Coast Gulf Of Mexico And International New Ventures, James L. (Jim) House, age 56, $600,000 total compensation
President And Ceo, John J. Christmann, age 51, $1,100,000 total compensation
Evp Corporate Reservoir Engineering, W. Kregg Olson, age 64, $625,000 total compensation
Region Vp North Sea Region And Managing Director Apache North Sea, Jon Graham, age 64
Senior Region Vp Permian Region, Faron J. Thibodeaux, age 58
Senior Region Vp North Sea And Canada, Grady L. Ables, age 57
Senior Region Vice President Delaware Basin Region, Steven J. Keenan, age 62
Svp North America Land Government Affairs And Real Estate, Timothy R. Custer, age 57
Evp And Cfo, Stephen J. Riney, age 58, $675,000 total compensation
Evp Operations Support, Timothy J. Sullivan, age 62, $625,000 total compensation
Region Vice President Egypt Region And General Manager Apache Egypt, David Chi, age 44
Svp Midstream And Marketing, Brian W. Freed
Executive Vice President And Chief Financial Officer Energy Minister, Brian Wilson
Vice President Corporate Communications And Public Affairs, Castlen Kennedy
Vice President, Robert Johnston
Vice President Information Technology, Phillip Vo
Vice President Planning Strategy And Investor Relations, Alfonso Leon
Vice President And Treasurer, Jim Kimble
Executive Vice President, P Lannie
Vice President Operations, Mark Trento
Executive Vice President, Jon A Jeppesen
Vice President Business Development Midstream And Marketing, Robert W Bourne
Chairman, John E. Lowe, age 60
Board Member, William Montgomery
Board Member, Rodman Patton
Board Member, Annell R Bay
Board Member, Charles Pitman
Board Member, Daniel Rabun
Auditors: Ernst & Young LLP

LOCATIONS

HQ: Apache Corp
One Post Oak Central, 2000 Post Oak Boulevard, Suite 100, Houston, TX 77056-4400
Phone: 713 296-6000
Web: www.apachecorp.com

2016 sales

	% of total
US	37
Egypt	38
UK (North Sea)	19
Canada	6
Total	**100**

PRODUCTS/OPERATIONS

2016 sales

	% of total
Oil	78
Gas	18
Natural gas liquids	4
Other	-
Total	**100**

COMPETITORS

Abraxas Petroleum	Hess Corporation
Adams Resources	Jones Energy
Anadarko Petroleum	Pioneer Natural
BP	Resources
Chesapeake Energy	Qatargas
Chevron	Range Resources
Devon Energy	Royal Dutch Shell
EOG	Santos Ltd
Exxon Mobil	XTO Energy
Helmerich & Payne	

HISTORICAL FINANCIALS

Company Type: Public

Income Statement   FYE: December 31

	REVENUE ($ mil.)	NET INCOME ($ mil.)	NET PROFIT MARGIN	EMPLOYEES
12/17	6,423	1,304	20.3%	3,356
12/16	5,354	(1,405)	—	3,727
12/15	6,366	(23,119)	—	3,860
12/14	13,851	(5,403)	—	4,950
12/13	16,054	2,232	13.9%	5,342
Annual Growth	(20.5%)	(12.6%)	—	(11.0%)

2017 Year-End Financials

Debt ratio: 38.70%	No. of shares (mil.): 380
Return on equity: 19.10%	Dividends
Cash ($ mil.): 1,668	Yield: 0.0%
Current ratio: 1.45	Payout: 29.3%
Long-term debt ($ mil.): 7,934	Market value ($ mil.): 16,084

	STOCK PRICE ($) FY Close	P/E High/Low	PER SHARE ($) Earnings	Dividends	Book Value
12/17	42.22	19 11	3.41	1.00	19.47
12/16	63.47	— —	(3.71)	1.00	16.44
12/15	44.47	— —	(61.20)	1.00	6.79
12/14	62.67	— —	(14.06)	0.95	68.89
12/13	85.94	17 12	5.50	0.77	84.38
Annual Growth	(16.3%)	— —	(11.3%)	6.8%	(30.7%)

Apple Inc

Ask Siri to name the most successful company in the world and it might respond: Apple. And it's not just out of familial pride. In terms of profit revenue market capitalization and consumer cachet it consistently ranks right up there. In 2018 the company became the first reach a trillion dollar market capitalization. The iPhone in its 11th year has been the company's golden goose generating tens of billions in revenue and profit. In addition to the iPhone other familiar Apple products and services include Mac computers and iPad tablets as well as iTunes the App store and Apple Music. Primarily a consumer-oriented company Apple has inked several alliances with Accenture General Electric and IBM to deepen its penetration of the enterprise market. About 60% of revenue comes from outside the Americas.

HISTORY

College dropouts Steve Jobs (1955-2011) and Steve Wozniak founded Apple in 1976 in California's Santa Clara Valley. After Jobs' first sales call brought an order for 50 units the duo built the Apple I in his garage and sold it without a monitor keyboard or casing. Demand convinced Jobs there was a distinct market for small computers and the company's name (a reference to Jobs' stint on an Oregon farm) and the computer's user-friendly look and feel set it apart from others.

By 1977 Wozniak added a keyboard color monitor and eight peripheral device slots (which gave the machine considerable versatility and inspired numerous third-party add-on devices and software). Sales jumped from $7.8 million in 1978 to $117 million in 1980 the year Apple went public. In 1983 Wozniak left the firm and Jobs hired PepsiCo's John Sculley as president. Apple rebounded from failed product introductions that year by unveiling the Macintosh in 1984. After tumultuous struggles with Sculley Jobs left in 1985 and founded NeXT a designer of applications for developing software. That year Sculley ignored Microsoft founder Bill Gates' appeal for Apple to license its products and make the Microsoft platform an industry standard.

Apple blazed the desktop publishing trail in 1986 with its Mac Plus and LaserWriter printers. The following year it formed the software firm that later became Claris (and ultimately FileMaker). The late 1980s brought new competition from Microsoft whose Windows operating system (OS) featured a graphical interface akin to Apple's. Apple sued but lost its claim to copyright protection in 1992.

In 1993 Apple unveiled the Newton handheld computer but sales were slow. Earnings fell drastically so the company trimmed its workforce. (Sculley was among the departed.) In 1994 Apple cried "uncle" and began licensing clones of its OS hoping a flurry of cheaper Mac-alikes would encourage software developers. By 1996 struggling Apple realized Mac clones were stealing sales. That year it hired Gilbert Amelio formerly of National Semiconductor as CEO.

The company bought NeXT in 1997 but sales kept dropping and it subsequently cut about 30% of its workforce canceled projects and trimmed research costs. Meanwhile Apple's board ousted Amelio and Jobs took the position back on an interim basis. The CEO forged a surprising alliance with Microsoft which included releasing a Mac version of Microsoft's popular office software. To protect market share Jobs also stripped the cloning license from chief imitator Power Computing and put it out of business.

In 1998 Apple jumped back into the race with its colorful cocktail of iMacs and its first server software the Mac OS X. That year the company also revamped its profitable Claris unit (by cutting 300 employees shifting most operations to Apple and renaming it FileMaker) and stopped making its Newton handheld device and printer products.

Apple in 1999 opened a new chapter in portable computing with the introduction of its iBook laptop and (taking a cue from Dell) began selling built-to-order systems online. In 2000 after two and a half years as the semipermanent executive in charge Jobs took the "interim" out of his title and revamped the company's Web site around a suite of consumer Internet services. Jobs unveiled overhauled desktop lines later that year including an eight-inch cube-shaped G4. The company ended 2000 on a sour note as an industrywide slowdown and poor response to the G4 cube resulted in Apple's first unprofitable quarter in years.

EXECUTIVES

Vp Worldwide Developer Relations, Ron Okamoto
Svp Worldwide Marketing, Philip W. Schiller, age 58, $494,942 total compensation
Svp Software Engineering, Craig Federighi, age 49
Svp General Counsel And Secretary, D. Bruce Sewell, age 60, $1,000,000 total compensation
Svp Retail And Online Stores, Angela Ahrendts, age 57, $1,000,000 total compensation
Vp Applications, Eduardo H. (Eddy) Cue, age 54, $1,000,000 total compensation
Chief Design Officer, Jonathan Ive
Svp And Cfo, Luca Maestri, age 55, $1,000,000 total compensation
Coo, Jeffrey E. (Jeff) Williams, age 54, $947,596 total compensation
Svp Hardware Engineering, Daniel (Dan) Riccio, age 56, $1,000,000 total compensation
Svp Hardware Technologies, Johny Srouji
Vp Technology, Kevin Lynch
Vice President Corp. Dev, Adrian Perica
Vp And Managing Director Greater China, Isabel Mahe
Vice President, Celia Vigil
Vp Advertising Platforms, Todd Teresi
Senior Vice President, Dan Whisenhunt
Vp Systems, Oconnor Niall
First Vice President Of Human Resources, Ann Bowers
Vice President Of Product Design, Doug Field
Vp Communications, Steve Dowling
First Vice President Of Human Resources, Ann Bowers
Svp Internet Software And Services, Eddy Cue
Vp People, Deirdre O'brien
Vp Product Marketing, Michael Tchao
Vp Apple Care, Tara Bunch
Vice President Hardware Engineering, Kate Bergeron
Vp Siri, Bill Stasior
Vice President Inclusion And Diversity, Denise Smith
Vice President Of Marketing, Nancy Macintosh
Vice President For Public Policy And Government Affairs Americas, Cynthia Hogan
Vice President Finance, Donal Conroy
Vice President Enterprise And Government, John Solomon
Vice President Visi. Hardware Engineering, Bob Mansfield
Vice President, Siobhan Murphy
Vice President Of Consumer Applications, Jeff Robbin
Chairman, Arthur D. (Art) Levinson, age 68
Svp General Counsel And Secretary, D. Bruce Sewell, age 60
Auditors: Ernst & Young LLP

LOCATIONS

HQ: Apple Inc
One Apple Park Way, Cupertino, CA 95014
Phone: 408 996-1010   **Fax:** 408 974-2483
Web: www.apple.com

2018 Sales

	$ mil.	% of total
Americas	112,093	42
Europe	62,420	24
Asia/Pacific		
China	51,942	20
Japan	21,733	8
Rest of Asia Pacific	17,404	6
Total	**265,595**	**100**

PRODUCTS/OPERATIONS

2018 Sales

	% of total
iPhone	63
Services	14
Mac	10
iPad	7
Other products	6
Total	**100**

Selected Products

Hardware
    Desktop computers (iMac Mac mini Mac Pro)
    Displays (Cinema Thunderbolt)
    External hard drives (Airport Time Capsule)
    Keyboards
    Media devices (Apple TV)
    Mice (Magic Mouse)
    Mobile phones (iPhone)
    Portable computers (MacBook MacBook Air MacBook Pro)
    Portable digital music player (iPod touch)
    Tablet computers (iPad)
    Wearable technology (Apple Watch)
    Webcams (iSight)
    Wireless networking systems (AirPort)
Software
    MultimediaDVD Studio Pro FinalCut GarageBand iDVD iLife suite iMovie Photo iTunes Quicktime Soundtrack)
    Networking (Apple Remote Desktop AppleShare IP)
    Operating systems (macOS iOS watchOS tvOS)
    Personal productivity (AppleWorks FileMaker iWork Keynote Pages)
    Server (Mac OS X Server)
    Web browser (Safari)
Online Services
    Applications for iPad iPhone iPod touch (App Store)
    Applications for Mac (Mac App Store)
    Music Streaming (Apple Music)
    Cloud service (iCloud)
    E-books (iBooks)
    Electronic greeting cards (iCard)
    E-mail (Webmail)
    Online multimedia store (iTunes)
    Personal Web page creation (HomePage)
    Remote network storage (iDisk)
    Software (antivirus backup)
    Technical support (AppleCare)

COMPETITORS

AT&T	Google
Acer	HP
Adobe Systems	HTC Corporation
Alphabet Inc.	IBM
Amazon.com	LG Electronics
Best Buy	Lenovo
BlackBerry	Microsoft
Bose	Netflix
CASIO COMPUTER	Nokia
Cisco Systems	PayPal
Comcast	Philips Electronics
Ericsson	Samsung Electronics
Facebook	Sony
Fitbit	Spotify
Garmin	Wal-Mart

HISTORICAL FINANCIALS

Company Type: Public

Income Statement   FYE: September 29

	REVENUE ($ mil.)	NET INCOME ($ mil.)	NET PROFIT MARGIN	EMPLOYEES
09/18	265,595	59,531	22.4%	132,000
09/17	229,234	48,351	21.1%	123,000
09/16	215,639	45,687	21.2%	116,000
09/15	233,715	53,394	22.8%	110,000
09/14	182,795	39,510	21.6%	97,000
Annual Growth	**9.8%**	**10.8%**	**—**	**8.0%**

2018 Year-End Financials

Debt ratio: 31.30%
Return on equity: 49.50%
Cash ($ mil.): 25,913
Current ratio: 1.12
Long-term debt ($ mil.): 93,735

Dividends
Yield: 0.0%
Payout: 22.8%
Market value ($ mil.): —

	STOCK PRICE ($) FY Close	P/E High/Low		PER SHARE ($) Earnings	Dividends	Book Value
09/18	225.74	19	13	11.91	2.72	22.53
09/17	154.12	18	11	9.21	2.40	26.15
09/16	112.71	15	11	8.31	2.18	24.03
09/15	114.71	14	10	9.22	1.98	21.39
09/14	100.75	100	14	6.45	1.81	19.02
Annual Growth	**22.3%**	**—**	**—**	**16.6%**	**10.7%**	**4.3%**

Applied Materials, Inc.

Applied Materials makes the machines that make computer chips flat panel TVs and solar energy devices. The company's equipment handles the complex processes of making chips from laying down patterns on silicon to packaging. Its display business produces equipment for manufacturing organic light-emitting diodes (OLEDs) and other display technologies for TVs personal computers and smart phones. The services business offers manufacuring consulting and automation software. Based in California Applied has factories around the world. Asian customers account for about 75% of revenue.

Operations

Applied operates in three segments: Semiconductor Systems Applied Global Services and Display.

Semiconductor Systems (65% of revenue) makes a wide range of manufacturing equipment used to fabricate integrated circuits.

Applied Global Services (25% of revenue) provides products that improve equipment and fab performance and productivity including spares upgrades services and factory automation software for semiconductor display and other products.

The Display segment (10% of revenue) engineers products for making liquid crystal displays (LCDs) organic light-emitting diodes (OLEDs) and other display technologies for TVs personal computers (PCs) tablets smart phones and other consumer-oriented devices as well as equipment for flexible substrates.

Geographic Reach

Applied has operations in the US Asia/Pacific and Europe. Customers in Korea account for nearly 30% of revenue and those in Taiwan and China each account for about a quarter of revenue. The US and Japan each supply about 10% of Applied?s revenue.

Products in Semiconductor Systems are manufactured in Santa Clara California; Austin Texas; Gloucester Massachusetts; Kalispell Montana; Rehovot Israel; and Singapore. Remanufactured equipment products in the Applied Global Services segment are handled primarily in Austin Texas. Products in the Display and Adjacent Markets segment are manufactured in Alzenau Germany; and Tainan Taiwan. Other products are manufactured in Treviso Italy.

Sales and Marketing

Due to the highly technical nature of its products Applied's direct sales force does most of the company's marketing and selling worldwide. Leading customers for Applied's chip making equipment include Samsung Electronics about 25% of revenue and Taiwan Semiconductor Manufacturing Company. US chipmakers Intel and Micron each account for less than 10% of Applied?s sales.

Financial Performance

Applied Materials has manufactured strong revenue gains in the past five years doubling its top line with average annual increases of about 18% driven by demand for semiconductors for use in an increasing number of devices. A 34% revenue increase in 2017 punctuated the trend.

Applied?s 2017 revenue and earnings were company records: Revenue hit $14.5 billion while profit doubled from 2016. The Semiconductor Systems segment?s sales rose 38% as memory manufacturers invested in technology upgrades and new capacity driven by the transition to newer NAND technology and demand for high performance storage in data centers and increasing smartphone content. Applied Global Services? sales increased 17% from Applied?s large installed base of manufacturing systems and customers? needs improve performance. In the Display segment customer investment in equipment to make mobile and TV displays drove revenue about 60% higher.

The jump in revenue filtered down to the bottom line to produce a $3.4 billion profit compared to a $1.7 billion profit in 2016. The 24% profit margin was another company record.

Applied?s cash increased to $5 billion in 2017 from $3.4 billion in 2016. Capital expenditures increased to build demonstration and test equipment and laboratory tools in North America. The company issued about $2.2 billion in debt and spent about $1.2 billion to buy back shares.

Strategy

Applied Materials sees growth in semiconductors driven by the expansion of the internet of things big data and artificial intelligence and technologies such as augmented and virtual reality. In displays the company sees continuing demand for big and small screens. The company is investing in research development and engineering to help its customers make more chips and with fewer defects. Applied?s R&D spending skews toward etch e-beam inspection and other materials engineering capabilities to improve chip performance and enable advanced displays.

Geographically Applied continues to focus on Asia the base of its two biggest customers Samsung Electronics and Taiwan Semiconductor Manufacturing Co. (TSMC). Samsung buys equipment from Applied to make its memory chips chips for its electronics products as well as the screens for its phone and TVs. TSMC is the biggest chip foundry and is intent on providing the latest chip-making equipment for its customers.

Mergers and Acquisitions

Applied Materials and Tokyo Electron halted their proposed merger in April 2015 because they decided they couldn't clear antitrust concerns of regulators. The deal would have combined the two biggest companies in their industry but allowed them to cut costs and increase efficiencies. Now Applied will have to find other ways to deal with the rising costs of equipping a semiconductor fab with increasingly sophisticated instruments.

HISTORY

Applied Materials was founded in 1967 in Mountain View California as a maker of chemical vapor deposition systems for fabricating semiconductors. After years of rapid growth the company went public in 1972. Two years later it purchased wafer maker Galamar Industries.

In 1975 Applied Materials suffered a 45% drop in sales as the semiconductor industry (and the US economy) contracted. Financial and managerial problems plagued the company following the recession so in 1976 James Morgan a former division manager for conglomerate Textron was chosen to replace founder Michael McNeilly as CEO. Two years later Morgan also became chairman.

After selling Galamar (1977) and other non-core units and extending the company's line of credit Morgan announced a plan to move into Japan. The company's first joint venture Applied Materials Japan was set up in 1979.

Applied got into the ion implanter market in 1980 through its acquisition of the UK's Lintott Engineering.

EXECUTIVES

Vice President And General Manager Etch And Cleans Business, Ellie Yieh

Svp Engineering, Gino Addiego, age 58, $457,692 total compensation

Group Vp; General Manager Transistor And Interconnect Group, Steve Ghanayem

Svp General Counsel And Secretary, Thomas F. Larkins, $489,231 total compensation

Group Vp; General Manager Imaging And Process Control Group, Robert J. Perlmutter, age 61

Svp And Cto; President Applied Ventures, Omkaram (Om) Nalamasu, age 59, $468,846 total compensation

Group Vp And Cio, Jay Kerley

Svp And Cfo, Daniel (Dan) Durn, age 51

President And Ceo, Gary E. Dickerson, age 60, $1,019,231 total compensation

Svp And General Manager Applied Global Services And Growth Markets, Ali Salehpour, age 56, $560,577 total compensation

Group Vp; General Manager Patterning And Packaging Group, Prabu G. Raja

Regional President, Russell Tham

Vp Global Operations And Planning Silicon Systems Group, Duane Loos

Vice President Human Resources, Blake Wolfe

Vice President, Shelly Zeigler

Vice President And Treasurer, Robert Friess

Corporate Vice President And General Manager Of Display Business Group, Brian Shieh

Vice President, Joe Nolan

Vice President, Karin Basilio

Vice President, Ramesh Viswanathan

Vice President And General Manager Of Front End Products Division, Sundar Ramamurthy

Senior Vice President And Chief Of Staff, Manfred Kerschbaum

Vice President, Mike Parcella

Vice President Technology Development, Cheri Lamotte

Vice President Intellectual Property, James Wilson

Vice President Service Information Systems, Chris Allan

Vice President And General Manager, Mukund Srinivasan

Svp General Counsel And Secretary, Thomas F. Larkins

Chairman, Thomas J. (Tom) Iannotti, age 62

Assistant Treasurer, Randy Webb

Assistant Treasurer Customer, Brad Mccurrie

Secretary, Yvonne Teo

Auditors: KPMG LLP

LOCATIONS

HQ: Applied Materials, Inc.
3050 Bowers Avenue, P.O. Box 58039, Santa Clara, CA 95052-8039
Phone: 408 727-5555
Web: www.appliedmaterials.com

2017 Sales

	$ mil.	% of total
Asia/Pacific		
Korea	4,052	28
Taiwan	3,291	23
China	2,746	19
Japan	1,518	10
Southeast Asia	640	4
US	1,474	10
Europe	816	6
Total	**14,537**	**100**

PRODUCTS/OPERATIONS

2017 Sales

	$ mil.	% of total
Silicon Systems	9,517	65
Applied Global Services	3,017	21
Display	1,900	13
Corporate & Other	103	1
Total	**14,537**	**100**

Products and Technologies
Semiconductor
Display
Solar
Roll to Roll WEB Coating
Emerging Technologies and Products
Automation Software
Product Library

Selected Products

Chemical mechanical polishing/planarization systems (wafer polishing)
Deposition systems (deposit layers of conducting and insulating material on wafers)
  Dielectric deposition (chemical vapor deposition or CVD)
  Metal (CVD electroplating or physical vapor deposition)
  Silicon and thermal deposition
  Sputtering (physical vapor deposition) for solar cells
  Thin-film silicon solar cells
  Web coating for flexible solar cells
Etch systems (remove portions of a wafer surface for circuit construction)
Inspection systems (defect review for reticles — patterned plates which hold precise images of chip circuit patterns — and wafers)
Ion implant systems (implant ions into wafer surface to change conductive properties)
Manufacturing process optimization software
Metrology systems
  CD-SEM (scanning electron microscope system)
Optical monitoring systems (for glass or web coating systems)
Rapid thermal processing systems (heat wafers to change electrical characteristics)

COMPETITORS

AIXTRON	Micronic Laser Systems
ASM International	Nanometrics
Axcelis Technologies	Nikon
EG Systems	Rennova Health
Ebara	Rudolph Technologies
FEI	SCREEN Holdings
GT Advanced Technologies	Spire Corp.
Hitachi	Sumitomo Heavy Industries
Hitachi Kokusai Electric	TEL FSI
Intevac	Tokyo Electron
KLA-Tencor	ULVAC
Lam Research	Veeco Instruments
Mattson Technology	Zygo

HISTORICAL FINANCIALS

Company Type: Public

Income Statement

FYE: October 28

	REVENUE ($ mil.)	NET INCOME ($ mil.)	NET PROFIT MARGIN	EMPLOYEES
10/18	17,253	3,313	19.2%	21,000
10/17	14,537	3,434	23.6%	18,400
10/16	10,825	1,721	15.9%	16,700
10/15	9,659	1,377	14.3%	15,500
10/14	9,072	1,072	11.8%	14,950
Annual Growth	17.4%	32.6%	—	8.9%

2018 Year-End Financials

Debt ratio: 29.87%	No. of shares (mil.): 967
Return on equity: 41.04%	Dividends
Cash ($ mil.): 3,440	Yield: 0.0%
Current ratio: 2.64	Payout: 18.5%
Long-term debt ($ mil.): 5,309	Market value ($ mil.): 31,292

	STOCK PRICE ($) FY Close	P/E High/Low		PER SHARE ($) Earnings	Dividends	Book Value
10/18	32.36	19	10	3.23	0.60	7.07
10/17	56.69	18	9	3.17	0.40	8.82
10/16	28.66	20	10	1.54	0.40	6.69
10/15	16.44	23	13	1.12	0.40	6.56
10/14	20.99	26	19	0.87	0.40	6.44
Annual Growth	11.4%	—	—	38.8%	10.7%	2.4%

Aramark

Keeping employees fed and clothed is a mark of this company. ARAMARK is one of the leading contract foodservice providers in the world and a high-ranking uniform supplier in the US. The company offers corporate dining services and operates concessions at sports arenas and other entertainment venues while its ARAMARK Refreshment Services unit is a leading provider of vending and beverage services. The firm also provides facilities management services. Through ARAMARK Uniform and Career Apparel the company supplies uniforms for healthcare public safety and technology workers. US customers generate about three-quarters of the company?s revenue.

Operations

ARAMARK operates in three segments: Food and Support Services (FSS) US FSS International and Uniform and Career Apparel.

FSS US which supplies nearly two-thirds of sales provides food refreshment specialized dietary and support services including facility maintenance and housekeeping in the US.

FSS International about a quarter of sales provides food and facility services to customers outside the US.

The Uniform and Career Apparel segment about 15% of sales offers personalized uniforms and accessories work clothing outerwear and particulate-free garments as well as mats shop towels and first aid supplies.

The company relies on one food distributor Sysco Corp. to deliver about half of its food and non-food products in the US and Canada.

Geographic Reach

ARAMARK has operations throughout the US and nearly 20 other countries. International markets such as Canada Chile Germany Ireland and the UK account for about 25% of the company's revenue. It also has operations in Japan through its 50% ownership of AIM Services Co.

The company has a diverse customer base in North America serving customers in about 45 states Puerto Rico Mexico and Canada from about 390 service facilities and distribution centers.

Sales and Marketing

ARAMARK serves businesses of all sizes in many industries. Like its outsourcing rivals ARAMARK competes primarily through bids to provide services to specific clients. It is generally engaged through long-term contracts that are renewed periodically. Most of ARAMARK's contracts allow the company to retain all revenue from its operations while paying a commission to the client; it also works under management-fee arrangements under which clients bear some of the risk for expenses. In addition the company's uniform and apparel division also sells products (outerwear safety gear work wear) directly to customers.

Financial Performance

Three years of increasing sales pushed ARAMARK?s top line past its previous revenue high of $14.8 billion reached in 2014 while its net income steadily rose over those five years.

In 2018 (ended September) ARAMARK served up an 8% sales increase to $15.8 billion from 2017 with higher sales in all segments. Organic sales accounted for half the increase and acquisitions and favorable currency exchange rates provided the other half. The uniform business boosted by the AmeriPride acquisition grew 28% accounting for 36% of the overall increase.

ARAMARK?s net income jumped about 50% to about $568 million in 2018 from 2017 as costs were stable as a percentage of sales from year-to-year.

The company had about $215 million in cash and equivalents on hand in 2018 compared to $238 million the year before. In 2018 the company?s operations generated $1 billion in cash investing activities used $2.8 billion and financing activities provided $1.8 billion.

The company has a heavy debt load of $7.2 billion which could limit its flexibility in funding acquisitions or other expenditures and lead to higher interest rates for new financing.

Strategy

ARAMARK is working on its menu and technology tools to drive growth. The company has partnered with the American Heart Association to develop menus that improve the nutrition offered to customers. Through the partnership called the Healthy by Life 20 by 20 campaign ARAMARK has reduced calories saturated fats and sodium across its menus and increased the presence of grains fruits and vegetables.

ARAMARK has installed technology tools including those that allow for self-ordering to provide a better customer experience and improve productivity.

Acquisitions continue to be a key part of ARAMARK?s strategy. The $1 billion deal for AmeriPride Services Inc. expanded the company?s uniform business in the US and established a strong position in Canada.

ARAMARK has been trying to consolidate its operations to become more efficient. The company sold its healthcare technologies business for $300 million in 2019 planning to use the proceeds to pay down debt.

Mergers and Acquisitions

In 2018 ARARK acquired AmeriPride Services Inc. a uniform and linen rental and supply company in the US and Canada for about $1 billion. Besides expanding the uniform business in the US AmeriPride?s operations put ARMARK?s Canadian business on a stronger foundation.

The 2017 acquisition of Avendra a hospitality procurement services provider in North America bolstered ARAMARK?s purchasing power and supply chain management capabilities. ARAMARK paid about $1.35 billion for Avendra.

During fiscal 2016 ARAMARK purchased Avoca Handweavers Limited an Irish retail and cafe business for approximately $65.8 million.

Company Background

ARAMARK was founded in 1959 and gone through several transitions over the years. In 1984 management and employees teamed up with investors to buy the company and 17 years later made an IPO. ARAMARK went private again in 2007 bought out by investors that included Goldman Sachs Capital Partners and CCMP Capital Advisors as well as some 250 senior managers. In 2013 ARAMARK returned to the public markets with an IPO.

HISTORY

Davre Davidson began his career in foodservice by selling peanuts from the backseat of his car in the 1930s. He landed his first vending contract with Douglas Aircraft (later McDonnell Douglas now part of Boeing) in 1935. Through that relationship Davidson met William Fishman of Chicago who had vending operations in the Midwest. Davidson and Fishman merged their companies in 1959 to form Automatic Retailers of America (ARA). Davidson became chairman and CEO of the new company; Fishman served as president.

Focusing on candy beverage and cigarette machines ARA became the leading vending machine company in the US by 1961 with operations in 38 states. Despite slimmer profit margins ARA moved into food vending in the early 1960s. It acquired 150 foodservice businesses between 1959 and 1963 quickly becoming a leader in the operation of cafeterias at colleges hospitals and work sites. The company (which changed its name to ARA Services in 1966) grew so rapidly that the FTC stepped in; ARA agreed to restrict future food vending acquisitions.

ARA provided foodservices at the 1968 Summer Olympics in Mexico City beginning a long-term relationship with the amateur sports event. The company also diversified into publication distribution that year and in 1970 it expanded into janitorial and maintenance services. A foray into residential care for the elderly began in 1973 (and ended in 1993 with the sale of the subsidiary). ARA also entered into emergency room staffing services (sold 1997). The company expanded into child care (National Child Care Centers) in 1980.

CFO Joseph Neubauer became CEO in 1983 and was named chairman in 1984. To avoid a hostile takeover shortly thereafter he led a $1.2 billion leveraged buyout. After the buyout ARA began refining its core operations. It acquired Szabo (correctional foodservices) in 1986 Children's World Learning Centers in 1987 and Coordinated Health Services (medical billing services) in 1993.

ARA changed its name to ARAMARK in 1994 as part of an effort to raise its profile with its ultimate customers the public. The company's concession operations suffered from long work stoppages in baseball (1994) and hockey (1995). ARAMARK acquired Galls (North America's #1 supplier of public safety equipment) in 1996 and in 1997 announced plans to become 100% employee-owned.

The following year ARAMARK entered into a joint venture with privately held Anderson News Company exchanging its magazine distribution operations for a minority stake in the new business. In 2000 the company was on hand to supply foodservices to the Olympic Games in Sydney.

With the new millennium the company was focused on expansion buying the food and beverage concessions business of conglomerate Ogden

Corp. for $236 million. The company penned a 10-year deal with Boeing in 2000 to supply food-services to about 100 locations one of the biggest foodservice contracts ever. It also bought the Correctional Foodservice Management division of G4S Secure Solutions (USA) then named The Wackenhut Corporation.

ARAMARK continued its expansion with the purchase of ServiceMaster's management services division in 2001 for about $800 million — opening doors in nonfood management groundskeeping and custodial services. However the company lost a bid to cater the 2002 Olympic Games in Salt Lake City to rival Compass Group. In late 2001 ARAMARK went public.

The company bought Hilton's 14 Harrison Conference Centers and university lodgings for about $49 million in 2002.

EXECUTIVES

Chairman President And Ceo, Eric J. Foss, age 60, $1,622,625 total compensation

Evp Human Resources, Lynn B. McKee, age 62, $666,475 total compensation

Svp Controller And Chief Accounting Officer, Joseph M. (Joe) Munnelly, age 54, $384,503 total compensation

Coo Uniform And Refreshment Services, Brad C. Drummond

Coo International, Brent J. Franks

Evp And Cfo, Stephen P. (Steve) Bramlage, age 47, $300,000 total compensation

Coo Europe, Harrald F. Kroeker, age 60

Coo Healthcare Education And Facilities, Victor L. Crawford, age 57

Coo Sports Leisure Corrections And Business Dining, Marc Bruno

Evp General Counsel And Secretary, Stephen R. (Steve) Reynolds, age 60, $517,650 total compensation

Coo Emerging Markets, Marty Welch

Senior Vice President Finance, Christina Morrison

Vice President And Associate General Counsel Litigation, Stephen A Mallozzi

Vice President Business Development, Diane Browne

Vice President Strategic Partnerships, Brian Drew

Vice President Human Resources And Public Affairs, Ivan Mergudich

Vice President Strategic Partnerships, Ed Snowden

Vice President Human Resources, Lynn Farrell

Vice President, Larry Weger

Associate Vice President, Alan Leo

Vice President Of Marketing, Mark S Mendes

Senior Vice President And Deputy General Counsel, James C Lee

Regional Vice President, Peter J Evola

Vice President Finance, Eric Brown

Vice President Business Development, Tim Grant

Vice President Of Sales, Betsy Kline

Vice President Supply Chain Fleet Manage, Art Wake

Vice President Of Global Business Servic, Brian Gabbard

Vice President Finance, Sandra Demas

Associate Vice President And Assistant General Counsel, Stephanie Walter

Regional Vice President, Jim Frost

Vice President Of Tax, Robert Deitz

Vice President Information Technology, Danielle Blanco

Vice President Of Business Development, Timothy Grant

Assistant Vice President, Paul Sizer

Associate Vice President Human Resources, Emanuel Maxwell

Vice President Compensation And Benefits, Scott Haverlock

Vice President Human Resources, Amna Shoro

Vice President Global Security, Edward Hanko

Regional Vice President, Winston Wright

Associate Vice President Marketing, Stephanie Provost

National Account Manager, David Romero

Vice President Operations, Dan Hagler

National Account Manager, Stephen J Dolph

Vice President Of Operations, Jim McLaughlin

Associate Vice President Consumer Insights, Jill Marchick

Vice President Strategic Development Aramark Healthcare, Mike Morgioni

Vice President, Carale Brown

Chairman President And Ceo, Eric J. Foss, age 60

Evp General Counsel And Secretary, Stephen R. (Steve) Reynolds, age 60

Auditors: KPMG LLP

LOCATIONS

HQ: Aramark
2400 Market Street, Philadelphia, PA 19103
Phone: 215 238-3000
Web: www.aramark.com

2018 Sales

	% of total
United States	75
International	25
Total	**100**

PRODUCTS/OPERATIONS

2018 Sales

	% of total
FSS United States	64
FSS International	23
Uniform	13
Total	**100**

Brands
Brands
WearGuard
Crest
Aramark

Services
Food hospitality and facilities
Rental sale and maintenance of uniform apparel and other items

Selected Operations
Food and support services
  ARAMARK Colleges and Universities
  ARAMARK Conference Centers
  ARAMARK Convention Centers
  ARAMARK Correctional Services
  ARAMARK Cultural Attractions
  ARAMARK Facility Services
  ARAMARK Food Services
  ARAMARK Healthcare
  ARAMARK Higher Education
  ARAMARK Innovative Dining Solutions
  ARAMARK Parks and Resorts
  ARAMARK Refreshment Services (vending services)
  ARAMARK Senior Living
  ARAMARK Sports and Entertainment
Uniform and career apparel
  ARAMARK Cleanroom Services
  ARAMARK Uniform & Career Apparel
  Galls (tactical equipment and apparel)

COMPETITORS

ABM Industries	G&K Services
Autogrill	Healthcare Services
Centerplate	ISS A/S
Cintas	SSP
Compass Group	Serco
Delaware North	Sodexo
Elior	UniFirst

HISTORICAL FINANCIALS
Company Type: Public

Income Statement FYE: September 28

	REVENUE ($ mil.)	NET INCOME ($ mil.)	NET PROFIT MARGIN	EMPLOYEES
09/18	15,789	567	3.6%	274,400
09/17	14,604	373	2.6%	260,500
09/16*	14,415	287	2.0%	266,500
10/15	14,329	235	1.6%	265,500
10/14	14,832	148	1.0%	269,500
Annual Growth	**1.6%**	**39.7%**	**—**	**0.5%**

*Fiscal year change

2018 Year-End Financials

Debt ratio: 52.80%	No. of shares (mil.): 246
Return on equity: 20.75%	Dividends
Cash ($ mil.): 215	Yield: 0.9%
Current ratio: 1.17	Payout: 20.9%
Long-term debt ($ mil.): 7,213	Market value ($ mil.): 10,615

	STOCK PRICE ($) FY Close	P/E High/Low		PER SHARE ($) Earnings	Dividends	Book Value
09/18	43.02	20	16	2.24	0.42	12.28
09/17	40.61	27	22	1.49	0.41	10.01
09/16*	38.03	32	25	1.16	0.38	8.83
10/15	30.83	34	26	0.96	0.35	7.85
10/14	26.44	45	34	0.63	0.23	7.34
Annual Growth	**12.9%**	**—**	**—**	**37.3%**	**16.9%**	**13.7%**

*Fiscal year change

Archer Daniels Midland Co.

Archer-Daniels-Midland (ADM) forges every link in the food chain from field to processing to store. One of the world's largest processors of agricultural commodities the company converts corn oilseeds and wheat into products for food animal feed industrial and energy uses at 280 processing plants worldwide. The company is also a leading manufacturer of protein meal vegetable oil corn sweeteners flour biodiesel ethanol and other value-added food and feed ingredients. ADM operates an extensive US grain elevator and global transportation network that buys stores transports and resells feed commodities for the agricultural processing industry connecting crops with markets on six continents.

Operations

Archer-Daniels-Midland (ADM) conducts its business through four operating segments: Agricultural Services Corn Processing Oilseeds Processing and Wild Flavors and Specialty Ingredients.

Agricultural Services accounts for nearly half of ADM's revenue and buys stores cleans and transports agricultural commodities such as oilseeds corn wheat milo oats rice and barley. It resells them as food and feed ingredients and as raw materials for the agriculture processing industry.

The Oilseeds segment generates nearly 45% of sales and processes soybeans and soft seeds (such as cottonseeds sunflower seeds canola rapeseed and flaxseed) into vegetable oils and protein meals. Vegetable oils are either sold as raw oils or further refined into salad oils or hydrogenated into margarine and shortening. Partly refined oils are also turned into biodiesel or sold to other manufacturers for use in industrial applications such as paint and chemicals. The protein meals are typically used as a food for livestock particularly poultry. In Europe and South America the segment operates "grain elevators" (storage facilities) port facilities and transport assets.

The Corn Processing segment accounts for 15% of sales and carries out corn wet and dry milling to convert corn into sweeteners starches syrups glucose dextrose and bioproducts. The bulk of its operations are in the mid-US but it also has operations in China Bulgaria Morocco and Turkey. It also ferments dextrose to produce alcohol and amino acids.

Wild Flavors and Specialty Ingredients brings in most of the remaining revenue and produces natural flavor ingredients flavor systems natural colors proteins emulsifiers and soluble fiber among other specialty products. Additionally it buys processes and sells edible beans and soy proteins; it also sells gluten-free and high-protein pastas.

In total ADM has 271 owned or leased US or non-US processing plants and 514 owned or leased US or non-US procurement facilities.

A big part of ADM's business is getting products from one place to another. It has developed a comprehensive transportation network that moves commodities and processed products around the world. It owns or leases thousands of trucks trailers railroad tank and hopper cars river barges towboats and ocean-going vessels.

Geographic Reach

The US is Archer-Daniels-Midlands's largest market accounting for more than 45% of total sales. Switzerland accounts for more than 20% and Germany around 5%. More than 160 other countries contribute the rest. ADM currently owns or leases 270 processing plants and more than 510 procurement facilities 25% of which are located outside of the US.

The company also has 230 warehouses and terminals primarily used as bulk storage facilities and around 40 innovation centers.

ADM has Agricultural Services processing plants in North America and Europe; Agricultural Services procurement facilities in North America South America and Europe; Corn Processing plants in North America South America Europe and Asia. Oilseeds processing plants in North America South America Europe Asia and Africa; Oilseeds Processing procurement facilities in North America South America and Europe; and Wild Flavors and Specialty Ingredients operations in North America South America Europe and Asia.

Sales and Marketing

Archer-Daniels-Midland's products are distributed mainly in bulk from processing plants or storage facilities directly to customers' facilities. ADM has developed transportation capability to move both commodities and processed products virtually anywhere in the world.

Financial Performance

Archer-Daniels-Midland's revenue has declined steadily since 2013. In fiscal 2016 revenue fell a further 8% to $62.3 billion mostly because of lower average sales prices and the disposal of the sugar ethanol and cocoa businesses partially offset by contributions from acquisitions.

Net income fell 30% to $1.3 billion due to gains recorded in the previous year on the sale of the cocoa and chocolate business and lower earnings in fiscal 2016 due to their sale. The company also recorded lower global crushing and origination margins and lower international merchandising results.

Cash from operations fell by $1 billion to $1.5 billion due to changes in working capital.

Strategy

To stay abreast of changes in consumer tastes Archer-Daniels-Midland made a number of acqui-

sitions in the gluten-free and high-protein space. Acquisitions include Harvest Innovations (minimally processed soy proteins and gluten-free ingredients) and Caterina Foods (gluten-free and high-protein pastas) integrated into the Wild Flavors segment.

The company's strategy involves expanding the volume and diversity of crops that it merchandises and processes expanding the global reach of its core model and expanding its value-added product portfolio. One of ADM's strategies is to expand the global reach of its core model may include expanding or developing its business in emerging market areas such as Asia Eastern Europe the Middle East and Africa. As the company adds new products to its portfolio it is keeps an eye on operations that fail to meet expectations. To that end in 2016 ADM sold its sugarcane ethanol operations in Limeira do Oeste in the Brazilian state of Minas Gerais and the year before that it sold its cocoa and chocolate business as well.

Mergers and Acquisitions

In early 2017 Archer-Daniels-Midland acquired Crosswind Industries a manufacturer of private label pet treats and foods as well as specialty ingredients.

The company made a number of acquisitions in 2016. In February it acquired Harvest Innovations an industry leader in minimally processed expeller-pressed soy proteins oils and gluten-free ingredients) for $84 million. In April it bought a 50% interest in Egyptian firm Medsofts Group that manages merchandising and supply chain operations; in September Caterina Foods a maker of gluten-free and high-protein pastas; and in May the remaining 60% interest in Amazon Flavors a Brazilian manufacturer of natural extracts emulsions and compounds. It also agreed to acquire from Tate & Lyle a Casablanca Morocco-based corn wet mill that produces glucose and native starch.

HISTORY

John Daniels began crushing flaxseed to make linseed oil in 1878 and in 1902 he formed Daniels Linseed Company in Minneapolis. George Archer another flaxseed crusher joined the company the following year. In 1923 the company bought Midland Linseed Products and became Archer Daniels Midland (ADM). ADM kept buying oil processing companies in the Midwest during the 1920s. It also started to research the chemical composition of linseed oil.

ADM entered the flour milling business in 1930 when it bought Commander-Larabee (then the #3 flour miller in the US). In the 1930s the company discovered a method for extracting lecithin (an emulsifier food additive used in candy and other products) from soybean oil significantly lowering its price.

The enterprise grew rapidly following WWII. By 1949 it was the leading processor of linseed oil and soybeans in the US and was fourth in flour milling. During the early 1950s ADM began foreign expansion in earnest.

In 1966 the company's leadership passed to Dwayne Andreas a former Cargill executive who had purchased a block of Archer family stock. Andreas focused ADM on soybeans including the production of textured vegetable protein a cheap soybean by-product used in foodstuffs.

EXECUTIVES

Svp Chief Risk Officer And President North America, Mark A. Bemis, age 57
Svp Agricultural Services Business Unit; President Europe, Joseph D. (Joe) Taets, age 52, $700,008 total compensation

Evp And Cfo, Ray G. Young, age 57, $825,048 total compensation
Svp General Counsel And Secretary, D. Cameron Findlay, age 59, $700,000 total compensation
Svp Chief Strategy Officer And Chief Sustainability Officer, Ismael Roig, age 51
Svp And President Corn Processing, Christopher M. (Chris) Cuddy, age 44
Chairman And Ceo, Juan R. Luciano, age 56, $1,283,340 total compensation
President Adm Europe Middle East And Africa (emea), Pierre-Christophe Duprat, age 50
Svp And Cto, Todd A. Werpy, age 55
Svp And President Oilseeds Processing Business Unit, Gregory A. (Greg) Morris, age 46, $650,004 total compensation
Svp And President Wild Flavors And Specialty Ingredients, Vince F. Macciocchi, age 52
President North Asia, Donald Chen, age 55
President Southeast Asia Australia And New Zealand And Global Destination Marketing, Ian Pinner, age 45
President Global Trade, Gary McGuigan
Vice President Of Research And Development, Leif Solheim
Executive Vice President And Chief Risk Officer, Roger Hoffman
Vice President Bio Products, John Hansen
Vice President Human Resources Canada And Cost Management, Crocifissa Mandraccia
Senior Vice President Human Resources, Michael D'Ambrose
Senior Vice President For The Research Division, Mark Matlock
Vice President Environmental, Mark E Calmes
Svp General Counsel And Secretary, D. Cameron Findlay, age 59
Chairman And Ceo, Juan R. Luciano, age 56
Auditors: Ernst & Young LLP

LOCATIONS

HQ: Archer Daniels Midland Co.
77 West Wacker Drive, Suite 4600, Chicago, IL 60601
Phone: 312 634-8100
Web: www.adm.com

2015 Sales

	$ mil.	% of total
US	31,828	47
Switzerland	11,681	17
Germany	3,436	5
Other countries	20,757	31
Total	**67,702**	**100**

PRODUCTS/OPERATIONS

2015 Sales

	$ mil.	% of total
Agricultural services	33,658	44
Oilseeds processing	29,393	39
Corn processing	10,051	13
Wild Flavors and Specialty Ingredients	2,423	3
Other	634	1
Intersegment Elimination	(8457)	-
Total	**67,702**	**100**

Selected Commodities

Barley
Corn
Milo (sorghum)
Oats
Oilseeds
Rice
Rye
Wheat

Selected Brands

Consumer food
Casa (canned refried beans)
Commander (wheat flour)
Five Roses (wheat flour)
Gigantic (wheat flour)

Midland Harvest (rice)
Novasoy (soy supplement)
Top King (wheat flour)
VegeFull (cooked ground beans)
Industrial food
Ambrosia (chocolate)
CardioAid (plant sterol)
EnviroStrip (dry-stripping)
Evolution Chemicals (sustainable alternative chemical)
NovaLipid (fats and oils)
NovaSoy (isoflavones)
VegeFull (dried bean-based food ingredient)

Selected Products

Agricultural
  Fertilizer
Feed ingredients
  Animal nutrition
  Corn co-products
  Milling products
  Oils/energy products
  Premixes
  Specialty feed ingredients
Food
  Acidulants
  Beverage alcohol
  Edible beans and bean ingredients
  Fiber
  Flour and whole grains
  Lecithin
  Natural-source vitamin E
  Oils
  Plant sterols
  Polyols and gums
  Proteins
  Rice
  Soy isoflavones
  Starches
  Sweeteners
Fuel
  Biodiesel
  Ethanol
Industrials
  Acidulants
  De-icers
  Dispersants
  Dust control products
  Emulsifiers and thickeners
  Fermentation nutrients
  Fertilizers
  Industrial oils
  Polyols
  Propylene glycol
  Solvents
  Starches
  Superabsorbents

Selected Services

Agriculture
  Grain merchandising
  Grain milling
  Grain processing
Information
  Billing and invoicing
  Inventory
  Logistics
  Payment
  Product search
Transportation
  Land
  Rail
  Truck
  Water
  Ocean
  River

Selected Subsidiaries Joint Ventures and Other Holdings

Almidones Mexicanos S.A. (50% wet corn milling plant Mexico)
Alfred C. Toepfer International (80% agricultural commodities trading and processed products Germany)
Compagnie Industrielle et Financiere des Produits Amylaces SA (Luxembourg) (42% joint venture investments in food feed ingredients and bioenergy)
Eaststarch C.V. (50% wet corn milling plants Netherlands)
Edible Oils Limited (50% procure package sell edible oils UK)

Golden Peanut LLC (100% peanut hulls oil meal and seed)
Gruma S.A.B. de C.V (23% corn flour and corn tortilla manufacturer Mexico)
Kalama Export Company (45% grain export elevator)
Red Star Yeast LLC (40% joint venture fresh and dry yeast manufacturer US and Canada)
Stratas Foods LLC (50% procure package sell edible oils North America)
Telles LLC (50% market sell corn-based bioplastic)

COMPETITORS

AGRI Industries	Liberty Vegetable Oil
Abengoa Bioenergy	LifeLine
Ag Processing Inc.	Little Sioux Corn
Ajinomoto	Processors
Andersons	Louis Dreyfus
Barry Callebaut	Commodities
Bartlett and Company	Louis Dreyfus Group
Bayer CropScience	MGP Ingredients
Brenntag North America	Malt Products
Bunge Limited	Corporation
CHS	Monsanto Company
CP Kelco	Nestlé
Cargill	Nisshin Oillio
Cosun	Northern Growers
Danisco A/S	Omega Protein
Dow AgroSciences	Pacific Ethanol
DuPont Agriculture	Pioneer Hi-Bred
General Mills	Renewable Energy Group
Green Brick Partners	Riceland Foods
Green Plains	Scoular
Hain Celestial	Syngenta
Hershey	S dzucker
Ingredion	Tate & Lyle

HISTORICAL FINANCIALS

Company Type: Public

Income Statement   FYE: December 31

	REVENUE ($ mil.)	NET INCOME ($ mil.)	NET PROFIT MARGIN	EMPLOYEES
12/17	60,828	1,595	2.6%	31,300
12/16	62,346	1,279	2.1%	31,800
12/15	67,702	1,849	2.7%	32,300
12/14	81,201	2,248	2.8%	33,900
12/13	89,804	1,342	1.5%	31,100
Annual Growth	(9.3%)	4.4%	—	0.2%

2017 Year-End Financials

Debt ratio: 18.75%
Return on equity: 8.99%
Cash ($ mil.): 804
Current ratio: 1.59
Long-term debt ($ mil.): 6,623

No. of shares (mil.): 557
Dividends
  Yield: 0.0%
  Payout: 45.8%
Market value ($ mil.): 22,325

	STOCK PRICE ($) FY Close	P/E High/Low		Earnings	Dividends	Book Value
12/17	40.08	17	14	2.79	1.28	32.88
12/16	45.65	22	14	2.16	1.20	29.97
12/15	36.68	18	11	2.98	1.12	30.08
12/14	52.00	16	11	3.43	0.96	30.73
12/13	43.40	22	13	2.02	0.76	30.59
Annual Growth	(2.0%)	—	—	8.4%	13.9%	1.8%

Arconic Inc

Arconic has a heavy presence in the global light-weight metals manufacturing scene. Its engineered products—primarily made from aluminum steel nickel and titanium— can help you fly drive build and generate power. Created in 2016 from the the aluminum giant Alcoa's spinoff Arconic has retained the parts businesses of its predecessor—engineered products like fastening systems or castings; rolled products like aluminum sheets and plates; and transportation and construction products. With operations in some 20 countries Arconic is a top provider of specialty materials to the aerospace commercial transportation automotive defense building and construction oil & gas and packaging industries.

HISTORY

In 1886 two chemists one in France and one in the US simultaneously discovered an inexpensive process for aluminum production. The American Charles Hall pursued commercial applications. Two years later with an investor group led by Captain Alfred Hunt Hall formed the Pittsburgh Reduction Company. Its first salesman Arthur Davis secured an initial order for 2000 cooking pots.

In 1889 the Mellon Bank loaned the company $4000. In 1891 the firm recapitalized with the Mellon family holding 12% of the stock.

Davis led the business after Hunt died in 1899 and stayed on until 1957 (he died in 1962 at age 95). The company introduced aluminum foil (1910) and found applications for aluminum in new products such as airplanes and cars. It became the Aluminum Company of America in 1907.

By the end of WWI Alcoa had integrated backward into bauxite mining and forward into end-use production. By the 1920s the Mellons had raised their stake to 33%.

The government and Alcoa had debated antitrust issues in court for years since the smelting patent expired in 1912. Finally a 1946 federal ruling forced the company to sell many operations built during WWII as well as its Canadian subsidiary (Alcan).

In the competitive aluminum industry of the 1960s Alcoa's lower-cost production helped it seize market share especially in beverage cans. In the 1970s Alcoa began offering engineered products such as aerospace components and in the 1980s it invested in research acquisitions and plant modernization.

Paul O'Neill (former president of International Paper) arrived as CEO in 1987 and shifted the company's focus back to aluminum. Sales and earnings set records the next two years but plunged afterward reflecting a weak global economy and record-low aluminum prices. Then the fall of the Soviet Union in the early 1990s led to a worldwide glut as Russian exports soared.

In 1994 Alcoa cut its production as part of a two-year accord with Western and Russian producers. That year the company agreed to pool its alumina and chemical operations with Australia's Western Mining Corp.

Alcoa formed a joint venture with Shanghai Aluminum Fabrication Plant in China. The company expanded in Europe in 1996 acquiring Italy's state-run aluminum business followed by the purchase of Inespal Spain's state-run aluminum operations in 1998. Alcoa also bought #3 US aluminum producer Alumax for $3.8 billion in 1998 but only after divesting its cast-plate operations.

Known by the nickname "Alcoa" since the late 1920s the company adopted that as its official name in 1999. O'Neill retired as CEO in 1999; COO Alain Belda succeeded him. Later that year Alcoa bought the 50% of aluminum auto parts maker A-CMI that it did not already own from Hayes Lemmerz International.

In 2000 Alcoa bought aluminum extrusion maker Excel Extrusions from Noranda (now called Falconbridge) and paid $4.5 billion for Reynolds Metals after agreeing to divest some assets — including all of Reynolds' alumina refineries — to satisfy regulators. The same month Alcoa acquired Cordant Technologies. Alcoa also assumed Cordant's 85% ownership of Howmet International (castings) as a result of the transaction — and later acquired the remainder of Howmet. Late in 2000 President-elect George W. Bush named Alcoa's chairman Paul O'Neill to be treasury secretary. (O'Neill subsequently resigned the post in December 2002.)

Alcoa sold its majority stake in the Worsley alumina refinery (Australia) to BHP Billiton in 2001 for about $1.5 billion as part of its

EXECUTIVES

Evp Corporate Development Strategy And New Ventures, Christoph Kollatz, age 57, $531,250 total compensation

Ceo And Director, Charles P. (Chip) Blankenship, age 52

President International Project Development And Asset Management, Kenneth (Ken) Wisnoski, age 63

Evp; Group President Alcoa Engineered Products And Solutions, Karl Tragl, age 56, $453,125 total compensation

Evp And Group President Alcoa Transportation And Construction Solutions, Tim D. Myers, age 52

President Arconic Global Rolled Products And Arconic Defense, Eric V. Roegner, age 49

Evp And Cto, Raymond J. (Ray) Kilmer

Evp And Cfo, Ken Giacobbe, $386,250 total compensation

Evp Human Resources And Environment Health Safety And Sustainability, Vas Nair, age 52

Evp Legal, Kate Ramundo

Vice President Finance, Jim Herring

Vice President Global Communications And Program Development Formerly Alcoa Foundation, Suzanne Van De Raadt

Vice President Controller, Paul Myron

Vice President Investor Relations, Patricia Figueroa

Vice President Compensation And Benefits, Brian Redmond

Chair, John C. Plant, age 65

Vice President Treasurer, Peter Hong

Ceo And Director, Charles P. (Chip) Blankenship, age 52

Chief Securities And Governance Counsel And Assistant Secretary, Margaret Lam

Auditors: PricewaterhouseCoopers LLP

LOCATIONS

HQ: Arconic Inc
390 Park Avenue, New York, NY 10022-4608
Phone: 212 836-2732
Web: www.arconic.com

2017 Sales

Country	$ mil.	% of total
United States	8,167	63
France	965	7
Hungary	739	6
United Kingdom	721	6
China	615	5
Russia	500	4
Germany	309	2
Brazil	285	2
Canada	262	2
Japan	141	1
Italy	37	-
Other	220	2
Total	**12,960**	**100**

PRODUCTS/OPERATIONS

2017 Sales by Segment

	$ mil.	% of total
Engineered Products and Solutions	5,935	46
Global Rolled Products	5,140	39
Transportation and construction Solutions	1,985	15
Total	**13,060**	**100**

2017 Sales by product

	$ mil.	% of total
Flat-rolled aluminum	4,992	39
Fastening systems	2,102	16
Investment castings	1,983	15
Other extruded and forged products	1,565	12
Architectural aluminum systems	1,065	8
Aluminum wheels	805	6
Other	448	4
Total	**12,960**	**100**

Selected Products

Engineered Products and Solutions
  Arconic Engines
  Arconic Engineered Structures
  Arconic Fastening Systems
Global Rolled Products
  Aerospace and Automotive Products
  Brazing Commercial Transportation and Industrial Solutions
Transportation and Construction Solutions
  Building and Construction Systems
  Arconic Wheel and Transportation Products
Certified Reference Material
  Spectrochemical Reference Materials

COMPETITORS

Accuride
Aleris Corp.
Allegheny Technologies
Apogee Enterprises
Berkshire Hathaway
Companhia Brasileira de Alum nio
Constellium
Eramet
Kaiser Aluminum
Kobe Steel
LISI
Nippon Steel & Sumitomo Metal Corporation
Novelis
VSMPO-AVISMA

HISTORICAL FINANCIALS

Company Type: Public

Income Statement

FYE: December 31

	REVENUE ($ mil.)	NET INCOME ($ mil.)	NET PROFIT MARGIN	EMPLOYEES
12/17	12,960	(74)	—	41,500
12/16	12,394	(941)	—	41,500
12/15	22,534	(322)	—	60,000
12/14	23,906	268	1.1%	59,000
12/13	23,032	(2,285)	—	60,000
Annual Growth	**(13.4%)**	**—**	**—**	**(8.8%)**

2017 Year-End Financials

Debt ratio: 36.56%
Return on equity: (-1.48%)
Cash ($ mil.): 2,150
Current ratio: 2.26
Long-term debt ($ mil.): 6,806
No. of shares (mil.): 481
Dividends
Yield: 0.0%
Payout: —
Market value ($ mil.): 13,119

	STOCK PRICE ($) FY Close	P/E High/Low	PER SHARE ($) Earnings	Dividends	Book Value
12/17	27.25	— —	(0.28)	0.24	10.20
12/16	18.54	— —	(2.31)	0.09	11.66
12/15	9.87	— —	(0.93)	0.00	27.58
12/14	15.79	28 16	0.63	0.00	30.34
12/13	10.63	— —	(6.42)	0.36	29.67
Annual Growth	**26.5% (23.4%)**			**(9.6%)**	

Arrow Electronics, Inc.

Arrow Electronics hits its target markets with a quiver of thousands of electronic products. The company is a leading global distributor of electronic components and computer products alongside rival Avnet. It sells semiconductors passive components interconnect products and computer peripherals to more than 150000 equipment manufacturers and commercial customers. Arrow also provides value-added services such as materials planning design and engineering inventory management and contract manufacturing. It distributes products from manufacturers that include Hitachi Foxconn Microsoft Dell Technologies and Intel. The company operates from more than 600 locations across the globe.

Operations

Arrow Electronics operates in two segments — global components and Enterprise Computing Solutions (ECS). Global components accounts for more than two-thirds of sales. Its product offerings consist of semiconductors passive electro-mechanical interconnect products (capacitors resistors potentiometers power supplies relays switches and connectors) and computing and memory products. More than two-thirds of the unit?s sales are from semiconductor products and related services.

Arrow's ECS business sells hardware software storage and security products to value-added resellers. ECS has expanded its offerings adding professional consulting cloud computing managed services and technical training. Software is the unit?s biggest seller accounting for more than 40% of revenue.

Geographic Reach

Arrow Electronics based in Englewood Colorado generates more than 45% of sales from the Americas (mostly the US) with Europe the Middle East and Africa (EMEA) accounting for nearly 30% and the Asia-Pacific region contributing 25%.

The company has 300 sales offices and 45 distribution centers in more than 80 countries.

Sales and Marketing

Arrow Electronics serves more than 125000 OEMs and contract manufacturers through its components business segment and value-added resellers through its ECS business segment. Most of its sales are made on an order-by-order basis rather than through long-term sales contracts.

The company's customers are in aerospace and defense alternative energy automotive computers gaming industrial equipment instrumentation medical and scientific devices networking optoelectronics and telecommunications equipment.

Financial Performance

After several years of low-single digit revenue growth Arrow Electronics? 2017 sales jumped 13% to $26.8 billion a company record from 2016. Its global components business supplied all but a small fraction of the $3 billion overall increase with higher sales in the Americas EMEA and Asia/Pacific on growth in the industrial transportation aerospace and defense consumer and communications markets. The ECS segment?s revenue was flat year-to-year.

Net income fell to $402 million in 2017 from about $523 million in 2016 because of spending about $60 million to pay off some debt restructuring charges that were about $20 million higher than 2016 and a federal income tax increase of about $97 million due to the US Tax Cuts and Jobs Act of 2017.

Arrow had about $730 million in cash in 2017 an increase from $534 million the year before.

Strategy

Arrow Electronics has implemented what it calls a ?sensor to sunset? strategy which means supplying the hardware and software that companies need to use the full range of cloud computing and the Internet of Things. The strategy encompasses the components that gather data the computing power and software that analyze data and offerings that put it to use.

The company maintains its competitive edge by offering more value-added services to diversify its revenue stream. It also keeps a large supplier base so that customers can procure from a one-stop shop rather than purchase from several different vendors.

Along with rival Avnet Arrow has made acquisitions to corral competition increase its footprint and multiply product offerings. The acquisition of eInfochips (and its 1500 engineers) was made to strengthen Arrow?s capability to staff large engineering jobs. The eInfochips engineers have expertise in chip design hardware and software and cloud-based tools.

More than 45% if Arrow?s revenue comes from semiconductor products and related services. Such dependence makes Arrow susceptible to the semiconductor industry?s boom-and-bust cycles as well as occasional shortages and surplus of products that can wreak havoc on pricing.

Mergers and Acquisitions
Arrow Electronics continues to expand its service capabilities and global presence primarily through acquisitions. Most of the activity has been in the global components segment which made more than 15 deals in the past several years expanding products and services offerings extending its geographic reach in the Asia/Pacific region and to boost its digital capabilities.

In 2018 Arrow Electronics acquired eInfochips a design and managed services company. Headquartered in San Jose California eInfochips also has locations in India and Europe. They company has customers in retail consumer goods industrial automation health care and aerospace.

In 2016 acquired the global internet media portfolio focused on technology and electronic design from UBM including EE Times EDN ESM Embedded EBN TechONline and Datasheets.com.

EXECUTIVES

Chairman President And Ceo, Michael J. (Mike) Long, age 60, $1,150,000 total compensation
Vp And Cio, Vincent P. (Vin) Melvin, age 54
President Global Components, Andrew D. (Andy) King, age 54, $500,000 total compensation
Svp And Chief Strategy Officer, M. Catherine (Cathy) Morris, age 59, $475,000 total compensation
President Global Enterprise Computing Solutions, Sean J. Kerins, age 55, $550,000 total compensation
Svp And Cfo, Christopher D. (Chris) Stansbury, age 52, $452,308 total compensation
Vice President And Treasurer, Michael Taunton
Senior Vice President Human Resources, John McMahon
Chairman President And Ceo, Michael J. (Mike) Long, age 60
Auditors: Ernst & Young LLP

LOCATIONS

HQ: Arrow Electronics, Inc.
9201 East Dry Creek Road, Centennial, CO 80112
Phone: 303 824-4000
Web: www.arrow.com

2016 Sales

	$ mil.	% of total
Americas	11,442	48
Europe Middle East & Africa	6,772	28
Asia/Pacific	5,609	24
Total	**23,825**	**100**

Selected Acquisitions
FY2015
immixGroup Inc.
FY2014
Data Mogul AG
FY 2013
ComputerLinks
FY 2012
ALTIMATE Group
Asset Recovery Corporation
Global Link Technology
Redemtech
Seed International
TechTurn

PRODUCTS/OPERATIONS

2016 Sales

	$ mil.	% of total
Global Components	15,408	65
Global Enterprise computing solutions (ECS)	8,416	35
Total	**23,825**	**100**

Selected Products and Services
Computer Products
  Communication control equipment
  Controllers
  Design systems
  Desktop computers
  Flat-panel displays
  Microcomputer boards and systems
  Monitors
  Printers
  Servers
  Software
  Storage products
  System chassis and enclosures
  Workstations
Electronic Components
  Capacitors
  Connectors
  Potentiometers
  Power supplies
  Relays
  Resistors
  Switches

Services
Analysis implementation and support
Component design
Contract manufacturing
Forecast and order management
Inventory management

COMPETITORS

Avnet	Richardson Electronics
Digi-Key	SYNNEX
Future Electronics	TTI Inc.
Heilind Electronics	Tech Data
Ingram Micro	WPG Holdings
N.F. Smith	Yosun
Newark Corporation	ePlus

HISTORICAL FINANCIALS
Company Type: Public

Income Statement				FYE: December 31
	REVENUE ($ mil.)	NET INCOME ($ mil.)	NET PROFIT MARGIN	EMPLOYEES
12/18	29,676	716	2.4%	20,100
12/17	26,812	401	1.5%	18,800
12/16	23,825	522	2.2%	18,700
12/15	23,282	497	2.1%	18,500
12/14	22,768	498	2.2%	17,000
Annual Growth	**6.8%**	**9.5%**	**—**	**4.3%**

2018 Year-End Financials

Debt ratio: 19.60%	No. of shares (mil.): 85
Return on equity: 13.94%	Dividends
Cash ($ mil.): 509	Yield: —
Current ratio: 1.55	Payout: —
Long-term debt ($ mil.): 3,239	Market value ($ mil.): 5,874

	STOCK PRICE ($) FY Close	P/E High/Low		PER SHARE ($) Earnings	Dividends	Book Value
12/18	68.95	11	8	8.10	0.00	62.51
12/17	80.41	19	15	4.48	0.00	56.47
12/16	71.30	13	8	5.68	0.00	49.64
12/15	54.18	12	10	5.20	0.00	45.56
12/14	57.89	12	9	4.98	0.00	43.32
Annual Growth	**4.5%**	**—**	**—**	**12.9%**	**—**	**9.6%**

Arrow Financial Corp.

Arrow Financial has more than one shaft in its quiver. It's the holding company for two banks: $2 billion-asset Glens Falls National Bank operates 30 branches in eastern upstate New York while $400 million-asset Saratoga National Bank and Trust Company has around 10 branches in Saratoga County. Serving local individuals and businesses the banks offer standard deposit and loan products as well as retirement trust and estate planning services and employee benefit plan administration. Its subsidiaries include: McPhillips Insurance Agency and Upstate Agency which offer property and casualty insurance; Capital Financial Group which sells group health plans; and North Country Investment Advisors which provides financial planning services.

Operations
Arrow Financial's loan portfolio consisted of residential real estate mortgages and home equity loans (40% of loan assets) commercial and commercial real estate loans (31%) and indirect auto loans (29%) at the end of 2015.

The banking group makes more than 70% of its revenue from interest income. About 58% of Arrow Financial's total revenue came from loan interest (including fees) during 2015 while another 14% came from interest on taxable and tax-exempt investment securities. The rest of its revenue came from insurance commissions (9% of revenue) customer service fees (9%) fiduciary activity income (8%) and other miscellaneous income sources.

Geographic Reach
Glens Falls National Bank has 30 branches in eastern upstate New York (in Warren Washington Saratoga Essex and Clinton Counties). Saratoga Springs-based Saratoga National Bank operates nine branches in Saratoga Albany and Rensselaer Counties.

Financial Performance
Arrow Financial Corporation's revenues and profits have been slowly rising since 2013 mostly as steady — and more creditworthy — loan growth has spurred more interest income.

The group's revenue climbed 4% to $98.86 million during 2015 mostly as 7%-plus growth in loan and other interest-earning assets continued to spur additional interest income.

Revenue growth in 2015 pushed Arrow Financial's net income up 6% to $24.66 million. The banking group's operating cash levels dipped 6% to $28.93 million despite earnings growth mostly due to unfavorable working capital changes.

Strategy
Arrow Financial has been working its loan portfolio quality by implementing smarter lending strategies with stronger underwriting and collateral control procedures and credit review systems.

It's also slowly expanding its business and branch network in the Capital District of New York which has been a key market for the bnak's growth. In September 2015 its Saratoga National Bank subsidiary opened its ninth branch in Troy. In June 2014 it opened a new branch in Colonie after opening two new branches in Queensbury and Clifton Park in 2013.

EXECUTIVES

Svp Arrow Financial Corporation And President And Ceo Saratoga National Bank And Trust Company, David S. (Dave) DeMarco, $178,500 total compensation

Director Arrow Financial Corporation And Chairman Saratoga National Bank And Trust, Raymond F. (Ray) O'Conor, $178,500 total compensation

President And Ceo, Thomas J. (Tom) Murphy, age 60, $300,000 total compensation

Svp And Cfo Arrow Financial Corporation And Evp And Cfo Glens Falls National Bank And Trust Company, Edward J. Campanella, age 50

Vice President, Jim Brown

Vice President, Paul Delzotto

Vice President Trust Officer, Laura Vamvalis

Vice President, Peter Capozzola

Chairman, Thomas L. Hoy, age 69

Director Arrow Financial Corporation And Chairman Saratoga National Bank And Trust, Raymond F. (Ray) O'Conor

Board Member, David Kruczlnicki

Board Member, Michael B Clarke

Board Member, Colin Read

Auditors: KPMG LLP

LOCATIONS

HQ: Arrow Financial Corp.
250 Glen Street, Glens Falls, NY 12801
Phone: 518 745-1000
Web: www.arrowfinancial.com

PRODUCTS/OPERATIONS

2015 Sales

	$ mil.	% of total
Interest and dividend income		
Interest and Fees on Loans	56	58
Fully Taxable	8	8
Exempt from Federal Taxes	5	6
Non-interest income		
Fees for Other Services to Customers	9	9
Insurance Commissions	9	9
Income From Fiduciary Activities	7	8
Other	2	2
Total	**98**	**100**

Selected Subsidiaries

Glens Falls National Bank and Trust Company
Arrow Properties Inc. (real estate investment trust)
Capital Financial Group Inc.
Glens Falls National Community Development Corporation
Glens Falls National Insurance Agencies LLC (dba McPhillips Agency)
Loomis & LaPann Inc.
NC Financial Services Inc.
North Country Investment Advisers Inc.
Upstate Agency LLC
Saratoga National Bank and Trust Company

COMPETITORS

Ballston Spa Bancorp	Community Bank System
Bank of America	KeyCorp
Citizens Financial Group	NBT Bancorp
	TrustCo Bank Corp NY

HISTORICAL FINANCIALS

Company Type: Public

Income Statement   FYE: December 31

	ASSETS ($ mil.)	NET INCOME ($ mil.)	INCOME AS % OF ASSETS	EMPLOYEES
12/17	2,760	29	1.1%	533
12/16	2,605	26	1.0%	524
12/15	2,446	24	1.0%	511
12/14	2,217	23	1.1%	513
12/13	2,163	21	1.0%	516
Annual Growth	**6.3%**	**7.7%**	**—**	**0.8%**

2017 Year-End Financials

Debt ratio: 0.72%
Return on equity: 12.16%
Cash ($ mil.): 72
Current ratio: —
Long-term debt ($ mil.): —

No. of shares (mil.): 14
Dividends
Yield: 0.0%
Payout: 46.5%
Market value ($ mil.): 487

	STOCK PRICE ($) FY Close	P/E High/Low	Earnings	Dividends	Book Value
12/17	33.95	20 15	2.04	0.95	17.38
12/16	40.50	22 14	1.86	0.92	16.26
12/15	27.17	17 15	1.75	0.90	15.07
12/14	27.49	17 15	1.66	0.88	14.20
12/13	26.56	18 15	1.56	0.87	13.58
Annual Growth	**6.3%**	**— —**	**7.0%**	**2.3%**	**6.4%**

Asbury Automotive Group Inc

Car dealership giant Asbury Automotive Group oversees around 93 new vehicle franchises representing around 80 dealership locations in about a dozen states including the Carolinas Florida Texas and Virginia. The dealerships sell some 30 different brands of US and non-US new and used vehicles. Asbury also offer parts servicing and collision repair from about 25 repair centers and two stand-alone used vehicle stores as well as financing insurance and warranty and service contracts. The auto dealer has grown by acquiring large locally branded dealership groups as well as smaller groups and individually owned dealerships throughout the US. Customers include individual buyers and fleet operators.

Operations

Asbury sells in the region of 100000 new vehicles each year representing around 55% of its total revenues. Used car sales bring in 30%. The company also operates a parts and services division (10% of revenue) and a finance and insurance division (5%).

Some 80% of Asbury's sales come from import brands. Honda represents around 15% of new vehicle revenue while Nissan and Toyota each account for slightly more than 10%.

Geographic Reach

Duluth Georgia-based Asbury Automotive operates dealerships in more than 15 metropolitan markets throughout the US. Aside from the Carolinas Florida Texas and Virginia Asbury has dealerships in Indiana Georgia Mississippi and Missouri.

Sales and Marketing

Asbury advertises on TV radio and newspaper as well as through internet-based campaigns including search engine marketing website optimization and through third-party websites.

Financial Performance

Six consecutive years of revenue growthstalled in fiscal 2016 flattening out at $6.5 billion.

A slight fall in new and used vehicle sales was mostly offset by an increase in parts and service revenue to a net negative effect of $60.6 million or less than 1% of total sales.

Net income was also virtually unchanged falling $2.2 million to $167.2 million.

Cash from operations fell 8% to $142.3 million.

Strategy

With revenue growth flagging and net income not much better Asbury's management bought back shares to boost its share price. It spent around $162 million on share repurchases in the first four months of 2017.

Asbury has been selling off underperforming dealerships. It exited Arkansas entirely and sold four stores representing five franchises. On the other hand it acquired a Chevrolet franchise and an Isuzu truck franchise in Indianapolis Indiana in 2017.

To help drive sales in a more cost effective manner Asbury is decreasing its advertising spend per vehicle while increasing its focus on digital. It has improved its e-commerce offering and now sells vehicles online.

Mergers and Acquisitions

In 2017 Asbury bought Hare Chevrolet a Chevrolet dealership that also runs a collision center and Isuzu dealership and a truck center.

EXECUTIVES

Svp Corporate Development And Real Estate, George C. Karolis, age 43, $397,728 total compensation

President And Ceo, David W. Hult, age 52, $745,182 total compensation

Vp And Cio, Barry Cohen

Svp And Cfo, Sean D. Goodman, age 53

Vice President Manufacturer Relations, Matthew Mees

Vice President Human Resources, Renee Mckenzie

Vice President Manufacturer Relations, Matthew Mees

Executive Vice President, Michael S Kearney

Vice President, Joe Parham

Senior Vice President Chro, Jed Milstein

Chairman, Thomas C. DeLoach, age 71

Vice Chairman, Craig T. Monaghan, age 61

Vice President And Treasurer, Matthew K Pettoni

Board Member, Joel Alsfine

Board Member, Dennis Clements

Auditors: Ernst & Young LLP

LOCATIONS

HQ: Asbury Automotive Group Inc
2905 Premiere Parkway N.W., Suite 300, Duluth, GA 30097
Phone: 770 418-8200
Web: www.asburyauto.com

PRODUCTS/OPERATIONS

2017 Sales

	$ mil.	% of total
New vehicles	3,561	55
Used vehicles	1,834	28
Parts & services	786	12
Finance & insurance	275	5
Total	**6,456**	**100**

2017 Sales

	% of total
Imports	46
Luxury	34
Domestic	20
Total	**100**

Selected Brands

Coggin Automotive Group
Courtesy Autogroup
David McDavid Auto Group
Gray-Daniels Auto Family
Nalley Automotive Group
Plaza Motor Company

COMPETITORS

AutoNation
Buchanan Automotive
CarMax
Ferman Automotive
Group 1 Automotive
Hendrick Automotive
Island Lincoln-Mercury

Penske Automotive
Group
Ron Tonkin Family of
Dealerships
Scott-McRae
Sonic Automotive

HISTORICAL FINANCIALS

Company Type: Public

Income Statement   FYE: December 31

	REVENUE ($ mil.)	NET INCOME ($ mil.)	NET PROFIT MARGIN	EMPLOYEES
12/17	6,456	139	2.2%	8,000
12/16	6,527	167	2.6%	7,900
12/15	6,588	169	2.6%	8,600
12/14	5,867	111	1.9%	8,300
12/13	5,334	109	2.0%	7,600
Annual Growth	4.9%	6.3%	—	1.3%

2017 Year-End Financials

Debt ratio: 68.21%
Return on equity: 41.28%
Cash ($ mil.): 4
Current ratio: 1.23
Long-term debt ($ mil.): 862

No. of shares (mil.): 20
Dividends
Yield: —
Payout: —
Market value ($ mil.): 1,332

	STOCK PRICE ($) FY Close	P/E High/Low		PER SHARE ($) Earnings	Dividends	Book Value
12/17	64.00	10	7	6.62	0.00	18.94
12/16	61.70	9	6	7.40	0.00	13.16
12/15	67.44	15	10	6.41	0.00	12.68
12/14	75.92	21	12	3.71	0.00	15.60
12/13	53.74	16	9	3.51	0.00	15.95
Annual Growth	4.5%	—	—	17.2%	—	4.4%

Ascena Retail Group Inc

Ascena Retail Group operates about 4900 specialty stores throughout the US Puerto Rico and Canada. Its 800-plus dressbarn stores court women ages 35 to 55. Maurices with some 990-plus locations targets 17-to-34-year-old females in towns with populations between 25000 and 100000. Its second-largest chain Justice and its Charming Shoppes subsidiary courts "tweens" at about 940 stores and online. In 2015 Ascena purchased upscale retailer ANN which became Ascena's largest segment and added Ann Taylor Lou & Grey and LOFT stores.

Operations

The company operates six business segments: ANN Justice Lane Bryant maurices dressbarn and Catherines.

ANN offers sells clothes for women under its Ann Taylor and LOFT brands and accounts for around a third of the company's revenue.

Justice makes clothes and related branded merchandise for girls age 6-12; Lane Bryant and mau-

rices specialize in plus-sized fashion for women in suburban and small towns; the three chains each bring in around 16% of net revenue.

Catherines offers mid-range wear-to-work and casual clothing and accessories and brings in some 6% of revenue.

Dressbarn accounts for 14% of sales.

Geographic Reach

New Jersey-based Ascena Retail Group's +4900 specialty stores are located across the US states as well as in Puerto Rico and Canada. The Justice and maurices chains operate 42 stores and 35 stores in Canada respectively. While more are planned they contribute an insignificant amount of sales at present.

ANN has stores in 47 states the District of Columbia Canada and Puerto Rico as well as six international franchise stores. Justice has stores in 48 states and Canada as well as 68 international franchise stores while maurices has stores in 45 states and Canada. dressbarn Lane Bryant and Catherines have stores located in 48 47 and 44 states respectively.

ANN segment had 13 company-operated stores in Canada. ANN had the highest number of stores of about over 1020 in fiscal 2015.

Sales and Marketing

Ascena Retail employs a variety of advertising and marketing strategies across its six retail brands. The company engages in customer research promotional events window and in-store marketing materials as well as direct mail online and magazine advertising. In fiscal 2016 (ended July) the company spent $271 million on advertising and marketing compared with $177 million the previous year and $160 million in fiscal 2014.

Financial Performance

The acquisition of ANN in August 2015 bumped up revenue a healthy 46% in fiscal 2016 to $7.0 billion. Comparable sales fell by $214 million. The company reduced its net loss from $236.8 million to $11.9 million partly due to higher net revenue and partly due to the absence of impairment goodwill relating to the write-down in Lane Bryant value.

Cash from operations increased 3% to $445.4 million.

Strategy

Ascena Retail Group mines different retail niches including younger women (ages 17 to 34) tween (ages seven to 14) girls plus-size women (sizes 12 to 32) and "mature" women through its various retail brands. The recent acquisition of ANN and its Anne Taylor and LOFT brands taps into the working women market.

Acquisitions are key to the holding company's successful growth strategy. Concurrently the company is working to right-size its store network closing underperforming Dress Barn locations and adding Maurice's shops and Justice stores including locations in Canada. While the company's international presence is relatively light it's exploring other international opportunities for its brands. Licensing presents an opportunity for overseas growth.

Another focus for the company is its omnichannel strategy which includes traditional stores in-store ordering capabilities and e-commerce operations. It made nearly $520 million from online sales in 2015 up 15%.

Mergers and Acquisitions

In 2015 the company doubled down on its plan to focus on older customers when it paid $2.2 billion for upscale retailer ANN parent of career-wear maker Ann Taylor and its more casual LOFT banner. The acquisition positioned Ascena as the third largest specialty apparel retailer and the single largest focused on women's apparel with a diverse brand portfolio that serves women of all ages sizes and demographics.

HISTORY

Roslyn Jaffe started The Dress Barn in 1962. Focusing on career women in need of reasonably priced wardrobes the store offered a 20%-50% discount from department store prices. By the mid-1970s Dress Barn had 18 stores and was expanding through acquisitions. It went public in 1983. The Dress Barn Woman division was introduced three years later. The company discontinued its casual apparel stores (SBX) in fiscal 1995.

The discount appeal of Dress Barn stores has been undermined in recent years by the increased use of moderately priced private-label brands by major department stores. Manufacturers such as Jones Apparel Group have also entered the retail market via factory outlets. In its rapid expansion during the 1990s Dress Barn countered this trend by focusing on combination stores offering both regular and larger-size merchandise. These larger stores (8000-9000 sq. ft.) provide the company a greater presence in shopping center locations and have lower operating costs.

Dress Barn added shoe departments and petite sizes in 1996 and 1997 and stepped up closures of poorly performing stores. It continued doing so in fiscal 1998 and 1999 while opening new combo stores and converting existing stores to the combo format. Dress Barn introduced a mail-order catalog in the fall of 1999 and launched a website the following year. The Jaffes' son David was named CEO in early 2002; Roslyn's husband Elliot remains chairman.

Dress Barn's longtime search for acquisition opportunities was consummated in January 2005 with the purchase of specialty chain Maurices which targets younger women (ages 17 to 34) in small to metro fringe markets with more fashion-forward merchandise.

In 2009 Dress Barn tapped into the teen market again with its purchase of Tween Brands and the retailer's Justice stores.

The company changed its name in January 2011 to Ascena Retail Group and adopted a holding company structure. In June 2012 the firm acquired plus-size retailer Charming Shoppes for about $900 million.

EXECUTIVES

Chairman And Ceo, David R. Jaffe, age 59, $1,019,231 total compensation
President And Ceo Ascena Brands, Gary P. Muto, age 58
Evp And Chief Human Resources Officer, John Pershing, age 47, $557,812 total compensation
President And Coo, Brian E. Lynch, age 61
Evp And Cfo, Robb Giammatteo, age 46, $509,615 total compensation
Evp And General Counsel, Duane D. Holloway, $215,385 total compensation
Vice President Of Global Sourcing, Carolyn Eberly
Svp Design Justice, Lucia Murillo
Vice President Infrastructure Security And Operations, Andre Gold
Vp Corporate Benefits Ascena Retail Group, Isabella Spiegel
Svp Stores And Store Operations Justice, Chris Kaighn
Chairman And Ceo, David R. Jaffe, age 59
Auditors: DELOITTE & TOUCHE LLP

LOCATIONS

HQ: Ascena Retail Group Inc
933 MacArthur Boulevard, Mahwah, NJ 07430
Phone: 551 777-6700   **Fax:** 845 369-8001
Web: www.ascenaretail.com

PRODUCTS/OPERATIONS

Selected Brands
Ann Taylor
Ann Taylor Loft
Cacique
Catherines
Dressbarn
Justice
Lane Bryant
Lane Bryant Outlet
Loft
Lou & Grey
Maurices
Right Fit

2016 Stores

	No.
ANN	1,022
Maurices	993
Justice	937
DressBarn	809
Lane Bryant	772
Catherines	373
Total	**4,906**

2016 Sales

	$ mil.	% of total
ANN	2,330	33
Justice	1,106	16
Lane Bryant	1,130	16
Maurices	1,101	16
Dress Barn	993	14
Catherines	333	5
Total	**6,995**	**100**

COMPETITORS

American Eagle	Kohl's
Outfitters	L Brands
Avenue Stores	Macy's
Aéropostale	Old Navy
Burlington Coat	Ross Stores
Factory	Saks
Christopher & Banks	Sears
Deb Shops	Stage Stores
Dillard's	Target Corporation
J. C. Penney	Wal-Mart

HISTORICAL FINANCIALS

Company Type: Public

Income Statement

FYE: August 4

	REVENUE ($ mil.)	NET INCOME ($ mil.)	NET PROFIT MARGIN	EMPLOYEES
08/18*	6,578	(39)	—	63,000
07/17	6,649	(1,067)	—	64,000
07/16	6,995	(11)	—	66,000
07/15	4,802	(236)	—	48,000
07/14	4,790	133	2.8%	48,000
Annual Growth	**8.3%**	**—**		**7.0%**

*Fiscal year change

2018 Year-End Financials

Debt ratio: 37.21%
Return on equity: (-4.82%)
Cash ($ mil.): 238
Current ratio: 1.25
Long-term debt ($ mil.): 1,328

No. of shares (mil.): 196
Dividends
Yield: —
Payout: —
Market value ($ mil.): 789

	STOCK PRICE ($) FY Close	P/E High/Low		PER SHARE ($) Earnings	Dividends	Book Value
08/18*	4.02	—	—	(0.20)	0.00	4.07
07/17	2.32	—	—	(5.48)	0.00	4.21
07/16	8.13	—	—	(0.06)	0.00	9.59
07/15	12.56	—	—	(1.46)	0.00	9.30
07/14	16.12	27	19	0.81	0.00	10.74
Annual Growth	**(29.3%)**	—	—	—		**—(21.6%)**

*Fiscal year change

ASCENSION HEALTH ALLIANCE

EXECUTIVES

Pres, Anthony R Tersigni
Sr Exec Advsr, Sister Bernice Coreil DC
Evp, John D Doyle
Evp, Robert J Henkel
Evp-Gen Coun, Joseph R Impicciche
Evp, Susan Nestor Levy
Evp, Sister Maureen McGuire DC
Evp, David B Pryor
Evp-Cfo, Anthony J Speranzo
Executive Assistant, Barbara Flick
Chief Information Oficer, Mark Barner
Auditors: ERNST & YOUNG LLP ST LOUIS M

LOCATIONS

HQ: ASCENSION HEALTH ALLIANCE
101 S HANLEY RD STE 450, SAINT LOUIS, MO
631053463
Phone: 314 733-8000
Web: WWW.HEALTHMART.COM

HISTORICAL FINANCIALS

Company Type: Private

Income Statement

FYE: June 30

	ASSETS ($ mil.)	NET INCOME ($ mil.)	INCOME AS % OF ASSETS	EMPLOYEES
06/17	34,320	1,638	4.8%	111,719
06/16	32,469	(339)	—	—
06/15	30,963	(42)	—	—
Annual Growth	**5.3%**	**—**	**—**	**—**

2017 Year-End Financials

Debt ratio: ——
Return on equity: 7.20%
Cash ($ mil.): 857
Current ratio: 0.70
Long-term debt ($ mil.): —

Dividends
Yield: —
Payout: —
Market value ($ mil.): —

Associated Banc-Corp

A lot of Midwesterners are associated with Associated Banc-Corp the holding company for Associated Bank. One of the largest banks based in Wisconsin the bank operates about 200 branches in that state as well as in Illinois and Minnesota. Catering to consumers and local businesses it offers deposit accounts loans mortgage banking credit and debit cards and leasing. The bank's wealth management division offers investments trust services brokerage insurance and employee group benefits plans. Commercial loans including agricultural construction and real estate loans make up more than 60% of bank's loan portfolio. The bank also writes residential mortgages consumer loans and home equity loans.

Operations

Associated Banc-Corp boasts total assets of more than $27 billion making it one of the 50 largest publicly traded US bank holding companies. More than 70% of revenue comes from interest income mostly from loans. Roughly 60% of Associated Banc-Corp's $18 billion loan portfolio

consists of commercial and industrial real estate construction commercial real estate loans and lease financing.

Nearly 30% of the company's income is from non-interest sources including: trust service fees service charges insurance commissions brokerage and annuity commissions and mortgage banking income among others. It also offers benefits consulting services through its Associated Financial Group subsidiary.

Geographic Reach

The company offers a full range of financial products and services in more than 200 banking locations serving more than 100 communities throughout Wisconsin Illinois and Minnesota and commercial financial services in Indiana Michigan Missouri Ohio and Texas.

Sales and Marketing

Associated Banc-Corp spent $26.1 million on business development and advertising in 2014 compared to $23.3 million in 2013 and $21.3 million in 2012.

Financial Performance

Associated Banc-Corp's revenue has remained flat for the past several years at just above $1 billion. Revenue in 2014 inched up by less than 1% to $1.03 billion mostly thanks to higher interest income as loan assets grew by 11% and as interest and dividends on investment securities also grew by double digits. Offsetting much of this growth the company's net mortgage banking income shrunk by $28 million (56%) driven by lower gains on sales and related income as secondary mortgage production declined.

Profit levels have been steadily rising over the past several years since losses in 2009 and 2010 with net income in 2014 rising by 1% to $190.51 million. Higher revenue combined with lower interest expenses on deposits and lower personnel costs all helped to boost the company's bottom line.

Despite higher earnings cash from operations fell 56% to $212.74 million primarily as the company made fewer net proceeds from the sale of its mortgage loans held for sale. The company's total loans grew by 11% to $17.6 billion in 2014 while total deposits rose by 9% to $18.77 billion.

Strategy

The company intends to continue pursuing a profitable growth strategy by carefully screening its prospective customers in light of the risks expenses and difficulties frequently encountered by companies in significant growth stages of development. Associated Banc-Corp hopes to keep its momentum going via organic growth including increasing its fee income and commercial deposits among other measures. It is also remodeling or relocating many of its branches.

Associated Banc-Corp also plans to continue strong loan business growth. For 2015 the company expects high single-digit annual average loan growth after posting loan double-digit loan growth across most categories in 2014.

Mergers and Acquisitions

Associated purchased BankMutual a Wisconsin-based bank in 2018.

In early 2015 subsidiary Associated Financial Group agreed to buy Minnesota-based Ahmann & Martin Co a risk and benefits consulting firm to gain new clients and expand its financial risk and insurance product and service lines.

Company Background

Hampered by one of the worst economic environments in recent history the bank saw an increase in nonperforming loans (particularly business- and housing-related loans) and more than tripled its provision for loan losses from 2008 to 2009. The company cut its losses in 2010 and nearly turned a profit as it concentrated on improving its credit quality. It moved away from construction lending and its nonperforming loans and its provisions for loan losses decreased. Even though 2011 revenues were down Associated Banc-Corp returned to profitability as credit quality continued to improve.

EXECUTIVES

Evp And Chief Risk Officer, Arthur G. (Art) Heise, age 60

President And Ceo, Philip B. (Phil) Flynn, age 60, $1,250,000 total compensation

Evp General Counsel And Corporate Secretary, Randall J. Erickson, age 59, $406,667 total compensation

Evp And Head Retail Banking, David L. Stein, age 54, $545,849 total compensation

Evp And Chief Human Resources Officer, Judith M. Docter, age 57

Evp And Chief Credit Officer, Scott S. Hickey, age 62, $644,531 total compensation

Evp And Chief Strategy Officer, Oliver Buechse, age 49

Evp And Head Commercial Real Estate, Breck F. Hanson

Evp And Head Corporate Banking, Donna N. Smith

Evp And Head Specialized Industries And Commercial Financial Services, John A. Utz, $348,417 total compensation

Evp And Head Community Markets, Timothy J. Lau

Evp And Cfo, Christopher J. Del Moral-Niles, $477,500 total compensation

Evp And Chief Audit Executive, Patrick J. Derpinghaus

Evp Cio And Coo, James Yee, $458,333 total compensation

Evp And Head Private Client And Institutional Services, William M. Bohn

President Southern Illinois, Phillip Hickman

Senior Vice President Investme, Sara Walker

Vice President Customer Care Program And Operations Manager, Wendy Kumm

Vice President Marketing Manager, Shawn Kesler

Vice President, Mark Vorel

Vice President Of Commercial Lending, Jon Hein

Vice President, Ed Parada

Vice President Atm Channel Manager, Deanna Helminiak

Vice President, Terry Zeske

Assistant Vice President Senior Bank Manager, Kim Klinkner

Senior Vice President, Angela O'neill

Vice President, Brad Amundsen

Senior Vice President, Diane Gantner

Senior Vice President Experiential Marketing, Ryan Taylor

Assistant Vice President Corporate, Robert Brothers

Senior Vice President Community Markets, Sandra Earp

Executive Vice President And Director Human Resources, Judy Docter

Vice President, Gina Frease

Vice President, Charles Garcia

Vice President Field Exams, Jeff Kohr

Vice President Public Relations Manager, Jennifer Kaminski

Underwriting Review Officer Ii Vice President, Shannon Little

Vice President Commercial Banking Portfo, Bradley Anderson

Senior Vice President And Trust Manager, Robert Skowronski

Executive Vice President Commercial Real Estate, Paul Schmidt

Senior Vice President Commercial Real Estate, Lisa Cunningham

Vice President Commercial Banking Relationship Manager, Ben Veach

Vice President Commercial Banking Relationship Manager, Scott Hoerth

Senior Vice President Marketing, Heidi Hahn

Vice President, Christian Bryant

Assistant Vice President Senior Loan Officer, Christine Howard

Assistant Vice President Branch Manager, Kenneth Alburg

Assistant Vice President Of Retail Marketing, Shannon Krohn

Vice President Portfolio Manager, Mark Buechler

Vice President And Trust Officer, John Kvamme

Assistant Vice President Branch Manager, Jared Cotto

Vice President Private Banker, Chad Otte

Vice President, Daniel Zettinger

Vice President, Amy Kolb

Vice President, Heather Wise

Vice President Private Banking, Scott Rannila

Assistant Vice President Residential Loan Officer Nmls#762823, Jason Smith

Senior Vice President And Manager: Chicago Private Banking Group, Doug Myers

Vice President, Tracy Session

Vice President, Ryun Van Cuyk

Vice President, Jessica Brandom

Vice President Business Development Officer, Paul Zahour

Senior Vice President Director Of Treasury Management Product And Strategy, Michael Dacko

Vice President Asset Based Lending, Mickey Moran

Assistant Vice President Systems Analyst, Jesse Oskey

Vice President Design And Construction Services, Anthony Ferro

Senior Vice President Senior Manager Interactive Consumer Marketing, Jennifer Ott

Vice President Project Manager Senior, Mary Zellner

Senior Vice President Market Manager, Kevin Jordan

Senior Vice President, Don Heath

Vice President Commercial Banking, Grant Schilling

Vice President Market Manager, Chris Davis

Senior Vice President, Farhan Iqbal

Vice President, Adam Demont

Vice President Senior Project Manager, Melissa Birling

Vice President Commercial Banking, Dean Rosencrans

Vice President, Dave Bolwerk

Assistant Vice President Certified Appraiser Residential Loan Officer, Debbie Schlager

Senior Vice President Regional Sales Manager, Tim Damato

Vice President Portfolio Manager, Steve Pipp

Vice President Portfolio Manager, Paul Henning

Senior Vice President, Anthony P Pecora

Vice President Experiential Marketing Manager, Jenny Strachota

Vice President And Multicultural And Affordable Sales Integration Manager, LaDonna Reed

Senior Vice President, Mike Waltz

Ctp Vice President, Melissa Fellows

Assistant Vice President Mortgage Lending, Mark Tripp

Senior Vice President, Shawn Bullock

Senior Vice President Interest Rate Derivatives And Foreign Exchange, Sue Johnson

Vice President Human Resource Business Partner, Lynn Smits

Assistant Vice President Certified Appraiser Residential Loan Officer, Andrea Lopezbartoszewicz

Vice President Private Banker, Gene Williams

Vice President Business Manager, Zachary Wolff

Vice President Telecommunications Services Lead, Don Cross

Vice President Private Banking Manager, Tracy Stansbury

Senior Vice President, Kathy Bozek

Vice President, David Reitz

Senior Vice President Commercial Team Leader, James Lynch

Chairman, William R. Hutchinson, age 75

Treasurer, Tim Watson

Auditors: KPMG LLP

LOCATIONS

HQ: Associated Banc-Corp
   433 Main Street, Green Bay, WI 54301
Phone: 920 491-7500
Web: www.associatedbank.com

PRODUCTS/OPERATIONS

2016 Sales

	$ mil.	% of total
Interest		
Loans including fees	659	58
Investment securities including dividends and Interest	127	11
Other	4	0
Noninterest		
Insurance Commissions	80	7
Service charges on deposit accounts	66	6
Card-based & other nondeposit fees	50	4
Trust Service fees	46	4
Other	108	10
Total	1,144	100

2016 Sales

	% of total
Community Consumer and Business	59
Corporate and Commercial Specialty	36
Risk Management and Shared Services	5
Total	100

COMPETITORS

Bank Mutual	Northern Trust
Harris	TCF Financial
KeyCorp	U.S. Bancorp

HISTORICAL FINANCIALS

Company Type: Public

Income Statement				FYE: December 31
	ASSETS ($ mil.)	NET INCOME ($ mil.)	INCOME AS % OF ASSETS	EMPLOYEES
12/17	30,483	229	0.8%	4,388
12/16	29,139	200	0.7%	4,441
12/15	27,715	188	0.7%	4,383
12/14	26,821	190	0.7%	4,300
12/13	24,226	188	0.8%	4,600
Annual Growth	5.9%	5.0%	—	(1.2%)

2017 Year-End Financials

Debt ratio: 1.63%	No. of shares (mil.): 152
Return on equity: 7.25%	Dividends
Cash ($ mil.): 683	Yield: 0.0%
Current ratio: —	Payout: 35.2%
Long-term debt ($ mil.): —	Market value ($ mil.): 3,882

	STOCK PRICE ($) FY Close	P/E High/Low		PER SHARE ($) Earnings	Dividends	Book Value
12/17	25.40	18	15	1.42	0.50	21.18
12/16	24.70	20	12	1.26	0.45	20.32
12/15	18.75	17	14	1.19	0.41	19.42
12/14	18.63	17	13	1.16	0.37	18.48
12/13	17.40	16	12	1.10	0.33	17.61
Annual Growth	9.9%	—		6.6%	10.9%	4.7%

ASSOCIATED WHOLESALE GROCERS, INC.

Associated Wholesale Grocers (AWG) knows its customers can't live on bread and milk alone. The second-largest retailer-owned distribution cooperative in the US (behind Wakefern Food Corporation) AWG supplies more than 3800 grocery retail outlets in more than half of the US states from 10 distribution centers which collectively have some 7 million square feet of space. In addition to its wholesale grocery operation AWG offers a variety of business services to its members including marketing and merchandising programs retail accounting supermarket development and access to low-cost merchandise through its Value Merchandisers subsidiary. AWG was founded by a group of independent grocers in 1924.

Geographic Reach

Kansas City-headquartered Associated Wholesale Grocers began in Missouri and its operations are generally centered on that state. It operates ten wholesale divisions in Missouri Nebraska Kansas Oklahoma Louisiana Alabama Tennessee and Wisconsin. Its distribution activities extend into another 25 states.

AWG?s Valu Merchandisers subsidiary is gaining a foothold in non-US regions such as the Caribbean Central & South America and the Middle East.

Sales and Marketing

As a cooperative AWG serves the needs of its members who collectively determine how best to utilize the co-ops operations. Its board of directors is made up of nearly 20 people each a key executive at a grocer retail chain which receives products from AWG.

AWG serves up several private label brands to stores. They include Superior Selections Clearly Organic Best Choice Always Save and IGA.

Financial Performance

Associated Wholesale Grocers (AWG) has grown net sales in recent years from $7.8 billion in 2016 to more recent results exceeding $9.0 billion. Net income has trended positively over the same period from $175 million in 2012 to a spiked of more than $225 million in 2014 to a current result near $190 million.

For the year 2016 net sales grew 3% to $9.2 billion. Product price deflation pushed sales lower as did the loss of Albertsons? membership in the distribution co-op. AWG gained 800 new member stores in conjunction with its unification with Affiliated Foods Midwest which increased sales sufficiently to overcome the negative influencers.

Net income for the year was $190 million 4% lower than the prior year due to a corresponding increase in the co-op?s general and administrative expenses.

Strategy

As a supplier to primarily independent and non-national grocers the co-op must retain size in order to compete with larger corporate firms. Years 2016 and 2017 saw its size shrink in Texas particularly in the hotly contested Dallas-Fort Worth market. Associated Wholesale Grocers lost two key members Albertsons (owner of Tom Thumb?s and Safeway) and WinCo. It countered this by uniting with Affiliated Foods Midwest a distribution co-op with some 800 retail stores but the loss of such notable members is expected influence AWG?s posturing within the North Texas area.

AWG continues to build sales of its billion-dollar private-label products line which includes the Best Choice IGA and Always Save brands. In addition to marketing the products as lower-cost alternatives to brand-name products the co-op has been investing in efforts to make sure the quality of its private-label items matches competing national brands. The company also owns and operates the Value Merchandisers Company (VMC) which offers some 22000 nonfood items to its members including health and beauty care general merchandise and seasonal and promotional products.

Operating in a fragmented business AWG competes with a large number of local and regional suppliers as well as distributors of specialty items. The food wholesale business also has its share of national giants including C & S Wholesale Nash-Finch and wholesale grocery and retail company SUPERVALU.

EXECUTIVES

Svp And Division Manager Nashville, Mike Danes
Evp And Chief Marketing Officer, Steve Arnold
Svp And Division Manager Memphis, Gary Jennings
Svp Finance, David Carl
Svp Distribution, Richard Kearns
Svp And Cio, Jon Payne
Svp And Division Manager Fort Worth, Linda Lawson
Svp Springfield, Tim Bellanti
President And Ceo, David Smith
Svp And Division Manager Oklahoma City, Danny Lane
Svp Grocery Products, Dan Funk
Svp Perishables, Jerry Edney
Svp And Division Manager Gulf Coast, Bob Durand
President Valu Merchandisers Company (vmc), Dave Sutton
President Always Fresh, Michael Schumacher
Vp Sales And Merchandising Memphis Division, David Gates
Senior Vice President, Maurice Henry
Vice President Of Sales Great Lakes, Sonny Leon
Director, Bob Hufford
Vice Chairman, Don Woods

LOCATIONS

HQ: ASSOCIATED WHOLESALE GROCERS, INC.
5000 KANSAS AVE, KANSAS CITY, KS 661061135
Phone: 913 288-1000
Web: WWW.AWGINC.COM

COMPETITORS

Affiliated Foods	GSC Enterprises
Affiliated Foods Midwest	H. T. Hackney
Albertsons	McLane
Alex Lee	SUPERVALU
C&S Wholesale	SpartanNash
Central Grocers	Wakefern Food
Dearborn Wholesale Grocers	Wal-Mart
	WinCo Foods

HISTORICAL FINANCIALS

Company Type: Private

Income Statement   FYE: December 31

	REVENUE ($ mil.)	NET INCOME ($ mil.)	NET PROFIT MARGIN	EMPLOYEES
12/17	9,703	199	2.1%	5,500
12/15	8,935	198	2.2%	—
12/14	8,934	226	2.5%	—
12/13	8,380	192	2.3%	—
Annual Growth	3.7%	0.8%	—	—

2017 Year-End Financials
Debt ratio: ——
Return on equity: 2.10%
Cash ($ mil.): 166
Current ratio: 0.50
Long-term debt ($ mil.): —
Dividends
Yield: —
Payout: —
Market value ($ mil.): —

Assurant Inc

From appliance protection to trailer park coverage Assurant aims to give its customers peace of mind. The company provides a diverse range of specialty insurance products such as manufactured home coverage creditor-placed homeowners insurance pre-need funeral policies and extended service contracts for electronics appliances and vehicles. Assurant's products are distributed through sales offices and independent agents across North America and in Latin America Europe and the Asia/Pacific region.

Operations

Assurant operates through three primary segments: Global Lifestyle Global Housing and Global Preneed. The largest segment Global Lifestyle provides mobile device protection and extended service contracts for consumer electronics and appliances vehicle protection and credit and related insurance. That segment accounts for more than half of the company's total revenues.

The Global Housing segment offers lender-placed insurance multi-family housing products (renters insurance and related offerings). Other products include homeowners flood and manufactured housing insurance. Assurant sold its mortgage solutions (such as property inspection valuation and title services) business for $35 million in mid-2018. Global Housing brings in about 35% of Assurant's revenues.

The Global Preneed segment offers pre-funded funeral insurance and annuities in the US and Canada. It accounts for more than 5% of total revenue.

Geographic Reach

More than 75% of Assurant's sales are in the US but the company also operates in Canada Latin America Europe and the Asia/Pacific region. It has locations in Argentina Brazil Canada Chile China Colombia France Germany Italy Ireland Mexico Peru Puerto Rico South Korea Spain and the UK. In all the company has 45 offices worldwide including 34 offices in North America.

Sales and Marketing

Assurant sells its products through independent brokers agents financial institution representatives and third-party marketing organizations as well as through retail outlets including mortgage loan offices funeral homes and retailers. It markets multi-family housing products through property management companies and affinity marketing partners.

Financial Performance

After years of modest growth Assurant's revenue declined 27% in 2016 and another 12% to $6.4 billion in 2017. This was partially driven by a 12% decline in net earned premiums in the housing and lifestyle businesses. Improving economic conditions have lessened demand for lender-placed insurance for example. The Global Lifestyle segment had an 8% revenue decline (to $3.8 billion) while Global Housing's revenue fell 5% to $2.3 billion. Net investment income also dropped that year. These declines were partially offset by an increase in Global Preneed's revenue which rose 3% to $443 million.

In 2016 net income nearly tripled largely due to a decline in losses and expenses related to the winding down of Assurant Health. The following year net income fell 8% to $519.6 million in 2017. This was largely due a reduction in net gains from the prior sale of the employee benefits arm as well as an increase in catastrophe-related losses from Hurricanes Harvey Irma and Maria. However net income for the Global Lifestyle segment rose 15% in 2017 as the company saw growth in its mobile and vehicle protection businesses.

Despite the drop in profits cash flow from operations rose a whopping 388% to $530.4 million that year. This increase was chiefly due to positive changes in insurance policy reserves and expenses which were again related to the divestiture of Assurant Health.

Strategy

Assurant works to develop innovative niche products within the lifestyle and housing markets. Its target areas for growth are connected living (primarily extended service contracts for mobile devices and consumer electronics and appliances) multi-family housing and vehicle protection services. To focus on these key markets Assurant exited the health insurance and employee benefits businesses in 2016. With a wary eye on US health care reform it divested the underperforming Assurant Health (which as an insurer focused on serving small employers and individuals struggled under the Affordable Care Act) that year. It sold certain Assurant Health assets to National General Holdings and shuttered the rest of the business.

Also that year the company sold Assurant Employee Benefits (another underperforming unit) to Sun Life Financial in a deal valued at some $975 million. That sale further allowed Assurant to focus on such products as property credit renters funeral and flood policies. In 2018 the company sold its mortgage solutions operations to Dallas-based Xome Holdings for $35 million.

In 2016 the company launched Assurant Product Protection which allows e-commerce businesses to offer extended protection plans to their customers. Other new products include small business protection against losses from data breaches (offered in partnerships with cybersecurity firms My DigitalShield and SnoopWall) and protection from cyberattacks to small business website owners (offered in partnership with another cybersecurity firm GamaSec).

Assurant typically expands by pursuing a conservative acquisition strategy investing in purchases that neatly complement its existing offerings. For example it is buying The Warranty Group to boost its vehicle and lifestyle product portfolio. The company has also grown through organic measures; its rental insurance customer base rose 20% during 2017.

In addition Assurant partners with other companies to expand its reach. In 2017 the company established partnerships with AppleCare Services Darty and KDDI further growing its lifestyle operations. Late that year it joined forces with Fair a property/casualty firm that allows customers to use an app to get a car on a temporary basis.

Mergers and Acquisitions

In 2018 Assurant bought a controlling stake in The Warranty Group. The $2.5 billion deal greatly expanded the number of automobiles Assurant covers as well as boosting its financial service contract and extended service contract numbers and growing its international operations.

In 2017 Assurant bought Green Tree Insurance Agency from Walter Investment Management for $125 million plus additional performance-based payouts. Green Tree sells housing protection products such as homeowners' and manufacturing housing insurance.

In 2016 Assurant acquired American Title (title and valuation services for home equity lenders) for $45 million.

Company Background

Assurant traces its roots to the LaCrosse Mutual Aid Association which was founded in 1892 to provide disability insurance in Wisconsin. The company formerly known as Fortis Inc. was spun off by the Fortis group (now known as Ageas) in 2004 and became publicly traded.

EXECUTIVES

Evp Chief Legal Officer And Secretary, Bart R. Schwartz, age 65, $595,000 total compensation
President Global Home, Michael P. Campbell
Evp And Chief Communication And Marketing Officer, Francesca Luthi
President And Ceo, Alan B. Colberg, age 56, $955,000 total compensation
Evp And Chief Risk Officer, Christopher J. Pagano, age 54, $639,583 total compensation
Evp Cfo And Treasurer, Richard S. Dziadzio, age 55, $283,205 total compensation
President And Ceo Assurant Specialty Property, Gene E. Mergelmeyer, age 59, $657,500 total compensation
Evp And Cto, Ajay Waghray, age 56, $338,335 total compensation
Evp And Chief Human Resources Officer, Robyn Price Stonehill, age 46
President Global Lifestyle, Keith W. Demmings
Evp And Chief Strategy Officer, Robert A. Lonergan
Senior Vice President Human Resources, Cynthia Lowden
Senior Vice President, Lynn Gelsomin
Senior Vice President Global Sales And Business Development, Allen Tuthill
Vice President Finance, James Shosh
Senior Vice President Portfolio Manager, Matthew Sosland
Vice President, John Sheehan
Evp Chief Legal Officer And Secretary, Bart R. Schwartz, age 65
Chair, Elaine D. Rosen, age 65
Evp Cfo And Treasurer, Richard S. Dziadzio, age 55
Auditors: PricewaterhouseCoopers LLP

LOCATIONS

HQ: Assurant Inc
28 Liberty Street, 41st Floor, New York, NY 10005
Phone: 212 859-7000
Web: www.assurant.com

2017 Sales

	$ mil.	% of total
US	4,980	78
Other countries	1,434	22
Total	**6,415**	**100**

PRODUCTS/OPERATIONS

2017 Sales by Segment

	$ mil.	% of total
Lifestyle	3,510	55
Housing	2,250	35
Preneed	443	7
Corporate & other	210	3
Total	**6,415**	**100**

COMPETITORS

Allstate	Home Buyers Warranty
AmTrust Financial	Homesteaders Life
American Home Shield	Maiden Holdings
Americo	Monumental Life
Asurion	NGL Insurance
Bankers Financial	Nationwide
First American	State Farm
Great American Insurance Company	Warrantech

HISTORICAL FINANCIALS
Company Type: Public

Income Statement
FYE: December 31

	ASSETS ($ mil.)	NET INCOME ($ mil.)	INCOME AS % OF ASSETS	EMPLOYEES
12/17	31,843	519	1.6%	14,750
12/16	29,709	565	1.9%	14,700
12/15	30,043	141	0.5%	16,700
12/14	31,562	470	1.5%	17,600
12/13	29,714	488	1.6%	16,600
Annual Growth	1.7%	1.5%	—	(2.9%)

2017 Year-End Financials

Debt ratio: 3.35%	No. of shares (mil.): 52
Return on equity: 12.42%	Dividends
Cash ($ mil.): 996	Yield: 0.0%
Current ratio: —	Payout: 22.9%
Long-term debt ($ mil.): —	Market value ($ mil.): 5,286

	STOCK PRICE ($) FY Close	P/E High/Low		PER SHARE ($) Earnings	Dividends	Book Value
12/17	100.84	11	9	9.39	2.15	81.47
12/16	92.86	10	7	9.13	2.03	73.26
12/15	80.54	42	29	2.05	1.37	68.70
12/14	68.43	11	9	6.44	1.06	74.77
12/13	66.37	10	5	6.30	0.96	67.29
Annual Growth	11.0%	—	—	10.5%	22.3%	4.9%

AT&T Inc

If there's a way to communicate there's a good chance AT&T Inc. provides it. The company offers services via wireless wireline satellite WiFi IP network Virtual Private Network and fiber optic cable. The company is the biggest wireline voice provider and the second biggest wireless provider (behind Verizon Communications) in the US with more than 140 million subscribers. It offers digital TV (as well as voice and internet service) through its U-verse brand and satellite Pay TV through DIRECTV. AT&T's acquired Time Warner Inc. in 2018 after winning a court challenge by the US government. The deal added Time Warner's content such as HBO and CNN to AT&T's distribution capabilities.

Operations

AT&T's Business Solutions segment is its biggest unit generating about 45% of revenue. The unit provides services to business governmental and wholesale customers and individual subscribers who purchase wireless services through employers.

The Entertainment Group accounts for about 30% of revenue by providing video internet interactive and targeted advertising services and voice services to US residential customers. The group includes AT&T?s DIRECTV and U-verse operations. The Consumer Mobility business about 20% of revenue provides wireless services to consumers and wireless wholesale and resale services in the US. The international unit which consists mostly of operations in Brazil and Mexico accounts for the remaining revenue.

Geographic Reach

Dallas Texas-based AT&T has spectrum licenses in all 50 US states Puerto Rico and Washington DC. About 95% of AT&T's revenue is generated in the US. Its wireless services and mobile broadband services are available in about 200 countries but most of its international revenue comes from Mexico and Brazil.

Sales and Marketing

AT&T is nothing if not ubiquitous. The company is a big advertiser to businesses and consumers with presence on TV print and online. The company operates its own retail stores where it offers smartphones from major manufacturers such as Apple and Samsung. The company spends more than $3.5 billion a year on advertising about $1 billion more than wireless rival Verizon Communications.

Financial Performance

AT&T's revenue marched steadily higher from 2013-2016 growing an average of about 7% a year before taking a step back in 2017.

AT&T's revenue slipped 2% in 2017 to $160 billion from 2016. Service revenue which account for about 90% of the company's total fell 2% on continued declines in legacy wireline voice and data products and lower wireless service revenues as customer move to unlimited plans. There were however higher revenue from video and strategic business services. Equipment sales rose slightly in 2017 from 2016 boosted by higher volume in Mexico.

AT&T posted $29 billion in revenue for 2017 a 120% increase from 2016. The company paid about $21 billion less in taxes in 2017 because of the enactment of the US Tax Cuts and Jobs Act late in the year.

Cash from operations dropped to $39.1 billion from $39.5 billion because the company issued about $1 billion in bonuses to employees following tax reduction legislation. Cash used in investing in 2017 was about $20 billion mostly for capital expenditures for networks and video services. Free cash flow was about $21 billion in 2017.

Strategy

As the US wireless phone market becomes saturated (AT&T and Verizon count more than 280 million subscribers between them) carriers are looking for ways to generate more traffic on their networks to generate revenue. AT&T Inc. bought a content carrier DIRECTV in 2015. AT&T added to it content capabilities with the 2018 acquisition of Time Warner and its properties such as HBO and CNN. The deal had been held up by a lawsuit filed by the US government over concentration concerns. A federal judge ruled that the deal could go through with no conditions.

With unremitting competition from its wireless rivals such as Verizon and Sprint as well as content providers like Netflix and Amazon AT&T sees the Time Warner deal as crucial to its future. It argues that having content to send over its pipes would make it a more effective competitor rather than a monopolist.

AT&T has spent billions in capital expenditures on its LTE network buying spectrum and extending fiber optic lines to more than 12 million locations. The company is implementing software-defined networking technologies so changes to the network can be done through software not hardware. That lowers costs of maintaining and upgrading the network. To make sure it all works AT&T had undertaken a massive retraining program to move workers to new roles and out of ones that are going the way of copper landlines.

In 2018 AT&T began work on FirstNet a government funded nationwide network for first-responders and public agencies. A possible bonus AT&T would be excess wireless capacity that it could use for its paying customers.

AT&T was testing 5G network technologies in 2018 and expected to have operational mobile 5G networks in 12 US cities by the end of the year. Besides providing faster speeds for mobile phones 5G could help driverless cars and smart cities technologies communicate. AT&T expanded an agreement with Crown & Castle to provide AT&T with access to cell towers to add 5G technologies.

As US companies enter the first full year under the US Tax Cuts and Jobs Act legislation AT&T expects more investment in communications technologies. The company said it would add $1 billion to its capital expenditures for 2018 as a result of the tax act.

Mergers and Acquisitions

AT&T acquired AppNexus a digital advertising firm in 2018 for a reported price of $1.6 billion. With AppNexus AT&T seeks to speed the growth of its advertising platform. The purchase brings to AT&T some 400 software engineers and product managers with experience in machine learning and predictive analytics advertising technology and video. AT&T intends to integrate AppNexus's technologies with AT&T's first-party data premium video content and distribution. The deal closed in the 2018 third quarter.

In 2018 AT&T acquired FiberTower Corp. for $207 million. AT&T plans to use the millimeter wave spectrum obtained in the deal to help meet its goal of being the first US company to introduce mobile 5G in a dozen markets by late 2018.

AT&T extended its efforts to use software to manage networks with its acquisition of the Vyatta network operating system from Brocade Communications. The deal reached in June 2017 includes the vRouter product line; AT&T intends to hire employees associated with the business. AT&T expects the Vyatta platform to help virtualize its network and control it with software. The deal was expected to close in summer 2017.

In April 2017 AT&T said it would spend $1.25 billion to buy Straight Path Communications which owns licenses to wireless spectrum. That is until rival Verizon Inc. swooped in with a $3.1 billion bid. Verizon gets Straight Path's large holdings of 28 GHz and 39 GHz millimeter wave spectrum used in mobile communications.

AT&T's acquisition of Time Warner for $85 billion a process that began in 2016 concluded in 2018. The closing was preceded by a lawsuit brought by the US Department of Justice which contended the deal would reduce consumer choice. AT&T won at trial and quickly concluded the transaction. The DoJ however filed another suit against the deal. As it stands the merger united a creator of popular content with a distribution network that would reach screens of all sizes. Time Warner's holdings include HBO CNN TNT TBS and the Warner Bros. Studio which produces movies such as the Harry Potter franchise and TV shows (such as the Big Bang Theory).

The deal for Time Warner followed AT&T's acquisition of satellite pay-TV provider DIRECTV for $48.5 billion in mid-2015. The combination enables AT&T to offer new packaged services and deliver content on mobile devices TVs laptops cars and airplanes.

EXECUTIVES

Ceo Business Solutions And International, F. Thaddeus Arroyo, age 54

President And Ceo Sbc Southwest, William A. (Bill) Blase, age 63

Sevp And Cfo, John J. Stephens, age 59, $870,833 total compensation

Chairman And Ceo, Randall L. Stephenson, age 58, $1,791,667 total compensation

Ceo At&t Entertainment And Internet Services At&t Services Inc., John T. Stankey, age 56, $965,833 total compensation

Executive Vice President - Home Solutions, Lori M. Lee, age 52

President Public Sector And Wholesale Solutions, Xavier Williams

Ceo At&t Communications, John M. Donovan, age 57, $858,833 total compensation

Sevp External And Legislative Affairs At&t Services Inc., Robert W. (Bob) Quinn, age 57

Senior Associate General Counsel, David R. McAtee, age 49

Sevp And Chief Compliance Officer, David S. Huntley, age 59

Ceo New Advertising & Analytics Company, Brian Lesser

President Business Operations At&t Business, Sorabh Saxena

Senior Vice President Business Marketing Sbc Operations Inc, Mark Keiffer

Vice President, Judy Phillips

Senior Vice President Of Emerging Devices, Chris Penrose

Sales Vice President Premier Client Group, Sean Murphy

Area Vice President Government Solutions Group, Tim Walsh

Senior Vice President Finance, David Muro

Senior Vice President Technology Management And Operations, Juan Flores

Assistant Vice President C And E Osp, James Keown

Vice President Of Workforce Development And Diversity, Belinda Grant-anderson

Regional Vice President, Craig Warbinton

Vice President Wholesale Wireline Sales, Joan Jambor

Senior Vice President U Verse Field Oprations, Randy Tomlin

Assistant Vice President Ran Engineering, Rajive Beri

Regional Vice President Business Integrated Solutions At At And T Mobility, Maurice Styles

Vice President Financial Planning, George Goeke

Senior Vice President Corporate Strategy, Steve McGaw

Eastern Region Sales Vice President, Annette Nunis

Vice President Of Acquisitions, James Bielar

Rvp, Meredith Caram

Associate Vice President, Tara Colon

Assistant Vice President Network Services, Raymond Perkins

Vice President Fleet Operations, Jerome Webber

Senior Vice President Global Solutions And Sales Operations, Alex Parker

Vice President Communication S, Monte Cely

Assistant Vice President Network Contracting, Roland Tunez

Assistant Vice President Business Advertising, Kelly Thengvall

Vice President And General Manager, Gary Lackhouse

Sales Vice President, Steve Williams

Regional Vice President Global Access Management, Bob Flappan

Vice President Att Com, Philip Bienert

Vice President, Michele Smith

Director Of Government Relations, Jane Sosebee

Regional Vice President Public Affairs, Sage Rhodes

Regional Vice President External Affairs, Brooke Thomson

Vice President Of Chemical Development, Damon Holzer

Vice President U Verse Product Managemetn, G W Shaw

Att Ravpn Contact, Sam Tuffaha

Senior Vice President, Bruce Goemaat

Vice President Head Product And Business Development At&t Adworks, Matthew Van Houten

Director Evpn, Gregory Feenstra

Vice President Bus Solutions Digital Experience, Laura Merling

Area Vice President At And T Mobility Smb, Jeff Goldstein

Rvp Business Integrated Solutions, Martha K Wells
Vice President, Michael Flanagan
Vice President Small Business Product Management, Tom Hughes
Regional Vice President, Stephen Vergine
Sales Center Vice President, Vicky Santangelo
Executive Vice President Wholesale And Gem Solutio, Sherry Morse
Assistant Vice President Project Program Management, William Schutts
Assistant Vice President (assistant Vice President) Accounting, Lonnie Shirey
Vice President Of Project Development, Jeff Lewis
National Account Manager, Kevin Moore
National Account Manager, Dean Ramsey
Sales Center Vice President, Steve D'Lugos
At And T Home Solutions Assistant Vice President, Valerie Scheder
Vice President, Dan Lafond
Vice President, Tim O'Brien
Vice President, Duff Armstrong
Assistant Vice President Accounting, James Lacy
Sales Vice President, Dan Roche
Vice President, Steve Mitchell
Mse And Vpn Engineering, Glenn Williman
Customer Network Operations Vice President, Marvonia Walker
Client Executive Vice President, Knute A Olson
Sales Vice President, Fred Monacelli
Vice President Audit Services, Gerry Chicoine
Senior Vice President External, Holly Reed
Vice President Broadband And Narrowband Operations, Diane Young
Vice President And Senior Counsel, Diana Fellure
Regional Vice President Mobility Customer Care, Jenifer Robertson
National Account Manager, Edward Hale
Vice President Business Development At And T Government Solutions, Robert Caffrey
Assistant Vice President Life Cycle Management Global Customer Service, Judy Miller
Senior Vice President Labor Relations Sbc Services, Michael Rodriguez
Assistant To Assistant Vice President Product Advertising, Pam Krueger
Vice President Antenna Solutions, Chad Townes
Executive Vice President Historian, Olga De La Vega
Senior Vice President Signature Global Client Groups, John Finnegan
Assistant Vice President Technical Project Management Antenna Solutions Group, Stephen McNamara
Vice President Supply Chain Operations, Jim McGuire
Vice President Corporate Strategy, Christopher Sambar
Assistant Vice President Information Technology, Joanne Pate
Vice President Platforms And Enablers, Brad Mohs
Senior Vice President Advanced Solutions, Abhi Ingle
Architecture And Vendor Vice President, Ron Fowinkle
Assistant Vice President Billing Operations, Wesley Carpenter
Vice President Market Insights, Helen McGrath
Vice President Service Platforms, Pari Bajpay
Assistant Vice President Life Cycle Management, Armond Suraci
Vice President Premier Client Group, Trish Renz
Vice President Ip Platform, Maria Dillard
Vice President General Manager, Bob Holliday
Vice President Glbl Managed Services And Outsourcing, Constance Diehl-boyle
Vice President, Jack Duffy
Assistant Vice President Digital Care Strategy, Kim Keating
Solution Implementation Manager At And T Vpn Tunneling Services, Brian Congleton

Senior Vice President Managed Services, Robin Young
Assistant Vice President National Security Network Regulatory, Brooks Fitzsimmons
Vice President At&t University, Nate Edwards
First Vice President Membership, Barry Winkler
Senior Vice President Employee Communications And Corporate Sponsorships, Gail Torreano
Rvp Sales, Jim Medenis
Vice President Sales, Kevin McKeand
Vice President Of U Verse Media Sales, Chris Monteferrante
Assistant Vice President External And Legislative Affairs, Gloria Corey
Vice President, Randy Cook
Senior Vice President Of Customer Experience, Carmen P Nava
Assistant Vice President Information Technology, Joseph Green
Intellectual Property Vice President, Ronald Sherman
Assistant Vice President Regulatory And External Affairs, Pat Wingo
Area Vice President Silicon Valley Growth Markets, Thomas McDonough
Vice President Platform Strategy And Solutions, Richard Batelaan
Vice Presdient, Trudy Vankirk
Regional Vice President Public Relations, Robert Schauer
Assistant Vice President Network Services, Robert Spieler
Regional Vice President Southeast, Ivan Somavilla-castro
Area Vice President, Karime Bavrica
Vice President Benefits, Susan Colburn
Assistant To Assistant Vice President Information Technology, Kathleen Wiegand
National Sales Manager, David Plante
National Account Manager, Dom Cimmino
Vpn Product Manager, Andrew Sullivan
Executive Vice President Client Services, Casey Coleman
Senior Vice President Business Product Management, Joe Lueckenhoff
Assistant Vice President Information Technology Architecture Solutions, Robert Kafka
Vice President Big Data Strategy And Business Development, Christopher G Parsons
Vice President, Bill Daumer
Rvp, Tom Bordeaux
Assistant Vice President Financial Analysis, Roger W Sloan
Executive Vice President Global Enterprise Solutions, Jose Gutierrez
Vice President Law And Litigation, Edward Barillari
Assistant Vice President Customer Experience Solutions Architect, Mary A Allen
Senior Vice President Consumer Self Service And Sales, Rick Welday
Senior Vice President Pacific Northwest, Jeff Hefflinger
Avp Strategic Pricing, Falguni Datta
Vice President And Gm, Dahna Hull
Auditors: Ernst & Young LLP

LOCATIONS

HQ: AT&T Inc
208 S. Akard St., Dallas, TX 75202
Phone: 210 821-4105
Web: www.att.com

2017 Sales

	$ mil.	% of total
United States	149,841	93
Latin America		
Brazil	2,948	2
Other	2,743	2
Mexico	2,913	2
Other	2,101	1
Total	**160,546**	**100**

PRODUCTS/OPERATIONS

2017 Sales

	% of total
Service	91
Equipment	9
Total	**100**

2017 Sales

	$ mil.	% of total
Business Solutions	69,406	43
Entertainment Group	50,698	31
Consumer Mobility	31,552	20
International	8,269	5
Corporate and Other	864	1
Certain Significant Items	(243)	-
Total	**160,546**	**100**

Selected Services

Voice
    Local
    Long-distance
    Wholesale
Data
    Application management
    Data equipment sales
    Data storage
    Database management
    Dedicated Internet service
    Digital television
    Directory and operator assistance
    Disaster recovery
    Enterprise networking
    Hardware and operating system management
    Internet access and network integration
    Managed Web hosting
    Network design
    Network implementation
    Network installation
    Network integration
    Network management
    Outsourcing
    Packet services
    Private lines
    Satellite video
    Switched and dedicated transport
    Voice-over-IP networks
    Wholesale networking
    WiFi

COMPETITORS

Altice USA	Level 3
América MÓvil	SAVVIS
CenturyLink	Sprint Communications
Charter Communications	T-Mobile USA
Comcast	TDS Metrocom
Consolidated Communications	TelefÓnica
Cox Communications	Telephone & Data Systems
DISH Network	Time Warner Cable
EarthLink	U.S. Cellular
Equinix	Verizon
Frontier Communications	XO Holdings

HISTORICAL FINANCIALS
Company Type: Public

Income Statement   FYE: December 31

	REVENUE ($ mil.)	NET INCOME ($ mil.)	NET PROFIT MARGIN	EMPLOYEES
12/17	160,546	29,450	18.3%	252,000
12/16	163,786	12,976	7.9%	268,000
12/15	146,801	13,345	9.1%	281,450
12/14	132,447	6,224	4.7%	253,000
12/13	128,752	18,249	14.2%	243,000
Annual Growth	**5.7%**	**12.7%**	**—**	**0.9%**

2017 Year-End Financials

Debt ratio: 37.01%—
Return on equity: 22.31%
Cash ($ mil.): 50,498
Current ratio: 0.97
Long-term debt ($ mil.): 125,972

Dividends
Yield: 0.0%
Payout: 41.1%
Market value ($ mil.): —

	STOCK PRICE ($) FY Close	P/E High/Low		PER SHARE ($) Earnings	Dividends	Book Value
12/17	38.88	9	7	4.76	1.96	22.94
12/16	42.53	21	16	2.10	1.92	20.06
12/15	34.41	15	13	2.37	1.88	19.96
12/14	33.59	31	27	1.19	1.84	16.65
12/13	35.16	12	10	3.39	1.80	17.41
Annual Growth	2.5%	—	—	8.9%	2.2%	7.1%

Atlantic Capital Bancshares Inc

Auditors: Ernst & Young LLP

LOCATIONS

HQ: Atlantic Capital Bancshares Inc
945 East Paces Ferry Road N.E., Suite 1600, Atlanta,
GA 30326
Phone: 404 995-6050
Web: www.atlanticcapitalbank.com

HISTORICAL FINANCIALS

Company Type: Public

Income Statement   FYE: December 31

	ASSETS ($ mil.)	NET INCOME ($ mil.)	INCOME AS % OF ASSETS	EMPLOYEES
12/17	2,891	(3)	—	353
12/16	2,727	13	0.5%	347
12/15	2,638	(1)	—	361
12/14	1,314	7	0.6%	106
12/13	1,229	5	0.4%	—
Annual Growth	23.8%			

2017 Year-End Financials

Debt ratio: 1.71%
Return on equity: (-1.22%)
Cash ($ mil.): 330
Current ratio: —
Long-term debt ($ mil.): —

No. of shares (mil.): 25
Dividends
Yield: —
Payout: —
Market value ($ mil.): 453

	STOCK PRICE ($) FY Close	P/E High/Low		PER SHARE ($) Earnings	Dividends	Book Value
12/17	17.60	—	—	(0.15)	0.00	11.99
12/16	19.00	35	22	0.53	0.00	12.10
12/15	14.98	—	—	(0.09)	0.00	11.79
Annual Growth	4.1%	—	—	—	—	0.4%

AURORA HEALTH CARE, INC.

EXECUTIVES

Ceo-Pres, Nick Turkal
Clinic Manager, Anna Biancuzzo
Supervisor Loss Prevention, Arthur Smith
Environmental Manager, Brad Winnie
Manager of Distribution, David Orlovsky
Recruiter, Debbie Gast
Certified Clinical Research Co, Debra Smith
Operations Manager, Ellen Whitehall
Director Hospice, Glenn Ragalie
Human Resources Assistant, Jean Yunker
Lead Project Coordinator, Michele Johnson
Auditors: DELOITTE & TOUCHE LLP MILWAUK

LOCATIONS

HQ: AURORA HEALTH CARE, INC.
750 W VIRGINIA ST, MILWAUKEE, WI 532041539
Phone: 414 647-3000

HISTORICAL FINANCIALS

Company Type: Private

Income Statement   FYE: December 31

	REVENUE ($ mil.)	NET INCOME ($ mil.)	NET PROFIT MARGIN	EMPLOYEES
12/17	5,334	437	8.2%	30,000
12/16	5,124	385	7.5%	—
12/15	4,930	428	8.7%	—
Annual Growth	4.0%	1.1%		

2017 Year-End Financials

Debt ratio: —
Return on equity: 8.20%
Cash ($ mil.): 192
Current ratio: 1.10
Long-term debt ($ mil.): —

Dividends
Yield: —
Payout: —
Market value ($ mil.): —

Autoliv Inc

The world's #1 manufacturer of car safety equipment Autoliv aims to save lives by increasing the survivability statistics of traffic accidents. It makes components such as seat belts airbags anti-whiplash systems and safety electronics. Other products include rollover protection systems steering wheels (with airbags) night vision systems radar systems and child seats. The company caters to about every car maker in the industry and has more than 100 locations around the globe. Car making giant GM Renault/Nissan is one of its largest customers. Autoliv was established in 1956.

Operations

Autoliv operates through two business segments: passive safety (75% of net sales; airbags and seatbelts) and electronics (25%; electronics and active safety). By product airbags account for around half of Autoliv's total revenue seatbelts 25% passive safety electronics 10% active safety products 5% and brake control systems 5%.

Geographic Reach

Autoliv has about 20 crash test tracks more than 20 technical centers and about 80 production facilities in more than 25 countries. Its US opera-

tions are overseen by Autoliv ASP Inc. Its revenue is well diversified geographically taking in broadly comparable amounts from its three regions. The Asia/Pacific region is the largest at more than 35% of sales while and the Americas and Europe regions both generate more than 30%.

Sales and Marketing

Autoliv is dependent on a small number of global automakers. Autoliv's top five customers account for more than half of total company sales and the ten largest 80%. Its largest customers are Renault/Nissan Honda Ford and Hyundai/Kia. Other customers include BWM Mercedes Volvo Volkswagen Toyota FCA PSA Group and Great Wall Motors.

Autoliv has a market share in the passive safety sector of around 40%

Financial Performance

Aside from a small dip in 2015 Autoliv has posted consistent revenue growth in recent years fueled by expanding global light-vehicle production (particularly in China) as well as acquisitions. On the flip side Autoliv has struggled to attain meaningful profit growth.

In fiscal 2017 sales grew 3% to $10.4 billion as higher global light vehicle production drove passive safety equipment growth. Seatbelt sales grew 5% and airbags 2%. In the Electronics segment brake control systems grew strongly thanks to demand for automotive radars cameras with driver assist systems and ADAS-ECU (driver assistance software) while restraint control systems faltered amid lower demand from North America Japan and South Korea. By geography Autolive grew everywhere except the Americas which shrank by 4% as GM (General Motors) shifted to a new vehicle platform.

Net income fell 26% to $427 million as goodwill impairments worth $234 million capacity optimization initiatives (costing $26 million) antitrust matters ($18 million) and business segment separation ($9 million) weighed on operating margins.

Cash inflow from operations increased 8% to $936 reflecting higher growth in the underlying business.

Strategy

Autoliv's growth strategy is based on geographical and technological developments. European Union road-fatality reduction targets are encouraging automakers to find new ways to improve car safety. With physical systems (airbags chassis design seatbelts) reaching a high level of sophistication automakers are looking to new technologies such as on-board sensors to reduce the frequency and impact of accidents further. In response to this demand-driver Autoliv increased its R&D spend in electronics and passive safety from $524 million in 2015 to $741 million in 2017 or in relative terms from 5.7% of total sales to 7.1%. As a result order intake for Active Safety products grew by 300% to $1.6 billion in 2017 while lifetime electronics order intake increased from $1.1 billion in 2015 to $4.0 billion in 2017.

Autoliv is developing its presence in autonomous driving and driver assistance via a joint venture named Zenuity with Volvo. It has also form partnerships with Seeing Machines for driver monitoring systems Velodyne for LiDAR solutions and NVIDA (with Zenuity) for AI computing systems.

Given the different skills and pace of technology advancement Autoliv plans to spin off its Electronics business in 2018.

The company also seeks to maintain balance between its three primary geographies although rapid growth in China made the Asia/Pacific region Autoliv's largest geography. It achieved balance by making timely investments and strengthening its technical and support capabilities. It has made substantial investments in its manufacturing capabilities in China and Japan.

Mergers and Acquisitions

Autoliv is focused on acquisitions in two key areas: active safety systems and growth markets.

In November 2017 Autoliv completed the $16.9 million acquisition of Fotonic i Norden (Fotonic) headquartered in Stockholm and SkellefteA? in Sweden.

In 2016 the company acquired a 51% interest in the entities that formed Autoliv-Nissin Brake Systems (ANBS) for approximately $263 million in cash. ANBS designs manufactures and sells products in the brake control and actuation systems business. Nissin Kogyo retained a 49% interest in ANBS.

HISTORY

Autoliv traces its origins back to 1956 when Autoliv AB a Swedish corporation pioneered automotive seat belt technology. By 1967 the company had invented the retractor belt. Granges Weda AB another maker of seat belt retractors acquired the company in 1975. Electrolux bought the Granges Group (later renamed SAPA) in 1989 and changed its name to Electrolux Autoliv. Throughout the 1980s and 1990s the company continued to grow through acquisitions buying seat belt manufacturing operations primarily in Europe but also in Australia and New Zealand. In 1994 the company changed its name to Autoliv AB and went public with Electrolux selling all its shares during the offering.

EXECUTIVES

Chairman President And Ceo, Jan Carlson, age 58, $1,376,766 total compensation
Cto, Steven (Steve) Fredin, age 56, $578,240 total compensation
President Passive Safety, Mikael Bratt, age 51
Group Vp Research And Development And Cto, Johan L ¶fvenholm, age 49
Group Vp Finance And Cfo, Mats Backman, age 50, $381,074 total compensation
Vice President Global Business Unit, Walter Guertler
Vice President, Erin Patrick
Vice President For Ford Business, Stefan Kroenung
Vice President Corporate Communications, Thomas Jonsson
Vice President, Karin Eliasson
Vice President Global Engineering, Michael Seeger
Chairman President And Ceo, Jan Carlson, age 58
Treasurer, Thomas Williams
Auditors: Ernst & Young AB

LOCATIONS

HQ: Autoliv Inc
Klarabergsviadukten 70, Section B7, Box 70381, SE-107 24, Stockholm SE-107 24
Phone: (46) 8 587 20 600
Web: www.autoliv.com

2016 Sales

	$ mil.	% of total
Asia		
China	1,766	18
Japan	949	9
Rest of Asia	901	9
Americas	3,380	34
Europe	3,075	30
Total	**10,073**	**100**

PRODUCTS/OPERATIONS

2017 Sales

	$ mil.	% of total
Passive Safety	8,134	78
Electronics	2,322	22
Corporate and other	5	-
Inter-segment sales	(66.6)	-
Total	**10,382**	**100**

2017 Sales

	$ mil.	% of total
Asia		
China	1,839	18
Japan	1,040	10
Rest of Asia	965	9
Americas	3,247	31
Europe	3,290	32
Total	**10,382**	**100**

Selected Products

Anti-whiplash seats
Child restraints
Electronics
Frontal airbags
Inflators
Leg airbags
Seat belts
Side-impact airbags
Steering wheels

Selected Subsidiaries and Affiliates

Airbags International Ltd (UK)
Autoflator AB
Autoliv AB
Autoliv Argentina SA
Autoliv ASP BV (The Netherlands)
Autoliv ASP Inc. (US)
Autoliv Australia Proprietary Ltd
Autoliv Autosicherheitstechnik GmbH (Germany)
Autoliv BKI SA (Spain)
Autoliv BV (The Netherlands)
Autoliv Canada Inc
Autoliv Cankor Otomotiv Emniyet Sistemleri Sanayi Ve (Turkey)
Autoliv China Electronics Co. Ltd
Autoliv do Brasil Ltda.
Autoliv East Europe AB
Autoliv Electronics AB
Autoliv Electronics SAS (France)
Autoliv France SNC
Autoliv Holding BV (The Netherlands)
Autoliv Holding Inc. (US)
Autoliv Holding Ltd. (UK)
Autoliv Italia S.P.A.
Autoliv Japan Ltd
Autoliv KFT (Hungary)
Autoliv KLE SAU (Spain)
Autoliv Ltd (UK)
Autoliv Nichiyo Co. (Japan)
Autoliv Overseas BV (The Netherlands)
Autoliv Poland Sp zoo
Autoliv Romania SA
Autoliv Safety Technology Inc. (US)
Autoliv Sicherheitstechnik GmbH (Germany)
Autoliv Southern Africa Pty Ltd
Autoliv Stakupress GmbH (Germany)
Autoliv Sverige AB
Autoliv Thailand Ltd
Autoliv UK Holding Ltd
Marling BV (The Netherlands)
Mei-An Autoliv Co. (59% Taiwan)
Nanjing Hongguang Autoliv Vehicle Safety Co. Ltd. (50% China)
NSK Safety Technology (Thailand) Co. Ltd.
OEA Inc. (US)
Svensk Airbag AB
Van Oerle Alberton BV (The Netherlands)
Van Oerle Alberton Holding BV (The Netherlands)
Van Oerle Webco Pty Ltd (Australia)

COMPETITORS

AISIN World Corp.	Key Safety Systems
ASHIMORI INDUSTRY CO. LTD.	Kongsberg Automotive
Autocam	Magna International
Bosch Corp.	Mitsubishi Electric
CASCO Products	NFA
DENSO	Neaton Auto Products
Delphi Automotive Systems	Nihon Plast
Ensign-Bickford	Nippon Kayaku
Gentex	Scqua
Hella	Special Devices
Honeywell International	Takata
International Textile Group	Toyoda Gosei
	Toyota Boshoku
	Valeo

HISTORICAL FINANCIALS

Company Type: Public

Income Statement

FYE: December 31

	REVENUE ($ mil.)	NET INCOME ($ mil.)	NET PROFIT MARGIN	EMPLOYEES
12/17	10,382	427	4.1%	72,000
12/16	10,073	567	5.6%	70,300
12/15	9,169	456	5.0%	64,100
12/14	9,240	467	5.1%	60,000
12/13	8,803	485	5.5%	56,500
Annual Growth	4.2%	(3.2%)	—	6.2%

2017 Year-End Financials

Debt ratio: 15.69%
Return on equity: 11.08%
Cash ($ mil.): 959
Current ratio: 1.58
Long-term debt ($ mil.): 1,321

No. of shares (mil.): 86
Dividends
Yield: 0.0%
Payout: 48.8%
Market value ($ mil.): 11,053

	STOCK PRICE ($) FY Close	P/E High/Low	PER SHARE ($) Earnings	Dividends	Book Value
12/17	127.08	27 20	4.87	2.38	46.39
12/16	113.15	20 15	6.42	2.30	41.68
12/15	124.77	25 19	5.17	2.22	39.22
12/14	106.12	21 17	5.06	2.12	38.63
12/13	91.80	19 13	5.07	2.00	42.18
Annual Growth	8.5%	— —	(1.0%)	4.4%	2.4%

Automatic Data Processing Inc.

EXECUTIVES

Pres-Ceo, Carlos A Rodriguez
Non Exec Chb, John P Jones
Cfo, Jan Siegmund
Cto, Dermot J O'Brien
Chief Hr Officer, Sreeni Kutam
Cao-Corp Contrl, Brock Albinson
Corp V Pres-General Counsel-SE, Michael A Bonarti
National Sales Manager, Al Simmons
Technology Consultant, Anthony Condegni
Client Manager, Anthony Monaco
Associate District Manager, Anthony Taliento
Auditors: DELOITTE & TOUCHE LLP

LOCATIONS

HQ: Automatic Data Processing Inc.
One ADP Boulevard, Roseland, NJ 07068
Phone: 973 974-5000   **Fax:** 973 974-5390
Web: www.adp.com

COMPETITORS

Avatar Systems	Insperity
CBIZ	Intuit
Ceridian	Oasis Outsourcing
Computer Sciences Corp.	Paychex
Enertia Software	Reynolds and Reynolds
Global Payments	Total System Services
HP Enterprise Services	TriNet Group
	Ultimate Software

HISTORICAL FINANCIALS

Company Type: Public

Income Statement

FYE: June 30

	REVENUE ($ mil.)	NET INCOME ($ mil.)	NET PROFIT MARGIN	EMPLOYEES
06/18	13,325	1,620	12.2%	57,000
06/17	12,379	1,733	14.0%	58,000
06/16	11,667	1,492	12.8%	57,000
06/15	10,938	1,452	13.3%	55,000
06/14	12,206	1,515	12.4%	61,000
Annual Growth	2.2%	1.7%	—	(1.7%)

2018 Year-End Financials

Debt ratio: 5.40%
Return on equity: 43.59%
Cash ($ mil.): 2,170
Current ratio: 1.05
Long-term debt ($ mil.): 2,002

No. of shares (mil.): 438
Dividends
  Yield: 0.0%
  Payout: 68.8%
Market value ($ mil.): 58,861

	STOCK PRICE ($) FY Close	P/E High/Low		PER SHARE ($) Earnings	Dividends	Book Value
06/18	134.14	38	28	3.66	2.52	7.88
06/17	102.46	27	22	3.85	2.24	8.94
06/16	91.87	28	22	3.25	2.08	9.83
06/15	80.23	29	23	3.05	1.95	10.31
06/14	79.28	26	22	3.14	1.88	13.89
Annual Growth	14.1%	—	—	3.9%	7.7%	(13.2%)

AutoNation, Inc.

AutoNation wants to instill patriotic fervor in the fickle car-buying public. The brainchild of entrepreneur Wayne Huizenga (Waste Management Blockbuster) AutoNation is the #1 auto dealer in the US (ahead of Penske Automotive Group and Sonic Automotive). The firm owns more than 370 new-vehicle franchises in 15 states and it conducts online sales through AutoNation.com and individual dealer websites. It sells 35 new brands of new vehicles. AutoNation acquires local retail brands and transitions them to the AutoNation name. In addition to auto sales AutoNation provides maintenance and repair services sells auto parts and finances and insures vehicles which together account for the majority of profits.

Operations

AutoNation divides the vehicle market into three segments: Domestic Import and Premium Luxury all of which generate around a third of sales each. Imports accounts for more than 35% of sales while Domestic brands represent more than 30%. Its core brands of new vehicles include Toyota Ford Honda Nissan and General Motors.

The Premium Luxury Segment which sells new vehicles manufactured primarily by Mercedes-Benz BMW and Lexus contributes more than 30% of AutoNation's sales.

Geographic Reach

AutoNation has more than 370 new-vehicle franchises in +15 US states. Florida Texas and California are its largest markets accounting for 26% 21% and 17% respectively .

Sales and Marketing

AutoNation sells vehicles through its online website and its stores.

Financial Performance

The company has reported an upward trend in revenues since 2011.

In fiscal 2016 sales increased a further 4% to $21.6 billion on the back of growth in all product categories including $260.8 million growth in new vehicle sales and $226.6 million growth in used vehicle sales. Growth in new car sales primarily came from contributions from acquired businesses; same store sales declined 3% due to lower unit sales partially offset by a shift towards higher-value vehicles such as trucks and sports utility vehicles.

Net income fell 3% to $430.5 million due to disruptive manufacturer marketing and a more competitive automotive retail environment.

Cash from operations increased 2% to $516.0 million due to a decrease in working capital requirements partially offset by a decrease in earnings.

Strategy

The auto dealer is banking on the cachA© of the AutoNation name to win sales and market share.

The company has invested and will continue to invest significantly in the AutoNation retail brand with the goals of enhancing its strong customer satisfaction and expanding its market share. It continues to make significant investments to build a seamless end-to-end customer experience in its stores and through its digital channels and to improve its ability to generate business through those channels.

A key element of the firm's business strategy is its diversified portfolio of 30-plus brands spanning imports premium luxury vehicles and domestic autos. Over the past decade AutoNation has increased the percentage of import and luxury cars it sells. It clusters dealerships within markets so that they can share inventory cross-sell to customers and reduce marketing costs — basically cutting and combining costs in an attempt to become the auto industry's Wal-Mart. As the economy improves AutoNation is looking for acquisition and new store opportunities.

In 2016 the company purchased 20 stores in Texas New York Colorado California and Maryland. It sold five Domestic stores and nine Import stores in the same year.

Hoping to capitalize on the possible takeover of self-driving cars in 2017 AutoNation signed a repair contract with Alphabet's self-drive unit Waymo. It will maintain and repair Waymo's Chrysler Pacific hybrid fleet as well as other brands that Waymo may develop in the future.

Mergers and Acquisitions

Historically AutoNation has been a driving force in the consolidation of the US car sales business. After an hiatus during the recession and credit crunch which put the brakes on acquisitions by mega dealers such as AutoNation the company is back in acquisition mode buying up around 20 stores and franchises each year.

In 2016 it acquired 20 stores in Texas New York Colorado California and Maryland. The acquisitions include Chrysler Dodge Jeep Ram Chevrolet Hyundai Mercedes-Benz Sprinter Jaguar Land Rover and BMW franchises.

HISTORY

AutoNation started in 1980 as Republic Resources which brokered petroleum leases did exploration and production and blended lubricants. In 1989 after oil prices crashed and a stockholder group tried to force Republic into liquidation Browning-Ferris Industries (BFI) founder Thomas Fatjo gained control of the company and refocused it on a field he knew well — solid waste. He renamed the firm Republic Waste.

Michael DeGroote founder of BFI rival Laidlaw bought into Republic in 1990. (Fatjo left the next year.) DeGroote's investment funded more acquisitions. Republic moved into hazardous waste in

1992 just before the industry nosedived due to stringent new environmental rules. In 1994 Republic spun off its hazardous-waste operations as Republic Environmental Systems and Republic's stock began rising immediately.

That attracted the attention of Wayne Huizenga who had founded Waste Management and Blockbuster Video. To him Republic was not merely a midsized solid-waste firm. No Huizenga saw Republic as a publicly traded vehicle that could allow him to tap into the stock market to fund his latest project: an integrated nationwide auto dealer — a first for the highly fragmented and localized industry.

In 1995 Republic bought Hudson Management a trash business owned by Huizenga's brother-in-law and Huizenga bought a large interest in Republic. As a result Huizenga took control of Republic's board. The firm became Republic Industries and DeGroote stepped back from active management.

Huizenga's investment helped Republic acquire more waste businesses and his name brought a flood of new investors. The firm diversified with electronic security acquisitions but growth in this field faltered with a failed bid to buy market leader ADT in 1996. (Republic sold its security division to Ameritech in 1997.)

By 1996 Huizenga's still-separate auto concept AutoNation was operational with 55 automobile franchises and seven used-car stores. Republic bought Alamo Rent A Car and National Car Rental System and in 1997 AutoNation was bought by Republic. The combined company continued buying dealerships and car rental firms at a sizzling rate.

Republic spun off its solid-waste operations to the public in 1998 as Republic Services. That year Republic bought or agreed to buy 181 new-car franchises opened nine AutoNation USA dealerships and opened 62 CarTemps USA insurance-replacement locations.

Republic became AutoNation in 1999.

Having survived a market downturn in the late 2000s in 2013 the company began marketing its domestic and import stores under the AutoNation retail brand in local markets. The re-branding of the stores which previously operated under various local market retail brands (including Mike Shad in Jacksonville Florida and GO in Colorado) was completed that year. (The exception is the company's luxury dealership business which will continue to operate under their existing retail brands.) Using its website store signage and media presence the car dealer is working to increase consumer awareness of the AutoNation brand.

In 2013 the company acquired 12 franchises.

EXECUTIVES

Executive Vice President Secretary And General Counsel, Jonathan Ferrando

Chairman And Ceo, Michael J. (Mike) Jackson, age 70, $1,250,000 total compensation

Evp And Chief Marketing Officer, Marc Cannon, age 56

Evp And Cfo, Cheryl Miller, age 45, $596,875 total compensation

Evp Franchise Operations Mergers & Acquisitions And Corporate Real Estate, Donna Parlapiano, age 53, $532,084 total compensation

Evp General Counsel And Corporate Secretary, Coleman Edmunds

President Eastern Region, Jim Bender

Evp And Cto, Thomas M. (Tom) Conophy, age 57

President Western Region, Lance Iserman

President Central Region, Ron Ardisonne

Evp Customer Care And Brand Extensions, Scott Arnold

Chairman And Ceo, Michael J. (Mike) Jackson, age 70

LOCATIONS

HQ: AutoNation, Inc.
200 S.W. 1st Avenue, Fort Lauderdale, FL 33301
Phone: 954 769-6000
Web: www.autonation.com

2017 Stores

	No.
Florida	5
Texas	47
California	39
Georgia	23
Colorado	15
Washington	16
Arizona	14
Nevada	11
Tennessee	8
Maryland	7
Illinois	7
Alabama	5
Ohio	4
New York	4
Virginia	2
Minnesota	1
Total	**253**

PRODUCTS/OPERATIONS

2017 Sales

	$ mil.	% of total
New vehicle	12,180	57
Used vehicle	4,878	23
Parts & services	3,398	16
Finance & insurance	939	4
Other	137	-
Total	**21**	**100**

2017 Sales

	$ mil.	% of total
Domestic	7,452	35
Import	6,873	32
Premium Luxury	6,832	32
Corporate & other	375	1
Total	**21,534**	**100**

COMPETITORS

Asbury Automotive	JM Family Enterprises
Brown Automotive	Lithia Motors
CarMax	Penske Automotive
Ed Morse Auto	Group
Group 1 Automotive	Potamkin Automotive
Hendrick Automotive	Sonic Automotive
Holman Enterprises	

HISTORICAL FINANCIALS

Company Type: Public

Income Statement

FYE: December 31

	REVENUE ($ mil.)	NET INCOME ($ mil.)	NET PROFIT MARGIN	EMPLOYEES
12/17	21,534	434	2.0%	26,000
12/16	21,609	430	2.0%	26,000
12/15	20,862	442	2.1%	26,000
12/14	19,108	418	2.2%	24,000
12/13	17,517	374	2.1%	22,000
Annual Growth	**5.3%**	**3.8%**	**—**	**4.3%**

2017 Year-End Financials

Debt ratio: 26.32%
Return on equity: 18.57%
Cash ($ mil.): 69
Current ratio: 0.85
Long-term debt ($ mil.): 1,959
No. of shares (mil.): 91
Dividends
  Yield: —
  Payout: —
Market value ($ mil.): 4,700

STOCK PRICE ($) / P/E / PER SHARE ($)

	STOCK PRICE ($) FY Close	P/E High/Low		Earnings	Dividends	Book Value
12/17	51.33	13	9	4.43	0.00	25.88
12/16	48.65	14	10	4.15	0.00	22.95
12/15	59.66	17	14	3.89	0.00	21.20
12/14	60.41	17	13	3.52	0.00	18.29
12/13	49.69	18	13	3.04	0.00	17.05
Annual Growth	**0.8%**	**—**	**—**	**9.9%**	**—**	**11.0%**

AutoZone, Inc.

With more than 5600 stores in the US and Puerto Rico AutoZone is one of the nation's leading auto parts chains. It also has more than 550 stores in Mexico and about two dozen in Brazil. AutoZone stores sell hard parts (alternators engines batteries) maintenance items (oil antifreeze) accessories (car stereos floor mats) and non-automotive merchandise under brand names and private labels. AutoZone's commercial sales program distributes parts and other products to garages dealerships and other businesses. The company operates an electronic parts catalog Z-net that provide a wide range of information on parts for employees and customers.

Operations

AutoZone operates through one primary segment Auto Parts Stores which accounts for more than 95% of revenue. Leveraging a consistent store format each AutoZone store boasts between 85% and 90% of selling space — up to 40% to 45% of which is dedicated to hard parts inventory. Stores are outfitted with Z-net AutoZone's proprietary electronic catalog that gives employees advice and information for customers' vehicles down to the year make model and engine type.

Other revenue is generated by e-commerce operations (autozone.com and autoanything.com) and diagnostic and other software (provided through the company's ALLDATA business) used in automotive repair. The company also has a smartphone app through which customers can find and buy parts.

One class of similar products accounted for about an eighth of AutoZone's sales and it depends on one vendor for about 12 percent of its purchases.

Geographic Reach

Based in Tennessee AutoZone operates about 5600 AutoZone stores in the 50 US states the District of Columbia and Puerto Rico. Texas California Florida Ohio and Illinois are the company's largest markets and together account for more than a third of locations. The company's fast-growing subsidiary in Mexico AutoZone de México operates more than 560 stores. AutoZone also has stores in Brazil.

AutoZone has distribution centers in the US (Arizona California Georgia Illinois Ohio Pennsylvania Tennessee Texas and Washington) and Mexico; store support centers are in Tennessee as well as Mexico and Brazil. In addition the company has operations in China which support the sourcing efforts in Asia.

Sales and Marketing

AutoZone sells to do-it-yourself (DIY) consumers as well as repair garages dealers service stations and other commercial customers.

The company relies on targeted advertising and promotions to build its brand offer advice about the overall importance of vehicle maintenance and

position its business as a great value. To drive traffic to its stores the retailer advertises on broadcast and Internet media. It works to educate consumers about which products they need through use of in-store signage and circulars as well as creative product placement and promotions.

Advertising expense for the company runs about $95 million a year.

Financial Performance

New locations drive revenue growth for AutoZone which has seen an average revenue increase of 5% per year since 2012 (similar to the 4% average location increase over the same period). Net income has also ticked up consistently since 2012 as the company keeps its net profit margin between 11%-12%.

In 2018 (ended August) the company reported revenue of $11.2 billion a company record and a 3.1% increase from $10.9 billion in 2017. New stores in the US provided $196.5 million while domestic same store sales rose about 2%. Domestic commercial sales increased $151.4 million about 7% year-to-year while auto parts sales rose 4% in 2018 from 2017 throughout the company.

AutoZone?s net income increased 4% to about $1.3 billion in 2018 from 2017 boosted by a lower income tax bill due to the US Tax Cuts and Jobs Act. The company?s net profit margin climbed to 12% in 2018 its highest in at least five years.

Cash at the end of 2018 was $218 million a decrease of about $75 million from the prior year. Cash from operations contributed $2.1 billion to the coffers while investing activities used about $522 million with increases the result of new distribution centers and additional investment in existing locations. Financing activities subtracted about $1.6 billion as AutoZone repaid about $250 million in debt and purchased about $1.6 billion in treasuries.

Strategy

AutoZone's core strategy includes expanding its store network and store inventory to meet customer needs. It added about 200 stores (net of closings) in fiscal 2018 (on top of 215 in 2017 and 205 in 2016) and is focusing on new-store development while also enhancing its existing stores and infrastructure. Nearly 50 of the new stores in 2018 were opened in Mexico and Brazil. The company also opened a distribution center in 2018.

With an eye on expanding inventory AutoZone is focused on hub and mega hub locations which offer inventory two to four times broader than typical stores. In 2018 it opened five hub stores for a total of nearly 195 and eight mega hub locations bringing that total to about 25. The company plans to have a total of 40 mega hub stores in operation over the next few years.

While AutoZone directly imports between 10% and 15% of parts many of its domestic vendors get supplies from overseas making the company subject to tariffs and other complications from international trade tensions.

Company Background

Joseph "Pitt" Hyde took over the family grocery wholesale business Malone & Hyde (established 1907) in 1968. He expanded into specialty retailing opening drugstores sporting goods stores and supermarkets but his fortunes began to race on Independence Day 1979 when he opened his first Auto Shack auto parts store in Forrest City Arkansas.

Using retailing behemoth Wal-Mart as a model Hyde concentrated on smaller markets in the South and Southeast emphasizing everyday low prices and centralized distribution operations. He stressed customer service to provide his do-it-yourself customers with expert advice on choosing parts. While a number of retailers have tried to copy Wal-Mart's successful model Hyde had an inside track: Before starting Auto Shack he served on Wal-Mart's board for seven years.

Auto Shack had expanded into seven states by 1980 and by 1983 it had 129 stores in 10 states. The next year Malone & Hyde's senior management with investment firm Kohlberg Kravis Roberts (KKR) took the company private in an LBO. Auto Shack continued to expand reaching 192 stores in 1984. The company was spun off to Malone & Hyde's shareholders in 1987 and Malone & Hyde's other operations were sold. The company changed its name to AutoZone in 1987 in part to settle a lawsuit with RadioShack.

To build its online presence AutoZone in 2013 acquired AutoAnything an online retailer of specialized automotive products.

HISTORY

Joseph "Pitt" Hyde took over the family grocery wholesale business Malone & Hyde (established 1907) in 1968. He expanded into specialty retailing opening drugstores sporting goods stores and supermarkets but his fortunes began to race on Independence Day 1979 when he opened his first Auto Shack auto parts store in Forrest City Arkansas.

Using retailing behemoth Wal-Mart as a model Hyde concentrated on smaller markets in the South and Southeast emphasizing everyday low prices and centralized distribution operations. He stressed customer service to provide his do-it-yourself customers with expert advice on choosing parts. While a number of retailers have tried to copy Wal-Mart's successful model Hyde had an inside track: Before starting Auto Shack he served on Wal-Mart's board for seven years.

Auto Shack had expanded into seven states by 1980 and by 1983 it had 129 stores in 10 states. The next year Malone & Hyde's senior management with investment firm Kohlberg Kravis Roberts (KKR) took the company private in an LBO. Auto Shack continued to expand reaching 192 stores in 1984. The company was spun off to Malone & Hyde's shareholders in 1987 and Malone & Hyde's other operations were sold. The company changed its name to AutoZone in 1987 in part to settle a lawsuit with RadioShack.

To build its online presence AutoZone in 2013 acquired AutoAnything an online retailer of specialized automotive products.

EXECUTIVES

Evp Finance Information Technology And Alldata And Cfo, William T. (Bill) Giles, age 59, $560,539 total compensation

Svp Supply Chain And Information Technology, William C. (Bill) Rhodes, age 53, $1,000,000 total compensation

Svp Commercial, Larry M. Roesel, age 61, $425,308 total compensation

Svp Merchandising And Store Development, Mark A. Finestone, age 57, $430,154 total compensation

Evp Mexico Brazil Imc And Store Development, William W. Graves, age 58, $430,154 total compensation

Evp Store Operations Commercial And Loss Prevention, Thomas B. Newbern, age 56, $430,154 total compensation

Svp And Cio, Ronald B. (Ron) Griffin, age 65, $407,692 total compensation

Svp Marketing And E-commerce, Albert (Al) Saltiel, age 55

Svp Supply Chain And Information Technology, William C. (Bill) Rhodes, age 53

Auditors: Ernst & Young LLP

LOCATIONS

HQ: AutoZone, Inc.
123 South Front Street, Memphis, TN 38103
Phone: 901 495-6500
Web: www.autozone.com

2018 Stores

	No.
US	5,618
Mexico	564
Brazil	20
Total	**6,202**

PRODUCTS/OPERATIONS

2018 Sales

	$ mil.	% of total
Auto Parts Locations	10,951	98
Other	269	2
Total	**11,221**	**100**

Selected Merchandise

Accessories
 Car stereos
 Floor mats
 Lights
 Mirrors
Hard Parts
 Alternators
 Batteries
 Brake shoes and pads
 Carburetors
 Clutches
 Engines
 Spark plugs
 Starters
 Struts
 Water pumps
Maintenance Items
 Antifreeze
 Brake fluid
 Engine additives
 Oil
 Power steering fluid
 Transmission fluid
 Waxes
 Windshield wipers
Other
 Air fresheners
 Dent filler
 Hand cleaner
 Paint
 Repair manuals
 Tools

Selected Brands

ALLDATA
AutoZone
Duralast
Duralast Gold
ProElite
SureBilt
Valucraft

COMPETITORS

Advance Auto Parts	Goodyear Tire & Rubber
Amazon.com	O'Reilly Automotive
CARQUEST	Pep Boys
Costco Wholesale	Sears Holdings
Fisher Auto Parts	Target Corporation
Genuine Parts	Wal-Mart

HISTORICAL FINANCIALS

Company Type: Public

Income Statement

FYE: August 25

	REVENUE ($ mil.)	NET INCOME ($ mil.)	NET PROFIT MARGIN	EMPLOYEES
08/18	11,221	1,337	11.9%	90,000
08/17	10,888	1,280	11.8%	87,000
08/16	10,635	1,241	11.7%	84,000
08/15	10,187	1,160	11.4%	81,000
08/14	9,475	1,069	11.3%	76,000
Annual Growth	**4.3%**	**5.7%**	**—**	**4.3%**

2018 Year-End Financials

Debt ratio: 54.12%
Return on equity: —
Cash ($ mil.): 217
Current ratio: 0.92
Long-term debt ($ mil.): 5,005
No. of shares (mil.): 25
Dividends
 Yield: —
 Payout: —
Market value ($ mil.): 19,835

	STOCK PRICE ($) FY Close	P/E High/Low	Earnings	PER SHARE ($) Dividends	Book Value
08/18	770.52	16 11	48.77	0.00	(59.06)
08/17	528.95	18 11	44.07	0.00	(51.32)
08/16	753.47	20 17	40.70	0.00	(61.39)
08/15	726.39	20 14	36.03	0.00	(55.49)
08/14	538.84	17 13	31.57	0.00	(50.21)
Annual Growth	**9.4%**	**— —**	**11.5%**	**—**	**—**

Avangrid Inc

Auditors: KPMG LLP

LOCATIONS

HQ: Avangrid Inc
180 Marsh Hill Road, Orange, CT 06477
Phone: 207 629-1200
Web: www.avangrid.com

HISTORICAL FINANCIALS

Company Type: Public

Income Statement

FYE: December 31

	REVENUE ($ mil.)	NET INCOME ($ mil.)	NET PROFIT MARGIN	EMPLOYEES
12/17	5,963	381	6.4%	6,570
12/16	6,018	630	10.5%	6,801
12/15	4,367	267	6.1%	6,809
12/14	4,594	424	9.2%	4,977
12/13	4,313	(65)	—	—
Annual Growth	**8.4%**	**—**	**—**	**—**

2017 Year-End Financials

Debt ratio: 19.47%
Return on equity: 2.52%
Cash ($ mil.): 41
Current ratio: 0.73
Long-term debt ($ mil.): 5,196
No. of shares (mil.): 309
Dividends
 Yield: 0.0%
 Payout: 140.4%
Market value ($ mil.): 15,629

	STOCK PRICE ($) FY Close	P/E High/Low	Earnings	PER SHARE ($) Dividends	Book Value
12/17	50.58	43 31	1.23	1.73	48.79
12/16	37.88	23 17	2.04	1.73	48.90
12/15	38.40	36 32	1.05	0.00	48.74
Annual Growth	**7.1%**	**— —**	**4.0%**	**—**	**0.0%**

Avery Dennison Corp

Avery Dennison has worked out how to make the most of a sticky situation. The company is a world-leader in sticky labels used by businesses to add their branding to products such as drinks food personal care and pharmaceuticals. Its adhesives also extend to vinyl wraps and specialty materials designed for digital imaging screen printing and sign cutting applications. Under the Avery Dennison and Fasson brands it makes papers films and foils coated with adhesive and sold in rolls to printers. It also makes retail branding and security tags printer systems and fasteners as well as medical adhesive products.

Operations

Avery Dennison has three operating segments: Label and Graphics the largest at around 70% of sales; Retail Branding and Information Solutions accounting for around 25% of sales; and Industrial and Healthcare Materials (under 10% of sales).

The Label and Graphics segment makes pressure-sensitive adhesives (PSAs) which are sticky labels that are applied via pressure rather than heat or other means. Through the Fasson JAC and Avery Dennison brands the segment makes papers plastic films metal foils fabrics and specially coated backing papers and films.

The Retail Branding and Information Solutions segment designs manufactures and sells a wide variety of branding and information products and services.

Industrial and Healthcare Materials sells branded tapes and fasteners pressure-sensitive medical devices and performance polymers.

Geographic Reach

The company operates about 180 manufacturing and distribution facilities in more than 50 countries. Asia is its largest market accounting for around 35% of Avery Dennison's total revenue; Europe brings in around 30% followed by the US which bring in another quarter of the revenue.

Sales and Marketing

The company's major customers include advertising agencies distributors designers government agencies graphic vendors label converters architecture & building electronics & electrical OEMs package designers packaging engineers and manufacturers printers and sign manufacturers.

The RBIS segment sells a variety of branding and information solutions to retailers food service grocery pharmaceutical supply chains and transportation companies.

Avery Dennison also sells durable cast and reflective films to the construction automotive and fleet transportation market segments; and reflective films for traffic and safety applications.

The company sells its products directly and via third-party distributors and retailers.

Financial Performance

Avery Dennison has seen revenue hover around the $6 billion mark for half a decade though the last couple of years have seen decent growth. Net income has been less stead over the same period of time with average profits north of $250 million per year.

Revenue at Avery Dennison increased $6 billion to $6.6 billion in the 2016-17 period. Majority of that growth came from the Label and Graphic materials segment ($325 million) due to organic sales growth in the emerging markets and Western Europe. Industrial and Healthcare Materials has also seen an impressive growth by adding $137 million more to the coffers year-over-year.

Net income reduced by some $40 million to $282 million in 2017 primarily due to highers income tax provisions employee-related costs and restructuring charges. Profit also declined due to lower margins in the Healthcare Materials segment driven by the impact of acquisitions growth investments near-term operational challenges and a program loss in personal care tapes.

Avery Dennison's cash holdings increased from $195 million in 2016 to $224 million in 2017. Net Cash provided by operating activities was $650 million in 2017. Investment activities used up some $548 million majority of which went towards acquisition costs and business investments; a further $84 million was utilized for financing activities.

Strategy

Avery Dennison's growth strategy is based on expanding its presence in high-value and emerging markets. The company is targeting the automotive segment through the acquired Yongle's wire harnessing business leveraging its OEM (original equipment manufacturer) relationships and increasing the scale of its commercial focus.

It also aims to return the Healthcare segment to growth and profitability by rebuilding customer relationships strengthening product pipeline and driving aggressive productivity improvements. It will also launch two new wound care technologies CHG (an antimicrobial agent) and TASA (Thin Absorbent Skin Adhesive).

The company focuses on emerging markets including countries in Asia Latin America and Eastern Europe; and continues to pursue acquisitions.

However acquisitions and heavy investments has presented the company with limited cash to fund new opportunities in the market or meet its short term debt obligations. Moreover rapid changes in the packaging industry may also force the company to divest many core assets in the years ahead especially as business try to move away from plastics and waste reduction in a more sustainable fashion.

Mergers and Acquisitions

In 2017 the company acquired Yongle Tape Company for $190 million. Yongle is China's largest producer of cable harnessing and insulation tape and supplies both Chinese and global customers.

It also acquired Hanita Coatings for $75 million and Irish wound care company Finesse Medical in 2017.

In 2016 it acquired Mactac Europe from Platinum Equity. Mactac complements Avery Dennison's existing graphics portfolio.

HISTORY

Avery Dennison was created in 1990 by the merger of Avery International and Dennison Manufacturing. In 1935 Stanton Avery founded Kum-Kleen Products which would become Avery International. After a fire destroyed the plant's equipment in 1938 Avery who had renamed the company Avery Adhesives improved the machinery used in making the labels.

During and after WWII Avery Adhesives shifted toward the industrial market for self-adhesives. The company incorporated in 1946. At that time Avery Adhesives sold 80% of its production consisting of industrial labels to manufacturers that labeled their own products. The company lost its patent rights for self-adhesive labels in 1952 transforming the firm and the entire industry. As a result a new division was created — the Avery Paper Company (later renamed Fasson) — to produce and market self-adhesive base materials. Avery Adhesives went public in 1961.

Dennison was started in 1844 by the father-and-son team of Andrew and Aaron Dennison to produce jewelry boxes. By 1849 Aaron's younger brother Eliphalet Whorf (E.W.) was running the business and expanding it into tags labels and tissue paper. Dennison was incorporated in 1878 with $150000 in capital.

EXECUTIVES

Svp And Chief Human Resources Officer, Anne Hill, age 59, $512,787 total compensation
President Materials Group, Georges Gravanis, age 61, $523,775 total compensation
President And Ceo, Mitchell R. Butier, age 47, $988,333 total compensation
Svp And Cfo, Gregory S. (Greg) Lovins, age 45
Vice President Communications Label And Graphic Materials, Amy White
Chairman, Dean A. Scarborough, age 63
Auditors: PricewaterhouseCoopers LLP

LOCATIONS

HQ: Avery Dennison Corp
207 Goode Avenue, Glendale, CA 91203
Phone: 626 304-2000
Web: www.averydennison.com

2016 Sales

	$ mil.	% of total
Asia	1,996	33
Europe	1,838	30
US	1,525	25
Latin America	450	7
Other regions	275	5
Total	**6,086**	**100**

PRODUCTS/OPERATIONS

2016 Sales

	$ mil.	% of total
Label and Graphic Materials	4,187	69
Retail Branding and Information Solutions	1,445	24
Industrial and Healthcare Materials	453	7
Total	**6,086**	**100**

Selected Brands

Avery
Avery Dennison
Avery Graphics
Fasson

COMPETITORS

3M	Checkpoint Systems
ACCO Brands	Esselte
Beam Suntory	H.B. Fuller
Bemis	Newell Brands
Bostik	UPM-Kymmene
Brady Corporation	

HISTORICAL FINANCIALS

Company Type: Public

Income Statement

FYE: December 30

	REVENUE ($ mil.)	NET INCOME ($ mil.)	NET PROFIT MARGIN	EMPLOYEES
12/17	6,613	281	4.3%	30,000
12/16*	6,086	320	5.3%	—
01/16	5,966	274	4.6%	—
01/15	6,330	248	3.9%	25,000
12/13	6,140	215	3.5%	26,000
Annual Growth	1.9%	6.9%	—	3.6%

*Fiscal year change

2017 Year-End Financials

Debt ratio: 30.79%	No. of shares (mil.): 88
Return on equity: 28.66%	Dividends
Cash ($ mil.): 224	Yield: 0.0%
Current ratio: 1.13	Payout: 56.2%
Long-term debt ($ mil.): 1,316	Market value ($ mil.): 10,109

	STOCK PRICE ($)	P/E		PER SHARE ($)	
	FY Close	High/Low	Earnings	Dividends	Book Value
12/17	114.86	37 22	3.13	1.76	11.89
12/16*	70.22	22 16	3.54	1.60	10.48
01/16	62.66	22 17	2.95	1.46	10.73
01/15	51.79	20 16	2.60	1.34	11.79
12/13	50.48	23 16	2.16	1.14	15.51
Annual Growth	22.8%	— —	9.7%	11.5%	(6.4%)

*Fiscal year change

Avis Budget Group Inc

Avis Budget Group (ABG) has a car rental brand for you. The company's core brands include: Avis Rent A Car which targets corporate and leisure travelers at the high end of the market; Budget Rent A Car and Payless Car Rental both marketed to those on a budget; and Zipcar a car-sharing service. The rental car operator operates through 5500 Avis and 4050 Budget branches across 180 countries in North America Europe Australia and New Zealand and generates nearly 70% of its revenue from its on-airport locations. Avis's Budget Truck is one of the leading truck rental businesses in the US.

HISTORY

Cendant began life through the 1997 merger of CUC International and HFS. A giant in hospitality HFS was cobbled together as Hospitality Franchise Systems by LBO specialist Blackstone Group in 1992. With brands including Days Inn Ramada and Howard Johnson HFS went public that year. In 1995 HFS bought real estate firm Century 21. The next year it added Electronic Realty Associates (ERA) and Coldwell Banker. Also in 1996 HFS acquired the Super 8 Motels brand as well as car-rental firm Avis (founded by Warren Avis in 1946 it went through a succession of owners until acquired by HFS). The next year HFS sold 75% of Avis' #1 franchisee to the public and later bought relocation service firm PHH.

In an attempt to leverage the power of his brands HFS CEO Henry Silverman began looking at direct marketing giant CUC International. CUC was founded in 1973 as Comp-U-Card America by Walter Forbes and other investors envisioning a computer-based home shopping network. During the 1980s CUC developed as a discount direct marketer and catalog-based shopping club. It went public in 1983 with 100000 members. CUC saw explosive growth as it signed up 7.6 million members between 1989 and 1993. In 1996 CUC acquired Rent Net an online apartment rental service and later bought entertainment software publishers Davidson & Associates and Sierra On-Line. In 1997 CUC bought software maker Knowledge Adventure and launched online shopping site Net-Market.

CUC and HFS completed their $14.1 billion merger in December 1997 with Silverman as CEO and Forbes as chairman. While the name Cendant was derived from "ascendant" the marriage quickly headed in the opposite direction. Accounting irregularities from before the merger that had inflated CUC's revenue and pretax profit by about $500 million were revealed in 1998. Cendant's stock price tumbled taking a $14 billion hit in one day. Forbes resigned that summer. Silverman quickly took action and began to sell off opera-

tions. Cendant Software National Leisure Group (now World Travel Holdings) National Library of Poetry and Match.com all were sold that year for a total of about $1.4 billion. The company also acquired Jackson Hewitt the US's #2 tax-preparation firm and UK-based National Parking.

Through 1999 the company continued to sell assets. Cendant sold its fleet business — including PHH Vehicle Management Services — to Avis Rent A Car for $5 billion and sold its Entertainment Publications unit the world's largest coupon book marketer and publisher to The Carlyle Group. Cendant later paid $2.8 billion in one of the largest shareholder class action lawsuit settlements. (Accounting firm Ernst & Young also settled with Cendant shareholders for $335 million.)

In 2000 Cendant introduced Move.com a relocation and real estate Internet portal. Also that year the company launched Cendant Internet Group to help cement its presence on the Web and bought the brand name and franchising rights of AmeriHost Inns from AmeriHost Properties. Later in 2000 cable programming company Liberty Media (now Liberty Interactive) invested $400 million in Cendant. The next year the company began licensing and outsourcing its Incentives and Marketing Services business (practically all of the businesses that made up the former CUC International) to Trilegiant a new company formed by the units' management.

In 2001 after selling Move.com to Homestore (later called Move) for $761 million Cendant sought to expand its travel holdings with a slew of acquisitions. Its purchases included timeshare resort firm Fairfield Communities ($690 million); travel services firm Galileo International ($2.4 billion); online travel reservation service Cheap Tickets ($425 million); and vacation timeshare marketer Equivest Finance ($100 million). In late 2001 Cendant cut some 6000 jobs to improve its bottom line and announced that during the next year or so it would cut an additional 10000 jobs and eliminate about 7% of its franchised hotels.

In 2002 the company sold its UK-based National Car Park unit which accounted for 3% of sales as part of its strategy to sell off noncore businesses. In June Cendant bought TRUST International from Bertelsmann and later that year purchased car-rental company Budget Rent A Car for about $110 million then slashed costs by closing facilities and laying off more than 450 employees. The company also purchased Novasol AS which rented out private vacation homes in Northern Europe.

Cendant terminated its licensing and services agreements with Trilegiant in January 2004 and in February Sotheby's Holdings sold its 15 Sotheby's International Realty offices (along with the brand's licensing rights) to the company for about $100 million. In March Cendant's Jackson Hewitt subsidiary filed for its IPO. In May the company purchased Dutch vacation rental company Landal Green Parks (LGP) for about $150 million. Also that month former chairman Walter Forbes and former vice chairman E. Kirk Shelton went on trial for federal fraud and conspiracy stemming from the pre-merger accounting irregularities. (Shelton was found guilty of multiple counts of fraud in early 2005.) In October CFO Ronald Nelson was named president taking over for Henry Silverman who remained chairman and CEO.

In 2004 Cendant acquired online travel firm Orbitz in a deal valued at about $1.25 billion. Quick on the heels of the Orbitz deal the company Cendant also purchased ebookers (a European online travel site now called Flightbookers) in a deal worth about $400 million and acquired two travel groups collectively known as Gullivers for about $1.1 billion.

As 2004 wound to a close Cendant completed the acquisition of the Ramada International Hotels

& Resorts brand and franchising operations from Marriott International. Cendant already owned the rights to the brand and franchising operations in the US and Canada which included some 820 US properties and about 70 Canadian properties. In 2005 Cendant acquired the Wyndham hotel brand from Wyndham International Inc. for $101 million. The deal included the franchise agreements for 82 hotels and the management contracts for another 29 hotels but not the actual properties which were located in the US Mexico and the Caribbean. The next year Cendant acquired the Baymont Inn & Suites brand of limited-service midscale lodging from Blackstone's La Quinta Corporation (now LQ Management). The Baymont Inn & Suites brand covered 115 franchised properties; the properties themselves were not included in the deal.

Cendant in 2005 spun off its mortgage operations PHH Mortgage (formerly Cendant Mortgage) and fleet management (PHH Arval) businesses under the PHH Corporation umbrella. Also that year Cendant spun off Wright Express (payment processing and information services for fleet management) in an IPO and sold its marketing services division to Apollo Management for about $1.8 billion.

The divestitures that began in 2005 culminated in the unwinding of the Cendant conglomerate the next year. The company spun off its hotel and real estate operations and sold its travel services division in 2006 reconfiguring itself around its rental car businesses and renaming itself Avis Budget Group. Silverman became chairman and CEO of the company's real estate business Realogy and Nelson took over as chairman and CEO of the slimmed-down Avis Budget Group which took on its new name in September 2006.

Warren Avis the founder of Avis Rent A Car died in April 2007 at the age of 92. In October the company acquired a 48% stake in chauffeured transportation company Carey International for $60 million. (In 2009 due to losses at Carey it wrote down its investment in the company to zero.)

Avis Budget Group acquired Avis Europe plc in October 2011. The purchase followed ABG's withdrawal from its battle with rival Hertz to acquire Dollar Thrifty Automotive Group (DTG). Instead the company turned to Europe for growth by reuniting with Avis Europe which was legally separated from Avis in 1986. The deal created what ABG says is the largest publicly traded rental car business in the world.

In 2012 in continuing to bulk up its global operations after its purchase of Avis Europe ABG in 2012 acquired New Zealand's largest independently-owned car rental company Apex Car Rentals. The purchase added more than 4000 rental cars and strengthened Avis's position in New Zealand and Australia.

EXECUTIVES

President International, Mark J. Servodidio, age 53, $596,538 total compensation
Interim Cfo, Martyn R. Smith, age 63
Evp And Chief Marketing Officer, W. Scott Deaver, age 67
Ceo And Coo, Larry D. De Shon, age 59, $1,000,000 total compensation
Evp And Cio, Gerard Insall
Evp General Counsel And Chief Compliance Officer, Michael K. Tucker, age 60
Svp North America Operations, Joseph A. (Joe) Ferraro, age 61, $623,269 total compensation
Svp And Chief Human Resources Officer, Edward P. (Ned) Linnen, age 48
Evp And Chief Innovation Officer, Arthur Orduna
Senior Vice President Of Fleet Services, Edward Gitlitz

Vice President Enterprise Applications, Steve Hoffman
Vice President Fleet Control, Neil Schamus
Vice President Human Resources, Gina Bruzzichesi
Vice President Human Resources, April Scavone
Vice President Area, Jeff Eisenbarth
Executive Vice President Strategy And Pricing, Scott Deaver
Vice President Sales And Marketing, John Barrows
Vice President Of Engineering, Jennifer Rodean
Senior Vice President Information Technology, Jeff Edwards
Vice President Global Account Sales, Matthew Tolan
Vice President Ecommerce, Joseph Kirrane
Vice President Sales, Joanne Cormier
Vice President Supply Chain Americas, Mark Haeussler
Senior Vice President Management Information Services, Suzzane Wetherington
Vice President Fleet Services, Gregg Nierenberg
Vice President Finance, Lynn Finkel
Chairman, Ronald L. (Ron) Nelson, age 66
Board Member, Robert Salerno
Auditors: DELOITTE & TOUCHE LLP

LOCATIONS

HQ: Avis Budget Group Inc
6 Sylvan Way, Parsippany, NJ 07054
Phone: 973 496-4700
Web: www.avisbudgetgroup.com

2016 Locations

	$ mil.	% of total
Company-operated	1,550	1,400
Licensees	700	650
International		
Company-operated	1,200	650
Licensees	2,050	1,350
Total	**5,550**	**4,050**

2016 Sales

	$ mil.	% of total
United States	5,674	66
All other countries	2,985	34
Total	**8,659**	**100**

2016 Sales

	% of total
Americas	71
International	29
Total	**100**

2016 Car Rental Sales

	% of total
On-Airport	70
Off-airport	30
Total	**100**

PRODUCTS/OPERATIONS

2016 Sales

	$ mil.	% of total
Vehicle rental	6,081	70
Others	2,578	30
Total	**8,659**	**100**

COMPETITORS

AMERCO	Penske Truck Leasing
Enterprise Rent-A-Car	Ryder System
Europcar	Sixt
Herc Holdings	

HISTORICAL FINANCIALS

Company Type: Public

Income Statement

FYE: December 31

	REVENUE ($ mil.)	NET INCOME ($ mil.)	NET PROFIT MARGIN	EMPLOYEES
12/17	8,848	361	4.1%	31,000
12/16	8,659	163	1.9%	30,000
12/15	8,502	313	3.7%	30,000
12/14	8,485	245	2.9%	30,000
12/13	7,937	16	0.2%	29,000
Annual Growth	**2.8%**	**117.9%**	**—**	**1.7%**

2017 Year-End Financials

Debt ratio: 72.43%
Return on equity: 90.93%
Cash ($ mil.): 611
Current ratio: 1.26
Long-term debt ($ mil.): 12,794

No. of shares (mil.): 81
Dividends
Yield: —
Payout: —
Market value ($ mil.): 3,554

	STOCK PRICE ($) FY Close	P/E High/Low		PER SHARE ($) Earnings	Dividends	Book Value
12/17	43.88	11	5	4.25	0.00	7.07
12/16	36.68	23	12	1.75	0.00	2.57
12/15	36.29	22	11	2.98	0.00	4.48
12/14	66.33	30	15	2.22	0.00	6.29
12/13	40.42	263	132	0.15	0.00	7.24
Annual Growth	**2.1%**	**—**	**—**	**130.7%**	**—**	**(0.6%)**

Avnet Inc

EXECUTIVES

Ceo, William J Amelio
Chb, Rodney C Adkins
Cfo, Thomas Liguori
Sr V Pres-Cto, Peter G Bartolotta
Sr V Pres-Chief Hr Officer, Maryann G Miller
Sr V Pres-Clo-General Counsel, Michael J O'Neill
Sr V Pres-CIO, Kevin V Summers
V Pres Global Fin-Cao-Contrl, Ken A Jacobson
Svp-Chf Strtgy & Innov Offcr, Therese M Bassett
Global Pres Core Dstrbtion, Philip R Gallagher
Director, Ayman Taha
Auditors: KPMG LLP

LOCATIONS

HQ: Avnet Inc
2211 South 47th Street, Phoenix, AZ 85034
Phone: 480 643-2000
Web: www.avnet.com

COMPETITORS

Arrow Electronics	Premier Farnell
Digi-Key	SYNNEX
Future Electronics	TTI Inc.
Heilind Electronics	Tech Data
Ingram Micro	WPG Holdings
N.F. Smith	

HISTORICAL FINANCIALS

Company Type: Public

Income Statement

FYE: June 30

	REVENUE ($ mil.)	NET INCOME ($ mil.)	NET PROFIT MARGIN	EMPLOYEES
06/18*	19,036	(156)	—	15,400
07/17	17,439	525	3.0%	15,700
07/16	26,219	506	1.9%	17,700
06/15	27,924	571	2.0%	18,800
06/14	27,499	545	2.0%	19,000
Annual Growth	**(8.8%)**	**—**	**—**	**(5.1%)**

*Fiscal year change

2018 Year-End Financials

Debt ratio: 17.24%
Return on equity: (-3.17%)
Cash ($ mil.): 621
Current ratio: 2.56
Long-term debt ($ mil.): 1,489

No. of shares (mil.): 115
Dividends
Yield: 0.0%
Payout: —
Market value ($ mil.): 4,968

	STOCK PRICE ($) FY Close	P/E High/Low		PER SHARE ($) Earnings	Dividends	Book Value
06/18*	42.89	—	—	(1.30)	0.74	40.45
07/17	38.88	12	9	4.08	0.70	42.10
07/16	40.27	12	10	3.80	0.68	36.84
06/15	42.09	11	9	4.12	0.64	34.58
06/14	43.71	12	9	3.89	0.60	35.37
Annual Growth	**(0.5%)**	**—**	**—**	**—**	**5.4%**	**3.4%**

*Fiscal year change

Avon Products, Inc.

Auditors: PricewaterhouseCoopers LLP

LOCATIONS

HQ: Avon Products, Inc.
Building 6, Chiswick Park, London W4 5HR
Phone: (44) 1604 232425
Web: www.avon.com

COMPETITORS

Alticor	Johnson Publishing
Amway China	Jostens
Bath & Body Works	Kracie
BeautiControl	L'Oreal
Beiersdorf	LJ International
Body Shop	LVMH
Carolee	Macy's
Chanel	Mary Kay
Clarins	Murad Inc.
Colgate-Palmolive	Nu Skin
Coty Inc.	Perrigo
Dana Classic Fragrances	Prestige Cosmetics
Dillard's	Procter & Gamble
Elizabeth Arden Inc	Revlon
Enesco	Sara Lee
Estee Lauder	Shaklee
Forever Living	Shiseido
Fossil Inc.	Target Corporation
Hanover Direct	Tiffany & Co.
J. C. Penney	Tupperware Brands
Jafra	Unilever
James Avery	Wal-Mart
Johnson & Johnson	Zale

HISTORICAL FINANCIALS
Company Type: Public

Income Statement
FYE: December 31

	REVENUE ($ mil.)	NET INCOME ($ mil.)	NET PROFIT MARGIN	EMPLOYEES
12/17	5,715	22	0.4%	25,000
12/16	5,717	(107)	—	26,400
12/15	6,160	(1,148)	—	28,300
12/14	8,851	(388)	—	33,200
12/13	9,955	(56)	—	36,700
Annual Growth	(13.0%)			(9.2%)

2017 Year-End Financials

Debt ratio: 51.32%	No. of shares (mil.): 440
Return on equity: —	Dividends
Cash ($ mil.): 881	Yield: 0.0%
Current ratio: 1.43	Payout: —
Long-term debt ($ mil.): 1,872	Market value ($ mil.): 947

	STOCK PRICE ($) FY Close	P/E High/Low	PER SHARE ($) Earnings	Dividends	Book Value
12/17	2.15	— —	(0.00)	0.00	(0.58)
12/16	5.04	— —	(0.29)	0.00	(0.92)
12/15	4.05	— —	(2.60)	0.24	(2.46)
12/14	9.39	— —	(0.88)	0.24	0.67
12/13	17.22	— —	(0.13)	0.24	2.56
Annual Growth	(40.6%)	—	—	—	—

AXA Equitable Holdings Inc

Auditors: PricewaterhouseCoopers LLP

LOCATIONS
HQ: AXA Equitable Holdings Inc
1290 Avenue of the Americas, New York, NY 10104
Phone: 212 554-1234
Web: www.axa.com

HISTORICAL FINANCIALS
Company Type: Public

Income Statement
FYE: December 31

	REVENUE ($ mil.)	NET INCOME ($ mil.)	NET PROFIT MARGIN	EMPLOYEES
12/17	12,514	850	6.8%	7,500
12/16	11,922	1,272	10.7%	—
12/15	10,079	333	3.3%	—
Annual Growth	11.4%	59.8%	—	—

2017 Year-End Financials

Debt ratio: 2.56%	No. of shares (mil.): 561
Return on equity: 6.82%	Dividends
Cash ($ mil.): 5,639	Yield: —
Current ratio: 1.72	Payout: —
Long-term debt ($ mil.): 4,174	Market value ($ mil.): —

	STOCK PRICE ($) FY Close	P/E High/Low	PER SHARE ($) Earnings	Dividends	Book Value
12/17	0.00	— —	1.51	0.00	24.04
12/16	0.00	— —	2.27	0.00	20.42
Annual Growth	—	— —	(18.5%)	—	8.5%

AXOS BANK

EXECUTIVES
Ceo, Greg Garrabants
Sr V Pres-Cfo, Andrew Micheletti
Evp-Chief Credit Offr-Chief RE, Tom Constantine
Gen Counsel, Eshel Bar-Adon
Exec V Pres, Brian Swanson
Svp-Business Banking Division, Robert Armstrong
Vice-President, Randall Becker
Account Executive, Cari Anderson
Manager, Judy Davidtz
Manager, Rudy Villa
Executive Vice-President, Adriaan Van Zyl

LOCATIONS
HQ: AXOS BANK
4350 LA JOLLA VILLAGE DR, SAN DIEGO, CA 921221243
Phone: 858 350-6200
Web: WWW.BOFIFEDERALBANK.COM

HISTORICAL FINANCIALS
Company Type: Private

Income Statement
FYE: December 31

	ASSETS ($ mil.)	NET INCOME ($ mil.)	INCOME AS % OF ASSETS	EMPLOYEES
12/17	8,908	150	1.7%	102
12/16	8,162	137	1.7%	—
12/15	6,656	104	1.6%	—
12/14	5,190	71	1.4%	—
Annual Growth	19.7%	28.1%		

2017 Year-End Financials

Debt ratio: ——	
Return on equity: 31.20%	Dividends
Cash ($ mil.): 617	Yield: —
Current ratio: —	Payout: —
Long-term debt ($ mil.): —	Market value ($ mil.): —

Axos Financial Inc

Skip the teller lines by banking with a branchless online-only bank Bofl Holding Inc. It is the holding company for Bofl Federal Bank which provides consumers and businesses a variety of banking choices for both deposits and loans. It conducts its business without any physical bank branches preferring to support its customers through a comprehensive online banking platform supported occasionally by physical retail locations of its partners. The majority of its business originates in its headquarter state of California though its online operations attract customers from every US state.

Operations
Bofl operates a single financial reporting segment. Its operations are generally divided into attracting money (deposits) and then lending it out (loans).

The lending business originates purchases and sometimes sells loans. The bank issues loans for single family homes commercial real estate (for example multi-family units) commercial & industrial needs small business operations and consumer purchases (such as for automobiles). Single family residential and multi-family mortgages make up more than 70% of its loan portfolio. About 85%

of its loan and lease holdings are adjustable rate loans.

The bank?s deposit operations attract money from consumers and businesses with about 50% held in checking and other demand deposit accounts roughly 35% in savings accounts and the rest in time deposits (CDs) and IRA accounts. The bank?s deposits have grown dramatically between 2013 and 2017 from $2.1 billion to $6.8 billion because of significant growth in business deposits (10X increase over the same time).

Behind the scenes Bofl operates a robust software platform that enables secure responsive banking interactions with nationwide customers who use smartphones and computers to access their accounts.

Geographic Reach

San Diego-based Bofl holds deposits from customers in every US state with large sources of balances in Florida the Mid-Atlantic states and the California coast. Nearly 70% of its loans are secured by real estate in California.

Sales and Marketing
Because the bank is branchless the traditional means of attracting customers ? such as local advertising a physical bank presence community charity sponsorship ? are not used. Rather the bank creates brand awareness through digital marketing ensures a productive and intuitive user experience and gathers analytical data about their customers to help cross-sell other products and generate ideas for product/service enhancements.

Financial Performance
In recent years Bofl experienced strong annual increases in revenue composed mainly of interest and non-interest income and in net income. Interest income jumped from $63 million in FY2009 (ending June 30) to more than $380 million in FY2017. Non-interest income typically fees and gains from loan sales rose from $1.4 million to more than $68 million in the same time. Net income experienced a similar rise swelling from $3.9 million in 2009 to almost $135 million in 2017.

For the fiscal year 2017 Bofl generated $387 million of interest income a 22% increase from FY2016. An increase in the bank?s net interest margin to 3.95% in FY2017 (versus 3.91% in the prior year) as well as a larger loan portfolio ($7.4 billion vs $6.4 billion) produced most of the increase. The bank also saw its non-interest income rise 3% to $68 million.

Net income rose 13% in FY2017 to $134 million compared to the prior year. The rise in interest income as the result of a larger loan portfolio was the primary reason for increased net income.

Cash and cash equivalents rose $156 million in FY2017 to $644 million. The cash buildup was the result of $753 million from financing activities (mainly from an increase in bank deposits) and $224 million from operations both offset by an $821 million use by investing activities (due to loan origination amounts higher than repayment amounts).

Strategy
Bofl?s strategy is simply to grow its loan portfolio ? and therefore its interest income ? through new products expanded distribution channels leveraged data mining and occasional acquisitions.

In FY2017 the bank introduced two new products: retail auto loans and unsecured lending offerings. It also established a US tax refund advance through H&R Block. It?s partnership with H&R Block began in 2015 when it acquired $419 million in deposits from tax preparer?s owned bank. From there the H&R Block distribution channel has blossomed to include several Bofl services made available to the tax preparer?s nearly 20 million customers including coordinating the US government?s electronically delivered tax refund and an offer made by H&R Block tax preparers to open a BofI-originated IRA account.

The amount of customer data gathered by BofI through its own customer base and through the H&R Block customers that choose to use BofI?s tax refund services is a significant data mining asset. The bank analyzes this information to help cross-sell other products & services and even anticipates deploying artificial intelligence to assist with the effort.

From time to time the bank purchases loans and leases from other entities. It did so in early 2016 with the acquisition of $140 million of equipment leases from Pacific Western Equipment Finance and with the 2015 acquisition of H&R Block Bank deposits.

EXECUTIVES

Evp And Cfo Bofi Holding Inc. And Bofi Federal Bank, Andrew J. Micheletti, age 61, $231,000 total compensation
President And Ceo Bofi Holding Inc. And Bofi Federal Bank, Gregory Garrabrants, age 47, $375,000 total compensation
Evp Specialty Finance And Chief Legal Officer Bofi Federal Bank, Eshel Bar-Adon, age 63, $250,000 total compensation
Evp And Chief Credit Officer Bofi Federal Bank, Thomas Constantine, age 56, $235,000 total compensation
Evp And Chief Lending Officer Bofi Federal Bank, Brian Swanson, age 38, $235,000 total compensation
Evp Chief Of Staff And Chief Performance Officer Bofi Federal Bank, Jan Durrans
Evp Chief Deposit Officer And Chief Marketing Officer Bofi Federal Bank, Eduardo Urdapilleta
Senior Vice President Warehouse Lending And Loan Operations, Darin Sullivan
Vice President Wholesale Banking, Johnson Raymond
Chairman, Paul J. Grinberg, age 57
Vice Chairman, Nicholas A. Mosich
Member Board Of Directors, Edward Ratinoff
Auditors: BDO USA, LLP

LOCATIONS

HQ: Axos Financial Inc
4350 La Jolla Village Drive, Suite 140, San Diego, CA 92122
Phone: 858 350-6200
Web: www.bofiholding.com

PRODUCTS/OPERATIONS

2016 Sales

	$ mil.	% of total
Interest and dividend income:		
Loans and leases including fees	358	79
Investments	28	6
Non-interest income	68	14
Total	**455**	**100**

COMPETITORS

Ally Bank	ISN Bank
California Bank & Trust	MUFG Americas Holdings
Discover	PacWest Bancorp
E*TRADE Bank	San Diego County Credit Union
First IB	Scottrade
HSBC USA	

HISTORICAL FINANCIALS

Company Type: Public

Income Statement
FYE: June 30

	ASSETS ($ mil.)	NET INCOME ($ mil.)	INCOME AS % OF ASSETS	EMPLOYEES
06/18	9,539	152	1.6%	801
06/17	8,501	134	1.6%	681
06/16	7,601	119	1.6%	647
06/15	5,823	82	1.4%	467
06/14	4,403	55	1.3%	366
Annual Growth	**21.3%**	**28.5%**	**—**	**21.6%**

2018 Year-End Financials

Debt ratio: 0.57%
Return on equity: 16.98%
Cash ($ mil.): 622
Current ratio: —
Long-term debt ($ mil.): —

No. of shares (mil.): 62
Dividends
Yield: —
Payout: —
Market value ($ mil.): 2,565

	STOCK PRICE ($) FY Close	P/E High/Low	PER SHARE ($) Earnings	Dividends	Book Value
06/18	40.91	19 10	2.37	0.00	15.32
06/17	23.72	16 7	2.07	0.00	13.13
06/16	17.71	77 7	1.85	0.00	10.81
06/15	105.71	79 49	1.34	0.00	8.59
06/14	73.47	109 48	0.96	0.00	6.41
Annual Growth	**(13.6%)**	**— —**	**25.3%**	**—**	**24.3%**

Baker Hughes, A GE Company

Auditors: KPMG LLP

LOCATIONS

HQ: Baker Hughes, A GE Company
17021 Aldine Westfield Road, Houston, TX 77073-5101
Phone: 713 439-8600
Web: www.bakerhughes.com

HISTORICAL FINANCIALS

Company Type: Public

Income Statement
FYE: December 31

	REVENUE ($ mil.)	NET INCOME ($ mil.)	NET PROFIT MARGIN	EMPLOYEES
12/17	17,259	(73)	—	64,000
12/16	13,269	403	3.0%	34,000
12/15	16,688	(606)	—	—
12/14	19,191	1,840	9.6%	—
Annual Growth	**(3.5%)**	**—**	**—**	**—**

2017 Year-End Financials

Debt ratio: 12.66%
Return on equity: (-0.50%)
Cash ($ mil.): 7,023
Current ratio: 2.08
Long-term debt ($ mil.): 6,312

No. of shares (mil.): 1,129
Dividends
Yield: 0.0%
Payout: —
Market value ($ mil.): 35,728

	STOCK PRICE ($) FY Close	P/E High/Low	PER SHARE ($) Earnings	Dividends	Book Value
12/17	31.64	— —	(0.17)	0.35	13.03
12/16	0.00	— —	(2.08)	0.00	(0.00)
Annual Growth	**—**	**— —**	**—**	**—**	**—**

BALFOUR BEATTY, LLC

EXECUTIVES

Mng MBR-Pres, Mark Crouser
V Pres, Peter Zinkin
V Pres, Leslie Cohn
V Pres-Asst SEC, Joanne Bonfiglio
Treas, Barry Crozier
SEC, Christine Schiltz
Asst Treas, Vicki Sizemore
Vp and Business Unit Leader Fo, Ed Prendergast
Auditors: DELOITTE & TOUCHE LLP DALLAS

LOCATIONS

HQ: BALFOUR BEATTY, LLC
1011 CENTRE RD STE 322, WILMINGTON, DE 198051266
Phone: 302 573-3873
Web: WWW.BALFOURBEATTYUS.COM

HISTORICAL FINANCIALS

Company Type: Private

Income Statement
FYE: December 31

	REVENUE ($ mil.)	NET INCOME ($ mil.)	NET PROFIT MARGIN	EMPLOYEES
12/15	4,690	(18)	—	2,200
12/12	4,378	43	1.0%	—
12/11	4,078	58	1.4%	—
Annual Growth	**3.6%**	**—**	**—**	**—**

2015 Year-End Financials

Debt ratio:
Return on equity: (-0.40%)
Cash ($ mil.): 391
Current ratio: 0.60
Long-term debt ($ mil.): —

Dividends
Yield: —
Payout: —
Market value ($ mil.): —

Ball Corp

The Ball Corporation is well-contained. The company produces sustainable metal packaging and containers for beverage food and household products. Ball's packaging revenue (more than 90% of its net sales) is derived from a relatively few major beverage-producing companies and brands such as Coca-Cola and Unilever. Additionally its aerospace segment provides an array of aerospace systems and services (such as spacecraft instruments and sensors and data solutions); 98% of these sales are to the US government. Ball Corporation operates through 85 locations in about 30 countries with the US its largest single market.

Operations

Ball Corporation divides its operations between five business segments. Its three beverage packaging segments ? North and Central America (about 40% of total revenue) Europe (more than 20%) and South America (about 15%) ? are all the leading provider of aluminum cans for soft drinks energy drinks beer and other beverages in their respective markets.

Food and aerosol packaging (10%) makes two- and three-piece steel food containers and ends for packaging food products steel and aluminum aerosol containers and aluminum slugs. Its facilities are in the US Europe Argentina Canada Mexico and India.

The company's smallest segment aerospace (almost 10%) makes and sells aerospace and related products for the civil commercial and national security aerospace markets.

Geographic Reach

The company operates more than 85 facilities spanning Asia Europe North America and South America. The US accounts for about half of total revenues and almost 15% of sales come from Brazil.

Ball Corporation?s headquarters as well as its aerospace segment offices are located in Broomfield CO. Regional offices for Europe are in Luton UK; Middle East and Asia operations are run out of Dubai and Hong Kong respectively; and South American offices are in Rio de Janeiro.

Sales and Marketing

Ball's packaging revenue is derived primarily from long-term contracts with a relatively few customers; Anheuser-Busch contributes about 15% of net sales with Coca-Cola Molson Coors and the US government each accounting for about 10%.

Financial Performance

Ball's revenues climbed by a whopping 21% from $9 billion in 2016 to almost $11 billion in 2017 its second consecutive historic high. The growth was fueled by increased sales volumes from beverage packaging including an entire 12 months of sales from the acquired Rexam business (Rexam represented just six months of sales in 2016). Also of note was an increased pass through of higher metal prices in North and Central America and South America and favorable currency exchange rates in the European segment.

Profits increased by $111 million in 2017. The increase is attributed to higher sales volumes and synergy realizations (2016 cost of sales included $84 million in inventory step-up related to Rexam).

Cash flows from operations in 2017 were higher compared to 2016 primarily due to improved earnings and working capital.

Strategy

Ball is continuing its ?Drive for 10? vision ? a 10-year initiative established in 2011 which is focused on key levers underpinning its corporate strategy. Ball is focused on growing its existing business while also adding new products to its portfolio.

The company is streamlining processes and systems and increasing the sustainability of its beverage cans. In 2018 it is continuing with its global finance transformation projects by opening shared service centers in Serbia and Mexico. To tighten its beverage and food can operations it closed several plants in the US and one in Germany. It opened new aluminum aerosol lines in India and the Czech Republic.

To increases aluminum strength and reduce weight in its beverage cans Ball is developing a new bottle-shaping technology. It is also leveraging cyber and data analytics to conduct predictive maintenance and redesign processes for better efficiency in its manufacturing operations enterprise-wide.

Ball hopes to anticipate customer needs such as increased demand for specialty beverage containers versus the standard 12-ounce can by expanding distribution channels and identifying new markets including craft brewers sparkling water fillers and wine producers.

To meet growing demand the company is constructing new plants in Arizona and Spain expanding facilities in Argentina Texas and Mexico and investing in joint ventures in Panama and Vietnam. Plans in 2018 include a new beverage can facility in Paraguay.

Mergers and Acquisitions

Ball's blueprint for growth has been pretty simple over the years: it acquires similar companies

around the world to widen its customer base and extend its geographical reach.

In a sweeping move for the industry the company in mid-2016 acquired Rexam one of its biggest rivals for around $6,1 billion. The deal created the world's largest maker of food and beverage cans. As part of the stipulations to complete the deal Ball sold a dozen plants in Europe and two in Brazil. The company also completed the required sale of eight aluminum-can plants and related assets in the US to Ardagh Group for $3.4 billion. Further it shut down Rexam's London headquarters in late 2016.

HISTORY

The Ball Corporation began in 1880 when Frank Ball and his four brothers started making wood-jacket tin cans to store and transport kerosene and other materials. In 1884 the company switched to tin-jacketed glass containers for kerosene lamps. The lamps however were soon displaced by Thomas Edison's electric light bulb.

The Ball brothers then learned that the patent to the original sealed-glass storage container (the Mason jar) had expired. By 1886 the brothers had entered the sealed-jar business and imprinted their jars with the Ball name. In their first year they made 12500 jars and sparked a patent war with the two reigning jar producers who asserted that they controlled the correct patents and threatened to sue. The Ball lawyers proved that the patents had expired and the jar remained Ball's mainstay for many years.

The company began diversifying but a 1947 antitrust ruling prohibited it from buying additional glass subsidiaries. Ball decided to take advantage of the space race by buying Control Cells (aerospace science research) in 1957; that operation became Ball Brothers Research Corporation (later Ball Aerospace Systems Division). The Soviets launched Sputnik that year igniting a massive US scientific effort in 1958 and Ball won federal contracts to make equipment for the US space program.

Ball established its metal beverage-container business in 1969 when it bought Jeffco Manufacturing of Colorado. The operation soon won contracts to supply two-piece cans to Budweiser Coca-Cola Dr Pepper Pepsi and Stroh's Beer.

EXECUTIVES

Svp And Cfo, Scott C. Morrison, age 55, $666,728 total compensation

Vice President, David L Taylor

Chairman President And Ceo, John A. Hayes, age 52, $1,238,615 total compensation

Svp Human Resources And Administration, Lisa A. Pauley, age 56, $464,443 total compensation

Svp And Coo Global Beverage Packaging, Daniel W. Fisher, age 45

Vp Technology, M. Andrew (Drew) Crouch

Vp General Counsel And Corporate Secretary, Charles E. Baker, age 60, $492,871 total compensation

Svp; President Ball Aerospace And Technologies, Robert D. (Rob) Strain, age 61

Vp Marketing And Corporate Affairs, James N. Peterson, age 49

Director Progam Development Chief Sales Officer, Jim Good

Vice President Operational Planning And Administra, Jim Curtin

Vice President And General Manager Advanced Technologies, Andrew Crouch

Vice President Operations, Mike Shuster

Vice President Legal Patents And Insurance Ball Packaging Europe, Clive Martyr

Information Technology Vice President, Scott Chrisbacher

Vice President, Art Morrissey

Vice President Engineering, Joseph Atwell

Vp Human Resources Metal Beverage Americas, John Olson

Vice President, Roy Nelson

Vice President Business Development, Drew Couch

Vice President Of Marketing, Bill Braun

Vice President Mission Assurance, Sherri Fike

Senior Vice President Of International Sales, David Fredericks

Group Vice President, John Haas

Senior Vice President Sales And Marketing, Neil Anderson

Vice President And General Manager Of National Security Space, Fred Doyle

Vice President Metal Food Container Operations, Brian Cardno

Vice President Of Information Technology, Fernando Diaz

Vice President Communications And Corporate Relations, Kathleen E Pitre

Vp Engineering Ball Aerospace And Technologies, Michael Gazarik

Vice President Global Business Services, Brian Gabbard

Vice President Information Technology And Services, Cheryl Martin

Vice President Information Technology And Services, Rod Hefford

Vice President, Alison Medbery

Chairman President And Ceo, John A. Hayes, age 52

Vp General Counsel And Corporate Secretary, Charles E. Baker, age 60

Board Member, Daniel Heinrich

Board Member, Cynthia Niekamp

Auditors: PricewaterhouseCoopers LLP

LOCATIONS

HQ: Ball Corp
10 Longs Peak Drive, P.O. Box 5000, Broomfield, CO 80021-2510
Phone: 303 469-3131
Web: www.ball.com

2017 Sales

	$ mil.	% of total
US	5,496	50
Brazil	1,427	13
Other	4,060	37
Total	**10,983**	**100**

PRODUCTS/OPERATIONS

2017 Sales

	$ mil.	% of total
Beverage packaging North and Central America	4,178	38
Beverage packaging Europe	2,360	22
Beverage packaging South America	1,692	15
Food and aerosol packaging	1,138	10
Aerospace	991	9
Other	624	6
Total	**10,983**	**100**

Selected Products

Packaging
  Aluminum beverage cans
  Metal food containers and ends
  Steel aerosol containers
  Extruded aluminum aerosol containers
  Aluminum slugs
  Paint and general line cans
Aerospace and technologies
  Aerospace hardware and components
  Antennas and video tactical systems
  Satellites and spacecraft
  Space-based instruments and sensors
  Radio frequency systems
  Technical services

COMPETITORS

Amcor	Saint-Gobain
Arconic	Containers
Ardagh Group	Sequa
Crown Holdings	Silgan
Reynolds Food Packaging	Teledyne Technologies
Rio Tinto Alcan	Tetra Laval

HISTORICAL FINANCIALS

Company Type: Public

Income Statement

FYE: December 31

	REVENUE ($ mil.)	NET INCOME ($ mil.)	NET PROFIT MARGIN	EMPLOYEES
12/17	10,983	374	3.4%	18,300
12/16	9,061	263	2.9%	18,450
12/15	7,997	280	3.5%	15,200
12/14	8,570	470	5.5%	14,500
12/13	8,468	406	4.8%	14,600
Annual Growth	6.7%	(2.1%)	—	5.8%

2017 Year-End Financials

Debt ratio: 40.60%
Return on equity: 10.14%
Cash ($ mil.): 448
Current ratio: 0.92
Long-term debt ($ mil.): 6,518

No. of shares (mil.): 349
Dividends
Yield: 0.0%
Payout: 34.7%
Market value ($ mil.): 13,243

	STOCK PRICE ($) FY Close	P/E High/Low		PER SHARE ($) Earnings	Dividends	Book Value
12/17	37.85	76	35	1.05	0.37	11.26
12/16	75.07	99	77	0.82	0.26	9.82
12/15	72.73	75	59	1.00	0.26	4.40
12/14	68.17	41	28	1.65	0.26	3.77
12/13	51.66	37	30	1.37	0.26	4.22
Annual Growth	(7.5%)	—	—	(6.3%)	8.9%	27.8%

Banc Of California Inc

Banc of California offers deposit and loan services at 35 branches in Southern California's Los Angeles Orange County and San Diego. Customers enjoy checking savings and money market accounts as well as mobile online and card payment services telephone banking automated bill payment safe deposit boxes direct deposit and wire transfers. Customers can also access their accounts through a nationwide network of 55000 surcharge-free ATMs. In addition to its branches the $9 billion-asset Banc of California operates around 70 mortgage loan production offices in California Arizona Oregon Indiana Idaho Nevada and Virginia.

Operations

Banc of California operates three core segments: Commercial Banking which offers commercial consumer and real estate secured loans as well as deposit accounts; Mortgage Banking which originates conforming SFR loans and sells the loans in the secondary market; and the Financial Advisory segment which purchases sells and manages SFR mortgage loans.

Unlike most retail banks Banc of California's income streams are less dependent on interest rates. The bank made 50% of its revenue from loan interest (including fees) during 2015 and another 5% from interest on investments. But it also made 29% of its revenue from its mortgage banking business while the rest came from other non-interest income sources.

Geographic Reach

The Irvine California-based bank has 90-plus banking locations in California including 35 branches in San Diego Orange Santa Barbara and Los Angeles Counties (as of mid-2016). It has 68 loan production offices in California Arizona Oregon Virginia Indiana Maryland Colorado Idaho and Nevada.

Sales and Marketing

The bank spent $6.2 million on advertising during 2015 or 23% more than in the prior year due to higher overall marketing costs tied to the bank's continued expansion.

Financial Performance

Banc of California's revenue has risen sevenfold since 2011 as a slew of bank acquisitions and organic growth have driven its loan and deposit business as well as its mortgage banking business.

The bank's revenue jumped 46% to $486.5 million during 2015 thanks to a 34% spike in loan interest income on more loan origination and loan and lease purchase activity; and thanks to a 52% rise in mortgage banking income as the bank originated and sold nearly twice as many mortgage loans on the secondary market than in 2014.

Strong revenue growth in 2015 caused Banc of California's net income to double to $62 million despite an uptick in salary and benefits cost that stemmed from additional hiring and commercial banking and mortgage banking expansion. The bank's operations used $45.24 million during the year or less than one-tenth as much cash as in 2014 mostly after adjusting its earnings for non-cash items related to proceeds of mortgage banking loans held-for-sale and proceeds from other loans held-for-sale.

Strategy

With its eye on becoming "California's Bank" Banc of California sometimes acquires smaller banks or bank branch networks to boost its loan and deposit business while expanding its branch network (mostly around California).

From 2010 through 2015 the bank has made seven acquisitions including three bank acquisitions (Gateway Bancorp Beach Business Bank and The Private Bank of California) and three other specialty financial firm acquisitions (Palisades Group which it divested in 2016; CS Financial; and Renovation Ready.)

Mergers and Acquisitions

In November 2014 the bank bought 20 branches in Southern California from Banco Popular North America (BPNA) along with $1.07 billion in loans and $1.08 billion in deposits for a total price of $24 million.

In January 2014 Banc of California purchased service contracts and intellectual property of RenovationReady a specialized loan services provider that served financial institutions and mortgage bankers that originated agency-eligible residential renovation and construction loan products.

Company Background

In 2012 it paid $15.5 million for Gateway Business Bank and $37 million for Beach Business Bank. The next year it took over The Private Bank of California for $25 million and bought The Palisades Group a residential mortgage investment advisory firm and specialty finance company CS Financial. In 2014 it announced plans to buy 20 branches of Banco Popular North America to reach California's Hispanic community.

In 2013 it sold eight branches to AmericanWest Bank in order to reshape its retail branch network to focus on servicing small - to midsized businesses and high net worth families.

EXECUTIVES

Evp Division General Counsel Lending, John F. Madden, age 57
Evp Enterprise Risk Analytics, Gilda Youdeem
Managing Director Institutional Banking And Fiduciary Services, Steven C. (Steve) Canup

Evp And Cfo Banc Of California Inc. And Banc Of California N.a., John A. Bogler
Evp And General Counsel Banking, Angelee J. Harris, age 48
Chief Investment Officer, Brian P. Kuelbs, age 55
Managing Director Community Banking, Gaylin D. Anderson
Vice Chairman And Evp, Jeffrey T. Seabold, age 51, $750,000 total compensation
President And Ceo, Douglas H. (Doug) Bowers, age 60
Chief Risk Officer, Hugh F. Boyle, age 58, $599,679 total compensation
Managing Director Warehouse Lending, Zoila Price
Evp And Chief Compliance Officer, Diane M. Summers
Evp Community Development, Gary S. Dunn
Evp And Cio, Ken Plummer
Evp Division General Counsel Banking, Manisha K. Merchant
Managing Director Construction Lending, Jim Fraser
Managing Director Cre Lending, Thomas Senske
Managing Director Sba Lending, Heather Endresen
Managing Director Commercial Banking, David Park
Chief Credit Officer, Paul Simmons
Managing Director Portfolio Lending, Julie Duong
Svp Operations, Robert Villaneda
Svp Marketing, Samantha Haugh
Managing Director Payment Solutions, Ben Kessler
Evp General Counsel And Secretary, John C. Grosvenor, age 68, $501,378 total compensation
Evp Private Banking, Jay D. Sanders
Assistant Vice President Senior Financial Analyst, Marianna Helton
Vice President Relationship Manager, Kristin Koptyra
Vice President Credit Administration, Edward Massey
Executive Vice President, Chang Liu
Vice President Loan Accounting, Barbara Curtis
Vice President Branch Manager, Rena Alekperova
Senior Vice President Residential Lending, Jon Irvine
Vice President Information Technology Infrastructure, Len Tateyama
Assistant Vice President Credit Portfolio Manager, Aida Rodriguez
Senior Vice President Treasury Management Sales Director, Gary Tackoor
Chairman, Robert D. Sznewajs, age 71
Vice Chairman And Evp, Jeffrey T. Seabold, age 51
Evp General Counsel And Secretary, John C. Grosvenor, age 68
Board Member, Jonah Schnel
Auditors: KPMG LLP

LOCATIONS

HQ: Banc Of California Inc
3 MacArthur Place, Santa Ana, CA 92707
Phone: 855 361-2262
Web: www.bancofcal.com

PRODUCTS/OPERATIONS

2013 Sales

	% of total
Interest and dividend income	
Loans including fees	53
Securities and others	2
Noninterest income	
Net gain on mortgage banking activities	31
Gain on sale of branches	6
Net gain on sale of loans	4
Loan servicing income	1
Customer service fees	1
Others	2
Total	100

COMPETITORS

American Business Bank	East West Bancorp
Bank of America	JPMorgan Chase
Bank of the West	MUFG Americas Holdings
BofI	PacWest Bancorp
California Bank &	Pacific Mercantile
Trust	Pacific Premier
City National	Simplicity Bancorp
Comerica	U.S. Bancorp

HISTORICAL FINANCIALS

Company Type: Public

Income Statement

FYE: December 31

	ASSETS ($ mil.)	NET INCOME ($ mil.)	INCOME AS % OF ASSETS	EMPLOYEES
12/17	10,327	57	0.6%	738
12/16	11,029	115	1.0%	1,797
12/15	8,235	62	0.8%	1,710
12/14	5,971	30	0.5%	1,470
12/13	3,628	0	0.0%	1,384
Annual Growth	29.9%	419.9%	—	(14.5%)

2017 Year-End Financials

Debt ratio: 1.67%	No. of shares (mil.): 50
Return on equity: 5.79%	Dividends
Cash ($ mil.): 387	Yield: 0.0%
Current ratio: —	Payout: 73.2%
Long-term debt ($ mil.): —	Market value ($ mil.): 1,045

	STOCK PRICE ($) FY Close	P/E High/Low	PER SHARE ($) Earnings	Dividends	Book Value
12/17	20.65	32 20	0.71	0.52	20.01
12/16	17.35	12 6	1.94	0.49	19.65
12/15	14.62	11 8	1.34	0.48	17.15
12/14	11.47	15 11	0.91	0.48	14.47
12/13	13.41	— —	(0.14)	0.48	16.13
Annual Growth	11.4%	— —	—	2.0%	5.5%

BancFirst Corp. (Oklahoma City, Okla)

This Oklahoma bank wants to be more than OK. It wants to be super . BancFirst Corporation is the holding company for BancFirst a super-community bank that emphasizes decentralized management and centralized support. BancFirst operates more than 100 branches in more than 50 Oklahoma communities. It serves individuals and small to midsized businesses offering traditional deposit products such as checking and savings accounts CDs and IRAs. Commercial real estate lending (including farmland and multifamily residential loans) makes up more than a third of the bank's loan portfolio while one-to-four family residential mortgages represent about 20%. The bank also issues business construction and consumer loans.

Operations

The company operates three core units: metropolitan banks community banks and other financial service. Metropolitan and community banks offer traditional banking products such as commercial and retail lending and a full line of deposit accounts in the metropolitan Oklahoma City and Tulsa areas. Community banks consist of banking locations in communities throughout Oklahoma. Other financial services are specialty product business units including guaranteed small business

lending residential mortgage lending trust services securities brokerage electronic banking and insurance.

The company's BancFirst Insurance Services arm sells property/casualty coverage while the bank's trust and investment management division oversees some $1.21 billion of assets on behalf of clients. Bank subsidiaries Council Oak Investment Corporation and Council Oak Real Estate focus on small business and property investments respectively.

Like other retail banks BancFirst makes the bulk of its money from interest income. More than 60% of its total revenue came from loan interest (including fees) during 2015 while another 2% came from interest on taxable securities. The rest of its revenue came from service charges on deposits (19% of revenue) insurance commissions (5%) trust revenue (3%) securities transactions (3%) and loan sales (1%).

Geographic Reach

BancFirst has 95 banking locations serving more than 52 communities across Oklahoma.

Sales and Marketing

The bank customers are generally small to medium-sized businesses engaged in light manufacturing local wholesale and retail trade commercial and residential real estate development and construction services agriculture and the energy industry.

BancFirst spent about $6.9 million for advertising and promotion during 2015 compared to $6.6 million in each of 2014 and 2013.

Financial Performance

BancFirst's annual revenues have risen 20% since 2011 thanks to continued loan asset and deposit growth (partly thanks to branch expansion). The company's annual profits have grown more than 40% over the same period as it's kept a lid on operating expenses and loan loss provisions.

BancFirst's revenue climbed 6% to $306.85 million during 2015 thanks to a combination of loan asset growth and gains on the sales of some of its securities.

Revenue growth in 2015 drove the company's net income up nearly 4% to $66.17 million. The bank's operating cash levels increased by almost 2% to $78.1 million with the rise in cash-based earnings.

Strategy

BancFirst's strategy focuses on providing a full range of commercial banking services to retail customers and small to medium-sized businesses in both the non-metropolitan trade centers and cities in the metropolitan statistical areas of Oklahoma. It operates as a 'super community bank' managing its community banking offices on a decentralized basis which permits them to be responsive to local customer needs. Underwriting funding customer service and pricing decisions are made by presidents in each market within the company's strategic parameters.

Mergers and Acquisitions

In October 2015 BancFirst purchased $196 million-asset CSB Banchsares and its Bank of Commerce branches in Yukon Mustang and El Reno in Oklahoma. The deal also added $148 million in new loan business and $170 million in deposits.

Company Background

The company has been buying smaller banks to expand in Oklahoma. In 2011 it acquired FBC Financial Corporation and its subsidiary bank 1st Bank Oklahoma with about five branches throughout the state. In 2010 BancFirst acquired Union Bank of Chandler Okemah National Bank and Exchange National Bank of Moore adding about another five branches. It acquired First State Bank Jones in 2009 to expand in eastern Oklahoma.

President and CEO David Rainbolt owns some 40% of BancFirst .

EXECUTIVES

Evp Investments Bancfirst, Robert M. Neville, age 62

Evp Financial Services Bancfirst, D. Jay Hannah, age 62

Evp And Chief Risk Officer, Randy P. Foraker, age 62, $174,423 total compensation

Evp Human Resources Bancfirst, J. Michael Rogers, age 74

Evp And Cio Bancfirst, Scott Copeland, age 53

Sevp And Chairman Executive Committee, Dennis L. Brand, age 70, $525,000 total compensation

Vice Chairman And Ceo Council Oak Investment Corporation And Council Oak Real Estate Inc., William O. Johnstone, age 70, $200,000 total compensation

Evp And Chief Credit Officer Bancfirst, Roy C. Ferguson, age 71

Regional Executive Bancfirst, Karen James, age 62

President And Ceo Bancfirst, Darryl Schmidt, age 56, $350,000 total compensation

Regional Executive Bancfirst, David M. Seat, age 67

Evp And Cto Bancfirst, David Westman, age 62

Ceo, David R. Harlow, age 55, $325,000 total compensation

Regional Executive Bancfirst, Harvey G. Robinson, age 59

Evp Cfo And Treasurer, Kevin Lawrence, age 39, $214,231 total compensation

President Bancfirst Frederick, Jason McQueen

Evp And Chief Internal Auditor, Paul Fleming, age 67

Regional Executive Bancfirst, John Anderson, age 62

Senior Vice President, Gail Norman

Senior Vice President, Patrick A Lippmann

Senior Vice President General Manager, Michael Kernan

Senior Vice President, Blane Allen

Senior Vice President Chief In, Scott Lewis

Vice President Treasury Management Sales, Ashlea Briggs

Senior Vice President, Denise Duffle

Vice President Mortgage Production Manager, Billy Parsley

Senior Vice President, Brian Renz

Vice President Mortgage Lending, Shelly Matthews

Senior Vice President, Blane Allen

Assistant Vice President Network Services, Dian Joysizemore

Senior Vice President, Bill Miller

Vice President Marketing, Ben Harrington

Executive Vice President, Sean Shadid

Executive Vice President, Janet W Gotwals

Senior Vice President, Kevin J Calabrese

Vice President, Alan Geiger

Assistant Vice President And Consumer Loan Officer, Jenny Gifford

Assistant Vice President, Dauna Dines

Senior Vice President Asset Quality Loan Compliance, Frances Peterson

Assistant Vice President Commercial Loan Officer, Mary Johnston

Evp And Chief Risk Officer, Randy P. Foraker, age 62

Vice Chairman, James R. Daniel, age 78

Vice Chairman, K. Gordon Greer, age 81

Chairman, David E. Rainbolt, age 62

Vice Chairman And Ceo Council Oak Investment Corporation And Council Oak Real Estate Inc., William O. Johnstone, age 70

Evp Cfo And Treasurer, Kevin Lawrence, age 39

Board Member, Ronald Norick

Auditors: BKD, LLP

LOCATIONS

HQ: BancFirst Corp. (Oklahoma City, Okla)
101 North Broadway, Oklahoma City, OK 73102-8405
Phone: 405 270-1086   **Fax:** 405 270-1089
Web: www.bancfirst.com

PRODUCTS/OPERATIONS

2015 Sales

	$ mil.	% of total
Interest		
Loans including fees	190	63
Securities	6	2
Interest-bearing deposit	4	1
Noninterest		
Service charges on deposits	57	18
Insurance commissions	14	5
Security transactions	9	3
Trust revenue	9	3
Income from sale of loans	2	1
Cash management	7	2
Other	5	2
Total	**306**	**100**

Selected Subsidiaries

BancFirst
  BancFirst Agency Inc. (credit life insurance)
  BancFirst Community Development Corporation
  Council Oak Investment Corporation (small business
   investments)
  Council Oak Real Estate Inc. (real estate investments)
Council Oak Partners LLC
BancFirst Insurance Services Inc.

COMPETITORS

Arvest Bank	Midland Financial
BOK Financial	Southwest Bancorp
Bank of America	UMB Financial
International	Wells Fargo
Bancshares	

HISTORICAL FINANCIALS

Company Type: Public

Income Statement
FYE: December 31

	ASSETS ($ mil.)	NET INCOME ($ mil.)	INCOME AS % OF ASSETS	EMPLOYEES
12/17	7,253	86	1.2%	1,782
12/16	7,018	70	1.0%	1,773
12/15	6,692	66	1.0%	1,744
12/14	6,574	63	1.0%	1,688
12/13	6,038	54	0.9%	1,653
Annual Growth	**4.7%**	**12.3%**	**—**	**1.9%**

2017 Year-End Financials

Debt ratio: 0.44%	No. of shares (mil.): 31
Return on equity: 11.63%	Dividends
Cash ($ mil.): 1,757	Yield: 0.0%
Current ratio: —	Payout: 30.1%
Long-term debt ($ mil.): —	Market value ($ mil.): 1,631

	STOCK PRICE ($) FY Close	P/E High/Low		PER SHARE ($) Earnings	Dividends	Book Value
12/17	51.15	40	18	2.65	0.80	24.32
12/16	93.05	42	23	2.22	0.74	22.49
12/15	58.62	32	26	2.09	0.70	21.01
12/14	63.39	33	25	2.02	0.65	19.65
12/13	56.06	32	22	1.75	0.60	18.16
Annual Growth	**(2.3%)**	**—**	**—**	**11.0%**	**7.5%**	**7.6%**

BancorpSouth Bank (Tupelo, MS)

Like Elvis Presley BancorpSouth has grown beyond its Tupelo roots. It's the holding company for BancorpSouth Bank which operates some 290 branches in nine southern and midwestern states. Catering to consumers and small and midsized businesses the bank offers checking and savings accounts loans credit cards and commercial banking services. BancorpSouth also sells insurance and provides brokerage investment advisory and asset management services throughout most of its market area. Real estate loans including consumer and commercial mortgages and home equity construction and agricultural loans comprise approximately three-quarters of its loan portfolio. BancorpSouth has assets of $13 billion.

Geographic Reach

Mississippi-based BancorpSouth Bank operates in Alabama Arkansas Florida Illinois Louisiana Mississippi Missouri Tennessee and Texas. BancorpSouth's insurance and financial advisory businesses also operate in Illinois and Florida respectively.

Financial Performance

BancorpSouth reported net income of $94.1 million in 2013 an increase of 12% versus 2012. The decreased provision for credit losses was the primary factor contributing to the rise. Net interest revenue — the bank's primary source of revenue — fell 4% year over year to $$398.9 million the fourth consecutive year of decline. Net interest revenue declined because the decrease in interest expense was more than offset by the decrease in interest revenue as the yield on earning assets declined by a greater amount than that of interest-bearing liabilities. Noninterest income also declined on lower mortgage origination revenue in 2013 versus 2012.

Strategy

The regional bank has grown via the acquisition of other banks and insurance agencies and by opening new branches most recently in Texas and Louisiana. To reduce its reliance on interest-related revenue BancorpSouth hopes to diversify its revenue stream by increasing the amount it generates from mortgage lending insurance brokerage and securities activities. To this end subsidiary BancorpSouth Insurance Services has acquired small insurance agencies in Arkansas Missouri and Texas.

Mergers and Acquisitions

In 2014 BancorpSouth agreed to acquire Central Community Corp. the holding company for First State Bank Central Texas headquartered in Austin Texas. First State Bank operates 31 branches in Austin Round Rock Killeen and several other Central Texas communities. BancorpSouth has also agreed to purchase Ouachita Bancshares Corp. with a dozen branches in Louisiana. Both deals were announced in January 2014 and were expected to close promptly. However they've been delayed because BancorpSouth needs more time to get regulatory approvals and to meet "closing conditions necessary to complete" the mergers.

EXECUTIVES

Sevp Cfo And Treasurer, John G. Copeland, age 65
Evp And Corporate Secretary Bancorpsouth And Bancorpsouth Bank, Cathy S. Freeman, age 53
Chairman And Ceo Bancorpsouth Inc. And Bancorpsouth Bank, James D. (Dan) Rollins, age 59, $840,000 total compensation

Evp Bancorpsouth Inc. And Vice Chairman And Chief Lending Officer Bancorpsouth Bank, James R. Hodges, $382,500 total compensation
President And Coo, Chris A. Bagley, $495,000 total compensation
President Equipment Finance And Leasing, Kyle Gilliam
Sevp And General Counsel, Chuck Pignuolo, age 62
Executive Vice President, Clyde Guyse
Sevp Cfo And Treasurer, John G. Copeland, age 65
Evp And Corporate Secretary Bancorpsouth And Bancorpsouth Bank, Cathy S. Freeman, age 53
Chairman And Ceo Bancorpsouth Inc. And Bancorpsouth Bank, James D. (Dan) Rollins, age 59
Auditors: KPMG LLP

LOCATIONS

HQ: BancorpSouth Bank (Tupelo, MS)
One Mississippi Plaza, 201 South Spring Street,
Tupelo, MS 38804
Phone: 662 680-2000
Web: www.bancorpsouth.com

PRODUCTS/OPERATIONS

2016 Sales

	$ mil.	% of total
Interest		
Loans & leases	440	58
Securities	41	5
Deposits with other banks	1	-
Noninterest		
Insurance commissions	115	15
Deposit service charges	43	6
Mortgage lending	41	5
Credit card debit card and merchant fees	37	5
Wealth management	21	3
Other	19	3
Total	**762**	**100**

Selected Subsidiaries

BancorpSouth Bank
  BancorpSouth Insurance Services Inc.
  BancorpSouth Investment Services Inc.
  BancorpSouth Municipal Development Corporation
  Century Credit Life Insurance Company
  Personal Finance Corporation

COMPETITORS

BBVA Compass	Hancock Holding
Bancshares	Regions Financial
Capital One	Renasant
First Horizon	SunTrust
Great Southern Bancorp	Trustmark

HISTORICAL FINANCIALS

Company Type: Public

Income Statement
FYE: December 31

	ASSETS ($ mil.)	NET INCOME ($ mil.)	INCOME AS % OF ASSETS	EMPLOYEES
12/17	15,298	153	1.0%	3,947
12/16	14,724	132	0.9%	3,998
12/15	13,798	127	0.9%	4,002
12/14	13,326	116	0.9%	3,820
12/13	13,029	94	0.7%	4,005
Annual Growth	**4.1%**	**12.9%**	**—**	**(0.4%)**

2017 Year-End Financials

Debt ratio: 0.20%	No. of shares (mil.): 90
Return on equity: 8.90%	Dividends
Cash ($ mil.): 220	Yield: 0.0%
Current ratio: —	Payout: 8.3%
Long-term debt ($ mil.): —	Market value ($ mil.): 2,840

	STOCK PRICE ($) FY Close	P/E High/Low	PER SHARE ($) Earnings	Dividends	Book Value
12/17	31.45	20 16	1.67	0.14	18.97
12/16	31.05	22 13	1.41	0.45	18.40
12/15	23.99	20 15	1.33	0.35	17.58
12/14	22.51	21 16	1.21	0.25	16.69
12/13	25.42	26 14	0.99	0.12	15.89
Annual Growth	5.5%	— —	14.0%	3.9%	4.5%

Bank First National Corp

EXECUTIVES

Chb, Robert S Weinert
Vice President Business Banking, Meghann Kasper
Vice President Marketing, Debbie Weyker
Vice President Business Banking, Christopher Stream
Auditors: Porter Keadle Moore, LLC

LOCATIONS

HQ: Bank First National Corp
402 North Eighth Street, P.O. Box 10, Manitowoc, WI 54220-0010
Phone: 920 652-3100   **Fax:** 920 652-3182
Web: www.bankfirstnational.com

HISTORICAL FINANCIALS

Company Type: Public

Income Statement   FYE: December 31

	ASSETS ($ mil.)	NET INCOME ($ mil.)	INCOME AS % OF ASSETS	EMPLOYEES
12/17	1,753	15	0.9%	—
12/16	1,316	14	1.1%	—
12/15	1,237	13	1.1%	—
12/14	1,105	12	1.1%	—
12/13	1,060	11	1.1%	—
Annual Growth	13.4%	7.3%	—	—

2017 Year-End Financials

Debt ratio: 1.14%	No. of shares (mil.): 6
Return on equity: 10.59%	Dividends
Cash ($ mil.): 53	Yield: 0.0%
Current ratio: —	Payout: 26.2%
Long-term debt ($ mil.): —	Market value ($ mil.): 304

	STOCK PRICE ($) FY Close	P/E High/Low	PER SHARE ($) Earnings	Dividends	Book Value
12/17	44.70	18 14	2.44	0.64	23.76
12/16	33.33	14 11	2.40	0.59	20.53
12/15	28.25	13 10	2.13	0.51	18.97
12/14	22.65	12 9	1.99	0.34	17.42
12/13	19.00	11 8	1.79	0.22	15.91
Annual Growth	23.8%	— —	8.1%	30.6%	10.6%

Bank of America Corp

Among the United States' largest banks by assets (alongside JPMorgan Chase and Citigroup) ubiquitous Bank of America Corporation operates one of the country's most extensive branch networks with some 4600 locations and 16000 ATMs. The bank's core services include consumer and small business banking corporate banking credit cards mortgage lending and asset management. Its online banking operation counts some 35 million active users and 24 million mobile users. Bank of America acquired Merrill Lynch in 2009 making it one of the world's leading wealth managers with about $2.3 trillion assets under management and boasting a beefed up trading and international businesses.

HISTORY

Bank of America predecessor NationsBank was formed as the Commercial National Bank in 1874 by citizens of Charlotte North Carolina. In 1901 George Stephens and Word Wood formed what became American Trust Co. The banks merged in 1957 to become American Commercial Bank which in 1960 merged with Security National to form North Carolina National Bank.

In 1968 the bank formed holding company NCNB which by 1980 was the largest bank in North Carolina. Under the leadership of Hugh McColl who became chairman in 1983 NCNB became the first southern bank to span six states.

NCNB profited from the savings and loan crisis of the late 1980s by managing assets and buying defunct thrifts at fire-sale prices. The company nearly doubled its assets in 1988 when the FDIC chose it to manage the shuttered First Republicbank then Texas' largest bank. The company renamed itself NationsBank in 1991.

In 1993 the company bought Chicago Research & Trading a government securities dealer and provider of oil and gas financing. A 1993 joint venture with Dean Witter and Discover to open securities brokerages in banks led to complaints that customers were not fully informed of the risks of some investments and that brokers were paying rebates to banking personnel for customer referrals. Dean Witter withdrew from the arrangement in 1994 and SEC investigations and a class-action lawsuit ensued. NationsBank settled the lawsuit for about $30 million the next year. (The company agreed to pay nearly $7 million to settle similar charges in 1998.)

NationsBank scooped up St. Louis-based Boatmen's Bancshares and Montgomery Securities (now Banc of America Securities) in 1997. The next year it bought Barnett Banks Florida's #1 bank.

Enter BankAmerica. Founded in 1904 as Bank of Italy BankAmerica had once been the US's largest bank but had fallen behind as competitors consolidated. The company's board of directors was pondering ways to become more competitive and in 1998 decided a merger was the best way. With the ink barely dry on its Barnett Banks deal NationsBank obliged.

After the merger the combined firm announced it would write down a billion-dollar bad loan to D.E. Shaw & Co. which followed the same Russian-investment-paved path of descent as Long-Term Capital Management. David Coulter (head of the old BankAmerica which made the loan) took the fall for the loss resigning as president; the balance of power shifted to the NationsBank side in 1999 when Kenneth Lewis took the post.

The Russian debacle and merger hiccups led the firm in early 1999 to reorganize and reduce overseas operations; it sold its private banking operations in Europe and Asia to UBS. Also that year it bought the recreational-vehicle financing unit of Associates First Capital (now part of Citigroup) 50% of Denver-based mutual fund firm Marsico Capital Management (it bought the rest in 2001) and BA Merchant Services. The bank also changed its name to Bank of America and began offering online banking through America Online. To avoid a court battle the bank settled charges that it retained proceeds from unclaimed bonds in California.

In 1999 the company earned the ire of labor officials for a program in which employees were recruited to maintain ATMs without being paid or provided supplies. EVP Frank Gentry who crafted the NationsBank/BankAmerica deal retired in 2000 signaling an end to the company's buying spree. Its focus turned inward as it set about the difficult integration of the two firms.

McColl retired as chairman in 2

EXECUTIVES

Chairman And Ceo, Brian T. Moynihan, age 58, $1,500,000 total compensation
Chief Operations And Technology Officer, Catherine P. (Cathy) Bessant, age 57
Coo, Thomas K. (Tom) Montag, age 62, $1,000,000 total compensation
President Preferred And Small Business Banking, Dean C. Athanasia, age 51
President Retail Banking And Co-head Consumer Banking, Thong M. Nguyen, age 59
Vice Chairman And Head Global Wealth And Investment Management, Terence P. (Terry) Laughlin, age 63, $850,000 total compensation
Chief Risk Officer, Geoffrey S. Greener, age 53, $850,000 total compensation
Cfo, Paul M. Donofrio, age 57, $850,000 total compensation
Head Of Merrill Lynch Wealth Management, John Thiel
Head Of Global Wealth And Retirement Solution, Andy Sieg
Vice President, Michael Young
Vice President, Victor Ward
Information Technology Team Manager Assistant Vice President, Leo Kaplin
Senior Vice President Program Manager, Jason Oliver
Assistant Vice President, Jennifer Satterthwaite
Vice President Operations Project Consultant, Carol Rogers
Vice President Senior Technical Manager, John Syper
Vice President Human Resources Manager, Michelle John
Senior Vice President, Toby Clifton
Senior Vice President;consumer Market Executive, Ventura Perez
Vice President; Market Information Manager I, Richard Baker
Vice President, Kumar Mithipati
Vice President, William Gilley
Vice President, Debbie Kirk
Vice President;gwim Senior Credit Underwriter, Erin H Grow
Vice President; Paralegal, David Guerrero
Vice President Global Information Security, Okan Demirmen
Senior Vice President Leadership Development Executive, Stephanie Asbury
Vice President Client Managed Sb Analytics, Maribel Johnston
Vice President Transaction Management, Adam Robitshek
Vice President, Myra Wardwell

Vice President, Jennifer Whitemyer

Vice President, John Waccard

Senior Vice President Compensation Executive, Rachel Kane

Assistant Vice President, Tracy Newman

Assistant Vice President;file Administrator Ii, Renee Beacham

Senior Vice President Corporate Treasury Insurable Risk Management, Brian Mower

Vice President Of Customer, Scott Prince

Vice President, Armida Warren

Senior Vice President;business Executive Technology, Henry Richers

Vice President, Samuel Willett

Vice President Cnslt Systems Engineer, Mihir Gandhi

Vice President Human Resources, Stacey Moninski

Senior Vice President Information Foundation For Competitive Analytics, Hans Schumacher

Vice President Senior Client Manager Commercial Real Estate Banking Cdb Bank Of America Merrill Lynch, Valerie Williams

Vice President Business Analyst, Magesh Arumugam

Vice President Learning Consultant, Debbi Johnston

Vice President;business Support Lead Iii, Terry Kennedy

Senior Vice President Senior Project Manager, Terry Lomas

Assistant Vice President;gwim Credit Service Associate, Jenelle Cadogan

Vice President, Patty Spooner

Senior Vice President User Experience Ecommerce, Abbey Katcher

Senior Vice President;credit Review Manager, Tricia Becker

Vice President Corporate Audit, Ruben Macias

Assistant Vice President, William Pagano

Assistant Vice President;gwim Loan Monitoring Specialist, Jacquelyn Capers

Vice President Project Test Manager, Yolanda Shorey

Senior Vice President, Robert Maloney

Assistant Vice President;gwim Document Administrator, Lorita Cagle

Assistant Vice President Operations Project Consultant, Shawna Taylor

Vice President Interactive Design, Robert Pothier

Vice President Document Imaging Engineering, James Mayers

Vice Presideni Gt And O Innovation Innovation Lab Director, Alicia Jones

Senior Vice President;compliance Program Executive, Paige Brockmann

Vice President Senior Audit Consultant Corporate Audit Global Technology, Romelle K Parsons

Vice President, Stacey Clark

Vice President Infrastructure, Chris Ritchie

Senior Vice President, Andrew Schauer

Vice President Enterprise Data Services, Giovanni Simeone

Vice President Operational Risk, Shawn Otto

Senior Vice President Senior Credit Products Officer, Bill Franey

Senior Vice President Market Manager Pennsylvania Corporate Social Responsibility, Deborah O'brien

Vice President Marketing, Michele Ekarius

Senior Vice President Small Business Banking Manager, Dean Bird

Vice President Existing Customer Marketing Strategies, Alex Wisniewski Alex Wisniewski

Vice President, Judd Glasco

Vice President, Pushpanjali Kottapalli

Vice President, Jason Dyckes

Vice President Commercial Information Officer, Julie Smith

Vice President Of Process Design, Paul Sheehan

Vice President Small Business Banking Technology, Gary Hammock

Senior Vice President, Joyce Taylor

Avp Assistant Manager, Corey Schissler

Assistant Vice President Credit Support Associate, Diane Baine

Vice President National Remarketing Manager, Jeannie Chiaromonte

Assistant Vice President, Christopher Hopkins

Assistant Vice President; Executive Support, Joe Louie

Vice President; Operations Project Consultant Transportation Services Commercial Services, Dina Scott

Vice President Campus Recruiter, Marisa Witherspoon

Vice President, Art Brito

Senior Card Account Manager Vice President, Janet Jernigan

Vice President, Sanjay Dhulia

Vice President Senior Investigator Corporate Security Background Screening Investigations, Paulette Brooks

Vice President, Vicki Svendsgaard

Vice President Process Design And Improvement, Charles Byron

Vice President; Operations Project Consultant, Charles Martinez

Vice President Consultant System Engineer, Prajwal Shetty Prajwal Shetty

Vice President Senior Operations Consultant, Sylvia Coats

Vice President;change Consultant, Julie Kreger

Assistant Vice President Senior Marketing Programs Development Manager I, Marcia Carneiro

Senior Vice President Business Control Manager, Christine Plankinton

Vice President Competitive Research, Himani Bahl

Assistant Vice President Process Design Consultant, Jennifer Montgomery

Vice President, Julie Wallis

Vice President, Allyson Webster

Vice President, Toni Westfall

Assistant Vice President; Senior Credit Support Associate, Gayle Sellitto

Vice President, Torivia Whiten

Vice President, Terrie Wilkerson

Vice President, Marry Wanchik

Vice President, Beth Watson

Vice President, Prashant Bidkar

Vice President Of Operations, Sethu Iyer

Vice President Quantative Modeling, Chunying Fan

Assistant Vice President Business Support, Shannon Hart

Vice President Risk Operations Manager, Terri Stallings

Vice Presidentconsumer Products Strategic Analyst, Dave Ellison

Vice President, Patrick Kamachi

Vp Software Product Management, Bridget Beavers

Senior Vice President, Kevin Deir

Vice President Software Test Team Manager, Bin Lu

Senior Vice President, Todd Chitester

Assistant Vice President, Pam West

Assistant Vice President;gwim Credit Service Associate, Anita Cannon

Assistant Vice President;gwim Loan Administrator, Crystal Shipp

Vice President Corporate Events Planner, Patricia Casper

Vice President, Frank Barrios

Vice President, Doug Lang

Senior Vice President Post Closing And Central Services Mortgage Loan Control, Edward Kralian

Vice President Compensation Manager, Allison Sarubbi

Vice President, Stephanie Barbee

Vice President Retail Store Planning, Warren Bowes

Vice President, Facheryl Williams

Vice President, Robyn Wilkins

Senior Vice President Senior Technology Manager, Tim Rohrbacher

Vice President Global Technology Manager, Raul Marquez

Senior Vice President Compliance, Charlene Logan

Vice President Business Support, Skip Winnebald Skip Winnebald

Vice President, Christian Stevens

Senior Vice President, Marge Sanders

Senior Vice President Consumer Products Strategy Executive, Ryan Rzucidlo

Vice President (global Markets Technology), Paresh Mohanty

Vice President Senior Financial Analyst, Ryan McKay

Vice President, Brian Cogan

Vice President, Scott Matarese

Vice President Systems Engineer, James Cook

Assistant Vice President;gwim Document Administrator, Frank J Taylor

Vice President, Richard Warner

Vice President Information Technology, Harsh Patel

Senior Vice President, Rhett Hardy

Svp; Senior Dwh Buyer Ii Manager, Ravi Maraka

Auditors: PricewaterhouseCoopers LLP

LOCATIONS

HQ: Bank of America Corp
Bank of America Corporate Center, 100 N. Tryon Street, Charlotte, NC 28255
Phone: 704 386-5681
Web: www.bankofamerica.com

2017 Sales by Region

	% of total
US	86
EMEA	9
Asia	4
Latin America	1
Total	100

PRODUCTS/OPERATIONS

2017 Sales

	$ mil.	% of total
Interest income	44,667	51
Non-interest income	42,685	49
Total	87,352	100

2017 sales

	% of total
Consumer Banking	39
Global Banking	22
Global Wealth & Investment Management	21
Global Markets	18
Total	100

Selected Products & Services

Capital raising and advisory
Card solutions
Equipment finance/leasing
Fraud prevention
Interest rate currency and commodity risk management
Investment solutions and management
Lending and financing
Liquidity management
Merchant services
Mergers and acquisitions
Payments/receivables management
Philanthropic management
Retirement and benefit plan services
Trade services

COMPETITORS

BB&T	JPMorgan Chase
Bank of New York Mellon	KeyCorp
	MUFG Americas Holdings

Capital One
Citigroup
Citizens Financial
  Group
Goldman Sachs
HSBC
HSBC USA

Morgan Stanley
PNC Financial
RBC Financial Group
State Street
SunTrust
U.S. Bancorp
Wells Fargo

HISTORICAL FINANCIALS

Company Type: Public

Income Statement

FYE: December 31

	ASSETS ($ mil.)	NET INCOME ($ mil.)	INCOME AS % OF ASSETS	EMPLOYEES
12/17	2,281,234	18,232	0.8%	209,000
12/16	2,187,702	17,906	0.8%	208,000
12/15	2,144,316	15,888	0.7%	213,000
12/14	2,104,534	4,833	0.2%	224,000
12/13	2,102,273	11,431	0.5%	242,000
Annual Growth	2.1%	12.4%	—	(3.6%)

2017 Year-End Financials

Debt ratio: 9.74%—
Return on equity: 6.83%
Cash ($ mil.): 157,434
Current ratio: —
Long-term debt ($ mil.): —

Dividends
  Yield: 0.0%
  Payout: 25.0%
Market value ($ mil.): —

	STOCK PRICE ($) FY Close	P/E High/Low		PER SHARE ($) Earnings	Dividends	Book Value
12/17	29.52	18	14	1.56	0.39	25.97
12/16	22.10	15	7	1.50	0.25	26.54
12/15	16.83	13	11	1.31	0.20	24.68
12/14	17.89	50	40	0.36	0.12	23.15
12/13	15.57	17	12	0.90	0.04	21.97
Annual Growth	17.3%	—	—	14.7%	76.7%	4.3%

Bank of Hawaii Corp

Bank of Hawaii Corporation is the holding company for Bank of Hawaii (familiarly known as Bankoh) which has about 70 branches and 380-plus ATMs in its home state plus an additional dozen in American Samoa Guam Palau and Saipan. Founded in 1897 the bank operates through four business segments: retail banking for consumers and small businesses in Hawaii; commercial banking including property/casualty insurance for middle-market and large corporations (this segment also includes the bank's activities beyond the state); investment services such as trust asset management and private banking; and treasury which performs corporate asset and liability management services.

Operations

Bank of Hawaii operates through four segments including retail banking and commercial banking (which together account for about 85% of total net income) and investment services and treasury. The retail banking and commercial baking segments offer a range of financial products and services to consumers and small businesses and middle-market and large enterprises respectively. The company's investment services include private banking trust services and investment advisory services while the treasury segment includes corporate asset and liability management activities.

Bank of Hawaii generates nearly 60% of total revenue from interest and fees on loans. About 60% of its loan portfolio is made up of consumer loans (residential mortgage is the largest) with

commercial loans accounting for the rest (commercial mortgage is the largest).

Geographic Reach

Bank of Hawaii provides a broad range of financial services and products to customers not only Hawaii but in Guam and other Pacific islands. Its principal offices are located in Honolulu.

Sales and Marketing

Bank of Hawaii spent about $6 million on advertising in 2017 and 2016 compared to $5.3 million in 2015.

Financial Performance

As Hawaii's real estate market continues to set records (in median sales prices for Oahu homes among other areas) Bank of Hawaii has seen consistent growth over the past five years with revenue up more than 15% since 2013. Net income has been on a similar trajectory rising just more than 20% during that time.

In 2017 the company reported revenue of $642.7 million which is up 5% from the prior year. The increase was powered by growth in the commercial and consumer lending portfolios as well as higher net interest margin; it was somewhat offset by a decline in noninterest income led by a nearly $7 million drop in mortgage banking income.

Net income rose 2% to $184.7 million in 2017 on the increase in revenue. The retail and commercial baking segments together account for 85% of total net income.

Cash at the end of fiscal 2017 was $447.8 million a decrease of $431.8 million from the prior year. Cash from operations contributed $175.1 million to the coffers while investing activities used $1 billion mainly because of net change in loans and leases and purchases of investment securities held-to-maturity. Financing activities provided another $415 million on a net change in deposits.

Strategy

A primary focus for Bank of Hawaii along with many other regional banks is modernizing and digitizing its business. It continues to renovate branches into what it calls the Branch of Tomorrow which includes updated technology interactive and private meeting spaces and more. In addition the company has introduced easy-deposit ATMs a Cardless Cash feature and enhancements to its mobile banking app.

Company Background

Bank of Hawaii traces its history to 1897 when businessman Peter Cushman Jones and friends Joseph Ballard Atherton and Charles Montague Cooke established a bank to serve the Hawaiian Islands. It was the first chartered and incorporated bank to do business in the Republic of Hawaii.

The company had branches on every major island in the archipelago by 1930. In 1971 it reorganized as a bank holding company.

EXECUTIVES

Sevp And Cfo, Dean Y. Shigemura
Chairman President And Ceo, Peter S. Ho, age 54, $776,077 total compensation
Vice Chairman And Chief Risk Officer, Mary E. Sellers, age 62, $427,565 total compensation
Vice Chairman Client Solutions Group, Sharon M. Crofts
Vice Chairman And Chief Administrative Officer, Mark A. Rossi, age 69, $433,776 total compensation
Vice Chairman; Chief Commercial Officer, Wayne Y. Hamano, $355,170 total compensation
Vice Chairman; Residential And Consumer Lending Group Manager, Derek J. Norris, age 68, $224,615 total compensation
Executive Vice President, Betty Brow
Vice President Of Operations, Andrew Boyles
Assistant Vice President And Operations Manager, Chris Onzuka

Senior Vice President, Kevin Baptist
Vice President, John Hulihee
Vice President Of Cash Management, Bernie Alama
Assistant Vice President, Gregory Biegen
Vice President Executive Loan Officer, Brenda Mitchell
Vice President Of Lending, Cindy Okamura
Assistant Vice President Dealer Marketing Relationship Officer, Craig Ito
Vice President And Audit Consultant, Irene E B Kwan
Senior Vice President And Senior Audit Manager, James P Garcia
Assistant Vice President, Dora Rivera
Vice President, Cheryl Minaai
Vice President And Assistant Service Manager, Tina Nakahara
Senior Vice President Card Products, Anthony DeSanctis
Vice President, Toshiya Matsumoto
Senior Vice President, Roberta Chu
Vice President, Dean Uyeda
Vice President And West Oahu Isb Area Manager Of Bank Of Hawaii, Charleen Deuprey
Vice President, Edison Kobayashi
Executive Vice President Human Resources, Lester Stiefel
Vice President, Miki Ikeda
Senior Vice President And Manager, Dirk Yoshizawa
Senior Vice President And Manager Cash Management Services, Coleen Fujimoto
Executive Vice President, David Oyadomari
Vice President And Credit Compliance Officer Iii, Janis Okamoto
Assistant Vice President And Compensation Manager, Kaleo Kekoolani
Vice President And Sales And Marketing And Client Development Manager, Dale Tanimoto
Vice President, Mario Subia
Vice President And Regional Manager East Oahu Region, Scott Yoshihara
Vice President, Tim Chang
Vice President, Robert Trent
Vice President, Malcom Lau
Vice President And Investment Services Group Compliance Manager, Catherine Fujisaki
Financial Consultant And Vice President, Christopher Otto
Senior Vice President And Manager, Teri Young
Senior Vice President Director Of Corporate Security, Brian Ishikawa
Executive Vice President And Chief Audit Executive, James Garcia
Vice President Private Client Services, Annalena Zanolini
Vice President, Arthur K Taniguchi
Senior Vice President, Leilani Williams
Vice President, Natalie Fogle
Assistant Vice President, Kathy Rodriguez
Executive Vice President, Cynthia Wyrick
Senior Vice President, Donovan Koki
Senior Vice President Commercial Banking, Robert Mancini
Assistant Vice President Corporate Risk Analyst, Arm Gregory Biegen
Vice President Administration, Pat Hulaton
Vice President And Private Banking Officer Private Banking Division, Davin Nakasato
Vice President And Service Manager, Lisa Revilla
Assistant Vice President And Branch Manager, Anne Banting
Vice President, Amy Honda
Vice President And International Private Banking Manager, Ken Niimura
Vice President Commercial Banking, Vincent Perez
Vp And Corporate Counsel, Val Ito
Assistant Vice President And Senior Auditor, Daniel Li

Executive Vice President And Manager, Dana Takushi

Vice President Manager, Mark Carkin

Assistant Vice President Service Manager, Kimberly Holani

Vice President Commercial Banking Officer, Christopher Frost

Vice President, Gunjan Doshi

Vice President, Helene B Davis

Vice President And Manager Corporate Sourcing And Accounts Payable Department, Calla Oda

Vice President And Financial Advisor, Naalei Keaunui

Vice Chairman And Chief Strategy Officer, Kent T. Lucien, age 64

Vice Chairman, Donna A. Tanoue, age 64

Chairman President And Ceo, Peter S. Ho, age 54

Vice Chairman And Chief Risk Officer, Mary E. Sellers, age 62

Vice Chairman Client Solutions Group, Sharon M. Crofts

Svp; Manager Commercial Credit Underwriting And Analysis Pacific Islands Division Bank Of Hawaii, James C. (Jim) Polk

Vice Chairman And Chief Administrative Officer, Mark A. Rossi, age 69

Vice Chairman; Chief Commercial Officer, Wayne Y. Hamano

Vice Chairman; Residential And Consumer Lending Group Manager, Derek J. Norris, age 68

Secretary, Jill Rotolo

Secretary, SHERRY SERRANO

Board Member, ROBERT WO

Board Director, Young Mary

Auditors: Ernst & Young LLP

LOCATIONS

HQ: Bank of Hawaii Corp
130 Merchant Street, Honolulu, HI 96813
Phone: 888 643-3888
Web: www.boh.com

PRODUCTS/OPERATIONS

2017 Sales

	% of total
Net Interest Income	
Interest and Fees on Loans and Leases	48
Income on Investment Securities	21
Other	-
Interest Expense	-
Non-interest Income	
Trust and Asset Management	8
Mortgage Banking	2
Service Charges on Deposit Accounts	6
Fees Exchange and Other Service Charges	9
Investment Securities Gains Net	2
Annuity and Insurance	1
Bank-Owned Life Insurance	1
Other	2
Total	**100**

Selected Products/Services

Personal
Banking Products
Checking
Savings
Special Packages
Loans & Lines
Mortgages
Credit Cards
Debit Cards
Online & Mobile Banking
IRAs
Small Business
Banking Products
Checking
Savings
Special Packages
Credit Card
Debit Card
Loans & Leasing
Trade & International

Business Services
Online Banking
Corporate & Commercial
Checking
Savings
Cash Management
Loans & Leasing
International Trade Services
Business Needs

COMPETITORS

American Savings Bank
Australia and New Zealand Banking
Bank of America
Central Pacific Financial
First Hawaiian
HSBC
Territorial Bancorp
Westpac Banking

HISTORICAL FINANCIALS

Company Type: Public

Income Statement
FYE: December 31

	ASSETS ($ mil.)	NET INCOME ($ mil.)	INCOME AS % OF ASSETS	EMPLOYEES
12/17	17,089	184	1.1%	2,132
12/16	16,492	181	1.1%	2,122
12/15	15,455	160	1.0%	2,200
12/14	14,787	163	1.1%	2,200
12/13	14,084	150	1.1%	2,200
Annual Growth	5.0%	5.2%	—	(0.8%)

2017 Year-End Financials

Debt ratio: 0.06%
Return on equity: 15.43%
Cash ($ mil.): 266
Current ratio: —
Long-term debt ($ mil.): —

No. of shares (mil.): 42
Dividends
Yield: 0.0%
Payout: 47.1%
Market value ($ mil.): 3,634

	STOCK PRICE ($) FY Close	P/E High/Low	PER SHARE ($) Earnings	Dividends	Book Value
12/17	85.70	21 17	4.33	2.04	29.05
12/16	88.69	21 13	4.23	1.89	27.24
12/15	62.90	19 15	3.70	1.80	25.79
12/14	59.31	17 14	3.69	1.80	24.13
12/13	59.14	18 13	3.38	1.80	22.75
Annual Growth	9.7%	— —	6.4%	3.2%	6.3%

Bank of Marin Bancorp

Bank of Marin supports the wealthy enclave of Marin County north of San Francisco. The bank operates more than 20 branches in the posh California counties of Marin Sonoma and Napa as well as in San Francisco and Alameda counties. Targeting area residents and small to midsized businesses the bank offers standard retail products as checking and savings accounts CDs credit cards and loans. It also provides private banking and wealth management services to high net-worth clients. Commercial mortgages account for the largest portion of the company's loan portfolio followed by business construction and home equity loans.

Geographic Reach

Bank of Marin has branches in Alameda Corte Madera Emeryville Greenbrae Mill Valley Napa Novato Oakland Petaluma San Francisco San Rafael Santa Rosa Sausalito Sonoma and Tiburon.

Sales and Marketing

Its customer base is made up of individuals small to midsized businesses professionals and not-for-profit organizations.

Financial Performance

The bank makes its money through interest income and non-interest income such as service charges and fees. Interest income accounts for almost 90% of overall revenues. The bank has seen its revenue levels fluctuate over the years and in 2013 revenues fell 5% to $68 million due to lower yields on investments and new loans with lower interest rates.

Mergers and Acquisitions

In 2013 the bank gained a branch in Alameda with the purchase of NorCal Community Bancorp the holding company of the Bank of Alameda.

EXECUTIVES

President Ceo And Director Bank Of Marin Bancorp And Bank Of Marin, Russell A. (Russ) Colombo, age 65, $400,355 total compensation

Evp Retail Banking Bank Of Marin, Peter Pelham, age 61, $214,725 total compensation

Evp And Cfo, Tani Girton, age 58, $239,500 total compensation

Evp And Chief Credit Officer Bank Of Marin, Elizabeth Reizman, age 59, $221,250 total compensation

Evp Commercial Banking Bank Of Marin, Timothy D. (Tim) Myers, age 47, $215,000 total compensation

Evp And Cio, James T. Burke, age 63

Vice President, Nancy Boatright

Assistant Vice President, Melanie Rempe

Executive Vice President And Chief Cre, Kevin Coonan

Fvp Business Banking Deposit Services Group Manager, Norma Saavedra

Vice President And Commercial Banking Officer, Jim Foot

Vice President, Lynn Zamora

Vice President Wealth Management Services, Deborah Smith

Assistant Vice President Branch Manager, Dan Ancheta

Vice President Human Resources Manager, Faye Garcia

Vice President Of Human Resources, Robert Gotelli

Vice President Compliance Manager, Barbara Collins

Vice President Commercial Banking Officer Middle Market, Ryan Pyne

Assistant Vice President And Assistant Corporate Secretary, Megan Garner

Vice President, Allison Spitzer

Vice President And Controller, Jan Freidig

Vice President Commercial Banking Officer, Phil Aghajanian

Vice President Senior Commercial Banking Officer, David Casassa

Assistant Vice President And Assistant Branch Manager, Eddie Roslin

Assistant Vice President Branch Manager, Kathy Madsen

Vice President Of Human Resources, Honey Garcia

First Vice President Cre Credit Administrator, Patrick McCarty

Chairman Bank Of Marin Bancorp And Bank Of Marin, Brian M. Sobel, age 63

President Ceo And Director Bank Of Marin Bancorp And Bank Of Marin, Russell A. (Russ) Colombo, age 65

Board Member, Michaela Rodeno

Board Member, Jan Yanehiro

Board Director, Rafelina Maglio

Board Member, James Hale

Auditors: Moss Adams LLP

LOCATIONS

HQ: Bank of Marin Bancorp
504 Redwood Blvd., Suite 100, Novato, CA 94947
Phone: 415 763-4520
Web: www.bankofmarin.com

PRODUCTS/OPERATIONS

2015 Sales

	% of total
Interest and fees on loan	78
Interest on investment securities	10
Non-Interest income	
Wealth management & trust services	3
Service charges on deposit accounts	3
Debit card interchange fees	2
Others	4
Total	**100**

Selected Services

Business checking
Cash management
Credit cards
Floating home loans
Home equity lines
Lending
Online and mobile
Personal checking
Personal savings

COMPETITORS

Bank of America	MUFG Americas Holdings
Bank of the West	Patelco Credit Union
Citibank	SVB Financial
Community Bank of the Bay	U.S. Bancorp
	Wells Fargo
FNB Bancorp (CA)	Westamerica
First Republic (CA)	

HISTORICAL FINANCIALS

Company Type: Public

Income Statement

FYE: December 31

	ASSETS ($ mil.)	NET INCOME ($ mil.)	INCOME AS % OF ASSETS	EMPLOYEES
12/17	2,468	15	0.6%	306
12/16	2,023	23	1.1%	262
12/15	2,031	18	0.9%	274
12/14	1,787	19	1.1%	278
12/13	1,805	14	0.8%	297
Annual Growth	**8.1%**	**2.9%**	**—**	**0.7%**

2017 Year-End Financials

Debt ratio: 0.23%
Return on equity: 6.06%
Cash ($ mil.): 203
Current ratio: —
Long-term debt ($ mil.): —

No. of shares (mil.): 13
Dividends
  Yield: 0.0%
  Payout: 87.8%
Market value ($ mil.): 941

	STOCK PRICE ($) FY Close	P/E High/Low	PER SHARE ($) Earnings	Dividends	Book Value
12/17	68.00	57 46	1.28	1.12	21.46
12/16	69.75	39 25	1.89	1.02	18.81
12/15	53.40	36 30	1.52	0.90	17.67
12/14	52.59	32 25	1.65	0.80	16.84
12/13	43.39	35 29	1.29	0.73	15.39
Annual Growth	**11.9%**	**— —**	**(0.2%)**	**11.3%**	**8.7%**

Bank of New York Mellon Corp

The Bank of New York Mellon (BNY Mellon) is one of the world's largest global asset servicing companies and a leader in asset management and corporate trust and treasury services. The firm boasts $32 trillion in assets under custody and administration and some $1.8 trillion in assets under management. BNY Mellon's state-chartered bank subsidiary Bank of New York Mellon offers asset issuer treasury broker-dealer and advisor services while its other main subsidiary BNY Mellon N.A. offers wealth management services. Alexander Hamilton a founding father of the US and icon of the US $10 bill helped establish in 1784 The Bank of New York which merged in 2007 with Pittsburgh?s Mellon Financial to form BNY Mellon.

HISTORY

In 1784 Alexander Hamilton (at 27 already a Revolutionary War hero and economic theorist) and a group of New York merchants and lawyers founded New York City's first bank The Bank of New York (BNY). Hamilton saw a need for a credit system to finance the nation's growth and to establish credibility for the new nation's chaotic monetary system.

Hamilton became US secretary of the treasury in 1789 and soon negotiated the new US government's first loan — for $200000 — from BNY. The bank later helped finance the War of 1812 by raising $16 million and the Civil War by loaning the government $150 million. In 1878 BNY became a US Treasury depository for the sale of government bonds.

The bank's conservative fiscal policies and emphasis on commercial banking enabled it to weather economic turbulence in the 19th century. In 1922 it merged with New York Life Insurance and Trust (formed in 1830 by many of BNY's directors) to form Bank of New York and Trust. The bank survived the crash of 1929 and remained profitable paying dividends throughout the Depression. In 1938 it reclaimed its Bank of New York name.

During the mid-20th century BNY expanded its operations and its reach through acquisitions including Fifth Avenue Bank (trust services 1948) and Empire Trust (serving developing industries 1966). In 1968 the bank created holding company The Bank of New York Company to expand statewide with purchases such as Empire National Bank (1980).

BNY relaxed its lending policies in the 1980s and began to build its fee-for-service side boosting its American Depositary Receipts business by directly soliciting European companies and seeking government securities business. The bank bought New York rival Irving Trust in a 1989 hostile takeover and in 1990 began buying other banks' credit card portfolios.

As the economy cooled in the early 1990s BNY's book of highly leveraged transactions and nonperforming loans suffered so the company sold many of those loans.

In the mid-1990s BNY bought processing and trust businesses and continued to build its retail business in the suburbs. It pared noncore operations selling its mortgage banking unit (and in 1998 moved its remaining mortgage operations into a joint venture with Alliance Mortgage); credit card business (1998); and factoring and asset-based lending operations (1999). In late 1997 and

again in 1998 the bank tried to woo Mellon Bank (now Mellon Financial) into a merger but was rejected; it had better luck in 2006.

The growth of the firm's custody services accelerated in the late 1990s. In 1997 BNY bought operations from Wells Fargo Signet Bank (later part of First Union) and NationsBank (now Bank of America). By 1998 BNY had bought some two dozen corporate trust businesses. Two years later it acquired the trust operations of Royal Bank of Scotland and Barclays Bank.

During this period BNY also built its other operations largely through purchases. It bought the Bank of Montreal's UK-based fiscal agency business (1998) and Eastbrook Capital Management which manages assets for businesses and wealthy individuals (1999).

Scandal rocked the firm in 1999 when the US began investigating the possible flow of money related to Russian organized crime; the following year a former bank executive admitted to having laundered about $7 billion through BNY. The bank reached a non-prosecution agreement in the US in 2005 and four years later agreed to a $14 million settlement with Russia.

In 2000 BNY bought the corporate trust business of Dai-Ichi Kangyo Bank (now part of Mizuho Financial) and Harris Trust and Savings Bank. It also purchased a trio of securities clearing and processing firms in addition to hedge fund manager Ivy Asset Management. The next year BNY bought the corporate trust operations of U.S. Trust.

Purchases in 2002 included equity research firm Jaywalk institutional trader Francis P. Maglio & Co. and a pair of Boston-area asset managers for high-net-worth individuals Gannet Welsh & Kotler and Beacon Fiduciary Advisors. BNY bought Pershing from Credit Suisse First Boston in 2003.

Fallout from the money laundering scandal lingered. In 2006 the Federal Reserve accused the bank of not tightening its own controls to prevent a recurrence of illegal activity. But there were apparently no hard feelings between BNY and the federal government who tapped the company in 2008 to act as custodian for the US Treasury's $700 million Troubled Asset Relief Program (TARP) meant to provide liquidity to banks.

The Bank of New York jettisoned much of its traditional banking services for more lucrative fee-based securities and financial services swapping virtually all its retail branches in metropolitan New York for JPMorgan Chase's corporate trust business in 2006. Both units were valued at more than $2 billion each and JPMorgan Chase paid an additional $150 million in cash to make up the difference.

In 2007 Bank of New York merged with Mellon Financial to create BNY Mellon). It was the New York company's third attempt to acquire the Pittsburgh-based firm. The deal cemented the company's status as one of the largest securities servicing companies in the world and augmented its other other areas of focus including asset management and corporate trust and treasury services.

The company followed that transaction with the sale of Mellon 1st Business Bank to U.S. Bancorp in 2008.

In 2009 the company acquired Insight Investment Management which specializes in liability-driven investment services fixed income products and alternative investments from Lloyds Bank for some $387 million. Also that year BNY Mellon bought analytics firm Portsmouth Financial Systems. The acquisition offered customers more transparency in structured credit portfolios.

In 2010 BNY Mellon sold one of the last remnants of Mellon Financial's banking operations the Florida-based Mellon United National Bank to Banco de Sabadell. Mellon had previously sold most of its retail business to Royal Bank of Scotland's US banking arm Citizens Financial Group in 2001.

EXECUTIVES

Chairman And Ceo, Gerald L. Hassell, age 66, $1,000,000 total compensation

Ceo Clearing Markets And Client Management, Thomas P. (Todd) Gibbons, age 61, $650,000 total compensation

Ceo Investment Management, Mitchell E. Harris, $625,000 total compensation

Sevp And General Counsel, J. Kevin McCarthy, age 54

Ceo Pershing, Lisa Dolly

Ceo Global Asset Servicing And Chairman Europe Middle East And Africa (emea), Hani Kablawi

Sevp And Chief Human Resources Officer, Monique R. Herena

Sevp And Head Client Service Delivery, Doug Shulman

Sevp And Chief Risk Officer, James S. (Jim) Wiener

Ceo Exchange Traded Funds, Jeff McCarthy

Chairman Asia Pacific, J. David Cruikshank

Ceo Issuer Services, Francis J. (Frank) La Salla

Ceo Alternative Investment Services (ais) And Structured Products, Chandresh Iyer

Sevp And Cio, Bridget E. Engle

Cfo, Michael P. Santomassimo

Ceo Bny Mellon Markets, Michelle M. Neal

Senior Vice President, John Weisenhorn

Assistant Vice President Systems And Technology, Rebecca Stalker

Vice President Relationship Manager, Mary Snyder

Vice President, Kevin Miles

Vice President, Larry Denbaum

Vice President Financial Regulatory Reporting, Tuhin Dasgupta

Assistant Vice President Systems, Kenneth Kenneth Newman Newman

Vice President Information Technology, Joseph Aboulafia

Vice President, Jeffrey McSteen

Vice President, Keith Koble

Vice President, Anthony Lalima

Senior Vice President And Director Of Employee Benefits, Robert Perego

Vice President, Patricia Gallagher

Vice President Global Trade Finance Servs Div, Andrea Ratay

Vice President, Randolph Medrano

Vice President, Cary Jones

Vice President, Ellie Whalen

Vice President, Raymond Connery

Assistant Vice President, Jeffrey Roe

Vice President, Joseph Schnorr

Senior Vice President Legal Affairs, Bill Robinson

Assistant Vice President Investments, Remy Quito

Vice President, Edward Dougherty

Assistant Vice President, John Rushmore

Vice President, David Sunderwirth

Assistant Vice President, Ann Lynch

Vice President, Gordon Wong

Vice President, Mary Milner

Vice President Customer Technology Solutions Delivery, Carl Hagelin

Vice President, Charles Baker

Vice President, Justin Verdesca

Vice President, Brian Stern

Assistant Vice President Information Security, Sam Dekay

Assistant Vice President, Panagiota Bouboulis

Vice President And Relationship Manager, Mark Hochgesang

Vice President Global Trade Financial Services Division, Toula Tavlarides

Vice President, Brian Weddington

Vice President, Melinda Valentine

Vice President Information Technology, Joseph Hole

Assistant Vice President Business Services Group, Danny Wong

Vice President, Paul Angotta

Vice President, Elizabeth Wagner

Vice President, Claudia Leslie

Vice President, Brenda Stone

Vice President North American Banks Division, Joseph Barnes

Vice President Business Solutions Group, Bradley Jones

Vice President, Reyne Macadaeg

Vice President Application Development, Brian Burton

Assistant Vice President, Glenn Obando

Vice President, Peter Helt

Vice President Mutual Funds Division, Linda Pizzuti

Assistant Vice President, Kerri Shenkin

Vice President, Paul Meskiewicz

Vice President, Rebecca Newman

Vice President, Derrick Cornelious

Vice President Relationship Manager Long Island Queens Brooklyn Regional Commercial Banking, Gail Rnian-bivona

Senior Vice President Customer Care, Bruce Falkin

Vice President, Larisa Turetsky

Vice President, Peter Holland

Executive Vice President, John Moore

Vice President Information Risk Management, Michael Lam

Vice President Of Information Solutions, Peter Farrell

Vice President Marketing Communications, Geraldine Lutzel

Vice President, David Cook

Vice President U S Corporate Banking, Mark O'Connor

Vice President, Lawrence Timmins

Vice President, Ron Giromonte

Vice President, Irene Kugel

Vice President, Carol Turi

Vice President, Joseph Sierra

Vice President Of Sales, Sarah Foster

Vice President Human Resources, Susan McFarlan

Vice President Of Information Technology Learning, Michael Dermody

Assistant Vice President Internal Audit, Maria Dolinski

Vice President Benefits Disbursements, Steve Coates

Vice President It Procurement Bank Of New York Mellon, Rich Castman

Assistant Vice President; Critical System Engineer, Dan Gaffney

Senior Vice President, Douglas Owen

Vice President Global Corporate Trust, Mike Maio

Vice President, Timothy Fitzgerald

Vice President, Wayne Ross

Assistant Vice President, Clarence Burleigh

Assistant Vice President, Karen O'Donohoe

Assistant Vice President Technology Global Markets And Ecommerce, Vadim Kazakevich

Assistant Vice President, Neil Grill

Assistant Vice President, Jeff Charmatz

Senior Vice President Chief Information Officer, Kurt Wetzel

Senior Vice President, James McTiernan

Assistant Vice President Corporate General Services, Patrick Koziol

Executive Vice President The Bank Of New York, John R Mohr

Executive Vice President The Bank Of New York, Thomas V Ford

Assistant Vice President Enterprise Bi Architect, Ron Van Der Laan

First Vice President Operations Strategy Group, Mary Hannon

Vice President Alternative Investment Services, Thomas Ryder

Vice President, Cebert Boothe

Vice President Us Structured Finance, Adam Metzinger

Vice President, Seth Crone

Executive Vice President The Bank Of New York, William Kerr

Vice President Securities Finance, Dennis Cahill

Vice President Senior Wealth Manager, Riyad Said

Vice President Private Banker, Bryan Monteverde

Vice President Alternative Investment Services, John Carbaugh

Vice President Senior Wealth Manager, Anthony Tanner

Vice President, Robert Nelson

Vice President, Jean McNicholas Earley

Vice President, Debold Kate

Vice President Ais Prime Custody, Maja Vandenbush

Vice President Leadership Talent Acquisition, Karthik Nath

Vice President, Jay Peaslee

Vice President Digital Workplace Technologies Digital Onsite Services Platinum Service, Ted Petromelis

Vice President, Christopher Adamo

Vice President Advisor Solutions, Devika Del Duca

Vice President, Steve Mccarten

Vice President, Jarvis Joseph

Vice President Regional Manager West Region Trust Real Estate, Liz Stultz

Vice President, Matthew Joyce

Vice President, Jim Treanor

Vice President Private Banker, Jay Serniak

Vice President Senior Wealth Director, Scott Strochak

Board Member, Thomas J Mastro

Chairman And Ceo, Gerald L. Hassell, age 66

Ceo Clearing Markets And Client Management, Thomas P. (Todd) Gibbons, age 61

Assistant Treasurer, Wendy Havener

Assistant Treasurer Of Information Security, Nicholas Aromando

Assistant Treasurer, Cheryl Baye

Assistant Treasurer, David Rocco

Assistant Treasurer, Daniel Giles

Assistant Treasurer, Nina Cheung

Assistant Treasurer, Denise Freytas

Assistant Treasurer, Marcus McGregor

Treasurer, Ruby Pizzini

Assistant Treasurer, Nicole Pelligra

Assistant Treasurer Asia Pacific Division, Xiaotong Jia

Auditors: KPMG LLP

LOCATIONS

HQ: Bank of New York Mellon Corp
240 Greenwich Street, New York, NY 10286
Phone: 212 495-1784
Web: www.bnymellon.com

PRODUCTS/OPERATIONS

2016 Revenue

	$ mil.	% of total
Investment servicing fees		
Asset servicing	4,244	27
Clearing services	1,404	9
Issuer services	1,026	7
Treasury services	547	3
Interest net	3,138	22
Investment management & performance fees	3,350	23
Foreign exchange & other trading revenue	701	4
Investment & other income	341	2
Financing-related fees	219	1
Distribution & servicing	166	1
Net securities gains	75	1
Income from consolidated investment management funds	26	-
Total	**15,237**	**100**

Selected Subsidiaries and Business Lines

BNY Capital Funding LLC - State of Organization: Delaware

BNY Capital Markets Holdings Inc. - State of Incorporation: New York

BNY Capital Resources Corporation - State of Incorporation: New York

BNY International Financing Corporation - Incorporation: United States

BNY Mellon Capital Markets LLC - State of Organization: Delaware

BNY Mellon Fund Managers Limited - Incorporation: England

BNY Mellon Global Management Limited - Incorporation: Ireland

BNY Mellon International Asset Management Group Limited - Incorporation: England

BNY Mellon International Asset Management (Holdings) Limited - Incorporation: England and Wales

BNY Mellon International Asset Management (Holdings) No. 1 Limited - Incorporation: England and Wales

BNY Mellon Investment Management Cayman Ltd. - Incorporation: Cayman Islands

BNY Mellon Investment Management EMEA Limited - Incorporation: England

BNY Mellon Investment Management Europe Holdings Limited - Incorporation: England

BNY Mellon Investment Management (Europe) Limited - Incorporation: England

BNY Mellon Investment Management (Jersey) Limited - Incorporation: Jersey

BNY Mellon Investment Servicing (US) Inc. - State of Incorporation: Massachusetts

BNY Mellon National Association - Incorporation: United States

BNY Mellon Securities Services (Ireland) Limited - Incorporation: Ireland

BNY Mellon Trust Company (Ireland) Limited - Incorporation: Ireland

BNYM GIS Funding I LLC - State of Organization: Delaware

BNYM GIS Funding III LLC - State of Organization: Delaware

BNYM GIS (UK) Funding II LLC - State of Organization: Delaware

Insight Investment Funds Management Limited - Incorporation: England

Insight Investment Management (Global) Limited - Incorporation: England

Insight Investment Management Limited - Incorporation: England

MAM (MA) Holding Trust - State of Incorporation: Massachusetts

MBC Investments Corporation - State of Incorporation: Delaware

Mellon Canada Holding Company - Incorporation: Canada

Mellon Overseas Investment Corporation - Incorporation: United States

Pershing Group LLC - State of Organization: Delaware

Pershing Holdings (UK) Limited - Incorporation: England

Pershing Limited - Incorporation: England

Pershing LLC - State of Organization: Delaware

Pershing Securities Limited - Incorporation: England

Standish Mellon Asset Management Company LLC - State of Organization: Delaware

The Bank of New York Mellon - State of Organization: New York

The Bank of New York Mellon (International) Limited - Incorporation: England

The Bank of New York Mellon (Luxembourg) S.A. - Incorporation: Luxembourg

The Bank of New York Mellon SA/NV - Incorporation: Belgium

The Dreyfus Corporation - State of Incorporation: New York

Walter Scott & Partners Limited - Incorporation: Scotland

COMPETITORS

Bank of America	JPMorgan Chase
Barclays	Morgan Stanley
BlackRock	Northern Trust
Charles Schwab	PNC Financial
Citigroup	Prudential
Credit Suisse (USA)	State Street
Deutsche Bank	U.S. Bancorp
Franklin Templeton	Wells Fargo
HSBC	

HISTORICAL FINANCIALS

Company Type: Public

Income Statement   FYE: December 31

	ASSETS ($ mil.)	NET INCOME ($ mil.)	INCOME AS % OF ASSETS	EMPLOYEES
12/17	371,758	4,090	1.1%	52,500
12/16	333,469	3,547	1.1%	52,000
12/15	393,780	3,158	0.8%	51,200
12/14	385,303	2,567	0.7%	50,300
12/13	374,310	2,111	0.6%	51,100
Annual Growth	(0.2%)	18.0%	—	0.7%

2017 Year-End Financials

Debt ratio: 7.53%
Return on equity: 10.22%
Cash ($ mil.): 108,871
Current ratio: —
Long-term debt ($ mil.): —

No. of shares (mil.): 1,013
Dividends
  Yield: 0.0%
  Payout: 23.1%
Market value ($ mil.): 54,584

	STOCK PRICE ($) FY Close	P/E High/Low	PER SHARE ($) Earnings	Dividends	Book Value
12/17	53.86	15 12	3.72	0.86	40.70
12/16	47.38	16 10	3.15	0.72	37.05
12/15	41.22	17 13	2.71	0.68	35.05
12/14	40.57	19 14	2.15	0.66	33.48
12/13	34.94	20 15	1.74	0.58	32.85
Annual Growth	11.4%	— —	20.9%	10.3%	5.5%

Bank OZK

Bank of the Ozarks is the holding company for the bank of the same name which has about 260 branches in Alabama Arkansas California the Carolinas Florida Georgia New York and Texas. Focusing on individuals and small to midsized businesses the $12-billion bank offers traditional deposit and loan services in addition to personal and commercial trust services retirement and financial planning and investment management. Commercial real estate and construction and land development loans make up the largest portion of Bank of the Ozarks' loan portfolio followed by residential mortgage business and agricultural loans. Bank of the Ozarks grows its loan and deposit business by acquiring smaller banks and opening branches across the US.

Operations

The bank makes three-fourths of its total revenue from interest income while the rest comes from fee-based sources. About 43% of Bank of the Ozark's total revenue came from non-purchased loan interest in 2014 while another 26% came from interest on purchased loans and a further 8% came from interest on its investment securities. The rest of its revenue came from service charges on deposit accounts (8% of revenue) mortgage lending income (1%) trust income (1%) and other non-recurring sources.

Geographic Reach

Bank of the Ozarks had 174 branches in eight states at the end of 2014 with 81 of them in Alabama and another 75 branches split among Georgia North Carolina and Texas. It has two loan offices in Houston and Manhattan that serve as an extension of the bank's Dallas-based Real Estate Specialties Group.

Sales and Marketing

The bank spent $3.03 million on advertising and public relations expenses in 2014 compared to $2.2 million and $4.09 million in 2013 and 2012 respectively.

Financial Performance

Bank of the Ozarks' annual revenues and profits have doubled since 2010 mostly as its loan assets have doubled from recent bank acquisitions spawning higher interest income.

The bank's revenue jumped 31% to $376 million during 2014 mostly thanks to strong purchased and non-purchased loan asset growth during the year from recent bank acquisitions. Its non-interest income grew 12% thanks to a 20% increase in deposit account service charges stemming from newly acquired deposit customers.

Strong revenue growth in 2014 boosted Bank of the Ozarks' net income by 30% to $119 million for the year. Its operating cash levels jumped 22% to $61 million during the year mostly thanks to higher cash earnings.

Strategy

Bank of the Ozarks continues its strategy of loan and deposit volume growth by acquiring smaller banks in new and existing geographic markets. It has also opened new branches and loan offices sparingly. During 2014 for example the bank opened retail branches in Bradenton Florida; Cornelius North Carolina; and Hilton Head Island South Carolina along with a new loan production office in Asheville North Carolina.

Mergers and Acquisitions

In July 2016 Bank of the Ozarks acquired Georgia-based Community & Southern Holdings and its Community & Southern Bank subsidiary. Adding some 45 branch locations in Georgia plus another in Florida it was the company's largest acquisition to-date.

Also in July 2016 the bank purchased C1 Financial along with its 32 CI Bank branches on the west coast of Florida and in Miami-Dade and Orange Counties. The deal added $1.7 billion in total assets $1.4 billion in loans and $1.3 billion in deposits. This transaction was the bank's fifteenth acquisition in the past six years.

In August 2015 the bank purchased Bank of the Carolinas Corporation (BCAR) — and its eight Bank of the Carolinas branches in North Carolina $345 million in total assets $277 million in loans and $296 million in deposits — for a total price of $65.4 million.

In February 2015 Bank of the Ozarks bought Intervest Bancshares Corporation and its seven Intervest National Bank branches in (five in Clearwater Florida and two more in New York City and Pasadena Florida) for $238.5 million. The deal added $1.5 billion in assets including $1.1 billion in loans and $1.2 billion in deposits.

In May 2014 it bought Arkansas-based Summit Bancorp Inc. and its 23 Summit Bank branches across Arkansas for $42.5 million though it closed more than a handful of them later in the year.

In March 2014 the company acquired Houston-based Bancshares Inc. and its subsidiary Omnibank N.A. for $21.5 million adding three branches in Houston Texas and a branch each in Austin Cedar Park Lockhart and San Antonio.

Company Background

The expansion strategy of Bank of the Ozarks - which had a mere five branches in Arkansas 20 years ago — centered on opening new locations in smaller communities in Arkansas. But with the financial crash the bank was able to expand to more states through a series of FDIC-assisted transactions to take over failed banks. It bought Chestatee State Bank First Choice Community Bank Horizon Bank Oglethorpe Bank Park Avenue Bank Unity National and Woodlands Bank.

Chairman and CEO George Gleason initially bought the bank more than three decades ago at age 25.

EXECUTIVES

Chief Credit Officer Bank Of The Ozarks, Darrel Russell, age 64, $252,308 total compensation

Chairman; Chief Executive Officer Of The Company And The Bank, George G. Gleason, age 64, $1,730,769 total compensation

President Leasing Division Bank Of The Ozarks, Scott Hastings, age 60, $181,925 total compensation

President Mortgage Division Bank Of The Ozarks, Gene Holman, age 70, $150,042 total compensation

President Trust And Wealth Management Division Bank Of The Ozarks, Rex Kyle, age 61, $241,674 total compensation

President Real Estate Specialties Group Bank Of The Ozarks, Dan Thomas, age 55, $1,242,308 total compensation

Cfo And Chief Accounting Officer Bank Of The Ozarks Inc. And Bank Of The Ozarks, Greg McKinney, age 50, $368,077 total compensation

Chief Operating Officer And Chief Banking Officer Of The Company And The Bank, Tyler Vance, age 43, $366,923 total compensation

President Western Division, Don Keesee

Senior Vice President Market Leader, Russell Hewatt

Senior Vice President Of Information Systems, Malcolm Hicks

Vice President Payment Systems, Paula Shaw

Senior Vice President, Chris Bragg

Senior Vice President Retail Banking Manager, Bob Moore

Vice President Regional Manager, Lisa Amato

Vice President Commercial Loan Officer, Austin Simpson

Vice President Lending, Erik Larson

Assistant Vice President Community Development Officer, Kimberly L Marshall

Vice President Marketing, Mark Greenhaw

Senior Vice President Treasury Management, Steve Woodruff

Assistant Vice President Branch Operations Manager, Fabian Garantiva

Senior Vice President Commercial Lender, Jeni Chokron

Vice President, Eric Teague

Senior Vice President, Ryan Tanner

Assistant Vice President Branch Manager, Pam Toney

Assistant Vice President Branch Manager, Derek Labrosse

Assistant Vice President Community Development Officer, Joann Smith

Executive Vice President, David Sarner

Executive Vice President, Martin Ball

Senior Vice President, Aram Zakian

Vice President Loan Officer, Dawn Speas

Vice President Treasury Management Wire Manager, Mona Kalchik

Chairman; Chief Executive Officer Of The Company And The Bank, George G. Gleason, age 64

President Real Estate Specialties Group Bank Of The Ozarks, Dan Thomas, age 55

Auditors: PricewaterhouseCoopers LLP

LOCATIONS

HQ: Bank OZK
17901 Chenal Parkway, Little Rock, AR 72223
Phone: 501 978-2265   **Fax:** 501 978-2224
Web: www.bankozarks.com

PRODUCTS/OPERATIONS

2014 Sales

	$ mil.	% of total
Interest income		
Non-purchased loans and leases	162	43
Purchased loans	98	26
Investment securities	30	8
Non-interest income		
Service charges on deposit accounts	26	8
Other income from purchased loans net	14	4
Others	43	11
Total	**376**	**100**

Selected Services

Personal Banking
Apple PayChecking AccountsCredit CardsFree Bill PayFREE Debit CardsCustom Debit CardsEMV Chip CardsMobile BankingMortgage LoansMy Change KeeperOnline BankingOverdraft ProtectionPersonal LoansReloadable Spending CardsRetirement PlanningReorder ChecksSafe
Business Banking
Business ProductsApple Pay for BusinessDebit CardEMV Chip CardsBusiness Credit CardsChecking & Money MarketCommercial LoansExpress DepositMerchant ProcessingOnline BankingOverdraft ProtectionReorder ChecksTreasury Management Services
Online & Mobile Banking
Online BankingMobile BankingMobile DepositOnline Bill Pay
Wealth Management Services
Investment ProgramsFinancial PlanningCustomer Service

COMPETITORS

Arvest Bank	IBERIABANK
BOK Financial	JPMorgan Chase
BancorpSouth	Regions Financial
Bank of America	Simmons First
Bear State Financial	SunTrust
Cullen/Frost Bankers	Wells Fargo
Home BancShares	

HISTORICAL FINANCIALS

Company Type: Public

Income Statement
FYE: December 31

	ASSETS ($ mil.)	NET INCOME ($ mil.)	INCOME AS % OF ASSETS	EMPLOYEES
12/17	21,275	421	2.0%	2,400
12/16	18,890	269	1.4%	2,315
12/15	9,879	182	1.8%	1,642
12/14	6,766	118	1.8%	1,479
12/13	4,787	87	1.8%	1,223
Annual Growth	**45.2%**	**48.3%**	**—**	**18.4%**

2017 Year-End Financials

Debt ratio: 1.71%
Return on equity: 13.50%
Cash ($ mil.): 440
Current ratio: —
Long-term debt ($ mil.): —

No. of shares (mil.): 128
Dividends
Yield: 0.0%
Payout: 10.9%
Market value ($ mil.): 6,216

	STOCK PRICE ($) FY Close	P/E High/Low		PER SHARE ($) Earnings	Dividends	Book Value
12/17	48.45	17	12	3.35	0.37	26.98
12/16	52.59	21	13	2.58	0.63	23.02
12/15	49.46	26	15	2.09	0.55	16.19
12/14	37.92	46	20	1.52	0.47	11.37
12/13	56.59	48	28	1.21	0.36	8.48
Annual Growth	**(3.8%)**	**—**	**—**	**29.1%**	**0.3%**	**33.6%**

BankFinancial Corp

If you need a BankNow to handle your BankBusiness try BankFinancial. The bank serves individuals and businesses through about 20 branches in Cook DuPage Lake and Will counties in northeastern Illinois including parts of Chicago. It offers standard products such as checking and savings accounts credit cards and loans; services such as account management are available online. Multifamily residential mortgage loans make up 40% of its loan portfolio while another 40% is made up of commercial leases and non-residential mortgage loans. The bank also writes one-to-four family residential mortgages and home equity loans and lines of credit business loans and construction and land loans.

Operations

BankFinancial sells auto business disability homeowners and life insurance through subsidiary Financial Assurance Services while BF Asset Recovery Corporation sells foreclosed real estate. The bank also offers investment products and services such as annuities bonds mutual funds and financial and retirement planning through an a agreement with third-party broker-dealer Cetera Financial Services.

Like other banks BankFinancial makes most of its revenue from interest from the loans it issues. About 85% of its revenue came from loan interest (including fees) during 2015 while another 3% came from interest income on securities. The rest of its revenue came from deposit service charges and fees (4% of revenue) other fee income (4%) insurance commissions and annuities income (1%) loan servicing fees (1%) and trust income (1%).

Sales and Marketing

The bank provides services to individuals families and businesses. It spent $991000 on advertising and public relations during 2015 compared to $1.1 million and $925000 in 2014 and 2013 respectively.

Financial Performance

The bank's annual revenues have fallen more than 25% since 2011 mostly due to shrinking interest margins from low market interest rates and yields and fierce competition for customers in the Chicago metropolitan area.

BankFinancial's revenue dipped 1% to $55.65 million during 2015 despite a three basis point uptick in net interest margins mostly as its average interest-earning asset balances fell slightly during the year. Its deposit service charges and fee income increased 14% thanks to higher deposit account fees while other fee income decreased 4% for the year on lower ATM surcharges and serve charges.

The company's net income plunged almost 80% to $8.7 million in 2015 mostly because in 2014 it had earned a non-recurring $35.1 million tax benefit related to a valuation allowance reversal. Excluding this item its earnings would have been 58% higher as the bank's loan provisions declined on a strengthened credit portfolio and as it spent less on non-interest expenses. BankFinancial's operating cash levels fell 17% to $14.9 million for the year mostly because of a decline in cash-based earnings.

Strategy

BankFinancial continued in 2016 to focus on boosting its core commercial loan and lease business by marketing its variety of services and growing its commercial banking officer talent in their respective markets. The bank regularly introduces new commercial loan and lease products as well as deposit products to better fit its customers' needs.

EXECUTIVES

Chairman President And Ceo Bankfinancial Corporation And Bankfinancial F.s.b., F. Morgan Gasior, age 54, $405,804 total compensation

Evp Corporate Affairs Corporate Secretary And General Counsel Bankfinancial Corporation And Bankfinancial F.s.b., James J. Brennan, age 67, $325,468 total compensation

Evp And Cfo, Paul A. Cloutier, age 54, $271,998 total compensation

Executive Vice President Marketing & Sales, Gregg T. Adams, age 59, $230,625 total compensation

President Commercial Real Estate Bankfinancial F.s.b., John G. Manos, age 57

President National Commercial Leasing Bankfinancial F.s.b., William J. Deutsch, age 50, $205,000 total compensation

Senior Vice President, Mary Tritsis

Vice President Research And Development, John Harrell

Vice President System Integration, Carol Johnson

Assistant Vice President, Jodi Long

Senior Vice President Client Services, Mary Livingstone

Vice President Internal Audit, Niki Pilotte

Executive Vice President Sales And Marketing, Amy Olson

Vice President Apartment Lending, John Rainbolt

Senior Vice President, Layne Burns

Senior Vice President Retail Loans, Noreen Demarie

Regional Senior Vice President, Rich Nieman

Chairman President And Ceo Bankfinancial Corporation And Bankfinancial F.s.b., F. Morgan Gasior, age 54

Evp Corporate Affairs Corporate Secretary And General Counsel Bankfinancial Corporation And Bankfinancial F.s.b., James J. Brennan, age 67

Board Member, Thomas O'Neill

Board Member, John Palmer

Auditors: Crowe Horwath LLP

LOCATIONS

HQ: BankFinancial Corp
15W060 North Frontage Road, Burr Ridge, IL 60527
Phone: 800 894-6900

PRODUCTS/OPERATIONS

2015 Sales

	$ mil.	% of total
Interest		
Loans including fees	47	85
Securities	1	2
Other	0	1
Noninterest		
Deposit service charges & fees	2	4
Other fee income	2	4
Other	2	4
Total	55	100

Selected Services

Checking
Savings & money market
Online banking & bill pay
CDs & IRAs services
Deposit accounts
Credit & loans
Merchant services
Retirement plans services

COMPETITORS

Banco Popular North America
Bank of America
Citizens Financial Group
Fifth Third
First Midwest Bancorp
HSBC North America
Harris
JPMorgan Chase
MB Financial
Northern Trust
Old Second Bancorp
U.S. Bancorp
Wintrust Financial

HISTORICAL FINANCIALS

Company Type: Public

Income Statement

FYE: December 31

	ASSETS ($ mil.)	NET INCOME ($ mil.)	INCOME AS % OF ASSETS	EMPLOYEES
12/17	1,625	9	0.6%	259
12/16	1,620	7	0.5%	264
12/15	1,512	8	0.6%	273
12/14	1,465	40	2.8%	290
12/13	1,453	3	0.2%	320
Annual Growth	2.8%	28.5%	—	(5.2%)

2017 Year-End Financials

Debt ratio: —
Return on equity: 2.23%
Cash ($ mil.): 127
Current ratio: —
Long-term debt ($ mil.): —
No. of shares (mil.): 17
Dividends
Yield: 0.0%
Payout: 100.0%
Market value ($ mil.): 275

	STOCK PRICE ($) FY Close	P/E High/Low	PER SHARE ($) Earnings	Dividends	Book Value
12/17	15.34	34 23	0.49	0.49	11.00
12/16	14.82	37 29	0.39	0.21	10.65
12/15	12.63	31 25	0.44	0.20	10.46
12/14	11.86	6 5	2.01	0.09	10.24
12/13	9.16	61 45	0.16	0.04	8.32
Annual Growth	13.8%	— —	32.3%	87.1%	7.2%

BankUnited Inc.

BankUnited is uniting the north and south again. It's the bank holding company for BankUnited N.A. which provides standard banking services to individuals and businesses through nearly 90 banking centers in about 15 Florida counties and five banking centers in the New York metro area. Deposit offerings include checking and savings accounts treasury management services and certificates of deposit. Commercial loans including multi-family residential mortgages account for some 80% of the bank's lending portfolio. In 2018 the company launched BankUnitedDirect an online division offering money market and CD accounts nationwide. BankUnited does not offer investment banking or wealth management services.

Sales and Marketing

BankUnited serves individuals growing companies and established middle-market companies. It markets its products through local television and radio ads digital and print ads and direct mail campaigns.

Financial Performance

BankUnited's revenue has been growing steadily for the last five years. Profits were relatively static until 2017 when they more than doubled. Cash flow has been somewhat volatile.

In 2017 revenue increased 14% to $1.1 billion as both interest and non-interest income grew. Interest on loans and securities rose while gains of sales of loans boosted non-interest income.

Net income rose 172% to $591 million that year. Part of that gain was due to a $327.9 million income tax benefit received.

The company ended 2017 with some $195 million in cash versus $448 million held at the end of 2016. Financing activities provided $1.9 billion in cash and operating activities provided $319 million. Investing activities used $2.5 billion in 2017

(the fifth straight year investments have used more than $2 billion).

Strategy

BankUnited has placed its bets on two large and growing markets — the Miami metro area and the Tri-State area of New York New Jersey and Connecticut. Because those geographic markets are so attractive though competition is fierce.

The company is also open to making strategic acquisitions of other financial firms or companies in complementary businesses.

Company Background

BankUnited was formed in 2009 following the demise of the former BankUnited FSB which collapsed under the weight of bad mortgages. A team of private investors bought BankUnited from the FDIC injected $900 million in fresh capital and in 2011 took the company public via an initial public offering (IPO); it was the first IPO of a rescued bank during the economic crisis.

In February 2012 BankUnited acquired Herald National Bank for $65 million in cash and stock. At the time of the purchase BankUnited converted to a bank holding company. It also converted the charter of subsidiary BankUnited from a thrift to a national commercial bank. Herald National was merged into BankUnited in mid-2012.

EXECUTIVES

President New York Region, Joseph (Joe) Roberto, age 61, $300,000 total compensation

Chief Risk Officer, Mark P. Bagnoli, age 66

President And Ceo, Rajinder P. (Raj) Singh, age 47, $500,000 total compensation

Cfo, Leslie N. Lunak, age 61, $400,000 total compensation

Coo, Thomas M. Cornish, age 60, $500,000 total compensation

Cio, Julio Jogaib

Senior Vice President Commercial Real Estate, Robert Hummel

Vice President Hub Manager, Amy Ouellette

Assistant Vice President Portfolio Manager, Tracey Snow

Vice President, Kenneth Lipke

Senior Vice President Treasury Management, Nicholas Schiralli

Senior Vice President Commercial Private Banking, Corey Prinz

Vice President, Bill Williams

Vice President, Peter Dumelle

Senior Vice President Associate General Counsel, Alina Pastiu

Vice President Treasury Management Relationship Manager Treasury Management, Mark Stevens

Vice President, Carol Hammond

Assistant Vice President Design And Development, Sonya Moro

Vice President Portfolio Manager For Commercial Real Estate, Sabine SE Bouchereau

Vice President, Frank Puccio

Senior Vice President Community Development Offic, Claire Raley

Vice President Banking Center Assistant Manager, Theresa Schuman

Vice President Accounting Department, Dorrett Boothe

Senior Vice President Bsa Officer, Scott Nathan

Senior Vice President Nyc Business Banking Team Leader, Gene Sullivan

Vice President Busines Banker, Nicholas Marrone

Senior Vice President Enterprise Stress Testing, Filippo Ghia

Vice President Financial Center Manager, John Hernandez

Senior Vice President, Stephen Hartigan

Senior Vice President Corporate Banking, Joseph Disanti

Vice President Corporate Banking, Justin Allbright

Vice President And Business Banking, Jose Alonso
Senior Vice President Relationship Manager Commercial Real Estate, Patricia Lubian
Vice President, Mireya Foster
Senior Vice President Associate General Counsel, Nancy Elia
Senior Vice President, Percy R Aguila
Vice President Commercial Banking, Ted Kunkel
Vice President, Carlos X Ramos
Vice President Commercial Real Estate, Jeremy Romine
Vice President Business Development Officer, Amy Rice
Senior Vice President Senior Business Development Officer, Scott Gilman
Senior Vice President, Michael Del Rocco
Senior Vice President Commercial Private Banking, Meghan Sheehan
Senior Vice President Senior Credit Officer Commercial Real Estate, John Kenyon
Senior Vice President, Jose Valdes
Assistant Vice President Regulatory Compliance Analyst Ii, Paula Gagnon
Assistant Vice President, Gloria Persaud
Senior Vice President Environmental Risk Manager, Michael Tartanella
Senior Vice President Business Banking Sales Manager, Gregory Milford
Vice President Branch Sales Leader, Milton Price
Vice President Commercial Real Estate, Chris Nielsen
Vice President Corporate Banking Division, Milciades Herrera
Executive Vice President, Gardner Semet
Senior Vice President, John Wamboldt
Senior Vice President, Larry Crowley
Vice President Operations Manager, Jose Alvarado
Vice President Corporate Banking, Jennifer Garcia-Barbon
Vice President Business Development Officer, Marissa Ames
Vice President Private Client Team Lead, Thomas Pla
Vice President Business Banking Lead Underwriter, Alexanders Saenz
Senior Vice President Corporate Team Leader, Christine Gerula
Assistant Vice President Project Administrator And Executive Assistant, Natalia Valenti
Vice President Commercial Real Estate, Chris Demeter
Avp Corporate Banking Portfolio Manager, Anthony Fulchi
Assistant Vice President, Shannie DeFreitas
Executive Vice President Mortgage Services, Ray Barbone
Vice President Branch Sales Leader, Monica Ribeiro
Vice President Business Development Officer, Stephen Speer
Vice President, Sul Hemani
Senior Vice President, Steve Markowski
Vice President Senior Analyst Business Development Officer, Tom Francis
Vice President Branch Sales Leader Downtown Delray Branch, Glenn Milspaugh
Avp Sba Loan Closer, Muni Chum
Senior Vice President, Brett Shulick
Vice President Business Banking Relationship Manager, Marshall Fulton
Vice President Business Development Officer Franchise Lending Specialist, Turner Gaw
Avp Sba Loan Closer, Leslie Giannantoni
Avp Recruiter Iii Hr Generalist, Tsahai Green
Svp Credit Review Group Manager, Nancy Lanzoni
Vice President Commercial Credit Review Officer Iii, Elizabeth Nader
Senior Vice President Senior Cre Credit Officer Florida Region, Raul Llanes
Vp Electronic Banking Manager, Daniel Cox
Senior Vice President, Candy Dugan

Senior Vice President Commercial Private Banking, Kelly Sleece
Avp Business Banking Portfolio Manager, Fredy Calderon
Vice President, Peter Anderson
Senior Vice President Corporate Banking, Jackson Young
Vice President Business Banking, Richard Rippy
Vice President Business Development Officer, Jared Johnson
Vice President Branch Sales Manager, Kathy Nemeth
Assistant Vice President Mortgage Warehouse Lending, Rosemarie Loparrino
Chairman, John A. Kanas, age 71
Auditors: KPMG LLP

LOCATIONS

HQ: BankUnited Inc.
14817 Oak Lane, Miami Lakes, FL 33016
Phone: 305 569-2000
Web: www.bankunited.com

COMPETITORS

BB&T	Ocean Bankshares
Bank of America	PNC Financial
Capital One	Regions Financial
Citibank	Signature Bank
Great Florida Bank	SunTrust
JPMorgan Chase	TD Bank USA
M&T Bank	Valley National
New York Community	Bancorp
Bancorp	Wells Fargo

HISTORICAL FINANCIALS

Company Type: Public

Income Statement

FYE: December 31

	ASSETS ($ mil.)	NET INCOME ($ mil.)	INCOME AS % OF ASSETS	EMPLOYEES
12/17	30,346	614	2.0%	1,763
12/16	27,880	225	0.8%	1,706
12/15	23,883	251	1.1%	1,741
12/14	19,210	204	1.1%	1,647
12/13	15,046	208	1.4%	1,623
Annual Growth	19.2%	30.9%	—	2.1%

2017 Year-End Financials

Debt ratio: 1.33%
Return on equity: 22.56%
Cash ($ mil.): 194
Current ratio: —
Long-term debt ($ mil.): —
No. of shares (mil.): 106
Dividends
Yield: 0.0%
Payout: 15.0%
Market value ($ mil.): 4,351

	STOCK PRICE ($) FY Close	P/E High/Low		PER SHARE ($) Earnings	Dividends	Book Value
12/17	40.72	7	5	5.58	0.84	28.32
12/16	37.69	18	13	2.09	0.84	23.22
12/15	36.06	17	11	2.35	0.84	21.65
12/14	28.97	18	14	1.95	0.84	20.19
12/13	32.92	16	12	2.01	0.84	19.09
Annual Growth	5.5%	—	—	29.1%	(0.0%)	10.4%

Bankwell Financial Group Inc

EXECUTIVES

Pres-Ceo, Christopher Gruseke
Chb, Blake S Drexler
Exec V Pres-Cfo, Ernest J Verrico Sr
Exec V Pres-Clo, Heidi S Dewyngaert
Exec V Pres-Cco, Christine Chivily
Evp-Cfo, Penko Ivanov
Information Technology Manager, John Adams
Vice-President, Susan Kornberg
Director, Courtney Sacchetti
Vice President Commercial Lend, Michael Sulkis
Senior Vice President, Robert J Palermo
Auditors: RSM US LLP

LOCATIONS

HQ: Bankwell Financial Group Inc
220 Elm Street, New Canaan, CT 06840
Phone: 203 652-0166
Web: www.mybankwell.com

HISTORICAL FINANCIALS

Company Type: Public

Income Statement

FYE: December 31

	ASSETS ($ mil.)	NET INCOME ($ mil.)	INCOME AS % OF ASSETS	EMPLOYEES
12/17	1,796	13	0.8%	141
12/16	1,628	12	0.8%	127
12/15	1,330	9	0.7%	125
12/14	1,099	4	0.4%	130
12/13	779	5	0.7%	—
Annual Growth	23.2%	27.9%	—	—

2017 Year-End Financials

Debt ratio: 1.40%
Return on equity: 9.01%
Cash ($ mil.): 70
Current ratio: —
Long-term debt ($ mil.): —
No. of shares (mil.): 7
Dividends
Yield: 0.0%
Payout: 15.7%
Market value ($ mil.): 266

	STOCK PRICE ($) FY Close	P/E High/Low		PER SHARE ($) Earnings	Dividends	Book Value
12/17	34.34	21	16	1.78	0.28	20.77
12/16	32.50	21	12	1.62	0.22	19.14
12/15	19.85	17	14	1.21	0.05	17.53
12/14	21.00	28	21	0.78	0.00	17.98
12/13	20.90	16	9	1.44	0.00	17.93
Annual Growth	13.2%	—	—	5.4%	—	3.8%

Banner Corp.

Flagging bank accounts? See Banner Corporation. Banner is the holding company for Banner Bank which serves the Pacific Northwest through about 100 branches and 10 loan production offices in Washington Oregon and Idaho. The company also owns Islanders Bank which operates three branches in Washington's San Juan Islands. The banks offer standard products such as deposit accounts credit cards and business and consumer loans. Commercial loans including business agriculture construction and multifamily mortgage loans account for about 90% of the company's portfolio. Bank subsidiary Community Financial writes residential mortgage and construction loans.

Geographic Reach

Washington-based Banner Bank is focused on five primary markets in the Northwest: the Puget Sound region of Washington; the greater Portland Oregon market; Boise Idaho; and Spokane Washington. The fifth is the bank's historical base in the agricultural communities in the Columbia Basin region of Washington and Oregon.

Sales and Marketing

Banner Corp. reported advertising and marketing expenses of $6.9 million in 2013 versus $7.2 million in 2012. Banner Bank launched a redesigned website and new ad campaign in Boise Seattle and Portland and on social media in fall 2014.

Financial Performance

The regional bank holding company reported revenue of $223 million in 2013 an increase of 4% versus 2012. The rise in revenue was due to increased operating income as a result of gains on the sale of securities and a fee received from the termination of the bank's proposed acquisition of Home Federal Bancorp. The bank's growing customer base led to increased income from deposit fees and other service charges of $1.3 billion (5%) in 2013 versus the prior year. Net income declined 28% in 2013 versus 2012 to $46.6 million primarily due to higher provision for income tax expenses. After three consecutive years of losses (2008 thru 2010) the bank returned to profitability in 2011 and has remained profitable.

Banner Corp. has total consolidated assets of about $4.5 billion.

Strategy

Historically Banner Corp. has grown by acquisition. Since going public (in 1995) Banner has acquired about 10 commercial banks. Islanders Bank was acquired in 2007 the same year Banner acquired F&M Bank and NCW Community Bank of Wenatchee both also based in Washington. After the spate of acquisitions the company focused on opening branches. The company continues to look for acquisition opportunities with an eye on banks shut down by regulators.

In 2013 however a plan to merge with Home Federal Bancorp was terminated when that bank received a better offer from Cascade Bancorp. Also the company abandoned plans to buy Idaho Banking Company out of bankruptcy after being outbid.

Mergers and Acquisitions

In August 2014 Banner Bank acquired Siuslaw Financial Group the holding company for Siuslaw Bank the operator of 10 branches along the coast of Oregon. In June 2014 Banner Bank purchased six branches in Oregon from Sterling Savings Bank.

EXECUTIVES

Evp And Cfo Banner Corporation, Lloyd W. Baker, age 69, $260,724 total compensation

Evp Retail Banking And Administration, Cynthia D. (Cindy) Purcell, age 60, $289,038 total compensation

Evp And Chief Lending Officer Banner Corporation And Banner Bank, Richard B. Barton, age 74, $264,895 total compensation

President And Ceo, Mark J. Grescovich, age 53, $716,415 total compensation

Evp And Real Estate Lending Manager Banner Bank, Douglas M. Bennett, age 65, $236,174 total compensation

Evp And Cio, Steven W. (Steve) Rust, age 70

Evp Retail Products And Services, Gary W. Wagers, age 57

Evp And Commercial Executive East Region, M. Kirk Quillin, age 55

Evp And Commercial Executive West Region, James T. (Jim) Reed, age 55

Evp And Cfo Banner Bank, Peter J. Conner, age 52

Evp Human Resources, Kayleen Kohler

Evp And Mortgage Banking Director, Kenneth A. (Ken) Larsen, age 48

Evp And General Counsel Banner Bank, Craig Miller

Evp And Chief Risk Officer Banner Bank, Judy Steiner

Evp And Commercial Executive (south Region), Keith A. Western, age 62

Senior Vice President Sba Manager, Walter Mclaughlin

Senior Vice President, Mark Brandon

Assistant Vice President And Senior Underwriter, Nancy Piestrack

Vice President And Portfolio Manager, Michael Thomas

Vice President Senior Commercial Relationship Manager, Jeanne Walker

Assistant Vice President Training Manager, Terri Anderson

Vice Chairman Banner Corporation And Banner Bank, Jesse G. Foster, age 80

Chairman Banner Corporation And Banner Bank, Gary L. Sirmon, age 75

Auditors: Moss Adams LLP

LOCATIONS

HQ: Banner Corp.
 10 South First Avenue, Walla Walla, WA 99362
Phone: 509 527-3636
Web: www.bannerbank.com

PRODUCTS/OPERATIONS

2016 Sales

	% of total
INTEREST INCOME:	
Loans receivable	75
Mortgage-backed securities	4
Securities and cash equivalents	3
NON-INTEREST INCOME:	
Deposit fees and other service charges	10
Mortgage banking operations	6
BOLI	1
Miscellaneous	1
Total	**100**

COMPETITORS

Bank of America	Sound Financial
Cascade Bancorp	U.S. Bancorp
Columbia Banking	Umpqua Holdings
FCA	Washington Federal
Glacier Bancorp	Wells Fargo
KeyCorp	

HISTORICAL FINANCIALS

Company Type: Public

Income Statement   FYE: December 31

	ASSETS ($ mil.)	NET INCOME ($ mil.)	INCOME AS % OF ASSETS	EMPLOYEES
12/17	9,763	60	0.6%	2,128
12/16	9,793	85	0.9%	2,137
12/15	9,796	45	0.5%	2,143
12/14	4,723	54	1.1%	1,193
12/13	4,388	46	1.1%	1,131
Annual Growth	**22.1%**	**6.9%**	**—**	**17.1%**

2017 Year-End Financials

Debt ratio: 1.99%	No. of shares (mil.): 32
Return on equity: 4.71%	Dividends
Cash ($ mil.): 261	Yield: 0.0%
Current ratio: —	Payout: 107.6%
Long-term debt ($ mil.): —	Market value ($ mil.): 1,804

	STOCK PRICE ($) FY Close	P/E High/Low		PER SHARE ($) Earnings	Dividends	Book Value
12/17	55.12	34	28	1.84	1.98	38.89
12/16	55.81	22	15	2.52	0.65	39.34
12/15	45.86	28	21	1.89	0.72	37.97
12/14	43.02	16	13	2.79	0.72	29.82
12/13	44.82	19	12	2.40	0.54	27.63
Annual Growth	**5.3%**	**—**	**—**	**(6.4%)**	**38.4%**	**8.9%**

BANNER HEALTH

Banner Health is one of the largest secular not-for-profit health systems in the US. The organization operates about 30 acute-care hospitals (with roughly 4000 beds). It also operates clinics nursing homes clinical laboratories ambulatory surgery centers home health agencies and other health care-related organizations including physician practices and a captive insurance company. Banner Health participates in medical research in areas such as Alzheimer's disease and spinal cord injuries through its Banner Sun Health Research division. The company which has more than 400000 members provides services in seven states in the western US; its largest concentration of facilities is in Arizona.

Operations

Banner Health is one of the first not-for-profit hospital operators to reinsure its employees through its captive insurance company Samaritan Insurance Funding. By offering this service Banner Health is able to diversify its risk improve cash flow and lower life insurance costs by about half a million dollars a year.

The multi-specialty system also operates a health plan in Arizona for Medicare-eligible patients. Its MediSunONE plan includes Medicare and Medicare Part D. The company has joined forces with Aetna in what is called an accountable care collaboration (ACO). An ACO uses technology and a team-based approach to care for the hospital's patients. Doctors and hospitals assume accountability for patient outcomes and are rewarded financially for achieving higher quality greater efficiency and overall better patient outcomes. The partnership also includes a new product called Aetna Whole Health that allows Banner's patients access to a line of Aetna services including their own electronic patient record.

The system's specialty centers include Banner Alzheimer's Institute Banner Concussion Center Banner Heart Hospital and the Western States Burn Center. In addition Banner Health trains 270 doctors per year at Banner Good Samaritan and Northern Colorado Medical Center.

Banner Health also partners with M.D. Anderson Cancer Center to operate a comprehensive cancer center in Phoenix. Services include medical oncology radiation oncology surgical oncology pathology laboratory diagnostic imaging as well as other supportive clinical services. M.D. Anderson has clinical oversight for all aspects of care delivery.

Education looms large on Banner Health's list of priorities — the hospital operates one of the country's largest simulation education centers at its Banner Corporate Center-Mesa. Simulation education is an expanding field in which medical students use computerized mannequins to improve their surgical and medical skills. The school's research has paid off and with Scottsdale Healthcare Osborn Medical Center Banner Health invented the Sapien Transcatheter Heart Valve an artificial heart valve that can replace a diseased aortic heart valve without the open heart surgery that previously was required.

Geographic Reach

Banner Health operates in Alaska Arizona California Colorado Nebraska Nevada and Wyoming.

The system's Banner Health Network is a group of health care providers located in Arizona's Maricopa and Pinal counties.

Financial Performance

Banner Health's income is generally derived through three channels: third-party payers such as commercial insurance managed care agreements Medicare and Medicaid and a small portion of self-pay patients as well as by borrowing funds and receiving philanthropic donations.

Its revenues grew by 29% in 2015 from $5.4 billion to $7 billion; higher net patient service medical insurance premium and other revenues drove that increase. However rising expenses and a $49.3 million loss for ACO Banner Health Network led to a drop in net income which fell 65% to $83.7 million.

Strategy

The health system has grown through construction. Banner Health is nearly always engaged in some sort of construction renovation or upgrading at its numerous facilities. The organization has more than $1 billion in construction projects in progress or completed in recent years. The system has expanded its facilities at Banner Baywood Medical Center Banner Del E. Webb Medical Center Banner Desert Medical Center Banner Thunderbird Medical Center Cardon Children's Medical Center and McKee Medical Center.

In 2015 Banner Health opened a Fort Collins facility on a 28-acre campus with a two-story hospital featuring an emergency department a 24-bed inpatient unit labor and delivery rooms medical imaging women's services surgical services and lab services.

Also that year the system merged with the University of Arizona Health Network (now named Banner - University Medicine) as well as establishing a 30-year affiliation with the University of Arizona. The moves align with its strategy of combining health care provision with medical schools and academic training as well as expanding operations into new markets (in this case the Tuscon region). Banner Health hopes to both improve access to health care through a consumer-focused system and to provide opportunities for medical professionals to remain in Arizona. As part of the merger the company plans to build a new hospital and renovate an existing ambulatory campus.

In 2017 Banner Health restructured operations including cutting some 500 employees' positions. The move was part of its efforts to become more consumer-focused and included changes to its leadership lineup. Later that year after the restructuring was completed the company began recruiting to fill 1000 positions including spots for specialty nurses and physical and occupational therapists.

Mergers and Acquisitions

Banner Health does occasionally pick up a new hospital through acquisition. For instance in 2015 the company acquired The University of Arizona Health Network (now Banner - University Medicine). As a result University Medicine is the new academic medicine division of Banner Health which includes three academic medical centers: Banner - University Medical Center Tucson Banner

- University Medical Center Phoenix and Banner - University Medical Center South.

In mid-2016 the company acquired more than 30 Arizona urgent-care centers from Urgent Care Extra. The centers to be rebranded under the Banner banner are among the expected 50 the company plans to have in Arizona by 2018.

In 2017 Banner Health acquired Medicare-certified home health agency SunLife Home Health which is based in Tucson Arizona. That deal allowed the system to expand its home care operations into southern Arizona.

Company Background

Banner Good Samaritan Medical Center first opened its doors as a 20-bed hospital in 1911. The medical center which is four months older than the state of Arizona marked its 100th anniversary in October 2011.

EXECUTIVES

Evp And Chief Administrative Officer, Ronald R. (Ron) Bunnell
President Ceo And Director, Peter S. Fine, age 66
Evp And Chief Clinical Officer, John Hensing
Evp University Medicine, Kathy Bollinger
Coo, Rebecca (Becky) Kuhn
Ceo Banner University Medical Center South And Banner University Medical Center Tucson, Tom Dickson
Cfo, Dennis L. Laraway
President Western Region, Jim Ferando
Ceo East Morgan County Hospital And Sterling Regional Medcenter, Linda Thorpe
President Arizona East Division, Todd S. Werner, age 50
Ceo Banner Desert Medical Center And Interim Ceo Cardon Children's Medical Center, Laura Robertson
Ceo Platte County Memorial Hospital And Community Hospital, Shelby Nelson
Ceo Banner Thunderbird Medical Center, Deb Krmpotic
Ceo Banner Research, Eric (Bill) Reiman
President Banner Health Network, Chuck Lehn
Ceo Banner Del E. Webb Medical Center And Banner Boswell Medical Center, Debbie Flores
Ceo University Medical Center Phoenix, Steve Narang
Ceo Banner Ironwood Medical Center And Banner Goldfield Medical Center, Sharon Lind
President And Ceo Banner Health Foundation And Banner Alzheimer's Foundation, Andy Kramer Petersen
Cio, Ryan Smith
Ceo Banner Casa Grande Medical Center, Rona Curphy
Ceo Banner Estrella Medical Center, Courtney Ophaug
Ceo Banner Gateway Medical Center Banner Md Anderson Cancer Center Banner Baywood Medical Center And Banner Heart Hospital, Lamont Yoder
Vp Post Acute Services And Ceo Banner Home Care/hospice, Lynn Rosenbach
Ceo Banner Lassen Medical Center, Catherine Harshbarger
Ceo Banner Churchill Community Hospital, Hoyt Skabelund
Ceo Washakie Medical Center, Jay Stallings
Ceo Ogallala Community Hospital, Drew Dostal
Ceo Banner Behavioral Health Hospital, Brian Beutin
Ceo Page Hospital, Brian Kellar
Interim Ceo Northern Colorado Service Area Including: Banner Fort Collins Medical Center Mckee Medical Center North Colorado Medical Center, Scott Baker
Vice President, Tony Blake

System Vice President Information Technology Business Services, Bryce Carder
Vice President Consumer Experience Center, Dave Kriesand
Director Of Pharmacy, E-J Chane
Director Of Pharmacy, Kurt Weibel
Vice Chair, Christopher H. (Chris) Volk
Chairman, Larry S. Lazarus
Auditors: ERNST & YOUNG LLP PHOENIX AZ

LOCATIONS

HQ: BANNER HEALTH
2901 N CENTRAL AVE # 160, PHOENIX, AZ 850122702
Phone: 602 747-4000
Web: WWW.BANNERHEALTH.COM

FEATURED SERVICES

Academic Medicine
Alzheimer's
Cancer
Heart
Insurance (Networks)
Maternity
Orthopedics
Pediatrics
Pharmacy
Physicians & Specialists
Research
Women's Health

COMPETITORS

Community Health Systems	Poudre Valley Health System
Dignity Health	Providence St. Joseph Health
HCA	
Inova	Scottsdale Healthcare
John C. Lincoln Health Network	Tenet Healthcare
	Texas Health Resources
Memorial Health System of East Texas	Wyoming Medical Center
Northern Arizona Healthcare	Yuma Regional Medical Center
Phoenix Children's Hospital	

HISTORICAL FINANCIALS

Company Type: Private

Income Statement   FYE: December 31

	REVENUE ($ mil.)	NET INCOME ($ mil.)	NET PROFIT MARGIN	EMPLOYEES
12/17	7,835	728	9.3%	35,000
12/16	7,633	309	4.1%	—
12/15	6,971	119	1.7%	—
12/14	5,397	261	4.8%	—
Annual Growth	13.2%	40.8%	—	—

2017 Year-End Financials

Debt ratio: ——
Return on equity: 9.30%
Cash ($ mil.): 292
Current ratio: 0.60
Long-term debt ($ mil.): —

Dividends
Yield: —
Payout: —
Market value ($ mil.): —

Bar Harbor Bankshares

Bar Harbor Bankshares which holds Bar Harbor Bank & Trust is a Maine -stay. Boasting $1.6 billion in assets the bank offers traditional deposit and retirement products trust services and a variety of loans to individuals and businesses through 15 branches in the state's Hancock Knox and Washington counties. Commercial real estate and residential mortgages loans make up nearly 80% of the bank's loan portfolio though it also originates business construction agricultural home equity and other consumer loans. About 10% of its loans are to the tourist industry which is associated with nearby Acadia National Park. Subsidiary Bar Harbor Trust Services offers trust and estate planning services.

Operations

Around 80% of the bank's loan assets are tied to real estate. About 41% of its loan portfolio was made up of residential real estate mortgages at the end of 2015 while another 37% was made up of commercial real estate mortgages. The rest of the portfolio was tied to commercial and industrial loans (8% of loan assets) home equity loans (5%) agricultural and farming loans (3%) commercial construction (3%) and other consumer loans (1%).

More than 80% of Bar Harbor's revenue comes from interest income. About 61% of its total revenue came from loan interest (including fees) during 2015 while another 25% came from interest income on investment securities. The remainder of its revenue came from trust and other financial services (6% of revenue) debit card service charges and fees (3%) deposit account service charges (1%) and other miscellaneous income sources.

Geographic Reach

The Bar Harbor Maine-based group operates 15 branches across the downeast midcoast and central regions of Maine more specifically in Bar Harbor Northeast Harbor Southwest Harbor Somesville Deer Isle Blue Hill Ellsworth Rockland Topsham South China Augusta Winter Harbor Milbridge Machias and Lubec.

Sales and Marketing

Bar Harbor serves individuals and retirees nonprofits municipalities as well as businesses that are vital to Maine's coastal economy including retailers restaurants seasonal lodging bio research laboratories.

Financial Performance

The group's annual revenues have risen more than 10% since 2011 as its loan assets have swelled over 35% to $990 million. Its profits have grown more than 30% over the same period as Bar Harbor has kept a lid on rising operating costs and as it's enjoyed low interest rates.

Bar Harbor's revenue climbed 4% to $64.2 million during 2015 mostly as its loan and other interest earning assets grew by more than 7%.

Revenue growth in 2015 drove the bank's net income up 4% to $15.15 million. Bar Harbor's operating cash levels spiked 31% to $20.33 million for the year mainly thanks to favorable working capital changes related to changes in other assets.

Strategy

Bar Harbor Bankshares looks to grow its loan and deposit business organically and through strategic bank acquisitions targeting the downeast midcoast and central Maine markets. It also continued in 2016 to focus on managing its operating expenses building upon its strong efficient ratio of 56.3% in 2015.

EXECUTIVES

Evp Business Banking Bar Harbor Bank & Trust, Gregory W. Dalton, age 58, $203,000 total compensation

Evp Retail Banking, Stephen M. Leackfeldt, age 61, $225,000 total compensation

Evp And Chief Risk Officer, Richard B. Maltz, $255,000 total compensation

Evp Cfo And Treasurer, Josephine Iannelli, age 46

President And Ceo Bar Harbor Bankshares And Bar Harbor Bank & Trust, Curtis C. Simard, age 47, $438,000 total compensation

Assistant Vice President And Senior Risk Management Analyst, John Williams

Vice President Regional Relationship Manager, Larissa Darcy

Senior Vice President Internal Audit, Johanne Lapointe

Vice President Regional Market Manager, Michelle Curtis

Chairman, David B. Woodside, age 66

Evp Cfo And Treasurer, Josephine Iannelli, age 46

Board Member, Matthew Caras

Auditors: RSM US LLP

LOCATIONS

HQ: Bar Harbor Bankshares
P.O. Box 400, 82 Main Street, Bar Harbor, ME 04609-0400

Phone: 207 288-3314 **Fax:** 207 288-4560
Web: www.bhbt.com

PRODUCTS/OPERATIONS

2015 sales

	$ mil.	% of total
Interest and dividend income		
Interest and fees on loans	39	61
Interest on securities	15	24
Dividends on FHLB stock	0	1
Non-interest income		
Trust and other financial services	3	6
Debit card service charges and fees	1	3
Net securities gains	1	2
Other operating income	1	2
Service charges on deposit accounts	0	1
Total	**64**	**100**

Selected Services

Retail Products and Services
Retail Brokerage Services
Electronic Banking Services
Commercial Products and Services

COMPETITORS

Bangor Savings Bank	TD Bank USA
Bank of America	The First Bancorp
Camden National	
People's United Financial	

HISTORICAL FINANCIALS

Company Type: Public

Income Statement

FYE: December 31

	ASSETS ($ mil.)	NET INCOME ($ mil.)	INCOME AS % OF ASSETS	EMPLOYEES
12/17	3,565	25	0.7%	423
12/16	1,755	14	0.9%	186
12/15	1,580	15	1.0%	221
12/14	1,459	14	1.0%	223
12/13	1,373	13	1.0%	185
Annual Growth	**26.9%**	**18.5%**	**—**	**23.0%**

2017 Year-End Financials

Debt ratio: 1.21%	No. of shares (mil.): 15
Return on equity: 10.17%	Dividends
Cash ($ mil.): 90	Yield: 0.0%
Current ratio: —	Payout: 43.9%
Long-term debt ($ mil.): —	Market value ($ mil.): 417

	STOCK PRICE ($) FY Close	P/E High/Low	PER SHARE ($) Earnings	Dividends	Book Value
12/17	27.01	28 15	1.70	0.75	22.96
12/16	47.33	30 18	1.63	0.73	17.19
12/15	34.42	22 18	1.67	0.67	17.10
12/14	32.00	24 15	1.63	0.60	16.40
12/13	39.99	27 23	1.48	0.56	13.70
Annual Growth	**(9.3%)**	**— —**	**3.4%**	**7.7%**	**13.8%**

Baxter International Inc

A medical products manufacturer Baxter International is a leading producer of intravenous (IV) fluids and systems. It also makes infusion pumps pre-filled syringes biological sealants and inhaled anesthetics as well as dialyzers and other products for the treatment of end-stage renal disease (ESRD). In 2015 Baxter split its operations into two companies — one focused on biopharmaceuticals (Baxalta) and the other on medical products (Baxter).The company traces its roots back to 1931 when it was founded as an intravenous products maker.

HISTORY

Idaho surgeon Ralph Falk his brother Harry and California physician Donald Baxter formed Don Baxter Intravenous Products in 1931 to distribute the IV solutions Baxter made in Los Angeles. Two years later the company opened its first plant located outside Chicago. Ralph Falk bought Baxter's interest in 1935 and began R&D efforts leading to the first sterilized vacuum-type blood collection device (1939) which could store blood for weeks instead of hours. Product demand during WWII spurred sales above $1.5 million by 1945.

In 1949 the company created Travenol Laboratories to make and sell drugs. Baxter went public in 1951 and began an acquisition program the next year. In 1953 failing health caused both Falks to give control to William Graham a manager since 1945. Under Graham's leadership Baxter absorbed Wallerstein (1957); Fenwal Labs (1959); Flint Eaton (1959); and Dayton Flexible Products (1967).

In 1975 Baxter's headquarters moved to Deerfield Illinois. In 1978 the company debuted the first portable dialysis machine and had $1 billion in sales. Vernon Loucks Jr. became CEO two years later. Baxter claimed the title of the world's leading hospital supplier in 1985 when it bought American Hospital Supply (a Baxter distributor from 1932 to 1962). Offering more than 120000 products and an electronic system that connected customers with some 1500 vendors Baxter captured nearly 25% of the US hospital supply market in 1988. That year it became Baxter International.

In 1992 Baxter spun off Caremark (home infusion therapy and mail-order drugs) but kept a division that controlled 75% of the world's dialysis machine market.

In 1993 Baxter pleaded guilty (and was temporarily suspended from selling to the Veterans Administration) to bribing Syria to remove Baxter from a blacklist for trading in Israel.

The company entered the US cardiovascular perfusion services market in 1995 with the purchases of PSICOR and SETA. Baxter along with two other silicone breast-implant makers agreed to settle thousands of claims (at an average of $26000 each) from women suffering side-effects from the implants. The next year Baxter spun off its cost management and hospital supply business as Allegiance (sold to Cardinal Health in 1999).

Buys in 1997 boosted Baxter's presence in Europe and its share of the open-heart-surgery devices market. That year it agreed to pay about 20% of a $670 million legal settlement in a suit relating to hemophiliacs infected with HIV from blood products.

In response to concerns posed by shareholders Baxter in 1999 said it would phase out the use of PVC (polyvinyl chloride) in some products by 2010. In 2000 the firm spun off its underperforming cardiovascular unit as Edwards Lifesciences.

To strengthen core operations it lined up a number of purchases including North American Vaccine.

Purchases in 2001 included the cancer treatment unit of chemicals firm Degussa. Also that year Baxter withdrew dialysis equipment from Spain and Croatia after patients who used its products died. It also ended production of two types of dialyzers that were sold there. As the number of deaths mounted to more than 50 in seven countries Baxter began facing lawsuits; it later settled with the families of many of the patients. In September 2002 the FDA issued a warning when several patients died after using Baxter's Meridian dialysis machines. The same year Baxter bought Fusion Medical to expand its BioScience unit.

Robert L. Parkinson Jr. took over as chairman and CEO in April 2004. Parkinson succeeded Harry M. Jansen Kraemer Jr. William Graham who remained on the Baxter board of directors as honorary chairman emeritus after his official retirement in 1996 died in 2006.

In 2005 the FDA seized Baxter's existing inventories of previously recalled 6000 Colleague Volumetric Infusion Pumps and nearly 1000 Syndeo PCA Syringe Pumps; the federal agency resorted to these measures after the company did not fix production and design problems with the pumps in a suitable amount of time after batches of the product had been recalled earlier that year.

Baxter's product troubles didn't end there. In 2008 Baxter halted production of heparin after hundreds of bad reactions (including several deaths) occurred in patients using the drug. Subsequent investigations focused on raw heparin supplied to Baxter by a Chinese factory which apparently added a cheaper ingredient into the drug which contaminated it. Heparin-related litigation continued for Baxter in following years.

In 2009 the company acquired the hemofiltration (renal replacement therapy) product line of Edwards Lifesciences in a $65 million deal.

To meet increasing demand Baxter also expanded its infusion systems portfolio that year by entering an agreement to distribute medical device maker SIGMA's Spectrum large volume infusion pumps domestically and internationally. The deal also gave Baxter a 40% stake in the company (with the option to buy the rest) as well as access to future products under development. In 2012 Baxter exercised its right to buy and paid $90 million in cash for the remaining 60% of the company.

The addition of the Spectrum system was especially helpful when the FDA ordered the company to recall all of its Colleague infusion pumps in the US market in 2010. Patients were given the option of receiving Spectrum pumps to replace the Colleague systems.

As part of restructuring efforts in 2010 the company sold its noncore US generic injectables business to Hikma Pharmaceuticals for about $112 million. Baxter divested the business to focus on its proprietary injectable formulation and packaging operations. The sale also included Baxter's manufacturing facility in New Jersey and a warehouse and distribution center in Tennessee.

The company grew its BioScience operations in 2010 by acquiring all of the hemophilia-related assets from privately-held Archemix in a deal worth up to $315 million. Archemix has products under development including a synthetic hemophilia treatment to improve the body's blood clotting capabilities. Then to jump into the bone grafting market the company spent some $330 million to acquire UK-based ApaTech which sells bone grafting materials in the US and Europe; the deal gave Baxter manufacturing and research facilities in Germany the UK and the US.

EXECUTIVES

Corporate Vp And Cio, Paul E. Martin
Chairman And Ceo, José E. (Joe) Almeida, age 56, $1,300,000 total compensation
Corporate Vp Human Resources, Jeanne K. Mason, age 62, $540,192 total compensation
Corporate Vp And Cfo, James K. Saccaro, age 45, $644,415 total compensation
Corporate Vp And President Hospital Products, Brik V. Eyre, age 54, $618,533 total compensation
Corporate Vp And Chief Scientific Officer, Marcus Schabacker, age 54
Corporate Vp And President International, Paul Vibert, age 58
Corporate Vp And President Renal, Giuseppe Accogli, age 47, $514,028 total compensation
Vice President, Michael Baughman
Global Vice President Application Services, Michael Hamill
Vice President Marketing, Cindy Huey
Vice President Renal Information Technology, Frank Bolata
Vice President Of Treasurer, Scott Bohaboy
Associate Medical Director, Carol Schermer
Vice President Life Science And Operations, Halit Bander
Vice President Sales For National Accounts, Gregg Boyer
Medical Director Medical Device Safety Operations, Daniel Jacob
Vice President Human Resources, Mike Edicola
Vice President Talent Management, Irina Konstantinovsky
Vice President Talent Management, Steve King
Vice President Sales, Mike Canzoneri
Vice President Manufacturing And Supply, Timothy Lawrence
Corporate Vice President And Chief Scientific Officer, Norbert Riedel
Vice President Of Global Research And Development, Noel Barrett
Vice President Sales, Joe Pudlo
Corporate Vice President And Cio, Karenann Terrell
Vice President Finance, Patrick Marschall
Human Resources Vice President Latin America, Paulo Bolgar
Vice President Employee Services, Faye Katt
Vice President Biosurgery Research And Development, Russ Holscher
Vice President Operations Of And Strategy, Donna Kopera
Vice President Global Supply Chain Strategic Initiatives, Prabir Sen-Gupta
Assistant Vice President And Business Development Officer, Nicholas Evans
Corporate Vice President Human Resources, Jeannie K Mason
Vice President Marketing Strategy And Operations, Tom Progar
Vice President Research And Development And Quality Information Technology, Andrew Worley
Vice President Quality, Katherine Azuara
Vice President Manufacturing Oncology, Burkhard Wichert
Medical Director, Farah Ali
Vice President And Head Baxter Ventures, Anne Sissel
Vice President Corporate Audit, Kim Roll-Wallace
Area Vice President Strategic Accounts, Alan Mavis
Vice President Of Digital Innovation, Jonathan Handler
Vice President And Global Head Of Clinical Research Hematology, Anne Prener
Vice President Strategy Hospital Products, David H Roman
Vice President Global Engineering (baxter Global Operations), Bass William
Vice President Strategic Initiatives And Business Development, Jay Saccaro

Vice President Commercial It, Marc T'hart
Corporate Vice President And Treasurer, Robert J Hombach
Chairman And Ceo, José E. (Joe) Almeida, age 56
Corporate Vp And Cfo, James K. Saccaro, age 45
Board Member, Peter Hellman
Board Member, John Forsyth
Board Member, Michael Mahoney
Assistant Treasurer, Jeff Schaible
Board Member, Munib Islam
Auditors: PricewaterhouseCoopers LLP

LOCATIONS

HQ: Baxter International Inc
One Baxter Parkway, Deerfield, IL 60015
Phone: 224 948-2000   **Fax:** 847 948-2964
Web: www.baxter.com

2017 Sales

	$ mil.	% of total
US	4,510	42
Europe	2,731	26
Asia/Pacific	2,110	20
Latin America & Canada	1,210	12
Total	**10,561**	**100**

PRODUCTS/OPERATIONS

2017 Sales

	$ mil.	% of total
Renal	3,480	33
Medical delivery	2,698	26
Pharmaceuticals	1,883	18
Nutrition	882	8
Advanced surgery	707	7
Acute therapies	456	4
Others	455	4
Total	**10,561**	**100**

COMPETITORS

Becton Dickinson	Genzyme
CSL	Grifols
CSL Behring	Hospira
CareFusion	Kimberly-Clark Health
Fresenius Medical Care	Terumo

HISTORICAL FINANCIALS

Company Type: Public

Income Statement
FYE: December 31

	REVENUE ($ mil.)	NET INCOME ($ mil.)	NET PROFIT MARGIN	EMPLOYEES
12/17	10,561	717	6.8%	47,000
12/16	10,163	4,965	48.9%	48,000
12/15	9,968	968	9.7%	50,000
12/14	16,671	2,497	15.0%	66,000
12/13	15,259	2,012	13.2%	61,000
Annual Growth	(8.8%)	(22.7%)	—	(6.3%)

2017 Year-End Financials

Debt ratio: 20.52%   No. of shares (mil.): 541
Return on equity: 8.23%   Dividends
Cash ($ mil.): 3,394   Yield: 0.0%
Current ratio: 2.57   Payout: 47.2%
Long-term debt ($ mil.): 3,509   Market value ($ mil.): 35,001

	STOCK PRICE ($) FY Close	P/E High/Low		PER SHARE ($) Earnings	Dividends	Book Value
12/17	64.64	50	34	1.29	0.61	16.85
12/16	44.34	5	4	9.01	0.51	15.36
12/15	38.15	41	18	1.76	1.27	16.15
12/14	73.29	17	14	4.56	2.05	14.97
12/13	69.55	20	17	3.66	1.92	15.58
Annual Growth	(1.8%)	—	—	(22.9%)	(24.9%)	2.0%

BAYLOR SCOTT & WHITE HOLDINGS

EXECUTIVES

Exec Dir, Paul E Madeley
Director of External Digital C, Jacob Sloan
Vice President of Corporate Co, Jamie Rambo
Auditors: PRICEWATERHOUSECOOPERS LLP DA

LOCATIONS

HQ: BAYLOR SCOTT & WHITE HOLDINGS
    350 N SAINT PAUL ST # 2900, DALLAS, TX
    752014234
Phone: 214 820-3151
Web: WWW.BAYLORSCOTTANDWHITE.COM

HISTORICAL FINANCIALS

Company Type: Private

Income Statement   FYE: June 30

	REVENUE ($ mil.)	NET INCOME ($ mil.)	NET PROFIT MARGIN	EMPLOYEES
06/18	9,476	754	8.0%	1
06/17	9,084	630	6.9%	—
06/15	7,535	356	4.7%	—
Annual Growth	7.9%	28.4%	—	—

2018 Year-End Financials

Debt ratio: ——
Return on equity: 8.00%
Cash ($ mil.): 1,263
Current ratio: 1.20
Long-term debt ($ mil.): —

Dividends
Yield: —
Payout: —
Market value ($ mil.): —

BB&T Corp.

BB&T Corporation provides traditional banking insurance investment banking and wealth management services through more than 2100 bank branches across the South and Southeastern US. The holding company's flagship subsidiary Branch Banking and Trust (BB&T) is one of North Carolina's oldest banks and a leading originator of residential mortgages in the Southeast. The company also operates investment bank Scott & Stringfellow. Boasting assets of around $220 billion BB&T is one of the largest financial services holding companies in the US. In February 2019 BB&T agreed to merge with retail and commercial banking services company SunTrust Banks in a $66 billion deal.

Operations

In addition to standard services like deposits and loans BB&T also offers insurance mutual funds discount brokerage wealth management financial planning and business services such as leasing and venture capital.

As part of its business BB&T operates through six segments: Community Banking Residential Mortgage Banking Dealer Financial Services Specialized Lending Insurance Holdings and Financial Services.

More than 50% of the bank's total revenue comes from loan interest while just less than 10% comes from interest and dividend income on investments. Non-interest income accounts for the remaining and consists of insurance income (some 15% of total) service charges on deposits (over 5%) mortgage banking income (5%) investment banking and brokerage fees and commissions (5%) trust and investment advisory revenues (2%) and various other fee-related incomes.

Geographic Reach

North Carolina-based BB&T has US offices in Virginia Florida Georgia Maryland the Carolinas West Virginia Kentucky Alabama Tennessee Texas Pennsylvania New Jersey and Washington DC. Its largest markets are Virginia North Carolina and Florida each home to more than 300 bank branches.

Sales and Marketing

BB&T though its network of subsidiaries serves its target retail and commercial clients. BB&T's primary markets offer a diverse employment base and consist of manufacturing general services agriculture wholesale and retail trade technology government and financial services.

Financial Performance

In fiscal 2016 BB&T's revenue increased 12% to $11.5 billion amid strong increases in both interest and non-interest income. The acquisition of National Penn is the main factor behind the revenue increase.

Net income increased 17% to $2.3 billion due to higher revenue and higher yields on loans and an improved funding mix.

Cash from operations fell 40% to $1.2 billion as higher net income was offset by net changes in loans held for sale.

Strategy

BB&T has in recent years been following a long-term strategy of growing its branch network reach and diversifying its revenue streams through strategic bank acquisition. In 2016 the company acquired two banks: National Penn a Pennsylvanian retail and commercial bank with 126 offices; and CGSC America Holdings Corporation. It has also recently acquired more than 60 branches in Texas from Citibank at the time doubling BB&T's branch size in the state and adding more than $200 million worth new loan business and $6.3 billion in new deposits.

The company has been carrying out layoffs as its consolidates the acquired businesses. The former Susquehanna Bank (acquired in 2015) call center was shut down in 2017 for the loss of 82 jobs; the remaining staff have been relocated to other offices. It has made other branch closures too as the viability of branches is eroded by the rise of internet banking which is also the cheaper option for bank.

Mergers and Acquisitions

In February 2019 BB&T agreed to merge with SunTrust Banks a retail and commercial banking services company with some 1300 offices primarily in Florida Georgia Virginia North Carolina Tennessee Maryland South Carolina and Washington DC. The all-stock deal is valued at $66 billion. SunTrust's middle market corporate and investment banking business and digital consumer lending platform will complement BB&T's community banking and insurance operations. With about $301 billion in loans the combined company will be the sixth largest US bank based on assets of around $442 billion and deposits of roughly $324 billion. A new name and brand for the company will be determined prior to the deal's close. BB&T shareholders will have a 57% stake in the combined company while SunTrust investors will receive 43%.

HISTORY

In 1872 Alpheus Branch son of a wealthy planter founded Branch and Company a mercantile business in Wilson North Carolina. He and Thomas Jefferson Hadley who was organizing a public school system created the Branch and Hadley bank later that same year. The private bank helped rebuild farms and small businesses after the Civil War.

In 1887 Branch bought out Hadley and changed the bank's name to Branch and Company Bankers. Two years later Branch secured a state trust charter for the Wilson Banking and Trust Company. He never got the business running however and died in 1893. The trust charter was amended to change the name to Branch Banking and Company and Branch and Company Bankers was folded into it in 1900.

In 1907 the bank finally got its trust operations running and began calling itself Branch Banking and Trust Company. In 1922 it opened its first insurance department; the next year it started its mortgage loan activities.

BB&T survived the 1929 stock market crash with the help of the Post Office. Nervous customers withdrew their funds from BB&T and other banks and deposited them in postal savings accounts unaware that BB&T was the local Post Office's bank and the withdrawn funds went right back to the bank. BB&T opened six more branches between 1929 and 1933.

After WWII consumerism skyrocketed resulting in more car loans and mortgages. During the 1960s and 1970s the bank embarked on a series of mergers and acquisitions forming the thin end of a buying wedge that would widen significantly in the coming decades.

By 1994 BB&T was the fourth-largest bank in North Carolina. In 1995 it merged with North Carolina's fifth-largest bank Southern National Corp. founded in 1897.

With banking regulations loosening to allow different types of operations BB&T in 1997 made several acquisitions including banks thrifts and securities brokerage Craigie.

BB&T's 1998 activities included three bank acquisitions that pushed it into metro Washington DC. The company also increased holdings in fields such as insurance sales venture capital for Southern businesses and investment banking (through its acquisition of Scott & Stringfellow Financial the South's oldest NYSE member).

In 1999 Craigie was melded into Scott & Stringfellow. That year BB&T bought several insurance companies and small banks. The company continued its march through the South the following year buying several Georgia banks and Tennessee's BankFirst. In 2001 BB&T purchased South Carolina's FirstSpartan Financial multibank holding company Century South Banks Maryland-based FCNB Corporation and western Georgia's Community First Banking Company. To bolster its presence in the Washington DC market it bought Virginia Capital Bancshares and F&M National.

BB&T purchased Alabama-based Cooney Rikard & Curtin a wholesale insurance broker active in 45 states in 2002. Also that year it added about 100 branches in Kentucky after buying MidAmerica Bancorp and AREA Bancshares and entered the coveted Florida market following its purchase of Regional Financial the privately held parent of First South Bank.

Acquisitions continued the following three years as the bank swallowed First Virginia Banks among other targets. It took a break in 2005 to assimilate its holdings before joining the acquisition hunt in 2006 with deals for banks in Georgia (Main Street B

EXECUTIVES

Chairman And Ceo, Kelly S. King, age 69, $1,075,000 total compensation

President And Coo Bb&t Corporation And Branch Banking & Trust Company, Christopher L. (Chris) Henson, age 56, $700,000 total compensation

Sevp And Manager Risk Management, Barbara F. Duck, age 51, $507,083 total compensation

Sevp And Deposit Services Manager, Donna C. Goodrich, age 55, $507,083 total compensation

Sevp And Chief Risk Officer, Clarke R. Starnes, age 59, $582,500 total compensation

Sevp And Cfo, Daryl N. Bible, age 56, $590,000 total compensation

Sevp And President Community Banking, David H. Weaver, age 52

Sevp General Counsel Secretary And Chief Corporate Governance Officer, Robert J. Johnson, age 45

Sevp President And Ceo Bb&t Securities Llc And Capital Markets Manager, W. Rufus Yates, age 60

President West Florida Region, Jim Daly, age 57

Sevp And Chief Digital Officer, W. Bennett Bradley, age 56

Sevp And Lending Group Manager, Brant J. Standridge, age 42

Sevp And Chief Client Experience Officer, Dont L. Wilson, age 41

Sevp And Deputy Chief Risk Officer, Jim D. Godwin, age 49

Vice President Dealer Finance Relationship Manager, Paul Johnson

Vice President, Cindy Powell

Senior Vice President Wealth Management Team Direc, Craig Frye

Senior Vice President, Ann Hardison

Vice President And Manager Is Section Bbandt Corporation, Bill Colon

Vice President Information Technology Strategy, Craig Moss

Vice President, Debrah More

Wealth Advisor Vice President, Tommy Rhyne

Vice President Bbandt Insurance, Ben Manning

Assistant Vice President, Libby Slaton

Assistant Vice President Financial Center Leader Hablo Espaiiol, Gil Rolon

Executive Vice President Chief Market And Liquidity Risk Officer, Steve Buisson

Vice President Sales And Service Leader, Kim Allen

Vice President, Karen Starnes

Vice President Personal Trust Specialist, Kim Lamm

Senior Vice President Credit Risk Review Team Leader, Nancy Ortkiese

Senior Vice President Senior Credit Officer, Thomas Findlay

Vice President, Scott Fisher

Vice President Regional Payments Consultant, Brenda Hudnall

Assistant Vice President, Steve Eng

Vice President Dealer Finance, Mark Cloyd

Svp And Market President Greensboro Winston Salem North Carolina Area, Jack Lynch

Vice President Regional Multicultural Banking Officer, David Ramos

Vice President Of Real Estate Acquisition, Brenda Shamloo

Senior Vice President Senior Credit Officer, Scott Carpenter

Senior Vice President, Bryan Thomas

Vice President Private Advisor, Haivyl Lopez

Vice President, Scott Snedeker

Vice President, Brian Westcott

Vice President, Lorie Garland

Vice President, Scott Snow

Senior Vice President And Chief Administrative Office Bb And T Commercial Finance, Neal Harm

Assistant Vice President, Paul McManus

Vice President, Abdul Labi

Residential Real Estate Lending Vice President, Keri Jackson

Wealth Management Vice President, Cole Benoit

Senior Vice President, Len Lewan

Vice President Customer Credit Manager, Michael Catapano

Financial Center Leader Assistant Vice President, Mike Maxwell

Executive Vice President, Tol Broome

Vice President Employee Benefits Agent, Will Stewart

Vice President, Steve Paulk

Vice President, Christopher Pearce

Vice President Financial Center Leader, Michelle Haines

Senior Vice President, Mildred Henry

Vice President, John Kincaid

Vice President, Theresa Arrighi

Vice President Channel Manager Direct Retail Lending, Steve Picard

Vice President, Kelly Fallen

Vice President, Jennifer Weaver

Vice President, Steve Jordan

Vice President Surety, Peter Holley

Electronic Delivery Channel Strategist Vice President, Ken Nixon

Vice President Mortgage Loan Officer, Vincent Spadea

Vice President, Abner Lowry

Assistant Vice President Information Technology Resource, Jill Deanhardt

Assistant Vice President Project Manager, Sharon McMichael

Team Lead Vice President, Monte Wheeler

Vice President Employee Benefits, Robert Davis

Vice President Operations, Kelly Ferguson

Vice President, Barbara McAllister

Vice President Enterprise Data Governance Bbandt Corporation, Jan England

Vice President, Jeffrey Hollon

Vice President, Doug Moore

Vice President, Allen Phinney

Vice President, Becky Barefoot

Vice President Major Accounts Division, William Glass

Vice President Fraud Technology Manager, Mark Steeber

Vice President, Sandra Braswell

Vice President, Jacqueline Bristor

Vice President, Vernon Brown

Senior Vice President, Adam Ogburn

Vice President It, Jim Ray

Senior Vice President Bb And T Capital Markets, Jim Hill

Senior Vice President, Randy McGann

Vice President, Diane Lyles

Commercial Banker Assistant Vice President, Patrick Poynor

Senior Vice President, Don Beam

Senior Vice President, David Wojdyla

Vice President, Pamela Watson

Vice President, Naomi Chizmar

Assistant Vice President Business Services Officer Portfolio Manager Team Leader, Shawn Millet

Retail Services Officer Vice President, Deana Cheek

Vice President Management Devt Program Human Systems, Pam Angle

Assistant Vice President, Francisco Guerrero

Vice President, Will Pierce

Vice President, Debbie Venanzio

Assistant Vice President, Deborah Richendollar

Vice President, Kathy Dunsmore

Vice President, John Settin

Senior Vice President, Stan Crawford

Senior Vice President, Bruce Sharp

Senior Vice President, James Ellison

Assistant Vice President It Problem Management Team Lead, Bobby Davenport

Senior Vice President Insurance Services Administration, Lori Herring

Assistant Vice President Information Technology Strategic Planning And Operations, Bill Schirf

Senior Vice President Comm'l Fin Loan Admin Manager, John Davis

Assistant Vice Presidentbusiness Deposit Officer, Vanessa Courtois

Vice President, Jeffrey Clemons

Assistant Vice President, John McGarvey

Assistant Vice President And Sales Consultant, Annette Shamblin

Vice President Business Insurance Agent, Scott Burns

Vice President Assistant General Counsel, William Conger

Senior Vice President, Liz Brown

Vice President Risk Control Consultant, Michelle Barker

Senior Vice President Agency Manager, Ed White

Vice President It Operations, Mark Freeman

Bb And T Assistant Vice President, Willie Karnes

Senior Vice President, David Wojdyla

Senior Vice President, Doug Smith

Vice President Enterprise Application Architecture, James Rakshys

Vice President, Tonya Vickers

Vice President, Darcee Neal

Senior Vice President Business Services, Shane Spray

Vice President Regional Operations Manager, Sondra Tustin

Senior Vice President, Jim Citrano

Vice President, John Lavin

Assistant Vice President Senior Marketing Specialist, Pam Taylor

Associate Vice President, Peter Zhang

Assistant Vice President, Pam McCoy

Vice President Wealth Team, Robin Thomas

Senior Vice President Private Regional Director, Margaret Larson

Vice President Senior Financial Analyst, Kristina Hodges

Executive Vice President And Director Financial Crimes Program, Richard Small

Senior Vice President Corporate Banker Capital Markets, Sandy Centa

Vice President, Wayne Barber

Senior Vice President Regional Corporate Banking Manager, Dan Summerford

Assistant Vice President Market Leader Iii, Esteban Calle

Senior Vice President, Ronald Barley

Vice President Information Technology Solutions Architect, Michael Moore

Assistant Vice President Risk Control Analyst, Cindy Hellmann

Auditors: PricewaterhouseCoopers LLP

LOCATIONS

HQ: BB&T Corp.
  200 West Second Street, Winston-Salem, NC 27101
Phone: 336 733-2000   **Fax:** 336 671-2399
Web: www.bbt.com

2017 sales

	No.
North Carolina	328
Virginia	319
Florida	298
Pennsylvania	246
Maryland	158
Georgia	144
Texas	117
South Carolina	102
Kentucky	99
Alabama	77
West Virginia	68
Tennessee	46
New Jersey	30
Washington D.C.	12
Total	**2,044**

PRODUCTS/OPERATIONS

2017 Sales

	$ mil.	% of total
Interest Income:		
Interest & fees on loans & leases	6,230	51
Interest & dividends on securities	1,092	9
Interest on other earning assets	52	1
Non-interest income:		
Insurance income	1,754	15
Service charges on deposits	706	6
Mortgage banking income	415	3
Investment banking & brokerage fees & commissions	410	3
Trust & investment advisory	278	2
Bankcard fees & merchant discounts	271	2
Checkcard fees	214	2
Operating lease income	146	1
Income from bank-owned life insurance	122	1
FDIC loss share income net - -		
Other income	467	4
Securities gains (losses) net	(1)	-
Total	**12,156**	**100**

Selected Services

Commercial
  Asset management
  Association services
  Capital markets services
  Commercial deposit services
  Commercial finance
  Commercial middle market lending
  Commercial mortgage lending
  Institutional trust services
  Insurance
  Insurance premium finance
  International banking services
  Leasing
  Merchant services
  Payment solutions
  Private equity investments
  Real estate lending
  Supply chain management
Retail
  Asset management
  Automobile lending
  Bankcard lending
  Consumer finance
  Home equity lending
  Insurance
  Investment brokerage services
  Mobile/online banking
  Payment solutions
  Retail deposit services
  Sales finance
  Small business lending
  Wealth management/private banking

Selected Subsidiaries & Affiliates

American Coastal Insurance Company
BB&T Equipment Finance Corporation
BB&T Financial FSB
  Sheffield Financial
BB&T Insurance Services Inc.
BB&T Investment Services Inc.
BB&T Securities LLC
Branch Banking and Trust Company
Clearview Correspondent Services
CRC Insurance Services
Grandbridge Real Estate Capital LLC
Lendmark Financial Services Inc.
McGriff Seibels & Williams Inc.
MidAmerica Gift Certificate Company
Prime Rate Premium Finance Corporation Inc.
  AFCO Credit Corporation
Regional Acceptance Corporation
Stanley Hunt DuPree & Rhine Inc.
Sterling Capital Management LLC

COMPETITORS

Bank of America	PNC Financial
Capital One	Regions Financial
Fifth Third	SunTrust
First Citizens	Synovus
BancShares	United Bankshares
First Horizon	Wells Fargo
JPMorgan Chase	

HISTORICAL FINANCIALS

Company Type: Public

Income Statement
FYE: December 31

	ASSETS ($ mil.)	NET INCOME ($ mil.)	INCOME AS % OF ASSETS	EMPLOYEES
12/17	221,642	2,394	1.1%	36,484
12/16	219,276	2,426	1.1%	37,500
12/15	209,947	2,084	1.0%	37,200
12/14	186,814	2,151	1.2%	33,400
12/13	183,010	1,679	0.9%	33,700
Annual Growth	4.9%	9.3%	—	2.0%

2017 Year-End Financials

Debt ratio: 9.55%
Return on equity: 8.04%
Cash ($ mil.): 3,083
Current ratio: —
Long-term debt ($ mil.): —
No. of shares (mil.): 782
Dividends
  Yield: 0.0%
  Payout: 45.9%
Market value ($ mil.): 38,881

	STOCK PRICE ($) FY Close	P/E High/Low	PER SHARE ($) Earnings	Dividends	Book Value
12/17	49.72	18 15	2.74	1.26	37.91
12/16	47.02	17 11	2.77	1.15	36.91
12/15	37.81	16 13	2.56	1.05	34.99
12/14	38.89	15 13	2.75	0.95	33.77
12/13	37.32	17 13	2.19	1.12	32.21
Annual Growth	7.4%	— —	5.8%	3.0%	4.2%

BCB Bancorp Inc

EXECUTIVES

Chb, Mark D Hogan
RES-Ceo, Thomas M Coughlin
Cfo, Thomas P Keating
V Pres-Gen Counsel, John J Brogan
Evp-Coo, Michael Lesler
Auditors: Wolf & Company, P.C.

LOCATIONS

HQ: BCB Bancorp Inc
  104-110 Avenue C, Bayonne, NJ 07002
Phone: 201 823-0700
Web: www.bcbcommunitybank.com

COMPETITORS

Bank of America	PNC Financial
City National	Provident Financial
Bancshares	Services
Hudson City Bancorp	Sterling Bank
Meridian Capital Group	Stewardship Financial
New York Community	
Bancorp	

HISTORICAL FINANCIALS

Company Type: Public

Income Statement
FYE: December 31

	ASSETS ($ mil.)	NET INCOME ($ mil.)	INCOME AS % OF ASSETS	EMPLOYEES
12/17	1,942	9	0.5%	314
12/16	1,708	8	0.5%	353
12/15	1,618	7	0.4%	331
12/14	1,301	7	0.6%	327
12/13	1,207	9	0.8%	249
Annual Growth	12.6%	1.5%	—	6.0%

2017 Year-End Financials

Debt ratio: 0.21%
Return on equity: 6.49%
Cash ($ mil.): 124
Current ratio: —
Long-term debt ($ mil.): —
No. of shares (mil.): 15
Dividends
  Yield: 0.0%
  Payout: 74.6%
Market value ($ mil.): 218

	STOCK PRICE ($) FY Close	P/E High/Low	PER SHARE ($) Earnings	Dividends	Book Value
12/17	14.50	22 16	0.75	0.56	11.73
12/16	13.00	21 16	0.63	0.56	11.63
12/15	10.40	18 14	0.69	0.56	11.91
12/14	11.73	17 14	0.81	0.54	12.18
12/13	13.45	14 8	1.06	0.48	12.01
Annual Growth	1.9%	— —	(8.3%)	3.9%	(0.6%)

Beacon Roofing Supply Inc

Not all products from Beacon Roofing Supply (BRS) are to be placed over your head. Along with roofing products Beacon distributes complementary building materials such as siding windows and waterproofing systems. One of North America's largest roofing materials distributors the company operates some 40 regional companies with 590 branches in the 50 US states and six Canadian provinces. BRS carries more than 90000 stock keeping units (SKUs) available for about 100000 customers. The company's customers include contractors home builders building owners and other resellers. Most of BRS's business involves reroofing existing homes because of age or weather damage.

Operations

Operating through one reportable segment BRS is focused on the wholesale distribution of building materials.

As the result of past purchases and its rapid growth rate acquisitive BRS operates its business under some 40 trade names. Its subsidiaries include Beacon Canada Beacon Roofing Supply Canada and Beacon Sales Acquisition. The residential and nonresidential roofing products BRS supplies to its customer base are sourced from companies such as Carlisle Johns Manville Malarkey Mid-States Asphalt and Owens Corning among others.

It caters to customers through 590 branch offices and a distribution infrastructure that has the capacity to make 2 million deliveries a year supported by a company-owned fleet of 2300 straight trucks 800 tractors and 1350 trailers. Typically each branch delivers roofing materials to customers within a two-hour radius; deliveries are made five days a week.

Residential roofing products comprise 45% of BRS' sales; nonresidential roofing products 25%; and siding waterproofing systems windows and other exterior building products 30%.

Geographic Reach

BRS enjoys a broad reach across the US serving mostly metropolitan areas in the 50 US states as well as half a dozen Canadian provinces. About 97% of the company's sales are in the US with the rest in Canada.

Sales and Marketing

BRS's customer base has grown to about 100000 home builders building owners resellers and contractors. The company's customers vary by end market with relatively small contractors in the residential market and small to large-sized contractors in the non-residential market.

BRS markets its products via its sales force newsletters direct mail social media and the internet.

Financial Performance

BRS has seen an upward trend in revenue over the last seven years.

In 2018 (ended September) sales jumped about 47% to $6.4 billion from 2017. While robust the increase was less than the 64% revenue jump in 2017 from 2016. A 400% increase in acquired market sales with a strong push from the Allied acquisition drove the overall growth of BRS's revenue in 2018 with existing market sales rising less than 1% year-to-year. Existing market sales suffered from comparison with previous years when more storm damage occurred. However the company saw higher selling prices across the company's major product lines and greater average sales volume for its complementary products. It also reported high demand in Florida and Texas following hurricanes Irma and Harvey.

BRS's net income slipped to $98.6 million in 2018 about $2.3 million less than the 2017 total of $100.9 million.

The company's cash rose to $138 million in 2018 from about $31 million in 2017. In 2018 operations generated $315 million while investing activities used $167 million and financing activities used about $40 million.

Strategy

Looking to increase its market share as one of the nation's top roofing materials distribution companies BRS is keenly focused on adding new names to its portfolio as it works to boost its bottom line. Acquisitions have been a key part of BRS's growth story. Since 2004 when it became a public company BRS has made nearly 50 acquisitions opened more than 80 new branches and broadened the scope of its product lines. In just 2018 the company acquired 215 branches and opened 3 new branches.

BRS made one of its biggest deals in 2018 buying Allied Building Products Corp. for about $2.9 billion. Allied distributed products from some 210 locations in more than 30 states. It had a strong presence in the populous states of New York New Jersey Florida and California as well as Hawaii and the upper Midwest.

Besides acquisitions BRS opens new operations in locations it doesn't serve with plans to open 10-15 branches in 2019. The new stores could focus on waterproofing insulation or interiors as well as roofing.

The company has expanded its online sales channels deploying technology to help contractors and consumers make purchases. BRS's Beacon Pro+ e-commerce portal introduced in 2017 enables online ordering and real time pricing and the capabilities to request and approve quotes and pay bills online. In 2018 the company rolled out Beacon 3D+ an application that allows residential customers to use their smartphone photos to generate a 3D models.

Mergers and Acquisitions

BRS acquired Allied Building Products Corp. for about $2.9 billion in 2018 adding significant geographic coverage in the US. Headquartered in East Rutherford New Jersey Allied was one of the country's largest exterior and interior building products distributors with some 210 locations in about 30 states in the US. Its major markets were New York New Jersey Florida California Hawaii and the upper Midwest.

Also in 2018 BRS acquired Tri-State Builder's Supply in Duluth Minnesota and Atlas Supply Inc. in the Pacific Northwest.

Company Background

BRS was started in 1928 in Charlestown Massachusetts one of the first distributors of commercial roofing materials in New England. In 1953 the company expanded its operations to a larger facility in Somerville and to Worcester and Lewiston Maine in the 1970s.

HISTORY

In 2014 BRS acquired All Weather Products Ltd. a distributor of residential roofing systems and related accessories with three branches in Canada; it also acquired Dallas-based Wholesale Roofing Supply a distributor of residential roofing materials.

In 2013 BRS relocated its corporate headquarters from Peabody Massachusetts to Herndon Virginia.

Adding to its roofing business the company in late 2012 acquired Pittsburgh-based McClure-Johnston Co. a distributor of residential and commercial roofing products; Ford Wholesale Co. of San Jose a distributor of residential and commercial roofing and related accessories; and Construction Materials Supply a distributor of mostly residential roofing products across Northern California.

The company bought Missouri-based Contractors Roofing & Supply Co. for about $14 million in 2012 as well as Southern California distributor Structural Materials which specializes in residential and commercial roofing products and operates six locations. It has also purchased Cassady Pierce a Pennsylvania-based distributor of roofing products for residential and commercial uses that logs some $52 million in sales each year. The deal gave BRS half a dozen locations in the Pittsburgh area. Concentrating on Canada BRS in 2011 acquired roofing distributor Enercon Products. With six locations in Western Canada Enercon extends from Edmonton to Vancouver giving BRS a presence in every major Canadian market.

BRS was formed in 1997 when investment firm Code Hennessy & Simmons acquired a controlling interest in Beacon Sales a commercial roofer founded in 1928.

EXECUTIVES

Vice President Of Sales And Marketing, John Massarelli

President And Ceo, Paul M. Isabella, age 62, $640,385 total compensation

Evp And Cfo, Joseph M. Nowicki, age 56, $440,419 total compensation

Evp Sales And Marketing, Jeff Willis

Evp North Division And Engineering, James I. MacKimm

Evp Acquisitions Operational Improvements Fleet And Safety; President Canada, John C. (Jack) Smith

Vp And Cio, Christopher (Chris) Nelson

Evp General Counsel And Secretary, Ross D. Cooper, age 53, $421,289 total compensation

Evp South Division, C. Munroe Best
Evp West Division, Kent C. Gardner
Evp East Division, C. Eric Swank
Evp And Chief Supply Chain Officer, Brendan P. Daly
Evp And Chief Human Resources Officer, Christopher Harrison
Vice President And Cio, Chris Nelson
Vice President Finance South Division, Rick Kosek
Executive Vice President, Munroe Best
Executive Vice President East Division, Eric Swank
Vice President, Scott Wade
Vice President, Bill Sarvis
Vice President Sales, Tommy Thompson
Vice President Human Resources West Division, David Chandler
Chairman, Robert R. Buck, age 70
Auditors: Ernst & Young LLP

LOCATIONS

HQ: Beacon Roofing Supply Inc
505 Huntmar Park Drive, Suite 300, Herndon, VA 20170
Phone: 571 323-3939
Web: www.becn.com

2018 Sales

	$ mil.	% of total
Net sales		
US	6,239	97
Canada	179	3
Total	**6,418**	**100**

PRODUCTS/OPERATIONS

2018 Sales

	$ mil.	% of total
Residential roofing products	2,799	44
Non-residential roofing products	1,636	25
Complementary building products	1,983	31
Total	**6,418**	**100**

Selected Trade Names

Alabama Roofing Supply
Beacon Roofing Supply Canada Company
Beacon Sales Company
Best Distributing Company
Coastal Metal Service
Dealer's Choice
Enercon Products
Entrepot de la Toiture
Fowler & Peth
GLACO
Groupe Bedard
JGA Beacon
Lafayette Wood Works
Louisiana Roofing Supply
Mississippi Roofing Supply
North Coast Commercial Roofing Systems
Pacific Supply Company
Posi-Slope
Posi-Pentes
Quality Roofing Supply Company
The Roof Center
Roof Depot
Roofing and Sheet Metal Supply
RSM Supply
Shelter Distribution
Southern Roof Center
West End Lumber Company
West End Roofing Siding and Windows
Wholesale Roofing Supply
Residential roofing products
Asphalt shingles
Clay tile
Concrete tile
Felt
Gutters and downspouts
Metal edgings and flashings
Metal roofing
Nail base insulation
Nails and fasteners
Prefabricated flashings
Slate

Synthetic slate and tile
Ridges and soffit vents
Wood shingles and shakes
Non-residential roofing products
Asphalt
Built-up roofing
Cements and coatings
Commercial fasteners
Insulation—flat stock and tapered
Metal
Metal edges and flashings
Modified bitumen
Single-ply roofing
Skylights smoke vents and roof hatches
Complementary building products
Doors windows and millwork
Residential insulation
Vinyl siding
Waterproofing systems
Wood and fiber cement siding

COMPETITORS

84 Lumber
ABC Supply
BMC Stock
Do it Best
F.W. Webb
Guardian Building Products Distribution
HD Supply
Lowe's
PrimeSource Building
Sutherland Lumber

HISTORICAL FINANCIALS

Company Type: Public

Income Statement				FYE: September 30
	REVENUE ($ mil.)	NET INCOME ($ mil.)	NET PROFIT MARGIN	EMPLOYEES
09/18	6,418	98	1.5%	8,356
09/17	4,376	100	2.3%	5,406
09/16	4,127	89	2.2%	5,042
09/15	2,515	62	2.5%	3,366
09/14	2,326	53	2.3%	3,179
Annual Growth	28.9%	16.3%	—	27.3%

2018 Year-End Financials

Debt ratio: 40.26%
Return on equity: 4.85%
Cash ($ mil.): 129
Current ratio: 1.59
Long-term debt ($ mil.): 2,600

No. of shares (mil.): 68
Dividends
Yield: —
Payout: —
Market value ($ mil.): 2,466

	STOCK PRICE ($) FY Close	P/E High/Low	PER SHARE ($) Earnings	Dividends	Book Value
09/18	36.19	62 33	1.05	0.00	33.51
09/17	51.25	31 24	1.64	0.00	26.32
09/16	42.07	32 22	1.49	0.00	22.10
09/15	32.49	29 18	1.24	0.00	17.74
09/14	25.48	38 23	1.08	0.00	16.54
Annual Growth	9.2%	— —	(0.7%)	—	19.3%

Becton, Dickinson & Co

Don't worry you'll only feel a slight prick if Becton Dickinson (BD) is at work. The company's BD Medical segment is one of the top global manufacturers of syringes and other injection and infusion devices. BD Medical also makes IV catheters and syringes pre-fillable drug delivery systems self-injection devices for diabetes patients and related supplies such as anesthesia trays and sharps disposal systems. The BD Life Sciences segment makes products for the safe collection and transportation of diagnostic specimens; it also makes instruments and reagent systems that detect cancers infectious diseases and health care associated infections (HAIs). BD Interventional provides vascular urology oncology and surgical specialty products.

Operations

BD operates through three reportable segments: BD Medical (more than half of total revenue) BD Life Sciences (more than 25% of revenue) and BD Interventional (some 20% of revenue).

BD Medical specializes in the manufacturing of syringes catheters and injection devices. Sales of its safety devices have experienced growth in recent years especially in international markets. Other products include pre-filled syringes and diabetic pen needles.

BD Life Sciences operates in three key areas: pre-analytical systems diagnostic systems and biosciences. Its products include safety-engineered equipment for the collection of blood automated diagnostic platforms and cell analysis equipment.

BD Interventional also operates in three key areas: surgery peripheral intervention and urology and critical care. That segment's products include catheters stents and grafts.

Geographic Reach

BD has manufacturing marketing and warehousing operations in about 50 countries in the US; Europe the Middle East and Africa (EMEA); Greater Asia; Latin America; and Canada.

Though the company is working to increase international sales (especially in emerging markets) the US remains its largest segment accounting for about 55% of sales. The EMEA is BD's second-largest operating region accounting for about 20% of revenue. Asia brings in some 15% of revenue.

Sales and Marketing

BD's customers include entities in health care (including hospitals and pharmacies) drug development medical research (including academic and government labs) clinical research (such as reference labs and blood banks) and agricultural or food analysis. The company uses a direct sales force and independent representatives to market and distribute its products in the US and abroad. In the US products are sold primarily to distributors who then resell to end-users.

Financial Performance

With the exception of fiscal 2017 (ended September) BD's revenue has been climbing for the past few years. Growth has been driven by acquisitions of other companies including C. R. Bard purchased in late 2017. Net income on the other hand has been quite volatile especially as operating expenses have risen.

In fiscal 2018 revenue increased 32% to $16 billion thanks largely to the acquisition of Bard. Overall product sales increased 6% that year; all the BD Medical segment's units saw growth — especially the medication delivery business which had a 30% sales increase. Additionally the BD Life Sciences segment had higher sales in all three of its businesses (especially the diagnostic systems unit which grew 12%).

Despite the higher revenue net income fell 85% to $159 million in fiscal 2018. Operating costs and expenses increased 36% and the company's $862 million income tax provision further cut into the bottom line.

The company ended fiscal 2018 with $1.1 billion in net cash some $13.2 billion less than it had at the end of fiscal 2017. Operating activities provided $2.9 billion while investing activities (business acquisitions primarily) used $15.8 billion and financing activities used another $58 million.

Strategy

BD's growth strategies include focusing on its core lines of products developing platform extensions and new types of products acquiring companies to supplement organic growth and expanding further into emerging markets all while improving the effectiveness of its operations. Its disease management focus is centered on conditions including diabetes women's health and cancer and infectious disease. The company continually invests in research and development; it spent $1 billion on R&D in 2018 compared to $774 million in 2017.

Through the BD Medical segment BD has been cashing in on the increased emphasis on safety in health care delivery by introducing a number of safety-engineered devices that prevent accidental needle sticks (and thus exposure to infected blood). BD Life Sciences is doing the same growing through sales of its safety-engineered blood collection equipment including the BD Vacutainer system.

In addition to improving safety BD is working to improve drug delivery methods increasing the speed of disease diagnosis and advancing pharmaceutical research techniques. The company supplements its internal R&D programs by forming partnerships and conducting acquisitions.

BD has also divested non-core operations in recent years to focus its resources on its faster-growing operations. In 2018 the company sold its Advanced Bioprocessing business to Thermo Fisher Scientific. The sale should help its Life Sciences segment focus more on disease and therapy research and clinical diagnostics. Also that year the company sold French subsidiary Cardial (vascular grafts valvulotomes and surgical glue) to LeMaitre Vascular for $2 million.

After a 2018 recall of BD syringes the FDA released a warning letter to the company for failing to prevent equipment contamination at its Franklin Wisconsin manufacturing plant.

Mergers and Acquisitions

In mid-2018 BD acquired TVA Medical which develops minimally invasive vascular access products for patients with chronic kidney disease requiring hemodialysis.

BD made a big splash when it acquired US peer C. R. Bard for some $25 billion in late 2017. That purchase strengthened BD's oncology and surgery device portfolios as the company continues to expand beyond its diabetes care operations. Most of Bard's products were added to the BD Interventional operating segment. BD sold its global core needle biopsy devices business as well as a tissue market product under development as a condition for the deal.

Company Background

Maxwell Becton and Fairleigh Dickinson established medical supply firm Becton Dickinson and Company in New York in 1897. In 1907 the company moved to New Jersey and became one of the first US firms to make hypodermic needles.

During WWI Becton Dickinson (BD) made all-glass syringes and introduced the cotton elastic bandage. After the war its researchers designed an improved stethoscope and created specialized hypodermic needles.

After the deaths of Dickinson (1948) and Becton (1951) their respective sons Fairleigh Jr. and Henry took over. BD went public in 1963 to raise money for new expansion.

HISTORY

Maxwell Becton and Fairleigh Dickinson established a medical supply firm in New York in 1897. In 1907 the company moved to New Jersey and became one of the first US firms to make hypodermic needles.

During WWI Becton Dickinson (BD) made all-glass syringes and introduced the cotton elastic bandage. After the war its researchers designed an improved stethoscope and created specialized hypodermic needles. The company supplied medical equipment to the armed forces during WWII. Becton and Dickinson helped establish Fairleigh Dickinson Junior College (now Fairleigh Dickinson University) in 1942. The company continued to develop products such as the Vacutainer blood-collection apparatus its first medical laboratory aid.

After the deaths of Dickinson (1948) and Becton (1951) their respective sons Fairleigh Jr. and Henry took over. The company introduced disposable hypodermic syringes in 1961. BD went public in 1963 to raise money for new expansion. In the 1960s the company opened plants in Brazil Canada France and Ireland and climbed aboard the conglomeration bandwagon by diversifying into such businesses as industrial gloves (Edmont 1966) and computer systems (Spear 1968). BD also went on a major acquisition spree in its core fields during the 1960s and 1970s buying more than 25 medical supply testing and lab companies by 1980.

Wesley Howe successor to Fairleigh Dickinson Jr. expanded the company's foreign sales in the 1970s. Howe thwarted a takeover by the diversifying oil giant Sun Company (now Sunoco) in 1978 and began to sell BD's non-medical businesses in 1983 ending with the 1989 sale of Edmont. Acquisitions including Deseret Medical (IV catheters surgical gloves and masks; 1986) sharpened BD's focus on medical and surgical supplies.

In the 1990s BD formed a number of alliances and ventures including a 1991 agreement to make and market Baxter International's InterLink needleless injection system which reduces the risk of accidental needle sticks and a 1993 joint venture with NeXagen (now part of Gilead Sciences) to make and market in vitro diagnostics. As tuberculosis reemerged in the US as a serious health threat the firm improved its TB-detection and drug-resistance test systems which cut testing time from as much as seven weeks to less than two.

In 1996 BD introduced GlucoWatch (a glucose monitoring device developed by Cygnus) and acquired the diagnostic business and brand name of MicroProbe (now Epoch Pharmaceuticals).

Previously known on Wall Street as a homely company that focused on cutting costs BD changed its image with a string of acquisitions beginning in 1997. The firm acquired PharMingen (biomedical research reagents) and Difco Laboratories (microbiology media) which broadened its product lines. BD also collaborated with Nanogen on diagnosis products for infectious disease.

EXECUTIVES

Chairman And Ceo, Vincent A. (Vince) Forlenza, age 65, $1,105,000 total compensation

Evp And President Global Health, Gary M. Cohen, age 60, $605,700 total compensation

Evp And General Counsel, Jeffrey S. Sherman, age 63, $560,333 total compensation

Evp Integrated Supply Chain Officer, Stephen (Steve) Sichak, age 60

Evp Cfo And Chief Administrative Officer, Christopher R. (Chris) Reidy, age 61, $746,568 total compensation

Evp Strategic Planning And Chief Marketing Officer, Nabil Shabshab, age 52

Evp And Chief Human Resource Officer, Linda M. Tharby, age 50

President, Thomas E. Polen, age 45, $651,000 total compensation

Evp; President Greater Asia, James Lim, age 53

President Pharmaceutical Systems, Alexandre Conroy, age 54, $530,334 total compensation

Evp And Chief Quality Officer, Pierre Boisier

Evp And President Life Sciences Segment, Alberto Mas, age 56

Evp Research And Development And Chief Medical Officer, Ellen R. Strahlman, age 60, $664,427 total compensation

Evp And Chief Regulatory Officer, Richard J. Naples

Senior Vice President Corporate Finance Controller And Treasurer, John Gallagher

Senior Vice President Human Resources, Jerry Hurwitz

Vp And Chief Ip Counsel, David Highet

Senior Vice President Corporate Secretary And Associate General Counsel, Gary DeFazio

Executive Vice President And Chief Integrated Supply Chain Officer, James Borzi

Vice President, J Natale

Vp Global Business Systems, Karen Baughman

Worldwide Vp Medical Affairs Diabetes Care, Larry Hirsch

Vice President Global Strategy And Development, Amit Bhalla

Executive Vice President And President Emea, Roland Goette

Vice President M And A Process, Tom Jaeger

Chairman And Ceo, Vincent A. (Vince) Forlenza, age 65

Assistant Secretary, Patricia Walesiewicz

Assistant Secretary, David Singer

Assistant Secretary, Robert Thibeault

Board Member, Claire Pomeroy

Board Member, Gary Mecklenburg

Board Member, Rebecca Rimel

Board Member, Catherine Burzik

Auditors: Ernst & Young LLP

LOCATIONS

HQ: Becton, Dickinson & Co
1 Becton Drive, Franklin Lakes, NJ 07417-1880
Phone: 201 847-6800
Web: www.bd.com

2018 Sales

	$ mil.	% of total
US	8,769	55
EMEA	3,298	21
Greater Asia	2,460	15
Other	1,457	9
Total	**15,983**	**100**

PRODUCTS/OPERATIONS

2018 Sales by Segment

	$ mil.	% of total
Medical	8,616	54
Life Sciences	4,330	27
Interventional	3,037	19
Total	**15,983**	**100**

Selected Products

Medical
 Anesthesia needles and trays
 Hypodermic needles and syringes
 Intravenous catheters
 Insulin syringes and pen needles
 Prefillable drug-delivery systems
 Prefillable IV flush syringes
 Safety needles and syringes
 Sharps disposal systems
Diagnostics
 Bar-code systems for patient identification and data capture
 Blood culturing systems
 Cytology systems (for cervical cancer screening)
 Drug susceptibility systems
 Immunodiagnostic test kits
 Microorganism identification systems
 Molecular diagnostics (for infectious disease and hospital infection testing)
 Plated media
 Rapid diagnostic assays
 Safety-engineered blood collection devices
 Sample collection products
 Specimen management systems

Biosciences
 Cell culture media
 Cell sorters and analyzers
 Cell growth and screening products
 Cellular imaging systems
 Clinical and research laboratory software
 Diagnostic assays
 Labware (tubes pipettes Petri dishes etc.)
 Molecular biology reagents (for study of genes)
 Monoclonal antibodies (for biomedical research)
 Other research reagents

COMPETITORS

Abbott Labs	Hospira
B. Braun Melsungen	Johnson & Johnson
Baxter International	Novo Nordisk
Boston Scientific	Roche Diagnostics
Dako	Terumo
Fresenius	Thermo Fisher
Gen-Probe	Scientific
Hologic	bioMérieux

HISTORICAL FINANCIALS

Company Type: Public

Income Statement

FYE: September 30

	REVENUE ($ mil.)	NET INCOME ($ mil.)	NET PROFIT MARGIN	EMPLOYEES
09/18	15,983	311	1.9%	76,032
09/17	12,093	1,100	9.1%	41,933
09/16	12,483	976	7.8%	50,928
09/15	10,282	695	6.8%	49,517
09/14	8,446	1,185	14.0%	30,619
Annual Growth	**17.3%**	**(28.4%)**	**—**	**25.5%**

2018 Year-End Financials

Debt ratio: 39.88%	No. of shares (mil.): 268
Return on equity: 1.83%	Dividends
Cash ($ mil.): 1,140	Yield: 0.0%
Current ratio: 1.03	Payout: 500.0%
Long-term debt ($ mil.): 18,894	Market value ($ mil.): 70,007

	STOCK PRICE ($) FY Close	P/E High/Low		PER SHARE ($) Earnings	Dividends	Book Value
09/18	261.00	423	312	0.60	3.00	78.27
09/17	195.95	44	35	4.60	2.92	56.82
09/16	179.73	40	29	4.49	2.64	35.79
09/15	132.66	45	33	3.35	2.40	34.00
09/14	113.81	20	16	5.99	2.18	26.32
Annual Growth	**23.1%**	**—**	**—**	**(43.7%)**	**8.3%**	**31.3%**

Bed, Bath & Beyond, Inc.

Bed Bath & Beyond (BBB) is the nation's #1 superstore domestics retailer with more than 1540 BBB stores throughout the US Puerto Rico and Canada. The stores' floor-to-ceiling shelves stock better-quality (brand-name and private-label) goods in two main categories: domestics (bed linens bathroom and kitchen items) and home furnishings (cookware and cutlery small household appliances picture frames and more). BBB also operates more than 275 Cost Plus and World Market stores and three smaller specialty chains: about 80 Christmas Tree Shops; 115 buybuy BABY stores; and more than 50 Harmon discount health and beauty shops.
Operations

Beyond its main BBB-branded chain of more than 1540 stores the retailer operates more than 275 stores under the names World Market Cost Plus World Market and World Market Stores banners. It also operates 115 buybuy BABY shops almost 80 Christmas Tree Shops and more than 50 stores under the names Harmon and Harmon Face Values. In Mexico BBB also has a joint venture with Mexican retailer Home & More where it currently operates seven stores under the BBB banner.

Sales of home furnishings generate more than 60% of the retailer's total revenue while domestic merchandise makes up almost 40% of total revenue each year.

Geographic Reach

Nearly all of the New Jersey-based retailer's more than 1540 stores are in the US though 55 of its stores are located across nine Canadian provinces while three are in Puerto Rico. About 40% of the company's stores are in five US states: California Texas Florida New York and New Jersey.

Sales and Marketing

BBB prefers to locate its stores in strip malls and power strip shopping centers in suburban areas of medium and large-sized cities. It also places its stores near major off-price and conventional malls. The chain relies exclusively on circulars mailings and word-of-mouth for advertising.

BBB purchases its merchandise from 10800 suppliers with the company's 10 largest suppliers accounting for almost 15% of such purchases. The company purchases substantially all of its merchandise in the US.

Financial Performance

BBB's sales have been steadily growing the last few years thanks to a strengthening US economy and increased business from acquisitions. In fiscal 2017 net sales increased by 1% to peak at a record-setting $12.2 billion due to higher sales driven by digital acquisitions and new store sales.

However BBB'snet income has steadily declined the last several years as it uses additional cash to improve its infrastructure and operations. Net income fell 9% from $842 million in 2016 to $685 million in 2017 due to additional expenditures for enhancements to its digital channels ongoing investments in its data warehouse and data analytics and expenditures for the continued development and deployment of new systems and equipment in stores.

Strategy

BBB strategy is to expand its market reach either through strategic acquisitions or organically by adding stores in both new and existing markets. To this end in fiscal 2016 the company opened 29 new stores closed 12 stores and opened a new customer contact center in Layton Utah and a new distribution facility in Las Vegas.

BBB also wants to further enhance its omnichannel capabilities through such initiatives as adding new functionality to its e-commerce and mobile sites and by opening new distribution centers for both direct to consumer and store fulfillment. Additionally it plans to expand specialty departments in its stores in areas such as health and beauty care baby specialty food and specialty beverage sections.

The retailer's decentralized structure allows store managers to have more control than their peers at other retailers (and the company has less manager turnover). BBB cuts costs by locating its stores in strip shopping centers freestanding buildings and off-price malls rather than in pricier regional malls. To cut costs further its vendors ship merchandise directly to the stores eliminating the expense of a central distribution center and reducing warehousing costs.

Mergers and Acquisitions

BBB has used acquisitions as a means for quickly bolstering its online presence as it faces mounting competition from online retailers like Amazon.

In early 2017 it acquired Decorist an online interior design platform that provides personalized home design services. Decorist also offers photo-realistic 3-D renderings of how items will look in their actual homes and offers additional online services.

In 2016 the company acquired online home goods retailer One Kings Lane Inc. in an all-cash deal. The deal the value of which was undisclosed bolstered BBB's furniture and home dA©cor offerings in the online space. One Kings offers an extensive collection of designer and vintage furniture rugs kitchenware lighting and other dA©cor for homes.

Also in 2016 the company acquired PersonalizationMall.com a online seller of personalized gifts for $190 in cash.

In 2015 BBB acquired Of a Kind an e-commerce website that features specially commissioned limited edition items from emerging fashion and home designers.

HISTORY

Warren Eisenberg and Leonard Feinstein both employed by a discounter called Arlan's brainstormed an idea in 1971 for a chain of stores offering only home goods. They were betting that customers were in Feinstein's words interested in a "designer approach to linens and housewares." The two men started two small linens stores (about 2000 sq. ft) named bed n bath one in New York and one in New Jersey.

Expansion came at a fairly slow pace as the company moved only into California and Connecticut by 1985. By then the time was right for such a specialty retailer: Department stores were cutting back on the more housewares lines to focus on the more profitable apparel segment and baby boomers were spending more leisure time at their homes (and more money on spiffing them up). Eisenberg and Feinstein opened a 20000-sq.-ft. superstore in 1985 that offered a full line of home furnishings. The firm changed its name to Bed Bath & Beyond (BBB) two years later in order to reflect its new offerings.

With the successful superstore format the company built all new stores in the larger design. BBB grew rapidly; square footage quadrupled between 1992 and 1996. The company went public in 1992. That year it eclipsed the size of its previous stores when it opened a 50000-sq.-ft. store in Manhattan. (It later enlarged this store to 80000 sq. ft.; the company's stores now average 42000 sq. ft.)

BBB's management has attributed its success in part to the leeway it gives its store managers who monitor inventory and have the freedom to try new products and layouts. One example often cited by the company is the case of a manager who decided to sell glasses by the piece instead of in sets. Sales increased 30% and the whole chain incorporated the practice.

The retailer opened 28 new stores in 1996 33 in 1997 (its first-ever billion-dollar sales year) and 45 in 1998.

In 1999 the company dipped a toe into the waters of e-commerce by agreeing to buy a stake in Internet Gift Registries which operates the WeddingNetwork website. The company later began offering online sales and bridal registry services. Keeping up its rapid expansion pace the company opened 70 stores in 1999 85 in 2000 and 95 in 2001.

In 2002 BBB acquired Harmon Stores a health and beauty aid retailer with 29 stores in three states. It acquired Christmas Tree Shops a giftware

and household items retailer with 23 stores in six states for $200 million in 2003.

In March 2007 BBB acquired buybuy BABY which operates eight stores on the East Coast for $67 million. The retailer opened its first Canadian location in Ontario north of Toronto in December. In 2008 BBB added three more stores in Canada and its first locations in Mexico via a joint venture there under the Home & More banner.

In June 2012 the company bought Cost Plus which operates nearly 260 stores in 30 states under the World Market Cost Plus World Market and Cost Plus Imports banners for $495 million in cash.

EXECUTIVES

LOCATIONS

HQ: Bed, Bath & Beyond, Inc.
650 Liberty Avenue, Union, NJ 07083
Phone: 908 688-0888   **Fax:** 908 810-8813
Web: www.bedbathandbeyond.com

2017 Stores

	No.
California	184
Texas	119
New York	101
Florida	96
New Jersey	91
Illinois	55
Ohio	49
Virginia	46
Massachusetts	44
Michigan	44
Pennsylvania	44
North Carolina	43
Arizona	42
Georgia	39
Washington	37
Colorado	35
Tennessee	29
Connecticut	25
Ontario Canada	25
Alabama	24
South Carolina	24
Indiana	23
Maryland	23
Missouri	23
Louisiana	20
Oregon	17
Utah	16
Wisconsin	16
Minnesota	15
Nevada	15
New Hampshire	14
Kansas	12
Alberta Canada	12
British Columbia Canada	12
Iowa	11
Kentucky	11
Idaho	10
New Mexico	10
Other	90
Total	**1,546**

PRODUCTS/OPERATIONS

2017 Stores

	No.
Bed Bath & Beyond	1,023
Cost Plus World Market	276
BABY Stores	113
Christmas Tree Shops	80
Harmon stores	54
Total	**1,546**

COMPETITORS

Amazon.com	Macy's
Art.com	Pier 1 Imports
Babies "R" Us	Ross Stores
Burlington Coat	Sears
Factory	Sensational Beginnings
Children's Place	TJX Companies
Container Store	Target Corporation
Dillard's	Tuesday Morning
Euromarket Designs	Corporation
Garden Ridge	Wal-Mart
Gymboree	Wayfair
J. C. Penney	Williams-Sonoma
Kmart	

HISTORICAL FINANCIALS

Company Type: Public

Income Statement

FYE: March 3

	REVENUE ($ mil.)	NET INCOME ($ mil.)	NET PROFIT MARGIN	EMPLOYEES
03/18*	12,349	424	3.4%	65,000
02/17	12,215	685	5.6%	65,000
02/16	12,103	841	7.0%	62,000
02/15	11,881	957	8.1%	60,000
03/14	11,503	1,022	8.9%	58,000
Annual Growth	1.8%	(19.7%)	—	2.9%

*Fiscal year change

2018 Year-End Financials

Debt ratio: 21.19%
Return on equity: 14.91%
Cash ($ mil.): 346
Current ratio: 1.83
Long-term debt ($ mil.): 1,492

No. of shares (mil.): 140
Dividends
Yield: 0.0%
Payout: 18.9%
Market value ($ mil.): 3,067

	STOCK PRICE ($) FY Close	P/E High/Low		PER SHARE ($) Earnings	Dividends	Book Value
03/18*	21.83	14	6	3.04	0.58	20.56
02/17	41.04	11	8	4.58	0.38	18.59
02/16	48.99	15	8	5.10	0.00	16.34
02/15	74.66	15	11	5.07	0.00	15.75
03/14	67.82	17	12	4.79	0.00	19.19
Annual Growth	(24.7%)	—	—	(10.7%)	—	1.7%

*Fiscal year change

Beneficial Bancorp Inc

Auditors: KPMG LLP

LOCATIONS

HQ: Beneficial Bancorp Inc
1818 Market Street, Philadelphia, PA 19103
Phone: 215 864-6000
Web: www.thebeneficial.com

HISTORICAL FINANCIALS

Company Type: Public

Income Statement

FYE: December 31

	ASSETS ($ mil.)	NET INCOME ($ mil.)	INCOME AS % OF ASSETS	EMPLOYEES
12/17	5,798	23	0.4%	779
12/16	5,738	25	0.4%	798
12/15	4,826	22	0.5%	809
12/14	4,751	18	0.4%	830
12/13	4,583	12	0.3%	842
Annual Growth	6.1%	17.4%	—	(1.9%)

2017 Year-End Financials

Debt ratio: 9.32%
Return on equity: 2.34%
Cash ($ mil.): 557
Current ratio: —
Long-term debt ($ mil.): —

No. of shares (mil.): 75
Dividends
Yield: 0.0%
Payout: 75.0%
Market value ($ mil.): 1,247

	STOCK PRICE ($) FY Close	P/E High/Low		PER SHARE ($) Earnings	Dividends	Book Value
12/17	16.45	56	43	0.32	0.24	13.64
12/16	18.40	56	37	0.34	0.12	13.40
12/15	13.32	49	37	0.29	0.00	13.45
12/14	12.27	56	43	0.24	0.00	8.12
12/13	10.92	66	49	0.17	0.00	7.98
Annual Growth	10.8%	—	—	17.1%	—	14.4%

Berkley (WR) Corp

Holding company W. R. Berkley offers an assortment of niche commercial property/casualty insurance across two segments — Insurance and Reinsurance. The Insurance segment comprising more than 60 operating companies underwrites commercial insurance coverage including excess and surplus lines and admitted lines. It also develops self-insuring programs aimed at employers and employer groups. The Reinsurance segment allows insurance companies to pool their risks in order to reduce their liability. Berkley serves customers in 60 countries in the Americas Europe and the Asia/Pacific region.

Operations

Berkley's Insurance segment accounts for more than 80% of the company's total revenue while the Reinsurance segment accounts for about 10%. (The remainder is brought in by other operations.)

In addition to insurance products Berkley offers a variety of fee-based services such as claims administrative and consulting services.

Geographic Reach

Berkley offers insurance and reinsurance through more than 60 operating units in 60 nations in North America South America Europe Africa and the Asia/Pacific region.

Sales and Marketing

Berkley primarily serves small to midsized business customers. The insurer sells its high-risk coverage products directly and through retail and wholesale agents brokers and managing general agents to a wide variety of clients. The regional products business' offerings are sold through a network of non-exclusive commission-based independent agents.

Financial Performance

Following a multi-year trend of steady growth Berkley's revenue rose less than 1% to $7.7 billion in 2017. That modest increase was primarily due to higher total premiums earned and net income but was partially offset by a decline in fees and commissions.

Net income has fluctuated a bit for the past five years and in 2017 it fell 9% to $549.1 million as a result of increased catastrophe losses. Operating cash flow also declined falling 16% to $710.9 million. This decline was driven by the lower net income as well as changes in working capital.

Strategy

Strategically Berkley's decentralized structure promotes the development of specialized expertise in a range of areas and enables the company to adapt to cyclical market conditions and insulate itself from great risk. While the company has made a handful of acquisitions through the years it prefers to expand by forming new operating units after identifying needs in specific areas. For example in 2017 Berkley split its Specialty Underwriting Managers unit into two separate firms — Berkley Entertainment & Sports and Berkley Environmental — to better allow the businesses to grow within their respective niches.

Other recent additions include firms specializing in cybersecurity and health care. In 2018 subsidiary Berkley One (formed in 2016) established a partnership with data defense services provider CyberScout to offer a suite of cyber solutions covering identity theft cyber bullying and system compromise. That same unit is also rolling out its platform serving high-net-worth customers in certain states.

The company focuses on growing world markets including Scandinavia South America Australia and the Asia/Pacific region. Additionally Berkley exercises insightful discretion in exiting insurance lines as demand diminishes.

Like most property/casualty insurers Berkley had losses related to natural disasters in 2017. Hurricanes Harvey Irma and Maria earthquakes in Mexico and California wildfires led to $184 million in catastrophe losses that year.

Additionally with the insurance market being so fragmented and new competitors entering the fray Berkley is under pressure to keep its prices down. This has led to a slowdown in premium growth for the company.

EXECUTIVES

Evp Investments, James G. Shiel, age 58, $650,000 total compensation
Senior Vice President, Robert Gosselink
Senior Vice President, Peter Kamford
Vice President, Michele Fleckenstein
Evp, C. Fred Madsen
Evp And Secretary, Ira S. Lederman, age 65, $650,000 total compensation
Evp, Eugene G. Ballard, age 65, $650,000 total compensation
President And Ceo, W. Robert (Rob) Berkley, age 45, $993,769 total compensation
Evp, Robert C. Hewitt, age 57
Evp, Philip S. Welt, age 59
Evp, Robert D. Stone, age 54
Evp, John K. Goldwater
Evp, William M. Rohde
Evp, Jeffrey M. (Jeff) Hafter
Evp, Lucille T. Sgaglione
Svp Cfo And Treasurer, Richard M. Baio, $497,981 total compensation
Evp, Kathleen M. Tierney
Vp And Chief Marketing Officer, Jonathan M. Levine
Svp And Cio, Richard M. Lowery
Evp, James P. Bronner
Svp And Chief Project Officer, Mir Mazhar
Evp, Kenneth P. Sroka
Vice President, Michael Harris
Evp, James Gilbert
Vice President And Investment Controller, Richard K Altorelli
Vice President And Corporate Actuary, Dana Frantz
Assistant Vice President And Corporate Actuary, Gene Zhang
Vice President And Chief Actuary, Julie Halper
Vice President, Nicholas Lang
Vice President Analytics, Robert McPherson
Vp And Head Corporate Catastrophe Analysis, Robert Sabio
Executive Vice President, Ricardo Gonzalez
Vice President Actuarial And Data Analysis, Debbie Savoie
Executive Vice President, Steven Walsh
Senior Vice President Information Technology, Kevin H Ebers
Vp And Corporate Actuary, Jessica Somerfeld
Senior Vice President, C Madsen
Vice President External Financial Communications, Karen Horvath
Senior Vice President Underwriting, Joseph Walsh

Senior Vice President International Operations, Steven W Taylor
Vice President And Chief Compliance Officer, Scott Mansolillo
Vice President, Joyce Krech
Vice President Marketing, John Bowen
Vice President And Corporate Controller, Andrea Kanefsky
Senior Vice President Corporate Strategy And Development, Jared Abbey
Vice President Insurance Risk Management, Laura Goodall
Vice President Enterprise Risk Management, Trish Conway
Senior Vice President Marketing, Christoph Ritterson
Senior Vice President Customer Experience Berkley One, Susan Vella
Senior Vice President Claims, Kevin Shea
Vice President Actuary, Dustin J Turner
Vice President Actuary, Dustin Turner
Evp And Secretary, Ira S. Lederman, age 65
Chairman, William R. (Bill) Berkley, age 72
Svp Cfo And Treasurer, Richard M. Baio
Auditors: KPMG LLP

LOCATIONS

HQ: Berkley (WR) Corp
475 Steamboat Road, Greenwich, CT 06830
Phone: 203 629-3000
Web: www.wrberkley.com

PRODUCTS/OPERATIONS

2017 Sales

	$ mil.	% of total
Insurance	6,229	81
Reinsurance	696	9
Net investment gains	335	4
Corporate other & adjustments	423	6
Total	**7,684**	**100**

Selected Property/Casualty Segments

Specialty (includes excess and surplus lines and admitted specialty lines)
Regional (commercial lines property/casualty)
Alternative markets (includes excess workers' compensation monoline workers' compensation accident and health and insurance services)
Reinsurance (facultative or treaty basis; participates in business written through Lloyd's of London)
International business (global underwriting)

COMPETITORS

AIG	Liberty Mutual
Allied World Assurance	Munich Re America
American Financial	Nationwide
Group	Old Republic
Arch Capital	PartnerRe
Berkshire Hathaway	Swiss Re
CNA Financial	Transatlantic
Chubb Limited	Reinsurance
Everest Re	Travelers Companies
Farmers Group	White Mountains
HCC Insurance	Insurance Group

HISTORICAL FINANCIALS

Company Type: Public

Income Statement   FYE: December 31

	ASSETS ($ mil.)	NET INCOME ($ mil.)	INCOME AS % OF ASSETS	EMPLOYEES
12/17	24,299	549	2.3%	7,722
12/16	23,364	601	2.6%	7,683
12/15	21,730	503	2.3%	7,621
12/14	21,716	648	3.0%	7,521
12/13	20,551	499	2.4%	7,247
Annual Growth	**4.3%**	**2.4%**	**—**	**1.6%**

2017 Year-End Financials

Debt ratio: 10.28%	No. of shares (mil.): 121
Return on equity: 10.50%	Dividends
Cash ($ mil.): 950	Yield: 0.0%
Current ratio: —	Payout: 36.3%
Long-term debt ($ mil.): —	Market value ($ mil.): 8,707

	STOCK PRICE ($) FY Close	P/E High/Low		PER SHARE ($) Earnings	Dividends	Book Value
12/17	71.65	17	14	4.26	1.55	44.53
12/16	66.51	14	10	4.68	1.51	41.65
12/15	54.75	14	12	3.87	0.47	37.31
12/14	51.26	11	7	4.86	1.43	36.21
12/13	43.39	12	10	3.55	0.39	32.79
Annual Growth	**13.4%**	**—**	**—**	**4.7%**	**41.2%**	**8.0%**

Berkshire Hathaway Inc

Berkshire Hathaway is the holding company where Warren Buffett one of the world's richest men makes his money and spreads his risk. The company invests in a variety of industries from insurance and utilities to apparel and food and from building materials and furniture retailers to jewelry shops. Its core insurance subsidiaries include GEICO National Indemnity and reinsurance giant General Re. The company's other large holdings include Marmon Group McLane Company MidAmerican Energy and Shaw Industries. Buffett holds a significant stake in Berkshire Hathaway which owns a majority of more than 50 firms in all and has equity stakes in about a dozen others.

Operations

Berkshire Hathaway operates as a holding company with a highly decentralized structure without integrated business functions (such as sales marketing purchasing legal and human resources). Practicing a minimal day-to-day management leadership style the firm owns a diverse group of companies from a variety of industries with its core subsidiaries being insurance reinsurance freight rail transportation utilities and energy generation companies.

The insurance businesses constitute about three quarters of total revenue and are composed of over a dozen large providers that insure for example automobiles boats commercial buildings businesses workers? compensation and medical practices. Its most recognizable holding is GEICO (auto insurance). Sales and service revenues make up almost 70% of the insurance business revenue while another 20% comes from insurance premiums.

Lesser known to most are the company?s investment in other industries. Berkshire Hathaway's holdings include a railroad transportation company (Burlington Northern Santa Fe) a real estate business (Berkshire Hathaway Property Advisors) a carpet manufacturer (Shaw Industries) a wholesale distributor of consumer goods (McLane) a manufacturer of clay bricks (Acme Brick) a battery company (Duracell) and a specialty chemicals producer (Lubrizol). Berkshire Hathaway provides capital and financial guidance ensures the companies are well managed and then takes a back seat to allow company leadership to run the entities.

More than 15% of Berkshire Hathaway revenue comes from its railroad utilities and energy subsidiaries and about 5% comes from its finance and financial product companies.

Additionally the company invests its treasure trove of excess cash (typically more than $60 billion) in shares of public companies or in commercial debt which it usually holds for a few years. Recent investments were in Wrigley Kraft Heinz Dow and Phillips 66.

Geographic Reach

Omaha Nebraska-headquartered Berkshire Hathaway operates primarily in the US although it does provide insurance (and reinsurance) to clients in the Asia Pacific and Western Europe geographies.

Financial Performance

Buffett's famed investment vehicle enjoyed upward trends in revenue and profit over recent years highlighting the legendary investors' knack for choosing financially successful companies over the long term. It grew revenue from $107 billion in 2008 to more than $223 billion in 2016. Net income expanded almost fivefold from $5 billion in 2008 to almost $25 billion in 2016.

In 2016 Berkshire's revenue climbed 6% to a record-setting $223 billion on increases in insurance and financial product revenue which more than overcame a slip in revenue from its railroad utilities and energy businesses. Its insurance business especially through higher demand for GEICO?s auto policies grew 7% year over year. The firm's Finance and Financial Products business revenue shot up 36% with higher home sales volumes and a significant jump in the segment?s investment gains.

Net income was flat in 2016 versus the prior year. A jump in insurance losses & adjustments coupled with higher costs for sales and services ate into the higher revenue leaving the firm with a still highly profitable $24 billion.

Cash on hand at the end of 2016 was $28 billion a decrease of $39 billion from 2015. While operating activities provided $32 billion and financing activities offered an additional $13 billion of cash investing activities (primarily the purchase of US Treasury Bills) used more than $84 billion.

Strategy

Berkshire Hathaway seeks out large companies with consistent earnings easy-to-understand business models and like-minded leadership. Most acquisitions are made with cash and most firms retain their management after the transaction. Buffett and longtime business partner Charlie Munger attempt to run Berkshire like a small business albeit on a much larger scale. It operates as a collection of individual enterprises; Buffett and Munger largely keep their hands off portfolio companies' day-to-day operations but allocate capital and control risk.

In a letter to shareholders Buffett once declared "Our elephant gun has been reloaded and my trigger finger is itchy." Hunting big game (i.e. acquiring big companies) has become somewhat of a necessity for Berkshire Hathaway to continue its growth trajectory but the company benefits from not being married to any industry as it seeks out its quarry. Following its ?big game? investment strategy Berkshire entered new markets with the 2017 purchase of 38% of Pilot Flying J truck stop company and the $32 billion 2016 acquisition of aerospace components giant Precision Castparts. It plans to purchase a further 41% of Pilot Flying J in 2023 as part of a long-term move to acquire majority ownership. Berkshire?s holds non-majority investment stakes in Apple ($19 billion) Bank of America ($16 billion) and many other household name companies.

Company Background

Chairman and CEO Warren Buffett along with associates slowly accumulated a majority of shares in the Berkshire Hathaway textile company in the early 1960s. To stabilize revenues and reduce financial risks Buffett diversified the company with a purchase of Indemnity and National Fire & Marine Insurance Company in 1967. Thus began the long prosperous road towards profitability and dozens of acquisitions. Buffett still owns about 20% of Berkshire Hathaway's shares.

HISTORY

Warren Buffett bought his first stock — three shares of Cities Service — at age 11. In the 1950s he studied at Columbia University under famed investor Benjamin Graham. Graham's axioms: Use quantitative analysis to discover companies whose intrinsic worth exceeds their stock prices; popularity is irrelevant; the market will vindicate the patient investor.

In 1956 Buffett then 25 founded Buffett Partnership. Its $105000 in initial assets multiplied as the company bought Berkshire Hathaway (textiles 1965) and National Indemnity (insurance 1967). When Buffett nixed the partnership in 1969 because he believed stocks were overvalued value per share had risen 30-fold.

In late 2012 the firm also acquired Omaha-based online party supplier Oriental Trading Company.

Berkshire Hathaway's $28-billion purchase of ketchup giant H.J. Heinz in 2013 is also a textbook example of the firm's investment strategy as the firm and its investment partner Brazil's 3G Capital took the ketchup maker private to speed its transformation into a global food business.

EXECUTIVES

Chairman Bnsf Railway., Matthew K. (Matt) Rose, age 59

Svp And Cfo, Marc D. Hamburg, age 68, $1,550,000 total compensation

Chairman And Ceo, Warren E. Buffett, age 88, $100,000 total compensation

Head Of Reinsurance, Ajit Jain, age 66

Head Of Berkshire Hathaway Energy, Greg Abel

Vice President Human Resources And Administration, Jennifer Johnson

Vice Chairman, Charles T. (Charlie) Munger, age 94

Chairman And Ceo, Warren E. Buffett, age 88

Board Member, Thomas Murphy

Treasurer And Controller, Janet Saar

Auditors: DELOITTE & TOUCHE LLP

LOCATIONS

HQ: Berkshire Hathaway Inc
3555 Farnam Street, Omaha, NE 68131
Phone: 402 346-1400
Web: www.berkshirehathaway.com

PRODUCTS/OPERATIONS

2016 sales

	% of total
Insurance and Other	
Sales and service revenues	53
Insurance premiums earned	21
Investment gains	2
Interest dividend and other investment income	2
Railroad Utilities and Energy	17
Finance and Financial Products	
Sales and service revenues	3
Investment gains	1
Interest dividend and other investment income	1
Derivative gains	0
Total	100

Subsidiaries and Selected Holdings
Acme Brick Company (bricks)
Applied Underwriters (workers' compensation)
Ben Bridge Jeweler (jewelry retailer)
Benjamin Moore (architectural and industrial paint)
Berkshire Hathaway Automotive
Berkshire Hathaway Energy Company
Berkshire Hathaway GUARD Insurance Companies
Berkshire Hathaway Homestate Companies
Berkshire Hathaway Life Insurance Company of Nebraska
BH Media Group (digital marketing publishing)
Boat U.S. (insurance)
Borsheim Jewelry Company (jewelry retailer)
Brooks (shoes)
The Buffalo News (newspaper)
Burlington Northern Santa Fe (railroad)
Business Wire Inc. (news service)
Central States Indemnity Co. of Omaha (credit and disability insurance)
Clayton Homes (manufactured housing and financing)
CORT Business Services Corp. (provider of rental furniture accessories and related services)
CTB International (manufacturer of equipment and systems for poultry hog and egg production)
The Fechheimer Brothers (uniforms and accessories)
FlightSafety International (high technology training to operators of aircraft and ships)
Forest River (recreational vehicles)
Fruit of the Loom (apparel)
Garan Inc. (apparel)
GEICO (property/casualty insurance)
General Re Corporation (property/casualty reinsurance)
H.H. Brown Shoe Company
Helzberg's Diamond Shops (jewelry retailer)
HomeServices of America (real estate services)
International Dairy Queen Inc. (licensing and servicing Dairy Queen Stores)
Johns Manville (building and equipment insulation)
Jordan's Furniture (retailing home furnishings)
Justin Brands (western footwear and apparel)
Kraft Heinz
Larson-Juhl
LiquidPower Speciality Products
Lubrizol (specialty chemicals)
Marmon Holdings (manufacturing and service)
McLane Company (wholesale distribution of groceries and non-food items)
MedPro Group (Med Pro; professional liability insurer)
MidAmerican Energy Holdings Company
 HomeServices of America Inc. (residential real estate brokerage)
 Kern River Gas Transmission Company
 Northern Electric
 Northern Natural Gas
 Pacific Power
 Rocky Mountain Power
 Yorkshire Electricity
MiTek (building components)
National Indemnity Company (specialty insurance)
Nebraska Furniture Mart (retailing home furnishings)
NetJets Inc. (fractional ownership programs for general aviation aircraft)
Oriental Trading Company (party supplies)
Pampered Chef Ltd. (kitchenware and housewares)
Precision Castparts Corp (aerospace parts manufacturer)
Precision Steel Warehouse (steel service center)
R.C. Willey Home Furnishings (home furnishings retailer)
Richline Group (jewelry manufacturer)
Scott Fetzer Company (manufacture and distribution of diversified products)
See's Candies (boxed chocolates and other confectionery products)
Shaw Industries (carpets and rugs)
Star Furniture Co. (home furnishings retailer)
TTI Inc. (electronics distribution)
United States Liability Insurance Group
XTRA Corporation (transportation equipment)

COMPETITORS

AEA Investors	Lincoln Financial
Allstate	Group
Apollo Global	Progressive
Management	Corporation
Bain Capital	State Farm
BlackRock	TPG
Blackstone Group	The Carlyle Group
CNA Financial	The Hartford
KKR	

HISTORICAL FINANCIALS

Company Type: Public

Income Statement
FYE: December 31

	ASSETS ($ mil.)	NET INCOME ($ mil.)	INCOME AS % OF ASSETS	EMPLOYEES
12/17	702,095	44,940	6.4%	377,000
12/16	620,854	24,074	3.9%	367,700
12/15	552,257	24,083	4.4%	331,000
12/14	526,186	19,872	3.8%	316,000
12/13	484,931	19,476	4.0%	32,000
Annual Growth	9.7%	23.2%	—	85.3%

2017 Year-End Financials

Debt ratio: 14.61%
Return on equity: 14.24%
Cash ($ mil.): 115,954
Current ratio: —
Long-term debt ($ mil.): —
No. of shares (mil.): 1
Dividends
Yield: —
Payout: —
Market value ($ mil.): 489,506

	STOCK PRICE ($) FY Close	P/E High/Low	PER SHARE ($) Earnings	Dividends	Book Value
12/17	297,600.00 211,749.91	11	927,326.00	0.00	
12/16	244,121.00 172,108.12	17	1314,645.00	0.00	
12/15	197,800.00 155,501.45	15	1314,656.00	0.00	
12/14	226,000.00 146,185.82	19	1412,092.00	0.00	
12/13	177,900.00 134,973.36	15	1111,850.00	0.00	
Annual Growth	13.7%	— —	23.2%	—	11.9%

Berkshire Hills Bancorp Inc

EXECUTIVES

Ceo-Pres, Richard M Marotta
Chb, William J Ryan
Sr Exec V Pres, Sean A Gray
Sr Exec V Pres-Cfo, James M Moses
Auditors: Crowe Horwath LLP

LOCATIONS

HQ: Berkshire Hills Bancorp Inc
60 State Street, Boston, MA 02109
Phone: 800 773-5601
Web: www.berkshirebank.com

COMPETITORS

Bank of America	RBS Citizens Financial
Hudson City Bancorp	Group
KeyCorp	Sovereign Bank
Pathfinder Bancorp	TD Bank USA

HISTORICAL FINANCIALS

Company Type: Public

Income Statement
FYE: December 31

	ASSETS ($ mil.)	NET INCOME ($ mil.)	INCOME AS % OF ASSETS	EMPLOYEES
12/17	11,570	55	0.5%	1,992
12/16	9,162	58	0.6%	1,731
12/15	7,831	49	0.6%	1,221
12/14	6,502	33	0.5%	1,091
12/13	5,672	41	0.7%	939
Annual Growth	19.5%	7.6%	—	20.7%

2017 Year-End Financials

Debt ratio: 0.87%
Return on equity: 4.27%
Cash ($ mil.): 248
Current ratio: —
Long-term debt ($ mil.): —
No. of shares (mil.): 45
Dividends
Yield: 0.0%
Payout: 60.4%
Market value ($ mil.): 1,658

	STOCK PRICE ($) FY Close	P/E High/Low	PER SHARE ($) Earnings	Dividends	Book Value
12/17	36.60	28 24	1.39	0.84	33.04
12/16	36.85	20 13	1.88	0.80	30.65
12/15	29.11	17 14	1.73	0.76	28.64
12/14	26.66	20 16	1.36	0.72	28.17
12/13	27.27	18 14	1.65	0.72	27.08
Annual Growth	7.6%	— —	(4.2%)	3.9%	5.1%

Berry Global Group Inc

With a portfolio that includes tapes tubes and trash bags Berry Global is a top maker of plastic products and engineered materials for customers across a broad range of industries. Its products include shrink wrap and other packaging films cloth and foil tapes plastic cups and lids components for diapers and other personal care items and prescription bottles. Key markets include the healthcare personal care and food and beverage industries. Berry Global operates worldwide but North America is by far its largest market.

Operations

Berry Global reports three operating segments: Engineered Materials; Health Hygiene and Specialties; and Consumer Packaging each contributing roughly a third of total revenue.

Engineered Materials manufactures tapes and adhesives polyethylene-based film products can liners printed films and laminated products.

The Health Hygiene and Specialties segment primarily consists of nonwoven specialty materials and films used in hygiene infection prevention personal care industrial construction and filtration applications.

The Consumer Packaging segment primarily consists of containers foodservice items closures overcaps bottles prescription containers and tubes.

Geographic Reach

Headquartered in Evansville Indiana Berry Global has some 130 manufacturing facilities primarily in North America but also in Europe the Middle East Asia and South America.

North America represents 80% of the company's sales.

Sales and Marketing

Berry Global sells its products to a very diverse customer base through a direct sales force and strategic distributors. Since many products are customized the sales team creates partnership with customers. The company?s top ten customers account for 20% of total revenue.

Financial Performance

Berry Global?s revenue has seen upward mobility increasing more than $2 billion in the last five years thanks to a string of acquisitions. In fiscal 2018 (ended September) the company reported net sales of $7.8 billion up 11% from the previous year. Acquisitions claimed the lion's share of revenue increase ($624 million) with the rest coming from organic sales ($92 million) and favorable impact of currency exchange ($58 million).

Berry has been profitable for five years straight but has enjoyed a sharp spike in the last couple of years. Profits increased 45% to $496 million in fiscal 2018 primarily due to a net income tax benefit of $19 million (compared to $109 million in expenses the prior year).

Cash holdings were at $381 million. Operations provided $1 billion offset by $1 billion going towards investment (mostly in acquisitions). Financial activities brought in $113 million.

Strategy

Enjoying half a decade of growing revenue and profits Berry Global is looking to turn competition up a notch. To that end the company is focusing on continuing strategic acquisitions on one hand and company restructuring to save money on the other.

In 2017-18 period Berry has shelled out $1.6 billion to acquire Laddawn Clopay AEP Industries and Adchem?s tapes businesses. A major area of focus has been to expand its custom bag film and flexible packaging products as well as adhesive tapes.

The company is aiming to expand its complementary product lines especially in the technical film production sector. Taken in total the company expects to save more than $120 million in cost synergies. In particular the company has tremendously expanded its Health Hygiene & Specialties segment through inorganic growth ($365 million more in revenue in 2018).

Berry's continued growth is all the more impressive due to an already-crowded competitive landscape dominated by big producers including Silgan Aptar Reynolds 3M and Fitesa. The company's large and diverse customer base its scale and common customers across segments enables the company to minimize sales and marketing costs. However with current levels of healthy cash flow and reasonably costs of plastic resin the company will focus on paying down its considerable debts ($5.8 billion in long-term debt) before further strategic acquisitions.

Mergers and Acquisitions

In 2018 Berry Global acquired Laddawn a manufacturer of blown polyethylene bags and films with a unique-to-industry e-commerce sales platform for $242 million. The company also completed its acquisition of Clopay for $475 million in November 2017. The acquisition is expected to bring $40 million in cost synergies while expanding Berry?s reach in the elastic films and laminates business.

In 2017 Berry acquired Adchem Corp?s tapes business for $49 million increasing its access to high performance adhesive tape business used in the automotive construction electronics and medical markets. Earlier that year the company completed the acquisition of AEP Industries for $791 million. AEP manufactures and markets flexible plastic packaging products with consumer industrial and agricultural applications.

Company Background

Berry Global was established in 1967 under the name of Imperial Plastics. In 1972 the injection molding company entered the container market and in 1983 Imperial plastics was purchased by Jerry Berry Sr. and renamed Berry Plastics. In

1988 it acquired some 40 companies. It began trading on the NYSE in 2012. In 2017 the company changed its name from Berry Plastics Group Inc. to Berry Global Inc.

EXECUTIVES

Evp Global Purchasing, Scott Farmer
Evp Strategic Corporate Development, Brett C. Bauer
Vp Finance And Business Planning, Rodgers K. Greenwalt
Cfo, Mark W. Miles, age 46, $453,380 total compensation
Chairman And Ceo, Thomas E. (Tom) Salmon, age 55, $499,617 total compensation
Evp Supply Chain, Terri Pitcher
Evp Human Resources, Ed Stratton
Evp General Counsel And Secretary, Jason K. Greene, age 47
President Engineered Materials, Curt L. Begle, age 42, $420,288 total compensation
President Flexible Packaging, Lawrence A. (Larry) Goldstein, age 55
Evp International, Jeffrey D. (Jeff) Thompson, age 46
Cio, Mark Freeman
President North America Avintiv, Scott Tracey, age 50
President Consumer Packaging, Jean-Marc Galvez
Chairman And Ceo, Thomas E. (Tom) Salmon, age 55
Evp General Counsel And Secretary, Jason K. Greene, age 47
Auditors: Ernst & Young LLP

LOCATIONS

HQ: Berry Global Group Inc
101 Oakley Street, Evansville, IN 47710
Phone: 812 424-2904
Web: www.berryplastics.com

2018 Sales

	$ mil.	% of total
North America	6,474	82
Europe	807	11
South America	332	4
Asia	256	3
Total	**7,896**	**100**

PRODUCTS/OPERATIONS

2018 Sales

	$ mil.	% of total
Consumer Packaging	2,463	31
Health Hygiene & Specialties	2,734	35
Engineered Materials	2,672	34
Total	**7,869**	**100**

Selected Products

Rigid Plastics
  Bottles
  Containers
  Closures
  Foodservice items
  Housewares
  Overcaps
  Prescription vials
  Tubes
Engineered Materials
  Can liners
  Corrosion protection
  Polyethylene-based film products
  Specialty tapes and adhesives
Flexible packaging
  Custom films
  Flexible packaging products
  Printed bags
  Pouches

Selected Brands

Versalite
Color Scents
Ruffies

Polyken
Nashua
Reemay
Stopaq
Qubic

COMPETITORS

3M
AptarGroup
Bemis
Intertape Polymer
Reynolds Food Packaging
Silgan Plastics
Tredegar

HISTORICAL FINANCIALS

Company Type: Public

Income Statement

FYE: September 29

	REVENUE ($ mil.)	NET INCOME ($ mil.)	NET PROFIT MARGIN	EMPLOYEES
09/18	7,869	496	6.3%	24,000
09/17*	7,095	340	4.8%	23,000
10/16	6,489	236	3.6%	21,000
09/15	4,881	86	1.8%	16,000
09/14	4,958	62	1.3%	16,000
Annual Growth	**12.2%**	**68.2%**	**—**	**10.7%**

*Fiscal year change

2018 Year-End Financials

Debt ratio: 64.00%
Return on equity: 40.72%
Cash ($ mil.): 381
Current ratio: 1.85
Long-term debt ($ mil.): 5,806

No. of shares (mil.): 131
Dividends
  Yield: —
  Payout: —
Market value ($ mil.): 6,358

	STOCK PRICE ($) FY Close	P/E High/Low	PER SHARE ($) Earnings	Dividends	Book Value
09/18	48.39	16 12	3.67	0.00	10.89
09/17*	56.65	22 16	2.56	0.00	7.73
10/16	43.85	24 15	1.89	0.00	1.79
09/15	30.29	51 32	0.70	0.00	(0.57)
09/14	24.71	49 34	0.51	0.00	(0.99)
Annual Growth	**18.3%**	**— —**	**63.8%**	**—**	**—**

*Fiscal year change

Best Buy Inc

Best Buy is one of the largest consumer electronics outlets in the US and beyond. The multinational retailer sells both products and services through roughly 1700 retail mobile stand-alone and smaller express stores under the Best Buy Best Buy Express Best Buy Mobile Five Star Future Shop Geek Squad Magnolia Audio Video and Pacific Kitchen and Home Sales banners. Its stores sell a variety of electronic gadgets and wearables tablets movies music computers mobile phones and appliances. On the services side it offers installation and maintenance technical support and subscriptions for mobile phone and Internet services.

HISTORY

Tired of working for a father who ignored his ideas on how to improve the business (electronics distribution) Dick Schulze quit. In 1966 with a partner he founded Sound of Music a Minnesota home/car stereo store. Schulze bought out his partner in 1971 and began to expand the chain. While chairing a school board Schulze saw declining enrollment and realized his target customer

group 15- to 18-year-old males was shrinking. In the early 1980s he broadened his product line and targeted older more affluent customers by offering appliances and VCRs.

After a 1981 tornado destroyed his best store (but not its inventory) Schulze spent his entire marketing budget to advertise a huge parking-lot sale. The successful sale taught him the benefits of strong advertising and wide selection combined with low prices. In 1983 Schulze changed the company's name to Best Buy and began to open larger superstores. The firm went public two years later.

Buoyed by the format change and the fast-rising popularity of the VCR Best Buy grew rapidly. Between 1984 and 1987 it expanded from eight stores to 24 and sales jumped from $29 million to $240 million. In 1988 another 16 stores opened and sales jumped by 84%. But Best Buy began to butt heads with many expanding consumer electronics retailers and profits took a beating.

To set Best Buy apart from its competitors in 1989 Schulze introduced the Concept II warehouse-like store format. Thinking that customers could buy products without much help Schulze cut payroll by taking sales staff off commission and reducing the number of employees per store by about a third. The concept proved to be such a hit in the company's home territory Minneapolis/St. Paul that it drove major competitor Highland Appliance to bankruptcy. Customers were happy but many of Best Buy's suppliers believing sales help was needed to sell products pulled their products from Best Buy stores. The losses didn't seem to hurt Best Buy; it took on Sears and Montgomery Ward in the Chicago market in 1989 and continued expanding.

In 1994 the company debuted Concept III an even larger store format. Best Buy opened 47 new stores in 1995 but found itself swimming in debt. Earnings plummeted in fiscal 1997 partly due to a huge PC inventory made obsolete by Intel's newer product. Best Buy started selling CDs on its website in 1997. That year it realized it had overextended itself with its expansion super-sized stores and financing promotions. Best Buy underwent a speedy massive makeover by scaling back expansion and doing away with its policy of "no money down no monthly payments no interest" (and next-to-no profits).

In 1999 Best Buy began to enter new markets (including New England) and introduced its Concept IV stores which highlighted digital products and featured stations for computer software and DVD demonstrations. Also in 1999 Best Buy formed a separate subsidiary for its online operations (BestBuy.com Inc.) and invested $10 million in consumer electronics information website etown.com (etown.com closed down in February 2001).

In 2000 Best Buy agreed to pay $88 million for Seattle-based Magnolia Hi-Fi a privately held chain of 13 high-end audio and video stores. In early 2001 Best Buy bought The Musicland Group (at the time operator of more than 1300 Sam Goody Suncoast On Cue and Media Play music stores) for about $425 million. The company began its international expansion in November 2002 with its $377 million acquisition of Future Shop Canada's leading consumer electronics retailer. Over the next year Best Buy opened eight of its own Best Buy stores in Ontario Canada.

In June 2002 Schulze turned over his responsibilities as CEO to vice chairman Brad Anderson; Schulze remained as chairman of the board. Best Buy acquired Geek Squad a computer support provider for $3 million the same year.

Best Buy shut down more than 100 Musicland stores (90 Sam Goody music stores and 20 Suncoast video stores) and laid off about 700 employees in January 2003; in June it sold the entire Musicland subsidiary (then about 1100 stores) to an affiliate of investment firm Sun Capital Partners. Three years later Best Buy purchased Pacific Sales Kitchen and Bath Centers which sells appliances and offers assistance on residential remodeling for $410 million.

Philip Schoonover a top executive in charge of customer segments defected to rival Circuit City in 2004. The company also dismissed Ernst & Young as its independent auditor after a former board member disclosed personal business dealings with the firm.

In 2006 the chain acquired home appliance and remodeling retailer Pacific Sales Kitchen and Bath Centers for about $410 million.

To facilitate its expansion in China Best Buy purchased a 75% stake in Jiangsu Five Star Appliance Co. in May 2006 and later opened the first Best Buy store in China in Shanghai.

To enhance its technology product offering for small businesses Best Buy in fiscal 2008 acquired Seattle-based Speakeasy a provider of broadband voice data and IT services. The deal valued at some $97 million made Speakeasy a wholly owned subsidiary that operates through the Best Buy for Business unit. Speakeasy CEO Bruce Chatterley as well as his management team was retained to run the Speakeasy operation once the deal closed. In a bid to add digital music downloads to its playlist Best Buy acquired a majority stake in Napster for about $127 million. The retailer's 2008 purchase of the music-swapping service included Napster's approximately 700000 digital entertainment subscribers.

In June 2008 Best Buy acquired a 50% stake in Carphone Warehouse's European and US retail interests for about $2.2 billion. In late October the company acquired digital music pioneer Napster for about $127 million via a tender offer for the firm's shares.

In early 2009 the retailer acquired the 25% of China's Jiangsu Five Star Appliance that it didn't already own. It also entered the Mexican market with its first store there.

CEO Brad Anderson retired in mid-2009 and COO and longtime employee Brian Dunn took over as CEO. Dunn's stint as chief executive lasted about three years. The 28-year company veteran stepped down in April 2012 handing his CEO title in the interim to board director Mike Mikan. In September 2012 the company named turnaround expert and Frenchman Hubert Joly to the position of CEO. Previously Joly served as head of T.G.I. Friday's and Radisson parent Carlson.

EXECUTIVES

Chairman And Ceo, Hubert Joly, age 59, $1,175,000 total compensation

Sevp And Chief Merchandising And Marketing Officer, R. Michael (Mike) Mohan, age 50, $833,654 total compensation

Sevp And President Multichannel Retail, Shari L. Ballard, age 51, $800,000 total compensation

President And Coo Best Buy Canada, Ron Wilson

Evp General Counsel And Secretary, Keith J. Nelsen, age 54, $650,000 total compensation

President Services, Trish Walker, age 51

Chief Strategic Growth Officer, Corie S. Barry, age 43, $713,462 total compensation

Vice President Sales Operations, Chris Schmidt

Chairman And Ceo, Hubert Joly, age 59

Evp General Counsel And Secretary, Keith J. Nelsen, age 54

Auditors: Deloitte & Touche LLP

LOCATIONS

HQ: Best Buy Inc
   7601 Penn Avenue South, Richfield, MN 55423
Phone: 612 291-1000
Web: www.bestbuy.com

2017 Sales

	$ mil.	% of total
Domestic	36,248	92
International	3,155	8
Total	**39,403**	**100**

PRODUCTS/OPERATIONS

2018 U.S. Stores by Brand

	No.
Best Buy	
U.S. Best Buy	1,008
Mobile Stand-Alone Stores	257
Pacific Sales	28
Total	**1,293**

2018 Sales

	$ mil.	% of total
Domestic	38 662.9	92
International	3 498.8	8
Total	**42,151**	**100**

2018 International Stores by Brand

	No.
Canada	
Best Buy	134
Best Buy Mobile	51
Mexico	
Best Buy	25
Express	6
Total	**216**

2018 Sales by Domestic Category

	% of total
Products	
Consumer Electronics	33
Computing & Mobile Phones	45
Entertainment	8
Appliances	10
Services	4
Total	**100**

2018 Sales by International Category

	% of total
Products	
Computing & mobile phones	46
Consumer electronics	32
Entertainment	7
Appliance	8
Services	5
Other	2
Total	**100**

Selected Brands

Domestic
   Best Buy
   Best Buy Mobile
   Geek Squad
   Magnolia Audio Video
   Pacific Sales
International
   Canada
   Best Buy
   Best Buy Mobile
   Cell Shop
   Connect Pro
   Future Shop
   Geek Squad
   China
   Five Star
   Europe
   The Carphone Warehouse
   The Phone House
   Geek Squad
   Mexico
   Best Buy
   Geek Squad

Selected Products

Consumer Electronics
   Audio
   Car stereos
   Home theater audio systems
   MP3 players
   Satellite radio systems
   Video
   Digital cameras and camcorders
   DVD players
   Televisions
Computing and mobile phones
   Computers
   Networking equipment
   Office furniture
   Printers
   Scanners
   Supplies
   Telephones
Entertainment
   CDs
   Computer software
   DVDs
   Subscription plans
   Video game hardware and software
Appliances
   Dishwashers
   Microwave ovens
   Refrigerators
   Stoves and ranges
   Vacuum cleaners
   Washers and dryers

COMPETITORS

ARTISTdirect	METRO AG
Amazon.com	MSN
Apple Inc.	MediaNet Digital
Audible Inc.	Myspace
Barnes & Noble	Office Depot
Brilliant Digital	OfficeMax
Entertainment	RadioShack
Brookstone	RealNetworks
Buy.com	Sears Holdings
Buzz Media	Sony Music
Conn's	Staples
Costco Wholesale	Systemax
Dell	Target Corporation
Fry's Electronics	Trans World
Gateway Inc.	Entertainment
HMV Retail	Virgin Group
Hastings Entertainment	Wal-Mart
Home Depot	Yahoo!
Lowe's	eMusic.com

HISTORICAL FINANCIALS

Company Type: Public

Income Statement

FYE: February 3

	REVENUE ($ mil.)	NET INCOME ($ mil.)	NET PROFIT MARGIN	EMPLOYEES
02/18*	42,151	1,000	2.4%	125,000
01/17	39,403	1,228	3.1%	125,000
01/16	39,528	897	2.3%	125,000
01/15	40,339	1,233	3.1%	125,000
02/14	42,410	532	1.3%	140,000
Annual Growth	(0.2%)	17.1%	—	(2.8%)

*Fiscal year change

2018 Year-End Financials

Debt ratio: 10.38%	No. of shares (mil.): 282
Return on equity: 23.65%	Dividends
Cash ($ mil.): 1,101	Yield: 0.0%
Current ratio: 1.26	Payout: 41.7%
Long-term debt ($ mil.): 811	Market value ($ mil.): 20,160

	STOCK PRICE ($) FY Close	P/E High/Low		PER SHARE ($) Earnings	Dividends	Book Value
02/18*	71.24	23	13	3.26	1.36	12.76
01/17	43.47	13	7	3.81	1.57	15.14
01/16	27.93	16	10	2.56	1.43	13.52
01/15	35.20	11	6	3.49	0.72	14.21
02/14	23.54	28	10	1.53	0.68	11.50
Annual Growth	31.9%			20.8%	18.9%	2.7%

*Fiscal year change

Big Lots, Inc.

One of North America's largest broadline closeout retailers Big Lots operates more than 1400 stores across the US. It sells a variety of brand-name products — including food and other consumables furniture housewares and decor seasonal items and toys — that have been overproduced returned discontinued or liquidated. Furniture represents the company's largest product line accounting for nearly a quarter of sales. Big Lots also has e-commerce operations and offers products via its website including some items only available online.

Operations

Big Lots sells merchandise in seven primary categories: furniture food consumables soft home seasonal hard home and electronics toys & accessories.

Furniture which includes upholstery mattresses case goods and ready-to-assemble items generates about a quarter of total sales. The food consumables (health items cosmetics plastics pet supplies) soft home (bedding frames rugs decor) and seasonal categories each account for about 15% of sales. The rest of sales is contributed by hard home (home appliances maintenance items) and electronics toys & accessories.

Geographic Reach

Big Lots has locations in nearly all US states with California Texas Florida and Ohio home to about a third of its stores and representing nearly 35% of sales.

The company boasts five regional distribution centers one each in Alabama California Oklahoma Ohio and Pennsylvania to receive process and distribute the majority of its merchandise to its retail locations across the US.

Sales and Marketing

Traditionally using television campaigns as its chief marketing channel Big Lots has shifted its marketing efforts to focus on capturing its customers' daily attention on mobile devices and digital media. It has significantly increased its presence in social and digital media outlets conducting entire campaigns on Facebook Instagram Pinterest Twitter and YouTube to drive increased brand awareness with its core customers and attract new customers.

In conjunction with those channels Big Lots still uses printed ad circulars in-store signage and television advertising to promote its brand and advertise special discounts in its stores.

Financial Performance

Amid store closures Big Lots has seen flat revenue over the past five years with growth between 0%-1%. Net income however has been trending upward a little more consistently during that time.

In fiscal 2017 (ended January 2018) the company reported revenue of $5.3 billion up 1% from the prior year. The increase is almost entirely because an extra week in the fiscal year as compared to 2016 offset by a net decrease of 16 stores.

Net income was $190 million that year up nearly 25% from fiscal 2016. Selling and administrative expenses and depreciation expense were both down in 2017 which combined with the slight uptick in revenue boosted the bottom line.

Cash at the end of fiscal 2017 was $51 million about the same as the prior year. Cash from operations contributed $250 million to the coffers while investing activities used $156 million mainly for capital expenditures. Financing activities used another $94 million for dividends to stockholders and treasury shares acquired.

Strategy

Big Lots is still focused on its Edit to Amplify strategy first introduced in 2013 and enhanced in 2016 to focus on merchandise categories it considers ownable and winnable. The company's attention investments and floor space are first dedicated to the segments it believes it can own (Furniture Seasonal) and next to the segments it believes it can win (Soft Home Food Consumables). Adjacent categories such as Hard Home and Electronics Toys & Accessories have been narrowed in recent years. (The bankruptcy of toy retailer Toys 'R' Us in 2018 caused Big Lots to rethink its decreased focus on toys at least temporarily as it looks to capture some of the holiday toy spending.)

The company's Store of the Future concept introduced in 2017 and scheduled to roll out over five to seven years (although not necessarily chainwide) further emphasizes the Edit to Amplify strategy with more prominent positioning of those ownable and winnable categories and a revamped product mix.

As with many of its competitors Big Lots is also strengthening its e-commerce platform and omnichannel services. It was somewhat late to the e-commerce game first launching its platform in 2016. It has continued to expand and enhance its online offerings in the years since.

HISTORY

As a kid growing up in Columbus Ohio Russian-born Sol Shenk (pronounced "Shank") couldn't stand to pay full price for anything. His frugality blossomed into a knack for buying low and wholesaling. After a failed effort to make auto parts Shenk began the precursor to Consolidated Stores in 1967 backed by brothers Alvin Saul and Jerome Schottenstein.

The company started by wholesaling closeout auto parts and buying retailers' closeout items to sell to other retailers. By 1971 Shenk had branched into retailing selling closeout auto parts through a small chain of Corvair Auto Stores.

One of Shenk's sons suggested they devote space in the Corvair stores to closeout merchandise other than car parts. Sales surged and Shenk decided to sell the Corvair outlets and focus on closeout stores. The first Odd Lots opened in 1982. Consolidated grew more than 100% annually for the next three years. By 1986 the year after it went public the company was opening two stores a week in midsized markets around the Midwest.

Shenk found that people would buy anything as long as the price was right. Two years after the mania for Rubik's Cubes ended Odd Lots bought 6 million of the puzzles (once priced at $8) at 8 cents apiece marked them up 500% and sold them all.

By 1987 the company had nearly 300 Odd Lots/Big Lots stores. But runaway growth had created massive inventory shortages and losses as disappointed customers stopped browsing the company's sparsely stocked shelves. The woes coincided with a falling-out with the Schottensteins. Shenk retired in 1989.

Apparel and electronics retail executive William Kelley was named chairman and CEO the next year. Kelley returned Consolidated to its closeout roots and increased sales through acquisitions and creating new discount chains.

Consolidated doubled its size in 1996 with the $315 million purchase of more than 1000 struggling Kay-Bee Toys (now KB Toys) stores from Melville Corp. The expansion continued with the 1998 purchase of top closeout competitor Mac Frugal's Bargains - Closeouts. (Mac Frugal's had nearly bought Consolidated in 1989 before Consolidated board members vetoed the deal.) The $1 billion acquisition of Mac Frugal's gave Consoli-

dated another 326 western stores under the Pic 'N' Save and Mac Frugal's names.

In 1999 Consolidated combined its online toy sales operations with those of BrainPlay.com to form KBkids.com. In mid-2000 Kelley was ousted as CEO handing the title over to CFO Michael Potter.

In December 2000 the company sold KB Toys (including KBkids.com) to a group led by KB management and global private equity firm Bain Capital for about $300 million. In mid-2001 the company changed its name to Big Lots and began converting all stores to that name to establish a national brand. Big Lots bought the inventory of bankrupt Internet home furnishings giant Living.com in June.

In 2002 the company completed converting 434 stores to the Big Lots banner including 380 stores previously operating under the names of Odd Lots Mac Frugal's and Pic 'N' Save. The name changes were part of a larger initiative to broaden the appeal of closeout retailing and to establish a unified national brand. During the year Big Lots opened 87 new stores and closed 42 others.

In 2003 Big Lots continued to remodel stores opened 86 new locations and closed 36 others. In 2004 the company opened about 100 new stores and continued to add furniture departments to its existing stores.

The company shuttered 174 stores in 2005 including 43 Big Lots Furniture stores and exited the frozen food business. Store closures continued in 2006 with a net loss of 25 locations.

In 2011 Big Lots acquired

EXECUTIVES

Evp Chief Merchandising And Operating Officer, Lisa M. Bachmann, age 56, $738,277 total compensation

Evp Human Resources And Store Operations, Michael A. (Mike) Schlonsky, age 51, $481,931 total compensation

Evp Chief Administrative Officer And Cfo, Timothy A. (Tim) Johnson, age 50, $578,317 total compensation

President Ceo And Director, David J. (Dave) Campisi, age 62, $1,092,308 total compensation

Svp And Cio, Stewart Wenerstrom, age 51

Vice President Of Transportation, Carlos Rodriguez

Vp Strategic Planning, Dan Yokum

Vice President Food Division, Michael PE Morales

Vice President Dmm, Robert Lebrun

Regional Vice President, Thomas R Myron

Regional Vice President, Gary E Huber

Vice President Home Texiles, Kevin Kuehl

Vp Advertising, Shelley Rubin

Vice President Merchandise Planning, Craig Hart

Vice President, Joshua Nanberg

Vice President, Deborah Kelley

Senior Vice President Merchandising, Michelle Christensen

Vice President Information Technology Program Management Office, Tom Czajkowski

Senior Vice President General Counsel And Corporate Secretary, Rocky Robins

Vice President Tax, Mike Watts

Vice President In Store Marketing And Merchandise Presentation, Louis Dorado

Vice President Store Projects, Gary Null Hubr

Chairman, Philip E. Mallott, age 60

President Ceo And Director, David J. (Dave) Campisi, age 62

Board Member, Marla Gottschalk

Auditors: Deloitte & Touche LLP

LOCATIONS

HQ: Big Lots, Inc.
300 Phillipi Road, P.O. Box 28512, Columbus, OH
43228-5311
Phone: 614 278-6800   **Fax:** 614 278-6666
Web: www.biglots.com

2017 Locations

	No.
California	151
Texas	112
Florida	104
Ohio	96
North Carolina	72
Pennsylvania	67
New York	63
Georgia	53
Tennessee	47
Indiana	44
Other states	607
Total	**1,416**

PRODUCTS/OPERATIONS

2017 Sales

	$ mil.	% of total
Furniture	1,237	23
Food	824	16
Consumables	822	16
Soft Home	790	15
Seasonal	766	15
Hard Home	429	8
Electronics Toys & Accessories	403	7
Total	**5,271**	**100**

COMPETITORS

99 Cents Only	Michaels Companies
Amazon.com	OllieÂ's Bargain
BJ's Wholesale Club	Outlet
Costco Wholesale	Ross Stores
Dollar General	Sears
Dollar Tree	TJX Companies
Family Dollar Stores	Target Corporation
Five Below	Tuesday Morning
Fred's	Corporation
J. C. Penney	Variety Wholesalers
Jo-Ann Stores	Wal-Mart
Kmart	

HISTORICAL FINANCIALS

Company Type: Public

Income Statement

FYE: February 3

	REVENUE ($ mil.)	NET INCOME ($ mil.)	NET PROFIT MARGIN	EMPLOYEES
02/18*	5,270	189	3.6%	34,800
01/17	5,200	152	2.9%	35,100
01/16	5,190	142	2.8%	35,900
01/15	5,177	114	2.2%	36,100
02/14	5,301	125	2.4%	38,100
Annual Growth	**(0.1%)**	**10.9%**	**—**	**(2.2%)**

*Fiscal year change

2018 Year-End Financials

Debt ratio: 12.10%
Return on equity: 28.29%
Cash ($ mil.): 51
Current ratio: 1.73
Long-term debt ($ mil.): 199

No. of shares (mil.): 41
Dividends
  Yield: 0.0%
  Payout: 22.8%
Market value ($ mil.): 2,421

	STOCK PRICE ($) FY Close	P/E High/Low	PER SHARE ($) Earnings	Dividends	Book Value
02/18*	57.74	14 10	4.38	1.00	15.97
01/17	48.67	17 11	3.32	0.84	14.70
01/16	38.78	18 13	2.80	0.76	14.67
01/15	45.91	24 12	2.06	0.51	14.92
02/14	26.79	18 12	2.16	0.00	15.66
Annual Growth	**21.2%**	**— —**	**19.3%**	**—**	**0.5%**

*Fiscal year change

Biogen Inc

With its pipeline full of biotech drugs Biogen aims to meet the unmet needs of patients around the world. The biotech giant is focused on developing treatments in the areas of immunology and neurology. Its product roster includes best-selling drugs Tecfidera and Avonex (interferon) for the treatment of relapsing multiple sclerosis (MS); Tysabri a drug treatment for MS and Crohn's disease; and Fampyra which improves walking in adults with MS. Other products include Plegridy for MS. Founded in 1978 Biogen serves customers in more than 90 countries.

Operations

Biogen's top selling drug Tecfidera is sold in markets around the globe and accounts for around 35% of annual revenues. It is an oral therapy marketed in the US for the treatment of patients with relapsing forms of MS. It is sold in Europe for patients with relapsing-remitting MS (RRMS).

The firm's next-best seller Avonex (interferon) accounts for some 25% of revenues. A treatment to improve walking in adults with MS the Avonex pen is a single-use auto-injector version of the drug for once-weekly dosing.

Another top-selling global drug is Tysabri bringing in more than 15% of revenues. Despite the drug's troubled regulatory history — the drug can only be prescribed under a strict risk management plan due to the possible side effect of a rare brain condition — the company continues to pursue additional uses for the drug.

Rituxan sales conducted through a partnership with Genentech account for another 10% of sales and are classified as "unconsolidated joint business" revenues. In addition to non-Hodgkin's lymphoma and rheumatoid arthritis Rituxan is approved to treat leukemia follicular lymphoma and vasculitis.

Another drug MS treatment Fampyra (also known as Ampyra) is sold in partnership with Acorda Therapeutics. Biogen is also co-marketing Zinbryta another MS treatment in US with AbbVie.

In addition to gaining revenue from the development and sales of its products (both directly and through partnerships) Biogen receives royalties on some patents it has licensed to other companies. For instance The Medicines Company pays royalties on sales of anticoagulant Angiomax.

Products in Biogen's pipeline include the anti-LINGO program for MS BAN2401 (in collaboration with Eisai) for Alzheimer's disease and STX-100 for idiopathic pulmonary fibrosis.

Geographic Reach

Biogen has offices in the US Australia Canada Japan the US and several European countries. It has direct sales operations in about 30 countries and operates through distribution partners in another 60 countries.

The US is Biogen's largest market bringing in more than 60% of total revenues. Europe follows with Germany alone representing more than 5% of revenues.

Sales and Marketing

Biogen primarily distributes its products in the US through wholesale pharmaceutical distributors mail-order specialty distributors and shipping service providers. Two wholesale distributors AmerisourceBergen and McKesson each bring in more than 10% of the firm's total revenues. Outside of the US distribution varies but includes wholesale pharmaceutical distributors and third-party distribution partners.

Avonex is marketed through Biogen's direct sales force to specialist physicians and hospitals in North America Europe and select other countries around the globe. The company also handles global marketing efforts for Tysabri. Genentech handles sales and marketing duties for Rituxan while marketing duties for Fampyra are split with Acorda (Biogen sells the drug in Europe and Canada).

In 2016 Biogen spent $106 million on advertising versus $108.6 million in 2015 and $92.9 million in 2014.

Financial Performance

Biogen's revenues and profits have steadily risen over the years as sales of its products have increased. In 2016 net revenue rose 6% to $11.4 billion largely due to higher sales of Tecfidera and Alprolix (which has since been spun off). Tecfidera sales rose 9% tto $4 billion that year as sales in existing markets increased; the drug also continues to be launched in new markets boosting sales even further. Alprolix sales rose 45% to $333.7 million that year.

In 2016 net income increased 4% to $3.7 billion due to the higher revenue and a relatively low increase in operating expenses. Cash flow from operations rose 22% to $4.5 billion that year primarily due to higher earnings and positive changes in current liabilities.

Strategy

Biogen is the industry leader in multiple sclerosis treatments and in Europe it has a strong business in biosimilars (Benepali a biosimilar version of Enbrel and Flixabi a biosimilar of Remicade). It launched four new therapies during 2016 and the approval of spinal muscular atrophy treatment Spinraza that year should provide the company with its next blockbuster.

Biogen's pipeline of drug candidates is focused on treatments for central nervous system ailments including Alzheimer's MS amyotrophic lateral sclerosis (ALS) neuropathic pain and lupus. In addition to proprietary candidates the company has collaborative development candidates with Genentech Portola Pharmaceuticals (lupus and rheumatoid arthritis) and other drugmakers and it continuously looks to expand its pipeline through acquisitions and partnerships.R&D expenses totaled $1.97 in 2016 down from $2.01 billion in 2015.

The company has had its share of setbacks though. In 2015 Tysabri failed in a late-stage clinical trial for secondary progressive MS. The company responded to the setback by initiating certain restructuring efforts including stopping tests for Tysabri's effectiveness against secondary progressive MS as well as stopping test for pipeline drug anti-TWEAK's effectiveness against lupus nephritis. Biogen also cut some 880 employees (about 11% of its workforce) that year. In 2016 the company's anti-LINGO MS drug failed in mid-stage trials; Biogen is exploring additional studies for the treatment.

In early 2017 Biogen spun off its growing hemophilia operations into a separate publicly traded company named Bioverativ. That business' marketed products include Eloctate and Alprolix; the new firm continues its activities around the discovery and development of hemophilia therapies utilizing XTEN technology.

Mergers and Acquisitions

Biogen has expanded its operations through purchases of drug development firms as well as by purchasing commercialized and development-stage drugs. In 2015 the company acquired UK-based Convergence Pharmaceuticals a clinical-stage biopharmaceutical for $200.1 million. The deal added Convergence's CNV1014802 candidate (for the treatment of trigeminal neuralgia and sciatica) to Biogen's pipeline.

HISTORY

Biogen Idec was formed out of the 2003 merger of IDEC Pharmaceuticals and Biogen.

The company began experiencing troubles with its lead product — Tysabri developed with partner Elan— soon after its formation. Sales were temporarily halted in 2005 after several patients died from a rare neurological condition. The companies were allowed to reintroduce Tysabri in 2006 (when it was also launched in Europe) under a strict risk management plan that insures sufficient doctor and patient education about risks and proper usage.

Activist investor Carl Icahn held a minority stake in the company for several years and kept a watchful eye over his investment. In 2007 he bullied the company to put itself up for sale but no buyer came through. Then he began a series of proxy battles in an attempt to stack the board with his own nominees to gain further control. By 2010 he had secured three seats on the board filled with his own representatives and resumed talks of seeing Biogen Idec broken into parts and/or sold to a larger pharmaceutical company.

Ichan's persistence might have contributed to the retirement of Biogen Idec's long-time CEO James Mullen in mid-2010 with George Scangos (former CEO of Exelixis) stepping in as Mullen's replacement. Scangos implemented sharp changes in late 2010 launching a reorganization plan aimed at reducing operational costs and increasing efficiencies. The plan included a 13% workforce reduction and a streamlining of R&D programs to focus primarily on neurological disease. Biogen Idec halted or licensed out its oncology and cardiovascular development programs and consolidated a number of US sites. As a sign that he was pleased with Mullen's work in early 2011 Icahn reduced his ownership stake and did not seek to gain control of more board seats; he sold his remaining interests in the firm in mid-2011.

EXECUTIVES

Evp Chief Legal Officer And Corporate Secretary, Susan H. Alexander, age 61, $697,721 total compensation
Evp And Cfo, Jeffrey D. (Jeff) Capello, age 53
Evp Human Resources, Kenneth A. (Ken) DiPietro, age 60, $648,023 total compensation
Ceo And Director, Michel Vounatsos, $519,231 total compensation
Evp And Head Of Research And Development, Michael D. (Mike) Ehlers, $491,827 total compensation
Evp Neurology Discovery And Development Center Neurodegeneration Therapeutic Area And Chief Medical Officer, Alfred W. Sandrock, age 60, $564,596 total compensation
Evp Pharmaceutical Operations And Technology, Paul McKenzie
Vp And Chief Accounting Officer And Interim Principal Financial Officer, Greg Covino, age 52
Evp And Head Of Global Marketing Market Access And Customer Innovation, Chirfi Guindo
Vice President Global Public Affairs, Katja Buller
Executive Vice President And Chief Medical Officer, Al Sandrock
Senior Vice President Corporate Development, Richard Brudnick
Vice President Customer Support, Janis Meyer
Vice President, Adam Adamson
Vice President Eu Market Access And Pricing, Chris Leibman
Vice President Global Engineering, Phillip McDuff
Medical Director, Martha Fournier
Senior Vice President Translational Medicine And Technology, Timothy Harris
Vice President Sales And Field Operations, Todd Nichols
Medical Director Clinical Development, Mark Beatty
Vice President Of Quality, Sid Senroy

Senior Vice President Program Management, Johnathan Palmer
Vice President Global Commercial Strategy, Adrian Gottschalk
Vice President Treasurer, Michael Dambach
Executive Vice President Human Resources, Scott Handren
Executive Vice President Of Human Resources, Kenneth Dipetrio
Vice President Of Global Medical Affairs Biogen Idec's Avonex, Thorsten Eickenhorst
Vice President Managing Director, Simon Jordan
Vice President Research And Development Technology, Andrew Allen
Vice President Executive Director Biogen Idec Innovation Incubator, Rainer Fuchs
Vice President Medical Research, Bradley Maroni
Vice President Alzheimers Disease, Samantha Haeberlein
Senior Vice President Research And Early Development, Anirvan Ghosh
Vice President Legal Chief Employment Counsel, Jo A Taormina
Vice President Legal Chief Employment Counsel, Jo Taormina
Director, Stelios Papadopoulos, age 70
Evp Chief Legal Officer And Corporate Secretary, Susan H. Alexander, age 61
Ceo And Director, Michel Vounatsos
Abm, Karmon Warren
Abm, Don Benson
Board Member, Eric Rowinsky
Member Of The Board, Bob Pangia
Auditors: PricewaterhouseCoopers LLP

LOCATIONS

HQ: Biogen Inc
225 Binney Street, Cambridge, MA 02142
Phone: 617 679-2000
Web: www.biogen.com

2017 Sales

	$ mil.	% of total
US	7,017	57
Europe	2,844	23
Asia	160	1
Other	332	3
Unconsolidated joint business	1,559	13
Other	360	3
Total	**12,273**	**100**

PRODUCTS/OPERATIONS

2017 Sales

	$ mil.	% of total
Products		
Tecfidera	4,214	34
Interferon	2,645	22
Tysabri	1,973	16
Spinraza	883	7
Benepali	370	3
Fampyra	91	1
Zinbryta	52	1
Eloctate	48	-
Fumaderm	39	-
Alprolix	26	-
Flixabi	9	-
Other products	360	3
Other	1,559	13
Total	**12,273**	**100**

Selected Products

Approved
  Avonex (multiple sclerosis)
  Fampyra (multiple sclerosis with Acorda Therapeutics)
  Fumaderm (severe psoriasis in Germany only)
  Rituxan (non-Hodgkin's lymphoma chronic lymphocytic leukemia follicular lymphoma rheumatoid arthritis vasculitis)
  Tecfidera (multiple sclerosis)
  Tysabri (multiple sclerosis Crohn's disease; with Elan Pharmaceuticals)
In development

GA101 (chronic lymphocytic leukemia non-Hodgkin's lymphoma)
Plegridy (PEGylated interferon beta 1a relapsing forms of multiple sclerosis)
Tysabri (secondary-progressive MS)

COMPETITORS

AbbVie	Johnson & Johnson
Abbott Labs	Merck KGaA
Amgen	Millennium: The Takeda
Bayer HealthCare	Oncology Company
Pharmaceuticals	Novartis
Bristol-Myers Squibb	Pfizer
Cephalon	Roche Holding
Genentech	Sanofi
Genmab	Teva
GlaxoSmithKline	UCB

HISTORICAL FINANCIALS

Company Type: Public

Income Statement   FYE: December 31

	REVENUE ($ mil.)	NET INCOME ($ mil.)	NET PROFIT MARGIN	EMPLOYEES
12/18	13,452	4,430	32.9%	7,800
12/17	12,273	2,539	20.7%	7,300
12/16	11,448	3,702	32.3%	7,400
12/15	10,763	3,547	33.0%	7,350
12/14	9,703	2,934	30.2%	7,550
Annual Growth	8.5%	10.8%	—	0.8%

2018 Year-End Financials

Debt ratio: 23.47%	No. of shares (mil.): 197
Return on equity: 34.54%	Dividends
Cash ($ mil.): 1,224	Yield: —
Current ratio: 2.32	Payout: —
Long-term debt ($ mil.): 5,936	Market value ($ mil.): 59,341

	STOCK PRICE ($) FY Close	P/E High/Low	PER SHARE ($) Earnings	Dividends	Book Value
12/18	300.92	18 12	21.58	0.00	66.12
12/17	318.57	29 21	11.92	0.00	59.63
12/16	283.58	19 13	16.93	0.00	56.23
12/15	306.35	31 17	15.34	0.00	42.88
12/14	339.45	29 22	12.37	0.00	46.08
Annual Growth	(3.0%)	— —	14.9%	—	9.4%

BJ's Wholesale Club Holdings Inc

LOCATIONS

HQ: BJ's Wholesale Club Holdings Inc
25 Research Drive, Westborough, MA 01581
Phone: Fax: 774 512-7400
Web: www.bjs.com

HISTORICAL FINANCIALS

Company Type: Public

Income Statement   FYE: February 3

	REVENUE ($ mil.)	NET INCOME ($ mil.)	NET PROFIT MARGIN	EMPLOYEES
02/18*	12,754	50	0.4%	26,520
01/17	12,350	44	0.4%	—
01/16	12,467	24	0.2%	—
Annual Growth	1.1%	44.5%		

2018 Year-End Financials

Debt ratio: 84.19% No. of shares (mil.): 87
Return on equity: — Dividends
Cash ($ mil.): 34 Yield: —
Current ratio: 0.91 Payout: 1,538.8%
Long-term debt ($ mil.): 2,534 Market value ($ mil.): —

	STOCK PRICE ($) FY Close	P/E High/Low		PER SHARE ($)	
			Earnings	Dividends	Book Value
02/18*	0.00	— —	0.54	8.31	(11.71)
01/17	0.00	— —	0.48	0.00	(3.89)
Annual Growth	—	— —	6.1%	—	—

*Fiscal year change

BlackRock Inc

With some $6.3 trillion in assets under management BlackRock is the world's largest public investment management firm. It specializes in equity and fixed income products as well as alternative and multi-class instruments which it invests in on behalf of institutional and retail investors worldwide. Clients include pension plans governments insurance companies mutual funds endowments foundations and charities. BlackRock also provides risk management services through BlackRock Solutions and is a leading provider of exchange-traded funds (ETFs) through iShares. The firm has offices in more than 30 countries. BlackRock serves around 90% of the Fortune 100 largest companies.

Operations

BlackRock manages some $6.3 trillion in assets through 135 investment teams. The BlackRock Solutions division provides risk management advisory and enterprise investment system services. iShares one of BlackRock's brands is a leading provider of exchange-traded funds (ETFs).

BlackRock's iShares is the world's largest ETF in the world with $1.3 trillion in assets under management.

BlackRock offers active and passive retail investment services. Mutual funds account for the majority of retail investment sums at around 80%. Retail has a US and an international arm.

The company possesses $3.4 trillion in institutional assets of which $2.3 trillion are index funds and $1.1 trillion active. Its clients consist of pensions foundations and endowments; official institutions; and financial and other institutions.

BlackRock's Asset Liability And Debt and Derivative Investment Network (or to use its snappier name Aladdin) is its enterprise resource management system which provides risk management portfolio management and trading and operation tools for other asset managers and institutional investors. Aladdin is used by around 25000 investment professionals around the world.

Geographic Reach

New York-based BlackRock has more than 70 offices in more than 30 countries. The company makes more than 65% of its revenue in the Americas. Europe accounts for nearly 30% and the Asia-Pacific region 5%. BlackRock has clients and investments in more than 100 countries.

Sales and Marketing

BlackRock serves 15 out of the 25 largest endowments and foundation organizations in the US. It also serves around 90 of the Fortune 100 companies and more than 90% of the largest US retirement plans.

BlackRock focuses on establishing and maintaining its investment management relationships by marketing its services through financial professionals pension consultants third-party distribution relationships or directly to investors themselves.

Clients include tax-exempt institutions (defined benefit pension plans charities and foundations); official institutions (central banks sovereign wealth funds supranationals and other government entities); and taxable institutions (insurance companies financial institutions corporations and third-party fund sponsors and retail investors). Two-thirds of BlackRock's assets are pension plan assets.

Financial Performance

Thanks to a rising stock market and a growing investor base BlackRock has nearly quintupled its assets under management since 2007 — from $1.3 trillion to $6.3 trillion at the end of 2017 — which has led strong fee and advisory income growth over the past few years.

In fiscal 2017 revenue surged 12% to $12.5 billion due to growth in base fees performance fees and technology and risk management revenue. The strongest gains were in fees from iShares exchange-traded fundswhich added $570 million to revenue while higher demand for Aladdin added $82 million to the top line.

The 2017 US Tax Cuts and Jobs Act produced a tax benefit of $1.2 billion for BlackRock in 2017 helping net income swell 56% to $5.0 billion.

Cash from operations increased 72% to $3.8 billion mostly due to higher net income.

Strategy

Even powerful fund managers' jobs are not immune to the threat of automation. In 2017 BlackRock sacked seven portfolio managers as part of a wider shift away from active stock pickers and towards a robot-led quantitative approach. Amid relative market stability active fund managers are less able to beat the market than passive trackers. Investors pulled some $40 billion from actively managed funds during 2016. The robo-funds can be offered at a lower price than the more expensive hand-picked investment funds.

Part of the shift to automation includes the transfer of $1 trillion in assets under custody of State Street to JP Morgan in 2017. BlackRock hopes the move will cut operating expenses; JP Morgan has been investing in automation technology enabling the cheaper provision of services.

The company aims to drive customer growth in its Aladdin enterprise risk management system as well as its wider solutions business. Its goal is to grow Aladdin and other solutions to 30% of total revenue by 2022.

Mergers and Acquisitions

In 2017 BlackRock acquired First Reserve's equity infrastructure franchise First Reserve Energy Infrastructure Funds. The acquisition will help connect BlackRock's clients with energy infrastructure projects.

Company Background

BlackRock is led by CEO Laurence Fink who has overseen a string of major acquisitions in recent years expanding into private equity real estate energy and hedge funds as investors look to diversify beyond stock and bond funds.

Fink engineered a blockbuster merger with Barclays Global Investors (BGI) in 2009. In the deal which was several years in the making BlackRock bought Barclays Global Investors from UK banking giant Barclays for some $15 billion. The deal resulted in a new company operating under the BlackRock name. Barclays Bank retained a 20% stake in the combined firm but Fink remained in charge of the enterprise. The merger nearly tripled BlackRock's assets under management and propelled the company to the top of the international money management industry by enhancing its investment and risk management capabilities. The deal also gave BlackRock a much larger footprint outside the US and added more than 3500 new employees.

EXECUTIVES

President And Director, Robert S. (Rob) Kapito, age 61, $750,000 total compensation

Chairman And Ceo, Laurence D. (Larry) Fink, age 65, $900,000 total compensation

Senior Managing Director, Robert W. (Rob) Fairbairn, age 52, $350,000 total compensation

Senior Managing Director And Chief Risk Officer, Bennett W. Golub, age 60

Senior Managing Director And Global Head Of Multi-asset Strategies, J. Richard (Rich) Kushel, age 51, $500,000 total compensation

Senior Managing Director And Head Of Trading Liquidity And Investments Platform, Richard L. (Richie) Prager

Chairman And Head Of Asia/pacific, Ryan D. Stork, age 46

Senior Managing Director Head Of Global Active Equities And Chairman Blackrock Alternative Investors, Mark Wiseman

Senior Managing Director And Global Head Of Ishares And Index Investments, Mark K. Wiedman

Senior Managing Director And Head Of Global Human Resources, Jeffrey A. Smith, age 47

Senior Managing Director Head Of The Americas Region And Global Head Of Blackrock Alternative Investors, Mark S. McCombe, age 52

Senior Managing Director And Head Of Europe Middle East And Africa (emea), David J. Blumer, age 49

Senior Managing Director And Cfo, Gary S. Shedlin, age 54, $500,000 total compensation

Senior Managing Director Coo And Global Head Blackrock Solutions, Rob L. Goldstein, age 44, $500,000 total compensation

Senior Managing Director And Global Head Business Operations And Technology, Derek K. Stein

Vice President, Ed Mallon

Vice President Human Resources, Katie Nedl

Vice President Database Administration, David Louie

Vice President, Marie McCarthy

Vice President Institutional Sales Benelux, Norbert Van Veldhuizen

Vice President Technology, Rob Smith

Vice President, Laura Tyrholm

Vice President, Derek Cook

Vice President Of Information Systems, Saba Anvar

Vice President, Robert Chiolan

Vice President, Vineet Gupta

Vice President Research And Development, Karen Definis

Vice President, John Kent

Vice President Crm Database Marketing Manager, Sorin Tudor

Vice President, Piyush Naik

Vice President, Paul Horowitz

Vice President, Duane Liedl

Senior Compliance Manager Vice President, Beth Moore

Vice President Corporate Communications, Farrell Denby

Vice President Recruiting, Ken Daponte

Vice President Risk And Quantitative, Fay Zhao

Vice President, Viola Dunne

Vice President, Sherrika Fuller

Vice President Access And Identity Management, Nikhil Mathur

Vice President, Gina Forziati

Vice President, Victor Glazer

Vice President Hr Business Partner, Anna Kim

Vice President, Nigel Benson
Vice President Desktop Engineering, David Gagliardotto
Vice President, Simon Chew
Vice President, Dana Aurora
Vice President Finance, Roger Castoral
Vice President, Ada Aromando
Vice President, Sharda Lekhraj
Vice President, Richard Steel
Vice President, Bridget Dean-Hammel
Vice President Program Management, Jennifer Galler
Vice President, Uri Morris
Vice President Sourcing, Michael Schnalzer
Vice President, Peter Hirsh
Vice President Professional Development, Enid Crystal
Vice President, Phil Green
Vice President, Brian Roberson
Vice President Fixed Income Portfolio Management Group, Sriram Reddy
Vice President, Richard Mejzak
Vice President Trader Portfolio Manager Cash Managment, Gene Meshechek
Vice President User Experience And Design, Devjit Basu
Vice President, David Kurapka
Vice President, Jeff Puntney
Vice President, Jason Devlin
Vice President Compliance, John Longhurst
Vice President, Benjamin Cunningham
Vice President Critical Infrastructure, Ed Cannon
Vice President Business Operations, David Birnbaum
Vice President Information Technology And Legal Sourcing, Hillary Grand
Vice President, Lauren Giametta
Vice President, Benjamin Friedlander
Vice President Market Research, Katie Herzog
Vice President, Amanda Huckle
Vice President, Brian Fitzpatrick
Vice President, Susan Lapczynski
Vice President, Loryn Sperber
Vice President, Ashish Sharma
Vice President, Kumar Duvvuri
Vice President, Aaron Kipnis
Vice President, David Edson
Vice President, Miranda Harrison
Vice President, Patricia Belcher
Vice President Securities, Jason Yanagihara
Vice President Legal And Compliance, Danny Riemer
Vice President, Ryan Shriber
Vice President, Sukhbir Gill
Vice President Of Human Resources, Toretha McGuire
Vice President, Kenny Ma
Vice President, Amy Goldfarb
Vicepresident, Rodrigo Castaneda
Vice President Access And Identity Management, Nikhil Mathur
Vice President Aladdin And Technology, Paul Dearman
Vice President, Matthew Roberts
Vice President Media Services, Lisa Sturdivant
Vice President, Vincent Dellaglio
Vice President, Julie Hoffman
Vice President Risk And Quantitative Analysis, Ben Wu
Vice President Institutional Client Business Institutional Sales, Guido Bridelli
Vice President, Heinrich Schutze
Vice President, Joanne Mavra
Ishares Governance Vice President, Leah Schoellkopf
Vice President Institutional Sales, Chantal Giles
Vice President, Davina Stickland
Vice President, Celia Chau
Vice President Internal Audit, Stella Yap

Vice President Director Account Management, Whitney Ehrlich
Vice President Service Center, Johnathan Keating
Vice President Governance Risk And Compliance, Bobby Singh
Vice President, Patricia Inlander
Vice President Investment Management Consultant, Robert Fakhry
Vice President Sma Portfolio Manager, David Dressel
Vice President, Elizabeth Schloemer
Vice President, Kirsten Filosa
Vice President, Nancy Dambrosio
Vice President Finance, Amit Soni
Vice President Business Development, Luis Garcia
Vice President Product Management (digital), Jennifer Rector
Vice President Digital Marketing, Ritesh Joseph
Vice President Risk Analytics, Sangeeta Pandey
Vice President And Compensation Consultant, Michael Lebowitz
Vice President Human Resources Systems And Analytics Business Analyst, Kyla M Donnelly
Vice President Blackrock, Brian Compton
Vice President Blackrock, Long Tran
Vice President Blackrock, Marc Chin
Vice President Blackrock, Raja Kurapati
Vice President, Sai Patnala
Vice President Blackrock, Scott Golub
Vice President Legal, Michelle Galvez
Vice President, Rupkumar Radhakrishnan
Vice President Security Risk Management, Janice Douglas
Vice President Security Engineering, Rebecca Quinn
Vice President Legal And Compliance, Eugene Drozdetski
Vice President, Ian Pinnavaia
Vice President, Vincent Van Der Meer
Vice President, Qiuting Pan
Vice President Portfolio Compliance, Niranjan Nagarkar
Vice President, Tim Wright
Vice President, Simon Barr
Vice President, Neneth Robledo
Vice President Asset Management, Gillian Tng
Vice President, Melanie Ng
Vice President Real Estate, Tatiana Tezel
Vice President, Naveen Shukla
Vice President, Gaurav Mahajan
Vice President, Sakthivel Thiyagarajan
Auditors: Deloitte & Touche LLP

LOCATIONS

HQ: BlackRock Inc
55 East 52nd Street, New York, NY 10055
Phone: 212 810-5300
Web: www.blackrock.com

2017 Sales

	$ mil.	% of total
Americas	8,406	67
Europe	3,432	28
Asia/Pacific	653	5
Total	12,491	100

PRODUCTS/OPERATIONS

2017 Sales

	$ mil.	% of total
Investment advisory administration fees & securities lending		
Equity	5,722	46
Fixed income	2,921	23
Multi-asset class	1,181	10
Alternative investments	1,105	9
Cash management	558	5
Black Rock Solutions & advisory	755	6
Distribution fees	24	—
Other revenue	225	2
Total	12,491	100

COMPETITORS

Allianz Global Investors	Federated Investors
Bank of New York Mellon	Legg Mason
	Morgan Stanley
Charles Schwab	Principal Global
Dimensional Fund Advisors	State Street
	UBS
	Waddell & Reed

HISTORICAL FINANCIALS

Company Type: Public

Income Statement

FYE: December 31

	REVENUE ($ mil.)	NET INCOME ($ mil.)	NET PROFIT MARGIN	EMPLOYEES
12/17	12,491	4,970	39.8%	13,900
12/16	11,155	3,172	28.4%	13,000
12/15	11,401	3,345	29.3%	13,000
12/14	11,081	3,294	29.7%	12,200
12/13	10,180	2,932	28.8%	11,400
Annual Growth	5.2%	14.1%	—	5.1%

2017 Year-End Financials

Debt ratio: 2.28%
Return on equity: 16.32%
Cash ($ mil.): 6,894
Current ratio: 2.89
Long-term debt ($ mil.): 5,014

No. of shares (mil.): 159
Dividends
Yield: 0.0%
Payout: 33.0%
Market value ($ mil.): 82,182

	STOCK PRICE ($) FY Close	P/E High/Low	PER SHARE ($) Earnings	Dividends	Book Value
12/17	513.71	17 12	30.23	10.00	198.93
12/16	380.54	21 15	19.04	9.16	180.13
12/15	340.52	19 15	19.79	8.72	174.37
12/14	357.56	19 15	19.25	7.72	166.07
12/13	316.47	18 12	16.87	6.72	158.83
Annual Growth	12.9%	— —	15.7%	10.4%	5.8%

Blackstone Group LP (The)

Throw a rock and you're bound to hit a Blackstone investment. The Blackstone Group is one of the world's largest real estate private equity and alternative asset managers in the world with around $430 billion in assets under management and such notable past holdings as Michaels Stores and SeaWorld. The firm manages investment vehicles including private equity funds funds of hedge funds and real estate funds. Clients include public and corporate pensions financial institutions and individuals.

Operations

The Blackstone Group is organized into four business segments: Private Equity Real Estate Credit and Hedge Fund Solutions.

The Private Equity segment produces about 30% of revenue and typically holds interests in more than 70 companies. It has some $100 billion in assets under management (about 75% of which are in the US) and has traditionally been involved in leveraged buyouts of developed companies investments in growth-oriented companies development projects and funding for smaller companies needing money and leadership to scale in fragmented industries.

The Real Estate segment is one of the largest real estate investment management operations in the world with $115 billion in assets under management. The operations focus on acquiring high quality well-located real estate that is undermanaged and for sale at attractive prices. It then addresses property or business issues through active management and once the property reaches potential it sells the real estate. Its portfolio include retail residential industrial office and hotel properties. It generated a bit more than 45% of Blackstone revenue.

The company's Credit business GSO Capital Partners accounts for a bit less than 15% of revenue. It focuses on credit-oriented financial arrangements in alternative assets using senior and subordinated debt preferred stock and even common stock as vehicles for its investment. Credit has about $140 billion in assets under management.

Blackstone's Hedge Fund Solutions business primarily made up of Blackstone Alternative Asset Management (BAAM) has more than $70 billion in assets under management and makes just more than 10% of revenue. Its clients include public and corporate pension funds and high net worth individuals.

Geographic Reach

New York-based Blackstone Group has 25 offices worldwide in the Americas the Asia Pacific region and in Europe. In the US the firm has branches in Houston Los Angeles and Santa Barbara. Its overseas offices are in Beijing Dubai Dublin Dusseldorf Hong Kong London Madrid Mexico City Montecito Mumbai Paris San Paulo Seoul Shanghai Singapore Sydney Tokyo and Toronto.

The firm holds real estate properties and portfolio (private equity) companies throughout the world. Investors also have a global presence.

Financial Performance

In recent years Blackstone?s revenue and income trends moved in unison both peaked dipped and pushed back upwards. Since 2012 it grew earnings considerably higher almost 7-fold on revenues that have improved more than 75%. The worldwide economic growth backdrop provided a nice tailwind for Blackstone whose business is providing credit and expertise in the growth of other businesses.

In 2017 Blackstone revenue jumped nearly 40% to $7.1 billion due to appreciation in the value of its private equity and real estate holdings whose carrying values increased some 15% each. Investment income ticked up $42 million on appreciation of its hedge fund holdings and management & advisory fees improved more than $300 million. Assets under management for all division in the Blackstone Group rose from $366 billion to $434 billion.

Earnings for 2017 grew 50% from the prior year. Helped by higher revenues the group also harvested a tax windfall of $404 million due to the reduction in US Federal tax rate from 35% to 21%.

Cash at year end was $2 billion an increase of $155 million. Financing activities contributed $2.8 billion mainly attributed to $7.6 billion that Blackstone took out in new loans. Investing activities used $188 million and operating activities depleted the stash by $2.4 billion primarily due to purchases of investments.

Strategy

Blackstone?s four segments each follow a set of investment policies to achieve their respective financial objectives. Depending on market conditions and anticipated economic activity one segment might be more active than others. In 2017 Blackstone?s Real Estate segment participated in a slew of transactions continuing a multi-year upward trend.

Real Estate has been growing at an even faster clip (and is now larger) than its Private Equity business over the past few years thanks to prudent property investments that have seen healthy valuation gains in the hot real estate market. In 2017 it committed a $500 million investment to refurbish and redevelop its Chicago-located 110 story Willis Tower. In that same year it purchased Hotel Investment Partners a Spanish owner of 14 tourist focused hotels on Spain?s southern coast. It also launched a non-publicly-traded Real Estate Investment Trust (REIT) targeted at individual investors; in December 2017 alone purchased nearly $375 million in properties.

Not to be forgotten Blackstone's legacy Private Equity division is known as a hands-on investor that builds up its portfolio companies' values before selling them off for large profits. However 2017 was a challenging year due to uncertainty in US Federal tax laws. Overall US M&A activity slid 16% and rest of world was largely flat compared to the prior year. With the tax law change in place Blackstone has a renewed positive outlook for M&A transactions.

Mergers and Acquisitions

In 2018 Blackstone agreed to purchase a majority stake in Thomson Reuters' Financial and Risk business for $20 billion.

In 2017 Anadarko Petroleum agreed to sell its South Texas oil and gas assets to Sanchez Energy and The Blackstone Group for $2.3 billion.In that same year Spanish company Banco Popular agreed to sell a majority stake in its ?30 billion ($33 billion) real estate asset portfolio to Blackstone.

Also in 2017 Blackstone acquired Aon's human resources outsourcing business for $4.8 billion. The business supplies some 15% of the United States' entire working population and conducts health retirement and HR services. Blackstone added to its UK portfolio with the purchase of Clarion Events an independent organizer of some 180 worldwide events for roughly A?600 million.

Company Background

In 2013 the firm purchased the Hughes Center complex in Las Vegas for $347 million to eventually benefit from the region's rebound. Blackstone was also part of an investor group that bought Extended Stay Hotels owner HVM which was in bankruptcy. All of the hospitality investment activity helped bring in a dramatic rise in revenues in 2013.

In China following its strategy to invest in high-growth Chinese companies through its partnership with the Shanghai-Pudong district government a consortium led by Blackstone agreed in late 2013 to acquire China-based global consulting and technology services company Pactera Technology International Ltd. for about $600 million. The move marked Blackstone's foray into China's technology outsourcing industry a sector traditionally dominated by Indian firms.

In 2012 in capitalizing on the boom in energy markets Blackstone completed fundraising for its first energy-focused private equity fund Blackstone Energy Partners L.P. with total fund commitments of $2.4 billion. The firm also raised $13.3 billion for its seventh global real estate fund BREP VII making it the biggest real estate fund in the world. In 2013 Blackstone acquired secondary private fund of funds unit Strategic Partners Fund Solutions in a deal that added some $9.4 billion in assets under management.

Founded in 1985 by industry veterans Peter Peterson and CEO Stephen Schwarzman the once-reclusive Blackstone went public in June 2007. The public offering which was a first among major US private equity firms valued Blackstone at upwards of $4 billion.

HISTORY

In 2013 the firm purchased the Hughes Center complex in Las Vegas for $347 million to eventually benefit from the region's rebound. Blackstone was also part of an investor group that bought Extended Stay Hotels owner HVM which was in bankruptcy. All of the hospitality investment activity helped bring in a dramatic rise in revenues in 2013.

In China following its strategy to invest in high-growth Chinese companies through its partnership with the Shanghai-Pudong district government a consortium led by Blackstone agreed in late 2013 to acquire China-based global consulting and technology services company Pactera Technology International Ltd. for about $600 million. The move marked Blackstone's foray into China's technology outsourcing industry a sector traditionally dominated by Indian firms.

In 2012 in capitalizing on the boom in energy markets Blackstone completed fundraising for its first energy-focused private equity fund Blackstone Energy Partners L.P. with total fund commitments of $2.4 billion. The firm also raised $13.3 billion for its seventh global real estate fund BREP VII making it the biggest real estate fund in the world. In 2013 Blackstone acquired secondary private fund of funds unit Strategic Partners Fund Solutions in a deal that added some $9.4 billion in assets under management.

Founded in 1985 by industry veterans Peter Peterson and CEO Stephen Schwarzman the once-reclusive Blackstone went public in June 2007. The public offering which was a first among major US private equity firms valued Blackstone at upwards of $4 billion.

EXECUTIVES

President And Coo, Hamilton E. (Tony) James, age 67, $350,000 total compensation

Chairman And Ceo, Stephen A. Schwarzman, age 71, $350,000 total compensation

Senior Managing Director And Head Of Private Equity Portfolio Operations, David L. (Dave) Calhoun, age 61

Senior Managing Director And Cfo, Michael S. Chae, age 49, $350,000 total compensation

Senior Managing Director Gso Capital Partners, Bennett J. Goodman, age 60

Senior Managing Director And Head Of Tactical Opportunities, David S. Blitzer, age 48

Senior Managing Director And Global Head Of Real Estate, Jonathan D. Gray, age 48

Senior Managing Director And Head Of Multi-asset Investing And External Relations, Joan Solotar, age 53, $350,000 total compensation

Vice Chairman And President And Ceo Blackstone Alternative Asset Management, J. Tomilson Hill, age 69, $350,000 total compensation

Senior Managing Director Private Equity London, Joseph P. Baratta, age 47

Senior Managing Director And Chief Legal Officer, John G. Finley, age 61, $350,000 total compensation

Senior Managing Director And Cto, William Murphy

Chairman Asia-pacific, Christopher (Chris) Heady

Senior Managing Director And President Gso, Dwight Scott, age 54

Senior Managing Director And Ceo Blackstone Insurance Solutions, Chris Blunt

Senior Vice President Of Facilities And Construction Management Global Corporate Services, Anthony Riccio

Vice President, Brian Batten

Vice President Information Technology, Andrew Scott

Senior Vice President Finance Group, Stanley Go

Vice President, Melanie Endo
Vice President Credit Business, Juliann O'Sullivan
Senior Vice President, Christine Cangir
Vice President, Rita Mangalick
Vice President, John Wander
Vice President, Alexis Sachin
Vice President Finance, Masako Sunada
Vice President Innovations And Infrastructure, Michael Scaturo
Vice President, Stephane Aubry
Vice President, John Tierney
Vice President, Ronald Lintag
Divisional Vice President, Byung U Choi
Vice President, Brij Kalaria
Vice President, Nentcho Nentchev
Vice President Credit Businesses, Justin Hall
Vice President, John Shields
Vice President, Raphael Kiam
Assistant Vice President, Satie Prashaud
Vice President, Michael Schlappig
Vice President, Brett Chalanick
Vice President, Thomas Procida
Assistant Vice President, Alexander Brezden
Vice President, Ilan Halal
Assistant Vice President, Kelly Yan
Vice President Strategic Partners, Emily Ho
Vice President, Justin Smith
Vice President, Thomas Kali
Vice President, Kevin Kresge
Vice President, Stephen O'Connor
Vice President, Michael Distefano
Assistant Vice President, Jason Drum
Assistant Vice President, Michael LaCerda
Vice President, Bryan Shelby
Vice President, Katie Brackenbury
Assistant Vice President, Eric Meyer
Vice President Business Analyst, Cindy Hwang
Assistant Vice President, Sophie Chen
Vice President Real Estate Legal And Compliance Group, Madeleine Russo
Vice President, Lauren Brescia
Vice President, Taylor Carvajal
Vice President, Kuohsin Chen
Assistant Vice President, Joshua Wallin
Vice President, Brett Crandall
Vice President, Christian Vardeleon
Vice President, Jack Pitts
Assistant Vice President, Frank Alleva
Vice President, Katherine Daco
Vice President, Sebastian Grasso
Vice President, Gregory Bilse
Senior Vice President Credit Businesses, Thomas Iannarone
Senior Vice President, Bryan Sullivan
Vice President, Kevin Gee
Vice President, Paul Sheaffer
Vice President, Mike Wilcox
Vice President, Matthew Pedley
Vice President, Mark Tornga
Vice President, Michelle Harika
Vice President, Roberta Osborne
Senior Vice President, Christopher Duff
Vice President Finance, Walter Dinsmore
Vice President Software Development, David Tanzer
Assistant Vice President, Amanda Hewitson
Vice President, Sal Aloia
Vice President, Daniel Chang
Vice President, Thomas Procida
Vice President, Gordon McKemie
Vice President, Cooper Wright
Vice President, Michael Pierog
Vice President, Michael Amoroso
Vice President, Milca Beltre
Vice President Real Estate Debt Strategies, Damiano Buffa
Vice President, Marni Blivice
Assistant Vice President, Mai LA
Vice President, Cj Brown
Assistant Vice President, Cornelia Andersson

Senior Vice President Data Governance And Portfolio Reporting, Jana Douglas
Vice President Hedge Fund Solutions, Sarah Acott
Senior Vice President, Susan Burkhardt
Vice President, Jennifer Chang
Senior Vice President, Martin Kamber
Senior Vice President Human Resources, Anna Mignot
Senior Vice President Treasury, Steven Swanson
Assistant Vice President, Jennifer Singh
Vice President Private Wealth Management, Brian Munson
Vice President, Paul Bozgo
Vice President, Eric Tam
Vice President Multi Asset Investing, John Donovan
Vice President, Brijesh Kalaria
Vice President, Bill Sheehan
Vice President, Ryan Chapman
Vice President, Simon Mahler
Senior Vice President, Cathleen Becker
Vice President, Davitt Kelly
Vice President, Mohamed El Beih
Assistant Vice President, Laura White
Vice President, Eugene Baek
Vice President, Ashley Kristoffersen
Vice President Private Wealth Solutions, John Bogosian
Assistant Vice President, Larry Vodopivec
Chairman And Ceo, Stephen A. Schwarzman, age 71
Vice Chairman And President And Ceo Blackstone Alternative Asset Management, J. Tomilson Hill, age 69
Auditors: DELOITTE & TOUCHE LLP

LOCATIONS

HQ: Blackstone Group LP (The)
345 Park Avenue, New York, NY 10154
Phone: 212 583-5000
Web: www.blackstone.com

PRODUCTS/OPERATIONS

2017 Sales by Business Segment

	% of total
Real Estate	44
Private Equity	28
Credit	13
Hedge fund solutions	10
Total	**100**

2016 Sales

	$ mil.	% of total
Management and advisory fees	2	48
Performance fees	3,705	52
Investment income	678	10
Interest & dividends &Other	6	-
Total	**0**	**100**

Selected Investments

Allcargo
Alliant Insurance Services
AlliedBarton Security Services
Antares Restaurant Group
Apria Healthcare
Axis Capital
BankUnited
Bayview Asset Management
Biomet
Caesars Entertainment (formerly Harrah's Entertainment)
Catalent Pharma Solutions
Celanese
Center Parcs
Charter Communications
China Animal Healthcare Ltd.
China National Bluestar Group
CMS Computers Ltd.
Crestwood Midstream Partners
CTI Holdings
Cumulus Media Partners
DJO
Dili Group

eAccess
Emcure
Equity Office Properties
Extended Stay America
Freescale Semiconductor Group
Gates Corporation
Gateway Rail Freight Ltd.
Gerresheimer Group
Gokaldas Exports Limited
Gold Toe-Moretz
Houghton Mifflin
Imperial Home Décor
Independent Clinical Services
Intelenet Global Services
Intertrust
Klöckner Pentaplast
Leica Camera
Maldivian Air
Michaels Stores
Mivisa Envases S.A.U.
Monnet
Montecito
Moser Baer Energy
MTAR Technologies Private
Nuziveedu Seeds
Osum Oil Sands Corp.
PBF Energy
People's Choice TV
Performance Food Group
Pinnacle Foods Corporation
Polymer Group Inc.
RGIS Inventory Specialists
Sonalike International Tractors
SeaWorld Parks & Entertainment
Summit Materials
Stiefel Laboratories
SunGard
Team Health
Texas Genco
Tragus
TRW Automotive
UCAR
United Biscuits
Vivint Inc.
The Weather Channel
Western Integrated Networks

COMPETITORS

AEA Investors	Haas Wheat
American Financial Group	Heico Companies
	Investcorp
Apollo Global Management	Jordan Company
	KKR
Bain Capital	Leonard Green
Berkshire Hathaway	MacAndrews & Forbes
BlackRock	Silver Lake
Clayton Dubilier & Rice	TPG
	The Carlyle Group
Goldman Sachs	Thomas H. Lee Partners

HISTORICAL FINANCIALS

Company Type: Public

Income Statement

FYE: December 31

	REVENUE ($ mil.)	NET INCOME ($ mil.)	NET PROFIT MARGIN	EMPLOYEES
12/17	7,119	1,470	20.7%	2,360
12/16	5,125	1,039	20.3%	2,120
12/15	4,646	709	15.3%	2,060
12/14	7,484	1,584	21.2%	2,190
12/13	6,613	1,171	17.7%	2,010
Annual Growth	**1.9%**	**5.9%**	**—**	**4.1%**

2017 Year-End Financials

Debt ratio: 43.03%
Return on equity: —
Cash ($ mil.): 3,922
Current ratio: 1.18
Long-term debt ($ mil.): 14,815
No. of shares (mil.): 659
Dividends
  Yield: 0.0%
  Payout: 104.9%
Market value ($ mil.): 21,118

STOCK PRICE ($)		P/E		PER SHARE ($)		
	FY Close	High/Low		Earnings	Dividends	Book Value
12/17	32.02	16	13	2.21	2.32	10.06
12/16	27.03	19	14	1.56	1.66	10.04
12/15	29.24	39	25	1.04	2.90	10.04
12/14	33.83	14	11	2.58	1.92	11.85
12/13	31.50	16	8	1.98	1.18	11.01
Annual Growth	0.4%	—	—	2.8%	18.4%	(2.2%)

Blue Hills Bancorp Inc

Auditors: Wolf & Company, P.C.

LOCATIONS

HQ: Blue Hills Bancorp Inc
500 River Ridge Drive, Norwood, MA 02062
Phone: 617 360-6520
Web: www.bluehillsbancorp.com

HISTORICAL FINANCIALS

Company Type: Public

Income Statement — FYE: December 31

	ASSETS ($ mil.)	NET INCOME ($ mil.)	INCOME AS % OF ASSETS	EMPLOYEES
12/17	2,668	16	0.6%	237
12/16	2,469	8	0.4%	228
12/15	2,114	7	0.3%	209
12/14	1,728	(0)	—	202
12/13	1,314	2	0.2%	147
Annual Growth	19.4%	57.7%	—	12.7%

2017 Year-End Financials

Debt ratio: 3.93%
Return on equity: 4.20%
Cash ($ mil.): 46
Current ratio: —
Long-term debt ($ mil.): —

No. of shares (mil.): 26
Dividends
  Yield: 0.0%
  Payout: 89.5%
Market value ($ mil.): 539

STOCK PRICE ($)		P/E		PER SHARE ($)		
	FY Close	High/Low		Earnings	Dividends	Book Value
12/17	20.10	32	24	0.67	0.60	14.83
12/16	18.75	54	38	0.35	0.11	14.46
12/15	15.31	59	46	0.28	0.04	14.00
12/14	13.58	—	—	(0.00)	0.00	14.46
Annual Growth	10.3%	—	—	—	—	0.6%

BNSF RAILWAY COMPANY

BNSF Railway operates one of the largest railroad networks in North America. A wholly-owned subsidiary of Burlington Northern Santa Fe itself a unit of Berkshire Hathaway the company provides freight transportation over a network of about 32500 route miles of track across two-thirds of the western US and two provinces in Canada. BNSF Railway owns or leases a fleet of about 8000 locomotives. It also has some 30 intermodal facilities that help to transport agricultural consumer and industrial products as well as coal. In addition to major cities and ports BNSF Railway serves smaller markets in alliance with short-line partners.

Operations
BNSF Railway serves more than 40 ports and 30 intermodal facilities and operates 1600 trains per day.

In 2014 it hauled nearly 1 million carloads of agricultural commodities; more than 5 million intermodal shipments (truck trailers or containers); nearly 2 million carloads of industrial products; and almost 2.3 million coal shipments. All told the company hauled more than 10 million carloads in 2014.

Geographic Reach
The company's network is spread across 28 US states and three Canadian provinces.

Sales and Marketing
BNSF Railway serves smaller markets by working closely with 200 shortline partners. It has also forms marketing agreements with other rail carriers expanding the marketing reach for each railroad and their customers.

Financial Performance
In 2014 the company's revenues rose by 5.6% due to increased capacity offset by the negative effects of severe winter weather conditions early in the year which dampened transportation activities.

BNSF Railway generated 31% of its revenues in 2014 from consumer products; 28% from industrial products; 22% from coal; and 19% from agricultural products.

It also reported a 1.8% increase in cars/units handled and a 3.5% increase in average revenue per car/unit for the year.

The company accounted for more than 56% of Burlington Northern Santa Fe's net revenues for 2014.

Strategy
As part of its capital plan of $6 billion for 2015 the company has planned some major capital projects to maintain and grow its rail network.

In its northern region the company has plans to invest $1.5 billion across eight states for engineering maintenance and line expansion projects of which $700 million is planned for projects to expand the rail lines and Positive Train Control (PTC advanced technologies designed to automatically stop or slow a train before accidents occur) in that region. In the southern region it plans to spend $800 million in nine states for engineering maintenance and line expansion projects of which $175 million is planned for line expansion initiatives and continued implementation of PTC.

The overall $6 billion investment for 2015 includes $2.9 billion to replace and maintain core network and related assets nearly $1.5 billion on expansion and efficiency projects $200 million for continued implementation of PTC and $1.4 billion for locomotives freight cars and other equipment acquisitions.

In 2014 the company made capital investments for line expansion system improvement projects additional equipment and new employee hires. BNSF Railway had a 2013 capital program (to strengthen its infrastructure) valued at $4.1 billion.

EXECUTIVES

President And Ceo, Carl R. Ice, age 61
Evp Law And Corporate Affairs, Roger Nober, age 53
Evp And Cfo, Julie A. Piggott
Evp And Chief Marketing Officer, Stevan B. Bobb
Evp Operations, Gregory C. Fox
Executive Chairman, Matthew K. (Matt) Rose, age 59

President And Ceo, Carl R. Ice, age 61
Evp Law And Corporate Affairs, Roger Nober, age 53
Evp And Cfo, Julie A. Piggott
Evp And Chief Marketing Officer, Stevan B. Bobb
Evp Operations, Gregory C. Fox
Executive Chairman, Matthew K. (Matt) Rose, age 59
Auditors: DELOITTE & TOUCHE LLP FORT WO

LOCATIONS

HQ: BNSF RAILWAY COMPANY
  2650 LOU MENK DR, FORT WORTH, TX 761312830
Phone: 800 795-2673
Web: WWW.BNSF.COM

COMPETITORS

American Commercial Lines	Kansas City Southern Railway
American Commercial Lines	Kansas City Southern Railway
Canadian National Railway	Kirby Corporation
Canadian National Railway	Kirby Corporation
Canadian Pacific Railway	Landstar System
Canadian Pacific Railway	Landstar System
Canadian Pacific Railway	Norfolk Southern
Ingram Industries	Norfolk Southern
Ingram Industries	Schneider National
J.B. Hunt	Schneider National
J.B. Hunt	Union Pacific Railroad
	Union Pacific Railroad
	Werner Enterprises
	Werner Enterprises

HISTORICAL FINANCIALS

Company Type: Private

Income Statement — FYE: December 31

	REVENUE ($ mil.)	NET INCOME ($ mil.)	NET PROFIT MARGIN	EMPLOYEES
12/17	20,747	12,119	58.4%	41,000
12/16	19,278	4,260	22.1%	—
12/14	22,714	4,397	19.4%	—
12/13	21,552	4,271	19.8%	—
Annual Growth	(0.9%)	29.8%	—	—

2017 Year-End Financials

Debt ratio: —
Return on equity: 58.40%
Cash ($ mil.): 516
Current ratio: 0.70
Long-term debt ($ mil.): —

Dividends
  Yield: —
  Payout: —
Market value ($ mil.): —

BOARD OF EDUCATION OF CITY OF CHICAGO

EXECUTIVES

Pres, Frank Clark
Technology, James V Dispensa
Coordinator, Samantha Treworgy
Information Technology Influen, Hallie Askuvich
Technology Manager, Denise Sangster
Chief Public Policy Officer, Frank Bilecki
Director, Ryan Crosby
Auditors: MCGLADREY LLP CHICAGO ILLINO

BOARD OF REGENTS OF THE UNIVERSITY SYSTEM OF GEORGIA

Boeing Co. (The)

Boeing has built a big name for itself as one of the world's largest aerospace companies. Its commercial jet aircraft models include the 737 narrow body; the fuel efficient 737 MAX; the 747 767 and 777 wide bodies; and the 787 Dreamliner. Serving the military science and space and sea exploration sectors the company also produces KC-46 aerial refueling aircraft the AH-64 Apache helicopter the 702 family of satellites CST-100 Starliner spacecraft and the Echo Voyager unmanned undersea vehicle. Major customers include the US Department of Defense and NASA. Additionally Boeing provides airplane financing and leasing services to both commercial and military customers.

Operations

Boeing's operations are divided into three business units: Commercial Airplanes; Defense Space & Security (DSS); and Boeing Global Services (BGS) which began operations in mid-2017. Supporting these segments is Boeing Capital its global financing operations.

Boeing Commercial Airplanes designs manufactures and services commercial jet aircraft for both passengers and cargo. Models include the 737 narrow body the fuel efficient 737 MAX and the 747 767 777 and 787 families. New product development initiatives include the Boeing 787-10 Dreamliner the 737 MAX and the 777X.

DSS provides design modification and support services for large-scale systems including missiles munitions aerial refuelers transporters and spacecraft. It acts as a systems integrator on several programs including NASA's International Space Station and Missile Defense Agency's Ground-based Midcourse Defense.

The newly formed BGS division caters to aerospace and defense needs across the following four areas: supply chain management engineering aircraft modification digital analytics and training and professional services. The division is also tasked with expanding Boeing's data analytics and information-based services capabilities.

Geographic Reach

Boeing's principal operations are in the US Canada and Australia with some key suppliers and subcontractors located in Europe and Japan. Boeing makes about 40% of its total revenues in the US and about 60% from international markets (primarily Europe Asia/Pacific and the Middle East).

Sales and Marketing

Boeing's main customer is the Department of Defense with approximately 65% of revenues (excluding foreign military sales through the US government). Other significant revenues are derived from international defense markets civil markets and the commercial satellite market.

Financial Performance

After posting record-setting revenues of $96 billion in 2015 Boeing saw its revenues slip 2% to $95 billion in 2016. This was attributed to declines across the majority of its segments.

Commercial Airplanes revenues decreased 1% in 2016 primarily due to lower deliveries. The DSS segment also experienced decreased revenues related to its Commercial Crew program lower milestone revenue related to fewer C-17 aircraft deliveries and lower volume on proprietary programs. In addition Boeing Capital's revenues plummeted due to lower lease income and lower end of lease settlement payments during 2016.

Boeing's profits fell 5% from $5.2 billion in 2015 to $4.9 billion in 2016 due to higher research and development costs related to 787 aircraft flight tests. Despite the revenue and profit declines

Being's operating cash flow climbed from nearly $9.4 billion in 2015 to $10.5 billion in 2016. The rise in cash flow was largely due to lower expenditures on commercial airplane program inventory primarily for its 787.

Strategy

Boeing's growth strategy is centered around its new product development initiatives. Flight testing of the 787-9 Dreamliner variant occurred in 2014 and its first delivery was in mid-2014. The 787-10 is on plan for first delivery in 2018 and will incorporate a high degree of shared design elements and parts commonality with the 787-9 to likewise minimize risk and lower development and fleet maintenance costs. The 777X (Boeing's newest twin-engine jet with 12% lower fuel consumption and 10% lower operating costs than its competitors) is slated for its first delivery in 2019.

In a significant move to make it less reliant on suppliers Boeing in 2017 created a new avionics and aircraft computer system manufacturing division that will produce aircraft electronics systems such as navigation flight controls communications sensors and displays. The move is part of Boeing?s strategy of growing its aftermarket services segment from $14 billion to $50 billion within five to 10 years. By creating its avionics components and systems itself Boeing can continue to reap sales from maintenance and upgrade contracts of its planes for years after they?re sold.

Mergers and Acquisitions

Boeing achieves growth by acquiring businesses that focus on specific technology products and target the needs of emerging markets. In 2018 the company acquired California small-satellite developer Millennium Space Systems allowing Boeing to offer high-performance satellites to its customers. Boeing also formed a partnership in 2018 with Brazil-based Embraer to take over its commercial aircraft operations (Embraer's defense division and business jet unit were not part of the deal). Boeing acquired an 80% interest in the venture and expects costs synergies of about $150 million by 2020.

Another 2018 deal was the purchase of aerospace and aviation parts and services provider KLX Aerospace Solutions. With KLX Boeing hopes to better compete in the aerospace services market and grow its service business.

In late 2016 Boeing acquired Liquid Robotics a manufacturer of Wave Glider the first wave and solar-powered autonomous ocean drone. Boeing made the deal to enhance its seabed-to-space autonomous capabilities. It also plans to meet the challenges facing defense commercial and science customers by making ocean data collection and communications easier and safer.

HISTORY

Bill Boeing who had already made his fortune in Washington real estate built his first airplane in 1916 with naval officer Conrad Westervelt. His Seattle company Pacific Aero Products changed its name to Boeing Airplane Company the next year. During WWI Boeing built training planes for the US Navy and began the first international airmail service (between Seattle and Victoria British Columbia). The company added a Chicago-San Francisco route in 1927 and established an airline subsidiary Boeing Air Transport. The airline's success was aided by Boeing's Model 40A the first plane to use Frederick Rentschler's new air-cooled engine.

Rentschler and Boeing combined their companies as United Aircraft and Transport in 1929 and introduced the all-metal airliner in 1933. The next year new antitrust rules forced United Aircraft and Transportation to sell portions of its operations as United Air Lines and United Aircraft (later United

Technologies). This left Boeing Airplane (as it was known until 1961) with the manufacturing concerns.

EXECUTIVES

Evp And Ceo Boeing Global Services, Stanley A. (Stan) Deal, age 54

Evp And General Counsel, J. Michael (Mike) Luttig, age 63, $903,673 total compensation

Svp Supply Chain And Operations, Patrick M. (Pat) Shanahan, age 56

Chairman President And Ceo, Dennis A. Muilenburg, age 54, $1,640,962 total compensation

President Phantom Works Boeing Defense Space And Security, Darryl W. Davis

Evp And President And Ceo Boeing Commercial Airplanes, Kevin G. McAllister, age 55, $92,308 total compensation

Svp Sales Asia Pacific And President Boeing India, Dinesh A. Keskar, age 64

Evp Business Development And Strategy And Cfo, Gregory D. (Greg) Smith, age 51, $911,442 total compensation

President Boeing Military Aircraft Boeing Defense Space And Security, Shelley K. Lavender, age 54

Svp And President Boeing International, Bertrand-Marc (Marc) Allen, age 44

Svp Information And Analytics And Cio, Theodore (Ted) Colbert, age 44

Vp And General Manager Boeing Research And Technology, Gregory L. (Greg) Hyslop, age 59

President Boeing Capital Corporation, Timothy Myers

Evp And President And Ceo Defense Space And Security (bds), Leanne G. Caret, age 51

President Network And Space Systems, Jim Chilton

President Boeing Defense Space And Security Development (bds), Patrick (Pat) Goggin

Vice President Commercial Sales And Marketing, Ihssane Mounir

Vice President Strategy Global Services, Dennis Floyd

Assistant Vice President, Sharon D Wilson

Vice President Global Trade Services, Haynes Arnett

Boeing Vice President Of Leasing Sales, Bill Collins

Vice President, Karen Tang

Vice President, Bill McSherry

Vice President Legislative Affairs, Steve Bachmann

Regional Vice President, David Cazer

Vice President Human Resources, Grace Miller

Vice President Australia And Pacific Sales, Rick Westmoreland

Vice President Corporate Strategy, Rik Geiersbach

Vice President Customer Support, Don Ruhmann

Vice President Sales, Mitzy Gough

National Account Manager, Jacqueline Stephenson

Vice President, Phyllis Ditocco

Vice President, Paula Nosca-lay

Vice President, James W Hoskinson

Vice President Of Sales For Digital Division, Keith P White

Vice President Integrated Defense System, Gregory Laxton

Vice President Customer Support Americas, Larry Slate

Vice President F A 18 Programs, Mike Gibbons

Vice President Business Systems And Administration, Renee L Stober

Vice President, Darrel Roby

Vice President Airplane Development Engineering, Ed Petkus

Vice President, Sherry Carbary

Vice President, Brad McMullen

Vice President, Jay Byunn

Vice President Business Development, Christopher Raymond

Vp Intellectual Property Management Engineering Operations And Technology, Peter Hoffman

Vice President Of Marketing And Sales, Lynn Johnson

Vice President And Program Manager, Joy Bryant

Vice President, Tim Sele

Vice President Accounting And Financial Reporting, Michael Cleary

Vice President, Randy Woolard

Vice President, Bruce Dennis

Vice President, Thomas Brennan

Vice President, Tobias Bright

Vice President And General Manager For Supplier Management, Steve Schaffer

Vice President Communications Global Services, Conrad Chun

Vice President Of Sales And Marketing, Harry W Gray

Vice President Navigation And Communication Systems Military Satellite Communica, Ken Torok

Vice President Manufacturing Safety And Quality Commercial Airplanes, Walter Odisho

Vice President, Michael Sloup

Senior Vice President Public Policy, Tim Keating

Vice President, Terry Kamm

Vice President, Catherine J Pruss-Jones

Vice President Engineering, Russell E Shue

Senior Vice President Sales, Sharon Y Santillanes

Vice President Supply Chain Boeing Global Services, Kenneth Shaw

Vice President Of Commercial Airplane Contracts, Thomas J Hyland

Vice President, Steve Wallace

Vice President Corporate Audit, Bavan Holloway

Vice President Edelman Employee Engagement Practice, Nicole Silva

Vice President And Program Manager Commercial Programs, Silvia I-Thieme

Vice President Of Decision Support, Rebecca Fasano

Vice President Of International Relations, Troy Thomason

Svp Global Sales And Marketing Defense Space And Security, Thomas Bell

Vice President, Michael Ford

Vice President Director Of Marketing, Paul Mittmann

Senior Vice President Supplier Management, Jim Morris

Vice President Business And Supply Chain Systems, Lakshmi Eleswarpu

Vice President Total Rewards And Human Resources Analytics, Jon Fliss

Vice President, Jeremy Griffin

Vice President, Michael Fleming

Vice President Communications, Linda Mills

Vice President, Stanley A Orr

Vice President Information Technology Business Partners Defense Space And Security, Denise Russell Fleming

Vice Chairman, Raymond L. (Ray) Conner, age 62

Chairman President And Ceo, Dennis A. Muilenburg, age 54

Board Member, Jack Commerford

Secretary, Mark Little

Assistant Treasurer, Ruud Roggekamp

Secretary, Bruce J Cadiz

Board Member, James W Powers

Board Member, Daniel Anderson

Assistant Treasurer, Verett Mims

Board Member, Nancy J Kaatman

Treasurer, Roger Pullman

Board Member, George Durham

Chapter Treasurer, Daniel Hill

Svp Finance And Treasurer, David Dohnalek

Secretary, Chris Tavares

Treasurer, Laura LU

Chapter Treasurer, Daniel Hill

Board Member, Charles Lee

Treasurer, Melinda Donaldson

Auditors: DELOITTE & TOUCHE LLP

LOCATIONS

HQ: Boeing Co. (The)
100 North Riverside Plaza, Chicago, IL 60606-1596
Phone: 312 544-2000
Web: www.boeing.com

2016 Sales

	$ mil.	% of total
US	38,765	41
Asia		
China	10,312	11
Other Asia	10,553	11
Europe	13,790	15
Middle East	13,297	14
Oceania	1,843	2
Canada	2,076	2
Africa	1,999	2
Latin American Caribbean & other	1,936	2
Total	**94,571**	**100**

PRODUCTS/OPERATIONS

2016 Sales

	$ mil.	% of total
Sales of products	84,399	89
Sales of services	10,172	11
Total	**94,571**	**100**

2016 Sales

	$ mil.	% of total
Commercial Airplanes	65,069	69
Defense Space & Security		
Military Aircraft	12,515	13
Global Services & Support	9,937	11
Network & Space Systems	7,046	7
Boeing Capital	298	-
Adjustments	(294)	-
Total	**94,571**	**100**

Selected Products and Services

Commercial Airplanes
Products
737 Next Generation (short-to-medium-range two-engine jet)
747 (long-range four-engine jet)
767 (medium-to-long-range two-engine jet)
777 (long-range two-engine jet)
Boeing Business Jet
787 Dreamliner (in development; long-range super-efficient 200-250 passenger capacity)
747-8 (in development;
Services
Engineering modification and logistics
Maintenance repair and overhaul
Boeing Training & Flight Services
Defense Space & Security
Military Aircraft
AH-64 Apache
B-1B Lancer
B-2 Spirit
F/A-18 Hornet
F-15E Strike Eagle
F-22 Raptor
T-45 Flight Training System
A160 Hummingbird
Harpoon
Insitu
C-17 Globemaster III
CH-47D/F Chinook
V-22 Osprey
Global Services & Support
Integrated logistics
Maintenance modifications and upgrades
Training systems
Government services
Network & Space Systems
Electronic and mission
Cyber security
Infrastructure
Intelligence
Logistics command and control
Satellite and ground operations
Space exploration

COMPETITORS

AgustaWestland	Lockheed Martin
Airbus	Northrop Grumman
Airbus Group	Raytheon
BAE SYSTEMS	Rockwell Collins
Dassault Aviation	Space Exploration
Embraer	Technologies
General Dynamics	Thales
Kaman	United Technologies
Leonardo	

HISTORICAL FINANCIALS

Company Type: Public

Income Statement — FYE: December 31

	REVENUE ($ mil.)	NET INCOME ($ mil.)	NET PROFIT MARGIN	EMPLOYEES
12/18	101,127	10,460	10.3%	153,000
12/17	93,392	8,197	8.8%	140,800
12/16	94,571	4,895	5.2%	150,500
12/15	96,114	5,176	5.4%	161,400
12/14	90,762	5,446	6.0%	165,500
Annual Growth	2.7%	17.7%	—	(1.9%)

2018 Year-End Financials

Debt ratio: 11.80%	No. of shares (mil.): 567
Return on equity: 3,014.41%	Dividends
Cash ($ mil.): 7,637	Yield: 2.1%
Current ratio: 1.08	Payout: 39.9%
Long-term debt ($ mil.): 10,657	Market value ($ mil.): 183,064

	STOCK PRICE ($) FY Close	P/E High/Low	PER SHARE ($) Earnings	Dividends	Book Value
12/18	322.50	22 16	17.85	6.84	0.60
12/17	294.91	22 12	13.43	5.68	0.60
12/16	155.68	20 14	7.61	4.36	1.32
12/15	144.59	21 17	7.44	3.64	9.50
12/14	129.98	19 16	7.38	2.92	12.26
Annual Growth	25.5%	— —	24.7%	23.7%	(53.0%)

BOK Financial Corp

With seven principal banking divisions in eight midwestern and southwestern states multi-bank holding company BOK offers a range of financial services to consumers and regional businesses. In addition to traditional deposit lending and trust services its banks provide investment management wealth advisory and mineral and real estate management services through a network of branches in Arizona Arkansas Colorado Kansas Missouri New Mexico Oklahoma and Texas. Brokerage subsidiary BOSC underwrites public private and municipal securities. BOK also owns electronic funds network TransFund and institutional asset manager Cavanal Hill.

Operations

BOK Financial operates through three primary segments: Commercial Banking Consumer Banking and Wealth Management. The Commercial Banking segment brings in more than 75% of BOK's total revenue with offerings including lending treasury and cash management and risk management products for small midsized and large companies. The Consumer Banking segment which brings in about 15% of total revenue is the retail arm providing lending and deposit services and all mortgage activities. The Wealth Management segment provides private bank and investment advisory services across all markets and it

has more than $16 billion in assets under management. The segment is also engaged in trading and it underwrites state and municipal securities.

Geographic Reach

Most of Tulsa-based BOK Financial's locations are located in and around Tulsa; Oklahoma City; Dallas/Fort Worth; Houston; Albuquerque New Mexico; Denver; Phoenix; and Kansas City in Kansas and Missouri. The company's primary operations facilities lare in Tulsa; Oklahoma City; Dallas; and Albuquerque New Mexico.

Sales and Marketing

In 2017 BOK Financials spent $28.9 million on promotional costs versus $26.6 million in 2016 and $27.9 million in 2015.

Financial Performance

Thanks largely to the improving US economy BOK's revenues have been trending upward for the past five years. Net income has been somewhat more volatile but reached a peak in 2017.

Revenue increased 9% to $1.5 billion in 2017 as interest income increased 17%. Loan trading securities and interest-bearing cash and cash equivalents revenues saw significant growth that year. Asset management income also rose gaining some 20%. These increases were partially offset by a decline in mortgage banking revenue.

With the higher revenue plus certain lower operating expenses (including mortgage banking costs and insurance expenses) net income rose 44% to $331.1 million in 2017.

The company ended 2017 with $2.3 billion in net cash some $220 million less than it had at the end of 2016. Operating activities provided $214.9 million and investing activities provided $739.6 million. Financing activities used $1.2 billion.

Strategy

BOK emphasizes local decision-making at its flagship subsidiary Bank of Oklahoma and its operating divisions Bank of Albuquerque Bank of Arizona Bank of Arkansas Bank of Texas Colorado State Bank and Trust and Mobank. Commercial loans primarily to the energy services health care and wholesale and retail industries make up the majority of the company's loan portfolio. Commercial real estate residential mortgage car and consumer loans round out its lending activities.

The company is also focused on diversifying its revenue stream by growing its mortgage banking brokerage and wealth management operations.

With banking operations in several major oil- and natural gas-producing states more than 15% of the group's lending portfolio is in the energy sector. Because the energy industry has been challenged with low commodity prices BOK's energy-related charge-offs have grown significantly. In Q2 of 2018 net charge-offs reached $10.5 million — more than half of which was attributed to a single energy customer.

Mergers and Acquisitions

In October 2018 BOK Financial acquired financial services company CoBiz Financial which provides commercial banking and other financial services to businesses in Arizona and Colorado through its Colorado Business Bank and Bank of Arizona subsidiaries. The deal valued at $1 billion more than doubled BOK Financial's deposit market share in the two states.

EXECUTIVES

President And Ceo, Steven G. (Steve) Bradshaw, age 58, $484,275 total compensation
Evp And Cfo, Steven E. Nell, age 56, $439,354 total compensation
Evp Corporate Banking, Stacy C. Kymes, age 47
Chief Credit Officer, Marc C. Maun, age 60
Chairman And Ceo Bank Of Texas, Norman P. Bagwell, age 55, $403,054 total compensation

Evp And Chief Human Resources Officer, Stephen D. Grossi
Evp And Cio, Donald T. Parker
Evp Consumer Banking, Patrick E. Piper
Evp Wealth Management And Ceo Bosc. Inc., Scott B. Grauer
Ceo Oklahoma City Market, John Higginbotham
Assistant Vice President Process Consultant, Diana Pruitt
Assistant Vice President Finance And Administration, Lanny L Randolph
Vice President Senior Petroleum Engineer, Sterling Kirk Condry
Senior Vice President, Michael Bickel
Vice President, Alice Worthington
Senior Vice President Credit Administration, Carol Cable
Senior Vice President, Lee Allen
Vice President, Debi Briscoe
Vice President Marketing, Margot McKoy
Senior Vice President, Jill Hall
Senior Vice President, Jeff Sanders
Vice President, Mary Campbell
Vice President Call Center, Gregg Jaynes
Senior Vice President Retirement Plan Services Manager, Cheryl Cranford
Vice President Accounting Control Reporting, Ed Disney
Chairman, George B. Kaiser, age 75
Auditors: Ernst & Young LLP

LOCATIONS

HQ: BOK Financial Corp
Bank of Oklahoma Tower, Boston Avenue at Second Street, Tulsa, OK 74192
Phone: 918 588-6000
Web: www.bokf.com

PRODUCTS/OPERATIONS

2017 Sales

	% of total
Commercial Banking	76
Consumer Banking	7
Wealth Management	17
Total	**100**

Selected Banking Subsidiaries

Bank of Albuquerque National Association
Bank of Arizona National Association
Bank of Arkansas National Association
Bank of Oklahoma National Association
Bank of Texas National Association
Colorado State Bank & Trust
Mobank

COMPETITORS

BBVA Compass	JPMorgan Chase
Bancshares	Regions Financial
Bank of America	UMB Financial
Bank of the West	Wells Fargo
Comerica	Zions Bancorporation
Commerce Bancshares	
First National of	
Nebraska	

HISTORICAL FINANCIALS

Company Type: Public

Income Statement — FYE: December 31

	ASSETS ($ mil.)	NET INCOME ($ mil.)	INCOME AS % OF ASSETS	EMPLOYEES
12/17	32,272	334	1.0%	4,930
12/16	32,772	232	0.7%	4,884
12/15	31,476	288	0.9%	4,789
12/14	29,089	292	1.0%	4,743
12/13	27,015	316	1.2%	4,632
Annual Growth	4.5%	1.4%	—	1.6%

Debt ratio: 0.56%	No. of shares (mil.): 65
Return on equity: 9.89%	Dividends
Cash ($ mil.): 2,317	Yield: 0.0%
Current ratio: —	Payout: 34.6%
Long-term debt ($ mil.): —	Market value ($ mil.): 6,037

	STOCK PRICE ($) FY Close	P/E High/Low		PER SHARE ($) Earnings	Dividends	Book Value
12/17	92.32	18	15	5.11	1.77	53.45
12/16	83.04	24	13	3.53	1.73	50.12
12/15	59.79	17	13	4.21	1.69	49.03
12/14	60.04	17	14	4.22	1.62	47.78
12/13	66.32	15	12	4.59	1.54	43.86
Annual Growth	8.6%	—	—	2.7%	3.5%	5.1%

Booking Holdings Inc

The Priceline Group is the princeling of online travel. It made its name through flights hotels and car rental website priceline.com but ascended to travel royalty after the purchase of booking.com in 2006 which now brings in billions of dollars each year. With Agoda KAYAK RentalCars and OpenTable filling out its portfolio the travel company offers an array of booking options for travelers worldwide. Priceline.com also employs its famous Name Your Own Price booking system that allows customers to haggle on prices for hotels and cars. In the case of airline tickets and hotel reservations it generates sales on the margin keeping the difference between the price paid by the individual and what it shelled out for the ticket or hotel room. Priceline was founded in 1997 .

Operations

Priceline operates an online global travel services network. It works to connect customers looking to make travel reservations with providers of travel services worldwide including more than 1.12 million hotels and accommodations. Hotel reservation services are conducted primarily under the Booking.com priceline.com and Agoda.com brands.

In the US the company offers reservations via its namesake priceline.com brand for rental cars airline tickets vacations packages destination services and cruises. Internationally the company offers a retail price-disclosed hotel and accommodation reservation service through global brands Booking.com (the world's largest online hotel and accommodation website) and Agoda.com (an online hotel reservation service with operations primarily in Asia). Priceline Group's OpenTable allows consumers to set up restaurant reservations online and provide reservation management services for restaurants.

About 75% of Priceline Group's total revenue comes from Agency revenue while Merchant revenue and Advertising revenue make up 20% and 5% of its total revenue respectively.

Geographic Reach

The Connecticut-based global online travel giant serves more than 220 countries. Its ownership of Amsterdam-based Booking.com means the company generates around 70% of its total revenue from the Netherlands. The US and other international markets generate around 15% each.

Priceline Group's Agoda.com is based in Bangkok; KAYAK is headquartered in Stamford Connecticut; OpenTable is based in San Francisco; and Rentalcars.com is located in Manchester UK. Additional offices and data centers are located in

the US UK Switzerland the Netherlands and Hong Kong.

Sales and Marketing

Priceline Group aggressively promotes its brands online relying on internet search engine (mostly Google) keyword purchases referrals from meta-search sites and travel research websites affiliate programs banner and pop-up advertisements and email campaigns to boost its business. The company is one of Google's biggest search marketing customers. The Priceline Group spent $3.5 billion on online advertising during 2016.

Financial Performance

Priceline Group's annual revenue has more than doubled since 2012 thanks to the rising popularity of the online travel booking business.The company is also immensely profitable consistently posting profit margins of around 20%.

In fiscal 2016 sales crested the $10-billion mark for the first time climbing a further 16% to $10.7 billion. Growth was concentrated in Agency revenue — travel reservation commissions mostly as well as travel insurance and global distribution system reservation booking fees — which grew $1.45 billion. Advertising revenue grew by $100 million while Merchant revenue slipped 2% due to lower "Name Your Own Price" reservations on Priceline.com.

Net income however fell for the first time in over a decade declining 16% to $2.1 billion due almost entirely to an impairment charge of $940.7 million relating to OpenTable after the business suffered a sharp write-down. OpenTable has not proved the revenue driver that was hoped for following its costly acquisition in 2014. Excluding this one significant item the company otherwise performed well succeeding in growing sales while reducing cost of revenue and only small increases in higher expenses in headcount and marketing as the company expands.

Cash from operations increased x% to $3.9 billion due to adjustments made to reconcile the asset impairment. Priceline also recorded favorable changes to working capital.

Strategy

Priceline Group reiterated in 2016 its long-term strategy for growth is to expand its service offerings and markets and become the market leader in online travel and travel-related services by "providing consumers better service partnering with travel service providers and restaurants to its mutual benefit and operating entrepreneurial independent brands that share best practices."In 2017 it added a flights section to Booking.com while the KAYAK business acquired two flight meta-search companies — Momondo Group and Mundi — in the same year.

Priceline is scaling backits renowned and sometimes controversial opaque bookings system Name Your Own Price (NYOP). The company's (successful) push to drive more mobile traffic brought about the demise of Priceline's original product — NYOP flights booking — as the bid system proved too cumbersome to port over to the smaller-screened smartphones and tablets. The NYOP flights service was brought to an end in fall 2016.

Mergers and Acquisitions

The Priceline Group strengthened its presence in Europe with the 2017 acquisition of Momondo Group for about $550 million. Momondo operates momondo a meta travel site and Cheapflight. They were folded into Priceline's Kayak brand. In the same year subsidiary KAYAK bought Brazilian meta-search company Mundi which ended its relationship with KAYAK rival Skyscanner.

Company Background

In April 2014 the company changed its name from Priceline.com to The Priceline Group to better reflect the growth of its business and all of its sub-

sidiaries and brands including Booking.com priceline.com KAYAK OpenTable and others.

HISTORY

Priceline founder Jay Walker launched a string of ventures before making the leap into e-commerce. In 1994 he founded Walker Digital an entrepreneurial think tank formed to develop business models that could germinate into new companies.

In 1996 Walker Digital found the impetus that would drive Priceline: Each day major airlines have more than 500000 empty seats. Walker's team reasoned that if the airlines were offered even a discounted price for these empty seats they'd jump at the chance to cut their losses. Based on that premise Walker Digital developed a "name your price" system and founded Priceline in 1997.

The company launched its airfare service in 1998 and obtained financing from General Atlantic Partners and Paul Allen's Vulcan Ventures (now called Vulcan Northwest). That year it expanded into hotel reservations and added a car-buying service. Richard Braddock became chairman and CEO in 1998.

Priceline added home financing services to its offerings in 1999. The company went public with a chart-busting IPO later that year. Priceline also launched a rental car service. Branching into the retail arena it licensed its technology to WebHouse Club for use in selling grocery products. The company sued Microsoft in 1999 claiming that company's Expedia unit's name-your-own-price hotel reservation service violated Priceline's patent.

In 2000 the company licensed its business model to several international ventures including General Atlantic Partners' Priceline.com Europe (headed by Dennis Malamatinas former Burger King CEO) SOFTBANK's Priceline.com Japan (a deal that was later cancelled) MyPrice in Australia and New Zealand (also cancelled) and Asian conglomerate Hutchinson Whampoa. In collaboration with Alliance Capital (now AllianceBernstein) Priceline created subsidiary pricelinemortgage to act as mortgage broker.

Daniel Schulman became CEO later that year. Jay Walker resigned as vice chairman at the end of 2000 after taking on the role of CEO at Walker Digital. After deciding it would probably never be profitable WebHouse Club shut down ending Priceline's foray into grocery sales. Known for its splashy ads Priceline dumped pop icon William Shatner as its TV spokesperson in favor of Sex and the City star Sarah Jessica Parker. (Shatner returned in 2002.) Later that year the company fired Schulman and reappointed Braddock as CEO.

In 2002 the company joined with National Leisure Group to offer cruises from its website. Later that year Priceline purchased the assets of discount travel site Lowestfare.com. It also announced plans to sell cars under a marketing agreement with Autobytel. In late 2002 Braddock passed his CEO responsibilities to president Jeffery Boyd. (Braddock remained as chairman.)

A handful of new international destinations (Australia Japan Indonesia Malaysia South Korea Taiwan) was added in 2003 to Priceline's hotel reservation service. In April 2004 chairman Richard Braddock (former president of Citicorp and one of the last remaining high-profile board members) resigned from the company. Director Ralph Bahna was then named chairman. The following month Priceline acquired most of Travelweb.com. That September it bought Active Hotels of Britain for about $161 million in cash. In December 2004 Priceline acquired the remaining stake in Travelweb for about $4 million.

EXECUTIVES

Ceo Priceline.com, Brett Keller, age 50

Svp And General Counsel, Peter J. Millones, age 48, $330,000 total compensation

Ceo, Glenn D. Fogel, age 56, $315,000 total compensation

Svp Cfo And Chief Accounting Officer, Daniel J. Finnegan, age 55, $315,000 total compensation

Ceo Agoda.com, Robert Rosenstein, age 51

Ceo Kayak, Steve Hafner

President And Ceo Booking.com, Gillian Tans, age 47, $498,356 total compensation

Ceo Rentalcars.com, Ian Brown

Ceo Opentable Inc., Christa Quarles

Vice President Associate General Counsel, Brian Macdonald

Senior Vice President Global Infrastructure, Glen Dalgleish

Chairman, Jeffery H. (Jeff) Boyd, age 61

Svp And General Counsel, Peter J. Millones, age 48

Auditors: DELOITTE & TOUCHE LLP

LOCATIONS

HQ: Booking Holdings Inc
800 Connecticut Avenue, Norwalk, CT 06854
Phone: 203 299-8000   **Fax:** 203 595-0160
Web: www.pricelinegroup.com

2016 Sales

	$ mil.	% of total
The Netherlands	7,783	72
US	1,680	16
Other	1,279	12
Total	**10,743**	**100**

PRODUCTS/OPERATIONS

2016 Sales

	$ mil.	% of total
Agency	7,982	74
Merchant	2,048	19
Advertising and other	712	7
Total	**10,743**	**100**

Selected Products

Airline tickets
Cruises
Hotel rooms
Rental cars
Restaurant reservations
Vacation packages

Selected Brands

agoda.com
Booking.com
KAYAK
OpenTable
priceline.com
rentalcars.com

COMPETITORS

Alibaba Group	Hotwire Inc.
Amazon.com	Internet Brands
American Express	Intuit
Apple Inc.	Microsoft
AutoNation	Orbitz Worldwide
AutoTrader	Prestige Travel
Autobytel	Restaurant.com
BCD Travel	SavvyDiner.com
Carlson Wagonlit	Travelocity
Expedia	Travelport
Facebook	Travelzoo
GetThere	TripAdvisor
Google	Yahoo!
Groupon	Yelp

HISTORICAL FINANCIALS

Company Type: Public

Income Statement

FYE: December 31

	REVENUE ($ mil.)	NET INCOME ($ mil.)	NET PROFIT MARGIN	EMPLOYEES
12/17	12,681	2,340	18.5%	22,900
12/16	10,743	2,134	19.9%	18,500
12/15	9,223	2,551	27.7%	15,500
12/14	8,441	2,421	28.7%	12,700
12/13	6,793	1,892	27.9%	9,500
Annual Growth	**16.9%**	**5.5%**		**24.6%**

2017 Year-End Financials

Debt ratio: 37.41%
Return on equity: 22.21%
Cash ($ mil.): 2,541
Current ratio: 2.58
Long-term debt ($ mil.): 8,809

No. of shares (mil.): 48
Dividends
  Yield: —
  Payout: —
Market value ($ mil.): 84,232

	STOCK PRICE ($) FY Close	P/E High/Low	PER SHARE ($) Earnings	Dividends	Book Value
12/17	1,737.74	43 31	46.86	0.00	232.31
12/16	1,466.06	37 23	42.65	0.00	199.64
12/15	1,274.95	29 20	49.45	0.00	177.29
12/14	1,140.21	30 22	45.67	0.00	164.96
12/13	1,162.40	32 17	36.11	0.00	132.86
Annual Growth	**10.6%**	**— —**	**6.7%**	**—**	**15.0%**

Booz Allen Hamilton Holding Corp.

For almost a century consultants at Booz Allen Hamilton have been helping US government agencies operate more efficiently at home and abroad. The firm provides a wide range of management consulting and technology integration services; its specialties include information technology operations organization and change program management strategy training programs cybersecurity and systems engineering. Booz Allen has long-established relationships with such agencies as the Department of Defense the National Security Agency and the Internal Revenue Service. Investment firm The Carlyle Group owns a majority interest in the consulting firm which was founded in 1914.

Operations

Booz Allen Hamilton typically works under three contract types. Cost-Reimbursable Contracts which account for half of revenue provide for the payment of costs racked up during the completion of a contract (up to a pre-determined ceiling) plus a fee. Under Time-and-Materials Contracts which account for 25% of Booz Allen's sales the company bills its clients for each labor hour and material costs and out-of-pocket expenses. Under Fixed-Price Contacts which also account for 25% of sales the company works to a pre-determined price.

Booz Allen carries out contracts ranging from sub-$1 million to $10 million plus; the latter category accounts for the largest chunk of its sales at around a third of the total. Around 25% of the company's contracts are classified.

Geographic Reach

Booz Allen's headquarters are located in McLean Virginia. The firm also has offices in Annapolis Junction Rockville and Laurel Maryland; San Diego California; Herndon Arlington and Alexandria Virginia; Charleston South Carolina; and Washington D.C.

Sales and Marketing

The majority (95%) of Booz Allen Hamilton's revenue comes from the US government. Defense clients including the US Army Navy/Marine Corps Air Force and Joint Combatant Commands account for around 45% of Booz Allen Hamilton's revenue. Intelligence agencies including the NSA National Geospatial Intelligence Agency and National Reconnaissance Office account for another 25% of sales. Its other customers are mostly civil government clients (energy and environment financial services health homeland security) and global commercial clients (non-US governments and commercial entities in the Middle East North Africa and the Asia/Pacific region).

Financial Performance

Booz Allen Hamilton's revenue has been trending up for the past four years. Fiscal 2018 (ended March 31) was the company's best ever year in terms of revenue which grew 6% to $6.2 billion thanks to higher client demand and billable expenses.

Net income grew 21% to $305.1 million on the back of higher revenue a 0.1 percentage point increase in operating margin and lower income tax paid. Cash from operations fell 3% to $369.1 million due to changes in accounts receivable partially offset by higher net income.

Strategy

Booz Allen Hamilton growth strategy is based on increasing the technical content of its services expanding in the commercial and international markets innovating on its capabilities and establishing a broad network of external partners and alliances. The strategy has been vindicated by strengthening backlog and headcount growth. Investment areas include machine intelligence and directed energy (high-energy lasers or microwaves) which are areas that the company expects to create integrated capabilities and drive demand in the long term. It also makes targeted acquisitions to expand capabilities.

Mergers and Acquisitions

In 2017 Booz Allen acquired technology firm Morphick Inc. The acquisition expands Booz Allen's managed security portfolio and strengthens the firm's capability to help clients counter advanced cyber threats. In the same year it also acquired eGov Holdings Inc. (Aquilent) an architect of IT solutions for the US Federal government for $253.6 million. The acquisition further blends Booz Allen's consulting with advanced technical expertise.

HISTORY

Edwin Booz graduated from Northwestern University in 1914 with degrees in economics and psychology and started a statistical analysis firm in Chicago. After serving in the army during WWI he returned to his firm renamed Edwin Booz Surveys. In 1925 Booz hired his first full-time assistant George Fry and in 1929 he hired a second James Allen. By then the company had a long list of clients including U.S. Gypsum the Chicago Tribune and Montgomery Ward which was losing a retail battle with Sears Roebuck and Co.

In 1935 Carl Hamilton joined the partnership and a year later it was renamed Booz Fry Allen & Hamilton. The firm prospered well into the next decade by providing advice based on "independence that enables us to say plainly from the outside what cannot always be said safely from within" according to a company brochure.

During WWII the firm worked increasingly on government and military contracts. Fry opposed the pursuit of such work for consultants and left in 1942. The firm was renamed Booz Allen &

Hamilton. Hamilton died in 1946 and the following year Booz retired (he died in 1951) leaving Allen as chairman. He successfully steered the firm into lucrative postwar work for clients such as Johnson Wax RCA and the US Air Force.

A separate company Booz Allen Applied Research Inc. (BAARINC) was formed in 1955 for technical and government consulting including missile and weaponry work as well as consulting with NASA. By the end of the decade Time had dubbed Booz Allen "the world's largest most prestigious management consultant firm." The partnership was incorporated as a private company in 1962 and in 1967 commissioner Pete Rozelle requested its services for the merger of the National Football League and American Football League.

When Allen retired in 1970 Charlie Bowen became the new chairman and the company went public. However as the economy stalled during the energy crisis spending for consultants plunged. Jim Farley replaced Bowen in 1975 and the company was taken private again in 1976. A turnaround was engineered and the firm was soon helping Chrysler through its 1979 bailout and developing strategies for the breakup of AT&T in 1984.

Booz Allen again experienced trouble in the 1980s after Farley instituted a competition to select his successor. Michael McCullough was eventually chosen in 1984 but the 10-month election process turned into a dogfight that pitted partner against partner taking an enormous toll on morale. McCullough began restructuring the firm along industry lines creating a department store of services in an industry characterized by boutique houses. The turmoil was too much and by 1988 nearly a third of the partners had quit.

William Stasior became chairman in 1991 and reorganized Booz Allen yet again splitting it down public and private sector lines. Allen died in 1992 the same year the firm moved to McLean Virginia. The company began privatization work in the former Soviet Union and in Eastern Europe in 1992 and continued to emphasize government business including contracts with the IRS (1995) for technology modernization and with the General Services Administration (1996) to provide technical and management support for all federal telecommunications users.

In 1998 the company won a 10-year $200 million contract with the US Defense Department to establish a scientific and technical data warehouse. Ralph Shrader was appointed CEO in early 1999; Stasior retired as chairman later th

EXECUTIVES

Evp Middle East And North Africa (mena), Nabih Maroun

Evp Digital Solutions, Gary D. Labovich

President And Ceo, Horacio D. Rozanski, age 50, $1,437,500 total compensation

Evp Justice And Homeland Security Business, Thad W. Allen

Evp Directed Energy Innovation, Henry A. (Trey) Obering

Evp Cfo And Treasurer, Lloyd W. Howell, age 56, $1,000,000 total compensation

Evp Chief Administrative Officer (cao) And Chief Information Security Officer (ciso), Joseph W. (Joe) Mahaffee, age 60, $765,000 total compensation

Evp Strategic Transformation, Michael M. (Mike) Thomas

Evp Homeland Security And Transportation, Patrick F. Peck, age 60

Evp Client Service Officer (cso) Justice Homeland Security And Transportation (jht), Fred K. Blackburn

Evp Digital Solutions, Gary C. Cubbage

Evp Civil Commercial Group (ccg), Karen M. Dahut, age 54, $1,000,000 total compensation

Evp, Maria Darby

Evp Joint Combatant Command, Judith H. (Judi) Dotson

Evp Infrastructure And Military Health, Laurene (Laurie) Gallo

Evp Engineering And Science And C4isr Crosscut, Patricia Goforth

Vp, Tom Greenspon

Evp Air Force Lead, Gregory Harrison

Evp Financial Services Group, David Kletter

Evp International Business, Christopher Ling

Evp Defense And Intelligence Group, Joseph (Joe) Logue, age 53, $1,250,000 total compensation

Evp Innovation Service Officer (iso) And Cyber Functional Service Officer (fso), Angela M. (Angie) Messer

Vp, Anthony (Tony) Mitchell

Vp, Susan L. Penfield

Evp Energy Business, Gary Rahl

Evp And Lead U.s. Defense And Military Intelligence And Operations, Joseph F. (Joe) Sifer

Evp Defense And Intelligence, Ted Sniffin

Vp, William (Bill) Stewart

Vp, Elizabeth M. (Betty) Thompson, age 63

Evp Strategic Innovation Group (sig), Gregory G. (Greg) Wenzel

Evp Cyber Business, Christopher Pierce

Vp, Joan A. Dempsey

Evp Civil Health Business, Kristine Martin Anderson

Evp Chief Legal Officer And Secretary, Nancy J. Laben, age 56

Vp And Cio, Kevin Winter

Evp Energy Chemicals And Utilities, Walid Fayad

Evp Middle East And North Africa, Ramez Shehadi

Evp Command Control Communications Computers Intelligence Surveillance And Reconnaissance (c4isr), Steve Soules

Evp Army Market, Brian M. McKeon

Evp Digital Practice Middle East And North Africa (mena), Raymond Khoury

Vice President And Group Administrative Officer Defense And Intelligence Market, Joan Wolfle

Senior Vice President Digital Solutions, Jeff Fossum

Vice President, Kevin Vigilante

Senior Vice President, Charles S Hamilton

Vice President, Theodore Kraemer

Senior Vice President And Digital Analytics And Strategy Lead, Julie Mcpherson

Vice President Security Sector, Patricia Hanback

Vice President, Khalid Syed

Vice President Army Business, Jay Dodd

Vice President, Larry Scheuble

Vice President, Ralph Lawrence

Senior Vice President Commercial Health, Lucy Stribley

Vice President, Lutfi Zakhour

Vice President, Adham Sleiman

Vice President, Donald Busson

Senior Vice President And Executive, Booz A Hamilton

Vice President, Chris Pierce

Vice President Sales And Marketing, Scott Barr

Senior Vice President, Jason Escaravage

Vice President Technical Services, Felix Yao

Vice President Civil And Commercial Market, Marlene Aquino

Senior Vice President, George Schu

Senior Vice President Application Workforce And People Solutions, Leslie Raimondo

Vice President, Terry Thompson

Vice President Defense Market, Brian Pickerall

Senior Vice President And Chief Administrative Officer, Samuel R Strickland

Vice President Of Information Technology, Joe Sifer

Vice President, Scott Welles

Vice President, Rob Silverman

Vice President Defense Market, James Gibbons

Senior Vice President, Ken Mills

Executive Vice President Portfolio Strategic Projects, Matthew Calderone

Vice President Human Capital Management, Abe Zwany

Vice President And Lead Contracting Officer, Linda Asher

Senior Vice President Global Defense Group And Crosscut Market Strategy, Andrea Inserra

Vice President Enterprise Cloud Computing Business, Munjeet Singh

Vice President Consulting Services, Craig Todd

Vice President Digital Transformation Programs And Opportunities, Ralph Wade

Vice President Civil Health Business, John Peterson

Vice President Technology Services, Raymond Melnyk

Vice President, Mark Hoffman

Vice President And Deputy General Counsel, Stanley Hillary

Senior Vice President Nextgen Finance Modernization (ngfm) Program, Tim Lawrence

Vice President Civil Health Business, Travis Burd

Vice President Energy Environment And Infrastructure, Johnny Ayoub

Vice President Air Force Military Intelligence And Cyber Business, Kim Bird

Senior Vice President Finance Energy And Economic Development, Mark Gamis

Vice President Finance Energy And Economic Development, Paul Tartaglione

Senior Vice President Health Business, Richard Crowe

Vice President International Cyber Practice, Sedar Labarre

Vice President Navy And Marine Corps Headquarters And Operations, Steve Moore

Vice President Finance Energy And Economic Development, Terence Mandable

Executive Vice President Joint Combatant Command, Judy Dotson

Senior Vice President Cf And Ao, Sam Strickland

Vice President, Chris Ellis

Chairman, Ralph W. Shrader, age 74

Evp Cfo And Treasurer, Lloyd W. Howell, age 56

Evp Chief Legal Officer And Secretary, Nancy J. Laben, age 56

Auditors: Ernst & Young LLP

LOCATIONS

HQ: Booz Allen Hamilton Holding Corp.
8283 Greensboro Drive, McLean, VA 22102
Phone: 703 902-5000
Web: www.boozallen.com

PRODUCTS/OPERATIONS

Selected Markets Served
Civil government
  Benefits and entitlements
  Federal finance
  International development and diplomacy
Defense
  Air Force
  Army
  Joint staff and combatant commands
  Navy and Marine Corps
  Office of the Secretary of Defense and defense agencies
  Space
Energy
Environment
Health
  Health informatics
  Health not-for-profit/nongovernmental organizations
  International public health
  US public health
Homeland security
Intelligence
Law enforcement
Not-for-profit/nongovernmental organizations

Transportation
  Aviation infrastructure
  Highways and automotive technology
  Passenger rail and mass transit

Selected Practice Areas
Assurance and resilience
Economic and business analysis
Information technology
Modeling and simulation
Organization and strategy
Supply chain and logistics
Systems engineering and integration

COMPETITORS

A.T. Kearney	IBM
Accenture	L3 Technologies
BAE SYSTEMS	Leidos
Bain & Company	Lockheed Martin
Boeing	MAXIMUS
Boston Consulting	ManTech
CACI International	McKinsey & Company
Capgemini	Northrop Grumman
Computer Sciences	PA Consulting
Corp.	PRTM Management
Deloitte Consulting	Raytheon
General Dynamics	Unisys
HP Enterprise Services	

HISTORICAL FINANCIALS

Company Type: Public

Income Statement   FYE: March 31

	REVENUE ($ mil.)	NET INCOME ($ mil.)	NET PROFIT MARGIN	EMPLOYEES
03/18	6,171	305	4.9%	24,600
03/17	5,804	252	4.4%	23,300
03/16	5,405	294	5.4%	22,600
03/15	5,274	232	4.4%	22,500
03/14	5,478	232	4.2%	22,700
Annual Growth	3.0%	7.1%	—	2.0%

2018 Year-End Financials

Debt ratio: 50.47%
Return on equity: 54.09%
Cash ($ mil.): 286
Current ratio: 1.44
Long-term debt ($ mil.): 1,755

No. of shares (mil.): 143
Dividends
  Yield: 0.0%
  Payout: 34.1%
Market value ($ mil.): 5,554

	STOCK PRICE ($) FY Close	P/E High/Low	PER SHARE ($) Earnings	Dividends	Book Value
03/18	38.72	19 15	2.05	0.70	3.87
03/17	35.39	23 16	1.67	0.62	3.85
03/16	30.28	16 12	1.94	0.54	2.76
03/15	28.94	19 13	1.52	1.46	1.25
03/14	22.00	14 8	1.54	2.40	1.15
Annual Growth	15.2%	— —	7.4%	(26.5%)	35.4%

BorgWarner Inc

If suburbanites need four-wheel-drive vehicles to turbocharge their urban drive that's OK with BorgWarner. The company is a leading maker of engine and drivetrain products for the world's major automotive manufacturers. Products include turbochargers air pumps timing chain systems four-wheel-drive and all-wheel-drive transfer cases (primarily for light trucks and SUVs) and transmission components. Its largest customers include Volkswagen Ford and Daimler. The company nets more than 75% of its sales from outside the US.

Operations

BorgWarner's two operating segments are Engine Products (more than 60% of total sales) and drivetrain products (nearly 40% of sales). The Engine division manufactures products to optimize engines for fuel efficiency reduce emissions and enhance performance and includes turbochargers electric boosting systems engine timing systems ignition systems air management and cooling and controls. Its Remy business makes starter motors alternators and hybrid electric motors for OEMs. The Drivetrain unit provides automotive transmission components all-wheel drive torque transfer systems and rotating electrical devices. Turbochargers for light vehicles is the company's largest product line representing around 30% of sales.

Key divisions and units include BorgWarner TorqTransfer Systems BorgWarner Transmission Systems BorgWarner Morse TEC and BorgWarner BERU Systems. BorgWarner also operates seven joint ventures located in Japan China India and South Korea including NSK-Warner KK a leading producer of friction plates and one-way clutches in Japan and China.

Geographic Reach

BorgWarner operates more than 60 manufacturing and technical facilities in some 20 countries (including more than a dozen in the US and about half a dozen each in Germany China and South Korea).

Europe is by far BorgWarner's largest market: Germany accounts for roughly 20% of total sales; Hungary accounts for around 10% and other Europe 15%. The US generates around 25% of its sales and South Korea and China together represent some 25%.

Sales and Marketing

BorgWarner markets its products to OEMs of light vehicles (passenger cars sport-utility vehicles vans and light trucks) through separate sales teams for its two product divisions. Volkswagen and Ford each generate around 15% of the company's overall sales. Other key customers include Chrysler Nissan and General Motors.

Financial Performance

Aside from a misfire in 2015 BorgWarner's Engine and Drivetrain revenue has been turbocharged in recent years.

In fiscal 2017 revenue increased 8% to $9.8 billion due to higher sales of light vehicle turbochargers thermal products engine timing systems and stronger international commercial vehicle markets. In the Drivetrain segment BorgWarner sold more all-wheel drive systems and transmission components.

Net income rebounded in 2017 to $439.9 million after an $878.3 million asbestos-related lawsuit charge dragged 2016 net income down to just $118.5 million. Despite the improvement profitability remained below the levels seen in 2013-15 due to restructuring and merger and acquisition-related expenses.

Cash from operations increased 14% to $1.2 billion due to higher earnings.

Strategy

BorgWarner's product strategy puts it in a position to capitalize on growth in hybrid and electric vehicles while continuing to grow in the steadily declining combustion market. Its combustion products are increasingly being used on hybrids: Turbochargers with hybrid applications account for more than 10% of its order backlog. Its eBooster system improved the performance of both combustion vehicles and hybrids and it will supply the FUSO eCanter truck — the world's first all-electric light-duty truck — with its HV250 electric motor and eGearDrive transmission.

The company also grows via regular acquisitions including Sevcon in 2017 and Remy in 2016.

Mergers and Acquisitions

BorgWarner has been generating additional revenue over the years through the use of acquisitions.

In 2017 BorgWarner acquired Sevcon a British producer of electrification technologies with global operations. Its products include motor controllers battery chargers and uninterrupted power source system for electric and hybrid vehicles industrial medical and telecom applications. The purchase price was $10 million.

In a milestone transaction in late 2015 the company acquired Remy International for $1.2 billion. Remy is a global producer of rotating electrical components with key technologies and operations spanning 10 countries. The deal enhanced BorgWarner's rapidly developing powertrain electrification technology line.It sold the Remy light vehicle aftermarket business a year later.

HISTORY

BorgWarner traces its roots to the 1928 merger of major Chicago auto parts companies Borg & Beck (clutches) Warner Gear (transmissions) Mechanics Universal Joint and Marvel Carburetor. The newly named Borg-Warner Corporation quickly began buying other companies including Ingersoll Steel & Disc (agricultural blades and discs) and Norge (refrigerators).

EXECUTIVES

Vice President, Pete Kohler
Vp General Counsel And Secretary, John J. Gasparovic, age 60, $477,250 total compensation
Vp; President And General Manager Borgwarner Transmissions Systems, Robin Kendrick, age 53, $406,250 total compensation
Vp Marketing Public Relations Communications And Government Affairs, Scott D. Gallett, age 52
Evp And Cfo, Ronald T. (Ron) Hundzinski, age 59, $665,750 total compensation
President And Ceo, James R. Verrier, age 55, $1,245,000 total compensation
Vp And President And General Manager Borgwarner Emissions Systems, Brady D. Ericson, age 46, $415,000 total compensation
Vp And President And General Manager Borgwarner Morse Systems, Joseph F. Fadool, age 51, $416,250 total compensation
Vp; President And General Manager Borgwarner Turbo Systems, Frédéric B. Lissalde, age 50, $606,630 total compensation
Vp And President And General Manager Borgwarner Powerdrive Systems, Stefan Demmerle, age 53, $442,750 total compensation
Vice President And Treasurer, Jan Bertsch
Vice President Of Finance, Jim Hohenadel
Vice President Information Technology, Andre Rothfuss
Vp Global Supply Management, Rob Deni
Vp Drivetrain It, Sandra Short
Vice President Sales And Marketing Turbo, Ulli Froehn
Vice President Human Resources, Monica Rottman
Vice President, Karsten Edel
Vice President Finance Morsetec, Daryl Gingell
Vice President Global Supply Chain Management, Thomas Babineau
Vice President, Dan Casasanta
Vice President Director Manager, Mary Srbu
Vice President Global Supply Chain Management, Marco Caputo
Vice President Sales And Engineering, Karl Wagner
Vice President Sales Emmissions Systems, Jean-Francois Savajols
Vice President Sales, Mike Mccabe
Vice President Strategic Risk Management, Michelle Logan

Vp Human Resources, Shelley Bridarolli
Vice President Global Engineering And Sales
  Commercial Vehicle, Wouter Nijenhuis
Vice President And Treasurer, Tom McGill
Vice President Investor Relations, Patrick Nolan
Vice President Finance Emission Systems,
  Frederic Vaillant
Vice President Global Transmission Engineering,
  Isabelle McKenzie
Chairman, Alexis P. Michas, age 60
Vp General Counsel And Secretary, John J.
  Gasparovic, age 60
Auditors: PricewaterhouseCoopers LLP

LOCATIONS

HQ: BorgWarner Inc
  3850 Hamlin Road, Auburn Hills, MI 48326
Phone: 248 754-9200
Web: www.borgwarner.com

2017 Sales

	$ mil.	% of total
United States	2,280	23
Europe		
Germany	1,652	17
Hungary	655	7
Other Europe	1,427	15
China	1,560	16
South Korea	877	9
Mexico	920	9
Other regions	425	4
Total	**9,799**	**100**

PRODUCTS/OPERATIONS

2017 Sales

	$ mil.	% of total
Engine	6,061	62
Drivetrain	3,790	38
Elimination	(52.4)	-
Total	**9,799**	**100**

Selected Products

Engine Group
  Air-control valves
  Chain tensioners and snubbers
  Complete engine induction systems
  Complex solenoids and multi-function modules
  Crankshaft and camshaft sprockets
  Diesel cabin heaters
  Diesel cold starting systems (glow plugs and instant
   starting systems)
  Electric air pumps
  Engine hydraulic pumps
  Exhaust gas-recirculation (EGR) coolers modules
   tubes and valves
  Fan clutches
  Fans and fan drives
  Front-wheel and four-wheel-drive chain and timing-
   chain systems
  High-temperature sensors (for exhaust gas
   aftertreatment systems)
  Ignition coils
  Intake manifolds
  On-off fan drives
  Single-function solenoids
  Throttle bodies
  Throttle position sensors
  Tire pressure sensors
  Transfer cases
  Turbochargers
Drivetrain Group
  Four-wheel-drive and all-wheel-drive transfer cases
  Friction plates
  One-way clutches
  Torque converter lock-up clutches
  Transmission bands

Selected Joint Ventures

BERU Korea Co. Ltd. (51% South Korea ignition coils
  and pumps)
Borg-Warner Shenglong (Ningbo) Co. Ltd. (70% China
  fans and fan drives)
BorgWarner TorqTransfer Systems Beijing Co. Ltd. (80%
  China transfer cases)

BorgWarner Transmission Systems Korea Inc. (60%
  South Korea transmission components)
BorgWarner United Transmission Systems Co. Ltd. (66%
  China transmission components)
BorgWarner-Vikas Emissions Systems India Private
  Limited (60% India EGR coolers)
Divgi-Warner Limited (60% India transfer cases and
  automatic locking hubs)
SeohanWarner Turbo Systems Ltd. (71% South Korea
  turbochargers)

COMPETITORS

American Axle &	Magna Powertrain
Manufacturing	Meritor
DENSO	Mitsubishi Heavy
Dana	Industries
Delphi Automotive	Modine Manufacturing
Systems	NGK SPARK PLUG
GKN	Renold
Honeywell	Robert Bosch
International	Schaeffler
IHI Corp.	Tsubaki Nakashima
JTEKT	Valeo
Kolbenschmidt Pierburg	Visteon

HISTORICAL FINANCIALS

Company Type: Public

Income Statement
FYE: December 31

	REVENUE ($ mil.)	NET INCOME ($ mil.)	NET PROFIT MARGIN	EMPLOYEES
12/17	9,799	439	4.5%	29,000
12/16	9,071	118	1.3%	27,000
12/15	8,023	609	7.6%	30,000
12/14	8,305	655	7.9%	22,000
12/13	7,436	624	8.4%	19,700
Annual Growth	**7.1%**	**(8.4%)**		**10.1%**

2017 Year-End Financials

Debt ratio: 22.36%	No. of shares (mil.): 210
Return on equity: 12.69%	Dividends
Cash ($ mil.): 545	Yield: 0.0%
Current ratio: 1.46	Payout: 28.3%
Long-term debt ($ mil.): 2,103	Market value ($ mil.): 10,770

	STOCK PRICE ($) FY Close	P/E High/Low	PER SHARE ($) Earnings	Dividends	Book Value
12/17	51.09	27 18	2.08	0.59	17.63
12/16	39.44	79 50	0.55	0.53	15.16
12/15	43.23	23 14	2.70	0.52	16.20
12/14	54.95	23 17	2.86	0.51	15.97
12/13	55.91	40 20	2.70	0.25	15.62
Annual Growth	**(2.2%)**	**— —**	**(6.3%)**	**23.9%**	**3.1%**

Boston Private Financial Holdings, Inc.

Boston Private Financial Holdings (BPFH) is a
holding company for firms engaged in wealth management and private banking including Boston
Private Bank & Trust which operates branches in
New England New York Los Angeles and the San
Francisco Bay Area. (The bank sold its branches
in the Pacific Northwest in 2013.) BPFH also owns
four other wealth advisory and investment management firms. The company offers private banking wealth advisory investment management deposits and lending and trust services to wealthy
individuals corporations and institutional clients.

All told BPFH and its affiliates have more than
$30 billion in managed or advised assets.

Operations

In addition to Boston Private Bank & Trust Co.
BPFH's other affiliates include: investment advisory
firms Anchor Capital Advisors and Dalton Greiner
Hartman Maher & Co.; wealth managers Bingham
Osborn & Scarborough and KLS Professional Ad-
visors Group; as well as newly-acquired Banyan
Partners a registered investment advisor. BPFH
sold its majority-owned affiliate Davidson Trust
Co. (DTC) in 2012. DTC was part of the holding
company's wealth advisory business.

Financial Performance

Boston Private Financial Holdings (BPFH) reported revenue of $339.5 million in 2013 an in-
crease of less than 1% versus 2012. The modest
uptick was due to increased recurring fees from
its investment management wealth advisory and
private banking wealth management and trust
businesses as well as other income and a gain on
the sale of loans. Assets under management and
advisory (AUM) increased 19% during 2013 due
to $3.7 billion of market appreciation and $0.2 billion of net flows. All three of the BPFH's segments
experienced gains in AUM.

Net income grew 32% in 2013 compared with
2012 to $70.5 million on a decline in interest ex-
pense on deposits partially offset by a 2% increase
in average balance. The lower interest rate environment in the US has allowed the company's
banking arm to lower interest rates on money markets accounts and certificates of deposit.

Strategy

Since its founding in 1987 Boston Private has
had a voracious appetite for acquiring smaller trust
companies private banks and wealth managers.
While the firm put the brakes on its expansion
and shifted strategies amid the economic recession.
Indeed it divested about a half-dozen money management subsidiaries as way to raise capital and
reduce risk. Also in 2011 the company consolidated its four banking charters into Boston Private
Bank & Trust to simplify its structure and cut
costs.

However with the economy and financial markets on the mend the company has resumed making acquisitions most recently to build its wealth
management business.

Mergers and Acquisitions

In October 2014 Boston Private Bank & Trust
Co. acquired Banyan Partners LLC an independent
registered investment advisory firm based in Palm
Beach Florida. With more than $4.5 billion in client
assets Banyan has offices in Boston Miami Naples
Atlanta Wisconsin Texas and California. The purchase furthered the bank's aim of expanding the
reach and accelerating the development of its
wealth management business.

In May 2013 Boston Private Bank & Trust sold
three offices in the Pacific Northwest to focus on
its banking business in California and New England. The bank recorded a $10.6 million pretax
gain on the sale.

EXECUTIVES

Evp And General Counsel, Margaret W. (Megan)
  Chambers, age 59, $360,000 total compensation
Evp And Coo, Anne L. Randall
**Evp Deposit And Cash Coo And Treasurer Deposit
  Management Boston Private Bank & Trust,**
  George G. Schwartz
**Svp And Chief Lending Officer Boston Private
  Bank & Trust,** James C. Brown
Evp Cfo And Chief Administrative Officer, David J.
  Kaye, age 54, $425,000 total compensation
Ceo; Ceo Boston Private Bank And Trust, Clayton
  G. (Clay) Deutsch, $675,000 total compensation

Evp And Chief Risk Officer, W. Timothy MacDonald, $350,000 total compensation
Ceo Boston Private Wealth Llc, Corey A. Griffin, $400,000 total compensation
Evp And Chief Human Resource Officer, Martha T. Higgins
President Boston Private Wealth Llc, Peter J. Raimondi
Co-president Private Banking Group, Torrance Childs
Evp Private Clients Group, Nicholas A.R. Hofer
Evp Commercial Banking Group, Robert J. Nentwig
Evp And Client Development Officer, Jacqueline S. Shoback
Svp And Chief Fiduciary Officer, Lynn Swenson
Assistant Vice President, Joe Lavigne
Senior Vice President Marketing, Allison Baird
Assistant Vice President Commercial Lending, Jonathan Willis
Vice President Manager Of Credit Administration, Susan Tackitt
Senior Vice President, Mary Rohan
Vice President Residential Lending, Richard Little
Vice President Office Manager, Mark Connor
Senior Vice President Residential Lending, Rob Kinasewich
Vice President Commercial Real Estate, Andrew Garfinkle
Senior Vice President Northern California Deposit Sales Manager, John Delaney
Senior Vice President Market Leader Residential Lending, Patrick Skovran
Senior Vice President Venture And Private Equity Group West Coast Leader, Mark Shang
Vice President Commercial Banking, Sean Burke
Chairman, Stephen M. Waters, age 71
Auditors: KPMG LLP

LOCATIONS

HQ: Boston Private Financial Holdings, Inc.
Ten Post Office Square, Boston, MA 02109
Phone: 617 912-1900
Web: www.bostonprivate.com

PRODUCTS/OPERATIONS

2015 Sales

	$ mil.	% of total
Interest and dividend income		
Loans	192	51
Mortgage-backed securities	10	3
Investment securities	9	2
Federal funds sold and other	1	1
Fees and other income		
Investment management & trust fees	45	12
Wealth advisory fees	50	14
Wealth management and trust fees	51	14
Other	13	3
Total	**374**	**100**

Selected Subsidiaries & Affiliates

Anchor Capital Advisors LLC
Bingham Osborn & Scarborough LLC
Boston Private Bank & Trust Company
Dalton Greiner Hartman Maher & Co. LLC
KLS Professional Advisors Group LLC

COMPETITORS

Bank of America	FMR
Brown Brothers	JPMorgan Chase
Harriman	Morgan Stanley
Central Bancorp	Sovereign Bank
Century Bancorp (MA)	TD Bank USA
Citigroup	TriState Capital
Citizens Financial	Wells Fargo
Group	

HISTORICAL FINANCIALS

Company Type: Public

Income Statement

FYE: December 31

	ASSETS ($ mil.)	NET INCOME ($ mil.)	INCOME AS % OF ASSETS	EMPLOYEES
12/17	8,311	40	0.5%	925
12/16	7,970	71	0.9%	888
12/15	7,542	64	0.9%	890
12/14	6,797	68	1.0%	875
12/13	6,437	70	1.1%	781
Annual Growth	6.6%	(12.9%)	—	4.3%

2017 Year-End Financials

Debt ratio: 1.28%	No. of shares (mil.): 84
Return on equity: 5.25%	Dividends
Cash ($ mil.): 120	Yield: 0.0%
Current ratio: —	Payout: 104.7%
Long-term debt ($ mil.): —	Market value ($ mil.): 1,301

	STOCK PRICE ($) FY Close	P/E High/Low	PER SHARE ($) Earnings	Dividends	Book Value
12/17	15.45	42 33	0.42	0.44	9.27
12/16	16.55	20 11	0.81	0.40	9.13
12/15	11.34	18 14	0.74	0.36	8.91
12/14	13.47	18 14	0.79	0.32	8.48
12/13	12.62	18 13	0.68	0.24	7.94
Annual Growth	5.2%	— —	(11.3%)	16.4%	4.0%

Boston Scientific Corp.

Boston Scientific makes medical supplies and devices used to diagnose and treat medical conditions with an emphasis on cardiovascular products and cardiac rhythm management (CRM). It also makes devices used for electrophysiology endoscopy pain management (neuromodulation) urology and women's health. Its roughly 13000 products — made in more than a dozen factories worldwide — include biopsy forceps catheters coronary and urethral stents defibrillators needles and pacemakers. Boston Scientific markets its products in around 120 countries.

Operations

Boston Scientific operates in three primary segments: Cardiovascular MedSurg and Rhythm Management.

Its largest segment Cardiovascular accounts for around 40% of annual revenues. That segment makes interventional cardiology products (coronary stents catheters guidewires) which account for more than 25% of the company?s sales and peripheral intervention products (non-coronary vascular stents) which bring in more than 10% of total sales.

The MedSurg segment (more than 35% of revenue) makes digestive and pulmonary systems devices for endoscopy urology and pelvic health and neuromodulation.

The Rhythm Management segment (some 25% of revenue) makes implantable devices (pacemakers and implanted coronary defibrillators or ICDs) for CRM and electrophysiology.

Geographic Reach

Boston Scientific operates in around 40 countries and markets its products in some 120 nations around the world. Based in Massachusetts it has seven manufacturing facilities in the US and six manufacturing facilities abroad (Ireland Costa Rica and Puerto Rico). The company also has physician training centers in France Germany Italy South Africa India and Japan and research operations in China Costa Rica Germany India Ireland and Puerto Rico.

While the US is still Boston Scientific's largest single market international sales have grown to make up about 45% of total sales. Its second-largest market is Japan which brings in some 10% of annual sales.

Sales and Marketing

Boston Scientific markets its products to some 35000 hospitals clinics outpatient facilities and medical offices around the world. In the US large group purchasing organizations (GPOs) hospital networks and other buying groups make up a significant portion of sales.

Boston Scientific markets products through direct disease-focused sales forces in the US and about 40 other major international markets; it also uses dealers and distributors in certain countries. Some products are marketed through partnerships; for instance Boston Scientific distributes urology laser systems made by Lumenis through a development and commercialization agreement.

Financial Performance

Boston Scientific revenues have remained relatively flat for the past five years but saw a 12% rise to $8.4 billion in fiscal 2016. This was driven by sales increases across all three segments including a 20% increase for MedSurg but was partially offset by the negative impact of foreign currency rates. Growth was driven by two areas — pelvic health and interventional cardiology. A new line of business gained from the 2015 acquisition of the American Medical Systems urology portfolio pelvic health revenue brought in $226 million in 2016. New product launches including the SYNERGY Stent and the Lotus Valve System in Europe boosted sales in interventional cardiology. The increased revenue helped the company enter the black after a number of years of posting net losses (including a $4 billion loss in 2012) due to expenses related to acquisitions litigation and other areas. The company netted profits of $347 million in 2016.

That increase in net income drove up operating cash flow which rose 62% to $972 million.

Strategy

Boston Scientific is focused on growth measures that drive innovation in core markets expansion of its global commercial presence and diversification into additional areas of disease. Its strategies include acquisitions research and development partnerships and internal development efforts.

Boston Scientific looks to expand geographically and is working to build an infrastructure to support growth in such emerging markets as China India and Brazil. (Emerging markets account for more than 10% of total sales.) In 2015 it entered a partnership with Frankenman Medical Equipment to develop manufacture and market products in China. It also opened Institutes for Advancing Science in Turkey China and South Africa and established a new R&D center in India focused on developing products for emerging markets.

In mid-2016 the company announced a restructuring plan expected to be complete by the end of 2018 which will allow it focus on international growth in the areas of commercialization manufacturing and technology. The plan should save the firm between $115 million and $150 million in annual operating expenses.

Rather than riding the medical device industry?s consolidation wave Boston Scientific tends to focus on internal growth over large mergers and acquisitions. It spends about 11% of its net sales (about $920 million in 2016) on R&D each year and strives to lead the market for minimally invasive medical devices that address unmet patient needs.

In 2016 the company launched the AXiOS Stent and Electrocautery Enhanced Delivery System for drainage of pancreatic pseudo cysts. Other new products that year included the Precision Montage MRI Spinal Cord Stimulator System and two new catheters (IntellaNav XP and Intella Nav MiFi XP) for use with the Rhythmia Mapping System. The company additionally received FDA approval for its ImageReady MR-Conditional Pacing System and its Blazer Open-Irrigated Catheter.

Mergers and Acquisitions

In late 2018 Boston Scientific agreed to buy UK-based health care firm BTG for $4.2 billion. It is particularly interested in BTG's interventional medicine assets. BTG also has a pharmaceuticals division but it is unclear what Boston Scientific will do with that business.

Also in 2018 Boston Scientific acquired Nx-Thera which makes the Rezum system for the treatment of enlarged prostrate in a deal valued at up to $406 million. In a separate deal it bought private firm Augmenix for $500 million. Augmenix developed the SpaceOAR Hydrogel System a treatment for the side effects of prostate-cancer radio-therapy. Boston Scientific is also buying startup Securus Medical Group which makes imaging technology for use in heart rhythm procedures for $40 million.

Another deal struck in 2018 was the company's agreement to buy the 65% of Cryterion Medical it doesn't already own for some $202 million. Cryterion is developing a single-shot cryoablation platform to treat atrial fibrillation. Along with its 2017 purchase of Apama Medical this transaction will make Boston Scientific the first company to own both cryothermal and radiofrequency single-shot balloon-based ablation therapies.

In 2017 the company bought Swiss company Symetis which makes minimally invasive trans-catheter aortic valve implantation devices for $435 million. That purchase brought Symetis' ACU-RATE systems which are sold in Europe and other non-US markets. Later that year Boston Scientific bought private manufacturer Apama Medical the developer of a radiofrequency balloon catheter system to treat atrial fibrillation for $175 million up-front plus up to $125 million in milestone payments.

In late 2016 Boston Scientific acquired Endo-Choice Holdings which focuses on developing infection control products and single-use devices for the treatment of gastrointestinal conditions for $210 million. It also purchased manufacturing assets and capabilities of Canada-based Neovasc for $75 million. That deal included a 15% stake in Neovasc and expanded Boston Scientific's structural heart capabilities which it will utilize in the manufacturing of heart valve products including its Lotus Valve System.

HISTORY

Many medical companies start near a hospital but Boston Scientific's roots sprouted at a children's soccer game where two dads found common ground. John Abele and Peter Nicholas had complementary interests: Wharton MBA Nichols wanted to run his own company; philosophy and physics graduate Abele wanted a job that would help people.

In 1979 the two men founded Boston Scientific to buy medical device maker Medi-Tech. Abele and Nicholas had to borrow half a million dollars from a bank and raise an additional $300000. Medi-Tech's primary product was a steerable catheter a soft-tipped device that could be maneuvered within the body. The catheter revolutionized gallstone operations in the early 1970s and Boston Scientific expanded on the success of the product. The com-

pany adapted it for a slew of new procedures for the heart lungs intestines and other organs.

Boston Scientific's sales were healthy in 1983 but the firm still lacked funds. It eagerly accepted $21 million from Abbott Laboratories in exchange for a 20% stake. New FDA regulations slowed product introduction and put a crimp in the company's growth. Boston Scientific found a legal loophole in the late 1980s to avoid lengthy delays: The company described its products in the vaguest possible terms so upgraded devices were considered similar enough to predecessors to escape the in-depth scrutiny of the new approval process. Still Abele and Nicholas had to mortgage their personal properties to stay afloat before this linguistic leg-erdemain helped to clear government red tape. Boston Scientific returned to profitability in 1991 and went public the next year buying back Abbott Laboratories' interest in the company as well.

Boston Scientific acquired a bevy of medical device companies throughout the late 1990's which expanded its range of cardiology products and doubled sales. Among them were SCIMED Life Systems Heart Technology Meadox Medicals EP Technologies and Symbiosis Target Therapeutics and Pfizer' s catheter stent and angioplasty equipment business.

EXECUTIVES

Chairman President And Ceo, Michael F. (Mike) Mahoney, age 53, $1,042,191 total compensation
Evp And President Rhythm Management, Joseph M. (Joe) Fitzgerald, age 54, $499,241 total compensation
Evp And Cfo, Daniel J. (Dan) Brennan, age 52, $544,421 total compensation
Svp And President Neuromodulation, Maulik Nanavaty, age 56
Evp And President Medical Surgery (medsurg), Michael P. (Mike) Phalen, age 59
Evp Chief Administrative Officer General Counseland Secretary, Timothy A. (Tim) Pratt, age 68, $640,017 total compensation
Evp And President Asia-pacific Middle East And Africa, Supratim Bose, age 65, $537,326 total compensation
Svp And President Endoscopy, David A. (Dave) Pierce, age 54
Svp And President Interventional Cardiology, Kevin J. Ballinger, age 45, $476,647 total compensation
Evp Operations, Edward F. Mackey, age 55, $410,548 total compensation
Svp Manufacturing And Supply Chain, John B. (Brad) Sorenson, age 50
Svp And President Europe, Eric Thépaut, age 56
Svp And President Endoscopy, Art Butcher
Evp And Global Chief Medical Officer, Ian Meredith
Svp And President Peripheral Interventions, Jeff Mirviss
Vice President Mg And Galway Operations, Aaron Milton
Vice President Operations, Daniel Zaic
Vice President Communications And Progra, Marilee Grant
Vice President Of Sales, Mike Jones
Vice President Corporate Accounting, Jon Monson
Vice President Manager Director, Ru Zheng
Vice President, Prabodh Mathur
Vice President Of Operations, Sean Aherne
Vice President Global Marketing Endoscopy, Meghan Scanlon
Vp And Managing Director India, Prabal Chakraborty
Vice President Of Information Technology And General Superintendent, Neha Khera
National Sales Manager, Rahul Garg
Executive Vice President Operations, Edward Macky

Svp And President Emea, Eric Thepaut
Vp Information Systems, Benjamin Amel
Vice President Is Global Infrastructure Services, Tom Woehrle
Vice President Global E Marketing, Eric Siebert
Vice President Information Technology And Chief Digital Health Officer, David Feygin
Chairman President And Ceo, Michael F. (Mike) Mahoney, age 53
Evp Chief Administrative Officer General Counseland Secretary, Timothy A. (Tim) Pratt, age 68
Board Member, Charles Dockendorff
Assistant Treasurer, Graeme Williamson
Auditors: Ernst & Young LLP

LOCATIONS

HQ: Boston Scientific Corp.
300 Boston Scientific Way, Marlborough, MA 01752-1234
Phone: 508 683-4000
Web: www.bostonscientific.com

PRODUCTS/OPERATIONS

Selected Products
Cardiovascular
  Interventional Cardiology
  PolarCath peripheral dilation system
  PROMUS drug-eluting stents
  TAXUS drug-eluting stents
  VeriFLEX bare-metal stents
  WALLSTENT carotid artery stents
  Cardiac Rhythm Management (CRM)
  ACUITY steerable ventricular leads
  COGNIS cardiac resynchronization defibrillator
  LATITUDE remote patient monitoring system
  TELIGEN implantable cardiac defbrillator
  Other cardiovascular
  Cutting Balloon dilation device
  FilterWire EZ embolic protection system
  iLab ultrasound imaging catheter system
  Maverick balloon catheters
Endoscopy
  Radial Jaw 4 single-use biopsy forceps (gastrointestinal)
  RX Biliary System (bile duct surgeries)
  SpyGlass direct visualization system (pancreatic system)
Urology/Pelvic health
  Genesys Hydro ThermAblator (endometrial ablation system)
Neuromodulation
  Precision Spinal Cord Stimulation system (chronic pain)
Electrophysiology
  Blazer Prime temperature ablation catheters

Selected Acquisitions

COMPETITORS

Abbott Labs	Hologic
American Medical Systems	Johnson & Johnson
Bard	LeMaitre Vascular
Cook Group	Medtronic
Edwards Lifesciences	ZOLL

HISTORICAL FINANCIALS

Company Type: Public

Income Statement				FYE: December 31
	REVENUE ($ mil.)	NET INCOME ($ mil.)	NET PROFIT MARGIN	EMPLOYEES
12/17	9,048	104	1.1%	29,000
12/16	8,386	347	4.1%	27,000
12/15	7,477	(239)	—	25,000
12/14	7,380	(119)	—	24,000
12/13	7,143	(121)	—	23,000
Annual Growth	6.1%	—		6.0%

2017 Year-End Financials

Debt ratio: 29.49% No. of shares (mil.): 1,373
Return on equity: 1.51% Dividends
Cash ($ mil.): 188 Yield: —
Current ratio: 0.68 Payout: —
Long-term debt ($ mil.): 3,815 Market value ($ mil.): 34,049

	STOCK PRICE ($) FY Close	P/E High/Low	PER SHARE ($) Earnings	Dividends	Book Value
12/17	24.79	373274	0.08	0.00	5.11
12/16	21.63	94 62	0.25	0.00	4.94
12/15	18.44	— —	(0.18)	0.00	4.69
12/14	13.25	— —	(0.09)	0.00	4.86
12/13	12.02	— —	(0.09)	0.00	4.95
Annual Growth	19.8%	— —	—	—	0.8%

BRAZOS EDUCATION LOAN AUTHORITY, INC

EXECUTIVES

Pres, Murray Watson Jr
Exec Vp - Ceo, Ricky Turman
Exec Vp, David Horner

LOCATIONS

HQ: BRAZOS EDUCATION LOAN AUTHORITY, INC
2600 WASHINGTON AVE, WACO, TX 767107449
Phone: 254 753-0915
Web: WWW.BRAZOSFOUNDATION.ORG

HISTORICAL FINANCIALS

Company Type: Private

Income Statement				FYE: June 30
	ASSETS ($ mil.)	NET INCOME ($ mil.)	INCOME AS % OF ASSETS	EMPLOYEES
06/18	2,224	8	0.4%	3
06/17	2,477	11	0.5%	—
06/16	2,770	19	0.7%	—
Annual Growth	(10.4%)	(34.7%)	—	—

BRE GLACIER L.P.

EXECUTIVES

Pres-ceo, Jack Cuneo

LOCATIONS

HQ: BRE GLACIER L.P.
90 PARK AVE FL 32, NEW YORK, NY 100161316
Phone: 212 297-1000
Web: WWW.GPTREIT.COM

HISTORICAL FINANCIALS

Company Type: Private

Income Statement			FYE: December 31
	ASSETS ($ mil.)	NET INCOME ($ mil.)	INCOME AS % OF ASSETS	EMPLOYEES
12/17	6,456	86	1.3%	109
12/16	5,603	33	0.6%	
12/15	5,840	(48)	—	—
Annual Growth	5.1%			

2017 Year-End Financials

Debt ratio: —
Return on equity: 15.80% Dividends
Cash ($ mil.): 30 Yield: —
Current ratio: — Payout: —
Long-term debt ($ mil.): — Market value ($ mil.): —

Bridge Bancorp, Inc. (Bridgehampton, NY)

Bridge Bancorp wants you to cross over to its subsidiary The Bridgehampton National Bank which operates about 25 branches on eastern Long Island New York. Founded in 1910 the bank offers traditional deposit services to area individuals small businesses and municipalities including checking savings and money market accounts and CDs. Deposits are invested primarily in mortgages which account for some 80% of the bank's loan portfolio. Title insurance services are available through bank subsidiary Bridge Abstract; wealth management services include financial planning estate administration and trustee services. Bridge Bancorp bought Hamptons State Bank in 2011 to fortify its presence on Long Island.

Geographic Reach

Bridgehampton New York-based Bridge Bancorp's market area is Suffolk County in eastern Long Island. The bank serves customers in the towns of East Hampton Southampton Southold and Riverhead. It also has branches in Brookhaven Babylon and Islip.

Financial Performance

The bank reported net income of $13.1 million in 2013 versus $12.8 million in 2012. Revenue increased 3% to $67.3 million on rising net interest income. Bridge Bancorp had total assets of $1.9 billion in 2013 an increase of 17% versus the prior year. Total deposits rose 9% in 2013 versus 2012 to $1.5 billion.

Mergers and Acquisitions

In February 2014 Bridge Bancorp acquired FNBNY Bancorp and its wholly-owned subsidiary the First National Bank of New York and converted its three branches to Bridgehampton National Bank (BNB) branches. The purchase expanded BNB's reach into Nassau County. Following the acquisition Bridge Bancorp's assets totaled approximately $2.1 billion with loans of approximately $1.1 billion and deposits of $1.7 billion with 26 branches throughout Long Island and one loan production office in Manhattan.

EXECUTIVES

President And Ceo, Kevin M. O'Connor, age 55, $300,000 total compensation
Evp And Chief Lending Officer, Kevin L. Santacroce, $180,000 total compensation
Svp And Cio Bridgehampton National Bank, Thomas H. Simson, $175,000 total compensation
President Ceo And Director, Kevin OConnor
Chief Financial Officer, Adam Hall
Evp And Chief Retail Banking Officer, James J. Manseau, $235,000 total compensation
Vice Chairman, Dennis A. Suskind, age 75
Chairman, Marcia Z. Hefter, age 74
Auditors: Crowe Horwath LLP

LOCATIONS

HQ: Bridge Bancorp, Inc. (Bridgehampton, NY)
2200 Montauk Highway, Bridgehampton, NY 11932
Phone: 631 537-1000
Web: www.bridgenb.com

COMPETITORS

Bank of America
Bank of New York Mellon
JPMorgan Chase
Suffolk Bancorp

HISTORICAL FINANCIALS

Company Type: Public

Income Statement				FYE: December 31
	ASSETS ($ mil.)	NET INCOME ($ mil.)	INCOME AS % OF ASSETS	EMPLOYEES
12/17	4,430	20	0.5%	480
12/16	4,054	35	0.9%	477
12/15	3,781	21	0.6%	433
12/14	2,288	13	0.6%	348
12/13	1,896	13	0.7%	271
Annual Growth	23.6%	11.9%	—	15.4%

2017 Year-End Financials

Debt ratio: 1.78% No. of shares (mil.): 19
Return on equity: 4.91% Dividends
Cash ($ mil.): 94 Yield: 0.0%
Current ratio: — Payout: 88.4%
Long-term debt ($ mil.): — Market value ($ mil.): 690

	STOCK PRICE ($) FY Close	P/E High/Low	PER SHARE ($) Earnings	Dividends	Book Value
12/17	35.00	37 29	1.04	0.92	21.78
12/16	37.90	19 13	2.00	0.92	21.36
12/15	30.43	22 17	1.43	0.92	19.62
12/14	26.75	23 20	1.18	0.92	15.03
12/13	26.00	19 14	1.36	0.92	14.10
Annual Growth	7.7%	— —	(6.5%)	(0.0%)	11.5%

Bridgewater Bancshares Inc

Auditors: CliftonLarsonAllen LLP

LOCATIONS

HQ: Bridgewater Bancshares Inc
3800 American Boulevard West, Suite 100, Bloomington, MN 55431
Phone: 952 893-6868
Web: www.bridgewaterbankmn.com

HISTORICAL FINANCIALS

Company Type: Public

Income Statement
FYE: December 31

	ASSETS ($ mil.)	NET INCOME ($ mil.)	INCOME AS % OF ASSETS	EMPLOYEES
12/17	1,616	16	1.0%	114
12/16	1,260	13	1.0%	
Annual Growth	28.3%	27.8%	—	—

2017 Year-End Financials

Debt ratio: 2.57%
Return on equity: 13.38%
Cash ($ mil.): 26
Current ratio: —
Long-term debt ($ mil.): —

No. of shares (mil.): 24
Dividends
Yield: —
Payout: —
Market value ($ mil.): —

	STOCK PRICE ($) FY Close	P/E High/Low		PER SHARE ($) Earnings	Dividends	Book Value
12/17	0.00	—	—	0.68	0.00	5.56
12/16	0.00	—	—	0.58	0.00	4.69
/0.00	—		—(0.00)	0.00	(0.00)	
Annual Growth	—	—	—	—	—	—

Brighthouse Financial Inc

Auditors: DELOITTE & TOUCHE LLP

LOCATIONS

HQ: Brighthouse Financial Inc
11225 North Community House Road, Charlotte, NC 28277
Phone: 980 365-7100
Web: www.brighthousefinancial.com

HISTORICAL FINANCIALS

Company Type: Public

Income Statement
FYE: December 31

	ASSETS ($ mil.)	NET INCOME ($ mil.)	INCOME AS % OF ASSETS	EMPLOYEES
12/17	224,192	(378)	—	1,260
12/16	221,930	(2,939)	—	1,100
12/15	226,725	1,119	0.5%	—
12/14	0	1,159	—	—
Annual Growth	—	—	—	—

2017 Year-End Financials

Debt ratio: 1.61%
Return on equity: 12.69%
Cash ($ mil.): 1,857
Current ratio: —
Long-term debt ($ mil.): —

No. of shares (mil.): 119
Dividends
Yield: —
Payout: —
Market value ($ mil.): 7,023

	STOCK PRICE ($) FY Close	P/E High/Low		PER SHARE ($) Earnings	Dividends	Book Value
12/17	58.64	—	—	(3.16)	0.00	121.19
12/16	0.00	—	—	(24.62)	0.00	(0.00)
Annual Growth	—	—	—	—	—	—

Brighthouse Life Insurance Co - Insurance Products

EXECUTIVES

Chb-Pres-Ceo, Eric T Steigerwalt
V Pres-Cfo, Anant Bhalla
V Pres-Cao, Lynn A Dumais
Consultant, Candace Hackney
Auditors: DELOITTE & TOUCHE LLP

LOCATIONS

HQ: Brighthouse Life Insurance Co - Insurance Products
11225 North Community House Road, Charlotte, NC 28277
Phone: 980 365-7100
Web: www.metlife.com

HISTORICAL FINANCIALS

Company Type: Public

Income Statement
FYE: December 31

	ASSETS ($ mil.)	NET INCOME ($ mil.)	INCOME AS % OF ASSETS	EMPLOYEES
12/17	212,045	(883)	—	—
12/16	199,273	(2,937)	—	—
12/15	202,362	839	0.4%	—
12/14	205,863	295	0.1%	—
12/13	188,039	720	0.4%	—
Annual Growth	3.0%	—	—	—

2017 Year-End Financials

Debt ratio: 0.02%
Return on equity: (-6.65%)
Cash ($ mil.): 1,363
Current ratio: —
Long-term debt ($ mil.): —

No. of shares (mil.): 0
Dividends
Yield: —
Payout: —
Market value ($ mil.): —

Bristol-Myers Squibb Co.

Pharmaceutical giant Bristol-Myers Squibb (BMS) treats an array of maladies through its vast lineup of therapies. The biopharmaceutical's blockbuster drugs include cancer treatment Opdivo rheumatoid arthritis treatment Orencia and Eliquis for stroke prevention. BMS also makes HIV treatments Reyataz and Sustiva. Most of the firm's sales come from products in the therapeutic areas of oncology cardiovascular care immunology and virology. BMS has global research facilities and manufacturing plants mainly in the US and Europe and its products are marketed to health care practitioners hospitals and managed care providers in 100 countries.

Operations

BMS's R&D efforts are focused on medicines that address serious unmet medical needs with a special emphasis on the immuno-oncology arena. Other core therapeutic areas include immunoscience (especially lupus rheumatoid arthritis and inflammatory bowel disease) cardiovascular and fibrotis disease.

Geographic Reach

While BMS serves a global customer base the US market accounts for more than half of its annual revenues. The company's major research and development facilities are in New Jersey and Connecticut; it plans to sell the Connecticut site but will open a new R&D facility in Massachusetts. BMS has other sites in the US the UK Belgium India Japan and other countries. It has about a dozen manufacturing facilities which are located in the US and Puerto Rico France Italy Ireland Japan Mexico and China.

Sales and Marketing

US wholesale drug distributors McKesson Cardinal Health and AmerisourceBergen together account for about 60% of BMS' annual sales. In addition to wholesalers the company also sells some products directly to customers including hospitals clinics physicians and nurse practitioners government agencies pharmacies pharmacy benefit managers (PBMs) and managed-care organizations (MCOs). BMS employs a direct sales force in certain markets; it also uses independent marketing representatives.

Annual advertising expense of some $740 million goes towards television radio print and digital promotion activities which target consumers medical professionals benefit managers and managed care organizations.

Financial Performance

The biggest financial story for BMS in 2016 and 2017 was the growing demand for cancer drug Opdivo which helped turn around the declining revenue seen in prior years. In fact the company had five other blockbuster drugs with rising sales in 2017 including Eliquis Orencia Sprycel Baraclude and Yervoy. Sales in the US and Europe also increased further boosting revenue that year.

However with rising expenses ranging from cost of products sold and higher R&D expenses to an increased provision for income taxes the company's net income declined 77% to 1 billion.

BMS ended 2017 with $5.4 billion in cash and cash equivalents — $1.2 billion more than it had at the end of 2016. Cash flow from operations including an increase in deferred income taxes and income taxes payable provided $5.3 billion. Investing and financing activities including securities purchases and the repurchasing of common stock used $66 million and $4.1 billion respectively.

Strategy

Following the loss of marketing rights to antipsychotic medication Abilify and patent expirations for drugs including HIV treatments Reyataz and Sustiva BMS is pinning its hopes on rising sales of newer medicines in fields including oncology neurology and metabolism. Its fastest-growing products include Opdivo (its biggest seller in 2017 bringing in $4.9 billion) Eliquis (its fastest grower with a 44% increase in sales) Orencia and Sprycel. In 2017 sales of Opdivo and Eliquis represented nearly 50% of total revenues.

Collaborations are an important part of BMS' development and marketing strategy. In the oncology arena BMS has been collaborating with others to expand Opdivo's usage (the drug was approved for seven new indications in 2017 alone) and it continues to invest in its pipeline of additional cancer treatments.

In terms of cardiovascular treatments an area in which the company has historically been a strong performer Eliquis brought the company nearly $4.9 billion in 2017.

The company sold its pipeline of investigational HIV medications to ViiV Healthcare in 2016. Two years later it agreed to sell its France-based OTC firm UPSA to Taisho Pharmaceuticals for $1.6 billion.

Mergers and Acquisitions

Acquisitions are a major piece of BMS's growth goals. In early 2019 the company agreed to buy Celgene Corporation for $74 billion. The combined company will have nine blockbuster drugs including Celgene's top asset Revlimid and six probable near-term product launches.

In 2017 it acquired IFM Therapeutics for $325 million further boosting its cancer program.

HISTORY

Bristol-Myers Squibb is the product of a merger of rivals.

Squibb was founded by Dr. Edward Squibb in New York City in 1858. He developed techniques for making pure ether and chloroform; he turned the business over to his sons in 1891.

Sales of $414000 in 1904 grew to $13 million by 1928. The company supplied penicillin and morphine during WWII. In 1952 it was bought by Mathieson Chemical which in turn was bought by Olin Industries in 1953 forming Olin Mathieson Chemical. Squibb maintained its separate identity.

From 1968 to 1971 Olin Mathieson went through repeated reorganizations and adopted the Squibb name. Capoten and Corgard two major cardiovascular drugs were introduced in the late 1970s. Capoten was the first drug engineered to attack a specific disease-causing mechanism. Squibb formed a joint venture with Denmark's Novo (now Novo Nordisk) in 1982 to sell insulin.

William Bristol and John Myers founded Clinton Pharmaceutical in Clinton New York in 1887 (renamed Bristol-Myers in 1900) to sell bulk pharmaceuticals. The firm made antibiotics after the 1943 purchase of Cheplin Biological Labs. It began expanding overseas in the 1950s and eventually bought Clairol (1959); Mead Johnson (drugs infant and nutritional formula; 1967); and Zimmer (orthopedic implants 1972). Bristol-Myers launched new drugs to treat cancer (Platinol 1978) and anxiety (BuSpar 1986). That year it acquired biotech companies Oncogen and Genetic Systems.

The firm bought Squibb in 1989. In 1990 the new company bought arthroscopy products and implant business lines and joined Eastman Kodak and Elf Aquitaine to develop new heart drugs in 1993. Despite these initiatives earnings slipped. In 1994 company veteran Charles Heimbold became CEO and moved to increase profits. BMS in 1995 bought wound and skin care products firm Calgon Vestal Laboratories. Also that year the company along with fellow silicone breast implant makers 3M and Baxter International agreed to settle thousands of personal injury claims at an average of $26000 per claim.

As the company entered the 21st century it began streamlining. It sold its Sea Breeze skin care brand (1999); Matrix Essentials hair care products unit (2000); and Clairol hair and personal care products business (2001). BMS also spun off its Zimmer orthopedic implant unit in 2001. More changes came in 2004: The firm sold its Mead Johnson Adult Nutritional business.

During 2005 the company cleaned out parts of its medicine cabinet. Analgesics Excedrin and Bufferin had made the company a household name but in 2005 the company sold its US and Canadian consumer products operations to Novartis. The deal also meant saying goodbye to such brands as Comtrex (cold medications) Choice (blood sugar monitoring supplies) and Keri (lotions skin care). Sales for the its US and Canadian consumer products operations reached about $270 million in 2004.

The company announced a reorganizational plan in 2007 named the string-of-pearls strategy. As part of its efforts to remake itself into a purely biopharmaceutical player BMS began jettisoning its non-pharmaceutical businesses. During 2008 the company sold its Medical Imaging unit to private equity firm Avista Capital Partners for $525 million and Avista Capital Partners and Nordic Capital paid $4.1 billion to acquire BMS' ConvaTec ostomy and wound-care subsidiary. Then in 2009 the company divested its Mead Johnson subsidiary which sold Enfamil infant formula and other nutritional products for children.

EXECUTIVES

Evp And General Counsel, Sandra Leung, age 57, $919,945 total compensation

Chairman And Ceo, Giovanni Caforio, age 54, $1,513,077 total compensation

Evp Cfo And Global Business Operations, Charles A. Bancroft, age 59, $966,115 total compensation

Svp And Cio, Paul von Autenried, age 56

President Global Manufacturing And Supply, Louis S. (Lou) Schmukler, age 62

Svp And Head Of Worldwide Markets, Murdo Gordon, age 51, $737,225 total compensation

Evp And Chief Scientific Officer R&d, Thomas J. Lynch

Svp And Head Business Development, Paul Biondi

Vice President, John Pinter

Senior Vice President And Chief Procurement Officer, Farryn Melton

Vice President, Harjit Banga

Svp And Deputy General Counsel, Henry Hadad

Medical Director, William Petkun

Svp And Chro, Ann Judge

Vice President Human Resources, Catherine Blachere

Vp Finance, David Brienza

Vp And Assistant General Counsel Global Strategic Corporate Transactions, Luis Vilarin

Medical Director, Xuemei Li

Vice President Research Informatics And Automation, Alastair Binnie

Vice President: Head Of Strategic Payer Marketing, Laurent Carter

Vice President Immuno Oncology Global Clinical Research, Louis Kayitalire

Senior Vice President Global Supply Chain, Ricardo Zayas

Vp Process Sciences, E Morrey Atkinson

Vice President And Head R And D And Commercial Communications, Danielle Halstrom

Chairman And Ceo, Giovanni Caforio, age 54

Assistant Treasurer, Scott R Massengill

Auditors: DELOITTE & TOUCHE LLP

LOCATIONS

HQ: Bristol-Myers Squibb Co.
430 E. 29th Street, 14th Floor, New York, NY 10016
Phone: 212 546-4000   **Fax:** 212 546-4020
Web: www.bms.com

2017 Sales

	$ mil.	% of total
US	11,358	55
Europe	4,988	24
Other	3,877	18
Other revenues	553	3
Total	**20,776**	**100**

PRODUCTS/OPERATIONS

2017 Sales

	$ mil.	% of total
Prioritized brands		
Opdivo	4,948	24
Eliquis	4,872	23
Orencia	2,479	12
Sprycel	2,005	10
Yervoy	1,244	6
Empliciti	231	1
Established brands		
Baraclude	1,052	5
Sustiva franchise	729	4
Reyataz franchise	698	3
Hepatitis C franchise	406	2
Other	2,112	10
Total	**20,776**	**100**

Selected Pharmaceuticals

Cardiovascular
Eliquis (atrial fibrillation with Pfizer)
Immunology
Nulojix (kidney rejection)
Orencia (rheumatoid arthritis)
Metabolism
Bydureon (type 2 diabetes)
Byetta (type 2 diabetes)
Neuroscience
Emsam (major depressive disorder)
Oncology
Erbitux (colorectal head and neck cancer with Lilly)
Sprycel (chronic myeloid leukemia with Otsuka)
Yervoy (metastatic melanoma)
Virology
Baraclude (chronic hepatitis B)
Reyataz (HIV)
Sustiva Franchise (includes Atripla and Sustiva for HIV with Gilead)

COMPETITORS

AbbVie	Johnson & Johnson
Allergan plc	Merck
Amgen	Mylan
Apotex	Novartis
AstraZeneca	Pfizer
Biogen	Roche Holding
Boehringer Ingelheim	Sandoz International
Eli Lilly	GmbH
Genentech	Sanofi
GlaxoSmithKline	Teva

HISTORICAL FINANCIALS

Company Type: Public

Income Statement

FYE: December 31

	REVENUE ($ mil.)	NET INCOME ($ mil.)	NET PROFIT MARGIN	EMPLOYEES
12/17	20,776	1,007	4.8%	23,700
12/16	19,427	4,457	22.9%	25,000
12/15	16,560	1,565	9.5%	25,000
12/14	15,879	2,004	12.6%	25,000
12/13	16,385	2,563	15.6%	28,000
Annual Growth	**6.1%**	**(20.8%)**	**—**	**(4.1%)**

2017 Year-End Financials

Debt ratio: 23.73%	No. of shares (mil.): 1,625
Return on equity: 7.21%	Dividends
Cash ($ mil.): 5,421	Yield: 0.0%
Current ratio: 1.55	Payout: 255.7%
Long-term debt ($ mil.): 6,975	Market value ($ mil.): 99,580

	STOCK PRICE ($) FY Close	P/E High/Low	PER SHARE ($) Earnings	Dividends	Book Value
12/17	61.28	107 77	0.61	1.56	7.23
12/16	58.44	29 18	2.65	1.14	9.72
12/15	68.79	75 61	0.93	1.49	8.55
12/14	59.03	51 39	1.20	1.45	8.94
12/13	53.15	35 21	1.54	1.41	9.19
Annual Growth	**3.6%**	**— —**	**(20.7%)**	**2.6%**	**(5.8%)**

Brookdale Senior Living Inc

Over the brook and through the dale to grandmother's house we go! Brookdale Senior Living operates assisted and independent living centers and retirement communities for middle- and upper-income elderly clients. The US' largest senior living provider Brookdale owns or manages more than 1000 facilities offering studio one-bedroom and two-bedroom units in 46 states. It has the capacity to serve some 101000 residents in all. Services for its residents include meals 24-hour emergency response housekeeping concierge services transportation and recreational activities. Brookdale's continuing care retirement centers include skilled nursing units that serve Alzheimer's patients and others who require ongoing care.

Operations

Brookdale operates in five segments: assisted living retirement centers continuing care retirement communities (CCRC) - rental ancillary services and management services. Its largest operating segment is its assisted living division which provides daily living services to residents and accounts for about half of all revenues. The retirement centers segment operates upscale independent living facilities for middle and upper-income seniors and accounts for some 15% of sales. The CCRC rental segment provides a mix of independent assisted and nursing care services within one location. It accounts for some 10% of revenue.

The remainder of Brookdale's sales comes from its management services and ancillary services segments. The management services segment (some 20% of revenue) receives fees for facilities that Brookdale operates on behalf of third parties. The ancillary services division (nearly 10% of revenue) provides outpatient therapy home health and hospice services to residents of Brookdale and non-Brookdale facilities as well as to seniors living in their own homes.

The company owns or leases nearly 800 communities with about 66600 units; it manages approximately 230 third-party-owned or partially owned communities with nearly 34000 units.

While some of Brookdale's facilities provide intensive nursing services that are reimbursed by third-parties including Medicare and Medicaid most of the company's facilities are independent or assisted-living centers that target higher-end clients with minimal medical needs.

About half of the company's sales come from its leased communities and another 40% are generated from owned communities.

Geographic Reach

Brookdale has more than 1000 communities in 46 states. Its largest markets Florida and Texas are home to almost 25% of its communities. Other key states include North Carolina California Ohio Oregon and Washington.

Sales and Marketing

For its retirement centers Brookdale targets residents of age 75 and older who are seeking a more supportive living situation. Its assisted living residents are primarily aged 80 and higher requiring daily assistance with two or more activities of daily living.

Due to Brookdale's focus on high-income customers more than 80% of its revenues come from private pay customers. By keeping its exposure to federal programs (Medicare and Medicaid) to a minimum the company is less vulnerable (though not immune) to changes in reimbursement levels.

Brookdale uses direct marketing teams to target potential residents and family members as well as referral sources including hospital discharge agents social workers physicians local agencies home health agents and clergy members. It also seeks to promote its brand through event sponsorships and online print signage and direct mail advertising programs.

Financial Performance

In recent years Brookdale had seen strong growth but revenue remained relatively flat in 2016 and it declined 5% to $4.7 billion in 2017. That decline was primarily due to a drop in resident fees a consequence of several community divestitures made in 2016 and 2017 as well as pressure from increased competition. This was slightly offset by a 20% increase in management services revenues which rose after the company took on management of several communities for Blackstone.

The company has reported losses over a period of several years due to unusual expenses such as lease terminations and asset impairments. Its net loss in 2017 totaled $571.6 million versus a $404.6 million loss in 2016.

Cash flow from operations remained relatively flat at $366.7 million that year.

Strategy

Brookdale has a newly defined strategy for operations beginning in 2018. This strategy is focused on three priorities: its shareholders its employees and its residents and patients and their families.

On behalf of its shareholders the company is striving to grow its revenue per room adjusted earnings and free cash flow. It has been streamlining operations to cut costs. It has removed certain layers of its organization and has been establishing corporate shared service centers of excellence to improve business effectiveness.

In terms of employees Brookdale is looking to create value in the areas of pay growth opportunities and meaningful work. It has already made improvements in this area by launching new training and development programs and by expanding its quality tracking initiatives. It is also evaluating innovative ideas and working models that could improve the ways it serves its residents.

Through those and other measures the company strives to serve its existing (and future) patients with compassion and respect. The company utilizes customized marketing campaigns in markets with strong growth potential and it is segmenting its communities to offer the right services amenities programs and price levels based on market needs. The company is also increasing its ancillary services revenues by extending those programs to new facilities as well as by introducing new services such as wellness and physical fitness programs.In terms of sales the company is working to improve coordination between different teams within their markets.

Although the company has a refined strategy its modus operandi remains the same: keeping an eagle eye on its holdings and seeking opportunities to buy existing communities or to sell and lease communities already in its portfolio. Brookdale intends to take advantage of its sheer size in partnership deals and to carefully invest in community expansions renovations and repositionings. In 2017 the company invested $28.8 million in expansion and conversion projects adding 103 units; it plans to continue with these projects ultimately adding another 70 net new units. The company regularly prunes its facility portfolio as well and it earmarked some 30 properties for sale during 2018. During 2016 and 2017 it divested 165 communities through sales or lease terminations.

Brookdale also explores possible acquisitions of other companies including care providers and ancillary service providers.

Increased competition in some markets has put some pressure on Brookdale which has in turn responded by offering discounts and other incentives to residents and increasing employees' salaries to prevent poaching. The company should benefit from an uptick in demand as the US population of seniors steadily increases.

In 2017 Brookdale was in talks to be acquired by Chinese real estate firm Zhonghong Zhuoye Group which had bid $3 billion for the company but those talks stalled without a deal being made. Other investors have also made moves to buy Brookdale but the company hopes to turn things around itself with the help of a new management team.

HISTORY

Brookdale Senior Living was formed through the 2005 merger of Brookdale Living Communities and Alterra Healthcare. The combined organization expanded through additional acquisitions in the following years.

Difficult economic conditions caused Brookdale to cut back on its spending during 2009 and 2010. During that time it turned its attention inward and worked to improve occupancy rates at existing facilities. The senior housing industry as a whole was affected by the downturn in the housing market causing a precipitous drop in occupancy rates industry-wide.

Sensing improved economic conditions in 2011 Brookdale acquired private facility operator Horizon Bay adding 90 residential facilities in the southern and midwestern US. Horizon Bay's independent and assisted living facilities complement Brookdale's existing properties as they cater to high-end customers. The acquisition also reinforced the company's existing presence in several markets and opened a few new markets. As part of the deal Brookdale entered restructured lease arrangements on certain facilities with Horizon Bay's former shareholders Chartwell Seniors Housing REIT and HCP.

In 2012 it partnered with online services firm Connected Living to increase Internet training and social networking capabilities at several Brookdale communities in California. In early 2012 the company paid $121 million for nine communities it had formerly operated through lease agreements. The facilities included a total of some 1300 living units.

In 2014 Brookdale purchased fellow senior living firm Emeritus for nearly $3 billion. The move gave Brookdale a nationwide network of senior care facilities adding 10 states and bringing its total number of communities to 1100.

EXECUTIVES

Evp Corporate Development, H. Todd Kaestner, age 63

Evp Finance And Treasurer, George T. Hicks, age 61

Evp And Chief Administrative Officer, Bryan D. Richardson, age 60, $432,115 total compensation

Cfo, Lucinda M. (Cindy) Baier, age 53, $552,115 total compensation

President And Ceo, T. Andrew (Andy) Smith, age 57, $953,654 total compensation

Evp And Chief People Officer, Cedric T. Coco, age 50

Evp Community And Field Operations, Mary Sue Patchett, age 55, $426,635 total compensation

Executive Vice President And Chief People Officer, Glenn Maul

Vice President Sales, Greg Martin

Vice President, James Alspaugh

Vice President Legal Employment Affairs, Jack Leebron

Regional Vice President Operations, Patty Luessenhop

Vice President, Marla Sovereign

Vice President Of Clinical Services, Brenda Calbow

Vice President Of Sales, Chris Bird

Physical Therapy Director, Becky Lemery

Vice President Of Benefits And Compensation, Pam Engle

Director Of Nursing Services, Christine Pepito

Vp Internal Audit, Kevin Potter

Executive Vice President Development, Todd Kaestner

Vice President Direct Response Marketing, Shelly Riera

Vice President, Randy Cyphers

Divisional Vice President Of Operations, Cindy Chastulik

Senior Vice President Procurement, Jeffrey M Patton

Senior Vice President Of Clinical Services, Kim Estes

Senior Vice President Human Resources, Liberty Stansberry

Vice President Total Rewards, Pamela Engle

Vp Financial Planning And Analysis, Steve Mcgill

Rvp, Sheri Garrett

Vice President Legal And Compliance Operations, Kirstin Baum Sumner

Senior Vice President Insights And Analytics, Kirk Gripenstraw

Division President, Anthony Mollica

Director Of Admissions, Erica Davis

Head Nurse, Amy Lubinskas

Chairman, Daniel A. Decker, age 65

Evp Finance And Treasurer, George T. Hicks, age 61

Auditors: Ernst & Young LLP

LOCATIONS

HQ: Brookdale Senior Living Inc
111 Westwood Place, Suite 400, Brentwood, TN 37027
Phone: 615 221-2250
Web: www.brookdale.com

PRODUCTS/OPERATIONS

2017 Sales

	$ mil.	% of total
Resident fees		
Assisted living	2,210	47
Retirement centers	654	14
CCRCs-rental	469	10
Ancillary services	446	9
Management services	967	20
Total	**4,747**	**100**

COMPETITORS

ACTS Retirement-Life Communities
Amedisys
American Baptist Homes of the West
Apria Healthcare
Atria Senior Living
BPM Senior Living
Capital Senior Living
Colson & Colson
Consulate Health Care
Enlivant
Evangelical Lutheran Good Samaritan Society
Five Star Senior Living
Golden Horizons
HCP
Horizon Bay
Life Care Centers
Life Care Services
SavaSeniorCare
Sunrise Senior Living
Ventas
Welltower

HISTORICAL FINANCIALS

Company Type: Public

Income Statement   FYE: December 31

	REVENUE ($ mil.)	NET INCOME ($ mil.)	NET PROFIT MARGIN	EMPLOYEES
12/17	4,747	(571)	—	75,600
12/16	4,976	(404)	—	77,600
12/15	4,960	(457)	—	81,300
12/14	3,031	(148)	—	82,000
12/13	2,891	(3)	—	49,000
Annual Growth	**13.2%**	—	—	**11.5%**

2017 Year-End Financials

Debt ratio: 67.00%
Return on equity: (-31.67%)
Cash ($ mil.): 514
Current ratio: 0.82
Long-term debt ($ mil.): 4,539
No. of shares (mil.): 191
Dividends
  Yield: —
  Payout: —
Market value ($ mil.): 1,855

	STOCK PRICE ($) FY Close	P/E High/Low	PER SHARE ($) Earnings	Dividends	Book Value
12/17	9.70	— —	(3.07)	0.00	8.00
12/16	12.42	— —	(2.18)	0.00	10.93
12/15	18.46	— —	(2.48)	0.00	13.06
12/14	36.67	— —	(1.01)	0.00	15.41
12/13	27.18	— —	(0.03)	0.00	7.99
Annual Growth	**(22.7%)**	— —	—	—	**0.0%**

Brookline Bancorp Inc (DE)

Boston-based Brookline Bancorp is the holding company for Brookline Bank Bank Rhode Island (BankRI) and First Ipswich Bank which together operate more than 50 full-service branches in eastern Massachusetts and Rhode Island. Commercial and multifamily mortgages backed by real estate such as apartments condominiums and office buildings account for the largest portion of the company's loan portfolio followed by indirect auto loans commercial loans and consumer loans. Established in 1997 as Brookline Savings Bank the bank went public five years later and changed its name to Brookline Bank in 2003.

Operations

Brookline Bancorp focuses its services and products to commercial enterprises. It offers commercial business and retail banking services such as cash management products on-line banking services consumer and residential loans and investment services. The holding company provides equipment financing through its Eastern Funding and Macrolease Corporation subsidiaries. Eastern Funding holds loans with higher-than-normal credit risk (and higher yields) due to the limited capital of its typical customers: coin-operated laundries dry cleaning businesses and convenience stores in the New York City metropolitan area.

Geographic Reach

Boston-based Brookline Bancorp operates primarily in Boston MA and Providence Rhode Island.

Financial Performance

Brookline Bancorp generated $263 million in interest & dividend income and another $32 million of non-interest income. Combined the $295 million of 2017 annual revenue exceeded the previous year?s result by 12% aided heavily by the bank?s one-time gain of $11 million on the sale of investment securities. Its loan portfolio grew 6% to $5.7 billion in 2017.

Despite the healthy improvement in revenue net income fell 4% to $50.5 million due in large part to an unusually high income tax bill triggered by the passing of the US Federal Tax Reform bill in late 2017.

Strategy

Brookline has grown from a sleepy suburban community savings bank to a publicly-traded commercial lender with loan volumes that put it among Massachusetts' top banks. Its operational approach of a holding company with local largely independent banks gives it certain advantages. The local banks are empowered to address local market needs whether in the form of products services or even interest rates on loans. This gives each bank the opportunity to build its own brand along with strong long-term relationships with commercial customers while leaving the corporate functions (IT risk management etc.) to the centralized holding company.

Mergers and Acquisitions

In 2018 the bank purchased for $264 million First Commons Bank N.A. to extend its reach into the western suburbs of Boston MA.

EXECUTIVES

President And Ceo, Paul A. Perrault, age 67, $715,000 total compensation

Coo, James M. Cosman, age 67, $265,000 total compensation

President And Ceo Bank Rhode Island, Mark J. Meiklejohn, age 54, $330,000 total compensation

Chief Risk Officer General Counsel And Secretary, Michael W. McCurdy, age 49

Chief Credit Officer, M. Robert Rose, age 66, $288,000 total compensation

President And Ceo The First National Bank Of Ipswich, Russell G. Cole, age 60

Cfo, Carl M. Carlson, age 54, $335,000 total compensation

Senior Vice President, Bill Mackenzie

Vice President Regional Manager, Cathy Pierce

Vice President, Tony Glazier

Vice President Of Commercial Lending, Tim Steiner

Vice President Underwriting And Operations, Gretchen Annese

Chairman, Joseph J. Slotnik, age 82

Treasurer, Reed H Whitman

Auditors: KPMG LLP

LOCATIONS

HQ: Brookline Bancorp Inc (DE)
131 Clarendon Street, Boston, MA 02116
Phone: 617 425-4600
Web: www.brooklinebancorp.com

PRODUCTS/OPERATIONS

2017 sales

	$ mil.	% of total
Interest and dividend income:		
Loans and leases	247	84
Debt securities	12	4
Marketable and restricted equity securities	3	1
Short-term investments	.4	-
Non-interest income:		
Deposit fees	10	3
Loan fees	1	-
Loan level derivative income net	2	1
Gain on sales of investment securities	11	4
Gain on sales of loans and leases held-for-sale	2	1
Other	4	2
Total	**295**	**100**

Selected Services

Personal
Checking
Savings
Borrowing
Investment Services
Business
Signature Business Banking
Business Checking Accounts
Business Savings
Business Lending
Business Online Banking
Cash Management
Service Center
Branch Locations
ATM Locations
Online Banking
Mobile Banking
Telephone Services
Mail Services
Order Checks
Order Foreign Currency
Overdraft Privilege Service

COMPETITORS

Bank of America	Citizens Financial
Berkshire Hills	Group
Bancorp	Eastern Bank
Boston Private	Sovereign Bank
Central Bancorp	TD Bank USA
Century Bancorp (MA)	

HISTORICAL FINANCIALS

Company Type: Public

Income Statement   FYE: December 31

	ASSETS ($ mil.)	NET INCOME ($ mil.)	INCOME AS % OF ASSETS	EMPLOYEES
12/17	6,780	50	0.7%	765
12/16	6,438	52	0.8%	743
12/15	6,042	49	0.8%	718
12/14	5,799	42	0.7%	725
12/13	5,325	35	0.7%	720
Annual Growth	6.2%	9.3%	—	1.5%

2017 Year-End Financials

Debt ratio: 1.93%	No. of shares (mil.): 77
Return on equity: 6.74%	Dividends
Cash ($ mil.): 61	Yield: 0.0%
Current ratio: —	Payout: 52.9%
Long-term debt ($ mil.): —	Market value ($ mil.): 1,211

	STOCK PRICE ($) FY Close	P/E High/Low		PER SHARE ($) Earnings	Dividends	Book Value
12/17	15.70	25	20	0.68	0.36	10.42
12/16	16.40	22	14	0.74	0.36	9.82
12/15	11.50	17	13	0.71	0.36	9.45
12/14	10.03	17	14	0.61	0.34	9.09
12/13	9.55	20	16	0.51	0.34	8.73
Annual Growth	13.2%	—	—	7.5%	1.4%	4.5%

Brunswick Corp.

Brunswick Corporation is a global manufacturer of marine recreation and fitness products. Its largest business segment marine engines makes outboard inboard and stern drive engines propellers and control systems. The company also makes pleasure craft offshore fishing boats and pontoons. Its fitness segment includes treadmills cross trainers stair climbers and stationary bicycles sold under the brands Life Fitness and Hammer

Strength. It also has a 49% stake in marine financing company Brunswick Acceptance Company; a Wells Fargo subsidiary holds the other 51%.

Operations

Brunswick has three operating segments: Marine Engine Boat and Fitness.

Marine generates some 55% of sales and manufactures and markets a full range of outboard sterndrive and inboard engines as well as marine parts and accessories.

The Boat segment accounts for some 25% of sales and designs manufactures and markets fiberglass pleasure boats yachts and sport yachts sport cruisers and sport boats as well as offshore fishing boats aluminum and fiberglass fishing boats pontoon boats utility boats deck boats inflatable boats and heavy-gauge aluminum boats.

The Fitness segment is the world's largest manufacturer of commercial fitness equipment and generates more than 20% of total revenue. It designs manufactures and markets a full line of cardiovascular fitness and strength equipment including treadmills total body cross-trainers stair climbers exercise bikes and strength-training equipment such as weight machines and free weights. Its brands are Life Fitness Cybex Hammer Strength SciFit and Indoor Cycling. The segment also includes games room equipment such as billiards tables.

Geographic Reach

Headquartered in Illinois Brunswick has manufacturing distribution warehouses sales offices and research and development facilities in some 14 countries across North America Europe and the Asia/Pacific region. The US generates some 70% of its total sales.

Sales and Marketing

Brunswick's marine engine segment's global sales network includes more than 6000 marine dealers distributors and marine retailers and service centers that sell its engines to end-users.

More than 2000 boat dealers and distributors market its lineup of boats. The business' largest dealer MarineMax Inc has multiple centers and delivers more than 15% of the Boat segment's sales. The Boat segment includes a commercial and governmental sales unit that sells products to commercial customers as well as to the US government and state local and foreign governments.

The Fitness segment serves health clubs corporations schools and universities hotels professional sports teams and more. Its principal customer is Planet Fitness. Its sales division consists of a direct sales force domestic dealers and international distributors. Its products can be found in specialty retailers select mass merchants sporting goods stores and on the Life Fitness website.

Financial PerformanceNote: Brunswick provides revenue figures for continuing operations excluding revenue from units held for sale. In 2017 this included the Sea Ray business which had revenue of around $387 million and incurred a net loss of $40.9 million.In fiscal 2017 Brunswick's sales increased 9% to $4.5 billion due to increases in all segments. The Marine Engine segment grew sales of outboard engines and marine parts and accessories. Sales of higher horsepower engines performed particularly well. Boat segment sales were buoyed by higher aluminum and fiberglass outboard boat sales while the Fitness segment grew mostly internationally. Cross-segment international sales increased 10%.Net income fell 31% to $187.3 million due to higher impairment charges and pension settlement expenses partially offset by a tax benefit from the 2017 US Tax Cuts and Jobs Act.Cash from operations was largely unchanged in 2017 at $417.2 million down 1% due to an increase in working capital.

Strategy

Brunswick has been selling off various of its underperforming businesses in recent years due to unsatisfactory sales or profitability. In 2018 it made the decision to float its Fitness business which has struggled to find growth in the US. It also made the decision to sell its Sea Ray outboard engines business in 2017 although after no satisfactory offer to buy was received it is progressing with refocusing on its 25-40ft sports boat and cruiser product lines and will no longer make boats over 40ft. In 2014 it sold the AMF bowling business and in 2015 it sold its bowling products business.

Mergers and Acquisitions

Brunswick uses acquisitions to find additional revenue growth.

In 2017 Brunswick acquired Lankhorst Taselaar a Netherlands- and Germany-based marine parts and accessories distribution company for about $15 million. The acquisition augments the marine parts and accessories businesses through a broader product line and an expanded distribution network. Lankhorst Taselaar was combined into Brunswick's Marine Engine segment.

Recently it has pursued transactions to extend its international reach and beef up its Life Fitness portfolio. In 2016 the company obtained Payne's Marine Group of Victoria British Columbia a wholesale distributor of marine parts and accessories (P&A) in Canada. It also acquired Germany-based Indoor Cycling Group (ICG) for $54 million. Based in Nuremburg Germany ICG specializes in the design of indoor cycling equipment and is now part of the company's Life Fitness division. The company's third acquisition in 2016 was of Cybex International a maker of commercial fitness equipment for $195 million.

HISTORY

Swiss immigrant woodworker John Brunswick built his first billiard table in 1845 in Cincinnati. In 1874 he formed a partnership with Julius Balke and a decade later they teamed with H. W. Collender to form Brunswick-Balke-Collender Company.

Following Brunswick's death son-in-law Moses Bensinger became president. The company diversified into bowling equipment during the 1880s. Bensinger's son B. E. followed as president (1904) and led the company into wood and rubber products phonographs and records. (Al Jolson recorded "Sonny Boy" on the Brunswick label.) Brunswick went public after WWI.

By 1930 Brunswick focused on bowling and billiards sports that had seedy reputations during the 1920s and 1930s. When B. E. died in 1935 his son Bob became CEO and launched a massive promotional campaign to make his meal tickets respectable.

Bob's brother Ted succeeded him as CEO in 1954. Bowling equipment rival AMF introduced the first automatic pinsetter in 1952 and Brunswick followed four years later capturing the lead by 1958. Brunswick diversified adding Owens Yacht MacGregor (sporting goods 1958) Aloe (medical supplies 1959) Mercury (marine products 1961) and Zebco (fishing equipment 1961). The company adopted its present name in 1960.

To focus exclusively on its marine engine and boat business Brunswick sold all of its bowling operations in 2014 and 2015.

EXECUTIVES

Vice President, William Seeley
Vp And President South America Mercury Marine, William J. Gress
Svp And Cfo, William L. Metzger, age 56, $505,000
total compensation

Chairman And Ceo, Mark D. Schwabero, age 65, $971,154 total compensation
Vp And President Mercury Marine, John C. Pfeifer, age 52, $475,000 total compensation
Vp And Cto, David M. Foulkes
Vp And President Fitness Division, Jaime A. Irick, age 43
President Boston Whaler Group, Huw S. Bower, age 43, $332,061 total compensation
Vp And Cio, Danielle Brown, age 48
Vice President New Business Development, Robert Staehle
Chairman And Ceo, Mark D. Schwabero, age 65
Auditors: DELOITTE & TOUCHE LLP

LOCATIONS

HQ: Brunswick Corp.
26125 N. Riverwoods Blvd., Suite 500, Mettawa, IL 60045-3420
Phone: 847 735-4700
Web: www.brunswick.com

2017 Sales

	$ mil.	% of total
US	2,972	66
International	1,537	34
Total	**4,501**	**100**

PRODUCTS/OPERATIONS

2017 Sales

	$ mil.	% of total
Marine		
Marine Engine	2,631	55
Boat	1,103	23
Marine eliminations	(258.5)	-
Fitness	1,033	22
Total	**4,510**	**100**

Selected Products

Billiards
  Air hockey
  Billiards tables and accessories
Fitness
  Commercial equipment
Marine - Boats
  Boat parts and accessories
  Freshwater fishing and utility boats
  General recreation boats
  Motor yachts
  Pontoon and deck boats
  Rigid inflatable and inflatable boats
Marine - Engines
  Engine parts and accessories
  Inboard stern drive and jet drive engines
  Trolling motors
  Outboard engines

COMPETITORS

Cigarette Racing Team	Honda
Fountain Powerboat	Marine Products Corp.
Giant Manufacturing	Yamaha

HISTORICAL FINANCIALS

Company Type: Public

Income Statement   FYE: December 31

	REVENUE ($ mil.)	NET INCOME ($ mil.)	NET PROFIT MARGIN	EMPLOYEES
12/17	4,510	146	3.2%	15,116
12/16	4,488	276	6.1%	14,415
12/15	4,105	241	5.9%	12,607
12/14	3,838	245	6.4%	12,165
12/13	3,887	769	19.8%	15,701
Annual Growth	**3.8%**	**(33.9%)**	**—**	**(0.9%)**

2017 Year-End Financials

Debt ratio: 13.02%   No. of shares (mil.): 87
Return on equity: 10.02%   Dividends
Cash ($ mil.): 458   Yield: 0.0%
Current ratio: 1.78   Payout: 42.2%
Long-term debt ($ mil.): 431   Market value ($ mil.): 4,834

	STOCK PRICE ($) FY Close	P/E High/Low		PER SHARE ($) Earnings	Dividends	Book Value
12/17	55.22	39	30	1.62	0.69	16.94
12/16	54.54	18	13	3.00	0.62	16.12
12/15	50.51	22	18	2.56	0.53	14.11
12/14	51.26	20	15	2.58	0.45	12.64
12/13	46.06	6	3	8.20	0.10	11.24
Annual Growth	**4.6%**	**—**	**—**	**(33.3%)**	**61.8%**	**10.8%**

Bryn Mawr Bank Corp

Bryn Mawr Bank Corporation stands atop a "big hill" in Pennsylvania. Bryn Mawr (which in Welsh translates as "big hill") is the bank holding company for Bryn Mawr Trust operates some 20 offices in Pennsylvania and Delaware. The bank offers traditional services as checking and savings accounts CDs mortgages and business and consumer loans in addition to insurance products equipment leasing investment management retirement planning tax planning and preparation and trust services. Founded in 1889 Bryn Mawr boasts more than $5 billion of assets under administration and management.

Operations

Bryn Mawr operates two business segments. Its Banking segment which makes up two-thirds of overall business provides commercial and retail banking services. The Wealth Management division which includes the Bryn Mawr Trust of Delaware and Lau Associates businesses makes up about one-third of the bank's overall revenue and provides a variety of custody investment management tax and brokerage services.

Broadly speaking the company generated 60% of its total revenue from interest and fees on loans and leases in 2014 while another 30% of its total revenue came from fees for wealth management services.

Bryn Mawr operated 19 full-service branches seven Life Care Community Offices five wealth offices and a full-service insurance agency in 2014.

Geographic Reach

The bank corporation has branches and offices across Montgomery Delaware Chester and Dauphin counties in Pennsylvania and New Castle county in Delaware.

Financial Performance

Bryn Mawr has enjoyed rising revenues and profits over the past several years reflecting strong growth in its loan business and wealth management business.

The bank's revenue rose by 4% to a record $131.23 million in 2014 mostly thanks to higher interest income from loans as it grew its loan assets by $153.9 million during the year. The company's Wealth Management services fees also grew by 5% thanks to new business acquisitions and solid market appreciation during the year which resulted in higher assets under management.

Higher revenue and a strong grip on costs in 2014 also boosted Bryn Mawr's net income by 14% to a record $27.84 million. Despite higher earnings the bank's operating cash declined by 6% to $37.68 million for the year as it made less

in net proceeds from the sales of its loans held for resale.

Strategy

Bryn Mawr Bank Corporation continued to push its acquisition strategy in 2015 designed to broaden its service offerings boost its loan and deposit business and expand its branch network. The bank looks to strategically acquire smaller insurance businesses small to mid-sized banks and community banks wealth management companies and advisory and planning services firm that complement its existing businesses.

Besides acquisitions the company has been growing its wealth management business through marketing campaigns to raise brand awareness.

Mergers and Acquisitions

In April 2015 to grow its wealth management business the bank purchased Robert J. McAllister Agency which provides insurance and risk management solutions to individuals and businesses in the Philadelphia region.

In January 2015 Bryn Mawr acquired the Continental Bank Holdings and its Plymouth Meeting-based flagship Continental Bank adding some $433 million in loans and $480 million in deposits along with 10 full-service branches located in key markets in Montgomery Chester and Philadelphia counties.

In October 2014 Bryn Mawr bought the Rosemont Pennsylvania-based insurance agency Powers Craft Parker & Beard Inc. (PCPB) for $7 million to enhance its own insurance business among individuals and commercial clients.

In 2012 as part of a strategy to build its wealth management division the company acquired Davidson Trust adding some $1 billion in assets under management.

Company Background

In 2011 the company bought the private wealth management business of Hershey Trust Company for more than $14.5 million; that deal brought in approximately $1 billion of assets under management. In 2010 the company purchased First Keystone Financial adding about 10 bank branches in Pennsylvania and some $2.7 billion in trust and investment assets.

EXECUTIVES

Evp And Coo, Alison E. Gers, age 60, $250,000 total compensation
Evp And Chief Lending Officer Bryn Mawr Trust, Joseph G. (Joe) Keefer, age 59, $238,500 total compensation
President And Ceo, Francis J. Leto, age 58, $310,000 total compensation
Evp Secretary And Chief Risk Officer, Geoffrey L. Halberstadt
Cfo And Treasurer Bryn Mawr Bank Corporation; Evp Cfo And Treasurer Bryn Mawr Bank, Michael W. (Mike) Harrington, age 55
Evp Wealth Management Division, Harry R. Madeira
Senior Vice President Of Wealth Management Division, Rande Whitham
Vice President, John Metz
Senior Vice President, Richard Gentile
Vice President Construction Real Estate, Michelle Wilson
Vice President, Martha Hilty
Vice President, John Roman
Senior Vice President Market Leader, Tony Poluch
Vice President Real Estate Lending, Kristin Reese
Vice President Wealth Management Division, J Keefer-Hugill
Vice President, Brian Snyder
Vice President Small Business Account Lending Division, Douglas Whalen
Vice President, Drew Smith

Vice President Relationship Manager, Shawn Williams

Vice President Director Of Investment Services, Bryan Andersen

Vice President Mortgage Division, Anne Stulpin

Vice President Comptrollers And Finance, Maral Kaloustian

Vice President Mortgage Division, Patrick McGowan

Senior Vice President Managing Partner, Robert McLaughlin

Assistant Vice President Service Manager Chadds Ford Branch, Leslie Paynter

Evp Secretary And Chief Risk Officer, Geoffrey L. Halberstadt

Cfo And Treasurer Bryn Mawr Bank Corporation; Evp Cfo And Treasurer Bryn Mawr Bank, Michael W. (Mike) Harrington, age 55

Chairman, Britton H. Murdoch

Assistant Treasurer, Linda McLaughlin

Auditors: KPMG LLP

LOCATIONS

HQ: Bryn Mawr Bank Corp
  801 Lancaster Avenue, Bryn Mawr, PA 19010
Phone: 610 525-1700
Web: www.bmtc.com

PRODUCTS/OPERATIONS

2014 Sales

	$ mil.	% of total
Interest		
Interest & fees on loans & leases	78	60
Investment securities	4	3
Cash & cash equivalents	0	-
Noninterest		
Fees for wealth management services	36	30
Service charges on deposits	2	2
Net gain on sale of residential mortgages	1	1
Loan Servicing and other fees	1	1
Other	5	3
Total	**131**	**100**

Selected Subsidiaries

Bryn Mawr Advisors Inc.
Bryn Mawr Asset Management Inc.
Bryn Mawr Brokerage Co. Inc.
Bryn Mawr Financial Services Inc.
Bryn Mawr Trust Company of Delaware
Joseph W. Roskos Co. Inc.
Lau Associates LLC
The Bryn Mawr Trust Company
  BMT Leasing Inc.
  BMT Mortgage Services Inc.
  BMT Settlement Services Inc.
  Insurance Counsellors of Bryn Mawr Inc.

COMPETITORS

Alliance Bancorp of Pennsylvania	Royal Bancshares
	Sovereign Bank
Firstrust Savings Bank	Wells Fargo
PNC Financial	

HISTORICAL FINANCIALS

Company Type: Public

Income Statement   FYE: December 31

	ASSETS ($ mil.)	NET INCOME ($ mil.)	INCOME AS % OF ASSETS	EMPLOYEES
12/17	4,449	23	0.5%	680
12/16	3,421	36	1.1%	544
12/15	3,031	16	0.6%	530
12/14	2,246	27	1.2%	444
12/13	2,061	24	1.2%	432
Annual Growth	**21.2%**	**(1.5%)**	**—**	**12.0%**

2017 Year-End Financials

Debt ratio: 2.69%	No. of shares (mil.): 20
Return on equity: 5.06%	Dividends
Cash ($ mil.): 60	Yield: 0.0%
Current ratio: —	Payout: 65.1%
Long-term debt ($ mil.): —	Market value ($ mil.): 891

	STOCK PRICE ($) FY Close	P/E High/Low		Earnings	PER SHARE ($) Dividends	Book Value
12/17	44.20	34	28	1.32	0.86	26.23
12/16	42.15	20	11	2.12	0.82	22.50
12/15	28.72	33	29	0.94	0.78	21.42
12/14	31.30	15	13	2.01	0.74	17.83
12/13	30.18	17	12	1.80	0.69	16.84
Annual Growth	**10.0%**	**—**	**—**	**(7.5%)**	**5.7%**	**11.7%**

BSB Bancorp Inc. (MD)

BSB Bancorp is the holding company for Belmont Savings Bank a community back with about half a dozen branches in southeastern Middlesex County in the suburbs of Boston. Serving local businesses and individuals the $2 billion-asset bank offers checking savings money market retirement accounts and a variety of lending products. Almost 50% of its loan portfolio is made up of one-to-four family residential mortgages while commercial real estate loans make up another 30%. While Belmont Savings Bank traces its roots back to 1885 BSB Bancorp was formed in 2011 to take the company public.

Operations

BSB Bancorp mostly originates one-to-four family residential mortgages and commercial real estate loans for office buildings owner-occupied commercial buildings industrial buildings and strip mall centers. About 46% of its loan portfolio was made up of one-to-four family residential mortgages at the end of 2015 while another 29% was made up of commercial real estate loans. The rest of the portfolio was made up of home equity loans (10% of loan assets) construction (4%) business loans (3.5%) auto loans (6%) and other consumer loans (less than 1%).

The bank also makes more than 90% of its revenue from interest income. About 87% of its total revenue came from loan interest (including fees) during 2015 while another 7% came from interest on investment securities. The remainder of its revenue came from non-interest income sources including customer service fees.

Geographic Reach

While its primary market area is in the greater Boston area the company serves southeastern Massachusetts in the Essex Middlesex Norfolk and Suffolk Counties from branches in Belmont Watertown Waltham Newton and Cambridge.

Sales and Marketing

BSB Bancorp has been cutting back on its marketing in recent years. It spent $926000 on marketing in 2015 down from $975000 and $999000 in 2014 and 2013 respectively.

Financial Performance

BSB Bancorp's annual revenues have doubled since 2011 as its loan assets have more than tripled to $1.53 billion as a result new branch openings and organic growth with the strengthening economy around Boston. The bank's net income has skyrocketed more than five-fold over the time period as it's kept a lid on rising operating costs and benefited from the low-interest environment.

The bank's revenue jumped 23% to $51.57 million during 2015 mostly as a 30% increase in loan assets spurred higher interest income.

Strong revenue growth in 2015 drove BSB Bancorp's net income higher by 61% to $6.91 million. The bank's operating cash levels fell 14% to $18.1 million for the year mostly after adjusting its earnings for non-cash items related to its net proceeds from loan sales.

Strategy

BSB Bancorp reiterated in 2016 that it planned to continue focusing on growing its one-to-four family residential mortgage commercial real estate and home equity lending business which made up more than 85% of its loan assets in 2015. With its eye on being the "Bank of Choice" for small businesses and municipalities in its core Boston market area it plans to organically grow its deposit and lending business in the parts of Eastern Massachusetts that weren't as affected by the most recent recession.

In 2013 BSB Bancorp expanded its reach by 50% after opening two branches inside Shaw's Supermarkets in Cambridge and Newton (its first supermarket branch was opened in Waltham in 2012).

EXECUTIVES

President Ceo And Director Bsb Bancorp Inc.; President And Ceo Belmont Savings Bank, Robert M. (Bob) Mahoney, age 69

Evp And Coo, Hal R. Tovin, age 62

Evp Consumer Lending And Auto Finance Belmont Savings Bank, Christopher Y. (Chris) Downs, age 67

Svp Cfo And Secretary Bsb Bancorp Inc. And Belmont Savings Bank, John A. Citrano, age 54

President Bob Mahoney, Belmont Bank

Senior Vice President, Morgan Cambern

Svp Cfo And Secretary Bsb Bancorp Inc. And Belmont Savings Bank, John A. Citrano, age 54

Board Member, Warren Farrell

Board Member, John Whittemore

Board Member, Richard Fougere

Board Member, Paul Petry

Auditors: Baker Newman & Noyes LLC

LOCATIONS

HQ: BSB Bancorp Inc. (MD)
  2 Leonard Street, Belmont, MA 02478
Phone: 617 484-6700
Web: www.belmontsavings.com

COMPETITORS

Bank of America	Hingham Institution
Boston Private	for Savings
Brookline Bancorp	Independent Bank (MA)
Century Bancorp (MA)	Meridian Bancorp
Citizens Financial	Middlesex Savings
Group	Peoples Federal
DCU	Bancshares Inc.
Eastern Bank	Sovereign Bank
Enterprise Bancorp	TD Bank USA

HISTORICAL FINANCIALS

Company Type: Public

Income Statement   FYE: December 31

	ASSETS ($ mil.)	NET INCOME ($ mil.)	INCOME AS % OF ASSETS	EMPLOYEES
12/17	2,676	14	0.5%	126
12/16	2,158	11	0.6%	125
12/15	1,812	6	0.4%	132
12/14	1,425	4	0.3%	128
12/13	1,054	1	0.2%	127
Annual Growth	**26.2%**	**64.6%**	**—**	**(0.2%)**

2017 Year-End Financials

Debt ratio: —
Return on equity: 8.49%
Cash ($ mil.): 113
Current ratio: —
Long-term debt ($ mil.): —

No. of shares (mil.): 9
Dividends
  Yield: —
  Payout: —
Market value ($ mil.): 284

	STOCK PRICE ($) FY Close	P/E High/Low		PER SHARE ($) Earnings	Dividends	Book Value
12/17	29.25	20	16	1.55	0.00	18.34
12/16	28.95	21	15	1.33	0.00	17.66
12/15	23.39	30	23	0.78	0.00	16.09
12/14	18.63	38	30	0.49	0.00	15.11
12/13	15.09	69	56	0.22	0.00	14.40
Annual Growth	18.0%	—	—	62.9%	—	6.2%

Builders FirstSource Inc.

Builders FirstSource makes and sells building materials and manufactured components for homebuilders contractors remodelers and DIY consumers. It also offers construction-related services. The company's products and services — which include lumber windows and doors and millwork as well as installation and shell construction — are offered through some 400 locations across the US. Homebuilders such as Pulte Homes and Lennar are among its largest customers. Builders FirstSource was founded in 1998 as BSL Holdings.

Operations

Builders FirstSource operates through half a dozen product categories. Its largest lumber & lumber sheet goods accounts for about 35% of revenue and includes plywood and oriented strand board among other items. Windows doors & millwork (windows interior and exterior doors trim) and manufactured products (roof trusses wall panels stairs) together contribute another 35% of revenue.

The company's other product categories include gypsum roofing & insulation; siding metal & concrete; and other products & services.

Geographic Reach

Builders FirstSource operates only in the US with sales reported by region. The western US is its largest region accounting for some 30% of sales; the South and the Southeast contribute more than 25% and about 20% respectively.

The company has facilities in about 40 US states and serves 75 of the top 100 Metropolitan Statistical Areas.

Sales and Marketing

Builders FirstSource serves a range of customers from individual consumers to repair and remodel contractors to large homebuilders. Its top 10 customers mostly large homebuilders such as D.R. Horton CalAtlantic and Hovnanian Enterprises account for more than 15% of sales.

The company markets its products and services through a locally focused sales force of some 1700.

Financial Performance

After five years of steady revenue growth Builders FirstSource has doubled or nearly doubled its sales the past two years. It reported revenue of $6.4 billion in 2016 up about 80% from the prior year due to the impact of the mid-2015 purchase of building materials supplier ProBuild. Sales increased across all product lines and all geographic regions.

Following revenue net income was also up in 2016 jumping to $144 million from a loss of $23 million the prior year. The company was helped by reduced selling general and administrative expenses as well as an income tax benefit of $123 million. Cash from operations fell about 10% to $158 million as working capital increased in 2016 (primarily related to the ProBuild acquisition) compared to a decrease the prior year.

Strategy

An aggressive acquisition strategy — some three dozen companies since 1998 — enabled Builders FirstSource to become a construction powerhouse. It is relying on its standing in the industry (particularly within the professional segment of the US residential building products market) to propel growth.

Amid continued improvement in the US housing market the company believes its "one-stop-shop" offering will be a draw for homebuilders focused on competitive pricing on-site services and an expansive product portfolio.This is especially important as customers reduce supplier relationships in search of efficiencies. In addition Builders First-Source continues to emphasize and invest in its value-added manufactured products category which again helps drive efficiencies for its customer base.

In 2017 the company has also made the expansion of its sales force a focus. Through mid-year it had added more than 100 new sales associates with additional hires planned.

Mergers and Acquisitions

Historically an acquisitive company Builders FirstSource made its last big purchase in mid-2015 when it paid some $1.6 billion for competitor ProBuild Holdings. The deal created a giant professional building materials company with more than $6 billion in combined sales and more than 400 locations across the US.

EXECUTIVES

Svp And General Counsel, Donald F. McAleenan, age 63, $415,481 total compensation
President And Ceo, M. Chad Crow, age 50, $625,000 total compensation
Svp And Cfo, Peter Jackson
Vice President Treasury, Mark Cooper
Area Vice President, Dave Rush
Vice President, Gary Raven
Vice President And Associate General Counsel, Jeff A Wier
Vice President Sales And Marketing, Randy Craine
Vice President Sales, Matt Liska
Senior Vice President And General Counsel, Don McAleenan
Vice President Sales, Chris Lemly
Svp Investor Relations, Jennifer Pasquino
Vice President Human Resources, John Foley
Vice President Development Seattle, Steve Yoon
Chairman, Paul S. Levy, age 70
Board Member, Kevin Kruse
Auditors: PricewaterhouseCoopers LLP

LOCATIONS

HQ: Builders FirstSource Inc.
2001 Bryan Street, Suite 1600, Dallas, TX 75201
Phone: 214 880-3500   **Fax:** 214 880-3599
Web: www.bldr.com

2017 Sales

	$ mil.	% of total
West	2,188	31
South	1,855	26
Southeast	1,542	22
Northeast	1,285	18
Other	162	3
Total	**7,034**	**100**

PRODUCTS/OPERATIONS

2017 Sales

	$ mil.	% of total
Lumber & lumber sheet goods	2,510	36
Manufactured products	1,208	17
Windows doors & millwork	1,360	19
Siding metal & concrete products	655	8
Gypsum roofing & insulation	538	9
Other building products & services	759	11
Total	**7,034**	**100**

Selected Products

Building Materials
  Concrete
  Concrete block
  Decking
  Gypsum
  Paint
  Roofing
  Sheathing
Interior Items
  Builder hardware
  Cabinets
  Cabinet hardware
  Countertops
  Fireplaces
Lumber and Related Products
  Dimensional lumber
  Engineered wood
  Oriented strand board
  Plywood
  Pressure-treated lumber
Manufactured Components
  Floor trusses
  I-Joist floor systems
  Interior and exterior doors
  Open wall panels
  Roof trusses
  Stairs
Millwork
  Columns
  Custom millwork
  Interior and exterior doors
  Moldings
  Special-order millwork
  Windows
Tools
  Pneumatic tools
  Power tools

COMPETITORS

84 Lumber	HD Supply
Ace Hardware	Lowe's
BMC Stock	McCoy Corp.
BlueLinx	Menard
Boise Cascade Company	True Value
Carter Lumber	Universal Forest
CertainTeed	Products

HISTORICAL FINANCIALS

Company Type: Public

Income Statement

FYE: December 31

	REVENUE ($ mil.)	NET INCOME ($ mil.)	NET PROFIT MARGIN	EMPLOYEES
12/17	7,034	38	0.6%	15,000
12/16	6,367	144	2.3%	14,000
12/15	3,564	(22)	—	14,000
12/14	1,604	18	1.1%	3,800
12/13	1,489	(42)	—	3,300
Annual Growth	47.4%	—	—	46.0%

2017 Year-End Financials

Debt ratio: 60.92%
Return on equity: 11.31%
Cash ($ mil.): 57
Current ratio: 1.75
Long-term debt ($ mil.): 1,771

No. of shares (mil.): 113
Dividends
  Yield: —
  Payout: —
Market value ($ mil.): 2,475

STOCK PRICE ($)		P/E		PER SHARE ($)		
	FY Close	High/Low		Earnings	Dividends	Book Value
12/17	21.79	64	32	0.34	0.00	3.31
12/16	10.97	11	5	1.27	0.00	2.78
12/15	11.08	—	—	(0.22)	0.00	1.36
12/14	6.87	48	26	0.18	0.00	0.41
12/13	7.13	—	—	(0.44)	0.00	0.16
Annual Growth	32.2%	—	—	—	—	—114.3%

Burlington Northern & Santa Fe Railway Co. (The)

BNSF Railway operates one of the largest railroad networks in North America. A wholly-owned subsidiary of Burlington Northern Santa Fe itself a unit of Berkshire Hathaway the company provides freight transportation over a network of about 32500 route miles of track across two-thirds of the western US and two provinces in Canada. BNSF Railway owns or leases a fleet of about 8000 locomotives. It also has some 30 intermodal facilities that help to transport agricultural consumer and industrial products as well as coal. In addition to major cities and ports BNSF Railway serves smaller markets in alliance with short-line partners.

Operations
BNSF Railway serves more than 40 ports and 30 intermodal facilities and operates 1600 trains per day.

In 2014 it hauled nearly 1 million carloads of agricultural commodities; more than 5 million intermodal shipments (truck trailers or containers); nearly 2 million carloads of industrial products; and almost 2.3 million coal shipments. All told the company hauled more than 10 million carloads in 2014.

Geographic Reach
The company's network is spread across 28 US states and three Canadian provinces.

Sales and Marketing
BNSF Railway serves smaller markets by working closely with 200 shortline partners. It has also forms marketing agreements with other rail carriers expanding the marketing reach for each railroad and their customers.

Financial Performance
In 2014 the company's revenues rose by 5.6% due to increased capacity offset by the negative effects of severe winter weather conditions early in the year which dampened transportation activities.

BNSF Railway generated 31% of its revenues in 2014 from consumer products; 28% from industrial products; 22% from coal; and 19% from agricultural products.

It also reported a 1.8% increase in cars/units handled and a 3.5% increase in average revenue per car/unit for the year.

The company accounted for more than 56% of Burlington Northern Santa Fe's net revenues for 2014.

Strategy
As part of its capital plan of $6 billion for 2015 the company has planned some major capital projects to maintain and grow its rail network.

In its northern region the company has plans to invest $1.5 billion across eight states for engineering maintenance and line expansion projects of which $700 million is planned for projects to expand the rail lines and Positive Train Control (PTC advanced technologies designed to automatically stop or slow a train before accidents occur) in that region. In the southern region it plans to spend $800 million in nine states for engineering maintenance and line expansion projects of which $175 million is planned for line expansion initiatives and continued implementation of PTC.

The overall $6 billion investment for 2015 includes $2.9 billion to replace and maintain core network and related assets nearly $1.5 billion on expansion and efficiency projects $200 million for continued implementation of PTC and $1.4 billion for locomotives freight cars and other equipment acquisitions.

In 2014 the company made capital investments for line expansion system improvement projects additional equipment and new employee hires. BNSF Railway had a 2013 capital program (to strengthen its infrastructure) valued at $4.1 billion.

EXECUTIVES

President And Ceo, Carl R. Ice, age 61
Evp Law And Corporate Affairs, Roger Nober, age 53
Evp And Cfo, Julie A. Piggott
Evp And Chief Marketing Officer, Stevan B. Bobb
Evp Operations, Gregory C. Fox
Executive Chairman, Matthew K. (Matt) Rose, age 59
President And Ceo, Carl R. Ice, age 61
Evp Law And Corporate Affairs, Roger Nober, age 53
Evp And Cfo, Julie A. Piggott
Evp And Chief Marketing Officer, Stevan B. Bobb
Evp Operations, Gregory C. Fox
Executive Chairman, Matthew K. (Matt) Rose, age 59
Auditors: Deloitte & Touche LLP

LOCATIONS

HQ: Burlington Northern & Santa Fe Railway Co. (The)
2650 Lou Menk Drive, Fort Worth, TX 76131-2830
Phone: 800 795-2673
Web: www.bnsf.com

COMPETITORS

American Commercial Lines	Kansas City Southern Railway
American Commercial Lines	Kansas City Southern Railway
Canadian National Railway	Kirby Corporation
Canadian National Railway	Kirby Corporation
Canadian Pacific Railway	Landstar System
Canadian Pacific Railway	Landstar System
Ingram Industries	Norfolk Southern
Ingram Industries	Norfolk Southern
J.B. Hunt	Schneider National
J.B. Hunt	Schneider National
	Union Pacific Railroad
	Union Pacific Railroad
	Werner Enterprises
	Werner Enterprises

HISTORICAL FINANCIALS
Company Type: Public

Income Statement				FYE: December 31
	REVENUE ($ mil.)	NET INCOME ($ mil.)	NET PROFIT MARGIN	EMPLOYEES
12/17	20,747	12,119	58.4%	41,000
12/16	19,278	4,260	22.1%	41,000
12/15	21,401	4,915	23.0%	44,000
12/14	22,714	4,397	19.4%	48,000
12/13	21,552	4,271	19.8%	43,000
Annual Growth	(0.9%)	29.8%	—	(1.2%)

2017 Year-End Financials

Debt ratio: 1.74%	No. of shares (mil.): 0
Return on equity: 20.75%	Dividends
Cash ($ mil.): 516	Yield: —
Current ratio: 1.01	Payout: —
Long-term debt ($ mil.): 1,355	Market value ($ mil.): —

Burlington Stores Inc

Burlington Stores (dba Burlington Coat Factory) takes the "Brrr!" out of your life. The clothing retailer which made its name selling coats operates more than 590 no-frills retail stores (averaging 76000 square feet) offering off-price current brand-name clothing in about 45 states plus Puerto Rico. Although it is one of the nation's largest coat sellers the stores also sells a full wardrobe of products including children's apparel bath items furniture gifts jewelry linens and shoes. Sister chains include a pair of higher-priced Cohoes Fashions shops and about a dozen MJM Designer Shoe stores. Burlington Stores was founded in 1972.

Operations
About 98% of the company's sales are rung up at its Burlington Coat Factory Warehouse stores. Women's ready-to-wear apparel is its biggest earner at 24% of sales followed by accessories and shoes (22%) menswear (20%) youth and baby apparel (16%) home (12%) and coats (6%).

Its three other smaller businesses — Cohoes Fashions (off-price designer apparel) MJM Designer Shoe and Super Baby Depot — account for the rest. As its name suggests Super Baby Depot's two stores sell baby clothing accessories furniture and everything else a baby might need in the middle to higher price range. The company's MJM Designer Shoe chain has stores in New Jersey and New York and several other states. Like its larger sister chain MJM Designer Shoes sells brand names at significant discounts. The company also sells merchandise online at burlingtoncoatfactory.com and babydepot.com.

Geographic Reach
The New Jersey-based off-price retail chain has stores in 45 states and Puerto Rico. Its two primarily distribution centers which ship about 95% of its merchandise are located in Edgewater Park New Jersey and San Bernardino California.

Sales and Marketing
The chain is known for its year-round selection of about 10000 to 20000 discounted coats (compared to about 1500 to 2000 coats at department stores). Burlington Coat Factory takes less of a markup than its department store competition and has lower profit margins than other clothing retailers. It buys the coats early in the season (up to five months before department stores) to lock in lower prices.

Financial Performance

The company has recorded increasing revenue in the last six years.

In fiscal 2017 (ending January) revenue climbed 9% to $5.6 billion with gains spread evenly between comparable and non-comparable store sales. The company attributes the increase in its comparable store sales to an improved execution of its business model and the transition of its fragrance business from leased department rental income to an owned business.

Net income ticked up 43% to $215.9 million due to higher revenue and a reduction in selling general and administrative expenses as a proportion of total sales.

Cash from operating activities leaped 84% to $602.4 million on the back of higher net income and lower income tax and compensation payments.

Strategy

Burlington's primary growth driver is store expansions. In 2016 the company added a further 25 stores taking its store base to nearly 600. Burlington's goal is to have 1000 stores in operation.

Burlington Coat Factory's off-price niche has resonated with consumers looking for bargains both during the recession and continuing during the recovery. To grow the company is focusing on its core customers: 25-49 year-old women.

HISTORY

Russian-Jewish immigrant Abe Milstein and a partner started coat wholesaler and manufacturer Milstein and Feigelson in 1924. Abe's son Monroe was a quick study. He graduated from New York University with a business degree in 1946 at age 19 and started his own coat and suit wholesaling business called Monroe G. Milstein Inc. His mother provided free labor at her son's company six days a week to keep the business alive. Abe ended his partnership in 1953 and joined his son's business.

Family relations were strained temporarily in 1972 when Monroe disregarded his father's advice not to buy a faltering coat factory outlet store in Burlington New Jersey. (Abe believed that his son did not have enough retailing experience.) Monroe however thought owning a retail store would provide a guaranteed sales outlet for their merchandise and he bought Burlington Coat Factory for $675000 (using $60000 of his wife Henrietta's savings). His company also adopted the Burlington Coat Factory Warehouse moniker as its own.

To become less dependent on the season-specific coat business the company soon expanded its merchandise mix by adding a children's division (started by Henrietta deceased in 2001) and subleased departments. It opened a second store in Long Island New York in 1975.

Settling a trademark dispute with fabric maker Burlington Industries in 1981 Burlington Coat Factory agreed to say in advertising — as it does to this day — that the two companies are not affiliated. The 31-store company went public two years later using the money it raised to open almost 30 stores that year. As part of its expansion in the 1980s Burlington Coat Factory opened stores in warmer climates such as Texas and Florida.

The firm tried to grow through acquisitions that decade but failed in its attempts to buy a number of department store retailers. It made a successful bid in 1989 for New York discount retailer Cohoes.

Burlington Coat Factory's sales topped the $1 billion mark for the first time in fiscal 1993. Also that year the company bought Boston-based off-price family apparel chain Decelle. It then opened its first store outside the US (in Mexico) and tried new stand-alone store concepts based on successful in-store departments such as Luxury Linens and Baby Depot. A warm winter in 1994 hurt the company: Profits fell by two-thirds and it sold off inventory for two years afterward.

The company pulled a line of men's parkas in late 1998 after a Humane Society investigation revealed that the coats were trimmed with hair from dogs killed inhumanely in China. Burlington Coat Factory launched a baby gift registry in 2000 and later that year opened a silk floral division in selected stores. In 2001 the company acquired 16 stores formerly occupied by bankrupt Montgomery Ward. Burlington Coat Factory began operating MJM Designer Shoes in fiscal 2002 opening nine of the stand-alone specialty shoe stores. The company closed its Decelle stores in 2003 but converted most of them to the Burlington Coat Factory and Cohoes names while launching 25 new stores in 2004 (most under the Burlington Coat Factory moniker).

In 2005 the company opened two Super Baby Depot stores. Burlington Coat Factory was acquired by the Boston-based private equity firm Bain Capital Partners in April 2006 for about $2.1 billion.

In fiscal year 2006 the company opened three MJM Designer Shoes stores. The company's two stand-alone Luxury Linens stores were shut down and instead operate as departments within Burlington Coat Factory stores.

In December 2008 Thomas Kingsbury was named president and CEO of Burlington Coat Factory Warehouse succeeding Mark Nesci who retired after 37 years with the retailer. Prior to joining the company Kingsbury was a SEVP at Kohl's.

In February 2010 the company changed its fiscal year end from May to January to better comply with its peers in the retail industry. In October Burlington Coat Factory agreed to pay $10 million to settle a long-running legal fight with Italian luxury goods maker Fendi over the sale of counterfeit handbags and other leather goods.

Burlington went public in 2013.

EXECUTIVES

Chairman President And Ceo, Thomas A. (Tom) Kingsbury, age 65, $1,164,257 total compensation
Evp Human Resources, Joyce Manning Magrini, age 63, $386,539 total compensation
Cfo And Principal, Marc D. Katz, age 53, $654,400 total compensation
Evp General Counsel And Corporate Secretary, Janet L. Dhillon, age 55
Chief Merchandising Officer And Principal, Jennifer Vecchio, age 52, $677,195 total compensation
Chief Customer Officer And Principal, Fred Hand, age 54, $654,400 total compensation
Evp And Chief Marketing Officer, Hobart (Bart) Sichel, age 53, $326,923 total compensation
Evp Supply Chain Corporate Services And Asset Protection, Mike Metheny, age 51
Evp Merchandising, Rick Seeger, age 56, $629,826 total compensation
Evp Stores, Forrest David Coder
Evp Planning & Allocation And Merchandise Information Operations (mio), Eliot M. Rosenfield
Vice President Dmm Men 's Sportswear, Dave Panyard
Vice President Supply Chain Support, Steven Bienstock
Regional Vice President, Marty Frent
Vice President Dmm, Heather Brown
Vice President Shortage Prevention, Bob Morris
Executive Vice President Human Resources, Joyce Manning
Vice President Planning And Allocation, Michael Cane
Executive Vice President Supply Chain, Charlie Guardiola
Vice President, Melanie Grant
Vice President Accounting Operations, Tony Hughes
Executive Vice President Chief Merchandising Officer, Stephen Milstein
Vice President Of Information Technology Transitional Services, Mike Prince
Senior Vice President Gmm Home, Kevin Griffin
Senior Vice President And Chief Accounting Officer, John Crimmins
Vice President Tax, Shobna Daga
Vice President Human Resources Corporate, Susan Katims
Chairman President And Ceo, Thomas A. (Tom) Kingsbury, age 65
Evp General Counsel And Corporate Secretary, Janet L. Dhillon, age 55
Board Member, Jordan Hitch
Auditors: Deloitte & Touche LLP

LOCATIONS

HQ: Burlington Stores Inc
2006 Route 130 North, Burlington, NJ 08016
Phone: 609 387-7800
Web: www.burlingtonstores.com

2017 Stores

	No.
Texas	67
California	66
Florida	46
New York	41
Illinois	34
Pennsylvania	33
New Jersey	31
Ohio	24
Georgia	19
Michigan	18
Virginia	18
Maryland	16
North Carolina	15
Massachusetts	14
Arizona	12
Indiana	12
Washington	12
Connecticut	11
Puerto Rico	11
Wisconsin	10
Missouri	9
Minnesota	8
South Carolina	8
Tennessee	8
Colorado	7
Louisiana	7
Nevada	7
Alabama	6
Arizona	5
Kansas	5
Kentucky	5
Rhode Island	5
Utah	5
Oregon	4
Delaware	3
Iowa	3
Mississippi	3
Nebraska	3
New Hampshire	3
New Mexico	3
Oklahoma	3
Arkansas	2
Idaho	2
Maine	2
North Dakota	1
South Dakota	1
Online Store	1
Total	**629**

PRODUCTS/OPERATIONS

2017 Sales

	% of total
Women's ready-to-wear apparel	23
Accessories & Footwear	22
Menswear	20
Youth Apparel/Babby	16
Home	14
Coats	5
Total	**100**

2017 Stores

	No.
Burlington Stores	614
MJM Designer Shoes	10
Cohoes Fashions	2
Super Baby Depot	2
Online Store	1
Total	**629**

Selected Store Banners

Burlington Coat Factory Warehouse (value-priced apparel accessories linens bath items gifts)
Cohoes Fashions (higher-priced apparel and accessories)
MJM Designer Shoes (designer and fashion shoes)
Super Baby Depot (baby clothing accessories furniture)

COMPETITORS

Ascena Retail	Nordstrom
Babies "R" Us	Payless ShoeSource
Bed Bath & Beyond	Ross Stores
Belk	Saks
Bon-Ton Stores	Sears
DSW	Stein Mart
Dillard's	TJX Companies
J. C. Penney	Target Corporation
Kohl's	Wal-Mart
Macy's	

HISTORICAL FINANCIALS
Company Type: Public

Income Statement
FYE: February 3

	REVENUE ($ mil.)	NET INCOME ($ mil.)	NET PROFIT MARGIN	EMPLOYEES
02/18*	6,110	384	6.3%	40,000
01/17	5,590	215	3.9%	40,000
01/16	5,129	150	2.9%	37,500
01/15	4,849	65	1.4%	34,000
02/14	4,461	16	0.4%	30,095
Annual Growth	**8.2%**	**120.9%**		**7.4%**

*Fiscal year change

2018 Year-End Financials

Debt ratio: 40.07%
Return on equity: 2,048.74%
Cash ($ mil.): 133
Current ratio: 0.98
Long-term debt ($ mil.): 1,113

No. of shares (mil.): 67
Dividends
  Yield: —
  Payout: —
Market value ($ mil.): 7,856

	STOCK PRICE ($) FY Close	P/E High/Low		Earnings	PER SHARE ($) Dividends	Book Value
02/18*	115.75	23	14	5.48	0.00	1.28
01/17	80.91	29	16	3.01	0.00	(0.71)
01/16	53.73	30	20	1.99	0.00	(1.37)
01/15	49.89	58	27	0.87	0.00	(0.88)
02/14	25.58	—	—	(0.39)	0.00	(2.04)
Annual Growth	**45.8%**			**—**	**—**	**—**

*Fiscal year change

Byline Bancorp Inc

Auditors: Moss Adams LLP

LOCATIONS

HQ: Byline Bancorp Inc
180 North LaSalle Street, Suite 300, Chicago, IL 60601
Phone: 773 244-7000
Web: www.bylinebank.com

HISTORICAL FINANCIALS
Company Type: Public

Income Statement
FYE: December 31

	ASSETS ($ mil.)	NET INCOME ($ mil.)	INCOME AS % OF ASSETS	EMPLOYEES
12/17	3,366	21	0.6%	844
12/16	3,295	66	2.0%	791
12/15	2,479	(14)	—	
Annual Growth	**16.5%**		**—**	

2017 Year-End Financials

Debt ratio: 0.82%
Return on equity: 5.16%
Cash ($ mil.): 58
Current ratio: —
Long-term debt ($ mil.): —

No. of shares (mil.): 29
Dividends
  Yield: —
  Payout: 108.2%
Market value ($ mil.): 673

	STOCK PRICE ($) FY Close	P/E High/Low		Earnings	PER SHARE ($) Dividends	Book Value
12/17	22.97	59	50	0.38	0.00	15.64
12/16	0.00	—	—	3.27	0.00	15.54
12/15	0.00	—	—	(0.86)	0.00	10.86
Annual Growth	**—**			**—**	**—**	**20.0%**

C & F Financial Corp.

C&F Financial Corporation is the holding company for C&F Bank (aka Citizens and Farmers Bank) which operates about 20 branches in eastern Virginia. The bank targets individuals and local businesses offering such products and services as checking and savings accounts CDs credit cards and trust services. Commercial industrial and agricultural loans account for the largest portion of the company's loan portfolio (about 40%) which also includes residential mortgages consumer auto loans and consumer and construction loans.

EXECUTIVES

Chb-Ceo, Larry G Dillon
Pres-SEC, Thomas F Cherry
Sr V Pres-Cfo, Jason E Long
Pres-Ceo C&f Mortgage, Bryan E McKernon
Svp-Cco C&f Bank, John A Seaman III
Auditors: Yount, Hyde & Barbour, P.C.

LOCATIONS

HQ: C & F Financial Corp.
802 Main Street, West Point, VA 23181
Phone: 804 843-2360   **Fax:** 804 843-3017
Web: www.cffc.com

COMPETITORS

BB&T	First Citizens
Bank of America	BancShares
Eastern Virginia	SunTrust
Bankshares	Union Bankshares Corp.

HISTORICAL FINANCIALS
Company Type: Public

Income Statement
FYE: December 31

	ASSETS ($ mil.)	NET INCOME ($ mil.)	INCOME AS % OF ASSETS	EMPLOYEES
12/17	1,509	6	0.4%	650
12/16	1,451	13	0.9%	636
12/15	1,405	12	0.9%	598
12/14	1,333	12	0.9%	616
12/13	1,312	14	1.1%	643
Annual Growth	**3.6%**	**(17.8%)**	**—**	**0.3%**

2017 Year-End Financials

Debt ratio: 9.76%
Return on equity: 4.68%
Cash ($ mil.): 119
Current ratio: —
Long-term debt ($ mil.): —

No. of shares (mil.): 3
Dividends
  Yield: 0.0%
  Payout: 70.7%
Market value ($ mil.): 203

	STOCK PRICE ($) FY Close	P/E High/Low		Earnings	PER SHARE ($) Dividends	Book Value
12/17	58.00	34	23	1.88	1.33	40.53
12/16	49.85	13	10	3.89	1.29	40.09
12/15	39.00	11	9	3.68	1.22	38.12
12/14	39.74	13	8	3.59	1.19	36.09
12/13	45.67	14	9	4.18	1.16	33.33
Annual Growth	**6.2%**			**(18.1%)**	**3.5%**	**5.0%**

Cadence Bancorporation

Auditors: Ernst & Young LLP

LOCATIONS

HQ: Cadence Bancorporation
2800 Post Oak Boulevard, Suite 3800, Houston, TX 77056
Phone: 713 871-4000
Web: www.cadencebank.com

HISTORICAL FINANCIALS
Company Type: Public

Income Statement
FYE: December 31

	ASSETS ($ mil.)	NET INCOME ($ mil.)	INCOME AS % OF ASSETS	EMPLOYEES
12/17	10,948	102	0.9%	1,206
12/16	9,530	65	0.7%	1,193
12/15	8,811	39	0.4%	—
12/14	0	44		
Annual Growth	**—**	**31.7%**	**—**	**—**

2017 Year-End Financials

Debt ratio: 2.92%
Return on equity: 8.39%
Cash ($ mil.): 721
Current ratio: —
Long-term debt ($ mil.): —

No. of shares (mil.): 83
Dividends
  Yield: —
  Payout: —
Market value ($ mil.): 2,268

	STOCK PRICE ($) FY Close	P/E High/Low		Earnings	PER SHARE ($) Dividends	Book Value
12/17	27.12	22	16	1.25	0.00	16.25
12/16	0.00	—	—	0.87	0.00	14.41
Annual Growth	**—**			**12.8%**	**—**	**4.1%**

Caesars Entertainment Corp

The palaces owned by this Caesar are part of a vast gaming empire. Through its operating subsidiaries Caesars Entertainment Corporation owns and operates nearly 50 casinos mostly in a dozen US states and the UK. Its major properties include Harrah's Horseshoe and Rio casinos as well as Caesars Palace Paris Las Vegas and Planet Hollywood on the Vegas Strip. Caesars Entertainment's operations which comprise hotels riverboat casinos and gaming establishments boast millions of square feet of casino space and thousands of hotel rooms. In addition to casinos and hotels the company owns the World Series of Poker brand and tournaments through its Caesars Interactive Entertainment business.

Operations

Caesars Entertainment Corporation's facilities include land-based and riverboat casinos as well as casinos combined with greyhound and horse racing racetracks.

The company earns more than half its revenue from its casino operations which comprise sales from some 36000 slot machines and 2700 table games. Its hotel properties with more than 36000 guest rooms generate 20% of the company's revenue. Caesars' food and beverage operations (15% of revenue) generate sales from some 150 buffets bars and restaurants and nightclubs located in its casinos.

Its entertainment operations represent an additional revenue stream. Caesars' entertainment venues include the Colosseum at Caesars Palace and Zappos Theather at Planet Hollywood. Its venues enjoy healthy ticket sales and have hosted prominent acts like Celine Dion and Jennifer Lopez.

Geographic Reach

The majority of Caesars Entertainment Corporation's casinos operate in the US primarily under the Caesars Harrah's and Horseshoe brand names. Outside of Las Vegas the company has casino resorts in Atlantic City NJ; Laughlin NV; New Orleans LA; and Baltimore MD. It also leases or manages a dozen casinos in 15 states.

Internationally Caesars operates casinos primarily in the UK and South Africa.

Financial Performance

Caesars Entertainment Corporation's main operating subsidiary emerged from bankruptcy in 2017 two years after filing for Chapter 11 bankruptcy protection. Consequently financial results between 2016 and 2017 are not comparable.

Casino and hotel operations continued business as usual throughout the restructuring. Results from revenue was $4.85 billion in fiscal 2017 an increase of 25% over 2016. Results were driven primarily by the consolidation of its entertainment and other operating results which was tied to its emergence from bankruptcy. Modest increases in casino and hotel sales also contributed to the increase.

Despite higher revenue figures the company reported a net loss of $375 million for fiscal 2017 driven by high operating costs and $2 billion in restructuring costs related to its 2015 bankruptcy.

The company saw a negative cash flow from operations; however its overall cash in 2017 stood at $2.7 billion.

Strategy

Caesars Entertainment Corporation's growth strategy includes investing in new and existing hotel properties as well as in entertainment and other non-gaming activities. Investments fund renovation and expansion of hotel properties as well as the construction of new properties. Non-gaming-related operations currently account for nearly half of the company's revenue.

The company does invest in its gaming operations as well primarily through acquisitions. In 2018 Caesars acquired two central Indiana casinos and sports betting properties for $1.7 billion and it intends to acquire additional casino properties in the future. To help fund the $1.7 billion acquisition the company sold the land under Harrah's

Las Vegas to VICI Properties. Caesars continues to operate Harrah's Las Vegas however.

Reducing operational costs is another key strategic priority for Caesars Entertainment. Operating casinos in water-limited desert locations like Las Vegas is an challenge that Caesars and other casinos aspire to meet year after year. To control costs the company is committed to environmental sustainability and energy conservation and leverages technologies and innovative approaches to cut down on water and energy consumption at its hotels and casinos. The company boasts that since 2008 it has reduced water consumption across its portfolio of companies by 20%.

Mergers and Acquisitions

Caesars Entertainment Corporation acquired Centaur Holdings LLC in 2018 for $1.7 billion in cash. The transaction included two central Indiana casinos and sports betting properties Hoosier Park Racing and Casino and the Indiana Grand Racing and Casino.

Company Background

The company traces its roots back to 1937 when William Harrah and his father founded their first bingo parlor in Reno Nevada. Using the income from that business Harrah opened his first casino Harrah's Club in downtown Reno in 1946. In 1955 and 1956 he bought several clubs in Stateline Nevada (near Lake Tahoe). Harrah built the company by using promotions to draw middle-class Californians to his clubs.

The company acquired Caesars Entertainment Inc. many years later in 2005 and in 2010 changed its name to from Harrah's to Caesars Entertainment Corporation. In 2015 the company — riddled with debt — filed for Chapter 11 bankruptcy protection; it subsequently emerged in 2017 and sold off its Harrah's real estate in Las Vegas to raise funds for an acquisition. To date it still operates Harrah's Las Vegas.

HISTORY

William Harrah and his father founded their first bingo parlor in Reno Nevada in 1937. Using the income from that business Harrah opened his first casino Harrah's Club in downtown Reno in 1946. In 1955 and 1956 he bought several clubs in Stateline Nevada (near Lake Tahoe). Harrah built the company by using promotions to draw middle-class Californians to his clubs.

During the 1960s the entrepreneur expanded his operations in Lake Tahoe and in 1968 he built a 400-room hotel tower in Reno. Harrah's went public in 1971. After Harrah's death in 1978 the company expanded outside Nevada by building a hotel and casino in Atlantic City New Jersey.

Holiday Inns bought Harrah's in 1980 for about $300 million. The hotelier already owned a 40% interest in River Boat Casino which operated a casino next to a Holiday Inn in Las Vegas. When Holiday Inns acquired the other 60% of the casino/hotel in 1983 Harrah's took over its management. Holiday Inns became Holiday Corporation in 1985. The following year UK brewer Bass PLC put up $100 million for 10% of Holiday Corporation.

In 1990 Bass acquired the Holiday Inn hotel chain for $2.2 billion. The rest of Holiday Corporation including Harrah's was renamed Promus under chairman Michael Rose.

In the early 1990s Harrah's built a casino on Ak-Chin Indian land near Phoenix and opened riverboat casinos in Joliet Illinois; Shreveport Louisiana; and North Kansas City Missouri. In 1995 Promus spun off its hotel operations as Promus Hotel Corporation and changed the name of its casino business to Harrah's Entertainment. (Promus was acquired by Hilton Hotels later called Hilton Worldwide in 1999.)

Also in 1995 Harrah's gambled and lost. Big. Its New Orleans casino was shelved even before it was finished — a victim of Louisiana's Byzantine politics. Eager for the right to build what would be a $395 million 200000-sq.-ft. casino in the heart of the city Harrah's had made a number of ill-advised concessions to state and municipal officials. It agreed not to offer hotel rooms or food at the casino (forgoing about 20% of anticipated revenues) and promised to make an annual $100 million minimum payment to the state in addition to 19% of the casino's revenues. In the end the fiasco's price tag reached $900 million (only half of which went to casino construction costs) and Harrah's put the project into bankruptcy to stop the bleeding. (It resumed construction in 1999 and finally opened the casino at the end of the year.)

In 1997 Rose retired as chairman and was replaced by CEO Philip Satre. In 1998 Harrah's bought competitor Showboat with properties in Las Vegas and Atlantic City and management of a New South Wales Australia casino. A Louisiana Supreme Court ruling that year allowed the company to resume work on the New Orleans casino (albeit with a stake of less than 45% which was later increased to 63%). Harrah's also invested in Las Vegas-based National Airlines that year.

In early 1999 Harrah's bought Rio Hotel & Casino (also a partner in National Airlines) which operates one upscale casino on the Las Vegas Strip for about $525 million. In 2000 the company bought riverboat casino operator Players International for $425 million. Also that year Harrah's had to write off about $39 million in investments and loans to National Airlines which filed for bankruptcy. The company had a 48% stake in the airline.

Harrah's continued its acquisition streak in 2001 with the purchase of Harveys Casino Resorts with four locations in Colorado Iowa and Nevada for $675 million. (It sold the Colorado location in 2002.) The 452-room Harrah's Atlantic City hotel tower was opened in 2002.

EXECUTIVES

Evp Government Relations And Corporate Responsibility, Janis L. (Jan) Jones Blackhurst, age 70

President And Ceo, Mark P. Frissora, age 62, $1,976,923 total compensation

Evp General Counsel And Chief Regulatory And Compliance Officer, Timothy R. (Tim) Donovan, age 62, $703,990 total compensation

Global President, Thomas M. (Tom) Jenkin, age 63, $1,206,841 total compensation

President Global Development And Chief Development Officer, Marco A. Roca, age 53

President Hospitality, Robert J. (Bob) Morse, age 62, $854,845 total compensation

Evp Human Resources, Mary H. Thomas, age 51

Evp Public Affairs And Communications, Richard D. Broome, age 59

Cfo, Eric Hession, age 44, $703,990 total compensation

President International Development, Steven M. Tight, age 62

Evp And Cio, Les Ottolenghi, age 56

Evp Gaming And Interactive Entertainment, Christian Stuart

Vice President, John Maddox

Executive Vice President And Chief Marketing Officer, Tariq M Shaukat

Senior Vice President Domestic Development, Gregory Miller

Vice President Brand Management, Kris Hart

Vice President Information Technology, Scott Campbell

National Sales Manager, Lindsay Myers

Vice President Finance, Jacqueline Beato

Vice President Of Human Resources, Jennifer Jennings
Senior Vice President Genl Manager, Michael Stpierre
Vice President Of Corporate Finance, Brad Belhouse
Vice President Corporate Human Resources Services, Michael O'Brien
Senior Vice President Partner And Channel Marketing, Annette Weishaar
Senior Vice President Development, Mike Salzman
Vice President Human Resources, Jan Chapman
Vice President Of Finance And Administra, Russell Deaver
Regional Assistant Vice President Of Marketing, Renee Nadeau
Vice President Of Csa, Terry Byrnes
Vice President Vip Sales And Operations, David Koloski
Vice President, Nora West
Vice President Of Slot Operations, Stephen Bimson
Vice President, Mike Stratton
Vp And Chief Procurement Officer, Mike Fath
National Sales Manager, Robin Eissinger
Vice President Information Technology Development, Charley Paelinck
Vice President Of Strategic Data, Dave Kowal
Vice President Of Hospitality Operations, Scott Lokke
Senior Vice President General Manager, Michael Rich
Vice President And Executive Associate To The Chief Marketing Officer, Matt Anfinson
Vice President And Associate Chief Counsel Employment Law, Jeffrey D Winchester
Vice President Of Player Development, Steve Moy
Vice President International Marketing, Bruce Bommarito
Vice President Hotel Operations, Steve Opdyke
Vice President Financial Assurance, Sam Rubenstein
Vice President Of Finance, Jim Janchar
Vice President Casino Operations, Mark Kelly
Vice President And Executive Associate, Spyro Costopoulos
Vice President Of National Marketing, Joseph Watson
Vice President Player Development, Gerry Green
Assistant Vice President International Marketing Click Here For Credit Application, Lorena Mota
Portfolio Vice President, Andrew Kesler
National Sales Manager, Judy Sereni
Vice President Of National Ticketing, Amy Graca
Vice President Of Finance At Sac And Bac And Cac, Karen Worman
Vice President Human Resources, Colleen Moore
Vice President Of Human Resources, Melinda Mackey
Vice President Casino Operations, William Kelly
Senior Vice President Chief Experience Officer, Michael Marino
Regional Vice President Government Relations, Joseph Tyrrell
Vice President Gaming Analytics, Nathan Armogan
National Sales Manager, Grant Kehler
Vice President Government Relations, Karlos Lasane
Vice President Player Development, Sandra Zobrist
Vice President Of Human Resources And Property Develo, Ricky Busey
Vice President Of Total Rewards And Promotions, Matthew Bowers
Vice President Casino Marketing, Eric Zilewicz
Vice President Of Finance Las Vegas Region, Boris Petkov
Vice President Assistant Controller, Kenneth Kuick
Corporate Vice President Of Human Resources, Jeff Wagner
Vice President International Marketing, Jose Lopez

Senior Vice President And General Manager Harrah 's Joliet, Darren Vandover
Vice President And Deputy General Counsel, Bill Buffalo
National Sales Manager, Stacey Purcell
National Sales Manager, Kelly Wildfong
Vice President Table Games, Dan Burdalski
Executive Vice President Government Relations And Corporate Responsibility, Janis J Blackhurst
Nnv Vice President Of Finance And Player Development, Bob Owens
Vice President Asian Marketing, Ernest Wu
Vice President Of Hospitality Marketing, Jared Rapier
Vice President Corporate Communications, Jennifer Forkish
National Sales Manager, Jennifer Flacke
Vice President National Marketing, Thomas Fiore
Vice President Of Food And Beverage, Jay Lattimer
Vice President Of Food, Sean DiCicco
Regional Vice President Government Relations, Aj Baker
Vice President Ess Credit, Bill Gormley
Vice President Of Beverage, Ryan Voss
Vice President Enterprise Project Management And Strategic Initiatives, Rias Attar
Vice President Of Marketing, Noah Hirsch
National Sales Manager, Lester Robinson
Vice President And Assistant General Manager, Jacqueline Grace
Assistant Vice President, Franco D'Angelo
Vice President Caesars Palace, Daniel Burdalski
Evp Public Policy And Corporate Responsibility, Jan Jones Blackhurst
Chairman, James Hunt
Pac Treasurer, Lindsay Garcia
Secretary, Rachel Reed
Auditors: DELOITTE & TOUCHE LLP

LOCATIONS

HQ: Caesars Entertainment Corp
  One Caesars Palace Drive, Las Vegas, NV 89109
Phone: 702 407-6000
Web: www.caesars.com

2017 Sales

	$ mil.	% of total
Las Vegas	2,897	60
Other US	1,756	36
All Other	199	4
Total	4,852	100

PRODUCTS/OPERATIONS

2017 Sales

	$ mil.	% of total
Casino	2,865	52
Hotel Rooms	1,054	19
Food and Beverage	938	17
Other	626	11
Reimbursed Management Costs	48	1
Casino Promotional Allowances	(679)	-
Total	4,852	100

COMPETITORS

Boyd Gaming	Mashantucket Pequot
Isle of Capri Casinos	Station Casinos
Kerzner International	Tropicana
Las Vegas Sands	Entertainment
MGM Resorts	Trump Resorts
MGP	Wynn Resorts

HISTORICAL FINANCIALS

Company Type: Public

Income Statement				FYE: December 31
	REVENUE ($ mil.)	NET INCOME ($ mil.)	NET PROFIT MARGIN	EMPLOYEES
12/17	4,852	(375)	—	65,000
12/16	3,877	(3,569)	—	31,000
12/15	4,654	5,920	127.2%	33,000
12/14	8,516	(2,783)	—	68,000
12/13	8,559	(2,948)	—	68,000
Annual Growth	(13.2%)	—	—	(1.1%)

2017 Year-End Financials

Debt ratio: 71.93%
Return on equity: (-1,562.50%)
Cash ($ mil.): 2,558
Current ratio: 1.83
Long-term debt ($ mil.): 18,278

No. of shares (mil.): 684
Dividends
  Yield: —
  Payout: —
Market value ($ mil.): 8,653

	STOCK PRICE ($) FY Close	P/E High/Low	PER SHARE ($) Earnings	Dividends	Book Value
12/17	12.65	— —	(1.35)	0.00	4.71
12/16	8.50	— —	(24.41)	0.00	(21.61)
12/15	7.89	0 0	40.26	0.00	6.81
12/14	15.69	— —	(19.53)	0.00	(34.46)
12/13	21.54	— —	(22.93)	0.00	(22.82)
Annual Growth	(12.5%)				

Cambridge Bancorp

Cambridge Bancorp is the nearly $2 billion-asset holding company for Cambridge Trust Company a community bank serving Cambridge and the Greater Boston area through about a dozen branch locations in Massachusetts. It offers standard retail products and services including checking and savings accounts CDs IRAs and credit cards. Residential mortgages including home equity loans account for about 50% of the company's loan portfolio while commercial real estate loans make up more than 40%. The company also offers commercial industrial and consumer loans. Established in 1892 the bank also offers trust and investment management services.

Operations

The commercial bank operates a traditional retail banking line focused on lending as well as its Wealth Management Group which investment management and trust business. The bank had $1.8 billion in total assets and $2.4 billion in client assets under management at the end of 2015.

As with other retail banks Cambridge Bancorp makes the bulk of its revenue from interest income. About 58% of its total revenue came from loan interest during 2015 while another 10% came from interest on taxable and tax-exempt investment securities. The rest of its revenue came from wealth management income (24% of revenue) deposit account fees (3%) ATM/Debit card income (1%) and other non-interest income sources.

Geographic Reach

Cambridge Bancorp has 12 branches in Massachusetts in Cambridge Boston Belmont Concord Lexington Lincoln and Weston. It also has wealth management offices in Boston as well as in New Hampshire in Concord Manchester and Portsmouth.

Sales and Marketing

The company spent $2.38 million on marketing during 2015 up from $2.12 million in 2014.

Financial Performance

Cambridge's annual revenues and profits have been steadily rising over the past several years thanks to continued commercial real estate mortgage growth and as its Wealth Management business has nearly doubled its managed assets since 2011 spurring higher fee revenue.

The bank's revenue climbed 7% to $80.2 million during 2015 on 10% loan growth mostly driven by commercial real estate loans which spurred higher interest income. The company's wealth management business income grew 7% as its client assets continued to grow with new investor inflows.

Revenue growth in 2015 drove Cambridge Bancorp's net income up 5% to $15.7 million. The bank's operating cash levels rose 24% to $20 million for the year with an increase in cash-based earnings and favorable changes in working capital mostly related to a change in accrued interest receivable deferred taxes and other assets and liabilities.

Strategy

Cambridge Bancorp continued in 2016 to lean on the success of its commercial mortgage business though it plans to pivot more to commercial and industrial lending to diversify its commercial lending portfolio.

To better prepare for rising interest rates Cambridge Bancorp in 2015 and 2016 modified its commercial loan strategy from long-term fixed-rate loans (which are vulnerable to interest rate risk) to a new interest rate derivative product to offer an alternative long-term financing for its customers while helping the bank earn a variable rate of interest on its loans. For its consumer banking unit the bank in 2015 began a plan to sell the majority of its long-term residential mortgage production including secondary loans to the secondary market.

EXECUTIVES

Chairman President And Ceo, Denis K. Sheahan, age 52

Svp And Chief Investment Officer, James F. Spencer

Svp Commercial Real Estate Cambridge Trust, Martin B. Millane

Evp And Cio Cambridge Trust, Lynne M. Burrow

Evp And Head Of Wealth Management Cambridge Trust, Michael A. Duca

Evp And Consumer Banking Director Cambridge Trust, Thomas A. Johnson

Cfo, Michael Carotenuto

Svp And President Cambridge Trust Company Of New Hampshire, Susan Martore-Baker

Svp And Marketing Director, Robert N. Siegrist

Assistant Vice President Bsa Officer, Marya Wall

Title Operations Manager And Assistant Vice President, Coates Peter

Chairman President And Ceo, Denis K. Sheahan, age 52

Auditors: KPMG LLP

LOCATIONS

HQ: Cambridge Bancorp
1336 Massachusetts Avenue, Cambridge, MA 02138
Phone: 617 876-5500
Web: www.cambridgetrust.com

PRODUCTS/OPERATIONS

2015 Sales

	% of total
Interest Income	
Interest on loans	58
Interest on taxable investment securities	7
Interest on tax exempt investment securities	3
Non-Interest Income	
Wealth Management Income	24
Deposits accounts fee	3
ATM/Debit card income	1
Bank Owned life insurance income	1
Gain on disposition on investment securities	1
Gain on loans held of sale	1
Other income	1
Loan related derivative income	-
Total	**100**

Products/Services

Personal Banking
Checking
Savings CDs & IRAs
Online Banking
Mobile Banking
Mortgages
Home Equity
Credit Cards
Personal Loans
More Services
Business Banking
Checking & Savings
Commercial Lending
Commercial Real Estate
Cash Management
Remote Deposit Capture
Online Banking
Mobile Banking
Professional Services Program
More Services
Wealth Management
Investment Process
Investment Management
Fiduciary & Planning Services
Estate Settlement
Wealth Management Personnel
Forums
Online Access

COMPETITORS

Bank of America
Cambridge Financial
Central Bancorp
Century Bancorp (MA)
Citizens Financial Group

Eastern Bank
Middlesex Savings
Peoples Federal Bancshares Inc.

HISTORICAL FINANCIALS

Company Type: Public

Income Statement

FYE: December 31

	ASSETS ($ mil.)	NET INCOME ($ mil.)	INCOME AS % OF ASSETS	EMPLOYEES
12/17	1,949	14	0.8%	247
12/16	1,849	16	0.9%	—
12/15	1,706	15	0.9%	—
12/14	1,573	14	0.9%	—
12/13	1,533	14	0.9%	123
Annual Growth	**6.2%**	**1.2%**	**—**	**19.0%**

2017 Year-End Financials

Debt ratio: —
Return on equity: 10.48%
Cash ($ mil.): 103
Current ratio: —
Long-term debt ($ mil.): —

No. of shares (mil.): 4
Dividends
 Yield: 0.0%
 Payout: 51.5%
Market value ($ mil.): 326

	STOCK PRICE ($) FY Close	P/E High/Low	PER SHARE ($) Earnings	Dividends	Book Value
12/17	79.80	24 17	3.61	1.86	36.24
12/16	62.29	15 11	4.15	1.84	33.36
12/15	47.40	13 11	3.93	1.80	31.26
12/14	46.50	13 10	3.78	1.68	29.50
12/13	40.01	12 10	3.62	1.59	28.13
Annual Growth	**18.8%**	**—**	**(0.1%)**	**4.0%**	**6.5%**

Camden National Corp. (ME)

Camden National Corporation is the holding company for Camden National Bank which boasts nearly 45 branches in about a dozen Maine counties and provides standard deposit products such as checking and savings accounts CDs and IRAs. Commercial mortgages and loans make up 50% of its loan portfolio while residential mortgages make up another 40% and consumer loans constitute the remainder. Subsidiary Acadia Trust provides trust fiduciary investment management and retirement plan administration services while Camden Financial Consultants offers brokerage and insurance services. The largest bank headquartered in Maine Camden National Bank was founded in 1875 and once issued its own US currency.

Operations

About 63% of Camden National's total revenue came from loan interest (including fees) in 2014 while another 15% came from interest on its US government and sponsored enterprise obligations (investment securities). The rest of its revenue came from deposit account service charges (5%) other service charges and fees (5%) income from fiduciary services (4%) brokerage and insurance commissions (2%) and other miscellaneous income sources. The bank had a staff of 471 employees at the end of 2014.

Geographic Reach

Camden National has around 45 branches in 12 counties throughout Maine with one commercial loan office in Manchester New Hampshire. Its primary markets are in the counties of Androscoggin Cumberland Hancock Kennebec Knox Lincoln Penobscot Piscataquis Somerset Waldo Washington and York.

Sales and Marketing

The company offers deposit and loan services to consumers institutions municipalities non-profits and commercial customers.

Financial Performance

The company has struggled to consistently grow its revenues and profits in recent years mostly due to shrinking interest margins on loans amidst the low-interest environment.

Camden National's revenue dipped by 3% to $112.8 million in 2014 mostly because the bank in 2013 had collected a non-recurring $2.7 million gain from the sale of its five Franklin County branches and because its mortgage banking income fell by $1.1 million as it decided to retain most of its 30-year fixed rate residential mortgage production in 2014.

Despite revenue declines in 2014 the bank's net income jumped by 8% to $24.6 million mostly because in 2013 it had recorded a non-recurring $2.8 million goodwill impairment charge related to its financial services reporting unit. Camden's operating cash levels rose by 1% to $29.9 million for the year on higher cash earnings.

Strategy

The bank competes with larger financial institutions by emphasizing customer service to build customer loyalty and long-term relationships. It also sometimes pursues acquisitions of banks and branches in its target markets in Maine to grow its loan and deposit business.

Camden may also be expanding its franchise beyond Maine in future years. In 2014 it opened a commercial loan office in Manchester New Hampshire enabling it to serve more customers across northern New England.

Mergers and Acquisitions

In March 2015 Camden National Corporation agreed to purchase SBM Financial along with its subsidiary The Bank of Maine subsidiary. The deal expected to be completed in late 2015 would add $813 million in assets and make Camden National Bank Maine's largest community bank.

In late 2012 the bank acquired 15 full-service branches from Bank of America for $12 million.

EXECUTIVES

Vice President Risk Management, Steve Matteo

Evp Coo And Cfo, Deborah A. Jordan, age 52, $223,327 total compensation

Evp Retail Banking, June B. Parent, age 54, $189,248 total compensation

Evp Risk Management, Joanne T. Campbell, age 55, $124,585 total compensation

President And Ceo, Gregory A. (Greg) Dufour, age 57, $398,077 total compensation

Svp Information Technology, Scott Buckheit

Evp Commercial Lending, Timothy P. Nightingale, age 60, $213,846 total compensation

Vice President Commercial Portfolio Manager Commercial Loan Administrator Team Leader, Libby Arrico

Vice President, Richard Nickerson

Vice President Retail Regional Manager Southern, Nancy Tracy

Vice President, Craig Day

Assistant Vice President, Jody Landrith

Vice President, Cynthia Bergin

Vice President Market Manager, Traci Tenney

Senior Vice President, Vera Rand Roberts

Vice President Commercial Loan Officer, Brent Folster

Vice President Information Security Manager, Anthony Mazzeo

Vice President Credit Risk Officer, Susan Weber

Vice President Commercial Portfolio Manager, Brooke Woodbury

Vice President Loan Servicing, Mark Richards

Senior Vice President, AL Butler

Vice President Of Mortgage Operations, Betsy Hauser

Vice President Of Mortgage Operations, Paul Palmer

Vice President Collections, Tim Crowe

Senior Vice President Director Of Corporate Services, Susan Giffard

Assistant Vice President Senior Client Services Specialist, Amanda Neuts

Vice President Commercial Portfolio Manager, Matthew Gilbert

Vice President Senior Retail Loan Officer, Donna Maynard

Avp It Systems Management, John Bentley

Senior Vice President Client Advisor, Zach Rubin

Chairman Camden National Corporation And Camden National Bank, Karen W. Stanley, age 72

Auditors: RSM US LLP

LOCATIONS

HQ: Camden National Corp. (ME)
2 Elm Street, Camden, ME 04843
Phone: 207 236-8821 **Fax:** 207 236-6256
Web: www.camdennational.com

PRODUCTS/OPERATIONS

2014 Sales

	$ mil.	% of total
Interest		
Loans including fees	70	63
US government & agency securities	17	14
Other investments	0	1
Noninterest		
Service charges on deposit accounts & others	12	11
Income from fiduciary services	5	4
Brokerage and insurance commission	1	2
Other	5	5
Total	**112**	**100**

COMPETITORS

Bangor Savings Bank
Bar Harbor Bankshares
KeyCorp
Northeast Bancorp
Norway Bancorp
People's United Financial
TD Bank USA
The First Bancorp

HISTORICAL FINANCIALS

Company Type: Public

Income Statement

FYE: December 31

	ASSETS ($ mil.)	NET INCOME ($ mil.)	INCOME AS % OF ASSETS	EMPLOYEES
12/17	4,065	28	0.7%	636
12/16	3,864	40	1.0%	631
12/15	3,709	20	0.6%	652
12/14	2,789	24	0.9%	471
12/13	2,603	22	0.9%	481
Annual Growth	11.8%	5.7%	—	7.2%

2017 Year-End Financials

Debt ratio: 1.47%
Return on equity: 7.16%
Cash ($ mil.): 102
Current ratio: —
Long-term debt ($ mil.): —

No. of shares (mil.): 15
Dividends
Yield: 0.0%
Payout: 50.5%
Market value ($ mil.): 654

	STOCK PRICE ($) FY Close	P/E High/Low	PER SHARE ($) Earnings	Dividends	Book Value
12/17	42.13	26 20	1.82	0.92	25.99
12/16	44.45	19 11	2.57	0.80	25.30
12/15	44.09	26 21	1.73	0.80	23.69
12/14	39.84	19 16	2.19	0.72	22.00
12/13	41.84	22 16	1.98	0.71	20.33
Annual Growth	0.2%	— —	(2.1%)	6.8%	6.3%

Campbell Soup Co

Soup boils down to   M'm! M'm! Money!   at the world's #1 soup maker Campbell Soup. The company's most popular selections among its extensive soup portfolio in the US include chicken noodle tomato and cream of mushroom. Campbell also makes many other simple foods snacks and beverages including SpaghettiOs canned pasta Pace picante sauce V8 beverages Aussie favorite Arnott's biscuits and Pepperidge Farm baked goods (including those popular tiny Goldfish crackers). Newer products for the soup company include

Garden Fresh Gourmet salsas and dips and Bolthouse Farms carrots and organic baby foods. Campbell sells its products worldwide.

HISTORY

Campbell Soup Company began in Camden New Jersey in 1869 as a canning and preserving business founded by icebox maker Abram Anderson and fruit merchant Joseph Campbell. Anderson left in 1876 and Arthur Dorrance took his place. The Dorrance family assumed control after Campbell retired in 1894.

Arthur's nephew John Dorrance joined Campbell in 1897. The young chemist soon found a way to condense soup by eliminating most of its water. Without the heavy bulk of water-filled cans distribution was cheaper; Campbell products quickly spread.

In 1904 the firm introduced the Campbell Kids characters. Entering the California market in 1911 Campbell became one of the first US companies to achieve national distribution of a food brand. It bought Franco-American the first American soup maker in 1915.

The company's ubiquity in American kitchens made its soup can an American icon (consider Andy Warhol's celebrated 1960 print) and brought great wealth to the Dorrance family.

With a reputation for conservative management Campbell began to diversify acquiring V8 juice (1948) Swanson (1955) Pepperidge Farm (1961) Godiva Chocolatier (33% in 1966 full ownership in 1974) Vlasic pickles (1978) and Mrs. Paul's seafood (1982). It introduced Prego spaghetti sauce and LeMenu frozen dinners in the early 1980s.

Much of Campbell's sales growth in the 1990s came not from unit sales but from increasing its prices. In 1993 it took a $300 million restructuring charge and over the next two years it sold poor performers at home and abroad. John Sr.'s grandson Bennett Dorrance took up the role of vice chairman in 1993 becoming the first family member to take a senior executive position in 10 years.

Two years later Campbell paid $1.1 billion for Pace Foods (picante sauce) and acquired Fresh Start Bakeries (buns and muffins for McDonald's) and Homepride (popular cooking sauce in the UK).

As part of its international expansion in 1996 the firm acquired Erasco a top German soup maker and Cheong Chan a food manufacturer in Malaysia. However back at home it sold Mrs. Paul's. In 1997 Campbell sold its Marie's salad dressing operations and bought Groupe Danone's Liebig (France's leading wet-soup brand). Also that year Dale Morrison a relative newcomer to the firm succeeded David Johnson as president and CEO. To reduce costs and focus on other core segments in 1998 Campbell spun off Swanson frozen foods and Vlasic pickles into Vlasic Foods International. (Vlasic later filed bankruptcy and was snapped up in a leveraged buyout.) In 1999 Campbell redesigned its soup can labels altering an American icon.

Morrison resigned abruptly as president and CEO in 2000; Johnson returned to the helm during the search for a permanent chief. In early 2001 Douglas Conant previously of Nabisco Foods joined Campbell as president and CEO. A fresh plan was introduced to spend up to $600 million on marketing product development and quality upgrades (at the expense of shareholder dividends). In 2001 Campbell also bought the Batchelors Royco and Heisse Tasse brands of soup as well as the OXO brand of stock cubes from Unilever for about $900 million. The deal made Campbell the leading soup maker in Europe. In 2003 Campbell bought Snack Foods Limited a leading snack food maker in Australia and Irish dry soup maker Erin Foods from Greencore.

Campbell reorganized its North American business in 2004 into the following units: US Soup Sauces and Beverages; Campbell Away From Home and Canada Mexico and Latin America; Pepperidge Farm; and Godiva Worldwide. (In response to dietary trends the company announced that year that it was removing all trans-fatty acids from its Pepperidge Farm breads.) The company retired the Franco-American brand in 2004; products that carried the brand (most notably SpaghettiOs) now bear the Campbell brand. Also that year company chairman George M. Sherman retired and was replaced by Harvey Golub.

In 2006 Campbell sold its UK and Irish businesses to Premier Foods for about $870 million. Brands involved in the sale included Homepride sauces OXO stock cubes and Batchelors McDonnells and Erin soups.

In 2012 the company purchased Bolthouse Farms for about $1.55 billion from Madison Dearborn Partners. Bolthouse known for selling fresh carrots beverages and salad dressings was expected to further fuel Campbell's US beverage division which had benefited from the rising popularity of the V8 juice brand.

In fiscal 2013 Campbell expanded its access to manufacturing and distribution capabilities in Mexico for its beverages soups broths and sauces after it signed a deal with Grupo Jumex and Conservas La CosteA±ato. That year it also sold its European simple meals business closing facilities in Belgium France Germany and Sweden.

In August 2013 the soup giant acquired the Denmark-based baked snack maker Kelsen Group for $325 million.

In June 2013 it bought Plum Organics one of the top brands of organic baby food in the US. The company makes organic foods and snacks for babies toddlers and children a fast-growing premium food category. It hoped the purchase would bring a new generation of consumers to Campbell.

EXECUTIVES

President And Ceo, Denise M. Morrison, age 64, $1,100,000 total compensation
Vp And Controller, Anthony P. DiSilvestro, age 59, $642,500 total compensation
President Americas Simple Meals And Beverages, Mark R. Alexander, age 54, $696,667 total compensation
Svp And General Counsel, Adam G. Ciongoli, age 50, $700,000 total compensation
President Campbell Fresh, Edward L. (Ed) Carolan, age 49
President Global Biscuits And Snacks, Luca Mignini, age 55, $674,042 total compensation
Svp Global Research And Development And Quality, Carlos J. Barroso, age 59, $470,000 total compensation
President Campbell Soup Foundation, Kim Fremont Fortunato
Vp And Chief Technology And Information Officer, Francisco Fraga
Svp Integrated Global Services, Bethmara Kessler
Vice President Marketing, Tom Wegmann
Vice President Initiatives And Network Optimization, Dave Parcher
Vice President Of Logistics, Skip Tappan
Senior Vice President And Chief Legal And Public Affairs Officer, Ellen O Kaden
Regional Vice President West, Joe McDonnell
Chairman, Les C. Vinney, age 69
Auditors: PricewaterhouseCoopers LLP

LOCATIONS

HQ: Campbell Soup Co
1 Campbell Place, Camden, NJ 08103-1799
Phone: 856 342-4800   **Fax:** 856 342-3878
Web: www.campbellsoupcompany.com

2016 Sales

	$ mil.	% of total
US	6,437	81
Australia	590	7
Other	934	12
Total	**7,961**	**100**

PRODUCTS/OPERATIONS

2016 Sales

	$ mil.	% of total
Americas Simple Meals and Beverages	4,380	55
Global Biscuits and Snacks	2,564	32
Campbell Fresh	1,017	13
Total	**7,961**	**100**

2016 Sales

	$ mil.	% of total
Soup	2,690	34
Baked snacks	2,479	31
Other simple meals	1,702	21
Beverages	1,090	14
Total	**7,961**	**100**

Selected Brand Names

Domestic
  Away From Home
  Bolthouse Farms
  Campbell
  Ecce Panis
  Pace
  Pepperidge Farm
  Plum Organics
  Prego
  Select Harvest
  StockPot
  Swanson
  V8 and V8 Splash
  Wolfgang Puck
International
  Arnott's (Australia)

Selected Subsidiaries

Arnott's Biscuits Limited (Australia)
Bolthouse Holding Corp. (US)
Ecce Panis Inc.
Pepperidge Farm Incorporated
Players Group Limited (Australia)
Sinalopasta S.A. de C.V. (Mexico)
Stockpot Inc.

COMPETITORS

Associated British Foods	Hanover Foods
B&G Foods	Harry's Fresh Foods
Barbara's Bakery	Heinz
Baxters	Hormel
Beech-Nut	Kellogg U.S. Snacks
Big Heart Pet Brands	Mondelez International
Bush Brothers	Morgan Foods
Canyon Creek Food	NORPAC
ConAgra	Nestlé
Dole Food	Odwalla
Frito-Lay	Pacific Coast Producers
General Mills	Peter Rabbit Farms
Gerber Products	Red Gold
Golden Enterprises	Reily Foods
Grimmway Enterprises	Renée's Gourmet Foods
H. J. Heinz Limited	Snyder's-Lance
Hain Celestial	Walkers Snack Foods

HISTORICAL FINANCIALS

Company Type: Public

Income Statement
FYE: July 29

	REVENUE ($ mil.)	NET INCOME ($ mil.)	NET PROFIT MARGIN	EMPLOYEES
07/18	8,685	261	3.0%	23,000
07/17	7,890	887	11.2%	18,000
07/16*	7,961	563	7.1%	16,500
08/15	8,082	691	8.5%	18,600
08/14	8,268	818	9.9%	19,400
Annual Growth	**1.2%**	**(24.8%)**	**—**	**4.3%**

*Fiscal year change

2018 Year-End Financials

Debt ratio: 68.10%
Return on equity: 17.44%
Cash ($ mil.): 226
Current ratio: 0.64
Long-term debt ($ mil.): 7,998
No. of shares (mil.): 323
Dividends
  Yield: 0.0%
  Payout: 162.7%
Market value ($ mil.): 13,224

	STOCK PRICE ($) FY Close	P/E High/Low		PER SHARE ($) Earnings	Dividends	Book Value
07/18	40.94	62	38	0.86	1.40	4.22
07/17	52.85	22	18	2.89	1.40	5.44
07/16*	62.27	37	25	1.81	1.25	4.95
08/15	49.31	22	19	2.21	1.25	4.45
08/14	41.96	18	15	2.59	1.25	5.16
Annual Growth	**(0.6%)**	**—**	**—**	**(24.1%)**	**2.9%**	**(4.9%)**

*Fiscal year change

Capital City Bank Group, Inc.

Capital City Bank Group is the holding company for Capital City Bank (CCB) which serves individuals businesses and institutions from some 70 branches in Florida Georgia and Alabama. CCB offers checking savings and money market accounts; CDs; IRAs; Internet banking; and debit and credit cards. Commercial real estate mortgages account for about 40% of its loan portfolio; residential real estate loans also hover near 40%. The bank also originates business loans and consumer loans including credit cards. Capital City also performs data processing services for other financial institutions in its market area.

Operations

In addition to its CCB bank subsidiary which accounts for about 94% of Capital City Bank Group's total revenue the holding company operates three other subsidiaries: Capital City Trust a provider of trust and asset management services; Capital City Banc Investments which offers investments retirement plans and life and long-term care insurance through an agreement with third-party provider INVEST Financial Corporation a subsidiary of Jackson National Life Insurance Company; and data processor Capital City Services Co.

Geographic Reach

Florida is CCB's largest market accounting for about 78% of its revenue. Georgia and Alabama account for 21% and 1% respectively.

Financial Performance

Capital City Bank Group's revenue has slid since the onset of the recession and housing crisis which battered the Florida market and during the uneven recovery. Revenue fell 5% in 2011 vs. 2010 marking the fourth consecutive year of decline. Indeed revenue plunged 74% between 2007 and 2011. However in 2011 the group returned to profitability with net income of $4.9 million following losses in 2010 and 2009.

Interest income decreased by 10% while non-interest income increased 4% in 2011 vs. 2010. Lower interest and fees on loans contributed to the decline in interest income. Growth in bank card and retail brokerage fees contributed to the rise in non-interest income.

Strategy

Capital City Bank Group was founded in 1982 to acquire six banks and has never looked back. While its growth has slowed the company has continued its acquisition strategy buying 15 banks since 1984; it has also expanded by opening new offices. However its home state of Florida was one of the hardest hit during the recession. High unemployment levels contributed to an increase in nonperforming loans in the bank's portfolio which in turn translated to net losses in 2009 and 2010. (Nonperforming loans totaled $75 million or 4.6% of the company's total loan portfolio at the end of 2011.) Capital City is focusing on diversifying its portfolio and reducing problem assets.

EXECUTIVES

Evp And Cfo, J. Kimbrough (Kim) Davis, age 64, $260,000 total compensation

Chairman President And Ceo, William G. (Bill) Smith, age 64, $350,000 total compensation

Credit Administration, Dale A. Thompson

Chief People Officer And President Capital Services Company, Bethany H. (Beth) Corum

President Capital City Banc Investments; President Capital City Trust Company, Bill Moor

President Leon County, Ed West

Residential Mortgage, Tom Allen

Commercial Banking, Ed Canup

Community Banking, Mitch Englert

Vice President Cre, Tolga Dincman

Assistant Vice President, Lisa Elam

Assistant Vice President Community Banker, Brian Timmons

Senior Vice President, David Caldwell

Assistant Vice President, Cindy Richardson

Assistant Vice President, Janette Wagner

Vice President And Community Banker, Valerie Hoffler

Vice President Of Digital Engagement, Craig Ellard

Vice President, Francis Rolfes

Vice President Marketing, Walter Hoskins

Assistant Vice President, Sylvia White

Assistant Vice President, Edie Frasier

Vice President, Karen C Meadows

Assistant Vice President And Community Banker, Janie Stewart

Executive Vice President Chief Financial Officer, Kim Davis

Senior Vice President Capital City Bank, Mark Strickland

Assistant Vice President Business Banker, Terry Huiskens

Senior Vice President, Jim Scarboro

Vice President, Catherine Sherman

Vice President And Compliance Manager, Sheila Reddick

Assistant Vice President, Francis M Rolfes

Senior Vice President, Lee Nichols

Senior Vice President, Brantley Henderson

Chairman President And Ceo, William G. (Bill) Smith, age 64

Auditors: Ernst & Young LLP

LOCATIONS

HQ: Capital City Bank Group, Inc.
217 North Monroe Street, Tallahassee, FL 32301
Phone: 850 402-7821
Web: www.ccbg.com

PRODUCTS/OPERATIONS

2015 Sales

	$ mil.	% of total
Interest		
Loans including fees	73	55
Investment securities	5	5
Funds sold	0	-
Noninterest income		
Deposit fee	22	17
Bank card fees	11	8
Wealth management fees	7	6
Mortgage Banking fees	4	3
Data processing fees	1	1
Other	6	5
Total	**133**	**100**

COMPETITORS

Ameris	Regions Financial
BBX Capital	SunTrust
Bank of America	Thomasville Bancshares
Delta Community Credit Union	

HISTORICAL FINANCIALS

Company Type: Public

Income Statement

FYE: December 31

	ASSETS ($ mil.)	NET INCOME ($ mil.)	INCOME AS % OF ASSETS	EMPLOYEES
12/17	2,898	10	0.4%	825
12/16	2,845	11	0.4%	853
12/15	2,797	9	0.3%	894
12/14	2,627	9	0.4%	937
12/13	2,611	6	0.2%	927
Annual Growth	2.6%	15.8%	—	(2.9%)

2017 Year-End Financials

Debt ratio: 2.31%	No. of shares (mil.): 16
Return on equity: 3.88%	Dividends
Cash ($ mil.): 285	Yield: 0.0%
Current ratio: —	Payout: 37.5%
Long-term debt ($ mil.): —	Market value ($ mil.): 390

	STOCK PRICE ($) FY Close	P/E High/Low	Earnings	Dividends	Book Value
12/17	22.94	41 28	0.64	0.24	16.73
12/16	20.48	32 19	0.69	0.17	16.34
12/15	15.35	31 26	0.53	0.13	15.99
12/14	15.54	30 22	0.53	0.09	15.62
12/13	11.77	37 30	0.35	0.00	15.92
Annual Growth	18.2%	— —	16.3%	—	1.2%

Capital One Financial Corp

Thanks to its ?What?s in Your Wallet? branding campaign Capital One Financial Corporation is one of the most recognizable issuers of Visa and MasterCard credit cards in the US. It also provides typical banking products such as mortgage loans and checking accounts and has a unit focused on auto financing. It also sells insurance and manages assets for institution and high-net-worth individuals. Capital One holds more than 65 million customer accounts in the US Canada and the UK and maintains a deposit portfolio worth over $200 billion. It boasts a banking network of hundreds of branches in about half a dozen US states and maintains a strong online presence with its internet and mobile banking applications.

HISTORY

Capital One Financial is a descendant of the Bank of Virginia which was formed in 1945. The company began issuing products similar to credit cards in 1953 and was MasterCard issuer #001. Acquisitions and mergers brought some 30 banks and several finance and mortgage companies under the bank's umbrella between 1962 and 1986 when Bank of Virginia became Signet Banking.

Signet's credit card operations had reached a million customers in 1988 when the bank hired consultants Richard Fairbank and Nigel Morris (Fairbank is now chairman and CEO) to implement their "Information-Based Strategy." Under the duo's leadership the bank began using sophisticated data-collection methods to gather massive amounts of information on existing or prospective customers; it then used the information to design and mass-market customized products to the customer.

In 1991 — after creating an enormous database and developing sophisticated screening processes and direct-mail marketing tactics — Signet escalated the credit card wars luring customers from its rivals with its innovative balance-transfer credit card. The card let customers of other companies transfer what they owed on higher-interest cards to a Signet card with a lower introductory rate.

The new card immediately drew imitators (by 1997 balance-transfer cards accounted for 85% of credit card solicitations). After skimming off the least risky customers Fairbank and Morris began going after less desirable credit customers who could be charged higher rates. The result was what they call second-generation products — secured and unsecured cards with lower credit lines and higher annual percentage rates and fees for higher-risk customers.

The credit card business had grown to 5 million customers by 1994 but at a high cost to Signet which had devoted most of its resources to finding and servicing credit card holders. That year Signet spun off its credit card business as Capital One to focus on banking. (Signet was later acquired by First Union.)

The company moved into Florida and Texas in 1995 and into Canada and the UK in 1996; that year it established its savings bank mainly to offer products and services to its cardholders. In 1997 the company used this unit to move into deposit accounts buying a deposit portfolio from J. C. Penney. In 1998 the company began marketing its products to such clients as immigrants and high school students (whose parents must co-sign for the card). The company also expanded in terms of products and geography acquiring auto lender Summit Acceptance and opening a new office in Nottingham England.

In 1999 the firm's growth continued. The company stepped up its marketing efforts and was rewarded with significant boosts to its non-interest income and customer base. The next year the company launched The Capital One Place an Internet shopping site. In 2001 the company acquired AmeriFee which provides loans for elective medical and dental surgery; and PeopleFirst Inc. the nation's largest online provider of direct motor vehicle loans.

In response to industry-wide concern over subprime lending Capital One agreed in 2002 to beef up reserves on its subprime portfolio. Also in 2002 the company's UK operations proved profitable for the first time.

The company expanded into banking in 2005 and 2006 with the acquisitions of Hibernia and North Fork Bancorporation respectively. The deals gave it a boost in the banking sector expanding its presence both geographically in the Northeast and in the South and turning the company into one of the top bank holding companies in the US. The $13.2 billion stock-and-cash North Fork deal gave the company more than 300 bank branches in New York New Jersey and Connecticut.

The 2005 purchase of New Orleans-based Hibernia was a stock-and-cash transaction valued at some $5 billion nearly 10% less than the originally agreed-upon price. The transaction was delayed then renegotiated after Hurricane Katrina devastated Hibernia's home city. Hibernia which relocated to Houston adopted the Capital One moniker.

Capital One closed wholesale lender GreenPoint Mortgage Funding acquired as part of its acquisition of North Fork in 2007. The unit suffered from the credit woes that have plagued the subprime mortgage industry.

The company expanded its franchise into the Washington DC market in 2009 by buying Chevy Chase Bank for some $475 million in cash and stock.

In 2011 the company boosted its credit card business with the acquisition of GE Capital's $1.3 billion Hudson's Bay credit card portfolio tripling the number of Canadian customer accounts Capital One services. That year Capital One also acquired Kohl's existing $3.7 billion private-label credit card portfolio.

Capital One grew its US credit card business once again with the 2012 acquisition of HSBC's US card portfolio for some $2.6 billion.

In 2013 Capital One introduced its Capital One Quicksilver credit card offering cardholders a simple way to earn and redeem higher-than-average cash back rewards.

EXECUTIVES

General Counsel And Corporate Secretary, John G. Finneran, age 68, $1,016,538 total compensation
Chairman And Ceo, Richard D. (Rich) Fairbank, age 67
Senior Vice President Manager, Gerald Shepard
Head Of Finance And Corporate Development, Stephen S. (Steve) Crawford, age 53, $1,592,692 total compensation
Cfo, R. Scott Blackley, age 50, $617,769 total compensation
Cio, Robert M. Alexander, age 53
President Commercial Banking, Michael C. Slocum, age 61
President Financial Services, Sanjiv Yajnik, age 61, $962,654 total compensation
President Retail And Direct Banking, Jonathan W. Witter, age 48, $870,769 total compensation
Chief Enterprise Services Officer And Chief Of Staff To The Ceo, Frank G. LaPrade, age 51, $974,577 total compensation
Chief Risk Officer, Kevin S. Borgmann, age 46
President U.s. Card, Michael J. Wassmer, age 48
President International And Small Business Card, Christopher T. Newkirk, age 47
Vp Atm Kiosk Channel Management, Max Doerfler
Vice President, Ashish Tandon
Vice President Senior Associate General Counsel, Kathryn Hu
Assistant Vice President Information S, Carl Pomplon
Assistant Vice President, Disnalda Cuevas

Senior Vice President, Richard Amador
Vice President, Anthony Fermo
Vice President, Brad Dolbec
Assistant Vice President, Karla Lastrap
Executive Vice President, Murray Abrams
Senior Vice President, Roy Aksdal
Vice President Human Resources, Guenet Beshah
Vp Digital Mobile It, Jeff Elgin
Vice President, Hamilton Blanton
Vice President, Ehab Awadallah
Vice President In Us Card Recoveries Division, Amanda N Aghdami
Vice President And Cra Business Development Officer, Lydia Jackson
Vice President Corporate Audit Services, Erika Ray
Vice President, Michael Lockery
Vice President Sales And Service Strategy, Shail Moorjani
Managing Vice President Treasury Balance, Jeffrey Kuzbel
Managing Vice President, Johan Gericke
Vice President Of Sales And Service, Rob Younger
Vice President Private Banking, Bob Sferrazza
Vice President And Senior Business Relationship Banker, Franklin Carrero
Senior Vice President, Gregory Horstman
Vice President And Manager Of Treasury Management Client Service, Marty Paris
Vice President Business Banking, Nate Hoffman
Senior Vice President, Bryan N Pynchon
Senior Vice President Capital One Equipment Finance Corp, Ellen Barry
Managing Vice President, John Walker
Senior Vice President Senior Director Mid Corporate And Healthcare Banking, Philip Davi
Vice President Business Banking, Maria Brosnahan
Vice President Bank Project Management Office, Jonathan Topp
Senior Vice President, Spencer Gagnet
Vice President, David P Blasini
Managing Vice President, Detelina Ivanova
Vice President Strategy, Sarah Strauss
Vice President Us Card, Emilia Lopez
Senior Vice President, Ric Kearny
Vice President And Trust Officer, Jean Moncla
Vice President Of Human Resources, Joel Martinez
Vice President Senior Audit Manager, Sandra Dato
Senior Vice President, Kristen Croxton
Vice President Investor Real Estate, Kevin Lemoine
Assistant Vice President, Lawren Allen
Assistant Vice President, Karen Eleser
Senior Vice President Commercial Real Estate, Jeff Wallace
Vice President Internet Services, Marie Kraus
Svp And Chief Scoring Officer, Scott Hallworth
Assistant Vice President, Danny Moore
Vice President Corporate Security, Timothy Rigg
Vice President Regional Operations Manager, Farina Hanif
Senior Vice President, Fran Nuchims
Vice President, Diana Macculley
Assistant Vice President, Marroy Michael
Senior Vice President, Louis Rosado
Senior Vice President, William Booth
Vice President, Shishir Singhania
Vice President, Ken Shah
Assistant Vice President Branch Manager, Jessica Kitzmann
Assistant Vice President, David Mialaret
Vice President Business Banking, Roger Watkins
Senior Vice President, Enrico Panno
Senior Vice President, Richard Wolbach
Vice President, Sal Fratanduono
Senior Vice President, Joshua Howes
Unit Manager Assistant Vice President, Michelle Jordan
Vice President, Bonnie Lowrimore
Assistant Vice President Branch Manager, Kristi Whaley

Vice President Senior Manager Strategy And Transformation, Aysun Cokyuksel
Assistant Vice President, Malcolm Ferrell
Vice President And Senior Trust Officer, Lorraine Gallagher
Executive Vice President Card Operations, Noelle Eder
Assistant Vice President Merchant Services Sales Advisor, Diane Slatkin
Senior Vice President, Jennifer Driscoll
Front Line Manager Assistant Vice President, Patricia Milton
Assistant Vice President, Cindy Lau
Vice President Director Commercial Real Estate Underwriting, Peter Ilovic
Senior Vice President, Jonathan Wood
Vice President, Julianne Low
Assistant Vice President, Stanley Liu
Vice President Business Banker, Joshua Prejean
Vice President, Haley Douds
Vice President Branch Manager Iii, Yenisel Gamez
Vice President Managing Underwriter, Albert Lopez
Assistant Vice President, Milos Milosevic
Vice President, Michael Tomek
Vice President, Dana Thompson
Vice President, Robert Plank
Assistant Vice President Proposal Manager, Paula Wiesner
Senior Vice President, Diane Dolce
Vice President, Christine Pascarella
Vice President, Lawrence Montz
Vice President, Daniel Mouadeb
Vice President Senior Business Banker, Kirk Ranzino
Vice President Commercial Real Estate, Michael Monroe
Vice President, Kirk Hudson
Assistant Vice President, Kyle Anglin
Vice President, Staci Harvey
Vice President, Luis Otoya
Senior Vice President, Jon Oldham
Vice President Of Finance, Steve Braskamp
Vice President, Ilene O'Tero
Executive Vice President, Paul Widuch
Assistant Vice President And Specialty Sales Process Manager, Darla Smith
Senior Vice President Chief Financial Officer Commercial Bank, Dan Hugo
Senior Vice President Northeast Team Leader, Lauren Kramer
Senior Vice President Deposit And Debit Products, Konrad Schwarz
Vice President Of Business Banking, Ryan Cash
Vice President Commerical Banking, Tom Shinn
Vice President Account Management, Kenneth Hund
Vice President Capital One, Brent Reynolds
Senior Vice President, Adam Ostrach
Vice President Finance, Darrell Alexander
Vice President Finance, Rena Friske
Managing Vice President, Michelle Moss
Vice President, Jamie Ludvigsen
Mvp Portfolio Management, Jeffrey Juliane
Vice President Of Credit, James Snyder
Vice President Loan Administration, Maryann Mastrantonio
Senior Vice President, David Denbina
Vice President Institutional Equity Sales, James Brady
Assistant Vice President And Manager, Catherine Deluca
Senior Vice President Commercial Real Estate, Clay Wright
Treasury Management Sales Vice President, Bonnie Rivera
Senior Vice President Relationship Manager, Shelby Davis
Senior Vice President Of Business Development, Paul Patrick

Vice President Deputy Chief Underwriter, Tina Quirin
Senior Vice President, Joel Willard
Vp Human Resources, Lisa Mays
Managing Underwriter Senior Vice President Commercial Banking, Gina White
Senior Vice President, Marsha Baumgarner
Vice President Retail Bank Operations, John Dudas
Vice President, Jamie Lutton
Vice President Data Product Innovation, Philip Kim
Vice President Software Engineering, Tarik Essawi
Assistant Vice President, Andrew Kwok
Auditors: Ernst & Young LLP

LOCATIONS

HQ: Capital One Financial Corp
1680 Capital One Drive, McLean, VA 22102
Phone: 703 720-1000
Web: www.capitalone.com

PRODUCTS/OPERATIONS

2016 Sales

	$ mil.	% of total
Interest		
Loans held for investment	21,203	77
Investment securities	1,599	6
Other	89	-
Non interest		
Interchange fees	2,452	9
Service charges & other customer fees	1,646	6
Other	541	2
Adjustments	(11)	-
Total	27,519	100

2016 Segment sales

	% of total
Credit card	62
Consumer banking	26
Commercial banking	11
Others	1
Total	100

Selected Products

Auto Loans
Business Credit Cards
Commercial Banking
Home Equity Lines
Home Loans
Investing
Personal Banking
Personal Credit Cards
Small Business Banking

COMPETITORS

Alliance Data Systems	GM Financial
American Express	HSBC USA
Bank of America	JPMorgan Chase
Citigroup	PNC Financial
Credit Acceptance	Regions Financial
Discover	Wells Fargo

HISTORICAL FINANCIALS

Company Type: Public

Income Statement

FYE: December 31

	ASSETS ($ mil.)	NET INCOME ($ mil.)	INCOME AS % OF ASSETS	EMPLOYEES
12/17	365,693	1,982	0.5%	49,300
12/16	357,033	3,751	1.1%	47,300
12/15	334,048	4,050	1.2%	45,400
12/14	308,854	4,428	1.4%	46,000
12/13	297,048	4,159	1.4%	41,951
Annual Growth	5.3%	(16.9%)	—	4.1%

2017 Year-End Financials

Debt ratio: 16.48%
Return on equity: 4.12%
Cash ($ mil.): 14,040
Current ratio: —
Long-term debt ($ mil.): —

No. of shares (mil.): 485
Dividends
 Yield: 0.0%
 Payout: 45.8%
Market value ($ mil.): 48,349

	STOCK PRICE ($) FY Close	P/E High/Low		PER SHARE ($) Earnings	Dividends	Book Value
12/17	99.58	29	22	3.49	1.60	100.37
12/16	87.24	13	8	6.89	1.60	98.94
12/15	72.18	13	10	7.07	1.50	89.68
12/14	82.55	11	9	7.59	1.20	81.41
12/13	76.61	11	7	6.96	0.95	72.89
Annual Growth	6.8%	—		(15.9%)	13.9%	8.3%

Capitol Federal Financial Inc

Dorothy and Toto may not be in Kansas anymore but Capitol Federal Financial is. The holding company owns Capitol Federal Savings Bank the largest bank headquarted there. The savings bankA serves metropolitan areasA of the Sunflower StateA as well asA Kansas City Missouri throughA aboutA 45 branches includingA nearly aA dozen inside retail stores such as Target Price Chopper and Dillons. Serving consumers and commercial customers theA thrift offers standard servicesA such as mortgages and loans depositsA and retail investments. Its Capitol Agency affiliate sells life liability homeowners renters and vehicle insurance.

EXECUTIVES

Chairman President And Ceo, John B. Dicus, age 57, $581,484 total compensation
Svp And Controller, Kent G. Townsend, age 56, $303,991 total compensation
Evp And Chief Lending Officer, Rick C. Jackson, $163,690 total compensation
Evp Corporate Services, Carlton A Ricketts
Evp General Counsel, Natalie Haag
Evp Retail Operations, Frank H. Wright, $202,362 total compensation
Vice President Information Technology Delivery Systems, Tamara Vande Velde
Vice President Consumer Lending, Kevin Morgison
Vice President Security Business, Kevin Moore
First Vice President, Rodney Martin
Vice President, David Richardson
Vice President Consumer Lending Man, Mike Cast
Vice President Security, Ed Cox
First Vice President Lending, Jacque Taylor
Vp Financial Reporting And Analysis, Phil Whalen
Senior Vice President, Deb Campos
First Vice President: Mortgage Lending, Kevin Brittain
First Vice President Principal Accounting Officer And Reporting Director Capitol Federal Financia, Tara Van Houweling
Assistant Vice President Network And Telecom Supervisor, Kevin Nelson
Vice President Deposit Services, Clint Devoe
Assistant Vice President Application Services, Travis Buchanan
Vice President Accounting Manager, Angie Whalen
First Vice President, Joel Oliver
Executive Vice President Corporate Services, Carl Ricketts

Board Member, Jeffrey Johnson
Auditors: DELOITTE & TOUCHE LLP

LOCATIONS

HQ: Capitol Federal Financial Inc
700 South Kansas Avenue, Topeka, KS 66603
Phone: 785 235-1341
Web: www.capfed.com

PRODUCTS/OPERATIONS

2016 Sales

	% of total
Interest Income	
Loans receivable	75
Mortgage backed securities	9
FHLB stock	4
Cash and cash equivalents	3
Investment securities	2
Non-Interest Income	
Retail fees and charges	4
Income from bank-owned life insurance	1
Other non-interest income	2
Total	100

COMPETITORS

Bank of America	Landmark Bancorp
Commerce Bancshares	U.S. Bancorp
First Federal of Olathe	UMB Financial

HISTORICAL FINANCIALS

Company Type: Public

Income Statement

FYE: September 30

	ASSETS ($ mil.)	NET INCOME ($ mil.)	INCOME AS % OF ASSETS	EMPLOYEES
09/18	9,449	98	1.0%	775
09/17	9,192	84	0.9%	708
09/16	9,267	83	0.9%	676
09/15	9,844	78	0.8%	691
09/14	9,865	77	0.8%	716
Annual Growth	(1.1%)	6.2%	—	2.0%

2018 Year-End Financials

Debt ratio: 1.16%
Return on equity: 7.17%
Cash ($ mil.): 139
Current ratio: —
Long-term debt ($ mil.): —

No. of shares (mil.): 141
Dividends
 Yield: 0.0%
 Payout: 120.5%
Market value ($ mil.): 1,799

	STOCK PRICE ($) FY Close	P/E High/Low		PER SHARE ($) Earnings	Dividends	Book Value
09/18	12.74	21	17	0.73	0.88	9.85
09/17	14.70	27	21	0.63	0.88	9.90
09/16	14.07	23	19	0.63	0.84	10.13
09/15	12.12	22	20	0.58	0.84	10.33
09/14	11.82	24	21	0.56	0.98	10.59
Annual Growth	1.9%	—		6.9%	(2.7%)	(1.8%)

Cardinal Health, Inc.

When your local pharmacy runs low on drugs or supplies it might just call Cardinal Health. The company is a top distributor of pharmaceuticals and other medical supplies and equipment in the US. Its pharmaceutical division provides supply chain services including branded generic and specialty pharmaceutical and OTC drug distribution. It also franchises Medicine Shoppe retail pharmacies. Cardinal's medical division parcels out medical laboratory and surgical supplies and provides logistics consulting and data management. Customers include retail pharmacies hospitals health care systems surgery centers nursing homes doctor's offices clinical labs and other health care businesses. The US accounts for the majority of Cardinal's sales.

HISTORY

Cardinal Health harks back to Cardinal Foods a food wholesaler named for Ohio's state bird. In 1971 Robert Walter then 26 and with the ink still fresh on his Harvard MBA acquired Cardinal in a leveraged buyout. He hoped to grow Cardinal by acquisitions but was frustrated when he found that the food distribution industry was already highly consolidated.

In 1980 Cardinal moved into pharmaceuticals distribution with the acquisition of Zanesville. It went public in 1983 as Cardinal Distribution and Walter began looking for more acquisitions. Cardinal soon expanded nationwide by swallowing other distributors. During the 1980s these purchases included two pharmaceuticals distributors headquartered in New York and a Massachusetts-based pharmaceuticals and food distributor.

In 1988 Cardinal sold its food group including Midland Grocery and Mr. Moneysworth to Roundy's and narrowed its focus to pharmaceuticals.

Drug distributors joined the rest of the pharmaceutical industry in its rush toward consolidation during the 1990s. Cardinal's acquisitions in those years included Ohio Valley-Clarksburg (1990 the Mid-Atlantic) Chapman Drug Co. (1991 Tennessee) PRN Services (1993 Michigan) Solomons Co. (1993 Georgia) Humiston-Keeling (1994 Illinois) and Behrens (1994 Texas).

One of Cardinal's most important acquisitions during this period was its cash purchase of Whitmire Distribution in 1994. Formerly Amfac Health Care Whitmire had been a subsidiary of Amfac one of Hawaii's "Big Five" landholders. When Amfac Health Care was spun off in 1988 its president Melburn Whitmire led a management group that acquired a majority interest. When Cardinal bought it Whitmire was the US's #6 drug wholesaler; the purchase bumped Cardinal up to #3. At that time the company changed its name to Cardinal Health and Melburn Whitmire became Cardinal's vice chairman.

In 1995 Cardinal made its biggest acquisition yet when it purchased St. Louis-based Medicine Shoppe International the US's largest franchisor of independent retail pharmacies. Founded by two St. Louis obstetricians in 1970 the Medicine Shoppe had 987 US outlets and 107 abroad at the time of its purchase by Cardinal (for $348 million in stock).

Over the next few years Cardinal continued to grow through acquisitions including automatic drug-dispensing system maker Pyxis pharmaceutical packaging company PCI Services and pharmacy management services company Owen Healthcare (which became Cardinal Health Pharmacy Management).

EXECUTIVES

Evp Customer Support Services And Cio, Patricia B. (Patty) Morrison, age 59
Chief Human Resources Officer, Pamela O. (Pam) Kimmet, age 59
President Nuclear Pharmacy Services, Tiffany P. Olson, age 59
Ceo And Director, Michael C. (Mike) Kaufmann, age 55, $721,311 total compensation

Ceo Medical Segment, Donald M. (Don) Casey, age 59, $671,311 total compensation
Chief Legal And Compliance Officer, Craig S. Morford, age 59, $531,311 total compensation
President Cardinal Health Specialty Solutions, Joseph I. DePinto, age 51
Ceo Pharmaceutical Segment, Jon Giacomin, age 53, $542,623 total compensation
Evp Global Sourcing, Craig Cowman
President Cordis, David J. Wilson
President Cardinal Health At Home, Steve Mason
President Global Commercial Solutions, Steve Blazejewski
Evp Strategy And Corporate Development, Michele Holcomb
Evp Deputy General Counsel And Corporate Secretary, Jessica L. Mayer
President Us Pharmaceutical Distribution, Debbie Weitzman
Cfo, Jorge M. Gomez
Vice President, Ryan Mcgraw
Vice President Alternate Care Sales, Jim Scott
Senior Vice President Global Sourcing, Stefan Grunwald
Pharmacy Manager, John Miller
Vice President Retail Independent Sale East Region, Marc DeLorenzo
Vice President And Associate General Counsel Finance, Rylan Rawlins
Vice President, Warren Hastings
Vice President Distribution Services, Paul Farnin
Pharmacy Manager, Jeremy Guthrie
Senior Vice President And Chief Scientific Officer, Robert Berus
Manager Government Relations, Laura Padgitt
Director Of Pharmacy, Michelle Dalton
Vice President, Colleen McGuffin
Director Of Pharmacy Operations And Account Manager, Sue Raymoure
Pharmacy Manager, Gene Nickman
Group Vice President Health Systems, Therese Grossi
Executive Vice President Packaging Service Group, Renard Pawlak
Vice President Managed Care Payer Relations And Business Development, Elie Bahou
Pharmacy Manager, Sherry Miller
Director Of Pharmacy, Jay Dyer
Director Of Pharmacy, Todd Worsham
Pharmacy Manager, Bevan Callicott
Director Of Pharmacy, Lynn Staggs
Pharmacy Manager, Mary Johnson
Pharmacy Manager, John Miano
Vice President And Executive Director Of Training, Lori Rivers
Director Of Pharmacy, Sharon Greasheimer
Vice President Business Development, Luke Augustine
Director Of Pharmacy, Rande Hempen
Vice President Enterprise Information Technology, Cyndi Carter
Vice President Business Development, Michelle Zaluzney
Pharmacy Manager, Chad Walker
Vice President Of Marketing And Strategic Business Development Innovative Delivery Solutions, Erika Jurrens
Pharmacy Manager, Abdul Kamara
Vice President Associate General Counsel, Cheryl Kahn
Vice President Enterprise Contracting, Jim Bonanni
Pharmacy Manager, Matt Champ
Vp Human Resources, Bill Rozich
Director Of Pharmacy, Thomas Deeds
Director Of Pharmacy Operations And Account Management Community Health, Curtis Hartin
Pharmacy Manager, Kelli Love
Pharmacy Manager, Martin Clemens

Senior Vice President General Counsel Medical Segment, Jennifer Spalding
Vice President Investor Relations, Lisa Capodici
Pharmacy Manager, Kevin Ryan
Vice President Engineering Fuse, Steve Langella
Vice President Of Operations, Martin Alires
Chairman, George S. Barrett, age 63
Ceo And Director, Michael C. (Mike) Kaufmann, age 55
Evp Deputy General Counsel And Corporate Secretary, Jessica L. Mayer
Secretary, Shelley Lebeck
Board Member, Colleen Arnold
Manager Treasurer Corporate Finance, Eric Zink
Board Member, Nancy Killefer
Auditors: Ernst & Young LLP

LOCATIONS

HQ: Cardinal Health, Inc.
7000 Cardinal Place, Dublin, OH 43017
Phone: 614 757-5000
Web: www.cardinalhealth.com

2018 Sales

	$ mil.	% of total
US	132,526	97
Other	4,283	3
Total	**136,809**	**100**

PRODUCTS/OPERATIONS

2018 Sales by Segment

	$ mil.	% of total
Pharmaceutical	121,241	89
Medical	15,581	11
Corporate	(13)	-
Total	**136,809**	**100**

COMPETITORS

AmerisourceBergen	Medline Industries
Becton Dickinson	Owens & Minor
CVS	PharMerica
Deroyal Industries	Rite Aid
Franz Haniel	Thermo Fisher
Henry Schein	Scientific
McKesson	Walgreen

HISTORICAL FINANCIALS

Company Type: Public

Income Statement

FYE: June 30

	REVENUE ($ mil.)	NET INCOME ($ mil.)	NET PROFIT MARGIN	EMPLOYEES
06/18	136,809	256	0.2%	50,200
06/17	129,976	1,288	1.0%	40,400
06/16	121,546	1,427	1.2%	37,300
06/15	102,531	1,215	1.2%	34,500
06/14	91,084	1,166	1.3%	34,000
Annual Growth	10.7%	(31.5%)	—	10.2%

2018 Year-End Financials

Debt ratio: 22.56%
Return on equity: 3.98%
Cash ($ mil.): 1,763
Current ratio: 1.07
Long-term debt ($ mil.): 8,012

No. of shares (mil.): 309
Dividends
Yield: 0.0%
Payout: 230.0%
Market value ($ mil.): 15,088

	STOCK PRICE ($) FY Close	P/E High/Low	PER SHARE ($) Earnings	Dividends	Book Value
06/18	48.83	96 60	0.81	1.86	19.61
06/17	77.92	21 16	4.03	1.81	21.54
06/16	78.01	21 17	4.32	1.61	20.35
06/15	83.65	25 19	3.62	1.41	19.07
06/14	68.56	22 14	3.38	1.25	18.99
Annual Growth	(8.1%)	— —	(30.0%)	10.5%	0.8%

Carmax Inc.

CarMax helps drivers find late-model used autos. Typically selling vehicles that are less than ten years old with less than 100000 miles the US's largest specialty used-car retailer buys reconditions and sells cars and light trucks through more than 170 superstores in 85-plus television markets (markets in which CarMax has a television advertising presence) mainly in the Southeast and Midwest. CarMax also operates two new-car franchises and sells older vehicles through more than 390000 in-store auctions each year at over 70 stores. Additionally it sells older cars and trucks with higher mileage and offers vehicle financing through its CarMax Auto Finance unit.

Operations

CarMax operates through two business segments: CarMax Sales Operations and CarMax Auto Finance (CAF).

CarMax Sales Operations which sells more than 670000 used cars per year represents the nation's largest used-car retailer. The company's finance arm CarMax Auto Financing (CAF) offers financing solely to CarMax customers and finances more around 45% of the company's retail vehicle unit sales. CAF also serviced over 800000 customer accounts in its $9.6 billion portfolio of managed receivables.

The company's used vehicle sales generate over 80% of total revenue wholesale vehicle sales nearly 15% and new vehicle sales less than 5%.

Geographic Reach

While Richmond-based CarMax sells cars in 39 US states it sells most of its vehicles in Florida Texas Southern California Virginia and the Washington DC/Baltimore area.

Sales and Marketing

CarMax focuses on developing brand awareness and detailing the advantages of shopping at its stores. It reaches customers through TV and radio broadcasts carmax.com search engine optimisation and online classified listings such as Pandora and Hulu. Additionally it looks to connect with consumers through Facebook Twitter and mobile apps.

CarMax's customers often take advantage of its transfer option which allows a customer to get a vehicle of their choice relocated to a more local CarMax store. About 30% of vehicles sold are transferred via customer request.

Financial Performance

CarMax has recorded a fairly sharply increasing net revenue trend for more than five years.

In fiscal 2017 (ended February) revenue increased 5% to $15.9 billion. The growth was concentrated in used car sales which grew $831 million; wholesale vehicle sales recorded a $106 million contraction. Used vehicle revenue was pushed up by an 8% increase in total unit sales partly due to acquisitions and partly due to higher same-store sales. The higher volume more than compensated for 2% lower average selling prices. Wholesale revenue was impacted by lower appraisal traffic and a reduction in cars aged 7-9 years old a long-term lag relating to lower car purchases during and after the 2008 global financial crisis.

Net income crept up less than 1% to $627 million as an increase in selling general and administrative expenses offset higher revenue.

Cash from operations fell 18% to $746.6 million due to changes in inventory.

Strategy

CarMax's main strategy is to "revolutionize the used auto retail market" by resolving the major sources of complaint that customers face at traditional used car retailers with superior customer service offerings. Some of these offerings include the 5-day money-back guarantee and the vehicle transfer service which allows a customer to get a vehicle of their choice relocated from a distant CarMax store to a more local one. CarMax is taking steps to distance itself from the much-maligned used car dealership image by shaping its selling around transparency and honesty so that customers don't go in expecting a battle with a salesperson. It wants to be a low risk place to buy a car.

Leveraging its successful "no-haggle" pricing business model CarMax has been aggressively expanding its geographic footprint over the past several years. The auto dealer has already tripled its store count from 58 locations in 2005 to 173 stores in 2017. As a rule CarMax aims to average around 15 store openings each year.

HISTORY

Looking for new retailing channels to conquer in 1993 Circuit City Stores began test-driving the used-car concept when it opened its first CarMax outlet in Richmond Virginia. Richard Sharp who was named Circuit City's CEO in 1986 became the chairman and CEO for CarMax Group as well.

A pioneer in the car industry CarMax offered computerized shopping play areas for children and no-haggle pricing. Competing car dealers criticized CarMax's TV ads which tarred rivals with a stereotype of sleaze and greed. Some dealers disputed CarMax's low-price claims.

The company extended its geographical reach into North Carolina Georgia and Florida in 1995 and 1996. In 1996 CarMax began selling new cars at an Atlanta store.

No longer riding it as a test-drive Circuit City spun off about 25% of CarMax to the public in 1997. The following year it moved into Illinois.

Also in 1998 CarMax bought a new-car Toyota dealership in Maryland and the multi-make Mauro Auto Mall of Wisconsin. It entered South Carolina that year and added a Georgia Mitsubishi dealership in early 1999. The company acquired two new-car franchises in the competitive Los Angeles market in mid-1999.

In mid-2001 Circuit City reduced its share in CarMax from 75% to about 65% having sold some stock to help remodel the company's electronics stores. Circuit City then spun off CarMax as an independent company in October 2002. President Austin Ligon took the CEO title at that time (Sharp remained chairman).

CarMax opened five superstores but sold four new-car dealerships in 2003.

EXECUTIVES

Vice President Marketing Carmax, Rob Sorenson
Region Vice President Merchandising Florida Region, William L McChrystal
Regional Vice President, Rodney Baker
Vice President Investor Relations, Katharine Kenny
Evp Strategy And Business Transformation, Edwin J. (Ed) Hill, age 58, $597,209 total compensation
Evp General Counsel And Secretary, Eric M. Margolin, age 65, $572,801 total compensation
Evp And Cfo, Thomas W. (Tom) Reedy, age 54, $699,039 total compensation
President Ceo And Director, William D. (Bill) Nash, age 49, $902,308 total compensation
Evp And Coo, William C. (Cliff) Wood, age 51, $699,039 total compensation
Svp And Chief Marketing Officer, James (Jim) Lyski, age 55
Svp And Cio, Shamim Mohammad, age 49
Svp Carmax Auto Finance, Jon G. Daniels, age 46
Vice President Human Resources, Peggy Philips

Vice President Operations, John Davis
Senior Vice President, Fred Hayton
Assistant Vice President Associate Relations, Greg Stewart
Vice President Finance, Enrique Mayor-Mora
Assistant Vice President Construction Design And Grand Opening, Scott Sawyer
Assistant Vice President Assistant Controller, Veronica Hinckle
Vice President Treasurer, Andy McMonigle
Senior Vice President And Chief Human Resources Officer, Diane Cafritz
Vice President, Anu Agarwal
Assistant Vice President Risk And Servicing Analytics, Kevin Duck
Vice President For The Atlanta Region, Kevin Cox
Avp Human Resources Services, Kim Ross
Vice President Treasurer, Tom Reedy
Regional Vice President, Chris Bartee
Vice President And Controller, Kim D Orcutt
Vice President Financial Services And Products, Robert W Mitchell
Assistant Vice President Information Technology, Greg Shull
Vice President Talent Management, Roberta Douma
Senior Vice President Service Operations, ED Hill
Vice President Security And Ciso, Cherri Heart
Vp Marketing Analytics, Gautam Puranik
Regional Vice President Purchasing, Bryan Windsor
Vice President Information Technology, Steve Allocco
Vice President Procurement And Strategic Sourcing, Julie Reed
Regional Vice President General Manager Xf Nashville Region, Dave Cantu
Chairman, Thomas J. (Tom) Folliard
Evp General Counsel And Secretary, Eric M. Margolin, age 65
President Ceo And Director, William D. (Bill) Nash, age 49
Board Member, Mitchell Steenrod
Board Member, Rakesh Gangwal
Auditors: KPMG LLP

LOCATIONS

HQ: Carmax Inc.
12800 Tuckahoe Creek Parkway, Richmond, VA 23238
Phone: 804 747-0422
Web: www.carmax.com

2017 Stores

	No.
California	23
Florida	16
Texas	16
Virginia	10
Georgia	9
Illinois	9
North Carolina	9
Tennessee	8
Maryland	6
Colorado	5
Ohio	5
Alabama	4
Massachusetts	4
Wisconsin	4
Arizona	3
Missouri	3
Nevada	3
Pennsylvania	3
South Carolina	3
Connecticut	2
Indiana	2
Kansas	2
Kentucky	2
Minnesota	2
Mississippi	2
New Jersey	2
New York	2
Oklahoma	2
Oregon	2
Delaware	1
Idaho	1

Iowa	1
Louisiana	1
Michigan	1
Nebraska	1
New Mexico	1
Rhode Island	1
Utah	1
Washington	1
Total	**173**

PRODUCTS/OPERATIONS

2017 Sales

	$ mil.	% of total
Used vehicles	13,270	84
Wholesale vehicles	2,082	13
Other sales & revenue	522	3
Total	**15,875**	**100**

COMPETITORS

Asbury Automotive	Holman Enterprises
AutoNation	Internet Brands
AutoTrader	JM Family Enterprises
Brown Automotive	KAR Auction Services
Cox Automotive	McCombs Enterprises
Danner Company	Penske Automotive
DriveTime Automotive	Group
Ed Morse Auto	Serra Automotive
Group 1 Automotive	Sonic Automotive
Hendrick Automotive	

HISTORICAL FINANCIALS

Company Type: Public

Income Statement   FYE: February 28

	REVENUE ($ mil.)	NET INCOME ($ mil.)	NET PROFIT MARGIN	EMPLOYEES
02/18	17,120	664	3.9%	25,110
02/17	15,875	626	3.9%	24,344
02/16	15,149	623	4.1%	22,429
02/15	14,268	597	4.2%	22,064
02/14	12,574	492	3.9%	20,171
Annual Growth	**8.0%**	**7.8%**	**—**	**5.6%**

2018 Year-End Financials

Debt ratio: 75.02%	No. of shares (mil.): 179
Return on equity: 20.67%	Dividends
Cash ($ mil.): 44	Yield: —
Current ratio: 2.61	Payout: —
Long-term debt ($ mil.): 12,752	Market value ($ mil.): 11,130

	STOCK PRICE ($) FY Close	P/E High/Low		PER SHARE ($) Earnings	Dividends	Book Value
02/18	61.92	21	15	3.60	0.00	18.45
02/17	64.54	21	14	3.26	0.00	16.66
02/16	46.26	24	14	3.03	0.00	14.92
02/15	67.11	25	15	2.73	0.00	15.11
02/14	48.43	24	17	2.16	0.00	14.96
Annual Growth	**6.3%**	—	—	**13.6%**		**5.4%**

Carolina Financial Corp (New)

EXECUTIVES

Pres-Ceo, Jerold L Rexroad
Chb, G Manly Eubank
Exec V Pres-Cfo, William A Gehman III
Exec V Pres-SEC, M J Huggins III
Exec V Pres, David L Morrow
Officer, Ashley Beebe

Senior Vice-President, Kevin Adams
Assistant Vice-President, Lisa Adams
Loan Officer, Katie Matthews
Customer Representativ, Michelle Ward
Commercial Lender, Brian Walker
Auditors: Elliott Davis, LLC

LOCATIONS

HQ: Carolina Financial Corp (New)
288 Meeting Street, Charleston, SC 29401
Phone: 843 723-7700

HISTORICAL FINANCIALS

Company Type: Public

Income Statement   FYE: December 31

	ASSETS ($ mil.)	NET INCOME ($ mil.)	INCOME AS % OF ASSETS	EMPLOYEES
12/17	3,519	28	0.8%	770
12/16	1,683	17	1.0%	441
12/15	1,409	14	1.0%	421
12/14	1,199	8	0.7%	394
12/13	881	16	1.9%	—
Annual Growth	**41.3%**	**14.2%**		

2017 Year-End Financials

Debt ratio: 0.92%	No. of shares (mil.): 21
Return on equity: 8.95%	Dividends
Cash ($ mil.): 81	Yield: 0.0%
Current ratio: —	Payout: 9.8%
Long-term debt ($ mil.): —	Market value ($ mil.): 781

	STOCK PRICE ($) FY Close	P/E High/Low		PER SHARE ($) Earnings	Dividends	Book Value
12/17	37.15	22	16	1.73	0.17	22.61
12/16	30.70	21	11	1.42	0.13	13.00
12/15	18.00	12	9	1.48	0.11	11.63
12/14	13.99	48	15	0.88	0.09	9.64
12/13	31.51	22	17	1.77	0.02	8.53
Annual Growth	**4.2%**	—	—	**(0.5%)**	**69.0%**	**27.6%**

Carter Bank & Trust (Martinsville, VA)

Auditors: Yount, Hyde & Barbour, P.C.

LOCATIONS

HQ: Carter Bank & Trust (Martinsville, VA)
1300 Kings Mountain Road, Martinsville, VA 24112
Phone: 276 656-1776

HISTORICAL FINANCIALS

Company Type: Public

Income Statement   FYE: December 31

	ASSETS ($ mil.)	NET INCOME ($ mil.)	INCOME AS % OF ASSETS	EMPLOYEES
12/17	4,112	(0)	—	963
12/16	4,505	15	0.4%	—
12/15	4,893	39	0.8%	964
12/14	4,629	33	0.7%	957
12/13	4,661	26	0.6%	970
Annual Growth	**(3.1%)**	**—**	**—**	**(0.2%)**

2017 Year-End Financials

Debt ratio: —	No. of shares (mil.): 26
Return on equity: (-0.16%)	Dividends
Cash ($ mil.): 268	Yield: —
Current ratio: —	Payout: —
Long-term debt ($ mil.): —	Market value ($ mil.): 461

	STOCK PRICE ($) FY Close	P/E High/Low		PER SHARE ($) Earnings	Dividends	Book Value
12/17	17.55	—	—	(0.03)	0.00	16.46
12/16	13.29	23	20	0.61	0.30	16.55
12/15	13.50	9	8	1.49	0.40	16.24
12/14	12.70	10	9	1.27	0.40	15.15
12/13	11.00	12	9	0.99	0.40	14.28
Annual Growth	**12.4%**	—	—	—	—	**3.6%**

Casey's General Stores, Inc.

Casey's provides convenience for small-town customers. One of the largest convenience store chains in the country Casey's General Stores owns some 2100 stores across 15-plus states primarily in the Midwest. Its stores most of which operate in areas with fewer than 5000 people offer gasoline prepared foods such as pizza and donuts and other food and nonfood items traditionally found in convenience stores. In addition to Casey's and Casey's General Store locations the company operates two tobacco stores two liquor stores and one grocery store. Gas sales account for about 60% of Casey's revenue.

Operations

Casey's generates some 60% of its revenue from fuel about 25% from grocery and other merchandise and more than 10% from prepared food and fountain drinks.

It has a broad selection of merchandise (from food staples to school supplies pet supplies and auto products) with stores typically stocking more than 3000 food and non-food items. The company sells nationally known brands as well as its own proprietary brands. Casey's has built up its selection of prepared foods over the years and now offers sandwiches and burgers pizza donuts chicken tenders and breakfast biscuits among other items.

Geographic Reach

Casey's operates stores in some 15 states including its largest markets — Iowa Illinois and Missouri — as well as Kansas Kentucky Minnesota Nebraska Wisconsin Indiana Michigan Ohio Oklahoma Arkansas Tennessee and the Dakotas.

It has distribution centers in Ankeny Iowa and Terre Haute Indiana.

Sales and Marketing

Casey's targets smaller communities by serving as both general and convenience stores including stocking a broader selection of products than typical of convenience stores.

Financial Performance

After falling for three years because of lower gas prices Casey's revenue has risen the past two years. Net income has been a little more sporadic but jumped significantly in fiscal 2018.

The comapny reported revenue of $8.4 billion in fiscal 2018 (ended April 2018) up 12% from the prior year. The results were driven by a rise in gas prices as well as more gas sold and an increase in grocery and other inside sales.

Net income that year jumped nearly 80% to $318 million from fiscal 2017 primarily as a result of a deferred tax benefit related to the 2017 Tax Act.

Cash at the end of fiscal 2018 was $53.7 million a decrease of $23 million from the prior year. Cash from operations contributed $419.8 million to the coffers while investing activities used $609.3 million mainly for capital expenditures. Financing activities provided $166.5 million primarily from long-term debt proceeds.

Strategy

In 2018 the year of Casey's 50th anniversary the company announced a long-term "Value Creation Plan." Key to that plan are three initiatives to improve store performance: its fleet car program price optimization and digital engagement.

Casey's has selected Fleetcor a provider of commercial payments services as a partner on its new commercial fuel card program. Fleetcor will handle all aspects of the program — which promises enhanced capabilities and convenience — from initial sales to payment processing billing and customer service. New card sales began in the summer of 2018 with existing customers being converted that fall.

The company has also selected partners for its price optimization initiative: PriceAdvantage for fuel optimzation and Dunnhumby for grocery items and other merchandise. Casey's with the help of its partners will use customer data as well as market data to centalize its pricing decisions to hopefully improve sales and margins across all categories. The rollout of this initiative is estimated to extend through fiscal 2020.

Lastly Casey's is looking to engage and interact with its customers through online and mobile channels as well as in stores. Plans include an enhanced website and revamped mobile app a new loyalty platform and in-store technology upgrades. As part of this initiative the company has staffed up in various marketing and digital functions and selected technology platforms from such heavyhitters as SAP MuleSoft and Salesforce.

Amid its "Value Creation Plan" the company continues opening or acquiring new stores. It ended fiscal 2018 with about 90 additional stores.

Mergers and Acquisitions

In fiscal 2018 Casey's acquired 26 stores of which it opened 20 (six will open in fiscal 2019). The comany will continue to acquire stores as the opportunity arises.

Company Background

Donald Lamberti who had run his family's grocery store founded Casey's General Stores with Kurvin C. "K. C." Fish. The men converted a gas station into the first Casey's convenience store in 1968. To expand and build brand recognition the company began franchising outlets two years later. By focusing on small towns the company avoided competition and expensive building and property costs. A significant growth spurt in 1979 took Casey's from 119 stores to 226. Fish retired the following year and the company went public in 1983.

EXECUTIVES

Svp And Cfo, William J. (Bill) Walljasper, age 57, $550,000 total compensation
Vp Marketing, Michael R. (Mike) Richardson, $195,000 total compensation
President And Ceo, Terry W. Handley, age 59, $770,000 total compensation
Svp General Counsel And Secretary, Julia L. (Julie) Jackowski, age 53, $530,000 total compensation
Vp Information Technology, Rich Schappert
Svp Operations, John C. (Jay) Soupene, age 50
Svp General Counsel And Secretary, Julia L. (Julie) Jackowski, age 53
Auditors: KPMG LLP

LOCATIONS

HQ: Casey's General Stores, Inc.
One SE Convenience Boulevard, Ankeny, IA 50021
Phone: 515 965-6100
Web: www.caseys.com

PRODUCTS/OPERATIONS

2018 Sales

	$ mil.	% of total
Fuel	5,146	61
Grocery & other merchandise	2,184	26
Prepared food & fountain	1,005	12
Other	55	1
Total	**8,391**	**100**

Selected Merchandise

Ammunition
Automotive products
Beverages
Food including fresh foods
Gasoline (self-service)
Health and beauty aids
Housewares
Pet products
Photo supplies
School supplies
Tobacco products

COMPETITORS

7-Eleven	Krause Gentle
Chevron	Kwik Trip
Couche-Tard	Martin & Bayley
Exxon Mobil	QuikTrip
Holiday Companies	Royal Dutch Shell
Hy-Vee	Thorntons Inc.

HISTORICAL FINANCIALS

Company Type: Public

Income Statement

FYE: April 30

	REVENUE ($ mil.)	NET INCOME ($ mil.)	NET PROFIT MARGIN	EMPLOYEES
04/18	8,391	317	3.8%	37,205
04/17	7,506	177	2.4%	35,014
04/16	7,122	225	3.2%	34,997
04/15	7,767	180	2.3%	31,766
04/14	7,840	134	1.7%	29,749
Annual Growth	**1.7%**	**24.0%**	**—**	**5.8%**

2018 Year-End Financials

Debt ratio: 38.81%
Return on equity: 25.83%
Cash ($ mil.): 53
Current ratio: 0.78
Long-term debt ($ mil.): 1,291

No. of shares (mil.): 36
Dividends
  Yield: 1.0%
  Payout: 12.4%
Market value ($ mil.): 3,562

	STOCK PRICE ($) FY Close	P/E High/Low		Earnings	PER SHARE ($) Dividends	Book Value
04/18	96.60	15	11	8.34	1.04	34.47
04/17	112.07	30	24	4.48	0.96	30.71
04/16	112.00	22	14	5.73	0.88	27.74
04/15	82.18	20	14	4.62	0.80	22.51
04/14	68.66	22	16	3.46	0.72	18.69
Annual Growth	**8.9%**			**24.6%**	**9.6%**	**16.5%**

Cashmere Valley Bank Washington (New)

EXECUTIVES

Pres, Greg Oakes
V Pres, Connie Fritz
Prin, Alex Cruz
Prin, Jana Flores
Sales and Marketing Executive, Taylor Stormo
Information Specialist, Kathy McGaughey
Supervisor, Shirley Reyes
Vice-President, Mike Kintner
Vice-President, Pam Wilson
Board of Directors, Claudia Robles
Director, Ron Olsen
Auditors: BDO USA, LLP

LOCATIONS

HQ: Cashmere Valley Bank Washington (New)
117 Aplets Way, Cashmere, WA 98815
Phone: 509 782-2624   **Fax:** 509 782-1643
Web: www.cashmerevalleybank.com

HISTORICAL FINANCIALS

Company Type: Public

Income Statement

FYE: December 31

	ASSETS ($ mil.)	NET INCOME ($ mil.)	INCOME AS % OF ASSETS	EMPLOYEES
12/17	1,516	18	1.2%	—
12/16	1,454	17	1.2%	—
12/15	1,381	16	1.2%	—
12/14	1,324	15	1.2%	—
12/13	1,283	14	1.1%	—
Annual Growth	**4.3%**	**6.7%**		

2017 Year-End Financials

Debt ratio: —
Return on equity: 10.63%
Cash ($ mil.): 52
Current ratio: —
Long-term debt ($ mil.): —

No. of shares (mil.): 4
Dividends
  Yield: 0.0%
  Payout: 24.1%
Market value ($ mil.): 238

	STOCK PRICE ($) FY Close	P/E High/Low		Earnings	PER SHARE ($) Dividends	Book Value
12/17	58.00	13	11	4.47	1.08	43.90
12/16	47.25	11	9	4.27	0.98	40.50
12/15	38.42	9	8	4.10	0.90	38.08
12/14	35.25	10	8	3.88	0.79	35.02
12/13	29.50	10	8	3.51	0.38	31.13
Annual Growth	**18.4%**			**6.2%**	**29.8%**	**9.0%**

Cass Information Systems Inc.

Cass Information Systems wants to pay your company's bills. The information services firm provides freight payment and information processing services to large manufacturing distribution and retail companies across the US. Its offerings include freight bill payment audit and rating services as well as outsourcing of utility bill processing and payments. Its telecommunications division manages telecom expenses for large companies. Cass grew out of Cass Commercial Bank (now a subsidiary) which provides banking services to private companies and churches as well as to consumers in the St. Louis area and Orange County California. Other major customer bases include Massachusetts Ohio and South Carolina.

Geographic Reach

Cass has locations in St. Louis Missouri; Columbus Ohio; Boston Massachusetts; Greenville South Carolina; Wellington Kansas; and Jacksonville Florida. It opened an office in Breda Netherlands — its first outside the US — in 2011 to support its multinational information processing clients.

Sales and Marketing

Cass lists some of the nation's largest companies including Macy's Dole and PepsiCo among its clients.

Financial Performance

Cass achieved record results in 2012 surpassing $115 million in revenues and earning $23 million in net profits. The firm's revenue increased 4% in 2012 vs. 2011 while net income rose by 1% over the same period. It was the third consecutive year of rising sales and profits for the company following a couple of lean years during the recession when businesses were either failing or more likely cutting back on outsourcing. The recent rise in revenue resulted from higher fees and other income including interest.

Strategy

Geographic expansion and technology improvements are on the list of goals for Cass as it looks to the future. The expense management firm is seeking new markets to enter in order to grow its customer base. Indeed Cass began 2012 with the acquisition of Jacksonville Florida-based Waste Reduction Consultants a provider of environmental expense management services. The deal expanded Cass' portfolio of services for controlling facility-related expenses. Previously Cass acquired telecom procurement technology from TelAdvisor Group in 2010. The technology allowed Cass to offer consulting services directly to clients.

EXECUTIVES

Executive Vice President Corporate Development, Harry Murray

Chairman President And Ceo, Eric H. Brunngraber, age 61, $557,874 total compensation

President Expense Management Services, Gary B. Langfitt, age 62, $236,862 total compensation

President Transportation Information Services, Mark A. Campbell, age 56, $206,157 total compensation

Evp Cfo And Secretary, P. Stephen (Steve) Appelbaum, age 60, $264,337 total compensation

President And Coo Cass Commercial Bank, Robert J. Mathias, age 65, $276,100 total compensation

Vice President Sales And Marketing, Gary Nutter

Chairman President And Ceo, Eric H. Brunngraber, age 61

Evp Cfo And Secretary, P. Stephen (Steve) Appelbaum, age 60

Board Member, Franklin Wicks

Board Member, James Lindemann

Board Member, Ralph Clermont

Auditors: KPMG LLP

LOCATIONS

HQ: Cass Information Systems Inc.
12444 Powerscourt Drive, Suite 550, St. Louis, MO 63131
Phone: 314 506-5500
Web: www.cassinfo.com

PRODUCTS/OPERATIONS

2016 Sales

	$ mil.	% of total
Fee Revenue and Other Income:		
Information services payment & processing revenue	83	66
Bank service fees	1	1
Gains on sales of securities	0	0
Other	0	1
Interest Income:		
Interest and fees on loans	29	23
Interest and dividends on securities:		
Taxable	0	-
Exempt from federal income taxes	9	8
Interest on federal funds sold and other short-term investments	1	1
Total	**126**	**100**

Products/Services
Transportation
Business Process
Freight Accounting
Freight Audit & Payment
Supply Chain Analysis
Utility
Energy Savings
Facility Cost Reporting
Utility Bill Payment
Telecom
Business Analytics
Procure To Pay
Telecom Consulting
Telecom Expense Management
Waste
Corporate Recycling
Industry Solutions
Waste Management
Waste Plans

COMPETITORS

ACCUSHIP	First Banks
Alliance Data Systems	MER Telemanagement
C.H. Robinson	Solutions
Worldwide	Pulaski Financial
CTSI	U.S. Bancorp
Data2Logistics	

HISTORICAL FINANCIALS

Company Type: Public

Income Statement

FYE: December 31

	ASSETS ($ mil.)	NET INCOME ($ mil.)	INCOME AS % OF ASSETS	EMPLOYEES
12/17	1,603	25	1.6%	1,116
12/16	1,504	24	1.6%	1,075
12/15	1,455	23	1.6%	989
12/14	1,500	24	1.6%	1,077
12/13	1,326	23	1.8%	1,087
Annual Growth	**4.9%**	**1.6%**	**—**	**0.7%**

2017 Year-End Financials

Debt ratio: —
Return on equity: 11.55%
Cash ($ mil.): 228
Current ratio: —
Long-term debt ($ mil.): —

No. of shares (mil.): 14
Dividends
  Yield: 0.0%
  Payout: 42.0%
Market value ($ mil.): 858

	STOCK PRICE ($) FY Close	P/E High/Low	PER SHARE ($) Earnings	Dividends	Book Value
12/17	58.21	43 34	1.68	0.70	15.27
12/16	73.57	45 28	1.63	0.67	14.09
12/15	51.46	38 28	1.52	0.77	13.86
12/14	53.25	43 25	1.56	0.74	13.20
12/13	67.35	44 25	1.53	0.67	12.52
Annual Growth	**(3.6%)**	**—**	**2.3%**	**1.2%**	**5.1%**

Caterpillar Inc.

EXECUTIVES

Ceo, D James Umpleby III
Chb, David L Calhoun
Cfo, Andrew Bonfield
Cao, Jananne A Copeland
Gen Counsel-Corp SEC, Suzette M Long
Chief Hr Officer, Cheryl C Johnson
Grp Pres Energy & Transportati, Ramin Younessi
Grp Pres Construction Industri, Thomas A Pellette
Grp Pres Cust & Dealer Support, Bob De Lange
Grp Pres, Denise C Johnson
Human Resources Manager, Julie Ammons
Auditors: PricewaterhouseCoopers LLP

LOCATIONS

HQ: Caterpillar Inc.
510 Lake Cook Road, Suite 100, Deerfield, IL 60015
Phone: 224 551-4000
Web: www.caterpillar.com

COMPETITORS

ALSTOM	Komatsu
Atlas Copco	Kubota
Bombardier	Kuehne + Nagel
CNH Global	MAN
Charles Machine Works	Menlo Worldwide
Cummins	Mitsubishi Heavy
DEUTZ	Industries
DHL	Multiquip
Deere	Navistar International
Detroit Diesel	Nortrak
Doosan Infracore	Rolls-Royce
Dresser Inc.	Sandvik
GE	Sany Heavy Industry
GE Capital	Siemens Energy
GENCO Distribution	Sumitomo Heavy
System	Industries
Generac Holdings	Terex
Hitachi Construction	Tognum
Machinery	UPS Supply Chain
Hyundai Heavy	Solutions
Industries	Volvo
J C Bamford Excavators	Vossloh
Joy Global	Wartsila
Joy Mining	Weichai Power
Kawasaki Heavy	Wells Fargo Equipment
Industries	Finance
Kohler	Woods Equipment

HISTORICAL FINANCIALS

Company Type: Public

Income Statement

FYE: December 31

	REVENUE ($ mil.)	NET INCOME ($ mil.)	NET PROFIT MARGIN	EMPLOYEES
12/17	45,462	754	1.7%	98,400
12/16	38,537	(67)	—	98,400
12/15	47,011	2,102	4.5%	105,700
12/14	55,184	3,695	6.7%	114,233
12/13	55,656	3,789	6.8%	118,501
Annual Growth	**(4.9%)**	**(33.2%)**	**—**	**(4.5%)**

2017 Year-End Financials

Debt ratio: 45.32%
Return on equity: 5.62%
Cash ($ mil.): 8,261
Current ratio: 1.35
Long-term debt ($ mil.): 23,847

No. of shares (mil.): 597
Dividends
  Yield: 0.0%
  Payout: 246.0%
Market value ($ mil.): 94,174

	STOCK PRICE ($) FY Close	P/E High/Low	Earnings	PER SHARE ($) Dividends	Book Value
12/17	157.58	125 72	1.26	3.10	22.92
12/16	92.74	— —	(0.11)	3.08	22.40
12/15	67.96	26 18	3.50	2.94	25.43
12/14	91.53	19 14	5.88	2.60	27.63
12/13	90.81	17 14	5.75	2.24	32.63
Annual Growth	14.8%	— —	(31.6%)	8.5%	(8.5%)

Cathay General Bancorp

Cathay General Bancorp is the holding company for Cathay Bank which mainly serves Chinese and Vietnamese communities from some 30 branches in California and about 20 more in Illinois New Jersey New York Massachusetts Washington and Texas. It also has a branch in Hong Kong and offices in Shanghai and Taipei. Catering to small to medium-sized businesses and individual consumers the bank offers standard deposit services and loans. Commercial mortgage loans account for more than half of the bank's portfolio; business loans comprise nearly 25%. The bank's Cathay Wealth Management unit offers online stock trading mutual funds and other investment products and services through an agreement with PrimeVest.

Geographic Reach

California state-chartered Cathay Bank has branches in California Illinois Massachusetts New Jersey New York Texas and Washington. Overseas it has a branch in Hong Kong and offices in Shanghai and Taipei.

Financial Performance

The bank's revenue is on a downward trend. In 2012 revenue declined more than 5% vs. 2011 after posting a 3% decline in the previous annual comparison. Indeed between 2008 and 2012 revenue dipped by about 17% on lower interest income and dividend income. However the bank's profit picture is improving with net income up in 2012 for the third consecutive year.

Strategy

With 60% of its branches in California — a state hard hit by the downturn in the housing market — Cathay Bank's real estate secured loan portfolio has suffered as the value of the underlying collateral plummeted. In 2010 the company entered into a memorandum of understanding with the FDIC to reduce its concentration of commercial real estate loans improve its capital ratios reduce overall risk and strengthen asset quality. The moves have helped the company to cut its losses. The bank has also been successful growing deposits.

Mergers and Acquisitions

In 2016 Cathay Bank agreed to buy SinoPac Bancorp from Taiwan's Bank SinoPac for $340 million. SinoPac's Far East National Bank operates nine branches including five in Los Angeles. After the deal closes Cathay plans to close a number of branches. The transaction will help boost the company's balance sheet.

EXECUTIVES

Sevp And Coo, Irwin Wong, age 69, $339,777 total compensation

Evp And Chief Credit Officer Cathay Bank, Donald S. Chow, age 67, $312,615 total compensation

Evp Cfo And Treasurer, Heng W. Chen, age 66, $416,542 total compensation

Chairman President And Ceo Cathay General Bancorp And Chairman And Ceo Cathay Bank, Pin Tai, $424,900 total compensation

Evp And Chief Risk Officer Cathy Bank, Kim R. Bingham, age 61

Assistant Vice President Marketing, Chris Lu

Board Member, Michael M Y Chang

Evp Cfo And Treasurer, Heng W. Chen, age 66

Chairman President And Ceo Cathay General Bancorp And Chairman And Ceo Cathay Bank, Pin Tai

Auditors: KPMG LLP

LOCATIONS

HQ: Cathay General Bancorp
777 North Broadway, Los Angeles, CA 90012
Phone: 213 625-4700
Web: www.cathaybank.com

2015 Branch offices

	No.
Southern California Branches	21
Northern California Branches	12
New York Branches	12
Illinois Branches	4
Washington Branches	3
Texas Branches	2
Massachusetts Branch	1
Nevada Branch	1
New Jersey Branch	1
Maryland Branch	1
Overseas Branch	1
Total	**59**

PRODUCTS/OPERATIONS

2015 sales

	$ mil.	% of total
Interest and Dividend income		
Loan receivable	427	88
Investment securities- taxable	21	4
Federal Home Loan Bank stock	3	1
Deposits with banks	1	-
Non-Interest income		
Securities losses net	(3.3)	-
Letters of credit commissions	5	1
Depository service fees	5	1
Other operating income	25	5
Total	**486**	**100**

Products/Services
Personal
Accounts
Checking Accounts
Savings Accounts
CDs
IRA CD
Debit Cards
Loans
Mortgage Loan
Home Equity Financing
Auto Loan
Credit Cards
Cathay Online Banking
Mobile Banking
Business/Commercial
Business Accounts
Business Checking Account
Business Savings Account
CDs
Cash Management Services
Merchant Deposit Capture
Zero Balance Account
Lockbox Service
Merchant Bankcard Services
Courier Deposit Service
Armored Transport Services
Cash Vault Services
Business Online Banking
Loans
Commercial Financing
Real Estate & Construction Financing
International Banking & Financing
Smart Capital Line
SBA Guaranteed Loan Program
Credit Cards

COMPETITORS

Bank of America	Grandpoint
Citibank	Hanmi Financial
East West Bancorp	Hope Bancorp
Far East National Bank	U.S. Bancorp

HISTORICAL FINANCIALS

Company Type: Public

Income Statement

	ASSETS ($ mil.)	NET INCOME ($ mil.)	INCOME AS % OF ASSETS	FYE: December 31 EMPLOYEES
12/17	15,640	176	1.1%	1,271
12/16	14,520	175	1.2%	1,129
12/15	13,254	161	1.2%	1,122
12/14	11,516	137	1.2%	1,074
12/13	10,989	123	1.1%	1,132
Annual Growth	9.2%	9.3%	—	2.9%

2017 Year-End Financials

Debt ratio: 1.35%
Return on equity: 9.26%
Cash ($ mil.): 539
Current ratio: —
Long-term debt ($ mil.): —
No. of shares (mil.): 80
Dividends
Yield: 0.0%
Payout: 40.0%
Market value ($ mil.): 3,411

	STOCK PRICE ($) FY Close	P/E High/Low	Earnings	PER SHARE ($) Dividends	Book Value
12/17	42.17	20 16	2.17	0.87	24.39
12/16	38.03	17 12	2.19	0.75	22.97
12/15	31.33	17 12	1.98	0.56	21.63
12/14	25.59	16 13	1.72	0.29	20.08
12/13	26.73	19 13	1.43	0.08	18.33
Annual Growth	12.1%	— —	11.0%	81.6%	7.4%

CATHOLIC HEALTH INITIATIVES

For Catholic Health Initiatives (CHI) returning sick people to good health is more than a business — it's a mission. Formed in 1996 through the merger of three Catholic hospital systems the giant not-for-profit organization is one of the largest Catholic hospital operators in the US. It covers more than 90 sites including hospitals and clinics as well as long-term care assisted-living and senior residential facilities in about 20 states from Washington to Maryland. Its hospitals range from large urban medical centers (many with educational and research programs) to small hospitals in rural areas. All told CHI has more than 14000 acute-care beds. It is sponsored by a dozen different congregations of nuns. In 2019 CHI merged with San Francisco-based hospital system Dignity Health to create the $29 billion not-for-profit organization CommonSpirit Health.

Change in Company Type

After the merger with Dignity Health CHI operates as a part of CommonSpirit Health which has more than 140 hospitals and serves 21 states. CommonSpirit Health is headquartered in Chicago.

Operations

CHI's network includes 105 hospitals four of which are academic and teaching facilities and 30 rural facilities with critical-care access as well as nursing colleges home-health agencies community health services organizations long-term care facilities assisted-care and residential senior homes research and development programs and labs.

Geographic Reach

CHI operates in Arkansas Colorado Indiana Iowa Kansas Kentucky Minnesota Nebraska New Jersey New Mexico North Dakota Ohio Oregon Pennsylvania South Dakota Tennessee Texas Washington and Wisconsin — 19 states in all.

Strategy

CHI whose mission covers "expressing Christ's love by caring for those in need" is issuing nearly $2 billion in taxable and tax-exempt bonds to fund several initiatives including a system-wide IT infrastructure upgrade (in part to facilitate its federally mandated conversion to universal electronic health records) virtual health programs (telemedicine) insurance products and clinic networks.

In 2016 the company announced plans to exit the health insurance business by selling its Qual-Choice Health insurance subsidiary acquired in 2014. The unit lost nearly $97 million in the first three quarters of fiscal 2016 (ended March) and CHI posted an operating loss of some $19 million.

Mergers and Acquisitions

After years of discussions CHI and Dignity Health merged in early 2019. The combined health system with 142 hospitals in 21 states is the largest not-for-profit hospital system in the US. The size of the system allows for it to provide expanded care to patients through such methods as virtual appointments a broader range of clinical programs and advanced technologies. The new organization named CommonSpirit Health is headquartered in Chicago. Individual hospitals continue to operate under their existing names.

HISTORY

In 1860 the Sisters of St. Francis established a hospital in Philadelphia laying the foundation for a larger health care organization. In 1981 Franciscan Health System was formally established to be a national holding company for Catholic hospitals and related organizations. By the mid-1990s the system consisted of 12 member and two affiliate hospitals and 11 long-term-care facilities located in the mid-Atlantic states and the Pacific Northwest.

Sisters of Charity of Cincinnati and the Sisters of St. Francis Perpetual Adoration of Colorado Springs co-sponsored The Sisters of Charity Health Care Systems incorporated in 1979 as a multi-institutional health care network. By the mid-1990s the system included 20 hospitals in Colorado Kentucky Nebraska New Mexico and Ohio.

Three congregations collaborated to form Catholic Health Corporation in 1980 one of the first such health care partnerships between religious communities within the Roman Catholic Church in the US. By 1996 this coalition operated 100 health care facilities in 12 states.

The development of modern managed care health care systems put pressure on the smaller Catholic hospital operations so the three systems established Catholic Health Initiatives (CHI) in 1996 as a national entity serving five geographic regions. Patricia Cahill a lay health care veteran who previously served the Archdiocese of New York was appointed president and CEO of CHI. The following year CHI absorbed the 10-hospital Sisters of Charity of Nazareth Health Care System based in Bardstown Kentucky (founded in a log cabin in 1812).

That year CHI continued to seek new partnerships to improve efficiency. With Alegent Health it formed provider network Midwest Select with nearly 200 hospitals marketing discounted rates to businesses. CHI allied with the Daughters of Charity to form for-profit joint venture Catholic Healthcare Audit Network to provide operational financial compliance and information systems audits as well as due diligence reviews. CHI also joined insurance joint venture NewCap Insurance with the Daughters of Charity and Catholic Health East; the firm allowed CHI to operate independently of commercial insurers.

CHI made a secular tie-in with the University of Pennsylvania Health System in 1998 whereby the university's system would offer care through five Catholic hospitals (CHI made plans to transfer these hospitals to Catholic Health East in 2001). The next year CHI announced its first loss due to lackluster performance in the Midwest. During 2000 the company responded by streamlining operations and changing management resulting in a positive bottom line. In 2001 it sold three hospitals in Pennsylvania one in Delaware and one in New Jersey to Catholic Health East.

EXECUTIVES

President Ceo And Trustee, Kevin E. Lofton, age 63
President Enterprise Business Lines And Cfo, J. Dean Swindle
Svp Divisional Operations (texas), Michael H. Covert
Svp Marketing And Communications, Joyce M. Ross
Executive Vice President Mission, Thomas R. Kopfensteiner
Svp Divisional Operations And Ceo Chi Memorial (tennessee), Larry Schumacher, age 60
Evp Corporate Affairs And Chief Legal Officer, Mitch H. Melfi
Evp Growth And Business Acquisitions, Paul W. Edgett
Svp Human Resources And Chief Human Resources Officer, Patricia G. (Pat) Webb
Svp Divisional Operations And Ceo Chi Health (nebraska And Southwest Iowa), Cliff A. Robertson
Senior Vice President And Division Executive Officer, Jeffrey S. Drop
Svp And Chief Nursing Officer, Kathleen D. Sanford
Svp Divisional Operations And Ceo Mercy Health Network (iowa), David H. Vellinga
Svp Divisional Operations And Ceo Chi Franciscan Health (tacoma), Ketul J. Patel
Svp And President And Ceo Kentuckyone Health, Ruth W. Brinkley
Ceo Chi St. Alexius Health, Matt Grimshaw, age 43
Interim Evp Operations, Anthony Jones
Svp And Chief Medical Officer, Robert J. Weil
Senior Vice President And Chief Medical Officer, Stephen L Moore
Senior Vice President Divisional Operationsceo, Robert Ratzi
Vice President Treasury, Linda Macdonald
Vice President Human Resource Business Practices, Thomas Sams
Vice President Supply Chain Data Analytics, Kevin Kakuda
Vice President Public Policy, Marcia Desmond
Vice President And Chief Nursing Informatics And Telehealth Officer, Ann Shepard
Vice President National Hospitalist, Amanda Trask
Vice President Legal Transactions And Tax, Cynthia Leon
Vice President Of Patient Care, Deb Haagenson
Vice President Outreach, Ellen Lee
Director Of Pharmacy, Nicki Bohl
Senior Vice President Performance Excellence, Robert Strickland
Vice President Real Estate, Dave Glasscock
Senior Vice President Strategy Development, Meta Dooley
Vice President Ministry Formation, Alan BowmanCHI
Svp Ciso, Sheryl Rose
Vice President, Deeanna Opstedahl
Senior Vice President Capital Finance, Nick Barto
Auditors: ERNST & YOUNG LLP DENVER CO

LOCATIONS

HQ: CATHOLIC HEALTH INITIATIVES
198 INVERNESS DR W, ENGLEWOOD, CO 801123637
Phone: 303 298-9100
Web: WWW.CATHOLICHEALTHINITIATIVES.ORG

Selected Facilities and Operations
Arkansas
St. Vincent Health System
St. Vincent Doctors Hospital (Little Rock)
St. Vincent Infirmary Medical Center (Little Rock)
St. Vincent Medical Center North (Sherwood)
St. Vincent Morrilton (formerly St. Anthony's Medical Center Morrilton)
St. Vincent Rehabilitation Hospital (Sherwood)
Colorado
Centura Health
Centura Senior Services
The Gardens at St. Elizabeth (Denver)
Medalion Retirement Center (Colorado Springs)
Namaste Alzheimer Center (Colorado Springs)
Progressive Care Center (Canon City)
Villa Pueblo (Pueblo)
The Villas at Sunny Acres (Thornton)
Mercy Regional Medical Center (Durango)
Penrose-St. Francis Health Services
Penrose Hospital (Colorado Springs)
St. Francis Health Center (Colorado Springs)
St. Francis Medical Center (Colorado Springs)
St. Anthony Hospitals
St. Anthony Central Hospital (Denver)
St. Anthony North Hospital (Westminster)
St. Anthony Summit Medical Center (Frisco)
St. Mary-Corwin Medical Center (Pueblo)
St. Thomas More Hospital (Canon City)
Iowa
Alegent Health
Alegent Health-Mercy Hospital (Corning)
Alegent Health-Mercy Hospital (Council Bluffs)
Mercy Health Network
Bishop Drumm Retirement Center (Johnston)
Mercy Clinics (Des Moines)
Mercy College of Health Sciences (Des Moines)
Mercy Court (Des Moines)
Mercy Franklin Center (Des Moines)
Mercy Medical Center - Centerville (Centerville)
Mercy Medical Center - West Lakes (Des Moines)
Mercy Park Apartments (Des Moines)
Kansas
St. Rose Ambulatory and Surgery Center (formerly Central Kansas Medical Center Great Bend)
St. Catherine Hospital (Garden City)
Kentucky
KentuckyOne Health
Jewish Hospital and St. Mary's HealthCare (with Jewish Hospital HealthCare Services)
Our Lady of Peace (Louisville)
Sts. Mary & Elizabeth Hospital (Louisville)
Saint Joseph Health System
Continuing Care Hospital Inc. (Lexington)
Flaget Memorial Hospital (Bardstown)
Saint Joseph Berea Hospital (Berea)
Saint Joseph Hospital (Lexington)
Saint Joseph Hospital East (Lexington)
Saint Joseph Hospital Mount Sterling (Mt. Sterling)
Marymount Medical Center (London)
Maryland
St. Joseph Medical Center (Towson)
Minnesota
LakeWood Health Center (Baudette)
St. Francis Healthcare Campus (Breckenridge)
St. Francis Home (Breckenridge)
St. Joseph's Area Health Services (Park Rapids)
Unity Family Healthcare (dba St. Gabriel's Healthcare)
Albany Area Hospital and Medical Center
Alverna Apartments (Little Falls)
St. Camillus Place (Little Falls)
St. Gabriel's Hospital (Little Falls)
Nebraska
Alegent Health (joint venture with Immanuel Healthcare System)
Alegent Health-Bergan Mercy Medical Center (Omaha)
Alegent Health-Mercy Hospital (Council Bluffs)
Good Samaritan Hospital (Kearney)
Richard H. Young Hospital (Kearney)
Saint Elizabeth Regional Medical Center (Lincoln)
Saint Francis Medical Center (Grand Island)
St. Mary's Community Hospital (Nebraska City)
New Jersey
Saint Clare's Health System (Denville)

Saint Clare's Hospital (Boonton)
Saint Clare's Hospital (Denville)
Saint Clare's Hospital (Dover)
Saint Clare's Hospital (Sussex)
New Mexico
St. Joseph Community Health (Albuquerque)
North Dakota
CHI North Dakota
Carrington Health Center (Carrington)
Lisbon Area Health Services
Mercy Hospital (Valley City)
Oakes Community Hospital
Mercy Hospital (Devils Lake)
Mercy Medical Center (Williston)
St. Joseph's Hospital and Health Center (Dickinson)
Villa Nazareth Corporation
Friendship (Fargo)
Riverview Place (Fargo)
Ohio
Premier Health Partners
Good Samaritan Hospital (Dayton)
The Maria-Joseph Center (Dayton)
TriHealth
Good Samaritan Hospital (Cincinnati)
Oregon
Mercy Medical Center
Linus Oakes Inc. (Roseburg)
St. Anthony Hospital (Pendleton)
Pennsylvania
St. Joseph Health Ministries (Lancaster)
St. Joseph Regional Health Network
St. Joseph Medical Center (Reading)
South Dakota
St. Mary's Healthcare Center
Gettysburg Medical Center
Maryhouse Long-term Care Facility (Pierre)
ParkWood Retirement Apartments (Pierre)
Oahe Manor (Gettysburg)
Oahe Villa (Gettysburg)
St. Mary's Hospital (Pierre)
Tennessee
Memorial Health Care System
Memorial Hospital (Chattanooga)
Memorial North Park Hospital (Hixson)
Washington
Franciscan Health System
Enumclaw Regional Hospital (Enumclaw)
St. Anthony Hospital (Gig Harbor)
St. Clare Hospital (Lakewood)
St. Francis Hospital (Federal Way)
St. Joseph Medical Center (Tacoma)
Wisconsin
Franciscan Villa (South Milwaukee)

COMPETITORS

Adventist Health System Sunbelt Healthcare
Allina Hospitals
Ascension Health
Baptist Health
Baptist Health (Arkansas)
BryanLGH Medical Center
Denver Health and Hospital Authority
Exempla Healthcare
Golden Horizons
HCA
Kettering Health Network
Life Care Centers
Memorial Health System (Colorado)
Methodist Health System
MultiCare Health System
OhioHealth
Tenet Healthcare
UC Health
Universal Health Services
University of Colorado Hospital

HISTORICAL FINANCIALS

Company Type: Private

Income Statement   FYE: June 30

	REVENUE ($ mil.)	NET INCOME ($ mil.)	NET PROFIT MARGIN	EMPLOYEES
06/18	14,982	222	1.5%	72,500
06/17	15,547	128	0.8%	—
06/16	15,942	(703)	—	—
06/07	7,731	902	11.7%	—
Annual Growth	6.2%	(12.0%)		

2018 Year-End Financials

Debt ratio: ——
Return on equity: 1.50%
Cash ($ mil.): 510
Current ratio: 0.60
Long-term debt ($ mil.): —

Dividends
Yield: —
Payout: —
Market value ($ mil.): —

CBRE Group Inc

CBRE is all about location location location — not to mention ubicaciA?n l'emplacement posizione and Standort. As the world's largest commercial real estate services company by revenue CBRE provides property and facilities management leasing brokerage appraisal and valuation asset management financing and market research services from more than 450 offices worldwide and manages 1.6 billion sq. ft. of commercial space for third-party owners and occupants. Subsidiary Trammell Crow provides property development services for corporate and institutional clients primarily in the US. CBRE Global Investors manages real estate investments for institutional clients.

HISTORY

Colbert Coldwell and Albert Tucker started real estate brokerage Tucker Lynch & Coldwell in 1906 in San Francisco. In 1922 the company expanded to Los Angeles where it began developing real estate in 1933 with a 60-acre subdivision in the burgeoning city.

Having profited from California's rapid growth in the 1950s and 1960s the firm expanded out of state. The partnership incorporated in 1962 as Coldwell Banker which went public in 1968. Sears Roebuck & Co. bought the company in 1981 for 80% above its market price. But by 1991 Sears had abandoned aims to become a financial services giant and sold Coldwell Banker's commercial operations to The Carlyle Group as CB Commercial Real Estate Services Group.

Free of Sears but $56 million in the red the company didn't return to profitability until 1993. Two years later it embarked on a shopping spree in real estate services buying tenant representatives Langon Rieder and Westmark Realty. In 1996 the company went public and bought mortgage banker L. J. Melody & Company (which was renamed CBRE | Melody); it purchased Koll Real Estate Services in 1997.

In 1998 the company widened its global scope with the acquisition of REI Limited the non-UK operations of Richard Ellis; it was renamed CB Richard Ellis Services. CB Richard Ellis also bought Hillier Parker May & Rowden (now operating in the UK as CB Hillier) a London-based provider of commercial property services.

CB Richard Ellis experienced a revenue crunch in 1999 and responded by restructuring its North American operations into three divisions (transaction financial and management services) and cutting management ranks by 30%. Growth continued in 1999 with the purchase of Pittsburgh-based Gold & Co. the addition of an office in Venezuela and a fat contract to manage more than 1100 locations for Prudential.

In 2000 the company committed significant resources to the Internet inking a deal to offer the lease management services of MyContracts.com and investing in Canadian real estate transaction tracker RealNet Canada.

A group of investors including then-CEO Ray Wirta chairman Richard Blum (and his BLUM Capital Partners) and Freeman Spogli took the company private in 2001. Blum Capital Partners bought the 60% of publicly traded CBRE that it did not already own forming CBRE Holding. Three years later the company went public once again.

In 2003 CBRE merged with top commercial real estate broker and property manager Insignia Financial. The next year the company changed its name to CB Richard Ellis Group and went public. It bought rival Trammell Crow in 2006 as well as a dozen or so other companies as it sought to fill in its holdings. The acquisitions deepened CBRE's outsourcing services especially project and facilities management for corporate and institutional clients in the US.

CBRE spun off former subsidiary Realty Finance Corporation in 2008 after the real estate investment trust continued to post losses in a troubled credit market.

Also in 2008 it opened its first offices in Bahrain and joined forces with Vanke to provide residential property management services in China. The following year CBRE expanded its existing UK-based investment banking business (advisory and restructuring services for real estate hospitality and gaming companies) to the Americas.

CBRE in 2011 made one of its largest deals in several years. The company bolstered its global real estate i

EXECUTIVES

President Ceo And Director, Robert E. (Bob) Sulentic, age 62, $990,000 total compensation
President Global Corporate Services, William F. (Bill) Concannon, age 62, $675,000 total compensation
Global President Capital Markets, Christopher R. Ludeman
Cfo And Global Director Of Corporate Development, James R. (Jim) Groch, age 56, $770,000 total compensation
Global Group President Geographies, Calvin W. (Cal) Frese, age 62, $680,000 total compensation
Executive Managing Director And Coo L. J. Melody & Company, Brian F. Stoffers
Ceo Asia Pacific, Steven A. (Steve) Swerdlow
Global Group President Lines Of Business & Client Care, Michael J. (Mike) Lafitte, age 57, $700,000 total compensation
Global Chief Investment Officer And Ceo Cbre Global Investors And Cbre Clarion Securities, T. Ritson Ferguson, age 58, $800,000 total compensation
Chairman Asia Pacific, Robert (Rob) Blain, age 63, $560,000 total compensation
Evp And General Counsel, Laurence H. Midler, age 53, $325,000 total compensation
Global Director Client Care, Tony Long
Ceo Trammell Crow Company., Matt Khourie
President Cbre Global Investors, Daniel (Danny) Queenan
Evp Global Brokerage And Sales Management, Laura OBrien
Ceo Americas, Jack Durburg

Ceo Cbre Europe Middle East And Africa (emea), Martin Samworth
Global President Occupier Advisory And Transaction Services, Whitley Collins
Global President Asset Services And Valuation And Advisory Services (vas), Mary Jo Eaton
President Cbre Southern California - Hawaii, Lewis Horne
Vice Chairman Capital Markets And Institutional Properties, Michael Hines
Chief Digital And Technology Officer, Chandra Dhandapani
Vice Chairman Cbre Capital Markets Debt And Structured Finance, Rocco Mandala
Senior Vice President And Head Econic Incentive Solutions Group, Eric Stavriotis
Senior Vice President, Gregg Haly
Senior Vice President, Steven Brabant
Senior Vice President Los Angeles, Richard Ratner
Executive Vice President, Jeffrey C Babikian
Senior Vice President, Jim Koenig
Senior Vice President, Michael Liss
Vice President, Nancy Johnson
Vice President Information Technology, Mike Washington
Senior Vice President, Ned Burns
Senior Vice President Of Brokerage Services, Jeffrey Counsell
Senior Vice President, Bradley Gingerich
Vice President Senior, Mary O'Connor
Executive Vice President Managing Director, Jason Ruegg
Vice President, Mitchell Stravitz
Executive Vice President, Thomas Bohlinger
Senior Vice President, Greg Geraci
Vice President, Matt Burnett
Senior Vice President, Rod Apodaca
Senior Vice President Investment Properties, Alex Kozakov
Senior Vice President, Bradley Gingerich
Vice President, Justin Mohler
Senior Vice President, Cal Wessman
First Vice President, John Boote
Senior Vice President Of Debt And Equity Finance, Pete Marino
Senior Vice President Based, Daniel Woodward
Senior Vice President, Mark McDermott
Senior Vice President, Alan Krueger
Senior Vice President, Hyoung Chon
Senior Vice President Of Industrial Properties, Mark Writt
Senior Vice President, Paul Stockwell
Senior Vice President, George Maragos
Vice President, Leonard Santoro
Senior Vice President Partner, Rob Walles
First Vice President, Gary Leone
Senior Vice President, Terry Reily
First Vice President, Lee Diamond
First Vice President, Steve Delaney
First Vice President, Patrick Wade
Vice President, Joseph Orscheln
Executive Vice President, Steven Gartner
Senior Vice President Global Corporate Services (gcs), Armando Nunez
Senior Vice President, Andy Felber
Senior Vice President, Bob Meehling
Senior Vice President, Gerald Cobb
First Vice President, Michael Hoeck
Senior Vice President, Pat Mulready
Vice President, Jim Angelotti
Senior Vice President, Bob Kadoori
First Vice President, Dave Giltner
Vice President, Andy Fosberg
First Vice President, Andy Hitchcock
Vice President, Benjamin Rojahn
First Vice President, Bob Hill
First Vice President, Bob Mihelich
Vice President, Dan Brandel
Vice President, Dan Buhrmann
Vice President, Dave Wolf

First Vice President, Debbie Royal
First Vice President, Ed Wujek
Executuve Vice President, Jim Gunning
Vice President, Jim Mecham
Vice President, Michael P Wall
First Vice President, Mike Kaider
Senior Vice President, Pat Gildea
Senior Vice President, Pete Kast
First Vice President, Richard Trott
First Vice President, Rick Bamonte
Senior Vice President, Ronald Lakin
Vice President, Russ Janicek
Senior Vice President, Clark Gore
Senior Vice President, Paul Chaput
Senior Vice President Global Occupier Services, Dave Fields
Senior Vice President, Michael Wilson
Sp Vice President, William Kuntz
Mai Vice President, Mark Mediavilla
Lp Senior Vice President, Van Wehr
Senior Vice President, Joe Franco
Vice President, Carter Kendall
Senior Vice President Institutional Properties Multifamily, Robert Dean
Executive Vice President, Michael Dash
Senior Vice President, Jeremy Ballenger
Executive Vice President, Traci Payette
Mai Vice President, Cheryl Scott
Senior Vice President, James Flinn
Vice President, John Makowski
Senior Vice President, Mike Fahey
Vice President, Bennett Johnson
Senior Principal Vice President, Timothy Jaeger
First Vice President, Mike Horne
Vice President, Marcus Cornelius
Executive Vice President, Bob Kraynak
Senior Vice President, Larry Dinner
Vice President, Marc Frederick
Senior Vice President, Jeff Kapcheck
Vice President, Sonya Schmidt
Senior Vice President, Matt Kroger
Vice President Leasing, Blake Bishop
Vice President Of Cbre, Matt Larson
First Vice President Investment Properties Private Client Group, Matt Berry
Executive Vice President San Francisco, John Cecconi
Spqrea Senior Vice President, Matt Marschall
Senior Vice President, Paul Slockwell
Vice President, Dan Yeilding
Senior Vice President, Paul Farry
Senior Vice President Southern Ontario, Mitchell Blaine
Vice President, Byron Ahmet
First Vice President, Jeremy Woods
Vice President Retail Property And Shopping Center Leasing And Investment Sales, Greg Abbott
Senior Vice President Advisory And Transaction Services, Pat Gamble
Vice President, Steve Lee
First Vice President, Mike Parker
Senior Vice President Agency Group, Gregg Rothkin
Vice President Debt And Structured Finance, Chris Carr
Senior Vice President, Steve Heffner
Spqrea Senior Vice President, Philip Woodford
Senior Vice President, Matthew Whitlock
Vice President, Michael Affronti
Senior Vice President, Jack Gosnell
Vice President, Constance Wilde
Executive Vice President Debt And Structured Finance, Jesse Zarouk
Senior Vice President, Joel Frank
Senior Vice President, Andrew Peeples
Vice President, Steve Kohls
Vice President National Senior Housing, Austin Sacco

Senior Vice President Strategy Global Workplace Solutions, Ron Haddock
Associate Vice President Retail, Gina Mastromonaco
Executive Vice President, Jeremy Kronman
Auditors: KPMG LLP

LOCATIONS

HQ: CBRE Group Inc
400 South Hope Street, 25th Floor, Los Angeles, CA 90071
Phone: 213 613-3333
Web: www.cbre.com

2016 Sales

	$ mil.	% of total
Americas	7,226	55
Europe Middle East & Africa	3,917	30
Asia/Pacific	1,485	11
Global investment management	369	3
Development services	71	1
Total	**13,071**	**100**

2016 Sales

	$ in mil.
% of total	
US	55
UK	18
Other countries	27
Total	**100**

PRODUCTS/OPERATIONS

Selected Industries
CBRE Hotels
Data Centers
Energy & Sustainability
Golf & Resort Properties
Healthcare
Industrial & Logistics
Labor Analytics
Multifamily
Office
Public Institutions & Education
Residential
Retail
Alternative Investments Practice
Labor Analytics
Life Sciences

Selected Subsidiaries
CBRE Inc.
CBRE Capital Markets Inc.
CB/TCC LLC
CBRE Global Holdings SARL
CBRE Finance Europe LLP
CBRE Limited
CBRE Services Inc.
Norland Managed Services Ltd.
Trammell Crow Company LLC
CBRE Luxembourg Holdings SARL
CBRE Global Acquisition Company SARL
Relam Amsterdam Holdings
CBRE Limited Partnership

Selected service Investors
Financing
Investment Administration
Investment Banking
Leasing & Advisory
Loan Servicing
Property Management
Property Sales
Valuation & Advisory

Selected services for occupiers
Facilities Management
Leasing & Advisory
Management Consulting
Project Management
Valuation & Advisory
Workplace

Selected Business Lines
Advisory & Transaction Services
Asset Services
Capital Markets
Global Workplace Solutions

Valuation & Advisory Services
Investment Management (CBRE Global Investors)
Development Services (Trammell Crow Company)
CB/TCC LLC
CBRE Finance Europe LLPCBRE Luxembourg Holdings
SARLCBRE Global Acquisition Company SARLRelam
Amsterdam HoldingsCBRE Limited Partnership

COMPETITORS

BGC Partners	Inland Group
Cassidy Turley	Jones Lang LaSalle
Colliers International	Lincoln Property
Colliers International Group	Marcus & Millichap
Cushman & Wakefield	Mitsui Fudosan
Eastdil Secured	Realogy Holdings
HFF	Savills Studley

HISTORICAL FINANCIALS
Company Type: Public

Income Statement				FYE: December 31
	REVENUE ($ mil.)	NET INCOME ($ mil.)	NET PROFIT MARGIN	EMPLOYEES
12/17	14,209	691	4.9%	80,000
12/16	13,071	571	4.4%	75,000
12/15	10,855	547	5.0%	70,000
12/14	9,049	484	5.4%	52,000
12/13	7,184	316	4.4%	44,000
Annual Growth	18.6%	21.6%	—	16.1%

2017 Year-End Financials

Debt ratio: 25.34%	No. of shares (mil.): 339
Return on equity: 19.66%	Dividends
Cash ($ mil.): 751	Yield: —
Current ratio: 1.18	Payout: —
Long-term debt ($ mil.): 1,999	Market value ($ mil.): 14,702

	STOCK PRICE ($) FY Close	P/E High/Low	PER SHARE ($) Earnings	Dividends	Book Value
12/17	43.31	22 15	2.03	0.00	11.84
12/16	31.49	20 14	1.69	0.00	8.94
12/15	34.58	24 19	1.63	0.00	8.12
12/14	34.25	24 17	1.45	0.00	6.79
12/13	26.30	27 21	0.95	0.00	5.71
Annual Growth	13.3%	—	20.9%	—	20.0%

CBS Corp

You might say this company has a real eye for broadcasting. CBS Corporation known by some as the "Eye Network" due to its eye logo is a leading mass media conglomerate with television radio online content and publishing operations. Its portfolio is anchored by CBS Broadcasting which operates the #1 rated CBS television network along with a group of local TV stations. CBS also owns cable network Showtime and produces and distributes TV programming through CBS Television Studios and CBS Television Distribution. Other operations include CBS Interactive and book publisher Simon & Schuster. Chairman Emeritus Sumner Redstone controls CBS Corporation through National Amusements.

Operations

CBS Corporation operates through four segments. Its Entertainment segment consists of the CBS Television Network CBS Television Studios CBS Studios International Network Ten CBS Films CBS Interactive and its digital streaming services

CBS All Access and CBSN. The Cable Networks segment consists of Showtime Networks The Movie Channel Flix CBS Sports Network and Smithsonian Networks.

The company's Publishing segment consists of Simon & Schuster's consumer book publishing business with imprints such as Simon & Schuster Pocket Books Scribner Gallery Books Touchstone and Atria Books. The Local Broadcasting segment consists of CBS Television Stations and CBS Local Digital Media with revenues generated primarily from advertising sales.

The Entertainment segment contributed 65% of the company's revenue in fiscal 2016 while the company's Cable Networks segment accounted for around 20%.

Geographic Reach

CBS Corporation has operations in the US and Canada. The US contributes around 85% of the company's total revenue.

Sales and Marketing

CBS Corporation continues to draw the largest number of TV viewers among broadcast networks with hit crime shows news sports and comedies. The high ratings allow CBS Corporation to charge advertisers more and more every year. Advertising accounts for more than 40% of the company's total revenues.

CBS Corporation has a presence online with such leading websites as CNET (technology news and reviews) GameSpot (video game information) and Last.fm (social networking for music fans). Its CBS Interactive segment focuses on selling advertising across its vast collection of properties.

Financial Performance

CBS Corporation's revenue has been on an upwards trend for several years. In fiscal 2017 revenue increased 4% to $13.7 billion as strong growth in affiliate and subscription fees and content licensing and distribution offset a 9% decrease in advertising revenue. The 26% rise in subscription fees was driven by one massive pay-per-view event — the record-setting fight between Floyd Mayweather and Conor McGregor — in addition to 27% growth in station affiliation fees and retransmission fees. Content Licensing revenue grew thanks to higher sales from NCIS: New Orleans Madam Secretary and several CSI titles. Advertising revenue was down due to the effect of televising the Super Bowl the previous year (television rights rotate between CBS Fox and NBC). Underlying advertising revenue was down 2% due to overall lower viewing figures partially offset by higher pricing.

Net income fell sharply to $357 million in 2017 from $1.3 billion the previous year due to a series of one-off items including a $105 million loss on the sale of its CBS Radio business a 4 percentage point increase in income tax paid a $49 million loss on early debt extinguishment a $63 million restructuring charge and a $352 million pension settlement (plus a discretionary contribution of $600 million).

Cash from operations fell 47% to $887 million on the back of the pension contribution and the tough comparable of the 2016 Super Bowl.

Strategy

It is clear now that traditional forms of television distribution (cable satellite) have been successfully "disrupted" by internet-based streaming services such as Netflix. CBS is continuing to fine-tune its "All Access" streaming bundle and has begun rolling it out abroad starting with Canada followed by Australia. The process has required CBS to revise its licensing strategies as the company risks getting tangled up by its current model: Currently CBS grants exclusive international streaming rights for its shows to companies such as Netflix obstructing CBS from showing its own content online in overseas territories. Indeed its licensing

strategy causes problems even in its domestic streaming service. Catalogs of flagship shows such as Big Bang Theory and 2 Broke Girls are either incomplete or not available at all on its All Access service. Other developments in the streaming domain include a new a sports-focused channel (news analysis and previews — but not live events) and the hire of an ex-Facebook exec to oversee its digital expansion efforts.

Mergers and Acquisitions

In late 2017 CBS acquired Network Ten one of three major commercial broadcast networks in Australia. In addition to core linear channel TEN the deal includes digital terrestrial television (DTT) channel ELEVEN which CBS already had a stake in as well as the DTT channel ONE and Network Ten's rapidly growing digital platform TENPLAY. The acquisition plays into CBS' digital-led international growth strategy.

HISTORY

The company that would eventually become CBS Corporation began as Viacom in 1970. It was the result of numerous mergers and acquisitions dating back nearly 90 years combining everything from a movie studio to a company that made car bumpers. CBS launched Viacom after the FCC ruled that TV networks could not own cable systems and TV stations in the same market. Viacom took over CBS's program syndication division and bought TV and radio stations in the late 1970s and early 1980s. In 1978 it co-founded pay-TV network Showtime. Viacom became full owner in 1982 and combined Showtime with The Movie Channel the following year to form Showtime Networks. Viacom also began producing TV series and bought MTV Networks in 1986.

After a bidding war with renowned financier Carl Icahn and a Viacom management group Sumner Redstone's National Amusements bought 83% of Viacom in 1987. Viacom bought King's Entertainment (theme parks) shortly thereafter and followed that with two mega-deals in 1994: it bought Paramount Communications for about $10 billion (which included Simon & Schuster) and Blockbuster for $8.4 billion (which included Spelling Entertainment). The next year along with Chris-Craft Viacom launched UPN (United Paramount Network) the fifth commercial-broadcast TV network in the US.

Chiseling away at a mountain of debt Viacom dumped its radio stations and sold its share in USA Networks (now named IAC/InterActiveCorp) to Universal for $1.7 billion in 1997. In 1998 it sold the reference and education publishing divisions of Simon & Schuster to Pearson for $4.6 billion and unloaded the unprofitable Blockbuster Music chain to Wherehouse Entertainment for $115 million.

Viacom created an Internet division (MTV Networks Online) in 1999 to house its MTV VH1 and Nickelodeon Web sites (later decentralized into The MTVi Group and Nickelodeon Online). Later that year it sold 18% of Blockbuster in an IPO and sold 10% of MTVi to TCI Music (later Liberty Digital) in exchange for the SonicNet websites.

Viacom bought Chris-Craft's 50%-stake in the struggling UPN Network for a paltry $5 million in 2000 by exercising a buy-sell clause in the contract. BHC Communications (Chris-Craft's 80%-owned subsidiary that actually owned the stake in UPN) filed suit to block Viacom's merger with CBS claiming that it violated a non-compete clause in the contract but the New York Supreme Court ruled in Viacom's favor. Its $45 billion merger with CBS went through (reuniting two companies split apart by the government 30 years ago) and Viacom was given one year to sell UPN. However a federal law prohibiting ownership of more than one TV network was overturned in 2001 allowing Viacom to keep the network.

Later that year Viacom's victory over Chris-Craft turned to sour grapes when News Corp. agreed to buy Chris-Craft. The deal could have forced UPN to fold if News Corp. had turned Chris-Craft's large-market UPN stations into FOX affiliates (a new pact later signed with Chris-Craft keeps UPN as the stations' network).

In 2001 Viacom bought the rest of Infinity Broadcasting that it didn't already own as well as Black Entertainment Television (the media company targeting African-Americans) for $3 billion. It also folded MTVi back into parent MTV Networks. Other cost cutting measures in 2002 included combining the

EXECUTIVES

Executive Vice President Worldwide Marketing Cbs Films, Debbie Miller

Chairman President And Ceo, Leslie (Les) Moonves, age 68, $3,500,000 total compensation

Sevp And Chief Communications Officer, Gil Schwartz, age 67, $896,923 total compensation

Sevp Chief Administrative Officer And Chief Human Resources Officer, Anthony G. Ambrosio, age 58, $964,423 total compensation

Sevp And Chief Legal Officer, Lawrence P. (Larry) Tu, age 63, $1,200,000 total compensation

Evp Government Affairs, John Orlando

Evp Investor Relations, Adam Townsend

Evp Deputy General Counsel And Secretary, Jonathan H. Anschell

Coo, Joseph R. Ianniello, age 51, $2,500,000 total compensation

Evp General Tax Counsel And Chief Veteran Officer, Richard M. Jones, age 53

Evp Controller And Chief Accounting Officer, Lawrence (Larry) Liding, age 49

Executive Vice President Cbs Marketing Group, Anne O'grady

Evp Communication, Dana Mcclintock

Vice President Government Relations, Bryce Harlow

Vice President Production, Al Kennedy

Vice President Advertising And Promotion, Michael Pollack

Vice President Of Sales, Betty E Berlamino

Vice President Sales, Alan Clack

Senior Vice President Current Programs, Jeanne Mau

Vice President Counsel, Michael Arseneault

Senior Vice President, Jonathan Sarrow

Vice President And Assistant General Counsel, Michael Rona

Evp Corporate Development, Bryon Rubin

Senior Vice President Western Regional Manager, Greg Guenther

Vice President And Assistant Treasurer, Jim Morrison

Vice President And General Manager, Tom Herschel

Vice President And Assistant General Counsel, Joseph Richburg

Executive Vice President Sales, Dean Kaplan

Vice President Senior Tax Counsel, Kenneth Koen

Vice President Of Web Development, Allan Bressler

Senior Vice President Creative, Jorge Ferreiro

Vice President Human Resources, Robin Bona

Seniorvice President, Sue Lamphear

Senior Vice President Workforce Development, Jennifer Suarez

Vice President Of Detroit Sales, Joe Butkovich

Vice President Finance, Steve Grosso

Vp Workforce Development, Bryn Berglund

Vice President Diversity And Communications, Fern Orenstein

Vice President Comedy Development, Edy Mendoza

Senior Vice President And Director Of Sales Analysis Operations, Bob Kaplan

Vice President And Assistant General Counsel, Mary Tischler

Vice President Of Sales, Kevin Barth

Senior Vice President Of Manufacturing, Marilyn Levatino

Vice President And News Director, Jeff Kiernan

Vice President, George Lewis

Vice President Distribution, Ken Hinshaw

Vice President Human Resources, Michael Niceberg

Vice President Drama Development, Bryan Seabury

Vice President Ad Operations, Mark Halstead

Vice President Executive Creative Director, James Shefcik

Vice President Executive Creative Director, James Shefcik

Senior Vice President Alt Series Development, Ghen Maynard

Vice President Business Development At Cbs Interactive, Adam London

Executive Vice President Cbs Marketing Group, Anne Ogrady

Vice President Finance, Denny McCormick

Vice President Client Services, Christoph Hesterbrink

Svp And Associate General Counsel Litigation, Anthony Bongiorno

Vice President Corporate Communications, Judy Dehaven

Senior Vice President For Standards And Special Projects, Linda Mason

Vice President West Coast, Josh Comay

Vp Internal Audit Operations, Jeffrey Meyer

Vice President Legal Affairs, Scott Birnbaum

Vice President Finance, Susan Varo

Vice President Media Advertising And Promotion, Kim Philo

Vice President Talent And Casting, Matt Skrobalak

Vice President Assistant General Counsel, Darlene Crump

Vice President Finance, Dennis Lowry

Global Vice President Of Sales, Laura Summers

Senior Vice President Human Resources Cbs Radio, Mark Zulli

Vice President Executive Search, Conway Shui

Vice President Research And Audience Measurement, Gary Heller

Senior Vice President Labor Relations, Edgar Yergeau

Vice President Business Affairs, Alison Choppelas

Vice President Senior Counsel, Maria Charon

Vice President Product Management And Marketing, Patrick Herde

Senior Vice President Communications, Phil Gonzales

Executive Vice President Communications, Kelli Raftery

Executive Vice President, Kurt Davis

Svp And Cio Cbs Interactive, Steve Comstock

Svp Tax Reporting And Operations, Richard Ciraulo

Svp Associate General Counsel Corporate And Securities, Kim Pittman

Svp Business Affairs Cbs Television Studios, Dan Kupetz

Vice President Health And Welfare Benefits, Robert Brandwene

Vice President Captioning And Video Description, Mark Turits

Vice President And General Manager, Scott Schuman

Vice President Business Affairs And Legal, Charles Gardner

Vice President Product, John Pacino

Vice President Comedy Development, Alex Botnick

Vice President Finance, Steven Haft

Vice President Information Systems And Technology, Elizabeth Gilmore

Senior Vice President Digital Sales, Andi Poch

Vice President And General Manager, Adam Levy

Senior Vice President Business Affairs And Legal, Peter Kane

Senior Vice President Communications, Laurie Metrose

Senior Vice President, Roni Mueller

Vice President Compensation, Julia Ambrose

Senior Vice President Business Development, Jeff Shultz

Vice President Associate General Counsel, Laura Burton

Senior Vice President And Market Manager, Dan Kearney

Vice President Search Strategies, Cameron Olthuis

Senior Vice President, Kim Metcalf

Vice President Affiliate Relations, David Comisar

Senior Vice President Current Programming, Amy Reisenbach

Vice President Current Programs, Marci Cooperstein

Vice President Artist Partnerships And Experiences, Noel Grey

Senior Vice President Specials, Courtney Conroy

Senior Vice President And Associate General Counsel, Naomi Waltman

Senior Vice President Supplier Category Management, Mike Smyklo

Executive Vice President Digital, JD Crowley

Senior Vice President, Jonathan Bingaman

Vice President Post Production, Jeff Henry

Vice President Strategic Partnerships, Michael Gulbin

Evp Diversity Inclusion And Communications, Tiffany Smith-anoa'i

Executive Vice President Communications Cbs Television Distribution, Scott Grogin

Vice President And Assistant General Counsel Labor And Employment Relations, Daniel Paretsky

Vice President Digital Sales, Trevor Frederickson

Vice President Short Term Capital Markets, Ken Woltersdorf

Senior Vice President Legal, Cindy Teele

Vice President Broadcast Distribution, Brent Stranathan

Chairman President And Ceo, Leslie (Les) Moonves, age 68

Vice Chair, Shari E. Redstone, age 64

Evp Deputy General Counsel And Secretary, Jonathan H. Anschell

Board Member, Linda M Griego

Board Member, Patrick Corr

Board Member, Charlie Gifford

Treasurer, Jacqueline Miller

Auditors: PricewaterhouseCoopers LLP

LOCATIONS

HQ: CBS Corp
51 W. 52nd Street, New York, NY 10019
Phone: 212 975-4321
Web: www.cbscorporation.com

2017 Sales

	$ mil.	% of total
United States	11,675	85
International	2,017	15
Total	**13,692**	**100**

PRODUCTS/OPERATIONS

2017 Sales

	$ mil.	% of total
Entertainment	9,164	66
Cable Networks	2,501	18
Local Media	1,668	12
Publishing	830	4
Corporate/Eliminations	(471)	-
Total	**13,692**	**100**

2017 Sales

	$ mil.	% of total
Advertising	5,753	42
Content licensing & distribution	3,952	29
Affiliate & subscription fees	3,758	27
Other	229	2
Total	**13,692**	**100**

Selected Operations

CBS Television Network
CBS Entertainment
CBS News
CBS Sports
CBS Television Stations
CBS Television Studios
CBS Studios International
CBS Television Distribution
CBS Home Entertainment
CBS Consumer Products
CBS Films
The CW
Showtime
Smithsonian Channel
CBS Sports Network
CBS Interactive
Simon & Schuster
CBS Scene
Watch! Magazine
EcoMedia
Pop
CBS VISION

COMPETITORS

21st Century Fox	Penguin Random House
AOL	SIRIUS XM
Cumulus Media	Sony Pictures
Disney	Entertainment
JCDecaux	Time Warner
Lamar Advertising	Yahoo!
NBCUniversal	iHeartCommunications
Netflix	

HISTORICAL FINANCIALS

Company Type: Public

Income Statement				FYE: December 31
	REVENUE ($ mil.)	NET INCOME ($ mil.)	NET PROFIT MARGIN	EMPLOYEES
12/17	13,692	357	2.6%	16,730
12/16	13,166	1,261	9.6%	21,270
12/15	13,886	1,413	10.2%	16,260
12/14	13,806	2,959	21.4%	17,310
12/13	15,284	1,879	12.3%	19,490
Annual Growth	(2.7%)	(34.0%)	—	(3.7%)

2017 Year-End Financials

Debt ratio: 48.75%
Return on equity: 12.60%
Cash ($ mil.): 285
Current ratio: 1.58
Long-term debt ($ mil.): 9,464

No. of shares (mil.): 383
Dividends
Yield: 0.0%
Payout: 81.8%
Market value ($ mil.): 22,597

	STOCK PRICE ($)	P/E		PER SHARE ($)		
	FY Close	High/Low		Earnings	Dividends	Book Value
12/17	59.00	78	61	0.88	0.72	5.16
12/16	63.62	23	15	2.81	0.66	8.95
12/15	47.13	22	13	2.89	0.60	12.02
12/14	55.34	13	9	5.27	0.54	13.75
12/13	63.74	21	12	3.01	0.48	16.72
Annual Growth	(1.9%)	—	—	(26.5%)	10.7%	(25.5%)

CBTX Inc

Auditors: GRANT THORNTON LLP

LOCATIONS

HQ: CBTX Inc
9 Greenway Plaza, Suite 110, Houston, TX 77046
Phone: 713 210-7600
Web: www.communitybankoftx.com

HISTORICAL FINANCIALS

Company Type: Public

Income Statement				FYE: December 31
	ASSETS ($ mil.)	NET INCOME ($ mil.)	INCOME AS % OF ASSETS	EMPLOYEES
12/17	3,081	27	0.9%	462
12/16	2,951	27	0.9%	472
12/15	2,882	24	0.8%	—
Annual Growth	3.4%	6.9%	—	—

2017 Year-End Financials

Debt ratio: 0.22%
Return on equity: 6.86%
Cash ($ mil.): 326
Current ratio: —
Long-term debt ($ mil.): —

No. of shares (mil.): 24
Dividends
Yield: 0.0%
Payout: 4.1%
Market value ($ mil.): 737

	STOCK PRICE ($)	P/E		PER SHARE ($)		
	FY Close	High/Low		Earnings	Dividends	Book Value
12/17	29.66	24	23	1.22	0.05	17.97
12/16	0.00	—	—	1.22	0.20	16.21
12/15	0.00	—	—	1.06	0.20	15.44
Annual Growth	—	—	—	7.3%	(50.0%)	7.9%

CDW Corp

Auditors: Ernst & Young LLP

LOCATIONS

HQ: CDW Corp
75 Tri-State International, Lincolnshire, IL 60069
Phone: 847 465-6000
Web: www.cdw.com

HISTORICAL FINANCIALS

Company Type: Public

Income Statement				FYE: December 31
	REVENUE ($ mil.)	NET INCOME ($ mil.)	NET PROFIT MARGIN	EMPLOYEES
12/17	15,191	523	3.4%	250
12/16	13,981	424	3.0%	8,516
12/15	12,988	403	3.1%	8,465
12/14	12,074	244	2.0%	7,211
12/13	10,768	132	1.2%	7,000
Annual Growth	9.0%	40.9%	—	(56.5%)

2017 Year-End Financials

Debt ratio: 46.51%
Return on equity: 51.57%
Cash ($ mil.): 144
Current ratio: 1.34
Long-term debt ($ mil.): 3,210

No. of shares (mil.): 153
Dividends
Yield: 0.0%
Payout: 20.8%
Market value ($ mil.): 10,632

	STOCK PRICE ($)	P/E		PER SHARE ($)		
	FY Close	High/Low		Earnings	Dividends	Book Value
12/17	69.49	21	15	3.31	0.69	6.42
12/16	52.09	21	13	2.56	0.48	6.52
12/15	42.04	20	14	2.35	0.31	6.52
12/14	35.17	25	16	1.42	0.20	5.44
12/13	23.36	29	22	0.84	0.04	4.14
Annual Growth	31.3%	—	—	40.9%	100.7%	11.6%

Celanese Corp (DE)

Celanese Corporation is a global technology and specialty materials company that manufactures building block chemicals like acetic acid and vinyl acetate monomers used in everything from inks and paints to agricultural products and chewing gum. The Texas-based also makes advanced plastics products such as precision molds for injection molding flame- and heat-resistance plastics and acetate film. Other products include acetate tow (used in cigarette filters) and industrial specialties like ethylene vinyl acetate.The company has dozens of industry-leading brands including polyacetal like Celcon and Hostaform thermoplastics under the GUR brand polyesters under Celanex and Impet brands Nylon under Nylfor Nimalid and Frianyl.

Operations

Celanese is one of the world's largest producers of acetyl products and a top global producer of engineered polymers.It operates through four business segments: Acetyl Intermediates Advanced Engineered Materials Consumer Specialties and Industrial Specialties.

Acetyl Intermediates bringing in around 40% of total company revenue produces acetic acid vinyl acetate monomer acetic anhydride and acetate esters. The segment's products are commonly used in colorants paints adhesives coatings and pharmaceuticals. It also produces organic solvents and intermediates for pharmaceutical agricultural and chemical products.

Advanced Engineered Materials worth more than 30% of sales makes high performance plastics mostly for automotive and medical applications.

Industrial Specialties accounts for 15% of sales and includes the emulsion polymers and EVA polymers businesses. The former's products find use in paints and coatings adhesives construction glass fiber textiles and paper. EVA polymers makes specialty ethylene vinyl acetate resins and compounds and low-density polyethylene for use in packaging lamination film hot melt adhesives auto parts and carpeting.

The Consumer Specialties segment brings in some 10% of sales and mostly makes acetate tow for use in cigarette filters. It also makes preservatives for the food and drink industries such as sorbic acid and potassium sorbate. It also makes Qorus and Sunett sweeteners.

Geographic Reach

Irving Texas-based Celanese has more than 30 production facilities across the world and 10 affiliate production sites.

Besides the US Celanese has properties plants or other operations in Belgium Brazil Canada China Germany Hungary Malaysia Mexico the Netherlands South Korea Sweden Singapore and the UK.

Germany account for around 30% of the company's sales followed by the US at 25%

Sales and Marketing

Celanese markets its products both directly to customers and through distributors. Sales to major global customers in a wide range of industries are usually made under multi-year contracts. The company serves a broad range of industries including consumer and industrial adhesives paints and coatings textiles food and beverage automotive applications consumer and medical applications performance industrial applications filter media paper and packaging chemical additives and construction applications.

Acetate tow is sold principally to the major tobacco companies that account for a majority of worldwide cigarette production. Customers of Clarifoil film include printers carton manufacturers retailers packaging buyers publishers designers and freezer door manufacturers. Food protection ingredients are primarily sold through regional distributors to small and medium sized customers and directly to large multinational customers in the food industry.

Financial Performance

In the last decade (2008-17) revenue at Celanese has hovered around the $5 billion to $6 billion mark. Although the company posted profits every year in that same period net income has fluctuated considerably between a low of $282 million (2008) and a peak of $1 billion (2013).

In 2017 Celanese revenue climbed some 15% to $6.1 billion stemming almost entirely from a 45% spike in additional volumes sold in the advanced engineered materials segment compared to the year prior. The growth was related SOFTER acquisition and the NILIT nylon compounding division.

Net income fell some 6% to $843 million mostly due to a year-over-year increase of some $90 million in SG&A costs and other charges. The $100 million SG&A spending increase comes from the merger acquisition and integration costs in the advanced engineered materials segment.

Celanese cash holdings decreased from $638 million in 2016 to $576 million in 2017. Operations generated $800 million. Investing activities used $550 million primarily in acquisitions and CAPEX. Financing took out a further $350 million due to a bulk purchase of treasury stocks costing some $500 million.

Strategy

The biggest advantage of Celanese is its continued name recognition across all the major industries on a global scale. It has over two-dozen high performance engineered materials that are readily recognized as top brands. The company maintains a large global production capacity. Its revenue stream also reflects an impressive geographic balance. This guards Celanese against sudden downturns as proven by its continued profitability despite a commodity price downturn in 2014-16 period.

The company spends top-dollar (averaging over $70 million a year) on research and innovation of new products and applications as well as an average CAPEX of $250 million in the 2015-17 period.

Ever expansive the company often acquires businesses with higher margins and lower exposure to price fluctuation. For example Celanese is pumping up its advanced materials business by making three acquisitions in 2015-18 period? SOFTER Nilit and Omni ? adding more nylon and thermoplastic end-products to its product lines.

Mergers and Acquisitions

In 2018 Celanese acquired Omni Plastics which specializes in custom compounding of various engineered thermoplastic materials. This particular material is in high demand in the automotive electrical and electronics consumer goods and industrial markets. The acquisition adds Celanese's compounding capacity in the Americas. The addition continues a recent trend of resin makers diversifying with compounding (both LyndondellBassel and Westlake Chemical pursued similar deals).

In 2017 Celanese acquired Nilit Plastics the nylon compounding division of Nilit an Israeli nylon manufacturer.

Company Background

Celanese Corporation was created in 2004 by the Blackstone Group which had acquired a majority share in Celanese AG turned it private and then flipped it in a 2005 public offering. Blackstone finally divested its remaining holdings in Celanese in 2007.

EXECUTIVES

Chairman And Ceo, Mark C. Rohr, age 66, $1,142,308 total compensation

Evp And Chief Administrative Officer, Lori A. Johnston, age 53, $475,000 total compensation

Evp And General Counsel, Peter G. Edwards, age 56

Evp And President Acetyl Chain And Integrated Supply Chain, Patrick D. (Pat) Quarles, age 50, $627,692 total compensation

Evp Coo And President Materials Solutions, Scott M. Sutton, age 53, $581,538 total compensation

Svp Finance And Cfo, Christopher W. (Chris) Jensen, age 51, $546,154 total compensation

Cio, Rajesh Nagarajan

Vice President Europe Region, Amy Hebert

Senior Vice President Acetyles, Todd Elliott

Vice President Global Communications And Corporate Social Responsibility, Gretchen Rosswurm

Vice President Global Sales Americas Region, John Caamano

Vice President Of Talent Development, Lisa Esparza

Vice President And Deputy General Counsel, Jay Felkins

Senior Vice President Supply Management, William Antonace

Vice President And Deputy General Counsel, Jay Felkins

Senior Vice President Chief Financial Officer, Steven Sterin

Executive Vice President, Sandy Lin

Vice President Business Develo, Marcel V Amerongen

Vice President Human Resources And Employment Law, Joseph Fox

Chairman And Ceo, Mark C. Rohr, age 66

Board Member, John Wulff

Assistant Treasurer, Thomas Liu

Board Member, Jean Blackwell

Board Member, Kathryn Hill

Board Member, William Brown

Auditors: KPMG LLP

LOCATIONS

HQ: Celanese Corp (DE)
222 West Las Colinas Blvd., Suite 900N, Irving, TX 75039-5421
Phone: 972 443-4000
Web: www.celanese.com

2016 sales

	$ mil.	% of total
Germany	1,540	29
US	1,451	27
China	758	14
Singapore	745	14
Belgium	408	8
Canada	214	4
Mexico	150	2
Others	123	2
Total	**5,389**	**100**

PRODUCTS/OPERATIONS

2016 sales

	$ mil.	% of total
Advanced Engineered Materials	1,444	27
Acetyl Intermediates	2,441	45
Industrial Specialties	979	18
Consumer Specialties	929	17
Adjustments (404) -7		
Total	**5,389**	**100**

Selected Products

Acetyl Intermediates
  Acetate esters
  Acetic acid
  Acetic anhydride
  Carboxylic acids
  Methanol
  Vinyl acetate monomer (VAM)
Industrial Specialties
  Emulsions
Consumer Specialties
  Acetate tow
  Sunett sweetener
Advanced Engineered Materials
  Polyacetal products (POM)
  Polyphenylene sulfide (Forton)
  UHMW-PE (GUR)

Selected Brand Names

AOPlus
BuyTiconaDirect
Celanex
Celcon
Celstran
Celvolit
Clarifoil
Compel
Erkol
GUR
Hostaform
Impet
Mowilith
Nutrinova
Riteflex
Sunett
Thermx
Vandar
Vectra
Vinamul

COMPETITORS

Asahi Kasei	LANXESS
BASF SE	Methanex
DSM	NutraSweet
Daicel Chemical	Rhodia
Dow Chemical	SABIC Innovative
DuPont	Plastics
Eastman Chemical	Solvay
Hexion	

HISTORICAL FINANCIALS

Company Type: Public

Income Statement

FYE: December 31

	REVENUE ($ mil.)	NET INCOME ($ mil.)	NET PROFIT MARGIN	EMPLOYEES
12/18	7,155	1,207	16.9%	7,684
12/17	6,140	843	13.7%	7,592
12/16	5,389	900	16.7%	7,293
12/15	5,674	304	5.4%	7,081
12/14	6,802	624	9.2%	7,468
Annual Growth	**1.3%**	**17.9%**	**—**	**0.7%**

2018 Year-End Financials

Debt ratio: 37.91%
Return on equity: 41.12%
Cash ($ mil.): 439
Current ratio: 1.62
Long-term debt ($ mil.): 2,970

No. of shares (mil.): 128
Dividends
  Yield: 2.3%
  Payout: 21.6%
Market value ($ mil.): 11,525

	STOCK PRICE ($) FY Close	P/E High/Low		PER SHARE ($) Earnings	Dividends	Book Value
12/18	89.97	13	9	8.91	2.08	23.30
12/17	107.08	18	13	6.09	1.74	21.26
12/16	78.74	13	9	6.18	1.38	18.40
12/15	67.33	36	26	2.00	1.15	16.20
12/14	59.96	16	12	4.00	0.93	18.43
Annual Growth	**10.7%**	**—**	**—**	**22.2%**	**22.3%**	**6.0%**

Celgene Corp

Celgene lines up cells and genes to create good health. The biopharmaceutical company's lead product is Revlimid which is approved in the US Europe and other select markets as a treatment for multiple myeloma (bone marrow cancer). Revlimid also is used to treat a blood disorder called myelodysplastic syndrome (MDS). The company's second-biggest seller is Pomalyst/Imnovid which is approved in various markets for the treatment of multiple myeloma. Other products include Otezla for the treatment of psoriatic arthritis and chemotherapy agent Abraxane. The firm has other drugs in development that combat inflammatory diseases and cancer. Bristol-Myers Squibb is buying Celgene in a $74 billion deal.

Change in Company Type

In early 2019 Celgene agreed to be acquired by pharmaceutical giant Bristol-Myers Squibb for some $74 million in cash and stock. After the transaction Celgene shareholders will own some 31% of the combined company.

Operations

Revlimid is by far Celgene's biggest seller making up nearly two-thirds of its annual sales. Its other top selling products — Pomalyst Otezla Abraxane and Vidaza — make up most of its remaining revenues.

Outside of blood cancers and diseases Celgene receives royalties on sales of ADHD drugs Focalin XR and Ritalin which are licensed to and sold by global drug maker Novartis. (Those drugs have lost sales due to competition from generics.)

Other therapies in the works include CC-122 and CC-220 which are being tested for hematological and solid tumor cancers MS and for neuro-inflammation.

Geographic Reach

The US is Celgene's largest market accounting for about 65% of revenues with Europe accounting for most of the rest of sales. However Celgene is working to expand its global presence. Its products reach customers in more than 50 countries.

In addition to global sales and service locations Celgene operates manufacturing plants in the US (Phoenix) and Switzerland (Boudry and Zofingen) that meet most of its needs though some of the firm's products are made by third-party manufacturers. The company also has sales and research offices in California Kansas Massachusetts New Jersey Texas and Washington DC.

Sales and Marketing

Celgene sells its products through a global direct sales force as well as via independent representatives in select markets (primarily in Latin America). In the US products are distributed primarily to wholesalers and in the case of Revlimid Pomalyst and Thalomid specialty pharmacies (the drugs must be handled under special risk-management programs due to blood clot risks associated with the drugs). Otezla is marketed directly to consumers through print and television advertising.

CVS and McKesson are the company's two largest customers representing more than 10% of sales each.

Financial Performance

Celgene's strategies of making select acquisitions finding new uses for existing drugs and conducting proprietary R&D to keep its pipeline well-stocked seem to be paying off. Celgene has achieved rapidly climbing revenues in recent years as its product offerings have grown. Net income fell 20% in 2015 but has rebounded in subsequent years.

In 2017 revenue increased 16% to $13 billion. Higher sales of Revlamid Otezla and Pomalyst both in the US and abroad helped strengthen the company's earning power. These gains were partially offset however by declines in sales of generic formula azacitidine and Thalomid.

Net income rose 47% to $2.9 billion in 2017. This was largely due to acquisition-related gains made as a result of the discontinuation of trials for GED-0301.

The higher net income plus a positive adjustment to income tax payable led to a 26% increase in operating cash flow which totaled $5.2 billion that year.

Strategy

Key focus areas for Celgene include protein homeostasis immuno-oncology epigenetics and neuro-inflammation and immunology. Though the company has a little breathing room before it loses market exclusivity on most of its products competitors are pushing to release generic versions of Revlimid Celgene's top moneymaker. The firm is working avidly to stay ahead of patent losses by adding or developing new drugs and pipeline candidates. The company has expanded its portfolio through internal development collaborations and acquisitions. It expects to move about 10 novel agents into testing within the next couple of years; Celgene also plans to release data from about 20 phase III trials within that time period.

Celgene often relies heavily on partners to develop drugs but that strategy doesn't always work out. In 2017 Celgene stopped developing GED-0301 (mongersen) for the treatment of Crohn's disease after the drug failed in trials. It had purchased the treatment for $710 million in an R&D deal with Irish firm Nogra Pharma; the agreement called for approval and tiered sales milestones that could have cost the company more than $1 billion more. Celgene is still studying the drug in combination with ozanimod.

Celgene acquired former R&D partner Juno Therapeutics for $9 billion in 2018. That deal gave it full access to Juno's experimental CAR-T therapy JCAR017 (liso-cel) which is expected to win approval for the treatment of lymphoma in 2019. Celgene is betting heavily on the treatment which is the nearest CAR-T asset it has to the market.

The company also has collaboration agreements with Lycera and Nurix among others.

Celgene was hit by some negative press in 2018 when the FDA named it with a handful of other drug makers as possibly blocking access to samples of its drugs to generic drug manufacturers. As the FDA pushes for more generics to be approved in order to lower costs for consumers samples of branded drugs are expected to be made available to other pharmaceuticals. Celgene contends that there are possible side effects to its products in question and that rigorous safety controls are necessary.

Mergers and Acquisitions

In 2018 Celgene bought Juno Therapeutics for $9 billion. Juno specializes in CAR-T therapies for cancer; Celgene has partnered with firms including Juno toward the development of CAR-T treatments. The acquisition gave Celgene access to Juno's lead asset JCAR017 which is expected to gain approval for the treatment of lymphoma in 2019.

Also in 2018 the company bought the privately held Impact Biomedicines in a deal that with milestone payments could be worth as much as $7 billion. The company paid $1.1 billion upfront to gain access to fedratinib Impact's experimental blood cancer treatment.

In early 2017 Celgene bought Delinia a private biotech with a focus on developing novel therapeutics for autoimmune diseases for an initial payment of $300 million plus a potential $475 million in milestone payments.

Company Background

Celgene was founded in 1986 as a spinoff entity; it was formerly part of Celanese Corporation.

EXECUTIVES

Evp And Cfo, Peter N. Kellogg, age 62, $845,667 total compensation

Evp General Counsel And Corporate Secretary, Gerald F. Masoudi, age 50

President And Coo, Scott A. Smith, age 56, $691,667 total compensation

Evp And President Research And Early Development, S.J. Rupert Vessey, $673,141 total compensation

Ceo And Director, Mark J. Alles, age 59, $1,062,583 total compensation

President Global Inflammation And Immunology (i&i) Franchise, Terrie Curran

President Hematology & Oncology, Nadim Ahmed

Vp Clinical Development And Medical Affairs Asia Pacific, Kevin Lynch

Senior Vice President Of Research And Development, Garth McGrath

Vice President Regulatory Policy And Strategy, Florence Houn

Vice President Chief Compliance Officer, Gabriel Flores

National Account Manager, Jeff Presson

Executive Vice President, Beatriz C Mateos

Vice President, Julie Mathew

Vice President And Chief Legal Counsel, Maria E Pasquale

Vice President Human Resources, Dorothea Klein

Vice President Clinical Pharmacology, Maria Palmisano

Vice President Corporate Communications, William Westlin

Vice President Of Oncology And Experimental Therap, Peter Worland

Vice President Of Clinical Trial Operations, Patricia Moenaert

Vice President, Robert Murdock

Vice President Information Technology, Xiao-ping Dai

Vice President Regulatory Affairs Emea, Patricia Pallier

Vice President Clinical Research And Development, Patricia Rohane

National Account Manager, Dave Orlando

Medical Director, Giovanni De Crescenzo

Medical Director, Alexander Bliev

Vice President, Stefan Gluck

Medical Director, Christina Ornauer

Vp Corporate Strategy, Katherine Kalin

Vice President Lead Counsel Inflammation And Immunology Franchise, Jill Andersen

Vice President Biotherapeutics, Ho Cho

National Account Manager Managed Care Specialty Pharmacy, Scott Lukasek

Corporate Vp Investor Relations, Patrick Flanigan Iii

Vice President Global Head Of Regulatory Affairs Inflammation And Immunology, Matthew Lamb

Chairman, Robert J. (Bob) Hugin, age 63

Ceo And Director, Mark J. Alles, age 59

Board Member, Stacy Deserio

Assistant Treasurer, Michael Bradley

Auditors: KPMG LLP

LOCATIONS

HQ: Celgene Corp
86 Morris Avenue, Summit, NJ 07901
Phone: 908 673-9000
Web: www.celgene.com

2017 Sales

	$ mil.	% of total
U.S.	8,324	64
Europe	3,327	26
Other regions	1,352	10
Total	13,003	100

PRODUCTS/OPERATIONS

2017 Sales

Products	$ mil.	% of total
Revlimid	8,187	63
Pomalyst/Imnovid	1,614	12
Otezla	1,279	10
Abraxane	992	8
Vidaza	628	5
Thalomid	132	1
Istodax	76	1
Azacitidine for injection	36	-
Idhifa	20	-
Other	9	-
Other	30	-
Total	**13,003**	**100**

Selected Products

Approved
  Abraxane (breast cancer treatment)
  Istodax (cancer treatment gained through Gloucester buy)
  Revlimid (multiple myeloma myelodysplastic syndromes)
  Pomalyst (multiple myeloma)
  Thalomid (complications from leprosy multiple myeloma)
  Vidaza (myelodysplastic syndromes)

COMPETITORS

AbbVie	Merck
Amgen	Millennium: The Takeda
AstraZeneca	Oncology Company
Biogen	Novartis
Bristol-Myers Squibb	Pfizer
Eisai	Roche Holding
Eli Lilly	Sanofi
Gilead Sciences	UCB
Johnson & Johnson	

HISTORICAL FINANCIALS

Company Type: Public

Income Statement

FYE: December 31

	REVENUE ($ mil.)	NET INCOME ($ mil.)	NET PROFIT MARGIN	EMPLOYEES
12/17	13,003	2,940	22.6%	7,467
12/16	11,229	1,999	17.8%	7,132
12/15	9,256	1,602	17.3%	6,971
12/14	7,670	1,999	26.1%	6,012
12/13	6,493	1,449	22.3%	5,100
Annual Growth	**19.0%**	**19.3%**	**—**	**10.0%**

2017 Year-End Financials

Debt ratio: 52.55%
Return on equity: 43.49%
Cash ($ mil.): 7,013
Current ratio: 4.99
Long-term debt ($ mil.): 15,838

No. of shares (mil.): 759
Dividends
Yield: —
Payout: —
Market value ($ mil.): 79,241

	STOCK PRICE ($) FY Close	P/E High/Low	PER SHARE ($) Earnings	Dividends	Book Value
12/17	104.36	39 26	3.64	0.00	9.11
12/16	115.75	48 37	2.49	0.00	8.48
12/15	119.76	69 52	1.94	0.00	7.52
12/14	111.86	69 33	2.39	0.00	8.15
12/13	168.97	98 45	1.69	0.00	6.82
Annual Growth	**(11.3%)**	**— —**	**21.2%**	**—**	**7.5%**

Centene Corp

Centene provides managed care and related services in more than a dozen states under names such as Managed Health Services (Wisconsin and Indiana) Superior HealthPlan (Texas) and Buckeye Community Health Plan (Ohio). Centene provides services to some 12.3 million low-income elderly and disabled people receiving benefits from programs including Medicaid Supplemental Security Income (SSI) and state Children's Health Insurance Program (CHIP). Centene also offers specialty services in areas such as behavioral health (through Cenpatico) vision benefits (OptiCare) and pharmacy benefits management (US Script).

Operations

Centene operates in two primary segments: Managed Care and Specialty Services.

The Managed Care segment provides services through Medicaid CHIP Long-Term Services and Supports (LTSS) LTC (long-term care) foster care and ABD (aged blind and disabled) programs. Centene's Medicaid contracts account for about 80% of total revenues. California accounts for about a fifth of revenues.

The Specialty Services segment is composed of companies offering a range of health care services and products to state programs health care organizations correctional facilities employer groups and other organizations. Offerings include telehealth advisory case management (CaseNet) and pharmacy services. Centene's Celtic Insurance subsidiary specializes in providing low-cost consumer-directed insurance policies to uninsured customers nationwide and its Bridgeway Health Solutions provides long-term care policies in select territories.

Geographic Reach

Centene serves hospitals and care facilities in more than 25 states including Arizona California Florida Louisiana and Texas. California and Texas are its two largest markets.

Sales and Marketing

Most of Centene's revenue comes under contract or subcontract with state Medicaid managed care programs. Its largest markets are California and Texas.

Financial Performance

Centene's revenue and net income have been rising significantly for the past five years as the company acquires other firms adds and retains state contracts and enters new business areas. Similarly net income has risen over the past few years.

Revenue grew 19% to $48.4 billion in 2017. The company's 2016 acquisition of Health Net boosted sales that year. Overall managed care membership increased 7% and premiums increased 22%. The company also secured numerous contracts with state corrections departments.

With the higher revenue net income rose 47% to $828 million in 2017. An increase in investment income and a decrease in income tax expenses also helped the bottom line.

The company ended 2017 with $4.1 billion in cash and cash equivalents a 4% increase from what it had at the beginning of the year. This was largely due to the higher earnings. Operating activities provided $1.5 billion in cash while investing activities (system enhancements and headquarters expansion) used $1.3 billion. Financing activities used another $82 million.

Strategy

Centene's primary growth strategies are to enter new markets and expand in existing markets via acquisitions and by gaining new contracts with state Medicaid agencies. The company is benefiting from the growing number of mandated managed care plans in states that are looking to control Medicaid spending. Since 2017 the firm has expanded its Medicare Advantage operations into more than a dozen existing states.

In addition to geographic expansion the company looks to grow its membership by adding new services in its existing state markets such as small business health plans and low-income individual plans. Centene has also done well in the challenging Affordable Care Act (ACA) exchange markets. It plans to enter the ACA markets in Pennsylvania North Carolina South Carolina and Tennessee in 2019.

The firm evaluates opportunities to grow in new fields such as health-related information technology and non-Medicaid health plans. It has a joint venture with MHM Services named Centurion which operates in the correctional facility managed care market; the company now plans to buy MHM and take full ownership of the Centurion venture.

Centene also occasionally divests or exits operations in smaller service areas to focus on its core growth regions. For example it exited the Arizona individual preferred provider organization (PPO) business in early 2017. The company has also lost certain contracts or market share where insurers have joined the Medicaid program.

Mergers and Acquisitions

Centene bought not-for-profit insurer Fidelis Care for $3.75 billion in mid-2018. Fidelis offers Medicaid CHIP and other affordable coverage to some 1.6 million individuals. Through that deal the company gained entry to the New York market.

In 2018 Centene agreed to buy MHM Services which specializes in providing health care to correctional systems and other government agencies. The deal includes MHM's 49% stake in the companies' Centurion joint venture which provides clinical programs for correctional systems. By investing in MHM Centene will have a more expansive presence in the correctional system health care market.

Also that year the company agreed to acquire Community Medical Holdings (dba Community Medical Group or CMG) an at-risk primary care provider serving more than 70000 patients in the Miami area. CMG provides health care and social services to Medicaid Medicare Advantage and Health Insurance Marketplace recipients. Centene is exploring the possibility of expanding CMG's business model into other areas.

In a similar move Centene acquired insurer Health Net in a $6.3 billion deal in 2016. That acquisition also broadened its presence in the Medicare Advantage and Medicaid programs. After that deal Centene became the nation's largest Medicaid Managed Care organization.

EXECUTIVES

Svp Products, Kevin J. Counihan

President And Coo, Cynthia J. (Cindy) Brinkley, age 58, $650,000 total compensation

Chairman And Ceo, Michael F. Neidorff, age 75, $1,500,000 total compensation

Evp Mergers & Acquisitions And Chief Strategy Officer, Jesse N. Hunter, age 42, $650,000 total compensation

President And Ceo Superior Healthplan, Christopher D. Bowers, age 62

Evp General Counsel And Secretary, Keith H. Williamson, age 65, $600,000 total compensation

Evp Cfo And Treasurer, Jeffrey A Schwaneke, age 43, $632,671 total compensation

Evp And Cio, Mark J. Brooks, age 48

Vice President Media Affairs, Deanne Lane

Senior Vice President Operations, Patricia Darnley

Vice President Sales Marketing And Business Development, Kristine Ziegler
Vice President Of Finance, Trip Peeples
Corporate Vice President Business Development, Wade Rakes
Senior Vice President Patient Services, Susan Ekvall
Vice President And Director, Marian Williams
Vice President And Director, Tiffany Smith
Vice President And Director, Sharon Casey
Vice President Health Plan Accounting, Darren Meyer
Vice President Operations, D Lewis
Vice President Member And Provider Solutions, Scott Ireland
Senior Vice President Individual Business, Anand Shukla
Senior Vice President Operations (comp Care Progs), Ceseley Rollins
Medical Director, David Gilchrist
Vice President Of Business Development, Stacey Hull
Vice President Internal Audit, Shannon Bagley
Senior Vice President Business Development, Debra Cooper
Vice President Of Human Resour, Jalie Cohen
Vice President Of Human Resources, Mary-Katherine Kutac
Senior Vice President Of Clinical Operations, Patricia Murray
Vice President Of Human Resources, Stephanie Hall
Vice President Of Payment Innovation, Ananth Lalithakumar
Vice President And Director, Karen Dockerty
Vice President Of Compliance And Regulatory Affairs, Cheyenne Ross
Vice President And Director, Carolyn Thomas
Vice President Of Business Operation, Ed Gallegos
Senior Vice President And Chief Communications Officer, Marcela Manjarrez-Williams
Vice President Pharmacy Operations, Justin Weiss
Senior Vice President, Edmund Kroll
Vice President Facility Management And Construction, Andrea Cruce
Vice President Of Medical Affairs, Ronald Charles
Medical Director, Randy Tompkins
Executive Vice President, Mark Eggert
Vice President Compliance, Jeff Torres
Vice President Product Solutions, Lisa McClellan
Vice President Customer Service, Rodney Long
Vp It Envolve Pharmacy Solutions, Matt Merlo
Vice President Marketing, John Howell
Director Of Pharmacy Operations, Martha Exton
Vice President Pharmacy Operations Federal Programs, Jeff Borowiecki
Senior Vice President Hoalth Services, Debra Smyers
Vice President Of Finance, Nitin Jain
Evp Sales And Account Management Envolve Pharmacy Solutions, Carmen Fontanez
Vice President Operations And Implementations Cenpatico Behavioral Health, McKensie DeRocher
Vice President Information Technology Operations Strategy And Business Development, Brian Holman
Senior Vice President And Chief Security Risk Officer, Louis Desorbo
Senior Vice President Of Medical Affairs, Marcus Wallace
Vice President Product Development Hemophilia Acariahealth, Charles Signorino
Senior Vice President Strategic Initiatives Nurtur Health, Bryan Mullen
Vp Clinical Pharmacy Solutions Envolve Pharmacy Solutions, Laurie Amirpoor
Senior Vice President Finance Us Script, Karen Rinehart
Vp Business Knowledge And Informatics, Sigal Dor

Vice President Multi Product Sales, Jason Patchen
Vp Business Intelligence Strategy Cenpatico Behavioral Health, Ryan Gregory
Vp Data Analytics Cenpatico, Michael Grover
Vice President Compliance And Government Affairs, Terrica Miller
Vice President Government Affairs And Marketing, Eric Poklar
Vice President Innovation And Commercialization, Fredrik Engelhardt
Vice President Medical Management Um Superior Health Plan, Janice Wierschke
Vp Pharma Relations And Business Development Acariahealth, Steve Granzyk
Vice President Finance Specialist Co, Sarah Baiocchi
Vice President, Joyce Larkln
Chairman And Ceo, Michael F. Neidorff, age 75
Evp General Counsel And Secretary, Keith H. Williamson, age 65
Evp Cfo And Treasurer, Jeffrey A Schwaneke, age 43
Auditors: KPMG LLP

LOCATIONS

HQ: Centene Corp
7700 Forsyth Boulevard, St. Louis, MO 63105
Phone: 314 725-4477   Fax: 314 725-5180
Web: www.centene.com

PRODUCTS/OPERATIONS

2017 Sales

	$ mil.	% of total
Premiums	43,353	89
Premium tax & health insurer fee	2,762	6
Service	2,267	5
Total	48,382	100

2017 Sales by Segment

	$ mil.	% of total
Managed Care	45,842	79
Specialty Services	12,055	21
Adjustments	(9515)	-
Total	48,382	100

COMPETITORS

AMERIGROUP	Kaiser Foundation
Aetna	Health Plan
Anthem	Molina Healthcare
Blue Cross and Blue	Scott & White Health
Shield of Texas	Plan
CIGNA	UnitedHealth Group
Humana	WellCare Health Plans

HISTORICAL FINANCIALS
Company Type: Public

Income Statement
FYE: December 31

	REVENUE ($ mil.)	NET INCOME ($ mil.)	NET PROFIT MARGIN	EMPLOYEES
12/17	48,382	828	1.7%	33,700
12/16	40,607	562	1.4%	30,500
12/15	22,760	355	1.6%	18,200
12/14	16,560	271	1.6%	13,400
12/13	10,863	165	1.5%	8,800
Annual Growth	45.3%	49.6%	—	39.9%

2017 Year-End Financials

Debt ratio: 21.50%
Return on equity: 12.99%
Cash ($ mil.): 4,072
Current ratio: 0.93
Long-term debt ($ mil.): 4,695

No. of shares (mil.): 346
Dividends
Yield: —
Payout: —
Market value ($ mil.): 34,993

STOCK PRICE ($) FY Close	P/E High/Low		PER SHARE ($) Earnings	Dividends	Book Value
12/17	100.88	43 24	2.35	0.00	19.75
12/16	56.51	43 29	1.72	0.00	17.14
12/15	65.81	81 35	1.44	0.00	8.96
12/14	103.85	92 48	1.13	0.00	7.36
12/13	58.95	87 54	0.74	0.00	5.58
Annual Growth	14.4%	— —	33.6%	—	37.2%

CenterPoint Energy Resources Corp.

EXECUTIVES

Chb-pres-ceo, Scott M Prochazka
Auditors: DELOITTE & TOUCHE LLP

LOCATIONS

HQ: CenterPoint Energy Resources Corp.
1111 Louisiana, Houston, TX 77002
Phone: 713 207-1111
Web: www.centerpointenergy.com

HISTORICAL FINANCIALS
Company Type: Public

Income Statement
FYE: December 31

	REVENUE ($ mil.)	NET INCOME ($ mil.)	NET PROFIT MARGIN	EMPLOYEES
12/17	6,603	745	11.3%	3,613
12/16	4,454	245	5.5%	3,467
12/15	4,527	(912)	—	3,421
12/14	6,367	323	5.1%	4,581
12/13	5,522	64	1.2%	4,714
Annual Growth	4.6%	84.7%	—	(6.4%)

2017 Year-End Financials

Debt ratio: 24.68%
Return on equity: 24.71%
Cash ($ mil.): 12
Current ratio: 0.96
Long-term debt ($ mil.): 2,457

No. of shares (mil.): 0
Dividends
Yield: —
Payout: 80.6%
Market value ($ mil.): —

CenterPoint Energy, Inc

CenterPoint Energy makes a point of selling energy through power and gas distribution utilities and natural gas pipeline gathering and marketing operations. CenterPoint Energy's regulated utilities distribute natural gas to nearly 3.5 million customers in six US states and electricity to more than 2.4 million customers on the Texas Gulf Coast. The company's main stomping ground is Texas where it has regulated power distribution operations through subsidiary CenterPoint Energy Houston Electric. CenterPoint Energy operates more than 53500 miles of power distribution lines and some 74000 miles of gas distribution mains.

HISTORY

CenterPoint Energy's earliest predecessor Houston Electric Lighting and Power was formed in 1882 by a group including Emanuel Raphael cashier at Houston Savings Bank and Mayor William Baker. In 1901 General Electric's financial arm United Electric Securities Company took control of the utility which became Houston Lighting & Power (HL&P). United Electric sold HL&P five years later; by 1922 HL&P ended up in the arms of National Power & Light Company (NP&L) a subsidiary of Electric Bond & Share (a public utility holding company that had been spun off by General Electric).

In 1942 NP&L was forced to sell HL&P in order to comply with the 1935 Public Utility Holding Company Act. As the oil industry boomed in Houston after WWII so did HL&P.

HL&P became the managing partner in a venture to build a nuclear plant on the Texas Gulf Coast in 1973. Construction on the South Texas Project with partners Central Power and Light and the cities of Austin and San Antonio began in 1975. In 1976 Houston Industries (HI) was formed as the holding company for HL&P.

By 1980 the nuke was four years behind schedule and over budget. HL&P and its partners sued construction firm Brown & Root in 1982 and received a $700 million settlement in 1985. (The City of Austin also sued HL&P for damages but lost.) The nuke was finally brought online in 1988 with the final cost estimated at $5.8 billion.

Meanwhile HI diversified into cable TV in 1986 by creating Enrcom (later Paragon Communications) through a venture with Time Inc. Two years later it bought the US cable interests of Canada's Rogers Communications. HI left the cable business in 1995 selling out to Time Warner.

Developing Latin fever HI joined a consortium that bought 51% of Argentinean electric company EDELAP in 1992. (However in 1998 HI sold its stake to AES.) On a roll HI acquired 90% of Argentina's electric utility EDESE (1995); joined a consortium that won a controlling stake in Light a Brazilian electric utility (1996); bought a stake in Colombian electric utility EPSA (1997); and bought interests in three electric utilities in El Salvador (1998). It also won a permit to develop and operate a natural gas system in Mexico (1998).

Back in the US HI acquired gas dealer NorAm for $2.5 billion in 1997. The next year it bought five generating plants in California from Edison International and laid plans to build merchant plants in Arizona (near Phoenix) Illinois Nevada (near Las Vegas in partnership with Sempra Energy) and Rhode Island. Overseas HI finished a power plant in India in 1998. It also bought a 65% interest in Colombian electric utilities Electricaribe and Electrocosta; EPSA bought about 55% of CET in Colombia and Light bought about 75% of Metropolitana (SA?o Paulo Brazil).

In 1999 HI became Reliant Energy and HL&P became Reliant Energy HL&P. That year the company bought a 52% stake in Dutch power generation firm UNA; it bought the remaining 48% the next year. Also in 2000 Reliant Energy paid Sithe Energies (now a part of Dynegy) $2.1 billion for 21 power plants in the mid-Atlantic states. It sold its operations in Brazil Colombia and El Salvador that year and transferred all of its nonregulated operations to subsidiary Reliant Resources. Reliant Energy also announced plans to spin off Reliant Resources that year.

Reliant Energy netted about $1.7 billion in 2001 from the sale to the public of nearly 20% of Reliant Resou

EXECUTIVES

Evp And President Electric Division, Tracy B. Bridge, age 59, $481,250 total compensation
President Ceo And Director, Scott M. Prochazka, age 51, $996,525 total compensation

Svp Electric Utility Business, Kenneth M. Mercado
Svp Gas Operations, Richard A. (Rick) Zapalac
Evp And Cfo, William D. (Bill) Rogers, age 57, $485,000 total compensation
Svp Natural Gas Distribution, Scott E. Doyle
Svp Energy Services, Joseph J. (Joe) Vortherms
Vice President Marketing, Carol Burchfield
Chairman, Milton Carroll, age 67
President Ceo And Director, Scott M. Prochazka, age 51
Auditors: DELOITTE & TOUCHE LLP

LOCATIONS

HQ: CenterPoint Energy, Inc
  1111 Louisiana, Houston, TX 77002
Phone: 713 207-1111
Web: www.centerpointenergy.com

PRODUCTS/OPERATIONS

2017 Sales

	$ mil.	% of total
Retail gas	3,634	37
Electric delivery	2,997	31
Wholesale gas	2,811	29
Energy products & services	1,432	3
Gas transportation & processing	(29)	-
Total	**9,614**	**100**

2017 Sales

	$ mil.	% of total
Energy Services	3,997	42
Electric Transmission & Distribution	2,997	31
Natural Gas Distribution	2,606	27
Other	(14)	-
Total	**9,614**	**100**

COMPETITORS

AEP	Exelon
AEP Texas Central	Koch Industries Inc.
AEP Texas North	Mississippi Power
Ameren	NextEra Energy
Avista	OGE Energy
CMS Energy	ONEOK
Cleco	Progress Energy
Constellation Energy	Southern Company
Group	Southwestern Electric
Dominion Energy	Power
Duke Energy	Southwestern Energy
Energy Future	Williams Companies
Entergy	Xcel Energy

HISTORICAL FINANCIALS

Company Type: Public

Income Statement   FYE: December 31

	REVENUE ($ mil.)	NET INCOME ($ mil.)	NET PROFIT MARGIN	EMPLOYEES
12/17	9,614	1,792	18.6%	7,977
12/16	7,528	432	5.7%	7,727
12/15	7,386	(692)	—	7,505
12/14	9,226	611	6.6%	8,540
12/13	8,106	311	3.8%	8,591
Annual Growth	**4.4%**	**54.9%**	**—**	**(1.8%)**

2017 Year-End Financials

Debt ratio: 38.88%
Return on equity: 43.99%
Cash ($ mil.): 260
Current ratio: 1.11
Long-term debt ($ mil.): 8,195

No. of shares (mil.): 431
Dividends
  Yield: 0.0%
  Payout: 25.9%
Market value ($ mil.): 12,224

	STOCK PRICE ($) FY Close	P/E High/Low		PER SHARE ($) Earnings	Dividends	Book Value
12/17	28.36	7	6	4.13	1.07	10.88
12/16	24.64	25	17	1.00	1.03	8.03
12/15	18.36	—	—	(1.61)	0.99	8.05
12/14	23.43	18	15	1.42	0.95	10.58
12/13	23.18	34	26	0.72	0.83	10.09
Annual Growth	**5.2%**	**—**	**—**	**54.8%**	**6.6%**	**1.9%**

CenterState Bank Corp

CenterState Banks is the holding company for CenterState Bank of Florida which serves the Sunshine State through about 60 branches. The bank offers standard deposit products such as checking and savings accounts money market accounts and CDs. Real estate loans primarily residential and commercial mortgages make up 85% of the company's loan portfolio while the rest is made up of business loans and consumer loans. The bank's correspondent division provides bond securities accounting and loans to small and mid-sized banks across the Southeast and Texas. It also sells mutual funds annuities and other investment products.

Operations

About 65% of CenterState Banks' total revenue came from loan interest in 2014 while another 10% came from interest on its investment securities. The rest of the bank's revenue came form correspondent banking capital markets revenue and related revenue (11%) deposit account service charges (5%) debit/ATM and merchant card fees (3%) wealth management fees (2%) and other miscellaneous income sources. The company had a staff of 785 employees by the end of 2014.

Geographic Reach

CenterState has nearly 60 branches across 20 counties in central southeast and northeast Florida. Its loan production offices are in Tampa Gainesville Crystal River and Ft. Meyers.

Sales and Marketing

CenterState offers consumer and commercial banking services to individuals businesses and industries across Florida.

Financial Performance

The company has struggled to consistently grow its revenues in recent years due to shrinking interest margins on loans amidst the low-interest environment. Its profits however have been rising thanks to declining loan loss provisions as its loan portfolio's credit quality has improved with higher property valuations in the strengthened economy.

CenterState had a breakout year in 2014 however with its revenue jumping 22% to $164.5 million thanks to higher interest income stemming from new loan business from its acquisitions of First Southern Bancorp and Gulfstream Bancshares during the year.

Higher revenue and stable costs in 2014 also drove the bank's net income higher by 6% to a record $12.96 million. CenterState's operating cash levels plummeted by 90% to $1.4 million after adjusting its earnings for non-cash items mostly related to the net proceeds from its trading securities sales.

Strategy

CenterState Banks continues to seek out additional acquisition opportunities to boost its loan and deposit business and expand into more markets across Florida. To this end the bank's 2014 acquisitions extended its reach into Broward Palm Beach and Martin counties for the first time while adding more than $1.3 billion in new deposits and over $600 million in new loan business to its books.

Struggling to grow its revenues the bank has also worked to become more efficient and profitable through selective branch closures. During 2014 the company closed seven smaller branches and a standalone drive-thru facility to free up resources for more profitable bank acquisitions.

Mergers and Acquisitions

CenterState is buying Platinum Bank Holding Company parent company of Platinum Bank for approximately $83.9 million. The acquisition will add seven banking branches in the Tampa-St. Petersburg-Clearwater and Lakeland-Winter Haven areas. It will also add some $584 million in assets.

In June 2014 CenterState purchased First Southern Bancorp which expanded its market reach into Broward County after adding a net of seven new branches. The deal also added some $600 million in new loan assets and $853 million in deposits.

In January 2014 the company expanded into Palm Beach and Martin counties after buying Gulfstream Bancshares and its four branches with $479 million in deposits.

EXECUTIVES

Svp And Cfo, James J. Antal, age 67, $312,750 total compensation
Senior Vice President, Rick Alspaugh
President Ceo And Director Centerstate Banks Inc. And Centerstate Bank Of Florida, John Corbett, age 49, $420,250 total compensation
Corporate Chief Risk Officer, Daniel E. Bockhorst, $217,500 total compensation
Treasurer, Stephen Young, $278,333 total compensation
First Vice President Business Development, Chris Wright
Assistant Vice President Residential Loan Operations Manager, Becky Chiasson
Vice President Retail Service Leader, Annette Fortunato-diaz
Senior Vice President And Commercial Lending Officer, Bill Daniels
Assistant Vice President Merchant Services Divison, Deborah Joyce
Assistant Vice President Business Analyst Ii, Chante Carlson
First Vice President, Stacey A Dunn
Senior Vice President And Chief Operations Officer, Stacy Byrd
Assistant Vice President, Mary Young
Vice President Retail Market Manager, Bretta Christakos
Assistant Vice President Human Resources Employee Relations Officer, Raquel Morales
Senior Vice President, Mark Tucker
Assistant Vice President Project Manager, Lexie Williams
Vice President, Gail Copa
First Vice President, Richard Skopick
Vice President Commercial Lender, Winn Keeton
Senior Vice President Commercial Banking, Garry Lubi
Senior Vice President Community President, Mark Stevens
Vice President, Elfa Mora
First Vice President Prepaid Cards Division, Bruce Davidson
Vice President Commercial Lender, Mike Clanton
Assistant Vice President And Fed Funds Trader, Rebecca Henderson
Assistant Vice President Branch Manager, Denise Tarafa
Chairman, Ernest S. (Ernie) Pinner, age 70
President Ceo And Director Centerstate Banks Inc. And Centerstate Bank Of Florida, John Corbett, age 49
Auditors: Crowe Horwath LLP

LOCATIONS

HQ: CenterState Bank Corp
1101 First Street South, Suite 202, Winter Haven, FL 33880
Phone: 863 293-4710
Web: www.centerstatebanks.com

PRODUCTS/OPERATIONS

2011 Sales

	$ mil.	% of total
Interest		
Loans	65	36
Investment securities available for sale	15	9
Other	0	-
Noninterest		
Bargain purchase gain	57	31
Correspondent banking & bond sales	24	13
Service charges on deposit accounts	6	3
Net gain on sale of securities	3	2
Other	10	6
Total	**184**	**100**

COMPETITORS

BB&T	Regions Financial
BBX Capital	Seacoast Banking
Bank of America	SunTrust
Fifth Third	Wells Fargo
JPMorgan Chase	

HISTORICAL FINANCIALS

Company Type: Public

Income Statement

FYE: December 31

	ASSETS ($ mil.)	NET INCOME ($ mil.)	INCOME AS % OF ASSETS	EMPLOYEES
12/17	7,123	55	0.8%	1,200
12/16	5,078	42	0.8%	952
12/15	4,022	39	1.0%	784
12/14	3,776	12	0.3%	785
12/13	2,415	12	0.5%	693
Annual Growth	**31.0%**	**46.1%**	—	**14.7%**

2017 Year-End Financials

Debt ratio: 2.82%
Return on equity: 7.66%
Cash ($ mil.): 280
Current ratio: —
Long-term debt ($ mil.): —

No. of shares (mil.): 60
Dividends
  Yield: 0.0%
  Payout: 25.2%
Market value ($ mil.): 1,548

	STOCK PRICE ($) FY Close	P/E High/Low	PER SHARE ($) Earnings	Dividends	Book Value
12/17	25.73	29 23	0.95	0.24	15.04
12/16	25.17	29 15	0.88	0.16	11.47
12/15	15.65	19 13	0.85	0.07	10.79
12/14	11.91	37 31	0.31	0.04	9.98
12/13	10.15	26 18	0.41	0.04	9.08
Annual Growth	**26.2%**	— —	**23.4%**	**56.5%**	**13.4%**

Central Pacific Financial Corp

When in the Central Pacific do as the islanders do. This may include doing business with Central Pacific Financial the holding company for Central Pacific Bank which operates more than 35 branch locations and 110 ATMs across the Hawaiian Islands. Targeting individuals and local businesses the $5 billion bank provides such standard retail banking products as checking and savings accounts money market accounts and CDs. About 70% of the bank's loan portfolio is made up of commercial real estate loans residential mortgages and construction loans though it also provides business and consumer loans.

Operations

Central Pacific Financial operates through two core segments. The Banking Operations segment provides construction and real estate development loans commercial loans residential mortgage loans consumer loans trust services retail brokerage services and traditional banking products and services. The Treasury segment manages the company's investment securities portfolio and wholesale funding activities.

Boasting total assets of $5 billion Central Pacific Bank ranked as the fourth-largest bank by deposits in the state of Hawaii in 2014. The bank makes nearly 60% of its total revenue from interest and fees on loans and leases and nearly 20% from interest and dividends on its investment securities. It makes about 10% on service charges on deposit accounts and other charges and fees while the small remainder of its revenue comes from a mix of loan servicing fees gains on sales of residential loans and foreclosed assets income from fiduciary activities and income from bank-owned life insurance.

Central Pacific Financial's other wholly-owned subsidiaries include CPB Capital Trust II; CPB Statutory Trust III; CPB Capital Trust IV; and CPB Statutory Trust V. Central Pacific Bank holds 50% stakes in Pacific Access Mortgage Gentry HomeLoans and Island Pacific HomeLoans.

Geographic Reach

Honolulu-based Central Pacific boasts more than 35 branches and 110 ATMs across Hawaii. The island of Oahu holds 28 branches while the Maui Hawaii and Kauai islands host the remaining branches.

Sales and Marketing

Central Pacific Financial spent $2.34 million on advertising in 2014 compared to $2.67 million and $3.52 million in 2013 and 2012 respectively.

Financial Performance

Central Pacific Financial's revenue performance has been mixed in recent years. Its mortgage banking business has suffered from lower residential mortgage origination volumes while its loan business has been growing at a healthy clip thanks to higher loan balances from added assets.

Following two years of modest top-line growth driven by growing loan business Central Pacific's revenue dipped by 1% to $193.63 million in 2014 as it collected lower net gains on sales of foreclosed assets and lower net gains on sales of residential mortgage loans. The bank's interest income from loans continued to grow however as the bank added more than $403 million in new loan assets.

Central Pacific's net income declined by 76% to $40.45 million in 2014 mostly because in 2013 the bank received a $112.25 million income tax benefit as it reversed a significant portion of its valuation allowance for its doubtful accounts from 2009. Beyond this non-recurring event the bank managed to cut its salaries and employee benefit expenses by 22% saving about $8 million for the year.

The bank's operating cash also fell by 15% during the year to $71.43 million primarily due to lower cash earnings.

Strategy

Central Pacific reiterated in 2015 that its strategy is to continue growing its loan business particularly focusing on providing more commercial loans and mortgages as well as construction loans and leases to small and mid-sized companies business professionals and real estate developers. Though its residential mortgage and consumer loans made up just 25% of its loan portfolio that year the bank will also continue its focus on extended those loans to more local homebuyers and individuals.

The bank's key to drumming up its commercial loan business has traditionally come from its community-oriented commercial real estate team and banking officers which are able to develop deep relationships with local communities and industries that they serve.

EXECUTIVES

President And Ceo, A. Catherine Ngo, age 58, $345,833 total compensation
Chairman, John C. Dean, age 71, $265,625 total compensation
Svp And Chief Marketing Officer Central Pacific Financial Corp. And Central Pacific Bank, Wayne H. Kirihara
Interim Vice Chairman And Coo, Denis K. Isono, age 67, $244,792 total compensation
Evp And Cio Central Pacific Financial Corp. And Central Pacific Bank, Lee Y. Moriwaki, age 59, $205,625 total compensation
Evp Cfo And Treasurer, David S. Morimoto, age 50, $201,208 total compensation
Evp Chief Legal Officer And Risk Management Division Manager Central Pacific Financial Corp. And Central Pacific Bank, K.C. (Glenn) Ching, age 59
Evp Community Banking Division Manager Central Pacific Financial Corp. And Central Pacific Bank, David W. Hudson, age 59, $220,000 total compensation
Svp And Commercial Real Estate Lending Division Manager Central Pacific Financial Corp. And Central Pacific Bank, Arnold D. Martines, age 53
Vice President Administration, Dayna Matsumoto
Assistant Vice President And Commercial Branch Manager, Jolene Kiyono
Vice President And Senior Commercial Banking Officer, Patrick Matsumoto
Vice President And Commercial Banking Officer, Chong Pak
Assistant Vice President And Branch Manager, Sharlene Chae
Senior Vice President, John Taira
Vice President And Commercial Real Estate Officer, Keith Wakamura
Vice President, Michael Waring
Vice President And Manager Call Center, Norman Nakasone
Vice President And Branch Manager, Miyuki Almario
Vice President And Manager Information Security Department, Emanuel Edmondson
Chairman, John C. Dean, age 71
Interim Vice Chairman And Coo, Denis K. Isono, age 67
Evp Cfo And Treasurer, David S. Morimoto, age 50
Board Member, Paul J Kosasa
Board Member, Wayne Kamitaki
Auditors: Crowe Horwath LLP

LOCATIONS

HQ: Central Pacific Financial Corp
220 South King Street, Honolulu, HI 96813
Phone: 808 544-0500   **Fax:** 808 531-2875
Web: www.centralpacificbank.com

PRODUCTS/OPERATIONS

2014 Sales

	$ mil.	% of total
Interest income		
Loans and leases	112	58
Securities	37	19
Non-interest income		
Other service charges and fees	11	6
Service Charges on deposit accounts	8	4
Loan Servicing fees	5	3
Others	18	10
Total	**193**	**100**

COMPETITORS

American Savings Bank	Mitsubishi UFJ
Bank of Hawaii	Financial Group
First Hawaiian	Territorial Bancorp

HISTORICAL FINANCIALS

Company Type: Public

Income Statement

FYE: December 31

	ASSETS ($ mil.)	NET INCOME ($ mil.)	INCOME AS % OF ASSETS	EMPLOYEES
12/17	5,623	41	0.7%	838
12/16	5,384	46	0.9%	837
12/15	5,131	45	0.9%	876
12/14	4,852	40	0.8%	841
12/13	4,741	172	3.6%	903
Annual Growth	4.4%	(30.0%)	—	(1.9%)

2017 Year-End Financials

Debt ratio: 1.65%
Return on equity: 8.20%
Cash ($ mil.): 82
Current ratio: —
Long-term debt ($ mil.): —

No. of shares (mil.): 30
Dividends
Yield: 0.0%
Payout: 52.2%
Market value ($ mil.): 896

	STOCK PRICE ($) FY Close	P/E High/Low		PER SHARE ($) Earnings	Dividends	Book Value
12/17	29.83	24	20	1.34	0.70	16.65
12/16	31.42	21	12	1.50	0.60	16.39
12/15	22.02	18	13	1.40	0.82	15.77
12/14	21.50	20	16	1.07	0.36	16.12
12/13	20.08	5	4	4.07	0.16	15.68
Annual Growth	10.4%	—	—	(24.3%)	44.6%	1.5%

Central Valley Community Bancorp

EXECUTIVES

Vice President Operations, Teresa Gilio
Vice President Cash Management Officer, Evey Amado
Vice President And Human Resources Director, Marci Madsen
Vice President And Compliance Officer, Denise Jereb
Vice President, Debra Walker
Vice President Sales, Shannon Reinard
Vice President Commercial Loan, Robert Walker
Vice President Branch Manager, Vicki Nino
Vice President Commercial Loan Officer, Chad Bringe
Vice President Commercial Banking, Brad Wible
Auditors: Crowe Horwath LLP

LOCATIONS

HQ: Central Valley Community Bancorp
7100 N. Financial Drive., Suite 101, Fresno, CA 93720
Phone: 559 298-1775
Web: www.cvcb.com

COMPETITORS

American River	Sierra Bancorp
Bankshares	TriCo Bancshares
Bank of America	United Security
Comerica	Bancshares
MUFG Americas Holdings	Westamerica
RCB Corp.	

HISTORICAL FINANCIALS

Company Type: Public

Income Statement

FYE: December 31

	ASSETS ($ mil.)	NET INCOME ($ mil.)	INCOME AS % OF ASSETS	EMPLOYEES
12/17	1,661	14	0.8%	316
12/16	1,443	15	1.1%	287
12/15	1,276	10	0.9%	282
12/14	1,192	5	0.4%	290
12/13	1,145	8	0.7%	290
Annual Growth	9.7%	14.2%		2.2%

2017 Year-End Financials

Debt ratio: 0.31%
Return on equity: 7.51%
Cash ($ mil.): 100
Current ratio: —
Long-term debt ($ mil.): —

No. of shares (mil.): 13
Dividends
Yield: 0.0%
Payout: 21.8%
Market value ($ mil.): 276

	STOCK PRICE ($) FY Close	P/E High/Low		PER SHARE ($) Earnings	Dividends	Book Value
12/17	20.18	21	16	1.10	0.24	15.30
12/16	19.96	15	8	1.33	0.24	13.51
12/15	12.03	13	10	1.00	0.23	12.67
12/14	11.08	28	22	0.48	0.20	11.93
12/13	11.25	16	10	0.77	0.20	11.00
Annual Growth	15.7%	—	—	9.3%	4.7%	8.6%

Century Bancorp, Inc.

Century Bancorp is the holding company for Century Bank and Trust which serves Boston and surrounding parts of northeastern Massachusetts from more than 25 branches. Boasting some $3.6 billion in total assets the bank offers standard deposit products including checking savings and money market accounts; CDs; and IRAs. Nearly two-thirds of its loan portfolio is comprised of commercial and commercial real estate loans. while residential mortgages and home equity loans make up around 30%. The bank also writes construction and land development loans business loans and personal loans. It offers brokerage services through an agreement with third-party provider LPL Financial.

Operations

Century Bank also provides cash management short-term financing and transaction processing services to municipalities in Massachusetts and Rhode Island. It offers automated lockbox collection services to its municipal customers as well as commercial clients. The bank also continues to open new branches in its traditional market area in metropolitan Boston.

The bank gets more than 80% of its revenue in the form of interest income (mostly from loans). It generated 32% of its total revenue from taxable loans in 2014 while another 18% came from non-taxable loans and 35% came from interest income on the bank's investment securities. On the non-interest side the bank made 8% of its overall revenue from service charges on deposit accounts 3% from lockbox fees and a negligible amount on brokerage commissions and gains on sales of securities or mortgage loans.

Geographic Reach

The bank operates more than 25 branches in 20 cities and towns across Massachusetts ranging from Braintree in the South to Andover in the northern part of the state.

Sales and Marketing

Most of Century Bank's business comes from small and medium-sized businesses needing commercial loans though the bank also serves retail customers as well as local governments and other institutions throughout Massachusetts.

The bank spent $1.79 million on advertising in 2014 compared to $1.75 million and $1.85 million in 2013 and 2012 respectively.

Financial Performance

Century Bancorp's revenues and profits have been steadily rising over the past few years thanks to increased loan business and declining loan loss provisions as its loan portfolio's credit quality has been improving in the strengthening economy.

The bank's revenue rose by more than 2% to a record $100.64 million in 2014 mostly as it collected more interest income from long-term securities and non-taxable loans during the year. The bank's earning securities assets grew by 8.5% during the year while the size of its loan business swelled by double-digits with increased tax-exempt lending and residential second mortgage lending; all of which boosted interest income during the year.

Higher revenue lower interest expenses on deposits and a continued dip in loan loss provisions in 2014 pushed Century's net income higher by 9% to a record $21.86 million. The bank's operating cash also grew by 7% to $22.39 million thanks to higher cash earnings.

Strategy

Century Bancorp has been growing organically through new branch openings and digital bank product launches in recent years. In 2014 for example the bank opened its new branch in Woburn Massachusetts and launched its all-new Century Bank Mobile App which boosted customer convenience and allowed the bank to better compete with larger banks with more expansive branch networks.

Showcasing its strong financial capitalization the bank received an "A" rating from the Standard and Poor's credit ratings agency in 2015 making Century Bank the only regional bank in the state to receive such a rating.

EXECUTIVES

Senior Vice President, Susan Delahunt

Evp Century Bank And Trust Company, Paul A. Evangelista, age 54, $337,614 total compensation

Evp Century Bank And Trust Company, David B. Woonton, age 62, $337,614 total compensation

President Ceo And Director, Barry R. Sloane, age 63, $569,207 total compensation

Cfo And Treasurer, William P. Hornby, age 51, $294,708 total compensation

Evp Century Bank And Trust Company, Linda Sloane Kay, age 56, $294,708 total compensation

Evp Century Bank And Trust, Brian J. Feeney, age 57, $294,708 total compensation

Vice President, Karen Martin

Vice President, Jim Smith

Senior Vice President, Janice Brandano

Vice President, Anna Gorska

Vice President, Nancy M Marsh

Chairman, Marshall M. Sloane, age 91

President Ceo And Director, Barry R. Sloane, age 63

Cfo And Treasurer, William P. Hornby, age 51

Board Member, Joseph Senna

Auditors: KPMG LLP

LOCATIONS

HQ: Century Bancorp, Inc.
400 Mystic Avenue, Medford, MA 02155
Phone: 781 391-4000
Web: www.centurybank.com

PRODUCTS/OPERATIONS

2014 Sales

	$ mil.	% of total
Interest		
Loans	50	50
Securities	2	3
Other	32	32
Noninterest		
Service charges on deposit accounts	8	8
Lockbox fees	3	3
Gains on sales of Mortgage loans	2	3
Other	1	1
Total	**100**	**100**

COMPETITORS

Boston Private	Eastern Bank
Brookline Bancorp	Middlesex Savings
Cambridge Financial	Peoples Federal
Capital Crossing	Bancshares Inc.
Central Bancorp	Sovereign Bank
Citizens Financial	
Group	

HISTORICAL FINANCIALS

Company Type: Public

Income Statement

FYE: December 31

	ASSETS ($ mil.)	NET INCOME ($ mil.)	INCOME AS % OF ASSETS	EMPLOYEES
12/17	4,785	22	0.5%	447
12/16	4,462	24	0.5%	438
12/15	3,947	23	0.6%	438
12/14	3,624	21	0.6%	440
12/13	3,431	20	0.6%	428
Annual Growth	**8.7%**	**2.7%**	**—**	**1.1%**

2017 Year-End Financials

Debt ratio: 8.02%	No. of shares (mil.): 5
Return on equity: 8.91%	Dividends
Cash ($ mil.): 356	Yield: 0.0%
Current ratio: —	Payout: 11.9%
Long-term debt ($ mil.): —	Market value ($ mil.): 436

	STOCK PRICE ($) FY Close	P/E High/Low		PER SHARE ($) Earnings	Dividends	Book Value
12/17	78.25	18	12	4.01	0.48	46.75
12/16	60.00	12	7	4.41	0.48	43.11
12/15	43.46	9	8	4.13	0.48	38.53
12/14	40.06	8	7	3.93	0.48	34.57
12/13	33.25	9	7	3.61	0.48	31.76
Annual Growth	**23.9%**	**—**	**—**	**2.7%**	**(0.0%)**	**10.1%**

CenturyLink Inc

CenturyLink provides cyber links throughout the country on one of the longest fiber networks in the US. Historically a regional wireline local and long-distance telephone provider it's connecting with the times by transforming into a broadband and network services provider for business residential and government clients. It spends around $3 billion a year on capital costs to further develop its network. The company is the one of the largest US wireline telecom companies by total access lines (it has about 11 million of them) and is the incumbent local carrier in nearly 40 states though three-quarters of its lines are in just a dozen. In 2017 CenturyLink and Level 3 Communications merged in a $34 billion deal.

Operations

CenturyLink operates in two main segments with the Business segment accounting for 60% of sales. It provides private line broadband Ethernet Multiprotocol Label Switching (MPLS) Voice over Internet Protocol (VoIP) network management services colocation and managed hosting and cloud hosting services for enterprise wholesale and governmental customers including other communication providers.

The Consumer segment about a third of sales offers broadband wireless and video services including Prism TV service and an over-the-top streaming service. It also offers local and long-distance phone service as well as satellite TV through DirecTV and wireless service through Verizon.

The company?s ?other? segment which includes federal payments for serving rural areas accounts for the rest of revenue.

CenturyLink operates a 265000-route-mile US fiber network in the US and a 360000-route-mile international transport network.

Geographic Reach

CenturyLink operates about 75% of its total access lines in portions of Arizona Colorado Florida Iowa Minnesota Missouri New Mexico Nevada North Carolina Oregon Utah and Washington (the company has paid a reported $75 million to put its name on the Seattle Seahawks stadium on the city's waterfront for 15 years).

It also provides local service in parts of Alabama Arkansas California Georgia Idaho Illinois Indiana Kansas Louisiana Ohio Michigan Mississippi Montana Nebraska New Jersey North Dakota Oklahoma Pennsylvania South Carolina South Dakota Tennessee Texas Virginia Wisconsin and Wyoming.

Financial Performance

CenturyLink?s revenue dropped about 2% in 2016 to $17.5 billion from 2015 continuing a string of incremental declines over the past five years. Business segment sales fell 3% in 2016 from 2015 mainly on declines in legacy services revenues from fewer in local service access lines and lower volumes of long-distance and access services. The continued erosion of legacy services (traditional phone service) also drove the consumer segment?s revenue 2% lower in 2016 from 2015. Revenue from strategic services rose in the business and consumer segments from increased MPLS Ethernet and VoIP services in business and rate increases and pricing initiatives for broadband and Prism TV in consumer.

The company reported net income of $626 million in 2016 a 29% drop from 2015. Although the company had lower expenses for the most part in 2016 they didn?t outweigh the drop in revenue.

Cash flow from operations slipped to $4.6 billion in 2016 from $5.1 billion in 2015 on lower net income.

Strategy

The network is at the heart of CenturyLink?s business and its strategy. Already big with 265000-route-miles of fiber in the US the network is poised to get even bigger with CenturyLink?s pending acquisition of Level 3 and its 200000 route miles of fiber. The company delivers video streaming applications and services related to the Internet of Things (IoT) and emerging technologies like virtual and augmented reality and still-to-come 5G wireless technology over the network.

Besides extending its network the Level 3 deal would add to the revenue CenturyLink gets from business customers. CenturyLink?s business revenue which is more stable and carries higher margins would rise to 75% of sales from 60%. Recently introduced products and services geared to businesses include cloud data analytics and security offerings.

The consumer remains an integral part of CenturyLink?s plans. The company is working to improve network speeds and the customer experience. It has invested in broadband to supply speeds of 100 Mbps to 1 Gbps to more service areas. The company also has simplified its pricing plans and offers an over-the-top (OTT) video service for cord-cutters.

On the operations side CenturyLink implemented cost-containment moves in 2016 that included reducing employee-related expenses up to 8%.

CenturyLink sold its data centers and colocation business in 2017 for about $1.8 billion to a consortium of investors who formed Cyxtera Technologies. CenturyLink maintained an ownership stake in the new business and can sell services to its customers.

Mergers and Acquisitions

The $34 billion-dollar merger of CenturyLink and Level 3 Communications which closed in November 2017 created one of the largest telecommunications service providers in the US. The combined company's network connects more than 350 metro areas in the US and it has a presence in more than 60 countries. While each company has a nationwide network they say their combination brings together complementary assets and not result in less competition. With Level 3 carrying some $10 billion in net operating losses the combined company's tax bill should be lower freeing up cash flow for developing more infrastructure.

CenturyLink expanded its capabilities in IT services with the acquisition of SEAL Consulting a provider of SAP tools for enterprise business and technology needs.

In 2016 CenturyLink added a security element to its networking business with the acquisition in 2016 of netAura. The company specializes in engineering developing and consulting on managed security technologies.

EXECUTIVES

Evp Controller And Assistant Secretary, David D. Cole, age 60, $482,687 total compensation

President And Ceo, Glen F. Post, age 65, $1,250,000 total compensation

Senior Vice President Business Service Delivery And Operations, Todd Schafer

President Small And Mid-size Business (smb) And Ges/sled, Vernon L. Irvin, age 56

Evp And Cfo, Sunit S. Patel, age 56

Evp Chief Administrative Officer General Counsel And Secretary, Stacey W. Goff, age 52, $540,758 total compensation

Evp And Cto, Aamir Hussain, $496,049 total compensation

President Consumer Markets, Maxine L. Moreau, age 56

Evp Human Resources, Scott A. Trezise, age 49

President Global Accounts Management And International, Laurinda Y. Pang, age 48

Svp Cyber Engineering And Technology Services, William E. (Bill) Bradley

President Advanced Solutions Group And Chief Enterprise Relationship Officer, Gary Gauba

President And Coo, Jeffrey K. (Jeff) Storey

President Wholesale Indirect Channels And Alliances, Lisa Miller

President Strategic Enterprise Federal Government And Ges/sled, Ed Morche

Vice President Of Sales, Harman Steve

Vice President Financial Planning And Analysis, Wes Gibson

Vice President And General Counsel, Laurie Korneffel

Vice President And Assistant Controller, Lyle Hippen

Vice President And General Manager, Guy Gunther

Vice President Idaho, Jim Schmit

Vice President Finance And Planning, Jerry Allen

National Account Manager, Frank Palazzo

Vice President Of External Relations Middle Atlantic Region, William Hanchey

Vice President Of Corporate Development And Strategy, Kenneth Dunn

Vice President Compensation And Analytics, Jill Turner

Executive Vice President Controller And Operations Support, Dave Cole

Vice President And Treasurer, Glynn Williams

Senior Vice President Information Technology And India Operations, Harsh Bhatnagar

Vice President Network Service Operations, Jeff Mitchell

Vice President Operational Transformation, Bob Reedy

Vice President Engineering And Construction, Dayl White

Vice President Corporate Tax, Jon Robinson

Vice President Product Strategy, Pasha Mohammed

Senior Vice President Product Development, Phillip Bronsdon

Vice President Information Technology Architecture, Anand Singh

Senior Vice President Innovation And Integration, Gnanasekaran Sekar Swaminathan

Vice President Consumer Markets, Christi Uhrig

Vice President Assistant General Counsel, Mark Stites

Vice President Operations, Karen Currington

Vice President Customer Care, Jeff Johnstone

Segment Vice President, Lynn Smullen-Volz

Vice President Real Estate And Fleet, LaRae Dodson

Vice President Public Markets, Shane Matson

Vice President Global Infrastructure Operations, Todd Miller

Vice President Global Assistant Special Delivery, Jinesh Jain

Senior Vice President Sales And Delivery Global Its, Badal Patel

Vice President Global Business Process Innovation, Beth Hannan

Senior Vice President Innovation And Integration, Sekar Swaminathan

Evp Controller And Assistant Secretary, David D. Cole, age 60

Chairman, Harvey P. Perry, age 73

President And Ceo, Glen F. Post, age 65

Vice Chairman, W. Bruce Hanks, age 63

Evp Chief Administrative Officer General Counsel And Secretary, Stacey W. Goff, age 52

Secretary, Melissa Brocato

Board Member, Andy Olson

Auditors: KPMG LLP

LOCATIONS

HQ: CenturyLink Inc
100 CenturyLink Drive, Monroe, LA 71203
Phone: 318 388-9000   **Fax:** 318 789-8656
Web: www.centurylink.com

PRODUCTS/OPERATIONS

2016 Sales by Category

	$ mil.	% of total
Strategic services	8,050	46
Legacy services	7,672	44
Data integration	533	3
Other	1,215	7
Total	**17,470**	**100**

2016 Sales

	% of total
Business segment	59
Consumer segment	34
Other	7
Total	**100**

Selected Products & Services

Local and long-distance voice
High-speed Internet
MPLS
Private line (including special access)
Data integration
Ethernet
Colocation
Managed hosting (including cloud hosting)
NetworkPublic access
Video
Wireless
Other ancillary servicesi

COMPETITORS

AT&T	Frontier
Cavalier Telephone	Communications
Comcast	Level 3
Cox Communications	Nsight
DISH Network	Sprint Communications
Equinix	Telephone & Data
FairPoint	Systems
Communications Inc.	Time Warner Cable
Farmers	Verizon
Telecommunications	XO Holdings

HISTORICAL FINANCIALS

Company Type: Public

Income Statement

FYE: December 31

	REVENUE ($ mil.)	NET INCOME ($ mil.)	NET PROFIT MARGIN	EMPLOYEES
12/17	17,656	1,389	7.9%	51,000
12/16	17,470	626	3.6%	40,000
12/15	17,900	878	4.9%	43,000
12/14	18,031	772	4.3%	45,000
12/13	18,095	(239)	—	47,000
Annual Growth	(0.6%)	—		2.1%

2017 Year-End Financials

Debt ratio: 49.89%	No. of shares (mil.): 1,069
Return on equity: 7.53%	Dividends
Cash ($ mil.): 556	Yield: 0.1%
Current ratio: 0.86	Payout: 97.7%
Long-term debt ($ mil.): 37,283	Market value ($ mil.): 17,834

	STOCK PRICE ($) FY Close	P/E High/Low		PER SHARE ($) Earnings	Dividends	Book Value
12/17	16.68	12	6	2.21	2.16	21.97
12/16	23.78	28	19	1.16	2.16	24.52
12/15	25.16	26	15	1.58	2.16	25.86
12/14	39.58	31	21	1.36	2.16	26.42
12/13	31.85	—	—	(0.40)	2.16	29.45
Annual Growth	(14.9%)	—	—	—	(0.0%)	(7.1%)

Cerner Corp.

Cerner Corp. provides health care organizations with health care IT (HCIT). The company develops and sells software systems designed to help improve processes and eliminate errors and waste for organizations ranging from single-doctor practices to the pharmaceutical and medical device industries. Its software combines clinical financial and administrative information management applications including tools for managing electronic health records (EHRs). Complementary services include support and maintenance implementation and training remote hosting data analytics and transaction processing. The company's products are licensed by some 25000 facilities around the globe although the US is by far its largest market.

Operations

About 50% of Cerner Corp.?s revenue comes from services which includes professional and managed services with system sales accounting for about 25% of revenue and support and maintenance bringing in about 20% of revenue.

The company offers its technologies on two main software platforms. The Cerner Millennium architecture includes integrated clinical financial and management information systems. It organizes and delivers information for physicians nurses laboratory technicians pharmacists front- and back-office professionals and consumers.

The HealtheIntent cloud-based platform is designed to grow with an institution?s patient population while facilitating care for patient and provider. The HealtheIntent platform offers applications that can run on any EHR system (including those that aren?t Cerner?s) for gathering and processing data across the continuum of care.

Cerner?s strong services segment is anchored by its CernerWorks managed services business which is designed to help customer spend more effectively. Other service products are Cerner IT-Works which helps customers manage IT functions and Cerner RevWorks which helps with customer revenue cycle functions.

Geographic Reach

Cerner has operations in about two dozen countries in Asia Australia Europe and North and South America. The company?s sales are split about 90% to customers in the US and about 10% to international customers.

Sales and Marketing

Although hospitals and health systems account for most of sales Cerner's clients include physician groups and networks blood banks home health agencies laboratories managed care organizations pharmacies pharmaceutical manufacturers and public health organizations. The company markets its offerings directly via industry seminars and trade shows as well as by leveraging current customers for new leads in addition to upsell and cross-sell opportunities.

Financial Performance

Cerner Corp. has ridden a wave of spending for healthcare technology to post five years of rising revenue and profit.

The company?s sales rose about 7% to $5.1 billion in 2017 from 2016 driven by customers? needs to keep pace with regulatory requirements deal with changing reimbursement protocols and provide better patient care.

Net income jumped 36% to $867 million in 2017 from 2016. While higher revenue aided the rise the booster came from a tax bill that was $180 million lower in 2017 from 2016 thanks to the US Tax Cuts and Jobs Act made law in late 2017.

Cerner maintained a strong cash position adding about $200 million to its cash holdings in 2017 ending the year with about $371 million on hand. The company also added to its free cash flow which rose to $671 million in 2017 from $492 million in 2016.

Strategy

Cerner's fundamental strategy is to create organic growth by continuing to make large investments in R&D. This strategy has proven itself over time as Cerner reports 10-year compound annual growth rates of 10% or more in revenue and 20% or more in earnings. With a strong foothold in many of its client markets part of the company's

strategy is to sell additional products and services to its customers.

The company has introduced new health care IT (HCIT) services as clients increase their IT spending. Cerner ITWorks is a service that helps hospitals meet their technology needs while Cerner RevWorks helps health care organizations improve their revenue cycle functions. Additionally the company has introduced applications used to automate information collection from medical devices as part of its integrated Smart Room software.

Another path to growth is outside the Cerner?s core HCIT market. Using its own experience the company has developed products for clinic pharmacy wellness and third-party administrator services that the company offers directly to employers.

Cerner also is targeting population health which involves the collection of large amounts of data from people who interact with health care systems. The collected data can be analyzed to provide new health care products and services. The company?s HealtheIntent cloud platform is its population health engine. About 100 customers use the platform building up more 6 petabytes of data.

Cerner is in the early stages of major contracts to provide healthcare IT services to the US Department of Defense and the Department of Veterans Affairs.

If there?s a market to sell more of your healthcare information to it?s the US. The country has some of the highest healthcare costs in the world and much of that spending goes for technology. Cerner gets about 90% of its revenue from clients in the US where sales rose 8% in 2017 compared to a 3% rise in its international sales.

However Cerner?s geographic concentration puts it as the mercy of US healthcare policy which has experienced a level of instability in recent years as elected officials struggle to define who pays for what. The company has made strides outside the US with international bookings rising 50% and landing contracts in the Middle East and Sweden.

Mergers and Acquisitions

After buying the hospital information system business of Siemens for $1.3 billion in early 2015 Cerner has been quiet on the acquisition front. The Siemens business brought technology for administrative hospital IT and electronic patient records to Cerner. It covered about 5000 client facilities in 40 countries.

EXECUTIVES

Evp And Chief Of Staff, Jeffrey A. (Jeff) Townsend, age 54, $657,596 total compensation

Chairman And Interim Ceo, Clifford W. (Cliff) Illig, age 67

Evp And Cfo, Marc G. Naughton, age 62, $524,712 total compensation

President, Zane M. Burke, age 51, $657,596 total compensation

Evp And Coo, Michael R. (Mike) Nill, age 53, $657,596 total compensation

Vp And General Manager United Kingdom, Donald D. Trigg

Evp And Chief People Officer, Julia M. (Julie) Wilson, age 55

Vp And General Manager Academic/children's Northeast, Debbie Yantis

Vice President Ambulatory Sales, Julie Kay

Vice President Compensation And Benefits, Todd Downey

Vice President Finance, Mickey Rajan

Chairman And Interim Ceo, Clifford W. (Cliff) Illig, age 67

Auditors: KPMG LLP

LOCATIONS

HQ: Cerner Corp.
2800 Rockcreek Parkway, North Kansas City, MO 64117
Phone: 816 221-1024
Web: www.cerner.com

2017 Sales

	$ mil.	% of total
Domestic	4,575	89
Global	567	11
Total	**5,142**	**100**

PRODUCTS/OPERATIONS

2017 Sales

	$ mil.	% of total
Services	2,639	51
System sales	1,355	26
Support & maintenance	1,046	21
Reimbursed travel	101	2
Total	**5,142**	**100**

Selected Services

Population Health Management
Clinical Solutions
Open & Interoperable
Revenue Cycle Management

Services & Technology

COMPETITORS

Accenture	Healthcare Holdings
Accretive Health	IBM Global Services
Allscripts	MEDHOST
CPSI	MEDITECH
Capgemini North	McKesson
America	MedAssets
CareFusion	NTT Data
Conceptual MindWorks	Omnicell
Dell	QuadraMed
Deloitte LLP	Quality Systems
Epic Systems	SSI Group
GE Healthcare	Sage Software
Greenway Medical	athenahealth
Technologies	e-MDs
HP	eClinicalWorks

HISTORICAL FINANCIALS

Company Type: Public

Income Statement

FYE: December 29

	REVENUE ($ mil.)	NET INCOME ($ mil.)	NET PROFIT MARGIN	EMPLOYEES
12/18	5,366	630	11.7%	29,200
12/17	5,142	866	16.9%	26,000
12/16*	4,796	636	13.3%	24,400
01/16	4,425	539	12.2%	22,200
01/15	3,402	525	15.4%	15,800
Annual Growth	**12.1%**	**4.6%**	**—**	**16.6%**

*Fiscal year change

2018 Year-End Financials

Debt ratio: 6.61%	No. of shares (mil.): 324
Return on equity: 13.01%	Dividends
Cash ($ mil.): 374	Yield: —
Current ratio: 2.41	Payout: —
Long-term debt ($ mil.): 438	Market value ($ mil.): 16,867

	STOCK PRICE ($) FY Close	P/E High/Low		PER SHARE ($) Earnings	Dividends	Book Value
12/18	52.01	38 26		1.89	0.00	15.20
12/17	67.39	28 18		2.57	0.00	14.39
12/16*	47.37	36 25		1.85	0.00	11.92
01/16	60.17	48 36		1.54	0.00	11.38
01/15	65.03	43 32		1.50	0.00	10.42
Annual Growth	**(5.4%)**	**— —**		**5.9%**	**—**	**9.9%**

*Fiscal year change

Charter Communications Inc (New)

LOCATIONS

HQ: Charter Communications Inc (New)
400 Atlantic Street, Stamford, CT 06901
Phone: 203 905-7801
Web: www.charter.com

COMPETITORS

AT&T	Mediacom
Apple Inc.	Communications
Bright House Networks	Netflix
Cablevision Systems	RCN Corporation
Clearwire	Skype
Comcast	Sprint Communications
Cox Communications	Suddenlink
DIRECTV	Communications
DISH Network	T-Mobile USA
EarthLink	Time Warner Cable
Frontier	United Online
Communications	Verizon
Hulu	Vonage
Insight Communications	YouTube
LodgeNet	

HISTORICAL FINANCIALS

Company Type: Public

Income Statement   FYE: December 31

	REVENUE ($ mil.)	NET INCOME ($ mil.)	NET PROFIT MARGIN	EMPLOYEES
12/18	43,634	1,230	2.8%	98,000
12/17	41,581	9,895	23.8%	94,800
12/16	29,003	3,522	12.1%	91,500
12/15	9,754	(271)	—	23,800
12/14	9,108	(183)	—	23,200
Annual Growth	47.9%	—	—	43.4%

2018 Year-End Financials

Debt ratio: 49.84%	No. of shares (mil.): 225
Return on equity: 3.26%	Dividends
Cash ($ mil.): 551	Yield: —
Current ratio: 0.23	Payout: —
Long-term debt ($ mil.): 69,537	Market value ($ mil.): 64,219

	STOCK PRICE ($) FY Close	P/E High/Low	Earnings	Dividends	Book Value
12/18	284.97	73 49	5.22	0.00	161.01
12/17	335.96	10 7	34.09	0.00	163.87
12/16	287.92	17 9	15.94	0.00	149.27
12/15	183.10	— —	(2.43)	0.00	(0.41)
12/14	166.62	— —	(1.70)	0.00	1.30
Annual Growth	14.4%		—	—	—233.4%

Chemical Financial Corp

Chemical Financial has banking down to a science. It's the holding company for Chemical Bank which provides standard services such as checking and savings accounts CDs and IRAs credit and debit cards and loans and mortgages to individuals and businesses through nearly 190 branches in the lower peninsula of Michigan. The majority of the bank's loan portfolio is made up of commercial loans while consumer loans make up the remainder. Boasting assets of $9 billion Chemical is the second largest bank in Michigan. The company also offers trust investment management brokerage and title insurance services through subsidiaries.

Operations

Its Wealth Management division which has some $4 billion in assets under custody offers trust services estate planning investment management and employee benefit programs. Chemical Financial Advisors offers mutual funds and marketable securities while CFC Title Services issues title insurance for mortgage properties. CFC Capital manages the company's municipal investment securities portfolio.

About 72% of Chemical Financial's total revenue came from loan interest (including fees) in 2014 while another 6% came from interest on its investment securities. The rest of its revenue came from deposit account service charges and fees (8%) wealth management revenue (6%) mortgage banking income (2%) and other miscellaneous sources of income.

Sales and Marketing

Chemical Financial spent $3.45 million on advertising in 2014 up from $2.97 million and $3.11 million in 2013 and 2012 respectively.

Financial Performance

Chemical Financial's revenues and profits have been rising over the past few years thanks growing loan and deposit business from acquisitions lower interest expenses on deposits and declining loan loss provisions as its loan portfolio's credit quality has improved with higher property valuations in the strengthened economy.

The bank's revenue rose by 6% to $290.4 million in 2014 as the bank as its acquisition of Northwestern Bancorp boosted its loan business during the year. Higher revenue lower interest expenses and a continued decline in loan loss provisions drove the bank's net income up by 9% to a record $62.1 million. The bank's operating cash levels inched higher to $89.9 million on higher cash earnings.

Strategy

The bank follows an aggressive acquisition strategy to boost its loan and deposit business while expanding its branch network into key parts of Michigan. Indeed its acquisitions in 2015 and 2014 boosted the bank's presence in northwestern Michigan and along the Michigan-Indiana border. By the end of 2014 the bank had acquired some 21 community banks and 36 branch bank offices.

Mergers and Acquisitions

Chemical Financial agreed in January 2019 to merge with Minnesota-based TCF Financial to form a Midwest bank with about $45 billion in assets $34 billion in total deposits and more than 500 branches in nine states. TCF's large deposit base and national wholesale lending business will complement Chemical's commercial lending and wealth management activities. The combined company which is to retain the TCF brand will have a more diversified deposit mix between retail and commercial lines and a more balanced loan portfolio across geographies asset classes and industries. Following the merger TCF shareholders will have a controlling interest in the combined company.

Company Background

In late 2012 the company acquired 21 branches in northeastern Michigan and Battle Creek from Independent Bank. That more than $8-million transaction further expands Chemical Bank's presence geographically. Additional acquisitions including FDIC-assisted takeovers of failed banks are possible.

EXECUTIVES

Svp Cfo And Treasurer, Lori A. Gwizdala, age 60, $344,720 total compensation
Vice Chairman And President Chemical Bank, Thomas C. (Tom) Shafer, age 59
Evp And Senior Credit Officer Chemical Bank, James E. Tomczyk, age 66, $225,504 total compensation
Vice Chairman Chemical Bank And Ceo Insite Capital Llc, Thomas W. Kohn, age 64, $329,174 total compensation
Evp Commercial Lending Chemical Bank, Daniel W. Terpsma, age 64
Evp And Cfo Chemical Financial And Chemical Bank, Dennis L. Klaeser, age 60, $183,483 total compensation
President And Ceo, David T. Provost
Director Chemical Financial And Chairman Chemical Bank, Franklin C. Wheatlake, age 70
Evp And Coo Business Operations Chemical Bank, Leonardo Amat, age 49, $309,477 total compensation
Evp And Chief Risk Officer Chemical Bank, Lynn M. Kerber, age 49
Evp General Counsel And Secretary, William C. Collins, age 65
Evp And Coo Customer Experience Chemical Bank, Robert S. Rathbun, age 54, $309,477 total compensation
Svp And Cio, Greg Meidt
Vice President Of Customer Service, Sue Lynde
Vice President, Robert O Burgess
Assistant Vice President Product Development, Jim Hubinger
Senior Vice President Head Of Personal Trust, James Blanchard
Vice President Commercial Loan Officer, Jeff Hyde
Executive Vice President Chief Operating Officer, James Milroy
Senior Vice President Senior Lender, Mike Williams
Vice President Information Systems, Laurie Soren
Senior Vice President And Trust Officer, Jude Patnaude
Vice President Commercial Lending, Kip Miller
Vice President Data Services, Brian Beall
First Vice President, David Vermilye
Vice President, Robin Grove
Vice President And Trust Investment Officer, Glen Matz
Vice President And Community Reinvestment Act Officer, Robert BurgessJr
Assistant Vice President, Jane Pontious
Vice President Secondary Market Manager, Robert Clark
Vice President, Kelly Hutchings
Assistant Vice President, Lorie Moriarty
Vice President Commercial Banking, Melissa Spranger
Vice President, Joseph Dick
Vice President, John Laman
Vice President Human Resources, David Ramaker
Vice President Retail Sales Manager, Jeff Sharpe
Vice President Mortgage Originator, Krista Martiny
Vice President Commercial Banking Relationship Manager Commerce Park Interim Vice, Ron Cordaro
Vice President First, Michael Debo
Vice Chairman And President Chemical Bank, Thomas C. (Tom) Shafer, age 59
Chairman, Gary H. Torgow, age 60
President And Ceo, David T. Provost
Director Chemical Financial And Chairman Chemical Bank, Franklin C. Wheatlake, age 70
Board Member, Larry Stauffer
Board Member, James Fitterling
Auditors: KPMG LLP

Chemical Financial Corp

LOCATIONS
HQ: Chemical Financial Corp
333 W. Fort Street, Suite 1800, Detroit, MI 48226
Phone: 800 867-9757
Web: www.chemicalbank.com

PRODUCTS/OPERATIONS

2014 Sales

	$ mil.	% of total
Interest		
Loans including fees	209	72
Investment securities	17	6
Other	0	-
Non-interest		
Service charges on deposit accounts	22	8
Wealth management revenue	16	6
Other customer service charges & fees	18	6
Other	6	2
Total	**290**	**100**

COMPETITORS

1st Source Corporation	Flagstar Bancorp
Bank of America	Huntington Bancshares
Comerica	Independent Bank (MI)
Fifth Third	Mercantile Bank
Firstbank	

HISTORICAL FINANCIALS
Company Type: Public

Income Statement — FYE: December 31

	ASSETS ($ mil.)	NET INCOME ($ mil.)	INCOME AS % OF ASSETS	EMPLOYEES
12/17	19,280	149	0.8%	3,000
12/16	17,355	108	0.6%	3,300
12/15	9,188	86	0.9%	2,100
12/14	7,322	62	0.8%	2,000
12/13	6,184	56	0.9%	1,700
Annual Growth	32.9%	27.4%	—	15.3%

2017 Year-End Financials

Debt ratio: 0.19%
Return on equity: 5.70%
Cash ($ mil.): 455
Current ratio: —
Long-term debt ($ mil.): —
No. of shares (mil.): 71
Dividends
Yield: 0.0%
Payout: 52.8%
Market value ($ mil.): 3,807

	STOCK PRICE ($) FY Close	P/E High/Low	PER SHARE ($) Earnings	Dividends	Book Value
12/17	53.47	27 21	2.08	1.10	37.48
12/16	54.17	25 13	2.17	1.06	36.57
12/15	34.27	15 12	2.39	1.00	26.62
12/14	30.64	17 13	1.97	0.94	24.32
12/13	31.67	16 12	2.00	0.87	23.38
Annual Growth	14.0%	— —	1.0%	6.0%	12.5%

Chemours Co (The)

Auditors: PricewaterhouseCoopers LLP

LOCATIONS
HQ: Chemours Co (The)
1007 Market Street, Wilmington, DE 19899
Phone: 302 773-1000
Web: www.chemours.com

HISTORICAL FINANCIALS
Company Type: Public

Income Statement — FYE: December 31

	REVENUE ($ mil.)	NET INCOME ($ mil.)	NET PROFIT MARGIN	EMPLOYEES
12/17	6,183	746	12.1%	7,000
12/16	5,400	7	0.1%	7,000
12/15	5,717	(90)	—	8,100
12/14	6,432	400	6.2%	9,000
12/13	6,859	423	6.2%	—
Annual Growth	(2.6%)	15.2%	—	—

2017 Year-End Financials

Debt ratio: 56.38%
Return on equity: 155.42%
Cash ($ mil.): 1,556
Current ratio: 2.12
Long-term debt ($ mil.): 4,097
No. of shares (mil.): 182
Dividends
Yield: 0.0%
Payout: 3.0%
Market value ($ mil.): 9,159

	STOCK PRICE ($) FY Close	P/E High/Low	PER SHARE ($) Earnings	Dividends	Book Value
12/17	50.06	14 5	3.91	0.12	4.70
12/16	22.09	674 78	0.04	0.12	0.55
12/15	5.36	— —	(0.50)	0.58	0.70
Annual Growth	74.8%	— —	—	(32.6%)	61.2%

Chemung Financial Corp.

EXECUTIVES
Vice President Private Banker, ED Morton
Assistant Vice President Bus Client Services, Mary Narosky
Vice President And Compliance Officer, Lucimar Escudero
Assistant Vice President, Theresa Wagner
Assistant Treasurer Branch Manager, Sherry Armstrong
Auditors: Crowe Horwath LLP

LOCATIONS
HQ: Chemung Financial Corp.
One Chemung Canal Plaza, Elmira, NY 14901
Phone: 607 737-3711
Web: www.chemungcanal.com

COMPETITORS

Astoria Financial	Financial Institutions
Citizens Financial Group	HSBC USA
Community Bank System	M&T Bank
Elmira Savings Bank	Tompkins Financial

HISTORICAL FINANCIALS
Company Type: Public

Income Statement — FYE: December 31

	ASSETS ($ mil.)	NET INCOME ($ mil.)	INCOME AS % OF ASSETS	EMPLOYEES
12/17	1,707	7	0.4%	371
12/16	1,657	10	0.6%	368
12/15	1,619	9	0.6%	377
12/14	1,524	8	0.5%	393
12/13	1,476	8	0.6%	390
Annual Growth	3.7%	(4.0%)	—	(1.2%)

2017 Year-End Financials

Debt ratio: 0.26%
Return on equity: 5.06%
Cash ($ mil.): 30
Current ratio: —
Long-term debt ($ mil.): —
No. of shares (mil.): 4
Dividends
Yield: 0.0%
Payout: 67.1%
Market value ($ mil.): 229

	STOCK PRICE ($) FY Close	P/E High/Low	PER SHARE ($) Earnings	Dividends	Book Value
12/17	48.10	35 21	1.55	1.04	31.53
12/16	36.35	17 12	2.11	1.04	30.51
12/15	27.50	14 13	2.00	1.04	29.40
12/14	27.66	20 15	1.74	1.04	28.87
12/13	34.17	19 15	1.87	1.04	30.11
Annual Growth	8.9%	— —	(4.6%)	(0.0%)	1.2%

Cheniere Energy Inc.

Gaseous form or liquid state are both OK with Cheniere Energy which is engaged in the development of a liquefied natural gas (LNG) receiving-terminal business. It owns and operates Sabine Pass LNG terminal in Louisiana (with a capacity of 16.9 billion cu. ft.) and the Creole Trail Pipeline which interconnects the Sabine Pass LNG terminal with North American natural gas markets. Cheniere Energy also operates an LNG and natural gas marketing business and has minor exploration and production assets. Its Cheniere Energy Partners unit (which Cheniere Energy agreed to buy in 2016 before dropping the idea) operates the Sabine Pass LNG terminal.

Operations

Cheniere Energy owns and operates the Sabine Pass LNG receiving terminal in Louisiana through its control of and management agreements with Cheniere Energy Partners L.P. It also owns and operates the Creole Trail Pipeline which interconnects the Sabine Pass LNG receiving terminal with downstream markets. Its Cheniere Marketing LLC subsidiary is developing a portfolio of contracts to monetize capacity at the Sabine Pass LNG receiving terminal and the Creole Trail Pipeline. Cheniere Energy is also developing projects to provide liquefaction and export services at its Sabine Pass terminal and at its site in Corpus Christi Texas.

Sales and Marketing

The company's major customers include BG Gulf Coast LNG LLC; Gas Natural Aprovisionamientos SDG S.A.; Korea Gas Corporation; and GAIL (India) Limited.

Financial Performance

Cheniere revenue increased substantially from $1.3 billion in 2016 to a whopping $5.6 billion in 2017 mostly due to increases in volume from Trains 23 and 4 coming online as well as increased revenues per MMBtu.

Despite a 300% increase in revenue the company posted net loss of $393 million compared to $610 million in losses the year prior. This the almost $220 million decrease came from income increases from operations offset by non-controlling interest share and increased interest expense.

Cash holdings improved to $2.6 billion. Operations generated $1.2 billion offset by $3.4 billion used in investing activities. Financing provided a further $2.9 billion.

Strategy

With oil & gas prices on the rise again Cheniere is looking to improve performance. Moreover by 2035 LNG is expected to reach 25% of the total energy mix being the only fossil fuel whose share grows according to the IEA.

It is already established as one the top companies in developing and maintaining LNG terminals with premium access to existing pipeline infrastructure and deepwater shipping channels especially in the US Gulf Coast. It has a global customers base that uses its sprawling infrastructure to conduct business through flexible competitive contracts. Its asset base includes Sabine Pass in Louisiana and the Creole Trail Pipeline interconnecting Sabine with interstate pipelines including Transcontinental Tennessee Gas Florida Gas and Texas Eastern Gas.

Cheniere is looking to further expand operations by constructing a 200 mile 36-inch interstate natural gas pipeline called the Midship Project with a 1.5 million dekatherm capacity per day of firm transportation to connect production from STACK and SCOOP resource plays in the Anadarko Basin in Oklahoma to Gulf Coast and Southeast markets.

In February 2018 the company entered into two LNG sale and purchase agreements with PetroChina for the sale of approximately 1.2 MMtpa of LNG through 2043.

EXECUTIVES

Svp International, Jean Abiteboul, age 66, $461,850 total compensation
President And Ceo, Jack A. Fusco, age 55
Evp Asset Group, R. Keith Teague, age 53, $565,385 total compensation
Director, Neal A. Shear, $38,462 total compensation
Svp And Cfo, Michael J. Wortley, age 41, $565,385 total compensation
Svp And General Counsel, Greg W. Rayford, $565,385 total compensation
Vice President Operations, Pat Yeater
Vice President Trading Cheniere International (uk Establishment), Nicolas Zanen
Senior Vice President Engineering And Construction, Ed Lehotsky
Senior Vice President Policy Government And Public Affairs, Chris Smith
Chairman, G. Andrea Botta, age 64
Board Member, John Gross
Auditors: KPMG LLP

LOCATIONS

HQ: Cheniere Energy Inc.
700 Milam Street, Suite 1900, Houston, TX 77002
Phone: 713 375-5000
Web: www.cheniere.com

PRODUCTS/OPERATIONS

2017 Sales

	$ mil.	% of total
LNG revenues	5,317	95
Regasification revenues	260	5
Other revenues	21	-
Other- related party	3	-
Total	**5,601**	**100**

Subsidiaries

Subsidiaries
Caldera LNG Holdings SpA Chile
Cheniere Cares Inc. Texas
Cheniere Chile SpA Chile
Cheniere CCH HoldCo I LLC Delaware
Cheniere CCH HoldCo II LLC Delaware
Cheniere Corpus Christi Holdings LLC Delaware
Cheniere Corpus Christi Pipeline L.P. Delaware
Cheniere Creole Trail Pipeline L.P. Delaware
Cheniere Energy Investments LLC Delaware
Cheniere Energy Operating Co. Inc. Delaware
Cheniere Energy Partners GP LLC Delaware
Cheniere Energy Partners LP Holdings LLC Delaware
Cheniere Energy Partners L.P. Delaware
Cheniere Energy Shared Services Inc. Delaware

Cheniere Field Services LLC Delaware
Cheniere GP Holding Company LLC Delaware
Cheniere Ingleside Marine Terminal LLC Delaware
Cheniere International Investments Holdings S.à.r.l Luxembourg
Cheniere International Investments S.à.r.l Luxembourg
Cheniere Land Holdings LLC Delaware
Cheniere Liquids LLC Delaware
Cheniere LNG Holdings GP LLC Delaware
Cheniere LNG O&M Services LLC Delaware
Cheniere LNG Terminals LLC Delaware
Cheniere Major Project Development LLC Delaware
Cheniere Marketing International HoldCo I L.P. Bermuda
Cheniere Marketing International HoldCo II Ltd. Bermuda
Cheniere Marketing International LLP United Kingdom
Cheniere Marketing LLC Delaware
Cheniere Marketing Ltd. United Kingdom
Cheniere Marketing PTE Ltd. Singapore
Cheniere Midship Holdings LLC Delaware
Cheniere Midstream Holdings Inc. Delaware
Cheniere Pipeline GP Interests LLC Delaware
Cheniere Pipeline Holdings LLC Delaware
Cheniere San Patricio Processing Hub LLC Delaware
Cheniere Southern Trail GP Inc. Delaware
Cheniere SPH Pipeline LLC Delaware
Cheniere Supply & Marketing Inc. Delaware
Concepción LNG Holding SpA Chile
Corpus Christi Liquefaction LLC Delaware
Corpus Christi Liquefaction Stage II LLC Delaware
Corpus Christi Liquefaction Stage III LLC Delaware
Corpus Christi LNG LLC Delaware
Corpus Christi Pipeline GP LLC Delaware
Corpus Christi Tug Services LLC Delaware
CQH Holdings Company LLC Delaware
CUI I LLC Delaware
Johnson Bayou Holdings LLC Delaware
Live Oak LNG Holdings LLC Delaware
Louisiana LNG Holdings LLC Delaware
Midship Holdings LLC Delaware
Midship Pipeline Company LLC Delaware
Nordheim Eagle Ford Gathering LLC Delaware
Sabine Pass Liquefaction LLC Delaware
Sabine Pass LNG-GP LLC Delaware
Sabine Pass LNG-LP LLC Delaware
Sabine Pass LNG L.P. Delaware
Sabine Pass Tug Services LLC Delaware

COMPETITORS

Ameren	PG&E Corporation
CMS Energy	Public Service
Calpine	Enterprise Group
DTE	Sempra Energy
Dominion Energy	TRII
Enbridge	TransCanada
ONEOK	

HISTORICAL FINANCIALS

Company Type: Public

Income Statement

FYE: December 31

	REVENUE ($ mil.)	NET INCOME ($ mil.)	NET PROFIT MARGIN	EMPLOYEES
12/17	5,601	(393)	—	1,230
12/16	1,283	(609)	—	911
12/15	270	(975)	—	888
12/14	267	(547)	—	642
12/13	267	(507)	—	423
Annual Growth	**114.0%**	**—**	**—**	**30.6%**

2017 Year-End Financials

Debt ratio: 90.79%
Return on equity: —
Cash ($ mil.): 722
Current ratio: 2.69
Long-term debt ($ mil.): 25,336
No. of shares (mil.): 237
Dividends
  Yield: —
  Payout: —
Market value ($ mil.): 12,792

	STOCK PRICE ($) FY Close	P/E High/Low	PER SHARE ($) Earnings	Dividends	Book Value
12/17	53.84	— —	(1.68)	0.00	(7.42)
12/16	41.43	— —	(2.67)	0.00	(5.87)
12/15	37.25	— —	(4.30)	0.00	(3.83)
12/14	70.40	— —	(2.44)	0.00	(0.69)
12/13	43.12	— —	(2.32)	0.00	0.78
Annual Growth	**5.7%**	**— —**	**—**	**—**	**—**

Chesapeake Energy Corp.

Chesapeake Energy builds hydrocarbon reserves through the acquisition and development of oil and gas assets across the US. The company one of the biggest natural gas producers in the US and the world has estimated proved reserves of some 6.5 trillion cu. ft. of natural gas equivalent. Chesapeake has exploration and production assets in Appalachia the Mid-Continent the Barnett Bossier and Haynesville shale plays the Permian Basin and the Rockies. The company boasts 22700 producing oil and natural gas wells that turn out 575000 barrels of oil equivalent per day. The company was founded in 1989 by fracking pioneer Aubrey McClendon who died in a car crash in 2016 shortly after being indicted for bid rigging.

Operations

The company has two reportable operating segments: marketing gathering and compression (MGC); and production and exploration.

MGC through Chesapeake Energy Marketing provides oil natural gas and NGL marketing services including commodity price structuring; securing and negotiating gathering hauling processing and transportation services; and marketing services for third party producers in wells in which it does not have an interest. It also conducts gas compression through subsidiary Compass Manufacturing and MidCon Compression. The segment accounts for some 60% of sales.

Production and exploration conducts natural gas oil and NGLs (natural gas liquids) mining. Natural gas accounts for about 65% of segment sales; oil 35%; and NGLs 5%.

Geographic Reach

Chesapeake Energy has natural gas resources in the Haynesville and Bossier Shales in northwestern Louisiana and East Texas; the Marcellus Shale in the northern Appalachian Basin of West Virginia and Pennsylvania; and the Barnett Shale in the Fort Worth Basin of north-central Texas. In addition it has built leading positions in the liquids-rich resource plays of the Eagle Ford Shale in South Texas; the Utica Shale in Ohio and Pennsylvania; the Granite Wash Cleveland Tonkawa and Mississippi Lime plays in the Anadarko Basin in western Oklahoma and the Texas Panhandle; and Utica Shale in the Powder River Basin in Wyoming.

Sales and Marketing

Chesapeake Energy Marketing provides natural gas oil and NGL marketing services including commodity price structuring contract administration and nomination services for Chesapeake its partners and other producers. By aggregating volumes it seeks to increase the value of products to be sold to in various intermediary markets end markets and pipelines. Chesapeake's oil and NGL production is sold under market sensitive short-term or spot price contracts while its natural gas production is sold to purchasers under spot price contracts or percentage-of-proceeds and percentage-of-index contracts.

Sales to BP and Exxon Mobil account for more than 10% each.

Financial Performance

The oversupply-related fall in natural gas prices in recent years put a hefty dent in Chesapeake's revenue.

In fiscal 2016 revenue fell a further 38% to $7.9 billion due to lower prices and a 6% fall in total hydrocarbon output relating to asset sales; oil sales fell 20% on prior year.

Chesapeake lost $4.9 billion in 2016 down from the $14.9 billion loss the previous year. The relative improvement was down to a reduction in impairments although derivative losses of $578 billion (versus gains of $624 million and $1.0 billion the previous two years) weighed heavily on the bottom line.

Cash from operations in 2016 constituted an outflow of $204 million compared to cash provided by operations of $1.2 billion the previous year. The fall was down to lower realized oil prices and lower volumes.

Strategy

Chesapeake may be one of the top gas producers but the once $40 billion-dollar company has reduced to one-tenth its original size due to plummeting heating and power-plant fuel prices. In 2018 saddled with debt the company sold its Ohio shale assets for about $2 billion to Encino Acquisitions. The company used proceeds from the sale to pay down debt.

The company is also focusing on its gathering and transportation agreements and reducing its production and G&A expenses. It downscaled drilling activities in 2016 from 18 to 10 operating rigs on average.

Mergers and Acquisitions

In October 2018 Chesapeake bought WildHorse Resource for nearly $4 billion adding 20000 net acres in the Eagle Ford shale and Austin Chalk formations in Texas. Synergies will be around $280 million over the first five years the company said. However the deal came as a surprise to stockholders who expected further sell-offs to improve profitability. Investors have punished shares of peers like Denbury Concho Resources and Diamondback after similar merger announcements.

HISTORY

Aubrey McClendon (who grew up near Maryland's Chesapeake Bay) and Tom Ward had been non-operating partners in about 600 wells in Oklahoma before forming their own company in 1989 to develop new fields in Texas and Oklahoma during the 1990s. The firm went public in 1993. In 1995 the company acquired oil and gas acreage in Louisiana as well as Princeton Natural Gas an Oklahoma City-based gas marketing firm.

Oil finds in Louisiana and strong production from its Texas and Oklahoma wells helped lift Chesapeake's sales in 1996. That year it acquired Amerada Hess' (later renamed Hess) half of their joint operations in two Oklahoma fields. In 1997 chairman McClendon and president Ward acquired control of Chesapeake.

The company's success was based on its "growth through the drillbit" strategy — developing new wells. But after a 1997 loss Chesapeake modified its strategy and sought to grow by acquiring other companies. That year it bought energy company AnSon Production. Chesapeake subsequently bought oil and gas explorer-producer Hugoton Energy and energy company DLB Oil & Gas.

In 1998 the company acquired a 40% stake in Canadian oil producer Ranger Oil and paid Occidental Petroleum$105 million for natural gas reserves in the Texas Panhandle. Chesapeake then began to transform itself from a hotshot driller to an acquirer of natural gas properties almost tripling its proved reserves. The company suffered a huge loss that year in part from the acquisitions and continuing lower gas prices.

With gas prices soaring again the company continued its buying spree into 2000 when it agreed to buy midcontinent natural gas producer Gothic Energy for $345 million in stock and assumed debt. The deal closed in 2001. The company also sold its Canadian assets that year in order to focus on its core US properties.

In 2002 Chesapeake acquired oil and gas producer Canaan Energy for about $118 million. Later that year the company announced plans to sell or trade its Permian Basin assets.

Chesapeake acquired in 2003 a 25% stake in Pioneer Drilling (which it subsequently sold). In 2004 the company acquired Barnett Shale assets from Hallwood Energy for $292 million. That year it also bought privately owned Concho Resources for $420 million. The next year the company acquired privately held BRG Petroleum which held assets of more than 450 wells with proved reserves of more than 275 billion cu. ft. of natural gas for $325 million.

In 2005 Chesapeake acquired 20% of Gastar Exploration (reduced to 15% by 2007). That year in a major move the company acquired Columbia Natural Resources for $2.2 billion.

To get better financial returns the company is selling assets to secure capital. Hurt by continuing low natural gas prices the company sold its midstream assets in 2012 and 2013 for $4.9 billion in three separate deals. As part of this move in 2012 the company sold its limited partner units and its general partner interests in Chesapeake Midstream Partners to Global Infrastructure Partners for $2 billion. That year the company also sold about $6.9 billion of its Permian basin properties in order to pay down debt.

To simplify its operations in 2012 Chesapeake spun off its oilfield service affiliate Chesapeake Oilfield Services.

In 2013 it also sold assets in the Northern Eagle Ford Shale and Haynesville Shale to an EXCO Resources subsidiary for $1 billion.

In 2013 the company sold its 50% undivided interest in 850000 acres in northern Oklahoma (its

EXECUTIVES

Svp Information Technology And Cio, Cathlyn L. (Cathy) Tompkins, age 57

Evp And Cfo, Domenic J. (Nick) Dell'Osso, age 42, $725,001 total compensation

Evp Exploration And Production, Frank J. Patterson, age 59, $600,000 total compensation

Evp General Counsel And Corporate Secretary, James R. Webb, age 50, $625,000 total compensation

President And Ceo, Robert D. (Doug) Lawler, age 51, $1,300,000 total compensation

Evp Operations And Technical Services, M. Jason Pigott, age 44, $574,999 total compensation

Vice President And Division Controller Operations, Randy Goben

Vice President Drilling, Dave Bert

Vice President Marine Information Technology, Steve A Melton

Vice President Human Resources, James jay Hawkins

Vice President, Mandy Duane

Vice President Information Technology, Steve Evans

Senior Vice President And Chief Accounting Officer, William Buergler

Vice President, Frank Gagliardi

Senior Vice President Information Technology And Cio, Cathy Tompkins

Vice President Of Human Resources, Jay james Hawkins

Vice President, Michael Harris

Vice President Marketing, Sarika Jewell

Vice President Internal Audit, John Christ

Evp And Cfo, Domenic Dell'osso Jr

Chairman, R. Brad Martin, age 66

Evp General Counsel And Corporate Secretary, James R. Webb, age 50

Assistant Secretary, Anita Brodrick

Auditors: PricewaterhouseCoopers LLP

LOCATIONS

HQ: Chesapeake Energy Corp.
6100 North Western Avenue, Oklahoma City, OK 73118
Phone: 405 848-8000
Web: www.chk.com

PRODUCTS/OPERATIONS

2016 Sales

	$ mil.	% of total
Marketing gathering & compression	4,584	58
Natural gas Oil and NGL	3,288	42
Total	**7,872**	**100**

COMPETITORS

Adams Resources	Koch Industries Inc.
Anadarko Petroleum	Noble Energy
Apache	OGE Energy
Ashland	Occidental Petroleum
BP	Par Pacific
Bonanza Creek	Patterson-UTI Energy
Chevron	Pioneer Natural
ConocoPhillips	Resources
Exxon Mobil	SandRidge Energy
Freeport-McMoRan Oil &	Southwestern Energy
Gas LLC	Unit Corporation

HISTORICAL FINANCIALS

Company Type: Public

Income Statement

FYE: December 31

	REVENUE ($ mil.)	NET INCOME ($ mil.)	NET PROFIT MARGIN	EMPLOYEES
12/17	9,496	949	10.0%	3,200
12/16	7,872	(4,401)	—	3,300
12/15	12,764	(14,685)	—	4,400
12/14	20,951	1,917	9.1%	5,500
12/13	17,506	724	4.1%	10,800
Annual Growth	**(14.2%)**	**7.0%**	**—**	**(26.2%)**

2017 Year-End Financials

Debt ratio: 80.27%	No. of shares (mil.): 906
Return on equity: —	Dividends
Cash ($ mil.): 5	Yield: —
Current ratio: 0.65	Payout: —
Long-term debt ($ mil.): 9,921	Market value ($ mil.): 3,590

	STOCK PRICE ($) FY Close	P/E High/Low		PER SHARE ($) Earnings	Dividends	Book Value
12/17	3.96	8	4	0.90	0.00	(0.55)
12/16	7.02	—	—	(6.45)	0.00	(1.63)
12/15	4.50	—	—	(22.43)	0.26	3.22
12/14	19.57	16	9	1.87	0.35	25.48
12/13	27.14	40	23	0.73	0.35	24.08
Annual Growth	**(38.2%)**	**—**	**—**	**5.4%**	**—**	**—**

Chevron Corporation

Chevron has earned its stripes as the #2 integrated oil company in the US behind Exxon Mobil. Its global operations explore for and produce oil and oil equivalents refines them into various fuels and other end products and sells them through gas stations airport fuel depots and industrial channels. Chevron boasts more than 11 billion barrels of proved reserves produces about 2.7 million barrels of oil per day and has refining capacity for nearly 1.7 million barrels per day. The company sells refined products branded under the Chevron Texaco and Caltex names through nearly 8000 gas stations in the US and almost 6000 outside the US.

HISTORY

Thirty years after the California gold rush a small firm began digging for a new product — oil. The crude came from wildcatter Frederick Taylor's well located north of Los Angeles. In 1879 Taylor and other oilmen formed Pacific Coast Oil attracting the attention of John D. Rockefeller's Standard Oil. The two competed fiercely until Standard took over Pacific Coast in 1900.

When Standard Oil was broken up in 1911 its West Coast operations became the stand-alone Standard Oil Company (California) which was nicknamed Socal and sold Chevron-brand products. After winning drilling concessions in Bahrain and Saudi Arabia in the 1930s Socal summoned Texaco to help and they formed Caltex (California-Texas Oil Company) as equal partners. In 1948 Socony (later Mobil) and Jersey Standard (later Exxon) bought 40% of Caltex's Saudi operations and the Saudi arm became Aramco (Arabian American Oil Company).

Socal exploration pushed into Louisiana and the Gulf of Mexico in the 1940s. In 1961 it bought Standard Oil Company of Kentucky (Kyso). The 1970s brought setbacks: Caltex holdings were nationalized during the OPEC-spawned upheaval and the Saudi Arabian government claimed Aramco in 1980.

In 1984 Socal was renamed Chevron and doubled its reserves with its $13 billion purchase of Gulf Corp. which had origins in the 1901 Spindletop gusher in Texas. Gulf became an oil power by developing Kuwaiti concessions but was hobbled when those assets were nationalized in 1975. After Gulf was rocked by disclosures that it had an illegal political slush fund Socal stepped in. The deal loaded the new company with debt and it cut 20000 jobs and sold billions in assets.

Chevron bought Tenneco's Gulf of Mexico properties in 1988 and in 1992 swapped fields valued at $1.1 billion for 15.7 million shares of Chevron stock owned by Pennzoil. It also moved into the North Sea in 1994.

In the 1990s Chevron gave its retailing units a tune-up. It allied with McDonald's (1995) to combine burger stands and gas stations in 12 western states. In addition the company sold 450 UK gas stations and a refinery to Shell (1997). Meanwhile Chevron sold its natural gas operation in 1996 for a stake in Houston-based NGC (later Dynegy ; sold in 2007) and it signed an onshore exploration contract in China the next year.

Poor economic conditions in Asia and slumping oil prices in 1998 forced Chevron to shed some US holdings including California properties. Looking for growth overseas in 1999 it bought Rutherford-Moran Oil increasing its interests in Thailand and Petrolera Argentina San Jorge Argentina's #3 oil company.

Chevron trimmed about 10% of its workforce in 1999 and 2000 in an effort to cut costs. As the rest of the industry consolidated Chevron discussed merging with Texaco but the talks collapsed in 1999. Later that year CEO Ken Derr retired and vice chairman Dave O'Reilly replaced him.

In 2000 Chevron formed a joint venture with Phillips Petroleum (later ConocoPhillips) that combined the companies' chemicals businesses as Chevron Phillips Chemical . That year talks with Texaco were revived and Chevron agreed to acquire its Caltex partner for about $35 billion in stock and about $8 billion in assumed debt. The deal completed in 2001 formed ChevronTexaco.

Part of the 2001 deal to acquire Texaco required Chevron to sell exclusive rights to the Texaco brand for a period of three years. A division of Royal Dutch Shell owned rights to the Texaco brand until 2004 and changed the name of the service stations to Shell. Once Chevron regained the rights to the Texaco name it revitalized the brand name by adding about 400 Texaco stations in the western US.

In 2002 ChevronTexaco divested its stakes in US downstream joint ventures Equilon (to Shell) and Motiva (to Shell and Saudi Aramco). It also sold part of a Gulf of Mexico pipeline and two natural gas plants in Louisiana to Duke Energy and its 12.5% stake in a natural gas liquids fractionator to Enterprise Products Partners. In 2004 ChevronTexaco sold 150 US natural gas and oil properties to XTO Energy for $912 million. The company changed its name to Chevron Corporation in 2005.

Chevron acquired Unocal in 2005 for more than $16 billion boosting its proved reserves by about 15%. Equally attractive to Chevron was the strategic position of Unocal's operations; at a time when industries are trying to get a foothold in China the reserves in Southeast Asia could easily be transported not only there but also to a surging India as well. Unocal's other operations easily supplied the US (from the Gulf of Mexico) and Europe (Caspian Sea) with gas and oil. Chevron bought a 5% stake in Indian refiner Reliance Petroleum for about $300 million in 2006. That year a company-led group of exploration firms announced a new successful oil strike in the Gulf of Mexico.

The company has also been growing its natural gas assets. In 2008 it announced plans to construct a $3.1 billion natural gas project in the Gulf of Thailand. The project will have the capacity to meet 14% of Thailand's natural gas needs.

Ultrapar acquired Chevron's Texaco-branded fuel distribution business in Brazil for $720 million in 2008 and the next year Chevron sold its Nigerian fuel marketing business.

A leading producer of viscous heavy oil in 2010 a Chevron-led consortium was awarded the rights to 40% of a heavy oil project in Venezuela's Orinoco Oil Belt.

In 2010 in the wake of the BP oil rig disaster in the Gulf of Mexico Chevron announced it was forming a $1 billion joint venture with Exxon Mobil Royal Dutch Shell and ConocoPhillips to create a rapid-response system capable of capturing and containing up to 100000 barrels of oil from an oil spill in water depths of 10000 feet.

Looking to develop a deepwater area unaffected by US regulations in 2010 the company acquired a 70% stake in three concessions in Liberia in West Africa. Other deepwater exploration asset acquisitions that year included purchases in China and the Turkish Black Sea.

In 2010 the company began to cut its US refining and marketing business staff by 20% and as part of this realignment it sold its 23% stake in Colonial Pipeline to a KKR affiliate.

In 2013 company acquired exploration interests in offshore Blocks EPP44 and EPP45 (more than 8 million acres in the Bight Basin off the South Australian coast).

Growing its LNG supply and export capacity in 2013 Chevron acquired a 50% operating interest in the Kitimat liquefied natural gas project and proposed Pacific Trail Pipeline and a 50% stake in 644000 acres of petroleum and natural gas rights in the Horn River and Liard Basins in British Columbia Canada. The company bought the assets from Apache for $405 million.

In a major move in 2011 Chevron acquired Atlas Energy in a $4.3 billion deal. The acquisition is part the company's strategy of finding new reserves to replace reserves lost from declining fields. It also marked Chevron's move to become a major player in the prolific Marcellus Shale play in Pennsylvania where a number of majors are seeking to cash in on the improved drilling technology that has made the exploitation of unconventional gas finds more commercially viable. The purchase gave Chevron Atlas Energy's 850 billion cu. ft. of proved natural gas reserves and 80 million cu. ft. of daily natural gas production. It also complements Chevron's earlier acquisitions of shale gas assets in Canada Poland and Romania as well as its purchase of an additional 228000 acres in the Marcellus Shale from Chief Oil & Gas LLC and Tug Hill Inc. (The acquisitions added up to 5 trillion cubic feet of natural gas resources to Chevron's existing Marcellus Shale operations.)

An earlier chapter of Chevron's history reemerged in 2011 when the company was slapped with a bill for $18 billion in fines and charges by a court in Ecuador regarding environmental damages allegedly caused by Texaco (acquired in 2001) in the 1970s and 1980s. Chevron challenged the findings as illegitimate and unenforceable.

Restructuring its refinery and retail businesses to cut costs in 2011 Chevron sold its Chevron Ltd. UK unit which operated the Pembroke refinery to Valero for $730 million. In addition Valero agreed to pay more that $1 billion for other Chevron Ltd. assets including 1000 gas stations. That year Chevron also sold its fuels marketing and aviation businesses in 16 countries in the Caribbean and Latin America and some marketing businesses in five African countries.

In 2012 the company signed a 20-year deal with Tohoku Electric Power for the delivery of liquefied natural gas (LNG) from the Chevron-operated Wheatstone natural gas project in Australia.

Growing its shale assets in 2013 Chevron agreed to a $1.24 billion investment in YPF to help YPF develop the world's second-largest shale gas deposit and fourth-largest shale oil reservoir located in Argentina's Vaca Muerta region. In 2013 and 2012 the company also announced new exploration and production deals to expand its assets in China Kurdistan the Republic of Congo Surinam and the US.

In 2013 50%-owned affiliate GS Caltex opened a 53000-barrel-per-day gas oil fluid catalytic cracking unit at the Yeosu Refinery in South Korea.

The company consolidated the supply and trading functions in 2013 into a single supply and trading group within Chevron's Gas and Midstream organization.

EXECUTIVES

Vp And Cfo, Patricia E. (Pat) Yarrington, age 61, $1,073,242 total compensation
Chairman And Ceo, Michael K. (Mike) Wirth, age 58, $1,094,492 total compensation

Evp Downstream And Chemicals, Pierre R. Breber, age 53

Vp And General Counsel, R. Hewitt (Hew) Pate, age 56, $867,000 total compensation

Evp Technology Projects And Services, Joseph C. (Joe) Geagea, age 58, $906,367 total compensation

Evp Upstream, James W. (Jay) Johnson, age 59, $1,012,417 total compensation

Managing Director Chevron Nigeria Mid-africa, Clay Neff, age 56

Vice President, John Oveson

Vice President Health Environment And Safety, Rhonda Zygocki

Vice President And General Cou, Wendy Daboval

Senior Vice President, Kevin Masson

Vice President Law, Tana Daughtrey

Vice President, Martin Donohue

Executive Vice President, Sandy Cab

Vice President Finance, Brenda Young

National Account Manager, Marcella Love

Vice President, Jay Byers

Vice Chairman Of The Board And Executive Vice President, Mike Wirth

Vice President Strategic Planning, Bruce Niemeyer

Vice President, Truett Enloe

Chairman And Ceo, Michael K. (Mike) Wirth, age 58

Vice Chairman Of The Board, Glenn F Tilton

Secretary, H Xun

Board Member, Thomas Hebert

Auditors: PricewaterhouseCoopers LLP

LOCATIONS

HQ: Chevron Corporation
6001 Bollinger Canyon Road, San Ramon, CA 94583-2324
Phone: 925 842-1000   **Fax:** 925 894-6017
Web: www.chevron.com

2016 sales

	$ mil.	% of total
US	56,187	42
International	72,843	55
Equity income and others	4,257	3
Adjustments	(18815)	-
Total	**144,472**	**100**

PRODUCTS/OPERATIONS

2016 Sales

	$ mil.	% of total
Downstream	94,743	71
Upstream	33,145	25
Equity income and others	4,257	3
Other	1,142	1
Adjustments	(18815)	-
Total	**114,472**	**100**

COMPETITORS

Anadarko Petroleum	Marathon Petroleum
BP	PEMEX
ConocoPhillips	PETROBRAS
Devon Energy	PetrÓleos de
Eni	Venezuela
Exxon Mobil	Repsol
Hess Corporation	Royal Dutch Shell
Imperial Oil	Sinopec Corp.
Koch Industries Inc.	TOTAL

HISTORICAL FINANCIALS

Company Type: Public

Income Statement

FYE: December 31

	REVENUE ($ mil.)	NET INCOME ($ mil.)	NET PROFIT MARGIN	EMPLOYEES
12/17	141,722	9,195	6.5%	51,900
12/16	114,472	(497)	—	55,200
12/15	138,477	4,587	3.3%	61,500
12/14	211,970	19,241	9.1%	64,700
12/13	228,848	21,423	9.4%	64,600
Annual Growth	(11.3%)	(19.1%)	—	(5.3%)

2017 Year-End Financials

Debt ratio: 15.27%
Return on equity: 6.26%
Cash ($ mil.): 4,813
Current ratio: 1.03
Long-term debt ($ mil.): 33,571

No. of shares (mil.): 1,904
Dividends
Yield: 0.0%
Payout: 89.0%
Market value ($ mil.): 238,450

	STOCK PRICE ($) FY Close	P/E High/Low		PER SHARE ($) Earnings	Dividends	Book Value
12/17	125.19	26	21	4.85	4.32	77.77
12/16	117.70	—	—	(0.27)	4.29	76.95
12/15	89.96	46	28	2.45	4.28	81.11
12/14	112.18	13	10	10.14	4.21	82.48
12/13	124.91	11	10	11.09	3.90	77.92
Annual Growth	0.1%	—	—	(18.7%)	2.6%	(0.0%)

CHEVRON PHILLIPS CHEMICAL COMPANY LLC

Among the world's largest petrochemical firms Chevron Phillips Chemical (CPChem) produces ethylene propylene polyethylene and polypropylene — sometimes used as building blocks for the company's other products such as pipe. Chevron Phillips Chemical also produces aromatics such as benzene and styrene specialty chemicals such as acetylene black (a form of carbon black) and mining chemicals. Chevron Phillips Chemical Company LP is CPChem's wholly-owned primary US operating subsidiary. CPChem is 50% owned by Chevron U.S.A. Inc. an indirect wholly-owned subsidiary of Chevron Corporation and 50% by wholly-owned subsidiaries of Phillips 66.

Operations

CPChem is a leading global producer of olefins and polyolefins (more than 80% of total sales) and a major supplier of aromatics alpha olefins styrenics specialty chemicals as well as piping material and other proprietary plastics. It is the Western Hemisphere's largest producer of high-density polyethylene — used in blow/injection molding plastic bags and pipes and films. CPChem also is near the top in styrene ethylene and aromatics production.

CPChem has several petrochemical joint ventures in the Middle East including Saudi Chevron Phillips Company (50%) and Qatar Chemical Company (not quite 50%). Subsidiary Chevron Oronite produces fuel additives.

The company's chemical products are used in more than 70000 consumer and industrial products. Its brands include Marlex Aromax Scentinel Soltex and K-Resin.

Geographic Reach

CPChem operates 35 manufacturing facilities and two research and development centers in Belgium China Colombia Qatar Saudi Arabia Singapore South Korea and the US.

Sales and Marketing

The company serves a range of markets including Adhesives and Sealants Agricultural Appliances Automotive Building and Construction Chemical Manufacturing Drycleaning Textiles Pharmaceuticals Paint and Coatings Imaging and Photography Packaging and Electronics.

Strategy

CPChem is growing its complex of chemical plants taking advantage of the deep pockets of its multinational parents increased demand for chemical products (especially in Asia) and the abundance of chemical raw materials generated by natural gas production in North American shale basins.

In 2015 the company completed an expansion of its normal alpha olefins capacity at its Cedar Bayou plant in Baytown. Alpha olefins are used in synthetic motor oils lubricants surfactants and other specialty applications.

Growing its infrastructure during 2014 CPChem completed the construction of a 1-hexene plant (the world's largest) at the company's Cedar Bayou complex in Baytown Texas with a design capacity of 250000 metric tons per year. The product 1-hexene is a component used in the manufacture of polyethylene a plastic resin commonly converted into film plastic pipe milk jugs detergent bottles and food and beverage containers.

In 2014 CPChem completed an ethylene expansion at its Sweeny complex in Old Ocean Texas.

That year to take advantage of chemical supply from nearby oil and gas basins the company committed $6 billion to build a 1.5-million-metric-tons/year (3.3 billion pounds/year) ethane cracker and two ethylene derivatives facilities on the US Gulf Coast. The two new polyethylene facilities will each have an annual capacity of 500000 metric tons (1.1 billion pounds). The projects are due to be completed in 2017.

To raise cash in 2015 the company sold its its Ryton polyphenylene sulfide business to Solvay for $220 million.

Company Background

In 2011 to expand its portfolio in Europe the company acquired a polyalphaolefin plant in Beringen Belgium from Neste Oil. The acquisition also added to the company's existing production of polyalphaolefins (PAOs) which are used in high-performance lubricants.

A coin toss determined whose name would go first when Chevron and Phillips Petroleum (now Phillips 66) formed 50-50 joint venture Chevron Phillips Chemical Company in 2000.

EXECUTIVES

Svp Petrochemicals, D. S. (Dave) Smith

President And Ceo, Mark E. Lashier

Vp And Cio, Peggy Colsman

Svp Cfo And Controller, Tim D. Leveille

Svp Projects And Supply Chain, R. E. (Ron) Corn

Svp Manufacturing, M. S. (Scott) Sharp

Svp Polymers, David Morgan

Vice President Of Human Resources, Greg Wagner

Vice President, Ken Hope

Vice President Human Resources, Donald Kremer

Vice President Manufacturing, Todd Monette

Auditors: ERNST & YOUNG LLP HOUSTON TX

LOCATIONS

HQ: CHEVRON PHILLIPS CHEMICAL COMPANY LLC
10001 SIX PINES DR, THE WOODLANDS, TX
773801498
Phone: 832 813-4100
Web: WWW.CPCHEM.COM

PRODUCTS/OPERATIONS

Selected Products

Olefins and polyolefins
  Ethylene
  Polyethylene
  Polyethylene pipe
  Polypropylene
  Propylene
Aromatics and styrenics
  Benzene
  Cumene
  Cyclohexane
  Paraxylene
  Styrene
Specialty products
  Acetylene black
  Alpha olefins
  Dimethyl sulfide
  Drilling specialty chemicals
  High-purity hydrocarbons and solvents
  Mining chemicals
  Neohexene
  Performance and reference fuels
  Polyalpha olefins
  Polystyrene

Selected Joint Ventures

Americas Styrenics (50%)
Chevron Phillips Singapore Chemicals (Private) Limited (50%)
KR Copolymer Co. Ltd. (60% South Korea)
Qatar Chemical Company Ltd. (Q-Chem 49%)
Saudi Chevron Phillips Company (50%)
Shanghai Golden Phillips Petrochemical Co. Ltd. (40%)

COMPETITORS

Dow Chemical	NOVA Chemicals
DuPont	SABIC
ExxonMobil Chemical	Sasol
Kraton	Total Petrochemicals
LyondellBasell	Westlake Chemical

HISTORICAL FINANCIALS

Company Type: Private

Income Statement   FYE: December 31

	REVENUE ($ mil.)	NET INCOME ($ mil.)	NET PROFIT MARGIN	EMPLOYEES
12/17	9,622	1,446	15.0%	5,000
12/16	8,769	1,687	19.2%	—
12/15	9,859	2,651	26.9%	—
12/14	14,148	3,288	23.2%	—
Annual Growth	(12.1%)	(24.0%)	—	—

2017 Year-End Financials

Debt ratio: ——
Return on equity: 15.00%
Cash ($ mil.): 676
Current ratio: 1.10
Long-term debt ($ mil.): —

Dividends
Yield: —
Payout: —
Market value ($ mil.): —

CHEVRON PHILLIPS CHEMICAL COMPANY LP

EXECUTIVES

Ceo, Peter L Cella
Exec V Pres, Mark E Lashier
Sr V Pres, Ron Corn
Sr V Pres, Tim Hill
V Pres, Mitch Eichelberger
Director of Operations, Tommy Gilligan
Coordinator, Aprile Turner
Finance Administrator, Jacqueline Ray
Marketing Manager, Lee Fixmer
Marketing Director, Marty Utterback
Technical Manager, Michael Rhodes
Auditors: ERNST & YOUNG LLP HOUSTON T

LOCATIONS

HQ: CHEVRON PHILLIPS CHEMICAL COMPANY LP
10001 SIX PINES DR, THE WOODLANDS, TX
773801498
Phone: 832 813-4100
Web: WWW.CPCHEM.COM

HISTORICAL FINANCIALS

Company Type: Private

Income Statement   FYE: December 31

	REVENUE ($ mil.)	NET INCOME ($ mil.)	NET PROFIT MARGIN	EMPLOYEES
12/17	7,919	841	10.6%	5,000
12/16	7,106	1,301	18.3%	—
12/15	7,990	2,020	25.3%	—
12/14	11,758	2,444	20.8%	—
Annual Growth	(12.3%)	(29.9%)	—	—

2017 Year-End Financials

Debt ratio: ——
Return on equity: 10.60%
Cash ($ mil.): 519
Current ratio: 1.00
Long-term debt ($ mil.): —

Dividends
Yield: —
Payout: —
Market value ($ mil.): —

Chipotle Mexican Grill Inc

Chipotle Mexican Grill is a popular quick-service restaurant chain. The company owns and operates more than 2350 quick-casual eateries popular for their burritos and other Mexican food items. Chipotle customers can build a 1-1/4 pound burrito from a lineup that includes chicken steak barbecue or free-range pork as well as beans rice guacamole and various other veggies and salsas. The company claims that with extras its menu offers thousands of choices. Chipotle restaurants also serve soft tacos crispy tacos chips and salsa beer and margaritas.

Operations
Chipotle no longer operates its ShopHouse Southeast Asian Kitchen locations.

Geographic Reach
Denver Colorado-based Chipotle sells its products in different types of locations such as in-line or end-cap locations in strip or power centers in regional malls and downtown business districts free-standing buildings food courts outlet centers airports military bases and train stations. The company categorizes its restaurants as end-caps (more than 1500 locations) free-standing units (almost 400) in-line (more than 350) and other (nearly 150). The average restaurant size is about 2500 square feet and seats about 60 people. About one-third of Chipotle?s restaurants are located in California Texas and Ohio.

Sales and Marketing
Despite food safety issues that have consumed the Chipotle in recent years the company still promotes the fact that it uses organically grown produce whenever possible and that its animal products are naturally raised and antibiotic free. Chipotle promotes its products through print outdoor transit and radio ads but it also incorporate digital advertising into the mix and conducts strategic promotions. It also has a dedicated team of field marketing staff that helps to connect its restaurants to local communities through fundraisers sponsorships and participation in local events.

The company's advertising and marketing expenses were approximately $106 million in 2017.

Financial Performance
Chipotle's revenue had been increasing year-over-year. However food safety problems caused revenue to slump in 2016. Its revenue bounced back in fiscal 2017. The company's revenue was $4.4 billion in fiscal 2017 up from $3.9 billion in fiscal 2016.

Chipotle's net income increased in fiscal 2017 compared to the prior fiscal year on the strength of its increased total revenue. The company's net income was $176.25 million in fiscal 2017 up from $22.9 million in fiscal 2016.

Strategy
While very much a quick-service restaurant chain Chipotle has successfully differentiated itself from other fast-food brands by focusing on its distinctive customer experience and food quality. Most of the restaurants feature a minimalist interior designed to appeal to the young adult segment while the made-to-order system sets the brand apart from other fast-food chains.Chipotle restaurants serve a focused menu of burritos tacos burrito bowls (a burrito without the tortilla) and salads.

Chipotle still has a long way to go to win back customers that were scared away by its food safety scares. The company has hired food safety experts as part of its effort to manage its public image.

EXECUTIVES

Chairman And Ceo, M. Steven (Steve) Ells, age 53, $1,540,000 total compensation
Cfo, John R. (Jack) Hartung, age 61, $792,308 total compensation
Chief Digital Officer And Cio, Curtis (Curt) Garner
Vice President Information Technology, Elvir Ibrahimpasic
Vice President, Karin Alexander
Chairman And Ceo, M. Steven (Steve) Ells, age 53
Auditors: Ernst & Young LLP

LOCATIONS

HQ: Chipotle Mexican Grill Inc
610 Newport Center Drive, Suite 1300, Newport Beach, CA 92660
Phone: 303 595-4000
Web: www.chipotle.com

COMPETITORS

ABP Corporation	Long John Silver's
Burger King	McDonald's
CKE Restaurants	Moe's Southwest Grill

Chick-fil-A	Panda Restaurant Group
Church's Chicken	Panera Bread
Del Taco	Popeyes
Einstein Noah	Qdoba Restaurants
Restaurant Group	Quiznos
El Pollo Loco	Red Robin
Fresh Enterprises	Subway
Jack in the Box	Taco Bell
KFC	Wendy's

HISTORICAL FINANCIALS

Company Type: Public

Income Statement
FYE: December 31

	REVENUE ($ mil.)	NET INCOME ($ mil.)	NET PROFIT MARGIN	EMPLOYEES
12/18	4,864	176	3.6%	73,000
12/17	4,476	176	3.9%	68,890
12/16	3,904	22	0.6%	64,570
12/15	4,501	475	10.6%	59,330
12/14	4,108	445	10.8%	53,090
Annual Growth	4.3%	(20.7%)	—	8.3%

2018 Year-End Financials

Debt ratio: —
Return on equity: 12.58%
Cash ($ mil.): 249
Current ratio: 1.81
Long-term debt ($ mil.): —

No. of shares (mil.): 27
Dividends
Yield: —
Payout: —
Market value ($ mil.): 11,959

	STOCK PRICE ($) FY Close	P/E High/Low	PER SHARE ($) Earnings	Dividends	Book Value
12/18	431.79	83 40	6.31	0.00	52.04
12/17	289.03	80 43	6.17	0.00	48.68
12/16	377.32	684461	0.77	0.00	48.67
12/15	479.85	50 32	15.10	0.00	69.58
12/14	684.51	48 33	14.13	0.00	64.86
Annual Growth	(10.9%)	— —	(18.3%)	—	(5.4%)

CHS Inc

EXECUTIVES

Pres-Ceo, Jay Debertin
Chb, Daniel Schurr
Exec V Pres-Cfo, Timothy Skidmore
Exec V Pres-Gen Counsel, James Zappa
Exec V Pres-Cso, Darin Hunhoff
V Pres Fin-Corp Contrl-Cao, Daniel Lehmann
Manager Sales, Jerome Irlmeier
Vice President, Mark Biedenfeld
Auditors: PricewaterhouseCoopers LLP

LOCATIONS

HQ: CHS Inc
  5500 Cenex Drive, Inver Grove Heights, MN 55077
Phone: 651 355-6000
Web: www.chsinc.com

COMPETITORS

ACH Food Companies	JR Simplot
ADM	Koch Industries Inc.
Ag Processing Inc.	Land O'Lakes Purina
Agrium	Feed
AmeriGas Partners	Louis Dreyfus Group
Andersons	Marathon Petroleum
BP	Marzetti
Bartlett and Company	Mondelez International
Bunge Limited	Mosaic Company
C.F. Sauer	Nestle

CGC	Riceland Foods
CITGO	Ridley Inc.
Cargill	Scoular
Columbia Grain	Shell Oil Products
ConAgra	Smucker
ConocoPhillips	U.S. Venture
Dakota Growers	US Soy
ExxonMobil Chemical	Unilever NV
Ferrellgas Partners	Valero Energy
Flint Hills	Western Petroleum
GROWMARK	Whole Harvest Foods
Gavilon Group	Wilbur-Ellis
Helena Chemical	

HISTORICAL FINANCIALS

Company Type: Public

Income Statement
FYE: August 31

	REVENUE ($ mil.)	NET INCOME ($ mil.)	NET PROFIT MARGIN	EMPLOYEES
08/18	32,683	775	2.4%	10,495
08/17	31,934	127	0.4%	11,626
08/16	30,347	424	1.4%	12,157
08/15	34,582	781	2.3%	12,511
08/14	42,664	1,081	2.5%	11,824
Annual Growth	(6.4%)	(8.0%)	—	(2.9%)

2018 Year-End Financials

Debt ratio: 25.65%
Return on equity: 9.67%
Cash ($ mil.): 450
Current ratio: 1.13
Long-term debt ($ mil.): 1,762

Dividends
Yield: 6.5%
Payout: —
Market value ($ mil.): —

	STOCK PRICE ($) FY Close	P/E High/Low	PER SHARE ($) Earnings	Dividends	Book Value
08/18	29.13	— —	(0.00)	2.00	(0.00)
08/17	29.47	— —	(0.00)	2.00	(0.00)
08/16	30.87	— —	(0.00)	2.00	(0.00)
08/15	28.39	— —	(0.00)	2.00	(0.00)
08/14	29.25	— —	(0.00)	1.50	(0.00)
Annual Growth	(0.1%)	— —	—	7.4%	—

Cigna Holding Co

With a significant position in the US health insurance market CIGNA covers some 16 million Americans with its various medical plans. The firm's offerings include PPO HMO point-of-service (POS) indemnity and consumer-directed products as well as specialty coverage in the form of dental vision pharmacy and behavioral health plans. It also sells group accident life and disability insurance. Customers include employers government entities unions Medicare recipients and other groups and individuals in North America. Internationally CIGNA sells life accident and health insurance in parts of Europe and Asia and provides health coverage to expatriate employees of multinational companies.

HISTORY

The Insurance Company of North America (INA) was founded in 1792 by Philadelphia businessmen. INA was the US's first stock insurance company and its first marine insurer. It later issued life insurance fire insurance and coverage for the contents of buildings. In 1808 it began using agents outside Pennsylvania. INA grew internationally in the late 1800s appointing agents in Canada as

well as in London and Vienna in Europe. It was the first US company to write insurance in China beginning in Shanghai in 1897.

In 1942 INA provided both accident and health insurance for men working on the Manhattan Project which developed the atomic bomb. It introduced the first widely available homeowner coverage in 1950. In 1978 INA bought HMO International which was then the largest publicly owned health maintenance organization in the US. INA merged with Connecticut General in 1982 to form CIGNA.

Connecticut General began selling life insurance in 1865 and health insurance in 1912. It wrote its first group insurance (for the Hartford Courant newspaper) in 1913 and the first individual accident coverage for airline passengers in 1926. In the late 1930s Connecticut General was a leader in developing group medical coverage. The company offered the first group medical coverage for general use in 1952 and in 1964 added group dental insurance.

After the merger CIGNA bought Crusader Insurance (UK 1983; sold 1991) and AFIA (1984). To begin positioning itself as a provider of managed health care the company sold its individual insurance products division to InterContinental Life in 1988 and its Horace Mann Cos. (individual financial services) to an investor group in 1989. To further its goal in 1990 CIGNA bought EQUICOR an HMO started by Hospital Corporation of America (now part of HCA Inc.) and what is now AXA Equitable Life Insurance.

In the early 1990s it began to withdraw from the personal property/casualty business to focus on small and midsized commercial clients in the US cutting sales overseas and combining them with life and health operations. It also exited such areas as airline insurance and surety bonds.

CIGNA expanded internationally in the mid-1990s opening a Beijing office in 1993 43 years after its departure from China. The next year the company bought 60% of an Indonesian insurance company. It also acquired 45% of Mediplan a managed health care organization in Mexico.

Reeling from unforeseen environmental liabilities (chiefly related to asbestos) CIGNA in 1995 split its remaining property/casualty business between a healthy segment that continued to write new policies and one for run-off business. Four years later it finally sold these operations (including Cigna Insurance Co. of Europe) to ACE Limited (later renamed Chubb Limited) in order to fund internal growth and acquisitions.

In the late 1990s the company continued to cultivate its health care segment acquiring managed care provider Healthsource in 1997. The company expanded its group benefits operations to India Brazil and Poland; at home it cut its payroll by 1300 in the US to counter rising costs. The company sold its domestic individual life insurance and annuity business in 1998 but began offering investment and pension products in Japan in 1999. In 2000 CIGNA settled a federal lawsuit over Medicare billing fraud. It also sold its reinsurance businesses that year to a subsidiary of Swiss Reinsurance Company while continuing to maintain some previous reinsurance policies on a runoff basis.

EXECUTIVES

Chief Medical Officer And Total Health & Network Lead, Alan M. Muney, age 65
Evp Human Resources And Services, John M. Murabito, age 60, $592,250 total compensation
Evp And Global Cio, Mark L. Boxer, age 59
President And Ceo, David M. Cordani, age 52, $1,200,000 total compensation

Evp And General Counsel, Nicole S. Jones, age 47, $581,137 total compensation
President U.s. Markets, Michael W. Triplett
President International Markets, Jason D. Sadler, age 49, $589,463 total compensation
Evp Chief Marketing And Customer Officer, Lisa R. Bacus, age 53
President Strategy Segments And Solutions, Christopher Hocevar
Evp And Cfo, Eric P. Palmer, age 42
President Mountain States (colorado New Mexico Utah And Wyoming), John Roble
Vice President Of Information Technolo, Jack Godsill
Vice President Corporate Communications At Cigna, Jon Sandberg
Vice President Sales, Sean Hughes
Vice President Middle Market Account Services, Paul Fruhwirth
National Account Manager, Marianne Byrne
Senior Vice President, Jack Wright
Vice President National Accounts, Kirk Drees
Vice President Pharmaceutical Contracting, Alex Krikorian
Regional Vice President, Tobin Hawkins
Senior Vice President Of Sales, Sasha Yamaguchi
National Accounts Manager, Jonathan Espinosa
National Account Manager, Steve Black
Vice President Talent Optimization, Charlene Parsons
Vice President National Accounts Dental, Karen Wever
Vice President, Antoinette Bonacci
Vice President, Joan Mastropaolo
Vice President National Account Executive, Melanie McCoy
Vice President, David Harman
Vice President Global Marketing Customer Relationship Management, Michele Paige
Vice President, Ed Eberhard
Vp Sales, Edgar Miranda
Assistant Vice President Global Storage And Backup Engineer, Anthony Szwankowski
Senior Vice President And Chief Actuary Cigna Supplemental Benefits, Tracy Maples
Senior Vice President And Associate Chief Counsel, Teresa Jordan
Vice President, Susan Quish
Vice President Clinical Operations, Jennifer Joy
Vice President Sales Northern California Cigna Healthcare, Kirby Hutson
Assistant Vice President Financial Control, Jim Bedard
Vice President Texas Sales, Chas Pierce
Assistant Vice President Operational Effectiveness And Bpo Strategy; Service Operations, Leeanne Engels
Vice President, Brian Smith
Vice President Sales Manager, Peter Gaddi
Assistant Vice President Network Operations, Maryanne Bourdier
Director Of Pharmacy Operations, Sunny Ogbonda
Vice President Information Strategy And Solutions, Daniel Carmody
Rvp Network Contracting, Susan Dennis-Buss
Vice President Global Product Strategy, Robert Wentling
Vice President Information Technology Infrastructure Services, Eric Reed
Vice President Sales And Account Services, Kevin Ritchie
Vp Corporate Development Cigna International, Rick Secchia
Vice President, William O'Donnell
Vice President National Account Executive, Barnett Michele
Vice President, Richard Secchia
Vp Medical Economics Cigna Healthcare, Christopher Whelan
Vice President, Kristen Gorodetzer

Vice President Head Of Direct To Consumer Channel, Marc Jeffreys
Vp Talent Optimization, Cindy Ryan
Vice President And Chief Information Security Officer, James Beeson
Vice President And Senior Director Strategic Operations, Jennifer Herz
Senior Vice President Information Technology, John Gabbert
Clinical Director Physician Assistant For Mohawk On Site Clinics, Cara Bramlett
National Account Manager, Patricia Lynn
Regional Vice President Government And Education, Sean Shepard
Medical Director, Melvin Watson
Senior Vice President Chief Clinical Officer Cigna, W Schaffer
Vice President Transformation National Accounts Team, Carol Gregor
Vice President Government And Education Florida And Caribbean, Yesenia Sanchez
Chairman, Isaiah (Ike) Harris, age 65
Board Member, John Partridge
Board Member, Eric Foss
Auditors: PricewaterhouseCoopers LLP

LOCATIONS

HQ: Cigna Holding Co
900 Cottage Grove Road, Bloomfield, CT 06002
Phone: 860 226-6000   Fax: 860 226-6741
Web: www.cigna.com

PRODUCTS/OPERATIONS

2017 Sales by Segment

	$ mil.	% of total
Global Health Care	32,753	79
Global Disability & Life	4,515	11
Global Supplemental Benefits	3,904	9
Other	463	1
Adjustments	(19)	-
Total	**41,616**	**100**

2017 Sales

	$ mil.	% of total
Premiums	32,307	78
Mail-order pharmacy	2,979	7
Net investment income	1,226	3
Net realized investment gains	237	-
Fees & other	4,867	12
Total	**41,616**	**100**

Selected Products and Services

Health care
  Behavioral health care benefits
  CareAllies (disease management and health advocacy)
  CIGNA Choice Fund (consumer-directed products)
  CIGNA Tel-Drug (mail order pharmacy)
  Dental insurance
  Managed care health plans (HMO PPO POS)
  Medicare Part D (prescription drug coverage)
  Prescription drug coverage
  Stop-loss coverage
  Voluntary plans
Disability and life
  Group disability insurance
  Group term life insurance
  Leave management services
  Workers' compensation case management
International
  Expatriate insurance
  Life accident and supplemental health insurance

COMPETITORS

AEGON	Kaiser Foundation
AIG	Health Plan
AMERIGROUP	MetLife
Aetna	Prudential
Anthem	The Hartford
BUPA	UnitedHealth Group
Blue Cross	Unum Group
Centene	WellCare Health Plans
Humana	

Company Type: Public

Income Statement   FYE: December 31

	ASSETS ($ mil.)	NET INCOME ($ mil.)	INCOME AS % OF ASSETS	EMPLOYEES
12/17	61,753	2,237	3.6%	46,000
12/16	59,360	1,867	3.1%	41,000
12/15	57,088	2,094	3.7%	39,300
12/14	55,898	2,102	3.8%	37,200
12/13	54,336	1,476	2.7%	36,500
Annual Growth	3.3%	11.0%	—	6.0%

2017 Year-End Financials

Debt ratio: 8.63%
Return on equity: 16.29%
Cash ($ mil.): 2,972
Current ratio: —
Long-term debt ($ mil.): —

No. of shares (mil.): 243
Dividends
  Yield: 0.0%
  Payout: 0.4%
Market value ($ mil.): 49,547

	STOCK PRICE ($) FY Close	P/E High/Low		PER SHARE ($) Earnings	Dividends	Book Value
12/17	203.09	24	15	8.77	0.04	56.30
12/16	133.39	20	16	7.19	0.04	53.42
12/15	146.33	21	12	8.04	0.04	46.91
12/14	102.91	13	9	7.83	0.04	41.55
12/13	87.48	17	10	5.18	0.04	38.35
Annual Growth	23.4%	—	—	14.1%	(0.0%)	10.1%

Cincinnati Financial Corp.

Cincinnati Financial Corporation (CFC) provides a wide range of financial security products and services primarily in the Midwest and Southeast United States. Its flagship firm Cincinnati Insurance (operating through four property/casualty subsidiaries) sells commercial property liability excess and surplus auto bond and fire insurance. The companies' personal lines include homeowners auto and liability products. Another CFC subsidiary Cincinnati Life sells life disability income and annuities. The company's CFC Investment unit provides commercial financing leasing and real estate services to its independent insurance agents. Its CSU Producers Resources offers insurance brokerage services to independent agencies. The Schiff family formed CFC in 1968.

Operations

CFC operates through five segments: Commercial Lines Insurance Personal Lines Insurance Excess and Surplus Lines Insurance Life Insurance and Investments. The Commercial Lines Insurance segment which accounts for about 55% of total sales provides coverage including commercial property/casualty workers' compensation and management liability. Personal Lines Insurance accounting for more than 20% of sales writes personal automobile and homeowner products.

Investment earnings represent nearly 15% of revenue while excess and surplus lines and life insurance make up the remainder.

Subsidiaries include standard property/casualty insurers Cincinnati Casualty Company Cincinnati Indemnity Company Cincinnati Life Insurance Company and Cincinnati Specialty Underwriters Insurance Company.

Geographic Reach

CFC markets its policies in more than 40 states but does most of its business in the Midwest and Southeast US. The company writes more than 15% of its business in Ohio and it is strong in Illinois Indiana Georgia Michigan North Carolina and Pennsylvania. It is licensed in 49 states the District of Columbia and Puerto Rico.

Sales and Marketing

CFC maintains a force of roughly 1700 field associates who provide local service to distributing independent agencies and policy holders.

The company's commercial lines segment targets primarily small to mid-sized businesses. CFC has tied its growth to expanding the territories in which it markets and to increasing the number of new agencies with which it strikes new relationships.

Financial Performance

CFC revenue which has been on the rise for the past five years rose 5% to $5.7 billion in 2017. That gain was largely due to higher earned premiums but the company also saw higher net investment income net realized investment gains and fee revenues that year. The Commercial Lines Personal Lines Excess and Surplus Lines and Life businesses all had increases in earned premiums that year.

Due to the company's growing revenues net income has generally been on the rise but it fell 7% to $591 million in 2016. The following year net income rose 77% to $1 billion. That gain was largely driven by a $495 million benefit related to US tax reforms that year as well as higher investment income after taxes.

Cash flow from operations fell 6% to $1.1 billion in 2017 primarily due to negative adjustments to deferred income tax expense.

Strategy

Going forward CFC plans to wring more profit out of policies by raising deductibles and conducting more site inspections of properties it insures. CFC also works on developing new products and helping its independent and captive agents better market existing policies. To further broaden its operations the company works toward deepening its penetration into each market it serves. For example it has been introducing workers' compensation coverage in more states and new types of coverage launched include cyber protection and management liability.

The year 2017 hit CFC and other US insurers hard with three major hurricanes and wildfires in California. To counteract the negative impact that can occur in years with numerous catastrophes the company plans to continue its geographic expansion and improve its underwriting activities. And to decrease the frequency and severity of auto losses — which have been rising across the industry — the company has partnered with software firm LifeSaver to help employers enforce safety policies and prevent fleet drivers from phone-related distracted driving practices.

With the goal of providing its agents with the best option for complex commercial coverage CFC has been hiring more underwriters buying risk data and implementing a risk-management information system.

The group is also expanding its products and services for wealthy individuals. Since 2015 it has introduced the Executive Capstone program in New York California Colorado and New Jersey; in 2017 it launched these offerings in additional markets including Washington Texas Massachusetts and Washington DC.

HISTORY

Jack Schiff spent three years with the Travelers Company before he joined the Navy in WWII. He returned to Cincinnati to start his own independent insurance agency in 1946 and was joined by his younger brother Robert; both were Ohio State graduates whose affection for the Buckeyes led them in later years to close company banquets with the school fight song. The brothers incorporated Cincinnati Insurance with $200000 from investors.

Under Harry Turner the company's first president the company offered property/casualty insurance to small businesses and homeowners through its network of agents. By 1956 the company had spread into neighboring Kentucky and Indiana. During the next decade Cincinnati Insurance expanded its products and network adding auto burglary and commercial all-risk lines and enlisting agents throughout the Midwest.

In 1963 Turner took the chairman's seat and Jack Schiff became president introducing a more aggressive leadership style. In 1969 the company reorganized and went public forming Cincinnati Financial Corporation as a holding company for the insurance operation. CFC used the money to pay off debts and buy new businesses forming two subsidiaries: CFC Investment Company in 1970 to deal in commercial real estate and financing; and Queen City Indemnity (later named The Cincinnati Casualty Company) in 1972 to offer direct-bill personal policies.

By 1973 operations included The Life Insurance Company of Cincinnati Queen City Indemnity and fellow Cincinnati giant Inter-Ocean Insurance Company. That year Jack Schiff added CEO to his title.

CFC continued to grow throughout the 1970s with a new emphasis on independent investments. In 1982 Cincinnati Financial veteran Robert Morgan became president and CEO. The company's conservative roots and investment base helped it shake off the early-1980s recession and a string of natural disasters that left many other insurers dangling in the wind.

Also during the 1980s the company started to shift its focus from personal to commercial lines. In 1988 it reorganized its life insurance subsidiaries under the Cincinnati Life banner and formed The Cincinnati Indemnity Company to offer workers' compensation and personal insurance.

EXECUTIVES

Senior Vice President Strategic Planning Cincinnati Insurance, Donald Doyle

Senior Vice President Commercial Lines, Charles Stoneburner

President Ceo And Director, Steven J. Johnston, age 58, $960,814 total compensation

Vice President Commercial, Anthony Henn

Svp Cfo And Treasurer, Michael J. (Mike) Sewell, age 54, $784,665 total compensation

Svp Chief Investment Officer Assistant Secretary And Assistant Treasurer, Martin F. Hollenbeck, age 58, $646,808 total compensation

Assistant Vice President Field Claims, Jack Kelley

Vice President, Craig Forrester

Senior Vice President, Lisa Love

Assistant Vice President Government Relations Of, Scott Gilliam

Vice President, Gary J Kline

Senior Vice President And Senior Marketing Officer, Glenn Nicholson

Assistant Vice President Information Technology, Michael Hingsbergen

Vice President Commercial Lines Central, Joel W Davenport

Vice President Marketing, Mark McBeath

Vice President Commercial Lines, Mark Wietmarschen

Vice President Information Technology, Rich Williamson

Assistant Vice President For Education, BradleyBrad Delaney

Assistant Vice President Commercial Lines, Elizabeth Stephens

Vice President Of Personal Lines, Stephen Leibel

Assistant Vice President Information Technology, Kim Beckman

Senior Vice President, Joan Shevchik

Vice President, Tom Scheid

Assistant Vice President, Carol Oler

Vice President And Manager Target Markets, Ronald Klimkowski

Vice President Marketing, Mike Terrell

Legal Secretary, Rebecca Alexander

Vice President Sales And Marketing, Duane Swanson

Assistant Vice President, Frank Obermeyer

Avp It, Ryan Osborn

Assistant Vice President Headquarters Claims, William Gregory

Vice President Sales And Marketing, Sean Givler

Vice President Sales And Marketing, Duane Swanson

Vice President And Chief Information Security Officer, Mike Dockery

Assistant Vice President Director Of Worksite Marketing, Eric Taylor

Executive Vice President, Blake D Slater

Assistant Vice President Commercial Lines Proper, David E McKinney

Vice President Assistant Secretary And Assistant Treasurer Pre, Kenneth Miller

Vice President, Richard Matson

Vice President Nformation Technology, Bill Geir

Vp Commercial Lines The Cincinnati Insurance Company, William Thomas

Vice President Commercial Lines Director Of Underwriting, Rick Ferris

Vice President, David Helmers

Vice President Target Markets, Klimkowski Ron

Executive Vice President, Jf Scherer

Vice President Field Claims, Charles Robinson

Vice President, Joseph Kinsey

Vice President Corporate Comminications, Elizabeth Ertel

Vice President Reinsured Assumed, John Davis

Assistant Vice President Headquarters Claims, John Crow

Assistant Vice President For Education, Bradley Delaney

Vice President Director Of Risk Management, Vicki Walno

Region Vice President, Pat Luchtel

Vice President, Mike Abrams

Chairman, Kenneth W. (Ken) Stecher, age 71

President Ceo And Director, Steven J. Johnston, age 58

Svp Cfo And Treasurer, Michael J. (Mike) Sewell, age 54

Svp Chief Investment Officer Assistant Secretary And Assistant Treasurer, Martin F. Hollenbeck, age 58

Secretary Life And Health Claims Cincinnati Life Insurance Company, Ann Binzer

Secretary, Susan Fitzgerald

Board Member, John Steele

Secretary Headquarters Claims The Cincinnati Insurance Company, Troy Reichers

Board Member, BRENDA GAGNON

Assistant Treasurer, William Loftis

Board Member, Kenneth Lichtendahl

Assistant Secretary Process Developmenteducation, David Pierce

Board Member, Linda Clement-Holmes

Secretary Commercial Lines The Cincinnati Insurance Company, Pamela Cooper

Assistant Secretary Headquarters Claims The Cincinnati Insurance Company, Dale Prisco

Auditors: DELOITTE & TOUCHE LLP

LOCATIONS

HQ: Cincinnati Financial Corp.
  6200 S. Gilmore Road, Fairfield, OH 45014-5141
Phone: 513 870-2000
Web: www.cinfin.com

PRODUCTS/OPERATIONS

2017 Sales

	$ mil.	% of total
Earned premiums	4,954	86
Net investment income	609	11
Realized investment gains	148	3
Fees	16	-
Other	5	-
Total	**5,732**	**100**

2017 Sales

	$ mil.	% of total
Commercial lines	3,170	55
Personal lines	1,246	22
Investment income	757	13
Life insurance	237	4
Excess & surplus	210	4
Other	112	2
Total	**5,732**	**100**

Selected Subsidiaries

CFC Investment Company
CSU Producer Resources Inc.
The Cincinnati Insurance Company
  The Cincinnati Casualty Company
  The Cincinnati Indemnity Company
  The Cincinnati Life Insurance Company
  The Cincinnati Specialty Underwriters Insurance
  Company

COMPETITORS

American Financial	Progressive
Group	Corporation
CNA Financial	Selective Insurance
Erie Indemnity	The Hartford
Farmers Group	Travelers Companies
Indiana Insurance	Westfield Insurance
Ohio Casualty	Zurich American
OneBeacon	

HISTORICAL FINANCIALS

Company Type: Public

Income Statement

FYE: December 31

	ASSETS ($ mil.)	NET INCOME ($ mil.)	INCOME AS % OF ASSETS	EMPLOYEES
12/17	21,843	1,045	4.8%	4,925
12/16	20,386	591	2.9%	4,754
12/15	18,888	634	3.4%	4,493
12/14	18,753	525	2.8%	4,305
12/13	17,662	517	2.9%	4,163
Annual Growth	**5.5%**	**19.2%**	**—**	**4.3%**

2017 Year-End Financials

Debt ratio: 3.90%
Return on equity: 13.66%
Cash ($ mil.): 657
Current ratio: —
Long-term debt ($ mil.): —

No. of shares (mil.): 163
Dividends
  Yield: 0.0%
  Payout: 39.7%
Market value ($ mil.): 12,288

	STOCK PRICE ($) FY Close	P/E High/Low	PER SHARE ($) Earnings	Dividends	Book Value
12/17	74.97	13 11	6.29	2.50	50.29
12/16	75.75	22 15	3.55	1.92	42.94
12/15	59.17	16 13	3.83	2.30	39.21
12/14	51.83	16 14	3.18	1.76	40.15
12/13	52.37	17 12	3.12	1.66	37.24
Annual Growth	**9.4%**	**—**	**19.2%**	**10.9%**	**7.8%**

Cintas Corporation

Cintas has a uniform approach to business. The #1 uniform supplier in the US boasts more than 1 million clients (McDonald's MGM Resorts) and some 5 million people wear its garb each day. Cintas — which sells leases and rents uniforms — operates 386 facilities in 288 cities across the US and Canada; it leases about half of them. Besides offering shirts jackets slacks and footwear the company provides clean-room apparel and flame-resistant clothing. Other products offered by Cintas include uniform cleaning first-aid and safety products and clean-room supplies. Richard Farmer founded the company in 1968. Cintas is run by his son CEO Scott Farmer.

Operations

In 2015 Cintas realigned its organizational structure and updated its reportable operating segments in light of certain changes in its business including the acquisition of ZEE Medical. It now has two segments - Uniform Rental and Facility Services and First Aid and Safety Services.

Uniform Rental and Facility Services (77% of total revenues in 2016) consists of the rental and servicing of uniforms and other garments including flame resistant clothing mats mops and shop towels and other ancillary items. In addition to these rental items it provides restroom cleaning services and supplies and carpet and tile cleaning services.

First Aid and Safety Services (9%) consists of first aid and safety products and services.

The remainder of Cintas' businesses (14%) consist primarily of Fire Protection Services and its Direct Sale business.

Geographic Reach

Cincinnati-based Cintas operates about 377 facilities including five manufacturing plants and eight distribution centers in some 286 cities across the US and Canada. It also serves businesses in Asia Europe and Latin America. The company has approximately 9000 local delivery routes.

Sales and Marketing

Cintas provides its products and services to more than 1 million businesses of all sizes. Cintas uses its corporate website www.cintas.com as a channel for routine distribution of important information including news releases analyst presentations and financial information.

Financial Performance

The company has seen an upward trend in its revenues since 2011.

In fiscal 2016 Cintas' net revenues increased by 10%.

Revenues from the Uniform Rental and Facility Services grew by 6.7% including an organic revenue increase of 6.4%. The amount of new business grew resulting from an increase in the number and productivity of sales representatives due to increased tenure and improved training which resulted in a higher number of products and services sold. Revenues also rose via acquisitions and increased working days in fiscal 2016.

First Aid and Safety Services and All Other revenues increased 20.3%. Some 8% was due to improved sales representative productivity. Acquisitions positively impacted the growth rate by 11.8% and two more workdays positively impacted growth.

Cintas has recorded an increasing trend net income over the last five years.

In fiscal 2016 net income increased by 61% due to income from discontinued operations (Shred-it).

Cash from operating activities decreased by 20% due to the $229.5 million payment of taxes due on the gain on the sale of Shred-it. Excluding the impact of this tax payment net cash provided by operations increased $115 million as a result of increased net income partially offset by changes in working capital.

Strategy

Cintas' strategy for adding to its customer base includes investing in its sales force across all business segments as well expanding geographically. Beyond its dominant position in uniform rental and sales Cintas is looking to emerging businesses such as First Aid Safety and Fire Protection Services for growth. While still relatively small representing 9% of sales the business is growing through acquisitions and the introduction of new services. It is looking to increase its penetration with existing customers and by broadening its customer base to include business segments to which it has not historically served. It will also continue to identify additional product and service opportunities for its current and future customers.

The company pursues the strategy of broadening its customer base in several ways. Cintas has a national sales organization introducing all of its products and services to prospects in all business segments. Its broad range of products and services allows its sales organization to consider any type of business a prospect. It also broadens its customer base through geographic expansion especially in its first aid and safety and fire protection businesses.

To raise cash to pay down debt and reinvest in its core businesses in 2015 Cintas sold its 42% stake in Shred-it International to JV partner Stericycle for about $600 million. In 2014 the company exited another line of business when it sold a portion of its document management operations for $180 million.

Mergers and Acquisitions

As part of the strategy in 2016 Cintas acquired two businesses included in the Uniform Rental and Facility Services segment two businesses included in the First Aid and Safety Services segment and six businesses included in All Other. The company also acquired Zee Medical for $130 million which expanded its footprint in van-delivered first aid safety training and emergency products.

In 2017 Cintas acquired rival G&K Services a top-five uniform rental company for $2.2 billion. The acquisition will bolster Cintas' business customer base broaden its service areas and strengthen its route operations. G&K Services now operates as a subsidiary of the company.

HISTORY

In 1929 onetime animal trainer boxer and blacksmith Richard "Doc" Farmer started a business of salvaging old rags cleaning them and then selling them to factories. Farmer later began renting the rags to his customers. He would pick up the dirty rags clean them and return them to the factory. By 1936 the Acme Overall & Rag Laundry had established itself in Cincinnati with plans to convert an old bathhouse into a laundry. Farmer along with his adopted son Herschell suffered a setback from flood damage in 1937 but the family rebuilt and continued to grow the business.

Doc Farmer died in 1952 and Herschell assumed command of the company. Five years later Herschell turned the reins over to his 23-year-old son Richard who immediately moved Acme into the uniform rental market and the company blossomed. Throughout the 1960s the company grew enormously aided by Richard's innovative leadership. (Acme was the first to use a polyester-cotton blend that lasted twice as long as normal cotton work uniforms.) Through a holding company Richard established a string of uniform plants in the Midwest starting with a factory in Cleveland in

1968. Four years later the company changed its name to Cintas.

At this time the company began tapping into the new corporate identity market pushing the idea that uniforms convey a sense of professionalism and present a cleaner safer image. The company began to custom-design the uniforms adding logos and distinctive colors. This aspect of the business compelled Cintas to expand to help accommodate its national clients; by 1972 the company had offices throughout Ohio and in Chicago Detroit and Washington DC. By 1975 Cintas was operating in 13 states.

The company went public in 1983. For the rest of the 1980s Cintas rode the wave of consolidation in the uniform rental industry making a slew of acquisitions. The company also expanded from its blue-collar base into the service industry and began to supply uniforms to hotels restaurants and banks. By the early 1990s Cintas was a presence in most major US cities and its share of the US market had climbed to about 10%. Farmer turned over the title of CEO to president Robert Kohlhepp in 1995. That year the company acquired Cadet Uniform Services a Toronto uniform rental business for $41 million.

Scott Farmer Richard's 38-year-old son was named president and COO in 1997. That year Cintas made a number of acquisitions including Micron-Clean Uniform Service and Canadian firms Act One Uniform Rentals and DW King Services. The company also moved into the first aid supplies industry with its purchase of American First Aid and added clean-room garments to its expanding list of uniform rentals. In 1998 Cintas acquired uniform rental company Apparelmaster as well as Chicago-based Uniforms To You a $150 million design and manufacturing company. In an effort to expand its corporate uniform business the company acquired rival Unitog in 1999 for about $460 million.

As part of the integration of Unitog in 2000 Cintas closed several of Unitog's uniform rental operations distribution centers and manufacturing plants. The company also established first aid supplies and safety equipment unit Xpect. In 2002 Cintas purchased Omni Services marking its largest acquisition to date.

Cintas purchased more than 10 document management businesses and three first-aid and fire protection businesses in fiscal 2009.

In fiscal 2013 it launched its AR Red Suiting Collection (made with renewable-sourced fiber) as well as its Signature Series line of designer soap and toilet paper dispensers and related products.

EXECUTIVES

Vp Research And Development, J. Phillip Holloman, age 63, $643,966 total compensation

Chairman And Ceo, Scott D. Farmer, age 59, $1,000,000 total compensation

Svp Secretary And General Counsel, Thomas E. Frooman, age 51, $499,550 total compensation

Vp Finance And Cfo, J. Michael (Mike) Hansen, age 50, $360,000 total compensation

Vp And Treasurer, Paul F. Adler, age 47, $250,000 total compensation

National Account Manager, John Shannon

Regional Vice President, Greg Eling

Senior Vice President Operations, Dave Pollack

National Account Manager, Eric Wermes

Vice President Corporate Development, Mike Mahoney

Vice President And Marriott Lodging Uniforms And Services, Donna L Williams

Executive Vice President Finance Principal Accounting Officer And Chief Financial Officer, Michael Hansen

Chairman And Ceo, Scott D. Farmer, age 59

Svp Secretary And General Counsel, Thomas E. Frooman, age 51

Vp And Treasurer, Paul F. Adler, age 47

Board Member, Lynn Burton

Treasurer, Mike Thompson

Auditors: Ernst & Young LLP

LOCATIONS

HQ: Cintas Corporation
6800 Cintas Boulevard, P.O. Box 625737, Cincinnati, OH 45262-5737

Phone: 513 459-1200   **Fax:** 513 573-4030

Web: www.cintas.com

PRODUCTS/OPERATIONS

2016 sales

	$ mil.	% of total
Uniforms Rental & Facility Services	3,777	77
First aid and safety services	461	9
All others	665	14
Total	**4,905**	**100**

Selected Products and Services

Clean-room supplies
Entrance mats
Fender covers
Fire protection
First aid and safety products and services
Linen products
Mops
Restroom supplies
Towels
Uniform cleaning
Uniform rental and sales

COMPETITORS

ARAMARK	NCH
Alsco	Superior Uniform Group
Angelica Corporation	UniFirst
Iron Mountain Inc	

HISTORICAL FINANCIALS

Company Type: Public

Income Statement

FYE: May 31

	REVENUE ($ mil.)	NET INCOME ($ mil.)	NET PROFIT MARGIN	EMPLOYEES
05/18	6,476	842	13.0%	41,000
05/17	5,323	480	9.0%	42,000
05/16	4,905	693	14.1%	35,000
05/15	4,476	430	9.6%	32,000
05/14	4,551	374	8.2%	33,000
Annual Growth	**9.2%**	**22.5%**	**—**	**5.6%**

2018 Year-End Financials

Debt ratio: 36.44%
Return on equity: 31.68%
Cash ($ mil.): 138
Current ratio: 2.55
Long-term debt ($ mil.): 2,535

No. of shares (mil.): 106
Dividends
Yield: 0.8%
Payout: 21.4%
Market value ($ mil.): 19,378

	STOCK PRICE ($) FY Close	P/E High/Low	PER SHARE ($) Earnings	Dividends	Book Value
05/18	182.25	24 16	7.56	1.62	28.37
05/17	125.88	28 20	4.38	1.33	21.85
05/16	94.80	15 13	6.21	1.05	17.68
05/15	86.09	23 17	3.63	1.70	17.30
05/14	62.12	20 15	3.05	0.77	18.74
Annual Growth	**30.9%**	**— —**	**25.5%**	**20.4%**	**10.9%**

Cisco Systems Inc

Cisco Systems makes the network gear — routers switches and servers as well as software — that moves information around the internet and corporate networks. The company which has dominated the market for internet protocol-based networking equipment also makes security devices internet conferencing systems set-top boxes and other networking equipment to businesses and government agencies. Software that controls networks has become an increasing focus for Cisco which also provides consulting services. Most sales come from customers in the Americas. Cisco's primary customers are large enterprises and telecommunications service providers but it also sells products designed for small businesses.

Operations

The meat-and-potatoes of Cisco has been its switching equipment which generates 30% of its revenue while its next-generation networking routing gear accounts for 15% of revenue. Services provide about a quarter of the company's revenue. The rest of the company's product lines are collaboration products (about 10% of revenue) data center (less than 10%) and wireless and security (about 5% each).

Cisco engages independent third-party contractors to make printed-circuit boards conduct in-circuit testing make product repairs and assemble products.

Geographic Reach

While the Americas is Cisco's largest market accounting for some 60% of its sales about half its employees reside outside of the US. European customers generate 25% of revenue and the Asia/Pacific region supplies about 15%.

Cisco's headquarters is in San Jose California. It also has regional headquarters in Amsterdam and Singapore. Cisco has a Globalization Center East campus in Bangalore India. The company has other significant operations in Belgium China France Germany India Israel Italy Japan Norway and the UK.

Financial Performance

Cisco Systems? revenue slipped 3% to $48 billion in 2017 (ended July) from 2016. Product revenue fell 4% while service revenue rose 3% year-to-year. Revenues from Switching and NGN Routing were off 5% and 4% respectively in 2017. Switching sales were hurt by lower sales of switches used in campus environments due to general economic uncertainty and competition. Sales in Security and Wireless grew by 9% and 5% respectively.

Net income dropped 11% to $9.6 billion in 2017 from 2016. While the company reduced costs in 2017 it had a higher effective tax rate for the year.

Cash flow from operations closed out 2017 at $13.8 billion compared to about $13.6 billion in 2016.

Strategy

Cisco has been a hardware company making the switches and routers and other devices that transfer information. But it is building up its software offerings for cloud computing and software-defined networks (SDN). Telecom service providers in particular are moving toward SDN to program their networks. In response Cisco is shifting its business to a more subscription and software-based model. To address the emergence of SDN the company offers its Application Centric Infrastructure (ACI) which delivers centralized application-driven policy automation management and visibility of both physical and virtual environments as a single system. The system is composed of Cisco's Nexus 9000 portfolio of switches improved versions of its NX-OS operating system and the Application Policy Infrastructure Controller (APIC).

In another software-centric strategy the company's Cisco DNA Center a centralized management dashboard for its intuitive network and ETA are available through subscriptions on the Cisco Catalyst 9000 Series Switches. Such moves get Cisco closer to cloud-managed products and services across its networking portfolio. In 2017 (ended July) the company's deferred product revenue related to software and subscriptions grew to $5 billion a 50% year-to-year increase and a doubling over two years.

The company is also addressing its software capabilities through acquisitions. In 2017 the company was to spend nearly $6 billion to shore up its software side in networking file systems and telecommunications.

In 2015 Cisco partnered with Ericsson to develop products and services in areas such as 5G cloud computing internet protocol and the Internet of Things. Their goal is to add $1 billion in revenue for each company by 2018. The deal helps Cisco and Ericsson counter the merger of Alcatel-Lucent and Nokia which created the second biggest provider of telecom equipment (Huawei is #1).

In 2017 Cisco teamed up with Google to build more efficient hybrid cloud offerings. They are to work on the security configuration and policy requirements of enterprises as well as capabilities for delivering real-time networking and performance data.

Mergers and Acquisitions

Cisco regularly acquires companies to expand technologies and fill gaps.

In 2018 Cisco said it would buy privately-held Luxtera which uses silicon photonics to make chips with optics capabilities for faster transmission for about $660 million. Cisco intends to use Luxtera's technology to increase the speed and capacity that its networking equipment can provide for webscale and enterprise data centers service provider market segments and other customers. The deal is expected to close in 2019.

Also in 2018 Cisco acquired Duo Security a developer of security software for about $2.3 billion. Duo develops two-factor authentication software which helps companies keep track of employees as they log in from multiple devices such as a computer at the office or a phone from home. The deal deepens Cisco's software portfolio and strengthens its security offerings.

Cisco started 2017 with the $3.7 billion acquisition of AppDynamics which develops software that monitors performance of applications. The acquisition further fills out Cisco's networking software lineup. Cisco's acquisition offer came just before AppDynamics sold stock to the public in an initial public offering. The deal concluded in March 2017 reinforced Cisco's software-centric strategy.

In mid-2017 Cisco agreed to acquire Springpath Inc. a developer of a distributed file system built for hyperconvergence that enables server-based storage systems for about $320 million in cash. The companies have had a relationship that includes development of HyperFlex an integrated hyperconvergence infrastructure. Cisco also was an investor in Springpath. Hyperconvergence integrates computing storage networking and virtualization resources in hardware. The deal further builds out Cisco's data center capabilities.

Cisco continued its software shopping spree later in 2017 with its agreement to buy BroadSoft a developer of telecommunications software for $1.9 billion. The deal would provide Cisco with a range of software and services that allow mobile fixed-line and cable service providers to offer unified communications over their internet protocol networks. The transaction closed in early 2018.

In another 2017 deal Cisco acquired MindMeld Inc. an artificial intelligence company that develops conversational interfaces for applications and devices for about $125 million. The acquisition would help Cisco build voice and text capabilities into its collaboration products.

In 2016 Cisco completed the acquisition of Jasper which develops a cloud-based Internet of Things (IoT) service platform for $1.4 billion. With the deal Cisco can provide more comprehensive range of IoT products and services.

In 2016 Cisco completed the acquisition of Jasper which develops a cloud-based Internet of Things (IoT) service platform for $1.4 billion. With the deal Cisco can provide more comprehensive range of IoT products and services.

EXECUTIVES

Vp; General Manager Broadband Edge And Midrange Routing Business Unit, Pankaj S. Patel, $749,135 total compensation

Svp Emea Sales, Chris Dedicoat, $691,490 total compensation

Svp Cloud Services And Platforms; Cto, Zorawar Biri Singh

Chairman And Ceo, Charles H. (Chuck) Robbins, age 52, $1,172,115 total compensation

President Asia Pacific, Owen Chan

Svp And Chief Operations, Rebecca J. Jacoby

Svp And General Manager Collaboration Technology Group, Rowan M. Trollope

President Cisco Capital, Kristine A. (Kris) Snow, age 58

President Latin America Theater, Jordi Botifoll

President Smart+connected Communities And Deputy Chief Globalization Officer, Anil Menon

Svp And General Manager Cisco Security Solutions, Bryan Palma

Evp And Cfo, Kelly A. Kramer, $749,135 total compensation

Svp And Cio, Guillermo Diaz

Svp And Chief Marketing Officer, Karen Walker

President Cisco India And Saarc, Sameer Garde

Vice President Legal Services Deputy General Counsel And Secretary, Evan Sloves

Vice President, Mark Gorman

Senior Vice President Marketing For The Insieme Business Unit, Soni Jiandani

Vice President Middle East And Turkey Operat, Mike Weston

Regional Vice President Northeast, Mei Ling

Vice President Corporate Marketing Cisco Canada, Willa Black

Vice President Of Business Development, Mario Mastromattei

Vice President Of Business Development, Bonnie Yang

Vice President Marketing Deutsche Telekom Ag, Hanswerner Neubert

Vice President, Arcangelo Fanelli

Vice President, Bruce Laird

Senior Vice President Global And Transformational Partner Organizati, Wendy Bahr

Vice President Product Management And Marketing, Tuqiang Cao

Vice President Canadian Services Operations, Derek Mak

Vice President Global Isv And Technology Partners, Denny Trevett

Vice President Corporate Affairs, Amy Christen

Vice President Market Development, Paul Bosco

Vice President Global Iot Service Operations, Cliff Johnson

Vice President Plant, Don McClaughlin

Vice President Global Video And Connected Life Solutions, Stephen Silva

Vice President Enterprise And Mid Market Solutions Marketing, Paul McNab

Vice President And Ct0, Bret Hartman

Senior Vice President Software, John Brigden

Regional Vice President Cisco Systems Administrator, Mark Guerrazzi

Vice President Advanced Services, Flint Brenton

Senior Vice President And General Manager: Server Access Virtualization Group, David Yen

Area Vice President Us Sales, Georges Antoun

Vice President, John Graham

Vpam Small Business Fl South North Carolina South Carolina, Richard Hinkley

Vpss Flexpod, Cesar Hurtado

Vice President Worldwide Manufacturing, Gregory Taylor

Vice President Of Marketing, Thomas Hooker

Vice President Federal Operations, Ed McCrossen

Vice President, Randy Harrell

Vice President Customer Value Chain Management, Jeff Devine

Vice President New Business Ventures, Sanjay Pol

Vice President Finance Operations, Debbie Normington

Area Vice President Us Sales, Roxann Swanson

Vice Presidentibsg, Richard Cantwell

Vice President Finance, Phil Roush

Senior Vice President Of Engineering, Sumeet Arora

Vice President Information Technology Customer Strategy And Success, Lance Perry

Consulting Systems Engineer Northeast Security Vpn Cisco Representative, Ken Kaminski

Vice President Broker, Rajeev Grover

Vice President Engineering Network Software And Systems, Amit S Phadnis

Vice President Of Marketing, Andy Blackburn

Vice President Of Software Engineering, Ramesh Bodapati

Vice President Sales, Timothy Hannon

Vice President Sales And Purchasing, Peter Buchmeier

Vice President, Marie Higa

Vice President Sales, Jeff Towson

Kfir Pravda Imtc Vice President Of Marketing, Cary Bryan

Area Vice President Commercial Sales S, David Ruggiero

Vice President Subscriber Networks Sector, Robert Beebe

Vice President Engineering, John Wakerly

Vice President Consumer Marketing, Ken Wirt

Major Vice President Marketing Cisco Systems, Mitch Connor

Vice President World Wide Supply Chain Management, Steve Darendinger

Vice President And General Manager Sales And Business Operations, Ruma Balasubramanian

Vice President Systems Engineering, Maria Cannon

Vice President Marketing Smb, Joseph Puthussery

Vice President Systems Development, Paul Sanchirico

Vice President Information Technology, Lance Perry

Vice President Of Business Development, Greg Hardy

Vice President Information Technology, Vc Gopalratnam

Vice Presidents, Adrian Lopez

Vice President United Kingdom And Ireland, Duncan Mitchell

Senior Vice President, Donald R Proctor

Vp Marketing, St Srikantan

Senior Vice President, Michael Ganser

Area Vice President For State And Local Government And Education, Tony Morelli

Vice President Of Operations For North America And Japan, Gaurav Saple

Vice President North American Center Of Excellence, Conrad Clemson

Svp And Gm Service Providers Business, Yvette Kanouff

Senior Vice President Customer Assurance, Curtis Hill

Regional Vice President Sales, Doug Chamberlain

Vice President Emea Security Sales, Elad Shaviv

Senior Vice President Global Service Provider Sales Emear, Peter Karlstromer

Senior Vice President Sales And Service Finance, Mike Mohn

Svp Engineering Security Business Group, Gee Rittenhouse

Vice President Finance, Brian Maddox

Senior Vice President Customer And Partner Experience, Gilles Leyrat

Virtual Sales Vpam, Mohamed Sharkawi

Vice President, Rajat Mishra

Vice President Engineering Enterprise Networking Group, Raviner Reddy Amanaganti

Vp Americas Technical Services, Denise Cox

Corporate Senior Vice President And President Of Subscriber Networks, Michael Harney

Vp Engineering, Maurilio De

Vice President Cloud Devops Cloud Platforms And Services, ULF BAUMANN

Vice President Public Policy And Government Affairs For Europe Middle East Africa And Russia, Pastora Valero

Vp, Uiopio Tertete

Vice President Finance Cisco Systems, Dylan Cannon

Senior Vice President, Tom Edsall

Regional Vice President Of Sales West Region, Mike Dabner

Vice President Of Human Resources, Christine Bastian

Vice President Middle East And Africa, David Meads

Board Member, Michael Capellas

Chairman And Ceo, Charles H. (Chuck) Robbins, age 52

Board Member, Steven West

Board Member, Richard Kovacevich

Board Member, Mary Cirillo

Board Member, Carol A Bartz

Board Member, Roderick McGeary

Auditors: PricewaterhouseCoopers LLP

LOCATIONS

HQ: Cisco Systems Inc
170 West Tasman Drive, San Jose, CA 95134-1706
Phone: 408 526-4000
Web: www.cisco.com

2017 sales

	$ mil.	% of total
Americas	28,341	60
Europe the Middle East& Africa	12,004	25
Asia-Pacific regionJapan & China	7,650	15
Total	**48,005**	**100**

PRODUCTS/OPERATIONS

2017 sales

	$ mil.	% of total
Product		
Switching	13,949	29
NGN Routing	7,831	16
Service provider video	946	2
Collaboration	4,352	9
Data Center	4,278	9
Wireless	2,766	6
Security	2,153	4
Other	554	-
Service	12,300	25
Total	**48,005**	**100**

Selected Products

Access servers
Blade servers
Cable modems
Cables and cords
Content delivery devices
Customer contact software
Digital video recorders
Ethernet concentrators hubs and transceivers
Interfaces and adapters
Network management software
Networked applications software
Optical platforms
Power supplies
Routers
Security components
Switches
Telephony access systems
Television set-top boxes
Video networking
Virtual private network (VPN) systems
Voice integration applications
Wireless networking

COMPETITORS

ARRIS	Huawei Technologies
Amazon.com	IBM
Aruba Networks	Juniper Networks
Avaya	LogMeIn
Belden	MRV Communications
Brocade Communications	Meru Networks
CA Inc.	Microsoft
Check Point Software	Motorola Mobility
Ciena	NETGEAR
Citrix Systems	NSN
D-Link	Nutanix
Dell	Pace
ECI Telecom	Palo Alto Networks
Ericsson	Polycom
Extreme Networks	Symantec
F5 Networks	Technicolor
Fortinet	Tellabs
Harris Corp.	VMware
Hewlett Packard Enterprise	ZTE

HISTORICAL FINANCIALS

Company Type: Public

Income Statement

FYE: July 28

	REVENUE ($ mil.)	NET INCOME ($ mil.)	NET PROFIT MARGIN	EMPLOYEES
07/18	49,330	110	0.2%	74,200
07/17	48,005	9,609	20.0%	72,900
07/16	49,247	10,739	21.8%	73,700
07/15	49,161	8,981	18.3%	71,833
07/14	47,142	7,853	16.7%	74,042
Annual Growth	**1.1%**	**(65.6%)**	**—**	**0.1%**

2018 Year-End Financials

Debt ratio: 23.50%—
Return on equity: 0.20%
Cash ($ mil.): 8,934
Current ratio: 2.29
Long-term debt ($ mil.): 20,331

Dividends
Yield: 0.0%
Payout: 6,200.0%
Market value ($ mil.): —

	STOCK PRICE ($) FY Close	P/E High/Low		PER SHARE ($) Earnings	Dividends	Book Value
07/18	42.57	23	15	0.02	1.24	9.36
07/17	31.52	18	15	1.90	1.10	13.27
07/16	30.53	14	11	2.11	0.94	12.64
07/15	28.40	17	13	1.75	0.80	11.74
07/14	25.97	18	13	1.49	0.72	11.09
Annual Growth	**13.2%**		**—**	**(66.0%)**	**14.6%**	**(4.1%)**

CIT Group Inc

A stalwart in the big-business landscape for over a century CIT Group is a financial holding company that offers lending leasing debt restructuring equipment financing and advisory services to small- and mid-sized businesses in such industries as energy health care retail communications manufacturing IT services and sports. It operates a physical branch network in southern California and spans the US with its online banking platform. Founded in 1908 CIT expanded is consumer presence with the 2015 acquisition of OneWest.

HISTORY

Henry Ittleson founded CIT Group as Commercial Credit and Investment Trust in St. Louis in 1908. Initially financing horse-drawn carriages it moved to New York in 1915 as Commercial Investment Trust (CIT) to participate in one of the milestones of modern consumer debt: Its auto financing program launched in collaboration with Studebaker was the first of its kind.

CIT diversified into industrial financing during the 1920s and went public in 1924 on the NYSE. Cars remained a strong focus though: When Ford Motor Co. ran into difficulties in 1933 it sold financing division Universal Credit Corp. to CIT. CIT continued to expand into industrial financing incorporating its industrial business as CIT Financial Corp. in 1942.

During the post-WWII boom CIT began financing manufactured home sales and offering small loans. In 1964 it consolidated factoring operations into Meinhard-Commercial Corp. By the end of the 1960s the firm started to retreat from auto financing focusing instead on industrial leasing factoring and equipment financing.

In 1980 RCA bought CIT seeking to buy financing to develop its other businesses. RCA found the debt from the purchase unwieldy however and sold CIT to Manufacturers Hanover Bank (Manny Hanny) in 1984. The bank bought CIT to expand outside its home state of New York: Though it could not open banks out of state Manny Hanny could still offer financial services through CIT which became The CIT Group in 1986.

Manny Hanny executives tried to bring aggressive management to staid top-heavy CIT. The company sold its Inventory Finance division in 1987 divested the consumer loan business in 1988 and consolidated the Meinhard-Commercial and Manufacturers Hanover factoring units in 1989. By then Manny Hanny was cash-strapped over losses incurred from foreign loans so it sold a 60% stake in CIT to The Dai-Ichi Kangyo Bank of Japan.

CIT gave Dai-Ichi entrA©e into US financial services and it began expanding CIT's range of services again including equity investment (1990) credit finance (from its purchase of Fidelcor Business Credit in 1991) and venture capital (1992). CIT also reentered the consumer loan market (including home equity lending) with a new Consumer Finance group (1992).

In 1995 Chemical Bank (Manny Hanny's successor; now part of JPMorgan Chase) sold an additional 20% share to Dai-Ichi bumping the Japanese bank's holdings to 80% and arranging to sell its remaining shares to Dai-Ichi. In 1997 instead of Dai-Ichi buying the rest of Chase's shares CIT bought them and spun them off to the public. In 1998 Dai-Ichi reduced its stake.

In 1999 CIT bought Newcourt Credit Group North America's #2 equipment finance and leasing firm; it also bought Heller Financial's commercial services unit. In 2000 the firm worked on integrating Newcourt and sold its Hong Kong consumer finance unit.

Tyco International bought CIT in 2001 renaming the new subsidiary Tyco Capital. Under Tyco's umbrella it sold its manufactured home loan portfolio to Lehman Brothers and recreational vehicle portfolio to Salomon Smith Barney in an effort to exit noncore businesses. Tyco however expanded too far too fast and the next year announced an about-face on its financial services subsidiary deciding to spin off the division and return it to its CIT identity.

Jeff Peek took the reins of the company from longtime chairman and CEO Al Gamper in 2004.

CIT Group's Student Loan Xpress unit was one of several companies in the student-lending industry that came under investigation for business practices in 2007. It discontinued its private student loans that year and in 2008 it stopped originating government-guaranteed student loans.

Amid losses the company also exited the consumer finance business to focus on commercial lending. In 2008 it sold its home loan unit to Lone Star Funds and its manufactured housing portfolio to Vanderbilt Mortgage and Finance. The previous year it sold its construction lending unit to Wells Fargo and its 30% stake in Dell Financial Services to Dell.

CIT was hit hard in the economic recession which nearly shut down the credit markets. The company struggled to stay afloat as liquidity levels sank (a situation exacerbated as nervous customers drew on their credit lines). It exited money-losing businesses sold units and secured $3 billion from company bondholders including PIMCO and Oaktree Capital. The company also converted to a bank holding company enabling it to access government bailout funds. Still struggling CIT filed for Chapter 11 in November 2009. The restructuring lasted six weeks and helped the company eliminate more than $10 billion in debt. None of CIT's operating subsidiaries were included in the bankruptcy.

Jeffrey Peek who oversaw CIT's untimely expansion activities stepped down as CEO in early 2010. He was succeeded by John Thain who has also led Merrill Lynch and New York Stock Exchange. No stranger to turning ailing companies around Thain is credited with bringing the NYSE into the modern era with electronic trading. He also merged NYSE with Euronext establishing the first trans-Atlantic exchange.

EXECUTIVES

President Cit Rail, George D. Cashman, age 64

Evp And Cfo, John J. Fawcett

Evp And Head Of Technology And Operations, Denise M. Menelly, age 56, $253,846 total compensation

Evp And Chief Marketing And Communications Officer, Gina M. Proia, age 46

President Cit Commercial Finance, James L. (Jim) Hudak, age 54, $503,526 total compensation

Evp And Chief Risk Officer, Robert C. Rowe, age 57

Evp General Counsel And Corporate Secretary, Stuart Alderoty, age 59

President Cit Real Estate Finance, Matthew E. (Matt) Galligan, age 64

Chairman And Ceo; President And Ceo Cit Bank, Ellen R. Alemany, age 62, $883,333 total compensation

Evp And Chief Strategy Officer, Kelley Morrell, age 38

President Consumer Banking Cit Business Capital And California, Steven (Steve) Solk, age 63

Evp And Chief Human Resources Officer, James J. (Jim) Duffy, age 63

President Aviation Lending, Jennifer Villa Tennity

Managing Director Aerospace Defense And Government Services, John Heskin

Senior Vice President And Corporate Controller, Carol Hayles

Assistant Vice President Senior Business Analyst Bi, Jennifer Repik

Senior Vice President, John Edel

Assistant Vice President Risk Management Reporting And Analytics, Maria ReCasino

Vice President, Julianne Allen

Vice President Strategic Marketing, Ann Crater

Assistant Vice President Fleet Operations, Charles Burdic

Vice President And Information Technology Manager Receibable Systems, Mike Noonan

Vice President Capital Equipment Finance, Bruce Fabian

Vice President Dealer Service, Rob Sureda

Vice President, Jeff Rushnak

Senior Vice President Bsa Aml And Ofac Sanctions Compliance Head, Michelle Goodsir

Vice President, George Fikaris

Senior Vice President National Manager, Kenneth Wendler

Vice President, Joel Wolitzer

Vice President National Accounts Manager, Mike Loconsolo

Vice President, Kristin Appelbaum

Vice President, Ronald Gibney

Executive Vice President Chief Credit And Risk Officer Corporate Credit Risk Management, Nancy Foster

Vice President Aml Compliance, Rachel Benjamin

Assistant Vice President Portfolio Manager, Carolle Sorel

Assistant Vice President, Joshua Hare

Assistant Vice President, Rosalyn Jones

Vice President, Sohail Khan

Assistant Vice President, Soheir Krauss

Vice President, Debra Brown

Assistant Vice President Sales Support, Haley Werle

Vice President, Patricia Matos

Vice President, David Howson

Vice President, Kai Liang

Vice President, William Riggin

Senior Vice President, Eugene Schwartz

Vice President Consumer Finance Operations, Krista Neal

Vice President Employment Human, Tammy Haynie

Vice President Threat And Vulnerability Management Information, Roman Brozyna

Vice President Sales, Thomas Gonnella

Vice President Finance, Frederick Rick

Operation Manager Vice President, Marvin Daniel

Vice President, Kristin Appelbaum

Assistant Vice President, Adam Schacter

Executive Vice President And Treasurer, Glenn Alan Votek

Assistant Vice President Corporate Finance, Nicole C Rapport

Vice President, Diane Harris

Vice President Project And Service Management, Russell Hansen

Vice President Facility Operations, Vincent Sorrentino

Senior Vice President, Mike Cleary

Vice President, Daniel Bernstein

Assistant Vice President Human Resources, Craig Harada

Assistant Vice President Content Marketing, Saryia Green

Assistant Vice President, Munindra Nath

Vice President, Paul Tufaro

Svp And General Manager Locomotives, Ken Pierson

Vice President Information Technology Security Engineering, Tom Brown

Vice President Information Technology .net Enterprise Architecture, Harvey Orloff

Senior Vice President Head Of Consumer And Internet Banking Technology, Kedar Sathe

Vice President Of Factoring Operations For Ny Region, Sam Macrillo

Vice President Information Technology For Equipment Finance Risk Management Systems, Khundnir Mohammed

Vice President Capital Markets, Elias Uribe

Avp, Rebecca Wong

Avp Sox, Liana Balseiro

Vp Regulatory Compliance And Controls, Nathan Lai

Avp Compliance Aml Edd, Cynthia Hernandez

Vice President, Manesh Chandwani

Assistant Vice President, Oscar Menendez

Vice President Financial Analytics And Modeling, Cynthia Kim

Avp Treasury Controllers, Robert Bickerstaff

Assistant Vice President Accounts Payable, Warren Allen

Vice President Brand Communications And Social Media, Debra Newton

Assistant Vice President Third Party Management, Jennifer Terribile

Vice President, William Sheridan

Assistant Vice President Accounting Manager, Irene Yang

Assistant Vice President Aml And Sanctions Program Strategy, Mark DiGaetani

Vice President Information Technology Security Assurance, Nicholas Zaky

Vice President Sponsor Finance, Joseph Longobardi

Senior Vice President Of Information Technology, Fred Mistretta

Evp General Counsel And Corporate Secretary, Stuart Alderoty, age 59

Chairman And Ceo; President And Ceo Cit Bank, Ellen R. Alemany, age 62

Auditors: DELOITTE & TOUCHE LLP

LOCATIONS

HQ: CIT Group Inc
11 West 42nd Street, New York, NY 10036
Phone: 212 461-5200
Web: www.cit.com

2016 Sales

	$ mil.	% of total
US	2,755	89
Europe	139	5
Rest of the world	198	6
Total	**3,093**	**100**

PRODUCTS/OPERATIONS

Products and Services

Account receivables collection
Acquisition and expansion financing
Asset management and servicing
Asset-based loans
Cash management and payment services
Credit protection
Debt restructuring
Debt underwriting and syndication
Deposits
Enterprise value and cash flow loans
Equipment leases
Factoring services
Financial risk management
Import and export financing
Insurance services
Letters of credit / trade acceptances
Merger and acquisition advisory services
Residential mortgage loans
Secured lines of credit
Small Business Administration loans

2016 Sales

	$ mil.	% of total
Commercial Banking	2,546	79
Consumer Banking	382	12
Non-Strategic Portfolios	26	1
Corporate & Other	252	8
Total	**3,207**	**100**

2017 Sales

	$ mil.	% of total
Interest income		
Interest & fees on loans	1,638	58
Other interest and dividends	197	4
Non-interest income		
Rental income on operating leases	1,007	33
Other income	364	5
Total	**3,207**	**100**

COMPETITORS

Ally Financial	ILFC
Citigroup	JPMorgan Chase
Comerica	ORIX
Deutsche Bank	Zions Bancorporation
First Republic (CA)	

HISTORICAL FINANCIALS

Company Type: Public

Income Statement

FYE: December 31

	ASSETS ($ mil.)	NET INCOME ($ mil.)	INCOME AS % OF ASSETS	EMPLOYEES
12/17	49,278	468	1.0%	4,167
12/16	64,170	(848)	—	4,410
12/15	67,498	1,056	1.6%	4,900
12/14	47,880	1,130	2.4%	3,360
12/13	47,139	675	1.4%	3,240
Annual Growth	1.1%	(8.8%)	—	6.5%

2017 Year-End Financials

Debt ratio: 10.71%	No. of shares (mil.): 131
Return on equity: 5.51%	Dividends
Cash ($ mil.): 1,718	Yield: 0.0%
Current ratio: —	Payout: 21.7%
Long-term debt ($ mil.): —	Market value ($ mil.): 6,467

	STOCK PRICE ($) FY Close	P/E High/Low	PER SHARE ($) Earnings	Dividends	Book Value
12/17	49.23	18 14	2.80	0.61	55.73
12/16	42.68	— —	(4.20)	0.60	49.50
12/15	39.70	9 7	5.67	0.60	54.61
12/14	47.83	9 7	5.96	0.50	50.13
12/13	52.13	15 11	3.35	0.10	44.78
Annual Growth	(1.4%)	— —	(4.4%)	57.2%	5.6%

CITGO PETROLEUM CORPORATION

From the get-go CITGO Petroleum has been refining and marketing petroleum products including jet fuel diesel fuel heating oils and lubricants. It markets CITGO branded gasoline through about 6500 independent retail outlets in 28 US states mainly east of the Rockies. CITGO Petroleum owns oil refineries in Illinois Louisiana and Texas. The company has the refining capacity to process more than 749000 barrels per day. It markets more than 600 types of lubricants and sold 15.5 billion gallons of refined products in 2015. CITGO Petroleum is the operating subsidiary of PDV America itself a subsidiary of Venezuela's national oil company PDVSA.

Operations

In addition to its refineries CITGO Petroleum has almost 50 storage terminals (which together process more than 10 billion gallons of fuel per year) and access to an additional 140 facilities. It also has three fully-owned pipelines and six jointly owned pipelines.

Geographic Reach

The company is based in Houston and operates three refineries in Lemont Illinois; Corpus Christi Texas; and Lake Charles Louisiana; and three lubricant blending plants in Cicero Illinois; Oklahoma City and Atlanta.

Sales and Marketing

The company markets automotive fuels to independent marketers which sell to nearly 6000 branded retail outlets. It markets jet fuel directly to airlines. CITGO Petroleum produces a variety of agricultural automotive industrial and private label lubricants which are sold to independent distributors mass marketers and industrial customers. It also sells petrochemicals and industrial products directly to various manufacturers and industrial companies across the US.

Company Background

The company had an agreement to access the St. Croix Virgin Islands refinery jointly owned by PDVSA and US-based Hess but the parties shut down the HOVENSA refinery in 2012 due to poor market conditions and high operating expenses.

Growing its retail network in 2011 the company converted 42 locally owned gas station in Maine and New Hampshire to the CITGO brand.

That year CITGO Petroleum completed and started up a 42500 barrel-per day unit at its Corpus Christi Texas refinery to produce Ultra Low Sulfur Diesel.

One of CITGO Petroleum's public relations initiatives is that it annually provides low-cost heating oil to selected low income communities as a way to offset high fuel prices. In early 2011 the company supplied 132000 low-income households in 25 states as well as 250 tribal communities and 234 homeless shelters. That year it invested more than $75 million in contributions for community activities.

CITGO Petroleum traces its history to Cities Service Company founded in Oklahoma in 1910. PDVSA took control of the company in 1990. In 2010 Venezuelan President Hugo Chavez announced a long term interest in selling CITGO Petroleum in order to generate cash for parent company PDVSA but PDVSA scrapped the idea in 2014.

EXECUTIVES

Chairman President And Ceo, Alejandro Granado
Vp Finance And Treasurer, Maritza Villanueva
Vp Refining And General Manager Lake Charles Manufacturing Complex, Eduardo Assef
Vp Supply And Marketing, Gustavo Vel ˜squez
Vp And General Manager Lemont Refinery, Jim Cristman
Vice President General Manager, Tomeu Vadell
Vice President And General Manager Corpus Christi Refinery, Randy Flowers
Vice President Manager Director, Bob Pennington
Vice President Supply Marketing, Fernando Valera
Vice President Finance, Jose Pereira
Chairman President And Ceo, Alejandro Granado
Vp Finance And Treasurer, Maritza Villanueva
Auditors: KPMG LLP HOUSTON TEXAS

LOCATIONS

HQ: CITGO PETROLEUM CORPORATION
1293 ELDRIDGE PKWY, HOUSTON, TX 770771670
Phone: 832 486-4000
Web: WWW.CITGOLUBES.COM

PRODUCTS/OPERATIONS

Selected Products

Lubricants and Oils
Petrochemicals
Retail Gasoline

COMPETITORS

BP	Motiva Enterprises
CRI/Criterion Catalyst	Shell Oil Products
Chevron	Sunoco
ConocoPhillips	TransMontaigne

Exxon Mobil	Partners
Kimber Petroleum	Valero Energy
Marathon Petroleum	

HISTORICAL FINANCIALS

Company Type: Private

Income Statement

FYE: December 31

	REVENUE ($ mil.)	NET INCOME ($ mil.)	NET PROFIT MARGIN	EMPLOYEES
12/17	24,100	715	3.0%	4,000
12/16	19,914	234	1.2%	—
/	0	0	—	—
Annual Growth	—	—	—	—

2017 Year-End Financials

Debt ratio: —	
Return on equity: 3.00%	Dividends
Cash ($ mil.): 276	Yield: —
Current ratio: 0.50	Payout: —
Long-term debt ($ mil.): —	Market value ($ mil.): —

Citigroup Inc

This is the Citi that never sleeps. One of the largest financial services firms known to man Citigroup (also known as Citi) has some 200 million customer accounts and serves clients around the globe. It offers deposits and loans (mainly through Citibank) investment banking brokerage wealth management and other financial services. Few other banks can equal Citigroup's global reach: In addition to Citibank it owns stakes in several international regional banks and has more than 140 million Citi-branded credit cards in circulation worldwide. Hit hard by the 2008 financial crisis Citi has been refocusing on its original mission — traditional banking.Citi has some $1.3 trillion in assets and some $640 billion in deposits.

HISTORY

Empire builder Sanford "Sandy" Weill who helped build brokerage firm Shearson Loeb Rhoades sold the company to American Express (AmEx) in 1981. Forced out of AmEx in 1985 Weill bounced back in 1986 buying Control Data's Commercial Credit unit.

Primerica caught Weill's eye next. Its predecessor American Can was founded in 1901 as a New Jersey canning company; it eventually expanded into the paper and retail industries before turning to financial services in 1986. The firm was renamed Primerica in 1987 and bought brokerage Smith Barney Harris Upham & Co.

Weill's Commercial Credit bought Primerica in 1988. In 1993 Primerica bought Shearson from AmEx as well as Travelers taking its name and logo.

Weill set about trimming Travelers. He sold life subsidiaries and bought Aetna's property/casualty business in 1995. In 1996 he consolidated all property/casualty operations to form Travelers Property Casualty and took it public. The next year Travelers bought investment bank Salomon Brothers and formed Salomon Smith Barney Holdings (now Citigroup Global Markets).

Weill sold Citicorp chairman and CEO John Reed on the idea of a merger in 1998 in advance of the Gramm-Leach-Bliley act which deregulated the financial services industry in the US. By the time the merger went through a slowed US economy and foreign-market turmoil brought significant losses to both sides. The renamed Citigroup consolidated in 1998 and 1999 laying off more than 10000 employees. So many executives (including co-chairmen and co-CEOs Weill and Reed) were paired through "co" titling that the company was dubbed "the ark."

In 1999 Citigroup moved deeper into subprime lending. Also that year former Treasury Secretary Robert Rubin joined Citigroup as a co-chairman.

In 2000 Reed retired and the company bought the investment banking business of British firm Schroders. Citigroup also bought subprime lender Associates First Capital (now part of CitiFinancial) for approximately $27 billion to expand its consumer product lines and its international presence. The deal however also brought Citigroup federal scrutiny regarding perceived predatory lending tactics. In 2001 the company bought New York-based European American Bank from ABN AMRO and purchased Grupo Financiero Banamex one of Mexico's biggest banks.

The company parlayed the $4 billion it netted from the 2002 spinoff of 20% of Travelers Property Casualty (it distributed most of the remaining stock to Citigroup shareholders) into a $5.8 billion purchase of California-based Golden State Bancorp the parent of the then-third-largest thrift in the US Cal Fed.

Also that year Citigroup paid some $215 million to settle federal allegations that Associates First Capital made customers unwittingly purchase credit insurance by automatically billing for the service. The agreement was one of the largest consumer-protection settlements ever.

The company also became embroiled in the Enron mess as regulators scrutinized short-term loans that Citigroup floated to the energy trader and were possibly used by Enron in transactions with offshore entities to mask debt and inflate cash flow figures. Citigroup neither confirmed nor denied allegations that it helped fudge Enron's books but in 2003 remitted more than $100 million earmarked to pay victims who lost money because of Enron's malfeasance.

A landmark ruling by the SEC in 2003 implied that Citigroup issued favorable stock ratings to companies in exchange for investment banking contracts (predictably the company neither confirmed nor denied the allegations). Also as part of the ruling erstwhile star analyst Jack Grubman agreed to pay some $15 million in fines for his overly rosy stock reports and accepted a lifetime ban from working in the securities industry. Citigroup forked over $400 million in fines the largest portion of a total of some $1.4 billion levied against 10 brokerage firms regarding conflicts of interest between analysts and investment bankers.

Amid the investigations Citigroup separated its stock-picking and corporate advisory businesses creating a retail brokerage and equity research unit called Smith Barney. In the SEC's 2003 ruling such a "Chinese Wall" between bankers and analysts was later made mandatory at all firms. Still Citigroup raked in net profits of nearly $18 billion (on revenues in excess of $94 billion) in 2003 one of the largest-ever yearly takes in US corporate history.

In 2004 the company — while admitting no wrongdoing — paid $2.65 billion to investors who were burned when WorldCom went bankrupt amid an accounting scandal. (Citigroup was one of the lead underwriters of WorldCom stocks and bonds.) The settlement was one of the largest ever for alleged securities fraud and compelled Citigroup to set aside an additional $5 billion to cover legal fees for this case and others involving Enron and spinning. The company eventually paid $2 billion in mid-2005 to investors who lost money on publicly traded Enron stocks and bonds again set-

tling the matter while denying it broke any laws. Enron shareholders had argued that Citigroup helped Enron to set up offshore companies and shady partnerships to exaggerate the energy trader's cash flow.

In Japan where Citigroup is one of the leading foreign banks regulators pulled the plug on the company's private banking operations in 2004 after determining that Citigroup misled customers regarding the sale of certain structured bonds. The closures led to the forced resignation of three top executives in the company's asset management and private banking units about a month later.

Citigroup sold The Travelers Life and Annuity Company (now MetLife Life and Annuity Company of Connecticut) plus most of its international insurance business to MetLife in 2005. Later that year a convoluted deal with Legg Mason netted Citigroup that company's retail brokerage and capital markets business (and $1.5 billion of Legg Mason stock) in exchange for most of Citigroup's asset management and mutual fund division; Citigroup concurrently sold Legg Mason's capital markets operations to Stifel Financial.

Seeking growth internationally Citigroup was part of a consortium that acquired a controlling stake in Guangdong Development Bank in 2006. Also that year the company opened more than 800 bank branches and consumer finance offices outside the US.

Weill ended years of speculation in 2003 by anointing corporate and investment bank head Chuck Prince as his successor. Weill retired as chairman in 2006 and Prince assumed that title as well. Prince resigned in 2007 as Citigroup dealt with losses on mortgage-related securities and other investments.

Prince was succeeded by Vikram Pandit a Morgan Stanley veteran who came to Citigroup when it acquired hedge fund and private equity manager Old Lane Partners in 2007. Pandit was at Citigroup only a few months before he was named CEO but during that time he oversaw the company's alternative investments and led its institutional clients group. The following year Citigroup disbanded Old Lane and wound up its flagship fund.

Citigroup further expanded its fund services operations via its 2007 acquisition of BISYS. As part of the deal the company sold BISYS' insurance services division to investment firm J.C. Flowers & Co.

Also that year it picked up remnants of the subprime mortgage collapse when it acquired ACC Capital Holding's wholesale mortgage origination operations as well as the servicing rights to some $5 billion in home loans. It also bought ABN AMRO Mortgage Group and shelled out more than $1 billion to buy Egg one of the largest online-only banks in the world from Prudential plc. The deal boosted its UK consumer operations by adding some 3 million customers.

The company sold its trademark red umbrella logo back to insurance firm Travelers which began using the symbol nearly 150 years before. Citigroup acquired the iconic logo when it bought the insurance company in 1993 and held onto it after it spun off Travelers in 2002. But the company ultimately decided that customers associated the umbrella with insurance and sold it in 2007.

In order to shore up its balance sheet Citigroup sold some 5% of itself to the Abu Dhabi Investment Authority a Middle Eastern sovereign fund for $7.5 billion in 2007. It later raised more than $12 billion by selling preferred shares to investors including a Singapore government-owned investment fund former CEO Sandy Weill and Saudi investor Prince Al-Walid bin Talal who owns roughly 5% stake of Citigroup.

Citigroup bought a majority stake in one of Japan's largest brokerages Nikko Cordial in 2007.

It acquired the remaining shares of Nikko Cordial in early 2008 and merged it with Citigroup Japan Holdings to form Nikko Citi Holdings.

In 2008 Citigroup sold several of its commercial finance lines to GE Capital. It sold its German consumer banking business to French bank Groupe CrA©dit Mutuel.

As the global credit crisis mounted in 2008 the US government injected some $700 billion into the nation's banking industry including $45 billion investment in Citigroup. It further stepped in to aid the faltering bank by backing more than $300 in loans and securities to boost confidence in the bank and protect its investments. In exchange the government took a 34% stake in Citigroup. The company received approval to pay the funds back in 2009 and the government began reducing its ownership.

Citigroup shed numerous noncore operations (grouped into its new Citi Holdings division) to raise money to repay the government bailout funds. In 2009 it sold Japanese brokerage Nikko Cordial (now SMBC Nikko) and other parts of Nikko Citi Holdings for $8.7 billion to Sumitomo Mitsui Financial Group. Also in 2009 Citigroup combined its Smith Barney and Quilter wealth management units with those of Morgan Stanley to create Morgan Stanley Smith Barney taking a 49% of the combined firm.

Sales in 2010 include its $1.93 billion Canadian MasterCard portfolio (to CIBC) a $3.5 billion real estate loan portfolio (to JPMorgan Chase) a $3.2 billion auto loan portfolio (to Santander) and a $1.6 billion portfolio of retail credit card assets (to GE). In 2011 it sold a $1.7 billion private equity portfolio to AXA. Also in 2010 the company spun off Primerica in an IPO selling remaining shares by 2011.

Furthermore Citigroup exited the student loan business in the wake of federal legislation eliminating subsidies for private lenders: It sold its 80% stake in Student Loan Corporation and much of its private student loans portfolio to Discover Financial Services and Sallie Mae. The company also sold three hedge fund businesses with a combined $4.2 billion in assets under management to New York-based SkyBridge Capital.

The firm began withdrawing from the consumer lending business in Europe by selling its Egg UK credit card business to Barclays in 2011 and its UK/Ireland Diners Club business to Affiniture Cards in 2012.

EXECUTIVES

Ceo Citibank N.a., Barbara J. Desoer, age 65
Ceo North America, William J. (Bill) Mills, age 62
President Citigroup Inc. And Ceo Institutional Clients Group, James A. (Jim) Forese, age 55, $500,000 total compensation
Managing Director And Head Global Corporate Bank Citi Markets And Banking, Michael L. Corbat, age 57, $1,500,000 total compensation
Managing Director And Global Head Emerging Markets Sales And Trading Corporate And Investment Banking, Paco Ybarra
Cfo, John C. Gerspach, age 65, $500,000 total compensation
Ceo North Asia; Head Consumer Banking And Global Cards Asia Pacific, Stephen Bird, age 51, $499,623 total compensation
Ceo Citi Holdings, Francesco Vanni d'Archirafi
Head Operations And Technology, Don Callahan, age 61, $500,000 total compensation
Evp Global Public Affairs, Edward Skyler, age 44
Ceo Latin America, Jane Fraser, age 50, $500,000 total compensation
Head Emea Markets Institutional Clients Group, James C. Cowles, age 62
Ceo Citi Cards, Jud Linville

Ceo Asia Pacific, Francisco A. Aristeguieta Silva, age 52

Chief Risk Officer, Bradford Hu, age 54

Ceo Citi Mexico And Banco Nacional De México (banamex), Ernesto Torres Cantu

Assistant Vice President And Business Information Security Officer, Veena Srinivasan

Senior Vice President Asset Management, Gustav Gollisz

Senior Vice President, Carol Williams

Senior Vice President, Ryan McCaughey

Vice President Technology, David Gubitosi

Senior Vice President, Linda Basher

Vice President Global Technology Sourcing Services, Charlotte Lawrence

Vice President Relationship Manager, Geetika Vats

Vice President, Brenna Makin

Senior Vice President, Fabricio Calderon

Vice President Treasury Sales Consultant, Teri Estes

Senior Vice President, Nareg Dermanuelian

First Vice President Wealth Management, Drew Newman

Senior Vice President Relationship Manager, Betty Silfa

Relationship Manager Vice President, Edia Cruz

Assistant Vice President Equity Derivatives Trading, Peter Plevritis

Assistant Vice President, Donna Chan

Vice President, John Gannon

Vice President, James DeLuise

Assistant Vice President, David Baker

Vice President Head Of Customer Engagement, Lisa Sagita

Senior Vice President Compliance, Joseph Morgo

Vice President, Brad Randlett

Senior Vice President Manager Of Regulatory Reporting Department For Derivatives (otc And Et), Yanina Kulchitskaya

Assistant Vice President, Anthony Thomas

Senior Vice President, Frank Zhang

Vice President Crm Process Manager, Brian Lilly

Assistant Vice President Recovery Senior Supervisor Litigation, John Linnenbrink

Senior Vice President, Tim Walter

Assistant Vice President At Citi Loan Syndications Group, Christopher Romanelli

Assistant Vice President, Timothy Seaton

Vice President, Diego Szuldman

Vice President, Kyle Moeller

Vice President, Donna McCafferty

Vice President Senior Relationship Manager Learning And Development, Jennifer Gabriele

Vice President Customer Engagement Risk, Pankaj Agarwal

Senior Vice President, Diana Alfonso

Vice President Sales Development Counsultant Cit, Leta Bajraktari

Assistant Vice President, Sharon Eng

Assistant Vice President, Cherry Tam

Vice President And Senior Quality Assurance, Stella Zhang

Vice President At Citibank, Ramon Cabrera

Vice President Executive Recruiter, Carlos Fernandez

Vice President And Compliance Officer, Yolette Mazile

Executive Vice President, Mark Morgenlender

Vice President Marketing And Revenue Services, Ben Bartscht

Vice President Of Commercial Real Estate Group, Beth Raba

Vice President Technology, James Carney

Vice President, Ganesh Jayaraman

Vice President, Jodi Rodgers

Assistant Vice President Transaction Services, Zirley Moyette

Assistant Vice President Change Management Shift Manager, Patrick Davis

Vice President Of Market Research Glob, Tim Teran

Vice President, Patrick Kosiek

Vice President Marketing, Reema Butala

Senior Vice President Risk Management, Peter You

Vice President, Kyle Finnerty

Vice President, Julian Stippig

Senior Vice President Citi Cards, Ron Guggenheimer

Assistant Vice President, Suleman Khan

Assistant Vice President Local Advanced, Mary Chin

Vice President Information Security Officer, Denise Zeigler

Vice President, Eric Levine

Assistant Vice President Mutual Funds And Annuities, Jamie Catalano

Senior Vice President Treasury Capital Markets, Pascal Weel

Vice President, Edward Montero

Vice President Information Technology, Jim Horn

Vice President Business Unit Manager, Sarah Bennett

Vice President, Mario Lanzi

Vice President Infrastructure, Rob Ampaw

Senior Vice President Cbs, Patrick Mentzer

Vice President Ibd, Jens Bender

Senior Vice President C And B, Vani Hung

Senior Vice President, William Johnson

Vice President Cash Management, Therese Schlossberg

Vice President And Program Marketing Manager, Jay Bernstein

Senior Vice President Human Resources Business Advisor, Jeffrey Friedman

Vice President Operations Support Senior Manager, Patricia Padilla

Senior Vice President, Michael Wilson

Citibank N A Senior Vice President, Ryan Beiser

Vice President Senior Manager Regulatory Reporting, Lenny Everett

Senior Vice President Fraud Prevention, Brian Todd

Vice President User Experience Group, Andrew Demers

Vice President, Parul Todai

Senior Vice President, Aniruddha Bhat

Vice President, Harihar Brahma

Senior Auditor Assistant Vice President, Carol Amesquita

Senior Vice President, Michael Megias

Vice President, Dirk Hatzmann

Assistant Vice President, Fern Langham

Vice President, Helen Guo

Assistant Vice President, Reevu Ghosh

Senior Vice President Relationship Manager, Gevork Markarian

Senior Vice President, Patrick Clark

Vice President, Peter Rozario

Vice President; Operational Risk Manager, Andrew Mensack

Senior Vice President Citi Community Development, Gregory Schiefelbein

Senior Vice President, David Viggiano

Vice President, Andi Williams

Vice President, Raghunath Gullapalli

Vice President, Junshuo Liao

Vice President, Juan Matta

Vice President, Ardian Haliti

Vice President Risk Manager, Yibai Cai

Vice President, Aileen Long

Vice President, Kumar Narayan

Vice President, Kimberly Archuleta

Vice President, Stephan Reinhard

Vice President Finance, Vikram Tewatia

Assistant Vice President, Arham Gupta

Senior Vice President, Cindy Heismeyer

Vice President Portfolio Manager, Laurie Kenski

Senior Vice President Client Development, Kade Walter

Assistant Vice President Of Public Relations, Michelle Knowles

Senior Vice President, Matt Allred

Vice President, Jason Howard

Senior Vice President, Jessica Gaspard

Assistant Vice President, Saroja Vallury

Vice President, Miok Joo

Senior Vice President, Lucia Chen

Vice President, Shweta Jain

Assistant Vice President Credit Analyst, Zubair Kazi

Assistant Vice President, Robin Jackson

Vice President, Robert Traverso

Assistant Vice President, Justin Edelstein

Senior Vice President, Catherine Garrity

Vice President, Fred Frillman

Vice President, Pallavi Saxena

Vice President, Samuil Shpits

Vice President, Chintan Parikh

Senior Vice President Compliance Testing, Alexis Chistik

Vice President, Ralph Gonzalez

Vice President Product Management, Xavier Pardo

Vice President, Kiran Bevinamar

Senior Vice President Area Director, Shanti Musacchia

Auditors: KPMG LLP

LOCATIONS

HQ: Citigroup Inc
388 Greenwich Street, New York, NY 10013
Phone: 212 559-1000
Web: www.citigroup.com

PRODUCTS/OPERATIONS

2017 Sales

	$ mil.	% of total
Net Interest	44,687	63
Non-interest		
Commissions & fees	12,939	18
Principal transactions	9,168	13
Administration & other fiduciary fees	3,079	4
Realized gains on sales of investments	778	1
Other	861	1
Adjustments	(63)	-
Total	**71,449**	**100**

2017 Sales

	% of total
Institutional Clients Group	50
Global Consumer Banking	46
Corporate/Other	4
Total	**100**

2017 Sales

	% of total
North America	47
Asia	20
Latin America	14
EMEA	15
Corporate/Other	4
Total	**100**

Selected Products

Banamex
Bill Consolidation
Checking
Citi Cards
Citi Private Bank
CitiMortgage
Commercial Real Estate Loans
Home Equity
Mortgages
Online Banking
Personal Loans
Savings
Student Loans

COMPETITORS

American Express	Goldman Sachs
Bank of America	HSBC
Bank of New York	JPMorgan Chase
Mellon	Mizuho Financial
Barclays	U.S. Bancorp
Capital One	UBS
Deutsche Bank	USAA
FMR	Wells Fargo
GE	

HISTORICAL FINANCIALS

Company Type: Public

Income Statement

FYE: December 31

	ASSETS ($ mil.)	NET INCOME ($ mil.)	INCOME AS % OF ASSETS	EMPLOYEES
12/17	1,842,465	(6,798)	—	209,000
12/16	1,792,077	14,912	0.8%	219,000
12/15	1,731,210	17,242	1.0%	231,000
12/14	1,842,530	7,313	0.4%	241,000
12/13	1,880,382	13,673	0.7%	251,000
Annual Growth	(0.5%)	—	—	(4.5%)

2017 Year-End Financials

Debt ratio: 12.85%—
Return on equity: (-3.19%)
Cash ($ mil.): 180,516
Current ratio: —
Long-term debt ($ mil.): —

Dividends
Yield: 0.0%
Payout: —
Market value ($ mil.): —

	STOCK PRICE ($) FY Close	P/E High/Low		PER SHARE ($) Earnings	Dividends	Book Value
12/17	74.41	—	—	(2.98)	0.96	78.11
12/16	59.43	13	7	4.72	0.42	81.20
12/15	51.75	11	9	5.40	0.16	75.12
12/14	54.11	26	21	2.20	0.04	69.62
12/13	52.11	12	9	4.35	0.04	67.46
Annual Growth	9 3%	—		—	121.3%	3.7%

Citizens Financial Group Inc (New)

Paper plastic or coin? No matter — Citizens Financial Group can handle it all. The company's main operating subsidiary is consumer bank Citizens Bank which spans some 1150 branches across eleven US states in the Northeast and the Midwest and boasts more than $150 billion in assets. The bank's branches are often found in supermarkets and offer standard retail and commercial services as well as investment services insurance employer-sponsored retirement plans student loans and vehicle lending. Citizens Financial also operates a network of non-branch banking offices.

Operations

Citizens Financial offers customers mortgage lending auto lending student lending and commercial banking services. Altogether its portfolio includes 1150 branches 130 non-branch offices and 3300 ATMs.

The bank operates two segments: Consumer Banking which serves individuals and counts for more than 60% of the bank's total revenue; and Commercial Banking which serves businesses and accounts for some 35% of revenue.

Interest income accounts for more than three-quarters of Citizens' revenue.

Geographic Reach

Rhode Island-based Citizens Financial operates branches in New England the Mid-Atlantic and the Midwest. Its largest markets are Boston Philadelphia Providence and Pittsburgh.

Sales and Marketing

Citizens Financial's customers include individuals small businesses middle-market companies large corporations and institutions. Its business clients typically operate out of the healthcare technology franchise and energy sectors.

Financial Performance

Citizens Financial has grown its revenue and profits more or less consistently since 2013. In fiscal 2017 the bank's net revenue (net interest income plus noninterest income) rose 9% to $5.7 billion as a $7.9 billion increase in interest-earning assets pushed up net interest income 11% to $4.2 billion. Total assets grew $2.8 billion to $152.3 billion while deposits expanded $5.3 billion to $115.1 billion.

Net income grew strongly in 2017 up 59% to $1.7 billion. A significant chunk of the growth was a one-time effect of the 2017 US Tax Cuts and Jobs Act worth $340 million; the rest of the increase came from stronger overall operating performance and higher interest rates.

The company's cash position weakened in 2017 with cash on hand falling $672 million to $3.0 million.

Strategy

Citizen Financial's growth strategy is based outperforming its rivals in terms of customer relationships. The company is leveraging analytics to target customers with customized products and offers with the goal of winning expanding and retaining customer relationships. It is working to increase convenience by investing in its digital channels (online mobile ATM) while implementing a more personal in-branch experience with "Citizens Checkup" consultations.

Citizens Financial is also tightening its focus on the Mass Affluent and Affluent customer segments which have higher growth potential. To do so the company is working on its Wealth Management business which includes improving its advice services (including digital advice) and product suite and services.

The company has been leaning on student lending and installment loans in recent years to drive growth. The group has launched several new products including student loan refinancing partnered with Apple on iPhone upgrade financing and launched a new credit card.

Company Background

In September 2014 Royal Bank of Scotland (RBS) sold a 25% ownership interest or 140 million shares of the regional US bank for $21.50 each (below the company's expected range of $23 to $25 per share). The deal which valued Citizens Financial Group (CFG) at $3 billion was one of the largest bank IPOs on record. In October 2015 RBS sold its remaining stake (the last 20.9% of Citizens common stock) for $23.38 per share raising some $2.6 billion.

After being bought by RBS in 1988 Citizens Financial went on an acquisition spree making more than two dozen deals. In 2000 and through later years the company gobbled up Mellon's retail banking network Medford Bancorp and Port Financial in Massachusetts and Pennsylvania's Commonwealth Bancorp and Thistle Group Holdings among others. The company expanded into the Midwest by buying superregional bank Charter One in 2004. Following its acquisition of Charter One its largest deal yet Citizens Financial retained the Charter One Bank name in Midwestern markets but converted the bank's branches to Citizens

Bank in New York and Pennsylvania. That was the company's last major acquisition however.

Like many banks the company was hamstrung by the mortgage crisis. It posted a nearly $1 billion loss in 2008 as its nonperforming loans roughly doubled. The developments compelled the company to re-evaluate its acquisition strategy and it has reversed its field: Citizens Financial sold 18 of its branches in northern New York to Community Bank System in 2008 and all 65 Charter One branches in Indiana to Old National Bancorp the following year. The company also pegged certain operations as noncore including its dealer finance program and portions of its auto lending business. In 2012 Citizens Financial unloaded more branches selling nearly 60 supermarket locations to People's United Financial. In 2013 it opted to unload its Chicago branches.

In 2015 RBS sold its remaining stake in Citizens Financial.

EXECUTIVES

Evp And Cfo, John F. Woods, age 53
Evp And Chief Risk Officer, Malcolm D. Griggs, age 57
Vice Chairman Commercial Banking, Donald H. (Don) McCree, age 56, $700,000 total compensation
Evp General Counsel And Chief Legal Officer, Stephen T. (Steve) Gannon, age 65, $600,000 total compensation
Vice Chairman Consumer Banking, Brad L. Conner, age 56, $700,000 total compensation
Chairman And Ceo, Bruce Van Saun, age 60, $1,487,000 total compensation
Chief Marketing Officer And Head Of Consumer Strategy, Beth Johnson
Head Of Technology Services, Brian OÂ'Connell
President Citizens Bank Rhode Island, Keith Kelly
Evp And Head Of Business Services, Mary Ellen Baker, age 59
Vice President Senior Risk Manager, Pat Coutu
Vice President And Regulatory Liaison Law Department, Pam Brown
Assistant Vice President Portfolio Manager, Laurie Charest
Vice Chairman Commercial Banking, Donald H. (Don) McCree, age 56
Vice Chairman Consumer Banking, Brad L. Conner, age 56
Chairman And Ceo, Bruce Van Saun, age 60
Auditors: DELOITTE & TOUCHE LLP

LOCATIONS

HQ: Citizens Financial Group Inc (New)
One Citizens Plaza, Providence, RI 02903
Phone: 401 456-7000   **Fax:** 401 455-5927
Web: www.citizensbank.com

2017 Branches

	Nos
Pennsylvania	340
Massachusetts	246
New York	133
Ohio	103
Michigan	93
Rhode Island	78
New Hampshire	66
Connecticut	41
Delaware	23
Vermont	16
New Jersey	11
Total	**1,150**

PRODUCTS/OPERATIONS

2017 Sales

	$ mil.	% of total
Interest income		
Interest on loans & fees	4,249	66
Investment securities	625	10
Others	46	1
Non-interest income		
Service charges & fees	517	8
Card fees	233	3
Trust & investment services fees	158	2
Capital markets fees	194	3
Letter of credit & loan fees	121	2
Others	320	5
Net security impairment loss	(7)	–
Total	**6,454**	**100**

2017 Sales

	% of total
Consumer Banking	62
Commercial Banking	34
Others	4
Total	**100**

COMPETITORS

Bank of America	M&T Bank
Bank of New York Mellon	PNC Financial
Citigroup	People's United Financial
Fifth Third	Sovereign Bank
HSBC USA	TD Bank USA
Huntington Bancshares	U.S. Bancorp
JPMorgan Chase	Wintrust Financial
KeyCorp	

HISTORICAL FINANCIALS

Company Type: Public

Income Statement

FYE: December 31

	ASSETS ($ mil.)	NET INCOME ($ mil.)	INCOME AS % OF ASSETS	EMPLOYEES
12/17	152,336	1,652	1.1%	17,600
12/16	149,520	1,045	0.7%	18,000
12/15	138,208	840	0.6%	17,700
12/14	132,857	865	0.7%	18,310
12/13	122,154	(3,426)	—	18,160
Annual Growth	**5.7%**	**—**	**—**	**(0.8%)**

2017 Year-End Financials

Debt ratio: 5.25%	No. of shares (mil.): 490
Return on equity: 8.26%	Dividends
Cash ($ mil.): 3,224	Yield: 0.0%
Current ratio: —	Payout: 19.6%
Long-term debt ($ mil.): —	Market value ($ mil.): 20,604

	STOCK PRICE ($) FY Close	P/E High/Low	PER SHARE ($) Earnings	Dividends	Book Value
12/17	41.98	13 10	3.25	0.64	41.30
12/16	35.63	19 9	1.97	0.46	38.57
12/15	26.19	18 15	1.55	0.40	37.22
12/14	24.86	16 14	1.55	0.10	35.30
Annual Growth	**14.0%**	**— —**	**20.3%**	**59.1%**	**4.0%**

Citizens, Inc. (Austin, TX)

Citizens aims to prepare its customers for two of life's certainties: living and dying. A holding company Citizens provides ordinary life insurance in niche markets through its various operating subsidiaries. Through its CICA Life Insurance Company it issues life insurance in US dollars to wealthy individuals in Latin America and Taiwan. On the other end of the economic and life spectrum its Home Service segment sells life insurance to lower-income individuals in the a few Midwest and southern states primarily to cover final expenses and burial costs. The company has $1.4 billion of assets and $4.7 billion of insurance in force.

Operations

Citizens operates two primary business segments: Life Insurance (73% of sales) and Home Service which accounts for most of the rest. The Home Service segment operates through subsidiaries Security Plan Life Insurance (SPLIC) and Security Plan Fire Insurance Co. (SPFIC). Both focus on the needs of middle and lower income earners primarily in Louisiana Mississippi and Arkansas.

Geographic Reach

The US accounts for about 30% of the firm's insurance sales. Colombia and Venezuela each account for around 15% of sales. Other foreign markets include Taiwan Ecuador and Argentina. In total the firm sells insurance in about 30 Latin American and the Pacific Rim countries.

Sales and Marketing

The policies are sold through some 300 field agents who make home visits and more than 200 funeral homes and independent agents. SPFIC writes a small amount of modest property/casualty insurance and is distributed through the same field agents that represent its life insurance products.

Its distribution strategy is conducted through marketing consultants comprised primarily of part-time second-career sales associates (such as teachers coaches community leaders and others) in rural and urban areas.

Financial Performance

The company has seen slow revenue growth in last five years. In 2014 revenues increased by 8% thanks to higher premium income from renewals and new sales in life insurance. Home Service Insurance premium growth was related to the acquisition of Magnolia Guaranty Life Insurance Company which offers industrial life policies.

Citizens' net investment income increased due to higher yields from new investments primarily in municipal and corporate issues and as the company experienced higher average invested assets as a result of the investment of new premium revenues.

In 2014 the company's net loss ($6.5 million compared to a net gain of $4.8 million in 2013) was due to higher insurance benefits paid or provided (including claims and surrenders and an increase in future policy benefit reserves commissions and other general expenses.

Operating cash flow has followed the revenue trend over the last five years. Operating cash flow increased by 20% in 2014 due to a rise in cash provided by future policy benefit reserves and federal income tax receivable.

Strategy

Citizens has been building its life insurance business in the US for several years having acquired about 17 life insurance companies since 1987. Despite its efforts revenue earned from its US life insurance business has been relatively flat in recent years.

Its strategy both international and domestic has kept the company operating in the black. As many insurance companies crumbled around it during the economic crisis Citizens has logged steady growth in insurance premium sales for the past four years.

The company's acquisition transition strategy focuses on the introduction of its cash accumulation ordinary whole life products to independent marketing consultants associated with companies it has acquired while continuing to service the needs of acquired policyholders.

Mergers and Acquisitions

In 2014 Citizens acquired Mississippi-based Magnolia Guaranty Life Insurance Company for $5.2 million. This company began writing business in 1992 and issues primarily industrial life policies through independent funeral homes in the state of Mississippi.

Company Background

The family of Harold E. Riley who founded Citizens in 1969 hold a controlling share of the company.

EXECUTIVES

Coo, Terry Festervand
President And Chief Corporate Officer, Kay E. Osbourn, age 51, $379,173 total compensation
Ceo, Geoffrey M. Kolander, age 42, $379,173 total compensation
Vp Cfo And Treasurer, David S. Jorgensen, age 54, $43,751 total compensation
Chairman, Rick D. Riley, age 64
Vice Chairman, E. Dean Gage, age 75
Vp Cfo And Treasurer, David S. Jorgensen, age 54
Auditors: Deloitte & Touche LLP

LOCATIONS

HQ: Citizens, Inc. (Austin, TX)
2900 Esperanza Crossing, 2nd Floor, Austin, TX 78758
Phone: 512 837-7100
Web: www.citizensinc.com

2014 Premium Earned

	% of total
US	28
Venezuela	16
Colombia	14
Taiwan	9
Ecuador	8
Other	25
Total	**100**

PRODUCTS/OPERATIONS

2014 Sales

	$ mil.	% of total
Life insurance	169	73
Home service	59	26
Other non-insurance enterprises	1	1
Total	**230**	**100**

Selected Subsidiaries

CICA Life Insurance Company of America (CICA)
Citizens National Life Insurance Company (CNLIC)
Computing Technology Inc.
Insurance Investors Inc.
Security Plan Fire Insurance Company (SPFIC)
Security Plan Life Insurance Company (SPLIC)

COMPETITORS

AIG	Monumental Life
BMI Financial Group	National Western
Guardian Holdings	Nationwide
Kemper Corp	Pan-American Life
MetLife	

HISTORICAL FINANCIALS

Company Type: Public

Income Statement

FYE: December 31

	ASSETS ($ mil.)	NET INCOME ($ mil.)	INCOME AS % OF ASSETS	EMPLOYEES
12/17	1,644	(38)	—	443
12/16	1,583	1	0.1%	730
12/15	1,484	(3)	—	620
12/14	1,417	(6)	—	306
12/13	1,216	4	0.4%	350
Annual Growth	**7.8%**	**—**	**—**	**6.1%**

Debt ratio: —	No. of shares (mil.): 50
Return on equity: (-16.13%)	Dividends
Cash ($ mil.): 46	Yield: —
Current ratio: —	Payout: —
Long-term debt ($ mil.): —	Market value ($ mil.): 368

	STOCK PRICE ($) FY Close	P/E High/Low	PER SHARE ($) Earnings	Dividends	Book Value
12/17	7.35	— —	(0.77)	0.00	4.46
12/16	9.82	292 154	0.04	0.00	4.97
12/15	7.43	— —	(0.07)	0.00	4.84
12/14	7.60	— —	(0.13)	0.00	5.16
12/13	8.75	115 60	0.10	0.00	4.91
Annual Growth	(4.3%)	— —	—	—	(2.3%)

City Holding Co.

"Take Me Home Country Roads" may be the (unofficial) state song of West Virginia but City Holding hopes all roads lead to its City National Bank of West Virginia subsidiary which operates more than 80 branches in the Mountaineer State and in neighboring areas of southern Ohio eastern Kentucky and northern Virginia. Serving consumers and regional businesses the nearly $4 billion bank offers standard deposit products loans credit cards insurance trust and investment services. Residential mortgages and home equity loans constitute more than half of City Holding's $2.5 billion loan portfolio though the bank also writes commercial industrial commercial mortgage and installment consumer loans.

Operations

City National Bank (CNB) operates four main business divisions: Commercial banking Consumer Banking Mortgage Banking and Wealth Management and Trust Services.

Commercial Banking provides traditional banking products commercial and industrial loans and different kinds of real estate loans to corporations and other business customers. Consumer Banking provides deposit products installment loans and real estate loans and lines of credit. The bank's Mortgage Banking division offers fixed and adjustable-rate mortgages construction financing production of conventional and government-backed mortgages secondary marketing and mortgage servicing.

Wealth Management and Trust Services offers personal trust and estate administration investment management and investment and custodial services for commercial and individual customers. This includes management of investment accounts for individuals employee benefit plans and charitable foundations.

Altogether the company earned 62% of its total revenue from interest and fees on loans in 2014 plus another 7% from interest on its investment securities. About 14% of revenue came from service charges 8% came from bankcard revenue and 2% came from trust and investment management fee income.

Geographic Reach

City boasts around 80 branches in four US states including more than 55 branches in West Virginia nearly 15 in Virginia around 10 in Kentucky and less than a handful of branches in Ohio.

Sales and Marketing

The bank spent $3.27 million on advertising in 2014 compared to $2.67 million and $2.59 million in 2013 and 2012 respectively.

Financial Performance

City Holding's revenues and profits have mostly been on the uptrend in recent years as the bank has grown its loan business through acquisitions.

The bank's revenue dipped by 4% to $188.29 million in 2014 mostly because it generated less in loan interest due to an expected drop in accretion from fair value adjustments related to its recent Virginia Savings Bank and Community Bank acquisitions. Interest margins also shrank amidst the low interest environment which caused further headwinds to interest income. The bank did have some bright spots with 16% growth in trust and investment fee income and 11% growth in bankcard revenue as it continued to push those services.

Despite lower revenue in 2014 City Holdings net income jumped by 10% to $52.96 million — the highest its profit has been since 2007. The rise was mostly thanks to a combination of a non-income based tax rebate (non-recurring) decreased legal and professional fees from lower legal settlements a $2.7 million decline in loan loss provisions as the credit quality of the bank's loan portfolio improved and a $1.3 million reduction in interest expense on deposits.

City's operating cash fell to $53.35 million despite higher earnings during the year primarily because the bank used more of its cash toward purchasing assets and generated less net cash proceeds from its loans held for sale.

Strategy

City Holding's flagship subsidiary City National Bank has been growing its loan business and branch network in target markets through acquisitions in recent years. In mid-2015 for example the bank agreed to acquire three bank branches in Lexington Kentucky from American Founders Bank boosting CNB's presence in the state to 11 branches while adding $164.2 million in new deposits and $125 billion in performing loans to its books.

Beyond buying just select branches the bank has also been known to buy smaller community banks outright in its target markets.

To free up resources for more investment in its core business City National sold its insurance operations to The Hilb Group in early 2015 netting an after-tax gain of $5.80 million.

Mergers and Acquisitions

In January 2013 City Holding acquired Community Financial Corporation holding company of the 11-branch Community Bank in Virginia.

In 2012 the company entered a new market in Virginia through its acquisition of Virginia Savings Bank which had five branches in the northern part of the state.

EXECUTIVES

Evp Marketing Human Resources And Retail Banking, Craig G. Stilwell, age 62, $330,000 total compensation

President And Ceo, Charles R. (Skip) Hageboeck, age 55, $500,000 total compensation

Evp Commercial Banking, John A. DeRito, age 68, $250,000 total compensation

Cfo, David L. Bumgarner, age 53, $207,000 total compensation

Cio, Jeffrey D. (Jeff) Legge, $175,000 total compensation

Assistant Vice President And Trust Officer, John Chandler

Executive Vice President Customer Service, Jack Cavender

Executive Vice President Marketing, Carolyn Hays

Vice President Of Customer Service, John Kelly

Assistant Vice President, Patricia Davis

Vice President Information Technology, Vince Workman

Vice President And Senior Trust Officer, P K Ellison

Senior Vice President Director Of Security, Joe Flueckiger

Vice President Treasury Management, Dewey Kuhns

Vice President Information Technology, David Payne

Vice President Human Resources, Lillian Komata

Senior Vice President Information Technology, Abigal Scott

Senior Vice President Retail Administration, Terry Childers

Avp, Pat Davis

Avp And Branch Manager, Massie Schemmel

President And Ceo, Charles R. (Skip) Hageboeck, age 55

Chairman, C. Dallas Kayser, age 66

Board Member, John Elliot

Board Member, Tracy Hylton

Board Member, Sharon Rowe

Board Member, James Rossi

Auditors: Ernst & Young LLP

LOCATIONS

HQ: City Holding Co.
25 Gatewater Road, Charleston, WV 25313
Phone: 304 769-1100
Web: www.bankatcity.com

PRODUCTS/OPERATIONS

2014 Sales

	$ mil.	% of total
Interest		
Loans including fees	116	62
Investment securities & other	13	7
Noninterest		
Service charges	265	14
Bankcard revenue	15	8
Other	171	9
Total	**188**	**100**

COMPETITORS

1st West Virginia Bancorp	Huntington Bancshares
BB&T	Ohio Valley Banc
Fifth Third	Premier Financial Bancorp
First Community Bancshares	United Bankshares
	WesBanco

HISTORICAL FINANCIALS

Company Type: Public

Income Statement — FYE: December 31

	ASSETS ($ mil.)	NET INCOME ($ mil.)	INCOME AS % OF ASSETS	EMPLOYEES
12/17	4,132	54	1.3%	839
12/16	3,984	52	1.3%	847
12/15	3,714	54	1.5%	853
12/14	3,461	52	1.5%	889
12/13	3,368	48	1.4%	923
Annual Growth	5.2%	3.0%	—	(2.4%)

2017 Year-End Financials

Debt ratio: 0.40%	No. of shares (mil.): 15
Return on equity: 11.49%	Dividends
Cash ($ mil.): 82	Yield: 0.0%
Current ratio: —	Payout: 50.2%
Long-term debt ($ mil.): —	Market value ($ mil.): 1,054

STOCK PRICE ($) FY Close	P/E High/Low		PER SHARE ($) Earnings	Dividends	Book Value
12/17	67.47	21 17	3.48	1.75	32.17
12/16	67.60	20 12	3.45	1.71	29.25
12/15	45.64	15 12	3.53	1.66	27.62
12/14	46.53	14 12	3.38	1.57	25.79
12/13	46.33	16 11	3.04	1.46	24.61
Annual Growth	9.9%	— —	3.4%	4.6%	6.9%

Civista Bancshares Inc

EXECUTIVES

Pres-Ceo, Dennis G Shaffer
Chb, James O Miller
Sr V Pres-Contrl, Todd A Michel
Sr V Pres-General Counsel-Sec, James E McGookey
Sr V Pres, Richard J Dutton
Sr V Pres, Charles A Parcher
Sr V Pres, Paul J Stark
Senior Vice President, Donna M Waltz-Jaskolski
Board Member, Allen R Maurice
Manager, Bruce Brinkerhoff
Board Member, Thomas A Depler
Auditors: S. R. Snodgrass, P.C.

LOCATIONS

HQ: Civista Bancshares Inc
100 East Water Street, Sandusky, OH 44870
Phone: 419 625-4121
Web: www.civb.com

COMPETITORS

Fifth Third	PNC Financial
Huntington Bancshares	U.S. Bancorp
KeyCorp	

HISTORICAL FINANCIALS

Company Type: Public

Income Statement   FYE: December 31

	ASSETS ($ mil.)	NET INCOME ($ mil.)	INCOME AS % OF ASSETS	EMPLOYEES
12/17	1,525	15	1.0%	350
12/16	1,377	17	1.3%	337
12/15	1,315	12	1.0%	326
12/14	1,213	9	0.8%	303
12/13	1,167	6	0.5%	313
Annual Growth	6.9%	26.6%	—	2.8%

2017 Year-End Financials

Debt ratio: 1.93%
Return on equity: 9.86%
Cash ($ mil.): 40
Current ratio: —
Long-term debt ($ mil.): —

No. of shares (mil.): 10
Dividends
  Yield: 0.0%
  Payout: 19.5%
Market value ($ mil.): 224

STOCK PRICE ($) FY Close	P/E High/Low		PER SHARE ($) Earnings	Dividends	Book Value
12/17	22.00	16 13	1.28	0.25	18.09
12/16	19.43	10 5	1.57	0.22	16.49
12/15	12.83	8 7	1.17	0.20	15.96
12/14	10.28	11 7	0.85	0.19	15.04
12/13	6.52	12 8	0.64	0.15	16.66
Annual Growth	35.5%	— —	18.9%	13.6%	2.1%

Clorox Co (The)

Bleach is the cornerstone of Clorox. The company's namesake household cleaning products are world leaders but the Clorox business reaches far beyond bleach. While it makes laundry and cleaning items (Formula 409 Pine-Sol Green Works) its vast products portfolio extends into dressings/sauces (Hidden Valley KC Masterpiece) plastic wrap and containers (Glad) cat litters (Fresh Step Scoop Away) and infection control items (HealthLink Aplicare Soy Vay). Other items include filtration systems (Brita in the Americas) charcoal briquettes (Kingsford Match Light) and natural personal care items (Burt's Bees). Clorox makes and sells its products worldwide.

HISTORY

Known first as the Electro-Alkaline Company The Clorox Company was founded in 1913 by five Oakland California investors who put up $100 apiece to make bleach using water from salt ponds around San Francisco Bay. The next year the company registered the brand name Clorox (the name combines the bleach's two main ingredients chlorine and sodium hydroxide). At first the company sold only industrial-strength bleach but in 1916 it formulated a household solution.

With the establishment of a Philadelphia distributor in 1921 Clorox began national expansion. The company went public in 1928 and built plants in Illinois and New Jersey in the 1930s; it opened nine more US plants in the 1940s and 1950s. In 1957 Procter & Gamble (P&G) bought Clorox. The Federal Trade Commission raised antitrust questions and litigation ensued over the next decade. P&G was ordered to divest Clorox and in 1969 Clorox again became an independent company.

Following its split with P&G the firm added household consumer goods and foods acquiring the brands Liquid-Plumr (drain opener 1969) Formula 409 (spray cleaner 1970) Litter Green (cat litter 1971) and Hidden Valley (salad dressings 1972). Clorox entered the specialty food products business by purchasing Grocery Store Products (Kitchen Bouquet 1971) and Kingsford (charcoal briquettes 1973).

Henkel a large West German maker of cleansers and detergents purchased 15% of Clorox's stock in 1974 as part of an agreement to share research. Beginning in 1977 Clorox sold off subsidiaries and brands such as Country Kitchen Foods (1979) to focus on household goods.

During the 1980s Clorox launched a variety of new products including Match Light (instant-lighting charcoal 1980) Tilex (mildew remover 1981) and Fresh Step (cat litter 1984). Clorox began marketing Brita water filtration systems in the US in 1988 (adding Canada in 1995). In 1990 it paid $465 million for American Cyanamid's household products group including Pine-Sol cleaner and Combat insecticide. (It sold Combat and Soft Scrub to Henkel in 2004.)

Clorox left the laundry detergent business in 1991 (begun in 1988) after it was battered by heavyweights P&G and Unilever. Household products VP Craig Sullivan became CEO the next year (stepping down in December 2003). In 1993 Clorox dumped its frozen food and bottled water operations. It began marketing its liquid bleach in Hungary through a Henkel subsidiary in 1994 and also bought S.O.S soap pads from Miles Inc.

A string of acquisitions brought the company into new markets as it built on existing brands. Clorox bought Black Flag and Lestoil in 1996 and car care product manufacturer Armor All in 1997. With its 1999 purchase of First Brands — for about $2 billion in stock and debt — Clorox added four more brands of cat litter and diversified into plastic products (Glad).

Despite adding 115 new products in 2000 the company said it would put more emphasis on core brands going forward; it pushed its struggling Glad brand with more trade promotions and coupons.

Clorox in January 2001 announced a joint venture with Bombril Brazil's leading name in steel wool to form Detergentes Bombril; however Clorox canceled the agreement in April 2001 claiming that various conditions of the deal had not been met. A year later Clorox further distanced itself from the Brazilian market selling its SBP insecticides business to Reckitt Benckiser. In 2002 Clorox announced that due to the difficult economic environment in the region it was selling its Brazil business.

In 2003 it jumpstarted a joint venture with P

EXECUTIVES

Evp General Counsel And Corporate Affairs, Laura Stein, age 57, $582,050 total compensation
Chairman And Ceo, Benno Dorer, age 54, $976,154 total compensation
Evp And Cfo, Stephen M. (Steve) Robb, age 53, $576,846 total compensation
Evp Product Supply Enterprise Performance And It, James Foster, age 55
Svp And Chief Innovation Officer, Denise Garner, age 54
Svp And Cio, Manjit Singh, age 48
Svp International Division, Michael Costello, age 51
Svp; General Manager Specialty Division, Jon Balousek, age 49
Evp And Coo, Dawn Willoughby, age 49, $515,154 total compensation
Svp And Chief Marketing Officer, Eric Reynolds, age 47
Chairman And Ceo, Benno Dorer, age 54
Auditors: Ernst & Young LLP

LOCATIONS

HQ: Clorox Co (The)
1221 Broadway, Oakland, CA 94612-1888
Phone: 510 271-7000
Web: www.thecloroxcompany.com

2016 sales

	% of total
United States	83
International	17
Total	**100**

PRODUCTS/OPERATIONS

2016 sales

	$ mil.	% of total
Cleaning	1,912	33
Household	1,862	33
International	997	17
Lifestyle	990	17
Total	**5,761**	**100**

Selected Mergers & Acquisitions

FY 2007
  Latin American and Canadian bleach brands (Javex Agua Jane Nevex) from Colgate-Palmolive Company ($126 million plus inventory)
  Burt's Bees line of natural skin and hair-care products ($925 million)
FY 2006
  Tom's of Maine natural oral care products

Selected Food-Related Products

Brita
Glad
Glad Press 'n Seal
GladWare
Hidden Valley
K.C. Masterpiece

Selected Household & Professional Cleaning Products

Aplicare
Clorox
Clorox 2
Clorox Clean-Up
Clorox Disinfecting Wipes
Clorox Dispatch
Clorox FreshCare
Clorox Healthcare
Clorox Oxi Magic
Clorox ReadyMop
Clorox Toilet Bowl Cleaner
Formula 409
Formula 409 Carpet Cleaner
Green Works
Handi-Wipes
HealthLink
Lestoil
Liquid-Plumr
Pine-Sol
S.O.S
Stain Out
Tilex
ToiletWand
Tuffy
Ultra Clorox Bleach

Selected International Products

Agua Jane (bleach Uruguay)
Ant Rid (insecticides)
Arela (waxes)
Astra (disposable gloves)
Bluebell (cleaners)
Chux (cleaning tools)
Clorisol (bleach)
Clorox Gentle (color-safe bleach)
Glad (containers)
Glad-Lock (resealable bags)
Guard (shoe polish)
Gumption (cleaners)
Home Mat (insecticides)
Home Keeper (insecticides)
Javex (bleach Canada)
Mono (aluminum foil)
Nevex (bleach Venezuela)
OSO (aluminum foil)
Prestone (coolant)
Selton (insecticides)
S.O.S (cleaners)
Super Globo (bleach)
XLO (sponges)
Yuhanrox (bleach)

Selected Specialty Products

BBQ Bag
Burt's Bees
EverClean
EverFresh
Fresh Step
Fresh Step Scoop
Kingsford
Match Light
Rain Dance
Scoop Away
Son of a Gun!
Tuff Stuff

COMPETITORS

Alticor	Kiehl's
Big Heart Pet Brands	Kiss My Face
Blistex	McBride plc
Bonne Bell	Mondelez International
CalCedar	Natural Health Trends
Campbell Soup	Nature's Sunshine
Church & Dwight	Newman's Own
Colgate-Palmolive	Oil-Dri
ConAgra	Pactiv
Diversey	Procter & Gamble
Dow Chemical	Reckitt Benckiser
Dr. Bronner's	S.C. Johnson
Estée Lauder	Seventh Generation
Forever Living	The Dial Corporation

HISTORICAL FINANCIALS

Company Type: Public

Income Statement

FYE: June 30

	REVENUE ($ mil.)	NET INCOME ($ mil.)	NET PROFIT MARGIN	EMPLOYEES
06/18	6,124	823	13.4%	8,700
06/17	5,973	701	11.7%	8,100
06/16	5,761	648	11.2%	8,000
06/15	5,655	580	10.3%	7,700
06/14	5,591	558	10.0%	8,200
Annual Growth	2.3%	10.2%	—	1.5%

2018 Year-End Financials

Debt ratio: 49.07%	No. of shares (mil.): 127
Return on equity: 129.81%	Dividends
Cash ($ mil.): 131	Yield: 0.0%
Current ratio: 1.09	Payout: 55.5%
Long-term debt ($ mil.): 2,284	Market value ($ mil.): 17,310

	STOCK PRICE ($) FY Close	P/E High/Low	PER SHARE ($) Earnings	Dividends	Book Value
06/18	135.25	23 18	6.26	3.48	5.67
06/17	133.24	26 21	5.33	3.20	4.20
06/16	138.39	27 21	4.92	3.08	2.30
06/15	104.02	25 19	4.37	2.96	0.92
06/14	91.40	22 19	4.23	2.84	1.20
Annual Growth	10.3%	— —	10.3%	5.2%	47.6%

CMS Energy Corp

Michigan relies on CMS Energy. The energy holding company's regulated utility subsidiary Consumers Energy serves 1.8 million electricity and 1.8 million natural gas customers. It has electric generating capacity of 5800 MW and purchases an additional 2700 MW from third party electricity providers. Another subsidiary CMS Enterprises operates the non-regulated businesses of CMS Energy and is an operator of independent power generating plants. CMS Enterprises' independent power plants (coal- gas- and biomass-fired) have a capacity of 1200 MW and are located in Michigan North Carolina and Wisconsin.

Operations

CMS Energy operates three reportable segments: Consumers Electric Utility (70%% of total sales) Consumers Gas Utility (25%) and CMS Enterprises. The Electric and Gas segments conduct their business primarily through a state regulated utility Consumers Energy.

The Consumers Electric business generates purchases transmits distributes and sells electricity. After shuttering seven smaller coal plants in 2016 the segment still has two coal-fired generation plants along with several oil/gas plants hydroelectric facilities and wind farms. It buys about one third of its electricity and produces the rest. The segment owns more than 10000 miles of underground and 56000 overhead electric distribution lines.

The Consumers Gas segment stores transmits distributes and sells natural gas. It owns 15 gas storage fields and nearly 28000 miles of distribution pipelines.

CMS Enterprises runs an energy marketing group to sell electricity and natural gas on behalf of CMS Enterprises and other Michigan producers.

Geographic Reach

The company serves residential commercial industrial and other customers. Though it is a regulated utility Consumers Energy is open to electricity competition in its service area at a rate of up to 10% of its previous year's retail sales. Gas competition also exists from Gulf Coast companies as well as alternative fuels such as propane oil and electricity. CMS Energy's non-regulated operations within the CMS Enterprise subsidiary experience competitive pressures by the very nature of its business model of buying and selling electricity on open markets.

Sales and Marketing

The company serves residential commercial industrial and other customers. Though it is a regulated utility Consumers Energy is open to electricity competition in its service area at a rate of up to 10% of its previous year?s retail sales. Gas competition also exists from Gulf Coast companies as well as alternative fuels such as propane oil and electricity. CMS Energy?s non-regulated operations within the CMS Enterprise subsidiary experience competitive pressures by the very nature of its business model of buying and selling electricity on open markets.

Financial Performance

In recent years CMS Energy?s revenue drifted between $6.2 billion and $6.5 billion although it had an unusual spike of $7.2 billion in 2014. Net income rose methodically each year since 2012 from $382 million to more than $550 million.

Despite growth in electricity revenues 2016 revenue fell less than 1% to $6.4 billion due to a $230 million decrease in gas revenue. Although the amount of gas delivered rose the average amount charged to customers dropped. Electricity deliveries were up incrementally as was the average customer billing rate.

CMS Energy had $257 million in cash at the end of 2016 $31 million lower than the prior year. Cash from operations contributed $1.6 billion while financing activities provided $255 million however they were overshadowed by the $1.9 billion used for investing activities (mainly capital expenditures).

Strategy

CMS Energy anticipates spending $9.0 billion in capital improvements between 2017 and 2021. While most of the funding is intended for maintenance and upgrades to existing infrastructure some money will help the company meet new air quality and renewable energy mandates.

Addressing new mandates the Consumers business is making big changes its energy generation mix mostly from coal to natural gas. In 2016 after retiring seven of its smaller coal-fired plants (representing 950 MW of capacity) the percent of power coming from the black commodity dropped from 79% to 58%. That same year Consumers adjusted a Power Purchase Agreement (PPA) with an Entergy nuclear plant to terminate the agreement in May 2018 four years ahead of schedule. The lost capacity will be replaced with the output of Consumers? 2015-acquired 540 MW gas-fueled plant in Jackson MI along with a reduction in consumer demand updated PPA agreements and power from renewable energy sources.

Consumers Electricity informed state regulators in 2017 that it is interested in acquiring an additional gas-fired plant in Michigan. As well it broke ground on its third wind energy project Cross Winds Energy Park II in Tuscola County. Phase I is expected to have 19 turbines capable of generating 44 MW of electricity and will commence service in early 2018. When completed it will have more than 80 wind turbines and 155 MW of energy production (enough to serve 60000 residents).

Consumers Gas business will receive nearly $4.0 of the multi-year capital investment. One benefactor of the funds is a $610 million 5-year project to replace 78 miles of gas pipe dating to the 1940s and located in Saginaw Genesee and Oakland counties. Construction began in mid-2017 and will continue until the end of 2022. Another use is focused on growth installing new pipes to serve an anticipated increase of nearly 8000 new business customers and 2500 residential customers in its service area.

The CMS Enterprise business which is non-regulated is also investing for the future. It purchased in late 2017 Delta Solar a 24 MW project whose power output will eventually be sold to Landing Board of Water & Light to power 3300 homes.

HISTORY

In the late 1880s W. A. Foote and Samuel Jarvis formed hydroelectric company Jackson Electrical Light Works in Jackson Michigan. After building plants in other Michigan towns Foote formed utility holding company Consumers Power. In 1910 the firm merged with Michigan Light to create Commonwealth Power Railway and Light (CPR&L) and began building a statewide transmission system.

Foote died in 1915 and after nine years of acquisitions successor Bernard Cobb sold the rail systems and split CPR&L into Commonwealth Power (CP) and Electric Railway Securities. In 1928 Cobb bought Southeastern Power & Light (SP&L) and merged CP with Penn-Ohio Edison to form Allied Power & Light. Commonwealth and Southern (C&S) was then created as the parent of Allied and SP&L.

In 1932 future GOP presidential nominee Wendell Willkie took the helm and became a national political figure by opposing the Public Utility Holding Company Act of 1935 which began 60 years of regulated monopolies. Consumers Power was divested from C&S after WWII.

Consumers brought a nuclear plant on line in 1962 and the next year began buying Michigan oil and gas fields. In 1967 it formed NOMECO (now CMS Oil and Gas) to guide its oil and gas efforts.

The completion of the Palisades nuke in 1971 began a 13-year run of chronic problems and lengthy shutdowns. Cost overruns and an environmental lawsuit killed the firm's third nuke (Midland) in 1984 — after $4.1 billion was spent.

A rate hike and new CEO William McCormick set the firm on a new path in 1985. McCormick formed a subsidiary to develop and invest in independent power projects in 1986 and created holding company CMS (short for "Consumers") Energy the next year. CMS Gas Transmission was formed in 1989.

Midland Cogeneration Venture (CMS Energy and six partners) completed converting Midland to a natural gas-fueled cogeneration plant in 1990 and CMS Energy wrote off $657 million from its losses at the former nuke. It regained profitability in 1993.

McCormick split the utilities into electric and gas divisions in 1995 and also issued stock for its gas utility and transmission businesses Consumers Gas Group. The next year CMS Energy formed an energy marketing arm.

In 1996 and 1997 CMS Energy invested in power plants in Morocco and Australia and bought a stake in a Brazilian electric utility. The next year it began developing a gas-fired plant in Ghana and won a bid to build a plant in India. CMS Energy also bought gas gathering and processing firms Continental Natural Gas and Heritage Gas Services in 1998.

Michigan's public service commission (PSC) issued utility restructuring orders in 1997 and 1998 but in 1999 the state Supreme Court ruled that the PSC lacked restructuring authority. Facing less-favorable proposed legislation CMS Energy and DTE Energy moved to implement competition per the PSC's guidelines.

CMS Energy bought Panhandle Eastern Pipe Line from Duke Energy for $2.2 billion in 1999. It also grabbed a 77% stake in another Brazilian utility and began building its Powder River Basin gas pipeline. In 2000 the company partnered with Marathon Ashland Petroleum (now Marathon Petroleum) and TEPPCO to operate a pipeline transporting refined petroleum from the US Gulf Coast to Illinois. Later that year CMS Energy announced plans for an IPO for its CMS Oil and Gas unit; however the IPO was withdrawn in 2001.

CMS Energy agreed in 2001 to sell Consumers' high-voltage electric transmission assets to independent transmission operator Trans-Elect for about $290 million; the deal which was the first of its kind in the US was completed in 2002. That year the company sold i

EXECUTIVES

Vice Chairman Cms Energy And Consumers Energy, Thomas J. (Tom) Webb, age 66, $705,000 total compensation

Svp Governmental Regulatory And Public Affairs, David G. Mengebier, age 61, $375,000 total compensation

Svp Energy Resources, Daniel J. (Dan) Malone, age 57, $490,000 total compensation

Svp And General Counsel, Catherine M. Reynolds, age 60, $516,667 total compensation

Evp And Cfo Cms Energy And Consumers Energy, Rejji P. Hayes, age 43

Svp Customer Experience And Cio, Brian F. Rich, age 43

President And Ceo, Patricia K. (Patti) Poppe, age 50, $775,000 total compensation

Vice President Gas Engineering And Supply Consumers Energy, Mary Palkovich

Vice President Electric Grid Integration Consumers Energy, Tim Sparks

Senior Vice President, John Butler

Senior Vice President, Jackson Hanson

Vp Enterprise Project Management And Environmental Services Consumers Energy, Dennis Dobbs

Senior Vice President Strategy And Business Planning Cms Energy And Consumers Energy., Venkat Rao

Senior Vice President Finance, Tim Kowaleski

Vice Chairman Cms Energy And Consumers Energy, Thomas J. (Tom) Webb, age 66

Chairman, John G. Russell, age 61

Svp And General Counsel, Catherine M. Reynolds, age 60

Auditors: PricewaterhouseCoopers LLP

LOCATIONS

HQ: CMS Energy Corp
One Energy Plaza, Jackson, MI 49201
Phone: 517 788-0550
Web: www.cmsenergy.com

PRODUCTS/OPERATIONS

2017 Sales

	$ mil.	% of total
Electric utility	4,448	68
Gas utility	1,774	27
Enterprises	229	3
Other reconciling items	132	2
Total	**6,583**	**100**

Selected Subsidiaries

Consumers Energy Company (electric and gas utility)
CMS Capital
  EnerBank USA (banking services)
CMS Enterprises Company (nonutility holding company)
EnerBank USA

COMPETITORS

AEP	Progress Energy
Alliant Energy	Resources Corp.
Calpine	SCANA
Con Edison	SEMCO ENERGY
DTE	TECO Energy
Edison International	WEC Energy
NextEra Energy	Xcel Energy
NiSource	

HISTORICAL FINANCIALS

Company Type: Public

Income Statement

FYE: December 31

	REVENUE ($ mil.)	NET INCOME ($ mil.)	NET PROFIT MARGIN	EMPLOYEES
12/18	6,873	657	9.6%	8,625
12/17	6,583	460	7.0%	7,952
12/16	6,399	551	8.6%	7,366
12/15	6,456	523	8.1%	7,804
12/14	7,179	477	6.6%	7,388
Annual Growth	(1.1%)	8.3%	—	3.9%

2018 Year-End Financials

Debt ratio: 47.62%
Return on equity: 14.29%
Cash ($ mil.): 153
Current ratio: 0.94
Long-term debt ($ mil.): 10,684

No. of shares (mil.): 283
Dividends
  Yield: 2.8%
  Payout: 74.0%
Market value ($ mil.): 14,070

	STOCK PRICE ($) FY Close	P/E High/Low	PER SHARE ($)		
			Earnings	Dividends	Book Value
12/18	49.65	23 18	2.32	1.43	16.78
12/17	47.30	31 25	1.64	1.33	15.77
12/16	41.62	23 18	1.98	1.24	15.23
12/15	36.08	20 17	1.89	1.16	14.21
12/14	34.75	21 15	1.74	1.08	13.34
Annual Growth	9.3%	— —	7.5%	7.3%	5.9%

CNA Financial Corp

CNA Financial is an umbrella organization for a wide range of insurance providers including Continental Casualty and Continental Insurance. It primarily provides commercial policies such as workers' compensation auto and general liability. CNA also sells specialty insurance including professional liability (doctors lawyers and architects) and vehicle warranty service contracts. The firm offers commercial surety bonds (through CNA Surety) risk management claims administration and information services. Its products are sold by independent agents and brokers in the US and through partners abroad. Holding company Loews owns 90% of CNA which was formed in 1897.

Operations

In late 2014 the company realigned its core property/casualty segments to Specialty (40% of sales) Commercial (40% of sales) and International. Its non-core business segments are Life & Group Non-Core and Corporate & Other Non-Core.

The Specialty segment provides professional financial and specialty products and services through independent agents brokers and managing general underwriters. The Commercial segment includes products sold to small and mid-market organizations primarily through an independent agency distribution system; it also sells commercial insurance and risk management products to large corporations primarily through insurance brokers. Meanwhile the International segment offers management and professional liability products and services outside of the US; distribution is via a network of brokers independent agencies and managing general underwriters. It also sells on the Lloyd's marketplace.

Most of CNA Financial's non-core insurance products are in run-off including a few remaining life annuity and pension products as well as accident and health insurance.

Geographic Reach

CNA is headquartered in Chicago and has offices throughout the US and Canada; it also has locations in Europe and Asia.

Sales and Marketing

In the US independent agents and brokers market CNA products while partners handle the coverage abroad. It primarily targets companies in the health care manufacturing education financial services and construction industries.

Financial Performance

CNA's revenue has seen slow growth over the past few years. In 2014 revenue decreased 2% to $9.6 billion on decreases in the Commercial segment which saw net written premiums decline $143 million. That slowdown was indicative of a lower level of new business in an increasingly competitive market although offset by rate increases. The decline in Commercial was partially offset by a $43 million increase in the Specialty segment. Net written premiums in the International segment fell $79 million largely due to changes in the recently acquired London-based Hardy subsidiary and the termination of a specialty product managing general underwriter relationship in Canada.

The lower revenue as well as a $211 million loss from discontinued operations from the 2014 sale of Continental Assurance Company led to a 26% decline in net revenue (to $691 million).

Cash flow from operations rose 20% to $1.4 billion in 2014 on lower net claim payments and other factors.

Strategy

CNA is focused on strengthening its core commercial operations through both enhanced customer retention efforts and new customer additions. In 2015 it expanded its Allied Vendor Program for law firms by adding three companies offering services to strengthen customers' risk control programs. Also that year the company expanded its specialty lines business into Canada.

CNA partnered with equipment maintenance and asset management service provider Remi in 2014. The company intends to offer a program to manage the risk of equipment maintenance and repair.

In 2014 the company began efforts to sell its run-off and pension deposit business. It also sold Continental Assurance Company a structured settlement and group annuity subsidiary.

EXECUTIVES

Evp General Counsel And Secretary, Jonathan D. (Jon) Kantor, age 62, $800,000 total compensation
President And Coo Cna Specialty, Mark I. Herman, age 59, $675,000 total compensation
Evp And Cfo, D. Craig Mense, age 66, $825,000 total compensation
President And Ceo Cna Canada, Nick Creatura
Ceo Cna Europe And Hardy Underwriting, David J. (Dave) Brosnan, age 55
Evp And Chief Underwriting Officer, Douglas M. (Doug) Worman
Evp Worldwide Property And Casualty Claim, Andrew J. Pinkes, age 55
Chairman And Ceo, Dino E. Robusto, age 59, $114,103 total compensation

Evp And Chief Actuary, Larry A. Haefner, age 61, $367,628 total compensation
President Worldwide Field Operations, Timothy J. (Tim) Szerlong, age 65, $700,000 total compensation
President Long Term Care, Albert J. (Al) Miralles, age 48
President And Coo Cna Commercial, Kevin Leidwinger, age 54
Evp Technology And Operations, Joseph (J.) Merten
Evp General Counsel And Secretary, Jonathan D. (Jon) Kantor, age 62
Chairman And Ceo, Dino E. Robusto, age 59
Auditors: DELOITTE & TOUCHE LLP

LOCATIONS

HQ: CNA Financial Corp
151 N. Franklin, Chicago, IL 60606
Phone: 312 822-5000   **Fax:** 312 822-6419
Web: www.cna.com

PRODUCTS/OPERATIONS

2014 Sales

	$ mil.	% of total
Commercial		
Middle market	1,631	17
Small business insurance	709	7
Other commercial insurance	1,343	14
Specialty		
Management & professional	2,818	29
Surety	509	5
Warranty & alternative risks	381	4
International		
Hardy	365	4
CNA Europe	335	3
Canada	273	3
Life & Group	1,279	13
Corporate & other	56	1
Adjustments	(7)	-
Total	**9,692**	**100**

Selected Solutions

Business interruption
Cargo (ocean marine)
CNA connect
CNA paramount
Commercial auto
Commercial general liability
Cyber liability
Directors & officers (d&o)
Employment practices liability (epl)
Epack extra
Equipment breakdown
Fidelity and crime insurance
Inland marine
International
Kidnap ransom and extortion
Professional liability (errors & omissions)
Property
Surety
Umbrella liability
Warranty
Workers' compensation

COMPETITORS

ACMAT	Nationwide
AIG	Old Republic
American Financial Group	State Farm
	The Hartford
Aspen Insurance	Travelers Companies
Assurant	United Fire
Berkshire Hathaway	W. R. Berkley
Cincinnati Financial	White Mountains
Everest Re	Insurance Group
Liberty Mutual	Zurich Insurance Group

HISTORICAL FINANCIALS

Company Type: Public

Income Statement   FYE: December 31

	ASSETS ($ mil.)	NET INCOME ($ mil.)	INCOME AS % OF ASSETS	EMPLOYEES
12/17	56,567	899	1.6%	6,300
12/16	55,233	859	1.6%	6,700
12/15	55,047	479	0.9%	6,900
12/14	55,566	691	1.2%	6,900
12/13	57,194	937	1.6%	7,035
Annual Growth	(0.3%)	(1.0%)	—	(2.7%)

2017 Year-End Financials

Debt ratio: 4.79%	No. of shares (mil.): 271
Return on equity: 7.43%	Dividends
Cash ($ mil.): 355	Yield: 0.0%
Current ratio: —	Payout: 93.9%
Long-term debt ($ mil.): —	Market value ($ mil.): 14,387

	STOCK PRICE ($) FY Close	P/E High/Low		PER SHARE ($) Earnings	Dividends	Book Value
12/17	53.05	17	12	3.30	3.10	45.15
12/16	41.50	13	9	3.17	3.00	44.25
12/15	35.15	25	19	1.77	3.00	43.50
12/14	38.71	17	14	2.55	2.00	47.39
12/13	42.89	12	8	3.47	0.80	46.90
Annual Growth	5.5%	—	—	(1.2%)	40.3%	(1.0%)

CNB Financial Corp. (Clearfield, PA)

CNB Financial is the holding company for CNB Bank ERIEBANK and FCBank. The banks and subsidiaries provide traditional deposit and loan services as well as wealth management merchant credit card processing and life insurance through nearly 30 CNB Bank- and ERIEBANK-branded branches in Pennsylvania and nine FCBank branches in central Ohio. Commercial industrial and agricultural loans make up more than one-third of the bank's loan portfolio while commercial mortgages make up another one-third. It also makes residential mortgages consumer and credit card loans. The company's non-bank subsidiaries include CNB Securities Corporation Holiday Financial Services Corporation and CNB Insurance Agency.

Operations

Commercial industrial and agricultural loans made up 36% of the bank's $16.74 billion loan portfolio at the end of 2015 while commercial mortgages made up another 33%. The rest of the portfolio was made up of residential mortgages (15% of loan assets) consumer (14%) overdrafts (less than 1%) and credit card loans (less than 1%).

The group makes more than 80% of its revenue from interest income. About 70% of its revenue came from loan interest during 2015 while another 15% came from interest income from taxable and tax-exempt securities. The remainder of its revenue came from deposit account service charges (4% of revenue) wealth and asset management fees (3%) and other miscellaneous income sources.

Geographic Reach

Clearfield Pennsylvania-based CNB Financial serves clients in its home state as well as in Ohio.

CNB Financial serves a specific market area such as the Pennsylvania counties of Cambria Cameron Centre Clearfield Crawford Elk Erie Indiana Jefferson McKean and Warren.

Sales and Marketing

The group serves individuals businesses government and institutional customers.

CNB Financial has been increasing its advertising spend in recent years. It spent $1.6 million during 2015 up from $1.5 million and $1 million in 2014 and 2013 respectively.

Financial Performance

CNB Financial's revenues have risen more than 30% since 2011 as its loan assets have nearly doubled to $1.58 billion. The firm's profits have grown nearly 50% over the same period as low-interest rates and declining loan loss provisions have lowered operating costs.

The group's revenue climbed 1% to $102 million during 2015 thanks to a modest rise in interest income stemming mostly from 16% loan asset growth.

Despite revenue growth in 2015 CNB Financial's net income dipped 4% to $22.2 million mostly due to nearly 10% rise in salary and employee benefit costs from new hires and more expensive benefits. The group's operating cash levels jumped 16% to $34 million for the year thanks to favorable working capital changes related to accrued interest payables and other liabilities.

Strategy

CNB Financial has been acquiring other banks and opening branches in new geographic markets in recent years to boost its loan and deposit business. As a sign of success the bank noted that its assets have nearly doubled in size since 2009 from $1.16 billion to $2.29 billion at the end of 2015.

Toward its branch expansion plans the group's ERIEBANK brand entered Ohio by opening a loan production office there in 2014 with plans to open another by the end of 2016. After opening an FCBank branch in Dublin Ohio in 2014 the group in 2016 also continued to push its FCBank brand which has been enjoying double-digit loan and deposit business growth in the Columbus and Lancaster regions in Ohio. It plans to open a new FCBank branch in Worthington Ohio by the end of 2016.

Mergers and Acquisitions

In 2016 CNB looked expanded into Northeast Ohio after buying Mentor Ohio-based Lake National Bank — and its $152 million in assets — for nearly $25 million. Lake National Bank's operations were folded into ERIEBANK's operations when the transaction closed.

In 2013 extending its reach in Ohio CNB Financial acquired FC Banc Corp. for $41.6 million. The deal gave CNB Financial Farmers Citizens Bank which serves the northern Ohio communities of Bucyrus Cardington Fredericktown Mount Hope and Shiloh as well as the greater Columbus Ohio area.

Company Background

In 2012 CNB Financial acquired an Ebensburg Pennsylvania-based consumer discount company which brought with it a loan portfolio valued at about $1 million.

EXECUTIVES

Evp Human Resources, Mary Ann Conaway
Sevp And Chief Credit Officer Cnb Bank, Mark D. Breakey, age 59, $211,000 total compensation
President And Ceo, Joseph B. Bower, age 54, $458,000 total compensation
Sevp And Coo Cnb Bank, Richard L Greslick, age 42, $221,000 total compensation

Evp Cfo And Treasurer Cnb Bank And Treasurer Principal Financial Officer And Principal Accounting Officer Cnb Financial Corporation, Brian W. Wingard, age 44, $210,000 total compensation
Evp And Chief Commercial Banking Officer Cnb Bank, Joseph E. Dell, age 62, $211,000 total compensation
Evp Customer Experience, Leanne D. Kassab
Assistant Vice President Of Credit Administration, Gregory Dixon
Assistant Vice President Of Mortgage Lending, Eileen Ryan
Assistant Vice President Of Regional Branch Administration, Vickie Baker
Vice Presidents Commercial Banking, Joseph Yaros
Assistant Vice President Compliance, Kylie Ogden
Vice President Commercial Lending, Brett Stewart
President And Ceo, Joseph B. Bower, age 54
Chairman, Peter F. Smith, age 63
Senior Vice President Operations And Assistant Secretary, Vincent C Turiano
Auditors: Crowe Horwath LLP

LOCATIONS

HQ: CNB Financial Corp. (Clearfield, PA)
1 South Second Street, P.O. Box 42, Clearfield, PA 16830
Phone: 814 765-9621
Web: www.cnbbank.bank

PRODUCTS/OPERATIONS

2015 Sales

	% of total
Interest and Dividend Income	
Loans including fees	70
Securities	
Taxable	10
Tax-exempt	4
Dividends	1
Non-Interest Income	
Wealth and asset management fees	3
Service charges on deposit accounts	4
Other service charges and fees	3
Other revenues	5
Total	**100**

Selected Services

Checking
Credit cards
Loans
Savings

COMPETITORS

AmeriServ Financial	M&T Bank
CBT Financial	Northwest Bancshares
Citizens Financial Group	PNC Financial
First Commonwealth Financial	S&T Bancorp

HISTORICAL FINANCIALS

Company Type: Public

Income Statement FYE: December 31

	ASSETS ($ mil.)	NET INCOME ($ mil.)	INCOME AS % OF ASSETS	EMPLOYEES
12/17	2,768	23	0.9%	528
12/16	2,573	20	0.8%	507
12/15	2,285	22	1.0%	454
12/14	2,189	23	1.1%	426
12/13	2,131	16	0.8%	395
Annual Growth	**6.8%**	**9.4%**	**—**	**7.5%**

2017 Year-End Financials

Debt ratio: 10.60%	No. of shares (mil.): 15
Return on equity: 10.47%	Dividends
Cash ($ mil.): 35	Yield: 0.0%
Current ratio: —	Payout: 42.0%
Long-term debt ($ mil.): —	Market value ($ mil.): 401

	STOCK PRICE ($) FY Close	P/E High/Low	PER SHARE ($) Earnings	Dividends	Book Value
12/17	26.24	19 13	1.57	0.66	15.98
12/16	26.74	20 12	1.42	0.66	14.64
12/15	18.03	12 11	1.54	0.66	14.01
12/14	18.50	12 10	1.60	0.66	13.09
12/13	19.00	16 12	1.29	0.66	11.43
Annual Growth	**8.4%**	**— —**	**5.0%**	**(0.0%)**	**8.7%**

CNO Financial Group Inc

Have a modest but stable income? Graying at the temples? CNO Financial Group finds that especially attractive and has life insurance and related products targeted at you and millions of others. With a focus on middle-income working families and seniors the holding company's primary units include Bankers Life and Casualty which provides Medicare supplement life annuities and long-term care insurance; Washington National which offers specified disease insurance accident insurance life insurance and annuities; and Colonial Penn which offers life insurance to consumers. The company also offers reinsurance. CNO Financial operates nationwide.

Operations

CNO operates through four segments: Bankers Life Washington National Colonial Penn and Long-term care in run-off. The Bankers Life segment accounts for about 70% of CNO's annual revenue and the Washington National segment accounts for more than 20%. Colonial Penn (nearly 10%) and Long-term care in run-off (1%) round out the group's sales.

CNO has some 3.5 million policies in force including third-party policies sold by its Bankers Life agents.

Geographic Reach

With operations throughout the US (including the District of Columbia and certain protectorates) CNO counts Florida Pennsylvania California and Texas among its largest markets. Together the four states account for more than a quarter of CNO's total premiums.

Sales and Marketing

CNO's largest segment Bankers Life sells products through its own team of around 4000 career agents; it also markets Medicare Advantage plans through distribution arrangements with Humana and United HealthCare. The Washington National segment uses a combination of brokers independent agents and worksite marketing programs. The smaller Colonial Penn segment sells policies through direct sales efforts including television advertising direct mail telemarketing and online sales campaigns.

The group's career agent distribution channel brings in the bulk of its business representing some three-fourths of premiums collected. Independent producers account for more than 15% of collected premiums and direct marketing accounts for some 10%.

CNO leases around 275 sales offices.

Financial Performance

CNO had steady single-digit growth until the 2014 sale of Conseco Life Insurance which brought revenue down for a couple of years. Revenue has been rising since but net income has been more turbulent.

In 2017 revenue increased 8% to $4.3 billion. This was largely due to increases in insurance policy and investment income but was partially offset by a decline in fees and other income. Subsidiary Bankers Life had higher collected premium and annuity account values that year. Washington National also had a strong year gaining a record in new annualized premium. Colonial Penn had a reduction in new annualized premium.

Despite the higher revenue in 2017 net income fell 51% to $175.6 million as operating expenses (primarily insurance policy benefits paid) and income tax expenses both rose.

The company ended 2017 with $578.4 million in net cash $100 million more than it had at the end of 2016. Operating activities provided $613.1 million in cash while financing activities used $274 million and investing activities used $239.6 million.

Strategy

CNO believes its target markets of seniors and middle-income families are often overlooked and underserved giving the company opportunity in the senior market which is expected to double over the next decade. One of its strategies is to market Medicare Supplement insurance which is popular among its target customers and cross-sell discretionary products such as life insurance and annuities.

A major priority is growth across a number of areas including broadening its product portfolio revamping its distribution channels to increase efficiency and reach and deepening its reach within certain of its target demographics. For example in 2016 the company launched its own broker-dealer (Bankers Life Securities) and registered investment advisor (Bankers Life Advisory Services) subsidiaries. Those financial services units are a direct response to Middle America 's increasing concern with financial security in retirement when health care costs typically increase.

The company is working to lower its relative exposure to the long-term care business which pose a higher level of tail risk. It stopped selling home health care long-term policies and comprehensive and nursing home long-term care policies with benefits exceeding three years. In 2018 CNO ceded the legacy (prior to 2003) comprehensive and nursing home long-term care policies of subsidiary Bankers Life and Casualty to Wilton Reassurance Company.

To increase profits CNO is working to reduce unnecessary costs across the entire organization while expanding its number of locations. It also works to attract and retain talented employees in part by offering professional development opportunities. For example it is dedicated to increasing the number of career agents holding a securities license which has already helped assets under administration and assets under management grow.

Company Background

In 2010 the company changed its name from Conseco to CNO Financial Group to reflect a broader identity. (The firm also sought to distance itself from historical financial instabilities associated with the Conseco brand.) The name change came after several years' worth of management efforts to conserve capital reduce complexity and debt and sequester or divest less profitable operations.

HISTORY

CNO Financial evolved from Security National an Indiana insurance company formed in 1979 by Stephen Hilbert. The former encyclopedia salesman and Aetna executive believed most insurance companies were bloated and the industry itself overcrowded as well as ripe for consolidation by a smart lean organization.

In 1982 the company began a growth-by-acquisition strategy with the purchase of Executive Income Life Insurance (renamed Security National Life Insurance). The next year it bought Consolidated National Life Insurance and renamed the expanded company Conseco.

The firm went public in 1985 using the proceeds to fund an acquisitions spree that included Lincoln American Life Insurance Lincoln Income Life (sold in 1990) Bankers National Life Insurance Western National Life Insurance (sold in 1994) and National Fidelity Life Insurance.

In 1990 the company formed Conseco Capital Partners (with General Electric and Bankers Trust) to finance acquisitions without seeming to burden the parent company with debt. This device financed the purchase of Great American Reserve and the 1991 acquisition of Beneficial Standard Life. The former Conseco bought Bankers Life Insurance in 1992 then sold 67% of the firm the next year. Also in 1993 the company formed the Private Capital Group to invest in non-insurance companies.

In 1994 the company tried to acquire the much larger Kemper Corp. but shied away from the debt load that the $2.6 billion deal would have entailed. The aborted deal cost $36 million in bank and accounting fees and spelled the end of the company's relationship with Merrill Lynch which had underwritten the company's IPO when a Merrill Lynch analyst downgraded its stock after the fiasco.

Meanwhile Private Capital's success led the company to form Conseco Global Investments. Other investments included stakes in racetrack and riverboat gambling operations in Indiana.

In 1996 and 1997 the firm absorbed eight life health property/casualty and specialty insurance companies and raised its interest in American Life Holdings to 100%.

Itching to move beyond insurance in 1998 the company bought Green Tree Financial the US's #1 mobile home financier. Charges of Green Tree's own fuzzy accounting practices helped torpedo the company's quest for a federal thrift charter. But the troubles had just begun. The mobile home finance industry took a dive as customers refinanced at lower rates and prepayments slammed Green Tree Financial reducing Conseco's earnings.

The company tried to recoup in 1999 by launching an ad campaign portraying the company as the "Wal-Mart of financial services." It also continued the acquisition spree. But Green Tree Financial (renamed Conseco Finance that year) couldn't stanch the flow of red ink: Buyers grew wary of the quality of the finance unit's loan securities and changes in accounting methods cost the parent company a $350 million charge against earnings for 1999.

In 2002 due to its financial woes the NYSE suspended trading in the company and its stock was moved to the OTC. The company also filed for Chapter 11 protection. As part of the reorganization agreement it agreed to sell Conseco Finance. The company's insurance operations were not subject to the Chapter 11 agreement.

In 2003 it finally unloaded the Conseco Finance unit to investor group CFN Investment Holdings and General Electric Co.'s consumer finance unit for $1 billion. The company emerged from bankruptcy in September 2003.

EXECUTIVES

Ceo And Director, Gary C. Bhojwani, age 50, $517,307 total compensation

Evp Coo And Cto, Bruce K. Baude, age 54, $559,487 total compensation

Chief Investment Officer And President 40|86 Advisors, Eric R. Johnson, age 58, $500,000 total compensation

Evp Human Resources, Susan L. (Sue) Menzel, age 52

President Bankers Life And Casualty Company, Scott L. Goldberg, age 47

Evp And Chief Actuary, Christopher J. (Chris) Nickele, age 62, $416,667 total compensation

Evp And General Counsel, Matthew J. (Matt) Zimpfer, age 51

Evp And Cfo, Erik M. Helding, age 45, $357,813 total compensation

President Washington National, Mike Heard

President Colonial Penn, Joel Schwartz

Vice President Technical Support, Gevan Arnett

Senior Vice President Underwriting And New Business, David Vega

Vice President Of Product Management, Blake Westerfield

Vice President Finance, John Rizzo

Vice President, Gregory Turner

Vice President Compensation And Benefits, Grace Brothers

Vice President Operations, Ken Kueber

Assistant Vice President Internet T Senior Director Customer Service, Ming Tong

Executive Vice President Government Relations, William Fritts

Vp Corporate Tax, David Humm

Vp Operational Risk And Performance Management, Tricia Borcherding

Vice President Human Resources Services, Mark Rawas

Vice President Customer Service, Jean Linnenbringer

Vp And General Auditor, Tom Kleyle

Vice President Human Resources Services, Mitch Schulz

Ceo And Director, Gary C. Bhojwani, age 50

Chairman, Neal C. Schneider, age 74

Auditors: PricewaterhouseCoopers LLP

LOCATIONS

HQ: CNO Financial Group Inc
11825 N. Pennsylvania Street, Carmel, IN 46032
Phone: 317 817-6100
Web: www.cnoinc.com

PRODUCTS/OPERATIONS

2017 Sales

	$ mil.	% of total
Insurance policy income	2,647	61
General account assets	1,285	30
Policyholder & reinsurer accounts & other special-purpose portfolios	265	6
Net realized investment gains excluding impairment losses	77	2
Fee revenue & other	48	1
Adjustments	(27.1)	-
Total	**4,297**	**100**

2017 Sales by Segment

	% of total
Bankers Life	67
Washington National	23
Colonial Penn	8
Long-term care in run-off	1
Corporate	1
Total	**100**

COMPETITORS

Aflac	MetLife
Allstate	Mutual of Omaha
Colonial Life &	New York Life
Accident	Northwestern Mutual
Gerber Life	Torchmark
MassMutual	

HISTORICAL FINANCIALS

Company Type: Public

Income Statement

FYE: December 31

	ASSETS ($ mil.)	NET INCOME ($ mil.)	INCOME AS % OF ASSETS	EMPLOYEES
12/17	33,110	175	0.5%	3,300
12/16	31,975	358	1.1%	3,400
12/15	31,125	270	0.9%	3,500
12/14	31,184	51	0.2%	4,200
12/13	34,780	478	1.4%	4,250
Annual Growth	(1.2%)	(22.1%)	—	(6.1%)

2017 Year-End Financials

Debt ratio: 12.00%	No. of shares (mil.): 166
Return on equity: 3.76%	Dividends
Cash ($ mil.): 757	Yield: 0.0%
Current ratio: —	Payout: 34.3%
Long-term debt ($ mil.): —	Market value ($ mil.): 4,120

	STOCK PRICE ($) FY Close	P/E High/Low	PER SHARE ($) Earnings	Dividends	Book Value
12/17	24.69	25 18	1.02	0.35	29.05
12/16	19.15	10 7	2.01	0.31	25.82
12/15	19.09	15 11	1.39	0.27	22.49
12/14	17.22	80 65	0.24	0.24	23.06
12/13	17.69	8 4	2.06	0.11	22.49
Annual Growth	8.7%	— —	(16.1%)	33.6%	6.6%

COBANK, ACB

You could say CoBank is dependent on its rural customers and vice versa. A member of the Farm Credit System (which is regulated by the FCA) the $110 billion cooperative bank provides seasonal and wholesale loans to agribusinesses as well as to rural power water and communications cooperatives across the US. The bank also leases vehicles farming equipment and agricultural facilities through various Farm Credit System affiliates. Its core agribusiness customers range from local and regional farmers' cooperatives to multinational food companies. It has counted Land O' Lakes Blue Diamond Almonds and National Beef as among its larger customers. Formed in 1989 CoBank merged with US AgBank in early 2012.

Operations

CoBank operates three main business segments: Strategic Relationships Agribusiness and Rural Infrastructure. Its Strategic Relationships loans made up 50% of its $80 billion loan portfolio at the end of 2014 while Agribusiness and Rural Infrastructure made up another 30% and 20% respectively.

About 76% of CoBank's total revenue came from loan interest in 2014 while another 16% came from interest income on investment securities. The rest of its revenue came from fee income (5% of revenue) prepayment income (1%) and other miscellaneous sources.

Geographic Reach

Based in Colorado the bank operates 15 regional offices throughout the US including locations in Iowa Georgia Texas Connecticut Kansas Missouri and Kentucky. It also has an international office in Singapore.

Sales and Marketing

CoBank mainly serves clients in rural America in the agribusiness water communications and power sectors.

Financial Performance

CoBank's annual revenues and profits have been rising over the past several years thanks to steady loan asset growth across all three of its target loan types (Strategic Relationships Agribusiness and Rural Infrastructure).

The bank's revenue jumped 5% to $2.2 million during 2014 mostly thanks to higher average loan volume and increased earnings from a strengthened balance sheet. CoBank's lending business grew with food and agribusiness customers Farm Credit Association customers and rural energy and communications customers which all in turn contributed to its top-line growth.

Revenue growth in 2014 drove CoBank's net income up 6% to $904.3 million for the year. The bank's operating cash levels dipped 2% to $883.1 million during the year due to unfavorable working capital changes related to accrued interest balance changes.

EXECUTIVES

Cfo, David P. Burlage
Chief Risk Officer, Lori L. O'Flaherty
Coo, Ann Trakimas
Evp Banking Services Group, Antony M. Bahr
Svp And Cio, James R. Bernsten
Evp Regional Agribusiness Banking Group, Amy H. Gales
Central Region President Regional Agribusiness Banking Group, Mike Hechtner
Chief Credit Officer, Daniel Key
Evp Corporate Agribusiness Banking Group, Jonathan B. Logan
Southern Region President Regional Agribusiness Banking Group, Lynn Scherler
Svp And Manager Communications Division, Robert F. (Rob) West
Eastern Region President Regional Agribusiness Banking Group, David Sparks
Western Region President Regional Agribusiness Banking Group, Leili Ghazi
Ceo, Robert B. Engel, $880,000 total compensation
President, Mary E. McBride
Chief Banking Officer; Member Management Executive Committee, Thomas Halverson
Vp And Managing Counsel Legal And Loan Processing Division, Chris Clayton
President Farm Credit Leasing, Mike Romanowski
Svp Power Energy And Utilities Banking Division, Todd E. Telesz
Svp Electric Distribution Water And Community Facilities, Nivin Elgohary
Regional Vice President, Todd Sogge
Senior Vice President, Karen Lowe
Vice President, Marshall Essig
Vice President Lead Relationship Manager, David James
Vice President, Andrew Haberern
Vice President Infrastructure, Shawn Dombowsky
Vice President, Bryan Ervin
Vice President Senior Relationship Manager, Natalya Rivkin
Regional Vice President Electric Distribution Division Acb, Tamra Reynolds
Regional Vice President, Brett Challenger
Senior Vice President Corporate Communications, Arthur Hodges
Sector Vice President Managing Director, Michael Tousignant
Vice President, Andy Glover
Vice President Energy Banking, Allison Dunn

Vice President, Tom Houser
Vice President Agribusiness Banking Group, Kurt Harris
Vice President, Marshall Essig
Sector Vice President, Dave Dornbirer
Vice President, James Matzat
Vice President Government Affairs, Sarah Tyree
Senior Vice President Of Operations, Horst Kisch
Vice President Appraisal Services, Ray Wagester
Vice President Project Finance, Jennifer Daurio
Senior Vice President, Brian Cavey
Vice President Digital Business Solutions Sales, Noelle Daghe
Sector Vice President Of Project Finance Group, Brian Goldstein
Second Vice Chair, Kevin A. Still
First Vice Chair, Daniel T. (Dan) Kelley
Chairman, Everett M. Dobrinski
Chief Banking Officer; Member Management Executive Committee, Thomas Halverson
Auditors: PRICEWATERHOUSECOOPERS LLP DE

LOCATIONS

HQ: COBANK, ACB
6340 S FIDDLERS GREEN CIR, GREENWOOD VILLAGE, CO 801114951
Phone: 303 740-6527
Web: WWW.COBANK.COM

Selected Regional Offices

Ames IA
Atlanta GA
Austin TX
Enfield CT
Fargo ND
Louisville KY
Lubbock TX
Minneapolis MN
Omaha NE
Roseville CA
Spokane WA
St. Louis MO
Washington D.C.
Wichita KS

COMPETITORS

AgFirst	Northwest Farm Credit
AgStar	Rabo AgriFinance
AgriBank	Wells Fargo
Bank of America	
Farm Credit Services of Mid-America	

HISTORICAL FINANCIALS

Company Type: Private

Income Statement

FYE: December 31

	ASSETS ($ mil.)	NET INCOME ($ mil.)	INCOME AS % OF ASSETS	EMPLOYEES
12/15	117,470	936	0.8%	500
12/14	107,428	904	0.8%	—
12/10	67,700	818	1.2%	—
12/09	58,160	565	1.0%	—
Annual Growth	12.4%	8.8%	—	—

2015 Year-End Financials

Debt ratio: —	
Return on equity: 39.40%	Dividends
Cash ($ mil.): 3,113	Yield: —
Current ratio: —	Payout: —
Long-term debt ($ mil.): —	Market value ($ mil.): —

Coca-Cola Co (The)

Coke is it — it being the #1 nonalcoholic beverage company in the world as well as one of the world's most recognizable brands. The Coca-Cola Company is home to more than 500 beverage brands some 20 of those billion-dollar-brands including four of the top five soft drinks: Coca-Cola Diet Coke Fanta and Sprite. In addition to soft drinks it markets waters juice drinks energy and sports drinks and ready-to-drink teas and coffees. Other top brands include Minute Maid Powerade Dasani and vitaminwater. With the world's largest beverage distribution system The Coca-Cola Company reaches thirsty consumers in more than 200 countries. Nearly 60% of its sales comes from outside the US.

HISTORY

Atlanta pharmacist John Pemberton invented Coke in 1886. His bookkeeper Frank Robinson named the product after two ingredients coca leaves (later cleaned of narcotics) and kola nuts. By 1891 druggist Asa Candler had bought The Coca-Cola Company and within four years the soda-fountain drink was available in all states; it was in Canada and Mexico by 1898.

Candler sold most US bottling rights in 1899 to Benjamin Thomas and John Whitehead of Chattanooga Tennessee for $1. The two designed a regional franchise bottling system that created more than 1000 bottlers within 20 years. In 1916 Candler retired to become Atlanta's mayor; his family sold the company to Atlanta banker Ernest Woodruff for $25 million in 1919. Coca-Cola went public that year.

The firm expanded overseas and introduced the slogans "The Pause that Refreshes" (1929) and "It's the Real Thing" (1941). To keep WWII soldiers in Cokes at a nickel a pop the government built 64 overseas bottling plants. Coca-Cola bought Minute Maid in 1960 and began launching new drinks — Fanta (1960) Sprite (1960) TAB (1963) and Diet Coke (1982).

In 1981 Roberto Goizueta became chairman. Four years later with Coke slipping in market share the firm changed its formula and introduced New Coke which consumers soundly rejected (thus Coca-Cola Classic was born). In 1986 it consolidated the US bottling operations it owned into Coca-Cola Enterprises and sold 51% of the new company to the public. Goizueta also engineered the company's purchase of Columbia Pictures in 1982. (Columbia earned Coke a $1 billion profit when it sold the studio to Sony in 1989.)

In 1995 it bought Barq's root beer. Goizueta died of lung cancer in 1997; while he was at the helm the firm's value rose from $4 billion to $145 billion. Douglas Ivester the architect of Coca-Cola's restructured bottling operations succeeded him. An agreement to buy about 30 Cadbury Schweppes beverage brands — including Canada Dry Dr Pepper and Schweppes — outside the US and France was scaled down because of antitrust concerns. Completed in 1999 the deal also excluded Canada much of continental Europe and Mexico. (Cadbury in 2008 spun off its beverage division which became Dr Pepper Snapple Group.)

A battered Ivester resigned in 2000; president and COO Douglas Daft was named chairman and CEO. Coca-Cola began its largest cutbacks ever slashing nearly 5000 jobs and later agreed to pay nearly $193 million to settle a race-discrimination suit filed by African-American workers.

To fortify its portfolio in the fast-growing noncarbonated drinks segment Coca-Cola acquired Mad River Traders (teas juices sodas) and Odwalla (juices and smoothies) in 2001. The company also bought a 35% interest (San Miguel Corporation owned the rest) in bottler Coca-Cola Philippines from Coca-Cola Amatil. (In 2005 Coke bought the remaining percentage of the Philippine bottler.) The company announced the creation of a huge beverage and snack distribution joint venture with Procter & Gamble but the multibillion-dollar operation fell apart before it could begin. Coca-Cola also announced that it would invest $150 million to build bottling facilities in China.

In 2002 Coca-Cola introduced Vanilla Coke its biggest new product launch since the disastrous New Coke debacle. The company also secured distribution rights to Danone's Evian brand in North America and paid about $128 million when it formed a joint venture (CCDA Waters LLC) with Danone to produce market and distribute Danone's bottled water in the North America (including Dannon and Sparkletts brands under license). Also

EXECUTIVES

Evp And President Bottling Investments And Supply Chain, Irial Finan, age 61, $908,108 total compensation

Evp And President Coca-cola North America, J. Alexander M. (Sandy) Douglas, age 57, $698,091 total compensation

Evp And Chief Marketing Officer, Marcos de Quinto, age 59, $778,379 total compensation

President Europe Middle East And Africa (emea), Brian J. Smith, age 62

Svp And Cio, Barry N. Simpson, age 57

President And Ceo, James R. Quincey, age 54, $923,625 total compensation

Evp And Cfo, Kathy N. Waller, age 60, $749,365 total compensation

President Coca-cola Refreshments North America, Paul Mulligan

Svp And Cto, Ed Hays, age 59

Svp And Chief Customer And Commercial Leadership Officer, Julie Hamilton, age 52

President Asia Pacific Group, John Murphy, age 56

President West Africa, Peter Njonjo

President South And East Africa, Kelvin Balogun

Svp And President The Mcdonaldâ's Division, Craig Williams

President Latin America Group, Alfredo Rivera, age 56

President Coca-cola Ltd., Shane Grant

Regional Director-india Bangladesh Sri Lanka And Nepal Hindustan Coca-cola Beverages Pvt Ltd., Vamsi Mohan

Vice President Government Relations, Connell Stafford

Vice President Of Tamacc, Ish Arebalos

Vice President Sprite Flavors, Kim Venkatesh

Vice President Environment, Jefferson Seabright

Chairman, Muhtar Kent, age 65

Auditors: Ernst & Young LLP

LOCATIONS

HQ: Coca-Cola Co (The)
One Coca-Cola Plaza, Atlanta, GA 30313
Phone: 404 676-2121   **Fax:** 404 676-6792
Web: www.coca-colacompany.com

2017 Sales

	$ mil.	% of total
US	14,727	42
Other countries	20,683	58
Total	**35,410**	**100**

2017 Sales

	% of total
Bottling Investments	28
North America	28
Europe Middle East & Africa	19
Asia Pacific	14
Latin America	11
Corporate	-
Eliminations	-
Total	**100**

PRODUCTS/OPERATIONS

2017 Sales

	% of total
Finished product operations	49
Concentrate operations	51
Total	**100**

Selected Brands

Sparkling Beverages
  Core sparkling
  Barq's
  Coca-Cola
  Coca-Cola Zero/Coke Zero
  Diet Coke/Coca-Cola Light
  Fanta
  Fresca
  Inca Kola
  Lift
  Schweppes
  Sprite
  Thums Up
  Energy drinks
  Burn
  Nos
  Real Gold
Still Beverages
  Coffee & teas
  Ayataka teas
  Dogadan teas
  Georgia coffees
  Leão/Matte Leão teas
  Nestea teas
  Sokenbicha teas
  Juices and juice drinks
  Cappy
  Del Valle
  Dobriy
  Hi-C
  Minute Maid
  Minute Maid Pulpy
  Simply
  Other still beverages
  glaceau vitaminwater
  Fuze
  Sports drinks
  Aquarius
  Powerade
  Waters
  Bonaqua/Bonaqa
  Ciel
  Dasani
  Ice Dew
  Kinley
  ZICO Pure Premium Coconut Water

COMPETITORS

Britvic	Kraft Heinz
Citrus World	Mondelez International
Clement Pappas	Mountain Valley
Cott	Naked Juice
Danone	National Beverage
Dole Food	Nestlé
Dr Pepper Snapple	Ocean Spray
Group	PepsiCo
Fiji Water	Pernod Ricard
Fresh Del Monte	Red Bull
Produce	Sun-Rype
Hawaiian Springs	Sunny Delight
Hornell Brewing	Suntory Holdings
IZZE	Tree Top
Jamba	Unilever PLC
Jones Soda	Welch's
Kirin Holdings Company	

HISTORICAL FINANCIALS

Company Type: Public

Income Statement

FYE: December 31

	REVENUE ($ mil.)	NET INCOME ($ mil.)	NET PROFIT MARGIN	EMPLOYEES
12/17	35,410	1,248	3.5%	61,800
12/16	41,863	6,527	15.6%	100,300
12/15	44,294	7,351	16.6%	123,200
12/14	45,998	7,098	15.4%	129,200
12/13	46,854	8,584	18.3%	130,600
Annual Growth	(6.8%)	(38.3%)	—	(17.1%)

2017 Year-End Financials

Debt ratio: 54.25%—
Return on equity: 6.22%
Cash ($ mil.): 6,006
Current ratio: 1.34
Long-term debt ($ mil.): 31,182

Dividends
Yield: 0.0%
Payout: 510.3%
Market value ($ mil.): —

	STOCK PRICE ($) FY Close	P/E High/Low	Earnings	PER SHARE ($) Dividends	Book Value
12/17	45.88	164 139	0.29	1.48	4.01
12/16	41.46	31 27	1.49	1.40	5.38
12/15	42.96	26 22	1.67	1.32	5.91
12/14	42.22	28 23	1.60	1.22	6.94
12/13	41.31	22 19	1.90	1.12	7.54
Annual Growth	2.7%	— —	(37.5%)	7.2%	(14.6%)

Codorus Valley Bancorp, Inc.

EXECUTIVES

Vice President Commercial Team Leader, Adam Bryner
Senior Vice President, Neil Brownawell
Auditors: BDO USA, LLP

LOCATIONS

HQ: Codorus Valley Bancorp, Inc.
105 Leader Heights Road, P.O. Box 2887, York, PA 17405
Phone: 717 747-1519
Web: www.peoplesbanknet.com

COMPETITORS

Citizens Financial Group	M&T Bank
Fulton Financial	Northwest Bancshares

HISTORICAL FINANCIALS

Company Type: Public

Income Statement

FYE: December 31

	ASSETS ($ mil.)	NET INCOME ($ mil.)	INCOME AS % OF ASSETS	EMPLOYEES
12/17	1,709	12	0.7%	339
12/16	1,611	13	0.8%	304
12/15	1,456	11	0.8%	292
12/14	1,213	11	1.0%	258
12/13	1,150	10	0.9%	248
Annual Growth	10.4%	3.2%	—	8.1%

2017 Year-End Financials

Debt ratio: 0.60%
Return on equity: 7.52%
Cash ($ mil.): 79
Current ratio: —
Long-term debt ($ mil.): —

No. of shares (mil.): 9
Dividends
Yield: 0.0%
Payout: 38.3%
Market value ($ mil.): 257

	STOCK PRICE ($) FY Close	P/E High/Low	Earnings	PER SHARE ($) Dividends	Book Value
12/17	27.53	27 19	1.28	0.49	17.56
12/16	28.60	21 14	1.41	0.45	16.68
12/15	20.34	14 13	1.51	0.42	17.28
12/14	19.68	14 11	1.67	0.38	16.71
12/13	19.53	13 9	1.67	0.34	17.57
Annual Growth	9.0%	— —	(6.5%)	9.3%	(0.0%)

Cognizant Technology Solutions Corp.

Cognizant Technology Solutions is aware of the desire to shift business processes to digital technologies and it wants to help. To help customers make the switch to digital operations the information technology outsourcing company provides intelligent systems automation cloud technologies and cyber security tools. In more traditional IT services Cognizant offers application maintenance business intelligence data warehousing software and systems development and integration and re-engineering services for legacy systems. The company targets companies in financial services health care manufacturing retail and logistics. Most of Cognizant's software development centers and employees are in India although it has development and delivery facilities around the world.

Operations

Cognizant offers a mix of on-site and near-shore and offshore service. Unlike competitors that provide no on-site assistance Cognizant typically locates technical and account management teams at its customers' locations with development work handled at dedicated development centers offshore. This boosts Cognizant's bottom line by taking advantage of cheaper labor costs while maintaining a close connection with its customers.

The company?s financial services business brings in about 40% of revenue; followed by the healthcare segment about 30%; the products and resources unit about 20%; and its communications media and technology operation some 10% of revenue.

Geographic Reach

Cognizant has more than 170 delivery centers in more than 30 countries along with business development offices in more than 80 cities and about 40 countries. Some 70% of its employees work in India. Although it has operations worldwide Cognizant relies heavily on its North American customers which generate more than 75% of its revenue. Combined Europe and the UK constitute the next biggest market accounting for about 15% of sales.

Sales and Marketing

Cognizant markets and sells through its direct sales force which operates from offices in the US and around the world. The sales process can last between two months to a year depending on the products or services under negotiation.

Cognizant's Top 10 customers account for about 15% of its revenue. It considers about 360 customers to be strategic in that they have the potential to generate $5 million-$50 million or more in annual revenue.

Financial Performance

Cognizant's revenue marched steadily higher for the past decade as did profit except for a recent slip.

Sales increased about 10% in 2017 to about $14.8 billion driven by increases in all segments and geographies but for the UK. The company cited higher customer spending on discretionary projects expansion of its service offerings including consulting and digital services and deeper penetration at existing customers including strategic customers. While sales in other segments grew at double-digit rates in 2017 financial services sales rose just 5% as Cognizant's banking customers tightened reins on their costs. The company saw higher growth in Europe with the help of recent acquisitions while sales in the Rest of the World category (primarily Asia) jumped 20%. UK revenue slipped about 2% on weakness in the banking sector.

Cognizant's net income ticked down about 3% to $1.5 billion in 2017 from 2016. The company had a higher tax bill in 2017 as it brought foreign earnings back to the US with the enactment of the US Tax Cuts and Jobs act in 2017.

The company had about $1.9 billion cash on hand at the end of 2017 off from about $2 billion the year before. It spent about $1.9 billion on stock buybacks in 2017 more than three times the amount spent in 2016.

Strategy

Cognizant has aligned its operations to pursue its digital strategy. The company?s Digital Business area is to help customers design and implement digital business models. In the Digital Operations area Cognizant provides digital tools for managing customers? business processes. And the Cognizant Digital Systems and Technology area helps customers simplify modernize and protect applications platforms and infrastructure. The company reported that digital-related revenue rose 30% in 2017 and accounts for about 27% of total revenue.

Cognizant has turned to acquisitions to beef up its digitization expertise and capabilities and to bolster its healthcare offerings. In 2017 and into 2018 the company made five deals to address those areas.

Operationally Cognizant focuses on increasing efficiency leveraging its growing size to shave costs. The company deploys automated tools to optimize its more traditional application infrastructure and process services.

Cognizant works in a competitive business where margins are thin and companies try to keep costs low. The industry?s practice of short-term contracts with customers makes it easy for customers to move to other service providers. Some of Cognizant?s competitors are bigger companies with more resources which can make a difference in hiring employees and bidding for acquisitions.

Mergers and Acquisitions

With recent acquisitions Cognizant has expanded its reach in international markets while adding to its digital capabilities.

Cognizant agreed to acquire Advanced Technology Group (ATG) a consultant on Salesforce.com implementations in 2018. Cognizant cited ATG's quote-to-cash capabilities in making the acquisition. ATG's customers include financial services healthcare communications and technology organizations. The deal was expected to close in the 2018 fourth quarter.

In 2018 Cognizant acquired Bolder Healthcare Solutions a developer of revenue cycle management software for healthcare facilities and physician practices. The deal helps Cognizant expand its healthcare and its digitization efforts.

The 2017 acquisition of TMG Health which provides business process services to Medicare and Medicaid markets was another move to build on healthcare.

The deal for Zone made in 2017 brought a UK-based digital agency specializing in customer experience digital strategy and content creation into Cognizant.

Cognizant also made inroads in the UK and Europe with the acquisition of Netcentric in 2017. Based in Zurich Netcentric's customers include Allianz Mercedes-Benz Swisscom and UBS. It offers services for personalizing customer interaction.

In another 2017 transaction Cognizant acquired Brilliant Service a Japan-based company that develops intelligent products. The acquisition adds to Cognizant's digital service offerings in Japan and expands its presence in Osaka and Tokyo.

Company Background

Cognizant Technology Solutions began as an in-house technology center for Dun & Bradstreet in 1994 and was spun off from D&B in 1996. Two years later Cognizant reorganized and spun off its market research operations into two public companies IMS Health and Nielsen Media Research in order to focus on IT services.

EXECUTIVES

President, Rajeev (Raj) Mehta, age 51, $574,100 total compensation
Evp Strategy And Marketing, Malcolm Frank, age 52, $417,000 total compensation
Executive Vice Chairman Cognizant India, Ramakrishnan Chandrasekaran, age 60, $152,925 total compensation
Cfo, Karen McLoughlin, age 53, $426,500 total compensation
Ceo And Director, Francisco D'Souza, age 49, $664,300 total compensation
Coo, Srinivasan Veeraghavachary
Evp And President Global Industries And Consulting, Ramakrishna Prasad Chintamaneni, age 48, $417,250 total compensation
Evp And President Global Client Services, Dharmendra Kumar Sinha, age 55, $356,504 total compensation
Assistant Vice President Projects, Ronald Trella
Senior Vice President And Head Of Life Sciences North America, Nagaraja Srivatsan
Vice Chairman, Lakshmi Narayanan, age 65
Chairman, John E. Klein, age 76
Ceo And Director, Francisco D'Souza, age 49
Auditors: PricewaterhouseCoopers LLP

LOCATIONS

HQ: Cognizant Technology Solutions Corp.
Glenpointe Centre West, 500 Frank W. Burr Blvd., Teaneck, NJ 07666
Phone: 201 801-0233   **Fax:** 201 801-0243
Web: www.cognizant.com

2017 Sales

	$ mil.	% of total
North America	11,450	77
Europe		
United Kingdom	1,150	8
Rest of Europe	1,248	8
Other	962	7
Total	**13,487**	**100**

PRODUCTS/OPERATIONS

Selected Services
Application design development integration and re-engineering
  Complex custom systems development
  Customer relationship management (CRM)
  Data warehousing/Business intelligence (BI)
  Enterprise resource planning (ERP)

Software testing services
IT consulting and technology services
  Business and knowledge process consulting
  IT strategy consulting
  Program management consulting
  Technology consulting
Outsourcing services
  Application maintenance
  Business and knowledge process outsourcing
  Cloud
  CRM and ERP maintenance
  Custom application maintenance
  IT infrastructure outsourcing
  Mobility

Selected Mergers and Acquisitions
FY2017
Brilliant Service (Intelligent Products and Solutions Company)
FY2016
KBACE Technologies Inc (global consulting and technology services company)
FY2014
TriZetto (Healthcare information processing services)
CoreLogic Global Services (business processing services)
FY2010
Galileo Performance (IT testing)
The PIPC Group (management consulting)
FY2009
UBS India Service Centre (financial-services outsourcing)
Pepperweed Advisors (IT consulting)
Active Intelligence (systems integration)

2017 Sales

	$ mil.	% of total
Financial services	5636	38
Health care	4263	29
Products and Resources	3040	20
Communications Media and Technology	1871	13
Total	**14810**	**100**

Industries
Banking & Financial Services
Communications
Consumer Goods
Education
Energy & Utilities
Healthcare
Information Services
Insurance
Life Sciences
Manufacturing
Media & Entertainment
Retail
Technology
Transportation & Logistics
Travel & Hospitality

COMPETITORS

3i Infotech	IBM Global Services
Accenture	ITC Infotech India
Atos	Infosys
Capgemini	Mastek
Computer Sciences Corp.	MindTree
	MphasiS
EPAM	Ness Technologies
Genpact	Tata Consultancy
HCL Technologies	Wipro
HP Enterprise Services	Zensar Technologies

HISTORICAL FINANCIALS

Company Type: Public

Income Statement   FYE: December 31

	REVENUE ($ mil.)	NET INCOME ($ mil.)	NET PROFIT MARGIN	EMPLOYEES
12/17	14,810	1,504	10.2%	260,000
12/16	13,487	1,553	11.5%	260,200
12/15	12,416	1,623	13.1%	221,700
12/14	10,262	1,439	14.0%	211,500
12/13	8,843	1,228	13.9%	171,400
Annual Growth	13.8%	5.2%	—	11.0%

2017 Year-End Financials

Debt ratio: 5.74%
Return on equity: 14.06%
Cash ($ mil.): 1,925
Current ratio: 3.21
Long-term debt ($ mil.): 698
No. of shares (mil.): 588
Dividends
  Yield: 0.0%
  Payout: 17.7%
Market value ($ mil.): 41,760

	STOCK PRICE ($) FY Close	P/E High/Low	PER SHARE ($) Earnings	Dividends	Book Value
12/17	71.02	30 20	2.53	0.45	18.14
12/16	56.03	25 19	2.55	0.00	17.64
12/15	60.02	26 19	2.65	0.00	15.23
12/14	52.66	45 18	2.35	0.00	12.70
12/13	100.98	49 30	2.02	0.00	10.10
Annual Growth	(8.4%)	— —	5.9%	—	15.8%

Colgate-Palmolive Co.

Colgate-Palmolive takes a bite out of grime. The company is a top global maker and marketer of toothpaste (it has more than 40% of the global market) and soap and cleaning products. Colgate-Palmolive also offers pet nutrition products through subsidiary Hill's Pet Nutrition which makes Science Diet Ideal Balance and Prescription Diet pet foods. Many of its oral care products fall under the Colgate brand and include toothbrushes mouthwash and dental floss. Its Tom's of Maine unit covers the natural toothpaste niche. Personal and home care items include Ajax brand household cleaner Palmolive dishwashing liquid Soft-soap shower gel and Sanex and Speed Stick deodorants. The company has operations in 80-plus countries and sells its products in more than 200 countries.

HISTORY

William Colgate founded The Colgate Company in Manhattan in 1806 to produce soap candles and starch. Colgate died in 1857 and the company was passed to his son Samuel who renamed it Colgate and Company. In 1873 the company introduced toothpaste in jars and in 1896 it began selling Colgate Dental Cream in tubes. By 1906 Colgate was making 160 kinds of soap 625 perfumes and 2000 other products. The company went public in 1908.

In 1898 Milwaukee's B. J. Johnson Soap Company (founded 1864) introduced Palmolive a soap made of palm and olive oils rather than smelly animal fats. It became so popular that the firm changed its name to The Palmolive Company in 1916. Ten years later Palmolive merged with Peet Brothers a Kansas City-based soap maker founded in 1872. Palmolive-Peet merged with Colgate in 1928 forming Colgate-Palmolive-Peet (shortened to Colgate-Palmolive in 1953). The stock market crash of 1929 prevented a planned merger of the company with Hershey and Kraft.

During the 1930s the firm purchased French and German soap makers and opened branches in Europe. Colgate-Palmolive-Peet introduced Fab detergent and Ajax cleanser in 1947 and the brands soon became top sellers in Europe. The company expanded to Asia in the 1950s and by 1961 foreign sales were 52% of the total.

Colgate-Palmolive introduced a host of products in the 1960s and 1970s including Palmolive dishwashing liquid (1966) Ultra Brite toothpaste (1968) and Irish Spring soap (1972). During the same time the company diversified by buying approximately 70 other businesses including Kendall hospital and industrial supplies (1972) Helena Rubinstein cosmetics (1973) Ram Golf (1974) and Riviana Foods and Hill's Pet Products (1976). The strategy had mixed results and most of these acquisitions were sold in the 1980s.

Reuben Mark became CEO of Colgate-Palmolive in 1984. The company bought 50% of Southeast Asia's leading toothpaste Darkie in 1985; it changed its name to Darlie in 1989 following protests of its minstrel-in-blackface trademark. Both Palmolive automatic dishwasher detergent and Colgate Tartar Control toothpaste were introduced in 1986. That year Colgate-Palmolive purchased the liquid soap lines of Minnetonka the most popular of which is Softsoap. In 1992 the company bought Mennen maker of Speed Stick (the leading US deodorant).

Increasing its share of the oral care market in Latin America to 79% in 1995 Colgate-Palmolive acquired Brazilian company Kolynos (from Wyeth for $1 billion) and 94% of Argentina's Odol Saic. The company also bought Ciba-Geigy's oral hygiene business in India increasing its share of that toothpaste market. At home however sales and earnings in key segments were dismal so in 1995 Colgate-Palmolive began a restructuring that included cutting more than 8% of its employees and closing or reconfiguring 24 factories in two years.

The company introduced a record 602 products in 1996 and continued to expand its operations in countries with emerging economies. In 1997 Colgate-Palmolive took the lead in the US toothpaste market for the first time in 35 years (displacing P&G).

In 1999 the company sold the rights to Baby Magic (shampoos lotions oils) in the US Canada and Puerto Rico to Playtex Products retaining the rights in all other countries. Two years later the company sold its heavy-duty laundry detergent business in Mexico (primarily the Viva brand) to Henkel one of Europe's leading detergent producers.

In 2002 Colgate-Palmolive introduced a teeth-whitening gel Simply White to compete with rival P&G's Crest Whitestrips. The company saw

EXECUTIVES

Vp And Controller, Dennis J. Hickey, age 69, $910,000 total compensation
Chairman President And Ceo, Ian M. Cook, age 66, $1,309,000 total compensation
President Global Oral Care, Suzan F. Harrison
Vp And General Manager Colgate South Pacific, Chris E. Pedersen
President Colgate Mexico, Ricardo (Ricky) Ramos
Chief Supply Chain Officer, Michael A. (Mike) Corbo
President Colgate Latin America, Panagiotis Tsourapas
Coo Global Innovation And Growth And Hill's Pet Nutrition, Noel R. Wallace
President And Ceo Hill's Pet Nutrition, Peter Brons-Poulsen
Coo North America Europe Africa/eurasia And Global Sustainability, P. Justin Skala, age 59, $734,333 total compensation
Vp And General Manager Colgate U.s., Derek A. Gordon
Vp Colgate-latin America, Bernal Saborio
Vp And Controller, Henning Jakobsen, age 58
President Colgate-africa/eurasia, Jean-Luc Fischer
Vp And General Manager Colgate Central Europe East, Wojciech Krol
Vp And General Manager Colgate Brazil, Andrea Lagioia
Vp And General Manager Colgate-russia, Francisco Munoz Ramirez
Cto, Patricia Verduin, age 58

President Colgate-north America, Juan Pablo Zamorano
Vp And General Manager Colgate Latin America, Massimo Poli
Vp; General Manager Colgate-venezuela, Ruben Young
President Colgate Asia Pacific, Vinod Nambiar
Vp And General Manager Colgate-north Africa Middle East, Burc Cankat
Vp And General Manager Colgate Northern Europe, Philip Durocher
Cio, Mike Crowe
Vp And General Manager Colgate India And South Asia, Issam Bachaalani
President Colgate Europe, Prabha Parameswaran
Vp And General Manager Colgate-philippines, Arvind Sachdev
Vp Hill's Pet Nutrition-eurasia, David Scharf
Vp And General Manager Colgate Central Europe West, Dany Schmidt
Vp And General Manager Greater China, Stephen Lau
Vp And General Manager Colgate North America, Bill Van de Graaf
Vp And Gm Colgate Andina Region, Hector Pedraza
Chief Information And Business Services Officer, Thomas (Tom) Greene
Vp And General Manager Global Toothbrush Division, Christopher Rector
Vp And General Manager Colgate-north America, Anne-Marie Motte
Vp And General Manager Colgate-north America, Julie Dillon
Vp And General Manager Tom's Of Maine, Nancy Pak
Vp And General Manager Colgate Western Europe, Andrew Shepard
Vp And General Manager Colgate South Africa, Orlando Tenorio
Vp And General Manager Global Personal Care, John Hazlin
Vp And General Manager Colgate Southern Cone, Adriana Leite
Vp And General Manager Hawley & Hazel, Eddie Niem
Vice President Colgate North America, John Kooyman
National Account Manager, Crystal Harris
Vice President Deputy General Counsel Operations, Rosemary Nelson
Vice President Global Analytics, Spencer Pingel
Vice President Global Toothbrush Division, Neil Stout
National Account Manager, Jenny Squier
Vice President Worldwide Shopper Marketing, Steve Fogarty
Vice President Colgate Africa Middle East, Robert Tatera
Vice President, Jack Haber
Vice President And Corporate Treasurer, Elaine Paik
Vice President Global Oral Care, Marsha Butler
Vp Global Legal, Nina Huffman
Vp Hill's Pet Nutrition Japan, Joy Klemencic
Vp Colgate Europe, Vangelis Spyridakos
Vice President Colgate Africa Eurasia, Rosario Carlino
Vice President Toothbrush Category Supply Chain, Manu Mehrotra
Senior Vice President Investor Relations, Jon Simon
National Account Manager, Susan Siao
Vice President Colgate Southern Europe, Riccardo Ricci
Vice President And Gm Colgate Malaysia, Corrado Giaquinto
Vice President Global Legal, Lisa Mather
Vice President Corporate Audit, Gregory Malcolm
Vice President Colgate Europe, Yves Briantais
Vp Global Legal, Cliff Wilkins

Vice President Chief Dental Officer, Maria Ryan
Vp And Gm Colgate Cace, Shekar Bharatwaj
Senior Vice President General Counsel, Andrew Hendry
Vp Manufacturing, Liz Sorota Orbuch
Vice President, Thomas Quinlan
National Account Manager, Amy Fewell
Vice President, Danielle Koffer
Vp Global Marketing Communications, Maria Elisa Carvajal
Vice President Colgate Latin America, Jose Fernando Fernando Serrano
Vice President And Gm Global Home Care, Lucie Claire Claire Vincent
Chairman President And Ceo, Ian M. Cook, age 66
Vice Chairman, Franck J. Moison, age 65
Auditors: PricewaterhouseCoopers LLP

LOCATIONS

HQ: Colgate-Palmolive Co.
300 Park Avenue, New York, NY 10022
Phone: 212 310-2000   **Fax:** 212 310-3284
Web: www.colgatepalmolive.com

2017 Sales

	$ mil.	% of total
Oral personal & home care		
Latin America	3,887	25
North America	3,117	20
Asia Pacific	2,781	18
Europe	2,394	16
Africa/Eurasia	983	6
Pet nutrition	2,292	15
Total	**15,454**	**100**

PRODUCTS/OPERATIONS

2017 Sales

	$ mil.	% of total
Oral personal & home care	13,162	85
Pet nutrition	2,292	15
Total	**15,454**	**100**

Selected Brands

Home Care
  Ajax
  Fabuloso
  Murphy Oil Soap
  Palmolive
  Suavitel
Oral Care
  Colgate
Personal Care
  Afta
  Irish Spring
  Sanex
  Skin Bracer
  Softsoap
  Speed Stick
Pet Nutrition
  Prescription Diet
  Science Diet

COMPETITORS

Amden	Henkel
Avon	Johnson & Johnson
Campbell Soup	Kimberly-Clark
Church & Dwight	Kraft Heinz
Clorox	Nestlé
ConAgra	Nu Skin
Dr. Fresh	Philips Oral
Estée Lauder	Procter & Gamble
General Mills	Reckitt Benckiser
GlaxoSmithKline	Sun Products
Hain Celestial	Unilever NV

HISTORICAL FINANCIALS

Company Type: Public

Income Statement — FYE: December 31

	REVENUE ($ mil.)	NET INCOME ($ mil.)	NET PROFIT MARGIN	EMPLOYEES
12/17	15,454	2,024	13.1%	35,900
12/16	15,195	2,441	16.1%	36,700
12/15	16,034	1,384	8.6%	37,900
12/14	17,277	2,180	12.6%	37,700
12/13	17,420	2,241	12.9%	37,400
Annual Growth	(2.9%)	(2.5%)	—	(1.0%)

2017 Year-End Financials

Debt ratio: 51.89%
Return on equity: —
Cash ($ mil.): 1,535
Current ratio: 1.36
Long-term debt ($ mil.): 6,566

No. of shares (mil.): 874
Dividends
Yield: 0.0%
Payout: 69.7%
Market value ($ mil.): 65,996

	STOCK PRICE ($) FY Close	P/E High/Low	PER SHARE ($) Earnings	Dividends	Book Value
12/17	75.45	34 28	2.28	1.59	(0.07)
12/16	65.44	27 23	2.72	1.55	(0.28)
12/15	66.62	47 39	1.52	1.50	(0.33)
12/14	69.19	30 25	2.36	1.42	1.26
12/13	65.21	52 23	2.38	1.33	2.51
Annual Growth	3.7%	— —	(1.1%)	4.6%	

COLORADO HOUSING AND FINANCE AUTHORITY

EXECUTIVES

Ceo, Cris A White
Chief Operating Officer, Jaime Gomez
Cfo, Patricia Hippe
Compliance Manager, Emily Jensik
Executive Officer, Julie Chelin
Compliance Staff, Shelia Anderson
Executive Officer, Margaret Miller
Quality Assurance Director, Sugin Sim
Manager, Beth Truby
General Counsel, Charles Knight
Public Relations Staff, Heather Johnson
Auditors: CLIFTON & GUNDERSON LLP GREEN

LOCATIONS

HQ: COLORADO HOUSING AND FINANCE AUTHORITY
1981 BLAKE ST, DENVER, CO 802021229
Phone: 303 297-2432
Web: WWW.CHFAINFO.COM

HISTORICAL FINANCIALS

Company Type: Private

Income Statement — FYE: December 31

	ASSETS ($ mil.)	NET INCOME ($ mil.)	INCOME AS % OF ASSETS	EMPLOYEES
12/17	2,192	52	2.4%	150
12/16	2,037	24	1.2%	—
12/09	3,671	(15)	—	—
12/08	4,059	13	0.3%	—
Annual Growth	(6.6%)	16.5%	—	—

2017 Year-End Financials

Debt ratio: —
Return on equity: 30.20%
Cash ($ mil.): 47
Current ratio: 0.10
Long-term debt ($ mil.): —

Dividends
Yield: —
Payout: —
Market value ($ mil.): —

Columbia Banking System Inc

Columbia Banking System (CBS) is the $8.5 billion-asset holding company for Columbia State Bank (also known as Columbia Bank). The regional community bank has about 150 branches in Washington from Puget Sound to the timber country in the southwestern part of the state as well as in northern Oregon and Idaho. Targeting retail and small and medium-sized business customers the bank offers standard retail services such as checking and savings accounts CDs IRAs credit cards loans and mortgages. Commercial and multifamily real estate loans make up more than 40% of the company's loan portfolio while business loans make up another 40%. CBS is expanding in the Pacific Northwest through acquisitions of other community banks.

Operations

The bank's Columbia Private Banking division offers customized financial services for businesses and affluent families. Subsidiary CB Financial Services provides investment products through a pact with third-party provider PrimeVest.

Like other retail banks Columbia makes most of its money from interest income. About 68% of its total revenue came from loan interest during 2015 while another 10% came from interest on taxable and tax-exempt securities. The rest of its revenue came from service charges and other fees (15% of revenue) merchant service fees (2%) and other non-interest income sources.

Geographic Reach

Tacoma-based Columbia Banking System has 149 bank branches (as of mid-2016) with about half in the state of Washington 60 across Oregon and 16 in Idaho.

Sales and Marketing

The bank spent $4.7 million on advertising and promotion in 2015 up from $3.9 million and $4.1 million in 2014 and 2013 respectively.

Financial Performance

Columbia Bank's annual revenues have nearly doubled since 2011 as its loan assets have more than doubled to $5.8 billion (at the end of 2015). Its profits have also doubled over the time period as it's kept a handle on costs.

The bank's revenue jumped 14% to $420.36 million during 2015 on higher interest income as it increased its loan business and interest-earning security assets. The company also earned more in service charges and other non-interest income thanks to its organically growing customer base and its Intermountain acquisition.

Revenue growth in 2015 drove the bank's net income up 21% to $98.83 million. Columbia Bank's operating cash levels dipped 2% to $134.76 million for the year mostly due to unfavorable working capital changes related to other liabilities.

Strategy

Columbia reiterated in 2016 that it would focus on expanding its branches into new markets (either on its own or through acquisitions) while focusing on high-quality loan growth. One of its most recent acquisitions — the purchase of Intermoun-

tain Community Bancorp — expanded its presence in Idaho for the first time.

Mergers and Acquisitions

In November 2014 the bank expanded its presence into Idaho after purchasing $960 million-asset Intermountain Community Bancorp and its Panhandle State Bank branches in the state.

In April 2013 Columbia acquired West Coast Bancorp— the parent company of West Coast Bank which operated nearly 60 bank branches in Oregon and Washington. The purchase boosted Columbia's total assets to more than $7 billion and furthered Columbia's goal of becoming the leading regional community bank in the Pacific Northwest.

Company Background

Columbia Banking System took advantage of the rash of bank failures in past years to increase its presence in the Pacific Northwest region. It added more than 30 branches in 2010 when it acquired most of the deposits and assets of failed banks Columbia River Bank and American Marine Bank a week apart. In similar transactions in 2011 it acquired most of the operations of the failed institutions Summit Bank First Heritage Bank and Bank of Whitman. Those deals added more than a dozen branches in Washington.

EXECUTIVES

Evp And Chief Credit Officer, Andrew L. (Andy) McDonald, age 59, $298,000 total compensation
Evp And Cfo, Clint E. Stein, age 47, $345,000 total compensation
Ceo, Hadley S. Robbins, age 61, $369,827 total compensation
Evp And General Counsel, Kumi Yamamoto Baruffi, age 48
Evp And Chief Human Resources Officer, David C. (Dave) Lawson, age 60, $247,500 total compensation
Vice President Senior Financial Advisor With Cb Financial, John Brunk
Vice President, Thomas Poole
Senior Vice President And Banking Solutions Manager, Bruce Morehead
Vice President Commercial Banking Officer, Antoine White
Senior Vice President, Gus Martin
Vice President, Jennifer Kinkade
Vice President, Harold Boucher
Vice President, Saira Russell
Vice President, Rhonda Seagraves
Chairman, William T. Weyerhaeuser, age 75
Auditors: DELOITTE & TOUCHE LLP

LOCATIONS

HQ: Columbia Banking System Inc
1301 "A" Street, Tacoma, WA 98402-2156
Phone: 253 305-1900
Web: www.columbiabank.com

2015 Branches

	No.
Washington	74
Oregon	59
Idaho	16
Total	**149**

PRODUCTS/OPERATIONS

2015 Sales

	$ mil.	% of total
Interest Income:		
Loans	286	68
Taxable securities	30	7
Tax-exempt securities	11	3
Deposits in banks	0	-
Non-interest Income:		
Service charges and other fees	61	15
Merchant services fees	9	2
Other	24	5
FDIC loss-sharing asset	(4.0)	-
Total	**420**	**100**

COMPETITORS

BECU	JPMorgan Chase
Bank of America	KeyCorp
Banner Corp	U.S. Bancorp
Heritage Financial	Washington Federal
HomeStreet	Wells Fargo

HISTORICAL FINANCIALS

Company Type: Public

Income Statement   FYE: December 31

	ASSETS ($ mil.)	NET INCOME ($ mil.)	INCOME AS % OF ASSETS	EMPLOYEES
12/17	12,716	112	0.9%	2,120
12/16	9,509	104	1.1%	1,819
12/15	8,951	98	1.1%	1,868
12/14	8,578	81	1.0%	1,844
12/13	7,161	60	0.8%	1,695
Annual Growth	15.4%	17.1%	—	5.8%

2017 Year-End Financials

Debt ratio: 0.35%
Return on equity: 7.05%
Cash ($ mil.): 342
Current ratio: —
Long-term debt ($ mil.): —

No. of shares (mil.): 73
Dividends
  Yield: 0.0%
  Payout: 47.3%
Market value ($ mil.): 3,172

	STOCK PRICE ($) FY Close	P/E High/Low		PER SHARE ($) Earnings	Dividends	Book Value
12/17	43.44	25	19	1.86	0.88	26.70
12/16	44.68	25	15	1.81	1.53	21.55
12/15	32.51	21	15	1.71	1.34	21.52
12/14	27.61	19	16	1.52	0.94	21.38
12/13	27.49	23	14	1.21	0.41	20.55
Annual Growth	12.1%	—	—	11.3%	21.0%	6.8%

Comcast Corp

EXECUTIVES

Chb-Pres-Ceo, Brian L Roberts
Sr Exec V Pres-Cfo, Michael J Cavanagh
Sr Exec V Pres, Stephen B Burke
Sr Exec V Pres, David L Cohen
Sr Exec V Pres, David N Watson
Exec V Pres-General Counsel-SE, Arthur R Block
Sr V Pres-Cao-Contrl, Daniel C Murdock
Auditors: Deloitte & Touche LLP

LOCATIONS

HQ: Comcast Corp
One Comcast Center, Philadelphia, PA 19103-2838
Phone: 215 286-1700
Web: www.comcastcorporation.com

COMPETITORS

21st Century Fox	ITC^DeltaCom
AT&T	Insight Communications
Blockbuster	Liberty Interactive
Cablevision Systems	Netflix
Charter Communications	RCN Corporation
Cox Communications	Time Warner Cable
DIRECTV	ValueVision Media
DISH Network	Verizon
Disney	Viacom
EarthLink	Xanadoo

HISTORICAL FINANCIALS

Company Type: Public

Income Statement   FYE: December 31

	REVENUE ($ mil.)	NET INCOME ($ mil.)	NET PROFIT MARGIN	EMPLOYEES
12/18	94,507	11,731	12.4%	184,000
12/17	84,526	22,714	26.9%	164,000
12/16	80,403	8,695	10.8%	159,000
12/15	74,510	8,163	11.0%	141,000
12/14	68,775	8,380	12.2%	139,000
Annual Growth	8.3%	8.8%	—	7.3%

2018 Year-End Financials

Debt ratio: 44.40%
Return on equity: 16.73%
Cash ($ mil.): 3,814
Current ratio: 0.79
Long-term debt ($ mil.): 107,345

Dividends
  Yield: 2.2%
  Payout: 14.8%
Market value ($ mil.): —

	STOCK PRICE ($) FY Close	P/E High/Low		PER SHARE ($) Earnings	Dividends	Book Value
12/18	34.05	17	12	2.53	0.76	15.82
12/17	40.05	16	7	4.75	0.47	14.77
12/16	69.05	39	30	1.79	0.68	11.35
12/15	56.43	39	32	1.62	0.49	10.70
12/14	58.01	36	30	1.60	0.44	10.37
Annual Growth	(12.5%)	—	—	12.1%	15.0%	11.1%

Comerica, Inc.

Comerica is the holding company for Comerica Bank which has around 460 branches primarily in five US states and Canada. The company is organized into three main segments. The Business Bank division is the largest offering loans deposits and capital markets products to middle-market large corporate and government clients. The Retail Bank serves small businesses and consumers while the Wealth Management arm provides private banking investment management financial advisory investment banking brokerage insurance and retirement services. Comerica boasts total assets of around $75 billion and total deposits of some $60 billion.

Operations

Broadly speaking Comerica generates nearly 55% of its revenue from loan interest and almost 10% from interest on investment securities and short-term investments. The remainder of the bank's revenue is fee-based coming mostly from card fees (10% of revenue) service charges on deposit accounts (more than 5%) fiduciary income (more than 5%) and commercial lending fees (less than 5%).

The bank divides its operations into several segments: The Business Bank (commercial loans and lines of credit to middle market businesses multinational corporations and government agencies) The Retail Bank (small business banking and personal financial services) and Wealth Management (fiduciary services private banking and retirement and investment management services). In addition to these segments Comerica manages a securities portfolio and offers asset and liability management services.

Geographic Reach

Comerica operates out of some 590 locations include 460 branches as well as banking centers trust services locations loan production or other financial services offices. It's biggest markets are Michigan Texas California Arizona and Florida but it also operates and Canada and has 25 other businesses in various other states.

Sales and Marketing

Beyond retail customers Comerica caters to businesses and others operating in the energy automotive production and real estate industries.

Financial Performance

After enduring several years of flat sales Comerica has recorded two years of strong growth.

In fiscal 2016 revenue grew 5% to $2.9 billion following on from an 8% jump the previous year. The increase in 2016 was down to higher interest rates loan growth and a larger securities portfolio. Noninterest income crept up $16 million due to an increase in customer-driven fees partially offset by a fall in non-fee items.

Net income fell 8% to $447 million due to restructuring charges and the release in 2015 of litigation reserves. Excluding these two significant one-off items noninterest expense decreased by $23 million due to lower salary and benefit expenses as a result of the restructuring.

Cash from operations fell 42% to $493 million due to net changes in other items.

Strategy

Comerica's management is grappling with the issue of a sharp deterioration in the performance of loans to the beleaguered oil industry. While a number of US banks are under pressure from oil weakness Comerica has the largest exposure of an US bank to the industry at about 6% of its total loans.

To deal with the issue the company is cutting costs to free up cash in preparation for heavy losses. Its GEARup program has consisted of layoffs renegotiated vendor contracts a reduction in real estate and lower executive bonuses. It has also reduced lending to oil drillers.

HISTORY

Comerica traces its history to 1849 when Michigan governor Epaphroditus Ransom tapped Elon Farnsworth to found the Detroit Savings Fund Institute. At that time Detroit was a major transit point for shipping between Lakes Huron and Erie as well as between the US and Canada. The bank grew with the town and in 1871 became Detroit Savings Bank.

By 1899 Detroit was one of the top 10 US manufacturing centers and thanks to a group of local tinkerers and mechanics that included Henry Ford was on the brink of even greater growth. Detroit Savings grew also fueled by the deposits of workers whom Ford paid up to $5 a day. Detroit Savings was not however the beneficiary of significant business with the auto makers; for corporate banking they turned first to eastern banks and then to large local banks in which they had an interest.

Detroit boomed during the 1920s as America went car-crazy but after the 1929 crash Detroiters defaulted on mortgages by the thousands. By 1933 Michigan's banks were in such disarray that the governor shut them down three weeks prior to the federal bank holiday. Detroit Savings was one of only four Detroit banks to reopen. None of the major banks associated with auto companies survived.

A few months later Manufacturers National Bank backed by a group of investors that included Edsel Ford (Henry's son) was founded. Although its start was rocky Manufacturers National was on firm footing by 1936; around the same time Detroit Savings Bank renamed itself the Detroit Bank to appeal to a more commercial clientele.

WWII and the postwar boom put Detroit back in gear. In the 1950s and 1960s both banks thrived. In the 1970s statewide branching was permitted and both banks formed holding companies

(DETROITBANK Corp. and Manufacturers National Corp.) and expanded throughout Michigan. As they grew they added services; when Detroit's economy was hit by the oil shocks of the 1970s these diversifications helped them through the lean years.

DETROITBANK opened a trust operation in Florida in 1982 to maintain its relationship with retired customers and renamed itself Comerica to be less area-specific. Manufacturers National also began operating in Florida (1983) and made acquisitions in the Chicago area (1987). Comerica went farther afield buying banks in Texas (1988) and California (1991).

Following the national consolidation trend in 1992 Comerica and Manufacturers National merged (retaining the Comerica name) but did not fully integrate until 1994 when the new entity began making more acquisitions. To increase sales and develop its consumer business the company reorganized in 1996. It sold its Illinois bank and its Michigan customs brokerage business and acquired Fairlane Associates to expand its property/casualty insurance line.

As part of its strategy to have operations in all three NAFTA countries Comerica opened a bank in Mexico in 1997 and one in Canada in 1998. That year it dropped $66 million for the naming rights to the Detroit Tigers' baseball stadium which opened as Comerica Park in 2000. It also started a Web-based payment system for its international trade business.

To fortify its business lending operations in California Comerica bought Imperial Bancorp in 2001. At the beginning of 2002 chairman Eugene Miller handed the CEO reins to Ralph Babb who had been CFO. Later that year Babb became chairman as well.

EXECUTIVES

Chairman President And Ceo Comerica Incorporated And Comerica Bank, Ralph W. Babb, age 69, $1,265,000 total compensation
Evp And President Comerica Bank (california Market), Judith S. Love, age 61
Evp And Chief Risk Officer Comerica Incorporated And Comerica Bank, Michael H. Michalak, age 60
Evp And Cio Comerica Incorporated And Evp Comerica Bank, Paul R. Obermeyer, age 60
Evp Governance Regulatory Relations And Legal Affairs Comerica Incorporated And Comerica Bank, John D. Buchanan, age 54, $573,846 total compensation
President Comerica Incorporated And Comerica Bank, Curtis C. Farmer, age 55, $700,000 total compensation
Evp And Cfo, Muneera S. Carr, age 50
Evp And President Comerica Bank Michigan Market, Michael T. Ritchie, age 49
Evp And Chief Human Resources Officer Comerica Incorporated And Comerica Bank, Megan D. Burkhart, age 46
Evp And Chief Credit Officer, Peter W. Guilfoile, age 57
Evp And President Comerica Bank Texas Market, Peter L. Sefzik, age 42
Evp And General Auditor, Christine Moore
Vice President, Lake McGuire
Vice President Business Continuity, Blair Alexander
First Vice President Regional Sales Manager, Darla Mick Darla Mick
Vice President Senior Portfolio Risk Manager, Walter Galloway
Assistant Vice President, Catherine Cornell
Vice President, Deanna Fietzer
Vice President, Jeff Treadway

Vice President Human Resources Staffing, Dan Dunn
Assistant Vice President Relationship Manager, Dave Sullivan
Vice President, Daniel Roesner
Vice President, Jon E Haffner
Vice President, Jenal Zak
Vice President Marketing, Jason Logan
Vice President Social Media, Nancy Huxen
Vice President Business Finance, Matthew Griffin
Vice President, Kelly McConnell
Vice President End User Technology Ser, Kim Martin
Vice President, Jake Friemel
Vice President Relationship Manager, Brad Bell
Vice President Western Market, Peter Wentworth
Vice President, Thomas Jones
Assistant Vice President, Padmanabhan Karatha
Vice President Senior Wealth Advisor, Matthew Orth
Vice President, Brett Jackson
Assistant Vice President Financial Consultant, Tony Stefani
Vice President, Rhonda D Dantzler
Vice President, Josie Fenech
Vice President, Lynn M Hough
Vice President Private Banking, Gary J Beyer
Treasury Management Vice President, Danette R Hames
Vice President Middle Market Banking, Bryan L Johnston
Vice President, Marc P Abello
Vice President, Lesley B Higginbotham
Vice President And Alternate Group Manager Commercial Real Estate, Cynthia V Porter
Banking Center Manager And Assistant Vice President, Alfonso J Ugarte
Vice President, Debbie Tuftee
Vice President, Doreen Boelstler
Vice President Treasury Management Global Sales Consultant, Sheila Ausberry
Assistant Vice President Treasury Management, Pamela G Porter
Vice President, Nancy Blake
Senior Vice President And Alternate Credit Administration Officer, Mike Hammond
Vice President, Kristy Denby
Vice President Portfolio Risk Analytics, Nicholas Teson
Vice President, Linda Vance
Vice President Middle Market Banking, Kelly L Mione
Vice President Estate Administration, Angela W Aycock
Vice President, Tien G Huynh
Vice President And Alternate Group Manager, Stephen G Wells
Vice President Market Planning, Kevin Cornell
Vice President, John Mckee
Banking Center Manager Vice President, Gordon McKinley
Vice President Agm, Matthew Breight
Vice President, Raffi Khelghatian
Vice President, Gary P Mach
Vice President, Lorraine Jackman
Vice President, Sharon Feigelson
Senior Vice President And Director Compensation, Sarah Stratton
First Vice President Western Market, Philip Diorio
Banking Center Manager Assistant Vice President, Henry Tran
Senior Vice President And Assistant General Counsel, Terrance Henderson
Vice President, Rona Khan
Senior Vice President Texas Market North Texas Region Manager, Barry Brundage
Senior Vice President Midwest Region Commercial Real Estate Finance, James Preston
Vice President Business Banking, Karen Gladney
Vice President, Kathy Pitton

Vice President Product Development, William Anderson
Vice President, Jason Olsen
Senior Vice President, Dan Evans
Vice President, Tom O'connell
Vice President, Peter Kennedy
Assistant Vice President, Bryndon Skelton
Vice President U S Banking Midwest, Brandon Welling
Vice President Regional Banking Officer Financial Services Division, Laura Reyes
Senior Vice President Division Finance Officer Wim, Sajid Siddiqi
Vice President, Madhuri Bandla
Vice President, Evan Huckabay
Vice President, Teresa Bosco
Senior Vice President, Thomas Higginbottom
Vice President, Maribeth Gomez
Vice President And Senior Counsel, Jennifer Perry
Vice President Sba Portfolio Management, Mario Nava
Vice President, Barry Carroll
Vice President Trust And Estate Advisor, Elisabeth Gregory
Assistant Vice President Private Banking, Leslie A Fletcher
Assistant Vice President, Ian Patterson
Vice President, Trent Sampson
Senior Vice President, David Ohanian
Vice President .s. Banking Sports Franchise Group, Thomas Vandermeulen
Assistant Vice President, Jacqueline O'connor
Vice President And Human Resources Counsel, Von Hays
Vice President Of Enterprise Project Management Office, Paul Gustafson
Vice President Investor Relations, Tracy Fralick
Vice President, Elizabeth Alvarado
Senior Vice President Middle Market Group, Alice Yang
Assistant Vice President Relationship Manager, Sara Trogdon
Vice President Texas Market, Jim Young
Vice President, Margie C Petru
Vice President, Laith Francis
Assistant Vice President Finance, Haiyan Li
Svptexas Marketing Gro, John Castellano
Vice President International Finance, Carlos Capetillo
Vice President, Douglas Smith
Vice President, Ira Brandon
Banking Center Manager Assistant Vice President, Vanessa Ochoa
Vice President Ets Server Engineering, Alex Gonzalez
Senior Vice President Credit Administration, Scott Wineman
Vice President And Banking Center Manager Iv, Linda K Landers
Assistant Vice President, David Miller
Vice President, Michael Cha
Vice President Project Manager, Hyla G Williams
Vice President Of Financial Systems, Steve Kort
Assistant Vice President, Joe Fisher
Vice President Institutional Sales, Rick Clancy
Vice President Of Finance, Jim Donohue Ctp
Vice President, Craig Weingarden
First Vice President, Anne Marie Coulter
Vice President Retail Product Management, Darrin Davis
Assistant Vice President, Megan Trapp
Vice President, Dennis Black
Assistant Vice President Branch Manager, Anna Quijano
Vice President Relationship Manager, Erik McKay
Vice President District Trust Manager, Corinne Sorey
Vice President, Danny Sanchez
Vice President, Theresa Barnett
Assistant Vice President Learning, Scott Blackman

Vice President, Larry McWhorter
Vice President, Mike VanderWeele
Vice President And Manager, Dennis Herbert
Vice President Regional Sales Manager, Stephanie
 Sealey
Senior Vice President, Jim Cavellier
Vice President Commercial Banking Officer, Adan
 Gonzalez
Banking Center Manager Assistant Vice President,
 Jasko Korajkic
Vice President Senior Systems Engineer, Tom
 Thayer
Vice President, Crystal Dennis
Vice President, Dustin Hollas
Senior Vice President, Norm Bird
Assistant Vice President Business Systems
 Operations Vendor Distributed Applications
 Comerica Bank, Brian Frost
Vice President, Embry Fura
Vice President Senior Counsel, Nicole Cheng
Auditors: Ernst & Young LLP

LOCATIONS

HQ: Comerica, Inc.
 Comerica Bank Tower, 1717 Main Street, MC 6404,
 Dallas, TX 75201
Phone: 214 462-6831
Web: www.comerica.com

2016 Banking Centers

	No.
Michigan	209
Texas	127
California	97
Other Markets	
Arizona	17
Florida	7
Canada	1
Total	**458**

Selected Markets

Arizona
California
Colorado
Florida
Illinois
Michigan
Nevada
Ohio
Texas
Washington

PRODUCTS/OPERATIONS

2016 Sales

	$ mil.	% of total
Interest		
Fees on Loans	1,635	55
Investment securities	247	8
Short-term investments	27	1
Noninterest		
Card fees	303	10
Service charges on deposit accounts	219	7
Fiduciary income	190	6
Commercial lending fees	89	3
Letter of credit fees	50	2
Foreign exchange	42	2
Bank-owned life insurance	42	2
Brokerage fee	19	1
Others	102	3
Net Securities(losses) gaints	(5)	0
Total	**2,960**	**100**

2016 Sales

	% of total
Business Bank	88
Wealth Management	11
Retail Bank	1
Total	**100**

Selected Subsidiaries

Comerica Bank
Comerica Bank & Trust National Association
Comerica Capital Advisors Incorporated

Comerica Financial Incorporated
Comerica Holdings Incorporated
Comerica Insurance Group Inc.
Comerica Insurance Services Inc.
Comerica Investment Services Inc.
Comerica Investments LLC
Comerica Leasing Corporation
Comerica Merchant Services Inc.
Comerica Securities Inc.
Wilson Kemp & Associates Inc.
World Asset Management Inc.

COMPETITORS

Bank of America	Regions Financial
Citigroup	SVB Financial
Cullen/Frost Bankers	SunTrust
Fifth Third	TCF Financial
Huntington Bancshares	U.S. Bancorp
JPMorgan Chase	Wells Fargo
MUFG Americas Holdings	

HISTORICAL FINANCIALS

Company Type: Public

Income Statement

FYE: December 31

	ASSETS ($ mil.)	NET INCOME ($ mil.)	INCOME AS % OF ASSETS	EMPLOYEES
12/17	71,567	743	1.0%	8,190
12/16	72,978	477	0.7%	8,149
12/15	71,877	521	0.7%	9,103
12/14	69,190	593	0.9%	9,115
12/13	65,227	541	0.8%	9,207
Annual Growth	**2.3%**	**8.3%**	**—**	**(2.9%)**

2017 Year-End Financials

Debt ratio: 2.55%
Return on equity: 9.43%
Cash ($ mil.): 5,845
Current ratio: —
Long-term debt ($ mil.): —

No. of shares (mil.): 172
Dividends
 Yield: 0.0%
 Payout: 26.3%
Market value ($ mil.): 15,006

	STOCK PRICE ($) FY Close	P/E High/Low		PER SHARE ($) Earnings	Dividends	Book Value
12/17	86.81	21	15	4.14	1.09	46.07
12/16	68.11	26	11	2.68	0.89	44.47
12/15	41.83	18	14	2.84	0.83	43.03
12/14	46.84	16	13	3.16	0.79	41.35
12/13	47.54	16	10	2.85	0.68	39.24
Annual Growth	**16.2%**	**—**	**—**	**9.8%**	**12.5%**	**4.1%**

Commerce Bancshares Inc

Commerce Bancshares owns bank branch operator Commerce Bank. The financial institution boasts a network of more than 360 locations across several US states including Missouri Kansas Illinois Oklahoma and Colorado. The bank focuses on retail and commercial banking services such as deposit accounts mortgages loans and credit cards. Commerce Bank also runs a wealth management division that offers asset management trust private banking brokerage and estate planning services and also manages proprietary mutual funds. As part of its operations Commerce Bank has subsidiaries devoted to insurance leasing and private equity investments.

Operations

The company operates three main segments: Consumer Commercial and Wealth.

The Commercial segment which collects roughly 65% of the bank's total revenue provides corporate lending merchant and commercial bank card products leasing and international services as well as business and government deposit and cash management services. Fixed income investments are sold to individuals and institutional investors through the segment's Capital Markets Group.

Another 20% of bank revenue is generated through the Consumer segment which includes the retail branch network consumer installment lending personal mortgage banking and consumer debit and credit bank card activities. It provides services through a network of more than 200 full-service branches a 400-machine ATM network and alternative delivery channels such as extensive on-line banking and telephone banking services.

The remaining bank revenue (around 15%) comes from the Wealth segment which manages investments with a market value of $20.4 billion and administers an additional $14.8 billion in non-managed assets provides traditional trust and estate tax-planning services brokerage services and advisory and discretionary investment portfolio management services targeted to personal and institutional corporate customers. The Wealth segment also manages Commerce Bank's proprietary mutual funds.

Broadly speaking interest income from the bank's portfolio of loans make up more than 40% of total revenue. Roughly 60% of the portfolio is comprised of commercial loans (mostly business real estate loans but also construction and land loans and other business-related loans). Personal banking loans make up the remaining 40% of the portfolio and mostly include real estate loans and consumer lines of credit but also consumer credit cards revolving home equity loans and some overdraft lines of credit.

Geographic Reach

Commerce Bancshares through its Commerce Bank business operates more than 360 branch banks in five central US states with major focus in Peoria and Bloomington Illinois; St. Louis; Kansas City and Wichita Kansas; Denver; Tulsa Oklahoma; Nashville; Cincinnati; and Dallas. The bank also has commercial offices in Cincinnati Nashville and Dallas. The company's two largest markets include St. Louis and Kansas City. To this end the cities serve as the central hubs for its operation.

Sales and Marketing

The bank spent $14.2 million on marketing in fiscal 2013 down 6% from $15.1 million in 2012 and down 15% from the $16.8 million it spent on marketing in 2011.

Financial Performance

In the recent low interest environment Commerce Bancshares has seen its revenue slowly decline over the past few years from declining interest income from its loans and investment securities. In fiscal 2013 revenue fell by $8.9 million to $1.08 billion as the bank earned lower rates on investment securities and loans (from smaller interest margins) despite higher loan balances and lower rates paid on deposits. The bank was able to offset some of its revenue losses by earning $18.8 million more from bank card transaction trust and brokerage fees.

The bank's net income also dipped by $8.4 million (or 3%) to $261 million in 2013. This is mostly from the drop in revenue but also because the bank paid $6 million more toward employee salaries and benefits (from higher salaries) and $4.4 million more toward data processing and software expenses as bank card processing costs went up. Profits are still up significantly from the bank's recovery period in 2009 and 2010 when it earned $169.1 million and $221.7 million respectively.

The amount of cash provided from operations fell for the third straight year to $360.9 million in 2013 down 6% from the $383.1 million provided in 2012. This was primarily because of lower net income but also because it paid $11.7 million more toward its income tax obligations than in the prior year.

Unlike its revenue and earnings Commerce's assets have been growing. Total loans were $10.96 billion in 2013 representing an increase of $1.13 billion or 11% over balances in 2012. While loan assets have increased across the board business loan assets contributed the most growing by $580.5 million in 2013 to a total of $3.7 billion. Deposit assets also rose by 4% to $19.05 billion in 2013.

Strategy

Commerce Bancshares serves its local retail markets through relationship banking and high touch service. It works to grow its core revenue by expanding new and existing customer relationships leveraging improved technology and enhancing customer satisfaction. To respond to changes in consumer banking preferences the bank will work to improve its distribution strategy by de-emphasizing the central role of traditional branch banking and providing more customers access to its services through ATMs call centers mobile and house lines internet. It will also work to develop new products and focus on expense reductions wherever possible to improve the company's bottom line.

To grow its commercial business segment which already provides two-thirds of all bank revenue Commerce plans to invest in distinctive lower-risk/higher return businesses to increase its loan business. In addition it intends to deepen its relationships with existing commercial customers and provide more products to them to increase profitability while taking on little additional risk or cost.

Thanks to higher brokerage and trust fees Commerce Bancshares' Wealth division saw the largest segment revenue growth in 2013. The bank is optimistic that its new hires in the division will contribute to higher sales productivity over the next few years particularly in the institutional and St. Louis Family Office. In addition management believes that the improving US economy and booming stock market will improve investor confidence and M&A activity which should help grow the segment in the years ahead.

Mergers and Acquisitions

Commerce Bancshares in May 2013 inked a merger agreement with Summit Bancshares whereby Summit merged into a wholly-owned subsidiary of Commerce Bancshares. The transaction valued at approximately $40.6 million consisted entirely of Commerce Bancshares' stock and added more than $200 million in new loans to the bank's portfolio. The deal significantly boosted Commerce Bank's foothold in the Tulsa Oklahoma market and allowed it to enter the Oklahoma City market.

EXECUTIVES

Svp; Director Operations And Information Services, Robert J. Rauscher, age 60

Cfo, Charles G. (Chuck) Kim, age 58, $415,080 total compensation

Evp Commercial Line Of Business; President And Coo Commerce Bank Kansas City Region, Kevin G. Barth, age 58, $408,705 total compensation

Evp; Chief Human Resources Officer And Director Internal Support Services, Sara E. Foster, age 58

Chairman And Ceo, David W. Kemper, age 67, $896,073 total compensation

Evp Trust Line Of Business; President The Commerce Trust Company A Division Of Commerce Bank, V. Raymond (Ray) Stranghoener, age 67, $235,900 total compensation

Evp; Chief Credit Officer And Chief Risk Officer, Daniel D. Callahan

Svp; Director Commercial Card And Merchant Services, Jeff Burik

Svp; Director Community Bank Administration, Michael J. Petrie

President And Coo, John W. Kemper, $462,207 total compensation

Vice President, Jason Boyer

Assistant Vice President Deposit Product Manager, Catherine Mills

Vice President, Paul Zietlow

Vice President Private Client Group, Joe Morris

Vice President Of Human Resources, Betty Maes

Senior Vice President Retail Group And Manager Operations, Darryl Collins

Assistant Vice President Regional Marketing, Jenny Stanley

Vice President, Jeffrey Turner

Senior Vice President, Mary McClain

Vice President, James Roman

Vice President Regional Retail Sales Manager, Jen Bradley

Senior Vice President Retail And Small Business Group Manager, Robin Wandschneider

Vice President, Trishia Baker

Senior Vice President Portfolio Manager, WM Cody

Senior Vice President And Director Operations, Eric Rauscher

Vice President Information Technology, Dino Spatoulis

Vice President Business Banking Relationship Manager, Rob Gillespie

Vice President Financial Advisor, Aaron Alexander

Vice President Treasury Sales, Chuck Peterson

Senior Vice President, Dee Joyner

Vice President Server Operations Manager Information Technology, Wanda Edgmond

Senior Vice President, Mark Tankesley

Senior Vice President Management Information Syste, John Blakeney

Vice President, Clive Veri

Vice President, Carissa Albers

Vice President, Susan McGee

Vice President, Pam Hill

Senior Vice President, William Gamewell

Vice President And Director Of Finance, Duane Locher

Executive Vice President, Gaylyn McGregor

Vice President, Ron Koenig

Vice President Information Technology, Thomas Cook

Vice President Accounts Payable Solutions, Marla Freeman

Vice President, Craig Duerksen

Vice President, James Fallon

Assistant Vice President Business Line Systems Manager, Kevin Belloma

Vice President, Frank Hill

Vice President, JO Hicks

Vice President, Barbara Mccaslin

Vice President, Lance Wright

Vice President, Dave Young

Senior Vice President, Gordon Roewe

Assistant Vice President Computer Operations Information Technology, Matt Pflugradt

Senior Vice President, Nick Fafoglia

Senior Vice President, Steve Sebade

Vice President Finance, Lynn McLaughlin

Vice President, Judy Shilling

Vice President Treasury Sales, Chuck Peterson

Vice President, Brendan Carmichael

Vice President Commercial Card Services, Rob Perdue

Vice President Of Commercial Banking, Sam Jarvis

Assistant Vice President, Jim Hanson

Vice President, Lyons Lon

Vice President Business Banking, Janelle Schneider

Vice President Mortgage Technology Manager, Sarah Vande

Vice President Senior Relationship Manager, Lee Tilghman

Vice President Team Leader, Matt Dority

Vice President Business Banking Center Manager, Jamie Huch

Senior Vice President, Richard Jankovich

Assistant Vice President Branch Manager Iv, Hank Koehly

Senior Vice President, John Meyer

Vice President Energy Finance, Parker Heikes

Assistant Vice President, Melissa Caputo

Vice President, Jack Stapleton

Vice President National Accounts, Venus Vega

Assistant Vice President, Cole Higginbotham

Vice President Retail Banking Manager, Kathy Wilkes

Assistant Vice President Small Business Banking, Sonya Tandy

Assistant Vice President Small Business Banking, Donald Reynolds

Assistant Vice President, Angela Wright-Jones

Senior Vice President Commercial Banking, Matt Gomric

Assistant Vice President, Amy Winter

Corporate Banking Senior Vice President, Steven Bloemer

Private Client Group Vice President Tax, Doug Nelson

Vice President C And I Relationship Manager, Chris Steuterman

Vice President Of Information Technology, Ken Isbell

Assistant Vice President, Isaac Mishler

Senior Vice President Commercial Loan Servicing, Jeremy Allen

Vice President, Niall Mooney

Vice Chairman, Seth M. Leadbeater, age 67

Vice Chairman, Jonathan M. Kemper, age 65

Chairman And Ceo, David W. Kemper, age 67

Treasurer, Michael Bude

Auditors: KPMG LLP

LOCATIONS

HQ: Commerce Bancshares Inc
1000 Walnut, Kansas City, MO 64106
Phone: 816 234-2000   **Fax:** 816 234-2369
Web: www.commercebank.com

2016 Sales by Market

	% of total
Kansas City	32
St. Louis	28
Other regions	40
Total	**100**

PRODUCTS/OPERATIONS

2016 Sales

	$ mil.	% of total
Interest Income		
Interest and fees on loans	490	42
Interest on investment securities	207	18
Interest on long-term securities purchased under agreements to resell	13	1
Interest on loans held for sale	1	0
Interest on federal funds sold and short-term securities purchased under agreements to resell	0	0
Interest on deposits with banks	1	0
Non-Interest Income		
Bank card transaction fees	181	15
Trust fees	121	10
Deposit account charges and other fees	86	7
Consumer brokerage services	13	1
Loan fees and sales	11	1
Capital market fees	10	1
Other	48	4
Total	**1,187**	**100**

Selected Services

Commercial Banking
  Financing
  Treasury Services
  Commercial Card Products
  Merchant Services
  International Services
  Capital Markets
  Investment Management
  Corporate Trust
Personal Banking
  Checking Accounts
  Savings Accounts
  Money Market Accounts & CDs
  Borrowing Solutions & Loans
  Mortgages
  Credit Cards
  Check Cards & Prepaid Cards
  Online Banking Services & Mobile Banking
Small Business Banking
  Small Business Checking Accounts
  Small Business Online Services
  Small Business Loans
  Business Credit Cards & Check Cards
  Business Resource Center
  Merchant Services
Wealth Management
  The Commerce Trust Company
  Investment Management
  Private Banking Services
  Financial Advisory Services
  Trust Services
  Institutional Trust Services
  Corporate Trust
  Brokerage Services
  Insurance Services

Selected Subsidiaries

Capital for Business Inc.
CBI-Kansas Inc.
CFB Partners LLC
CFB Venture Fund L.P.
Clayton Financial Corp.
Clayton Holdings LLC
Clayton Realty Corp.
Commerce Bank National Association
Commerce Brokerage Services Inc.
Commerce Insurance Services Inc.
Commerce Investment Advisors Inc.
Commerce Mortgage Corp.
Illinois Financial LLC
Illinois Realty LLC
Tower Redevelopment Corporation

COMPETITORS

BOK Financial	First National of
Bank of America	Nebraska
Bank of the West	Great Western Bancorp
Capitol Federal	INTRUST
Financial	U.S. Bancorp
Dickinson Financial	UMB Financial
First Banks	Wells Fargo

HISTORICAL FINANCIALS

Company Type: Public

Income Statement — FYE: December 31

	ASSETS ($ mil.)	NET INCOME ($ mil.)	INCOME AS % OF ASSETS	EMPLOYEES
12/17	24,833	319	1.3%	4,857
12/16	25,641	275	1.1%	4,877
12/15	24,604	263	1.1%	4,859
12/14	23,994	261	1.1%	4,866
12/13	23,072	260	1.1%	4,889
Annual Growth	1.9%	5.2%	—	(0.2%)

2017 Year-End Financials

Debt ratio: 0.01%
Return on equity: 12.25%
Cash ($ mil.): 487
Current ratio: —
Long-term debt ($ mil.): —
No. of shares (mil.): 112
Dividends
  Yield: 0.0%
  Payout: 31.1%
Market value ($ mil.): 6,262

	STOCK PRICE ($) FY Close	P/E High/Low	PER SHARE ($) Earnings	Dividends	Book Value
12/17	55.84	22 19	2.75	0.86	24.22
12/16	57.81	25 16	2.37	0.82	22.27
12/15	42.54	22 18	2.21	0.74	20.95
12/14	43.49	22 19	2.15	0.71	19.87
12/13	44.91	22 16	2.13	0.67	18.04
Annual Growth	5.6%	— —	6.6%	6.3%	7.6%

Commercial Metals Co.

EXECUTIVES

Chb-Pres-Ceo, Barbara R Smith
Exec V Pres-Coo, Tracy L Porter
Sr V Pres-Cfo, Mary A Lindsey
V Pres-Gen Counsel-Corp SEC, Paul K Kirkpatrick
V Pres Fin, Paul J Lawrence
V Pres-Cao, Adam R Hickey
Auditors: DELOITTE & TOUCHE LLP

LOCATIONS

HQ: Commercial Metals Co.
  6565 North MacArthur Blvd., Irving, TX 75039
Phone: 214 689-4300   **Fax:** 214 689-5886
Web: www.cmc.com

COMPETITORS

AK Steel Holding	Roanoke Bar Division
Corporation	Ryerson
BHP Billiton	Schnitzer Steel
Blue Tee	Severstal North
Connell LP	America
David J. Joseph	Simec
Gerdau Ameristeel	Steel Dynamics
Indel	Tube City IMS
Keywell	United States Steel
Metals USA	Universal Forest
Mueller Industries	Products
Nucor	Worthington Industries
OmniSource	
Quanex Building	
Products	

HISTORICAL FINANCIALS

Company Type: Public

Income Statement — FYE: August 31

	REVENUE ($ mil.)	NET INCOME ($ mil.)	NET PROFIT MARGIN	EMPLOYEES
08/18	4,643	138	3.0%	8,900
08/17	4,569	46	1.0%	8,797
08/16	4,610	54	1.2%	8,388
08/15	5,988	141	2.4%	9,126
08/14	7,039	115	1.6%	9,293
Annual Growth	(9.9%)	4.6%	—	(1.1%)

2018 Year-End Financials

Debt ratio: 34.80%
Return on equity: 9.57%
Cash ($ mil.): 622
Current ratio: 3.83
Long-term debt ($ mil.): 1,138
No. of shares (mil.): 117
Dividends
  Yield: 2.2%
  Payout: 41.0%
Market value ($ mil.): 2,528

CommScope Holding Co., Inc.

Auditors: Ernst & Young LLP

LOCATIONS

HQ: CommScope Holding Co., Inc.
  1100 CommScope Place, S.E., Hickory, NC 28602
Phone: 828 324-2200
Web: www.commscope.com

HISTORICAL FINANCIALS

Company Type: Public

Income Statement — FYE: December 31

	REVENUE ($ mil.)	NET INCOME ($ mil.)	NET PROFIT MARGIN	EMPLOYEES
12/17	4,560	193	4.2%	20,000
12/16	4,923	222	4.5%	25,000
12/15	3,807	(70)		23,000
12/14	3,829	236	6.2%	13,000
12/13	3,480	19	0.6%	13,000
Annual Growth	7.0%	77.8%	—	11.4%

2017 Year-End Financials

Debt ratio: 62.05%
Return on equity: 12.74%
Cash ($ mil.): 453
Current ratio: 2.69
Long-term debt ($ mil.): 4,369
No. of shares (mil.): 190
Dividends
  Yield: —
  Payout: —
Market value ($ mil.): 7,222

	STOCK PRICE ($) FY Close	P/E High/Low	PER SHARE ($) Earnings	Dividends	Book Value
12/17	37.83	42 31	0.98	0.00	8.63
12/16	37.20	32 17	1.13	0.00	7.19
12/15	25.89	— —	(0.37)	0.00	6.39
12/14	22.83	22 14	1.24	0.00	6.96
12/13	18.93	154 124	0.12	0.00	5.85
Annual Growth	18.9%	— —	69.0%	—	10.2%

	STOCK PRICE ($) FY Close	P/E High/Low	PER SHARE ($) Earnings	Dividends	Book Value
08/18	21.60	22 15	1.17	0.48	12.76
08/17	18.89	61 37	0.39	0.48	12.10
08/16	15.52	38 27	0.47	0.48	11.93
08/15	15.70	15 11	1.20	0.48	11.41
08/14	17.28	21 15	0.97	0.48	11.44
Annual Growth	5.7%	— —	4.8%	(0.0%)	2.8%

Community Bank System Inc

Community Bank System is right up front about what it is. The holding company owns Community Bank which operates about 195 branches across upstate New York and northeastern Pennsylvania where it operates as First Liberty Bank and Trust.

Focusing on small underserved towns and non-urban markets the bank offers standard products and services such as checking and savings accounts certificates of deposit and loans and mortgages to consumer business and government clients. Boasting over $11.0 billion in assets the bank's loan portfolio consists of mostly business loans residential mortgages and consumer loans. Community Bank System's subsidiaries offer employee benefit services wealth management and insurance products and services.

Operations

Community Bank System operates three business segments. The Banking segment which made up 83% of the company's total revenue during 2015 provides lending and deposit services to individuals businesses and municipalities. Employee Benefit Services (12% of revenue) offers trust investment fund retirement plan actuarial healthcare consulting and other administrative services through Benefit Plan Administrative Services (BPAS). The All Other segment (5% of revenue) includes its Wealth Management (operating through Community Investment Services) and Insurance businesses (operating through CBNA Insurance Agency).

Nearly 70% of the company's revenue comes from interest income. About 49% of its revenue came from loan interest during 2015 while another 19% came from interest on taxable and nontaxable investments. The rest of its revenue came from deposit service fees (14% of revenue) employee benefit services (12%) wealth management and insurance services (5%) and other banking revenues (1%).

Geographic Reach

Community Bank System operated 194 branches and six back-office operating facilities in 36 counties in upstate New York and six counties in northeastern Pennsylvania at the end of 2015.

Sales and Marketing

The bank has been ramping up its advertising spend in recent years. It spent $3.6 million on advertising during 2015 up from $3.2 million and $3.0 million in 2014 and 2013 respectively.

Financial Performance

Community Bank System's annual revenues have been slowly trending higher since 2013 despite a decline in loan interest mostly as it's been building its non-interest related business lines. Meanwhile its net income has risen more than 15% as it's had to pay less in interest expenses on deposits amidst the low interest environment.

The bank's revenue grew 2% to $382.92 million during 2015 thanks to a combination of employee benefit services business growth from new customers and expanding business relationships with existing customers as well as from new service offerings; higher interest income from loans and taxable investments as such interest-earning asset balances grew modestly; and a 13% jump in wealth management and insurance services revenue stemming from the acquisition of OneGroup from the Oneida Financial Group acquisition.

Despite revenue growth in 2015 Community's net income dipped less than 1% to $91.23 million for the year due to costs related to the Oneida acquisition. The company's operating cash levels shrank 5% to $116.46 million mostly due to unfavorable working capital changes related to deferred income tax provisions and changes in other assets and liabilities.

Strategy

Community Bank System looks to continue building its loan and deposit business as well as its non-interest service lines organically and through strategic acquisitions of other banks and financial companies. The financial company in 2015 began exploring expansion opportunities into neighboring markets in eastern Ohio upper New England and New Jersey and in 2017 acquired Northeast Retirement Services (NRS) for around $146 million. NRS provides institutional transfer agency master recordkeeping services custom target date fund administration trust product administration and customized reporting services to institutional clients.

Mergers and Acquisitions

Community Bank System agreed to acquire Kinderhook Bank for $93.4 million. Kinderhook has 11 offices in five New York counties (including in the Capital District of upstate New York) and holds nearly $640 million in assets and about $560 million in deposits. The deal extends Community Bank's reach into the Capital District markets.

In spring 2017 Community Bank acquired Vermont-based Merchants Bancshares. Merchants operates nearly 35 branches and has assets in excess of $1.8 billion; the acquisition will expand Community Bank's operations into Vermont and western Massachusetts.

Company Background

In mid-2012 the bank purchased about 20 branches in upstate New York from HSBC. The deal which was made to satisfy antitrust concerns regarding First Niagara's purchase of 195 branches in New York from HSBC strengthened Community Bank Systems' geographic footprint.

In 2011 the company bought bank holding company The Wilber Corporation adding about 20 locations in the Catskills Mountains region of central New York.

In 2011 expanding its trust and benefits administration business it bought retirement plan administrator CAI Benefits which has offices in New York and Northern New Jersey.

EXECUTIVES

Evp And Cfo, Scott A. Kingsley, age 53, $422,500 total compensation

President Ceo And Director, Mark E. Tryniski, age 57, $725,000 total compensation

Evp And Chief Banking Officer, Brian D. Donahue, age 62, $350,000 total compensation

Svp And Cto, J. Michael Wilson, age 47

Svp Retail Banking Sales And Marketing, Harold M. (Harry) Wentworth, age 53

Svp And Chief Investment Officer, Joseph J. Lemchak, age 56

President Pennsylvania Banking, Robert P. Matley, age 66

Svp Municipal Banking Director, Joseph E. Sutaris, age 50

Svp And Senior Commercial Lending Officer Northern New York, Nicholas S. (Nick) Russell, age 50

Svp And Chief Credit Administrator, Stephen G. Hardy, age 63

Evp And General Counsel, George J. Getman, age 61, $375,000 total compensation

Svp And Chief Risk Officer, Paul J. Ward

Svp And Chief Credit Officer, Joseph Serbun, $248,107 total compensation

Vice President And Security Officer, Stuart Smith

Assistant Vice President Marketing An, Mary K Barnette

Executive Vice President Marketing, Aaron Kurtz

Vice President, Patrick Gorman

Executive Vice President Marketing, Deborah Fitch

Vice President Marketing, Art Gentry

Executive Vice President, Barbara Call

Vice President And Manager Financial Analysis, Robert Frost

Vice President Director Mortgage Lending, George J Burke

Vice President And Information Technology Manager, James Wilson

Vice President Administration, Eric Wollman

Senior Vice President And Chief Credit Officer, Joe Serbun

Finance Senior Vice President, Richard Heidrick

Vice President Commercial Banker, Allison Mosher

Vice President Commercial Banking, Craig Stevens

Assistant Vice President And General Accounting Ma, Laura Mattice

President Ceo And Director, Mark E. Tryniski, age 57

Chair, Sally A. Steele, age 62

Auditors: PricewaterhouseCoopers LLP

LOCATIONS

HQ: Community Bank System Inc
5790 Widewaters Parkway, DeWitt, NY 13214-1883
Phone: 315 445-2282
Web: www.communitybankna.com

PRODUCTS/OPERATIONS

2015 Sales

	$ mil.	% of total
Interest Income:		
Interest and fees on loans	187	49
Taxable investments	52	14
Nontaxable investments	19	5
Noninterest		
Deposit service fees	52	14
Employee benefit services	45	12
Wealth management	20	5
Other	5	1
Total	**382**	**100**

Selected Subsidiaries & Affiliates

Benefit Plans Administrative Services Inc.
Benefit Plans Administrative Services LLC
Brilie Corporation
CBNA Insurance Agency Inc.
CBNA Preferred Funding Corp.
CBNA Treasury Management Corporation
Community Bank N.A. (also dba First Liberty Bank & Trust)
Community Investment Services Inc.
First of Jermyn Realty Company
First Liberty Service Corporation
Flex Corporation
Hand Benefit & Trust Company
Hand Securities Inc.
Harbridge Consulting Group LLP
Nottingham Advisors Inc.
Town & Country Agency LLC
Western Catskill Realty Inc.

COMPETITORS

Arrow Financial	Financial Institutions
Bank of America	HSBC USA
Canandaigua National	JPMorgan Chase
Chemung Financial	KeyCorp
Citizens Financial Group	M&T Bank
Elmira Savings Bank	NBT Bancorp

HISTORICAL FINANCIALS

Company Type: Public

Income Statement				FYE: December 31
	ASSETS ($ mil.)	NET INCOME ($ mil.)	INCOME AS % OF ASSETS	EMPLOYEES
12/17	10,746	150	1.4%	2,874
12/16	8,666	103	1.2%	2,499
12/15	8,552	91	1.1%	2,490
12/14	7,489	91	1.2%	2,182
12/13	7,095	78	1.1%	2,215
Annual Growth	**10.9%**	**17.6%**	**—**	**6.7%**

2017 Year-End Financials

Debt ratio: 1.16%	No. of shares (mil.): 50
Return on equity: 10.64%	Dividends
Cash ($ mil.): 221	Yield: 0.0%
Current ratio: —	Payout: 43.5%
Long-term debt ($ mil.): —	Market value ($ mil.): 2,725

STOCK PRICE ($) FY Close	P/E High/Low		PER SHARE ($) Earnings	Dividends	Book Value
12/17	53.75	20 16	3.03	1.32	32.26
12/16	61.79	27 15	2.32	1.26	26.96
12/15	39.94	20 15	2.19	1.22	26.06
12/14	38.13	18 15	2.22	1.16	24.24
12/13	39.68	21 14	1.94	1.10	21.66
Annual Growth	7.9%	— —	11.8%	4.7%	10.5%

Community Financial Corp (The)

EXECUTIVES

Assistant Vice President, Donna Goldey
Assistant Vice President, Cathy Thompson
Auditors: Dixon Hughes Goodman LLP

LOCATIONS

HQ: Community Financial Corp (The)
   3035 Leonardtown Road, Waldorf, MD 20601
Phone: 301 645-5601
Web: www.cbtc.com

COMPETITORS

American Bank Holdings	M&T Bank
BB&T	Old Line Bancshares
Burke & Herbert Bank	WSB Holdings
Independence Federal	

HISTORICAL FINANCIALS

Company Type: Public

Income Statement — FYE: December 31

	ASSETS ($ mil.)	NET INCOME ($ mil.)	INCOME AS % OF ASSETS	EMPLOYEES
12/17	1,405	7	0.5%	165
12/16	1,334	7	0.5%	162
12/15	1,143	6	0.6%	171
12/14	1,082	6	0.6%	172
12/13	1,023	6	0.6%	165
Annual Growth	8.3%	2.0%	—	0.0%

2017 Year-End Financials

Debt ratio: 6.44%
Return on equity: 6.72%
Cash ($ mil.): 15
Current ratio: —
Long-term debt ($ mil.): —

No. of shares (mil.): 4
Dividends
   Yield: 0.0%
   Payout: 25.6%
Market value ($ mil.): 178

STOCK PRICE ($) FY Close	P/E High/Low		PER SHARE ($) Earnings	Dividends	Book Value
12/17	38.30	26 18	1.56	0.40	23.65
12/16	29.00	19 12	1.59	0.40	22.54
12/15	20.96	18 14	1.35	0.40	21.48
12/14	20.07	18 15	1.35	0.40	24.79
12/13	20.71	12 8	1.88	0.50	23.83
Annual Growth	16.6%	— —	(4.6%)	(5.4%)	(0.2%)

Community Health Systems, Inc.

Community Health Systems (CHS) isn't much of a city dweller. The hospital operator prefers small-town America owning or leasing more than 100 hospitals — mostly in rural areas or small cities — in about 20 states. Its hospitals (which house roughly 21000 beds) typically act as the sole or primary acute health care provider in a service area and offer a variety of medical surgical and emergency services (though a handful are specialty centers). Its portfolio primarily includes acute care hospitals as well as a couple of stand-alone rehabilitation or psychiatric facilities. The hospitals generally have ancillary facilities including doctors' offices surgery centers and diagnostic imaging facilities. CHS also operates outpatient care centers surgery centers cancer and imaging centers and occupational medicine clinics.

Operations

CHS operates through a single segment — hospital operations. The segment's holdings include inpatient centers and their related outpatient care facilities. CHS recently exited the home health business by selling those assets to Almost Family in early 2017.

Altogether CHS employs some 20000 physicians and their medical staffs.

Geographic Reach

CHS has hospitals in about 20 states with its largest market concentrations in Florida Indiana Texas and Pennsylvania.

Sales and Marketing

CHS receives more than half of its revenues from commercial insurance companies through managed care contracts. Approximately 35% of revenues come from Medicare and Medicaid reimbursements for patient services and the rest of revenue comes from self-pay patients.

Financial Performance

CHS revenue rose significantly in 2014 when the company acquired rival Health Management Associates and expanded its network of facilities. Revenues have since struggled growing a modest 4% in 2015 and then slipping 5% to $18.4 billion in 2016. Net operating revenue fell another 17% to $15.4 billion in 2017; this decline was primarily due to the divestiture of hospitals during 2016 and 2017.

Net income hovered at around $150 million until 2016 when CHS posted a net loss of $1.7 billion. CHS's net loss widened the following year reaching $2.8 billion. Lower revenues in those years drove the losses and an increase in operating expenses as a percentage of net operating revenues put further pressure on the company. Severance payments and surgical supplies purchased as a result of a higher surgical case mix contributed to the relatively higher expenses.

Cash flow from operations which has been fairly turbulent fell 32% to $773 million in 2017. Negative adjustments to reconcile net income including deferred income taxes and depreciation and amortization contributed to that drop.

Strategy

CHS has been shedding non-core assets in light of financial struggles — it reported a net loss of $1.7 billion in fiscal 2016 and a net loss of $2.4 billion in 2017. In 2016 the company spun off nearly 40 of its hospitals along with its Quorum Health Resources unit (a provider of management services to non-affiliated hospitals) forming a new public company named Quorum Health Corporation. That split created two distinct companies with their own strategies and opportunities for growth. In 2017 it sold 30 hospitals for a total of some $1.7 billion. Also that year CHS sold an 80% stake in its home health and hospice operations to Almost Family for $128 million. The company is still divesting hospitals as it focuses on its stronger holdings.

Historically CHS has expanded by acquiring hospitals especially in growing non-urban markets. It expects to ultimately return to that strategy once its portfolio of holdings is streamlined through divestitures. The company now believes it is better positioned to focus on some of the larger markets it serves a bit of a turnaround from its previous trajectory.

To promote future growth the company has a number of strategies in place. It plans to grow and strengthen its care networks in certain markets aligning its expanding suite of services with larger hospitals to establish a broad continuum of care. Within those networks it is working to increase revenues at its facilities through such efforts as hiring additional physicians expanding services such as its orthopedic program and free-standing emergency departments and evaluating opportunities to participate in managed care contracts.

Additionally CHS is standardizing and centralizing operations across its facilities to improve efficiency and contain costs. (For instance it trims supply costs through its membership in group purchasing organization HealthTrust.) All the while the company emphasizes patient safety and quality care through systematic improvements that improve physician and employee satisfaction as well as provide a patient-centric experience.

However due to the drop in earnings CHS has been weighing various options it has going forward. In September 2016 it revealed that it was exploring a possible sale of itself; shortly thereafter it threw up a temporary block (a "poison pill") to prevent any buyer from taking a controlling stake in CHS. The company is still open to the idea of a full buyout though.

Mergers and Acquisitions

You don't become one of the largest for-profit hospital operators in the nation without a pretty aggressive acquisition strategy and CHS certainly has had that. Historically CHS has targeted hospitals in non-urban locations poised for growth. Because such areas have fewer people they generally have fewer hospitals (meaning less competition for patients and for managed care contracts). CHS typically purchases a number of small community hospitals each year though it also sometimes conducts larger acquisitions of hospital operating groups.

However CHS posted steep net losses in 2016 and 2017; in response it has been selling hospitals and exiting other operations (home care and hospice).

In 2016 the company acquired a majority stake in the 20-bed Arkansas-based Physicians' Specialty Hospital. It operates the facility in a joint venture with Indiana University Health.

HISTORY

Community Health Systems (CHS) was founded in 1985.

In 1996 it was acquired by investment firm Forstmann Little & Co. in a leveraged buyout transaction worth some $1.1 billion. It also moved its headquarters from Houston to Nashville Tennessee that year.

CHS once again became a public entity through an IPO in 2000. It engaged is engaged in a flurry of acquisition activity of small regional hospitals each year following its IPO.

However CHS limited its purchases somewhat after plunking down $7 billion in 2007 to acquire

Triad Hospitals (and its more than 50 hospitals). After conducting integration efforts at the former Triad hospitals CHS fully resumed its acquisition activity when it purchased five hospitals during 2010 including the Marion Regional Hospital in South Carolina the Forum Health (later Valley-Care) hospitals in Ohio and the Bluefield Hospital in West Virginia.

Buoyed by those purchases CHS launched a campaign to acquire fellow hospital operator and rival Tenet in late 2010 in a deal worth some $7.3 billion in cash stock and debt. However after much back and forth between the firms — including lawsuits and hostile tender offers — CHS halted its acquisition attempts the following year due to a lack of response from Tenet's shareholders and board members.

CHS instead completed several smaller purchases that year including the acquisition of the Mercy Health Partners Scranton operations in Pennsylvania from Catholic Health Partners. The company also purchased Tomball Regional Medical Center (TRMC) located near Houston.

As part of its periodic practice of divesting non-core centers in 2011 it sold two Oklahoma facilities SouthCrest Hospital and Claremore Regional Hospital to Ardent Health Services' Hillcrest Health-Care System unit for an undisclosed price. It also sold a Texas hospital Cleveland Regional Medical Center that year to New Directions Health Systems.

EXECUTIVES

Evp And Cfo, W. Larry Cash, age 70, $850,000 total compensation

Chairman And Ceo, Wayne T. Smith, age 72, $1,600,000 total compensation

President Division Ii Operations, Michael T. Portacci, age 60, $663,341 total compensation

Evp Administration, Martin G. (Marty) Schweinhart, age 63

Svp Corporate Communications Marketing And Public Affairs, Tomi Galin

President And Coo, Tim L. Hingtgen, age 51, $655,007 total compensation

Svp And Chief Purchasing Officer, Tim G. Marlette

President Division Iii Operations, P. Paul Smith, age 55

Svp And Cio, Manish Shah

President Division Iv Operations, John W. McClellan

Chief Quality Officer; President Clinical Services, Lynn T. Simon, age 55

President Division I Operations, Martin J. Bonick, age 45

Svp And Chief Nursing Officer, Pamela T. Rudisill

Cfo, Thomas J. (Tom) Aaron

Vice President, Terry Hendon

Vice President Division Operations, Christopher Costello

Medical Director, Scott Wagner

Clinic Manager, Amanda Anderton

Vice President, Laurence Bludau

Chairman And Ceo, Wayne T. Smith, age 72

Auditors: Deloitte & Touche LLP

LOCATIONS

HQ: Community Health Systems, Inc.
4000 Meridian Boulevard, Franklin, TN 37067
Phone: 615 465-7000
Web: www.chs.net

PRODUCTS/OPERATIONS

2017 Sales

	% of total
Managed care & other third-party payors	54
Medicare	23
Self-pay	13
Medicaid	10
Total	**100**

COMPETITORS

Adventist Health System Sunbelt Healthcare
Adventist Health System West
Ascension Health
Banner Health
CHRISTUS Health
Carolinas HealthCare System
Catholic Health Initiatives
Dignity Health
Encompass Health
HCA
LifePoint Health
Mercy Health
SSM Health Care
SunLink Health Systems
Sutter Health
Tenet Healthcare
Texas Health Resources
Trinity Health (Novi)
Universal Health Services
University Health Services
WellStar Health System

HISTORICAL FINANCIALS

Company Type: Public

Income Statement

FYE: December 31

	REVENUE ($ mil.)	NET INCOME ($ mil.)	NET PROFIT MARGIN	EMPLOYEES
12/17	15,353	(2,459)	—	95,000
12/16	18,438	(1,721)	—	120,000
12/15	19,437	158	0.8%	137,000
12/14	18,639	92	0.5%	167,000
12/13	12,997	141	1.1%	87,000
Annual Growth	**4.3%**	**—**	**—**	**2.2%**

2017 Year-End Financials

Debt ratio: 79.73%
Return on equity: (-579.95%)
Cash ($ mil.): 563
Current ratio: 1.73
Long-term debt ($ mil.): 13,880

No. of shares (mil.): 114
Dividends
Yield: —
Payout: —
Market value ($ mil.): 488

	STOCK PRICE ($) FY Close	P/E High/Low		PER SHARE ($) Earnings	Dividends	Book Value
12/17	4.26	—	—	(22.00)	0.00	(6.69)
12/16	5.59	—	—	(15.54)	0.00	14.18
12/15	26.53	46	18	1.37	0.00	35.64
12/14	53.92	70	43	0.82	0.00	34.29
12/13	39.27	34	20	1.51	0.00	32.29
Annual Growth	**(42.6%)**			**—**	**—**	**—**

Community Trust Bancorp, Inc.

Community Trust Bancorp is the holding company for Community Trust Bank one of the largest Kentucky-based banks. It operates 70-plus branches throughout the state as well as in northeastern Tennessee and southern West Virginia. The bank offers standard services to area businesses and individuals including checking and savings accounts credit cards and CDs. Loans secured by commercial properties and other real estate account for nearly 70% of the bank's portfolio which also includes business consumer and construction loans. Subsidiary Community Trust and Investment Company provides trust estate retirement

brokerage and insurance services through a handful of offices in Kentucky and Tennessee.

Operations
Community Trust Bancorp's lending activities include making commercial construction mortgage and personal loans. It also offers lease-financing lines of credit revolving lines of credit term loans and other specialized loans including asset-backed financing.

Some 69% of Community Trust Bancorp's portfolio of loans is secured real estate (36% of which consists of commercial real estate).

Geographic Reach
Kentucky-based Community Trust Bancorp operates more than 70 banking locations across Kentucky West Virginia and Tennessee. Its trust offices are located in Kentucky and Tennessee.

Sales and Marketing
Community Trust Bancorp specializes in serving both small and medium-sized businesses.

Financial Performance
Despite weak loan demand Community Trust Bancorp has grown its revenue from 2009 to 2011 followed by a marginal decline in 2012. Thanks to a decline in both interest expenses and provisions for loan losses Community Trust Bancorp has seen its net income rise during the past five years.

While Community Trust Bancorp logged marginal decreases (1%) in revenue in fiscal 2012 vs. 2011 the financial institution posted net income increases of 16% to $45 million during the reporting period.

Mergers and Acquisitions
Community Trust Bancorp bought LaFollette First National Corporation the holding company for First National Bank of LaFollette for some $16 million. The 2010 acquisition gave the company its first four bank branches and first trust office in Tennessee.

Community Trust is considering additional acquisitions of smaller competitors. It also grows by opening new branches.

EXECUTIVES

Senior Vice President Human Resources, Howard W Blackburn

Chairman President And Ceo And Chairman Community Trust Bank, Jean R. Hale, age 72, $548,077 total compensation

Evp And Cfo Community Trust Bancorp And Evp And Treasurer Community Trust Bank, Kevin J. Stumbo, age 58, $231,539 total compensation

Evp And Secretary Community Trust Bancorp President And Ceo Community Trust Bank And Vp Community Trust And Investment Company, Mark A. Gooch, age 60, $397,000 total compensation

Evp Community Trust Bancorp And Evp And Chief Credit Officer Community Trust Bank, James J. (Jim) Gartner, age 77

Evp Community Trust Bancorp And Evp Operations Community Trust Bank, James B. (Jim) Draughn, age 59, $241,231 total compensation

Evp Community Trust Bancorp And Evp And South Central Region President Community Trust Bank, Ricky D. Sparkman, age 55

Evp Community Trust Bancor And Evp And Eastern Region President Community Trust Bank, Richard W. (Rick) Newsom, age 63

Evp Community Trust Bancorp And Evp And President Central Kentucky Region Community Trust Bank Inc., Larry W. Jones, age 71, $249,231 total compensation

Evp Community Trust Bancorp And Evp And Chief Internal Audit And Risk Officer Community Trust Bank, Steven E. (Steve) Jameson, age 61

Evp Community Trust Bancorp And Evp And President North East Region Community Trust Bank Inc., D. Andrew Jones, age 55

Evp Community Trust Bancorp And President And Ceo Community Trust And Investment Co., Andy D. Waters, age 52

Evp Community Trust Bancorp Inc. And Evp And Senior Staff Attorney Community Trust Bank Inc., C. Wayne Hancock, age 43

Chairman President And Ceo And Chairman Community Trust Bank, Jean R. Hale, age 72

Evp And Cfo Community Trust Bancorp And Evp And Treasurer Community Trust Bank, Kevin J. Stumbo, age 58

Evp And Secretary Community Trust Bancorp President And Ceo Community Trust Bank And Vp Community Trust And Investment Company, Mark A. Gooch, age 60

Auditors: BKD, LLP

LOCATIONS

HQ: Community Trust Bancorp, Inc.
346 North Mayo Trail, Pikeville, KY 41501
Phone: 606 432-1414
Web: www.ctbi.com

PRODUCTS/OPERATIONS

2016 Sales

	% of total
Interest income	
Interest and fees on loans	69
Interest and dividends on securities	6
Noninterest income	
Service charges on deposit accounts	13
Gains on sales of loans	1
Trust and wealth management income	5
Loan related fees	2
Bank owned life insurance	1
Brokerage revenue	1
Securities gains (losses)	
Other noninterest income	2
Total	**100**

Selected Products & Services

Business Banking
  Business CDs
  Business Checking
  Corporate Services
  Lending
  Merchant Services
  Online Services
  Savings & Money Market
Financial Services
Personal Banking
  Card Services
  CDs & IRAs
  Consumer Loans
  Home Equity
  Interest Checking
  Mobile Banking
  Mortgages
  Personal Checking
  Savings & Money Market
Wealth & Trust Management

COMPETITORS

BB&T	Republic Bancorp
Fifth Third	U.S. Bancorp
Home Federal	
Premier Financial	
Bancorp	

HISTORICAL FINANCIALS

Company Type: Public

Income Statement

FYE: December 31

	ASSETS ($ mil.)	NET INCOME ($ mil.)	INCOME AS % OF ASSETS	EMPLOYEES
12/17	4,136	51	1.2%	990
12/16	3,932	47	1.2%	996
12/15	3,903	46	1.2%	984
12/14	3,723	43	1.2%	1,012
12/13	3,581	45	1.3%	1,022
Annual Growth	**3.7%**	**3.3%**	**—**	**(0.8%)**

2017 Year-End Financials

Debt ratio: 1.43%		No. of shares (mil.): 17		
Return on equity: 9.99%		Dividends		
Cash ($ mil.): 185		Yield: 0.0%		
Current ratio: —		Payout: 44.5%		
Long-term debt ($ mil.): —		Market value ($ mil.): 833		

	STOCK PRICE ($) FY Close	P/E High/Low	PER SHARE ($) Earnings	Dividends	Book Value
12/17	47.10	18 14	2.92	1.30	30.00
12/16	49.60	18 12	2.70	1.26	28.40
12/15	34.96	14 12	2.66	1.22	27.12
12/14	36.61	18 13	2.49	1.18	25.64
12/13	45.16	17 12	2.62	1.15	23.70
Annual Growth	**1.1%**	**—**	**2.8%**	**3.0%**	**6.1%**

COMMUNITYBANK OF TEXAS NATIONAL ASSOCIATION

EXECUTIVES

Prin, George Casseb
Fo, Donna Dillon
Manager, Trudy Jones
Senior Vice-President, Michael Mallette
Senior Vice-President, Paul Broussard
Senior Vice-President, N Felan

LOCATIONS

HQ: COMMUNITYBANK OF TEXAS NATIONAL ASSOCIATION
5999 DELAWARE ST, BEAUMONT, TX 777067607
Phone: 409 861-7200
Web: WWW.COMMUNITYBANKOFTX.COM

HISTORICAL FINANCIALS

Company Type: Private

Income Statement

FYE: December 31

	ASSETS ($ mil.)	NET INCOME ($ mil.)	INCOME AS % OF ASSETS	EMPLOYEES
12/17	3,079	28	0.9%	60
12/16	2,950	28	1.0%	—
12/15	2,881	25	0.9%	—
12/14	2,629	23	0.9%	—
Annual Growth	**5.4%**	**6.2%**	**—**	**—**

2017 Year-End Financials

Debt ratio: —		
Return on equity: 21.70%	Dividends	
Cash ($ mil.): 326	Yield: —	
Current ratio: —	Payout: —	
Long-term debt ($ mil.): —	Market value ($ mil.): —	

COMPUTER SCIENCES CORPORATION

Computer Sciences Corporation (CSC) has been one of the world's leading providers of systems integration and other information technology services. It offers application development data center management communications and networking development IT systems management and business consulting. It also provides business process outsourcing (BPO) services in such areas as billing and payment processing customer relationship management (CRM) and human resources. CSC boasts 2500 clients in more than 70 countries. In 2017 CSC merged with the Enterprise Services segment of Hewlett-Packard Enterprise to form DXC Technology Co. This report is based on CSC's last year as an independent company.

Change in Company Type

DXC is the result of mixing and matching of downsizing and upsizing corporate units. Computer Sciences Corp. spun out its government service unit several years ago which reduced CSC's revenue. Hewlett Packard Enterprise Services was part of Hewlett Packard Enterprise one of two companies created with Hewlett-Packard split up. The combination of HP Enterprise Services and CSC began in 2016 and concluded in April 2017 when DXC formally began operations. The new company is expected to have annual revenue of about $26 billion. This report reflects the final year of CSC as an independent company.

Operations

Prior to the creation of DXC CSC conducted business in through Global Business Services (GBS) and Global Infrastructure Services (GIS). GBS (55% of revenue) addresses key business challenges such as consulting applications services and software. GIS (45% of revenue) provides IT infrastructure services such as managed and virtual desktop solutions unified communications and collaboration services data center management cyber security and cloud-based offerings.

Geographic Reach

CSC has major operations throughout North America Europe Asia and Australia. The company has clients in more than 70 countries. About 40% of sales are made in the US and about 20% are in the UK the second biggest market.

Sales and Marketing

CSC's clients have included AboveNet Communications Deutsche Telekom DirecTV Vodafone and Ryman Hospitality Properties (formerly Gaylord Entertainment).

Financial Performance

After seven straight years of revenue declines CSC's sales rebounded in 2017 (ended March) to $7.6 billion a 7% increase from 2016. The increase was driven by the Global Business Services unit?s business processing services offerings and contributions from recent acquisitions in the Digital Applications business. The Global Infrastructure Services unit posted a small revenue increase from new business and sales from acquisitions.

CSC lost about $123 million in 2017 down from a $251 million profit in 2016 mainly due to large restructuring charges.

Cash flow from operating activities rose to $978 million in 2017 from $802 million in 2016. The increase flowed from an increase in trade payables and a decrease in net account receivables.

Strategy

After going through corporate breakups DXC Technology bets that bigger will be better and stronger in competing in the worldwide market for IT services. The companies have a wide footprint and with some $26 billion in annual revenue and will have some weight to throw around. A question will be if the company can effectively compete with companies that provide similar services such as Cognizant WiPro Accenture IBM Global Service and Dell Technologies.

DXC has bulked up to ride the wave of digital transformation that its customers and potential customers are going through. The company's range of services could lead customers from legacy systems to private or public or hybrid cloud systems.

Mergers and Acquisitions

In 2016 CSC acquired Xchanging plc provider of technology-enabled business services for $633 million. Xchanging brings its Xuber software which is used by commercial insurance companies around the world.

Also in 2016 CSC acquired Aspediens a European provider in the service-management sector and a preferred partner of ServiceNow. The deal extended CSC?s reach in software-as-a-service in Europe.

EXECUTIVES

Vice President Of Global Human Resources And Trans, Mike Darcy
Division Director Deputy Vice President General Manager, Richard Morrow
Vice President Global Sales Excellence, Cherie Gartner
Vice President, Brad Canel
Auditors: DELOITTE & TOUCHE LLP MCLEAN

LOCATIONS

HQ: COMPUTER SCIENCES CORPORATION
1775 TYSONS BLVD STE 1000, TYSONS, VA
221024284
Phone: 703 245-9675
Web: WWW.DXC.TECHNOLOGY

2017 Sales

	$ mil.	% of total
United States	2,986	40
United Kingdom	1,482	19
Australia	921	12
Other Europe	1,594	21
Other International	624	8
Total	**7,607**	**100**

PRODUCTS/OPERATIONS

2017 Sales

	$ mil.	% of total
Global Business Services	4,173	55
Global Infrastructure Services	3,434	45
Total	**7,607**	**100**

Selected Service Areas

Application outsourcing
Business process outsourcing
Customer relationship management
Data hosting
Enterprise application integration
Knowledge management
Management consulting
Risk management
Security
Supply chain management

Selected Solutions

Application Services
Big Data & Analytics
Business & Technology Consulting
Cloud Solutions & Services
Cybersecurity
Industry Software & Solutions
Infrastructure Services
Managed Services & Outsourcing
Mobility Solutions

COMPETITORS

ADP
Accenture
Atos
Booz Allen
CACI International
CIBER
Capgemini
Cognizant Tech Solutions
Computacenter
Convergys
Dell
Deloitte Consulting
Dimension Data
General Dynamics Information Technology
Getronics
HCL Technologies
Honeywell International
IBM Global Services
Infosys
Leidos
ManTech
NTT Data
Northrop Grumman
Siemens AG
Tata Consultancy
Tech Mahindra
Unisys
Wipro
Wipro Technologies

HISTORICAL FINANCIALS

Company Type: Private

Income Statement   FYE: March 31

	REVENUE ($ mil.)	NET INCOME ($ mil.)	NET PROFIT MARGIN	EMPLOYEES
03/17*	7,607	(100)	—	66,000
04/16	7,106	263	3.7%	—
04/15	12,173	7	0.1%	—
03/14	12,998	690	5.3%	—
Annual Growth	(16.4%)	—	—	—

*Fiscal year change

2017 Year-End Financials

Debt ratio: ——
Return on equity: (-1.30%)
Cash ($ mil.): 1,263
Current ratio: 1.00
Long-term debt ($ mil.): —

Dividends
Yield: —
Payout: —
Market value ($ mil.): —

Conagra Brands Inc

ConAgra Foods fills the refrigerators freezers and pantries of most households. The company makes and markets name-brand packaged and frozen foods that are sold in most retail outlets. ConAgra's cornucopia of America's best-known brands includes Banquet Chef Boyardee Egg Beaters Healthy Choice and Marie Callender. It is also one of the biggest producers of seasoning and grain ingredients for the US food service food manufacturing and industrial markets. ConAgra Foods sold its private-label food business to TreeHouse Foods for $2.7 billion in early 2016. In July 2016 the company filed with the SEC to split into two public companies: Lamb Weston Holdings and Conagra Brands.

HISTORY

Alva Kinney founded Nebraska Consolidated Mills in 1919 by combining the operations of four Nebraska grain mills. It did not expand outside Nebraska until it opened a mill and feed processing plant in Alabama in 1942.

Consolidated Mills developed Duncan Hines cake mix in the 1950s. But Duncan Hines failed to raise a large enough market share and the company sold it to Procter & Gamble in 1956. Consolidated Mills used the proceeds to expand opening a flour and feed mill in Puerto Rico the next year. In the 1960s while competitors were moving into prepared foods the firm expanded into animal feeds and poultry processing. By 1970 it had poultry processing plants in Alabama Georgia and Louisiana. In 1971 the company changed its name to ConAgra (Latin for "in partnership with the land"). During the 1970s it expanded into the fertilizer catfish and pet accessory businesses.

Poorly performing subsidiaries and commodity speculation caused ConAgra severe financial problems until 1974 when Mike Harper a former Pillsbury executive took over. Harper trimmed properties to reduce debt and had the company back on its feet by 1976. ConAgra stayed focused on the commodities side of the business but was thus tied to volatile price cycles. In 1978 it bought United Agri Products (agricultural chemicals).

ConAgra moved into consumer food products in the 1980s. It bought Banquet (frozen food 1980) and within six years had introduced almost 90 new products under that label. Other purchases included Singleton Seafood (1981) Armour Food Company (meats dairy products frozen food; 1983) and RJR Nabisco's frozen food business (1986). ConAgra became a major player in the red meat market with the 1987 purchases of E.A. Miller (boxed beef) Monfort (beef and lamb) and Swift Independent Packing.

Confident it had found the right path ConAgra continued with acquisitions of consumer food makers including Beatrice Foods (Orville Redenbacher's popcorn Hunt's tomato products) in 1991. In 1997 the company agreed to pay $8.3 million to settle federal charges of wire fraud and watering down grain. That year ConAgra named vice chairman and president Bruce Rohde as CEO; he became chairman in 1998. Also in 1998 the company bought GoodMark Foods maker of Slim Jim and Nabisco's Egg Beaters and table spread unit(Parkay). ConAgra bought Holly Ridge Foods (pastries) in 1999 and announced a major restructuring.

ConAgra bought Emerge an agricultural and land-use information software provider from Litton Industries in 2000. It also acquired Seaboard's poultry division and refrigerated meat alternatives maker Lightlife (Tofu pups Smart Dogs) before buying major brand holder International Home Foods from HM Capital Partners (known as Hicks Muse Tate & Furst at the time) for about $2.9 billion. The company then became ConAgra Foods.

During 2001 the company drew SEC attention and was forced to restate earnings for the previous three years due to accounting no-no's in its United Agri Products division.

In 2002 the USDA forced ConAgra to recall 19 million pounds of ground beef because of possible E. coli contamination making it the second-largest food recall in US history. (The largest recall occurred in 1997 when Hudson Foods later purchased by Tyson Foods withdrew 35 million pounds of beef.) Later in 2002 ConAgra sold its fresh beef and pork processing business — one of the largest in the US — to Booth Creek Management and HM Capital Partners and it was renamed Swift & Company Swift & Company . (Swift was acquired by Brazilian beef giant JBS in 2007.)

In 2003 the company began supplying packaged meat products for grilling to George Foreman

Foods which sells them via its Web site. That year it sold its Bumble Bee canned seafood business to members of Bumble Bee management and private investment firm Centre Partners Management and its blue cheese brands (Treasure Cave Nauvoo) to Canada's Saputo Inc. for undisclosed prices. It also sold its chicken processing business to Pilgrim's Pride for a stock and cash deal worth about $550 million in 2003.

Also in 2003 ConAgra agreed to pay $1.5 million in cash and job offers to settle an EEOC lawsuit charging bias against disabled workers at the company's California-based Gilroy Foods plant. The agreement involves the largest disability settlement in the agriculture industry. The dispute dated back to 1999 when Gilroy Foods then owned by Basic Vegetable Products (ConAgra bought the facility in 2000) after a strike failed to recall disabled workers who were on leaves of absence due to illness or pregnancy or who had a history of illness or injury.

In keeping with its strategy to focus on its branded and value-added food business in 2003 ConAgra sold United Agri Products to Apollo Management for stock and securities. The deal was worth about $600 million. In 2004 it sold its minority interest in the beef and pork processing operations of Swift Foods to HM Capital Partners. The deal was worth $194 million. ConAgra also sold Swift's feedlot operations to Smithfield Foods for an undisclosed amount.

ConAgra sold its turkey hatchery and breeding business to Ag Forte in 2004. It sold its Canadian and US crop inputs businesses and its Spanish feed and Portuguese poultry businesses that year as well. In addition it sold Casa de Oro Foods (the US's third-largest tortilla maker) to the Plaza Belmont Fund II. Also that year ConAgra introduced Golden Cuisine a line of frozen meals designed for seniors. The company began manufacturing and supplying Golden Cuisine to Meals On Wheels which distributes the meals which are formulated for seniors to the homebound elderly. That year ConAgra also introduced a high-fiber flour called Ultragrain that has the taste and texture of refined flour but the nutrition of whole grain.

In 2005 ConAgra sold its remaining 15 million shares of Pilgrim's Pride to that company for about $480 million. That year CEO Bruce Rhode retired. His replacement was former chairman and CEO of PepsiCo Beverages and Foods North America Gary Rodkin who began a company-wide restructuring. The company reorganized its business structure from three channels to two: Foodservice was merged with Food Ingredients and became ConAgra Foods Commercial ; the ConAgra Retail channel remained the same.

ConAgra agreed to pay a $14 million shareholder settlement in 2005 regarding a lawsuit claiming fictitious sales and mis-reported earnings at its former subsidiary United Agri Products.

In a move to demonstrate its commitment to the humane treatment of animals in 2006 ConAgra urged its poultry suppliers to consider slaughtering chickens in a more humane manner called controlled-atmosphere killing. The process which ConAgra has only suggested to its suppliers is approved by the People for the Ethical Treatment of Animals.

Rodkin continued the company redo focusing on portfolio trimming when in early 2006 he announced plans to sell a large part of ConAgra's refrigerated-meats business. The brands involved in the sale include some of the company's best-known: Armour Butterball and Eckrich. (The Brown 'N Serve Healthy Choice Hebrew National Pemmican and Slim Jim brands were not included in the portfolio reduction.) It sold its Cook's ham business to Smithfield Foods for $260 million that year.

Not long after that it agreed to sell of the rest of its refrigerated meats business that it had for sale to Smithfield as well. The deal which became final in October 2006 cost Smithfield $571 million in cash. That same month it sold its Butterball Turkey unit to Carolina Turkeys for $325 million. (Carolina subsequently changed its company name to Butterball LLC .)

Divesting almost faster than one can keep track of one day after the Butterball deal was completed ConAgra sold its MaMa Rosa's Pizza operations to investment firm the Plaza Belmont Management Group. (MaMa Rosa's is refrigerated — not frozen pizza — and competes in a different market than other pizzas albeit frozen powerhouses such as Di Giorno Tombstone or Tony's .)

In another move to improve long-term operating performance ConAgra announced its intention to sell off its seafood and domestic and imported cheese businesses. To that end the company sold its surimi business including the Louis Kemp brand to Trident Seafoods and its Singleton Seafood and Meridian Seafood to Singleton Fisheries. It sold its specialty and imported cheese operation Swissrose International to investment company Fairmount Food Group. Late in 2006 the company sold its oat-milling business to investment companies Sequel Holdings and Falcon Investment Advisors.

The company added to its Lamb Weston branded potato products with the 2008 acquisition of Watts Brothers. With operations in Washington and Oregon Watts is a vegetable-processing company that has annual sales of some $100 million. It has retail foodservice and industrial customers throughout the US as well as in Mexico Japan China and other Far East countries. The deal also included Watts' organic dairy fertilizer cold storage packaging and agricultural farming businesses.

In early 2007 salmonella was found in some of the company's Peter Pan and Great Value (a Wal-Mart product) brands of peanut butter forcing a nationwide recall of the peanut butter bearing the product code involved. Salmonella food poisoning was linked to some 600 people in 47 states. No deaths related to the peanut better were confirmed. The recall eventually included products made as far back as October 2004. ConAgra shut down the Sylvester Georgia plant that was involved in the outbreak and reopened it in Auguts 2007 having spent $15 million on renovation which included repairing the roof installing new equipment and creating a manufacturing process that better separated raw materials from the finished peanut butter.

Just two months later the company voluntarily stopped production at the Missouri plant that makes its Banquet and generic brands of frozen turkey and chicken pot pies after learning that the were linked to some 140 cases of salmonella in 30 states. ConAgra did not recall the pies but offered mail-in refunds and store returns. The USDA began an investigation and advised consumers not to eat the pies.

As part of its strategy to add to its brand-name offerings in 2007 ConAgra acquired Alexia Foods a maker of natural frozen potatoes appetizers and artisan breads for about $50 million in cash. Later that year the company paid a penalty of $45 million in the wake of SEC charges that alleged the company had misreported its profits for the fiscal years 1999 2000 and 2001.

The company acquired Lincoln Snacks Company in 2007. Lincoln's well-known brands such as Fiddle Faddle and Poppycock extended ConAgra's name-brand lineup which is in line with company strategy. That year it also announced the removal of the chemicals from its microwave popcorn products that are suspected of causing lung ailments in popcorn-plant workers.

ConAgra sold its trading and merchandising operations (ConAgra Trade Group) in 2008 to a group of investors that included the Ospraie Special Opportunities Fund for $2.8 billion. The sale was part of the company's long-term strategy to exit the commodities business and concentrate on its consumer food products. Saying it couldn't give the brand the attention it needs in 2008 the company sold its Knott's Berry Farm jam and jelly business to J. M. Smucker .

In a tragedy that made the evening news three ConAgra workers were killed and some 40 were injured in an explosion and fire at a company Slim Jim manufacturing plant in Garner North Carolina in June 2009. It was later determined that the blast was caused by a natural-gas leak. ConAgra partnered with the United Way forming the Garner Plant Fund that raised money to assist the victims and their families. The company also continued to pay workers salaries while the plant remained closed for investigation. ConAgra was fined $106000 by the government in 2010 and the plant was eventually closed.

During 2010 ConAgra unloaded its Gilroy Foods & Flavors business-to-business unit to Olam International for $250 million. The sale excluded Gilroy's seasonings and flavors businesses.

In 2011 ConAgra Foods made an unsolicited takeover bid to buy Ralcorp Holdings a leading maker of private-label snack foods cereals and condiments. After proffering an initial bid of $82 per share ConAgra ultimately offered $94 (valuing Ralcorp at more than $5 billion). However Ralcorp spurned all bids saying they were not in the best interests of shareholders.

In May 2012 the company completed the acquisition of Odom's Tennessee Pride the #2 producer of frozen breakfast sandwiches in the US.

In January 2013 ConAgra completed its $6.8 billion purchase of Ralcorp Holdings.

In September 2013 it purchased the frozen dessert producer business of Harlan Bakeries which made frozen fruit pies cream pies pastry shells and loaf cakes.

In early 2013 ConAgra acquired Ralcorp the nation's #1 maker of private-label food in a deal valued at about $6.8 billion (including debt). The combined company was expected to generate $18 billion in sales and made ConAgra the largest private-brand packaged foods business in North America with annual private brand sales of about $4.5 billion a year. The private brands segment makes private-label ready-to-eat cereals cereal bars snack mixes cookies crackers and other products for retailers under their own brand names.

EXECUTIVES

Senior Vice President And Chief Litigation Counsel, Leo Knowles
Evp General Counsel And Corporate Secretary, Colleen Batcheler, age 44, $521,635 total compensation
Evp And Cfo, John F. Gehring, age 57, $643,269 total compensation
Ceo, Sean M. Connolly, $1,100,000 total compensation
President Consumer Foods, Thomas M. (Tom) McGough, age 53, $636,538 total compensation
Evp And President Sales, Derek De La Mater
President Commercial Foods, Tom Werner, $438,654 total compensation
Evp And Chief Supply Chain Officer, Dave Biegger
Evp And Chief Human Resources Officer, Charisse Brock
Cio, Mindy Simon
Vice President Human Resources, Kelly Schaefer
Vice President General Manager, Taylor Strubell

Vice President Organization Development, Lucy Dinwiddie
Vice President Of Marketing, Andy Johnston
National Account Manager, Chad Yuza
Vice President Research Quality And Innovation, Christian Rhynalds
Vice President General Manager Spicetec, Mark Duffy
Senior Vice President Marketing, Karen E Carey
Vice President Internal Audit, Allen Cooper
Chairman, Steven F. (Steve) Goldstone, age 73
Evp General Counsel And Corporate Secretary, Colleen Batcheler, age 44
Ceo, Sean M. Connolly
Board Member, Jennifer Hudson
Auditors: KPMG LLP

LOCATIONS

HQ: Conagra Brands Inc
222 Merchandise Mart Plaza, Suite 1300, Chicago, IL 60654
Phone: 312 549-5000
Web: www.conagrafoods.com

PRODUCTS/OPERATIONS

2016 Sales

	% of total
Consumer foods	62
Commercial foods	38
Total	**100**

2016 Sales

	% of total
Consumer Foods	
Grocery	29
Frozen	25
International	7
Other Brands	1
Commercial Foods	
Specialty potatoes	25
Food services	13
Total	**100**

Selected Brands

Commercial foods
ConAgra Mills
Lamb Weston
Spicetec Flavors & Seasonings
Consumer foods
Act II
Alexia
Banquet
Bertolli
Blue Bonnet
Chef Boyardee
DAVID Seeds
Egg Beaters
Healthy Choice
Hebrew National
Hunt's
Marie Callender's
Odom's Tennessee Pride
Orville Redenbacher's
PAM
Peter Pan
P.F. Chang's
Reddi-wip
Slim Jim
Snack Pack
Swiss Miss
Van Camp's
Wesson

COMPETITORS

American Pop Corn	Jenny Craig
B&G Foods	Kellogg
Big Heart Pet Brands	Link Snacks
Boulder Brands	MOM Brands
Bush Brothers	Manischewitz Company
Campbell Soup	McCain Foods
Clorox	McIlhenny
Eden Foods	Monterey Gourmet Foods

Frito-Lay	Mott's
General Mills	Nestlé
Gilster-Mary Lee	Newman's Own
Goya	Nutrisystem
H. J. Heinz Limited	Pinnacle Foods
Hain Celestial	Schwan's
Hanover Foods	Seneca Foods
Heinz	Slim-Fast
Hormel	Smucker
Inventure foods	Snappy Popcorn
J-OIL MILLS	Weaver Popcorn Company
JR Simplot	

HISTORICAL FINANCIALS
Company Type: Public

Income Statement
FYE: May 27

	REVENUE ($ mil.)	NET INCOME ($ mil.)	NET PROFIT MARGIN	EMPLOYEES
05/18	7,938	808	10.2%	12,400
05/17	7,826	639	8.2%	12,600
05/16	11,642	(677)	—	20,900
05/15	15,832	(252)	—	32,900
05/14	17,702	303	1.7%	32,800
Annual Growth	**(18.2%)**	**27.8%**	**—**	**(21.6%)**

2018 Year-End Financials

Debt ratio: 36.73%	No. of shares (mil.): 390
Return on equity: 21.15%	Dividends
Cash ($ mil.): 128	Yield: 0.0%
Current ratio: 0.83	Payout: 42.9%
Long-term debt ($ mil.): 3,231	Market value ($ mil.): 14,621

	STOCK PRICE ($) FY Close	P/E High/Low		PER SHARE ($) Earnings	Dividends	Book Value
05/18	37.41	20	16	1.98	0.85	9.41
05/17	39.03	33	23	1.46	0.90	9.58
05/16	45.29	—	—	(1.56)	1.00	8.48
05/15	38.61	—	—	(0.60)	1.00	10.57
05/14	31.61	52	39	0.70	1.00	12.46
Annual Growth	**4.3%**		**—**	**29.7%**	**(4.0%)**	**(6.8%)**

Conduent Inc

Auditors: PricewaterhouseCoopers LLP

LOCATIONS

HQ: Conduent Inc
100 Campus Drive, Suite 200, Florham Park, NJ 07932
Phone: 844 663-2638
Web: www.conduent.com

HISTORICAL FINANCIALS
Company Type: Public

Income Statement
FYE: December 31

	REVENUE ($ mil.)	NET INCOME ($ mil.)	NET PROFIT MARGIN	EMPLOYEES
12/17	6,022	181	3.0%	90,000
12/16	6,408	(983)	—	96,000
12/15	6,662	(414)	—	93,700
12/14	6,938	(81)	—	—
12/13	6,879	182	2.6%	—
Annual Growth	**(3.3%)**	**(0.1%)**	**—**	**—**

2017 Year-End Financials

Debt ratio: 27.31%	No. of shares (mil.): 210
Return on equity: 5.10%	Dividends
Cash ($ mil.): 658	Yield: —
Current ratio: 1.98	Payout: —
Long-term debt ($ mil.): 1,979	Market value ($ mil.): 3,401

	STOCK PRICE ($) FY Close	P/E High/Low		PER SHARE ($) Earnings	Dividends	Book Value
12/17	16.16	21	16	0.83	0.00	17.44
Annual Growth	**—**		**—**	**—**	**—**	**—**

ConnectOne Bancorp Inc (New)

ConnectOne Bancorp (formerly Center Bancorp) is the holding company for ConnectOne Bank which operates some two dozen branches across New Jersey. Serving individuals and local businesses the bank offers such deposit products as checking savings and money market accounts; CDs; and IRAs. It also performs trust services. Commercial loans account for about 60% of the bank's loan portfolio; residential mortgages account for most of the remainder. It also has a subsidiary that sells annuities and property/casualty life and health coverage. The former Center Bancorp acquired rival community bank ConnectOne Bancorp in 2014 and took that name.

Geographic Reach

ConnectOne has 24 branches in Bergen Essex Hudson Manhattan Mercer Monmouth Morris and Union Counties in New Jersey.

Mergers and Acquisitions

In 2014 Center Bancorp acquired ConnectOne Bancorp in an all-stock deal valued at approximately $243 million. The merged bank with nearly $4 billion in assets now does business under the ConnectOne brand name.

EXECUTIVES

Chb-Ceo, Frank Sorrentino III
Exec V Pres-Cfo, William S Burns
Exec V Pres-Coo, Christopher Ewing
Exec V Pres-Clo, Elizabeth Magennis
Sr V Pres-Cco, Michael McGrover
Board Member, Alexander Bol
Board Member, Frank W Baier
Board Member, Frank Huttle
Board Member, Frederick Fish
Board Member, Harold Schechter
Board Member, Joseph Parisi
Auditors: Crowe Horwath LLP

LOCATIONS

HQ: ConnectOne Bancorp Inc (New)
301 Sylvan Avenue, Englewood Cliffs, NJ 07632
Phone: 201 816-8900
Web: www.centerbancorp.com

COMPETITORS

BCB Bancorp	New York Community
Bank of America	Bancorp
Citizens Financial	Oritani Financial
Corp.	PNC Financial
Fulton Financial	Provident Financial
Hudson City Bancorp	Services
Investors Bancorp	Sovereign Bank
JPMorgan Chase	Valley National
Kearny Financial	Bancorp
Lakeland Bancorp	Westamerica

HISTORICAL FINANCIALS

Company Type: Public

Income Statement
FYE: December 31

	ASSETS ($ mil.)	NET INCOME ($ mil.)	INCOME AS % OF ASSETS	EMPLOYEES
12/17	5,108	43	0.8%	—
12/16	4,426	31	0.7%	—
12/15	4,016	41	1.0%	—
12/14	3,448	18	0.5%	—
12/13	1,673	19	1.2%	166
Annual Growth	32.2%	21.4%	—	—

2017 Year-End Financials

Debt ratio: 14.19%
Return on equity: 7.88%
Cash ($ mil.): 149
Current ratio: —
Long-term debt ($ mil.): —

No. of shares (mil.): 32
Dividends
Yield: 0.0%
Payout: 22.3%
Market value ($ mil.): 826

	STOCK PRICE ($) FY Close	P/E High/Low		PER SHARE ($) Earnings	Dividends	Book Value
12/17	25.75	21	16	1.34	0.30	17.63
12/16	25.95	26	15	1.01	0.30	16.62
12/15	18.69	16	13	1.36	0.30	15.87
12/14	19.00	25	21	0.79	0.30	15.03
12/13	18.76	16	10	1.21	0.26	10.30
Annual Growth	8.2%			2.6%	3.6%	14.4%

ConocoPhillips

EXECUTIVES

Ceo, Ryan M Lance
Chb-Ceo, J J Mulva
Exec V Pres-Cfo-Treas, John A Carrig
V Pres, Matt Fox
Supervisor, Brian Tran
Executive Assistant, Carol Riddell
Information Specialist, Diana Noteboom
Project Director, Garrett Rychlik
Counsel, Hans Holmen
Director, Jeff D Gow
Auditors: El Sayed El Ayouty & Co.

LOCATIONS

HQ: ConocoPhillips
  600 North Dairy Ashford, Houston, TX 77079
Phone: 281 293-1000   Fax: 281 661-7636
Web: www.conocophillips.com

HISTORICAL FINANCIALS

Company Type: Public

Income Statement
FYE: December 31

	REVENUE ($ mil.)	NET INCOME ($ mil.)	NET PROFIT MARGIN	EMPLOYEES
12/17	32,584	(855)	—	11,400
12/16	24,360	(3,615)	—	13,300
12/15	30,935	(4,428)	—	15,900
12/14	55,517	6,869	12.4%	19,100
12/13	58,248	9,156	15.7%	18,400
Annual Growth	(13.5%)	—		(11.3%)

2017 Year-End Financials

Debt ratio: 26.86%
Return on equity: (-2.61%)
Cash ($ mil.): 6,325
Current ratio: 1.76
Long-term debt ($ mil.): 17,128

No. of shares (mil.): 1,177
Dividends
Yield: 0.0%
Payout: —
Market value ($ mil.): 64,611

	STOCK PRICE ($) FY Close	P/E High/Low		PER SHARE ($) Earnings	Dividends	Book Value
12/17	54.89	—	—	(0.70)	1.06	26.00
12/16	50.14	—	—	(2.91)	1.00	28.27
12/15	46.69	—	—	(3.58)	2.94	32.17
12/14	69.06	16	11	5.51	2.84	42.16
12/13	70.65	10	8	7.38	2.70	42.49
Annual Growth	(6.1%) (11.6%)	—	—	—	(20.8%)	

Consolidated Edison Co. of New York, Inc.

Consolidated Edison Company of New York (Con Edison of New York) keeps the nightlife pulsing in The Big Apple. The utility a subsidiary of Consolidated Edison distributes electricity throughout most of New York City and Westchester County. The company distributes electricity to 3.4 million residential and business customers in New York City; it also delivers natural gas to about 1.1 million customers. The utility also provides steam services to 1703 customers in portions of the New York metropolitan area. Con Edison of New York owns and operates more than 133900 miles of overhead and underground power distribution lines.

Operations
The company has three segments: electric gas and steam — which contributed 79% 15% and 6% of total revenues in 2015.

Its assets include more than 4300 miles of gas distribution mains a gas liquefaction and storage facility and electric and steam generating stations. It also owns a range of power transmission assets which are operated by the New York Independent System Operator. Con Edison of New York's electric generating facilities consist of plants located in New York City with an aggregate capacity of 724 MW.

The company's distribution system had a transformer capacity of 29762 MVA with 36929 miles of overhead distribution lines and 97286 miles of underground distribution lines. The underground distribution lines represent the single longest underground electric delivery system in the United States.

Geographic Reach
Con Edison of New York has distribution facilities throughout New York City and Westchester County and operates manufactured gas plants at 51 sites.

Sales and Marketing
Con Edison of New York delivers electricity to state and municipal customers of NYPA and economic development customers of municipal electric agencies. Its customers include residential commercial industrial public authorities retail choice customers.

Financial Performance
In fiscal 2015 its net revenues decreased by 4% due to the lower gas steam and electric sales.

Revenues from electric decreased due to lower purchased power expenses and lower fuel expenses offset in part by higher revenues from the electric rate plan.

Con Edison of New York's gas revenues declined due to a decrease in gas purchased for resale expenses offset in part by higher revenues from the gas rate plan (reflecting higher delivery volumes attributable to oil-to-gas conversions). However revenues from steam increased due primarily to higher fuel expenses and higher revenues from the steam rate plan offset by the weather impact on revenues and lower purchased power costs.

In fiscal 2015 net income increased by 2% due to lower gas purchased for resale and purchased power.

Cash from operating activities increased by 16% due to lower income taxes paid net of refunds received offset in part by increased pension contributions.

Strategy
In 2016 Con Edison of New York filed a request with the New York State Public Service Commission for an electric rate increase of $482 million. It also entered into an agreement to sell certain electric transmission projects to NY Transco.

The company (in 2015) partnered with Drive Electric Vehicle Research Forward to help promote electric vehicles.

In 2014 Con Edison of New York was in the middle of a four-year $1 billion storm hardening program in the wake of 2012's Superstorm Sandy. Investments include the installation of 3000 devices that isolate and clear temporary faults on overhead electric systems and more than 150 smart switches that minimize outages caused by fallen trees. More than a mile of flood walls and 260 pieces of submersible equipment also have been installed. For its efforts the utility was named as the winner of the 2014 Outstanding System Reliability Award by the PA Consulting Group. The award recognizes the PA Consulting Group ReliabilityOne regional award recipient that demonstrated superior annual system-wide reliability performance for its customers. Con Edison of New York was also named best in the Northeast Region.

Company Background
Citing a 20% growth rate during the 2000s Con Edison of New York in 2011 spent almost $1.8 billion ($2 billion in 2010) to upgrade the company's aging electrical delivery systems (new high-voltage transmission cables) in New York City and surrounding areas. In 2010 Con Edison of New York and sister company Orange and Rockland also received $200 million in federal grants to install smart grid technology (automated more efficient meters and other systems) across their service area. By mid-2011 the company had also supported the installation of 8.5 MW of solar power units across its service region.

EXECUTIVES

Chairman And Ceo, Kevin Burke, age 68, $1,107,200 total compensation
Svp And Cro, Robert N. Hoglund, age 57, $584,200 total compensation
President Of Consolidated Edison Company Of New York; Inc., Craig S. Ivey, age 55
President And Ceo Orange And Rockland Utilities Inc., John T. McAvoy, age 57
Owner, Linda Goldberg
Chairman And Ceo, Kevin Burke, age 68
Auditors: PricewaterhouseCoopers LLP

LOCATIONS

HQ: Consolidated Edison Co. of New York, Inc.
  4 Irving Place, New York, NY 10003
Phone: 212 460-4600
Web: www.coned.com

Commerce Energy Group
Delmarva Power
Green Mountain Energy
Integrys Energy
  Services
NYSEG
National Grid USA

New York Power
  Authority
Public Service
  Enterprise Group
Rochester Gas and
  Electric

HISTORICAL FINANCIALS

Company Type: Public

Income Statement

	REVENUE ($ mil.)	NET INCOME ($ mil.)	NET PROFIT MARGIN	EMPLOYEES
12/17	10,468	1,104	10.5%	14,010
12/16	10,165	1,056	10.4%	13,531
12/15	10,328	1,084	10.5%	13,393
12/14	10,786	1,058	9.8%	13,200
12/13	10,430	1,020	9.8%	13,235
Annual Growth	0.1%	2.0%	—	1.4%

FYE: December 31

2017 Year-End Financials

Debt ratio: 32.79%
Return on equity: 9.10%
Cash ($ mil.): 730
Current ratio: 0.74
Long-term debt ($ mil.): 12,065

No. of shares (mil.): 235
Dividends
  Yield: —
  Payout: 72.1%
Market value ($ mil.): —

Consolidated Edison Inc

Utility holding company Consolidated Edison (Con Edison) is the night light for the city that never sleeps. Con Edison's main subsidiary Consolidated Edison Company of New York distributes electricity to 3.4 million residential and business customers in a 604-mile service territory centered on New York City. It delivers natural gas to about 1.1 million customers and operates the country?s largest steam distribution service to deliver energy to parts of Manhattan. Subsidiary Orange and Rockland Utilities serves more than 300000 electric and gas customers in New York and New Jersey. Con Edison also owns or operates renewable energy facilities and advises large clients on energy efficiency programs.

HISTORY

Several professionals led by Timothy Dewey formed The New York Gas Light Company in 1823 to illuminate part of Manhattan. In 1884 five other gas companies joined New York Gas Light to form the Consolidated Gas Company of New York.

Thomas Edison's incandescent lamp came on the scene in 1879 and The Edison Electric Illuminating Company of New York was formed in 1880 to build the world's first commercial electric power station (Pearl Street) financed by a group led by J.P. Morgan. Edison supervised the project and in 1882 New York became the first major city with electric lighting.

Realizing electricity would replace gas Consolidated Gas acquired electric companies including Anthony Brady's New York Gas and Electric Light Heat and Power Company (1900) which joined Edison's Illuminating Company in 1901 to form the New York Edison Company. More than 170

purchases followed including that of the New York Steam Company (1930) a cheap source of steam for electric turbines.

The Public Utility Holding Company Act of 1935 ushered in the era of regulated regional monopolies. The next year New York Edison combined its holdings to form the Consolidated Edison Company of New York (Con Ed).

Con Ed opened its first nuclear station in 1962. By then Con Ed had a reputation for inefficiency and poor service and shareholders were angry about its slow growth and low earnings. Environmentalists joined the grousers in 1963 when Con Ed began constructing a pumped-storage plant in Cornwall near the Hudson River. Charles Luce a former undersecretary with the Department of Interior was recruited to rescue Con Ed in 1967. He added power plants and beefed up customer service.

In the 1970s inflation and the energy crisis drove up oil prices (Con Ed's main fuel source) and in 1974 Luce withheld dividends for the first time since 1885. He persuaded the New York State Power Authority to buy two unfinished power plants saving Con Ed $200 million. In 1980 Luce ended the Cornwall controversy and donated the land for park use. He retired in 1982.

The utility started buying power from various suppliers and in 1984 began a two-year price freeze a boon to rate-hike-weary New Yorkers. The New York State Public Service Commission didn't approve another rate increase until 1992.

In 1997 Con Ed government officials consumer groups and other energy firms outlined the company's deregulation plan which included the formation of the Consolidated Edison Inc. holding company (known as Con Edison) and a power marketing unit in 1998. The next year Con Edison sold New York City generating facilities to KeySpan Northern States Power and Orion Power for a total of $1.65 billion.

Also in 1999 Con Edison bought Orange and Rockland Utilities for $790 million to increase its New York base and expand into New Jersey and Pennsylvania. In an effort to push into New England the company that year agreed to buy Northeast Utilities (NU since renamed Eversource Energy) for $3.3 billion in cash and stock and $3.9 billion in assumed debt. But the deal broke down in 2001. NU accused Con Edison of improperly trying to renegotiate terms while Con Edison accused NU of concealing information about unfavorable power supply contracts.

Con Edison's Indian Point Unit 2 nuclear plant was shut down temporarily in 2000 after a radioactive steam leak; later that year it agreed to sell Indian Point Units 1 and 2 to Entergy for $502 million. The sale was completed in 2001. That year Con Edison also incurred an estimated $400 million in costs related to emergency response and asset damage from the September 11 terrorist attacks on New York City.

In 2013 Con Edison announced plans to make it easier and less expensive for customers to convert from heating oil to lower cost natural gas in Manhattan and the Bronx. Its gas infrastructure expansion program includes investing a $100 million on new mains regulators and other upgrades in several neighborhoods.

It also plans to develop 25 MW of solar energy resources in New York City by the end of 2015. The solar power generated in the New York project would annually offset about 16000 tons of carbon dioxide.

EXECUTIVES

Vice President Human Resources, Claude Trahan, age 67
President And Ceo Con Edison Transmission Inc., Joseph P. Oates, age 57
Svp And Cfo Con Edison And Cecony, Robert N. Hoglund, age 57, $721,242 total compensation
Chairman And Ceo Coned And Cecony, John T. McAvoy, age 57, $1,220,767 total compensation
Svp Central Operations, Timothy P. Cawley, age 53, $409,033 total compensation
Svp And General Counsel Consolidated Edison And Cecony, Elizabeth D. Moore, age 63, $608,017 total compensation
President And Ceo Con Edison Clean Energy Businesses Inc., Mark Noyes, age 53
Office Of The Vice President Central Engineering, Laurens Irizarry
Chairman And Ceo Coned And Cecony, John T. McAvoy, age 57
Auditors: PricewaterhouseCoopers LLP

LOCATIONS

HQ: Consolidated Edison Inc
  4 Irving Place, New York, NY 10003
Phone: 212 460-4600
Web: www.conedison.com

PRODUCTS/OPERATIONS

2016 Sales

	$ mil.	% of total
Electric	8,741	72
Gas	1,692	14
Non-utility	1,091	9
Steam	551	5
Total	**12,075**	**100**

2016 sales

% of total	$ mil
CECONY	84
Clean Energy Business	9
O&R (Orange and Rockland)	7
Other	0
Total	**100**

Selected Subsidiaries

Consolidated Edison Inc. (Con Edison)
Consolidated Edison Company of New York Inc. (CECONY)
Con Edison Clean Energy Businesses Inc.
  Consolidated Edison Development Inc.
  Consolidated Edison Energy Inc.
  Consolidated Edison Solutions Inc.
Con Edison Transmission Inc.
  Consolidated Edison Transmission LLC (CET Electric)
  Consolidated Edison Gas Pipeline and Storage LLC (CET Gas)
Orange and Rockland Utilities Inc. (O&R)
Pike County Light & Power Company
Rockland Electric Company (RECO)

COMPETITORS

AEP
Avangrid
CH Energy
Green Mountain Energy
NSTAR
National Fuel Gas
National Grid USA

PPL Corporation
Public Service
  Enterprise Group
South Jersey
  Industries
USPowerGen

HISTORICAL FINANCIALS

Company Type: Public

Income Statement

FYE: December 31

	REVENUE ($ mil.)	NET INCOME ($ mil.)	NET PROFIT MARGIN	EMPLOYEES
12/17	12,033	1,525	12.7%	15,591
12/16	12,075	1,245	10.3%	14,960
12/15	12,554	1,193	9.5%	14,806
12/14	12,919	1,092	8.5%	14,601
12/13	12,354	1,062	8.6%	14,648
Annual Growth	(0.7%)	9.5%	—	1.6%

2017 Year-End Financials

Debt ratio: 33.32%
Return on equity: 10.26%
Cash ($ mil.): 797
Current ratio: 0.72
Long-term debt ($ mil.): 14,731

No. of shares (mil.): 310
Dividends
  Yield: 0.0%
  Payout: 55.8%
Market value ($ mil.): 26,335

	STOCK PRICE ($) FY Close	P/E High/Low	PER SHARE ($) Earnings	Dividends	Book Value
12/17	84.95	18 15	4.94	2.76	49.74
12/16	73.68	20 15	4.12	2.68	46.88
12/15	64.27	18 14	4.05	2.60	44.55
12/14	66.01	18 14	3.71	2.52	42.94
12/13	55.28	18 15	3.61	2.46	41.81
Annual Growth	11.3%	— —	8.2%	2.9%	4.4%

CONSOLIDATED GRAIN & BARGE COMPANY

EXECUTIVES

Ceo, Kevin D Adams
V Pres, Gregory Beck
Credit Manager, Randolph Hart
Information Technology, Sean Goodrion
Controller, Robin Gerarve
Accounting Assistant, Melody Bradfoot
Manager, Bill McBee
Human Resources Director, Judy Keitel
Manager, Paul Kelly
Auditors: KPMG LLP NEW ORLEANS LA

LOCATIONS

HQ: CONSOLIDATED GRAIN & BARGE COMPANY
1127 HWY 190 E SERVICE RD, COVINGTON, LA
704334929
Phone: 985 867-3500

HISTORICAL FINANCIALS

Company Type: Private

Income Statement

FYE: May 31

	REVENUE ($ mil.)	NET INCOME ($ mil.)	NET PROFIT MARGIN	EMPLOYEES
05/17	6,430	16	0.3%	2,000
05/16	5,759	21	0.4%	—
05/14	7,093	44	0.6%	—
05/12	5,996	50	0.8%	—
Annual Growth	1.4%	(20.4%)	—	—

2017 Year-End Financials

Debt ratio: —
Return on equity: 0.30%
Cash ($ mil.): 0
Current ratio: 0.10
Long-term debt ($ mil.): —

Dividends
  Yield: —
  Payout: —
Market value ($ mil.): —

Constellation Brands Inc

Constellation Brands is the world's largest premium wine producer. It offers more than 100 brands including Robert Mondavi Clos du Bois and Meiomi. The company is also the US's third-largest beer distributor and the sole US distributor for Mexican beer giant Grupo Modelo the brewer of Corona Modelo Especial Negra Modelo and other beers. Constellation Brands also markets premium spirits including Black Velvet whiskey and SVEDKA vodka. Constellation Brands' wine beer and spirits are sold in countries throughout the world. Brothers Richard and Robert Sands control the company which was founded by the late Marvin Sands.

Operations

Constellation Brands reports its business in two main segments: Beer and Wine & Spirits. The beer segment accounting for nearly 60% of group revenue has an exclusive license to import and sell Grupo Modelo's Corona Modelo and other brands. Wine & Spirits accounting for the remaining revenue covers a wide range of wine types brands and price points. Wine brands include Charles Smith Wines Meiomi and Ruffino while spirits brands include SVEDKA a Swedish import and the largest imported vodka brand in the US.

It has operations in the US New Zealand Italy and Canada.

Geographic Reach

New York-based Constellation Brands sells its products in roughly 100 countries. That being said the company gets virtually all its revenue from two countries: its generates over 90% of its sales in the US and most of the rest comes from Canada. The company is also a leading wine company in New Zealand.

Sales and Marketing

Constellation Brands staffs in-house marketing sales and customer service teams to increase its sales. These teams deploy a variety of marketing strategies conducting market research consumer and trade advertising price promotions point-of-sale materials event sponsorship on-premise promotions and public relations activities.

Financial Performance

Constellation set record revenue figures in fiscal 2017. At $8.1 billion revenue was 11% higher than the previous year. Sales growth was largely as a result of a series of acquisitions including Ballast Point Prisoner and Meiomi. Sales were also boosted by strong consumer demand across wine spirits and beer. The sale of the Canadian wine business weighed on growth.

Net income increased a strong 46% to $1.5 billion due to the favorable impact of pricing and lower cost of sales in the Mexican beer portfolio and gross profits from the acquired Ballast Point brand of $53.4 million.

Cash from operating activities increased 20% or $283 million to $1.7 billion due to strong cash generation in both the Beer and Wine and Spirits

segments. Beer was aided by volume growth and favorable pricing and wine by a favorable timing of payments from accounts payable.

Strategy

Constellation's long-term growth strategy is to increase its mix of premium brands improve profit margins expand distribution of key brands and create operating efficiencies. The company sold its Canadian wine business in 2016 due to inadequate profitability. The business which holds the largest share of the wine market in Canada was sold to Ontario Teachers' Pension Plan for C$1 billion. The sale included brands like Jackson-Triggs and Inniskillin.

To increase its number of premium brands the company made a raft of acquisitions in 2016. It bought no less than six beer or wine and spirits brands in 2015-16: Charles Smith (ultra-premium wine) and High West (high-end whiskeys) in October 2016 Prisoner (high margin wines) in April 2016 Ballast Point (craft beer) in December 2015 and Meiomi (red wine) in August 2015.

It also acquired Obregon Brewery in December 2016 to expand its brewing capacity.

Mergers and Acquisitions

Constellation has been through a heavy-acquisition period.

In December 2016 it acquired Obregon Brewery for $568.7 million to provide immediate brewing capacity to support its fast-growing Mexican beer portfolio.

In October 2016 it acquired Charles Smith and its collection of five super and ultra-premium wines (including Kung Fu Girl Riesling and Velvet Devil Merlot) $120 million. In the same month it bought fast-growing high-end craft whiskey maker High West for $160 million.

In August 2016 it acquired Prisoner which owns five super-luxury wine brands for $285 million.

In late 2017 in a move outside the realm of alcoholic beverages but in line with the company's strategy of staying on top of consumer trends Constellation agreed to pay C$245 million for a nearly 10% stake in medicinal cannabis provider Canopy Growth Corporation.

HISTORY

Marvin Sands the son of winemaker Mordecai (Mack) Sands exited the Navy in 1945 and entered distilling by purchasing an old sauerkraut factory in Canandaigua New York. His business Canandaigua Industries struggled while making fruit wines in bulk for local bottlers in the East. Aiming at regional markets the company began producing its own brands two years later. Marvin opened the Richards Wine Cellar in Petersburg Virginia in 1951 and put his father in charge of the unit. In 1954 Marvin developed his own brand of "fortified" wine — boosted by 190-proof brandy — and named it Richards Wild Irish Rose after his son Richard.

The company slowly expanded buying a number of small wineries in the 1960s and 1970s. It went public in 1973 changing its name to Canandaigua Wine. A year later the company expanded to the West Coast thus gaining access to the growing varietal market.

Canandaigua continued to grow through acquisitions and new product introductions in the early 1980s. In 1984 when wine coolers became popular the company introduced Sun Country Coolers doubling sales to $173 million by 1986.

The short-lived wine cooler fad made Canandaigua realize that its distribution network could handle more volume so it began looking for additional brands. After a flurry of acquisitions in the late 80s and 90s the company changed its name in 1997 to Canandaigua Brands.

Founder Marvin Sands died in 1999. His son Richard who had been CEO since 1993 succeeded his father as chairman. In 2000 the firm changed its name to Constellation Brands.

In June 2013 Constellation Brands completed its acquisition of Grupo Modelo's US beer business from Anheuser-Busch InBev for approximately $5.23 billion. The transaction included full ownership of Crown Imports LLC which provided Constellation with complete independent control of all aspects of the US commercial business; a state-of-the-art brewery in Nava (Piedras Negras) Mexico; and an exclusive perpetual brand license in the US to import market and sell Corona and the Modelo brands. The deal gave Constellation ownership of six of the top 20 imported beer brands in the US.

EXECUTIVES

President And Ceo, Robert S. (Rob) Sands, age 59, $1,310,383 total compensation

Evp And Coo, William A. (Bill) Newlands, age 59

Evp And General Counsel, Thomas J. (Tom) Mullin, age 67, $497,663 total compensation

Evp And President Beer, F. Paul Hetterich, age 55, $600,000 total compensation

Evp And President Wine And Spirits Division, Christopher (Chris) Stenzel, age 50

Evp And Chairman Beer, William F. (Bill) Hackett, age 66, $607,046 total compensation

Svp And Cio, Joseph D. (Joe) Bruhin

Evp And Chief Human Resources Officer, Thomas M. (Tom) Kane, age 57

Evp And Cfo, David Klein, age 54, $600,000 total compensation

Vice President Latin America, Erwin Petznek

Vice President Strategic Accounts, Mark Elder

Vp Digital Marketing, Karena Breslin

Vice President General Manager, Glenn Workman

Vice President Human Resources, Melina Param

Vice President And Legal Counsel Beer Division Mexico, Abdon Hernandez

Vice President And Controller, Deb Price

Senior Vice President Public Affairs, Ginny Clark

Vice President Strategic Accounts, Phil Parker

Vice President Financial Services, Paula Fitzgerald

Vice President Assistant Treasurer, Sandy Dominach

Senior Vice President General Manager, John Clemens

Vice President Engineering, Michael Drewel

Svp Ir, Patty Yahn-urlaub

Vice President Sales, Marty McCafferty

Vice President Facilities Management, Nikki Wojtalewicz

Senior Vice President Operations, Martin Van Der Merwe

Senior Vice President Operations Services, John Kester

National Account Manager, Chris Beletti

National Account Manager, Eric Ramey

National Account Manager, Paul Hays

Vice President Of Financial, Elizabeth Choate

Svp Bi, Julian Cohen

Senior Vice President Corporate Affairs, Jim Ryan

Vice President National Accounts, Shawn Keller

Executive Vice President Business Development, Tom Wyness

National Account Manager, Fred Ashenbrenner

Vice President Asia Middle East And Africa Technical Innovation And Head Greater China Research And Development, Julie Bassett

Vice President Of Sales, William Renspie

Vice President And Associate General Counsel, K Kristann Carey

Vice President Europe, Tim Fogarty

Senior Vice President Sales, Matt Deegan

National Account Manager, Matt Pinchera

Vice President Associate General Counsel, Tiffanie De Liberty

Senior Vice President, Bert Silk
Chairman, Richard Sands, age 67
Auditors: KPMG LLP

LOCATIONS

HQ: Constellation Brands Inc
  207 High Point Drive, Building 100, Victor, NY 14564
Phone: 585 678-7100
Web: www.cbrands.com

2017 Sales

	$ mil.	% of total
US	6,807	93
International	523	7
Total	**7,331**	**100**

PRODUCTS/OPERATIONS

2017 Sales

	$ mil.	% of total
Beer	4,229	58
Wine	2,739	37
Spirit	362	5
Total	**7,331**	**100**

Selected Subsidiaries and Operations

Constellation Spirits Inc.
Constellation Wines U.S.
Crown Imports LLC (beer)
Vincor International Inc. (wine Canada)

Selected Brands

Wine
  Black Box
  Clos du Bois
  Estancia
  Franciscan Estate
  Inniskillin
  Kim Crawford
  Mark West
  Mount Veeder
  Nobil
  Robert Mondavi
  Ruffino
  SIMI
  Wild Horse
Beer
  Corona Extra
  Corona Light
  Modelo Especial
  Negra Modelo
  Pacifico
Spirits
  SVEDKA Vodka

COMPETITORS

Andrew Peller	Lion
Anheuser-Busch InBev	MillerCoors
Bacardi	Patrón Spirits
Beam Suntory	Pernod Ricard
Boston Beer	SABMiller
Bronco Wine Co.	Scheid Vineyards
Brown-Forman	Sebastiani Vineyards
Carlsberg	Taittinger
Diageo	Terlato Wine
E. & J. Gallo	Treasury Wine Estates
GIV	Trinchero Family
Halewood	Estates
Heineken	W.J. Deutsch
Jackson Family Wines	Willamette Valley
Korbel	Vineyards
LVMH	Wine Group

HISTORICAL FINANCIALS

Company Type: Public

Income Statement

FYE: February 28

	REVENUE ($ mil.)	NET INCOME ($ mil.)	NET PROFIT MARGIN	EMPLOYEES
02/18	7,585	2,318	30.6%	9,600
02/17	7,331	1,535	20.9%	8,700
02/16	6,548	1,054	16.1%	9,000
02/15	6,028	839	13.9%	7,200
02/14	4,867	1,943	39.9%	6,300
Annual Growth	**11.7%**	**4.5%**	**—**	**11.1%**

2018 Year-End Financials

Debt ratio: 49.60%	No. of shares (mil.): 191
Return on equity: 31.05%	Dividends
Cash ($ mil.): 90	Yield: 0.9%
Current ratio: 1.79	Payout: 18.0%
Long-term debt ($ mil.): 9,417	Market value ($ mil.): 41,223

	STOCK PRICE ($) FY Close	P/E High/Low		PER SHARE ($) Earnings	Dividends	Book Value
02/18	215.48	19	13	11.55	2.08	42.06
02/17	158.81	22	18	7.52	1.60	35.41
02/16	141.43	28	20	5.18	1.24	32.89
02/15	114.72	26	18	4.17	0.00	29.66
02/14	81.03	8	4	9.83	0.00	26.02
Annual Growth	**27.7%**	**—**	**—**	**4.1%**	**—**	**12.8%**

Consumers Energy Co.

Consumers Energy Company makes sure that energy consumers in Michigan have the power to crank up their heaters and the gas to fire up their stoves. The company's operating area includes all 68 counties of Michigan's lower peninsula. All told Consumers Energy (the primary operating unit of CMS Energy) has a generating capacity of more than 5600 MW (primarily fossil-fueled) and distributes electricity to 1.8 million customers and natural gas to 1.8 million customers. Included in the utility's arsenal of power production is electricity generated from coal natural gas wind and hydroelectric power plants. Utility customers are a mix of residential commercial and diversified industrial clients.

Operations

Consumers Energy is the regulated utility subsidiary of CMS Energy.

Electric utility operations (70% of revenue) include the generation purchase distribution and sale of electricity. It owns some dozen power generation facilities and purchased some 2700 MW from third parties. It shuttered seven of its smaller coal-fired plants in 2016 and is replacing some of the lost capacity with gas-fired facilities. The company's electric distribution system has more than 60000 miles of electric lines.

Its gas utility operations (30%) include the purchase transmission storage distribution and sale of natural gas. The gas distribution system delivers roughly 350 billion cubic feet of natural gas per year

Geographic Reach

Consumers provides electric service to 275 cities and villages in 61 counties in Michigan. Principal cities served are Battle Creek Bay City Cadillac Flint Grand Rapids Jackson Kalamazoo Midland Muskegon and Saginaw.

Consumers gas business purchases about 5% of its gas from Canadian sources and the rest from US suppliers including several along the US Gulf Coast. It serves a 13000-square mile area that includes more than 200 cities and villages. More than one half of its customers are in metro Detroit.

Sales and Marketing

The company serves 1.8 million electric customers and 1.8 million gas customers in Michigan's Lower Peninsula.

The company serves residential commercial industrial and other customers. Though it is a regulated utility Consumers Energy is open to electricity competition in its service area at a rate of up to 10% of its previous year?s retail sales. Gas competition also exists from Gulf Coast companies as well as alternative fuels such as propane oil and electricity.

Financial Performance

Consumers Energy's overall revenue decreased by almost 2% (reflecting lower gas prices and sales volumes) in 2016 to $6.1 billion and its net income increased by about 4% to $616 million.

From a net income perspective electric operating revenues increased by $122 million reflecting $91 million from rate increases and a $62 million increase in sales due to favorable weather. These increases were partially offset by a $25 million net decrease in securitization revenue and a $6 million drop in other revenue.

Gas operating revenue increased by $15 million reflecting $33 million from a 2016 rate increase offset partially by an $18 million decrease in sales due to milder winter weather.

Net cash provided by operating activities dropped from $1.8 million to $1.7 million. This decline was due to lower customer collections offset partially by higher income tax payments to CMS Energy lower post-retirement benefits contributions and higher net income.

Strategy

Addressing new regulatory mandates Consumers is making big changes its energy generation mix mostly from coal to natural gas. In 2016 after retiring seven of its smaller coal-fired plants (representing 950 MW of capacity) the percent of power coming from the black commodity dropped from 79% to 58%. That same year Consumers adjusted a Power Purchase Agreement (PPA) with an Entergy nuclear plant to terminate the agreement in May 2018 four years ahead of schedule. The lost capacity will be replaced with the output of Consumers? 2015-acquired 540 MW gas-fueled plant in Jackson MI along with a reduction in consumer demand updated PPA agreements and power from renewable energy sources.

Consumers informed state regulators in 2017 that it is interested in acquiring an additional gas-fired electricity plant in Michigan. As well the utility broke ground on its third wind energy project Cross Winds Energy Park II in Tuscola County. Phase I is expected to have 19 turbines capable of generating 44 MW of electricity and will commence service in early 2018. When completed it will have more than 80 wind turbines and 155 MW of energy production (enough to serve 60000 residents).

Consumers gas business is working on a $610 million 5-year project to replace 78 miles of gas pipe dating to the 1940s and located in Saginaw Genesee and Oakland counties. Construction began in mid-2017 and will continue until the end of 2022. Additional capital is being deployed to address anticipated growth installing new pipes to serve an increase of nearly 8000 new business customers and 2500 residential customers in its service area.

To improve its bottom line and the efficiency of its operations and in an effort to stem the tide of commercial and residential customers jumping

ship for other electricity providers Consumers Energy is looking at options to reform its rate structures.

The company is being guided by its "Balanced Energy Initiative" a comprehensive 20 year plan (introduced in 2007). The plan calls for the utility to develop new power plants increase the efficiency of its operations and expand its renewable energy projects.

Consumers anticipates a continued rise in industrial production in its service territory will drive its total electric deliveries to increase annually by 0.5% through 2021. Excluding the impacts of energy efficiency programs the company expects its total electric deliveries to increase by 1% a year over the same time period. It also expects that its gas deliveries will remain stable through 2021 reflecting growth in gas demand being offset by energy efficiency and conservation activities.

The company's planned base capital investments of $4.6 billion in 2017 include $2.6 billion to preserve electric utility reliability and capacity and $2 billion at the gas utility to sustain the delivery system and enhance pipeline integrity.

Between 2012 and 2017 the company installed smart meters (advanced meters that allow customers to have better control over their energy use) across its electric power distribution system.

EXECUTIVES

Evp And Cfo, Thomas J. (Tom) Webb, age 66, $695,000 total compensation

Svp Energy Resources, Daniel J. (Dan) Malone, age 57, $465,000 total compensation

Svp, John M. Butler, age 54, $470,000 total compensation

Svp Customer Experience And Cio, Brian F. Rich, age 43

President And Ceo, Patricia K. (Patti) Poppe, age 50, $430,000 total compensation

President Electric And Gas, John G. Russell, age 61

Auditors: PricewaterhouseCoopers LLP

LOCATIONS

HQ: Consumers Energy Co.
One Energy Plaza, Jackson, MI 49201
Phone: 517 788-0550
Web: www.consumersenergy.com

PRODUCTS/OPERATIONS

2016 Sales

	$ mil.	% of total
Electric	4,379	72
Gas	1,685	28
Total	**6,064**	**100**

COMPETITORS

DTE Electric	SEMCO ENERGY
DTE Gas Company	We Energies
Indiana Michigan Power	Xcel Energy

HISTORICAL FINANCIALS

Company Type: Public

Income Statement   FYE: December 31

	REVENUE ($ mil.)	NET INCOME ($ mil.)	NET PROFIT MARGIN	EMPLOYEES
12/17	6,222	632	10.2%	7,496
12/16	6,064	616	10.2%	7,366
12/15	6,165	594	9.6%	7,394
12/14	6,800	567	8.3%	7,388
12/13	6,321	534	8.4%	7,435
Annual Growth	**(0.4%)**	**4.3%**	**—**	**0.2%**

2017 Year-End Financials

Debt ratio: 29.32%	No. of shares (mil.): 84
Return on equity: 10.17%	Dividends
Cash ($ mil.): 44	Yield: 0.0%
Current ratio: 0.92	Payout: 82.8%
Long-term debt ($ mil.): 5,652	Market value ($ mil.): 8,743

	STOCK PRICE ($) FY Close	P/E High/Low	PER SHARE ($) Earnings	Dividends	Book Value
12/17	103.96	— —	(0.00)	4.50	77.15
12/16	102.90	— —	(0.00)	4.50	70.62
12/15	97.00	— —	(0.00)	4.50	65.95
12/14	104.51	— —	(0.00)	4.50	62.75
12/13	96.32	— —	(0.00)	4.50	57.75
Annual Growth	**1.9%**	**— —**	**—**	**(0.0%)**	**7.5%**

Core Mark Holding Co Inc

Smokes and snacks are at the center of Core-Mark Holding's cosmos. The company distributes packaged consumables (including cigarettes and other tobacco products candy snacks grocery items perishables nonalcoholic beverages and health and beauty aids) to about 43000 convenience stores; mass merchandisers; supermarkets; and drug liquor and specialty retailers. Cigarettes and other tobacco products are its top sellers generating about 80% of net sales. Core-Mark serves customers in all 50 US states as well as five Canadian provinces. Its 10 biggest clients (which include Murphy U.S.A Couche-Tard and CST Brands) contribute about 45% of sales.

Operations

Core-Mark supplies its customers with consumable items from a network of nearly 30 distribution centers in the US and Canada. It also operates dedicated facilities for its largest customers Couche-Tard and CST Brands in Phoenix and San Antonio respectively.

The company also conducts marketing research to provide its convenience store customer base with consumer and market insight it might otherwise be unable to obtain.

Geographic Reach

South San Francisco California -based Core-Mark operates in the US where it generates more than 90% of its revenue. The company's remaining revenue of about 10% comes from Canada.

The company operates a network of about 28 distribution centers in the US and Canada (excluding two distribution facilities it operates as a third party logistics provider). Of its distribution centers around 25 are located in the US and the rest are located in Canada.

Sales and Marketing

Canadian convenience store operator Murphy U.S.A is Core-Mark's largest customer representing around 12% of sales while Alimentation Couche-Tard Inc accounted around 11%.

The company's primary customer base consists of traditional convenience stores as well as alternative outlets selling consumer packaged goods. Its traditional convenience store customers include many of the major national and super-regional convenience store operators as well as independently owned convenience stores. Its alternative outlet customers comprise a variety of store formats including grocery stores drug stores liquor stores cigarette and tobacco shops hotel gift shops military exchanges college and corporate campuses casinos hardware stores airport concessions and other specialty and small format stores that carry convenience products.

Its trucking fleet consists of around 2000 tractors trailers trucks and vans. More than 95% of its trailers were tri-temp with the remainder capable of delivering refrigerated and non-refrigerated foods.

Financial Performance

Core-Mark's net sales increased 31.3% in fiscal 2016 or $34 billion to $14.5 billion compared to $11 billion for 2015. The increase in net sales was driven primarily by market share gains including the addition of Murphy U.S.A. the acquisition of Pine State Convenience (Pine State) in June 2016 and the continued success of Core-Mark's core strategies.

Core-Mark's gross profit increased $99.0 million in fiscal 2016 or 15.5% to $736.9 million from $637.9 million in 2015 driven primarily by the increase in sales. Gross profit margin was 5.1% of total net sales in fiscal 2016 compared to 5.8% in 2015. The decrease in gross profit margin was due primarily to market share gains including the addition of Murphy U.S.A.

The company's operating expenses in fiscal 2016 increased 17.3% or $95.6 million to $646.8 million from $551.2 million in 2015. Increases in the amount of cubic feet of product handled incremental customer deliveries the acquisition of Pine State and costs related to the on-boarding of significant new customers contributed to higher operating expenses in 2016.

Core-Mark's net income in fiscal 2016 was $54.2 million compared to $51.5 million in 2015. Despite the strong revenue and net income in fiscal 2016 the company ended the year with negative cash from operations.

Strategy

During fiscal 2016 Core-Mark's continued to grow its market share and increase its food/nonfood sales and gross profit through its core strategies including its Vendor Consolidation Initiative (VCI) leveraging its ?Fresh? product solutions and providing category management expertise in order to make our customers more relevant and profitable.

Core-Mark's business model is to increase supply chain efficiency for convenience stores. It does this by consolidating the numerous daily deliveries from disparate product segments received by convenience stores into multiple unified weekly deliveries of the bulk of their products.

The company is leaning more towards fresh produce which has a higher margin and strong growth potential as consumers buy more fresh food and dairy products from convenience stores. To keep perishables fresh on the way to market the company has an upgraded refrigerated capacity chilling docks and other systems designed to deliver fresh goods quickly.

The company's Focused Marketing Initiative conducts marketing research to provide its customers with consumer insight. It is Core-Mark's interest for its customers to generate sales growth.

Mergers and Acquisitions

To grow market share and extend its geographic reach Core-Mark has been active on the acquisition front. In June 2016 Core-Mark acquired Convenience Division of Pine State Trading Company for $88 million. Based in Gardiner Maine Pine State markets and distributes convenience and beverage products. The acquisition widened Core-Mark's geographic footprint in an area where it has a limited presence and offered Pine State customers a new spectrum of products and marketing programs.

In 2015 Core-Mark paid $8 million for the assets of Karrys Bros a regional distributor in Ontario and surrounding provinces.

Company Background

The company's roots reach back to 1888 when it was known as Glaser Bros. a family-run candy and tobacco distribution business in San Francisco.

EXECUTIVES

Svp And Cfo, Christopher M. (Chris) Miller, age 57, $312,885 total compensation
President And Coo, Scott E. McPherson, age 48, $296,640 total compensation
Ceo And Director, Thomas B. Perkins, age 59, $515,412 total compensation
President Core-mark Canada, Eric J. Rolheiser, age 47
Svp Us Distribution-west, Christopher K. (Chris) Hobson, age 49, $270,375 total compensation
Svp Us Distribution East, William G. Stein, age 48, $263,718 total compensation
Chairman, Randolph I. Thornton, age 72
Ceo And Director, Thomas B. Perkins, age 59
Auditors: Deloitte & Touche LLP

LOCATIONS

HQ: Core Mark Holding Co Inc
395 Oyster Point Boulevard, Suite 415, South San Francisco, CA 94080
Phone: 650 589-9445
Web: www.core-mark.com

2016 Sales

	$ mil.	% of total
United States	13,133	91
Canada	1,356	9
Corporate	40	—
Total	**14,529**	**100**

PRODUCTS/OPERATIONS

2016 Sales

	$ mil.	% of total
Cigarettes	10,335	71
Food	1,422	10
Candy	620	3
Fresh	389	4
Other tobacco products	1,133	8
Health beauty & general	446	3
Beverages	176	1
Equipment/other	4	—
Total	**14,529**	**100**

COMPETITORS

800-JR Cigar	H. T. Hackney
AMCON Distributing	McLane
Associated Food	Roundy's
BJ's Wholesale Club	SUPERVALU
C&S Wholesale	Sam's Club
Coca-Cola	Southern Glazer's Wine
Costco Wholesale	and Spirits
Eby-Brown	Stephenson Wholesale
Frito-Lay	Company
GSC Enterprises	Wal-Mart

HISTORICAL FINANCIALS

Company Type: Public

Income Statement				FYE: December 31
	REVENUE ($ mil.)	NET INCOME ($ mil.)	NET PROFIT MARGIN	EMPLOYEES
12/17	15,687	33	0.2%	8,413
12/16	14,529	54	0.4%	7,688
12/15	11,069	51	0.5%	6,655
12/14	10,280	42	0.4%	5,933
12/13	9,767	41	0.4%	5,617
Annual Growth	**12.6%**	**(5.3%)**	**—**	**10.6%**

2017 Year-End Financials

Debt ratio: 28.77%
Return on equity: 6.18%
Cash ($ mil.): 41
Current ratio: 2.13
Long-term debt ($ mil.): 512

No. of shares (mil.): 46
Dividends
Yield: 0.0%
Payout: 51.3%
Market value ($ mil.): 1,458

	STOCK PRICE ($) FY Close	P/E High/Low		PER SHARE ($) Earnings	Dividends	Book Value
12/17	31.58	60	37	0.72	0.37	12.03
12/16	43.07	79	28	1.17	0.33	11.48
12/15	81.94	81	47	1.11	0.28	10.71
12/14	61.93	101	47	0.92	0.23	9.99
12/13	75.93	84	51	0.90	0.20	9.42
Annual Growth	**(19.7%)**	**—**	**—**	**(5.3%)**	**17.0%**	**6.3%**

Corning Inc

The source of Corning Inc.'s revenue is transparently obvious: it's glass. Once known for kitchenware and lab products the company makes glass ceramic and other components for the consumer electronics telecommunications automotive and life sciences industries. Its products include substrates for flat-panel displays and computer monitors optical fiber and cable substrates and filters for automotive emissions control products labware and scientific equipment and glass and optical materials for a wide range of industries. Corning operates about 100 manufacturing and processing facilities in nearly 20 countries. More than half of its sales come from the Asia/Pacific region.

Operations

Corning operates in five segments. Its largest Display Technologies accounts for about a third of sales and includes glass substrates for flat-panel liquid crystal displays. Optical Communications which includes fiber and cable and other components for the telecom industry also brings in about a third of sales. The Specialty Materials business about an eighth of sales is powered by superstar product Gorilla Glass which is used in consumer electronics devices such as notebook computers mobile phones and TVs.

Other Corning segments are Environmental Technologies (substrates and filters for automotive and diesel products) and Life Sciences (glass and plastic equipment for labs and other scientific applications) which each account for about 10% of sales.

Geographic Reach

Corning?s customers based in the US generate 30% of its revenue followed by China and South Korea which account for more than 20% and about 15% of sales respectively. The Asia-Pacific region accounts more than half of revenue.

The company operates manufacturing facilities in three US states and in Europe Brazil China India Australia and Israel.

Sales and Marketing

Corning has a concentrated set of customers with two or three accounting for about half or more of revenue in four of the company?s five segments. Among its biggest customers are Korean LCD panel makers including Samsung Display Co. (11% of revenue) and LG Display Co.

Financial Performance

Corning Inc. displayed a 3% revenue increase to about $9.4 billion in 2016 with growth in each segment but Environmental Technologies. The biggest increase 5% was in Display Technologies boosted by a volume increase and a stronger Japanese yen. The Optical Segment?s sales were slowed in the first half of the year by problems with new manufacturing software. The company also reported higher sales of Gorilla Glass 5 and advanced optics products. Slower sales of diesel products in the US automotive market helped reduce sales for Environmental Technologies.

The company?s profit for 2016 was $3.7 billion a 175% increase from 2015. Corning realized a $2.7 billion gain from a tax adjustment on the strategic realignment of its ownership in Dow Corning in 2016. On the operations side net income from the Display Technologies segment dropped 15% because of lower LCD glass prices.

Cash generated by operations fell to $2.5 billion in 2016 from $2.8 billion in 2015 on an increase in accounts receivable in the Optical Communications and Specialty Materials segments. That was somewhat offset by an increase in accounts payable and other current liabilities.

Strategy

Corning Inc. thinks that the Glass Age is at hand — and on the desk and on the wall and in the car. It's got a point: People interact with technology through a glass screen whether to view or touch or both. The company's R&D process came up with Gorilla Glass its protective cover glass used in thousands of consumer products such as cell phones computers and TVs. The company will keep up the R&D tradition by pumping $10 billion into the search for and development of new products. It will look for advances in products for optical communications mobile consumer electronics displays automotive and life sciences vessels.

Corning continues its drive into the automotive market beginning production of its first windshield sunroof and backlite windows in 2016. Beyond customer contact areas Corning makes gas particulate filters for automotive engines.

Getting into the automotive market could blunt Corning?s biggest weakness: Concentration of customers. Three customers for its Display Technologies segment generated about two-thirds of the unit?s while three customers account for more than 50% of sales for Specialty Materials. To find even more room in vehicles the company has formed a joint venture with Saint-Gobain Sekurit normally one of its many competitors to produce lightweight auto glazing that could be use throughout a vehicle.

In automotive as well as other markets Corning faces stiff competition. Asahi Glass Company one of Corning's key competitors has entered the automotive market even building a plant for automotive glass in Mexico.

Mergers and Acquisitions

Corning Inc.?s recent acquisitions have been made to strengthen its Optical Communications business. In late 2017 the company agreed to acquire 3M's Communications Markets Division which consists of optical fiber and copper passive connectivity tools for about $900 million. The 3M operations will be part of Corning's Optical Communications unit. The 3M assets expand Corning's reach in global markets and its high-bandwidth portfolio. The deal is expected to close in 2018.

Also in 2017 the company acquired SpiderCloud Wireless Inc. a provider of in-building wireless technologies. SpiderCloud?s products would help extend the Corning?s fiber optic cables in building networks.

In 2016 Corning acquired Stran Technologies which makes interconnect products for use in harsh environments. Besides adding to its product line the deal gives Corning greater exposure to military and aerospace and oil and gas customers.

In another 2016 deal Corning acquired Alliance Fiber Optic Products which makes high-performance passive optical components for cloud data center operators and data communications and telecommunications OEMs.

EXECUTIVES

Chairman And Ceo, Wendell P. Weeks, age 59, $1,337,740 total compensation
Vice Chairman And Corporate Development Officer, Lawrence D. (Larry) McRae, age 60, $731,971 total compensation
Svp And Cfo, R. Tony Tripeny, age 59, $504,808 total compensation
Evp And Corning Innovation Officer, Martin J. (Marty) Curran, age 59
Evp Corning Optical Telecommunications, Clark S. Kinlin, age 58
President Corning Glass Technologies (cgt), James P. Clappin, age 61, $686,538 total compensation
Evp Corning Technologies And International, Eric S. Musser, age 59
Evp And Cto, David L. Morse, age 66, $631,010 total compensation
Vice President Flat Glass Photovoltaics Program, Marc Giroux
Vice President New Opportunity Development New Business Development, Robert Ritchie
Vice President Of Sales, Allen Smith
Vice President Of Sales, Eric Marinakis
Vice President Of Product Management, Jeff Kunst
Senior Vice President And Chief Strategy Officer, Jeffrey Evenson
Vice President Of Chemical Engineering, Thomas Capek
Senior Vice President, Alan Eusden
Vice President, Adriane Brown
Vice President Of Communications, Joe Dunning
Senior Vice President Global Benefits And Compensation, John P MacMahon
Senior Vice President, David Bassett
Division Vice President And Director Of Strategy And Marketing, John Geniviva
Senior Vice President Of Sales, Rodney Lewis
Vice President Corporate Controller, Ed Schlesinger
Vice President Commercial Technology, Bill Cune
Vice President Marketing And Technical Support, Dave Purwin
Vice President And Gm Corning Life Sciences, Richard Eglen
Vice President, David Watson
Senior Vice President And General Manager, Mike Bell
Chairman And Ceo, Wendell P. Weeks, age 59
Vice Chairman And Corporate Development Officer, Lawrence D. (Larry) McRae, age 60
Treasurer, Lee Starnes
Board Member, Lisa Emel
Us Treasurer, Ida Meadows
Secretary, Kathy McClure
Auditors: PricewaterhouseCoopers LLP

LOCATIONS

HQ: Corning Inc
   One Riverfront Plaza, Corning, NY 14831
Phone: 607 974-9000
Web: www.corning.com

2017 Sales

	$ mil.	% of total
North America		
United States	3,146	31
Canada	287	3
Mexico	27	1
Asia Pacific		
Japan	455	4
Taiwan	846	8
China	2,230	22
Korea	1,286	13
Other	378	4
Europe		
Germany	426	4
Other	701	7
All other	334	3
Total	10,116	100

PRODUCTS/OPERATIONS

2017 Sales

	$ mil.	% of total
Optical Communications	3,545	35
Display Technologies	2,997	30
Specialty Materials	1,403	14
Environmental Technologies	1,106	11
Life Sciences	879	9
All Other	186	1
Total	**10,116**	**100**

Selected Products

Display technologies
   Liquid crystal displays (LCD)
   Organic light-emitting diode (OLED) displays
Telecommunications
   Optical fiber and cable
   Optical networking components
Environmental technologies
   Industrial and stationary emissions products
   Mobile emissions and automotive catalytic converter products
Life sciences
   Genomics and laboratory equipment
Specialty Materials
   Gorilla Glass
Other
   Polarized glass
   Semiconductor materials

COMPETITORS

3M	Nippon Electric Glass
Alcatel-Lucent	Nippon Sheet Glass
Amphenol	Nortel Networks
Asahi Glass	Oerlikon
Becton Dickinson	Prysmian
Belden	SCHOTT
Carl-Zeiss-Stiftung	SWCC SHOWA
CommScope	Saint-Gobain
DENSO	Shin-Etsu Chemical
Dai Nippon Printing	Sumitomo Electric
Fujikura Ltd.	Superior Essex
Furukawa Electric	TE Connectivity
General Cable	Thermo Fisher
Heraeus Holding	Scientific
Hoya Corp.	Thomas & Betts
IBIDEN	Toppan Printing
NGK INSULATORS	Viavi Solutions
Nikon	

HISTORICAL FINANCIALS

Company Type: Public

Income Statement

FYE: December 31

	REVENUE ($ mil.)	NET INCOME ($ mil.)	NET PROFIT MARGIN	EMPLOYEES
12/17	10,116	(497)	—	46,200
12/16	9,390	3,695	39.4%	40,700
12/15	9,111	1,339	14.7%	35,700
12/14	9,715	2,472	25.4%	34,600
12/13	7,819	1,961	25.1%	30,400
Annual Growth	6.7%	—	—	11.0%

2017 Year-End Financials

Debt ratio: 18.65%
Return on equity: (-2.96%)
Cash ($ mil.): 4,317
Current ratio: 2.75
Long-term debt ($ mil.): 4,749
No. of shares (mil.): 858
Dividends
   Yield: 0.0%
   Payout: —
Market value ($ mil.): 27,447

	STOCK PRICE ($) FY Close	P/E High/Low		PER SHARE ($) Earnings	Dividends	Book Value
12/17	31.99	—	—	(0.66)	0.62	18.30
12/16	24.27	7	5	3.23	0.54	19.32
12/15	18.28	25	16	1.00	0.48	16.63
12/14	22.93	13	9	1.73	0.40	16.94
12/13	17.82	13	9	1.34	0.39	15.13
Annual Growth	15.8%	—	—	—	12.3%	4.9%

Costco Wholesale Corp

Operating more than 760 membership warehouse stores Costco is the nation's largest wholesale club operator (ahead of Wal-Mart's SAM'S CLUB). Primarily under the Costco Wholesale banner it serves nearly 95 million cardholders in 44 US states Washington DC and Puerto Rico and some 10 other countries. Stores offer discount prices on an average of about 3700 products (many in bulk packaging) ranging from alcoholic beverages and appliances to fresh food pharmaceuticals and tires. Certain club memberships also offer products and services such as car and home insurance real estate services and travel packages. Costco generates most of its sales in the US.

Operations

Costco generates revenue from five major product categories: food & sundries hardlines fresh food softlines and ancillary. It generates about 40% of its revenue from food & sundries which includes dry and packaged foods groceries snacks candy alcoholic and nonalcoholic beverages and cleaning supplies. Another 15% each stem from hardlines (major appliances electronics hardware garden & patio items) and fresh foods (meat produce deli bakery). Softline product sales (apparel and small appliances) account for about 10% of sales with the ancillary gas and pharmacy operations bringing in the last 20%.

To shop at Costco customers must be members — a policy the company believes reinforces customer loyalty and provides a steady source of fee revenue (to the tune of about 2% of yearly sales). Three types of annual memberships are available: Business ($60 each); Gold Star ($60 for individuals and their spouses); and Executive ($120 allows members to purchase products and services including insurance mortgage services and long-distance phone service at reduced rates). Costco also operates the e-commerce site costco.com which offers products not found in its stores.

Geographic Reach

More than 70% of Costco's revenues come from the US while about 15% stem from Canada. The majority of its stores are located in the US and Puerto Rico although about 100 are in Canada. Other markets include Mexico the UK Japan Korea Taiwan Australia France Iceland and Spain. Costco operates in Taiwan and Korea through majority-owned subsidiaries.

Sales and Marketing

Costco uses several marketing and promotional tactics to reach existing and prospective members. It typically promotes new warehouse openings sends direct mail pieces to potential new members and employs a regular direct-marketing program. The program which targets existing members to promote selected merchandise consists of The Costco Connection magazine coupon mailers handouts and promotional emails to members.

The company sells products in China through Alibaba's Tmall site. Other e-commerce businesses such as Google Express Instacart and Jet.com offer Costco products for delivery via their online services.

Financial Performance

Costco's revenues and profits have seen strong growth over the past several years as the company has expanded its store count and in-store amenities. Revenue is up 25% since fiscal 2014 (ended August) and net income is up more than 50%.

In fiscal 2018 the company reported revenue of $142 billion up 10% from the prior year driven by sales at newly opened warehouses and a 9% spike in comparable sales. Changes in gasoline prices contributed positively thanks to an 19% increase in the average sales price per gallon. In addition membership fees increased by 10% in 2018 due to membership sign-ups at existing and new warehouses and an annual fee increase.

Net income that year jumped 17% to $3.1 billion primarily due to the higher revenues as well as a jump in interest income.

Cash at the end of fiscal 2018 was $6 billion an increase of about $1.5 billion from the prior year. Cash from operations contributed $5.8 billion to the coffers while investing activities used $2.9 billion mainly for property and equipment. Financing activities used another $1.3 billion primarily for stock buyback and dividends paid.

Strategy

Costco aims to offer its members a broad range of high-quality merchandise at consistently lower prices than they can find elsewhere. To keep inventory costs low its merchandising strategy is to limit certain items to fast-selling models sizes and colors. By doing this Costco is able to limit its number of stock keeping units (SKUs) to about 3700 per warehouse enabling it to hold significantly fewer items than other discount retailers supermarkets and supercenters. Its product lines are not static however as it continues to expand its own Kirkland Signature brand (which grew more than 10% in fiscal 2018).

Along with merchandise management Costco is focused on expansion. It has opened more than 100 new wholesale clubs in the last five years and has plans for about 25 new locations in 2019 including its first store in China. In addition the company has plans to relocate four warehouses in 2019 to more ideal spots within existing markets and it continues to add gas stations and other ancillary services to existing locations.

As is the case with many retailers the warehouse giant is also investing in digital initiatives as consumer preferences and technological advancements alter the landscape. The company's ecommerce sales jumped more than 30% in fiscal 2018 amid improved online ordering capabilities ecommerce product showcases and grocery delivery. Continued focus here is key for Costco as the competition is intense from traditional warehouse clubs and grocery stores as well as discount grocers such as Aldi and of course from online behemoth Amazon.

Company Background

Price Club's first location opened in 1976 in a converted airplane hangar in San Diego. It originally served only small businesses but soon found its engine for growth by serving non-business members as well. In 1983 the first Costco warehouse location was opened in Seattle; it went public in 1985.

The two chains merged in 1993 as Price/Costco. It changed its name to Costco later that decade.

HISTORY

From 1954 to 1974 retailer Sol Price built his Fed-Mart discount chain into a $300 million behemoth selling general merchandise to government employees. Price sold the company to Hugo Mann in 1975 and the next year with son Robert Rick Libenson and Giles Bateman opened the first Price Club warehouse in San Diego to sell in volume to small businesses at steep discounts.

Posting a large loss its first year prompted Price Club's decision to expand membership to include government utility and hospital employees as well as credit union members. In 1978 it opened a second store in Phoenix. With the help of his father Sol's other son Laurence began a chain of tire-mounting stores (located adjacent to Price Club outlets on land leased from the company and using tires sold by the Price Clubs).

The company went public in 1980 with four stores in California and Arizona. Price Club moved into the eastern US with its 1984 opening of a store in Virginia and continued to expand including a joint venture with Canadian retailer Steinberg in 1986 to operate stores in Canada; the first Canadian warehouse opened that year in Montreal.

Two years later Price Club acquired A. M. Lewis (grocery distributor Southern California and Arizona) and the next year it opened two Price Club Furnishings offering discounted home and office furniture.

Price Club bought out Steinberg's interest in the Canadian locations in 1990 and added stores on the East Coast and in California Colorado and British Columbia. However competition in the East from ensconced rivals such as SAM'S CLUB and PACE forced the closure of two stores two years later. A 50-50 joint venture with retailer Controladora Comercial Mexicana led to the opening of two Price Clubs in Mexico City one each in 1992 and 1993.

Price Club merged with Costco Wholesale in 1993. Founded in 1983 by Jeffrey Brotman and James Sinegal (a former EVP of Price Company) Costco Wholesale went public in 1985 and expanded into Canada.

In 1993 Price/Costco opened its first warehouse outside the Americas in a London suburb. Merger costs led to a loss the following year and Price/Costco spun off its commercial real estate operations as well as certain international operations as Price Enterprises (now Price Legacy). In 1995 the company launched its Kirkland Signature brand of private-label merchandise. Two years later the company changed its corporate name to Costco Companies.

Costco began online sales and struck a deal to buy two stores in South Korea in 1998 and opened its first store in Japan in 1999. Under industrywide pressure over the way members-only chains record fees Costco took a $118 million charge for fiscal 1999 to change accounting practices. That year the company made yet another name change to Costco Wholesale (emphasizing its core warehouse operations).

In 2000 the company purchased private retailer Littlewoods' 20% stake in Costco UK increasing Costco's ownership to 80%. Costco began expanding into the Midwest in 2001 as part of plans to open 40 new clubs a year including ones in China.

During fiscal 2002 Costco opened 29 new warehouse clubs. In December 2002 the retailer opened its first home store — called Costco Home — in Kirkland Washington stocked with mostly high-end furniture. A second Costco Home store opened in Tempe Arizona in December 2004.

Costco increased its equity interest in Costco Wholesale UK in October 2003 to 100% when it purchased Carrefour Nederland's 20% stake.

In 2006 Costco began offering more than 200 generic prescription medicines (100 count) for $10 or less. The following year Costco.com logged sales i

EXECUTIVES

Svp Operations, Roger A. Campbell

Evp Costco Wholesale Industries, Timothy L. Rose, age 65

Evp Information Systems, Paul G. Moulton, age 67, $602,519 total compensation

Evp Administration And Human Resources, Franz E. Lazarus, age 71

Evp And Coo Eastern And Canadian Divisions, Joseph P. (Joe) Portera, age 66, $645,297 total compensation

President And Ceo, W. Craig Jelinek, age 66, $699,810 total compensation

Evp And Coo Southwest And Mexico Divisions,
Dennis R. Zook, age 69, $642,618 total compensation

Evp And Cfo, Richard A. Galanti, age 62, $712,888 total compensation

Evp International, James P. (Jim) Murphy, age 65

Evp And Coo Northern Division And Midwest Region, John D. McKay, age 61

Svp And General Manager Northeast Region, Jeffrey R. Long

Svp And General Manager Midwest Region, John B. Gaherty

Svp And General Manager Mexico, Jaime Gonzalez

Evp And Coo Merchandising, Douglas W. (Doug) Schutt, age 59

Svp And General Manager Bay Area Region, Jeffrey Abadir

Svp And General Manager Northwest Region, Mario Omoss

Svp And General Manager San Diego Region, Yoram Rubanenko

Svp And General Manager Eastern Canada Region, Pierre Riel

Svp And General Manager Los Angeles Region, Caton Frates

Svp And General Manager Western Canada Region, Russ Miller

Pharmacy Manager, Hassan Awada

Vice President Of Operations, Julie Cruz

Senior Vice President E Commerce And Publishing, Don Burdick

Pharmacy Manager, Jeff Mrowczynski

Senior Executive Vice President, Richard Dicerchio

Vice President Finance Loan Ac, Joseph Cawley

Pharmacy Manager, Bill Jones

Auditors: KPMG LLP

LOCATIONS

HQ: Costco Wholesale Corp
999 Lake Drive, Issaquah, WA 98027
Phone: 425 313-8100
Web: www.costco.com

2018 Sales

	$ mil.	% of total
US	102,286	72
Canada	20,689	15
Other	18,601	13
Total	**141,576**	**100**

PRODUCTS/OPERATIONS

2018 Sales

	$ mil.	% of total
Sales	138 434	98
Membership fees	3,142	2
Total	**141,576**	**100**

2018 Sales

	% of total
Food & Sundries (dry & institutionally packaged candy snacks beverages cleaning products)	41
Hardlines (major appliances electronics health & beauty hardware garden & patio)	16
Fresh food (meat bakery deli & produce)	14
Softlines (apparel small appliances)	11
Ancillary (pharmacy fuel)	18
Total	**100**

COMPETITORS

Amazon.com	Office Depot
BJ's Wholesale Club	Safeway
Best Buy	Sam's Club
Big Lots	Staples
Dollar General	Target Corporation
Dollar Tree	Wal-Mart
Home Depot	Walgreens Boots
Kroger	

Company Type: Public

Income Statement   FYE: September 2

	REVENUE ($ mil.)	NET INCOME ($ mil.)	NET PROFIT MARGIN	EMPLOYEES
09/18	141,576	3,134	2.2%	245,000
09/17*	129,025	2,679	2.1%	231,000
08/16	118,719	2,350	2.0%	218,000
08/15	116,199	2,377	2.0%	205,000
08/14	112,640	2,058	1.8%	195,000
Annual Growth	**5.9%**	**11.1%**	**—**	**5.9%**

*Fiscal year change

2018 Year-End Financials

Debt ratio: 15.89%	No. of shares (mil.): 438
Return on equity: 26.66%	Dividends
Cash ($ mil.): 6,055	Yield: 0.0%
Current ratio: 1.02	Payout: 30.1%
Long-term debt ($ mil.): 6,487	Market value ($ mil.): 102,155

	STOCK PRICE ($) FY Close	P/E High/Low	Earnings	Dividends	Book Value
09/18	233.13	33 22	7.09	2.14	29.21
09/17*	158.24	30 23	6.08	8.90	24.65
08/16	163.93	32 26	5.33	1.70	27.61
08/15	139.95	29 22	5.37	6.51	24.24
08/14	121.08	27 23	4.65	1.33	28.11
Annual Growth	**17.8%**	**— —**	**11.1%**	**12.6%**	**1.0%**

*Fiscal year change

Coty, Inc.

For perfume giant Coty the sweet smell of success is on retail shelves worldwide. The company is one of the leading makers of fragrances and beauty products for men and women across the globe. Its lineup ranges from moderately priced scents and cosmetics sold by mass retailers to prestige fragrances and premium skincare products found in department stores and upscale boutiques. Coty also make hair and nail care products for professional salons. The company's 75-plus owned or licensed brands include some of the world's most well-known including COVERGIRL Max Factor philosophy Escada Calvin Klein and Stetson. It generates most of its revenue outside North America. With a history that dates to 1904 Coty has used acquisitions to power its growth.

Operations

Coty divides its activities among three product segments: consumer beauty luxury and professional beauty.

The consumer beauty segment accounts for about 45% of total revenue and includes color cosmetics retail hair coloring and styling products body care products and mass fragrances. Brands include Clairol CoverGirl Max Factor Rimmel and Sally Hansen.

The company generates about 35% of revenue from the prestige fragrances premium skincare and premium cosmetics of its luxury segment which includes Burberry Calvin Klein Escada and philosophy among its brands.

With brands such as Sassoon Professional and Clairol Professional Coty generates the remainder of its revenue with sales to hair and nail salons and salon professionals.

The company generates about 40% of revenue from its licensed brands.

Geographic Reach

Truly a global company Coty generates nearly 70% of revenue outside North America; Europe accounts for about 45%.

It has offices in more than 35 countries and distributes products in some 150 countries. The company's major facilities are located in Brazil China France Germany Mexico Monaco Russia Spain Switzerland Thailand the UK and the US.

Sales and Marketing

Coty's products are sold in retail stores from drug stores to prestige boutiques as well as through hair and nail salons and travel retail sales channels such as duty-free shops airlines cruise ships and other tax-free zones. The company also has an e-commerce presence which accounts for about 10% of revenue. Its top retailer Walmart accounts for about 5% of total revenue.

The company has dedicated sales and marketing teams in most of its major markets and seeks to attract customers via traditional media in-store and in-salon displays digital and social media and collaborations product placements and events. Celebrity endorsers are also key for Coty; recent ad campaigns have included Lupita Nyong'o Kate Moss Jake Gyllenhaal Gwen Stefani and Jared Leto.

Advertising and promotional costs for fiscal years 2018 2017 and 2016 were $2.2 billion $1.9 billion and nearly $1 billion respectively.

Financial Performance

Acquisitions have driven Coty's strong growth over the past five years with revenue more than doubling since fiscal 2014. Net income has been less consistent with losses in three of the last five years.

In fiscal 2018 (ended June 2018) the company reported revenue of $9.4 billion up nearly 25% from the prior year. The increase was driven almost entirely by acquisitions including the Procter & Gamble Beauty Business the Burberry Beauty Business and others. Without acquisitions its revenue rose 4% on positive impacts from pricing and foreign currency exchange translations.

Coty had a net loss that year of nearly $170 million an improvement from a loss of about $420 million in fiscal 2017. The company has net profit margins that hover in the low single digits.

Cash at the end of fiscal 2018 was $362 million a decrease of $208 million from the prior year. Cash from operations contributed $414 million to the coffers while investing activities used $688 million mainly for capital expenditures. Financing activities added $69 million as proceeds from loans slightly outweighed repayments.

Strategy

Coty's growth strategy is focused around the areas of core brands and innovation digital transformation and emerging market expansion.

The company is putting its energy and investment dollars behind its strongest brands which include some of the world's most recognizable beauty names (CoverGirl Clairol Gucci Calvin Klein Burberry) as well as the smaller brands positioned for growth (Bourjois Younique Chloe). In addition to relaunches of select brands (including the opening of a CoverGirl flagship store) it has discarded about a dozen brands (GUESS Cerruti Playboy) as part of a portfolio rationalization. With core brands as the foundation Coty is introducing new fragrance products such as Gucci Bloom Gucci Guilty and Chloe Nomade as part of its innovation initiative. The focus on stabilizing core brands is especially critical for its consumer beauty business which excluding the impact of acquisitions has been on the decline.

On the digital transformation front the company is investing in talent acquisition data and product management systems and in-house content creation capabilities as it works to grow e-commerce capabilities. Online sales rose 50% in fiscal 2018 to 10% of total revenue (excluding Younique which is an e-commerce-only business). Coty launched a digital accelerator program in mid-2018 that allows tech start-ups to present at quarterly summits and earn the opportunity to work with Coty's vendor brands. It also introduced a personal beauty assistant app for the Amazon Echo that year.

Lastly growth in emerging markets in Latin America and Asia particularly are key to Coty's strategy. An acquisition moved the company into Brazil where it continues to gain market share. Although currently a small market for Coty China is a major focus. In 2018 the company had a successful launch of the Tiffany brand in China where it also has a business partnership with Asian e-commerce giant Alibaba. Mexico and Middle East are also target markets.

Mergers and Acquisitions

Coty has kickstarted revenue added new product categories and moved into new geographies through major acquisitions over the past several years.

In 2017 it bought a majority stake in privately held Younique a peer-to-peer online cosmetics retailer for about $600 million. The move accelerates the company's e-commerce operations moves it into social selling and broadens its appeal to younger consumers. It also acquired that year long-term global licensing rights for Burberry fragrances cosmetics and skincare which will enhance its luxury segment.

In a pivotal year for Coty in 2016 it acquired premium hair-care brand ghd (Good Hair Day) for about $510 million. Also that year it purchased Procter & Gamble Company's Specialty Beauty Business and the beauty business of Hypermarcas S.A.

The P&G deal included the CoverGirl and Max Factor cosmetics brands and the Hugo Boss and Gucci fragrance brands. Valued at a hefty $11.4 billion the move bolstered Coty's market presence as a beauty products company ranking it third behind L'Oréal and Unilever. Its geographic presence was also significantly expanded. The Hypermarcas business bought for about $1 billion provided Coty with a critical mass platform in the Brazilian beauty market. Its leading brands include Monange Risqué Bozzano Paixão and Biocolor.

Company Background

Coty was founded in Paris in 1904 after François Coty created his first perfume La Rose Jacqueminot.

EXECUTIVES

President Global Markets, Edgar O. Huber
Svp General Counsel And Secretary, Jules P. Kaufman, age 60, $525,000 total compensation
Svp Global Research And Development And Chief Scientific Officer, Ralph Macchio, age 61
Chairman And Interim Ceo, Lambertus J. H. (Bart) Becht, age 61
Evp And Cfo, Patrice de Talhouet, age 52, $784,100 total compensation
Evp Supply Chain, Mario Reis, age 58, $609,560 total compensation
Evp Category Development, Camillo Pane, age 48, $592,320 total compensation
Vice President Marketing, Lori Singer
Vice President Sales Rite Aid, Maggie Handel
Vice President Research, William Wohland
National Account Manager, Sarah Rack
Senior Vice President American Fragrances Coty Prestige, Catherine Walsh
Vice President Marketing, Trent Hurst
Vice President Global Marketing (coty Presitige Skincare), Rachel Shelowitz
Vice President Corporate Finance, Jerome Estampes
Vice President Packaging Concept Development, Bernard Quennessen
Vice President Marketing, Laura Weinstein
Vice President Sales, David Russell

Vice President Sales National Accounts, Mary Van-praag
Senior Vice President Human Resources, Gtraudmarie Lacassagne
Vice President Marketing, Barry Miller
Vice President Infrastructure Services, Glen Dalgleish
Vice President Global Information Technology, Natalie Stone
Vice President Global Information Technology, Natalie Elgart
Vice President Global Public Relations Social Media And Charity (philosophy), Tiffani Carter-Thompson
Senior Vice President Of Business Development, Bryan Falcone
Vice President Field Sales, Valerie Correiro
Senior Vice President Human Resources, Raul Valentin
Vice President Human Resources, Keri-Lynne Shaw
National Account Manager, Carolyn Goodrow
Vice President Creative And Design Excellence, Joseph Salah
National Account Manager, Nancy Petro
Vice President Legal Patents, David Joyal
Chairman And Interim Ceo, Lambertus J. H. (Bart) Becht, age 61
Board Member, Paul Michaels
Auditors: DELOITTE & TOUCHE LLP

LOCATIONS

HQ: Coty, Inc.
350 Fifth Avenue, New York, NY 10118
Phone: 212 389-7300
Web: www.coty.com

2018 Sales

	$ mil.	% of total
Europe	4,201	45
North America	2,966	31
ALMEA (Asia Latin America Middle East Africa)	2,230	24
Total	**9,398**	**100**

PRODUCTS/OPERATIONS

2018 Sales

	$ mil.	% of total
Consumer Beauty	4,268	45
Luxury	3,210	34
Professional Beauty	1,919	21
Total	**9,398**	**100**

Selected Brands by Segment

Consumer Beauty
  Adidas
  Beckham
  Beyonce
  Clairol
  CoverGirl
  Jovan
  Max Factor
  Rimmel
  Sally Hansen
  Stetson
Luxury
  Balenciaga
  Burberry
  Calvin Klein
  Chloe
  Escada
  Gucci
  Joop!
  Marc Jacobs
  Miu Miu
  philosophy
  Stella McCartney
  Tiffany & Co.
Professional Beauty
  Clairol Professional
  ghd
  Kadus Professional
  Sassoon Professional
  Wella Professionals

COMPETITORS

Avon	LVMH
Body Shop	Markwins International
Chanel	Mary Kay
Elizabeth Arden Inc	Nu Skin
Estée Lauder	Parlux Fragrances
Inter Parfums	Revlon
L'Oréal	

HISTORICAL FINANCIALS

Company Type: Public

Income Statement

FYE: June 30

	REVENUE ($ mil.)	NET INCOME ($ mil.)	NET PROFIT MARGIN	EMPLOYEES
06/18	9,398	(168)	—	20,000
06/17	7,650	(422)	—	22,000
06/16	4,349	156	3.6%	10,060
06/15	4,395	232	5.3%	8,100
06/14	4,551	(97)	—	9,000
Annual Growth	**19.9%**	**—**		**22.1%**

2018 Year-End Financials

Debt ratio: 33.25%
Return on equity: (-1.86%)
Cash ($ mil.): 331
Current ratio: 0.90
Long-term debt ($ mil.): 7,305
No. of shares (mil.): 750
Dividends
  Yield: 0.0%
  Payout: —
Market value ($ mil.): 10,585

	STOCK PRICE ($) FY Close	P/E High/Low		PER SHARE ($) Earnings	Dividends	Book Value
06/18	14.10	—	—	(0.23)	0.50	11.79
06/17	18.76	—	—	(0.66)	0.65	12.45
06/16	25.99	73	48	0.44	0.25	1.07
06/15	31.97	49	24	0.64	0.20	2.69
06/14	17.13	—	—	(0.26)	0.20	2.38
Annual Growth	**(4.7%)**	**—**	**—**	**—**	**25.7%**	**49.1%**

Crown Holdings Inc

Crown Holdings is a leading global manufacturer of consumer packaging products including steel and aluminum food and beverage cans. Its portfolio includes aerosol cans and various metal vacuum closures marketed under brands Liftoff SuperEnd and Easylift as well as specialty packaging products such as novelty containers and industrial cans. Crown also supplies can-making equipment and parts. Its roster of customers has included Coca-Cola SC Johnson Unilever and Procter & Gamble which owns Gillette another customer.Crown traces its historical roots all the way back to 1892.

Operations

Crown is focused on growing on a global scale and has divided its business along geographic lines. The company?s reportable segments are Americas Beverage North America Food European Beverage European Food and Asia Pacific. Its segments make steel and aluminum food/ beverage cans and ends glass bottles steel crowns and metal vacuum closures.

Geographic Reach

Crown operates roughly 150 plants in 35 countries with about 75% of net sales coming from outside the US.

Crown's US headquarters is stationed in Philadelphia while its European headquarters is in Baar Switzerland. In addition its Asia/Pacific headquarters resides in Singapore and it has additional research facilities in Alsip Illinois; and Wantage England.

Sales and Marketing

Crown markets and sells products to customers through its own sales and marketing staffs. In some instances contracts with customers are centrally negotiated but products are ordered through and distributed directly by its local facilities. Its top 10 global customers collectively represent more than 30% of its overall revenue.

Financial Performance

Crown's revenues have decreased the last two years dipping 4% from $8.8 billion in 2015 to $8.3 billion in 2016. The decline was attributed to unfavorable foreign currency translations and the pass-through of lower material costs. This was partially offset by a 6% increase in sales unit volumes from its Americas Beverage segment.

From 2015 to 2016 Crown's net income increased 26% from $393 million to $496 million mainly due to a reduction in restructuring expenses and a decrease in the cost of products sold. In addition cash provided by operating activities decreased from $956 million in 2015 to $930 million in 2016 primarily due to a spike in pension contributions premiums paid to retire debt and lower contributions from working capital changes.

Strategy

Crown grows its businesses in specific international growth markets while improving its operations and results in more mature markets through disciplined pricing and improvements in manufacturing and productivity. However with international expansion Crown like its rivals risks exposure to unfavorable foreign-currency exchange rates of the euro pound sterling and Canadian dollar as well as cyclical consumer spending on food and beverages. Its net sales are also impacted by the rise or decrease in the cost of aluminum and steel which is passed on to customers.

However the company believes that technological innovation will help mitigate for usual risks and cycles. Not content with making containers the same old way Crown Holdings operates research development and engineering centers in the US and the UK. Its mission is to design cost-efficient manufacturing processes reduce material content while maintaining freshness and develop new products with the application of new technologies.

Crown is specifically targeting Asia/Pacific as a region ripe with growth opportunities. In 2016 Crown opened a third new plant in Cambodia. It also plans to open two new can facilities in Indonesia and Vietnam in 2017 and a new beverage can plant in Myanmar in 2018 to support further growth in the region.

Mergers and Acquisitions

In 2018 Crown agreed to acquire Signode Industrial Group a global leader in transit packaging for $3.9 billion. The Illinois-based firm has operations in 40 countries across 6 continents and makes sales in some 60 countries.

HISTORY

Formed as Crown Cork & Seal Co. (CC&S) of Baltimore in 1892 the company was consolidated into its present form in 1927 when it merged with New Process Cork and New York Patents. The next year CC&S expanded overseas and formed Crown Cork International. In 1936 CC&S acquired Acme Can and benefited from the movement at the time from home canning to processed canning. A decade later the company launched its new product in 1946 — the first aerosol can.

EXECUTIVES

President Ceo And Director, Timothy J. Donahue, age 56, $915,000 total compensation
Svp And Cfo, Thomas A. Kelly, age 59, $575,000 total compensation
President Crown Technology, Daniel A. Abramowicz
Evp And Coo, Gerard H (Jerry) Gifford, age 63, $600,000 total compensation
President Crown Aerosol Packaging North America, C. Anderson (Andy) Bolton
President Crown Food Packaging North America Crown Closures And Specialty Packaging, James D. (Jim) Wilson
President Americas Division, Djalma Novaes, age 57, $510,000 total compensation
President Crown Beverage Packaging South America, Wilmar Arinelli
President Crown Beverage Packaging Mexico, Abel Coello Quintanilla
President Crown Beverage Packaging North America, Timothy J. (Tim) Lorge
Svp Crown Beverage Packaging China And Hong Kong, Robert H. Bourque, age 48, $302,413 total compensation
President Crown Europe, Didier Sourisseau, age 52
Vice President, Randall Chaffins
Vice President And Treasurer, Kevin C Clothier
Vice President Steel Sourcing, Daniel Shackell
Vice President Sales, Alvin Thornton
Executive Vice President, Ronald Thoma
Vice President Corporate Affairs And Public Relations, Michael F Dunleavy
Vice President Labor And Employee Relations, Vince Pepenelli
Vice President Sales Account Executive, Cliff Waddington
President Ceo And Director, Timothy J. Donahue, age 56
Chairman, John W. Conway, age 72
Auditors: PricewaterhouseCoopers LLP

LOCATIONS

HQ: Crown Holdings Inc
770 Township Line Road, Yardley, PA 19067
Phone: 215 698-5100
Web: www.crowncork.com

2017 Sales

	$ mil.	% of total
US	1,931	22
Mexico	699	8
Brazil	652	8
Spain	649	7
UK	600	7
Other regions	4,167	48
Total	**8,698**	**100**

PRODUCTS/OPERATIONS

2017 Sales

	$ mil.	% of total
Metal beverage cans & ends	5,085	58
Metal food cans & ends	2,331	27
Other metal packaging	887	10
Other products	395	5
Total	**8,698**	**100**

2017 Sales

	$ mil.	% of total
Americas beverage	2,928	34
European food	1,935	22
European beverage	1,457	17
Asia Pacific	1,177	13
North America food	679	8
Non-reportable segments	522	6
Total	**8,698**	**100**

Selected Products

Metal packaging
 Aerosol cans
 Beverage cans

Closures and caps
Crowns
Ends
Food cans
Plastics packaging
Other products
 Can making equipment and spares

Selected Markets

Food and beverage
Health and beauty
Household / Industrial
Luxury Goods
Promotional

COMPETITORS

Amcor
AptarGroup
Arconic
Ardagh Group
BWAY
Ball Corp.
Berry Global
Metal Container Corporation
Owens-Illinois
Silgan
Sonoco Products
Tetra Laval

HISTORICAL FINANCIALS

Company Type: Public

Income Statement

				FYE: December 31
	REVENUE ($ mil.)	NET INCOME ($ mil.)	NET PROFIT MARGIN	EMPLOYEES
12/17	8,698	323	3.7%	24,000
12/16	8,284	496	6.0%	24,000
12/15	8,762	393	4.5%	24,000
12/14	9,097	387	4.3%	23,000
12/13	8,656	324	3.7%	21,300
Annual Growth	0.1%	(0.1%)	—	3.0%

2017 Year-End Financials

Debt ratio: 50.11%
Return on equity: 66.80%
Cash ($ mil.): 424
Current ratio: 0.95
Long-term debt ($ mil.): 5,217

No. of shares (mil.): 134
Dividends
 Yield: —
 Payout: —
Market value ($ mil.): 7,553

	STOCK PRICE ($) FY Close	P/E High/Low		PER SHARE ($) Earnings	Dividends	Book Value
12/17	56.25	26	22	2.38	0.00	4.48
12/16	52.57	16	12	3.56	0.00	2.62
12/15	50.70	20	16	2.82	0.00	1.03
12/14	50.90	19	14	2.79	0.00	0.86
12/13	44.57	19	16	2.30	0.00	0.03
Annual Growth	6.0%	—	—	0.9%	—	-252.6%

CSX Corp

Through its main subsidiary CSX Transportation (CSXT) CSX Corporation operates a major rail system of some 21000 route miles in the eastern US. The freight carrier links 23 states 70 ports 240 short-line railroads the District of Columbia and two Canadian provinces (Ontario and Quebec). Freight hauled by the company includes a wide variety of merchandise (food chemicals and consumer goods) coal and automotive products. CSX also transports via intermodal containers and trailers (Intermodal freight hauling uses multiple modes of transportation). CSX's rail segment also includes units that operate motor vehicle distribution centers and bulk cargo terminals.

Operations

CSX's transportation services operate through three lines of businesses: merchandise (its largest segment by revenue) coal and intermodal. The company's subsidiary CSX Real Property handles real estate sales leasing acquisition and management and development activities. CSX Intermodal Terminals provides intermodal terminal and trucking services though more than 50 terminals across the eastern US.

CSXT operates with a fleet of more than 4400 locomotives (98% are owned by CSXT) and around 83300 railcars (gondolas hoppers and box/flat cars). Other CSX holdings include Total Distribution Services a storage and distribution company for the automotive industry; Transflo Terminal Services a logistics company for transferring shipments from rail to truck; and CSX Technology which provides IT services to its parent company.

Geographic Reach

CSX operates in two dozen states primarily in the Eastern US and along the Eastern Seaboard. It also operates in Washington DC and the two Canadian provinces of Ontario and Quebec.The company has representative offices in strategic parts of the world including Mexico City Monterrey Buenos Aires Sao Paolo Rio de Janeiro and Munich.

Sales and Marketing

CSX operates sales representative offices in strategic parts of the world including Mexico City Monterrey Buenos Aires Sao Paolo Rio de Janeiro and Munich. Noteworthy customers include Ascend Performance Materials Aux Sable Liquid Products Cargill Dow Corning MarkWest Hydrocarbon SABIC Americas and United Refining.

Financial Performance

CSX has posted revenue declines the last two years with revenues falling 6% to $11.1 billion in 2016. Profits also fell 15% to $1.71 billion in 2016. In addition its operating cash flow decreased from $3.37 billion in 2015 to $3.04 billion in 2016 mainly due to contributions it made to pension plans for the year.

The revenue decline for 2016 was primarily due to slumping fuel surcharges as a result of the ongoing steep decline in oil prices. For several years in a row CSX experienced a decline in coal business revenue as a result of mild weather high stockpiles and low natural gas prices favoring natural gas power generation. In addition its merchandise revenue in 2016 dipped due to lower volumes of agricultural industrial and forest products shipped.

Strategy

Citing fuel prices and environmental efficiency CSX hopes to persuade more shippers to shift freight from trucks to trains especially for cross-country journeys. It has invested almost $400 million and is working with several states and the federal government to outfit tunnels bridges and overpasses to accommodate the taller railcars.

To combat years of sagging coal volumes negatively affecting its balance sheet CSX in 2016 introduced a new operating plan that will restructure how the railroad manages its trains and resources. Its "CSX of Tomorrow? plan will realign its network to de-emphasize coal traffic and optimize the volume-growth potential of the more promising intermodal sector and solid merchandise segment. It will also deploy more high tech equipment and information systems to establish a highly automated and more modernized railroad.

HISTORY

CSX Corporation was formed in 1980 when Chessie System and Seaboard Coast Line (SCL) merged in an effort to improve the efficiency of their railroads. Chessie's oldest railroad the Balti-more & Ohio (B&O) was chartered in 1827 to help Baltimore compete against New York and Philadelphia for freight traffic. By the late 1800s the railroad served Chicago Cincinnati New York City St. Louis and Washington DC. Chesapeake & Ohio (C&O) acquired it in 1962.

C&O originated in Virginia with the Louisa Railroad in 1836. It gained access to Chicago Cincinnati and Washington DC and by the mid-1900s was a major coal carrier. After B&O and C&O acquired joint control of Baltimore-based Western Maryland Railway (1967) the three railroads became subsidiaries of newly formed Chessie System (1973).

One of SCL's two predecessors Seaboard Air Line Railroad (SAL) grew out of Virginia's Portsmouth & Roanoke Rail Road of 1832. SCL's other predecessor Atlantic Coast Line Railroad (ACL) took shape between 1869 and 1893 as William Walters acquired several southern railroads. In 1902 ACL bought the Plant System (railroads in Georgia Florida and other southern states) and the Louisville & Nashville (a north-south line connecting New Orleans and Chicago) giving ACL the basic form it was to retain until 1967 when it merged with SAL to form SCL.

EXECUTIVES

Vice President And Chro, Diana Sorfleet
President Ceo And Director, James M. Foote
President Csx Technology Inc., Frank A. Lonegro, age 49, $500,000 total compensation
President Csx Technology, Kathleen Brandt
Vp And Chief Transportation Officer, Mike Pendergrass
President Csx Real Property Inc., Shantel Davis
Evp Chief Legal Officer And Corporate Secretary, Nathan D. Goldman
Evp Corporate Affairs And Chief Of Staff, Mark K. Wallace
Vice President Network Operations, Steve Potter
Vp Strategic Business Development, Derrick Smith
Svp Chief Transportation Officer, Jermaine Swafford
Avp Labor Relations, David Ingoldsby
Vice President, Tom Holmes
Vice President Legal Affairs, Peter Shudtz
Regional Vice President, Bryan Rhode
Assistant Vice President Advanced Engineering, Timothy Male
Vice President Finance Commercial, Fred Eliasson
Vice President Strategic Infrastructure Initiatives, Louis Renjel
Senior Vice President And Chief Administrative Officer, Lisa A Mancini
Vice President And Chief Transportation Officer, Cindy Sandborn
Vice President Network Operations, Cary Helton
Regional Vp State Government Affairs Philadelphia Nj And Ny City, Rodney Oglesby
Vice President Treasurer, David Baggs
Senior Vice President Suddath Government Services, Wright Allon
Vice President Corporate Development, Hart William
President Ceo And Director, James M. Foote
Chairman, Edward J. (Ned) Kelly, age 65
Evp Chief Legal Officer And Corporate Secretary, Nathan D. Goldman
Board Member, Donald Shepard
Auditors: Ernst & Young LLP

LOCATIONS

HQ: CSX Corp
  500 Water Street, 15th Floor, Jacksonville, FL 32202
Phone: 904 359-3200
Web: www.csx.com

PRODUCTS/OPERATIONS

2017 Sales

	$ mil.	% of total
Merchandise	7,068	62
Coal	2,107	18
Intermodal	1,799	16
Other	434	4
Total	**11,408**	**100**

Selected Services

Commodities
Industrial Development
Intermodal
International
Load Engineering and Design Services
Product Transloading and Distribution
Property Services
Property/Real Estate
Specialized Rail Training

COMPETITORS

APL Logistics	Hub Group
Burlington Northern	J.B. Hunt
Santa Fe	Norfolk Southern
Canadian National	Schneider National
Railway	Union Pacific
Canadian Pacific	Washington Companies
Railway	

HISTORICAL FINANCIALS

Company Type: Public

Income Statement   FYE: December 31

	REVENUE ($ mil.)	NET INCOME ($ mil.)	NET PROFIT MARGIN	EMPLOYEES
12/18	12,250	3,309	27.0%	22,500
12/17	11,408	5,471	48.0%	24,000
12/16	11,069	1,714	15.5%	27,000
12/15	11,811	1,968	16.7%	29,000
12/14	12,669	1,927	15.2%	31,511
Annual Growth	(0.8%)	14.5%	—	(8.1%)

2018 Year-End Financials

Debt ratio: 40.18%
Return on equity: 24.27%
Cash ($ mil.): 858
Current ratio: 1.34
Long-term debt ($ mil.): 14,739

No. of shares (mil.): 818
Dividends
  Yield: 1.4%
  Payout: 11.9%
Market value ($ mil.): 50,834

	STOCK PRICE ($) FY Close	P/E High/Low		PER SHARE ($) Earnings	Dividends	Book Value
12/18	62.13	20	13	3.84	0.88	15.35
12/17	55.01	10	6	5.99	0.78	16.53
12/16	35.93	21	12	1.81	0.72	12.58
12/15	26.13	19	12	2.00	0.70	12.07
12/14	36.68	20	13	1.92	0.63	11.25
Annual Growth	14.1%	—	—	18.9%	8.7%	8.1%

Cullen/Frost Bankers, Inc.

One of the largest independent bank holding companies in Texas Cullen/Frost Bankers owns Frost Bank and other financial subsidiaries through a second-tier holding company The New Galveston Company. The community-oriented bank serves individuals and local businesses as well as clients in neighboring parts of Mexico through 120-plus branches in Texas metropolitan areas. It offers commercial and consumer deposit products and loans trust and investment management services mutual funds insurance brokerage and leasing. Subsidiaries include Frost Insurance Agency Frost Brokerage Services Frost Investment Advisors and investment banking arm Frost Securities. Cullen/Frost has total assets of $26.5 billion.

Geographic Reach
San Antonio-based Cullen/Frost Bankers has branches throughout Texas including the Austin Corpus Christi Dallas Fort Worth Houston Permian Basin the Rio Grande Valley and San Antonio regions.

Financial Performance
Cullen/Frost reported revenue of $945.3 million in 2013 an increase of 3% versus 2012 on increased interest income on loans and deposits and an increase in trust and investment management fees. Net income was $237.9 a flat comparison with the prior year. 2013 marked the third consecutive year of rising revenue following a dip in 2010. The bank's fortunes are rising along with the thriving energy and technology sectors in Texas.

Strategy
Cullen/Frost has built its insurance business through acquisitions in recent years; since 2009 it has bought agencies in Dallas Houston San Antonio and San Marcos that provide group employee benefit plans. The company continues to seek out acquisition opportunities while it also looks for ways to expand and diversify within its existing markets. To reduce its reliance on interest rate spreads Cullen/Frost wants to grow its income from fees such as insurance commissions trust investment fees and service charges on deposit accounts.

Mergers and Acquisitions
In June 2014 Frost Bank acquired Odessa Texas-based Western National Bank (WNB) increasing its presence in the oil-rich Permian Basin Midland and Odessa markets in West Texas. Seven of WNB's eight branches were converted to the Frost name (an office in San Antonio was closed) increasing the number of Frost branches statewide to more than 120. The acquisition of WNB added $1.8 billion in assets $1.6 billion in deposits and $668 million in total loans to Cullen/Frost. The purchase of WNB was the first time in nearly seven years that Frost acquired another bank.

EXECUTIVES

Chairman And Ceo, Phillip D. Green, age 63, $565,000 total compensation

President Frost Bank; Evp Frost Wealth Advisors, Patrick B. (Pat) Frost, age 58, $485,000 total compensation

President, Paul H. Bracher, age 61, $500,000 total compensation

Evp And Cfo, Jerry Salinas, $400,000 total compensation

Vice President Of Marketing, Bobby Jacob

Vice President Of Marketing, Howard Kasanoff

Senior Vice President It, Harvey Gutierrez

Senior Vice President Director Of Investor Relatio, Greg Parker

Vice President Of Finance, Vicki Ball

Vice President Community Development, Betty Davis

Assistan Vice President, Maralessa Gonzales

Vice President Sales, Jeffrey Tarr

Senior Vice President Treasury Management, Darlene Selsor

Executive Vice President, John Robb

Vice President Of Operation, Cliff McCauley

Vice President Of Finance, Gregory Dreier

Vice President, Oscar Molina

Senior Vice President, Michael Alcantar

Senior Vice President, Cliff Perez

Senior Vice President, Vennesa Starr

Vice President, Jonathan Pursch

Senior Vice President, Casey Maxfield

Vice President Corporate Communications, Sheri Rosen

Vice President Executive Benni, Darleen Schauer

Senior Vice President, Jill Stacy

Vice President Sales, Talal Tay

Vice President Of Marketing, Wendy Erickson

Vice President Of Finance, Wayne Baker

Vice President Marketing, Ericka Pullin

Executive Vice President, Michael S Cain

Senior Vice President, Mark Seeberger

Senior Vice President, Edward Porras

Senior Vice President, James Valdez

Senior Vice President, Scott Tellkamp

Senior Vice President Commercial Lending, Glenn Thomas

Assistant Vice President, Kelly Shanteau

Senior Vice President, David Seitze

Vice President Marketing, Erica Noriega

Senior Vice President Capital Markets, Mark Brell

Senior Vice President, Gene Witter

Vice President Administration, Gary Roney

Vice President, Clay Jones

Vice President Private Banking Officer, Beverly Hankinson

Senior Vice President, Diane Madalin

Senior Vice President Project Manager, Terrie Ramirez

Senior Vice President, Leigh Olejer

Vice President Collections, Alan McCabe

Senior Vice President Corporate Banking, Floyd Wilson

Executive Vice President, Jerold Yost

Vice President Research And Strategy Marketing Department Rb7, Tammy Herrera

Senior Vice President, Michael Nutter

Senior Vice President, Ronnie Miksch

Vice President, Todd Weber

Senior Vice President, Mike Davis

Vice President Of Employee Benefits, Tony Zavala

Senior Vice President, Carl A Mclaughlin

Vice President, Maro Rodriguez

Vice President, Susan Carruthers

Vice President Internal Audit, Natalie McCabe

Regional Vice President, Lorraine Neff

Senior Vice President, Olga Harrison

Assistant Vice President, Austin Burns

Assistant Vice President, Hope S Molina

Senior Vice President, Larry Inman

Vice President, Matt Badders

Senior Vice President Institutional Trust Administration, Steven A Klein

Senior Vice President, Terry Frank

Senior Vice President, Letty Dominguez

Vice President, Yolanda Maness

Senior Vice President Wealth Advisor Private Trust, John Sands

Vice President Mineral Asset Management Frost Banking Investments, Robert Turnbull

Vice President Of Marketing, Daryl Hoffmann

Executive Vice President, Sue Turnage

Vice President Sales, Dorothy Wood

Senior Vice President Of Investment Division, Jeanne Glorioso

Senior Vice President, Michael Williams

Senior Vice President Application Support, Jeff Sanders

Assistant Vice President, Elsie Boone

Senior Vice President Investments, Linnie Phebus

Executive Vice President Marketing, Debbie Danmeter

Vice President, Ben Kavanagh

Vice President, Omar Quintanilla

Vice President Sales, Anthony Vallejo

Senior Vice President, Carol Lampier

Assistant Vice President, Beth Pence

Senior Vice President, Gina Prill

Vice President Private Banking, Brannon Kroll

Assistant Vice President, Rene Ramirez

Senior Vice President, Melissa Adams

Vice President And Relationship Manager, Paul R Haney

Vice President Energy Finance, Alex Zemkoski

Vice President, Duncan Morrow

Vice President, Zada Cisneros

Executive Vice President, Roderick Washington

Vice President Finance, Charles Stockton

Vice President Of Marketing, John Greenwood

Executive Vice President Compliance Manager, Cindy Reeves

Senior Executive Vice President, James Allen

Senior Vice President Of Private Trust Services, Debbie Eippert

Senior Vice President, Mark Ritter

Vice President, Chris Brower

Assistant Vice President, J Rosow Jaroszewski

Executive Vice President Retail Loans, Genny Rakowitz

Vice President Marketing, Ericka Pullin

Assistant Vice President, Patricio Perez

Assistant Vice President Commercial Banking, Jennifer Grimes

Assistant Vice President, Yolanda Gonzales

Senior Vice President, Daniel O'Connor

Senior Vice President Professional And Executive Banking Frost Banking Investments, David Landry

Vice President, Anna Sanchez

Senior Vice President, Brent Bike

Vice President Corporate Banking Frost Banking Investments, Luke Healy

Vice President, Sallie Newman

Vice President, Margaret Velasquez

Assistant Vice President, Justin Steinbach

Assistant Vice President, Samuel Lopez

Senior Vice President, Carole Kilpatrick

Assistant Vice President, Karla Riley

Assistant Vice President, Trey McCord

Vice President Sales, Anthony White

Vice President And Sba Manager, Linda Wileman

Vice President Sba Loan Coordinator, Kathy Raia

Vice President, Allison Byers

Vice President, Lou Kissling

Vice President In Human Resources Department, Janet Lane

Vice President, Albert Shannon

Senior Vice President Technology, Ray Zapata

Vice President, Susie Smith

Executive Vice President And General Counsel, Stanley McCormick

Executive Vice President, Chas Mella

Senior Vice President, Sue Frye

Executive Vice President, Jerry Yost

Senior Vice President, Kaye Carpenter

Vice President, Ileana Payne

Vice President Business Services, Gloria Kopycinski

Vice President, Susan Essex

Vice President, Adrian Cadena

Vice President, Cindy Jacobs

Executive Vice President, Bill Sirakos

Senior Executive Vice President, Tom Frost

Vice President Administration, Marie Sanchez

Executive Vice President, Keith Donahoe

Vice President Research And Strategy Marketing Department Rb7, Tammy Herrera

Vice President Energy Finance, Erica Spencer

Senior Vice President, Richard Murray

Senior Vice President, Tim Mccormick

Vice President Relationship Manager, Carlos Gutierrez

Senior Vice President, Patti Ayala

Senior Vice President Director Of Investor Relations, Gregory Parker

Senior Vice President And International Operations Manager, Vangie Leal

Assistant Vice President Commercial Lending,
Alison Boyd
Auditors: Ernst & Young LLP

LOCATIONS

HQ: Cullen/Frost Bankers, Inc.
100 W. Houston Street, San Antonio, TX 78205
Phone: 210 220-4011   **Fax:** 210 220-5578
Web: www.frostbank.com

PRODUCTS/OPERATIONS

2016 Sales

	% of total
Interest	
Loans including fees	40
Securities	28
Interest-bearing deposits	1
Federal funds sold and resell agreements	-
Non-interest	
Trust and investment management fees	9
Service charges on deposit accounts	7
Insurance commissions & fees	4
Interchange and debit card transaction fees	2
Other charges commissions and fees	4
Net gain (loss) on securities transactions	1
Other	4
Total	100

2016 Sales

	% of total
Banking	88
Frost Wealth Advisors	12
Total	100

Selected Subsidiaries

Carton Service Corporation
Cullen BLP Inc.
Cullen/Frost Capital Trust II
Frost Bank
Frost Brokerage Services Inc.
Frost Insurance Agency Inc.
Frost Investment Advisors Inc.
Main Plaza Corporation
Tri-Frost Corporation

COMPETITORS

BBVA Compass Bancshares	JPMorgan Chase
Bank of America	Lone Star Bank
Broadway Bancshares	PlainsCapital
Capital One	Prosperity Bancshares
Comerica	Texas Capital Bancshares
Extraco	Wells Fargo
First Financial Bankshares	Woodforest Financial
International Bancshares	

HISTORICAL FINANCIALS

Company Type: Public

Income Statement

FYE: December 31

	ASSETS ($ mil.)	NET INCOME ($ mil.)	INCOME AS % OF ASSETS	EMPLOYEES
12/17	31,747	364	1.1%	4,270
12/16	30,196	304	1.0%	4,217
12/15	28,567	279	1.0%	4,211
12/14	28,277	277	1.0%	4,154
12/13	24,312	237	1.0%	3,979
Annual Growth	6.9%	11.2%	—	1.8%

2017 Year-End Financials

Debt ratio: 0.74%	No. of shares (mil.): 63
Return on equity: 11.56%	Dividends
Cash ($ mil.): 4,893	Yield: 0.0%
Current ratio: —	Payout: 40.8%
Long-term debt ($ mil.): —	Market value ($ mil.): 6,008

STOCK PRICE ($) FY Close	P/E High/Low		PER SHARE ($) Earnings	Dividends	Book Value
12/17	94.65	18 15	5.51	2.25	51.95
12/16	88.23	19 9	4.70	2.15	47.30
12/15	60.00	19 14	4.28	2.10	46.63
12/14	70.64	19 16	4.29	2.03	45.15
12/13	74.43	20 14	3.80	1.98	41.51
Annual Growth	6.2%	— —	9.7%	3.2%	5.8%

Cummins, Inc.

Cummins makes diesel and natural gas powered engines for the heavy and mid-duty truck RV automotive and industrial markets along with marine rail mining and construction. In addition to its flagship Engine segment other business segments include Components (filtration products and fuel systems) Power Systems (vehicle and residential generators) and Distribution (product distributors and servicing). Major customers include OEMs Chrysler Daimler Ford Komatsu PACCAR Navistar and Volvo. The company traces its historical roots back to 1919 when it was founded by Clessie Cummins.

Operations

The company's 49 to 5500 horsepower engines are made under the Cummins brand name. The Components segment manufactures products that are complementary to commercial diesel applications; more than 8300 filtration products are offered some branded as Fleetguard. Other products within this segment include turbo technologies for air handling in engines and exhaust after-treatment technology as well as new used and remanufactured fuel systems.

Power Systems' standby power products (alternators transfer switches and controls) serve commercial and consumer needs as well as those of the military. Brands include Onan (generator sets) and Stamford (alternators).

Cummins' Distribution segment comprises a network of more than 600 company owned and independent distributors that serve 190 countries worldwide.

Geographic Reach

Cummins has main domestic operating facilities in Columbus Indiana; Nashville Tennessee; and Washington DC. Key international locations reside in Beijing; Shanghai; Pune India; and Staines and Stanton UK. The US generates about 55% of its total sales.

Sales and Marketing

Cummins serves customers through a network of 600 wholly owned and independent distributor locations and more than 7400 dealer locations spanning more than 190 countries and territories. Major customer PACCAR accounts for almost 15% of the company's net sales.

Financial Performance

Cummins' revenues have declined the last two years dipping 8% from $19.1 billion in 2015 to $17.5 billion in 2016.

Engine segment sales declined 10% due to lower demand within the North American heavy-duty and medium-duty on-highway markets and lower demand in most North American off-highway markets partially offset by a spike in sales in the light-duty automotive market.

Power Systems segment sales also decreased 14% primarily due to lower demand across all product lines and decreased sales in most regions

including North America Asia China Latin America the Middle East Africa and Western Europe.

Cummins' profits remained static from 2015 to 2016 hovering around the $1.5 billion mark for both years. This was attributed to lower sales volumes and unfavorable foreign currency fluctuations (primarily from the Brazilian real South African rand and Canadian dollar).

Strategy

The company's fortunes are shaped in large part by the cyclical booms and busts of the on-highway construction and industrial markets. Its customers are particularly sensitive to the general economic climate interest rates and access to credit as well as regulatory issues (environmental and emissions standards) and political shifts.

In an effort to mitigate a slump in demand in any one market or region Cummins is continuing to transform itself from a company concentrated in North America to one whose business is seizing up opportunities in developing countries. Following the US China Brazil Russia and India are Cummins' largest markets.

To increase its market penetration the company also relies on joint ventures that allow it to reduce capital spending streamline its supply chain management and boost its technology development. Some of the partnering companies include Dongfeng Automotive and Beijing Foton Motor in China Tata Motors in India and Japan's Komatsu.

On the technological front Cummins in mid-2017 announced its entrance into the burgeoning electrical vehicle market. It unveiled a Class 7 heavy-duty truck cab that features an advanced 140 kWh battery pack that it will sell to bus operators and commercial truck fleets starting in 2019. Cummins is not building the trucks however but will instead supply the fully integrated battery electronics system and will buy the cells from an unnamed provider. The move signals that Cummins intends to remain a key player in the commercial truck sector even if that business shifts away from its core diesel engine business. It aims to be well-positioned against competition from new players like Tesla Proterra and Nikola Motor Company.

HISTORY

Chauffeur Clessie Cummins believed that Rudolph Diesel's cumbersome and smoky engine could be improved for use in transportation. Borrowing money and work space from his employer — Columbus Indiana banker W. G. Irwin — Cummins founded Cummins Engine in 1919. Irwin invested more than $2.5 million and in the mid-1920s Cummins produced a mobile diesel engine. Truck manufacturers were reluctant to switch from gas to diesel so Cummins used publicity stunts (such as racing in the Indianapolis 500) to advertise his engine.

The company was profitable by 1937 the year Irwin's grandnephew Irwin Miller took over. During WWII the Cummins engine was used in cargo trucks. Sales jumped from $20 million in 1946 to more than $100 million by 1956. That year Cummins started its first overseas plant in Scotland and bought Atlas Crankshafts in 1958. By 1967 it had 50% of the diesel-engine market.

EXECUTIVES

Vice President, Tony Satterthwaite
Vice President High Horsepower Engines, Ed Pence
Chairman And Ceo, N. Thomas (Tom) Linebarger, age 55, $1,375,000 total compensation
Vp And Chief Administrative Officer, Marya M. Rose, age 56, $634,000 total compensation

Vp And General Manager Powercare And Distribution Engine Business, Richard J. (Rich) Freeland, age 61, $848,000 total compensation
Vp And President Distribution Business, Livingston L. (Tony) Satterthwaite, age 57, $570,000 total compensation
Group Vp China And Russia, Steven M. (Steve) Chapman, age 63
Vp And Cio, Sherry A. Aaholm, age 55
Managing Director International India, Anant Talaulicar, age 57, $537,500 total compensation
Vp And President Engine Business, Srikanth Padmanabhan, age 54
Vp And Cfo, Patrick J. (Pat) Ward, age 54, $726,000 total compensation
President Cummins Turbo Technologies (ctt), Tracy A. Embree, age 44
Vp And President Power Systems, Norbert Nusterer, age 49
Vp Engineering Cummins Engine Business, Jennifer Rumsey, age 44
Vice President Chief Manufacturing And Procurement Officer, Ignacio Garcia
Vp Engineering, Jeff Jones
Vice President Information Technology, William Waller
Vice President Global Sales Marketing Logistics And Distribution Filtration, Pamela Carter
Vice President Information Technology, Joe D Mills
Vice President Corporate Controller, Marsha L Hunt
Vice President Engine Business, Seth Erdman
Vpi Sourcing Manager Engine Business Glo, Kurt Metzloff
Vice President Sales, Barry Kreuzer
Vpi Sourcing Director, Michelle Stall
Vice President East Asia, John Watkins
Vpi Manufacturing Program Manager, Hamilton Harper
Senior Vice President, Pam Fischvogt
Vice President Engine Business Quality, Robert Weimer
Vice President Government Relations, Stephen May
National Account Manager, Jeff Poferl
Vice President Oem S Human Resources Manager, Robert Shockman
Vice President Nebraska And South Dakota Operations, Rick Gomel
Ppt And Vpi Sourcing Manager, Tom Rager
Executive Vice President President Power Generation Business, Thomas Linebarge
Vp Diversity Initiaves Operations, Lori Thompson
Vp And Controller Engine Business, Michael Miller
Vice President Of Finance, Ariene Policarpio
Vice President Engineering, Jim Trueblood
Vice President Advanced Product Development, Julius Perr
Executive Vice President, J T White
Vice President Manufacturing Heavy Duty Mid Range And Light Duty Diesel, Dana Vogt
Vice President, Victor Meek
Vpi Manufacturing Engineer, Brent Nelson
Vice President, Gary Van Natten
Vice President Of Finance, Michael Doherty
Vpi Sourcing Manager, Mildred Louidor
Vice President General Manager, Greg Gilmore
Chairman And Ceo, N. Thomas (Tom) Linebarger, age 55
Board Member, Stephen Dobbs
Board Member, Thomas Lynch
Auditors: PricewaterhouseCoopers LLP

LOCATIONS

HQ: Cummins, Inc.
500 Jackson Street, P.O. Box 3005, Columbus, IN 47202-3005
Phone: 812 377-5000   **Fax:** 812 377-4937
Web: www.cummins.com

2017 Sales

	$ mil.	% of total
United States	11,010	54
International	9,418	46
Total	**20,428**	**100**

PRODUCTS/OPERATIONS

2017 Sales

	$ mil.	% of total
Engine	8,953	34
Distribution	7,058	27
Components	5,889	23
Power Generation	4,058	16
Intersegment eliminations	(5530)	-
Total	**20,428**	**100**

Selected Products

Components business
  Emission solutions
  Filtration (heavy-duty air fuel hydraulic and lube filtration and chemicals)
  Fuel systems (new fuel systems remanufactured electronic control modules)
  Turbo technologies (turbochargers)
Emissions solutions
Engine business
  Bus engines
  Heavy- and medium-duty truck engines
  Industrial engines for construction mining agricultural rail and marine equipment
  Light commercial vehicle engines
  Marine diesels (recreational and commercial)
Filtration business
  Air system
  Cooling system (crankcase ventilation)
  Diesel emission additives
  Fuel system (hydraulic)
  Lube system (transmission)
Fuel systems
  CELECT electronically controlled unit injection system
  Common rail pump
  Extreme pressure injection system
  High Pressure Injection (HPI) system
  Remanufactured products
Power generation business
  Diesel and alternative-fuel electrical generator sets (PowerCommand Onan Newage AVK SEG G-Drive)
Turbo technologies Holset (medium and heavy-duty diesel engines)

COMPETITORS

BorgWarner	Mack Trucks
Briggs & Stratton	Mitsubishi Heavy
Power Products	Industries
CLARCOR	Navistar International
Caterpillar	PACCAR
China Yuchai	Parker-Hannifin
DENSO	Regal Beloit
DEUTZ	Robert Bosch
Danaher	Rolls-Royce Power
Donaldson Company	Systems
Eaton	Tenneco
Emerson Electric	Textron
Fiat Chrysler	Volvo
MAN	

HISTORICAL FINANCIALS

Company Type: Public

Income Statement   FYE: December 31

	REVENUE ($ mil.)	NET INCOME ($ mil.)	NET PROFIT MARGIN	EMPLOYEES
12/17	20,428	999	4.9%	58,600
12/16	17,509	1,394	8.0%	55,400
12/15	19,110	1,399	7.3%	55,200
12/14	19,221	1,651	8.6%	54,600
12/13	17,301	1,483	8.6%	47,900
Annual Growth	**4.2%**	**(9.4%)**	**—**	**5.2%**

2017 Year-End Financials

Debt ratio: 11.10%
Return on equity: 14.14%
Cash ($ mil.): 1,369
Current ratio: 1.57
Long-term debt ($ mil.): 1,588
No. of shares (mil.): 165
Dividends
Yield: 0.0%
Payout: 70.5%
Market value ($ mil.): 29,269

	STOCK PRICE ($) FY Close	P/E High/Low		PER SHARE ($) Earnings	Dividends	Book Value
12/17	176.64	30	23	5.97	4.21	43.81
12/16	136.67	18	10	8.23	4.00	40.87
12/15	88.01	19	11	7.84	3.51	42.27
12/14	144.17	18	14	9.02	2.81	42.53
12/13	140.97	18	13	7.91	2.25	40.22
Annual Growth	**5.8%**	**—**	**—**	**(6.8%)**	**17.0%**	**2.2%**

Customers Bancorp Inc

Customers Bancorp makes it pretty clear who they want to serve. Boasting some $8.5 billion in assets the bank holding company operates about 15 branches mostly in southeastern Pennsylvania but also in New York and New Jersey. It offers personal and business checking savings and money market accounts as well as loans certificates of deposit credit cards and concierge or appointment banking (they come to you seven days a week). Around 95% of the bank's loan portfolio is made up of commercial loans while the rest consists of consumer loans. It was formed in 2010 as a holding company for Customers Bank which was created in 1994 as New Century Bank.

Operations
Customers Bancorp operates two main business lines: Commercial Lending and Consumer Lending. Its Commercial Lending business provides commercial and industrial loans small and middle-market business banking and small business administration (SBA) loans multi-family and commercial real estate loans and commercial loans to mortgage originators. Its Consumer Lending division mostly makes local market mortgage loans and home equity loans. More than 95% of the bank's loan portfolio was made up of commercial loans at the end of 2015 while the rest consisted of consumer loans.

Broadly speaking the bank makes roughly 90% of its revenue from interest income. About 66% of its revenue came from loan interest during 2015 while another 19% came from interest loans held for sale and 4% came from interest on investment securities. The remainder of its revenue came from mortgage warehouse transactional fees (4%) and other miscellaneous and non-recurring sources.

Geographic Reach
The bank had 14 branches at the end of 2015 including nine in Philadelphia and Southeastern Pennsylvania; four in Berks County Pennsylvania; one in Westchester County New York; and one in Mercer County New Jersey. It also had a handful of additional offices in Boston; New York City; Portsmouth New Hampshire; Providence Rhode Island; and Suffolk County New York.

Sales and Marketing
Customers Bancorp's customers include private businesses business customers non-profits and consumers. Its commercial lending division typically makes loans to companies with revenues between $1 million to $50 million needing between $0.5 million to $10 million in credit.

The bank has been ramping up its advertising spend in recent years. It spent $1.48 million on advertising in 2015 up from $1.33 million and $1.27 million in 2014 and 2013 respectively.

Financial Performance

The bank's annual revenues have nearly quadrupled since 2011 as its loan assets have more than tripled (its loan assets reached $5.45 billion by of the end of 2015). Meanwhile growing revenues strong cost controls and low interest rates have pushed the bank's annual profits up almost 15-fold over the same period.

Customers Bancorp's revenue jumped 29% to $277.5 million during 2015 mostly as its average balance of interest-earning loan and securities assets rose by 31% to $6.7 billion for the year.

Revenue growth in 2015 drove the bank's net income up 36% to $58.5 million. Customer Bancorp's operating cash levels declined sharply to $356.6 million for the year as the bank originated more loans held for sale than it actually sold.

Strategy

With its eye on becoming the leading regional bank holding company Customers Bancorp continued in 2016 to focus on expanding its market share with its high-touch personalized Concierge Banking services and its "high-tech" BankMobile offerings which include remote account opening remote deposit capture and mobile banking. The BankMobile and online banking channels allow Customers Bancorp to slow expensive branch-expansion plans and cut operating costs significantly while giving customers faster access to banking services.

But even with digital banking the bank occasionally opens new branches (and selectively acquire others) to grow its loan and deposit business. In January 2016 it opened and replaced an existing branch in Hamilton New Jersey onto Route 33 in the same city. In June 2015 Customers opened a new Long Island location in Mellville New York to expand its private and commercial banking services to local clients there.

Mergers and Acquisitions

In December 2015 Customers Bank expanded its deposit business and added 2 million new student customers after buying the One Account Student Checking and Refund Management Disbursement Services business from higher education refund disbursement provider Higher One Inc for $42 million.

Company Background

In late 2011 Customers purchased Berkshire Bancorp and picked up five branches in Berks County Pennsylvania for about $11.3 million.

EXECUTIVES

Chairman And Ceo, Jay S. Sidhu, age 66, $300,000 total compensation
President And Coo, Richard A. Ehst, age 72, $225,000 total compensation
Executive Vice President President Of Community Banking, Warren Taylor, age 60, $190,000 total compensation
Evp And Chief Credit Officer, Thomas Jastrem
Evp And Chief Administrative Officer, Jim Collins
Evp And Chief Lending Officer, Timothy D. Romig
Evp And President Special Assets Group, Robert A. White
Evp And And Director Enterprise Risk Management, James D. Hogan
Evp And Director Multi-family And Investment Cre Lending, Kenneth A. Keiser
Executive Vice President And Chief Financial Officer, Robert Wahlman
Vice President Assistant Loan Administration Manager And Loan Operations Manager, Michael McCarrie
Vice President, John Gerhart
Assistant Vice President And Appraisal Review Officer, Richard Nagy

Senior Vice President Berks County Commercial Banking Group, Mary Moffitt
Vp Assistant Bsa Officer, Melissa Krueger
Senior Vice President. Credit Officer, Barbara Bergman
Senior Vice President, William Hirst
Vice President Collections Manager, Robert Deyoung
Executive Vice President Market Chief Lending Officer, George Maroulis
Vice President Of Operations, Richard Kirk
Vice President Government Guaranteed Lending, Lisa Kennedy
Vice President Government Guaranteed Lending, Michele Vervlied
Assistant Vice President Capital Markets, Dana Galvin
Assistant Vice President And Assistant Branch Manager, Lisa Gearheart
Assistant Vice President Sox Internal Control Manager, Frank Bommentre
Senior Vice President, Kevin Cornwall
Assistant Vice President, Terry Meehan
Assistant Vice President And Credit Analyst, Angela Edwards
Assistant Vice President Client Relations, Benjamin Harris
Senior Vice President Ne Director Of Pla, Paula Pais
Senior Vice President, Michael Solomon
Senior Vice President Philadelphia Market Leader, Varsovia Fernandez
Vice President And Government Guaranteed Lender, Stephanie Schwandt
Senior Vice President Commercial Finance Group, Sam Smith
Vice President Sba Loan Specialist, Stacey Kuzniasz
Vice President, Laura Simon
Vice President, Elizabeth Le
Senior Vice President Regional Chief Lending Officer, Robert Fischer
Senior Vice President And Loan Review Director, David Dowd
Vice President Commercial Lending Philadelphia Market, Edwin Roman
Assistant Vice President Member Services And Talent Acquisition, Amy Shaughnessy
Business Development Officer Vice President, Sunita Raina
Senior Vice President, Veder Reddick
Senior Vice President And Director Of Corporate Planning, Tammy Sibalic
Vice President Commercial Lending, Brett V Long
Vice President And Credit Officer, Gary Arnold
Senior Vice President Director Of Operations Deposit Administration, Robert J Diegel
Vice President Special Assets Financial Reporting, Doan Dang
Assistant Vice President And Lead Information Technology Auditor, Patrick Direnzo
Vice President, S Gates
Assistant Vice President, John Chung
Vice President, Diane Billman
Vice President, Keith Munley
Vice President Consumer Lending Compliance, Matt Kachurka
Vice President Manager Of Network Administration, Joseph Thren
Vice President And Senior Analyst, Joann Zerbo
Senior Vice President Of Warehouse Lending, Kenneth Blume
Chairman And Ceo, Jay S. Sidhu, age 66
Auditors: BDO USA, LLP

LOCATIONS

HQ: Customers Bancorp Inc
1015 Penn Avenue, Suite 103, Wyomissing, PA 19610
Phone: 610 933-2000
Web: www.customersbank.com

PRODUCTS/OPERATIONS

2015

	% of total
Interest income	
Loans receivable including fees	66
Loans held for sale	19
Investment securities	4
Other	2
Non interest income	
Mortgage warehouse transnational fees	4
Bank-owned life insurance	3
Gains on sales of loans	1
Deposit fees	0
Mortgage loan and banking income	0
Gain (loss) on sale of investment securities)	0
Other	1
Total	**100**

Products include

Equipment Loans
Mortgage Warehouse Loans
Multi-Family And Commercial Real Estate Loans
Residential Mortgage Loans
Small Business Loans

COMPETITORS

Bank of America	Huntington Bancshares
Capital One	JPMorgan Chase
Citigroup	KeyCorp
Comerica	PNC Financial
Fifth Third	U.S. Bancorp
HSBC	Wells Fargo

HISTORICAL FINANCIALS

Company Type: Public

Income Statement

FYE: December 31

	ASSETS ($ mil.)	NET INCOME ($ mil.)	INCOME AS % OF ASSETS	EMPLOYEES
12/17	9,839	78	0.8%	765
12/16	9,382	78	0.8%	739
12/15	8,401	58	0.7%	517
12/14	6,825	43	0.6%	426
12/13	4,153	32	0.8%	388
Annual Growth	24.1%	24.6%	—	18.5%

2017 Year-End Financials

Debt ratio: 3.00%	No. of shares (mil.): 31
Return on equity: 8.87%	Dividends
Cash ($ mil.): 146	Yield: —
Current ratio: —	Payout: —
Long-term debt ($ mil.): —	Market value ($ mil.): 816

	STOCK PRICE ($) FY Close	P/E High/Low		PER SHARE ($) Earnings	Dividends	Book Value
12/17	25.99	17	12	1.97	0.00	29.35
12/16	35.82	15	9	2.31	0.00	28.26
12/15	27.22	15	9	1.96	0.00	20.59
12/14	19.46	14	11	1.55	0.00	16.57
12/13	20.46	15	11	1.30	0.00	14.51
Annual Growth	6.2%	—	—	11.0%	—	19.3%

CVB Financial Corp

CVB Financial is into the California Vibe Baby. The holding company's Citizens Business Bank offers community banking services to primarily small and midsized businesses but also to consumers through nearly 50 branch and office locations across central and southern California. Boasting more than $7 billion in assets the bank offers checking money market CDs and savings accounts trust and investment services and a variety of loans. Commercial real estate loans account for about two-thirds of the bank's loan portfolio which is rounded out by business consumer and construction loans; residential mortgages; dairy and livestock loans; and municipal lease financing.

Operations

In addition to its 40 business financial centers CVB operates seven Commercial Banking Centers (CBCs). The CBCs operate primarily as sales offices and focus on business clients professionals and high-net-worth individuals. The bank also has three trust offices.

Citizens Business Bank provides auto and equipment leasing and brokers mortgage loans through its Citizens Financial Services Division; CitizensTrust offers trust and investment services.

Overall the bank made 63% of its total revenue from interest income on loans and leases in 2014 with another 24% of total revenue coming from interest income on the bank's investment securities. About 5% of total revenue came from service charges on deposit accounts and 3% came from trust and investment services income.

Geographic Reach

CVB Financial has 40 Business Financial Centers located in the Inland Empire Los Angeles County Orange County San Diego County and the Central Valley regions in California.

Sales and Marketing

CVB Financial provides services to companies from a variety of industries including: industrial and manufacturing dairy and livestock agriculture education nonprofit entertainment medical professional services title and escrow government and property management.

Financial Performance

CVB's revenue has been in decline in recent years due to shrinking interest margins on loans amidst the low-interest environment. The firm's profits however have been rising thanks to declining loan loss provisions as its loan portfolio's credit quality has been improving in the strengthening economy.

CVB enjoyed a breakout year in 2014 with revenue rebounding by 12% to $289.32 million mostly thanks to higher interest income as the bank grew its loan and lease assets by 7% during the year and grew its investment security assets by 18%. Most of its loan growth came from commercial real estate loans while SFR mortgage loans consumer loans and construction loans also helped boost the company's top line. The bank's non-interest income also jumped by 44% during the year thanks to a $6 million gain on loans held-for-sale and a net $3.6 million decrease in its FDIC loss sharing asset.

Higher revenue and a $16.1 million loan loss provision recapture in 2014 also drove the bank's net income higher by 9% to $104.02 million.

Despite higher earnings for the year CVB's operating cash levels shrank by 22% to $87.70 million as the bank used more cash toward employee payments and income taxes.

Strategy

CVB Financial continues to seek out acquisitions of smaller banking trust and investment companies to grow its loan and deposit business as well as its geographic reach in key markets in (mostly Southern) California. With its 2014 acquisition of American Security Bank for example CVB boosted its assets by 6% to over $7 billion while adding branches in more than a handful of key markets in Southern California.

Remaining profitable throughout the economic downturn CVB Financial credits its success in part to its strict loan underwriting standards. The bank targets family-owned or other privately held businesses with annual revenues of up to $200 million

with the goal of maintaining its client relationships for decades.

Mergers and Acquisitions

In March 2014 CVB Financial through its Citizens Business Bank (CBB) subsidiary purchased Southern California-based American Security Bank (the flagship subsidiary of American Bancshares) for a total of $57 million. The deal would add American Security Bank's $431 million in assets and boost CBB's branch presence across key markets in Newport Beach Corona Laguna Niguel Lancastar Victorville and Apple Valley.

In 2016 CVB Financial agreed to buy the $416 million-asset Valley Commerce Bancorp the holding company for Valley Business Bank. Valley Business has four banking locations in California's Visalia Tulare Fresno and Woodlake.

Company Background

In 2009 CVB Financial healthier than most California banks acquired the failed San Joaquin Bank after the FDIC took it over. The deal added five branches banking centers in the Bakersfield area.

EXECUTIVES

Executive Vice President, Jay Coleman
Evp And General Counsel Cvb Financial Corporation And Citizens Business Bank, Richard H. Wohl, age 59
President And Ceo Cvb Financial And Citizens Business Bank, Christopher D. (Chris) Myers, age 55, $800,000 total compensation
Evp And Cfo, E. Allen Nicholson, age 51
Evp And Cio, Elsa I. Zavala
Evp And Dairy And Livestock Industries Group Manager Citizens Business Bank, G. Larry Zivelonghi
Svp And Regional Manager Citizens Business Bank, Ted J. Dondanville
Evp Sales Citizens Business Bank, David A. Brager, $300,000 total compensation
Evp And Coo Citizens Business Bank, David C. Harvey, $300,000 total compensation
Evp; Head Citizenstrust, R. Daniel Banis
Evp And Chief Risk Officer Citizens Business Bank, Yamynn De Angelis
Evp Ventura/santa Barbara, Donald R. Toussaint
Executive Vice President, Richard C Thomas
Vice President Relationship Manager, Jason Gould
Vice President Senior Product Manager, John Outwater
Executive Vice President, Angelis Yamynn
Vice President Administration, Joe Pacis
Vice President Marketing And Communications Manager, Jim Burns
Vice Chairman, George A. Borba, age 85
Chairman, Raymond V. OÂ'Brien
Auditors: KPMG LLP

LOCATIONS

HQ: CVB Financial Corp
701 North Haven Ave., Suite 350, Ontario, CA 91764
Phone: 909 980-4030
Web: www.cbbank.com

Selected Branch Locations
Fresno County
Kern County
Los Angeles County
Madera County
Orange County
Riverside County
San Bernardino County
Tulare County

PRODUCTS/OPERATIONS

2014 Sales

	$ mil.	% of total
Interest		
Loans including fees	181	62
Investment securities	68	24
Other	2	1
Noninterest		
Service charges on deposit accounts	15	5
Trust & investment services	8	3
Bankcard services	3	1
BOLI income	2	1
Other	10	3
Adjustments	(3.6)	-
Total	**289**	**100**

COMPETITORS

Bank of America	Popular Inc.
Bank of the West	Provident Financial
City National	Holdings
Comerica	U.S. Bancorp
JPMorgan Chase	Wells Fargo
MUFG Americas Holdings	

HISTORICAL FINANCIALS

Company Type: Public

Income Statement				FYE: December 31
	ASSETS ($ mil.)	NET INCOME ($ mil.)	INCOME AS % OF ASSETS	EMPLOYEES
12/17	8,270	104	1.3%	—
12/16	8,073	101	1.3%	—
12/15	7,671	99	1.3%	—
12/14	7,377	104	1.4%	—
12/13	6,664	95	1.4%	784
Annual Growth	**5.5%**	**2.2%**	**—**	**—**

2017 Year-End Financials

Debt ratio: 0.31%	No. of shares (mil.): 110
Return on equity: 10.14%	Dividends
Cash ($ mil.): 162	Yield: 0.0%
Current ratio: —	Payout: 54.7%
Long-term debt ($ mil.): —	Market value ($ mil.): 2,596

	STOCK PRICE ($) FY Close	P/E High/Low	PER SHARE ($) Earnings	Dividends	Book Value
12/17	23.56	26 21	0.95	0.52	9.70
12/16	22.93	25 15	0.94	0.36	9.15
12/15	16.92	20 16	0.93	0.48	8.68
12/14	16.02	17 14	0.98	0.40	8.29
12/13	17.07	19 11	0.91	0.39	7.33
Annual Growth	**8.4%**	**— —**	**1.1%**	**7.8%**	**7.3%**

CVR Energy Inc

CVR has built a solid CV around refining and marketing high value transportation fuels to retailers railroads and farm cooperatives and other refiners/marketers in Kansas Oklahoma and Illinois. Located within 100 miles of Cushing Oklahoma (a major crude oil trading and storage hub) the company's two oil refineries—in Coffeyville Kansas (115k bpcd) and Wynnewood Oklahoma (70k bpcd)—represent close to a quarter of the region's refining capacity. Through a limited partnership the company also produces and distributes ammonia and ammonium nitrate to farmers in Illinois Iowa Kansas Nebraska and Texas.

Operations

The company reports two segments based on its two primary products— Petroleum and Nitrogen Fertilizer. Petroleum segment (accounts for 95% of total revenue) produces gasoline diesel fuel jet fuel natural gas liquids asphalt and petroleum refining by-products including petroleum coke. The Nitrogen Fertilizer segment produces and distributes nitrogen fertilizer products used primarily by farmers to improve the yield and quality of their crops. The principal products are UAN and ammonia. The company's operations include two ammonia units (2400 ton/day capacity) and two UAN units (4400 ton/day).

Geographic Reach

Headquartered in Texas CVR has most of its properties in Kansas Oklahoma and Illinois. The petroleum business has marketing efforts in the central Mid-continent and Rockies due to its proximity to the refinery and pipeline access. The company also directly supplies customers in close geographic proximity to its two refineries through tanker trucks and customers at throughput terminals on the refined products distribution systems of Magellan and NuStar. The Nitrogen Fertilizer business sells to farmers in Iowa Illinois Kansas Nebraska and Texas.

Sales and Marketing

CVR customers include other retailers refiners convenience store chains railroads and farm cooperatives. Its Petroleum business' top ten customers accounted for more than half of the segment's revenue with one accounting for almost 20% of its total sales. Nitrogen fertilizer business' top five customers accounted for about 30% of the segment's revenue.

Financial Performance

CVR revenue rose from $3 billion in 2009 to decade-peak of $9 billion in 2014 only to decline again to below $5 billion by 2016. The company has not posted losses in the last decade with typical net profits averaging around $200 million.

In 2017 CVR annual revenue increased 25% to almost $6 billion. Most of this growth came from about 20% higher average sales price per gallon of gasoline ($1.59) and a corresponding 22% spike in distillates ($1.66) bringing in $1.2 billion more over 2016.

Net income surged from $25 million in 2016 to $235 million a year later thanks to a spike in refining margin due to higher sales prices for transportation fuels and by-products partially offset by increases in direct operating expense depreciation and amortization and selling and general and administrative expenses.

Cash holdings at the end of 2017 declined to $482 million. Operations provided $167 million but was offset by $195 million used up by investments and a further $225 million going towards financial activities.

Strategy

CVR is predicting improving financial and operating results from its core petroleum segment due to strong Group 3 crack spreads and lower RIN prices and increased internal RIN generation wide crude oil differentials and minimal loss opportunities. CVR made its reduction to RIN exposure a priority for example starting to blend B5 across RX resulting in a 5% increase in internally produced RINs of total renewable volume obligation.

The company is equally keen on improvements in netback prices for its fertilizer segment which had grown by 20% for UAN and 30% for ammonia by third quarter 2018 compared to a year prior. The company has earmarked around $100 million in CAPEX for 2018.

The company is also eyeing increasing its WCS shale oil and natural gas processing at its Coffeyville refinery for a 30% increase in return. However the project required a $350 million CAPEX plan that will be implemented in phases. At the

Wynnewood refinery CVR is also planning a Brent-free repositioning which should increase the liquid yield by approximately 1%.

Company Background

CVR Energy was formed in September 2006 as a subsidiary of Coffeyville. Its nitrogen business held an IPO in 2011 for $350 million followed by Refining IPO fetching $90 million in 2013.

EXECUTIVES

President And Ceo, John J. (Jack) Lipinski, age 67, $950,000 total compensation

Evp Refining Operations, Robert W. Haugen, age 60, $315,000 total compensation

Cfo And Treasurer, Susan M. Ball, age 55, $360,000 total compensation

Senior Vice President, John Walter

Vice President Technical Services, John Huggins

Vice President Government Relations, Gina Bowman

Vice President Human Resources, Jerry Reed

Vice President Logistics, Reed Copeland

Vice President Of Finance, Jay Finks

Executive Vice President, Bill White

Vice President Business Development, Angie Dasbach

Vice President, David Andreth

Vice President Refined Products, Mike Puddy

Vice President Economics And Planning, David LLandreth

Vice President And General Manager Refining, Darin Rains

Chairman, Carl C. Icahn

Board Member, Bob Alexander

Board Member, Stephen Mongillo

Auditors: Grant Thornton LLP

LOCATIONS

HQ: CVR Energy Inc
2277 Plaza Drive, Suite 500, Sugar Land, TX 77479
Phone: 281 207-3200
Web: www.cvrenergy.com

PRODUCTS/OPERATIONS

2017 Sales

	$ mil.	% of total
Petroleum	5,664	95
Nitrogen Fertilizer	330	5
Intersegment elimination	(6.6)	-
Total	**5,988**	**100**

COMPETITORS

CF Industries	Koch Industries Inc.
CHS	Phillips 66
ConocoPhillips	Terra Nitrogen
Flint Hills	Valero Energy
HollyFrontier	

HISTORICAL FINANCIALS

Company Type: Public

Income Statement   FYE: December 31

	REVENUE ($ mil.)	NET INCOME ($ mil.)	NET PROFIT MARGIN	EMPLOYEES
12/17	5,988	234	3.9%	1,440
12/16	4,782	24	0.5%	1,487
12/15	5,432	169	3.1%	1,332
12/14	9,109	173	1.9%	1,298
12/13	8,985	370	4.1%	1,192
Annual Growth	(9.6%)	(10.8%)	—	4.8%

2017 Year-End Financials

Debt ratio: 30.64%	No. of shares (mil.): 86
Return on equity: 26.38%	Dividends
Cash ($ mil.): 481	Yield: 0.0%
Current ratio: 2.01	Payout: 74.0%
Long-term debt ($ mil.): 1,164	Market value ($ mil.): 3,234

	STOCK PRICE ($) FY Close	P/E High/Low		PER SHARE ($) Earnings	Dividends	Book Value
12/17	37.24	14	6	2.70	2.00	10.58
12/16	25.39	141	45	0.28	2.00	9.88
12/15	39.35	25	17	1.95	2.00	11.33
12/14	38.71	25	18	2.00	5.00	11.38
12/13	43.43	16	8	4.27	14.25	13.69
Annual Growth	(3.8%)	—	—	(10.8%)	(38.8%)	(6.2%)

CVS Health Corporation

CVS Health Corp. is a leading pharmacy benefits manager with nearly 90 million plan members as well as the nation's largest drugstore chain (pipping Walgreens). It runs more than 9700 retail and specialty drugstores under the CVS Navarro and Longs Drug banners. In addition to its stand alone pharmacy operations the company operates CVS locations inside Target stores and runs a prescription management company Caremark Pharmacy Services. The company also offers specialty pharmainfusion services business as well as walk-in health services through its retail network of MinuteClinics that are located in around 1000 CVS stores. In late 2018 CVS acquired health insurer Aetna in a $70 billion megadeal..

Operations

CVS Health operates through two main segments: Pharmacy Services and Retail/LTC (long-term care).

Pharmacy Services which accounts for around 60% of sales is the company's pharmacy benefits management (PBM) division. It dispenses drugs through nearly 25 retail specialty pharmacy stores more than 13 specialty mail order pharmacies and four mail order dispensing pharmacies. It also operates around 85 medical branches most of which are ambulatory infusion sites but also include specialist infusion and enteral service facilities. Its other offerings include plan design and administration formulary management discounted drug purchase arrangements and a slew of other services. All told the division fills more than 1.2 billion prescriptions per year.

CVS's Retail/LTC segment (40% of sales) operates around 9700 pharmacies (including 1675 pharmacies located in Target stores) as well as 1140 MinuteClinic locations long-term care pharmacy operations and online operations (CVS.com Onofre.com.brTM and Navarro.com). The pharmacy accounts for more than two-thirds of sales in this segment while "front store" retail merchandise accounts for the rest. CVS' MinuteClinics which are primarily located in CVS stores are staffed by nurse practitioners and physician assistants who treat minor conditions perform health screenings and deliver vaccinations; some locations also treat chronic conditions.

Geographic Reach

CVS retail locations drugstores and clinics are located in 50 US states the District of Columbia Brazil and Puerto Rico. The company also operates pharmacies under the Longs Drugs banner in California Hawaii Nevada and Arizona. MinuteClinics are located in around 1000 store locations across

31 states and Washington DC. The company is present in all the top 100 drugstore markets in the US.

Sales and Marketing

Pharmacy Services' clients include employers insurance companies unions and other health care plan sponsors. The segment makes direct sales of its prescription drugs through its mail service dispensing pharmacies. It also sells indirectly through its retail pharmacy network.

Financial Performance

CVS Health's annual revenues and profits have risen sharply since 2011 surpassing that of competitor Walgreens thanks to aggressive store openings/acquisitions and expansion into new business lines.

In fiscal 2016 revenue increased a further 16%to $177.5 billion on the back of the acquisition of Omnicare in mid-2015 and the pharmacies and clinics of Target at the end of 2015. It also recorded net new business in the Pharmacy Services Segment.

Net income grew 2% to $5.3 billion as acquisition-related costs put a dent in profits relative to the strident revenue growth. Cash from operations grew 20% to $10.1 billion due to revenue growth and timing of payments for its Medicare Part D operations.

Strategy

In December 2017 CVS struck a deal to acquire health insurer Aetna in what might be a move to fend off potential competitor Amazon. The deal will allow CVS to further expand the health care services it offers as well as providing it with more leverage in negotiations for drug prices.

The planned acquisition of Aetna continues CVS' efforts to expand beyond retail pharmacy into health care provision. Its mid-2015 acquisition of Omnicare moved it into nursing home pharmacy while its acquisition of Coram the previous year brought the company into the specialty pharmainfusion services business for the first time. Its infusion business offers ambulatory infusion suites which offer patients an alternative to a hospital environment with IV infusions and other infusion therapy services in a safe monitored area.

The company's Retail Pharmacy Store Development plan — focused on entering new markets adding stores in existing markets and relocating stores to more convenient sites — has been a key growth driver. The acquisition of Target's pharmacies in late 2015 carried CVS past Walgreens in terms of annual revenue.

In addition to opening new stores CVS has made efforts to increase sales at existing ones. Prescription drugs account for more than two-thirds of its sales and the retailer is attempting to grow revenues from over-the-counter medications and general merchandise through its growing private-label product offering. CVS and Cardinal Health have a 50:50 generic sourcing joint venture to provide generic drugs in the US; they also extended their existing pharmaceutical distribution agreement through mid-2019.

Mergers and Acquisitions

At the end of 2018 CVS acquired healthcare insurer Aetna for $70 billion. The deal created a new giant in the prescription drugs industry and is seen as a defensive move with players such as Amazon eyeing a move into the prescription drug space.

HISTORY

Brothers Stanley and Sid Goldstein who ran health and beauty products distributor Mark Steven branched out into retail in 1963 when they opened up their first Consumer Value Store in Lowell Massachusetts with partner Ralph Hoagland.

The chain grew rapidly amassing 17 stores by the end of 1964 (the year the CVS name was first used) and 40 by 1969. That year the Goldsteins sold the chain to Melville Shoe to finance further expansion.

Melville had been founded in 1892 by shoe supplier Frank Melville. Melville's son Ward grew the company creating the Thom McAn shoe store chain and later buying its supplier. By 1969 Melville had opened shoe shops in Kmart stores (through its Meldisco unit) launched one apparel chain (Chess King sold in 1993) and purchased another (Foxwood Stores renamed Foxmoor and sold in 1985).

In 1972 CVS bought the 84-store Clinton Drug and Discount a Rochester New York-based chain. Two years later when sales hit $100 million CVS had 232 stores — only 45 of which had pharmacies. The company bought New Jersey-based Mack Drug (36 stores) in 1977. By 1981 CVS had more than 400 stores.

CVS's sales hit $1 billion in 1985 as it continued to add pharmacies to many of its older stores. In 1987 Stanley's success was recognized companywide when he was named chairman and CEO of CVS's parent company which by then had been renamed Melville.

CVS bought the 490-store Peoples Drug Stores chain from Imasco in 1990 giving it locations in Maryland Pennsylvania Virginia West Virginia and Washington DC. CVS created PharmaCare Management Services in 1994 to take advantage of the growing market for pharmacy services and managed-care drug programs. Pharmacist Tom Ryan was named CEO that year.

With CVS outperforming Melville's other operations in 1995 Melville decided to concentrate on the drugstore chain. By that time Melville's holdings had grown to include discount department store chain Marshalls and furniture chain This End Up both sold in 1995; footwear chain Footaction spun off as part of Footstar in 1996 along with Meldisco; the Linens 'n Things chain spun off in 1996; the Kay-Bee Toys chain sold in 1996; and Bob's Stores (apparel and footwear) sold in 1997.

Melville was renamed CVS in late 1996. Amid major consolidation in the drugstore industry in 1997 CVS — then with about 1425 stores — paid $3.7 billion for Revco D.S. which had nearly 2600 stores in 17 states mainly in the Midwest and Southeast. The next year the company bought Arbor Drugs (200 stores in Michigan later converted to the CVS banner) for nearly $1.5 billion.

CVS opened about 180 new stores and relocated nearly 200 in 1998 as it shifted from strip malls to freestanding stores. (It also closed nearly 160 stores.) Stanley retired as chairman in 1999 and was succeeded by Ryan.

In 1999 the company bought online drugstore pioneer Soma.com renamed CVS.com. It also launched the CVS ProCare pharmacy to serve customers in need of complex drug therapies. A year later CVS bought Stadtlander Pharmacy of Pittsburgh from Bergen Brunswig (now Amerisource-Bergen) for $124 million.

In early 2001 Wolverine Equities paid $288 million for 96 stores which CVS said it would continue to operate. In 2001 CVS opened 43 stores in new markets including Miami and Fort Lauderdale Florida; Las Vegas; and Dallas Houston and Fort Worth Texas. As part of a strategic restructuring begun in 2001 CVS closed more than 200 stores and moved others from strip malls to freestanding locations.

In July 2002 CVS was among the winning bidders for the remaining assets of bankrupt rival Ph

PRODUCTS/OPERATIONS

2016 Retail Sales

	% of total
Prescription drugs	75
Over-the-counter & personal care	10
Beauty/cosmetics	4
General merchandise & other	11
Total	**100**

2016 Sales

	% of total
Pharmacy services	60
Retail/LTC Segment	40
Adjustments	-
Total	**100**

COMPETITORS

A&P	MedImpact
Aetna	Medicine Shoppe
Anthem	OptumRx
BioScrip	PharMerica
CIGNA	Prime Therapeutics
Costco Wholesale	Rite Aid
Express Scripts	Target Corporation
H-E-B	UnitedHealth Group
Humana	Wal-Mart
Kmart	Walgreen
Kroger	

HISTORICAL FINANCIALS

Company Type: Public

Income Statement				FYE: December 31
	REVENUE ($ mil.)	NET INCOME ($ mil.)	NET PROFIT MARGIN	EMPLOYEES
12/17	184,765	6,622	3.6%	246,000
12/16	177,526	5,317	3.0%	250,000
12/15	153,290	5,237	3.4%	243,000
12/14	139,367	4,644	3.3%	217,800
12/13	126,761	4,592	3.6%	208,000
Annual Growth	**9.9%**	**9.6%**	**—**	**4.3%**

2017 Year-End Financials

Debt ratio: 28.38%
Return on equity: 17.77%
Cash ($ mil.): 1,696
Current ratio: 1.02
Long-term debt ($ mil.): 22,181

No. of shares (mil.): 1,014
Dividends
Yield: 0.0%
Payout: 31.0%
Market value ($ mil.): 73,515

	STOCK PRICE ($) FY Close	P/E High/Low		PER SHARE ($) Earnings	Dividends	Book Value
12/17	72.50	13	10	6.44	2.00	37.17
12/16	78.91	22	15	4.90	1.70	34.71
12/15	97.77	24	20	4.63	1.40	33.78
12/14	96.31	25	16	3.96	1.10	33.30
12/13	71.57	19	13	3.74	0.90	32.15
Annual Growth	**0.3%**	**—**	**—**	**14.6%**	**22.1%**	**3.7%**

Dacotah Banks Inc.

EXECUTIVES

Ceo, Richard Westra
Pres, Michael Hollan
SEC, Kenneth L Gosch
Cfo, Chad Bergan
Sr V Pres, Joe Senger
Sr V Pres, Robert Fouberg
Dir, Tom Heisler
Sr V Pres, Bob Compton

V Pres, Steven Schaefer
V Pres, Kent Edson
Vice-President, Richard Holland
Auditors: Eide Bailly LLP

LOCATIONS

HQ: Dacotah Banks Inc.
401 South Main, Suite 212, Aberdeen, SD 57402
Phone: 605 225-4850   **Fax:** 605 225-4929
Web: www.dacotahbank.com

HISTORICAL FINANCIALS

Company Type: Public

Income Statement				FYE: December 31
	ASSETS ($ mil.)	NET INCOME ($ mil.)	INCOME AS % OF ASSETS	EMPLOYEES
12/17	2,406	17	0.7%	—
12/16	2,297	22	1.0%	—
12/08	1,588	14	0.9%	—
12/07	1,391	12	0.9%	441
12/06	1,306	12	0.9%	424
Annual Growth	**5.7%**	**3.5%**		

2017 Year-End Financials

Debt ratio: 1.33%
Return on equity: 6.56%
Cash ($ mil.): 74
Current ratio: —
Long-term debt ($ mil.): —

No. of shares (mil.): 14
Dividends
Yield: 0.0%
Payout: 27.3%
Market value ($ mil.): 471

	STOCK PRICE ($) FY Close	P/E High/Low		PER SHARE ($) Earnings	Dividends	Book Value
12/17	33.00	25	18	1.57	0.43	19.17
12/16	28.25	135	12	2.07	0.40	18.20
12/08	147.00	118	105	1.32	0.23	13.34
12/07	150.00	142	121	1.13	0.22	12.20
12/06	175.00	165	148	1.06	0.21	10.80
Annual Growth	**(14.1%)**	**—**	**—**	**3.6%**	**6.7%**	**5.4%**

DAIRY FARMERS OF AMERICA, INC.

Dairy Farmers of America (DFA) is one of the world's largest dairy cooperatives with nearly 15000 member farmers across the US. Millions of cows belonging to member farmers produce 64 billion pounds of milk a year (roughly 30% of milk production in the US) which DFA markets. Along with fresh and shelf-stable fluid milk the co-op produces cheese butter dried milk powder and other dairy products for industrial wholesale and retail customers. It also offers contract manufacturing services. The co-op owns more than 40 manufacturing plants nationwide. DFA whose profits are shared based on member contribution is a major supplier to dairy giant Dean Foods as well as joint venture partners such as Hiland Dairy.

Operations

DFA owns more than 40 manufacturing plants nationwide. The facilities are focused on several functions and product categories including consumer cheese and butter consumer fluid ingredient cheese and protein and contract manufacturing.

The company's brands include Borden and Cache Valley for consumer cheese; Keller?s Creamery Plugra Breakstone?s Falfurrias and Hotel Bar for butter; and other dairy products under Sport

Shake (sports beverage) La Vaquita (queso) Kemps Guida?s Dairy and Dairy Maid Dairy.

Geographic Reach

DFA is based in Kansas City Missouri and divides the US into seven areas: Central (which shares the main headquarters) Mideast (Medina OH) Mountain (Salt Lake City UT) Northeast (East Syracuse NY) Southeast (Knoxville TN) Southwest (Grapevine TX) and Western (Corona CA).

Sales and Marketing

DFA's customers include big names in the dairy food and retail businesses including Hiland Dairy Borden supermarket giant Kroger Dean Foods Kraft Foods Nestle and many others.

Financial Performance

In 2017 DFA reported revenue of $14.7 billion up nearly 10% from the prior year due to unit sales growth as well as higher milk prices.

Net income that year was $127.4 million.

Strategy

In a statement that could be written about most companies across most industries DFA's strategic focus is on technology and innovation. In late 2018 it invested in SomaDetect a startup that promotes artificial intelligence as way for dairy farmers to more closely monitor herd health and improve milk quality. Also that year it partnered with startup ripe.io to evaluate the usefulness of blockchain technology in the food supply chain.

As far as product innovation DFA introduced a new cheese brand (Craigs Creamery) in early 2019 and invested in a whey protein-infused yogurt (MOPRO) in 2018.

The cooperative also continues to invest in its facilities expanding existing plants and acquiring new ones.

Mergers and Acquisitions

In late 2018 DFA agreed to purchase a St. Paul Minnesota facility from Canada-based dairy cooperative Agropur which will expand DFA's extended shelf-life capabilities and introduce aseptic processing into its business portfolio.

Company Background

DFA was established in 1998 by leaders of four of the nation?s leading milk cooperatives: Associated Milk Producers Mid-America Dairymen Milk Marketing and Western Dairymen Cooperative.

HISTORY

Mid-America Dairymen (Mid-Am) the largest of the cooperatives that merged to form Dairy Farmers of America (DFA) was born in 1968. At that time several Midwestern dairy co-ops banded together to attack common economic problems such as reduced government subsidies price drops resulting from a rising milk surplus dealer consolidation and improvements in production processing and packaging. The merging organizations — representing 15000 dairy farmers — were Producers Creamery Company (Springfield Missouri) Sanitary Milk Producers (St. Louis) Square Deal Milk Producers (Highland Illinois) Mid-Am (Kansas City Missouri) and Producers Creamery Company of Chillicothe (north central Missouri).

During the early 1970s Mid-Am struggled with internal restructuring. Most dairy farmers and co-ops were hit hard by the energy crisis and the government's decision to allow increased dairy imports in 1973 the same year the US Justice Department filed an antitrust suit against Mid-Am. (A judge cleared the co-op 12 years later.)

In 1974 Mid-Am lost almost $8 million on revenues of $625 million chalked up to record-high feed prices a weakened economy a milk surplus and a massive inventory loss. Co-op veteran Gary Hanman was named CEO that year. Over the next two years Mid-Am cut costs sold corporate frills downsized management and began marketing more of its own products under the Mid-America

Farms label thus reducing dependency on commodity sales.

Mid-Am expanded its research and development efforts throughout the 1980s. The co-op opened its services to farmers in California and New Mexico in 1993 and a series of mergers in 1994 and 1995 nearly doubled its size. In 1997 it purchased some of Borden's dairy operations including rights to the valuable Elsie the Cow and Borden's trademarks.

Wary of falling milk prices Mid-Am merged with Western Dairymen Cooperative Milk Marketing and the Southern Region of Associated Milk Producers at the end of 1997 to form DFA. Hanman moved into the seat of CEO at the new co-op. DFA began a series of joint ventures with the #1 US dairy processor Suiza Foods (now Dean Foods).

DFA added California Gold (more than 330 farmers 1998) and Independent Cooperative Milk Producers Association (730 dairy farmer members in Michigan and parts of Ohio and Indiana 1999). In another joint venture with Suiza in early 2000 DFA sold its 50% stake in the US's #3 fluid milk processor Southern Foods in exchange for 34% of a new company named Suiza Dairy Group.

After mollifying the government's antitrust fears DFA acquired the butter operations of Sodiaal North America in 2000. It then molded all its butter businesses into a new entity Keller's Creamery. However another acquisition did not fare as well. The same year DFA acquired controlling interest in Southern Belle Dairy only to have the merger challenged three years later by the Department of Justice. Arguing that the merger formed a monopoly in school milk sales in several states the Department of Justice filed suit which a federal judge later dismissed.

During 2001 the cooperative went in with Land O'Lakes 50/50 to purchase a cheese plant from Kraft. Later in the year as Suiza Foods acquired Dean Foods (and took on its name) DFA sold back its stake in Suiza Dairy Group to the new Dean Foods. DFA then teamed up with a group of dairy investors to form a new 50/50 joint venture National Dairy Holdings which received 11 processing plants from Dean Foods as part of the exchange for Suiza Dairy.

EXECUTIVES

Senior Adviser; President Affiliate Division, Alan J. Bernon, age 63
Coo Northeast Area, Gregory I. (Greg) Wickham
Coo And Ceo Dairylea, Richard P. (Rick) Smith
President Branded Cheese, Mark Korsmeyer
Svp Finance, David Meyer
Executive Vice President Of Commercial Operations, Doug Glade
Coo And Ceo Dairylea, Richard P. (Rick) Smith
Vice Chairman, Bill Siebenborn
First Vice Chairman, Randy Mooney
Vice Chairman, Wayne Palla
Svp Finance, David Meyer
Vice Chairman, George Mertens
Auditors: KPMG LLP KANSAS CITY MO

LOCATIONS

HQ: DAIRY FARMERS OF AMERICA, INC.
1405 N 98TH ST, KANSAS CITY, KS 661111865
Phone: 816 801-6455
Web: WWW.DFAMILK.COM

PRODUCTS/OPERATIONS

Selected Products and Brands
Consumer brands
  Borden cheese
  Breakstone's butter
  Cache Valley cheese

Keller's Creamery butter
Plugrá butter
Sport Shake energy milk shake
Contract manufacturing
  Cheese dips
  Cheese powders & flavors
  Coffee-based flavored drinks
  Instant formula
  Sour cream
  Sports drinks
Dairy ingredients
  Cheeses (American & Italian)
  Nonfat dry milk powder
  Skim milk powder
  Sweetened condensed milk

COMPETITORS

Arla Foods	Glanbia plc
Associated Milk	Great Lakes Cheese
Producers	HP Hood
Berkeley Farms	Humboldt Creamery
California Dairies	Lactalis
Inc.	Land O'Lakes
ConAgra	Marathon Cheese
Darigold Inc.	Mayfield Dairy Farms
Dean Foods	Northwest Dairy
Farmland Dairies	Prairie Farms Dairy
Foremost Farms	Quality Chekd
Friendship Dairies	Sargento
Garelick Farms	

HISTORICAL FINANCIALS

Company Type: Private

Income Statement   FYE: December 31

	REVENUE ($ mil.)	NET INCOME ($ mil.)	NET PROFIT MARGIN	EMPLOYEES
12/15	13,803	98	0.7%	7,000
12/14	17,856	48	0.3%	—
12/13	12,826	58	0.5%	—
12/12	12,082	(126)	—	—
Annual Growth	4.5%	—	—	—

2015 Year-End Financials

Debt ratio: —
Return on equity: 0.70%
Cash ($ mil.): 228
Current ratio: 0.70
Long-term debt ($ mil.): —
Dividends
  Yield: —
  Payout: —
Market value ($ mil.): —

Dana Inc

EXECUTIVES

Pres-Ceo, James K Kamsickas
Non Exec Chb, Keith E Wandell
Exec V Pres-Cfo, Jonathan M Collins
Chief Technical & Quality Offi, George T Constand
Sr V Pres-Cto, Christophe Dominiak
Sr V Pres-Cao, Rodney R Filcek
Sr V Pres-General Counsel-Sec, Marc S Levin
Quality Supervisor, Kim Yake
Unix Administrator, Kimberly Justinger
District Sales Manager Upper M, Leni Woodley
Quality Engineer, Leoline Cannon
Auditors: PricewaterhouseCoopers LLP

LOCATIONS

HQ: Dana Inc
3939 Technology Drive, Maumee, OH 43537
Phone: 419 887-3000   **Fax:** 419 887-5200
Web: www.dana.com

COMPETITORS

AISIN World Corp.	Magna International
American Axle &	Mahle International
Manufacturing	Mark IV
AxleTech International	Martinrea
Boler	International
BorgWarner	Meritor
Carraro	Metaldyne
Chrysler	Modine Manufacturing
DENSO	Neapco
ElringKlinger	Tower International
Federal-Mogul	Valeo
Freudenberg-NOK	Visteon
GKN	Wanxiang
Hitachi Automotive	ZF Friedrichshafen
Systems Americas	

HISTORICAL FINANCIALS

Company Type: Public

Income Statement   FYE: December 31

	REVENUE ($ mil.)	NET INCOME ($ mil.)	NET PROFIT MARGIN	EMPLOYEES
12/17	7,209	111	1.5%	30,100
12/16	5,826	640	11.0%	24,900
12/15	6,060	159	2.6%	23,100
12/14	6,617	319	4.8%	22,600
12/13	6,769	244	3.6%	23,000
Annual Growth	1.6%	(17.9%)	—	7.0%

2017 Year-End Financials

Debt ratio: 31.87%
Return on equity: 10.23%
Cash ($ mil.): 603
Current ratio: 1.69
Long-term debt ($ mil.): 1,759
No. of shares (mil.): 144
Dividends
  Yield: 0.0%
  Payout: 33.8%
Market value ($ mil.): 4,641

	STOCK PRICE ($) FY Close	P/E High/Low		Earnings	PER SHARE ($) Dividends	Book Value
12/17	32.01	46	24	0.71	0.24	6.99
12/16	18.98	5	2	4.36	0.24	8.04
12/15	13.80	23	13	0.99	0.23	4.85
12/14	21.74	12	9	1.84	0.20	6.50
12/13	19.62	—	—	(0.09)	0.20	9.01
Annual Growth	13.0%	—	—	—	4.7%	(6.2%)

Danaher Corp

Danaher is a well-diversified industrial and medical conglomerate whose products test analyze and diagnose. Its subsidiaries design manufacture and market products and offer services geared to worldwide professional medical and dental industrial and commercial markets. Danaher operates through four segments: Life Sciences Diagnostics (research and clinical tools) Environmental & Applied Solutions (turbine pumps and air/water analysis and treatment equipment) and Dental (orthodontic bracket systems and lab products). More than 35% of revenue comes from US customers.

Change in Company Type

Danaher acquired Pall Corporation a major supplier of filtration separation and purification technologies for $13.6 billion in mid-2015. A year later Danaher spun off the Test & Measurement Industrial Technologies and Retail/Commercial Petroleum businesses into a separate publicly traded company Fortive. Brands that went with Fortive include Fluke Qualitrol Tektronix Gilbarco Veeder-Root Kollmorgen and Matco Tools. The spin-off was completed in 2016.

Operations

Built largely through acquisitions Danaher's four business segments reflect a well-balanced portfolio. Top segments Diagnostics and Life Sciences account for more than 30% of revenue each. The Diagnostics segment offers clinical lab critical care and anatomical pathology. The Life Sciences segment's products include mass spectrometry; cellular analysis and lab automation; filtration; and microscopy. The remaining revenue comes from the Dental and Environmental & Applied Solutions units.

Key Danaher subsidiaries include Beckman Coulter X-Rite EskoArtwork Linx Printing Technologies Sybron Dental Specialtiesand Trojan Technologies.

Geographic Reach

Danaher has around 250 manufacturing and distribution facilities worldwide. More than 110 are in the US in more than 25 states; another 140 locations are in more than 50 other countries throughout Asia Europe North America South America and Australia. The company generates about 40% of its revenue from North America primarily the US (more than 35% of sales).

Financial Performance

Danaher Corp.'s sales have ebbed and flowed over the past five years at it has re-engineered itself with a major spinoff and major and minor acquisitions. Revenue rose 42% from a low of $12.6 billion in 2014 to $18.3 billion in 2017.

The 2016-2017 revenue growth was 8% with increases supplied by core business and acquired businesses. The Cepheid acquisition in 2016 drove Diagnostics revenue 16% higher in 2017 with help from immunoassay products in the clinical lab business and consumables in the acute diagnostic business. Sales in the Life Sciences segment rose about 7% in 2017 boosted by mass spectrometers food and forensics instruments flow cytometry equipment and particle counting products. Sales in the Environmental and Applied Solutions segment were up a bout 8% on higher sales in the analytical instrumentation product line from stronger demand in the industrial and municipal end-markets. Dental segment sales were flat year-to-year.

Danaher reported a 2% decline in net income to $2.1 billion in 2017 from 2016. A major difference was income from discontinued operations which was $400 million in 2016 and $22 million in 2017.

The company had about $630 million in cash at the end of 2017 down from more than $960 million for 2016.

Strategy

Even after spending some $20 billion to buy Cepheid Pall and Nobel Biocare in the past several years Danaher Corp. is still in acquisition mode. In 2017 the company bought 10 companies (for a measly $386 million) to fill in product gaps in some cases and to expand to adjacent markets in others.

If the most recent deals work out half as well as the big acquisitions have then it will be money well spent. Danaher has reported that the acquisitions have played a significant role in its rising revenue in terms of products sold as well as in geographies were sales are made. The company posted higher sales in emerging and developed markets in 2017.

The acquisitions have provided Danaher with a large installed base of instruments and equipment that provide increasing amounts of recurring revenue for consumables.

Mergers and Acquisitions

In 2017 Danaher acquired 10 companies for a total of close to $390 million in cash. The acquisitions complement businesses in the Life Sciences Dental and Environmental & Applied Solutions segments.

HISTORY

Danaher (from the Celtic word dana meaning "swift flowing") is named for a fishing stream off the Flathead River in Montana. The term is also an appropriate description of the spotlight-averse Rales brothers. The two have proven to be fishers not only of trout but also of companies buying underperforming companies with strong market shares and recognizable brand names.

Once dubbed "raiders in short pants" by Forbes Steven and Mitchell Rales began making acquisitions in their 20s. In 1981 they bought their father's 50% stake in Master Shield a maker of vinyl building products. The brothers bought tire manufacturer Mohawk Rubber the following year. In 1983 they acquired control of publicly traded DMG a distressed Florida real-estate firm; the next year they sold DMG's real estate holdings and folded Mohawk and Master Shield into the company which they renamed Danaher.

EXECUTIVES

Senior Vice President Finance And Tax, James Ditkoff

Evp And Cfo, Daniel L. Comas, age 54, $862,357 total compensation

President And Ceo, Thomas P. Joyce, age 57, $1,100,000 total compensation

Evp Diagnostics And Dental, William K. (Dan) Daniel, age 53, $730,144 total compensation

Svp Human Resources, Angela S. Lalor, age 52, $603,986 total compensation

Evp Life Sciences, Rainer M. Blair, age 53

Corporate Vice President And Chief Financial Officer Asia, Samuel Liao

Vice President Internal Audit, Christopher Sandberg

Vice President And Bu Manager, Raj Karanam

Vice President And Chief Counsel Mergers And Acquisitions, Attila Bodi

National Sales Manager, Jim White

Vice President Business Development And Strategy Dental, Mischa Reis

Vice President Sales (tektronix Division), Eben Jenkins

Chairman, Steven M. Rales, age 66

Board Member, Alan Spoon

Board Member, Elias A Zerhouni

Auditors: Ernst & Young LLP

LOCATIONS

HQ: Danaher Corp
2200 Pennsylvania Avenue, N.W., Suite 800W, Washington, DC 20037-1701
Phone: 202 828-0850 **Fax:** 202 828-0860
Web: www.danaher.com

2017 Sales

	$ mil.	% of total
United States	6,837	37
China	2,011	11
Germany	1,161	6
Japan	872	5
All other	7,466	41
Total	**18,329**	**100**

PRODUCTS/OPERATIONS

2017 Sales

	$ mil.	% of total
Diagnostics	5,839	32
Life Sciences	5,710	31
Environmental & Applied Solutions	3,968	22
Dental	2,810	15
Total	**18,329**	**100**

2017 Sales

	$ mil.	% of total
Research and medical products	11,512	63
Dental products	2,810	15
Analytical and physical instrumentation	2,232	12
Product identification	1,773	10
Total	**18,329**	**100**

COMPETITORS

ABB	National Instruments
Advantest	Parker-Hannifin
Bosch Rexroth Corp.	PerkinElmer
Datamax-O'Neil	Rockwell Automation
Emerson Electric	SPX
GE	Schneider Electric
Greenlee Textron	Siemens Water
Hitachi	Technologies
Johnson & Johnson	Snap-on
Medical	Stanley Black and
Keysight	Decker
Labfacility	Thermo Fisher
Makita	Scientific
Mettler-Toledo	Wayne

HISTORICAL FINANCIALS

Company Type: Public

Income Statement

FYE: December 31

	REVENUE ($ mil.)	NET INCOME ($ mil.)	NET PROFIT MARGIN	EMPLOYEES
12/17	18,329	2,492	13.6%	67,000
12/16	16,882	2,553	15.1%	62,000
12/15	20,563	3,357	16.3%	81,000
12/14	19,913	2,598	13.0%	71,000
12/13	19,118	2,695	14.1%	66,000
Annual Growth	(1.0%)	(1.9%)	—	0.4%

2017 Year-End Financials

Debt ratio: 22.56%
Return on equity: 10.10%
Cash ($ mil.): 630
Current ratio: 1.43
Long-term debt ($ mil.): 10,327

No. of shares (mil.): 696
Dividends
Yield: 0.0%
Payout: 15.8%
Market value ($ mil.): 64,658

	STOCK PRICE ($) FY Close	P/E High/Low	PER SHARE ($) Earnings	Dividends	Book Value
12/17	92.82	26 22	3.53	0.56	37.84
12/16	77.84	28 21	3.65	0.57	33.23
12/15	92.88	20 17	4.74	0.54	34.49
12/14	85.71	24 19	3.63	0.40	33.19
12/13	77.20	20 14	3.80	0.10	32.07
Annual Growth	4.7%	— —	(1.8%)	53.8%	4.2%

Darden Restaurants, Inc.

You could call this company Olive Darden. After all Darden Restaurants' spot as the No. 1 casual-dining company has been fueled by its Olive Garden chain of nearly 850 Italian-themed restaurants. But Darden is more than garden operating more than 1750 restaurants in the US and Canada. Its other concepts are LongHorn Steakhouse The Capital Grille (upscale steakhouse) Bahama Breeze (Caribbean food and drinks) Eddie V's (seafood) Yard House (American food) and Seasons 52 (casual grill and wine bar). The company added Cheddar's Scratch Kitchen chain to its menu in 2017. Most of the company's restaurants cater to families in suburban locations. Overall Darden restaurants serve about 390 million guests a year.

Operations

Darden's Olive Garden restaurants dish up about 50% the company's revenue followed by Long-Horn Steakhouse locations providing about 20% of revenue. Another 20% of revenue comes from the Other segment composed of the Yard House Bahama Breeze Cheddars and Seasons 52 restaurants. Darden's fine-dining segment of Capital Grille and Eddie V's restaurants with higher-priced menus (steak and seafood entrees in the $30-$50 range) provides less than 10% of revenue.

The company runs 850 Olive Garden restaurants about 500 LongHorn Steakhouses some 70 Yard House locations about 60 Capital Grilles 40 each Seasons 52 and Bahama Breeze and 20 Eddie V's restaurants.

Geographic Reach

Darden operates more than 1750 restaurants in the US and Canada. The three most populous US states have the most Darden locations: Florida about 200 Texas more than 180; and California more than 100. The company operates restaurants in all 50 states and the District of Columbia as well as six in Canada.

Sales and Marketing

Olive Garden has come to epitomize the chain restaurant experience. Olive Garden offers a version of Italian cuisine designed for mass appeal and affordability.

Darden spends heavily on research and development to roll out a succession of new menu items that are heavily promoted through television advertising. The chains also use discount pricing and special offers to win business against the competition which includes Applebee's Chili's (operated by Brinker International) and Outback Steakhouse (OSI Restaurant Partners).

Financial Performance

Darden's revenue has increased six years in a row rising at a 6% annual rate over that time.

In 2018 (ended May) sales rose 12% to $8.1 billion from $7.2 billion in 2017 driven by the strongest sales increases in each brand in at least four years. Sales at Olive Garden which accounts for half of revenue rose about 4% for the year. Overall the company benefited from the acquisition of Cheddar's a 2.3% increase in same-store sales and sales from 40 new company-owned restaurants.

Net income rose to $596 million in 2018 a 24% increase from $479 million in 2017. Food and beverage costs were lower as a percent of sales but labor costs increased as a percent of sales due to wage-rate inflation and the impact of Cheddar's higher labor costs compared to Darden's legacy brands.

Darden finished 2018 with $147 million in cash compared to $233 million in 2017. Cash from operations totaled $1 billion in 2017. Investing and financing activities in 2018 used $451 million and $636 million respectively.

Strategy

Darden has built its dining empire without the aid of franchising a strategy that allows the company the highest degree of control for maintaining food and service quality. The major downside is the cost of operating and maintaining all those restaurants. The company is constantly focused on improving margins by negotiating lower prices for food and other ingredients.

One cost that's hard to contain is labor. The national unemployment rate has been below 4% leading to competition between employers for workers. Darden's labor costs increased 15% in 2018 from 2017. The company said it has raised pay for its workers (it has some 180000 overall) and it provides health insurance benefits and retirement plan contributions.

Darden has invested in technology to strengthen its marketing and analytics capabilities. Its efforts include an online and mobile ordering system for Olive Garden and LongHorn Steakhouse and developing customer relationship management programs data analytics and data-driven marketing.

Darden is looking outside of the US for growth including plans to develop Olive Garden and LongHorn Steakhouse locations in Brazil Colombia the Dominican Republic Panama and Puerto Rico. Most of the company's international growth emphasis has been on its Olive Garden and LongHorn Steakhouse chains.

Mergers and Acquisitions

In 2017 Darden acquired the Cheddar's casual dining chain from private equity firms L Catterton and Oak Investment Partners among other owners. The $780 million deal brings some 160 locations across more than two dozen states to Darden.

EXECUTIVES

Ceo And Director, Eugene I. (Gene) Lee, age 57, $953,750 total compensation
Svp And Chief Human Resources Officer, Danielle Kirgan, $378,462 total compensation
Evp And President Olive Garden, David C. (Dave) George, age 62, $576,539 total compensation
Svp And Cfo, Ricardo (Rick) Cardenas, age 50, $474,539 total compensation
President Yard House, Michael (Mike) Kneidinger
Vp Operations The Capital Grille, Brian Foye
President Longhorn Steakhouse, Todd Burrowes, $442,211 total compensation
Svp And Cio, Chris Chang
President The Capital Grille And Eddie V's, John Martin
Senior Vice President, Melissa Baker
Senior Vice President Division, Sam Pereira
Senior Vice President Human Resource Olive Garden, Paula Manchester
Vice President, Kathy Janiga
Senior Vice President Division, Paula Britton
Vice President Quality Assurance, Ana Hooper
Senior Vice President Franchising And President International Operations, Michael Beacham
Svp And Chief Supply Chain Officer, Doug Milanes
Vice President Culinary Operations Olive Garden, Timothy Blaise
Vice President Enterprise Beverage Strategy And Innovation, Helen Mackey
Ceo And Director, Eugene I. (Gene) Lee, age 57
Chairman, Charles M. (Chuck) Sonsteby
Auditors: KPMG LLP

LOCATIONS

HQ: Darden Restaurants, Inc.
   1000 Darden Center Drive, Orlando, FL 32837
Phone: 407 245-4000
Web: www.darden.com

PRODUCTS/OPERATIONS

Restaurant Brands
Bahama Breeze
Eddie V's
LongHorn Steakhouse
Olive Garden
The Capital Grille
Yard House
Seasons 52
Cheddar's Scratch Kitchen

2018 Sales

	$ mil.	% of total
Olive Garden	4,082	51
LongHorn Steakhouse	1,703	21
Fine Dining	575	7
Other Business	1,720	21
Total	**8,080**	**100**

COMPETITORS

Bob Evans	DineEquity
Brinker	Hooters
Carlson Restaurants	OSI Restaurant
Cheesecake Factory	Partners
Cracker Barrel	Perkins & Marie
Denny's	Callender's

HISTORICAL FINANCIALS

Company Type: Public

Income Statement

FYE: May 27

	REVENUE ($ mil.)	NET INCOME ($ mil.)	NET PROFIT MARGIN	EMPLOYEES
05/18	8,080	596	7.4%	180,656
05/17	7,170	479	6.7%	178,729
05/16	6,933	375	5.4%	150,000
05/15	6,764	709	10.5%	150,000
05/14	6,285	286	4.6%	206,489
Annual Growth	**6.5%**	**20.1%**	**—**	**(3.3%)**

2018 Year-End Financials

Debt ratio: 16.94%	No. of shares (mil.): 123
Return on equity: 27.82%	Dividends
Cash ($ mil.): 146	Yield: 0.0%
Current ratio: 0.40	Payout: 53.2%
Long-term debt ($ mil.): 926	Market value ($ mil.): 10,853

	STOCK PRICE ($) FY Close	P/E High/Low	PER SHARE ($) Earnings	Dividends	Book Value
05/18	87.88	21 16	4.73	2.52	17.77
05/17	87.95	23 16	3.80	2.24	16.76
05/16	67.48	25 18	2.90	2.10	15.47
05/15	65.54	13 8	5.47	2.20	18.42
05/14	49.55	25 21	2.15	2.20	16.30
Annual Growth	**15.4%**	**— —**	**21.8%**	**3.5%**	**2.2%**

DaVita Inc

DaVita gives life in the form of dialysis treatments to patients suffering from end-stage renal disease (ESRD chronic kidney failure). Through its Kidney Care division the firm is one of the US' largest providers of dialysis providing administrative services to more than 2380 outpatient centers across the US; it serves some 189000 patients. The company also offers home-based dialysis services as well as inpatient dialysis in about 900 hospitals. It operates two clinical laboratories that specialize in routine testing of dialysis patients and serve the company's network of clinics.

Operations

DaVita operates through two divisions — Kidney Care (dialysis and related lab and support services) and DaVita Medical Group (DMG formerly known as HealthCare Partners or HCP).

Dialysis and lab services account for around 60% of the company's revenues. DaVita and its main competitor Fresenius Medical Care together control nearly three-fourths of the US dialysis clinic market. (DaVita controls about 35% of the market while Fresenius controls another 45%. Fresenius actually manufactures dialysis supplies and DaVita is a customer.)

A portion of DaVita's dialysis and lab-related revenues comes from administering specialty pharmaceuticals to patients receiving dialysis. The pharmaceuticals include vitamin D iron supplements and EPO — a genetically engineered protein that stimulates the production of red blood cells. EPO is used during dialysis to treat anemia (a common complication). Amgen is the only company manufacturing EPO and to buffer against price fluctuations or shortages DaVita has a multi-year agreement with Amgen to secure its supply of EPO at discounted pricing.

DMG is a patient- and physician-focused integrated health care delivery and management company. DMG has roughly 750000 members under its care in Southern California Central and South Florida southern Nevada central New Mexico and central Arizona through capitation contracts. Sales from the DMG business accounts for about 30% of revenues. In late 2017 the company announced plans to sell DMG to health insurer UnitedHealth for $4.34 billion.

Geographic Reach

California Florida and Texas are home to about 30% of all DaVita dialysis centers though the firm has locations in more than 45 US states and Washington DC. The DMG unit operates and manages medical groups and physician practice networks in California Colorado Florida Georgia Nevada New Mexico and Washington.

While its international operations (150 outpatient dialysis centers in more than 10 countries) are still a tiny fraction of its total business the company is involved in a long-term strategy to expand into overseas markets for growth through acquisitions and partnerships. The company has established a presence in select international markets including Europe Latin America the Middle East and the Asia/Pacific region. Colombia Germany India and Malaysia together account for more than 70% of DaVita's outpatient dialysis centers outside of the US.

Sales and Marketing

Almost 90% of DaVita's dialysis patients are covered by government-based health plans including Medicare and Medicaid agencies and the VA making DaVita particularly vulnerable to changes in government reimbursement rates (which are regularly under threat of being lowered by state and federal governments facing budget pressures). Government plan reimbursements account for about 65% of the company's annual revenues; the balance of the income comes from commercial insurance payers (including hospital dialysis services) as their primary payor.

DMG provides medical services through a network of about 700 primary care physicians as well as several thousand specialists in some 200 hospitals. Its teammates employed clinicians and affiliated clinicians provide care for some 1.7 million patients. DaVita is selling the unit to UnitedHealth.

One commercial payor Humana accounts for roughly 10% of DaVita's total consolidated net revenues each year.

Financial Performance

DaVita has achieved unprecedented growth the last few years with revenues peaking at a record-setting $14.8 billion in 2016. The most recent growth was fueled by increased treatment volume primarily from non-acquired growth at existing and new dialysis centers cost control initiatives and payor mix improvements within its dialysis business.

In addition to the historic revenue growth DaVita's profits more than tripled from $270 million in 2015 to $880 million in 2016 another company milestone. This was attributed to the increase in revenues and the absence of debt refinancing and redemption charges it incurred the previous year.

Strategy

While DaVita has primarily grown through acquisitions over the years it also expands its operations through joint ventures and partnerships. In 2015 it formed a joint venture to operate kidney care specialty hospitals in Shadong Province China. Also that year it entered the Brazilian market and it opened an outpatient vascular access center in Saudi Arabia.

In late 2017 DaVita announced plans to sell its DMG segment to UnitedHealth for $4.34 billion. The company will focus on its core kidney care business but is also exploring options to enter other areas of health care.

Mergers and Acquisitions

Historically DaVita has grown its network of facilities through acquisition of outpatient dialysis centers.

In 2017 it bought Colorado-based Renal Ventures for $415 million. Renal Ventures operates 36 dialysis clinics in six states; it also has units that operate infusion and vascular centers.Also that year the company acquired Nevada-based WellHealth Quality Care operator of about a dozen centers specializing in such areas as anesthesiology and obstetrics/gynecology.

During 2016 DaVita achieved a net increase of 99 US dialysis centers and 36 international dialysis centers.

HISTORY

Hospital chain National Medical Enterprises (NME now Tenet) formed Medical Ambulatory Care in 1979 to run its in-hospital dialysis centers. The unit bought other centers in NME's markets. In 1994 the subsidiary's management backed by a Donaldson Lufkin & Jenrette — now Credit Suisse First Boston (USA) — investment fund bought the dialysis business and renamed it Total Renal Care (TRC).

To become a leader in its consolidating field TRC began buying other centers and soon added clinical laboratory and dialysis-related pharmacy services and home dialysis programs. It went public in 1995.

The next year the firm added 66 facilities 32 from its acquisition of Caremark International's dialysis business. In 1997 TRC expanded abroad buying UK-based Open Access Sonography (vein care) and partnering with UK-based Priory Hospitals Group.

In 1998 TRC bought Renal Treatment Centers nearly doubling its size. But the acquisition costs caused a loss that year and sparked shareholder lawsuits (settled in 2000) over alleged misleading statements. The firm also became embroiled in a reimbursement dispute with Florida's Medicare program. Problems continued into 1999 as the company struggled to meld operations. The company took a charge to cover a billing shortfall and chairman and CEO Victor Chaltiel and COO/CFO John King resigned. New management began improving billing procedures and took other cost-cutting measures.

The company changed its name in 2000 to DaVita an Italian phrase loosely translated as "he/she gives life." It also sold its international operations to competitor Fresenius.

In 2005 the company acquired Gambro's US dialysis operations for about $3 billion adding some 565 dialysis clinics to its operations. To meet FTC requirements for the deal DaVita sold about 70 clinics to RenalAmerica a company founded by former Gambro Healthcare executive Michael Klein.

In 2007 DaVita expanded its health care offerings by acquiring a majority stake in HomeChoice Partners a provider of home infusion services. The company added about 80 new centers through acquisitions in 2009.

DaVita significantly widened its domestic network of dialysis centers when it acquired regional dialysis chain DSI Renal for $690 million in 2011. To secure approval for the deal from the FTC DaVita agreed to divest 30 clinics but overall the acquisition added more than 100 dialysis centers to its holdings.

Elsewhere around the world DaVita entered Germany with the 2011 purchase of DV Care. It also expanded into the Middle East through the acquisition of a majority stake in Lehbi Care a leading Riyadh-based kidney care company with three clinics.

The company has also been looking to branch out into new areas of health care including medical practice management a mission it accomplished through the 2012 purchase of private medical group management firm HealthCare Partners through a merger transaction worth some $4.4 billion.

Following the deal the company changed its legal name from DaVita to DaVita HealthCare Partners to reflect its broadened operations; the dialysis division continues to operate under the DaVita name while HealthCare Partners operates as an independent subsidiary of DaVita HealthCare Partners. The two companies both count California and Florida as key markets and DaVita HealthCare Partners has used HealthCare Partners' integrated care model to help it offer a wider range of health care services.

Internationally the company entered China in 2012 through a joint venture to provide dialysis se

EXECUTIVES

Executive Chair Davita Medical Group, Charles G. (Chuck) Berg, age 61
Chairman And Ceo, Kent J. Thiry, age 62, $1,273,077 total compensation
Cfo, Joel Ackerman, age 53
Group Vp Purchasing And Public Affairs, LeAnne M. Zumwalt, age 59, $400,000 total compensation
Chief Compliance Officer, Jeanine M. Jiganti, age 59
Chief Accounting Officer, James K. (Jim) Hilger, age 56, $375,000 total compensation
Ceo Davita Kidney Care, Javier J. Rodriguez, age 47, $865,385 total compensation
Chief Medical Officer Davita Kidney Care, Allen R. Nissenson, age 71
President Colorado Springs Health Partners, Oraida Roman
Ceo Davita International, Robert Lang
Medical Director, John Burns
Vice President Revenue Management, David Corlett
Vp Operations, Ray Follett
Divisional Vice President, Vicki Burrier
Vice President Integration, Douglas Allen
Vice President Finance, Chitra Goswami
Vice President, Stuart Bachelder
Vice President Federal Government Affairs, Joelle Thornhill
Group Vice President, Martha Wofford
Division Vice President Crossroads Division, Roxanne Ramoutar
Chairman And Ceo, Kent J. Thiry, age 62
Auditors: KPMG LLP

LOCATIONS

HQ: DaVita Inc
2000 16th Street, Denver, CO 80202
Phone: 303 405-2100
Web: www.davita.com

PRODUCTS/OPERATIONS

2016 Revenues by Payer

	% of total
Government-based programs	
Medicare & Medicare-assigned plans	55
Medicaid	5
Other government-based programs	4
Commercial	36
Total	**100**

2016 Dialysis Revenues

	% of total
Outpatient hemodialysis centers	79
Peritoneal dialysis & home-based hemodialysis	16
Hospital inpatient hemodialysis	5
Total	**100**

2016 Sales

	$ mil.	% of total
US dialysis & related lab services	9,138	61
DaVita Medical Group (DMG)	4,113	28
Ancillary services	1,621	11
Adjustments	(127.9)	-
Total	**14,745**	**100**

Selected Operations

Astro Hobby West Mt. Renal Care Limited Partnership
Austin Dialysis Centers L.P.
Beverly Hills Dialysis Partnership
Brighton Dialysis Center LLC
Capital Dialysis Partnership
Carroll County Dialysis Facility L.P.
Central Carolina Dialysis Centers LLC
Chicago Heights Dialysis LLC
Continental Dialysis Center Inc.
Dallas-Fort Worth Nephrology L.P.
Dialysis of Des Moines LLC
Dialysis Specialists of Dallas Inc.
Downriver Centers Inc.
Downtown Houston Dialysis Center L.P.
Durango Dialysis Center LLC
DVA Healthcare of Maryland Inc.
East End Dialysis Center Inc.
Elberton Dialysis Facility Inc.
Empire State DC Inc.
Greenwood Dialysis LLC
Hawaiian Gardens Dialysis LLC
HealthCare Partners LLC
HuntingtonPark Dialysis LLC
Indian River Dialysis Center LLC
Jedburg Dialysis LLC
Kidney Centers of Michigan L.L.C.
Lincoln Park Dialysis Services Inc.
Mason-Dixon Dialysis Facilities Inc.
Middlesex Dialysis Center LLC
Natomas Dialysis
Nephrolife Care (India) Pte. Ltd.
North Colorado Springs Dialysis LLC
Open Access Lifeline LLC
Palomar Dialysis LLC
Physicians Choice Dialysis of Alabama LLC
Physicians Dialysis of Houstin LLP
Renal Life Link Inc.
Renal Treatment Centers Inc.
RMS Lifeline Inc.
Rocky Mountain Dialysis Services LLC
Shining Star Dialysis Inc.
Soledad Dialysis Center LLC
Summit Dialysis Center L.P.
Tortugas Dialysis LLC
Total Renal Care Inc.
Total Renal Laboratories Inc.
Total Renal Research Inc.
TRC West Inc.
Tulsa Dialysis Center LLC
Upper Valley Dialysis L.P.

COMPETITORS

Apria Healthcare	Lincare Holdings
Critical Care Systems	Molina Healthcare
International	Permanente Medical
Dialysis Clinic Inc	Groups
FMCNA	Quest Diagnostics
Gentiva	U.S. Renal Care
LabCorp	UnitedHealth Group

HISTORICAL FINANCIALS

Company Type: Public

Income Statement

FYE: December 31

	REVENUE ($ mil.)	NET INCOME ($ mil.)	NET PROFIT MARGIN	EMPLOYEES
12/17	10,876	663	6.1%	74,500
12/16	14,745	879	6.0%	70,300
12/15	13,781	269	2.0%	60,400
12/14	12,795	723	5.7%	57,900
12/13	11,764	633	5.4%	57,400
Annual Growth	**(1.9%)**	**1.2%**	**—**	**6.7%**

2017 Year-End Financials

Debt ratio: 49.27%
Return on equity: 14.21%
Cash ($ mil.): 508
Current ratio: 2.88
Long-term debt ($ mil.): 9,158
No. of shares (mil.): 182
Dividends
  Yield: —
  Payout: —
Market value ($ mil.): 13,183

	STOCK PRICE ($) FY Close	P/E High/Low		PER SHARE ($) Earnings	Dividends	Book Value
12/17	72.25	21	15	3.47	0.00	25.70
12/16	64.20	18	13	4.29	0.00	23.89
12/15	69.71	66	53	1.25	0.00	23.22
12/14	75.74	23	18	3.33	0.00	23.98
12/13	63.37	43	18	2.95	0.00	20.79
Annual Growth	**3.3%**	**—**	**—**	**4.1%**	**—**	**5.4%**

DCP Midstream LP

DCP Midstream is one of the largest natural gas gatherers in North America and also the top producer and a primary marketer of natural gas liquids (NGLs). It also engages in natural gas compressing treating processing transporting and selling. DCP Midstream also transports and sells NGLs and distributes propane wholesale. The company operates natural gas gathering systems (11200 miles of pipe) in seven states (including Arkansas Louisiana Oklahoma and Texas) seven processing plants four NGL pipelines and nine propane storage terminals. DCP Midstream Partners LP merged with DCP Midstream LLC in 2017 to become DCP Midstream LP.

Change in Company Type

In 2017 DCP Midstream LLC a 50/50 joint venture between Phillips 66 and Spectra Energy and DCP Midstream Partners LP combined all of the assets and debt of the two companies simplifying its corporate structure and creating the largest NGL producer and gas processor in the US. The combined company was renamed DCP Midstream LP.

Operations

DCP Midstream operates three segments: Natural Gas Services (gathering compressing treating processing transporting and storing natural gas and fractionating NGLs); NGL Logistics (transportation storage and fractionation of NGLs); and Wholesale Propane Logistics (receipt of propane by pipeline rail or ship to its terminals that store and deliver product to distributors).

Natural Gas Services accounted for 85% of total net sales in 2015; Wholesale Propane Logistics 11%; and NGL Logistics 4%.

Geographic Reach

DCP Midstream operates assets in seven states in the continental US: Arkansas Colorado Louisiana MichiganOklahoma Texas and Wyoming.

The company operates its NGL logistics business in Colorado Kansas Louisiana Michigan Oklahoma and Texas and its wholesale propane logistics business in Maine Massachusetts Pennsylvania Vermont and Virginia.

Its NGL storage facility is located in Marysville Michigan.

The natural gas supply for its gathering pipelines and processing plants is derived primarily from natural gas wells located in Arkansas Colorado Louisiana Michigan Oklahoma Texas Wyoming and the Gulf of Mexico.

Sales and Marketing

The company typically sells propane to propane distributors under annual sales agreements. It had two third-party customers in its Wholesale Propane segment that accounted for greater than 10% of its segment revenues for 2015.

DCP Midstream sells natural gas to marketing affiliates of natural gas pipelines integrated oil companies national wholesale marketers industrial end-users and gas-fired power plants. It typically sells natural gas under market index related pricing terms. The NGLs extracted from the natural gas at its processing plants are sold at market index prices.

Financial Performance

In 2015 the company's net sales decreased by $1.7 billion compared to 2014. The primary reason was due to $1.5 billion decrease for its Natural Gas Services segment primarily due to decreased commodity prices lower NGL sales volumes lower volumes at natural gas storage and pipeline assets at the Southeast Texas system unfavorable commodity derivative activity a change in the contract structure at its Lucerne 1 plant and a favorable contractual producer settlement in 2014.

Net income decreased by $195 million due to lower sales partially offset by decreased purchases of natural gas propane and NGLs.

In 2015 DCP Midstream's net cash provided by the operating activities increased by 24% due to a change in accounts receivable.

Strategy

A consolidator in the fragmented natural gas gathering NGLs and wholesale propane industry segments the company has been expanding its gas supply base and its propane wholesale network in recent years through strategic complementary acquisitions and joint ventures.

The company continually evaluates economically attractive organic expansion opportunities to construct midstream systems in new or existing operating areas. It plans to execute its strategy in part through pursuing economically attractive drop down opportunities from DCP Midstream.

The company pursues economically attractive and strategic third party acquisition opportunities within the midstream energy industry both in new and existing lines of business and geographic areas of operation. Experiencing the downturn in the energy industry caused by the volatility in the commodity prices it is currently focusing on sustaining the per unit distribution on its units.

In 2015 DCP Midstream executed a reduction in force with the corporate restructuring. DCP Midstream closed its Oklahoma City regional office and reduced its workforce in its Tulsa and Midland offices relocating functions in those locations primarily to its Denver headquarters and Houston regional office.

Company Background

In 2013 DCP Midstream bought a 47% stake in an Eagle Ford joint venture from the owner of its general partner for $626 million bringing its ownership interest in the joint venture to 80%.

In 2012 DCP Midstream acquired the Texas-based Crossroads processing plant and gathering system from Penn Virginia Resource Partners for $63 million. The bolt-on acquisition allows the company to expand its market position in East Texas and provide services to drillers in the Haynesville shale and Cotton Valley regions.

In 2011 DCP Midstream acquired the Seaway Products Pipeline Co. from ConocoPhillips. The pipeline now called Southern Hills Pipeline and being converted to NGL service is expected to be operational by mid-2013. It will provide NGL access from the Midcontinent to the Texas Gulf Coast.

Expanding in Michigan in 2009 the company acquired gas gathering and treating assets for $45.1 million. In 2010 it acquired a 350-mile interstate natural gas liquids pipeline system in Colorado's Denver-Julesburg Basin from Buckeye Partners for $22 million.

In 2010 DCP Midstream moved to extend its Northeast wholesale propane business into the MidAtlantic region acquiring UGI's Atlantic Energy for $49 million. That year it also purchased of NGL storage company Marysville Hydrocarbon Holdings (in Michigan) for about $95 million.

In terms of the company's origins the D in DCP Midstream Partners (formerly Duke Energy Field Services) is for Duke Energy; the CP ConocoPhillips. These two energy majors formed DCP Midstream Partners in 2005. Following the spinoff of Spectra Energy from Duke Energy in 2007 Spectra Energy assumed Duke Energy's 50% holding in DCP.

EXECUTIVES

Group Vp And Chief Environmental Health And Safety Officer, Jerry Barnhill, age 56

Group Vp And Chief Transformation Officer, Bill Johnson

President Commercial, Don Baldridge, age 48, $182,077 total compensation

Chairman President And Ceo, Wouter T. van Kempen, age 48

Group Vp And Cfo, Sean P. OÂ'Brien, age 48

President Asset Operations, Brian Frederick

Vice President, Paul Kennedy

Vice President Of Quality Information Technology And Regulatory Affairs, Rusty Bondeson

Executive Vice President, Richard Cargile

Executive Vice President, Mark Borer

Vice President Procurement, Bill Prentice

Vice President Of Information Technology, Quay Chan

Vice President Of Information Technology, Susie Sjulin

Executive Vice President Of Marketing, William Johnson

Vice President Of Technology Systems, Timothy Yearous

Vice President Of Information Systems, Lori Martinez

Vice President, Mark Krabbe

Vp Engineering, Chris Root

Vice President Operations, Dan Tarpley

Senior Vice President Of North Region, Kevin Williams

Vice President Public Affairs And Investor Relations, Roz Elliott

Vice President Regulatory And Government Affairs, Bryant Kinney

Vice President And Deputy General Counsel, Steve Van Hooser

Chairman President And Ceo, Wouter T. van Kempen, age 48

Board Member, Billy Waycaster

Board Member, William Kimble

Auditors: DELOITTE & TOUCHE LLP

LOCATIONS

HQ: DCP Midstream LP
370 17th Street, Suite 2500, Denver, CO 80202
Phone: 303 595-3331
Web: www.dcpmidstream.com

PRODUCTS/OPERATIONS

2016 Sales

	$ mil.	% of total
Natural gas services	1,269	85
Wholesale propane logistics	146	10
NGL logistics	85	5
Intra-segment eliminations	(3)	-
Total	**1,497**	**100**

2016 Sales

	$ mil.	% of total
Sales of natural gas propane NGLs and condensate	1,093	72
Transportation processing and other	424	28
(Losses) gains from commodity derivative activity net	(20)	-
Total	**1,497**	**100**

COMPETITORS

BP NGL	Martin Midstream
Crestwood Midstream	Partners
Partners LP	SandRidge Energy
Enterprise Products	Williams Companies
Kinder Morgan	XTO Energy
Magellan Midstream	

HISTORICAL FINANCIALS

Company Type: Public

Income Statement

FYE: December 31

	REVENUE ($ mil.)	NET INCOME ($ mil.)	NET PROFIT MARGIN	EMPLOYEES
12/17	8,462	229	2.7%	—
12/16	1,497	312	20.8%	—
12/15	1,898	228	12.0%	—
12/14	3,642	423	11.6%	7
12/13	2,980	181	6.1%	7
Annual Growth	**29.8%**	**6.1%**	**—**	**—**

2017 Year-End Financials

Debt ratio: 33.92%
Return on equity: —
Cash ($ mil.): 156
Current ratio: 0.89
Long-term debt ($ mil.): 4,707

No. of shares (mil.): 143
Dividends
Yield: 0.0%
Payout: 725.5%
Market value ($ mil.): 5,206

	STOCK PRICE ($) FY Close	P/E High/Low	Earnings	Dividends	Book Value
12/17	36.33	97 69	0.43	3.12	51.69
12/16	38.38	24 10	1.64	3.12	22.67
12/15	24.67	52 23	0.91	3.12	24.16
12/14	45.43	20 15	2.84	3.01	26.27
12/13	50.35	43 30	1.34	2.82	21.84
Annual Growth	**(7.8%)**	**—**	**(24.7%)**	**2.6%**	**24.0%**

Dean Foods Co.

Dean Foods is the nation's largest milk bottler. The company markets fluid milk ice cream cultured dairy products and beverages (juices teas and bottled water) under more than 50 local regional and private-label brands including DairyPure Borden Pet Country Fresh Meadow Gold and TruMoo a leading national flavored milk brand. Dean Foods owns and operates a number of smaller regional dairy companies including Friendly's Berkeley Farms and Garelick Farms. The company distributes dairy products across the US from regional manufacturing facilities.

Operations

About 70% of Dean Foods' revenue comes from its fluid milk while ice cream products account for about 15%. The rest of the company's sales come from fresh cream cultured products extended shelf-life dairy and other products and other beverages. The company's reliance on fluid milk puts it at the mercy of milk prices consumer demand and competition. Changes in any of those forces could affect the company's operations.

The company has a wide reach around the US operating more than 60 production facilities around the country. It ships most of its products directly to stores in a fleet of refrigerated trucks. It buys milk produced by more than 930000 cows from some 4350 farms.

Geographic Reach

Dean Foods rings up 99% of its sales in the US where it operates manufacturing facilities in 32 states (and distributes across all 50 states). The company?s nationwide manufacturing and distribution capacity could be strengths as it tries to roll out products such as Friendly?s and Mayfield ice creams across bigger regions and countrywide.

Outside of the US the dairy giant has some operations in Europe.

Sales and Marketing

Dean Foods markets its products through advertising and other promotions including media coupons trade shows and other promotional activities. The company has significantly increased its advertising spending in the past several years to drive consumer awareness of its national brands.

Dean Foods' customers include food retailers distributors foodservice operators educational institutions (some 32500 schools) and governmental entities throughout the US. Walmart and its subsidiaries including Sam's Club is the company's largest customer accounting for more than 15% of revenue. The next four biggest customers account for less than 20% of sales.

The company's products are sold primarily on a local or regional basis through local and regional sales forces although some national customer relationships are coordinated by a centralized corporate sales department.

Financial Performance

After a couple years of declining revenue Dean Foods' sales inched up 1% in 2017 from 2016. The rise was attributed to higher prices for fluid milk which were caused by higher commodity prices. The company also had contributions from the Friendly's and Mayfield ice cream acquisitions. Increases were offset to a degree by lower fluid milk volume from overall category softness and reductions in private label fluid milk volume due to competitive pressures. Dean Foods also blamed an increase in retailers investing more in their own private label products.

Dean Foods' profit fell to about $61 million in 2017 from about $120 million in 2016. The company had higher expenses for several items in 2018 including increased commodity prices costs associated with closing facilities and reorganization and impairment charges for long-lived assets.

The company's cash and cash equivalents fell to $16.5 million in 2017 from $18 million in 2016. It had lower cash from operations because of reduced operating income and a discretionary payment made to the company-sponsored pension plan.

Strategy

Dean Foods is trying to move into higher margin products such as ice cream to lessen its dependence on low-margin milk products particularly private-label products. The transition has been interrupted however by rising milk prices declining demand and looming competition from Walmart the company's biggest customer.

Dean Foods looks to its size and scale to provide flexibility to serve customers the country with private label and branded products. The company counts on its national brands such as DairyPure TruMoo Organic Valley and Friendly's to win space in grocery dairy sections. It began selling extensions of the brands such as DairyPure cottage cheese that includes a mix-in product as well as DairyPure sour cream.

Another challenge on the horizon is Wal-Mart's construction of its own dairy processing plant in Indiana. The plant is to supply dairy products to some 600 stores in the Midwest. Walmart will shift an estimated 90 million gallons of production from Dean to the plant in 2018 and 2019 reducing Dean's annual volume by about 4%. Dean will continue to supply Walmart in other parts of the country.

Dean Foods is responding to these challenges with cost cutting measures plant closures and the shift to a more profitable product mix. In a program the company calls OPEX 2020 it plans to cut expenses to bring them into line with revenue and give the company flexibility to respond the market opportunities and challenges.

With fluid milk volumes declining Dean Foods believes a switch to more profitable branded products and reducing its large-format private label business will provide higher gross margins. Increased sales of products such as ice cream and cottage cheese is to improve profitability.

Dean Foods' strengthened its ice cream offerings with the 2016 acquisition of Friendly's. Friendly's bolstered Dean Foods' market position in the Northeast US and provides a platform for nationwide expansion. Dean Foods also is looking to expand the Mayfield Creamery product line in the southern US. Another step to sell higher margin products is Dean's 50-50 production and distribution partnership with Organic Valley and its line of organic dairy products.

Mergers and Acquisitions

In 2016 the company bolstered its ice cream product lineup after it acquired Friendly's Ice Cream's retail and manufacturing ice cream business for $155 million in cash. Prior to the acquisition Friendly's made and distributed a variety of ice cream products; it also operates a restaurant chain in the northeastern US that was not part of the acquisition. The Friendly's brand complements Dean's line-up of ice cream brands including Mayfield and Dean's Country Fresh.

HISTORY

Investment banker Gregg Engles formed a holding company in 1988 with other investors including dairy industry veteran Cletes Beshears to buy the Reddy Ice unit of Dallas-based Southland (operator of the 7-Eleven chain). The company also bought Circle K's Sparkle Ice and combined it with Reddy Ice. By 1990 it had acquired about 15 ice plants.

The company changed its name to Suiza Foods when it bought Suiza Dairy in 1993 for $99 million. The Puerto Rican dairy was formed in 1942 by Hector Nevares Sr. and named for the Spanish word for "Switzerland." By 1993 it was Puerto Rico's largest dairy controlling about 60% of the island's milk market.

Suiza Foods bought Florida's Velda Farms manufacturer and distributor of milk and dairy products in 1994. The company went public in 1996 the same year it bought Swiss Dairy (dairy products California and Nevada) and Garrido y CompaA±Aa (coffee products Puerto Rico).

The company became one of the largest players in the North American dairy industry through its acquisitions in 1997. It paid $960 million for Morningstar (Lactaid brand lactose-free milk Second Nature brand egg substitute) which — like Suiza Foods itself — was a Dallas-based company formed in 1988 through a Southland divestiture. The company entered the Midwest with its $98 million purchase of Country Fresh and the Northeast with the Bernon family's Massachusetts-based group of dairy and packaging companies including Garelick Farms and Franklin Plastics (packaging).

Suiza Foods strengthened its presence in the southeastern US in 1998 with its $287 million acquisition of Land-O-Sun Dairies operator of 13 fluid-dairy and ice-cream processing facilities. Also that year Suiza Foods purchased Continental Can (plastic packaging) for about $345 million and sold Reddy Ice to Packaged Ice for $172 million.

After settling an antitrust lawsuit brought by the US Department of Justice in 1999 Suiza Foods bought dairy processors in Colorado Ohio and Virginia. That year Suiza Foods combined its US packaging operations with Reid Plastics to form Consolidated Containers retaining about 40% of the new company.

In 2001 Suiza Foods announced it had agreed to purchase rival Dean Foods for $1.5 billion and the assumption of $1 billion worth of debt. Dean Foods had begun as Dean Evaporated Milk founded in 1925 by Sam Dean a Chicago evaporated-milk broker. By the mid-1930s it had moved into the fresh milk industry. The company went public in 1961 and was renamed Dean Foods in 1963.

Suiza Foods completed the acquisition and took on the Dean Foods name later in 2001. The new Dean Foods bought out Dairy Farmers of America's interest in Suiza Dairy and merged it with the "old" Dean's fluid-dairy operations to create its internal division Dean Dairy Group.

Along with the purchase of "old" Dean came a 36% ownership of soy milk maker WhiteWave and in 2002 Dean Foods purchased the remaining 64% for approximately $189 million. By the end of the year Dean had sold off some smaller businesses (boiled peanuts and contract hauling) and its Puerto Rico operations for $119 million in cash.

EXECUTIVES

Ceo, Ralph P. Scozzafava, age 59, $850,000 total compensation

Evp General Counsel Corporate Secretary And Government Affairs, Russell F. Coleman

Evp And Chief Human Resources Officer, Kimberly (Kim) Warmbier, age 56, $432,000 total compensation

Svp Logistics, S. Craig McCutcheon, age 57

Evp Supply Chain, Brad Cashaw, age 54, $343,674 total compensation

Interim Cfo, Scott K. Vopni, age 50

Vice President Business Development Group, Christopher Anderson

Vice President Finance, Kim Lechner

Vice President Research And Development Fresh Dairy Direct, Kathleen Dacunha

Vice President Finance, Eddie Tollison

Vice President, Scott Toth

Senior Vice President Operations Dean Branded Products Group, Wayne Allen

Vice President Of Finance, Brian Scheffler

Vice President And Corporate Treasurer, James Kenwood

Senior Vice President Industry Relations, Marty Devine

Vice President Sales South Region, Marvin Monroe

Vice President Prc, Gary Tritt

Vice President Corporate Development, Steve Schultz

Vice President Tax Planning, Shan Luton

Executive Vice President Chief Human Resources Officer, Kim Warmbier

Vice President Of Finance, Tim Jones

Vice President, David Hurst

Vice President Of Sales National Accounts, Tim Heil

Vice President National Warehouse Sales, John White

Chairman, Jim L. Turner, age 72

Ceo, Ralph P. Scozzafava, age 59

Auditors: DELOITTE & TOUCHE LLP

LOCATIONS

HQ: Dean Foods Co.
2711 North Haskell Avenue, Suite 3400, Dallas, TX 75204
Phone: 214 303-3400
Web: www.deanfoods.com

2017 Sales

	% of total
Domestic	99
Foreign	1
Total	**100**

PRODUCTS/OPERATIONS

2017 Sales

	$ mil.	% of total
Fluid milk	5,316	68
Ice cream	1,108	14
Fresh cream	389	5
Cultured	282	4
Other beverages	291	4
Extended shelf life and other dairy products	196	2
Other	213	3
Total	**7,795**	**100**

2017 Fresh Dairy Direct Sales

	% of total
Private-label brands	51
Company brands	49
Total	**100**

Selected Brands

Alpro (Europe)
Alta Dena
Berkeley Farms
Borden (licensed)
Brown Cow
Brown's Dairy
Dean's
Friendly's
Garelick Farms
Gandy's
Hershey's (licensed)
Horizon Organic
Knudsen (licensed)
LAND O'LAKES (licensed)
Mayfield Creamery
Oak Farms
Over the Moon
Pet (licensed)
Provamel (Europe)
Robinson Dairy
Silk
Swiss Premium
Tru Moo
Tuscan
WhiteWave

Selected Products

Bottled waters
Eggnog
Eggs
Cottage cheese
Half-and-half
Ice cream
Juice
Milk
Pudding
Sour cream
Soymilk
Whipping cream

COMPETITORS

Associated Milk Producers
Aurora Organic Dairy
Ben & Jerry's
Blue Bell
Brewster Dairy
California Dairies Inc.
ConAgra
Crystal Farms Refrigerated Distribution Company
Dairy Farmers of America
Danone
Darigold Inc.

Dreyer's
Foster Dairy Farms
Galaxy Nutritional Foods
Grupo LALA
H-E-B
HP Hood
Hain Celestial
Hiland Dairy
Lactalis
Lifeway Foods
Maryland & Virginia Milk Producers
Mondelez International
National Dairy
Nestlé USA
Northwest Dairy
Organic Valley
Prairie Farms Dairy
Quality Chekd
Rockview Dairies
Stonyfield Farm
Tillamook County Creamery Association
Vitasoy International
Wal-Mart

HISTORICAL FINANCIALS

Company Type: Public

Income Statement

FYE: December 31

	REVENUE ($ mil.)	NET INCOME ($ mil.)	NET PROFIT MARGIN	EMPLOYEES
12/17	7,795	61	0.8%	16,000
12/16	7,710	119	1.6%	17,000
12/15	8,121	(8)	—	16,960
12/14	9,503	(20)	—	17,246
12/13	9,016	813	9.0%	18,040
Annual Growth	(3.6%)	(47.5%)	—	(3.0%)

2017 Year-End Financials

Debt ratio: 36.47%
Return on equity: 9.73%
Cash ($ mil.): 16
Current ratio: 1.52
Long-term debt ($ mil.): 912

No. of shares (mil.): 91
Dividends
 Yield: 0.0%
 Payout: 53.7%
Market value ($ mil.): 1,053

	STOCK PRICE ($) FY Close	P/E High/Low		PER SHARE ($) Earnings	Dividends	Book Value
12/17	11.56	32	13	0.67	0.36	7.20
12/16	21.78	17	12	1.31	0.36	6.74
12/15	17.15	—	—	(0.09)	0.28	5.97
12/14	19.38	—	—	(0.22)	0.28	6.67
12/13	17.19	2	1	8.58	0.00	7.53
Annual Growth	(9.4%)	—	— (47.1%)		—	(1.1%)

Deere & Co.

Deere & Co. is interested in seeing its customers go to seed and grow. The company one of the world's largest makers of farm equipment is also a major producer of construction forestry and commercial and residential lawn care equipment. Deere operates through three business segments: the agriculture and turf and construction and forestry segments make up its equipment operations; a credit segment provides financial services. Deere famous for its "Nothing Runs Like A Deere" marketing sells John Deere and other brands through retail dealer networks and also makes products for outlets Home Depot and Lowes.

Operations

Deere's largest operating segment is agriculture and turf which accounts for 70% of revenue. Consolidated into five product platforms — crop har-

vesting turf and utility hay and forage crop care and tractors — the segment makes such products as loaders combines corn pickers cotton and sugarcane pickers and golf course equipment and outdoor power products. Besides John Deere brands include Frontier Kemper Green Systems Hagie Mazzotti and Monosem as well as SABO in Europe and Benye in China.

The company's construction and forestry segment generates 20% of revenue. Making 90% of the types of construction equipment used in North America this segment distributes backhoe loaders crawler dozers motor graders log skidders and skid-steer loaders.

Besides equipment the company's other main operational division financial services (10% of revenue) provides credit services for Deere dealers and wholesalers.

Geographic Reach

Deere is based in Moline Illinois which is in the middle of the US?s corn and soybean country. Accordingly North America (the US and Canada) accounts for about 60% of the company?s revenue each year. The Moline Illinois-based company doesn?t break out revenue from other specific regions but it operates manufacturing facilities around the world. To get equipment and parts where they need to go Deere has a centralized parts distribution center and eight regional parts depots and distribution centers throughout North America. It also has distribution operations in Europe South America Africa Asia Australia and India.

Sales and Marketing

Deere operates through roughly 25 sales and marketing locations and nearly 20 warehousing locations in Argentina Australia Brazil Chile China Ecuador France India Israel Italy Mexico Russia Spain Turkey and the US.

Through US and Canadian facilities Deere markets products to about 2360 dealer locations most of which are independently owned and operated. Of these about 1520 sell agricultural equipment while some 425 sell construction earthmoving material handling and forestry equipment. Some dealer locations are owned by Deere?s Nortrax subsidiary. Outside the US and Canada Deere agriculture and turf equipment is also sold to distributors and dealers for resale and lawn and garden equipment is sold through Home Depot and Lowe?s.

Financial Performance

Deere & Company?s sales dropped about 30% from its high-water mark of almost $38 billion in 2013 to 2016. The steepest year-to-year fall was 21% from 2014 from 2015 when farmers cut back spending because of lower commodity prices and currency exchange rates were particularly unfavorable.

In 2017 (ended October) sales perked up about 12% to nearly $30 billion from 2016 led by the agriculture and turf segment?s 21% sales jump. The segment shipped more pieces of equipment and benefitted from better currency exchange rates. Construction and forestry turned in a 17% sales increase on the same factors.

Net income rose more than 40% to more than $2 billion in 2017 from 2016. Besides higher sales Deere received about $400 million from the sale of the Site One Landscape Supply business.

Deere had about $9.3 billion in cash in 2017 a steep increase from $2.4 billion in 2016. The company issued about $4.6 billion in debt in 2017 compared to retiring some $1.4 billion the year before.

Strategy

Deere & Company is seeding its future with research and develop using a large dose of technology. The company is developing machinery that uses technologies such as machine learning and

high-speed wireless communications to automate planting and harvesting and tasks in between. This involves equipment and machinery used to monitor and measure crop yield moisture content or seeding population in real time. Other products generate prescriptions for planting seeds and applying fertilizer or pesticide with better accuracy. All of this helps farmers manage costs and increase revenue through improved productivity and higher yields. The company?s S700 line of combines introduced in 2017 brings many of those technologies to the field. Deere has spent an average of about $1.4 billion on research and development from 2015-2017.

The company supplements its R&D with acquisitions to extend its technology expertise as well as its lines of products and geographic reach.

Mergers and Acquisitions

In 2017 Deere & Company acquired Wirtgen Group a leading manufacturer of road construction equipment for $5.2 billion. Wirtgen Deere?s neighbor in Moline Illinois sells in more than 100 countries through a network of company-owned and independent dealers. Deere gained six brands across the global road-construction sector.

In another 2017 deal Deere bought Blue River Technology a developer of integrated computer-vision and machine-learning technology that helps growers reduce the use of herbicides for $284 million. Blue River?s technologies help optimize the use of farm inputs. Its Machine learning technologies could be applied to a wide range of Deere?s products.

Deere bought Mazzotti a sprayer manufacturer based in Italy. The deal adds to Deere?s sprayer technologies and brings more customers in Europe.

In 2016 the company acquired Hagie Manufacturing Company a manufacturer of high-clearance sprayers located in Clarion Iowa for $53 million. The deal accelerated John Deere's market reach in precision planting equipment and added engineering expertise to further develop planting technology.

Looking to grow internationally Deere in 2016 also picked up Monosem a European market leader in precision planters. The purchase included four facilities in France and two in the US.

HISTORY

Vermont-born John Deere moved to Grand Detour Illinois in 1836 and set up a blacksmith shop. Deere and other pioneers had trouble with the rich black soil of the Midwest sticking to iron plows designed for sandy eastern soils so in 1837 Deere used a circular steel saw blade to create a self-scouring plow that moved so quickly it was nicknamed the "whistling plow." He sold only three in 1838 but by 1842 he was making 25 a week.

Deere moved his enterprise to Moline in 1847. His son Charles joined the company in 1853 beginning a long tradition of family management. (All five Deere presidents before 1982 were related by blood or marriage.) Charles eventually set up an independent dealership distribution system and added wagons buggies and corn planters to the product line.

EXECUTIVES

Vice President Information Technology, Ganesh Jayaram
Vice President Worldwide Supply Management Logistics, Thomas Knoll
Chairman President And Ceo, Samuel R. (Sam) Allen, age 65, $1,500,000 total compensation

President Agriculture And Turf Americas Australia And Global Harvesting And Turf Platforms, James M. Field, age 55, $686,266 total compensation

President Worldwide Construction And Forestry Global Labor Relations And Security, Max A. Guinn, age 60

President Agriculture And Turf Division Europe Asia Africa And Global Tractor Platform, Mark von Pentz, age 55

Svp And Cfo, Rajesh (Raj) Kalathur, age 50, $615,312 total compensation

President Agricultural Solutions And Cio, John C. May, age 49, $599,840 total compensation

Vp Global Supply Management And Logistics, Pierre Guyot

Svp John Deere Power Systems Worldwide Parts Services Advanced Technology And Engineering And Global Supply Management And Logistics, Jean H. Gilles, age 61, $614,823 total compensation

Svp And Chief Administrative Officer, Marc A. Howze, age 55

President John Deere Financial, Cory J. Reed, age 47

Vice President Worldwide Supply Management, David Nelson

Vice President Strategic Partnerships Worldwide Construction And Forestry Division, Douglas Gage

Vice President Of Sales, Vanessa Stifferclaus

Vice President Information Technology, Dave Garrison

Vice President Of Finance, Jesus Rasgado

Vice President Marketing, Chris Arnold

Senior Vice President, Randy Sergesketter

Vice President, Pam Brandt

Vice President, John Mann

Vice President Information Systems, Ray Lybarger

Vice President, Arthur Woodcock

Vice President H R, Heather Rogers

Senior Vice President Agricultural Marketing North Ame, Douglas Devries

Vice President Taxes, Thomas K Jarrett

Vice President, Ted Norton

Senior Vice President Global Tractor Platform, Bernhard Haas

Vice President Information Technology, Daniel Mairet

Vice President Human Resources, Jeffrey Peterson

Vice President Of Planning And Corporate Development, Dan Reilly

Vice President Engineering And Manufacturing John Deere Power Systems, Michael Weinert

Vice President Global Service Delivery, Robert Boyle

Vp Internal Audit, Luann Rickert

Vice President International Finance For Europe Commonwealth Of Independent States North Africa, Stefan Von Stegmann

Vice President Corporate Communications Global Brand Man, Frances Emerson

Vice President Assistant Sec, Danny Langston

Vice President Of Management Informati, Richard Townsend

Vice President Of Finance, Cristina Pagliari

Vice President Operations, Bryan Bossert

Vice President Marketing, James Anderson

Vice President Taxes, Margaret Curry

Vice President Worldwide Parts Services, Kimberly Beardsley

Vice President And Deputy General Counsel Deere And Company And Senior Vice President And Chief Couns, Matthew Haney

Vice President Taxes, James Mccabe

Vice President Of Information Technology, Marty Wilkinson

Senior Vice President And Finance Director John Deere Financial, Steven Owenson

Director Of Nursing Services, Kimberly Campbell

Chairman President And Ceo, Samuel R. (Sam) Allen, age 65

Board Member, Crandall Bowles

Secretary, Victoria Graves

Board Member, Sherry Smith

Vice President And Treasurer, Thomas Spitzfaden

Vice President And Treasurer, Jenny Kimball

Board Member, Shukla Abhishek

Secretary, Paul Nagel

Board Member, Brian Krzanich

Board Member, Michael Johanns

Auditors: DELOITTE & TOUCHE LLP

LOCATIONS

HQ: Deere & Co.
  One John Deere Place, Moline, IL 61265
Phone: 309 765-8000   Fax: 309 765-9929
Web: www.johndeere.com

2017 Sales

	$ mil.	% of total
US & Canada	17,557	59
Outside U.S. and Canada	11,263	38
Other	918	3
Total	**29,738**	**100**

PRODUCTS/OPERATIONS

2017 Sales

	$ mil.	% of total
Agriculture & turf	20,167	68
Construction & forestry	5,718	19
Financial services	29,354	10
Other	918	3
Total	**29,738**	**100**

Selected Products and Services

Agricultural and turf equipment
  Balers
  Combines
  Cotton harvesting equipment
  Golf course equipment
  Harvesters
  Hay and forage equipment
  Irrigation
  Landscape and nursery
  Loaders
  Mowers (commercial riding lawn equipment and walk-behind mowers)
  Planting and seeding equipment
  Power products (outdoor)
  Sprayers
  Tillage
  Tractors (large medium and utility)
  Utility vehicles
Construction and forestry equipment
  Articulated dump trucks
  Backhoe loaders
  Crawler dozers
  Crawler loaders
  Excavators
  Landscape loaders
  Log skidders and loaders
  Material handling equipment
  Motor graders
  Skid-steer loaders
Credit
  Leasing
  Retail and wholesale financing
Power systems
  Diesel and natural gas engines (marine industrial mining)
  Powertrain components
  Transmissions

COMPETITORS

AGCO	Kubota
Briggs & Stratton	Mahindra
Buhler Industries	Navistar International
Caterpillar	PACCAR
Great Plains	Terex
Manufacturing	Toro Company
Honda	Valmont Industries
Komatsu	Volvo

HISTORICAL FINANCIALS

Company Type: Public

Income Statement
FYE: October 28

	REVENUE ($ mil.)	NET INCOME ($ mil.)	NET PROFIT MARGIN	EMPLOYEES
10/18	37,357	2,368	6.3%	74,413
10/17	29,737	2,159	7.3%	60,476
10/16	26,644	1,523	5.7%	56,800
10/15	28,862	1,940	6.7%	57,200
10/14	36,066	3,161	8.8%	59,623
Annual Growth	0.9%	(7.0%)	—	5.7%

2018 Year-End Financials

Debt ratio: 60.27%
Return on equity: 22.79%
Cash ($ mil.): 3,904
Current ratio: 0.69
Long-term debt ($ mil.): 27,237

No. of shares (mil.): 318
Dividends
  Yield: 0.0%
  Payout: 35.6%
Market value ($ mil.): 42,355

	STOCK PRICE ($) FY Close	P/E High/Low	PER SHARE ($) Earnings	Dividends	Book Value
10/18	133.00	23 18	7.24	2.58	35.45
10/17	133.25	20 13	6.68	2.40	29.70
10/16	88.30	18 15	4.81	2.40	20.71
10/15	78.00	17 13	5.77	2.40	21.29
10/14	85.54	11 9	8.63	2.22	26.23
Annual Growth	11.7%	— —	(4.3%)	3.8%	7.8%

Delek US Holdings Inc (New)

EXECUTIVES

Chb-Pres-Ceo, Ezra Uzi Yemin
Exec V Pres-Cfo, Kevin L Kremke
Exec V Pres-Coo, Frederec Green
Exec V Pres-Cco, Avigal Soreq
Exec V Pres Hr, Donald N Holmes
Unknown, Blake Waterson
Project Coordinator, Alexandra Dalton
Director Financial and SEC Rep, Heather Denham
Project Director, Randy Goodspeed
Technical Manager, Allen Kaiser
Manager of Training, Bob Gonzales
Auditors: Ernst & Young LLP

LOCATIONS

HQ: Delek US Holdings Inc (New)
  7102 Commerce Way, Brentwood, TN 37027
Phone: 615 771-6701
Web: www.Delekus.com

COMPETITORS

7-Eleven	Motiva Enterprises
CITGO	Murphy Oil
Chevron	Publix
ConocoPhillips	Racetrac Petroleum
Costco Wholesale	The Pantry
Cumberland Farms	Wal-Mart
Exxon Mobil	Winn-Dixie
Gate Petroleum	

HISTORICAL FINANCIALS

Company Type: Public

Income Statement

FYE: December 31

	REVENUE ($ mil.)	NET INCOME ($ mil.)	NET PROFIT MARGIN	EMPLOYEES
12/17	7,267	288	4.0%	3,941
12/16	4,197	(153)	—	1,326
12/15	5,762	19	0.3%	4,584
12/14	8,324	198	2.4%	4,361
12/13	8,706	117	1.4%	4,366
Annual Growth	(4.4%)	25.2%	—	(2.5%)

2017 Year-End Financials

Debt ratio: 24.69%
Return on equity: 21.86%
Cash ($ mil.): 931
Current ratio: 0.98
Long-term debt ($ mil.): 875

No. of shares (mil.): 80
Dividends
Yield: 0.0%
Payout: 7.5%
Market value ($ mil.): 2,822

	STOCK PRICE ($) FY Close	P/E High/Low		PER SHARE ($) Earnings	Dividends	Book Value
12/17	34.94	9	5	4.00	0.30	20.44
12/16	24.07			(2.49)	0.60	16.01
12/15	24.60	128	70	0.32	0.60	18.56
12/14	27.28	11	8	3.35	1.00	17.49
12/13	34.41	20	10	1.96	0.95	15.79
Annual Growth	0.4%	—	—	19.5%	(25.0%)	6.7%

Dell Technologies Inc

Auditors: PricewaterhouseCoopers LLP

LOCATIONS

HQ: Dell Technologies Inc
One Dell Way, Round Rock, TX 78682
Phone: 800 289-3355
Web: www.delltechnologies.com

HISTORICAL FINANCIALS

Company Type: Public

Income Statement

FYE: February 2

	REVENUE ($ mil.)	NET INCOME ($ mil.)	NET PROFIT MARGIN	EMPLOYEES
02/18	78,660	(3,728)	—	145,000
02/17*	61,642	(1,672)	—	138,000
01/16	50,911	(1,104)	—	—
01/15	54,142	(1,221)	—	—
Annual Growth	13.3%	—	—	—

*Fiscal year change

2018 Year-End Financials

Debt ratio: 42.42%
Return on equity: (-32.25%)
Cash ($ mil.): 13,942
Current ratio: 0.85
Long-term debt ($ mil.): 43,998

No. of shares (mil.): 769
Dividends
Yield: —
Payout: —
Market value ($ mil.): 54,522

	STOCK PRICE ($) FY Close	P/E High/Low		PER SHARE ($) Earnings	Dividends	Book Value
02/18	70.90	—	—	(0.00)	0.00	12.63
02/17*	64.35	44	30	1.43	0.00	17.32
01/16	0.00	—	—	(2.72)	0.00	3.88
Annual Growth	—	—	—	—	—	48.2%

*Fiscal year change

Delta Air Lines Inc (DE)

Delta Air Lines is one of the world's largest airlines by traffic. Through its regional carriers the company serves about 320 destinations in about 60 countries and it operates a mainline fleet of 800-plus aircraft as well as maintenance repair and overhaul (MRO) and cargo operations. The airline serves nearly 180 million customers each year and offers more than 15000 daily flights. Delta is a founding member of the SkyTeam marketing and code-sharing alliance (airlines extend their networks by selling tickets on flights) which includes carriers Air France KLM and Alitalia.

Operations

Delta divides its operations into two chief segments: airline and refinery. The airline segment provides scheduled air transportation for passengers and cargo throughout the US and around the world and other ancillary airline services including maintenance and repair services for third parties.

The refinery segment provides jet fuel to the airline segment from its own production and through jet fuel obtained through agreements through third parties. The costs included in the refinery segment are primarily for the benefit of the airline segment.

Geographic Reach

Delta operates from domestic hubs in Atlanta Boston Detroit London Los Angeles Minneapolis/St. Paul New York Seattle and Salt Lake City. Delta has international hubs in Amsterdam Paris and Tokyo. The US market is its largest representing about 70% of net sales.

Sales and Marketing

Delta's tickets are sold through various distribution channels including telephone reservations Delta.com and traditional brick and mortar and online travel agencies. It spent about $277 million on advertising in 2016.

Financial Performance

After peaking at a record-setting $40.7 billion in 2015 Delta's revenues dipped 3% to $39.6 billion in 2016. This was attributed to a 5% decline in passenger revenue per available seat mile (PRASM) on 2% higher capacity compared to 2015. The decrease in PRASM was largely driven by competitive pressure within the low fuel price environment and the impact of US dollar strength on tickets sold in international markets which are largely priced in local currency.

In addition to the revenue decline profits fell 3% from $4.5 billion in 2015 to $4.4 billion in 2016 as lower passenger revenue and higher salaries and related costs offset the benefits of lower fuel prices. Cash flow from operations also fell from $7.9 billion in 2015 to $7.2 billion in 2016 mainly due to unfavorable changes in accounts receivable and fuel inventories.

Strategy

The airline industry is fueled by strategic alliances that allow individual carriers to extend their service without physically flying into new territory. Delta's alliance with SkyTeam allows the airline's reach to extend to more than 900 destinations in 170-plus countries around the globe. The company gets a boost in global coverage with airlines around the world coming aboard the SkyTeam alliance.

To boost its position in the important region of China Delta in 2015 expanded its global network with China Eastern one of the leading airlines in China. The agreement included a $450 million investment by Delta to acquire an almost 4% stake in China Eastern. The move allowed Delta and China Eastern to compete more effectively on routes between the US and China and provided more travel options for customers in both countries.

Looking to Europe Delta plans to build its presence in its strategically advantaged hubs in London Paris and Amsterdam while de-emphasizing higher Europe point-of-sale markets. Its 49% equity investment in Virgin Atlantic has improved its presence in London one of the largest revenue markets from the US while also enhancing its transatlantic network including its existing joint venture relationship with Air France-KLM and Alitalia.

Targeting the Asia/Pacific region for growth in mid-2017 Delta and Korean Air announced a joint venture that will create a combined network serving more than 290 destinations in the Americas and more than 80 in Asia. The increase in scale between the carriers includes expanded codesharing in the trans-Pacific market joint sales and marketing initiatives in Asia and the US and co-location at key hubs.

Another important key growth component for airlines that has made headlines recently is customer satisfaction. Delta has significantly invested in its business since 2010 to improve its operational performance which it states consistently ranks first among the major US carriers. During 2016 the carrier operated 241 days with zero mainline canceled flights a nearly 50% improvement over its 2015 performance.

HISTORY

Delta Air Lines was founded in Macon Georgia in 1924 as the world's first crop-dusting service Huff-Daland Dusters to combat boll weevil infestation of cotton fields. It moved to Monroe Louisiana in 1925. In 1928 field manager C. E. Woolman and two partners bought the service and renamed it Delta Air Service after the Mississippi Delta region it served. About 80 years later Delta became one of the world's largest airlines by traffic after its $2.8 billion acquisition of Northwest Airlines in 2008.

EXECUTIVES

Ceo, Edward H. (Ed) Bastian, age 60, $741,669 total compensation
President, Glen W. Hauenstein, age 57, $604,997 total compensation
Evp And Cfo, Paul A. Jacobson, age 46, $525,000 total compensation
Sevp And Coo, Wayne G. (Gil) West, $617,977 total compensation
Evp And Chief Human Resources Officer, Joanne Smith
Svp And Cio, Rahul Samant
Evp Global Sales; President International, Steve Sear
Evp And Chief Legal Officer, Peter W. Carter, $500,000 total compensation
Vice President Corporate Real Estate, Shane Jones
Vp State And Local Government Affairs, Jeff Davidman
Vice President Learning, Sharon Mickelson
Svp Global Sales, Bob Somers
Executive Vice President And Chro, Anne Smith
Senior Vice President Operations And Customer Center, Dave Holtz
Vice President And Chief Accounting Officer, Craig Meynard
Vice President Facilities And Maintenanc, Robert Anderson
Vp Customer Experience Integration, Charisse Evans
Vice President Global Human Resources Services, Chris Collins
Vice President And Treasurer, Kenneth Morge
Assistant Vice President Retail Information Technology, Timothy W Harms
Svp Hr, Rob Kight
Vice President Information Systems, Robert Olson

Senior Vice President Delta Connection, Don
Bornhurst
Senior Vice President Delta Connection, Donald
Bornhorst
National Account Manager, Laura Cascino
Vice President, Shreve Lee
Senior Vice President Flight Operations, Steve
Dickson
Vice President Global Distribution And Digital
Strategy, Rhonda Crawford
Svp Supply Chain Management And Fleet
Strategy, Greg May
Vice President Womens Employee Network, Toni
Wysong
Vice President Of Business Operations, Thomas E
Schull
Vice President Corporate Real Estate Lax, Mary
Loeffelholz
Regional Vice President, Richard R Marr
Vp Airport Customer Service Detroit, John
Fechushak
Vice President, Sandeep Dube
Vice President Partner Development, Jeff Arinder
Senior Vice President And Deputy General
Counsel, Matthew Knopf
Vice President Channel Technology, Matthew Matt
Cincera
Aa To Senior Vice President, Laurie Jones
Vice President Total Rewards And Information
Technology Human Resources, Greg Tahvonen
Svp Worldport Operations, Greg Kennedy
Svp Legal Regulatory And International, Christine
Wilson
Vp Pricing And Revenue Management Trans
Pacific, Roberto Ioriatti
Vp Airport Operations New York Jfk International
Airport, Hussein Berry
Senior Vice President Safety Engineering And
Compliance, Kimberly Hill
Senior Vice President Central Region, Trevor O
Pickle
National Account Manager, Amy Shaw
Atg Vice President Fld Stns Xy, Kristin K Rice
Atg Vice President Human Resources Xy, Jannie
Richardson
Chairman, Francis S. (Frank) Blake, age 68
Board Member, Mickey Foret
Secretary, Wendy Tistinic
Auditors: Ernst & Young LLP

LOCATIONS

HQ: Delta Air Lines Inc (DE)
Post Office Box 20706, Atlanta, GA 30320-6001
Phone: 404 715-2600
Web: www.delta.com

2016 Sales

	$ mil.	% of total
Domestic	28,108	71
Atlantic	5,919	15
Pacific	2,939	7
Latin America	2,673	7
Total	39,639	100

PRODUCTS/OPERATIONS

2016 Sales

	$ mil.	% of total
Passenger		
Mainline	28,105	71
Regional carriers	5,672	14
Cargo	668	2
Other	5,194	13
Total	39,639	100

2016 Sales

	$ mil.	% of total
Airline	39,406	91
Refinery	3,843	9
Intersegment Sales/Other	(3610)	-
Total	39,639	100

Selected Aircraft

Type
B-717-200
B-737-700
B-737-800
B-737-900
ERB-747-400
B-757-200
B-767-300
B-777-200
ERE190-100
MD-88

COMPETITORS

Air Canada	Lufthansa
AirTran Airways	Qantas
American Airlines	SAS
Group	Singapore Airlines
British Airways	Southwest Airlines
Cathay Pacific	United Continental
Japan Airlines	Virgin Atlantic
JetBlue	Airways

HISTORICAL FINANCIALS

Company Type: Public

Income Statement

FYE: December 31

	REVENUE ($ mil.)	NET INCOME ($ mil.)	NET PROFIT MARGIN	EMPLOYEES
12/17	41,244	3,577	8.7%	87,000
12/16	39,639	4,373	11.0%	84,000
12/15	40,704	4,526	11.1%	83,000
12/14	40,362	659	1.6%	80,000
12/13	37,773	10,540	27.9%	78,000
Annual Growth	2.2%	(23.7%)	—	2.8%

2017 Year-End Financials

Debt ratio: 16.58%
Return on equity: 27.31%
Cash ($ mil.): 1,814
Current ratio: 0.42
Long-term debt ($ mil.): 6,592

No. of shares (mil.): 707
Dividends
Yield: 0.0%
Payout: 20.5%
Market value ($ mil.): 39,603

	STOCK PRICE ($) FY Close	P/E High/Low		PER SHARE ($) Earnings	Dividends	Book Value
12/17	56.00	11	9	4.95	1.02	19.67
12/16	49.19	9	6	5.79	0.68	16.81
12/15	50.69	9	7	5.63	0.45	13.93
12/14	49.19	62	35	0.78	0.30	10.68
12/13	27.47	2	1	12.29	0.12	13.67
Annual Growth	19.5%	—	—	(20.3%)	70.5%	9.5%

Devon Energy Corp.

As an independent energy company Devon explores develops and produces oil gas bitumen and NGLs onshore the US and Canada. It is especially focused in developing projects in the Delaware Basin and STACK assets. Devon also owns Enlink an MLP with substantial midstream operations in the US but agreed to sell it in 2018. The company manages some 6500 net wells with about 200 mmboe in annual production.

OperationsDevon had a total production output of 198 mmboe in 2017 (compared to 223 mmboe in 2016). The company reported more than 12350 producing gross wells and around 6470 net wells with some 4.3 million net acres to its name.Devon's daily production includes approximately 250000 barrels of oil 1.2 billion cubic feet of natural gas and about 100000 barrels NGL.

Geographic ReachDevon's assets are concentrated around STACK Delaware Basin in the US and heavy oil assets in Alberta Canada. The company also has properties in Texas (Eagle Ford & Barnett Shale) as well as the Powder River Basin & Wind River Basin in the Rockies. At Delaware Basin Devon is especially present in oil-rich Bone Spring Delaware Wolfcamp and Leonard formations. At STACK in Oklahoma Devon is busy in the Woodford Shale and the Meramec zones.In Canada Devon's Alberta oil assets include the Jackfish complex an industry-leading thermal heavy oil operation in the non-conventional oil sands of east central Alberta undeveloped Pike oil sands acreages southeast of Jackfish as well as acreage and producing assets in the Bonnyville region south and east of Jackfish.

Sales and MarketingDevon sells its products under both long-term (one year or more) and short-term (less than one year) agreements at prices negotiated with third parties. Majority of its products are sold at variable market-sensitive prices. Devon also enters into financial hedging arrangements or fixed-price contracts (146 mmboe in 2017).

Financial PerformanceRevenue in 2017 climbed 35% to $13.9 billion primarily from a $2.3 billion increase in marketing and midstream revenues thanks to EnLink's throughput of gas processing & transmission volumes. However Devon's margins were negatively impacted by downstream marketing commitments. The upstream segment also improved sales by an impressive $1.4 billion due to higher unhedged realized prices across Devon's portfolio even though divestitures led to production declines by some $427 million. After years of significant losses (almost $14 billion in 2015-16 years) Devon posted $898 million in profits in 2017 primarily due to higher gross margin linked directly to higher commodity prices and volumes sold. Cash holdings increased to $2.7 billion at the end of 2017. Operations provided $2.9 billion offset by $2.2 billion going towards investments. Financial activities contributed $9 million in cash inflows. CAPEX in 2017 was $2.8 billion.

StrategyDevon has returned to profitability in 2017 thanks to recovering commodity prices and major asset sell-offs. In June 2018 Devon sold EnLink to Global Infrastructure Partners for approximately $3.1 billion 12 times its current cash flow. Furthermore Devon's margins were being negatively impacted by downstream marketing commitments explaining its eagerness to offload Enlink. Devon also sold off its 50% interest in the Access Pipeline in Canada for $3 billion plus US upstream assets back in 2016 followed by further divestitures worth $415 million in 2017. In 2017 the company generated a healthy $2.7 billion from operations. Yields are at a 46-year high doubling output since 2012. Initial 90-day production rates have also skyrocketed 400% in the same period. A deep inventory and a healthy replacement rate (150% in 2017) adds future potential. Current activities are centered around the Bone Springs (Delaware Basin) Woodford Shale and the Meramec zones (STACK). With $1.4 billion in CAPEX earmarked for 2018 Devon is treating these assets as low-risk multi-decade growth platforms. For 2018 the company is aiming top-oil production growth by some 10% while well drilling & completion rate is expected to surge 25%. Yet significant challenges threaten recovery. Price pressures and volatility remain—NYMEX WTI oil prices have ranged from a high of over $100/ bbl to a low of $26/ bbl in less than a decade. The company also carries significant debt ($10.4 billion at 2017 end) taking away cash flows towards debt service payments.

Mergers and Acquisitions

In June 2018 Devon announced the sale of all its stake in EnLink Midstream Partners to Global Infrastructure Partners for approximately $3.1 billion. Total final divestiture value is expected to exceed Devon's $5 billion target.In 2016 Devon acquired Felix Energy for $1.9 billion. The transaction secures 80000 net acres in the most economic portion of the STACK oil play in Western Oklahoma. Devon holds one of the leading positions in the play.

Company Background

Devon was founded in 1971 by John Nichols and his son Larry. It became a public company in 1988 and the next year pioneered in the production of coalbed natural gas in the San Juan Basin. Over the next decades it steadily acquired big oil & gas companies with the US and abroad to become of the top independent oil companies.

HISTORY

Larry Nichols (a lawyer who clerked for US Supreme Court Chief Justice Earl Warren) and his father John founded Devon Energy in 1969. John Nichols was a partner in predecessor company Blackwood and Nichols an oil partnership formed in 1946.

In 1981 the company bought a small stake in the Northeast Blanco Unit of New Mexico's San Juan Basin. To raise capital Devon formed the limited partnership Devon Resource Investors and took it public in 1985. In 1988 Devon consolidated all of its units into a single publicly traded company.

The firm increased its stake in Northeast Blanco in 1988 and again in 1989 ending up with about 25%. By 1990 Devon had drilled more than 100 wells in the area and had proved reserves of 58 billion cu. ft. of natural gas.

During the 1990s the company launched a major expansion program using a two-pronged strategy: acquiring producing properties and drilling wells in proven fields. In 1990 it bought an 88% interest in six Texas wells; two years later Devon snapped up the US properties of Hondo Oil & Gas. After its 1994 purchase of Alta Energy which operated in New Mexico Oklahoma Texas and Wyoming Devon had proved reserves of more than 500 billion cu. ft. of gas.

Between 1992 and 1997 the company also drilled some 840 successful wells. Buoyed by new seismic techniques that raise the odds of finding oil Devon devoted more resources to pioneering fields in regions where it already had expertise.

Continuing its buying spree Devon bought Kerr-McGee's onshore assets in 1997. Two years later it bought Alberta Canada-based Northstar for $775 million creating a company with holdings divided almost evenly between oil and gas.

Also in 1999 Devon grabbed its biggest prize when it purchased PennzEnergy of Houston in a $2.3 billion stock-and-debt deal that analysts called a bargain. PennzEnergy spun off from Pennzoil in 1998 dates back to the Texas oil boom after WWII. In addition to new US holdings the deal gave Devon a number of international oil and gas assets in such places as Azerbaijan Brazil Egypt Qatar and Venezuela.

On a roll Devon in 2000 bought Santa Fe Snyder for $2.35 billion in stock and $1 billion in assumed debt. The deal increased Devon's proved reserves by nearly 400 million barrels of oil equivalent.

In 2001 the company agreed to a major deal to supply Indonesian natural gas to Singapore. It also made an unsuccessful bid for rival Barrett Resources that was trumped by a bid from Williams Companies. Undaunted that year Devon acquired Anderson Exploration for $3.4 billion in cash and $1.2 billion in assumed debt. It also purchased Mitchell Energy & Development for $3.1 billion in cash and stock and $400 million in assumed debt.

As part of its strategy to refocus on core operations in 2002 the company sold its Indonesian assets to PetroChina for $262 million. By mid-year the company had raised about $1.2 billion through the disposition of oil properties worldwide.

Over this decade Devon Energy bought its way into the big leagues as a North American producer through a series of multibillion-dollar acquisitions of oil and gas producers including Ocean Energy in 2003 for $3.5 billion and US-based Chief Holdings LLC in 2006 for $2.2 billion.

In 2007 Devon began to divest all of its assets in West Africa. It sold its oil and gas business in Egypt to Dana Petroleum for $375 million and its Gabon assets for $206 million. In 2008 it

EXECUTIVES

Evp Administration, R. Alan Marcum, age 51, $550,000 total compensation

President And Ceo, David A. (Dave) Hager, age 62, $1,275,000 total compensation

Evp And General Counsel, Lyndon C. Taylor, age 60, $625,000 total compensation

Vp And Cio, Ben Williams, age 46

Coo, Tony D. Vaughn, age 61, $735,192 total compensation

Svp Canadian Operations And President Devon Canada, Rob Dutton, age 48

Vp Southern Business Unit, Gregg Jacob, age 57

Vp Anadarko Basin Business Unit, Todd Moehlenbrock, age 53

Vp Delaware Basin Business Unit, Frank Schroeder, age 47

Svp Exploration And Production, Richard A. (Rick) Gideon, age 42

Svp Exploration And Production, Kevin Lafferty, age 43

Vp Rockies Business Unit, John Raines, age 35

Evp And Cfo, Jeff L. Ritenour, age 44

Svp Exploration And Production, David G. Harris, age 44

Vice President Supply Chain And Marketing, Mike Dionisio

Senior Vice President Us Operations, Rick Gideon

Assistant To Rick Gideon Senior Vice President Of Us Operations, Heather Powell

Senior Vice President Communications And Investor Relations, Howard Thill

Vp Policy And Government Affairs, Rebecca Rosen

Vp Texas Business Unit, Gregg Jacobs

Evp Administration, R Alan Marcum

Chairman, John Richels, age 67

Auditors: KPMG LLP

LOCATIONS

HQ: Devon Energy Corp.
333 West Sheridan Avenue, Oklahoma City, OK 73102-5015
Phone: 405 235-3611
Web: www.devonenergy.com

2017 Sales

	% of total
US	53
EnLink	36
Canada	11
Total	**100**

PRODUCTS/OPERATIONS

2017 Sales

	$ mil.	% of total
Marketing & midstream	8,642	62
Upstream	5,307	38
Total	**13,494**	**100**

COMPETITORS

Abraxas Petroleum	Exxon Mobil
Apache	Hess Corporation
BP	JKX
Bonanza Creek	Jones Energy
Cabot Oil & Gas	Marathon Oil
Chesapeake Energy	Occidental Petroleum
Chevron	Royal Dutch Shell
ConocoPhillips	Williams Companies
EOG	XTO Energy
Encana	

HISTORICAL FINANCIALS

Company Type: Public

Income Statement

FYE: December 31

	REVENUE ($ mil.)	NET INCOME ($ mil.)	NET PROFIT MARGIN	EMPLOYEES
12/17	13,949	898	6.4%	4,900
12/16	12,197	(3,302)	—	5,000
12/15	13,145	(14,454)	—	6,600
12/14	19,566	1,607	8.2%	6,600
12/13	10,397	(20)	—	5,900
Annual Growth	7.6%	—	—	(4.5%)

2017 Year-End Financials

Debt ratio: 34.41%	No. of shares (mil.): 525
Return on equity: 11.83%	Dividends
Cash ($ mil.): 2,673	Yield: 0.0%
Current ratio: 1.45	Payout: 14.1%
Long-term debt ($ mil.): 10,291	Market value ($ mil.): 21,735

	STOCK PRICE ($) FY Close	P/E High/Low		PER SHARE ($) Earnings	Dividends	Book Value
12/17	41.40	29	17	1.70	0.24	17.63
12/16	45.67	—	—	(6.52)	0.42	11.33
12/15	32.00	—	—	(35.55)	0.96	16.86
12/14	61.21	20	13	3.91	0.94	52.66
12/13	61.87	—	—	(0.06)	0.86	50.49
Annual Growth	(9.6%)	—	—	(23.1%)	—	(27.3%)

Dick's Sporting Goods, Inc

Dick's Sporting Goods sells a full range of sports and outdoor merchandise from A (adidas cleats) to uh Y (Yeti coolers). The company's more than 725 namesake stores across the US feature sporting goods apparel and footwear for leisure pursuits ranging from football golf and cycling to hunting and camping. In addition to well-known brand names Dick's carries exclusive brands such as Walter Hagen Second Skin and Top-Flite. The company also operates more than 90 Golf Galaxy and some three dozen Field & Stream stores as well as associated e-commerce sites.

Operations

Dick's reports through three primary merchandise categories: hardlines apparel and footwear. Hardlines which includes equipment and gear is the largest segment and accounts for about 45% of sales. Apparel and footwear bring in about 35% and 20% respectively.

The company purchases merchandise from some 1300 vendors including Nike (its largest) which represents nearly 20% of the total. Beyond Nike and other well-known national and international brands it sells products under its private-label brands such as Cobra (youth golf sets) Field & Stream Fitness Gear Lady Hagen and Quest. Dick's own brands contribute more than 10% of sales.

Geographic Reach

Dick's has a total of more than 850 stores in 45-plus US states; its largest markets are California Florida New York North Carolina Ohio Pennsylvania and Texas which together account for nearly 40% of total stores.

It also has distribution centers in Arizona Georgia Indiana New York and Pennsylvania.

Sales and Marketing

Dick's generates nearly 90% of sales through its network of retail stores with the remainder coming from its e-commerce sites. The company is focused on developing its omni-channel offering designed to serve customers however they prefer to shop — in stores online or through a combination of both.

It markets its products through traditional channels such as newspaper and direct mail pieces but is increasingly moving toward digital and personalized appeals enabled by its customer marketing database and ScoreCard loyalty program. Its Dick's Team Sports HQ business is a digital platform for youth sports meant to cultivate current and future customers.

Dick's spent $330 million on advertising in fiscal 2017 compared to about $305 million in 2016 and $276 million in 2015.

Financial Performance

Dick's has seen robust growth over the past decade with revenue doubling during that time as it expands its network of stores. Net income has generally grown over those 10 years but has been a little more sporadic.

In fiscal 2017 (ended January 2018) the company reported revenue of $8.6 billion up 8% from the prior year. Although same-store sales were essentially flat growth was driven by new stores (about 55 in 2017) as well as a 53rd week in the fiscal year. New stores have been powering Dick's for several years as organic growth has been anemic.

Net income that year rose about 13% to $323 million on the improved revenue performance as well as lower pre-opening expenses (which can fluctuate based on the timing and number of new store openings) and about $15 million more in investment and other income than in fiscal 2016.

Cash at the end of fiscal 2017 was $101 million a decrease of about $64 million from the prior year. Cash from operations contributed $746 million to the coffers while investing activities used $486 million mainly for property and equipment used in the buildout of new stores. Financing activities used another $324 million for dividends to stockholders and Dick's stock repurchase program.

Strategy

Dick's is operating in a highly competitive tough retail environment at a time when foot traffic in stores is on the decline as more consumers turn to Amazon and other online destinations for purchases. For that reason the company has made improving its omni-channel and e-commerce capabilities a key element of strategy alongside more traditional initiatives such as expanding its store network and boosting sales of its private-label brands.

E-commerce sales as a percent of total revenue inched up less than half a percent in fiscal 2017 (to 12.4%) considerably lower than the 2% rise in 2016 and the 1% increase in 2015. In 2018 Dick's is looking to boost this growth with an improved design of online product pages enhanced customer checkout and personalization. It also plans to improve its shipping and fulfillment functions.

Dick's also continues to expand its store network; it has plans for about 20 new Dick's Sporting Goods locations in 2018. The company is hoping to expand in markets left underserved by competitors such as Sports Authority who have gone out of business or entered bankruptcy. It has added about 200 locations since fiscal 2013.

Lastly Dick's continues to focus on its private-label brands which it feels is a differentiator and competitive advantage. The growth of the private-label business outpaced the company average in fiscal 2017 when it surpassed more than $1 billion in sales. The company expects private brands to outpace the average again in 2018 as it invests in marketing design and technology behind key brands such as CALIA Walter Hagen and Fitness Gear.

Mergers and Acquisitions

Dick's made several small purchases throughout 2016 as part of its Dick's Team Sports HQ business a digital platform for youth sports that includes mobile apps live scorekeeping and league management services. Those acquisitions include Blue Sombrero (team and league uniforms) Affinity Sports (league registration software) and GameChanger Media (team information sharing and management software).

Company Background

Dick's was founded in 1948 when Dick Stack father of company chairman and CEO Edward Stack opened a bait and tackle shop.

EXECUTIVES

V Pres-controller, Oliver Joseph
Chairman And Ceo, Edward W. (Ed) Stack, age 63, $1,000,000 total compensation
Cto, Paul J. Gaffney, age 47
Evp And Cfo, Lee J. Belitsky, age 57, $541,983 total compensation
President, Lauren R. Hobart, age 49, $520,000 total compensation
Evp And Chief Merchant, Keri Jones
Svp Information Technology And Cio, Kurt J. Schnieders
Evp And Chief Strategy Officer, Michele B. Willoughby, age 52, $538,024 total compensation
Svp Operations, Don Germano
Vice President Ecommerce, Traci Hayes
Svp Dick's Team Sports Hq, Ed Plummer
Senior Vice President Operations, Donald Germano
Vice President Total Rewards, Todd Lombardi
Vp Strategy And Innovation, Ryan Eckel
Vice President Gmm, Alan Epler
Vp Tax, Todd Hipwell
Vice President Of Marketing, Tom Hassett
Svp Real Estate, Dave Barnes
Senior Vice President Real Estate, Karin Bolcshazy
Vice President Of Brand Marketing, Ryan Eckle
Vice President Customer Innovation Technology, Rafeh Massod
Vice President, Meredith Laginess
Senior Vice President Product Development, Alexander Tomey
Vice President Talent Management, Adrienne Sims
Senior Vice President And General Merchandising Manager Hardlines, Wendy Fritz
Chairman And Ceo, Edward W. (Ed) Stack, age 63
Vice Chairman, William J. (Bill) Colombo, age 62
Board Member, Emanuel Chirico
Auditors: DELOITTE & TOUCHE LLP

LOCATIONS

HQ: Dick's Sporting Goods, Inc
345 Court Street, Coraopolis, PA 15108
Phone: 724 273-3400
Web: www.DICKS.com

2017 Locations

	No.
California	66
Pennsylvania	52
Texas	51
Florida	50
Ohio	50
New York	49
North Carolina	41
Virginia	35
Illinois	34
Michigan	28
Georgia	24
Indiana	21
Massachusetts	21
New Jersey	21
Tennessee	20
Other states	282
Total	**845**

PRODUCTS/OPERATIONS

2017 Sales

	% of total
Hardlines	45
Apparel	34
Footwear	20
Other	1
Total	**100**

Selected Categories

Archery
Backpacking
Baseball
Basketball
Boating
Bowling
Camping
Cycling
Exercise
Fishing
Football
Golf
Hockey (ice and roller)
Hunting
In-line skating
Lacrosse
Optics/telescopes
Paintball
Racquetball/squash
Running
Skateboarding
Snow sports
Soccer
Tennis
Volleyball
Water sports

COMPETITORS

Academy Sports	Kmart
Amazon.com	L.L. Bean
Big 5	Modell's
Cabela's	Olympia Sports
Costco Wholesale	REI
Dunham's	Sears
Finish Line	Sportsman's Warehouse
Foot Locker	Target Corporation
Hibbett Sports	Wal-Mart
J. C. Penney	Zumiez

HISTORICAL FINANCIALS

Company Type: Public

Income Statement

FYE: February 3

	REVENUE ($ mil.)	NET INCOME ($ mil.)	NET PROFIT MARGIN	EMPLOYEES
02/18*	8,590	323	3.8%	45,200
01/17	7,921	287	3.6%	40,500
01/16	7,270	330	4.5%	37,200
01/15	6,814	344	5.1%	37,600
02/14	6,213	337	5.4%	34,300
Annual Growth	**8.4%**	**(1.1%)**	**—**	**7.1%**

*Fiscal year change

Debt ratio: 1.55%	No. of shares (mil.): 103	
Return on equity: 16.44%	Dividends	
Cash ($ mil.): 101	Yield: 0.0%	
Current ratio: 1.41	Payout: 22.5%	
Long-term debt ($ mil.): 60	Market value ($ mil.): 3,244	

	STOCK PRICE ($) FY Close	P/E High/Low		PER SHARE ($) Earnings	Dividends	Book Value
02/18*	31.49	18	8	3.01	0.68	18.84
01/17	51.01	24	14	2.50	0.61	17.49
01/16	39.08	21	12	2.83	0.55	16.01
01/15	51.65	20	14	2.84	0.50	15.51
02/14	52.50	21	16	2.69	0.50	13.99
Annual Growth	(12.0%)	—	—	2.8%	8.0%	7.7%

*Fiscal year change

Diebold Nixdorf Inc

Cash never gets old at Diebold Nixdorf the leading global producer of automated teller machines (ATMs) with about a million in operation around the world. In addition it offers remote teller systems cash dispensers and check cashing machines. The company offers an array of services and software for mobile banking and managing payment systems and customer loyalty programs at retailers and banks. The company's related services range from traditional maintenance to remote monitoring transaction processing and currency management. Diebold Nixdorf gets about three-quarters of its sales outside the US. The company became Diebold Nixdorf when Diebold bought Wincor Nixdorf in 2016.

Operations

Diebold Nixdorf?s largest segment accounting for more than half of revenue is Services. These services make sure its machines ? ATMs point-of-sale and others ? maintain working order. Diebold Nixdorf services machines remotely or by sending technicians to the field. The company also offers managed services and outsourcing for managing the end-to-end business processes technology integration and day-to-day operation of self-service channels and bank branch and retail store networks.

The company?s systems segment nearly 40% of sales consists of it hardware that customers interact with the ATMs point-of-sales machines and ordering kiosks. Systems include the Extreme ATM which is less than 10-inches wide and conducts transactions via mobile phones. Also through the systems segment the sells peripherals such as printers scales and mobile scanners as well as banknote and coin processing systems.

In its software segment 10% of revenue Diebold Nixdorf provides applications that keep its equipment and those of other manufacturer running. The segment includes the company Vynamic platform that allows for connections between financial institutions retailers and payment providers offering omnichannel delivery.

Diebold Nixdorf make most of its systems in its production plants.

Geographic Reach

Diebold Nixdorf isn?t overly dependent on any one market. The US is the company?s single biggest market supplying almost a quarter of revenue. The addition of the German-based Wincor Nixdorf operations made Germany the second biggest market with about an eighth of sales. Other single markets broken by the company are Brazil 5% and China 2%. Other geographic markets covering Europe Asia South America provide nearly 60% of revenue.

The company has corporate offices in North Canton Ohio and Paderborn Germany. Manufacturing operations are the US Brazil China India and Germany. The company conducts software development in Canada.

Financial Performance

A full year of sales from the Nixdorf side of the company boosted Diebold Nixdorf?s revenue 40% to $4.6 billion in 2017 from 2016. Revenue might have been higher but sales declines in the services and systems segments reduced the Nixdorf contribution by some $220 million. Decreased sales were blamed on the winding down of multi-vendor service contracts in the Americas and fewer sales of big systems.

Diebold Nixdorf company posted a net loss of $233 million in 2017 compared to a $33 million loss in 2016. The company had higher expenses in 2017 including those associated with integrating Diebold and Nixdorf.

Diebold?s cash on hand fell to $535 million in 2017 from $652 million in 2016 as the company used cash for integration initiatives restructuring programs interest on debt and income taxes.

Strategy

Diebold bought Wincor Nixdorf to develop size scale and depth of product as well as worldwide geographic reach. Diebold positioned the merger as a match between companies with strong services and software components areas that Diebold emphasizes as it changes its business model from a hardware orientation to a software focus.

With the deal done and integration the company aims to make transactions friction free to buyer seller and middleman through integration of hardware software and services. While the company seeks to operate through technology it?s 15000-member service force (65% of the company's headcount) is a key part of its strategy. The service personnel are to quickly fix machines in hands-on visits or through remote access.

With Nixdorf the company expanded in Europe in a big way. Diebold Nixdorf is the top provider of point-of-sale systems on the continent and it sees retail as a growing business. Retail accounts for more than 10% of the company?s revenue all of it coming with Nixdorf. The company also seeks to develop customers for mobile banking applications in Europe where mobile banking has proved popular with consumers.

The company continues to work on integration and finding areas to save money as part of the acquisition process. It plans about $240 million in savings through consolidation and increasing efficiency by 2020. In 2016 the company sold its electronic security business in the US and Canada to Securitas for about $350 million.

Diebold Nixdorf has about $2.6 billion in debt some of it from the Wincor Nixdorf transaction. Maintaining payments on the debt could prevent the company from making investments in the company and limit its flexibility to respond to opportunities and threats.

Mergers and Acquisitions

In 2015 Diebold acquired Phoenix Interactive Design a software developer for ATMs and other financial self-service applications. The purchase was made to accelerate Diebold's growth in managed services and branch automation.

EXECUTIVES

Vp And Chief Human Resources Officer, Sheila M. Rutt, age 50, $348,801 total compensation

Svp And Chief Integration Officer, J rgen Wunram, age 60, $230,553 total compensation

Svp And Managing Director Asia Pacific, Neil Emerson

Svp And Managing Director Americas, Octavio Marquez

Vp Global Finance, Christopher A. Chapman, age 43, $500,000 total compensation

President And Ceo, Andreas W. (Andy) Mattes, age 57, $937,500 total compensation

Svp Corporate Strategy And Development, Stefan E. Merz, $400,000 total compensation

Svp Chief Legal Officer And Secretary, Jonathan B. Leiken, $440,000 total compensation

Cio, Murat Ekinci

Svp And Managing Director Emea, Christian Weisser

Vp And Chief Marketing Officer, Devon R. Watson

Vice President Software Services Solutioning, Hormuzd Karkaria

Senior Vice President North America Sales, Tom Signorello

Vice President Global Oracle Center Of Excellence, Douglas Yenor

Vice President Professional And Managed Services, Chuck Somers

Vice President Corporate Strategy And Development, Patrick Tournoy

National Accounts Manager, Bob Alder

National Account Manager Electronic Security, John May

Vice President Information Systems, Chuck Bechtel

Svp And Chief Integration Officer, J rgen Wunram, age 60

Svp Chief Legal Officer And Secretary, Jonathan B. Leiken

Auditors: KPMG LLP

LOCATIONS

HQ: Diebold Nixdorf Inc
5995 Mayfair Road, P.O. Box 3077, North Canton, OH 44720-8077
Phone: 330 490-4000
Web: www.diebold.com

2017 Sales

	$ mil.	% of total
Europe Middle East & Africa	2,380	52
Americas	1,605	35
Asia/Pacific	623	13
Total	**4,609**	**100**

2017 Sales

	$ mil.	% of total
United States	1,038	23
Germany	564	12
Brazil	218	5
China	96	2
Other international	2,691	58
Total	**46,096**	**100**

PRODUCTS/OPERATIONS

2017 Sales

	$ mil.	% of total
Banking	3,429	74
Retail	1,180	26
Total	**4,609**	**100**

2017 Sales

	$ mil.	% of total
Services	2,397	52
Systems	1,735	38
Software	476	10
Total	**4,609**	**100**

Selected Services Software and Systems

Services

Maintenance and Availability
Total Implementation
Managed Mobility
Store Lifecycle Management

Physical Security
Software
Vynamic Connection Points
Vynamic Transaction Engine
Vynamic Engagement
Vynamic Operations
Vynamic Analytics
Vynamic Digital
Postal
Service Station
Systems
POS Systems
Pay Tower
Interactive Kiosk
Reverse Vending
Electronic Shelf Labeling
Postal Systems
Resource Library

COMPETITORS

ACI Worldwide	Hart InterCivic
ADT	Hyosung
Cardtronics	Itautec
De La Rue	NCR
Election Systems &	OMRON
Software	Oki Electric
Fujitsu	Siemens AG
GRG Banking Equipment	Thales
Co. Ltd.	Triton Systems
Gemalto	

HISTORICAL FINANCIALS

Company Type: Public

Income Statement — FYE: December 31

	REVENUE ($ mil.)	NET INCOME ($ mil.)	NET PROFIT MARGIN	EMPLOYEES
12/17	4,609	(233)	—	23,000
12/16	3,316	(33)	—	25,000
12/15	2,419	73	3.0%	16,000
12/14	3,051	114	3.8%	16,000
12/13	2,857	(181)	—	16,000
Annual Growth	12.7%	—	—	9.5%

2017 Year-End Financials

Debt ratio: 35.31%	No. of shares (mil.): 75
Return on equity: (-43.92%)	Dividends
Cash ($ mil.): 535	Yield: 0.0%
Current ratio: 1.39	Payout: —
Long-term debt ($ mil.): 1,787	Market value ($ mil.): 1,235

	STOCK PRICE ($) FY Close	P/E High/Low	PER SHARE ($) Earnings	Dividends	Book Value
12/17	16.35	— —	(3.09)	0.40	6.22
12/16	25.15	— —	(0.48)	0.96	7.87
12/15	30.09	33 26	1.12	1.15	6.34
12/14	34.64	23 18	1.76	1.15	8.23
12/13	33.01	— —	(2.85)	1.15	9.31
Annual Growth	(16.1%)	— —	—	(23.2%)	(9.6%)

Dillard's Inc.

Tradition is trying to catch up with the times at Dillard's. Sandwiched between retail giant Macy's and discount chains such as Kohl's Dillard's is rethinking its strategy and trimming its store count. The department store chain operates about 290 locations (down from 330 in 2005) in some 30 US states covering the Sunbelt and the central US. Its stores cater to middle- and upper-middle-income women selling name-brand and private-label merchandise with a focus on apparel and home furnishings. Founded in 1938 by William Dillard family members through the W. D. Company control the company.

HISTORY

At age 12 William Dillard began working in his father's general store in Mineral Springs Arkansas. After he graduated from Columbia University in 1937 the third-generation retailer spent seven months in the Sears Roebuck manager training program in Tulsa Oklahoma.

With $8000 borrowed from his father William opened his first department store in Nashville Arkansas in 1938. Service was one of the most important things he had to offer he said and he insisted on quality — he personally inspected every item and would settle for nothing but the best. William sold the store in 1948 to finance a partnership in Wooten's Department Store in Texarkana Arkansas; he bought out Wooten and established Dillard's the next year.

Throughout the 1950s and 1960s the company became a strong regional retailer developing its strategy of buying well-established downtown stores in small cities; acquisitions in those years included Mayer & Schmidt (Tyler Texas; 1956) and Joseph Pfeifer (Little Rock Arkansas; 1963). Dillard's moved its headquarters to Little Rock after buying Pfeifer. When it went public in 1969 it had 15 stores in three states.

During the early 1960s the company began computerizing operations to streamline inventory and information management. In 1970 Dillard's added computerized cash registers which gave management hourly sales figures.

The chain continued acquiring outlets (more than 130 over the next three decades including stores owned by Stix Baer & Fuller Macy's Joske's and Maison Blanche). In a 1988 joint venture with Edward J. DeBartolo Dillard's bought a 50% interest in the 12 Higbee's stores in Ohio (buying the other 50% in 1992 shortly after Higbee's bought five former Horne's stores in Ohio).

In 1991 Vendamerica (subsidiary of Vendex International and the only major nonfamily holder of the company's stock) sold its 8.9 million shares of Class A stock (25% of the class) in an underwritten public offering.

Dillard's purchase of 12 Diamond stores from Dayton Hudson in 1994 gave it a small-event ticket-sales chain in the Southwest which it renamed Dillard's Box Office. A lawsuit filed by the FTC against Dillard's that year claiming the company made it unreasonably difficult for its credit card holders to remove unauthorized charges from their bills was dismissed the following year.

Dillard's continued to grow; it opened 11 new stores in 1995 and 16 more in 1996 (entering Georgia and Colorado). The next year it opened 12 new stores and acquired 20 making its way into Virginia California and Wyoming.

William retired in 1998 and William Dillard II took over the CEO position while brother Alex became president. The company then paid $3.1 billion for Mercantile Stores which operated 106 apparel and home design stores in the South and Midwest. To avoid redundancy in certain regions Dillard's sold 26 of those stores and exchanged seven others for new Dillard's stores. The assimilation of Mercantile brought distribution problems that cut into earnings for fiscal 1999. In late 2000 with a slumping stock price and declining sales Dillard's said it would de-emphasize its concentration on name-brand merchandise and offer deep discounts on branded items already in stock. Despite these efforts sales and earnings continued to slide in 2001.

Founder and patriarch William Dillard (the company's guiding force) died in February 2002. Son William II became chairman of the company which has been family-controlled for half a century. Dillard's opened four new stores and closed nine in 2002. Sales declined 3% versus the previous year.

In 2003 Dillard's shuttered 10 stores and opened five new store locations.

In November 2004 Dillard's completed the sale of Dillard National Bank the retailer's credit card portfolio to GE Consumer Finance for about $1.1 billion (plus debt). Dillard's had said it would use the proceeds to reduce debt repurchase stock and to achieve general corporate purposes.

In the spring of 2005 Dillard's shuttered the last of 16 home and furniture stores acquired when the department store chain acquired Mercantile Stores Co. in 1998. Hurricanes Katrina Rita and Wilma took a toll on Dillard's in 2005 interrupting business in about 60 of the company's stores at various times.

In August 2008 Dillard's purchased the 50% stake in the Arkansas-based construction firm CDI Contractors that it didn't already own for about $9.8 million. CDI is a general contactor that also builds stores for Dillard's. In November Dillard's announced 500 job cuts including about 60 at headquarters.

Amid falling sales and rising investor discontent Dillard's bowed to pressure from hedge funds Barington Capital Group and Clinton Group and appointed four new directors in April 2008 to avoid a proxy fight.

In February 2012 Dillard's acquired Acumen Brands an e-commerce company located in Fayetteville Arkansas.

EXECUTIVES

Evp, Drue Matheny, age 71, $735,000 total compensation
Evp, Mike Dillard, age 66, $735,000 total compensation
President, Alex Dillard, age 68, $1,000,000 total compensation
Chairman And Ceo, William (Bill) Dillard, age 73, $1,000,000 total compensation
Svp Co-principal Financial Officer And Principal Accounting Officer, Phillip R. Watts, age 55, $500,000 total compensation
Svp And Co-principal Financial Officer, Chris B. Johnson, age 46, $500,000 total compensation
Regional Vice President, Michael Hubbell
Vice President Advertising, Christine Rowell
Vp, Mike Mcniff
Upper Management Vice President, Kristin Jacobson
Vice President, Mike Shields
Vice President Accounting, Steve Gelwix
Executive Vice President And Director, Drue Corbusier
Vice President Merchanising, Mike McNiff
Corporate Vice President Stores, Mike Litchford
Vice President Merchandising St Louis Division, Mark Killingsworth
Vice President Sales Promotion, Louise Platt
Executive Vice President And Director, Drue Corbusier
Svp, Denise Mahaffy
Corporate Vice President Ladies ' Juniors ' And Children 's Exclusive Brands, Alexandra Lucie
Vice President Online Experience, Annemarie Jazic
Chairman And Ceo, William (Bill) Dillard, age 73
Secretary, Suzanne Stewart
Secretary, Shirley Wallace
Board Member, Lee Hastings
Board Member, Reynie Rutledge
Auditors: KPMG LLP

LOCATIONS

HQ: Dillard's Inc.
1600 Cantrell Road, Little Rock, AR 72201
Phone: 501 376-5200
Web: www.dillards.com

2017 Stores

	No.
Texas	58
Florida	42
Arizona	17
Louisiana	15
North Carolina	14
Ohio	14
Georgia	12
Oklahoma	10
Tennessee	10
Alabama	9
Missouri	9
Arkansas	8
Colorado	7
South Carolina	7
Kansas	6
Kentucky	6
Mississippi	6
New Mexico	6
Virginia	6
Iowa	5
Nevada	5
Utah	4
California	3
Illinois	3
Indiana	3
Nebraska	3
Idaho	2
Montana	2
Wyoming	1
Total	**293**

PRODUCTS/OPERATIONS

2017 Sales

	% of total
Ladies' apparel	22
Men's apparel & accessories	17
Shoes	16
Ladies' accessories & lingerie	16
Cosmetics	14
Juniors' & children's apparel	8
Home & furniture	4
Construction segment	3
Total	**100**

COMPETITORS

Abercrombie & Fitch	Macy's
American Eagle	Mattress Firm
Outfitters	Neiman Marcus
Ann Taylor	Nordstrom
Bed Bath & Beyond	Sears
Belk	Stein Mart
Bon-Ton Stores	TJX Companies
Burlington Coat	Tailored Brands
Factory	Talbots
Caleres	Target Corporation
Eddie Bauer LLC	The Gap
Foot Locker	Tuesday Morning
J. C. Penney	Corporation
J. Crew	Von Maur
Kohl's	Walgreen
Lands' End	

HISTORICAL FINANCIALS

Company Type: Public

Income Statement

FYE: February 3

	REVENUE ($ mil.)	NET INCOME ($ mil.)	NET PROFIT MARGIN	EMPLOYEES
02/18*	6,422	221	3.4%	40,000
01/17	6,418	169	2.6%	40,000
01/16	6,754	269	4.0%	40,000
01/15	6,780	331	4.9%	40,000
02/14	6,691	323	4.8%	40,000
Annual Growth	(1.0%)	(9.1%)	—	0.0%

*Fiscal year change

2018 Year-End Financials

Debt ratio: 19.88%
Return on equity: 12.71%
Cash ($ mil.): 187
Current ratio: 1.66
Long-term debt ($ mil.): 568

No. of shares (mil.): 28
Dividends
Yield: 0.0%
Payout: 4.5%
Market value ($ mil.): 1,790

	STOCK PRICE ($) FY Close	P/E High/Low		PER SHARE ($) Earnings	Dividends	Book Value
02/18*	63.68	11	6	7.51	0.34	60.77
01/17	54.65	18	11	4.93	0.28	53.41
01/16	70.41	21	9	6.91	0.26	49.98
01/15	113.60	16	11	7.79	0.24	49.02
02/14	87.30	14	11	7.10	0.22	45.33
Annual Growth	(7.6%)	—	—	1.4%	11.5%	7.6%

*Fiscal year change

Dime Community Bancshares, Inc

Dime Community Bancshares is in a New York state of mind. It is the holding company for Dime Community Bank (formerly The Dime Savings Bank of Williamsburgh) which boasts $4.5 billion in assets and operates more than 25 branches in Brooklyn Queens and the Bronx as well as Nassau County on Long Island. Founded in 1864 the bank provides standard products and services including checking savings retirement money market and club accounts accounts. Multifamily residential and commercial real estate loans comprise the vast majority of the bank's loan portfolio. Subsidiary Dime Insurance Agency (formerly Havemeyer Investments) offers life policies fixed annuities and wealth management services.

Operations

Multifamily residential real estate loans accounted for 80% of Dime Savings' $4 billion loan portfolio in 2014; most of these were secured by properties in Brooklyn Queens and Manhattan. Another 18% of the portfolio was made up of commercial real estate loans. The community-oriented bank believes that multifamily residential and mixed-use loans in the New York City area produce higher yields than securities with similar maturities.

The bank generated 93% of its total revenue from interest income on loans secured by real estate in 2014 while interest on mortgage-backed securities service charge fees mortgage banking income and other miscellaneous fees made up the rest of revenues.

Geographic Reach

The Brooklyn-based bank operates 25 branches in New York City in the boroughs of Brooklyn Queens and the Bronx as well as in Nassau County in New York.

Sales and Marketing

Dime Community's primary lending area is in the New York Metro area though its total lending area spans 50 miles from its headquarters' radius.

Financial Performance

Dime Community's revenue has been in decline in recent years due to shrinking interest margins on loans amidst the low-interest environment. The firm's profits however have been rising since 2012 thanks to declining loan loss provisions as its loan portfolio's credit quality has improved with the strengthened economy.

Dime's revenue dipped by less than 1% to $182 million in 2014 as the bank's interest income continued to decline on shrinking interest margins on both real estate loans and mortgage-backed securities. The bank blamed fierce mortgage refinancing competition for much of the 49 basis point-reduction of interest yields on its loan portfolio which led to lower interest income.

Despite lower revenue in 2014 the company's net income rose by nearly 2% to $44.25 million thanks to a continued decline in the provision for loan losses. Dime Community's operating cash fell by 23% to $47.26 million during the year due to lower cash earnings.

Strategy

Dime Community Bancshares has been moving toward digital banking channels that are quickly taking the industry by storm allowing the bank to slow expensive branch-expansion plans and cut operating costs significantly while giving customers faster access to banking services. In 2014 as part of its eBanking platform initiative to expand into online banking mobile banking bill pay and remote deposit the bank launched its Dime Mobile Banking platform which allowed customer to deposit checks pay bills transfer funds and check account balances and status from their smartphones.

EXECUTIVES

Evp And Chief Risk Officer, Timothy B. King, age 59, $342,000 total compensation
President And Ceo, Kenneth J. Mahon, age 67, $550,000 total compensation
Secretary, Lance J. Bennett, age 66
Sevp Business Banking, Stuart H. Lubow, age 60
Sevp And Coo, Robert S. Volino, age 46
Evp And Cto, Timothy K. Lenhoff, age 60
Evp And Chief Retail Officer, William E. Brown, age 51
Evp And Chief Administrative Officer, Anthony J. Rose, age 47
Evp Business Banking, Conrad J. Gunther, age 71
Principal Financial Officer Dime Community Bancshares Inc. And Dime Community Bank, James L. Rizzo
Vice President, Tom Dippolito
Vice Chairman, Michael P. Devine, age 71
Chairman, Vincent F. Palagiano, age 77
Auditors: Crowe Horwath LLP

LOCATIONS

HQ: Dime Community Bancshares, Inc
300 Cadman Plaza West, 8th Floor, Brooklyn, NY 11201
Phone: 718 782-6200
Web: www.dime.com

PRODUCTS/OPERATIONS

2014 Sales

	$ mil.	% of total
Interest		
Loans secured by real estate	169	93
Mortgage-backed securities	0	1
Other	2	1
Noninterest		
Service charges & other fees	3	2
Bank-owned life insurance	1	1
Other	4	2
Total	**182**	**100**

COMPETITORS

Astoria Financial	HSBC
Carver Bancorp	JPMorgan Chase
Citigroup	Valley National
First of Long Island	Bancorp
Flushing Financial	

HISTORICAL FINANCIALS

Company Type: Public

Income Statement

FYE: December 31

	ASSETS ($ mil.)	NET INCOME ($ mil.)	INCOME AS % OF ASSETS	EMPLOYEES
12/17	6,403	51	0.8%	421
12/16	6,005	72	1.2%	386
12/15	5,032	44	0.9%	388
12/14	4,497	44	1.0%	409
12/13	4,028	43	1.1%	413
Annual Growth	**12.3%**	**4.5%**	**—**	**0.5%**

2017 Year-End Financials

Debt ratio: 1.77%
Return on equity: 8.91%
Cash ($ mil.): 169
Current ratio: —
Long-term debt ($ mil.): —

No. of shares (mil.): 37
Dividends
  Yield: 0.0%
  Payout: 40.5%
Market value ($ mil.): 784

	STOCK PRICE ($) FY Close	P/E High/Low	Earnings	Dividends	Book Value
12/17	20.95	16 13	1.38	0.56	16.00
12/16	20.10	10 8	1.97	0.56	15.11
12/15	17.49	15 12	1.23	0.56	13.22
12/14	16.28	14 11	1.23	0.56	12.47
12/13	16.92	14 11	1.23	0.56	11.86
Annual Growth	**5.5%**	**— —**	**2.9%**	**(0.0%)**	**7.8%**

Discover Financial Services

EXECUTIVES

Pres-Ceo, Roger C Hochschild
Exec Chb, David W Nelms
Exec V Pres-Cfo, R Mark Graf
Exec V Pres-Cro, Brian D Hughes
Exec V Pres-CIO, Glenn P Schneider
Exec V Pres-General Counsel-SE, Kathryn McNamara Corley
Voice, Aaron Murray
Information Technology Manager, Bill Fronk
Senior Manager Information TEC, Darryl Wingate
Physical Security Manager, Gary McGarvin
Director, Lori Lenard
Auditors: Deloitte & Touche LLP

LOCATIONS

HQ: Discover Financial Services
2500 Lake Cook Road, Riverwoods, IL 60015
Phone: 224 405-0900
Web: www.discover.com

COMPETITORS

Ally Financial	JPMorgan Chase
American Express	MasterCard
Bank of America	Sallie Mae
Capital One	USAA
Citigroup	Visa Inc
First Data	Wells Fargo

HISTORICAL FINANCIALS

Company Type: Public

Income Statement

FYE: December 31

	ASSETS ($ mil.)	NET INCOME ($ mil.)	INCOME AS % OF ASSETS	EMPLOYEES
12/17	100,087	2,099	2.1%	16,500
12/16	92,308	2,393	2.6%	15,549
12/15	86,936	2,297	2.6%	15,036
12/14	83,126	2,323	2.8%	14,676
12/13	79,340	2,470	3.1%	14,128
Annual Growth	**6.0%**	**(4.0%)**	**—**	**4.0%**

2017 Year-End Financials

Debt ratio: 26.30%
Return on equity: 18.90%
Cash ($ mil.): 13,306
Current ratio: —
Long-term debt ($ mil.): —

No. of shares (mil.): 357
Dividends
  Yield: 0.0%
  Payout: 23.9%
Market value ($ mil.): 27,531

	STOCK PRICE ($) FY Close	P/E High/Low	Earnings	Dividends	Book Value
12/17	76.92	14 11	5.42	1.30	30.43
12/16	72.09	13 7	5.77	1.16	29.13
12/15	53.62	13 10	5.13	1.08	26.74
12/14	65.49	14 11	4.90	0.92	24.79
12/13	55.95	11 8	4.96	0.74	22.89
Annual Growth	**8.3%**	**— —**	**2.2%**	**15.1%**	**7.4%**

Discovery Inc

Discovery allows viewers to go on safari without ever having to leave their couch. The company is the world's #1 non-fiction media company with dozens of worldwide cable TV networks including Discovery Channel Animal Planet Oprah Winfrey Network (OWN) Eurosport and The Learning Channel (TLC). Discovery's various networks reach 3 billion subscribers in more than 220 countries. Its network has evolved to include digital streaming services and the company participates in joint ventures including Group Nine Media and The Enthusiast Network. In addition the company offers educational products and services to school; a diverse set of digital media services; and online content through Discovery.com and AnimalPlanet.com.

Operations

Discovery operates through two reportable segments US Networks and International Networks which each generate half of the company's sales.

Six of Discovery's networks are broadcast globally: Discovery Channel (91 million US and 340 million international subscribers) TLC (89 million US and 375 million international subscribers) An-

imal Planet (87 million US and 263 million international); ID (84 million/167 million); SCI (65 million/117 million) and Velocity (73 million/114 million). US-only networks include OWN Discovery Family AHC Destination America and Discovery Life.

In the US Discovery generates revenue from fees charged to distributors of its television networks' first-run content fees from licensed content advertising fees fees from sales representation and fees from licensing its brands for consumer products.

Geographic Reach

Headquartered in Maryland Discovery has operations in 85 locations. It has offices in New York California Florida Virginia Miami London Warsaw Milan and Singapore. It distributes customized content in the U.S. and over 220 other countries and territories in over 40 languages. The US is Discovery's largest market accounting for 50% of revenue.

Sales and Marketing

Discovery cites the popularity of non-fiction programming as a key factor in its success; Discovery has carved out its leading position in the TV business by focusing on non-fiction and reality-based shows that mix entertainment and educational content.

The company has contracts with distributors representing most cable and satellite service providers around the world including the largest operators in the US and major international distributors. In the US more than 90% of distribution revenues come from the top 10 distributors. Outside of the US approximately 45% of distribution revenue comes from the top 10 distributors.

Financial Performance

Discovery has seen its revenue trending upward across recent fiscal years. In fiscal 2017 sales grew 6% to $6.9 billion on the back of higher affiliate fee rates and advertising revenue partially offset by a decline in affiliate subscribers. US portfolio subscribers fell 5%. Growth in Europe was led by investment in sports content.

The company incurred a loss of $337 million in 2017 compared to a $1.2 billion profit the previous year. The loss was a result of a $1.3 billion impairment of goodwill after a downwards reassessment of expected international viewership. Without that single large item profitability would have been comparable with prior year.

Cash from operations grew $249 million almost entirely due to a $235 million decrease in tax paid.

Strategy

Discovery's content development strategy is designed to increase viewership maintain innovation and quality leadership and provide value for its network distributors and advertising customers. Like rival cable programmers such as Viacom and A&E Television Networks Discovery uses its portfolio of channels to segment its audience by programming each network around specific interests. The strategy gives each of Discovery's channels a distinct identity and simplifies the company's marketing efforts. It also increases the value of commercial air time for advertisers trying to reach those audiences. Discovery generates the lion's share of its revenue through advertising and carriage fees paid by cable system operators. Additionally Discovery is extending its content distribution platforms to take in new media channels such as direct streaming (known as "over-the-top" distribution as it bypasses the middleman to reach the customer directly) mobile-device enabled content for apps such as Snapchat and other video-on-demand and broadband channels.

Mergers and Acquisitions

In 2018 Discovery acquired Scripps Networks Interactive Inc. in deal worth $14.6 billion. Knoxville-headquarted Scripps owns cable channels such as the Food Network HGTV Travel

Channel and DIY Network. The combined company will have a 20% share of ad-supported pay-TV audiences in the US.

In late 2017 the company spent $70 million on buying a controlling interest in the OWN network from Harpo Inc. increasing Discovery's ownership stake in OWN from 49.50% to 73.99%. OWN is a pay-TV network and website that provides adult lifestyle and entertainment content which is focused on African Americans.

HISTORY

John Hendricks a history graduate who wanted to expand the presence of educational programming on TV founded Cable Educational Network in 1982. Three years later he introduced the Discovery Channel. Devoted entirely to documentaries and nature shows the channel premiered in 156000 US homes. After dodging bankruptcy (it had $5000 cash and $1 million in debt to the BBC) within a year the Discovery Channel had 7 million subscribers and a host of new investors including Cox Communications and TCI (later AT&T Broadband). It expanded its programming from 12 hours to 18 hours a day in 1987.

Discovery continued to attract subscribers reaching more than 32 million by 1988. The next year it launched Discovery Channel Europe to more than 200000 homes in the UK and Scandinavia. The company began selling home videos in 1990 and entered the Israeli market. The following year Discovery Communications Inc. (DCI) was formed to house the company's operations and it bought The Learning Channel (TLC founded 1980). The company revamped TLC's programming and in 1992 introduced a daily six-hour commercial-free block of children's programs. The next year it introduced its first CD-ROM title In the Company of Whales based on the Discovery Channel documentary.

DCI increased its focus on international expansion in 1994 moving into Asia Latin America the Middle East North Africa Portugal and Spain. The next year the company introduced its website and began selling company merchandise such as CD-ROMs and videos. DCI solidified its move into the retail sector in 1996 with the acquisition of The Nature Company and Scientific Revolution chains (renamed Discovery Channel Store). Also that year it launched its third major cable channel Animal Planet.

The company continued expanding internationally throughout the mid-1990s establishing operations in Australia Canada India New Zealand and South Korea (1995); Africa Brazil Germany and Italy (1996); and Japan and Turkey (1997). DCI also added to its stable of cable channels with the purchase of 70% of the Travel Channel from Paxson Communications (later ION Media Networks) in 1997. (It acquired the remaining 30% interest in 1999.) The company's 1997 original production "Titanic: Anatomy of a Disaster" attracted 3.2 million US households setting a network ratings record.

The following year DCI and the BBC launched Animal Planet in Asia through a joint venture and agreed to market and distribute new cable channel BBC America. It also bought CBS's Eye on People renaming the channel Discovery People (DCI shut the channel down in 2000). DCI spent $330 million launching its new health and fitness channel Discovery Health in 1999 and formed partnerships with high-speed online service Road Runner (to provide interactive information and services to Road Runner customers) and Rosenbluth Travel (to provide vacation packages based on DCI programming).

DCI reorganized its Internet activities into one unit called Discovery.com in 2000 with plans to eventually take it public. Later that year the Discovery Channel set back-to-back records ever on cable "Raising the Mammoth" (10.1 million people) and "Walking With Dinosaurs" (10.7 million people). In 2001 the company cut about 50 jobs as part of a restructuring. Later that year Discovery Communications struck a three-year deal to lease time from NBC on Saturday mornings (paying $6 million per season) to show its Discovery Kids programs.

In 2002 the company launched a 24-hour high-definition television network called Discovery HD Thea

EXECUTIVES

President Ceo And Director, David M. Zaslav, age 59, $3,000,000 total compensation
Group President Discovery Channel Animal Planet And Science Channel, Rich Ross, age 57
President Own: Oprah Winfrey Network And Harpo Studios, Erik Logan
Chief Commercial Officer, Paul (Guyardo) Guagliardo, age 54, $1,400,000 total compensation
Group President Investigation Discovery American Heroes Channel And Destination America, Henry S. Schleiff, age 69
Cto, John Honeycutt
President Discovery Networks International, Jean-Briac (JB) Perrette, $1,381,557 total compensation
President And Managing Director Discovery Networks Asia-pacific, Arthur Bastings
Ceo Domestic Content Distribution And President And Ceo Of Discovery Education, Bill Goodwyn
President International Development Digital And Discovery Nordics, Michael (Mike) Lang, age 53
Chief Corporate Operations And Communications Officer, David C. Leavy
Chief Development Distribution And Legal Officer, Bruce L. Campbell, age 51, $1,544,423 total compensation
Vp Development And Production Discovery Studios, Nancy Daniels
President And Managing Director Discovery Networks Latin America/u.s. Hispanic And Canada, Enrique R. (Henry) Mart nez
Chief Human Resources And Global Diversity Officer, Adria Alpert-Romm, age 63, $801,058 total compensation
President And Managing Director Discovery Networks Central & Eastern Europe Middle East And Africa, Kasia Kieli
Cfo, Gunnar Wiedenfels
Ceo Eurosport, Peter Hutton
President Domestic Distribution, Eric Phillips
President And Managing Director Discovery Networks Southern Europe, Marinella Soldi
President International Content Group, Susanna Dinnage
Vice President Operations And Prod Development Partnerships, Kevin Malone
Vice President Operations, Toni Herbert
Vice President Financial Planning And Analysis, Matthew Deprey
Executive Vice President Advertising Sales Mtv Networks Kids And Family Group, Jim Perry
Vice President Technology, Jim Boyle
Carrie D Storer Senior Vice President Human Resources And Compliance Legal, Carrie Storer
Senior Vice President Of Operations, Veronica Cajigas
Vice President, John Saag
Vice President, Michela Giorelli
Senior Vice President Investor Relations, Craig Felenstein
Senior Vice President Distribution, Meg Lowe
Senior Vice President Us Media Operations, Don Johnson

Vice President Strategy And Account Management, Todd Richards
President Ceo And Director, David M. Zaslav, age 59
Chairman, Robert J. (Bob) Miron, age 81
Auditors: PricewaterhouseCoopers LLP

LOCATIONS

HQ: Discovery Inc
One Discovery Place, Silver Spring, MD 20910
Phone: 240 662 2000
Web: www.discoverycommunications.com

PRODUCTS/OPERATIONS

2017 Sales

	$ mil.	% of total
Distribution	3,474	51
Advertising	3,073	45
Other	326	4
Total	**6,873**	**100**

2017 Sales

	$ mil.	% of total
US networks	3,434	50
International networks	3,281	48
Education & other	158	2
Corporate & adjustments	(2)	-
Total	**6,873**	**100**

Selected Mergers and Acquisitions

FY2012
Revision3 ($30 million; San Francisco CA; digital video provider)

Selected Operations

Cable channels
  Animal Planet
  Discovery Channel
  Discovery Kids
  Investigation Discovery
  Planet Green
  Science Channel
  TLC (The Learning Channel)
Commerce and education
  Discovery Education
  DiscoveryStore.com
Business and Brands
U.S. Networks
Discovery Networks International
Discovery Education
Discovery Commerce
Discovery Digital Media
Revision3
Discovery Enterprises International
Discovery Studios

COMPETITORS

A&E Networks	NBCUniversal
AMC Networks	PBS
CBS Corp	Turner Broadcasting
Disney	Viacom
E! Entertainment Television	

HISTORICAL FINANCIALS

Company Type: Public

Income Statement

FYE: December 31

	REVENUE ($ mil.)	NET INCOME ($ mil.)	NET PROFIT MARGIN	EMPLOYEES
12/17	6,873	(337)	—	7,000
12/16	6,497	1,194	18.4%	7,000
12/15	6,394	1,034	16.2%	7,000
12/14	6,265	1,139	18.2%	6,800
12/13	5,535	1,075	19.4%	5,700
Annual Growth	**5.6%**	**—**	**—**	**5.3%**

2017 Year-End Financials

Debt ratio: 65.55%
Return on equity: (-6.89%)
Cash ($ mil.): 7,309
Current ratio: 5.34
Long-term debt ($ mil.): 14,755

No. of shares (mil.): 381
Dividends
Yield: —
Payout: —
Market value ($ mil.): 8,547

	STOCK PRICE ($) FY Close	P/E High/Low	PER SHARE ($) Earnings	Dividends	Book Value
12/17	22.38	— —	(0.59)	0.00	12.07
12/16	27.41	15 12	1.96	0.00	13.29
12/15	26.68	22 16	1.58	0.00	13.30
12/14	34.45	54 19	1.66	0.00	12.75
12/13	90.42	60 42	1.49	0.00	13.23
Annual Growth	(29.5%)	— —	—	—	(2.3%)

Dish Network Corp

DISH Network believes entertainment (and news and sports) is a dish best served from the sky and over the internet. The company is the fourth biggest pay-TV provider in the US serving more than 13 million household subscribers as well as hotels restaurants retail spots and other commercial accounts. Programming includes premium movies on-demand video service regional and specialty sports local and international channels and pay-per-view in addition to basic video programming. Its Sling TV offering provides streaming video over the internet. DISH generates almost all sales in the US.

Operations

DISH Network?s revenue comes from its satellite and streaming pay-TV subscriptions. The satellite service relies on satellite dishes that are set up on customers? structures (homes and commercial buildings) to receive signals. The company also leases set-top boxes and video recorders to subscribers.

The Sling streaming service is transmitted over the internet and is geared to consumers who don?t subscribe to cable or satellite services. Sling branded pay-TV services consist of live streaming in versions for the US and international markets.

DISH Network counts more than 13 million pay-TV subscribers. About 11 million are satellite subscribers and about 2.2 million have Sling TV.

The company also owns spectrum licenses for wireless service but it has yet to offer service. It has spent about $20 billion on spectrum licenses since 2008.

Geographic Reach

While virtually all of DISH Network?s revenue is from US customers the company does get a fraction of sales from Canada and Mexico. The company operates about a dozen call centers in the US.

Sales and Marketing

DISH Network gains new subscribers through third parties including national retailers and telecommunications firms local and regional electronics stores and small satellite retailers among other channels.

Financial Performance

DISH Network?s revenue peaked in 2015 after seven years of steady growth. Revenue has declined in the past two years in the face of increasing competition from over-the-top services.

DISH Network?s revenue dropped 5% to $14.4 billion in 2017 from 2016 due to a net loss of 211000 subscribers. Nearly 1 million subscribers dropped the company?s satellite pay-TV service in 2017 compared to about 1.3 million droppers in 2016. While DISH Network gained more than 710000 subscribers to Sling TV that was less than nearly 880000 who signed up in 2016. The monthly average revenue per user (for satellite and Sling TV) fell to $86.43 in 2017 from $88.66 in 2016 due to the lower customer cost of a Sling TV payment.

Net income increased 40% to $2.1 billion in 2017 from 2016 boosted by a tax benefit from the US Tax Cuts and Jobs Acts of 2017. Overall the company held expenses steady as a percentage of revenue.

DISH Network?s cash on hand fell to $1.5 billion in 2017 from about $5.3 billion in 2016 because it paid about $4.7 billion to the Federal Communications Commission to license spectrum.

Strategy

DISH Network has focused much of its attention on its Sling TV packages aimed at customers who have cut their subscription to cable and satellite TV services. The company expanded its Sling packages to offer consumers more choices: The Sling TV Blue service offers streaming over multiple devices while the original service now Sling TV Orange streams to one device. It is working on a cloud-based DVR system that enable Sling subscribers to record programs. First aimed at millennials the company has expanded Sling's scope to target other groups of consumers interested in cutting the pay TV cord as well as other populations becoming more comfortable with technology.

Sling TV helped DISH Network reduced its customer turnover (churn) to about 1.7% in 2017 from 1.9% in 2016. The company also credited a focus on acquiring and retaining higher quality satellite subscribers.

While Sling TV has helped DISH Network is it enough to enable it to compete with increasingly fierce rivals? Rival satellite TV provider DirecTV has the backing of giant telecom AT&T which is trying to buy the Time Warner news and entertainment offerings (such as HBO CNN and TNT). Cable provider Comcast is taking advantage of its NBCUniversal division to bolster its offerings. Netflix Hulu and Amazon.com?s Prime video have put pressure on DISH Network and its competitors.

In 2017 DISH Network swapped some assets with EchoStar that gave DISH greater control over Sling and satellite hardware and software development. The move allows DISH to integrate DISH and Sling customer experiences which should include operating efficiencies.

DISH Network which has been stockpiling wireless spectrum licenses (about $20 billion worth over 10 years) said it would but has yet to deploy services such as phone service a 5G-capable network to support narrowband Internet of Things devices. The company plans to complete the first phase of the deployment by March 2020. In 2017 Charlie Ergen DISH Network chairman turned the CEO post over to another executive to concentrate on wireless developments.

EXECUTIVES

Evp Strategic Planning, Bernard L. (Bernie) Han, age 53, $500,000 total compensation
Evp, James (Jim) DeFranco, age 66, $374,640 total compensation
Chairman And Ceo, Charles W. (Charlie) Ergen, age 64, $1,000,000 total compensation
Evp Corporate Development, Thomas A. (Tom) Cullen, age 58, $450,000 total compensation
President And Coo, W. Erik Carlson, age 48, $515,000 total compensation
Evp General Counsel And Secretary, R. Stanton Dodge, age 50, $296,155 total compensation
Evp And Cto, Vivek Khemka, age 45
Evp Operations, John W. Swieringa, age 40
Evp Customer Acquisition And Retention, Brian V. Neylon, age 52
Svp And Cfo, Steven E. (Steve) Swain, age 50, $357,539 total compensation
Svp Media Sales And Analytics, Warren W. Schlichting, age 56, $372,885 total compensation
Svp And Cio, Rob Dravenstott
Svp And Chief Marketing Officer, Jay Roth
Vice President Corporate Development, Theodore Henderson
Senior Vice President Programming, Andrew Lecuyer
Vice President Wireless Development, David Zufall
Vice President, Melissa Gonzalez
Vice President Dns Operations, Dennis Newman
National Sales Manager, Glen Smith
Senior Vice President Deputy General Counsel And Corporate Secretary, Brandon Ehrhart
National Sales Manager, Milena Bontcheva
Vice President Corporate Taxes, Matthew Sheers
Senior Vice President Public Policy And Government Affairs, Jeffrey Blum
National Sales Manager, Juan Colmenares
Vp Marketing, Melanie Polvoriza
Vice President Of Corporate Initiatives, Rex Povenmire
National Account Manager, Laura Haessler
Svp Manufacturing, Jim Larocque
Svp In Home Services, Nick Rossetti
Vice President, Shannon Picchione
Chief Human Resources Officer And Executive Vice President, Michael McClaskey
Senior Vice President Software Engineering, Daniel Minnick
Vice President Operations, Jeremy Mccarty
Vice President Of Local Sales Director Of Sales National And Major Accounts, Doug Mohr
Senior Vice President Supply Chain And Operations, Gareth Hughes
Chairman And Ceo, Charles W. (Charlie) Ergen, age 64
Board Member, Charles Lillis
Auditors: KPMG LLP

LOCATIONS

HQ: Dish Network Corp
9601 South Meridian Boulevard, Englewood, CO 80112
Phone: 303 723-1000   Fax: 303 723-1499
Web: www.dishnetwork.com

2017 Sales

	% of total
United States	100
Services	-
Total	100

PRODUCTS/OPERATIONS

2017 Sales

	$ mil.	% of total
Subscriber-related revenue	14,260	99
Equipment sales and other revenue	131	1
Total	14,391	100

COMPETITORS

AMC Networks	Grande Communications
AT&T	Hulu
Altice USA	Netflix
Amazon.com	RCN Corporation
Charter Communications	Roku
Comcast	Time Warner Cable
Cox Communications	Verizon
DIRECTV	

HISTORICAL FINANCIALS

Company Type: Public

Income Statement

	REVENUE ($ mil.)	NET INCOME ($ mil.)	NET PROFIT MARGIN	EMPLOYEES
12/17	14,391	2,098	14.6%	17,000
12/16	15,094	1,449	9.6%	16,000
12/15	15,068	747	5.0%	18,000
12/14	14,643	944	6.5%	19,000
12/13	13,904	807	5.8%	25,000
Annual Growth	0.9%	27.0%	—	(9.2%)

FYE: December 31

2017 Year-End Financials

Debt ratio: 54.42%
Return on equity: 36.26%
Cash ($ mil.): 1,479
Current ratio: 0.68
Long-term debt ($ mil.): 15,134

No. of shares (mil.): 466
Dividends
Yield: —
Payout: —
Market value ($ mil.): 22,274

	STOCK PRICE ($) FY Close	P/E High/Low	PER SHARE ($) Earnings	Dividends	Book Value
12/17	47.75	15 10	4.07	0.00	14.87
12/16	57.93	19 13	3.05	0.00	9.97
12/15	57.18	49 35	1.61	0.00	5.92
12/14	72.89	39 26	2.04	0.00	4.36
12/13	57.92	33 19	1.76	0.00	2.13
Annual Growth	(4.7%)	— —	23.3%	—	62.5%

Disney (Walt) Co. (The)

The monarch of this magic kingdom is no man but a mouse: Mickey Mouse. The Walt Disney Company is the world's largest media conglomerate with assets encompassing movies television publishing and theme parks. Its Disney/ABC Television Group includes the ABC television network and 10 broadcast stations as well as a portfolio of cable networks including ABC Family Disney Channel and ESPN (80%-owned). Walt Disney Studios produces films through imprints Walt Disney Pictures Disney Animation and Pixar. It also owns Marvel Entertainment and Lucasfilm two extremely successful film producers. In addition Walt Disney Parks and Resorts runs its popular theme parks including Walt Disney World and Disneyland.

HISTORY

After getting started as an illustrator in Kansas City Walt Disney and his brother Roy started Disney Brothers Studio in Hollywood California in 1923. Walt directed the first Mickey Mouse cartoon Plane Crazy in 1928 (the third Steamboat Willie was the first cartoon with a soundtrack). The studio produced its first animated feature film Snow White and the Seven Dwarfs in 1937. Walt Disney Productions went public in 1940 and later produced classics such as Fantasia and Pinocchio. The Disneyland theme park opened in 1955.

Roy Disney became chairman after Walt died of lung cancer in 1966. Disney World opened in Florida in 1971 the year Roy died. His son Roy E. became the company's principal individual shareholder. Walt's son-in-law Ron Miller became president in 1980. Two years later Epcot Center opened in Florida. In 1984 the Bass family of Texas in alliance with Roy E. bought a controlling interest in the company. New CEO Michael Eisner (from Paramount) and president Frank Wells

(from Warner Bros.) ushered in an era of innovation prosperity and high executive salaries.

The company later launched The Disney Channel and opened new theme parks including Tokyo Disneyland (1984) and Disney-MGM Studios (1989; eventually renamed Hollywood Studios). In 1986 the company changed its name to The Walt Disney Company. The Disney Store retail chain debuted in 1987. Disneyland Paris (originally Euro Disney) opened in 1992. The following year Disney expanded its movie studio with the purchase of independent film company Miramax the brainchild of producers Bob and Harvey Weinstein.

Following Wells' death in a helicopter crash in 1994 boardroom infighting led to the acrimonious departure of studio head Jeffrey Katzenberg. (He was awarded $250 million in compensation in 1999.) The next year Eisner appointed Hollywood agent Michael Ovitz as president. (Ovitz left after 16 months with a severance package of more than $100 million.) Disney bought Capital Cities/ABC (now ABC Inc.) for $19 billion in 1996 and two years later it bought Web services firm Starwave from Microsoft co-founder Paul Allen. It later acquired 43% of Internet search engine Infoseek for $70 million and together they launched the GO Network in 1999. Disney bought the remaining 57% of Infoseek later that year and formed GO.com (later Disney Online) which began trading as a separate tracking stock.

In early 2000 ABC chairman Robert Iger was named Disney's president and COO. Later that year Time Warner Cable briefly suspended ABC broadcasts during a dispute over re-broadcasting rights drawing the ire of some 3.5 million cable customers. (The FCC later ruled that Time Warner violated rules against dropping a station from cable systems during sweeps periods.)

The company expanded its theme parks in Anaheim in 2001 opening Downtown Disney and Disney's California Adventure. It also announced a further restructuring of its Internet business including closing the GO.com search site and converting its Internet tracking stock back into Disney common stock. That year Disney formed a joint venture with Wenner Media (US Weekly LLC) and took a 50% stake in entertainment magazine US Weekly (sold in 2006) . Later Disney bought Fox Family Channel which it renamed ABC Family from News Corporation and Haim Saban for $2.9 billion in cash and assumption of $2.3 billion in debt.

In 2003 Disney began its exit from the sports world by selling the Anaheim Angels. (The company had acquired a 25% stake in the baseball team in 1995 and purchased the remaining interest four years later.) At Disney's annual shareholder meeting in 2004 about 45% of stock owners voted to not re-elect the embattled Eisner to the board. In response Disney directors stripped Eisner of the chairman title and named director and former US senator George Mitchell to that position.

Disney sold its under-performing chain of Disney Store retail outlets to The Children's Place in 2004. Amid all the strife the company boosted its children's entertainment properties by purchasing the Muppet and Bear in the Big Blue House characters along with their film and television libraries from The Jim Henson Company.

Several big executive shakeups occurred at Walt Disney in late 2005. Eisner finally passed the CEO torch after more than 20 years to former COO Iger. That same year Disney Parks opened Hong Kong Disneyland the company's biggest foray into the world's most populated country. In addition the Weinstein brothers left Miramax to form The Weinstein Company ending two of the most successful tenures of the independent film movement. (Disney ceased the operations of Miramax in a

cost-cutting move in 2010 and announced plans to sell the Miramax label later that year.)

In mid-2006 Walt Disney completed a crucial acquisition — the $7.4 billion purchase of Pixar Animation. Disney almost lost Pixar as a production partner in the animation house's blockbuster films but Iger successfully dodged the bullet. Disney Studios' release of Pirates of the Caribbean: Dead Man's Chest that year topped box office records when it brought in $132 million during its opening weekend. The mark was broken by the third installment of the series Pirates of the Caribbean: At World's End which took in $156 million when it was released the next year. Also in 2007 Disney spun off ABC's radio broadcasting operations to Citadel Broadcasting for $2.7 billion in cash and stock.

Disney re-acquired the Disney Store chain in 2008 from Hoop Holdings a subsidiary of retailer The Children's Place in an effort to save the stores from closing. Hoop Holdings had filed bankruptcy that year citing continued losses and rising debt. (The Children's Place was not involved in the bankruptcy filing.) Also in 2008 the company reorganized its digital holdings with the formation of Disney Interactive Media Group. The following year the company purchased a 30% stake in video streaming website Hulu.

Roy E. died in late 2009 at age 79. Also that year Disney acquired Marvel Entertainment bringing Spider-Man Iron Man and other comic book characters into the Magic Kingdom. The deal was worth a whopping $4 billion and changed the course of its movie-making strategy reducing the number of films the studio releases each year while significantly ramping up production of costly big-budget franchises.

In attempts to cut costs Disney Studios in 2010 sold its venerable Miramax production unit (producer of films as Pulp Fiction and Shakespeare in Love) in 2010 to a group of investors (including Ron Tutor private equity firm Colony Capital and Qatar Holdings) for some $663 million. Also that year the company spent $563.2 million to acquire Playdom a popular social game company on Facebook in order to boost its DIMG holdings. Meanwhile Pixar's Toy Story 3 was the top grossing summer release in 2010.

Jobs who stepped down as CEO of Apple in 2011 for medical reasons and died of pancreatic cancer later that year had been Disney's largest individual stockholder with a 7% stake he acquired when the company purchased Pixar. (Jobs had bought Pixar from Lucasfilm in 1986.) Upon his death his Disney shares were converted to the Steven P. Jobs Trust led by his widow Laurene Powell Jobs.

Disney's 2012 box office bomb John Carter lost some $200 million and is reported to be one of the biggest money-losing films of all time.

EXECUTIVES

Evp Corporate Communications, Zenia Mucha
Sevp General Counsel And Secretary, Alan N. Braverman, age 69, $1,549,000 total compensation
Senior Vice President, Steven Bardwill
Chairman And Ceo, Robert A. (Bob) Iger, age 65, $2,500,000 total compensation
President Espn And Co-chairman Disney Media Networks, John Skipper
Sevp And Cfo, Christine M. McCarthy, age 62, $1,287,692 total compensation
Evp Controllership Financial Planning And Tax, Brent A. Woodford
Chairman The Walt Disney Studios, Alan F. Horn
Chairman Walt Disney Parks And Resorts, Robert (Bob) Chapek

Chairman Walt Disney International, Andy Bird, age 55
Sevp Chief Strategy Officer, Kevin A. Mayer, age 55, $1,287,692 total compensation
Chairman Disney Consumer Products And Interactive Media, James A. (Jimmy) Pitaro
Evp And Chief Human Resources Officer, Mary Jayne Parker, age 56, $826,385 total compensation
President The Walt Disney Company Europe Middle East And Africa (emea), Rebecca Campbell
Co-chair Disney Media Networks And President Disney/abc Television Group, Ben Sherwood
President Disney Cruise Line And New Vacation Operations, Anthony Connelly
Senior Vice President Human Resources, Steven Milovich
Senior Vice President Chief Financial Officer Disney Consumer Products, Robert Langer
Senior Vice President Of Marketing, David Sameth
Executive Assistant Supporting Jb Orecchia Vice President Marketing, Holly Franks
Vp Human Resources, Rochelle Holden
Vice President, Kris Theiler
Senior Vice President Human Re, Marjorie Randolph
Senior Vice President Advertising Sales, Irv Schulman
Vice President Human Resources Business Partner, Josefina Leon
Vice President Employee And Organization Development, Carolyn Wilson
Senior Vice President Human Resources And Diversity And Inclusion Walt Disney Parks And Resorts, Tami Garcia
Vice President Creative Marketing, Tom Connor
Vice President Financial Controller, Richard Brookbanks
Vice President Finance, Graham Burridge
Vice President Human Resources Walt Disney Studio, Kathy Locketti
Vp Engineering Services Disney Technology Solutions And Services Team, Eric Lippke
Vice President Sales, Jeremiah Tachna
Vice President Finance, Tim Adam
Vice President, Margaret Malone
Senior Vice President Sales And Marketing, Patrick Scanlan
Vice President Dca Park And Guest Services, Mary M Niven
Senior Vice President Corporate Strategy, Nick Van Dyk
Executive Vice President, Paul Gregg
Vice President Global Publicity, Andrew Bernstein
Vice President Of Human Resources, Jayne Parker
Vp Of Art Development, Jeff Bunker
Vice President, Greg Head
Vice President International Theatrical Sales And Distribution, David Kornblum
Vice President Mobile Broadband And Operations Abc News Digital, Elizabeth Barrett
Vice President Of Retail Sales, Chip Lister
Regional Vice President Human Resources, Bill Frew
Vice President Counsel, Suet Lai
Vice President Finance And Business Development, Sherri Lombra
Vice President Marketing, Paul Baribault
Vice President Media Relations, Charissa Gilmore
Vice President, Darlene Papalini
Vice President Dcl Shoreside Travel Operations, Joann Arndt
Vice President Resort Sale, Anne Hamilton-Chehab
Vice President Research And Brand Strategy, Elizabeth Sloan
Vice President, Tom Stauffer
Vice President Corporate Financial Planning And Analysis, Blair Boyle
Vice President Casting Original Movies, Judy Taylor
Vp Systems, Chris Kaiser

Senior Vice President Business Affairs And Legal Counsel, John D Olson
Vice President And General Manager Jap, Kazuo Nakazawa
Vice President Product Design And Development, Kelli Coleman
Legal Secretary, Ivy Iacono
Vice President Digital Marketing Walt Disney Parks And Resorts, Tom Aronson
Vice President And Chief Information, Bruno Brocheton
Senior Vice President National Sales Manager, Mark Rejtig
Senior Vice President Global Security, Ron Iden
Manager Government Relations, Adam E Babington
Senior Vice President Corporate Real Estate, Martha Welborne
Vp Multicultural Initiatives, Christine Cadena
Vice President Global Licensing And Digital Business Development, Tonya Agurto
National Account Manager, Dorothy Kemper
Vp Original Movies Disney Channel, Naketha Mattocks
Legal Secretary, Alexa Perez
Vice President Global Retail Product Design And Development, Lisa Baldzicki
Assistant Vice President Controller, Pooja Zand
Vice President Engineering, Kathy De
Vice President, Eric Velez
Vice President Affiliate Marketing, Kimberly Wilson
Vice President Supply Chain Solutions, Jeff Bethel
Senior Vice President, Ketcham Jerry
Vp Broadcast Operations, Bob Witkowski
Vice President Information Technology, Laura Hall
Sr Vp Sales, Jim Brehm
Vp Strategic Marketing And Promotions, Aaron Simon
Vice President And General Manager, Maciek Bral
Vice President, FRAN VIESTI
Chairman And Ceo, Robert A. (Bob) Iger, age 65
Secretary Boardwalk Catering, Brenda Gernay
Secretary I, Sheryl Doss
Board Member, Debbie Mookini
Secretary, Sheila McTarsney-Horne
Secretary Magic Kingdommain Street Restaurants, Julie McMannen
Secretary, Chrissy Sumi
Secretary, Tommy Ehrenberg
Secretary, Eileen Buckles
Secretary I, Karla Salansky
Secretary, Melody Rousey
Secretary I, Carolyn Woolfork
Secretary I, Kellie Atwell
Secretary Iv, Amber Morales
Secretary, Linda Serracin
Secretary I, Celia Satterwhite
Secretary, Tammy Faulkner
Secretary I, Wendy Brown
Secretary I, Kelli Mongeon
Secretary I, Robin Chase
Secretary I, Brigitte Murray
Secretary I, Debra Favinger
Secretary I, Aydin Rivera
Secretary I, Deanna Gilmore
Secretary 1, Noelle Spikes
Secretary I, Chris Punahele
Secretary Iv, Jennik Apikian
Secretary I, Joyce Fair
Secretary, Diggy Hopkins
Secretary I, Helen Lannuier
Secretary, Erika Zeigler
Secretary I, Evelyn Crespo-almond
Secretary I, Margarita Rementeria
Secretary, Lisa Hooper
Secretary, Carmen Vessells
Secretary I, Jorda Gwyneth
Auditors: PricewaterhouseCoopers LLP

LOCATIONS

HQ: Disney (Walt) Co. (The)
500 South Buena Vista Street, Burbank, CA 91521
Phone: 818 560-1000
Web: www.disney.com

2016 Sales

	$ mil.	% of total
US & Canada	42,616	77
Europe	6,714	12
Asia/Pacific	4,582	8
Latin America & other regions	1,720	3
Total	**55,632**	**100**

PRODUCTS/OPERATIONS

2016 Sales

	$ mil.	% of total
Media networks	23,689	43
Parks & resorts	16,974	30
Studio entertainment	9,441	17
Consumer products & Interactive media	5,528	10
Total	**55,632**	**100**

2016 Sales

	$ mil.	% of total
Service	47,130	85
Product	8,502	15
Total	**55,632**	**100**

Selected Operations

Consumer products
  Disney Publishing Worldwide
  Disney Stores (retail outlets)
Interactive media
  Disney Interactive Studios (video games)
  Club Penguin (social networking for children)
  Disney Online
  Disney.com
  DisneyFamily.com
Media networks
  A&E Television Networks (42%)
  A&E
  Bio (The Biography Channel)
  The History Channel
  History International
  Lifetime
  Lifetime Movie Network
  Lifetime Real Women
  The Military History Channel
  ABC Family Channel
  ABC Television Network
  Disney Channel
  ESPN (80%)
  ESPN2
  ESPN Classic
  ESPNEWS
  JETIX Europe
  SOAPnet
  Television broadcast stations
  KABC (Los Angeles)
  KFSN (Fresno CA)
  KGO (San Francisco)
  KTRK (Houston)
  WABC (New York City)
  WJRT (Flint MI)
  WLS (Chicago)
  WPVI (Philadelphia)
  WTVD (Raleigh-Durham NC)
  WTVG (Toledo OH)
  Toon Disney
Studio entertainment
  Dimension
  Disney Music Group (music production and distribution)
  Disney Theatrical Group (live entertainment events)
  Lucasfilm
  Marvel Entertainment
  Pixar
  Touchstone Pictures
  Walt Disney Pictures
Theme parks and resorts
  Adventures by Disney (vacation packages)
  Disney Cruise Line
  Euro Disney (40%)
  Disney Village
  Disneyland Paris

The Walt Disney Studios Park (Marne-La-Vallee
France)
Disneyland Resort (Anaheim CA)
Disneyland
Disney's California Adventure
Hong Kong Disneyland (47%)
Tokyo Disney Resort (owned and operated by Oriental
Land Co.; Disney earns royalties)
Tokyo Disneyland
Tokyo DisneySea
Walt Disney Imagineering (planning and development)
Walt Disney World Resort (Orlando FL)
Disney Vacation Club
Disney's Animal Kingdom
Disney's Hollywood Studios
Disney's Wide World of Sports
Downtown Disney
Epcot
Magic Kingdom

COMPETITORS

21st Century Fox	SeaWorld
AOL	Six Flags
CBS Corp	Sony Pictures
Comcast	Entertainment
Discovery	Time Warner
DreamWorks Animation	Viacom
Liberty Interactive	Yahoo!
MGM	

HISTORICAL FINANCIALS
Company Type: Public

Income Statement				FYE: September 29
	REVENUE ($ mil.)	NET INCOME ($ mil.)	NET PROFIT MARGIN	EMPLOYEES
09/18	59,434	12,598	21.2%	201,000
09/17*	55,137	8,980	16.3%	199,000
10/16	55,632	9,391	16.9%	195,000
10/15	52,465	8,382	16.0%	185,000
09/14	48,813	7,501	15.4%	180,000
Annual Growth	5.0%	13.8%	—	2.8%

*Fiscal year change

2018 Year-End Financials

Debt ratio: 21.17%
Return on equity: 28.05%
Cash ($ mil.): 4,150
Current ratio: 0.94
Long-term debt ($ mil.): 17,084

Dividends
Yield: 0.0%
Payout: 20.1%
No. of shares (mil.): 1,488
Market value ($ mil.): 174,007

	STOCK PRICE ($) FY Close	P/E High/Low		PER SHARE ($)		
				Earnings	Dividends	Book Value
09/18	116.94	14	12	8.36	1.68	32.78
09/17*	98.57	20	16	5.69	1.56	27.23
10/16	92.86	21	15	5.73	1.42	27.09
10/15	103.00	25	17	4.90	1.81	26.81
09/14	88.74	21	15	4.26	0.86	26.34
Annual Growth	7.1%	—	—	18.4%	18.2%	5.6%

*Fiscal year change

DLL FINANCE LLC

EXECUTIVES

Mng MBR, Dave Roszak
MBR, Dan Kronlage
Business Manager, Gustavo Lichtenberger
Director, Eugene Purcell
Relationslrip Manager, Geoffrey Hoffman
Sales Representati, Stewart Ibsen
Senior Sales Repre, Chris Seymour
Business Manager, John Sugden
Financial Advisor, Josh Nielsen
Marketing Executive, Kelly Whitelaw

LOCATIONS

HQ: DLL FINANCE LLC
8001 BIRCHWOOD CT STE C, JOHNSTON, IA
501312889
Phone: 800 873-2474
Web: WWW.AGRICREDIT.COM

HISTORICAL FINANCIALS
Company Type: Private

Income Statement				FYE: December 31
	ASSETS ($ mil.)	NET INCOME ($ mil.)	INCOME AS % OF ASSETS	EMPLOYEES
12/16	2,327	14	0.6%	250
12/15	1,578	10	0.7%	—
12/14	1,454	14	1.0%	—
12/13	1,321	17	1.3%	—
Annual Growth	20.8%	(5.8%)	—	—

2016 Year-End Financials

Debt ratio: ——
Return on equity: 19.40%
Cash ($ mil.): 13
Current ratio: 0.70
Long-term debt ($ mil.): —

Dividends
Yield: —
Payout: —
Market value ($ mil.): —

Dollar General Corp

EXECUTIVES

Ceo, Todd J Vasos
Chb, Michael M Calbert
Exec V Pres-Cfo, John W Garratt
Exec V Pres-Gen Counsel, Rhonda M Taylor
Exec V Pres-CIO, Carman R Wenkoff
Sr V Pres-Cao, Anita C Elliott
Manager, Amanda Hamilton
Senior Manager Apparel Allocat, Amanda Whited
Senior Claims Representative R, Bobbie Ray
Senior Programmer Analyst, Chris Johnson
Demand Chain Management Analys, Derrick Black
Auditors: Ernst & Young LLP

LOCATIONS

HQ: Dollar General Corp
100 Mission Ridge, Goodlettsville, TN 37072
Phone: 615 855-4000   Fax: 615 855-5527
Web: www.dollargeneral.com

COMPETITORS

99 Cents Only	Kmart
Big Lots	Rite Aid
CVS Caremark	TJX Companies
Costco Wholesale	Target Corporation
Dollar Tree	Variety Wholesalers
Family Dollar Stores	Wal-Mart
Fred's	Walgreen

HISTORICAL FINANCIALS
Company Type: Public

Income Statement				FYE: February 2
	REVENUE ($ mil.)	NET INCOME ($ mil.)	NET PROFIT MARGIN	EMPLOYEES
02/18	23,470	1,538	6.6%	129,000
02/17*	21,986	1,251	5.7%	121,000
01/16	20,368	1,165	5.7%	113,400
01/15	18,909	1,065	5.6%	105,500
01/14	17,504	1,025	5.9%	100,600
Annual Growth	7.6%	10.7%	—	6.4%

*Fiscal year change

2018 Year-End Financials

Debt ratio: 24.02%
Return on equity: 26.76%
Cash ($ mil.): 267
Current ratio: 1.43
Long-term debt ($ mil.): 2,604

No. of shares (mil.): 268
Dividends
Yield: 1.0%
Payout: 18.4%
Market value ($ mil.): 26,723

	STOCK PRICE ($) FY Close	P/E High/Low		PER SHARE ($)		
				Earnings	Dividends	Book Value
02/18	99.44	19	12	5.63	1.04	22.80
02/17*	73.14	22	15	4.43	1.00	19.64
01/16	75.06	21	15	3.95	0.88	18.76
01/15	67.06	20	15	3.49	0.00	18.82
01/14	56.32	20	14	3.17	0.00	17.04
Annual Growth	15.3%	—	—	15.4%	—	7.5%

*Fiscal year change

Dollar Tree Inc

Dollars may not grow on trees but Dollar Tree brings in the green. The fast-growing company operates more than 15000 Dollar Tree and Family Dollar discount stores across the US and in five provinces in Canada. The stores carry a mix of housewares toys seasonal items food health and beauty aids and books. At Dollar Tree shops most goods are priced at $1 or less while Family Dollar merchandise is usually less than $10. The stores are generally located in high-traffic strip centers and malls often in midsized cities and small towns.

Operations

Dollar Tree reports its operations through the Dollar Tree and Family Dollar brands. Each brand generates about half of the company's overall revenue.

The Dollar Tree division built around merchandise at the $1 price point has about 6650 stores with some 8000 - 10000 sq. ft. of sales space each. Family Dollar operates through nearly 8200 stores which are a bit smaller at 6000-8000 sq.ft. of sales space; it offers competitively priced merchandise often less than $10.

From a product standpoint the consumables category (candy food health and beauty products household paper products) accounts for about half of sales and variety merchandise (toys housewares gifts) accounts for about 45%. The company's holiday and seasonal offerings category brings in the remainder of sales.

Geographic Reach

Dollar Tree operates stores in 48 US states and the District of Columbia. Its largest markets are Texas Florida Ohio North Carolina and California which together account for about a third of locations. It has more than 225 stores in Canada with about half in Ontario.

The Dollar Tree segment has about a dozen distribution centers in the US two distribution centers in Canada and a store support center in Chesapeake Virginia. The Family Dollar segment has more than 10 distribution centers across the US and a store support center in Matthews North Carolina.

Sales and Marketing

The Dollar Tree brand primarily serves middle income customers in suburban locations with Family Dollar serving lower income customers in urban and rural locations.

The company's advertising costs jumped to more than $106 million in fiscal 2017 from about $60 million in 2016 and $32 million in 2015.

Financial Performance

Dollar Tree saw its revenue nearly double in fiscal 2016 as a result of the acquisition of Family Dollar and the growth has only continued as the company opens new stores each year. Net income sank the year of the acquisition but has risen substantially since then. The company took on quite a bit of debt related to the Family Dollar acquisition although it has been reduced by about a third in just the past two years amid strong free cash flow.

In fiscal 2017 (ended January 2018) the company reported record revenue of $22.2 billion up 7% from the prior year. The results were driven mostly by new stores but also an increase of nearly 2% in same-store sales and a 53rd week in the fiscal year. The weak spot financially for Dollar Tree is the flat same-store sales for Family Dollar (0.4% in 2017); the company has struggled to get that brand growing at a faster clip.

Net income was also up that year about 90% hitting $1.7 billion. Along with the increase in revenue much lower provision for income taxes related to the 2017 Tax Cuts and Jobs Act boosted the bottom line.

Cash at the end of fiscal 2017 was $1.1 billion an increase of $231 million from the prior year. Cash from operations contributed $1.5 billion to the coffers while investing activities used $628 million mainly for capital expenditures. Financing activities used another $651 million for payments on long-term debt primarily.

Strategy

Fast-growing Dollar Tree opens hundreds of new locations each year. In fiscal 2017 it opened more than 600 new stores and relocated or expanded another 100-plus locations and plans similarly sized initiatives in fiscal 2018. The company envisions some 26000 stores across North America ultimately.

With its strong store portfolio Dollar Tree is focused on adding new merchandise options and refreshing locations. It has been adding coolers and freezers to its Dollar Tree stores (more than 400 in 2017) to boost the consumables business including frozen and refrigerated foods and more directly compete with convenience and grocery stores. In addition the company has introduced Snack Zones which provides easy access to immediately consumable goods to hundreds of stores. Within the Family Dollar brand Dollar Tree is investing in renovation with some 375 stores revamped in 2017 and another 450 planned for the following year; improvements include more productive endcaps more beverage and snack offerings updated hair care assortments and in some stores expanded adult beverages.

Unlike many retailers dollar stores are a bit more immune to competitive pressure from Amazon and other online sites. For that reason the company has not had to invest in building a robust omnichannel experience with e-commerce platforms and apps. It is however cutting costs as it works to jumpstart the stalled Family Dollar business. In late 2018 Dollar Tree announced it would close Family Dollar's North Carolina corporate office and eliminate about 200 jobs as a result (the other 700 positions will be relocated to the company's Virginia headquarters).

Company Background

In 1953 K. R. Perry opened a variety store in Norfolk Virginia called Ben Franklin; it was later renamed K&K 5&10. By 1970 Perry and two other men established a mall concept store called K&K Toys also in Virginia although it eventually grew to some 130 locations along the East Coast. A third chain Only $1.00 was started in 1986 with stores located alongside K&K Toys stores.

K&K Toys was sold in the early 1990s to KB Toys and proceeds from the sale were used to expand the dollar store chain. By 1995 that chain Only $1.00 had become Dollar Tree and gone public.

Dollar Tree expanded through new store openings and acquisitions culminating in the 2015 purchase of North Carolina-based Family Dollar for about $9 billion.

EXECUTIVES

Chief Supply Chain Officer, Gary A. Maxwell, age 56

Cfo, Kevin S. Wampler, age 55, $690,385 total compensation

President Ceo And Director, Gary M. Philbin, age 61, $1,121,154 total compensation

Cio, Joshua R. (Josh) Jewett, age 48

President And Coo Family Dollar Stores, Duncan C. Mac Naughton, age 56, $61,538 total compensation

Chief Administrative Officer, Michael (Mike) Matacunas, age 51, $537,500 total compensation

Chief Merchandising Officer, Robert H. (Bob) Rudman, age 67, $740,385 total compensation

President And Coo Dollar Tree, Michael Witynski, age 55

President Ceo And Director, Gary M. Philbin, age 61

Chairman, Bob Sasser, age 66

Auditors: KPMG LLP

LOCATIONS

HQ: Dollar Tree Inc
500 Volvo Parkway, Chesapeake, VA 23320
Phone: 757 321-5000
Web: www.dollartree.com

2017 Canadian Stores

	No.
Ontario	109
British Columbia	51
Alberta	38
Saskatchewan	15
Manitoba	12
Total	**225**

2017 US Stores

	No.
Texas	1,551
Florida	1,087
Ohio	737
North Carolina	705
California	705
Georgia	640
New York	630
Michigan	623
Pennsylvania	613
Other states	7,319
Total	**14,610**

PRODUCTS/OPERATIONS

2017 Sales

	% of total
Consumables	49
Variety categories	46
Seasonal	5
Total	**100**

2017 Sales

	% of total
Dollar Tree	50
Family Dollar	50
Total	**100**

Selected Products

Books
Candy
Cards
Food
Gifts
Health and beauty care products
Housewares
Party goods
Personal accessories
Seasonal goods
Stationery
Toys

COMPETITORS

99 Cents Only	Rite Aid
ALDI	SUPERVALU
Big Lots	Save-A-Lot Food Stores
CVS	Savers Inc.
Dollar General	Target Corporation
Five Below	Wal-Mart
Fred's	Walgreen
Kmart	Winn-Dixie
OllieÂ's Bargain Outlet	

HISTORICAL FINANCIALS

Company Type: Public

Income Statement

FYE: February 3

	REVENUE ($ mil.)	NET INCOME ($ mil.)	NET PROFIT MARGIN	EMPLOYEES
02/18*	22,245	1,714	7.7%	176,100
01/17	20,719	896	4.3%	176,800
01/16	15,498	282	1.8%	167,800
01/15	8,602	599	7.0%	90,000
02/14	7,840	596	7.6%	87,400
Annual Growth	**29.8%**	**30.2%**	**—**	**19.1%**

*Fiscal year change

2018 Year-End Financials

Debt ratio: 34.76%	No. of shares (mil.): 237
Return on equity: 26.83%	Dividends
Cash ($ mil.): 1,097	Yield: —
Current ratio: 1.60	Payout: —
Long-term debt ($ mil.): 4,762	Market value ($ mil.): 25,828

	STOCK PRICE ($) FY Close	P/E High/Low		PER SHARE ($) Earnings	Dividends	Book Value
02/18*	108.83	16	9	7.21	0.00	30.26
01/17	74.05	26	19	3.78	0.00	22.82
01/16	81.32	66	48	1.26	0.00	18.76
01/15	71.10	25	17	2.90	0.00	8.68
02/14	50.52	22	14	2.72	0.00	5.62
Annual Growth	**21.1%**	**—**	**—**	**27.6%**	**—**	**52.3%**

*Fiscal year change

Dominion Energy Inc (New)

Dominion Energy dominates the American energy market as one of its top producers and transporters of electricity and natural gas. It serves some 6 million utility and retail energy customers across 12 US states with a special concentration in Ohio Virginia West Virginia and Pennsylvania. The company boasts an impressive energy portfolio with approximately 26000 MW of generating capacity as well as one of the largest underground natural gas storage systems with 1 trillion cu. ft. capacity. Formerly Dominion Resources the company changed its name to Dominion Energy in 2017.

Change in Company Type

In November 2018 Dominion Energy Midstream announced its merger plan with Dominion Energy.

However the proposed merger might be investigated by authorities for final approval.

Operations

Dominion operates through three segments: Power Generation Gas Infrastructure and Power Delivery.

Power Generation (55% of revenue) includes Virginia Power?s regulated utility and its related energy supply operations. Under Dominion Energy it also includes Virginia power?s utility generation operation as well as Dominion's merchant fleet energy marketing and risk management services.

Gas Infrastructure (20% of revenue) consists of both Dominion Energy businesses and well as Dominion Energy Gas businesses. As a result this umbrella segment includes LNG operations Questar (a subsidiary) operations as well as natural gas marketing.

Power Delivery which brings in a further 20% of sales includes Virginia Power's regulated electric transmission and distribution operations which serve more than 2.5 million residential commercial industrial and governmental customers in Virginia and North Carolina.

In electricity it has some 6600 miles of transmission and 58000 distribution lines. In the natural gas business the company operates 14800 miles of transmission gathering and storage pipelines and 52000 miles distribution pipelines.

Geographic Reach

In addition to distributing power to customers in North Carolina West Virginia and Virginia through Dominion Virginia Power Dominion serves retail energy customers in 12 US states.

The company's merchant non-renewable generation facilities are located in Connecticut Pennsylvania and Rhode Island with a majority of that capacity concentrated in New England.

Dominion's merchant renewable generation facilities include a fuel cell generation facility in Connecticut solar generation facilities in Indiana Georgia California North & South Carolina Tennessee Utah and Connecticut and wind generation facilities in Indiana and West Virginia.

Sales and Marketing

Dominion sells electricity to the wholesale market local distribution companies utilities distribution network and end-users. The company serves 6 million utility and retail energy customers.

Virginia Power sells electricity and provides distribution and transmission services to customers in Virginia and northeastern North Carolina. Virginia Power has 6600 miles of electric transmission lines of 69 kV or more.

Dominion's ten largest gas customers provides approximately 40% of the company's total storage and transportation revenue and the thirty largest nearly 70%.

Financial Performance

In the past decade (2008-17) Dominion Energy has seen revenue shrink by some $3.3 billion dollars with an average yearly revenue around $13 billion. During the same period net income fluctuated between $300 million (2012) and $3 billion (2017).

In 2017 revenue rose about 10% to $9.6 billion. Majority of that increase came from the Quester acquisition ($663 million) but was aided by higher electricity capacity benefits in non-utility generators and volume increases in the solar projects and electric utility sectors.

Net Income in 2017 increased more than 40% to $3 billion mostly due to the favorable corporate tax rate introduced for the year an absence of 2016 landfill closure charges ($197 million) and $115 million decrease in electric transmission expenses.

Dominion's 2017 cash holdings reduced more than half year-over-year to $120 million the lowest since 2012. In contrast cash from operations was

the highest in a decade at $4.5 billion while financing activities contributed $1.3 billion. Investment used some $6 billion. Property plant and equipment has averaged $5.5 billion in the 2012-17 period.

Strategy

Dominion is following a five-year investment plan that outlines more than $8 billion during the 2018-22 period for new energy generation capacity and upgrading facilities—from electric lines to gas storage lines and aging nuclear facilities. A $1 billion-plus construction project in Greensville County is also nearing completion.

Solar projects have emerged as a main source of investment at Dominion. This strengthens the company's already impressive diversified portfolio of fuel sources that includes nuclear coal oil solar and other renewables.

In 2014-17 period the company has added almost 850 MW capacity from solar generation alone most of it through acquisition and new developments. However the reduction in solar investment tax credits may hamper growth of these projects.

Dominion is banking on normal weather to increase growth in its electric utility operations and additional revenue stemming from new projects coming online. A lower effective tax rate due to the tax reform should also benefit the company.

However Dominion's working capital deficit ($5.2 billion in 2017) raises serious concerns about its short-term obligations as the company's current liabilities increased approach $10 billion. The company has tried to boost inorganic growth through major acquisitions in the last three years.

Mergers and Acquisitions

After no acquisitions during the 2008-13 period Dominion has pursued several costly acquisitions since.

In 2018 Dominion agreed to acquire Scana Corporation the parent company of South Carolina Electric & Gas Company for $7.9 billion adding a million customers to Dominion's already massive base.

Betting on stable revenues from natural gas distribution at a time when power demand is in decline in 2016 Dominion bought Questar Corp. for $4.4 billion. The combined companies have 2.5 million electric utility customer accounts in Virginia and North Carolina; 2.3 million natural gas utility customer accounts in Idaho Ohio Utah West Virginia and Wyoming; and 1.3 million retail energy and related services customer accounts in 13 states.

In 2017 Dominion Energy also completed several acquisitions of wholly-owned merchant solar projects in California North Carolina and Virginia for $356 million. The same year Virginia Power also entered into agreements to acquire two solar development projects in North Carolina. The projects are slated to complete in 2019 with a total expected cost of $280 million once constructed including the initial acquisition cost and will generate approximately 155 MW combined.

HISTORY

In 1781 the Virginia General Assembly established a group of trustees including George Washington and James Madison to promote navigation on the Appomattox River. The group (named the Appomattox Trustees) formed the Upper Appomattox Company in 1795 to secure its water rights. The company eventually began operating hydroelectric plants on the river and by 1888 it had added a steam-powered plant to its portfolio.

The Virginia Railway and Power Company (VR&P) led by Frank Jay Gould purchased the Upper Appomattox Company (which had changed its name) in 1909. The next year the firm acquired

several electric and gas utilities as well as some electric streetcar lines.

In 1925 New York engineering company Stone & Webster acquired VR&P. The company became known as Virginia Electric and Power Company (Virginia Power) and was placed under Engineers Public Service (EPS) a new holding company. Virginia Power purchased several North Carolina utilities following its acquisition.

During the 1930s the Depression (and the popularity of the automobile) led the company to exit the trolley business. The Public Utility Holding Company Act of 1935 (repealed 2005) which ushered in an era of regulated utility monopolies forced EPS to divest all of its operations except Virginia Power. However the utility soon merged with the Virginia Public Service Company thus doubling its service territory.

The company added new power plants to keep up with growing customer demand in the 1950s. Always an innovator it also built an extra-high-voltage transmission system the first in the world.

In the 1970s Virginia Power's first nuclear plants became operational. By 1980 however the firm was near bankruptcy. That year William Berry who had completed a 23-year rise through the ranks to become president canceled two other nuclear units. He also became an early supporter of competition in the electric utility industry. In 1983 he formed Dominion Resources as a parent company for Virginia Power and halted nearly all plant construction. Two additional subsidiaries were soon formed: Dominion Capital in 1985 and Dominion Energy in 1987.

In 1990 the year Thomas Capps took over as CEO Dominion sold its natural gas distribution business and in 1995 Dominion Energy began developing natural gas reserves through joint ventures and by purchasing three natural gas exploration and production companies.

EXECUTIVES

LOCATIONS

HQ: Dominion Energy Inc (New)
120 Tredegar Street, Richmond, VA 23219
Phone: 804 819-2000 **Fax:** 804 775-5819
Web: www.dom.com

PRODUCTS/OPERATIONS

2016 Sales

	$ mil.	% of total
Dominion Generation	6,757	55
Dominion Energy	2,766	22
DVP	2,233	18
Corporate and Other	602	5
Adjustments & Eliminations	(621)	-
Total	**11,737**	**100**

2016 Sales

	$ mil.	% of total
Electric Sales	8,867	76
Gas transportation and Storage	1,636	14
Gas Sales	854	7
Other	380	3
Total	**11,737**	**100**

Selected Subsidiaries and Business Units

Dominion Generation Corporation (power plant management)
Dominion Energy (energy marketing gas and power transmission)
Dominion Transmission Inc. (natural gas pipelines)
Dominion Virginia Power
Consolidated Natural Gas
Dominion East Ohio (or The East Ohio Gas Company gas distribution)
Dominion Hope (or Hope Gas Inc. West Virginia gas distribution)
Dominion North Carolina Power (or Virginia Electric and Power Company electricity distribution)
Dominion Retail Inc. (retail energy marketing)
Virginia Electric and Power Company (electricity distribution)

COMPETITORS

AEP	Exelon
CenterPoint Energy	Koch Industries Inc.
Duke Energy	NiSource
Entergy	Piedmont Natural Gas

HISTORICAL FINANCIALS

Company Type: Public

Income Statement

FYE: December 31

	REVENUE ($ mil.)	NET INCOME ($ mil.)	NET PROFIT MARGIN	EMPLOYEES
12/17	12,586	2,999	23.8%	16,200
12/16	11,737	2,123	18.1%	16,200
12/15	11,683	1,899	16.3%	14,700
12/14	12,436	1,310	10.5%	14,400
12/13	13,120	1,697	12.9%	14,500
Annual Growth	**(1.0%)**	**15.3%**	**—**	**2.8%**

2017 Year-End Financials

Debt ratio: 44.72%
Return on equity: 18.89%
Cash ($ mil.): 120
Current ratio: 0.45
Long-term debt ($ mil.): 30,948

No. of shares (mil.): 645
Dividends
Yield: 0.0%
Payout: 64.3%
Market value ($ mil.): 52,284

	STOCK PRICE ($) FY Close	P/E High/Low		PER SHARE ($) Earnings	Dividends	Book Value
12/17	81.06	18	15	4.72	3.04	26.58
12/16	76.59	23	20	3.44	2.80	23.26
12/15	67.64	25	20	3.20	2.59	21.25
12/14	76.90	36	28	2.24	2.40	19.75
12/13	64.69	23	18	2.93	2.25	20.48
Annual Growth	**5.8%**	**—**	**—**	**12.7%**	**7.8%**	**6.7%**

Domtar Corp

Auditors: PricewaterhouseCoopers LLP

LOCATIONS

HQ: Domtar Corp
234 Kingsley Park Drive, Fort Mill, SC 29715
Phone: 803 802-7500
Web: www.domtar.com

HISTORICAL FINANCIALS

Company Type: Public

Income Statement

FYE: December 31

	REVENUE ($ mil.)	NET INCOME ($ mil.)	NET PROFIT MARGIN	EMPLOYEES
12/17	5,157	(258)	—	10,000
12/16	5,098	128	2.5%	10,000
12/15	5,264	142	2.7%	9,850
12/14	5,563	431	7.7%	9,800
12/13	5,391	91	1.7%	9,400
Annual Growth	**(1.1%)**	**—**	**—**	**1.6%**

2017 Year-End Financials

Debt ratio: 21.68%
Return on equity: (-10.00%)
Cash ($ mil.): 139
Current ratio: 2.24
Long-term debt ($ mil.): 1,129

No. of shares (mil.): 62
Dividends
Yield: 0.0%
Payout: —
Market value ($ mil.): 3,105

	STOCK PRICE ($) FY Close	P/E High/Low		PER SHARE ($) Earnings	Dividends	Book Value
12/17	49.52	—	—	(4.11)	1.66	39.60
12/16	39.03	21	15	2.04	1.65	42.76
12/15	36.95	21	16	2.24	1.60	42.20
12/14	40.22	17	5	6.64	1.40	45.15
12/13	94.34	70	48	1.36	1.05	42.91
Annual Growth	**(14.9%)**	**—**	**—**	**—**	**12.1%**	**(2.0%)**

Donegal Group Inc.

Risk is Donegal Group's middle name. Through its subsidiaries including Atlantic States Insurance and Southern Insurance Company of Virginia Donegal Group provides personal farm and commercial property/casualty insurance products. It is active in about two dozen states in the mid-Atlantic Midwest New England and South. The group's personal insurance offerings range from auto and boat policies to homeowners and fire coverage; its commercial insurance products include business owners multi-peril and workers' compensation. Donegal's financial services arm owns Union Community Bank with about 15 branches in Pennsylvania. Donegal Mutual Insurance controls more than 70% of the company's voting stock.

Operations

Donegal Group operates through four segments: personal lines of Insurance commercial lines of insurance investment function and Donegal Financial services Corporation. Some 95% of the group's revenue comes from net insurance premiums.

The personal lines of insurance are primarily composed of homeowners and automobile policies.

That business brings in more than half of Donegal's total revenue.

Commercial lines consist primarily of commercial automobile workers' compensation and commercial multi-peril policies. The segment brings in more than 40% of total revenue.

Geographic Reach

Donegal is headquartered in Pennsylvania; it operates several locations in Iowa Maryland Virginia and Wisconsin.

The group primarily does business in the mid-Atlantic Midwest South and New England.

Sales and Marketing

Donegal's insurance businesses target customers in small to mid-sized regional communities to allow for local market knowledge and more personal services. Pennsylvania is the company's largest market accounting for more than a third of revenues.

Personal auto policies account for about 35% of Donegal's written net premiums.

The company exclusively distributes it products through some 2400 independent agencies.

Donegal spends about $700000 on advertising each year.

Financial Performance

Donegal's revenue has been increasing over the past few years as the group expands its operations into new territories. Net income has been more turbulent though rising and falling depending on factors such as weather catastrophe losses.

In 2017 revenue increased 7% to $739 million thanks to a 7% increase in net premiums written that year. That was driven by premium rate increases and more new business acquired.

Despite the higher revenue net income fell 77% to $7.1 million in 2017. Although the group tends to limit its exposure to regions that are prone to natural disasters that year proved to be one of the worst on record in terms of catastrophes. Donegal's severe weather losses totaled $58.4 million some $20 million higher than its average.

The company ended 2017 with $37.8 million in net cash $13.2 million more than it had at the end of 2016. Operating activities provided $81 million in cash while investing activities and financing activities used $58.4 million and $9.3 million respectively.

Strategy

Donegal Group's growth strategy is to acquire property/casualty insurance companies to augment its organic growth in existing markets and to expand into new markets. Majority shareholder Donegal Mutual acquired Mountain States Mutual Casualty Company in mid-2017; although that deal didn't directly impact Donegal Group it does provide an opportunity for expansion into the Southwest in future years.

The group actively tracks the performance of its various businesses so that it can change course as it sees fit. For example it is been working to limit new automobile insurance business in underperforming states.

EXECUTIVES

Vice President, Francis J Haefner
Svp Claims, Robert G. Shenk, age 64, $292,000 total compensation
President And Ceo, Kevin G. Burke, age 52, $305,000 total compensation
Svp And Cfo, Jeffrey D. Miller, age 53, $310,000 total compensation
Svp And Chief Underwriting Officer, Cyril J. Greenya, age 73, $280,000 total compensation
Vp Marketing And Advertising, David S. Krenkel
Svp And Chief Actuary, Chester J. Szczepanski
Svp And Cio, Sanjay Pandey, age 51, $280,000 total compensation

Svp And Chief Investment Officer, V. Anthony
Viozzi

President And Treasurer Sheboygan Falls
Insurance Company, Lee F. Wilcox

President Peninsula Insurance Group, G. Eric
Crouchley

President Michigan Insurance Company, Ermil L.
Adamson

President And Treasurer Southern Mutual
Insurance Company, Allen R. Green

Assistant Vice President Personal Lines
Underwriting, Karen Colwill

Vice President Internal Audit, Perry Keith

Vice President Casualty Claims, Thomas Richards

Vice President Vice President Engineering R Vice
President Engineering R Research, Ken Dull

Vice President, Teresa Shertzer

Vice President Regional, James Stiegler

Assistant Vice President Research And
Development, Jason McAfee

Assistant Vice President Regional Sales Manager,
Keith Captain

Vice President Casualty Claims Donegal Mutual,
Steven P Klia

Assistant Vice President And Manager Siu, Jim
Seibert

President And Ceo, Kevin G. Burke, age 52

Chairman, Donald H. Nikolaus, age 75

Assistant Treasurer, Jerry Demastus

Secretary, Rebecca Simowitz

Auditors: KPMG LLP

LOCATIONS

HQ: Donegal Group Inc.
  1195 River Road, P.O. Box 302, Marietta, PA 17547
Phone: 717 426-1931
Web: www.donegalgroup.com

PRODUCTS/OPERATIONS

2017 Sales

	$ mil.	% of total
Personal lines premiums	384	52
Commercial lines premiums	318	43
Net investment income	23	3
Realized investment gains	5	1
Equity in earnings of DFSC	1	-
Other	5	1
Total	**739**	**100**

Selected Subsidiaries

Atlantic States Insurance Company
Donegal Financial Services Corporation (48%)
  Union Community Bank
Le Mars Insurance Company
Michigan Insurance Company
The Peninsula Insurance Company
  Peninsula Indemnity Company
Sheboygan Falls Insurance Company
Southern Insurance Company of Virginia

COMPETITORS

AIG	GEICO
Allstate	Liberty Mutual
American National	Penn National Mutual
Insurance	Casualty
Berkley Mid-Atlantic	Penn-America
Group	Progressive
COUNTRY Financial	Corporation
Erie Indemnity	State Farm

HISTORICAL FINANCIALS

Company Type: Public

Income Statement

FYE: December 31

	ASSETS ($ mil.)	NET INCOME ($ mil.)	INCOME AS % OF ASSETS	EMPLOYEES
12/17	1,737	7	0.4%	—
12/16	1,623	30	1.9%	—
12/15	1,537	20	1.4%	—
12/14	1,458	14	1.0%	—
12/13	1,385	26	1.9%	—
Annual Growth	**5.8%**	**(27.9%)**		

2017 Year-End Financials

Debt ratio: 0.29%
Return on equity: 1.60%
Cash ($ mil.): 37
Current ratio: —
Long-term debt ($ mil.): —

No. of shares (mil.): 28
Dividends
  Yield: 0.0%
  Payout: 214.4%
Market value ($ mil.): 487

	STOCK PRICE ($) FY Close	P/E High/Low		PER SHARE ($) Earnings	Dividends	Book Value
12/17	17.30	67	54	0.26	0.56	15.95
12/16	17.48	15	11	1.16	0.55	16.21
12/15	14.08	21	17	0.77	0.54	15.66
12/14	15.98	29	25	0.55	0.52	15.40
12/13	15.90	16	13	1.02	0.51	15.02
Annual Growth	**2.1%**	**—**	**—**	**(28.9%)**	**2.5%**	**1.5%**

Donnelley (RR) & Sons Company

If you can read it R.R. Donnelley & Sons (RRD) can print it and since this is the 21st century it can digitize it too. The company provides printing services for direct mail labels forms and other commercial and digital printing jobs. It also offers digital technologies that include content management data analytics and multichannel distribution. The formerly huge printing firm split itself up into three smaller companies with separate management teams in 2016. RRD with about $7 billion in revenue and more than 42000 employees is the biggest of the three companies. About three-quarters of RRD's revenue comes from the US.

Change in Company Type

Donnelley split itself into three companies in order to better focus on certain markets. The other companies resulting from the breakup are LSC Communications which serves retail and merchandise clients from the pre-split company and Donnelley Financial Solutions which focuses on financial investment and legal printing.

Operations

RRD operates in three segments: Variable Print Strategic Services and International.

The Variable Print segment which provides about 45% of revenue is the company's short-run and transactional printing operation. It handles commercial and digital print direct mail labels statement printing and forms. The Commercial & Digital unit was the biggest business within Variable Print accounting for nearly 25% of total RRD revenue.

The Strategic Services segment 25% of revenue offers logistics sourcing and digital and creative services. Logistics accounts for close to 10% of overall RRD revenue.

About 30% of revenue comes from the International segment which consists of printing operations in Asia Canada Latin America and Europe as well as its Global Turnkey Solutions and business process outsourcing units. The Asia market supplies about an eighth of RRD's total sales.

Geographic Reach

RRD headquartered in Chicago operates about 240 facilities in the US and more than 90 facilities in Asia Europe Canada and Latin America. The US accounts for about 75% of its sales with Asia adding about an eighth of revenue and Europe contributing more than 5%.

Sales and Marketing

RRD claims more than 50000 customers including 99 of the Fortune 100 companies. The company's five largest clients account for about 10% of sales. After the corporate split RRD continues to provide logistics pre-media production and sales services to LSC and Donnelley Financial and their customers.

Financial Performance

The separation of Donnelley into three companies in 2016 cut RRD's revenue from $10.5 billion in 2013 to $6.8 billion in 2016. Sales rose about 2% in 2017 to $6.9 billion.

The company in 2017 had higher volume in Asia which was somewhat countered by lower volume in the Variable Print segment and units within the International segment and lower postage pass-through sales in the logistics unit. The company also experienced price pressures across all segments during the year.

RRD took a big step toward recovering from the costs of separation and restructuring in 2017 reporting a net loss of $34.4 million compared to a net loss of $495.9 million in 2016. The company also took a $104 million non-cash provision because of the US Tax Cuts and Jobs Act of 2017.

The company's cash holdings fell to $301.5 million in 2017 from $335.9 million in 2016. Cash generated by operations in 2017 increased to $217.9 million about $90 million more than 2016 on improvements in working capital lower interest expense and lower spinoff-related transaction payments. RRD reduced debt by $278 million in 2017.

Strategy

In 2017 RRD pretty much closed out restructuring activities resulting from the company's three-way split in 2016. Restructuring included the closing of manufacturing facilities reducing headcount reorganization and consolidation.

In 2018 the company changed its reporting structure to two more outwardly focused segments from three segments that were internally based. The new segments are Marketing Solutions a provider of multichannel marketing activation programs and Business Services a provider of business communications services.

RRD said the new structure organized by common strategic purposes would help it better meet the rapidly changing needs of its customers and allow stakeholders to better assess the company's progress. For RRD the segments should enable each business to focus on the best opportunities in their markets.

RRD's business markets are fiercely competitive with larger companies and smaller regional firms vying for customers' attention. The competition forces prices lower. Bigger firms buying smaller ones could increase price pressures as remaining competitors lower prices.

Mergers and Acquisitions

In 2016 RRD acquired Precision Dialogue Holdings a provider of email marketing direct mail marketing and other services for $59.2 million. The acquisition expanded the company's ability to help its clients measure communications effectiveness and audience engagement.

EXECUTIVES

Evp And Cfo, Terry D. Peterson, age 53, $168,750 total compensation

Ceo, Daniel L. (Dan) Knotts, age 54, $781,250 total compensation

Evp And Chief Administrative Officer, Thomas M. Carroll, age 52, $450,000 total compensation

Cio, Ken O'Brien

Evp Global Markets, John P. Pecaric, age 52, $396,250 total compensation

Evp Domestic Operations, Glynn Perry

President Dls, Charles Fattore

Chairman, John C. (Jack) Pope, age 68

Auditors: Deloitte & Touche LLP

LOCATIONS

HQ: Donnelley (RR) & Sons Company
35 West Wacker Drive, Chicago, IL 60601
Phone: 312 326-8000
Web: www.rrdonnelley.com

2017 sales

	$ mil.	% of total
U.S	5,233	75
Asia	857	12
Europe	455	7
Other	394	6
Total	**6,939**	**100**

PRODUCTS/OPERATIONS

2017 Sales

	$ mil.	% of total
Variable Print	3,113	45
Strategic Services	1,765	25
International	2,060	30
Total	**6,939**	**100**

2017 Sales

	$ mil.	% of total
Product	5,326	77
Services	1,613	23
Total	**6,939**	**100**

Selected Operations

US print and related services
Book (consumer religious educational and specialty and telecommunications)
Direct mail (content creation database management printing personalization finishing and distribution in North America)
Directories (yellow and white pages)
Logistics (consolidation and delivery of printed products; expedited distribution of time-sensitive and secure material; print-on-demand warehousing and fulfillment services)
Magazine catalog and retail inserts
Short-run commercial print (annual reports marketing brochures catalog and marketing inserts pharmaceutical inserts and other marketing retail point-of-sale and promotional materials and technical publications)
International
Business process outsourcing
Global Turnkey Solutions (product configuration customized kitting and order fulfillment)

Selected Capabilities:

Digital
Print
Consulting & Execution
Logistics & supply chain
Industry solutions

COMPETITORS

Accenture	Merrill
Arandell	Penn Lithographics
Capgemini	Quad/Graphics
Cenveo	St Ives
Dai Nippon Printing	St. Joseph
Deluxe Corporation	Communications
EBSCO	Taylor Corporation

Harte-Hanks
IBM Global Services
Infosys
M & F Worldwide

Toppan Printing
Transcontinental Inc.
Valassis

HISTORICAL FINANCIALS

Company Type: Public

Income Statement

FYE: December 31

	REVENUE ($ mil.)	NET INCOME ($ mil.)	NET PROFIT MARGIN	EMPLOYEES
12/17	6,939	(34)	—	42,700
12/16	6,895	(495)	—	44,360
12/15	11,256	151	1.3%	68,400
12/14	11,603	117	1.0%	68,000
12/13	10,480	211	2.0%	57,000
Annual Growth	(9.8%)	—	—	(7.0%)

2017 Year-End Financials

Debt ratio: 54.03%
Return on equity: —
Cash ($ mil.): 273
Current ratio: 1.43
Long-term debt ($ mil.): 2,098

No. of shares (mil.): 70
Dividends
Yield: 0.0%
Payout: —
Market value ($ mil.): 652

	STOCK PRICE ($) FY Close	P/E High/Low		PER SHARE ($) Earnings	Dividends	Book Value
12/17	9.30	—	—	(0.49)	0.56	(3.10)
12/16	16.32	—	—	(7.09)	0.14	(1.51)
12/15	14.72	9	7	2.19	3.12	9.81
12/14	16.81	12	8	1.77	3.12	8.92
12/13	20.28	6	3	3.45	3.12	10.43
Annual Growth	(17.7%)	—	—	—(34.9%)		—

Dover Corp

The "D" in Dover could stand for diversity. The global manufacturer makes a whole range of equipment ranging from car wash systems to fridges. Dover operates in four segments: engineered systems (products for printing and identification transportation waste handling and industrial markets) energy (extraction and handling of oil and gas); fluids (fluid handling products for retail fueling oil and gas chemical and hygienic markets); and refrigeration and food equipment (systems and products serving the commercial refrigeration and food service industries). It generates around 45% of revenue outside the US. Dover traces its historical roots back to 1955.

Operations

Dover operates through four segments: Engineered Systems Fluids Refrigeration and Food and Energy.

The Engineered Systems segment accounts for around a third of total revenue and makes precision marking and coding digital textile printing and soldering and dispensing equipment. It also serves the vehicle service industrial automation and waste and recycling sectors with products such as light and heavy duty vehicle lifts vehicle diagnostics and module automation components such as clamps conveyors and more. Brands include Destaco TWG and Dover Digital Printing.

Fluids makes products to handle fluids in the retail fueling chemical hygienic oil and gas and industrial markets. It can transport fuel from refineries to gas stations via chemical processing plants. Brands include CPC Dover Fueling Solutions and Maag. It generates nearly 30% of sales.

Refrigeration & Food Equipment generates 20% of sales and makes the kind of fridges found in supermarkets and other refrigeration systems as well as food preparation equipment for the food service industry. Brands inclde Anthony SWEP Unified Brands and Dover Food Retail.

Energy generates under 20% of sales and makes drilling and extraction products bearings and compressor parts for natural gas production and automated drilling chemical injection and hybrid electronics products.

Geographic Reach

Dover has a significant worldwide presence and operates in Australia Brazil Canada China Eastern Europe France Germany India Malaysia Mexicothe Middle East the Netherlands Switzerland Sweden the UK and the US.

The US generates about 55% of its revenue while Europe accounts for nearly 20%. Other countries in the Americas generate around 10% as does the Asia/Pacific region.By segment Dover's geographic spread is uneven: Fluids generates 55% of its revenue outside the US while non-US sales in the Energy segment account for just 25%.

Sales and Marketing

Dover sells directly to customers as well as through a network of distributors. It caters to the supermarket industry including big-box retail and convenience stores the commercial/industrial refrigeration industry institutional and commercial food service and food production markets and beverage can-making industries.

Its products are sold to national dealership networks original equipment manufacturers national multi-shop operations groups independent repair and service shops large national accounts and government/transit customers through a network of distributors and channel partners.

Financial Performance

Dover has posted uneven revenue and profit growth over the last five years.

After in fell it 2016 in fiscal 2017 Dover's revenue grew 15% to $7.8 billion. The Engineered Systems segment found organic growth and benefited from additional revenue from acquired businesses while Energy grew 27% thanks to an uptick in the US oil and gas industry. Fluids grew an impressive 32% most of which related to acquisitions but organic growth was found in higher industrial pump activity and solid hygienic and pharma markets. Refrigeration & Food Equipment was the only segment to decline as divestments outweighed organic revenue growth. By geography the US Europe and China all grew organically.

Despite growth of 60% to $811 million net income remained below recent highs. Contributing to growth were higher gross revenue due to margin improvements in Engineered Systems and Energy a $172.6 million gain on disposals and a $50.9 million tax benefit resulting from the 2017 US Tax Cuts and Jobs Act. These were partially offset by higher acquisition-related administrative expenses and streamlining expenses.

Cash from operations fell 5% to $821.6 million driven by the timing of year-end revenue increased tax payments and $9.5 million paid in cash for the Wellsite separation.

Strategy

Dover relies on a steady stream of divestitures and acquisitions as its principal means for growth. It goes for bolt-ons that enhance existing businesses (through global reach or products strategy) or more rarely larger standalone businesses that provide synergies or bring innovative technologies in growth spaces. Between 2015 and 2017 Dover spent $2.2 billion across 13 such purchases. On the other hand in the same period it sold seven businesses for a total of $1.3 billion. These included Performance Motorsports International Texas Hydraulics and Sargent Aerospace.

Mergers and Acquisitions

Dover's acquisition activity is significant.

In 2018 it acquired Ettlinger Group a German manufacturer of filtering solutions for the recycling industry for €50.0 million. The company opens Dover to the virgin and higher-growth recycled plastics processing market. It also acquired Rosario Handel a Dutch manufacturer of decorator and base coating machinery used in the production of drink food and aerosol cans. It spent €13.5 million on the purchase which will grant Dover technical market and operations leadership in the space.

Between 2015 and 2017 it acquired 13 businesses for a total of $2.2 billion. It spent $43.1 million on three businesses in 2017; $1.6 billion on six businesses in 2016 including Tokheim Group Fairbanks Environmental ProGauge and Wayne Fueling Systems; and $567.8 million in 2015 on companies including Gala Industries and Reduction Engineering Scheer.

HISTORY

George Ohrstrom a New York stockbroker formed Dover in 1955 and took it public that year. Originally headquartered in Washington DC Dover consisted of four companies: C. Lee Cook (compressor seals and piston rings) Peerless (space-venting heaters) Rotary Lift (automotive lifts) and W.C. Norris (components for oil wells). In 1958 Dover made the first of many acquisitions and entered the elevator industry by buying Shepard Warner Elevator.

EXECUTIVES

Vp; President And Ceo Dover Fluids, William W. (Bill) Spurgeon, age 60, $650,000 total compensation

President And Ceo, Robert A. (Bob) Livingston, age 64, $1,030,000 total compensation

President And Ceo Dover Energy, Sivasankaran (Soma) Somasundaram, age 53, $502,000 total compensation

Svp And Cfo, Brad M. Cerepak, age 59, $670,000 total compensation

President And Ceo Dover Engineered Systems, C. Anderson Fincher, age 47, $530,000 total compensation

President And Ceo Refrigeration And Food Equipment, William T. Bosway

President Dover Business Services, S. Gary Kennon

Vice President Integration, Gary Campbell

Chairman, Michael F. (Mike) Johnston, age 70

Auditors: PricewaterhouseCoopers LLP

LOCATIONS

HQ: Dover Corp
3005 Highland Parkway, Downers Grove, IL 60515
Phone: 630 541-1540
Web: www.dovercorporation.com

2017 Sales

	$ mil.	% of total
Americas		
United States	4	57
Other Americas	735	9
Europe	1,504	19
Asia	774	10
Other	391	5
Total	**6,830**	**100**

PRODUCTS/OPERATIONS

2017 Sales

	$ mil.	% of total
Engineered Systems	2,576	33
Fluids	2,250	29
Refrigeration & Food Equipment	1,599	20
Energy	1,406	18
Intra-segment eliminations	(1.3)	-
Total	**6,794**	**100**

Selected Brands

Engineered Systems
Caldera
Destaco
JK Group
Fluids
PC
Dover Fueling Solutions
Hydro
Energy
Accelerated
Cook Compression
Dover Artifical Lift
Refrigeration & Food Equipment
Anthony
Belvac
Hillphoenix

COMPETITORS

Alfa Laval	Middleby
Brother Industries	Navistar
Carlisle Companies	Oshkosh Truck
Crane Co.	PACCAR
Danaher	Paul Mueller
Danfoss	RAKON LIMITED
Dayco Products	SPX
Domino Printing	Sequa
Fortive	Siemens AG
Franklin Electric	Smith Bits
Gardner Denver	Snap-on
Hussmann International	Swagelok
IDEX	Tatung
Illinois Tool Works	Thermador Groupe
Ingersoll-Rand	Vesuvius
KEMET	Wastequip
KSB AG	Weatherford
Kaydon	International
Lufkin Industries	Zebra Technologies
Manitowoc	

HISTORICAL FINANCIALS

Company Type: Public

Income Statement				FYE: December 31
	REVENUE ($ mil.)	NET INCOME ($ mil.)	NET PROFIT MARGIN	EMPLOYEES
12/17	7,830	811	10.4%	29,000
12/16	6,794	508	7.5%	29,000
12/15	6,956	869	12.5%	26,000
12/14	7,752	775	10.0%	27,000
12/13	8,729	1,003	11.5%	37,000
Annual Growth	(2.7%)	(5.2%)	—	(5.9%)

2017 Year-End Financials

Debt ratio: 33.48%
Return on equity: 19.84%
Cash ($ mil.): 753
Current ratio: 1.40
Long-term debt ($ mil.): 2,986

No. of shares (mil.): 154
Dividends
Yield: 0.0%
Payout: 35.3%
Market value ($ mil.): 15,636

	STOCK PRICE ($) FY Close	P/E High/Low	Earnings	PER SHARE ($) Dividends	Book Value
12/17	100.99	19 15	5.15	1.82	28.31
12/16	74.93	24 16	3.25	1.72	24.45
12/15	61.31	14 10	5.46	1.64	23.51
12/14	71.72	21 15	4.59	1.55	22.70
12/13	96.54	16 11	5.78	1.45	31.65
Annual Growth	1.1%	— —	(2.8%)	5.8%	(2.7%)

DowDuPont Inc

Auditors: PricewaterhouseCoopers LLP

LOCATIONS

HQ: DowDuPont Inc
c/o The Dow Chemical Company, 2211 H.H. Dow Way, Midland, MI 48674
Phone: 989 636-1000
Web: www.dow-dupont.com

HISTORICAL FINANCIALS

Company Type: Public

Income Statement				FYE: December 31
	REVENUE ($ mil.)	NET INCOME ($ mil.)	NET PROFIT MARGIN	EMPLOYEES
12/18	85,977	3,844	4.5%	98,000
12/17	62,484	1,460	2.3%	98,000
Annual Growth	37.6%	163.3%	—	0.0%

2018 Year-End Financials

Debt ratio: 21.52%—
Return on equity: 3.94%
Cash ($ mil.): 13,482
Current ratio: 2.01
Long-term debt ($ mil.): 37,662

Dividends
Yield: 2.8%
Payout: 447.0%
Market value ($ mil.): —

	STOCK PRICE ($) FY Close	P/E High/Low	Earnings	PER SHARE ($) Dividends	Book Value
12/18	53.48	46 30	1.65	1.52	41.68
12/17	71.22	80 70	0.91	0.38	43.11
/0.00	—	—(0.00)	0.00	(0.00)	
/0.00	—	—(0.00)	0.00	(0.00)	
/0.00	—	—(0.00)	0.00	(0.00)	
Annual Growth	—	—	—	—	—

DTE Electric Company

Ford Motors is not the only powerhouse operating in Detroit — DTE Electric is another. The utility (formerly known as Detroit Edison) generates and distributes electricity to 2.2 million customers in Michigan mainly around Detroit with expansion north to Lake Huron and east to Ann Arbor. The company a unit of regional power player DTE Energy has more than 11000 MW of generating capacity from its interests in primarily fossil-fueled nuclear and hydroelectric power plants. It operates more than 46000 circuit miles of distribution lines and owns and operates more than 670 distribution substations.

Operations

The largest electric utility in Michigan DTE Electric has a 1 million utility poles 671 distribution substations and 430600 line transformers.

The utility operates nine fossil fuel-(coal and oil) fired generating plants and one nuclear power plant (which accounts for 30% of Michigan's nuclear power output). It also co-owns a hydroelectric pumped storage plant with Consumers Energy.

Geographic Reach

The company serves customers across a 7600-sq. ml. service area in southeastern Michigan.

Financial Performance

Reflecting a stronger economy and growing demand in 2012 DTE Electric's revenues increased by 3% to $5.3 billion due to an 8% jump in residential segment sales 11% growth in commercial segment revenues and a 13% increase in industrial segment sales. Net income increased 11% in 2012 due to stronger sales and a 13% jump in other income.

The company has seen consistent revenue growth over the past five years.

Strategy

To meet the state requirements for reducing carbon emissions in 2009 the company announced plans to add 1200 MW of renewable power by 2015 half through contracts with third-parties and the remainder through its own renewable energy projects (primarily wind farms). In 2011 the company was working on developing a 200 MW wind farm.

In 2010 the company began operating a 60-kW solar energy plant in Scio Township in Washtenaw County the first installation to produce power for the grid under DTE Electric's SolarCurrents program. Its 270 solar panels include 60 that track the sun's movement.

EXECUTIVES

Chb-Ceo, Gerard M Anderson
Sr V Pres-Cfo, Peter B Oleksiak
Cao, Donna M England
Operator, Efrain Rivera
Mechanical Engineer, Emily Yatch
Quality Consultant, Matt Klucevek
Engineer, Mohammed Jalil
Plant Manager, Russ Presswood
Senior Electrical Super, Bryan Fowler
Strategic Category Manager, Michelle Underwood
Operations Analyst, Georgetta Davis
Auditors: PricewaterhouseCoopers LLP

LOCATIONS

HQ: DTE Electric Company
One Energy Plaza, Detroit, MI 48226-1279
Phone: 313 235-4000
Web: www.dteenergy.com

PRODUCTS/OPERATIONS

2016 Sales

	$ mil.	% of total
Residential	2,477	47
Commercial	1,754	34
Industrial	654	12
Interconnection sales	50	1
Other	290	6
Total	**5,225**	**100**

COMPETITORS

Consumers Energy	WEC Energy
Indiana Michigan Power	Xcel Energy

HISTORICAL FINANCIALS

Company Type: Public

Income Statement

FYE: December 31

	REVENUE ($ mil.)	NET INCOME ($ mil.)	NET PROFIT MARGIN	EMPLOYEES
12/17	5,102	601	11.8%	4,700
12/16	5,225	622	11.9%	4,600
12/15	4,900	544	11.1%	4,500
12/14	5,282	532	10.1%	4,900
12/13	5,197	487	9.4%	4,800
Annual Growth	**(0.5%)**	**5.4%**	**—**	**(0.5%)**

2017 Year-End Financials

Debt ratio: 29.49%	No. of shares (mil.): 138
Return on equity: 9.80%	Dividends
Cash ($ mil.): 15	Yield: —
Current ratio: 1.36	Payout: 71.8%
Long-term debt ($ mil.): 6,018	Market value ($ mil.): —

DTE Energy Co

DTE Energy provides Detroit with a reliable spark. The holding company's main subsidiary DTE Electric (formerly Detroit Edison) distributes electricity to some 2.2 million customers in southeastern Michigan. The utility's power plants have a generating capacity of more than 11600 MW. The company's DTE Gas unit distributes natural gas to 1.3 million customers throughout Michigan. DTE Energy runs non-regulated businesses in gas storage & pipelines power & industrial operations and energy trading which together have a presence in more than 15 US states.

HISTORY

DTE Energy's predecessor threw its first switch in 1886 when George Peck and local investors incorporated the Edison Illuminating Company of Detroit. Neighboring utility Peninsular Electric Light was formed in 1891 and both companies bought smaller utilities until they merged in 1903 to form Detroit Edison. A subsidiary of holding company North American Co. Detroit Edison was incorporated in New York to secure financing for power plants.

Detroit's growth in the 1920s and 1930s led the utility to build plants and buy others in outlying areas. Detroit Edison acquired Michigan Electric Power which had been divested from its holding company under the Public Utility Holding Company Act of 1935 and was itself divested from North American in 1940.

The post-WWII boom prompted Detroit Edison to build more plants most of them coal-fired. In 1953 it joined a consortium of 34 companies to build Fermi 1 a nuclear plant brought on line in 1963. Still strapped for power Detroit Edison built the coal-fired Monroe plant which began service in 1970. In 1972 Fermi 1 had a partial core meltdown and was taken off line.

Detroit Edison began shipping low-sulfur Montana coal through its Wisconsin terminal in 1974 which reduced the cost of obtaining the fuel. The next year it began building another nuke Fermi 2. The nuke had cost more than $4.8 billion by the time it went on line in 1988. That year the utility began its landfill gas recovery operation (now DTE Biomass Energy).

A recession pounded automakers in the early 1990s leading to cutbacks in electricity purchases. In 1992 Congress passed the Energy Policy Act allowing wholesale power competition. In 1993 a fire shut down Fermi 2 for almost two years. Michigan's public service commission (PSC) approved retail customer-choice pilot programs for its utilities in 1994. Detroit Edison and rival Consumers Energy (now CMS Energy) took the PSC to court.

DTE Energy became Detroit Edison's holding company in 1996. The next year it formed DTE Energy Trading (to broker power) and DTE-Co-Energy (to provide energy-management services and sell power to large customers). It also formed Plug Power with Mechanical Technology to develop fuel cells that convert natural gas to power without combustion.

In 1997 and 1998 the PSC bolstered by state court decisions issued orders to restructure Michigan's utilities. The transition to retail competition began in 1998. That year DTE Energy and natural gas provider Michigan Consolidated Gas (MichCon) began collaborating on some operations including billing and meter reading. DTE and GE formed a venture to sell and install Plug Power fuel cell systems.

A higher court shot down the PSC's restructuring orders in 1999 but DTE Energy and CMS Energy decided to implement customer choice using PSC guidelines. That year the US Department of Energy selected DTE Energy to install the world's first super power-cable which could carry three times as much electricity as conventional copper. Also in 1999 DTE Energy agreed to acquire MCN Energy MichCon's parent.

In 2000 DTE Energy formed subsidiary International Transmission (ITC) to hold Detroit Edison's transmission assets; the next year ITC joined the Midwest Independent System Operator which began to manage ITC's network. It also completed its $4.3 billion purchase of MCN Energy in 2001. Full deregulation of Michigan's electricity market was completed in 2002. International Transmission was sold in 2003 to affiliates of Kohlberg Kravis Roberts and Trimaran Capital Partners for $610 million.

In 2007 it sold its Michigan Antrim Shale gas exploration and production assets to Atlas Energy Resources.

EXECUTIVES

Chairman And Ceo, Gerard M. Anderson, $1,293,519 total compensation
President Dte Gas And Oil And Dte Gas Resources, Richard L. Redmond, age 61
Chairman And President Dte Energy Foundation, Faye A. Nelson, age 65
President And Coo Dte Electric, Trevor F. Lauer, age 54
President And Coo, Gerardo (Jerry) Norcia, $650,926 total compensation
President And Coo Dte Gas, Mark W. Stiers, age 56
President Power And Industrial Dte Energy Resources, David Ruud, age 51
President Dte Biomass Energy, Mark Cousino
Svp And Cfo, Peter B. Oleksiak, age 52, $553,519 total compensation
President Dte Energy Trading, Steven Mabry
Vp And Cio, Steve Ambrose
President Dte Gas Stprage And Pipelines, David Slater
President Dte Energy Foundation, Lynette Dowler
Executive Vice President Major Enterprise Projects, Ron May
Vp And Chief Tax Officer, Joann Chavez
Vice President Regulatory Affairs, Daniel Brudzynski
Vp Environmental Management And Resources, Skiles Boyd
Vice Chairman And Chief Administrative Officer, David E. (Dave) Meador, age 61
Chairman And Ceo, Gerard M. Anderson
Board Member, David Thomas
Secretary, Francesca Racz
Auditors: PricewaterhouseCoopers LLP

LOCATIONS

HQ: DTE Energy Co
One Energy Plaza, Detroit, MI 48226-1279
Phone: 313 235-4000
Web: www.dteenergy.com

PRODUCTS/OPERATIONS

2017 Sales

	$ mil.	% of total
Electric utility	5,102	38
Gas utility	1,388	11
Energy trading	4,277	32
Power & industrial products	2,089	16
Gas storage & pipeline	453	3
Adjustments	(704)	-
Corporate and Other	2	-
Total	**12,607**	**100**

2017 Sales

	$ mil.	% of total
Utility	6,434	51
Non-utility	6,173	49
Total	**12,607**	**100**

COMPETITORS

AEP	Indiana Michigan Power
CMS Energy	Nicor Gas
CMS Enterprises	PG&E Corporation
Consumers Energy	SEMCO ENERGY
DPL	WEC Energy
Dairyland Power	Xcel Energy
Exelon Energy	

HISTORICAL FINANCIALS

Company Type: Public

Income Statement   FYE: December 31

	REVENUE ($ mil.)	NET INCOME ($ mil.)	NET PROFIT MARGIN	EMPLOYEES
12/18	14,212	1,120	7.9%	10,600
12/17	12,607	1,134	9.0%	10,200
12/16	10,630	868	8.2%	10,000
12/15	10,337	727	7.0%	10,000
12/14	12,301	905	7.4%	10,000
Annual Growth	**3.7%**	**5.5%**	—	**1.5%**

2018 Year-End Financials

Debt ratio: 39.25%
Return on equity: 11.34%
Cash ($ mil.): 71
Current ratio: 0.73
Long-term debt ($ mil.): 12,134

No. of shares (mil.): 181
Dividends
Yield: 3.2%
Payout: 53.3%
Market value ($ mil.): 20,066

	STOCK PRICE ($) FY Close	P/E High/Low	PER SHARE ($) Earnings	Dividends	Book Value
12/18	110.30	19 15	6.17	3.59	56.27
12/17	109.46	18 15	6.32	3.36	53.03
12/16	98.51	21 16	4.83	3.06	50.22
12/15	80.19	23 18	4.05	2.84	48.88
12/14	86.37	18 13	5.10	2.69	47.05
Annual Growth	**6.3%**	— —	**4.9%**	**7.5%**	**4.6%**

Duke Energy Carolinas LLC

Auditors: DELOITTE & TOUCHE LLP

LOCATIONS

HQ: Duke Energy Carolinas LLC
526 South Church Street, Charlotte, NC 28202-1803
Phone: 704 382-3853

HISTORICAL FINANCIALS

Company Type: Public

Income Statement   FYE: December 31

	REVENUE ($ mil.)	NET INCOME ($ mil.)	NET PROFIT MARGIN	EMPLOYEES
12/17	7,302	1,214	16.6%	—
12/16	7,322	1,166	15.9%	—
12/15	7,729	1,081	15.0%	—
12/14	7,351	1,072	14.6%	—
12/13	6,954	976	14.0%	—
Annual Growth	**1.2%**	**5.6%**	—	—

2017 Year-End Financials

Debt ratio: 26.78%
Return on equity: 10.97%
Cash ($ mil.): 16
Current ratio: 0.61
Long-term debt ($ mil.): 8,898

Dividends
Yield: —
Payout: —
Market value ($ mil.): —

Duke Energy Corp

Duke Energy serves electricity to 7.6 million customers covering 95000 square miles in southeastern US. Annually the company generates 50000 MW of electricity primarily from coal nuclear and natural gas sources. It also supplies natural gas via its 60000 miles of pipelines to around 1.5 million customers. Its government-regulated utilities have a solid presence in the Carolinas Florida Ohio Indiana and Kentucky. The company also boasts a small commercial renewables portfolio generating clean energy through utility-scale wind and solar assets.

HISTORY

Surgeon Gill Wylie founded Catawba Power Company in 1899; its first hydroelectric plant in South Carolina was on line by 1904. The next year Wylie and James "Buck" Duke (founder of the American Tobacco Company and Duke University's namesake) formed Southern Power Company with Wylie as president.

In 1910 Buck Duke became president of Southern Power and organized Mill-Power Supply to sell electric equipment and appliances. He also began investing in electricity-powered textile mills which prospered as a result of the electric power and continued to bring in customers. He formed the Southern Public Utility Company in 1913 to buy other Piedmont-region utilities. Wylie died in 1924 the same year the company was renamed Duke Power; Buck Duke died the next year.

Growing after WWII the company went public in 1950 and moved to the NYSE in 1961. It also formed its real estate arm Crescent Resources in the 1960s. Insulating itself from the 1970s energy crises Duke invested in coal mining and three nuclear plants the first completed in 1974.

In 1988 Duke began to develop power projects outside its home region and it also bought neighboring utility Nantahala Power and Light. The next year it formed a joint venture with Fluor's Fluor Daniel unit to provide engineering and construction services to power generators. Mill-Power Supply was sold in 1990.

By the 1990s Duke had moved into overseas markets acquiring an Argentine power station in 1992. It also tried its hand at telecommunications creating DukeNet Communications in 1994 to build fiber-optic systems and in 1996 it joined oil giant Mobil to create a power trading and marketing business. As the US power industry traveled toward deregulation Duke also sought natural gas operations. It targeted PanEnergy which owned a major pipeline system in the eastern half of the US. Duke Power bought PanEnergy in 1997 to form Duke Energy Corporation.

Seeing an opportunity in 1998 Duke formed Duke Communication Services to provide antenna sites to the fast-growing wireless communications industry. It also acquired a 52% stake in Electroquil an electric power generating company in Guayaquil Ecuador. That year it purchased a pipeline company in Australia from PG&E; it also bought three PG&E power plants to compete in California's deregulated electric utility marketplace.

Duke merged its pipeline business Duke Energy Trading and Transport with TEPPCO Partners and acquired gas processing operations from Union Pacific Resources. It sold Panhandle Eastern Pipe Line and gas-related assets in the Midwest to CMS Energy in 1999 to reduce operations in the region and made plans to build a pipeline extending from Alabama to Florida (completed in 2002).

To further enhance natural gas operations in other regions Duke bought El Paso's East Tennessee Natural Gas pipeline unit in 2000 and a 20% stake in Canadian 88 Energy; it also purchased $1.4 billion in South American generation assets including assets from Dominion Resources and the gas trading operations of Mobil (now Exxon Mobil) in the Netherlands. Also in 2000 Duke and Phillips Petroleum (now ConocoPhillips) merged their gas gathering and processing and NGL operations into Duke Energy Field Services.

In 2001 Duke announced the $8 billion acquisition of

EXECUTIVES

Evp And Cfo, Steven K. Young, age 58, $625,000 total compensation

Svp Global Risk Management And Insurance And Chief Risk Officer, Keith G. Butler, age 58

Evp Chief Legal Officer And Corporate Secretary, Julie S. Janson, age 53, $520,833 total compensation

Evp; President Natural Gas Business, Franklin H. Yoho, age 59

Svp And Chief Distriution Officer, Michael A. Lewis, age 56

Evp Regulated Utilities, Lloyd M. Yates, age 57, $661,458 total compensation

Chairman President And Ceo, Lynn J. Good, age 58, $1,291,667 total compensation

Evp And President Midwest And Florida, Douglas F. (Doug) Esamann, age 60

Evp And Coo, Dhiaa M. Jamil, age 61, $737,500 total compensation

Svp Midwest Distribution Operations, Melody Birmingham-Byrd

State President North Carolina, David B. Fountain

State President Ohio And Kentucky, James P. (Jim) Henning

Svp And Chief Nuclear Officer, John W. (Bill) Pitesa

Vp And Cio, Christopher B. (Chris) Heck

Evp Administration And Chief Human Resources Officer, Melissa H. Anderson, age 53

State President South Carolina, Kodwo Ghartey-Tagoe

State President Florida, Harry K. Sideris

Svp Financial Planning And Analysis, Bill Currens

Vp Legal And Assistant Corporate Secretary, David Maltz

Vice President Of Marketing, Jack Farley

Vice President Human Resources Business Partners, Jim O'Connor

Vice President, David Litchfield

Vice President Process Technology, Mag Fouad

Executive Vice President, John McArthur

Vice President, Jay Alvaro

Senior Vice President, William Tyndall
Senior Vice President, John Enloe
Vice President Finance, Bill Dickey
Vice President, Angeline Clinton
Vice President Business Development, John
  Upchurch
Site Vice President, Dave Baxter
Vice President, John Stowell
Senior Vice President Government Relations,
  David Dave Marventano
Svp And Chief Communications Officer, Selim
  Bingol
Senior Vice President Business Development And
  Strategy Infrastructure, Robert Bob Prieto
Vice President Asset Management, Ron Snead
Vp Corporate Public Affairs, Hilda Pinnix-ragland
Vp Western Carolinas Modernization, Robert Sipes
Vice President, Arthur Raymond
Vice President Talent Management, Lisa Marcuz
Vice President Indiana Government Affairs, Stan
  Pinegar
Svp State And Federal Regulatory Legal Support,
  R Alexander Glenn
Vp Community Relations And Economic
  Development, Laura Boisvert
Vice President And Chief Ethics And Compliance
  Officer, Sandra Wyckoff
Vice President Technology Development, Rob
  Miller
Chairman President And Ceo, Lynn J. Good, age 58
Pac Treasurer, William Mayhew
Board Member, Charles Moorman
Board Of Directors, John Herron
Board Member, Michael Angelakis
Board Member, Carlos Saladrigas
Board Member, Tom Skains
Auditors: Deloitte & Touche LLP

LOCATIONS

HQ: Duke Energy Corp
  550 South Tryon Street, Charlotte, NC 28202-1803
Phone: 704 382-3853
Web: www.duke-energy.com

PRODUCTS/OPERATIONS

2017 Sales

	$ mil.	% of total
Electric Utilities and Infrastructure	21,331	90
Gas Utilities and Infrastructure	1,836	8
Commercial Renewables	460	2
Other	117	1
Eliminations	(200)	-
Total	**23,565**	**100**

2017 Sales

	$ mil.	% of total
Regulated electric	21,177	90
Regulated natural gas	1,734	7
Nonregulated electric and other	654	3
Total	**22,743**	**100**

COMPETITORS

AEP	PG&E Corporation
AES	Piedmont Natural Gas
Avista	SCANA
CenterPoint Energy	Southern Company
Energy Future	TVA
Entergy	Williams Companies
Exelon	

HISTORICAL FINANCIALS
Company Type: Public

Income Statement
FYE: December 31

	REVENUE ($ mil.)	NET INCOME ($ mil.)	NET PROFIT MARGIN	EMPLOYEES
12/17	23,565	3,059	13.0%	29,060
12/16	22,743	2,152	9.5%	28,798
12/15	23,459	2,816	12.0%	29,188
12/14	23,925	1,883	7.9%	28,344
12/13	24,598	2,665	10.8%	27,948
Annual Growth	**(1.1%)**	**3.5%**	**—**	**1.0%**

2017 Year-End Financials

Debt ratio: 39.48%
Return on equity: 7.39%
Cash ($ mil.): 358
Current ratio: 0.68
Long-term debt ($ mil.): 49,035

No. of shares (mil.): 700
Dividends
  Yield: 0.0%
  Payout: 80.0%
Market value ($ mil.): 58,877

	STOCK PRICE ($) FY Close	P/E High/Low	Earnings	PER SHARE ($) Dividends	Book Value
12/17	84.11	21 18	4.36	3.49	59.63
12/16	77.62	28 23	3.11	3.36	58.62
12/15	71.39	22 16	4.05	3.24	57.74
12/14	83.54	33 25	2.66	3.15	57.81
12/13	69.01	20 17	3.76	3.09	58.54
Annual Growth	**5.1%**	**— —**	**3.8%**	**3.1%**	**0.5%**

Duke Energy Florida LLC

Sometimes the sunshine state just isn't bright enough and that's when Florida Power (doing business as Progress Energy Florida) really shines. The utility transmits and distributes electricity to 1.6 million customers and oversees 10025 MW of generating capacity from interests in 14 nuclear and coal- oil- and gas-fired power plants. Additionally Florida Power purchases about 20% of the energy it provides. Florida Power operates 5100 miles of transmission lines and 52000 miles of overhead and 18700 miles of underground distribution cable. It also has 500 electric substations. A subsidiary of holding company Duke Energy the company also sells wholesale power to other utilities and marketers.

Operations
The company is a regulated public utility primarily engaged in the generation transmission distribution and sale of electricity. Its power grid is interconnected with 22 municipal power systems and with nine rural electric cooperative systems.

Geographic Reach
Florida Power's service territory covers 20000 square miles in west-central Florida and includes the densely populated areas around Orlando as well as the cities of St. Petersburg and Clearwater.

Sales and Marketing
The company's wholesale customers include Seminole Electric Cooperative Reedy Creek Improvement District the city of Gainesville the city of Winter Park and the city of Homestead.

Financial Performance
Revenue decreased by 17% in 2011 primarily due to the unfavorable impact of weather and lower wholesale base revenues. The unfavorable

impact of weather was driven by 61% lower heating-degree days than in the previous year.

Net income decreased by 31% in 2011 primarily due to the charge for the amount to be refunded to customers through the fuel clause in accordance with a settlement agreement and the less favorable impact of weather.

EXECUTIVES

Ceo, Lynn J Good
Exec V Pres-Cfo, Steven K Young
V Pres-Cao-Contrl, Brian D Savoy
Sr Vice President, E Michael Williams
Supervisor, Barbara Moore
Coordinator, April Harley
Manager, Bill Tyner
Coordinator, Tim White
Information Specialist, Aja Grant
Smartgrid, George Willis
Leadership, Jothen Kinney
Auditors: DELOITTE & TOUCHE LLP

LOCATIONS

HQ: Duke Energy Florida LLC
  299 First Avenue North, St. Petersburg, FL 33701
Phone: 704 382-3853

COMPETITORS

Florida Power & Light	Orlando Utilities
Florida Public	Commission
Utilities	Seminole Electric
Gulf Power	Southern Company Gas
JEA	Tampa Electric

HISTORICAL FINANCIALS
Company Type: Public

Income Statement
FYE: December 31

	REVENUE ($ mil.)	NET INCOME ($ mil.)	NET PROFIT MARGIN	EMPLOYEES
12/17	4,646	712	15.3%	—
12/16	4,568	551	12.1%	—
12/15	4,977	599	12.0%	—
12/14	4,975	548	11.0%	—
12/13	4,527	325	7.2%	—
Annual Growth	**0.7%**	**21.7%**	**—**	**—**

2017 Year-End Financials

Debt ratio: 39.27%—
Return on equity: 13.54%
Cash ($ mil.): 13
Current ratio: 0.91
Long-term debt ($ mil.): 6,327

Dividends
  Yield: —
  Payout: —
Market value ($ mil.): —

E*TRADE Financial Corp.

E*TRADE wants you to use its services for nearly everything financial. Known for its brokerage services the firm provides the products tools services and advice to individual investors and stock plan participants wanting to manage their own investments. For corporate clients it offers market making trade clearing and employee stock option plan administration services. Subsidiary E*TRADE Bank offers deposits savings and credit cards online and from 30 financial centers in major

US cities. E*TRADE Clearing offers securities clearing and settlement while E*TRADE Securities the bank's broker-dealer arm offers mutual funds options fixed income products exchange-traded funds and portfolio management services.

Operations

E*TRADE operates one unified segment. Its core brokerage business is split out into three product areas: Trading Investing and Corporate Services. It also offers banking and cash management offering debit cards online and mobile bill pay mobile check deposit and Apple Pay.

Trading products cover investment vehicles including US equities exchange-traded funds options bonds futures and non-proprietary mutual funds. It also provides margin solutions including calculators and requirement lookup and analysis. It serves self-directed investors and active traders with products delivered through web desktop and mobile digital channels.

Investing products and services include retirement accounts including Roth IRAs virtual advice managed investment portfolios and unified and separately managed accounts. It also offers retirement planning through teams at its 30 regional branches and through two national branches by phone and email.

Corporate Services provides stock plan administration and public and private companies. Its Equity Edge Online platform offers employee stock option management stock repurchase plans and accounting reporting and scenario modeling tools.

Geographic Reach

New York-based E*TRADE Financial has 30 branch offices across the US. E*TRADE currently maintains about a dozen retail brokerage websites in Europe the Middle East and the Pacific Rim in addition to the US.

Sales and Marketing

The company sells and provides customer support from its branches online and by telephone. Its financial advisors also promote the firm's products and services.

Financial Performance

After several years of decline E*TRADE's revenue picked up in fiscal 2016 climbing 30% to $2.0 billion. Growth was concentrated in non-interest income which returned to a level closer to previous years after the company incurred a $413 million charge on the termination of $4.4 billion of wholesale funding obligations in 2015. Net interest revenue increased $127 million mostly as a result of lower interest expense

Net income rose by 105% to $552 million due to a jump in gains on securities and higher net interest income offset by an increase in income tax expense. Cash from operations rose 95% to $1.6 billion on the back of higher net income and a 25% increase in customer payables relating to sales of securities to brokerage customer accounts.

Strategy

E*TRADE in 2016 reiterated its focus on growing its customer's wallet share in retirement investing and savings through its retail brokerage business by offering innovative solutions for trading margin lending and cash management. It also hopes its competitive pricing will attract new customers and that its wide variety of corporate services will allow it to build existing relationships via cross-selling.

E*TRADE continues its interest in mobile innovation to attract new customers as well. IT launched its custom Apple Watch market data app in 2015 following on from an iOS 8 app released the previous year that provides market and watch list information.

In order to spruce up its balance sheet E*TRADE shed $4.4 billion in legacy wholesale funding obligations in 2015 to cut its profits free.

Mergers and Acquisitions

In early 2018 E*TRADE acquired Trust Company of America (TCA) a custodian of independent investment advisors that it supports with tehcnology solutions consultative services and back-office operations. TCA had $18.3 billion in institutional assets under custody at the time of the purchase.

Company Background

A disastrous decision to move more strongly into banking (originally aiming to triple its loan business) just as the credit crisis struck down banks and lenders around the world led to large losses at the company. The firm was forced to hoard reserves to counter loan losses and exited both its wholesale lending and direct lending operations. The company also shuttered its institutional brokerage business. Its strategy to do improve results revolves around focusing on its online brokerage business and enhancing its position in retirement and investing while continuing to mitigate credit losses in its loan portfolio.

HISTORY

In 1982 physicist William Porter created Trade Plus an electronic brokerage service for stockbrokers; clients included Charles Schwab & Co. and Fidelity Brokerage Services. A decade later subsidiary E*TRADE Securities became CompuServe's first online securities trader.

In 1996 E*TRADE moved from the institutional side to retail when it launched its website. Christos Cotsakos (a Vietnam and FedEx veteran) became CEO and took the firm public. But there were problems: E*TRADE covered $1.7 million in customer losses and added backup systems after computer failure stymied user access. In 1997 it formed alliances with America Online and BANK ONE and ended the year with 225000 accounts.

The firm began to position itself globally in 1997 and 1998 opening sites for Australian Canadian German Israeli and Japanese customers. It offered its first IPO (Sportline USA) in 1997. Volume grew as Internet trading increased but technical glitches dogged E*TRADE. In 1999 day trading became fashionable and the company began running ads promoting prudent trading to counter criticism that online trading fosters a get-rich-quick mentality.

The company also continued to add services. In 1999 it teamed with Garage.com to offer affluent clients venture capital investments in young companies and launched online investment bank E*OFFERING with former Robertson Stephens & Co. chairman Sanford Robertson. (E*TRADE sold its stake in the bank to Wit Soundview — which later became SoundView Technology Group — the next year.) It also bought TIR Holdings which executes and settles multi-currency securities transactions.

Retail banking was a major focus in 2000. The company bought Telebanc Financial (now E*TRADE Financial) owner of Telebank an online bank with more than 100000 depositors and started E*TRADE Bank which offers retail banking products on the E*TRADE website. To provide clients with "real-world" access to their money it bought Card Capture Services an operator of more than 9000 ATMs across the US.

Continuing to expand its global reach E*TRADE bought the part of its E*TRADE UK joint venture it didn't already own; acquired Canadian firm VERSUS Technologies a provider of electronic trading services; and teamed with UBS Warburg to allow non-US investors to buy US securities without needing to trade in dollars. Later its E*Trade International Capital announced plans to offer IPOs to European investors.

In 2001 E*TRADE entered consumer lending when it bought online mortgage originator LoansDirect (now E*TRADE Mortgage). Also that year

the company bought online brokerage Web Street and moved to the NYSE. In late 2002 E*TRADE Bank purchased Ganis Credit Corp. (a US-based unit of Germany's Deutsche Bank) to boost its consumer finance business.

E*TRADE purchased the online trading operations of Tradescape in mid-2002. The deal which cost E*TRADE $280 million was hashed out the previous April — just days after rival Ameritrade announced its acquisition of online brokerage Datek.

Cotsakos resigned in early 2003 days after the company issued a gloomy forecast (he also had been criticized for his 2001 pay of $80 million although he subsequently gave up about $20 million). He was replaced by company president Mitch Caplan who had been viewed as instrumental in the company's effort to integrate brokerage and banking operations.

In 2005 E*TRADE bought US-based online brokerage Harris direct from Bank of Montreal as well as the former J.P. Morgan Invest unit BrownCo which served experienced online traders. The acquisitions expanded its client base and helped the company to keep pace with TD Ameritrade (the result of the 2006 merger of rivals Ameritrade and TD Waterhouse).

E*TRADE built its wealth management operations in 2005 and 2006 by purchasing several money managers including Boston-area investment advisory firm Kobren Insight Management.

After E*TRADE got snared in the subprime mortgage crisis in 2007 Caplan stepped down. He was replaced in 2008 by Donald Layton a former executive with JPMorgan Chase.

Layton retired the following year. Company director Robert Druskin took over as chairman while Steven Freiberg became CEO. Freiberg was formerly a co-CEO of Citigroup's global consumer operations.

To raise additional cash it sold its Canadian operations to Scotiabank for more than $440 million in 2008. The following year it raised some $733 million in three separate stock offerings and exchanged another $1.7 billion in debt for convertible debentures.

EXECUTIVES

Chief Brokerage Officer, Michael J. Curcio, age 56, $450,000 total compensation

Ceo, Karl A. Roessner, age 50, $800,000 total compensation

Evp And Chief Administrative Officer, Michael E. Foley, age 66, $592,308 total compensation

Evp And Cfo, Michael A. Pizzi, $484,615 total compensation

Evp And Chief Risk Officer, Ellen Koebler

Chairman, Rodger A. Lawson, age 71

Auditors: Deloitte & Touche LLP

LOCATIONS

HQ: E*TRADE Financial Corp.
11 Times Square, 32nd Floor, New York, NY 10036
Phone: 646 521-4300
Web: www.etrade.com

PRODUCTS/OPERATIONS

2016 Sales

	$ mil.	% of total
Interest income	1,233	61
Commissions	442	22
Fees & service charges	268	13
Gains on loans and securities net	42	2
Other revenue	41	2
Total	**2,026**	**100**

Selected Subsidiaries

E*TRADE Bank (federally chartered savings bank)
E*TRADE Clearing LLC (clearing house)
E*TRADE Securities (registered broker-dealer)
G1 Execution Services LLC (registered broker-dealer and market maker)

COMPETITORS

Charles Schwab	ShareBuilder
FMR	Siebert Financial
Morgan Stanley	TD Ameritrade
Scottrade	UBS Financial Services

HISTORICAL FINANCIALS

Company Type: Public

Income Statement

FYE: December 31

	ASSETS ($ mil.)	NET INCOME ($ mil.)	INCOME AS % OF ASSETS	EMPLOYEES
12/17	63,365	614	1.0%	3,600
12/16	48,999	552	1.1%	3,600
12/15	45,427	268	0.6%	3,400
12/14	45,530	293	0.6%	3,200
12/13	46,279	86	0.2%	3,009
Annual Growth	8.2%	63.5%	—	4.6%

2017 Year-End Financials

Debt ratio: 3.00%
Return on equity: 9.30%
Cash ($ mil.): 1,803
Current ratio: —
Long-term debt ($ mil.): —
No. of shares (mil.): 266
Dividends
　Yield: —
　Payout: —
Market value ($ mil.): 13,227

	STOCK PRICE ($) FY Close	P/E High/Low		PER SHARE ($) Earnings	Dividends	Book Value
12/17	49.57	23	15	2.15	0.00	25.98
12/16	34.65	18	10	1.98	0.00	22.89
12/15	29.64	34	24	0.91	0.00	19.90
12/14	24.26	25	19	1.00	0.00	18.58
12/13	19.64	65	30	0.29	0.00	16.90
Annual Growth	26.0%	—	—	65.0%	—	11.3%

Eagle Bancorp Inc (MD)

For those nest eggs that need a little help hatching holding company Eagle Bancorp would recommend its community-oriented EagleBank subsidiary. The bank serves businesses and individuals through more than 20 branches in Maryland Virginia and Washington DC and its suburbs. Deposit products include checking savings and money market accounts; certificates of deposit; and IRAs. Commercial real estate loans represent more than 70% of its loan portfolio while construction loans make up another more than 20%. The bank which has significant expertise as a Small Business Administration lender also writes business consumer and home equity loans. EagleBank offers insurance products through an agreement with The Meltzer Group.

Operations

Like other retail banks Eagle Bancorp makes the bulk of its money from loan interest. About 86% of its total revenue came from loan interest (including fees) during 2015 while another 4% came from interest on investment securities. The rest of its revenue came from deposit account service charges (2% of revenue) and non-recurring income sources.

The bank has two direct subsidiaries: Bethesda Leasing LLC which holds the bank's foreclosed real estate (owned and acquired); and Eagle Insurance Services LLC which provides commercial and retail insurance products through a referral arrangement with insurance broker The Meltzer Group.

Geographic Reach

The Bethesda Maryland-based bank operates 21 branches in Maryland Virginia and Washington DC (as of mid-2016) including nine in Northern Virginia seven in Montgomery County and five in the District of Columbia.

Sales and Marketing

Eagle Bancorp serves local businesses professional clients individuals sole proprietors small and medium-sized businesses non-profits and investors. Other clients are from the healthcare accountant and attorney markets.

The bank spent $2.7 million on marketing and advertising during 2015 up 38% from the $2 million it spent in 2014 mostly due to higher digital and print advertising and sponsorship costs.

Financial Performance

Eagle Bancorp's annual revenue has more than doubled since 2011 mostly thanks to strong loan growth with the addition of new branches. Meanwhile its net income has more than tripled as the bank has kept a lid on credit loss provisions and overhead costs.

The bank's revenue jumped 33% to $279.8 million during 2015 largely thanks to a rise in interest income as its loan assets grew 16%.

Strong revenue growth in 2015 coupled with an absence of merger expenses drove Eagle Bancorp's net income up 55% to $84.1 million. The bank's operating cash levels spiked 66% to $98.5 million for the year thanks to a strong rise in cash-based earnings.

Strategy

The company has been focused on growing within its existing markets. Its strategy for further growth includes continuing to seek opportunities to open or acquire new banking locations while waiting out record low interest rates. Eagle's strict loan underwriting standards — it didn't write subprime residential mortgages and didn't buy securities backed by subprime mortgages — has helped it have fewer problem loans the downfall for many banks.

Beyond its core lending and deposit businesses Eagle Bancorp continues to expand its other product offerings as well. In 2015 it introduced a Full Service Equipment Leasing program which provided alternative and convenient financing for all types of business equipment for customers.

Mergers and Acquisitions

In November 2014 Eagle Bancorp significantly expanded its presence in Northern Virginia after it purchased Fairfax County-based Virginia Heritage. The deal added six Virginia Heritage Bank branches (renamed as EagleBank) in northern Virginia along with $917.4 million in assets — including $715 million in loans and $737 million in deposits.

EXECUTIVES

Evp; Sevp And Coo Eaglebank, Susan G. Riel, age 69, $478,806 total compensation
Chairman President And Ceo; Chairman And Ceo Eaglebank; President Ronald D. Paul Cos., Ronald D. Paul, age 63, $863,565 total compensation
Evp; Evp And Chief Credit Officer Eaglebank, Janice L. Williams, age 61, $391,758 total compensation
Evp And General Counsel Eagle Bancorp And Eaglebank, Laurence E. Bensignor, age 62

Evp; Evp And Chief Lending Officer Commercial Real Estate Eaglebank, Antonio F. Marquez, age 60, $368,256 total compensation
Evp; Evp And Chief Lending Officer Commercial And Industrial Eaglebank, Lindsey S. Rheaume, age 58
Evp And Cfo, Charles D. Levingston, age 38
Vice President, Joan Grant
Senior Vice President Commercial Banking Team Leader, Derek Whitwer
Vice President Facilities Operations Manager, Shawn Cox
Executive Vice President Chief Real Estate, Tony Marquez
Chairman President And Ceo; Chairman And Ceo Eaglebank; President Ronald D. Paul Cos., Ronald D. Paul, age 63
Vice President Treasurer, Scott Clark
Auditors: Dixon Hughes Goodman LLP

LOCATIONS

HQ: Eagle Bancorp Inc (MD)
7830 Old Georgetown Road, Third Floor, Bethesda, MD 20814
Phone: 301 986-1800
Web: www.eaglebankcorp.com

PRODUCTS/OPERATIONS

Selected Subsidiaries

EagleBank
　Bethesda Leasing LLC
　Eagle Insurance Services LLC
　Fidelity Mortgage Inc.
Eagle Commercial Ventures LLC

COMPETITORS

BB&T	OBA Financial Services
Bank of America	PNC Financial
Capital One	Sandy Spring Bancorp
M&T Bank	SunTrust

HISTORICAL FINANCIALS

Company Type: Public

Income Statement

FYE: December 31

	ASSETS ($ mil.)	NET INCOME ($ mil.)	INCOME AS % OF ASSETS	EMPLOYEES
12/17	7,479	100	1.3%	466
12/16	6,890	97	1.4%	469
12/15	6,076	84	1.4%	434
12/14	5,247	54	1.0%	427
12/13	3,771	47	1.2%	386
Annual Growth	18.7%	20.8%	—	4.8%

2017 Year-End Financials

Debt ratio: 2.90%
Return on equity: 11.18%
Cash ($ mil.): 174
Current ratio: —
Long-term debt ($ mil.): —
No. of shares (mil.): 34
Dividends
　Yield: —
　Payout: —
Market value ($ mil.): 1,979

	STOCK PRICE ($) FY Close	P/E High/Low		PER SHARE ($) Earnings	Dividends	Book Value
12/17	57.90	23	17	2.92	0.00	27.80
12/16	60.95	22	15	2.86	0.00	24.77
12/15	50.47	22	13	2.50	0.00	22.07
12/14	35.52	18	15	1.95	0.00	20.60
12/13	30.63	18	11	1.76	0.00	15.22
Annual Growth	17.3%	—	—	13.5%	—	16.3%

East West Bancorp, Inc

East West Bancorp banks in both hemispheres of the world. It's the holding company for East West Bank which provides standard banking services and loans through more than 130 branches in major US metropolitan areas and about 10 offices across in China Hong Kong and Taiwan. Boasting $29 billion in assets East West Bank focuses on making commercial and industrial real estate loans which account for the majority of the company's loan portfolio. Catering to the Asian-American community it also provides international banking and trade financing to importers/exporters doing business in the Asia/Pacific region. East West Bank offers multilingual service in English Cantonese Mandarin Vietnamese and Spanish.

Operations

East West Bancorp operates two business segments. The commercial banking segment (which generated 62% of its total revenue in 2014) includes commercial industrial and commercial real estate primarily generates commercial and industrial real estate loans and offers a wide variety of international finance and trade services and products. The retail banking segment (33% of total revenue) focuses primarily on retail operations through the East West Bank's branch network. The bank also offers insurance products through East West Insurance.

Broadly speaking the bank made 93% of its revenue from loan interest (including fees) in 2014 and another 7% from interest on investment securities investment in Federal Home Loan Bank and Federal Reserve Bank Stock and short-term investments. It had a staff of roughly 2700 employees at the end of 2014.

Geographic Reach

East West's bank network in the US is mainly in California (in and around Los Angeles the San Francisco Bay area Orange County and Silicon Valley) and in the Atlanta Boston Houston New York and Seattle metropolitan areas. Internationally the bank has five branches in Hong Kong and Greater China (Shanghai Shantou and Shenzhen) and five representative offices in Beijing Chongqing Guangzhou Xiamen and Taiwan.

Sales and Marketing

East West Bancorp caters its banking and loan business to companies in the manufacturing wholesale trade and service sectors.

Financial Performance

The bank has struggled to consistently grow its revenues in recent years due to shrinking interest margins on loans amidst the low-interest environment. Its profits however have been rising thanks to declining loan loss provisions as its loan portfolio's credit quality has improved with higher property valuations in the strengthened economy.

East West had a breakout year in 2014 as its revenue climbed by 17% to $1.14 billion mostly thanks to an increase in non-covered loan volumes. Higher revenue in 2014 drove East West Bancorp's net income higher by 16% to $342.5 million. Lower income tax provisions resulting from additional purchases of affordable housing partnerships and tax-credited investments also help pad the bank's bottom line.

The bank's operating cash levels dipped by 8% to $392.9 million mostly due to unfavorable working capital changes related to accrued interest receivables and other asset balances.

Strategy

East West Bancorp's long-term vision reiterated in 2015 is to "serve as the financial bridge between the United States and Greater China" by reaching more customers with its cross-border products and capabilities. Its full-service branches in Greater China offer traditional letters of credit and trade finance between businesses while also providing the bank a way to serve existing clients and establish new business relationships.

Toward its international expansion plans the company opened two new branches in Greater China's Shenzhen and Shanghai Pilot Free Trade Zone during 2014 which would better position it to help its customers and facilitate their financial needs between Greater China and the US.

The bank may also occasionally pursue acquisitions of other banks to broaden its market reach and grow its loan and deposit business.

Mergers and Acquisitions

In 2014 East West Bancorp expanded its presence in Texas and California after it purchased Metrocorp along with its 19 MetroBank and Metro United Bank branches in the Houston Dallas and San Diego markets. The deal also added $1.7 billion in assets and $1.4 billion in new loan assets.

Company Background

East West Bancorp was founded in 1998.

In 2009 the company acquired more than 60 branches and most of the banking operations of larger rival United Commercial Bank which had been seized by regulators. The deal gave East West Bank about 40 more California branches plus some 20 additional US locations beyond the state.

EXECUTIVES

Evp Chief Risk Officer General Counsel And Secretary East West Bancorp And East West Bank, Douglas P. Krause, age 62, $403,090 total compensation

Chairman And Ceo East West Bancorp And East West Bank, Dominic Ng, age 59, $1,000,000 total compensation

Vice Chairman East West Bancorp And East West Bank, John M. Lee, age 86

Evp And Head Of International And Commercial Banking, Andy Yen, age 60, $370,977 total compensation

Evp And Cfo East West Bancorp And East West Bank, Irene H. Oh, age 40, $403,090 total compensation

Evp And Chief Credit Officer East West Bank, Albert Sun, age 63

President And Coo East West Bancorp And East West Bank, Gregory L. Guyett, age 54

Evp Head Of U.s. Eastern And Texas Regions And Head Of Consumer And Business Banking, Wendy Cai-Lee

Vice President, Sue Chao

First Vice President Consumer Banking Regional Manager, Renee Chang

First Vice President Relationship Manager, Dorothy Zhao

Vice President Business Development Officer, Ellen Chiang

Avp Loan Portfolio Manager, Sheng-ta Tsai

Avp Loan Documentation And Funding, Jacquelynn Forte

Vice President, Ann Huynh

Assistant Vice President Credit Analyst, Joseph Au

Evp Chief Risk Officer General Counsel And Secretary East West Bancorp And East West Bank, Douglas P. Krause, age 62

Chairman And Ceo East West Bancorp And East West Bank, Dominic Ng, age 59

Vice Chairman East West Bancorp And East West Bank, John M. Lee, age 86

Auditors: KPMG LLP

LOCATIONS

HQ: East West Bancorp, Inc
135 North Los Robles Ave., 7th Floor, Pasadena, CA 91101
Phone: 626 768-6000
Web: www.eastwestbank.com

PRODUCTS/OPERATIONS

2011 Sales

	$ mil.	% of total
Commercial lending	619	57
Retail banking	358	33
Other & adjustments	112	10
Total	**1,091**	**100**

COMPETITORS

Bank of America	Hanmi Financial
Bank of East Asia	Hope Bancorp
Cathay General Bancorp	JPMorgan Chase
Citibank	U.S. Bancorp
City National	Wells Fargo
Comerica	

HISTORICAL FINANCIALS

Company Type: Public

Income Statement

FYE: December 31

	ASSETS ($ mil.)	NET INCOME ($ mil.)	INCOME AS % OF ASSETS	EMPLOYEES
12/17	37,150	505	1.4%	3,000
12/16	34,788	431	1.2%	2,873
12/15	32,350	384	1.2%	2,833
12/14	28,738	342	1.2%	2,709
12/13	24,730	295	1.2%	2,542
Annual Growth	**10.7%**	**14.4%**	**—**	**4.2%**

2017 Year-End Financials

Debt ratio: 0.46%	No. of shares (mil.): 144
Return on equity: 13.91%	Dividends
Cash ($ mil.): 2,573	Yield: 0.0%
Current ratio: —	Payout: 23.0%
Long-term debt ($ mil.): —	Market value ($ mil.): 8,793

	STOCK PRICE ($) FY Close	P/E High/Low		PER SHARE ($) Earnings	Dividends	Book Value
12/17	60.83	18	14	3.47	0.80	26.58
12/16	50.83	17	9	2.97	0.80	23.78
12/15	41.56	17	13	2.66	0.80	21.70
12/14	38.71	16	13	2.38	0.72	19.85
12/13	34.97	17	10	2.10	0.60	17.18
Annual Growth	**14.8%**	**—**	**—**	**13.4%**	**7.5%**	**11.5%**

Eastman Chemical Co

Eastman Chemical Company is a major international producer of acetate tow for cigarette filters. From manufacturing sites in the US and six European countries (including the UK Germany and France) it also turns out chemicals fibers plastics rubber materials polymers and solvents. Eastman's products include such items as food and medical packaging films and toothbrushes. Its end markets include transportation building and construction tobacco consumer durables food and agriculture and health and wellbeing. The company was once part of film giant Eastman Kodak.

Operations

Eastman Chemical operates through four segments: Additives and Functional Products (AFP) Advanced Materials (AM) Fibers and Chemical Intermediates (CI).

Additives and Functional Products generates some 35% of total sales. It manufactures for transportation consumables building and construction animal nutrition crop protection energy personal and home care markets.

Chemical Intermediates segment brings in nearly 30% of sales and supports Eastman's specialty businesses via its vertical integration into the cellulose acetyl olefins and alkylamines streams.

Advanced Materials accounts for about 25% of sales and produces polymers films and plastics for downstream industries such as transportation building and construction durable goods and health and wellness.

The Fibers segment accounts for 10% of sales and consists primarily of the acetate tow and triacetin plasticizers for use in the manufacture of cigarette filters. It also makes dyed acetate yarns for use in clothing furniture and industrial fabrics; and cellulose acetate flake and acetyl raw materials for other acetate fiber products.

Geographic Reach

Eastman has operations in Belgium Estonia France Germany Netherlands the UK and the US. Eastman has about 50 manufacturing sites and equity interests in three manufacturing joint ventures in some 15 countries that supply chemicals plastics and fibers products to customers throughout the world.

The US is Eastman Chemical's largest territory at around 45% of total sales. The EMEA region (Europe Middle East and Africa) accounts for around a quarter of sales as does the Asia-Pacific region. Latin America generates the remaining roughly 5% of sales.

Sales and Marketing

Eastman Chemical markets and sells products in more than 100 countries through a global marketing and sales organization which has a presence in the US and around 30 other countries.

The company's products are also marketed through indirect channels which include distributors and contract representatives primarily outside of the US. Products are shipped to customers directly from Eastman's manufacturing plants and from distribution centers worldwide.

Some of the markets the company serves are Adhesives Appliances Agriculture Building & Construction Childcare items Coatings Consumer Durable Goods Personal Care & Cosmetics and Electronics.

With a relatively diversified customer base its top 100 customers account for around 55% of Eastman's total sales.

Financial Performance

Eastman earned $9.6 billion in revenues in 2017 (2016: $9 billion). The 6% increase came from the AFP CI and AM segments (primarily higher sales volumes followed by higher selling prices of chemical products) more than offsetting a decline in the Fibers segment. The decline in Fibers came from operation disruptions relating to an explosion in the Kingsport coal gasification area (estimated above $110 million in damage costs).

Net income also climbed to $1.4 billion from $854 million the year prior primarily from a $100 million benefit from income tax provisions compared to $190 million expense the year before. Results further improved from the absence of a $85 million pay out in 2016 for early debt extinguishment and almost $40 million less in asset impairment charges.

Cash holdings went up slightly to $190 million. Operations generated $1.7 billion offset by $1 billion in financing activities and $640 million in investments.

Strategy

Eastman aims to drive 1-2% revenue growth in 2016-18 through innovation and market development initiatives. It has invested in two manufacturing sites (in Germany and Malaysia) to capitalize on advances in the manufacture of Crystex insoluble sulfur.

An unfortunate glitch came in the fourth quarter of 2017 when operation were disrupted due to an explosion in the Kingsport coal gasification area that will cost the company upwards of $110 million in damages.

However the company successfully completed the retrofit of its Nienburg Germany manufacturing facility and continued work on the expansion of the rubber additives facility in Malaysia. Eastman also commercialized its Tertrashield performance polyester resins providing improved performance for the automotive coatings industrial and food packaging markets.

Other developments include work on 60000 tons of extra capacity in the Eatman Tritan copolyester plant in Kingsport Tennessee and further construction on a polyvinyl butyral resin plant in Malaysia.

Eastman is also adding emphasis to its specialty businesses and products by divesting or monetizing its excess ethelyne capacity and restructuring following the Taminco acquisition.

HISTORY

Eastman Chemical went public in 1994 but the company traces its roots to the 19th century. George Eastman after developing a method for dry-plate photography established the Eastman Dry Plate and Film Company in 1884 in Rochester New York (the name was changed to Eastman Kodak in 1892).

In 1886 Eastman hired scientist Henry Reichenbach to help create and manufacture new photographic chemicals. As time passed Reichenbach and the company's other scientists came up with chemicals that were either not directly related to photography or had uses in addition to photography.

Eastman bought a wood-distillation plant in Kingsport Tennessee in 1920 and formed the Tennessee Eastman Corporation to make methanol and acetone for the manufacture of photographic chemicals. The company by this time called Kodak introduced acetate yarn and Tenite a cellulose ester plastic in the early 1930s. During WWII the company formed Holston Defense to make explosives for the US armed forces.

Kodak began to vertically integrate Tennessee Eastman's operations during the 1950s acquiring A. M. Tenney Associates Tennessee Eastman's selling agent for its acetate yarn products in 1950. It also established Texas Eastman opening a plant in Longview to produce ethyl alcohol and aldehydes raw materials used in fiber and film production. At the end of 1952 Kodak created Eastman Chemical Products to sell alcohols plastics and fibers made by Tennessee Eastman and Texas Eastman. Also that year Tennessee Eastman developed cellulose acetate filter tow for use in cigarette filters. In the late 1950s the company introduced Kodel polyester fiber.

Kodak created Carolina Eastman Company in 1968 opening a plant in Columbia South Carolina to produce Kodel and other polyester products. It also created Eastman Chemicals Division to handle its chemical operations.

In the late 1970s Eastman Chemicals Division introduced polyethylene terephthalate (PET) resin used to make containers. It acquired biological and molecular instrumentation manufacturer International Biotechnologies in 1987.

Eastman Chemicals Division became Eastman Chemical Company in 1990. In 1993 it exited the polyester fiber business. When Kodak spun off Eastman Chemical in early 1994 the new company was saddled with $1.8 billion in debt.

Eastman's 1996 earnings were reduced when oversupply lowered prices for PET. Eastman opened plants in Argentina Malaysia and the Netherlands in 1998.

Eastman added to its international locations in 1999 by opening a plant in Singapore and an office in Bangkok. It also bought Lawter International (specialty chemicals for ink and coatings) with locations in Belgium China and Ireland. In 2000 the company began restructuring into two business segments (chemicals and polymers) and acquired resin and colorant maker McWhorter Technologies.

In 2001 Eastman acquired most of Hercules' resins business. In November the company announced that it had postponed plans to split into two companies (one focusing on specialty chemicals and plastics the other concentrating on polyethylene plastics and acetate fibers) until mid-2002 due to the weak economy. In early 2002 the company announced that it had cancelled those plans altogether and would operate the two as separate divisions.

The following year Eastman announced it would split off part of its coatings adhesives specialty polymers and inks (CASPI) segment. The division had been underperforming and had been hit particularly hard by the high costs of raw materials and a general overcapacity in the marketplace. Eastman sold a portion of CASPI to investment firm Apollo Manageme

EXECUTIVES

Evp And Cfo, Curtis E. (Curt) Espeland, age 53, $736,887 total compensation

Chairman And Ceo, Mark J. Costa, age 51, $1,102,895 total compensation

Svp And Chief International Ventures Officer, Michael H. K. Chung, age 64

Svp And Cto, Stephen G. (Steve) Crawford, age 53, $484,892 total compensation

Evp And Chief Commercial Officer, Brad A. Lich, age 50, $611,007 total compensation

Svp And Chief Manufacturing Supply Chain And Engineering Officer, Mark K. Cox, age 52

Senior Vice President Fibers And Global Supply Chain, Richard Johnson

Vice President, Don Cleek

Chairman And Ceo, Mark J. Costa, age 51

Auditors: PricewaterhouseCoopers LLP

LOCATIONS

HQ: Eastman Chemical Co
200 South Wilcox Drive, Kingsport, TN 37662
Phone: 423 229-2000
Web: www.eastman.com

2016 Sales

	$ mil.	% of total
US & Canada	4,025	45
Europe Middle East & Africa	2,305	24
Asia/Pacific	2,163	25
Latin America	515	6
Total	**9,008**	**100**

PRODUCTS/OPERATIONS

2016 Sales

	$ mil.	% of total
Additives & Functional Products	2,979	33
Chemical Intermediates	2,534	28
Advanced Materials	2,457	27
Fibers	992	11
Other	46	1
Total	**9,008**	**100**

Selected Brands and Products

ABALYN rosin resins
ABITOL hydroabietyl alcohols
ADMEX plasticizers
ASPIRA family of resins
BENZOFLEX plasticizers
BIOEXTEND high performance additives
CADENCE resins for calendered films
CELLOLYN synthetic resins
CHROMSPUN acetate yarn
CRYSTEX insoluble sulfur
CYPHREX microfibers
DRESINATE rosin soaps
DURASTAR polymer
DYMEREX rosins
EASTAPURE electronic chemicals
EASTAR copolyesters
EASTEK polymer dispersion
EASTMAN AQ polymers
EASTMAN cellulose esters
EASTMAN coalescents
EASTMAN G polymers
EASTMAN low volatile pure monomer resins
EASTMAN NPG glycol
EASTMAN plasticizers
EASTMAN solvents
EASTMAN TXIB formulation additive
EASTOFLEX amorphous polyolefins
EASTOTAC resins
ECDEL elastomers
EMBRACE family of resins
ENDEX hydrocarbon resins
ENERLOGIC low-e window film
ESTRON acetate yarn
FLEXVUE film
FORAL hydrogenated rosins
FORALYN hydrogenated rosin esters
FORMULAONE high performance auto tint
GILA DIY window film
HUPER OPTIK & DESIGN film
IQUE film
KRISTALEX hydrocarbon resins
LLUMAR window film
METALYN rosin esters
NANOLUX film
NEOSTAR elastomer
OPTIFILM family of products
PAMOLYN fatty acids
PENTALYN synthetic resins
PERENNIAL WOOD
PERMALYN resins
PICCO hydrocarbon resins
PICCOLASTIC hydrocarbon resins
PICCOTAC hydrocarbon resins
PICCOTEX hydrocarbon resins
PLASTOLYN hydrocarbon resins
POLY-PALE rosin resins
PROBENZ sodium benzoate
PROVISTA copolymer
REGALITE hydrocarbon resins
REGALREZ hydrocarbon resins
SAFLEX PVB polymers
SANTOFLEX antidegradants
SKYDROL aviation hydraulic fluids
SKYKLEEN solvents
SOLUS performance additive
SPECTAR copolyester
STAYBELITE-E hydrogenated rosins
SUN-X film
SUSTANE SAIB
TACOLYN resin dispersions
TENITE cellulosics
TENOX antioxidants
TEXANOL ester alcohol
THE GLASS POLYMER
THERMINOL heat transfer fluids
TiGLAZE copolyester
TMPD glycol
TRITAN copolyester
VANCEVA PVB polymers
VELATE coalescents
VISTA window film
V-KOOL film
XIR coated PET

COMPETITORS

Akzo Nobel	Dow Chemical
BASF SE	DuPont
Celanese	ExxonMobil Chemical
Clariant	Huntsman Corp
DIC Corporation	Solvay
DSM	

HISTORICAL FINANCIALS

Company Type: Public

Income Statement
FYE: December 31

	REVENUE ($ mil.)	NET INCOME ($ mil.)	NET PROFIT MARGIN	EMPLOYEES
12/17	9,549	1,384	14.5%	14,000
12/16	9,008	854	9.5%	14,000
12/15	9,648	848	8.8%	15,000
12/14	9,527	751	7.9%	15,000
12/13	9,350	1,165	12.5%	14,000
Annual Growth	0.5%	4.4%	—	0.0%

2017 Year-End Financials

Debt ratio: 40.88%	No. of shares (mil.): 142
Return on equity: 27.86%	Dividends
Cash ($ mil.): 191	Yield: 0.0%
Current ratio: 1.59	Payout: 22.0%
Long-term debt ($ mil.): 6,147	Market value ($ mil.): 13,240

	STOCK PRICE ($) FY Close	P/E High/Low		PER SHARE ($) Earnings	Dividends	Book Value
12/17	92.64	10	8	9.47	2.09	37.81
12/16	75.21	13	10	5.75	1.89	30.95
12/15	67.51	15	11	5.66	1.66	26.67
12/14	75.86	18	14	4.97	1.45	23.62
12/13	80.70	11	8	7.44	1.25	24.91
Annual Growth	3.5%	—	—	6.2%	13.7%	11.0%

EATON CORPORATION

EXECUTIVES

Chb-Ceo-Pres, Alexander Cutler
Cfo, Richard Fearon
Exec V Pres, Mark McGuire
Sr V Pres-SEC, Thomas Moran
Sr V Pres-Contrl, Billie Rawot
Sr V Pres Corp Devt & Treas, David Foster
Senior Engineer, Fred James
Manager, Gordon Harmon
Sales Manager, Jim Lago
Executive Officer, Matt Greene
Coordinator, Sandy Benzin
Auditors: ERNST & YOUNG LLP CLEVELAND

LOCATIONS

HQ: EATON CORPORATION
 1000 EATON BLVD, CLEVELAND, OH 441226058
Phone: 440 523-5000
Web: WWW.EATON.COM

HISTORICAL FINANCIALS

Company Type: Private

Income Statement
FYE: December 31

	REVENUE ($ mil.)	NET INCOME ($ mil.)	NET PROFIT MARGIN	EMPLOYEES
12/15	6,925	821	11.9%	736
12/14	6,990	170	2.4%	—
Annual Growth	(0.9%)	382.9%	—	—

eBay Inc.

eBay is a well-known e-commerce platform for online auctions. Trading goods every second of every day eBay offers an online forum for buying and selling merchandise worldwide from fine antiques to the latest video games. eBay generates revenue through listing and selling fees and through advertising and boasts more than 177 million users and more than 1 billion listings globally. The company sells tickets to concerts sporting events and other entertainment via its Stubhub platform. eBay is available across digital platforms including mobile. More than half of eBay's sales are outside the US.

Operations

eBay generates revenue from net transactions about 80% of the total and from marketing services and other about 20%.

Net transaction revenue consists of final value fees (fees payable on transactions closed in the Marketplace and StubHub platforms) listing fees and other service fees. Marketing services and other revenue consists of sales from Marketplace StubHub and Classified principally from the sale of advertisements revenue sharing arrangements classifieds fees marketing service fees and lead referral fees.

Geographic Reach

About 55% of eBay's revenue is generated outside the US. The company has a strong focus on Europe with Germany and the UK each providing about 15% of revenue. The company's classified websites are available in more than 1000 cities around the world.

The company has offices data centers product development offices fulfillment centers and customer service offices in about 35 countries.

Sales and Marketing

eBay's online marketing efforts go to traffic acquisition in paid search affiliates marketing and display advertising. Offline advertising includes brand campaigns and buyer and seller communications.

Financial Performance

Although uneven eBay's revenue has trended higher for the past five years.

In 2017 sales rose about 7% to $9.5 billion driven by a 6% increase in net transaction revenue and a 7% rise in marketing services and other revenue. US revenue was up 6% and international revenue was up 7%.

The company posted a net loss of $1 billion in 2017 compared to a $17.2 million profit in 2016. The company recognized a tax charge of $3.1 billion in 2017 related to the US Tax Cuts and Jobs Act.

Cash in eBay's coffers totaled about $2.1 billion in 2017 compared to $1.8 billion in 2016. In 2017 the company generated $3.1 billion from operations and used $1.3 billion in investing activities and $1.8 billion in financing activities.

Strategy

Whether online through the mobile channel or offline eBay's monetization strategy remains the same. The company is primarily a transaction-based business model that generates revenue through its e-commerce platforms. The company also generates revenue through marketing services classifieds and advertising.

eBay has made changes to enhance experiences for buyers and sellers. It allows users to search for products by image using artificial intelligence technology. For buyers of high-end goods the company introduced an authentication program to increase consumer confidence. Another new service has been guaranteed delivery in three days or less for tens of millions of items.

The company activated a global branding campaign called Fill Your Cart With Color to drive more traffic and new buyers to its sites. It rolled out local campaigns to increase brand awareness of eBay in North America Europe and Australia using television digital and social media channels.

Mergers and Acquisitions

In 2017 eBay and Flipkart concluded a three-part transaction. eBay sold its business in India to Flipkart and made a $500000 investment in the company. The companies also agreed to make their inventories available to each other's customers.

In 2018 eBay acquired Giosis' Japan business including the Qoo10.jp platform. With the close of the transaction eBay relinquished its investment in Giosis' non-Japanese businesses. The transaction expanded eBay's footprint in Japan one of the largest e-commerce markets in the world.

Company Background

Pierre Omidyar created a flea market in cyberspace when he launched online auction service Auction Web on Labor Day weekend in 1995. Making a name for itself largely through word of mouth the company incorporated in 1996 the same year it began to charge a fee to auction items online. That year it enhanced its service with Feedback Forum (buyer and seller ratings).

The company changed the name to eBay in 1997 and began promoting itself through advertising. By the middle of that year eBay was boasting nearly 800000 auctions each day and Benchmark Capital came on board as a significant financial backer.

HISTORY

Pierre Omidyar created a flea market in cyberspace when he launched online auction service Auction Web on Labor Day weekend in 1995. Making a name for itself largely through word of mouth the company incorporated in 1996 the same year it began to charge a fee to auction items online. That year it enhanced its service with Feedback Forum (buyer and seller ratings).

The company changed the name to eBay in 1997 and began promoting itself through advertising. By the middle of that year eBay was boasting nearly 800000 auctions each day and Benchmark Capital came on board as a significant financial backer.

Margaret ("Meg") Whitman a former Hasbro executive replaced Omidyar as CEO in early 1998. eBay made a blockbuster debut as a public company later that year.

eBay showed its acquisitive streak in 1999 with purchases of Alando (online auctions in Germany) and Billpoint (person-to-person credit card technology). It also made one of its first investments in an outside company with the purchase of 6% of TradeOut.com an online seller of corporate surplus materials. The company set the jewel in its 1999 acquisition crown when it acquired upscale auction house Butterfield & Butterfield (now just Butterfields). eBay also expanded down under through a joint venture with Australia-based ecorp (formerly PBL Online). A bit of the bloom came off the rose in 1999 when online service interruptions (one "brownout" in June persisted for 22 hours) revealed a chink in eBay's armor. The company called its top 10000 users to convey its apologies and pledged to improve its website's performance.

In 2000 eBay agreed to develop person-to-person and merchant-to-person auction sites for Disney's GO Network began distributing information through wireless products and joined with banking giant Wells Fargo to offer eBay sellers the option of accepting online checks. Also that year the US

Department of Justice began an investigation to determine if eBay had violated antitrust laws in its dealings with competitors. In other legal news a class-action lawsuit was filed against the company claiming that eBay was an auctioneer and therefore must authenticate the items on its site. (A trial court dismissed the case in early 2001.)

Also in 2000 the company expanded into Japan through eBay Japan with computer firm NEC acquiring 30% of the Japanese subsidiary and eBay owning the rest; it also launched Canadian and Austrian sites. In addition eBay took an equity stake in online used-car dealer AutoTrader.com and launched a co-branded used-car auction website and it acquired online trading community Half.com.

eBay strengthened its European position in 2001 through the purchase of French Internet auction firm iBazar. It also launched sites in Ireland New Zealand and Switzerland. eBay made a deal that year to provide its e-commerce capabilities to Microsoft developers and to add business-to-business auctions to its consumer operations. In addition the company began offering virtual storefronts for retailers to sell fixed-price items and purchased auctioneer of foreclosed property HomesDirect. In late 2001 eBay sold its iBazar's Brazilian subsidiary to MercadoLibre Latin America's leading auction site in exchange for a 19.5% stake (now 18%) in MercadoLibre.

Disappointed with the performance of eBay Premiere (fine art and other high-end merchandise) in 2002 the company partnered with Sotheby

EXECUTIVES

Senior Vice President, Alan Marks
President And Ceo, Devin N. Wenig, age 51, $1,000,000 total compensation
President Stubhub, Scott Cutler
Svp And General Counsel, Marie Oh Huber, age 57, $389,462 total compensation
Svp Ebay North America, Harry A. (Hal) Lawton, age 44, $650,000 total compensation
Svp And Cto, Stephen (Steve) Fisher, age 53, $625,000 total compensation
Svp And Cfo, Scott F. Schenkel, age 50, $650,000 total compensation
Svp Global Operations, Wendy Jones
Svp Ebay Europe, Paul Todd
Svp Ebay Asia Pacific, Jay Lee
Svp And Chief Product Officer, Raymond J. (R.J.) Pittman, age 48, $580,000 total compensation
Svp And Chief People Officer, Kristin Yetto
Chief Accounting Officer And Vice President, Brian Doerger
Vice President Intellectual Property, Jay Monahan
Senior Vice President Operations, Ryan Downs
Vp Of Applied Research, Tom Pinckney
Vice President Talent Acquisition Management And Development, Lou Sanchez
Senior Vice President Of Marketing, Jae Lee
Vice President Sales, Todd Pearson
National Account Manager, Jessica Schrenker
Vp Product And Engineering, Lucius DiPhillips
Senior Vice President Finance Chief Financial Officer, Bob Swan
Vice President, Don Albert
Vice President Global Customer Experience Ebay Europe, Jean-marc Codsi
Vice President Investor Relations, Thomas Hudson
Vice President Legal, John Muller
Vice President Of Compensation Benefits And Human Resources, Robin Colman
Vice President Human Resources Business Partner, Donna Zontos
Vice President, Maureen Loftus
Vice President And Chief Architect, Sanjeev Katariya

Vice President And General Manager Selling Experience, Sunil Rajasekar
Chairman, Thomas J. (Tom) Tierney, age 64
Board Member, Bonnie Hammer
Board Member, Logan Green
Board Member, Fred Anderson
Board Member, Perry Traquina
Auditors: PricewaterhouseCoopers LLP

LOCATIONS

HQ: eBay Inc.
2025 Hamilton Avenue, San Jose, CA 95125
Phone: 408 376-7008
Web: www.ebay.com

2017 Sales

	$ mil.	% of total
US	4,091	43
Germany	1,450	15
UK	1,359	14
Rest of world	2,667	28
Total	**8,567**	**100**

2017 Sales

	$ mil.	% of total
Net transaction revenues:		
Marketplace	6,450	67
StubHub	1,010	11
Marketing services and other revenues:		
Marketplace	1,192	13
Classifieds	897	9
StubHub Corporate and other	18	-
Total	**9,567**	**100**

COMPETITORS

Alibaba.com	HSN
Amazon.com	Naspers
Apple Inc.	Overstock.com
Buy.com	Schibsted
Costco Wholesale	Spectrum Group
Digital River	Target Corporation
Etsy	Tickets.com
Facebook	Walmart.com
Google	

HISTORICAL FINANCIALS

Company Type: Public

Income Statement

FYE: December 31

	REVENUE ($ mil.)	NET INCOME ($ mil.)	NET PROFIT MARGIN	EMPLOYEES
12/18	10,746	2,530	23.5%	14,000
12/17	9,567	(1,016)	—	14,100
12/16	8,979	7,266	80.9%	12,600
12/15	8,592	1,725	20.1%	11,600
12/14	17,902	46	0.3%	36,500
Annual Growth	**(12.0%)**	**172.3%**	**—**	**(21.3%)**

2018 Year-End Financials

Debt ratio: 40.45%	No. of shares (mil.): 915
Return on equity: 35.28%	Dividends
Cash ($ mil.): 2,202	Yield: —
Current ratio: 1.60	Payout: —
Long-term debt ($ mil.): 7,685	Market value ($ mil.): 25,684

	STOCK PRICE ($) FY Close	P/E High/Low		PER SHARE ($) Earnings	Dividends	Book Value
12/18	28.07	18	10	2.55	0.00	6.86
12/17	37.74	—	—	(0.95)	0.00	7.84
12/16	29.69	5	3	6.35	0.00	9.70
12/15	27.48	46	17	1.42	0.00	5.55
12/14	56.12	1483	1197	0.04	0.00	16.26
Annual Growth	**(15.9%)**	**—**		**—182.6%**	**—**	**(19.4%)**

Ecolab Inc

Ecolab cleans up by cleaning up. The company offers cleaning sanitation pest-elimination and maintenance products and services to the energy healthcare hospitality and industrial sectors among others. Its cleaning and sanitizing operations serve hotels schools commercial and institutional laundries and quick service restaurants. Other units focus on products for textile care water care healthcare food and beverage processing and pest control. It also makes chemicals used in water treatment for industrial processes including in the paper and energy industries. The company is expanding its services to the offshore and international energy market.

Operations

Ecolab provides cleaning and sanitizing programs and products equipment repair and pest elimination for markets such as food service food and beverage processing chemical processing oil and gas production healthcare government and education and textile care.

Ecolab's chemicals and services are used in water treatment pollution control oil and gas steelmaking papermaking mining and other industrial processes. It is also one of the top suppliers of chemical dishwashing products to institutions in the US.

Ecolab has three operating segments: Global Industrial (consisting of the Global Water Global Food & Beverage Global Paper and Global Textile Care operating units); Global Institutional (Global Institutional Global Specialty and Global Healthcare operating units); and Global Energy (operating under the Nalco Champion name).

The Global Industrial segment (accounting for some 35% of sales) provides water treatment and cleaning and sanitizing services to large industrial clients in the chemical commercial laundry food manufacturing and paper industries. Global Institutional also generates around 35% of sales; and Global Energy around 25%.

Geographic Reach

St. Paul Minnesota-based Ecolab operates in more than 170 countries. Outside the US its largest operations are in Europe the Asia/Pacific region and Latin America. Smaller operations are in Canada Africa and the Middle East.

The US accounts for more than 50% of the company's total revenue. Europe accounts for nearly 20% the Asia/Pacific region around 15%; Latin America less than 10% the Middle East and Africa 5% and Canada 5%.

The company directly operates in some 100 countries outside the US through wholly-owned subsidiaries or in some cases through a joint venture with a local partner.

Sales and Marketing

The company serves customers in a range of segments including Buildings and Facilities Chemical Processing Education Facility Care Food and Beverage Processing Food Retail Foodservice Government Healthcare Lodging and Oil and Gas.

Selected Ecolab's products are sold to distributors agents or licensees. Deliveries to customers are made from manufacturing plants and a network of distribution centers and third-party logistics service providers using common carriers Ecolab's own delivery vehicles and distributors' vehicles.

Financial Performance

In the last decade (2008-17) Ecolab?s revenue has fluctuated significantly from a low of $6 billion (2009) to a high of $14.3 billion (2014) with an average revenue just above $10 billion a year. Company profits however have had a strong up-

ward trajectory. From posting $448 million in profits in 2009 it has grown some 240% to $1.5 billion in 2017 its highest in a decade.

Revenue in 2017 was $13.8 billion more than 5% growth from the year prior. Sales increased due to a combination of increases in volumes pricing and additional revenue flow from acquisitions.

Net income increased more than 20% since 2016 to $1.5 billion thanks to a $4 million in net gains from special charges likes restructuring activities and acquisition costs (compared to $450 million in charges in 2015-16 period combined) as well as some $200 million reduction in income tax provisions from the year prior.

Cash holdings reduced from $327 million in 2016 to $211 million in 2017. Operating activities provided $2.9 billion. By contrast Investment activities used up $1.6 billion (mostly in acquisition of $990 million and CAPEX of $790 million); a further $523 million was utilized by investment activities mainly in long-term debt payments and share repurchases.

Strategy

Ecolab grows through acquisitions. The company's global reach and expanded line of products and services will enable it to provide total water processing management to food and beverage hospitality and laundry customers worldwide. It continues to target key acquisitions to complement its businesses and to focus on key growth areas. In July 2016 it acquired a minority stake in a water treatment company and in February 2017 it acquired a French hygiene and disinfectant product maker.

Ecolab's strategy for growth also includes investing organically in its businesses including equipment used by customers to dispense its cleaning and sanitizing products as well as in process control and monitoring equipment.

Ecolab's 2020 growth strategy rests on integrating digital into its back end and products and positioning the company as a desirable destination for talent. To do so Ecolab is clarifying its story offering diverse career paths and promoting learning via performance management career framework and formal learning.

However the company?s Energy Business segment remains volatile despite a $100 million increase in revenue in the 2016-17 period. Moreover with a possible trade war looming in the global markets Ecolab may suffer from higher raw material costs needed for its products that include an array of organic and inorganic chemicals.

Mergers and Acquisitions

Ecolab acquired food hygiene and cleaning products firm Holchem Group in 2018. The company serves food and beverage and food service customers in Ireland the U.K. and mainland European countries. It made $56 million in revenue last year. Financial details were not disclosed. Additionally it has made an offer to acquire Bioquell a leading provider of hydrogen peroxide vapor bio-decontamination systems and services for the life sciences and healthcare industries. Based in the UK Bioquell's 2017 sales were approximately £29 million.

In 2017 Ecolab acquired Laboratoires Anios from co-owners Bertrand and Thierry Letartre and private investment company Ardian for about $800 million. Anios is a European manufacturer and marketer of hygiene and disinfection products for the healthcare food service and food and beverage processing industries. Based in Lille France Anios has a presence in more than 85 countries. Anios' innovative product line expands the solutions Ecolab can offer while also providing a complementary geographic footprint.

Also in 2017 the company acquired Abednego Environmental Services a Novi Michigan-based provider of water solutions for automotive cus-

tomers. The acquisition adds to the suite of products and services Ecolab provides to automobile manufacturers to re-cycle water reduce energy usage and reduce waste.

In 2016 the company purchased certain assets of Keedak Limited an oilfield chemical distributor in Nigeria. Ecolab also bought a 33% stake in Aquatech International a water treatment solutions company.

HISTORY

Salesman Merritt Osborn founded Economics Laboratory in 1924 as a specialty chemical maker; its first product was a rug cleaner for hotels. It added industrial and institutional cleaners and consumer detergents in the 1950s. The company went public in 1957. By 1973 it had been organized into five divisions: industrial (cleaners and specialty chemical formulas) institutional (dishwasher products sanitation formulas) consumer (dishwasher detergent and laundry aids coffee filters floor cleaners) food-processing (detergents) and international (run by future CEO Fred Lanners).

EXECUTIVES

Chairman And Ceo, Douglas M. (Doug) Baker, age 60, $1,187,500 total compensation

Cfo, Daniel J. (Dan) Schmechel, age 58, $581,250 total compensation

Evp And Cio, Stewart H. McCutcheon

President And Coo, Thomas W. (Tom) Handley, age 63, $581,250 total compensation

Assistant Secretary, Michael C. McCormick

Evp; President Global Institutional, Michael A. (Mike) Hickey, age 56, $543,125 total compensation

Evp And Cto, Larry L. Berger, age 57

Evp; President International Regions, Christophe Beck, age 50, $548,125 total compensation

Vp And General Manager Healthcare North America, Paul B. Chaffin

Evp; President Global Water And Process Services, Timothy P. Mulhere, age 55

Evp Human Resources, Laurie M. Marsh, age 54

Evp; President Global Energy, Stephen M. (Steve) Taylor, age 56, $518,818 total compensation

Evp; President Global Services And Specialty, Roberto D. (Bobby) Mendez

Evp General Counsel And Secretary, James J. (Jim) Seifert, age 61

Evp And President Europe, Darrell Brown

Evp Global Textile Care, Andreas Weilinghoff

Evp; President Global Food And Beverage, Jill S. Wyant, age 46

Evp And Chief Supply Chain Officer, Alex Blanco, age 57, $450,000 total compensation

Svp Global Marketing And Communications, Elizabeth A. (Beth) Simermeyer

Svp And President Middle East And Africa, Vishal Sharma

Evp; President Asia Pacific, Sean Toohey

Evp And General Manager Global Food And Beverage, Nicholas (Nick) Alfano

Svp And President Latin America, John Guttery

Assistant Vice President Corporate Accounts, Cargile Kelly

Vice President Of Finance, Anil Arcalgud

Vice President Human Resources Talent, Sue Metcalf

Chairman And Ceo, Douglas M. (Doug) Baker, age 60

Assistant Secretary, Michael C. McCormick

Evp General Counsel And Secretary, James J. (Jim) Seifert, age 61

Auditors: PricewaterhouseCoopers LLP

LOCATIONS

HQ: Ecolab Inc
  1 Ecolab Place, St. Paul, MN 55102
Phone: 800 232-6522
Web: www.ecolab.com

2016 Sales

	$ mil.	% of total
United States	7,035	53
Europe	2,361	18
Asia Pacific excluding Greater China	1,159	9
Latin America	852	7
MEA	667	5
Canada	576	4
Greater China	499	4
Total	**13,152**	**100**

PRODUCTS/OPERATIONS

2016 Sales

	$ mil.	% of total
Global Industrial	4,617	35
Global Institutional	4,495	34
Global Energy	3,035	23
Other	806	6
Effect of foreign currency translation	197	2
Total	**13,152**	**100**

Selected Services

Equipment Care
Facility Cleaning
Food Retail Solutions
Food Safety Specialties
Foodservice Water Management
Front and Back of House
Housekeeping — Guest Rooms
HVAC Performance Services
Laundry
Pest Elimination
Pool and Spa
Restaurants
Water Safety
Water Treatment

COMPETITORS

3M Purification	ISS A/S
Ashland	Medline Industries
Chemed	Rollins Inc.
Diversey	STERIS
GE Water and Process	ServiceMaster
Technologies	Zep Inc.
Healthcare Services	

HISTORICAL FINANCIALS

Company Type: Public

Income Statement

FYE: December 31

	REVENUE ($ mil.)	NET INCOME ($ mil.)	NET PROFIT MARGIN	EMPLOYEES
12/17	13,838	1,508	10.9%	48,400
12/16	13,152	1,229	9.3%	47,565
12/15	13,545	1,002	7.4%	47,000
12/14	14,280	1,202	8.4%	47,430
12/13	13,253	967	7.3%	45,415
Annual Growth	**1.1%**	**11.7%**	**—**	**1.6%**

2017 Year-End Financials

Debt ratio: 36.68%	No. of shares (mil.): 289
Return on equity: 20.78%	Dividends
Cash ($ mil.): 211	Yield: 0.0%
Current ratio: 1.34	Payout: 29.6%
Long-term debt ($ mil.): 6,758	Market value ($ mil.): 38,821

	STOCK PRICE ($) FY Close	P/E High/Low		PER SHARE ($) Earnings	Dividends	Book Value
12/17	134.18	26	23	5.13	1.52	26.33
12/16	117.22	30	24	4.14	1.42	23.65
12/15	114.38	36	29	3.32	1.34	23.35
12/14	104.52	29	24	3.93	1.16	24.40
12/13	104.27	33	22	3.16	0.97	24.39
Annual Growth	**6.5%**	**—**	**—**	**12.9%**	**12.0%**	**1.9%**

Edison International

Edison International is a power player in Southern California through its largest subsidiary Southern California Edison (SCE) which distributes electricity to of about 14 million people in central coastal and southern California. It is also the top purchaser of renewable energy in the US. The utility's system consists of more than 12780 circuit miles of transmission lines and more than 91800 circuit miles of distribution lines. SCE also has about 6325 MW of generating capacity from interests in nuclear hydroelectric and fossil-fueled power plants. Through its Edison Energy subsidiary the company owns and operates solar power projects.

HISTORY

In 1896 a group including Elmer Peck and George Baker organized West Side Lighting to provide electricity in Los Angeles. The next year the company merged with Los Angeles Edison Electric which owned the rights to the Edison name and patents in the region and Baker became president. Edison Electric installed the first DC-power underground conduits in the Southwest.

John Barnes Miller took over the top spot in 1901. During his 31-year reign the firm bought many neighboring utilities and built several power plants. In 1909 it took the name Southern California Edison (SCE).

SCE doubled its assets by buying Southern California electric interests from rival Pacific Light & Power in 1917. However in 1912 the City of Los Angeles had decided to develop its own power distribution system and by 1922 SCE's authority in the city had ended. A 1925 earthquake and the 1928 collapse of the St. Francis Dam severely damaged SCE's facilities.

SCE built 11 fossil-fueled power stations (1948-1973) and moved into nuclear power in 1963 when it broke ground on the San Onofre plant with San Diego Gas & Electric (brought online in 1968). It finished consolidating its service territory with the 1964 purchase of California Electric Power. In the late 1970s SCE began to build solar geothermal and wind power facilities.

Edison Mission Energy (EME) was founded in 1986 to develop buy and operate power plants around the world. The next year investment arm Edison Capital was formed as well as a holding company for the entire group SCEcorp. EME began to build its portfolio in 1992 when it snagged a 51% stake in an Australian plant and bought hydroelectric facilities in Spain. In 1995 it bought UK hydroelectric company First Hydro; it also began building plants in Italy Turkey and Indonesia.

The 1994 Northridge earthquake that cut power to a million SCE customers was nothing compared to the industry's seismic shifts. In 1996 SCEcorp became the more worldly Edison International. California's electricity market opened to competition in 1998 and the utility began divesting SCE's generation assets; it sold 12 gas-fired plants. Overseas EME picked up 25% of a power plant being built in Thailand and a 50% stake in a cogeneration facility in Puerto Rico.

SCE got regulatory approval to offer telecom services in its utility territory in 1999. That year EME snapped up several plants in the Midwest from Unicom for $5 billion. Overseas it purchased two UK coal-fired plants from PowerGen (which it sold to American Electric Power in 2001 for $960 million). The next year EME CEO Edward Muller (who had held the post since 1994) abruptly resigned and Edison bought Citizens Power from the Peabody Group.

In 2000 SCE got caught in a price squeeze brought on in part by deregulation. Prices on the wholesale power market soared but the utility was unable to pass along the increase to customers because of a rate freeze. The company gained some prospect of relief in 2001 when California's governor signed legislation to allow a state agency to buy power from wholesalers under long-term contracts. In addition the California Public Utilities Commission (CPUC) approved a substantial increase in retail electricity rates and the Federal Energy Regulatory Commission approved a plan to limit wholesale energy prices during periods of severe shortage in 11 western states.

To reduce debt Edison International agreed to sell its transmission grid to the state for $2.8 billion. While the California legislature debated the agreement however the CPUC announced a settlement in which SCE would be allowed to keep its current high rates in place until its debts are paid off. The settlement which was approved in 2002 eliminated the need for the sale of the company's transmission grid.

Also in 2001 the company sold most of its Edison Enterprises businesses including home security services unit Edison Select which was sold to ADT Security Services.

In 2004 Edison International committed to taking a lead position in developing comprehensive national programs to reduce greenhouse gas emissions primarily carbon dioxide.

In 2006 SCE signed the largest wind energy deal ever completed by a US utility providing for 1500 MW of wind power from plants in the Tehachapi area of California.

EME marketed energy in the US and Turkey and had interests in more than 40 power plants in the US and one in Turkey that gave it a net physical generating capacity of about 10780 MW. EME filed for bankruptcy protection in 2012 citing high operating losses due to low realized energy and capacity prices high fuel costs and low generation at its Midwest Generation plants.

In 2013 SCE decided to permanently retire Units 2 and 3 of its San Onofre Nuclear Generating Station. Unit 2 was taken out of service January 2012 for a planned routine outage. Unit 3 was also taken offline a few weeks later after station operators found a small leak in a tube inside a steam generator.

In 2013 Edison Energy acquired SoCore Energy a Chicago-based solar portfolio development and commercial rooftop installation company focusing on the solar energy needs of multisite retailers REITs and industrial clients and bought a minority stake in Clean Power Finance a financial services and software provider for the solar industry.

EXECUTIVES

President Edison Energy, Ronald L. Litzinger, age 59, $600,000 total compensation

President Ceo And Director, Pedro J. Pizarro, age 53, $836,782 total compensation

Vp And Cio Southern California Edison, Todd L. Inlander

Ceo Southern California Edison Company (sce), Kevin M. Payne, age 57, $421,171 total compensation

Svp Commercial Operations Edison Energy And President Edison Transmission Llc, Steven D. Eisenberg

Evp And Cfo, Maria Rigatti, age 54, $392,891 total compensation

Evp And General Counsel, Adam S. Umanoff, age 58, $548,391 total compensation

President Socore Energy, Rob Scheuermann

President Southern California Edison (sce), Ronald O. Nichols, age 64

Vice President Human Resources, Jenene Wilson

Vice President Of Information Technology, Jodi Collins

Vice President, Weston Williams

Vice President Regulatory Operations, Akbar Jazayeri

Senior Vice President Human Resources, John Kelly

Svp Government Affairs Edison International And Sce, Gaddi Vasquez

Vp And Corporate Controller, Aaron Moss

Senior Vice President, Drew Murphy

Vice President Local Public Affairs Sce, Christopher Thompson

Vice President Tax Edison International And Sce, Andrea Wood

Chairman, William P. (Bill) Sullivan, age 68

President Ceo And Director, Pedro J. Pizarro, age 53

Secretary, Beth Do

Auditors: PricewaterhouseCoopers LLP

LOCATIONS

HQ: Edison International
2244 Walnut Grove Avenue, P.O. Box 976, Rosemead, CA 91770
Phone: 626 302-2222
Web: www.edisoninvestor.com

PRODUCTS/OPERATIONS

Selected Subsidiaries
Edison Energy (solar power activities)
Southern California Edison Company (SCE electric utility)

COMPETITORS

AES	NV Energy
Avista	NextEra Energy
Berkshire Hathaway Energy	PG&E Corporation
CMS Energy	PacifiCorp
Calpine	Portland General Electric
Constellation Energy Group	Sacramento Municipal Utility
Electricité de France	Sempra Energy
Los Angeles Water and Power	

HISTORICAL FINANCIALS

Company Type: Public

Income Statement   FYE: December 31

	REVENUE ($ mil.)	NET INCOME ($ mil.)	NET PROFIT MARGIN	EMPLOYEES
12/17	12,320	565	4.6%	12,521
12/16	11,869	1,311	11.0%	12,390
12/15	11,524	1,020	8.9%	12,768
12/14	13,413	1,612	12.0%	13,690
12/13	12,581	915	7.3%	13,677
Annual Growth	(0.5%)	(11.4%)	—	(2.2%)

2017 Year-End Financials

Debt ratio: 27.61%
Return on equity: 4.77%
Cash ($ mil.): 1,091
Current ratio: 0.53
Long-term debt ($ mil.): 11,642

No. of shares (mil.): 325
Dividends
  Yield: 0.0%
  Payout: 129.8%
Market value ($ mil.): 20,604

	STOCK PRICE ($) FY Close	P/E High/Low	PER SHARE ($) Earnings	Dividends	Book Value
12/17	63.24	48 37	1.72	2.23	35.82
12/16	71.00	20 14	0.97	1.98	30.82
12/15	59.21	22 18	3.10	1.73	34.89
12/14	65.48	14 9	4.89	1.48	33.64
12/13	46.30	19 16	2.78	1.37	30.50
Annual Growth	8.1%	—	(11.3%)	13.0%	4.1%

Electronic Arts, Inc.

Electronic Arts (EA) puts gamers in action on the gridiron the pitch the battlefield and in outer space with its most popular games. Its leading titles are Madden NFL (American football) FIFA (football/soccer) and Star Wars (all of which are licensed) and its own Battlefield Mass Effect and The Sims. While EA generates increasing sales for games on mobile devices it still makes most of its revenue from games played on consoles from Sony and Microsoft and on personal computers. EA also provides online social games such as those licensed from Hasbro which include Monopoly. The company is moving into competitive gaming and eS ports with its Competitive Gaming Division.

Operations

Electronic Arts collects revenue from sales of its games on disc digital downloads (onto several platforms) subscription fees and in-game transactions.

Digital has become increasingly important for EA bringing in more than 65% of revenue. Packaged games account nearly 35% of revenue. Its digital products and services are delivered via Sony's PlayStation Network Microsoft's Xbox Store Apple's App Store and the Google Play store. About 40% of revenue comes from the sale of live services (extra content subscription advertising and other services).

Perennially popular games are FIFA Madden NFL Star Wars Titanfall Battlefield and Sim City. FIFA is a top seller generating some 11% of the company's total revenue.

Geographic Reach

California-based Electronic Arts operates development studios in North America and leases properties for R&D sales and administration in Europe and Asia. North America is its largest market accounting for more than 40% of sales. International customers supply the rest.

Sales and Marketing

As Electronic Arts' business becomes increasingly digital more of its products sales are generated through the internet. Such channels include Origin the company's direct-to-consumer platform digital downloads from third-party retailers and mobile applications.

EA sells directly to console makers Sony and Microsoft which account for more than 25% and more than 15% respectively of total revenue. The company also sells packaged games to retailers including mass merchants (Walmart) consumer electronics stores (Best Buy) and specialty game shops (GameStop). EA has partnerships with Ten-

cent Holdings Limited in China and Nexon Co. Ltd. to sell FIFA Online 3 in Korea.

Financial Performance

Electronic Arts? up-and-down revenue was up in 2018 (ended March) rising 6% to about $5.1 billion from 2017 results. Stronger sales of its FIFA franchise and first-person shooter franchise Mass Effect drove the increase. Digital rose about 20% reflecting players increased interest in digitally delivered games and engagement with EA?s live services. Driving the spike in Digital live game services net revenue rose 31% due in large part to increases in Battlefield 1 Premium and Ultimate Team services sales.

EA?s net income rose to $1 billion up 8% in 2018 from 2017 year-over-year. Higher overall revenue as well as a lower cost percentage for product and service revenue drove the increase.

Total cash on hand was $1.6 billion in in 2018. A $385 million sales increase in the sale of Ultimate Team and Mass Effect: Andromeda launched in 2017 increased cash flow from operations to $1.7 billion in 2018 from $1.4 billion in 2017.

Strategy

Electronic Arts has discovered the value of connection. By connecting players through its Ultimate Team mode and live services which allow players to interact in real time EA's player network has captured more of its customers? time and established lucrative revenue streams. The more players it attracts and keeps playing in its networks the more money the company brings in.

In fact the company derives a significant portion of total revenue (more than 20%) from its Ultimate Team game mode a feature that breathes new life and player interest in EA's FIFA Madden NFL and other long-running franchises . Live game services also provide additional revenue streams for EA that includes extra digital content subscriptions and advertising.

Aside from its player network EA is investing heavily in its technology infrastructure for both external-facing and internal systems. On the customer side the company is extending many of its console and PC games to digital platforms to increase EA's presence in the mobile game market which has captured more market share in recent years.

To improve internal operational efficiently EA has moved nearly all of its development activity to one game engine. This allows the company's developers to work across platforms which in turn accelerates development and streamlines technology operations.

Mergers and Acquisitions

In late 2017 Electronic Arts acquired independent game development studio Respawn Entertainment LLC creators of AAA shooter and action games including the critically acclaimed Titanfall? franchise.

Company Background

After four years with Apple video game pioneer Trip Hawkins left in 1982 raised $5 million and founded Electronic Arts to explore the entertainment potential of PCs. The company went public in 1989 and sales exploded the next year when EA began designing games for SEGA's Genesis video game system. Hawkins stepped down as CEO in 1991 and was replaced by president Larry Probst. (Hawkins remained chairman until 1994; he left to devote time to another game company 3DO which later went bankrupt.) The company bought game developer ORIGIN Systems in 1992 and began marketing its games in Japan with partner JVC. That year Sony introduced its PlayStation game system in the US.

EXECUTIVES

Evp And Cfo, Blake J. Jorgensen, age 58, $762,981 total compensation

Evp Business And Legal Affairs, Joel Linzner, age 67

Ceo, Andrew Wilson, age 43, $1,083,846 total compensation

Evp Ea Studios, Patrick S ¶derlund, age 44, $611,291 total compensation

Cto, Kenneth (Ken) Moss, age 52, $619,104 total compensation

Evp Global Publishing, Laura Miele, age 48

Svp General Counsel And Corporate Secretary, Jacob (Jake) Schatz

Chief People Officer, Mala Singh

Vice President Social Marketing And Media, Chris Thorne

Senior Vice President Of Corporate Affairs, Regina Heenan

Vice President, Erika Peterson

International Vice President Development Services, Jaime Gine

Vice President Finance Worldwide Controller, Eric Kelly

Vice President Online Marketing, Chip Lange

Vice President Marketing, Richard Williams

Vice President General Counsel And Corporate Secretary, Steve Bena

Vice President English Insurance Group, Bonnie Buhnerkempe

Vice President Legal Affairs, Kyuli Oh

Vice President, Vivian MacDonald

Svp Ea Mobile And Maxis, Samantha Ryan

Vice President Global Talent Acquisition, Jesse Connell

Executive Vice President Of Human Resources, Greg Graybill

Senior Vice President, Scott Forrest

Vice President Of Mrktng, Kip Morgan

Vice President Tax, Keith Kallweit

Vp Investor Relations, Rob Sison

Vice President, Paul Cairns

Vp People Mobile Maxis Bioware, Christina Sawyer

Executive Chairman, Lawrence F. (Larry) Probst, age 69

Board Member, Vivek Paul

Auditors: KPMG LLP

LOCATIONS

HQ: Electronic Arts, Inc.
209 Redwood Shores Parkway, Redwood City, CA 94065
Phone: 650 628-1500
Web: www.ea.com

2018 Sales

	$ mil.	% of total
North America	2,090	41
Rest of world	3,060	59
Total	**5,150**	**100**

PRODUCTS/OPERATIONS

2018 Sales

	% of total
Xbox One PlayStation 4 Switch	68
PC/Browser	16
Mobile	13
Other consoles	3
Others	1
Total	**100**

2018 Sales

	$ mil.	% of total
Product	2,586	50
Service & other	2,564	50
Total	**5,150**	**100**

Selected Game Titles by Studio & Label

BioWare
  Command & Conquer
  Dragon Age
  Mass Effect
  Star Wars: Battlefield
EA Games
  DICE (Sweden)
  Battlefield
  Criterion (UK)
  Burnout
  Need for Speed
  Visceral
  Dante's Inferno
  Dead Space
  Various EA studios
  Medal of Honor
  Third-party
  Crysis (Crytek)
  Half-Life (Valve)
  Rock Band (Harmonix)
Maxis
  The Sims
  Spore
EA SPORTS
  FIFA
  Madden NFL
  NASCAR
  NBA Street
  NHL
  Skate 3
  SSX
  Tiger Woods PGA Tour

COMPETITORS

Activision Blizzard
Atari
Capcom
DIMG
DeNA
Glu Mobile
King Digital Entertainment
Konami
Lucasfilm Entertainment
Microsoft
NCsoft
NEXON CO.LTD.
Namco Limited
Nintendo
Rovio Entertainment
SEGA
Square Enix
Take-Two
Tencent Holdings
Ubisoft
ZeniMax Media
Zynga

HISTORICAL FINANCIALS

Company Type: Public

Income Statement

FYE: March 31

	REVENUE ($ mil.)	NET INCOME ($ mil.)	NET PROFIT MARGIN	EMPLOYEES
03/18	5,150	1,043	20.3%	9,300
03/17	4,845	967	20.0%	8,800
03/16	4,396	1,156	26.3%	8,500
03/15	4,515	875	19.4%	8,400
03/14	3,575	8	0.2%	8,300
Annual Growth	**9.6%**	**237.9%**	**—**	**2.9%**

2018 Year-End Financials

Debt ratio: 11.56%
Return on equity: 24.10%
Cash ($ mil.): 4,258
Current ratio: 2.41
Long-term debt ($ mil.): 992
No. of shares (mil.): 306
Dividends
  Yield: —
  Payout: —
Market value ($ mil.): 37,144

	STOCK PRICE ($) FY Close	P/E High/Low	PER SHARE ($) Earnings	Dividends	Book Value
03/18	121.24	38 26	3.34	0.00	15.00
03/17	89.52	29 19	3.08	0.00	13.17
03/16	66.11	21 15	3.50	0.00	11.30
03/15	58.82	21 9	2.69	0.00	9.80
03/14	29.01	1008564	0.03	0.00	7.78
Annual Growth	**43.0%**	**—**	**—224.8%**	**—**	**17.8%**

EMC Insurance Group Inc.

EXECUTIVES

Svp And Cfo, Mark E. Reese, age 60, $265,557 total compensation

Evp Corporate Development, Ronald W. Jean, age 68, $488,402 total compensation

President Ceo And Director, Bruce G. Kelley, age 63, $845,070 total compensation

Evp And Coo, Kevin J. Hovick, age 63, $406,419 total compensation

Svp Productivity And Technology, Rodney D Hanson, $235,620 total compensation

Chairman, Stephen A. Crane

Auditors: Ernst & Young LLP

LOCATIONS

HQ: EMC Insurance Group Inc.
717 Mulberry Street, Des Moines, IA 50309
Phone: 515 345-2902
Web: www.emcins.com

2016 Premiums Written by Pool Participants by State

	% of total
Iowa	13
Kansas	8
Wisconsin	6
Nebraska	5
Minnesota	5
Michigan	5
Illinois	4
Texas	4
North Carolina	4
Other states	46
Total	**100**

PRODUCTS/OPERATIONS

2016 Revenues

	$ mil.	% of total
Premiums earned	592	92
Net investment income	47	7
Realized investment gains	4	1
Other income	1	0
Total	**645**	**100**

2016 Premiums Earned

	% of total
Property/casualty	77
Reinsurance	23
Total	**100**

Selected Products

Property and Casualty Insurance
  Commercial Lines
  Automobile
  Liability
  Property
  Workers' compensation
  Other
  Aircraft and marine
  Fidelity and surety bonds
  Theft protection
  Personal Lines
  Automobile
  Liability
  Property
Reinsurance

Selected Subsidiaries

Dakota Fire Insurance Company
EMC Reinsurance Company
EMCASCO Insurance Company
  EMC Underwriters LLC
Illinois EMASCO Insurance Company

AIG	Nationwide
Allstate	Progressive
American Family	Corporation
Insurance	SECURA
Auto-Owners Insurance	State Farm
Farmers Group	The Hartford
GEICO	White Mountains
Liberty Mutual	Insurance Group

HISTORICAL FINANCIALS

Company Type: Public

Income Statement
FYE: December 31

	ASSETS ($ mil.)	NET INCOME ($ mil.)	INCOME AS % OF ASSETS	EMPLOYEES
12/17	1,681	39	2.3%	—
12/16	1,588	46	2.9%	—
12/15	1,535	50	3.3%	—
12/14	1,497	29	2.0%	—
12/13	1,378	43	3.2%	—
Annual Growth	5.1%	(2.6%)		

2017 Year-End Financials

Debt ratio: —	No. of shares (mil.): 21
Return on equity: 6.78%	Dividends
Cash ($ mil.): 23	Yield: 0.0%
Current ratio: —	Payout: 46.2%
Long-term debt ($ mil.): —	Market value ($ mil.): 616

	STOCK PRICE ($) FY Close	P/E High/Low	PER SHARE ($) Earnings	Dividends	Book Value
12/17	28.69	17 14	1.84	0.85	28.14
12/16	30.01	14 10	2.20	0.78	26.07
12/15	25.30	15 9	2.43	0.69	25.26
12/14	35.46	24 18	1.49	0.63	24.72
12/13	30.62	15 11	2.22	0.57	22.81
Annual Growth	(1.6%)	— —	(4.6%)	10.3%	5.4%

EMCOR Group, Inc.

Electrical and mechanical construction specialist EMCOR Group is one of the world's largest specialty construction firms. It designs installs operates and maintains complex mechanical and electrical systems. These include systems for power generation and distribution lighting water and wastewater treatment voice and data communications fire protection plumbing and heating ventilation and air-conditioning (HVAC). EMCOR also provides facilities services including management and maintenance support. Through some 75 subsidiaries and joint ventures the company serves a range of commercial industrial institutional and utility customers.

Operations

EMCOR Group operates four main business segments based on service type that together account for 96% of company revenue: Mechanical Construction and Facilities; Electrical Construction and Facilities; Building Services; and Industrial Services. It also operates a building services business in the UK accounting for the remaining 4%.

The Mechanical Construction and Facilities division generates some 40% of total sales. It makes systems for central air refrigeration and clean-room process ventilation; fire protection; plumbing and piping; controls and filtration; water and wastewater treatment and central plant heating and cooling; cranes and rigging; and steel-related work.

EMCOR's Electrical Construction and Facilities division (around 25% of sales) handles and installs systems for electrical power; on-premise electrical and lighting systems; low-voltage systems such as fire alarm security and process control; voice and data communication; roadway and transit lighting; and fiber optic lines.

The US Building Services business (around 25% of revenue) offers operation maintenance and services for everything from a company's electrical and mechanical systems for commercial and government sites to janitorial services landscaping and snow removal services.

The Industrial Services segment (10% of sales) provides industrial and maintenance services such as refinery turnaround planning and engineering; specialty welding; overhaul and maintenance; and refinery and petrochemical plant maintenance and services.

The UK Building Services operation supports and maintains customers' facilities including commercial and government sites in the UK.

Geographic Reach

More than 95% of Norwalk Connecticut-based EMCOR's revenue comes from work performed in the US. The remainder is derived from the UK.

Sales and Marketing

Some of EMCOR's largest institutional industrial and commercial projects include water treatment plants hospitals correctional facilities research labs manufacturing plants oil refineries data centers hotels shopping malls and office buildings.

Large projects (those larger than $10 million) account for around 30% of total sales. These are often multi-year projects.

Projects of less than $10.0 million account for 70% of sales. These smaller value projects are often one-off in nature such as a modification or construction to serve a specific purpose and are less dependent on the wider construction market.

Financial Performance

EMCOR's revenue and profits have grown steadily in recent years.

After an impressive 2016 in fiscal 2017 EMCOR's sales growth slowed to 2% although total sales of $7.7 billion was still a company record.

Growth was uneven across EMCOR's operating units as $320 million growth in US mechanical construction and $125 million growth in electrical construction was offset by contractions in US building services and US industrial services. The US mechanical construction segment was boosted by higher revenue from healthcare commercial and hospitality construction projects as well as contributions from acquired businesses. In EMCOR's UK business a $14.4 million revenue increase included an unfavorable exchange rate impact of $15.9 million as the Brexit vote dragged on the pound sterling.

Net income grew 25% to $227.2 million largely due to a tax benefit from the 2017 US Tax Cuts and Jobs Act as well as higher revenue.

Cash from operations increased 39% to $366.1 million due to higher net income and improved cash from accounts payable.

Strategy

EMCOR has grown by diversifying its services and expanding geographically within the US. With the US economy on the upswing EMCOR is reaping the benefits of being a more efficient operator. The company has continued its longstanding practice of building out its portfolio of services through acquisitions.Recently this has included three small purchases in 2017 and a larger purchase in 2016.

Mergers and Acquisitions

In 2017 EMCOR made three bolt-on acquisitions: one company that provides fire protection and alarms in the Southern region of the US; one that provides millwright services for manufacturers across the US; and one that offers mobile mechanical services in the Western US. The first two were combined into EMCOR's US mechanical construction and facilities services segment and the third into its US building services segment.

In 2016 EMCOR bought Ardent Services and subsidiary Rabalais Constructors providers of electrical and instrumentation services to the energy infrastructure market in North America for $205 million. Ardent is active in the US industrial and refinery electrical and instrumentation service business. It includes refiners petrochemical companies midstream operators integrated oil companies and other energy operators.

HISTORY

EMCOR's forerunner Jamaica Water Supply Co. was incorporated in 1887 to supply water to some residents of Queens and Nassau Counties in New York. In 1902 it bought Jamaica Township Water Co. and by 1906 it was generating revenue — reaching $1.6 million by 1932. Over the next 35 years the company kept pace with the population of its service area.

In 1966 the enterprise was acquired by Jamaica Water and Utilities which then bought Sea Cliff Water Co. In 1969 and 1970 it acquired Welsbach (electrical contractors) and A to Z Equipment (construction trailer suppliers); it briefly changed its name in 1974 to Welsbach Corp. before becoming Jamaica Water Properties in 1976.

Diversification proved unprofitable however and in 1977 Martin Dwyer and his son Andrew took over the management of the struggling firm. Despite posting million-dollar losses in 1979 it was profitable by 1980.

The Dwyers acquired companies in the electrical and mechanical contracting security telecommunications computer energy and environmental businesses. In 1985 Andrew Dwyer became president and the firm changed its name the next year to JWP.

Between 1986 and 1990 JWP acquired more than a dozen companies including Extel (1986) Gibson Electric (1987) Dynalectric (1988) Drake & Scull (1989) NEECO and Compumat (1990) and Comstock Canada (1990).

In 1991 JWP capped its strategy of buying up US computer systems resellers by acquiring Businessland. It then bought French microelectronics distributor SIVEA. Later that year JWP bought a 34% stake in Resource Recycling Technologies (a solid-waste recycler).

JWP's shopping spree extended the firm's reach but the company began to struggle when several sectors turned sour. A price war in the information services business and a weak construction market led to a loss of more than $600 million in 1992. That year president David Sokol resigned after questioning JWP's accounting practices. He turned over to the SEC a report that claimed inflated profits.

Cutting itself to about half its former size the company sold JWP Information Services in 1993. (JWP Information Services later became ENTEX Information Services which was acquired by Siemens in 2000.) However JWP continued to struggle and in early 1994 it filed for bankruptcy. Emerging from Chapter 11 protection in December 1994 the reorganized company took the name EMCOR. That year Frank MacInnis former CEO of electrical contractor Comstock Group stepped in to lead EMCOR.

In 1995 the SEC using Sokol's information charged several former JWP executives with accounting fraud claiming they had overstated profits to boost the value of their company stock and their bonuses. EMCOR later reached a non-monetary settlement with the SEC. The company sold Jamaica Water Supply and Sea Cliff in 1996; it also achieved profitability that year.

Focusing on external growth EMCOR acquired a number of firms in 1998 and 1999 including Marelich Mechanical Co. and Mesa Energy Systems BALCO Inc. and the Poole & Kent group of mechanical contracting companies based in Baltimore and Miami. To meet increased demands for facilities services in 2000 EMCOR consolidated the operations of three of its mechanical contractors (BALCO J.C. Higgins and Tucker Mechanical) into one company EMCOR Services which operates in New England.

That year about six years after emerging from bankruptcy EMCOR began trading on the New York Stock Exchange. In 2002 EMCOR bought 19 subsidiaries from its financially troubled rival Comfort Systems USA including its largest unit Shambaugh & Son. Later that year it expanded its facilities services operations with the acquisition of Consolidated Engi

EXECUTIVES

Evp And Cfo, Mark A. Pompa, age 54, $670,000 total compensation
Evp Shared Services, R. Kevin Matz, age 60, $530,000 total compensation
Ceo Emcor Uk, Keith Chanter, age 59
President Ceo And Director, Anthony J. (Tony) Guzzi, age 53, $1,071,000 total compensation
Vp Marketing And Communications, Mava K. Heffler
President And Ceo Emcor Construction Services, Michael J. (Mike) Parry, age 69
President And Ceo Emcor Building Services, Michael P. (Mike) Bordes
President And Ceo Emcor Industrial Services And Ohmstede, Bill Reid
Executive Vice President, Shelly Cammaker
Vice President Of Sales And Marketing Emcor Group Inc, Jeff Budzinski
Vice President Information Systems And Technology, Peter Baker
Vice President Massachusetts Operations, Gary Picco
Vice President Field Operations, Johnathan Doessel
Vice President, Charlie Hadsell
Vice President And Controller, William Feher
Vice President Facility Services, Anthony Scalise
Chairman, Stephen W. Bershad, age 76
President Ceo And Director, Anthony J. (Tony) Guzzi, age 53
Auditors: Ernst & Young LLP

LOCATIONS

HQ: EMCOR Group, Inc.
301 Merritt Seven, Norwalk, CT 06851-1092
Phone: 203 849-7800
Web: www.emcorgroup.com

PRODUCTS/OPERATIONS

Selected Services
EMCOR Construction Services
Electrical Construction
Mechanical Construction
Fire Protection
EMCOR Building Services
EMCOR Facilities Services
EMCOR Mechanical Services
EMCOR Government Services
EMCOR Energy Services
Customer Solutions Centers
EMCOR Industrial Services
Turnarounds
Heat Exchangers
Towers
Refractory

2017 Sales

	% of total
United States mechanical construction and facilities services	39
United States building services	23
United States electrical construction and facilities services	24
United States industrial services	10
Less intersegment revenues	0
United Kingdom building services	4
Total	**100**

Selected Operations

Mechanical and Electrical Construction
  Building plant and lighting systems
  Data communications systems
  Electrical power distribution systems
  Energy recovery
  Heating ventilation and air-conditioning (HVAC) systems
  Lighting systems
  Low-voltage systems (alarm security communications)
  Piping and plumbing systems
  Refrigeration systems
  Voice communications systems
Facilities Services
  Facilities management
  Installation and support for building systems
  Mobile maintenance and service
  Program development and management for energy systems
  Remote monitoring
  Site-based operations and maintenance
  Small modification and retrofit projects
  Technical consulting and diagnostic services

Selected Subsidiaries

Dyn Specialty Contracting Inc.
EMCOR Construction Services Inc.
EMCOR-CSI Holding Co.
EMCOR Facilities Services Inc.
EMCOR Group (UK) plc
EMCOR International Inc.
EMCOR (UK) Limited
EMCOR Mechanical/Electrical Services (East) Inc.
  EMCOR (UK) Limited
FR X Ohmstede Acquisitions Co.
MES Holdings Corporation

COMPETITORS

ABM Industries	Johnson Controls Power
AECOM	Solutions
APi Group	Jones Lang LaSalle
ARAMARK	Limbach Facility
CBRE Group	Services
Comfort Systems USA	MYR Group
Cushman & Wakefield	MasTec
Dycom	Quanta Services
Fluor	Schneider Electric
Hoffman Corporation	Siemens AG
Honeywell	Sodexo USA
International	SteelFab
IES Holdings	Trane Inc.
ISS GROUP LIMITED	Tutor Perini
Jacobs Technology	

HISTORICAL FINANCIALS

Company Type: Public

Income Statement

FYE: December 31

	REVENUE ($ mil.)	NET INCOME ($ mil.)	NET PROFIT MARGIN	EMPLOYEES
12/17	7,687	227	3.0%	32,000
12/16	7,551	181	2.4%	31,000
12/15	6,718	172	2.6%	29,000
12/14	6,424	168	2.6%	27,000
12/13	6,417	123	1.9%	27,000
Annual Growth	**4.6%**	**16.4%**	**—**	**4.3%**

2017 Year-End Financials

Debt ratio: 7.82%
Return on equity: 14.15%
Cash ($ mil.): 467
Current ratio: 1.38
Long-term debt ($ mil.): 294
No. of shares (mil.): 58
Dividends
  Yield: 0.0%
  Payout: 8.3%
Market value ($ mil.): 4,807

	STOCK PRICE ($) FY Close	P/E High/Low	PER SHARE ($) Earnings	Dividends	Book Value
12/17	81.75	22 16	3.82	0.32	28.46
12/16	70.76	24 14	2.97	0.32	25.64
12/15	48.04	19 15	2.72	0.32	24.18
12/14	44.49	19 15	2.52	0.32	22.48
12/13	42.44	24 19	1.82	0.49	21.92
Annual Growth	**17.8%**	**— —**	**20.4%**	**(10.1%)**	**6.7%**

Emerson Electric Co.

Emerson Electric goes with the flow and measures the flow as it goes. The company makes a range of electrical electromechanical and electronic products used to control gases liquids and electricity. Emerson also makes measurement and analytical instruments that provide data about the physical properties of gases and liquids. Want another example of an Emerson product? Look in your kitchen sink. Its InSinkErator unit is a maker of food waste disposers and hot water dispensers. Emerson operates more than 210 manufacturing locations with about 140 outside of the US. International markets make up over 50% of Emerson's sales.

Operations
Emerson Electric operates within two segments: Automation Solutions and Commercial & Residential Solutions.

Automation Solutions about two thirds of sales is made up of several product divisions. Measurement & Analytical Instrumentation makes valves actuators and regulators. Industrial Solutions produces things like fluid power and control mechanisms electrical distribution equipment and materials joining products. Process Control Systems & Solutions provides digital systems that control plant processes by communicating with and adjusting the “intelligent” plant devices that Emerson makes.

The Commercial & Residential Solutions business about a third of revenue consists of the Climate Technologies and Tools & Home Products segments. This business provides products that promote energy efficiency enhance household and commercial comfort and protect food quality and sustainability through heating air conditioning and refrigeration technology.

Across both segments the company has dozens of brand names including ASCO Aventics Bettis DeltaV Fisher Fusite InSinkErator Keystone Klauke KTM RIDGID and TopWorx.

Geographic Reach
The US and Canada form Emerson Electric's largest market representing almost half its sales. Asia generates nearly 25% of its revenue while Europe accounts for more than 15%. Other target markets include the Middle East and Africa region and Latin America splitting the remaining revenue. The company has over 210 manufacturing locations worldwide.

Sales and Marketing
Emerson Electric sells its products through a variety of distribution channels including its direct sales force a network of independent sales representatives and distributors to end-users and original equipment manufacturers (OEMs). Emerson serves industries such as oil and gas pulp and paper chemicals power food and beverage and life sciences.

Financial Performance

After two years of declines Emerson Electric's revenue rose 5% to $15.3 billion in fiscal 2017 (ended September) and another 14% to $17.4 billion in 2018. Most of the increase in 2018 came from higher sales in the Automation Solutions segment. About 5% is attributed to sales from acquisitions. Growth was led by the US (with a 9% increase to $7.9 billion) and strong performance in Asia specifically China.

Although cost of sales and expenses rose slightly net income jumped 15% to $2.2 billion in fiscal 2018 (the highest level in the past five years) primarily due to increased revenue.

Cash at the end of fiscal 2018 was $1.1 billion a decrease of $2.0 billion from the prior year. Cash from operations contributed $2.9 billion to the coffers while investing activities used $2.7 billion mainly for acquisitions. Financing activities used another $2.1 billion for dividends to stockholders and the company's stock repurchase program.

Strategy

Emerson has a history of achieving growth through acquisitions and by divesting underperforming non-core units to streamline its operations. Focusing on its two core segments—Automation Solutions and Commercial & Residential Solutions—Emerson is on a buying spree of complementary businesses having made about seven acquisitions in 2018 alone for a total of $2.2 billion. Geographically the company aims to expand its presence in Europe with a focus on key markets like Germany.

In Automation Solutions Emerson continues to enhance its industrial Internet of Things (IoT) technologies such as smart instrumentation and valves cloud applications and connected services. Its Plantweb digital ecosystem includes an installed base of 32000 wireless networks and 26000 asset management systems. The company plans to add new technologies to its portfolio such as location awareness to enhance safety and digital technologies to improve processes and reliability.

The Commercial & Residential Solutions segment is focused on developing technologies for energy and cost efficiencies for its customers. The company has invested in a $100 million state-of-the-art heating and cooling headquarters in Sidney Ohio and $18 million in a research center in Suzhou China. In Suzhou Emerson is developing technologies and compressors for next-generation refrigerants (the segment recently introduced Sensi Hydro a residential variable water volume heating and air conditioning system in China). This segment is also addressing "cold-as-a-service" food-delivery trends by developing technologies that monitor temperatures across the supply chain (or what it refers to as the cold chain) helping its customers comply with ever increasing regulatory standards.

Mergers and Acquisitions

Emerson Electric made several acquisitions in 2018 starting with ProSys which supplies software and services for production and safety for the chemical oil and gas pulp and paper and refining industries. The purchase of Textron's Tools & Test business for $810 million adds diagnostics test and measurement instruments to its arsenal and will be integrated with Emerson's Ridge Tool Company. Aventics acquired for €527 million expands Emerson's reach in the fluid automation market (particularly in Europe) with its smart pneumatics technologies for machine and factory automation. Emerson also acquired GE's Intelligent Platforms division and its programmable logic controller (PLC) technologies adding machine control capabilities for applications in industries such as metals and mining life sciences food and beverage and packing.

Also in 2018 Emerson acquired Ireland-based HTE Engineering Services a producer of heat stak-

ing equipment used to join plastic parts. HTE will operate within Emerson's Assembly Technologies business adding joining applications in market segments such as medical equipment packaging and automotive assembly. Its last acquisition for the year was Advanced Engineering Valves (A.E. Valves) a maker of valve technology that helps LNG customers operate more efficiently realizing Emerson's goal of being the premier supplier of final control solutions for the LNG industry.

Emerson also made multiple acquisitions in 2017 including Pentair's Valves & Controls business for $3.15 billion—the largest in its history. The complementary acquisition establishes Emerson's global presence in control isolation pressure relief valves and actuation as part of a larger strategy to build a broader automation product portfolio.

HISTORY

Emerson Electric was founded in 1890 in St. Louis by brothers Alexander and Charles Meston inventors who developed uses for the alternating-current electric motor which was new at the time. The company was named after former Missouri judge and US marshal John Emerson who financed the enterprise and became its first president. Emerson's best-known product was an electric fan introduced in 1892. Between 1910 and 1920 the company helped develop the first forced-air circulating systems.

EXECUTIVES

Svp And Cto, Randall D. Ledford, age 69
Chairman And Ceo, David N. Farr, age 63, $1,300,000 total compensation
Evp And Coo, Edgar Purvis
Evp Emerson Appliance Solutions, James J. (Jim) Lindemann, age 62
Evp Emerson Storage Solutions & Professional Tools, Patrick J. (Pat) Sly
Evp And Cfo, Frank J. Dellaquila, age 60, $620,000 total compensation
President, Edward L. Monser, age 67, $720,000 total compensation
Vp Planning, Mark J. Bulanda
Chairman Automated Solutions, Steven A. (Steve) Sonnenberg, age 66
Evp And Coo, Steve J. Pelch
Vp Profit Planning, Robert T. (Bob) Sharp
Evp; Group Business Leader Automated Solutions, Michael H. Train
Vice President Global Security, Tony Vermillion
Vice President Sales North America, Tim Erman
Vice President Product Safety, Steve Bryant
National Sales Manager, Dan Myers
Vice President Human Resources Americas, Tom Sheehan
Vice President Business Development, Matthew Fox
Vice President, Meiyin Lim
Vice President Sales And Services Rosemount Measurement And Analytical, Andrew White
Vice President Americas, John Turner
Vice President Global Sales And Marketing, Bruce Penning
Vice President Global Human Resources, Timothy M Volk
Vice President Operations, Kent Schultz
Vice President And General Manager Magnetic And Vortex Flowmeters, Kelly Klein
National Account Manager, Traci Olmstead
Senior Vice President Materials And Logistics, Larry Lawrence
Vice President Global Supply Chain, Ken Poczekaj
Senior Vice President Information Technology Servicing Operations, Ana Victoria
Vice President Engineering, Robert Jantz

Vice President And Chief Information Officer, Deb Miller
Vice President Global Logistics, Greg Fromknecht
Vice President It Emerson Process Management, Lisa Nelson
National Accounts Manager, Al Schuler
Senior Vice President Of Marketing, Dave Beckmann
Vice President, Michael Keating
Vice President And General Manager, Demetrios Georgacopoulos
Vice President Technology Development, Chuck Ketterer
Vice President And General Management In Brazil, Rafael Jaramillo
Vice President Controller And Chief Accounting Officer, Rick Schlueter
Vice President Global Operations, Dan Ackermann
National Account Manager, Monica Huminski
Vp Flow Europe, Stephane Tritz
Vice President Technology, Bill Butler
Svp Secretary And General Counsel, Sara Yang Bosco
Executive Vice President Fisher Division, Mike Mason
Vice President Of Sales And Marketing, Brian Sponsler
Vice President Of Engineering, Jon Piasecki
Chairman And Ceo, David N. Farr, age 63
Regional Treasurer, Martin Benedict Fernandez
Secretary Iii Emerson Process Management, Susan Amberson
Board Member, Joshua Bolten
Auditors: KPMG LLP

LOCATIONS

HQ: Emerson Electric Co.
8000 W Florissant Avenue, P.O. Box 4100, St. Louis, MO 63136
Phone: 314 553-2000
Web: www.emerson.com

2018 Sales

	$ mil.	% of total
United States and Canada	8,620	49
Asia	3,936	23
Europe	2,898	17
Middle East/Africa	1,105	6
Latin America	849	5
Total	**17,408**	**100**

PRODUCTS/OPERATIONS

2018 Sales

	$mil.	% of total
Automation Solutions		
Valves actuators and regulators	3769	
Measurement and analytical instrumentation	3604	
Process control systems and solutions	2121	
Industrial solutions	1947	
Total	11,441	66
Commercial & Residential Solutions		
Climate technologies	4454	
Tools and home products	1528	
Total	5,982	34
Eliminations	(15)	-
Total	**17,408**	**100**

PRODUCTS

Automation Solutions
Density & Viscosity Measurement
Flame & Gas Detection
Flow Measurement
Gas Analysis
Level Measurement
Liquid Analysis
Marine Measurement & Analytical
Pipeline Integrity
Pressure
Tank Gauging System
Temperature Measurement
Wireless Acoustic & Discrete
Wireless Infrastructure

Commercial & Residential Solutions
Ceiling Fans & Lighting
Construction & Plumbing Tools
Food Waste Disposers
Grind2Energy
Heating & Air Conditioning
Home Repair & Maintenance
Indoor Outdoor Heating Cables
Instant Hot Water Dispensers
Monitoring Systems & Facility Control
Refrigeration
Sensing & Protection Devices
Thermostats
Vacuum Equipment
Industries
AUTOMATION SOLUTIONS INDUSTRIES
Automotive
Chemical
Downstream Hydrocarbons
Food & Beverage
Industrial Energy & Onsite Utilities
Life Sciences & Medical
Marine
Mining Minerals & Metals
Oil & Gas
Packaging
Power Generation
Pulp & Paper
Water & Wastewater
COMMERCIAL & RESIDENTIAL SOLUTIONS
Commercial Buildings & Construction
Energy & Utilities
Facility Management & Maintenance
Food Retail
Food Service & Hospitality
Residential Construction & Home Improvement
Transportation

Selected Brands

AMS Suite
Baumann
Bettis
Bristol
CSI
Emerson Process Management

COMPETITORS

ABB
Danaher
Honeywell
 International
Mitsubishi Electric
OMRON

Rockwell Automation
Rolls-Royce
Siemens AG
TE Connectivity
United Technologies
Yokogawa Electric

HISTORICAL FINANCIALS

Company Type: Public

Income Statement   FYE: September 30

	REVENUE ($ mil.)	NET INCOME ($ mil.)	NET PROFIT MARGIN	EMPLOYEES
09/18	17,408	2,203	12.7%	87,500
09/17	15,264	1,518	9.9%	76,500
09/16	14,522	1,635	11.3%	103,500
09/15	22,304	2,710	12.2%	110,800
09/14	24,537	2,147	8.8%	115,100
Annual Growth	(8.2%)	0.6%	—	(6.6%)

2018 Year-End Financials

Debt ratio: 23.34%
Return on equity: 24.94%
Cash ($ mil.): 1,093
Current ratio: 1.07
Long-term debt ($ mil.): 3,137

No. of shares (mil.): 629
Dividends
  Yield: 0.0%
  Payout: 56.0%
Market value ($ mil.): 48,184

	STOCK PRICE ($) FY Close	P/E High/Low	PER SHARE ($) Earnings	Dividends	Book Value
09/18	76.58	23 17	3.46	1.94	14.22
09/17	62.84	27 21	2.35	1.92	13.59
09/16	54.51	22 17	2.52	1.90	11.77
09/15	44.17	16 11	3.99	1.88	12.34
09/14	62.58	23 20	3.03	1.72	14.53
Annual Growth	5.2%	— —	3.4%	3.1%	(0.5%)

Employers Holdings Inc

Because workers' compensation is nothing to gamble with small business owners can turn to Employers Holdings. The Reno-based holding company provides workers' compensation services including claims management loss prevention consulting and care management to small businesses in low and medium hazard industries including retailers and restaurants. The company provides workers' compensation through its Employer Insurance Company of Nevada (EICN) and Employers Compensation Insurance Company. Employers Holdings also operates Employers Assurance and Employers Preferred Insurance Company both of which also offer workers' compensation.

Geographic Reach

While Employers Holdings distributes its products in more than 35 states and the District of Columbia more than half of its premiums come from California.

Sales and Marketing

Employers Holdings uses a network of more than 5100 independent agencies to brings its wares to the public; these agencies bring in about three-fourths of the company's in-force premiums. The company also markets its products through brokers and local trade groups and associations. Furthermore it markets its products along with ADP's payroll services in several states. Employers Holdings is forging additional distribution partners in other markets.

Financial Performance

Employers Holdings' revenue has been relatively stable for the past few years. In fiscal 2016 revenue rose 4% to $779.8 million. That change was primarily driven by gains on investments as premiums earned saw just a modest increase.

The higher revenue and a drop in losses and loss adjustments led to higher profits that year. Employers Holdings' net income which has been recovering since taking a bit of a dip in 2013 increased 13% to $106.7 million in 2016. This in turn led to a 5% increase in operating cash flow which totaled $122.8 million.

Strategy

Employers Holdings targets small businesses as there are fewer competitors in that space. The firm operates in low-to-medium hazard industries to keep its losses under control. Its top sectors served include restaurants the clerical side of physician offices automobile service or repair centers and colleges (professional employees and clerical). The company also spreads its risk around and is not dependent upon any one customer for a significant portion of its income.Similarly although California is the firm's largest market it focuses on expanding geographically to diversify its revenue stream.

Additionally Employer Holdings is investing in its IT infrastructure to improve customer service increase efficiency and expand its operating capacity.

EXECUTIVES

President And Ceo, Douglas D. Dirks, $927,569 total compensation

Evp Chief Legal Officer And General Counsel, Lenard T. Ormsby, $485,708 total compensation

Evp Corporate And Public Affairs, Ann W. Nelson, $354,501 total compensation

Svp And Chief Administrative Officer Eicn And Ecic, John P. Nelson, $334,391 total compensation

Evp And Coo, Stephen V. Festa, $488,299 total compensation

Evp And Cio, Tracey L. Berg

Svp And Chief Underwriting Officer, Lawrence S. (Larry) Rogers

Evp And Cfo, Michael S. Paquette, age 55

Vice President Corporate Marketing, Ty Vukelich

Vice President Government And Regulatory Affairs, Jim Werbeckes

Vice President Of Treasury And Investments, Matthew Hendricksen

Vice President Sales East Region, Martha Collins

Vice President, Sam King

Vice President, James Cleymaet

Chairman, Michael D. (Mike) Rumbolz, age 65

Auditors: Ernst & Young LLP

LOCATIONS

HQ: Employers Holdings Inc
10375 Professional Circle, Reno, NV 89521
Phone: 888 682-6671

2015 Premiums In-force

	% of total
California	57
others	43
Total	**100**

PRODUCTS/OPERATIONS

2015 Sales

	$ mil.	% of total
Net premiums earned	690	91
Net investment income	72	9
Realized losses on investments	(10.7)	—
Other income	0	-
Total	**752**	**100**

Selected Products & Services

Claims Management
Fraud Prevention
Loss Control
Loss Run Report
Managed Care Services
PrecisePay (Pay-As-You-Go)
Premium Audit
Return to Work Program
Safety Promotion Programs
Workers' Compensation Insurance

Selected Subsidiaries

AmSERV Inc.
EIG Services Inc.
Elite Insurance Services Inc.
Employers Assurance Company
Employers Compensation Insurance Company
Employers Group Inc.
Employers Insurance Company of Nevada
Employers Occupational Health Inc.
Employers Preferred Insurance Company
Pinnacle Benefits Inc.

COMPETITORS

AMERISAFE
AmTrust Financial
Baldwin & Lyons
Berkshire Hathaway
CNA Financial
Donegal
EMC Insurance
Liberty Mutual
Meadowbrook Insurance
Navigators
ProAssurance
RLI

Republic Indemnity
Safety Insurance
SeaBright Insurance
Selective Insurance
State Auto Financial
State Compensation
 Insurance Fund
The Hartford
TowerGroup
Travelers Companies
United Fire
Zurich Insurance Group

HISTORICAL FINANCIALS

Company Type: Public

Income Statement

FYE: December 31

	ASSETS ($ mil.)	NET INCOME ($ mil.)	INCOME AS % OF ASSETS	EMPLOYEES
12/17	3,840	101	2.6%	672
12/16	3,773	106	2.8%	693
12/15	3,755	94	2.5%	716
12/14	3,769	100	2.7%	709
12/13	3,643	63	1.8%	723
Annual Growth	1.3%	12.2%	—	(1.8%)

2017 Year-End Financials

Debt ratio: 0.52%	No. of shares (mil.): 32
Return on equity: 11.32%	Dividends
Cash ($ mil.): 73	Yield: 0.0%
Current ratio: —	Payout: 19.6%
Long-term debt ($ mil.): —	Market value ($ mil.): 1,447

	STOCK PRICE ($) FY Close	P/E High/Low		PER SHARE ($) Earnings	Dividends	Book Value
12/17	44.40	16	12	3.06	0.60	29.07
12/16	39.60	12	7	3.24	0.36	26.16
12/15	27.30	10	7	2.90	0.24	23.62
12/14	23.51	10	6	3.14	0.24	21.81
12/13	31.65	16	10	2.00	0.24	18.17
Annual Growth	8.8%	—	—	11.2%	25.7%	12.5%

Energy Transfer LP

Energy Transfer Equity transfers natural gas and other energy resources through its massive network of US-based pipelines. The company?s operations occur primarily through subsidiaries Energy Transfer Partners (ETP) and Sunoco LP although it has interests in a number of LPs and other subsidiaries. Structured as a Master Limited Partnership it owns 71000 miles of pipelines that transport natural gas natural gas liquids refined products and crude oil across more than 35 US states. It also owns and operates associated terminalling storage and fractionation facilities. Sunoco supplies nearly 8 billion gallons of fuel to consumer and wholesale customers. An effort to purchase Tulsa-based Williams Companies in a $37.7 billion deal fell through in 2016.

Operations

Energy Transfer Equity (ETE) reports financial results according to its major investments in Energy Transfer Partners Sunoco LP and Lake Charles LNG.

Its largest segment is Energy Transfer Partners. ETP gathers processes compresses treats and transports natural gas. These midstream services occur in some of the most prolific shale plays in the US such as Eagle Ford Marcellus Utica Bone Spring and Avalon. ETP is one of the largest movers of natural gas in the country and does so through its 71000 miles of pipeline. It also possesses a controlling interest in a limited partnership that owns and operates a logistics business consisting of crude oil natural gas liquids (NGLs) and refined products pipelines. ETP generates roughly 60% of revenue.

Its investment in Sunoco LP brings in some 40% of revenue. Sunoco LP operates almost 50000 gas stations and convenience stores in the Eastern US. It produces revenue through fuel sales which typically top 2.5 billion gallons in a given year. It generates a few billion dollars from merchandise sales in its gas station convenience stores. Sunoco sells about 5 billion gallons of fuel wholesale through nearly 8000 dealers distributors and commercials customers. In 2017 this segment?s pipeline and product terminals were merged into the ETP entity.

Lake Charles LNG generates a small amount of total revenue by storing and re-gasifying natural gas in its facility in Lake Charles LA.

Geographic Reach

Dallas TX is home to Energy Transfer Equity?s and Energy Transfer Partners? headquarters. ETP along with the recently merged pipeline and terminal assets of Sunoco have significant operations in Texas Louisiana Oklahoma West Virginia Pennsylvania and New York. Its pipelines reach as far as North Dakota Arizona and Idaho.

The Sunoco LP subsidiary is headquartered in Philadelphia PA and operates nearly 5000 gas stations in 26 states mostly in the Eastern US and Texas.

Sales and Marketing

Energy Transfer Equity via Energy Transfer Partners sells natural gas to utilities industrial consumers other marketers and pipeline companies. Its Sunoco segment sells gasoline and diesel in addition to a broad mix of merchandise such as groceries fast foods and beverages at its convenience stores. A sizable portion of Sunoco?s gasoline and diesel sales are to wholesale customers.

Financial Performance

In recent years Energy Transfer Equity?s revenue growth has been excellent rising from a $5.4 billion low in 2009 to a $55.7 billion peak in 2014 (driven by the Sunoco acquisition) before sliding back to $37.5 billion in 2016. Net income was rangebound between 2010 and 2013 ($200 million - $300 million) before spiking to $1.2 billion in 2015 and then falling in 2016.

In 2016 revenue decreased 11% to $37.5 billion due to a 20% fall in crude oil sales and lower refined product sales both partially offset by higher NGL sales.

Net income in 2016 fell 17% to $983 million the result aided by a $954 million windfall from a noncontrolling interest adjustment. Without the adjustment net income from operations came in at a paltry $41 a 96% plummet from the prior year. Although in dollar terms operating expenses fell when viewed as a percent of revenue the expenses did not fall in line with revenue and therefore had a negative effect on earnings. Included in expenses was a goodwill impairment loss exceeding $1.0 billion.

Cash available at the end of 2016 was $483 million a decrease of $123 million from 2015. Large uses of cash came from $8.0 billion of capital expenditures and a $1.6 billion outlay for acquisitions. Operations contributed $3.4 billion to cash and financing activities added almost $6.0 billion mainly through issuance of debt and notes.

Strategy

Energy Transfer Equity has been busy in recent years. Its strategy is playing out through partnership restructuring divestitures capital raises and the build out of several midstream projects.

Announced in 2016 and closed in early 2017 ETE orchestrated a merger of its two primary subsidiaries ? Energy Transfer Partners and the midstream assets of its Sunoco LP ? into a surviving entity that kept the Energy Transfer Partners name. The deal cleans up its partnership structure and is anticipated to help with credit ratings going forward. Operational synergies are expected to be minimal.

Sunoco LP has been on an acquisition spree since 2014 spending over $700 million between then and mid-2017. Its retail acquisitions brought on board more than 120 new gas stations from previous owners Pico Petroleum Aziz Quick Stops Valentine Stores Denny Oil Aloha Petroleum among others. It purchased a wholesaler in the US Northeast and obtained midstream assets in Alabama Hawaii and Texas.

To help raise capital for its acquisitions and project expenses ETE sold in late 2017 half of its interests in ET Rover Pipeline to Blackstone Energy Partners for approximately $1.6 billion. ETE through its ETP subsidiary will remain operator of the Marcellus and Utica shale Rover Pipeline. ETE sold off partial interests in its Bakken holdings in late 2016 for $2 billion. ETE also issued perpetual preferred stock in late 2017 raising $1.5 billion.

ETE is building out its already expansive midstream network of assets. In the Permian Basin it brought online an additional 600 mm cubic feet/day in processing capacity and anticipates 200 mmcf/d more by mid-2018. Its Mariner East system in the Marcellus Shale is receiving capital to expand its NGLs transport line from Ohio & Western Pennsylvania to the Marcus Hook Industrial Complex on the Eastern Atlantic coast. ETE is also expanding its Mont Belvieu fractionation facility adding more than 250 mmbpd capacity by mid 2019. In total the company spent about $4.0 billion on capital expenditures in 2016 and is on track to spent $3.5 billion in 2017.

Mergers and Acquisitions

ETE?s ETP subsidiary purchased PennTex which provides natural gas gathering and processing and residue gas and natural gas liquids transportation services to producers in the Terryville Complex in northern Louisiana.

ETE Sunoco retail division purchased a number of retail gas stations throughout mainland US and Hawaii between 2014 and 2017. The Sunoco Logistics division purchased in late 2016 for $760 million certain west Texas crude oil assets from Vitol Inc.

Company Background

In 2012 Energy Transfer Equity bought diversified gas player Southern Union for $9.4 billion (including $3.7 billion in debt). The acquisition made Energy Transfer Equity one of the largest natural gas infrastructure companies in the US.

That year the company also completed a $2 billion merger of a wholly owned Energy Transfer Partners subsidiary with and into Southern Union subsidiary CrossCountry Energy LLC which owns an indirect 50% interest in Citrus Corp. the owner of the Florida Gas Transmission pipeline system. After the merger CrossCountry Energy remained as the surviving entity a wholly owned subsidiary of Energy Transfer Partners.

In 2010 Energy Transfer Equity acquired the general partner stake of Regency Energy Partners and sold a 49.9% stake in its Midcontinent Express Pipeline to that company. The move was seen as a way for the company to diversify its general partner operations with the aim of getting a better return for shareholders. Regency Energy Partners focuses on the gathering processing marketing and transportation of natural gas and natural gas liquids in Arkansas Kansas Louisiana and Texas.

Energy Transfer Equity was formed in 2002 as La Grange Energy a Texas limited partnership. In early 2005 it changed its name to Energy Transfer Company. In August 2005 it converted from a Texas limited partnership to a Delaware limited partnership and became Energy Transfer Equity.

EXECUTIVES

President, John W. McReynolds, age 66, $577,280 total compensation

Cfo, Thomas E. (Tom) Long, age 62, $454,154 total compensation

Evp And General Counsel, Thomas P. Mason, age 61, $571,729 total compensation

President And Coo Etp, Marshall S. (Mackie) McCrea, $1,009,231 total compensation

Evp And Head Tax, Bradford D. (Brad) Whitehurst, $503,354 total compensation

Vice President Human Resources And Administration, Robert Kerrigan

Vice President Market Services, Bradley Holmes

Vice President Engineering, Charles Frey

Vice President Lng Operations, Jeffrey Brightwell

Vice President Lng Operations, Jeff Brightwell

Vice President Business Development, Martin Anthony

Senior Vice President Business Development, Hank Alexander

Auditors: Grant Thornton LLP

LOCATIONS

HQ: Energy Transfer LP
8111 Westchester Drive, Suite 600, Dallas, TX 75225
Phone: 214 981-0700
Web: www.energytransfer.com

PRODUCTS/OPERATIONS

2016 Sales

	% of total
Investment in ETP	58
Investment in Sunoco LP	41
Investment in lake Charles LNG	1
Adjustments	-
Total	**100**

2016 Sales

	$ mil.	% of total
Refined product sales	14,020	37
Crude sales	6,766	18
NGL sales	4,841	13
Gathering transportation and other fees	4,172	11
Natural gas sales	3,619	10
Other	4,086	11
Total	**37,504**	**100**

Selected Subsidiaries and Operating Units

EASTERN GULF CRUDE ACCESS LLC
ETP- Energy Transfer Partners L.P.
ETP GP- Energy Transfer Partners GP L.P. the general partner of ETP
ETP LLC- Energy Transfer Partners L.L.C. the general partner of ETP GP
Holdco- ETP Holdco Corporation
Regency GP- Regency Energy Partners GP LP the general partner of Regency
Regency LLC- Regency Energy Partners GP LLC the general partner of Regency GP
Regency- Regency Energy Partners LP
Southern Union- Southern Union Company
Sunoco Logistics- Sunoco Logistics Partners L.P.
Sunoco- Sunoco Inc.

COMPETITORS

AmeriGas Partners	Exxon Mobil
Atmos Energy	Ferrellgas Partners
Chevron	Kinder Morgan
Crestwood Midstream Partners LP	Magellan Midstream
DCP Midstream Partners	ONEOK
Enbridge	Star Gas Partners
	Suburban Propane

HISTORICAL FINANCIALS

Company Type: Public

Income Statement

FYE: December 31

	REVENUE ($ mil.)	NET INCOME ($ mil.)	NET PROFIT MARGIN	EMPLOYEES
12/17	40,523	954	2.4%	29,486
12/16	37,504	995	2.7%	30,992
12/15	42,126	1,189	2.8%	30,078
12/14	55,691	633	1.1%	27,605
12/13	48,335	196	0.4%	13,573
Annual Growth	**(4.3%)**	**48.5%**	**—**	**21.4%**

2017 Year-End Financials

Debt ratio: 51.11%
Return on equity: —
Cash ($ mil.): 336
Current ratio: 1.35
Long-term debt ($ mil.): 43,671

No. of shares (mil.): 1,079
Dividends
Yield: 0.0%
Payout: 138.5%
Market value ($ mil.): 18,626

	STOCK PRICE ($) FY Close	P/E High/Low		PER SHARE ($) Earnings	Dividends	Book Value
12/17	17.26	23	18	0.83	1.15	(1.11)
12/16	19.31	21	4	0.92	1.14	(1.62)
12/15	13.74	63	10	1.11	1.02	(0.89)
12/14	57.38	146	69	0.58	0.75	0.61
12/13	81.74	471	260	0.18	0.65	0.96
Annual Growth	**(32.2%)**	**—**	**—**	**47.6%**	**15.2%**	**—**

Energy Transfer Operating LP

Sunoco Logistics Partners acquires owns and operates a large swath of midstream and downstream assets primarily in tandem with former parent and current affiliate Sunoco. This includes ownership of more than 7900 miles of crude oil refined product and oil gathering pipelines and minority interests in four refined product pipelines as well as more than 40 terminals and other storage assets related to Sunoco's refining and marketing operations. In 2016 the company agreed to buy Vitol's crude oil assets in the Permian basin for $760 million. In 2017 the company bought Energy Transfer Partners in a deal valued at $19.9 billion.

Operations

Sunoco Logistics Partners operates in industry segments including crude oil acquisition and marketing refined products pipelines terminal facilities and crude oil pipeline. The company's refined products pipelines segment consists of 2500 miles of petroleum products pipeline and serves customers primarily in the Northeast and Midwest regions of the US. Through its terminal facilities unit Sunoco Logistics Partners is capable of storing 42 million barrels of refined products and crude oil. The crude oil pipeline segment consisting of about 4900 miles of crude oil pipelines primarily serves customers in Oklahoma and Texas. It also has 500 miles of crude oil gathering lines that supply the trunk pipelines.

The company gets the bulk of its revenues from crude oil acquisition and marketing activities.

Financial Performance

Higher oil and refined product prices helped to lift Sunoco Logistics Partners' revenue by 39% in 2011 thanks to an increase in revenues from terminal facilities (up 52%) crude oil pipelines (44%) and crude oil acquisition and marketing (40%) segments. Net income dropped by 7% in 2011 due to an increase in operating expenses other interest costs and debt expense.

Except for a revenue slump in 2009 (caused by the drop in demand for oil and oil products as a result of the global recession) Sunoco Logistics Partners saw an upward trend in revenues from 2007 to 2011.

Strategy

The company pursues a strategy of growing its businesses organically and through complementary acquisitions (more than 20 since 2002). Expanding its pipeline assets in 2011 the company acquired control of Inland Corp. (which has a 350-mile refined-products pipeline and related facilities) for $100 million. It also acquired the Eagle Point tank farm and related assets in Westville New Jersey from Sunoco for $100 million.

That year Sunoco Logistics Partners acquired a crude oil acquisition and marketing business from Texon. The purchase consists of a lease crude business and gathering assets in 16 states primarily in the western US. (It had acquired the butane blending business of Texon in 2010 for $140 million plus inventory).

EXECUTIVES

Ceo, Kelcy L Warren
Pres-Coo, Matthew S Ramsey
L.P., Gen Ptnr, Energy T GP
Auditors: Grant Thornton LLP

LOCATIONS

HQ: Energy Transfer Operating LP
8111 Westchester Drive, Suite 600, Dallas, TX 75225
Phone: 214 981-0700
Web: www.energytransfer.com

PRODUCTS/OPERATIONS

2011 Sales

	% of total
Crude oil acquisition & marketing	92
Terminal facilities	4
Crude oil pipelines	3
Refined product pipelines	1
Total	**100**

COMPETITORS

Buckeye Partners	Magellan Midstream
CITGO	Marathon Petroleum
Enbridge Energy	Plains All American
Enterprise Products	Pipeline
Kinder Morgan Energy Partners	RKA Petroleum
Kinder Morgan	TransMontaigne
Management	TransMontaigne Partners

HISTORICAL FINANCIALS

Company Type: Public

Income Statement

FYE: December 31

	REVENUE ($ mil.)	NET INCOME ($ mil.)	NET PROFIT MARGIN	EMPLOYEES
12/17	29,054	2,081	7.2%	506,829
12/16	9,151	705	7.7%	2,575
12/15	10,486	393	3.7%	2,500
12/14	18,088	291	1.6%	2,250
12/13	16,639	463	2.8%	2,000
Annual Growth	**15.0%**	**45.6%**	**—**	**299.0%**

2017 Year-End Financials

Debt ratio: 42.45%
Return on equity: —
Cash ($ mil.): 306
Current ratio: 0.93
Long-term debt ($ mil.): 32,687

No. of shares (mil.): 1,164
Dividends
Yield: —
Payout: —
Market value ($ mil.): —

EnLink Midstream LLC

Auditors: KPMG LLP

LOCATIONS

HQ: EnLink Midstream LLC
1722 Routh St., Suite 1300, Dallas, TX 75201
Phone: 214 953-9500
Web: www.enlink.com

HISTORICAL FINANCIALS
Company Type: Public

Income Statement
FYE: December 31

	REVENUE ($ mil.)	NET INCOME ($ mil.)	NET PROFIT MARGIN	EMPLOYEES
12/17	5,739	212	3.7%	1,494
12/16	4,252	(460)	—	1,472
12/15	4,452	(355)	—	1,432
12/14	3,500	126	3.6%	1,148
12/13	2,390	115	4.8%	—
Annual Growth	24.5%	16.5%	—	—

2017 Year-End Financials

Debt ratio: 33.61%
Return on equity: 11.19%
Cash ($ mil.): 31
Current ratio: 0.78
Long-term debt ($ mil.): 3,542

No. of shares (mil.): 180
Dividends
Yield: 0.0%
Payout: 87.1%
Market value ($ mil.): 3,179

	STOCK PRICE ($) FY Close	P/E High/Low		PER SHARE ($) Earnings	Dividends	Book Value
12/17	17.60	17	13	1.17	1.02	10.64
12/16	19.05	—	—	(2.56)	1.02	10.45
12/15	15.09	—	—	(2.17)	0.99	13.92
12/14	35.56	77	55	0.55	0.63	16.91
Annual Growth	(16.1%)	—	—	20.8%	12.8%	(10.9%)

Entegra Financial Corp

LOCATIONS

HQ: Entegra Financial Corp
14 One Center Court, Franklin, NC 28734
Phone: 828 524-7000
Web: www.entegrabank.com

HISTORICAL FINANCIALS
Company Type: Public

Income Statement
FYE: December 31

	ASSETS ($ mil.)	NET INCOME ($ mil.)	INCOME AS % OF ASSETS	EMPLOYEES
12/17	1,581	2	0.2%	272
12/16	1,292	6	0.5%	245
12/15	1,031	23	2.3%	219
12/14	903	5	0.7%	189
12/13	784	(0)	—	184
Annual Growth	19.2%	—	—	10.3%

2017 Year-End Financials

Debt ratio: 1.46%
Return on equity: 1.81%
Cash ($ mil.): 109
Current ratio: —
Long-term debt ($ mil.): —

No. of shares (mil.): 6
Dividends
Yield: —
Payout: —
Market value ($ mil.): 201

	STOCK PRICE ($) FY Close	P/E High/Low		PER SHARE ($) Earnings	Dividends	Book Value
12/17	29.25	78	52	0.39	0.00	22.00
12/16	20.60	21	17	0.98	0.00	20.57
12/15	19.36	5	4	3.64	0.00	20.08
12/14	14.39	16	14	0.91	0.00	16.39
Annual Growth	19.4%	—	—	(19.1%)	—	7.6%

Entergy Corp

Entergy is into energy. The integrated utility holding company's subsidiaries distribute electricity to some 2.9 million customers in four southern states (Arkansas Louisiana Mississippi and Texas) and provide natural gas to about 200000 customers in Louisiana. The company has interests in regulated and non-regulated power plants in North America that have a combined generating capacity of about 30000 MW. Entergy is also one of the largest nuclear power generators in the US (nearly 9000 MW). The company's regulated utilities have little retail competition as they are deemed by state regulators as the sole providers of electricity in their service areas.

Operations

The company operates two business segments: Utility and Wholesale Commodities.

The Utility segment produces 85% of revenue by generating transmitting distributing and selling electric power to customers in its regulated service areas in the US Gulf States region. The segment is composed of several regulated utility companies including: Entergy Arkansas Inc. Entergy Louisiana LLC Entergy Mississippi Inc. Entergy New Orleans Inc. and Entergy Texas. Four nuclear power plant sites with capacity of some 5200 MW are owned and operated by corporations that roll up into this segment. It also runs a small natural gas distribution business. Of its generation capacity about 65% is from gas oil and hydroelectric sources about 25% is from nuclear and the rest comes from coal-fired plants.

Entergy Wholesale Commodities segment produces 15% of total revenue through its ownership and operation of nuclear power plants (nearly 4200 MW of capacity) and fossil fuel plants (some 400 MW of capacity) and the sale of its electricity on the wholesale market. It also provides management services to Nebraska's Cooper Nuclear Station (800 MW of capacity). More than 90% of this segment's generation portfolio is nuclear-sourced.

Geographic Reach

Entergy's Utility segments operates power plants in Arkansas Mississippi and its headquarters in Louisiana. It provides power to customers in those states plus Texas. Entergy New Orleans distributes and transports natural gas within New Orleans and Louisiana through approximately 2500 miles of gas pipeline.

The Wholesale Commodities segment has power plants and customers in New York Michigan Massachusetts Nebraska Arkansas and Louisiana.

Sales and Marketing

Entergy delivers electricity to about 700000 customers in Arkansas about 1.3 million in Louisiana

some 450000 in Mississippi and some 450000 in Texas. It provides natural gas to about 100000 customers in New Orleans and nearly another 100000 throughout the rest of Louisiana. Entergy's retail business (mostly through the regulated utility companies) generates some 40% of sales volume from industrial businesses nearly 25% from commercial enterprises more than 25% from residential and the rest from government agencies wholesale and other customers.

Entergy Wholesale Commodities segment sells both energy and capacity from its nuclear plants to retail power providers utilities electric power cooperatives power trading organizations and other power generation companies. These customers include Consolidated Edison and Consumers Energy companies from which Entergy purchased plants with the promise to continue providing energy to them. It also sells to transmission-sharing entities such as ISO New England NYISO and MISO.

The company's regulated utilities have little retail competition as they are deemed by state regulators as the sole providers of electricity in their service areas.

Financial Performance

In recent years Entergy's revenue remained steadfast within a range of $10 billion and $12 billion with a $12.5 billion peak in 2014. Net income over the same period has generally been going down with sharp decreases in 2015 and 2016.

In 2017 revenue crept up 2% to $11 billion thanks to $412 million addition in electric sales increases offset by a 10% fall in competitive business segment sales.

Net income improved from a loss of $565 million in 2016 to a profit of $425 million in 2017. The turnaround in performance was primarily due to a YOY reduction of $2.3 billion in special charges relating to asset write-offs.

Cash holdings at the end of 2017 reduced to $781 million from $1.2 billion the year prior. Operations generated a net inflow of $2.6 billion in cash which was more than offset by $3.8 billion used in investing activities. Financial activities brought in a net cash inflow of $810 million thanks to a net issuance of $1.4 billion in new debt.

Strategy

Entergy wants to expand its investments in regulated utility firms while winding down all its wholesale commodities businesses. The company plans to invest around $10 billion between 2017 and 2019 in utilities almost half of it earmarked for distribution and transmission upgrades. Generation plants will get some 45% of the pot.

The company recently completed the Ninemile 6 plant at the Union Power Station and received approval for work on its St. Charles Lake Charles and Montgomery County Power Stations. The company also joined the MISO transmission-sharing agreement to expand its own network. Finally it is awaiting approval to build a new New Orleans Power Station.

Entergy's Wholesale Commodities business has run into significant headwinds in recent years. The shale boom has resulted in nuclear power being pricier than plants running on shale-sourced natural gas. The New York state is also pressuring the company to decommission its Indian Point Energy Center by 2021. Other nuclear plants await similar fates.

Company Background

Entergy has had a colorful and varied start in the beginning of the 20th Century. Its roots can be traced back to Arkansas Power & Light (1913) New Orleans Public Service Inc (1922) Louisiana Power & Light and Mississippi Power & Light (both formed in 1927). In 1949 these four companies along with other utilities were combined into a Maine holding company Electric Power and Light. In 1949 after a small phase when the unified company was dissolved a new holding company Middle South Utilities emerged that year to take over the four utilities' assets. In 1989 following a badly botched construction plan of two nuclear facilities (behind schedule and over budget)– whereby Middle South tried to pass on the costs to customers but eventually settled the disputes— the company changed its name to Entergy to distance itself from the controversy.

HISTORY

Arkansas Power & Light (AP&L founded in 1913) consolidated operations with three other Arkansas utilities in 1926. Also that year New Orleans Public Service Inc. (NOPSI founded in 1922) merged with two other Big Easy electric companies. Louisiana Power & Light (LP&L) and Mississippi Power & Light (MP&L) were both formed in 1927 also through consolidation of regional utilities.

AP&L LP&L MP&L NOPSI and other utilities were combined into a Maine holding company Electric Power and Light which was dissolved in 1949. A new holding company Middle South Utilities emerged that year to take over the four utilities' assets.

In 1971 the company bought Arkansas-Missouri Power. In 1974 it brought its first nuclear plant on line and formed Middle South Energy (now System Energy Resources) to develop two more nuclear facilities Grand Gulf 1 and 2. Unfortunately Grand Gulf 1 was completed behind schedule and about 400% over budget. When Middle South tried to pass on the costs to customers controversy ensued. Construction of Grand Gulf 2 was halted and the CFO Edwin Lupberger took charge in 1985. Two years later nuke-related losses took the company to the brink of bankruptcy.

The company moved to settle the disputes by absorbing a $900 million loss on Grand Gulf 2 in 1989. To distance itself from the controversy Middle South changed its name to Entergy. In 1991 NOPSI settled with the City of New Orleans over Grand Gulf 1 costs.

That year Entergy anticipating deregulation branched out into nonregulated industries and looked abroad for growth opportunities. In 1993 a consortium including Entergy acquired a 51% interest in Edesur a Buenos Aires electric utility. In 1995 Entergy agreed to buy a 20% stake in a power plant under construction in India but the state government soon halted the project accusing the participating US companies of exploiting India.

Entergy completed its acquisition of CitiPower an Australian electric distributor in 1996 and the next year it bought the UK's London Electricity.

But diversification had drained funds. Lupberger resigned in 1998 and a new management team began selling noncore businesses such as CitiPower and London Electricity. NYMEX began trading electricity futures in 1998 using Entergy and Cinergy as contract-delivery points.

EXECUTIVES

Group President Utility Operations, Theodore H. (Theo) Bunting, age 60, $607,806 total compensation
Chairman And Ceo, Leo P. Denault, age 59, $1,191,462 total compensation
Svp And Coo, Paul D. Hinnenkamp
Evp, Roderick K. (Rod) West, age 50, $654,514 total compensation
President And Ceo Entergy Mississippi Inc, Haley R. Fisackerly, $248,346 total compensation
Evp Nuclear Operations And Chief Nuclear Officer, A. Christopher (Chris) Bakken, $426,990 total compensation
Evp And Cfo, Andrew S. (Drew) Marsh, age 45, $553,284 total compensation

President And Ceo Entergy New Orleans Inc, Charles Rice
President And Ceo Entergy Arkansas Inc., Rick Riley
Svp And General Counsel, Marcus V. Brown, age 56, $563,208 total compensation
President And Ceo Entergy Texas Inc, Sallie Rainer
President And Ceo Entergy Louisiana Llc And Entergy Gulf States Louisiana L.l.c., Phillip R. May
Evp Shared Services And Human Resources; Chief Diversity Officer, Don Vinci
Executive Vice President External Affairs, Curtis Hebert
Senior Vice President Of Nuclear Business Development, Randy Hutchinson
Vice President, Charles Fink
Vice President Performance Management, Jeanne Kenney
Vice President Utility Support, Laura Mcmanus
Vp Regulatory And Governmental Affairs Entergy Texas, Deanna Rodriguez
Vice President, William Maguire
Vice President, Eddie Peebles
Vp Customer Experience, Ed Melendreras
Site Vice President Vermont Yankee, Chris Wamser
Vice President Engineering, Mike Knight
Svp And Chief Accounting Officer, Alyson Mount
Vice President Federal Governmental Affairs, Daniel Turton
Vice President Credit, Wayne J Leonard
Vice President Finance, Bob Cushman
Vice President, Michael R Kansler
Vice President Customer Experience Strategy Entergy Services, Tracie Boutte
Vp Government And Regulatory Affairs, Kenneth Theobalds
Vice President Critical Infrastructur, Chris Peters
Vice President And Associate Broker, Mike Wilson
Senior Vice President Human Resources Chro And Chief Diversity Officer, Andrea Rowley
Executive Vice President Nuclear Operations; Chief Nuclear Officer Entergy Nuclear, Chris Bakken
Vice President Investor Relations, David Borde
Vp External Affairs Wholesale, Mike Twomey
Vice President Energy Technology And Analytics, Raiford Smith
Chairman And Ceo, Leo P. Denault, age 59
Secretary, Kim Leddy
Board Member, Donald Hintz
Secretary, Cheryl Morse
Board Member, Perry Rodrigue
Board Member, Charles E Watkins
Board Of Directors, Dave McElwee
Board Member, Kirkland Donald
Board Member, Doris Minter
Board Member, Philip Frederickson
Board Member, Blanche L Lincoln
Board Member, Karen Puckett
Auditors: Deloitte & Touche LLP

LOCATIONS

HQ: Entergy Corp
   639 Loyola Avenue, New Orleans, LA 70113
Phone: 504 576-4000
Web: www.entergy.com

PRODUCTS/OPERATIONS

2017 Sales

	$ mil.	% of total
Utility	9,417	85
Entergy Wholesale Commodities	1,656	15
Eliminations	(0.1)	-
Total	**11,074**	**100**

2017 Sales

	$ mil.	% of total
Electric	9,278	84
Competitive businesses	1,656	15
Natural gas	1,389	1
Total	**11,074**	**100**

Selected Subsidiaries

Entergy Arkansas Inc. (electric utility)
Entergy Louisiana LLC (electric utility)
Entergy Mississippi Inc. (electric utility)
Entergy New Orleans Inc. (electric and gas utility)
Entergy Nuclear Inc. (nuclear plant operation)
Entergy Operations Inc. (plant management and maintenance for Entergy utilities)
Entergy Services Inc. (management services for Entergy utilities)
System Energy Resources Inc. (plant management and supply to Entergy utilities)
System Fuels Inc. (fuel storage and delivery to Entergy utilities)

COMPETITORS

AEP	Oncor Electric
Atmos Energy	Delivery
CenterPoint Energy	Southern Company
OGE Energy	

HISTORICAL FINANCIALS

Company Type: Public

Income Statement
FYE: December 31

	REVENUE ($ mil.)	NET INCOME ($ mil.)	NET PROFIT MARGIN	EMPLOYEES
12/17	11,074	425	3.8%	13,504
12/16	10,845	(564)	—	13,513
12/15	11,513	(156)	—	13,579
12/14	12,494	960	7.7%	13,393
12/13	11,390	730	6.4%	13,808
Annual Growth	(0.7%)	(12.6%)		(0.6%)

2017 Year-End Financials

Debt ratio: 35.71%
Return on equity: 5.16%
Cash ($ mil.): 781
Current ratio: 0.65
Long-term debt ($ mil.): 14,337

No. of shares (mil.): 180
Dividends
   Yield: 0.0%
   Payout: 153.5%
Market value ($ mil.): 14,692

	STOCK PRICE ($) FY Close	P/E High/Low		Earnings	PER SHARE ($) Dividends	Book Value
12/17	81.39	38	31	2.28	3.50	45.37
12/16	73.47	—	—	(3.26)	3.42	46.25
12/15	68.36	—	—	(0.99)	3.34	53.67
12/14	87.48	17	12	5.22	3.32	57.53
12/13	63.27	18	15	3.99	3.32	55.71
Annual Growth	6.5%	—	—	(13.1%)	1.3%	(5.0%)

Enterprise Bancorp, Inc. (MA)

Enterprise Bancorp caters to more customers than just entrepreneurs. The holding company owns Enterprise Bank and Trust which operates more than 20 branches in north-central Massachusetts and southern New Hampshire. The $2 billion-asset bank offers traditional deposit and loan products specializing in lending to businesses professionals high-net-worth individuals and not-for-profits. About half of its loan portfolio is tied to commercial real estate while another one-third is tied to commercial and industrial and commercial construction loans. Subsidiaries Enterprise Investment Services and Enterprise Insurance Services provide investments and insurance geared to the bank's target business customers.

Operations
More than 50% of Enterprise Bancorp's $1.86 billion loan portfolio was tied to commercial real estate loans at the end of 2015 while commercial and industrial and commercial construction loans made up another 25% and 11% of the bank's loan assets. The rest of the bank's portfolio was tied to residential mortgages (9% of loan assets) home equity loans and lines of credit (4%) and consumer loans (less than 1%).

Nearly 80% of the bank's total revenue comes from loan interest while investment advisory fees and deposit and interchange fees each make up another 5%.

Geographic Reach
The Lowell Massachusetts-based bank operated 23 branches mostly located in the greater Merrimack Valley and North Central regions of Massachusetts and Southern New Hampshire at the end of 2015.

Sales and Marketing
Enterprise spent $2.7 million on advertising and public relations during 2015 down from $2.9 million in 2014.

Financial Performance
The bank's annual revenues have risen more than 40% since 2011 as its loan assets have swelled by 50% to $1.86 billion. Meanwhile its net income has grown more than 50% as it's kept a lid on loan loss provisions and operating costs.

Enterprise Bancorp's revenue climbed 8% to $98.4 million during 2015 thanks to 11% loan asset growth driven by a "seasoned" lending team a sales and service culture and geographic market expansion. Commercial construction loans grew the fastest rate during the year though all loans grew albeit at a slightly slower rate.

Revenue growth in 2015 drove the bank's net income up 10% to $16.1 million despite higher salary and employee benefit expenses. Enterprise Bancorp's operating cash levels nearly doubled to $25.7 million for the year largely thanks to positive changes in working capital mainly related to prepaid expenses and other assets.

Strategy
Enterprise Bancorp has traditionally expanded its loan and deposit business by opening new branches rather than by acquiring other banks. Enterprise hopes to take advantage of the trend to switch from larger banks to smaller community-oriented institutions. The company has also invested in upgrading its branches and operations systems.

EXECUTIVES

Evp And Cfo Enterprise Bancorp And Enterprise Bank And Trust, James A. (Jim) Marcotte, age 60, $194,806 total compensation

Ceo Enterprise Bancorp And Enterprise Bank And Trust, John P. (Jack) Clancy, age 60, $400,000 total compensation

President Enterprise Bancorp And Enterprise Bank And Trust, Richard W. (Dick) Main, age 70, $258,918 total compensation

Evp And Coo Enterprise Bank And Trust, Stephen J. Irish, age 63, $194,804 total compensation

Svp And Chief Commercial Lender, Brian H. Bullock, age 60

Evp And Chief Banking Officer Enterprise Bank And Trust, Steven R. Larochelle, age 54

Evp And Chief Sales And Marketing Officer Enterprise Bank And Trust, Chester J. (Chet) Szablak, age 60

Vice President, Paul Rousseau

Vice Chairman Enterprise Bancorp And Enterprise Bank And Trust, Arnold S. Lerner, age 88

Chairman Enterprise Bancorp And Enterprise Bank And Trust, George L. Duncan, age 77

Auditors: RSM US LLP

LOCATIONS

HQ: Enterprise Bancorp, Inc. (MA)
222 Merrimack Street, Lowell, MA 01852
Phone: 978 459-9000

PRODUCTS/OPERATIONS

2015 Sales

	$ mil.	% of total
Interest and dividend income:		
Loans and loans held for sale	77	79
Investment securities	5	5
Other interest-earning assets	0	-
Non-interest income:		
Investment advisory fees	4	5
Deposit and interchange fees	4	5
Net gains on sales of investment securities	1	2
Income on bank-owned life insurance net	0	1
Gains on sales of loans	0	1
Other income	2	3
Total	**98**	**100**

Products and Services
Lending Products:
Residential Loans
Home Equity Loans and Lines of Credit
Consumer Loans
Credit Risk and Allowance for Loan Losses
Deposit Products:
Cash Management Services
Product Delivery Channels
Investment Services
Insurance Services

COMPETITORS

Bank of America	Peoples Federal
Citizens Financial	Bancshares Inc.
Group	Sovereign Bank
Eastern Bank	TD Bank USA

HISTORICAL FINANCIALS
Company Type: Public

Income Statement

FYE: December 31

	ASSETS ($ mil.)	NET INCOME ($ mil.)	INCOME AS % OF ASSETS	EMPLOYEES
12/17	2,817	19	0.7%	482
12/16	2,526	18	0.7%	468
12/15	2,285	16	0.7%	426
12/14	2,022	14	0.7%	412
12/13	1,849	13	0.7%	398
Annual Growth	**11.1%**	**9.4%**	**—**	**4.9%**

2017 Year-End Financials

Debt ratio: 0.53%	No. of shares (mil.): 11
Return on equity: 8.68%	Dividends
Cash ($ mil.): 54	Yield: 0.0%
Current ratio: —	Payout: 32.5%
Long-term debt ($ mil.): —	Market value ($ mil.): 395

	STOCK PRICE ($) FY Close	P/E High/Low	PER SHARE ($) Earnings	Dividends	Book Value
12/17	34.05	23 18	1.66	0.54	19.97
12/16	37.56	22 12	1.70	0.52	18.72
12/15	22.85	16 13	1.55	0.50	17.38
12/14	25.25	18 12	1.44	0.48	16.35
12/13	21.17	16 11	1.36	0.46	15.14
Annual Growth	**12.6%**	**— —**	**5.1%**	**4.1%**	**7.2%**

Enterprise Financial Services Corp

Enterprise Financial Services wants you to boldly bank where many have banked before. It's the holding company for Enterprise Bank & Trust which mostly targets closely-held businesses and their owners but also serves individuals in the St. Louis Kansas City and Phoenix metropolitan areas. Boasting $3.8 billion in assets and 16 branches Enterprise offers standard products such as checking savings and money market accounts and CDs. Commercial and industrial loans make up over half of the company's lending activities while real estate loans make up another 45%. The bank also writes consumer and residential mortgage loans. Bank subsidiary Enterprise Trust offers wealth management services.

Operations
Enterprise Trust the company's wealth management unit targets business owners wealthy individuals and institutional investors providing financial planning business succession planning and related services. The unit also invests in Missouri state tax credits from funds for affordable housing development which it then sells to clients and others.

About 82% of Enterprise Financial's total revenue came from loan interest (including fees) in 2014 while another 7% came from interest on its taxable and tax-exempt investment securities. The rest of its revenue came from wealth management income (4%) service fees (3%) gains on state tax credits (1%) and other miscellaneous income sources. The bank had a staff of 452 full-time employees at the end of 2014.

Geographic Reach
Enterprise Bank & Trust operates eight banking locations in or around Kansas City six banking locations and a support center in the St. Louis area and two banking locations in the Phoenix metro area.

Financial Performance
The company has struggled to consistently grow its revenues in recent years mostly due to shrinking interest margins on its loans amidst the low-interest environment. Its profits however have mostly trended higher thanks to declining loan loss provisions as its loan portfolio's credit quality has improved with higher property valuations in the strengthened economy.

Enterprise Financials' revenue fell by 9% to $148.4 million in 2014 mostly due to double-digit declines in interest income as its purchased credit-impaired (PCI) loan balances and accelerated payments declined and as interest margins on its loans continued to shrink. The bank's portfolio loan balances increased however helping to offset some of its interest income decline.

Lower revenue and higher loan loss provisions (it received a loan loss benefit of $642 thousand in 2013) in 2014 caused the bank's net income to dive 18% to $27.2 million. Enterprise Financial's operating cash levels rose by 7% to $31.5 million despite lower earnings for the year mostly thanks to favorable changes in its working capital related to a $12-million change in other asset balances.

Strategy
Enterprise Financial Services planned in 2015 to continue its long-term strategy of keeping a "relationship-oriented distribution and sales approach"; growing its fee income and niche businesses; practicing "prudent" credit and interest rate risk management; and using advanced technology and controlled-expense growth. The company

added that it planned on "operating branches with larger average deposits and employing experienced staff who are compensated on the basis of performance and customer service."

Though it just had two branches in Phoenix in 2015 the bank believes the fast-growing Phoenix market offers long-term growth opportunities for the company with its underlying demographic and geographic factors. Indeed at the end of 2014 the market had over 90000 privately-held businesses and 80000-plus households each with investable assets of more than $1 million.

Mergers and Acquisitions
In 2017 Enterprise Financial Services completed the acquisition of Jefferson County Bancshares the holding company of Eagle Bank and Trust Company in Missouri. The deal added 13 branches in metropolitan St. Louis and Perry County Missouri. The acquisition expanded EFS's assets to nearly $5 billion.

Company Background
In a restructuring move Enterprise Financial Services sold life insurance arm Millennium Brokerage in 2010 five years after investing in the company.

EXECUTIVES

President Enterprise Bank And Trust, Scott R. Goodman, age 54, $318,150 total compensation

Evp And Cfo, Keene S. Turner, age 38, $333,125 total compensation

Ceo, James B. Lally, age 50, $331,342 total compensation

Chief Credit Officer Enterprise Bank & Trust, Douglas N. Bauche, age 49, $253,270 total compensation

Senior Vice President Loan Review, Jeremy Jameson

Vice President Relationship Manager, Brian Glarner

Vice President Branch Manager, Hidy Ortiz

Assistant Vice President Relationship Manager, Tom Noel

Assistant Vice President Business Banking Specialist, Arnold Otero

Avp Relationship Manager, Bob Sivewright

Vice President Relationship Manager, Michael Hasenkamp

Assistant Vice President Business Banking, Molly McKay

Assistant Vice President Business Banking Specialist, Jessica Nollett

Assistant Vice President Business Banking Specialist, Brandy Kimble

Assistant Vice President Relationship Manager, John Garrett

Chairman, John S. Eulich, age 67

Auditors: DELOITTE & TOUCHE LLP

LOCATIONS

HQ: Enterprise Financial Services Corp
150 North Meramec, Clayton, MO 63105
Phone: 314 725-5500
Web: www.enterprisebank.com

PRODUCTS/OPERATIONS

2011 Sales

	$ mil.	% of total
Interest		
Loans including fees	130	79
Securities	11	7
Other	0	1
Noninterest		
Wealth management	6	4
Service charges on deposit accounts	5	3
Gain on state tax credits net	3	2
Other service charges and fee income	1	1
Other	4	3
Adjustments	(3.5)	-
Total	161	100

HISTORICAL FINANCIALS
Company Type: Public

Income Statement
FYE: December 31

	ASSETS ($ mil.)	NET INCOME ($ mil.)	INCOME AS % OF ASSETS	EMPLOYEES
12/17	5,289	48	0.9%	635
12/16	4,081	48	1.2%	479
12/15	3,608	38	1.1%	459
12/14	3,277	27	0.8%	452
12/13	3,170	33	1.0%	455
Annual Growth	13.7%	9.8%	—	8.7%

2017 Year-End Financials

Debt ratio: 2.23%	No. of shares (mil.): 23
Return on equity: 10.30%	Dividends
Cash ($ mil.): 152	Yield: 0.0%
Current ratio: —	Payout: 21.2%
Long-term debt ($ mil.): —	Market value ($ mil.): 1,042

	STOCK PRICE ($) FY Close	P/E High/Low	PER SHARE ($) Earnings	Dividends	Book Value
12/17	45.15	22 18	2.07	0.44	23.76
12/16	43.00	18 10	2.41	0.41	19.31
12/15	28.35	16 10	1.89	0.26	17.53
12/14	19.73	15 12	1.35	0.21	15.94
12/13	20.42	12 7	1.73	0.21	14.47
Annual Growth	21.9%	— —	4.6%	20.3%	13.2%

Enterprise Products Partners L.P.

Enterprise Products Partners has the energy to go the distance. The limited partnership's primary operating subsidiary Enterprise Products Operating LLC (EPO) is a leading player in the North American midstream services to producers and consumers of natural gas natural gas liquids (NGL) crude oil petrochemicals and refined products. Operations include natural gas processing NGL fractionation petrochemical services and crude oil transportation. It owns some 50000 miles of pipelines 14 billion cu. ft. of natural gas storage and 260 million barrels of storage for NGLs refined products and crude oil. It owns some 27 natural gas processing plants and 18 deep water docks used to export product. The hub of EPO's business is Houston's Mont Belvieu refinery complex. Substantially all of the company's consolidated revenues are earned in the US and derived from a wide customer base.

Operations
Enterprise has four business segments: NGL Pipelines and Services Crude Oil Pipelines and Services Petrochemical and Refined Products Services Natural Gas Pipelines and Services.

The NGL Pipelines and Services segment produces some 45% of overall revenue with its natural gas processing plants and related natural gas liquid (NGL) marketing activities. At the core of its business are 25 processing plants that collect natural

gas and remove NGLs and impurities in preparation for transportation and eventual end-user purchase. It owns nearly 20000 miles of NGL pipelines NGL and related product storage facilities and 15 NGL fractionators. The segment also includes the company's NGL import and LPG export terminal operations. NGL marketing activities use a fleet of roughly 800 railcars to deliver feedstocks to its facilities and distribute NGLs to customers throughout the US and Canada.

Crude Oil Pipelines & Services brings in about 30% of revenue and includes about 6000 miles of crude oil pipelines and related operations crude oil storage and marine terminals and crude oil marketing activities. Of its pipelines the Seaway pipeline is notable in that it connects the Cushing OK crude oil hub (major industry hub where price settlement for West Texas Intermediate (WTI) occurs) with markets in southeast Texas.

The Petrochemical and Refined Products Services segment is engaged in petrochemical and refined products transportation and services. It fractionates propylene to create the building blocks of carpet fibers molded plastic parts for appliances cars and medical products and packaging film. It accounts for approximately 15% of revenue.

Natural Gas Pipelines and Services segment includes 19000 miles of pipeline used to gather and transport natural gas from shale plays Eagle Ford Haynesville Barnett Permian and others. It leases underground salt dome natural gas storage facilities in Texas and Louisiana. The segment is also home to natural gas marketing activities. It accounts for approximately 10% of revenue.

Geographic Reach
Houston TX-based Enterprise Products operates the vast majority of its facilities in Texas along the Gulf Coast with particular emphasis in the Mont Belvieu refinery and transport complex. Key locations from which it gathers natural gas and crude oil include Colorado Louisiana New Mexico Texas and Wyoming. It has a presence in shale plays: Eagle Ford Haynesville Barnett Permian Piceance San Juan and Greater Green River supply basins. Its NGL pipelines extend throughout the US Midwest and Gulf Coast including states such as Georgia New York Oklahoma and Minnesota.

Sales and Marketing
Enterprise Products sells product and services to refineries industrial companies commercial customers and regional natural gas processing plants. It generates much of its revenue from fees calculated by the volume of product it transports. Vitol accounted for more than 10% of the company's revenue. The company also performs significant intersegment sales.

Financial PerformanceRevenue increased some 30% to $29 billion. The $6 billion increase came primarily due to the higher sales price as well as higher volumes sold of crude oil natural gas petrochemicals refined products and octane additives.Net income increased more than 10% to $2.8 billion primarily from higher gross income (revenue increased more than expenses) as well as a $60 million increase in equity income of unconsolidated affiliates.Cash holdings reduced drastically from $417 million in 2016 to $70 million at the end of 2017. Operations generated $4.7 billion in cash inflows offset by $3.3 billion for investment and a further $1.7 billion in financing activities. CAPEX was $3.1 billion for 2017.

Strategy
Enterprise's strategy is focused on building and managing an integrated network of midstream energy assets (including salt domes and fractionation and natural gas processing plants) to take advantage of growing US market demand for natural gas NGLs crude oil and refined products.

The company's business strategies are to capitalize on expected increases in the production of natural gas NGLs and crude oil from development activities in various US production basins. Part of this strategy involves expansion through growth capital projects. It plans to continue to expand its assets through the construction of new facilities and to capitalize on expected increases in natural gas NGL and crude oil production resulting from development activities in the Rocky Mountains Mid-Continent Northeast and US Gulf Coast regions including the Niobrara Barnett Eagle Ford Permian Haynesville Marcellus and Utica Shale plays.

Enterprise began commercial service in 2016 on approximately $2.2 billion of growth capital projects. The projects included its Morgan?s Point Ethane Export Terminal Waha and South Eddy natural gas processing facilities and the completion of over 2 MMBbls of additional crude oil storage capacity at terminals in Houston and Mont Belvieu.

The company has approximately $6.7 billion of growth capital projects scheduled to be completed by 2020 including two processing facilities the Midland-to-Sealy segment of its Midland-to-ECHO Pipeline System and a joint venture-owned dock infrastructure project in Corpus Christi designed to accommodate crude oil volumes. In early 2017 it purchased assets from bankrupt Azure Midstream to extend its capabilities in East Texas and Northern Louisiana.

To raise cash to both weather the market downturn and fund capital expenditures Enterprise sold its entire Offshore Pipelines & Services segment to Genesis Energy for $1.5 billion. It also raised $2.5 billion with a secondary offering of its stock units.

Mergers and Acquisitions
In 2017 Enterprise Products purchased the midstream business and assets of bankrupt Azure Midstream which has operations in East Texas and Northern Louisiana. Enterprise gained nearly 1000 miles of natural gas gathering pipelines and three natural gas processing facilities.

Company Background
The company is investing heavily in serving shale plays especially the Eagle Ford in South Texas and is building midstream facilities to serve the surge in natural gas production. In 2012 it opened a fifth NGL fractionator at its Mont Belvieu facility to process Eagle Ford hydrocarbons and a fifth in 2012.

That year Enterprise joined Enbridge Energy Partners and Anadarko Petroleum in advancing development of the Texas Express Pipeline by the companies' joint venture. The 20-inch diameter pipeline will extend about 580 miles from Skellytown Texas to the Mont Belvieu NGL fractionation complex. The pipeline also provides access to other producers in several regions: West Texas the Rocky Mountains southern Oklahoma and the Mid-continent area.

In 2010 in a move to increase its footprint in the lucrative Haynesville/Bossier Shale play Enterprise acquired two natural gas gathering and treating systems in northwest Louisiana and East Texas from M2 Midstream LLC for $1.2 billion.

In a major expansion move in 2009 the company acquired rival TEPPCO Partners L.P. in a $26 billion all-stock deal which boosted its pipelines and oil refined products and NGL storage capacity. The TEPPCO Partners purchase made the company the largest publicly traded energy partnership in the US. The expanded company's assets include 60 liquid storage terminals 25 natural gas storage facilities 17 fractionation facilities and six offshore hub platforms.

That year the company acquired Enterprise GP Holdings which controlled the general partner of Enterprise. The $8 billion deal was aimed at reducing long-term capital costs and simplifying the business structure of Enterprise Products Partners.

The family of Chairman Dan Duncan controls a 35% stake in Enterprise.

EXECUTIVES

President, W. Randall (Randy) Fowler, age 62, $521,178 total compensation
Ceo, A. James (Jim) Teague, age 72, $800,000 total compensation
Evp Commercial, William (Bill) Ordemann, age 59, $451,150 total compensation
Svp And Cfo, Bryan F. Bulawa, age 49
Svp And Cio, Paul G. Flynn
Evp Operations And Engineering, Graham W. Bacon, age 54, $375,000 total compensation
Svp Liquid Hydrocarbons Marketing, Brent Secrest
Vice President, Tony Chovanec
Vp Internal Audit, Charles Stovall
Senior Vice President, Rudy Nix
Vice President Project Management, Craig Roper
Senior Vice President Enterprise General Partner, James Cisrik
Vice President, Darrell Kainer
Vice President Operations And Finance Mbd Apac, Troy A Rousse
Vp Government Affairs, Delbert Fore
Svp Regulatory Affairs, Craig Murray
Senior Vice President, Charles Brabson
Senior Vice President Human Resources, Karen Taylor
Senior Vice President Ngl Marketing And Supply, Albert Al Martinez
Senior Vice President Asset Optimization, Robert Sanders
Svp Unregulated Ngl Fractionation Storage And Unregulated Pipelines, Laurie Argo
Vice President Of Environmental Health And Training, Bryan Oliver
Senior Vice President, Carolyn Stone
Svp Accounting And Risk Control, R Daniel Boss
Senior Vice President Petrochemicals, F Christopher D'Anna
Chairman, Randa D. Williams, age 56
Auditors: DELOITTE & TOUCHE LLP

LOCATIONS

HQ: Enterprise Products Partners L.P.
 1100 Louisiana Street, 10th Floor, Houston, TX 77002
Phone: 713 381-6500
Web: www.enterpriseproducts.com

PRODUCTS/OPERATIONS

2016 Sales

	$ mil.	% of total
NGL Pipelines & Services	10,242	45
Crude Oil Pipelines & Services	6,515	28
Petrochemical & Refined Products Services	3,721	16
Natural Gas Pipelines & Services	2,543	11
Total	**23,022**	**100**

COMPETITORS

Anadarko Petroleum	Kinder Morgan
CenterPoint Energy	Magellan Midstream
Crestwood Midstream Partners LP	ONEOK
Dominion Energy	Occidental Petroleum
Duke Energy	Plains All American Pipeline
Enbridge	Spectra Energy
Energy Transfer Equity	TRII
Exxon Mobil	Williams Companies

HISTORICAL FINANCIALS
Company Type: Public

Income Statement				FYE: December 31
	REVENUE ($ mil.)	NET INCOME ($ mil.)	NET PROFIT MARGIN	EMPLOYEES
12/17	29,241	2,799	9.6%	—
12/16	23,022	2,513	10.9%	—
12/15	27,027	2,521	9.3%	—
12/14	47,061	2,707	5.0%	—
12/13	47,727	2,596	5.4%	—
Annual Growth	(11.5%)	1.9%	—	—

2017 Year-End Financials

Debt ratio: 45.15%—
Return on equity: —
Cash ($ mil.): 5
Current ratio: 0.70
Long-term debt ($ mil.): 21,713

Dividends
Yield: 0.0%
Payout: 128.2%
Market value ($ mil.): —

	STOCK PRICE ($) FY Close	P/E High/Low	PER SHARE ($) Earnings	Dividends	Book Value
12/17	26.51	23 18	1.30	1.67	10.43
12/16	27.04	25 16	1.20	1.59	10.41
12/15	25.58	29 17	1.26	1.51	10.08
12/14	36.12	53 21	1.47	1.43	9.32
12/13	66.30	45 35	1.41	1.35	8.13
Annual Growth	(20.5%)	— —	(2.0%)	5.4%	6.4%

EOG Resources, Inc.

Large-scale shale is the Holy Grail for oil prospector EOG Resources. It engages in exploration development and marketing of natural gas and crude oil originating in the Eagle Ford Shale and Barnett Shale in Texas and the Bakken formation in North Dakota. Of its 2.5 million boe reserves EOG holds 1.3 million barrels in crude oil and condensates with a roughly 4.3 billion cubic feet of natural gas. The US is the company's largest market.

Operations
EOG is the biggest operator (by volume produced) in the lucrative Eagle Ford Shale play in South Texas. The company also has a presence in the Delaware Basin owning about 160000 net acres in the Leonard Shale and over 345000 net acres in the Wolfcamp Shale. Additionally EOG has acreage in the Wolfcamp Shale within the Midland Basin.

Sales of crude oil and crude condensates account for around 55% of total sales natural gas sales account for roughly 10% and NGLs (natural gas liquids) over 5%.

EOG also conducts gas gathering processing and marketing which together bring in nearly 30% of the company's sales. It sells oil and natural gas in local downstream markets transported either by pipeline or truck.

EOG operates its own sand mine and sand processing plants in Hood County Texas to reduce costs and to help fulfill EOG's sand needs for its well completion operations in Texas.

Geographic Reach
EOG has a presence in three major shale plays of the US– the Eagle Ford Shale and Barnett Shale in Texas and the Bakken Formation in North Dakota. Though most of its assets are in the US EOG also has operations in Canada off-

shore Trinidad the UK North Sea and East Irish Sea and the Sichuan Basin in China.

The US accounts for over 95% of the company's proved reserves.

Sales and Marketing

EOG sells two major products—wellhead crude oil & condensates and natural gas. To sell beyond its local market EOG markets these products to downstream customers via extensive pipelines. Crude is also distributed by rail and truck. Its major sales points include Midwest the Permian Basin Cushing Oklahoma St. James Louisiana and other Gulf Coast locations.

The company's Trinidad natural gas operations were sold to the National Gas Company of Trinidad and Tobago while its Chinese natural gas operations were sold to PetroChina.

Financial Performance

EOG has seen revenue climb from $4.8 billion in 2009 to a peak of $12.6 billion by 2014 only to fall drastically to $5.5 billion by 2016. Though EOG has posted handsome profits (typically north of $1 billion) on most years a severe commodity price downturn led to a two-year loss of $5.6 billion in the 2015-16 period.

In 2017 revenue climbed an impressive 47% to $11.2 billion mostly coming from a 45% increase in wellhead crude oil and condenstate revenue higher composite average prices ($1.1 billion) plus higher production ($815 million). Natural gas revenue went up 24% to $922 million due to higher prices as well.

Net income shot up from a loss of $1.1 billion to a net profit of $2.6 billion. This was primarily due to a $2.1 billion improvement in operating income followed by an almost $1.5 billion YOY increase in income tax benefit for 2017.

Cash holdings declined $765 million to $834 million at the end of 2017. Operations generated $4.2 billion which was offset by $3.9 billion used for investments (mostly in additions of new oil & gas properties) plus $1 billion of outflows to financing activities (primarily in debt repayments).The company was able to reduce its debt by some $950 million during 2017 and its outstanding debt was just over $6 billion at the year end.

Strategy

EOG has recovered nicely from a rough commodity price downturn when it lost $5.6 billion in two short years (2015-16). Since then buoyed by recovering oil and gas prices Trump administration tax cuts and operational excellence the company has reported expectation-beating financial and production levels in the 2017-18 period. The key to its success has been two-fold— avoiding acquisition-driven growth and successful diversification into the Powder River Basin. EOG followed that with the spin-off of its UK business to London-based Tailwind Energy an oil and gas venture. This includes the Conwy oil field a 25% non-operated interest in the Columbus gas development project and other minor asset interests in the North Sea.

Since EOG has been acquisition averse it has only focused on low-cost exploration acreage as opposed to purchasing higher-cost acreage where oil has already been discovered. This has allowed EOG to maintain nearly $1 billion in cash holdings while only having some $6 billion in debt.

One of its biggest strategic gambles was exploring the Powder River Basin in Wyoming. South Texas' Eagle Ford shale remains EOG's top producing region and the company also has significant presence in the Permian Basin. And yet while most of its peers were keen to boost output at the Permian Basin of West Texas recognizing pipeline limitations creating a bottleneck EOG wanted to diversify.

It focused on E&P at the Powder Basin as early as 2015 which paid off initially with the discovery of the Turner formation. However the true jackpot came in 2018 when the company announced the stunning discovery of the Mowry and Niobrara shale plays in the Basin which holds some 1.9 billion BOE of recoverable resources a more than tenfold increase for EOG.

The company has also had an equally excellent production run. With a $6 billion capital spending budget EOG is aiming to complete 720 wells by the end of the year 20 more than originally expected. It also reported a record 415000 boe/day production rate up 27 percent from a year ago. It has also made considerable progress lowering costs and improving well performance which helps explain the company's $4.8 billion in revenue by September.

Mergers and Acquisitions

In 2016 EOG acquired Yates Petroleum Corporation Abo Petroleum Corporation MYCO Industries Inc. and certain other entities (collectively Yates) in a deal valued at $2.5 billion.

HISTORY

In 1987 Enron formed Enron Oil & Gas from its existing InterNorth and Houston Natural Gas operations to concentrate on exploration for oil and natural gas and their production. Enron maintained full ownership until 1989 when it spun off 16% of Enron Oil & Gas to the public raising about $200 million. Later offerings reduced its holdings to just over 50%.

Enron Oil & Gas in 1992 was awarded a 95% working interest in three fields off Trinidad that previously had been held by government-owned companies. Two years later the company assumed the operations of three drilling blocks off Bombay (including the Tapti field) as well as a 30% interest in them. Natural gas prices fell in the winter of 1994 causing Enron Oil & Gas to focus its 1995 drilling on crude oil exploitation and the enhancement of its natural gas reserves. Natural gas prices rebounded in 1996. That year Enron Oil & Gas was awarded a 90% interest in an offshore area of Venezuela. In 1997 the company inked a 30-year production contract with China. The company made a major discovery of natural gas in offshore Trinidad in 1998. That year Mark Papa succeeded Forrest Hoglund as CEO (Papa became chairman in 1999).

In 1999 Enron traded most of its remaining stake in Enron Oil & Gas to the company in exchange for Enron Oil & Gas' operations and assets in India and China. Consequently the company changed its name from Enron Oil & Gas to EOG Resources.

The next year EOG won contracts to develop properties in Canada's Northwest Territories. It also moved into the Appalachian Basin in 2000 through the acquisition of Somerset Oil & Gas. Buoyed by a strong performance that year the company increased its capital spending on North American exploration by more than 30% and in 2001 it bought Energy Search a small natural gas exploration and production company that operated in the Appalchian Basin.

EXECUTIVES

Chairman And Ceo, William R. Thomas, age 66, $925,000 total compensation

President And Coo, Gary L. Thomas, age 69, $835,000 total compensation

Svp And Chief Information And Technology Officer, Sandeep Bhakhri

Vp Human Resources Administration, Patricia L. Edwards

Evp And Cfo, Timothy K. Driggers, age 57, $480,000 total compensation

Vp And General Manager Fort Worth, Kenneth E. Dunn

Vp And General Manager Canada Shale Project, Lloyd W. (Bill) Helms, age 60, $470,000 total compensation

Vp Drilling, Robert C. Smith

Vp And General Manager San Antonio, Sammy G. Pickering

Evp Exploration And Production, David W. Trice, age 47

Vp And General Manager Forth Worth, J. Pat Woods

Vp And General Manager Midland, Ezra Y. Yacob

Svp Operations, John J. Boyd

Vp Land, Steven D. Wentworth

Evp General Counsel And Corporate Secretary, Michael P. Donaldson, $475,000 total compensation

Vp And General Manager Oklahoma City, Nathan J. Andrews

Vp And General Manager Corpus Christi, Kenneth D. Marbach

Vp And General Manager Denver, Kenneth W. Boedeker

Vp And General Manager Artesia, Reese T. Lantrip

Vice President Land, Bill Orchard

Senior Vice President And Chief Accounting Officer, Ann Janssen

Vice President, Sara Miller

Vp Audit, Kevin Hanzel

Vice President Business Development, Joe Korenek

Vp And Gm International, J Pat Woods

Chairman And Ceo, William R. Thomas, age 66

Auditors: Deloitte & Touche LLP

LOCATIONS

HQ: EOG Resources, Inc.
 1111 Bagby, Sky Lobby 2, Houston, TX 77002
Phone: 713 651-7000
Web: www.eogresources.com

2017 sales

	$ mil.	% of total
United States	10,872	97
Trinidad	284	3
Other International	51	-
Total	**11,208**	**100**

PRODUCTS/OPERATIONS

2017 sales

	$ mil.	% of total
Crude oil & condensate	6,256	55
Natural Gas Liquids	729	7
Natural Gas	921	8
Gains on Mark-to-Market Commodity Derivative Contracts	19	-
GatheringProcessing and Marketing	3,298	29
Gains on Asset DispositionsNet	(99.1)	-
OtherNet	81	1
Total	**11,208**	**100**

COMPETITORS

Anadarko Petroleum	Occidental Petroleum
Chevron	Parsley Energy LLC
ConocoPhillips	Pioneer Natural
Enerplus	Resources
Newfield Exploration	Royal Dutch Shell
Oasis Petroleum	

HISTORICAL FINANCIALS

Company Type: Public

Income Statement
FYE: December 31

	REVENUE ($ mil.)	NET INCOME ($ mil.)	NET PROFIT MARGIN	EMPLOYEES
12/17	11,208	2,582	23.0%	2,664
12/16	7,650	(1,096)	—	2,650
12/15	8,757	(4,524)	—	2,760
12/14	18,035	2,915	16.2%	3,000
12/13	14,487	2,197	15.2%	2,800
Annual Growth	(6.2%)	4.1%		(1.2%)

2017 Year-End Financials

Debt ratio: 21.41%
Return on equity: 17.07%
Cash ($ mil.): 834
Current ratio: 1.20
Long-term debt ($ mil.): 6,030

No. of shares (mil.): 578
Dividends
Yield: 0.0%
Payout: 15.0%
Market value ($ mil.): 62,423

	STOCK PRICE ($) FY Close	P/E High/Low	PER SHARE ($) Earnings	Dividends	Book Value
12/17	107.91	24 19	4.46	0.67	28.15
12/16	101.10	— —	(1.98)	0.67	24.24
12/15	70.79	— —	(8.29)	0.67	23.54
12/14	92.07	35 15	5.32	0.51	32.30
12/13	167.84	46 28	4.02	0.37	28.23
Annual Growth	(10.5%)	— —	2.6%	16.3%	(0.1%)

EQUINOR MARKETING & TRADING (US) INC.

EXECUTIVES

Vice President Human Resources, Shild Larsen
Vice President Legal, Paul Owen
Vice President Business Development, Ase Staupe
Vice President Project Management, Erik Westad
Vice President Project Management, Johnny Wollberg
Vice President Internal Communication, Kjell Hugvik
Senior Vice President International Exploration, Nicholas Maden
Vice President Drilling Americas, Erling Meyer
Vice President Organisational Change, Geir Husoy
Vice President Troll A Tpc34 Project, Karl Ulveseth
Vice President International Gas, Philippe Mathieu
Vice President Operations, Anita Solheim
Vice President Operations, Lars Hier
Vice President Operations, Dag Johnsgaard
Vice President Information Technology, Andreas Sollie
Executive Vice President, Arne Nylund
Vp Tax, Tom Geczik
Vice President Drilling And Well Engineering, Erik Kirkemo
Auditors: KPMG LLP STAMFORD CONNECTICU

LOCATIONS

HQ: EQUINOR MARKETING & TRADING (US) INC.
120 LONG RIDGE RD 3EO1, STAMFORD, CT 069021839
Phone: 203 978-6900
Web: WWW.STATOIL.COM

COMPETITORS

Global Partners
Gulf Oil
Hess Corporation

Irving Oil Limited
Shell Oil
Tauber Oil

HISTORICAL FINANCIALS

Company Type: Private

Income Statement
FYE: December 31

	REVENUE ($ mil.)	NET INCOME ($ mil.)	NET PROFIT MARGIN	EMPLOYEES
12/17	9,874	(28)	—	85
12/16	5,984	(259)	—	—
12/15	6,947	(132)	—	—
12/14	12,075	(140)	—	—
Annual Growth	(6.5%)			

2017 Year-End Financials

Debt ratio: —
Return on equity: (-0.30%)
Cash ($ mil.): 46
Current ratio: 0.70
Long-term debt ($ mil.): —

Dividends
Yield: —
Payout: —
Market value ($ mil.): —

Equity Bancshares Inc

Auditors: Crowe Chizek LLP

LOCATIONS

HQ: Equity Bancshares Inc
7701 East Kellogg Drive, Suite 300, Wichita, KS 67207
Phone: 316 612-6000
Web: www.equitybank.com

HISTORICAL FINANCIALS

Company Type: Public

Income Statement
FYE: December 31

	ASSETS ($ mil.)	NET INCOME ($ mil.)	INCOME AS % OF ASSETS	EMPLOYEES
12/17	3,170	20	0.7%	526
12/16	2,192	9	0.4%	415
12/15	1,585	10	0.6%	297
12/14	1,175	8	0.8%	262
12/13	1,140	7	0.7%	—
Annual Growth	29.1%	27.3%	—	—

2017 Year-End Financials

Debt ratio: 0.50%
Return on equity: 6.53%
Cash ($ mil.): 51
Current ratio: —
Long-term debt ($ mil.): —

No. of shares (mil.): 14
Dividends
Yield: —
Payout: —
Market value ($ mil.): 517

	STOCK PRICE ($) FY Close	P/E High/Low	PER SHARE ($) Earnings	Dividends	Book Value
12/17	35.41	22 18	1.62	0.00	25.62
12/16	33.64	34 19	1.07	0.00	22.09
12/15	23.39	16 15	1.54	0.00	20.37
Annual Growth	10.9%	— —	1.3%	—	5.9%

Erie Indemnity Co.

Erie Indemnity may be near a lake but it prefers pools. Founded in 1925 as an auto insurer it now provides management services that relate to the sales underwriting and issuance of policies of one customer: Erie Insurance Exchange. The Exchange is a reciprocal insurance exchange that pools the underwriting of several property/casualty insurance firms. It offers coverage ranging from homeowners to boat policies through independent representatives with a reach that extends to a dozen states east of the Mississippi River. Erie Indemnity charges a management fee of 25% of all premiums written or assumed by the Exchange.

Operations

Management fees account for more than 95% of Erie Indemnity's revenue; service agreements and investment income account for the remainder.

The Exchange and its subsidiaries (Erie Insurance Erie Insurance Company of New York Erie Insurance Property and Casualty and Flagship City Insurance) together operate as a property/casualty insurer and are collectively referred to as the Property and Casualty Group. The group also owns Erie Family Life Insurance.

Personal lines — primarily private passenger automobile and homeowners products — comprise some 70% of the direct and assumed premiums written; commercial lines — primarily multi-peril workers' compensation and commercial automobile — make up the rest.

Geographic Reach

Erie Indemnity operates in a dozen midwestern mid-Atlantic and southeastern states (Illinois Indiana Kentucky Maryland New York North Carolina Ohio Pennsylvania Tennessee Virginia West Virginia and Wisconsin) as well as in the District of Columbia.

Sales and Marketing

Erie Indemnity's distribution network includes about 12000 independent agents.

Financial Performance

Erie Indemnity's revenue which has been rising for the past five years increased 6% to $1.7 billion in 2017. This was driven by an increase in net management fee income (Erie Insurance Exchange raised its property/casualty premiums earning by 6% that year) and investment income but offset by a slight decline in service agreement income.

Net income declined 6% to $197 million in 2017 partially due to increased commission personnel and IT fee expenses. Cash flow from operations dropped 22% to $197 million.

Strategy

Through careful risk selection and pricing practices as well as by maintaining a diverse product mix Erie Indemnity seeks to maintain long-term underwriting profit growth for the Exchange. It also seeks to provide consistent support services to policyholders and agents. Towards that end the company is upgrading its technology platforms (such as its claims management system). Additionally it was an early adopter of drone technology which it uses to deploy drones to hard-to-reach claims sites.

Chief among Erie Indemnity's strategies for growth are efforts to increase its property/casualty group premiums. Furthermore it is working to improve its competitive position by expanding the size of its agency force and increasing market penetration in existing territories. It also intends to expand geographically and broaden the types of products it offers. For example in 2016 it began providing small to midsized companies with protection against cloud computing risks.

Erie Indemnity develops innovative products to address new types of risks as the world increasingly modernizes and to provide itself with new revenue sources. It was one of the first insurers to offer coverage for ride-sharing drivers and it now offers expanded home coverage for those who provide short-term property rentals through services such as Airbnb. The company is keeping an eye on additional new opportunities presented by such areas as self-driving cars blockchain technology the Internet of Things big data and cybersecurity.

Because of its reliance on sole customer Erie Insurance Exchange Erie Indemnity's performance is ultimately tied to that of the Exchange. That makes the company somewhat vulnerable to that firm's ability to withstand catastrophic losses or the possibility that the Exchange will lower its management fee rates.

Company Background

Erie Indemnity's structure and relationship to other parts of the larger Erie Insurance Group are complex to say the least. The company operated as a property/casualty insurer through its wholly-owned subsidiaries Erie Insurance Co. Erie New York and Erie Insurance Property and Casualty throughout 2010. At year-end however Erie Indemnity sold all of its outstanding capital stock and voting shares of these subsidiaries to the Exchange. As a result now all of its former property/casualty insurance operations are owned by the Exchange and Erie Indemnity serves as the management company. The sale of the subsidiaries did not affect its pooling agreement. The company also sold its approximate 22% ownership in Erie Family Life to the Exchange which became Erie's' full parent.

EXECUTIVES

President And Ceo, Timothy G. NeCastro, $492,085 total compensation

Evp And Cio, Robert C. (Bob) Ingram, age 59, $456,923 total compensation

Evp Claims And Customer Service, Lorianne Feltz

Svp And Chief Investment Officer, Bradley G. Postema, $418,558 total compensation

Evp And General Counsel, Sean J. McLaughlin, age 63, $426,923 total compensation

Svp And Controller, Gregory J. (Greg) Gutting, age 54, $406,885 total compensation

Evp Sales And Products, Doug Smith

Executive Vice President Sales And Marketing, John Kearns

Vice President Information Technology Operations And Service Management, Andrew Abramczyk

Vice Chairman, Jonathan Hirt Hagen, age 55

Chairman, Thomas B. Hagen, age 82

Board Member, Thomas Palmer

Auditors: Ernst & Young LLP

LOCATIONS

HQ: Erie Indemnity Co.
100 Erie Insurance Place, Erie, PA 16530
Phone: 814 870-2000
Web: www.erieinsurance.com

PRODUCTS/OPERATIONS

2017 Sales

	$ mil.	% of total
Operating revenue		
Net management fees	1,662	97
Service agreements	29	2
Investment income	28	1
Total	**1,720**	**100**

COMPETITORS

ACE USA	Navigators
Alleghany Corporation	Old Republic
Gallagher	Transatlantic Holdings
Marsh & McLennan	Travelers Companies

HISTORICAL FINANCIALS

Company Type: Public

Income Statement

FYE: December 31

	ASSETS ($ mil.)	NET INCOME ($ mil.)	INCOME AS % OF ASSETS	EMPLOYEES
12/17	1,665	197	11.8%	5,300
12/16	1,548	210	13.6%	5,000
12/15	1,407	174	12.4%	4,800
12/14	17,758	168	0.9%	4,700
12/13	16,676	163	1.0%	4,450
Annual Growth	**(43.8%)**	**4.9%**	**—**	**4.5%**

2017 Year-End Financials

Debt ratio: 4.49%
Return on equity: 23.53%
Cash ($ mil.): 215
Current ratio: —
Long-term debt ($ mil.): —
No. of shares (mil.): 46
Dividends
  Yield: 0.0%
  Payout: 83.2%
Market value ($ mil.): 5,628

	STOCK PRICE ($) FY Close	P/E High/Low		PER SHARE ($) Earnings	Dividends	Book Value
12/17	121.84	30	26	3.76	3.13	18.56
12/16	112.45	25	20	4.01	2.19	17.69
12/15	95.64	27	21	3.33	2.77	16.66
12/14	90.77	26	19	3.18	2.54	15.22
12/13	73.12	24	20	3.08	4.37	15.80
Annual Growth	**13.6%**	**—**	**—**	**5.1%**	**(8.0%)**	**4.1%**

ESSA Bancorp Inc

EXECUTIVES

Executive Vice President And Chief Operating Officer Of Company And Essa Bank, Charles Hangen

Vice President Commercial Loan Officer Iii, Henry Kush

Auditors: S.R. Snodgrass, P.C.

LOCATIONS

HQ: ESSA Bancorp Inc
200 Palmer Street, Stroudsburg, PA 18360
Phone: 570 421-0531
Web: www.essabank.com

COMPETITORS

First National	Norwood Financial
Community Bancorp	PNC Financial
Fulton Financial	Sovereign Bank

HISTORICAL FINANCIALS

Company Type: Public

Income Statement

FYE: September 30

	ASSETS ($ mil.)	NET INCOME ($ mil.)	INCOME AS % OF ASSETS	EMPLOYEES
09/18	1,833	6	0.4%	277
09/17	1,785	7	0.4%	323
09/16	1,772	7	0.4%	326
09/15	1,606	9	0.6%	303
09/14	1,574	8	0.5%	303
Annual Growth	**3.9%**	**(6.4%)**	**—**	**(2.2%)**

2018 Year-End Financials

Debt ratio: 6.47%
Return on equity: 3.61%
Cash ($ mil.): 44
Current ratio: —
Long-term debt ($ mil.): —
No. of shares (mil.): 11
Dividends
  Yield: 0.0%
  Payout: 60.0%
Market value ($ mil.): 192

	STOCK PRICE ($) FY Close	P/E High/Low		PER SHARE ($) Earnings	Dividends	Book Value
09/18	16.26	28	24	0.60	0.36	15.21
09/17	15.70	24	19	0.69	0.36	15.76
09/16	13.83	19	17	0.73	0.36	15.48
09/15	12.96	14	12	0.93	0.34	15.09
09/14	11.30	15	13	0.79	0.26	14.44
Annual Growth	**9.5%**	**—**	**—**	**(6.6%)**	**8.5%**	**1.3%**

Eversource Energy

Eversource Energy uses Yankee ingenuity power and gas to keep its customers happy. The largest energy delivery company in New England Eversource serves 3.6 million electric and gas customers via its six distinct utility companies in Connecticut Massachusetts and New Hampshire. Eversource delivers its energy over nearly 4000 miles of power transmission lines 40000 miles of electric distribution lines and more than 6500 miles of gas distribution lines. Its electricity-focused utility companies include Public Service Company of New Hampshire (PNSH) and Western Massachusetts Electric. Eversource?s gas utilities are NSTAR Gas and Yankee Gas the latter of which supplies natural gas to nearly 230000 customers in more than 70 cities and towns in Connecticut. Although PNSH generates its own power Eversource buys most of its electricity from third parties before distributing it to its customers.

HISTORY

In 1966 three old intertwined New England utilities merged. One was The Hartford Electric Light Company (HELCO) founded in 1883 by Austin Dunham in Hartford Connecticut. In 1915 the company signed the first power exchange agreement in the US with Connecticut Power (CP) which HELCO acquired in 1920.

The second founded in 1886 was Western Massachusetts Electric (WMECO) which merged with Western Counties in the 1930s to become WMECO. The third was Connecticut Light and Power (CL&P). Founded as Rocky River Power in 1905 it took the CL&P name in 1917. In 1929 it built the US's first large-scale pumped-storage hydroelectric plant.

In the 1950s HELCO formed Yankee Atomic Electric with CL&P WMECO and others to build an experimental nuclear reactor. In 1965 members of the group began jointly building the Connecticut Yankee nuke (on line in 1968). After years of cooperation CL&P HELCO and WMECO merged in 1966 and Northeast Utilities (NU) was born. It was the first multistate utility holding company created since the Public Utility Holding Company Act of 1935 had broken up the old utility giants. Holyoke Water Power joined NU the following year.

The 1970s energy crisis spurred NU to continue building nukes including Maine Yankee Vermont Yankee and two Millstone units. But by the 1980s construction delays had raised the cost of the final unit Millstone 3.

Regulators forced CL&P to spin off its gas utility Yankee Energy System in 1989. The next year

NU acquired bankrupt utility Public Service Company of New Hampshire (PSNH) and its new Seabrook nuke. (PSNH emerged from bankruptcy in 1991.)

The 1995 shutdown of Millstone 1 began NU's nuclear troubles. In 1996 regulators closed all of its nukes except Seabrook because of safety concerns and NU mothballed Connecticut Yankee. The next year Michael Morris replaced CEO Bernard Fox who left after federal regulators ordered NU to comply with regulations and fix management problems — NU managers had routinely retaliated against whistleblowers — the first time a utility had been given such an order. New managers came in including a former whistleblower but NU couldn't avoid a record-setting $2.1 million fine. NU received permission to restart the Millstone units in 1998-99. But it had to absorb the $1 billion in power replacement associated with the shutdown.

Meanwhile as deregulation loomed NU created a retail marketer (now Select Energy) and a telecommunications arm (Mode 1 Communications) in 1996. Two years later retail competition began in Massachusetts and deregulation legislation was passed in Connecticut (deregulation went into effect there in 2000).

In 1999 NU sold its Massachusetts plants to New York's Consolidated Edison and auctioned off its non-nuclear plants in Connecticut to its subsidiary Northeast Generation and Northern States Power (now Xcel Energy). NU agreed to plead guilty to 25 federal felony counts and pay $10 million in penalties for polluting water near Millstone and lying to regulators.

That year Consolidated Edison agreed to buy NU for $3.3 billion in cash and stock and $3.9 billion in assumed debt. The deal broke down in 2001 however; Con Edison charged NU with misrepresenting information about power-supply contracts and NU charged Con Edison with improperly attempting to renegotiate the terms of the acquisition.

Bringing an old family member home NU bought Yankee Energy System for $679 million in 2000. Later that year Dominion Resources which had helped NU restart Millstone 2 and Millstone 3 (Millstone 1 had been taken out of service) agreed to buy the Millstone complex for $1.3 billion. The sale closed in 2001.

Also in 2001 NU subsidiary Select Energy bought Niagara Mohawk's energy marketing unit NU sold the distribution business of its Holyoke Water Power utility to the City of Holyoke for $18 million and retail electric competition began in New Hampshire. The company agreed to sell CL&P's 10% stake in the Vermont Yankee nuclear facility to Entergy in 2001; the deal was completed the following year.

NU sold its 40% interest in the Seabrook Nuclear Generating facility in 2002 to FPL Group.

In 2006 NU sold nonregulated subsidiary Select Energy which marketed and traded energy to wholesale and retail customers to Hess Corporation. That year the company also sold its competitive generation assets in Connecticut and Massachusetts to Energy Capital Partners for $1.34 billion.

In 2007 Connecticut Light and Power Company completed the installation of electric service to Yankee Gas Services Company's new liquefied natural gas facility in Waterbury.

To give better access and service to its customers in 2009 NU relocated its headquarters from Berlin Connecticut to a larger building in downtown Hartford.

The 2012 acquisition of NSTAR (with 1.1 million power and 300000 gas customers) for $4.2 billion boosted the financial resources of Eversource to pay for planned transmission projects aimed at bringing cleaner power from northern New England and Canada to population centers in southern New England. The "merger of equals" (NSTAR and Eversource) created a major energy player in the US Northeast which serves more than half the total utility customers in New England. NSTAR shareholders hold about 44% of the expanded company.

EXECUTIVES

Evp And Coo, Werner J. Schweiger, age 58, $592,108 total compensation

Evp And General Counsel, Gregory B. Butler, age 60, $514,494 total compensation

President And Ceo, James J. (Jim) Judge, age 62, $959,690 total compensation

Evp Enterprise Energy Strategy And Business Development Eversource Energy And Eversource Service, Leon J. (Lee) Olivier, age 70, $1,232,250 total compensation

Evp Customer And Corporate Relations Eversource Energy And Eversource Service, Joseph R. (Joe) Nolan, age 54, $419,364 total compensation

Evp Human Resources And Information Technology Eversource Energy And Eversource Service, Christine M. (Chris) Carmody, age 55

Svp And Cfo, Philip J. (Phil) Lembo, age 62, $439,208 total compensation

Vice President Energy Supply, James Daly

Vice President Operations Executive, Robert S Coates

Vice President Operations Yankee Gas, Marc Andrukiewicz

Vice President New Hampshire Electric Operations, Joseph Purington

Vice President Communications, Beth Foley

Chairman, Thomas J. (Tom) May, age 71

Board Member, Dennis Harrington

Secretary, Richard Morrison

Auditors: Deloitte & Touche LLP

LOCATIONS

HQ: Eversource Energy
300 Cadwell Drive, Springfield, MA 01104
Phone: 800 286-5000
Web: www.eversource.com

PRODUCTS/OPERATIONS

2016 Sales

	$ mil.	% of total
Electric:		
Residential	3,448	45
Commercial	2,465	32
Wholesale	426	4
Industrial	328	6
Other	93	1
Natural Gas	854	12
Other	23	-
Total	**7,639**	**100**

2016 Sales

	$ mil.	% of total
Electric distribution	5,594	66
Electric transmission	1,210	10
Natural gas distribution	857	14
Other	870	10
Eliminations	(893.3)	-
Total	**7,639**	**100**

Selected Subsidiaries & Affiliates

The Connecticut Light and Power Company (CL&P eletric utility)
NSTAR Electric Company (electric utility)
NSTAR Gas Company (natural gas utility)
Public Service Company of New Hampsire (PSNH electric utility)
Western Massachusetts Electric Company (WMECO electric utility)
Yankee Gas Services Company (natural gas utility)

HISTORICAL FINANCIALS

Company Type: Public

Income Statement
FYE: December 31

	REVENUE ($ mil.)	NET INCOME ($ mil.)	NET PROFIT MARGIN	EMPLOYEES
12/17	7,751	988	12.7%	8,084
12/16	7,639	942	12.3%	7,762
12/15	7,954	878	11.0%	7,943
12/14	7,741	819	10.6%	8,248
12/13	7,301	786	10.8%	8,697
Annual Growth	1.5%	5.9%	—	(1.8%)

2017 Year-End Financials

Debt ratio: 37.03%
Return on equity: 9.07%
Cash ($ mil.): 38
Current ratio: 0.69
Long-term debt ($ mil.): 11,775

No. of shares (mil.): 316
Dividends
  Yield: 0.0%
  Payout: 61.0%
Market value ($ mil.): 20,021

	STOCK PRICE ($) FY Close	P/E High/Low		PER SHARE ($)		
				Earnings	Dividends	Book Value
12/17	63.18	21	17	3.11	1.90	34.98
12/16	55.23	20	17	2.96	1.78	33.80
12/15	51.07	20	16	2.76	1.67	32.64
12/14	53.52	22	16	2.58	1.57	31.47
12/13	42.39	18	16	2.49	1.47	30.49
Annual Growth	10.5%	—	—	5.7%	6.6%	3.5%

Exchange Bank (Santa Rosa, CA)

Exchange Bank serves personal and business customers from some 20 branch offices throughout Sonoma County California. It also has a branch in nearby Placer County. The bank provides standard products including checking and savings accounts Visa credit cards online banking and a variety of real estate business and consumer loans. It also offers investment services such as wealth management personal trust administration employee benefits plans and individual retirement accounts. Effective early 2014 Exchange Bank is on its eighth president since its inception in 1890. The Doyle Trust which was established by co-founder Frank Doyle owns a majority of the bank.

Operations

Exchange Bank's lending activity is concentrated in Sonoma County. Commercial real estate loans represent more than half of its loan portfolio. Exchange Bank believes it will continue to benefit from growth in the local technology and biomedical industries and lower unemployment increased tourism and a decline in commercial real estate vacancies in Sonoma County.

Geographic Reach

Based in Santa Rosa California Exchange Bank operates primarily in Sonoma County but also in Placer and Contra counties.

Sales and Marketing

Exchange Bank counts some 25000 customers among its clients serving them through about 20 branch offices. It caters to customers online as well through its website which in fiscal 2013 earned 1.5 million customer visits.

Financial Performance

Revenue dropped 4% in fiscal 2013 to $85.9 million as compared to $89.1 million in 2012. Exchange Bank attributes the decrease to lower interest income resulting from a decline in interest received on term loans offset in part by increased interest on securities. From $12.26 million in 2012 the firm's net income grew some 28% to $15.73 million. Exchange Bank points to noteworthy drops in the provision for loan and lease losses and a decrease in interest and non-interest income for the net income gains.

EXECUTIVES

Vice President Commercial, Connie Mcmannus
Vice President Human Resources, Diana Angell
Vice President Sba Loan Department, Scott Dykstra
Vice President, Laura Buhrer
Vice President Business Development, Ronald Malnati
Assistant Vice President And Bank Operations Analyst, Jane Daniel
Vice President And Real Estate Loan Officer, Wynn Spain
Senior Vice President Corporate And Business Development Manager, Howard Daulton
Assistant Vice President, Patty Brookins
Senior Vice President, Steve Herron
Senior Vice President Real Estate Loan, Louise Mason
Vice President, Joseph Huang
Executive Vice President Cco, Mark Crawford
Vice President And Employee Benefit Trust Officer, Susan Preston
Vice President, Jason Hinde
Vice President Business Banking Officer And Commercial Loan Officer, Bill Espindola
Vice President, Richard Carlson
Business Development Officer Vice President, Brian Kilkenny
Vice President And Trust Operations And Compliance Manager, SungWon Kang
Vice President Investment Officer, William Sullivan
Auditors: KPMG LLP

LOCATIONS

HQ: Exchange Bank (Santa Rosa, CA)
545 Fourth Street, Santa Rosa, CA 95401
Phone: 707 524-3301
Web: www.exchangebank.com

COMPETITORS

Bank of America	U.S. Bancorp
First Northern	Wells Fargo
JPMorgan Chase	Westamerica
MUFG Americas Holdings	

HISTORICAL FINANCIALS

Company Type: Public

Income Statement

FYE: December 31

	ASSETS ($ mil.)	NET INCOME ($ mil.)	INCOME AS % OF ASSETS	EMPLOYEES
12/17	2,584	19	0.8%	—
12/16	2,179	21	1.0%	—
12/15	2,062	21	1.0%	—
12/14	1,887	17	0.9%	—
12/13	1,783	15	0.9%	—
Annual Growth	9.7%	5.5%	—	—

2017 Year-End Financials

Debt ratio: —	No. of shares (mil.): 1
Return on equity: 9.94%	Dividends
Cash ($ mil.): 360	Yield: 0.0%
Current ratio: —	Payout: 29.8%
Long-term debt ($ mil.): —	Market value ($ mil.): 261

	STOCK PRICE ($) FY Close	P/E High/Low		PER SHARE ($) Earnings	Dividends	Book Value
12/17	152.00	14	11	11.38	3.40	118.53
12/16	125.00	11	6	12.54	2.80	110.35
12/15	89.00	7	6	12.27	2.20	100.98
12/14	84.00	8	7	10.25	1.55	93.37
12/13	69.00	8	6	8.60	1.10	90.42
Annual Growth	21.8%	—	—	7.3%	32.6%	7.0%

Exelon Corp

Exelon is lighting up the utility industry with high-powered energy generation and extensive electricity delivery. The utility holding company does enough of both to be designated one of the largest in the US. Its Exelon Generation subsidiary holds power-generating assets of almost 35000 MW (some 2000 MW is produced at 23 nuclear plants). Exelon distributes electricity and gas to 10 million customers in Illinois Maryland the District of Columbia Delaware New Jersey and Pennsylvania through its regulated utility companies. Its Constellation subsidiary provides energy products and services to 2.2 million business customers. In a major expansion Exelon acquired three regulated utilities for $7.1 billion in 2016

HISTORY

Thomas Dolan and local investors formed the Brush Electric Light Company of Philadelphia in 1881 to provide street and commercial lighting. Competitors sprang up and in 1885 Brush merged with the United States Electric Lighting Company of Pennsylvania to form a secret "electric trust" or holding company. Dolan became president in 1886 and bought four other utilities.

In 1895 Martin Maloney formed Pennsylvania Heat Light and Power to consolidate the city's electric companies. By the next year it had acquired among other businesses Columbia Electric Light Philadelphia Edison and the electric trust. In 1899 a new firm National Electric challenged Maloney by acquiring neighboring rival Southern Electric Light. Before retiring Maloney negotiated the merger of the two firms forming Philadelphia Electric in 1902.

Demand rose rapidly into the 1920s fueled in part by the company's promotion of electric appliances. In 1928 the year after it completed the Conowingo Hydroelectric Station Philadelphia Electric was absorbed by the much larger United Gas Improvement. United Gas avoided large layoffs during the Depression but passage of the Public Utility Holding Company Act (PUHCA) in 1935 sounded its death knell. (PUHCA was repealed in 2005.) In 1943 the SEC forced United Gas to divest Philadelphia Electric.

Philadelphia Electric built several plants in the 1950s and 1960s in response to a postwar electricity boom. A small experimental nuclear reactor was completed at Peach Bottom Pennsylvania in 1967 and in 1974 the company placed two nuclear units in service at the plant. The Salem (New Jersey) nuke (Unit 1) followed in 1977. The company

relied on these plants during the OPEC oil crisis. Another one Limerick Unit 1 began operations in 1986 and Unit 2 went on line in 1990 but the Peach Bottom plant was shut down from 1989 to 1991 because of management problems (later resolved).

The company began reorganizing in 1993 and changed its name the next year to PECO Energy Company. It also sold Maryland retail subsidiary Conowingo Power retaining the hydroelectric plant. In 1995 rival PP&L rejected PECO's acquisition bid citing PECO's nuclear liabilities.

A year later PECO teamed with AT&T Wireless to offer PCS in Philadelphia (service was launched in 1997). EnergyOne a national venture formed in 1997 by PECO UtiliCorp United (now Aquila) and AT&T offered consumers a package of power phone and Internet services on one bill. However the slow deregulation process caused the venture to fail.

PECO also joined with British Energy in 1997 to form AmerGen hoping to buy nukes at rock-bottom prices from utilities eager to unload them. AmerGen purchased three nuclear facilities in 1999 and 2000: Unit 1 of the Three Mile Island (Pennsylvania) facility; a plant in Clinton Illinois; and an Oyster Creek (New Jersey) location.

In 1999 PECO announced plans to acquire Chicago's Unicom the parent company of Commonwealth Edison (ComEd). After the deal was completed in 2000 the combined company took the name Exelon and established its headquarters in Chicago.

Pennsylvania's utility markets were fully deregulated in 2000. To expand its power generation business Exelon that year bought 49.9% of Sithe Energies for $682 million. In 2001 Exelon agreed to buy two gas-fired power plants (2300 MW) in Texas from TXU for $443 million; the deal was completed in 2002.

Also in 2002 Exelon purchased Sithe Energies' stakes in six New England power plants with 2000 MW of capacity (plus 2400 MW under construction) for $543 million plus the assumption of $1.15 billion in debt. The company also sold its Philadelphia PCS venture interest to former partner AT&a

EXECUTIVES

President And Ceo, Christopher M. (Chris) Crane, age 59, $1,255,515 total compensation
Svp And Chief Information And Digital Officer, Mike Koehler, age 51
President Exelon Power, Ronald J. (Ron) DeGregorio, age 55
Evp; Coo Excelon Generation, Michael J. Pacilio, age 57
Sevp And Cfo, Jonathan W. (Jack) Thayer, age 46, $784,802 total compensation
Evp Customer Operations Regulatory And External Affairs Comed, Anne R. Pramaggiore, age 59
Sevp And Chief Commercial Officer And President And Ceo Exelon Generation, Kenneth W. (Ken) Cornew, age 52, $857,477 total compensation
Evp And Ceo Constellation, Joseph (Joe) Nigro, age 53
Sevp And Chief Strategy Officer, William A. (Bill) Von Hoene, age 64, $831,350 total compensation
President And Ceo Pepco Holdings, David M. (Dave) Velazquez, age 59
President And Chief Nuclear Officer Exelon Nuclear, Bryan C. Hanson, age 52
Evp; President And Ceo Peco, Craig L. Adams, age 65
Ceo Baltimore Gas And Electric, Calvin G. Butler, age 48
Evp And Chief Enterprise Risk Officer, Paymon Aliabadi, age 55

Evp Governmental And Regulatory Affairs And
Public Policy, Joseph Dominguez, age 54
Sevp And Ceo Exelon Utilities, Denis P. OÂ'Brien,
age 57, $800,378 total compensation
Evp Corporate Operations, M. Bridget Reidy
Senior Vice President State Governmental And
Regulatory Affairs, David Fein
Senior Vice President Operations Support,
Christopher Mudrick
Vice President, Chris Symonds
Svp And Chief Investment Officer, Douglas Brown
Vpres Clinton Power Station, Mark Newcomer
Senior Vice President Portfolio Management And
Strategy Constellation, Ravi Ganti
Vice President Global Business Development,
Roger Burke
Senior Vice President And Chro, Amy Best
Senior Vice President Corporate Affairs
Philanthropy And Customer Engagement, Maggie
Fitzpatrick
Vice President Engineering And Project
Management, Michelle Blaise
Vice President Regulatory Policy And S, Michael
Guerra
Dresden Site Vice President, Shane Marik
Chairman, Mayo A. Shattuck, age 63
Board Member, Brian Boggetto
Auditors: PricewaterhouseCoopers LLP

LOCATIONS

HQ: Exelon Corp
10 South Dearborn Street, P.O. Box 805379, Chicago,
IL 60680-5379
Phone: 800 483-3220
Web: www.exeloncorp.com

PRODUCTS/OPERATIONS

2016 Sales

	$ mil.	% of total
Generation	17,751	54
ComEd	5,254	16
PECO	2,994	9
BGE	3,233	10
PHI	3,643	11
Other	(1515)	-
Total	**31,360**	**100**

2016 Sales

	$ mil.	% of total
Competitive businesses revenues	16,324	52
Rate-regulated utility revenues	15,036	48
Total	**31,360**	**100**

Selected Operating Units Subsidiaries and Affiliates

Exelon Energy Delivery
Baltimore Gas and Electric (BGE electric and gas utility)
Commonwealth Edison Company (ComEd electric
utility)
PECO Energy Company (PECO electric and gas utility)
Pepco Holdings LLC (PHI)
Potomac Electric Power Company (Pepco electric utility)
Delmarva Power & Light Company (DPL electric and gas
utility)
Atlantic City Electric Company (ACE electric utility)
Exelon Generation Company LLC
 Constellation
 Exelon Power
 Exelon Hydro
 Exelon Solar
 Exelon Wind
 Exelon Power Team
 Exelon Energy (nonregulated retail power sales)
 Exelon Nuclear (nuclear power generation)
Exelon Transmission Company

COMPETITORS

AES	FirstEnergy
Alliant Energy	Green Mountain Energy
Ambit Energy	Jersey Central Power &
Ameren	Light

American Transmission	NextEra Energy
Dominion Energy	PPL Corporation
Duke Energy	Public Service
Duquesne Light	Electric and Gas
Holdings	UGI

HISTORICAL FINANCIALS

Company Type: Public

Income Statement

FYE: December 31

	REVENUE ($ mil.)	NET INCOME ($ mil.)	NET PROFIT MARGIN	EMPLOYEES
12/18	35,985	2,010	5.6%	33,383
12/17	33,531	3,770	11.2%	34,621
12/16	31,360	1,134	3.6%	34,396
12/15	29,447	2,269	7.7%	29,762
12/14	27,429	1,623	5.9%	28,993
Annual Growth	**7.0%**	**5.5%**	**—**	**3.6%**

2018 Year-End Financials

Debt ratio: 30.52%	No. of shares (mil.): 968
Return on equity: 6.63%	Dividends
Cash ($ mil.): 1,349	Yield: 3.0%
Current ratio: 1.17	Payout: 35.5%
Long-term debt ($ mil.): 34,465	Market value ($ mil.): 43,665

	STOCK PRICE ($) FY Close	P/E High/Low		PER SHARE ($) Earnings	Dividends	Book Value
12/18	45.10	23	17	2.07	1.38	31.77
12/17	39.41	11	8	3.97	1.31	30.99
12/16	35.49	30	22	1.22	1.26	27.96
12/15	27.77	15	10	2.54	1.24	28.25
12/14	37.08	20	14	1.88	1.24	26.52
Annual Growth	**5.0%**	**—**	**—**	**2.4%**	**2.7%**	**4.6%**

Exelon Generation Co LLC

Exelon Generation Company has built an excellent reputation by generating electricity. The company a subsidiary of Exelon Corporation is one of the largest electric wholesale and retail power generation companies in the US. In 2013 Exelon Generation had a generation capacity of more than 44560 MW (primarily nuclear but also fossil-fired and hydroelectric and other renewable energy-based plants). Subsidiary Exelon Nuclear operates the largest fleet of nuclear power plants in the US. Exelon Generation's Exelon Power unit oversees a fleet of more than 100 fossil- and renewable-fueled plants (more than 15875 MW of capacity) in Illinois Maryland Massachusetts Pennsylvania and Texas.

Operations

The company operates as an integrated business leveraging its owned and contracted electric generation capacity to market and sell power to wholesale and retail customers. It has ownership interests in eleven nuclear generating stations currently in service consisting of 19 units with an aggregate of 17263 MW of capacity. It also owns a 50% interest in CENG a joint venture with EDF. CENG is governed by a board of ten directors five of which are appointed by Generation and five by EDF.

Geographic Reach

The Mid-Atlantic represents operations in the eastern half of PJM and accounted for 37% of Exelon Generation's generating capacity in 2013;

Midwest (western half of PJM the entire US footprint of MISO 34%); New England (the operations within the ISO-NE 8%); New York (ISO-NY 3%); ERCOT (Texas) 12%; and Other areas 6%).

The Mid-Atlantic region includes Pennsylvania New Jersey Maryland Virginia West Virginia Delaware the District of Columbia and parts of North Carolina. Midwest includes portions of Illinois Indiana Ohio Michigan Kentucky and Tennessee; and the United States footprint of MISO excluding MISO's Southern Region which covers all or most of North Dakota South Dakota Nebraska Minnesota Iowa Wisconsin and the remaining parts of Illinois Indiana Michigan and Ohio not covered by PJM; and parts of Montana Missouri and Kentucky.New England represents the operations within ISO-NE covering the states of Connecticut Maine Massachusetts New Hampshire Rhode Island and Vermont. New York represents the operations within ISO-NY which covers the state of New York in its entirety. ERCOT represents operations within Electric Reliability Council of Texas covering most of the state of Texas. "Other Regions" is an aggregate of other geographic regions not considered individually significant.

Sales and Marketing

Exelon Generation's customers include distribution utilities municipalities cooperatives financial institutions and commercial industrial governmental and residential customers in competitive markets. The company also sells natural gas and renewable energy and other energy-related products and services and engages in natural gas exploration and production activities.

Financial Performance

The company's revenues increased by 8% in 2013 primarily due to increased capacity prices and higher nuclear volume partially offset by lower realized energy prices higher nuclear fuel costs and lower mark-to-market gains.

Net income increased by 90% in 2013 primarily due to higher revenues net of purchased power and fuel expense lower operating and maintenance expense and higher earnings from Exelon Generation's interest in CENG; partially offset by impairment of certain generating assets and higher depreciation costs property taxes and interest expenses.

Strategy

Exelon Generation leverages owned and contracted electric generation capacity to market and sell power wholesale. The company's integrated business operations include the physical delivery and marketing of power obtained through its generation capacity and through long-term intermediate-term and short-term contracts. Exelon Generation maintains an effective supply strategy through ownership of generation assets and power purchase and lease agreements. The company has also contracted for access to additional generation through bilateral long-term power agreements.

Exelon Generation's electricity generation strategy is to pursue opportunities that provide generation to load matching and that diversify the generation fleet by expanding Generation's regional and technological footprint. The company leverages its energy generation portfolio to ensure delivery of energy to both wholesale and retail customers under long-term and short-term contracts and in wholesale power markets.

In 2012 a subsidiary of Exelon Generation sold three coal-fired plants (Brandon Shores and H.A. Wagner generating station in Anne Arundel County Maryland and the C.P. Crane plant in Baltimore County Maryland) to Raven Power Holdings LLC a subsidiary of Riverstone Holdings LLC to comply with certain of the regulatory approvals required by the company's merger with Constellation Energy for net proceeds of $371 million which resulted in a pre-tax loss of $272 million.

Exelon Nuclear operates the largest nuclear fleet in the US (10 stations with 17 nuclear units) and has about 20% of the industry's total capacity. Exelon Generation has submitted an application to the Nuclear Regulatory Commission to build a new nuclear generating facility in Texas. The company hasn't made the decision to build the facility but wanted to get a start on the potentially onerous process. The last license to result in the construction of a new nuclear facility in the US was granted in 1973. However the Fukushima nuclear plant disaster in early 2011 placed nuclear power expansion plans under serious scrutiny from regulators.

Mergers and Acquisitions

In a major move to grow its retail operations in 2012 parent Exelon Corporation bought Constellation Energy in a $7.9 billion stock deal. The purchase of Constellation Energy (which gets 17% of its power from nuclear plants) helped the company boost its nuclear-generated power plant assets.

Company Background

Growing its cleaner-burning plant fleet in Texas in 2011 Exelon Corporation bought the 720 MW capacity Wolf Hollow plant in north Texas from Sequent Wolf Hollow for $305 million.

In 2010 to grow its renewable energy unit the company acquired wind power developer John Deere Renewables for about $860 million. The purchase adds 735 MW of operating wind power capacity to its generation capacity.

EXECUTIVES

MBR, John W Rowe
MBR, John Young
MBR-Ceo, Christopher M Crane
Chm, Mayo A Shattuck III
Svp, Bryan Hanson
Paralegal, Jenifer Newman
Svp, Generation Development, Thomas S O'Neill
Svp, Doyle N Beneby
Svp and President and Chief Nu, Bryan C Hanson
Maintenance Supervisor, Carl Kelly
Records Management Specialist, Christine Bell
Auditors: PricewaterhouseCoopers LLP

LOCATIONS

HQ: Exelon Generation Co LLC
300 Exelon Way, Kennett Square, PA 19348-2473
Phone: 610 765-5959
Web: www.exeloncorp.com

PRODUCTS/OPERATIONS

2013 Sales

	% of total
Mid-Atlantic	33
Midwest	27
New England	8
ERCOT	8
Other Regions	6
New York	5
Others	13
Total	**100**

COMPETITORS

AES	Duke Energy
AMP	NextEra Energy
Buckeye Power	Wolverine Power Supply
CMS Energy	

HISTORICAL FINANCIALS

Company Type: Public

Income Statement

FYE: December 31

	REVENUE ($ mil.)	NET INCOME ($ mil.)	NET PROFIT MARGIN	EMPLOYEES
12/17	18,466	2,694	14.6%	15,011
12/16	17,751	496	2.8%	14,717
12/15	19,135	1,372	7.2%	14,512
12/14	17,393	835	4.8%	14,370
12/13	15,630	1,070	6.8%	11,973
Annual Growth	**4.3%**	**26.0%**	—	**5.8%**

2017 Year-End Financials

Debt ratio: 19.42%—
Return on equity: 21.46%
Cash ($ mil.): 416
Current ratio: 1.63
Long-term debt ($ mil.): 8,644

Dividends
Yield: —
Payout: —
Market value ($ mil.): —

Expedia Group Inc

Expediting your expedition often begins by accessing a travel web site. Expedia a market leader in online travel services (with rival Booking Holdings) is often the go-to online trip-planner. It offers tools that allow users to book airline tickets hotel reservations car rentals cruises and vacation packages. Expedia's portfolio of brands could fill a boutique hotel. They include flagship Expedia.com online travel bookers Travelocity and Orbitz accommodations manager Hotels.com vacation rental site HomeAway travel discounter Hotwire hotel meta-searcher Trivago luxury package provider Classic Vacations and several sites focused on international destinations. More than 665000 hotels and alternative accommodations properties can be booked through Expedia.

Operations

Expedia operates through four segments: Core OTA (online travel agency) Trivago HomeAway and Egencia.

Core OTA accounts for 75% of Expedia's total revenue and includes the brands Hotwire and Hotels.com. Trivago which generates 10% of total revenue is a hotel price-comparison platform that scans prices across 400 booking websites. HomeAway offers vacation rentals through HomeAway.com VRBO and Vacationrentals.com and also brings in some 10% of revenue. Egencia the smallest segment at 5% of sales is a full-service travel management company that offers travel products and services to businesses and their corporate travelers.

Geographic Reach

Based in Bellevue Washington Expedia has offices throughout the Americas Europe and Asia/Pacific region and operates in about 200 countries. The company operates call centers around the world including outsourced centers in the Philippines El Salvador Egypt and India.

The US accounts for about 55% of revenue.

Sales and Marketing

"Hotel? Trivago" is a refrain familiar to millions thanks to Expedia's extensive Trivago advertising campaigns on television radio print and online. The company spends a massive $3 billion a year on advertising.

Financial Performance

Expedia has traveled a long way in the past decade with revenue rising from $2.6 billion in 2007 to $10 billion in 2017.

The company's revenue leaped 15% to $10.1 billion amid strong growth in all four of Expedia's business lines. The Core OTA segment witnessed the strongest growth on the back of good performances in the Brand Expedia. hotels.com and EAN (Expedia Affiliate Network) units. Lodging revenue which includes hotels and HomeAway was up 14% thanks to a 16% increase in room nights partially offset by a 2% fall in revenue per room night.

Net income also grew strongly up 34% to $378.0 million due to higher revenue and a relatively lower cost of revenue partially offset by a $931 million increase in selling and marketing expenses. The company's direct costs including online and offline marketing expenses at Brand Expedia EAN and Hotels.com rose $830 million while indirect costs such as personnel growth at Egencia were up $101 million.

Cash inflow from operations increased $235 million to $1.8 billion due to increased benefits from working capital changes.

Strategy

Expedia's goal is to generate two-thirds of its revenue outside the US. International customers accounted for 45% of 2017 revenue up significantly from 30% in 2008. Building its image globally and expanding its brand portfolio have been key in its efforts to reach a wide slice of consumers (including budget-conscious luxury and business travelers). Expedia has grown internationally with the acquisition of several online travel sites around the world.

Expedia faces stiff competition in the shape of Booking Holdings (formerly Priceline.com and the owner of Booking.com) Airbnb TripAdvisor and more recently Google Travel. While HomeAway has its work cut out wresting the urban market from Airbnb Expedia is adding independent hotels from the Expedia.com to HomeAway listings. The company hopes a greater diversity in number and property types will improve conversion. Meanwhile its Trivago hotels business fell to a loss in 2017 as increased business from its advertising campaign failed to make up for the massive outlay. Trivago set up a marketing and sales subsidiary for its business software services to persuade independent hoteliers to take control of their own online marketing including via its Hotel Manager platform. The platform allows hoteliers manage their hotel profile and upload content; Trivago has around 310000 hotels signed up to the service.

Mergers and Acquisitions

Expedia isn't shy about acquiring parts of the travel planning experience that it doesn't already have. The approach has brought some well-recognized travel sites under its corporate umbrella.

In 2017 Expedia acquired a majority stake in SilverRail a provider of technology for rail travel. The companies have worked together since 2010. SilverRail expands the number of travel products through Expedia adding rail travel to online options.

Company Background

Originally a division of Microsoft Expedia was sold to IAC/InterActiveCorp which acquired the computer maker's majority stake in 2002 and the minority interest it did not already own in 2003. Two years later IAC spun off Expedia into a separate publicly traded firm.

EXECUTIVES

Head Of Customer Operations, J. Tucker Moodey
President Hotwire Group, Henrik V. Kjellberg, age 48
President Hotels.com And Ean, Johan Svanstrom, age 47
President Expedia Lodging Partner Services, Cyril Ranque

President Egencia, Rob Greyber
President Ceo And Director, Mark D. Okerstrom, $750,000 total compensation
Evp General Counsel And Secretary, Robert Dzielak, $575,000 total compensation
President Brand Expedia Group, Aman Bhutani, age 42
Chief People Officer, Nikki Krishnamurthy
President Homeaway, John Kim
Svp And General Manager Expedia Affiliate Network, Ariane Corin
Vice President Of Employee Engagement, Kristin Graham
Senior Vice President Marketing Packages And Canada, Sean C Shannon
Vice President And Associate Corporate Counsel, Angela Niemann
Vice President, Lisa Youel
Vice President Global Supply Operations, Sean Huberty
Global Vice President Expedia Media Solutions, Noah Tratt
Vice President Transport Americas, Julie Kyse
Global Senior Vice President, Hari Nair
Senior Vice President Sales, Bruce Freeman
Vice President Of Finance, Bank Rec
Senior Vice President Commercial Strategy And Services, Gregory Schulze
Associate Vice President Lifecycle Manager, Nicole Jubie
Vice President Government And Corporate Affairs, Amanda Pedigo
Vice President Global Product, Keela Robison
Senior Vp Technical Recruiter, Ryan Rodriguez
Vice Chairman, Victor A. Kaufman, age 74
Chairman, Barry Diller, age 76
President Ceo And Director, Mark D. Okerstrom
Evp General Counsel And Secretary, Robert Dzielak
Auditors: Ernst & Young LLP

LOCATIONS

HQ: Expedia Group Inc
333 108th Avenue N.E., Bellevue, WA 98004
Phone: 425 679-7200
Web: www.expediainc.com

2017 Sales

	$ mil.	% of total
United States	5,534	55
All other countries	4,525	45
Total	**10,059**	**100**

PRODUCTS/OPERATIONS

2017 Sales

	$ mil.	% of total
Core OTA	7,880	75
trivago	1,166	11
HomeAway	906	9
Egencia	520	5
Corporate & Eliminations	(413.8)	-
Total	**10,059**	**100**

2017 Sales

	% of total
Merchant	53
Agency	27
Advertising and media	11
HomeAway	9
Total	**100**

BRANDS

BRANDS
CarRentals.com
Classic Vacations
Egencia
Expedia
Expedia Affiliate Network (EAN)
Expedia CruiseShipCenters
Expedia Local Expert
Expedia Media Solutions
HomeAway

Hotels.com
Hotwire
Orbitz
SilverRail
Traveldoo
Travelocity
trivago
Wotif Group

SELECTED SUBSIDIARIES

Classic Vacations LLC
Cruise LLC
EAN.com LP
Egencia France SAS
Egencia LLC
EXP Holdings Luxembourg S.A.
Expedia Asia Holdings Mauritius
Expedia do Brasil Agencia de Viagens e Turismo Ltda.

COMPETITORS

Airbnb	Priceline
American Express	Sabre
BCD Travel	Travelport
Carlson Wagonlit	TripAdvisor
Concur Technologies	Uniglobe Travel
GetThere	WorldRes
Google	ebookers.com
Pegasus Solutions	last minute network
Prestige Travel	

HISTORICAL FINANCIALS

Company Type: Public

Income Statement
FYE: December 31

	REVENUE ($ mil.)	NET INCOME ($ mil.)	NET PROFIT MARGIN	EMPLOYEES
12/18	11,223	406	3.6%	24,500
12/17	10,059	377	3.8%	22,615
12/16	8,773	281	3.2%	20,075
12/15	6,672	764	11.5%	18,730
12/14	5,763	398	6.9%	18,210
Annual Growth	**18.1%**	**0.5%**	**—**	**7.7%**

2018 Year-End Financials

Debt ratio: 20.61%
Return on equity: 9.41%
Cash ($ mil.): 2,443
Current ratio: 0.64
Long-term debt ($ mil.): 3,717

No. of shares (mil.): 147
Dividends
Yield: 1.1%
Payout: 42.9%
Market value ($ mil.): 16,575

	STOCK PRICE ($) FY Close	P/E High/Low	PER SHARE ($) Earnings	Dividends	Book Value
12/18	112.65	51 37	2.65	1.24	27.89
12/17	119.77	64 45	2.42	1.16	29.80
12/16	113.28	70 49	1.82	1.00	27.54
12/15	124.30	23 13	5.70	0.84	32.37
12/14	85.36	30 20	2.99	0.66	14.04
Annual Growth	**7.2%**	**— —**	**(3.0%)**	**17.1%**	**18.7%**

Expeditors International of Washington, Inc.

As a freight forwarder Expeditors International of Washington keeps cargo moving. The company purchases air and ocean cargo space on a volume basis and resells that space to its customers at lower rates than they could obtain directly from the carriers. The company also acts as a customs broker for air and ocean freight shipped by its customers and offers supply chain management services. Customers include global businesses engaged in retailing and wholesaling electronics and manufacturing. How much does Expeditors ship? The company annually moves about 800 million kilograms of freight by air 900 million kilograms by ground and one million standard measurement shipping containers by sea.

Operations

Expeditors operates in three segments none of which supplies an outsized percentage of the company's revenue.

Expeditors' airfreight services segment more than 40% of revenue represents airlines as an agent in addition to providing freight consolidation for shippers. Besides shipping on scheduled flights the company sometimes charters aircraft for the delivery of backlogs. By not purchasing its own aircraft the company avoids the costs of large capital expenditures and operating costs.

Ocean freight and ocean services about 30% of revenue operates as a non-vessel operating common carrier which is a contractor with ocean shipping lines for a set amount of containers. Expeditors also obtains less-than container load freight to fill containers. The segment additionally provides such order management services as document management and SKU visibility.

Customs brokerage and other services almost 30% of revenue aids in the movement of shipments across borders by providing such services as adding up duties and taxes and arranging inspections. Beyond the border entry the segment provides additional services including warehousing product distribution and time-definite transportation. Expeditors provides these services not only for its own shipping customers but also for businesses that have not hired the company as a forwarder a class of client that accounts for a significant portion of the segment's revenue.

Geographic Reach

Expeditors is headquartered in Seattle Washington and has regional headquarters in London Dubai Singapore and Shanghai. It operates from more than 300 facilities in more than 100 countries.

North Asia is its largest market generating about 35% of revenue followed by the US with more than a quarter of revenue and Europe about 15% of revenue.

Sales and Marketing

Expeditors caters to its customers' supply chains. Therefore its marketing efforts target people in their company's logistics international and domestic transportation customs compliance and purchasing departments. It employs district managers who are responsible for marketing sales coordination and implementation in their area. The company primarily targets the aviation and aerospace health care oil and energy and retail sectors.

Financial Performance

Expeditors' revenue marched higher for several years before dropping in 2016. At the same time net income remained robust even if it didn't rise each year.

The company's revenue rebounded in 2017 rising 13% to $6.9 billion. Airfreight services turned in a 17% revenue increase because of higher tonnage and sell rates. Ocean freight and ocean services revenue rose 10% in 2017 from 2016 on higher container volume and sell rates. Higher shipping volumes drove revenue from customs brokerage and other services 12% higher.

The higher revenue helped Expeditors post a $59 million gain in net income to $490 million in 2017 from 2016.

The company's cash crested $1 billion in 2017 compared to $974 million in 2016. Cash generated by operating activities was $489 million in 2017 while cash used by investing and financing activities was $12 million and $425 million respectively.

Strategy

In its rapid development Expeditors has favored internal growth over expansion by acquisition (though it has also selectively made some strategic acquisitions) and the company continues to open new offices and to invest in its information technology infrastructure. By eschewing acquisitions as its main form of growth the company has been able to develop a common hardware platform that lets the entire company use the same accounting and transportation software.

The company is focused on diversifying its product mix through focused investments in its distribution services transcon and ocean export products. It also aims to diversify its market verticals by investing further in the pharmaceutical and automotive markets.

Expeditors wants to leverage its long presence in China to build a stronger import presence in the country. It is making investments to build its import infrastructure and its local delivery and support capabilities in China an effort that could be slow by trade disputes between the US and China remains to be seen. The company said it believes it can weather the current dispute and can adjust if manufacturers seek alternative sources for good and products.

EXECUTIVES

Evp Europe, Timothy C. Barber, age 58, $100,000 total compensation

President Global Services, Eugene K. Alger, age 57, $100,000 total compensation

Svp And Cfo, Bradley S. (Brad) Powell, age 58, $100,000 total compensation

President Global Products, Daniel R. Wall, age 49, $100,000 total compensation

President And Ceo, Jeffrey S. Musser, age 52, $100,000 total compensation

President Global Geographies And Operations, Richard H. Rostan

Svp And Cio, Christopher J. McClincy, age 43

Svp Global Sales And Marketing, J. Jonathan Song

Senior Vice President Corporate Controller Expeditors Int'l Of Washington, Charles Lynch

Director, Robert R. Wright, age 58

Auditors: KPMG LLP

LOCATIONS

HQ: Expeditors International of Washington, Inc. 1015 Third Avenue, 12th Floor, Seattle, WA 98104
Phone: 206 674-3400   **Fax:** 206 674-3459
Web: www.expeditors.com

2016 Sales

	$ mil.	% of total
Asia		
North Asia	2,598	36
South Asia	684	9
North America		
US	1,962	27
Other North America	268	4
Europe	1,115	16
Middle East Africa and India	426	6
Latin America	111	2
Eliminations	(2463)	-
Total	**6,920**	**100**

PRODUCTS/OPERATIONS

2017 Sales

	$ mil.	% of total
Airfreight services	2,877	42
Ocean freight & ocean services	2,107	30
Customs brokerage & other services	1,936	28
Total	**6,920**	**100**

Selected Products and Services

Air freight consolidation
Air freight forwarding
Customs brokerage services
Warehousing and Distribution Services
Direct Ocean Forwarding
Order Management
Transcom

COMPETITORS

APL Logistics	NYK Line
C.H. Robinson	Nippon Express
Worldwide	Panalpina
CEVA Logistics	Schenker
DHL	Sino-Global
FedEx Trade Networks	Sinotrans
Kintetsu World Express	UPS Supply Chain
Kuehne + Nagel	Solutions
International	Yamato Holdings
Mitsui-Soko	

HISTORICAL FINANCIALS

Company Type: Public

Income Statement   FYE: December 31

	REVENUE ($ mil.)	NET INCOME ($ mil.)	NET PROFIT MARGIN	EMPLOYEES
12/17	6,920	489	7.1%	16,500
12/16	6,098	430	7.1%	16,000
12/15	6,616	457	6.9%	15,397
12/14	6,564	376	5.7%	14,670
12/13	6,080	348	5.7%	13,910
Annual Growth	**3.3%**	**8.9%**	—	**4.4%**

2017 Year-End Financials

Debt ratio: —	No. of shares (mil.): 176
Return on equity: 25.51%	Dividends
Cash ($ mil.): 1,051	Yield: 0.0%
Current ratio: 2.32	Payout: 31.2%
Long-term debt ($ mil.): —	Market value ($ mil.): 11,410

	STOCK PRICE ($) FY Close	P/E High/Low	PER SHARE ($) Earnings	Dividends	Book Value
12/17	64.69	24 19	2.69	0.84	11.29
12/16	52.96	24 18	2.36	0.80	10.26
12/15	45.10	21 18	2.40	0.72	9.29
12/14	44.61	24 20	1.92	0.64	9.75
12/13	44.25	28 21	1.68	0.60	10.29
Annual Growth	**10.0%**	— —	**12.5%**	**8.8%**	**2.3%**

Exxon Mobil Corp

ExxonMobil is the world?s largest publicly traded oil company. It has a vast infrastructure of oil reserves refineries and petrochemical plants whose scale and reach is only rivaled by Royal Dutch Shell BP and Total. With 20 billion BOE of proven reserves ExxonMobil engages in oil & gas exploration production supply transportation and marketing. The corporation has 20 refineries spread across 14 countries and operates some 100 major exploration projects worldwide. It supplies refined products to more than 19000 global gas stations and is a major petrochemical producer.

HISTORY

Exxon's 1999 acquisition of Mobil reunited two descendants of John D. Rockefeller's Standard Oil Company. Rockefeller a commodity trader started his first oil refinery in 1863 in Cleveland. Realizing that the price of oil at the well would shrink with each new strike Rockefeller chose to monopolize oil refining and transportation. In 1870 he formed Standard Oil and in 1882 he created the Standard Oil Trust which allowed him to set up new ostensibly independent companies including the Standard Oil Company of New Jersey (Jersey Standard); Rochester New York-based Vacuum Oil; and Standard Oil of New York (nicknamed Socony).

Initially capitalized at $70 million the Standard Oil Trust controlled 90% of the petroleum industry. In 1911 after two decades of political and legal wrangling the Supreme Court broke up the trust into 34 companies the largest of which was Jersey Standard.

Walter Teagle who became president of Jersey Standard in 1917 secretly bought half of Humble Oil of Texas (1919) and expanded operations into South America. In 1928 Jersey Standard joined in the Red Line Agreement which reserved most Middle East oil for a few companies. Teagle resigned in 1942 after the company was criticized for a prewar research pact with German chemical giant I.G. Farben.

The 1948 purchase of a 40% stake in Arabian American Oil Company combined with a 7% share of Iranian production bought in 1954 made Jersey Standard the world's #1 oil company at that time.

Meanwhile Vacuum Oil and Socony reunited in 1931 as Socony-Vacuum and the company adopted the Flying Red Horse (Pegasus — representing speed and power) as a trademark. The fast-growing diversifying company changed its name to Socony Mobil Oil in 1955 and became Mobil in 1976.

Other US companies still using the Standard Oil name objected to Jersey Standard's marketing in their territories as Esso (derived from the initials for Standard Oil). To end the confusion in 1972 Jersey Standard became Exxon a name change that cost $100 million.

Nationalization of oil assets by producing countries reduced Exxon's access to oil during the 1970s. Though it increased exploration that decade and the next Exxon's reserves shrank.

Oil tanker *Exxon Valdez* spilled some 11 million gallons of oil into Alaska's Prince William Sound in 1989. Exxon spent billions on the cleanup and in 1994 a federal jury in Alaska ordered the company to pay $5.3 billion in punitive damages to fishermen and others affected by the spill. (Exxon appealed and in 2001 the jury award was reduced to $2.5 billion and in 2008 to $507.5 million).

With the oil industry consolidating Exxon merged its worldwide oil and fuel additives business with that of Royal Dutch/Shell in 1996. The next year under FTC pressure Exxon agreed to run ads refuting claims that its premium gas enabled car engines to run more efficiently. Another PR disaster followed in 1998 when CEO Lee Raymond upset environmentalists by publicly questioning the global warming theory.

Still Exxon was unstoppable. It acquired Mobil for $81 billion in 1999; the new company had Raymond at the helm and Mobil's Lucio Noto as vice chairman. (Noto retired in 2001.) To get the deal done Exxon Mobil had to divest $4 billion in assets. It agreed to end its European gasoline and lubricants joint venture with BP and to sell more than 2400 gas stations in the US.

In 2000 Exxon Mobil sold 1740 East Coast gas stations to Tosco for $860 million. It sold a California refinery and 340 gas stations to Valero Energy for about $1 billion.

More than a decade after the *Exxon Valdez* wreaked environmenta

EXECUTIVES

Svp And Principal Financial Officer, Andrew P. (Andy) Swiger, age 62, $1,287,500 total compensation

President Exxonmobil Chemical Company, John R. Verity

Chairman And Ceo, Darren W. Woods, age 53, $1,000,000 total compensation

Vp And President Exxonmobil Upstream Ventures, B. W. Corson

Vp And General Counsel, R. M. Ebner

Vp Human Resources, M. A. Farrant

President Exxonmobil Production Company, N. W. Duffin

President Exxonmobil Fuels Lubricants And Specialties Marketing Company, B. W. Milton

President Exxonmobil Refining And Supply Company, D. G. Wascom

President Exxonmobil Research And Engineering Company, T. J. Wojnar

President Exxonmobil Global Services Company, L. D. DuCharme

Senior Vice President Exxonmobil Lubricants, Nigel Searle

Vice President Human Resources, Malcolm Farrant

National Accounts Manager, Juan Rodriguez

Senior Vice President, Jack Williams

Vice President, Pat Doolan

Vice President, Elijah White

Senior Vice President Permian Integrated Development Xto Energy, Staale Gjervik

National Account Manager, Richard Bowen

Department Head, Michael Hotaling

Vice President And President Exxonmobil Exploration Company Upstream, Stephen Greenlee

Vice President And President Exxonmobil Production Company, Thomas Walters

Vice President Upstream Engineering, Gerry Gabriel

Vice President Engineering, Erika Anzaldua

Vice President, Jim Parsons

Vice President Investor Relations And Secretary, David Rosenthal

Vp And President Exxonmobil Upstream Ventures, Brad Corson

Vice President, Evelyn Miller

Vice President, Lee Willis

Vice President, Tina Fitts

Vice President Research And Development Exxonmobil Research And Engineering, Vijay Swarup

Government Relations, Alfredo Balena

Executive Vice President Exxonmobil Exploration Company, Mike Cousins

Vice President And President Exxonmobil Gas And Power Marketing Upstream, Peter Clarke

Vp And General Tax Counsel, James Spellings

Chairman And Ceo, Darren W. Woods, age 53

Treasurer???s ??? Benefits Finance And Investments, Cindy Kessel

Secretary, Suzanne Manahan-smith

L And S Downstream Treasurers Credit Analyst, Patricia Beckwith

Financial Advisor Upstream Treasurers, Todd Norman

Assistant Treasurer, Kate Shae

Auditors: PricewaterhouseCoopers LLP

LOCATIONS

HQ: Exxon Mobil Corp
5959 Las Colinas Boulevard, Irving, TX 75039-2298
Phone: 972 940-6000 **Fax:** 972 444-1505
Web: www.exxonmobil.com

2016 Sales

	% of total
U.S.	34
Non-U.S.	66
Total	**100**

PRODUCTS/OPERATIONS

2016 Sales

	% of total
Downstream	79
Chemical	12
Upstream	9
Total	**100**

2016 Sales

	$ mil.	% of total
Sales and Other Operating Revenue	218,608	97
Income From Equity Affiliates	4,806	2
Other Income	2,680	1
Total	**226,094**	**100**

COMPETITORS

7-Eleven	Marathon Oil
Ashland	Norsk Hydro ASA
BHP Billiton	Occidental Petroleum
BP	PEMEX
Chevron	PETROBRAS
ConocoPhillips	PetrÓleos de
Costco Wholesale	Venezuela
Dow Chemical	Racetrac Petroleum
DuPont	Repsol
Eastman Chemical	Royal Dutch Shell
Eni	Saudi Aramco
Hess Corporation	Sinopec Corp.
Huntsman International	Sunoco
JXTG Holdings	TOTAL
Koch Industries Inc.	Valero Energy

HISTORICAL FINANCIALS

Company Type: Public

Income Statement

FYE: December 31

	REVENUE ($ mil.)	NET INCOME ($ mil.)	NET PROFIT MARGIN	EMPLOYEES
12/17	244,363	19,710	8.1%	69,600
12/16	226,094	7,840	3.5%	71,100
12/15	268,882	16,150	6.0%	73,500
12/14	411,939	32,520	7.9%	75,300
12/13	438,255	32,580	7.4%	75,000
Annual Growth	(13.6%)	(11.8%)	—	(1.9%)

2017 Year-End Financials

Debt ratio: 12.14%—
Return on equity: 11.10%
Cash ($ mil.): 3,177
Current ratio: 0.82
Long-term debt ($ mil.): 24,406

Dividends
Yield: 0.0%
Payout: 66.0%
Market value ($ mil.): —

	STOCK PRICE ($) FY Close	P/E High/Low	PER SHARE ($) Earnings	Dividends	Book Value
12/17	83.64	20 16	4.63	3.06	44.28
12/16	90.26	51 39	1.88	2.98	40.34
12/15	77.95	24 18	3.85	2.88	41.10
12/14	92.45	14 11	7.60	2.70	41.51
12/13	101.20	14 12	7.37	2.46	40.14
Annual Growth	(4.7%)	— —	(11.0%)	5.6%	2.5%

Facebook Inc

Facebook is the face of social media for good and bad. The social networking juggernaut which continues to grow quickly even as it struggles with public relations and other issues lets users share information post photos and videos play games and otherwise connect with one another through online profiles. The site which allows outside developers to build apps that integrate with Facebook boasts more than two billion monthly active users. In addition to its namesake platform Facebook owns Instagram (photo/video sharing) Messenger and WhatsApp (instant messaging and payments services) and Oculus (virtual reality technology and content). The company generates revenue through advertising; the US accounts for about 45% of total sales.

Operations

In addition to the more than 2 billion monthly Facebook users WhatsApp and Messenger together claim nearly 3 billion monthly users and Instagram counts about 800 million monthly users.

Beyond these offerings the company has investments in longer-term technology initiatives such as artificial intelligence augmented and virtual reality and connectivity efforts.

Geographic Reach

Global in its reach Facebook generates about 55% of its revenue from outside of the US. The majority of its international business comes from customers located in western Europe Australia Brazil Canada and China.

The company has offices and data center facilities located all over the world.

Sales and Marketing

Facebook uses a global sales force in more than 40 offices worldwide to attract and retain advertisers (advertising accounts for nearly all of revenue). It also serves advertising customers through a self-service ad platform.

Users have generally found the site through word-of-mouth as well as internal marketing efforts. Facebook spent $324 million on its own advertising and promotional expenses during 2017 compared to $310 million and $281 million in 2016 and 2015 respectively.

Financial Performance

Facebook has experienced exponential growth over the past few years enabling it to dominate the social networking world as the most trafficked site of its kind in the US. Its revenue has grown from nearly $8 billion to more than $40 billion since 2013 while its net income has grown from $1.5 billion to $16 billion.

In 2017 the company reported revenue of $40.6 billion up nearly 50% from the prior year. Monthly active users grew nearly 15% and the average price per ad increased by about 30%.

Net income that year hit $16 billion up 55% year-over-year on the jump in revenue.

Cash at the end of 2017 was $8 billion a decrease of $824 million from the prior year. Cash from operations contributed $24 billion to the coffers while investing activities used $20 billion mainly for purchases of marketable securities. Financing activities used another $5 billion for stock repurchase and taxes related to net share settlement of equity awards.

Strategy

Facebook owes the bulk of its growth to its ability to lure more and more visitors to its site and keeping them engaged. As a result the growth in Facebook's advertising business driven by mobile ads customized for individuals has been staggering. The company will continue to invest in and expand its service offerings in an effort to keep growth strong as it grapples with both internal and external issues including new data protections in Europe which have driven away some 1 million users.

India is a particular region of interest for Facebook where in early 2018 it successfully tested a beta version of its WhatsApp payments feature. The company is also rolling out new video features (including live video) and original video content through Facebook Watch and continues to improve and enhance its Oculus virtual reality hardware and software.

The company however has had to pivot in recent months to focus more on privacy and security. It has suffered through several years of negative press since it was discovered that the Facebook News Feed included fake user accounts and millions of fraudulent stories meant to impact the 2016 US election cycle. In addition an outside researcher was able to collect and use for political purposes data on as many as 87 million users without Facebook's permission. The company is under investigation by several government agencies and has been criticized for its slow response to the issues. Debate continues over how Facebook should handle misinformation on its platform.

The change in strategy is already having an impact at least financially. In Q2 2018 the company said that security investments among other initiatives will impact the company's profitability; that combined with slower than expected growth in Q2 (and similar predictions for Q3 and Q4) wiped out some $150 billion in Facebook's market value as its stock suffered its biggest one-day drop.

Company Background

The firm was launched in 2004 by Harvard student Mark Zuckerberg as an online version of the Harvard Facebook. (The name comes from books of freshmen's faces majors and hometowns that are distributed to students.) In 2012 Facebook began publicly trading after filing one of the largest IPOs in US history.

EXECUTIVES

Coo, Sheryl K. Sandberg, age 49, $738,077 total compensation

Chairman And Ceo, Mark Zuckerberg, age 34, $1 total compensation

Cto, Michael (Mike) Schroepfer, age 43, $658,846 total compensation

Cio, Atish Banerjea, age 52

Cfo, David M. (Dave) Wehner, age 49, $662,692 total compensation

Chief Product Officer, Christopher K. (Chris) Cox, age 35, $658,846 total compensation

Senior Vice President Production Services, Ellis Collins

Chairman And Ceo, Mark Zuckerberg, age 34

Auditors: Ernst & Young LLP

LOCATIONS

HQ: Facebook Inc
1601 Willow Road, Menlo Park, CA 94025
Phone: 650 543-4800
Web: www.facebook.com

2017 Sales

	$ mil.	% of total
US	17,734	44
International	22,919	56
Total	**40,653**	**100**

PRODUCTS/OPERATIONS

2017 Sales

	$ mil.	% of total
Advertising	39,942	98
Payments & other fees	711	2
Total	**40,653**	**100**

Selected Products and Features

Products for Users
 Timeline
 News feed
 Photos & videos
 Messages
 Groups
 Lists
 Events
 Places
 Notifications
Facebook Pages
Products for Developers
 Open Graph
 Social plugins
 Like button
 Recommendations
 Comments
 Facebook Payments
 Apps on Facebook
Products for Advertisers & Marketers
 Facebook Ads
 Sponsored Stories
 Ad analytics

COMPETITORS

Bebo	Pinterest
Friendster	Snapchat
Google	Tencent Holdings
IAC	Tumblr
LiveJournal	Twitter
Meetup	Yelp
Memory Lane	craigslist
Microsoft	

HISTORICAL FINANCIALS

Company Type: Public

Income Statement

FYE: December 31

	REVENUE ($ mil.)	NET INCOME ($ mil.)	NET PROFIT MARGIN	EMPLOYEES
12/18	55,838	22,112	39.6%	35,587
12/17	40,653	15,934	39.2%	25,105
12/16	27,638	10,217	37.0%	17,048
12/15	17,928	3,688	20.6%	12,691
12/14	12,466	2,940	23.6%	9,199
Annual Growth	**45.5%**	**65.6%**	**—**	**40.2%**

2018 Year-End Financials

Debt ratio: ——
Return on equity: 27.91%
Cash ($ mil.): 10,019
Current ratio: 7.19
Long-term debt ($ mil.): —

Dividends
 Yield: —
 Payout: —
Market value ($ mil.): —

	STOCK PRICE ($) FY Close	P/E High/Low	PER SHARE ($) Earnings	Dividends	Book Value
12/18	131.09	28 16	7.57	0.00	29.48
12/17	176.46	33 21	5.39	0.00	25.58
12/16	115.05	37 26	3.49	0.00	20.47
12/15	104.66	83 57	1.29	0.00	15.54
12/14	78.02	73 48	1.10	0.00	12.91
Annual Growth	**13.9%**	**— —**	**62.0%**	**—**	**22.9%**

FAIRFAX COUNTY VIRGINIA

EXECUTIVES

City Exec, Anthony H Griffin
Staff, Mark Young
Manager, Matthew Vaughan
Director of Communications, Stephen Brundage
Business Dir, Angela Shaw
Telecommunications Staff, Alton Drew
Program Manager, Robert Grabowski
Information, Tanya Quinonez
Captain, Roger Arnn
Captain, John Piper
Coordinator, Kelly Bachand
Auditors: KPMG LLP WASHINGTON DC

LOCATIONS

HQ: FAIRFAX COUNTY VIRGINIA
 12000 GOVERNMENT STE 214, FAIRFAX, VA 22035
Phone: 703 324-3126
Web: WWW.FAIRFAXCOUNTYEDA.ORG

HISTORICAL FINANCIALS

Company Type: Private

Income Statement

FYE: June 30

	REVENUE ($ mil.)	NET INCOME ($ mil.)	NET PROFIT MARGIN	EMPLOYEES
06/18	4,806	71	1.5%	12,000
06/17	4,695	171	3.6%	—
06/16	4,469	49	1.1%	—
06/15	0	60	—	—
Annual Growth	**—**	**5.8%**	**—**	**—**

2018 Year-End Financials

Debt ratio: ——
Return on equity: 1.50%
Cash ($ mil.): 1,364
Current ratio: —
Long-term debt ($ mil.): —

Dividends
 Yield: —
 Payout: —
Market value ($ mil.): —

FAIRVIEW HEALTH SERVICES

EXECUTIVES

Ceo, Rulon F Stacey
Sr V Pres-Cfo, James M Fox
Sr V Pres, Daniel Fromm
V Pres, Bob Beacher
Exec V Pres, Carolyn Wilson
Manager of Lan, D Ick Neubaur
Director, Roby Thompson Jr
Chief of Emergency Room, Kevin S Meyer
Scientist, Gerald August
Scientist, Scott Crow
Family Practitioner, Kimberly De Roche
Auditors: ERNST & YOUNG LLP MINNEAPOLI

LOCATIONS

HQ: FAIRVIEW HEALTH SERVICES
 2450 RIVERSIDE AVE, MINNEAPOLIS, MN 554541450
Phone: 612 672-6300
Web: WWW.SONUSMETROMKE.COM

COMPETITORS

Abbott Northwestern Hospital	Mayo Clinic
Allina Hospitals	North Memorial Health Care
Bethesda Hospital	Park Nicollet Health Services
Catholic Health Initiatives	Regions Hospital
CentraCare Health	St. John's Hospital
HealthEast Care System	(Minnesota)

HISTORICAL FINANCIALS

Company Type: Private

Income Statement

FYE: December 31

	REVENUE ($ mil.)	NET INCOME ($ mil.)	NET PROFIT MARGIN	EMPLOYEES
12/17	5,275	511	9.7%	18,000
12/12	3,218	168	5.2%	—
12/11	2,575	4	0.2%	—
Annual Growth	**12.7%**	**120.0%**	**—**	**—**

2017 Year-End Financials

Debt ratio: —
Return on equity: 9.70%
Cash ($ mil.): 51
Current ratio: 0.80
Long-term debt ($ mil.): —

Dividends
Yield: —
Payout: —
Market value ($ mil.): —

Fannie Mae

The Federal National Mortgage Association or Fannie Mae has helped more than 50 million low- to middle-income families realize the American Dream of owning a home. Like its brother Freddie Mac the government-supported enterprise (GSE) provides liquidity in the mortgage market by buying mortgages from lenders and packaging them for resale transferring risk from lenders and allowing them to offer mortgages to those who may not otherwise qualify. It owns or guarantees more than $2.6 trillion in single family home loans (nearly 30% of US total) and about $230 billion in multifamily mortgages (nearly 20% of US total). Due to losses caused largely by the subprime mortgage crisis the government seized both Fannie and Freddie in 2008. Government plans to divest the firms into private ownership have proven difficult; they remain GSEs.

HISTORY

In 1938 President Franklin Roosevelt created Fannie Mae as part of the government-owned Reconstruction Finance Corporation; its mandate was to buy FHA (Federal Housing Administration) loans. Fannie Mae began buying VA (Veterans Administration) mortgages in 1948. It was rechartered as a public-private mixed-ownership corporation in 1954.

The Housing Act of 1968 divided the corporation into the Government National Mortgage Association (Ginnie Mae which retained explicit government backing) and Fannie Mae which went public (with only an implicit US guarantee). Fannie Mae retained its treasury backstop authority whereby the secretary of the treasury can purchase up to $2.24 billion of the company's obligations.

The company introduced uniform conventional loan mortgage documents in 1970 began to buy conventional mortgages in 1972 and started buying condo and planned-unit development mortgages in 1974. By 1976 it was buying more conventional loans than FHA and VA loans.

As interest rates rose in the 1970s Fannie Mae's profits declined and by 1981 it was losing more than $1 million a day. Then it began offering mortgage-backed securities (MBSs) — popular as an investment product because of their implicit guarantee from the government. By 1982 the company funded 14% of US home mortgages.

Fannie Mae began borrowing money overseas and buying conventional multifamily and co-op housing loans in 1984. The next year it tightened credit rules and began issuing securities aimed at foreign investors such as yen-denominated securities. Fannie Mae issued its first real estate mortgage investment conduit (REMIC) securities (shares in mortgage pools of specific maturities and risk classes) and introduced a program to allow small lenders to pool loans with other lenders to create MBSs in 1987.

After CEO David Maxwell's 1991 retirement with a reported $29 million pension package Fannie Mae's powerful Washington lobby squelched calls to limit executive salaries. Other attempts to make the company more competitive with private concerns were more successful. In 1992 Fannie Mae's capital requirements were raised; a new mandate also required the organization to lend greater support to inner-city buyers. A new client/server computer system helped the company handle the deluge of new and refinanced loans that came in 1993 (Fannie Mae had struggled to improve its information systems in the 1980s pouring more than $100 million into a mainframe system that was obsolete before it went online).

In 1997 Fannie Mae officially adopted its long-time nickname. The next year Fannie Mae named White House budget chief Franklin Raines to succeed CEO James Johnson.

Fannie Mae is no stranger to bad news or bad press. In 1999 the Department of Housing and Urban Development began investigating charges that the company's automated underwriting systems were racially biased. The next year the agency released a study that found it to be negligent in promoting homeownership in low-income neighborhoods. In response Fannie Mae eased credit requirements in an effort to boost minority home-ownership (1999) and announced plans to loan some $2 trillion to minority and low-income home-buyers (2000). This move however invoked criticism that the company was exposing itself to increased risk from buyers more likely to default.

Following the lead of rival Freddie Mac in 2000 Fannie Mae offered securities for sale over the Internet. In 2002 it tightened standards for mortgage refinance cash-out loans it would buy as mortgage defaults rose (even as home sales and mortgage refinancings were helping prop up the sagging US economy).

In response to those who thought it was in bed with the federal government Fannie Mae kicked off the covers and put one foot on the floor. In 2003 it fulfilled a voluntary commitment to register its common stock with the SEC and came permanently under that organization's disclosure and oversight requirements.

But the move did not stop controversy from swirling around the lender. Chairman and CEO Franklin Raines CFO Timothy Howard and auditor KPMG were ousted in December 2004 after the SEC determined Fannie Mae had violated accounting rules. The inquiry was prompted by accusations Fannie Mae had manipulated earnings; earnings from 2001 through 2003 were restated and those from 2004 and 2005 were each released more than a year late.

In 2006 federal regulators hit the firm with a whopping $400 million fine. Investigators claimed that its former executives willfully overstated earnings by more than $10 billion — and then tried to impede an investigation into the discrepancies — in order to reap performance bonuses. Chairman Stephen Ashley and CEO Daniel Mudd who'd been brought in to replace Franklin Raines in late 2004 were brought to task by the Senate Banking Committee in regard to accounting misdeeds.

Though the Justice Department eventually dropped criminal charges against the firm Fannie Mae agreed to major changes in its accounting internal controls and management practices. It additionally agreed to appoint an independent chief risk officer as well as an organizational review overseen by a compliance committee. Meanwhile the lender suspended its home construction loan program — worth about $10 billion — while it got its financial house in order.

Fannie suffered huge losses in 2007 and 2008 as a result of the subprime mortgage crisis which saw a tremendous increase in loan defaults. The government stepped in loans and in 2008 seized both Fannie and Freddie. It also shuffled their management teams: Fannie CEO Mudd was replaced by Herbert Allison former TIAA-CREF. Allison was later tapped by the Obama administration to run the Treasury Department's financial recovery program. Former COO Michael Williams was named CEO in 2009.

The Federal Housing Finance Agency (FHFA) was created in 2008 to oversee both Fannie and Freddie as well as the 12 Federal Home Loan Banks. The FHFA was granted more authority than its predecessor agencies the Federal Housing Finance Board and the Office of Federal Housing Enterprise Oversight.

In an historic move the government in 2008 placed the two GSEs in conservatorship which is a legal status similar to bankruptcy rather than risk the possibility that the companies might fail. The government assumed a nearly 80% stake in the troubled companies in a $111 billion bailout (with a commitment of up to $400 billion). In 2011 the Obama administration proposed to restructure the housing market in a plan that will reduce the government's role and eventually eliminate the GSEs.

In 2009 the Making Home Affordable Program was introduced to provide assistance to borrowers in default through refinancings and other loan modifications.

EXECUTIVES

President Ceo And Director, Timothy J. (Tim) Mayopoulos, age 59, $600,000 total compensation
Evp And Head Multifamily, Jeffery R. Hayward, age 62, $475,000 total compensation
Svp And Treasurer Capital Markets, David C. Benson, age 59, $600,000 total compensation
Svp Capital Markets - Lender Channel, Andrew Bon Salle, $500,000 total compensation
Evp General Counsel And Corporate Secretary, Brian P. Brooks, $500,000 total compensation
Evp And Chief Risk Officer, Kimberly H. Johnson
Svp Operations And Technology, Bruce Lee
Vice President Finance And Corporate Technology, Ramon Richards
Vice President Information Technology, Beth Applegate
Vice President Of Internal Audit Technology, Don Farineau
President Ceo And Director, Timothy J. (Tim) Mayopoulos, age 59
Chairman, Egbert L. J. Perry, age 62
Board Member, Kenneth Duberstein
Auditors: Deloitte & Touche LLP

LOCATIONS

HQ: Fannie Mae
1100 15th Street, NW, Washington, DC 20005
Phone: 800 232-6643
Web: www.fanniemae.com

Selected Locations
Atlanta
Chicago
Dallas
Pasadena
Philadelphia
Washington DC

PRODUCTS/OPERATIONS

2016 Sales

	% of total
Interest income	
Mortgage loans	97
Available-for-sale securities	1
Trading securities	-
Others	-
Non interest income	
Investment gains net	1
Fair value losses net	-
Fee and other income	1
Total	**100**

2016 Sales

	% of total
Single-Family	88
Multifamily	12
Total	**100**

Selected Business Segments
Single-Family Credit Guaranty
Multifamily

COMPETITORS

Freddie Mac	VBA
Ginnie Mae	Wells Fargo

HISTORICAL FINANCIALS
Company Type: Public

Income Statement
FYE: December 31

	ASSETS ($ mil.)	NET INCOME ($ mil.)	INCOME AS % OF ASSETS	EMPLOYEES
12/17	3,345,529	2,463	0.1%	7,200
12/16	3,287,968	12,313	0.4%	7,000
12/15	3,221,917	10,954	0.3%	7,300
12/14	3,248,176	14,208	0.4%	7,600
12/13	3,270,108	83,963	2.6%	7,400
Annual Growth	0.6%	(58.6%)	—	(0.7%)

2017 Year-End Financials
Debt ratio: 99.54%
Return on equity: 206.54%
Cash ($ mil.): 32,110
Current ratio: —
Long-term debt ($ mil.): —
No. of shares (mil.): 1,158
Dividends
Yield: —
Payout: —
Market value ($ mil.): 3,069

	STOCK PRICE ($) FY Close	P/E High/Low	PER SHARE ($) Earnings	Dividends	Book Value
12/17	2.65	— —	(1.12)	0.00	(3.18)
12/16	3.90	449 110	0.01	0.00	5.24
12/15	1.64	— —	(0.05)	0.00	3.48
12/14	2.06	— —	(0.19)	0.00	3.18
12/13	3.01	— —	(0.25)	0.00	8.24
Annual Growth	(3.1%)	— —	—	—	—

FARM CREDIT BANK OF TEXAS

EXECUTIVES

Vice President, Steve Donnell
Vice President And Controller, Vicki Rodriguez
Vice President, Paul Rudd
Vice President Business Systems Unit Manager, Ed Benson
Vice President, Darren Cannon
Vice President Regional Manager, Chris Amend
Vice President Collateral Risk Management, Brad Swinney
Assistant Vice President Operations, William Foley
Vice President, Ronnie Sellers
Board Member, Larry Fairchild
Auditors: PRICEWATERHOUSECOOPERS LLP AU

LOCATIONS

HQ: FARM CREDIT BANK OF TEXAS
4801 PLAZA ON THE LK # 1200, AUSTIN, TX 787461081
Phone: 512 330-9060
Web: WWW.FARMCREDITBANK.COM

HISTORICAL FINANCIALS
Company Type: Private

Income Statement
FYE: December 31

	ASSETS ($ mil.)	NET INCOME ($ mil.)	INCOME AS % OF ASSETS	EMPLOYEES
12/16	21,222	192	0.9%	200
12/13	16,212	179	1.1%	—
Annual Growth	—	—	—	—

2016 Year-End Financials
Debt ratio: —
Return on equity: 36.20%
Cash ($ mil.): 195
Current ratio: —
Long-term debt ($ mil.): —
Dividends
Yield: —
Payout: —
Market value ($ mil.): —

FARM CREDIT OF THE VIRGINIAS ACA

EXECUTIVES

Ceo, David Lawrence
Cfo, David Sauer
SEC, Carolyn Hite
Auditors: PRICEWATERHOUSECOOPERS LLP FO

LOCATIONS

HQ: FARM CREDIT OF THE VIRGINIAS ACA
106 SANGERS LN, STAUNTON, VA 244016711
Phone: 540 899-0989

HISTORICAL FINANCIALS
Company Type: Private

Income Statement
FYE: December 31

	ASSETS ($ mil.)	NET INCOME ($ mil.)	INCOME AS % OF ASSETS	EMPLOYEES
12/16	1,858	43	2.3%	142
12/15	1,757	44	2.5%	—
12/14	1,654	50	3.1%	—
12/13	1,560	51	3.3%	—
Annual Growth	6.0%	(5.5%)	—	—

2016 Year-End Financials
Debt ratio: —
Return on equity: 38.30%
Cash ($ mil.): 5
Current ratio: —
Long-term debt ($ mil.): —
Dividends
Yield: —
Payout: —
Market value ($ mil.): —

FARM CREDIT SERVICES OF AMERICA, PCA

EXECUTIVES

Pres-Ceo, Doug Stark
Exec V Pres, Neil Olsen
Sr V Pres-Cfo, Eugene College
Sr V Pres, Michelle Mapes
Sr V Pres, David Martin
Turner Youth Initiative Direct, Twila Phillips
Auditors: PRICEWATERHOUSECOOPERS LLP M

LOCATIONS

HQ: FARM CREDIT SERVICES OF AMERICA, PCA
5015 S 118TH ST, OMAHA, NE 681372210
Phone: 800 884-3276
Web: WWW.FCSAMERICA.COM

HISTORICAL FINANCIALS
Company Type: Private

Income Statement
FYE: December 31

	ASSETS ($ mil.)	NET INCOME ($ mil.)	INCOME AS % OF ASSETS	EMPLOYEES
12/15	24,772	514	2.1%	10,000
12/04	8,475	294	3.5%	—
12/03	7,633	114	1.5%	—
12/02	0	132	—	—
Annual Growth	—	11.0%	—	—

2015 Year-End Financials
Debt ratio: —
Return on equity: 46.80%
Cash ($ mil.): 60
Current ratio: —
Long-term debt ($ mil.): —
Dividends
Yield: —
Payout: —
Market value ($ mil.): —

Farmers & Merchants Bancorp (Lodi, CA)

EXECUTIVES

Chb-pres-ceo, Kent A Steinwert
Vice President, Denise Goodell
Assistant Vice President, Benea Schmidt
Vice President, Chris Winek
Executive Vice President Senior Credit Officer, Ken Smith
Executive Vice President, Deborah Hodkin
Vice President And Chief Appraiser, Jon Schrader
Vice President Commercial Loan Officer, Claire Forsythe
Vice President Treasury Relationship Manager, Mike Caselli
Senior Vice President, Carol Murray
Senior Vice President Human Resources, Charles Broom
Assistant Vice President Operations Supervisor, Carrie Henshaw
Auditors: Moss Adams LLP

LOCATIONS

HQ: Farmers & Merchants Bancorp (Lodi, CA)
111 W. Pine Street, Lodi, CA 95240
Phone: 209 367-2300
Web: www.fmbonline.com

HISTORICAL FINANCIALS
Company Type: Public

Income Statement
FYE: December 31

	ASSETS ($ mil.)	NET INCOME ($ mil.)	INCOME AS % OF ASSETS	EMPLOYEES
12/17	3,075	28	0.9%	330
12/16	2,922	29	1.0%	339
12/15	2,615	27	1.0%	316
12/14	2,360	25	1.1%	310
12/13	2,076	24	1.2%	299
Annual Growth	10.3%	4.2%	—	2.5%

	STOCK PRICE ($) FY Close	P/E High/Low	PER SHARE ($) Earnings	Dividends	Book Value
12/17	676.00	20 17	35.03	13.55	368.90
12/16	610.00	17 13	37.44	13.10	340.00
12/15	540.00	17 13	34.82	12.90	318.46
12/14	463.00	14 13	32.64	12.70	297.39
12/13	417.00	16 12	30.93	12.50	269.84
Annual Growth	12.8%	— —	3.2%	2.0%	8.1%

Farmers & Merchants Bank of Long Beach (CA)

Auditors: KPMG LLP

LOCATIONS

HQ: Farmers & Merchants Bank of Long Beach (CA)
302 Pine Avenue, Long Beach, CA 90802
Phone: 213 437-0011
Web: www.fmb.com

HISTORICAL FINANCIALS

Company Type: Public

Income Statement   FYE: December 31

	ASSETS ($ mil.)	NET INCOME ($ mil.)	INCOME AS % OF ASSETS	EMPLOYEES
12/17	6,991	64	0.9%	747
12/16	6,729	71	1.1%	—
12/15	6,153	64	1.1%	—
12/14	5,581	62	1.1%	—
12/13	5,214	62	1.2%	—
Annual Growth	7.6%	1.0%	—	—

	STOCK PRICE ($) FY Close	P/E High/Low	PER SHARE ($) Earnings	Dividends	Book Value
12/17	7,860.00	16 14	494.65	119.00	7,325
12/16	6,800.00	13 11	546.16	119.00	6,95
12/15	6,240.00	13 12	496.06	119.00	6,532
12/14	6,060.00	13 11	476.67	114.00	6,160
12/13	5,226.00	11 9	474.80	114.00	5,798
Annual Growth	10.7%	— —	1.0%	1.1%	6.0%

Farmers National Banc Corp. (Canfield,OH)

Farmers National Banc is willing to help even nonfarmers grow their seed income into thriving bounties of wealth. The bank provides commercial and personal banking from nearly 20 branches in Ohio. Founded in 1887 Farmers National Banc offers checking and savings accounts credit cards and loans and mortgages. Farmers' lending portfolio is composed of real estate mortgages consumer loans and commercial loans. The company also includes Farmers National Insurance and Farmers Trust Company a non-depository trust bank that offers wealth management and trust services.

Geographic Reach

Farmers National Banc operates 19 branches located throughout Mahoning Trumbull Columbiana Stark and Cuyahoga Counties. Farmers Trust Company operates two offices located in Boardman and Howland Ohio.

Financial Performance

The company's revenues have ranged from $40 million to $60 million in the past decade. In 2013 overall sales fell 1% to $54 million; the slight dip was due to lessened interest income on loans and taxable securities. (Financial institutions make their money on interest income from loans and non-interest income from fees.) Its non-interest income experienced growth from service charges insurance agency commissions and consulting fees for retirement planning.

Profits decreased by 22% to $8 million in 2013 due to increase in a provision for loan losses and non-interest expenses such as salary and employee benefits.

Mergers and Acquisitions

In 2013 the bank added retirement planning services to their portfolio with the acquisition of Cleveland-based National Associates Inc. for $4.4 million. The acquisition was part of its plan to boost noninterest income and complement its existing retirement services.

EXECUTIVES

Assistant Vice President, Francis Gallagher
Vice President And Treasury Manager, Bobbi Harding
Vice President Commercial Lending Relationship Manager, James Rhodes
Vice President Commercial Lending Relationship Manager, Andrew Estock
Vice President Commercial Lending Relationship Manager, Darrell Smucker
Vice President Commercial Lending Relationship Manager, Suzanne Rinehart
Assistant Vice President Small Business Lender, Dean Karhan
Senior Vice President Commercial Lending Team Leader, Thomas Stocksdale
Assistant Vice President Relationship Manager Treasury Management, Jessica Kane
Auditors: CliftonLarsonAllen, LLP

LOCATIONS

HQ: Farmers National Banc Corp. (Canfield,OH)
20 South Broad Street, Canfield, OH 44406
Phone: 330 533-3341
Web: www.farmersbankgroup.com

PRODUCTS/OPERATIONS

Selected Products

Personal
Certificate of Deposit
Checking Accounts
Children's Accounts
Consumer Loans
Home Equity Loans & Lines
Mortgage Loans
Online Banking
Personal Credit Card
Personal Debit Card
Phone Banking
Retirement
Savings Accounts
Business
Business Credit Card
Business Debit Card
Business Deposits
Business Loans
Cash Management
Remote Deposit Capture
Wealth Management and Insurance
Farmers Trust Company
Farmers National Investments
Farmers National Insurance
On-line banking

COMPETITORS

CSB Bancorp	JPMorgan Chase
Central Federal	Killbuck Bancshares
Consumers Bancorp	National Bancshares
Cortland Bancorp	Ohio Legacy
FFD Financial	Tri-State 1st Banc
Fifth Third	United Community
First Financial	Financial
Bancorp	Wayne Savings
First Niles Financial	Bancshares
Home Loan Financial	

HISTORICAL FINANCIALS

Company Type: Public

Income Statement   FYE: December 31

	ASSETS ($ mil.)	NET INCOME ($ mil.)	INCOME AS % OF ASSETS	EMPLOYEES
12/17	2,159	22	1.1%	445
12/16	1,966	20	1.0%	441
12/15	1,869	8	0.4%	432
12/14	1,136	8	0.8%	327
12/13	1,137	7	0.7%	328
Annual Growth	17.4%	30.7%	—	7.9%

	STOCK PRICE ($) FY Close	P/E High/Low	PER SHARE ($) Earnings	Dividends	Book Value
12/17	14.75	19 15	0.82	0.22	8.79
12/16	14.20	20 11	0.76	0.16	7.88
12/15	8.60	24 20	0.36	0.12	7.35
12/14	8.35	18 14	0.48	0.12	6.71
12/13	6.55	17 14	0.41	0.12	6.02
Annual Growth	22.5%	— —	18.9%	16.4%	9.9%

Fastenal Co.

Fastenal makes for a snug fit. The industrial and fastener distributor sells almost 1.4 million products in about a dozen categories including threaded fasteners (such as screws nuts and bolts) which represent more than 35% of overall sales. Other sales come from fluid-transfer parts for hydraulic and pneumatic power; janitorial electrical and welding supplies; material handling items; metal-cutting tool blades; and power tools. Founded in 1967 as a fastener shop Fastenal now operates more than 2500 stores in all 50 US states and in Canada Mexico Asia Africa and Europe. Its customers include construction manufacturing and other industrial professionals.

Operations

Products manufactured by other companies account for more than 95% of Fastenal's total sales. The remainder of sales come from items custommade or modified by Fastenal. Threaded fasteners accounted for 90% of product line sales and more than 30% of overall net sales in 2016. The company's FAST Solutions vending machines are equipped with such products as cutting tools inserts round tools and all way to refrigerated drinks for workshop personnel.

Geographic Reach

Fastenal is headquartered in Winona Minnesota. While it sells products in more than 20 countries the company rang more than 85% of its sales in the US during 2016. Canada is its second-largest market accounting for more than 5% of sales. Fastenal has 14 distribution centers 11 of which are in the US. It also has two distribution centers in Canada and one in Mexico.

Sales and Marketing

Fastenal promotes its products using in-store signage catalogs events email radio and online marketing and direct mailing (including promotional flyers). Sponsorship activities include NASCAR Fastenal Racing while its marketing partners include 3M Honeywell Ansell Apex Sprayway Loctite Red Head and Norton (during 2016).

Most of Fastenal's customers operate in the manufacturing and non-residential construction markets. Other major customers include farmers truckers railroads oil exploration production and refinement companies mining companies federal state and local governmental entities schools and select retail trades. The company boasted 400000 active customer accounts in 2016.

Financial Performance

Fastenal has enjoyed strong results from the company's FAST Solutions program higher sales in older stores and to a lesser extent new store openings.

The distributor's revenue climbed to $3.96 billion in fiscal 2016 up from $3.87 billion during 2015. The increase was mostly thanks to higher unit sales from its older store locations with an increase in customer traffic and stronger sales with each customer. Sales from new store openings also helped boost the company's top-line to a lesser degree.

Despite the increase in revenue Fastenal's net income dropped from $516 million in fiscal 2015 down to $499.48 million in fiscal 2016. The drop in net income affected Fastenal's cash on hand. The company's cash from operations declined from $546.94 million at the end of fiscal 2015 down to $514 million at the end of fiscal 2016.

Strategy

Fastenal grows by continuously adding customers and by increasing the activity with each customer. The company has been slowing down store openings in recent years in favor of adding more sales personnel to boost revenues. Fastenal continued this strategy through 2016 aimed at increasing labor hours adding district and regional leadership personnel and generating more 'sales energy' within the business.

The distributor has also been relocating stores in the US while slowly adding new stores abroad. It has continued to expand its store count in in Mexico South Africa South America China and India and countries in Central and Eastern Europe. Fastenal also continues to invest aggressively in its distribution infrastructure to support long-term growth.

Mergers and Acquisitions

In March 2017 Fastenal entered into an agreement to acquire the assets of Manufacturer?s Supply Company (Mansco) manufacturer of hydraulic products for $50 million.

In October 2015 the company purchased Washington-based regional industrial and construction supply distributor Fasteners Inc along with its store locations in Washington Idaho Oregon and Montana.

In October 2014 Fastenal acquired Texas-based aerospace product distributor Av-Tech Industries.

HISTORY

Peace Corps veteran Robert Kierlin led four friends and Winona Cotter High School classmates in founding Fastenal in 1967 as a distributor of threaded fasteners. (Kierlin's inspiration was customers' inquiries at his father's auto parts store.) The company and its lone store lost money its first two years but it was able to open another store by 1970. Fastenal then changed its retail focus from regular consumers to contractors and professionals.

The company expanded locating stores on the outskirts of small and medium-sized cities where real estate and operating costs are lower. By 1987 it had 58 stores. Fastenal went public that year using some 40% of the IPO proceeds to establish the Hiawatha Education Foundation to support private high school education especially the founders' financially troubled alma mater.

EXECUTIVES

Vp Manufacturing, Tim Borkowski

Sevp Human Resources, Reyne K. Wisecup, age 56, $327,500 total compensation

President And Ceo, Daniel L. (Dan) Florness, age 55, $577,500 total compensation

Sevp Operations, Nicholas J. (Nick) Lundquist, age 61, $322,917 total compensation

Sevp Sales, Leland J. (Lee) Hein, age 58, $439,167 total compensation

Evp Manufacturing, James C. (Cory) Jansen, age 48, $220,829 total compensation

Evp Fast Solutions, Gary A. Polipnick, age 56, $300,000 total compensation

Evp Sales Operations And Support, John L. Soderberg, age 48

Evp E-business, Terry M. Owen, $430,000 total compensation

Evp Sales, Charles S. Miller

Controller Chief Accounting Officer And Treasurer, Sheryl A. Lisowski, age 52, $250,000 total compensation

Evp National Accounts Sales, William J. Drazkowski, age 47

Evp And Cfo, Holden Lewis, age 49, $120,002 total compensation

Evp Information Technology, John L. Soderburg, age 47

Evp International Sales, Jeffery M. Watts, age 46, $207,596 total compensation

Vice President Director Purchasing, Mike Thompson

Vice President Human Resources, Bonnie Zeinert

Vice President Product Development, Mike Rusk

Vice President Information Technology Infrastructure And Security, Craig Weatherhead

Vice President Of Ecommerce, Kirk Talmontas

Executive Vice President Internal Operations, Corey Jansen

Vice President Global Accounts, Steve Berra

National Account Manager, Eric Schulz

National Accounts Manager, Greg Turner

Senior Vice President Human Re, John Barrera

Regional Vice President, JT Kuntz

Vice President Finance, Tony Banks

Assistant Vice President Vendor Relations, Cody Webb

National Account Manager, Matt Hagen

National Accounts Manager, Patrick Tompkins

National Accounts Manager, Patrick Logan

National Account Manager, Nicole Danner

National Accounts Manager, Carl Bruhn

Regional Vice President, Erik McCluskey

Regional Vice President, Ron Kitcher

Executive Vice President National Accounts Sales, Bill Drazkowski

Vice President Of Transportation And Safety, Chris Duffenbach

Chairman, Willard D. (Will) Oberton, age 60

Auditors: KPMG LLP

LOCATIONS

HQ: Fastenal Co.
2001 Theurer Boulevard, Winona, MN 55987-0978
Phone: 507 454-5374 **Fax:** 507 453-8049
Web: www.fastenal.com

2016 stores

	No.of stores
United States	2,194
Canada	198
Mexico	52
Puerto Rico and Dominican Republic	8
Central and south America	8
Asia	10
Southeast Asia	7
Europe	24
Africa	2
Total	**2,503**

2016 sales

	$ mil.	% of total
United States	3,493	88
Canada	228	6
Other foreign countries	239	6
Total	**3,962**	**100**

PRODUCTS/OPERATIONS

Selected Brands Products and Services

Blackstone (welding supplies and cutting tools)
Clean Choice (janitorial supplies)
Dynaflo (hydraulics and pneumatics)
EquipRite (material handling janitorial supplies tools and cutting tools)
Fastenal (fasteners tools hydraulics and pneumatics safety supplies and metals)
FMT (tools and cutting tools)
FNL G9 (fasteners)
Holo-Krome (fasteners)
PowerPhase (electrical supplies and fasteners)
Profitter (hydraulics and pneumatics)
Rock River (fasteners and tools)
Tritan (cutting tools)
Threaded Fasteners
Bolts
Nuts
Screws
Studs
Related washers Miscellaneous supplies and hardware
Pins and machinery keys
Concrete anchors
Metal framing systems
Wire rope
Strut Rivets
Related accessories

COMPETITORS

Ace Hardware	Menard
Align Aerospace	Noland
Applied Industrial	Park-Ohio Holdings
Technologies	PennEngineering
Do it Best	Production Tool Supply
HD Supply	Snap-on
Home Depot	True Value
Lawson Products	W.W. Grainger
Lowe's	WinWholesale
MSC Industrial Direct	

HISTORICAL FINANCIALS

Company Type: Public

Income Statement
FYE: December 31

	REVENUE ($ mil.)	NET INCOME ($ mil.)	NET PROFIT MARGIN	EMPLOYEES
12/18	4,965	751	15.1%	21,644
12/17	4,390	578	13.2%	20,565
12/16	3,962	499	12.6%	19,624
12/15	3,869	516	13.3%	20,746
12/14	3,733	494	13.2%	18,417
Annual Growth	7.4%	11.1%	—	4.1%

2018 Year-End Financials

Debt ratio: 15.05%
Return on equity: 34.18%
Cash ($ mil.): 167
Current ratio: 5.30
Long-term debt ($ mil.): 497

No. of shares (mil.): 285
Dividends
 Yield: 2.9%
 Payout: 59.9%
Market value ($ mil.): 14,950

	STOCK PRICE ($) FY Close	P/E High/Low		PER SHARE ($) Earnings	Dividends	Book Value
12/18	52.29	23	18	2.62	1.54	8.05
12/17	54.69	27	20	2.01	1.28	7.29
12/16	46.98	29	21	1.73	1.20	6.69
12/15	40.82	27	20	1.77	1.12	6.22
12/14	47.56	31	24	1.66	1.00	6.47
Annual Growth	2.4%	—	—	12.1%	11.4%	5.6%

FB Financial Corp

Auditors: Crowe Horwath LLP

LOCATIONS

HQ: FB Financial Corp
 211 Commerce Street, Suite 300, Nashville, TN 37201
Phone: 615 564-1212
Web: www.firstbankonline.com

HISTORICAL FINANCIALS

Company Type: Public

Income Statement
FYE: December 31

	ASSETS ($ mil.)	NET INCOME ($ mil.)	INCOME AS % OF ASSETS	EMPLOYEES
12/17	4,727	52	1.1%	1,386
12/16	3,276	40	1.2%	1,108
12/15	2,899	47	1.7%	1,038
12/14	2,428	32	1.3%	—
12/13	2,258	26	1.2%	—
Annual Growth	20.3%	18.1%	—	—

2017 Year-End Financials

Debt ratio: 0.65%
Return on equity: 11.30%
Cash ($ mil.): 53
Current ratio: —
Long-term debt ($ mil.): —

No. of shares (mil.): 30
Dividends
 Yield: 0.0%
 Payout: —
Market value ($ mil.): 1,282

	STOCK PRICE ($) FY Close	P/E High/Low		PER SHARE ($) Earnings	Dividends	Book Value
12/17	41.99	23	13	1.86	0.00	19.54
12/16	35.95	19	9	2.10	4.03	13.71
Annual Growth	12.8%	—	—	(3.0%)	—	9.3%

FBL Financial Group Inc

Insurance holding company FBL Financial Group (FBL) is the parent of Farm Bureau Life Insurance Company. Through its subsidiary the firm sells life insurance annuities and investment products to farmers ranchers and agricultural businesses. Farm Bureau Life sells insurance and annuities through an exclusive network of about 2000 agents across some 15 states in the Midwest and West. (In Colorado it operates as Greenfields Life Insurance.) The company markets its products through an affiliation with the American Farm Bureau Federation. FBL also manages for a fee two Farm Bureau-affiliated property/casualty insurance companies. The Iowa Farm Bureau Federation owns close to 60% of the company.

Operations

FBL divides its business into two segments annuity and life insurance. Traditional and universal life insurance products sold primarily in Iowa Kansas and Oklahoma account for about 60% of sales. Annuities including fixed rate and index are also big in Iowa and Kansas and account for about 30% of revenue.

The two Farm Bureau-affiliated property/casualty insurers that FBL manages are Farm Bureau Property & Casualty and Western Agricultural Insurance. The two affiliates underwrite auto crop and other property/casualty policies for individuals and groups under FBL's corporate and other segment which accounts for about 10% of revenue.

Geographic Reach

FBL offers its services in 15 western and midwestern states. Iowa Kansas Oklahoma and Wyoming are key markets.

Financial Performance

After a few rocky years FBL has been back on track the last two years. In 2013 it reported a 5% increase in revenue from $656 million to $691 million as both annuity and life segments reported increases in the volume of business. Net income has been on a steady rise and increased 36% in 2013 from $80 million to $109 million due to the improved revenue and increased equity income. Cash from operations however has been declining for years and continued its trend with a $24 million drop to $182 million due to cash used for paying out and administering claims.

Strategy

Strategically FBL expands its penetration in both the life and property/casualty markets by encouraging existing policyholders to purchase other insurance products through the agents they already know. Its cross-selling technique has led the industry as a whole. Additionally FBL depends on the talent of the agents it engages and its overall ability to provide products that meet changing needs as well as superior customer service and market knowledge. It continually invests in training and supporting existing agents and recruiting new ones. FBL also launches new products like index annuities in 2012 and takes steps like decreasing commissions for some products that aren't profitable during this time of low interest rates.

EXECUTIVES

Ceo, James P. (Jim) Brannen, age 56, $700,000 total compensation
Cfo And Treasurer, Donald J. (Don) Seibel, age 54, $360,706 total compensation
Chief Investment Officer, Charles T. Happel, age 56, $353,496 total compensation
Coo Life Companies, Raymond W. Wasilewski, age 59
Cio, Casey Decker
Coo Property Casualty Companies, Daniel D. Pitcher, age 56, $383,778 total compensation
Vice President Assistant General Counsel, Karl Olson
Vice Chairman, Jerry L. Chicoine, age 75
Chairman, Craig D. Hill, age 62
Cfo And Treasurer, Donald J. (Don) Seibel, age 54
Auditors: Ernst & Young LLP

LOCATIONS

HQ: FBL Financial Group Inc
 5400 University Avenue, West Des Moines, IA 50266-5997
Phone: 515 225-5400
Web: www.fblfinancial.com

Selected Areas of Operation

Farm Bureau Life Insurance Company
 Multi-line (life and property/casualty)
 Arizona
 Iowa
 Kansas
 Minnesota
 Nebraska
 New Mexico
 South Dakota
 Utah
 Life only
 Idaho
 Montana
 North Dakota
 Oklahoma
 Wisconsin
 Wyoming
Farm Bureau Property & Casualty Insurance Company
 and Western Agricultural Insurance Company
 Arizona
 Iowa
 Kansas
 Minnesota
 Nebraska
 New Mexico
 South Dakota
 Utah

PRODUCTS/OPERATIONS

2015 Sales

	$ mil.	% of total
Life Insurance	409	57
Annuity	212	29
Gains on derivatives	10	1
Losses on investments	(2.7)	-
Corporate & other	93	13
Total	**722**	**100**

Selected Subsidiaries

Insurance
 Farm Bureau Life Insurance Company
Noninsurance
 5400 Holdings L.L.C.
 FBL Assigned Benefit Company
 FBL Financial Group Capital Trust
 FBL Financial Group Capital Trust II
 FBL Financial Services Inc.
 FBL Investment Management Services Inc.
 FBL Leasing Services Inc.
 FBL Marketing Services L.L.C.

COMPETITORS

AIG
Allstate
American Equity Investment Life Holding Company
American Farmers & Ranchers Mutual Insurance Co.
COUNTRY Financial
Farm Family Holdings
Farmers & Merchants Investment
Great American Financial Resources
MetLife
Midland National Life
Nationwide
Prudential
State Farm
Thrivent Investment Management

HISTORICAL FINANCIALS

Company Type: Public

Income Statement
FYE: December 31

	ASSETS ($ mil.)	NET INCOME ($ mil.)	INCOME AS % OF ASSETS	EMPLOYEES
12/17	10,066	194	1.9%	1,692
12/16	9,566	107	1.1%	1,644
12/15	9,132	113	1.2%	1,637
12/14	9,064	109	1.2%	1,628
12/13	8,461	108	1.3%	1,589
Annual Growth	4.4%	15.7%	—	1.6%

2017 Year-End Financials

Debt ratio: 0.96%
Return on equity: 15.08%
Cash ($ mil.): 52
Current ratio: —
Long-term debt ($ mil.): —

No. of shares (mil.): 24
Dividends
  Yield: 0.0%
  Payout: 42.0%
Market value ($ mil.): 1,736

	STOCK PRICE ($) FY Close	P/E High/Low		PER SHARE ($) Earnings	Dividends	Book Value
12/17	69.65	10	8	7.75	3.26	55.71
12/16	78.15	19	13	4.28	3.68	47.73
12/15	63.64	15	11	4.53	3.60	45.73
12/14	58.03	13	8	4.39	1.40	50.69
12/13	44.79	11	8	4.21	2.52	42.20
Annual Growth	11.7%	—	—	16.5%	6.6%	7.2%

Federal Agricultural Mortgage Corp

Farmer Mac (Federal Agricultural Mortgage Corporation) is Fannie Mae and Freddie Mac's country cousin. Like its city-slicker kin it provides liquidity in its markets (agricultural real estate and rural housing mortgages) by buying loans from lenders and then securitizing the loans into Farmer Mac Guaranteed Securities. Farmer Mac buys both conventional loans and those guaranteed by the US Department of Agriculture. Farmer Mac was created by Congress in 1987 to establish a secondary market for agricultural mortgage and rural utilities loans. It is a stockholder-owned publicly-traded corporation based in Washington DC with an underwriting office in Iowa.

Operations

Farmer Mac operates four segments: Farm & Ranch which accounted for 39% of revenue during 2015 purchases mortgage loans secured by first liens on agricultural real estate including part-time farms and rural housing; Institutional Credit (28%

of revenue) which buys or guarantees general lender obligations secured by eligible pools of loans; the USDA Guarantees segment (18%) which buys USDA-backed agricultural rural development business and industry and community facilities loans; and Rural Utilities (10%) which buys mortgages tied to eligible rural utilities loans. The organization generates more than 90% of its revenue from interest income stemming from a roughly even mix of loans and backed loan securities. About 47% of its revenue came from interest on Farmer Mac Guaranteed or USDA securities during 2015 while another 41% came from interest on loans. The rest came from interest on other investments (5% of revenue) guarantee and commitment fees (5%) and gains on financial derivatives and hedging activities (1%).

Geographic Reach

The Washington DC-based group serves the US from satellite operations in Ames Iowa; Boise Idaho; Canton Michigan; Fresno California; Johnston Iowa; and Scottsdale Arizona.

Sales and Marketing

Farmer Mac markets its services personally and directly to agricultural lenders by participating regularly in events such as state and national banking conferences. It also has alliances with the American Bankers Association and the Independent Community Bankers of Alliances and has a business relationship with the members of the Farm Credit System.

Financial Performance

Farmer Mac's annual revenues have risen more than 25% since 2011 thanks to a stronger agricultural economy as well as product developments which have driven customer and overall loan asset growth over the years. Its annual profits have also trended higher but have fluctuated more due to the volatility of the gains it's made from financial derivatives hedging activities and other trading securities.

The group's revenue climbed 4% to $284 million during 2015 mostly thanks to double-digit interest income growth as its loan assets grew 12% to $3.96 billion and as its Farm & Ranch loans USDA Securities and AgVantage securities balances grew as well. Farmer Mac's non-interest income shrank 39% as it collected $37.4 million less in trading securities gains as it did in 2014.

Revenue growth and a decline in interest expenses in 2015 drove Farmer Mac's net income up 43% to $68.7 million. The lender's operating cash levels jumped 19% to $184 million as its cash-based earnings rose and as working capital increased with changes in other assets.

Strategy

Farmer Mac seeks to improve the availability of long-term credit at stable interest rates to rural communities. To this end its primary strategy for managing interest rate risk is to fund asset purchases with liabilities that have similar duration and cash flow characteristics so that they will perform similarly as interest rates change.

EXECUTIVES

President And Ceo, Timothy L. (Tim) Buzby, age 49, $643,750 total compensation
Evp Cfo And Treasurer, R. Dale Lynch, age 51, $375,950 total compensation
Svp Agricultural Finance, J. Curtis Covington, age 62
Svp General Counsel And Secretary, Stephen P. Mullery, age 51, $340,930 total compensation
Vice President Corporate Affairs, Chris Bohanon
Senior Vice President Agricultural Finance, Curt Covington
Chairman, Lowell L. Junkins, age 74
Evp Cfo And Treasurer, R. Dale Lynch, age 51

Vice Chairman, Myles J. Watts, age 67
Svp General Counsel And Secretary, Stephen P. Mullery, age 51
Auditors: PricewaterhouseCoopers LLP

LOCATIONS

HQ: Federal Agricultural Mortgage Corp
  1999 K Street, N.W., 4th Floor, Washington, DC 20006
Phone: 202 872-7700   Fax: 202 872-7713
Web: www.farmermac.com

PRODUCTS/OPERATIONS

2015 Sales

	% of total
Interest income	
Farmer Mac Guaranteed Securities and USDA Securities	47
Loans	41
Investments and cash equivalents	5
Noninterest income	
Guarantee and commitment fees	5
Gains on financial derivatives and hedging activities	1
Other	1
Total	**100**

2015 Sales

	% of total
Farm & Ranch	39
USDA Guarantees	28
Rural Utilities	18
Institutional Credit	10
Corporate	4
Reconciling Adjustments	1
Total	**100**

Selected Operations

Farm & Ranch (Farmer Mac I)
USDA Guarantees (Farmer Mac II)
Rural Utilities

COMPETITORS

AgFirst
AgStar
AgriBank
Bank of America
Citigroup

Fannie Mae
Farm Credit Services
  of Mid-America
Freddie Mac

HISTORICAL FINANCIALS

Company Type: Public

Income Statement
FYE: December 31

	ASSETS ($ mil.)	NET INCOME ($ mil.)	INCOME AS % OF ASSETS	EMPLOYEES
12/17	17,792	84	0.5%	88
12/16	15,606	77	0.5%	81
12/15	15,540	68	0.4%	71
12/14	14,287	48	0.3%	71
12/13	13,361	75	0.6%	67
Annual Growth	7.4%	2.9%	—	7.1%

2017 Year-End Financials

Debt ratio: 87.24%
Return on equity: 12.50%
Cash ($ mil.): 302
Current ratio: —
Long-term debt ($ mil.): —

No. of shares (mil.): 10
Dividends
  Yield: 0.0%
  Payout: 21.8%
Market value ($ mil.): 831

	STOCK PRICE ($) FY Close	P/E High/Low		PER SHARE ($) Earnings	Dividends	Book Value
12/17	78.24	12	8	6.60	1.44	66.69
12/16	57.27	10	4	5.97	1.04	61.05
12/15	31.57	8	5	4.19	0.64	51.79
12/14	30.34	10	8	3.37	0.56	49.90
12/13	34.25	6	4	6.41	0.48	30.55
Annual Growth	22.9%	—	—	0.7%	31.6%	21.5%

Federal Home Loan Bank New York

Federal Home Loan Bank of New York (FHLBNY) provides funds for residential mortgages and community development to more than 330 member banks savings and loans credit unions and life insurance companies in New York New Jersey Puerto Rico and the US Virgin Islands. One of a dozen Federal Home Loan Banks in the US it is cooperatively owned by its member institutions and supervised by the Federal Housing Finance Agency. FHLBNY like others in the system is privately capitalized; it receives no taxpayer funding. The bank instead raises funds mainly by issuing debt instruments in the capital markets.

Operations

FHLBNY is a secured lender that requires collateral for its advances which are typically used by members to underwrite residential mortgages or to invest in US Treasury and agency securities mortgage-backed securities and other real estate-related assets.

A large part of FHLBNY's business is in making collateralized loans or advances to members. It serves the public through its mortgage programs. Three members — Citibank (25%) Met Life (14%) and New York Community Bank (11%) — accounted for half of total advances.

Geographic Reach

Based in New York FHLBNY serves not only New York but New Jersey Puerto Rico and the US Virgin Islands.

Sales and Marketing

FHLBNY caters to more than 330 member banks credit unions life insurance companies and savings and loans.

Financial Performance

Revenue dropped by 14% to $801 million in fiscal 2013 from 2012's $934.9 million. FHLBNY attributes the decline to a decrease in interest income and other income. Net income also dropped some 16% in 2013 to $304.6 million vs. $360.7 million in 2012. It attributes net income decreases to declining revenue and rising other expenses. Operating cash flow decreased in fiscal 2013 to $525.6 million compared to 2012's $678.9 million.

Strategy

Credit unions are a possible area of growth for FHLBNY. The bank has identified more than 50 credit unions and banks that are not members but are eligible. To be under consideration an institution must have more than $50 million in assets ($100 million for banks) be an established wholesale lender maintain a high deposit-to-loan ratio and have management that has done business with an FHLB in the past.

Beginning in 2014 it's also funding — with the help of $35.5 million in subsidies — 48 affordable housing initiatives throughout New Jersey New York Puerto Rico the US Virgin Islands Florida Maryland and Pennsylvania. The effort involves the creation or rehabilitation of more than 3000 affordable housing units.

EXECUTIVES

Vice President Director Of Human Resources, Mildred Tse-Gonzalez
Assistant Vice President, Diahann Rothstein
Senior Vice President Director Of Bank Relations, Eric Amig
Vice President Sales And Marketing And C, Alfred O'Connell
Vice President Manager Business Research And Devolpment, John Brandon
Senior Vice President Chief Capital Markets Officer, Phil Scott
Vice President, Eugene Khesin
Assistant Vice President, Kristen Lalama
Assistant Vice President Fina, Kimberly Whitenack
Auditors: PricewaterhouseCoopers LLP

LOCATIONS

HQ: Federal Home Loan Bank New York
101 Park Avenue, New York, NY 10178
Phone: 212 681-6000
Web: www.fhlbny.com

PRODUCTS/OPERATIONS

2013 Sales

	$ mil.	% of total
Interest		
Advances	444	55
Long-term securities	244	30
Mortgage loans held for portfolio	68	9
Available-for-sale securities	16	2
Other	14	2
Non-interest	13	2
Total	**801**	**100**

HISTORICAL FINANCIALS
Company Type: Public

Income Statement				FYE: December 31
	ASSETS ($ mil.)	NET INCOME ($ mil.)	INCOME AS % OF ASSETS	EMPLOYEES
12/17	158,918	479	0.3%	308
12/16	143,606	401	0.3%	280
12/15	123,248	414	0.3%	273
12/14	132,825	314	0.2%	258
12/13	128,332	304	0.2%	258
Annual Growth	5.5%	12.0%	—	4.5%

2017 Year-End Financials

Debt ratio: 62.48%
Return on equity: 6.04%
Cash ($ mil.): 127
Current ratio: —
Long-term debt ($ mil.): —

No. of shares (mil.): 67
Dividends
 Yield: —
 Payout: 72.3%
Market value ($ mil.): —

Federal Home Loan Bank Of Cincinnati

Auditors: PricewaterhouseCoopers LLP

LOCATIONS

HQ: Federal Home Loan Bank Of Cincinnati
600 Atrium Two, P.O Box 598, Cincinnati, OH 45201-0598
Phone: 513 852-7500
Web: www.fhlbcin.com

HISTORICAL FINANCIALS
Company Type: Public

Income Statement				FYE: December 31
	ASSETS ($ mil.)	NET INCOME ($ mil.)	INCOME AS % OF ASSETS	EMPLOYEES
12/17	106,895	313	0.3%	226
12/16	104,635	268	0.3%	211
12/15	118,796	248	0.2%	203
12/14	106,640	244	0.2%	204
12/13	103,180	261	0.3%	—
Annual Growth	0.9%	4.7%	—	—

2017 Year-End Financials

Debt ratio: 93.90%
Return on equity: 6.18%
Cash ($ mil.): 26
Current ratio: —
Long-term debt ($ mil.): —

No. of shares (mil.): 42
Dividends
 Yield: —
 Payout: 66.3%
Market value ($ mil.): —

Federal Home Loan Bank Of Dallas

Auditors: PricewaterhouseCoopers LLP

LOCATIONS

HQ: Federal Home Loan Bank Of Dallas
8500 Freeport Parkway South, Suite 600, Irving, TX 75063-2547
Phone: 214 441-8500

HISTORICAL FINANCIALS
Company Type: Public

Income Statement				FYE: December 31
	ASSETS ($ mil.)	NET INCOME ($ mil.)	INCOME AS % OF ASSETS	EMPLOYEES
12/17	68,524	150	0.2%	205
12/16	58,212	79	0.1%	218
12/15	42,083	67	0.2%	207
12/14	38,045	48	0.1%	192
12/13	30,221	87	0.3%	—
Annual Growth	22.7%	14.4%	—	—

2017 Year-End Financials

Debt ratio: 45.79%
Return on equity: 4.77%
Cash ($ mil.): 88
Current ratio: —
Long-term debt ($ mil.): —

No. of shares (mil.): 23
Dividends
 Yield: —
 Payout: 21.6%
Market value ($ mil.): —

Federal Home Loan Bank Of Des Moines

Auditors: PricewaterhouseCoopers LLP

LOCATIONS

HQ: Federal Home Loan Bank Of Des Moines
909 Locust Street, Des Moines, IA 50309
Phone: 515 412-2100
Web: www.fhlbdm.com

HISTORICAL FINANCIALS
Company Type: Public

Income Statement
FYE: December 31

	ASSETS ($ mil.)	NET INCOME ($ mil.)	INCOME AS % OF ASSETS	EMPLOYEES
12/17	145,099	518	0.4%	351
12/16	180,605	649	0.4%	307
12/15	137,381	131	0.1%	279
12/14	95,523	121	0.1%	228
12/13	73,004	109	0.2%	—
Annual Growth	18.7%	47.4%	—	—

2017 Year-End Financials

Debt ratio: 93.44%
Return on equity: 7.18%
Cash ($ mil.): 504
Current ratio: —
Long-term debt ($ mil.): —

No. of shares (mil.): 51
Dividends
  Yield: —
  Payout: 24.9%
Market value ($ mil.): —

Federal Home Loan Bank Of San Francisco

The city by the bay is the home to the Federal Home Loan Bank of San Francisco one ofA a dozenA regional banks in the Federal Home Loan Bank System chartered by Congress inA 1932 to provide credit to residential mortgage lenders. TheA government-sponsored enterpriseA is privately owned by its members which include some 400 commercial banks credit unions industrial loan companies savings and loans insurance companies and housing associatesA headquartered in Arizona California and Nevada. The bank links members to worldwide capital markets which provide them with low-cost funding. Members then pass these advances along to their customers in the form of affordable home mortgage and economic development loans.

EXECUTIVES

Assistant Vice President Compliance, Jamie Leong
Auditors: PricewaterhouseCoopers LLP

LOCATIONS

HQ: Federal Home Loan Bank Of San Francisco
600 California Street, San Francisco, CA 94108
Phone: 415 616-1000
Web: www.fhlbsf.com

PRODUCTS/OPERATIONS

2013

	$ mil.	% of total
Interest income	1,086	97
Other income	5	3
Total	**1,091**	**100**

HISTORICAL FINANCIALS
Company Type: Public

Income Statement
FYE: December 31

	ASSETS ($ mil.)	NET INCOME ($ mil.)	INCOME AS % OF ASSETS	EMPLOYEES
12/17	123,385	376	0.3%	287
12/16	91,941	712	0.8%	274
12/15	85,707	638	0.7%	263
12/14	75,807	205	0.3%	255
12/13	85,774	308	0.4%	262
Annual Growth	9.5%	5.1%	—	2.3%

2017 Year-End Financials

Debt ratio: 93.61%
Return on equity: 6.09%
Cash ($ mil.): 1,146
Current ratio: —
Long-term debt ($ mil.): —

No. of shares (mil.): 32
Dividends
  Yield: —
  Payout: 49.7%
Market value ($ mil.): —

Federal Reserve Bank of Atlanta, Dist. No. 6

One of 12 regional banks in the Federal Reserve System the Federal Reserve Bank of Atlanta oversees Fed member banks and thrifts and their holding companies throughout the Southeast including Alabama Florida Georgia and parts of Louisiana Mississippi and Tennessee. It conducts examinations and investigations of member institutions distributes cash issues savings bonds and Treasury securities and assists the Fed in setting monetary policy such as interest rates. The bank also processes checks and acts as a clearinghouse for payments between banks. Fed Reserve Banks are independent arms within the government and return earnings (gleaned mostly from investments in government bonds) to the US Treasury.

Operations
Of the 12 regional banks in the Federal Reserve System only the Atlanta bank processes both paper and electronic checks for the system.

Financial Performance
In 2012 FRB Atlanta reported about $5.5 billion in total current income about 7% of the $81.6 billion in total income for the Federal Reserve System.

Company Background
The Federal Reserve Bank of Atlanta was established in 1914.

EXECUTIVES

Senior Vice President, William Estes
First Vp And Coo, Marie C. Gooding
Evp, Cheryl L. Venable
Evp, David E. Altig
President And Ceo, Raphael W. Bostic
Evp, Michael Johnson
Vice President, Michael Chriszt
Assistant Vice President, Nancy Montoya
Vice President Information Technology, Vicki Kosydor
Assistant Vice President, Jennifer Gibilterra
Assistant Vice President Systems, Brad Joiner
Vice President And General Auditor, Brian Bowling
Vice President And Regional Executive, Chris Oakley
Vice President, Robert Schenk
Vice President Marketing, Hanh Dong

Vice President, Mary Kepler
Senior Vice President And General Auditor, Lois Berthaume
Vice President Of Regional Research, John Robertson
Vice President Marketing, Christopher Oakley
Vice President, Doug Tillett
Vice President, Sheryl Britsch
Assistant Vice President And Information Security Officer, Keith Morales
Assistant Vice President And Information Security Officer, Allen Sautter
Vice President Information Technology, Gregory Johnston
Assistant Vice President Information Technology, Shilpa Dutt
Vice President, Prabal Chakrabarti
Vice President, Shonda Clay
Assistant Vice President Community And Economic Development, Karen Leonedenie
Assistant Vice President, Paula Armstrong
Executive Vice President, Julie Stackhouse
Vice President Public Affairs, Catherine Bourke
Senior Vice President, Todd Aadland
Assistant Vice President, Jim Fuchs
Vice President Architecture And Common Services, Colin Wynd
Vice President Global Brand, Sue Costello
Assistant Vice President, Meghan Wlaz
Vice President And Regional Economist, Rae Rosen
Senior Vice President, Chris Haley
Assistant Vice President, Michael Coldwell
Deputy Chairman, Michael J. (Mike) Jackson
Chairman, Thomas A. (Tom) Fanning
Board Member, Lee Thomas
Auditors: KPMG LLP

LOCATIONS

HQ: Federal Reserve Bank of Atlanta, Dist. No. 6
1000 Peachtree Street, N.E., Atlanta, GA 30309-4470
Phone: 404 498-8500
Web: www.frbatlanta.org

HISTORICAL FINANCIALS
Company Type: Public

Income Statement
FYE: December 31

	REVENUE ($ mil.)	NET INCOME ($ mil.)	NET PROFIT MARGIN	EMPLOYEES
12/17	6,971	48	0.7%	—
12/16	6,502	66	1.0%	—
12/15	6,562	(992)	—	—
12/14	6,861	156	2.3%	—
12/13	6,105	89	1.5%	—
Annual Growth	3.4%	(14.3%)	—	—

2017 Year-End Financials

Debt ratio: 74.47%
Return on equity: 2.02%
Cash ($ mil.): 289,653
Current ratio: 4.07
Long-term debt ($ mil.): 220,248

No. of shares (mil.): 36
Dividends
  Yield: —
  Payout: —
Market value ($ mil.): —

Federal Reserve Bank of Chicago, Dist. No. 7

The Federal Reserve Bank of Chicago regulates banks and bank holding companies in northern

Illinois northern Indiana southern Wisconsin the Lower Peninsula of Michigan and all of Iowa. It supervises more than 850 bank holding companies and state member banks distributes money issues savings bonds and Treasury securities and assists the Fed in setting monetary policy. The Chicago Fed also processes checks and acts as a clearinghouse for payments between banks. Like the 11 other regional banks in the Federal Reserve System it returns its profits (earned largely from investments in government and federal agency securities) to the US Treasury.

Geographic Reach

The Chicago Fed serves the Seventh Federal Reserve District a region that includes all of Iowa and most of the states of Illinois Indiana Michigan and Wisconsin. The bank's head office is in Chicago and it has a branch office in Detroit. Overall it has 2230 depository institutions across its district; these include banks credit unions savings and loans institutions and others.

Financial Performance

From 2011 to 2012 the bank's total revenues dropped by 3% from nearly $5.6 billion to $5.4 billion. However its net income surged by nearly 30% increasing from $94 million to $122 million during that same time period. Treasury securities accounted for 57% of its total revenue in 2012 while federal agency mortgage-backed securities generated nearly 40%.

Company Background

The Federal Reserve Bank of Chicago is one of the 12 Federal Reserve Banks created by Congress under the Federal Reserve Act of 1913 which established the central bank of the US.

EXECUTIVES

Executive Vice President Customer Relati, William Barouski
Vice President, Anna M Voytovich
President And Ceo, Charles L. (Charlie) Evans
Vp Institutions Supervision, Catharine (Cathy) Lemieux
Vp And General Auditor, Margaret K. (Peg) Koenigs
Research Director, Daniel G. Sullivan
First Vp And Coo, Ellen J. Bromagen
Vice President Consumer And Community Affairs, Alicia Williams
Vice President Financial Markets Group, Edward Nosal
Senior Vice President Financial Markets, David Marshall
Senior Vice President Customer Services, Barbara Benson
Senior Vice President Risk Specialists, Carl Tannenbaum
Assistant Vice President, Joan Fischmann
Vice President Industry Relations, Dan Gonzalez
Vice President, Ted Kurdes
Vice President District Cash Operations, Donna Dziak
Vice President, Kimberly Clark
Vice President Economic Research And Programs, Daniel Aaronson
Senior Vice President, Robert Wiley
Senior Vice President Supervision Regulation, Steve Durfey
Assistant Vice President, Kathrine Kielma
Chairman, Gregory Q. (Greg) Brown
Deputy Chair, Anne R. Pramaggiore
Member Board Of Directors, Spencer Krane
Auditors: KPMG LLP

LOCATIONS

HQ: Federal Reserve Bank of Chicago, Dist. No. 7
230 South La Salle Street, Chicago, IL 60604-1413
Phone: 312 322-5322
Web: www.chicagofed.org

PRODUCTS/OPERATIONS

2016 sales

	% of total
Interest Income	
Treasury securitiesnet	56
Government-sponsored enterprise debt securitiesnet	1
Federal agency and government-sponsored enterprise mortagage -backed securities net	40
Non Interest Income	
Income from services	2
Compensation received for service costs provided	1
Other -	
Total	**100**

HISTORICAL FINANCIALS

Company Type: Public

Income Statement				FYE: December 31
	REVENUE ($ mil.)	NET INCOME ($ mil.)	NET PROFIT MARGIN	EMPLOYEES
12/17	4,902	41	0.8%	—
12/16	4,458	183	4.1%	—
12/15	4,423	(473)	—	—
12/14	5,176	66	1.3%	—
12/13	5,001	(12)	—	—
Annual Growth	(0.5%)	—	—	—

2017 Year-End Financials

Debt ratio: 43.00%	No. of shares (mil.): 26
Return on equity: 2.38%	Dividends
Cash ($ mil.): —	Yield: —
Current ratio: 1.76	Payout: —
Long-term debt ($ mil.): 105,195	Market value ($ mil.): —

Federal Reserve Bank of New York, Dist. No. 2

The Federal Reserve Bank of New York is the largest in the Federal Reserve System to oversee US bank activities. It issues currency clears money transfers and lends to banks in its district. In addition to the duties it shares with 11 other regional Federal Reserve Banks the New York Fed trades US government securities to regulate the money supply intervenes on foreign exchange markets and stores monetary gold for foreign central banks and governments. The New York Fed's district is relatively small (made up of New York Puerto Rico the US Virgin Islands northern New Jersey and Fairfield County Connecticut) but the bank is the largest in the Federal Reserve System in assets and volume of transactions.

Operations

Secured in a vault 80 feet below street level in the New York Fed's Manhattan headquarters is billions of dollars worth of gold — some 25% to 30% of the world's official monetary gold reserves. The vault rests on Manhattan Island's bedrock considered to be one of the few foundations adequate enough to support the weight of the vault and its contents.

Financial Performance

The New York Fed's total revenue for 2015 surged by 37% compared to 2014. The growth was mainly due to increased investment returns from treasury securities.

EXECUTIVES

Corporate Secretary And Vice President, Michael Held
Evp; Head Emerging Markets And International Affairs Group, Terrence J. Checki
First Vice President, Christine M. Cumming
Executive Vice President, Roseann Stichnoth
Executive Vice President Risk Group, Sandra C. (Sandy) Krieger
Evp And Head Research And Statistics Group, James J. McAndrews
Evp Markets Group, Brian P. Sack
Evp And General Auditor, Edward C. Smith
Evp Corporate, Edward F. Murphy
President And Ceo, William C. Dudley
Executive Vice President, William T. Christie
Executive Vice President, Susan W. Mink
Evp And Head Communications, Krishna Guha
Executive Vice President Markets Group, Simon M. Potter
Chief Of Staff And Vice President, James P. Bergin
Executive Vice President And Chief Risk Officer, Joshua Rosenberg
Vice President, Stephanie Heller
Senior Vice President Financial Institution Supervision Group, Caroline Frawley
Assistant Vice President Accounting, Robert Pofsky
Assistant Vice President Of Financial Services Gro, Christopher Armstrong
Assistant Vice President, Hunter Clark
Vice President, Yoonhi Greene
Vice President, Jonathan Polk
Assistant Vice President, Rona Stein
Assistant Vice President Markets Group Automation Services, Michael Burk
Vice President Corporate Recruitment, Bettyann Griffith
Assistant Vice President, Sarah Adelson
Vice President, Dina Maher
Senior Vice President Federal Reserve Police, Nicholas Proto
Assistant Vice President Of Financial Institution Supervision Group, Louis Braunstein
Assistant Vice President, Louis Scenti
Vice President Andamp; Assistant General Counsel, Jen Wolgemuth
Assistant Vice President, Keith Pulsifer
Assistant Vice President And Senior Advisor, Ethan Buyon
Vice President And Counsel In The Legal Group, Michele Kalstein
Assistant Vice President, Mayra Gonzalez
Assistant Vice President Of Financial Institution Supervision Group, Glen Reppy
Senior Vice President, Nancy Bercovici
Assistant Vice President, Patrick Coyne
Senior Vice President And Assistant General Counse, Haeran Kim
Senior Vice President Human Resources, Elaine Mauriello
Assistant Vice President Of Legal Group, Brett Phillips
Vice President And Chief Technology Offi, Nathaniel Wuerffel
First Vice President, Jamie B Stewart
Senior Vice President, Chris McCurdy
Assistant Vice President, Matt Nemeth
Assistant Vice President, GERALD MCCRINK
Senior Vice President And Chief Information Security Officer, Joeseph Leonard
Executive Vice President And Chief Technology And Strategy Officer, James Lammers
Assistant Vice President, Ewan St Clair
Chairman, Lee C. Bollinger
Chairman, Emily K. Rafferty
President And Ceo, William C. Dudley
Auditors: KPMG LLP

LOCATIONS

HQ: Federal Reserve Bank of New York, Dist. No. 2
33 Liberty Street, New York, NY 10045-0001
Phone: 212 720-5000
Web: www.newyorkfed.org

Selected Offices
Buffalo New York
East Rutherford New Jersey
New York City
Utica New York

HISTORICAL FINANCIALS
Company Type: Public

Income Statement   FYE: December 31

	REVENUE ($ mil.)	NET INCOME ($ mil.)	NET PROFIT MARGIN	EMPLOYEES
12/17	65,090	(503)	—	—
12/16	64,509	328	0.5%	—
12/15	68,534	(5,604)	—	—
12/14	68,824	2,398	3.5%	—
12/13	50,355	(1,397)	—	—
Annual Growth	6.6%	—	—	—

2017 Year-End Financials

Debt ratio: 21.21%
Return on equity: (-3.87%)
Cash ($ mil.): 2,459,689
Current ratio: 1.69
Long-term debt ($ mil.): 528,663

No. of shares (mil.): 197
Dividends
Yield: —
Payout: —
Market value ($ mil.): —

Federal Reserve Bank of Richmond, Dist. No. 5

One of 12 regional banks in the Federal Reserve System the Federal Reserve Bank of Richmond oversees the Fifth District's system member banks and bank holding companies in Virginia; Maryland; the Carolinas; Washington DC; and most of West Virginia from branches in Maryland North Carolina and Virginia. It conducts examinations and investigations of member institutions distributes money issues savings bonds and Treasury securities and assists the Federal Reserve System in setting monetary policy. The bank also processes checks and acts as a clearinghouse for payments between banks. Federal Reserve Banks return earnings (mostly from investments in government bonds) to the US Treasury.

Operations
The Richmond Fed employs economists scholars and research associates to conduct economic study regarding the Fifth District economy and also to support the Federal Reserve System's policymakers. It was organized in 1914 subsequent to the enactment of the Federal Reserve Act in 1913.

Geographic Reach
The organization has its headquarters in Virginia. It serves the Fifth Federal Reserve District which includes Maryland North Carolina South Carolina Virginia District of Columbia and portions of West Virginia.

Financial Performance
Revenues increased 9% from 2013 to 2014. The growth was do to increased interest income and

additional government-sponsored enterprise mortgage-backed securities partially offset by non-interest losses.

EXECUTIVES

Vice President Federal Reserve Information Technology Audit, Gregory Johnson
Assistant Vice President Public Affairs, Steve Malone
Assistant Vice President, Edward Norfleet
Interim President And Ceo, Mark L. Mullinix
Svp And Cto Currency Technology Office And Cash Product Office, Roland Costa
Svp And Regional Executive Baltimore, David E. (Dave) Beck
Svp Supervision Regulation And Credit, Jennifer J. Burns
Svp And Cio, Janice E. Clatterbuck
Svp And Regional Executive Charlotte, Matthew A. Martin
Evp And Director Of Research, Kartik Athreya
Vice President, Edgar A Martindale
Vice President, James Hayes
Vice President Communications, Barbara Moss
Vice President, Steven Bareford
Assistant Vice President Of Information Technology, Johnnie Moore
Assistant Vice President, Joyce Romito
Isoc And Vice President Information, Tom Weber
Vice President Internal Audit, Cathy Howdyshell
Vice President, Sherri Thorne
Assistant Vice President, Bob Minteer
Assistant Vice President, Pinkaj Klokkenga
Assistant Vice President Information Technology, Keith Malatesta
Vice President Operations, Jack Mccolgan
Senior Vice President Procurement, Jeff Crow
Vice President, R Ahern
Vice President Credit Risk Management, Christy Cleare
Assistant Vice President Information Technology, Niranjan Chandramowli
Assistant Vice President Information Security, Bary Dalton
Assistant Vice President, Markus Summers
Vice President And General Manager, Michael Serrato
Vice President Senior Payments Advisor, Chad Harper
Senior Vice President Enterprise Information Security, Chris Tignor
Vice President Business Banker, Ott Dennis
Chairman, Margaret G. Lewis
Deputy Chair, Kathy J. Warden
Auditors: KPMG LLP

LOCATIONS

HQ: Federal Reserve Bank of Richmond, Dist. No. 5
Post Office Box 27622, Richmond, VA 23261
Phone: 804 697-8000
Web: www.richmondfed.org

PRODUCTS/OPERATIONS

2014 sales

	$ mil	% of contribution
Interest Income		
Treasury securities net	3,622	53
Government-sponsored enterprise debt securities net	92	2
Federal agency and government-sponsored enterprise mortgage-backed securities net	2,950	44
Foreign currency denominated investments net	16	0
Central bank liquidity swaps	0	0
Non-interest loss		
System Open Market Account	(600)	0
Compensation received for service costs provided	15	0
Reimbursable services to government agencies	50	1
Other	3	0
Total	**6,148**	**100**

HISTORICAL FINANCIALS
Company Type: Public

Income Statement   FYE: December 31

	REVENUE ($ mil.)	NET INCOME ($ mil.)	NET PROFIT MARGIN	EMPLOYEES
12/17	7,217	165	2.3%	—
12/16	6,604	67	1.0%	—
12/15	5,989	(3,955)	—	—
12/14	6,148	1,202	19.6%	—
12/13	5,666	284	5.0%	—
Annual Growth	6.2%	(12.7%)	—	—

2017 Year-End Financials

Debt ratio: 36.12%
Return on equity: 1.87%
Cash ($ mil.): 255,934
Current ratio: 1.62
Long-term debt ($ mil.): 105,982

No. of shares (mil.): 135
Dividends
Yield: —
Payout: —
Market value ($ mil.): —

Federal Reserve Bank of San Francisco, Dist. No. 12

One of 12 regional banks in the Federal Reserve System the Federal Reserve Bank of San Francisco through four branch offices oversees hundreds of banks and thrifts in nine western states and American Samoa Guam and the Northern Mariana Islands - the largest of the 12 districts. It conducts examinations and investigations of member institutions distributes money issues savings bonds and Treasury securities and assists the Federal Reserve in setting monetary policy. The bank also processes checks and acts as a clearinghouse for payments between banks. Federal Reserve Banks are not-for-profit and return earnings (mostly from investments in government bonds) to the US Treasury.

Geographic Reach
The bank oversees the Twelfth Federal Reserve District which includes the nine western states of Alaska Arizona California Hawaii Idaho Nevada Oregon Utah and Washington and also the American Samoa Guam and the Commonwealth of the Northern Mariana Islands.

Branch offices reside in Los Angeles; Portland Oregon; Salt Lake City; and Seattle. It also has a cash processing center in Phoenix.

EXECUTIVES

First Vp And Coo, Mark A. Gould
President And Ceo, John C. Williams
Svp, Teresa M. Curran
Svp Information And Technology And Cio, Gopa Kumar
Group Vice President, Fred Furlong
Vice President, William O Riley
Vice President Examinations Group, Tracy Basinger
Chairman, Roy A. Vallee
Deputy Chairman, Alexander R. (Alex) Mehran
Auditors: KPMG LLP

HQ: Federal Reserve Bank of San Francisco, Dist. No. 12
101 Market Street, San Francisco, CA 94105
Phone: 415 974-2000
Web: www.frbsf.org

HISTORICAL FINANCIALS

Company Type: Public

Income Statement				FYE: December 31
	REVENUE ($ mil.)	NET INCOME ($ mil.)	NET PROFIT MARGIN	EMPLOYEES
12/17	14,660	116	0.8%	—
12/16	13,437	51	0.4%	—
12/15	12,696	(2,426)		—
12/14	11,704	470	4.0%	—
12/13	8,507	323	3.8%	—
Annual Growth	14.6%	(22.6%)	—	—

2017 Year-End Financials

Debt ratio: 34.32%	No. of shares (mil.): 92
Return on equity: 1.93%	Dividends
Cash ($ mil.): 558,019	Yield: —
Current ratio: 1.57	Payout: —
Long-term debt ($ mil.): 195,221	Market value ($ mil.): —

Federal Reserve System

Where do banks go when they need a loan? To the Federal Reserve System which sets the discount interest rate the base rate at which its member banks may borrow. Known as the Fed the system oversees a network of 12 Federal Reserve Banks located in major US cities; these in turn regulate banks in their districts and ensure they maintain adequate reserves. The Fed also clears money transfers issues currency and buys or sells government securities to regulate the money supply. Through its powerful New York bank the Fed conducts foreign currency transactions trades on the world market to support the US dollar's value and stores gold for foreign governments and international agencies.

Operations

By setting the discount rate and the federal funds rate (the rate at which banks borrow from each other) the Board influences the pace of lending and many believe the pace of the economy itself. In response to the economic downturn in 2008 the Fed aggressively cut the discount interest rate in an effort to jump-start the US economy.

Fed board members are appointed by the US president and confirmed by the Senate for one-time 14-year terms staggered at two-year intervals to prevent political stacking. Seven governors comprise the majority of the 12-person Federal Open Market Committee which determines monetary policy. The five remaining members are reserve bank presidents who rotate in one-year terms with New York always holding a place. National member banks must own stock in their Federal Reserve Bank though it is optional for state-chartered banks.

A seven-member Board of Governors oversees the Fed's activities. The board was chaired by Alan Greenspan from the Reagan administration until 2006. As chairman under four different presidents Greenspan wielded more power than perhaps any Fed chief in history and securities markets rose

and fell on his every word. Greenspan was replaced by former chairman of President George W. Bush's Council of Economic Advisers and Fed board member Ben Bernanke who himself was replaced by former Vice Chair of the Board of Governors Janet L. Yellen on February 3 2014.

Geographic Reach

The company's banks are located in Boston New York Philadelphia Cleveland Richmond Atlanta Chicago St. Louis Minneapolis Kansas City Dallas and San Francisco.

Financial Performance

The Reserve Banks' income in 2015 was $114 billion. The total expenses for the entire Federal Reserve System for 2015 were $13 billion.

HISTORY

When New York's Knickerbocker Trust Company failed in 1907 it brought on a panic that was stemmed by J. P. Morgan who strong-armed his fellow bankers into supporting shaky New York banks. The incident showed the need for a central bank.

Morgan's actions sparked fears of his economic power and spurred congressional efforts to establish a central bank. After a six-year struggle between Eastern money interests and populist monetary reformers the 1913 Federal Reserve Act was passed. Twelve Federal Reserve districts were created but New York's economic might ensured it would be the most powerful.

New York bank head Benjamin Strong dominated the Fed in the 1920s countering the glut of European gold flooding the US in 1923 by selling securities from the Fed's portfolio. After he died in 1928 the Fed couldn't stabilize prices. Such difficulty along with low rates encouraging members to use Fed loans for stock speculation helped set the stage for 1929's crash.

During the Depression and WWII the Fed yielded to the demands of the Treasury to buy bonds. But after WWII it sought independence using Congress to help free it from Treasury demands. This effort was led by chairman William McChesney Martin with the assistance of New York bank president Alan Sproul (also a rival for the chairmanship). Martin diluted Sproul's influence by governing by consensus with the other bank leaders.

The Fed managed the economy successfully in the postwar boom but it was stymied by inflation in the late 1960s. In the early 1970s the New York bank also faced the collapse of the fixed currency exchange-rate system and the growth of currency trading. Its role as foreign currency trader became even more crucial as the dollar's value eroded amid rising oil prices and a slowing economy.

The US suffered from double-digit inflation in 1979 as President Jimmy Carter appointed New York Fed president Paul Volcker as chairman. Volcker believing that raising interest rates a few points would not suffice allowed the banks to raise their discount rates and increased bank reserve requirements to reduce the money supply. By the time inflation eased Ronald Reagan was president.

During the 1980s and 1990s US budget fights limited options for controlling the economy through spending decisions so the Fed's actions became more important. Its higher profile brought calls for more access to its decision-making processes. Alan Greenspan took over as chairman in 1987 after being designated by Reagan (and reappointed by presidents George H. W. Bush Bill Clinton and George W. Bush). He stepped down during the second Bush administration and was replaced by Ben Bernanke.

While the US economy seemed immune to the Asian currency crisis of 1997 and 1998 the Federal Reserve remained relatively quiescent. But when

Russia defaulted on some of its bonds in 1998 leading to the near-collapse of hedge fund Long-Term Capital Management the New York Federal Reserve Bank brokered a bailout by the fund's lenders and investors.

This led in 1999 to new guidelines for banks' risk management. The next year the Fed faced up to the Internet age taking a look at e-banking supervision. After raising interest rates to stave off inflation during the go-go late 1990s the Fed cut rates an unprecedented 11 times in 2001 (to a 40 year low of 1.75%) to help spur the flagging post-boom economy.

Rate changes and subsequent economic changes continued with a low of 1% in 2003. In all rates were adjusted a total of 18 times between 2002 and 2006.

In 2008 the US faced an economic crisis as severe as any seen since the Great Depression that claimed numerous victims including Bear Stearns (the Fed brokered and assisted its purchase by JPMorgan Chase) and Lehman Brothers. Together with former Secretary of the Treasury Henry Paulson chairman Ben Bernanke pushed for the passage of a $700 billion rescue plan — the largest in history. Through the plan the government purchased toxic assets including troubled mortgages and distressed properties. As his predecessor did during the economic downturn earlier this decade Bernanke also aggressively cut the discount interest rate in an effort to jump-start the economy.

EXECUTIVES

President Federal Reserve Bank Of Dallas, Robert S. (Rob) Kaplan
President Federal Reserve Bank Of Atlanta, Dennis P. Lockhart
President Federal Reserve Bank Of Chicago, Charles L. (Charlie) Evans
President Federal Reserve Bank Of Richmond, Jeffrey M. (Jeff) Lacker
Chairman, Janet L. Yellen
President Federal Reserve Bank Of Boston, Eric S. Rosengren
President And Ceo Federal Reserve Bank Of St. Louis, James B. Bullard
President Federal Reserve Bank Of New York, William C. Dudley
President Federal Reserve Bank Of Minneapolis, Neel T. Kashkari
President Federal Reserve Bank Of Philadelphia, Patrick T. Harker
President Federal Reserve Bank Of Kansas City, Ester L. George
President Federal Reserve Bank Of San Francisco, John C. Williams
President Federal Reserve Bank Of Cleveland, Loretta J. Mester
Vice President Information Technology, Jeffrey Blye
Vice President, Paul Rimmereid
Assistant Vice President It, Isaac Obstfeld
Vice President Treasury Services, Harvey Mitchell
Vice President, Patrick Defontnouvelle
Executive Vice President, Paul DeBruce
Chairman, Janet L. Yellen
Vice Chairman, Stanley Fischer
Auditors: KPMG LLP

LOCATIONS

HQ: Federal Reserve System
20th Street and Constitution Avenue N.W.,
Washington, DC 20551
Phone: 202 452-3245   **Fax:** 202 728-5886
Web: www.federalreserve.gov

HISTORICAL FINANCIALS

Company Type: Public

Income Statement   FYE: December 31

	REVENUE ($ mil.)	NET INCOME ($ mil.)	NET PROFIT MARGIN	EMPLOYEES
12/17	116,764	133	0.1%	—
12/16	112,207	894	0.8%	—
12/15	113,468	(17,195)	—	—
12/14	114,299	4,363	3.8%	—
12/13	90,540	(492)	—	—
Annual Growth	6.6%	—	—	—

2017 Year-End Financials

Debt ratio: 35.30%
Return on equity: 0.33%
Cash ($ mil.): 4,368,266
Current ratio: 1.95
Long-term debt ($ mil.): 1,570,727

No. of shares (mil.): 627
Dividends
  Yield: —
  Payout: —
Market value ($ mil.): —

FEDERAL-MOGUL HOLDINGS LLC

Auditors: GRANT THORNTON LLP
SOUTHFIELD

LOCATIONS

HQ: FEDERAL-MOGUL HOLDINGS LLC
  27300 W 11 MILE RD # 101, SOUTHFIELD, MI
  480346193
Phone: 248 354-7700
Web: WWW.FEDERALMOGUL.COM

HISTORICAL FINANCIALS

Company Type: Private

Income Statement   FYE: December 31

	REVENUE ($ mil.)	NET INCOME ($ mil.)	NET PROFIT MARGIN	EMPLOYEES
12/16	7,434	90	1.2%	53,700
12/15	7,419	(104)	—	—
12/14	7,317	(161)	—	—
Annual Growth	0.8%	—	—	—

2016 Year-End Financials

Debt ratio: —
Return on equity: 1.20%
Cash ($ mil.): 300
Current ratio: 0.90
Long-term debt ($ mil.): —

Dividends
  Yield: —
  Payout: —
Market value ($ mil.): —

FedEx Corp

Holding company FedEx hopes its package of subsidiaries will keep delivering significant market share. Its FedEx Express unit is the world's #1 express transportation provider delivering more than 4 million packages daily to more than 220 countries and territories from about 1800 FedEx Office shops. It maintains a fleet of more than 655 aircraft and roughly 58000 motor vehicles and trailers. To complement the express delivery business FedEx Ground provides small-package ground delivery in North America and less-than-truckload (LTL) carrier FedEx Freight hauls larger shipments. FedEx Office stores offer a variety of document-related and other business services and serve as retail hubs for other FedEx units.In addition its TNT Express subsidiary is an international express transportation and small-package ground delivery company.

Operations

FedEx offers a broad portfolio of transportation e-commerce and business services through subsidiary companies which operate independently and are managed collaboratively under the FedEx brand.

FedEx Express is the world's largest express transportation company. Its business operations include FedEx Trade Networks (international trade services) and FedEx SupplyChain Systems (supply chain solutions).

FedEx Ground is a North American provider of small-package ground delivery services. This segment includes FedEx SmartPost a business-to-consumer package delivery using the US Postal Service.

FedEx Freight offers less-than-truckload (LTL) freight services throughout Canada Mexico Puerto Rico and the US Virgin Islands. (LTL carriers consolidate freight from multiple shippers into a single truckload.) This unit's offerings include FedEx Freight Priority FedEx Freight Economy and FedEx Custom Critical.

FedEx Services provides sales marketing information technology communications and back-office support for other FedEx companies. This unit includes FedEx TechConnect (US billings and collections support) and FedEx Office and Print Services (document and business services for FedEx Express and FedEx Ground shipping services).

The company in 2016 added a new subsidiary to its operations through the purchase of TNT Express B.V. an international express transportation small-package ground delivery and freight transportation company. TNT Express operates road transportation networks and delivers to over 200 countries.

Geographic Reach

FedEx operates in or delivers goods to more than 220 countries and territories from over 1800 locations. Its sorting and handling facilities are located in Memphis Tennessee; Indianapolis Indiana; Fort Worth Texas; Newark New Jersey; Oakland and Los Angeles California; Greensboro North Carolina; Chicago Illinois; Anchorage Alaska; Paris France; Cologne Germany; Guangzhou China; and Osaka Japan. The US accounts for roughly 70% of net sales each year.

Sales and Marketing

FedEx promotes its brands through television print digital advertising sponsorships and special events. It also serves customers in more than 375 airports worldwide.

TNT Express?s customers are primarily large companies and multinationals as well as small and medium-sized enterprises. It mainly targets the industrial automotive high-tech and healthcare sectors.

Financial Performance

FedEx has achieved seven straight years of unprecedented growth. Revenues jumped 20% from $50.4 billion in 2016 to peak at $60.3 billion in 2017 — a historic milestone for the company. The growth for 2017 was led by a 9% increase in FedEx Ground sales fueled by volume growth in its residential services coupled with rate increases and full-year results from its GENCO acquisition. FedEx also experienced a 3% bump in FedEx Express sales mainly due to its TNT Express acquisition.

Profits surged by 65% from $1.8 billion in 2016 to $3 billion in 2017 another landmark total. This was attributed to a $24 million gain on a retirement plans market-to-market adjustment compared to an almost $1.5 billion loss for this item the previous year. FedEx's cash flow from operating activities however decreased from $5.71 billion to $4.93 billion due to almost $1.7 billion it spent on pension plans in 2017 compared to $346 million in 2016.

Strategy

In addition to making strategic acquisitions FedEx has signaled that it is ready to enhance its automation infrastructure to compete with industry leaders like Amazon and Uber. In 2017 the company announced it is exploring launching driverless small vehicles that could drive around neighborhoods and make deliveries. It has partnered with several automakers that specialize in autonomous trucking and expects to see a major ramp-up of automated vehicles in the shipping industry within the next ten years. However it plans to be selective about where it invests its money and will deploy technology in areas it sees will provide the best payoff and value.

In the meantime e-commerce continues to be a crucial growth engine for FedEx. Even though the company's residential e-commerce revenues are much smaller than its business-to-business revenues it is still its fastest-growing market and FedEx will continue to enhance and extend its global transportation and technology networks. In 2017 FedEx announced it increased its ground facilities by 10 million sq. ft. or 15% during the past year to meet increased demand for orders over the internet.

Mergers and Acquisitions

FedEx has achieved historic growth over the years through the use of acquisitions. In 2016 it acquired rival TNT Express for a purchase price of $4.9 billion. The major deal was the largest in FedEx's history and vastly improved its European footprint and its strength in other regions including North America and Asia.The full integration of FedEx Express and TNT Express is projected to be completed by the end of 2020.

Previously in 2015 FedEx expanded its e-commerce and supply chain portfolio through the purchase of GENCO a leading North American third-party logistics provider for $1.4 billion. The deal bolstered FedEx's expertise in the targeted vertical markets of technology health care and retail.

HISTORY

From his undergraduate classes at Yale and his experience as a charter airplane pilot Fred Smith got the idea that increased automation of business processes would create the need for a reliable overnight delivery service and he presented his case in a term paper in 1965. After serving in the Marine Corps in Vietnam Smith began raising money to develop the overnight delivery idea. He founded Federal Express in 1971 with $4 million inherited from his father and $80 million from investors. Overnight and second-day delivery to two dozen US cities began in 1973.

Several factors contributed to FedEx's early success: Airlines turned their focus from parcels to passengers; United Parcel Service (UPS) union workers went on strike in 1974; and competitor REA Express went bankrupt. FedEx went public in 1978.

EXECUTIVES

Evp Market Development And Corporate Communications, T. Michael Glenn, age 62, $850,028 total compensation

Evp And Cfo, Alan B. Graf, age 62, $920,840 total compensation

Chairman And Ceo, Frederick W. (Fred) Smith, age 74, $1,279,632 total compensation

President And Coo, David J. Bronczek, age 64, $960,936 total compensation

Evp Information Services And Cio, Robert B. (Rob) Carter, age 58, $778,216 total compensation

Coo Fedex Express; President International, Michael L. Ducker, age 65

Evp General Counsel And Secretary, Christine P. Richards, age 63, $617,640 total compensation

President And Ceo Fedex Express, David L. Cunningham

President And Ceo Fedex Ground, Henry J. Maier

Vice President Customer Services, Casey Zettler

Vice President Wro, Betty Hale

Senior Vice President Fedex Solutions, Mark J Colombo

Vice President Products Services And Network Planning, Jeff Euler

Vice President Customer Access Services, Rajesh Singh

Vp Finance And Administration Fedex Smartpost, Gopal Krishnamurthi

Svp Operations, Scott Ray

Vice President Internal Audit, Karl Stingily

Vp Global Operations Fedex Office, David Sutter

Vice President Strategic Planning And Support, Dale Chrystie

Corporate Vice President And Principal Accounting Officer, John Merino

Vice President Finance Fedex Services, Jane Amaba

Vice President Administration Ec Marketing, Shana Hyman

Executive Vice President, Rosa Rangel

Vice President Corporate Sales, Michael Moriarty

Corporate Vice President And Chief Information Security Officer, Denise Wood

Vice President Information Technology Emea, Michael Foster

Vice President Digital Access Marketing, Tom Wicinski

Vice President Marketing, Lawrence Lanier

Executive Vice President, Dottie Berry

Vice President, Don Gibson

Svp Sales, Dan Mullally

Vice President Customer Engagement Marketing, Rebecca Huling

Senior Marketing Vice President, Kim Winstead

Vice President Human Resources Fedex Freight, Lori Henry

Vice President Brand Experience And Marketing, Monica Skipper

Marketing Vice President, Randy Pepper

Vice President Retail Marketing, Randy Scarborough

Vice President, Graham Smith

Vice President Finance, Tom Holland

Senior Vice President Operations, Sev Mcmurtry

Vice President Operations Planning And Engineering Fedex Freight, Gary Bouch

Vice President Admin, Debby Davis

Vice President Global Operations Planning Fedex Office, Jerod Littlefield

Vp Litigation Fedex Ground, Joe Milcoff

Sr Vp Information Technology, Ken Spangler

Cvp Human Resources, Judy Edge

Vice President Information Technology Fedex Services, Jeff Roemer

Vice President Of Human Resources, Sean McNamee

Senior Vice President Global Product Marketing, Jill Brown

Vice President, Michael Macyauski

Senior Vice President Admin, Mary Macon

Vice President Legal, Sean S Mcnamee

Vice President Healthcare, Kevin J Mcpherson

Senior Vice President Sales, Aimee L Dicicco

First Vice President, Brandon Gill

Vice President Regulatory Affairs And Compliance, Cynthia D Allen

Executive Vice President Teammate Services, Dale Dudik

Vice President Senior Assistant, Demetra Walton

Executive Vice President Global Sales And Solutions, Donald F Colleran

Vice President Of Marketing, Donald J Miller

Vice President Human Resources, Tom Tannehill

Vp Assistant, Lillian Ventura

Svp Integrated Marketing And Communications, Patrick Fitzgerald

Senior Vice President Finance International Fedex Express, Helena Jansson

Vice President Information Technology Supply Chain Services, Rebecca McLendon

Corporate Vice President Customer And Business Transactions Legal, Jim Ferguson

Vp Senior Assistant, Saba Khan

Chairman And Ceo, Frederick W. (Fred) Smith, age 74

Evp General Counsel And Secretary, Christine P. Richards, age 63

Auditors: Ernst & Young LLP

LOCATIONS

HQ: FedEx Corp
942 South Shady Grove Road, Memphis, TN 38120
Phone: 901 818-7500
Web: www.fedex.com

2017 Sales

	$ mil.	% of total
US	40,269	67
Other countries	20,050	33
Total	**60,319**	**100**

PRODUCTS/OPERATIONS

2017 Sales

	$ mil.	% of total
FedEx Express	27,358	45
FedEx Ground	18,075	30
TNT Express	7,401	12
FedEx Freight	6,443	11
FedEx Services	1,621	2
Corporate eliminations and other	(579)	-
Total	**60,319**	**100**

Services
FedEx Trade Networks
FedEx Supply Chain Systems
FedEx SmartPost
GENCO

COMPETITORS

ABF Freight System	Pitney Bowes
Allegra Network	PostNL
AlphaGraphics	Ricoh USA
ArcBest	Ryder System
Canada Post	The UPS Store
DHL	UPS
Japan Post	US Postal Service
Nippon Express	Xerox
Office Depot	YRC Worldwide
Old Dominion Freight	

HISTORICAL FINANCIALS

Company Type: Public

Income Statement

FYE: May 31

	REVENUE ($ mil.)	NET INCOME ($ mil.)	NET PROFIT MARGIN	EMPLOYEES
05/18	65,450	4,572	7.0%	227,000
05/17	60,319	2,997	5.0%	169,000
05/16	50,365	1,820	3.6%	168,000
05/15	47,453	1,050	2.2%	166,000
05/14	45,567	2,097	4.6%	162,000
Annual Growth	**9.5%**	**21.5%**	**—**	**8.8%**

2018 Year-End Financials

Debt ratio: 31.69%
Return on equity: 25.77%
Cash ($ mil.): 3,265
Current ratio: 1.39
Long-term debt ($ mil.): 15,243

No. of shares (mil.): 265
Dividends
  Yield: 0.8%
  Payout: 11.9%
Market value ($ mil.): 66,247

	STOCK PRICE ($) FY Close	P/E High/Low	PER SHARE ($) Earnings	Dividends	Book Value
05/18	249.12	16 12	16.79	2.00	73.01
05/17	193.84	18 13	11.07	1.60	59.92
05/16	164.97	28 19	6.51	1.00	51.91
05/15	173.22	49 38	3.65	0.80	53.09
05/14	144.16	21 14	6.75	0.60	48.04
Annual Growth	**14.7%**	**— —**	**25.6%**	**35.1%**	**11.0%**

Fidelity National Financial Inc

To make sure that buying a dream home doesn't become a nightmare Fidelity National Financial (also known as FNF) provides title insurance escrow home warranties and other services related to real estate transactions. It is now the top dog in the residential and commercial title insurance sectors (the second-largest is First American) and issues more title insurance policies than any other title company in the US. The company operates through underwriters including Fidelity National Title Insurance Commonwealth Land Title Alamo Title and National Title of New York. It sells its products both directly and through independent agents. In 2018 FNF agreed to buy Stewart Information Services another Big Four title insurance firm.

Operations

FNF is organized into two segments: Title and Corporate and Other. The Title segment brings in most of the group's revenues; it includes title insurance and related closing services. Through subsidiary ServiceLink FNF provides mortgage transaction services such as facilitating the production and management of mortgage loans.

In late 2017 the company split off Cannae Holdings part of its former Fidelity National Finance Ventures (FNFV) segment. Now a publicly traded entity Cannae owns stakes in numerous firms including payroll and HR services firm Ceridian Holding restaurant owner American Blue Ribbon Holdings and medical software company T-System Holding.

Geographic Reach

FNF's insurance businesses operate exclusively within the US. Naturally the biggest markets are in states with the greatest populations: California

Texas Florida New York and Illinois combined account for more than 45% of its title insurance premiums.

The company leases offices in more than 40 states and Washington DC as well as in Canada and India.

Sales and Marketing

FNF uses direct sales representatives and independent agents to market its title and escrow products to residential and commercial real estate customers. The company maintains some 1400 retail offices to provide residential title insurance. It markets its commercial title insurance through a network of 5200 agents in major urban real estate markets.

Financial Performance

While the company is basically sound FNF's revenues can be hampered by stiffness in the residential mortgage lending market. With the exception of 2015 revenue has been on the rise. Even more steadily net income has been rising for the past few years.

Revenue rose 6% to $7.7 billion in 2017 as title insurance premiums and escrow title-related and other fees all increased. Existing home sales increased that year but mortgage interest rates inched upward leading refinance transactions to fall.

Thanks largely to the higher revenue net income rose 19% to $771 million in 2017. However higher agent commissions expenses and personnel costs did cut into profits that year.

FNF ended 2017 with $635 million in cash and cash equivalents which was $357 million less than it had at the beginning of the year. Operating activities provided $737 million in cash financing activities (primarily long-term debt reduction) used $999 million and investing activities used another $95 million.

Strategy

Title insurance is typically one of the most stable types of insurance written. It is folded into the piles of paperwork home buyers sign during closings with little or no fuss. Even when US home sales become sluggish FNF stays active from refinancing of existing mortgages. However when interest rates rise refinancing activities tend to slow down. In the current economic cycle FNF expects that mortgage originations will slow down through 2019 but lower unemployment rates and rising consumer confidence should help offset the impact of higher interest rates. Additionally commercial real estate transactions tend to be less reliant on interest rates which should help boost the company's sales.

To stay at the top of the title insurance game FNF's core strategies include building on its various well-known brand names including Fidelity National Title Commonwealth Land Title and Alamo Title. It is also focused on delivering superior customer service and maintaining operations that can withstand the cyclical title insurance industry. For the latter it monitors its corporate organization and office network (consolidating operations as necessary) and strikes a balance between residential and commercial transactions. The company also introduces new products and technologies to remain competitive.

In a similar vein transaction services unit ServiceLink entered the auction business when FNF acquired Hudson & Marshall in mid-2017. The new ServiceLink Auction offering provides foreclosure and real estate-owned auction services.

Historically FNF and its operating subsidiaries have grown through numerous acquisitions in the title insurance space as well as by adding new offerings to attract more customers. While keeping its eye on strengthening its existing title insurance operations the company has made some moves to diversify by buying up non-insurance related businesses. In 2017 for example it acquired health care technology firm T-System for $200 million.

However in a major turnaround the company divested most of its non-insurance holdings in 2017. It separated from its Black Knight technology services arm and holding company Cannae (both of which are now public companies). The transactions helped streamline FNF's corporate structure allowing it to focus on the title insurance sector.

Mergers and Acquisitions

FNF plans to buy another Big Four title insurance firm Stewart Information Services. The $1.2 billion deal will make the nation's largest title company even bigger with some 44% of the market share.

The company made a number of acquisitions during 2017. It bought Hudson & Marshall a leading property and real estate auction firm. FNF subsidiary ServiceLink entered the auction business through that transaction; Hudson & Marshall now powers the new ServiceLink Auction offering. Also that year FNF acquired Real Geeks which provides a customer relationship management (CRM) platform and other internet tools to the real estate industry. The company then acquired control of Title Guaranty of Hawaii the state's oldest title insurance company which was previously an unaffiliated agent of Chicago Title. FNF also acquired a majority stake in SkySlope which provides digital transaction management technology to the real estate sector.

Further boosting its technology capabilities in 2016 FNF acquired Georgia-based Commissions (which provides web-based real estate marketing and CRM software) for $229 million.

Company Background

Like all title insurers Fidelity National Financial shivered when the big chill hit the real estate market in 2008. But while the company slowed it remained quick enough to take advantage of opportunities. When its ailing rival LandAmerica Financial Group filed Chapter 11 in 2008 the company bought up the choice bits for $235 million. This purchase helped make it into the largest title insurer in the US and caught the attention of the FTC prompting the company to divest a few holdings to soothe the agency's nerves. The 2009 sale of Fidelity National Capital only brought in $50 million but took $214 million of debt off company ledgers. The 2010 sale of its 32% stake in Sedgwick Claims Management brought in some $225 million.

The current company arose in 2006 when a previous company also named Fidelity National Financial split apart its title insurance operations from its information services business. What had been Fidelity National Title Group took on its former parent's name while Fidelity National Information Services took on the former parent's remaining operations. The two companies share a history and some stray holdings but are otherwise separate.

EXECUTIVES

Evp And Chief Legal Officer, Peter T. Sadowski, age 64, $431,671 total compensation

Ceo, Raymond R. (Randy) Quirk, age 72, $831,692 total compensation

Evp General Counsel And Corporate Secretary, Michael L. (Mike) Gravelle, age 57, $550,500 total compensation

Evp Corporate Strategy, Brent B. Bickett, age 54, $550,500 total compensation

Coo, Roger S. Jewkes, age 60, $630,000 total compensation

President Fidelity National Title Group National Agency Operations, Erika Meinhardt, age 60

Evp And Cfo, Anthony J. (Tony) Park, age 52, $483,000 total compensation

President, Michael J. (Mike) Nolan, age 59, $557,308 total compensation

Vice President Regional Controller, Sylvia Freyling

Assistant Vice President And Administrative Assistant, Jennifer Edwards

Vice President And Counsel, Nathaniel Yingling

Avp Director Of Social Strategy Fidelity National Title Agency, Chelsea Peitz

Assistant Vice President West Chester Production M, Joseph Harkins

Senior Vice President Fidelity National Financial Inc, Woody Girion

Assistant Vice President Agency Auditor, Mary Rooney

Assistant Vice President Trial Counsel, Brian Linkowski

Vice President, Chris Martin

Assistant Vice President And Senior Claims Counsel, Stephanie Thomas

Vice President Brand Director Fntg Commercial Operations, Karim Moullemaaz

Assistant Vice President And Nw Indiana Escrow Manager, Susan Miedema

Assistant Vice President Information Technology Strategy Manager, Janine DaPaah

Assistant Vice President And Director 401k Plan, Eva Chavis

Vice President, Amy Tueckes

Senior Claims Counsel And Vice President, Scott Aronowitz

Vice President, Beth Rennie

Vice President Of Business Development, Ryan Pulliam

Vice President, Tabitha Campbell

Managing Counsel Vice President, Ray Aaronian

Executive Vice President, Phil Shea

Assistant Vice President, Pati Walter

Vice President And Litigation Attorney, Tiziana Scaccia

Senior Vice President And Manager New York National Commercial Services, Joanna Patilis

Vice President Sales, John Ravita

Avp Education And Marketing Services, Brian Boronat

Assistant Vice President Associate Branch Counsel, Francis Hoffman

Vice President And Senior Litigation Counsel, Simone Kenyon

Assistant Vice President Analyst Corporate Compliance, Gina Stanley

Vice President, Dorry Bragg

Vice President, Gerry Grady

Assistant Vice President, Lois Watson

Assistant Vice President And Agency Account Manager, John Stilla

Vice President, Sam Kitamura

Senior Vice President And Sales Manager, Tine Dickey

Executive Vice President And National Sales Manager, Joey Mitchell

Vice President And Manager Web Based Leveraged Solutions, John Berry

Vice President Managing Director, Scott Morgano

Vice President And Senior Escrow Officer, Lisa Wikert

Vice President And Executive Director, Grant Miller

Senior Vice President Field Operations Manager, Ruth Stolhanske

Vice President Financial Officer, Shawn Cassidy

Vice President Counsel, Douglas Whitaker

Vice President And Major Transactions Counsel, Sarah Webb

Vice President Agency Counsel, Tom Bartlett

Vice President Trial Counsel, Angie Shin

Vice President, Montha Guatero

Vice President, Cindy Heidel

Vice President Associate Counsel, Michael Tompkins

Assistant Vice President Director Of Education And Creative Services, Erin Tracy
Vice President National Business Development, Jen Reyes
Assistant Vice President, Kristopher Do
Senior Vice President Branch Manager And Escrow Officer, Vicki Mckie
Assistant Vice President, Karin Eberhard
Assistant Vice President, Jody Kelly
Vice President Builder And Commercial, Dustin Gaskey
Senior Vice President And Operations Manager Fidelity National Title, Diane Day
Senior Vice President Operations And Sales Manager, Lance Capel
Vice President Of Geographic Information Services, Jeff Asbury
Claims Counsel Avp, Djenita Svinjar
Vice President Sales Fidelity National Home Warranty, Sue Thomas
Avp Corporate It Project Operations Manager, Jane Powell
Assistant Vice President Sales Executive Fidelity National Title, Debbie Amend-Campbell
Vice President Denver Metro Sales, Louis Italiano
Vice President And Senior Commercial Escrow Officer, Valerie Vona Rapp
Assistant Vice President, Rich Christensen
Assistant Vice President Senior Escrow Officer, Cissy Martin
Vice President And Assistant Regional Counsel, Jerry Castro
Assistant Vice President, Nicole Goulet
Assistant Vice President, Heather Clark
Chairman, William P. (Bill) Foley, age 74
Evp General Counsel And Corporate Secretary, Michael L. (Mike) Gravelle, age 57
Secretary, Patricia Whitty
Secretary, Kelly Morley
Board Member, Michele Cavallaro
Auditors: Ernst & Young LLP

LOCATIONS

HQ: Fidelity National Financial Inc
601 Riverside Avenue, Jacksonville, FL 32204
Phone: 904 854-8100
Web: www.fnf.com

PRODUCTS/OPERATIONS

2017 Sales

	$ mil.	% of total
Agency title insurance premiums	2,723	36
Escrow title-related & other fees	2,637	34
Direct title insurance premiums	2,170	28
Interest & investment income	131	2
Net realized gains	2	-
Total	**7,663**	**100**

COMPETITORS

American Coast Title
Equity Title Company
First American
Investors Title
North American Title
Old Republic
Old Republic National Title

Stewart Information Services
Title Resource Group
United General Title Insurance

HISTORICAL FINANCIALS

Company Type: Public

Income Statement

FYE: December 31

	ASSETS ($ mil.)	NET INCOME ($ mil.)	INCOME AS % OF ASSETS	EMPLOYEES
12/17	9,151	771	8.4%	24,367
12/16	14,463	650	4.5%	55,219
12/15	13,931	527	3.8%	54,091
12/14	13,868	583	4.2%	56,883
12/13	10,524	402	3.8%	63,861
Annual Growth	(3.4%)	17.7%	—	(21.4%)

2017 Year-End Financials

Debt ratio: 8.29%
Return on equity: 14.77%
Cash ($ mil.): 1,110
Current ratio: —
Long-term debt ($ mil.): —

No. of shares (mil.): 274
Dividends
Yield: 0.0%
Payout: 42.8%
Market value ($ mil.): 10,769

	STOCK PRICE ($) FY Close	P/E High/Low		PER SHARE ($) Earnings	Dividends	Book Value
12/17	39.24	20	14	2.38	1.02	16.20
12/16	33.96	16	12	2.34	0.88	17.71
12/15	34.67	21	17	1.89	0.80	16.53
12/14	34.45	47	34	0.75	0.37	16.12
Annual Growth	3.3%	—	—	33.5%	28.9%	0.1%

Fidelity National Information Services Inc

At Fidelity National Information Services (FIS) the check will never get lost in the mail. The company helps financial institutions and their clients conduct transactions through its range of software and services. It also offers outsourcing and IT consulting for the financial services industry. For banks and other financing entities the company's offerings address financial functions such as core processing decision and risk management and retail channel operations. FIS also provides payment services such as electronic funds transfer check and ticket processing and credit card production and activation. The company's 20000 customers aren't just the largest private financial institutions but also small businesses and government entities. FIS was founded in 2018.

Operations

The Integrated Financial Solutions (IFS) segment supplies about half of Fidelity National Information Services? revenue. The unit provides services to regional and community banks and savings institutions in North America. Services include transaction and account processing payment tools lending and wealth management services mobile and digital banking technologies credit and debit card technologies and fraud risk management and compliance tools and services.

The Global Financial Solutions (GFS) segment provides about 45% of the company?s revenue. Its portfolio which includes the acquired SunGard businesses includes customers that are large global financial institutions. GFS provides securities processing and finance technologies and services asset

management and insurance retail banking and payments services and strategic consulting.

The Corporate and Other segment 5% of revenue includes corporate overhead expense other functions and some non-strategic businesses.

Geographic Reach

Fidelity National Information Services based in Jacksonville Florida operates through some 185 owned or leased locations in Brazil India Africa Southeast Asia and the Middle East. The company develops products and services in San Francisco London and Bangalore India.

FIS?s North American operations generate most of its revenue with just about 25% generated from contracts executed outside of North America. The company has business in more than 130 countries but most of its international revenue comes from customers in Brazil the UK France Australia and Germany.

Sales and Marketing

Fidelity National Information Services markets its products and services through direct and indirect field sales as well as inbound and outbound lead generation and telesales. It claims about 20000 clients around the world some of who are Credit Suisse Atom Bank Centennial Bank Kitsap Bank and Landesbank Baden-Wuerttemberg.

Financial Performance

Fidelity National Information Services got a big boost to more than $9 billion in revenue in 2016 from $6.5 billion in 2015 from its Sungard acquisition. But revenue was flat in 2017 as FIS absorbed Sungard and divested some assets.

The Integrated Financial Solutions segment posted a 2% revenue increase in 2017 on higher demand for banking and wealth services and growth in payment services. Card production revenue diminished with the slowdown in EMV (chip-equipped credit cards) deployment in 2017. The Global Financial Solutions segment reported sales fell about 3% due to the sale of the Capco consulting business. But growth in payment services in Brazil and in post-trade derivative services for existing clients took some of the sting out of the loss of Capco income.

FIS posted about $1.3 billion in net income in 2017 about a 130% higher than 2016. The company not only had some lower operating costs in 2017 but it had acquisition-related costs in 2016 that didn?t repeat.

FIS had cash on hand totaling $665 million at the end of 2017 compared to $683 million for the year before.

Strategy

Fidelity National Information Services (FIS) is working to run its businesses more efficiently as well as to obtain new customers and sell additional products to current customers.

On the efficiency side FIS is moving from a legacy server-based technology to cloud technologies to gain the benefits of speed efficiency and scale. The switch would help the company maintain and even increase margins. The company expected that by the end of 2018 more than half of its US-based services would be offered through its secure private cloud.

The acquisition of SunGard provided FIS with a more comprehensive product and services portfolio and resources that it intends to exploit.

FIS relies on strong free cash flow for flexibility in pursuing opportunities. The company had $1.2 billion in free cash flow in 2017 which it used to invest in the business pay down debt and return capital to shareholders.

The $8.8 billion in debt that FIS carries could limit its ability to borrow and restrict its flexibility in pursuing opportunities. Some of the debt has variable interest rates which could mean higher debt payments if interest rates rise.

FIS has pared away operations that were outside its focus on financial services. In 2017 FIS sold majority ownership in Capco to Clayton Dubilier & Rice. FIS also sold the SunGard Public Sector and Education in 2017 and in 2018 its China-based business Kingstar.

Mergers and Acquisitions

The 2015 acquisition of SunGard Data Systems made Fidelity National Information Systems (FIS) the biggest financial services company. The Sun-Gard assets cost about $9 billion and brought more than $4 billion in debt. The combined company produced $9.2 billion in revenue in 2015 its first full year. SunGard expanded FIS?s geographic reach and enriched its Global Financial Services unit with $1.8 billion in annual revenue. FIS was on track to clear about $257 million in savings by the end of 2017 as it consolidated and elimination duplicate functions.

EXECUTIVES

Corporate Evp And Coo Institutional And Wholesale, Marianne C. Brown, age 59, $700,000 total compensation

Cio, Ido Gileadi

President And Ceo, Gary A. Norcross, age 53, $1,000,000 total compensation

Evp North American Financial Solutions, Anthony M. Jabbour, age 50, $700,000 total compensation

Corporate Evp Chief Administrative Officer And Corporate Secretary, Michael P. Oates, age 59, $475,000 total compensation

Evp And Cfo, James W. (Woody) Woodall, age 48, $605,000 total compensation

Corporate Evp And Chief Risk Officer, Gregory G. (Greg) Montana, age 49, $365,000 total compensation

Evp International Markets, Raja Gopalakrishnan

Ceo Capco, Lance Levy

Evp And Chief Legal Officer, Marc Mayo

Coo Integrated Financial Solutions, Bruce Lowthers

Senior Vice President Global Commercial Services Supply Chain And Real Estate, Kevin Gouin

Senior Vice President And Legal Executive, Duncan Mitchell

Vice President Marketing And Strategy, Linda Netherton

Vice President Business Line Executive, Scott Morgano

Vice President Product Management, Dominique Stevens

Vice President Sales And Marketing, Robert Boitano

Vice President Operations, John Oleon

Assistant Vice President Treasury, Alex Alley

Assistant Vice President, Kimberly Sadler

Senior Vice President And Chief Division Counsel Check Services, Lynn Cravey

Vice President Advanced Technology Solutions, Hank Godwin

Vice President Business Recovery Services Advanced Technology Solutions, Ovid Babb

Assistant Vice President Global Midrange Applications, Alex Pisieczko

Senior Vice President Channel Architecture And Strategy, Bernie Schramm

Vice President New Solutions Architecture, Will Starnes

Vice President Acbs Global Sales, Gregg Cerniglia

Senior Vice President Operations, Mike Amble

Vice President Channels Delivery, Sethu Thottikamath

Senior Vice President And General Manager, Michelle Bowen

Vice President And Managing Director, Jim Gorski

Vice President Sales, Michael Daugherty

Vice President Client Relations, Jim Sheahan

Vice President Customer Service, Christopher Hermann

Vice President Infrastructure Services, David Plante

Vice President And Managing Director, Cathy David

Vice President Product And Systems Development, Michael Lovett

Senior Vice President Information Technology Security, Ivana Cojbasic

Senior Vice President Business Development, Max Balfour

Vice President Sales, Ryan Fetzer

Vice President Of Facilities, Cal Bampton

Vice President Product Management, Somesh Chablani

Vice President Product Management, Paul zur Nieden

Vice President Software Development, Jim English

Chief People Officer, Denise Williams

Senior Vice President Business Development, Chad Davis

Vice President Product Implementation And Support, David Murray

Vice President Global Networks And Security Engineering, Chris Young

Division Vice President Global Compensation, Gary Watts

Vice President And General Manager Merchant Services, Dawn Murray

Vp Global Voice And Network Services, Tim Ferguson

National Account Manager, Steven Romeo

Vice President Product Strategy, Dan Peacock

Vice President Application Development Services, Sam Ashton

Vice President Corporate And Executive Communications, Jen Becker

Vice President Professional Services, Ryan Forshee

Senior Vice President, Erik Hoag

Vice President, Patrick Hogan

Vice President Corporate Controller, Thomas Warren

Chairman, Frank R. Martire, age 70

Corporate Evp Chief Administrative Officer And Corporate Secretary, Michael P. Oates, age 59

Auditors: KPMG LLP

LOCATIONS

HQ: Fidelity National Information Services Inc
601 Riverside Avenue, Jacksonville, FL 32204
Phone: 904 438-6000
Web: www.fisglobal.com

PRODUCTS/OPERATIONS

2017 Sales

	$ mil.	% of total
IFS	4,630	51
GFS	4,138	45
Corporate & Other	355	4
Total	**9,123**	**100**

SOLUTIONS

SOLUTIONS
Banking and Wealth
Institutional and Wholesale
Management Consulting
Payments

COMPETITORS

ACI Worldwide	Infosys
Accenture	Jack Henry
Alliance Data Systems	MasterCard
D+H USA	Misys
DST Systems	Open Solutions
Fair Isaac	Oracle Financial
First Data	Services Software
Fiserv	SEI Investments
Global Payments	TEMENOS Group AG
HP Enterprise Services	TeleCheck
Heartland Payment Systems	Total System Services
IBM	Visa Inc

HISTORICAL FINANCIALS

Company Type: Public

Income Statement

FYE: December 31

	REVENUE ($ mil.)	NET INCOME ($ mil.)	NET PROFIT MARGIN	EMPLOYEES
12/17	9,123	1,319	14.5%	53,000
12/16	9,241	568	6.1%	55,000
12/15	6,595	631	9.6%	55,000
12/14	6,413	679	10.6%	40,000
12/13	6,070	493	8.1%	38,000
Annual Growth	10.7%	27.9%	—	8.7%

2017 Year-End Financials

Debt ratio: 35.74%	No. of shares (mil.): 333
Return on equity: 12.82%	Dividends
Cash ($ mil.): 665	Yield: 0.0%
Current ratio: 0.92	Payout: 29.5%
Long-term debt ($ mil.): 7,718	Market value ($ mil.): 31,332

	STOCK PRICE ($) FY Close	P/E High/Low		PER SHARE ($) Earnings	Dividends	Book Value
12/17	94.09	24	19	3.93	1.16	32.54
12/16	75.64	46	32	1.72	1.04	29.70
12/15	60.60	33	26	2.19	1.04	28.72
12/14	62.20	27	21	2.35	0.96	23.01
12/13	53.68	31	20	1.68	0.88	22.64
Annual Growth	15.1%	—	—	23.7%	7.2%	9.5%

Fidelity Southern Corp

Fidelity Southern Corp. is the holding company for Fidelity Bank which boasts over $3 billion in assets and some 45 branches in the Atlanta metro and in northern Florida markets. The bank offers traditional deposit services such as checking and savings accounts CDs and IRAs. Consumer loans primarily indirect auto loans which the company purchases from auto franchises and independent dealers throughout the Southeast make up more than 50% of its loan portfolio. Real estate construction commercial real estate business residential mortgage and other consumer loans round out Fidelity Southern's lending activities. Subsidiary LionMark Insurance Company offers consumer credit-related insurance products.

Operations

About 50% of Fidelity Southern's total revenue came from loan interest (including fees) in 2014 while another 2% came from interest on its investment securities. The rest of its revenue came from mortgage banking income (28%) indirect lending activities (9%) SBA Lending (3%) service charges on deposit accounts (2%) and other miscellaneous income sources. The bank had a staff of roughly 1040 employees at the end of 2014.

Geographic Reach

While the company mostly has a branch presence in Georgia and Florida it also offers mortgage loans indirect auto loans and Small Business Administration (SBA) loans in a dozen Southern states.

Sales and Marketing

Fidelity Southern mostly serves individuals and small to medium-sized businesses. The company spent $2.34 million on advertising and promotions in 2014 up from $1.69 million and $1.13 million in 2013 and 2012 respectively.

Financial Performance

Fidelity Southern's revenues and profits have risen over the past several years thanks to growing loan and deposit business from branch openings and acquisitions lower interest expenses and declining loan loss provisions as its loan portfolio's credit quality has improved with higher property valuations in the strengthened economy.

The company's revenue inched higher by 1% to $197 million in 2014 mostly as its loan balances grew organically by 8% during the year with higher loan originations and market expansion.

Higher revenue and lower interest expenses in 2014 boosted Fidelity Southern's net income by 9% to a record $30 million. Its cash levels plummeted during the year with operations using a net $141 million for the year after adjusting its earnings for non-cash items related to its net proceeds from its loans held for sale.

Strategy

Fidelity Southern has focused on building and diversifying its loan portfolio including originating more residential mortgages commercial loans and consumer installment loans. The bank has been opening new branches as part of this organic growth strategy. During 2014 it opened 12 new branches including five in Georgia and seven in Florida.

It's also pursued small bank and branch acquisitions to grow its loan and deposit business while expanding its geographic reach in Florida and Georgia.

Mergers and Acquisitions

In October 2015 the Fidelity Bank agreed to purchase The Bank of Georgia including its $295 million in total assets $280 million in deposits and seven branches in Peachtree City Fayetteville Tyrone Sharpsburg Newnan and Fairburn.

September 2015 Fidelity Southern purchased eight branches in Florida from First Bank including $154 million in deposits and $31.6 million in loans. The deal expanded Fidelity's presence in counties surrounding Bradenton Palmetto and Longboat Key.

In September 2014 the company purchased six branches of CenterState Bank of Florida including $174.2 million in deposits. The deal expanded Fidelity's presence in counties surrounding Orlando and Jacksonville.

HISTORY

WWII veteran Clark Harrison and five others founded Fidelity National Bank in 1973. The first office opened in downtown Decatur Georgia the next year. Fidelity National Bank opened its second branch and formed Fidelity Southern Corporation as a holding company in 1979; it formed Fidelity National Mortgage a year later. In 1984 the company received trust powers opened two new branches and began a major credit card marketing program.

The acquisition of two branches from the Resolution Trust Corporation in 1992 brought the number of branches to 10 and increased assets to $257 million. Fidelity National Capital Investors a retail brokerage was incorporated that year. In 1993 Fidelity National Bank began a consumer sales finance department to buy auto loans from car dealers.

The company opened an office in Jacksonville in 1995 to offer mortgage car and construction lending. Also that year the firm changed the name of its holding company to Fidelity National Corporation.

Fidelity National acquired Friendship Community Bank in Florida and bought six branches from First Union and NationsBank in 1996; rapid expansion and unexpectedly high credit card chargeoffs that year slashed earnings and prevented Fidelity National from opening three of its newly

acquired branches. Under the scrutiny of federal regulators the bank discontinued its high-default card program the next year and shored up its finances raising capital through a stock offering.

In 1998 Fidelity National focused on maintaining capital levels and recovering from its losses while other banks expanded. Fidelity National Bank finally gained regulatory approval to open the three remaining branches acquired from NationsBank and First Union later that year. Regulators released the bank from capital and dividend restrictions in 1999 but Fidelity National had to restate its earnings for 1997 citing overestimation of an asset's value.

Fidelity National experienced moderate growth in 2001. Inspections by the Federal Reserve Board in 2000 and 2001 led to Fidelity National's adoption of a resolution that prohibits Fidelity National from redeeming its capital stock paying dividends on its common stock or incurring debt without prior approval of the Federal Reserve Board. In light of a softening economy in 2001 Fidelity National placed greater significance on credit risk management and building the secured portion of its consumer loan portfolio. The company sold its credit card business to Bank One in December.

In 2003 the company changed its name back to Fidelity Southern Corporation and its branches converted to the shortened Fidelity Bank; the bank also switched from a national to a state charter.

EXECUTIVES

President Fidelity Southern; Ceo Fidelity Bank, H. Palmer Proctor, age 50, $500,000 total compensation
Chairman And Ceo, James B. Miller, age 78, $800,000 total compensation
Vp; Evp Fidelity Bank; President Lionmark Insurance, David Buchanan, age 60, $400,000 total compensation
Cfo, Charles D. Christy
Senior Vice President, Sam Mathis
Vice President Business Bankin, Scott Wright
Vice President Commercial Banking, Kevin Lubitz
Executive Vice President, Michael Pierson
Vice President, Ron Hendrix
Vice President, Josh Savage
Senior Vice President Regional Manager, John Andrews
Vice President Assistant Compliance Officer, Neda Tabaridunn
Vice President Loan Operations Manager, Maria Becerra
Senior Vice President Wealth Management, Dave Johnston
Vice President, Christine Hobert
Vice President Corporate Insurance And Accounting Operations Manager Fidelity Bank, Laura Eastman
Vice President, Nina Efird
Senior Vice President, Michelle McCorvey
Senior Vice President, Gerald Kemp
Vice President Mortgage Accounting, Joshua Savage
Chairman And Ceo, James B. Miller, age 78
Auditors: Ernst & Young LLP

LOCATIONS

HQ: Fidelity Southern Corp
   3490 Piedmont Road, Suite 1550, Atlanta, GA 30305
Phone: 404 639-6500
Web: www.FidelitySouthern.com

PRODUCTS/OPERATIONS

2014 Sales

	$ mil.	% of total
Interest		
Loans including fees	96	50
Investment securities	4	2
Federal funds sold & bank deposits	0	-
Noninterest		
Mortgage banking activities	55	28
Indirect lending activities	18	9
SBA lending activities	5	3
Service charges on deposit accounts	4	2
Bank owned life insurance	1	1
Other fees & charges	4	2
Other	5	3
Total	**197**	**100**

COMPETITORS

BB&T
Bank of America
Citizens Bancshares
Regions Financial
SunTrust
Synovus
Wells Fargo

HISTORICAL FINANCIALS

Company Type: Public

Income Statement

FYE: December 31

	ASSETS ($ mil.)	NET INCOME ($ mil.)	INCOME AS % OF ASSETS	EMPLOYEES
12/17	4,576	39	0.9%	1,394
12/16	4,389	38	0.9%	1,284
12/15	3,849	39	1.0%	1,242
12/14	3,085	30	1.0%	1,038
12/13	2,564	27	1.1%	890
Annual Growth	15.6%	9.5%	—	11.9%

2017 Year-End Financials

Debt ratio: 2.63%
Return on equity: 10.41%
Cash ($ mil.): 137
Current ratio: —
Long-term debt ($ mil.): —
No. of shares (mil.): 27
Dividends
   Yield: 0.0%
   Payout: 32.2%
Market value ($ mil.): 589

	STOCK PRICE ($) FY Close	P/E High/Low		Earnings	PER SHARE ($) Dividends	Book Value
12/17	21.80	17	13	1.49	0.48	14.86
12/16	23.67	16	9	1.50	0.48	13.78
12/15	22.31	13	9	1.64	0.39	13.03
12/14	16.11	12	9	1.28	0.30	12.40
12/13	16.61	13	7	1.21	0.05	11.07
Annual Growth	7.0%	—	—	5.3%	76.0%	7.7%

Fifth Third Bancorp (Cincinnati, OH)

Fifth Third Bancorp strives to be first in the hearts and minds of its customers. The holding company of Fifth Third Bank boasts assets of more than $140 billion and nearly 1200 branches across Ohio Michigan Florida and several other states in the Midwest and Southeast. Fifth Third offers branch banking (deposit accounts and loans for consumers and small businesses) commercial banking (lending leasing and syndicated and trade finance for corporations) consumer lending (residential mortgages home equity loans and credit cards) and wealth and asset management (private banking brokerage and asset management). Fifth

Third owns part of Vantiv one of the country's largest payment processing firms.

HISTORY

In 1863 a group of Cincinnati businessmen opened the Third National Bank inside a Masonic temple to serve the Ohio River trade. Acquiring the Bank of the Ohio Valley (founded 1858) in 1871 the firm progressed until the panic of 1907. Third National survived and in 1908 consolidated with Fifth National forming the Fifth Third National Bank of Cincinnati. The newly organized bank acquired two local banks in 1910.

A second bank consolidation in 1919 resulted in Fifth Third's affiliation with Union Savings Bank and Trust Company permitting the bank to establish branches theretofore forbidden by regulators. The company acquired the assets and offices of five more banks and thrifts that year operating them as branches.

In 1927 the bank merged its operations with the Union Trust Company forming the Fifth Third Union Trust. With its combined strength it weathered the Great Depression and acquired three more banks between 1930 and 1933. However the Depression also brought massive banking regulations to the industry limiting Fifth Third's acquisitions.

In the postwar years and during the 1950s and 1960s the bank expanded its consumer banking services offering traveler's checks. Under CEO Bill Rowe son of former CEO John Rowe the firm emphasized the convenience of its locations and increased hours of operations.

In the 1970s Fifth Third shifted its lending program's emphasis from commercial loans to consumer credit and launched its ATM and telephone banking services. Aware that the bank was technologically unprepared for the onslaught of electronic information Fifth Third expanded its data processing and information services resources forming the basis for its Midwest Payment Systems division.

The company formed Fifth Third Bancorp a holding company and began to branch within Ohio (branching had previously been limited to the home county) in 1975. Ten years later more deregulation allowed the bank to move into contiguous states. Focused on consumer banking and with cautious underwriting policies Fifth Third weathered the real estate bust and leveraged-buyout problems of the 1980s and acquired new outlets cheaply by buying several small banks as well as branches from larger banks. It acquired the American National Bank in Kentucky and moved further afield with its purchase of the Sovereign Savings Bank in Palm Harbor Florida in 1991.

The company continued to expand buying several banks and thrifts in Ohio in 1997 and 1998. In 1999 Fifth Third moved into Indiana in a big way with its purchase of CNB Bancshares then solidified its position in the state with the acquisition of Peoples Bank of Indianapolis. Fifth Third also moved into new business areas buying mortgage banker W. Lyman Case broker-dealer The Ohio Company (1998) and Cincinnati-based commercial mortgage banker Vanguard Financial (1999). The company began to offer online foreign exchange via its FX Internet Trading Web in 2000.

In 2001 Fifth Third bought money manager Maxus Investments and added some 300 bank branches with its purchase of Capital Holdings (Ohio and Michigan) and Old Kent Financial (Michigan Indiana and Illinois) its largest-ever acquisition.

Fifth Third exited the property/casualty insurance brokerage business in 2002 selling its operations to Hub International. Also that year Fifth Third arranged to enter Tennessee via its planned purchase of Franklin Financial. But the deal was stalled as industry regulators investigated Fifth Third's risk management procedures and internal controls. A moratorium on acquisitions was placed on the bank during the investigation. It was lifted in 2004 and the purchase of Franklin was completed not long afterwards. That opened the door for Fifth Third's acquisition of First National Bankshares of Florida in 2005. Two years later it continued growing with its purchase of R-G Crown Bank from R&G Financial which added some 30 branches in Florida in addition to locations in Georgia.

EXECUTIVES

President Ceo And Director, Greg D. Carmichael, age 56, $994,287 total compensation

Evp And Coo, Lars C. Anderson, age 57, $675,002 total compensation

Evp And Chief Risk Officer, Frank R. Forrest, age 63, $519,713 total compensation

Evp, Philip R. McHugh, age 53

Evp And Chief Corporate Responsibility And Reputation Officer, Brian Lamb

Evp And Chief Administrative Officer, Teresa J. Tanner, age 49

Evp And Cfo, Tayfun Tuzun, age 53, $519,342 total compensation

Evp, Chad M. Borton, age 47, $491,260 total compensation

Evp And Treasurer, James C. Leonard, age 48

Evp And Chief Strategy Officer, Timothy N. Spence, age 39, $450,008 total compensation

Evp And Chief Operations And Technology Officer, Aravind Immaneni

Evp Chief Legal Officer And Corporate Secretary, Jelena McWilliams

Evp, Richard Stein

Assistant Vice President Information Technology, Wes Debord

Vice President Finance, Dan Flanigan

Vice President Information Technology, Ken Valentine

Senior Vice President Market Manager, John Sieg

Vice President, Robert Weaver

Assistant Vice President Principal Application Developer, Aaron Stockmeister

Senior Vice President, William Thurman

Assistant Vice President Residential Lending, Chris Fink

Vice President, Fred Abblett

Assistant Vice President, Steve Hegele

Vice President Recruiting, Nancy Pinckney

Vice President, Robert Mancini

Portfolio Risk Segment Manager Assistant Vice President, Jason Arseneault

Director Marketing And Vice President, Tricia Eltonhead

Senior Vice President, Jeffrey Leithauser

Vice President Acquisitions, Jim Rose

Assistant Vice President Branch Manager, Cory Kent

Vice President, Morris Marlin

Vice President, Kevin Zgonc

Vice President Mortgage, Alisa Hunter

Assistant Vice President, Michelle Knight

Senior Vice President, Doug Riddle

Vice President, Thomas Merkle

Senior Vice President, Randy Schwarzman

Vice President Director Of Project And Quality Management, Tonja Specht

Vice President Commercial Lending, Jerry Hartley

Vice President Chief Operational Risk Officer, John Wallace

Mortgage Loan Originator Assistant Vice President Fifth Third Mortgage, Michael Cole

Financial Center Manager Assistant Vice President, Jim Hunter

Vice President And Trust Officer, David Garber

Vice President, Timothy Pace

Vice President Manager Project Manager, Colleen Foster

Vice President Of Enterprise Architecture, Gary Schnettler

Vice President, Greg Vollmer

Vice President, Tab Demita

Vice President And Director Commercial Analytics, Stephen Boras

Vice President And Chief Financial Officer Of Eastern Michigan, John Worthington

Senior Vice President Director Risk Strategies, Joseph Heller

Vice President Manager Financial Services, Terrence Lyons

Vice President Information Technology Compliance, Jeffrey A Jones

Vice President, Alfred Mancuso

Vice President, Douglas Schuchter

Vice President Treasury Management Officer, Alicia Mattice

Senior Vice President And Director Operations, Paul Moore

Vice President Consumer Collections, Mona Erickson

Vice President, Tim Tierney

Vice President, William Hummel

Vice President Regional Manager, Lynne Leece

Vice President Institutional Real Estate, Brad Boersma

Assistant Vice President, Brad Pinson

Vice President, Keith Goodpaster

Vice President, Libby Chapin

Vice President, Craig Ellis

Senior Vice President, Steven Slee

Senior Vice President, David Pearce

Vice President, Mark Telles

Vice President, Karen Mundy

Assistant Vice President, Anoopa McKim

Vice President Middle Market, Kathleen Mekesa

Senior Vice President, Peg Jula

Vice President Indirect Originations, Edward Mcelveen

Vice President, Dan Driscoll

Assistant Vice President Senior Market Intelligence Analyst, Ashley Wyant

Assistant Vice President, Gregory Hahn

Investment Executive Vice President, Jeffrey Noeker

Vice President Legal Counsel, Peter Jurs

Vice President, Jennifer Dunigan-wernke

Vice President Business Banking, Tracey Siarkowski

Vice President National Healthcare Finance, William Priester

Vice President Commercial Banking, Mary Weldon

Vice President Commercial Portfolio Manager, Jonathan Roe

Vice President Product And Risk Manager, April Cothran

Vice President, Donald McGill

Vice President, Mark Ransom

Vice President, Joe Acito

Vice President Sales, Russ Schnurr

Vice President, Herbert Kidd

Assistant Vice President Portfolio Manager, Jean Phelan

Vice President Senior Trust Officer, Lisa Laidler

Vice President, Tom Palermo

Vice President Professional Services, John Huber

Vice President, Rod Brown

Solutions Architect And Assistant Vice President, Michaela Schleifer

Vice President Employee Benefits Manager, Joy Byrwa

Assistant Vice President, Debra L Guisinger

Vice President Investment Executive, Michelle Griffith

Assistant Vice President Fiancial Center Manager I, Jim Goodfriend

Vice President, Phil Steenbergen

Vice President, William Krummen
Vice President Private Bank, David W Herrenbruck
Vice President, Maggie Sigler
Vice President And Counsel, H Lind
Vice President, Joanne Hindel
Structured Finance Group Assistant Vice
  President, Paul Bahra
Vice President, Sonia Sonecha
Vice President, Roger Luksik
Vice President Treasury Management, Kate Nagy
Vice President, Joc Szymanowski
Vice President Of Marketing, Richard Steimer
Vice President, Patrick Farnan
Financial Center Manager Assistant Vice
  President, Archard Mathis
Vice President Enterprise Qa, William Nearhood
Vice President, John Sharp
Vice President, Michael Olinsky
Senior Vice President, Tom Plodzeen
Vice President Officer, George Hunter
Vice President, Michael Hossack
Finance Manager Vice President, Janet Wolffis
Vice President Treasury Management Officer,
  Douglas Henderson
Vice President, Tammy Schaefer
Vice President Sba Alternative Lending, Chris
  Intemann
Vice President, Jason Fronheiser
Fcm Vice President, Rubia Marins
Vice President And Director Of Accounting, Glen
  Napolitano
Trust Officer Assistant Vice President, Kristi
  Nimsgern
Vice President, Thomas Begam
Vice President Group Manager, Tim Fergan
Assistant Vice President Portfolio Manager,
  Carolyn Dearmond
Vice President Employee Relations, Kathie Davis
Vice President, Shannon Paul
Vice President Recovery Manager, Jeremy Hejl
Vice President Area Investment Manager, Crystal
  Kolcz
Vice President And Senior Portfolio Ma, Frank
  Wojcik
Vice President Middle Market Corporate Banking,
  Yasmeen Jasey
Senior Vice President Commercial Banking, Tom
  Witt
Vice President Senior Wealth Management
  Advisor, Craig Vaness
Vice President Capital Markets Senior Manager,
  Michael Sams
Vice President, Jon Powell
Vice President, Jeffrey R Gardner
Vice President, Brian Lynd
Vice President Healthcare Treasury Management,
  Lynne Pearson
Vice Presidentandtrust Officer, Frank Rhodarmer
Assistant Vice President Special Assets Group,
  Monique Suranye
Loan Sales Senior Vice President, John Edwards
Financial Center Manager And Vice President,
  Adrian Mendieta
Senior Vice President Director Regional Portfolio
  Management, Sean Casey
Vice President Commercial Credit Risk Review,
  Andrew Kerr
Vice President Of Business Banking, Lisa
  Sammons
Auditors: Deloitte & Touche LLP

LOCATIONS

HQ: Fifth Third Bancorp (Cincinnati, OH)
  Fifth Third Center, Cincinnati, OH 45263
Phone: 800 972-3030
Web: www.53.com

Selected Markets

Florida
Georgia
Indiana
Illinois
Kentucky
Michigan
North Carolina
Ohio
Tennessee
West Virginia

PRODUCTS/OPERATIONS

2017 Sales

	$ mil.	% of total
Interest		
Loans & leases including fees	3,478	45
Securities & other	996	13
Interest on other short-term investments	15	-
Non-Interest		
Service charges on deposits	554	7
Wealth and asset management revenue	419	5
Corporate banking revenue	353	5
Mortgage banking net revenue	224	3
Card & processing revenue	313	4
Securities gains net	2	-
Other	1,357	18
Total	**7,713**	**100**

Selected Subsidiaries

Fifth Third Capital Trust VII
Fifth Third Financial Corporation
  Fifth Third Bank
  GNB Management LLC
  GNB Realty LLC
  ClearArc Capital Inc.
  Fifth Third Funding LLC
  Fifth Third Holdings LLC
  Fifth Third Insurance Agency Inc.
  Fifth Third International Company
  Fifth Third Trade Services Limited (Hong Kong)
  Fifth Third Equipment Finance Company (formerly
  The Fifth Third Leasing Company)
  The Fifth Third Auto Leasing Trust
  Fifth Third Mortgage Company
  Fifth Third Real Estate Investment Trust Inc.
  Fifth Third Real Estate Capital Markets Company
  Old Kent Mortgage Services Inc.
  Fifth Third Community Development Corporation
  Fifth Third New Markets Development Co. LLC
  Fifth Third Investment Company
  Fountain Square Life Reinsurance Company Ltd.
  (Turks and Caicos Islands)
  Vista Settlement Services LLC

COMPETITORS

Bank of America	KeyCorp
Citigroup	Northern Trust
Comerica	PNC Financial
Harris	U.S. Bancorp
Huntington Bancshares	Wells Fargo
JPMorgan Chase	

HISTORICAL FINANCIALS

Company Type: Public

Income Statement   FYE: December 31

	ASSETS ($ mil.)	NET INCOME ($ mil.)	INCOME AS % OF ASSETS	EMPLOYEES
12/17	142,193	2,194	1.5%	18,125
12/16	142,177	1,564	1.1%	17,844
12/15	141,082	1,712	1.2%	18,261
12/14	138,706	1,481	1.1%	18,351
12/13	130,443	1,836	1.4%	19,446
Annual Growth	**2.2%**	**4.6%**	**—**	**(1.7%)**

2017 Year-End Financials

Debt ratio: 10.46%
Return on equity: 13.47%
Cash ($ mil.): 3,376
Current ratio: —
Long-term debt ($ mil.): —

No. of shares (mil.): 693
Dividends
  Yield: 0.0%
  Payout: 21.2%
Market value ($ mil.): 21,050

	STOCK PRICE ($) FY Close	P/E High/Low		PER SHARE ($) Earnings	Dividends	Book Value
12/17	30.34	11	8	2.83	0.60	23.59
12/16	26.97	14	7	1.93	0.53	21.59
12/15	20.10	11	8	2.01	0.52	20.18
12/14	20.38	14	11	1.66	0.51	18.96
12/13	21.03	10	7	2.02	0.47	17.06
Annual Growth	**9.6%**	**—**	**—**	**8.8%**	**6.3%**	**8.4%**

Financial Institutions Inc.

Financial Institutions may not have a luxurious name but they specialize in five star service. The holding company owns Five Star Bank which provides standard deposit products such as checking and savings accounts CDs and IRAs to retail and business customers through some 50 branches across western and central New York. Indirect consumer loans originated through agreements with area franchised car dealers account for the largest percentage of the company's loan portfolio (35%) followed by commercial mortgages. The company also sells insurance while its Five Star Investment Services subsidiary offers brokerage and financial planning services.

Operations
Financial Institutions operates through two business segments: banking which includes the bank's retail and commercial banking operations; and insurance which sells insurance to both personal and business clients through its Scott Danahy Naylon Co (SDN) subsidiary.

About 65% of the company's total revenue came from loan interest (including fees) in 2014 while another 15% came from interest on its investment securities. The rest of its revenue came from deposit account service charges (7%) ATM and debit card fees (4%) insurance income (2%) investment advisory (2%) and other miscellaneous income sources.

Geographic Reach
Five Star Bank boasts 50 branches and an ATM network across Western and Central New York in the counties of Allegany Cattaraugus Cayuga Chautauqua Chemung Erie Genesee Livingston Monroe Ontario Orleans Schuyler Seneca Steuben Wyoming and Yates.

Sales and Marketing
The company offers financial and banking services to individuals municipalities and businesses in Western and Central New York.

Financial Performance
Financial Institution's revenues and profits have been rising over the past few years thanks to growing loan business (organically and from 2012 acquisitions) lower interest expenses and rising fee-based revenue.

The company's revenue rose by 2% to $126.4 million in 2014 mostly thanks to the addition of insurance income from stemming from the bank's acquisition of SDN. Financial's loan interest grew by 1% on organic loan business growth while interest on investment securities grew by 7% as it purchased more interest-earning assets.

Higher revenue and a decline in loan loss provisions from a more credit-worthy loan portfolio in 2014 drove Financial Institution's net income higher by 15% to a record $29.4 million. The company's operating cash levels dipped by 5% to $35.2 million during the year due to unfavorable changes in working capital related to its contributions to its defined benefit pension plan.

Strategy

Financial Institutions' long-term strategy reiterated in 2015 has been to "maintain a community bank philosophy which consists of focusing on and understanding the individualized banking needs of individuals municipalities and businesses of the local communities surrounding their primary service area." The firm believes this focus will enable it to better respond to customer needs and provide a higher level of personalized services giving it a competitive advantage over larger competitors.

The company has also pursued acquisitions to bolster its service lines to grow its non-interest business. Its 2014 acquisition of a New-York based full-service insurance agency for example launched it beyond banking into the insurance business.

Mergers and Acquisitions

In January 2015 Financial Institutions bolstered its investment service business after acquiring Courier Capital which offers customized investment management investment consulting and retirement plan services to some 1100 individuals businesses and institutions.

In 2014 Financial Institutions expanded its services into the insurance business after acquiring Buffalo-based Scott Danahy Naylon Co. (SDN) a full-service insurance agency for a total of $16.9 million plus a promise of $3.4 million in future payments contingent on SDN meeting revenue performance goal targets through 2017.

Company Background

In 2012 Five Star Bank acquired four retail branches owned by HSBC Bank and four owned by First Niagara Bank in upstate New York.

Five Star Bank was formed in 2005 when the company consolidated its four banking subsidiaries (First Tier Bank & Trust National Bank of Geneva Wyoming County Bank and Bath National Bank) into a single entity. First Tier Bank & Trust absorbed the other three banks and changed its name to Five Star Bank.

EXECUTIVES

Assistant Vice President Investment Services, David Macintyre

Evp Cfo And Treasurer, Kevin B. Klotzbach, age 65, $230,000 total compensation

President And Ceo, Martin K. Birmingham, $420,000 total compensation

Evp Commercial Executive And Regional President, Jeffrey P. Kenefick, $209,100 total compensation

Svp And Director Of Human Resources And Enterprise Planning, Paula D. Dolan, $140,000 total compensation

Evp And Chief Risk Officer, Kenneth V. Winn

Senior Vice President And Treasurer, Marc Swanson

Senior Vice President And Chief Development Officer, Emily Reynolds

Senior Vice President And Manager Work, Steven Ambrose

Vice Presidenti Information Technology, R McLaughlin

Senior Vice President Consumer Lending Manager, Jonathan Chase

Senior Vice President And Administrator Loan Revie, David Squire

Board Member, Samuel Gullo

Evp Cfo And Treasurer, Kevin B. Klotzbach, age 65

Chairman, Robert N. Latella, age 75

Board Member, Andrew Dorn

Board Member, Robert Glaser

Auditors: KPMG LLP

LOCATIONS

HQ: Financial Institutions Inc.
220 Liberty Street, Warsaw, NY 14569
Phone: 585 786-1100
Web: www.fiiwarsaw.com

PRODUCTS/OPERATIONS

2013 Sales

	$ mil.	% of total
Interest income		
Loans including fees	81	66
Investment securities	17	14
Noninterest income		
Service charges on deposits	9	9
ATM & debit card	5	4
Investment advisory	2	2
Other	7	5
Total	**123**	**100**

COMPETITORS

Astoria Financial	HSBC USA
Citibank	KeyCorp
Community Bank System	M&T Bank
ESL Federal Credit Union	

HISTORICAL FINANCIALS

Company Type: Public

Income Statement

FYE: December 31

	ASSETS ($ mil.)	NET INCOME ($ mil.)	INCOME AS % OF ASSETS	EMPLOYEES
12/17	4,105	33	0.8%	656
12/16	3,710	31	0.9%	654
12/15	3,381	28	0.8%	691
12/14	3,089	29	1.0%	645
12/13	2,928	25	0.9%	645
Annual Growth	**8.8%**	**7.0%**	**—**	**0.4%**

2017 Year-End Financials

Debt ratio: 0.95%
Return on equity: 9.56%
Cash ($ mil.): 99
Current ratio: —
Long-term debt ($ mil.): —

No. of shares (mil.): 15
Dividends
Yield: 0.0%
Payout: 39.9%
Market value ($ mil.): 495

	STOCK PRICE ($) FY Close	P/E High/Low	PER SHARE ($) Earnings	Dividends	Book Value
12/17	31.10	17 12	2.13	0.85	23.94
12/16	34.20	16 12	2.10	0.81	22.02
12/15	28.00	15 12	1.90	0.80	20.71
12/14	25.15	13 10	2.00	0.77	19.80
12/13	24.71	15 10	1.75	0.74	18.43
Annual Growth	**5.9%**	**— —**	**5.0%**	**3.5%**	**6.8%**

FINCANTIERI MARINE SYSTEMS NORTH AMERICA, INC.

EXECUTIVES

Ceo, Dario Deste
Pres, Domenico Sorvillo
V Pres-Gen Mgr, Richard Dinsmore
Treas, Paolo Pezzulo

Contrl, Martha Rosbrough
Manager, Pamela Thomas
Human Resources Coordinator, Ashley Morningstar

LOCATIONS

HQ: FINCANTIERI MARINE SYSTEMS NORTH AMERICA, INC.
800 PRINCIPAL CT STE C, CHESAPEAKE, VA 233203681
Phone: 757 548-6000
Web: WWW.FINCANTIERIMARINESYSTEMS.COM

HISTORICAL FINANCIALS

Company Type: Private

Income Statement

FYE: December 31

	REVENUE ($ mil.)	NET INCOME ($ mil.)	NET PROFIT MARGIN	EMPLOYEES
12/17	35,833	6,670	18.6%	56
12/16	37,567	6,365	16.9%	—
12/14	34,753	2,898	8.3%	—
12/13	0	1,229	—	—
Annual Growth	**—**	**52.6%**	**—**	**—**

2017 Year-End Financials

Debt ratio: —
Return on equity: 18.60%
Cash ($ mil.): 1,877
Current ratio: 1.20
Long-term debt ($ mil.): —

Dividends
Yield: —
Payout: —
Market value ($ mil.): —

First American Financial Corp

First American Financial knows that when you're buying real estate you'll probably want some insurance to go along with it. In addition to good old title insurance from its First American Title subsidiary the company's financial services arm also provides specialty property/casualty insurance and home warranties through First American Home Buyers Protection. Its First American Trust unit offers banking and trust services to the escrow and real estate industries. Other offerings include settlement title plant management valuation and investment advisory services.

Operations

First American Financial is one of the largest title insurers in the US. Its title insurance and services segment accounts for more than 90% of revenues. The unit is focused on issuing title insurance for commercial and residential real estate transactions in the US and abroad; it also provides escrow closing exchange documentation banking and other title insurance-related services. The company also provides real property-related data services to mitigate risk and facilitate transactions.

The remainder of revenue comes from the specialty insurance segment which offers property/casualty policies including homeowners renters and property hazard coverage. It also markets home warranties.

Geographic Reach

With headquarters in California First American Financial serves customers in over 40 countries around the globe. The US market where the specialty business is licensed in all 50 states and the District of Columbia accounts for about 95% of revenues.

The company has regional offices in countries including Australia Canada and the UK. Through acquisitions (partial and total) of existing businesses and through partnerships with local companies First American Financial is carefully moving into emerging markets in central and eastern Europe.

Sales and Marketing

First American Financial distributes its title insurance and related products through a direct sales force and via agent channels. For residential products it markets to real estate agents and brokers as well as mortgage originators and brokers real estate attorneys homebuilders and escrow service providers. Refinance business is marketed to mortgage originators and servicers and government-sponsored entities. Commercial lines are primarily marketed to investors including real estate investment trusts (REITs) as well as law firms banks investment banks mortgage brokers and commercial property owners.

Property/casualty insurance is marketed through direct distribution channels (including cross-selling to existing customers) and through a network of independent brokers.

Financial Performance

With the exception of 2014 First American Financial's net sales have been on the rise for the past five years. In 2016 net sales increased 8% to $5.6 billion as all lines of revenue (direct premiums and escrow fees agent premiums information and other net investment income and net realized investment gains) grew. In particular 9% increase in agent premiums drove the overall increase. Direct premiums and escrow fees rose 4% that year largely due to an increase in residential transactions.

Net income has been increasing since 2013. In 2016 the higher net sales helped net income rise 19% to $343 million but that was partially offset by an increase in most expenses.

Cash flow from operations slipped 11% to $489.4 million in 2016 primarily due to an $85 million contribution to the firm's termination of its legacy pension plan.

Strategy

First American Financial operates through three primary strategic lenses: growing its core title and settlement businesses strengthening its business with data and managing and buying complementary businesses that expand or support its core activities. In terms of growing its core operations the company works to bring greater efficiency to the business including seeking innovative growth drivers and making strategic acquisitions. To increase its stores of data First American Financial has made a number of purchases such as RedVision Systems and TD Service Financial. Those and other acquisitions have helped the company streamline the title process and improve the services it offers clients. And with the sheer volume of data the company has at its disposal (its data covers 100% of the counties in the US for example) First American Financial is positioned to benefit from the improving economy and expected rise in real estate transactions.

Mergers and Acquisitions

First American Financial continues to grow through a number of strategic acquisitions. In 2015 it bought New York-based title agency TitleVest Holdings. Then in 2016 it acquired New Jersey-based title data firm RedVision Systems which became part of First American's Data and Mortgage Solutions division. Further adding to its mortgage solutions operations the company bought TD Service Financial Corporation and its subsidiaries including TD Service Company Security Connections and TD Quality Control Services. Those firms provide technology services such as

lien releases audits document retrieval and post-closing services to the mortgage banking industry.

Company Background

Previously known as First American Corporation the company spun off its real estate information services into CoreLogic in 2010.

Chairman Parker Kennedy is a descendant of the founder of the company C. E. Parker.

HISTORY

In 1889 when Los Angeles was on its way to becoming a real city the more countrified residents to the south (including The Irvine Company's founding family) formed Orange County a peaceful realm of citrus groves where land transactions were assisted by title companies Orange County Abstract and Santa Ana Abstract. In 1894 the firms merged under the leadership of local businessman C. E. Parker. For three decades the resulting Orange County Title limited its business to title searches.

In 1924 as real estate transactions became more complex (in part because of mineral-rights issues related to Southern California's oil boom) Orange County Title began offering title insurance and escrow services. The company remained under Parker family management until 1930 when H. A. Gardner took over and guided it through the Depression. In 1943 the company returned to Parker family control.

In 1957 the company began a major expansion beyond Orange County. The new First American Title Insurance and Trust name acknowledged the firm's expansion into trust and custody operations. Donald Kennedy (C. E. Parker's grandson) took over in 1963 and took the company public the next year.

In 1968 First American Corporation was formed as a holding company for subsidiaries First American Title Insurance and First American Trust. This structure facilitated growth as the firm began opening new offices and buying all or parts of other title companies including Title Guaranty Co. of Wyoming Security Title & Trust (San Antonio) and Ticore Inc. (Portland Oregon) all purchased in 1968.

The 1970s were a quiet time for the company but it began growing again in the 1980s as savings and loan deregulation jump-started the commercial real estate market in Southern California. First American diversified into home warranty and real estate tax services. In 1988 on the brink of the California meltdown the company bought an industrial loan corporation to make commercial real estate loans.

EXECUTIVES

Evp, Kenneth D. DeGiorgio, age 46, $749,615 total compensation

Ceo And Director, Dennis J. Gilmore, age 59, $949,231 total compensation

Coo Mortgage Information Services Group, Christopher M. Leavell, age 55, $699,615 total compensation

Evp And Cfo, Mark E. Seaton, age 42, $574,231 total compensation

Vp And Chief Accounting Officer, Matthew F. Wajner, age 42, $274,769 total compensation

Vice President Southern California Area Operations Director, Chris Clemens

Vice President And Manager, Jordan Dunn

Senior Vice President National Accounts Director, Michael Hall

Vice President Corporate Information Technology, Desai Priti

Vice President, Michael Kennedy

Vice President And State Counsel, Leonard Prescott

Senior Vice President, George Gauger

Vice President National Accounts, Valerie Kolytiris

Senior Vice President Sales, Caitlin Stearns

Vice President, Trish Brown

Assistant Vice President Trust Services, Kathy Vian

Vice President, Paul Boccardi

Executive Vice President, Scott Callender

Vice President, Jeanne LaBelle

Vice President And Underwriting Counsel, Mitch Gluck

Vice President Of Sales Miami, Karun Mard

Vice President Director Of Title Operations, Maureen Garvey

Vice President Of Sales, Tori Robinson

Vice President Sales, Omar Kubba

Chairman, Parker S. Kennedy

Ceo And Director, Dennis J. Gilmore, age 59

Auditors: PricewaterhouseCoopers LLP

LOCATIONS

HQ: First American Financial Corp
1 First American Way, Santa Ana, CA 92707-5913
Phone: 714 250-3000   **Fax:** 714 250-3151
Web: www.firstam.com

2016 Sales

	% of total
US	94
International	6
Total	**100**

PRODUCTS/OPERATIONS

2016 Sales

	$ mil.	% of total
Direct premiums & escrow fees	2,416	43
Agent premiums	2,286	41
Information & other	724	13
Net investment income	126	2
Net realized investment losses	23	1
Total	**5,575**	**100**

2016 Sales

	% of total
Title Insurance and Services	92
Specialty Insurance	8
Corporate	-
Eliminations	-
Total	**100**

Selected Services

Property/Casualty Insurance
  Home Warranty
Title Insurance and Services
  1031 Tax-Deferred Exchange Services
  Banking and Investment Management
  Default Services
  Homebuilder Services
  National Commercial Services
  Origination Services
  Professional Real Estate Services
  Property Information and Recorded Documents
  Title Insurance and Closing Services
  Title Technology Solutions
  UCC Insurance Search and Filing Services
  Valuation Services

COMPETITORS

American Home Shield	North American Title
Fidelity National Financial	Old Republic
Home Buyers Warranty	Stewart Information Services
Investors Title	Ticor Title Co.

HISTORICAL FINANCIALS

Company Type: Public

Income Statement

FYE: December 31

	ASSETS ($ mil.)	NET INCOME ($ mil.)	INCOME AS % OF ASSETS	EMPLOYEES
12/17	9,573	423	4.4%	18,705
12/16	8,831	342	3.9%	19,531
12/15	8,254	288	3.5%	17,955
12/14	7,666	233	3.0%	17,103
12/13	6,520	186	2.9%	17,292
Annual Growth	10.1%	22.7%	—	2.0%

2017 Year-End Financials

Debt ratio: 7.65%
Return on equity: 13.04%
Cash ($ mil.): 1,387
Current ratio: —
Long-term debt ($ mil.): —

No. of shares (mil.): 110
Dividends
 Yield: 0.0%
 Payout: 38.3%
Market value ($ mil.): 6,216

	STOCK PRICE ($) FY Close	P/E High/Low		PER SHARE ($) Earnings	Dividends	Book Value
12/17	56.04	15	10	3.76	1.44	31.37
12/16	36.63	14	10	3.09	1.20	27.36
12/15	35.90	16	12	2.62	1.00	25.28
12/14	33.90	16	11	2.15	0.84	23.92
12/13	28.20	16	12	1.71	0.48	23.16
Annual Growth	18.7%	—	—	21.8%	31.6%	7.9%

FIRST AMERICAN TRUST COMPANY

EXECUTIVES

Chm-Ceo, Thomas M Kelley
SEC, Pat Lucado
Sr V Pres-Cfo, Teri Pierce
Sr V Pres-Coo, Kelly Dudley
Sr V Pres Personal Trust, Darliene Evans
V Pres Corporate Council, Dimetria Jackson
Exec V Pres, Robert Daniel Banis
Evp-Chief Fiduciary Officer, Eric R McMullen
Vp-Wealth Management, Mark Monaco
Vice-President, Michael Hinkle
Customer, Barbara Boomgarden
Auditors: PRICEWATERHOUSECOOPERS LLP O

LOCATIONS

HQ: FIRST AMERICAN TRUST COMPANY
 5 FIRST AMERICAN WAY, SANTA ANA, CA 927075913
Phone: 714 560-7856
Web: WWW.FIRSTAMTRUST.COM

HISTORICAL FINANCIALS

Company Type: Private

Income Statement

FYE: December 31

	ASSETS ($ mil.)	NET INCOME ($ mil.)	INCOME AS % OF ASSETS	EMPLOYEES
12/17	3,431	27	0.8%	106
12/16	3,124	29	0.9%	—
12/15	2,982	24	0.8%	—
12/14	2,627	18	0.7%	—
Annual Growth	9.3%	13.7%	—	—

Debt ratio: —
Return on equity: 33.40%
Cash ($ mil.): 674
Current ratio: —
Long-term debt ($ mil.): —

Dividends
 Yield: —
 Payout: —
Market value ($ mil.): —

First Bancorp

Not to be confused with North Carolina's First Bancorp this First BanCorp is the holding company for FirstBank Puerto Rico which provides business and retail banking services through more than 50 branches in Puerto Rico and about two dozen more in Florida and the Virgin Islands. Puerto Rico's second-largest bank gets more than one-third of its business from its Commercial and Corporate Banking loans and services. Residential mortgages make up nearly one-third of FirstBank's $9 billion loan portfolio while commercial mortgages make up another one-fifth. First BanCorp also owns FirstBank Insurance Agency Firstbank Puerto Rico Securities and the consumer loan company Money Express La Financiera.

Operations

Generating more than 80% of its revenue from loan interest First BanCorp operates through six business segments: Commercial and Corporate Banking; Consumer (Retail) Banking; Mortgage Banking; Treasury and Investments; United States Operations; and Virgin Islands Operations.

Commercial and Corporate Banking which made up roughly 35% of the company's total revenue in 2014 provides lending and other services for organizations in the public sector as well as for large and specialized middle-market businesses operating in a variety of industries.

The Consumer (Retail) Banking segment (22% of revenue) provides consumer lending and deposit services mainly through FirstBank's branch network and loan centers in Puerto Rico. FirstBank's loans include auto boat and personal loans credit cards and lines of credit.

The Mortgage Banking (18% of revenue) business buys and sells home loans through FirstBank and the company's mortgage origination subsidiary First Mortgage.

Treasury and Investments (1% of revenue) manages securities and lends funds to the company's three banking segments to finance their respective lending activities. It also borrows from those segments and from the United States Operations segment.

United States Operations (20% of revenue) consists of FirstBank's 10 retail and corporate banking businesses in the US mainland mostly in southern Florida.

Virgin Islands Operations (3% of revenue) counts FirstBank's banking business (mostly consumer commercial lending and deposit account activities) in the US Virgin Islands (USVI) and British Virgin Islands (BVI) through 12 branches in the USVI (St. Thomas St. Croix and St. John and the islands) and the BVI (Tortola and Virgin Gorda).

Geographic Reach

San Juan-based FirstBank boasts more than 50 branches across Puerto Rico around a dozen branches in the USVI and BVI and 10 US branches in southern Florida. The bank also has 27 First First Federal Finance Corp (dba Money Express La Financiera) offices in Puerto Rico.

Financial Performance

First BanCorp ended its multi-year revenue decline in 2014 with revenue rebounding by 10% to $695.3 million for the year. This is mostly because the bank in 2013 had suffered more than $200 million from a combination of losses on sales from non-performing assets and losses from a write-off of assets pledged as collateral to Lehman Brothers Inc. Despite earning lower interest income during 2014 the bank's net interest income managed to climb slightly thanks to lower interest expenses on deposits amidst the continued low-interest environment.

The company's profit jumped sharply to $392.29 million in 2014 (compared to a net loss of $164.49 million in 2013) mostly thanks to a drop in loan loss provisions as its loan portfolio's credit quality improved as the economy strengthened but also thanks to a combination of higher revenue and lower interest and non-interest expenses.

Despite higher earnings in 2014 First BanCorp's operating cash declined as the company generated less cash from proceeds on its loans held for sale.

Strategy

First BanCorp has followed an acquisition strategy to grow its loan business and bank clientele in recent years. In early 2015 for example flagship subsidiary FirstBank purchased 10 bank branches in Puerto Rico from its rival Doral Bank which added some $600 million in new deposits $300 million in new mortgage loan business and 140000 new clients. The acquisition also grew FirstBanCorp's total branch network by 20% while expanding its market presence in geographic areas with room for deposit and mortgage loan business growth. The year before in 2014 FirstBank expanded its loan business through the purchase of a $242-million portfolio of mortgage loans from Doral for some $232.9 million.

Company Background

Scotiabank a Canadian bank with operations throughout the Caribbean acquired a 10% stake in First BanCorp in 2007.

EXECUTIVES

Evp Business Group Executive, Cassan Pancham, age 58, $399,815 total compensation
Evp And Chief Risk Officer, Nayda Rivera-Batista, age 44
President And Ceo, Aurelio Aleman-Bermudez, $850,102 total compensation
Evp And Cfo, Orlando Berges-Gonzalez, $600,101 total compensation
Evp And Florida Region Executive, Calixto Garcia-Velez, $486,115 total compensation
Evp And Coo, Donald L. Kafka
Evp Retail And Business Banking Executive, Ginoris Lopez-Lay
Evp And Chief Lending Officer, Emilio Martino-Valdes
Evp And Business Group Director, Michael McDonald
Evp; General Counsel And Secretary, Lawrence Odell, $550,110 total compensation
Evp And Consumer Lending Business Executive, Carlos Power Pietrantoni
Assistant Vice President, Hiram Rivas
Vice President, Rafael Perez
Vice President Of Commercial Department, Francisco Pascual
Senior Vice President Commercial Lending, Alfred Massheder
Chairman, Roberto R. Herencia, age 58
Auditors: Crowe Horwath LLP

LOCATIONS

HQ: First Bancorp
  1519 Ponce de Leon Avenue, Stop 23, Santurce 00908
Phone: 787 729 8200
Web: www.firstbankpr.com

PRODUCTS/OPERATIONS

2014 Sales

	$ mil.	% of total
Interest		
Loans	579	82
Investment securities	52	8
Money market investments	1	-
Noninterest		
Service charges on deposit accounts	16	2
Mortgage banking activities	14	2
Insurance income	6	1
Others	30	5
Adjustments	(7.7)	-
Total	**695**	**100**

2014 Sales by Segments

	% of total
Commercial and corporate banking	35
Consumer(Retail) banking	22
United State Operations	21
Mortgage Banking	18
Virgin Island Operations	3
Treasury and Investments	1
Total	**100**

Selected Subsidiaries

FirstBank Puerto Rico
  FirstBank Overseas Corporation
  FirstBank Puerto Rico Securities Corp.
  First Federal Finance Corp. (d/b/a Money Express La Financiera)
  First Insurance Agency Inc.
  First Mortgage Inc.
FirstBank Insurance Agency Inc.
Grupo Empresas de Servicios Financieros (d/b/a PR Finance)

COMPETITORS

Citigroup	Popular Inc.
OFG Bancorp	Santander BanCorp

HISTORICAL FINANCIALS

Company Type: Public

Income Statement				FYE: December 31
	ASSETS ($ mil.)	NET INCOME ($ mil.)	INCOME AS % OF ASSETS	EMPLOYEES
12/17	12,261	66	0.5%	2,553
12/16	11,922	93	0.8%	2,701
12/15	12,573	21	0.2%	2,758
12/14	12,727	392	3.1%	2,617
12/13	12,656	(164)	—	2,458
Annual Growth	**(0.8%)**	**—**	**—**	**1.0%**

2017 Year-End Financials

Debt ratio: 1.70%
Return on equity: 3.66%
Cash ($ mil.): 716
Current ratio: —
Long-term debt ($ mil.): —
No. of shares (mil.): 216
Dividends
  Yield: —
  Payout: —
Market value ($ mil.): 1,103

	STOCK PRICE ($) FY Close	P/E High/Low	Earnings	PER SHARE ($) Dividends	Book Value
12/17	5.10	23 16	0.30	0.00	8.64
12/16	6.61	16 5	0.43	0.00	8.21
12/15	3.25	67 31	0.10	0.00	7.88
12/14	5.87	3 2	1.87	0.00	7.85
12/13	6.19	— —	(0.80)	0.00	5.87
Annual Growth	**(4.7%)**	**— —**	**—**	**—**	**10.1%**

First Bancorp (NC)

EXECUTIVES

Evp And Cfo First Bancorp And First Bank, Eric P. Credle, age 49, $325,000 total compensation
President And Director First Bancorp And President And Ceo First Bank, Michael G. Mayer, age 58, $425,000 total compensation
President Ceo And Director, Richard H. Moore, age 57, $525,000 total compensation
Senior Vice President Legal Division, Kirsten Foyles
Vice President, Jason Williams
Chairman First Bancorp And First Bank, James C. Crawford, age 61
President And Director First Bancorp And President And Ceo First Bank, Michael G. Mayer, age 58
President Ceo And Director, Richard H. Moore, age 57
Auditors: Elliott Davis, PLLC

LOCATIONS

HQ: First Bancorp (NC)
  300 S.W. Broad Street, Southern Pines, NC 28387
Phone: 910 246-2500
Web: www.localFirstbank.com

PRODUCTS/OPERATIONS

2016 Sales

	$ mil.	% of total
Interest Income	130	84
Non-interest Income	25	16
Total	**156**	**100**

COMPETITORS

BB&T	NewBridge Bancorp
BNC Bancorp	PNC Financial
Bank of America	South Street Financial
CommunityOne Bancorp	SunTrust
First Citizens BancShares	Wells Fargo

HISTORICAL FINANCIALS

Company Type: Public

Income Statement				FYE: December 31
	ASSETS ($ mil.)	NET INCOME ($ mil.)	INCOME AS % OF ASSETS	EMPLOYEES
12/17	5,547	45	0.8%	1,166
12/16	3,614	27	0.8%	861
12/15	3,362	27	0.8%	840
12/14	3,218	25	0.8%	825
12/13	3,185	20	0.6%	873
Annual Growth	**14.9%**	**22.1%**		**7.5%**

2017 Year-End Financials

Debt ratio: 0.97%
Return on equity: 8.67%
Cash ($ mil.): 489
Current ratio: —
Long-term debt ($ mil.): —
No. of shares (mil.): 29
Dividends
  Yield: 0.0%
  Payout: 17.5%
Market value ($ mil.): 1,047

	STOCK PRICE ($) FY Close	P/E High/Low	Earnings	PER SHARE ($) Dividends	Book Value
12/17	35.31	21 15	1.82	0.32	23.38
12/16	27.14	21 13	1.33	0.32	17.66
12/15	18.74	15 12	1.30	0.32	17.33
12/14	18.47	16 13	1.19	0.32	19.67
12/13	16.62	17 12	0.98	0.32	18.90
Annual Growth	**20.7%**	**— —**	**16.7%**	**(0.0%)**	**5.5%**

First Bancorp Inc (ME)

It may not actually be the first bank but The First Bancorp (formerly First National Lincoln) was founded over 150 years ago. It is the holding company for The First a regional bank serving coastal Maine from more than 15 branches. The bank offers traditional retail products and services including checking and savings accounts CDs IRAs and loans. Residential mortgages make up about 40% of the company's loan portfolio; business loans account for another 40%; and home equity and consumer loans comprise the rest. Bank subsidiary First Advisors offers private banking and investment management services. Founded in 1864 the bank now boasts more than $1.4 billion in assets.

Operations

Subsidiary First Advisors acts as the bank's Trust and Investment services division which managed some $740 million in investor assets as of late 2014.

The First Bancorp generated 57% of its total revenue from interest income on loans (including fees) while another 25% came from interest and dividends on its investments. Service charges on deposit accounts (4%) Fiduciary and investment management income (3%) mortgage origination (2%) and net securities gains (2%) made up most of the rest of its total revenue.

Geographic Reach

The Damariscotta-based bank boasts more than 15 branches in Mid-Coast Eastern and Down East regions of Maine in Lincoln Knox Hancock Washington and Penobscot counties.

Sales and Marketing

The community-oriented bank concentrates on marketing to small businesses and individuals within its local markets.

Financial Performance

The First Bancorp's revenues have slowly declined over the past few years mostly with as its loan business has stagnated and as its interest margins on loans and investments have been shrinking in the low-interest rate environment. Its profits however have been steadily rising thanks to declining loan loss provisions as its loan portfolio's credit quality has improved with the strengthened economy.

The company's revenue inched up by less than one-tenth of a percent to $62.07 million in 2014 mostly as the bank carried more interest-earning investment assets during the year. The bank's noninterest income however declined by 9% as it collected less from the origination and sale of refinanced mortgage loans into the secondary market.

The First Bancorp's net income jumped by 13% to $14.7 million in 2014 thanks primarily to a continued decline in loan loss provisions as its portfolio's credit quality improved. Slightly higher revenue and lower interest expenses on deposits also helped pad the company's bottom line. The bank's operating cash levels fell by 18% to $20.5 million after adjusting its earnings for non-cash items related to its loan loss provisions and its net proceeds from the sale of its mortgage loans held for sale.

Strategy

As management reiterated in early 2015 remaining well capitalized "remains a top priority for The First Bancorp" and has been key to its profit growth over the past several years. Indeed its de-risking initiatives for its loan portfolio assets have taken the bank's risk-based capital ratio from 11.13% in 2008 to 16.27% at the end of 2014 well above the FDIC's suggested threshold of 10%. As a result the bank's loan loss provisions have declined over the period and its profits have blossomed despite a lack of revenue growth.

Company Background

First National Lincoln acquired competitor FNB Bankshares and its First National Bank of Bar Harbor subsidiary in 2005. It merged that bank into its own subsidiary The First National Bank of Damariscotta which was renamed The First.

EXECUTIVES

Treasurer The First Bancorp Inc. And Evp And Cfo First National Bank, F. Stephen Ward, age 65, $254,400 total compensation

Evp And Clerk The First Bancorp Inc. And Evp Banking Services And Senior Loan Officer The First National Bank, Charles A. Wootton, age 61, $241,100 total compensation

Evp And Chief Administrative Officer First National Bank, Susan A. Norton, age 58, $210,000 total compensation

Evp And Treasurer First National Bank, Richard M. Elder, age 52, $179,400 total compensation

Evp And Cio The First, Tammy L. Plummer, age 52

President And Ceo The First Bancorp And The First N.a., Tony C. McKim, age 51, $430,000 total compensation

Executive Vice President Branch Administration, Sarah Tolman

Senior Vice President, Rick Elder

Treasurer The First Bancorp Inc. And Evp And Cfo First National Bank, F. Stephen Ward, age 65

Chairman, David B. Soule, age 73

Evp And Treasurer First National Bank, Richard M. Elder, age 52

Vice Chairman, Mark N. Rosborough, age 70

Auditors: Berry Dunn McNeil & Parker, LLC

LOCATIONS

HQ: First Bancorp Inc (ME)
Main Street, Damariscotta, ME 04543
Phone: 207 563-3195
Web: www.thefirstbancorp.com

PRODUCTS/OPERATIONS

2007 Sales

	$ mil.	% of total
Interest		
Loans including fees	60	74
Investments & other	11	14
Noninterest		
Service charges on deposit accounts	2	3
Fiduciary & investment management income	1	1
Other	6	8
Total	**81**	**100**

COMPETITORS

Bangor Savings Bank	KeyCorp
Bar Harbor Bankshares	Northeast Bancorp
Camden National	TD Bank USA

HISTORICAL FINANCIALS

Company Type: Public

Income Statement

FYE: December 31

	ASSETS ($ mil.)	NET INCOME ($ mil.)	INCOME AS % OF ASSETS	EMPLOYEES
12/17	1,842	19	1.1%	235
12/16	1,712	18	1.1%	235
12/15	1,564	16	1.0%	223
12/14	1,482	14	1.0%	235
12/13	1,463	12	0.9%	233
Annual Growth	**5.9%**	**10.9%**	**—**	**0.2%**

2017 Year-End Financials

Debt ratio: 6.25%
Return on equity: 11.07%
Cash ($ mil.): 20
Current ratio: —
Long-term debt ($ mil.): —

No. of shares (mil.): 10
Dividends
Yield: 0.0%
Payout: 58.5%
Market value ($ mil.): 295

	STOCK PRICE ($) FY Close	P/E High/Low		PER SHARE ($) Earnings	Dividends	Book Value
12/17	27.23	18	14	1.81	1.06	16.74
12/16	33.10	20	11	1.66	0.90	15.98
12/15	20.47	15	11	1.51	0.86	15.58
12/14	18.09	13	11	1.37	0.83	15.06
12/13	17.42	15	13	1.20	0.78	13.69
Annual Growth	**11.8%**	**—**	**—**	**10.8%**	**8.0%**	**5.2%**

First Bancshares Inc (MS)

EXECUTIVES

Vice President, Kevin Miller
Vice President, Ken Kennedy
Auditors: Crowe Horwath LLP

LOCATIONS

HQ: First Bancshares Inc (MS)
6480 U.S. Highway 98 West, Suite A, Hattiesburg, MS 39402
Phone: 601 268-8998
Web: www.thefirstbank.com

COMPETITORS

BancorpSouth	Peoples Financial
Community Bancshares of Mississippi	Renasant
	Trustmark
Hancock Holding	

HISTORICAL FINANCIALS

Company Type: Public

Income Statement

FYE: December 31

	ASSETS ($ mil.)	NET INCOME ($ mil.)	INCOME AS % OF ASSETS	EMPLOYEES
12/17	1,813	10	0.6%	487
12/16	1,277	10	0.8%	315
12/15	1,145	8	0.8%	305
12/14	1,093	6	0.6%	278
12/13	940	4	0.5%	266
Annual Growth	**17.8%**	**23.0%**	**—**	**16.3%**

2017 Year-End Financials

Debt ratio: 1.45%
Return on equity: 5.63%
Cash ($ mil.): 91
Current ratio: —
Long-term debt ($ mil.): —

No. of shares (mil.): 11
Dividends
Yield: 0.0%
Payout: 13.5%
Market value ($ mil.): 382

	STOCK PRICE ($) FY Close	P/E High/Low		PER SHARE ($) Earnings	Dividends	Book Value
12/17	34.20	31	24	1.11	0.15	19.92
12/16	27.50	15	8	1.64	0.15	17.19
12/15	18.34	11	8	1.62	0.15	19.24
12/14	14.51	12	11	1.25	0.15	18.10
12/13	14.02	16	9	1.06	0.15	16.70
Annual Growth	**25.0%**	**—**	**—**	**1.2%**	**(0.0%)**	**4.5%**

First Bank (Williamstown, NJ)

EXECUTIVES

Coo, Ryan K Manville
Vice President Compliance And Cra Officer, Luisa Franco
Auditors: RSM US LLP

LOCATIONS

HQ: First Bank (Williamstown, NJ)
2465 Kuser Road, Hamilton, NJ 08690
Phone: 609 643-4211
Web: www.FirstBankNJ.com

HISTORICAL FINANCIALS

Company Type: Public

Income Statement

FYE: December 31

	ASSETS ($ mil.)	NET INCOME ($ mil.)	INCOME AS % OF ASSETS	EMPLOYEES
12/17	1,452	6	0.5%	153
12/16	1,073	6	0.6%	110
12/15	855	3	0.5%	101
12/14	677	5	0.9%	96
12/13	466	1	0.4%	60
Annual Growth	**32.8%**	**42.2%**	**—**	**26.4%**

2017 Year-End Financials

Debt ratio: 1.50%
Return on equity: 5.55%
Cash ($ mil.): 47
Current ratio: —
Long-term debt ($ mil.): —

No. of shares (mil.): 17
Dividends
Yield: 0.0%
Payout: 16.6%
Market value ($ mil.): 242

	STOCK PRICE ($) FY Close	P/E High/Low		PER SHARE ($) Earnings	Dividends	Book Value
12/17	13.85	30	23	0.48	0.08	9.36
12/16	11.60	20	10	0.61	0.00	7.78
12/15	6.61	17	14	0.41	0.00	7.26
12/14	6.24	11	9	0.63	0.00	6.88
12/13	6.34	20	15	0.33	0.00	6.16
Annual Growth	**21.6%**	**—**	**—**	**9.8%**	**—**	**11.0%**

First Busey Corp

First Busey Corporation keeps itself busy taking care of deposits and making loans. It's the holding company for Busey Bank which boasts $4 billion in assets and 40 branches across Illinois Florida and Indiana. The bank offers standard deposit products and services using funds from deposits to originate primarily real estate loans and mortgages. Subsidiary Busey Wealth Management which manages $5 billion in assets provides asset management trust brokerage and related services to individuals businesses and foundations while FirsTech provides retail payment processing services. Most of Busey Bank's branches are located in downstate Illinois.

Operations

First Busey Corporation operates three business segments Busey Bank which generated more than 99% of its total revenue in 2014 and serves retail and corporate customers; FirsTech which provides remittance processing for online bill payments lock box and walk-in payments; and Busey Wealth Management which provides asset management tax preparation philanthropic advisory services and investment and fiduciary services to individuals businesses and foundations.

Real estate loans including commercial and residential mortgages accounted for 70% of the bank's loan portfolio in 2014 while commercial loans (25%) construction loans (4%) and consumer installments and other loans (0.5%) comprised the rest.

About 55% of First Busey's total revenue came from loan interest (including fees) while another 10% came from interest income on taxable and non-taxable investment securities. The rest of its revenue came from trust fees (11%) deposit account service charges (7%) remittance processing fees (6%) commissions and brokers' fees (2%) and various types of gains on securities and loan sales.

Geographic Reach

Busey Bank has nearly 30 branches in Illinois seven locations in southwest Florida and another office in Indianapolis. Its FirsTech subsidiary accepts payments from its 3000 agent locations across 36 US states.

Sales and Marketing

The bank which staffed 801 employees at the end of 2014 serves individuals businesses and foundations.

Financial Performance

First Busey's revenues have declined in recent years due to shrinking interest margins on loans amidst the low-interest environment. Its profits however have been rising thanks to lower interest expenses on deposits and declining loan loss provisions as its loan portfolio's credit quality has improved with higher property valuations in the strengthened economy.

The bank's revenue dipped by 2% to $167 million mostly as it collected smaller gains from loan sales due to lower refinancing volumes as interest rates began to rise. The bank's loan interest income also continued to decline with lower yields on loan and security assets in the low-interest environment.

Despite generating less revenue in 2014 First Busey's net income jumped by 14% to $32.8 million thanks to continued declines in interest expenses on deposits and lower loan loss provisions. The company's operating cash levels fell by 31% to $68.1 million after adjusting its earnings for non-cash items related to its net proceeds from its loans held-for-sale.

Strategy

First Busey sometimes strategically acquires smaller banks in its target markets to boost its market share broaden its service offerings and boost its loan and deposit business.

Mergers and Acquisitions

In December 2015 First Busey Corporation expanded into Missouri for the first time after it agreed to buy Pulaski Financial Corporation—along with its $1.5 billion in assets (including $1.3 billion in loans $1.1 billion in deposits) and 13 Pulaski Bank branches in the St. Louis metro area — for around $210.7 million.

In January 2015 First Busey boosted its market share in Illinois after purchasing Pekin-based Herget Financial and its three Herget Bank branches in the area. The $34.1 million-deal extended Busey Bank's presence in Pekin and the greater Peoria market added Herget Financials "dominant" deposit market position in its community and bolstered its service offerings with trust estate and asset management services as well as competitive commercial loan and mortgage offerings.

EXECUTIVES

Evp And Chief Risk Officer, Barbara J. Harrington, age 58

President Ceo And Director, Van A. Dukeman, age 59, $537,308 total compensation

Chief Credit Officer, Robert F. (Bob) Plecki, age 57, $268,654 total compensation

President And Ceo Firstech, Howard F. Mooney, age 53, $240,216 total compensation

Evp And Regional President Busey Bank, Christopher M. (Chris) Shroyer, age 52, $268,654 total compensation

Evp And General Counsel, John J. Powers

Coo And Cfo, Robin N. Elliott, $256,731 total compensation

Assistant Vice President Advisor Wealth Busey Wealth Management, Melissa Hendricks

Vice President Senior Retirement Plan Services Advisor, Charlee Seaton

Assistant Vice President Special Assets, Shana Reed-harper

Executive Vice President Managing Director Busey Wealth Management, Mark Wisniewski

Senior Vice President, Cheryl Chisholm

Vice President Retail Market Manager, Tami Crouch

Assistant Vice President Risk Management Analyst, Annie Feleccia

Senior Vice President Relationship Manager, David Bealke

Vice President Senior Mortgage Originator, Kent Hackstadt

Vice President, Briggett Carter

Assistant Vice President Wealth Advisor Assistant, Monya Russell

Vice President Mortgage Operations Manager, Kevin Hoogeveen

Assistant Vice President Wire Services Manager, Karen Aulph

Senior Vice President Cash Management Executive, Brian Hintz

Assistant Vice President, Valerie Garrett

Senior Vice President, Harry Mcsteen

Vice President Commercial Lending, Ross Rotherham

President Ceo And Director, Van A. Dukeman, age 59

Chairman, Gregory B. (Greg) Lykins, age 70

Auditors: RSM US LLP

LOCATIONS

HQ: First Busey Corp
100 W. University Ave., Champaign, IL 61820
Phone: 217 365-4544
Web: www.busey.com

PRODUCTS/OPERATIONS

2014 Sales

	$ mil.	% of total
Interest		
Loans including fees	92	55
Interest & dividends on securities	15	10
Noninterest		
Trust fees	19	11
Service charges on deposit accounts	12	7
Remittance processing	9	6
Gain on sales of loans	4	3
Commissions and broker's fees net	2	2
Other	10	6
Total	**167**	**100**

COMPETITORS

Bank of America	First Midwest Bancorp
CIB Marine Bancshares	JPMorgan Chase
Fifth Third	Mercantile Bancorp
First Mid-Illinois	PNC Financial
Bancshares	Wintrust Financial

HISTORICAL FINANCIALS

Company Type: Public

Income Statement
FYE: December 31

	ASSETS ($ mil.)	NET INCOME ($ mil.)	INCOME AS % OF ASSETS	EMPLOYEES
12/17	7,860	62	0.8%	1,347
12/16	5,425	49	0.9%	1,295
12/15	3,998	39	1.0%	795
12/14	3,665	32	0.9%	801
12/13	3,539	28	0.8%	849
Annual Growth	**22.1%**	**21.6%**	**—**	**12.2%**

2017 Year-End Financials

Debt ratio: 2.23%	No. of shares (mil.): 48
Return on equity: 8.20%	Dividends
Cash ($ mil.): 353	Yield: 0.0%
Current ratio: —	Payout: 49.6%
Long-term debt ($ mil.): —	Market value ($ mil.): 1,458

	STOCK PRICE ($) FY Close	P/E High/Low		Earnings	Dividends	Book Value
12/17	29.94	22	19	1.45	0.72	19.21
12/16	30.78	22	13	1.40	0.68	15.54
12/15	20.63	17	5	1.32	0.17	13.01
12/14	6.51	6	5	1.11	0.57	14.98
12/13	5.80	7	5	0.87	0.36	14.36
Annual Growth	**50.7%**	**—**	**—**	**13.6%**	**18.9%**	**7.5%**

First Business Financial Services, Inc.

Business comes first at First Business Financial Services which serves small and midsized companies entrepreneurs professionals and high-networth individuals through First Business Bank and First Business Bank - Milwaukee. The banks offer deposits loans cash management and trust services from a handful of offices in Wisconsin and Kansas. Over 60% of the company's loan portfolio is made up of commercial real estate loans. Subsidiary First Business Capital specializes in asset-based lending while First Business Equipment Finance provides commercial equipment financing. First Business Trust & Investments offers investment management and retirement services.

Operations

First Business Financial Services backs its subsidiaries with low-cost corporate services such as human resources finance IT and marketing. First Business Credit Cards provides revolving lines of credit and term loans for financial and strategic acquisitions capital expenditures working capital used to support rapid growth bank debt refinancing debt restructuring and other corporate financing needs.

The company generated 80% of its total revenue from interest on loans and leases in 2014 and another 5% from interest on its securities. About 7% of revenue came from trust and investment services fee income while service charges on deposits and loan fees made up 4% and 2% of revenue respectively.

Geographic Reach

The company's primary market areas are in Wisconsin Kansas and Missouri. First Business's loan production offices are in Wisconsin in Oshkosh Green Bay Appleton and Kenosha while its two Kansas offices are in Leawood and Overland Park. In Wisconsin it targets Madison Milwaukee Appleton Green Bay Oshkosh and their surrounding communities.

Sales and Marketing

Beyond individual customers the bank generally targets businesses with annual sales between $2 million and $75 million.

Financial Performance

The company has struggled to consistently grow its revenues in recent years due to shrinking interest margins on loans amidst the low-interest environment. Its profits however have been rising thanks to declining loan loss provisions as its loan portfolio's credit quality has improved with higher property valuations in a strengthened economy.

First Business had a breakout year in 2014 however as its revenue rose 9% to $67.8 million on higher loan interest as its commercial and industrial loans comercial real estate and other mortgage loans and direct financing leases businesses all enjoyed "favorable volume variances." The bank's non-interest income also jumped by 20% which was mostly driven by growth in trust and investment services fee income on higher assets under management.

Higher revenue and lower interest expenses on deposits in 2014 pushed the company's net income up by 3% to $14.1 million. First Business' operating cash levels fell by 25% to $11.9 million due to unfavorable changes in working capital related to an increase in accrued interest payable and other liabilities.

Strategy

First Business Financial Services continued in 2015 to focus on maintaining its loan asset quality while organically growing its loan and lease portfolio in addition to growing its customer account based to increase its fee-based revenues on its variety of treasury management trust and investment services and SBA loans. It also planned to boost its investment in utilizing technology to support these initiatives while staying efficient as the business grows.

The company occasionally opens new offices or strategically acquires other banks and financial companies to extend its reach into its target markets and to grow its loan and deposit business. In 2014 its FBB-Milwaukee bank subisidary expanded more into the southeastern area of Wisconsin after opening a loan production office in Kenosha; while its acquisition of Aslin Group and Alterra Bank furthered its exposure to new markets and loan and deposit business in Kansas.

Mergers and Acquisitions

In November 2014 First Business Financial Services expanded its Midwest market and extended its reach into Kansas after its acquisition of Leawood-based Aslin Group including its Alterra Bank subsidiary. The deal added $223 million in total assets including $182 million in new loan assets and $192 million in new deposits.

EXECUTIVES

President And Ceo, Corey A. Chambas, age 55, $416,000 total compensation
Svp And Chief Credit Officer, Michael J. Losenegger, age 60, $221,950 total compensation
President And Ceo First Business Capital, Charles H. (Chuck) Batson, age 64, $242,927 total compensation
President And Ceo First Business Bank - Madison, Mark J. Meloy, age 56, $201,800 total compensation
President First Business Trust & Investments, Joan A. Burke, age 66
President And Ceo First Business Bank - Milwaukee, David J. (Dave) Vetta, age 63
Cfo, Edward G. (Ed) Sloane, age 57
President Kenosha Region, Wesley Ricchio
Svp And Coo First Business Capital Corp., Peter Lowney
Coo And Interim President And Ceo Alterra Bank, David R. Seiler
Cio, Daniel S. Ovokaitys, age 44
Vice President Business Development, Tom Rude
Vice President Operations Manager First Business Factors, Jorge Varela
Vice President, Cymbre Van Fossen
Vice President, Josh Hoesch
Assistant Vice President Treasury Management, Wade Hanna
Vice President Business Development, Greg Lherault
Vice President, Mark Buchert
Vice President Private Wealth Management, Monica Schlicht
Senior Vice President, Bill Blenderman
Vice President Business Development Officer, Chris Mckernan
Vice President Business Development Officer, Jay Peterson
Vice President Internal Loan Review, Gretchen Griffin
Vice President, Nancy Johnshoy
Assistant Vice President Treasury Management, Laura Shoemaker
Vice President Commercial Banking, Jessica Meier
Chairman, Jerome R. (Jerry) Smith, age 67
Board Member, Jim Hartlieb
Auditors: KPMG LLP

LOCATIONS

HQ: First Business Financial Services, Inc.
401 Charmany Drive, Madison, WI 53719
Phone: 608 238-8008
Web: www.firstbusiness.com

COMPETITORS

Associated Banc-Corp	TCF Financial
Bank Mutual	U.S. Bancorp
Harris	

HISTORICAL FINANCIALS

Company Type: Public

Income Statement   FYE: December 31

	ASSETS ($ mil.)	NET INCOME ($ mil.)	INCOME AS % OF ASSETS	EMPLOYEES
12/17	1,794	11	0.7%	264
12/16	1,780	14	0.8%	272
12/15	1,782	16	0.9%	258
12/14	1,629	14	0.9%	231
12/13	1,268	13	1.1%	164
Annual Growth	9.0%	(3.5%)	—	12.6%

2017 Year-End Financials

Debt ratio: 12.15%
Return on equity: 7.19%
Cash ($ mil.): 52
Current ratio: —
Long-term debt ($ mil.): —

No. of shares (mil.): 8
Dividends
  Yield: 0.0%
  Payout: 38.2%
Market value ($ mil.): 194

	STOCK PRICE ($) FY Close	P/E High/Low	PER SHARE ($) Earnings	Dividends	Book Value
12/17	22.12	21 15	1.36	0.52	19.32
12/16	23.72	15 11	1.71	0.48	18.55
12/15	25.01	25 12	1.90	0.44	17.34
12/14	47.91	28 21	1.76	0.42	15.88
12/13	37.63	22 13	1.75	0.32	13.85
Annual Growth	(12.4%)	— —	(6.0%)	13.4%	8.7%

First Citizens BancShares Inc (NC)

First Citizens BancShares owns First-Citizens Bank which operates more than 550 branches in 20 states mainly in the southeastern and western US and urban areas scattered nationwide. The $32 billion-asset bank provides standard services such as deposits loans mortgages and trust services in addition to processing and operational support to other banks. Real estate loans including commercial residential and revolving mortgages and construction and land development loans comprise most of its loan portfolio. Subsidiaries First Citizens Investor Services First Citizens Securities Corporation and First Citizens Asset Management offers investment and discount brokerage services to bank clients.

Operations

The company provides consumer business and commercial banking wealth investments and insurance through a network of branch offices internet banking mobile banking telephone banking and ATMs.

More than 60% of the bank's total revenue came from loan and lease interest during 2015 while another 6% came from interest income on investment securities. The rest of its revenue came from merchant services (6% of revenue) service charges on deposit accounts (6%) wealth management services (6%) cardholder services (4%) mortgage income (1%) insurance commissions (1%) and other miscellaneous income sources.

Geographic Reach

First Citizens BancShares has nearly 560 branches in almost 20 states (Arizona California Colorado Florida Georgia Kansas Maryland Missouri New Mexico North Carolina Oklahoma Oregon South Carolina Tennessee Texas Virginia Washington and West Virginia) and Washington DC.

Sales and Marketing

First Citizens BancShares serves both individuals and commercial entities operating in the healthcare dental practices legal services property management agribusiness nonprofit and trade association markets.

The bank has been ramping up its advertising spend in recent years. It spent $12.4 million in 2015 up from $11.4 million and $8.2 million in 2014 and 2013 respectively.

Financial Performance

First Citizens BancShares' annual revenues have risen more than 35% since 2013 thanks to growth in its variety of non-banking business. Its profits have also been trending higher thanks to declining loan loss provisions as its loan portfolio's credit quality has improved with higher property valuations in the strengthened economy.

The bank's revenue jumped 30% to $1.44 billion during 2015 mostly thanks to higher loan and lease interest income stemming from added loan business from the acquisition of First Citizens Bancorporation. Its non-interest income sources grew 36% during the year as well.

Strong revenue growth in 2015 drove First Citizen's net income up 52% to $210.3 million. The bank's operating cash levels rose 28% to $233 million with the rise in cash-based earnings.

Strategy

FCB has expanded its branch network into new markets while bolstering its loan and deposit business by acquiring small community banks in new territory.

Mergers and Acquisitions

In May 2016 the bank made an agreement with the FDIC to buy select assets and liabilities of First Cornerstone Bank of King of Prussia in Pennsylvania. It made a similar FDIC transaction to buy North Milwaukee State Bank in March 2016. Later that year the company acquired Cordia Bancorp and its six-branch subsidiary Bank of Virginia.

In February 2015 also through the FDIC First Citizens bought select assets and deposits of Capitol City Bank & Trust (CCBT) expanding into Georgia with eight branches in Atlanta Albany Augusta Stone Mountain and Savannah.

In January 2015 First Citizens BancShares expanded its loan business and expanded into South Carolina after buying First Citizens Bancorporation and its subsidiary First Citizens Bank and Trust Company.

Company Background

First Citizens BancShares has been fortifying its presence along the West Coast by snapping up failed financial institutions. Since 2009 it has acquired most of the banking operations of Temecula Valley Bank Washington-based Venture Bank and First Regional Bank in Southern California. It also acquired the failed Florida-based bank Sun American and entered Colorado through the acquisitions of United Western Bank and Colorado Capital Bank. All were FDIC-assisted transactions and each acquired institution became branches of First-Citizens Bank. The deals added about 50 branches to the bank's network. First Citizens BancShares continues to seek out acquisitions of other seized institutions.

Though the company has been able to grow geographically thanks to the economic downturn its IronStone Bank division which focused on business customers suffered from weakened markets in Florida and Georgia. (First Citizens Bancshares merged IronStone into First-Citizens Bank in 2011 to increase efficiency and unify the company's brand.) It has remained profitable thanks in part to its acquisitions which include loss-sharing agreements with the FDIC but has had to increase its provisions for loan losses each of the last five years.

The Holding family which occupies several positions in the company's board room and executive suite controls First Citizens BancShares.

EXECUTIVES

Coo Bancshares And First-citizens Bank & Trust Company, Edward L. (Ed) Willingham, age 63, $585,125 total compensation
President And Corporate Sales Executive Of Bancshares And First-citizens Bank & Trust Company, Peter M. Bristow, age 52

Chairman And Ceo First Citizens Bancshares First-citizens Bank & Trust And Ironstone Bank, Frank B. Holding, age 57, $902,875 total compensation
Evp Finance And Cfo, Craig L. Nix, age 46
Evp Business Banking Segment Manager And Director First-citizens Bank & Trust; President Ironstone Bank, Hope Holding Connell, age 55, $563,750 total compensation
Chief Human Resources Officer; Executive Vice President Of Fcb, Lou J. Davis, age 65
Evp And Chief Credit Officer First-citizens Bank & Trust; Group Vp And Chief Credit Officer Ironstone, Ricky T. Holland, age 64
Executive Vice President And General Auditor Of Fcb, Donald Preskenis
Vice President, Rhonda Chapman
Vice President Marketing, Christine Thompson
Vice President, Scott German
Assistant Vice President Of Information Technology, Kim Whalen
Vice President Commercial Banking, Drew Schiavone
Chairman And Ceo First Citizens Bancshares First-citizens Bank & Trust And Ironstone Bank, Frank B. Holding, age 57
Executive Vice Chairman First Citizens Bancshares And First-citizens Bank & Trust, Frank B. Holding, age 57
Evp Business Banking Segment Manager And Director First-citizens Bank & Trust; President Ironstone Bank, Hope Holding Connell, age 55
Auditors: Dixon Hughes Goodman LLP

LOCATIONS

HQ: First Citizens BancShares Inc (NC)
4300 Six Forks Road, Raleigh, NC 27609
Phone: 919 716-7000
Web: www.firstcitizens.com

2013 Branches

	No.
North Carolina	253
Virginia	48
California	21
Florida	18
Georgia	14
Washington	7
Texas	7
Colorado	6
Tennessee	6
West Virginia	5
Arizona	2
New Mexico	2
Oklahoma	2
Oregon	2
District of Columbia	1
Kanas	1
Maryland	1
Missouri	1
Total	**397**

PRODUCTS/OPERATIONS

2013 Sales

	$ mil.	% of total
Interest		
Loans & leases	757	72
Investment securities including dividends	36	3
Overnight investments	2	-
Noninterest		
Service charges on deposit accounts	60	5
Wealth management services	59	5
Merchant services	56	4
Cardholder services	48	4
Fees from processing services	22	1
Other service charges and fees	15	1
Adjustments	(72.3)	-
Other	72	5
Total	**1,060**	**100**

COMPETITORS

BB&T	JPMorgan Chase
BBVA Compass Bancshares	PNC Financial
Bank of America	Regions Financial
Capital One	SunTrust
Citibank	Synovus
First Horizon	Wachovia Corp
	Wells Fargo

HISTORICAL FINANCIALS

Company Type: Public

Income Statement

FYE: December 31

	ASSETS ($ mil.)	NET INCOME ($ mil.)	INCOME AS % OF ASSETS	EMPLOYEES
12/17	34,527	323	0.9%	6,799
12/16	32,990	225	0.7%	6,296
12/15	31,475	210	0.7%	6,232
12/14	30,075	138	0.5%	6,440
12/13	21,199	167	0.8%	4,875
Annual Growth	**13.0%**	**17.9%**	**—**	**8.7%**

2017 Year-End Financials

Debt ratio: 2.56%	No. of shares (mil.): 12
Return on equity: 10.20%	Dividends
Cash ($ mil.): 1,724	Yield: 0.0%
Current ratio: —	Payout: 4.6%
Long-term debt ($ mil.): —	Market value ($ mil.): 4,840

	STOCK PRICE ($) FY Close	P/E High/Low	PER SHARE ($) Earnings	Dividends	Book Value
12/17	403.00	16 12	26.96	1.25	277.60
12/16	355.00	19 12	18.77	1.20	250.82
12/15	258.17	15 12	17.52	1.20	239.14
12/14	252.79	20 16	13.56	1.20	223.77
12/13	222.63	13 9	17.43	1.20	215.89
Annual Growth	**16.0%**	**— —**	**11.5%**	**1.0%**	**6.5%**

First Commonwealth Financial Corp (Indiana, PA)

First Commonwealth Financial is the holding company for First Commonwealth Bank which provides consumer and commercial banking services from nearly 115 branches across 15 central and western Pennsylvania counties as well as in Columbus Ohio. The bank's loan portfolio mostly consists of commercial and industrial loans including real estate operating agricultural and construction loans. It also issues consumer loans such as education automobile and home equity loans and offers wealth management insurance financial planning retail brokerage and trust services. The company has total assets of some $6.7 billion with deposits of roughly $4.5 billion.

Operations

The bank made 65% of its total revenue from interest and fees on loans in 2014 while another 12% came from interest and dividends on its investments. Another 6% of First Commonwealth's revenue came from service charges on deposit accounts while trust income and insurance and retail brokerage commissions each made up 2% of the bank's total revenue.

Geographic Reach

The bank boasts nearly 115 branch offices in western and central Pennsylvania and Columbus Ohio. It also has loan production offices in downtown Pittsburgh Pennsylvania and Cleveland Ohio.

Sales and Marketing

First Commonwealth Financial spent $2.95 million on advertising in 2014 compared to $3.13 million and $4.16 million in 2013 and 2012 respectively.

Financial Performance

First Commonwealth's revenues have been slowly decline over the past few years due to shrinking interest margins on loans amidst the low-interest environment. The firm's profits however have been rising thanks to declining loan loss provisions as its loan portfolio's credit quality has been improving in the strengthening economy.

The bank's revenue dipped by more than 1% to $263.04 million in 2014 mostly as interest margins on loans continued to decline as it issued new loans with lower rates in the low-interest environment.

Despite lower revenue in 2014 the bank's net income jumped by 7% to $44.45 million for the year mostly thanks to further decreases in loan loss provisions with a strengthening credit portfolio and lower interest expenses on deposits. First Commonwealth's operating cash fell by 4% to $82.14 million despite higher earnings mostly as the bank collected less in cash proceeds from the sales of its mortgage loans held for sale.

Strategy

First Commonwealth Financial has historically expanded its branch reach through the acquisition smaller banks and thrifts in its market area. However in recent years the company has also been adding non-banking businesses such as insurance firms to bolster its existing non-banking service lines.

Mergers and Acquisitions

First Commonwealth Bank acquired 13 branches in Canton and Ashtabula Ohio from FirstMerit Bank in 2016. The acquisition related to FirstMerit's acquisition by Huntington Bancshares added some $735 million in deposits and some 34000 customers. It is also buying Ohio's DCB Financial parent company of Delaware County Bank & Trust for some $106 million. That deal will add nine full-service branches in central Ohio.

In 2014 First Commonwealth Bank entered the Columbus Ohio market for the first time with its purchase of the Ohio-based First Community Bank for $14.75 million cash.

Also in 2014 the bank bolstered its insurance business through its acquisition of Thompson/McLay Insurance Associates which boasted long-term client relationships in the home auto commercial and specialty insurance lines. The deal added the insurance firm's experienced sales and account management personnel as well as the popular Thompson/McLay Insurance Associates brand which it would keep as a division of its own insurance agency.

EXECUTIVES

Evp And Chief Revenue Officer, Jane Grebenc, $355,833 total compensation

Evp And Chief Credit Officer, I. Robert (Bob) Emmerich, $274,500 total compensation

President And Ceo, Thomas Michael (Mike) Price, age 55, $435,567 total compensation

Evp Cfo And Treasurer, James R. Reske, $237,372 total compensation

Evp And Chief Audit Executive, Leonard V. Lombardi, age 58

Evp Business Integration, Norman J. Montgomery, $261,792 total compensation

Evp Chief Risk Officer General Counsel And Secretary, Matthew C. (Matt) Tomb
Evp Human Resources, Carrie Riggle
Assistant Vice President, Kris Levan
Vice President Administration, Wendy Reynolds
Vice President, Kevin Cribbs
Senior Vice President And Senior Operations Audit Manager, John M Heise
Vice President, Chuck Bennett
Vice President And Office Manager Of Murrysville And Export Offices, John Mango
Vice President And Commercial Real Estate, Brian Pukylo
Vice President Cash Management Services, Michael Thomas
Assistant Vice President Operations, Mona Straw
Vice President And Commercial Real Estate, Brian Pukylo
Vice President Office Manager Ii, David Louis
Executive Vice President, David Buckiso
Senior Vice President Relationship Manager, David McGowan
Assistant Vice President Benefits Administration, Natalie Felix
Assistant Vice President Office Manager, Jody Shepler
Senior Vice President Internal Audit, Steven Melletz
Business Banker Vice President, Susan Henigin
Executive Vice President Chief Credit Officer, Brian Karrip
Vice President Senior Corporate Banker First Commonwealth Bank, Matthew Zuro
Senior Vice President Corporate Banking, Joe Hynds
Senior Vice President Senior Treasury Managment Officer, Valarry Frymoyer
Senior Vice President Commercial Banking, Mary Patton
Assistant Vice President And Foreclosure Oreo Officer, Mark Oresick
Chairman, David S. (Dave) Dahlmann, age 68
Evp Chief Risk Officer General Counsel And Secretary, Matthew C. (Matt) Tomb
Auditors: KPMG LLP

LOCATIONS

HQ: First Commonwealth Financial Corp (Indiana, PA)
601 Philadelphia Street, Indiana, PA 15701
Phone: 724 349-7220
Web: www.fcbanking.com

PRODUCTS/OPERATIONS

2014 Sales

	$ mil.	% of total
Interest		
Loans including fees	171	65
Taxable investments	31	12
Noninterest		
Service charges on deposit accounts	15	7
Insurance & retail brokerage commissions	6	2
Trust income	6	2
Others	32	12
Total	**263**	**100**

Selected Subsidiaries

First Commonwealth Bank
  First Commonwealth Insurance Agency
  First Commonwealth Home Mortgage LLC (49.9%)
First Commonwealth Financial Advisors Incorporated

COMPETITORS

Allegheny Valley Bancorp	F.N.B. (PA)
AmeriServ Financial	Fidelity Bancorp (PA)
Citizens Financial Group	Northwest Bancshares
Dollar Bank	PNC Financial
	S&T Bancorp

HISTORICAL FINANCIALS

Company Type: Public

Income Statement

FYE: December 31

	ASSETS ($ mil.)	NET INCOME ($ mil.)	INCOME AS % OF ASSETS	EMPLOYEES
12/17	7,308	55	0.8%	1,476
12/16	6,684	59	0.9%	1,376
12/15	6,566	50	0.8%	1,311
12/14	6,360	44	0.7%	1,363
12/13	6,214	41	0.7%	1,437
Annual Growth	4.1%	7.4%	—	0.7%

2017 Year-End Financials

Debt ratio: 1.09%	No. of shares (mil.): 97
Return on equity: 6.74%	Dividends
Cash ($ mil.): 107	Yield: 0.0%
Current ratio: —	Payout: 55.1%
Long-term debt ($ mil.): —	Market value ($ mil.): 1,396

	STOCK PRICE ($) FY Close	P/E High/Low	PER SHARE ($) Earnings	Dividends	Book Value
12/17	14.32	26 21	0.58	0.32	9.11
12/16	14.18	21 12	0.67	0.28	8.43
12/15	9.07	18 14	0.56	0.28	8.09
12/14	9.22	20 16	0.48	0.28	7.81
12/13	8.82	22 16	0.43	0.23	7.47
Annual Growth	12.9%	— —	7.8%	8.6%	5.1%

First Community Bankshares Inc (VA)

First Community Bancshares doesn't play second fiddle to other area banks. The firm is the holding company for First Community Bank which provides traditional services like checking and savings accounts CDs and credit cards and serves communities through some 55 branches across Virginia West Virginia North Carolina and Tennessee. Commercial real estate loans make up 45% of its loan portfolio while commercial business loans make up another 5%. First Community Bancshares offers insurance through subsidiary Greenpoint Insurance and wealth management and investment advisory services through Trust Services and First Community Wealth Management.

Operations

First Community Bancshares operates through four main business activities: commercial and consumer banking lending activities wealth management and insurance services. Its Trust Services and First Community Wealth Management subsidiary had managed assets with a market value of nearly $700 million in 2014.

The bank which had a staff of 678 employees at the end of 2014 generated 70% of its total revenue from loan interest (including fees and loans held for investment) in 2014 and another 8% from interest on taxable and non-taxable securities. The rest of its revenue came from deposit account service charges (9%) insurance commissions (4%) wealth management (1%) and other miscellaneous sources of income.

Sales and Marketing

The bank serves individuals and businesses across several industries including: manufacturing mining services construction retail healthcare military and transportation.

Financial Performance

The company has struggled to grow its revenues in recent years due to shrinking interest margins on loans amidst the low-interest environment. Its profits however have been rising thanks to falling interest expenses and declining loan loss provisions as its loan portfolio's credit quality has improved with higher property valuations in the strengthened economy.

First Community Bancshares's revenue dipped by 2% to $136.1 million in 2014 as its interest income on loans and securities declined with fewer assets and because it took on a $1.39 million loss from the sale of its investment securities during the year.

Despite revenue declines in 2014 the bank's net income jumped 9% to $25.5 million thanks to continued declines in interest expenses on deposits and loan loss provisions. First Community's operating cash levels fell by 6% to $41.7 million for the year after adjusting its earnings for non-cash items related to its loan loss provisions and the proceeds of its mortgage loan sales.

Strategy

Faced with shrinking revenues in recent years First Community has been strategically changing its geographic positioning selling off some of its branches in certain areas and acquiring new branches in others. In late 2014 it acquired seven branches from Bank of America in Southwestern Virginia and Central North Carolina and sold 13 of its branches to Charleston-based CresCom Bank including 10 of its branches in Southeastern North Carolina and three in South Carolina.

Mergers and Acquisitions

In 2014 First Community purchased seven branches from Bank of America including six branches in Southwestern Virginia and one in Central North Carolina. The deal also added $318.9 million in new deposits as well as real estate and assumed leases associated with the branches.

Company Background

After slowing its acquisition activity during the economic downturn First Community resumed in 2012 buying Peoples Bank of Virginia which added four branches in the Richmond area. The company also acquired the failed Waccamaw Bank in a FDIC-facilitated transaction. That deal brought in 16 branches in North Carolina.

EXECUTIVES

Evp And Coo, E. Stephen (Steve) Lilly, age 59, $252,000 total compensation

Chairman And Ceo, William P. Stafford, age 54, $200,013 total compensation

Cfo, David D. Brown, age 43, $225,000 total compensation

President; Ceo First Community Bank, Gary R. Mills, $300,000 total compensation

President First Community Bank, Martyn A. Pell, $255,000 total compensation

Vice President Director Of Operations, Garry Stutts

Senior Vice President Chief Risk Officer And Secretary Of First Community Bank, Jason Belcher

Assistant Vice President Credit Administration, Jeff Noble

Senior Vice President Market President, Mark Evans

Senior Vice President On The Corporate Staff, John Spracher

Vice President And Sales And Service Leader, Brad Ferguson

Vice President, Robert Partrea

Vice President, Adam Jante

Vice Chairman, William P. Stafford, age 54

Chairman And Ceo, William P. Stafford, age 54

Auditors: Dixon Hughes Goodman LLP

LOCATIONS

HQ: First Community Bankshares Inc (VA)
P.O. Box 989, Bluefield, VA 24605-0989
Phone: 276 326-9000
Web: www.firstcommunitybank.com

PRODUCTS/OPERATIONS

2011 Sales

	$ mil.	% of total
Interest		
Loans including fees	80	61
Securities	13	10
Deposits in banks	0	-
Noninterest		
Service charges on deposit accounts	13	10
Insurance commissions	6	5
Net gains on sales of securities	5	4
Wealth management	3	3
Other service charges commissions & fees	5	4
Other	3	3
Adjustments	(2.3)	-
Total	**129**	**100**

COMPETITORS

BB&T	Huntington Bancshares
Bank of America	SunTrust
City Holding	United Bankshares
First Citizens	WesBanco
BancShares	
Highlands Bankshares	
Inc.	

HISTORICAL FINANCIALS

Company Type: Public

Income Statement

FYE: December 31

	ASSETS ($ mil.)	NET INCOME ($ mil.)	INCOME AS % OF ASSETS	EMPLOYEES
12/17	2,388	21	0.9%	562
12/16	2,386	25	1.1%	580
12/15	2,462	24	1.0%	673
12/14	2,607	25	1.0%	678
12/13	2,602	23	0.9%	729
Annual Growth	(2.1%)	(2.0%)	—	(6.3%)

2017 Year-End Financials

Debt ratio: —
Return on equity: 6.23%
Cash ($ mil.): 38
Current ratio: —
Long-term debt ($ mil.): —

No. of shares (mil.): 17
Dividends
  Yield: 0.0%
  Payout: 53.9%
Market value ($ mil.): 488

	STOCK PRICE ($) FY Close	P/E High/Low		PER SHARE ($) Earnings	Dividends	Book Value
12/17	28.73	24	19	1.26	0.68	20.63
12/16	30.14	22	12	1.45	0.60	19.95
12/15	18.63	16	11	1.31	0.54	18.95
12/14	16.47	13	10	1.31	0.50	19.09
12/13	16.70	16	13	1.11	0.48	17.75
Annual Growth	14.5%	—	—	3.2%	9.1%	3.8%

First Data Corp (New)

EXECUTIVES

Chb-Ceo, Frank J Bisignano
V Chb, Joseph J Plumeri
Pres, Guy Chiarello
Exec V Pres-Coo, Christine E Larsen
Exec V Pres-Cfo, Himanshu A Patel

Exec V Pres-General Counsel-SE, Adam L Rosman
Human Resources Director, Caroline Dobson
Information Specialist, Duc Nguyen
Director, Gary Breeton
Auditing Manager, Joanne West
Human Resources Manager, Kellie Cordeaux
Auditors: Ernst & Young LLP

LOCATIONS

HQ: First Data Corp (New)
225 Liberty Street, 29th Floor, New York, NY 10281
Phone: 800 735-3362
Web: www.firstdata.com

HISTORICAL FINANCIALS

Company Type: Public

Income Statement

FYE: December 31

	REVENUE ($ mil.)	NET INCOME ($ mil.)	NET PROFIT MARGIN	EMPLOYEES
12/17	12,052	1,465	12.2%	22,000
12/16	11,584	420	3.6%	24,000
12/15	11,451	(1,481)	—	24,000
12/14	11,151	(457)	—	23,000
12/13	10,808	(869)	—	23,000
Annual Growth	2.8%	—		(1.1%)

2017 Year-End Financials

Debt ratio: 39.77%
Return on equity: 67.02%
Cash ($ mil.): 498
Current ratio: 1.00
Long-term debt ($ mil.): 17,927

No. of shares (mil.): 925
Dividends
  Yield: —
  Payout: —
Market value ($ mil.): 15,457

	STOCK PRICE ($) FY Close	P/E High/Low		PER SHARE ($) Earnings	Dividends	Book Value
12/17	16.71	12	9	1.56	0.00	3.41
12/16	14.19	34	18	0.46	0.00	1.34
12/15	16.02	—	—	(7.70)	0.00	0.74
Annual Growth	1.1%	—	—	—	—	46.3%

First Defiance Financial Corp

Named for its hometown not its attitude First Defiance Financial is the holding company for First Federal Bank of the Midwest which operates more than 30 branches serving northwestern Ohio western Indiana and southern Michigan. The thrift offers standard deposit products including checking savings and money market accounts and CDs. Commercial real estate loans account for more than half of the bank's loan portfolio; commercial loans make up another quarter of all loans. The company's insurance agency subsidiary First Insurance Group of the Midwest which accounts for some 7% of the company's revenues provides life insurance property/casualty coverage and investments.

Strategy

First Defiance Financial has boosted its non-banking product lines via acquisitions. It bought the employee benefits insurance business of another local agency Andres O'Neil & Lowe in 2010; and property/casualty agency Payak-Dubbs Insurance Agency in 2011. Both additions became part of First Insurance Group of the Midwest (formerly named First Insurance & Investments).

In 2016 the company agreed to buy another bank serving northwest Ohio Commercial Bancshares. The deal is valued at some $63 million and adds seven branches and $342 million in assets.

EXECUTIVES

Evp Business Banking First Federal Bank, Dennis E. Rose, age 49, $144,077 total compensation

President And Ceo First Defiance Financial And First Federal Bank, Donald P. Hileman, age 65, $400,000 total compensation

Evp General Counsel And Chief Risk Officer First Defiance Financial Corp And First Federal Bank, John R. Reisner, age 62, $180,147 total compensation

Evp And Community Banking President Â– First Federal Bank, Gregory R. Allen, age 54, $200,000 total compensation

Evp And President Western Market Area First Federal Bank, James R. Williams, age 50

Evp And President Eastern Market Area First Federal Bank, Timothy K. (Tim) Harris, age 59

Svp Credit Administration First Federal Bank Of The Midwest, Michael D. Mulford, age 53, $149,387 total compensation

Evp And President Northern Market Area First Federal Bank, Marybeth Shunck, age 48

Evp And Cfo First Defiance Financial Corp. And First Federal Bank, Kent T. Thompson, age 64, $218,360 total compensation

Evp And Director Human Resources First Defiance Financial Corp. And First Federal Bank, Sharon L. Davis, age 36

Evp And President Southern Market Area First Federal Bank, Amy L. Hackenberg, age 47

Vice President, Gary Verhoff

Assistant Vice President Human Resources, Diane Beam

Assistant Vice President, Julie Harris

Senior Vice President, Lisa R Christy

Vice President Senior Accountant, Steve Giesige

Executive Vice President Eastern Market Area President, Tim Harris

Chairman, William J. (Bill) Small, age 67

Vice Chairman, Stephen L. Boomer, age 67

Auditors: Crowe Horwath LLP

LOCATIONS

HQ: First Defiance Financial Corp
601 Clinton Street, Defiance, OH 43512
Phone: 419 782-5015
Web: www.fdef.com

PRODUCTS/OPERATIONS

2016 Sales

	$ mil.	% of total
Interest		
Loans	80	66
Investment securities		
Taxable	3	3
Tax-exempt	3	2
Interest-bearing deposits	0	-
FHLB stock dividends	0	1
Non-interest		
Service fees & other charges	10	9
Insurance commissions	10	9
Mortgage banking income	7	6
Trust income	1	1
Gain on sale of non-mortgage loans	0	1
Income from bank owned life insurance	0	1
Gain on sale or call of securities	0	1
Other	1	1
Total	121	100

COMPETITORS

Farmers National	Huntington Bancshares
Fifth Third	KeyCorp
First Citizens Banc Corp	PNC Financial
First Financial Bancorp	SB Financial Group

HISTORICAL FINANCIALS

Company Type: Public

Income Statement

FYE: December 31

	ASSETS ($ mil.)	NET INCOME ($ mil.)	INCOME AS % OF ASSETS	EMPLOYEES
12/17	2,993	32	1.1%	674
12/16	2,477	28	1.2%	581
12/15	2,297	26	1.2%	586
12/14	2,178	24	1.1%	555
12/13	2,137	22	1.0%	549
Annual Growth	8.8%	9.8%	—	5.3%

2017 Year-End Financials

Debt ratio: 1.21%
Return on equity: 9.69%
Cash ($ mil.): 58
Current ratio: —
Long-term debt ($ mil.): —

No. of shares (mil.): 20
Dividends
  Yield: 0.0%
  Payout: 31.0%
Market value ($ mil.): 1,056

	STOCK PRICE ($) FY Close	P/E High/Low	PER SHARE ($) Earnings	Dividends	Book Value
12/17	51.97	35 29	1.61	0.50	18.38
12/16	50.74	32 22	1.60	0.44	16.31
12/15	37.78	29 21	1.41	0.39	15.39
12/14	34.06	27 19	1.22	0.31	15.13
12/13	25.97	25 17	1.10	0.23	14.00
Annual Growth	18.9%	— —	10.1%	22.1%	7.0%

First Financial Bancorp (OH)

First Financial Bancorp spreads itself thick. The holding company's flagship subsidiary First Financial Bank operates nearly 110 branches in Ohio Indiana and Kentucky. Founded in 1863 the bank offers checking and savings accounts money market accounts CDs credit cards private banking and wealth management services through its First Financial Wealth Management subsidiary. Commercial loans including real estate and construction loans make up more than 50% of First Financial's total loan portfolio; the bank also offers residential mortgage and consumer loans. First Financial Bancorp boasts more than $7 billion in assets including nearly $5 billion in loans.

Operations

The company's private banking business First Financial Wealth Management had $2.4 billion in assets under management in early 2015.

Sales and Marketing

First Financial spent $3.60 million on marketing in 2014 compared to $4.27 million and $5.55 million in 2013 and 2012 respectively.

Financial Performance

First Financial's revenue has been in decline in recent years due to shrinking interest margins on loans amidst the low-interest environment. The company has also struggled to grow its profits much past the $65 million-mark though profit levels are more than twice as high as they were prior to 2009.

The company's revenue dipped by 2% to $311.82 million in 2014 mostly as its loan interest income declined by nearly 4% as interest margins continued to shrink in the low-interest environment. First Financial's non-interest income fell by double-digits mostly due to lower FDIC loss sharing income lower income from the accelerated discount on prepaid covered loans and smaller gains on investment securities sales.

Despite lower revenue in 2014 First Financial's net income rebounded by 34% to $65 million for the year mostly thanks to an 80% reduction in loan and lease loss provisions as the bank's loan portfolio's credit quality improved with the strengthening economy. The company's non-interest expenses also declined by double-digits mostly because the bank in 2013 incurred a non-recurring $22.4 million FDIC indemnification valuation adjustment.

First Financial's operating cash declined by 66% to $56.65 million after adjusting its earnings for non-cash items related to the indemnification asset decrease and net sales proceeds on its loans held for sale.

Strategy

First Financial has been focusing on branch expansion (on its own or through acquisitions) in three core metropolitan markets: Cincinnati Dayton and Indianapolis. In 2014 for example First Financial acquired three Ohio-based banks and their branches in 2014 expanding its branch network in Central Ohio while adding new loan and deposit business at the same time.

Mergers and Acquisitions

In 2017 First Financial agreed to acquire MainSource Financial Group with an expected deal completion in 2Q 2018. The purchase extends its reach in Indiana (80 branches) Ohio Illinois and Kentucky.

In 2014 to expand further into key markets in Columbus and Central Ohio First Financial purchased The First Bexley Bank which served commercial and consumer bank clients from its one branch location in Bexley Ohio. Similarly that year it purchased Insight Bank operated a branch in Worthington Ohio and a mortgage origination office in Newark Ohio; and bought Worthington-based Guernsey Bancorp and its three branches in Central Ohio.

Company Background

In the past the bank acquired 16 branches in western Ohio from Liberty Savings Bank and bought 22 Indianapolis-area branches from Flagstar Bank in 2011. Together the two acquisitions furthered the bank's growth strategy for the key markets of Dayton and Indianapolis.

EXECUTIVES

President Western Markets Commercial Banking And Wealth Management, C. Douglas (Doug) Lefferson

President And Ceo, Claude E. Davis

President And Coo, Anthony M. (Tony) Stollings

Chief Credit Officer, Richard S. Barbercheck

Svp And Cfo, John Gavigan

President Mortgage Banking, Jill A. Stanton

Evp And Chief Compliance Officer, Holly M. Foster

President Corporate Banking, Brad Ringwald

Vice President Commercial Underwriter, Brian Englert

First Vice President Information Technology, Bard Lowry

Assistant Vice President Sales Center Manager Iii, Cooley Andrew

Vice President Of Mortgage Lending, Wade Spain

Senior Vice President, Robert Mason

Vice President, Chris Peffly

Vice President Network, Brad Stroeh

Vice President Information Technology Support Services, Roland Lima

Regional Market Manager Vice President, Shane Wilken

First Vice President, Jeffrey Weingartner

Vice President Commercial Real Estate, Steve Tanner

Assistant Vice President Loan Operations, Barbara A Sensibaugh

Assistant Vice President Mortgage Lending, Michael Reeve

First Vice President Deposit Operations And Processing Services, Peter Beccaccio

Vice President Digital Sales Channel Manager, Brano Tomic

Vice President, Mark Bicker

Senior Vice President Chief Talent Officer, Mary Findley

First Vice President Commercial Banking, Steve Murphy

Vice President Commercial Banking First Financial Bank, Jason King

Vice President Commercial Market Manager, Zac Nelson

Chairman, Murph Knapke

Vice Chairman, J. Wickliffe Ach

Board Member, John Neighbours

Board Member, Peter Geier

Auditors: Crowe Horwath LLP

LOCATIONS

HQ: First Financial Bancorp (OH)
255 East Fifth Street, Suite 700, Cincinnati, OH 45202
Phone: 877 322-9530
Web: www.bankatfirst.com

PRODUCTS/OPERATIONS

2014 Sales

	$ mil.	% of total
Interest		
Loans including fees	208	66
Investment securities	44	14
(Adjustment)	(5.5)	-
Noninterest		
Service charges on deposit accounts	20	7
Trust and wealth management fees	13	5
Bankcard income	10	3
Net gains from sales on loans	4	1
Accelerated discount on covered/formerly covered loans	4	1
Others	10	3
Total	**311**	**100**

COMPETITORS

AMB Financial	Logansport Financial
Commercial Bancshares	MutualFirst Financial
Farmers National	PNC Financial
Fifth Third	Peoples Community
First Defiance	Bancorp
Financial	Peoples-Sidney
First Franklin	SB Financial Group
LCNB	U.S. Bancorp
Liberty Capital	

HISTORICAL FINANCIALS

Company Type: Public

Income Statement

FYE: December 31

	ASSETS ($ mil.)	NET INCOME ($ mil.)	INCOME AS % OF ASSETS	EMPLOYEES
12/17	8,896	96	1.1%	1,366
12/16	8,437	88	1.0%	1,521
12/15	8,147	75	0.9%	1,471
12/14	7,217	65	0.9%	1,442
12/13	6,417	48	0.8%	1,422
Annual Growth	**8.5%**	**18.9%**	**—**	**(1.0%)**

2017 Year-End Financials

Debt ratio: 1.34%
Return on equity: 10.78%
Cash ($ mil.): 184
Current ratio: —
Long-term debt ($ mil.): —
No. of shares (mil.): 62
Dividends
Yield: 0.0%
Payout: 43.5%
Market value ($ mil.): 1,636

	STOCK PRICE ($) FY Close	P/E High/Low	PER SHARE ($) Earnings	Dividends	Book Value
12/17	26.35	19 15	1.56	0.68	14.99
12/16	28.45	20 10	1.43	0.64	13.96
12/15	18.07	17 13	1.21	0.64	13.13
12/14	18.59	17 14	1.09	0.61	12.76
12/13	17.43	21 17	0.83	0.94	11.86
Annual Growth	**10.9%**	**— —**	**17.1%**	**(7.8%)**	**6.0%**

First Financial Bankshares, Inc.

Texas hold 'em? Well sort of. First Financial Bankshares is the holding company for eleven banks consolidated under the First Financial brand all of which are located in small and midsized markets in Texas. Together they have about 50 locations. The company maintains a decentralized management structure with each of the subsidiary banks having their own local leadership and decision-making authority. Its First Financial Trust & Asset Management subsidiary administers retirement and employee benefit plans in addition to providing trust services. First Financial Bankshares also owns an insurance agency.

EXECUTIVES

Chairman President And Ceo; Chairman First Financial Bank N.a., F. Scott Dueser, age 65, $754,167 total compensation

Evp And Cfo, J. Bruce Hildebrand, age 63, $445,000 total compensation

Evp And Chief Administrative Officer, Ronald D. (Ron) Butler, age 57, $405,000 total compensation

Evp Lending, Marna Yerigan

Evp Lending, T. Luke Longhofer

Evp And Cio, Thomas S. (Stan) Limerick

Evp And Lending Officer, Gary S.Gragg, age 58, $325,000 total compensation

Evp Retail And Training, Monica Houston

Evp Chief Risk Officer, Randy Roewe

Vice President Of Commercial Loans, Chris Evatt

Senior Vice President, Kay Berry

Assistant Vice President Human Resources, Racheal Carter

Senior Vice President Consumer Lending, Chris Schjetnan

Senior Vice President And Credit Administration, Clay Trumble

Vice President, Wade Spain

Vice President, Isabel Montoya

Chairman President And Ceo; Chairman First Financial Bank N.a., F. Scott Dueser, age 65

Board Member, Tim Lancaster

Auditors: Ernst & Young LLP

LOCATIONS

HQ: First Financial Bankshares, Inc.
400 Pine Street, Abilene, TX 79601
Phone: 325 627-7155
Web: www.ffin.com

PRODUCTS/OPERATIONS

2015 sales

	$ mil.	% of total
Interest Income		
Interest and fees on loans	151	51
Interest on investment securities	69	24
Interest on federal funds sold and interest-bearing deposits in banks	0	
Non-Interest Income		
ATM interchange and credit card fees	21	7
Trust fees	10	4
Service charges on deposit accounts	17	6
Real estate mortgage operations	10	4
Net gain on sale of available-for-sale securities	0	-
Net gain on sale of foreclosed assets	0	-
Net loss on sale of assets	(0.8)	-
Other	4	2
Total	**295**	**100**

Products/ServicesPersonal
Learn
Online Banking
Mobile Banking
Consumer Education
FAQS
Privacy & Security Information
Resources
Testimonials
Tools
Bank
Checking
Savings
Invest
CDS & IRAS
Broker Services
Borrow
Mortgage Loans
Mortgage Lenders
Auto Loans
Recreational Loans
Home Equity Loans
Personal Line of Credit
CD Secured Loans
Banking with First Financial
Mobile Banking
Online Banking
Pay Bills
Get Cash
Make Deposit
Move Money
Keep Track
Business
Learn
Online Banking
Mobile Banking
Business Education
Starting your Business
Growing your Business
Tools
Business Banking Services
Manage Cash
Send Payments
Receive Payments
Manage Fraud and Risk
Other Services
Trust & Wealth Management
Investment Management
Trust Management
Estate Management
Oil & Gas Management
Real Estate and Property Management
Company Retirement Plans

Selected Subsidiaries

First Financial Bank National Association Abilene Texas.
First Technology Services Inc. Abilene Texas (wholly owned subsidiary of First Financial Bank National Association Abilene Texas).
First Financial Trust & Asset Management Company National Association Abilene Texas.
First Financial Insurance Agency Inc. Abilene Texas.
First Financial Investments Inc. Abilene Texas.

COMPETITORS

BBVA Compass Bancshares	JPMorgan Chase
Bank of America	Wells Fargo
Cullen/Frost Bankers	Woodforest Financial

HISTORICAL FINANCIALS

Company Type: Public

Income Statement

FYE: December 31

	ASSETS ($ mil.)	NET INCOME ($ mil.)	INCOME AS % OF ASSETS	EMPLOYEES
12/17	7,254	120	1.7%	1,300
12/16	6,809	104	1.5%	1,300
12/15	6,665	100	1.5%	1,270
12/14	5,848	89	1.5%	1,140
12/13	5,222	78	1.5%	1,100
Annual Growth	8.6%	11.1%	—	4.3%

2017 Year-End Financials

Debt ratio: —
Return on equity: 13.67%
Cash ($ mil.): 373
Current ratio: —
Long-term debt ($ mil.): —

No. of shares (mil.): 65
Dividends
  Yield: 0.0%
  Payout: 41.4%
Market value ($ mil.): 2,963

	STOCK PRICE ($) FY Close	P/E High/Low	PER SHARE ($) Earnings	Dividends	Book Value
12/17	45.05	27 20	1.81	0.75	14.03
12/16	45.20	29 15	1.59	0.70	12.78
12/15	30.17	23 16	1.54	0.62	12.30
12/14	29.88	47 20	1.39	0.55	10.72
12/13	66.11	54 31	1.24	0.52	9.26
Annual Growth	(9.1%)	— —	10.0%	9.9%	10.9%

First Financial Corp. (IN)

Which came first the First Financial in Indiana Ohio South Carolina or Texas? Regardless this particular First Financial Corporation is the holding company for First Financial Bank which offers traditional banking deposit accounts and loans as well as trust private banking wealth management and investment services through more than 70 branches in west-central Indiana and east-central Illinois. About 60% of its loan portfolio is tied to commercial loans while the rest is split between residential and consumer loans. Subsidiary Forrest Sherer sells personal and commercial insurance while subsidiary Morris Plan originates indirect auto loans through dealerships in the bank's market area.

Operations

About 59% of the bank's $1.76 billion loan portfolio was tied to commercial business loans to finance business asset purchases and expansion at the end of 2015 while the remainder of the portfolio was tied to 1-4 family residential real estate mortgages (25% of loan assets) and consumer loans (16%).

Nearly 75% of First Financial's revenue comes from interest income. About 57% of its total revenue came from loan interest (including fees) during 2015 while another 16% came from interest income on taxable and tax-exempt investment securities. The rest of its revenue came from deposit account service charges (7% of revenue) insurance commissions (5%) trust and financial services (4%) gains on mortgage loan sales (2%) and other miscellaneous income sources.

Geographic Reach

The Terre Haute Indiana-based bank operated 71 branches in west-central Indiana and east-central Illinois at the end of 2015.

Financial Performance

First Financial Corporation's annual revenues and profits have been trending lower over the past several years due to shrinking margins in the low-interest environment and as its loan assets have declined more than 5% since 2011.

The bank's revenue fell 4% to $147.86 million during 2015 mostly as its interest-earning loan and investment assets and the interest margins they command continued to decline. Its non-interest income tumbled at a similar rate due to reduced investment service and insurance agency income.

Revenue declines in 2015 caused First Financial's net income to dive nearly 11% to $30.2 million. The bank's operating cash levels plunged almost 30% to $41.26 million for the year as cash earnings shrank.

Strategy

First Financial Corporation continued in 2016 to expand its branch network in hopes to build its loan and deposit business. Indeed its branch network has steadily grown from 65 branches at the end of 2011 to 71 branches at the end of 2015.

Mergers and Acquisitions

In January 2019 First Financial agreed to purchase HopFed Bancorp in a deal valued at nearly $130 million. The Hopkinsville Kentucky-based company has 18 branches and three loan production offices in Kentucky and Tennessee new markets for First Financial.

Company Background

In 2011 First Financial bought Freestar Bank adding more than a dozen branches in central Illinois. It was the largest acquisition in the company's history.

With roots dating back to 1834 First Financial Bank is not only one of the oldest banks in Indiana but also the entire country. It is also one of the oldest continually operating businesses in its hometown of Terre Haute. Another local business Princeton Mining Company owns nearly 10% of First Financial Corporation.

EXECUTIVES

Vice Chairman And Ceo, Norman D. Lowery, age 50, $630,297 total compensation
Vice President, Jim Nichols
Personal Trust Department Assistant Vice Presiden, Carol Myers
Vice President Collections, Jeff Nickels
Personal Trust Department Assistant Vice Presiden, Carol Myers
Vice President, Thom Frantz
Vice President Director Of Consumer Lending, Carl Britton
Assistant Vice President Cra Officer, Chris Shaw
Vice President, Eric Feathers
Vice Chairman And Ceo, Norman D. Lowery, age 50
Board Member, Gregory L Gibson
Chairman, B. Guille Cox
Board Member, Anton H Tony George
Auditors: Crowe Horwath LLP

LOCATIONS

HQ: First Financial Corp. (IN)
  One First Financial Plaza, Terre Haute, IN 47807
Phone: 812 238-6000
Web: www.first-online.com

PRODUCTS/OPERATIONS

2011 Sales

	$ mil.	% of total
Interest		
Loans including related fees	91	61
Securities	22	15
Other	2	1
Noninterest		
Service charges & fees on deposit accounts	9	6
Other service charges & fees	8	6
Insurance commissions	7	5
Trust & financial services	4	3
Other	4	3
Total	149	100

COMPETITORS

FFW	Huntington Bancshares
Fifth Third	JPMorgan Chase
First Midwest Bancorp	Old National Bancorp
First Robinson Financial	PNC Financial

HISTORICAL FINANCIALS

Company Type: Public

Income Statement

FYE: December 31

	ASSETS ($ mil.)	NET INCOME ($ mil.)	INCOME AS % OF ASSETS	EMPLOYEES
12/17	3,000	29	1.0%	847
12/16	2,988	38	1.3%	846
12/15	2,979	30	1.0%	896
12/14	3,002	33	1.1%	952
12/13	3,018	31	1.0%	954
Annual Growth	(0.1%)	(2.0%)	—	(2.9%)

2017 Year-End Financials

Debt ratio: —
Return on equity: 7.04%
Cash ($ mil.): 74
Current ratio: —
Long-term debt ($ mil.): —

No. of shares (mil.): 12
Dividends
  Yield: 0.0%
  Payout: 105.0%
Market value ($ mil.): 555

	STOCK PRICE ($) FY Close	P/E High/Low	PER SHARE ($) Earnings	Dividends	Book Value
12/17	45.35	22 18	2.38	2.50	33.77
12/16	52.80	17 10	3.12	0.99	33.92
12/15	33.97	16 14	2.35	0.98	32.21
12/14	35.62	14 12	2.55	0.97	30.46
12/13	36.56	16 12	2.37	0.96	28.94
Annual Growth	5.5%	— —	0.1%	27.0%	3.9%

First Foundation Inc

Auditors: Vavrinek, Trine, Day & Co., LLP

LOCATIONS

HQ: First Foundation Inc
  18101 Von Karman Avenue, Suite 700, Irvine, CA 92612
Phone: 949 202-4160
Web: www.ff-inc.com

HISTORICAL FINANCIALS

Company Type: Public

Income Statement

FYE: December 31

	ASSETS ($ mil.)	NET INCOME ($ mil.)	INCOME AS % OF ASSETS	EMPLOYEES
12/17	4,541	27	0.6%	394
12/16	3,975	23	0.6%	335
12/15	2,592	13	0.5%	295
12/14	1,355	8	0.6%	207
12/13	1,037	7	0.8%	187
Annual Growth	44.6%	36.9%	—	20.4%

2017 Year-End Financials

Debt ratio: 14.93%
Return on equity: 8.12%
Cash ($ mil.): 120
Current ratio: —
Long-term debt ($ mil.): —

No. of shares (mil.): 38
Dividends
 Yield: —
 Payout: —
Market value ($ mil.): 708

	STOCK PRICE ($) FY Close	P/E High/Low		PER SHARE ($) Earnings	Dividends	Book Value
12/17	18.54	36	17	0.78	0.00	10.34
12/16	28.50	41	28	0.70	0.00	8.69
12/15	23.59	41	29	0.58	0.00	8.13
12/14	18.14	37	33	0.52	0.00	6.34
Annual Growth	0.5%	—	—	10.9%	—	13.0%

First Guaranty Bancshares, Inc.

EXECUTIVES

V Chb-Pres-Ceo, Alton B Lewis Jr
Chb, Marshall T Reynolds
Cfo-Sec-Treas, Eric J Dosch
Vice Chairman Board, Alton Lewis
Auditors: Castaing, Hussey & Lolan, LLC

LOCATIONS

HQ: First Guaranty Bancshares, Inc.
 400 East Thomas Street, Hammond, LA 70401
Phone: 985 345-7685
Web: www.eguaranty.com

HISTORICAL FINANCIALS

Company Type: Public

Income Statement

FYE: December 31

	ASSETS ($ mil.)	NET INCOME ($ mil.)	INCOME AS % OF ASSETS	EMPLOYEES
12/17	1,750	11	0.7%	349
12/16	1,500	14	0.9%	304
12/15	1,459	14	1.0%	289
12/14	1,518	11	0.7%	272
12/13	1,436	9	0.6%	278
Annual Growth	5.1%	6.5%	—	5.9%

2017 Year-End Financials

Debt ratio: 2.14%
Return on equity: 8.76%
Cash ($ mil.): 37
Current ratio: —
Long-term debt ($ mil.): —

No. of shares (mil.): 8
Dividends
 Yield: 0.0%
 Payout: 43.5%
Market value ($ mil.): 220

	STOCK PRICE ($) FY Close	P/E High/Low		PER SHARE ($) Earnings	Dividends	Book Value
12/17	25.00	22	17	1.37	0.60	16.35
12/16	23.93	14	9	1.68	0.58	14.86
12/15	18.75	12	9	1.83	0.54	14.12
12/14	19.00	14	10	1.42	0.53	18.34
12/13	14.02	14	12	1.11	0.53	16.21
Annual Growth	15.6%	—	—	5.5%	3.0%	0.2%

First Hawaiian Inc

Auditors: DELOITTE & TOUCHE LLP

LOCATIONS

HQ: First Hawaiian Inc
 999 Bishop Street, 29th Floor, Honolulu, HI 96813
Phone: 808 525-7000
Web: www.fhb.com

HISTORICAL FINANCIALS

Company Type: Public

Income Statement

FYE: December 31

	ASSETS ($ mil.)	NET INCOME ($ mil.)	INCOME AS % OF ASSETS	EMPLOYEES
12/17	20,549	183	0.9%	2,300
12/16	19,661	230	1.2%	2,200
12/15	19,352	213	1.1%	2,250
12/14	18,133	216	1.2%	
Annual Growth	4.3%	(5.4%)	—	

2017 Year-End Financials

Debt ratio: 0.00%
Return on equity: 7.33%
Cash ($ mil.): 1,034
Current ratio: —
Long-term debt ($ mil.): —

No. of shares (mil.): 139
Dividends
 Yield: 0.0%
 Payout: 66.6%
Market value ($ mil.): 4,073

	STOCK PRICE ($) FY Close	P/E High/Low		PER SHARE ($) Earnings	Dividends	Book Value
12/17	29.18	26	20	1.32	0.88	18.14
12/16	34.82	21	15	1.62	0.20	17.75
12/15	0.00	—	—	1.53	0.00	19.63
Annual Growth	—	—	—	(4.8%)	—	(2.6%)

First Horizon National Corp

First Horizon National would like to be on banking consumers' horizons in the Volunteer State and beyond. The bank holding company operates more than 170 First Tennessee Bank branches in its home state and neighboring markets. Boasting roughly $26 billion in total assets it offers traditional banking services like loans deposit accounts and credit cards as well as trust asset management financial advisory and investment services. Subsidiary FTN Financial performs securities sales and trading fixed-income underwriting and other investment banking services through more than 25 offices in more than 15 states as well as in Hong Kong.

Operations

First Horizon operates two core business segments: Regional Banking and Capital Markets.

Regional Banking is the company's largest division (it generated 73% of the bank's total revenue in 2014) and provides traditional banking products and services to retail and commercial customers mostly in Tennessee but also in neighboring markets. The division also provides investments financial panning trust services and asset management as well as correspondent banking services such as credit depository and other banking related services for financial institutions.

The Capital Markets segment which contributed 18% to total revenues in 2014 serves mainly institutional clients in the US and overseas. Its services consist of fixed-income sales trading loan sales portfolio advisory and derivative sales.

First Horizon's two non-core segments include a Corporate division which collects gains and losses related to the bank's debt and investment activities; and the non-strategic segment (11% of total revenues in 2014) which consists of the wind down of the company's national consumer lending activities its legacy mortgage banking elements including service fees its trust preferred loan portfolio and exited businesses.

The company has diversified revenue streams generating about 56% of its total revenue from interest income (mostly from loans) in 2014 16% from capital markets-related fees nearly 10% from deposit transactions and cash management fees about 6% from its Mortgage Banking business and 6% from a combination of brokerage fees and trust services and management fees.

Geographic Reach

First Horizon National boasts more than 180 branch locations across seven US states. More than 90% of the branches are in Tennessee while just over a dozen are in the states of Georgia (northwestern) Mississippi (northwestern) North Carolina Virginia South Carolina and Florida. It also has more than 25 financial offices in 16 states across the US plus a financial office in Hong Kong.

Sales and Marketing

The company spent $18.68 million on advertising and public relations in 2014 up from $18.24 million and $17.44 million in 2013 and 2012 respectively.

Financial Performance

First Horizon's revenue has been in decline in recent years due to shrinking interest margins on loans amidst the low-interest environment. The firm's profits however have been rising thanks to declining loan loss provisions as its loan portfolio's credit quality has been improving in the strengthening economy.

The company's revenue fell by 4% to $1.26 billion in 2014 mostly as the Capital Markets business shrank by 26% as fixed-income markets suffered from low rates low market volatility and uncertainty around the Federal Reserve's monetary policy. The bank's interest income also fell by 3% despite rising commercial loan business mostly due to a combination of continued run-off of non-strategic loan portfolios lower-yielding commercial loans and lower strategic loan balances. Offsetting some of the top-line decline First Horizon's mortgage banking revenue more than doubled for the year mostly thanks to a nearly $40 million gain on the sale of its mortgage loans held-for-sale.

Despite revenue declines in 2014 First Horizon's net income skyrocket nearly seven-fold to $219.52 million thanks to a combination of lower interest and non-interest expenses and a significant decline in loan loss provisions as its loan portfolio's credit condition improved.

The company's operating cash also jumped by 63% to $704.7 million during the year as cash earnings rose and as net cash proceeds from the bank's mortgage loans held-for-sale increased.

Strategy

First Horizon National's flagship First Tennessee Bank has been expanding its geographic reach in recent years through both branch openings and strategic acquisitions of smaller banks and branches in target markets. In 2014 the bank opened its first office in Florida (in Jacksonville) as it continued its plans for growth in the Mid-Atlantic region which includes North Carolina South Carolina Virginia and northern parts of Florida. Also that year the bank agreed to purchase 13 bank branches located in the Middle and East Tennessee for a total of nearly $438 million which would add some $437 million worth of new deposits and expand its reach in its home state.

Mergers and Acquisitions

In 2014 First Horizon agreed to purchase TrustAtlantic Financial Corporation along with its five TrustAtlantic Bank branches in North Carolina (mostly in the Raleigh-Cary metro area). The deal matched First Horizon's objectives to expand in North Carolina's fast-growing Research Triangle region of the state.

In mid-2013 First Tennessee bank acquired Mountain National Bank from the FDIC adding 12 new branch locations in Sevier and Blount counties in Eastern Tennessee as well as $249 million in loan assets and $362 million in deposits.

In 2012 the company added to FTN Financial with the purchase of Las Vegas-based Main Street Capital Advisors which provides investment management and consulting services mainly to state and local municipalities.

Company Background

At the start of the recession First Horizon began selling non-core assets and refocused growth closer to home. First Horizon exited the Baltimore-Washington DC and Atlanta markets. The company also sold some 230 First Horizon Home Loan offices as well as the unit's loan origination and servicing operations outside of Tennessee to MetLife. After the sale First Horizon Financial outsourced some its mortgage origination processing and servicing operations within Tennessee to PHH Mortgage.

In 2008 the bank discontinued its specialty construction and consumer lending activities beyond Tennessee. It exited the institutional equity research business in 2010 and sold its First Horizon Insurance unit to Brown & Brown the following year. Also in 2011 First Horizon sold a subsidiary that provided administrative services for health savings accounts.

EXECUTIVES

Evp And Chief Human Resources Officer, John M. Daniel, age 63

Evp Regional Banking; Coo First Tennessee Bank, David T. Popwell, age 57, $450,000 total compensation

Chairman President And Ceo, D. Bryan Jordan, age 56, $815,000 total compensation

Evp And General Counsel, Charles T. Tuggle, age 69, $475,000 total compensation

Evp Corporate Communications, Kimberley C. (Kim) Cherry

Evp Technology And Operations And Cio, Bruce A. Livesay

Evp And Cfo, William C. (BJ) Losch, age 47, $425,000 total compensation

Evp And Chief Risk Officer, Yousef A. Valine, age 58, $362,692 total compensation

President Ftn Financial, Michael E. Kisber, age 58, $600,000 total compensation

Evp And Chief Credit Officer, Susan L. Springfield, age 53

Evp And Chief Operating And Financial Officer Ftn Financial, Michael K. Waddell

Evp Consumer Banking First Tennessee Bank, David W. Miller

Evp Corporate Banking, Steve J. Hawkins

President First Tennessee Bank Mid-atlantic Region, Billy Frank, age 47

Chairman First Tennessee Bank Mid-atlantic Region, John Fox, age 65

Regional President First Tennessee Bank Tennessee Banking Group, Richard Shaffer, age 53

Evp And Chief Audit Executive, Vernon H. Stafford

Vice President Risk Management, Kathleen Mooney

Senior Vice President And Chief Investment.., Karen Kruse

Senior Vice President And Counsel (2004), John Arthur Niemoeller

Senior Vice President Cash Management, Taylor Vaughn

Vice President, David Ward

Chairman President And Ceo, D. Bryan Jordan, age 56

Auditors: KPMG LLP

LOCATIONS

HQ: First Horizon National Corp
165 Madison Avenue, Memphis, TN 38103
Phone: 901 523-4444
Web: www.firsthorizon.com

PRODUCTS/OPERATIONS

2014 Sales

	$ mil.	% of total
Interest		
Loans including fees	571	45
Investment securities	93	7
Trading securities	32	3
Loans held for sale	11	1
Other	1	-
Noninterest		
Capital markets	200	16
Deposit transactions & cash management	112	9
Mortgage banking	71	6
Brokerage management fees & commissions	49	4
Trust services and investment management	27	2
Bankcard income	23	2
Bank owned life insurance	16	1
Other	49	4
Total	**1,259**	**100**

COMPETITORS

Athens Federal Community Bank	JPMorgan Chase
BB&T	Regions Financial
Bank of America	SunTrust
Citigroup	Trustmark
	Wells Fargo

HISTORICAL FINANCIALS

Company Type: Public

Income Statement				FYE: December 31
	ASSETS ($ mil.)	NET INCOME ($ mil.)	INCOME AS % OF ASSETS	EMPLOYEES
12/17	41,423	165	0.4%	5,984
12/16	28,555	227	0.8%	4,288
12/15	26,195	85	0.3%	4,293
12/14	25,672	219	0.9%	4,310
12/13	23,789	29	0.1%	4,340
Annual Growth	**14.9%**	**53.8%**	**—**	**8.4%**

2017 Year-End Financials

Debt ratio: 2.94%	No. of shares (mil.): 326
Return on equity: 4.94%	Dividends
Cash ($ mil.): 1,824	Yield: 0.0%
Current ratio: —	Payout: 55.3%
Long-term debt ($ mil.): —	Market value ($ mil.): 6,531

	STOCK PRICE ($) FY Close	P/E High/Low		PER SHARE ($)		
			Earnings	Dividends	Book Value
12/17	19.99	31 24	0.65	0.36	13.11
12/16	20.01	22 12	0.94	0.28	10.31
12/15	14.52	48 36	0.34	0.24	9.83
12/14	13.58	15 12	0.91	0.20	9.80
12/13	11.65	126 97	0.10	0.20	9.33
Annual Growth	**14.5%**	**— —**	**59.7%**	**15.8%**	**8.9%**

First Internet Bancorp

EXECUTIVES

Vice President Treasury Management, Maria Bryce

Vice President Commercial Lender, Carl Osberg

Vice President Commercial Lending, Jim Laine

Vice President Commercial Lending, Kevin Lynch

Vice President Commercial Banking, Christy Smith

Vice President Commercial Banking, Suzy Sottong

Vp Human Resources, Angie Redmon

Vp Of Information Technology, Craig Fortner

Vice President Of Appraisal Review, John Reed

Auditors: BKD, LLP

LOCATIONS

HQ: First Internet Bancorp
11201 USA Parkway, Fishers, IN 46037
Phone: 317 532-7900
Web: www.firstinternetbancorp.com

COMPETITORS

Bank of America	Citibank
BofI	E*TRADE Bank

HISTORICAL FINANCIALS

Company Type: Public

Income Statement				FYE: December 31
	ASSETS ($ mil.)	NET INCOME ($ mil.)	INCOME AS % OF ASSETS	EMPLOYEES
12/17	2,767	15	0.6%	206
12/16	1,854	12	0.7%	192
12/15	1,269	8	0.7%	152
12/14	970	4	0.4%	143
12/13	802	4	0.6%	130
Annual Growth	**36.3%**	**34.9%**		**12.2%**

2017 Year-End Financials

Debt ratio: 1.33%	No. of shares (mil.): 8
Return on equity: 8.05%	Dividends
Cash ($ mil.): 47	Yield: 0.0%
Current ratio: —	Payout: 11.2%
Long-term debt ($ mil.): —	Market value ($ mil.): 321

STOCK PRICE ($)		P/E		PER SHARE ($)		
	FY Close	High/Low		Earnings	Dividends	Book Value
12/17	38.15	19	12	2.13	0.24	26.65
12/16	32.00	14	10	2.30	0.24	23.76
12/15	28.69	18	7	1.96	0.24	23.28
12/14	16.74	26	16	0.96	0.24	21.80
12/13	22.50	22	13	1.51	0.22	20.44
Annual Growth	14.1%	—	—	9.0%	2.2%	6.9%

First Interstate BancSystem Inc

This Treasure State bank wants to be your treasury. First Interstate BancSystem is the holding company for First Interstate Bank which has about 80 branches in Montana western South Dakota and Wyoming. Serving area consumers businesses and municipalities the bank provides traditional services including deposit accounts wealth management and loans. Commercial loans including mortgages make up more than half of the bank's loan portfolio; residential real estate agricultural and construction loans round out its lending activities. On the wealth management side the bank has more than $8 billion in trust assets held in a fiduciary or agent capacity.

Financial Performance
The company's revenue decreased in fiscal 2013 compared to the previous period. It reported $369.3 million in revenue for fiscal 2013 down from $388.8 million in fiscal 2012. However despite the decreased annual revenue the company's net income increased in fiscal 2013 to $86 million up from a net income of $58 million the prior fiscal year. Cash flow increased by about $15 million in fiscal 2013 compared to 2012 levels.

Strategy
The company is always looking for opportunities for expansion including organic growth as well as growth through acquisitions. It expanded into the northwest growth market with the acquisition of Cascade Bancorp for around $589 million.

EXECUTIVES

Svp And Cio, Kevin J. Guenthner, age 54, $205,385 total compensation
President And Ceo, Kevin P. Riley, age 58, $307,270 total compensation
Evp And Chief Banking Officer, Bill Gottwals
Evp And Cfo, Marcy D. Mutch, age 58
Executive Vice President And Chief Banking Officer, Michael Huston
Chairman, James R. Scott, age 68
President And Ceo, Kevin P. Riley, age 58
Auditors: RSM US LLP

LOCATIONS

HQ: First Interstate BancSystem Inc
401 North 31st Street, Billings, MT 59116-0918
Phone: 406 255-5390
Web: www.fibk.com

PRODUCTS/OPERATIONS

Selected ServicesBanking
Checking Accounts
Credit Cards
Debit Cards
Escrow Services
Foreign Currency
Overdraft Protection
Personal Resources
Prepaid Cards
Savings Accounts
Borrowing
AdvanceLine
Auto & Recreation
Debt Consolidation
Home Equity
Home Mortgage
Personal Loans
Create & Build Wealth
Long-Term Planning
Planning for the Unexpected
Saving for College
Saving for Retirement
Wealth Resources
Protect & Preserve Wealth
Asset Management
Employee Exit Strategies
Health Concerns
Investment Services
Retirement Plan Services

Sales 2015

	$ mil.	% of total
Interest income	282	70
Non-interest income	121	30
Total	403	100

COMPETITORS

Bank of the West	Great Western Bancorp
Crazy Woman Creek	U.S. Bancorp
Eagle Bancorp	Wells Fargo
Glacier Bancorp	

HISTORICAL FINANCIALS
Company Type: Public

Income Statement
FYE: December 31

	ASSETS ($ mil.)	NET INCOME ($ mil.)	INCOME AS % OF ASSETS	EMPLOYEES
12/17	12,213	106	0.9%	2,207
12/16	9,063	95	1.1%	1,721
12/15	8,728	86	1.0%	1,742
12/14	8,609	84	1.0%	1,705
12/13	7,564	86	1.1%	1,635
Annual Growth	12.7%	5.5%	—	7.8%

2017 Year-End Financials

Debt ratio: 0.78%	No. of shares (mil.): 56
Return on equity: 8.84%	Dividends
Cash ($ mil.): 758	Yield: 0.0%
Current ratio: —	Payout: 46.8%
Long-term debt ($ mil.): —	Market value ($ mil.): 2,261

STOCK PRICE ($)		P/E		PER SHARE ($)		
	FY Close	High/Low		Earnings	Dividends	Book Value
12/17	40.05	22	16	2.05	0.96	25.28
12/16	42.55	20	12	2.13	0.88	21.87
12/15	29.07	16	12	1.90	0.80	20.92
12/14	27.82	16	13	1.87	0.64	19.85
12/13	28.37	15	8	1.96	0.54	18.15
Annual Growth	9.0%	—	—	1.1%	15.5%	8.6%

First Merchants Corp

First Merchants is the holding company that owns First Merchants Bank which operates some 120 branches in Indiana Illinois and western Ohio. Through its Lafayette Bank & Trust and First Merchants Private Wealth Advisors divisions the bank provides standard consumer and commercial banking services including checking and savings accounts CDs check cards and consumer commercial agricultural and real estate mortgage loans. First Merchants also provides trust and asset management services. Founded in 1982 First Merchants has nearly $9.4 billion worth of consolidated assets.

Operations
Real estate loans made up about 70% of First Merchants's loan portfolio while commercial and industrial agricultural and consumer loans account for the remainder of the bank's lending activity.

Geographic Reach
Muncie Indiana-based First Merchants's 120-plus bank branches are located across Indiana and in two counties each in Illinois and Ohio.

Sales and Marketing
First Merchants's marketing expense was $3.73 million in 2017 $3 million (2016) and $3.5 million (2015).

Financial Performance
Revenue jumped by 19% to $348.2 million in 2017 driven by higher interest income from more organic and inorganic loan business and more investment security income following the bank's recent acquisitions. The bank also collected significantly more non-interest income from deposit account service charges electronic card fees and insurance-related gains as it grew its customer base through acquisitions. Higher revenue drove the bank's net income up 18% to $96 million.

Total cash on hand at the end of fiscal 2017 stood at $154.9 million which was $27 million higher than cash at the start of the year. Cash from operations contributed $126 million and cash generated through financing activities added $535.8 while investments in securities and other uses used $635.3 million.

Strategy
A key part of the First Merchants's growth strategy is to expand geographically through acquisitions of small community banks operating in its key Indiana Illinois and western Ohio markets.

In 2017 and 2018 First Merchants added more nearly 3 dozen branches to its banking network after acquiring Michigan-based Monroe Bank & Trust Ohio-based Arlington Bank and Independent Alliance Banks located in Indiana. The bank has in recent years acquired 1-2 community banks operating in these states each year often adding a handful of branches as well as loans and other assets through each transaction.

Mergers and Acquisitions
In 2018 First Merchants acquired MBT Financial Corporation the holding company for Monroe Bank & Trust and its 20 branches serving Monroe Michigan and the southeastern Michigan area.

In 2017 First Merchants bought Columbus Ohio-based Arlington Bank. for $82.6 million. The same year it spent $238.8 million to acquire a majority stake in Independent Alliance Banks and IAB's 16 banking centers located in and around Fort Wayne Indiana.

EXECUTIVES

Evp And Cfo, Mark K. Hardwick, age 47, $317,347 total compensation
Cto, Stephan H. Fluhler, $205,268 total compensation
President And Ceo, Michael C. (Mike) Rechin, age 59, $502,181 total compensation
Evp And Chief Banking Officer, Michael J. (Mike) Stewart, age 52, $310,077 total compensation
Evp And Chief Credit Officer, John J. Martin, age 51, $249,193 total compensation
Svp And Chief Risk Officer, Jeffery B. Lorentson
Vice President, Brad Wise

First Vice President And Director Investor Relations, David Ortega
Vice President Of Marketing, Deanne Beard
Vice President, Tom Dunson
Vice President Of Loans, Christopher Allen
Vice President Marketing Manager, Dana Talaga
Vice President, Lentz Gregory
Executive Vice President Mortgage Operations, Debra Rynearson
Vice President And Purchasing Director, Lisa Brothers
Senior Vice President Chief Accounting Officer, Jami Bradshaw
Vice President, Joseph Keyler
Vice President, Alex Jones
Assistant Vice President Relationship Manager, Michael Kahne
Vice President, Margaret Hoke
Avp Review Appraiser, Joanilla Barker
Vice President Manager Small Business Credit, Robert Spencer
Vice President Business Banking, Chris Chatfield
Senior Vice President Chief Sales Officer Lakeshore Region, Dale Clapp
Senior Vice President And Director Of Human Resources, Kim A Ellington
Vice President Retail Market Leader, Roberta Salway
Vice President Structured Finance, Dave Decraene
Vice President Retail Lending Leader, Jill Engerer
Senior Vice President And Director Of Human Resources, Kim A Ellington
Assistant Vice President, Tammy Hall
First Vice President, Mark Stevenson
Vice President, Jeffrey Lorentson
Vice President, Josh McKenney
Assistant Vice President, Jacob Crouch
Vice President, Adam Treibic
Vice President Manager Mortgage Sales, Elizabeth Chenore
Assistant Vice President Business Banking Officer, Duane Kamminga
Assistant Vice President, Jeffrey Chadwell
Vice President Human Resources Manager, Agnes Lasics
Assistant Vice President, Rob Garrett
Vice President, William Robertson
Vice President And Client Advisor, Rita K Smith
Vice President, Benjamin J Hartings
Assistant Vice President Manager Facilities Projects And Planning, Lindsay S Sweet
Vice President Relationship Manager Iii, Kevin M Orourke
Vice President Regional Sales Manager Muncie East And Ohio Region, Scott Vermillion
Vice President, Bill Robertson
Vice President Manager Commercial Lending, Scott Casbon
Vice President, Benjamin Hartings
Senior Vice President, Joseph Peterson
Assistant Vice President Manager Facilities Projects And Planning, Lindsay Sweet
First Vice President Director Talent Development, Sharissa Ulrey
Vice President, Hohl Matt
Board Member, Terry Walker
Chairman, Charles E. Schalliol, age 71
Board Member, Patrick Sherman
Auditors: BKD, LLP

LOCATIONS

HQ: First Merchants Corp
200 East Jackson Street, Muncie, IN 47305-2814
Phone: 765 747-1500
Web: www.firstmerchants.com

PRODUCTS/OPERATIONS

2017 Sales

	$ mil.	% of total
Interest		
Loans	274	71
Investment Securities	38	10
Federal Reserve and Federal Home Loan Bank stock	.9	-
Interest Expense/Other	(36.9)	-
Non-interest		
Service charges on deposits	18	5
Fiduciary activities	11	3
Other customer fees	20	5
Earnings on cash surrender value of life insurance	3	1
Net gains and fees on sales of loans	7	2
Net realized gains on sales of available for sale securities	2	1
Others	5	2
Total	**348**	**100**

COMPETITORS

Ameriana Bancorp	NorthWest Indiana
Bank of America	Bancorp
Citigroup	Old National Bancorp
Harris	STAR Financial Group
JPMorgan Chase	U.S. Bancorp
MutualFirst Financial	

HISTORICAL FINANCIALS

Company Type: Public

Income Statement

FYE: December 31

	ASSETS ($ mil.)	NET INCOME ($ mil.)	INCOME AS % OF ASSETS	EMPLOYEES
12/17	9,367	96	1.0%	1,684
12/16	7,211	81	1.1%	1,449
12/15	6,761	65	1.0%	1,529
12/14	5,824	60	1.0%	1,415
12/13	5,437	44	0.8%	1,449
Annual Growth	14.6%	21.2%	—	3.8%

2017 Year-End Financials

Debt ratio: 1.49%
Return on equity: 8.71%
Cash ($ mil.): 189
Current ratio: —
Long-term debt ($ mil.): —
No. of shares (mil.): 49
Dividends
Yield: 0.0%
Payout: 32.5%
Market value ($ mil.): 2,068

	STOCK PRICE ($) FY Close	P/E High/Low		Earnings	PER SHARE ($) Dividends	Book Value
12/17	42.06	21	17	2.12	0.69	26.52
12/16	37.65	19	11	1.98	0.54	22.04
12/15	25.42	16	13	1.72	0.41	20.92
12/14	22.75	14	12	1.65	0.29	19.29
12/13	22.72	16	10	1.41	0.18	17.68
Annual Growth	16.6%	—	—	10.7%	39.9%	10.7%

First Mid-Illinois Bancshares Inc

EXECUTIVES

Vice President Branch Operations And Cashier, Rhonda Rawlings
Senior Vice President Of Business Development, Clay Dean
Senior Management (senior Vice President General Manager Director), Jason Tucker
Vice President And Chief Audit Executive, Melissa Wilhelm
Assistant Vice President Mortgage Lending, Mary White
Senior Vice President, Andrew Zavarella
Assistant Vice President And Dep Statement Services, Joan Kirk
Assistant Vice President Mortgage Loan Administration, Sue Radloff
Vice President, Nancy Zike
Vice President Director Of Marketing, Laura Zuhone
Vice President, Gant Harper
Assistant Vice President Human Resource Generalist Ii, Tyla Larson
Auditors: BKD, LLP

LOCATIONS

HQ: First Mid-Illinois Bancshares Inc
1421 Charleston Avenue, Mattoon, IL 61938
Phone: 217 234-7454   Fax: 217 258-0485
Web: www.firstmid.com

PRODUCTS/OPERATIONS

Selected Subsidiaries
The Checkley Agency Inc. (dba First Mid Insurance Group)
First Mid-Illinois Bank & Trust N.A.
First Mid-Illinois Statutory Trust I II
Mid-Illinois Data Services Inc.

COMPETITORS

Bank of America	Northern Trust
Fifth Third	PNC Financial
First BancTrust	U.S. Bancorp
First Busey	

HISTORICAL FINANCIALS

Company Type: Public

Income Statement

FYE: December 31

	ASSETS ($ mil.)	NET INCOME ($ mil.)	INCOME AS % OF ASSETS	EMPLOYEES
12/17	2,841	26	0.9%	592
12/16	2,884	21	0.8%	598
12/15	2,114	16	0.8%	513
12/14	1,607	15	1.0%	400
12/13	1,605	14	0.9%	406
Annual Growth	15.3%	16.0%	—	9.9%

2017 Year-End Financials

Debt ratio: 1.21%
Return on equity: 9.07%
Cash ($ mil.): 88
Current ratio: —
Long-term debt ($ mil.): —
No. of shares (mil.): 12
Dividends
Yield: 0.0%
Payout: 30.9%
Market value ($ mil.): 488

	STOCK PRICE ($) FY Close	P/E High/Low		Earnings	PER SHARE ($) Dividends	Book Value
12/17	38.54	20	14	2.13	0.66	24.32
12/16	34.00	17	11	2.05	0.62	22.51
12/15	26.00	14	10	1.81	0.59	24.25
12/14	18.55	13	9	1.85	0.55	23.45
12/13	22.00	14	12	1.73	0.46	25.39
Annual Growth	15.0%	—	—	5.3%	9.4%	(1.1%)

First Midwest Bancorp, Inc. (Naperville, IL)

There's a lot of cabbage in corn country. Just ask First Midwest Bancorp the holding company for First Midwest Bank. Through nearly 110 branches the bank mainly serves suburban Chicago though its market extends into central and western Illinois and neighboring portions of Iowa and Indiana. Focusing on area small to mid-sized businesses it offers deposit products loans trust services wealth management insurance and retirement plan services; it has $7.2 billion of client trust and investment assets under management. Commercial real estate loans account for more than half of the company's portfolio.

Operations

More than 85% of the company's loan portfolio consists of corporate loans (the majority of which are secured by commercial real estate) while the remainder of the portfolio consists of consumer loans (which include home equity loans lines of credit and 1-4 family mortgages). Illustrative of its commitment to business lending First Midwest does not originate sub-prime lending or investment banking activities.

The bank's subsidiaries include: equipment leasing and commercial financier First Midwest Equipment Finance Co.; investment security managers First Midwest Securities Management LLC and First Midwest Holdings Inc.; Section 8 housing venture investor LIH Holdings; and Synergy Property Holdings LLC which manages the bank's OREO properties.

Geographic Reach

The company operates 109 banking offices largely located in various communities throughout the suburban metropolitan Chicago market as well as central and western Illinois and eastern Iowa. It owns 145 automated teller machines most of which are housed at banking locations. First Midwest and Allpoint together provide access to more than 50000 free ATMs worldwide.

Sales and Marketing

The company serves different industry segments including manufacturing health care pharmaceutical higher education wholesale and retail trade service and agricultural. First Midwest spent about $8.2 million on advertising and promotions in 2014 up from $7.8 million in 2013 and $5.1 million in 2012.

Financial Performance

Following a modest rebound in 2013 First Midwest's revenue in 2014 dipped by less than 1% to $426.48 million mostly because of a 76% drop in net securities gains as the bank in 2013 was able to collect a non-recurring equity investment sale gain of $34 million. Lower mortgage banking income resulting from lower market pricing also contributed to the modest dip in revenue. The bank did however report higher interest income as its loan business grew higher wealth management fees with growth in assets under management and higher service charge fees as deposit accounts grew.

After healthy profit growth in 2013 net income fell by nearly 13% to $69.31 million in 2014 mostly as the bank incurred higher costs associated with the acquisition and integration of Popular and Great Lakes and because the bank had higher loan loss provision expenses. In 2013 First Midwest had posted a large jump in net income thanks to higher revenue a decrease in the provision for loan and covered loan losses and lower interest and non-interest expenses.

Continuing its annual cash declines the bank's operations provided $122.93 million (or 10% less cash than in 2013) mostly due to lower earnings.

Mergers and Acquisitions

In 2014 First Midwest acquired south suburban Chicago-based Great Lakes Financial Resources Inc. the holding company for Great Lakes Bank National Association. As part of the $58 million deal the company gained eight locations $490 million in deposits and $234 million in loans.

That year it also bought the Chicago banking operations of Popular Community Bank a subsidiary of Popular Inc. (12 full-service retail branches and its small business and middle market commercial lending activities in the Chicago metropolitan area which included $726 million in deposits and $562 million in loans).

In early 2017 the company completed the acquisition of another Chicago-area bank Standard Bancshares. The deal will add 35 branches $2.3 billion in assets $2.1 billion in deposits and $1.9 million in loans.

Company Background

First Midwest capitalized on the rash of bank failures that have occurred in the Chicago area amid the recessionary economy. Its relative financial soundness put it in a position to acquire three failed Illinois banks through separate FDIC-facilitated transactions in 2009 and 2010: First DuPage Bank Peotone Bank and Trust and Palos Bank and Trust. The deals which included loss-sharing agreements with the regulator added a total of nearly 10 branches. In 2012 the company acquired the deposits and loans of Waukegan Savings Bank in another FDIC-assisted deal that added two more branches to its network. First Midwest will continue to consider acquisitions of failed banks in the Chicago area.

EXECUTIVES

President Ceo And Director; Chairman And Ceo First Midwest Bank, Michael L. Scudder, age 57, $750,000 total compensation

Evp Cio And Coo First Midwest Bank, Kent S. Belasco, age 67, $224,000 total compensation

Evp And Cfo First Midwest Bancorp Inc. & First Midwest Bank, Paul F. Clemens, age 66, $376,000 total compensation

Sevp And Coo; Vice Chairman And President First Midwest Bank, Mark G. Sander, age 59, $545,000 total compensation

Evp And Treasurer First Midwest Bancorp Inc. & First Midwest Bank, James P. Hotchkiss, age 61

Evp And Chief Risk Officer First Midwest Bancorp Inc. & First Midwest Bank, Kevin L. Moffitt

Evp Corporate Secretary And General Counsel, Nicholas J. Chulos

Vice President, Juan Cortez

Executive Vice President Bank Operations Director, David Kullander

Executive Vice President And Director Commercial Banking First Midwest Bank, Victor Carapella

Vice President, Ed Garner

Senior Vice President, Rob Schultz

Executive Vice President Director Of Employee Resources First Midwest Bank, Caryn Guinta

Vice President, Cheri Rubocki

Vice President Administration, Connie Steinke

Senior Vice President, Carlos Touza

Vice President, Jodie Speers

Senior Vice President Director Applic, John Hudak

Senior Vice President Financial Planning, Rich Padula

Vice President Area Sales Manager, Evan Klee

Assistant Vice President Branch Manager, Josie Pacheco

Vice President Public Funds, Susan Wade

Vice President, Tami Johnson

Vice President, Chris Sawyer

Senior Vice President Businessbanking Group Manager, Chris Esposito

Vice President, Brian Ruos

Assistant Vice President Branch Manager Ii, Michael Barbari

Vice President Treasury Management, Ala Swais

Vice President, Phillip Greiner

Vice President Business Banking, Dave Kurow

Vice President, Chad Lyons

Vice President Commercial Banking, Abdullah Tadros

Vice President Community Banking Officer Community Real Estate Group, Richard Rischall

Senior Vice President And Commercial Banking Manager, John Twohy

Executive Vice President Chro, Michelle Hoskins

Vice President, Angela Hart

Executive Vice President Chief Credit Officer, Mike Kozak

Senior Vice President Commercial Banking, James Schramm

Assistant Vice President, Andrew Trasatt

Senior Vice President, Aaron Markos

Vice President Cra Manager, Mary Morstadt

Vice President, Robert Rodie

Senior Vice President Manager Business Banking, Brian Burke

Vice President Group Sales Manager, Joseph Palazzolo

Vice President Senior Human Resources Consultant, Anita Dwyer

Senior Vice President, Phil Ostroski

Senior Vice President, Neil Prendergast

Avp Hr Consultant (business Partner), Amy Crabbe

Senior Vice President Healthcare Banking Coverage Group, James Goody

Executive Vice President And Senior Counsel, James Carroll

Chairman, Robert P. (Bob) O'Meara, age 80

President Ceo And Director; Chairman And Ceo First Midwest Bank, Michael L. Scudder, age 57

Evp And Treasurer First Midwest Bancorp Inc. & First Midwest Bank, James P. Hotchkiss, age 61

Evp Corporate Secretary And General Counsel, Nicholas J. Chulos

Board Member, Phupinder Gill

Board Member, Frank Modruson

Board Member, Kathryn Hayley

Auditors: Ernst & Young LLP

LOCATIONS

HQ: First Midwest Bancorp, Inc. (Naperville, IL)
8750 West Bryn Mawr Avenue, Suite 1300, Chicago, IL 60631-3655
Phone: 703 831-7483
Web: www.firstmidwest.com

PRODUCTS/OPERATIONS

2016

	$ mil.	% of total
Interest Income		
Loans	338	63
Investment securities - taxable	28	5
Investment securities - tax-exempt	8	2
Other short-term investments	2	0
Noninterest Income		
Service charges on deposit accounts	40	8
Wealth management fees	33	6
Card-based fees	29	5
Merchant servicing fees	12	2
Mortgage banking income	10	2
Capital market products income	10	2
Other service charges commissions and fees	9	2
Net gain on sale-leaseback transaction	5	1
BOLI income	3	1
Net securities gains	1	0
Other income	3	1
Total	**537**	**100**

COMPETITORS

Bank of America	Meta Financial Group
BankFinancial	Northern Trust
Cummins-Allison	PrivateBank
Fifth Third	QCR Holdings
First Busey	West Suburban Bancorp
Harris	Wintrust Financial
JPMorgan Chase	

HISTORICAL FINANCIALS
Company Type: Public

Income Statement
FYE: December 31

	ASSETS ($ mil.)	NET INCOME ($ mil.)	INCOME AS % OF ASSETS	EMPLOYEES
12/17	14,077	98	0.7%	2,152
12/16	11,422	92	0.8%	1,882
12/15	9,732	82	0.8%	1,790
12/14	9,445	69	0.7%	1,788
12/13	8,253	79	1.0%	1,647
Annual Growth	14.3%	5.5%		6.9%

2017 Year-End Financials

Debt ratio: 1.39%	No. of shares (mil.): 102
Return on equity: 6.30%	Dividends
Cash ($ mil.): 346	Yield: 0.0%
Current ratio: —	Payout: 40.6%
Long-term debt ($ mil.): —	Market value ($ mil.): 2,466

	STOCK PRICE ($) FY Close	P/E High/Low	PER SHARE ($) Earnings	Dividends	Book Value
12/17	24.01	27 22	0.96	0.39	18.16
12/16	25.23	22 14	1.14	0.36	15.46
12/15	18.43	19 15	1.05	0.36	14.70
12/14	17.11	19 17	0.92	0.31	14.17
12/13	17.53	17 11	1.06	0.16	13.34
Annual Growth	8.2%	— —	(2.4%)	25.0%	8.0%

First National Bank Alaska

First National Bank Alaska is a financial anchor in Anchorage. Founded in 1922 the bank is one of the state's oldest and largest financial institutions. With about 30 branches throughout The Last Frontier (and about 20 ATMs in rural communities) the bank offers traditional deposit products such as checking and savings accounts CDs and IRAs as well as loans and mortgages credit and debit cards and trust and investment management services. The family of longtime president Daniel Cuddy owns a majority of First National Bank Alaska; he took the helm of the bank in 1951.

Geographic Reach
In order to help serve clients in remote locales First National Bank Alaska opened its first branch with a full-service customer kiosk at a joint air force/army base outside of Anchorage where customers can make routine banking transactions without teller assistance. The bank may add such kiosks at other branches.

Financial Performance
The company's total annul revenue has slowly declining across recent fiscal years. However it has managed to stay profitable.

EXECUTIVES

Senior Vice President, David Stringer
Vice President Information Systems, Larry Chen
Senior Vice President Commercial Lending, Bill Inscho
Assistant Vice President, Becky Monterosso
Senior Vice President And Chief Financial Officer, Michele Schuh
Vice President, Lita Beck
Senior Vice President And Specialty Lending Director, Stacy Tomuro
Auditors: Crowe Horwath LLP

LOCATIONS

HQ: First National Bank Alaska
101 West 36th Avenue, P.O. Box 100720, Anchorage, AK 99510-0720
Phone: 907 777-4362   **Fax:** 907 265-3528
Web: www.FNBAlaska.com

COMPETITORS

Alaska Pacific Bancshares	KeyCorp
Alaska USA	Northrim BanCorp
	Wells Fargo

HISTORICAL FINANCIALS
Company Type: Public

Income Statement
FYE: December 31

	ASSETS ($ mil.)	NET INCOME ($ mil.)	INCOME AS % OF ASSETS	EMPLOYEES
12/17	3,653	36	1.0%	—
12/16	3,609	41	1.1%	—
12/15	3,569	36	1.0%	—
12/14	3,312	32	1.0%	—
12/13	3,102	32	1.0%	—
Annual Growth	4.2%	3.0%	—	—

2017 Year-End Financials

Debt ratio: —	No. of shares (mil.): 3
Return on equity: 7.36%	Dividends
Cash ($ mil.): 134	Yield: 0.0%
Current ratio: —	Payout: 870.5%
Long-term debt ($ mil.): —	Market value ($ mil.): 6,548

	STOCK PRICE ($) FY Close	P/E High/Low	PER SHARE ($) Earnings	Dividends	Book Value
12/17	2,065.00	210 144	11.49	100.00	156.70
12/16	1,750.00	134 97	13.04	85.00	155.37
12/15	1,403.00	142 124	11.30	50.00	153.43
12/14	1,588.00	174 157	10.14	50.00	147.21
12/13	1,751.00	183 166	9.98	50.00	140.38
Annual Growth	4.2%	— —	3.6%	18.9%	2.8%

First of Long Island Corp

When it comes to banking The First of Long Island wants to be the first thing on Long Islanders' minds. The company owns The First National Bank of Long Island which offers a variety of lending investment and deposit services through around 45 commercial and retail branches on New York's Long Island and the boroughs of Manhattan and Queens. Residential and Commercial Mortgages (particularly tied to multifamily properties) make up more than 90% of the bank's loan portfolio though the bank also writes revolving home equity business and consumer loans. Its two bank subsidiaries include insurance agency The First of Long Island Agency and investment firm FNY Service.

Operations
The First National Bank of Long Island also operates an investment management division that offers trust and investment management estate and custody services.

The bank makes more than 90% of its revenue from interest income. About 70% of its total revenue came from loan interest during 2015 while another 21% came from interest income on taxable and non-taxable investment securities. The rest of its revenue came from deposit account service charges (3% of revenue) investment management division income (2%) gains on securities sales (1%) and other income sources.

Geographic Reach
The New York City-based bank operated 45 branches at the end of 2015 including 41 in Long Island and two each in Manhattan and Queens.

Sales and Marketing
First serves individuals professionals corporations institutions and governmental clients through its branches.

The bank markets its services through customer service personnel tele-sales lending relationships referral sources and advertisements. It spent $877000 on marketing during 2015 compared to $927000 and $670000 in 2014 and 2013 respectively.

Financial Performance
The First of Long Island's annual revenues have risen more than 20% since 2011 as its loan assets have more than doubled to $2.25 billion. Meanwhile the bank's profits have swelled more than 30% thanks to revenue growth and low interest expenses.

First's revenue jumped 13% to $101 million during 2015 mostly thanks to higher interest income as its average loan balances grew 26% and as its non-taxable security assets rose by 6%. The bulk of the loan asset growth was tied to residential mortgages while most of the rest came from multi-family commercial mortgage growth.

Double-digit revenue growth drove the bank's net income up 12% to $25.9 million. First's operating cash levels dipped 1% to $35 million despite the rise in earnings due to unfavorable working capital changes mostly related to a decrease in accrued expenses and other liabilities.

Strategy
The bank has been opening new branches utilizing "effective relationship management" using targeted solicitation efforts and expanding its product and service offerings to boost its loan and deposit business in recent years.

In early 2016 the company planned to open between eight and 12 more The First National Bank of Long Island branches in Queens after opening two branches there in Howard Beach and Whitestone in 2015. It also planned to open branches in Brooklyn. Expanding its branch network on Long Island the bank in 2015 launched new branches in Patchogue and Melville.

EXECUTIVES

Svp And Evp And Senior Lending Officer Commercial Lending The First National Bank Long Island, Donald L. Manfredonia, age 66, $222,500 total compensation
Svp, Richard Kick, age 60, $230,100 total compensation

Svp And Treasurer; Evp Cfo And Cashier The First National Bank Of Long Island, Mark D. Curtis, age 63, $242,700 total compensation

President And Ceo The First Of Long Island Corporation And The First National Bank Of Long Island, Michael N. Vittorio, age 65, $468,000 total compensation

Svp And Secretary; Sevp The First National Bank Of Long Island, Sallyanne K. Ballweg, age 62, $264,000 total compensation

Evp And Chief Risk Officer First National Bank Of Long Island, Christopher Becker

Vice President, Jane Reed

Assistant Vice President, Giuseppe Sparacino

Vice President, Robert Eisen

Vice President Sales Manager, Rick Hughes

Vice President Director Of Human Resources, Sue Hempton

Vice President, Susan Donovan

Vice President Financial Reporting Manager, Dina Cascione

Vice President Of Marketing, Laura Ierulli

Vice President And Controller, Maria Doyle

Chairman The First Of Long Island Corporation And The First National Bank Of Long Island, Walter C. Teagle, age 68

Svp And Secretary; Sevp The First National Bank Of Long Island, Sallyanne K. Ballweg, age 62

Auditors: Crowe Horwath LLP

LOCATIONS

HQ: First of Long Island Corp
10 Glen Head Road, Glen Head, NY 11545
Phone: 516 671-4900
Web: www.fnbli.com

PRODUCTS/OPERATIONS

2015 Sales

	$ mil.	% of total
Interest and dividend income:		
Loans	70	70
Investment securities		
Taxable	8	8
Nontaxable	13	13
Noninterest income		
Investment Management Division income	2	2
Service charges on deposit accounts	2	3
Net gains on sales of securities	1	1
Other	2	3
Total	**100**	**100**

Selected Services

Checking
Savings
Saving for Retirement & Education
Online Banking & Bill Pay
FirstLink Online Banking
Quicken/Quickbooks
FirstPay Bill Pay
PopMoney
Account to Account Transfers

COMPETITORS

Astoria Financial	JPMorgan Chase
Bank of America	New York Community
Citibank	Bancorp
Dime Community	Ridgewood Savings Bank
Bancshares	Suffolk Bancorp
Flushing Financial	

HISTORICAL FINANCIALS

Company Type: Public

Income Statement
FYE: December 31

	ASSETS ($ mil.)	NET INCOME ($ mil.)	INCOME AS % OF ASSETS	EMPLOYEES
12/17	3,894	35	0.9%	333
12/16	3,510	30	0.9%	314
12/15	3,130	25	0.8%	302
12/14	2,721	23	0.8%	284
12/13	2,399	21	0.9%	260
Annual Growth	**12.9%**	**13.3%**	**—**	**6.4%**

2017 Year-End Financials

Debt ratio: 0.13%
Return on equity: 10.64%
Cash ($ mil.): 69
Current ratio: —
Long-term debt ($ mil.): —

No. of shares (mil.): 24
Dividends
Yield: 0.0%
Payout: 40.5%
Market value ($ mil.): 703

	STOCK PRICE ($) FY Close	P/E High/Low	PER SHARE ($) Earnings	Dividends	Book Value
12/17	28.50	22 18	1.43	0.58	14.37
12/16	28.55	30 19	1.34	0.55	12.90
12/15	30.00	26 19	1.22	0.52	11.85
12/14	28.37	39 21	1.10	0.47	11.20
12/13	42.87	41 27	1.03	0.45	10.04
Annual Growth	**(9.7%)**	**— —**	**8.5%**	**6.4%**	**9.4%**

First Republic Bank (San Francisco, CA)

No not the original Roman Republic but rather a modern-day haven for the elite. Founded in 1985 First Republic Bank offers private banking wealth management trust and brokerage services for businesses and high-net-worth clients though about 75 branches. Its main geographic focus is on urban markets including San Francisco Los Angeles New York Boston Portland and San Diego. The bank's lending focuses on commercial and residential real estate and personal loans including vacation home mortgages and aircraft and yacht financing. Trust services are offered through the bank's First Republic Trust Company division. First Republic Bank has some $83.6 billion of assets under management.

Operations

First Republic's wealth management services consists of various investment strategies and products trust and custody services online brokerage financial and estate planning access to alternative investments (private equity venture capital hedge and real estate funds) socially responsible investing insurance and foreign exchange. First Republic has a number of operating subsidiaries: it operates its wealth management through First Republic Investment Management; brokerage through First Republic Securities; trust services through First Republic Trust (a division of the bank) and First Republic Trust Company.

Geographic Reach

First Republic operates some 75 offices around 70 of which are Preferred Banking locations in Boston; Los Angeles; New York; Palm Beach Florida; Palo Alto Newport Beach San Diego San Francisco and Santa Barbara California; and Port-

land Oregon. The other five locations offer lending wealth management or trust services.

California accounts for around 60% of First Republic's outstanding loans.

Sales and Marketing

First Republic Bank advertises via digital media and newspaper and radio ads; its primary marketing goal is to attract deposits in its Preferred Banking offices. The vast majority of new clients are referred by word of mouth from existing clients.

Financial Performance

First Republic has recorded steady interest and non-interest revenue growth since 2010. In fiscal 2016 revenue increased 19% to $2.4 billion due to higher loan origination (particularly in single and multifamily loans) and increases in investment income relating to purchases of new investments. Offsetting factors include lower interest rates and lower investment yields.

Net income rose 29% to $673.4 million on the back of strong performances in Commercial Banking and Wealth Management. Cash from operations increased 36% to $852.5 million thanks to higher net income and adjustments to other assets.

Strategy

First Republic takes a conservative approach to banking issuing loans to high-net-worth individuals that it can work with in the long term. To support this the company ensures a low employee turnover to create deep and long-lasting relationships with its clients. Top class service is essential to the growth of the business: the majority of First Republic's new clients are sourced by word-of-mouth from within high-net-worth networks.

Mergers and Acquisitions

In 2016 First Republic acquired Gradifi a Boston-based company that helps employers offer student-loan repayment as an employee perk.

EXECUTIVES

Evp Secretary And General Counsel, Edward J. Dobranski, age 67

President Ceo And Director, James H. Herbert

Evp And Chief Credit Officer, David B. Lichtman

President First Republic Securities, David Tateosian

Sevp And Chief Banking Officer, Michael D. (Mike) Selfridge, age 50

Chairman First Republic Trust Company, Michael J. Harrington

Evp And President Private Wealth Management, Bob Thornton

Evp And Chief Marketing Officer, Dianne Snedaker

Svp Chief Deposit Officer And Chief Investment Officer, Hafize Gaye (Gaye) Erkan

Evp And Cfo, Michael J. (Mike) Roffler

Evp; Chief Bsa And Aml And Security Officer, Bill Ward

Evp And Cio, Dale A. Smith

Evp And Coo, Jason C. Bender

President First Republic Trust Company, Kelly Johnston

Senior Vice President Foreign Exchange, Kate Kent-Sheehan

Cfa Cpa Vice President Wealth Manager, Stephen Marotto

Vice President Business Analysis, Greg Boudreaux

Vice President Compliance Risk Manager, Steven Sears

Vice President Residential Lending, Lionel Antunes

Vice President, Michael Curley

Vice President, Todd Brantley

Vice President, Margaret AE Zywicz

Vice President And Assistant General Counsel, Janisha Sabnani

Vice President, Karen Conway

Vice President Strategic Planning And Special Projects, Tim Maguire

Executive Vice President, Brian Riley
Vice President Of Retail Marketing, Gwenn Murphy
Vice President, Peter Chang
Vice President Lending Services, Pj Pamulo
Vice President, DAVID WEITGENANT
Senior Vice President, Bradley Finn
Vice President Finance, Erwin Hom
Vice President Of Operations, Seth Bermel
Vice President Wealth Manager, Jeff Greene
Vice President, Andrew Gibson
Senior Vice President, Helene Jepson
Vice President Compensation, Mea Kwon
Vice President Trading, Ann Northrop
Vice President And Associate General Counsel, Hilary Gevondyan
Senior Vice President Technology Strategy, Ken Chou
Vice President And Assistant General Counsel Private Wealth Management, Debra Achkire
Senior Vice President Platform Optimization Private Wealth Management, Marjorie Qualey
Assistant Vice President Media And Entertainment Finance, Jeff Hammond
Senior Vice President, David Breslin
Vice President Info Security Programs Information Security, David Estabrook
Vice Chair, Katherine August-deWilde, age 67
President Ceo And Director, James H. Herbert
Assistant Treasurer, Aaron Frank
Auditors: KPMG LLP

LOCATIONS

HQ: First Republic Bank (San Francisco, CA)
111 Pine Street, 2nd Floor, San Francisco, CA 94111
Phone: 415 392-1400
Web: www.firstrepublic.com

PRODUCTS/OPERATIONS

2016 Sales

	% of total
Interest income other	83
Noninterest income	17
Total	**100**

Selected Affiliates
First Republic Investment Management Inc.
First Republic Securities Company LLC
First Republic Trust Company

COMPETITORS

Bank of Marin	City National
Bank of New York Mellon	JPMorgan Private Bank
	MUFG Americas Holdings
Boston Private	Morgan Stanley
Citigroup Private Bank	TriState Capital

HISTORICAL FINANCIALS

Company Type: Public

Income Statement   FYE: December 31

	ASSETS ($ mil.)	NET INCOME ($ mil.)	INCOME AS % OF ASSETS	EMPLOYEES
12/17	87,780	757	0.9%	4,025
12/16	73,277	673	0.9%	3,566
12/15	58,981	522	0.9%	—
12/14	48,353	487	1.0%	2,506
12/13	42,112	462	1.1%	2,388
Annual Growth	**20.2%**	**13.2%**	**—**	**13.9%**

2017 Year-End Financials

Debt ratio: 1.90%   No. of shares (mil.): 161
Return on equity: 10.29%   Dividends
Cash ($ mil.): 2,297   Yield: 0.0%
Current ratio: —   Payout: 15.5%
Long-term debt ($ mil.): —   Market value ($ mil.): 14,009

	STOCK PRICE ($) FY Close	P/E High/Low	PER SHARE ($) Earnings	Dividends	Book Value
12/17	86.64	24 20	4.31	0.67	48.35
12/16	92.14	23 14	3.93	0.63	44.78
12/15	66.06	21 15	3.18	0.59	39.05
12/14	52.12	18 14	3.07	0.54	34.56
12/13	52.35	16 10	3.10	0.46	31.33
Annual Growth	**13.4%**	**— —**	**8.6%**	**9.9%**	**11.5%**

FirstEnergy Corp

FirstEnergy's first goal is to generate and deliver power but its second goal is to stay profitable in a market undergoing deregulation. Its ten utilities provide electricity to 6 million customers in the Midwest and the Mid-Atlantic. The company's domestic power plants have a total generating capacity of more than 16000 MW an amount expected to diminish as the company winds down its deregulated business. Subsidiary FirstEnergy Solutions trades energy commodities in deregulated US markets. FirstEnergy's other nonregulated operations include electrical and mechanical contracting and energy planning and procurement.

Operations
FirstEnergy has three primary operating segments: Regulated Distribution Regulated Transmission and Competitive Energy Services (CES). About 65% of total revenue comes from Regulated Distribution roughly 25% from Competitive Energy Services and the rest from Regulated Transmission.

The Regulated Distribution segment distributes electricity through FirstEnergy's ten utilities which serve 6 million customers in a service area with a total population of 13.3 million. It has a controlling interest in 3800 MWs of generation capacity in West Virginia Virginia and New Jersey. It fulfills the additional electricity needs of its customers through power purchase agreements.

The Competitive Energy Services segment through its subsidiaries FES and AE Supply supplies electricity through retail and wholesale arrangements including competitive retail sale to customers primarily in Ohio Pennsylvania Illinois Michigan New Jersey and Maryland. It controls some 12300 MW of capacity.

The Regulated Transmission segment transmits electricity through transmission facilities owned and operated by American Transmission Systems Trans-Allegheny Interstate Line Company and a number of FirstEnergy's utilities. Transmission operations include approximately 24500 miles of lines and two regional transmission operation centers.

Geographic Reach
FirstEnergy operates and serves customers in a service area of 65000 square miles in Maryland New Jersey New York Ohio Pennsylvania and West Virginia.

Its power generating assets are located in Pennsylvania Ohio West Virginia New Jersey and Maryland.

Sales and Marketing
The Regulated Distribution segment sells roughly equal amounts of electricity to its residential and industrial customers and slightly less to its commercial customers. Generally there is no competition for electric distribution service in its service territories in Ohio Pennsylvania West Virginia Maryland New Jersey and New York.

FirstEnergy's CES segment participates in deregulated energy markets in Ohio Pennsylvania Maryland Michigan New Jersey and Illinois through FES and AE Supply. CES competes to provide retail generation service directly to end users to provide wholesale generation service to utilities municipalities and co-operatives which in turn resell to end users and in the electricity wholesale market.

Financial Performance
Until 2016 the company's financial performance was steady through trending slightly downward. Revenue peaked at $16.1 billion in 2011 and since slid to below $15 billion in 2016. Net income slipped from $885 million in 2011 to below $300 million in 2014 before an upward tick in 2015 which preceded a massive fall in 2016.

In 2017 revenue decreased 4% to $14 billion mostly coming from CES ($1 billion less) which saw a 10 million MWH decline in contract sales at lower prices as well as lower capacity auction prices offset by better performance from Transmission and Distribution segments.

The company posted a loss of $1.7 billion for 2017 a marked improvement from some $6.2 billion in losses the year before due to $8.3 billion reduction in impairment charges related to its exit from commodity-exposed generation at CES. In 2017 $2 billion in impairments came from nuclear generating assets.

It has $590 million in cash holdings. Operations generated $3.8 billion offset by $2.7 billion in investing cash outflow and a further $700 million going towards financing activities.

Strategy
The overriding long-term objective for FirstEnergy is to transition its business model from being a holding company of competitive energy wholesaler subsidiaries into one that holds solely regulated utilities. As an energy wholesaler the CES subsidiary is tossed about by the volatile pricing of energy products (oil coal etc.) and therefore carries a high risk with volatile financial results. The move to wind down CES and focus on regulated utilities brings with it a much lower risk profile and predictable steady cash flows.

Part of its plan includes divestitures. In 2017 FirstEnergy?s CES segment agreed to sell four natural gas generating plants in Pennsylvania its ownership interests in a Virginia hydroelectric power station and gas/oil-fired facility to a subsidiary of LS Power Equity Partners III LP for $925 million. In total it is selling off more than 1600 MW of generation capacity. Additionally it plans to retire by 2020 720 MW of capacity at its Sammis Plant and 136 MW at its Bay Shore plant both in Ohio.

Meanwhile First Energy continues to invest in its regulated companies. To date it?s installed 550000 smart meters across its Pennsylvania market and plans to replace them for all 2 million of the state?s customers by 2019. It is working with Ohio regulator agencies to pursue a similar grid modernization effort in that state. In total it plans to spend roughly $1 billion/year on its utilities companies between 2017 and 2020.

HISTORY

FirstEnergy came to light in 1893 as the Akron Electric Light and Power Company. After several mergers the business went bankrupt and was sold in 1899 to Akron Traction and Electric Company which became Northern Ohio Power and Light (NOP&L).

In 1930 Commonwealth and Southern (C&S) bought NOP&L and merged it with four other Ohio utility holding companies to form Ohio Edison. The new firm increased sales during the Depression by selling electric appliances.

The Public Utility Holding Company Act of 1935 (passed to rein in uncontrolled utilities) caught up with C&S in 1949 forcing it to divest Ohio Edison. Rival Ohio Public Service was also divested from its holding company and in 1950 Ohio Edison bought it.

In 1967 after two decades of expansion Ohio Edison and three other Ohio and Pennsylvania utilities formed the Central Area Power Coordination Group (CAPCO) to share new power-plant costs including the construction of the Beaver Valley nuclear plant (1970-76). Although the CAPCO partners agreed in 1980 to cancel four planned nukes in 1985 Ohio Edison took part in building the Perry Unit 1 and Beaver Valley Unit 2 nuclear plants.

The federal Energy Policy Act of 1992 allowed wholesale power competition and to satisfy new federal requirements Ohio Edison formed a six-state transmission alliance in 1996 with fellow utilities Centerior Energy Allegheny Power System and Dominion Resources' Virginia Power to coordinate their grids.

Ohio Edison paid about $1.5 billion in 1997 for Centerior Energy formed in 1986 as a holding company for Toledo Edison and Cleveland Electric. Ohio Edison and Centerior both burdened by high-cost generating plants merged to cut costs and the expanded energy concern was renamed FirstEnergy Corp.

Looking toward deregulation FirstEnergy began buying mechanical construction contracting and energy management companies in 1997 including Roth Bros. and RPC Mechanical. In 1998 it added nine more. FirstEnergy then ventured into natural gas operations by purchasing MARBEL Energy. The company also created separate subsidiaries for its nuclear and transmission assets.

In 2000 FirstEnergy agreed to acquire New Jersey-based electric utility GPU in an $11.9 billion deal; it became one of the largest US utilities in 2001 when it completed the acquisition which added three utilities (Jersey Central Power & Light Metropolitan Edison and Pennsylvania Electric) serving 2.1 million electricity customers.

Beefing up its generation assets in 2011 the company acquired Allegheny Energy in a $8.5 billion deal. The acquisition increased FirstEnergy's power generation capacity by 70% and its customer base by 35% dramatically boosting its position as a leading regional energy provider focused on both regulated utility operations and a competitive generation business.

EXECUTIVES

President Maryland Operations, James A. Sears
Evp Corporate Strategy Regulatory Affairs And Chief Legal Officer, Leila L. Vespoli, age 59, $758,606 total compensation
Plant Manager, Donald R. (Donny) Schneider, age 57, $552,404 total compensation
Svp Corporate Services And Cio, Bennett L. Gaines, age 64
Regional President The Cleveland Electric Illuminating Company, Dennis M. Chack, age 67
Svp And President Utilities Business, Steven E. (Steve) Strah, age 54, $553,286 total compensation
President Ceo And Director, Charles E. (Chuck) Jones, age 63, $1,133,840 total compensation
Evp And Cfo, James F. (Jim) Pearson, age 64, $659,884 total compensation
Evp And President Firstenergy Generation, James H. (Jim) Lash, age 67, $583,187 total compensation
Regional President The Cleveland Electric Illuminating Company, John E. Skory
Regional President Metropolitan Edison Company, Edward L. Shuttleworth
Regional President Ohio Edison Company, Randall A. Frame

Regional President West Penn Power Company, David W. McDonald
President Jersey Central Power And Light, James V. Fakult
Regional President Pennsylvania Electric Company, Scott R Wyman
President West Virginia Operations, Holly C Kauffman
President Pennsylvania Operations, Linda L. Moss, age 53
President And Chief Nuclear Officer Firstenergy Nuclear Operating Company (fenoc), Samuel L. Belcher
Regional President Toledo Edison Company, Richard S. Sweeney
Vp Investor Relations, Irene Prezelj
Vice President Corporate Affairs, Dee Lowery
Executive Vice President, Charles Lasky
Vice President Energy Efficiency, John Dargie
Regional Vice President, Jeffrey Elser
Senior Vice President Strategic Planning And Opera, Mark Clark
Vice President East Fleet Operations, Peter Kotsenas
Vice President Of Information System, Jeffrey Steiner
Vp And Treasurer, Steve Staub
Vice President Transmission, Carl Bridenbaugh
Vp East Fleet Operations, Daniel Rossero
Vice President And General Counsel, Robert Reffner
Vp Fe Products, Dennis Reynolds
Chairman, George M. Smart, age 72
President Ceo And Director, Charles E. (Chuck) Jones, age 63
Assistant Treasurer, Bill Wang
Board Member, Michael Anderson
Secretary, Diana Chambers
Auditors: PricewaterhouseCoopers LLP

LOCATIONS

HQ: FirstEnergy Corp
76 South Main Street, Akron, OH 44308
Phone: 800 736-3402
Web: www.firstenergycorp.com

PRODUCTS/OPERATIONS

2016 Sales

	$ mil.	% of total
Regulated Distribution	9,629	63
Competitive Energy Services	4,549	30
Regulated Transmission	1,151	7
Corporate/Other and Reconciling Adjustments	(767)	-
Total	**14,562**	**100**

COMPETITORS

AEP	Exelon
Avista	National Fuel Gas
CMS Energy	NiSource
Constellation Energy	PPL Corporation
Group	PSEG Energy Holdings
DPL	Peoples Natural Gas
Delmarva Power	Pepco Holdings
Dominion Energy	Public Service
Duquesne Light	Enterprise Group
Duquesne Light	TVA
Holdings	Vectren
EnergySolve	WGL Holdings

Income Statement   FYE: December 31

	REVENUE ($ mil.)	NET INCOME ($ mil.)	NET PROFIT MARGIN	EMPLOYEES
12/17	14,017	(1,724)	—	15,617
12/16	14,562	(6,177)	—	15,707
12/15	15,026	578	3.8%	15,781
12/14	15,049	300	2.0%	15,557
12/13	14,917	392	2.6%	15,754
Annual Growth	(1.5%)	—		(0.2%)

2017 Year-End Financials

Debt ratio: 53.24%
Return on equity: (-33.92%)
Cash ($ mil.): 589
Current ratio: 0.76
Long-term debt ($ mil.): 21,115

No. of shares (mil.): 445
Dividends
Yield: 0.0%
Payout: —
Market value ($ mil.): 13,636

	STOCK PRICE ($) FY Close	P/E High/Low	Earnings	Dividends	Book Value
12/17	30.62	— —	(3.88)	1.44	8.81
12/16	30.97	— —	(14.49)	1.44	14.11
12/15	31.73	30 21	1.37	1.44	29.33
12/14	38.99	57 43	0.71	1.44	29.49
12/13	32.98	50 34	0.94	2.20	30.32
Annual Growth (26.6%)	(1.8%)	— —		—	(10.1%)

Fiserv Inc

EXECUTIVES

Pres-Ceo, Jeffery W Yabuki
Chb, Glenn M Renwick
Cfo-Treas, Robert W Hau
Clo-SEC, Lynn S McCreary
Chief ADM Officer, Byron Vielehr
Grp Pres, Billin & Payments, Devin B McGranahan
Pres, Digital Banking Grp, Kevin J Schultz
Grp Pres, Depository Instituti, Byron C Vielehr
Pres-Card Services, Kim Crawford Goodman
Manager, Benjamin Cooper
Client Manager, Brian Scheet
Auditors: DELOITTE & TOUCHE LLP

LOCATIONS

HQ: Fiserv Inc
255 Fiserv Drive, Brookfield, WI 53045
Phone: 262 879-5000   **Fax:** 262 879-5013
Web: www.fiserv.com

COMPETITORS

Accenture	Intuit Financial
Banc of America	Services
Merchant Services	Jack Henry
CGI Group	MasterCard
DST Systems	Online Resources
Fidelity National	Open Solutions
Information Services	SunGard
First Data	Total System Services
Harland Financial	Visa Inc
Solutions	Western Union

Company Type: Public

Income Statement				FYE: December 31
	REVENUE ($ mil.)	NET INCOME ($ mil.)	NET PROFIT MARGIN	EMPLOYEES
12/17	5,696	1,246	21.9%	24,000
12/16	5,505	930	16.9%	23,000
12/15	5,254	712	13.6%	22,000
12/14	5,066	754	14.9%	21,000
12/13	4,814	648	13.5%	21,000
Annual Growth	4.3%	17.8%	—	3.4%

2017 Year-End Financials

Debt ratio: 47.62%
Return on equity: 47.27%
Cash ($ mil.): 325
Current ratio: 1.02
Long-term debt ($ mil.): 4,897

No. of shares (mil.): 415
Dividends
Yield: —
Payout: —
Market value ($ mil.): 54,445

	STOCK PRICE ($) FY Close	P/E High/Low	PER SHARE ($) Earnings	Dividends	Book Value
12/17	131.13	45 36	2.89	0.00	6.58
12/16	106.28	53 41	2.08	0.00	5.90
12/15	91.46	64 46	1.50	0.00	5.90
12/14	70.97	48 36	1.49	0.00	6.86
12/13	59.05	92 46	1.22	0.00	6.98
Annual Growth	22.1%	— —	24.1%	—	(1.5%)

Flagstar Bancorp, Inc.

Flagstar Bancorp is the holding company for Flagstar Bank which operates around 110 branches (including 10 in retail stores) mostly in Michigan. Beyond offering traditional deposit and loan products Michigan's largest bank specializes in originating purchasing and servicing one-to-four family residential mortgage loans across all 50 states through a network of brokers and correspondents. Around 70% of the Flagstar's revenue is linked to mortgage origination and servicing while another 25% comes from its community banking business. Boasting $14 billion in assets Flagstar is one of the nation's 10 largest savings banks.

Operations

Flagstar Bancorp operates four business segments: Mortgage Originations which made up 58% of its total revenue during 2015 and acquires and sells one-to-four family residential mortgage loans; Mortgage Servicing (12% of revenue) which charges a fee to service and sub-service mortgage loans for its own community bank and other parties; and Community Banking (24%) which provides deposit and loan products (including warehouse lending) to businesses individuals government entities and held-for-investment portfolio groups.

Unlike traditional banks which focus on interest income Flagstar makes most of its revenue from its mortgage banking business. Only about 43% of its revenue came from interest during 2015 (mostly from loans) while most of the rest came from gains on mortgage loan sales (36% of revenue) loan fees and charges (8%) and other mortgage-banking related fees (10%).

Geographic Reach

The Troy Michigan-based company had 99 branches in Michigan and another 10 locations in retail locations in nine highly-populous states. Its mortgage banking business does business in all 50 states.

Sales and Marketing

Flagstar spent $9 million on advertising in 2015 compared to $10 million and $9 million in 2014 and 2013 respectively.

Financial Performance

As with other mortgage bankers Flagstar has struggled to grow its revenues over the past few years as many borrowers have already refinanced their loans to take advantage of low interest rates. The lender has also been in and out of the red in recent years suffering losses in 2014 and 2011.

Flagstar Bancorp's revenue rebounded 28% to $825 million during 2015 however thanks to a combination of higher interest income and mortgage sales. On the mortgage side a 40% jump in loan sale gains were driven by higher fallout-adjusted lock volumes improved margins and lower representation and warranty provisions. The company's interest income grew 24% as it continued to build its average loans held-for-sale loans held-for-investment and investment security assets.

Strong revenue growth in 2015 and a sharp decline in loan loss provisions on an improving quality credit portfolio drove the company's net income up 28% to $158 million (compared to a $70 million loss in 2014). Despite earnings growth Flagstar's operations used $9.55 billion in cash or about 17% more than in 2014 mostly as it used more cash to originate mortgage loans.

Strategy

While home mortgage lending remains key to Flagstar the company hopes to diversify its revenue streams so the business eventually accounts for about a third of sales. Over the past few years the company has been transforming its branches into full-service community banks and moving toward cross-selling an expanded suite of retail commercial and government banking services.

In February 2016 the company expanded and diversified more into commercial lending after launching its national homebuilder lending platform designed to offer financing to residential developers and homebuilders across the US. In past years it introduced a line of consumer loans such as credit cards and home equity lines of credit and added services for small and midsized businesses like treasury management and specialty lending.

Company Background

In 2011 to raise capital after suffering the effects of the housing bust the company sold 27 bank branches in the suburbs north of Atlanta along with their deposits to PNC. The company also sold its 22 Indiana branches to First Financial Bancorp later that year. In addition to bringing in some cash the divestitures help Flagstar focus on its Michigan operations.

MP Thrift an affiliate of private equity firm MatlinPatterson Global Advisors assumed a controlling stake of Flagstar in 2009. Today it owns 64% of the company.

EXECUTIVES

Evp And Director Performing Servicing, Mark Landschulz, age 53
President Mortgage Banking, Leonard (Len) Israel
President Ceo And Director, Alessandro P. DiNello, age 63
Evp And Senior Deputy General Counsel, Paul D. Borja, age 57, $749,982 total compensation
Evp And Treasurer, Brian D.J. Boike, age 41
Evp And Coo, Lee M. Smith
Evp And Cfo, James K. Ciroli
Evp And Chief Risk Officer, Steve Figliuolo
Evp And Director Mis And Analytics, William D. Belekewicz
Evp And Cio, Tony Buttrick
Evp Secondary Marketing, Palmer T. Heenan
Evp And Director Mortgage Fulfillment, Donna M. Krall
Evp And Chief Lending Officer Commercial Banking, Thomas R. Kuslits
Evp And Chief Human Resources Officer, Cynthia M. Myers
Evp And Chief Credit Officer, Joseph M. Redoutey
Evp And Chief Compliance Officer, Karen A. Sabatowski
Chairman, John D. Lewis
President Ceo And Director, Alessandro P. DiNello, age 63
Auditors: PricewaterhouseCoopers LLP

LOCATIONS

HQ: Flagstar Bancorp, Inc.
5151 Corporate Drive, Troy, MI 48098-2639
Phone: 248 312-2000
Web: www.flagstar.com

PRODUCTS/OPERATIONS

2015 Sales

	$ mil.	% of total
Interest income		
Loans	295	36
Investment securities	59	7
Interest-earning deposits and other	1	-
Non interest income		
Net gain on loan sales	288	36
Loan fees & charges	67	8
Deposit fees and charges	25	3
Loan administration income	26	3
Net return on mortgage serving assets	28	3
Net (loss) gain on sale of assets	(1)	-
Representation and warranty benefit (provision)	19	2
Other non-interest income	18	2
Total	825	100

2015 Sales

	% of total
Mortgage origination	58
Community Banking	24
Mortgage Servicing	12
Others	6
Total	100

Selected Products/Services

Personal Banking
Banking
Checking Accounts
Checking
Savings Accounts
Savings Accounts: Personal
Banking Goals
View All Rates
Online Banking Login: Personal Accounts
Mobile Banking
Detroit Red Wings Partnership
Foreign Currency
Loans
Home Loans
Refinance
Home Equity Solutions
Credit Cards
Money Market
Investment Accounts: Personal

COMPETITORS

Bank of America	JPMorgan Chase
Comerica	KeyCorp
Fifth Third	Northern Trust
Harris	PNC Financial
Huntington Bancshares	

HISTORICAL FINANCIALS
Company Type: Public

Income Statement
FYE: December 31

	ASSETS ($ mil.)	NET INCOME ($ mil.)	INCOME AS % OF ASSETS	EMPLOYEES
12/17	16,912	63	0.4%	3,525
12/16	14,053	171	1.2%	2,886
12/15	13,715	158	1.2%	2,713
12/14	9,839	(69)	—	2,739
12/13	9,407	266	2.8%	3,253
Annual Growth	15.8%	(30.3%)		2.0%

2017 Year-End Financials

Debt ratio: 2.92%
Return on equity: 4.61%
Cash ($ mil.): 204
Current ratio: —
Long-term debt ($ mil.): —

No. of shares (mil.): 57
Dividends
  Yield: —
  Payout: —
Market value ($ mil.): 2,145

	STOCK PRICE ($) FY Close	P/E High/Low		PER SHARE ($) Earnings	Dividends	Book Value
12/17	37.42	35	23	1.09	0.00	24.41
12/16	26.94	11	6	2.66	0.00	23.51
12/15	23.11	11	6	2.24	0.00	27.07
12/14	15.73	—	—	(1.72)	0.00	24.37
12/13	19.62	5	3	4.37	0.00	25.40
Annual Growth	17.5%		— —	(29.3%)	—	(1.0%)

FLORIDA HOUSING FINANCE CORP

EXECUTIVES

Exec Dir, Stephen Auger
Executive Officer, Vicki Robinson
Auditors: ERNST & YOUNG LLP ORLANDO FL

LOCATIONS

HQ: FLORIDA HOUSING FINANCE CORP
227 N BRONOUGH ST # 5000, TALLAHASSEE, FL 323011367
Phone: 850 488-4197
Web: WWW.FLORIDAHOUSING.ORG

PRODUCTS/OPERATIONS

Selected Programs
First Time Homebuyer Program
Down Payment Assistance
Homeownership Loan Program
Mortgage Credit Certificate
Multifamily Development Programs
Multifamily Mortgage Revenue Bonds
Florida Affordable Housing Guarantee Program
HOME Investment Partnerships
Elderly Housing Community Loan Program
Low Income Housing Tax Credits
State Apartment Incentive Loan
Predevelopment Loan Program
State Housing Initiative Partnerships
Demonstration Loans
Affordable Housing Catalyst Program

HISTORICAL FINANCIALS
Company Type: Private

Income Statement
FYE: December 31

	ASSETS ($ mil.)	NET INCOME ($ mil.)	INCOME AS % OF ASSETS	EMPLOYEES
12/17	4,764	206	4.3%	130
12/16	4,567	141	3.1%	—
12/14	5,079	23	0.5%	—
12/12	5,721	0		—
Annual Growth	(3.6%)	—	—	—

2017 Year-End Financials

Debt ratio: —
Return on equity: 111.20%
Cash ($ mil.): 239
Current ratio: 0.70
Long-term debt ($ mil.): —

Dividends
  Yield: —
  Payout: —
Market value ($ mil.): —

Florida Power & Light Co.

Florida Power & Light (FPL) sheds extra light onto the Sunshine State. The company a subsidiary of utility holding company NextEra Energy serves some 5 million electricity customers in eastern and southern Florida. FPL has more than 74800 miles of transmission and distribution lines as well as interests in fossil-fueled nuclear and solar power plants that give it a generating capacity of about 26000 MW. FPL also purchases and sells energy commodities to wholesale customers. FPL's has one of the cleanest power plant fleets across the US.

Operations

FPL's power generations relies on a mix of fuel sources which includes Fossil Operations (primarily uses fossil fuels natural gas and a joint ownership interest in 3 coal units) Nuclear Operations (supply of uranium and the conversion enrichment and fabrication of nuclear fuel) and Solar Operations (utility-owned and customer-owned or leased). In Solar Operations the energy generated goes directly to the location it is serving. In addition FPL also purchases a small amount of power and capacity from non-utility generators and other utilities.

It generates about 70% of its energy with oil/gas-sourced power plants an additional roughly 20% from four nuclear plants and the rest from coal oil and solar.

Geographic Reach

Juno Beach FL-headquartered FPL serves retail customers along Florida?s Atlantic and southern Gulf Coasts.

Sales and Marketing

FPL provides service to its customers through an integrated transmission and distribution system that links its generation facilities to its customers. As a state-regulated utility its market is largely restricted to other entrants although niche project such as rooftop solar provide negligible competition.

Financial Performance

FPL produced $10.9 billion in 2016 operating revenues down 6% from the prior year due to lower fuel cost recoveries.

Despite lower revenue the utility generated $1.7 billion in net income up 5% from 2015. Lower interest expense and tighter control over operating expenses boosted the year's earnings.

Strategy

Florida Power and Light has a 2017-2020 budget of some $18 billion to pursue its strategic endeavors. About half of the capital expenditures are targeted for improvements and expansion of its transmission and distribution segment. It plans to invest heavily into solar farms envisioning nearly $3.0 billion to construct new facilities the first of which is expected to open in early 2018. Capacity expansion and modernization of generation facilities will receive the remaining funds.

In 2016 FPL and the Daytona International Speedway completed FPL Solar Circuit a system of more than 7000 solar panels with capacity of 2.1 MW to generate power for the Speedway's operations. It is one of the largest solar panel installed for US professional sports. The company also intends to build three new solar photovoltaic power plants.

Mergers and Acquisitions

In 2015 FPL and Office of Public Counsel acquired the coal-fired Cedar Bay plant and phased out 90% of its operations to will eventually phase the plant out of service. This saved FPL about a $70 million in operating costs and avoids nearly 1 million tons of carbon dioxide emissions annually.

Company Background

In 2013 FPL began installing solar panels at about 100 schools in 23 counties. It also agreed to a plan whereby more than 400 homes being built or refurbished by Habitat for Humanity and other non-profits would be fitted with solar-powered water heaters.

Between 2011 to 2013 FPL invested $9 billion to strengthen and improve its electric generation and delivery system. The company has revived a $2 billion plan to convert a plant in Port St. John and a plant in Riviera Beach from heavy fuel to natural gas. It also got a further 510 MW of capacity from its Turkey Point and St. Lucie nuclear power plants in 2012 and 2013.

In 2010 the Florida Public Service Commission turned down the company's proposed 30% retail rate hike or $1.3 billion. FPL adjusted its expansion programs accordingly.

Moving further to meet federal requirements for green energy production in 2010 the company commissioned the Space Coast Next Generation Solar Energy Center at the Kennedy Space Center three solar farms built in tandem with NASA to produce 10 MW of clean energy enough to serve 1100 homes. It also brought into service the 75-MW Martin Next Generation Solar Energy Center designed to power about 11000 homes. The hybrid facility connects more than 190000 solar thermal mirrors to an existing combined-cycle natural gas power plant.

EXECUTIVES

Evp Engineering Construction And Corporate Services, Robert L. (Bob) McGrath, age 65
Evp Finance And Cfo, Moray P. Dewhurst, age 63
Evp, Charles E. Sieving, age 45
President And Ceo, Eric E. Silagy
Evp Human Resources, Shaun J. Francis
Chairman, Lewis (Lew) Hay, age 62
Auditors: DELOITTE & TOUCHE LLP

LOCATIONS

HQ: Florida Power & Light Co.
700 Universe Boulevard, Juno Beach, FL 33408
Phone: 561 694-4000
Web: www.nexteraenergy.com

PRODUCTS/OPERATIONS

2016 Operating Revenues

	% of total
Residential	89
Commercial	11
Total	**100**

2016 Sales

	$ mil.	% of total
Retail base	5,807	53
Fuel cost recovery	3,120	29
Other	1,962	18
Total	**10,114**	**100**

COMPETITORS

Clay Electric	Progress Energy
Florida Public	Florida
Utilities	Seminole Electric
Gulf Power	Southern Company Gas
JEA	Sumter Electric
Orlando Utilities	Tampa Electric
Commission	

HISTORICAL FINANCIALS

Company Type: Public

Income Statement				FYE: December 31
	REVENUE ($ mil.)	NET INCOME ($ mil.)	NET PROFIT MARGIN	EMPLOYEES
12/17	11,972	1,880	15.7%	8,700
12/16	10,895	1,727	15.9%	8,900
12/15	11,651	1,648	14.1%	8,800
12/14	11,421	1,517	13.3%	8,700
12/13	10,445	1,349	12.9%	8,900
Annual Growth	**3.5%**	**8.7%**	**—**	**(0.6%)**

2017 Year-End Financials

Debt ratio: 26.65%	No. of shares (mil.): 0
Return on equity: 11.18%	Dividends
Cash ($ mil.): 33	Yield: —
Current ratio: 0.46	Payout: —
Long-term debt ($ mil.): 11,236	Market value ($ mil.): —

Fluor Corp.

EXECUTIVES

Chb-Ceo, David T Seaton
Exec V Pres-Cfo, Bruce A Stanski
Exec V Pres-Clo-Sec, Carlos M Hernandez
Sr V Pres-Cao-Contrl, Robin K Chopra
Sr V Pres Hr, Mark A Landry
Evp Systems & Supply Chain, Ray F Barnard
Grp Pres Energy & Chemicals, James F Brittain
Evp Bus Dev't & Strategy, Jose-Luis Bustamante
Grp Pres, Gov't, Thomas P D'Agostino
Grp Pres, Diversified Svcs, Taco De Haan
Evp, Garry W Flowers
Auditors: Ernst & Young LLP

LOCATIONS

HQ: Fluor Corp.
6700 Las Colinas Boulevard, Irving, TX 75039
Phone: 469 398-7000
Web: www.fluor.com

COMPETITORS

AMEC	JGC
ARCADIS	Jacobs Engineering
Balfour Construction	KBR

Bechtel	McDermott
Bilfinger Berger	POSCO
Black & Veatch	Parsons Corporation
Bouygues	Raytheon
CH2M HILL	Shaw Group
Chicago Bridge &	Technip
Iron	Tetra Tech
Chiyoda Corp.	URS
Foster Wheeler	WorleyParsons Corp.
Hitachi	
Hyundai Engineering and Construction	

HISTORICAL FINANCIALS

Company Type: Public

Income Statement				FYE: December 31
	REVENUE ($ mil.)	NET INCOME ($ mil.)	NET PROFIT MARGIN	EMPLOYEES
12/17	19,520	191	1.0%	56,706
12/16	19,036	281	1.5%	61,551
12/15	18,114	412	2.3%	38,758
12/14	21,531	510	2.4%	37,508
12/13	27,351	667	2.4%	38,129
Annual Growth	**(8.1%)**	**(26.8%)**	**—**	**10.4%**

2017 Year-End Financials

Debt ratio: 17.36%	No. of shares (mil.): 139
Return on equity: 5.92%	Dividends
Cash ($ mil.): 1,804	Yield: 0.0%
Current ratio: 1.57	Payout: 61.7%
Long-term debt ($ mil.): 1,591	Market value ($ mil.): 7,227

	STOCK PRICE ($) FY Close	P/E High/Low	PER SHARE ($) Earnings	Dividends	Book Value
12/17	51.65	42 27	1.36	0.84	23.89
12/16	52.52	28 20	2.00	0.84	22.44
12/15	47.22	21 14	2.81	0.84	21.56
12/14	60.63	26 17	3.20	0.84	20.93
12/13	80.29	19 13	4.06	0.64	23.29
Annual Growth	**(10.4%)**	**—**	**—(23.9%)**	**7.0%**	**0.6%**

Flushing Financial Corp.

Flushing Financial Corp. (FFC) is the holding company for Flushing Bank which operates more than 15 branches in the New York City metropolitan area. The bank offers services catering to the sizable populations of Asians and other ethnic groups in Queens where it has the most full-service offices. Deposit products include CDs and checking savings money market and negotiable order of withdrawal (NOW) accounts. Mortgages secured by multifamily residential commercial and mixed-use real estate account for most of the company's $5.2 billion loan portfolio.

Operations

Flushing Financial generates some 85% of revenue from fees and interest on loans. About 85% of the company's lending is for mortgages including more than 40% for multifamily residences followed by commercial real estate (around 25%) and one-to-four family mixed-use properties (around 10%). Business loans account for the remainder of its lending activity.

Its deposits are equally dominated by negotiable order of withdrawal (NOW) accounts and CDs which comprise about 60% of its $4.4 billion total.

Geographic Reach

Flushing Bank operates solely in the New York City metropolitan area including Nassau County. The company's NYC branches are in Brooklyn Manhattan and Queens. Around half of its banking offices are in Queens where the company is focused on fostering its links to Asian communities.

Sales and Marketing

Flushing's marketing activities revolve primarily around promoting its online banking services which attracted nearly 10% of deposits in 2017 and outreach to Asian communities at its branches in the Queens borough of New York City.

The company has two online banking brands: iGObanking.com (offering savings and checking accounts among other traditional products) and BankPurely (positioned as an environmental sustainable philanthropic banking solution).

Flushing also has an advisory board to promote awareness of the bank's role in the Asian communities of Queens which account for more than $500 million in deposits and $450 million in loans and lines of credit outstanding. The company's employees also speak Cantonese and Mandarin in its locations that serve primarily Chinese customers.

Financial Performance

Although Flushing's revenue and net income fell by double-digits in 2017 both metrics have trended positively over the last five years as the economic environment strengthened in the New York City region and the bank expanded its asset base.

In 2017 the company reported revenue of $183.5 million down 18% from the previous year despite an increase in interest from assets. Net income was also down falling 37% to $41.1 million. Both declines resulted from an uncharacteristic $48 million bump earned in 2016 from the sale of three branch buildings.

The company's cash increased by $15.7 in 2017 to $51.5 million. Cash from operations added $83.5 million to the coffers while investing activities used $254.1 million for purchases of securities available for sale loan purchases and net originations of loans. Financing activities provided $186.3 million as a result of a net increase in interest-bearing deposits and proceeds from borrowings.

Strategy

Flushing's business strategy is centered on improving net interest income and automating bank services. The company is also working to further its presence in New York City-area Asian communities which make up a large portion of its customer base.

In its efforts increase net interest income the company is continuing a strategy which seeks higher loan prices instead of greater volume. The company is focused on growing multifamily residence mortgage loans non-owner occupied commercial mortgages and commercial business loans while pulling back on loans for one-to-four family mixed-use properties and construction. Results in 2017 showed evidence of this strategy with two of Flushing's three focus areas ticking up a point or two and both of the deemphasized areas declining.

As part of its automation push Flushing expects a 20% expense savings following the rollout of its Universal Banker model which is designed to improve efficiency at its physical branches. The technology — which Flushing has deployed at about 60% of its locations — utilizes automated bank telling from assisted service kiosks that include an option to video chat with a banker for assistance.

The bank also continues to invest in services for NYC's Asian populations. In 2018 Flushing announced plans to open a Universal Banker branch in the city's Chinatown area.

Company Background

Flushing Bank was founded as a mutual savings bank in 1929 and converted to a holding company structure in 1994.

EXECUTIVES

Sevp And Chief Of Real Estate Lending Flushing Financial And Flushing Savings Bank, Francis W. (Frank) Korzekwinski, age 55, $418,111 total compensation

President Ceo And Director Flushing Financial And Flushing Savings Bank, John R. Buran, age 68, $899,176 total compensation

Sevp Coo And Corporate Secretary Flushing Financial And Flushing Savings Bank, Maria A. Grasso, age 53, $481,222 total compensation

Evp Residential Mixed-use And Small Multi-family Real Estate Lending, Jeoung (A. J.) Jin, age 51

Evp And Cio, Allen M. Brewer, age 65

Evp And Chief Audit Officer, Robert G. (Bob) Kiraly, age 62

Evp And Director Of Government Banking, Patricia Mezeul, age 58

Evp Commercial Real Estate Lending, Ronald Hartmann, age 62

Evp Business Banking Flushing Financial And Flushing Savings Bank, Theresa Kelly, age 56, $285,704 total compensation

Evp And Chief Risk Officer, Gary P. Liotta, age 58

Evp Cfo And Treasurer, Susan Cullen

Evp And Director Of Distribution And Client Development, Michael Bingold, age 55

Evp And Chief Of Staff, John F. Stewart

Svp And Chief Investment Officer, Frank J. Akalski, age 63

Vice President Business Development, Steven Glass

Vice President Information Security, Joe Rinaldi

Vice President, Rhonda Delorenzo

Assistant Vice President Loan Servicing, Marcia Witter

Vice President Business Banking, Louis Matti

Senior Vice President, Michael Nedder

Vice President Business Banking, Denis Healy

Vice President Business Banking, Jonathan Stern

Assistant Vice President Bsa Department, Karen Williams

Senior Vice President Team Leader Business Banking, Gus Buitrago

Vice President Credit Relationship Manager, Joanne Nasuti

Senior Vice President And Accounting, Timothy Aletrakis

Vice President And Loan Review Officer, James Kumpas

Vice President And Audit Manager, Josephine Amoroso

Vice President, Jin Kim

Vice President And Budget And Financial Foreca, Edward Zekraus

Vice President And Credit Relationship Manager, Elizabeth Carroll

Assistant Vice President And Training Specialist Ii, Marva Webb

Assistant Vice President And Review Appraiser, Stanley Dziorny

Chairman Flushing Financial And Flushing Savings Bank, John E. Roe, age 84

Sevp Coo And Corporate Secretary Flushing Financial And Flushing Savings Bank, Maria A. Grasso, age 53

Evp Cfo And Treasurer, Susan Cullen

Board Member, Caren Yoh

Auditors: BDO USA, LLP

LOCATIONS

HQ: Flushing Financial Corp.
220 RXR Plaza, Uniondale, NY 11556
Phone: 718 961-5400
Web: www.flushingbank.com

PRODUCTS/OPERATIONS

2017 Sales

	$ mil.	% of total
Interest and dividend income		
Interest and fees on loans	209	84
Interest and dividends on securities		
Interest	24	10
Dividends	0	-
Other interest income	0	-
Total	**0**	**0**
Non-interest income		
Banking services fee income	4	2
Net gain on sale of loans	0	-
Net loss on sale of securities	(0.2)	-
Net loss from fair value adjustments	(3.5)	-
Federal Home Loan Bank of New York stock dividends	3	1
Gains from life insurance proceeds	1	1
Bank owned life insurance	3	1
Other income	1	1
Total	**183**	**100**

COMPETITORS

Apple Bank for Savings
Astoria Financial
Bank of America
Bank of New York Mellon
Citigroup
Dime Community Bancshares
First of Long Island
HSBC USA
JPMorgan Chase
Korea Exchange Bank
New York Community Bancorp

HISTORICAL FINANCIALS

Company Type: Public

Income Statement

	ASSETS ($ mil.)	NET INCOME ($ mil.)	INCOME AS % OF ASSETS	EMPLOYEES
12/17	6,299	41	0.7%	467
12/16	6,058	64	1.1%	470
12/15	5,704	46	0.8%	442
12/14	5,077	44	0.9%	424
12/13	4,721	37	0.8%	378
Annual Growth	**7.5%**	**2.2%**	**—**	**5.4%**

FYE: December 31

2017 Year-End Financials

Debt ratio: 1.76%
Return on equity: 7.86%
Cash ($ mil.): 51
Current ratio: —
Long-term debt ($ mil.): —

No. of shares (mil.): 28
Dividends
Yield: 0.0%
Payout: 51.0%
Market value ($ mil.): 786

	STOCK PRICE ($) FY Close	P/E High/Low	PER SHARE ($) Earnings	Dividends	Book Value
12/17	27.50	22 18	1.41	0.72	18.63
12/16	29.39	13 8	2.24	0.68	17.95
12/15	21.64	14 11	1.59	0.64	16.41
12/14	20.27	14 12	1.48	0.60	15.52
12/13	20.70	17 12	1.26	0.52	14.36
Annual Growth	**7.4%**	**— —**	**2.9%**	**8.5%**	**6.7%**

FNB Corp

F.N.B. Corporation is the holding company for First National Bank of Pennsylvania which serves consumers and small to midsized businesses though almost 290 bank branches in Pennsylvania northeastern Ohio and Maryland. The company also has more than 70 consumer finance offices operating as Regency Finance in those states as well as Tennessee and Kentucky. In addition to community banking and consumer finance F.N.B. also has segments devoted to insurance and wealth management. It also offers leasing and merchant banking services. F.N.B. has extended its reach in its target states through acquisitions of banks including Metro Bancorp Annapolis Bancorp and PVF Capital Corp.

Operations

F.N.B operates four segments. The Community Banking segment which made up almost 90% of the company's total revenue during 2015 provides commercial and consumer banking services including corporate banking small business banking investment real estate financing asset-based lending capital markets services and lease financing as well as traditional consumer banking products.

The company's Wealth Management segment (5% of revenue) offers trust and other fiduciary services while the Insurance segment (2% of revenue) offers commercial and personal insurance through major carriers. F.N.B.'s Consumer Finance segment (6% of revenue) which operates through subsidiary Regency Finance Company provides installment loans to individuals and buys installment loans from retail merchants.

Like other retail banks F.N.B. makes the bulk of its money from interest income. Nearly 70% of the bank's total revenue came from loan and lease interest (including fees) during 2015 while 9% came from interest on taxable and non-taxable securities. The rest of money came from service charges (10% of revenue) trust income (3%) insurance commissions and fees (2%) securities commissions and fees (2%) mortgage banking (1%) and other non-interest income sources.

Geographic Reach

Most of the Pittsburgh-based company's branches are concentrated in Pennsylvania with the next largest markets being in Ohio Maryland and West Virginia. Its consumer finance offices are mostly in Pennsylvania and Tennessee with others in Kentucky and Ohio.

Sales and Marketing

F.N.B. boosted its advertising and promotional spend by 7% to $8.4 million during 2015 mostly because of higher expenses associated with the bank's recent acquisitions as it worked to get the name out in new territories such as in Cleveland Ohio and Baltimore.

Financial Performance

F.N.B. Corporation's annual revenues have risen nearly 40% since 2011 as its loan assets have nearly doubled with new branch openings and acquisitions. Its profits have doubled as well over the period as the company has kept a lid on growing costs.

The bank's revenue climbed 6% to $709.21 million during 2015 thanks to continued loan business growth stemming from recent bank acquisitions.

Revenue growth in 2015 drove F.N.B.'s net income up 11% to $159.65 million. The company's operating cash levels plunged 50% to $223.48 million for the year due to unfavorable changes in working capital related to securities classified as trading in business combination and sold.

Strategy

F.N.B. Corporation grows its loan and deposit business while expanding into new markets by acquiring smaller banks and select bank branches. In 2016 it agreed to buy North Carolina-based Yadkin Financial for $1.4 billion. That deal will add around 100 banking locations in the Carolinas and some $7.5 billion in assets. The combined bank will have some 400 branches across the Mid-Atlantic and Southeast US.

Mergers and Acquisitions

In April 2016 the company bought 17 branch locations in the Pittsburgh area from Fifth Third Bank as well as $100000 in loans and over $300000 in deposits.

In February 2016 F.N.B. Corporation purchased Metro Bancorp along with its $3 billion in assets and more than 30 Metro Bank branches in south-central Pennsylvania. The deal effectively merged Metro Bank into F.N.B.'s First National Bank of Pennsylvania subsidiary.

In September 2015 the bank purchased five branches in southeastern Pennsylvania from Bank of America along with almost $155000 in associated deposits.

In October 2013 F.N.B. moved to expand its presence in the greater Cleveland area by purchasing PVF Capital Corp. which owned Park View Federal Savings Bank with some 20 offices in Cleveland and northeastern Ohio.

In April 2013 F.N.B. purchased Annapolis Bancorp the parent company of BankAnnapolis in an all-stock transaction valued at about $51 million. The deal expanded F.N.B.'s reach into Maryland.

Company Background

F.N.B. which moved its headquarters from Pennsylvania to Florida in 2001 spun off First National Bankshares of Florida at the start of 2004 and returned to the Pittsburgh area. F.N.B. still operates two loan offices in Florida but these primarily manage the company's legacy loan portfolio there.

The bank is again rooted firmly in the Keystone State and bordering markets. After returning it expanded via several acquisitions prior to the Parkvale deal including bank holding companies NSD Bancorp Slippery Rock Financial North East Bancshares Omega Financial and Iron and Glass Bancorp. In 2011 F.N.B. expanded in northeastern Pennsylvania through the acquisition of Comm Bancorp. The deal valued at some $70 million brought in 15 branches.

EXECUTIVES

Svp And Corporate Controller, Timothy G. Rubritz, age 65, $215,016 total compensation

Chief Legal Officer, James G. Orie, age 59, $165,000 total compensation

Cfo, Vincent J. Calabrese, age 55, $385,008 total compensation

Chief Credit Officer, Gary Guerrieri, age 57, $350,016 total compensation

President And Ceo; Ceo First National Bank, Vincent J. (Vince) Delie, age 53, $770,016 total compensation

President First National Bank, John C. Williams, $385,008 total compensation

President Charlotte Region, Gregory L. (Greg) Heaton

Vice President Business Development Officer, Leslie Harrison

Vice President, Gregory Robb

Senior Vice President, Craig Muthler

Vice President, Michael Griffo

Vice President Private Banking, Donna Logan

Vice President, Mike DeRosa

Vice President Wealth Advisor Maryland Region, Nick Ey

Senior Vice President Managing Director, Nick Bellino

Chairman, Stephen J. (Steve) Gurgovits, age 74

Board Member, Stephen Martz

Board Member, Heidi Nicholas

Auditors: Ernst & Young LLP

LOCATIONS

HQ: FNB Corp
One North Shore Center, 12 Federal Street, Pittsburgh, PA 15212
Phone: 800 555-5455
Web: www.fnb-online.com

PRODUCTS/OPERATIONS

2015 Sales by Segment

	$ mil.	% of total
Community banking	616	87
Consumer finance	42	6
Wealth management	35	5
Insurance	13	2
parent & other	1	–
Total	**709**	**100**

2015 Sales

	$ mil.	% of total
Interest		
Loans including fees	482	68
Securities including dividends	64	9
Other	0	–
Non-interest		
Service charges	70	10
Trust Services	20	3
Insurance commissions & fees	16	2
Securities commissions & fees	13	2
Other	40	6
Total	**709**	**100**

Selected Subsidiaries

F.N.B. Capital Corporation (merchant banking)
First National Bank of Pennsylvania
　Bank Capital Services LLC (also dba F.N.B. Commercial Leasing)
　First National Trust Company
　F.N.B. Investment Advisors
　First National Investment Services Company
First National Insurance Agency LLC
Regency Finance Company
　Citizens Financial Services Inc.
　F.N.B. Consumer Discount Company
　Finance and Mortgage Acceptance Corporation

COMPETITORS

Bank of America	Huntington Bancshares
Citizens Financial Group	M&T Bank
Dollar Bank	Northwest Bancshares
Fifth Third	PNC Financial
First Commonwealth Financial	S&T Bancorp
Fulton Financial	Sandy Spring Bancorp
Glen Burnie Bancorp	Sovereign Bank
	United Community Financial

HISTORICAL FINANCIALS

Company Type: Public

Income Statement

FYE: December 31

	ASSETS ($ mil.)	NET INCOME ($ mil.)	INCOME AS % OF ASSETS	EMPLOYEES
12/17	31,417	199	0.6%	4,748
12/16	21,844	170	0.8%	3,821
12/15	17,557	159	0.9%	3,205
12/14	16,127	144	0.9%	3,145
12/13	13,563	117	0.9%	3,103
Annual Growth	**23.4%**	**14.0%**	**—**	**11.2%**

2017 Year-End Financials

Debt ratio: 1.14%	No. of shares (mil.): 323
Return on equity: 5.71%	Dividends
Cash ($ mil.): 479	Yield: 0.0%
Current ratio: —	Payout: 76.1%
Long-term debt ($ mil.): —	Market value ($ mil.): 4,470

	STOCK PRICE ($) FY Close	P/E High/Low		PER SHARE ($) Earnings	Dividends	Book Value
12/17	13.82	26	19	0.63	0.48	13.63
12/16	16.03	21	14	0.78	0.48	12.18
12/15	13.34	17	14	0.86	0.48	11.95
12/14	13.32	17	14	0.80	0.48	11.62
12/13	12.62	16	13	0.80	0.48	11.16
Annual Growth	**2.3%**	**—**	**—**	**(5.8%)**	**(0.0%)**	**5.1%**

Foot Locker, Inc.

Foot Locker leads the footrace to capture the biggest retail share of the global athletic footwear market. It is a leading retailer of athletic shoes and apparel with more than 3360 specialty stores mostly in US malls but also in 23 countries in North America and Europe as well as in Australia and New Zealand. Its 1796-store namesake Foot Locker chain is the #1 seller of name-brand (NIKE) athletic footwear in the US. Other store brands include Lady Foot Locker Kids Foot Locker Footaction Champs Sports SIX:02 Runners Point and Sidestep. Beyond its bricks-and-mortar business Foot Locker markets sports gear through direct-to-customer units (catalog retailer Eastbay and Footlocker.com).

HISTORY

With the idea of selling merchandise priced at no more than five cents Frank Woolworth opened the Great Five Cent Store in Utica New York in 1879; it failed. That year he moved to Lancaster Pennsylvania and created the first five-and-dime. Woolworth moved his headquarters to New York City (1886) and spent the rest of the century acquiring other dime-store chains. He later expanded to Canada (1897) England (1909) France (1922) and Germany (1927).

The 120-store chain with $10 million in sales incorporated as F.W. Woolworth & Company in 1905 with Woolworth as president. In 1912 the company merged with five rival chains and went public with 596 stores making $52 million in sales the first year. The next year paying $13.5 million in cash Woolworth finished construction of the Woolworth Building then the world's tallest building (792 feet). When he died in 1919 the chain had 1081 stores with sales of $119 million.

Woolworth became more competitive after WWII by advertising establishing revolving credit and self-service moving stores to suburbs and expanding merchandise selections. In 1962 it opened Woolco a US and Canadian discount chain.

From the 1960s through the 1980s the company grew by acquiring and expanding in the US and abroad. It picked up Kinney (shoes 1963) Richman Brothers (men's clothing 1969) Holtzman's Little Folk Shop (children's clothing 1983) Champs Sports (sporting goods 1987) and Mathers (shoes Australia 1988).

The company introduced Foot Locker the athletic shoe chain in 1974 later developing Lady Foot Locker (1982) and Kids Foot Locker (1987). In 1993 Woolworth launched an ambitious restructuring plan focusing on specialty stores (mostly apparel and shoes). It also closed 400 US stores and sold 122 Canadian Woolco stores to Wal-Mart that year. Former Macy's president Roger Farah became CEO in 1994. Farah eliminated 16 divisions and dozens of executives.

A year later the firm sold its Kids Mart/Little Folks children's wear chain. In 1996 Woolworth began a major remodeling program that included removing its venerable lunch counters. (Another alleged renovation at the Woolworth chain — the firing of older workers who were replaced by teenagers — led to an Equal Employment Opportunity Commission lawsuit against the company in 1999.) The changes failed and the next year the company closed its US Woolworth stores and bought athletic-products catalog company Eastbay.

In 1998 Woolworth changed its name to Venator Group and sold the Woolworth Building a national landmark (headquarters remained in the building). The company then shed itself of more than 1400 stores including Kinney shoes and Footquarters (both closed).

Internet site eVenator was launched in 1999 to sell Eastbay Champs and Foot Locker merchandise. Venator came out the champ in a proxy fight against investment group Greenway Partners in July 1999. Shortly thereafter Farah was replaced as CEO (he remained chairman) by president Dale Hilpert.

In 2000 Venator slashed 7% of its workforce in the US and Canada (a small part of the planned 30% cut) and closed 465 stores. COO Matt Serra became president and Hilpert became chairman when Farah resigned later that year.

In March 2001 Hilpert resigned replaced by Carter Bacot as chairman and Serra added CEO to his title. Venator later sold its Canadian Northern Group unit to investment firm York Management Services and closed its Northern Reflections stores in the US. Venator changed its name to Foot Locker in November. It also sold gift retailer San Francisco Music Box Co. and its hospitality division's fast-food franchises before the end of the year.

In early 2004 chairman Bacot become lead director and president and CEO Serra added chairman to his title.

In 2004 Foot Locker capitalizing on the Chapter 11 filing of Footstar Inc. purchased from the company 350 of its Footaction stores. The company also acquired 11 stores in Ireland from Champion Sports Group later in the same year.

The company's short-lived family footwear retail concept — called Footquarters — launched in early 2007 but was quickly discontinued due to poor performance. The locations were converted to Foot Lockers and Champs Sports outlet stores. Also in early 2007 Foot Locker made an unsolicited $1.2 billion bid for rival Genesco that was rejected by Genesco's board. Foot Locker closed about 275 mostly underperforming stores in 2007.

In 2008 the company reduced its store count by about 145 locations across its five chains in a bid to boost profitability by focusing on its most profitable locations and improving operations. In November Foot Locker acquired the CCS brand from dELia*s for about $103 million. The CCS brand includes skateboarding and snowboarding equipment apparel and footwear targeting primarily teenage boys.

J.C. Penney executive Kenneth Hicks was recruited to succeed Serra as president and CEO in August 2009. Serra who had held the CEO title since 2001 retained the chairman's title until his retirement in January 2010. At that time Hicks became chairman.

In July 2013 Foot Locker acquired Germany's Runners Point Group a specialty athletic store and online retailer based in Recklinghausen in a deal valued at ?72 million Euros ($94 million). The move gave Foot Locker shops in Germany that operated under the Runners Point and Sidestep banners as well as stores in the Netherlands Austria and Switzerland.

EXECUTIVES

Evp And Cfo, Lauren B. Peters, age 56, $657,500 total compensation
Chairman President And Ceo, Richard A. (Dick) Johnson, age 60, $1,087,500 total compensation
President And Ceo Foot Locker Europe, Lewis P. Kimble, age 59, $642,460 total compensation
Evp And Ceo North America, Stephon D. (Jake) Jacobs, age 55, $844,445 total compensation
Svp And Chief Human Resources Officer, Paulette R. Alviti, age 47, $486,250 total compensation
Svp And Cio, Pawan Verma, age 41, $216,071 total compensation
Vp And General Manager Asia Pacific, Natalie Ellis
Vice President Brand Marketing, Jed Berger
Vice President Global Supply Chain, Saadi Majzoub
Vp Leasing, Rita Dickerson
Chairman President And Ceo, Richard A. (Dick) Johnson, age 60
Auditors: KPMG LLP

LOCATIONS

HQ: Foot Locker, Inc.
330 West 34th Street, New York, NY 10001
Phone: 212 720-3700
Web: www.footlocker-inc.com

2017 Sales

	$ mil.	% of total
US	5,562	72
International	2,204	28
Total	**7,766**	**100**

PRODUCTS/OPERATIONS

2017 Stores

stores	No of stores
Foot Locker US	948
Foot Locker Europe	622
Champs Sports	545
Kids Foot Locker	411
Footaction	261
Lady Foot Locker	124
Runners Point	122
Foot Locker Canada	119
Foot Locker Asia Pacific	95
Sidestep	86
SIX:02	30
Total	**3,363**

2017 Sales

	$ mil.	% of total
Athletic Stores	6,744	87
Direct-to-Customers	1,022	13
Total	**7,766**	**100**

COMPETITORS

Academy Sports	Modell's
Caleres	Pacific Sunwear
DSW	Quiksilver
Dick's Sporting Goods	Sears
Dillard's	Shoe Carnival
FGL Sports	Sports Authority
Finish Line	TJX Companies
Genesco	Target Corporation
Hibbett Sports	The Gap
J. C. Penney	Wal-Mart
Kmart	Zappos.com
L.L. Bean	shoebuy.com
Macy's	

HISTORICAL FINANCIALS

Company Type: Public

Income Statement				FYE: February 3
	REVENUE ($ mil.)	NET INCOME ($ mil.)	NET PROFIT MARGIN	EMPLOYEES
02/18*	7,782	284	3.6%	49,209
01/17	7,700	004	0.0%	50,100
01/16	7,412	541	7.3%	47,025
01/15	7,151	520	7.3%	44,568
02/14	6,505	429	6.6%	43,518
Annual Growth	**4.6%**	**(9.8%)**	**—**	**3.1%**

*Fiscal year change

2018 Year-End Financials

Debt ratio: 3.16%
Return on equity: 10.69%
Cash ($ mil.): 849
Current ratio: 4.14
Long-term debt ($ mil.): 125

No. of shares (mil.): 119
Dividends
  Yield: 0.0%
  Payout: 55.8%
Market value ($ mil.): 5,797

	STOCK PRICE ($) FY Close	P/E High/Low	PER SHARE ($)		
			Earnings	Dividends	Book Value
02/18*	48.38	35 13	2.22	1.24	21.02
01/17	68.01	16 10	4.91	1.10	20.61
01/16	67.56	19 13	3.84	1.00	18.64
01/15	53.22	16 10	3.56	0.88	17.72
02/14	38.60	14 11	2.85	0.80	17.16
Annual Growth	**5.8%**	**— —**	**(6.1%)**	**11.6%**	**5.2%**

*Fiscal year change

Ford Motor Co. (DE)

Ford Motor is striving to build smart vehicles for a smart world. One of the ?Big Three? automakers in the US (with GM and Fiat Chrysler) the company manufactures cars trucks and SUVs under the Ford and Lincoln brands ? the F-150 the Escape and the Fusion among its most popular models ? and finances sales through Ford Motor Credit. Ford which does business worldwide is making significant investments in line with a strategic shift to move it from solely an automaker to a leader in vehicle technology and mobility services.

Operations

Ford?s Automotive segment represents more than 90% of revenue and includes the sale of Ford and Lincoln brand vehicles. The Financial Services segment contributes more than 5% of revenue and includes vehicle-related financing and leasing through Ford Motor Credit Company; outside the US Europe is Ford Credit?s largest operation with nearly 60% of that region's receivables in the UK and Germany

Other operations include Central Treasury (which manages the company?s investment portfolio) and the growing Ford Smart Mobility (which invests in emerging technologies).

Geographic Reach

Ford's business units span the five regions of North America South America Europe the Middle East and Africa and Asia-Pacific. More than half of its 60-plus plants are in North America with about 25% in Europe.

The US accounts for more than 60% of Ford's revenue; other major markets include the UK Canada and Germany each accounting for about 5% of sales.

Sales and Marketing

Ford's vehicles parts and accessories are sold through more than 11000 dealerships worldwide most independently-owned. In addition to retail sales these dealerships sell vehicles to commercial fleet customers rental car companies and governments.

Financial Performance

Ford has seen strong growth for four consecutive years since 2013 with revenue up nearly 9% over that time. The company's total revenue for 2017 hit $156.8 billion an increase of more than 3% from the previous year. The Automotive segment was up about 3% with Asian sales up 17% (powered by strong growth in China and India). Financial Services revenue jumped more than 8% compared with 2016.

Net income increased to $7.6 billion a $3 billion increase from 2016 due a much lower tax pension remeasurement loss.

Cash at the end of fiscal 2017 was $18.5 billion an increase of $2.6 billion from the prior year. Cash from operations contributed $18.1 billion to the coffers while investing activities used $19.4 billion mainly for capital spending for product development restructuring and company infrastructure. Financing activities used another $3.4 billion for dividends to stockholders and the company's stock repurchase program.

Strategy

After an evaluation of its operations in 2016 Ford has several initiatives in place to increase efficiency cut costs and increase profits. The company plans to update factories speed up product development and facilitate decision-making within the management ranks with fewer direct reports to the CEO.

In an effort to cut materials costs by $10 billion by 2022 Ford is making new deals with suppliers simplifying its designs and available options and sharing parts between vehicles.

With increased demand for SUVs and trucks Ford is reallocating $7 billion to support production of those vehicles. The company's F-150 truck has been the best-selling model in the US for decades; it is offering a diesel F-150 in 2018 and has plans for a hybrid version. Ford also plans to add the midsized Ranger to its North American pickup portfolio.

In other areas of its automotive business Ford has boosted its luxury Lincoln brand with a new Continental and an aluminum-body Navigator. It has also launched a smaller value model the India-made KA+. In 2017 Ford announced plans to introduce 15 electric or hybrid vehicles in China (the world?s biggest auto market) by 2025.

Ford is also making huge investments in emerging opportunities such as electrification autonomy and mobility. In addition to new electric vehicles models and hybrid versions of existing models the company is expanding its test fleet of 30 autonomous vehicles and has begun testing in Europe (it plans to have a fully autonomous vehicle in commercial production in 2021). A 2017 partnership with Lyft ride sharing service and a $1 billion investment in artificial intelligence startup Argo AI will pave the way for the development of software for self-driving vehicles. Ford is also working on establishing its Transportation Mobility Cloud an open cloud-based platform to manage a city?s transportation ecosystem.

Mergers and Acquisitions

In 2018 Ford agreed to acquire two transportation software companies Autonomic and TransLoc ? part of its plan to speed up the development of new products such as microtransit services and self-driving cars.

Ford's $65 million acquisition of app-based crowd-sourced shuttle service Chariot (completed in 2017) is allowing it to use data algorithms to schedule trips in real time. Chariot uses 100 Ford Transit 15-seat vans; its 28 routes have been based on demand from riders. Ford is expanding the service from two cities (San Francisco and Austin) to eight with at least one outside the US.

HISTORY

Henry Ford started the Ford Motor Company in 1903 in Dearborn Michigan. In 1908 Ford introduced the Model T produced on a moving assembly line that revolutionized both carmaking and manufacturing. By 1920 some 60% of all vehicles on the road were Fords.

After Ford omitted its usual dividend in 1916 stockholders sued. Ford responded by buying back all of its outstanding shares in 1919 and didn't allow outside ownership again until 1956.

Ford bought Lincoln Motor Company in 1922 and discontinued the Model T in 1927. Its replacement the Model A came in 1932. With Henry Ford's health failing his son Edsel became president that year. Despite the debut of the Mercury (1938) market share slipped behind General Motors and Chrysler. After Edsel's death in 1943 his son Henry II took over and decentralized Ford following the GM model. Henry Ford died in 1947 at the age of 83. In 1950 the carmaker recaptured second place. Ford rolled out the infamous Edsel line in 1958 and launched the Mustang in 1964.

Ford acquired Hertz in 1994 and two years later bought #3 rental agency Budget Rent a Car (sold 1997). Also in 1996 it sold a 19% stake in finance unit Associates First Capital in an IPO and increased its stake in Mazda to one-third. The next year Ford sold its heavy-duty truck unit to Daimler's Freightliner subsidiary (since renamed Daimler Trucks North America) for about $200 million and spun off 19% of Hertz in an IPO. Also in 1997 it launched automotive systems supplier Visteon (formerly Ford Automotive Products Operations) at the Frankfurt Motor Show.

Decades later in order to focus on its struggling automotive operations Ford sold its Hertz car rental business in 2005 to a private equity group made up of Clayton Dubilier & Rice The Carlyle Group and Merrill Lynch Global Private Equity for $5.6 billion and the assumption of nearly $10 billion of Hertz debt.

In mid-2009 the US Department of Energy approved $5.9 billion in low-interest loans to Ford for converting its US plants to making cleaner more efficient engines transmissions and vehicles. As a result Ford reported it would spend $550 million to convert its Michigan Assembly Plant where Ford Expedition and Lincoln Navigator SUVs were produced into a modern facility for making its next-generation Focus small car. The new Focus rolled off the assembly line in 2010 with an all-electric version of the Focus to follow in 2011. Ford consolidated operations from its Wayne Assembly Plant as part of the project and worked with the UAW on more flexible work rules for the Michigan Assembly Plant. In addition Ford converted its Cuautitlan Assembly Plant in Mexico from SUV production to assembly of small cars commencing in 2011. The Mexican plant began building the new Fiesta subcompact in 2010.

With the automotive industry reeling from the Great Recession companies made decisions to streamline their operations for survival. In mid-2010 Ford sold all of Volvo Car Corporation to Geely Automotive a subsidiary of China-based Zhejiang Geely Holding Group. Volvo's headquarters and manufacturing operations remain in Sweden and Belgium with Stefan Jacoby (former CEO of Volkswagen Group of America) serving as president and CEO of Volvo Cars. At the onset of 2011 Ford's Mercury model production was discontinued.

EXECUTIVES

Group Vice President Human Resources And Corporate Services, Felicia J Fields
Evp And Cfo, Robert L. (Bob) Shanks, age 65, $858,000 total compensation
President Ford Motor Company Fund & Community Services, James G. (Jim) Vella
Chairman And Ceo Ford China, Jason Luo, age 52
Evp And President Global Markets, James D. (Jim) Farley, age 55, $918,750 total compensation
Evp And President Global Operations, Joseph R. (Joe) Hinrichs, age 52, $1,053,500 total compensation
Chairman And Ceo Ford China, Dave L. (Dave) Schoch, age 66
Vp And Coo Ford Europe, Steven Armstrong
Chief Marketing Officer And President Lincoln, A. Kumar Galhotra
Executive Director Material Planning & Logistics, Frederiek Toney, age 62
Group Vp And President Asia Pacific, Peter Fleet
Vp; President Changan Ford Automotive, Nigel Harris, age 57
Evp Product Development And Cto, Raj Nair, age 53
Evp And President Mobility, Marcy Klevorn, age 58
President Ford Middle East And Africa, Jacques Brent
President Ford South America, Lyle Watters
President And Ceo Ford Motor Company Of Canada Limited, Mark Buzzell
Group Vp; Chairman And Ceo Ford Motor Credit Company, Joy Falotico
Ceo, Jim Hackett, age 63
President And Ceo Ford Motor Company Southern Africa (fmcsa), Jeffery Nemeth
Director Marketing And Sales Ford Asean And Managing Director Ford Thailand, Yukontorn (Vickie) Wisadkosin
Vp Quality And New Model Launch, Linda Cash
Executive Director Hr Global Markets, Kiersten Robinson
Ric Pte Navp Portfolio Manager Vehicle Solutions, Mark Anders
Vice President Marketing, Lee Jelenic
Vice President Quality Ford Europe, Gunnar Herrmann
Vice President, Ken Washington
Executive Vice President; President Global Markets, Jim Farley
National Accounts Manager, Katherine Garland
Vice President, Michael Null Parente
Vice President Marketing Sales And Service, Roelant Dewaard
Vp Vehicle Component And System Engineering, Jim Holland
Group Vp Sustainability Environment And Safety Engineering, Kimberly Pittel
National Account Manager, Mark Lowrey
Executive Vice President Marketing And Sales Executive Vice President Asia Pacific, David McClelland
Government Relations, Marilee Chlebicki
Vp And Treasurer, Kenneth R Kent
Executive Chairman, William C. (Bill) Ford, age 60
Financial Strategy Treasurers Office, Mark Turner
Auditors: PricewaterhouseCoopers LLP

LOCATIONS

HQ: Ford Motor Co. (DE)
One American Road, Dearborn, MI 48126
Phone: 313 322-3000
Web: www.corporate.ford.com

2017 Sales

	$ mil.	% of total
US	93,844	60
United Kingdom	9,619	6
Canada	10,580	7
Germany	7,265	5
All Others	35,468	22
Total	**156,776**	**100**

PRODUCTS/OPERATIONS

Selected Products
Automotive Products
  Automotive relays
  Camera modules
  Car navigation systems
  Car speakers
  Charging systems
  Cockpit systems
  EV relays
  Head up displays
  Instrument panel switches
  Lithium-ion batteries
  Telematics control units
Cars
  C-Max
  Fiesta
  Focus
  Fusion
  Mustang
  Taurus
Crossovers and SUVs
  EcoSport
  Escape
  Edge
  Flex
  Explorer
  Expedition
Commercial Vehicles
  Chassis Cab
  E-Series Cutaway
  F-650
  F-750
  Stripped Chassis
  Super Duty Pickup
  Transit Chassis Cab and Cutaway
  Transit Connect
Hybrids and Electric Vehicles
  C-Max Hybrid
  C-Max Energi
  Focus Electric
  Fusion Hybrid
  Fusion Energi
Performance Vehicles
  F-150 Raptor
  Fiesta ST
  Focus RS
  Focus SST
  GT
  Mustang Shelby GT350
Trucks and Vans
  F-150
  Super Duty
  Transit Connect
  Transit Passenger Wagon

2017 Sales

	$ mil.	% of total
Automotive	145,653	93
Financial services	11,113	7
Other	10	-
Total	**156,776**	**100**

COMPETITORS

BMW	Mitsubishi Motors
Daimler	Nissan
Fiat Chrysler	Peugeot
General Motors	Renault
Honda	Suzuki Motor
Hyundai Motor	Tata Motors
Isuzu	Toyota
Kia Motors	Volkswagen
Mazda	Volvo

HISTORICAL FINANCIALS
Company Type: Public

Income Statement   FYE: December 31

	REVENUE ($ mil.)	NET INCOME ($ mil.)	NET PROFIT MARGIN	EMPLOYEES
12/17	156,776	7,602	4.8%	202,000
12/16	151,800	4,596	3.0%	201,000
12/15	149,558	7,373	4.9%	199,000
12/14	144,077	3,187	2.2%	187,000
12/13	146,917	7,155	4.9%	181,000
Annual Growth	**1.6%**	**1.5%**	**—**	**2.8%**

2017 Year-End Financials

Debt ratio: 59.85%
Return on equity: 23.73%
Cash ($ mil.): 18,492
Current ratio: 1.23
Long-term debt ($ mil.): 102,666

Dividends
  Yield: 0.0%
  Payout: 34.2%
Market value ($ mil.): —

	STOCK PRICE ($) FY Close	P/E High/Low		Earnings	PER SHARE ($) Dividends	Book Value
12/17	12.49	7	6	1.90	0.65	8.78
12/16	12.13	12	10	1.15	0.85	7.34
12/15	14.09	9	7	1.84	0.60	7.22
12/14	15.50	22	17	0.80	0.50	6.27
12/13	15.43	10	7	1.76	0.40	6.69
Annual Growth	**(5.1%)**	**—**	**—**	**1.9%**	**12.9%**	**7.0%**

Fortive Corp

Auditors: Ernst & Young LLP

LOCATIONS

HQ: Fortive Corp
6920 Seaway Blvd, Everett, WA 98203
Phone: 425 446-5000
Web: www.fortive.com

HISTORICAL FINANCIALS
Company Type: Public

Income Statement   FYE: December 31

	REVENUE ($ mil.)	NET INCOME ($ mil.)	NET PROFIT MARGIN	EMPLOYEES
12/17	6,656	1,044	15.7%	26,000
12/16	6,224	872	14.0%	24,000
12/15	6,178	863	14.0%	22,000
12/14	6,337	883	13.9%	—
12/13	5,961	830	13.9%	—
Annual Growth	**2.8%**	**5.9%**	**—**	**—**

2017 Year-End Financials

Debt ratio: 38.63%
Return on equity: 32.25%
Cash ($ mil.): 962
Current ratio: 1.83
Long-term debt ($ mil.): 4,056

No. of shares (mil.): 347
Dividends
  Yield: 0.0%
  Payout: 9.4%
Market value ($ mil.): 25,163

	STOCK PRICE ($) FY Close	P/E High/Low		Earnings	PER SHARE ($) Dividends	Book Value
12/17	72.35	25	18	2.96	0.28	10.90
12/16	53.63	22	19	2.51	0.14	7.77
Annual Growth	**7.8%**	**—**	**—**	**4.2%**	**18.9%**	**8.8%**

Fortune Brands Home & Security, Inc.

Fortune Brands Home & Security (FBHS) holds the keys to the kitchen and the garden shed. With about 45 plants worldwide the consumer products manufacturer makes and sells kitchen and bathroom cabinets faucets entry doors trim and padlocks. Its well-known brands include Moen faucets MasterBrand Cabinets SentrySafe and Therma-Tru entry doors along with Master Lock and American Lock padlocks and other security products. Most of the company's products are the top sellers in their respective markets. FBHS was formed in 2011 when its former parent company Fortune Brands spun off its alcohol and home and security brands as separate businesses.

Operations
Fortune Brands Home & Security (FBHS) operates four business segments: Cabinets Plumbing Security and Doors.

The Cabinets segment generates nearly 50% of sales and ranks as the #1 maker of such cabinetry in North America. Its brands include Aristokraft Mid-Continent Diamond Kitchen Classics among others. The Plumbing business brings in around 30% of sales and manufactures Moen Cleveland Faucet Group and Waste King brand faucets the leading brands in North America and China. Doors accounts for 10% of sales and makes doors and vinyl windows; and Security which also brings in around 10% of sales is the #1 maker of padlocks in North America and Europe.

Geographic Reach
Illinois-based Fortune Brands Home & Security (FBHS) rang up almost 85% of its sales in the US in 2015. Canada is the company's largest international market representing about 10% of sales. China and other countries account for the rest. Other major markets for FBHS include Europe Southeast Asia South America and Mexico. The company operates some 30 US manufacturing facilities in 16 states and has around 15 international plant locations in Mexico Asia Europe and Canada.

Sales and Marketing
Fortune Brands Home & Security (FBHS) two largest customers are Home Depot and Lowe's Companies together accounting for about 30% of annual sales. The company sells directly through its own sales force and indirectly through independent manufacturers' representatives. Other sales channels include kitchen and bath dealers wholesalers catering to builders or professional remodelers industrial distributors and other retail outlets including mass merchants. Sales to all US home centers in the aggregate account for approximately 25% of net sales.

Financial Performance
The improving US home products market market share gains growth overseas and acquisitions have collectively driven Fortune Brands Home & Security (FBHS)'s sales up in recent years.

In fiscal 2016 sales grew a further 9% to $5.0 billion due to continued expansion in the housing market acquisitions in the Cabinets and Plumbing segments. and higher prices.

Net income grew 31% to $413.2 million as increases in revenue outpaced the relative increase in selling costs. The company achieved productivity gains and benefited from the positive contributions from the acquired businesses.

Cash from operations grew 52% to $650.5 million due to a reduction in working capital in 2016 and higher net income.

Strategy

Fortune Brands Home Security (FBHS) is focused on expanding internationally. It is developing its relationships with its dealers and distributors and their Moen branded stores throughout China India and South America. Master Lock expanded its presence further in Europe and Asia (primarily Japan) while Therma-Tru made inroads in Canada as consumers transitioned from traditional entry door materials to more advanced and energy-efficient fiberglass doors.

FBHS is also focused on expanding its product portfolio. Its Norcraft Companies expands regional market presence and enhances frameless cabinetry. In 2016 MasterBrand Cabinets launched new cabinet door designs color palettes and features in a range of styles; exclusive laminate door & finish options. Its Moen brand introduces hand showers featuring the Magnetix magnetic docking system a new line of garbage disposals Spot Resist finish touchless Motionsense electronic faucets and pull-out and pull-down faucets with Reflex self-retraction. Its Therma-Tru released a portfolio of on-trend door and glass collections.

Signaling its intent to boost its plumbing business the company in late 2016 created Global Plumbing Group. Its goal is to increase plumbing sales to $2.5 billion by 2020 (from $1.5 billion in 2016). The division will become a multi-brand -channel and -geography business and will grow organically and through acquisitions; its first such acquisitions were Riobel a Canadian premium showroom brand; ROHL a Californian luxury brand; and TCL Manufacturing which gave it control of Perrin & Rowe a UK manufacturer of luxury kitchen and bathroom plumbing products.

Mergers and Acquisitions

In 2016 Fortune Brands Home Security made a number of acquisitions to add meat to its new Global Plumbing Group division. It bought Riobel a Canadian premium showroom brand with annual sales of $40 million which it followed up with the acquisitions of ROHL and TCL Manufacturing. ROHL is a manufacturer of high-end faucets and TCL owns Perrin & Rowe a UK luxury kitchen plumbing company.

Company Background

Formed in 1988 as a Fortune Brands subsidiary the company was spun off in 2011.

In 2013 FBHS' Kitchen & Bath Cabinetry business acquired WoodCrafters a manufacturer of bathroom vanities and tops for about $302 million. The purchase expanded the company's bathroom cabinetry products offering.

EXECUTIVES

Evp, E. Lee Wyatt, age 65, $770,333 total compensation
President The Master Lock Co., Michael P. (Mike) Bauer, age 53
Ceo, Christopher J. (Chris) Klein, age 54, $1,093,333 total compensation
President Masterbrand Cabinets, David M. Randich, age 56, $585,269 total compensation
President Therma-tru, Brett Finley, age 47
Svp Global Growth And Development, Tracey Belcourt
President Global Plumbing Group, Nicholas I. Fink, age 43, $505,833 total compensation
President U.s. Businesses Moen, Troy Shay
Svp And Cfo, Patrick D. Hallinan
Vice President Investor Relations Home And Security, Brian Lantz
Vice President Treasurer, Matt Lenz
Vice President Tax, Kathleen Weston
Vice President Associate General Counsel, Scott D'Angelo
Vice President Corporate Development, Wayne Partington
Vp Total Rewards, Margaret Reddick

Chairman, David M. Thomas
Board Member, Ann Hackett
Assistant Secretary, Angela Pla
Auditors: PricewaterhouseCoopers LLP

LOCATIONS

HQ: Fortune Brands Home & Security, Inc.
520 Lake Cook Road, Deerfield, IL 60015-5611
Phone: 847 484-4400
Web: www.fbhs.com

2016 Sales

	$ mil.	% of total
US	4,258	86
Canada	406	8
China & other international	320	6
Total	**4,984**	**100**

PRODUCTS/OPERATIONS

2016 Sales

	$ mil.	% of total
Cabinets	2,397	48
Plumbing	1,534	31
Security	579	12
Doors	473	9
Total	**4,984**	**100**

Selected Brands

Aristokraft
Diamond
Homecrest
Kitchen Classics
Kitchen Craft
Master Lock
MasterBrand Cabinets
Mid-Continent
Moen
Omega
Schrock
Sentry
SafeStar
Mark
Therma-Tru Doors
Thomasville
Ultracraft
Selected Products Cabinets
Stock cabinetry
Vanities
Plumbing Accessor

COMPETITORS

American Woodmark	Kwikset Corporation
Andersen Corporation	Masco
Armstrong World Industries	Pella
	Pfister
B.J. Tidwell Industries	Republic National Cabinet
Conestoga	Stanley Black and Decker
Delta Faucet	Sterilite
Elkay Manufacturing	US Home Systems
JELD-WEN	Wood-Mode
Kohler	

HISTORICAL FINANCIALS

Company Type: Public

Income Statement

FYE: December 31

	REVENUE ($ mil.)	NET INCOME ($ mil.)	NET PROFIT MARGIN	EMPLOYEES
12/17	5,283	472	8.9%	23,800
12/16	4,984	413	8.3%	22,700
12/15	4,579	315	6.9%	21,400
12/14	4,013	158	3.9%	18,000
12/13	4,157	229	5.5%	19,500
Annual Growth	**6.2%**	**19.8%**	**—**	**5.1%**

2017 Year-End Financials

Debt ratio: 27.35%
Return on equity: 19.05%
Cash ($ mil.): 323
Current ratio: 1.77
Long-term debt ($ mil.): 1,507

No. of shares (mil.): 151
Dividends
  Yield: 0.0%
  Payout: 23.7%
Market value ($ mil.): 10,397

	STOCK PRICE ($) FY Close	P/E High/Low	PER SHARE ($) Earnings	Dividends	Book Value
12/17	68.44	23 17	3.03	0.72	17.11
12/16	53.46	24 17	2.62	0.64	15.39
12/15	55.50	29 22	1.93	0.56	15.33
12/14	45.27	49 38	0.95	0.48	14.29
12/13	45.70	33 21	1.34	0.30	15.90
Annual Growth	**10.6%**	**— —**	**22.6%**	**24.5%**	**1.9%**

Franklin Financial Network Inc

EXECUTIVES

Chb-Pres, Richard E Herrington
Exec V Pres-Cfo, Sarah L Meyerrose
Exec V Pres-Chief ADM Officer, Sally P Kimble
Board Member, Gregory Waldron
Board Member, Henry Brockman
Lead Independent Director, Melody Sullivan
Board Member, Pamela Stephens
Board Member, Paul Pratt
Evp Strategy, Chris Black
Auditors: Crowe Horwath LLP

LOCATIONS

HQ: Franklin Financial Network Inc
722 Columbia Avenue, Franklin, TN 37064
Phone: 615 236-2265
Web: www.franklinsynergybank.com

HISTORICAL FINANCIALS

Company Type: Public

Income Statement

FYE: December 31

	ASSETS ($ mil.)	NET INCOME ($ mil.)	INCOME AS % OF ASSETS	EMPLOYEES
12/17	3,843	28	0.7%	281
12/16	2,943	28	1.0%	268
12/15	2,167	16	0.7%	226
12/14	1,355	8	0.6%	220
12/13	796	4	0.6%	—
Annual Growth	**48.2%**	**57.5%**		

2017 Year-End Financials

Debt ratio: 1.52%
Return on equity: 9.77%
Cash ($ mil.): 1,466
Current ratio: —
Long-term debt ($ mil.): —

No. of shares (mil.): 13
Dividends
  Yield: —
  Payout: —
Market value ($ mil.): 451

	STOCK PRICE ($) FY Close	P/E High/Low	PER SHARE ($) Earnings	Dividends	Book Value
12/17	34.10	20 14	2.04	0.00	23.01
12/16	41.85	17 10	2.42	0.00	20.73
12/15	31.38	20 11	1.54	0.00	17.86
12/14	17.30	17 13	1.27	0.00	15.70
12/13	12.90	11 11	1.10	0.00	13.40
Annual Growth	**27.5%**	**— —**	**16.7%**	**—**	**14.5%**

Franklin Resources, Inc.

Operating as Franklin Templeton Investments Franklin Resources manages mutual funds that invest in international and domestic stocks taxable and tax-exempt money market instruments and corporate municipal and US government bonds. Franklin Resources also offers separately managed accounts closed-end funds insurance product funds and retirement and college savings plans. Its open-end US funds are offered through about 1100 banks and securities and financial adviser firms; about 2700 banks and securities and financial adviser firms offer shares of its cross-border non-US funds. The products are housed under the company's Franklin Templeton Franklin Mutual Series Franklin Bissett Fiduciary Trust Darby Balanced Equity Management K2 LibertyShares and Edinburgh Partners brands. The US is the company's largest market.

Operations

Most of Franklin Resources' revenue (nearly 70%) come from investment management fees which are directly tied to its assets under management. Sales and distribution fees generate about 25% of revenue and are made up of sales charges and commissions derived from sales and distribution of the company's sponsored investment products (SIPs).

In addition to its core business Franklin Resources also provides shareholder services and manages investments for high-net-worth clients and institutional investors. These services make up less than 5% of overall revenue.

Franklin Resources and its subsidiaries boast roughly $720 billion in assets under management.

Geographic Reach

Based in San Mateo California Franklin Resources boasts an extensive global presence with offices in more than 30 countries and clients reaching across 170-plus countries. The firm has operations in the Americas; Europe the Middle East and Africa (EMEA); and the Asia-Pacific region.

Of its assets under management about two-thirds are in the US; EMEA and the Asia-Pacific region each account for nearly 15%. Most of its revenue comes from the US (more than $3.7 billion) while a significant portion comes from Luxembourg (about $1.7 billion); together the two countries account for more than 85% of total company revenue.

Sales and Marketing

Franklin Resources relies on a large network of independent financial intermediaries to be the front end of the sales process. In the US approximately 1100 local regional and national banks securities firms and financial adviser firms offer shares in Franklin's US funds. Outside the US Franklin Resources leverages about 2700 banks securities firms and financial adviser firms to sell its non-US funds to the investing public.

The company sells its investment products and services under a variety of brand names such as Franklin Templeton Franklin Mutual Series Franklin Bissett Fiduciary Trust Darby Balanced Equity Management K2 LibertyShares and Edinburgh Partners.

The company generates brand awareness through advertisements in major financial publications television internet through sporting event sponsorship and social media marketing.

Financial Performance

Franklin Resources' revenue has decreased every year since fiscal 2014 ending the period down about 25% as investment management fees fell along with average assets under management and effective fee rates. Sales and distribution fees

also receded due to reduced assets under management and lower commissionable sales. Net income fell more than two-thirds in that time on the poor revenue performance. The company's cash stores lost about 10% as it slashed its long-term debt by about two-thirds.

Franklin's revenue slipped 1% to $6.3 billion in 2018 compared with the prior year. Investment management fees (which account for about $4.4 billion – nearly 70% — of the company's revenue) ticked up only $8.3 million on a slight increase in average assets under management. Sales and distribution fees which provide about 25% of revenue decreased 6% on lower average US assets under management and a reduction in total commissionable sales.

The company's net income fell 55% to $764 million in 2018 owing to an income tax charge related to the enactment of the Tax Cuts and Jobs Act.

Franklin's cash dropped $1.8 billion to $6.9 billion in 2018. Operations provided $2.2 billion as net trading in securities of consolidated investment products decreased and income taxes payable increased. Investments and financings used $290.4 million and $3.8 billion respectively. Investment spend was mainly for purchase of investments and net additions of property and equipment. Major financing activities included dividend payments and common stock repurchases.

Strategy

Franklin Resources' strategy includes stemming the tide of net fund redemptions by its clientele growing its distribution network outside the US taking advantage of a global return to value investing (as opposed to growth investing which has led the charge in recent years) and acquiring companies that complement its business.

Despite its key tenet to sell more shares in its funds than it redeems Franklin has experienced net fund outflows in past years. As part of its correction efforts the firm is expanding its distribution network (particularly outside the US) to address the growing population of middle class investors in emerging markets. International institutional long-term sales increased more than 40% in Franklin's fiscal 2018 compared with the previous year.

A headwind buffeting Franklin for the last decade is a widespread investment strategy focusing on growth stocks. Franklin's equity funds typically are value oriented which have lagged the market in recent years. With the rising interest rate environment in the US and similar raises in other countries Franklin believes the headwind will turn into a tailwind as value investing returns to favor.

In early 2018 the company entered three business acquisition agreements for US alternative credit manager Benefit Street Partners data science and non-bank marketplace lending investment firm Random Forest Capital and independent value investment management firm Edinburgh Partners. The Benefit Street purchase will expand Franklin's alternative credit offerings which have seen increased demand in the last decade. Random Forest provides the company with extended data science capabilities including machine learning and statistical algorithms to solve for expected gains in financial instruments. Edinburgh brought $10 billion in global and emerging markets equities to the firm.

Mergers and Acquisitions

In 2018 Franklin Resources agreed to acquire US alternative credit manager Benefit Street Partners for $683 million in cash of which $130 million will be used to retire debt Benefit Street debt. The acquisition expected to close in Franklin's fiscal 2Q19 will bolster Franklin Templeton's alternative credit offerings which have seen increased demand

in the last decade from middle market companies and investors seeking assets with higher yields and lower volatility compared with traditional fixed-income products. Based in New York with five other US offices Benefit Street had $26.2 billion in assets under management at the end of 2018.

Franklin also agreed to purchase data science and non-bank marketplace lending investment firm Random Forest Capital in 2018. Random Forest uses machine learning and statistical algorithms to solve for expected gains on financial instruments.

Furthermore Franklin acquired independent value investment management firm Edinburgh Partners in 2018. Based in Edinburgh UK with an office in London and two in the United States Edinburgh Partners managed about $10 billion in global and emerging markets equities at the end of 2017.

Company Background

Rupert Johnson Sr. founded Franklin Distributors (capitalizing on Benjamin Franklin's reputation for thrift) in New York in 1947; it launched its first fund Franklin Custodian in 1948. Custodian grew into five funds including conservatively managed equity and bond funds. In 1968 Johnson's son Charles (who had joined the firm in 1957) became president and CEO. The company went public in 1971 as Franklin Resources.

EXECUTIVES

Chairman And Ceo, Gregory E. Johnson, age 58, $783,633 total compensation

President, Jennifer M. Johnson, age 55, $527,356 total compensation

Evp And Cfo, Kenneth A. Lewis, age 58, $527,356 total compensation

Evp Alternative Strategies, William Y. Yun, age 59, $525,000 total compensation

Evp Investment Management, John M. Lusk, $527,356 total compensation

Evp And General Counsel, Craig S. Tyle, age 59

Svp And Cio, Priscilla Moyer

Chairman And Ceo, Gregory E. Johnson, age 58

Vice Chairman, Rupert H. Johnson, age 79

Auditors: Pricewaterhouse Coopers LLP

LOCATIONS

HQ: Franklin Resources, Inc.
One Franklin Parkway, San Mateo, CA 94403
Phone: 650 312-2000   **Fax:** 650 312-3655
Web: www.franklinresources.com

2018 Sales by Geography

	$ mil.	% of total
United States	3,722	59
Luxembourg	1,730	27
Canada	250	4
Asia-Pacific	297	5
The Bahamas	208	3
Europe the Middle East and Africa excluding Luxembourg	97	2
Latin America	13	-
Total	**6,319**	**100**

PRODUCTS/OPERATIONS

2018 Sales by Type

	$ mil.	% of total
Investment management fees	4,367	69
Sales & distribution fees	1,599	25
Shareholder servicing fees	221	4
Other	129	2
Total	**6,319**	**100**

2018 Average Assets Under Management by Asset Class

	% of total
Equity	43
Fixed-income	37
Hybrid	19
Cash management	1
Total	**100**

Selected Subsidiaries

Balanced Equity Management Pty. Limited
Darby - Hana Infrastructure Fund Management Co. Ltd.
Fiduciary Trust Company of Canada
Fiduciary Trust (International) Sàrl
Franklin Mutual Advisers LLC
Franklin Templeton Services LLC
ITI Capital Markets Limited
Riva Financial Systems Limited
Templeton Asset Management Ltd.

COMPETITORS

AllianceBernstein	Legg Mason
American Century	Morgan Stanley
BlackRock	Old Mutual (US)
Capital Group	PIMCO
Dodge & Cox	Principal Financial
FMR	Putnam
Invesco	T. Rowe Price
John Hancock Financial Services	The Vanguard Group

HISTORICAL FINANCIALS

Company Type: Public

Income Statement
FYE: September 30

	REVENUE ($ mil.)	NET INCOME ($ mil.)	NET PROFIT MARGIN	EMPLOYEES
09/18	6,319	764	12.1%	9,700
09/17	6,392	1,696	26.5%	9,400
09/16	6,618	1,726	26.1%	9,100
09/15	7,948	2,035	25.6%	9,500
09/14	8,491	2,384	28.1%	9,300
Annual Growth	(7.1%)	(24.8%)	—	1.1%

2018 Year-End Financials

Debt ratio: 5.06%
Return on equity: 6.79%
Cash ($ mil.): 6,910
Current ratio: 3.71
Long-term debt ($ mil.): 728

No. of shares (mil.): 519
Dividends
Yield: 0.1%
Payout: 282.0%
Market value ($ mil.): 15,787

	STOCK PRICE ($) FY Close	P/E High/Low	PER SHARE ($) Earnings	Dividends	Book Value
09/18	30.41	33 22	1.39	3.92	19.07
09/17	44.51	16 11	3.01	0.80	22.74
09/16	35.57	14 10	2.94	0.72	20.93
09/15	37.26	18 11	3.29	1.10	19.62
09/14	54.61	15 13	3.79	0.48	18.60
Annual Growth	(13.6%)	— —	(22.2%)	69.0%	0.6%

Freddie Mac

These siblings know there's no place like home. Government-sponsored enterprises (GSEs) Freddie Mac (officially Federal Home Loan Mortgage Corporation) and Fannie Mae were established to buy residential mortgages and boost the housing market. They do so by purchasing mortgages from lenders and packaging them for resale thereby mitigating risk and allowing lenders to provide mortgages to those who may not otherwise qualify. The agency also provides assistance for affordable rental housing. Together Fannie and Freddie guarantee some 70% of all new home loans in the US. Due to losses related to the subprime mortgage crisis the government seized Fannie and Freddie in 2008. Government plans to divest the firms into private ownership have proven difficult; they remain GSEs.

HISTORY

Ah the '60s — free love great tunes and a war nobody wanted to pay for with taxes. By the '70s inflation was rising and real income was starting to fall. To divert a construction industry recession Congress created a new entity to buy home mortgages and boost the flow of money into the housing market.

Fannie Mae had been buying mortgages since 1938 but focused on Federal Housing Administration (FHA) and Veterans Administration loans. In 1970 Congress created Freddie Mac and enlarged Fannie Mae's field of action to include conventional mortgages. Still rising interest rates in the 1970s were brutal to the US real estate market.

In the early 1980s dealers devised a way to securitize the company's loans — seen as somewhat frumpy investments — by packaging them into more alluring bond-like investments made even sexier by the implicit government guarantee. When three major government securities dealers collapsed in 1985 ownership of some Freddie Mac securities was in doubt and the Federal Reserve Bank of New York quickly automated registration of government securities.

In 1984 Freddie Mac issued shares to members of the Federal Home Loan Bank (the overseer of US savings and loans). By 1989 the shares had been converted to common stock and were traded on the NYSE. Freddie Mac's board expanded from three political appointees to 18 members.

Nationwide real estate defaults (rampant in the wake of the late 1980s crash) kindled concern about Freddie Mac's reserve levels and whether it might need to tap its US Treasury line of credit. In response Congress in 1992 created the Office of Federal Housing Enterprise Oversight to regulate Freddie Mac and Fannie Mae. Initial examinations sounded no alarms. A 1996 Congressional Budget Office report questioned whether the government should continue its implicit guarantees of the pair's debt securities.

In 1997 Freddie Mac officially adopted its longtime nickname. The next year it launched a system to cut loan approval time from weeks to minutes (it agreed to develop a similar version for the FHA). The streamlining was crucial to pacts in which mortgage lenders (including one of the US's largest Wells Fargo) promised to sell Freddie Mac their loan originations. In 1999 Freddie Mac hired former House Speaker Newt Gingrich as a consultant.

Freddie Mac made a major Internet push in 2000 with its first online taxable bond offering. A wired venture involving Freddie Mac Microsoft and such big lenders as Chase Manhattan (now part of JPMorgan Chase & Co.) Bank of America and Wells Fargo drew fire from small banks that said it would push them out of the online lending business.

In 2001 Freddie Mac bought Tuttle Decision Systems a loan-pricing software system provider. Critics responded that Freddie Mac overstepped its government charter with such a move.

In a move initiated by its auditor Freddie Mac re-audited its earnings from 2000 to 2003 uncovering accounting irregularities and employee misconduct. Further investigations executive oustings restructuring and numerous lawsuits followed. In late 2003 Freddie Mac announced the findings of its re-audit. The company admitted to understating earnings by $4.4 billion between 2000 and 2002 and overstating profits by $989 million in 2001 all in an attempt to smooth out results and show steady profit growth.

In 2006 the company paid a record $3.8 million fine to settle allegations by the Federal Election Commission that the company made illegal campaign c

EXECUTIVES

Evp General Counsel And Corporate Secretary, William H. (Bill) McDavid, age 70, $500,000 total compensation
Ceo, Donald H. (Don) Layton, age 67, $600,000 total compensation
Vice President, James Bowden
Evp And Chief Administrative Officer, Jerry Weiss, age 57, $450,000 total compensation
Evp Multifamily Business, David M. Brickman
Chairman, Christopher S. Lynch, age 60
Evp And Cio, Stacey Goodman, age 55
Evp Single-family Business, David B. (Dave) Lowman, age 57, $500,000 total compensation
Evp And Cfo, James G. Mackey, age 51, $500,000 total compensation
Evp Investments And Capital Markets, Michael Hutchins
Evp And Chief Enterprise Risk Officer, Anil Hinduja, $500,000 total compensation
Senior Vice President And National Head Multifamily Underwriting And Credit, Deborah Jenkins
Vice President Executive Compensation, Daniel Scheinkman
Vice President Call Centers, Jeanmarie Puglisi
Vice President Information Technology And Chief Administrative Officer, Tammy Hoffman
Vp And Chief Tax Officer, Gregory Metz
Vice President Underwriting, Stephen Lansbury
Executive Vice President General Counsel Corporate Secretary, Robert Bostrom
Senior Vice President, John Cannon
Vice President Risk Process And Governance, Ken Moskowitz
Vice President Sourcing, Sally W Baker
Vice President Servicing Operations, Ken Burke
Vice President Of Tax Accounting And Compliance, Michael Culhane
Vice President Multiclass Issuance, Mike Dawson
Vice President Singlefamily Customer Care, Kelly Steele
Svp Enterprise Chief Risk Officer Investments And Capital Markets, Jorge Reis
Senior Vice President Sales And Relationship Mgt, Chris Boyle
Vice President Change Management, Bill Cary
Vice President Multifamily Asset Management, Pamela Dent
Vp Targeted Affordable Sales And Investment Multifamily, David Leopold
Vice President, Ty Miller
National Account Manager, Steve Pattee
Vice President Customer Technology Integration, Rick Lang
Chairman, Christopher S. Lynch, age 60
Vice Chair, Mark Friend
Auditors: PricewaterhouseCoopers LLP

LOCATIONS

HQ: Freddie Mac
   8200 Jones Branch Drive, McLean, VA 22102-3110
Phone: 703 903-2000
Web: www.freddiemac.com

PRODUCTS/OPERATIONS

2017 Sales

	$ mil.	% of total
Interest		
Mortgage loans	63,735	85
Securities	3,415	5
Other	657	1
Non-interest	6,869	9
Adjustments	(53643)	-
Total	20,692	100

HISTORICAL FINANCIALS

Company Type: Public

Income Statement   FYE: December 31

	ASSETS ($ mil.)	NET INCOME ($ mil.)	INCOME AS % OF ASSETS	EMPLOYEES
12/17	2,040,770	5,025	0.3%	6,185
12/16	2,023,376	7,815	0.4%	6,004
12/15	1,986,050	6,376	0.3%	5,462
12/14	1,945,539	7,690	0.4%	5,007
12/13	1,966,061	48,668	2.5%	5,112
Annual Growth	1.0%	(41.7%)	—	4.9%

2017 Year-End Financials

Debt ratio: 96.56%
Return on equity: 236.20%
Cash ($ mil.): 9,811
Current ratio: —
Long-term debt ($ mil.): —

No. of shares (mil.): 650
Dividends
 Yield: —
 Payout: —
Market value ($ mil.): 1,638

	STOCK PRICE ($) FY Close	P/E High/Low		PER SHARE ($)	
			Earnings	Dividends	Book Value
12/17	2.52	— —	(1.00)	0.00	(0.48)
12/16	3.74	147 36	0.03	0.00	7.81
12/15	1.62	— —	(0.01)	0.00	4.52
12/14	2.06	— —	(0.72)	0.00	4.08
12/13	2.90	— —	(1.09)	0.00	19.74
Annual Growth	(3.5%)	— —	—	—	—

Freeport-McMoRan Inc

Freeport McMoran (FCX) is one of the world's major mining companies with holdings in copper molybdenum and gold. It is a leading copper producer with proven or probable reserves of more than 85 billion pounds; the company also has nearly 25 million ounces of gold reserves and about 3 billion pounds of molybdenum reserves. FCX's mines are in the Americas and Indonesia. The US accounts for about 40% of company revenue.

HISTORY

The Freeport Sulfur Company was formed in Texas in 1912 by Francis Pemberton banker Eric Swenson and several investors to develop a sulfur field. The next year Freeport Texas was formed as a holding company for Freeport Sulfur and other enterprises.

During the 1930s the company diversified. In 1936 Freeport pioneered a process to remove hydrocarbons from sulfur. The company joined Consolidated Coal in 1955 to establish the National Potash Company. In 1956 Freeport formed an oil and gas subsidiary Freeport Oil.

Internationally Freeport formed an Australian minerals subsidiary in 1964 and a copper-mining subsidiary in Indonesia in 1967. The company changed its name to Freeport Minerals in 1971 and merged with Utah-based McMoRan Oil & Gas (formerly McMoRan Explorations) in 1982.

McMoRan Explorations had been formed in 1969 by William McWilliams Jim Bob Moffett and Byron Rankin. In 1973 McMoRan formed an exploration and drilling alliance with Dow Chemical and signed a deal with Indonesia to mine in the re-mote Irian Jaya region. McMoRan went public in 1978.

Moffett became chairman and CEO of Freeport-McMoRan in 1984. The company formed Freeport-McMoRan Copper in 1987 to manage its Indonesian operations. The unit assumed the Freeport-McMoRan Copper & Gold name in 1991. Two years later Freeport-McMoRan acquired Rio Tinto Minera a copper-smelting business with operations in Spain.

To support expansion in Indonesia Freeport McMoRan spun off its copper and gold division in 1994. In 1995 Freeport-McMoRan Copper & Gold (FCX) formed an alliance with the UK's RTZ Corporation to develop its Indonesian mineral reserves. Local riots that year closed the Grasberg Mine and FCX's political risk insurance was canceled. Despite these setbacks higher metal prices and growing sales in 1995 helped the company double its operating income.

An Indonesian tribal leader filed a $6 billion lawsuit in 1996 charging FCX with environmental human rights and social and cultural violations. The company called the suit baseless but offered to set aside 1% of its annual revenues or about $15 million to help local tribes. Tribal leaders rejected the offer and in 1997 a judge dismissed the lawsuit.

In 1997 FCX pulled out of Bre-X Minerals' Busang gold mine project which independent tests later proved to be a fraud of historic proportions. Amid widespread rioting Indonesia's embattled president Suharto was forced out of office in 1998. The new government investigated charges of cronyism involving FCX.

FCX received permission from the Indonesian government in 1999 to expand the Grasberg Mine and increase ore output up to 300000 metric tons per day. However the next year an overflow accident killed four workers in Grasberg and as a result of the accident the Indonesian government ordered FCX to reduce its production at the mine by up to 30%. Normal production at the mine resumed in early 2001.

FM Services (administrative legal and financial services) was added as a subsidiary in 2002. In 2003 FCX bought an 86% stake in PT Puncakjaya Power a supplier of power to PT-FI.

The $26 billion acquisition of Phelps Dodge in 2007 brought that company's global copper gold and molybdenum business into the fold. The deal placed FCX in a position to thrive as a global competitor in the rank just below metals and mining giants such as BHP Billiton Rio Tinto and Vale. A year later FCX sold the wire and cable business it acquired in the Phelps Dodge deal to General Cable Corporation for $735 million.

Following the

EXECUTIVES

Evp And Chief Administrative Officer, Michael J. Arnold, age 66, $550,000 total compensation
Vice Chairman President And Ceo, Richard C. Adkerson, age 71, $1,250,000 total compensation
Vice President Taxes, Hugh O Donahue
Evp Cfo And Treasurer, Kathleen L. Quirk, age 54, $650,000 total compensation
President Americas And Africa Mining, Harry M. (Red) Conger, age 86, $500,000 total compensation
Vp And Cio, Bertrand (Bert) Odinet
Vice Chairman President And Ceo, Richard C. Adkerson, age 71
Chairman, Gerald J. Ford, age 74
Evp Cfo And Treasurer, Kathleen L. Quirk, age 54
Auditors: Ernst & Young LLP

LOCATIONS

HQ: Freeport-McMoRan Inc
 333 North Central Avenue, Phoenix, AZ 85004-2189
Phone: 602 366-8100
Web: www.fcx.com

2017 Sales

	$ mil.	% of total
North America Copper mines	4,565	23
Rod & Refining	4	23
Indonesia mining	4,445	23
South America mining	3,694	19
Atlantic Copper Smelting & Refining	2,032	11
Molybdenum mines	268	1
Corporate other & eliminations	(3083)	-
Total	**16,403**	**100**

PRODUCTS/OPERATIONS

2017 Sales

	$ mil.	% of total
Copper in concentrates	5,373	33
Copper Cathode	4,557	28
Refined copper products	2,272	14
Gold	2,032	12
Molybdenum	889	5
Oil	73	1
Other products	1,207	7
Total	**16,403**	**100**

Selected subsidiaries

Atlantic Copper Holding SA (smelting and refining Spain)
Chino Mines Company
Climax Molybdenum Company
FM Service Company (administrative and financial services)
Missouri Lead Smelting Company
Plains Exploration & Production (oil and gas US)
PT Freeport Indonesia Co. (91% mining)
 PT Smelting (Gresik) Co. (25% smelting Indonesia)
PT Irja Eastern Minerals Corp. (mining Indonesia)
PT Puncakjaya Power (86% supplies power to PT Freeport Indonesia)

COMPETITORS

Anglo American
Antofagasta
BHP Billiton
Codelco
First Quantum Minerals
Glencore
KGHM Polska Miedz
Rio Tinto Limited
Southern Copper
Vale Limited

HISTORICAL FINANCIALS

Company Type: Public

Income Statement   FYE: December 31

	REVENUE ($ mil.)	NET INCOME ($ mil.)	NET PROFIT MARGIN	EMPLOYEES
12/17	16,403	1,817	11.1%	53,200
12/16	14,830	(4,315)	—	59,100
12/15	15,877	(12,195)	—	72,000
12/14	21,438	(1,268)	—	81,300
12/13	20,921	2,680	12.8%	74,500
Annual Growth	(5.9%)	(9.3%)	—	(8.1%)

2017 Year-End Financials

Debt ratio: 35.16%
Return on equity: 25.91%
Cash ($ mil.): 4,447
Current ratio: 2.14
Long-term debt ($ mil.): 11,703

No. of shares (mil.): 1,448
Dividends
 Yield: —
 Payout: —
Market value ($ mil.): 27,454

STOCK PRICE ($)	P/E		PER SHARE ($)		
FY Close	High/Low		Earnings	Dividends	Book Value
12/17	18.96	15 9	1.25	0.00	5.51
12/16	13.19	— —	(3.16)	0.00	4.19
12/15	6.77	— —	(11.31)	0.57	6.28
12/14	23.36	— —	(1.26)	1.25	17.60
12/13	37.74	14 10	2.64	2.25	20.17
Annual Growth	(15.8%)	— —	(17.0%)		—(27.7%)

Frontier Communications Corp

Serving city dwellers and country folk alike Frontier Communications provides phone internet video and satellite TV (through a partnership with DISH Network) services in about 30 US states. The company has more than 5.4 million residential and business voice subscribers about 4.35 million broadband internet customers and some 1.4 million video subscribers. Frontier is active mostly in rural and small to mid-sized markets where it is the incumbent local-exchange carrier (ILEC). About 7% of the company?s revenue comes from government support for serving rural areas. In 2016 Frontier acquired the wireline operations of Verizon Communications in California Texas and Florida for about $10.5 billion.

Operations

Frontier Communications' data and internet services contribute more than 40% of revenue while local and long distance services account for about a third of the company's revenue followed by switched access and subsidy revenue about 10% and other services less than 5%.

The company offers broadband video voice and other services and products to residential customers over a combination of fiber and copper-based networks. For business customers Frontier offers broadband Ethernet traditional circuit-based services and voice services. The company also sells customer premise equipment and related maintenance services.

Geographic Reach

Frontier Communications based in Norwalk Connecticut has operations in Alabama Arizona California Connecticut Florida Georgia Idaho Illinois Indiana Iowa Michigan Minnesota Mississippi Montana Nebraska Nevada New Mexico New York North Carolina Ohio Oregon Pennsylvania South Carolina Tennessee Texas Utah Washington West Virginia and Wisconsin. The acquisition of Verizon?s wireline operations in California Texas and Florida expanded Frontier?s activities in those states.

Sales and Marketing

Frontier Communication dials in new customers through its broadband offerings and tries to sell other services such as voice and video to them. However Frontier ran into a churn saw in 2018. The monthly rate of turnover of residential customers (known as churn) grew 10% to 2.17%. All in all the company lost subscribers in video broadband and video during the year.

Financial Performance

After several years of fluctuating revenue Frontier Communications got a boost with the acquisition of Verizon assets in 2016 driving revenue to $8.9 billion up 60% from 2015. A full year of the operations in California Florida and Texas pro-

duced a 5% revenue gain to $9.1 billion. The rise in revenue came mostly from the added three months of sales supplied by the acquired operations. Otherwise revenue fell as did the number of subscribers.

Frontier lost $1.8 billion in 2017 about six times bigger than the $373 million loss of 2016. The company took a $2.7 billion goodwill impairment charge to reflect its financial performance and stock price and align the enterprise value of the company with its fair value.

At the end of 2017 Frontier had a working capital deficit of about $1.2 billion which included $656 million of long-term debt due within one year. The working capital deficit was $788 million in 2016. The difference came from $293 million in long-term debt within a year.

Strategy

Frontier Communications has worked to integrate the California Texas and Florida (CTF) operation it bought from Verizon in 2016 into its own operations. The company highlights the high-speed FiOS service that the CTF brought to the company. It also has tried to quell customer concern about service from Frontier with improved customer service.

The company is investing in technologies to improve service and user experience for its consumer and business customers. It plans to roll out fiber-to-the-home (FTTH) to 50000-100000 residences over the next two years starting with new subdivisions which are less expensive for build out than established neighborhoods. Frontier is also deploying technology fixes to offer higher speeds over the copper wire that still connect most of its customers.

To gather cash to pay for network improvements Frontier suspended its common stock dividend to devote money to reducing debt. The suspension will supply $250 million of additional cash a year that it will use pay down debt faster and give it more financial room to implement its strategy.

Mergers and Acquisitions

The Frontier Communications acquisition of Verizon Communications? wireline operations in California Texas and Florida for $10.5 billion closed in 2016. The acquisition brought about 3.3 million voice connections 2.1 million broadband connections and 1.2 million FiOS video subscribers and the related incumbent local exchange carrier businesses to Frontier. The deal expanded Frontier?s presence large but still fast-growing states and improved the revenue mix by increasing the percentage of revenue generated by segments with promising potential.

EXECUTIVES

Evp Field Operations, John J. Lass, age 61, $436,156 total compensation
Evp Consumer Sales Marketing And Product, John Maduri
President And Ceo, Daniel J. McCarthy, age 53, $981,251 total compensation
Evp And Chief People Officer, Kathleen Weslock, age 62
Evp General Counsel And Corporate Secretary, Mark D. Nielsen, age 53, $387,500 total compensation
Evp And Cto, Steve Gable, age 44, $458,750 total compensation
Evp And Cfo, R. Perley McBride, $199,432 total compensation
Evp Commercial Sales Operations, Kenneth A. Arndt
Evp Operational Transformation, Tim Travaille
Senior Vice President Deputy General Counsel, Nancy Rights
Svp And Gm Connecticut Operations, Paul Quick
Svp-gen Mgr Pennsylvania, Elena Kilpatrick

Vp It Strategy And Planning, Nick Cory
Executive Vice President Of Customer Service, Jennifer Brown
Senior Vice President West Region, Denise Baumbach
Vice President, David Schwartz
Vp Investor Relations, Luke Szymczak
Chairman, Pamela D. A. Reeve, age 69
President And Ceo, Daniel J. McCarthy, age 53
Auditors: KPMG LLP

LOCATIONS

HQ: Frontier Communications Corp
401 Merritt 7, Norwalk, CT 06851
Phone: 203 614-5600   Fax: 203 614-4602
Web: www.frontier.com

PRODUCTS/OPERATIONS

2017 Sales

	$ mil.	% of total
Customer revenue		
Business	4,476	49
Residential	3,876	42
Switched access and subsidy	776	9
Total	**9,128**	**100**

2017 Sales

	$ mil.	% of total
Customer Revenue		
Data and internet services	3,862	42
Voice Services	2,864	31
Video services	1,304	14
Others	322	4
Switched access and subsidy	776	9
Total	**9,128**	**100**

COMPETITORS

AT&T	Hulu
Altice USA	Integra Telecom
Amazon.com	Netflix
CenturyLink	Time Warner Cable
Charter Communications	U.S. TelePacific
Comcast	Verizon
Cox Communications	Vonage
FairPoint Communications Inc.	XO Holdings

HISTORICAL FINANCIALS

Company Type: Public

Income Statement

FYE: December 31

	REVENUE ($ mil.)	NET INCOME ($ mil.)	NET PROFIT MARGIN	EMPLOYEES
12/17	9,128	(1,804)	—	22,700
12/16	8,896	(373)	—	28,300
12/15	5,576	(196)	—	19,200
12/14	4,772	132	2.8%	17,400
12/13	4,761	112	2.4%	13,650
Annual Growth	17.7%	—	—	13.6%

2017 Year-End Financials

Debt ratio: 70.83%
Return on equity: (-53.11%)
Cash ($ mil.): 362
Current ratio: 0.53
Long-term debt ($ mil.): 16,970

No. of shares (mil.): 78
Dividends
  Yield: 0.1%
  Payout: —
Market value ($ mil.): 530

STOCK PRICE ($)	P/E		PER SHARE ($)		
FY Close	High/Low		Earnings	Dividends	Book Value
12/17	6.76	— —	(25.99)	1.20	28.99
12/16	3.38	— —	(7.65)	6.30	57.81
12/15	4.67	— —	(4.35)	6.30	72.09
12/14	6.67	4 2	1.95	6.00	54.73
12/13	4.65	3 2	1.65	6.00	60.86
Annual Growth	9.8% (16.9%)	— —		—(33.1%)	

Fulton Financial Corp. (PA)

Fulton Financial is a financial holding company with $20 billion in assets that owns four community banks in semi-rural and suburban areas of Pennsylvania Maryland Delaware New Jersey and Virginia. Through some 240 branches the banks offer standard products such as checking savings and credit accounts CDs retirement accounts mortgages and loans. Commercial loans — including for real estate and industrial financial and agricultural loans — account for most of the company's loan portfolio.? The company owns several non-banking units including Fulton Insurance an agency selling life insurance and related products.

Operations

More than 70% of Fulton Financial's revenue comes from net interest income particularly from loans including fees. The remainder is derived from non-interest income mostly from service charges on deposit accounts investment management and trust services and other service charges and fees. Commercial real estate loans account for about 40% of the company's nearly $16 billion loan portfolio; industrial financial and agricultural commercial loans contribute more than 25% to that lineup. Residential mortgages and home equity each account for around 10% of the portfolio.

Fulton Financial's four subsidiary banks include Fulton Bank Fulton Bank of New Jersey The Columbia Bank and Lafayette Ambassador Bank. Fulton Bank (120-plus branches) accounts for about 60% of the holding company's total assets while Fulton Bank of New Jersey (some 65 branches) contributing about 20% and the other two banks accounting for some 10% each. In October 2018 Fulton merged subsidiary banks FNB Bank and Swineford National Bank (which each held less than 2% of its total assets) into lead bank Fulton Bank.

Geographic Reach

Fulton Financial and its subsidiary banks operate about 240 branches in suburban and semi-rural markets in the northeastern US. Lead bank Fulton Bank serves customers in Pennsylvania Delaware and Virginia. Fulton Bank of New Jersey Lafayette Ambassador Bank and The Columbia Bank serve New Jersey Pennsylvania and Maryland respectively.

Headquartered in Lancaster Pennsylvania the holding company has operations centers in East Petersburg Pennsylvania and Mantua New Jersey.

Sales and Marketing

Fulton Financial increased its marketing spend by 14% in 2017 compared with 2016 primarily for promotions to increase deposits. Commercial customers are the holding company's leading customer segment.

Financial Performance

Amid its expansion into new markets Fulton Financial saw its revenue tick up about 10% to more than $780 million between 2013 and 2017 thanks mostly to increased net interest income particularly loans including fees. Net income trended up more than 5% to about $170 million. However its cash stores were halved to less than $110 million (owing to increased use for financings and decreased proceeds from sales of mortgage loans held for sale); its debt also went up almost 20% to about $1 billion in that time.

The company's revenue gained 10% in 2017 to $783.3 million driven primarily by increased income from loans including fees in Fulton's commercial and residential mortgage commercial loan construction and leasing portfolios. Increased loan revenues also drove the company's 2017 net income up 6% to $172 million.

Fulton had cash of $108.3 million at the end of 2017 down $10.5 million from the prior year. Operations contributed $258.8 million and investments used $1.2 billion related mostly to a net increase in loans. Financings added $897.1 million due to a net increase in demand and savings deposits.

Strategy

Fulton Financial is shifting its strategy away from allowing its subsidiary banks autonomy in their regions to instead focus on consolidation of its banks expansion without geographic restriction and alignment with its customer segments. The company believes such a strategy will enable it to more efficiently manage risk through centralized risk management and compliance operations. In October 2018 Fulton merged subsidiary banks FNB Bank and Swineford National Bank into lead bank Fulton Bank. The company plans to absorb its remaining subsidiary banks into Fulton Bank by the end of 2019.

Fulton's near-term strategy is to invest in Philadelphia Pennsylvania a quickly growing urban market. The company hired a regional president and a commercial team for the area in 2016 and opened a mortgage loan production office in May 2018. The company also has regulatory approval to open two full service branches in the area which are targeted to open in early 2019. The company also plans to grow its presence in Baltimore Maryland.

Mergers and Acquisitions

In early 2019 Fulton Financial agreed to buy the wealth management business of Altoona Pennsylvania-based Forney Financial Solutions. The deal broadens Fulton's services for clients in the central part of the state.

Company Background

Fulton Financial traces its history back to the creation of Fulton National Bank in Lancaster Pennsylvania in 1882. It began acquiring other banks in the late 1940s and launched a holding company structure in 1982.

EXECUTIVES

Sevp Community Banking, Craig A. Roda, $398,805 total compensation
Sevp Coo And Interim Cfo, Philmer H. (Phil) Rohrbaugh, age 66, $478,543 total compensation
Sevp; President And Coo Fulton Bank, Curtis J. Myers, $371,347 total compensation
Sevp And Chief Credit Officer, Meg R. Mueller
Sevp And Cio, Angela M. Sargent
Chairman President And Ceo, E. Philip (Phil) Wenger, $944,103 total compensation
Sevp And Chief Risk Officer, Beth Ann L. Chivinski
President Small Business Administration Lending, Lynn Ozer
President And Coo Fulton Mortgage Company, Jeffrey J. Scheuren
Senior Vice President Loan Operations, Georgina Condran
Senior Vice President And Retail Sales Leader, Smokey Glover
Vice President And Corporate Training Director, William Glover
Vice President, Constance Beck
Vice President Of Loan Administration, Patricia Royer
Vice President Of Customer Service, Yadira Rivera
Executive Vice President Treasurer, James Radick
Vice President Senior Cash Management Sales Officer, Steve Schreiber Steve Schreiber
Vice President And Corporate Training Director, Kay Burky
Sr Vice President, Forest Crigler
Senior Vice President Director Of Retail, Randy Metz
Vice President, Marc Ryan
Vice President Residential And Consumer Defauls, Tonya Samuel
Senior Vice President Bank Controller, Linda Schroeder
Senior Vice President Funds Management, Keith Paich
Vice President And Corporate Training Director, William Glover
Vice President, Joe Warner
Vice President, Christopher Bigos
Vice President, Tammy Snyder
Vice President Information Technology Service And Support, Linda Suarez
Vice President Of Cash Management, Angie Harcum
Senior Vice President Audit Director, Jennifer Lauver
Senior Vice President, James Bush
Vice President Relationship Manager, Drummond Sandra
Senior Vice President Regional Manager, Iwona Shillingford
Vice President Tax Accounting And Planning Officer, David Rorabaugh
Vice President Senior Relationship Manager, William Maeglin
Vice President, Michael Thompson
Vice President Consumer Loan Review, Domenick Vitale
Senior Vice President Trust Manager, Stuart Juppenlatz
Vice President Lending Compliance Officer, Eileen Moyer
Senior Vice President Senior Credit Officer, Paul Phillips
Senior Vice President, Sal Marone
Vice President And Regional Sales Manager, Becky Lanzino
Senior Vice President Commercial Lending Team Leader, Joseph Valenzuela
Senior Vice President Commercial Team Leader, Mac Weems
Vice President Portfolio Manager, Theodore Walden
Senior Vice President And Corporate Tax Director, Brian Demild
Senior Vice President And Senior Portfolio Manager, Walter J Banta
Senior Vice President, Willie A Maddox
Vice President And Portfolio Manager, Laurie Bodisch
Senior Vice President, Richard J Mason
Vice President And Senior Leasing Sales Officer, Sharon Wingenroth
Vice President Vendor Risk And Relations, Gregory Lampe
Senior Vice President, John D Harding
Vice President And Senior Leasing Officer, Jason D Ibach
Executive Vice President And Chief Investment Officer, Keith P Aleardi
Vice President Product Implementation And Process Manager, Angela Schadt
Vice President Manager, Colleen A Lukacs
Vice President, Debbie Truckermiller
Senior Vice President, Richard Mason
Senior Vice President, John Harding
Vice President And Senior Leasing Officer, Jason Ibach
Vice President Manager, Colleen Lukacs
Vice President Loan Documentation, Rebecca Chamberlain
Senior Vice President And Senior Portfolio Manager, Walter Banta
Senior Vice President, Willie Maddox
Chairman President And Ceo, E. Philip (Phil) Wenger
Auditors: KPMG LLP

LOCATIONS

HQ: Fulton Financial Corp. (PA)
One Penn Square, P.O. Box 4887, Lancaster, PA 17604
Phone: 717 291-2411
Web: www.fult.com

PRODUCTS/OPERATIONS

2017 Sales

	$ mil.	% of total
Interest		
Loans including fees	604	69
Investment securities	59	7
Other	5	1
Expense	(93.5)	
Non interest		
Service charges on deposit accounts	51	6
Other service charges & fees	52	6
Investment management & trust services	49	5
Mortgage banking income	19	2
Investment securities gains	9	1
Other	25	3
Total	**783**	**100**

COMPETITORS

First Commonwealth Financial	Mid Penn Bancorp
Investors Bancorp	PNC Financial
M&T Bank	Sovereign Bank
	TD Bank USA

HISTORICAL FINANCIALS

Company Type: Public

Income Statement

FYE: December 31

	ASSETS ($ mil.)	NET INCOME ($ mil.)	INCOME AS % OF ASSETS	EMPLOYEES
12/17	20,036	171	0.9%	3,700
12/16	18,944	161	0.9%	3,500
12/15	17,914	149	0.8%	3,460
12/14	17,124	157	0.9%	3,560
12/13	16,934	161	1.0%	3,620
Annual Growth	**4.3%**	**1.5%**	**—**	**0.5%**

2017 Year-End Financials

Debt ratio: 1.93%	No. of shares (mil.): 175
Return on equity: 7.89%	Dividends
Cash ($ mil.): 402	Yield: 0.0%
Current ratio: —	Payout: 47.9%
Long-term debt ($ mil.): —	Market value ($ mil.): 3,136

	STOCK PRICE ($) FY Close	P/E High/Low	PER SHARE ($) Earnings	Dividends	Book Value
12/17	17.90	20 17	0.98	0.47	12.73
12/16	18.80	21 13	0.93	0.41	12.18
12/15	13.01	17 13	0.85	0.38	11.72
12/14	12.36	15 12	0.84	0.34	11.16
12/13	13.09	16 11	0.83	0.32	10.71
Annual Growth	**8.1%**	**— —**	**4.2%**	**10.1%**	**4.4%**

Gallagher (Arthur J.) & Co.

One of the world's largest insurance brokers Arthur J. Gallagher provides commercial insurance products and risk management services through a network of subsidiaries and agencies. It places (arranges directly with underwriters) traditional and niche property/casualty lines in addition to offering retirement solutions and managing employee benefits programs. Risk management services include claims management loss control consulting and workers' compensation investigations. Gallagher UK places insurance with the Lloyd's of London exchange. The global company operates more than 600 sales and service locations in more than 30 nations and through correspondent brokers and consultants does business in more than 90 countries. Most of Gallagher's revenue comes from the US.

Operations

Gallagher has grown to become one of the world's top five insurance brokers based on revenue as well as a top property/casualty claims administrator. It also ranks among the top employee benefits consulting firms.

The company operates through three reportable segments: Brokerage Corporate and Risk Management.

The Brokerage segment which provides both retail and wholesale services accounts for more than 60% of annual revenue. A majority of Gallagher's brokerage income comes from commissions paid by insurance companies (upon placement of their policies). Retail insurance brokerage accounts for more than 80% of the segment's revenue.

Gallagher's Corporate segment accounts for about a quarter of total revenue; it primarily generates income from refined fuel operations. The segment's managed investments include a 46.5% stake in pollutant reduction firm Chem-Mod and a 12% stake in private carbon dioxide emissions reduction outfit C-Quest Technology.

The smaller Risk Management segment (more than 10% of sales) provides contract claim settlement and administration services for enterprises; it earns fees from insurance companies and self-insured clients. The segment primarily works with workers' compensation claims and auto liability and property claims.

Geographic Reach

Gallagher gets more than 75% of its revenue from the US but the company is working to expand its international operations. The company operates in more than 30 nations and through a brokerage and consultant network serves more than 150 nations. Its largest overseas markets include Australia Bermuda Canada the Caribbean New Zealand Singapore and the UK.

Sales and Marketing

Most of Gallagher's brokerage business comes from retail customers which include commercial industrial not-for-profit government and religious organizations. Gallagher's wholesale brokerage centers provide insurance placement assistance to affiliated and independent agents.

The company manages its brokerage operations through a network of more than 600 sales and service offices.

Financial Performance

Gallagher's growth efforts in both the brokerage segment and the risk management segment have helped the company to increase new customer volumes and has created substantial annual revenue and net income increases in recent years. Cash flow has also risen over the past few years.

In 2017 revenue rose 10% to $6.2 billion as all three segments saw growth: Brokerage earnings increased 9% Corporate earnings increased 16% and Risk Management earnings increased 7% that year. The Corporate segment primarily generates income from refined fuel operations; overall commissions fees and revenue from clean coal activities grew that year.

With the higher revenue net income rose 12% to $463.1 million in 2017.

The company ended 2017 with $2.3 billion in net cash nearly 20% more than it had at the end of 2016. Operating activities mostly from the Brokerage and Risk Management segments provided $854.2 million in cash during 2017. Investing activities — primarily business acquisitions — used $511 million and financing activities used $47.8 million.

Strategy

A key component of Gallagher's growth strategy is the ongoing acquisition of small regional insurance agencies and benefits consulting firms. The company targets strong sales organizations with a focus on middle-market clients or expertise in niche property/casualty lines (such as aviation energy hospitality and health care).

In addition to growth through acquisitions Gallagher has influenced the growth of its business by expanding and strengthening its relationships with independent brokerage partners increasing cross-selling opportunities and pursuing niche markets such as employee benefit risk management. Unfortunately the group has lagged behind its competition in introducing new types of business such as cyber protection.

Additionally the company has been successful at countering declining property/casualty insurance rates by securing new business and improving retention rates. Gallagher sees strong potential in a growing insurance market and an increasingly risky and complex world.

Gallagher was named one of the world's most ethical companies by the Ethisphere Institute for the seventh straight year in 2018; it was the only insurance brokerage named to the list. As part of the company's 90th anniversary that year the company's employees committed to perform 90000 hours of volunteer work in 2018. The firm also invests in clean energy owning some 35 commercial clean coal production facilities that emit less mercury sulfur dioxide and other chemicals. (Gallagher could lose money on it coal interests if other cleaner sources of energy increase in demand.)

Mergers and Acquisitions

A core strategy of Gallagher is to expand through acquisitions. Purchases typically cost between $1 million and $60 million.

In 2018 the company acquired more than a dozen firms including Thomas Costello Insurance Agency Pronto Insurance McGregor & Associates and Williams Insurance Agency.

Gallagher spent some $550 million on around 40 acquisitions during 2017. Companies purchased that year included Construction Risk Solutions Presidio Group GPL Assurance and Lutgert Insurance.

In 2016 Gallagher completed more than 35 acquisitions spending nearly $400 million in the process. Some of the firms acquired in that period included Kane's Insurance Management Altman & Cronin Benefit Consultants McNeary and Victory Insurance Agency.

Company Background

Gallagher is led by J. Patrick Gallagher grandson of founder Arthur Gallagher who formed the company back in 1927.

EXECUTIVES

Corporate Vice President And President U.s. Wholesale Brokerage, David McGurn

Chairman Employee Benefits Consulting And Brokerage, James W. (Jim) Durkin, age 68, $725,000 total compensation

Chairman President And Ceo, J. Patrick (Pat) Gallagher, age 65, $1,000,000 total compensation

Cfo, Douglas K. (Doug) Howell, age 56, $850,000 total compensation

President U.s. Wholesale Brokerage, Joel D. Cavaness, age 56

Chairman Brokerage Services, James S. (Jim) Gault, age 66, $800,000 total compensation

President And Ceo Risk Management Services, Scott R. Hudson, age 56

Corporate Vp And Chairman International Brokerage, Thomas J. (Tom) Gallagher, age 60, $750,000 total compensation

Global Chief Service Officer, Vishal Jain

Ceo Employee Benefits Consulting And Brokerage, William F. Ziebell, age 55

Ceo Arthur J. Gallagher Australia, Sarah Lyons

Executive Vice President, Mike Temple

Senior Vice President, Diana Bertoni

Vice President, David Perry

Senior Area Vice President, Bill Dickenson

Area Vice President Global Human Resources Services, Kristin M Sampson

Area Senior Vice President, David D Kempton

Area Senior Vice President, Barb Galuppi

Area Vice President, Rob Erzen

Area Senior Vice President, Maureen O'Connell

Vice President, Bruce Beardsley

Vice President Corporate Ethics And Sustainability, Tom Tropp

Division Vice President, Michael McKee

Area Executive Vice President, Tim Gonsior

Area Senior Vice President, Kevin Gregory

Assistant Vice President Real Estate And Hospitality, Sandy Gilder

Area Vice President Marine, Marc Dunn

Area Vice President, Jack Zogg

Aavp And Director Of Operations Tampa Bay Branch, Randi Watson

Senior Vice President, Susan Ruvolo

Division President, Teresa Koster

Area Executive Vice President, Daniel Johnson

Area Executive Vice President, Eric Olson

Area Vice President, Kelly Bonanno

Area Vice President, Cindy Caslin

Vice President Sourcing And Services, Cara Richardson

Area Vice President Of Business Insurance Sales And Risk Management Consulting, John Sence

Area Assistant Vice President Property Loss Control, Scott Quackenbush

Area Vice President And Consultant, Janet Brendis

Area Vice President Human Capital And Employee Benefits, Bobby Desai

Area Vice President, Victoria Dowling

Area Senior Vice President, Rusty Russell

Vp Global Cash Management, Patricia Hinton

Area Assistant Vice President, Jill Keidel

Area Vice President, Paul Nelson

Area Vice President, Judy Worrall

Senior Vice President, Daniel R'bibo

Area Vice President, Greg Fine

Area Executive Vice President, Marc Wagman

Chairman President And Ceo, J. Patrick (Pat) Gallagher, age 65

Auditors: Ernst & Young LLP

LOCATIONS

HQ: Gallagher (Arthur J.) & Co.
2850 W. Golf Road, Rolling Meadows, IL 60008-4050
Phone: 630 773-3800
Web: www.ajg.com

2017 Sales

	$ mil.	% of total
U.S.	4,737	77
U.K.	717	12
Australia	270	4
Canada	155	3
New Zealand	150	2
Other foreign	127	2
Total	6,159	100

PRODUCTS/OPERATIONS

2017 Sales

	$ mil.	% of total
Brokerage		
Commissions	2,627	43
Fees	868	14
Supplemental commissions	163	3
Contingent commissions	111	2
Investment income	59	1
Risk management		
Fees	760	10
Investment income	0	
Corporate		
Clean energy & other investment income	1,560	25
Total	6,159	100

Selected Subsidiaries

AJG Financial Services Inc.
    AJG Coal Inc.
Arthur J. Gallagher & Co. (Bermuda) Limited (insurance & reinsurance placement captive risk services)
    Artex Risk Solutions (Bermuda) Ltd.
Arthur J. Gallagher & Co. (Canada) Ltd.
Arthur J. Gallagher Australasia Holdings Pty Ltd (Australia)
Arthur J. Gallagher Brokerage & Risk Management Services LLC
    Arthur J. Gallagher Risk Management Services Inc.
Arthur J. Gallagher Service Company
Arthur J. Gallagher (UK) Limited (Lloyd's of London brokerage)
    Risk Management Partners Ltd. (customized insurance & risk management)
Gallagher Bassett Services Inc. (risk analysis)
    Gallagher Bassett International Ltd. (UK)
    Gallagher Bassett Services Pty Ltd. (Australia)
Gallagher Benefit Services Inc. (employee benefit program management)
Heath Lambert Limited (Gallagher Heath UK)
Protected Insurance Company
Risk Placement Services Inc.

COMPETITORS

ACE USA	Liberty Mutual
Aon	Marsh & McLennan
BroadSpire	Sedgwick Claims
Brown & Brown	Management Services
Chubb Limited	Travelers Companies
Hub International	Willis Towers Watson
Jardine Lloyd	

HISTORICAL FINANCIALS

Company Type: Public

Income Statement   FYE: December 31

	REVENUE ($ mil.)	NET INCOME ($ mil.)	NET PROFIT MARGIN	EMPLOYEES
12/18	6,934	633	9.1%	30,362
12/17	6,159	463	7.5%	26,800
12/16	5,594	414	7.4%	24,800
12/15	5,392	356	6.6%	21,500
12/14	4,626	303	6.6%	20,200
Annual Growth	10.6%	20.2%	—	10.7%

2018 Year-End Financials

Debt ratio: 22.10%
Return on equity: 14.73%
Cash ($ mil.): 607
Current ratio: 1.06
Long-term debt ($ mil.): 3,091

No. of shares (mil.): 184
Dividends
    Yield: 2.2%
    Payout: 48.9%
Market value ($ mil.): 13,561

	STOCK PRICE ($) FY Close	P/E High/Low	PER SHARE ($) Earnings	Dividends	Book Value
12/18	73.70	23 18	3.40	1.64	24.45
12/17	63.28	26 20	2.54	1.56	22.68
12/16	51.96	22 16	2.32	1.52	20.17
12/15	40.94	24 19	2.06	1.48	20.57
12/14	47.08	25 22	1.97	1.44	19.62
Annual Growth	11.9%	—	14.6%	3.3%	5.7%

GameStop Corp

GameStop holds the top score in video game retailing. The largest retailer of new and used games hardware entertainment software and accessories boasts roughly 4000 GameStop EB Games and Micromania branded stores in the US and 2000-plus stores in Europe Australia and Canada. Its stores and e-commerce websites stock more than 6000 video game related items with more than half of its sales coming from new video game hardware and software. GameStop also sells downloadable add-on content from publishers operates 1300 smartphone retail locations under the AT&T Cricket Wireless Simply Mac and Spring Mobile banners (which it is selling) and publishes video game magazine Game Informer.

HISTORY

NeoStar Retail Group resulted from the 1994 combination of software retailers Babbage's and Software Etc. Babbage's had been founded by James McCurry and Gary Kusin in 1983. Named for 19th-century mathematician Charles Babbage (considered the father of the computer) it went public in 1988.

Software Etc. began as a division of B. Dalton Bookseller in 1984. Bookstore chain Barnes & Noble and Dutch retailer Vendex acquired B. Dalton two years later. Software Etc. went public in 1992.

Both companies focused on mall retailing: Babbage's on game software and Software Etc. on a broader variety of PC software. Both saw growth spurred by the rising popularity of Nintendo and Sega game systems and by falling PC prices. The two merged in 1994 in an effort to stave off growing competition from big retail chains such as Best Buy and Wal-Mart. NeoStar opened 122 stores in 1995.

Amid flat sales the following year several senior executives left. Also in 1996 NeoStar lost its contract to operate software departments at 136 Barnes & Noble sites and it soon filed for Chapter 11. Late that year a group led by Barnes & Noble's head honcho Leonard Riggio purchased about 460 of NeoStar's 650 stores for $58.5 million and renamed the company Babbage's Etc. Former Software Etc. chief Dick Fontaine was named CEO.

By 1997 the company began concentrating on popular games and software and in 1999 it formed its e-commerce site GameStop.com. In late 1999 Barnes & Noble paid Riggio's group $210 million for Babbage's Etc. In June 2000 the company fortified its position and became the #1 US video game retailer with the purchase of rival game retailer Funco (about 400 stores) for $161.5 million. The company changed its name to GameStop in August 2001 and filed to go public which it accomplished in February 2002. Though public it was still under the majority control of Barnes & Noble until 2004 when GameStop bought back its shares.

GameStop bought rival Electronics Boutique in 2005 more than doubling its size from 2000 to about 4500 stores. Steven R. Morgan a former executive with Electronics Boutique became president of GameStop later that year.

A new CEO took the controls at GameStop in 2008 — its first CEO change since the company's inception in 1996. Dick Fontaine gave up the title of chief executive to Daniel DeMatteo who had served as COO since 1996 and vice chairman of the company since 2004. Also Paul Raines formerly with Home Depot joined the company as COO in September 2008. Fontaine retained the chairman's title and focused on international operations and acquisitions.

GameStop focused on international expansion in 2008 driven primarily by a pair of acquisitions. The largest of those was its $629 million purchase of video game retailer Micromania which brought with it some 330 stores in France. South of the equator GameStop acquired The Gamesman the largest independent gaming retailer in New Zealand. The deal included eight Gamesman video game stores and brought GameStop's total store count in the country to 38.

In June 2010 DeMatteo was promoted to executive chairman of the company while Raines was named CEO.

In late 2013 the company acquired the 50.1% of Simply Mac that it didn't already own boosting its Technology Brands segment. The $9.5 million deal added Apple specialty retail stores in Utah and Wyoming. Also that year GameStop bought Spring Communications for $62.6 million.

EXECUTIVES

Coo, Tony D. Bartel, age 54, $924,923 total compensation
Ceo, J. Paul Raines, age 54, $1,285,077 total compensation
Cfo, Robert A. (Rob) Lloyd, age 56, $707,385 total compensation
Evp Strategic Business And Brand Development, Michael P. (Mike) Hogan, age 59, $613,923 total compensation
Evp; President U.s. Stores, Michael T. (Mike) Buskey, age 69
President Kongregate, Emily Greer
Svp Supply Chain And Refurbishment, Michael K. (Mike) Mauler, age 57, $571,846 total compensation
Svp Information Technology And Cio, Michael Cooper
Vice President Marketing And Sales, Art Doud
Svp International Technology And Support, Kevin Weimerskirch
Chairman, Daniel A. DeMatteo, age 70
Auditors: DELOITTE & TOUCHE LLP

LOCATIONS

HQ: GameStop Corp
625 Westport Parkway, Grapevine, TX 76051
Phone: 817 424-2000
Web: www.gamestop.com

2017 Sales

	% of total
US	64
Europe	15
Australia	7
Canada	4
Technology Brands	9
Total	**100**

PRODUCTS/OPERATIONS

2017 Sales

	% of total
New video game software	29
Pre-owned and value video game products	26
New video game hardware	16
Technology Brands	9
Video game accessories	8
Collectables	6
Digital	3
Other	3
Total	**100**

Selected Websites

www.ebgames.com.au
www.gamestop.ca
www.gamestop.co.uk
www.gamestop.com
www.gamestop.com/pcgames

www.gamestop.de
www.gamestop.es
www.gamestop.ie
www.gamestop.it
www.kongregate.com
www.micromania.fr

Selected Merchandise

Accessories
  PC entertainment accessories
  Video game accessories
  Other
Internet streaming technology & digital distribution
Online games
PC entertainment software & other software
Used video games
Video game hardware
Video game software

COMPETITORS

Amazon.com	GameFly
Best Buy	Kmart
Buy.com	Target Corporation
Carrefour	Wal-Mart
Costco Wholesale	Zones
Fry's Electronics	eBay

HISTORICAL FINANCIALS

Company Type: Public

Income Statement

FYE: February 3

	REVENUE ($ mil.)	NET INCOME ($ mil.)	NET PROFIT MARGIN	EMPLOYEES
02/18*	9,224	34	0.4%	67,000
01/17	8,607	353	4.1%	68,000
01/16	9,363	402	4.3%	82,000
01/15	9,296	393	4.2%	73,000
02/14	9,039	354	3.9%	69,000
Annual Growth	**0.5%**	**(44.1%)**	**—**	**(0.7%)**

*Fiscal year change

2018 Year-End Financials

Debt ratio: 16.22%
Return on equity: 1.53%
Cash ($ mil.): 864
Current ratio: 1.33
Long-term debt ($ mil.): 817

No. of shares (mil.): 101
Dividends
  Yield: 0.0%
  Payout: 447.0%
Market value ($ mil.): 1,644

	STOCK PRICE ($) FY Close	P/E High/Low		PER SHARE ($) Earnings	Dividends	Book Value
02/18*	16.23	78	47	0.34	1.52	21.86
01/17	24.31	10	6	3.40	1.48	22.32
01/16	26.21	12	7	3.78	1.44	20.15
01/15	35.25	13	9	3.47	1.32	19.20
02/14	35.07	19	8	2.99	1.10	19.53
Annual Growth	**(17.5%)**	**—**	**—**	**(41.9%)**	**8.4%**	**2.9%**

*Fiscal year change

GEISINGER HEALTH

Geisinger Health System provides health care to a large portion of the Keystone State. The health care system serves more than 3 million residents of nearly 50 counties spanning central and northeastern Pennsylvania. Founded in 1915 the organization's flagship facility is Geisinger Medical Center a 400-bed medical-surgical hospital located in Danville. It includes the Janet Weis Children's Hospital. With joint venture partner HealthSouth Geisinger also runs a rehabilitation hospital in Danville. As part of its operations the health system runs the 240-bed Geisinger Wyoming Valley Med-

ical Center as well as numerous outpatient facilities and doctors' offices located throughout the region.

Geographic Reach

Geisinger Health System extends the reach of its health care system to millions of central and northeastern Pennsylvania residents across about 50 counties.

Financial Performance

In fiscal 2014 the hospital reported net revenue of $9.8 billion a $1 billion increase over the prior year.

Strategy

Geisinger Health System has been working to standardize its procedural operations to improve the quality of care at its facilities and cut costs. Initiatives include assigning care coordinators and providing home visits for high-risk patients to avoid repeat hospitalizations. The health network also implemented an electronic medical records system and began using networking technology to reach into rural markets. Known as "telemedicine" the system's networking technologies are used among other things to facilitate remote two-way consultations between system physicians and rural patients. Additionally Geisinger runs the Geisinger Health Plan a not-for-profit HMO with some 230000 members.

In addition to its clinical operations Geisinger Health System also pursues industry partnerships and licensing opportunities through Geisinger Ventures its business development unit. The unit works to commercialize (and sometimes spin off) medical and technology-related innovations.

Mergers and Acquisitions

Geisinger has grown through several strategic acquisitions as of late. The health care system purchased central Pennsylvania's Cancer Care Centers in late 2014 adding four facilities to its network.

EXECUTIVES

Evp And Coo, Frank Trembulak
Evp Finance And Cfo, Kevin F. Brennan
Evp And Chief Medical Officer, Albert Bothe
Evp And Managing Partner Geisinger Consulting Services, Bruce H. Hamory
Evp And System Chief Nursing Officer, Susan M. Robel
Evp Clinical Operations, Lynn Miller
Evp And Chief Scientific Officer, David H. Ledbetter
President And Ceo, David T. Feinberg
President And Ceo Geisinger Health Plans, Steven R. Youso
Chief Medical Executive Geisinger Northeast Region, Robert J. Weil
Vice President Supply Chain Services, Deborah Templeton
Associate Vice President Nursing, Denise Venditti
Vice President Of Media, Wendy Wilson
Assistant To Greg Snow Vice President Of Revenue Cycle, Denise Baylor
Vice President Clinical Informatics, Joan Topper
Associate Vice President Resource, Nancy G Lawton
Vice President Of Sales, Chris Fanning
Vice President Faculty And Curriculum Development, Nicole Woll
Medical Director Government Programs, Perry Meadows
Auditors: KPMG LLP PHILADELPHIA PA

LOCATIONS

HQ: GEISINGER HEALTH
100 N ACADEMY AVE, DANVILLE, PA 178229800
Phone: 800 275-6401
Web: WWW.GEISINGER.ORG

PRODUCTS/OPERATIONS

Selected Services
Adolescent & Young Adult Medicine
Allergy
Anesthesia
Audiology
Bariatric Surgery
Cancer Institute
Cardiology
Colorectal Surgery
Cosmetics Program
Critical Care
Dental Medicine
Dermatology
Ear Nose & Throat
Emergency Medicine
Endocrinology & Metabolism
Fertility Center
Gastroenterology
Gynecology
Gynecologic Oncology
Heart Services
Hip & Knee Center
Imaging Services
Infectious Disease
Internal Medicine
Joint Replacement
Laboratory Medicine
LASIK Surgery
Mammography
Maternal Fetal Medicine
Mental Health
Minimally Invasive Surgery
Mohs Surgery
Neonatology
Nephrology
Neurodevelopmental Pediatrics
Neuroscience Institute
Neurology
Neurosurgery
Obstetrics
Ophthalmology
Orthopaedics
Osteoporosis
Pain Management
Palliative Medicine
Pediatrics (General)
Pediatric Allergy & Immunology
Pediatric Anesthesia & Sedation
Pediatric Cardiology
Pediatric Dental Surgery
Pediatric Dentistry
Pediatric Dermatology
Pediatric Endocrinology
Pediatric Gastroenterology
Pediatric General Surgery
Pediatric Genetics
Pediatric Hematology/Oncology
Pediatric Hospitalists
Pediatric Infectious Disease
Pediatric Intensive Care
Pediatric Interventional Radiology
Pediatric Nephrology
Pediatric Neurology
Pediatric Neuropsychology
Pediatric Neurosurgery
Pediatric Ophthalmology
Pediatric Orthopaedics
Pediatric Otolaryngology
Pediatric Plastic Surgery
Pediatric Psychology & Psychiatry
Pediatric Pulmonology
Pediatric Rehabilitation
Pediatric Rheumatology
Pediatric Transplant Surgery
Pediatric Trauma
Pediatric Urology
Pediatric Weight Management & Nutrition
Plastic & Reconstructive Surgery
Podiatry
Psychiatry
Pulmonary Medicine
Radiology
Rehabilitation
Rheumatology
Sleep Services
Spine Medicine
Sports Medicine
Surgery

Thoracic Surgery
Transplant Surgery
Trauma Center
Urogynecology
Urology
Vascular Surgery
Weight Management Clinic
Women's Health

Selected Facilities
Geisinger HealthSouth Rehabilitation Hospital
    (Danville)
Geisinger Medical Center (Danville)
    The Janet Weis Children's Hospital
Geisinger Wyoming Valley Medical Center (Wilkes-Barre)
    Pearsall Heart Hospital
Geisinger South Wilkes-Barre Outpatient Center
Shamokin Area Community Hospital

COMPETITORS

Ascension Health
Blue Cross of Northeastern Pennsylvania
Capital BlueCross
Community Health Systems
HealthAmerica
Highmark
PinnacleHealth System
UPMC
Universal Health Services
Wyoming Valley Health Care System

HISTORICAL FINANCIALS
Company Type: Private

Income Statement   FYE: June 30

	REVENUE ($ mil.)	NET INCOME ($ mil.)	NET PROFIT MARGIN	EMPLOYEES
06/18	6,536	359	5.5%	13,030
06/17	6,337	552	8.7%	—
06/10	47	31	65.7%	—
Annual Growth	**85.1%**	**35.8%**	—	—

2018 Year-End Financials

Debt ratio: —
Return on equity: 5.50%
Cash ($ mil.): 363
Current ratio: 0.80
Long-term debt ($ mil.): —

Dividends
Yield: —
Payout: —
Market value ($ mil.): —

General Dynamics Corp

General Dynamics is a prime military contractor to the Pentagon (the US government accounts for about 60% of sales). The company's military operations include information systems and technology (information technology and collection as well as command control systems); marine systems (warships commercial tankers and nuclear submarines); and combat systems (battle tanks wheeled combat/tactical vehicles munitions and rockets and gun systems). Its aerospace unit which is composed of Gulfstream Aerospace and Jet Aviation designs makes and refurbishes business jets primarily for civilian customers.

Operations
Unlike some of its rivals who cater only to the military market that is at the mercy of government budgetary fluctuations General Dynamics caters to military and civilian sectors manufacturing both combat systems and high-tech systems with each side buffering the other in times of market downturn. The Combat Systems division is composed of Armament and Technical Products; European Land Systems; Land Systems; and Ordnance and Tactical Systems.

General Dynamic's Marine Systems group is a major shipbuilder for the US Navy and it provides MRO (maintenance/repair/overhaul) services to keep those vessels ship-shape. Marine Systems manufactures the Virginia-class nuclear-powered submarine the Arleigh Burke-class guided-missile destroyer (DDG-51) and the Lewis and Clark-class dry cargo/ammunition combat-logistics ship (T-AKE). Subsidiary Electric Boat builds nuclear submarines (Seawolf Ohio and Los Angeles classes) while Bath Iron Works builds DDG-51 and DDG-1000 destroyers.

On the civilian side of the business the company's Aerospace segment produces mid- and large-cabin business jet aircraft for which the company provides maintenance refurbishment and outfitting.

Last but not least — serving both the military and civilian sides — the company's Information Systems and Technology business unit provides cyber security tactical communication systems sensors and cameras ruggedized computers (for use in harsh environments such as those with strong vibrations extreme temperatures and wet or dusty conditions) and antennas to customers in the DoD the Department of Homeland Security the intelligence community federal civilian agencies and international customers.

Geographic Reach
General Dynamics operates around the world serving government and commercial customers on six continents spanning more than 45 countries. North America represents its largest market generating around 75% of sales.

Sales and Marketing
General Dynamics' main customer is the US Department of Defense (DoD). The company conducts business with government customers around the world with operations in Australia Brazil Canada France Germany Mexico Spain Switzerland and the UK. About 60% of its revenues stem from the US government and 15% come from US commercial customers.

Financial Performance
General Dynamics' revenues and profits remained static during 2015 and 2016 hovering around the $31 billion and $3 billion marks for both years respectively

The company's revenues for 2016 reflected fewer aircraft deliveries in its Aerospace group offset largely by additional US Navy engineering and ship construction work within its Marine Systems segment.

C4SIR (Command Control Communications Computers Intelligence Surveillance and Reconnaissance) sales surged in 2016 due to higher volume across the business including its Warfighter Information Network-Tactical (WIN-T) mobile communications program and several programs in Canada and the UK.

Strategy
With US defense spending changing with each administration General Dynamics' business strategy addresses programs that the military continues to emphasize including the need for warfighters and the need to replace resources lost in Iraq and Afghanistan. As the first US submarine to be configured for a post-Cold War defense landscape General Dynamics' Virginia-class submarine continues to meet the needs of the US Navy.

The company in late 2017 received a $5 billion contract from the US Navy to complete the design of its next-generation ballistic missile submarine the Columbia-class submarine. The Columbia-class submarines are nuclear-armed ballistic missile submarines that are designed to ensure a second strike capability in the event of a nuclear attack on the US.

Mergers and Acquisitions

In 2018 General Dynamics acquired CRSA a provider of information technology services to the federal government for about $9.7 billion in cash and the assumption of debt. The acquisition was made to beef up the IT offerings of General Dynamics catapulting it to the No. 2 spot among large government IT contractors. The combined company would have close to $10 billion in revenue from government IT services. The move comes as government spending was expected to increase with a strong push from the White House and the US Congress.

In 2016 it acquired Bluefin Robotics a manufacturer of unmanned undersea vehicles (UUVs) that perform a wide range of missions for the US military and commercial customers. Bluefin Robotics became part of General Dynamics Mission Systems' Maritime and Strategic Systems line of business.

HISTORY

In 1899 John Holland founded Electric Boat Company a New Jersey ship and submarine builder. The company built ships PT boats and submarines during WWII but when faced with waning postwar orders CEO John Jay Hopkins diversified with the 1947 purchase of aircraft builder Canadair. Hopkins formed General Dynamics in 1952 merging Electric Boat and Canadair and buying Consolidated Vultee Aircraft (Convair) a major producer of military and civilian aircraft in 1954.

EXECUTIVES

Senior Vice President Planning Develop, Robert Helm

Evp Marine Systems, John P. Casey, age 63, $747,500 total compensation

Vp Strategic Planning, Phebe N. Novakovic, age 60, $1,585,000 total compensation

Vp And President General Dynamics Mission Systems, Christopher (Chris) Marzilli, age 58

Vp And President Electric Boat, Jeffrey S. Geiger, age 56

Vp; President Bath Iron Works, Dirk Lesko

Vp And President Gulfstream Aerospace Corp., Mark L. Burns, age 58

Vp And President Jet Aviation, Robert E. (Rob) Smith

Evp Combat Systems, Mark C. Roualet, age 60, $747,500 total compensation

Vp; President Nassco, Kevin M. Graney

Evp General Dynamics Information Systems And Technology Group; President General Dynamics Information Technology, S. Daniel (Dan) Johnson, age 71, $713,750 total compensation

Vp And President European Land Systems, Alfonso J. Ramonet

Svp And Cfo, Jason W. Aiken, age 45, $701,250 total compensation

Vp And President Land Systems, Gary L. Whited, age 57

President General Dynamics Information Technology, M. Amy Gilliland

Corporate Vice President For Communications And Government Relations, Teresa Gaines

Director Government Relations, Jen Navarro

Director Of Government Relations, Gerry Lamb

Vp Manufacturing, Howard Bruce

Vice President Information Technology, Tommy Augustsson

Director Of Surgery, Todd Tarby

Senior Vice President, Marcus Collier

Senior Vice President Human Resources And Administration, Kimberly Kuryea

Vice President Financial Planning, Randy Collins

Vice President And Treasurer, David H Fogg

Vice President New Marketing, Chris Trella

Vice President, Vincent Shugrue

Vp Strategic Planning, Phebe N. Novakovic, age 60

Board Member, Laura Schumacher

Board Member, Mark Malcolm

Board Member, Peter Wall

Auditors: KPMG LLP

LOCATIONS

HQ: General Dynamics Corp
2941 Fairview Park Drive, Suite 100, Falls Church, VA 22042-4513
Phone: 703 876-3000
Web: www.generaldynamics.com

2016 Sales

	$ mil.	% of total
North America	24,122	77
Europe	2,355	8
Africa/Middle East	2,668	8
Asia/Pacific	1,914	6
South America	294	1
Total	**31,353**	**100**

PRODUCTS/OPERATIONS

2016 Sales

	$ mil.	% of total
Information Systems and Technology	9,187	29
Aerospace	8,362	27
Marine Systems	8,202	26
Combat Systems	5,602	18
Total	**31,353**	**100**

2016 Sales

	$ mil.	% of total
Products	19,885	63
Services	11,468	37
Total	**31,353**	**100**

COMPETITORS

Airbus	Leidos
BAE SYSTEMS	Lockheed Martin
Boeing	Motorola Solutions
Bombardier	Navistar International
Cisco Systems	Nokia
DRS Technologies	Northrop Grumman
Dassault Aviation	Peugeot
Day & Zimmermann	Raytheon
FLIR Systems	Renco
HP Enterprise Services	Rockwell Collins
Harris Corp.	Textron
ITT Corp.	United Technologies
L3 Technologies	

HISTORICAL FINANCIALS

Company Type: Public

Income Statement

FYE: December 31

	REVENUE ($ mil.)	NET INCOME ($ mil.)	NET PROFIT MARGIN	EMPLOYEES
12/17	30,973	2,912	9.4%	98,600
12/16	31,353	2,955	9.4%	98,800
12/15	31,469	2,965	9.4%	99,900
12/14	30,852	2,533	8.2%	99,500
12/13	31,218	2,357	7.6%	96,000
Annual Growth	**(0.2%)**	**5.4%**	**—**	**0.7%**

2017 Year-End Financials

Debt ratio: 11.36%
Return on equity: 25.99%
Cash ($ mil.): 2,983
Current ratio: 1.40
Long-term debt ($ mil.): 3,980

No. of shares (mil.): 296
Dividends
 Yield: 0.0%
 Payout: 34.3%
Market value ($ mil.): 60,403

	STOCK PRICE ($) FY Close	P/E High/Low		PER SHARE ($) Earnings	Dividends	Book Value
12/17	203.45	22	18	9.56	3.28	38.52
12/16	172.66	18	13	9.52	2.97	36.29
12/15	137.36	17	14	9.08	2.69	34.31
12/14	137.62	19	12	7.42	2.42	35.61
12/13	95.55	14	10	6.67	2.19	41.03
Annual Growth	**20.8%**	**—**	**—**	**9.4%**	**10.6%**	**(1.6%)**

General Electric Co

From turbines and oilfield equipment to aircraft engines and power plants General Electric (GE) is plugged in to industrial equipment businesses that shape the modern world. The company produces aircraft engines locomotives and other transportation equipment generators and turbines and oil and gas exploration and production equipment. GE also is a major healthcare products provider. GE still owns GE Capital but has gradually divested the majority of its non-industrial business assets. To accelerate growth for its oil and gas business in 2017 GE spent $25 billion to acquire Baker Hughes and merged it with its GE Oil & Gas division.

HISTORY

General Electric (GE) was established in 1892 in New York the result of a merger between Thomson-Houston and Edison General Electric. Charles Coffin was GE's first president and Thomas Edison who left the company in 1894 was one of the directors.

GE's financial strength (backed by the Morgan banking house) and its research focus contributed to its initial success. Early products included such Edison legacies as light bulbs elevators motors toasters and other appliances under the GE and Hotpoint labels. In the 1920s GE joined AT&T and Westinghouse in a radio broadcasting venture Radio Corporation of America (RCA) but GE sold off its RCA holdings in 1930 because of an antitrust ruling.

By 1980 GE had reached $25 billion in revenues from plastics consumer electronics nuclear reactors and jet engines. But it had become rigid and bureaucratic. Jack Welch became president in 1981 and shook up the company. He decentralized operations and adopted a strategy of pursuing only high-achieving ventures and dumping those that didn't perform. GE shed air-conditioning (1982) housewares (1984) and semiconductors (1988) and with the proceeds acquired Employers Reinsurance (1984); RCA including NBC (1986 but sold RCA in 1987); CGR medical equipment (1987); and investment banker Kidder Peabody (1990).

In the early 1990s GE grew its lighting business. It bought mutual fund wholesaler GNA in 1993 and GE Investment Management (now GE Financial Network) began selling mutual funds to the public.

GE sold scandal-plagued Kidder Peabody to Paine Webber in 1994. General Electric Capital Services (GECS) expanded its lines buying Amex Life Insurance (Aon's Union Fidelity unit) and Life Insurance Co. of Virginia in 1995 and First Colony the next year. The company sold its struggling GEnie online service in 1996 and formed an NBC and Microsoft venture the MSNBC cable news channel. In 1997 GE Engine Services bought aircraft engine maintenance firms Greenwich Air Services and UNC.

GE acquired Lockheed Martin's medical imaging unit in 1997 and added to the medical systems business with the 1998 purchase of Marquette Medical Systems. In 1998 GECS became the first foreign company to enter Japan's life insurance market when it bought assets from Toho Mutual Life Insurance and set up GE Edison Life.

In 1999 GECS bought the 53% of Montgomery Ward it didn't already own along with the retailer's direct-marketing arm as Montgomery Ward emerged from bankruptcy. (Ward declared bankruptcy again in 2000.) In 2000 it reorganized GE Information Systems to form an e-commerce unit Global eXchange Services (GXS). (GE sold 90% of GXS to buyout firm Francisco Partners in 2002.)

Later in 2000 the company announced its biggest acquisition of the Welch era. Moving in at the last minute GE trumped a rival bid from United Technologies and agreed to pay $45 billion in stock for manufacturing giant Honeywell International and to assume $3.4 billion in Honeywell debt.

Welch by then viewed as one of the best corporate leaders in the US had agreed to postpone his retirement from April 2001 until the end of that year in order to oversee the completion of the Honeywell acquisition. But European regulators concerned about the potential strength of the combined GE-Honeywell aircraft-related businesses blocked the Honeywell deal that summer. Welch then stepped down and Jeff Immelt formerly president and CEO of GE Medical Systems succeeded him in September 2001.

Immelt initially set about reshaping GE by spinning off its life and mortgage insurance businesses into a new entity Genworth Financial which went public in 2004 (completely divested in 2006). GE acq

EXECUTIVES

Chairman And Ceo, John L. Flannery, age 56
Svp; Chairman And Ceo Ge Capital, Richard A. (Rich) Laxer
President And Ceo Current Powered By Ge, Maryrose T. Sylvester
Svp And President And Ceo Ge Aviation, David L. Joyce, age 61, $1,333,333 total compensation
Svp And Cto, Victor (Vic) Abate, age 49
Svp And President And Ceo Ge Power, Steve Bolze, age 55
Cfo, Jamie S. Miller, age 49
President And Ceo Ge Africa, Jay W. Ireland
President And Ceo Ge Europe And Alstom Integration Leader, Mark Hutchinson, age 58
Svp And Chairman President And Ceo Ge Asset Management, Dmitri L. Stockton, age 54
President And Ceo Ge Korea, Chris Khang
Svp And President And Ceo Power Services, Paul A. McElhinney
President And Ceo Baker Hughes A Ge Company, Lorenzo Simonelli, age 45
Svp And President And Ceo Ge Power, Russell Stokes, age 47
Svp And Chief Digital Officer Ge And Ceo Ge Digital, William (Bill) Ruh, age 57
President And Ceo Ge Renewable Energy, Jérôme Pécresse
Vp Global Services Organization (gso), Pete McCabe
Ceo Ge Malaysia, Datuk Mark Rozario
Ceo Ge Australia, Max York
Ceo Ge New Zealand And Ge Papua New Guinea, Kevin Hart
President And Ceo Ge Apac, Wouter Van Wersch
Ceo Ge Japan, Eriko Asai
Vice President, Kevin Czarnecki

Assistant Vice President, Valerie Bouchereau
Vpres-gen Counsel Government A, Fengming Liu
Vp And Gm Global Sales And Marketing Ge Aviation, Chaker Chahrour
Vice President Of Sales, Michael Sylstra
Vice President For Clinical And Regulatory Affairs, Mei Barselou
Vice President Strategic Initiatives, Allison Garrigan
Senior Vice President Vice Public Relations, Rene Buhay
Senior Vice President, Kathleen Chomienne
Legal Secretary, Marlene Gerardi
Senior Vice President, Matthew Pauley
Senior Vice President, Thomas Costello
Vice President Engineering, Luciano Cerone
Vice President, John Laws
Vice President National Direct Sales, David Robinson
Vice President Risk, Dennis Duffany
Vice President Speciality Solutions Sales Southeast, Randy Goins
Assistant Vice President: Franchiefinance, Vince Malizia
Vice President Retail Finance, Stephen Motta
National Account Manager Sears, Gary Howard
Assistant Vice President, Dennis Leonard
Senior Vice President, Bob Vail
Senior Vice President, David Richman
National Account Manager, Jack Hodes
Vp And Senior Counsel International Government Relations And Policy, Karan Bhatia
Vp Global Simplification Controllership And Risk Management Ge Healthcare, Thomas Westrick
Vice President Inside Sales, Jennifer Brandenburg
Vice President, Christopher Macke
Chairman And Ceo, John L. Flannery, age 56
Board Member, Shannon Winlove-smith
Board Member, Heather Bunyard
Advisory Board Member, Jill Johnson
Board Member, Elisa Morales
Board Member, Linda Reynolds
Board Member, Jessica Gee
Board Member, Jody Engel
Board Member, Jiahong Wang
Board Member, Mike Klein
Board Member, Michael Tengelin
Vice Chairman, Jesse Rock
Board Member, Michele Zizzi
Board Member, Eric Denoyel
Auditors: KPMG LLP

LOCATIONS

HQ: General Electric Co
41 Farnsworth Street, Boston, MA 02210
Phone: 617 443-3000
Web: www.ge.com

Sales 2016

	% of total
US	43
Europe	17
Asia	17
Americas	9
Middle East & Africa	14
Total	**100**

PRODUCTS/OPERATIONS

2016 Sales

	$ mil.	% of total
Power	26,827	22
Aviation	26,261	21
Healthcare	18,291	15
Oil & Gas	12,898	10
Energy Connections & Lighting	15,133	12
Capital	10,905	9
Renewable Energy	9,033	7
Transportation	4,713	4
Corporate items & eliminations	(368)	-
Total	**123,693**	**100**

COMPETITORS

ABB	Rockwell Automation
ALSTOM	Rolls-Royce
Agilent Technologies	Schneider Electric
Atlas Copco	Siemens AG
Caterpillar	Textron
Emerson Electric	ThyssenKrupp
FANUC	Toshiba
ITT Corp.	United Technologies
Raytheon	

HISTORICAL FINANCIALS

Company Type: Public

Income Statement

FYE: December 31

	REVENUE ($ mil.)	NET INCOME ($ mil.)	NET PROFIT MARGIN	EMPLOYEES
12/17	122,092	(5,786)	—	313,000
12/16	123,693	8,831	7.1%	295,000
12/15	117,386	(6,126)	—	333,000
12/14	148,589	15,233	10.3%	305,000
12/13	146,045	13,057	8.9%	307,000
Annual Growth	**(4.4%)**	**—**	**—**	**0.5%**

2017 Year-End Financials

Debt ratio: 35.09%—
Return on equity: (-8.26%)
Cash ($ mil.): 43,299
Current ratio: 1.62
Long-term debt ($ mil.): 108,575

Dividends
Yield: 0.0%
Payout: —
Market value ($ mil.): —

	STOCK PRICE ($) FY Close	P/E High/Low		PER SHARE ($) Earnings	Dividends	Book Value
12/17	17.45	—	—	(0.72)	0.84	7.40
12/16	31.60	37	31	0.89	0.93	8.67
12/15	31.15	—	—	(0.61)	0.92	10.48
12/14	25.27	19	16	1.50	0.89	12.74
12/13	28.03	22	16	1.27	0.79	12.98
Annual Growth	**(11.2%)**	—	—	**—**	**1.5%**	**(13.1%)**

GENERAL ELECTRIC INTERNATIONAL, INC.

EXECUTIVES

Pres, Giuseppe Recchi
V Pres, Candace F Carson
V Pres, Daniel Janki
SEC, Pierrot Christophe
SEC, Kristen Urso-Rio
Treas, Michael J Geary
Senior Specialist, A Carbone
Power Performance Mana, Jerry King
Fbw Integrator, Joseph Desormeaux
Auditors: KPMG LLP CINCINNATI OHIO

LOCATIONS

HQ: GENERAL ELECTRIC INTERNATIONAL, INC.
191 ROSA PARKS ST, CINCINNATI, OH 452022573
Phone: 617 443-3000
Web: WWW.GE.COM

HISTORICAL FINANCIALS

Company Type: Private

Income Statement				FYE: December 31
	REVENUE ($ mil.)	NET INCOME ($ mil.)	NET PROFIT MARGIN	EMPLOYEES
12/17	14,100	685	4.9%	125
12/16	13,364	1,339	10.0%	—
12/15	13,288	82	0.6%	—
12/14	12,884	(304)	—	—
Annual Growth	3.1%	—	—	—

2017 Year-End Financials

Debt ratio: ——
Return on equity: 4.90%
Cash ($ mil.): 961
Current ratio: 0.20
Long-term debt ($ mil.): —

Dividends
Yield: —
Payout: —
Market value ($ mil.): —

General Mills Inc

General Mills is high in the ranks of consumer packaged goods companies. Some of its #1 and #2 market-leading brands include Betty Crocker dessert mixes Gold Medal flour Pillsbury cookie dough and Yoplait yogurt. It competes with Kellogg to be the top cereal maker with a brand arsenal that includes Kix Chex Cheerios Lucky Charms and Wheaties. While most of the firm's sales come from the US General Mills is working to extend the reach and position of its brands globally. It has picked up natural foods maker Annie's premium meat snack maker EPIC Provisions and premium pet food maker Blue Buffalo in recent years.

HISTORY

Cadwallader Washburn built his first flour mill in 1866 in Minneapolis which eventually became the Washburn Crosby Company. After winning a gold medal for flour at an 1880 exposition the company changed the name of its best flour to Gold Medal Flour.

In 1921 advertising manager Sam Gale created fictional spokeswoman Betty Crocker so that correspondence to housewives could go out with her signature. The firm introduced Wheaties cereal in 1924. James Bell named president in 1925 consolidated the company with other US mills in 1928 to form General Mills the world's largest miller. The companies operated independently of one another with corporate headquarters coordinating advertising and merchandising.

General Mills began introducing convenience foods such as Bisquick (1931) and Cheerios (1941). During WWII it produced war goods such as ordnance equipment and developed chemical and electronics divisions.

When Edwin Rawlings became CEO in 1961 he closed half of the flour mills and divested such unprofitable lines as electronics. This cost $200 million in annual sales but freed resources for such acquisitions as Kenner Products (toys 1967) and Parker Brothers (board games 1968) which made General Mills the world's largest toy company.

During the next 20 years the company made many acquisitions including Gorton's (frozen seafood 1968) Monet (jewelry 1968) Eddie Bauer (outerwear 1971) and The Talbots (women's clothing 1973). It bought Red Lobster in 1970 and acquired the US rights to Yoplait yogurt in 1977.

When the toy and fashion divisions' profits fell in 1984 they were spun off as Kenner Parker Toys and Crystal Brands (1985). Reemphasizing food in 1989 the firm sold many businesses including Eddie Bauer and Talbots.

To expand into Europe General Mills struck two important joint ventures: Cereal Partners Worldwide (with NestlA© in 1989) and Snack Ventures Europe (with PepsiCo in 1992).

As part of a cereal price war in 1994 the company cut coupon promotion costs by $175 million and lowered prices on many cereals. But some retailers did not pass on the price cuts to consumers due to shortages that developed after the FDA found an unauthorized pesticide in some cereals. General Mills destroyed 55 million boxes of cereal at a cost of $140 million. Stephen Sanger became CEO in 1995. That year the company sold Gortons to Unilever and spun off its restaurant businesses as Darden Restaurants.

Focused on a food-only future in the late 1990s General Mills picked up several smaller businesses including Ralcorp Holdings' Chex snack and cereal lines and Gardetto's Bakery snack mixes as well as the North American rights to Olibra an appetite suppressant food additive made by Scotia Holdings. Entering the natural foods market in 2000 General Mills launched Sunrise organic cereal and bought organic foods producer Small Planet Foods.

Big changes came in 2001 when General Mills became the #1 cereal maker in the US overtaking Kellogg for the first time since 1906. The company then completed its $10.5 billion purchase of Pillsbury from Diageo in October 2001. A month later General Mills sold competing product lines to International Multifoods. Also that year the company launched a 50-50 joint venture with DuPont to develop soy beverages marketed under the 8th Continent brand name. While busily integrating Pillsbury in 2002 General Mills saw its income fall and watched as Kellogg regained the lead in the cereal market. In 2003 the SEC began an investigation into the company's sales and accounting practices (which it terminated in 2005 taking no action against General Mills).

In 2004 General Mills filed a universal shelf registration with the SEC the result of which is that Diageo had to register the common shares of General Mills that it owns before it could sell those shares in a public offering. Also as a result of the shelf registration two Diageo-designated members of General Mills' board (including Diageo CEO Paul Walsh) resigned as a result of a change in the two companies' stockholders agreement that terminated Diageo's right to designate two General Mills' board members. Diageo sold part of its approximate 20% stake in General Mills. General Mills in turn sold an $835 million stake to an affiliate of Lehman Brothers Holding and used $750 million to buy back the Diageo shares and $85 million to pay down debt.

Also in 2004 the company sold its US HA¤agen-Dazs ice cream shop franchise business to Dreyer's Grand Ice Cream. In 2005 it sold its stake in Snack Ventures Europe joint venture to PepsiCo for $750 million. That year the company introduced Yoplait Healthy Heart which contains cholesterol-lowering plant sterols.

Diageo sold two-thirds of its 20% stake in General Mills in 2005. Later that year General Mills announced the sale of Lloyd's barbecue business to Hormel Foods. In 2006 Cereal Partners Worldwide (its joint venture with NestlA©) acquired the Australian breakfast cereal operations of Uncle Tobys from Burns Philp.

After more than 10 years of being ignored the Jolly Green Giant came out of retirement in 2005 as part of a multi-million dollar marketing campaign by General Mills to up its veggie sales. The

next year General Mills declined to renew its licensing agreement with Archer Daniels Midland regarding the sale and marketing of Pillsbury Bakery Flour to the industrial and foodservice sectors. General Mills integrated the brand which consists of mixes and frozen bakery products into its bakery ingredients segment.

In order to develop healthier products in 2006 the company entered a supply agreement for DHA (an omega-3 fatty acid said to play a role in mental and cardiovascular health) with Martek Biosciences maker of DHA (which is already widely used in infant formula).

General Mills pulled its reduced-sugar children's cereal from the market in 2007 due to poor sales. Sweetened with SPLENDA the cereals never took off with consumers perhaps due to resistance to the sugar replacement. (Kellogg and Kraft use sugar in their reduced-sugar cereal offerings.) That year the company acquired UK chilled pastry company Saxby Bros.

Also in 2007 CEO Sanger stepped down. President and COO Ken Powell replaced him. The following year General Mills and DuPont sold their soy-milk joint venture 8th Continent to Stremicks Heritage Foods.

To better focus on its core brands and foodservice offerings the company in mid-2010 sold its Delicity chain of bakeries in Argentina to Tentissimo Group which also operates restaurants under the Tentissimo banner in the country. The deal included the Delicity brand five company-owned bakeries and franchiser rights which apply to the roughly 55 bakery locations operated by franchisees. General Mills also agreed to continue supplying dough products to the chain. It had owned Delicity since acquiring Pillsbury in 2001.

In 2008 the company sold its PopA·Secret operations to Diamond Foods for some $190 million in cash. PopA·Secret is the second-largest-selling branded popcorn in the US after Orville Redenbacher which is made by ConAgra. (ConAgra also makes Act II microwaveable popcorn.) While General Mills said it is concentrating its efforts on increasing the sales of its more lucrative core brands the high price of corn most probably also figured into the decision to jettison PopA·Secret.

General Mills made no divestures in 2009 but in 2010 the company ceased making Perfect Portions refrigerated biscuits and exited the kids' refrigerated yogurt beverage and microwave soup segments in its US retail operations; internationally it also stopped the manufacture of foodservice breadcrumbs with the sale of its Brazilian bread and pasta plant for $6 million. These product cessations were made in response to its declining financial results particularly in its international segment.

To better focus on its retail sales channels in late 2010 General Mills sold its Croissant King (acquired in 2005) and van den Bergh's (acquired in 1999) frozen bakery business in Australia to Ireland's Kerry Group. The sale includes frozen dough and pastry products sold to professional bakers.

Following that divestiture General Mills in 2011 acquired Australia's Pasta Master a maker of chilled Italian meals pasta and sauces. The purchase valued at nearly $40 million broadened General Mills' ready-to-cook pasta offerings.

To help offset weakness in its core cereal business General Mills is beefing up its yogurt empire through acquisitions such as its $1.2 billion purchase of a controlling stake in Yoplait in 2011 a brand that it had licensed for several decades. The company acquired the 50% stake in Yoplait owned by French investment firm PAI Partners plus 1% from dairy cooperative Social. Additionally General Mills acquired a 50% share of a related firm that owns Yoplait's global branding rights. General Mills aims to expand Yoplait's operations in France

Europe and the rest of the world. Also in 2011 General Mills acquired Dean Foods' Mountain High all-natural yogurt business for about $85 million. The brand became part of General Mills' Yoplait USA division.

In line with its strategy to grow its business in global markets General Mills acquired Parampara's ready-to-cook spice and sauce mixes made and marketed in India and also exported to the US Canada and Japan. In 2012 it bought Brazilian food maker Yoki Alimentos which makes and markets more than 600 items under nine brands including Yoki and Kitano. The deal doubles General Mills' annual sales in Latin America.

EXECUTIVES

Svp; Ceo Cereal Partners Worldwide, David P. (Dave) Homer

Evp And Coo International, Christopher D. (Chris) O'Leary, age 59, $730,133 total compensation

Vp; President Annieâ's Foods, John M. Foraker, age 55

Svp External Relations; President General Mills Foundation, Kimberly A. (Kim) Nelson, age 55

Svp; President Greater China, Gary Chu

Vp Treasurer, Donal L. (Don) Mulligan, age 58, $736,050 total compensation

Svp; President Big G Cereals, James H. (Jim) Murphy

Evp Supply Chain, John R. Church, age 52, $577,767 total compensation

Svp; President Meals, Michele S. Meyer

Svp; President Sales And Channel Development, Shawn P. O'Grady, age 54

Ceo, Jeffrey L. Harmening, age 51, $775,000 total compensation

Evp Innovation Technology And Quality, Peter C. Erickson, age 57

Svp; President Latin America, Sean N. Walker

Svp; President Europe Australia And New Zealand, Jonathon J. (Jon) Nudi

Vp; President Snacks, Anton Vincent

Vp; President International Yogurt And Ice Cream Strategic Business Unit, Olivier Faujour

Vp; President Asia Middle East And Africa, Christina Law

Vp; President Yoplait Usa, David Clark

Vp; President Convenience And Foodservice, Bethany C. Quam

Vp And President Small Planet Foods, Elizabeth M. Nordlie

Vice President Information Technology Global Business Solutions (gbs), Don Monk

Vice President Finance North American Retail, Brett White

Vice President Marketing Big G, John Haugen

Vice President It, Jodi Benson

Vp Mergers And Acquisitions, Doug Power

Senior Vice President Chief Human Resources Officer, Jacqueline Williams-Roll

Vice President And Deputy General Counsel, Eric Wedepohl

National Account Manager, Kurt Schuitema

Vice President Of Human Resources, Victor Huang

National Account Manager, Ted Mizerak

Vice President And Controller, Kofi Bruce

Vice President Information Technology, Zachariah Watne

National Account Manager, Dudley Whiteley

Vice President Innovation Technology And Quality Global Cereal Platform, Mayank Patel

Vice President Of Human Resources, Joseph Mucha

Vp Finance, Tito Wouda

Vice President Managing Director Yoplait Canada, Patrick Simmons

Vp Talent And Organization Capabilities, Mike Benson

Vice President And Chief Tax Officer, Jerry Morris

National Sales Manager Foodservice, Esme Plessis

Vice President Legal And External Affairs, Alice Lee

Vice President, Michael Trembley

Vice President Connectivity Solutions, Munson Dan

Vice President Marketing Big G, Becky O'grady

Chairman, Kendall J. (Ken) Powell, age 65

Board Member, Heidi Miller

Secretary, Christopher Rauschl

Board Member, Tim Clurcak

Board Member, David Cordani

Board Member, Eric Sprunk

Board Member, Henrietta Fore

Board Member, Roger Ferguson

Board Member, Maria Henry

Board Member, Jorge Uribe

Auditors: KPMG LLP

LOCATIONS

HQ: General Mills Inc
Number One General Mills Boulevard, Minneapolis, MN 55426
Phone: 763 764-7600   **Fax:** 763 764-8330
Web: www.generalmills.com

2016 sales

	$ mil.	% of total
US	11,930	72
International		
Europe	1,998	12
Canada	929	6
Asia/Pacific	995	6
Latin America	709	4
Total	**16,563**	**100**

PRODUCTS/OPERATIONS

2016 sales

	$ mil.	% of total
Snacks	3,297	20
Yogurt	2,760	17
Cereal	2,731	17
Convenient meals	2,779	17
Baking mixes & integrates	1,704	10
Dough	1,820	11
Vegetables	532	3
Super-premium ice cream	731	4
Other	206	1
Total	**16,563**	**100**

2016 sales

	$ mil.	% of total
US Retail	10,007	60
International	4,632	28
Convenience Stores & Foodservice	1,923	12
Total	**16,563**	**100**

Selected Brands

Dessert and baking mixes
  Betty Crocker
  Bisquick
  Gold Medal
  SuperMoist
  Warm Delights
Dry dinners and shelf stable and frozen vegetable products
  Annie's
  Bac*O's
  Betty Crocker
  Chicken Helper
  Diablitos
  Green Giant
  Hamburger Helper
  Old El Paso
  Potato Buds
  Simply Steam
  Suddenly Salad
  Valley Selections
  Tuna Helper
  Wanchai Ferry
Frozen pizza and pizza snacks
  Jeno's
  Party Pizza
  Pillsbury Pizza Minis
  Pillsbury Pizza Pops
  Pizza Rolls
  Totino's
Grain fruit and savory snacks
  Annie's
  Bugles
  Chex Mix
  Fiber One
  Fruit By The Foot
  Fruit Roll-Ups
  Gardetto's
  Gushers
  Larabar
  Nature Valley
  Stickerz
Ice cream and frozen desserts
  Häagen-Dazs
Organic products
  Annie's
  Cascadian Farm
  Muir Glen
Ready-to-eat cereals
  Basic 4
  Cheerios
  Chex
  Cinnamon Toast Crunch
  Clusters
  Cocoa Puffs
  Cookie Crisp
  Fiber One
  Golden Grahams
  Kix
  Lucky Charms
  Oatmeal Crisp
  Reese's Puffs
  Total
  Trix
  Wheaties
Ready-to-serve soup
  Progresso
Refrigerated and frozen dough products
  Big Deluxe
  Golden Layers
  Grands!
  Jus-Rol
  La Salte?a
  Latina
  Pasta Master
  Pillsbury
  Savorings
  Toaster Scrambles
  Toaster Strudel
  V.Pearl
  Wanchai Ferry
Refrigerated yogurt
  Go-GURT
  Fiber One
  Mountain High
  Trix
  Yoplait
  Yoplait Kids
  Yoplait Whips!
  YoPlus

COMPETITORS

B&G Foods	Hain Celestial
Barbara's Bakery	Hanover Foods
Bay State Milling	Heinz
Ben & Jerry's	Kellogg
Big Heart Pet Brands	King Arthur Flour
Birds Eye	Lakeside Foods
Blue Bell	MOM Brands
Bob's Red Mill Natural Foods	Manischewitz Company
Campbell Soup	McKee Foods
Carvel	Mondelez International
Chelsea Milling	Mrs. Fields
Cold Stone Creamery	Nature's Path
ConAgra	Nestlé
Dairy Queen	Pinnacle Foods
Danone	Pro-Fac
Dole Food	Procter & Gamble
Dreyer's	Ralston Food
Fresh «ns	Seneca Foods
Friendly's Ice Cream	Stonyfield Farm
Frito-Lay	Victoria Packing
Gilster-Mary Lee	YoCream

HISTORICAL FINANCIALS

Company Type: Public

Income Statement

FYE: May 27

	REVENUE ($ mil.)	NET INCOME ($ mil.)	NET PROFIT MARGIN	EMPLOYEES
05/18	15,740	2,131	13.5%	40,000
05/17	15,619	1,657	10.6%	38,000
05/16	16,563	1,697	10.2%	39,000
05/15	17,630	1,221	6.9%	42,000
05/14	17,909	1,824	10.2%	43,000
Annual Growth	(3.2%)	4.0%	—	(1.8%)

2018 Year-End Financials

Debt ratio: 51.65%
Return on equity: 40.82%
Cash ($ mil.): 399
Current ratio: 0.56
Long-term debt ($ mil.): 12,668

No. of shares (mil.): 593
Dividends
Yield: 0.0%
Payout: 53.8%
Market value ($ mil.): 25,290

	STOCK PRICE ($) FY Close	P/E High/Low	PER SHARE ($) Earnings	Dividends	Book Value
05/18	42.64	16 11	3.64	1.96	10.35
05/17	57.32	26 20	2.77	1.92	7.50
05/16	62.87	23 19	2.77	1.78	8.26
05/15	56.15	28 24	1.97	1.67	8.35
05/14	53.81	19 16	2.83	1.55	10.67
Annual Growth	(5.7%)	— —	6.5%	6.0%	(0.8%)

General Motors Co

General Motors (GM) one of the world's largest auto manufacturers makes cars and trucks with well-known brands such as Buick Cadillac Chevrolet and GMC. GM also builds cars through its GM Daewoo and Holden units. The company operates through three business segments. GM North America and GM International handle the automotive end of the business while General Motors Financial Co. provides financing. Looking toward the future of transportation the company is investing in developing electric vehicles and autonomous vehicles and it has established a ride-sharing service. GM sells about 9.6 million vehicles throughout the world. It's biggest single market is the US which accounts for about 30% of sales by volume.

Operations

GM operates through GM North America (GMNA) about 75% of revenue GM International about 15% of revenue and GM Financial about 10% of revenue.

GM Financial is an automotive finance company and global provider of retail loan and lease lending products and services. Additionally GM Financial offers commercial products to dealers that include new and used vehicle inventory financing inventory insurance working capital capital improvement loans and storage center financing.

The company cut back its operations in Europe with the sale of its Opel and Vauxhuall businesses to France-based PSA Group for $2.2 billion in 2017.

Geographic Reach

GM has more than 100 locations engaged in manufacturing assembly distribution warehousing engineering and testing in the US. It has locations with similar functions more than 35 countries.

GM Financial has about 40 facilities of which some 25 are in the US. Its major facilities outside the US are in Argentina Brazil Canada China Colombia Ecuador Mexico South Korea Thailand and Vietnam.

The US generates about three quarters of GM's overall revenue.

Sales and Marketing

GM sells cars and trucks directly to fleet customers including daily rental car companies commercial fleet customers leasing companies and governments.

Consumers buy GM vehicles through a network of more than 12500 independent distributors dealers and authorized sales service and parts outlets. GM is a constant presence on television and other media spending about $5 billion a year on advertising.

Financial Performance

Since hitting a post-recession high of nearly $156 billion in revenue in 2014 GM's sales have fluctuated at lower levels. In 2017 revenue slipped 2.4% to $145.6 billion from $149.2 billion in 2016. Sales of mid-size and compact passenger cars fell in 2017 from 2016 and the company sold fewer vehicles to rental car agencies. Sales dropped 6.5% in GM's North American unit its largest leading the automotive operations to an overall decline of about 5% despite higher revenue in its international unit. GM Financial's revenue increased 35% in 2017 on a larger lease portfolio and increased finance charge income.

GM claimed a $3.8 billion net loss in 2017 compared to a $9.4 billion profit in 2016 due to charges related to the US Tax Cuts and Jobs Act and the sale of the Opel/Vauxhaul business.

The automaker had $17.8 billion parked in cash and equivalents in 2017 $2.7 billion more than it had in 2016. Cash from operations generated $17.3 billion in 2017 while investing activities used $27.5 billion and financing activities provided $12.6 billion.

Strategy

In late 2018 GM signaled a significant shift in its operations announcing that it would stop production at five North American manufacturing plants in 2019. The company also said it would reorganize its global product development staffs and reduce the size of its salaried workforce. Other measures include increasing component sharing between vehicles expanding use of virtual tools to reduce development time and costs and integrating vehicle and propulsion engineering teams.

It said the moves would enable it to stay ahead of changing market conditions that have seen sales of compact and mid-sized cars decline as consumers prefer trucks and crossover vehicles. The changes were intended to provide financial flexibility to double investment in developing electric and autonomous vehicles.

In the electric car market GM aims to launch at least 10 clean-energy vehicles in China by 2020; this includes its Cadillac CT6 plug-in Buick Velite 5 and Baojun E100 models. GM's previous efforts to develop energy-saving models included the Chevrolet Volt an electric car (with a backup gas tank) powered by a lithium-ion battery able to drive 38 miles on one charge introduced in late 2010. In 2015 the auto maker introduced the second-generation Chevrolet Volt. It also launched the Chevrolet Bolt EV which can drive 238 miles on a full charge.

Signaling the importance of the Cruise autonomous unit GM named its corporate president to head it. Cruise works with Honda which committed $2 billion to the venture to develop autonomous vehicles and it has a significant investment from Softbank. It tests self-driving cars in California Arizona and Michigan.

To adapt to the changing transportation landscape GM offers a car-sharing service called Maven. The service which offers several car sharing services under one brand is available in about 20 cities in the US Canada and Australia.

Geographically GM will focuses on investing in China and the Americas. In China it aims to increase the number of nameplates under the Buick Chevrolet and Cadillac brands and continue to grow its business under the Baojun Jiefang and Wuling brands. It has also singled out the luxury segment as a springboard for growth in China buoyed by strong sales of Cadillac vehicles.

While it tries to increase its market share in China GM has been caught in the crossfire of the trade battles between the US and China. In 2018 the company said tariffs on steel and other trade-related charges cost it about $1 billion.

Late in 2018 General Motors announced a massive layoff that includes idling five factories in North America and cutting roughly 14000 jobs—roughly 10% of its workforce there. The layoffs were prompted by a slowdown in new car sales and increased trade tariffs. Plans to make smaller cars are also being scrapped as consumers are gravitating toward larger vehicles like SUVs and pickup trucks due to lower gas prices.

Mergers and Acquisitions

GM often uses acquisitions as a means to fortify its technological expertise and grow rapidly in cutting-edge markets. As such the company in 2016 acquired California-based Cruise Automation Inc. (Cruise) an autonomous vehicle technology company. GM paid $581 million for Cruise in order to accelerate its development of autonomous vehicles. GM has recently tested autonomous vehicles on public roads in San Francisco; Scottsdale Arizona; and Warren Michigan.

Company Background

In the early years of the auto industry hundreds of carmakers each produced a few models. William Durant who bought a failing Buick Motors in 1904 reasoned that manufacturers could benefit from banding together and formed the General Motors Company in Flint Michigan in 1908.

The auto giant went through a six-week period of bankruptcy protection in 2009. GM was split into two companies when it emerged from Chapter 11 — General Motors and Motors Liquidation (the name for leftover assets). In 2011 Motors Liquidation sold the majority of its assets which encompassed almost 90 industrial sites in 14 states which cleared the way for GM bondholders to receive stock in the new company.

EXECUTIVES

Svp; President And Ceo Gm Financial, Daniel E. (Dan) Berce, age 65

Evp Legal And Public Policy And General Counsel, Craig B. Glidden, age 60, $583,333 total compensation

Evp; President Europe; Chairman Management Board Opel Group, Karl-Thomas Neumann, age 57, $822,133 total compensation

Evp; President Cadillac, Carel Johannes de Nysschen, age 57

Evp Global Product Development Purchasing And Supply Chain, Mark L. Reuss, age 54, $1,100,000 total compensation

Chairman And Ceo, Mary T. Barra, age 57, $1,750,000 total compensation

Evp; President Gm China, Matthew (Matt) Tsien, age 57

Evp And President Gm International, Barry Engle, age 55

Evp Global Manufacturing, Alicia Boler Davis

Evp; President North America, Alan S. Batey, age 54

President, Daniel (Dan) Ammann, age 46, $1,200,000 total compensation

Svp Global Information Technology And Cio, Randall D. (Randy) Mott

Evp And Cfo, Charles K. (Chuck) Stevens, age 58, $1,000,000 total compensation

President And Managing Director General Motors India, Sanjiv Gupta

Vp Global Purchasing And Supply Chain, Robert E Socia, age 66

User Services. Vice President, Kurt Mcneil

Vice President, Ken Morris

U.s. Vice President Of Customer Experience, Alicia Bolerdavis

Vice President Of Sales Marketing And Aftersales Service Chevrolet Sales Thailand, Antonio Zara

Vice President, Travis Hester

Vice President, Carlos Diaz

Vice President Global Quality, Grace Lieblein

Senior Vice President Global Human Resources, Kim Brycz

Executive Assistant To Chief Finance Officer (chief Financial Officer) And Vice President, Esha Trikha

Senior Vice President Global Human Resources General Motors, Kimberly kim Brycz

Chairman And Ceo, Mary T. Barra, age 57

Board Member, Joe McHugh

Treasurer's Office, Nick Coupe

Auditors: DELOITTE & TOUCHE LLP

LOCATIONS

HQ: General Motors Co
300 Renaissance Center, Detroit, MI 48265-3000
Phone: 313 667-1500
Web: www.gm.com

PRODUCTS/OPERATIONS

2017 Sales

	$ mil.	% of total
GMNA	111	77
GMI	22	15
GM Financial	12	8
Corporate	0	-
Eliminations	0	-
Total	**145,588**	**100**

2017 Sales

	$ mil.	% of total
Automotive		
U.S.	100	69
Non-U.S.	32	23
GM Financial		
U.S.	10	7
Non-U.S.	1	1
Total	**145,588**	**100**

Selected Brands

Buick
Cadillac
Chevrolet
GMC
Holden
Isuzu
Baojun
Jiefang
Wuiling

COMPETITORS

BMW	Mitsubishi Motors
Chery Automobile	Navistar International
Daimler	Nissan
FCA US	Peugeot
Fiat Chrysler	Renault
Ford Motor	SAIC Motor
Geely Automobile	Subaru
Honda	Suzuki Motor
Hyundai Motor	Tata Motors
Kia Motors	Tesla Motors
Land Rover	Toyota
Lyft	Uber
Mazda	Volkswagen

HISTORICAL FINANCIALS

Company Type: Public

Income Statement

FYE: December 31

	REVENUE ($ mil.)	NET INCOME ($ mil.)	NET PROFIT MARGIN	EMPLOYEES
12/18	147,049	8,014	5.4%	173,000
12/17	145,588	(3,864)	—	180,000
12/16	166,380	9,427	5.7%	225,000
12/15	152,356	9,687	6.4%	215,000
12/14	155,929	3,949	2.5%	216,000
Annual Growth	**(1.5%)**	**19.4%**	**—**	**(5.4%)**

2018 Year-End Financials

Debt ratio: 46.16%
Return on equity: 21.70%
Cash ($ mil.): 26,810
Current ratio: 0.92
Long-term debt ($ mil.): 73,060

No. of shares (mil.): 1,409
Dividends
Yield: 4.5%
Payout: 223.5%
Market value ($ mil.): 47,147

	STOCK PRICE ($) FY Close	P/E High/Low		PER SHARE ($) Earnings	Dividends	Book Value
12/18	33.45	8	5	5.53	1.52	27.57
12/17	40.99	—	—	(2.60)	1.52	24.95
12/16	34.84	6	4	6.00	1.52	29.26
12/15	34.01	6	4	5.91	1.38	25.81
12/14	34.91	23	17	1.65	1.20	22.02
Annual Growth	**(1.1%)**	**—**	**—**	**35.3%**	**6.1%**	**5.8%**

Genesis Healthcare Inc

Genesis Healthcare helps seniors begin to thrive again after suffering a medical setback. Through some 500 skilled nursing facilities and assisted-living centers the company specializes in providing intensive medical care for weakened elderly patients such as those recovering from stroke or hip replacement therapy. Its facilities located in 30 states across the US house more than 55000 beds in all. Genesis also has subsidiaries that provide third-party services including rehab and respiratory therapy administrative services and consulting. Rehab services include speech pathology physical therapy and occupational therapy. These units serve more than 1700 clients in 45 states the District of Columbia and China.

Operations

Genesis operates through two primary segments — Inpatient Services and Rehabilitation Therapy Services. The larger segment Inpatient Services operates the group's skilled nursing centers and assisted-living facilities and accounts for nearly 80% of revenue. Rehabilitation Therapy Services provides third-party rehab and respiratory therapy services; it accounts for about 20% of revenue.

The company also provides some specialized services including staffing management services physician services and other medical offerings.

Geographic Reach

Genesis is based in California and has an executive office in Kennett Square Pennsylvania. It has other corporate offices in California Maryland Massachusetts and New Mexico.

The company operates its own network of facilities in 30 states throughout the US. It provides third-party services in 45 states the District of Columbia Hong Kong and China.

Sales and Marketing

Genesis' Rehabilitation Therapy Services segment is heavily reliant on its top four customers

which bring in about 70% of its gross outstanding contract receivables.

Financial Performance

Genesis revenues had been rising for the past few years until 2017 when revenue slipped 6%. The company has lost money most years over the past decade and in 2017 it warned that its debt levels may force it to file for bankruptcy protection.

In 2017 revenue fell to $5.4 billion. The company had declines across the board from inpatient services income at its skilled nursing facilities to its rehabilitation therapy services. Much of this decline was due to the divestitures of dozens of underperforming facilities as well as a decline in occupancy rates. Those declines were partially offset by increased payment rates. The sale of Genesis' hospice and homecare operations led to a decline in other services income. However the company is seeing growth in its staffing services operations.

The company's net loss increased eightfold to $579 million that year. That loss included a $360 million write-down for all of the goodwill associated with its inpatient services operations.

Genesis ended 2017 with $54.5 million in net cash which was $3.1 million more than it had at the end of 2016. Operating activities provided $120.5 million and investing activities provided $55.5 million. Financing activities such as repayments under revolving credit facilities used $172.8 million.

Strategy

Genesis' growth strategies include continually improving the quality of care its facilities provide and focusing on providing skilled nursing care for elderly patients. The company has been positioning itself to take advantage of the growing need for post-acute care services as Medicare and other payors look to shift patients away from stays at costlier hospitals and long-term acute care facilities. Rehabilitation therapy is another area of focus for Genesis as the company works to expand the types of services it offers its existing patients.

Genesis is also focusing on increasing value through its conservative management strategy. It utilizes its network size to secure better prices from suppliers for example.

The company seeks strategic acquisitions of short-stay facilities to expand its presence geographically. As the nation's largest operator of skilled nursing facilities it has somewhat of an advantage in its ability to acquire smaller competitors. Genesis is also open to establishing partnerships for further expansion. In early 2017 the company established a collaboration with Kindred Healthcare which is exiting its nursing home business to promote economies of scale through growth.

Faced with declining reimbursement rates paid by Medicare for its core skilled nursing business the company has worked to diversify its operations. Fast-growing areas such as hospice and home care helped fill the gap temporarily but the company sold those businesses in 2016 to pay down debt. The company also sold 40 underperforming facilities that year as well as its stake in a pharmacy company joint venture. It sold 35 facilities and exited four non-strategic states during 2017 recognizing losses totaling more than $12 million. In 2018 Genesis sold 15 skilled nursing facilities in Texas with plans to sell the rest of its Texas holdings and exit the state completely. The firm is exploring other strategic divestitures.

Mergers and Acquisitions

In 2016 Genesis completed the purchasing of 24 skilled nursing facilities for $240 million from Revera Assisted Living.

Company Background

In early 2015 Skilled Healthcare Group merged with Genesis Healthcare to become one of the nation's largest long-term care providers. Prior to the merger Skilled Healthcare Group operated nearly 100 skilled nursing and assisted living facilities while Genesis specialized in long-term care and rehabilitation centers. The combined firm operated more than 500 facilities.

EXECUTIVES

Ceo And Director, George V. Hager, age 63, $822,263 total compensation

Evp And President West Division, David C. (Dave) Almquist, age 64

Evp And President Northeast Division, Richard P. (Dick) Blinn, age 64

Svp And Cio, Richard L. (Rich) Castor

Evp And Coo, Paul D. Bach, age 60

Svp And Chief Human Resources Officer, Jeanne Phillips

Evp Clinical Operations And Chief Nursing Officer, JoAnne Reifsnyder, age 59, $364,998 total compensation

Svp And Cfo, Thomas (Tom) DiVittorio, age 49, $429,998 total compensation

Svp And General Counsel, Michael (Mike) Sherman

Vice President Operations, Cyndee Jackson

Vice President Senior Centers Operations, Christopher Evans

Senior Vice President Commercial Operations, Ami Faria

Director Of Pharmacy, Eric Mowery

Ceo And Director, George V. Hager, age 63

Auditors: KPMG LLP

LOCATIONS

HQ: Genesis Healthcare Inc
101 East State Street, Kennett Square, PA 19348
Phone: 610 444-6350
Web: www.genesishcc.com

PRODUCTS/OPERATIONS

2017 Sales by Payer

	% of total
Medicaid	56
Medicare	23
Insurance	12
Private & other	9
Total	**100**

2017 Sales by Segment

	$ mil.	% of total
Inpatient Services	4,627	80
Rehabilitation Therapy Services	983	17
Other Services	178	3
Corporate	0	-
Adjustments	(416.0)	-
Total	**5,373**	**100**

Selected Subsidiaries

SHG Resources LP
Summit Care Corporation
SunBridge Healthcare LLC
Genesis Administrative Services LLC

COMPETITORS

American HomePatient	Extendicare
Brookdale Senior Living	Five Star Senior Living
Covenant Care	Golden Horizons
Diversicare Healthcare Services	NHC
	SavaSeniorCare
Encompass Health	Sunrise Senior Living
Enlivant	Tenet Healthcare
Ensign Group	

HISTORICAL FINANCIALS

Company Type: Public

Income Statement

FYE: December 31

	REVENUE ($ mil.)	NET INCOME ($ mil.)	NET PROFIT MARGIN	EMPLOYEES
12/17	5,373	(578)	—	68,700
12/16	5,732	(64)	—	82,000
12/15	5,619	(426)	—	88,700
12/14	833	(0)	—	13,025
12/13	842	(10)	—	15,050
Annual Growth	**58.9%**	**—**		**46.2%**

2017 Year-End Financials

Debt ratio: 105.19%
Return on equity: —
Cash ($ mil.): 91
Current ratio: 1.05
Long-term debt ($ mil.): 5,005

No. of shares (mil.): 159
Dividends
Yield: —
Payout: —
Market value ($ mil.): 122

	STOCK PRICE ($) FY Close	P/E High/Low	Earnings	PER SHARE ($) Dividends	Book Value
12/17	0.76	— —	(6.15)	0.00	(6.80)
12/16	4.25	— —	(0.82)	0.00	(3.17)
12/15	3.47	— —	(4.97)	0.00	(2.84)
12/14	8.57	— —	(0.02)	0.00	2.38
12/13	4.81	— —	(0.28)	0.00	2.32
Annual Growth	**(36.9%)**				

Genuine Parts Co.

What do spark plugs hydraulic hoses paper clips and magnet wire have in common? They're all Genuine Parts. The diversified company is the sole member and majority owner of National Automotive Parts Association (NAPA) a voluntary trade association that distributes auto parts nationwide. Genuine Parts Company (GPC) operates about 1100 NAPA Auto Parts stores in more than 45 US states. It also distributes parts through chains in Canada Mexico and across Europe. Other subsidiaries include auto parts distributor Balkamp industrial parts supplier Motion Industries and office products distributor S.P. Richards.

HISTORY

Genuine Parts Company (GPC) got its start in Atlanta in 1928 when Carlyle Fraser bought a small auto parts store. That year GPC had the only loss in its history. Three years earlier a group that included Fraser had founded the National Automotive Parts Association (NAPA) an organization of automotive manufacturers remanufacturers distributors and retailers.

The Depression was a boon for GPC because fewer new-car sales meant more sales of replacement parts. During the 1930s GPC's sales rose from less than $350000 to more than $3 million. One tool it developed to spur sales during the Depression was its monthly magazine Parts Pups which featured pretty girls and corny jokes (discontinued in the 1990s). GPC acquired auto parts rebuilder Rayloc in 1931 and established parts distributor Balkamp in 1936.

WWII boosted sales at GPC because carmakers were producing for the war effort but scarce resources limited auto parts companies to producing functional parts. GPC went public in 1948.

The postwar boom in car sales boosted GPC's sales in the 1950s and 1960s. It expanded during this period with new distribution centers across the country. GPC bought Colyear Motor Sales (NAPA's West Coast distributor) in 1965 and introduced a line of filters and batteries in 1966 that were the first parts to carry the NAPA name.

GPC moved into Canada in 1972 when it bought Corbetts a Calgary-based parts distributor. That acquisition included Oliver Industrial Supply. During the mid-1970s GPC began to broaden its distribution businesses adding S.P. Richards (office products 1975) and Motion Industries (industrial replacement parts 1976). In the late 1970s GPC acquired Bearing Specialty and Michigan Bearing as part of Motion Industries.

In 1982 the company introduced its now familiar blue-and-yellow NAPA logo. Canadian parts distributor UAP (formerly United Auto Parts) and GPC formed a joint venture UAP/NAPA in 1988 with GPC acquiring a 20% stake in UAP.

During the 1990s GPC diversified its product lines and its geographic reach. Its 1993 acquisition of Berry Bearing made the company a leading distributor of industrial parts. The next year GPC formed a joint venture with Grupo Auto Todo of Mexico.

NAPA formed an agreement in 1995 with Penske Corporation to be the exclusive supplier of auto parts to nearly 900 Penske Auto Centers. GPC purchased Horizon USA Data Supplies that year adding computer supplies to S.P. Richards' product mix.

A string of acquisitions in the late 1990s increased GPC's industrial distribution business (including Midcap Bearing Power Drives & Bearings and Amarillo Bearing).

GPC paid $200 million in 1998 for EIS a leading wholesale distributor of materials and supplies to the electrical and electronics industries. Late in 1998 after a 10-year joint venture it bought the remaining 80% of UAP it didn't already own. GPC continued to expand its auto parts distribution network in 1999 acquiring Johnson Industries an independent distributor of auto supplies for large fleets and car dealers. GPC also acquired Oklahoma City-based Brittain Brothers a NAPA distributor that serves about 190 auto supply stores in Arkansas Missouri Oklahoma and Texas.

In 2000 the company bought a 15% interest in Mitchell Repair Information (MRIC) a subsidiary of Snap-on Incorporated that provides diagnostic and repair information services. The next year Johnson Industries acquired Coach and Motors a distribution center in Detroit.

GPC acquired NAPA Hawaii which serves more than 30 independently owned NAPA stores and four company-owned ones in Hawaii and Samoa in 2003. Also that year the company sold its interest in the partnership that distributes industrial parts in Mexico Refacciones Industriales de M©xico.

President Thomas Gallagher became the company's fourth CEO in more than 75 years when he was named to the position in August 2004. Former CEO Larry Prince remained as chairman until early in 2005 when Gallagher was elected chairman; Prince remains on the board. Also during 2005 the company acquired a 25% interest in Altrom Canada Corp.

GPC subsidiary Motion Industries in mid-2006 acquired Lewis Supply Co. a provider of casters cutting tools machinery accessories and other general mill supplies. In October the company merged HorizonUSA Data Supplies previously a wholly owned subsidiary of S.P. Richards into S.P. Richards.

In early 2008 the company sold its Johnson Industries subsidiary which provided automotive supplies to fleets and new car dealers. In October GPC's S.P. Richards unit acquired ActionEmco's business assets in the midwestern US including its Grand Rapids Michigan distribution center. Also that year Motion Industries acquired Texas-based Drago Supply Company Mill Supply Corp. and Monroe Rubber and Plastic Supply.

In 2009 GPC added eight companies to its industrial and automotive operations for about $70 million and snapped up the remaining 11% interest in Balkamp that it did not already control for some $60 million making it a wholly owned subsidiary. These deals compare to a broader acquisition strategy in 2008 which added a dozen companies to all four of GPC's business segments (automotive industrial office products and electrical and electronic) for nearly $135 million.

Also in 2010 it acquired Canada's BC Bearing a distributor of bearing and power transmission components.

In late 2013 Motion acquired AST Bearings an industrial distributor specializing in high-precision miniature and specialty bearing with locations in New Jersey and California as well as Paragon Service & Supply (PS&S) of Lima Ohio. PS&S distributes industrial cutting tools abrasives and metalworking equipment.

In 2013 GPC acquired the remaining 70% of Melbourne-based Exego Group for approximately $800 million. (In January 2012 it purchased a 30% share in the company for around $150 million in cash). Exego an aftermarket distributor of automotive replacement parts and accessories has about 430 stores across Australia and New Zealand. The Exego stake allows GPC an entry point into Asia.

In 2012 GPC bought rival auto parts distributor Quaker City Motor Parts Co. for $343 million and thus became the only member of NAPA. Delaware-based Quaker was a long-standing NAPA distributor with annual sales of about $300 million and some 270 auto parts stores.

EXECUTIVES

Evp Cfo And Corporate Secretary, Carol B. Yancey, age 55, $507,500 total compensation

Svp Human Resources, James R. (Jim) Neill, age 56, $319,000 total compensation

President And Ceo, Paul D. Donahue, age 62, $840,000 total compensation

President And Coo U.s. Automotive Parts Group, Lee A. Maher, $489,670 total compensation

President And Ceo Motion Industries, Timothy P. (Tim) Breen, age 57, $456,000 total compensation

Evp Cfo And Corporate Secretary, Carol B. Yancey, age 55

Chairman, Thomas C. (Tom) Gallagher, age 71

Auditors: Ernst & Young LLP

LOCATIONS

HQ: Genuine Parts Co.
2999 Wildwood Parkway, Atlanta, GA 30339
Phone: 678 934-5000
Web: www.genpt.com

2016 Sales

	$ mil.	% of total
US	12,822	83
Canada	1,390	9
Australasia	1,104	7
Mexico	112	1
Adjustments	(91.0)	-
Total	**15,339**	**100**

PRODUCTS/OPERATIONS

2016 Sales

	$ mil.	% of total
Automotive	8,111	52
Industrial	4,634	30
Office products	1,969	13
Electrical & electronic materials	715	5
Adjustments	(91.0)	-
Total	**15,339**	**100**

Selected Operations

Automotive Parts Group
  Altrom Canada Corp. (distribution of import automotive parts Canada)
  Balkamp (majority-owned subsidiary; distribution of replacement parts and accessories for cars heavy-duty vehicles motorcycles and farm equipment)
  Grupo Auto Todo S.A. de C.V. (Mexico)
  UAP Inc. (auto parts distribution Canada)
Electrical/Electronic Materials Group
  EIS Inc. (products for electrical and electronic equipment including adhesives copper foil and thermal management materials)
Industrial Parts Group
  Motion Industries (Canada) Inc.
  Motion Industries Inc.
Office Products Group
  S.P. Richards Company

COMPETITORS

Advance Auto Parts	General Parts
Applied Industrial Technologies	Gould Paper
	Graybar Electric
Arrow Electronics	Hahn Automotive
AutoZone	Ingersoll-Rand
Avnet	Kaman Industrial Technologies
CARQUEST	
Coast Distribution	MSC Industrial Direct
Cole Office Products	O'Reilly Automotive
Complete Office	Office Depot
D & H Distributing	Pep Boys
Essendant	Staples
Ford Motor	W.W. Grainger
General Motors	

HISTORICAL FINANCIALS

Company Type: Public

Income Statement

FYE: December 31

	REVENUE ($ mil.)	NET INCOME ($ mil.)	NET PROFIT MARGIN	EMPLOYEES
12/17	16,308	616	3.8%	48,000
12/16	15,339	687	4.5%	40,000
12/15	15,280	705	4.6%	39,600
12/14	15,341	711	4.6%	39,000
12/13	14,077	684	4.9%	37,500
Annual Growth	**3.7%**	**(2.6%)**	**—**	**6.4%**

2017 Year-End Financials

Debt ratio: 26.59%	No. of shares (mil.): 146
Return on equity: 18.67%	Dividends
Cash ($ mil.): 314	Yield: 0.0%
Current ratio: 1.34	Payout: 64.5%
Long-term debt ($ mil.): 2,605	Market value ($ mil.): 13,933

	STOCK PRICE ($) FY Close	P/E High/Low		PER SHARE ($) Earnings	Dividends	Book Value
12/17	95.01	24	19	4.18	2.70	23.27
12/16	95.54	23	17	4.59	2.63	21.52
12/15	85.89	23	17	4.63	2.46	20.97
12/14	106.57	23	17	4.61	2.30	21.56
12/13	83.19	19	14	4.40	2.15	21.78
Annual Growth	**3.4%**	**—**	**—**	**(1.3%)**	**5.9%**	**1.7%**

Genworth Financial, Inc. (Holding Co)

Insurance and investment specialist Genworth Financial specializes in life insurance and retirement investments in the US market. Internationally Genworth offers mortgage insurance and other payment protection products. The firm also provides private residential mortgage insurance in the US. Genworth focuses its retirement investment products including fixed annuities and mutual funds on affluent individuals. Genworth serves customers in 25 countries. Chinese conglomerate China Oceanwide Holdings is buying Genworth for $2.7 billion.

Change in Company Type

In October 2016 Genworth agreed to be acquired by China Oceanwide Holdings a family-owned holding company based in Beijing. China Oceanwide plans to contribute an additional $1.1 billion to support Genworth as it restructures its life insurance operations including divesting certain annuity businesses and meeting maturing debt obligations.

Operations

Genworth operates in five segments: US Life Insurance US Mortgage Insurance Canada Mortgage Insurance Australia Mortgage Insurance and Runoff.

The US Life Insurance segment is Genworth's largest unit bringing in some 75% of total revenue. It provides long-term coverage products and services traditional life insurance policies and fixed annuity products in the US.

The three mortgage insurance segments primarily offer prime mortgage insurance coverage for individually underwritten loans; they also offer selective bulk mortgage insurance. US Life Insurance provides long-term care coverage products and services traditional life insurance policies and fixed annuity products in the US. The runoff segment managed products that are no longer actively marketed including variable annuity variable life and corporate-owned life policies.

Geographic Reach

While US operations account for more than 85% of revenues Genworth's international operations include significant mortgage insurance businesses in Australia Canada and Mexico. The firm is looking to expand its mortgage insurance operations into emerging markets.For example it has a minority stake in a joint venture in India.

Sales and Marketing

Genworth's products are sold through direct sales brokerage general agencies and independent marketing organizations as well as by banks and financial advisors. Long-term care insurance products are sold through a variety of sales channels — independent producers financial intermediaries and sales specialists.

The company markets its mortgage products to financial groups and mortgage lenders that require mortgage insurance for customer financing. It has a field sales force throughout the US and a telephone sales force that primarily works with smaller lenders. Genworth also has a call center to support all customer segments.

Financial Performance

Genworth's revenue has been trending downward over the past five years. In 2016 it fell 2% to $8.4 billion as US life insurance and fixed annuities sales declined.

The company has been recovering from a $1.2 billion net loss in 2014 caused largely by an increase in benefits and other changes in policy reserves. In 2015 the company cut its losses to $629 million as expenses related to changes in policy reserves declined. Losses in 2016 totaled an even more palatable $277 million as losses from continuing operations declined. Genworth also had an $18 million gain that year from the sale of its European mortgage operations.

Cash flow from operations which fell 35% in 2015 rose 16% to $1.9 billion in 2016. This was primarily due to the decrease in net losses.

Strategy

Genworth is streamlining its operations through asset sales which allow the company to improve its cash position and focus on its core offerings. Additionally it is working to improve returns in the international mortgage units by reducing exposure in certain markets: It sold its European mortgage insurance business to AmTrust Financial in 2016 and sold part of the Australian unit in 2015. Also in 2015 it sold its European lifestyle protection insurance business to France's AXA for some $510 million. In early 2016 Genworth sold certain blocks of term life insurance policies to Protective Life Insurance Company.

The company is also restructuring its US life insurance segment. In early 2016 it announced it would suspend sales of its traditional life and fixed annuity products to cut expenses. It also began unwinding existing products from Bermuda-based subsidiary Brookfield Life and Annuity Insurance to its US life insurance units that year; it dissolved the Bermuda unit once that process was complete. Finally it has been separating its troubled long-term care insurance business for ultimate isolation.

To boost its core operations the company has realigned and expanded its sales team dedicated to serving mortgage originators. Genworth is also focused on increasing the value of new and existing policies through pricing initiatives and changes in product distribution and design practices across all of its business units.

In October 2016 the company agreed to be acquired by China Oceanwide Holdings for $2.7 billion. China Oceanwide has committed another $1.1 billion to help Genworth as it restructures its operations. The acquisition will assist Genworth as it tackles another strategic initiative — reducing debt.

HISTORY

The company was formed in 2004 to acquire certain insurance and financial services business from General Electric (GE). GE retained a controlling stake in Genworth Financial after its stock offering but sold its remaining stake in 2006.

During the downturn in the US housing market (starting in 2008) the company faced losses in its US mortgage insurance segment. After considering divestitures Genworth instead simply yanked hard on those operations making its underwriting criteria more stringent and restricting new business. The company also conducted extensive restructuring programs including a 15% workforce reduction in 2009 and a de-risking of its investment portfolio to recover from the economic downturn. Nonetheless the company saw income and cash flow losses during those years as a result of poor returns on investments.

In 2009 the company launched an IPO of its Canadian mortgage insurance business.

In late 2010 Genworth expanded its asset management operations with the purchase of hedge fund and managed futures producer Altegris Capital. The purchase brought in alternative investments and $2.2 billion in assets under management.

Despite steady growth in the sales of its Medicare supplemental products in 2011 the company sold the block of products (held by the former Continental Life Insurance Company unit) to Aetna for $290 million. In addition in 2011 the company stopped offering mortgage insurance policies in New Zealand.

EXECUTIVES

President And Ceo, Thomas J. (Tom) McInerney, age 62, $996,804 total compensation
President And Ceo Us Mortgage Insurance, Rohit Gupta
Evp Human Resources, Michael S. Laming, age 67, $491,692 total compensation

Evp And Chief Strategy Officer, Scott J. McKay, age 57
Evp And Coo, Kevin D. Schneider, age 56, $722,683 total compensation
President And Ceo Genworth Mortgage Insurance Canada, Stuart Levings
President And Ceo U.s. Life Insurance, David OÁ'Leary
Evp And Chief Investment Officer, Daniel J. (Dan) Sheehan, age 52, $598,083 total compensation
Evp And Chief Risk Officer, Lori M. Evangel, age 55, $455,271 total compensation
Evp And General Counsel, Ward E. Bobitz, age 53, $423,642 total compensation
Evp And Cfo, Kelly L. Groh, age 49, $538,657 total compensation
President And Ceo Genworth Mortgage Insurance Australia, Georgette C. Nicholas
Senior Vice President Of Sales, Matt Young
Senior Vice President, Joseph Mccusker
Vice President And Investments Counsel, Michael Shepherd
Senior Vice President Of Finance, Matt Farnay
Assistant Vice President Finance, Beth Adcock
Vice President And Investments Counsel, Philip Hart
Vice President International Government Relations, Scott Quesenberry
Vice President Accounting Policy, Mitch Rosen
Associate Vice President And Actuary, Vanesa Barbera
Vice President And Associate General Counsel, David Dodd
Divisional Vice President, Stan J Mensing
Vice President Products And Services Marketing, Miller Tammy
Vice President Model Development Annuities, Scott Rocco
Vice President Corporate Accounts, David Stagnitti
Medical Director, James Wright
Commercial Senior Vice President Mortgage Insurance Manager Information Technology, Alejandro Espinosa
Vice President Regional Sales, Tracie Michaud
Chairman, James S. (Jim) Riepe, age 75
Auditors: KPMG LLP

LOCATIONS

HQ: Genworth Financial, Inc. (Holding Co)
6620 West Broad Street, Richmond, VA 23230
Phone: 804 281-6000
Web: www.genworth.com

2016 Revenues

	$ mil.	% of total
US	7,270	87
Canada	645	8
Australia	440	5
Other countries	14	-
Total	**8,369**	**100**

PRODUCTS/OPERATIONS

2016 Revenues

	$ mil.	% of total
US Life	6,250	74
U.S. Mortgage Insurance	726	9
Canada Mortgage Insurance	645	8
Australia Mortgage Insurance	440	5
Runoff	302	4
Corporate & other	6	-
Total	**8,369**	**100**

2016 Revenues

	$ mil.	% of total
Premiums	4,160	50
Net Investment income	3,159	37
Net investment losses	72	1
Policy fees and other income	978	12
Total	**8,369**	**100**

Selected Products and Services
Fixed annuities
Life insurance
Long-term care insurance
Mortgage
Retirement solutions
Wealth management solutions

COMPETITORS

AEGON USA	MetLife
AIG	Nationwide
Great American	New York Life
Financial Resources	Northwestern Mutual
John Hancock Financial	PMI Group
Services	Prudential
MGIC Investment	Radian Group
MassMutual	The Hartford
Medamerica Insurance	

HISTORICAL FINANCIALS
Company Type: Public

Income Statement
FYE: December 31

	ASSETS ($ mil.)	NET INCOME ($ mil.)	INCOME AS % OF ASSETS	EMPLOYEES
12/17	105,297	817	0.8%	3,500
12/16	104,658	(277)	—	3,400
12/15	106,431	(615)	—	4,100
12/14	111,358	(1,244)	—	5,300
12/13	108,045	560	0.5%	5,000
Annual Growth	(0.6%)	9.9%	—	(8.5%)

2017 Year-End Financials

Debt ratio: 4.31%
Return on equity: 6.27%
Cash ($ mil.): 2,875
Current ratio: —
Long-term debt ($ mil.): —
No. of shares (mil.): 499
Dividends
Yield: —
Payout: —
Market value ($ mil.): 1,552

	STOCK PRICE ($) FY Close	P/E High/Low	Earnings	Dividends	Book Value
12/17	3.11	3 2	1.63	0.00	26.89
12/16	3.81	— —	(0.56)	0.00	25.39
12/15	3.73	— —	(1.24)	0.00	25.75
12/14	8.50	— —	(2.51)	0.00	30.03
12/13	15.53	14 7	1.12	0.00	29.08
Annual Growth	(33.1%)	— —	9.8%	—	(1.9%)

Georgia Power Co

Georgia Power is the largest subsidiary of US utility holding company Southern Company. The regulated utility provides electricity to about 2.4 million residential commercial and industrial customers throughout most of Georgia. It has interests in about 20 fossil-fueled 2 nuclear and 20 hydro-electric power plants that give it about 22000 MW of generating capacity. When necessary the company purchases excess power from nine small power producers. Georgia Power sells wholesale electricity to several cooperatives and municipalities in the region. The utility also offers energy efficiency surge protection and outdoor lighting products and services.

Operations

Georgia Power generates purchases transmits distributes and sells electricity in Georgia. It generates power from coal and natural gas as well as from renewable sources such as solar hydroelectric and wind.

In 2012 the company purchased about 440 kilowatt hours of power from other providers.

On the financing front the company invests in domestic equity international equity fixed income trust-owned life insurance special situations real estate investments and private equity.

Geographic Reach

The company serves retail customers in Georgia. It also sells power to wholesale customers across the US Southeast.

Financial Performance

Georgia Power's revenues grew by 3% in 2013 due to increase in retail base revenues as the result of higher rates (to help pay for placing new generating units at Plant McDonough-Atkinson in service and collecting financing costs related to the construction of Plant Vogtle Units 3 and 4 as well as higher market-driven contributions from commercial and industrial customers.

Net income was flat in 2013 at stayed at $1.2 million as an increase in operating expenses (the result of a 9.9% increase in the volume of KWHs generated as a result of higher prices for purchased power and an 8.1% increase in the average cost of fuel per KWH generated for all types of fuel generation) was offset by a decrease in other expenses due to the decline in interest expenses as a result of refinancing activity.

Strategy

As part of the company's integrated resource plan in addition to a renewables push it is looking to building two additional nuclear power units at its power plant in Vogtle near Waynesboro Georgia (the country's first nuclear power plants in more than 30 years). In 2012 it secured US Nuclear Regulatory Commission approval to go ahead and build these units.

To upgrade its coal plants between 1990 and 2015 Georgia Power plans to invest $7 billion on environmental control technologies.

The company is committed to diversifying its portfolio to include more green energy. To that end in 2013 it signed a contract with EDP Renewables North America for 250 MW of wind energy which it will begin receiving in 2016. That year Georgia Power opened its Water Research Center that will look for ways to reduce its power plant water use and improve the quality of water it releases from plants.

In 2012 it opened the Piedmont Green Power Plant in Barnesville Georgia and signed a 20-year agreement with Rollcast Energy to purchase about 54 MW of biomass energy.

Company Background

The company was founded in 1927.

EXECUTIVES

Senior Vice President Metro Atlanta Region, Richard Holmes

Evp Cfo Treasurer And Comptroller, W. Ron Hinson, age 61

Evp And Chief Production Officer Southern Company Generation, Theodore J. (Ted) McCullough, age 55

Chairman President And Ceo, Paul Bowers

Svp Marketing, Kenny Coleman

Evp External Affairs, Chris Cummiskey

Evp Customer Service And Operations, Pedro Cherry

Chief Accounting Officer Vice President And Comptroller, Ann Daiss

Vice President And Senior Production Officer Gulf Power, Michael Burroughs

Region Vice President, Cathy Hill

Vice President Of Corporate Communi, Jason Cuevas

Executive Vice President External Affairs, Craig Barrs

Vice President, Brian Ivey

Vice President Information Resources, Clare Blalock

Executive Vice President; President External Affairs, Chris Womack

Executive Vice President, Charles D McCrary

Executive Vice President, James H Miller

Vice President And Comptroller Georgia Power, David Poroch

Svp Customer Service And Sales, Douglas Jons

Evp Cfo Treasurer And Comptroller, W. Ron Hinson, age 61

Chairman President And Ceo, Paul Bowers

Vice Chairman, Keith Hadid

Board Member, Allan Bense

Board Member, William Smith

Auditors: DELOITTE & TOUCHE LLP

LOCATIONS

HQ: Georgia Power Co
241 Ralph McGill Boulevard, N.E., Atlanta, GA 30308
Phone: 404 506-6526
Web: www.georgiapower.com

PRODUCTS/OPERATIONS

Selected Services

Residential Customers
My Account
Pay My Bill
Turn On/Off Power
Payment Arrangements
Paperless Billing
Budget Billing
Prices/Rate
Save Money and Energy
Energy Audits
Money-Saving Tips
Rebates & Incentives
Electric Vehicles
Products & Programs
Water Heaters
Heat Pumps
Lighting
Power Credit
Green Energy
Smart Meter
Multifamily
Business Customers
My Account
Pay My Bill
Turn On/Off Power
Budget Billing
Prices/Rates
Save Money and Energy
Energy Audits
Money-Saving Tips
Rebates & Incentives
Electric Vehicles
Programs & Services
Water Heaters
Heat Pumps
Outdoor Lighting
Electric Cooking
Forklifts
Green Energy
Smart Meter
Energydirect

2016 Sales

	$ mil.	% of total
Retail		
Residential	3,318	40
Commercial	3,077	37
Industrial	1,291	15
Other retail	86	1
Wholesale	217	2
Other	394	5
Total	**8,383**	**100**

COMPETITORS

Atmos Energy	Progress Energy
Duke Energy Progress Inc.	SCANA
Energen	Sawnee EMC
	South Carolina
Entergy	Electric & Gas
Flint Energies	Southern Company Gas
MEAG Power	TECO Energy
Oglethorpe Power	Walton EMC

HISTORICAL FINANCIALS

Company Type: Public

Income Statement

	REVENUE ($ mil.)	NET INCOME ($ mil.)	NET PROFIT MARGIN	EMPLOYEES
12/17	8,310	1,428	17.2%	6,986
12/16	8,383	1,347	16.1%	7,527
12/15	8,326	1,277	15.3%	7,989
12/14	8,988	1,242	13.8%	7,909
12/13	8,274	1,191	14.4%	7,886
Annual Growth	0.1%	4.6%	—	(3.0%)

FYE: December 31

2017 Year-End Financials

Debt ratio: 32.84%	No. of shares (mil.): 9
Return on equity: 12.13%	Dividends
Cash ($ mil.): 852	Yield: 0.0%
Current ratio: 0.87	Payout: 90.5%
Long-term debt ($ mil.): 11,073	Market value ($ mil.): —

	STOCK PRICE ($) FY Close	P/E High/Low	Earnings	PER SHARE ($) Dividends	Book Value
12/17	0.00	— —	(0.00)	1.25	
1,288.24					
12/16	25.59	— —	(0.00)	1.53	
1,254.87					
12/15	29.43	— —	(0.00)	1.53	
1,186.09					
12/14	27.55	— —	(0.00)	1.53	
1,153.92					
Annual Growth	—	—	—	(5.0%)	2.8%

German American Bancorp Inc

German American Bancorp is the holding company for German American Bank which operates some 65 branches in southern Indiana and Kentucky. Founded in 1910 the bank offers such standard retail products as checking and savings accounts certificates of deposit and IRAs. It also provides trust services while sister company German American Investment Services provides trust investment advisory and brokerage services. German American Bancorp also owns German American Insurance which offers corporate and personal insurance products. The group's core banking operations provide more than 90% of its total sales.

Geographic Reach

German American is headquartered in Jasper Indiana. Its subsidiaries operate from more than 60 locations in southern Indiana and Kentucky.

Sales and Marketing

German American Bancorp spent $3.5 million on advertising in 2017. Advertising expenses totaled $2.7 million in 2016 and $3.7 million in 2015.

Financial Performance

German American's revenue has been climbing steadily for the past five years thanks to the company's acquisitions of other area banks. Similarly net income has also been on the rise. In 2017 the company marked its eighth consecutive year of record earnings.

In 2017 revenue increased 4% to $131.8 million. That increase was partially due to the addition of River Valley Financial Bank which German American acquired in 2016. Growth in the company's loan portfolio also boosted net interest income. This was slightly offset by a 1% decline in non-interest income. Although trust and insurance operations rose other operating income declined $1.1 million (29%).

Net income rose 16% to $35.2 million in 2017; in addition to having higher revenue the company recognized a benefit related to the reduced corporate tax rate that year.

German American ended 2017 with $70.4 million in net cash $5.5 million more than it had at the end of 2016. Operating activities provided $54.9 million in cash and financing activities provided $139.9 million. Investing activities used $189.3 million.

Strategy

German American Bancorp has grown recently through a number of acquisitions including bank branches an insurance office and other bank holding companies. These acquisitions have also helped the company grow into new geographic markets including locations in Kentucky.

Growth by acquisition can be somewhat risky though. The company could unknowingly acquire problem assets or have difficulties integrating other banks it purchases. These issues could bring down its financial performance.

German American operates in a relatively small region which leaves it vulnerable to economic downturns in that area. If economic conditions in its market decline German American faces the risk of increased delinquencies and charge-offs. The company's larger more widespread competitors would be less impacted in such a case.

Mergers and Acquisitions

In October 2018 German American Bancorp acquired Kentucky's First Security Bank for $101 million. With that deal the company expanded into Kentucky's Owensboro Bowling Green and Lexington markets.

Earlier that year the company purchased five Indiana branches from First Financial Bank. That acquisition helped quell regulatory concerns about the merger between First Financial and MainSource Bank.

In 2016 German American acquired River Valley Bancorp and its River Valley Financial Bank subsidiary. It entered the Kentucky market through that purchase.

EXECUTIVES

Vice President, Lisa Matheis
General Technical; Senior Vice President, Floyd Alsman
Chairman And Ceo, Mark A. Schroeder, age 65, $342,500 total compensation
President, Clay W. Ewing, age 63, $250,000 total compensation
Evp Cfo And Senior Administrative Officer, Bradley M. Rust, age 52, $210,000 total compensation
Svp And Chief Credit Officer, Keith A. Leinenbach, age 59, $180,000 total compensation
Svp And Head Of Retail Banking, Randall L. Braun, age 58, $180,000 total compensation
Senior Vice President Trust Officer, Dave Mitchell
Vice President Deposit Services Secruity, Dale Altstadt
Senior Vice President Of Technology And Operations, Clay Barrett
Senior Vice President Commercial Banking, Joe Hauersperger
Senior Vice President Commercial Banking, Julie Donham
Regional Senior Vice President, Jim Thomas
Vice President, Christina Lebeau

Senior Vice President Commercial Lender, Jane Thoma
Regional Vice President, Jean Emery
Vice President Private Banking, Sherri Alley
Vice President Senior Wealth Advisor, Jim Godsey
Executive Vice President Head Of Trust, Brent Sternberg
Vice President, John Schroeder
Regional Vice President Commercial Lending, Doug Bell
Vice President Commercial Banking, Rob Bingham
Vice President Commercial Banking, John Newcomer
Senior Vice President Commercial Banking, Greg Cardinal
Vice President Commercial Banking, Randy Goodman
Senior Vice President Senior Wealth Advisor, Alan VanCleef
Vice President Agriculture And Commercial Banking, Gaven Oexmann
Regional Senior Vice President, Steve Walker
Chairman And Ceo, Mark A. Schroeder, age 65
Board Member, Chris Ramsey
Auditors: Crowe Horwath LLP

LOCATIONS

HQ: German American Bancorp Inc
711 Main Street, Jasper, IN 47546
Phone: 812 482-1314
Web: www.germanamerican.com

PRODUCTS/OPERATIONS

2017 Sales

	$ mil.	% of total
Interest		
Loans including fees	91	64
Securities including dividends	19	13
Short-term investments	0	-
Non-interest		
Insurance	8	6
Service charges on deposit accounts	6	4
Trust & investment product fees	5	4
Other	12	9
Adjustments	(11.1)	-
Total	**131**	**100**

COMPETITORS

Fidelity Federal	Home Financial Bancorp
Fifth Third	Old National Bancorp
First Bancorp of Indiana	Porter Bancorp
First Capital	SVB&T

HISTORICAL FINANCIALS

Company Type: Public

Income Statement

FYE: December 31

	ASSETS ($ mil.)	NET INCOME ($ mil.)	INCOME AS % OF ASSETS	EMPLOYEES
12/17	3,144	40	1.3%	614
12/16	2,955	35	1.2%	597
12/15	2,373	30	1.3%	596
12/14	2,237	28	1.3%	484
12/13	2,163	25	1.2%	480
Annual Growth	9.8%	12.5%	—	6.3%

2017 Year-End Financials

Debt ratio: 0.47%	No. of shares (mil.): 22
Return on equity: 11.71%	Dividends
Cash ($ mil.): 70	Yield: 0.0%
Current ratio: —	Payout: 29.1%
Long-term debt ($ mil.): —	Market value ($ mil.): 810

STOCK PRICE ($) FY Close	P/E High/Low	PER SHARE ($) Earnings	Dividends	Book Value
12/17	35.33	30 17	1.77	0.52	15.90
12/16	52.61	34 19	1.57	0.48	14.43
12/15	33.32	23 18	1.51	0.45	12.67
12/14	30.52	22 17	1.43	0.43	11.54
12/13	28.42	23 15	1.32	0.40	10.13
Annual Growth	5.6%	— —	7.6%	6.6%	11.9%

GILBANE BUILDING COMPANY

Gilbane Building Company has built a big business constructing for equally large customers. The firm provides construction services consulting subcontracting and facilities management to commercial institutional and governmental markets. Operating as the construction arm of Gilbane the company builds schools hospitals laboratories and prisons serving both the public and private sectors. Its completed projects include the Stroh Center at Bowling Green State University and the National WWII Memorial in Washington DC. Founded in 1873 as a carpentry and general contracting shop the family-owned Gilbane Building Company operates from more than 50 offices around the world.

Operations

The company has worked on a wide range of projects including: the Worcester Recovery Center & Hospital El Paso Corporation Building Renovation New York State Capital Restoration Georgia Tech Carbon Neutral Energy Solutions Laboratory University of North Florida Student Wellness and Sports Albert Einstein Health Network Elmhurst Memorial Healthcare and the University of Puerto Rico Molecular Sciences Building.

As part of its business Gilbane Building Company operates ITSI Gilbane a major provider of engineering and construction services to the US federal government including the Department of Defense Environmental Protection Agency and Department of Energy.

Geographic Reach

With more than 50 offices and 1000 projects underway around the world Gilbane Building Company enjoys a geographic footprint that extends from the US to Japan the United Arab Emirates Ireland South Korea and Afghanistan.

Sales and Marketing

Gilbane Building Company serves several sectors such as healthcare higher education K-12 schools federal and public entities mission critical corporate and sports and recreation. In 2014 the company boasted a 98.4% client satisfaction rate and reported that 65% of its work comes from repeat clients.

Some of its clients have included: Einstein Healthcare Network Google Inc. Operations Mane Inc Wilmington Public School Uihlein Wilson Architects City of Phoenix Crime Lab and the Operating Forces D&C Division.

Strategy

Gilbane Building Company has been busy working on projects in all parts of the country. In 2014 Gilbane secured a $43 million contract for historical renovation work on Pomerene and Oxley Halls on the Ohio State University campus. The firm's 2013 projects included the 131000-sq.-ft. Bergen County Justice Center in Hackensack New Jersey; the Columbus Regional Airport Authority's modernization of concourses B and C at Port Columbus international airports; and Miami University's Kreger Hall Rehabilitation & Addition Project which included the reorganization of 33372 sq. ft. of interior spaces and upgrades to the building's infrastructure as well as a major rehabilitation.

The company also continues to be recognized for its environment-conscious building designs particularly with schools. In early 2015 the company's completed Dunbar High School project — equipped with an advanced geothermal system a 482 kW array of photovoltaic panels and 20000-gallon cisterns — was awarded the LEED for Schools v2009 Platinum certification taking home the highest LEED score on record worldwide. Also in early 2015 the company was awarded the #1 ranking for Education K-12 Building Design and Construction and ranked within the top 5 of green contractor engineers.

It has also extended its reach in Europe in recent years. In 2012 the company formed a joint venture with Ed. ZA?blinAG known as ZA?blin Gilbane to pursue and execute projects in Europe.

EXECUTIVES

President And Ceo, Michael C. (Mike) McKelvy, age 58
Vice Chairman, William J. (Bill) Gilbane, age 71
Chairman, Thomas F. (Tom) Gilbane, age 70
Auditors: RSM US LLP BOSTON MASSACHUSE

LOCATIONS

HQ: GILBANE BUILDING COMPANY
7 JACKSON WALKWAY STE 2, PROVIDENCE, RI 029033694
Phone: 401 456-5800
Web: WWW.GILBANECO.COM

PRODUCTS/OPERATIONS

Selected Markets
Convention/cultural
Corporate
Criminal justice
Federal/public
Health care
  Children's hospitals
  Women's centers
  Cardiac-care centers
  Cancer centers
  Clinical and research facilities
Higher education
  Research laboratories
  Academic facilities
  Admissions buildings
  Residence halls
  Performing arts centers
  Sports and recreational centers
  Libraries and technology centers
  Student unions
K-12 schools
Life sciences
Mission critical
Sports/recreation
Transportation
Water/wastewater

Selected Services
Pre-construction
  Transition planning and management
  Building information modeling
  Conceptual cost modeling
  High-performance building & energy modeling
  Interdisciplinary document coordination
Consulting
  CAT-response
  Facilities management services
  Schedule & risk analysis
  Transition planning & management
Construction
  Construction management at risk
  Construction management as agent
  Lump sum general contracting
  Integrated project delivery

COMPETITORS

Barton Malow	McCarthy Building
Batson-Cook	Peter Kiewit Sons'
Bechtel	Skanska USA Building
Bernards Brothers	Swinerton
Clark Construction	The Pike Company
Group	Thos. S. Byrne
Dimeo Construction	Turner Construction
Fluor	Turner Corporation
KBR	Tutor Perini
L.F. Driscoll	Walbridge Aldinger
MEDCO Construction	Whiting-Turner

HISTORICAL FINANCIALS
Company Type: Private

Income Statement
FYE: December 31

	REVENUE ($ mil.)	NET INCOME ($ mil.)	NET PROFIT MARGIN	EMPLOYEES
12/17	4,899	63	1.3%	2,500
12/14	3,840	0	—	—
12/13	4,100	0	—	—
12/12	3,386	0	—	—
Annual Growth	7.7%	—	—	—

2017 Year-End Financials

Debt ratio: ——
Return on equity: 1.30%
Cash ($ mil.): 252
Current ratio: 1.00
Long-term debt ($ mil.): —

Dividends
  Yield: —
  Payout: —
Market value ($ mil.): —

Gilead Sciences Inc

Gilead Sciences has biotech balms for infectious diseases including hepatitis HIV and infections related to AIDS. The company's HIV franchise includes Truvada a combination of two of its other drugs Viread and Emtriva. It co-promotes another HIV treatment called Atripla in the US and Europe with Bristol-Myers Squibb (BMS). Other products on the market include AmBisome used to treat systemic fungal infections such as those that accompany AIDS or kidney disease; and hepatitis B antiviral Hepsera. Beyond HIV/AIDS Gilead also markets cardiovascular drugs as well as respiratory and ophthalmic medicines and the Yescarta CAR-T cell therapy for cancer.

Operations
Gilead primarily focuses on producing treatments for HIV liver diseases including hepatitis B and hepatitis C cancer and inflammation and cardiovascular and respiratory conditions. Although the company is steadily working to expand in medicines in various fields its main source of revenue continues to be its antiviral franchise which contributes more than 90% of product sales and primarily consists of HIV medications.

Aside from the Atripla partnership with BMS Gilead has collaborations with other companies including Japan Tobacco which promotes HIV drugs Truvada Viread and Emtriva in Japan; and with GlaxoSmithKline which markets Hepsera Viread and Volbris in select international markets. Additionally Gilead receives royalties on influenza treatment Tamiflu which it developed with Roche and on Macugen an ophthalmologic drug developed by Eyetech using Gilead's technology. In addition to distributing AmBisome in Canada and the US Astellas Pharma pays royalties on US sales of Lexiscan which is used in stress tests for coronary artery disease.

Gilead continues to advance its R&D pipeline; the company had more than 165 active clinical studies at the end of 2016. It has more than 60 trials in Phase III.

The company's portfolio of more than 20 marketed products contains a number of firsts such as the first complete treatment regimens for HIV and chronic hepatitis C available in a once-daily single pill.

Geographic Reach
The US market accounts for some 65% of Gilead's annual revenues. The company operates in more than 30 countries worldwide with a significant presence in Europe (France the UK Spain Italy Germany and Switzerland); Europe accounts for more than 20% of its annual revenue. Gilead also operates in Africa South America and the Asia/Pacific region.

Gilead has R&D facilities in Oceanside and Fremont California; Alberta; and Seattle. It has manufacturing sites in San Dimas and La Verne California; Foster City Alberta; and Cork Ireland. Commercial operations are located in 20 offices throughout Europe 10 in North America seven in Asia two in South America and one each in the Middle East Australia and Africa.

Sales and Marketing
Gilead promotes its antiviral drugs through its own commercial infrastructure in North America some European and Asian countries and in Australia and New Zealand; products are promoted through third-party distributors and partnerships in other regions. Gilead sells and distributes products including Atripla Sovaldi and Viread exclusively through wholesale channels in the US; Letairis and Cayston are distributed through specialty pharmacies. Customers include physicians hospitals clinics and other health care facilities. The company's product distribution processes are handled primarily by wholesalers including McKessonAmerisourceBergen and Cardinal Health.

In 2016 Gilead spent $618 million on advertising versus $601 million in 2015 and $393 million.

Financial Performance
Increased sales of antiviral products have provided healthy revenue increases for Gilead in recent years. After rising 31% in 2015 revenue fell 7% to $30.4 billion in 2016 as antiviral product sales dropped 7% and royalty contract and other revenue declined 10%. Top sellers Harvoni and Sovaldi had lower sales (by 34% and 24% respectively) that year as did Atripla (which fell by 17%). However these declines were offset by growing sales of other products including HIV treatments Genvoya and Odefsey and the launch of new hepatitis blockbuster Epclusa.

Net income has also seen significant growth in recent years more than tripling in 2014 and then rising another 50% in 2015. In 2016 net income fell 25% to $13.5 billion largely as a result of higher research and development expenses.

Like revenue and net income cash flow from operations dipped after seeing rapid growth. It declined 18% to $16.7 billion in 2016 due to the lower net income and negative changes in operating assets and liabilities.

Strategy
One of the pitfalls of the pharma manufacturing business is patent expirations where older medications see a decline in sales as they begin to face generic competition. Other medications struggle to penetrate highly saturated markets. To offset potential losses from these challenges Gilead is working to increase sales of top selling products in new territories. In addition Gilead works to get existing medications approved for new medical indications.

The company also works to launch new or next-generation drugs to freshen its lineup of patent-protected offerings. Although it is focused on remaining a leader in anti-virals treating HIV and hepatitis C Gilead is increasingly turning toward oncology and inflammation research. Non-alcoholic steatohepatitis (NASH) treatments present significant opportunity for the company which has already seen some success in related trials. In cancer research Gilead is focused on immuno-oncology cellular therapies and targeted therapies.

In 2015 the company launched Genvoya for the treatment of HIV-1 infections. The following year the company launched Epclusa (a single-table regiment for adults with genotype 1-6 chronic hepatitis C) Descovy (a combination for the treatment of HIV) and Odefsey (for HIV-1).

In 2016 Gilead partnered with Galapagos to develop and commercialize filgotinib which is being investigated for inflammatory disease.

In 2017 the company's Yescarta treatment was the second CAR-T cell therapy to be given FDA approval. These new therapies reprogram immune cells' DNA to attack cancers and could change the way certain cancers are treated going forward.

The company opened a new manufacturing campus in La Verne California in mid-2017.

Mergers and Acquisitions

As a way of fending off losses from patent expirations Gilead has diversified its product line through acquisitions. In 2015 Gilead acquired EpiTherapeutics a developer of novel cancer drugs based on epigenetics for $65 million.

Also in 2015 the company entered into an agreement with Phenex Pharmaceuticals in 2015; under the deal Gilead acquired Phenex's FXR program for the treatment of liver diseases for some $470 million. That transaction accelerated Gilead's efforts to develop new treatments for fibrotic liver diseases.

In 2016 the company bought Nimbus Therapeutics subsidiary Nimbus Apollo for $400 million; the deal included Nimbus' Acetyl-CoA Carboxylase (ACC) inhibitor program for the treatment of liver disease.

In 2017 the company bought Kite Pharma a leader in the development of cell therapy treatments for cancer for $11.9 billion. That purchase provided Gilead with a pipeline of CAR-T therapy products including Yescarta which was shortly thereafter approved by the FDA. It was the second CAR-T cell therapy to receive approval in the US.

HISTORY

Dr. Michael Riordan started Gilead Sciences in 1987 backed by venture capital firm Menlo Ventures. The name was derived from the Biblical phrase "Is there no balm in Gilead?" In 1990 Glaxo Wellcome (now GlaxoSmithKline) agreed to fund Gilead's research into code-blocking treatments for cancer. Gilead went public in 1992.

In 1994 the company formed an alliance with American Home Products' Storz Instruments (now part of Bausch & Lomb) to develop and market a topical treatment for an ophthalmic virus. Two years later Gilead joined forces with Roche to develop treatments for influenza.

Vistide was approved in the US in 1996 and in Europe in 1997. But more-effective HIV therapies brought declining demand for Vistide.

The company bounced back with Tamiflu (the fruit of its Roche partnership) which was approved in 1999. Sales were brisk during that flu season. Also that year Gilead expanded its pipeline and geographic reach with the $550 million all-stock acquisition of NeXstar Pharmaceuticals which focused on antifungals antibiotics and cancer treatments.

In 2000 Gilead sought approval for Tamiflu in Japan and Europe (it withdrew the European application after regulators there asked for more information) and also sought approval for pediatric uses for the drug which was granted. The following year it resubmitted Tamiflu for approval in Europe.

Chairman Donald Rumsfeld resigned in 2001 to become US secretary of defense and was replaced by retired Sears Roebuck executive James Denny. Perhaps the Defense connection helped: Vistide became one of the many drugs that researchers began studying as possible alternatives to vaccines should a smallpox bio-attack occur in the US.

EXECUTIVES

Evp Pharmaceutical Development And Manufacturing, Taiyin Yang, age 64
Evp Research, William A. Lee, age 62, $363,333 total compensation
Evp Research And Development And Chief Scientific Officer, Norbert W. Bischofberger, age 62, $1,044,231 total compensation
President And Ceo, John F. Milligan, age 57, $1,465,385 total compensation
Coo, Kevin Young, $787,645 total compensation
Evp And Cfo, Robin L. Washington, age 55, $900,385 total compensation
Evp Commercial And Access Operations (asia Latin America And Africa) And Corporate And Medical Affairs, Gregg H. Alton, age 52, $925,385 total compensation
Evp Clinical Research And Development Operations, Andrew Cheng
Evp Clinical Research, John G. McHutchison
Evp Strategy, Martin B. Silverstein, age 63
Evp And General Counsel, Brett Pletcher
Evp Human Resources, Katie L. Watson
Vice President Of U S Marketing And Sales, Jean Kress
V P Risk Management, Marti Dodson
Vice President, Choung Kim
Chairman, John C. Martin, age 66
Auditors: Ernst & Young LLP

LOCATIONS

HQ: Gilead Sciences Inc
333 Lakeside Drive, Foster City, CA 94404
Phone: 650 574-3000
Web: www.gilead.com

2016 Sales

	$ mil.	% of total
US	19,354	64
Europe	6,365	21
Japan	2,527	8
Other countries & regions	2,144	7
Total	**30,390**	**100**

PRODUCTS/OPERATIONS

2016 Sales

	$ mil.	% of total
Antiviral products:		
Harvoni	9,081	30
Sovaldi	4,001	13
Truvada	3,566	12
Atripla	2,605	9
Stribild	1,914	6
Epclusa	1,752	6
Genvoya	1,484	5
Complera/Eviplera	1,457	5
Viread	1,186	4
Odefsey	329	1
Descovy	298	1
Other antiviral	72	-
Other products:		
Letaris	819	2
Ranexa	677	2
AmBisome	356	1
Zydelig	168	1
Other	188	1
Royalties Contract & other	437	1
Total	**30,390**	**100**

Selected Products

Antiviral
Atripla (HIV with Bristol-Myers Squibb)
Complera/Eviplera (HIV)
Emtriva (HIV)
Harvoni (HCV infection)
Hepsera (hepatitis B)
Sovaldi (HCV infection)
Stribild (HIV)
Tamiflu (flu treatment royalties from Roche)
Truvada (fixed-dose combination of Viread and Emtriva for HIV)
Viread (HIV chronic hepatitis B with liver disease)
Vistide (AIDS-related cytomegalovirus retinitis)
Other products
AmBisome (antifungal with Astellas)
Cayston (cystic fibrosis)
Flolan (pulmonary hypertension)
Letairis (pulmonary arterial hypertension)
Lexiscan/Rapiscan (cardiovascular with Astellas)
Macugen (age-related macular degeneration royalties from Eyetech)
Ranexa (chronic angina)
Products in development
Aztreonam (cystic fibrosis)
Cobicistat (HIV/AIDS)
Elvitegravir (HIV/AIDS)
GS-1101 (leukemia and lymphoma)
GS-7977 (hepatitis C)
Intesgrase (HIV)
Ranolazine (cardiovascular diabetes)

COMPETITORS

AbbVie	GlaxoSmithKline
Abbott Labs	Janssen
Actelion	Pharmaceuticals
AstraZeneca	Merck
BioCryst	Novartis
Pharmaceuticals	Pfizer
Boehringer Ingelheim	Roche Holding
Bristol-Myers Squibb	Shire
Enzon	

HISTORICAL FINANCIALS

Company Type: Public

Income Statement

FYE: December 31

	REVENUE ($ mil.)	NET INCOME ($ mil.)	NET PROFIT MARGIN	EMPLOYEES
12/17	26,107	4,628	17.7%	10,000
12/16	30,390	13,501	44.4%	9,000
12/15	32,639	18,108	55.5%	8,000
12/14	24,890	12,101	48.6%	7,000
12/13	11,201	3,074	27.4%	6,100
Annual Growth	23.6%	10.8%	—	13.2%

2017 Year-End Financials

Debt ratio: 47.72%	No. of shares (mil.): 1,308
Return on equity: 23.53%	Dividends
Cash ($ mil.): 7,588	Yield: 0.0%
Current ratio: 2.74	Payout: 59.2%
Long-term debt ($ mil.): 30,795	Market value ($ mil.): 93,705

	STOCK PRICE ($) FY Close	P/E High/Low		PER SHARE ($) Earnings	Dividends	Book Value
12/17	71.64	24	18	3.51	2.08	15.63
12/16	71.61	10	7	9.94	1.84	14.42
12/15	101.19	10	8	11.91	1.29	13.03
12/14	94.26	14	8	7.35	0.00	10.29
12/13	75.10	39	20	1.81	0.00	7.41
Annual Growth	(1.2%)	—	—	18.0%	—	20.5%

Glacier Bancorp, Inc.

Glacier Bancorp is on a Rocky Mountain high. The holding company owns about a dozen community bank divisions with about 100 locations in Montana Idaho Utah Washington Arizona Colorado and Wyoming. Serving individuals small to midsized businesses not-for-profits and public entities the banks offer traditional deposit products and credit cards in addition to retail brokerage and investment services through agreements with third-party providers. Its lending activities consist of commercial real estate loans (about half of the company's loan portfolio) as well as residential mortgages business loans and consumer loans.

Financial Performance

Glacier's financial results are on a steady upward swing since 2012 with yearly increases in interest income and near-annual improvement in non-interest income and net income.

In 2017 the company generated $375 million in interest income and $112 million in non-interest income for total revenue of $487 million. Its loan portfolio grew by $601 million or 11% in the year bringing the size of its loan portfolio to just less than $6.5 billion.

Net income for the year was $116 million 4% more than 2016 due to the higher revenue partially offset by an increase in loan loss provisions employee compensation and income tax expense.

Glacier Bancorp ended 2017 with $200 million in cash an increase of nearly $50 million over the previous year. Financing activities used $230 million for loan repayments stock dividends and a decrease in deposits. Investing activities added $24 million to the coffers and operating activities contributed $255 million mostly from net income a deferred tax expense and proceeds from selling some of its loan portfolio.

Strategy

Glacier Bancorp hopes to capitalize on additional acquisition opportunities that it expects to arise as small banks deal with new industry regulations. To this end it has been on a buying spree in recent years. In early 2018 it acquired Inter-Mountain Bancorp (Montana) Columbine Capital Corporation (Colorado); in 2017 it purchased TFB Bancorp (Arizona); in 2016 it bought Treasure State Bank (Montana) and in 2015 Glacier acquired Canon Bank Corporation (Colorado) and Montana Community Banks (Montana). In total these purchases cost $377 million.

The company is also banking on organic growth with the populations of the states in its market area growing faster than the national average thanks to an influx of retiring Baby Boomers and an increase in energy- and natural resource-related jobs.

EXECUTIVES

Evp And Cfo, Ron J. Copher, $352,651 total compensation
Evp And Chief Administrative Officer, Don J. Cherry, $299,950 total compensation
President And Ceo, Randall M. (Randy) Chesler, age 60, $153,846 total compensation
Vice President And Cra And Compliance Officer, Lanette Marcum
Senior Vice President, Robert Taylor
Vice President Internal Auditor, Judy Overcast
Vice President Marketing North America, Martha Tannehill
Vice President, Ryan T Screnar
Assistant Vice President, Judy Gohsman
Vice President, Donald Mccarthy

Executive Vice President Chief Admin Officer, Don Chery
Senior Vice President Of Human Resources, Robin S Roush
Vice President Of Human Resources, Christopher Murphy
Vice President Internal Auditor, Leslie Thompson
Vice President, Melody Pieri
Vp Corporate Bsa Officer, Mary Strozzi
Vice President And Risk Manager, Emily Lamb
Senior Vice President Enterprise Wide Risk Manager, T Frickle
Assistant Vice President Benefits Administrator, Jill Klocke
Vice President Risk Management, T J Frickle
Real Estate Lender Vice President, Toby Gilchrist
Board Member, Craig A Langel
Chairman, Dallas I. Herron, age 73
Board Member, Sherry Cladouhos
Board Member, Annie Goodwin
Board Member, Douglas Mcbride
Board Member, James English
Board Member, Mark Semmens
Auditors: BKD, LLP

LOCATIONS

HQ: Glacier Bancorp, Inc.
49 Commons Loop, Kalispell, MT 59901
Phone: 406 756-4200
Web: www.glacierbank.com

PRODUCTS/OPERATIONS

2016 Sales

	% of total
Interest income	
Commercial loans	47
Investment securities	17
Residential real estate loans	7
Consumer and other loans	7
Non-interest income	
Service charges and other fees	14
Gain on sale of loans	6
Miscellaneous loan fees and charges	1
(Loss) gain on sale of investments	-
Other income	2
Total	**100**

Selected Services

Commercial loan
Consumer loan
Deposits
Mortgage origination services
Real estate loan
Retail brokerage services
Transaction and savings

Selected Bank Divisions

1st Bank (Wyoming)
Bank of the San Juans (Colorado)
Big Sky Western Bank (Montana)
Citizens Community Bank (Idaho)
Collegiate Peaks Bank
First Bank of Montana
First Bank of Wyoming
First Security Bank (Montana)
First State Bank (Wyoming)
Foothills Bank
Glacier Bank (Montana)
Mountain West Bank (Idaho)
North Cascades Bank (Washington)
Valley Bank of Helena (Montana)
Western Security Bank (Montana)

COMPETITORS

Eagle Bancorp	U.S. Bancorp
First Citizens Banc Corp	Wells Fargo
First Interstate	Zions Bancorporation

HISTORICAL FINANCIALS

Company Type: Public

Income Statement

FYE: December 31

	ASSETS ($ mil.)	NET INCOME ($ mil.)	INCOME AS % OF ASSETS	EMPLOYEES
12/17	9,706	116	1.2%	2,354
12/16	9,450	121	1.3%	2,291
12/15	9,089	116	1.3%	2,245
12/14	8,306	112	1.4%	2,030
12/13	7,884	95	1.2%	1,919
Annual Growth	5.3%	5.0%	—	5.2%

2017 Year-End Financials

Debt ratio: 1.30%	No. of shares (mil.): 78
Return on equity: 10.05%	Dividends
Cash ($ mil.): 200	Yield: 0.0%
Current ratio: —	Payout: 96.0%
Long-term debt ($ mil.): —	Market value ($ mil.): 3,073

	STOCK PRICE ($) FY Close	P/E High/Low	PER SHARE ($) Earnings	Dividends	Book Value
12/17	39.39	27 21	1.50	1.44	15.37
12/16	36.23	24 14	1.59	1.10	14.59
12/15	26.53	20 14	1.54	1.05	14.15
12/14	27.77	20 16	1.51	0.68	13.70
12/13	29.79	24 11	1.31	0.60	12.95
Annual Growth	7.2%	— —	3.4%	24.5%	4.4%

Global Partners LP

Global Partners imports petroleum products from global sources but its marketing is largely regional. The company wholesales heating oil residual fuel oil diesel oil kerosene distillates and gasoline to commercial retail and wholesale customers in New England and New York. A major player in the regional home heating oil market Global Partners operates storage facilities at 25 bulk terminals each with a storage capacity of more than 50000 barrels and with a collective storage capacity of 12.2 million barrels. It also owns and supplies a network of gasoline stations. Wholesale revenues accounts for the bulk of the company's sales.

Operations

Global Partners consists of three operating segments: Wholesale Gasoline Distribution and Station Operations (GDSO) and Commercial.

Wholesale accounts for around 50% of total sales and sells unbranded gasoline and diesel to unbranded gasoline customers and other resellers of transportation fuels. It also sells home heating oil diesel kerosene and residual oil to home heating oil retailers and wholesale distributors; as well as crude oil to refiners.

GDSO generates more than 40% of total sales and sells branded and unbranded gasoline to gasoline stations and other sub-jobbers such as gasoline convenience store car wash and other ancillary services at company operated stores and leased gas stations.

Commercial brings in the remaining nearly 10% of sales and sells unbranded gasoline custom blended fuels home heating oil diesel kerosene residual oil renewable fuels and natural gas. Its customers are public sector and large commercial and industrial end users. The segment also includes the sale of custom blended distillates and residual oil delivered by barge or from a terminal dock to ships through its bunkering activity.

The company owns storage facilities at 25 petroleum product bulk terminals each with the capacity of more than 50000 barrels including 22 refined product terminals located throughout the Northeast.

Through gas station company Global Montello Group the company sells food beverages snacks grocery and non-food merchandise at its convenience store locations.

Geographic Reach

Global Partners has a network of refined petroleum products and renewable fuels terminals throughout the Northeast region and into the Mid-Atlantic States (Connecticut Florida Georgia Indiana Louisiana Maine Maryland Massachusetts Michigan New Hampshire New Jersey New York North Dakota Ohio Oregon Pennsylvania Rhode Island Tennessee Texas Vermont and Virginia).

It has some 1460 owned leased and/or supplied gas stations including 248 convenience stores in the Northeast Maryland and Virginia. It also owns transload and storage terminals in North Dakota and Oregon.

Sales and Marketing

Global Partners gets its revenue primarily from convenience store sales at its directly operated stores and rental income from dealer leased or commission agent leased gasoline stations. Global Partners also is one of the largest distributors of gasoline distillates residual oil and renewable fuels to wholesalers retailers and commercial customers in New England and New York

In the Commercial segment it serves customers in the public sector and large commercial and industrial end users of unbranded gasoline home heating oil diesel kerosene residual oil bunker fuel and natural gas. In the case of public sector commercial and industrial end user customers Global Partners sell products through a competitive bidding process or through contracts of various terms. It generally arranges for the delivery of the product to the customer's designated location and responds to publicly-issued requests for product proposals and quotes. The Commercial segment also includes sales of custom blended fuels delivered by barges or from a terminal dock to ships through bunkering activity.

Nearly 10% of the volume of home heating oil Global Partners sold to wholesale distributors is Heating Oil Plus. It sells home heating oil including Heating Oil Plus to about 790 wholesale distributors and retailers. About 35% of the home heating oil volume was sold using forward fixed price contracts.

Global Partners has a long term relationship with Exxon Mobil which accounts for about 15% of total sales.

Financial Performance

Global Partner's (GP) revenue has crashed since a high of $19.6 billion in 2013. In fiscal 2016 total sales of $8.2 billion represented a 20% fall on prior year. GP is vulnerable to changes in the global oil price and the sharp fall in prices beginning in 2014 is the primary factor in the sales decline. The company sold 5.1 billion gallons of product in 2016 versus 5.6 billion in 2015. The Wholesale segment's crude oil and gasoline blendstocks bore the brunt of the decline in volume sales while the Gasoline Distribution and Station Operations (GDSO) and Commercial segments grew product volume sales by 74 million and 72 million gallons respectively due to the full year contribution from the acquired Capitol business.

GP made a loss of $238.6 million in 2016 versus net income of $43.4 million in 2015. The poor performance was linked to the low oil price and resultant asset impairments in the Wholesale business.

GP used $119.9 million in its operating activities compared to net cash provided by operating activ-

ities of $62.5 million the previous year. The worsening was down to lower net income higher accounts receivable and $80.7 million lease exit expenses.

Strategy

Global Partner's management's primary concern is navigating the low oil price environment that has battered revenue and profits since 2014. To support profitability and better position for future growth the company has sold off a number of its less profitable assets. These include 31 gas stations and convenience stores its natural gas and electricity brokerage business and the termination of a sublease for more than 1600 rail cars. It is also seeking a buyer for six refined petroleum terminals.

Mergers and Acquisitions

In July 2018 the company acquired Champlain Oil of Vermont for $135 million approximately. It includes about 40 gas stations with Jiffy Mart-branded convenience stores approximately 25 fuel sites as well as term fuel supply agreements to about 65 gas stations primarily in Vermont and New Hampshire.

The acquisition increases retail portfolio and geographic footprint of Global Partners in New England and provides additional volume to strategically located terminals in New York and Vermont.

Company Background

Through AE Holdings the Slifka family controls about 21% of Global Partners; Kayne Anderson Capital Advisors L.P 12%.

Global Partners was founded in 1933 as a one-truck heating oil retailer by current CEO Eric Slifka's grandfather Abraham Slifka.

In 2010 in order to expand its wholesale supply business the company acquired about 190 retail gas stations in three states in the Northeast from Exxon Mobil and some of its dealers for $202.3 million. Pursuing a strategy of growing its storage capacity in 2010 Global Partners also acquired three terminals in Newburgh New York from Warex Terminals for $47.5 million.

In 2012 the company signed a long-term lease agreement with Getty Realty to supply gasoline to and operate about 90 of Getty's gas station in Queens Manhattan and the Bronx as well as in Long Island and Westchester County.

Boosting its gas station network in 2012 Global Partners acquired Alliance Energy a gasoline distributor and gas stations/convenience store operator controlled by the Slifka family for $180 million.

Growing its portfolio in 2013 Global Partners acquired Cascade Kelly Holdings LLC (a crude oil and ethanol facility near Portland Oregon) for $95 million. That year it also acquired 60% of Basin Transload LLC (which operates two crude oil transloading facilities in Columbus and Beulah North Dakota with a combined rail loading capacity of 160000 barrels per day) for $85 million. The transaction complements its purchase of West Coast crude oil transload and ethanol facility near Portland.

EXECUTIVES

Coo, Mark A. Romaine, age 49, $500,000 total compensation

Evp Chief Accounting Officer And Co-director Mergers And Acquisitions, Charles A. (Chuck) Rudinsky, age 70, $273,000 total compensation

Svp Marketing, Joseph (Joe) DeStefano

President Ceo And Director, Eric Slifka, age 52, $800,000 total compensation

Evp General Counsel And Secretary, Edward J. Faneuil, age 65, $450,000 total compensation

Cfo, Daphne H. Foster, age 60, $400,000 total compensation

Evp Director And President Alliance Gasoline, Andrew Slifka, age 49, $425,000 total compensation

Svp Information Technology, Bill Gifford

Vice President Of Marketing Information Technology, Mary McCarty

Vice President Of Business Development, Bruce Atkins

Vice President Project Management And Development, Jack Frost

Vice President National Business Group, Ken Whalley

Vice President Heavy Oil Marketing, Dennis Bowersox

Vice President Credit, Robert J Fraczkiewicz

Vice President Health And Safety Operations, Tom Keefe

Senior Vice President Marketing, Joe Destefano

Senior Vice President, Mark Cosenza Mark Cosenza

Vice President, Eileen Sweeney

Vice President Of Commercial Fuels, Miles Allen

Board Member, Robert McCool

President Ceo And Director, Eric Slifka, age 52

Chairman, Richard Slifka, age 77

Evp General Counsel And Secretary, Edward J. Faneuil, age 65

Evp Director And President Alliance Gasoline, Andrew Slifka, age 49

Senior Executive Assistant To Edward J. Faneuil Vice President Group Chief Officer And Secretary, Lillian Santangelo

Auditors: Ernst & Young LLP

LOCATIONS

HQ: Global Partners LP
P.O. Box 9161, 800 South Street, Waltham, MA 02454-9161
Phone: 781 894-8800
Web: www.globalp.com

PRODUCTS/OPERATIONS

2016 Sales

	$ mil.	% of total
Wholesale	4,107	50
Gasoline distribution & station operations	3,443	42
Commercial	689	8
Total	**8,239**	**100**

Selected Products

Biofuels
Bunker oil
Diesel oil
Distillates
Gasoline
Home heating oil
Kerosene
Residual fuel oil

COMPETITORS

Bayside Fuel	Koch Industries Inc.
Exxon Mobil	Sprague Resources
George Warren	Tauber Oil
Gulf Oil	Warren Equities
Highlands Fuel Delivery	

HISTORICAL FINANCIALS

Company Type: Public

Income Statement · FYE: December 31

	REVENUE ($ mil.)	NET INCOME ($ mil.)	NET PROFIT MARGIN	EMPLOYEES
12/17	8,920	58	0.7%	2,000
12/16	8,239	(199)	—	1,770
12/15	10,314	43	0.4%	1,890
12/14	17,269	114	0.7%	1,154
12/13	19,589	42	0.2%	943
Annual Growth	(17.9%)	8.4%	—	20.7%

Debt ratio: 46.74% No. of shares (mil.): 33
Return on equity: — Dividends
Cash ($ mil.): 24 Yield: 0.1%
Current ratio: 1.31 Payout: 106.3%
Long-term debt ($ mil.): 957 Market value ($ mil.): 566

	STOCK PRICE ($) FY Close	P/E High/Low		PER SHARE ($) Earnings	Dividends	Book Value
12/17	16.70	12	9	1.74	1.85	11.54
13/16	10.45			(6.01)	1.06	11.60
12/15	17.57	37	14	1.11	2.74	19.20
12/14	32.99	11	8	3.95	2.53	19.03
12/13	35.39	28	18	1.42	2.34	15.10
Annual Growth	(17.1%)	—	—	5.2%	(5.7%)	(6.5%)

Goldman Sachs Group Inc

Goldman Sachs has long possessed the Midas touch in the investment banking world. One of the world's most powerful investment banks Goldman Sachs offers a gamut of investment banking and asset management services to corporate and government clients worldwide as well as institutional and wealth individual investors. It is a world leader in merger and acquisitions advice and equities and debt underwriting. Through its Institution Client Services division Goldman Sachs is a major market maker offering fixed income equities currency and commodity products. The bank boasts some $1.5 trillion in assets under supervision covering all major asset classes. Goldman Sachs was founded in 1869.

HISTORY

German immigrant-cum-Philadelphia retailer Marcus Goldman moved to New York in 1869 and began buying customers' promissory notes from jewelers to resell to banks. Goldman's son-in-law came aboard in 1882 and the firm became Goldman Sachs & Co. in 1885.

Two years later Goldman Sachs began offering US-UK foreign exchange and currency services. To serve such clients as Sears Roebuck it expanded to Chicago and St. Louis. In 1896 it joined the NYSE.

While the firm increased its European contracts Goldman's son Henry made it a major source of financing for US industry. In 1906 it co-managed its first public offering United Cigar Manufacturers (later General Cigar). By 1920 it had underwritten IPOs for Sears B.F. Goodrich and Merck.

Sidney Weinberg made partner in 1927 and stayed until his death in 1969. In the 1930s Goldman Sachs entered securities dealing and sales. After WWII it became a leader in investment banking co-managing Ford's 1956 IPO. In the 1970s it pioneered buying blocks of stock for resale.

Under Weinberg's son John Goldman Sachs became a leader in mergers and acquisitions. The 1981 purchase of J. Aron gave the firm a significant commodities presence and helped it grow in South America.

Seeking capital after 1987's market crash Goldman Sachs raised more than $500 million from Sumitomo for a 12% nonvoting interest in the firm (since reduced to 3%). The Kamehameha

Schools/Bishop Estate of Hawaii an educational trust also invested.

The 1994 bond crash and a decline in new debt issues led Goldman Sachs to cut staffing for the first time since the 1980s. But problems went deeper. Partners began leaving and taking their equity. Cost cuts a stronger bond market and the long bull market helped the firm rebound; firm members sought protection through limited liability partnership status. The firm also extended the period during which partners can cash out (slowing the cash drain) and limited the number of people entitled to a share of profits. Overseas growth in 1996 and 1997 focused on the UK and Asia.

After three decades of resistance the partners in 1998 voted to sell the public a minority stake in the firm but market volatility led to postponement. Goldman Sachs also suffered from involvement with Long-Term Capital Management ultimately contributing $300 million to its bailout.

In 1999 Jon Corzine then co-chairman and co-CEO announced that he would leave the group after seeing it through its IPO and Goldman Sachs finally went public that year in an offering valued at close to $4 billion. In 2000 Corzine was elected to a US Senate seat. The New Jersey Democrat spent more than $64 million on his campaign (a record) nearly $61 million of it from his own personal wealth (also a record). Corzine went on to win New Jersey's gubernatorial race in 2005.

In early 2004 Goldman president and COO John Thain left the firm to assume the helm of the New York Stock Exchange. Lloyd Blankfein was named his successor and became chairman and CEO in 2006 when his predecessor Henry "Hank" Paulson was named secretary of the US Treasury.

At the height of the economic crisis Goldman Sachs converted to a bank holding company. It formed subsidiary Goldman Sachs Bank USA (GS Bank USA) to manage bank loan trading mortgage originations and other activities. The Federal Reserve mandated the change for Goldman Sachs and fellow investment bank Morgan Stanley. The shift marked a monumental change on Wall Street as it put an end to the independent brokerage firm model that had been a mainstay in the US since reform measures were implemented during the Great Depression. Rivals Merrill Lynch Lehman Brothers and Bear Stearns had already merged with larger banks or filed for bankruptcy. The bank holding company structure brought increased regulation but allowed Goldman Sachs to acquire commercial banks — all in an effort to shore up the company's balance sheet.

In the days following the Federal Reserve announcement Warren Buffett's Berkshire Hathaway invested $5 billion in Goldman Sachs and acquired an option to assume $5 billion more of the company's common shares. Goldman Sachs made an additional $5 billion worth of stock available in a public offering. Additionally the US government stepped in with funding for Goldman Sachs in late 2008 when it announced an economic stimulus plan to buy some $250 billion worth of preferred shares of the nation's top banks; approximately $10 billion went to Goldman Sachs.

The capital infusions helped but didn't completely shield Goldman Sachs from the financial crisis the effects of which were felt worldwide. To cut costs the company trimmed some 10% of its workforce. It eventually returned to profitability in 2009 and paid back the money it received from the government but still drew ire from politicians over what have been perceived to be extravagant pay packages for its top employees. (The firm's extravagant year-end bonuses had become the stuff of legend.)

Goldman Sachs opened a new $1.8-billion headquarters building in New York City's lower Manhattan in 2009.

In 2012 Goldman spent some $5.65 billion to buy back preferred shares that Warren Buffet's Berkshire Hathaway acquired in 2008. The repurchase would save the firm money as it had been paying some 10% interest on the shares (or some $500 million annually).

Also in 2012 Goldman acquired the Bermuda-based insurance and reinsurance operations of Ariel Reinsurance; an addition that should bring in a steady stream of fees. Additionally that year the company arranged to sell hedge fund administrator Goldman Sachs Administration Services to State Street for some $550 million.

In 2013 Goldman Sachs Asset Management acquired the Global Treasury Funds assets which consists of a variety of money market funds from RBS Asset Management to strengthen its strong fixed income and liquidity management businesses in Europe and around the world.

Goldman bought the remaining 20% stake it didn't already own in Endesa Gas T&D in 2013. It purchased the natural gas transport firm from Spanish power utility Endesa for about $174 million.

In January 2013 Goldman sold approximately 45% of its ordinary shares of ICBC.

EXECUTIVES

Head Merchant Banking Division, Richard A. Friedman, age 60
Evp General Counsel And Secretary, Gregory K. Palm, age 69
Chairman Goldman Sachs Bank Usa And Goldman Sachs International Bank, Esta E. Stecher, age 61
Cio, R. Martin Chavez, age 54
Chairman And Ceo, Lloyd C. Blankfein, age 63, $2,000,000 total compensation
Evp And Head Of Global Compliance, Sarah E. Smith
Vice Chairman Ceo Goldman Sachs International And Co-head Investment Banking Division, Richard J. Gnodde, age 58
President And Co-coo, David M. Solomon, age 56
President Goldman Sachs Japan, Masanori Mochida
President Asia/pacific Outside Japan, Kenneth W. Hitchner
Evp Chief Of Staff And Secretary, John F.W. Rogers, age 61
Global Co-head Investment Management Division, Timothy J. O'Neill
Evp And Global Head Human Capital Management, Edith W. Cooper, age 56
Global Co-coo Equities Franchise, Michael D. Daffey
Head Conflicts Resolution Group, Gwen R. Libstag
President And Co-coo, Harvey M. Schwartz, age 53, $1,850,000 total compensation
Global Co-head Securities Division, Isabelle Ealet
Vice Chairman And Global Co-head Securities Division, Pablo J. Salame, age 52
Head Global Investment Research, Steven H. Strongin
Global Co-head Investment Management Division, Eric S. Lane
Chief Strategy Officer And Ceo Goldman Sachs Bank Usa, Stephen M. Scherr
Global Co-head Securities Division, Ashok Varadhan
Chief Risk Officer, Craig W. Broderick
Co-head Investment Banking Division, John Waldron
Global Head Credit Trading, Justin G. Gmelich
Co-head Of Global Mergers And Acquisitions, Gregg R. Lemkau
Head Of The Global Financing Group And Head Of Latin America, Marc Nachmann
Chairman Global Financial Institutions Group (fig), Mike Esposito

Co-head Global Financial Institutions Group (fig), Luke Sarsfield

Co-head Global Financial Institutions Group, Todd Leland

Global Co-coo Equities Franchise, Paul M. Russo

Head Of The Global Special Situations Group (gssg), Julian Salisbury

Ceo Goldman Sachs Singapore Pte., Jason Moo

Vice President Technology, Ted Najjar

West Coast Technology Vice President, Brandon Johnson

Vice President Private Wealth Management, Brandy Warren

Vice President In Technology, David Olivares

Vice President Gsam Insurance Asset Management Relationship Manager, Brian Rapino

Vice President, Jill Toporek

Vice President, Jonathan Fallin

Vice President Regional Director, Evan Recht

Vice President, Roger Gardiner

Vice President, Lindsay Chock

Vice President, James Wilcox

Vice President, Anuraag Verma

Vice President Technology, Krishnamurthy Vaidyanathan

Vice President, Curtis L Ambrose

Vice President, Robyn Wade

Vice President, Caitlin Walsh

Vice President Investment Banking, Siddharth Shrivastava

Vice President, Jim Gabriel

Vice President, Richard Skidmore

Vice President Private Wealth Management Investment Management Division, Cristin Dalecki

Vice President Leveraged Finance Investment Banking, Jamie Tam

Vice President, Tim Halladay

Vice President, Karen Ho

Vice President, Nancy Benchoff

Vice President, Puneet Awasthi

Vice President, Carrie Gannon

Vice President, Gitika Gumbar

Vice President, Lindsey Morfin

Vice President In Asset Management Operations, Maureen Hill

Vice President, Brian Krawczyk

Vice President Information Technology Manager, Greg Killeen

Vice President, David Rothenberg

Vice President In Goldman Sachs, Krishnan Narayanan

Vice President, Jessie Sinden

Vice President, Barbara Williams

Vice President, Alex Topkins

Vice President Investment Management Division, Ryan Sobeck

Vice President, Gary Godshaw

Vice President, Christopher Higgins

Vice President, Dugan Lawrence

Vice President, Narayanan Radhakrishnan

Vice President, Kevin Carmody

Vice President, Brian Dong

Vice President, Linda Avery

Vice President, Eric Riley

Vice President Technology, Eugene Gauthier

Vice President Private Wealth Management Investment Management Division, Neil Stone

Vice President, Matthew Korenberg

Vice President Technology, Stephen Chan

Vice President, Allison Marsh

Vice President, Sean Butkus

Vice President Systems Management, Jeff Levine

Vice President, Christopher Wright

Vice President Investment Banking Division, Thomas Lynch

Vice President, Jeffrey Gido

Vice President, Robert Leggett

Vice President, Andre Benjamin

Vice President, Michael Darling

Vice President, Kathryn Boyles

Vice President, Richard Jiang

Vice President Of Information Technology, Prasert Chirachanakul

Vice President, Joseph Pozzi

Executive Vice President And Global Head Human Capital Management, Dane Holmes

Vice President, WILLIAM CARINCI

Vice President Information Security, Anita Nandakumar

Vice President, JARRETT SCHUBE

Vice President, Joe Mella

Vice President Goldman Sachs Asset Management, Keyur Modi

Vice President, David Bao

Vice President And Tax Counsel, James Nolan

Vice President, Andy Andreo

Vice President, SYLVIE TRUDEL

Vice President Strategic Marketing, Vicky Angelos

Vice President, Giovanni Sansalone

Vice President Technology Engineering Campus Recruiting, Mallory Leib

Vice President, Caitlin DeSantis

Vice President And Associate General Counsel, Jamie Greenberg

Vice President, Brandon Brown

Vice President Software Engineer, Javier Vazquez

Vice President And Associate General Counsel, Adam Heft

Vice President Legal Department Technology Intellectual Property And Contracts Group, Marie Willemsen

Vice President, Nita Birla

Vice President Of Fxpb, Michael McCreesh

Vice President Information Systems, Reto Frei

Vice President, Greg Larson

Vice President, Michael Watts

Vice President, Stephen Blumenfeld

Vice President Information Technology, David Goldman

Vice President Information Security, Donald Callahan

Vice President, Ira Powell

Vice President Credit Risk Information Technology, Ofer Imanuel

Vice President Information Technology Infrastructure, Leonid Tsvayberg

Vice President, Sabrina Khan

Vice President Tax, Joyce Hsu

Tax Vice President Transfer Pricing, Benjamin Sun

Vice President, Greg York

Vice President Information Technology, Jayish Jivrajani

Vice President, Rich Mason

Vice President, Jonathan Rousse

Vice President Security Risk And Controls, Matthew White

Vice President In The Finance Division, Thomas Morin

Vice President Wealth Management, Charles Michaels

Vice President, Alland Sy

Vice President, Kristin Vonnes

Vice President, Gargi Banerjee

Vice President, Kathleen Burt

Vice President Global Communications Group Investment Banking Division, Bryan Slotkin

Vice President Hudson Street, Darren Cohen

Vice President Realty Management Division, Lauren Swinden

Vice President, Ronnie Wexler

Vice President, Joshua Leonardi

Vice President Fx Prime Brokerage, Keith Coyne

Vice President Ficc Mortgage Technology, Tito George

Vice President, Brian Spellman

Vice President, Steve Miller

Vice President Equities Division, Tara Pardo

Vice President Software Development, Marty Pauley

Vice President Investment Banking Division, Matt McClure

Auditors: PricewaterhouseCoopers LLC

LOCATIONS

HQ: Goldman Sachs Group Inc
200 West Street, New York, NY 10282
Phone: 212 902-1000   **Fax:** 212 902-3000
Web: www.gs.com

2017 Sales

	% of total
Americas	61
Europe the Middle East & Africa	24
Asia	15
Total	**100**

PRODUCTS/OPERATIONS

2017 Sales

	$ mil.	% of total
Interest income	13,113	31
Non Interest income		
Market making	7,660	18
Investment banking	7,371	18
Investment management	5,803	14
Commissions & fees	3,051	7
Other	5,256	12
Total	**42,254**	**100**

2017 Sales

	% of total
Institutional Client Services	37
Investment Banking	23
Investment Management	19
Investing & Lending	21
Total	**100**

Selected Subsidiaries

Goldman Sachs & Co.
Goldman Sachs Bank USA
Goldman Sachs Credit Partners L.P. (Bermuda)
Goldman Sachs Financial Markets L.P.
Goldman Sachs International (UK)
Goldman Sachs Japan Co. Ltd.
Goldman Sachs Mortgage Company
GSTM LLC
    Goldman Sachs Execution & Clearing L.P.
J. Aron & Company

COMPETITORS

BMO Capital Markets	FMR
Barclays	JPMorgan Chase
CIBC World Markets	Lazard
Citigroup Global	Merrill Lynch
Markets	Morgan Stanley
Credit Suisse	Nomura Securities
Credit Suisse (USA)	RBC Capital Markets
Deutsche Bank	UBS

HISTORICAL FINANCIALS

Company Type: Public

Income Statement

FYE: December 31

	ASSETS ($ mil.)	NET INCOME ($ mil.)	INCOME AS % OF ASSETS	EMPLOYEES
12/17	916,776	4,286	0.5%	36,600
12/16	860,165	7,398	0.9%	34,400
12/15	861,395	6,083	0.7%	36,800
12/14	856,240	8,477	1.0%	34,000
12/13	911,507	8,040	0.9%	32,900
Annual Growth	0.1%	(14.6%)	—	2.7%

2017 Year-End Financials

Debt ratio: 29.73%   No. of shares (mil.): 374
Return on equity: 5.07%   Dividends
Cash ($ mil.): 110,051   Yield: 0.0%
Current ratio: —   Payout: 32.1%
Long-term debt ($ mil.): —   Market value ($ mil.): 95,486

STOCK PRICE ($)	P/E		PER SHARE ($)		
FY Close	High/Low	Earnings	Dividends	Book Value
12/17	254.76	29 23	9.01	2.90	219.43
12/16	239.45	15 8	16.29	2.60	221.31
12/15	180.23	18 14	12.14	2.55	206.75
12/14	193.83	11 9	17.07	2.25	192.44
12/13	177.26	11 8	15.46	2.05	175.79
Annual Growth	9.5%	— —	(12.6%)	9.1%	5.7%

Goodyear Tire & Rubber Co.

Goodyear Tire & Rubber is working to unseat tire industry leaders Bridgestone and Michelin (by total sales). Goodyear sells mainly new tires under the Goodyear Dunlop Kelly Fulda Debica Just Tires and Sava brand names. Goodyear makes markets and sells Dunlop tires across the Americas the EMEA and the Asia/Pacific. In Japan the tire makers own businesses that sell tires separately to OEMs and to aftermarket companies. Goodyear sells more than 55% of its products outside the US.

HISTORY

In 1898 Frank and Charles Seiberling founded a tire and rubber company in Akron Ohio and named it after Charles Goodyear (inventor of the vulcanization process 1839). The debut of the Quick Detachable tire and the Universal Rim (1903) made Goodyear the world's largest tire maker by 1916.

Goodyear began manufacturing in Canada in 1910 and over the next two decades it expanded into Argentina Australia and the Dutch East Indies. The company established its own rubber plantations in Sumatra (now part of Indonesia) in 1916.

Financial woes led to reorganization in 1921 and investment bankers forced the Seiberlings out. Succeeding caretaker management Paul Litchfield began three decades as CEO in 1926 a time in which Goodyear emerged to become the world's largest rubber company.

Goodyear blimps served as floating billboards nationwide by the 1930s. During that decade Goodyear opened company stores acquired tire maker Kelly-Springfield (1935) and began producing tires made from synthetic rubber (1937). After WWII Goodyear was an innovative leader in technologies such as polyester tire cord (1962) and the bias-belted tire (1967).

By 1980 Goodyear had introduced radial tire brands such as the all-weather Tiempo the Eagle and the Arriva as it led the US market.

Thwarting British financier Sir James Goldsmith's takeover attempt in 1986 CEO Robert Mercer raised $1.7 billion by selling the company's non-tire businesses (Motor Wheel Goodyear Aerospace) and by borrowing heavily.

Recession overcapacity and price-cutting in 1990 led to hard times for tire makers. After suffering through 1990 its first money-losing year since the Depression Goodyear lured Stanley Gault out of retirement. He ceased marketing tires exclusively through Goodyear's dealer network by selling tires through Wal-Mart Kmart and Sears. Gault also cut costs through layoffs plant closures and spending reductions and returned Goodyear to profitability in 1991.

The company increased its presence in the US retail market in 1995 when it began selling tires through 860 Penske Auto Centers and 300 Montgomery Ward auto centers. President Samir Gibara succeeded chairman Gault as CEO in 1996. That year Goodyear bought Poland's leading tire maker T C Debica and a 60% stake in South African tire maker Contred (acquiring the rest in 1998).

In 1997 Goodyear formed an alliance with Sumitomo Rubber Industries under which the companies agreed to make and market tires for one another in Asia and North America. The next year Goodyear sold its Celeron Oil subsidiary which operated the All American Pipeline and acquired the remaining 26% stake in tire distributor Brad Ragan (commercial and retail outlets in the US) for $20.7 million.

The company acquired Sumitomo Rubber Industries' North American and European Dunlop tire businesses in 1999. The acquisition returned Goodyear to its #1 position in the tire-making industry. However the company recorded drastically low profits that year because it had cut tire production and was unable to meet supplier demands.

To improve profitability Goodyear increased tire prices in 2000 and began consolidating its manufacturing operations. Goodyear also announced plans to combine its commercial tire service centers with those of Treadco through a joint venture named Wingfoot Commercial Tire Systems. Despite record sales in 2000 the company's profits hit some hard road prompting Goodyear to lay off 10% of its workforce and implement other cost-cutting efforts.

Early in 2001 the company announced that it would close its Mexican tire plant. The same year the company agreed to replace Firestone Wilderness AT tires with Goodyear tires for Ford owners as part of Ford's big Firestone tire recall.

Early in 2002 Goodyear announced that its recent job cuts and manufacturing consolidation resulted in an $85 million decrease in annual operating costs. Later in the year the tire maker became embroiled in an age discrimination lawsuit claiming unfair job evaluations for the company's older employees. Blaming a slow US economy Goodyear announced plans to cut 450 jobs at its Union City Tennessee manufacturing plant. The job cuts were just the beginning of what would be a series of operational adjustments made as part of a Capital Structure Improvement Plan formally launched in 2003.

Although Goodyear once owned about 10% of its Sumitomo Rubber Industries it sold more than 20 million shares of its Japanese counterpart stock back to the tire maker in 2003. Later in the year as the company was embroiled in a lengthy debate with the United Steelworkers union it was announced that the Huntsville Alabama tire manufacturing plant would be closed. Goodyear also announced that it would cut 500 non-union salaried employees in North America. Later that same year it was announced that Goodyear was chosen by Volvo to be the truck manufacturer's primary tire supplier in North America; Goodyear had a similar contract with Mack Trucks.

Qantas Airways announced in early 2004 that it chose Goodyear to provide tires for the Australia-based company's Jetstar Airways. Later in the year Goodyear acquired the shares of Slovenia-based Sava Tires it did not already own and the company's Goodyear Dunlop Tires Europe unit purchased the Sweden-based Dackia retail tire stores. The company announced more job cuts in the non-tire sector in 2004 affecting Goodyear's engineered products and chemical units.

In 2005 Goodyear sold its stake in Goodyear Sumatra Plantations (rubber plantations in Indone-sia) to rival Bridgestone for $62 million. Later that year the company sold its Wingtack adhesive resin business to Sartomer Company Inc. (a subsidiary of France's TOTAL S.A.) for about $65 million. As 2005 wound to a close the company sold its farm tire business to Titan International for $100 million.

Goodyear called off plans to sell its Chemical Products division. Instead the company integrated its chemical operations with those of its North American Tire division to take greater advantage of operational synergies. The company did however move forward with plans to jettison its Engineered Products division. In 2005 Goodyear secured the services of J.P. Morgan Securities and Goldman Sachs to help it explore opportunities for the sale of Engineered Products. The company struck a deal for The Carlyle Group in 2007 to buy its Engineered Products division for about $1.5 billion.

In 2011 Goodyear sold its tire reinforcement wire business (located in Luxembourg and North Carolina) to South Korea-based Hyosung for $50 million. The same year it sold its farm tire business in Latin America to a Titan International unit for $99 million. In 2010 Goodyear had agreed to sell its farm tire business in Europe as well as Latin America to Titan but the European part of the deal fell through and Goodyear does not have a time frame for making that sale. (In 2005 Titan had purchased Goodyear's North American farm tire business.) Also in 2011 Goodyear closed a facility in Union City Tennessee.

Intent on making more tires at lower-cost facilities Goodyear relocated its tire-making operations from Dalian China to Pulandian China in 2012. Additionally Goodyear is expanding or modernizing plants in Brazil Chile Germany and the US.

EXECUTIVES

Chairman President And Ceo, Richard J. (Rich) Kramer, age 54, $1,233,333 total compensation
Svp General Counsel And Secretary, David L. (Dave) Bialosky, age 61, $565,000 total compensation
Evp And Cfo, Laura K. Thompson, age 53, $621,667 total compensation
Vp Consumer Tires North American Tire, Stephen R. (Steve) McClellan, age 52, $610,000 total compensation
Svp Global Operations And Technology, Joseph (Joe) Zekoski, age 66
President North America Consumer, R. Scott Rogers, age 49
President Europe Middle East And Africa (emea), Chris Delaney, age 57
Svp Global Human Resources And Chief Human Resources Officer, John T. Lucas, age 58, $547,333 total compensation
Svp Global Sales And Marketing, Richard Kellam, age 57
Vp And Cto, Christopher Helsel, age 53
President Asia Pacific, Ryan Patterson, age 44
Vp Global It Sap, Horst Ebert
Vice President Human Resources North American Tire, Gary Vanderlind
Vice President Global Labor Relations, Jim Allen
Vice President Total Rewards At The Goodyear Tire And Rubber Company, Annie Granchi
Vice President And General Auditor, Kristian Hoeh
Chairman President And Ceo, Richard J. (Rich) Kramer, age 54
Svp General Counsel And Secretary, David L. (Dave) Bialosky, age 61
Secretary Marketing Department, Marilyn Chapanar
Auditors: PricewaterhouseCoopers LLP

LOCATIONS

HQ: Goodyear Tire & Rubber Co.
  200 Innovation Way, Akron, OH 44316-0001
Phone: 330 796-2121 Fax: 330 796-4099
Web: www.goodyear.com

2016 Sales

	$ mil.	% of total
Americas	8,172	54
Europe Middle East and Africa	4,880	32
Asia Pacific	2,106	14
Total	**15,158**	**100**

2016 Sales

	$ mil.	% of total
United States	6,724	44
Germany	1,853	12
Other international	6,581	44
Total	**15,158**	**100**

PRODUCTS/OPERATIONS

Selected Products

Automotive repair services
Chemical products
Natural rubber
Tires
  Automotive
  Aviation
  Buses
  Construction
  Farm
  Mining
  Motorcycles
  Trucks
Tread rubber
Wholesale tires

Selected Subsidiaries

Celeron Corporation
Dunlop Grund und Service Verwaltungs GmbH
  (Germany)
Dunlop Tyres Limited (UK)
Goodyear Canada Inc.
Goodyear Dalian Tire Company Ltd. (China)
Goodyear de Chile S.A.I.C.
Goodyear de Colombia S.A.
Goodyear do Brasil Produtos de Borracha Ltda (Brazil)
Goodyear Dunlop Tires Austria GmbH
Goodyear Dunlop Tires Belgium N.V.
Goodyear Dunlop Tires Czech s.r.o.
Goodyear Dunlop Tires Danmark A/S
Goodyear Dunlop Tires Espana S.A. (Spain)
Goodyear Dunlop Tires Finland OY
Goodyear Dunlop Tires Hellas S.A.I.C. (Greece)
Goodyear Dunlop Tires Hungary Ltd.
Goodyear Dunlop Tires Ireland Ltd
Goodyear Dunlop Tires Italia SpA (Italy)
Goodyear Dunlop Tires Polska Sp z.o.o. (Poland)
Goodyear Dunlop Tires Portugal Unipessoal Lda
Goodyear Dunlop Tires Slovakia s.r.o.
Goodyear Dunlop Tires Suisse S.A. (Switzerland)
The Kelly-Springfield Tyre Company Ltd (UK)
Wingfoot Corporation

COMPETITORS

Bridgestone	Pep Boys
Continental AG	Pirelli
Cooper Tire & Rubber	Sime Darby
Hankook Tire	Titan International
Kumho Tire	Toyo Tire & Rubber
Marangoni	Yokohama Rubber
Michelin	Zeon
Midas	

HISTORICAL FINANCIALS

Company Type: Public

Income Statement
FYE: December 31

	REVENUE ($ mil.)	NET INCOME ($ mil.)	NET PROFIT MARGIN	EMPLOYEES
12/18	15,475	693	4.5%	64,000
12/17	15,377	346	2.3%	64,000
12/16	15,158	1,264	8.3%	66,000
12/15	16,443	307	1.9%	66,000
12/14	18,138	2,452	13.5%	67,000
Annual Growth	**(3.9%)**	**(27.1%)**	**—**	**(1.1%)**

2018 Year-End Financials

Debt ratio: 34.16%
Return on equity: 14.64%
Cash ($ mil.): 801
Current ratio: 1.24
Long-term debt ($ mil.): 5,110

No. of shares (mil.): 232
Dividends
  Yield: 2.8%
  Payout: 52.7%
Market value ($ mil.): 4,739

	STOCK PRICE ($) FY Close	P/E High/Low		Earnings	PER SHARE ($) Dividends	Book Value
12/18	20.41	12	7	2.89	0.58	20.95
12/17	32.31	27	21	1.37	0.44	19.17
12/16	30.87	7	5	4.74	0.31	17.91
12/15	32.67	31	21	1.12	0.25	14.68
12/14	28.57	3	2	8.78	0.22	13.40
Annual Growth	**(8.1%)**	**—**	**—**	**(24.3%)**	**27.4%**	**11.8%**

Grainger (W.W.) Inc.

Grainger is no stranger to industrial products. W.W. Grainger distributes more than 1.9 million industrial products from supplies to equipment and tools. The short list has electrical devices fasteners fleet maintenance equipment hand tools hardware janitorial lighting office supplies power and plumbing tools and safety security and test instruments. Its 1.1 million customers are contractors maintenance and repair shops manufacturers and commercial government and educational facilities. Grainger sells through a network of branches distribution centers catalogs and websites.

Operations

Grainger's US business is its largest operating segment representing around 75% of net sales. The segment's product lines include lighting and electrical equipment power and hand tools pumps and plumbing and cleaning and maintenance supplies. The US business purchases products from more than 2600 key suppliers most of which are manufacturers.

Acklands-Grainger the company's core Canadian business focuses on distributing industrial and safety products via about 150 domestic branches and distribution centers.

Through a global sourcing operation Grainger procures competitively priced high-quality products produced outside the US from some 400 suppliers.

Besides a wide range of products Grainger also provides services that include inventory management and energy efficiency assistance for lower maintenance costs. The company's KeepStock program offers on-site services and vendor-managed inventory. Since the program's launch in 2006 KeepStock has grown to serve more than 21000 customers. It completes more than 11000 installations each year.

Geographic Reach

About 75% of Grainger's sales stem from the US 10% in Canada and the rest in Europe Asia and Latin America. With locations in all 50 states the US business has about 280 branches and almost 20 distribution centers and roughly 40 contact centers.

Sales and Marketing

Grainger offers its services to a range of industries such as manufacturing hospitality transportation government retail healthcare and education. It markets its products through sales representatives direct marketing materials catalogs and eCommerce and also through contact centers inventory management and its branches.

The company also operates its international business through Fabory a European distributor of fasteners tools and industrial supplies; and in Japan through its 51% stake in MonotaRO Co.

Its Zoro Tools unit is an online distributor serving US businesses and consumers through its website Zorotools.com.

Financial Performance

Grainger has enjoyed seven straight years (2010-2016) of unprecedented growth. Revenues increased 2% to peak at $10.1 billion in 2016. This was driven by 3% growth from acquisitions and 1% sales growth offset by a 2% decline in price deflation exceeding cost deflation and an unfavorable customer mix.

In addition to experiencing sales growth from government retail and light manufacturing customers during 2016 Grainger saw its eCommerce sales grow by 15%. This was driven by stronger sales via electronic purchasing platforms in the US and Japan.

Grainger's profits however declined 21% from $769 million in 2015 to $606 million in 2016 mainly due to a 2% rise in operating expenses. This percentage included almost $90 million collectively in restructuring and impairment charges.

Strategy

To grow its already burgeoning eCommerce operations Grainger is targeting global economies with robust IT systems and a developed infrastructure. These include North America Japan and Western Europe. Stating that more than 65% of its orders currently originate digitally (and that number will continue to surge) Grainger has also made investing in its own technological infrastructure a priority.

Grainger is also open to using acquisitions to strengthen its online operations. In 2015 the company bought Cromwell Group Limited a broad line distributor of MRO supplies in the UK for A?310 million. The acquisition enhanced Grainger's supply chain and eCommerce offerings and will enable Grainger to profitably scale its single channel online business Zoro Germany.

HISTORY

In 1919 William W. Grainger a motor designer and salesman saw the opportunity to develop a wholesale electric-motor sales and distribution company. He set up an office in Chicago in 1927 and incorporated the business a year later. With sales generated primarily through postcard mailers and an eight-page catalog called   MotorBook Grainger started shipping motors to mail-order customers.

Utilities and factories began to shift from direct-current to alternating-current power systems in the late 1920s. Uniform DC-powered assembly lines gave way to individual workstations each powered by a separate AC motor. This burgeoning market opened the way for distributors such as W.W. Grainger to tap into segments that high-volume manufacturers found difficult to reach. In the early 1930s W.W. Grainger opened offices in Atlanta Dallas Philadelphia and San Francisco; by 1936 it had 15 sales branches.

W.W. Grainger entered a boom period after WWII and by 1949 it had branches in 30 states. The company continued to expand in the 1950s and 1960s then went public in 1967.

William Grainger retired in 1968 and his son David succeeded him as CEO. The company expanded into electric motor manufacturing with the purchase of the Doerr Companies in 1969. Ten years later it opened its 150th branch.

Grainger's distribution became decentralized with the 1983 opening of its 1.4-million-sq.-ft. automated regional distribution center in Kansas City. The next year Grainger surpassed $1 billion in sales. The company sold its Doerr Electric subsidiary to Emerson Electric in 1986. It added 91 branches in 1987 and 1988.

After a 17-year hiatus the company started making acquisitions again buying Vonnegut Industrial Products in 1989; Bossert Industrial Supply and Allied Safety in 1990; Ball Industries a distributor of sanitary and janitorial supplies in 1991; and Lab Safety Supply in 1992. Grainger began integrating its sanitary supply business with its core activities in 1993.

For the first time in company history no Grainger held the CEO position when president Richard Keyser was appointed in 1995 replacing David Grainger. That year the company moved its headquarters to Lake Forest Illinois.

EXECUTIVES

Svp And General Counsel, John L. Howard, age 61, $673,828 total compensation

Svp And Chief People Officer, Joseph C. High, age 65, $495,250 total compensation

Svp And Cfo, Ronald L. Jadin, age 58, $721,885 total compensation

Chairman And Ceo, Donald G. (D.G.) Macpherson, age 51, $875,000 total compensation

Svp Global Supply Chain Branch Network Contact Centers And Corporate Strategy, Paige K. Robbins, age 49, $441,769 total compensation

Vice President Manager Director, Patrick ONeal

Vp Global Talent Acquisition Inclusion And Diversity, Marty Belle

Regional Sales Vice President, Daniel Moscaritolo

Vice President Marketing, Jim Penvillo

Regional Sales Vice President, Lloyd Peterson

Vice President Corporate Strategy And Continuous Improvement, Elizabeth Ubell

Chairman And Ceo, Donald G. (D.G.) Macpherson, age 51

Auditors: Ernst & Young LLP

LOCATIONS

HQ: Grainger (W.W.) Inc.
100 Grainger Parkway, Lake Forest, IL 60045-5201
Phone: 847 535-1000   **Fax:** 847 535-0878
Web: www.grainger.com

2016 Sales

	$ mil.	% of total
US	7,834	77
Canada	739	7
Other countries	1,563	16
Total	**10,137**	**100**

PRODUCTS/OPERATIONS

2016 Sales

	$ mil.	% of total
US-based businesses	7,522	74
Canada-based businesses	733	7
Other businesses	1,880	19
Total	**10,137**	**100**

Selected Products

Adhesives
Air compressors
Air-filtration equipment
Electric motors
Electrical products
Fasteners
Fleet and vehicle maintenance products
Hand tools
Heating and ventilation equipment
Janitorial and plumbing supplies
Lab supplies
Library equipment
Lighting equipment
Material handling
Pneumatics and hydraulics
Power tools
Pumps
Safety products
Security products
Spray paints
Test Instruments

COMPETITORS

Ace Hardware	International Library
Applied Industrial	Furniture
Technologies	Kaman Industrial
Fastenal	Technologies
Genuine Parts	Lowe's
Gexpro	MSC Industrial Direct
Graybar Electric	McMaster-Carr
Industrial	WESCO International
Distribution Group	Wilson

HISTORICAL FINANCIALS

Company Type: Public

Income Statement

FYE: December 31

	REVENUE ($ mil.)	NET INCOME ($ mil.)	NET PROFIT MARGIN	EMPLOYEES
12/17	10,424	585	5.6%	25,700
12/16	10,137	605	6.0%	25,600
12/15	9,973	769	7.7%	25,800
12/14	9,964	801	3.0%	23,600
12/13	9,437	797	8.4%	23,700
Annual Growth	**2.5%**	**(7.4%)**	**—**	**2.0%**

2017 Year-End Financials

Debt ratio: 40.36%	No. of shares (mil.): 56
Return on equity: 33.58%	Dividends
Cash ($ mil.): 326	Yield: 0.0%
Current ratio: 2.13	Payout: 50.5%
Long-term debt ($ mil.): 2,248	Market value ($ mil.): 13,308

	STOCK PRICE ($) FY Close	P/E High/Low		PER SHARE ($) Earnings	Dividends	Book Value
12/17	236.25	26	16	10.02	5.06	30.00
12/16	232.25	24	18	9.87	4.83	30.57
12/15	202.59	22	16	11.58	4.59	36.54
12/14	254.89	23	20	11.45	4.17	47.60
12/13	255.42	24	18	11.13	3.59	47.21
Annual Growth	**(1.9%)**	**—**	**—**	**(2.6%)**	**9.0%**	**(10.7%)**

Graybar Electric Co., Inc.

Graybar Electric is one of the largest distributors of electrical products in the US. The employee-owned company distributes more than 1 million electrical communications and data networking products through a network of around 260 distribution facilities. Its diversified lineup includes a myriad of wire cable and lighting products from thousands of manufacturers and suppliers. It also offers supply chain management and logistics services. Affiliate Graybar Financial Services provides equipment leasing and financing. Graybar Electric sells to construction contractors industrial plants power utilities and telecommunications providers primarily in the US.

Operations

The company mainly operates through its subsidiaries of Graybar Canada Advantage Industrial Automation Cape Electrical Supply and Commonwealth Controls.

Geographic Reach

Graybar's business is primarily based in the US as its headquarters are located in St. Louis Missouri. Other operations include distribution facilities in Canada and Puerto Rico. The company serves its customers through a a network of over 260 locations across the US and Canada.

It also operates in 13 geographical districts in the US each of which maintains multiple distribution facilities that consist primarily of warehouse space. The number of facilities excluding distribution centers in its designated districts varies from 11 to 22 totaling 218 for all districts.

Sales and Marketing

Among the company's strengths is a diverse and large customer base with more than 140000 clients. Graybar gets nearly half of its sales from the construction sector. Other customers come from the institutional commercial and government (23%) and industrial and utility (21%) sectors. The company has expanded its sales presence to support its government business which continues to see strong growth.

Graybar distributes one million products purchased from more than 4600 manufacturers and suppliers. The company sells approximately 50% of the products from its top 25 suppliers.

Financial Performance

Graybar's revenue climbed 5% from $6.1 billion in 2015 to peak at a record-setting $6.4 billion in 2016. In addition Graybar's profits increased 2% from $91 million to $93 million during that same time period. The historic growth for 2016 was fueled by a 9% surge in sales from its construction vertical and a marginal uptick from the industrial and utility markets.It also generated additional revenue from previous acquisitions.

Strategy

Graybar plans to continue adding physical locations to expand its presence and service offerings. In addition Graybar is broadening its e-commerce and mobility capabilities to enhance its online presence and expand its digital marketing to grow sales with new and existing customers.

In 2015 Graybar established a branch in Utah and two branches in California. The company in 2014 opened a branch in Texas two in North Dakota and one in Oregon.

Mergers and Acquisitions

Graybar has achieved historic growth over the last few years through the help of acquisitions. In the summer of 2016 it purchased Cape Electrical Supply a regional distributor serving electrical contractors and large engineering construction firms as well as industrial institutional and utility customers. The previous year Graybar obtained Advantage Industrial Automation a provider of control and automation equipment catering to industrial users.

HISTORY

After serving as a telegrapher during the Civil War Enos Barton borrowed $400 from his widowed mother in 1869 and started an electrical equipment shop in Cleveland with George Shawk. Later that year Elisha Gray a professor of physics at Oberlin College who had several inventions (including a printing telegraph) to his credit bought Shawk's interest in the shop and the firm of Gray & Barton moved to Chicago where a third partner joined.

The company incorporated as the Western Electric Manufacturing Co. in 1872 with two-thirds of the company's stock held by two Western Union executives. As the telegraph industry took off the enterprise grew rapidly providing equipment to towns and railroads in the western US.

Western Electric then formed a new distribution business in 1926 Graybar Electric Co. (from "Gray" and "Barton") the world's largest electrical supply merchandiser. In 1929 employees bought the company from Western Electric for $3 million in cash and $6 million in preferred stock. During the 1930s it marketed a line of appliances and sewing machines under the Graybar name.

EXECUTIVES

Regional Vp Western Region, Dennis E. DeSousa, age 60, $276,571 total compensation

Regional Vp Eastern Region, Robert C. Lyons, age 62, $268,435 total compensation

Svp Marketing, William P. Mansfield, age 56, $256,288 total compensation

Svp And Cfo, Randall R. Harwood, age 62, $280,000 total compensation

Svp Sales And Director, David G. Maxwell

Chairman President And Ceo, Kathleen M. Mazzarella, age 57, $854,921 total compensation

Svp Secretary And General Counsel, Matthew W. Geekie, age 56, $313,119 total compensation

Svp Human Resources And Director, Beverly L. Propst, age 48, $284,632 total compensation

Vp And Cio, David Meyer

Svp Supply Chain Management, Scott S. Clifford, age 47

Vice President Education Graybar Electric, Chris Althauser

Vice President Of Marketing, Rob Bezjak

District Vice President, Joseph Lamotte

Regional Vp Western Region, Dennis E. DeSousa, age 60

Svp Sales And Director, David G. Maxwell

Chairman President And Ceo, Kathleen M. Mazzarella, age 57

Svp Secretary And General Counsel, Matthew W. Geekie, age 56

Svp Human Resources And Director, Beverly L. Propst, age 48

Auditors: Ernst & Young LLP

LOCATIONS

HQ: Graybar Electric Co., Inc.
34 North Meramec Avenue, St. Louis, MO 63105
Phone: 314 573-9200
Web: www.graybar.com

2015 Sales

	% of total
US	95
Other countries	5
Total	**100**

PRODUCTS/OPERATIONS

2015 Sales

	% of total
Construction	56
Commercial Institutional and Government	23
Utility & Industrial	21
Total	**100**

Selected Products

Ballasts
Batteries
Cable
Conduit
Connectors
Emergency lighting
Enclosures
Fiber-optic cable
Fittings
Fluorescent lighting
Fuses
Hand tools
Hangers/fasteners
Heating and ventilating equipment
Industrial fans
Lighting
Lubricants
Paints
Patch cords
Smoke detectors
Testing and measuring instruments
Timers
Transfer switches
Transformers
Utility products
Wire

Selected Subsidiaries

Commonwealth Controls Corporation
Distribution Associates Inc.
Graybar Business Services Inc.
Graybar Canada Limited
Graybar Commerce Corporation
Graybar Electric Canada Limited
Graybar Financial Services Inc.
Graybar International Inc.
Graybar Services Inc.

COMPETITORS

Anixter International	Rexel Canada
Border States Electric	Rexel Inc.
Communications Supply	Richardson Electronics
Consolidated Electrical	SUMMIT Electric Supply
Gexpro	Sonepar USA
HD Supply	United Electric Supply
HWC	W.W. Grainger
Premier Farnell	WESCO International

HISTORICAL FINANCIALS

Company Type: Public

Income Statement

FYE: December 31

	REVENUE ($ mil.)	NET INCOME ($ mil.)	NET PROFIT MARGIN	EMPLOYEES
12/17	6,631	71	1.1%	8,500
12/16	6,385	93	1.5%	8,500
12/15	6,110	91	1.5%	8,300
12/14	5,978	87	1.5%	8,250
12/13	5,659	81	1.4%	7,600
Annual Growth	**4.0%**	**(3.1%)**	**—**	**2.8%**

2017 Year-End Financials

Debt ratio: 7.90%	No. of shares (mil.): 19
Return on equity: 9.64%	Dividends
Cash ($ mil.): 42	Yield: —
Current ratio: 1.41	Payout: 54.0%
Long-term debt ($ mil.): 7	Market value ($ mil.): —

Great Southern Bancorp, Inc.

Despite its name Great Southern Bancorp is firmly entrenched in the heartland. It is the holding company for nearly 200-year-old Great Southern Bank which offers loans deposit accounts CDs IRAs and credit cards through more than 75 branches in Missouri plus more than two dozen locations in Iowa Kansas Nebraska Minnesota and Arkansas. The firm's Great Southern Travel division is one of the largest travel agencies in Missouri. It serves both leisure and corporate travelers through about a dozen offices. Great Southern Insurance offers property/casualty and life insurance while Great Southern Financial provides investment products and services through an agreement with Ameriprise.

Operations

Great Southern loan portfolio is mostly made up of real estate loans. Commercial real estate mortgages and construction and land development loans accounted for around half of its loan portfolio at the end of 2015 while single-family residential mortgages made up another roughly 15%. The bank also writes consumer (including home equity) construction and business loans.

The bank made 82% of its total revenue from loan interest during 2015 while the rest of its revenue came from service charges and fees (9% of revenue) and other non-interest income sources.

Sales and Marketing

The bank served more than 169000 households mostly in Missouri but also in Arkansas Iowa Kansas Minnesota and Nebraska. It spent $2.3 million on advertising during 2015 compared to $2.4 million and $2.17 million in 2014 and 2013 respectively.

Financial Performance

Great Southern has struggled to consistently grow its revenues in recent years despite a 30% rise in loan assets since 2011 mostly as it's been selling off more of its interest-earning mortgage-backed securities assets. Its profits have been rising thanks to declining loan loss provisions as its loan portfolio's credit quality has improved with higher property valuations in the strengthened economy.

The bank's revenue dipped less than 1% to $197.93 million during 2015 as the bank continued to sell more of its mortgage-backed securities which led to lower interest income. It also earned $2.14 million less in gains from security sales than it did in 2014.

Despite modest revenue declines in 2015 Great Southern's net income climbed 7% to $46.5 million mostly as in 2014 it incurred prepayment penalties when it repaid $130 million of its FHLB advances. The bank's operating cash levels rose 6% to $71.42 million thanks to the increase in cash-denominated earnings.

Strategy

Great Southern Bancorp continues to expand its bank network to grow its loan and deposit business either through new branch openings or by acquiring branches in new geographic markets. Its branch network has grown from 104 branches in 2011 to 110 at the end of 2015.

Mergers and Acquisitions

In 2015 the bank purchased 12 branches and related deposit and loan business in the St. Louis area from Cincinnati-based Fifth Third Bank more than doubling its branch presence in the St. Louis area.

EXECUTIVES

Vp Operations And Secretary Great Southern Bank, Douglas W. (Doug) Marrs, age 60, $122,602 total compensation
Vice President, Bob Ogden
Svp And Chief Lending Officer Of The Bank, Steven G. Mitchem, age 66, $227,429 total compensation
President Ceo And Director Great Southern Bancorp And Great Southern Bank, Joseph W. (Joe) Turner, age 53, $299,237 total compensation
Svp And Cfo Great Southern Bank, Rex A. Copeland, age 53, $235,201 total compensation
Vp Information Systems, Linton J. (Lin) Thomason, age 61
Vice President, Jennifer Cook
Vice President, Scott Brekke
Assistant Vice President, Denit Patrick
Vice President Commercial Lending, Kent Lammers
Vp Operations And Secretary Great Southern Bank, Douglas W. (Doug) Marrs, age 60
Board Member, Larry D Frazier
President Ceo And Director Great Southern Bancorp And Great Southern Bank, Joseph W. (Joe) Turner, age 53
Chairman Great Southern Bancorp And Great Southern Bank, William V. Turner, age 85
Board Member, Julie T Brown
Board Member, Douglas Pitt
Auditors: BKD, LLP

LOCATIONS

HQ: Great Southern Bancorp, Inc.
1451 E. Battlefield, Springfield, MO 65804
Phone: 417 887-4400
Web: www.greatsouthernbank.com

COMPETITORS

Arvest Bank	Hawthorn Bancshares
BancorpSouth	NASB Financial
Bank of America	Scottrade
Commerce Bancshares	U.S. Bancorp
First Bancshares (MO)	UMB Financial
Guaranty Federal	Wells Fargo

HISTORICAL FINANCIALS
Company Type: Public

Income Statement				FYE: December 31
	ASSETS ($ mil.)	NET INCOME ($ mil.)	INCOME AS % OF ASSETS	EMPLOYEES
12/17	4,414	51	1.2%	1,225
12/16	4,550	45	1.0%	1,263
12/15	4,104	46	1.1%	1,270
12/14	3,951	43	1.1%	1,252
12/13	3,560	33	0.9%	1,163
Annual Growth	5.5%	11.2%	—	1.3%

2017 Year-End Financials

Debt ratio: 2.25%
Return on equity: 5.71%
Cash ($ mil.): 242
Current ratio: —
Long-term debt ($ mil.): —
No. of shares (mil.): 14
Dividends
  Yield: 0.0%
  Payout: 50.0%
Market value ($ mil.): 728

	STOCK PRICE ($) FY Close	P/E High/Low	PER SHARE ($) Earnings	Dividends	Book Value
12/17	51.65	16 9	3.64	1.82	33.48
12/16	54.65	17 11	3.21	0.88	30.77
12/15	45.26	16 11	3.28	0.86	28.67
12/14	39.67	13 9	3.10	0.80	30.52
12/13	30.41	13 9	2.42	0.72	27.84
Annual Growth	14.2%	— —	10.7%	26.1%	4.7%

Great West Life & Annuity Insurance Co - Insurance Products

Great-West Life & Annuity Insurance is the southern arm of a northern parent. The company a subsidiary of Canada's Great-West Lifeco and a member of the Power Financial family represents the Great-West group's primary US operations. It offers life insurance and annuities to individuals and employer groups. Under the Great-West Retirement Services brand it administers employer-sponsored retirement products including defined-benefit pension and 401(k) plans. Additional Great-West services include investment consulting and fund management. Great-West Life & Annuity markets products through its sales representatives and regional offices as well as independent brokers. The company is being acquired by Protective Life Insurance for $1.2 billion.

Operations

Great-West Life & Annuity also distributes its individual life insurance and annuity products through partnerships with banking institutions and financial advisors including Bank of America Citigroup and Charles Schwab. Outside of its own retirement products which are marketed to corporate not-for-profit health care educational and government organizations the Great-West Retirement Services unit provides business services including record-keeping for plans offered by other financial institutions. Its recordkeeping subsidiary FASCore LLC serves 4.7 million participant accounts. Great-West Life & Annuity's Individual Markets Division offers individual retirement accounts (IRAs) individual term and single-premium life insurance individual annuity products as well as executive benefits and business-owned life insurance products.

Geographic Reach

Great-West Life & Annuity has offices in more than 50 locations throughout the US Puerto Rico Guam and the US Virgin Islands.

Sales and Marketing

Great-West Life & Annuity markets its products and services through sales and service professionals brokers consultants advisors financial institutions and third-party administrators.

EXECUTIVES

Evp Individual Markets, Robert K. Shaw, age 63, $458,100 total compensation
Svp Investments, Ernie Friesen
Svp And Chief Investment Officer Separate Accounts, Catherine S. Tocher
President And Ceo, Robert L. Reynolds
President Empower Retirement, Edmund F. Murphy
Evp Great West Lifeco U.s. Inc., Charles B. McDevitt
Svp And Cio, Jeffrey W. Knight
Svp And Cfo, Louis J. Mannello
Svp Product Management, David G. McLeod
Executive Vice President Great-west Lifeco U.s, Charles B. McDevitt
Vice President, Eve Hampton
Vice President Investment Operations, Mary C Maiers
Assistant Vice President, Terry Homenuik
Senior Vice President, Brett Ford
Auditors: DELOITTE & TOUCHE LLP

LOCATIONS

HQ: Great West Life & Annuity Insurance Co - Insurance Products
8515 East Orchard Road, Greenwood Village, CO 80111
Phone: 303 737-3000
Web: www.greatwest.com

PRODUCTS/OPERATIONS

Selected Products and Services

Annuities
Life insurance
Retirement services
  Retirement plans for government corporate and not-for-profit employers
  Communication and education services
  Enrollment services
  Investment options
  Third-party administrative and record-keeping services (FASCore)

COMPETITORS

AXA Financial
Allstate
Industrial Alliance Insurance and Financial Servic
John Hancock Financial Services
Liberty Mutual
Lincoln Financial Group
Manulife Financial
MetLife
Mutual of Omaha
Nationwide Financial
Pacific Mutual
Prudential
State Farm
Sun Life
The Hartford

HISTORICAL FINANCIALS
Company Type: Public

Income Statement				FYE: December 31
	ASSETS ($ mil.)	NET INCOME ($ mil.)	INCOME AS % OF ASSETS	EMPLOYEES
12/17	62,461	369	0.6%	5,800
12/16	60,308	231	0.4%	5,800
12/15	57,899	190	0.3%	5,400
12/14	58,348	317	0.5%	4,500
12/13	55,323	128	0.2%	3,300
Annual Growth	3.1%	30.1%	—	15.1%

2017 Year-End Financials

Debt ratio: 0.89%
Return on equity: 16.55%
Cash ($ mil.): 17
Current ratio: —
Long-term debt ($ mil.): —
No. of shares (mil.): 7
Dividends
  Yield: —
  Payout: 39.3%
Market value ($ mil.): —

Great Western Bancorp Inc

Auditors: Ernst & Young LLP

LOCATIONS

HQ: Great Western Bancorp Inc
225 South Main Avenue, Sioux Falls, SD 57104
Phone: 605 334-2548
Web: www.greatwesternbank.com

HISTORICAL FINANCIALS

Company Type: Public

Income Statement

FYE: September 30

	ASSETS ($ mil.)	NET INCOME ($ mil.)	INCOME AS % OF ASSETS	EMPLOYEES
09/18	12,116	157	1.3%	1,664
09/17	11,690	144	1.2%	1,689
09/16	11,531	121	1.1%	1,649
09/15	9,798	109	1.1%	1,475
09/14	9,371	104	1.1%	1,492
Annual Growth	6.6%	10.8%	—	2.8%

2018 Year-End Financials

Debt ratio: 3.16%
Return on equity: 8.78%
Cash ($ mil.): 298
Current ratio: —
Long-term debt ($ mil.): —

No. of shares (mil.): 58
Dividends
　Yield: 0.0%
　Payout: 33.7%
Market value ($ mil.): 2,486

	STOCK PRICE ($) FY Close	P/E High/Low	PER SHARE ($) Earnings	Dividends	Book Value
09/18	42.19	17 14	2.67	0.90	31.24
09/17	41.28	18 13	2.45	0.74	29.83
09/16	33.32	16 11	2.14	0.56	28.34
09/15	25.37	14 9	1.90	0.36	26.43
Annual Growth	13.6%	— —	8.9%	25.7%	4.3%

Group 1 Automotive, Inc.

Group 1 Automotive is the third largest of a group of new and used car retailers (behind #1 AutoNation and #2 Penske Automotive Group) striving to consolidate US auto sales. The company owns more than 155 dealerships around 210 franchises and about 35 collision service centers operating under their own branding in the US UK and Brazil. The US is the biggest market and the company is present in 14 US states. Group 1 sells more than 30 car and light truck brands of which Toyota BMW and Ford are the biggest sellers. It also offers financing provides maintenance and repair services and sells replacement parts.

Operations

Group 1 Automotive's operations include five core business segments: New Vehicles (around 55% of sales) Used Vehicles (25%) Parts & Service (10%) Used Vehicles wholesale (5%) and Finance & Insurance (5%). In the UK the auto dealer operates through its subsidiary Group 1 Automotive UK Ltd.

Geographic Reach

The auto dealer rings up about 80% of its sales in the US; the remainder comes from the UK (15%) and Brazil (5%). More than half of Group 1's dealerships are located in Texas Oklahoma and California. In the UK Group 1 Automotive has about 40 franchises 30 dealerships and nearly 10 collision centers; and in Brazil nearly 25 franchises 20 dealerships and one collision center.

The company's US operations are located primarily major metropolitan areas. It is present 20 towns and cities in the UK and has a presence in Brazil in key metropolitan areas in the states of Sao Paulo Parana and Mato Grosso do Sul.

Financial Performance

Group 1's recent strong revenue growth continued in fiscal 2016 albeit at a slower pace than pre-viously increasing 2% to $10.9 billion. Growth in the UK new car market relating to acquisitions and overall market strength was partially offset by new car declines in the US and Brazil. Weakness in the US was concentrated in Group 1's significant Houston market as the oil city's workers have reduced their spending as the industry-wide squeeze continued. Used car sales rose 5% due to good performance in the US and UK. The Parts & Services business also grew.

Net income ticked up 56% to $147 million due mostly to higher net sales.

Cash from operations climbed 172% to $384.9 million due to higher net income and an increase in accounts payable and inventories.

Strategy

Group 1 is looking to capitalize on growth opportunities in the UK (where it already has an established presence) and in Brazil a relatively new market for the company. It acquired 12 dealerships and opened two additional dealerships in the UK in fiscal 2016. The company's strategy also includes growing its higher margin parts and services business growing its share of the new and used vehicle market taking advantage of its size to boost efficiency and continuing to make strategic acquisitions. In recent years Group 1 has seen import and luxury brands account for an increased share of its business.

Mergers and Acquisitions

In 2016 Group 1 acquired London-based Spire Automotive Group's twelve dealerships including four Audi dealerships and three BMW/MINI dealerships which will continue to use the Spire brand name. The acquired dealerships are expected to bring in approximately $575 million per year. The acquisition could also further Group 1's relationships with BMW and the Volkswagen Group in the UK.

EXECUTIVES

President Ceo And Director, Earl J. Hesterberg, age 65, $1,100,000 total compensation
Vp Manufacturer Relations Financial Services And Public Affairs, Peter C. DeLongchamps, age 57, $456,300 total compensation
Svp Human Resources Training And Operations Support, Frank Grese, age 66, $540,000 total compensation
Svp And Cfo, John C. Rickel, age 57, $583,500 total compensation
Vp And General Counsel, Darryl M. Burman, age 60, $440,300 total compensation
Vp Information Systems, James R. Druzbik
Vice President Information Technology Chief Information Officer, Wade Hubbard
Vice President Human Resources, Brooks O'hara
Vp Corporate Development, Mark Iuppenlatz
Vice President Human Resources, Brooks OHara
Vice President, Larry Caudill
President Ceo And Director, Earl J. Hesterberg, age 65
Chairman, Stephen D. Quinn, age 63
Corporate Treasurer, Kim Craig
Auditors: Ernst & Young LLP

LOCATIONS

HQ: Group 1 Automotive, Inc.
　800 Gessner, Suite 500, Houston, TX 77024
Phone: 713 647-5700　　**Fax:** 713 647-5858
Web: www.group1auto.com

2016 Sales

	$ mil.	% of total
U.S.	8,734	80
U.K.	1,723	16
Brazil	429	4
Total	10,887	100

Dealership presence

Dealership presence
United States
　Alabama
　California
　Florida
　Georgia
　Kansas
　Louisiana
　Maryland
　Massachusetts
　Mississippi
　New Hampshire
　New Jersey
　Oklahoma
　South Carolina
　Texas
United Kingdom
　Brighton
　Chelmsford
　Chingford
　Farnborough
　Hailsham
　Harold Wood
　Hindhead
　Southend
　Stansted
　Worthington
Brazil
　Sao Paolo
　Parana
　Mato Grosso do Sul

2015 Sales

	% of total
Finished goods and merchandise	53
Service revenue	22
Construction revenue	14
Gain on valuation by equity method	7
Other revenue	4
Total	100

Selected Subsidiaries and Affiliates

Chemicals
　LG Chem
　LG DOW Polycarbonate
　SEETEC
　LG Household & Healthcare
　Coca-Cola Beverage Company
　Diamond Pure Water
　LG Hausys
　LG Life Sciences
　LG MMA
Electronics
　LG Electronics Inc.
　Hi Logistics
　Hiplaza
　LG Display
　LG Innotek Co. Ltd.
　System Air-Con Engineering
　Lusem
　Siltron
Telecommunications & Services
　G2R
　Alchemedia
　Bugs Com Ad
　G Outdoor
　HS Ad
　L. Best
　TAMS Media
　W Brand Connection
　LG CNS
　Biztech & Ektimo
　LG N-Sys
　Uccess Partners
　V-ENS
　LG Management Development Institute
　LG Solar Energy
　LG Sports
　LG U+
　AIN Teleservice
　CS Leader
　CS ONE Partner
　Dacom Crossing
　Dacom Multimedia Internet
　SERVEONE
　Konjiam Yewon

PRODUCTS/OPERATIONS

2016 Sales

	$ mil.	% of total
New vehicle retail	6,046	55
Used vehicle retail	2,757	25
Used vehicle wholesale	401	4
Parts & service	1,261	12
Finance insurance & other	420	4
Total	**10,887**	**100**

Selected Brands

Domestic
 Ford
 Chevrolet
 Dodge
 Jeep
 GMC
 Chrysler
 Buick
 RAM
Import
 Toyota
 Nissan
 Honda
 Volkswagen
 Hyundai
 Mazda
 Subaru
 Scion
 Kia
 Peugeot
 Renault
Luxury
 BMW
 Acura
 MINI
 Land Rover
 Lexus
 Mercedes
 Audi
 Volvo
 Cadillac
 Lincoln
 Porsche
 Sprinter
 smart
 Jaguar

COMPETITORS

Ancira	Lookers
Asbury Automotive	Pendragon
AutoNation	Penske Automotive
CarMax	Group
David McDavid Auto	Phil Long Dealerships
Group	Sonic Automotive
Herb Chambers	Sytner
Lithia Motors	

HISTORICAL FINANCIALS

Company Type: Public

Income Statement

FYE: December 31

	REVENUE ($ mil.)	NET INCOME ($ mil.)	NET PROFIT MARGIN	EMPLOYEES
12/17	11,123	213	1.9%	14,108
12/16	10,887	147	1.4%	13,500
12/15	10,632	94	0.9%	12,886
12/14	9,937	93	0.9%	11,978
12/13	8,918	113	1.3%	11,510
Annual Growth	**5.7%**	**17.0%**	**—**	**5.2%**

2017 Year-End Financials

Debt ratio: 60.04%
Return on equity: 20.78%
Cash ($ mil.): 28
Current ratio: 1.06
Long-term debt ($ mil.): 1,318

No. of shares (mil.): 20
Dividends
 Yield: 0.0%
 Payout: 9.6%
Market value ($ mil.): 1,483

	STOCK PRICE ($) FY Close	P/E High/Low		PER SHARE ($) Earnings	Dividends	Book Value
12/17	70.97	8	5	10.08	0.97	53.80
12/16	77.94	12	7	6.67	0.91	43.46
12/15	75.70	25	19	3.90	0.83	39.22
12/14	89.62	24	16	3.60	0.70	40.18
12/13	71.02	17	12	4.32	0.65	43.77
Annual Growth	**(0.0%)**	**—**	**—**	**23.6%**	**10.5%**	**5.3%**

GROWMARK, INC.

Retail farm-supply and grain-marketing cooperative GROWMARK can mark its growth by the grain. A member-owed agricultural co-op GROWMARK has more than 100000 members. Under the FAST STOP name the co-op runs more than 250 fuel stations and convenience stores in the Midwest. Its Seedway subsidiary sells commercial vegetable seed and farm seed for turf and grains including alfalfa corn wheat and soybeans. GROWMARK also offers fertilizer seeds ethanol biodiesel and farm financing. Its MID-CO COMMODITIES subsidiary trades grain and offers advice regarding futures and options.

Geographic Reach

GROWMARK is headquartered in Bloomington Illinois and serves customers in more than 40 states and Ontario Canada. SEEDWAY maintains eight office and warehouse locations in Vermont New York Pennsylvania and Florida.

Strategy

Cooperation is important within and among agricultural cooperatives. A strong believer in the latter part of this principle GROWMARK has marketing agreements and alliances with among others fertilizer maker and distributor CF Industries pet-food producer PRO-PET agribusiness company Syngenta and rural financial services provider CoBank.

Mergers and Acquisitions

GROWMARK acquires fertilizer storage terminals and transportation infrastructure on a regular basis.

EXECUTIVES

Vice Chairman, John Reifsteck
Ceo, Jeff Solberg
Vp And General Counsel, Brent Bostrom
Vp Eastern Retail Operations, Steve Buckalew
Vp And Cfo, Marshall Bohbrink
Vp Energy, Kevin Carroll
Vp Midwest Retail And Acquisitions, Shelly Kruse
Vp Grain, Brent Ericson
Vice President Human Resources & Compliance, Gary Swango
Vp Agronomy, Mark Orr
Vp Financial And Risk Management, Mike Woods
Vp Member Services, Denny Worth
Vice President Systems, George Key
Vice President, Ron Milby
Vice President Of Information Technology, Rick Norton
Vice President Member Services, Dennis Farmer
Vice Presidnet Of Finance, Jeffrey Solberg
Vice Chairman, John Reifsteck
Vice Chairman, Rick Nelson
Vice Chairman, Chet Esther
Board Member Administration Executive, Bob Phelps
Auditors: ERNST & YOUNG LLP CHICAGO I

LOCATIONS

HQ: GROWMARK, INC.
 1701 TOWANDA AVE, BLOOMINGTON, IL 617012057
Phone: 309 557-6000
Web: WWW.GROWMARK.COM

PRODUCTS/OPERATIONS

Selected Retail Products and Operations

COMFORT PRO (propane heating oil)
FAST STOP (fuel facilities)
FS (farm supplies)
Green Yard (turf seed fertilizer)
Seedway (farm turf and vegetable seed)

Selected Member Cooperatives and Subsidiaries

AgVantage FS Inc.
AgView Grain LLC
Evergreen FS Inc.
GROWMARK FS LLC
MID-CO COMMODITIES
Northern Grain Marketing LLC
Seedway LLC
Total Grain Marketing LLC
Western Grain Marketing LLC

COMPETITORS

ADM	Marathon Oil
AGRI Industries	NC Hybrids
Ag Processing Inc.	Orscheln Farm and Home
BP	Pfister Hybrid Corn
Barkley Seed	Pioneer Hi-Bred
Bayer CropScience	Rabo AgriFinance
CHS	Sakata Seed
Cargill	Seed Enterprises
Chevron	Southern States
Costco Wholesale	Terra Nitrogen
DeBruce Grain	Wal-Mart
Exxon Mobil	Wilbur-Ellis

HISTORICAL FINANCIALS

Company Type: Private

Income Statement

FYE: August 31

	REVENUE ($ mil.)	NET INCOME ($ mil.)	NET PROFIT MARGIN	EMPLOYEES
08/18	8,522	65	0.8%	7,000
08/17	7,291	115	1.6%	—
08/16	7,031	101	1.4%	—
08/15	8,727	113	1.3%	—
Annual Growth	**(0.8%)**	**(16.6%)**	**—**	**—**

2018 Year-End Financials

Debt ratio: —
Return on equity: 0.80%
Cash ($ mil.): 99
Current ratio: 0.70
Long-term debt ($ mil.): —

Dividends
 Yield: —
 Payout: —
Market value ($ mil.): —

Guaranty Bancshares Inc

EXECUTIVES

Chb-Ceo, Tyson T Abston
Pres, Kirk L Lee
Sr Exec V Pres-Cfo, Clifton A Payne
V Pres-General Counsel, Randall R Kucera
Snr Vice President, Kirk Lee
Auditors: Whitley Penn LLP

LOCATIONS

HQ: Guaranty Bancshares Inc
  201 South Jefferson Avenue, Mount Pleasant, TX
  75455
Phone: 903 572-9881
Web: www.gnty.com

PRODUCTS/OPERATIONS

2008 Sales

	$ mil.	% of total
Interest		
Loans including fees	31	70
Securities	6	13
Other	1	2
Noninterest		
Service charges	4	8
Other	3	7
Total	**46**	**100**

COMPETITORS

BancorpSouth
Bank of America
Capital One
Cullen/Frost Bankers
Southside Bancshares
Wells Fargo
Woodforest Financial

HISTORICAL FINANCIALS

Company Type: Public

Income Statement

FYE: December 31

	ASSETS ($ mil.)	NET INCOME ($ mil.)	INCOME AS % OF ASSETS	EMPLOYEES
12/17	1,962	14	0.7%	407
12/16	1,828	12	0.7%	397
12/15	1,682	10	0.6%	—
12/14	1,334	9	0.7%	—
12/13	1,247	14	1.2%	—
Annual Growth	12.0%	(0.6%)	—	—

2017 Year-End Financials

Debt ratio: 0.70%
Return on equity: 8.27%
Cash ($ mil.): 65
Current ratio: —
Long-term debt ($ mil.): —

No. of shares (mil.): 11
Dividends
  Yield: 0.0%
  Payout: 28.5%
Market value ($ mil.): 339

	STOCK PRICE ($) FY Close	P/E High/Low	PER SHARE ($) Earnings	Dividends	Book Value
12/17	30.65	25 20	1.40	0.40	18.75
12/16	26.50	— —	1.35	0.52	16.22
12/15	26.50	— —	1.15	0.50	15.47
12/14	26.50	— —	1.25	1.50	14.01
12/13	26.50	— —	2.40	1.90	13.25
Annual Growth	3.7%	— —	(12.6%)	(32.3%)	9.1%

Halliburton Company

One of the largest oilfield services companies in the world Halliburton serves the global upstream oil and gas industry with a broad array of products and services. It manufactures drill bits and other downhole and completion tools; provides pressure pumping services; locates hydrocarbons and manages geological data; drills new wells; and optimizes production once the well is operational. It maintains advantages in the highly competitive market by combining tried-and-true well drilling and optimization techniques with high-tech analysis and modeling software and services. The US accounts for some 55% of company revenue.

HISTORY

Erle Halliburton began his oil career in 1916 at Perkins Oil Well Cementing. He moved to oil boomtown Burkburnett Texas to start his Better Method Oil Well Cementing Company in 1919. Halliburton used cement to hold a steel pipe in a well which kept oil out of the water table strengthened well walls and reduced the risk of explosions. Though the contribution would later be praised his technique was considered useless at the time.

In 1920 Halliburton moved to Oklahoma. Incorporating Halliburton Oil Well Cementing Company in 1924 he patented its products and services forcing oil companies to employ his firm if they wanted to cement wells.

Erle died in 1957 and his company grew through acquisitions between the 1950s and the 1970s. In 1962 it bought Houston construction giant Brown & Root an expert in offshore platforms. After the 1973 Arab oil embargo Halliburton benefited from the surge in global oil exploration and later as drilling costs surged it became a leader in well stimulation.

When the oil industry slumped in 1982 the firm halved its workforce. Three years later a suffering Brown & Root coughed up $750 million to settle charges of mismanagement at the South Texas Nuclear Project.

In the 1990s Halliburton expanded abroad entering Russia in 1991 and China in 1993. The next year Brown & Root was named contractor for a pipeline stretching from Qatar to Pakistan. Halliburton drilled the world's deepest horizontal well (18860 ft.) in Germany in 1995.

That year Dick Cheney a former US defense secretary became CEO. Brown & Root began providing engineering and logistics services to US Army peacekeeping troops in the Balkans in 1995 and won a major contract to develop an offshore Canadian oil field the next year.

In 1997 Halliburton completed a major reorganization started in 1993 uniting 10 businesses under the Halliburton Energy Services umbrella. The company nearly doubled in size in 1998 with its $7.7 billion acquisition of oil field equipment manufacturer Dresser Industries. The purchase coupled with falling oil prices in 1998 and 1999 prompted Halliburton to ax more than 9000 workers. (Even after oil prices rebounded in 2000 Halliburton had to wait for the effects of the upturn to reach the oil field services sector.)

Brown & Root Energy Services won a contract to provide logistics support for the US Army in Albania in 1999. Halliburton also invested in oil field emergency-response firm Boots & Coots and took a stake in Japanese engineering firm Chiyoda.

The company began to sell off portions of its Dresser acquisition in 1999. Partner Ingersoll-Rand bought Halliburton's stake in Ingersoll-Dresser Pump for $515 million and bought its stake in Dresser-Rand (industrial compressors) for $579 million in 2000. Cheney resigned as chairman and CEO that year after he was chosen as George W. Bush's vice presidential running mate. President and COO David Lesar was named to succeed him.

A group consisting of investment firms First Reserve and Odyssey Investment Partners and Dresser managers paid $1.55 billion in 2001 for Dresser Equipment Group. That year a number of multimillion-dollar verdicts against Halliburton in asbestos cases sparked rumors that the company was going to file for bankruptcy (flatly denied by Halliburton) and caused the firm's stock price to tumble.

In 2002 in part to protect the company's assets from the unresolved asbestos claims issue Lesar announced plans to restructure Halliburton into two independent subsidiaries separating the Energy Services Group from Halliburton's KBR eng

EXECUTIVES

Evp Administration And Chief Human Resources Officer, Lawrence J. Pope, age 49, $535,000 total compensation
Evp And General Counsel, Robb L. Voyles, age 60
President Eastern Hemisphere, Joseph D. (Joe) Rainey, age 61, $809,950 total compensation
President Western Hemisphere, James S. (Jim) Brown, age 63, $873,000 total compensation
President And Ceo, Jeffrey A. (Jeff) Miller, age 54, $970,000 total compensation
Evp And Cfo, Christopher T. (Chris) Weber, age 45
Evp Global Business Lines, Eric Carre
Regional Vice President Apac, Rao Abdullah
Vice President Mergers And Acquisitions, Michael Cheeseman
Vp Production Enhancement, Richard Gonzalez
Legal Secretary, Sharkila Hassim
Vice President, Mark Dawson
Chairman, David J. (Dave) Lesar, age 65
Secretary, Elisabeth Skeie
Secretary, Jihan Jinin
Secretary, Nienke Lenters
Secretary, Robin Raber
Office Assistance Secretary, Vera Febriyanti
Auditors: KPMG LLP

LOCATIONS

HQ: Halliburton Company
  3000 North Sam Houston Parkway East, Houston, TX
  77032
Phone: 281 871-2699
Web: www.halliburton.com

2016 Sales

	$ mil.	% of total
North America	11,564	56
Middle East/Asia	4,159	20
Europe/Africa/CIS	2,781	14
Latin America	2,116	10
Total	**20,620**	**100**

PRODUCTS/OPERATIONS

2017 Sales

	$ mil.	% of total
Completion and Production	13,077	63
Drilling and Evaluation	7,543	37
Total	**20,620**	**100**

2017 Sales

	$ mil.	% of total
Services	15,408	75
Product sales	5,212	25
Total	**20,620**	**100**

Areas of Expertise

Areas of Expertise
Clean Energy
Deepwater
Heavy Oil
High Pressure/Temperature
Mature Fields
Unconventional Resources

Selected Products and Services

Artificial Lift
Cementing
Consulting
Coring
Drill Bits
Drilling
Fluid Services
Formation Evaluation
Hole Enlargement
Pipeline & Process Services
Project Management
Real Time Services
Reservoir Testing / Analysis

Sand Control
Wellbore Service Tools
Software and Services
Stimulation
Subsea
Well Completions
Well Intervention
Wireline and Perforating

Selected Brands
Baroid
Landmark
Multi-Chem
Pinnacle
Sperry Drilling

COMPETITORS

Baker Hughes	RPC
McDermott	TechnipFMC
National Oilwell Varco	

HISTORICAL FINANCIALS
Company Type: Public

Income Statement

FYE: December 31

	REVENUE ($ mil.)	NET INCOME ($ mil.)	NET PROFIT MARGIN	EMPLOYEES
12/17	20,620	(463)	—	55,000
12/16	15,887	(5,763)	—	50,000
12/15	23,633	(671)	—	65,000
12/14	32,870	3,500	10.6%	80,000
12/13	29,402	2,125	7.2%	77,000
Annual Growth	(8.5%)	—	—	(8.1%)

2017 Year-End Financials

Debt ratio: 43.62%	No. of shares (mil.): 873
Return on equity: (-5.22%)	Dividends
Cash ($ mil.): 2,337	Yield: 0.0%
Current ratio: 2.22	Payout: —
Long-term debt ($ mil.): 10,430	Market value ($ mil.): 42,664

	STOCK PRICE ($) FY Close	P/E High/Low	Earnings	PER SHARE ($) Dividends	Book Value
12/17	48.87	— —	(0.53)	0.72	9.53
12/16	54.09	— —	(6.69)	0.72	10.86
12/15	34.04	— —	(0.79)	0.72	18.06
12/14	39.33	18 9	4.11	0.63	19.18
12/13	50.75	24 15	2.36	0.53	16.00
Annual Growth	(0.9%)	— —	—	8.2%	(12.1%)

Hancock Whitney Corp

EXECUTIVES

President Ceo And Director, John M. Hairston, age 55, $707,000 total compensation
Coo, D. Shane Loper, age 52, $400,000 total compensation
Cfo, Michael M. Achary, age 57, $400,000 total compensation
President Whitney Bank, Joseph S. Exnicios, age 62, $375,000 total compensation
Chief Credit Officer Whitney Bank, Suzanne C. Thomas, age 63
Chief Credit Risk Officer, Samuel B. Kendricks, age 58
Chief Investment Officer, David J. Lundgren
Vice President And Private Banker, Larry Cuervo
Senior Vice President Financial And Estate Planner, Emile Koury

Assistant Vice President, Kim Gibson
Assistant Vice President, Jimmy Campbell
Vice President Project Manager Enterprise Project Office, Heather Argent
Senior Vice President, David Cooper
Vice President, Billy Price
Vice President Deposit Services Manager, Jeff Carnes
Assistant Vice President Merchant Services Sales Specialist, Lisa Parks
Chairman, James B. Estabrook, age 74
President Ceo And Director, John M. Hairston, age 55
Auditors: PricewaterhouseCoopers LLP

LOCATIONS

HQ: Hancock Whitney Corp
One Hancock Plaza, 2510, 14th Street, Gulfport, MS 39501
Phone: 228 868-4000
Web: www.hancockbank.com

PRODUCTS/OPERATIONS

2017 Sales

	$ mil.	% of total
Interest income		
Loans including fees	772	66
Securities	124	11
Other	4	-
Interest expense	(108.3)	-
Non interest income		
Service charges on deposit accounts	83	7
Bank card and ATM fees	53	5
Trust fees	44	4
Investment and annuity fees	20	2
Secondary mortgage market operations	15	1
Insurance commissions and fees	3	-
Other	49	4
Total	**1,062**	**100**

Selected Services
Banking
Checking
Credit Cards
Currency Exchange
Home Equity Loans and Lines
Investment Services
Investments
Loans & Credit
Mobile Banking
Mortgage
Online & Mobile Banking
Online Banking
Personal Loans and Lines
Savings

COMPETITORS

BancorpSouth	MidSouth Bancorp
Capital One	Regions Financial
First Horizon	Renasant
IBERIABANK	Trustmark
Investar	

HISTORICAL FINANCIALS
Company Type: Public

Income Statement

FYE: December 31

	ASSETS ($ mil.)	NET INCOME ($ mil.)	INCOME AS % OF ASSETS	EMPLOYEES
12/17	27,336	215	0.8%	3,887
12/16	23,975	149	0.6%	3,724
12/15	22,839	131	0.6%	3,921
12/14	20,747	175	0.8%	3,794
12/13	19,009	163	0.9%	3,978
Annual Growth	9.5%	7.2%	—	(0.6%)

2017 Year-End Financials

Debt ratio: 1.12%	No. of shares (mil.): 85
Return on equity: 7.69%	Dividends
Cash ($ mil.): 479	Yield: 0.0%
Current ratio: —	Payout: 38.7%
Long-term debt ($ mil.): —	Market value ($ mil.): 4,217

	STOCK PRICE ($) FY Close	P/E High/Low	Earnings	PER SHARE ($) Dividends	Book Value
12/17	49.50	21 17	2.48	0.96	33.86
12/16	42.10	24 11	1.87	0.96	32.29
12/15	25.17	20 15	1.64	0.96	31.14
12/14	30.70	18 14	2.10	0.96	30.74
12/13	36.68	19 14	1.93	0.96	29.49
Annual Growth	7.8%	— —	6.5%	(0.0%)	3.5%

HanesBrands Inc

Hanesbrands can't wait 'til it gets its Hanes on you. The company designs makes and sells bras hosiery men's boxers socks and other intimate apparel under brand names such as Bali Champion barely there Just My Size Hanes L'eggs Playtex and Wonderbra. Its bras are tops in the US and its underwear legwear and activewear units are market leaders as well. Hanesbrands also makes basic outerwear such as T-shirts and licensed logo apparel for collegiate bookstores legwear for Donna Karan and underwear for Polo Ralph Lauren. The lineup is sold to wholesalers major retail chains (Wal-Mart Target and Kohls) and through Hanesbrands' value outlets and Internet site.

Operations
Hanesbrands divides its operations into four segments including innerwear (intimate apparel men's and children's underwear and socks) activewear direct to consumer and international. Innerwear is the largest by far accounting for more than 50% of revenue in 2015 while Activewear generated more than 25%.

The company operates nearly 40 distribution centers with 16 in the US and 21 located internationally near manufacturing regions.

Geographic Reach
Hanesbrands sells in roughly 35 countries and rings up roughly 80% of its sales in the US (during 2015). Its largest international markets include Europe (12% of sales) Canada Japan Mexico Brazil and China.

Sales and Marketing
Wal-Mart Target and Kohls are the company's largest customers accounting for 23% 15% and 5% of 2015 sales respectively. Mass merchandise stores are vital to the company's performance accounting for about half of Hanesbrands' total sales. Hanesbrands also allies with mid-tier stores including J. C. Penney Macy's and Kohls which are adding its lower-priced labels. It's L'eggs and Hanes brand underwear are also sold in food drug and variety stores. Hanesbrands also sell apparel to the US military for sale to soldiers and through discount chains including Dollar General and Family Dollar Stores.

Financial Performance
Hanesbrands' annual sales and profits have been growing over the past few years as new brand acquisitions have spurred more sales in more geographic markets.

The company's sales rose nearly 8% to $5.73 billion during fiscal 2016 (ended January 2016) mostly thanks to 40%-plus International segment growth. The International segment's Europe operation was boosted by its late 2014 acquisition of DBApparel. Its Activewear sales also grew as its Knights Apparel acquisition led to higher sports apparel sales.

Sales growth in FY2016 drove Hanesbrands' net income up 6% to $428.2 million despite higher selling general and administration costs associated with acquisition and integration charges. The apparel maker's operating cash levels plunged 55% to $227 million for the year as it used more cash to build its inventory levels paid $100 million in pension contributions and decreased its accounts receivables collections due to the timing of sales in the fourth quarter.

Strategy

Hanesbrands has been expanding its business overseas by acquiring top brands in its less-tapped markets. In 2016 for example the company expanded in Australia after buying top intimates maker Pacific Brands in Australia. Pacific Brands adds to the 2014 acquisition of DBApparel Group of France licensed to sell the Wonderbra and Playdex trademarks in the EU and South Africa.

The company also hopes to identify and capitalize on the long-term megatrends related to their top product lines over the next five to 10 years. To this end in early 2015 the company purchased Knights Apparel to expand its sports licensed collegiate apparel business with a goal of appealing to college students as that market grows over the next years and decades.

Beyond growth Hanesbrands has been reducing production costs by improving operating efficiencies in using a low-cost global supply chain based upon a combination of owned contracted and sourced manufacturing.

Mergers and Acquisitions

In 2016 the company acquired leading Australian undergarment company Pacific Brands Limited in a cash deal valued at $800 million. The acquisition gave Hanesbrands the top market position in Australia for intimate apparel. In addition to its core products Pacific Brands Limited also operates pillow business Tontine and flooring business Dunlop. Hanesbrands intends to divest both businesses.

Hanesbrands also acquired Champion Europe which owned the Champion brand in Europe Middle East and Africa in 2016 for $228 million in cash. The company operates Champion Europe as a division of Hanes' global Champion organization.

In 2015 the company bought Knights Apparel a leading retailer of licensed collegiate logo apparel to enrich its own Gear for Sports licensed collegiate apparel business.

EXECUTIVES

Vice President Global Human Resources, Jim Flynn

Ceo, Gerald W. Evans, age 58, $912,500 total compensation

Group President Innerwear Americas, W. Howard Upchurch, age 54, $525,000 total compensation

Cfo, Barry A. Hytinen, age 43

President Chief Supply Chain And Information Technology Officer, Michael E. Faircloth, age 52, $510,000 total compensation

President Activewear, John T. Marsh, age 52

Vice President Marketing, Richard Heller

Vice President Distribution, Chuck Allen

Vice President Textiles E Hilos, Keith Huskins

Chairman, Richard A. (Rich) Noll, age 61

Auditors: PricewaterhouseCoopers LLP

LOCATIONS

HQ: HanesBrands Inc
1000 East Hanes Mill Road, Winston-Salem, NC 27105
Phone: 336 519-8080
Web: www.Hanes.com

2016 Sales

	$ mil.	% of total
US	4,489	74
France	290	5
Austrila	278	5
Japan	182	3
Italy	174	3
Germany	110	2
Europe (other)	96	2
Canada	90	1
Spain	65	1
Mexico	60	1
United Kingdom	32	1
Brazil	28	0
China	5	0
Central America & the Caribbean Basin	3	0
Other	120	2
Total	**6,028**	**100**

2016 Sales

	$ mil.	% of total
Innerwear	2,609	43
Activewear	1,570	26
Direct to Consumer	315	5
International	1,531	26
Total	**6,028**	**100**

PRODUCTS/OPERATIONS

Selected Brands

Bali
barely there
C9 by Champion
Champion
Gear for Sports
Just My Size
Hanes
L'eggs
Maidenform
Outer Banks
Playtex
Rinbros
Sol y Oro
Wonderbra
Zorba

COMPETITORS

Calvin Klein	Russell Brands
Frederick's of	The Gap
Hollywood Group	Tommy Hilfiger
Fruit of the Loom	Top Form
Gerber Childrenswear	Triumph Apparel
Gildan Activewear	Under Armour
J. Crew	Victoria's Secret
Jockey International	Stores
L Brands	Wacoal
PremiumWear	Warnaco Group
Redcats USA	Warnaco Swimwear

HISTORICAL FINANCIALS

Company Type: Public

Income Statement

FYE: December 29

	REVENUE ($ mil.)	NET INCOME ($ mil.)	NET PROFIT MARGIN	EMPLOYEES
12/18	6,803	553	8.1%	68,000
12/17	6,471	61	1.0%	67,200
12/16*	6,028	539	8.9%	67,800
01/16	5,731	428	7.5%	65,300
01/15	5,324	404	7.6%	59,500
Annual Growth	**6.3%**	**8.1%**	**—**	**3.4%**

*Fiscal year change

2018 Year-End Financials

Debt ratio: 54.86%
Return on equity: 66.96%
Cash ($ mil.): 433
Current ratio: 1.73
Long-term debt ($ mil.): 3,534

No. of shares (mil.): 361
Dividends
  Yield: 0.0%
  Payout: 39.4%
Market value ($ mil.): 4,405

	STOCK PRICE ($) FY Close	P/E High/Low		PER SHARE ($) Earnings	Dividends	Book Value
12/18	12.19	15	8	1.52	0.60	2.69
12/17	20.91	151	112	0.17	0.60	1.91
12/16*	21.57	22	15	1.40	0.44	3.23
01/16	29.43	120	25	1.06	0.40	3.26
01/15	110.61	86	48	1.32	0.30	4.61
Annual Growth	**(42.4%)**	**—**	**—**	**3.5%**	**18.9%**	**(12.7%)**

*Fiscal year change

Hanmi Financial Corp.

Hanmi Financial owns Hanmi Bank which serves Korean-American and other ethnic communities in California Colorado Georgia Illinois New Jersey New York Texas Virginia and Washington. The company which holds $5.5 billion in assets offers traditional banking services to small and midsized businesses from about 40 branches and eight loan offices. Real estate loans — including for retail hospitality mixed-use apartment office industrial gas station faith-based facility and warehouse properties — account for about 80% of its loan portfolio; commercial and industrial loans and leases receivable make up most of the rest.

Operations

Hanmi Financial originates real estate loans (including commercial construction and residential property) commercial and industrial loans (including commercial term commercial lines of credit and international) equipment lease financing consumer loans and Small Business Administration (SBA) loans. The bank also offers traditional deposit products including checking savings negotiable order of withdrawal (NOW) and money market accounts and CDs.

Hanmi's $4.6 billion loan portfolio is made up mostly of real estate loans — particularly commercial property loans including retail (about 20% of total portfolio) hospitality (20%) and other loans (30%). Other loans include loans for mixed-use apartment office industrial gas station faith-based facility and warehouse properties. Residential property loans comprise around 10%.

Commercial and industrial loans and leases receivable together make up about 15% of the bank's portfolio.

Geographic Reach

Headquartered in a penthouse suite on Los Angeles' Wilshire Boulevard Hanmi Financial has one bank branch in each of New Jersey New York and Virginia; some five branches in Illinois; about 10 branches in Texas; and around 25 branches in California. The majority of its loan and deposit concentration is in Southern California.

Sales and Marketing

Hanmi Financial's lending is concentrated in real estate loans commercial loans and leases and Small Business Administration (SBA) loans for small and middle market businesses in California Texas Illinois and New York — primarily among Korean-American and other multi-ethnic communities.

Financial Performance

Since 2013 Hanmi Financial has grown its revenue and net income by about 60% and 40% respectively thanks to increasing net interest income. But the company also depleted its cash stores by about 15% and more than doubled its long-term debt in that time mostly due to Federal Home Loan Bank advances in 2016.

The bank's revenue increased 9% in 2017 compared with 2016 reaching $210.2 million. Higher interest and fees on loans and leases drove the improvement which was partially offset by higher expense for interest on deposits. Average loans and leases and the percentage of loans and leases in Hanmi's mix of interest-earning assets both increased in 2017.

Net income slipped 3% to $54.7 million owing mostly to an increase in the bank's income tax provision which included a $3.9 million charge for a one-time revaluation adjustment connected with the Tax Cuts and Jobs Act (TCJA).

Hanmi added $6.6 million to its cash stores in 2017 for a total of $153.8 million. Operations and financings provided $79.9 million and $445.1 million respectively. Investment activity used $518.4 million.

Strategy

Hanmi Financial is working to diversify its loan portfolio to reduce its reliance on commercial real estate and increase its composition of leases and commercial industrial and residential real estate loans. Since 2014 the company has increased the proportion of its portfolio made up of leases and residential real estate while maintaining the proportion of commercial and industrial loans.

After a review of its cost structure and operating efficiency in 2018 the company is moderating its growth expectations lowering its non-interest expenses and consolidating about 10% of its branches.

Hanmi also hired a Chief Technology officer in 2018 to implement a strategy to improve the company's use of technology including using it to increase efficiency of regulatory compliance activities (for which the company heavily relies on human capital).

Mergers and Acquisitions

In its first foray outside of California in late 2013 Hanmi agreed to acquire Central Bancorp Inc. the parent of Texas-based United Central Bank. United Central Bank serves multi-ethnic communities in Texas Illinois Virginia California New York and New Jersey through some two dozen branches. Once the acquisition is complete Hanmi will have about 50 branches and two loan production offices serving a broad range of ethnic communities in California Texas Illinois New York New Jersey Virginia and Georgia.

Company Background

Hanmi Financial was founded in 1982.

EXECUTIVES

Sevp And Coo, Bonita I. (Bonnie) Lee, age 55
Chief Compliance And Bsa Officer, Jean Lim
Evp And Cfo, Michael W. McCall
President Ceo And Director, Chong Guk (C. G.) Kum
Evp And Chief Credit Officer, Randall G. Ewig
Evp And Chief Administrative Officer, Greg D. Kim
Evp And Chief Banking Officer, Peter Yang
Evp And Chief Lending Officer, Anthony Kim
Vice President And Loan Officer, Yong Park
Assistant Vice President Compliance Officer, Michael Santiago
Assistant Vice President Treasury Management, Debby Sassoon
Senior Vice President Senior Credit Administrator, Oliver Kim
Vice President Loss Share Accounting Manager, Brian Rogers
Assistant Vice President Andamp; Sba Loan Officer, Sharon Min

Vice President Human Resources Officer, Ashley Sowa
Vice President And Accounting Officer Accounting Department, Jin Shin
Chairman, Joseph K. Rho, age 77
President Ceo And Director, Chong Guk (C. G.) Kum
Auditors: KPMG LLP

LOCATIONS

HQ: Hanmi Financial Corp.
3660 Wilshire Boulevard, Penthouse Suite A, Los Angeles, CA 90010
Phone: 213 382-2200
Web: www.hanmi.com

PRODUCTS/OPERATIONS

2017 Sales

	$ mil.	% of total
Net interest income	176	84
Non-interest income	33	16
Total	**210**	**100**

COMPETITORS

Bank of America	Far East National Bank
Broadway Financial	Hope Bancorp
Cathay General Bancorp	JPMorgan Chase
East West Bancorp	Woori

HISTORICAL FINANCIALS

Company Type: Public

Income Statement   FYE: December 31

	ASSETS ($ mil.)	NET INCOME ($ mil.)	INCOME AS % OF ASSETS	EMPLOYEES
12/17	5,210	54	1.0%	642
12/16	4,701	56	1.2%	638
12/15	4,234	53	1.3%	622
12/14	4,232	49	1.2%	699
12/13	3,055	39	1.3%	499
Annual Growth	**14.3%**	**8.2%**	**—**	**6.5%**

2017 Year-End Financials

Debt ratio: 5.13%	No. of shares (mil.): 32
Return on equity: 10.00%	Dividends
Cash ($ mil.): 153	Yield: 0.0%
Current ratio: —	Payout: 47.3%
Long-term debt ($ mil.): —	Market value ($ mil.): 984

	STOCK PRICE ($) FY Close	P/E High/Low	PER SHARE ($) Earnings	Dividends	Book Value
12/17	30.35	21 15	1.69	0.80	17.34
12/16	34.90	20 11	1.75	0.66	16.42
12/15	23.72	16 12	1.68	0.47	15.45
12/14	21.81	16 12	1.56	0.28	14.21
12/13	21.89	18 11	1.26	0.14	12.63
Annual Growth	**8.5%**	**— —**	**7.6%**	**54.6%**	**8.2%**

Hanover Insurance Group Inc

Founded in 1852 The Hanover Insurance Group is one of the oldest property/casualty insurance holding companies around. Through Hanover Insurance Company the group provides personal and commercial automobile homeowners and workers' compensation coverage as well as commercial multi-peril insurance and professional liability coverage. The group sells its products through a network of independent agents throughout the US; Michigan Massachusetts and New York account for about 40% of its business. In Michigan it operates as Citizens Insurance Company. Hanover's Opus Investment Management subsidiary provides institutional investment management services.

Operations

Hanover's primary domestic segments are Commercial Lines Personal Lines and Other while its international segment is Chaucer.

Primarily through the Hanover Insurance Company unit Hanover writes more than $5 billion in gross premiums each year. Commercial policies account for nearly half of annual revenues while personal lines account for 30%. Former subsidiary Chaucer operated two Lloyd's of London syndicates which manage and underwrite global property/casualty policies; the subsidiary also offered specialty insurance and reinsurance coverage. In late 2018 Hanover sold Chaucer which generated about 20% of the group's revenues.

Hanover's Other segment comprises Opus Investment Management which provides investment advisory services to affiliates; it also manages assets for unaffiliated clients including insurance companies retirement plans and foundations.

Geographic Reach

Hanover is licensed to sell property/casualty insurance in all 50 US states and the District of Columbia. It actively markets commercial policies in 37 states and personal lines policies in 18 states. The group is highly dependent on three states: Michigan is the company's largest market accounting for some 20% of all commercial and personal lines. Massachusetts and New York account for about 10% each. Altogether US operations account for some 85% of annual premiums.

In addition to its headquarters in Worcester Massachusetts the company has more than 40 regional offices in cities across the US and about 10 overseas locations. It has an office in London and other global offices for sales underwriting and claims processing activities as well as offices of acquired companies in select nations.

Sales and Marketing

Hanover sells through a network of agents and brokers including about 2100 agent partners. The company's customers include individuals families and businesses.

Financial Performance

Hanover's revenues have been slightly erratic over the past five years. In 2017 revenue increased 5% to $5.2 billion as premiums and net investment income rose. Commercial lines net premiums grew by 4% that year while personal lines net premiums written grew by 8%. Chaucer net premiums written increased 4% as well.

Net income rose 20% to $186.2 million that year thanks primarily to the higher revenue and an increase in operating income. However Hanover's bottom line was impacted by catastrophe losses totaling some $382.6 million (versus $125.1 million in 2016). Hurricanes Harvey Irma and Maria wildfires in California and a heavy windstorm in the Midwest all contributed to the company's catastrophe losses.

Operating cash flow declined 5% to $704.6 million in 2017.

Strategy

One of Hanover's strategies is to build partnerships with other insurers and agents while expanding its product offerings and geographic presence beyond its three historical core markets of Massachusetts New York and Michigan. The company pursues growth in a conservative manner to preserve long-term financial and operational stability.

It also intends to build on its agent-centered distribution strategy by expanding its agency network into new geographic markets. In terms of personal lines the firm is making a push to convert more of its customers into multi-policy consumers; more than 80% of its personal lines customers already fall into that bucket. In addition Hanover is working to increase efficiencies through technology upgrades.

Written premiums are balanced between personal and commercial products but competition is fierce in personal insurance so the company has placed more emphasis on expanding its commercial offerings. It does this by deepening its relationships with agents through diverse product offerings.

Wriggling into a niche is one method of expanding and Hanover has moved into several areas of specialty insurance in recent years such as health care and engineering. The company has launched several niche insurance programs such as coverage for not-for-profit youth organizations community services organizations and religious institutions. In 2017 the company launched Hanover Fusion a life sciences product that includes coverage for errors and omissions information security media and content and operations liability. Also that year Chaucer established Chaucer Dublin to write international specialty insurance. And in 2016 Chaucer partnered with another leading insurer AXA to develop specialty business in Africa.

However Hanover sold Chaucer to China Reinsurance in late 2018. It had been exploring strategic alternatives related to the UK unit. Selling Chaucer diminished its geographic diversity though which limits its growth potential.

Mergers and Acquisitions

In 2017 Hanover's international subsidiary Chaucer acquired SLE Holdings a Lloyd's managing general underwriting agency operating in Australia. SLE focuses on the sports entertainment and leisure sectors. The purchase broadened Chaucer's Australian operations as well as widening its specialty product lines. (Hanover sold Chaucer in late 2018.)

HISTORY

In 1842 a group of Worcester Massachusetts businessmen tried to form a mutual life insurance company. After a failed first attempt they succeeded with the help of lobbyist Benjamin Balch. In 1844 the State Mutual Life Assurance Co. of Worcester set up business in the back room of secretary Clarendon Harris' bookstore. The first president was John Davis a US senator. The company issued its first policy in 1845.

In the early years State Mutual reduced risk by issuing policies only for residents of such "civilized" areas as New England New Jersey New York Pennsylvania and Ohio. It also restricted movement requiring policyholders to get permission for travel outside those areas. By the 1850s the company had begun issuing policies in the Midwest (with a 25% premium surcharge) the South (for 30% extra) and California (for a pricey extra $25 per $1000) with a maximum coverage of $5000.

The Civil War was a problem for many insurers who had to decide what to do about Southern policyholders and payment on war-related claims. State Mutual chose to pay out its Northern policyholders' benefits despite the extra cost. In 1896 the firm began offering installment pay-out plans for policyholders concerned that their beneficiaries would fritter away the whole payment.

The first 30 years of the 20th century were for the company a time of growth that was stopped short by the Depression. But despite a great increase in the number of policy loans and surren-ders for cash value State Mutual's financial footing remained solid.

After WWII the company entered group insurance and began offering individual sickness and accident coverage. In 1957 it was renamed State Mutual Life Assurance Co. of America. The firm added property/casualty insurance in the late 1950s through alliances with such firms as Worcester Mutual Fire Insurance. During the 1960s State Mutual continued to develop property/casualty buying interests in Hanover Insurance and Citizens Corp.

The firm followed the industrywide shift into financial services in the 1970s adding mutual funds a real estate investment trust and an investment management firm. This trend accelerated in the 1980s and State Mutual began offering financial planning services as well as administrative and other services for the insurance and mutual fund industries (the mutual fund administration operations were sold in 1995). Managing this growth was another story: Its acquisitions left it bloated and disorganized. Technical systems were in disarray by the early 1990s and the agency force had grown to more than 1400. In response the company began a five-year effort to upgrade systems cut fat and reduce sales positions.

In view of its shifting focus State Mutual became Allmerica Financial in 1992. Three years later it demutualized. In 1997 it bought the 40% of Allmerica Property & Casualty it didn't already own.

EXECUTIVES

Evp General Counsel And Assistant Secretary, J. Kendall Huber, age 63, $498,077 total compensation

Evp And Cfo, Jeffrey M. (Jeff) Farber, age 53, $150,000 total compensation

Evp And Chief Claims Officer, Mark Welzenbach, age 58

President And Ceo, John C. (Jack) Roche, age 54, $470,385 total compensation

Chief Growth Innovation Officer, Richard W. (Dick) Lavey

Chief Investment Officer; President Opus Investment Management, Ann K. Tripp, age 59

Ceo And Chief Underwriting Officer Chaucer, John Fowle, age 48

Chief Technology Innovation Officer, Mark L. Berthiaume, age 61

Evp And Chief Human Resources Officer, Christine Bilotti-Peterson, age 47

Evp Corporate Development And Strategy, Mark L. Keim, age 52

Evp; President Specialty, Bryan J. Salvatore

Vice President Management Liability Of Commercial Lines Business, Helen Savaiano

Vice President And General Auditor, Don Gilbert

Vice President, Charles Kingsbury

Vice President Investor Relations, Oksana Lukasheva

Vice President Commercial Surety, Carrick Bligh

Assistant Vice President Program Director, Dennis Warren

Assistant Vice President Program Director, Mark Fikucki

Vice President Claims, James McSheffrey

Regional Vice President, John Buckalew

Vice President Technology Niche, Anthony Levy

Vice President Of Corporate Real Estate, James Johnson

Regional Vice President, SCOTT BETLESKY

Vice President Risk Management, Cheryl Nesta

Vice President And Chief Product Officer Personal Lines, Gavin Blair

Assistant Vice President Business Integration, Kevin D Pray

Assistant Vice President Marine Uw Development, Mary Corcoran

Assistant Vice President Sales Effectiveness Sales Training Field Operations, Larry Kaczmarek

Director Media Relations, Emily Trevallion

Assistant Vice President Product Management, Joseph Brophy

Vice President Marketing And Comm., Jennifer F Luisa

Assistant Vice President Property Large Loss, Joe Green

Vice President Of Information Technology, Patty Kularski

Branch Vice President, Mark E Mcgregor

Regional Vice President, Gregory L Parr

Regional Vice President, Steve Schaeberle

Assistant Vice President And Financial Officer, Randy Dinjian

Assistant Vice President, Lisa Binnie

Vice President, Anurag Bairathi

Vice President Business Development, Daniel Mastrototaro

Branch Vice President, Carla Northcutt

Assistant Vice President Human Resources, Liz Berry

Vice President Chief Information Security Officer, Brian Haugli

Assistant Vice President Human Resources Business Partner, Tina Achorn

Zonal Vice President Pl, Kendra Schenkel

Assistant Vice President Human Resources Strategic Business Partner, Kelly Villanueva

Branch Vice President, Michael Sharr

Avp Liability Strategist, Doug Kratzer

Assistant Vice President Marketing And Distribution, Sari Cook

Assistant Vice President Strategic Initiatives, Taylor MacFarlane

Vice President Casualty Underwriting Commercial Lines, Coleman Johnson

Vice President Excess And Surplus Lines, Daniel Kearney

Evp General Counsel And Assistant Secretary, J. Kendall Huber, age 63

Chairman, Michael P. Angelini, age 75

Auditors: PricewaterhouseCoopers LLP

LOCATIONS

HQ: Hanover Insurance Group Inc
440 Lincoln Street, Worcester, MA 01653
Phone: 508 855-1000   **Fax:** 508 855-6332
Web: www.hanover.com

PRODUCTS/OPERATIONS

2017 Sales

	$ mil.	% of total
Net premiums earned		
Commercial lines	2,399	46
Personal lines	1,580	31
Chaucer	853	16
Net investment income	298	6
Net realized investment gains	23	-
Fees & other	29	1
Total	**5,184**	**100**

Selected Products

Personal Lines
  Auto Insurance
  Companion Products
  Dwelling Fire
  Home Care Services
  Homeowners Insurance
  Identity Integrity
  Umbrella
  Valuable Items
  Watercraft
Small Commercial and Middle Market Core Products
  Business Owner's Policy
  Commercial Automobile
  Commercial Package
  General Liability
  Property
  Umbrella

Workers' Compensation
Specialized Products
  AIX Specialty Programs
  Commercial Umbrella and Excess
  Healthcare
  Industrial Property Risk
  Management Liability
  Marine (inland and ocean)
  Professional Liability
  Surety (commercial and contract)

COMPETITORS

Alleghany Corporation	Liberty Mutual
Allstate	Markel Insurance
American Automobile	Nationwide
Association (AAA)	Progressive
American Financial	Corporation
Group	State Farm
Auto-Owners Insurance	Travelers Companies
GEICO	USAA

HISTORICAL FINANCIALS

Company Type: Public

Income Statement   FYE: December 31

	ASSETS ($ mil.)	NET INCOME ($ mil.)	INCOME AS % OF ASSETS	EMPLOYEES
12/17	15,469	186	1.2%	4,600
12/16	14,220	155	1.1%	4,900
12/15	13,790	331	2.4%	4,800
12/14	13,759	282	2.0%	5,100
12/13	13,378	251	1.9%	5,100
Annual Growth	3.7%	(7.2%)	—	(2.5%)

2017 Year-End Financials

Debt ratio: 5.09%
Return on equity: 6.36%
Cash ($ mil.): 376
Current ratio: —
Long-term debt ($ mil.): —
No. of shares (mil.): 42
Dividends
  Yield: 0.0%
  Payout: 47.1%
Market value ($ mil.): 4,593

	STOCK PRICE ($) FY Close	P/E High/Low		PER SHARE ($) Earnings	Dividends	Book Value
12/17	108.08	25	18	4.33	2.04	70.53
12/16	91.01	25	20	3.59	1.88	67.39
12/15	81.34	11	9	7.40	1.69	66.15
12/14	71.32	11	8	6.28	1.52	64.78
12/13	59.71	11	7	5.59	1.36	59.37
Annual Growth	16.0%	—	—	(6.2%)	10.7%	4.4%

HarborOne Bancorp Inc

LOCATIONS

HQ: HarborOne Bancorp Inc
  770 Oak Street, Brockton, MA 02301
Phone: 508 895-1000
Web: www.harborone.com

HISTORICAL FINANCIALS

Company Type: Public

Income Statement   FYE: December 31

	ASSETS ($ mil.)	NET INCOME ($ mil.)	INCOME AS % OF ASSETS	EMPLOYEES
12/17	2,684	10	0.4%	581
12/16	2,448	5	0.2%	614
12/15	2,163	5	0.3%	387
12/14	2,041	2	0.1%	—
Annual Growth	9.6%	59.2%	—	—

2017 Year-End Financials

Debt ratio: 9.18%
Return on equity: 3.09%
Cash ($ mil.): 80
Current ratio: —
Long-term debt ($ mil.): —
No. of shares (mil.): 32
Dividends
  Yield: —
  Payout: —
Market value ($ mil.): 626

	STOCK PRICE ($) FY Close	P/E High/Low		PER SHARE ($) Earnings	Dividends	Book Value
12/17	19.16	67	49	0.33	0.00	10.52
12/16	19.34	—	—	(0.00)	0.00	10.25
12/15	0.00	—	—	(0.00)	0.00	(0.00)
Annual Growth	—	—	—	—	—	—

Harley-Davidson Inc

Harley-Davidson is a major US maker of motorcycles and seller of heavyweight cruisers. The company offers touring and custom Harleys through a worldwide network of more than 1460 dealers. The company manufactures and markets six families of motorcycles: Touring Dyna Softail Street Sportster and V-Rod. It also makes three-wheeled motorcycles. Harley-Davidson sells attitude with its brand-name products which include a line of clothing and accessories (MotorClothes). Harley-Davidson Financial Services (HDFS) offers financing to dealers and consumers in the US and Canada.

Operations

The company operates through two segments. Its core motorcycle manufacturing operations generate around 90% of its revenue each year; Harley-Davidson Financial Services contributes the remainder of revenue.

Harley-Davidson's Touring Dyna Softail Street and Sportster are equipped with air-cooled twin-cylinder engines (in a 45-degree "V" configuration) while its V-Rod sports a 60-degree "V" configuration twin-cylinder engine that is liquid cooled.

The company also makes special editions for peace officers and firefighters. Its products and related lifestyle are supported by H.O.G. (Harley Owners Group). Harley also supports a rental and tour program market and a rider training program known as Riders Edge.

Geographic Reach

Harley-Davidson generates 60% of its total sales from the US. Its operations are located in the Asia/Pacific Europe the Middle East Africa Latin America and the US. Manufacturing and regional offices reside in Brazil India Australia New Zealand Singapore and the UK.

Sales and Marketing

Harley-Davidson's motorcycles are sold to customers through a network of independent distributors. The company spends around $130 million each year on advertising. Its products are marketed to retail customers worldwide primarily through advertising and promotional activities via various broadcast print and electronic channels. The company targets young adults ages 18-34 women African-Americans and Hispanics as well as Caucasian men ages 35-plus.

Financial Performance

Harley-Davidson's revenues remained static for both 2015 and 2016 hovering around the $6 billion mark for both years. The company's profits also fell 8% from $752 million in 2015 to $692 million in 2016. Cash flow from operations increased from $1.1 billion to $1.17 billion during that same time period due to lower net cash out-

flows from wholesale lending and favorable changes in working capital driven by a reduction in inventory.

Wholesale shipments of Harley-Davidson motorcycles were down 2% in 2016 compared to the prior year; this was in line with a 2% decrease in dealer retail sales of new Harley-Davidson motorcycles. Its motorcycles segment was also affected by unfavorable manufacturing costs and unfavorable foreign currency exchange rates. In addition its Financial Services segment experienced decreased sales primarily due to a higher provision for credit losses.

Strategy

In the midst of a soft US industry driven by weak oil-dependent region sales Harley-Davidson is focused on growing internationally. To support this initiative it has two CKD (complete knock down) assembly plants which assemble motorcycles from component kits produced by its US plants and by its suppliers. Its first CKD plant is located in Brazil and has been in operation since 1999 and its second CKD resides in India and has been in operation since 2011.

As a primary means of growth the company adds new dealerships to its network each year. In 2016 it added 40 new international dealerships and it plans to add a total of 150 to 200 from 2016 through 2020.

Tapping an important new market Harley-Davidson has introduced its prototype Livewire electric bike and has plans to launch it to the market within the next five years. In total the company plans to introduce 100 new motorcycles over the next 10 years including an entire range of electric vehicles.

HISTORY

In 1903 William Harley and the Davidson brothers (Walter William and Arthur) of Milwaukee sold their first Harley-Davidson motorcycle which essentially was motor-assisted bicycle that required pedaling uphill. Demand was high and most sold before leaving the factory. Six years later the company debuted its trademark two-cylinder V-twin engine. By 1913 it had 150 competitors.

EXECUTIVES

Vp Communications; President Harley-davidson Foundation Inc., Joanne M. Bischmann, age 56
President And Coo Harley-davidson Financial Services, Lawrence G. Hund, age 61, $596,668 total compensation
Vp General Counsel And Secretary, Paul J. Jones, age 48, $546,667 total compensation
President And Ceo, Matthew S. (Matt) Levatich, age 53, $1,041,667 total compensation
Svp And Cfo, John A. Olin, age 57, $651,500 total compensation
Coo Harley-davidson Motor Company, Michelle A. Kumbier, $560,000 total compensation
Svp Global Demand, Sean J. Cummings, age 55
Vice President Marketing Harley Davidson Financial Services, Eduardo Bravo
Vice President Operations, Leah Mann
Vp General Counsel And Secretary, Paul J. Jones, age 48
Chairman, Michael J. (Mike) Cave, age 58
Auditors: Ernst & Young LLP

LOCATIONS

HQ: Harley-Davidson Inc
  3700 West Juneau Avenue, Milwaukee, WI 53208
Phone: 414 342-4680
Web: www.harley-davidson.com

2016 Sales

	$ mil.	% of total
US	3,579	60
EMEA	798	13
Canada	212	4
Australia	181	3
Japan	200	3
Other	299	5
Financial Services	725	12
Total	**5,996**	**100**

PRODUCTS/OPERATIONS

2016 Sales

	$ mil.	% of total
Motorcycle & related parts	5,271	88
Financial services	725	12
Total	**5,996**	**100**

Selected Motorcycles

Harley-Davidson
  CVO (custom vehicle operations)
  Road Gllide Ultra
  Softail Convertible
  Street Glide
  Ultra Classic Electroglide
  Dyna
  Fat BOB
  Street BOB
  Super Glide Custom
  Wide Glide
  Softail
  Black Line
  Cross Bones
  Fat Boy
  Heritage Softail Classic
  Night Train
  Rocker C
  Softail Deluxe
  Sportster
  883 (Low and Custom)
  1200 (Custom and Low)
  Forty Eight
  Iron 883
  Nightster
  SuperLow
  XR1200X
  Touring
  Electra Glide (Standard Classic and Ultra Classic)
  Road Glide Ultra
  Road King (and Classic)
  Street Glide
  Tri Glide Ultra Classic
  Trike
  Street Glide Trike
  Tri Glide Ultra Classic
  VRSC
  Night Rod Special
  V-Rod (and V-Rod Muscle)

Selected Operations

Motorcycles
  Harley-Davidson Motor Company
Financial services
  Harley-Davidson Financial Services Inc.
  Harley-Davidson Credit
  Harley-Davidson Insurance

COMPETITORS

BMW	Polaris Industries
Ducati	Triumph Motorcycles
Honda	Ultra Motorcycle
Indian Motorcycle	Viper Motorcycle

HISTORICAL FINANCIALS

Company Type: Public

Income Statement

FYE: December 31

	REVENUE ($ mil.)	NET INCOME ($ mil.)	NET PROFIT MARGIN	EMPLOYEES
12/17	5,647	521	9.2%	5,800
12/16	5,996	692	11.5%	6,000
12/15	5,995	752	12.5%	6,300
12/14	6,228	844	13.6%	6,500
12/13	5,899	733	12.4%	6,400
Annual Growth	(1.1%)	(8.2%)	—	(2.4%)

2017 Year-End Financials

Debt ratio: 70.07%
Return on equity: 27.72%
Cash ($ mil.): 687
Current ratio: 1.23
Long-term debt ($ mil.): 4,587

No. of shares (mil.): 168
Dividends
  Yield: 0.0%
  Payout: 48.3%
Market value ($ mil.): 8,552

	STOCK PRICE ($) FY Close	P/E High/Low	Earnings	Dividends	Book Value
12/17	50.88	21 15	3.02	1.46	10.97
12/16	58.34	16 10	3.83	1.40	10.91
12/15	45.39	18 12	3.69	1.24	9.96
12/14	65.91	19 14	3.88	1.10	13.73
12/13	69.24	21 15	3.28	0.84	13.68
Annual Growth	(7.4%)	— —	(2.0%)	14.8%	(5.4%)

Harris Corp.

Harris Corp. keeps customers communicating on the battlefield in the air and space and just about everywhere else. The company develops communications products for government and commercial customers in more than 100 countries. It makes radio-frequency (RF) and satellite communications and other wireless network transmission equipment; air traffic control systems; and digital network management systems. About three-quarter of Harris' revenue comes from US government agencies particularly the Department of Defense. Its commercial clients come from the construction energy health care maritime oil transportation and utilities industries. In 2018 Harris agreed to merge with L3 Technologies to form what would be the sixth biggest defense contracting firm in the US.

Change in Company Type

Harris agreed in 2018 to merge with L3 Technologies to form L3 Harris Technologies a company that would have $16 billion in revenue. The combined company would have complementary products and services and deeper resources that would enable it to bid on large-scale Department of Defense projects. The all-stock deal would result in Harris shareholders owning 54% of the company and L3 shareholders owning the rest. The company would fall in line behind Lockheed Martin Boeing General Dynamics and Northrop Grumman as one of the biggest defense contractors in the US and in the top 10 internationally. The companies expect the deal to close in mid-2019.

Operations

Harris Corp. has reorganized its divisions following divestitures and to better reflect its operations.

Its Communication Systems segment about 30% of revenue develops and makes tactical communications and defense products including tactical ground and airborne radio communications equipment and night vision technology and equipment for public safety networks.

The Electronic Systems 40% of revenue provides electronic warfare avionics and command control communications computers intelligence surveillance and reconnaissance equipment for the defense industry. It also makes air traffic management systems for civil aviation.

Space and Intelligence Systems 30% of revenue provides intelligence space protection geospatial complete Earth observation universe exploration positioning navigation and timing and environmental equipment for national security defense civil and commercial customers. Among its products are advanced sensors antennas and payloads as well as ground processing and information analytics.

Geographic Reach

Harris Corp. operates some 170 locations in Canada Europe the Middle East Central and South America Africa Asia Caribbean Latin American and the US. Exports account for about 20% of revenue; no foreign customer accounts for more than 5% of revenue.

Sales and Marketing

Harris Corp.?s primary customers are US government agencies including prime contractors and supported foreign defense organizations accounting for about 75% of sales.

Financial Performance

Harris Corp.?s revenue fell is 2017 (ended June) no matter how it?s figured. The company has made divestitures and made its past financials reflect current operations. Without that refiguring revenue fell 21% in 2017 from 2016. With the company?s recalculation revenue dropped just 2%. The rest of this report will use Harris? recalculated numbers.

The decrease company attributed the revenue drop to lower Tactical Communications revenue in the Communication Systems segment and lower revenue due to the impact of the divestiture of the Aerostructures business in the fourth quarter of 2016. Other factors were environmental and commercial space programs in the Space and Intelligence Systems segment that moved from build-out to sustainment. Bringing in more revenue were the ramp up of the United Arab Emirates integrated battle management system program electronic warfare in the Electronic Systems segment and a $36 million revenue increase from classified customers in the Space and Intelligence Systems segment.

Harris reported a 70% jump in net income to $553 million in 2017 from 2016. The big difference was a lower loss from discontinued operations in 2017 $85 million compared to loss of $287 million in 2016.

Cash flow from operations fell to $569 million in 207 from $924 million in 2016 because of a $415 million payment to the company pension plan and $127 million less of impairment of goodwill and other assets.

Strategy

Harris Corp. has reconfigured its operations through a series of five divestitures in the past four years. That has provided the company with the resources to focus on what it considers growth opportunities: managed satellite communications public safety and professional communications health care IT and emerging national markets particularly in the energy maritime and government sectors.

The company has rolled out several products that reflect the new focus. They include an HF manpack radio that provides soldiers with 10 times faster data rates than other equipment an advanced wideband phased-array antenna with improved anti-jamming electronic warfare capabilities and an environmental sensor that more precisely detects greenhouse gas emissions and a robotic system with human-like dexterity for ease of use in bomb disposal and other applications.

Harris? changes have increased its sales to and dependence on government and particularly defense-related customers. Sales to federal agencies account for about three-quarters of revenue up from about two-thirds in 2015. Not all of it is defense however. Some government work is related to civil agencies in law enforcement and aviation.

Mergers and Acquisitions

While most of Harris Corp.?s focus has been on divesting operations that no longer fit into its product mix it has made one significant acquisition. In 2015 it bought Exelis provider of communications products catering to the government in a transaction worth $4.7 billion. The deal beefed up Harris' presence in the government sector.

EXECUTIVES

Chairman President And Ceo, William M. (Bill) Brown, age 55, $1,172,913 total compensation
Svp And Chief Global Business Development Officer, Dana A. Mehnert, age 56, $527,770 total compensation
Svp Integration And Engineering, Sheldon J. Fox, age 60, $521,346 total compensation
President Critical Networks, Carl D'Alessandro, age 54
Svp Human Resources And Administration, Robert L. Duffy, age 50, $459,885 total compensation
Cio, Henry Debnam
President Electronic Systems, Edward J. (Ed) Zoiss, age 52
President Space And Intelligence Systems, William H. (Bill) Gattle, age 56
President Communication Systems, Christopher D. (Chris) Young, age 57, $411,749 total compensation
Svp And Cfo, Rahul Ghai, age 46, $376,238 total compensation
Senior Vice President Of Business Development, Alex Heidt
Vice President Of Supply Chain Management And Operations, Janice Lindsay
Vice President Corporate Technology, Kent Buchanon
Vice President Controller, Daniel Heneghan
Vice President Operations, Paul North
Vice President Sales, John Koening
Broker And Vice President, George Hurst
Vice President Products And Systems, Shawn Baerlocher
Vice President Large Account Sales, Kevin Lombardo
Vice President Investor Relations, Pamela Padgett
Senior Vice President, Neal Serven
Vice President Information Technology, Michele St Mary
Vice President, Brett Kleefisch
Vice President, Daniel Flugstad
Vice President General Counsel, Eugene Cavallucci
Vice President Information Technology, Mark Gawron
Vice President, Paul Eisner
Vice President Human Resources, Ken Laprade
Vice President Lean Six Sigma, Phil Burroughs
Vice President Finance Public Safety And Professional Communications, William Cullen
Vice President, Erick Sanz
Chairman President And Ceo, William M. (Bill) Brown, age 55
Engineering Team Manager Treasurer, David Bruder
Treasurer, Steve Thompson
Treasurer, Harmon David
Auditors: Ernst & Young LLP

LOCATIONS

HQ: Harris Corp.
 1025 West NASA Boulevard, Melbourne, FL 32919
Phone: 321 727-9100
Web: www.harris.com

2017 sales

	$ mil.	% of total
US	5,639	95
Other countries	261	5
Total	**5,900**	**100**

PRODUCTS/OPERATIONS

2017 sales

	$ mil.	% of total
Communication systems	1,753	30
Space and intelligence systems	1,902	30
Electronic systems	2,251	40
Adjustments	(6)	-
Total	**5,900**	**100**

Selected Product Groups

Government Communications Systems
 Civil programs
 Aviation
 Weather
 IT services
 Mission command-and-control
 National intelligence programs
Radio-frequency (RF) Communications
 Antennas and accessories
 Information assurance
 Internet protocol voice and data networks
 Public safety
 Tactical radio communications

COMPETITORS

Advisory Board	Lockheed Martin
Airbus Group	ManTech
Alcatel-Lucent	Motorola Solutions
Amper	NCI
Avid Technology	NEC
BAE Systems Inc.	NSN
Boeing	Nortel Networks
CACI International	Northrop Grumman
Ceragon Networks	Orion HealthCorp
ChyronHego	Pilat Media
Cisco Systems	Raytheon
Computer Sciences	RigNet
Corp.	Rockwell Collins
Dell	Rohde & Schwarz
Elbit Systems	SELEX SI
Ericsson	Sony
General Dynamics	Technicolor
Globecomm	Tektronix
HP	Telos
Harmonic	Thales
IBM	UNICOM Government
L3 Technologies	Vizrt
Leidos	WideOrbit

HISTORICAL FINANCIALS

Company Type: Public

Income Statement   FYE: June 29

	REVENUE ($ mil.)	NET INCOME ($ mil.)	NET PROFIT MARGIN	EMPLOYEES
06/18	6,182	718	11.6%	17,500
06/17*	5,900	553	9.4%	17,000
07/16	7,467	324	4.3%	21,000
07/15	5,083	334	6.6%	22,300
06/14	5,012	534	10.7%	14,000
Annual Growth	**5.4%**	**7.6%**	**—**	**5.7%**

*Fiscal year change

2018 Year-End Financials

Debt ratio: 38.52%	No. of shares (mil.): 118
Return on equity: 23.04%	Dividends
Cash ($ mil.): 288	Yield: 1.5%
Current ratio: 1.24	Payout: 43.8%
Long-term debt ($ mil.): 3,408	Market value ($ mil.): 17,096

	STOCK PRICE ($) FY Close	P/E High/Low		PER SHARE ($) Earnings	Dividends	Book Value
06/18	144.54	28	18	5.92	2.28	28.09
06/17*	109.08	25	18	4.44	2.12	34.48
07/16	82.59	34	27	2.59	2.00	24.52
07/15	77.74	26	20	3.11	1.88	27.47
06/14	75.98	16	10	4.95	1.68	17.31
Annual Growth	**17.4%**	—	—	**4.6%**	**7.9%**	**12.9%**

*Fiscal year change

Hartford Financial Services Group Inc.

The Hartford Financial Services Group is an insurer offering a range of commercial and personal property/casualty insurance and financial products. Its commercial operations include auto liability and workers' compensation policies as well as group benefits and specialty commercial coverage for large companies. The Hartford also offers consumer homeowners and auto coverage. The group has been the direct auto and home insurance writer for AARP's members for more than 30 years. Through its mutual fund division the company offers wealth management products and services. The Hartford has been in business since 1810.

HISTORY

In 1810 a group of Hartford Connecticut businessmen led by Walter Mitchell and Henry Terry founded the Hartford Fire Insurance Co. Frequent fires in America's wooden cities and executive ignorance of risk assessment and premium-setting often left the firm on the edge of insolvency. (In 1835 stockholders staged a coup and threw management out.) Still each urban conflagration — including the Great Chicago Fire of 1871 — gave The Hartford an opportunity to seek out and pay all its policyholders thus teaching the company to underwrite under fire as it were and to use such disasters to refine its rates.

The company's stag logo was initially a little deer as shown on a policy sold to Abraham Lincoln in 1861. A few years later however Hartford began using the majestic creature (from a Landseer painting) now familiar to customers. By the 1880s Hartford operated nationwide as well as in Canada and Hawaii.

The company survived both world wars and the Depression but emerged in the 1950s in need of organization. It set up new regional offices and added life insurance buying Columbian National Life (founded 1902) which became Hartford Life Insurance Co.

In 1969 Hartford was bought by ITT (formerly International Telephone and Telegraph) whose CEO Harold Geneen was an avid conglomerateur. Consumer advocate Ralph Nader strongly opposed the acquisition — he fought the merger in court for years and felt vindicated when ITT spun off Hartford in 1995. Others opposed it too because ITT had engineered the merger based on an IRS ruling (later revoked) that Hartford stockholders wouldn't have to pay capital gains taxes on the purchase price of their stock.

Insurance operations consolidated under the Hartford Life Insurance banner in 1978. Through the 1980s Hartford Life remained one of ITT's strongest operations. A conservative investment policy kept Hartford safe from the junk bond and real estate manias of the 1980s.

Hartford reorganized its property/casualty operations along three lines in 1986 and in 1992 it organized its reinsurance business into one unit. The company faced some liability in relation to Dow Corning's breast-implant litigation but underwriting standards after 1985 reduced long-term risk. In 1994 the company began selling insurance products to AARP members under an exclusive agreement. In 1996 the company finished its spin-off from ITT which was acquired by Starwood Hotels & Resorts two years later.

To grow its reinsurance operation Hartford acquired the reinsurance business of Orion Capital (now Royal & SunAlliance USA) in 1996. It posted a loss of $99 million due in large part to asbestos and pollution liabilities. Late that year the firm changed its name to The Hartford Financial Services Group.

To shore up reserves and fund growth in 1997 the company spun off 19% of Hartford Life. The Hartford expanded into nonstandard auto insurance in 1998 by buying Omni Insurance Group (since sold in 2006). The company also sold its London & Edinburgh Insurance Group in 1998 to Norwich Union (now part of Aviva formerly CGNU). In 1999 The Hartford acquired the reinsurance business of Vesta Fire Insurance a subsidiary of Vesta Insurance Group.

In 2000 Hartford bought back the part of Hartford Life it had spun off. The Hartford also bought the financial products and excess and surplus specialty insurance lines of Reliance Group Holdings. Assurances GA©nA©rales de France bought the company's Dutch subsidiary Zwolsche Algemeene. In 2001 the company bought Fortis Financial a US subsidiary of Belgian insurer Fortis and sold Hartford Seguros its Spanish sub

EXECUTIVES

President, Douglas G. (Doug) Elliot, age 58, $918,750 total compensation

Evp Group Benefits, Michael (Mike) Concannon, age 56

Chairman And Ceo, Christopher J. Swift, age 57, $1,075,000 total compensation

Chief Investment Officer, Brion Johnson, age 58, $525,000 total compensation

Evp Digital Commerce And Customer Analytics, Jonathan R. Bennett, age 54

Evp And Property And Casual Chief Underwriting Officer, A. Morris (Mo) Tooker

Cfo, Beth A. Bombara, age 50, $687,500 total compensation

Evp Human Resources, Martha (Marty) Gervasi, age 56

President Hartford Funds, James E. (Jim) Davey, age 53

Evp And Chief Risk Officer, Robert R. Rupp, age 65, $600,000 total compensation

Evp Operations Technology And Data, William A. (Bill) Bloom, age 54

Svp And Secretary, David C. Robinson, age 53

Evp Personal Lines, Raymond J. (Ray) Sprague, age 59

Evp Small Commercial, Stephanie Bush

Chief Claims Officer, John Kinney

Vice President Marketing Communications And Sponsorships, Laura Marzi

Senior Vice President Treasure, John Giamalis

Vice President, Debra Fox

Assistant Vice President Service Strategy, Sue Sweeney

Vice President Underwriting And Operations Small Commercial At The Hartford, Jim Williamson

Assistant Vice President Human Resources, Daniel O'Shea

Assistant Vice President Corporate Communications, Paula McGinley

Assistant Vice President Server And Storage Engineering, Ryan Wilhelm

Senior Vice President Product And Strategy, Mike Fish

Assistant Vice President Loss Control Product And Strategy, Dorothy Doyle

Vice President Strategy And Corporate Development, Devi Mohanty

Assistant Vice President Risk Management, John Rogers

Assistant Vice President Security, Daniel Lewis

Avp Enterprise Model Risk Management, Joanne Courtright

Assistant Vice President, Carolyn L Kopper

Assistant Vice President Senior Counsel And Assistant Secretary, Terence Shields

Assistant Vice President Claim Account Management, Sean Faherty

Vice President Marketing Analytics And Media Execution, Gary Coleman

Vice President Strategy, Kari Ratajczak

Vice President Construction Insurance, Thomas M Boudreau

Divisional Vice President, Augie Chella

Regional Vice President, Anthony Phifer

National Account Manager, Shelly Birkholz

Assistant Vice President And Counsel, Andrew Golden

National Account Manager Group Benefits, Kevin Goff

Assistant Vice President Industry Practices, Melissa Zaparanick

Vice President Of Communications, Donna Gendreau

National Account Manager Group Benefits, Sarah Berard

Assistant Vice President Group Benefits Relationship Management, Alison Colli

Vice President Enterprise Process Improvement, Troy Nagel

Senior Vice President And General Auditor, Michael Hession

Assistant Vice President Uw Small Comm, Kenneth Zygiel

Assistant Vice President, Jeanne Fenster

Assistant Vice President And Actuary, Ken Kasner

Vice President Integrated Marketing, Lori Allen

Senior Vice President Procurement, Jahn Surette

Vice President Houston, Jeffrey Lange

Mbr 1st Vice President, Mayer Goldberger

Assistant Vice President And Senior Risk Manager, Xiangrong Cai

Legal Secretary, Sandra Branz

Assistant Vice President And Senior Counsel, Jason Kuselias

Assistant Vice President Assistant General Counsel, Liz Steigman

Vice President And Assistant General Counsel, Laura Santirocco

Senior Vice President Sales And Distribution Commercial Markets Division, Mathew Kirk

Assistant Vice President Commercial Markets Technology, Ann Nemphos

Vice President Sales And Distribution Operations, Matthew Montminy

Assistant Vice President Counsel, Brian Fresher

Senior Tax Counsel Assistant Vice President, William Elwell

Assistant Vice President, Susan D Bencher

Vice President And General Cou, Danielle Woolsey

Assistant Vice President Senior Counsel, Cedric Delacruz

Assistant Vice President Finance Business Lead, Steven Paccioretti

Assistant Vice President And Senior Risk Manager, Michael Nguyen

Assistant Vice President And Counsel, Deborah A Millum

Regional Vice President, Mark Shears

Vice President Auto And Property Strategy, Mike Lawlor

Assistant Vice President Property Line Lead, Eric Cannon

Assistant Vice President Human Resources, Daniel Oshea

Executive Vice President, David Johnson

Assistant Vice President And Assistant Treasurer, Mike Fixer

Assistant Vice President Information Technology Program Management, Steven Hatch

Vice President Internal Audit, Robin Generous

Assistant Vice President Financial Planning And Analysis, Stephen Logan

Regional Vice President Hartford Mutual Funds, Curtis Ranta

Assistant Vice President, Gurunatham Pellakuru

Assistant Vice President Product Management, Chad Mirock

Vice President Government Affairs, Cliff Leach

Vice President Research, Isaac Adams

Vice President And Assistant General Counsel, Kevin LaFreniere

Assistant Vice President, Tracy Charbonneau

Assistant Vice President And Counsel, Andrew Daly

Vice President, Alice Pellegrino

Assistant Vice President, James Plante

Assistant Vice President Claims, Barbara Agulnek

Vice President Of Committees, Sharon Havrilak

Assistant Vice President Information Technology Operations And Back Office, Sam Balasubramaniyam

Assistant Vice President Information Technology Quality, Dianne Bertolet-Duff

Assistant Vice President Internal Communication, Kristin Tetreault

Assistant Vice President Claims, Debbie Kane

Vice President Project Management Office, Ellen Below

Assistant Vice President Project Management And Planning, Bob Leyden

Assistant Vice President Product Management, Sean Meehan

Assistant Vice President And Counsel, Michael Petropoulos

Assistant Vice President And Actuary, Greg Larsson

Senior Vice President And Controller, Scott Lewis

Vice President Large Loss, Charlene Ridgeway

Assistant Vice President Reinsurance, Salvatore Morelli

Assistant Vice President, Steve Thompson

Associate Vice President Shared Infrastructure Services, Steven Blum

Assistant Vice President Information Technology, Benjamin Davidson

Senior Vice President Small Commercial Sales, Lisa Morgan

Vice President Finance, Thomas Peloquin

Vice President Applied Research And Analytics, Peter Bothwell

Assistant Vice President, Tracey Kamenash

Assistant Vice President, Deb Szaraburak

Vice President Eso, Srini Krishnamurthy

Assistant Vice President Information Technology, Carolyn Small

Vice President Of Operations, Marc Mailloux

Assistant Vice President Prod Development, Bryan R Smith

Assistant Vice President Small Commercial
Information Technology, Brian Pierz
Vice President Product Management, Brent
Radeloff
Senior Vice President And Controller Pandc
Operations, Fred Jones
Assistant Vice President Small Commercial Sales,
Kim Stuhr
Assistant Vice President Agency Compensation,
Keith Lawler
Vice President Claims Operations, Matthew Scott
Regional Senior Vice President, Michael Parker
Vice President E Business Delivery, Thomas
Nogles
Vice President Digital Strategy, Kevin Keller
Assistant Vice President Finance Executive
Management, Anthony Horvath
Avp Enterprise Process Improvement, Doug Muzzy
Avp Personal Auto Data Science, Josh Grunin
Vice President Internal Communications And
Corporate Sustainability, Paula Angelo
Assistant Vice President Security, Daniel J Lewis
Vice President Liability Field Claims, Richard
Bowman
Vice President And Actuary, Robert FSA
Assistant Vice President Group Benefits Claim
Practices, Sally Monson
Avp Enterprise Strategy And Business
Development, Ariadna Khafizova
Assistant Vice President, Maria Manuele
Avp And Director It And Customer Service For
Europe, Joanne Stjames
Vice President Enterprise Operations, Michelle
Buswell
Vice President Sales And Distribution, Andrew
Plousi
Vice President Bond, Richard Ciullo
Vice President Marketing, Tracy Wade
Assistant Vice President, Timothy Scully
Vice President And Deputy Associate Counsel For
Co, Ronald Apter
Assistant Vice President Northeast Region
Underwriting, Chuck Gill
Assistant Vice President Senior Counsel, Pauline
Wallace
Assistant Vice President Oper Initiatives, Douglas
Muzzy
Assistant Vice President And Actuary, Jenni Prior
Assistant Vice President Risk Management, Daniel
Oconnell
Assistant Vice President Commercial Compliance,
Melissa Baribault
Avp Claims Solutions, Stephanie Polzella
Vice President Claim Continuous Performance
Improvement, Karmela Malone
Assistant Vice President Information Technology
Operations And Back Office, Thirugnanap
Balasubramaniyam
Assistant Vice President Construction Group,
Shelli Hamilton
Avp Compensation, Lynn Faraca-bond
Auditors: DELOITTE & TOUCHE LLP

LOCATIONS

HQ: Hartford Financial Services Group Inc.
One Hartford Plaza, Hartford, CT 06155
Phone: 860 547-5000
Web: www.thehartford.com

PRODUCTS/OPERATIONS

2017 Sales by Segment

	$ mil.	% of total
Commercial Lines	7,954	47
Group Benefits	4,092	24
Personal Lines	3,975	23
Mutual Funds	807	5
Property & Casualty Other Operations	120	1
Corporate	26	-
Total	**16,974**	**100**

COMPETITORS

AIG	Nationwide
Allstate	State Farm
Berkshire Hathaway	Travelers Companies
CNA Financial	Unum Group
Liberty Mutual	Zurich Insurance Group
MetLife	

HISTORICAL FINANCIALS

Company Type: Public

Income Statement

FYE: December 31

	ASSETS ($ mil.)	NET INCOME ($ mil.)	INCOME AS % OF ASSETS	EMPLOYEES
12/17	225,260	(3,131)	—	16,400
12/16	223,432	896	0.4%	16,900
12/15	228,348	1,682	0.7%	17,400
12/14	245,013	798	0.3%	17,500
12/13	277,884	176	0.1%	18,800
Annual Growth	(5.1%)	—	—	(3.4%)

2017 Year-End Financials

Debt ratio: 2.08%
Return on equity: (-20.60%)
Cash ($ mil.): 180
Current ratio: —
Long-term debt ($ mil.): —

No. of shares (mil.): 356
Dividends
Yield: 0.0%
Payout: —
Market value ($ mil.): 20,083

	STOCK PRICE ($) FY Close	P/E High/Low		PER SHARE ($) Earnings	Dividends	Book Value
12/17	56.28	—	—	(8.61)	0.94	37.82
12/16	47.65	21	16	2.27	0.86	45.20
12/15	43.46	12	10	3.96	0.78	43.91
12/14	41.69	23	18	1.73	0.66	44.11
12/13	36.23	99	61	0.34	0.50	41.71
Annual Growth	11.6%			17.1%	(2.4%)	

Hasbro, Inc.

It's all fun and games at Hasbro the #2 toy maker in the US (after Mattel) and the producer of such childhood favorites as G.I. Joe Play-Doh Tonka toys Transformers Mr. Potato Head Nerf balls and My Little Pony. Hasbro has a significant relationship with Disney producing merchandise for the entertainment giant's megabrands including Star Wars Marvel (including Spider-Man Thor and Captain America) and Frozen and other Dreamworks features. Besides toys Hasbro makes board games such as Scrabble Monopoly and Trivial Pursuit as well as trading cards including Magic: The Gathering (through its Wizards of the Coast unit) and Dungeons & Dragons .

Operations

Hasbro divides its products into four brand categories: Franchise Brands Partner Brands Hasbro Gaming and Emerging Brands.

Franchise Brands are the company's core growth drivers and consist of seven brands that offer sustained revenue for the long term: Littlest Pet Shop Magic: the Gathering Monopoly My Little Pony Nerf Play-Doh and Transformers. Franchise Brands account for around half of total revenue.

Partner Brands encompasses Hasbro's licensed brands (principally from Disney) for which it makes toys and games. These include Marvel Star Wars Disney's Descendants Dreamworks' Trolls and Sesame Street.

Hasbro's Gaming portfolio counts such well known board games as Pie Face Connect 4 Elefun & Friends Jenga The Game of Life Operation Scrabble Trivial Pursuit and Twister. The category also includes trading cards and digital games.

Emerging Brands consists of those brands Hasbro believes have potential to become Franchise Brands but need further development and investment. These include Baby Alive Furby Furreal Friends Playskool and Playskool Heroes.

Geographic Reach

More than 50% of Rhode Island-based Hasbro's total sales come from the US and Canada. Europe is its largest international market accounting for nearly two-thirds of overseas sales while emerging markets (including Brazil China and Russia) made up the rest. The toy maker operates in 40-plus countries across the Americas Europe and Asia though almost all of its products were sourced from third-party facilities the Far East (mostly in China).

Sales and Marketing

Hasbro's products are sold through wholesalers distributors chain stores discount stores drug stores mail order houses catalog stores and department stores among other outlets. The company's top three customers are Wal-Mart (which accounts for nearly 20% of sales) Toys "R" Us (nearly 10%) and Target (nearly 10%). In the US around 60% of the toy maker's revenue is derived from these top three chains.

Hasbro markets products via television and digital devices (including Netflix and iTunes). It also showcases certain new products at the American International Toy Fair held each February in New York City.

Financial Performance

Hasbro's sales and profits have been steadily rising in recent years as demand for toys (especially preschool brands) has been buoyed by strong economic and population growth in North America and abroad.

In fiscal 2016 sales grew a further 13% to $5.0 billion amid growth in almost all segments and geographies. Particular highlights include 15% growth in the US and Canada 9% growth in Gaming and 28% growth in Partner Brands. The important Franchise Brands segment recorded 2% growth. The only product category to decline was Preschool which fell by $7.6 million or about 1%.

Net income grew 22% to $551.4 million due to higher revenue and improved margins partially offset by a $32.9 million impairment charge relating to Hasbro's investment in Backflip.

Cash from operations increased 40% to $774.9 million due to higher net income and changes in impairment deferred income taxes and accounts receivable.

Strategy

Hasbro recently extended its Marvel and Star Wars licenses when it signed deals for all properties through 2020. The move has paid off big: the two franchises continue to generate box office-topping sales figures with the annual December Star Wars release now all but assured to be that year's highest-grossing feature. The success of Disney's motion picture IPs has driven consistent year-on-year growth in Hasbro's Partner Brands segment.

Hasbro has also entirely revised its advertising approach. The company de-emphasised its advertising stalwart — television — in favor of digital channels. The social media platforms of Facebook Instagram Twitter and others have helped Hasbro create communities of millions of fans and subscribers. Additionally in 2016 Hasbro increased its ownership stake in mobile game maker Backflip from 70% to 100% to further increase its brand touchpoints; and has teamed up with gaming titan Electronic Arts to create digital versions of Monopoly Scrabble and Yahtzee. Hasbro has also pivoted away from its famous mantra of "to sell to the parents market to the kids" — the wealth of data produced by digital showed that millennials now entering parenthood were likely to buy toys they themselves used as kids.

Mergers and Acquisitions

In 2016 Hasbro acquired Dublin-based Boulder Media an animation company. Hasbro lacked an in-house cartoon creator; the acquisition will allow the company to expand its animation and storytelling.

In 2017 Hasbro increased its ownership in mobile games company Backflip from 70% to 100%.

HISTORY

Henry and Helal Hassenfeld formed Hassenfeld Brothers in Pawtucket Rhode Island in 1923 to distribute fabric remnants. By 1926 the company was manufacturing fabric-covered pencil boxes and shortly thereafter pencils.

Hassenfeld Brothers branched into the toy industry during the 1940s by introducing toy nurse and doctor kits. The company's toy division was the first to use TV to promote a toy product (Mr. Potato Head in 1952).

Expansion continued in the mid-1960s with the introduction of the G.I. Joe doll which quickly became its primary toy line. Hassenfeld Brothers went public in 1968 and changed its name to Hasbro Industries. It bought Romper Room (TV productions) the next year.

In the 1970s the toy and pencil divisions led by different family members disagreed over the company's finances future direction and leadership. The dispute caused the company to split in 1980. The toy division continued to operate under the Hasbro name; the pencil division (Empire Pencil Corporation in Shelbyville Tennessee led by Harold Hassenfeld) became a separate corporation.

EXECUTIVES

Chairman And Ceo, Brian D. Goldner, age 55, $1,300,000 total compensation
Evp And Chief Global Operations And Business Development Officer, Duncan J. Billing, age 60, $545,910 total compensation
Evp And Chief Content Officer, Stephen J. Davis, age 56
President, Johnathan A. (John) Frascotti, age 57, $772,308 total compensation
President Wizards Of The Coast, Chris Cocks
Svp And Head Corporate Finance, Deborah M. (Deb) Thomas, age 54, $690,385 total compensation
Svp Human Resources, Dolph Johnson
Evp Chief Legal Officer And Secretary, Barbara Finigan, age 57
Evp And Chief Commercial Officer, Wiebe Tinga, age 57, $592,787 total compensation
Evp Global Operations, Tom Courtney
Vice President Investor Relations, Debbie Hancock
Svp And Gm Power Rangers Franchise, Simon Waters
Senior Vice President And Cio, Steve Zoltick
Senior Vice President International Distribution And Development Hasbro Studios, Finn Arnesen
Senior Vice President Global Human Resources, Claudia Mellet
Vice President Global Tax, Edward Houde
Business Operations Vice President Director Manager, David Pomer
Vice President Legal, Michael Cashton
Vice President, David Fergenbaum
Senior Vice President Global Planning And Logistics, Ramesh Murthy
Vice President Technical Services, Jack Popp
Vice President Finance, Paul Alexander
Vice President Global Brand Management, Derryl Depriest
Vice President Benefits And Hris, Briana Sullivan

Vice President Sales Walmart, Chad Miller
Vice President Global Legal Compliance, Jaime Laporte
Vp Of Global It Operations, Steven Melanson
Vice President Finance, Tony Simms
Vice President Design And Development, Daizo Uehara
Vice President Global Ecommerce, Scott Stroud
Senior Vice President Hasbro Digital Media And Gaming Hasbro Games, Mark Blecher
Senior Vice President General Manager Hasbro Asia Pacific, Tomasz Micek
Vice President Human Resources, Robert Kiely
Vice President Marketing, Greg Ferguson
National Account Manager, Courtney I Chahal
Vice President Franchise Lead, Tyla Bucher
Chairman And Ceo, Brian D. Goldner, age 55
Secretary, Pauline Casey
Assistant Treasurer, Joanne Haworth
Auditors: KPMG

LOCATIONS

HQ: Hasbro, Inc.
  1027 Newport Avenue, Pawtucket, RI 02861
Phone: 401 431-8697
Web: www.hasbro.com

2016 Sales

	$ mil.	% of total
US & Canada	2,559	51
International	2,194	44
Entertainment & licensing	265	5
Global operations	0	-
Total	**5,019**	**100**

PRODUCTS/OPERATIONS

2016 Sales

	$ mil.	% of total
Boys	1,849	37
Games	1,387	27
Girls	1,193	24
Preschool	589	12
Total	**5,019**	**100**

Selected Product Categories

Action Battling
Action Figures & Collectibles
Apparel
Arts & Crafts
Books & Comics
Creative & Pretend Play
Dolls & Plush
Electronic Toys & Games
Games
Parts & Refills
Party Supplies
Sports & Outdoor Play
Vehicles

Selected Brands

HASBRO GAMING
Clue
Monopoly
Scrabble
Twister
Yahtzee
GIRLS
Nerf Rebelle
My Little Pony
My Little Pony Equestria Girls
Littlest Pet Shop
Furby BOYS
Nerf
Beyblade
Star Wars
B-Daman
Transformers
PRESCHOOL
Play-Doh
Playskool
FurReal Friends
Baby Alive
Elefun

COMPETITORS

Build-A-Bear	Playmates Toys
Cartoon Network	Playmobil
Enesco	Poof-Slinky
Graco Children's Products	RC2 Corporation
	Radio Flyer
JAKKS Pacific	Sanrio
LEGO	Simba Dickie Group
LeapFrog	Smoby
MGA Entertainment	Spin Master
Marvel Entertainment	TakaraTomy
Mattel	Toy Quest
Nakajima USA	Ty
Namco Bandai	VTech Holdings
Nickelodeon	WHAM-O
Ohio Art	

HISTORICAL FINANCIALS

Company Type: Public

Income Statement

	REVENUE ($ mil.)	NET INCOME ($ mil.)	NET PROFIT MARGIN	EMPLOYEES
12/17	5,209	396	7.6%	5,400
12/16	5,019	551	11.0%	5,400
12/15	4,447	451	10.2%	5,000
12/14	4,277	415	9.7%	5,200
12/13	4,082	286	7.0%	5,000
Annual Growth	**6.3%**	**8.5%**	**—**	**1.9%**

FYE: December 31

2017 Year-End Financials

Debt ratio: 34.94%
Return on equity: 21.13%
Cash ($ mil.): 1,581
Current ratio: 2.90
Long-term debt ($ mil.): 1,693
No. of shares (mil.): 124
Dividends
  Yield: 0.0%
  Payout: 71.1%
Market value ($ mil.): 11,311

	STOCK PRICE ($) FY Close	P/E High/Low	PER SHARE ($) Earnings	Dividends	Book Value
12/17	90.89	37 24	3.12	2.22	14.70
12/16	78.36	20 15	4.34	1.99	14.96
12/15	67.62	23 14	3.57	1.81	13.33
12/14	55.54	18 15	3.20	1.69	11.77
12/13	54.40	25 16	2.17	1.20	12.84
Annual Growth	**13.7%**	**— —**	**9.5%**	**16.6%**	**3.5%**

Hawthorn Bancshares Inc

EXECUTIVES

Ceo, James E Smith
Sr V Pres, Gene Henry
Sr V Pres, Ernie Spaashelm
Exec Dir, David Garnett
Coo, Kathleen Bruegenhemke
Human Resources Coordinator, Jennifer Lamb
Senior Vice-President, Chris Schrimpf
Vice-President, Todd Hoien
Regional President, Keith Asel
Loan Officer, Dan Lewis
Vice-President, David Clithero
Auditors: KPMG LLP

LOCATIONS

HQ: Hawthorn Bancshares Inc
132 East High Street, P.O. Box 688, Jefferson City, MO 65102
Phone: 573 761-6100
Web: www.hawthornbancshares.com

HISTORICAL FINANCIALS

Company Type: Public

Income Statement   FYE: December 31

	ASSETS ($ mil.)	NET INCOME ($ mil.)	INCOME AS % OF ASSETS	EMPLOYEES
12/17	1,429	3	0.2%	349
12/16	1,287	7	0.6%	343
12/15	1,200	8	0.7%	371
12/14	1,169	7	0.7%	358
12/13	1,140	4	0.4%	372
Annual Growth	5.8%	(9.0%)	—	(1.6%)

2017 Year-End Financials

Debt ratio: 11.96%
Return on equity: 3.74%
Cash ($ mil.): 62
Current ratio: —
Long-term debt ($ mil.): —

No. of shares (mil.): 6
Dividends
Yield: 0.0%
Payout: 44.9%
Market value ($ mil.): 125

	STOCK PRICE ($) FY Close	P/E High/Low	PER SHARE ($) Earnings	Dividends	Book Value
12/17	20.75	40 30	0.57	0.25	15.15
12/16	17.70	15 11	1.19	0.19	14.98
12/15	15.75	13 10	1.25	0.17	14.26
12/14	14.25	13 10	1.25	0.17	13.16
12/13	12.15	20 10	0.72	0.16	12.15
Annual Growth	14.3%	— —	(5.6%)	12.1%	5.7%

HCA Healthcare Inc

HCA dispenses TLC for a profit. HCA Healthcare (formerly HCA Holdings) through its HCA Inc. (Hospital Corporation of America) unit operates 185 hospitals — mostly acute care centers as well as three psychiatric facilities and one rehabilitation hospital — located in the US and UK. It also runs about 120 ambulatory surgery centers — as well as cancer treatment urgent care and outpatient rehab centers — that form health care networks in many of the communities it serves. In total its hospitals are home to some 44300 beds. HCA's facilities are located in more than 20 states; roughly half of its hospitals are in Florida and Texas. The HCA International unit operates the company's hospitals and clinics in the UK.

Operations

HCA is the largest for-profit hospital operator in the US providing about 5% of all the nation's hospital services. Primarily located in high-growth urban and suburban markets most of its hospitals are general acute care facilities that offer a full range of inpatient services in medical fields such as internal medicine general surgery cardiology oncology neurosurgery orthopedics and obstetrics. HCA ranks first or second in terms of inpatient market share in many of its key markets.

The hospital group also operates a handful of psychiatric rehabilitation and other specialty hospitals as well as outpatient care facilities providing a vast array of services. HCA counts on a diversified service line and revenue base to help spread its financial risk around; diversification also helps

limit the company's exposure to increased competition.

HCA typically has more than 26 million patient encounters more than 8 million emergency department visits and delivers some 218000 babies each year. The system has approximately 37000 active physicians.

Geographic Reach

HCA divides its US hospitals into two groups: The National Group covers facilities in Alaska California Florida southern Georgia Idaho Indiana northern Kentucky Nevada New Hampshire North Carolina South Carolina Utah and Virginia. The American Group covers hospitals in Colorado northern Georgia Kansas southern Kentucky Louisiana Mississippi Missouri Oklahoma Tennessee and Texas. Each group operates some 80 hospitals while the international unit runs six facilities in the UK.

The company has its highest concentration of hospitals in Florida (43 hospitals) and Texas (40).

Sales and Marketing

Managed care contracts with insurance firms account for about half of HCA's total revenue. Medicare accounts for more than 20% of revenue while Medicaid accounts for about 5%.

Financial Performance

HCA's revenues have increased steadily in recent years due to a combination of more patient admissions and increased billings per admission. Revenues rose to $41.5 billion in 2016 up 5% from 2015 after the deduction of provisions for the doubtful accounts of patients who could not pay their bills. Both equivalent admissions and revenue per equivalent admissions increased that year.

Net income rose 36% to $2.9 billion in 2016 largely due to benefits (versus costs) in legal claim costs. The rise in profits helped lead to an increase in cash flow from operations which rose 19% to $5.7 billion in 2016. Also boosting cash flow that year were positive adjustments providing by operating activities primarily the aforementioned legal claim benefits.

Strategy

HCA's strategy for growth includes five overall priorities. The first is to expand its presence in existing markets. It accomplishes this by expanding the types of service lines offered within its hospitals especially in high-margin fields such as oncology women's services and cardiology. It also aims to develop more outpatient care centers such as urgent care clinics surgery centers and freestanding emergency departments.

Secondly HCA is focused on providing the highest quality care to have the most satisfied patients. The group takes cues from its best-performing hospitals to discover ways to innovate and improve operations. Recent initiatives have been a push to reduce infections implementing hospitalist programs investing in technology and utilizing evidence-based medicine programs.

A third component of the company's strategy is to attract and recruit physicians by offering high-quality facilities with modern technologies. It also continues to expand its specialty care offerings and its outpatient facilities bringing in a variety of physicians.

Next HCA takes advantage of its national scale and its position as the leading health care provider in many communities. For example its size helps it negotiate advantageous purchasing contracts with its suppliers. Entering into favorable reimbursement terms with managed care companies also helps the company's bottom line. Current related initiatives include hiring more care navigators investing in clinical data exchange and centralizing patient transfer operations for improved coordination of care.

Finally the company is disciplined in its development efforts. It selectively buys or develops new

care facilities where the opportunity proves promising but it is also positioned to consolidate operations as the hospital industry faces new challenges. To keep operations nimble HCA also occasionally divests facilities that it deems non-core to its strategy. Additionally HCA enters into joint ventures to further expand its reach. For example in joined together with Guy's NHS Foundation Trust to open a new private care cancer facility in the UK.

Mergers and Acquisitions

Periodic acquisitions have been core to HCA's growth strategy. For instance in 2019 it bought Mission Health System which operates seven hospitals in western North Carolina for $1.5 billion. In mid-2017 it bought three hospitals (two in Texas the other in Florida) from Community Health Systems. It also agreed to buy three Houston hospitals from Tenet Healthcare.

HISTORY

In 1987 Dallas lawyer Rick Scott and Fort Worth Texas financier Richard Rainwater founded Columbia Hospital Corp. to buy two hospitals in El Paso Texas. The partners eventually sold 40% of the hospitals to local doctors hoping that ownership would motivate physicians to increase productivity and efficiency.

The company entered the Miami market the next year and by 1990 had four hospitals. After merging with Smith Laboratories that year Columbia went public and then acquired Sutter Laboratories (orthopedic products). By the end of 1990 it had 11 hospitals.

Columbia moved into Florida in 1992 with the purchase of several hospitals and facilities. The next year it acquired Galen Health Care which operated 73 hospitals and had been spun off from health plan operator Humana earlier in the year. The merger thrust the hospital chain into about 15 new markets.

Columbia bought Hospital Corporation of America (HCA) in 1994. Thomas Frist his son Thomas Frist Jr. and Jack Massey (former owner of Kentucky Fried Chicken now part of TRICON) founded HCA in Nashville Tennessee in 1968. By 1973 the company had grown to 50 hospitals.

Meanwhile the medical industry was changing — insurers Medicare and Medicaid began scrutinizing payment procedures while the growth of HMOs (which aimed to restrict hospital admissions) cut hospital occupancy rates. HCA began paring operations in the late 1980s selling more than 100 hospitals. In 1989 the younger Frist led a $5.1 billion leveraged buyout of the company. He sold more assets and in 1992 took HCA public again but losses and a tumbling stock price made it a takeover target.

Later in 1994 the newly christened Columbia/HCA acquired the US's largest operator of outpatient surgery centers Dallas-based Medical Care America. A year later it bought 117-hospital HealthTrust a 1987 offshoot of HCA. Columbia/HCA was unstoppable in 1996 with some 150 acquisitions.

In 1997 the government began investigating the company's business practices. After executive indictments the company fired Scott and several other top officers. Frist Jr. became chairman and CEO pledging to shrink the company and tone down its aggressive approach. Columbia/HCA sold its home care business more than 100 of its less-desirable hospitals and almost all the operations of Value Health a pharmacy benefits and behavioral health care management firm it had recently bought.

The trimming continued in 1998: The company sold nearly three dozen outpatient surgery centers and more than a dozen hospitals. That year Columbia/HCA sued former financial executive Samuel Greco and several vendors accusing them of defrauding the company of several million dollars. In 1999 it spun off regional operators Life-Point Health (23 facilities) and Triad Hospitals (34) to trim its holdings. The next year it sold some 120 medical buildings to MedCap Properties a joint venture formed with First Union Capital Partners.

During 2000 the company bought out partner Sun Life and Provincial Holdings' (now AXA UK) interest in several London hospitals and bought three hospitals there from St. Martins Healthcare. It also renamed itself HCA - The Healthcare Company. While continuing a strategy of consolidating and streamlining operations (and resolving remaining legal matters) in 2001 the company streamlined its name even further to simply HCA Inc.

By 2002 HCA began shaking off its shaky past. Profits stabilized allowing it to reinvest millions into modernizing facilities and equipment at its hospitals and surgery centers. It entered the Kansas City market in 2003 by acquiring a local hospital chain

EXECUTIVES

Chairman And Ceo, R. Milton Johnson, age 61, $1,391,667 total compensation

President And Coo, Samuel N. (Sam) Hazen, age 58, $995,834 total compensation

President Service Line And Operations Integration, A. Bruce Moore, age 58, $574,989 total compensation

Cfo Eastern Group, William B. (Bill) Rutherford, age 54, $793,750 total compensation

President American Group, Jon M. Foster, age 56, $762,781 total compensation

President Clinical Services And Chief Medical Officer, Jonathan B. (Jon) Perlin, age 57, $795,833 total compensation

President National Group, Charles J. (Chuck) Hall, age 65, $797,088 total compensation

Svp Marketing And Corporate Affairs, Jana J. Davis, age 59

Svp And Cio, P. Martin (Marty) Paslick, age 58

President Physician Services Group, Michael S. Cuffe, age 52

Svp And Chief Nursing Officer, Jane D. Englebright, age 59

Director Of Physical Therapy Physical Therapy Director, Angie Brown

Physical Therapy Director, Mary B Peterson

Assistant Vice President Risk, Joseph Haase

Vice President, Michael Marotta

Director Of Radiology Services, Phyllis Barker

Vice President Field Operations, Jay Levy

Assistant Vice President Technical Services, Bill Fitzgerald

Assistant Vice President Development, Bobby Stokes

Assistant Vice President Owned Hospitals, Ron Redding

Director Of Pharmacy, Ron Nagata

Assistant Vice President Information Technology Strategy And Planning, David Catino

Vice President Human Resources Operations Support, Yonnie Chesley

Vice President Human Resources Midwest Division, Rich Lowe

Vice President Information Technology, Cyndi Talley

Chairman And Ceo, R. Milton Johnson, age 61

Auditors: Ernst & Young LLP

LOCATIONS

HQ: HCA Healthcare Inc
One Park Plaza, Nashville, TN 37203
Phone: 615 344-9551
Web: www.hcahealthcare.com

2016 Locations

	No.
US	
Florida	43
Texas	40
Tennessee	13
Virginia	11
Utah	8
Colorado	7
Georgia	7
Missouri	5
California	5
Kansas	4
Louisiana	4
Nevada	3
South Carolina	3
Idaho	2
Kentucky	2
New Hampshire	2
Oklahoma	2
Alaska	1
Indiana	1
Mississippi	1
UK	6
Total	**168**

Selected US Facilities

Alaska
Alaska Regional Hospital (Anchorage)
California
Good Samaritan Hospital (San Jose)
Los Robles Medical Center (Thousand Oaks)
Regional Medical Center of San Jose
Riverside Community Hospital
West Hills Hospital & Medical Center
Colorado
Centrum Surgical Center (Greenwood Village)
Medical Center of Aurora
North Suburban Medical Center (Thornton)
Presbyterian/St. Luke's Medical Center (Denver)
Rose Medical Center (Denver)
Sky Ridge Medical Center (Lone Tree)
Spalding Rehabilitation Hospital (Aurora)
Swedish Medical Center (Englewood)
Florida
Aventura Hospital and Medical Center
Blake Medical Center (Bradenton)
Brandon Regional Hospital
Capital Regional Medical Center (Tallahassee)
Central Florida Regional Hospital (Sanford)
Columbia Hospital (West Palm Beach)
Doctors Hospital of Sarasota
Edward White Hospital (St. Petersburg)
Fawcett Memorial Hospital (Port Charlotte)
Gulf Coast Medical Center (Panama City)
JFK Medical Center (Atlantis)
Kendall Regional Medical Center (Miami)
Lake City Medical Center
Largo Medical Center
Memorial Hospital Jacksonville
Memorial Hospital of Tampa
North Florida Regional Medical Center (Gainesville)
Northwest Medical Center (Margate)
Ocala Regional Medical Center
Osceola Regional Medical Center (Kissimmee)
Palms of Pasadena Hospital (St. Petersburg)
Palms West Hospital (Loxahatchee)
South Bay Hospital (Sun City Center)
St. Lucie Medical Center (Port St. Lucie)
Town and Country Hospital (Tampa)
Twin Cities Hospital (Niceville)
University Hospital and Medical Center (Tamarac)
West Florida Hospital (Pensacola)
Westside Regional Medical Center (Plantation)
Georgia
Atlanta Outpatient Surgery Center (Atlanta)
Cartersville Medical Center
Coliseum Medical Centers (Macon)
Doctors Hospital (Augusta)
Eastside Medical Center (Snellville)
Fairview Park Hospital (Dublin)
Northlake Surgical Center (Tucker)
Polk Medical Center (Cedartown)
Redmond Regional Medical Center (Rome)
Idaho
Eastern Idaho Regional Medical Center (Idaho Falls)
West Valley Medical Center (Caldwell)
Indiana
Terre Haute Regional Hospital
Kansas
Allen County Hospital (Iola)

Galichia Heart Hospital (Wichita)
Menorah Medical Center (Overland Park)
Overland Park Regional Medical Center
Wesley Medical Center (Wichita)
Kentucky
Frankfort Regional Medical Center
Greenview Regional Hospital (Bowling Green)
Louisiana
Dauterive Hospital (New Iberia)
Lafayette Surgicare
Lakeview Regional Medical Center (Covington)
Rapides Regional Medical Center (Alexandria)
Tulane Medical Center (Metarie)
Tulane University Hospital & Clinic (New Orleans)
Women's & Children's Hospital (Lafayette)
Mississippi
Garden Park Medical Center (Gulfport)
Missouri
Centerpoint Medical Center (Independence)
Lafayette Regional Health Center (Lexington)
Lee's Summit Hospital
Research Medical Center (Kansas City)
Research Psychiatric Center (Kansas City)
Nevada
Flamingo Surgery Center (Las Vegas)
MountainView Hospital (Las Vegas)
Southern Hills Hospital and Medical Center (Las Vegas)
Sunrise Hospital and Medical Center (Las Vegas)
New Hampshire
Parkland Medical Center (Derry)
Portsmouth Regional Hospital
Salem Surgery Center
Oklahoma
Edmond Medical Center
Oklahoma Surgicare (Oklahoma City)
Oklahoma University Medical Center (Oklahoma City)
South Carolina
Colleton Medical Cemter (Walterboro)
Grand Dunes Surgery Center (Myrtle Beach)
Grand Strand Regional Medical Center (Myrtle Beach)
Summerville Medical Center
Trident Regional Medical Center (Charleston)
Tennessee
Centennial Medical Center (Nashville)
Hendersonville Medical Center
Horizon Medical Center (Dickson)
Parkridge East Hospital (Chattanooga)
Parkridge Valley Hospital (Chattanooga)
Skyline Medical Center (Nashville)
StoneCrest Medical Center (Smyrna)
Summit Medical Center (Hermitage)
Texas
Bailey Square Surgery Center (Austin)
Bayshore Medical Center (Pasadena)
Clear Lake Regional Medical Center (Webster)
Conroe Regional Medical Center
Corpus Christi Medical Center
Del Sol Medical Center (El Paso)
Denton Regional Medical Center
Green Oaks Hospital (Dallas)
Kingwood Medical Center
Las Colinas Medical Center (Irving)
Mainland Medical Center (Texas City)
Medical Center of Arlington
Medical Center of Lewisville
Medical Center of McKinney
Medical Center of Plano
Medical City Dallas Hospital
Methodist Hospital (San Antonio)
Metropolitan Methodist Hospital (San Antonio)
North Austin Medical Center
North Hills Hospital (North Richland Hills)
Plaza Medical Center of Fort Worth
Rio Grande Regional Hospital (McAllen)
Round Rock Medical Center
South Austin Hospital
St. David's Medical Center (Austin)
Valley Regional Medical Center (Brownsville)
West Houston Medical Center
Woman's Hospital of Texas (Houston)
Utah
Brigham City Community Hospital
Lakeview Hospital (Bountiful)
Ogden Regional Medical Center
St. Mark's Hospital (Salt Lake City)
Timpanogos Regional Hospital (Orem)
Virginia
CJW Medical Center (Richmond)
Dominion Hospital (Falls Church)
Henrico Doctors' Hospital (Richmond)

John Randolph Medical Center
LewisGale Medical Center (Salem)
Pulaski Community Hospital
Reston Hospital Center
Spotsylvania Regional Medical Center (Fredricksburg)

Selected International Facilities

UK
Harley Street Clinic (London)
Lister Hospital (London)
London Bridge Hospital (London)
The Portland Hospital for Women and Children (London)
Princess Grace Hospital (London)
The Wellington Hospital (London)

PRODUCTS/OPERATIONS

2016 Revenue

	$ mil.	% of total
Payer sources		
Managed care & other insurers	23,441	52
Medicare	8,895	20
Managed Medicare	4,355	10
Managed Medicaid	2,478	5
Medicaid	1,597	4
International (managed care & other insurers)	1,195	3
Uninsured	1,135	2
Other	1,651	4
Provisions for doubtful accounts)	(3257)	-
Total	**41,490**	**100**

2016 Revenues

	$ mil.	% of total
National Group	19,845	48
American Group	19,648	47
Corporate & other	1,997	5
Total	**41,490**	**100**

COMPETITORS

Adventist Health System Sunbelt Healthcare
Adventist Health System West
Ascension Health
Banner Health
CHRISTUS Health
Catholic Health Initiatives
Children's Medical Center of Dallas
Community Health Systems
Encompass Health
LifePoint Health
SSM Health Care
Saint Thomas Midtown Hospital
Sutter Health
Tenet Healthcare
Texas Health Resources
Trinity Health (Novi)
United Surgical Partners
Universal Health Services

HISTORICAL FINANCIALS

Company Type: Public

Income Statement				FYE: December 31
	REVENUE ($ mil.)	NET INCOME ($ mil.)	NET PROFIT MARGIN	EMPLOYEES
12/17	43,614	2,216	5.1%	253,000
12/16	41,490	2,890	7.0%	241,000
12/15	39,678	2,129	5.4%	233,000
12/14	36,918	1,875	5.1%	225,000
12/13	34,182	1,556	4.6%	215,000
Annual Growth	**6.3%**	**9.2%**	**—**	**4.2%**

2017 Year-End Financials

Debt ratio: 90.34%
Return on equity: —
Cash ($ mil.): 732
Current ratio: 1.62
Long-term debt ($ mil.): 32,858
No. of shares (mil.): 350
Dividends
Yield: —
Payout: —
Market value ($ mil.): 30,752

STOCK PRICE ($) FY Close	P/E High/Low	PER SHARE ($) Earnings	Dividends	Book Value
12/17	87.84	15 12	5.95	0.00 (19.44)
12/16	74.02	11 8	7.30	0.00 (19.71)
12/15	67.63	18 13	4.99	0.00 (19.06)
12/14	73.39	17 11	4.16	0.00 (18.77)
12/13	47.71	14 9	3.37	0.00 (18.81)
Annual Growth	**16.5%**	**— —**	**15.3%**	**—**

HD Supply Holdings Inc

EXECUTIVES

Pres-Ceo, Joseph J Deangelo
Cfo, Evan Levitt
Sr V Pres, Ronald J Domanico
Sr V Pres-Hr Mktg & Communicat, Margaret Newman
Exec V Pres, John Stegeman
Sr V Pres-Gen Counsel-Corp SEC, Ricardo J Nunez
Chb, James G Berges
Auditors: PricewaterhouseCoopers LLP

LOCATIONS

HQ: HD Supply Holdings Inc
3400 Cumberland Boulevard SE, Atlanta, GA 30339
Phone: 770 852-9000
Web: www.hdsupply.com

HISTORICAL FINANCIALS

Company Type: Public

Income Statement				FYE: January 28
	REVENUE ($ mil.)	NET INCOME ($ mil.)	NET PROFIT MARGIN	EMPLOYEES
01/18	5,121	970	18.9%	11,000
01/17	7,439	196	2.6%	14,000
01/16*	7,388	1,472	19.9%	14,000
02/15	8,882	3	0.0%	15,000
02/14	8,487	(218)	—	15,500
Annual Growth	**(11.9%)**	**—**	**—**	**(8.2%)**

*Fiscal year change

2018 Year-End Financials

Debt ratio: 48.66%
Return on equity: 80.19%
Cash ($ mil.): 558
Current ratio: 3.02
Long-term debt ($ mil.): 2,090
No. of shares (mil.): 185
Dividends
Yield: —
Payout: —
Market value ($ mil.): 7,361

STOCK PRICE ($) FY Close	P/E High/Low	PER SHARE ($) Earnings	Dividends	Book Value
01/18	39.64	9 6	5.01	0.00	7.89
01/17	42.69	45 23	0.97	0.00	4.77
01/16*	26.27	5 3	7.31	0.00	3.72
02/15	28.83	1509 1045	0.02	0.00	(3.88)
02/14	21.47	— —	(1.31)	0.00	(3.97)
Annual Growth	**16.6%**	**— —**	**—**	**—**	**—**

*Fiscal year change

Heartland Financial USA, Inc. (Dubuque, IA)

Heartland Financial USA is an $11.3 billion multi-bank holding company that owns flagship subsidiary Dubuque Bank and Trust (Iowa) and ten other banks that together operate more than 120 branches in about a dozen states primarily in the West and Midwest. In addition to standard deposit loan and mortgage services the banks also offer retirement wealth management trust insurance and investment services. Heartland also owns consumer lender Citizens Finance which has about a dozen offices in Illinois Iowa and Wisconsin.

Operations

Heartland Financial USA operates two main segments: community and other banking and retail mortgage banking services which account for about 90% and 10% of revenue respectively. The community banking business generates revenue from interest earned on loans and investment securities and fees from deposit services. Its retail mortgage banking services division collects revenue from interest from mortgage loans held for sale gains on sales of loans on the secondary market the servicing of mortgage loans for investors and loan origination fee income.

About three-quarters of Heartland's loan portfolio comes from commercial and commercial real estate loans but — in keeping with the bank's Midwestern identity — it also makes agricultural residential mortgage and consumer loans.

Heartland's subsidiaries include: Citywide Banks (approximately $1.9 billion total deposits) New Mexico Bank & Trust ($1.2 billion) Dubuque Bank and Trust Company ($1.1 billion) Wisconsin Bank & Trust ($890 million) First Bank & Trust ($820 million) Premier Valley Bank ($710 million) Illinois Bank & Trust ($690 million) Morrill & Janes Bank and Trust ($560 million) Arizona Bank & Trust ($520 million) Rocky Mountain Bank ($420 million) and Minnesota Bank & Trust ($180 million).

Geographic Reach

Dubuque Iowa-based Heartland Financial USA operates through about 145 locations (including branches and loan production offices) in local communities in Iowa Illinois Wisconsin New Mexico Arizona Montana Colorado Minnesota Kansas Missouri Texas and California. The company's three largest bank subsidiaries by number of locations are Colorado's Citywide Banks with about 25 and Wisconsin Bank & Trust and New Mexico Bank & Trust with about 20 each.

Sales and Marketing

Heartland Financial USA offers its banking services to businesses public sector and non-profit entities and individuals.

The company's Commercial Card team works with its commercial clients to help cut manual processes and costs from employee travel entertainment spending and vendor payments.

Financial Performance

As it grows its assets and loan portfolio via acquisitions Heartland Financial USA had positive overall performance in the last five years increasing revenue by some 70% and net income by more than 100% — all while expanding its cash by about 55% and reducing long-term debt by nearly 20%.

Revenue ticked up 6% to $432.3 million in 2017 on increased interest income mostly from interest and fees on a larger loan portfolio following the company's acquisitions of Citywide Banks and Founders Bancorp.

Net income trended down 6% to $75.3 million owing to higher income taxes salaries employee benefits and professional fees.

Heartland added $37.3 million to its cash stores in 2017 to end the year with $196 million. Operations and investments brought in $155.9 million and $27.3 million respectively. Financing activities used up $145.9 million due to a net decrease from savings accounts and repayments of short term Federal Home Loan Bank advances.

Strategy

Heartland Financial USA's strategy for the past two decades is centered on expanding through acquisitions in its existing and adjacent markets while balancing growth in newer western markets with the stability of its established midwestern markets. The company's goal is to have at least $1 billion in assets in each state where it operates.

Mergers and Acquisitions

Heartland added its eleventh subsidiary in May 2018 through its acquisition of Lubbock Texas-based First Bank Lubbock Bancshares for $189.9 million. Operating under the name First Bank & Trust (which Heartland retained) the bank held $681.1 million in gross loans held to maturity and deposits of $893.8 million. First Bank & Trust has eight branches in West Texas and eight mortgage lending services offices throughout Texas.

In February 2018 the company acquired Minnetonka Minnesota-based Signature Bancshares for $61.4 million and incorporated it into its Minnesota Bank & Trust subsidiary. Signature had two branches in the Twin Cities metropolitan area with $324.5 million in gross loans held to maturity and deposits of $357.3 million.

Heartland acquired Citywide Banks (headquartered in Aurora Colorado) in July 2017 for $211.2 million. At the time of purchase Citywide had $985.4 million in net loans outstanding and $1.2 billion in deposits. Following incorporation of Citywide into its Centennial Bank and Trust subsidiary (which then adopted Citywide's name) Heartland had more than 25 branches in Colorado.

In February 2017 Heartland Financial USA acquired San Luis Obispo California-based Founders Bancorp which it incorporated into its Premier Valley Bank subsidiary for $31 million. The company's Founders Community Bank held loans totaling $96.4 million and the purchase increased Heartland's total number of branches in California from five to nine.

Company Background

Heartland Financial USA was founded in 1981 although it traces its roots back to the 1935 establishment of Dubuque Bank and Trust. It made its first bank acquisition in in 1989 – Key City Bank – and has continued acquiring community banks since.

EXECUTIVES

President And Ceo Minnesota Bank & Trust, Catherine T. (Kate) Kelly

Chairman President And Ceo Heartland Financial Usa Inc.; Vice Chairman Dubuque Bank & Trust Wisconsin Bank & Trust New Mexico Bank & Trust Arizona Bank & Trust Rocky Mountain Bank Centennial Bank And Trust(1) Minnesota Bank & Trust And Premier Valley Bank, Lynn B. Fuller, age 68, $486,388 total compensation

Evp Lending, Douglas J. Horstmann, age 64, $275,156 total compensation

President And Ceo New Mexico Bank & Trust, R. Greg Leyendecker

President And Ceo Wisconsin Bank & Trust, Kevin S. Tenpas

President Of Heartland Director Rocky Mountain Bank And President Heartland Financial Usa Inc. Insurance Services, Bruce K. Lee, age 57, $383,519 total compensation

Evp Human Resources And Organizational Development, Mark G. Murtha, age 56

Svp Chief Accounting Officer, Janet M. Quick

President And Ceo Riverside Community Bank, Steven E. Ward

Evp Wealth Management, Bruce C. Rehmke

Evp Commercial Sales, Frank E. Walter, age 71

Evp Senior General Counsel And Corporate Secretary, Michael J. Coyle, age 72

Evp Operations, Brian J. Fox, age 69, $190,000 total compensation

Evp And Chief Risk Officer, Rodney L. Sloan, age 58

Evp And Cfo Heartland Financial Usa Treasurer Citizens Finance Parent Co.. And Director Heartland Financial Usa Inc. Insurance Services, Bryan R. McKeag, age 57, $305,625 total compensation

Evp Finance And Corporate Strategy, David L. Horstmann, age 68

President And Ceo Arizona Bank & Trust, Jerry L. Schwallier

President And Ceo Rocky Mountain Bank, Curtis Chrystal

President And Ceo Morrill & Janes Bank And Trust Co., Kurt M. Saylor

Evp Private Client Services, Kelly J. Johnson, age 56

President And Ceo Illinois Bank And Trust, Jeff Hultman

Chief Investment Officer, Nancy Tengler

Evp And Chief Credit Officer, Drew Townsend

Evp And Private Wealth Management Director, Rick O. Terry

President And Ceo Heartland Mortgage, Paul Johnstun

Ceo Centennial Bank And Trust, Jim Basey

President Heartland Mortgage, Jack Lloyd

Vice President Finance, Sandra Wild

Vice President Administrative Services, Joseph V Berretta

Vice President, Jean Harkey

Assistant Vice President Commercial Services, Lynn Stoffregen

Vice President, Shelley Phillips

Vice President, Craig Sciara

Senior Vice President Credit Administration, Brian McCarthy

Assistant Vice President, Michelle Schoen

Assistant Vice President Information Services, Brent Wilke

Vice President Director Financial Planning And Performance Management, Michael G Flood

Credit Admin Officer Iv Senior Vice President, Ralph Atkinson

Credit Admin Officer Iv Senior Vice President, Jeffery Viviano

Pcs Director Of Financial Planning Vice President, Chrisanna Elser

Vice President Director Financial Planning And Performance Management, Michael Flood

Vice Chairman Of The Board Of Heartland Financial Usa Inc.; Chairman And Director Of Dubuque Bank And Trust, Mark C. Falb, age 70

Vice Chairman Of The Board Of Heartland Financial Usa Inc.; Director And Vice Chairman Of The Board Of Dubuque Bank And Trust, Thomas L. Flynn, age 62

Board Member, Duane White

Auditors: KPMG LLP

LOCATIONS

HQ: Heartland Financial USA, Inc. (Dubuque, IA)
  1398 Central Avenue, Dubuque, IA 52001
Phone: 563 589-2100   **Fax:** 563 589-2011
Web: www.htlf.com

PRODUCTS/OPERATIONS

2017 Sales

	$ mil.	% of total
Interest		
Loans & leases including fees	304	65
Securities	58	13
Other	1	-
Interest expense	(33.3)	-
Noninterest		
Gains on sales of loans	22	5
Service charges and fees	39	8
Trust fees	15	3
Loan serving income	5	1
Brokerage & insurance commissions	4	1
Security gains	7	2
Other	8	2
Total	**432**	**100**

Selected Subsidiaries

Arizona Bank & Trust
Citywide Banks (Colorado)
Dubuque Bank and Trust Company (Iowa)
  DB&T Community Development Corp.
  DB&T Insurance
Illinois Bank & Trust
Minnesota Bank & Trust
Morrill & Janes Bank and Trust Company (Kansas)
New Mexico Bank & Trust
Premier Valley Bank (California)
Rocky Mountain Bank (Montana)
Wisconsin Bank & Trust

COMPETITORS

Associated Banc-Corp	First Banks
BBVA Compass	U.S. Bancorp
Bancshares	Wells Fargo
Bank of America	Zions Bancorporation
Bank of the West	

HISTORICAL FINANCIALS

Company Type: Public

Income Statement

FYE: December 31

	ASSETS ($ mil.)	NET INCOME ($ mil.)	INCOME AS % OF ASSETS	EMPLOYEES
12/17	9,810	75	0.8%	2,008
12/16	8,247	80	1.0%	1,864
12/15	7,694	60	0.8%	1,799
12/14	6,052	41	0.7%	1,631
12/13	5,923	36	0.6%	1,676
Annual Growth	13.4%	19.6%	—	4.6%

2017 Year-End Financials

Debt ratio: 2.84%	No. of shares (mil.): 29
Return on equity: 8.69%	Dividends
Cash ($ mil.): 205	Yield: 0.0%
Current ratio: —	Payout: 19.2%
Long-term debt ($ mil.): —	Market value ($ mil.): 1,607

	STOCK PRICE ($) FY Close	P/E High/Low	PER SHARE ($) Earnings	Dividends	Book Value
12/17	53.65	20 16	2.65	0.51	33.10
12/16	48.00	15 8	3.22	0.50	28.37
12/15	31.36	14 9	2.83	0.45	29.56
12/14	27.10	13 10	2.19	0.40	26.81
12/13	28.79	14 11	2.04	0.50	23.88
Annual Growth	16.8%	— —	6.8%	0.5%	8.5%

HENRY FORD HEALTH SYSTEM

Built around a hospital founded by Detroit's favorite son the not-for-profit Henry Ford Health System (HFHS) is a hospital network that is also involved in medical research and education. The system's half-dozen hospitals — including the flagship Henry Ford Hospital as well as Henry Ford Wyandotte Hospital and mental health facility Kingswood Hospital — are home to roughly 2200 beds. HFHS also operates a 1200-doctor-strong medical group (with more than 40 specialties) as well as nursing homes hospice and a home health care network. The system's Health Alliance Plan of Michigan provides managed care and health insurance to more than half a million members.

Operations

Along with its hospitals large and small the system also operates more than 30 medical centers and maintains partnerships with community health services. About 20% of ambulatory care and 10% of acute care services in the region are provided by HFHS. In 2013 its hospitals took in more than 89000 patients and delivered more than 7900 babies. It also had 3.2 million outpatient visits and performed more than 88000 surgical procedures. HFHS conducts more than 285000 home health care visits annually.

For patients who need more than an ambulance to get them to the hospital the Henry Ford Hospital provides air ambulance transportation. The flagship hospital provides transport for critically ill and trauma patients within a 150-mile radius of Detroit (in Michigan Ohio and Ontario) via its Air Med 1 aeromedical helicopter.

Affiliated with Wayne State University's School of Medicine the health system is a leading education and research center with ongoing research in areas such as stroke heart disease cancer and diabetes. Wayne State and HFHS have agreed to expand their affiliation by increasing the number of medical students who train at Henry Ford working together on research projects and opening a new research center. HFHS trains more than 1500 future physicians every year. Henry Ford Hospital is responsible for many of those providing about 45 accredited programs to medical students.

Flagship facility Henry Ford Hospital is an 877-bed tertiary care hospital education and research complex. Kingswood Hospital is a 100-bed hospital offering inpatient care for individuals with acute episodes of mental illness. Henry Ford Macomb Hospital has 349 beds while Henry Ford West Bloomfield Hospital has 191 beds. Henry Ford Wyandotte Hospital is 401-bed acute care facility.

Geographic Reach

HFHS serves patients in Detroit and southeastern Michigan.

Sales and Marketing

Medicare accounted for 45% of payors in 2014 followed by Blue Cross (23%) Medicaid (17%) and self-pay and other (15%).

Financial Performance

Revenue increased 4% to $4.7 billion in 2014 as net patient services and health care premiums rose. However the system reported a net loss of $54.6 million that year as it used cash in pension and other post-retirement net adjustments and lost money on investments.

Cash flow from operations more than doubled to $142 million due to a decline in pension and health care premium receivables and changes in trading securities and accounts payable.

Strategy

HFHS grows organically and through partnerships. In 2012 it teamed up with Presbyterian Villages of Michigan forming a joint venture to operate the Center for Senior Independence. The Center is now a separate not-for-profit organization expected to increase the number of seniors it serves from 230 to nearly 1000 by 2016.

HFHS has increased its physician base by launching a subsidiary the Henry Ford Physician Network which is composed of private practice and hospital employed physicians as well as the existing Henry Ford Medical Group.

In 2014 the system launched a clinical trial to investigate a new drug to treat tinnitus a chronic ringing of the head or ears.

Company Background

Automaker Henry Ford founded Henry Ford Hospital in 1915.

EXECUTIVES

Evp; President And Ceo Health Alliance Plan, James M. Connelly
Ceo, Nancy M. Schlichting
Coo, Robert G. (Bob) Riney
President, Wright L. Lassiter, age 55
Evp And Chief Medical Officer; President And Ceo Henry Ford Hospital, John Popovich
President And Ceo Community Care Services, John J. Polanski
Evp And Cfo, Edward G. (Ed) Chadwick
Evp; Ceo Henry Ford Medical Group, William A. Conway
President And Ceo Henry Ford West Bloomfield Hospital, Lynn M. Torossian
President And Ceo Henry Ford Wyandotte Hospital, Denise Brooks-Williams
Chief Nursing Officer; Coo Henry Ford Hospital, Veronica M. Hall
President And Ceo Henry Ford Macomb Hospitals, Barbara W. Rossmann
Svp Community Health And Equity; Chief Wellness Officer, Kimberlydawn Wisdom
Svp And Cio, Mary Alice Annecharico
Director Of Radiology, Mark C Diamond
Director Of Radiology, Xia Wang
Senior Vice President Is Clinical Integration And Transformation, Michelle Schreiber
Director Of Radiology, Scott G Sturza
Director Of Radiology, John W Bonnett
Vice President Corporate Strategic Planning, Joel Keiper
Vice President, Mary Whitbread
Vice President Clinical Transformation And Information Technology Integration, Matt Walsh
Director Of Radiology, Jay Pearlberg
Director Of Radiology, Manuel L Brown
Director Of Radiology, Peter J Feczko
Director Of Radiology, Randall R Walter
Director Of Radiology, Riffat K Ahmed
Director Of Radiology, Sampath Ramachandran
Director Of Radiology, Suresh C Patel
Director Of Radiology, Todd R Aho
Vice President Information Technology, Veeresh Nama
System Vice President Risk Finance And Insurance Services, John Mucha
Medical Director Of Perioperative Services, Gaylord Alexander
Vp Of It Applications, Josephine Molle
Director Of Radiology, Daniel Croteau
Vice President, Gregory Solecki
Senior Vice President, Henry W Lim
Medical Records Director, SUSAN GLEASON
Vice President Finance, Paul Kolpasky
Vice President Physician Development, Timothy Ryan
Executive Vice President And Chief Strategy Officer, Seth Frazier

Chair Department Of Anesthesiology, Michael Lewis
Director Of Radiology, Zachary Delpropoto
Vice President Revenue Cycle, Kevin Oneill
Vice Chair Radiology, William Sanders
Secretary, Barbara Paul
Auditors: DELOITTE & TOUCHE LLP DETROI

LOCATIONS

HQ: HENRY FORD HEALTH SYSTEM
1 FORD PL, DETROIT, MI 482023450
Phone: 313 916-2600
Web: WWW.HFHS.ORG

HOSPITAL LOCATIONS

Henry Ford Allegiance Health
Henry Ford Hospital
Henry Ford Kingswood Hospital
Henry Ford Macomb Hospital - Clinton Township
Henry Ford West Bloomfield Hospital
Henry Ford Wyandotte Hospital

PRODUCTS/OPERATIONS

SELECTED SERVICES

Bariatric Surgery
Cancer
Heart & Vascular
Neurology & Neurosurgery
OptimEyes
Orthopedic Surgery
Primary Care
Transplant Services

COMPETITORS

Ascension Health	Mount Clemens Regional
Beaumont Health System	Medical Center
Blue Cross Blue Shield	OmniCare Health Plan
of Michigan	St. John Health
Crittenton Hospital	Total Health Care
Detroit Medical Center	Trinity Health (Novi)
Garden City Hospital	University of Michigan
Harper-Hutzel Hospital	Health System
McLaren Health Care	

HISTORICAL FINANCIALS

Company Type: Private

Income Statement   FYE: December 31

	REVENUE ($ mil.)	NET INCOME ($ mil.)	NET PROFIT MARGIN	EMPLOYEES
12/17	5,977	203	3.4%	23,000
12/14	1,513	(13)	—	—
12/13	4,517	135	3.0%	—
12/09	2,118	26	1.3%	—
Annual Growth	13.8%	28.8%	—	—

2017 Year-End Financials

Debt ratio: ——
Return on equity: 3.40%
Cash ($ mil.): 774
Current ratio: 1.20
Long-term debt ($ mil.): —

Dividends
  Yield: —
  Payout: —
Market value ($ mil.): —

Heritage Commerce Corp

EXECUTIVES

Evp And Cfo, Lawrence D. McGovern, age 63, $260,753 total compensation

President And Ceo, Walter T. (Walt) Kaczmarek, age 66, $368,509 total compensation

Evp And Director Business Development, Robert P. (Bob) Gionfriddo, age 72

Evp Banking Division, Michael E. Benito, $244,826 total compensation

Coo, Keith A. Wilton, $243,025 total compensation

Evp And Chief Credit Officer, David E. Porter, $260,738 total compensation

Evp And Corporate Secretary, Deborah K. (Debbie) Reuter

Evp Hoa And Deposit Services, Teresa Powell

Vice President Business Development Officer, David Beronio

Vice President Cash Management Officer, Kelly Swanson

Chairman, Jack W. Conner, age 78

Auditors: Crowe Horwath LLP

LOCATIONS

HQ: Heritage Commerce Corp
150 Almaden Boulevard, San Jose, CA 95113
Phone: 408 947-6900
Web: www.heritagecommercecorp.com

PRODUCTS/OPERATIONS

2017 Sales

	$ mil.	% of total
Interest		
Loans including fees	86	74
Taxable securities	13	12
Other	6	6
Interest expense	(5.4)	-
Noninterest		
Service charges & fees on deposit accounts	3	3
Increase in cash surrender value of life insurance	1	1
Gain on sales of SBA loans	1	1
Servicing income	1	1
Other	2	2
Total	**111**	**100**

COMPETITORS

Bank of America	JPMorgan Chase
Bank of the West	MUFG Americas Holdings
Citibank	SVB Financial
Comerica	U.S. Bancorp
First Republic (CA)	Wells Fargo

HISTORICAL FINANCIALS

Company Type: Public

Income Statement

FYE: December 31

	ASSETS ($ mil.)	NET INCOME ($ mil.)	INCOME AS % OF ASSETS	EMPLOYEES
12/17	2,843	23	0.8%	278
12/16	2,570	27	1.1%	263
12/15	2,361	16	0.7%	260
12/14	1,617	13	0.8%	242
12/13	1,491	11	0.8%	193
Annual Growth	**17.5%**	**19.9%**	**—**	**9.6%**

2017 Year-End Financials

Debt ratio: 1.38%	No. of shares (mil.): 38
Return on equity: 8.97%	Dividends
Cash ($ mil.): 316	Yield: 0.0%
Current ratio: —	Payout: 64.5%
Long-term debt ($ mil.): —	Market value ($ mil.): 585

	STOCK PRICE ($) FY Close	P/E High/Low	PER SHARE ($) Earnings	Dividends	Book Value
12/17	15.32	26 21	0.62	0.40	7.10
12/16	14.43	20 13	0.72	0.36	6.85
12/15	11.96	26 17	0.48	0.32	7.64
12/14	8.83	21 19	0.42	0.18	6.96
12/13	8.24	23 18	0.36	0.06	6.58
Annual Growth	**16.8%**	**— —**	**14.6%**	**60.7%**	**1.9%**

Heritage Financial Corp (WA)

Heritage Financial is ready to answer the call of Pacific Northwesterners seeking to preserve their heritage. Heritage Financial is the holding company for Heritage Bank which operates more than 65 branches throughout Washington and Oregon. Boasting nearly $4 billion in assets the bank offers a range of deposit products to consumers and businesses such as CDs IRAs and checking savings NOW and money market accounts. Commercial and industrial loans account for over 50% of Heritage Financial's loan portfolio while mortgages secured by multi-family real estate comprise about 5%. The bank also originates single-family mortgages land development construction loans and consumer loans.

Operations

The bank also does business under the Central Valley Bank name in the Yakima and Kittitas counties of Washington and under the Whidbey Island Bank name on Whidbey Island.

About 79% of Heritage Financial's total revenue came from loan interest (including fees) in 2014 while another 7% came from interest on its investment securities. The rest of its revenue came from service charges and other fees (8%) Merchant Visa income (1%) and other miscellaneous fees. The company had a staff of 748 employees at the end of that year.

Geographic Reach

The Olympia-based bank operates more than 65 branches across Washington and the greater Portland area. It has additional offices in eastern Washington mostly in Yakima county.

Sales and Marketing

Heritage targets small and medium-sized businesses along with their owners as well as individuals.

Financial Performance

Fueled by loan and deposit growth from a series of bank acquisitions Heritage Financial's revenues and profits have been on the rise in recent years.

The company's revenue jumped 70% to a record $137.6 million in 2014 mostly thanks to new loan business stemming from its acquisition of Washington Banking Company. Deposit service charge income also increased thanks to new deposit business from the acquisition.

Higher revenue in 2014 allowed Heritage Financial's net income to more than double to a record $21 million while its operating cash levels rose 66% to $51.3 million on higher cash earnings and net proceeds from the sale of its loans.

Strategy

The bank reiterated in 2015 that it would continue to pursue strategic acquisitions of community banks to grow market share across the Pacific Northwest (its region of expertise) expand its business lines and grow its loan and deposit business.

With its focus on business and commercial lending the bank also in 2015 emphasized the importance of seeking high asset quality loans lending to familiar markets that have a historical record of success. Recruiting and retaining "highly competent personnel" to execute its strategies was also key to its long-term agenda.

Mergers and Acquisitions

In May 2014 Heritage acquired Washington Banking Company and its Whidbey Island Bank subsidiary for $265 million which "significantly expanded and enhanced" its product offerings across its core geographic market.

In July 2013 the bank acquired Puyallup Washington-based Valley Community Bancshares and its eight Valley Bank branches for $44 million.

In January 2013 the company purchased Lakewood Washington-based Northwest Commercial Bank along with its two branch locations in Washington state for $5 million.

EXECUTIVES

President Ceo And Director Heritage Financial And Ceo Heritage Bank, Brian L. Vance, age 63, $494,316 total compensation

Evp And Cfo Heritage Financial And Heritage Bank, Donald J. Hinson, age 57, $255,084 total compensation

Evp And Chief Credit Officer Heritage Bank, David A. Spurling, age 65, $237,342 total compensation

Evp Heritage Financial And President And Coo Heritage Bank, Jeffrey J. (Jeff) Deuel, $291,516 total compensation

Evp And Chief Lending Officer Heritage Bank, Bryan D. McDonald, age 46, $261,374 total compensation

Vice President And Financial Reporting Manager, Patrice Hernandez

Chairman, Brian S. Charneski, age 56

Auditors: Crowe Horwath LLP

LOCATIONS

HQ: Heritage Financial Corp (WA)
201 Fifth Avenue S.W., Olympia, WA 98501
Phone: 360 943-1500
Web: www.HF-WA.com

PRODUCTS/OPERATIONS

2014 Sales

	$ mil.	% of total
Interest income		
Interest and fees on loans	110	79
Investment securities	10	7
Others	0	-
Non-interest income		
Service charges and others	11	8
Merchant Visa income	1	1
Others	4	5
Total	**137**	**100**

COMPETITORS

Bank of America	U.S. Bancorp
Columbia Banking	Washington Federal
FS Bancorp	Wells Fargo
KeyCorp	

HISTORICAL FINANCIALS

Company Type: Public

Income Statement

FYE: December 31

	ASSETS ($ mil.)	NET INCOME ($ mil.)	INCOME AS % OF ASSETS	EMPLOYEES
12/17	4,113	41	1.0%	735
12/16	3,878	38	1.0%	760
12/15	3,650	37	1.0%	717
12/14	3,457	21	0.6%	748
12/13	1,659	9	0.6%	373
Annual Growth	25.5%	44.5%	—	18.5%

2017 Year-End Financials

Debt ratio: 0.49%
Return on equity: 8.44%
Cash ($ mil.): 103
Current ratio: —
Long-term debt ($ mil.): —

No. of shares (mil.): 29
Dividends
Yield: 0.0%
Payout: 43.8%
Market value ($ mil.): 922

	STOCK PRICE ($) FY Close	P/E High/Low		PER SHARE ($) Earnings	Dividends	Book Value
12/17	30.80	23	16	1.39	0.61	16.98
12/16	25.75	20	13	1.30	0.72	16.08
12/15	18.84	16	12	1.25	0.69	15.68
12/14	17.55	23	19	0.82	0.50	15.02
12/13	17.10	29	22	0.61	0.42	13.31
Annual Growth	15.8%	—	—	22.9%	9.8%	6.3%

Heritage Insurance Holdings Inc

Auditors: Plante & Moran, PLLC

LOCATIONS

HQ: Heritage Insurance Holdings Inc
2600 McCormick Drive, Suite 300, Clearwater, FL 33759
Phone: 727 362-7200
Web: www.heritagepci.com

HISTORICAL FINANCIALS

Company Type: Public

Income Statement

FYE: December 31

	ASSETS ($ mil.)	NET INCOME ($ mil.)	INCOME AS % OF ASSETS	EMPLOYEES
12/17	1,771	(1)	—	431
12/16	1,033	33	3.3%	311
12/15	837	92	11.0%	247
12/14	615	47	7.7%	133
12/13	281	34	12.1%	90
Annual Growth	58.3%	—	—	47.9%

2017 Year-End Financials

Debt ratio: 10.41%
Return on equity: (-0.30%)
Cash ($ mil.): 174
Current ratio: —
Long-term debt ($ mil.): —

No. of shares (mil.): 25
Dividends
Yield: 0.0%
Payout: —
Market value ($ mil.): 466

	STOCK PRICE ($) FY Close	P/E High/Low		PER SHARE ($) Earnings	Dividends	Book Value
12/17	18.02	—	—	(0.04)	0.24	14.67
12/16	15.67	19	10	1.14	0.23	12.41
12/15	21.82	9	6	3.05	0.05	11.71
12/14	19.43	10	6	1.82	0.00	8.56
Annual Growth	(1.9%)	—	—	—	—	14.4%

Hershey Company (The)

The Hershey Company works to spread Almond Joy and lots of Kisses. With its portfolio of more than 80 global brands the #1 chocolate producer in North America has built a big business manufacturing such well-known chocolate and candy brands as Hershey's Kisses Reese's peanut butter cups Twizzlers Mounds and Almond Joy candy bars (under a license) York peppermint patties and Kit Kat wafer bars. Hershey also makes grocery goods including baking chocolate chocolate syrup cocoa mix cookies snack nuts breath mints and bubble gum. Beyond candy Hershey's has expanded into the snacks category. Products from the chocolate king are sold to a variety of wholesale distributors and retailers throughout North America and exported overseas.

Operations

Hershey's operations consist of two business segments North America 90% of revenue and International and Other 10% of revenue. The company makes and sells more than 80 name brands led by Hershey's and Reese's as well as Krackle Kit Kat and York. Other popular brand franchises are Twizzlers Mounds York Ice Breakers and Bubble Yum which fall within the company's sweets and refreshment business unit. Through acquisitions Hershey has added snack brands such as Skinny Pop popcorn and other "better-for-you" snacks and Krave meat snacks (jerky).

Geographic Reach

Hershey's North America segment accounts for 90% of revenue and it caters to the traditional chocolate and non-chocolate confectionery market as well as grocery and growing snacks markets in the US and Canada.

International and Other (10% of revenue) has operations in China Mexico Brazil India and Malaysia primarily for consumers in these regions. The segment also distributes and sells confectionery products in export markets within Asia Latin America Middle East Europe Africa and other regions. It also includes global retail operations including Hershey's Chocolate World stores in Hershey Pennsylvania; New York; Las Vegas; Niagara Falls (Ontario); Dubai; and Singapore as well as operations associated with licensing the use of certain of Hershey's trademarks and products to third parties around the world.

Sales and Marketing

Two customers account for 40% of Hershey's sales. The biggest is McLane Co. 30% of revenue the primary distributor of Hershey products to Walmart while Target supplies another 10% of Hershey's sales.

Hershey leverages a staff of full-time sales representatives and food brokers to peddle its products to customers. In general the confectionery company counts wholesale distributors chain gro-

cery stores mass merchandiser chain drug stores vending companies wholesale clubs convenience stores dollar stores concessionaires and department stores among its vast customer set. Hershey's distribution network ships its products from its manufacturing plants to strategically located distribution centers using common carriers to deliver products from there to customers.

The company makes a point to launch new versions of old favorites such as Jolly Rancher lollipops and bite-sized chocolate bars. Although chocolate bars take center stage it offers sugar-free chocolate to tempt the growing number of diabetic and overweight consumers. Moving into the snack aisle Hershey has rolled out cookies 100-calorie treats and granola bars.

Financial Performance

Hershey's revenue has trended steadily higher over the past 10 years except for a slip in sales in 2015. Sales rose about 5% a year over the decade.

The rate slowed to 1% 2017 when sales totaled $7.5 billion from 2016 sales. The company benefited from favorable currency exchange rates and from new products such as Hershey's Cookie Layer Crunch Hershey's Gold and Hershey's and Reese's Popped Snack Mix and Chocolate Dipped Pretzels.

Net income reached $783 million in 2017 a 9% increase from 2016 due to lower costs in 2017.

Hershey added about $83 million to its cash holdings to reach $380 million in 2017. Its operations generated $1.2 billion while investing and financing activities used $328.6 million and $843 million respectively.

Strategy

Hershey's growth strategy includes expanding its snack foods business while continuing to invest in its core confectionery business. The chocolate maker is bolstering its snack food line up to capitalize on US consumers' growing appetite for healthier snacks. With consumers in the US snacking more than in years past Hershey has begun offering more mixed snack options including nut pretzel and chocolate mixes. The company plans to introduce additional snack categories and might pursue acquisitions of companies that produce protein-based and other types of snacks it hasn't traditionally offered. Hershey also continues to invest in its iconic brands including Hershey's Reese's and Hershey's Kisses.

To compete with online sweets and snacks purveyors Hershey in 2017 announced plans to significantly ramp up its e-commerce operations through potential collaborations with brick-and-mortar retailers and invest more money in its technology infrastructure.

In addition to its growth initiatives the company is also cutting costs to improve profitably particularly in international markets. In 2017 Hershey announced it would lay off about 15% of its global workforce. The employee reduction intended to improve operating margins between 2017 and 2019 affected about 2700 mostly hourly workers outside of the US.

Mergers and Acquisitions

Hershey's strategic focus is on expanding its global presence as it jockeys to capture market share from rivals Mars and Kraft which owns Cadbury.

In early 2018 Hershey acquired Amplify Snack Brands a high-growth snack food company that makes SkinnyPop its market leading healthy popcorn brand. The transaction was valued at $1.6 billion and helped Hershey develop a broader portfolio of consumer snacking brands especially as they pertain to "better-for-you" products that feature clean simple and transparent ingredients. Later that year it announced plans to buy Pirate Brands from B&G Foods for $420 million. Pirate

Brands includes Pirate's Booty cheese puffs along with the Smart Puffs and Original Tings brands.

In 2016 the company acquired Ripple Brand Collective LLC a privately held company based in Congers New York that owns the barkTHINS mass premium chocolate snacking brand for approximately $285 million. The acquisition was made to broaden the company's product offerings in the premium and portable snacking categories.

Company Background

The Hershey Company is the legacy of Milton Hershey of Pennsylvania Dutch origin. Apprenticed in 1872 at age 15 to a candy maker Hershey started Lancaster Caramel Company at age 30. In 1893 at the Chicago Exposition he saw a new chocolate-making machine and in 1900 he sold the caramel operations for $1 million to start a chocolate factory. Chocolate proved to be a wise decision as the company made the name Hershey synonymous with American chocolate over the century.

HISTORY

The Hershey Company is the legacy of Milton Hershey of Pennsylvania Dutch origin. Apprenticed in 1872 at age 15 to a candy maker Hershey started Lancaster Caramel Company at age 30. In 1893 at the Chicago Exposition he saw a new chocolate-making machine and in 1900 he sold the caramel operations for $1 million to start a chocolate factory.

The factory was completed in 1905 in Derry Church Pennsylvania and renamed Hershey Foods the next year. Chocolate Kisses individually hand-wrapped in silver foil were introduced in 1907. Two years later the candy man founded the Milton Hershey School an orphanage; the company was donated to a trust in 1918 and for years existed solely to fund the school. Hershey went public in 1927.

EXECUTIVES

Vice President And Chief Accou, David Tacka
Senior Vice President, Thomas Hernquist
President North America, Michele G. Buck, age 57
Svp And Chief Product Supply And Technology Officer, Terence L. O'Day, age 68, $590,061 total compensation
Svp And Cfo, Patricia A. Little, age 58, $629,412 total compensation
President International, Steven C. Schiller
President U.s., Todd W. Tillemans
Vice President Us Finance, Todd Cunfer
Vice President, Joe Beck
National Account Manager, Mike Jauch
Senior Vice President Chief Research And Development Officer, William Papa
Vice President Finance, Gayla Molinelli
Vice President Corporate Communications And Corporate Social Responsibility, Leigh E Horner
Chairman, John P. (J.P.) Bilbrey, age 61
Vp Treasurer, Rosa Stroh
Vice Chairman For Finance And Informatics, Doug Eggli
Assistant Secretary, Kathleen Purcell
Board Member, Robert Malcolm
Auditors: Ernst & Young LLP

LOCATIONS

HQ: Hershey Company (The)
100 Crystal A. Drive, Hershey, PA 17033
Phone: 717 534-4200   **Fax:** 717 531-6161
Web: www.hersheys.com

2017 Sales

	$ mil.	% of total
North America	6,621	88
International and Other	894	12
Total	**7,515**	**100**

2017 Sales

	$ mil.	% of total
United States	6,263	83
Other	1,251	17
Total	**7,515**	**100**

COMPETITORS

Ferrero	Mondelez International
Flowers Foods	Nestlé
Ghirardelli Chocolate	Otis Spunkmeyer
Godiva Chocolatier	Russell Stover
Guittard	Smucker
Kellogg	Tootsie Roll
Lindt & Spr ngli	Wrigley
Mars Incorporated	

HISTORICAL FINANCIALS

Company Type: Public

Income Statement

FYE: December 31

	REVENUE ($ mil.)	NET INCOME ($ mil.)	NET PROFIT MARGIN	EMPLOYEES
12/17	7,515	782	10.4%	16,910
12/16	7,440	720	9.7%	17,980
12/15	7,386	512	6.9%	20,710
12/14	7,421	846	11.4%	22,450
12/13	7,146	820	11.5%	14,800
Annual Growth	**1.3%**	**(1.2%)**	**—**	**3.4%**

2017 Year-End Financials

Debt ratio: 52.59%
Return on equity: 92.05%
Cash ($ mil.): 380
Current ratio: 0.96
Long-term debt ($ mil.): 2,061
No. of shares (mil.): 210
Dividends
  Yield: 0.0%
  Payout: 69.6%
Market value ($ mil.): 23,935

	STOCK PRICE ($) FY Close	P/E High/Low		PER SHARE ($) Earnings	Dividends	Book Value
12/17	113.51	31	27	3.66	2.55	4.34
12/16	103.43	33	24	3.34	2.40	3.70
12/15	89.27	46	35	2.32	2.24	4.60
12/14	103.93	28	23	3.77	2.04	6.58
12/13	97.23	27	19	3.61	1.81	7.17
Annual Growth	**3.9%**	**—**	**—**	**0.3%**	**8.9%**	**(11.8%)**

Hertz Global Holdings Inc (New)

LOCATIONS

HQ: Hertz Global Holdings Inc (New)
8501 Williams Road, Estero, FL 33928
Phone: 239 301-7000
Web: www.hertz.com

HISTORICAL FINANCIALS

Company Type: Public

Income Statement

FYE: December 31

	REVENUE ($ mil.)	NET INCOME ($ mil.)	NET PROFIT MARGIN	EMPLOYEES
12/17	8,803	327	3.7%	37,000
12/16	8,803	(491)	—	36,000
12/15	9,017	273	3.0%	—
12/14	9,475	(82)	—	—
Annual Growth	**(2.4%)**	**—**	**—**	**—**

2017 Year-End Financials

Debt ratio: 74.11%
Return on equity: 25.20%
Cash ($ mil.): 1,072
Current ratio: 1.42
Long-term debt ($ mil.): 14,865
No. of shares (mil.): 84
Dividends
  Yield: —
  Payout: —
Market value ($ mil.): 1,856

	STOCK PRICE ($) FY Close	P/E High/Low		PER SHARE ($) Earnings	Dividends	Book Value
12/17	22.10	7	2	3.94	0.00	18.10
12/16	21.56	—	—	(5.85)	0.00	12.95
12/15	0.00	—	—	3.00	0.00	4.77
Annual Growth	**—**	**—**	**—**	**9.5%**	**—**	**55.9%**

Hess Corp

Oil and gas company Hess can profess to owning no less than 1.1 billion barrels of oil equivalent worldwide. Crude oil is the company's primary output resource but it also produces natural gas and NGLs (natural gas liquids). Its primary operations are in the US but it also has producing interests in Denmark Malaysia and Thailand. It also offers midstream services including gathering compressing and transporting hydrocarbons as well as propane storage. Hess has been prospecting for oil since the 1920s.

HISTORY

In 1919 British oil entrepreneur Lord Cowdray formed Amerada Corporation to explore for oil in North America. Cowdray soon hired geophysicist Everette DeGolyer a pioneer in oil geology research. DeGolyer's systematic methods helped Amerada not only find oil deposits faster but also pick up fields missed by competitors. DeGolyer became president of Amerada in 1929 but left in 1932 to work independently.

After WWII Amerada began exploring overseas and during the 1950s entered pipelining and refining. It continued its overseas exploration through Oasis a consortium formed in 1964 with Marathon Shell and Continental to explore in Libya.

Leon Hess began to buy stock in Amerada in 1966. The son of immigrants he had entered the oil business during the Depression selling "resid" — thick refining leftovers that refineries discarded — from a 1929 Dodge truck in New Jersey. He bought the resid cheap and sold it as heating fuel to hotels. Hess also speculated buying oil at low prices in the summer and selling it for a profit in the winter. He later bought more trucks a transportation network refineries and gas stations and went into oil exploration. Expansion pushed up debt so in 1962 Leon's company went public as Hess Oil and Chemical after merging with Cletrac Corporation.

Hess acquired Amerada in 1969 after an ownership battle with Phillips Petroleum. During the Arab oil embargo of the 1970s Amerada Hess began drilling on Alaska's North Slope. Oilman T. Boone Pickens bought up a chunk of Amerada Hess stock during the 1980s spurring takeover rumors. They proved premature.

Amerada Hess completed a pipeline in 1993 to carry natural gas from the North Sea to the UK. In 1995 Leon Hess stepped down as CEO (he died in 1999) and his son John took the position. Amerada Hess sold its 81% interest in the Northstar oil field in Alaska to BP and the next year Petro-

Canada bought the company's Canadian operations. In 1996 the company acquired a 25% stake (sold in 2002) in UK-based Premier Oil.

The company teamed with Dixons Stores Group in 1997 to market gas in the UK. It also purchased 66 Pick Wick convenience store/service stations.

In 1998 Amerada Hess signed production-sharing contracts with a Malaysian oil firm as part of its strategy to move into Southeast Asia and began to sell natural gas to retail customers in the UK.

To offset losses brought on by depressed oil prices Amerada Hess sold assets worth more than $300 million in 1999 including its southeastern pipeline network gas stations in Georgia and South Carolina and Gulf Coast terminals. It also moved into Latin America acquiring stakes in fields in offshore Brazil.

In 2000 Amerada Hess acquired Statoil Energy Services which markets natural gas and electricity to industrial and commercial customers in the northeastern US. It also announced its intention to buy LASMO a UK-based exploration and production company before Italy's Eni topped the Amerada Hess offer.

Undeterred in 2001 the company bought Dallas-based exploration and production company Triton Energy for $2.7 billion in cash and $500 million in assumed debt. Amerada Hess also acquired the Gulf of Mexico assets of LLOG Exploration Company for $750 million. That year however stiff competition prompted Amerada Hess to put its UK gas and electricity supply business on the auction block. The unit was sold to TXU (now Energy Future Holdings) in 2002.

In 2003 Amerada Hess sold 26 oil and gas fields in the Gulf of Mexico to Anadarko Petroleum. Amerada Hess was granted permission by the Equatorial Guinea government in 2004 to develop 29 new wells in that country. That year Amerada Hess acquired a 65% stake in Trabant Holdings International a Russia-based production and exploration company.

The company re-entered its former oil and gas production operations in the Waha concessions in Libya in 2006. Also that year it changed its name to Hess Corporation.

Looking to grow its position in the lucrative Bakken oil shale play in North Dakota in 2010 the company acquired American Oil and Gas in a $450 million stock deal that added 85000 net acres to Hess' holdings. It also bought 167000 acres in the Bakken play from TRZ Energy LLC for $1 billion.

Hess' former refinery in the US Virgin Islands was operated as a joint venture with Venezuela's state oil company PetrA?leos de Venezuela S.A (PDVSA). However the loss-making HOVENSA refinery was shut down in 2012 and converted to an oil storage terminal. In 2013 Hess announced that it completed its exit from the refining business by closing its Port Reading New Jersey refinery.

As part of its strategy of unwinding its refining and marketing assets in 2013 Hess sold Russian subsidiary Samara-Nafta to LUKOIL for $2.05 billion. It also sold its energy marketing business to Direct Energy for a $1.2 billion.

To raise cash it also sold its 2.7% interest in India's Azeri Chirag and Guneshli Fields and its 2.4% stake in the associated BTC pipeline to ONGC Videsh for $1 billion. It also sold its Indonesian oil and gas assets for $1.3 billion.

That year it also sold 20 liquid petroleum products terminals along the US East Coast with total storage capacity of 39 million barrels to Buckeye Partners for $850 million.

The Utica Shale in Ohio was a growth area. However in 2014 low gas prices prompted Hess agreed to sell 74000 acres of dry gas acreage in the Utica Shale for $924 million in order to focus on more lucrative oil plays.

That year it also sold its oil and gas assets in Thailand to PTT Exploration and Production for $1 billion.

EXECUTIVES

Chairman And Ceo, John B. Hess, age 64, $1,500,000 total compensation
Svp And Cfo, John P. Rielly, age 55, $775,000 total compensation
President And Coo, Gregory P. (Greg) Hill, age 56, $1,100,000 total compensation
Svp Global Production, Michael R. (Mike) Turner, age 58, $575,000 total compensation
Svp Global Services, Brian D. Truelove, age 59
Svp Developments Drilling And Completions, Richard Lynch
Svp Exploration, Barbara Lowery-Yilmaz, age 61
Senior Vice President Of Human Resources, Mykel Ziolo
Vice President, Paul Fejer
Vice President Distribution, Chip Small
Vp And Treasurer, Eric Fishman
Executive Vice President, David Chaimengyew
Vice President Global Supply Chain, Dennis Creech
Vice President Exploration Capture, Timothy Chisholm
Vice President Natural Gas Sales, Todd Porter
Executive Assistant Vice President Global Supply Chain, Robin T Hensley
Vice President Of Sales And Marketing, Patrick A Dunn
Vice President Human Resources Operations, Helena Deal
Executive Vice President Exploration And Productio, Eloise Castillo
Vice President Information Technology And Knowledge Management, Marfiza Muhammad
Vice President Retail Field Operations, David Klavsons
Senior Vice President Development And Technical Su, Janice Flaherty
Vice President International Exploration, Grant Gilchrist
Vice President Mobile Communications, Bambang Prasodjo
Senior Vice President Operations And Marketing, Joseph Serafino
Executive Vice President, Greg Hill
Vice President Government And External Affairs, Drew Maloney
Vice President Exploration, Bob Spinieo
Vice President Secretary And Deputy General Counsel, George Barry
Vice President Corporate Tax, Martin Dunagin
Vp Controller, Kevin Wilcox
Senior Vice President Human Resources, Andrew Slentz
Assistant Vice President, Benjamin Yau
Senior Vice President Strategy Commercial And New Business Development, Scott Sloan
Vice President Audit And Compliance, J C Whitley
Vice President Asst. Controller, Kevin Daley
Vice President Benefits And Human Resources Services, Dave G Lutterbach
Vice President, Bill Hanna
Vp Global Offshore Production, Gerbert Schoonman
Director, James H. (Jim) Quigley, age 66
Assistant Treasurer, Christopher Molinaro
Board Member, Bill Schrader
Secretary, Grace Garcia
Auditors: Ernst & Young LLP

LOCATIONS

HQ: Hess Corp
1185 Avenue of the Americas, New York, NY 10036
Phone: 212 997-8500
Web: www.hess.com

2016 sales

	% of total
US	65
Europe	13
Africa	12
Asia & other regions	10
Total	**100**

PRODUCTS/OPERATIONS

2016 sales

	% of total
Exploration and Production	90
Bakken Midstream	10
Total	**100**

2016 Sales

	% of total
Crude oil	76
Natural gas	16
Natural gas liquids	6
Other	2
Total	**100**

COMPETITORS

Abraxas Petroleum	Gastar Exploration
BP	Koch Industries Inc.
CMA CGM	Marathon Oil
Chevron	Norsk Hydro ASA
ConocoPhillips	Occidental Petroleum
Continental Energy	PEMEX
Devon Energy	PETROBRAS
Dominion Energy	Petr leos de
Double Eagle Petroleum	Venezuela
ERHC	Pioneer Oil and Gas
Encana Oil & Gas (USA)	Royal Dutch Shell
Inc.	Serica Energy
Eni	TOTAL
Exxon Mobil	

HISTORICAL FINANCIALS

Company Type: Public

Income Statement

FYE: December 31

	REVENUE ($ mil.)	NET INCOME ($ mil.)	NET PROFIT MARGIN	EMPLOYEES
12/17	5,405	(4,074)	—	2,075
12/16	4,844	(6,132)	—	2,304
12/15	6,561	(3,056)	—	2,770
12/14	11,439	2,317	20.3%	3,045
12/13	24,421	5,052	20.7%	12,225
Annual Growth	(31.4%)	—		(35.8%)

2017 Year-End Financials

Debt ratio: 30.19%
Return on equity: (-31.85%)
Cash ($ mil.): 4,847
Current ratio: 2.53
Long-term debt ($ mil.): 6,397

No. of shares (mil.): 315
Dividends
  Yield: 0.0%
  Payout: —
Market value ($ mil.): 14,956

	STOCK PRICE ($) FY Close	P/E High/Low		Earnings	PER SHARE ($) Dividends	Book Value
12/17	47.47	—	—	(13.12)	1.00	35.08
12/16	62.29	—	—	(19.92)	1.00	45.92
12/15	48.48	—	—	(10.78)	1.00	67.77
12/14	73.82	13	9	7.53	1.00	77.68
12/13	83.00	6	4	14.82	0.70	75.99
Annual Growth	(13.0%)	—	—		9.3%	(17.6%)

Hewlett Packard Enterprise Co

HP Enterprise (HPE) once part of the storied Hewlett-Packard Corporation has whittled itself down to focus its business on what it calls HybridIT. It recently spun off its $9 billion Software division and its 100000-person $13.5 billion Enterprise Services business. The remaining business designs manufactures and sells servers storage and networking equipment and provides technology services to help its large enterprise customers architect and deploy IT solutions. HPE focuses its efforts on software-defined IT offerings for private and public cloud environments as well as solutions for industrial Internet of Things (IoT) applications. HPE is a global company and about two thirds of its revenue comes from outside the US. Its technology has a rich history and maintains a cache of nearly 11000 patents.

Operations

HPE operates a corporate investments segment and two business segments. The Enterprise Group is the primary operational segment and within it are its server storage networking and technology services divisions. Financial Services offers leasing financing and other means to help customers pay for HPE purchases. Corporate Investments include the research organization HP Labs and certain cloud-related business incubation projects.

The Enterprise Group generates a little more than 85% of total revenue and within the segment the server division accounts for nearly 50% of revenue while technology services brings in 30%. The segment provides secure software-defined technology and services that enable customers to move data seamlessly across hybrid IT environments (private & public cloud connected to traditional data centers for example) and to provide solutions for non-core computing environments that run campus branch and Internet of Things (IoT) applications.

The Financial Services segment provides flexible investment solutions such as leasing financing IT consumption and utility programs and asset management services. It helps customers create unique technology deployment models and acquire complete IT solutions including hardware software and services from Hewlett Packard Enterprise and others. The segment accounts for roughly 15% of total revenue.

Corporate Investments is a cost-centered segment focused on research & development projects. From its efforts come new technologies and ideas that HPE eventually turns into products and services. Its revenue is negligible and earnings are typically small losses.

Geographic Reach

Palo Alto CA-based HPE is a global organization with a global customer base. Its physical operations include offices manufacturing facilities and HP Labs R&D centers. It has nearly 20 locations in the US and Puerto Rico and about 10 outside the US such as in the UK India Brazil China and Taiwan. As part of its HPE Next 2020 initiative it appears poised to shutter some sites.

Approximately two thirds of revenue originate outside the US.

Sales and Marketing

HPE customers are mostly large companies and government agencies. The company reaches them through its own sales staff and resellers distribution partners OEMs independent software vendors system integrators and consulting services companies. HPE account managers maintain relationships between the company's businesses and large enterprise customers.

HPE not only sells its own products and services but partners with a plethora of technologies companies to supplement its own offerings when designing and deploying customer solutions.

Financial Performance

HPE?s size and revenue generation dwindled along with the divestiture of its two large segments HP Software and HP Enterprise Services. In reviewing the remaining continuing operations of HPE revenue decreased marginally in each of FY2016 and FY2017 (fiscal year ends October 31).

For FY2017 revenue fell 4% to $28.9 billion. HPE?s largest segment Enterprise Group saw its revenue decline nearly 6% due to across-the-board decreases in its servers storage networking and technical services divisions. The greatest impacts came from a decline in the number of servers sold and the loss of revenue from its divested H3C network products operations. Those actions were partially offset by new revenue from two acquisitions SGI and Nimble Storage. A positive contribution came from HPE?s Financial Services segment whose revenue increased 13% compared to FY2016.

Net income in FY2017 crashed to $344 million from $3.2 billion the prior year. The fall was the result of various extraneous charges including $93 million in costs related to damages to its Puerto Rico and Houston facilities from Hurricane Harvey. It also spent nearly $800 million on restructuring and transformation charges. Finally the prior year had a $2.4 billion gain on divestitures causing an unfavorable comparison between FY2017 and FY2016.

Cash on hand at the end of FY2017 was $9.6 billion down $3.4 billion from the previous year. Operating activities contributed some $900 million to cash through net earnings and large adjustments for depreciation and amortization. Investing activities used nearly $5.0 billion of cash due primarily to $2.5 billion of investments in property plant and equipment along with $2.2 for business acquisitions. Despite large layouts for stock repurchases and debt repayment financing activities provided $600 million due to large dividend payments to HPE from the sale of its Software and Enterprise Services segments.

Strategy

HPE has undergone tremendous change in the past few years first split off from Hewlett Packard Corporation followed by its subsequent divestitures of large entities HP Software and HP Enterprise Services. In 2014 it was part of a 350000 person $120 billion conglomerate and by the end of 2017 HPE employed less than 50000 people and generated just under $30 billion in revenue.

With the corporate reshaping largely complete the company is focused on transforming itself to match the demands of its customers ? from a product portfolio perspective a geographic presence perspective and from a competitive posture perspective.

Its Enterprise Group continues to experience challenges with revenue growth due to the shifting of computing workloads to cloud deployment models instead of in-house data centers the emergence of software-defined architectures which reduces the needs for server and networking hardware and an increasingly competitive pricing environment. It is combating these trends with investments in its portfolio of solutions for the data center cloud and edge computing environments; all with an emphasis on software-defined infrastructure which is aided by its 2017 acquisition of SimpliVity. It has a sweeping set of technologies and services making it an ideal candidate for customers who want a one-stop-shop for all things enterprise computing.

In 2017 the company launched an initiative called HPE Next through which it plans to simplify its operating model by streamlining its offerings and business processes to support investments in high growth and higher margin solutions & services. It includes consolidating its manufacturing and support services locations streamlining its business systems and reducing the number of countries in which it has a direct sales presence while migrating to a channel-only model in the remaining countries. The initiative will continue through FY2020 and will incur expenses for staff reductions upgrading its IT infrastructure and plant closures. It expects to partially offset the expenses with proceeds from real estate sales. When it is complete HPE expects the initiative will drive down annual costs by $800 million.

HPE doesn't lack for competitors in enterprise IT. Longtime rival Dell is in the process of buying storage system company EMC to get even bigger. Other competitors across HPE's portfolio include Cisco Systems Lenovo Group Ltd. Oracle Fujitsu Ltd. Inspur Co. Huawei Technologies NetApp Hitachi Ltd. Juniper Networks and Arista Networks.With the wave of cloud services changing the way customers implement their computing solutions HPE is also competing against Amazon and Google.

Mergers and Acquisitions

In 2018 HPE agreed to buy BlueData a developer of visualization software for artificial intelligence and analytics applications. HPE intends to combine BlueData's technology with its software-defined infrastructure to provide customers with faster visualizations of data. The deal is expected to close in early 2019.

Also in 2018 HPE acquired Cape Networks which develops tools for monitoring and measuring networks. HPE slotred Cape Networks in its Aruba subsidiary where the acquired technologies expanded Aruba's artificial intelligence-powered networking capabilities. Cape Networks brings tools for testing availability and performance of services and applications and issuing alerts when something is wrong. Terms were not disclosed.

HPE acquired three companies in 2017: Cloud Technology Partners a cloud consulting design and advisory services company; Nimble Storage a provider of all-flash and hybrid storage solutions for a little more than $1 billion; SimpliVity a provider of software-defined computing infrastructure solutions for $650 million.

In August 2016 HPE bought SGI (formerly Silicon Graphics) for $275 million. SGI's high performance computing products are used for data analytics and data management. The plan is to combine SGI's supercomputing capabilities to beef up HPE's enterprise offerings to provide faster and higher capacity analytics to customers. The deal is expected to close in early 2017. SGI reported a loss of $39 million on revenue of $529 million in 2015.

EXECUTIVES

President And Ceo, Margaret C. (Meg) Whitman, age 62, $1,500,058 total compensation

Evp And Chief Marketing And Communications Officer, Henry Gomez, age 55

Evp General Counsel And Secretary, John F. Schultz, age 54

Evp And Coo, Christopher P. (Chris) Hsu, age 47, $675,026 total compensation

Evp Human Resources, Alan May, age 60

Evp And General Manager Enterprise Group, Antonio Neri, age 51, $725,028 total compensation

Evp And Cfo, Timothy C. (Tim) Stonesifer, age 51, $675,026 total compensation

National Accounts Manager, Darienne Zamis

Vice President And General Manager Campus And Branch Networking Business Unit, Tom Black

Vice President Quality Enterprise Group, Jim Cosco

Vice President Strategy And Operations (enterprise Group), Mark Linesch

Senior Vice President Global Sales Operations, Tommy Geary

Vice President Technology Strategy Software Defined And Cloud Group, David Hunter

Vice President Helion Cloud Security, Ed Reynolds

Vp And Ciso, Elizabeth Joyce

Svp And Gm Hybrid It Group, Alain Andreoli

Vice President And Associate General Counsel Global Supply Chain And Strategic Alliances, Jonathan Sturz

Vice President Global Healthcare Services, Mary Mirabelli

Vice President, Jeff Nuckols

Vice President, Dominic Wilde

Vice President, Lou Berger

Vice President Global Pursuit Strategist, Ron Knauer

Vice President Dxc Technology, Barry Weiss

Vice President Executive Assistant, Jeff Dolce

Senior Vice President And General Manager Hewlett Packard Enterprise U.s. Public Sector, Marilyn Crouther

Vice President Product Management, Stephen Spellicy

Vice President Sales (global Accounts West Region), Lee Wilkerson

Ww Vice President Sales Big Data, Bruce Jones

Vice President Global Benefits And Employee Mobility, Samanntha Dubridge

Vice President And Managing Director, Thomas Adams

Vice President Federal Health Segment, William Lovell

Vice President, Jim O'grady

Chairman, Patricia F. (Pat) Russo, age 65

Senior Vice President Finance And Treasurer, Kirt Karros

Board Member, Michael Angelakis

Board Member, Ray Ozzie

Auditors: Ernst & Young LLP

LOCATIONS

HQ: Hewlett Packard Enterprise Co
3000 Hanover Street, Palo Alto, CA 94304
Phone: 650 687-5817
Web: www.hpe.com

COMPETITORS

Amazon.com	IBM
Arista Networks	Juniper Networks
Brocade Communications	Lenovo
Cisco Systems	Microsoft
Dell	NetApp
Fujitsu	Oracle
Hitachi	salesforce.com

HISTORICAL FINANCIALS

Company Type: Public

Income Statement   FYE: October 31

	REVENUE ($ mil.)	NET INCOME ($ mil.)	NET PROFIT MARGIN	EMPLOYEES
10/18	30,852	1,908	6.2%	60,000
10/17	28,871	344	1.2%	66,000
10/16	50,123	3,161	6.3%	195,000
10/15	52,107	2,461	4.7%	240,000
10/14	55,123	1,648	3.0%	252,000
Annual Growth	(13.5%)	3.7%	—	(30.1%)

2018 Year-End Financials

Debt ratio: 21.88%	No. of shares (mil.): 1,423
Return on equity: 8.54%	Dividends
Cash ($ mil.): 4,880	Yield: 2.4%
Current ratio: 1.00	Payout: 30.4%
Long-term debt ($ mil.): 10,136	Market value ($ mil.): 21,705

	STOCK PRICE ($) FY Close	P/E High/Low		PER SHARE ($) Earnings	Dividends	Book Value
10/18	15.25	16	10	1.23	0.38	14.92
10/17	13.92	118	62	0.21	0.32	14.71
10/16	22.47	13	7	1.82	0.22	18.87
10/15	14.72	13	11	1.34	0.00	19.25
Annual Growth	0.9%	—	—	(2.1%)	—	(6.2%)

Hills Bancorporation

EXECUTIVES

Vice President Of Investments Trust And Wealth Management, Aaron Schaefer

Auditors: BKD LLP

LOCATIONS

HQ: Hills Bancorporation
131 Main Street, Hills, IA 52235
Phone: 319 679-2291
Web: www.hillsbank.com

COMPETITORS

Ames National	MidWestOne
Bank of America	Regions Financial
Citigroup	U.S. Bancorp
Iowa First	Wells Fargo
Meta Financial Group	West Bancorporation

HISTORICAL FINANCIALS

Company Type: Public

Income Statement   FYE: December 31

	ASSETS ($ mil.)	NET INCOME ($ mil.)	INCOME AS % OF ASSETS	EMPLOYEES
12/17	2,963	28	0.9%	499
12/16	2,655	31	1.2%	503
12/15	2,493	28	1.1%	464
12/14	2,334	26	1.2%	428
12/13	2,167	25	1.2%	421
Annual Growth	8.1%	2.0%	—	4.3%

2017 Year-End Financials

Debt ratio: —	No. of shares (mil.): 9
Return on equity: 8.19%	Dividends
Cash ($ mil.): 154	Yield: 0.0%
Current ratio: —	Payout: 23.2%
Long-term debt ($ mil.): —	Market value ($ mil.): 504

	STOCK PRICE ($) FY Close	P/E High/Low		PER SHARE ($) Earnings	Dividends	Book Value
12/17	54.00	18	16	3.01	0.70	38.03
12/16	48.11	17	13	3.40	0.65	35.63
12/15	45.00	27	14	3.04	0.63	33.23
12/14	82.50	29	25	2.87	0.58	30.93
12/13	72.00	26	25	2.75	0.55	28.91
Annual Growth	(6.9%)	—	—	2.3%	6.2%	7.1%

Hilltop Holdings, Inc.

Hilltop Holdings sits on top of a mound of money-related businesses. The company's PlainsCapital subsidiary operates more than 80 branches in Texas and an offshore branch in the Caymans offers residential mortgages through 200 PrimeLending offices in 40-plus and provides securities brokerage and investment banking through HilltopSecurities. Subsidiary National Lloyds Corporation (NLC) offers fire and home-owners' coverage for low-value and manufactured homes and insurance through independent agents in Texas and more than 25 other (mostly) southern states. NLC operates as National Lloyds Insurance and American Summit Insurance. Hilltop has more than $13 billion in assets under management.

Operations

The purchase of PlainsCapital in a transaction valued at about $700 million moved Hilltop from insurance as its primary revenue generator to banking. It now operates in banking mortgage origination insurance and financial advisory services.

The PlainsCapital entities serve niche markets such as midsized businesses investors and high-net worth individuals. NLC's operating subsidiaries primarily write the kind of lower-cost homeowners' policies that only pay out cash value instead of replacement costs and most of its policies exclude coverage for water or mold damage. Texas accounts for over 70% of the company's premiums. While personal lines account for more than 90% of its premiums the company does write a small amount of commercial insurance covering builders' risk sports liability and transportation insurance which is known as "inland marine" policies.

Geographic Reach

PlainsCapital's banking operations are in Texas and its mortgages are secured by property in Texas mostly in or around major cities. NLC is licensed in 42 states and sells in 27 but primarily does business in Texas Oklahoma Arizona Tennessee Georgia and Louisiana with Texas accounting for more than 60% of sales. PrimeLending concentrates on nine states and does most of its business in Texas California and North Carolina.

Financial Performance

The PlainsCapital acquisition did what it was meant to do - gave the company a shot in the arm. For 2013 revenue rose nearly 350% to $1.3 billion. Net loss in 2012 became a net income of $125 million and cash from operations grew 71%.

Strategy

After the 2012 purchase of PlainsCapital Hilltop began to focus on being a Texas-based bank and financial services company. It plans to continue expanding its empire through organic growth and acquisitions. To that end in 2013 PlainsCapital purchased First National Bank a Texas-based company and its 51 branches. The same year Hilltop subsidiary NLASCO changed its name to National Lloyds Corporation or NLC as part of an overall re-branding effort.

Mergers and Acquisitions

Through its PlainsCapital subsidiary Hilltop in 2018 agreed to acquire The River Oaks Bank located in a posh region of Houston TX for $85 million.

In 2015 Hilltop purchased Dallas-based SWS Group Inc. which was comprised of Southwest Securities FSB (a $1.2 billion bank) Southwest Securities Inc. (broker-dealer subsidiaries) and SWS Financial Services Inc.

In 2013 the company purchased Texas-based First National Bank with about 50 branches mostly in South Texas. It followed that up in early 2015 with the acquisition of Dallas-based securities brokerage SWS Group. In 2016 Hilltop merged its broker-dealer subsidiaries First Southwest Company and Hilltop Securities (formerly Southwest Securities) to create HilltopSecurities. (HilltopSecurities division FirstSouthwest will continue to offer municipal advisory services.)

Company Background

The company began life as Affordable Residential Communities (ARC) and spent its early days as a real estate investment trust (REIT). It went public in 2004 dropped its REIT status in 2006 and built up its collection of manufactured housing communities through acquisitions.

After several years of losses in the housing business the company chose to transition into another industry. It acquired NLASCO a niche provider of fire and homeowners insurance for manufactured homes and other low-value properties at the start of 2007. The company then renamed itself Hilltop Holdings.

EXECUTIVES

President And Co-ceo, Jeremy B. Ford, age 43, $700,000 total compensation

Vice Chairman And Co-ceo; Chairman Plainscapital Bank, Alan B. White, age 69, $1,350,000 total compensation

Coo Subsidiaries, James R. Huffines, age 67, $690,000 total compensation

Chief Administrative Officer, Darren E. Parmenter, age 55, $335,000 total compensation

Chairman And Ceo Hilltop Securities, Hill A. Feinberg, age 71, $500,000 total compensation

President And Ceo Plainscapital Bank, Jerry L. Schaffner, age 60

Cfo, William B. Furr, age 40, $143,438 total compensation

Ceo Primelending, Todd L. Salmans, age 69, $750,000 total compensation

Cio, Toby Pennycuff

Executive Vice President Chief Financial Officer Of Plainscapital, John A Martin

Senior Vice President Corporate Development, Erik Yohe

Senior Vice President, David Commons

Senior Vice President, Ashlee Miller

Vice President, Matthew Weaver

Executive Vice President, Thomas Dallam

Chairman, Gerald J. Ford, age 74

Board Member, Charles R Cummings

Board Of Directors, Markham Green

Board Member, Andrew Littlefair

Board Member, Lee Lewis

Board Member, Robert Taylor

Auditors: PricewaterhouseCoopers LLP

LOCATIONS

HQ: Hilltop Holdings, Inc.
2323 Victory Avenue, Suite 1400, Dallas, TX 75219
Phone: 214 855-2177
Web: www.hilltop-holdings.com

PRODUCTS/OPERATIONS

2016 Sales

	% of total
Interest income	
Loans including fees	22
Securities borrowed	2
Taxable Securities	2
Tax-exempt securities	-
Other	-
Non-interest income	
Net gains from sale of loans and other mortgage production income	35
Net insurance premiums earned	9
Securities commissions and fees	9
Investment and securities advisory fees and commissions	7
Mortgage loan origination fees	5
Other	9
Total	**100**

Selected Services

Financial Advisory
Clearing
Retail Brokerage
Investment Banking Services
Internet Banking
Business Check Cards

Selected Subsidiaries

PlainsCapital Bank
PrimeLending
HilltopSecurities
National Lloyds Corporation

COMPETITORS

American Modern Insurance	International Bancshares
BBVA Compass Bancshares	JPMorgan Chase
Bank of America	Morgan Keegan
Comerica	Raymond James Financial
Costco Wholesale	Republic Group
Cullen/Frost Bankers	Texas Capital Bancshares
Fannie Mae	Travelers Companies
Foremost Insurance	Wells Fargo
Freddie Mac	
ING	

HISTORICAL FINANCIALS

Company Type: Public

Income Statement   FYE: December 31

	ASSETS ($ mil.)	NET INCOME ($ mil.)	INCOME AS % OF ASSETS	EMPLOYEES
12/17	13,365	132	1.0%	5,500
12/16	12,738	145	1.1%	5,400
12/15	11,867	210	1.8%	5,300
12/14	9,242	111	1.2%	4,400
12/13	8,903	125	1.4%	4,550
Annual Growth	10.7%	1.4%	—	4.9%

2017 Year-End Financials

Debt ratio: 2.06%	No. of shares (mil.): 95
Return on equity: 7.01%	Dividends
Cash ($ mil.): 486	Yield: 0.0%
Current ratio: —	Payout: 17.6%
Long-term debt ($ mil.): —	Market value ($ mil.): 2,431

	STOCK PRICE ($) FY Close	P/E High/Low	PER SHARE ($) Earnings	Dividends	Book Value
12/17	25.33	22 16	1.36	0.24	19.92
12/16	29.80	20 10	1.48	0.06	18.98
12/15	19.22	12 8	2.09	0.00	17.56
12/14	19.95	22 16	1.17	0.00	16.19
12/13	23.13	17 9	1.40	0.00	14.54
Annual Growth	2.3%	— —	(0.7%)	—	8.2%

Hilton Worldwide Holdings Inc

If you need a bed for the night Hilton has a few hundred thousand of them. The company is one of the world's largest hoteliers with a lodging empire that includes about 5285 hotels and resorts in more than 100 countries operating under such names as Doubletree Embassy Suites and Hampton Inn as well as its flagship Hilton brand. Many of its hotels serve the mid-market segment though its Hilton and Conrad hotels offer full-service upscale lodging. In addition its Homewood Suites chain offers extended-stay services. The company

franchises many of its hotels; it owns the Waldorf-Astoria brand and the New York Hilton. Hilton became a public company again in 2013.

HISTORY

Conrad Hilton got his start in hotel management by renting out rooms in his family's New Mexico home. He served as a state legislator and started a bank before leaving for Texas in 1919 hoping to make his fortune in banking. Hilton was unable to shoulder the cost of purchasing a bank however but recognized a high demand for hotel rooms and made a quick change in strategy buying his first hotel in Cisco Texas. Over the next decade he bought seven more Texas hotels.

Hilton lost several properties during the Depression but began rebuilding his empire soon thereafter through the purchase of hotels in California (1938) New Mexico (1939) and Mexico (1942). He even married starlet Zsa Zsa Gabor in 1942 (they later divorced of course). Hilton Hotels Corporation was formed in 1946 and went public. The company bought New York's Waldorf-Astoria in 1949 (a hotel Hilton called "the greatest of them all") and opened its first European hotel in Madrid in 1953. Hilton paid $111 million for the 10-hotel Statler chain the following year.

Hilton took his company out of the overseas hotel business in 1964 by spinning off Hilton International and began franchising the following year to capitalize on the well-known Hilton name. Barron Hilton Conrad's son was appointed president in 1966 (he became chairman upon Conrad Hilton's death in 1979). Hilton bought two Las Vegas hotels (the Las Vegas Hilton and the Flamingo Hilton) in 1970 and launched its gaming division. The company returned to the international hotel business with Conrad International Hotels in 1982 and opened its first suite-only Hilton Suites hotel in 1989.

In the 1990s Hilton expanded its gaming operations buying Bally's Casino Resort in Reno in 1992 and launching its first riverboat casino the Hilton Queen of New Orleans in 1994. Two years later it acquired all of Bally Entertainment making it the largest gaming company in the world. Also that year Stephen Bollenbach the former Walt Disney CFO who had negotiated the $19 billion acquisition of Capital Cities/ABC was named CEO — becoming the first nonfamily-member to run the company.

Hilton formed an alliance with Ladbroke Group in 1997 (later Hilton Group owner of Hilton International and the rights to the Hilton name outside the US) to promote the Hilton brand worldwide. Hilton also put in a bid that year to acquire ITT owner of Sheraton hotels and Caesars World but was thwarted when ITT accepted a higher offer from Starwood Hotels & Resorts. Hilton was foiled once again in 1998 when a deal with casino operator Circus Circus (now part of MGM Resorts International) that would have separated Hilton's hotel and casino operations fell through. With a downturn in the gambling industry translating into sluggish results in Hilton's gaming segment the company spun off its gaming interests as Park Place Entertainment later that year.

In 1999 Hilton made a massive acquisition with the $3.7 billion purchase of Promus Hotel Corp. The following year Hilton sold its Flamingo Casino-Kansas City a remaining casino property left over from the Park Place spinoff to Isle of Capri Casinos for $33.5 million. In 2001 it sold 56 of its leases and management contracts to RFS Hotel Investors for about $60 million.

Hilton continued selling properties in 2002 with the sales of two Doubletree hotels and all 41 Red Lion locations to WestCoast Hospitality (now Red Lion Hotels) for about $51 million. It also sold its

Harrison Conference Center portfolio (14 conference centers and university hotels) to ARAMARK for $55 million. At the end of that same year the company formed a $400 million venture with CNL Hospitality (now CNL Hotels & Resorts) to buy and refurbish hotel properties.

Following an extended downturn in the hospitality business brought on by recession and post-9/11 fears about terrorism Hilton began to invest in refurbishments for many of its properties and added about 150 locations in 2004.

Hilton Hotels acquired Hilton International from Hilton Group (now Ladbrokes) for about $5.7 billion in 2006. The deal re-unified the Hilton brand globally and added about 400 new locations to the company's portfolio. The year after the acquisition Hilton Hotels sold its Scandic Hotels business to private equity firm EQT for $1.1 billion and later sold LivingWell Health Clubs to Bannatyne Fitness; both brands had been included in the Hilton International transaction.

Also in 2007 the company was taken private by The Blackstone Group through a $26 billion buyout. The acquisition included about $6 billion in debt. Christopher Nassetta later replaced Bollenbach as CEO. Hilton Hotels was renamed Hilton Worldwide in 2009. Through a financial restructuring in 2010 Hilton was able to cut about $4 billion of its $20 billion debt. In early 2011 its newest brand Home2 Suites by Hilton opened its first property.

Hilton sold its Waldorf Astoria New York hotel for $1.95 billion in 2015.

EXECUTIVES

Evp And President Development Architecture And Construction, Ian R. Carter, age 56, $739,302 total compensation

President Ceo And Director, Christopher J. (Chris) Nassetta, age 56, $1,200,000 total compensation

Evp And Chief Human Resources Officer, Matthew W. (Matt) Schuyler, age 52

Evp And General Counsel, Kristin A. Campbell, age 56, $638,308 total compensation

Evp Global Brands, James E. (Jim) Holthouser, age 59, $600,000 total compensation

Evp And Cfo, Kevin J. Jacobs, age 45, $743,404 total compensation

Evp And President Americas, Joe Berger

Evp And President Europe Middle East And Africa, Simon Vincent

Evp And Chief Commercial Officer, Chris Silcock

Head Architecture Design And Construction, Matt Richardson

Evp And President Asia Pacific (apac), Alan Watts

Chairman, Jonathan D. Gray, age 48

Auditors: Ernst & Young LLP

LOCATIONS

HQ: Hilton Worldwide Holdings Inc
7930 Jones Branch Drive, Suite 1100, McLean, VA 22102
Phone: 703 883-1000
Web: www.hiltonworldwide.com

2017 sales

	% of total
U.S.	77
All other	23
Total	**100**

PRODUCTS/OPERATIONS

2017 sales

	% of total
Other revenues from managed and franchised properties	62
Owned and leased hotels	16
Franchise Fees	15
Other fees and revenues	7
Total	**100**

Selected Brands

Conrad Hotels & Resorts
Doubletree
Embassy Suites Hotels
Hampton Inn
Hampton Inn & Suites
Hilton
Hilton Garden Inn
Hilton Grand Vacations Club
Homewood Suites by Hilton
Waldorf Astoria Hotels & Resorts

Selected Hotels

Chicago's Palmer House Hilton
Hilton Barcelona
Hilton Bora Bora Nui Resort & Spa
The Hilton Hawaiian Village on Waikiki Beach
Hilton Manchester Deansgate
Hilton Orlando
Hilton San Francisco on Union Square
Hilton Sedona
The New York Hilton

COMPETITORS

Accor	Interstate Hotels
Best Western	Loews
Carlson Hotels	Marriott
Choice Hotels	Omni Hotels
FRHI Hotels and Resorts	Red Lion Hotels
	Ritz-Carlton
Four Seasons Hotels	Starwood Hotels & Resorts
Hyatt	
InterContinental Hotels	Wyndham Destinations

HISTORICAL FINANCIALS

Company Type: Public

Income Statement

FYE: December 31

	REVENUE ($ mil.)	NET INCOME ($ mil.)	NET PROFIT MARGIN	EMPLOYEES
12/17	9,140	1,259	13.8%	163,000
12/16	11,663	348	3.0%	169,000
12/15	11,272	1,404	12.5%	164,000
12/14	10,502	673	6.4%	157,000
12/13	9,735	415	4.3%	152,000
Annual Growth	**(1.6%)**	**32.0%**	**—**	**1.8%**

2017 Year-End Financials

Debt ratio: 46.14%
Return on equity: 31.59%
Cash ($ mil.): 570
Current ratio: 0.90
Long-term debt ($ mil.): 6,556

No. of shares (mil.): 317
Dividends
Yield: 0.0%
Payout: 15.5%
Market value ($ mil.): 25,349

	STOCK PRICE ($) FY Close	P/E High/Low		PER SHARE ($) Earnings	Dividends	Book Value
12/17	79.86	21	7	3.85	0.60	6.53
12/16	27.20	26	16	1.05	0.84	17.91
12/15	21.40	7	5	4.26	0.42	18.18
12/14	26.09	13	10	2.04	0.00	14.48
12/13	22.25	17	16	1.35	0.00	13.29
Annual Growth	**37.6%**	—	—	**30.0%**	—	**(16.3%)**

Hingham Institution for Savings

The Hingham Institution for Savings serves businesses and retail customers in Boston's south shore communities operating more than 10 branches in Massachusetts in Boston Cohasset Hingham Hull Norwell Scituate South Hingham and South Weymouth. Founded in 1834 the bank offers traditional deposit products such as checking and savings accounts IRAs and certificates of deposit. More than 90% of its loan portfolio is split between commercial mortgages and residential mortgages (including home equity loans) though the bank also originates construction business and consumer loans. More than 95% of the company's revenue comes from loan interest.

Operations

The Hingham Institution for Savings made 96% of its total revenue from loan interest during 2015 while about 2% came from interest in equities CODs and other investments. The rest of its revenue mostly came from service fees on deposit accounts.

Of its $1.4 billion loan portfolio (at the end of 2015) about 48% was made up of commercial real estate mortgages (including multi-family housing) while 45% was tied to residential mortgages (including home equity). The remainder of the portfolio was made up of residential and commercial construction loans (7% of loan assets) and commercial business loans and consumer loans (1%).

Subsidiary Hingham Unpledged Securities Corporation holds title to certain securities available for sale.

Geographic Reach

The company mostly serves clients in Boston the South Shore and the island of Nantucket. Its branches are in Boston Cohasset Hingham Hull Nantucket Norwell Scituate South Hingham and South Weymouth Massachusetts.

Sales and Marketing

The Hingham Institution for Savings serves both individuals and small businesses in its three target markets in Massachusetts. Some of its clients (as of mid-2016) include Lyons Associates The Hub TCR Development SYA+FH Steven Young Architect + Fine Home Builder and Park Drive Inc.

The bank spent $489000 on marketing expenses during 2015 down from $557000 in each of 2014 and 2013.

Financial Performance

The bank's annual revenues have slowly trended higher over the past several years as the promising Boston real estate market has fueled its commercial real estate and residential loan business growth.

Hingham's revenue dipped 1% to $64.34 million during 2015 despite 13% mortgage loan growth mostly because in 2014 it earned a gains on life insurance distributions. The bank also continued to lose fee income as it has eliminated many fees on its deposit products to simplify offerings and attract customer deposits.

Revenue declines and higher income tax provisions in 2015 (in 2014 it earned non-taxed death benefit proceeds) caused the bank's net income to fall 13% to $19.34 million. Hingham's operating cash levels rose 11% to $20.2 million for the year thanks to a jump in cash-based earnings.

Strategy

The Hingham Institution for Savings continued in 2016 to focus on originating commercial multi-family and single-family mortgage loans in its target markets of Boston the South Shore and the island of Nantucket in Massachusetts especially as the healthy real estate market in and around Boston has provided a tailwind for its lending business.

EXECUTIVES

Chief Executive Officer; President; Director, Robert H. Gaughen, $319,615 total compensation
Assistant Vice President Retail Lending, Pat Talbot
Auditors: Wolf & Company, P.C.

LOCATIONS

HQ: Hingham Institution for Savings
55 Main Street, Hingham, MA 02043
Phone: 781 749-2200   **Fax:** 781 740-4889
Web: www.hinghamsavings.com

COMPETITORS

Bank of America	Independent Bank (MA)
Citizens Financial	Peoples Federal
Group	Bancshares Inc.
Eastern Bank	Sovereign Bank

HISTORICAL FINANCIALS

Company Type: Public

Income Statement   FYE: December 31

	ASSETS ($ mil.)	NET INCOME ($ mil.)	INCOME AS % OF ASSETS	EMPLOYEES
12/17	2,284	25	1.1%	101
12/16	2,014	23	1.2%	103
12/15	1,768	19	1.1%	111
12/14	1,552	22	1.4%	121
12/13	1,356	13	1.0%	131
Annual Growth	13.9%	17.8%	—	(6.3%)

2017 Year-End Financials

Debt ratio: 0.04%
Return on equity: 14.84%
Cash ($ mil.): 10
Current ratio: —
Long-term debt ($ mil.): —

No. of shares (mil.): 2
Dividends
Yield: 0.0%
Payout: 13.7%
Market value ($ mil.): 441

	STOCK PRICE ($) FY Close	P/E High/Low	PER SHARE ($) Earnings	Dividends	Book Value
12/17	207.00	19 14	11.81	1.62	87.29
12/16	196.78	18 11	10.89	1.52	75.50
12/15	119.80	15 9	9.02	2.14	64.83
12/14	87.01	9 7	10.44	1.37	57.08
12/13	78.49	13 10	6.28	1.32	48.49
Annual Growth	27.4%	— —	17.1%	5.3%	15.8%

HOBBY LOBBY STORES, INC.

If something wicker this way comes Hobby Lobby Stores may be the source. Across more than 45 states the company operates more than 600 stores that sell arts and crafts supplies baskets beads candles frames home-decorating accessories and silk flowers. It also operates in China Hong Kong and the Philippines. The #3 craft and fabric retailer (behind Michaels Stores and Jo-Ann Stores) boasts sister companies: Mardel a seller of Christian and educational products and Hemispheres a supplier of home furnishings and other merchandise to Hobby Lobby stores. CEO David Green who owns the company founded Hobby Lobby in 1972 and operates it according to biblical principles including closing shop on Sunday.

Operations

Hobby Lobby operates about 600 stores in 45-plus US states. Its portfolio of 67000 products spans needle art to jewelry and scrapbooking supplies.

The company's operations are supported by a sole Oklahoma manufacturing and distribution center that measures some 3.4 million sq. ft. Affil-

iate Mardel Christian and Education Stores run by Green's son Mart is also based there. Mardel operates about 35 stores in Arkansas Colorado Kansas Oklahoma and Texas. Hemispheres imports and sells high-end furniture and home dÁ©cor accessories from Europe and Asia. In addition to supplying Hobby Lobby with select imports Hemispheres operates a store in Oklahoma and a handful in Texas. Its other affiliated companies include Ethno-Graphic Media a non-profit ministry that develops interactive learning materials and Every Tribe Entertainment. Every Tribe founded in 2003 produced the motion picture End of the Spear in 2006.

Geographic Reach

Based in Oklahoma City Oklahoma Hobby Lobby operates retail shops nationwide under the banners Hobby Lobby Mardel and Hemispheres. It sources some of its 67000 products from Europe and Asia. The company maintains an onsite manufacturing plant in Oklahoma that makes store fixtures candles scented products art canvases and picture frames. The facility also features product-packaging capabilities.

Strategy

One of America's largest private companies fast-growing Hobby Lobby has been busy expanding its network of stores which average 55000 sq. ft. The company has plans to reach a stores count of about 625 by the end of 2014. It's extending its reach in Oregon Vermont and Minnesota to supplement recently added stores in Virginia Wisconsin Kansas California and New York in 2013.

President Steven Green the son of founder David Green is typically the executive who is tasked with scouting new locations for the company. In general Hobby Lobby sets up shop in second-generation retail sites such as vacated supermarkets and superstores.

EXECUTIVES

Executive Vice President Assistant, Bill Owens
Asst Vp Advertising, John Schumacher
Ceo, David Green
Cfo, Jon Cargill
President, Steve Green
Executive Vice President, Stan Lett
Assistant Vice President Construction, Bob Mackey
Assistant Vice President, Deloris Miller
Department Head, Andrea Bruner
Department Head, Christi Claxon
Assistant Vice President Risk Management, Becky Robinson
Vice President Finance, Mandy Rodriguez
Seniorvice President Distribution, Bill Woody
Vice President Finance, Jerry Ballard
Vice President Art And Creative Department Greens Daughter, Darsee Green-Lett
Vice President Marketing And Advertising, Dolois Smith
Assistant Vice President Controller, Barbara Walke
Assistant Vice President Risk Manager, Rebecca Robinson
Department Head, JEAN STEPHENSON
Regional Vice President Region 2, Eddy McLaughlin
Regional Vice President Region 9, Joe Guerra
Vice President International Relations, Allen Quine
Assistant Vice President Of Accounting, Barbara A Walke
Administrative Assitant To Vice President Of Information And Interactive Sys, Sherri R Fisher
Executive; Sec Treas; Treasurer, Mart Green

LOCATIONS

HQ: HOBBY LOBBY STORES, INC.
7707 SW 44TH ST, OKLAHOMA CITY, OK 731794899
Phone: 405 745-1100
Web: WWW.HOBBYLOBBY.COM

PRODUCTS/OPERATIONS

Selected Products

Arts and crafts supplies
Baskets
Candles
Cards
Furniture
Home accent pieces
Jewelry-making supplies
Needlework
Party supplies
Picture frames and framing
Scrapbooking supplies
Seasonal items
Sewing materials (fabric patterns notions)
Silk flowers
Toys
Wearable art

Selected Affiliates

Hemispheres (home furnishings and accessories stores)
Mardel Christian Office & Educational Supply (Christian materials office supplies and educational products)

COMPETITORS

A.C. Moore	Kirkland's
Burnes Home Accents	Michaels Companies
Garden Ridge	Old Time Pottery
Hancock Fabrics	Target Corporation
Jo-Ann Stores	Wal-Mart

HISTORICAL FINANCIALS

Company Type: Private

Income Statement   FYE: December 31

	REVENUE ($ mil.)	NET INCOME ($ mil.)	NET PROFIT MARGIN	EMPLOYEES
12/17	4,544	352	7.8%	30,218
12/06	196	58	29.5%	—
12/04	1,363	88	6.5%	—
12/03	150	58	39.0%	—
Annual Growth	27.5%	13.7%	—	—

2017 Year-End Financials

Debt ratio: —
Return on equity: 7.80%
Cash ($ mil.): 0
Current ratio: 0.10
Long-term debt ($ mil.): —

Dividends
Yield: —
Payout: —
Market value ($ mil.): —

HollyFrontier Corp

HollyFrontier refines crude oil to produce gasoline diesel and jet fuel and sells it in erstwhile American frontier territories: the Southwest northern Mexico Kansas and the Rockies. Its major assets are a 52000 barrels-per-day (bpd) refinery in Wyoming; the 135000 bpd El Dorado Kansas refinery; a45000 bpd Utah refinery; a 125000 bpd Tulsa refinery; and subsidiary Navajo Refining (New Mexico) which has a capacity of 100000 bpd. The company also has a 36% stake in Holly Energy Partners (HEP) which operates crude oil and petroleum product pipelines. .

Operations

HollyFrontier operates two businesses: the refining business which accounts for the vast majority of total revenue and HollyFrontier Energy Partners (HEP).

The refining segment produces products such as gasoline diesel fuel jet fuel specialty lubricant products and specialty and modified asphalt. It turns out around 46000 barrels per day of product from its El Dorado Tulsa Navajo Cheyenne and Woods Cross refineries. It also produces asphalt via the HFC Asphalt business that makes asphalt in Arizona New Mexico and Oklahoma.

By product gasoline accounts for half its HollyFrontier's sales volume; diesel fuel accounts for around 35%; and jet fuel and specialty lubricants less than 5% each.

The HEP segment generates revenues by charging tariffs for transporting petroleum products and crude oil through its pipelines.

Geographic Reach

Dallas-based HollyFrontier's refinery operations (Cheyenne Wyoming; El Dorado Kansas; Navajo New Mexico; Tulsa Oklahoma; and Woods Cross Utah) serve customers in the US Mid-Continent Rocky Mountain and Southwest regions of the US.

Sales and Marketing

HollyFrontier's principal customers for gasoline include other refiners convenience store chains independent marketers and retailers. Diesel fuel is sold to other refiners truck stop chains wholesalers and railroads. Jet fuel is sold for commercial airline use. Specialty lubricant products are sold in both commercial and specialty markets. LPG's are sold to LPG wholesalers and LPG retailers. They produce and purchase asphalt products that are sold to governmental entities paving contractors or manufacturers. Asphalt is also blended into fuel oil and is either sold locally or is shipped to the Gulf Coast.

Sales to Shell Oil represented 10% of HollyFrontier's sales as did sales to Sinclair Oil.

The primary markets for the El Dorado Refinery's refined products are Colorado and the Plains States. The Woods Cross Refinery's primary market is Utah. The Cheyenne Refinery primarily markets its products in eastern Colorado including metropolitan Denver eastern Wyoming and western Nebraska. It also sells a significant portion of its diesel directly from the truck rack at the refinery eliminating transportation costs.

Asphalt products are marketed in Arizona New Mexico Oklahoma Kansas Missouri Texas and northern Mexico. Products are shipped via third-party trucking companies to commercial customers that provide asphalt based materials for commercial and government projects.

Financial Performance

The collapse in the global oil price since 2014 has reduced net revenue by nearly half and pushed HollyFrontier into the red.

In fiscal 2016 revenue fell a further 20% to $10.5 billion relating to lower average prices across the year while a curtailing of activity at its Woods Cross refinery due to insufficient crude supply from the Plains Rocky Mountain Pipeline was also a factor.

The company lost $260.5 million mostly as a result of non-cash good will and asset impairment charges totaling $654.1 million. Additionally margins were eroded 48% as selling prices fell further than raw material costs.

Cash from operations fell 29% to $602.3 million on the back of lower net income and revenue.

Strategy

With the refining business suffering under the low oil price HollyFrontier is diversifying its operations and seeking higher margins. In 2017 it closed the acquisition of Canadian lubricants business Suncor Energy increasing its lubricants position — particularly in high-margin Group III base

oils of which Suncor is the only North American producer. It is now the fourth-larges lubricants producers on the continent.

To raise cash the company on occasion carries out "drop-down" asset sales to subsidiary HollyFrontier Energy Partners. In 2016 it sold Woods Cross Refinery Units — including crude fluid catalytic cracking and polymerization units — constructed as part of the Woods Cross expansion for $275 million.

Mergers and Acquisitions

In 2017 HollyFrontier completed the $1.1 billion acquisition of Canadian lubricants company Petro-Canada Lubricants a subsidiary of Suncor. The company produces 15600 barrels per day of lubricants including specialty lubricants and white oils.

HISTORY

HollyFrontier was founded in 1947 as General Appliance Corp. to process other companies' crude oil; the current name was adopted in 1952. As Holly the company grew with the number of gas-guzzling cars in the 1950s and 1960s and in the 1970s it developed its Navajo refinery in New Mexico. In 1981 Holly began producing higher-grade gasoline and started an asphalt company at Navajo.

In 1984 Holly became a partner in Montana Refining and later bought the entire business. It upgraded the Navajo refinery in the early 1990s to meet the demand for unleaded gasoline. In 1995 Amoco Mapco and Holly formed a joint venture the 265-mile Rio Grande Pipeline (completed in 1997) to transport natural gas liquids to Mexico.

Also in 1997 FINA and Holly allied to expand and use Holly's pipelines in the southwestern US. A proposed merger with another southwestern refiner Giant Industries died in 1998 because of federal antitrust concerns and a billion dollar lawsuit filed against Holly by Longhorn Partners Pipeline. Court papers revealed in 2000 that Holly had paid $4 million to fight Longhorn's request for a permit to transport gasoline in its Houston-to-El Paso pipeline. The permit if approved would compete with Holly's own interests in western Texas.

Later in 2000 Holly cut its workforce by about 10% mostly at Navajo Refining. The next year Navajo Refining secured a $122 million contract to provide JP-8 jet fuel to the Defense Department.

In a move to expand its production capacity in 2003 Holly acquired ConocoPhillips' Woods Cross refinery and related assets for $25 million. Holly agreed to be acquired by Frontier Oil for about $450 million that year but the companies terminated the agreement and litigation between the parties resulted.

In 2004 the company spun off its Navajo refinery-related refined petroleum pipeline and other distribution assets as Holly Energy Partners L.P.; it retains a 45% interest in the company.

In 2005 the Delaware Chancery Court ruled that Frontier Oil had not proved that Holly had repudiated the merger agreement and awarded Frontier Oil only $1 in damages. Also that year Holly acquired the remaining 51% of NK Asphalt Producers that it did not already own. The company sold its intermediate feedstock pipelines connecting two refining facilities in Lovington and Artesia New Mexico to Holly Energy Partners for $81.5 million.

To free up cash in 2008 it sold 136 miles of crude oil trunk lines and some tankage assets to Holly Energy Partners for $180 million.

To expand market share in 2011 the company acquired regional rival Frontier Oil and Holly changed its corporate name to HollyFrontier.

The all-stock deal created an enterprise valued at $7 billion and added Frontier's Kansas and Wyoming refineries to the company's portfolio. The acquisition which boosted HollyFrontier's re-

fining capacity to 443000 barrels a day is expected to create cost savings of at least $30 million per year.

The purchase was part of a multi-year strategy of expanding refinery capacity through selective acquisitions of complementary assets. (Earlier the company bought Sunoco's 85000-barrels-per-day Tulsa refinery. Building the largest refinery complex in the Midcontinent the company also acquired Sinclair Oil's 75000-barrels-per-day Tulsa refinery for $138.5 million).

Responding to increased demand in 2012 HollyFrontier announced planned to expand the capacity of its Woods Cross Utah refinery from 31000 barrel per day to 45000 barrel per day.

Building up its infrastructure to create greater efficiencies in 2013 HollyFrontier and Holly Energy Partners agreed to build a rail facility to enable crude oil loading and unloading near HollyFrontier's Artesia and/or Lovington New Mexico refining facilities. The rail project which will be connected to Holly Energy's crude oil pipeline transportation system in southeastern New Mexico will have a capacity of up to 70000 barrels per day and will enable access to a variety of crude oil types.

EXECUTIVES

LOCATIONS

HQ: HollyFrontier Corp
  2828 N. Harwood, Suite 1300, Dallas, TX 75201
Phone: 214 871-3555
Web: www.hollyfrontier.com

PRODUCTS/OPERATIONS

2016 Sales

	$ mil.	% of total
Refining	10,467	96
HEP	402	4
Corporate & other	0	-
Elimination	(333.7)	-
Total	**10,535**	**100**

COMPETITORS

BP	Sunoco
Crown Central	Tesoro
Exxon Mobil	Valero Energy
George Warren	Williams Companies
Marathon Petroleum	

HISTORICAL FINANCIALS

Company Type: Public

Income Statement   FYE: December 31

	REVENUE ($ mil.)	NET INCOME ($ mil.)	NET PROFIT MARGIN	EMPLOYEES
12/17	14,251	805	5.7%	3,522
12/16	10,535	(260)	—	2,676
12/15	13,237	740	5.6%	2,704
12/14	19,764	281	1.4%	2,686
12/13	20,160	735	3.6%	2,662
Annual Growth	(8.3%)	2.3%	—	7.2%

2017 Year-End Financials

Debt ratio: 23.37%
Return on equity: 16.02%
Cash ($ mil.): 630
Current ratio: 2.15
Long-term debt ($ mil.): 2,498

No. of shares (mil.): 177
Dividends
  Yield: 0.0%
  Payout: 29.2%
Market value ($ mil.): 9,087

	STOCK PRICE ($) FY Close	P/E High/Low	Earnings	PER SHARE ($) Dividends	Book Value
12/17	51.22	11 5	4.52	1.32	30.27
12/16	32.76	— —	(1.48)	1.32	26.40
12/15	39.89	14 8	3.90	1.31	29.15
12/14	37.48	37 25	1.42	3.26	28.17
12/13	49.69	16 11	3.64	3.20	30.17
Annual Growth	0.8%	— —	5.6%	(19.9%)	0.1%

Home Bancorp Inc

Making its home in Cajun Country Home Bancorp is the holding company for Home Bank a community bank which offers deposit and loan services to consumers and small to midsized businesses in southern Louisiana. Through about two dozen branches the bank offers standard savings and checking accounts as well as lending services such as mortgages consumer loans and credit cards. Its loan portfolio includes commercial real estate commercial and industrial loans as well as construction and land loans. Home Bancorp also operates about half a dozen bank branches in west Mississippi which were formerly part of Britton & Koontz Bank.

Geographic Reach

Home Bancorp serves the Louisiana areas of Greater Lafayette Baton Rouge Greater New Orleans and Northshore (of Lake Pontchartrain). Its markets in Mississippi include Vicksburg and Natchez.

Financial Performance

Although the company saw assets and loans grow in 2013 net income fell 20% that year to $7.3 million on lower operating income.

Mergers and Acquisitions

In early 2014 Home Bancorp spent about $35 million on Britton & Koontz Capital Corporation the holding company of Britton & Koontz Bank; the deal added five branches in west Mississippi to Home Bancorp's operations.

EXECUTIVES

Executive Vice President, Darren Guidry
Auditors: Porter Keadle Moore, LLC

LOCATIONS

HQ: Home Bancorp Inc
  503 Kaliste Saloom Road, Lafayette, LA 70508
Phone: 337 237-1960   **Fax:** 337 264-9280
Web: www.home24bank.com

COMPETITORS

Capital One	MidSouth Bancorp
IBERIABANK	Regions Financial
JPMorgan Chase	Teche Holding
Louisiana Bancorp	

HISTORICAL FINANCIALS

Company Type: Public

Income Statement   FYE: December 31

	ASSETS ($ mil.)	NET INCOME ($ mil.)	INCOME AS % OF ASSETS	EMPLOYEES
12/17	2,228	16	0.8%	—
12/16	1,556	16	1.0%	—
12/15	1,551	12	0.8%	—
12/14	1,221	9	0.8%	—
12/13	984	7	0.7%	—
Annual Growth	22.7%	23.2%	—	—

2017 Year-End Financials

Debt ratio: —
Return on equity: 7.35%
Cash ($ mil.): 152
Current ratio: —
Long-term debt ($ mil.): —

No. of shares (mil.): 9
Dividends
  Yield: 0.0%
  Payout: 24.1%
Market value ($ mil.): 406

	STOCK PRICE ($) FY Close	P/E High/Low	Earnings	PER SHARE ($) Dividends	Book Value
12/17	43.22	19 14	2.28	0.55	29.57
12/16	38.61	17 10	2.25	0.41	24.47
12/15	25.98	14 11	1.79	0.37	22.80
12/14	22.94	15 12	1.42	0.07	21.64
12/13	18.85	17 15	1.06	0.00	19.99
Annual Growth	23.1%	— —	21.1%	—	10.3%

Home BancShares Inc

Home BancShares is the holding company for Centennial Bank which operates some 160 branches in Arkansas Florida and Alabama with an additional branch in each of New York City and Los Angeles (through which the company is building out a national lending platform). With $14.9 billion in assets the bank offers traditional services such as checking savings and money market accounts and CDs. About 60% of its lending portfolio is focused on commercial real estate loans — including non-farm and non-residential and construction and land development. The bank also writes residential mortgages and business and consumer loans. Through a subsidiary Home BancShares offers insurance services.

Operations

About 80% of Home Bancshares' $10.8 billion loan portfolio comprises real estate loans including non-farm and non-residential commercial loans which make up more than 40% of the total. Residential one-to-four-family loans and commercial construction and land development loans contribute about 20% and 15% respectively. Commercial and industrial loans make up around 10%.

The holding company has built a $6.3 billion portfolio of non-farm and non-residential commercial real estate loans primarily secured by commercial real estate. Around 50% 30% and 15% of the company's commercial real estate loan portfolio is in Florida Arkansas and with its Centennial Finance Group (CFG). Home Bancshares established the group in 2015 to manage loans acquired in the company's acquisition of the Florida Panhandle business of Banco Popular and to originate new loans (with a focus on commercial real estate and commercial and industrial loans) via a national lending platform.

About 30% and 60% of the company's $2.6 billion residential real estate loan portfolio are for one-to-four-family properties and non-owner occupied one-to-four family properties respectively.

The company's commercial and industrial loans account for about $1.3 billion of the portfolio; Arkansas Florida and Centennial CFG house about 40% 35% and 25% of that segment respectively.

Geographic Reach

Conway Arkansas-based Home Bancshares' holding company's Centennial Bank operates about 90 branches in Florida more than 75 in Arkansas around five in Southern Alabama and one in each of New York City and Los Angeles.

Sales and Marketing

Home Bancshares' non-farm and non-residential lending (comprising about 40% of the total) is made up of loans for shopping and retail centers hotels and motels offices industrial warehouses churches marinas and nursing homes.

Residential one-to-four-family residential mortgages for individuals make up some 20% of the company's portfolio. About 30% and 60% of its residential mortgage loans are for one-to-four-family owner-occupied and non-owner-occupied properties respectively.

The holding company also lends heavily to residential and commercial developers to construct commercial properties and develop land. Construction and land development loans make up about 15% of its portfolio.

Around 10% of the value of Home Bancshares' loans go to commercial and industrial clients.

Financial Performance

Home Bancshares reported revenue of $555.5 million in 2017 up 174% from 2013 and net income of $135.1 million up 103% over the same period. The company's cash stores and long-term debt both about tripled during that time to $635.9 million and $1.7 billion respectively.

The holding company's revenue increased 13% in 2017 compared with 2016 owing to increased interest income from loans.

Home Bancshares' net income fell 24% due mostly to an increase in income tax expense related to the passage of the Tax Cuts and Jobs Act.

The company's $419.3 million to its cash in 2017. Operating activities provided $176.9 million down from the previous year based on decreased net income and increased charges from indemnification and other assets and accrued interest payable on other liabilities. Investments used $355.5 million while financings added $597.8 million driven mostly by proceeds from issuance of subordinated debentures.

Strategy

Home Bancshares' strategy is focused on expanding in its core Florida market through the purchase of local managed community banks including four in 2017 and 2018.

In addition to growing its geographic footprint Home Bancshares is also diversifying its product offerings through acquisitions. In 2018 the company bought the Shore Premier Finance division of Union Bankshares. Shore originated direct consumer loans for high-end sail and power boats in southeast Florida.

Mergers and Acquisitions

Home Bancshares acquired Giant Holdings The Bank of Commerce and Stonegate Bank in 2017 as well as former Union Bankshares subsidiary Shore Premier Finance in 2018.

The holding company purchased Giant Holdings for $96 million. Giant operated six branches in the Ft. Lauderdale Florida area and had $398.1 million in total assets $327.8 million in loans and $304 million in deposits.

Home Bancshares acquired The Bank of Commerce from Bank of Commerce Holdings as part of that company's bankruptcy for $4.2 million. Bank of Commerce – which had $182.5 million in assets $127.5 million in loans and $141.7 million in deposits – operated three branches in the Sarasota Florida area.

Home Bancshares bought Stonegate Bank for $820 million adding the company's $3.1 billion in total assets $2.4 billion in loans and $2.6 billion in deposits to its books. Stonegate had 24 offices in Florida markets including Broward and Sarasota counties.

In 2018 the company acquired the Shore Premier Finance division of Union Bankshares for $374.5 million in cash and 1.3 million shares. Shore originates direct consumer loans for high-end sail and power boats at 16 locations in southeast Florida. At the deal's close Shore had $384.2 million in assets including $383.4 million in total loans.

Company Background

Home Bancshares formed in 1998 as First State Bank.

EXECUTIVES

Cfo And Treasurer And Director, Randy E. Mayor, age 53, $300,000 total compensation

President And Ceo, C. Randall (Randy) Sims, age 63, $390,000 total compensation

Regional President Centennial Bank, Robert F. Birch, age 68, $290,000 total compensation

President And Ceo Centennial Bank, Tracy M. French, age 56, $290,000 total compensation

Chief Lending Officer, Kevin D. Hester, age 54

Coo Home Bancshares Inc. And Centennial Bank, John (Stephen) Tipton

Vice President Security, Jenni Holbrook

Vice President, Brian Jackson

Chairman, John W. Allison, age 71

Vice Chairman, Robert H. Adcock, age 69

Board Member, Alex Lieblong

Board Member, James G Hinkle

Board Member, Thomas Longe

Board Member, Mike Beebe

Auditors: BKD, LLP

LOCATIONS

HQ: Home BancShares Inc
719 Harkrider, Suite 100, Conway, AR 72032
Phone: 501 339-2929
Web: www.homebancshares.com

COMPETITORS

Arvest Bank	Bear State Financial
BB&T	Regions Financial
BBX Capital	Simmons First
Bank of America	Woodforest Financial
Bank of the Ozarks	

HISTORICAL FINANCIALS

Company Type: Public

Income Statement
FYE: December 31

	ASSETS ($ mil.)	NET INCOME ($ mil.)	INCOME AS % OF ASSETS	EMPLOYEES
12/17	14,449	135	0.9%	1,744
12/16	9,808	177	1.8%	1,503
12/15	9,289	138	1.5%	1,424
12/14	7,403	113	1.5%	1,376
12/13	6,811	66	1.0%	1,497
Annual Growth	20.7%	19.4%	—	3.9%

2017 Year-End Financials

Debt ratio: 11.54%	No. of shares (mil.): 173
Return on equity: 7.65%	Dividends
Cash ($ mil.): 635	Yield: 0.0%
Current ratio: —	Payout: 44.9%
Long-term debt ($ mil.): —	Market value ($ mil.): 4,037

	STOCK PRICE ($) FY Close	P/E High/Low	PER SHARE ($) Earnings	Dividends	Book Value
12/17	23.25	33 24	0.89	0.40	12.70
12/16	27.77	35 15	1.26	0.34	9.45
12/15	40.52	46 28	1.01	0.28	8.55
12/14	32.16	44 33	0.85	0.18	7.51
12/13	37.35	75 36	0.57	0.18	6.46
Annual Growth	(11.2%)	—	11.8%	22.5%	18.4%

Home Depot Inc

When embarking on household projects many start their journey at The Home Depot. As the world's largest home improvement chain and one of the largest retailers in the US the company operates nearly 2300 stores in North America. It targets the do-it-yourself (DIY) and professional markets with its selection of some 40000 items including lumber flooring plumbing supplies garden products tools paint and appliances. Home Depot also offers installation services for carpeting cabinetry and other products for its do-it-for-me (DIFM) customers. It conducts e-commerce operations through its websites (including thecompanystore.com) and mobile apps.

HISTORY

Bernard Marcus and Arthur Blank founded The Home Depot in 1978 after they were fired (under disputed circumstances) from Handy Dan Home Improvement Centers. They joined Handy Dan coworker Ronald Brill to launch a "new and improved" home center for the do-it-yourselfer (DIY). In 1979 they opened three stores in the fast-growing Atlanta area and expanded to four stores in 1980.

Home Depot went public opened four stores in South Florida and posted sales of $50 million in 1981. The chain entered Louisiana and Arizona next. By 1983 sales were more than $250 million.

In 1984 Home Depot's stock was listed on the NYSE and the company acquired nine Bowater Home Centers in the South. Through subsequent stock and debenture offerings Home Depot continued to grow entering California (Handy Dan's home turf) with six new stores in 1985.

Back on track in 1986 sales exceeded $1 billion in the firm's 60 stores. Home Depot began the current policy of "low day-in day-out pricing" the following year achieving Marcus' dream of eliminating sales events. The company entered the competitive northeastern market with stores in Long Island New York in 1988 and opened its first EXPO Design Center in San Diego.

Home Depot's sales continued to rise during the 1990-92 recession and the retailer kept opening stores. It entered Canada in 1994 when it acquired a 75% interest in Aikenhead's a DIY chain that it converted to the Home Depot name (it bought the remaining 25% in 1998).

A series of gender-bias lawsuits plagued the company in 1994 as female workers claimed they were not treated on an equal basis with male employees. Home Depot reached a $65 million out-of-court settlement in 1997 but not before the company was ordered to pay another female employee $1.7 million in a case in California.

Troubles aside Home Depot roared past the 500-store mark in 1997. That year Blank succeeded Marcus as the company's CEO; Marcus remained chairman. Home Depot bought National Blind & Wallpaper Factory (a mail-order firm) and Maintenance Warehouse (a direct-mail marketer) that year.

The company introduced its 40000-sq.-ft. Villager's Hardware stores designed to compete with smaller hardware shops in 1999 in New Jersey. It also bought Georgia Lighting an Atlanta lighting designer distributor and retailer. Home Depot later began adding large appliances to some stores following competitor Lowe's (most stores had them by 2000).

In 2000 Home Depot bought Apex Supply (a 20-plus-location plumbing distributor in Georgia South Carolina and Tennessee) and opened a flooring-only test store in Texas. Later that year the company named General Electric executive Robert Nardelli as its president and CEO. Marcus and Blank were named co-chairmen.

The company opened 200 new stores in 2001 and bought Total HOME a home improvement chain with four stores in Mexico. Additionally Marcus was named chairman after Blank stepped down. Later in the year Marcus retired and Nardelli became chairman. Also that year the company said it was scrapping its Villager's Hardware experiment to test a small-store concept in urban areas.

In 2002 Home Depot opened its first small store a 61000-sq.-ft. outlet in New York City. Further increasing its presence in Mexico the company acquired the four-store Del Norte chain in Ciudad JuA?rez that year.

Also in 2002 Home Depot created a new subsidiary HD Builder Solutions through the acquisition of Floors Inc. Arvada Hardwood Floor Company and FloorWorks Inc. The next year the company acquired roofing installer IPUSA and replacement windows and siding installer RMA Home Services.

Home Depot expanded its business in the homebuilder market in January 2004 by purchasing Creative Touch Interiors a floor and counter installer in California and Nevada. Additionally early that year Home Depot opened its largest store ever — 205000 sq. ft. — in wealthy Anaheim Hills California. It also announced in February 2004 that it had partnered with AARP to hire people older than 50.

In addition that month Home Depot became the exclusive retailer of Maytag's SkyBox a home beverage dispenser. It acquired Home Mart a 20-unit Mexican chain in that June giving it a total of more than 40 stores in Mexico. Also in 2004 the company acquired White Cap Construction Supply; agreed to settle discrimination claims of some Colorado employees for $5.5 million; opened two trend-setting urban-oriented stores in Manhattan; and bought 18 stores from Kmart.

In mid-2005 Home Depot acquired National Waterworks Holdings (now National Waterworks Inc.) and Williams Bros. Lumber of Georgia and folded them both into its The Home Depot Supply business (called HD Supply until it was sold). In September Home Depot Direct launched 10 Crescent Lane a high-end home decorating catalog and Web site offering furniture lighting and decorative accessories housewares and more. While some Home Depot locations in Louisiana and Texas were temporarily shut down by hurricanes Katrina and Rita its stores (and those of rival Lowe's and other building suppliers) are among the first places people visited in the wake of the disaster. In the immediate aftermath of the storms Home Depot stocked nontraditional items such as food and diapers in affected areas. Also in 2005 the company shuttered 15 EXPO Design Center stores which cater to affluent homeowners and converted five others to The Home Depot format. In all in 2005 Home Depot spent about $2.5 billion to acquire 21 companies.

The company's direct-to-consumer division launched a pair of high-end catalogs in 2005: 10 Crescent Lane and Paces Trading Company. However the catalogs which featured home furnishings and lighting products were discontinued in 2006 and selected products were folded back into the main Home Depot store catalog and website.

In January 2006 Home Depot acquired carpet and upholstery cleaning franchisor Chem-Dry and folded it into its At-Home Services division. (Chem-Dry has some 4000 franchises worldwide including 2500 in the US). In March the company completed its largest acquisition to date: the construction repair and maintenance products distributor Hughes Supply Inc. for $3.2 billion. That purchase was followed in May by the acquisition of Cox Lumber Co. a Tampa-based provider of trusses doors and lumber-related products. Also Home Depot acquired Home Decorators Collection a company specializing in catalog and online sales of home decor merchandise in 2006. Lured by the growth potential of the vast Chinese market the retailer purchased a majority stake in Taiwan-based Home-Way for about $100 million in late 2006. Home-Way operates DIY warehouse stores in northern China.

Joining the trend of big-box retailers adding gasoline and convenience store services to fuel sales Home Depot opened its first Home Depot Fuel locations in Tennessee and Georgia in 2006.

In early 2007 Nardelli left the company and vice chairman and EVP Frank Blake took the top spot. Home Depot decided to close its handful of flooring-only stores that year. The apparent nail in Nardelli's coffin was his autocratic management style and hefty compensation package (strategically based on options rather than shareholder returns and estimated at $245 million over five years). Nardelli left Home Depot with a $210 million severance package.

The company sold its HD Supply business in 2007 to Bain Capital Carlyle Group and Clayton Dubilier & Rice. The retailer used the proceeds to help it make a $10 billion stock repurchase of more than 15% of its market capitalization.

The Home Depot closed two stores in China in fiscal 2011. In fiscal 2013 it closed the last of its big-box stores there.

EXECUTIVES

President Southern Division, Tim Hourigan
Evp Corporate Services And Cfo, Carol B. Tomé, age 61, $1,079,231 total compensation
President The Home Depot Mexico, Ricardo E. Saldivar, age 65
Chairman President And Ceo, Craig A. Menear, age 60, $1,300,000 total compensation
Evp Supply Chain And Product Development, Mark Q. Holifield, age 61, $775,385 total compensation
Evp And Cio, Matthew A. (Matt) Carey, age 53, $730,385 total compensation
Svp Talent Organization And Performance Systems, Timothy M. (Tim) Crow, age 62, $586,308 total compensation
Evp U.s. Stores, Ann-Marie Campbell, age 52, $665,385 total compensation
President The Home Depot Canada, Jeff Kinnaird
Evp Outside Sales And Service, William G. (Bill) Lennie, age 62
Evp General Counsel And Corporate Secretary, Teresa W. Roseborough, age 59
President Western Division, Aaron Flowe
President Online; Chief Marketing Officer, Kevin Hofmann
Evp Merchandising, Edward P. (Ted) Decker, age 55
President Northern Division, Crystal Hanlon
Vice President Information Technology Chief Architect, Barbara Sanders
Vice President Human Resources, Michael Hagan
Vice President Employment Practices And Associate Relations, Derek W Bottoms
Vp Marketing, Lisa Orebaugh
Regional Vice President, Quonta Vance
Vice President Service Operations And Home Renovation Services, Chuyu Xi
Merchandising Vice President, Mike Hogenmiller
Senior Vice President Supply Chain, Thomas Shortt
Vice President Operations, Ann Campbell
Senior Vice President Supply Chain, Tom Shortt
Vice President Of Pro Business, JT Rieves
Senior Vice President Of Operations, Tim Applebee
Vice President Marketing, Lisa DeStefano
Vice President And General Manager Home Depot Exteriors, Aaron Carmack
Vice President Online, Prat Vemana
Executive Vice President Cio, Matt Carey
Vice President Learning And Development, Tom Spahr
Department Head, William Morgan
Board Member, Albert Carey
Auditors: KPMG LLP

LOCATIONS

HQ: Home Depot Inc
2455 Paces Ferry Road, Atlanta, GA 30339
Phone: 770 433-8211   **Fax:** 770 431-2707
Web: www.homedepot.com

2017 Sales

	$ mil.	% of total
US	92,413	92
Other	8,491	8
Total	**100,904**	**100**

2017 Stores

	No.
US	1,980
Canada	182
Mexico	122
Total	**2,284**

PRODUCTS/OPERATIONS

2017 Sales

	$ mil.	% of total
Indoor garden	9,639	10
Appliances	8,147	8
Paint	7,990	8
Lumber	7,790	8
Tools	7,379	7
Kitchen and bath	7,377	7
Plumbing	7,356	7
Building materials	7,342	7
Flooring	7,078	7
Outdoor garden	7,030	7
Hardware	5,891	6
Millwork	5,382	5
Electrical	5,037	5
Other	7,466	8
Total	**100,904**	**100**

Selected Private Labels and Proprietary Brands

EcoSmart (lighting)
Glacier Bay (fixtures)
Hampton Bay (lighting)
Husky (hand tools)
LifeProof (flooring)
RIDGID (power tools)
Vigoro (lawn care products)

COMPETITORS

84 Lumber	Pacific Coast Building
Ace Hardware	Products
Amazon.com	RH
BMC Stock	RONA
Best Buy	Sears Holdings
CCA Global	Sherwin-Williams
Costco Wholesale	Sutherland Lumber
Do it Best	Target Corporation
Kelly-Moore	Tractor Supply
Lowe's	True Value
Lumber Liquidators	W.E. Aubuchon
Menard	Wal-Mart
Northern Tool	Wayfair

HISTORICAL FINANCIALS

Company Type: Public

Income Statement

FYE: January 28

	REVENUE ($ mil.)	NET INCOME ($ mil.)	NET PROFIT MARGIN	EMPLOYEES
01/18	100,904	8,630	8.6%	413,000
01/17	94,595	7,957	8.4%	406,000
01/16*	88,519	7,009	7.9%	385,000
02/15	83,176	6,345	7.6%	371,000
02/14	78,812	5,385	6.8%	365,000
Annual Growth	**6.4%**	**12.5%**	**—**	**3.1%**

*Fiscal year change

2018 Year-End Financials

Debt ratio: 60.70%
Return on equity: 299.07%
Cash ($ mil.): 3,595
Current ratio: 1.17
Long-term debt ($ mil.): 24,267

No. of shares (mil.): 1,158
Dividends
  Yield: 0.0%
  Payout: 48.8%
Market value ($ mil.): 239,972

	STOCK PRICE ($) FY Close	P/E High/Low		PER SHARE ($) Earnings	Dividends	Book Value
01/18	207.23	28	19	7.29	3.56	1.26
01/17	138.33	21	17	6.45	2.76	3.60
01/16*	125.76	25	19	5.46	2.36	5.04
02/15	104.42	23	16	4.71	1.88	7.13
02/14	76.85	22	17	3.76	1.56	9.07
Annual Growth	**28.1%**	—	—	**18.0%**	**22.9%**	**(39.0%)**

*Fiscal year change

HomeStreet Inc

HomeStreet aims to offer home and business mortgages to all in the Pacific Northwest and Hawaii. Its subsidiary HomeStreet Bank offers traditional consumer banking accounts as well as commercial and private banking investment and insurance products and services through 45 branches and 65 loan offices in the Pacific Northwest California and Hawaii. Specializing in residential and commercial mortgages the bank and fellow subsidiary Homestreet Capital Corp originate home loans both directly and through a joint venture Windermere Real Estate which operates about 40 offices in Washington and Oregon. HomeStreet also provides specialty financing for income-producing properties.

Operations

HomeStreet operates two lines of business: Commercial and Consumer Banking and Mortgage Banking which originates residential mortgage loans for wale in the secondary markets to be securitized by GSAs. Its primary subsidiaries are HomeStreet Bank and HomeStreet Capital Corp. (HCC). HCC sells and services multifamily mortgage loans in conjunction with HomeStreet Bank.

HomeStreet gets most of its business from mortgage originations and sales. About 53% of the company's revenue came from its mortgage banking business (origination and sales) during 2015 while another 6% came from mortgage servicing income. Another 34% of its revenue came from loan interest.

Geographic Reach

Seattle-based HomeStreet operates bank branches in Arizona California Colorado Hawaii Idaho Oregon Utah and Washington.

Sales and Marketing

HomeStreet provides financial services for small- and middle-market businesses as well as consumers.

Financial Performance

HomeStreet's annual revenues and profits have more than doubled since 2011 thanks to strong mortgage banking and loan business growth driven by a strengthening housing market.

The company's revenue spiked 50% to $446.35 million during 2015 mostly thanks to a 64% increase in gains on mortgage loan origination sales resulting from a rise in single family mortgage interest rate lock commitments.

Strong revenue growth in 2015 caused HomeStreet's net income to nearly double to $41.32 million. The company's operating cash levels spiked to $8.31 million for the year (operations had used $348.6 million in 2014) mostly because it collected more in cash-denominated proceeds from its mortgage loan sales than it did in 2014.

Strategy

HomeStreet has been moving more toward commercial mortgage and SBA originations in recent years launching its HomeStreet commercial capital business in Orange County California in 2015. It also continues to acquire other small community banks in its region to grow its loan and deposit business and expand into new geographic markets.

Additionally it's been expanding its retail operations its own opening two new branches in San Diego's Mission Gorge and Kearny Mesa markets in March 2016. To boost profitability HomeStreet looked in 2016 to enhance productivity and cut costs by streamlining operations.

Mergers and Acquisitions

The company plans to buy two Southern California banks from Boston Private Bank & Trust. Through that acquisition HomeStreet will gain some $110 million in deposit accounts. It will then have a dozen retail branches in Southern California.

In February 2016 the company purchased Orange County Business Bank for $55 million extending its reach into "one of the premier commercial and consumer banking markets in the country" according to HomeStreet CEO and chairman Mark Mason.

In March 2015 HomeStreet expanded into Southern California's retail banking market after acquiring Simplicity Bancorp and its seven Simply Bank retail deposit branches in the greater Los Angeles area. Beyond geographic expansion the deal added valuable retail deposit and loan assets.

In November 2013 HomeStreet acquired Fortune Bank a community bank with two branches in Seattle and Bellevue for about $27 million. Concurrently it purchased YNB Financial Services Corp. the parent company of Yakima National Bank which operates four branches in Yakima Selah Sunnyside and Kennewick for about $10.3 million. The twin purchases along with the acquisition of two branches from AmericanWest Bank increased the number of retail deposit branches operates by HomeStreet to 29.

Company Background

HomeStreet went public in February 2012 with an offering worth $55 million. The company sold 1.6 million shares priced at $44 each. HomeStreet had postponed two previous attempts to go public in 2011 that had planned to sell many more shares. Proceeds from the 2012 IPO were used to meet capital-ratio requirements required by regulators in the wake of allegations that the bank engaged in unsafe practices.

HomeStreet was hit hard by the economic downturn and slowdown in the housing market. Trouble in its core mortgage lending business led to losses in 2009 and 2010 and the bank entered into agreements with regulators to improve its capital position earnings and management. It brought in a new management team and launched a turnaround plan to stabilize the business which included tightening its lending standards restructuring troubled loans when necessary and the sale of real estate backed by nonperforming loans. The measures helped HomeStreet return to profitability in 2011 and remain in the black for several years thereafter.

EXECUTIVES

Chairman President And Ceo Homestreet Inc. And Homestreet Bank, Mark K. Mason, age 58, $537,500 total compensation

Evp Chief Administrative Officer General Counsel And Corporate Secretary Homestreet Inc. And Homestreet Bank, Godfrey B. Evans, age 64, $247,200 total compensation

Sevp Commercial Banking Homestreet Bank, David H. Straus, age 71

Evp Homestreet Inc. And Evp Residential Construction And Affiliated Businesses Homestreet Bank, Richard W. H. (Rich) Bennion, age 68, $203,000 total compensation

Evp And Retail Banking Director Homestreet Bank, Paulette Lemon, age 61

Evp And Human Resources Director Homestreet Bank, Pamela J. (Pam) Taylor, age 66

Evp Chief Risk Officer And Chief Credit Officer Homestreet Inc. And Homestreet Bank, Jay C. Iseman, age 58, $200,000 total compensation

Sevp Mortgage Lending Director, Rose Marie David, age 54, $200,000 total compensation

Evp Commercial Real Estate And Commercial Capital President Homestreet Bank, William D. Endresen, age 63

Evp And Residential Construction Lending Director Homestreet Bank, Jeff Todhunter

Evp Chief Investment Officer And Treasurer Homestreet Inc. And Homestreet Bank, Darrell S. van Amen, age 52

Vice President Commercial Lending Manager, George Brace

Vice President Loan Officer, Carmen Esteban

Auditors: DELOITTE & TOUCHE LLP

LOCATIONS

HQ: HomeStreet Inc
601 Union Street, Suite 2000, Seattle, WA 98101
Phone: 206 623-3050
Web: www.homestreet.com

PRODUCTS/OPERATIONS

2015 Sales

	$ mil.	% of total
Interest		
Loans	152	34
Investment securities available for sale	11	3
Other	0	-
Non-interest		
Net gains on mortgage origination & sales activities	236	53
Mortgage servicing	24	6
Depositor & other retail banking fees	5	1
Gain on sale of investment securities available for sale	2	1
Bargain purchase gain	7	2
Insurance agency commission Income from WMS Series LLC and other	4	-
Total	**446**	**100**

Selected Services

Personal Banking
Home LoansInvestmentInsurancePrivate Bank
Commercial Banking
Builder Financing/Residential ConstructionCommercial LendingCommercial Real EstatePartnership Programs

COMPETITORS

American Savings Bank	KeyCorp
Bank of America	Sound Financial
Bank of Hawaii	U.S. Bancorp
Banner Corp	Umpqua Holdings
First Hawaiian	Washington Federal
JPMorgan Chase	Wells Fargo

HISTORICAL FINANCIALS

Company Type: Public

Income Statement

FYE: December 31

	ASSETS ($ mil.)	NET INCOME ($ mil.)	INCOME AS % OF ASSETS	EMPLOYEES
12/17	6,742	68	1.0%	2,419
12/16	6,243	58	0.9%	2,552
12/15	4,894	41	0.8%	2,139
12/14	3,535	22	0.6%	1,611
12/13	3,066	23	0.8%	1,502
Annual Growth	21.8%	30.4%	—	12.7%

2017 Year-End Financials

Debt ratio: 1.86%
Return on equity: 10.34%
Cash ($ mil.): 72
Current ratio: —
Long-term debt ($ mil.): —

No. of shares (mil.): 26
Dividends
Yield: —
Payout: —
Market value ($ mil.): 778

	STOCK PRICE ($) FY Close	P/E High/Low		PER SHARE ($) Earnings	Dividends	Book Value
12/17	28.95	13	9	2.54	0.00	26.20
12/16	31.60	14	8	2.34	0.00	23.48
12/15	21.71	12	9	1.96	0.00	21.08
12/14	17.41	14	11	1.49	0.44	20.34
12/13	20.00	17	11	1.61	0.33	17.97
Annual Growth	9.7%		—	12.1%	—	9.9%

HomeTrust Bancshares Inc.

EXECUTIVES

Chb-Pres-Ceo, Dana L Stonestreet
Exec V Pres-Cfo-Treas, Tony J Vuncannon
Exec V Pres-CIO, Howard L Sellinger
Exec V Pres-Cbo, C Hunter Westbrook
Exec V Pres-Chief ADM Officer-, Teresa White
Exec V Pres-Cro, R Parrish Little
Evp-Commercial Banking Group E, Mark Demarcus
President, Market, Robert D Gray
Vp, Commercial Relationship MA, Jeffery Chad Davis
Evp and Commercial Banking Gro, W Mark Demarcus
Deposit Operations Supervisor, Brenda Houck
Auditors: Dixon Hughes Goodman LLP

LOCATIONS

HQ: HomeTrust Bancshares Inc.
10 Woodfin Street, Asheville, NC 28801
Phone: 828 259-3939
Web: www.hometrustbancshares.com

HISTORICAL FINANCIALS

Company Type: Public

Income Statement

FYE: June 30

	ASSETS ($ mil.)	NET INCOME ($ mil.)	INCOME AS % OF ASSETS	EMPLOYEES
06/18	3,304	8	0.2%	520
06/17	3,206	11	0.4%	486
06/16	2,717	11	0.4%	465
06/15	2,783	8	0.3%	505
06/14	2,074	10	0.5%	471
Annual Growth	12.3%	(5.5%)	—	2.5%

2018 Year-End Financials

Debt ratio: 0.06%
Return on equity: 2.04%
Cash ($ mil.): 366
Current ratio: —
Long-term debt ($ mil.): —

No. of shares (mil.): 19
Dividends
Yield: —
Payout: —
Market value ($ mil.): 536

	STOCK PRICE ($) FY Close	P/E High/Low	PER SHARE ($) Earnings	Dividends	Book Value
06/18	28.15	65 50	0.44	0.00	21.49
06/17	24.40	41 27	0.65	0.00	20.96
06/16	18.50	32 26	0.65	0.00	20.00
06/15	16.76	40 35	0.42	0.00	19.04
06/14	15.77	31 28	0.54	0.00	18.28
Annual Growth	15.6%	— —	(5.0%)	—	4.1%

Honeywell International Inc

Jet engines and Muck Boots seem worlds apart but they coexist at Honeywell International. More than a century old the company is a diverse industrial conglomerate its four segments making and selling products from aircraft engines flight safety and landing systems to smart controls for commercial buildings to personal safety products such as gas masks and footwear. In late 2018 Honeywell completed the spin-off of its vehicle turbo charger operations and home heating and security businesses to create two new publicly-listed companies—Garrett Motion Inc. (turbo charger technology) and Resideo for home comfort and security products (formerly its Homes and ADI Distribution business). The company does business worldwide although the US generates more than half its sales.

Operations

Honeywell is organized across four segments: Aerospace; Performance Materials and Technologies; Building Technologies; and Safety and Productivity Solutions.

The Aerospace segment accounts for more than 35% of the company's revenue. It provides products and services for aircraft and vehicles sold to OEMs and other customers in a variety of end markets—air transport; regional business and general aviation aircraft; airlines and aircraft operators; defense and space contractors; and automotive and truck manufacturers.

Performance Materials and Technologies (more than 25% of revenue) operates in three divisions. Honeywell UOP provides process technology for fuel production for the petroleum refining gas processing and petrochemical industries; Process Solutions sells automation controls and software for the oil and gas pulp and paper industrial power and several other industries; and Advanced Materials manufactures high-performance products such as fluorocarbons specialty films waxes additives and advanced fibers to name a few.

The company's former Home and Building Technologies segment—now just Building Technologies—(almost 25%) sells building automation controls for commercial customers.

The Safety and Productivity Solutions segment (15%) offers products that improve productivity workplace safety and asset performance. Safety products include personal protection equipment and footwear. Productivity solutions include gas detection technology mobile devices and software for computing and data collection supply chain and warehouse automation equipment and sensors switches and controls.

Geographic Reach

The company's principal executive offices are located in Morris Plains NJ. Honeywell has approximately 1300 locations of which some 300 are manufacturing sites. The US accounts for more than 55% of total revenue.

Sales and Marketing

Honeywell's Aerospace business sells its products and services to original equipment manufacturers (OEMs) and other end markets like regional business and general aviation aircraft; airlines and aircraft operators; defense and space contractors; and automotive and truck manufacturers. The Building Technologies segment sells to commercial building owners. Performance Materials and Technologies targets several industries including oil and gas pulp and paper industrial power generation petrochemicals life sciences and mining. The Safety and Productivity Solutions business sells its products globally to a variety of industries.

Financial Performance

Honeywell's revenues increased 3% from $39.3 billion in 2016 to $40.5 billion in 2017. This growth was led by a 22% increase in its Safety and Productivity Solutions business.

Honeywell's net income plummeted to $1.7 billion in 2017 a $3.2 billion decrease from 2016. The decrease is attributed to the impact of additional tax expense from the Tax Cuts and Jobs Act. The company is working to better align its operating structure to benefit from the new tax system.

Cash at the end of fiscal 2017 was $7.0 billion a decrease of $784 million from the prior year. Cash from operations contributed $6.0 billion to the coffers while investing activities used $3.6 billion which included a net $2 billion increase in investments (mostly in marketable securities). Financing activities used another $3.5 billion for loan payments dividends to stockholders and the company's stock repurchase program.

Strategy

For all its segments Honeywell is focused on several initiatives to spur growth including R&D activities to develop new technologies. The company aims to become an industrial software company offering products for the connected plane home building and factory. Other initiatives that target lower costs are process improvements in its manufacturing and administrative operations and cost control efforts for asbestos and environmental remediation and pension and retirement benefits.

Honeywell's strategy for growth includes both acquisitions and the divestiture of under-performing units. In order to streamline its operations Honeywell in late 2018 completed the spin-off of its turbo charger unit and home heating and security businesses to create two new publicly traded companies. The new business featuring its turbo charger technology (formerly the Transportation Systems business) is now Garrett Motion Inc. Its former Homes and ADI Global Distribution business is now Resideo a company providing home comfort and security systems. After the spin-offs Honeywell believes its remaining portfolio will consist of high-growth businesses each aligned to the global megatrends of energy efficiency infrastructure investment urbanization and safety.

Mergers and Acquisitions

In 2018 Honeywell acquired the warehouse automation business Transnorm for approximately €425 million from IK Investment Partners. The acquisition enhances Honeywell's presence in the growing e-commerce market in Europe as Transnorm does more than half its business there. With Transnorm Honeywell hopes to build on the success of its 2016 acquisition of Intelligrated a maker of material handling equipment including conveyors sorters and airport baggage handling equipment as well as order fulfillment and warehouse control software.

Mid-2017 saw the company complete the purchase of Nextnine a provider of security management solutions and technologies for industrial cybersecurity. The addition of Nextnine's security solutions and secure remote service capabilities is meant to shore up Honeywells's existing range of cybersecurity technologies and increase its Connected Plant cybersecurity customer base.

HISTORY

During WWI Germany controlled much of the world's chemical industry causing dye and drug shortages. In response Washington Post publisher Eugene Meyer and scientist William Nichols organized the Allied Chemical & Dye Corporation in 1920.

Allied opened a synthetic ammonia plant in 1928 near Hopewell Virginia and became the world's leading producer of ammonia. After WWII Allied began making nylon refrigerants and other products. The company became Allied Chemical Corporation in 1958.

Seeking a supplier of raw materials for its chemical products Allied bought Union Texas Natural Gas in 1962. In the early 1970s CEO John Connor sold many of the firm's unprofitable businesses and invested in oil and gas exploration. By 1979 when Edward Hennessy became CEO Union Texas produced 80% of Allied's income.

Hennessy led the company into the electronics and technical markets. Under a new name Allied Corporation (1981) it bought the Bendix Corporation an aerospace and automotive company in 1983. In 1985 Allied merged with Signal Companies (founded by Sam Mosher in 1922) to form AlliedSignal. The company spun off more than 40 unprofitable chemical and engineering businesses over the next two years.

Larry Bossidy hired from General Electric in 1991 as the new CEO began to cut waste and buy growth businesses. In 1998 alone the company made 13 acquisitions. Late in 1999 the company acquired Honeywell (which dated back to 1906) in a deal valued at $15 billion and changed its name to Honeywell International. Honeywell after trying to make a go of it in the computer and telecommunications industries had refocused on its core products lines — thermostats security systems and other automation equipment.

In 2016 Honeywell was engaged in talks to merge with industry powerhouse United Technologies Corp. in a merger valued at around $90 billion. The talks ended however after United Technologies refused to explore the deal further fearing that the massive transaction could not clear steep regulatory hurdles.

EXECUTIVES

President And Ceo Aerospace, Timothy O. (Tim) Mahoney, age 61, $917,019 total compensation
President And Ceo Global High Growth Regions, Shane Tedjarati
President And Ceo Home And Building Technologies (hbt), Terrence S. Hahn, age 52
Svp Engineering Operations And Information Technology, Krishna Mikkilineni, age 58, $717,678 total compensation
President And Ceo Performance Materials And Technologies, Rajeev Gautam, age 65
President And Ceo Safety And Productivity Solutions (sps), John Waldron, age 42
Svp And Cfo, Thomas A. (Tom) Szlosek, age 54, $840,000 total compensation
President And Ceo, Darius Adamczyk, age 52, $1,120,383 total compensation
President And Ceo Honeywell Transportation Systems, Olivier Rabiller
President Honeywell Intelligrated, Pieter Krynauw
President Honeywell Thailand, Mai Trang Thanh
Vice President General Manager Resins And Chemicals, Qamar S Bhatia
Vice President Marketing, Brian Holliday
Vice President Electrical Sourcing, Lawrence Polizzotto
Vice President Marketing, Athanasios Karras
Vice President Americas Htt, Anthony Schultz
Chairman, David M. (Dave) Cote, age 65
Auditors: DELOITTE & TOUCHE LLP

LOCATIONS

HQ: Honeywell International Inc
115 Tabor Road, Morris Plains, NJ 07950
Phone: 973 455-2000   **Fax:** 973 455-4807
Web: www.honeywell.com

2017 Sales

	$ mil.	% of total
US	22,722	56
Europe	10,400	26
Other International	7,412	18
Total	**40,534**	**100**

PRODUCTS/OPERATIONS

2017 Sales

	$ mil.	% of total
Aerospace	14,779	36
Performance Materials and Technologies	10,339	26
Home and Building Technologies	9,777	24
Safety and Productivity Solutions	5,639	14
Total	**40,534**	**100**

2017 Sales

	$ mil.	% of total
Product sales	32,317	80
Service sales	8,217	20
Total	**40,534**	**100**

Selected Products and Services

Aerospace
  Aircraft engines
  Auxiliary turbine power unites
  Cockpit systems and displays
  Cabin management and entertainment
  Air and thermal management
  Biofuel for aviation
  BendixKing avionics
Buildings
  Building automation systems
  Software and controls
  Construction and maintenance
  Security and fire services
  Combustion controls
Footwear
  Oliver safety footwear
  Muck boots
  Xtratuf boots
Healthcare
  Workflow automation for hospitals
  Patient monitoring systems
  Pharmaceutical laboratory products
  Pharmaceutical packaging films
Industrial
  Facility security and maintenance
  Energy solutions
  Honeywell Smart Energy for utilities
  Instrumentation for measurement and control
  Fuels and chemicals for clean power
Manufacturing
  Sensors and switches
  Advanced fibers and composites
  Renewable energy from biomass
  Honeywell MXProLine Quality Control System
  Honeywell HydroBlock anti-graffiti barrier film
Oil and Gas
  Refining technology
  Petrochemicals
  Gas processing equipment
  Adsorbents for contaminant removal
  Honeywell Green Diesel fuel
  Industrial water treatment
  Gas tank terminal operations controls
  Personal protective equipment
  Rope and performance fibers
Performance Materials
  Catalysts
  Refrigerants
  Honeywell Electronic Materials
  Research chemicals
  Honeywell Aclar barrier film for pharmaceutical packaging
  Honeywell Spectra fiber for braided fishing line
  Honeywell Specialty Additives
Productivity
  Barcode scanners
  Mobile computer devices
  Printers and media for RFID labels tags etc.
  Wearable devices
  OEM scan engines and modules
  Workflow solutions
  Vocollect voice technology for data collection
  Global tracking and messaging
  Search and rescue technology and services
Safety
  Protective equipment
  Honeywell Instant Alert cloud-based notification and emergency messaging

COMPETITORS

3M	Kion Group
Albemarle	MSA Safety
BASF SE	Rockwell Automation
BorgWarner	Rockwell Collins
Dow Chemical	Schneider Electric
DuPont	Siemens AG
Emerson Electric	TE Connectivity
GE	Thales
Garmin	United Technologies
Itron	Zebra Technologies
Johnson Controls Power Solutions	

HISTORICAL FINANCIALS

Company Type: Public

Income Statement
FYE: December 31

	REVENUE ($ mil.)	NET INCOME ($ mil.)	NET PROFIT MARGIN	EMPLOYEES
12/18	41,802	6,765	16.2%	114,000
12/17	40,534	1,655	4.1%	131,000
12/16	39,302	4,809	12.2%	131,000
12/15	38,581	4,768	12.4%	129,000
12/14	40,306	4,239	10.5%	127,000
Annual Growth	**0.9%**	**12.4%**	**—**	**(2.7%)**

2018 Year-End Financials

Debt ratio: 28.07%
Return on equity: 38.15%
Cash ($ mil.): 9,287
Current ratio: 1.29
Long-term debt ($ mil.): 9,756

No. of shares (mil.): 729
Dividends
  Yield: 2.3%
  Payout: 89.6%
Market value ($ mil.): 96,327

	STOCK PRICE ($) FY Close	P/E High/Low		PER SHARE ($) Earnings	Dividends	Book Value
12/18	132.12	18	14	8.98	3.06	24.94
12/17	153.36	72	54	2.14	2.74	23.01
12/16	115.85	19	15	6.20	2.45	25.46
12/15	103.57	18	15	6.04	2.15	24.11
12/14	99.92	19	16	5.33	1.87	22.85
Annual Growth	**7.2%**	**—**	**—**	**13.9%**	**13.1%**	**2.2%**

Hope Bancorp Inc

EXECUTIVES

Vice President And Systems Support Manager, Joshua Chu
Senior Vice President And Chief Credit Officer, Peter Koh
Senior Vice President And Manager Loan Center Iii We Are Now Bank Of Hope, Christie Yoo
Vice President Information Technology Procurement Manager, Karina Moran
Fvp And Manager General Services Department, Brandon Lee
Vice President Desktop Analyst Ii, Eunmoo Choi
Vice President Desktop Manager We Are Now Bank Of Hope, Charles Yoo
Senior Vice President Institutional Banking Director Business Aircraft, Scott Schaidle
Senior Vice President Manager Vendor Risk Management, Bradley Martin
Aap Senior Vice President Tms Operations Manager, Rachel Lim
Senior Vice President And Director Of Investment Banking Operations, Charuka Sinhabahu
Vice President And Operational Risk Management Assistant, Katelyn Kang

First Vice President And Senior Financial Analyst, Joonhyok Shin
Avp And Loan Officer Bank Of Hope, James Chong
Senior Vice President And Marketing Manager Senior Business Analyst Loan Department, Gene Pak
Auditors: Crowe Horwath LLP

LOCATIONS

HQ: Hope Bancorp Inc
3200 Wilshire Boulevard, Suite 1400, Los Angeles, CA 90010
Phone: 213 639-1700   **Fax:** 213 235-3033
Web: www.bankofhope.com

PRODUCTS/OPERATIONS

2015 Sales

	$ mil.	% of total
Interest income	313	88
Non-interest income	43	12
Total	**357**	**100**

COMPETITORS

Bank of America	Grandpoint
Broadway Financial	Hanmi Financial
Cathay General Bancorp	U.S. Bancorp
East West Bancorp	Wells Fargo
Far East National Bank	Woori

HISTORICAL FINANCIALS

Company Type: Public

Income Statement   FYE: December 31

	ASSETS ($ mil.)	NET INCOME ($ mil.)	INCOME AS % OF ASSETS	EMPLOYEES
12/17	14,206	139	1.0%	1,470
12/16	13,441	113	0.8%	1,372
12/15	7,912	92	1.2%	938
12/14	7,140	88	1.2%	915
12/13	6,475	81	1.3%	835
Annual Growth	**21.7%**	**14.3%**	**—**	**15.2%**

2017 Year-End Financials

Debt ratio: 0.71%
Return on equity: 7.37%
Cash ($ mil.): 492
Current ratio: —
Long-term debt ($ mil.): —

No. of shares (mil.): 135
Dividends
  Yield: 0.0%
  Payout: 48.5%
Market value ($ mil.): 2,473

	STOCK PRICE ($) FY Close	P/E High/Low		Earnings	PER SHARE ($) Dividends	Book Value
12/17	18.25	22	15	1.03	0.50	14.23
12/16	21.89	20	13	1.10	0.45	13.72
12/15	17.22	17	11	1.16	0.42	11.79
12/14	14.38	16	12	1.11	0.35	11.10
12/13	16.59	16	11	1.03	0.25	10.19
Annual Growth	**2.4%**	**—**	**—**	**(0.0%)**	**18.9%**	**8.7%**

Horace Mann Educators Corp.

Naming itself in honor of Horace Mann considered the father of public education Horace Mann Educators is an insurance holding company that primarily serves K-12 school teachers and other public school employees throughout the US.

Through its operating subsidiaries the company offers homeowners auto (majority of revenue) and individual and group life insurance as well as retirement annuities. Horace Mann employs some 735 agents many of whom are former teachers themselves. Writing business in 48 states and Washington DC the company derives about a third of its direct premiums and contract deposits from five states — California Illinois Texas North Carolina and Florida.

Operations

Horace Mann maintains a long-standing relationship with the country's biggest education association the National Education Association which has around 3.2 million members. It has also established a number of advertising and sponsorship agreements with a host of smaller educator groups as a way to drum up new business leads.

The company divides it business into property/casualty insurance annuities and life insurance. Property/casualty is the largest contributor to revenue with auto being the largest component of that group. The propertycasualty annuity and life segments account for some 48% 44% and 8% respectively of the company's insurance premiums and contract deposits.

Geographic Reach

The company is based in Springfield Illinois.

Financial Performance

Horace Mann's net revenue has been increasing steadily in recent years and in fiscal 2015 climbed a further 2% to $1.1 billion. The company was able to charge higher average premiums per policy for homeowners and automobiles.

Net income however has been falling consistently in the past five years and in fiscal 2015 fell 10% to $93.5 million due to an increase in property/casualty loss severity (particularly in automobile) as well as catastrophe costs and life mortality costs. Cash from operating activities fell 7% to $207.0 million due to an increase in claims and policyholder benefits paid.

Strategy

In recent years the company has moved away from single-person agency operations to an agency business model (ABM) with multiple sales agents licensed product specialists and other support personnel based together in outside offices. The company saw enough success with the ABM model that it began migrating agents over to an exclusive agent agreement through which the agents become independent contractors that only sell Horace Mann products. Nearly all its agents now operate in this manner.

Mergers and Acquisitions

In early 2019 Horace Mann acquired retirement plan coordinator Benefits Consultants Group further expanding its operations in the retirement market.

EXECUTIVES

Executive Vice President Service And Technology Operations And Financial Services, George J Zock
Evp And Cfo, Dwayne D. Hallman, age 55, $444,000 total compensation
President And Ceo, Marita Zuraitis, age 57, $742,333 total compensation
Evp Annuity And Life, Matthew P. Sharpe, $394,000 total compensation
Evp Property And Casualty, William J. Caldwell, $325,000 total compensation
Assistant Vice Presi, Paul Wappel
Vice President Human Resources, Kathi Karr
Vice President Chief Actuary, Robert Rich
Assistant Vice President Claims Training, Jill Kilroy
Chairman, Gabriel L. Shaheen, age 65
Auditors: KPMG LLP

LOCATIONS

HQ: Horace Mann Educators Corp.
1 Horace Mann Plaza, Springfield, IL 62715-0001
Phone: 217 789-2500
Web: www.horacemann.com

PRODUCTS/OPERATIONS

2016 Sales

	$ mil.	% of total
Insurance premiums & contract charges earned	759	67
Net investment income	361	32
Net realized investment gains	4	-
Other income	4	1
Total	**1,128**	**100**

COMPETITORS

AIG	Nationwide
AXA	Progressive
Allstate	Corporation
Farmers Group	Security Benefit Group
GEICO	State Farm
ING Americas	TIAA
LSW	USAA
Liberty Mutual Agency	VALIC
MetLife	

HISTORICAL FINANCIALS

Company Type: Public

Income Statement   FYE: December 31

	ASSETS ($ mil.)	NET INCOME ($ mil.)	INCOME AS % OF ASSETS	EMPLOYEES
12/17	11,198	169	1.5%	1,496
12/16	10,576	83	0.8%	2,061
12/15	10,059	93	0.9%	2,034
12/14	9,768	104	1.1%	2,008
12/13	8,826	110	1.3%	2,095
Annual Growth	**6.1%**	**11.2%**	**—**	**(8.1%)**

2017 Year-End Financials

Debt ratio: 2.66%
Return on equity: 12.12%
Cash ($ mil.): 7
Current ratio: —
Long-term debt ($ mil.): —

No. of shares (mil.): 40
Dividends
  Yield: 0.0%
  Payout: 26.9%
Market value ($ mil.): 1,796

	STOCK PRICE ($) FY Close	P/E High/Low		Earnings	PER SHARE ($) Dividends	Book Value
12/17	44.10	12	8	4.08	1.10	36.88
12/16	42.80	21	14	2.02	1.06	32.15
12/15	33.18	17	14	2.20	1.00	31.18
12/14	33.18	13	11	2.47	0.92	32.65
12/13	31.54	11	7	2.66	0.78	27.14
Annual Growth	**8.7%**	**—**	**—**	**11.3%**	**9.0%**	**8.0%**

Horizon Bancorp Inc

For those in Indiana and Michigan Horizon Bancorp stretches as far as the eye can see. The company is the holding company for Horizon Bank (and its Heartland Community Bank division) which provides checking and savings accounts IRAs CDs and credit cards to customers through more than 50 branches in north and central Indiana and southwest and central Michigan. Commercial financial and agricultural loans make up the largest segment of its loan portfolio which also includes mortgage warehouse loans (loans earmarked for sale into the secondary market) consumer loans and residential mortgages. Through subsidiaries the bank offers trust and investment management services; life health and property/casualty insurance; and annuities.

Operations

Horizon boasted more than $2.08 billion in total assets and $1.48 billion in deposits in 2014. Commercial loans made up 49% of the bank's total loan portfolio. The bank employed nearly 450 full and part time employees that year.

Horizon's subsidiaries include: Horizon Investments which manages the bank's investment portfolio; Horizon Properties which manages the real estate investment trust; Horizon Insurance Services which sells through the company's Wealth Management; and Horizon Grantor Trust which holds title to certain company-owned life insurance policies.

The bank generated 61% of its revenue from interest income on loans in 2014 while another 13% came from interest on its taxable and tax-exempt investments. About 8% of revenues came from gains on its mortgage sales while the remainder of revenues were mostly generated by a mix of service charges on deposit accounts interchange fees and fiduciary activities fees.

Geographic Reach

The bank's more than 30 branches serve customers in north and central Indiana and southwest and central Michigan. Its mortgage-banking services are offered across the Midwest.

Financial Performance

Horizon Bancorp's revenues and profits have been trending higher over the past few years mostly as it's continued to grow its loan business and deposit customer base through acquisitions.

The bank's revenue rose by 2% to $102.5 million in 2014 mostly as the bank increased its interest-earning assets during the year. Its non-interest income also increased thanks to higher service charges on deposits and interchange fee income resulting from the growth in transactional deposit accounts and volume.

Despite higher revenue in 2014 the company's net income fell by 9% to $18.1 million for the year on higher provisions for loan losses due to loan growth and a write off of a commercial account coupled with an increase in transaction costs related to its Summit acquisition and an increase in salaries and employee benefits due to growth. Horizon's operating cash levels fell by 62% to $17.7 million after adjusting its earnings for non-cash items related to its net proceeds on the sale of its held-for-sale loans.

Strategy

Horizon Bancorp continues to expand its geographic reach and loan business through acquisitions and new branches. It acquired several banks and opened new branches throughout 2016 and 2017.

Mergers and Acquisitions

In 2017 Horizon Bancorp agreed to buy Wolverine Bancorp for $92 million and Lafayette Community Bancorp for $32 million

In 2016 Horizon Bancorp bought LaPorte Bancorp for $98.9 million boosting its total assets by 20% to more than $3.24 billion while expanding its branch reach into the LaPorte area of Indiana. It also agreed to buy CNB Bancorp which operates Central National Bank & Trust in Attica Indiana.

In 2015 Horizon Bancorp agreed to buy Peoples Bancorp and subsidiary Peoples Federal Savings Bank of DeKalb County.

In April 2014 the company purchased SCP Bancorp including subsidiary Summit Community Bank and its two branches.

EXECUTIVES

President Ceo Chief Administrative Officer And Director; Chairman And Ceo Horizon Bank, Craig M. Dwight, age 61, $300,000 total compensation

Evp; President And Coo Horizon Bank, Thomas H. Edwards, age 65, $187,000 total compensation

Cfo, Mark E. Secor, age 52, $131,921 total compensation

President Laporte County Indiana Horizon Bank, Steven C. Kring

President Southwest Michigan Horizon Bank, Donald E. (Don) Radde, age 65, $166,000 total compensation

President Porter County Indiana Horizon Bank, David G. Rose

Vice President Data Processing, Bradford Smith

Chairman, Robert C. Dabagia, age 79

Auditors: BKD, LLP

LOCATIONS

HQ: Horizon Bancorp Inc
   515 Franklin Square, Michigan City, IN 46360
Phone: 219 879-0211
Web: www.horizonbank.com

PRODUCTS/OPERATIONS

Selected Subsidiaries

Horizon Bank National Association
   Horizon Insurance Services Inc.
   Horizon Investments Inc.
   Horizon Trust & Investment Management N.A.

COMPETITORS

1st Source Corporation	Farmers Mutual of NE
American United Mutual	Fifth Third
Bank of America	First Merchants
Brotherhood Mutual	Indiana Farmers Mutual

HISTORICAL FINANCIALS

Company Type: Public

Income Statement   FYE: December 31

	ASSETS ($ mil.)	NET INCOME ($ mil.)	INCOME AS % OF ASSETS	EMPLOYEES
12/17	3,964	33	0.8%	701
12/16	3,141	23	0.8%	665
12/15	2,652	20	0.8%	558
12/14	2,076	18	0.9%	448
12/13	1,758	19	1.1%	421
Annual Growth	**22.5%**	**13.6%**	**—**	**13.6%**

2017 Year-End Financials

Debt ratio: 1.27%	No. of shares (mil.): 38
Return on equity: 8.30%	Dividends
Cash ($ mil.): 76	Yield: 0.0%
Current ratio: —	Payout: 33.5%
Long-term debt ($ mil.): —	Market value ($ mil.): 1,065

	STOCK PRICE ($) FY Close	P/E High/Low		PER SHARE ($) Earnings	Dividends	Book Value
12/17	27.80	30	26	0.95	0.32	11.94
12/16	28.00	40	26	0.79	0.27	10.25
12/15	27.96	33	26	0.84	0.25	9.93
12/14	26.14	30	22	0.84	0.23	9.38
12/13	25.33	26	19	0.96	0.19	8.47
Annual Growth	**2.4%**	**—**	**—**	**(0.3%)**	**14.4%**	**8.9%**

Hormel Foods Corp.

The maker of such thrifty pantry staples as SPAM lunch meat and Dinty Moore stew Hormel Foods produces a slew of refrigerated processed meats and deli items ethnic entrees and frozen foods sold under the flagship Hormel brand as well as Don Miguel and MegaMex (Mexican) and Lloyd's (barbeque). Food service offerings include Hormel Natural Choice meats CafA© H Austin Blues and Bread Ready pre-sliced meats. Hormel is also a major US turkey and pork processor churning out Jennie-O turkey Cure 81 hams and Always Tender pork. More than 30 Hormel brands are ranked #1 or #2 in their respective markets.

HISTORY

George Hormel opened his Austin Minnesota slaughterhouse in an abandoned creamery in 1891. By 1900 Hormel had modernized his facilities to compete with larger meat processors. In 1903 the enterprise introduced its first brand name (Dairy Brand) and a year later began opening distribution centers nationwide. The scandal that ensued after the discovery in 1921 that an assistant controller had embezzled over $1 million almost broke the company causing Hormel to initiate tighter controls. By 1924 it was processing more than a million hogs annually. Hormel introduced canned ham two years later.

Jay Hormel George's son became president in 1929; under his guidance Hormel introduced Dinty Moore beef stew (1936) and SPAM (1937). A Hormel executive won a contest and $100 by submitting the name a contraction of "spiced ham." During WWII the US government bought over half of Hormel's output; it supplied SPAM to GIs and Allied forces.

In 1959 Hormel introduced its Little Sizzlers pork sausage and sold its billionth can of SPAM. New products rolled out in the 1960s included Hormel's Cure 81 ham (1963). By the mid-1970s the firm had more than 750 products.

The company survived a violent nationally publicized strike triggered by a pay cut in 1985. In the end only 500 of the original 1500 strikers returned to accept lower pay scales.

Sensing the consumer shift toward poultry Hormel purchased Jennie-O Foods in 1986. Later acquisitions included the House of Tsang and Oriental Deli (1992) Dubuque (processed pork 1993) and Herb-Ox (bouillon and dry soup mix 1993). After more than a century as Geo. A. Hormel & Co. the company began calling itself Hormel Foods in 1993 to reflect its expansion into non-pork foods. Former General Foods executive Joel Johnson was named president and CEO that year (and chairman two years later).

Hormel proved it could take a joke with the 1994 debut of its tongue-in-cheek SPAM catalog featuring dozens of SPAM-related products. But when a 1996 Muppets movie featured a porcine character named Spa'am Hormel sued Jim Henson Productions; a federal court gave Spa'am the go-ahead.

Also in 1996 Hormel teamed up with Mexican food processor Grupo Herdez to sell Herdez sauces and other Mexican food products in the US. It then formed a joint venture with Indian food producer Patak Spices (UK) to market its products in the US. Late that year Hormel paid $64 million for a 21% interest in Spanish food maker Campofrio Alimentacion.

Earnings fell in 1996 due in part to soaring hog prices. The company was hit hard again in 1998 when production contracts with hog growers meant it wound up paying premium rates despite a market glut. In 1998 the Smithsonian Institution accepted two cans of SPAM (one from 1937 the other an updated 1997 version) for its History of Technology collection.

SPAM sales soared in 1999 as nervous consumers stockpiled provisions for the millennium. To build its growing HealthLabs division Hormel acquired Cliffdale Farms (2000) and Diamond Crystal Brands nutritional products (a division of Imperial Sugar) in 2001 — boosting its share of the market for easy-to-swallow foods sold to hospitals and nursing homes.

In early 2001 Hormel acquired family-owned The Turkey Store for approximately $334 million and folded it into its Jennie-O division.

Hormel produced its 6 billionth can of SPAM in 2002 and traded $115 million in stock to acquire the rest of Imperial Sugar's Diamond Crystal Brands unit which packages single-serve packets of sugar sweeteners seasonings and plastic cutlery for the foodservice industry.

To further diversify in 2003 Hormel acquired food manufacturer Century Foods International (whey-based protein powders beverages and nutrition bars) and added it to its burgeoning specialty foods group. In 2004 Hormel sold off its stake in Campofrio to Smithfield Foods.

Its last act of business in 2004 was to purchase Southern California's Clougherty Packing for about $186 million. The pork processor's facilities help extend Hormel's capacity for further-processed foods in the southwestern US.

In 2005 the company purchased Mexican food manufacturer Arriba Foods for $47 million in cash. Later that year it bought Lloyd's Barbeque Company from General Mills.

Responding to the growing trend of the US population to dine out Hormel expanded its foodservice segment (which it refers to as its specialty foods business) with the 2005 purchase of foodservice food manufacturer and distributor Mark-Lynn Foods. Mark-Lynn's products include salt and pepper packets ketchup mustard sauces and salad dressings creamers and sugar packets as well as jellies desserts and drink mixes.

Adding to its grocery product offerings in 2006 the company acquired canned ready-to-eat chicken producer Valley Fresh Foods for $78 million. It also bought pepperoni and pasta maker Provena Foods and sausage and sliced meat maker Saag's Products. It added another to its list of countries in which it has joint ventures in 2006 when it formed a JV with San Miguel to raise and market hogs and animal feed in Vietnam. The JV is 49%-owned by Hormel.

Hormel acquired Burke Corporation a maker of pizza toppings and other fully cooked meat items in 2007 for $115 million in cash. The acquisition allowed Hormel to extend its pizza-topping operations into the foodservice sector. The following year it acquired Boca Grande Foods for $23.5 in cash. Boca Grande makes Poco Pac branded jams jellies and pancake syrup portion-control products for foodservice operators.

EXECUTIVES

Group Vice President; President Hormel Foods International, Richard A Bross
Vice President, David Longacre
Vice President Marketing For Foodservice Group, David F Weber
Evp And President Hormel Business Units, Steven G. Binder, age 61, $500,965 total compensation
Group Vp And President Hormel Foods International, Larry L. Vorpahl, age 55
Vp And Chief Accounting Officer, James N. Sheehan, age 63

Group Vp Refrigerated Foods, Thomas R. Day, age 60, $337,900 total compensation
Svp Supply Chain, Bryan D. Farnsworth, age 61
Group Vp And President Consumer Products Sales, Deanna T. Brady, age 53
Group Vp Specialty Foods, Donald H. (Don) Kremin, age 58
Chairman President And Ceo, James P. Snee, age 50, $509,595 total compensation
Group Vp And President Jennie-o Turkey Store, Glenn R. Leitch, age 57, $380,500 total compensation
Group Vp Foodservice, Jeffrey R. Baker, age 53
Group Vp Grocery Products, Luis G. Marconi, age 51
Vp Information Technology Services, Mark D. Vaupel
Vice President Engineering, Tyler Hulsebus
Vice President, Alan Rasell
Vice President Supply Chain, William Snyder
National Sales Manager Case Ready Meats, Jeff Schultz
National Sales Manager, Mark Engelhardt
National Sales Manager, Michael Dougherty
Svp External Affairs And General Counsel, Lori Marco
Vice President And Corporate Secretary, Brian Johnson
Vice President Corporate Communications, Juile Craven
Vice President Corporate Development, Fred Halvin
Vice President Farm Operations, Jose Rojas
National Sales Manager, Julie A Kerr
Vice President Treasurer, Rollie Gentzler
Vice President And Director Of Marketing And Administration, Tim Barinka
Vice President Supply Chain, Bill Snyder
Vp Corporate Innovation And Consumer Insights, D Scott Aakre
Vp Operations Refrigerated Foods, Donald Temperley
Board Member, Robert Nakasone
Board Member, Susan K Nestegard
Board Member, Dakota Pippins
Board Member, Gary Bhojwani
Board Member, Glenn Forbes
Board Member, Sally Smith
Vice President Finance And Treasurer, Gary Jamison
Auditors: Ernst & Young LLP

LOCATIONS

HQ: Hormel Foods Corp.
1 Hormel Place, Austin, MN 55912-3680
Phone: 507 437-5611   **Fax:** 507 437-5489
Web: www.hormel.com

FY2017 sales

	$ mil.	% of total
US	8	94
Foreign	536	6
Total	**9,167**	**100**

PRODUCTS/OPERATIONS

FY2017 sales

	$ mil.	% of total
Grocery Products	1,761	19
Refrigerated Foods	4,403	48
Jennie-O Turkey Store	1,663	18
Specialty Foods	794	9
International & Other	545	6
Total	**9,167**	**100**

Selected Products and Brands

Refrigerated
Country Crock Side Dishes
Hormel
Hormel Always Tender flavored pork and beef products
Hormel Black Label and Microwave Ready bacon
Hormel Cure 81 ham
Hormel Fresh Pantry meats

Hormel Little Sizzlers pork sausage
Hormel Natural Choice meats
Hormel pepperoni minis and stix
Hormel refrigerated entrees
Hormel Wranglers franks
Hormel Snac Cups
Lloyd's Barbeque products
Saag's sausages
Jennie-O Turkey Store
Bratwursts and breakfast/dinner sausages
Breast meat products
Deli
Di Lusso deli meats
Farmer John deli meats
Hormel 100 percent natural deli meats
Hormel Deli beef dry sausage ham and turkey
Hormel party trays
Ground turkey
Marinated turkey tenderloins
So-Easy Entrees
Turkey burger patties and franks
Whole turkeys
Grocery products
Dinty Moore stew Hearty Meals varieties microwave-ready products
Herb-Ox bouillon
Herdez Salsa
Hormel
Hormel bacon toppings
Hormel Chili Master
Hormel chunk meats
Hormel Compleats microwave meals
Hormel corned beef and roast beef with gravy
Hormel dried beef
Hormel Kid's Kitchen microwave cups
Hormel Mary Kitchen hash
Hormel microwave cups
Not-So-Sloppy-Joe sloppy joe sauce
Skippy peanut butter
SPAM products (classic hickory smoke flavored hot and spicy lite low-sodium spread singles and oven-roasted turkey)
Stagg chili
Valley Fresh chunk meats and broths
Specialty Foods
Century Foods International (dairy and vegetable proteins nutraceuticals)
Diamond Crystal Brands (salts sugar substitutes)
Hormel Foods Ingredients (sauces powders broths oils Omega-3 additives)
Private Label products (canned meats prepared foods and desserts bouillon sweeteners salts seasonings)
Other
MegaMex Mexican brands
Bufalo hot sauces
CHI-CHI'S Mexican hot sauces taco tubs dips seasoning mixes and tortillas
Do?a María Authentic Mexican products
Don Miguel burritos appetizers empanadas taquitos tacos flautas chimichangas enchiladas
El Torito sauces dressings and corn cakes
Embasa Mexican peppers salsas
Herdez imported salsas
La Victoria Mexican salsas taco sauces enchilada sauces green chile peppers
Wholly Guacamole
World Food ethnic brands
House of Tsang entrees sauces and oils
Marrakesh Express Mediterranean products (couscous risotto)
Peloponnese Greek foods olives

Selected Foodservice Brands

Always Tender Pork
Austin Blues barbeque meats
Authentic Barbeque
Bread Ready pre-sliced meats
Café H ethnic meats
Cure 81 Ham
Dry Sausage
Fast 'N Easy Fully Cooked Meats
Hormel Chili
Masterpieces Toppings
Natural Choice meats
Old Smokehouse bacon
Old Tyme breakfast sausage
Old Tyme ham
Special Recipe Sausage
Stagg Chili

COMPETITORS

B&G Foods	H. J. Heinz Limited
Boar's Head	JBS USA
Bob Evans	Perdue Incorporated
Bridgford Foods	Pilgrim's Pride
Bush Brothers	Pinnacle Foods
Butterball	Plainville Farms
Campbell Soup	Sanderson Farms
Cargill	Seaboard
ConAgra	Smithfield Foods
Cooper Farms	Smucker
Foster Farms	The Dial Corporation
General Mills	Tyson Foods

HISTORICAL FINANCIALS

Company Type: Public

Income Statement

FYE: October 28

	REVENUE ($ mil.)	NET INCOME ($ mil.)	NET PROFIT MARGIN	EMPLOYEES
10/18	9,545	1,012	10.6%	20,100
10/17	9,167	846	9.2%	20,200
10/16	9,523	890	9.3%	21,100
10/15	9,263	686	7.4%	20,700
10/14	9,316	602	6.5%	20,400
Annual Growth	0.6%	13.8%	—	(0.4%)

2018 Year-End Financials

Debt ratio: 7.67%
Return on equity: 19.26%
Cash ($ mil.): 459
Current ratio: 1.80
Long-term debt ($ mil.): 624
No. of shares (mil.): 534
Dividends
Yield: 0.0%
Payout: 40.3%
Market value ($ mil.): 21,990

	STOCK PRICE ($) FY Close	P/E High/Low	PER SHARE ($) Earnings	Dividends	Book Value
10/18	41.17	22 16	1.86	0.75	10.49
10/17	30.38	24 19	1.57	0.68	9.34
10/16	38.22	49 20	1.64	0.58	8.42
10/15	68.33	53 39	1.27	0.50	7.57
10/14	52.54	46 37	1.12	0.40	6.84
Annual Growth	(5.9%)	— —	13.6%	17.0%	11.3%

Horton (DR) Inc

The largest US homebuilder by volume D.R. Horton constructs single-family homes that range in size from 1000 sq. ft. to more than 4000 sq. ft. and sell for an average price of about $300000 under the D.R. Horton Emerald Homes Express Homes and Freedom Homes brand names. Texas-based D.R. Horton is active in about 80 markets in nearly 30 states and generates about 75% of its revenue from the Southeast South Central and Western regions of the US. Beyond single-family detached homes which account for nearly 90% of sales D.R. Horton builds duplexes townhomes and condominiums. It also provides mortgage title and closing services through its DHI Mortgage subsidiary.

HISTORY

Donald R. Horton was selling homes in Fort Worth Texas when he hit upon a strategy for increasing sales — add options to a basic floor plan. In 1978 he borrowed $33000 to build his first home added a bay window for an additional charge and sold the home for $44000. Donald soon added floor plans and options that appealed to regional preferences.

The depressed Texas market drove the company to expand beyond the Dallas/Fort Worth area in 1987 when it entered the then-hot Phoenix market. It continued to expand into the Southeast Mid-Atlantic Midwest and West in the late 1980s and early 1990s. By 1991 Horton and his family owned more than 25 companies that were combined as D.R. Horton which went public in 1992.

D.R. Horton acquired six geographically diverse construction firms in 1994 and 1995. In 1996 the company started a mortgage services joint venture expanded its title operations and added three more firms.

In 1998 the company bought four builders including Scottsdale Arizona-based Continental Homes. Continental had been expanding beyond its Arizona and Southern California base and had entered the lucrative retirement community market. After the Continental purchase Donald Horton stepped down as president remaining chairman. Richard Beckwitt took over as president and Donald Tomnitz became CEO. In 1999 the company acquired Century Title and Midwest builder Cambridge Properties.

D.R. Horton sold its St. Louis assets to McBride & Son Enterprises in 2000 after spending five years trying to break into the St. Louis homebuilding market. Tomnitz also took over the duties of president in 2000 when Beckwitt retired.

D.R. Horton gained homebuilding operations in Houston and Phoenix when it bought Emerald Builders in 2001. In February 2002 the company acquired Schuler Homes for $1.2 billion including debt.

Sales continued to climb in fiscal 2003 and 2004. D.R. Horton experienced its 27th consecutive year of earnings and revenue growth in 2004 and broke records by being the first residential homebuilder to sell more than 45000 homes in the US in a fiscal year; in fiscal 2005 the company closed 51172 homes. By 2007 however it was evident that the heady days were over with a rise in cancellations and a larger value of backlog orders.

CEO Donald Tomnitz summed up the housing market crash when he said "I don't want to be too sophisticated here but '07 is going to suck all 12 months of the calendar year." Indeed the company suffered a loss that year and the next when sales orders declined and cancellation rates rose due to tightened mortgage markets and severe liquidity shortages. Adding to homebuilders' difficulties an influx of foreclosed homes on the market brought down the demand for new homes.

D.R. Horton responded to the downturn in 2008 by reducing land and housing inventory controlling construction and inventory costs and using its cash to reduce debt. Despite drops in many markets D.R. Horton saw improvements in its eastern market where home affordability and employment led to a higher demand for new homes.

EXECUTIVES

President West Region, J. Matt Farris
Evp And Cfo, William W. (Bill) Wheat, age 52, $500,000 total compensation
President Financial Services, Randall C. (Randy) Present
Vp And Cio, Rick Rawlings
President Central Region, Rick Horton
President Southeast Region, David V. Auld, age 61, $700,000 total compensation
Evp And Coo, Michael Murray, $500,000 total compensation
President East Region, Tom Hill
President North Region, Doug Brown
President Florida Region, Paul Romanowski
Vice President And Division Counsel, Carolyn Mitchell
Vice President Of Construction, David Gude
Chairman, Donald R. Horton, age 68
Auditors: Ernst & Young LLP

LOCATIONS

HQ: Horton (DR) Inc
1341 Horton Circle, Arlington, TX 76011
Phone: 817 390-8200
Web: www.drhorton.com

2018 Homebuilding Sales by Region

	% of total
West	24
South central	24
Southeast	33
East	12
Midwest	5
Southwest	4
Total	**100**

PRODUCTS/OPERATIONS

2018 Homebuilding Sales by Region

	% of total
West	24
South Central	24
Southeast	29
East	12
Midwest	6
Southwest	5
Total	**100**

2018 Sales by Service

	$ mil.	% of total
Home building		
Home sales	15502.0	96
Land/lot sales	121	1
Financial services	375	2
Forestar	109	1
Eliminations	(39.1)	-
Other adjustments	(1.2)	-
Total	**16,068**	**100**

COMPETITORS

Beazer Homes	NVR
David Weekley Homes	PulteGroup
Hovnanian Enterprises	TRI Pointe
KB Home	Taylor Morrison
Lennar	Toll Brothers
M.D.C.	Weyerhaeuser Real
M/I Homes	Estate
Meritage Homes	William Lyon Homes

HISTORICAL FINANCIALS

Company Type: Public

Income Statement

FYE: September 30

	REVENUE ($ mil.)	NET INCOME ($ mil.)	NET PROFIT MARGIN	EMPLOYEES
09/18	16,068	1,460	9.1%	8,437
09/17	14,091	1,038	7.4%	7,735
09/16	12,157	886	7.3%	6,976
09/15	10,824	750	6.9%	6,230
09/14	8,024	533	6.6%	5,621
Annual Growth	19.0%	28.6%	—	10.7%

2018 Year-End Financials

Debt ratio: 22.70%
Return on equity: 17.46%
Cash ($ mil.): 1,473
Current ratio: 9.50
Long-term debt ($ mil.): 3,203
No. of shares (mil.): 376
Dividends
Yield: 0.0%
Payout: 13.1%
Market value ($ mil.): 15,871

	STOCK PRICE ($)	P/E		PER SHARE ($)		
	FY Close	High/Low	Earnings	Dividends	Book Value
09/18	42.18	14 10	3.81	0.50	23.88
09/17	39.93	14 10	2.74	0.40	20.66
09/16	30.20	14 10	2.36	0.32	18.21
09/15	29.36	16 10	2.03	0.25	15.99
09/14	20.52	16 11	1.50	0.14	14.03
Annual Growth	19.7%	— —	26.2%	38.1%	14.2%

Host Hotels & Resorts Inc

Host Hotels & Resorts is home to luxury hotel properties around the world. It's the largest hospitality real estate investment trust (REIT) in the US and one of the top owners of luxury and upscale hotels. It owns more than 95 luxury and "upper upscale" hotels mostly in the US but also in Canada Australia Mexico and Brazil totaling some 53900 rooms. Properties are managed by third parties; most operate under the Marriott brand and are managed by sister firm Marriott International. Other brands include Hyatt Ritz-Carlton Sheraton and Westin. To maintain its status as a REIT which carries tax advantages Host operates through majority-owned Host Hotels & Resorts LP.

HISTORY

That's right — The Four Seasons started as a root beer stand.

Newlyweds John and Alice Marriott left Marriott Utah (founded by John's grandparents) in 1927 and opened a root beer stand in Washington DC. As a way to attract customers during the winter they began selling tamales and tacos — recipes came from a cook at the Mexican Embassy. Dubbed the Hot Shoppe the Marriotts built the business into a regional chain.

In 1937 the Marriotts began providing boxed lunches for airlines. Hot Shoppes entered the hospital food service business in 1955 and two years later opened its first hotel in Arlington Virginia. John and Alice's son Bill became president in 1964. The company which operated four hotels 45 Hot Shoppes and the airline catering business became Marriott-Hot Shoppes.

In the 1960s the company acquired Bob's Big Boy restaurant chain (sold 1987) started Roy Rogers fast-food restaurants (sold 1990) and changed its name to Marriott Corp. Later Marriott bought an Athenian cruise line (Oceanic; sold 1987). Bill became CEO in 1972.

Marriott diversified its hotel operations in the 1980s moving into limited-service middle-priced hotels with the launch of Courtyard by Marriott in 1983. To accelerate growth the company began building hotels for sale retaining their control through management contracts. In 1987 it acquired Residence Inn Co. which targeted extended-stay travelers. The company also expanded its airline catering business and moved into retirement facilities. To fund the expansion Marriott formed limited partnerships and issued corporate bonds; when the late 1980s recession hit the company was deeply in debt.

In 1993 Marriott Corp. divided into Marriott International (hotel management services) and Host Marriott (real estate and food service) leaving Host Marriott with most of the corporation's debt. Host Marriott began focusing on full-service hotels. It raised money to buy more hotels (many of which belonged to its old limited partnerships) by taking loans from Marriott International and selling assets (including 14 retirement properties and 30 Fairfield Inns). In late 1995 the company further refined its focus by spinning off its food service and concessions business as Host Marriott Services (later acquired by Italy-based restaurant operator Autogrill).

Host Marriott acquired three Ritz-Carlton hotels in 1995 through Marriott International which owns the Ritz-Carlton name and in 1997 acquired the Forum Group owner of 29 retirement communities. The next year it spun off Crestline Capital (now Barcelo Crestline Corp.) to own its retirement properties and to lease its hotels.

In 1999 the company expanded its hotel brands adding controlling stakes in 13 luxury Ritz-Carlton Four Seasons SwissA?tel and Hyatt properties bought from the Blackstone Group investment firm in exchange for a stake in Host Marriott. It also restructured as a real estate investment trust or REIT.

Host Marriott and Marriott International were slapped with an investor fraud lawsuit in 2000 relating to its capital-raising efforts in the late 1980s; they reached a tentative settlement under which they would buy back the partnerships. The bulk of the settlements were awarded to about 2000 investors in two of the six limited partnerships in question. That year Marriott matriarch Alice died.

Host Marriott's New York Marriott World Trade Center hotel located at Three World Trade Center was completely devastated on September 11 2001. Two blocks south the New York Marriott Financial Center hotel sustained heavy damage.

Even before September 11 brought the hotel industry to a screeching halt the company had curtailed the buying binge that saw it add more than 100 hotels to its portfolio since 1994. It decided to sell less posh noncore hotels and focus on renovating remaining holdings. Crashing per-room revenue had the company waiting for the slow return of the health of the industry and when it had the company began a cautious acquisition spree.

After a tourism industry downturn made worse by the September 11 2001 terrorist attacks the company made a key acquisition in 2006: It purchased a portfolio of 25 domestic and 3 international hotels from Starwood Hotels & Resorts for more than $4 billion and changed its name to Host Hotels & Resorts in conjunction with that buy. The package expanded the company's reach into Europe South America and the South Pacific.

In 2009 Host sold its leasehold interest in CBM Joint Venture Partnership which owned 115 Courtyard by Marriott hotels. The deal earned Host about $13 million.

In late 2011 the company sold its 95% interest in the Toronto Airport Marriott Hotel for CAD$30.6 million ($30.7 million).

Host in 2011 bought the New York Helmsley Hotel from Helmsley Enterprises and announced plans to renovate the 775-room property and reopen it under the Westin brand. In a separate deal Host acquired the Manchester Grand Hyatt San Diego's largest hotel for $570 million.

In 2012 it bought 888-room Grand Hyatt Washington for about $400 million and its acquisition of land in Rio de Janeiro to develop two hotels with a total count of 405 rooms that opened in time for the FIFA World Cup in 2014.

In 2013 the company acquired fee-simple interest in the 426-room Hyatt Place Waikiki Beach in Honolulu Hawaii from an affiliate of Chartres Lodging Group and Morgan Stanley Real Estate Fund VII Global for $138.5 million.

EXECUTIVES

Ceo, James F. Risoleo, age 62, $576,800 total compensation

Evp And Cfo, Gregory J. (Greg) Larson, age 53, $503,950 total compensation

Evp General Counsel And Secretary, Elizabeth A. Abdoo, age 59, $488,050 total compensation

Evp Asset Management, Minaz B. Abji, age 64, $546,400 total compensation

Managing Director Investments East Coast, Nathan S. Tyrrell, age 45

Evp Human Resources, Joanne G. Hamilton, age 60

Managing Director Development, Mike E. Lentz

Senior Vice President, Bill Kelso

Senior Vice President International Cap Ex, Alastair McPhail

Vice President Asset Management, Patrick Webber

Vice President And Assistant General Counsel, Karen Grubber

Vice President Asset Management, Doug Mcleod

Vp Asset Management, Charles Satkewich

Vp Capital Expenditures, Jim Marthinsen

Svp And Head Enterprise Analytics Group, Sourav Ghosh

Vice President Risk Management, Gus Napoli

Vice President Design And Procurement, Helen Jorgensen

Senior Vice President Tax, Jeff Clark

Vice President Human Resources, Lisa Whittington

Vice President Asset Management, Kerry Gaber

Vice President Capital Expenditures Design Development And Construction, Larry Oleck

Vice President Of Tax, Doug Link

Svp And Corporate Controller, Brian Macnamara

Chairman, Richard E. Marriott, age 79

Auditors: KPMG LLP

LOCATIONS

HQ: Host Hotels & Resorts Inc
6903 Rockledge Drive, Suite 1500, Bethesda, MD 20817
Phone: 240 744-1000
Web: www.hosthotels.com

2016 Sales

	$ mil.	% of total
US	5,259	97
Canada	54	1
Others	117	2
Total	5,430	100

2016 Hotel Locations

	Nos
United States	89
Brazil	3
Canada	2
Mexico	1
Australia	1
Total	96

PRODUCTS/OPERATIONS

2016 Sales

	$ mil.	% of total
Rooms	3,492	64
Food & Beverage	1,599	30
Other	339	6
Total	5,430	100

2016 Brands

	No. of hotels
Marriott:	
Marriott	38
Westin	13
Ritz-Carlton	6
Sheraton	6
JW Marriott	5
W	3
Autograph Collection	1
St. Regis	1
Luxury Collection	1
Residence Inn	1

Courtyard	
Hyatt:	
Hyatt Regency	5
Grand Hyatt	3
Hyatt Place	1
Hilton:	
Hilton	2
Curio	1
Embassy Suites	1
AccorHotels:	
Swissôtel	1
Fairmont	1
ihis	1
Novotel	1
Other/Independent	3
Total	**96**

COMPETITORS

Ashford Hospitality Trust	LaSalle Hotel Properties
Carlson Companies	Lodgian
FelCor	Pebblebrook
Hospitality Properties Trust	Strategic Hotels
InterContinental Hotels	Sunstone Hotel Investors

HISTORICAL FINANCIALS

Company Type: Public

Income Statement

FYE: December 31

	REVENUE ($ mil.)	NET INCOME ($ mil.)	NET PROFIT MARGIN	EMPLOYEES
12/17	5,387	564	10.5%	205
12/16	5,430	762	14.0%	220
12/15	5,387	558	10.4%	240
12/14	5,354	732	13.7%	251
12/13	5,166	317	6.1%	242
Annual Growth	1.1%	15.5%	—	(4.1%)

2017 Year-End Financials

Debt ratio: 33.82%	No. of shares (mil.): 739
Return on equity: 8.08%	Dividends
Cash ($ mil.): 913	Yield: 0.0%
Current ratio: 3.23	Payout: 111.8%
Long-term debt ($ mil.): 3,954	Market value ($ mil.): 14,671

	STOCK PRICE ($) FY Close	P/E High/Low	PER SHARE ($) Earnings	Dividends	Book Value
12/17	19.85	27 23	0.76	0.85	9.43
12/16	18.84	19 12	1.02	0.85	9.48
12/15	15.34	33 21	0.74	0.80	9.41
12/14	23.77	25 19	0.96	0.75	9.71
12/13	19.44	45 36	0.42	0.46	9.58
Annual Growth	0.5%	— —	16.0%	16.6%	(0.4%)

HP Inc

Just about every office — from home to big business — has two basic items: a computer and printer. That's pretty much the business of HP Inc. one of two companies created from the breakup of Hewlett-Packard Co. HP makes a full line of computing devices from desktops and laptops for commercial and consumer use to tablets and point-of-sale systems. Its printers include large format commercial printers and inkjet and laser printers as well as 3D printers. And don't forget printer supplies such as ink cartridges. HP Inc. is the No. 1 printer company and No. 1 PC maker in the world.

Operations

HP Inc. reports its operations through three business segments: Personal Systems Printing and Corporate Investments.

Personal Systems makes and sells commercial PCs consumer PCs workstations thin clients commercial tablets and mobility devices retail point-of-sale systems displays and accessories software and support. The segment generates more than 60% of HP?s revenue.

Printing produces consumer and commercial printers supplies media services as well as scanning devices. About 40% of the company?s revenue rolls out of the unit.

Corporate Investments includes HP Labs and business incubation projects. As a research-oriented unit it contributes a negligible amount of revenue.

HP Inc. buys some components from other companies. That includes the laser printer engines and laser toner cartridges it obtains from Canon. Processors for the company?s computers come from Intel and AMD and the machines runs on Microsoft software. Most of HP?s mobile devices are based on the Android operating system.

While the company operates some of its own manufacturing it outsources a significant portion of the work to third party companies.

Geographic Reach

Although about 60% of HP Inc.'s revenue comes from customers outside the US no one country accounts for more than 10% of revenue. The company has operations throughout the world with significant facilities in the Singapore Malaysia and Israel as well its US operations.

Sales and Marketing

HP Inc. markets its products directly as well as through a wide range of third-party channels including retailers resellers and distributors and original equipment manufacturers and systems integrators.

Financial Performance

HP Inc. posted about an 8% increase in revenue to in 2017 (ended October) from 2016 driven by its core computer and printing supply products. Revenue rose 7% in the US and 8% elsewhere.

An increase in the number of notebooks and workstation sold and prices lifted revenue. Consumer revenue increased 16% in fiscal year 2017 driven by growth in Notebooks and Desktops as a result of higher unit volume combined with higher ASPs. Commercial revenue increased 9% in fiscal year 2017 driven by growth in Notebooks and Workstations. Net revenue increased 16% in Notebooks 9% in Workstations and 3% in Desktops in fiscal year 2017.

A rise of about 5% in Supplies revenue boosted Printing sales 3% in 2017 from 2016. Supplies growth was due to the change in the Supplies sales model in the prior-year period and better discount management. The company also sold more printers to consumers.

Net income inched about 1% higher in 2017 to $2.5 billion. The company spent more on sales and market in 2017 while cutting back on research and development. It also had more than $150 million in restructuring costs during the year.

HP has about $7 billion in cash on hand at the end of 2017 compared to about $6.3 billion in 2016.

Strategy

HP Inc. found life as a PC-and-printer company refreshing in 2017. PC sales rose for the year and brought printer and printer supply sales with them. In 2017 HP Inc. sold more PCs to businesses and consumers than in 2016 and sold them on average at higher prices. The company gained market share in taking over the top spot in overall PC sales from Lenovo. While PC sales are expected their long-term decline in 2018 HP sees opportunity to gain more market share from its rivals.

The company has released what it calls the most powerful and first detachable PC workstations and the OMEN X laptop for gaming. HP is also beefing up the security built into its systems.

HP?s move into 3D printing produced revenue (the company didn?t say how much) in 2017 as well as repeat orders and an expanding partner and materials ecosystem. The company pumps about $65 million a year into 3D printing research.

The company says its PC-as-a-service offerings have gained traction in the market producing sales for it and channel partners. By selling PCs and services by subscription HP appeals to smaller companies that can?t afford major computing upgrades.

While HP bolsters its PC and printer offerings the company has failed to field products in the smart phone and wearables markets. Wearables a category that includes exercise trackers help PC companies spread their resources into other categories.

Instead of stuffing the supply line with ink and toner it changed to making ink cartridges and shipping them as demand occurred. At the same time the company said it would end price promotions in favor of consistent pricing. HP Inc.'s supplies business has been under pressure from competitors? prices and reduced printing by businesses and consumers. HP?s supplies business is based on what it calls the ?four-box model.? The boxes are: increase the installed base drive use increase its share of supplies and optimize pricing.

Mergers and Acquisitions

In 2018 HP Inc. bought Corp. a UK-based printing company for about £380 million. The deal should help HP expand in managed print services leveraging Apogee's long-term contracts for providing printing and publishing services. HP leads the overall printer market with a 40% market share according to IDC.

HP Inc. in 2017 bought Samsung's printer business for about $1 billion. HP gets Samsung's laser printer portfolio and thousands of patents for printing technologies as well as an increased presence in Asia. The deal particularly strengthens HP in combination printer-copier machines which helps it compete with companies such as Xerox and Canon in the enterprise and office markets. The companies expect the deal to close in 2017.

In related 2016 deals HP Inc. bought David Vision Systems GmbH and David 3D Solutions which make 3-D scanning technology.

EXECUTIVES

Chief Supply Chain Officer, Stuart C. Pann, age 59
Coo, Jon E. Flaxman, age 61, $700,027 total compensation
President 3d Printing Business, Stephen (Steve) Nigro
Cto, Shane D. Wall, age 53
President Personal Systems Business, Ron Coughlin
Evp And Cfo, Catherine A. (Cathie) Lesjak, age 59, $850,033 total compensation
Vp And General Manager Inkjet Commercial Division Hp Imaging And Printing Group; Site Manager Barcelona, Enrique Lores, age 53
President Americas, Christoph Schell
President Asia Pacific And Japan (apj), Richard Bailey
President And Ceo, Dion J. Weisler, $1,200,046 total compensation
President Europe Middle East And Africa (emea), Nick Lazaridis
Chief Human Resources Officer, Tracy S. Keogh, $600,023 total compensation
Managing Director And General Manager Hp India, Sumeer Chandra
Vice President Big Data, Pankaj Dugar

Vice President Americas Channels And Alliances, Archie Miller
National Account Manager, Amy Hilfiker
Vice President Of Mobility Products, Keith Hartsfield
Assistant Vice President Operations, Sushanto Das
National Account Manager, Devin Pool
Chairman, Charles V. (Chip) Bergh, age 60
Auditors: Ernst & Young LLP

LOCATIONS

HQ: HP Inc
1501 Page Mill Road, Palo Alto, CA 94304
Phone: 650 857-1501
Web: www.hp.com

2017 Sales

	$ mil.	% of total
US	19,321	37
Other countries	32,735	63
Total	**52,056**	**100**

PRODUCTS/OPERATIONS

2017 Sales

	$ mil.	% of total
Notebook PCs	19,782	38
Desktop PCs	102,986	20
Workstations	2,042	4
Other	1,252	2
Supplies	12,416	24
Commercial Hardware	3,973	8
Consumer Hardware	2,412	4
Adjustments	(127)	-
Total	**52,056**	**100**

Selected Products and Services

Personal Systems
  Calculators
  Desktop PCs
  Digital entertainment centers
  DVD writers
  Handheld computers
  Notebook computers
  Televisions (LCD plasma)
  Workstations
Imaging and Printing
  Commercial printing
  Digital presses
  Printers
  Digital imaging
  Projectors
  Scanners
  Personal printing
  All-in-ones (copier fax printer scanner)
  Ink jet printers
  Laser printers
  Shared printing
  Networked inkjet laser and multifunction printers
  Office all-in-ones
  Services
  Supplies

Selected Acquisitions

2011
Autonomy (UK; data repurposing software)
Printelligent (managed print services)
2010
ArcSight (security software)
3PAR (storage software and hardware)
Fortify Software (data security software)
Stratavia (database and application automation)

COMPETITORS

ADP	Hitachi
ASUSTeK	Konica Minolta
Acer	Lenovo
Apple Inc.	Lexmark
Brother Industries	NCR
CACI International	NEC
CGI Group	Océ
Canon	Oki Electric
Dell	Panasonic Corp
Eastman Kodak	Ricoh Company

Epson	Samsung Electronics
First Data	Sharp Corp.
Fiserv	Sony
Fuji Xerox	Symantec
Fujitsu	Teradata
Fujitsu Technology Solutions	Toshiba
	Unisys
Heidelberger Druckmaschinen	Wipro Technologies
	Xerox

HISTORICAL FINANCIALS

Company Type: Public

Income Statement

FYE: October 31

	REVENUE ($ mil.)	NET INCOME ($ mil.)	NET PROFIT MARGIN	EMPLOYEES
10/18	58,472	5,327	9.1%	55,000
10/17	52,056	2,526	4.9%	49,000
10/16	48,238	2,496	5.2%	49,000
10/15	103,355	4,554	4.4%	287,000
10/14	111,454	5,013	4.5%	302,000
Annual Growth	**(14.9%)**	**1.5%**	**—**	**(34.7%)**

2018 Year-End Financials

Debt ratio: 17.29%
Return on equity: —
Cash ($ mil.): 5,166
Current ratio: 0.85
Long-term debt ($ mil.): 4,524

No. of shares (mil.): 1,560
Dividends
  Yield: 2.3%
  Payout: 17.0%
Market value ($ mil.): 37,658

	STOCK PRICE ($) FY Close	P/E High/Low		PER SHARE ($) Earnings	Dividends	Book Value
10/18	24.14	8	6	3.26	0.56	(0.41)
10/17	21.55	15	10	1.48	0.53	(2.07)
10/16	14.49	11	6	1.43	0.50	(2.27)
10/15	26.96	16	10	2.48	0.67	15.39
10/14	35.88	14	9	2.62	0.61	14.53
Annual Growth	**(9.4%)**	**—**	**—**	**5.6%**	**(2.3%)**	**—**

HSBC USA, Inc.

HSBC USA a subsidiary of British banking behemoth HSBC Holdings operates HSBC Bank USA one of the largest foreign-owned banks in the country. Boasting $200 billion in assets and 230-plus branches across 10 US states (including 145 in New York making it one of the state's largest banks by branches) the bank offers personal commercial and mortgage banking services as well as wealth management investment banking private banking brokerage and trust services. Its largest markets are in New York California New Jersey and Florida. Roughly 75% of HSBC USA's loan portfolio is made up of commercial loans and around 70% of its total revenue comes from interest income.

Operations

The company operates four business segments: Retail Banking and Wealth Management (RBWM); Commercial Banking which serves small and multinational businesses in five hubs where 50% of US corporate imports and exports happen (California Florida Illinois New York and Texas); Global Banking and Markets which offers advisory services and trading services for major government corporate and institutional clients; and Private Bank which serves high net worth and ultra-high net worth individuals and their families particularly focusing on multi-generational families business owners and entrepreneurs.

About 75% of HSBC USA's $82.92 billion-loan portfolio was made up of commercial loans (including global banking business and corporate banking and construction and other real estate loans) at the end of 2015. The rest of its portfolio was made up of consumer loans especially residential mortgages with some home equity credit card and other loans.

The bank makes around 70% of its revenue from interest income. About 41% of its total revenue came from loan interest during 2015 while another 27% came from interest on securities trading securities and short-term investments. The rest of its revenue came from trust and investment management fees (3% of revenue) credit card fees (1%) trading revenue (1%) residential mortgage banking revenue (1%) other fees and commissions (15%) gains on securities at fair value (5%) and other miscellaneous sources.

Geographic Reach

HSBC USA serves customers nationwide with the highest concentration of its bank branches located in New York City Los Angeles San Francisco Chicago Atlanta Houston Seattle Miami and Washington DC. The company operates foreign branches and representative offices in the Caribbean Canada Latin America Europe and Asia.

Sales and Marketing

HSBC USA serves a variety of customers such as individuals (including high net worth individuals) small businesses corporations institutions and governments. It boasted 2.4 million customers at the end of 2015 30% of which live in New York and 29% in California.

The bank has been ramping up its advertising spend in recent years. It spent $60 million on advertising in 2015 up from $53 million and $43 million in 2014 and 2013 respectively.

Financial Performance

The US division of HSBC has been struggling to grow its revenue over the past several years as low interest rates have continued to eat away at its interest margins and as its non-interest revenues have been in decline. The bank has been recovering from losses in 2013 and 2012 caused by goodwill impairments and regulatory expenses.

HSBC USA's revenue turned a corner in 2015 jumping 11% to $5.17 billion during the year mostly thanks to higher interest income on 8% commercial loan asset growth and double-digit security asset growth.

Despite strong revenue growth in 2015 the company's net income fell 7% to $330 million mainly because its credit loss provisions increased by $173 million mostly as it made more commercial loans with exposure to the oil and gas industry. HSBC USA's operating cash levels dropped 22% to $4.65 billion for the year due to unfavorable working capital changes primarily related to changes in trading assets and liabilities.

Strategy

HSBC USA as part of the broader HSBC group aims to become the world's leading international bank and seeks to connected emerging economies with developed markets. The US division like parent HSBC also continued in 2016 to look for ways to cut operating costs to boost efficiency and overall profits.

In 2014 HSBC USA became one of the nation's first major banks to roll out a new fraud protection device which employs two-factor authentication for its personal Internet customers.

Company Background

HSBC and HSBC USA restructured their operations in 2011 which included divesting operations and cutting staff. As part of the restructuring HSBC sold 195 retail branches in New York and Connecticut to First Niagara for $1 billion. Through HSBC USA and its HSBC Finance affiliate HSBC also sold its card and retail services business to Capital One Financial. In 2010 HSBC USA exited its noncore wholesale banknotes business. The company also closed and consolidated about a dozen branches in Connecticut and New Jersey. The moves are part of the company's strategy to focus more on commercial and corporate banking in New York and other key urban markets itself part of HSBC's restructuring to create a leaner group.

EXECUTIVES

Chairman President And Ceo Hsbc North America Holdings Inc. And Hsbc Bank Usa, Patrick J. (Pat) Burke, age 56

Sevp And Cfo, Mark A. Zaeske

Sevp And Coo Usa, Vittorio M. Severino

Sevp And Head Of Global Banking And Markets Americas, Thierry Roland

Sevp And Head Of Strategy And Planning, Loren C. Klug, age 57

Evp And Head Of Private Banking Americas, Marlon Young, age 62, $389,423 total compensation

Sevp And Chief Risk Officer, Rhydian H. Cox

Sevp And Head Of Commercial Banking, Wyatt E Crowell

Evp And Head Of Human Resources Usa, Maureen A. Gillan-Myer

Evp And Head Of Regulatory Remediation, Stephen R. Nesbitt

Sevp And Chief Auditor, Richard E. O'Brien

Evp And Corporate Secretary, Karen Pisarczyk

Sevp And Head Of Retail Banking And Wealth Management, Pablo Sanchez

Sevp And General Counsel, Mark Steffensen

Evp And Chief Accounting Officer, William Tabaka

Senior Vice President Compensation, Deanna Larkin

Auditors: PricewaterhouseCoopers LLP

LOCATIONS

HQ: HSBC USA, Inc.
452 Fifth Avenue, New York, NY 10018
Phone: 212 525-5000
Web: www.us.hsbc.com

PRODUCTS/OPERATIONS

2013 Sales

	$ mil.	% of total
Interest		
Loans	1,876	39
Securities	876	19
Other	227	4
Non-interest		
Other fees & commissions	706	14
Trading revenue	474	9
Servicing and other fees from HSBC affiliates	202	4
Other securities gains	202	4
Trust income	123	3
Other	150	4
Total	**4,836**	**100**

COMPETITORS

Astoria Financial	KeyCorp
Bank of America	M&T Bank
Capital One	New York Community
Citibank	Bancorp
Citizens Financial	PNC Financial
Group	TD Bank USA
JPMorgan Chase	Wells Fargo

HISTORICAL FINANCIALS

Company Type: Public

Income Statement

	ASSETS ($ mil.)	NET INCOME ($ mil.)	INCOME AS % OF ASSETS	EMPLOYEES
				FYE: December 31
12/17	187,235	(179)	—	5,107
12/16	201,301	129	0.1%	6,114
12/15	188,278	330	0.2%	6,173
12/14	185,539	354	0.2%	6,400
12/13	185,487	(338)	—	6,500
Annual Growth	0.2%	—	—	(5.9%)

2017 Year-End Financials

Debt ratio: 17.02%
Return on equity: (-0.89%)
Cash ($ mil.): 28,422
Current ratio: —
Long-term debt ($ mil.): —

No. of shares (mil.): 0
Dividends
Yield: —
Payout: —
Market value ($ mil.): —

	STOCK PRICE ($) FY Close	P/E High/Low	PER SHARE ($) Earnings	Dividends	Book Value
12/17	0.00	— —	(0.00)	0.00	
28,142,857.00					
12/16	0.00	— —	(0.00)	0.49	
28,508,403.00					
12/15	23.99	— —	(0.00)	1.02	
28,746,498.00					
Annual Growth	—		—	—	(0.5%)

Humana Inc.

Medicare has made Humana a big-time player in the insurance game. One of the largest Medicare providers and a top health insurer Humana provides Medicare Advantage plans and prescription drug coverage to more than 7.7 million members throughout the US. It also administers managed care plans for other government programs including Medicaid plans in Florida and Puerto Rico and TRICARE (for military personnel) in the South. Additionally Humana offers commercial health plans and specialty (life dental and vision) coverage; it also provides health management services and operates outpatient care clinics. All told it covers more than 21 million members in the US.

HISTORY

In 1961 Louisville Kentucky lawyers David Jones and Wendell Cherry bought a nursing home as a real estate investment. Within six years their company Extendicare was the largest nursing home chain in the US (with only eight homes).

Faced with a glutted nursing home market the partners noticed that hospitals received more money per patient per day than nursing homes so they took their company public in 1968 to finance hospital purchases (one per month from 1968 to 1971). The company then sold its 40 nursing homes. Sales rose 13 times over in the next five years and in 1973 the firm changed its name to Humana.

By 1975 Humana had built 27 hospitals in the South and Southwest. It targeted young privately insured patients and kept its charity caseload and bad-debt expenses low. Three years later #3 for-profit hospital operator Humana moved up a notch when it bought #2 American Medicorp.

In 1983 the government began reimbursing Medicare payments based on fixed rates. Counting

on its high hospital occupancy in 1984 the company launched Humana Health Care Plans rewarding doctors and patients who used Humana hospitals. However hospital occupancy dropped and the company closed several clinics. When its net income fell 75% in 1986 the firm responded by lowering premiums to attract employers.

In 1991 co-founder Cherry died. With hospital profits down in 1993 Jones spun off Humana's 76 hospitals as Galen Healthcare which formed the nucleus of what is now HCA - The Healthcare Company. Humana used the cash to expand its HMO membership buying Group Health Association (an HMO serving metropolitan Washington DC) and CareNetwork (a Milwaukee HMO). The next year Humana added 1.3 million members when it bought EMPHESYS and the company's income which had stagnated since the salad days of the late 1980s and early 1990s seemed headed in the right direction.

In the mid-1990s cutthroat premiums failed to cover rising health care costs as members' hospital use soared out of control particularly in the company's new Washington DC market. Profits dropped 94% and Humana's already tense relationship with doctors and members worsened. President and COO Wayne Smith and CFO Roger Drury resigned as part of a management shake-up and newly appointed president Gregory Wolf offered to drop the company's gag clause after the Florida Physicians Association threatened to sue.

A reorganized Humana rebounded in 1997. The company pulled out of 13 unprofitable markets including Alabama (though it did not drop TRICARE its military health coverage program in that state) and Washington DC. Refocusing on core markets in the Midwest and Southeast Humana bought Physician Corp. of America (PCA) and ChoiceCare a Cincinnati HMO. Wolf replaced Jones as CEO in 1997.

To cut costs Humana agreed in 1998 to be bought by United HealthCare (now UnitedHealth Group). The deal was abandoned however when United HealthCare took a $900 million charge in advance of the purchase. Humana found savings by pruning its Medicare HMO business.

Humana did everything but party in 1999. The company faced RICO charges for allegedly overcharging members for co-insurance; it agreed to repay $15 million in Medicare overpayments to the government; and it became the first health insurance firm to be slapped with a class-action suit over its physician incentives and other coverage policies.

Humana sold PCA in 2000 saying that it had paid too much for the company; subsidiary PCA Property & Casualty was also sold marking the company's exit from the workers' compensation business. That year Humana also sold its underperforming Florida Medicaid HMO to Well Care HMO and agreed to pay

EXECUTIVES

President And Ceo, Bruce D. Broussard, age 55, $1,235,446 total compensation

Svp And Chief Consumer Officer, Jody L. Bilney, age 56, $573,452 total compensation

Svp And Chief Medical Officer, Roy A. Beveridge, age 60

Svp And Cio, Brian P. LeClaire, age 57

Svp And Chief Human Resources Officer, Timothy S. (Tim) Huval, age 51, $573,453 total compensation

Svp And Cfo, Brian A. Kane, age 45, $636,254 total compensation

Svp And Chief Strategy Officer, Christopher H. (Chris) Hunter, age 49, $465,865 total compensation

President And Intermountain Region Market Leader Senior Products, Catherine Field

Segment Vice President, Mark A McCullough
Vice President Marketing, Phyllis Anderson
Vice President Marketpoint Sales, Jim Van Valin
Vice President Information Technology, Michael Richmond
Vice President Sales, Nelson Tawasha
Third Vice President, Tom Ryan
Vice President Compensation, Matthew Saxon
Vice President And Assistant General Counsel (2000), Ralph Martin Wilson
Health Services Director, Yvonne Shell
Segment Vice President, John Delorimier
Health Services Director, Ricardo Menchaca
Medical Director, Teresita Hernandez
Market Vice President, Anita Holloway
Vice President Information Technology Transformation And Shared Services, Faheem Zuberi
Enterprise Vice President Talent And Org, Roger Cude
Vice President, Gary Williams
Vice President Of Market Development Northeast Region, Denise Smith
Vice President Of Marketing, Jd Denny
Medical Director, Amy Fendrich
Vice President Marketing, Kristin Russel
Enterprise Vice President, Amin Kassem
Vice President And Chief Financial Officer Of Senior Products, Alisa Coppock
Medical Director, Jackie Germain
Market Vice President, Barry Boster
Medical Director, Bryan Carr
Srvpnr Lan Operating Systems, Wes Johnson
Vice President Retail Service Operations Contact Centers, Alyssa Reynolds
Market Vice President Dfw And Houston Senior Products, Lesli C Young
Vice President Of Clinical Compliance, Meliss A Koellner
Segment Vice President, Thoma P Klammer
Vice President, Kristin Martin
Medical Director, Cind M Dunn
National Sales Manager, Mallor Strange
Regional Vice President West Region, Charle Ritz
Field Vice President, Meredit Williams
Vice President Operations Provider Development Center Of Excellence, Patrici Laughren
National Sales Manager, Chin Chinigo
Regional Vice President National Contracting Southeast And Central Divisions, Pau Davis
Vice President Customer Analytics And Data Strategy, Bernar Lefang
Chairman, Kurt J. Hilzinger, age 57
Board Member, Jerry Valentine
Board Member, Martha Northcutt
Secretary Treasurer, Jeff Fernandez
Auditors: PricewaterhouseCoopers LLP

LOCATIONS

HQ: Humana Inc.
  500 West Main Street, Louisville, KY 40202
Phone: 502 580-1000
Web: www.humana.com

PRODUCTS/OPERATIONS

2016 Sales

	$ mil.	% of total
Premiums		
Individual Medicare Advantage	31,863	59
Fully insured commercial	8,897	16
Group medicare advantage	4,283	8
Medicare stand-alone PDP	4,009	7
Specialty commercial	1,279	2
Medicaid & other premiums	2,690	5
Services	969	2
Investment income	389	1
Total	**54,379**	**100**

2016 Sales by Segment

	$ mil.	% of total
Retail	46,655	59
Healthcare Services	25,122	32
Group	7,249	19
Other	114	-
Adjustments	(24761)	-
Total	**54,379**	**100**

Selected Products and Services

Government
  Medicaid managed care plans
  Medicare Advantage plans
  Medicare prescription drug plans
  TRICARE (military personnel)
Commercial
  Administrative services only (ASO)
  HMO plans
  HumanaOne (individual insurance)
  POS (point-of-service) plans
  PPO plans
  Specialty products
  Dental insurance
  Life insurance
  Short-term disability insurance

COMPETITORS

AMERIGROUP	First Health Group
Aetna	Florida Blue
Anthem	HCSC
Assurant	Health Net
Blue Cross and Blue Shield of Texas	HealthSpring
	Highmark
CIGNA	Kaiser Foundation
Caremark Pharmacy Services	Health Plan
	Molina Healthcare
Centene	UnitedHealth Group
Coventry Health Care	Universal American
Express Scripts	WellCare Health Plans

HISTORICAL FINANCIALS

Company Type: Public

Income Statement

FYE: December 31

	ASSETS ($ mil.)	NET INCOME ($ mil.)	INCOME AS % OF ASSETS	EMPLOYEES
12/17	27,178	2,448	9.0%	47,900
12/16	25,396	614	2.4%	54,200
12/15	24,705	1,276	5.2%	51,700
12/14	23,466	1,147	4.9%	57,000
12/13	20,735	1,231	5.9%	52,000
Annual Growth	**7.0%**	**18.8%**	**—**	**(2.0%)**

2017 Year-End Financials

Debt ratio: 18.07%
Return on equity: 23.85%
Cash ($ mil.): 4,042
Current ratio: —
Long-term debt ($ mil.): —

No. of shares (mil.): 137
Dividends
  Yield: 0.0%
  Payout: 11.2%
Market value ($ mil.): 34,154

	STOCK PRICE ($) FY Close	P/E High/Low		PER SHARE ($) Earnings	Dividends	Book Value
12/17	248.07	15	12	16.81	1.89	71.49
12/16	204.03	53	37	4.07	0.87	71.56
12/15	178.51	25	16	8.44	1.15	69.77
12/14	143.63	20	13	7.36	1.11	64.48
12/13	103.22	13	8	7.73	1.07	60.48
Annual Growth	**24.5%**	**—**	**—**	**21.4%**	**15.3%**	**4.3%**

Hunt (J.B.) Transport Services, Inc.

When it comes to hauling freight J.B. Hunt Transport Services knows how to deliver. Its intermodal unit the company's largest maintains about 4580 tractors; 5400 drivers; and more than 84500 pieces of trailing equipment and moves customers' cargo by combinations of truck and train. JBI's dedicated contract services unit supplies customers with drivers and equipment; it operates about 6970 company-owned trucks. The company's truckload transportation unit provides dry freight transportation with a fleet of about 1460 tractors. A fourth business segment integrated capacity solutions (ICS) manages freight transportation via third-party carriers as well as J.B. Hunt equipment.The company traces its roots back to 1961 when it was founded by Johnnie Bryan (J.B.) Hunt.

Operations

Freight transported by J.B. Hunt includes automotive parts building materials chemicals electronics food and beverages forest and paper products and general merchandise. The company divides its operations across four segments. JBI offers intermodal freight services to customers in Canada Mexico and the US and generates almost 60% of the company's net sales.

Dedicated contract services (DCS) provides supply chain services supplementing a variety of different types of transportation and accounted for almost 25% of total sales. Other segments include JBT (trucking) and ICS (integrated capacity solutions). The latter segment often arranges specialty trucking services such as transporting freight that requires the use of flatbed or refrigerated trailers.

Geographic Reach

J.B. Hunt is headquartered in Lowell Arkansas and its principal facilities are located throughout the US. Its JBI segment offers intermodal freight services to customers in the US Canada and Mexico.

Sales and Marketing

J.B. Hunt markets its services through a nationwide sales and marketing network. It uses a specific sales force within its DCS segment due to the length and complexity of the sales cycle. In addition the ICS segment utilizes its own local branch of salespeople.

Financial Performance

J.B. Hunt has enjoyed unprecedented growth in the receding wake of the recession. From 2015 to 2016 revenues increased 6% from $6.19 billion in 2015 to $6.56 billion in 2016 a company milestone. The recent growth was due to overall increased load volume partially offset by lower revenue per load in its JBI ICS and JBT segments. Its ICS segment revenue increased the most (22%) due to an overall volume increase of 57% mainly due to new offerings.

Profits also surged from $427 million in 2015 to peak at a record-setting $432 million in 2016.

Strategy

J.B. Hunt hopes to continue its pathway to growth by concentrating on its operating segments as separate but overlapping businesses and by selling more value-added services to its customers. It has continued to expand its intermodal unit which has agreements with major North American railroads including Burlington Northern Santa Fe and Norfolk Southern railways. The arrangement also allows J.B. Hunt to cut down on costs.

To keep pace with the rapid progress of technology and meet modern-day customer demands J. B. Hunt plans to invest heavily in its operating infrastructure. In 2016 it announced plans to fully equip its highway trailer and intermodal container fleets with tracking systems by the end of 2018. These systems will provide location tracking services and load information services for each of its trailers and containers. J.B. hunt believes the initiative will give it a competitive edge providing improvements in areas of asset utilization as well as providing meaningful advances in customer service load management and planning. Throughout 2016 it also launched multiple mobile applications for its drivers carrier partners and customers.

HISTORY

Johnnie Bryan (J.B.) Hunt's life was a classic tale of rolling from rags to riches — with a little help from a Rockefeller. Hunt grew up in a family of sharecroppers during the Depression and he left school at age 12 to work for his uncle's Arkansas sawmill. In the late 1950s after driving trucks for more than nine years Hunt noticed that the rice mills along his eastern Arkansas route were burning rice hulls. Believing the hulls could be used as poultry litter Hunt got a contract to haul away the hulls and began selling them to chicken farmers.

In 1961 he began the J.B. Hunt Company with help from future Arkansas governor Winthrop Rockefeller who owned Winrock grass company where Hunt bought sod for one of his side businesses. Hunt developed a machine to compress the rice hulls which made their transportation profitable and within a few years the company was the world's largest producer of rice hulls for poultry litter.

Still looking for new opportunities Hunt bought some used trucks and refrigerated trailers in 1969 though the company continued to focus on its original business. In the 1980s J.B. Hunt's trucking division grew dramatically and became lucrative as the trucking industry was being deregulated. In 1981-82 the Hunt trucking business had higher margins than most trucking firms. In 1983 when J.B. Hunt Transport Services went public Hunt sold the rice hull business to concentrate on trucking.

EXECUTIVES

Evp Operations And Coo, Craig Harper, age 61, $375,000 total compensation
President And Ceo, John N. Roberts, age 53, $807,747 total compensation
Vice President Finance, Richie Henderson
Evp And Cio, Stuart L. Scott, age 52
Evp; President Intermodal, Terrence D. (Terry) Matthews, age 60, $478,819 total compensation
Evp Finance And Administration Cfo And Corporate Secretary, David G. Mee, age 58, $480,660 total compensation
Evp And Chief Commercial Officer; President Highway Services, Shelley Simpson, age 46, $476,923 total compensation
Evp; President Dedicated Contract Services, Nicholas (Nick) Hobbs, age 55, $454,808 total compensation
Vice President Of Transportation, Tami Allensworth
Vice President Business Development, Brian Webb
Vice President Memphis, John Flynt
National Account Manager, Chris Putnam
National Account Manager, Michelle Timmermans
National Sales Manager, Keith Brown
Vp Marketing, Cecilia Gann
Vice President Strategic Accounts, Clay Cox
National Account Manager, Kevin Boortz
National Sales Manager, Brandon Parker
Vice President Of Maintenance, Derek Kennemer
Controller And Svp Finance, Kevin Bracy

Vice President Of Sales And Marketing, Jessica Brooks
National Account Manager, Linda Peak
National Account Manager, Christopher Trout
Vice President National Accounts, Bill Copelin
Vice President Maintenance Maintenance Manager, Charles Radcliffe
National Sales Manager, Scott Coleman
Senior Vice President Sales, Spencer Frazier
Senior Vice President, Ken Mangold
Vice President Sales Southern Region, Shannon Foley
National Account Manager, Rick Thurow
Vice President Of Finance And Accounting, Stephen Guenther
Vp Human Resources, Mark Greenway
National Sales Manager, Markis Randall
Vice President Operations, David Keefauver
Vice President Of Operations, Steve Rogers
National Sales Manager, Ben Mallard
Vice President Of Sales, Bill Carver
Senior Vice President Operations, Bradley Hicks
National Sales Manager, Jack Page
Senior Vice President Engineering, Margaret Townsend
Chairman, Kirk Thompson, age 65
Auditors: Ernst & Young LLP

LOCATIONS

HQ: Hunt (J.B.) Transport Services, Inc.
615 J.B. Hunt Corporate Drive, Lowell, AR 72745
Phone: 479 820-0000
Web: www.jbhunt.com

PRODUCTS/OPERATIONS

2016 Sales

	$ mil.	% of total
Intermodal (JBI)	3,796	58
Dedicated contract services (DCS)	1,533	23
Integrated capacity solutions (ICS)	852	13
Trucking (JBT)	388	6
Adjustments	(14)	-
Total	**6,555**	**100**

Selected Trucking Services
Dedicated
Expedited
Final Mile
Flatbed
Intermodal
Less Than Truckload
Refrigerated
Truckload

COMPETITORS

APL Logistics	Ryder System
CSX	Schneider National
Canadian National Railway	Swift Transportation
Hub Group	U.S. Xpress
Kansas City Southern	Union Pacific
Landstar System	Werner Enterprises
Old Dominion Freight	YRC Worldwide

HISTORICAL FINANCIALS

Company Type: Public

Income Statement

FYE: December 31

	REVENUE ($ mil.)	NET INCOME ($ mil.)	NET PROFIT MARGIN	EMPLOYEES
12/17	7,189	686	9.5%	24,681
12/16	6,555	432	6.6%	22,190
12/15	6,187	427	6.9%	21,562
12/14	6,165	374	6.1%	20,158
12/13	5,584	342	6.1%	18,467
Annual Growth	**6.5%**	**19.0%**	**—**	**7.5%**

2017 Year-End Financials

Debt ratio: 24.31%	No. of shares (mil.): 109
Return on equity: 42.19%	Dividends
Cash ($ mil.): 14	Yield: 0.0%
Current ratio: 1.45	Payout: 14.8%
Long-term debt ($ mil.): 1,085	Market value ($ mil.): 12,619

	STOCK PRICE ($) FY Close	P/E High/Low		PER SHARE ($) Earnings	Dividends	Book Value
12/17	114.98	19	13	6.18	0.92	16.76
12/16	97.07	26	17	3.81	0.88	12.70
12/15	73.36	25	19	3.66	0.84	11.41
12/14	84.25	27	22	3.16	0.80	10.33
12/13	77.30	27	20	2.87	0.60	8.64
Annual Growth	10.4%	—	—	21.1%	11.3%	18.0%

Huntington Bancshares Inc

Huntington Bancshares is the holding company for The Huntington National Bank which operates around 1100 branches in Ohio Michigan Illinois Indiana Kentucky Pennsylvania West Virginia and Wisconsin. In addition to traditional retail and commercial banking services the bank offers mortgage banking capital market services equipment leasing brokerage services investment management recreational vehicle and marine financing and trust and estate services. The company's automobile finance business provides car loans to consumers and real estate and inventory finance to car dealerships throughout the Midwest and Northeast. Founded in 1966 the company boasts total assets of more than $70 billion.

Operations

Huntington Bancshares operates through five main business segments: Consumer and Business Banking Commercial Banking Commercial Real Estate and Vehicle Finance Regional Banking and The Huntington Private Client Group (RBHPCG) and Home Lending.

Huntington's Consumer and Business Banking division which contributes more than 40% to total sales provides traditional banking products and services to consumer and small business customers as well as investment insurance foreign exchange hedging and treasury management services.

Its Commercial Banking division (almost 25% of total sales) is made up of seven business units: middle-market large corporate government public sector specialty banking asset finance capital markets treasury management and insurance brokerage.

The Commercial Real Estate and Vehicle Finance division (nearly 25%) provides lending and other banking services to customers outside of its traditional retail and commercial banking segments mostly offering new and used car financing for franchised automotive dealerships as well as their customers. Other vehicles include light-duty trucks and boats. The segment also offers financing for land buildings and other commercial real estate owned or constructed by real estate developers automobile dealerships or other customers needing real estate project financing.

RBHPCG (Regional Banking and The Huntington Private Client Group) accounts for under 10% of sales and provides specialized private banking trust investment and financial services for high net-worth customers under the Huntington brand name. The Home Lending division originates and services consumer loans and mortgages for the bank's retail and business banking divisions.

The small Home Lending segment (2% of sales) originates loans and mortgages for customers mainly in its primary banking markets.

Geographic Reach

Huntington Bancshares operates around 25 private client offices and nearly 1100 branches in the Midwest and Northeast US. Over 50% of the bank's branches were located in Ohio with Michigan hosting another 30%-plus.

Sales and Marketing

In addition to traditional bank branches Huntington distributes its products and services through convenience branches (in grocery stores and retirement centers for example) and an expansive ATM network as well as via internet and mobile services. The bank's branches can be found in Michigan's Meijer and Ohio's Giant Eagle grocery stores.

Financial Performance

A blip in 2013 aside Huntington has recorded steadily climbing growth for more than five years. In fiscal 2016 revenue climbed 16% to $3.8 billion. The company's interest income grew by over $500 million while non-interest income rose by $111 million.

Interest income was boosted by 21% earning asset growth and 22% interest-bearing liability growth largely down to the acquisition of First-Merit during the year. Non-interest income grew amid higher service charges on deposit accounts and card and payment processing due to new customer acquisition. Mortgage banking was also up due to higher mortgage origination.

Net income increased 3% to $712 million due to higher revenue partially offset by outsized growth in non-interest expense (i.e. expense grew faster than revenue). The increase was down to acquisition related expenses totaling $282 million.

Cash from operations rose 18% to $1.2 billion due to higher provision for credit losses and net changes in accrued income and other assets.

Strategy

Huntington is focused on expanding its market share through branch openings and strategic acquisitions to better compete in its target markets. In 2016 the company bought FirstMerit Corporation boosting total assets by 41% swelling its branch network by nearly 50% and making it Ohio's largest bank. Prior to the FirstMerit acquisition the bank opened 67 branches in Michigan and increased its deposit business by $750 million.

Mergers and Acquisitions

In August 2016 Huntington Bancshares paid $3.7 billion to buy Akron-based rival FirstMerit Corporation making it Ohio's largest bank and boosting its total assets by 41% to $100 billion. The acquisition also expanded Huntington's branch network by nearly 50% to some 1000 branches extending into the surrounding states of Michigan and Pennsylvania.

Company Background

With the economy in the Midwest wracked by the recession Huntington posted losses in 2008 and 2009 — more than $3 billion in the latter year alone — mainly attributable to credit losses due to nonperforming assets and the write down of goodwill related to past acquisitions. It returned to profitability in 2010 thanks in part to higher interest margins as a result of the company's focus on lower-cost customer checking accounts.

HISTORY

Pelatiah Webster (P. W.) Huntington descendant of both a Revolutionary War leader and a Declaration of Independence signer went to work at sea in 1850 at age 14. He returned to go into banking and in 1866 founded what would become Huntington National Bank of Columbus. As the business grew he conscripted four of his five sons. The bank took a national charter in 1905 and became The Huntington National Bank of Columbus. It survived the hard times of 1907 and 1912 through the Huntington philosophy of sitting on piles of cash.

P. W. died in 1918 and his son Francis became president. Francis expanded the company into trust services. Unlike many bankers in the 1920s he refused to make speculative loans based on the stock market. Francis died in 1928 and was succeeded by brother Theodore. By 1930 Huntington's trust assets accounted for more than half of the total. The family's conservative philosophy helped the bank sail through the 1933 bank holiday although when it reopened the amount of cash it could pay out was restricted to 10% of deposits.

P. W.'s son Gwynne chaired the bank during its post-WWII expansion. His death in 1958 ended the Huntington family reign. The bank began opening branches and adding new services such as mortgage and consumer loans. In 1966 in order to expand statewide the bank formed a holding company Huntington Bancshares. In the 1960s and 1970s the corporation added new operations including mortgage and leasing companies and an international division to help clients with foreign exchange.

In 1979 the company consolidated its 15 affiliates into The Huntington National Bank. Three years later the company bit off more than it could chew with the acquisitions of Reeves Banking and Trust Company of Dover and Union Commerce Corporation of Cleveland. The latter purchase loaded the company with debt. Nevertheless it continued to expand particularly after 1985 when banking regulations allowed interstate branch banking and it soon had operations in Florida Indiana Kentucky Michigan and West Virginia.

Huntington Bancshares was largely insulated from the real estate problems of the late 1980s and early 1990s thanks to its continuing conservative lending policies. But the company was at risk from the nationwide consolidation of the banking industry which made it a potential takeover target. It increased its service offerings and bolstered its place in the market through acquisitions. In 1996 Huntington Bancshares bought life insurance agency Tice & Associates and began cross-selling bank and insurance products. Important banking acquisitions in 1997 included First Michigan Bank and several Florida companies.

Also in 1997 the company took advantage of deregulation to consolidate its interstate operations (except for The Huntington State Bank) into a single operating company. In 1998 Huntington Bancshares continued to build its Huntington insurance services unit with the acquisition of Pollock & Pollock. In 1999 the bank launched a mortgage program aimed at wealthy clients and sold its credit card receivables portfolio to Chase Manhattan (now JPMorgan Chase & Co.). In 2000 the company bought Michigan's Empire Banc Corporation.

Former BANK ONE executive Thomas Hoaglin was named president and CEO in 2001. Later that year he became chairman when Frank Wobst retired after leading the company for 20 years.

In 2002 the company consolidated some branches in the Midwest to cut costs and exited the retail banking market in Florida selling some 140 retail branches there to SunTrust. After the mid-2007 acquisition of Sky Financial Sky's CEO Marty Adams became president and COO of Huntington Bancshares. He retired at the end of 2007 and Hoaglin resumed the president's role until his own retirement in 2009; Stephen Steinour then took the helm.

EXECUTIVES

Executive Vice President And Director Corporate Tax, Edward Kane

President Northwest Ohio The Huntington National Bank, Sharon S. Speyer

Evp General Counsel And Secretary, Richard A. Cheap, age 66, $279,833 total compensation

Chairman President And Ceo, Stephen D. (Steve) Steinour, age 60, $1,061,538 total compensation

Sevp And Managing Director Auto Finance Commercial Real Estate And Community Development Lending And Investment, Nicholas G. (Nick) Stanutz, age 63, $465,000 total compensation

Sevp Retail And Business Banking, Mary W. Navarro, age 62, $541,154 total compensation

Sevp And Chief Risk Officer, Helga S. Houston, age 57, $542,308 total compensation

Sevp And Director Regional Banking And The Huntington Private Client Group, James E. (Jim) Dunlap, age 65, $518,333 total compensation

Region President Central Ohio/west Virginia, James E. Kunk

Sevp And Director Corporate Operations And Corporate Services, Mark E. Thompson, age 59, $315,340 total compensation

President Central Ohio Region, Sue E. Zazon

President West Virginia Region, Andrew J. Paterno

President Western Pennsylvania And Ohio Valley Region, Susan (Susie) Baker Shipley

Sevp And Cfo, Howell D. (Mac) McCullough, age 60, $596,538 total compensation

President Greater Cleveland Region, Sean P. Richardson

President Chicago Region, Peter K. Gillespie

Vp Commercial Banking Greater Akron/canton Region, William C. Shivers

Sevp And Chief Credit Officer, Daniel J. Neumeyer, age 58

Sevp Chief Technology And Operations Officer, Paul G. Heller, age 54, $590,385 total compensation

President West Michigan Region, John Irwin

President Southern Ohio And Northern Kentucky Region, Kevin Jones

Sevp And Director Commercial Banking, Richard (Rich) Remiker, age 60

Sevp And Chief Human Resources Officer, Rajeev (Raj) Syal, age 52

President Akron Region, Nicholas Browning

President Indiana Region, John Corbin

President Wisconsin Region, Kevin Leissring

President East Michigan, David Lochner

Sevp Private Bank; Regional Banking Director And Chair Michigan, Sandra E. Pierce, $222,789 total compensation

Evp And Chief Communications And Marketing Director, Julie C. Tutkovics

Senior Vice President Treasury Management Sales Manager, Robin Triplett

Evp And Assistant Treasurer, Todd Beekman

Executive Vice President And Chief Public Affairs Officer, Barbara Benham

Vice President, Denise Stone

Senior Vice President Chief Sourcing Officer, Debbie Manos-Mchenry

Vice President Employee Benefits At Huntington National Bank, Kristin Janutolo

Vice President, Bruce Sautter

Vice President, Couturier Jan

Assistant Vice President And Senior Product Manage, Amy Beck

Vice President, Geoffrey Mowery

Vice President Sec Reporting Manager, Jeff Endres

Vice President, James Matousek

Assistant Vice President Section Manager, Gayla Strickler

Vice President And Community Development Director, Staci Glenn

Vice President National Sales Manager And Key Accounts, Patrick Prato

Assistant Vice President Mortgage Lending, James Boots

Treasury Management Sales Advisor Assistant Vice President, Heather Kubasak

Vice President Enterprise Technology Systems, Carolyn Jones

Senior Vice President Information Technology Risk, Christine Holland

Senior Vice President And Director Government Relations, Todd Bailey

Senior Vice President Credit Card Services, Scott Abramowitz

Assistant Vice President, Jenny Nickles

Vice President, Brad Udy

Assistant Vice President 1 Portfolio Manager, Nick Markovich

Vice President, Sheryl Palmer

Senior Vice President, Neil S Clark, age 67

Vice President And Manager Ecommerce Channel, Tenzin Alexander

Senior Vice President, Thomas Cirincione

Vice President Region Marketing Manager, Patricia Barton

Vice President General Manager, Kendra Musgrave

Credit Risk Executive Vice President, Fred Manning

Senior Vice President Credit Risk Management, Tim Barber

Vice President Tm Liquidity And Fraud Group Product Manager, Ashley Sanders

Vice President Business Unit Controller, Scott Dupler

Assistant Vice President, Sandra Clarke

Vice President, Rob Koogler

Vice President, Chris Shimala

Vice President Treasury Management Sales, John Tremoulis

Vice President Huntington Private Financial Group, Darryl Lycourt

Vice President Collections Mis, Willie Tackett

Vice President, Joseph Ahee

Senior Vice President Treasury Management, Steve Veach

Senior Vice President Commercial Lending, Daniel Erlandson

Vice President, Terry Kuney

Senior Vice President Corporate Benefits Director, Sarah A Hall

Vice President, Diana Ferrara

Assistant Vice President Home Lending Compliance Section Manager, Omar Ramsay

Business Banking Specialist Assistant Vice President, Tara Murphy

Senior Vice President Deposit Product Pricing And Fees Director, David Schamer

Senior Vice President, Roy Dsa

Vice President Human Resources Senior Staffing Specialist, Karis Spence

Vice President Senior Sourcing Manager, Jay Gomer

Senior Vice President Retail Marketing, Karen Maruna

Assistant Vice President, Tony Ruberg

Assistant Vice President Regional Property Manager, Cheryl Pitzer

Vice President Of The Mortgage Group, Linda Zack

Vice President, Renee Ross

Vice President, William Mokma

Vice President, Dan Lowrie

Assistant Vice President, Schlosser James

Vice President, Terri Whitman

Vice President, William Denehy

Executive Vice President Marketing, Chandra Kimble

Vice President Commercial Loans, John Leuhmann

Vice President Portfolio Manager, Matthew Alexander

Vice President Treasury Management Customer Care Manager, Raquel Ribe

Vice President, David Konik

Senior Executive Vice President And Director Commercial Banking, Rick Remiker

Vice President Business Banking, Herb Sawtell

Assistant Vice President And Branch Manager, Amber Babik

Vice President Retirement Plan Services Consultant, Douglas Scharphorn

Assistant Vice President Third Party, Michael Adams

Vice President Franchise Finance Group, Jared Hill

Vice President And Manager Customer Information And Market Research, Joyce Smith

Vice President, Bill Crum

Vice President Senior Relationship Manager, Jason Ratkovich

Assistant Vice President Deposit Pricing And Product Lead Analyst, Dominic Monley

Vice President, Bill Hise

Vice President Payments And Channels, Michael Becher

Senior Vice President, Tom Nist

Vice President, Charlie Groux

Vice President District Manager, Eric Kelemen

Assistant Vice President Scrum Master, Laura Elliott

Vice President Credit Administration, Bruce Brown

Assistant Vice President Auto Finance Credit Rep Senior, Jeremy Menning

East Area Business Banking Manager Senior Vice President, Sam Huston

Vice President General Manager, Mark Soccorsi

Assistant Vice President And Assistant Team Leader And Financial Advisor, Chay Rankin

Vice President, Michael Strabele

Vice President Business Banking, Julie Roth

Vice President, Thomas Hannaford

Vice President And Team Leader Special Assets Division, Alfred Casino

Assistant Vice President Senior Risk Man, Na Jin

Senior Vice President Segment Risk Officer, Mindy Ball

Assistant Vice President; Senior Product Manager Mobile Banking, Jill Tubaugh

Vice President Sales Executive, Justin Townsend

Senior Vice President Retail And Business Banking Risk Manager, David Mehrle

Assistant Vice President Business Banking Underwriter, John Hogue

Vice President, Andy Thomas

Senior Vice President Managing Director Lender Finance, Dennis Conway

Senior Vice President, Robyn Griffin

Information Technology Project Leader Assistant Vice President, Jeff Thompson

Vice President Associate Counsel, Dana Farthing

Vice President Mortgage Collections, Shane Rito

Vice President, Jeff Cholley

Senior Vice President, Monique Legris

Vice President; Senior Financial Advisor Team Leader, Patrick Riepenhoff

Vice President Product Manager Commercial Deposits And Fees, Larry Matteson

Vice President Lending, Miccau McClelland

Vice President And Senior Financial Advisor, Terresa Pratt

Vice President Tax, Michael Mayer

Senior Vice President Credit Manager, Becky Bandelaria

Vice President, Donna Smith

Assistant Vice President Senior Financial Analyst, Mike Valeri

Assistant Vice President, Susan Pelzer

Assistant Vice President Talent Acquisition Consultant Senior, Pam Burlingame

Vice President, Cheryl Hardwick

Vice President Portfolio Risk Specialist Senior, Yianni Vitellas

Vice President Senior Community Development Banker At Huntington National Bank, Christina Tracy

Vice President General Manager, Lisa Jameson

Vice President Senior Infrastructure Manager, Mark Hildebrand

Senior Vice President, Mark Palazzo

Auditors: PricewaterhouseCoopers LLP

LOCATIONS

HQ: Huntington Bancshares Inc
  41 South High Street, Columbus, OH 43287
Phone: 614 480-2265
Web: www.huntington.com

2016 Bank Branches

	No.
Ohio	523
Michigan	353
Pennsylvania	53
Indiana	46
Illinois	39
Wisconsin	37
West Virginia	30
Kentucky	10
Total	**1,091**

2016 sales

	No.
Consumer and Business Banking	43
Commercial Banking	23
Commercial Real Estate and Vehicle Finance	24
Regional Banking and The Huntington Private Client Group	8
Home Lending	2
Total	**100**

PRODUCTS/OPERATIONS

2016 Sales

	$ mil.	% of total
Interest		
Loans & leases	2,178	58
Available-for-sale and other securities	280	7
Held-to-maturity securities	138	4
Other	35	1
Noninterest		
Service charges on deposit accounts	324	9
cards and payment processing income	169	4
Mortgage banking income	128	3
Trust services	108	3
Insurance income	64	2
Brokerage income	61	2
Capital markets fees	59	2
Bank owned life insurance income	57	2
Gain on sales of loans	47	1
Net gains on sales of securities	2	-
Other	129	3
Impairment losses recognized in earnings on available-for-sale securities	(2.1)	
Total	**3,781**	**100**

COMPETITORS

Citizens Financial Group	PNC Financial
Comerica	Park National
Fifth Third	Regions Financial
JPMorgan Chase	TFS Financial
KeyCorp	U.S. Bancorp
	Wells Fargo

HISTORICAL FINANCIALS

Company Type: Public

Income Statement

	ASSETS ($ mil.)	NET INCOME ($ mil.)	INCOME AS % OF ASSETS	EMPLOYEES
12/17	104,185	1,186	1.1%	15,770
12/16	99,714	711	0.7%	15,993
12/15	71,044	692	1.0%	12,243
12/14	66,298	632	1.0%	11,873
12/13	59,476	638	1.1%	11,964
Annual Growth	15.0%	16.7%	—	7.1%

FYE: December 31

2017 Year-End Financials

Debt ratio: 8.83%
Return on equity: 11.23%
Cash ($ mil.): 1,567
Current ratio: —
Long-term debt ($ mil.): —

No. of shares (mil.): 1,072
Dividends
Yield: 0.0%
Payout: 35.0%
Market value ($ mil.): 15,609

	STOCK PRICE ($) FY Close	P/E High/Low	PER SHARE ($) Earnings	Dividends	Book Value
12/17	14.56	15 12	1.00	0.35	10.09
12/16	13.22	19 11	0.70	0.29	9.49
12/15	11.06	14 12	0.81	0.25	8.30
12/14	10.52	15 12	0.72	0.21	7.80
12/13	9.65	13 9	0.72	0.19	7.34
Annual Growth	10.8%	— —	8.6%	16.5%	8.3%

Huntington Ingalls Industries, Inc.

For 40 years Huntington Ingalls Industries (HII) has been the sole builder of the US Navy's nuclear aircraft carriers. Rivaling nuclear submarine builder General Dynamics HII is the largest naval shipbuilder in the world; it also maintains refuels and repairs nuclear aircraft carriers and submarines. In addition HII supplies expeditionary warfare ships surface combatants submarines commercial oil hull tankers and Coast Guard surface ships as well as provides aftermarket fleet support. Almost all its offerings are sold to the US government.

Operations

The shipbuilder divides its work between a few divisions: Newport News (nuclear-powered submarines; almost 60% of net sales) Ingalls (warship production for the US Navy; roughly 30%) and Technical Solutions (fleet support services; 10%). In addition subsidiary AMSEC offers a wide variety of naval architecture and marine engineering services.

Its carrier Gerald R. Ford (CVN 78) is the first ship of its class and is scheduled for delivery to the Navy in 2017. Its last-of-the- Nimitz -class predecessor the USS George H.W. Bush was commissioned in early 2009.

Geographic Reach

Headquartered in Newport News Virginia HII has offices in Huntsville Alabama; San Diego California; Broomfield Colorado; Avondale (New Orleans) Louisiana; Pascagoula Mississippi; Houston; Fairfax Hampton Newport News Suffolk and Virginia Beach Virginia; and Washington DC.

Sales and Marketing

HII provides services to the governmental energy oil and gas private sector companies in addition to commercial industries. The US government is its largest customer with the US Navy accounting for almost 90% of its net sales. The US Coast Guard generates around 5%.

Financial Performance

HII has achieved unprecedented growth over the years with revenues climbing 1% to peak at a record-setting $7.07 billion in 2016. Profits also surged 42% to reach $573 million in 2016 another company milestone.

The historic growth for 2016 was attributed to a 9% rise in Ingalls sales and a 12% spike in Technical Solutions sales. Ingalls experienced higher revenues in surface combatants and amphibious assault ships in 2016. Its Technical Solutions posted higher nuclear and environmental and fleet support revenues as well as additional revenue from its Camber acquisition.

The surge in profits for 2016 was driven by the absence of about $75 million in goodwill and intangible asset impairment charges stemming from its Technical Solutions segment it posted the previous year.

Strategy

One way HII grows is by signing multi-year contracts. The company bets on the fact that the longer a contract runs the more likely contract modifications for certain upgrades will occur resulting in enhanced contract value. In 2013 HII was awarded a multi-year contract totaling $3.3 billion for the construction of five additional DDG-51 Arleigh Burke-class destroyers as a part of a larger US Navy order for nine DDG-51 Arleigh Burke-class destroyers. HII indeed received a modification for this contract in mid-2017 to incorporate some of the latest radar upgrades.

Adhering to this strategy further in late 2017 HII's Newport News segment clinched a $2.8 billion contract to support the refueling and complex overhaul of the USS George Washington. This ship is a Nimitz-class aircraft and is one of the largest nuclear-powered warships that can accommodate up to 6000 personnel on board. HII manages the only private shipyard capable of refueling and overhauling nuclear-powered aircraft carriers. Work for this deal will be completed by August 2021.

Mergers and Acquisitions

HII often uses acquisitions in order to bolster its core offerings.

In late 2016 HII picked up Camber Corporation a provider of information technology and training services to the armed services for $372 million. The acquisition allowed it to form HII Technical Solutions a professional services segment catering to a wide variety of government and commercial customers worldwide. The division offers expertise in agile software development and network engineering training systems logistics support information technology fleet maintenance and modernization and unmanned undersea systems.

In mid-2015 HII acquired the engineering solutions division of The Columbia Group in a deal that enabled it to compete more strongly in the unmanned underwater vehicle market.

EXECUTIVES

President And Ceo, C. Michael (Mike) Petters, age 58, $328,847 total compensation

Evp Communications, Jerri Fuller Dickseski

Evp; President Newport News Shipbuilding, Matthew J. (Matt) Mulherin, age 58, $515,000 total compensation

Evp And General Counsel, Kellye L. Walker, age 51, $505,096 total compensation

Evp And Chief Human Resources Officer, William R. (Bill) Ermatinger

Evp And President Technical Solutions, Andy Green

Evp; President Ingalls Shipbuilding, Brian Cuccias, $514,906 total compensation

Evp Business Management And Cfo, Christopher D. Kastner, age 54, $463,462 total compensation

Evp Government And Customer Relations, Mitchell B. (Mitch) Waldman

Evp Strategy And Development, Michael S. Smith

Vp Quality Newport News Shipbuilding, Ron Murray

Corp Vice President Benefits And Compensatio, Jim Taylor

Vice President Operations, Danny Hunley

Corporate Vice President Internal Audit, Jeanne Callahan

Vp Manufacturing And Material Distribution Newport News Shipbuilding, Rob Hogan

Corporate Vice President Benefits And Compensation, Karen Velkey

Vp Legistlative Affairs, Andrew Hicks

Evp And Chief Human Resource Officer, Bill Ermatinger

Corporate Vice President Government And Customers Relations, Mitch Waldman

Vice President Legislative Affairs, Carrie Apostolou

Vp And Controller Newport News Shipbuilding, Carolyn Pittman

Vp Supply Chain Management Ingalls Shipbuilding, Lori Harper

Corporate Vice President Associate General Counsel And Secretary, Charles Chuck Monroe

Vice President Construction John F. Kennedy (cvn79) Newport News Shipbuilding, Lucas Hicks

Vp Human Resources And Administration Ingalls Shipbuilding, Edmond E Hughes

Vp Quality Engineering And Ils Ingalls Shipbuilding, Dave Belanger

Chairman, Thomas B. Fargo, age 70

Board Member, Anastasia Kelly

Board Member, Victoria Harker

Board Member, Thomas Schievelbein

Board Member, John Welch

Auditors: DELOITTE & TOUCHE LLP

LOCATIONS

HQ: Huntington Ingalls Industries, Inc.
4101 Washington Avenue, Newport News, VA 23607
Phone: 757 380-2000
Web: www.huntingtoningalls.com

PRODUCTS/OPERATIONS

2016 Sales

	$ mil.	% of total
Newport News	4,089	57
Ingalls	2,389	33
Technical Solutions	691	10
Intersegment eliminations	(101)	-
Total	**7,068**	**100**

2016 Sales

	$ mil.	% of total
Product sales	5,631	80
Service revenues	1,437	20
Total	**7,068**	**100**

Selected Products

Aircraft carriers (nuclear-powered)
Amphibious assault ships
Coast Guard cutters
Destroyers
Fleet services
Submarines (nuclear-powered)

COMPETITORS

BAE SYSTEMS
Direction des Constructions Navales
Electric Boat
General Dynamics
Northrop Grumman
Todd Shipyards

HISTORICAL FINANCIALS

Company Type: Public

Income Statement

	REVENUE ($ mil.)	NET INCOME ($ mil.)	NET PROFIT MARGIN	EMPLOYEES
12/17	7,441	479	6.4%	38,000
12/16	7,068	573	8.1%	37,000
12/15	7,020	404	5.8%	36,000
12/14	6,957	338	4.9%	38,000
12/13	6,820	261	3.8%	3,800
Annual Growth	2.2%	16.4%	—	77.8%

FYE: December 31

2017 Year-End Financials

Debt ratio: 20.07%
Return on equity: 28.09%
Cash ($ mil.): 701
Current ratio: 1.58
Long-term debt ($ mil.): 1,279

No. of shares (mil.): 45
Dividends
Yield: 0.0%
Payout: 24.0%
Market value ($ mil.): 10,630

	STOCK PRICE ($) FY Close	P/E High/Low		PER SHARE ($) Earnings	Dividends	Book Value
12/17	235.70	24	18	10.46	2.52	38.98
12/16	184.19	15	10	12.14	2.10	35.78
12/15	126.85	17	12	8.36	1.70	31.77
12/14	112.46	17	13	6.86	1.00	28.26
12/13	90.01	17	8	5.18	0.50	31.23
Annual Growth	27.2%	—	—	19.2%	49.8%	5.7%

Huntsman Corp

Operating its businesses through subsidiary Huntsman International global chemical manufacturer Huntsman Corporation makes a broad range of products that include MDI (methylene diphenyl diisocyanate) amines surfactants epoxy-based polymers and polyurethanes. Huntsman's chemicals are sold worldwide to a variety of customers in the adhesives construction products electronics medical and packaging industries. Huntsman operates manufacturing and research and development facilities in about 30 countries worldwide. In 2017 the company agreed to merge with Clariant AG in a $20 billion deal; however both companies mutually terminated the merger later in the year.

Operations

Huntsman makes differentiated organic chemical products and inorganic chemical products. Its products comprise a broad range of chemicals and formulations which it markets globally to a diversified group of consumer and industrial customers. Its key product lines include MDI (methylene diphenyl diisocyanate) amines surfactants maleic anhydride epoxy-based polymer formulations textile chemicals dyes titanium dioxide and color pigments.

The company operates through five business segments: Advanced Materials (10% of net sales) Performance Products (more than 20%) Pigments and Additives (almost 20%) Polyurethanes (almost 40%) and Textile Effects (roughly 10%).

The largest segment is the Polyurethanes unit which makes MDI propylene oxide and propylene glycol for automotive interiors footwear and furniture cushioning. It is one of the largest producers of MDI which is used in producing rigid and other types of polyurethanes.

Other segments are Advanced Materials (epoxy acrylic and polyurethane-based polymers) Textile Effects (epoxy resins and adhesives) Performance Products (mostly ethylene-based chemicals used in detergents paints and fuel additives) and Pig-

ments and Additives (the whitening agent titanium dioxide).

Geographic Reach

Huntsman operates more than 100 manufacturing and R&D facilities in more than 30 countries.

The company's MDI production facilities are located in Geismar Louisiana; Rotterdam The Netherlands; and through joint ventures in Caojing China. It operates synthesis formulating and production facilities in North America Europe Asia South America and Africa.

Pigments and Additives operate more than 25 manufacturing facilities have ten titanium dioxide manufacturing plants in Europe and roughly 20 color pigments manufacturing and processing facilities in the US. It also operates five facilities producing water treatment timber treatment chemicals and functional additives.

Sales and Marketing

Huntsman markets polyurethane chemicals to more than 3500 customers in about 90 countries. Major customers include companies in the appliance automotive footwear furniture and coatings construction products adhesives sealants and elastomers industries. It sells more than 1500 products to more than 3000 customers though the Performance Products marketing groups.

Huntsman sells iron oxides through its global sales force. The company's ultramarine sales are predominantly through specialty distributors. It sell the majority of its timber treatment products directly to end customers via Viance.

About 75% of Hunstman's sales are generated from 2050 direct customers through its global sales and technical services network and the remaining 25% is generated through distribution partners.

Financial Performance

Huntsman's revenues have declined the last two years dipping 6% from $10.3 billion in 2015 to $9.7 billion in 2016 due to lower average selling prices in all its segments and lower sales volumes in its Performance Products and Advanced Materials segments.

The decrease in revenues in Performance Products segment was primarily due to lower average selling prices and lower sales volumes. Sales volumes decreased due to competitive market conditions softer demand in China and for oilfield applications and the impact of weather related and other production outages.

The Advanced Materials segment revenue drop was due to lower sales volumes and lower average selling prices. Sales volumes decreased primarily in the Americas region due to competitive pressure and soft demand. Asia Pacific and European sales decreased primarily due to price concessions in its electrical electronic and wind markets and the foreign currency exchange impact of a stronger US dollar against major international currencies.

Huntsman's net income has fluctuated wildly over the years; after declining to $93 million in 2015 net income skyrocketed by more than 250% to $326 million in 2016. This was due to a 6% decline in operating expenses related to the impact of translating foreign currency amounts to the US dollar and a decrease in selling general and administrative expenses as a result of cost savings from restructuring programs within its Pigments and Additives segment.

Similarly cash from operating activities almost doubled from $575 million in 2015 to $1.1 billion in 2016. This was attributed to the massive net income growth coupled with a $473 million favorable variance in operating assets and liabilities for 2016.

Strategy

In mid-2017 Huntsman agreed to merge with Clariant AG one of the world's largest specialty

chemicals companies in a $20 billion deal; however both companies mutually terminated the merger later in the year as a block of shareholders were not satisfied with the terms of the transaction. Clariant and Huntsman initially planned the merger to give Clariant 52% of the combined entity stating the combination would produce around $400 million in annual cost synergies and establish itself as the world's second-biggest specialty chemicals maker behind Germany's Evonik.

Moving forward Huntsman's strategy is to increase sales to its current customers while seeking growth in emerging international markets such as India and China. Huntsman has relocated the headquarters of some of its divisions overseas to be closer to critical markets putting its Polyurethanes operation in Hong Kong and its Textile Effects unit in Singapore. Huntsman has also expanded its manufacturing capabilities overseas by expanding its current operations and acquiring other companies. The company believes that by integrating its different product operations in large facilities close to its customers it can cut transportation costs and exposure to cyclical prices.

In 2016 Huntsman sold its European Differentiated Surfactants business valued at about $225 million to Innospec.It is still focused on its global surfactants business primarily in the US and Australia.

EXECUTIVES

Senior Vice President Deputy General Counsel, Russ Stolle

Evp Strategy And Investment, J. Kimo Esplin, age 56, $686,575 total compensation

President And Ceo, Peter R. Huntsman, age 55, $1,700,000 total compensation

Evp And Cfo, Sean Douglas, age 54

Division President Performance Products, Monte G. Edlund, age 63

Vp And Cio, Delaney M. Bellinger

Ceo Asia/pacific; Division President Polyurethanes, Anthony P. Hankins, age 61, $865,650 total compensation

Evp General Counsel Chief Compliance Officer And Secretary, David M. Stryker, age 60, $505,900 total compensation

Division President Pigments, Simon Turner, age 55, $544,616 total compensation

Vp Europe Advanced Materials, Scott J. Wright

Division President Textile Effects, Rohit Aggarwal

Managing Director Indian Subcontinent, Harshad Naik

Vice President, David Hester

Vice President And General Manager, Eric Phillips

Executive Vice President Strategy And Investment, J Kimo Esplin

Vice President, Russell Healy

Vice President Investor Relations And Finance, Kurt Ogden

Vice President Performance Chemicals, Stu Monteith

Vice President, Brian Pellon

Vice President Research And Development Performance Products, Ralph Diguilio

Vice President Financial Planning And Analysis, Nooshin Vaughn

Vice President Global Supply Chain Polyurethanes, Mike Fowles

National Sales Manager, Katy Zukis

Vice Chairman, Nolan D. Archibald

Executive Chairman, Jon M. Huntsman, age 81

Auditors: DELOITTE & TOUCHE LLP

LOCATIONS

HQ: Huntsman Corp
10003 Woodloch Forest Drive, The Woodlands, TX 77380
Phone: 281 719-6000
Web: www.huntsman.com

2016 Sales

	$ mil.	% of total
US	3,005	31
China	1,021	10
Germany	676	7
Mexico	453	5
Other	4,502	47
Total	**9,657**	**100**

PRODUCTS/OPERATIONS

2016 Sales

	$ mil.	% of total
Polyurethanes	3,667	38
Performance Products	2,126	22
Pigments and Additives	2,139	22
Advanced Materials	1,020	10
Textile Effects	751	8
Corporate and eliminations	(46)	-
Total	**9,657**	**100**

Segments & Selected Products
Polyurethanes
  Aniline
  MDI (methylene diphenyl diisocyanate)
  MTBE (methyl tertiary-butyl ether)
  PG (propylene glycol)
  PO (propylene oxide)
  Polyols
  TPU (thermoplastic polyurethane)
Performance Products
  Ethylene glycol
  Ethylene oxide
  Ethanolamines
  Ethyleneamines
  Maleic anhydride
  Polyetheramines
  Surfactants
Materials & Effects
  Adhesives
  Acrylic
  Polyurethane-based
  Epoxy
  Epoxy resin compounds
Pigments
  Titanium dioxide

COMPETITORS

Akzo Nobel	DuPont
BASF SE	Evonik Degussa
Bayer AG	LyondellBasell
Covestro	Wanhua Chemical Group
Dow Chemical	Co. Ltd.

HISTORICAL FINANCIALS

Company Type: Public

Income Statement
FYE: December 31

	REVENUE ($ mil.)	NET INCOME ($ mil.)	NET PROFIT MARGIN	EMPLOYEES
12/17	8,358	636	7.6%	10,000
12/16	9,657	326	3.4%	15,000
12/15	10,299	93	0.9%	15,000
12/14	11,578	323	2.8%	16,000
12/13	11,079	128	1.2%	12,000
Annual Growth	**(6.8%)**	**49.3%**	**—**	**(4.5%)**

2017 Year-End Financials

Debt ratio: 22.43%	No. of shares (mil.): 240
Return on equity: 32.56%	Dividends
Cash ($ mil.): 470	Yield: 0.0%
Current ratio: 1.83	Payout: 19.1%
Long-term debt ($ mil.): 2,258	Market value ($ mil.): 7,997

	STOCK PRICE ($) FY Close	P/E High/Low		PER SHARE ($) Earnings	Dividends	Book Value
12/17	33.29	13	7	2.61	0.50	10.91
12/16	19.08	15	6	1.36	0.50	5.44
12/15	11.37	64	25	0.38	0.50	6.08
12/14	22.78	22	16	1.31	0.50	7.30
12/13	24.60	46	30	0.53	0.50	8.24
Annual Growth	**7.9%**	—	—	**49.0%**	**(0.0%)**	**7.3%**

Hyatt Hotels Corp

Hyatt Hotels is one of the world's top operators of luxury hotels and resorts. The company has more than 710 managed franchised and owned properties in some about 55 countries. Its core Hyatt Regency brand offers hospitality services targeted primarily to business travelers and upscale vacationers. The firm's hotel chains include the upscale full service Hyatt Grand Hyatt and Andaz brands as well as Park Hyatt (luxury) and Hyatt Place (select service). Hyatt also operates resorts under the names Hyatt Zilara and Hyatt Ziva and the company's Hyatt Residence Club sells timeshare properties.

HISTORY

Nicholas Pritzker left Kiev for Chicago in 1881 where his family's ascent to the ranks of America's wealthiest families began. His son A. N. left the family law practice in the 1930s and began investing in a variety of businesses. He turned a 1942 investment (Cory Corporation) worth $25000 into $23 million by 1967. A. N.'s son Jay followed in his father's wheeling-and-dealing footsteps. In 1953 with the help of his father's banking connections Jay purchased Colson Company and recruited his brother Bob an industrial engineer to restructure a company that made tricycles and US Navy rockets. By 1990 Jay and Bob had added 60 industrial companies with annual sales exceeding $3 billion to the entity they called The Marmon Group.

The family's connection to Hyatt hotels was established in 1957 when Jay Pritzker bought a hotel called Hyatt House located near the Los Angeles airport from Hyatt von Dehn. Jay added five locations by 1961 and hired his gregarious youngest brother Donald to manage the hotel company. Hyatt went public in 1967 but the move that opened new vistas for the hotel chain was the purchase that year of an 800-room hotel in Atlanta that both Hilton and Marriott had turned down. John Portman's design incorporating a 21-story atrium a large fountain and a revolving rooftop restaurant became a Hyatt trademark.

The Pritzkers formed Hyatt International in 1969 to operate hotels overseas and the company grew rapidly in the US and abroad during the 1970s. Donald Pritzker died in 1972 and Jay assumed control of Hyatt. The family decided to take the company private in 1979. Much of Hyatt's growth in the 1970s came from contracts to manage Hyatt hotels built by other investors. When Hyatt's earnings on those contracts shrank in the 1980s the company launched its own hotel and resort developments under Nick Pritzker a cousin to Jay and Bob. In 1988 with US and Japanese partners it built the Hyatt Regency Waikoloa on Hawaii's Big Island for $360 million — a record at the time for a hotel.

The Pritzkers took a side-venture into air travel in 1983 when they bought bedraggled Braniff Airlines through Hyatt subsidiaries as it emerged from bankruptcy. After a failed 1987 attempt to merge the airline with Pan Am the Pritzkers sold Braniff in 1988.

Hyatt opened Classic Residence by Hyatt a group of upscale retirement communities in 1989. The company joined Circus Circus (now part of MGM Resorts International) in 1994 to launch the Grand Victoria the nation's largest cruising gaming vessel. The next year as part of a new strategy to manage both freestanding golf courses and those near Hyatt hotels the company opened its first freestanding course: an 18-hole par 71 championship course in Aruba.

President Thomas Pritzker Jay's son took over as Hyatt chairman and CEO following his father's death in early 1999. In 2000 Hyatt announced plans to join rival Marriott International in launching an independent company to provide an online procurement network serving the hospitality industry. The Pritzker family that year led a buyout of U.S. Franchise Systems (sold to Wyndham Worldwide in 2008). The following year the company announced plans to build a 47-story skyscraper in downtown Chicago. Construction for the new building named the Hyatt Center began at the end of 2002.

In 2004 the Pritzker family consolidated its hospitality holdings to form Global Hyatt Corporation. The following year the company bought the AmeriSuites limited-service hotel chain from Prime Hospitality and rebranded it as Hyatt Place. And in 2006 Hyatt acquired the Summerfield Suites from The Blackstone Group. It converted the brand to Hyatt Summerfield Suites an upscale all-suite/extended stay brand.

Mark Hoplamazian president of The Pritzker Organization a merchant-banking firm serving the family's business activities took over as president and CEO in 2006; Thomas Pritzker remained chairman. In 2007 the company launched the Andaz chain a luxury brand with rates at about $300 a night and up.

Hyatt sold its U.S. Franchise Systems subsidiary in 2008 to Wyndham Worldwide for about $150 million in order to focus on its global growth and luxury brands. The unit acquired in 2000 operated the smaller Hawthorn Suites and Microtel Inns & Suites chains.

In 2009 the company changed its name from Global Hyatt Corporation to Hyatt Hotels Corporation. Later that year it filed an IPO. The timing of the public offering was questionable given the weak economy and a hotel industry suffering from decreased occupancy levels. However Hyatt's IPO had been years in the making as a way for the Pritzkers to raise cash as they split up the family's assets among 11 adult cousins. (Though the Pritzkers remain in control the IPO gave several family members the chance to cash out allowing for an end to the feuds within the family.)

Proceeds from the IPO were used for expansion through new hotel openings and acquisitions as well as renovation efforts at existing properties. In 2010 the company opened 16 new Hyatt Place hotels and 4 new Hyatt Summerfield Suites hotels in North America most of which were franchised properties.

EXECUTIVES

Evp And Global President Operations, H. Charles (Chuck) Floyd, age 58, $746,667 total compensation
Global Head Of Data Innovation And Business Transformation, Alex D. Zoghlin, age 48
President And Ceo, Mark S. Hoplamazian, age 55, $1,135,833 total compensation

Evp And Global Chief Marketing Officer, Maryam Banikarim, age 49, $584,936 total compensation

Evp And Global Head Of Capital Strategy Franchising And Select Service, Stephen G. (Steve) Haggerty, age 50, $687,500 total compensation

Evp And Chief Human Resources Officer, Anne-Marie Law, age 51

Evp General Counsel And Secretary, Rena Hozore Reiss, age 58

Evp And Cfo, Patrick J. (Pat) Grismer, age 56, $613,542 total compensation

Evp And Group President Europe Africa Middle East (eame) And Southwest Asia, Peter Fulton, age 60

Evp And Group President Asia Pacific (aspac), David Udell, age 57

Evp And Group President Americas, Peter J. (Pete) Sears, age 53

Vice President Sales And Marketing, Sara Kearney

Regional Vice President Acquisitions And Development Sub Saharan Africa, Tejas Shah

Vice President Finance, Tracy Gainer

Vice President, Suzanne Saunders

Vice President Of Human Resources, Monique Pinney

Regional Vice President Hotel Finance, Sal Galioto

Executive Chairman, Thomas J. (Tom) Pritzker, age 67

Auditors: Deloitte & Touche LLP

LOCATIONS

HQ: Hyatt Hotels Corp
150 North Riverside Plaza, 8th Floor, Chicago, IL 60606
Phone: 312 750-1234
Web: www.hyatt.com

2017 Sales

	$ mil.	% of total
US	3,771	80
Other countries	914	20
Total	**4,685**	**100**

PRODUCTS/OPERATIONS

2017 Sales

	$ mil.	% of total
Owned and leased hotels	2,192	47
Other revenues from managed & franchised properties	1,918	41
Management & franchised fees	505	11
Other revenues	70	1
Total	**4,685**	**100**

Selected Brands

Andaz (simple sophisticated luxury hotels)
Grand Hyatt Hotels (large-scale luxury format)
Hyatt Regency Hotels (core hotel format)
Hyatt Resorts (local culture including spas and cuisine)
Hyatt Summerfield Suites (extended stay)
Hyatt Vacation Ownership (timeshares)
Park Hyatt Hotels (smaller-scale luxury hotels)

Selected Properties

Andaz West Hollywood
Grand Hyatt New York
Grand Hyatt San Antonio
Grand Hyatt San Francisco
Grand Hyatt Seattle
Grand Hyatt Tampa Bay
Hyatt Place Atlanta/Perimeter Center
Hyatt Place Baltimore/Owings Mills
Hyatt Place Birmingham/Inverness
Hyatt Place Boise/Towne Square
Hyatt Place Charlotte Airport/Tyvola Road
Hyatt Place Chicago/Itasca
Hyatt Place Chicago/Lombard/Oak Brook
Hyatt Place Cincinnati - Northeast
Hyatt Regency Atlanta
Hyatt Regency Baltimore
Hyatt Regency Bellevue
Hyatt Regency Boston
Hyatt Regency Buffalo

Hyatt Regency Cincinnati
Hyatt Regency Cleveland at The Arcade
Hyatt Regency Coconut Point Resort & Spa
Hyatt Summerfield Suites Boston/Waltham
Hyatt Summerfield Suites Denver Tech Center
Hyatt Summerfield Suites Miami Airport
Hyatt Summerfield Suites Morristown
Hyatt Summerfield Suites Parsippany/Whippany
Park Hyatt Chicago
Park Hyatt Philadelphia at Bellevue
Park Hyatt Toronto
Park Hyatt Washington

COMPETITORS

Accor	Marriott
Carlson Hotels	Millennium & Copthorne
Club Med	Hotels
Four Seasons Hotels	Sonesta International
Hilton Worldwide	Hotels
InterContinental	Starwood Hotels &
Hotels	Resorts
LXR Luxury Resorts	Wyndham Destinations

HISTORICAL FINANCIALS

Company Type: Public

Income Statement

FYE: December 31

	REVENUE ($ mil.)	NET INCOME ($ mil.)	NET PROFIT MARGIN	EMPLOYEES
12/17	4,685	249	5.3%	45,000
12/16	4,429	204	4.6%	45,000
12/15	4,328	124	2.9%	45,000
12/14	4,415	344	7.8%	45,000
12/13	4,184	207	4.9%	45,000
Annual Growth	**2.9%**	**4.7%**	**—**	**0.0%**

2017 Year-End Financials

Debt ratio: 18.91%
Return on equity: 6.70%
Cash ($ mil.): 503
Current ratio: 1.37
Long-term debt ($ mil.): 1,440

No. of shares (mil.): 118
Dividends
  Yield: —
  Payout: —
Market value ($ mil.): 8,750

	STOCK PRICE ($) FY Close	P/E High/Low	PER SHARE ($) Earnings	Dividends	Book Value
12/17	73.54	37 25	1.98	0.00	29.71
12/16	55.26	38 23	1.52	0.00	29.84
12/15	47.02	71 53	0.86	0.00	29.30
12/14	60.21	28 20	2.23	0.00	31.04
12/13	49.46	38 30	1.30	0.00	30.55
Annual Growth	**10.4%**	**—**	**11.1%**	**—**	**(0.7%)**

IBERIABANK Corp

Holding company IBERIABANK Corporation through its flagship bank subsidiary IBERIABANK operates some 230 branches in Louisiana and about 10 other states. It also has about 30 title insurance offices in Louisiana Arkansas and Tennessee in addition to some 90 mortgage loan offices in a dozen states and about 20 wealth management offices in four states. Offering deposit products such as checking and savings accounts CDs and IRAs the bank uses funds gathered mainly to make loans. Commercial loans and leases make up around two-thirds of the company's $22.3 billion loan portfolio which also includes consumer loans and residential mortgages. IBERIABANK Corp. has $30.1 billion in assets.

Operations

IBERIABANK operates through its IBERIA-BANK mortgage and LTC segments.

The IBERIABANK segment — which includes commercial and retail banking wealth management capital markets and other corporate functions — accounts for about 90% of revenue. Net interest income comprises about 85% of the segment's revenue. Commercial loans provide about 70% of the holding company's loan interest income; consumer and other loans generate about 20% of its loan interest income.

The mortgage segment accounts for nearly 10% of revenue. Through that business IBERIABANK originates funds and sells one-to-four family residential mortgages. Such loans accounts for about 10% of the company's loan interest income.

IBERIABANK offers title insurance and loan closing services through its LTC segment.

Geographic Reach

IBERIABANK operates about 330 combined offices including around 230 bank branch offices and two loan production offices in Louisiana Arkansas Tennessee Alabama Texas Florida Georgia South Carolina New York and North Carolina; about 30 title insurance offices in Arkansas Tennessee and Louisiana; and mortgage representatives at some 90 locations in 12 US states.

Some 40% 20% and 10% of the company's loans are in Florida Louisiana and Texas respectively.

Financial Performance

IBERIABANK has seen strong revenue and net income growth from 2013 to 2017 adding 82% and 119% respectively. Cash stores increased 60% to $625.7 million while long-term debt ballooned by 433% to $1.5 billion.

The holding company's revenue trended up 15% to $1 billion in 2017 compared with 2016 thanks to increased interest and fees from loans caused by improvements in loan yields and average earning assets. The growth was offset slightly by a decline in non-interest income primarily from the residential mortgage business.

Net income however fell 24% to $142.4 million in that time owing to non-interest expenses related to IBERIABANK's acquisition of southeastern Florida bank chain Sabadell United Bank and a $51 million increase in income tax expense caused by the 2017 Tax Cuts and Jobs Act.

The bank's cash stores were depleted by $736.4 million in 2017. Operations added $263.6 million and investments used $1.9 billion including $490.4 million for acquisitions. Financings added another $908.5 million from proceeds from long-term debt and common stock issuances.

Strategy

IBERIABANK announced its 2020 strategic goals in April 2018 which include improving operating efficiency using a “branch-lite” approach that involves digitalization of client services and back-office processes. Since 2012 the company has increased the proportion of its alternative transactions — including via online digital and smart device delivery systems — by 10 percentage points. The bank opened 28 offices and closed 11 branches in 2017 and scheduled more than 20 branch closures or consolidations for 2018.

In 2018 IBERIABANK also launched a mobile banking app introduced robotic process automation back offices created a mortgage self-fulfillment application and announced plans to update its internet banking website.

IBERIABANK is working to increase its presence in Miami Florida which holds $226 billion in total market deposits. IBERIABANK acquired Southeast Florida-based Sabadell United Bank in July 2017. The deal gave IBERIABANK 25 offices serving the Miami metropolitan area and three offices in Naples Sarasota and Tampa. In March

2018 the bank acquired Gibraltar Private Bank & Trust another Florida bank with seven offices in the Miami Key West and Naples metropolitan areas and one in New York City.

The bank owns around 90 branches in Florida with about $9 billion total deposits. The company has significantly increased its presence in Florida; since 2014 it has grown the share of its portfolio comprising loans and deposits in that state by 13 and 22 percentage points respectively. Other growth markets for the company include Dallas and Houston as well as Atlanta Orlando and Tampa.

Mergers and Acquisitions

Since 2008 IBERIABANK has made more than 20 acquisitions of live and failing banks branches and wealth management and title insurance companies.

IBERIABANK acquired Gibraltar Private Bank & Trust another Florida bank in March 2018 for about $214.7 million. Gibraltar had seven offices in the Miami Key West and Naples metropolitan areas and one in New York City prior to the acquisition. The agreement conferred $1.5 billion in loans and $1.1 billion in deposits to IBERIA-BANK's portfolio.

The bank acquired SolomonParks Title & Escrow in January 2018 for $3.3 million thereby gaining eight title offices in the Nashville Tennessee area.

In July 2017 IBERIABANK acquired Southeast Florida-based Sabadell United Bank for $809.2 million in cash and 2.6 million IBERIABANK shares. The deal gave IBERIABANK $4 billion in loans and $4.4 billion in deposits as well as 25 offices serving the Miami metropolitan area and three offices in Naples Sarasota and Tampa.

Company Background

IBERIABANK was founded in 1887 in New Iberia Louisiana. It operated in just two states – Louisiana and Arkansas – until 2008 when it began spreading across the Southeast.

EXECUTIVES

President And Ceo, Daryl G. Byrd, age 63, $1,015,000 total compensation

Sevp Mergers And Acquisitions Finance And Investor Relations; Director Financial Strategy And Mortgage, John R. Davis, age 57, $456,154 total compensation

Vice Chairman And Managing Director Of Brokerage Trust And Wealth Management, Jefferson G. (Jeff) Parker, age 65, $480,192 total compensation

Sevp And Director Communications Facilities And Human Resources, Elizabeth A. (Beth) Ardoin, age 49

Sevp And Cfo, Anthony J. Restel, age 48, $480,385 total compensation

Vice Chairman; Sevp And Coo, Michael J. (Mike) Brown, age 54, $598,269 total compensation

President And Ceo Iberiabank Mortgage, Bill Edwards

Evp And Director Retail Small Business And Mortgage, Robert M. (Bob) Kottler, age 59

Evp And Executive Credit Officer, H. Spurgeon Mackie, age 67

Evp And Chief Risk Officer, J. Randolph Bryan, age 50

Evp Corporate Secretary And General Counsel, Robert B. Worley, age 58

President And Ceo Lender's Title Company, David B. Erb

Assistant Vice President Retail Support Specialist, Sheila Montgomery

Senior Vice President, Steve Krueger

Assistant Vice President, Dolores Hernandez

Vice President, Tom Chelewski

Vice President Bcs Ore Officer, Neel Stacy

Vice President, Bruce Reid

Vice President Support Services, Jerry Prejean

Vice President And Senior Business Relationship Manager, Ty Powell

Executive Vice President, Ken Brown

Vice President Commercial Lending, Jeremy Young

Assistant Vice President, Misty Labat

Vice President, Mary Rice

Senior Vice President Network Support Manager, Chris Berthaut

Vice President, Nancy Dost

Vice President Business Banking, Shannon Pemberton

Senior Vice President, Missy S Krantz

Vice President, Craig Peak

Senior Vice President, Greg Mendez

Vice President Of Product Management, Paula Allred

Senior Vice President, Eric Movassaghi

Vice President Retail Administration, Linda Swinkey

Vice President Ore Property Manager, Brian Buczko

Senior Vice President Corporate Banking, C Mizelle

Vice President, Michael Hallmark

Vice President Branch Manager Business Development Officer, Pedro Diaz

Vice President Business Credit Services Officer, Michael Schaefer

Vice President Business Credit Services, Timothy Wilson

Vice President Human Resources, Jayne Socotch

Vice President, Howard Mary

Senior Vice President Commercial Banking, Holly Popham

Vice President Finance, Joel Jewell

Vice President Human Resources And Employee Development And Training, Mike Pelletier

Vice President Controllera, Angela Robert

Senior Vice President, Pat Yates

Vice President Business Credit Services, David Krage

Bank Manager Vice President, Melanie Savell

Executive Vice President And Director Enterprise Risk Ma, Elise Latimer

Senior Vice President And Commercial Rel, Jamey Vaught

Vice President Corporate Security, Warren Bujol

Executive Vice President, Beth Ardoin

Vice President Benefits And Recruiting Director, Greg Rizzuto

Senior Vice President, Richard Perdue

Executive Vice President, Norman Vascocu

Vice President Business Banking, William Biossat

Vice President Compliance Officer, Winifred Stamps

Treasury Management Consultant And Vice President, Steven Perez

Mortgage Executive Vice President, Susie Boudreaux

Senior Vice President And Business And Retail Market Manger, Maurice Butler

Senior Vice President Consumer Credit Risk Director, Wayne Stone

Vice President, William Morrow

Senior Vice President Business Credit Se, Fred Malzahn

Senior Vice President And Manager Of Financial Analytics, Shawn Jordan

Vice President Branch Manager, Samantha McDermott

Vice President Commercial Relationship Manager, Layne Dodd

Vice President Mortgage Executive, Mark Young

Senior Vice President Special Assets Manager, Karen Repas

Vice President Mortgage Executive, Connie Fernandez

Senior Vice President Treasury Management, Kathaleen Parks

Assistant Vice President, Felesha Finch

Vice President Central Retail Administration, Donna Pye

Vice President Corporate Counsel, Lynn Dodd

Assistant Vice President Relationship Manager, Millard Morrison

Senior Vice President, Mary Morgan

Vice President, Linda Rodriguez

Vice President Private Banking Relationship Manager, Carrie Standlee

Vice President Business Banking, Tim Finn

Vice President, Cody Walker

Vice President, Leigh Seago

Vice President, Matthew Rink

Vice President Deposit Operations, Felicia Weeks

Senior Vice President, Doug Woodman

Vice President Quality Control, Cheryl Terry

Vice President, Marc Massad

Senior Vice President Commercial Relationship Manager Assistant Rebecca Oberg, Kelly Gegerson

Vice President, Karen Hardy

Vice President Manager Commercial Cash Vault, Anna Taylor

Business Intelligence Analyst Assistant Vice President, Kevin Cagle

Assistant Vice President Business Banking Relationship Manager, Deborah Sefcik

Senior Vice President Private Lending Relationship Manager, Maria Ferrer

Assistant Vice President Retail Support Specialist, Heather Wade

Assistant Vice President, Christie Bell

Asst. Vice President Branch Manager, Tamela Leger

Vice President Treasury Management Operations Manager, Kevin Northcutt

Assistant Vice President, Erica Murphy

Vice President Private Banking, Casey Lawhead

Vice President Treasury Management Product Management, Cindy Wolbach

Assistant Vice President Branch Manager, Colleen Lemoine

Vp Business Banking Relationship Manager, Kristen Strickland

Vice President Retail Support Lead, Terri Bridges

Executive Vice President And Commercial Group Manager, John Reingardt

Senior Vice President Compliance Manager Central Florida Cra Liaison, Susan DeFreese

Vice President, Glenn O'Leary

Vice President Human Resources Manager, Karla Newan

Vice President Treasury Management Implementations Manager, Megan Alesci

Vice President And Commercial Relationship Manager, Kevin Tarleton

Vice President Senior Business Analyst Development Officer, Martin Chapman

Assistant Vice President Branch Manager, Heather Ross

Senior Vice President, Michael Alcantar

Vice President Relationship Manager, Amy Moore

Senior Vice President Commercial Manager Collin County, Shannon Bettis

Chairman, William H. Fenstermaker, age 69

Vice Chairman, E. Stewart Shea, age 66

Board Member, Angus Cooper

Board Member, Rick Maples

Auditors: Ernst & Young LLP

LOCATIONS

HQ: IBERIABANK Corp
200 West Congress Street, Lafayette, LA 70501
Phone: 337 521-4003
Web: www.iberiabank.com

COMPETITORS

BancorpSouth	Investar
Bank of America	JPMorgan Chase
Bank of the Ozarks	Louisiana Bancorp
Capital One	MidSouth Bancorp
Hancock Holding	Regions Financial
Home Banc	Teche Holding

HISTORICAL FINANCIALS

Company Type: Public

Income Statement

FYE: December 31

	ASSETS ($ mil.)	NET INCOME ($ mil.)	INCOME AS % OF ASSETS	EMPLOYEES
12/17	27,904	142	0.5%	3,604
12/16	21,659	186	0.9%	3,155
12/15	19,504	142	0.7%	3,216
12/14	15,758	105	0.7%	2,825
12/13	13,365	65	0.5%	2,638
Annual Growth	20.2%	21.6%	—	8.1%

2017 Year-End Financials

Debt ratio: 0.59%	No. of shares (mil.): 53
Return on equity: 4.29%	Dividends
Cash ($ mil.): 625	Yield: 0.0%
Current ratio: —	Payout: 56.3%
Long-term debt ($ mil.): —	Market value ($ mil.): 4,175

	STOCK PRICE ($) FY Close	P/E High/Low	PER SHARE ($) Earnings	Dividends	Book Value
12/17	77.50	33 27	2.59	1.46	68.62
12/16	83.75	21 10	4.30	1.40	65.62
12/15	55.07	19 15	3.68	1.36	60.74
12/14	64.85	22 18	3.30	1.36	55.39
12/13	62.85	29 20	2.20	1.36	51.40
Annual Growth	5.4%	— —	4.2%	1.8%	7.5%

Icahn Enterprises LP

Icahn Enterprises has a can-do attitude when it comes to making money. The holding company has stakes in firms in a diverse array of industries including metals manufacturing energy real estate gaming and home fashion. Holdings include car parts maker Federal-Mogul; energy refinery and production company CVR; PSC Metals one of the largest scrap yard operators in the US; residential developer Bayswater which is active in Florida and Massachusetts; and WestPoint Home a maker of bed bath and other home products. Billionaire corporate raider Carl Icahn and his affiliates control his namesake firm. The US is the company's largest market accounting for about 70% of the revenue.

Operations

Icahn Enterprises holds and operates companies across several industries each of which is called out as a distinct segment in its financial statements. Automotive Energy and Railcar segments comprise more than 85% of annual company revenue. The remaining industry segments each generate between 0.5% and 4% of revenue and are: Gaming/Casinos Metals Mining Food Packaging Real Estate and Home Fashion. Icahn Enterprises also runs an Investment segment which invests money in private investment funds for the benefit of Icahn and his affiliates.

The Automotive segment generates nearly 50% of revenue and operates mainly through its Federal-Mogul holding. It also owns IEH Auto and

Pep Boys: Manny Moe and Jack. The Energy segment (more than 25% of revenue) operates through the CVR Energy Inc. subsidiary and is engaged in petroleum refining and nitrogen fertilizer manufacturing. The Railcar segment (about 10%) is run through the American Railcar Industries Inc. subsidiary which designs and manufactures hopper and tank railcars and then sells or leases them to customers.

Geographic Reach

The New York-headquartered company owns stakes in a number of companies operating worldwide. Federal-Mogul operates more than 250 facilities globally including manufacturing technical sales and administration and distribution centers. Icahn Enterprises' Energy segment holdings are mainly in Kansas and Oklahoma and its Railcar operations are in Missouri Arkansas and Texas.

Sales and Marketing

Icahn Enterprises' Federal-Mogul customers include automotive and heavy-duty vehicle manufacturers agricultural off-highway marine railroad aerospace high performance and industrial application manufacturers.

Its CVR subsidiary's petroleum customers include retailers railroads and farm cooperatives while its nitrogen fertilizer customers include retailers and distributors (for UAN products) and agricultural and industrial businesses (for ammonia products). It supplies jet fuel to the U.S. Department of Defense. One customer accounted for approximately 20% of CVR Refining's sales and more than 50% of CVR Refining's sales were made to its 10 largest customers.

Financial Performance

Icahn Enterprises has resumed generating rising revenue for the past two years after a sales drop in 2015 ended a six-year string of increases.

Revenue jumped 33% to $21.7 billion in 2017 from $16.3 billion in 2016 while the company turned in a $2.6 billion profit in 2017 after posting a $2.2 billion loss the year before. Automotive provided the bulk of Icahn's revenue (48%) in 2017 but the railcar unit delivered 48% of the profit due to the sale of the American Rail Leasing unit for $1.8 billion. All other segments posted higher revenue except for Home Fashion.

Cash at the 2017 year-end was $1.7 billion a decrease of $151 million compared to 2016. Cash used by operations was $1.4 billion. Cash provided by investing activities was $41 million and cash provided by financing activities was $743 million.

Strategy

Icahn Enterprises' strategy known as The Icahn Formula and named after its lead investment strategist Carl Icahn is to seek undervalued or bankrupt assets improve their operations enhance their valuation and sell them for a profit. The firm typically purchases substantial stakes in companies with an eye toward gaining control of them often by waging proxy battles for seats on their boards of directors. Icahn — famous for his activism — is known for his ability to force underperforming management teams to maximize value for shareholders.

In recent years Icahn Enterprises increased its holdings in the Automotive and Energy businesses and repositioned its investment in its Railcar segment.

Icahn Enterprises' diversification across multiple industries and geographies acts as a natural hedge against cyclical and general economic swings. Through its investment segment the firm has held significant positions in various companies including Dell Inc. Herbalife Chesapeake Energy Hain Celestial Group Forest laboratories and Transocean.

Mergers and Acquisitions

In 2018 Icahn Enterprises continued a push into automotive by purchasing four independently-

owned service centers in Metro Detroit: Belanger Tire & Auto Service in Westland Novi Motive Goodyear in Novi and Fix N Go Auto Centers in Troy and Oxford. The locations will convert to Pep Boys Service and Tire Centers.

In 2017 the company sold for $2.8 billion its American Railcar Leasing LLC to a subsidiary of Sumitomo Mitsui Banking Corporation. Icahn still owns its American Railcar Industries subsidiary.

In 2016 Icahn Enterprises purchased the Trump Taj Mahal Atlantic City casino fresh out of bankruptcy. Citing New Jersey political gamesmanship and workers' compensation demands as the cause Icahn shuttered the casino later that year and sold the property to Hard Rock Café in early 2017.

Also in 2016 the firm acquired The Pep Boys for some $1.03 billion which provided "excellent synergistic opportunities for Auto Plus" its automotive aftermarket company.

In June 2015 subsidiary IEH Auto bought Uni-Select USA (the US auto parts assets of auto parts distributor Uni-Select Inc.) and Beck/Arnley Worldparts Inc. for a purchase price of $340 million. The firm acquired all 39 distribution centers and satellite locations and 240 corporate-owned jobber stores in the US. The business became part of Icahn Enterprises' automotive segment with Federal-Mogul.

EXECUTIVES

Cfo And Director, SungHwan Cho, age 43, $822,616 total compensation
Chief Accounting Officer, Peter Reck, age 51, $300,000 total compensation
President Ceo And Director, Keith Cozza, age 39, $1,557,736 total compensation
Vice President And Secretary, Gail Golden
Vice President Corporate Technology And Cybersecurity, Dustin Goodwin
Chairman, Carl C. Icahn, age 82
Treasurer, John Saldarelli
Auditors: GRANT THORNTON LLP

LOCATIONS

HQ: Icahn Enterprises LP
  767 Fifth Avenue, Suite 4700, New York, NY 10153
Phone: 212 702-4300
Web: www.ielp.com

2017 Sales

	% of total
United States	69
Germany	9
Other countries	22
Total	**100**

PRODUCTS/OPERATIONS

2017 Sales

	% of total
Automotive	48
Energy	27
Railcar	11
Gaming	4
Real Estate	2
Metal	2
Home Fashion	1
Mining	-
Holding company	-
Investment	1
Total	**100**

Selected Subsidiaries

Ace Nevada Corp.
American Entertainment Properties Corp.
American Railcar Industries
AREP Oil & Gas Holdings LLC
AREP Real Estate Holdings LLC
Atlantic Coast Entertainment Holdings Inc.

Bayswater Development LLC
Federal-Mogul Corporation
Icahn Capital LP
Icahn Capital Management LP
Icahn Enterprises Holdings L.P.
Icahn Offshore LP
Icahn Onshore LP
New Seabury Properties L.L.C.
PEP Boys: Manny Moe and jack
PSC Metals Inc.
Tropicana Entertainment Inc.
Trump Taj Mahal
Viskase Companies Inc.
WestPoint Home LLC

COMPETITORS

Apollo Global	Leucadia National
Management	MSD Capital
Berkshire Hathaway	Soros Fund Management
Blackstone Group	The Trump Organization
Clark Enterprises	Vulcan
D. E. Shaw	Wesco Financial
KKR	

HISTORICAL FINANCIALS

Company Type: Public

Income Statement   FYE: December 31

	REVENUE ($ mil.)	NET INCOME ($ mil.)	NET PROFIT MARGIN	EMPLOYEES
12/17	21,744	2,430	11.2%	89,034
12/16	16,348	(1,128)	—	90,960
12/15	15,272	(1,194)	—	73,786
12/14	19,157	(373)	—	66,559
12/13	20,682	1,025	5.0%	59,565
Annual Growth	1.3%	24.1%	—	10.6%

2017 Year-End Financials

Debt ratio: 35.17%
Return on equity: —
Cash ($ mil.): 2,468
Current ratio: 2.28
Long-term debt ($ mil.): 11,185

No. of shares (mil.): 173
Dividends
Yield: 0.1%
Payout: 40.5%
Market value ($ mil.): 9,199

	STOCK PRICE ($) FY Close	P/E High/Low		PER SHARE ($) Earnings	Dividends	Book Value
12/17	53.00	4	3	14.80	6.00	29.42
12/16	59.92	—	—	(8.07)	6.00	14.88
12/15	61.30	—	—	(9.29)	6.00	30.32
12/14	92.47	—	—	(3.08)	6.00	44.21
12/13	109.41	16	5	9.07	4.50	52.56
Annual Growth	(16.6%)	—	—	13.0%	7.5%	(13.5%)

IHC HEALTH SERVICES, INC.

EXECUTIVES

Pres-Ceo, William Nelson
Svp-Cfo, Bert Zimmerli
V Pres-Pres, Charles Sorenson
Orthopedist, Zachary Leitze
Doctor, April Larson
Human Resources Consultant, Gail Burns
Emergency Medicine, Gerald Rowland
Diagnostic Radiologist, Steven Davis
Chief Staff, Steven Vannorman
Auditors: KPMG LLP SALT LAKE CITY UT

LOCATIONS

HQ: IHC HEALTH SERVICES, INC.
  1380 E MEDICAL CENTER DR, ST GEORGE, UT
  847902123
Phone: 435 251-2992
Web: WWW.SELECTHEALTH.ORG

HISTORICAL FINANCIALS

Company Type: Private

Income Statement   FYE: December 31

	REVENUE ($ mil.)	NET INCOME ($ mil.)	NET PROFIT MARGIN	EMPLOYEES
12/17	5,483	884	16.1%	4,000
12/16	5,275	564	10.7%	—
12/14	394	55	14.2%	—
Annual Growth	140.5%	150.9%	—	—

2017 Year-End Financials

Debt ratio: —
Return on equity: 16.10%
Cash ($ mil.): 164
Current ratio: 0.50
Long-term debt ($ mil.): —

Dividends
Yield: —
Payout: —
Market value ($ mil.): —

iHeartMedia Inc

iHeartMedia is the #1 radio company in the US. The firm formerly known as CC Media owns and operates more than 855 radio stations in about 160 markets through iHeartCommunications. With more than 245 million listeners a month its stations generate revenue by selling advertising and subscriptions. The company also owns outdoor advertising giant Clear Channel Outdoor Holdings. Clear Channel Outdoor Holdings sells advertising space on billboards public transportation buildings and other outdoor environments throughout the US and more than 35 other countries.

Operations

iHeartMedia operates in three reportable segments. Its iHM segment (54% of total revenue in fiscal 2016) provides media and entertainment services via broadcast and digital delivery. It also includes the company's national syndication business. iHeartMedia's America?s outdoor advertising segment and its International outdoor advertising segment both provide outdoor advertising services.

Geographic Reach

Headquartered in San Antonio Texas United States iHeartMedia's broadcast stations are available on AM/FM HD digital radio satellite radio Internet smartphones iPads and tablets auto dashboards smart TVs and gaming consoles. Its iHeartRadio has more than 100 million registered users.

The company does business throughout North and South America Europe and the Asia/Pacific region. The majority of revenue comes from the Americas.

Sales and Marketing

iHeartMedia's top five customers in Americas outdoor were from the business services automotive technology beverage and travel industries. The company's top five customers in International outdoor were in the retail entertainment telecommunications food and food products automotive accessories and equipment industries.

Advertising partners are the iHeartRadio Music Festival the iHeartRadio Music Awards the

iHeartRadio Ultimate Pool Party and the iHeartRadio Jingle Ball Tour. The company's advertising expenses were $132.7 million in fiscal 2016.

Financial Performance

iHeartMedia's revenue has been consistent across recent fiscal years. It reported $6.2 billion in revenue for fiscal 2016 after claiming $6.2 in revenue the prior fiscal year.

Even with billions in revenue the company has suffered net losses in recent fiscal periods. iHeartMedia claimed a net loss of $296 million in fiscal 2016 which was an improvement compared to the roughly $755 million net loss the company reported in fiscal 2015. The net losses have been caused by the iHeartMedia's extremely high cost of doing business.

Strategy

iHeartMedia's growth strategy includes investing in digital platforms. It is developing the next generation of iHeartRadio an integrated digital radio platform. The company is also working on the ongoing deployment of more digital outdoor displays.iHeartMedia expects to continue to expand its reach deeper into mobile social live events and on-demand entertainment.

EXECUTIVES

President Coo And Cfo, Richard J. Bressler, age 60, $1,200,000 total compensation
President Entertainment Enterprises, John Sykes, age 57
Chairman And Ceo, Robert W. (Bob) Pittman, age 64, $1,200,000 total compensation
Ceo Clear Channel International, C. William Eccleshare, age 62, $927,601 total compensation
Ceo Clear Channel Outdoor America, Scott R. Wells, age 49, $750,000 total compensation
Evp And Chief Communications Officer, Wendy Goldberg, age 54
Evp And General Counsel, Robert H. Walls, age 57, $750,000 total compensation
Evp And Chief Marketing Officer, Gayle Troberman
Global Cio, Steve Mills
Senior Vice President Real Estates, Chad Dan
Vice President Of Information Technology, Jeff Cage
Vice President Of Sales Atlanta Division, Jonathan Graviss
Vice President Corporate Communications Clear, Jason King
Vice President Sales, Lisa Djafari
Vice President Human Resources Ccme, Scott Logeman
Senior Vice President Human Resources, William Feehan
Vice President, Elizabeth Bethea
Vice President And Information Technology Sales, Trisha Dall
Vice President Business Operations, Barbara Caraballo
Vice President Corporate Reporting, Susan Krieg
Vice President Finance, Dina Odak
Vice President Product Management, R O Catalfo
Vice President And Market Manager, Jackie Rinker
Vice President Marketing Solutions, Tara Adamos
Vp Government And Public Affiars Clear Channel Outdoor, Mitchell Schwartz
Vice President Of Marketing, Eileen Woodbury
Vice President Of Sales Denver Market, Tim Hager
Vice President Las Vegas Operations And Partnerships, Edward Sheftel
Senior Vice President Corporate Relations, Kathryn Johnson
Vice President Treasurer, Brian Coleman
Senior Vice President And Chief Accounting Officer, Herbert Hill
Vice President Level, Vice president sales Diane Veres
Vice President, Susan Holshouser

Executive Vice President Automotive Business Development And Partnerships, John Karpinski

Senior Vice President Chief Accounting Officer, Scott Hamilton

Vice President Sales Digital And Alternative, Dean Peterson

National Sales Manager, Guy Goldschmidt

Vice President Sales, Joe Madden

National Account Manager, Michelle Dannaher

Vice President Sales, Scott Clark

Vice President Test Engineering, Aj Almanzor

Vice President And Sales, Damon Gunkel

Senior Vice President Of Sales Northeast Region, Robert Schachter

Vice President Director Of Sales, Michael Newman

Vice President, Bridgett Knupp

Vice President Director Of Sales, Michelle Olivera

Vice President, Britt Levine

Vice President Director Of Sales, Staci Verzera-Fair

Vice President Sales, Lisa Neugarten

Vice President, Bill Mcmartin

Vice President Of Business Development, Greg Yelverton

Vice President And Director Of Sales, Paul Masse

Senior Vice President Of Sales, Scott Hogle

Vice President Of Sales, Jeff Luckoff

Vice President Director Of Sales, Brian Callahan

Vice President Dos National Sales, Raul Calvo

National Sales Manager, Josh Brooks

Vice President Sales, Kevin O'Malley

Vice President Of Sales, Melody Caldwell

Vice President And Director Of Sales, David Scott

Vice President Of Sales, Joel Kelly

Vice President Sales, Ray Tejeda

Vice President Sales Kfi Klac Keib Radio Los Angeles, Bill Denton

Vice President Finance, Steve Trubiano

Senior Vice President Corporate Finance, Chris Skillin

Executive Vice President Programming Operations, Jon Zellner

Vice President Network Sales, Kelly Gittleman

Vice President Talent Management, Joyce Keilen

Executive Vice President Sales Total Traffic And Weather Network, Gary Larkin

Vice President Marketing And Content, Andy Kelly

Senior Vice President Of Sales, Ann Postell

Senior Vice President Of Sales, Claudia Bays

Senior Vice President Sales, Sabrena Martin

National Sales Manager, Jeff Howard

Senior Vice President Of Sales, Vicki Ward

Vice President Sales, Darren McMillan

Vice President General Manager, Charles Cotton

Vice President Strategic Partnerships, Heather Baumli

Vice President Connections, Joe Shields

Vice President And Associate General Counsel, Christopher Cain

Vice President Connections, Victoria Pollard

Vice President Media Planning, Kevin Ryan

Senior Vice President Marketing Solutions, Amy Newman

Vice President Of Sales, Shari Gonzalez

Vice President West Coast Digital Sales, Melanie Gensler

Vice President Director Of Sales Connections, Erin Collier

Vice President Creative Services Group, Dave Savage

Vice President Of Real Estate, Cody Rutschman

Vice President Real Estate And Public Affairs, Stewart M Howe

Vice President Revenue Strategy And Analytics, James Liao

Executive Vice President And Gm, Brad Hardin

Executive Vice President Us Hispanic Strategy And Sales Iheartmedia, Liz Saracheck

Senior Vice President Of Sales, Judy Copier

Vice President Of Online Content And Design, Alexus Dominguez

Svp Product Innovation Iheartradio Networks, Steven Radley

Senior Vice President Accounting, Jason Dilger

Vice President Of Sales, Catherine Nye

Vice President, Stephanie Stein

Vice President Product Innovation, Leonard Cervantes

Vice President Connections, Kyle Blank

Vice President Of Sales Las Vegas West Division, Stacey Eisenberg

Senior Vice President I Programmatic, Ross Geier

Vice President Content Partnerships Entertainment Enterprises, Rachel Herskovitz

Vice President Client Solutions, Lisa Kruglov

National Account Manager, Michelle Brown

Vice President National Sales Premiere Networks, John Buckley

Senior Vice President Programming, Gator Harrison

National Sales Manager, Sharon Moses

Vice President Talent Management, Julio Manso

Executive Vice President Tech, Lasse Hamre

Vice President Finance, Marc Goldstein

Vice President Automotive Business Development And Partnerships, Julie Beaty

Vice President Connections East, Ethan Turner

Vice President Of Financial Planning And Analysis, Brennan Gerster

Vice President Connections, Michael Keohane

Regional Vice President Programming, Greg Swedberg

Vice President Landlease Div, Mary Groves

Senior Vice President Engineering, Michael Guidotti

Senior Vice President Programming, Eddie Rupp

Senior Vice President Programming, Mike Killabrew

Vice President Sales And Partnerships, David Saunders

National Account Manager, Joan Selfa

Senior Vice President Programming, Mark Murphy

Vice President, Mark Preble

Senior Vice President Programming, Tom Hanrahan

Vice President Artist Relations, Morris Marissa

Senior Vice President Live Entertainment And Events National Programming Group, Dennis Oheron

Vice President Digital Monetization, Jeff Silber

Vice President Npg Strategic Services Marketing, Marc Chase

Senior Vice President Sales San Francisco Region, Ed Diller

National Account Manager, David Rowley

Vice President Information Technology Clear Channel Outdoor Latin America, Ean Hernandez

Board Member, Gary Sullivan

Treasurer, Jerry Burnham

Auditors: Ernst & Young LLP

LOCATIONS

HQ: iHeartMedia Inc
  20880 Stone Oak Parkway, San Antonio, TX 78258
Phone: 210 822-2828
Web: www.iheartmedia.com

PRODUCTS/OPERATIONS

2016 Sales

	$ mil.	% of total
iHM	3,403	54
Americas Outdoor Advertising	1,278	20
Internationl Outdoor Advertising	1,423	23
Other	171	3
Eliminations	(3.4)	-
Total	**6,273**	**100**

Sales - 2016

Source of revenue		% of total
Billboards:		
Bulletins		59
Posters		10
Street furniture displays		7
Transit displays		16
Spectaculars/walls capes		4
Other		4
Total		**100**

COMPETITORS

CBS Corp	Live Nation
Cumulus Media	Entertainment
JCDecaux	Radio One Inc.
Lamar Advertising	

HISTORICAL FINANCIALS

Company Type: Public

Income Statement

	REVENUE ($ mil.)	NET INCOME ($ mil.)	NET PROFIT MARGIN	FYE: December 31 EMPLOYEES
12/17	6,170	(393)	—	17,900
12/16	6,273	(296)	—	18,700
12/15	6,241	(754)	—	18,700
12/14	6,318	(793)	—	19,200
12/13	6,243	(606)	—	20,800
Annual Growth	(0.3%)	—	—	(3.7%)

2017 Year-End Financials

Debt ratio: 168.42%
Return on equity: —
Cash ($ mil.): 267
Current ratio: 0.13
Long-term debt ($ mil.): 5,676

No. of shares (mil.): 91
Dividends
  Yield: —
  Payout: —
Market value ($ mil.): 46

	STOCK PRICE ($) FY Close	P/E High/Low		PER SHARE ($) Earnings	Dividends	Book Value
12/17	0.50	—	—	(4.64)	0.00	(124)
12/16	1.11	—	—	(3.50)	0.00	(121)
12/15	0.90	—	—	(8.95)	0.00	(120)
12/14	7.35	—	—	(9.46)	0.00	(111)
12/13	6.53	—	—	(7.31)	0.00	(102)
Annual Growth	(47.4%)			—	—	—

Illinois Tool Works, Inc.

Illinois Tool Works (ITW) hammers out more than just basic tools. With operations in about 55 countries ITW manufactures and services equipment for the automotive construction electronics food beverage power system decorative surfaces and medical components industries. The largest of its segments is Automotive OEM which provides metal and plastic fasteners components and chassis used in light vehicles automobiles and industrial applications. Other major segments include Food Equipment (cooking equipment such as ovens ranges and broilers) and Test & Measurement and Electronics (equipment and software for testing and measuring materials structures gases and fluids). Customers in the US supply about 45% of ITW's revenue.

Operations

ITW operates through seven segments each providing ample revenue. The segments are Test & Measurement and Electronics about 15% of revenue; Automotive OEM about 25% of revenue; Polymers & Fluids about 10% of revenue; Food Equipment 15% of revenue; Construction Products about 10%; Welding 10%; and Specialty Products close to 15%.

Subsidiaries include Instron Vulcan-Hart CFC International Quipp FB Johnston Graphics Miller Electric Manufacturing Hobart Corp. Wynn's Avery Weigh-Tronix RainX Vitronics Soltec and Zip Pack.

Innovation is a big selling point for ITW's products. The company holds about 11600 US and foreign patents as well as 6100 patents pending. R&D is executed cooperatively with customers seeking specific applications.

Geographic Reach

ITW operates more than 300 plants and offices in about 55 countries notably China France Germany and the UK. The US represents ITW's largest market generating 45% of net sales. Other major markets include EMEA about 30% of revenue and Asia/Pacific about 15% of revenue.

Sales and Marketing

ITW distributes its products directly to industrial manufacturers and through independent distributors. It serves customers in a range of industries including automotive manufacturers automotive aftermarket general industrial commercial food equipment and construction.

Financial Performance

ITW has posted two years of revenue gains after several years of uneven sales. Even with the gains the company has not returnd to its six-year sales high of about $14.8 billion in 2012.

In 2017 the Automotive OEM segment led the company to a 5% sales increase to $14.3 billion from $13.6 billion in 2016. The Automotive segment's sales rose 14% on organic growth in China and Europe and help from the EF&C acquisition made in 2016. The other segments reported higher sales ranging from less than 1% to about 5%. Overall organic growth was 3% in 2017.

Net income slipped to $1.7 billion in 2017 from $2 billion in 2016. ITW had an additional expense of about $658 million in 2017 from 2016 related to the US Tax Cuts and Jobs Act of 2017.

ITW's coffers held $3.1 billion in cash in 2017 compared to $2.47 billion in 2016. Operations generated cash totaling $2.4 billion in 2017 while investing and financing activities used $251 million and $1.6 billion respectively.

Strategy

ITW focuses on a five-year enterprise strategy with key initiatives that include portfolio management business structure simplification and strategic sourcing. This entails making internal investments that support organic growth to sustain its core businesses. The strategy is driven by the company's 80-20 rule that calls for focusing resources on the 80% of its biggest and most rewarding opportunities and reducing expenses for less profitable opportunities which comprise the other 20%.

ITW's portfolio management initiative includes divesting businesses that are no longer aligned with the company's long-term objectives. This strategy which reduced the company's global workforce from 59000 to 50000 over nine years which has cuts expenses and increased operating income despite slowly shrinking revenue totals.

As the US and China have engaged in trade disputes ITW maintains it has been largely unaffected with about 10%-15% of its cost inflation in 2018 was related to tariffs. The company makes most of its products in the markets in which they are used and it sources just 2% of it goods in China.

Mergers and Acquisitions

ITW has focused on organic growth and has been quiet on the acquisition side since it bought Engineered Fasteners and Components (EF&C) business from ZF TRW for approximately $450 million in 2016. EF&C is a global supplier of engineered fastening systems and interior technical components to the automotive OEM market operating about a dozen manufacturing facilities glob-ally. The deal bolstered the ITW's Automotive OEM segment.

Company Background

In the early years of the 20th century Byron Smith founder of Chicago's Northern Trust Company recognized that rapid industrialization was outgrowing the capacity of small shops to supply machine tools. Smith encouraged two of his four sons to launch Illinois Tool Works (ITW) in 1912. Harold C. Smith became president of ITW in 1915 and expanded its product line into automotive parts.

ITW developed the Shakeproof fastener the first twisted-tooth lock washer in 1923. When Harold C. died in 1936 his son Harold B. took up the torch and he decentralized the company and exhorted salesmen to learn customers' businesses so they could develop products before customers recognized they needed them. Smith plowed profits back into research as WWII spurred demand.

EXECUTIVES

Evp Test And Measurement And Electronics, Steven L. (Steve) Martindale, age 61

Chairman And Ceo, E. Scott Santi, age 56, $1,205,313 total compensation

Evp Specialty Products, Roland M. Martel, age 64, $534,434 total compensation

Evp Polymers And Fluids, Juan Valls, age 57

Svp And Cfo, Michael M. Larsen, age 49, $702,152 total compensation

Evp Automotive Oem, Sundaram (Naga) Nagarajan, age 55, $520,456 total compensation

Evp Welding, John R. Hartnett, age 58

Vp And Cio, Mike Parisi

Evp Construction Products, Michael R. Zimmerman, age 57

Evp Food Equipment, Lei Zhang Schlitz, age 51

Executive Vice President, Jane Warner

Executive Vice President, Mike Zimmerman

Vice President Of Marketing, Lee Burtelson

Vice Chairman, Christopher (Chris) O'Herlihy, age 54

Auditors: DELOITTE & TOUCHE LLP

LOCATIONS

HQ: Illinois Tool Works, Inc.
155 Harlem Avenue, Glenview, IL 60025
Phone: 847 724-7500
Web: www.itw.com

2017 Sales

	$ mil.	% of total
North America		
United States	6,243	43
Canada/Mexico	996	7
Europe Middle East and Africa	4,102	29
Asia Pacific	2,577	18
South America	396	3
Total	**14,314**	**100**

PRODUCTS/OPERATIONS

2017 Sales

	$ mil.	% of total
Automotive OEM	3,271	23
Food Equipment	2,123	15
Test & Measurement and Electronics	2,069	14
Specialty Products	1,938	14
Polymers & Fluids	1,724	12
Construction Products	1,672	12
Welding	1,538	10
Intersegment revenue	(21)	-
Total	**14,314**	**100**

Selected Products

Construction products
  Anchors for concrete applications
  Anchors for retail
  Fasteners concrete applications
  Fasteners for retail
  Fasteners for wood and metal applications
  Metal plate truss components
  Packaged hardware for retail
Decorative surfaces
  Decorative high-pressure laminate for furniture office and retail space and countertops
  High-pressure laminate worktops
Food equipment
  Cooking equipment
  Ovens
  Ranges
  Broilers
  Food processing equipment
  Slicers
  Mixers
  Scales
  Kitchen exhaust systems
  Pollution-control systems
  Refrigeration equipment
  Refrigerators
  Freezers
  Prep tables
  Ventilation Systems
  Warewashing equipment
Industrial packaging
  Metal jacketing
  Paper products that protect goods in transit
  Plastic products that protect goods in transit
  Plastic strapping
  Plastic stretch film
  Steel strapping
Polymers and fluids
  Adhesives
  Industrial
  Construction
  Consumer
  Chemical fluids that clean or add lubrication to machines
  Epoxy and resin-based coating products for industrial applications
  Hand wipes and cleaners for industrial applications
  Pressure-sensitive adhesives and components
  Telecommunications
  Electronics
  Medical
  Transportation
  Resin-based coating products for industrial applications
Power systems and electronics
  Airport ground support equipment
  Arc welding equipment
  Component packaging
  Electronic components
  Equipment for microelectronics assembly
  Metal arc welding consumables
  Metal solder materials for PC board fabrication
Transportation
  Fillers for auto body repair
  Fluids for auto aftermarket maintenance and appearance
  Metal components for automobiles and light trucks
  Patch products for the marine industry
  Plastic components for automobiles and light trucks
  Polyester coatings for the marine industry
  Polymers for auto aftermarket maintenance and appearance
  Putties for auto body repair
Other
  Equipment and related software for testing and measuring of materials and structures
  Film used to decorate consumer products
  Foil used to decorate consumer products
  Plastic reclosable packaging for consumer food storage
  Plastic consumables that multi-pack cans and bottles and related equipment
  Plastic for appliances and industrial applications
  Metal fasteners for appliances and industrial applications

COMPETITORS

3M	Marmon Group
BASF SE	NCH
Cummins	Nordson
DuPont	Park-Ohio Holdings
ESAB	PennEngineering
Emerson Electric	Snap-on
Federal Screw Works	Stanley Black and
GE	Decker
Graco	Textron

IBIDEN
Koch Enterprises
Lincoln Electric
Manitowoc

TriMas
Victor Technologies
W. R. Grace

HISTORICAL FINANCIALS
Company Type: Public

Income Statement   FYE: December 31

	REVENUE ($ mil.)	NET INCOME ($ mil.)	NET PROFIT MARGIN	EMPLOYEES
12/17	14,314	1,687	11.8%	50,000
12/16	13,599	2,035	15.0%	50,000
12/15	13,405	1,899	14.2%	48,000
12/14	14,484	2,946	20.3%	49,000
12/13	14,135	1,679	11.9%	51,000
Annual Growth	0.3%	0.1%	—	(0.5%)

2017 Year-End Financials

Debt ratio: 49.63%
Return on equity: 38.17%
Cash ($ mil.): 3,094
Current ratio: 2.38
Long-term debt ($ mil.): 7,478

No. of shares (mil.): 341
Dividends
  Yield: 0.0%
  Payout: 58.8%
Market value ($ mil.): 56,979

	STOCK PRICE ($) FY Close	P/E High/Low	PER SHARE ($) Earnings	Dividends	Book Value
12/17	166.85	35 25	4.86	2.86	13.43
12/16	122.46	22 14	5.70	2.40	12.26
12/15	92.68	19 16	5.13	2.07	14.36
12/14	94.70	13 10	7.28	1.81	17.81
12/13	84.08	22 16	3.74	1.60	22.55
Annual Growth	18.7%	— —	6.8%	15.6%	(12.2%)

Independent Bank Corp (MA)

Independent Bank wants to rock the northeast. Its banking subsidiary Rockland Trust operates almost 75 retail branches as well as investment and lending offices in Eastern Massachusetts and Rhode Island. Serving area individuals and small to midsized businesses the bank offers standard services such as checking and savings accounts CDs and credit cards in addition to insurance products financial planning trust services. Commercial loans including industrial construction and small business loans make up more than 70% of Rockland Trust's loan portfolio. Incorporated in 1985 the bank boasts total assets of some $7.5 billion.

Operations

About 28% of Independent Bank's loan portfolio is made up of consumer real estate loans which include residential mortgages and home equity loans and lines; while personal loans and auto loans make up around 1% of the portfolio. Through an agreement with LPL Investment Holdings Rockland Trust offers investment products such as securities and insurance.

Independent Bank generated 70% of its total revenue from interest and fee income on loans in 2014 and another 6% from interest and dividends on investment securities. Investment management fees made up 6% of total revenue for the year while deposit account fees and interchange and ATM fees combined made up 11%.

Geographic Reach

Rockland Trust boasts nearly 75 retail branches and three limited-services branches located in Eastern Massachusetts in the counties of Barnstable Bristol Middlesex Norfolk Plymouth and Worcester.

Sales and Marketing

The company's borrowers include consumers and small-to-medium sized businesses with credit needs up to $250000 and revenues of less than $2.5 million. Independent Bank spent $3.86 million on advertising in 2014 compared to $4.28 million and $3.95 million in 2013 and 2012 respectively.

Financial Performance

Independent Bank Corp's revenues and profits have trended higher in recent years thanks to continued loan business growth from both acquisitions and through organic expansion higher deposit account and ATM fee income from customer base growth and thanks to a decline in loan loss provisions as the credit quality of its loan portfolio has improved with the strengthened economy.

The bank's revenue rose by 5% to $286.40 million in 2014 mostly thanks to higher interest income as its loan business growth continued to outpace the margin-eating impacts of low interest rates. Independent's non-interest income also rose by 3% thanks to a combination of higher interchange and ATM fees and investment management fees.

Higher revenue and lower interest expenses on deposits in 2014 drove Independent Bank Corp's net income up by 19% to $59.85 million. Despite higher earnings the company's operating cash dove sharply primarily because of working capital changes related to its loans held for sale and changes in other assets.

Strategy

Independent Bank planned in 2015 to grow its loans organically between 4-6% for the year while growing its deposits between 3% and 4%. The company has also been expanding its fee-based revenue business especially in its investment management segment with expectations of growing the business by another 3% to 4% in 2015.

In addition to organic growth in other financial services areas Independent Bank has expanded via acquisitions.

Mergers and Acquisitions

In October 2016 the company agreed to buy Island Bancorp and its Edgartown National Bank subsidiary which operates four branches on Massachusetts' Martha's Vineyard island. The transaction is valued at some $24.5 million.

In 2015 in expanding its Eastern Massachusetts presence and strengthening its position in the greater Boston market Independent Bank Corp purchased Peoples Federal Bancshares along with its flagship subsidiary Peoples Federal Savings Bank for $130.6 million. The deal added $606 million in total assets $435 million in deposits and $497 million in new loan business.

In November 2013 Independent Bank acquired Mayflower Bancorp along with Mayflower Co-operative Bank for a total of $40.3 million adding deposits and loan assets and expanding its product and service offerings.

In 2012 the company agreed to buy Central Bancorp parent of Central Bank. That deal added nine branches in Maryland's Middlesex County.

Company Background

In past years Independent Bank launched institutional asset managers Bright Rock Capital Management (2010) and Compass Exchange Advisors (2006) and formed a handful of mutual funds.

EXECUTIVES

Executive Vice President Director Of Retail Delivery Business Banking & Home Equity Lending, Jane L. Lundquist, age 61, $262,981 total compensation
President Ceo And Director Independent Bank Corp. And Rockland Trust, Christopher (Chris) Oddleifson, age 59, $589,616 total compensation
Cfo, Robert D. Cozzone
Executive Vice President Commercial Banking, Gerard F. Nadeau, age 60, $322,308 total compensation
Chief Information Officer, Barry Jensen
Chairman, Donna L. Abelli
Auditors: Ernst & Young LLP

LOCATIONS

HQ: Independent Bank Corp (MA)
  2036 Washington Street, Hanover, MA 02339
Phone: 781 878-6100
Web: www.RocklandTrust.com

PRODUCTS/OPERATIONS

2012 Sales

	$ mil.	% of total
Interest		
Loans	178	69
Taxable securities including dividends	16	6
Other	1	-
Noninterest		
Service charges on deposit accounts	16	6
Wealth management	14	6
Interchange & ATM fees	9	4
Other	21	9
Adjustments	(0.1)	-
Total	258	100

COMPETITORS

Bank of America
Citizens Financial
  Group
Eastern Bank

Hingham Institution
  for Savings
Sovereign Bank
TD Bank USA

HISTORICAL FINANCIALS
Company Type: Public

Income Statement   FYE: December 31

	ASSETS ($ mil.)	NET INCOME ($ mil.)	INCOME AS % OF ASSETS	EMPLOYEES
12/17	8,082	87	1.1%	1,108
12/16	7,709	76	1.0%	1,103
12/15	7,210	64	0.9%	1,051
12/14	6,364	59	0.9%	980
12/13	6,099	50	0.8%	984
Annual Growth	7.3%	14.8%	—	3.0%

2017 Year-End Financials

Debt ratio: 1.33%
Return on equity: 9.64%
Cash ($ mil.): 213
Current ratio: —
Long-term debt ($ mil.): —

No. of shares (mil.): 27
Dividends
  Yield: 0.0%
  Payout: 40.1%
Market value ($ mil.): 1,917

	STOCK PRICE ($) FY Close	P/E High/Low	PER SHARE ($) Earnings	Dividends	Book Value
12/17	69.85	24 19	3.19	1.28	34.38
12/16	70.45	24 14	2.90	1.16	32.02
12/15	46.52	21 15	2.50	1.04	29.40
12/14	42.81	17 14	2.49	0.96	26.69
12/13	39.12	18 13	2.18	0.88	24.85
Annual Growth	15.6%	— —	10.0%	9.8%	8.5%

Independent Bank Corporation (Ionia, MI)

Independent Bank Corporation is the holding company for Independent Bank which serves rural and suburban communities of Michigan's Lower Peninsula from more than 100 branches. The bank offers traditional deposit products including checking and savings accounts and CDs. Loans to businesses account for about 40% of the bank's portfolio; real estate mortgages are more than a third. Independent Bank also offers additional products and services like title insurance through subsidiary Independent Title Services and investments through agreement with third-party provider PrimeVest.

Operations

The company also owns Mepco Finance which acquires and services payment plans for extended automobile warranties.

Financial Performance

The company's revenue has been trending down year-over-year. However its net income and cash on hand have both been spiking up across recent fiscal years.

Strategy

As Michigan's economy has exhibited signs of stabilizing and the company's results have relatively improved as well. Independent Bank has reduced its number of high-risk loans non-performing loans and delinquency rates.

EXECUTIVES

Assistant Vice President Senior Business Analyst, Phil Hamlin
Vice President Commercial Lending, Angela Sanborn
Vice President Commercial Lending, Phil Clacko
Vice President Sales Manager, Sue Fulk
Assistant Vice President Loan Servicing Risk Managa, Gayle Brooke
Assistant Vice President, Denise Geers
Senior Vice President, Hank B Risley
Auditors: Crowe Horwath LLP

LOCATIONS

HQ: Independent Bank Corporation (Ionia, MI)
4200 East Beltline, Grand Rapids, MI 49525
Phone: 616 527-5820
Web: www.independentbank.com

COMPETITORS

Bank of America	Flagstar Bancorp
Chemical Financial	Huntington Bancshares
Fifth Third	JPMorgan Chase
Firstbank	Mercantile Bank

HISTORICAL FINANCIALS

Company Type: Public

Income Statement — FYE: December 31

	ASSETS ($ mil.)	NET INCOME ($ mil.)	INCOME AS % OF ASSETS	EMPLOYEES
12/17	2,789	20	0.7%	911
12/16	2,548	22	0.9%	885
12/15	2,409	20	0.8%	831
12/14	2,248	18	0.8%	876
12/13	2,209	77	3.5%	896
Annual Growth	6.0%	(28.3%)	—	0.4%

2017 Year-End Financials

Debt ratio: 1.28%	No. of shares (mil.): 21
Return on equity: 7.97%	Dividends
Cash ($ mil.): 57	Yield: 0.0%
Current ratio: —	Payout: 44.2%
Long-term debt ($ mil.): —	Market value ($ mil.): 477

	STOCK PRICE ($) FY Close	P/E High/Low	Earnings	Dividends	Book Value
12/17	22.35	24 20	0.95	0.42	12.42
12/16	21.70	21 13	1.05	0.34	11.71
12/15	15.23	18 14	0.86	0.26	11.28
12/14	13.05	18 15	0.77	0.18	10.91
12/13	12.00	2 1	3.55	0.00	10.15
Annual Growth	16.8%	—	(28.1%)	—	5.2%

Independent Bank Group Inc.

It makes sense that a company that calls itself Independent Bank Group (IBG) would do business in a state that was once its own country. The bank holding company does business through subsidiary Independent Bank which operates about 40 banking offices and 70 branches in North and Central Texas Houston and Colorado. The banks offer standard personal and business accounts and services including some focused on small business owners. IBG has total assets of nearly $8.9 billion and loans of about $6.4 billion. The company traces its roots back 100 years but took its current shape in 2002.

Operations

In addition to its banking activities Independent Bank Group (IBG)also owns IBG Adriatica a mixed use development in the Dallas-Fort Worth area. The company does not intend to move into real estate but purchased the development where one of its branches is located to help maintain business in the area. It had also made commercial loans to several tenants of the development and saw the purchase as a way to protect its investments rather than have the entire property go into foreclosure.

Financial Performance

Independent Bank Group has shown increasing net income for several years and in fiscal 2016 grew revenue a further 20% to $210.0 million. Net income has likewise been consistently growing reaching $53.5 million up 39%. Cash from operations increased 85% to $80.3 million.

Strategy

Independent Bank Group's strategy is all about growth. It seeks organic growth in loans and deposits in existing locations by developing customer relationships while maintaining the quality of its loan portfolio. It also makes acquisitions: since 2010 it has made nine acquisitions most recently of Carlile Bancshares and its subsidiary Northstar Bank and Grand Bank in Dallas.

Mergers and Acquisitions

Independent Bank Group acquired Carlile Bancshares and its subsidiary Northstar Bank for around $434 million in 2017.

EXECUTIVES

Chairman President And Ceo, David R. Brooks, age 60, $650,000 total compensation
Evp And Coo, James C. (Jim) White, age 53
Vice Chairman And Chief Lending Officer And President Independent Bank Central Texas, Brian E. Hobart, age 53, $350,000 total compensation
Executive Vice President And Chief Financial Officer, Michelle S. Hickox, age 51, $265,000 total compensation
Evp And Secretary And Evp And Senior Operations Officer Independent Bank, Jan C. Webb, age 60
Vice President Commercial Banking, Ethan Everett
Vice President Market Manager, Tisha Reyes
Senior Vice President, Kaitlin Mahard
Senior Vice President Director Of Financial Reporting, Leslie Beseda
Assistant Vice President, Scott Daniels
Senior Vice President, Jenny Steelman
Vice President Commercial Lending, Ozzie Martinez
Avp Area Banking Manager, Marcey Bench
Svp Director Hr, Lisa Murray
Svp Hr Director Texas, Pam Murray
Executive Vice President, Duane Reaves
Senior Vice President, Julie Crump
Vice Chairman And Chief Risk Officer, Daniel W. Brooks, age 58
Auditors: RSM US LLP

LOCATIONS

HQ: Independent Bank Group Inc.
1600 Redbud Boulevard, Suite 400, McKinney, TX 75069-3257
Phone: 972 562-9004
Web: www.ibtx.com

PRODUCTS/OPERATIONS

2012 Loan Portfolio

	% of total
Real estate	
Commercial	47
Residential	23
Construction land & land development	7
Single-family interim construction	5
Commercial	12
Agricultural	3
Consumer	3
Total	**100**

Selected Acquisition

Town Center Bank (2010 North Texas)
Farmersville Bancshares Inc. (2010 North Texas)
I Bank Holding Company Inc. (2012 Austin/Central Texas)
The Community Group Inc. (2012 Dallas/North Texas)

COMPETITORS

BBVA Compass Bancshares	HSBC International Bancshares
Bank of America	
Broadway Bancshares	JPMorgan Chase
Capital One	Lone Star Bank
Citigroup	PlainsCapital
Comerica	Prosperity Bancshares
Cullen/Frost Bankers	Texas Capital Bancshares
Extraco	
First Financial Bankshares	Wells Fargo Woodforest Financial

HISTORICAL FINANCIALS

Company Type: Public

Income Statement — FYE: December 31

	ASSETS ($ mil.)	NET INCOME ($ mil.)	INCOME AS % OF ASSETS	EMPLOYEES
12/17	8,684	76	0.9%	924
12/16	5,852	53	0.9%	577
12/15	5,055	38	0.8%	587
12/14	4,132	28	0.7%	511
12/13	2,163	19	0.9%	340
Annual Growth	41.5%	40.2%	—	28.4%

2017 Year-End Financials

Debt ratio: 1.89%
Return on equity: 7.62%
Cash ($ mil.): 431
Current ratio: —
Long-term debt ($ mil.): —

No. of shares (mil.): 28
Dividends
  Yield: 0.0%
  Payout: 13.4%
Market value ($ mil.): 1,910

	STOCK PRICE ($) FY Close	P/E High/Low	PER SHARE ($) Earnings	Dividends	Book Value
12/17	67.60	24 18	2.97	0.40	47.28
12/16	62.40	22 0	2.00	0.34	05.63
12/15	32.00	21 13	2.21	0.32	34.09
12/14	39.06	33 21	1.85	0.24	31.75
12/13	49.66	28 16	1.77	0.12	18.96
Annual Growth	8.0%	— —	13.8%	35.1%	25.7%

Ingredion Inc

Sweet sodas and diet desserts alike get their taste and feel from Ingredion's ingredients. The company makes food ingredients and industrial products from corn and other starch-based raw materials. It serve customers in some 60 markets including food brewing and paper companies. Ingredion's largest product line is starches used in food for stabilization feel and texture and in paper packaging and other materials for quality strength and a host of other attributes. Its other product lines include sweeteners (high-fructose corn syrup dextrose) specialty ingredients (products focused on health affordability and sustainability) and co-products (refined corn oil corn gluten feed and meal). Ingredion operates worldwide but generates most of its sales in North America.

Operations

Cornstarch and other starch products account for about 45% of Ingredion's revenue and are used in processed foods as well as in paper and packaging adhesives textiles pharmaceuticals make-up and other products.

Sweeteners used in a wide range of foods — from condiments to candy — generate another 40% of sales with specialty ingredients designed to capitalize on consumer trends bringing in about a quarter.

The company's smallest product segment co-products includes refined corn oil sold to a variety of food producers and corn gluten feed and meal used for pet food. It accounts for about 15% of revenue.

Geographic Reach

Well-covered geographically Ingredion serves customers in more than 100 countries worldwide. North America is its largest market accounting for some 60% of sales. South America represents about 20% of sales followed by the Asia Pacific and EMEA (Europe Middle East and Africa) regions which each contribute about 10%.

Ingredion has some 45 manufacturing plants in about a dozen countries (the US is home to about a third of them).

Sales and Marketing

Ingredion exploits the versatility of corn in supplying a customers across some 60 industries. Food is the company's largest industry segment generating more than 50% of revenue; however the beverage animal nutrition paper and brewing industries each contribute about 10%.

Ingredion sells its products through its own sales force directly to manufacturers and distributors.

Financial Performance

Although Ingredion's revenue stabilized slightly in 2016 and net income rose more substantially the company has seen a general decline in both measures since 2012. Revenue has fallen nearly $1 billion in the past four years.

The company reported revenue of $5.7 billion in 2016 up 1% on improved performance in North America where price increases and a more favorable product mix offset a slight decline in volume. Reduced cost of sales because of the effects of currency translation and lower restructuring/impairment charges allowed Ingredion to post net income of $485 million up 20% from the from $402 million reported in 2015.

Cash provided by operations also rose in 2016 increasing 12% to $771 million primarily as a result of the company's improved net income.

Strategy

Ingredion's "Strategic Blueprint" for growth is built around six areas: market relevance innovation broadening ingredient portfolio continuous improvement sustainability and geographic diversity.

Three of those areas — market relevance innovation and broadening portfolio — are focused on the company's desire to adapt to changing consumer tastes and capitalize on trends such as simplicity health convenience and affordability. To that end Ingredion employs some 350 scientists in more than two dozen Ingredion Idea Labs across the globe and spends about $40 million on research and development.

In 2016 the company expanded its portfolio of gums and resins. It also partnered with Alliance Grain Traders to market pulse flours and plant protein ingredients and became a global distributor of stevia sweetener SweeGen.

Through acquisitions investments and product launches Ingredion also bolstered its global presence. It acquired businesses in China and Thailand in 2017 and 2016 launched a new sweetener (SWEETIS) across the Asia-Pacific region and invested some $300 million in plant improvements worldwide.

Mergers and Acquisitions

Ingredion bought the rice starch and flour business of Thailand's Sun Flour Industries in 2017 which boosts the company's specialty ingredients segment.

In late 2016 it paid nearly $400 million for Maryland-based TIC Gums which provides gums and resins to improve the texture of foods and beverages. The deal expands Ingredion's customer base and again adds to its specialty ingredients segment. Also that year the company acquired state-owned Shandong Huanong Specialty Corn Development Co. in China's Shandong Province to increase its manufacturing capacity in the country.

Ingredion in March 2015 acquired Iowa-based Penford Corp. a maker of carbohydrate-based specialty starches used by the paper packaging and food industries. The deal was valued at around $330 million and extended Ingredion's core offerings and geographical footprint; Penford has offices and plants in Colorado Idaho Iowa Pennsylvania South Carolina Washington and Wisconsin.

EXECUTIVES

Svp And Chief Innovation Officer, Anthony P. (Tony) Delio, age 62
Evp Global Specialties; President North America And Emea, James P. Zallie, age 56, $600,000 total compensation
Svp Operating Excellence Sustainability Information Technology And Chief Supply Chain Officer, Robert J. (Bob) Stefansic, age 56
Svp And President Asia/pacific And Emea, Jorgen Kokke, age 49, $403,340 total compensation
Evp And Cfo, James D. (Jim) Gray, age 51

Vp And Corporate Treasurer, Kevin Wilson
Vp Business Development South America, Jose Bertoli
Vice President Marketing Us And Canada, Jim Low
Vice President Manufacturing Na, Mark Madsen
Vice President Applications Research And Technical Services, Ron Deis
National Accounts Manager, James Gilbert
Vice President Investor Relations And Corporate Communications, Heather Kos
Vice President Compensation Benefits And Hris, Robert Simitz
Vice President And Managing Director Canada, Rob Kee
Chairman, Ilene S. Gordon, age 64
Auditors: KPMG LLP

LOCATIONS

HQ: Ingredion Inc
  5 Westbrook Corporate Center, Westchester, IL 60154
Phone: 708 551-2600   **Fax:** 708 551-2700
Web: www.ingredion.com

2016 Sales

	$ mil.	% of total
North America	3,447	60
South America	1,010	18
Asia Pacific	709	12
EMEA	538	10
Total	**5,704**	**100**

PRODUCTS/OPERATIONS

2016 Sales

	% of total
Starch products	46
Sweetener products	37
Co-products & others	17
Total	**100**

Selected Products

Sweetener products
  Dextrose
  Glucose corn syrups
  High fructose corn syrup
  High maltose corn syrup
  Maltodextrins
  Polyols
Starch products
  Corn starch (consumer and industrial)
  Specialty Starches
Co-products and others
  Corn gluten feed
  Corn gluten meal
  Refined corn oil
Specialty Ingredients
  Delivery systems
  Green Solutions
  Nutrition
  Sweetness
  Texture
  Wholesome

COMPETITORS

ACH Food Companies	Malt Products
ADM	Corporation
Ajinomoto	Merisant
Cargill	NutraSweet
Cumberland Packing	PureCircle
DSM	Roquette Fr ¨res
Global Bio-chem	Sweet Green Fields
Grain Processing	S dzucker
Corporation	Tate & Lyle
Imperial Sugar	Ingredients

HISTORICAL FINANCIALS

Company Type: Public

Income Statement

FYE: December 31

	REVENUE ($ mil.)	NET INCOME ($ mil.)	NET PROFIT MARGIN	EMPLOYEES
12/17	5,832	519	8.9%	11,000
12/16	5,704	485	8.5%	11,000
12/15	5,621	402	7.2%	11,000
12/14	5,668	355	6.3%	11,400
12/13	6,328	396	6.3%	11,300
Annual Growth	(2.0%)	7.0%	—	(0.7%)

2017 Year-End Financials

Debt ratio: 30.66%
Return on equity: 19.02%
Cash ($ mil.): 595
Current ratio: 2.52
Long-term debt ($ mil.): 1,744

No. of shares (mil.): 72
Dividends
Yield: 0.0%
Payout: 31.1%
Market value ($ mil.): 10,065

	STOCK PRICE ($) FY Close	P/E High/Low	PER SHARE ($) Earnings	Dividends	Book Value
12/17	139.80	20 16	7.06	2.20	40.16
12/16	124.96	21 13	6.55	1.90	35.42
12/15	95.84	18 14	5.51	1.74	29.94
12/14	84.84	18 12	4.74	1.68	30.52
12/13	68.46	14 12	5.05	1.56	32.35
Annual Growth	19.5%	— —	8.7%	9.0%	5.6%

Insight Enterprises Inc.

With Insight Enterprises around the end of a customer's technology woes could be in sight. The company distributes computer hardware and software and provides IT services for businesses schools and government agencies and departments. Insight offers thousands of products from major manufacturers (including Hewlett-Packard IBM and Cisco) and provides networking and communications services through subsidiaries Insight Networking in the US and UK-based MINX. The company uses direct telesales field sales agents and an e-commerce site to reach its clients in North America and about 200 other countries across Europe the Middle East Africa and the Asia-Pacific region.

Operations

In North America and Western Europe Insight sells hardware software and services. In the rest of the world it sells just software and related services.

Hardware accounts for more than half of the company's revenue and software 40%. Services revenue accounts for the remainder.

Insight purchases products and software from over 5100 partners. These include Cisco HP Lenovo Dell EMC NetApp Apple and IBM. More than 65% were from manufacturers and software publishers; the remainder was bought through distributors.

Geographic Reach

Insight rings up more than 70% of its sales in the US and Canada. The EMEA region (Europe the Middle East and Africa contributes almost 25% of which the UK brings in 10%. The Asia-Pacific (APAC) region accounts for the rest. The company has locations in the US Canada and the UK.

Sales and Marketing

Microsoft accounts for over 25% of Insight's revenue; HP 10%; and Cisco 10%.

Its five biggest manufacturers/publishers combined (including Lenovo and Dell) account for 60% of total sales.

Financial Performance

Insight has struggled to add pep to its top line in recent years. In fiscal 2016 revenue grew 2% to $5.5 billion. The only region to record growth was North America which grew 4% due to the BlueMetal acquisition and high demand for client devices servers and storage products. The EMEA and APAC regions both recorded 2% falls. Currency movements played a role: adjusting for FX fluctuations EMEA grew 4% and APAC was flat.

Net income increased 12% to $84.7 million due to higher revenue and better margins. Cash from operating activities fell 47% to $95.8 million due to a large ($160 million) receivable collected by a client in Q4 2016 offset by higher sales.

Strategy

Insight is growing at home and abroad by upgrading its technology expanding its product line entering new markets and making acquisitions.

To maintain a local market presence in select cities the company has invested in sales technical and service delivery resources (particularly in the large account client space).

The company is also focusing on growing its business with mid-sized and large clients in select vertical markets (including Federal government state and local K-12 education healthcare and service providers).

In EMEA and APAC the company is looking to increase its share in the mid-market and public sector including leveraging strategic relationships with partners and service delivery vendors to bring additional software Cloud and collaboration solutions to clients.

In APAC the company is growing its sales in the mid-market and enterprise space and on the developing specialized software services particularly in the areas of software license optimization and the Cloud.

Insight is putting more energy (and money) into its services offerings as hardware sales naturally ease amid market maturity. The company is advancing its Cloud-based solutions to help with the assessment migration integration of Cloud uptake.

Mergers and Acquisitions

In 2017 Insight acquired Datalink a Minnesota-based IT service and enterprise data center solutions provider for $257.5 million. The acquisition addresses market opportunities in hybrid cloud and other data center categories.

In 2016 it acquired Ignia an Australian digital mobile and cloud company with a foot in application design digital solutions cloud mobility and business analytics. The acquisition will also further Insight's reach into the APAC market.

In 2015 Insight acquired Boston-based BlueMetal (an interactive design and technology architecture firm with offices in Chicago and New York) for $44 million. This acquisition helped the company to expand its service capabilities in the area of application design mobility and big data.

HISTORY

Eric Crown worked for a small computer retail chain in the mid-1980s before leaving to market PCs. In 1986 he and his brother Tim pooled $2000 from credit cards and $1300 in savings and anticipating a drop in hard drive prices placed an ad for low-cost hard drives in a computer magazine. The ad pulled in $20000 worth of sales and since costs did indeed drop the profit was enough to start a new company Hard Drives International. In 1988 they changed the name to Insight Enterprises; by 1991 the Crowns also sold Insight-branded PCs software and peripherals (discontinued in 1995). The company passed the $100 million revenue mark in 1992.

Insight shifted its marketing focus to catalogs in 1993 and had a circulation of more than 7 mil-

lion by 1995. The company went public that year and entered an alliance with Computer City (acquired by CompUSA in 1998) to handle its mail-order fulfillment. It also launched its website. The next year subsidiary Insight Direct began to offer on-site service warranties and in 1997 retailing subsidiary Direct Alliance was chosen to provide product fulfillment for Internet software firm Geo Publishing. That year the company began sponsoring the Copper Bowl a college football game played in Arizona which was renamed the Insight.com Bowl (and later the Insight Bowl).

Looking beyond the US in 1998 Insight established operations in Canada and acquired direct marketers Choice Peripherals (UK) and Computerprofis Computersysteme (Germany). At home it added direct marketer Treasure Chest Computers. Sales passed the billion-dollar mark that year.

The company formed an alliance with Daisytek International in 1999 that expanded its product line by more than 10000. Soon thereafter Insight walked away from a merger with UK-based computer wholesaler Action Computer Supplies when Action's profits slumped.

Insight withdrew its planned IPO and spinoff of Direct Alliance in 2001 due to poor market conditions. Also that month Eric became chairman and Tim became CEO (they had previously shared the title of co-CEO). Insight ended up buying Action Computer Supplies in 2001. It also shut down its German operations and acquired computer direct marketers in both the UK and Canada in late 2001.

In April 2002 Insight acquired Comark a leading private reseller of computers peripherals and computer supplies in the US and began integrating its operations into Insight North America's existing operational structure.

Tim stepped down as president and CEO and became chairman in late 2004 while Eric assumed the title of chairman emeritus. The company appointed IBM veteran Richard Fennessy to the position of president and CEO. That year Insight spun off its UK-based Internet service provider PlusNet.

In 2006 Insight Enterprises bought software and mobile solutions firm Software Spectrum.

EXECUTIVES

President And Ceo, Kenneth T. (Ken) Lamneck, age 63, $800,000 total compensation

Cio, Michael Guggemos, age 53, $398,989 total compensation

Cfo, Glynis A. Bryan, age 59, $466,140 total compensation

President Insight Us, Steven W. Dodenhoff, age 55, $488,625 total compensation

President Insight Emea, Wolfgang Ebermann, age 53, $578,726 total compensation

Vice President Sales, Rob McConnell

Vice President Sales, Luke Purdon

Vice President Sales, Collin Ryan

Vice President Marketing, Bill Daly

Vice President Sales, Christy Arnold

Vp And Gm Digital Innovation, Stan Lequin

Vice President Sales, Jason Sullivan

Assistant Vice President Marketing Div, Karla Herder

Senior Vice President Na And Apac Software, Andrea Mattea

Svp Product Management, Bob Kane

Vice President Infrastructure And Security, Curt Cornum

Vp Sales And Marketing Emea, Alexander Kaatz

Vp Services Emea, Rolf Adam

Vp Hr, Jennifer Fernandez-vasin

President Ceo And Director, Timothy A. (Tim) Crown, age 54

Auditors: KPMG LLP

LOCATIONS

HQ: Insight Enterprises Inc.
6820 South Harl Avenue, Tempe, AZ 85283
Phone: 480 333-3000
Web: www.insight.com

2016 Sales

	$ mil.	% of total
North America	3,971	73
Europe Middle East & Africa	1,338	24
Asia/Pacific	175	3
Total	**5,485**	**100**

2016 Sales

	$ mil.	% of total
United States	3,776	69
United Kingdom	672	12
Others Foreign	1,037	19
Total	**5,485**	**100**

PRODUCTS/OPERATIONS

2016 Sales

	$ mil.	% of total
Hardware	2,955	54
Software	2,189	40
Services	340	6
Total	**5,485**	**100**

Selected Products

Computer memory and processors
Desktop computers
Monitors
Networking equipment
Notebook computers
Printers and printing consumables
Servers
Software
Storage devices
Tablet computers

Selected Services

Business optimization software
  Business productivity
  Core infrastructure
  Software asset management
Collaboration
  Call/contact center
  Unified communications/messaging
  Video collaboration/conferencing
Cloud services
  Collaboration
  Infrastructure
  Messaging
  Security
Data center
  Infrastructure solutions
  Server solutions
  Storage solutions
Infrastructure and security
  Network infrastructure
  Security infrastructure
Managed services
  Business process outsourcing
  Connected real estate and sports
  Financing and leasing
  IT asset disposal
  Maintenance
  Product provisioning
  Remote network operations
  Telecom expense management
  Warehouse/integration
  Mobility
  Big Data
  Creativity
  Data protection

COMPETITORS

Amazon.com	Microsoft
Best Buy	Newegg
Buy.com	Office Depot
CDW	OfficeMax
CompuCom	PC Connection
Convergys	PC Mall
Dell	PFSweb
Digital River	RadioShack

Fry's Electronics
Gateway Inc.
HP
HP Enterprise Services
IBM
Lenovo
Micro Electronics

SHI International
Softchoice
Staples
Symantec
Systemax
Zones

HISTORICAL FINANCIALS

Company Type: Public

Income Statement

FYE: December 31

	REVENUE ($ mil.)	NET INCOME ($ mil.)	NET PROFIT MARGIN	EMPLOYEES
12/17	6,703	90	1.4%	6,697
12/16	5,485	84	1.5%	5,930
12/15	5,373	75	1.4%	5,761
12/14	5,316	75	1.4%	5,406
12/13	5,144	71	1.4%	5,202
Annual Growth	**6.8%**	**6.3%**	—	**6.5%**

2017 Year-End Financials

Debt ratio: 11.66%
Return on equity: 11.65%
Cash ($ mil.): 105
Current ratio: 1.54
Long-term debt ($ mil.): 296

No. of shares (mil.): 35
Dividends
  Yield: —
  Payout: —
Market value ($ mil.): 1,372

	STOCK PRICE ($) FY Close	P/E High/Low	PER SHARE ($) Earnings	Dividends	Book Value
12/17	38.29	19 14	2.50	0.00	23.54
12/16	40.44	18 9	2.32	0.00	20.11
12/15	25.12	16 12	1.98	0.00	18.48
12/14	25.89	17 11	1.83	0.00	17.96
12/13	22.71	15 10	1.64	0.00	17.06
Annual Growth	**14.0%**	— —	**11.1%**	—	**8.4%**

Intel Corp

Intel Corp. is the brains of the operation. One the biggest computer chip companies Intel controls roughly 90% of the market for microprocessors that act as the brains of desktop notebook and server computers. It has dominated the PC chip market from the early x86 processors to Pentiums to today's Core technology. Intel also makes chips for smartphones and tablets as well as embedded semiconductors for the industrial medical and automotive markets. The company develops its chips and makes most of them itself in one of the industry's biggest manufacturing systems. As PC sales have declined Intel has shifted focus and resources to chips for the data centers that power cloud computing.

Operations

Intel Corp.'s Client Computing Group is the company's workhorse and cash generator delivering about 55% of its revenue and more than 70% of operating income. The business churns out chips for notebooks 2-in-1 systems desktops tablets phones wireless and wired connectivity products and mobile communication components.

The Data Center Group generates about 30% of Intel's revenue with chips for server-platforms and related products designed for the enterprise cloud and communication infrastructure market.

The Internet of Things Group makes chips for connected devices in retail transportation industrial video buildings smart cities and other markets. It accounts for about 5% of revenue.

Taken together the Programmable Solutions and Non-Volatile Memory Solutions groups provide about 10% of the company's revenue.

Intel makes most of its products in its own manufacturing facilities which allows the company to control the process for quality speed and flexibility. For some communications connectivity networking field programmable and memory components the company outsources manufacturing to third parties. Intel handles test and assembly in-house and through contractors.

Geographic Reach

Intel Corp. has more than 150 locations around the globe with assembly and test facilities in China Costa Rica Malaysia and Vietnam. Customers in China (including Hong Kong) and Singapore each generate about a quarter of Intel's sales followed by US customers who supply 20% of revenue and customers in Taiwan who kick in more than 15% of revenue.

Sales and Marketing

Intel sells its products primarily to original equipment manufacturers (OEMs) and original design manufacturers (ODMs). ODMs provide design and manufacturing services to branded and unbranded private label resellers. In addition Intel products are sold to makers of industrial and communications equipment.

Its customers also include those who buy PC components and other products through distributor reseller retail and OEM channels. Intel's worldwide reseller sales channel consists of thousands of indirect customers who are systems builders that purchase microprocessors and other products from distributors.

Intel's three largest customers account for nearly 40% of the total revenue. The biggest are Dell Technologies and Lenovo Group with 15% of sales each and HP Inc. with about 10%.

Financial Performance

Intel's sales have grown 20% a year over the past five years as the company had maintained revenue from computer-related products and its lineup of newer products for data centers and cloud computing has grown.

In 2017 revenue rose 6% to $62.8 billion from 2016 driven by growth in all parts of its business. Intel's data-related businesses posted a 16% jump (after adjusting for the divestment of the security unit) in 2017. Higher sales in the Data Center group were driven by cloud service and communication service providers. The Client Computer Group's revenue grew 3% in 2017 on higher notebook sales from gaming and commercial accounts. Shipment volume and average selling prices of notebook computers were higher in 2017 than 2016 while desktop computer volume dropped. The Non-volatile Memory Solutions Group's sale rose about 35% on data center demand. The Internet of Things Group posted a 20% increase in sales while the Progammable Solutions Group's sales were 12% higher.

Intel reduced costs for research and development and sales and marketing as a percentage of revenue leading to a higher gross margin of 62% in 2017 from 61% in 2016. But a one-time tax charge due to the US Tax Cuts and Jobs Act reduced Intel's profit to $9.6 billion a 7% decline from 2016.

In 2017 Intel spent about $14 billion on acquisitions $12 billion on capital expenditures $8 billion in debt payments and about $3 billion on stock buybacks. The company ended the year with about $14 billion in cash and cash equivalents compared to about $17 billion in 2016.

Strategy

Although Intel had higher sales of PC chips in 2016 and 2017 (as overall PC sales declined) the company realizes that the business is in long-term decline. But even as it diminishes there's still a lot of money Intel which supplies about 90% of the chips for PCs can pull out of it. The company maintains a level of investment in developing and making PC chips to squeeze out as much revenue as it can.

Intel is investing in its data-related processors and supplying them for growing markets such as data centers cloud computing 5G communications artificial intelligence and autonomous driving. The units that address those markets are growing quickly.

Intel's acquisition of Mobileye stakes out a prominent position for providing technology for self-driving cars. Mobileye's sensor technologies combined with Intel's semiconductors should make for a formidable competitor in developing autonomous vehicles. Intel has teamed with BMW AG and Delphi Automotive for developing driverless vehicle technology and had an ongoing relationship with Mobileye.

With annual revenue north of $60 billion Intel has deep resources. It had close to $12 billion in capital investment in 2017 with most it devoted to equipment and facilities to produce advanced chips. However Intel had a hiccup on its path to advanced manufacturing when it announced that full-scale 10-nanometer production would be pushed back from 2018 to 2019. The smaller size enables higher yields per wafer which reduces costs.

Intel faces challenges from other semiconductor companies that offer strong products in growing markets. Samsung Electronics' chip business has grown in recent years and the company is running neck-and-neck for the title of biggest chipmaker. Longtime rival AMD has released high-performance chips at price points that could undercut Intel's offerings. NVIDIA is growing quickly from its graphics chips that are well-suited to artificial intelligence applications.

In 2017 security flaws were discovered in Intel chips that could make computers vulnerable to hackers. Intel took steps to mitigate the flaws and doesn't expect material financial impact from the matter.

Mergers and Acquisitions

In 2018 Intel acquired Netspeed Systems which make tools for designing system-on-chip (SoC) devices. Intel is one of several chip companies that include NVIDIA and Qualcomm increasingly making circuits that handle multiple functions. Netspeed's tools speed up the design of SoCs through automation. Netspeed becomes part of Intel's Silicon Engineering Group. Intel has been a Netspeed customer and its venture arm had invested in the company. Terms of the acquisition were not disclosed.

In 2017 Intel acquired Mobileye for more than $15 billion. Mobileye based in Israel develops sensors and cameras for vehicles. The acquisition broadens Intel's offerings for makers of driverless vehicles beyond the chips that are brains of such vehicles. Mobileye's technologies provide more of the critical capabilities that autonomous autos need to maneuver safely. The deal closed in August 2017.

The acquisition of Altera provides Intel with key technology for dealing with data center cloud and the Internet of Things. Altera makes chips that can be reprogrammed after installation. Intel will combine its powerful Xeon processors which handle dedicated tasks with Altera's more chips to give customers more flexibility.

In 2105 Intel completed the acquisition of Lantiq a supplier of broadband access and home networking technologies. With the acquisition Intel moves further into DSL and fiber markets. It made two other acquisitions of companies with IOT-related technologies.

Also in 2015 Intel invested nearly $1 billion in Beijing UniSpreadtrum Technology a subsidiary of Tsinghua Holdings to jointly develop chips for mobile phones based on Intel architectures.

EXECUTIVES

Evp Corporate Strategy, Thomas M Kilroy, age 62
Interim Ceo, Robert H. (Bob) Swan, age 58, $194,800 total compensation
Vp Technology And Manufacturing Group; General Manager Systems Manufacturing, Leslie S. Culbertson
Svp, Gregory R. (Greg) Pearson, age 58, $545,000 total compensation
Group President Manufacturing Operations And Sales, Stacy J. Smith, age 56, $800,000 total compensation
Vp Intel Communications Group; General Manager Network Processor Division, Douglas L. (Doug) Davis, age 57
Vp Technology And Manufacturing Group; Director Logic Technology Development, Sohail U. Ahmed
Svp And General Manager Non-volatile Memory (nvm) Solutions Group, Robert B. Crooke
Svp And General Manager Client Computing Group, Diane M. Bryant, age 57, $618,700 total compensation
Svp And Managing Director Intel Labs And Cto, Michael C. (Mike) Mayberry, age 61
Svp And General Manager Intel Product Assurance And Security Engineering Group, Joshua M. (Josh) Walden, age 56
Svp And General Manager Platform Engineering Group, Amir Faintuch
Svp And General Manager Software And Services Group (ssg), Douglas W. (Doug) Fisher
Evp And General Counsel, Steven R. (Steve) Rodgers
Evp And General Manager Data Center Group, Navin Shenoy
Svp And Chief Marketing Officer, Steven L. Fund
Svp And Chief Strategy Officer, Aicha S. Evans
Svp And General Manager Internet Of Things (iot) Group, Thomas P. (Tom) Lantzsch
Corporate Vp And President Mergers And Acquisitions, Wendell M. Brooks
Corporate Vp And Cio, Paula C. Tolliver
Group President Technology Systems Architecture And Client Group And Chief Engineering Officer, Venkata M. (Murthy) Renduchintala, age 53, $900,000 total compensation
Corporate Vp And General Manager Technology And Manufacturing Group, Ann B. Kelleher
Corporate Vp And General Manager Programmable Solutions Group (psg), Daniel R. (Dan) McNamara
Corporate Vp And General Manager Artificial Intelligence Products Group, Naveen G. Rao
Vice President Law And Policy Group And Associate General Counsel Director Intel Standards Group, Ann K Armstrong
Vice President Intel Capital And Managing Director New Technologies, Ameet Bhansali
Intel Information Technology Vpro Amt Product Manager, Omer Livne
Vice President Nsg End User Solutions Marketing, Laura Crone
Vice President Technology And Manufacturing Group And Director Yield Technology, Melton C Bost
Senior Vice President, Arun Chandrasekhar
Northeast Regional Vice President, Praveen Kundurthy
Vice President Finance And Controller Corporate Planning And Reporting, Todd Underwood
Vice President Of Industrial And Motor Services, James A Kovacs
Vice President, Sanjiv Shah
Vice President Intel Labs And Director Integrated Platform Research Lab, Vida Ilderem

Vice President Platform Engineering Group, Noel Murphy
Executive Vice President And Chief Development Officer, Gadi Oren
Vpg Hardware, Anita Rao
Technical Advisor To Intel Vice President (sales Marketing Group), Iris WU
Vp Sales And Marketing Group Director Emea Marketing, Bernadette Andrietti
Vice President Applications And Support, John Kreatsoulas
Vice President Tmg Plant Manager Nm Site Fab 11x, Kirby Jefferson
Vice President, Ralph Schweinfurth
Assistant Vice President Of Sales, Heather Thomas
Vice President Human Resources, Michael Forrest
Vice President Software And Services Group And Director Open Source Technology Center Core Operati, Hillarie Prestopine
Vice President Mergers And Acquisitions Counsel, Daniel Vaughn
Vice President, Armin Sarstedt
Vice President Consumer Product Management, Alan LeFort
Vice President Sales And Marketing, Gilberto Vargas
Vice President Global Marketing And Communications, Alyson Griffin
Vice President Information Technology And Gm Enterprise Applications And Application Strategy, Aziz Safa
Vice President Platform Engineering Group, Anwar Awad
Vice President, Anil Rao
Vice President Engineering, Raheel Khan
Vice President Of Visual Technology Architecture Group, Martin Ashton
Vice President Platform Engineering Group And Director Product Development Itgs Devices Developme, Boyd Phelps
Vice President Sales And Marketing Group And General Manager Sales Non Volatile Memory Solutions Group, John Vossoughi
Vice President, Rahul Goyal
Vp Intel Capital And Director Mergers And Acquisition, Raheel A Shah
Vice President Client Computing Group And Gm Client Planning And Architecture, Adam King
Vice President Non Volatile Memory Solutions Group And Intel Co Executive Officer Intel Micron Fla, Albert Blaha
Vice President Law And Policy Group And Associate General Counsel Data Center Group, C Matt Swafford
Corporate Vice President Chief Financial Officer Data Center, Chris Min
Vice President Technology And Manufacturing Group And Director Specialized Technologies, Bernhard Sell
Chairman, Andy D. Bryant, age 67
Board Member, Haripriya Prakasam
Treasurer, Mahendra Malliwal
Board Member, Kai Wang
Board Member, Edison F Rodrigues
Secretary, Rosidah Ahmad
Auditors: Ernst & Young LLP

LOCATIONS

HQ: Intel Corp
2200 Mission College Boulevard, Santa Clara, CA 95054-1549
Phone: 408 765-8080   **Fax:** 408 765-2633
Web: www.intc.com

2017 Sales

	$ mil.	% of total
China (including Hong Kong)	14,796	23
Singapore	14,285	23
US	12,543	20
Taiwan	10,518	17
Other	10,619	17
Total	**62,761**	**100**

PRODUCTS/OPERATIONS

2017 Sales

	$ mil.	% of total
Client computing Group	34,003	54
Data Center Group	19,064	30
Internet of Things Group	3,169	5
Non-Volatile Memory Solutions Group	3,520	6
Programmable Solutions Group	1,902	3
All others	1,103	2
Total	**62,761**	**100**

Selected Products

Chipsets (communications consumer electronics desktop embedded handheld netbook notebook server storage workstation)

Communication infrastructure components
Network processors
Networked storage products

Device software optimization products (embedded handheld)

Digital home (chips for cable modems digital TVs high-definition media players set-top boxes and home network integration)

Microprocessors (communications consumer electronics desktop embedded handheld network netbook notebook server storage workstation)
Atom
Celeron
Centrino
Core i3 i5 i7
Core Duo
Core Quad
Itanium
Pentium
Xeon

Motherboards (desktop server workstation)

NAND flash memory (all-in-one desktop digital camera memory card portable memory storage device solid-state drive tablet computer)

Software products (software development tools middleware operating systems software tools)

Ultra-Mobility (chips for high-end smartphones handheld devices)

Wired and wireless connectivity components (embedded wireless cards network adapters)

COMPETITORS

AMD	Oracle
ARM Holdings	QUALCOMM
Apple Inc.	SK Hynix
Atmel	STMicroelectronics
Cisco Systems	Samsung Electronics
Conexant Systems	SanDisk
Fujitsu Semiconductor	Silicon Integrated
GLOBALFOUNDRIES	Systems
IBM	Sony
Maxim Integrated	Symantec
Products	TSMC
MediaTek	Texas Instruments
Microchip Technology	Toshiba Semiconductor
Micron Technology	& Storage Products
NVIDIA	VIA Technologies

HISTORICAL FINANCIALS

Company Type: Public

Income Statement — FYE: December 29

	REVENUE ($ mil.)	NET INCOME ($ mil.)	NET PROFIT MARGIN	EMPLOYEES
12/18	70,848	21,053	29.7%	107,400
12/17	62,761	9,601	15.3%	102,700
12/16	59,387	10,316	17.4%	106,000
12/15	55,355	11,420	20.6%	107,300
12/14	55,870	11,704	20.9%	106,700
Annual Growth	**6.1%**	**15.8%**	**—**	**0.2%**

2018 Year-End Financials

Debt ratio: 20.60%—
Return on equity: 29.15%
Cash ($ mil.): 3,019
Current ratio: 1.73
Long-term debt ($ mil.): 25,098

Dividends
Yield: 0.0%
Payout: 26.7%
Market value ($ mil.): —

	STOCK PRICE ($) FY Close	P/E High/Low	Earnings	Dividends	Book Value
12/18	46.75	12 9	4.48	1.20	16.60
12/17	46.16	23 16	1.99	1.08	14.91
12/16	36.27	17 13	2.12	1.04	14.19
12/15	34.98	16 11	2.33	0.96	13.12
12/14	37.55	16 10	2.31	0.90	11.96
Annual Growth	**5.6%**	**— —**	**18.0%**	**7.5%**	**8.6%**

Intercontinental Exchange Inc

EXECUTIVES

Chb-Ceo, Jeffrey C Sprecher
Vice Chb, Charles Vice
President, Benjamin Jackson
Cfo, Scott A Hill
Cso, David S Goone
General Counsel-Corp SEC, Johnathan H Short
Coo, Mark Wassersug
Information Technology Auditor, Benjamin Barry
Senior Director, Bill Meyers
Manager, Brent Wilkinson
Creative Director, Cecilia Sortino
Auditors: Ernst & Young LLP

LOCATIONS

HQ: Intercontinental Exchange Inc
5660 New Northside Drive, Atlanta, GA 30328
Phone: 770 857-4700   **Fax:** 770 937-0020
Web: www.theice.com

HISTORICAL FINANCIALS

Company Type: Public

Income Statement — FYE: December 31

	REVENUE ($ mil.)	NET INCOME ($ mil.)	NET PROFIT MARGIN	EMPLOYEES
12/18	6,276	1,988	31.7%	5,161
12/17	5,834	2,514	43.1%	4,952
12/16	5,958	1,422	23.9%	5,631
12/15	4,682	1,274	27.2%	5,549
12/14	4,221	981	23.2%	2,902
Annual Growth	**10.4%**	**19.3%**		**15.5%**

2018 Year-End Financials

Debt ratio: 8.02%
Return on equity: 11.65%
Cash ($ mil.): 724
Current ratio: 1.01
Long-term debt ($ mil.): 6,490

No. of shares (mil.): 569
Dividends
Yield: 1.2%
Payout: 21.7%
Market value ($ mil.): 42,863

	STOCK PRICE ($) FY Close	P/E High/Low	Earnings	Dividends	Book Value
12/18	75.33	24 19	3.43	0.96	30.23
12/17	70.56	17 13	4.23	0.80	29.03
12/16	56.42	119 22	2.37	0.68	26.42
12/15	256.26	115 89	2.28	0.58	24.89
12/14	219.29	132 107	1.71	0.52	21.88
Annual Growth	**(23.4%)**	**— —**	**19.0%**	**16.6%**	**8.4%**

INTERMOUNTAIN HEALTH CARE INC

If you whoosh down the side of one of Idaho's majestic mountains and take a nasty spill Intermountain Health Care (dba Intermountain Healthcare) can pick you up and put you back together. From air ambulance services to urgent care clinics and general hospitals Intermountain has all the tools to mend skiers (and non-skiers alike) in Utah and southern Idaho. With about 1600 physicians the not-for-profit health system operates 22 hospitals and some 180 clinics as well as urgent care centers and rehabilitation centers. Intermountain also has an insurance arm named SelectHealth.

Operations

Intermountain Healthcare's hospitals range from general surgical to specialty care including orthopedic and pediatric facilities. Along with the full spectrum of physical health care services Intermountain also offers comprehensive mental health and substance abuse programs for patients of all ages. The organization's spectrum of care includes acute inpatient residential treatment day treatment chemical dependency inpatient/detoxification and intensive outpatient programs.

The system conducts cancer research through its partnership with Huntsman Cancer Institute at the University of Utah. The two share data best practices funding and co-conduct clinical trials. They also operate a number of cancer-specific treatment centers including multi-disciplinary tumor-specific clinics designed to provide one-stop service for cancer patients to meet with different cancer specialists on the same day for a more comprehensive treatment plan. Other areas of research include cardiovascular intensive medicine surgical care and behavioral health.

On the physician side the Intermountain Medical Group administers multi-specialty health care services in clinics located throughout the region. The group also operates urgent care clinics under the InstaCare and KidsCare banners.

Entering itself into the "what doesn't Intermountain do?" category the health system also provides health and dental insurance plans through its SelectHealth division.

Geographic Reach

Intermountain Healthcare serves the health care needs of Utah and Idaho residents.

Financial Performance

In 2016 Intermountain Healthcare's revenue grew 14% to $7.6 billion in fiscal 2016. This was due to increases in net patient services income non-patient activity income and investment income. Net patient services accounted for 63% of the system's total revenue that year.

The company used $7 billion of that revenue towards operating expenses including salaries and benefits medical supplies and facilities maintenance and other business services as well as towards funds dedicated to future needs.

Strategy

Intermountain Healthcare uses its dedicated supply chain organization to continuously improve system efficiency. In addition to delivering medical supplies the unit also oversees hospital vehicles.

The system partners with several leading IT companies (including Xi3 Intel Dell and NetApp) to operate its Healthcare Transformation Lab on the campus of its flagship hospital Intermountain Medical Center in Murray Utah. The lab researches develops and measures new ideas to improve patient care.

In 2016 the system launched Navican Genomics its genomics research and testing arm. Also that year it partnered with the Stanford Genome Technology Center to establish a collaborative research program.

Intermountain has a number of projects underway to add expand or replace existing facilities.

Company Background

Intermountain was formed in 1975 when the Church of Jesus Christ of Latter Day Saints donated 15 hospitals to local communities.

EXECUTIVES

Senior Vice President, Greg Poulsen
Ceo Intermountain Medical Group And Vp Physician Division, Linda C. Leckman
President And Ceo Selecthealth, Patricia R. Richards
Evp And Cfo, Bert R. Zimmerli
Evp And Coo, Laura S. Kaiser
Regional Vp Central Region, Moody L. Chisholm
Vp And Cio, Marc Probst
President And Ceo, A. Marc Harrison, age 54
Regional Vp Soutwest Region, Terri Kane
Ceo Park City Medical Center, Robert Allen
Vp Clinical Operations And Chief Nursing Officer, Kim Henrichsen
Ceo Urban North Region And Mckay-dee Hospital Center, Timothy T. Pehrson
Chief Medical Officer, Brent E. Wallace
Ceo Primary Childrenâ's Medical Center, Katherine A. (Katy) Welkie
Regional Vp South Region, Steve Smoot
Vp Supply Chain And Support Services, Joe Walsh
Assistant Vice President Of Risk Management Services, Harlan Hammond
Vice President Management, Jim Darrington
Vice President Marketing And Communication, Todd Frehse
Director Media Relations, Daron Cowley
Medical Director, Scott Whittle
Assistant Vice President Research, Raj Srivastava
Medical Director Epilepsy Program, Tawnya Constantino
Medical Director, Kristian Kemp
Vice President Business Ethics And Compliance, Suzie Draper
Vice President Human Resources, Dan Zuhlke
Vice President And General Counsel, Doug Hammer
Vice President Rural Region, Rob Allen
Pharmacy Manager, Robb Dengg
Cota L, Celeste Marsh
Assistant Vice President Telehealth Services, Brian Wayling
Medical Director Clinical Genetics Institute, Steven Bleyl
Clinical Director Primary Children's Pediatric Behavioral Health Clinic, Nancy Cantor
Vice President Of Underwriting, Mike Brown
Occupational Therapy Director, Andrew Bracken
Medical Director Information Technology, Ed Clark
Medical Director Informatics, Farukh Usmani
Operating Room Dir, DEBRA ESPLIN
Vice Chairman, Bruce T. Reese
Chairman, A. Scott Anderson
Secretary, Nicole Houghton
Secretary, Jeri Lay
Secretary, Stephanie Stromberg
Secretary, Jodi Simmons
Auditors: KPMG LLP SALT LAKE CITY UT

LOCATIONS

HQ: INTERMOUNTAIN HEALTH CARE INC
36 S STATE ST STE 1600, SALT LAKE CITY, UT 841111633
Phone: 801 442-2000
Web: WWW.INTERMOUNTAINHEALTHCARE.ORG

PRODUCTS/OPERATIONS

2016 Sales

	$ mil.	% of total
Net patient services	4,368	57
Non-patient activities	3,010	40
Non-operating income	237	3
Total	**7,617**	**100**

Selected Hospitals

Alta View Hospital (Sandy UT)
American Fork Hospital (Utah)
Bear River Valley Hospital (Tremonton UT)
Cassia Regional Medical Center (Burley ID)
Delta Community Medical Center (Utah)
Dixie Regional Medical Center (St. George UT)
Fillmore Community Medical Center (Utah)
Garfield Memorial Hospital (Panguitch UT)
Heber Valley Medical Center (Heber City UT)
Intermountain Medical Center (Murray UT)
LDS Hospital (Salt Lake City)
Logan Regional Hospital (Orem UT)
McKay-Dee Hospital Center (Ogden UT)
 McKay-Dee Behavioral Health Institute
Orem Community Hospital (Utah)
Park City Medical Center (Park City UT)
Primary Children's Medical Center (Salt Lake City)
Riverton Hospital (Riverton UT)
Sanpete Valley Hospital (Mt. Pleasant UT)
Sevier Valley Hospital (Richfield UT)
TOSH - The Orthopedic Specialty Hospital (Murray UT)
Utah Valley Regional Medical Center (Provo UT)
Valley View Medical Center (Cedar City UT)

COMPETITORS

CHRISTUS Health	Regence BlueCross
Encompass Health	BlueShield of Utah
HCA	St. Mark's
LifePoint Health	University of Utah
Ogden Regional Medical Center	Hospitals & Clinics

HISTORICAL FINANCIALS

Company Type: Private

Income Statement

FYE: December 31

	REVENUE ($ mil.)	NET INCOME ($ mil.)	NET PROFIT MARGIN	EMPLOYEES
12/17	6,940	1,061	15.3%	35,000
12/16	6,716	606	9.0%	—
12/15	6,058	155	2.6%	—
12/14	5,573	(156)	—	—
Annual Growth	7.6%	—	—	—

2017 Year-End Financials

Debt ratio: ——
Return on equity: 15.30%
Cash ($ mil.): 204
Current ratio: 0.40
Long-term debt ($ mil.): —

Dividends
 Yield: —
 Payout: —
 Market value ($ mil.): —

International Bancshares Corp.

International Bancshares is leading post-NAFTA banking in South Texas. One of the state's largest bank holding companies it does business through nearly 200 locations of International Bank of Commerce (IBC) IBC-Oklahoma Commerce Bank IBC Zapata and IBC Brownsville. The company facilitates trade between the US and Mexico and serves Texas' growing Hispanic population; about 30% of its deposits come from south of the border. In addition to commercial and international banking services for small and midsized businesses International Bancshares provides retail deposit services insurance and investment products mortgages and consumer loans. The bulk of the company's portfolio is made up of commercial financial and agricultural loans and real estate loans for construction.

Operations

Operating under a single segment International Bancshares garners around 70% of its revenue from interest income particularly loans including fees. Non-interest income – mostly from service charges on deposit accounts and other banking service charges commissions and fees – accounts for the rest.

Commercial financial and agricultural loans represent half of International Bancshares' $6.5 billion portfolio. Mortgages and construction real estate loans comprise roughly 20% and 30% of that total respectively.

Geographic Reach

Based in the border city of Laredo Texas International Bancshares has many customers living in Mexico especially northern Mexico. The holding company has nearly 200 branches in South Central and Southeast Texas and Oklahoma. Its primary market area in Texas is bordered on the east by the Galveston area the northwest by Dallas the southwest by Del Rio and to the southeast by Brownsville.

The branches are in the regions of Laredo San Antonio Austin Dallas Houston Zapata Eagle Pass the Rio Grande Valley of Texas the Coastal Bend area of Texas and throughout the State of Oklahoma.

Sales and Marketing

A large proportion of International Bancshares' business is with customers in Mexico; deposits from such clients comprise around 30% of its deposit base.

Financial Performance

International Bancshares has seen modest sputtering growth since 2013 adding approximately 5% to its revenue and 25% to its net income. Cash and long-term debt have fallen less than 5% and about 15% respectively in that time.

International Bancshares' revenue ticked up 4% to $526.6 million in 2017 owing to increased interest income caused by higher loan volume and overall yield. The company's interest expense also decreased following early termination of long-term repurchase agreements by its lead subsidiary bank.

The holding company's net income increased 18% to $157.4 million based on the same interest income improvement and a reduction in its provision for probable loan losses and a tax refund.

Cash stores fell $3.8 million to $265.4 million. Operations provided $196.8 million down slightly from 2016; financing provided $203.1 million mostly due to a net increase in other borrowed funds (which include Federal Home Loan Bank borrowings). Investments used $403.8 million owing primarily a large net decrease in loans.

Strategy

International Bancshares is attempting to shift its focus from commercial banking for small and midsized businesses to consumer and retail banking including mortgage lending and opening branches in retail properties and shopping malls. About 52% of the company's portfolio comprised commercial financial and agricultural loans compared with 56% in 2013. The share accounted for by mortgages increased from 16% in 2013 to 18% in 2017.

Company Background

International Bancshares was founded in 1966.

EXECUTIVES

Vp And Director; President And Ceo International Bank Of Commerce Mcallen, R. David Guerra, age 65, $245,668 total compensation

Chairman And Ceo; Ceo International Bank Of Commerce Laredo, Dennis E. Nixon, age 75, $659,632 total compensation

President Coo And Cfo International Bank Of Commerce Laredo, Imelda Navarro, age 60, $235,960 total compensation

President And Ceo Commerce Bank Laredo Texas, Ignacio Urrabazo

President And Ceo International Bank Of Commerce Eagle Pass Texas, Hector J. Cerna

Chairman And Ceo International Bank Of Commerce Houston Texas, Jay Rogers

Chairman And Ceo International Bank Of Commerce Zapata Texas, Renato Ramirez

President And Ceo International Bank Of Commerce Austin Texas, Robert B. (Bob) Barnes

Svp, Eliza Gonzalez

President International Bank Of Commerce Houston Texas, Jeff Samples

President And Ceo International Bank Of Commerce San Antonio, Mike K. Sohn

President And Ceo International Bank Of Commerce Port Lavaca, Derek Schmidt

President And Ceo Corpus Christi, Harold Shockley

President And Ceo International Bank Of Commerce Brownsville, Al Villareal

Ceo San Antonio Service Center, Julie Tarvin

President Southwest Region International Bank Of Commerce, Brian Henry

President International Bank Of Commerce Tulsa, Andrew Levinson

President International Bank Of Commerce Zapata, Ricardo Ramirez

Evp Corporate International, Gerardo (Gerald) Schwebel

President And Ceo International Bank Of Commerce Oklahoma, Bill Schonacher

Evp And International Loan Officer, Natividad Lozano

Senior Vice President Of Commercial Lending, Craig Bunk

First Vice President Auditor, Ramiro Herrera

Executive Vice President, Guillermo Garcia

Vice President, Jennifer Alvarado

Vice President Of Accounting, Alvaro Martinez

Vice President Human Resources, Rosie Ramirez

Senior Vice President Of Electronic Services, Kevin Mullins

Vice President Accounting And Operations, David Shinn

Vice President, Mirta Salcedo

Executive Vice President, Lee Reed

Vice President Life Sales, Markham Benn

Assistant Vice President Commercial Lender, Bernardo De La Garza

Auditors: RSM US LLP

LOCATIONS

HQ: International Bancshares Corp.
1200 San Bernardo Avenue, Laredo, TX 78042-1359
Phone: 956 722-7611
Web: www.ibc.com

PRODUCTS/OPERATIONS

2017 Sales

	% of total
Interest income	
Loans including fees	57
Investment securities	16
Other	-
Interest expense	-
Non interest income	
Service charges on deposit accounts	13
Other service charges commissions & fees	9
Other investments net	3
Other	2
Net investment securities transactions	-
Total	**100**

Selected Services

Business Investors
Business Online Banking Services
Checking Options
Commercial Insurance
Home and Personal Loans
IBC First Equity
IBC Investment Services
Individual Investors
Life And Health
Manage Your Account
Mobile Banking
Online Banking Center
Online Banking Services
Other Personal Services
Overdraft Courtesy
Personal
Personal Insurance

COMPETITORS

BancFirst
Bank of America
Broadway Bancshares
Citigroup
Cullen/Frost Bankers
Falcon Bancshares
First Victoria
  National Bank

JPMorgan Chase
Lone Star National
  Bancshares
Midland Financial
Wells Fargo

HISTORICAL FINANCIALS

Company Type: Public

Income Statement

FYE: December 31

	ASSETS ($ mil.)	NET INCOME ($ mil.)	INCOME AS % OF ASSETS	EMPLOYEES
12/17	12,184	157	1.3%	3,273
12/16	11,804	133	1.1%	3,216
12/15	11,772	136	1.2%	3,218
12/14	12,196	153	1.3%	3,256
12/13	12,079	126	1.0%	3,223
Annual Growth	0.2%	5.7%	—	0.4%

2017 Year-End Financials

Debt ratio: 11.13%
Return on equity: 8.84%
Cash ($ mil.): 265
Current ratio: —
Long-term debt ($ mil.): —

No. of shares (mil.): 66
Dividends
  Yield: 0.0%
  Payout: 27.9%
Market value ($ mil.): 2,623

	STOCK PRICE ($) FY Close	P/E High/Low	PER SHARE ($) Earnings	Dividends	Book Value
12/17	39.70	18 14	2.36	0.66	27.83
12/16	40.80	21 11	2.02	0.60	26.14
12/15	25.70	15 11	2.05	0.58	25.13
12/14	26.54	12 9	2.28	0.52	23.78
12/13	26.36	14 10	1.88	0.43	21.19
Annual Growth	10.8%	— —	5.8%	11.3%	7.0%

International Business Machines Corp

International Business Machines (IBM) bets that cognition is the ignition for growth. The company is investing in it what is calls cognitive computing systems led by the Watson artificial intelligence platform that help customers analyze massive amounts of data to make better decisions. Among other areas the company is betting on for growth are security cloud and blockchain. The company's information technology business services and software units are among the largest in the world. While IBM has placed less emphasis on hardware the company maintains enterprise server and data storage product lines that are among industry leaders. As the perennial leader in the number of US patents granted IBM maintains a steady pipeline of potential products. In 2018 IBM agreed to buy Red Hat for about $34 billion to boost its cloud computing business.

Operations

IBM manages its sprawling operations in five segments.

Technology Services and Cloud Platforms which generates about 45% of revenue provides a portfolio of cloud outsourcing and other managed services focused on clients? enterprise IT infrastructure. Offerings include maintenance for IBM products and other technology platforms as well as support.

Cognitive Solutions which provides about a quarter of revenue includes Watson IBM?s cognitive computing project. Major Watson initiatives are Watson Platform Watson Health and Watson Internet of Things. Another part of the unit is the company?s security platform which provides detection and protection against cyber threats across a customer?s operations.

Global Business Services about 20% of revenue provides consulting application management services and global process services to help customers move their businesses to digital platforms.

Systems about 10% of revenue is IBM?s hardware business. It provides technologies for hybrid cloud and cognitive workloads. The unit sells servers storage systems and operating systems software.

Global Financing provides credit arrangements for customers to buy IBM products. It accounts for about 2% of revenue.

Geographic Reach

The international in IBM has become increasingly important to its bottom line. With clients in about 175 countries sales outside the US account for more than 50% of revenue. Customers in Europe the Middle East and Africa (EMEA) generate about 30% of sales and Asia/Pacific about 20%.

Sales and Marketing

IBM operates country-based units where consultants product specialists and other workers (most hired locally) facilitate the adoption and fulfillment of its products and services. It serves clients across most industries; leading industry groups include financial services industrial and communications.

Financial Performance

Over the past five years IBM has lost about $20 billion in revenue as it tries to reposition itself to capitalize on cognitive computing data analytics and cloud computing. So far sales declines tied to older products have outpaced sales of its newer offerings.

Revenue slipped about 1% to $79.2 billion in 2017 from 2016. Sales were about 2% higher in Cognitive Solutions from offerings in security industry platforms and Watson systems (the company reported double-digit growth for its Watson Health products). Systems sales rose about 6% driven by strong response to its z14 mainframe.

Technology Services & Cloud Platforms segment sales dropped about 3% overall but IBM reported growth in the segment's cloud analytics mobile and security elements grew. In Global Business Services growth in strategic initiatives was offset by declines in large ERP and on-premise enterprise application implementation.

IBM?s profit dropped by half to about $5.7 billion in 2017 from 2016. The biggest difference was a one-time tax bill of about $5.5 billion because of changes in US tax laws enacted in late 2017.

The company had about $12 billion in cash in 2017 compared to about $7.8 billion in 2016. The company banked more cash from favorable exchange rates and spent less on acquisitions in 2017.

Strategy

IBM halted its string of quarterly revenue declines at 22 quarters in the fourth quarter of 2017 when sales rose almost 4% from the same quarter in 2016. For the year IBM's revenue was down about 1.5% the sixth straight year of lower annual revenue.

IBM thinks indicators are pointing in the right direction and that its investments in cognitive computing cloud security big data and analytics are beginning to pay off. Together these helped IBM's Cognitive Solutions business generate more than $18 billion in revenue in 2017. The company highlighted a 24% increase in cloud revenue as well as contributions from the Watson platform including its health initiative.

Besides those areas IBM is investing in emerging technologies such as blockchain and those in earlier stages of research such as quantum computing.

In cloud computing the company competes with market leaders Amazon Google (a unit of Alphabet) and Microsoft. IBM focuses on hybrid cloud the mixture of keeping data on IBM computers and the customer's own systems. In 2017 the company introduced a Z series mainframe with encryption capabilities which is part of its security focus. The proposed acquisition of Red Hat (for about $34 billion) is to turbocharge IBM's hybrid cloud business. IBM intends to offer companies moving data to cloud environments a model that's not dependent on hardware but more so on Red Hat's open source software. The companies intend to offer customers a fast and secure path to cloud computing through the hybrid model. IBM is betting that the focus on the hybrid cloud will appeal to customers who need to keep some data under wraps while putting some out on the public cloud. IBM and Red Hat have partnered to offer software services for about 20 years. The deal was expected to close in late 2019.

To make way for the newer technologies it's developing IBM sometimes sells off technology that no longer fits. It did that in selling collaboration marketing and commerce software assets to HCL Technologies based in Noida India for $1.8 billion in late 2018. In the deal HCL picked up Appscan BigFix Unica Commerce Portal Notes and Domino and Connections.

Mergers and Acquisitions

IBM continues to use an aggressive acquisition strategy to augment its own R&D as it expands and refines its mix of business software and IT services. Many of the acquisitions have been made to provide data and services for the Watson system. IBM has earmarked $100 million to acquire startups that could expand Watson's capabilities.

IBM began a major acquisition to charge up its cloud computing capabilities in agreeing to buy Red Hat for about $34 billion one of the biggest technology acquisitions in history. The deal brings Red Hat's open source software to IBM's cloud computing division. Red Hat would become a distinct unit in IBM's hybrid cloud division.

The company's acquisition activity slowed in 2017 to five deals for a total of $134 million. In 2016 IBM bought spent about $6 billion in 15 companies. The 2017 transactions were for smaller companies that filled in niches in IBM cognitive and cloud businesses.

In 2016 the company made nearly 15 acquisitions. The biggest acquisition of 2016 was of Truven Health Analytics which provides data and analysis technologies for $2.6 billion. IBM seeks to put data and analysis together with Watson's cognitive capabilities to help health care professionals accomplish better patient outcomes.

In another Watson-related acquisition that closed in 2016 was of the Weather Company. IBM bought the company's business-to-business mobile and cloud-based web-properties weather.com Weather Underground The Weather Company brand and WSI its global business-to-business brand. The transaction did not include the Weather Channel but it licenses weather forecast data and analytics from IBM under a long-term contract. The deal provides a wealth of data for processing through Watson to help companies make better decisions that are affected by the weather.

EXECUTIVES

Svp Ibm Watson And Cloud Platform, David W. Kenny, age 56

Vice President Of Legal, Martha Rendeiro

Svp Solutions Portfolio And Research, John E. Kelly, age 65, $754,000 total compensation

Chairman President And Ceo, Virginia M. (Ginni) Rometty, age 60, $1,600,000 total compensation

Svp Ibm Cloud, Robert J. LeBlanc, age 59

Svp Global Business Services, Mark Foster, age 59

Svp Global Markets And Chairman Ibm Europe, Erich Clementi, age 59, $703,500 total compensation

Svp Global Markets, Martin J. Schroeter, age 53, $754,000 total compensation

Svp Ibm Watson Group, Michael D. (Mike) Rhodin, age 57, $630,000 total compensation

Svp Ibm Systems, Thomas W. (Tom) Rosamilia, age 57

Svp Global Markets, Bruno V. Di Leo, age 60

Svp Ibm Analytics, Robert J. (Bob) Picciano, age 59

Svp And Cfo, James J. Kavanaugh, age 51

Svp Ibm Industry Platforms, Bridget A. van Kralingen, age 54, $665,000 total compensation

Svp Ibm Global Technology Services, Martin Jetter, age 58, $650,000 total compensation

Cio, Fletcher Previn

Vice President Information Technology, Bryan Adair

Vice President Strategic Alliance And Chief Technologist Officer, Bernard Meyerson

Vice President, John Kirkwood

Vice President And Chief Technology Officer Distribution Sector, Cathy Lasser

Vice President Mergers And Acquisitions, Kareem Yusuf

Vice President Finance And Operations Ibm Channels, David Colistra

Vice President Finance And Director, James W Boyken

Executive Vice President, Surjit Chana

Vice President Marketing, Annie Cheung

Vice President And Partner, Srinivas Attili

Vice President Strategic Services, Randall Dalia

Vice President Telecommunications Industry Americas, Dave Mancl

Vice President Client Sales Ibm Digital Sales North America, Gregory Tavalsky

Vice President Of Global Sales Operations, Dzung Bui

Vice President Software Business Partners And Midmarket, Mark Register

Vice President Mkt Channels Websphere, Kristen Lauria

Vice President Operations, Emilio Griman

Vice President North America Microelectronics Sales, David Faircloth

Vice President Sales, Arlene Garcia

Vice President Human Resources Sales Incentive Compensation, Richard Rabjohn

Vice President Business Development, Mark Bytner

Vice President Marketing And Communications, Robyn Bennett

Vice President Semiconductor Research And Development Center, Gary Patton

Vice President Ar Bcs, Christine Kinser

Vice President Technology, Jay Cook

Vice President, David Simms

Vice President Integrated Marketing Communications, Ed Abrams

Vice President Marketing And Communications, Maria Reeves Hayes

Ibm Fellow Global Technology Services Vice President, Luba Cherbakov

Senior Vice President Marketing Storage Technologies, Jim Kely

Vice President Partner Enablement, William Bill Liebler

Senior Vice President, Bob Moffat

Vice President Iseries Marketing, Peter Bingaman

Vice President Information Security Strategy, John Hsieh

Vice President Workforce Strategy, Domenic Tripoli

Senior Vice President Human Resources, Jonathan R Zalisk

Vice President Ibm Enterprise Storage Ds8870 And Tape, Calline Sanchez

Vice President Manager Director, Christopher Goudreau

Vice President Marketing And Business Development, Gregory Adams

Vice President Of Global Community Initiatives, Paula Baker

Vice President Information Technology, Dennis Jay

Assistant Vice President Services Overall, Jen Noble

Worlwide Vice President Of Sales Systems And Tech, Bob Hoey

Vice President Sales, Peter Andino

Vice President Marketing Software Group, Buell Duncan

Vice President Product Management Watson Health, Cory Wiegert

Vice President Global Lead Account Partner General Manager, Donna Satterfield

Vice President Security Growth Initiatives Security Services, Shelley Westman

Vice President Sales And Marketing Western Region, Scott Ferber

Vice President For Software Standards And Cloud Co, Angel Thompson

Vice President Of Marketing Communication, Lisa Baird

Vice President Partner Enablement, Bill Liebler

Vice President Diversity Employee Experience, Patricia Lewis

Vice President Of Marketing, Katharyn White

Vice President Of Sales: East Smb, John Schultz

Vice President And Chief Techn, Jason Wilkinson

Vice President Of Strategy Global Business Services, Ian Watson

Vice President Of Supply Chain Management, Tom Edwards

Vice President And Treasurer, Jesse J Greene

Senior Vice President Worldwide Sales Netezza Product And Services, Ray Tacoma

Senior Vice President And Trust Officer, George Araujo

Vice President Business Development Its, Anil Philip

Vice President Marketing Ibm Security, Lindsey Lurie

Vice President Development Websphere, Buff Jones

Vice President Cloud Services North America, Philippe Oliva

Vice President Strategic Business Growth Markets Unit, Eduardo Joia

Vice President Deep Computing, Dave Turek

Vice President Bi Solutions, Karen Parrish

Vice President And General Manager Strategic Sourcing, Joseph Msays

Vice President Zseries Software Sales Swg, Raymond Jones

Vice President And Partner Ibm Watson Health Consulting Group, Matt Porta

Vice President Software Sales Strategy And Transformation, Robert Guidotti

Vice President Integrated Marketing For The Ibm Software Group, Mark Rosen

Assistant To John Manasso General Manager Kathy Bennett Vice President, Alexandria Kornegay

Vice President Marketing, Joe Damassa

Vice President Global Logistics, Gregory Smith

Michael Kula Vice President Barbara Kerr, Karen Karriker

Vice President C And N Global Development, Janice McGinty-polito

Secretary To Chris King Vice President Of Wired Comm, Patti Downey

Vice President Technology Solutions, Jing Shyr

Vice President, Janet Dahlberg

Vice President Of Global Strategy Business Partner And Midmarket, Valmor Bratz

Vice President Treasurer, Jeffrey Serkes

Vice President Quality And Operations Microelectronics Division, Kathleen Hall

Vice President Workforce Communications, Mary Barton

Vice President Of Systems And Technology Developme, Dexter Henderson

Vice President Ww Solution Sales, John Parillo

Vice President Woldwide Sales And Marketing, Lou D'Ambrosio

Vice President Human Resources Operations, Robert Gonzales

Vice President Systems And Software Products????????integrated Supply Chain, Stu Reed

Vice President, William May

Vice President Of Sensor And Actuator Solutions, Robert Mayberry

Vice President Of Global Midmarket, Crystal Holmes

Vice President, Mark O'Riley

Senior Vice President, Nicholas Donofrio

Vice President Strategy Business Performance Management, Hassan Khorshid

Chief Information Officer And Senior Vice President Of Information Technology, Michael Harkins

Vice President, Federico Castellano

Vice President Marketing Ibm Americas, Diane Brink

Vice President Global Information Technology Infra, John Whittington

Vice President Distributors And Influencers, Kevin Quarantello

Vice President, Herschel Weintraub

Vice President Worldwide Customer Support, Bill Foster

Vice President Tivoli, Paul Gigg

Vice President Aim Business Development Ibm Software Group, Lorenzo De La Vega

Vice President Of Technology Distinguished Engineer, George Welleck

Vice President, Harvey Ezrol

Vice President Partner Bcs, Mike Askew

Vice President Americas Custimer Fulfillment, Annette Haile

Vice President Marketing, Brent Bussell

Vice President Energy And Utilities Global Technology Services, Robert Miller

Vice President Support And Services Platform Computing, Andrew Giblon

Vice President Xseries Bladecenter And Retail Store Solutions Development, Jeffrey Benck

Vice President Horizon Transition And Transformation, Ron Atkins

Vice President For Worldwide Information Management Marketing, David Laverty

Vice President Bd And Strategy, Jim Liang

Vice President, Charles Varvaro

Vice President, Sanjeev Gosavi

Vice President, Rich Branch

Vice President Sales And Marketing, Louis Gerstner

Vice President Of Human Resources, Jonathan Schoonmaker

Vice President Human Resources, Mary Murphy

Vice President Remote Technical Support Global Technology Services, Hallie Myers

Vice President, Nicolas Sekkaki

Vice President Client Insights, Ari Sheinkin

Vice President Corporate Development And Strategy, B J Johnson

Vice President Strategic Alliances, Lester McHargue

Vice President Marketing And Strategy, Andrew Elix

Vice President Bpo, Melissa Amerson

Senior Vice President It, Linda Sanford

Vice President, Chew Guan

Vice President Corporate Strategy, John Metzger

Vice President Human Resource, James Carney

Vice President Marketing, Linda Ryan

Assistant Vice President, Steven Kalmar

Auditors: PricewaterhouseCoopers LLP

LOCATIONS

HQ: International Business Machines Corp
One New Orchard Road, Armonk, NY 10504
Phone: 914 499-1900   **Fax:** 914 765-4190
Web: www.ibm.com

2017 Sales

	$ mil.	% of total
Americas	37,479	47
Europe/Middle East/Africa	24,345	30
Asia Pacific	16,970	21
Total	**79,139**	**100**

PRODUCTS/OPERATIONS

2017 Sales

	$ mil.	% of total
Services	50,709	64
Sales	26,715	34
Financing	1,715	2
Total	**79,139**	**100**

2017 Sales

% of total	$ mill
Technology Services & Cloud Platforms	44
Cognitive Solutions	23
Global Business Services	21
Systems	10
Global financing	2
Other	-
Total	**100**

Selected Services

Business services
  Application management
  E-business
  Strategic consulting
  Systems integration
Financing
Technology services
  Business process outsourcing
  Infrastructure
  Maintenance
  Outsourcing
  Software integration
  Systems management
  Web hosting
Training

Selected Products

Printing systems
Servers
Software
  Application development
  Database and data management
  E-commerce
  Graphics and multimedia
  Groupware
  Networking and communication
  Operating systems
  Product life cycle management
  Security
  Speech recognition
  System management
  Transaction system
  Web application servers
Storage
  Hard drive systems
  Optical libraries
  Storage networking
  Tape drives systems and libraries

Selected Acquisitions

Cloudigo 2017
Agile 3 Solutions 2017
Vivant Digital 2017
XCC Web Content & Custom Apps Extension 2017
The Weather Company 2016
Truven Health Analytics 2016
Sanovi Technologies 2016
Resource/Ammirati 2016
ecx International AG 2016
Optevia Limited 2016
Bluewolf Group 2016
Resilient Systems 2016
EZ Legacy 2016
Promontory Financial Group 2016
Alchemy API (2015 data collection and analysis)
Lighthouse Security (2014 cloud computing)
Cloudant (2014 cloud computing)
Silverpop (2014 cloud computing)
CrossIdeas (2014 security software)
Aspera (2013 high-speed data transfer)
SoftLayer (2013 cloud-computing infrastructure)
Fiberlink Communications (2013 mobile management)
Xtify (2013 cloud-based mobile messaging)
Kenexa (2012 cloud-based recruiting and talent management)
Tealeaf Technology (2012 customer experience analytics software)
Vivisimo (2012 analytics software)
TRIRIGA (2011 real estate management software)
Netezza (2010 data storage and analysis devices)
BLADE Network Technologies (2010; network servers switches and software)
OpenPages (2010 financial risk and compliance management software)
Clarity Systems (2010 financial data management software)
PSS Systems (2010 legal software)
Unica (2010 enterprise marketing software)
Storwize (2010 data compression software)
Sterling Commerce (2010 business integration software)
Datacap (2010 document digitization and data management software)
Coremetrics (2010 Web analytics software)
BigFix (2010 corporate security software)
Lombardi (2010 business process management software)
SPSS (2009 enterprise data analysis software)
ILOG (2008 enterprise resource management software)
Telelogic (2008 embedded systems software)
Cognos (2008 business intelligence software)
Softek Storage Solutions (2007 storage management software)
NovusCG (2007 enterprise resource planning software)
DataMirror (2007 data integration software)
WebDialogs (2007 Web conferencing services)
Princeton Softech (2007 data management software)
Watchfire (2007 website management software)
Vallent (2007 network management software)
Consul Risk Management (2007 risk management software)

COMPETITORS

AWS	Hewlett Packard
Accenture	Enterprise
Alcatel-Lucent	Hitachi
Apple Inc.	Infosys
BMC Software	Intel
CA Inc.	Lexmark
Capgemini	Microsoft
Cisco Systems	Motorola Solutions
Cognizant Tech	NEC
Solutions	NTT DATA
Computer Sciences	Novell
Corp.	Oracle
Dell	Panasonic Corp
Deloitte Consulting	Ricoh Company
Deloitte Global	SAP
Services	Sony
EMC	TSMC
Epson	Tata Consultancy
Ericsson	Texas Instruments
Fujitsu	Toshiba
GE	Unisys
Google	Wipro Technologies
HCL Technologies	

HISTORICAL FINANCIALS

Company Type: Public

Income Statement

FYE: December 31

	REVENUE ($ mil.)	NET INCOME ($ mil.)	NET PROFIT MARGIN	EMPLOYEES
12/17	79,139	5,753	7.3%	366,600
12/16	79,919	11,872	14.9%	380,300
12/15	81,741	13,190	16.1%	377,757
12/14	92,793	12,022	13.0%	379,592
12/13	99,751	16,483	16.5%	431,212
Annual Growth	(5.6%)	(23.1%)	—	(4.0%)

2017 Year-End Financials

Debt ratio: 37.35%	No. of shares (mil.): 922
Return on equity: 32.10%	Dividends
Cash ($ mil.): 11,972	Yield: 0.0%
Current ratio: 1.33	Payout: 96.0%
Long-term debt ($ mil.): 39,837	Market value ($ mil.): 141,481

	STOCK PRICE ($) FY Close	P/E High/Low		Earnings	Dividends	Book Value
12/17	153.42	29	23	6.14	5.90	19.08
12/16	165.99	14	9	12.38	5.50	19.29
12/15	137.62	13	10	13.42	5.00	14.77
12/14	160.44	17	13	11.90	4.25	11.98
12/13	187.57	14	11	14.94	3.70	21.62
Annual Growth	(4.9%)	—	—	(19.9%)	12.4%	(3.1%)

International Paper Co

International Paper (IP) is one of the world's largest manufacturers of printing papers. Products include uncoated paper used in printers market pulp for making towels and tissues and coated paper and uncoated bristols (heavyweight art paper). In the US IP is #1 in containerboard production 80% of which is used in industrial corrugated boxes. A consumer packaging arm makes board to box cosmetics and food. IP owns recycling plants mainly in the US and a pulp and paper business in Russia via a 50/50 venture with Ilim Holding.

Operations

IP operates in four segments: Industrial Packaging (67% of net sales) Printing Papers (19%) Consumer Packaging (9%) and Global Cellulose Fibers (5%).

Industrial Packaging is the largest manufacturer of containerboard in the US with a production capacity of more than 13 million tons annually. Products include linerboard medium whitetop recycled linerboard recycled medium and saturating kraft.

Printing Papers produces printing and writing papers and Consumer Packaging makes solid bleached sulfate board with an annual US production capacity of about 1.2 million tons. Global Cellulose Fibers' product portfolio includes fluff market and specialty pulps.

Geographic Reach

IP has manufacturing operations in Asia Europe Latin America North America Africa the Middle East and Russia. In the US it operates nearly 30 pulp paper and packaging mills roughly 170 converting and packaging plants more than 15 recycling plants and three bag facilities. In Europe Asia Latin America and South America the company operates 16 pulp paper and packaging mills roughly 70 converting and packaging plants and two recycling plants.

The US is by far its largest market representing nearly 75% of its total sales each year. EMEA is its second-largest market generating around 15% followed by the Asia/Pacific almost 5%.

Sales and Marketing

IP?s products are used in copiers desktop and laser printers and digital imaging food cosmetics pharmaceuticals filtration construction material paints and coatings. End-use applications include advertising and promotional materials such as brochures pamphlets greeting cards books annual reports and direct mail.

Financial Performance

IP has experienced revenue declines the last three years. Its revenues dipped 6% from $22.4 billion in 2015 to $21.1 billion in 2016. The declines were driven by a 34% drop in Consumer Packaging sales. In North America coated paperboard sales volumes in 2016 for this segment were lower than in 2015 primarily due to IP's exit from the coated bristols market. Average sales price realizations also decreased year over year due to competitive pressures.

IP's profits have fluctuated over the years; after rising $938 million in 2015 profits declined 5% to $904 million in 2016. The erosion of profits was attributed to an operating loss of $180 million stemming from its Global Cellulose Fibers segment which recognized lower average sales price realizations and mix higher operating costs and higher maintenance outage costs throughout 2016.

While changes in key cash operating costs — such as energy raw material and transportation costs — do have an effect on IP's operating cash flow the company believes its focus on pricing and cost controls has improved its cash flow generation over an operating cycle. Focusing on these key factors IP's cash flows from operations remained consistent in 2015 and 2016 hovering around the $2.5 billion mark for both years.

Strategy

As the world's biggest paper company IP has experienced a sharp decline in demand as more media is consumed digitally. In order to get back on track IP is focused on products that are spiking in other markets. It has zeroed in on the aging baby boomers generation as the adult diaper market is predicted to explode in the years ahead. As a global maker of fluff — a primary ingredient in adult incontinence products — IP is poised to take advantage of this swiftly growing market. It already took steps to strengthen its capabilities in this area through the $2.2 billion purchase of Canada-based Weyerhaeuser's pulp business in late 2016. After the purchase it formed its new Global Cellulose Fibers segment as a springboard for future growth.

Mergers and Acquisitions

In late 2016 IP added a new operating segment when it purchased Canada-based Weyerhaeuser's pulp business for $2.2 billion in cash. The company combined the newly acquired business with its own legacy pulp operations to form its Global Cellulose Fibers segment. The acquisition included five pulp mills and two converting facilities that produce fluff pulp softwood pulp and specialty pulp products for a number of consumer applications including diapers other hygiene products tissue and textiles. Perhaps more importantly the purchase strengthened IP's position in the rapidly growing adult incontinence products market.

HISTORY

In 1898 nearly 20 northeastern pulp and paper firms consolidated to lower costs. The resulting International Paper had 20 mills in Maine Massachusetts New Hampshire New York and Vermont. The mills relied on forests in New England and Canada for wood pulp. When Canada enacted legislation to stop the export of pulpwood in 1919 International Paper formed Canadian International Paper.

During the 1940s and 1950s the company bought Agar Manufacturing (shipping containers 1940) Single Service Containers (Pure-Pak milk containers 1946) and Lord Baltimore Press (folding cartons 1958). It diversified in the 1960s and 1970s buying Davol (hospital products 1968; sold to C. R. Bard 1980) American Central (land development 1968; sold to developers 1974) and General Crude Oil (gas and oil 1975; sold to Mobil Oil 1979).

Decades later International Paper picked up Shorewood Packaging for $850 million in 2000. That year it made an unsolicited $6.2 billion bid for Champion International— which had previously agreed to be acquired by UPM-Kymmene— igniting a bidding war. UPM withdrew its offer however and International Paper acquired Champion for about $9.6 billion.

After surviving the Great Recession IP made one of its most significant acquisitions to date in 2012 when it acquired Temple-Inland one of North America's top producers of corrugated packaging in a transaction valued at $4.5 billion.

EXECUTIVES

National Account Manager, Todd J Taylor

Svp Human Resources Government Relations And Global Citizenship, Thomas G. (Tom) Kadien, age 62, $629,167 total compensation

Svp Consumer Packaging, Catherine I. Slater, age 54

Svp Industrial Packaging The Americas, Timothy S. (Tim) Nicholls, age 57, $710,000 total compensation

Chairman And Ceo, Mark S. Sutton, age 57, $1,200,000 total compensation

Svp Manufacturing Technology Ehs And Global Sourcing, Tommy S. Joseph, age 58, $600,000 total compensation

Svp Pulp, Jean-Michel Ribieras, age 55, $420,000 total compensation

Svp And Cfo, Glenn R. Landau, age 49

Svp Paper The Americas, W. Michael Amick, age 54, $500,000 total compensation

Svp And President Europe The Middle East Africa And Russia, John V. Sims, age 55

Svp North American Container, Gregory T. Wanta, age 52

Svp Global Cellulose Fibers, Jean-Michel Ribiéras, age 55

National Account Manager, Jennifer Mugavero

Vp Information Technology, Frank Bevan

Vice President Supply Chain North American
Papers Pulp And Coated Paperboard, Fred Towler
Svp Corporate Development, Carleton Ealy
National Account Manager, Doug Arters
Vice President And General Manager Xpedx
Illinois Division, Thomas Plath
National Account Manager, Thomas Hendricks
Vice President West Area Nac, Gary Gavin
Vice President Pulp, John Fisher
National Sales Manager, Tom Jackson
Vice President, Pamela Hollingsworth
Vice President Mill Operations, Anitra Collins
Vice President Talent Management And Corporate
Human Resources, Shiela P Vinczeller
Vp Industrial Packaging Group Strategy And
Finance, September Blane
Vice President, Pat Leggett
National Accounts Manager, Michael T Murphy
Senior Vice President Consumer Pkg, Catherine I
Slater
Senior Vice President, Debbie Ellington
National Accounts Manager, Mark Mang
National Account Manager, Mike Nelson
Svp Paper The Americas, W Michael Amick Jr
Board Member, Stacey Mobley
Auditors: DELOITTE & TOUCHE LLP

LOCATIONS

HQ: International Paper Co
6400 Poplar Avenue, Memphis, TN 38197
Phone: 901 419-7000
Web: www.internationalpaper.com

2016 Sales

	$ mil.	% of total
Americas		
US	15,918	76
Other countries	1,581	7
EMEA	2,862	14
Pacific Rim & Asia	718	3
Total	21,079	100

PRODUCTS/OPERATIONS

2016 Sales

	$ mil.	% of total
Industrial packaging	14,191	67
Printing papers	4,058	19
Consumer packaging	1,954	9
Global Cellulose Fibers	1,092	5
Adjustments	(216)	-
Total	21,079	100

Selected Operations and Products

Consumer Packaging
Cold cups and lids
Consumer-ready packaging (Shorewood Packaging
folding carton set-up box)
Folding carton board
Food buckets and lids
Hot cups and lids
Milk container and lids
Starcote tobacco board
Distribution North America (xpedx)
Building services and away-from-home markets with
facility supplies
Commercial printers with printing papers and graphic
pre-press printing presses post press equipment
Manufacturers with packaging supplies and equipment
Warehousing and delivery services
Industrial Packaging
Automotive packaging
Corrugated pallet
Die-cut package
Flapless
Kraft linerboard
Laminated bulk bin
Liquid bulk
Litho lamination
Medium paper
Retail displays
Saturating kraft
Slotted container
White top liner

Papers
HP (Hewlett-Packard) home and commercial papers
Office papers
Pulp
Fluff pulp
Paper and tissue pulp
Recycling products
Old corrugated containers and kraft corrugated
cuttings
Old newspaper

COMPETITORS

Amcor	M-real
Cascades Inc.	Mondi
Domtar	Nippon Paper
ENCE Energia y	Packaging Corp. of
Celulosa SA	America
Environmental Mill &	Smurfit Kappa
Supply	Stora Enso
Georgia-Pacific	UPM-Kymmene
Louisiana-Pacific	

HISTORICAL FINANCIALS

Company Type: Public

Income Statement

				FYE: December 31
	REVENUE ($ mil.)	NET INCOME ($ mil.)	NET PROFIT MARGIN	EMPLOYEES
12/17	21,743	2,144	9.9%	56,000
12/16	21,079	904	4.3%	55,000
12/15	22,365	938	4.2%	56,000
12/14	23,617	555	2.4%	58,000
12/13	29,080	1,395	4.8%	69,000
Annual Growth	(7.0%)	11.3%	—	(5.1%)

2017 Year-End Financials

Debt ratio: 32.91%
Return on equity: 39.47%
Cash ($ mil.): 1,018
Current ratio: 1.62
Long-term debt ($ mil.): 10,846

No. of shares (mil.): 412
Dividends
Yield: 0.0%
Payout: 36.3%
Market value ($ mil.): 23,926

	STOCK PRICE ($) FY Close	P/E High/Low		PER SHARE ($) Earnings	Dividends	Book Value
12/17	57.94	11	10	5.13	1.86	15.79
12/16	53.06	25	15	2.18	1.78	10.56
12/15	37.70	26	16	2.23	1.64	9.42
12/14	53.58	43	35	1.29	1.45	12.18
12/13	49.03	16	13	3.11	1.25	18.58
Annual Growth	4.3%	—	—	13.3%	10.5%	(4.0%)

Interpublic Group of Companies Inc.

The Interpublic Group of Companies is one of
the world's largest advertising and marketing services conglomerates. Its flagship creative agencies
include McCann Worldgroup and Lowe & Partners
while such firms as Deutsch and Hill Holliday are
leaders in the US advertising business. Interpublic
also offers direct marketing media services and
public relations through such agencies as Initiative
and Weber Shandwick. Its largest have clients included General Motors Johnson & Johnson Microsoft Samsung and Unilever.

HISTORY

Standard Oil advertising executive Harrison Mc-
Cann opened the H. K. McCann Company in 1911
and signed Standard Oil of New Jersey (later
Exxon) as his first client. McCann's ad business
boomed as the automobile became an integral part
of American life. His firm merged with Alfred Erickson's agency (created 1902) in 1930 forming
the McCann-Erickson Company. At the end of the
decade the firm hired Marion Harper a top Yale
graduate as a mailroom clerk. Harper became president in 1948.

Harper began acquiring other ad agencies and
by 1961 controlled more than 20 companies. That
year he unveiled a plan to create a holding company that would let the ad firms operate separately
allowing them to work on accounts for competing
products but giving them the parent firm's financial
and information resources. He named the company
Interpublic Inc. after a German research company
owned by the former H. K. McCann Co. The conglomerate continued expanding and was renamed
The Interpublic Group of Companies in 1964.
Harper's management capabilities weren't up to
the task however and the company soon faced
bankruptcy. In 1967 the board replaced him with
Robert Healy who saved Interpublic and returned
it to profitability. The company went public in
1971.

The 1970s were fruitful years for Interpublic;
its ad teams created memorable campaigns for
Coke ("It's the Real Thing" and "Have a Coke and
a Smile") and Miller Beer ("Miller Time" and Miller
Lite ads). After Philip Geier became chairman in
1980 the company gained a stake in Lowe
Howard-Spink (1983; it later became The Lowe
Group) and bought Lintas International (1987).
Interpublic bought the rest of The Lowe Group in
1990.

Interpublic bought Western International Media
(now known as Initiative) and Ammirati & Puris
(which was merged with Lintas to form Ammirati
Puris Lintas) in 1994. As industry consolidation
picked up in 1996 Interpublic kept pace with acquisitions of PR company Weber Group and Draft-
Worldwide. Interpublic bought a majority stake in
artist management and film production company
Addis-Wechsler & Associates (now Industry Entertainment) in 1997 and later formed sports marketing and management group Octagon.

Interpublic acquired US agencies Carmichael
Lynch and Hill Holliday Connors Cosmopulos in
1998. It also boosted its PR presence with its purchase of International Public Relations (UK) the
parent company of public relations networks
Shandwick and Golin/Harris. Interpublic strengthened its position in the online world in 1999 when
it bought 20% of Stockholm-based Internet services company Icon Medialab International. That
year the company merged agencies Ammirati and
Lowe & Partners Worldwide to form Lowe Lintas
& Partners Worldwide (in 2002 they changed the
name to just Lowe & Partners Worldwide).

Interpublic bought market research firm NFO
Worldwide for $580 million in 2000 and merged
Weber Public Relations with Shandwick International to form Weber Shandwick Worldwide one
of the world's largest PR firms. Later that year the
company bought ad agency Deutsch for about
$250 million. John Dooner took the position of
chairman and CEO at the end of the year after
Geier resigned. His first move proved a big one:
Interpublic acquired True North Communications
for $2.1 billion in stock in 2001.

The honeymoon was short lived; facing a recession the mounting debt from its buying spree
and with the revelation of accounting discrepancies
at McCann-Erickson WorldGroup (renamed Mc-
Cann Worldgroup in 2004) Dooner stepped aside

as chairman and CEO in 2003. Interpublic chose vice chairman David Bell (former CEO of True North) as Dooner's replacement. After almost two years of work to improve Interpublic's balance sheet Bell was replaced by former MONY Group chief Michael Roth.

In 2005 Roth was tasked with straightening out Interpublic's financial controls and improving its balance sheet. Later that year the company revealed extensive bookkeeping problems primarily in its overseas operations leading to a financial restatement going back to 2000.

In order to simplify its operating structure in 2006 Interpublic integrated direct marketer Draft Inc. with advertising agency Foote Cone & Belding (forming DraftFCB). A year later it restructured its vast network of media brands to report under a single management structure (Mediabrands).

Looking to India in mid-2007 Interpublic bought all the shares of FCB Ulka a top-five ad agency in the country that operated from six offices. Interpublic integrated the Indian agency with its DraftFCB operations. At the same time it acquired the remaining 51% stake it didn't hold in Lintas India Private Limited at a cost of $50 million in cash and integrated it into its Lowe Worldwide network.

In 2010 Interpublic acquired Brazilian creative advertising strategy firm CUBOCC and London-based marketing agency Delaney Lund Knox Warren & Partners (DLKW). During 2011 the company acquired several marketing agencies. In early 2012 Interpublic obtained German consumer lifestyle agency Nicole Weber Communications (NWC) and UK-based digital and interactive agency FUSE.

EXECUTIVES

Svp And Managing Director, Terry D. Peigh
Chairman And Ceo, Michael I. Roth, age 72, $1,500,000 total compensation
Evp And Cfo, Frank Mergenthaler, age 57, $1,000,000 total compensation
Evp And Chief Strategy And Talent Officer, Philippe Krakowsky, age 56, $1,000,000 total compensation
Svp And Managing Director, Peter Leinroth
Svp General Counsel And Secretary, Andrew Bonzani, age 54, $800,000 total compensation
Svp Controller And Chief Accounting Officer, Christopher F. Carroll, age 51, $587,714 total compensation
Svp And Cio, John Halper
Svp And Chief Growth Officer, Simon Bond
Auditors: PricewaterhouseCoopers LLP

LOCATIONS

HQ: Interpublic Group of Companies Inc.
909 Third Avenue, New York, NY 10022
Phone: 212 704-1200
Web: www.interpublic.com

COMPETITORS

Dentsu	Omnicom
Dentsu Aegis	Publicis Groupe
Hakuhodo	WPP
Havas	

HISTORICAL FINANCIALS

Company Type: Public

Income Statement   FYE: December 31

	REVENUE ($ mil.)	NET INCOME ($ mil.)	NET PROFIT MARGIN	EMPLOYEES
12/17	7,882	579	7.3%	50,200
12/16	7,846	608	7.8%	49,800
12/15	7,613	454	6.0%	49,200
12/14	7,537	477	6.3%	47,400
12/13	7,122	267	3.8%	45,400
Annual Growth	2.6%	21.2%	—	2.5%

2017 Year-End Financials

Debt ratio: 10.81%	No. of shares (mil.): 383
Return on equity: 27.45%	Dividends
Cash ($ mil.): 790	Yield: 0.0%
Current ratio: 0.97	Payout: 49.3%
Long-term debt ($ mil.): 1,285	Market value ($ mil.): 7,725

	STOCK PRICE ($) FY Close	P/E High/Low		PER SHARE ($) Earnings	Dividends	Book Value
12/17	20.16	17	12	1.46	0.72	5.74
12/16	23.41	16	13	1.49	0.60	5.15
12/15	23.28	21	16	1.09	0.48	4.87
12/14	20.77	18	14	1.12	0.38	5.11
12/13	17.70	28	18	0.61	0.30	5.22
Annual Growth	3.3%	—	—	24.4%	24.5%	2.4%

INTL FCStone Inc.

Going global is the name of the game for commodities broker INTL FCStone. The company specializes in the physical trade of commodities such as corn gold renewable fuels and livestock though its primary activities are hedging securities trading and clearing. It offers clearing and execution services of listed futures and options on futures and serves as a market-maker for some 5000 foreign securities. It operates in international markets offering commodity risk management consulting asset management and commodity financing. Its client base includes financial institutions corporations and charitable organizations in the US and abroad.

Operations

INTL FCStone garners a diverse revenue stream across five operating segments. Its global platform provides execution market intelligence and post-trade services across all its asset classes and markets.

Although the Physical Commodities segment accounts for 99% of overall revenue it is the only segment that has significant operating costs (the costs of traded commodities) and therefore contributes only about 5% of operating revenue. It provides trading and hedging capabilities for precious metals and physical agricultural and energy commodities and commits its own capital for buying and selling on a spot and forward basis. The company's preferred performance metric is operating revenue as it removes dramatic multi-year price swings in commodities.

The CES segment matches customer trades with the relevant commodity or stock exchange collects and manages customer margin deposits and accounts for and reports on transactions for all major futures and securities exchanges globally. CES provides about 35% of INTL's operating revenue.

Commodity pricing is susceptible to a great many variables and therefore producers consumers and investors institute hedging strategies to soften the vagaries of the financial risk. The Commercial Hedging segment provides assesses risk and designs and executes hedging strategies particularly for agricultural and energy commodities and base metals. The segment produces about 30% of INTL's operating revenue.

Accounting for some 20% of operating revenue the Securities segment facilitates cross-border currency stock share and debt instrument trades.

Global Payments (which contributes around 10% to operating revenue) provides cross-border money movement services to banks businesses charities and non-government and government organizations in approximately 170 countries and 140 currencies.

Geographic Reach

New York City-headquartered INTL FCStone serves 20000 customers in more than 130 countries around the world. The company operates through a network of more than 20 offices in the US. Just as many international offices support the company's business in the rest of the world with about half of them in the commodity-active region of South America. London and Dublin house its European facilities Sydney hosts its Australian operations and Shanghai Beijing Singapore and Hong Kong are home to its Asia offices.

The US provides about 70% of INTL's operating revenue. Europe and South America account for approximately 20% and 10% of operating revenue. Despite contributing less than 5% to operating revenue Asia represents about 95% of the company's total revenue.

Sales and Marketing

With more than 20000 customers INTL FCStone utilizes a direct sales force of risk management consultants who are organized by commodity verticals such as agriculture energy metals and livestock.

Its clients include commercial customers asset managers broker-dealers insurance companies brokers institutional and professional investors commercial and investment banks and governmental and non-governmental organizations.

Financial Performance

While INTL FCStone produces eye-popping revenue numbers – almost $28 billion in its fiscal 2018 – its preferred performance metric is operating revenue as it removes dramatic multi-year price swings in commodities. Operating revenue has risen year after year since 2014 from roughly $80 million in FY2009 to about $975 million in FY2017.

For 2018 revenue was $27.6 billion; operating revenue was $975.8 million. Operating revenue grew 24% from the prior year owing to record performance in all five of the company's segments. The growth was spurred by periods of increased market volatility that bolstered client activity and widened spreads as well as higher short-term interest rates and average client balances.

INTL's net income ended 2018 at $56 million regaining ground lost in 2017 when it fell to $6 million from $55 million the previous year. The 2017 losses stemmed from charges recorded to allow for doubtful accounts related to bad debt incurred by its coal business in Singapore. Gains in 2018 were driven by operating revenue growth and bad debt reduction.

Cash at the end of the year was $342.3 million an increase of $27.4 million from the prior year. Operations used $74 million and financing activities added $120.9 million. Investing activities used $15.4 million for property and equipment purchases and net acquisitions. Currency fluctuations reduced stores another $4.1 million.

Strategy

INTL FCStone is focused on broadening its customer base in new markets by offering more services. It continues to improve platforms and tools for internal and customer-facing functions. In its fiscal 2018 INTL expanded its OTC interest rates swap trading and advisory offerings to include cap and floor options on the London Interbank Offered Rate (LIBOR). Earlier that year the company soft-launched FXePrice a web-based platform that allows its local currency liquidity providers to feed the company local currency live prices electronically. That year the company also partnered with Allfunds Bank to gain direct access to Allfunds' offshore mutual fund distribution platform. The platform provides INTL's customers with access to more than 57000 offshore funds.

INTL is also expanding its offerings and footprint through acquisitions. In November 2018 the company acquired Luxembourg-based Carl Kliem an independent interdealer broker providing foreign exchange interest rate and fixed income products to more than 400 institutional customers throughout the EU. In January 2019 the company purchased the US-based broker-dealer subsidiary of GMP Capital GMP Securities. The deal extended INTL's fixed income product offerings to include high yield convertible and emerging market debt and brought more than 2400 institutional customers in the company's fold.

Mergers and Acquisitions

INTL FCStone bought the US-based broker-dealer GMP Securities a subsidiary of GMP International Holdings in January 2019. The purchase expanded INTL's fixed income product portfolio to include high yield convertible and emerging market debt gave the company more than 2400 institutional customers.

In November 2018 INTL acquired Luxembourg-based interdealer broker Carl Kliem which provides foreign exchange interest rate and fixed income products to more than 400 institutional customers throughout the EU.

Company Background

INTL FCStone which traces its roots to 1924 was created after the 2009 merger of FCStone Group and International Assets Holding.

EXECUTIVES

President And Ceo, Sean M. O'Connor, age 56, $400,000 total compensation
Cfo, William J. (Bill) Dunaway, age 47, $275,000 total compensation
Coo, Xuong Nguyen, age 50, $325,000 total compensation
Chief Risk Officer, Tricia Harrod, age 59
Ceo Europe Middle East Africa And Asia, Philip A. Smith, age 46, $324,105 total compensation
Executive Chairman Europe Middle East Africa And Asia, Malcolm Wilde, age 67
Ceo Intl Fcstone Markets, Mark Maurer, age 42
Vice President Equity Trading, AL Barbella
Senior Vice President Base Metals Lead, Tom Gramlich
Vice President, Ryan Smith
Vice President Latin America Payments Division, Fernando Mazzanti
Senior Vice President, Emily Barnes
Chairman, John Radziwill
Board Member, Bruce Krehbiel
Board Member, Brent Bunte
Treasurer, Bruce Fields
Auditors: KPMG LLP

LOCATIONS

HQ: INTL FCStone Inc.
708 Third Avenue, Suite 1500, New York, NY 10017
Phone: 212 485-3500
Web: www.intlfcstone.com

2018 Sales

	% of total
US	6
Asia	93
Europe	1
South America	0
Other	0
Total	**100**

PRODUCTS/OPERATIONS

2018 Total Revenue

	% of total
Commercial Hedging	1
Global Payments	0
Securities	1
Clearing & Execution Services	1
Physical Commodities	97
Corporate unallocated	0
Total	**100**

Selected Subsidiaries

FCC Futures Inc.
INTL Asia Pte. Ltd.
INTL FCStone Pte. Ltd.
FCStone do Brazil Ltda.
FCStone Financial Inc.
FCStone Group
FCStone Merchant Services LLC
FCStone Paraguay S.R.L.
FCStone LLC
Gainvest Asset Management Ltd.
Gainvest S.A.
Gainvest Uruguay Asset Management S.A.
Gletir S.A.
INTL Capital S.A. (Argentina)
INTL CIBSA Sociedad de Bolsa S.A.
INTL Commodities DMCC
INTL Custody & Clearing Solutions Inc.
INTL FCStone (Europe) Ltd.
INTL FCStone Financial
INTL FCStone (Netherlands) B.V.
INTL Netherlands B.V.
INTL Participacoes Ltda.
SA Stone Investment Advisors Inc.
Westown Commodities LLC

COMPETITORS

ADM
BGC Partners
CAPIS
Citigroup Global Markets
Credit Suisse (USA)
Glencore
Goldman Sachs
Interactive Brokers
J.P. Morgan Clearing
Morgan Stanley
NEX
R.J. O'Brien
Rosenthal Collins
Susquehanna International Group LLP
Wedbush Securities

HISTORICAL FINANCIALS

Company Type: Public

Income Statement   FYE: September 30

	REVENUE ($ mil.)	NET INCOME ($ mil.)	NET PROFIT MARGIN	EMPLOYEES
09/18	27,542	55	0.2%	1,701
09/17	29,381	6	0.0%	1,607
09/16	14,726	54	0.4%	1,464
09/15	34,676	55	0.2%	1,231
09/14	34,011	19	0.1%	1,141
Annual Growth	**(5.1%)**	**30.2%**	**—**	**10.5%**

2018 Year-End Financials

Debt ratio: 4.54%   No. of shares (mil.): 18
Return on equity: 11.62%   Dividends
Cash ($ mil.): 1,213   Yield: —
Current ratio: 0.73   Payout: —
Long-term debt ($ mil.): —   Market value ($ mil.): 914

	STOCK PRICE ($) FY Close	P/E High/Low		PER SHARE ($) Earnings	Dividends	Book Value
09/18	48.32	19	13	2.87	0.00	26.72
09/17	38.32	138	107	0.31	0.00	24.02
09/16	38.85	13	8	2.90	0.00	23.53
09/15	24.69	13	6	2.87	0.00	21.11
09/14	17.32	21	17	0.98	0.00	18.29
Annual Growth	**29.2%**	**—**	**—**	**30.8%**	**—**	**9.9%**

Intuit Inc

Intuit?s fact is: It handles other people?s taxes ? and their bookkeeping and other financial management tasks. The company is a leading developer of software used for small business accounting (QuickBooks) and consumer tax preparation (TurboTax). Mint the online service helps manage personal finances and budgeting. Professional accountants boot up Intuit?s Lacerte ProSeries and Intuit Tax Online products. More than 70% of revenue comes from products hosted on Intuit?s servers what the company calls connected services. Intuit claims more than 61 million users for its products and services. Not surprisingly about half of annual revenue comes in the quarter that includes April 15.

Operations

Intuit generates half its sales from small business clients with consumers representing another 42%. Professional accountants — who use the company's Lacerte ProSeries and Intuit Tax Online products — account for the remainder of revenue.

Geographic Reach

California-based Intuit has offices in the US Australia Canada India Singapore and the UK. The company's software and services are available in the US Canada the UK Australia India and Singapore. International sales consistently account for less than 5% of Intuit's sales.

Sales and Marketing

Intuit relies on web marketing and targeted advertising such as search engine optimization and purchasing key words from major search engine companies; placing its mobile application in proprietary online stores (including Google's Play Store and Apple's App Store) direct-response mail and email campaigns telephone solicitations TV radio and print advertisements social media and coordinated promotional offers with major retailers. Its TurboTax tax preparation software is displayed prominently in stores such as Office Depot Best Buy and Sam's Club through April 15 each year. Intuit ramped up advertising spending to $480 million in 2017 (ended July) from $394 million in 2016.

Financial Performance

Intuit reported 2017 (ended July) sales of $5.2 billion up 10% from the prior year. Each segment posted revenue gains in 2017 paced by a 13% increase in the Small Business segment?s sales because of a 30% rise in Small Business Online Ecosystem revenue and changes to QuickBooks Desktop software products that were implemented in 2015. Consumer Tax sales increased 9% in 2017 on growth in TurboTax federal units and a shift to higher end products. ProConnect segment?s sale rose 2% in 2017.

Intuit?s net income fell to $971 million in 2017 from $979 million in 2016. The company had about $170 million income in 2015 from discontinued operations that was not repeated in 2016. Operating income rose 12% in 2017 from the year before.

Cash flow from operations rose to about $1.6 billion in 2017 from $1.5 billion in 2016.

Strategy

Intuit has declared it intends to double its small business customer base by 2019 and it wants to make sure that its products are accessible online and can be accessed via desktops laptops and mobile devices. It also wants accessibility through social websites such as online forums and social media sites. The company generated nearly three-quarters of its revenue from connected services in 2017 up from 50% nine years ago.

Intuit has turned its applications into platforms open its products to third-party applications that users can integrate with Intuit software such as QuickBooks to more closely meet their specific needs. American Express for example offers an app for its business credit card holders that transfers transactions automatically to the user?s Quick-Books Online account.

While the company sells more than 37 million units of its TurboTax do-it-yourself software Intuit wants to carve out a bigger spot in the assisted tax preparation market. Of the nearly 180 million annual returns filed in the US and Canada some 82 million are filed by professional accountants on behalf of clients. The company has added its own assistance to tax preparation with its Smart-Look service which connects preparers with Intuit experts. The company also offered a feature that connects small businesses that use QuickBooks with accountants. That has helped customer retention.

Further Intuit is investing more in artificial intelligence and machine learning to take advantage of the massive amounts of data in its systems to help consumer and businesses prepare tax returns more effectively.

Mergers and Acquisitions

In 2017 Intuit agreed to buy TSheets a platform that small and medium businesses self-employed and accountants use to automate time tracking and scheduling. The deal formalizes a deal that some customers of both companies have already done: about 12000 customers use QuickBooks and TSheets in tandem. By buying TSheets Intuit will create a more seamless experience for those users.

HISTORY

After earning his MBA from Harvard founder Scott Cook spent three years in marketing at Procter & Gamble and four years with consultancy Bain & Company before establishing Intuit in 1983. Research showed that consumers wanted an easy-to-use personal finance software package. Quicken was introduced in 1984.

Intuit was near collapse in 1986 when it received its first big order from software retailer Egghead.com. Intuit released QuickBooks in 1992 and went public in 1993. The next year it acquired a number of firms including tax preparation software developer ChipSoft which brought TurboTax onboard.

In 1995 Microsoft's $2 billion bid to buy Intuit was halted by a Justice Department antitrust lawsuit. Also that year Intuit launched an online banking service and forged its first ties with the Web by bundling a browser and free Internet access with Quicken. It sold its online banking and bill presentation business to CheckFree in 1997. In

1998 the company bought Lacerte Software a provider of software and services to tax professionals.

EXECUTIVES

Evp And Chief People Officer, Sherry Whiteley
Chairman And Ceo, Brad D. Smith, age 54, $1,000,000 total compensation
Svp General Counsel And Corporate Secretary, Laura A. Fennell, age 57, $575,000 total compensation
Evp And General Manager Small Business Group, Sasan K. Goodarzi, age 50, $625,000 total compensation
Evp And General Manager Proconnect Group, CeCe Morken
Svp And Cto, H. Tayloe Stansbury, age 57, $625,000 total compensation
Evp And General Manager Consumer Tax Group, Daniel A. (Dan) Wernikoff, age 46, $725,000 total compensation
Svp And General Manager Consumer Ecosystem Group, Al Ko
Evp And Chief Marketing And Sales Officer, Lucas Watson
Evp And Cfo, Michelle Clatterbuck, age 50
Senior Vice President And Chief Communications Officer, Rob Lanesey
Senior Vice President Product Development Intuit Proconnect Group, Marilyn Jones
Vice President Of Product Management, Barry Saik
Vp Of Platform And Core Services Chief Architect, Brian Ellison
Vice President Corporate Development, Erika Swanson
Senior Vice President And Chief Technology Officer, Tayloe Stansbury
Vice President Marketing, Patti Newcomer
Board Member, Raul Vazquez
Auditors: Ernst & Young LLP

LOCATIONS

HQ: Intuit Inc
  2700 Coast Avenue, Mountain View, CA 94043
Phone: 650 944-6000
Web: www.intuit.com

PRODUCTS/OPERATIONS

2017 Sales

	$ mil.	% of total
Small Business	2,597	50
Consumer Tax	2,143	41
ProConnect	437	9
Total	**5,177**	**100**

2017 Sales

	$ mil.	% of total
Product	1,376	27
Service and other	3,808	73
Total	**5,177**	**100**

Products and services

Individuals
Manage budgeting and taxes with confidence
Mint Budgeting
Quicken Personal Finance
QuickBooks Self-Employed
TurboTax Tax Preparation
Small Businesses
The tools you need to run your company
Checks & Supplies
Demandforce Marketing
Intuit Payroll Services
QuickBooks Business Finance
QuickBooks Payments
Accountants
Pro software for the range of client needs
Intuit Tax Online
Lacerte Pro Tax Software
ProSeries Pro Tax Software
QuickBooks for Accountants

COMPETITORS

ADP	JPMorgan Chase
Bank of America	Jackson Hewitt
CA Inc.	MYOB
CCH Incorporated	Microsoft Dynamics
Elavon	NetSuite
Fidelity National Information Services	Paychex
	SAP
First Data	Sage Group
Fiserv	Thomson Reuters
Global Payments	Universal Tax
H&R Block	Wells Fargo

HISTORICAL FINANCIALS

Company Type: Public

Income Statement

	REVENUE ($ mil.)	NET INCOME ($ mil.)	NET PROFIT MARGIN	FYE: July 31 EMPLOYEES
07/18	5,964	1,211	20.3%	8,900
07/17	5,177	971	18.8%	8,200
07/16	4,694	979	20.9%	7,900
07/15	4,192	365	8.7%	7,700
07/14	4,506	907	20.1%	8,000
Annual Growth	**7.3%**	**7.5%**	**—**	**2.7%**

2018 Year-End Financials

Debt ratio: 8.46%	No. of shares (mil.): 258
Return on equity: 65.32%	Dividends
Cash ($ mil.): 1,464	Yield: 0.7%
Current ratio: 1.14	Payout: 33.6%
Long-term debt ($ mil.): 388	Market value ($ mil.): 52,820

	STOCK PRICE ($) FY Close	P/E High/Low	PER SHARE ($) Earnings	Dividends	Book Value
07/18	204.24	46 28	4.64	1.56	9.10
07/17	137.21	38 28	3.72	1.36	5.30
07/16	110.99	31 21	3.69	1.20	4.50
07/15	105.77	83 60	1.28	1.00	8.40
07/14	81.97	26 20	3.12	0.76	10.80
Annual Growth	**25.6%**	**— —**	**10.4%**	**19.7%**	**(4.2%)**

Invesco DB Commodity Index Tracking Fund

EXECUTIVES

Prin, Sonja Olsen
Auditors: PricewaterhouseCoopers LLP

LOCATIONS

HQ: Invesco DB Commodity Index Tracking Fund
  c/o Invesco PowerShares Capital Management LLC,
  3500 Lacey Road, Suite 700, Downers Grove, IL 60515
Phone: 800 983-0903
Web: www.invescopowershares.com

Company Type: Public

Income Statement				FYE: December 31
	ASSETS ($ mil.)	NET INCOME ($ mil.)	INCOME AS % OF ASSETS	EMPLOYEES
12/17	2,263	(1)	—	—
12/16	2,559	(13)	—	—
12/15	2,011	(25)	—	—
12/14	4,948	(45)	—	—
12/13	6,799	(53)	—	—
Annual Growth	(24.0%)			

2017 Year-End Financials

Debt ratio: —
Return on equity: (-0.06%)
Cash ($ mil.): 5
Current ratio: —
Long-term debt ($ mil.): —

No. of shares (mil.): 136
Dividends
Yield: —
Payout: —
Market value ($ mil.): 2,259

	STOCK PRICE ($) FY Close	P/E High/Low	PER SHARE ($) Earnings	Dividends	Book Value
12/17	16.61	— —	(0.01)	0.00	16.63
12/16	15.84	— —	(0.09)	0.00	15.83
12/15	13.36	— —	(0.15)	0.00	13.35
12/14	18.45	— —	(0.21)	0.00	18.40
12/13	25.66	— —	(0.21)	0.00	25.61
Annual Growth	(10.3%)	— —	—	—	(10.2%)

Investar Holding Corp

Auditors: Ernst & Young LLP

LOCATIONS

HQ: Investar Holding Corp
7244 Perkins Road, Baton Rouge, LA 70808
Phone: 225 227-2222

HISTORICAL FINANCIALS

Company Type: Public

Income Statement				FYE: December 31
	ASSETS ($ mil.)	NET INCOME ($ mil.)	INCOME AS % OF ASSETS	EMPLOYEES
12/17	1,622	8	0.5%	258
12/16	1,158	7	0.7%	152
12/15	1,031	7	0.7%	951
12/14	879	5	0.6%	179
12/13	634	3	0.5%	171
Annual Growth	26.4%	26.8%	—	10.8%

2017 Year-End Financials

Debt ratio: 1.48%
Return on equity: 5.75%
Cash ($ mil.): 30
Current ratio: —
Long-term debt ($ mil.): —

No. of shares (mil.): 9
Dividends
Yield: 0.0%
Payout: 7.5%
Market value ($ mil.): 229

	STOCK PRICE ($) FY Close	P/E High/Low	PER SHARE ($) Earnings	Dividends	Book Value
12/17	24.10	26 20	0.96	0.07	18.15
12/16	18.65	18 12	1.10	0.04	15.88
12/15	17.60	18 14	0.97	0.03	15.05
12/14	13.85	15 13	0.93	0.01	14.24
Annual Growth	14.9%	— —	0.8%	51.1%	6.3%

Investors Bancorp Inc (New)

Investors Bancorp is the holding company for Investors Savings Bank which serves New Jersey and New York from more than 130 branch offices. Founded in 1926 the bank offers such standard deposit products as savings and checking accounts CDs money market accounts and IRAs. Nearly 40% of the bank's loan portfolio is made up of residential mortgages while multi-family loans and commercial real estate loans make up more than 50% combined. The bank also originates business industrial and consumer loans. Founded in 1926 Investors Bancorp's assets now exceed $20 billion.

Operations

About 86% of Investors Bancorp's revenue came from interest income from loans and loans held-for sale in 2014 while another 8% came from interest income on the bank's mortgage-backed securities municipal bonds and other debt. The remainder of its revenue came from fees and service charges (3%) and other miscellaneous income sources. Investors Bancorp boasted a staff of more than 1700 at the end of 2014.

Geographic Reach

Based in Short Hills New Jersey Investors Bancorp has more than 130 branches across New Jersey and New York. It also has lending offices in New York City Short Hills Spring Lake Newark Astoria and Brooklyn. Its operation center is in Iselin New Jersey.

Sales and Marketing

The company offers retail and commercial banking services to individuals professional service firms municipalities small and middle-market companies commercial and industrial firms and other businesses.

Financial Performance

Investors Bancorp's revenues and profits have been rising thanks to strong loan growth from bank acquisitions falling interest expenses on deposits and declining loan loss provisions as its loan portfolio's credit quality has improved with higher property valuations in the strengthened economy.

The bank's revenue jumped by 21% to a record $702.7 million in 2014 mostly thanks to loan asset growth stemming from the bank's 2014 acquisition of Gateway Community Financial.

Higher revenue and a continued decline in loan loss provisions in 2014 drove the bank's net income higher by 18% to a record $131.7 million. Investor Bancorp's operating cash levels spiked by 58% to $277.4 million for the year on higher cash earnings and favorable changes in its working capital.

Strategy

Investors Bancorp continues to expand its geographic reach in its core New Jersey and New York markets and boost its loan and deposit business mainly through select bank and branch acquisitions. Indeed the bank noted in 2015 that it had made eight bank or branch acquisitions since 2008 adding that they have counted for "a significant portion" of the bank's historic growth.

The company's 2014 and 2013 bank acquisitions bolstered its expansion in New Jersey into the suburbs of Philadelphia the boroughs of New York City the Nassau and Suffolk Counties on Long Island and historic markets throughout New Jersey.

Mergers and Acquisitions

In May 2016 Investors Bancorp agreed to purchase the $1 billion-asset The Bank of Princeton along with its 13 branches in the greater Princeton New Jersey and Philadelphia Pennsylvania areas. The added locations would grow Investors Bancorp's branch network by almost 10% to 156 branches in the Philadelphia to New York City corridor.

In January 2014 Investors Bancorp purchased Gateway Community Financial Corp along with its four branches in Gloucester County New Jersey. The deal added nearly $255 million in customer deposits and $195 million in new loan business to its books.

In December 2013 the company bought Roma Financial Corporation and its 26 branches in Burlington Ocean Mercer Camden and Middlesex counties in New Jersey. The deal added $1.34 billion in deposits and $991 million in loan assets while expanding the company's reach into the Philadelphia suburbs of New Jersey.

Company Background

In late 2012 the company acquired Marathon Banking Corporation (a subsidiary of Greece-based Piraeus Bank) for $135 million adding 13 branches in the New York metro area and more than doubling its branches in New York. The deal also would mark Investors Bancorp's entry into Manhattan and Staten Island.

EXECUTIVES

Sevp And Coo, Domenick A. Cama, age 62, $621,000 total compensation
President And Ceo, Kevin Cummings, age 63, $935,000 total compensation
Evp And Chief Lending Officer, Richard S. Spengler, age 56, $400,000 total compensation
Evp And Chief Retail Banking Officer, Paul Kalamaras, $375,000 total compensation
Svp And Cfo, Sean Burke
Senior Vice President, Jawad Chaudhry
Vice President Information Security Officer
Director Of Information Security, David Van
Vice President Systems, Charles Little
Chairman, Robert M. Cashill, age 75
Auditors: KPMG LLP

LOCATIONS

HQ: Investors Bancorp Inc (New)
101 JFK Parkway, Short Hills, NJ 07078
Phone: 973 924-5100
Web: www.myinvestorsbank.com

PRODUCTS/OPERATIONS

2014 Sales

	$ mil.	% of total
Interest		
Loans receivable and held-for-sale	603	86
Mortgage-backed securities	44	6
Federal Home Loan Bank stock	6	1
Municipal bonds & other debt	5	1
Other	0	-
Non-interest		
Fees & service charges	19	3
Gain on loan transaction	5	2
Others	17	1
Total	702	100

COMPETITORS

Bank of America	M&T Bank
Bank of New York Mellon	New York Community Bancorp
Citigroup	OceanFirst Financial
ConnectOne Bancorp	PNC Financial
Fulton Financial	

HISTORICAL FINANCIALS
Company Type: Public

Income Statement
FYE: December 31

	ASSETS ($ mil.)	NET INCOME ($ mil.)	INCOME AS % OF ASSETS	EMPLOYEES
12/17	25,129	126	0.5%	1,959
12/16	23,174	192	0.8%	1,829
12/15	20,888	181	0.9%	1,768
12/14	18,773	131	0.7%	1,708
12/13	15,623	112	0.7%	1,597
Annual Growth	12.6%	3.1%	—	5.2%

2017 Year-End Financials
Debt ratio: 17.75%
Return on equity: 4.06%
Cash ($ mil.): 618
Current ratio: —
Long-term debt ($ mil.): —

No. of shares (mil.): 306
Dividends
Yield: 0.0%
Payout: 76.7%
Market value ($ mil.): 4,249

	STOCK PRICE ($) FY Close	P/E High/Low	PER SHARE ($) Earnings	Dividends	Book Value
12/17	13.88	34 29	0.43	0.33	10.21
12/16	13.95	22 16	0.64	0.26	10.09
12/15	12.44	24 19	0.55	0.25	9.89
12/14	11.23	74 26	0.38	0.08	9.99
12/13	25.58	64 44	0.40	0.00	3.78
Annual Growth	(14.2%)	— —	2.1%	—	28.2%

IOWA FINANCE AUTHORITY

EXECUTIVES
Eo, David Jamison
Coo*, Steven Harvey
Coordinator, Amber Lewis
General Counsel, Mark Thompson
Accounting Manager, Michelle Thomas
General Manager, Carolann Jensen
Government Relations Director, Wes Peterson
Director, Janet Phipps
Officer, Samantha Day
Clerk, Amanda Jenkins
Investment Manager, Mark Fairley
Auditors: KPMG LLP DES MOINES IA

LOCATIONS
HQ: IOWA FINANCE AUTHORITY
2015 GRAND AVE STE 200, DES MOINES, IA
503124903
Phone: 515 725-4900
Web: WWW.IOWAFINANCEAUTHORITY.GOV

HISTORICAL FINANCIALS
Company Type: Private

Income Statement
FYE: June 30

	ASSETS ($ mil.)	NET INCOME ($ mil.)	INCOME AS % OF ASSETS	EMPLOYEES
06/16	2,565	42	1.7%	89
06/10	2,914	63	2.2%	—
06/09	2,519	85	3.4%	—
06/08	0	80	—	—
Annual Growth	—	(7.7%)	—	—

2016 Year-End Financials
Debt ratio: —
Return on equity: 49.60%
Cash ($ mil.): 386
Current ratio: 4.00
Long-term debt ($ mil.): —

Dividends
Yield: —
Payout: —
Market value ($ mil.): —

IOWA STUDENT LOAN LIQUIDITY CORPORATION

EXECUTIVES
Pres, Steven W McCullough
SEC*, Mary Kay Debolt
Treas*, Erin Lacey
Auditors: KPMG LLP DES MOINES IOWA

LOCATIONS
HQ: IOWA STUDENT LOAN LIQUIDITY CORPORATION
6775 VISTA DR, WEST DES MOINES, IA 502669305
Phone: 515 243-5626
Web: WWW.STUDENTLOAN.ORG

HISTORICAL FINANCIALS
Company Type: Private

Income Statement
FYE: June 30

	ASSETS ($ mil.)	NET INCOME ($ mil.)	INCOME AS % OF ASSETS	EMPLOYEES
06/17	1,675	29	1.8%	214
06/16	1,659	7	0.5%	—
06/10	3,748	(28)	—	—
06/09	4,046	17	0.4%	—
Annual Growth	(10.4%)	7.1%	—	—

2017 Year-End Financials
Debt ratio: —
Return on equity: 35.90%
Cash ($ mil.): 11
Current ratio: 0.10
Long-term debt ($ mil.): —

Dividends
Yield: —
Payout: —
Market value ($ mil.): —

IQVIA Holdings Inc

IQVIA Holdings (formerly Quintiles) has plenty to CRO about. One of the world's largest contract research organizations (CROs) it helps pharmaceutical biotechnology and medical device companies develop and sell their products. The firm provides a comprehensive range of clinical trials management services including patient recruitment data analysis laboratory testing and regulatory filing assistance. Its consulting offerings include the provision of strategic advice at every stage of drug discovery and development. The company also provides data analytics technology and expertise to medical researchers government agencies and health care payers. Quintiles Transnational merged with IMS Health in October 2016 to create IQVIA Holdings a $23 billion life science company.

Operations
IQVIA operates through three primary segments: Research & Development Solutions Commercial Solutions and Integrated Engagement Services.

The Research & Development and Commercial segments each account for about 45% of total revenue. Research & Development offers project management clinical monitoring clinical trial support and strategic planning and design services. The Commercial segment offers technology insight workflow analytics and consulting national and sub-national information and reference information; it has access to data on the treatments and outcomes of more than 530 million unidentified patients.

The Integrated Engagement segment (about 10% of total revenue) provides health care provider and patient engagement services as well as medical affairs services.

The company has a 60% stake in a joint venture with Quest Diagnostics; the venture named Q2 Solutions is a clinical trials lab services provider.

Geographic Reach
IQVIA is co-headquartered in Durham North Carolina and Danbury Connecticut. It has some 280 offices in more than 80 countries in the Americas Europe Africa and the Asia/Pacific region. In recent years the company has been focusing on international expansion especially in Asia. It has a presence in all major biopharmaceutical markets including the US Japan and Europe as well as Russia India and China.

The Americas account for more than a third of all revenues.

Sales and Marketing
IQVIA serves large multinational and regional/domestic biopharmaceutical firms in the US Europe Asia Japan Canada and Latin America.It markets its offerings through a number of channels including retail hospital and mail order.

Financial Performance
Quintiles' (and now IQVIA's) revenues have been on the rise for the past five years. The company's revenue rose 42% to $9.7 billion in 2017 largely due to growth in the Commercial Solutions segment (which more than doubled its revenue). Other contributing factors included a positive impact from foreign currency fluctuations and growth in the Research & Development segment; these were partially offset by a slight decline in the Integrated Engagement Services segment. Sales increased in all geographic regions (Americas Europe and Africa and the Asia/Pacific region).

Net income had been trending upward until 2016 when expenses from the merger between Quintiles and IMS Health caused profits to decline 70%. Thanks to the higher revenue in 2017 net income rose some tenfold to more than $1.3 billion. Cost of revenue relative to revenue also declined a few percentage points.

Operating cash flow continued its growth trajectory in 2017 when it rose 13% to $970 million. This was primarily driven by the increase in net income that year.

Strategy
IQVIA is benefiting from its expertise in clinical trials and its information and technology capabilities. It it tapping into these assets to continue innovating and offering its clients new ways to bring their drugs to market quickly and efficiently. For example in 2017 it launched ePromo a cloud-based content management offering for life sciences companies. The company also plans to take advantage of acquisition opportunities to further build out its platform. It is working to leverage that growth to expand into a broader swath of the health care market with a focus on connected health care.

To its advantage demand for outsourced clinical development services has been growing: Belt-tightening pharma and biotech companies look to trim costs even as they are desperate to find and develop new products. Key to its success IQVIA has focused efforts on developing services that help its clients reduce risk and time-to-market. For instance its Cenduit subsidiary a joint venture with Thermo Fisher Scientific helps control clinical trials costs by automating delivery of supplies among other things. And in 2017 the company began offering a social media technology service which monitors hundreds of thousands of outlets to identify and validate any adverse events on its clients' products.

Additionally the company continues to invest in quality data and electronic health records. It has acquired data analytics products and services as well as personnel and created a proprietary data integration tool to manage data from multiple sources.Altogether the group owns more than 30 petabytes (one petabyte is equal to a million gigabytes) of unique data.

The company is also trimming itself of non-core operations after the merger. In 2017 it sold its recently acquired health information analytics unit Encore Health Resources which it had acquired in 2014 but which ultimately underperformed. IQVIA has also closed certain facilities cut some staff and is exploring opportunities to divest other assets. One area it may exit is its contract sales business as pharmaceuticals companies increasingly use their own sales teams.

Because IQVIA serves clients that conduct clinical trials it is vulnerable to the loss of business when trials go awry. Negative results can lead the firm's customers to shut down those research activities thereby terminating their contracts with IQVIA. Even successfully getting a drug to market can mean the loss of a contract. Therefore it is important for IQVIA to maintain a strong backlog of R&D jobs.

Additionally the company could face pricing pressures as drug developers themselves face competitive challenges from generics manufacturers.

Mergers and Acquisitions

In October 2016 Quintiles joined forces with health care data firm IMS Health Holdings in what it described as a merger of equals. (Upon closure of the deal IMS Health shareholders owned 51.4% of the merged company while Quintiles shareholders owned 48.6%.) The combined firm IQVIA benefits from increased efficiencies and cost savings. For example IMS's data is being utilized to improve Quintiles' clinical trial processes.

HISTORY

Quintiles was founded by Dennis Gillings a British biostatistician who had worked with Hoechst (later part of Sanofi) on data analysis in the 1970s. Gillings set up Quintiles (Quantitative Information Technology In The Life and Economic Sciences) in 1982 at the University of North Carolina where he was then teaching. The company grew as drug companies began outsourcing some of the more irksome tasks of drug development. Quintiles went public in 1994.

The company used the proceeds of the IPO to expand its health economics segment with the purchases of Benefit International (1995) and Lewin Group (1996). These purchases introduced it to such new clients as governments and HMOs. Quintiles' 1996 purchase of Innovex (unrelated to the computer hardware maker of the same name) made it the world's largest CRO. The buying spree continued in 1997 and 1998. Among the purchases were some intended to strengthen Quintiles' marketing services (Data Analysis Systems Inc. Q.E.D. International and France-based Serval).

The firm also formed new collaborations with such academic research organizations as Johns Hopkins Medicine.

In 1999 Quintiles expanded its marketing arm with the purchase of Pharmaceutical Marketing Services (parent of the leading pharmaceuticals industry research company Scott-Levin) and jumped headlong into data mining with its purchase of ENVOY — which processed insurance claims. Quintiles found the core business uninspiring and sold it to Healtheon (now Emdeon formerly WebMD) the next year. But it kept rights to ENVOY's stream of treatment outcome and insurance data gleaned from health care providers hospitals payers and pharmacies — a treasure house of information useful to salespeople and health providers.

The company continued in 2000 to add offices in Europe Asia and Latin America. It also opened additional offices in the US and Europe to help Japanese pharmaceutical companies market their products in those regions. Late in the year Quintiles bought the clinical development unit of Pharmacia.

In 2001 Quintiles became embroiled in a legal dispute with WebMD involving the availability of data associated with ENVOY; the company challenged WebMD's efforts to withhold such data. The two companies settled the squabble later that year and agreed to sever all ties. Also in 2001 Quintiles streamlined operations and cut about 5% of its workforce.

The future structure of the CRO came into question at the end of 2002. Gillings presented the company with a buyout offer; he planned to take the company private so he could pursue a new growth strategy Wall Street would surely find risky. The board rejected that offer in October 2002 but it opened up an auction. Some leading equity firms reportedly made offers but Gillings — with backing from Blackstone Group and BANK ONE's One Equity Partners (later part of JPMorgan Chase) — placed another offer for Quintiles and won the prize in April 2003. Some five months later Quintiles went private.

EXECUTIVES

Chairman And Ceo, Ari Bousbib, age 56, $390,137 total compensation
Cfo, Michael R. (Mike) McDonnell, age 54, $650,000 total compensation
Svp And Executive Director Quintilesims Institute, Murray L. Aitken
President Research And Development Solutions, W. Richard Staub, age 55, $485,923 total compensation
President Clinical Operations Research And Development Solutions, Cynthia L. Verst
Evp And Chief Customer Officer, Paul Spreen
President Information And Technology Solutions, Kevin C. Knightly, age 56, $119,399 total compensation
President Asia/pacific, Anand Tharmaratnam
President Central East And South Europe, Elisabeth Beck
President North Europe Middle East And Africa, Alistair Grenfell
President Japan, Norihiko Minato
President Latin America, Nilton Paletta
Evp And General Counsel, James H. (Jim) Erlinger, age 59, $468,333 total compensation
President Real-world Insights (rwi), Jon Resnick
President Integrated Engagement Services, W. Scott Evangelista
Svp And Cio, Karl Guenault
President United States And Canada, Hossam Sadek

President Data Sciences Safety And Regulatory Research And Development Solutions, Margaret Keegan
Ceo Qâ̦ Solutions, Costa Panagos
Vp Administration And Chief Of Staff To The Ceo Ims Health, Trudy Stein
Svp Strategy Marketing And Communications, Marla Kessler
President Global Services, José Luis Fernández
Vice President And Global Head Of Risk Management, Stella Blackburn
Vice President Commercial Sales, Jay Schwartz
Auditors: PricewaterhouseCoopers LLP

LOCATIONS

HQ: IQVIA Holdings Inc
 4820 Emperor Blvd., Durham, NC 27703
Phone: 919 998-2000
Web: www.quintiles.com

2017 Sales

	$ mil.	% of total
Americas		
US	3,282	34
Other	325	3
Europe & Africa		
UK	586	6
Other	2,532	26
Asia/Pacific		
Japan	763	8
Other	572	6
Reimbursed expenses	1,679	17
Total	**9,739**	**100**

PRODUCTS/OPERATIONS

2017 Sales by Segment

	% of total
Research & Development Solutions	45
Commercial Solutions	45
Integrated Engagement Services	10
Total	**100**

Selected Therapeutic Specialties

Cardiovascular
Central nervous system
Gastrointestinal/NASH
Infectious diseases
Internal medicine
Oncology
Pediatrics
Rheumatology
Women's health

COMPETITORS

Albany Molecular Research	PDI Inc.
Charles River Laboratories	Pharmaceutical Product Development
Covance	Premier Research Group
ICON	Quest Diagnostics
INC Research	UDG Healthcare
PAREXEL	WuXi PharmaTech
	inVentiv Health

HISTORICAL FINANCIALS

Company Type: Public

Income Statement — FYE: December 31

	REVENUE ($ mil.)	NET INCOME ($ mil.)	NET PROFIT MARGIN	EMPLOYEES
12/17	9,739	1,309	13.4%	55,000
12/16	6,878	115	1.7%	50,000
12/15	5,737	387	6.7%	36,100
12/14	5,460	356	6.5%	32,600
12/13	5,099	226	4.4%	28,200
Annual Growth	**17.6%**	**55.0%**	**—**	**18.2%**

2017 Year-End Financials

Debt ratio: 44.96%
Return on equity: 15.64%
Cash ($ mil.): 959
Current ratio: 1.19
Long-term debt ($ mil.): 10,122

No. of shares (mil.): 208
Dividends
  Yield: —
  Payout: —
Market value ($ mil.): 20,373

	STOCK PRICE ($) FY Close	P/E High/Low		PER SHARE ($) Earnings	Dividends	Book Value
12/17	97.90	18	13	5.88	0.00	38.97
12/16	76.05	105	73	0.76	0.00	36.67
12/15	68.66	25	18	3.08	0.00	(4.73)
12/14	58.87	22	16	2.72	0.00	(5.67)
12/13	46.34	25	23	1.77	0.00	(5.15)
Annual Growth	20.6%	—		35.0%	—	—

IRC RETAIL CENTERS LLC

IRC Retail Centers (formerly Inland Real Estate Corporation) buys leases and operates retail properties mainly in the Midwest with a concentration in the Chicago and Minneapolis/St. Paul metropolitan markets. The self-managed real estate investment trust (REIT) owns about 150 properties most of which are strip shopping centers anchored by a grocery or big-box store. It also invests in single-tenant retail properties and develops properties usually through joint ventures. The REIT's portfolio totals about 14 million sq. ft. of leasable space in a dozen states. IRC Retail Centers was acquired by DRA Advisors in early 2015.

Operations

As a REIT IRC Retail Centers is exempt from paying federal income tax so long as it distributes quarterly dividends to shareholders. Most tenants of its investment properties are responsible for paying real estate taxes as insurance as well as maintaining the properties.

Financial Performance

Overall revenues fell 4% in 2012 to $160 million. That year the company had decreased income across the board from rent property fees and joint venture fees despite buying 20 new properties and divesting eight. However it posted profits of almost $18 million in 2012 thanks to one-time earnings on continuing operations and a gain on equity in joint ventures.

Strategy

In 2013 the company announced plans for a new joint venture with an affiliate of Australia-based MAB Corporation. The project calls for developing about 20 grocery-anchored shopping centers that would include a 50000-sq.-ft. supermarket with another 20000 sq. ft. of retail space. The JV will extend IRC Retail's reach to the eastern US namely Florida Georgia North and South Carolina Virginia and Washington DC.

Another joint venture with Dutch pension fund administrator PGGM (established 2010) calls for acquiring grocery-anchored and community retail centers in the Midwest. In 2013 the JV bought three Wal-Mart shopping centers in the Milwaukee area for $24.2 million a 139000-sq.-ft. Whole Foods/CVS shopping center in Cleveland for $25 million and is building a 92000-sq.-ft. shopping center in Evergreen Park Illinois.

EXECUTIVES

Senior Vice President, William Anderson
Auditors: KPMG LLP CHICAGO ILLINOIS

LOCATIONS

HQ: IRC RETAIL CENTERS LLC
  814 COMMERCE DR STE 300, OAK BROOK, IL
  605238823
Phone: 877 206-5656
Web: WWW.IRCRETAILCENTERS.COM

2015 Properties (excluding joint ventures)

	No.
Illinois	62
Minnesota	16
Wisconsin	7
Indiana	5
Ohio	2
Alabama	1
Florida	1
Nebraska	1
North Carolina	1
Total	**96**

PRODUCTS/OPERATIONS

2015 Sales

	$ mil.	% of total
Rents	135	66
Tenant recoveries	57	28
Other property income	5	3
Fee income from unconsolidated joint ventures	5	3
Total	**203**	**100**

COMPETITORS

Brixmor
CBL & Associates Properties
Canal Capital
DDR
Federal Realty Investment
Horizon Group Properties
Kimco Realty
Macerich
Noddle Development
Pennsylvania Real Estate
Ramco-Gershenson
Realty Income
Retail Properties of America
Rubloff Development
Schottenstein
Taubman Centers
Weingarten Realty

HISTORICAL FINANCIALS

Company Type: Private

Income Statement

FYE: December 31

	ASSETS ($ mil.)	NET INCOME ($ mil.)	INCOME AS % OF ASSETS	EMPLOYEES
12/15	1,521	25	1.7%	129
12/14	1,572	39	2.5%	—
12/13	1,529	111	7.3%	—
12/12	1,243	17	1.4%	—
Annual Growth	7.0%	13.0%	—	—

2015 Year-End Financials

Debt ratio: —
Return on equity: 12.50%
Cash ($ mil.): 9
Current ratio: —
Long-term debt ($ mil.): —

Dividends
  Yield: —
  Payout: —
Market value ($ mil.): —

Isabella Bank Corp

EXECUTIVES

President - Breckenridge Division Of Isabella Bank, Timothy Miller
Auditors: Rehmann Robson LLC

LOCATIONS

HQ: Isabella Bank Corp
  401 N. Main St., Mt. Pleasant, MI 48858
Phone: 989 772-9471
Web: www.isabellabank.com

HISTORICAL FINANCIALS

Company Type: Public

Income Statement

FYE: December 31

	ASSETS ($ mil.)	NET INCOME ($ mil.)	INCOME AS % OF ASSETS	EMPLOYEES
12/17	1,813	13	0.7%	376
12/16	1,732	13	0.8%	372
12/15	1,668	15	0.9%	374
12/14	1,549	13	0.9%	361
12/13	1,493	12	0.8%	360
Annual Growth	5.0%	1.4%	—	1.1%

2017 Year-End Financials

Debt ratio: —
Return on equity: 6.92%
Cash ($ mil.): 30
Current ratio: —
Long-term debt ($ mil.): —

No. of shares (mil.): 7
Dividends
  Yield: 0.0%
  Payout: 61.8%
Market value ($ mil.): 222

	STOCK PRICE ($) FY Close	P/E High/Low		PER SHARE ($) Earnings	Dividends	Book Value
12/17	28.25	17	16	1.65	1.02	24.81
12/16	27.85	17	15	1.73	0.98	24.02
12/15	29.90	14	11	1.90	0.94	23.59
12/14	22.50	14	12	1.74	0.89	22.45
12/13	23.85	16	13	1.59	0.84	20.80
Annual Growth	4.3%	—		0.9%	5.0%	4.5%

Jabil Inc

Jabil Inc. makes a jabillion different kinds of electronics. The company is one of the leading providers of outsourced electronics manufacturing services (EMS) in the world. It makes electronics components and parts on a contract basis for computers smartphones printers and other consumer electronics as well as more complex specialized products for the aerospace automotive and healthcare industries. The company's services range from product design and component procurement to product testing order fulfillment and supply chain management. US-based Jabil operates more than 100 plants in about 30 countries with international customers accounting for about 90% of sales.

Operations

Jabil conducts business in two segments: Electronics Manufacturing Services (EMS) and Diversified Manufacturing Services (DMS).

The EMS segment (about 55% of revenue) focuses on IT supply chain design and engineering for all things electronic. The products Jabil makes for its customers are used in the automotive digital home industrial and energy networking and telecommunications point of sale printing and storage businesses.

The DMS segment (about 45% of revenue) focuses on manufacturing services for material sciences and technologies. It works with customers to develop and manufacture products for consumer wearable technologies defense and aerospace emerging growth healthcare mobility and packaging.

Geographic Reach

Jabil has manufacturing plants in the US Canada and Mexico as well as Europe Asia South Africa Asia and South America.

Singapore and China are its largest markets accounting for about 35% and more than 20% of sales respectively. Mexico accounts for about 15% of revenue.

Sales and Marketing

Jabil depends on a small number of customers for a significant percentage of revenue - five customers account for just less than 50% of sales. Its top customer is Apple (about 30% of sales) and other significant customers are Cisco Systems Dell Technologies HP Inc. LM Ericsson General Electric Ingenico NetApp Valeo and Zebra Technologies.

Financial Performance

Jabil's string of annual revenue increases continued for a fourth year in 2018 (ended August) with a 16% jump from 2017.

The company reported sales of $22.1 billion in 2018 up $3.1 billion from 2017 propelled by a 23% increase in the DMS segment on strong demand from mobility customers and higher sales to existing healthcare customers. The EMS segment's revenue rose 11% year-to-year boosted by customers in industrial and energy digital home and capital equipment.

The company's profit fell to $86.3 million in 2018 from $129 million in 2017 due to a $142 million tax expense related to the US Tax Cuts and Jobs Act.

Jabil had about $1.3 billion in cash and equivalents in 2018 compared to $1.2 billion in 2017. Operations generated about $933 million in cash in 2018 while investing and financing activities used $798 million and $47 million respectively.

Strategy

To compete in a rapidly consolidating industry Jabil provides production on a global scale and operates through semi-autonomous business units that are dedicated to individual customers. The company continues to add services and to expand globally through acquisitions including deals to acquire manufacturing operations from customers looking to reduce costs through outsourcing. The company tends to place manufacturing plants close to its customers.

Jabil had expanded its work in the health care device market and it has been a strong performer for the company. Operating income from production for health-related products which include drug-delivery systems continues to grow at better-than-expected levels.

Apple has been a long and profitable customer for Jabil a key supplier for Apple's iPhone. However Apple warned that sales of its phones slowed in emerging markets which would affect Jabil's revenue.

Jabil implemented a restructuring program in 2017 to realign costs and consolidate manufacturing in lower cost areas. The program included job cuts and cost the company about $160 million in 2017 and about $37 million in 2018. It plans to save up to $90 million a year with the moves.

Mergers and Acquisitions

Acquisitions have extended Jabil's product portfolio and its geographic reach.

In 2017 Jabil acquired True-Tech Corp. to expand its capital equipment division. True-Tech specialized in high-precision machining mechanical assembly and clean room assembly for semiconductor and aerospace customers.

In January 2016 Jabil acquired Inala a South African energy products provider and systems integrator. The deal acquisition expanded Jabil's presence in the market for remote location energy products and marked its first venture in Africa.

Company Background

Jabil Circuit was named for founders James Golden and Bill Morean. The duo who originally ran an excavation business started Jabil in suburban Detroit in 1966 to provide assembly and reworking services to electronics manufacturers. Jabil incorporated in 1969 and began making printed circuit boards for Control Data Corporation (later renamed Control Data Systems) that year.

William D. Morean the founder's son who had worked summers at Jabil while in high school joined the company in 1977. The next year the younger Morean took over Jabil's day-to-day operations. The company had entered the automotive electronics business in 1976 through a $12 million contract with General Motors.

During the 1980s Jabil began building computer components adding such customers as Dell NEC Sun Microsystems and Toshiba. Jabil moved its headquarters to St. Petersburg Florida in 1983. William Morean became Jabil's chairman and CEO in 1988.

EXECUTIVES

Ceo And Director, Mark T. Mondello, age 54, $1,100,000 total compensation

Evp And Coo, William D. (Bill) Muir, age 50, $700,000 total compensation

Evp Corporate Development And Chief Of Staff, Courtney J. Ryan, age 48

Cfo, Forbes I. J. Alexander, age 58, $700,000 total compensation

Vp Business Development, Steven D. (Steve) Borges, age 49

Evp General Counsel And Corporate Secretary, Robert L. (Bobby) Katz, age 56

Svp Materials Technology, Hwai Hai (HH) Chiang, $445,000 total compensation

Evp And Ceo Jabil Packaging Solutions, Erich Hoch, age 48

Svp High Velocity, Michael J. Loparco, age 47

Evp And Ceo Enterprise And Infrastructure, Alessandro Parimbelli, age 50, $444,392 total compensation

President, William E. (Bill) Peters, age 55, $700,000 total compensation

Svp And Cio, Gary L. Cantrell

Evp Human Resources And Human Development, Scott D Slipy, age 52

Executive Vice President National Operations, Mark Butler

Vice President Of Finance After Market Services Division, Brian Greff

Vice President Real Estate And Construction, Jacky Lau

Vice President After Market Services, Hartmut Liebel

Assistant Vice President Sales National Accounts, Dennis Maddock

Chairman, Timothy L. (Tim) Main, age 61

Vice Chairman, Thomas A. Sansone, age 69

Auditors: Ernst & Young LLP

LOCATIONS

HQ: Jabil Inc
10560 Dr. Martin Luther King, Jr. Street North, St. Petersburg, FL 33716
Phone: 727 577-9749
Web: www.jabil.com

2018 Sales

	$ mil.	% of total
Singapore	7	33
China	4,585	21
Mexico	3,533	16
U.S.	1,844	8
Malaysia	1,389	6
Hungary	897	4
Other	2,651	12
Total	**22,095**	**100**

PRODUCTS/OPERATIONS

2018 Sales

	$ mil.	% of total
Electronics Manufacturing Services	12,268	56
Diversified Manufacturing Services	9,826	44
Total	**22,095**	**100**

Services
Component selection sourcing and procurement
Design and prototyping
Engineering
Order fulfillment
Printed circuit board and backplane assembly
Product testing
Repair and warranty
Systems assembly
Test development
Tooling design (molds and dies)

COMPETITORS

ASUSTeK	Flextronics
AptarGroup	Hon Hai
BenQ	Inventec
Benchmark Electronics	Key Tronic
CATCHER TECHNOLOGY CO.	Plexus
LTD.	Sanmina
Celestica	Venture Corp.
Compal Electronics	Wistron

HISTORICAL FINANCIALS

Company Type: Public

Income Statement

FYE: August 31

	REVENUE ($ mil.)	NET INCOME ($ mil.)	NET PROFIT MARGIN	EMPLOYEES
08/18	22,095	86	0.4%	199,000
08/17	19,063	129	0.7%	170,000
08/16	18,353	254	1.4%	138,000
08/15	17,899	284	1.6%	161,000
08/14	15,762	241	1.5%	142,000
Annual Growth	**8.8%**	**(22.7%)**	**—**	**8.8%**

2018 Year-End Financials

Debt ratio: 20.91%
Return on equity: 4.01%
Cash ($ mil.): 1,257
Current ratio: 1.04
Long-term debt ($ mil.): 2,493
No. of shares (mil.): 164
Dividends
  Yield: 1.0%
  Payout: 65.3%
Market value ($ mil.): 4,865

	STOCK PRICE ($) FY Close	P/E High/Low		Earnings	PER SHARE ($) Dividends	Book Value
08/18	29.56	63	49	0.49	0.32	11.85
08/17	31.35	44	29	0.69	0.32	13.24
08/16	21.19	19	13	1.32	0.32	13.04
08/15	19.35	17	12	1.45	0.32	12.05
08/14	21.58	20	13	1.19	0.32	11.55
Annual Growth	**8.2%**	**—**	**—**	**(19.9%)**	**(0.0%)**	**0.6%**

Jacobs Engineering Group, Inc.

Jacobs Engineering Group provides technical professional and construction services for industrial government and commercial clients throughout the world. Jacobs handles project design and engineering construction operations maintenance and scientific consultation. Typical projects include oil refineries manufacturing plants infrastructure & telecommunications and aerospace facilities.

About two-thirds of revenue comes from the US while the rest originates in other countries primarily in Europe. Founded in 1947 Jacobs Engineering has more than 200 global offices. In 2018 the company agreed to sell its Energy Chemicals and Resources segment to WorleyParsons for $3.3 billion in cash and stock.

HISTORY

Joseph Jacobs graduated from the Polytechnic Institute of Brooklyn in 1942 with a doctorate in engineering. He went to work for Merck designing processes for pharmaceutical production. Later he moved to Chemurgic Corp. near San Francisco where he worked until 1947 when he founded Jacobs Engineering as a consulting firm. Jacobs also sold industrial equipment avoiding any apparent conflict of interest by simply telling his consulting clients.

When equipment sales outstripped consulting work by 1954 Jacobs hired four salesmen and engineer Stan Krugman who became his right-hand man. Two years later the company got its first big chemical design job for Kaiser Aluminum. Jacobs incorporated his sole proprietorship in 1957.

In 1960 the firm won its first construction contract to design and build a potash flotation plant and Jacobs Engineering became an integrated design and construction firm. In 1967 it opened its first regional office but kept management decentralized to replicate the small size and hard-hitting qualities of its home office. Three years later Jacobs Engineering went public.

The firm merged with Houston-based Pace Companies which specialized in petrochemical engineering design in 1974. Also that year the firm became Jacobs Engineering Group and began building its first major overseas chemical plant in Ireland.

By 1977 sales had reached $250 million. A decade of lobbying paid off that year when the firm won a contract for the Arab Potash complex in Jordan. Jacobs began to withdraw from his firm's operations in the early 1980s but the 1982-83 recession and poor management decisions pounded earnings. Jacobs returned from retirement in 1985 fired 14 VPs cut staff in half and pushed the firm to pursue smaller process-plant jobs and specialty construction.

After abandoning a 1986 attempt to take the company private Jacobs began making acquisitions to improve the firm's construction expertise. In 1992 he relinquished his role as CEO to president Noel Watson. The next year the company expanded its international holdings by acquiring the UK's H&G Process Contracting and H&G Contractors.

The firm's $38 million purchase of CRS Sirrine Engineers and CRSS Constructors in 1994 was the company's largest buy at that point and added new markets in the paper and semiconductor industries. By 1995 Jacobs Engineering was working on a record backlog.

Continuing its acquisition drive the company bought a 49% interest in European engineering specialist Serete Group in 1996; it bought the rest the next year. Also in 1997 it gained control of Indian engineering affiliate Humphreys & Glasgow (now Jacobs H&G) increasing its 40% stake to 70% and bought CPR Engineering a pulp and paper processing specialist. It also formed a joint venture with Krupp UHDE to provide design engineering and construction management services in Mexico.

In 1999 the company paid $198 million for St. Louis construction and design firm Sverdrup which had completed projects in some 65 countries. The next year Jacobs Engineering purchased half of Dutch firm Stork Engineering's business (it

acquired the rest in 2001). But the company's bid to buy the assets of bankrupt power plant construction company Stone & Webster in 2000 was topped by Shaw Group.

After being accused of overcharging the US government Jacobs Engineering settled a whistle-blower lawsuit (for $35 million) in 2000 while continuing to deny the allegations. However the next year Jacobs continued to receive federal contracts including contracts for boosting security at the US Capitol complex and providing logistics to the US Special Operations Command. Jacobs completed its acquisition of the UK-based GI

EXECUTIVES

Group Vice President, Walter Barber
Svp Information Technology, Cora L. Carmody, age 61
Chairman President And Ceo, Steven J. Demetriou, age 59, $125,000 total compensation
Evp And Cfo, Kevin C. Berryman, age 59, $544,832 total compensation
President Industrial, Robert V. (Bob) Pragada, age 50
Evp Operations, Joseph G. Mandel, age 58, $699,996 total compensation
Evp Operations, Phillip J. Stassi, age 63, $639,423 total compensation
President Aerospace And Technology, Terence D. Hagen, age 53
Gvp Consulting Operations, Robert McWhinney
Vice President Information Technology, Pete Young
Division Vice President Director Construction Services, Joseph Franco
Vice President, Albert Pozotrigo
Gvp Federal Operations, James Thiesing
Vice President Global Information Technology Security, George Hull
Auditors: Ernst & Young LLP

LOCATIONS

HQ: Jacobs Engineering Group, Inc.
1999 Bryan Street, Suite 1200, Dallas, TX 75201
Phone: 214 583-8500
Web: www.jacobs.com

2018 Sales

	$ mil.	% of total
US	9,519	64
Europe	2,768	18
Canada	863	6
Asia	316	2
India	212	1
Australia and New Zealand	719	5
South America and Mexico	159	1
Middle East and Africa	425	3
Total	**14,984**	**100**

PRODUCTS/OPERATIONS

2018 Sales by Segment

	$ mil.	% of total
Aerospace Technology Environmental and Nuclear	4,372	29
Buildings Infrastructure and Advanced Facilities	6,184	41
Energy Chemicals and Resources	4,427	30
Total	**14,984**	**100**

COMPETITORS

AECOM	HOK
Aker Solutions	KBR
Amec Foster Wheeler	Leidos
BWX Technologies	Lockheed Martin
Bechtel	Tetra Tech
Fluor	Turner Construction
HDR	WS Atkins
HNTB Companies	

HISTORICAL FINANCIALS

Company Type: Public

Income Statement

FYE: September 28

	REVENUE ($ mil.)	NET INCOME ($ mil.)	NET PROFIT MARGIN	EMPLOYEES
09/18	14,984	163	1.1%	80,800
09/17	10,022	293	2.9%	54,700
09/16*	10,964	210	1.9%	54,900
10/15	12,114	302	2.5%	64,000
09/14	12,695	328	2.6%	66,300
Annual Growth	**4.2%**	**(16.0%)**	**—**	**5.1%**

*Fiscal year change

2018 Year-End Financials

Debt ratio: 17.02%
Return on equity: 3.19%
Cash ($ mil.): 793
Current ratio: 1.45
Long-term debt ($ mil.): 2,146
No. of shares (mil.): 142
Dividends
Yield: 0.7%
Payout: 27.4%
Market value ($ mil.): 10,880

	STOCK PRICE ($) FY Close	P/E High/Low	PER SHARE ($) Earnings	Dividends	Book Value
09/18	76.50	66 47	1.17	0.60	41.16
09/17	58.27	26 20	2.42	0.45	36.78
09/16*	51.72	32 20	1.73	0.00	35.26
10/15	37.40	20 15	2.40	0.00	34.85
09/14	49.68	27 20	2.48	0.00	33.92
Annual Growth	**11.4%**	**— —**	**(17.1%)**	**—**	**5.0%**

*Fiscal year change

JARDEN CORPORATION

EXECUTIVES

Ceo, Michael B Polk
Information Specialist, Gragg Miller
Auditors: PRICEWATERHOUSECOOPERS LLP NE

LOCATIONS

HQ: JARDEN CORPORATION
221 RIVER ST, HOBOKEN, NJ 070305989
Phone: 201 610-6600
Web: WWW.JARDENCS.COM

COMPETITORS

AZZ	Johnson Outdoors
Academy Sports	Kaz
Amazon.com	Kellwood
Amer Sports	Lasko Products
Andis	Lifetime Brands
BWAY	Lowe's
Bass Pro Shops	MEGA Brands
Bauer Hockey	Mattel
Bed Bath & Beyond	Mayborn Group
Burton	Mizuno
Cabela's	NACCO Industries
CalCedar	NIKE
Canadian Tire	New Balance
Carrefour	Newell Rubbermaid
Church & Dwight	Owens-Illinois
Conair Consumer	Patch Products
Products	Philips Avent
Costco Wholesale	Procter & Gamble
Crayola	Quiksilver
Daiwa	REI
De'Longhi	Richco
Deswell	Rollerblade
Dick's Sporting Goods	Rossignol
EBSCO	Russell Hobbs
Easton-Bell Sports	SEB

Elmer's Products
Energizer Holdings
Evenflo
Female Health
Gaming Partners
  International
Gerber Products
Habasit America
Hamilton Beach
Hanesbrands
Head N.V.
Hillerich &
  Bradsby
HoMedics
Home Depot
Honeywell ACS
Igloo Products
Intex DIY
Invensys
Johnson & Johnson

Sealy
Simmons
Spectrum Brands
Suncast
Target Corporation
Tecnica
Tegrant
UTC Climate Controls
  & Security
Universal Security
  Instruments
VF Corporation
W.C. Bradley Co.
Wahl Clipper
West Pharmaceutical
  Services
Whirlpool
Worthington Industries
adidas

HISTORICAL FINANCIALS

Company Type: Private

Income Statement

FYE: December 31

	REVENUE ($ mil.)	NET INCOME ($ mil.)	NET PROFIT MARGIN	EMPLOYEES
12/15	8,603	146	1.7%	17,000
12/14	8,287	242	2.9%	—
12/13	7,355	203	2.8%	—
12/12	6,696	243	3.6%	—
Annual Growth	8.7%	(15.6%)	—	—

2015 Year-End Financials

Debt ratio: —
Return on equity: 1.70%
Cash ($ mil.): 1,298
Current ratio: 1.10
Long-term debt ($ mil.): —

Dividends
Yield: —
Payout: —
Market value ($ mil.): —

JetBlue Airways Corp

Airline JetBlue Airways offers one-class service — with leather seats satellite TV from DIRECTV satellite radio from XM and movies — to more than 38 million passengers a year and taking them to more than 100 cities. It has 1000 daily flights in nearly 30 US states Puerto Rico and 21 countries in the Caribbean and Latin America. Most of its flights arrive or depart from Boston; Los Angeles; New York; Orlando and Fort Lauderdale Florida; and San Juan Puerto Rico. JetBlue's fleet of about 230 aircraft consists mainly of Airbus A320s and A321s but also includes Embraer 190s.

Operations

The New York-based carrier is the largest domestic airline at New York's JFK International Airport — the US's biggest travel market. Operating primarily out of Terminal 5 or T5 JetBlue also serves New Jersey's Newark Liberty International Airport New York's LaGuardia Airport Newburgh New York's Stewart International Airport and White Plains New York's Westchester County Airport.

The company operates a fleet consisting of 37 Airbus A321 aircraft 130 Airbus A320 aircraft and 60 Embraer 190 aircraft. Its in-flight entertainment system include 36 channels of free DIRECTV 100 channels of free SiriusXM satellite radio and premium movie channel offerings from JetBlue Features a source of first run films.

Geographic Reach

JetBlue flies to more than 100 cities with 1000 daily flights to 100 cities in 21 countries through-

out the Americas with one-third of its route network in the Caribbean and Latin America. It concentrates primarily on the cities of Boston; New York; Long Beach California; Fort Lauderdale and Orlando Florida; and San Juan Puerto Rico.

The US represents nearly 70% of total sales while Latin America and the Caribbean account for the remainder.

Sales and Marketing

JetBlue markets its services through advertising and promotions in various media forms including social media outlets. It also engages in large multi-market programs local events and sponsorships across route network as well as mobile marketing programs. The company sells its services across several major global distribution systems and on-line travel agents. It also sells vacation packages through JetBlue Vacations a one-stop value-priced vacation service for self-directed packaged travel planning.

Financial Performance

JetBlue has experienced unprecedented revenue growth over the years. In 2016 its revenues jumped 4% to peak at a record-setting $6.6 billion. Its profits also surged by 12% to reach $759 million another company milestone primarily due to a major decrease in fuel prices and the higher passenger revenue.

The historic growth for 2016 was due to higher passenger revenues mainly attributable to increased capacity and yield. Ancillary revenue continues to be a source of significant revenue growth primarily driven by customer demand for JetBlue's Even More Space products as well as changes to its fee structure.

Strategy

Traditionally focused on the leisure traveler JetBlue has been developing more service for the business customer to offset the seasonal limitations of the vacation market. Also to develop more business beyond vacation travelers JetBlue has been growing its operations in Latin America and the Caribbean (LACA) which has a strong presence of visiting-friends-and-relatives (VFR) travelers in addition to vacationers. LACA now accounts for about 30% of JetBlue's revenues.

During 2016 JetBlue launched its first commercial US flight to Cuba in 50 years with its inaugural flight from Fort Lauderdale-Hollywood to Santa Clara. It also launched services to CamagA?ey and Holguin Cuba. Overall in 2016 JetBlue commenced service to eight new cities including four destinations in Cuba and Quito Ecuador.

JetBlue entered an agreement with Airbus in mid-2016 to add 30 incremental Airbus A321 aircraft to its order book. The aircraft are scheduled to be delivered between 2017 and 2023. The carrier believes the aircraft will allow it to continue to grow profitably particularly in the transcontinental market.

HISTORY

JetBlue took to the skies in 2000 as the third airline start-up for founder and CEO David Neeleman. The first airline Neeleman helped create Morris Air was formed in 1984. Named after his business partner June Morris the discount airline was operating 22 planes out of Salt Lake City by 1993. While with Morris Air Neeleman pioneered ticketless travel which a decade later would become an industry standard.

Impressed with Morris Air's efficient and strategic network its e-ticket system and Neeleman Southwest Airlines acquired its smaller rival in 1993. Neeleman left Southwest after just six months but not without signing a non-compete clause that prevented him from attempting to repeat his Morris Air success in the US for five years.

Not willing to sit still for long (a characteristic he attributes to attention deficit disorder) Neeleman partnered with David Evans to create Open Skies an integrated e-ticket Internet booking and sales management tool that they began to market to smaller airlines.

Meanwhile Neeleman had skirted the terms of his non-compete agreement to help the founders of Canadian low-fare carrier WestJet get their project off of the ground serving as a consultant and a board member.

In 1999 a year after his non-compete agreement expired Neeleman sold Open Skies to Hewlett-Packard and set to work creating a new airline. In a matter of weeks he had managed to gather $130 million the most ever raised for a start-up airline from investors that included Chase Capital and financier George Soros. Neeleman immediately began acquiring new Airbus A320 jets and fitting them with satellite TV.

JetBlue's first flight was from New York to Fort Lauderdale in 2000. During the year the airline added nine more destinations in California Florida New York Utah and Vermont. By 2001 the airline was operating 20 new A320s with an ambitious 131 on order.

On September 11 of that year terrorists commandeered four passenger aircrafts and turned them into instruments of destruction killing some 3000 people. The events shocked the world and crippled the airline industry. Despite the climate however JetBlue continued to expand its network and it went public in 2002.

The industry star took some heat in 2003 for violating its own privacy policy when it gave the personal information of 1.1 million customers to the Department of Defense as part of anti-terrorism project.

JetBlue added nine new destinations in 2004 including Boston — a major market not dominated by a single carrier and lacking what the company deemed to be sufficient low-fare domestic service.

Consecutive losses in the fourth quarter of 2005 and the first quarter of 2006 — caused in part by rising fuel costs— led the carrier to raise fares on some routes redouble its efforts to keep expenses down and slow some of its expansion plans.

As part of the effort to improve the company's operations JetBlue's board in May 2007 asked David Neeleman to step down as CEO in favor of former president Dave Barger. Neeleman remained with the company as nonexecutive chairman until May 2008.

To grow JetBlue increased capacity at its base at New York's JFK airport with the opening of a new terminal in October 2008. The 630000 sq. ft. Terminal 5 has 26 gates solely used by JetBlue and can accommodate 250 daily departures. The $875 million renovation took three years; it has the largest single security checkpoint in the US and an adjacent 1500-space parking lot.

JetBlue expanded service in 2009 to Bogota Colombia and the Caribbean islands of St. Maarten and Jamaica.

In 2010 JetBlue ink a limited partnership with AMR Corp.'s legacy airline American; the two are sharing activities in New York and Boston including customer "interline" service one-stop booking and check-in and bag transfers for connecting flights. The partnership gives the younger low-cost carrier eight pairs of the Texas-based carrier's take-off and landing slots at Ronald Reagan Washington National Airport and swells American Airlines' New York market with 12 pairs of JetBlue's slots at John F. Kennedy International Airport.

In early 2011 the airline signed an interline agreement with Virgin Atlantic that allows passengers to make connecting flights on transatlantic routes using a single itinerary and baggage check.

EXECUTIVES

Vice President, Jim Hnat
Evp Corporate Affairs General Counsel And Secretary, James G. (Jim) Hnat, age 47, $425,000 total compensation
President And Ceo, Robin Hayes, age 51, $550,000 total compensation
Evp Customer Experience, Joanna Geraghty
Evp Operations, Jeff Martin
Cio, Eash Sundaram
Evp People, Mike Elliott
Evp Commercial And Planning, Martin (Marty) St. George, $400,000 total compensation
Evp And Cfo, Stephen J. (Steve) Priest, age 48
Vice President Flight Operations, Andres Sandoval
Vice President And Associate General Counsel Corporate Governance, Eileen McCarthy
Vp Inflight Experience, John Culp
Executive Vice President Commercial And Planning, Martin St George
Vice President Flight Operations, Bart Roberts
Senior Vice President Airline Planning, Scott Laurence
Senior Vice President System Operations, Alex Battaglia
Vice President Compensation Benefits And Corporate Social Responsibility, Harry Spencer
Vice President Network Planning, John Checketts
Evp And Cfo, Steve Priest
Vice President Customer Support, Frankie Littleford
Vice President Flight Operations, John Ross
Vice President Marketing, Elizabeth Windram
Vice President Infrastructure Properties And Development, Lisa Reifer
Executive Vice President Commercial And Planning, Marty Stgeorge
Vice Chairman, Frank V. Sica, age 67
Chairman, Joel C. Peterson, age 71
Auditors: Ernst & Young LLP

LOCATIONS

HQ: JetBlue Airways Corp
27-01 Queens Plaza North, Long Island City, NY 11101
Phone: 718 286-7900
Web: www.jetblue.com

2016 Sales

	$ mil.	% of total
Domestic	4,751	72
Caribbean & Latin America	1,881	28
Total	**6,632**	**100**

PRODUCTS/OPERATIONS

2016 Sales

	$ mil.	% of total
Passenger	6,013	91
Other	619	9
Total	**6,632**	**100**

COMPETITORS

AirTran Airways	Frontier Airlines
Alaska Air	Southwest Airlines
American Airlines Group	United Continental
Delta Air Lines	Virgin America
	WestJet

HISTORICAL FINANCIALS

Company Type: Public

Income Statement

FYE: December 31

	REVENUE ($ mil.)	NET INCOME ($ mil.)	NET PROFIT MARGIN	EMPLOYEES
12/17	7,015	1,147	16.4%	19,978
12/16	6,632	759	11.4%	18,406
12/15	6,416	677	10.6%	16,862
12/14	5,817	401	6.9%	15,334
12/13	5,441	168	3.1%	14,883
Annual Growth	**6.6%**	**61.6%**	—	**7.6%**

2017 Year-End Financials

Debt ratio: 12.26%
Return on equity: 25.93%
Cash ($ mil.): 303
Current ratio: 0.50
Long-term debt ($ mil.): 1,003

No. of shares (mil.): 321
Dividends
  Yield: —
  Payout: —
Market value ($ mil.): 7,171

	STOCK PRICE ($) FY Close	P/E High/Low		PER SHARE ($) Earnings	Dividends	Book Value
12/17	22.34	7	5	3.47	0.00	15.06
12/16	22.42	10	7	2.22	0.00	11.91
12/15	22.65	13	7	1.98	0.00	9.97
12/14	15.86	12	6	1.19	0.00	8.16
12/13	8.54	15	10	0.52	0.00	7.22
Annual Growth	**27.2%**	—	—	**60.7%**	—	**20.2%**

JEWISH COMMUNAL FUND

EXECUTIVES

Pres, Zoya Raynes
V Pres, Susan F Dickman
Sr V Pres, Jose Virella
Offc Mgr, Wanda Gutierrez
Manager, Hilda Beck
Associate Director, Igor Musayev
Coordinator, Claudia Pinto
Chief Operations Officer, Beth Wohlgelernter
Director of Grants, Karla Floris
Freelance Journalist, Tamar Snyder
Auditors: EISNERAMPER LLP NEW YORK NY

LOCATIONS

HQ: JEWISH COMMUNAL FUND
575 MADISON AVE STE 703, NEW YORK, NY 100228591
Phone: 212 752-8277
Web: WWW.JEWISHCOMMUNALFUND.ORG

HISTORICAL FINANCIALS

Company Type: Private

Income Statement

FYE: June 30

	ASSETS ($ mil.)	NET INCOME ($ mil.)	INCOME AS % OF ASSETS	EMPLOYEES
06/17	1,558	55	3.6%	14
06/13	1,179	110	9.3%	—
06/12	1,012	(57)	—	—
06/11	1,086	42	3.9%	—
Annual Growth	**6.2%**	**4.6%**	—	—

2017 Year-End Financials

Debt ratio: ——
Return on equity: 12.00%
Cash ($ mil.): 404
Current ratio: 625.40
Long-term debt ($ mil.): —

Dividends
  Yield: —
  Payout: —
Market value ($ mil.): —

JOHNS HOPKINS HEALTH SYS CORP

Named after philanthropist Johns Hopkins the Johns Hopkins Health System (JHHS) gifts Baltimore residents with an array of health care services. The health system is an affiliate of world-renowned Johns Hopkins Medicine and oversees six hospitals: All Children's Hospital Johns Hopkins Hospital Bayview Medical Center Howard County General Hospital Sibley Memorial Hospital and Suburban Hospital. The not-for-profit teaching hospitals offer inpatient and outpatient health services that include general medicine emergency/trauma care pediatrics maternity care senior care and numerous specialized areas of medicine. JHHS also operates community health and satellite care facilities.

Operations

JHHS facilities handle 2.8 million patient encounters each year including 115000 inpatient admissions and 350000 emergency room visits. In addition to the six Johns Hopkins Medicine hospitals (which combined house more than 2600 beds) the JHHS organization includes four surgery centers two dozen primary care clinics associated with the Johns Hopkins Community Physicians practice organization and a home health care services agency. JHHS offers unified shared services to its members including advertising purchasing finance legal and other administrative functions.

The Johns Hopkins name is well-known for health care but is probably equally as well-known for its medical education and research initiatives. The health system's hospitals are affiliated with Johns Hopkins University offering physicians-in-training a whole host of residency options.

Geographic Reach

The JHHS inpatient and outpatient facilities are located throughout Maryland and the Washington DC-area as well as in Florida. The system operates a handful of outpatient surgery and imaging centers as well. The group's hospitals serve visitors from all over the world.

Strategy

The organization regularly expands through small to large construction efforts as well as through acquisitions. For example it has acquired two hospitals (All Children's Hospital in Florida and Sibley Memorial Hospital in Washington DC) since 2010.

EXECUTIVES

Pres, Ronald R Peterson
Chb*, C Micheal Amstrong
V Pres Fin-Cfo*, Ronald J Werthman
V Pres-Medical Affairs*, Beryl Rosenstein
Corp SEC*, Hannah Jones
Accountant, Donna Deinish
Assistant Director, Renee Genco
Programmer Analyst, Keith Haggard
Manager, Bridget Carver
Coordinator, Matthew Trojanowski
Senior Vice-President, Bertrand M Emerson
Auditors: PRICEWATERHOUSECOOPERS LLP BA

LOCATIONS

HQ: JOHNS HOPKINS HEALTH SYS CORP
600 N WOLFE ST, BALTIMORE, MD 212870005
Phone: 410 955-5000
Web: WWW.JINHEMD.COM

PRODUCTS/OPERATIONS

Selected Facilities
All Children's Hospital (St. Petersburg FL)
Bayview Medical Center (Baltimore MD)
Howard County General Hospital (Columbia MD)
Johns Hopkins at Cedar Lane (Columbia MD)
Johns Hopkins at Greenspring Station (Lutherville MD)
Johns Hopkins at Odenton (Odenton MD)
Johns Hopkins at White Marsh (White Marsh MD)
Johns Hopkins Hospital (Baltimore MD)
Johns Hopkins Outpatient Center (Baltimore MD)
Sibley Memorial Hospital (Washington DC)
Suburban Hospital (Bethesda MD)

COMPETITORS

Anne Arundel Medical Center	LifeBridge Health
Ascension Health	MedStar Health
Bon Secours Health	MedStar Union Memorial Hospital
Carilion Clinic	Sinai Hospital of Baltimore
Christiana Care	St. Agnes HealthCare
Dimensions Healthcare	St. Joseph Medical Center
Franklin Square Hospital Center	University of Maryland Medical System
GBMC	
Good Samaritan Hospital of Maryland	Upper Chesapeake Health
Harbor Hospital	
Levindale Hospital	

HISTORICAL FINANCIALS

Company Type: Private

Income Statement   FYE: June 30

	REVENUE ($ mil.)	NET INCOME ($ mil.)	NET PROFIT MARGIN	EMPLOYEES
06/18	6,558	308	4.7%	13,000
06/17	6,153	412	6.7%	—
06/07	2,438	163	6.7%	—
06/06	0	0	2.5%	—
Annual Growth	122.9%	134.8%	—	—

2018 Year-End Financials

Debt ratio: ——
Return on equity: 4.70%
Cash ($ mil.): 579
Current ratio: 1.00
Long-term debt ($ mil.): —

Dividends
Yield: —
Payout: —
Market value ($ mil.): —

JOHNS HOPKINS UNIVERSITY

Founded in 1876 with a $7 million bequest from its namesake The Johns Hopkins University has established its reputation by molding itself in the image of a European research institution. While renowned for its School of Medicine the private university offers 260 academic programs spanning fields of study including arts and sciences business and international studies. The university enrolls more than 24000 full- and part-time students. Johns Hopkins has about a half-dozen campuses in Maryland and Washington DC as well as facilities in China and Italy. The student-teacher ratio is 13:1. The affiliated Johns Hopkins Health Sys-

tem provides health care from its three Baltimore-area hospitals.

Operations

Johns Hopkins University a private and non-profit institution with 1700 non-medical and 2800 medical faculty members offers education research and professional medical services. Its research and related services are offered through about 1800 government and private sponsors.

Keenly focused on research Johns Hopkins is engaged in a range of disciplines including health and medicine social sciences humanities the arts natural sciences engineering and technology. Projects include researching alternatives to animal testing disease treatments and chemical and biomolecular engineering topics among others.

The Johns Hopkins University offers graduate programs in business finance and real estate through its relatively new Carey Business School. Trustee emeritus William Polk Carey chairman of W. P. Carey & Co. partially funded the $100 million development of the school with $50 million which was completed in 2007.

Notable alumni of the school include 28th US president Woodrow Wilson Michael Bloomberg and horror film director Wesley Craven.

Geographic Reach

The university boasts three major campuses in Baltimore as well as single campus locations in (Montgomery County) Maryland and Washington DC. Johns Hopkins also operates facilities in the Baltimore-Washington area and abroad in China and Italy.

Strategy

Johns Hopkins is mid-way through its Ten By Twenty program — comprising 10 goals to achieve by 2020 — launched in 2013. The 10 goals are divided into four categories: One University (forging collaboration across disciplines); Individual Excellence (supporting faculty students and staff); Commitment to Our Communities (enriching ties to Baltimore the US and the world); and Institution Building (building a stronger university). In its 2017 progress report some of the achievements listed are more robust mental health resources; smaller class sizes; around 25 (out of a goal of 50) hires of interdisciplinary scholars; improved diversity and inclusion; and raised $4.6 billion in donations.

EXECUTIVES

Cio And Vice Provost Information Technology, Stephanie L. Reel
President, Ronald J. (Ron) Daniels
Svp Finance And Administration, Daniel G. Ennis
Svp Academic Affairs And Provost, Sunil Kumar
Vice President, Thomas Lewis
Vice President, Joseph Zolenas
Vice President Finance, Debbie Palmerino
Medical Director, Haig Kazazian
Senior Vice President Patient Care Services, Laura Wood
Vice President, Ben Myers
Medical Director Wilmer Eye Instructor At Columbia, Dean Glaros
Medical Director, Jeanette Nazarian
Clinical Director, Peter Hill
Vice President Chief Strategy Officer, Jackie Crain
Medical Director Of Care Coordination, Joseph Perno
Vice President For Population Health And Advancement, Elizabeth Kromm
Vice President And Chief Administrator, Sowell Ashlyn
Vice President Human Resources, Marcos Deleon
Director Of Nursing, Laurie Saletnik
Medical Director, Ekaterina Stepanova
Vice President Human Resources, Jon Oravec
Senior Vice President Health Care Transformation And Strategic Planning, John Colmers

Medical Director, Anne Ruble
Secretary, Beth Six
Assistant Secretary, Judith Moss
Secretary, Laura Cornelius
Secretary, Keisha Guice

LOCATIONS

HQ: JOHNS HOPKINS UNIVERSITY
3400 N CHARLES ST, BALTIMORE, MD 212182680
Phone: 410 516-8000
Web: WWW.JHU.EDU

PRODUCTS/OPERATIONS

Selected Schools and Colleges
Bloomberg School of Public Health
Carey Business School
Krieger School of Arts and Sciences
Peabody Institute
School of Advanced International Studies
School of Education
School of Medicine
School of Nursing
Whiting School of Engineering

Selected Centers and Institutes
American Institute for Contemporary German Studies
Bloomberg School of Public Health Department of Health Policy and Management Fall Institute in Barcelona Spain
Bloomberg School of Public Health Research Centers
Center for Africana Studies
Center for Communication Programs
Center for Constitutional Studies and Democratic Development
Center for Clinical Global Health Education
Center for Global Health
Center for International Business and Public Policy
Center for Language Education
Center for Talented Youth
Center for Transatlantic Relations
Central Asia Caucasus Institute
Foreign Policy Institute
Hopkins Nanjing Center
Institute for Global Studies in Culture Power and History
Institute for Policy Studies
Johns Hopkins SAIS Bologna Center
Office of Global Nursing
SAIS Research Centers
Summer Language Institute
The Institute for Johns Hopkins Nursing
Yeung Center for Collaborative China Studies

Selected Campuses
Columbia Center - Columbia Maryland
East Baltimore Campus - Baltimore
Harbor East - Downtown Baltimore
Homewood Campus - Baltimore
Hopkins-Nanjing Center - Nanjing Jiangsu Province People's Republic of China
Johns Hopkins University Applied Physics Laboratory - Laurel MD; Baltimore and Washington
Johns Hopkins University Zanvyl Krieger School of Arts & Sciences Advanced Academic Programs - Washington DC
Montgomery County Center - Rockville Maryland
Nitze School of Advanced International Studies (SAIS) - Washington D.C
Peabody Campus - Baltimore
School of Advanced International Studies - Bologna Italy

HISTORICAL FINANCIALS

Company Type: Private

Income Statement   FYE: June 30

	REVENUE ($ mil.)	NET INCOME ($ mil.)	NET PROFIT MARGIN	EMPLOYEES
06/18	6,020	705	11.7%	37,600
06/13	4,793	526	11.0%	—
06/11	4,369	826	18.9%	—
Annual Growth	4.7%	(2.2%)	—	—

2018 Year-End Financials

Debt ratio: —
Return on equity: 11.70%
Cash ($ mil.): 262
Current ratio: —
Long-term debt ($ mil.): —

Dividends
Yield: —
Payout: —
Market value ($ mil.): —

Johnson & Johnson

It's difficult to get well without Johnson & Johnson (J&J). The diversified health care giant operates in three segments through more than 260 operating companies located in more than 60 countries. Its Medical Devices division offers surgical equipment monitoring devices orthopedic products and contact lenses among other items. J&J's Pharmaceuticals division makes drugs for an array of ailments such as neurological conditions blood disorders autoimmune diseases and pain. Top sellers are psoriasis and arthritis drugs Remicade and Stelara. Finally J&J's Consumer business makes over-the-counter (OTC) drugs and products for baby skin and oral care as well as first-aid and nutritional uses. The company operates worldwide but makes more than half of its revenues in the US.

HISTORY

Brothers James and Edward Mead Johnson founded their medical products company in 1885 in New Brunswick New Jersey. In 1886 Robert joined his brothers to make the antiseptic surgical dressings he developed. The company bought gauze maker Chicopee Manufacturing in 1916. In 1921 it introduced two of its classic products the Band-Aid and Johnson's Baby Cream.

Robert Jr. became chairman in 1932 and served until 1963. A WWII Army general he believed in decentralization; managers were given substantial freedom a principle still used today. Product lines in the 1940s included Ortho (birth control products) and Ethicon (sutures). In 1959 Johnson & Johnson bought McNeil Labs which launched Tylenol (acetaminophen) as an OTC drug the next year. Foreign acquisitions included Switzerland's Cilag-Chemie (1959) and Belgium's Janssen (1961). The company focused on consumer products in the 1970s gaining half the feminine protection market and making Tylenol the top-selling painkiller.

Trouble struck in 1982 when someone laced Tylenol capsules with cyanide killing eight people. The company's response is now a damage-control classic: It immediately recalled 31 million bottles and totally redesigned its packaging to prevent future tampering. The move cost $240 million but saved the Tylenol brand. The next year prescription painkiller Zomax was linked to five deaths and was pulled.

New products in the 1980s included ACUVUE disposable contact lenses and Retin-A. The company bought LifeScan (blood-monitoring products for diabetics) in 1986. In 1989 it began a joint venture with Merck to sell Mylanta and other drugs bought from ICI Americas.

The firm continued its acquisition and diversification strategy in the 1990s. After introducing the first daily-wear disposable contact lenses in 1993 it bought skin-care product maker Neutrogena (1994) to enhance its consumer lines. To diversify its medical products and better compete for hospital business it bought Mitek Surgical Products (1995) and heart disease product maker Cordis (1996). The FDA cleared J&J's Renova wrinkle and fade cream in 1996. The company also began selling at-home HIV test Confide but pulled it the next year after low sales and other problems.

EXECUTIVES

Evp And Cfo, Dominic J. Caruso, age 61, $909,500 total compensation

Evp And Worldwide Chairman Consumer Group, Jorge S. Mesquita, age 56

Evp And Group Worldwide Chairman, Sandra E. Peterson, age 60, $963,462 total compensation

Chairman And Ceo, Alex Gorsky, age 57, $1,600,000 total compensation

Company Group Chairman Consumer Medical Devices, Ashley A. McEvoy

Evp And Chief Scientist Officer, Paulus (Paul) Stoffels, age 56, $1,144,000 total compensation

Evp And Worldwide Chairman Pharmaceuticals, Joaquin Duato, age 55, $875,000 total compensation

Evp And Chief Human Resources Officer, Peter M. Fasolo, age 55

Evp And General Counsel, Michael H. Ullmann, age 59, $645,385 total compensation

Evp And World Chairman Medical Devices, Gary Pruden, age 56

Company Group Chairman Pharmaceuticals The Americas, Jennifer Taubert

Vp Hr, Martha Liano

Vice Chairman Executive Vice President And Chief Scientific Officer, Paul Stoffels

Corporate Vice President Worldwide Government Affairs And Policy, Clifford Holland

Vice President North America For Global Marketing Group, Darryl Nicholson

Vice President Oncology Sci Innovation, Pamela Carroll

Vice President Research And Development, Steven Catani

Vice President Of Human Resources, Michael Ehret

Vice President Research And Development Healthcare Compliance, Frank Konings

Vice President Global Medical Affairs, Craig Tendler

Vice President Comm And Public Affairs Med Dev, Tom Sanford

Vice President Global Engineering, Michael Maggio

Vice President Business Transformation, Angie Caswell

Area Vice President Northeast, Travis Williams

Ww Vice President Research And Development Mcneil Nutritionals, Tom Ells

Vice President Of Global Health, Scott Ratzan

Vice President Prod Stewardship, Susan Nettesheim

Vice President Quality Assurance J And J Consumer Group Of Companies, Teresa Gorecki

Vice President Global Account Management, Jack Gelman

Vice President Global Pharmaceutical Communications, Craig Rothenberg

Vice President Sterile Process Technolog, Rainer Newman

Vice President Director Manager, Ken Solognier

Vice President Global Strategic Marketing, Aldo Denti

Vice President Strategic Business Support, James Rider

Vice President Business Development, Robert Havard

Vice President Marketing Mcneil Consumer Healthcare, Catherine Devine

Vice President U.s. Sales, David Venner

Vice President Marketing, Elle Green

Vice President Immunology Marketing, Catherine Owen

Vice President Information Technology Consumer Emea, Diane Levin

Vice President Business Operations, Mike Mountan

Vice President, Mike Rose

Vice President Health Policy And Advocacy, John Hoffman

Vice President State Govt Affairs, Don Bohn

Vice President Customer Management, Scott Chilson

Vice President Ecommerce, Sri Rajagopalan

Vice President Communication And Public Affairs, Efen Huang

Vice President Medical Affairs, Andree Amelsberg

Vice President Marketing, Ganesh Bangalore

Vice President Alliance Management, Cindy Warren

Vice President Human Resources Worldwide, Mary Fink

Vice President Global Medical Affairs Cvm, Robert Cuddihy

Ww Vice President Marketing, Timothy Czartoski

Vice President Immunology Research And Development, Dan Baker

Regional Vice President, Mark Sienkiewicz

Vice President Integrated Networks, Donald Delaney

Vpcx Infrastructure Services, Nick Fisher

Vice President, Li Mao

Vp Cfo Global Consumer Supply Chain, Jill Freedman

Vice President And Head Cardiovascular And Metabolic Disease Areas Global Regulatory Affairs, Craig Ostroff

Senior Vice President, Instructor Sunywcc

Vice President Supply Chain North America Otc, Gaspar Zuniga

Vp Health System Innovation, Brad Moore

Vice President Global Medical Affairs Regional L, Suzanne Anderson

Vice President Us Sales Marketing And Ww Services, Sandor Palfi

Vice President Commercial Innovation And Operations, Fred Canterberry

Board Member, Dirk Collier

Auditors: PricewaterhouseCoopers LLP

LOCATIONS

HQ: Johnson & Johnson
One Johnson & Johnson Plaza, New Brunswick, NJ 08933
Phone: 732 524-0400   **Fax:** 732 214-0332
Web: www.jnj.com

2017 Sales

	$ mil.	% of total
US	39,863	52
Europe	17,126	22
Asia/Pacific & Africa	13,420	18
Western hemisphere excluding US	6,041	8
Total	**76,450**	**100**

PRODUCTS/OPERATIONS

2017 Sales by Segment

	$ mil.	% of total
Pharmaceutical	36,356	47
Medical Devices	26,592	35
Consumer	13,602	18
Total	**76,450**	**100**

COMPETITORS

3M Health Care	Genzyme
Abbott Labs	GlaxoSmithKline
Alcon	Kimberly-Clark Health
Allergan plc	L'Oréal USA
Amgen	Medtronic
ArthroCare	Mentholatum Company
AstraZeneca	Merck
B. Braun Melsungen	Mylan
Bard	Novartis
Bausch & Lomb	NutraSweet
Baxter International	Perrigo
Bayer AG	Pfizer
Beckman Coulter	Procter & Gamble
Becton Dickinson	Roche Holding

Biogen
Boehringer Ingelheim
Boston Scientific
Bristol-Myers Squibb
Chattem
Colgate-Palmolive
Cook Incorporated
Dr. Reddy's
Edwards Lifesciences
Eli Lilly

Sanofi
Shire
Smith & Nephew
St. Jude Medical
Stryker
Terumo
Teva
The Dial Corporation
UCB
Zimmer Biomet

HISTORICAL FINANCIALS

Company Type: Public

Income Statement   FYE: December 31

	REVENUE ($ mil.)	NET INCOME ($ mil.)	NET PROFIT MARGIN	EMPLOYEES
12/17*	76,450	1,300	1.7%	134,000
01/17	71,890	16,540	23.0%	126,400
01/16	70,074	15,409	22.0%	127,100
12/14	74,331	16,323	22.0%	126,500
12/13	71,312	13,831	19.4%	128,100
Annual Growth	1.8%	(44.6%)	—	1.1%

*Fiscal year change

2017 Year-End Financials

Debt ratio: 21.98%—
Return on equity: 2.00%
Cash ($ mil.): 17,824
Current ratio: 1.41
Long-term debt ($ mil.): 30,675

Dividends
Yield: 0.0%
Payout: 706.3%
Market value ($ mil.): —

	STOCK PRICE ($) FY Close	P/E High/Low	PER SHARE ($) Earnings	Dividends	Book Value
12/17*	139.72	299 233	0.47	3.32	22.43
01/17	115.21	21 16	5.93	3.15	26.02
01/16	102.72	19 16	5.48	2.95	25.82
12/14	105.06	19 15	5.70	2.76	25.06
12/13	92.35	19 14	4.81	2.59	26.25
Annual Growth	10.9%	—	(44.1%)	6.4%	(3.9%)

*Fiscal year change

JOHNSON CONTROLS, INC.

EXECUTIVES

Pres-Coo, George R Oliver
Exec V Pres-Cfo*, Brian Stief
V Pres-Gen Counsel-Sec*, Brian J Cadwallader
V Pres-Corp Contrl*, Suzanne M Vincent
Cpo-V Pres of Controls Operati*, Michael Bartschat
Coordinator, Bob Anders
Designer, Ed Stevens
Coordinator, Debra Morley
Coordinator, Mary Moore
Compliance Staff, Melissa Goetz-Krummel
Coordinator, Patricia Kettner
Auditors: PRICEWATERHOUSECOOPERS LLP MI

LOCATIONS

HQ: JOHNSON CONTROLS, INC.
5757 N GREEN BAY AVE, MILWAUKEE, WI 532094408
Phone: 414 524-1200
Web: WWW.JCI.COM

COMPETITORS

3M
A123 Systems
Addison

Honeywell
International
Illinois Tool Works

Alcoa
Building Technologies
Caterpillar
Comfort Systems USA
DENSO
Deere
Delphi Automotive
  Systems
Dow Chemical
DuPont
Eagle-Picher
East Penn
  Manufacturing
Eaton
Emerson Electric
Exide
Faurecia
GS Yuasa
General Dynamics
General Motors
Goodman Global
Goodyear Tire &
  Rubber

Inci Aku
International Paper
Invensys
Lear Corp
Lennox
Lockheed Martin
Magna International
Northrop Grumman
Paloma Group
Raytheon
Rieter Automotive
  North America
Robert Bosch
SPX
Trane Inc.
United Technologies
Valeo
Visteon
Whirlpool
Yazaki North America

HISTORICAL FINANCIALS

Company Type: Private

Income Statement   FYE: September 30

	REVENUE ($ mil.)	NET INCOME ($ mil.)	NET PROFIT MARGIN	EMPLOYEES
09/15	37,179	1,679	4.5%	139,000
09/14	42,828	1,335	3.1%	—
09/13	42,730	1,297	3.0%	—
Annual Growth	(6.7%)	13.8%	—	—

2015 Year-End Financials

Debt ratio: —
Return on equity: 4.50%
Cash ($ mil.): 597
Current ratio: 0.60
Long-term debt ($ mil.): —

Dividends
Yield: —
Payout: —
Market value ($ mil.): —

Jones Financial Companies LLLP

LOCATIONS

HQ: Jones Financial Companies LLLP
12555 Manchester Road, Des Peres, MO 63131
Phone: 314 515-2000

HISTORICAL FINANCIALS

Company Type: Public

Income Statement   FYE: December 31

	REVENUE ($ mil.)	NET INCOME ($ mil.)	NET PROFIT MARGIN	EMPLOYEES
12/17	7,506	872	11.6%	45,000
12/16	6,557	746	11.4%	43,000
12/15	6,619	838	12.7%	41,000
12/14	6,278	770	12.3%	40,000
12/13	5,656	674	11.9%	39,000
Annual Growth	7.3%	6.6%	—	3.6%

2017 Year-End Financials

Debt ratio: —
Return on equity: —
Cash ($ mil.): 2,010
Current ratio: 1.13
Long-term debt ($ mil.): —

No. of shares (mil.): 0
Dividends
Yield: —
Payout: —
Market value ($ mil.): —

Jones Lang LaSalle Inc

Jones Lang LaSalle (JLL) provides real estate without borders. Its services include commercial leasing real estate brokerage management advisory and financing through nearly 300 corporate offices in more than 80 countries around the world; almost 45% of its business is in the US. The company's LaSalle Investment Management arm is a diversified real estate management firm with about $60 billion in assets under management. JLL has commercial real estate expertise across office retail hotel health care industrial cultural and multifamily residential properties. It manages more than 4.5 billion sq. ft. worldwide.

HISTORY

Jones Lang Wootton had roots in London's Paternoster Row auction houses in 1783. LaSalle Partners originally known as IDC Real Estate was founded in El Paso Texas in 1968. The two companies could not have started out in a more disparate fashion yet their combined force is now one of the largest real estate services firms in the world.

Richard Winstanley opened an auction house in 1783 and his son James joined him in that business in 1806. In 1840 the Joneses entered the picture — the Winstanleys created a partnership with one James Jones. The business moved to King Street (in the Guildhall section of London) in 1860 and remained in that location for some 100 years in various incarnations — James' son Frederick took over the business renaming it Frederick Jones and Co. When James retired in 1872 the firm was again renamed to Jones Lang and Co. and was controlled by C. A. Lang. Jones Lang merged with Wootton and Son in 1939 becoming Jones Lang Wootton and Sons.

Jones Lang Wootton was active in redrawing the property lines in London after the Blitz. In 1945 the firm began contacting small landowners and by combining small parcels of land secured development leasing and/or purchase contracts. When the rebuilding of London began in 1954 Jones Lang Wootton was in a secure place to be right at the forefront of that new development. The firm began engaging in speculative development in the West End and in the City of London.

The year 1958 saw the expansion of Jones Lang Wootton into Australia; the firm had offices throughout the Asia/Pacific region by 1968. Further expansion took place closer to home in Scotland (1962) and Ireland (1965) and the first continental European office in Brussels (also 1965). The firm moved into the Manhattan market in 1975.

On the other side of the story IDC Real Estate (the name change to LaSalle Partners came in 1977) was a group of partnerships initially focused on investment banking investment management and land. The firm began offering development management services in 1975; it moved into property management leasing and tenant representation in 1978 and facility management operations in 1980.

It built market share by buying other firms including Kleinwort Benson Realty Advisors Corp. (1994) and UK-based investment adviser CIN Property Management (1996).

The firm leveraged its experience and long-term client base to pursue an acquisition strategy taking advantage of trends shaping commercial real estate — globalization consolidation and merchant banking. LaSalle went public in 1997 amalgamating the Galbreath Company (a property and development management firm with which it merged that year) with its other partnerships and becoming a corporation.

In 1998 it acquired the project management business of Satulah Group and two retail management business units from Lend Lease and took real estate investment trust LaSalle Hotel Properties public. In 1999 the firm strengthened its world position by merging with Jones Lang Wootton; the company was renamed Jones Lang LaSalle.

The merger with Jones Lang Wootton combined Wootton's strength in Asia and Europe with LaSalle Partners' large presence in North America to create a worldwide real estate services firm. In 2006 the company acquired Spaulding & Slye strengthening operations in the Mid-Atlantic and New England. Also that year it opened an office in Dubai and acquired RSP Group which operates in North Africa and the Middle East. In 2007 Jones Lang LaSalle bought German property advisory firm Kemper's Holding and took a stake in the former Trammell Crow Meghraj one of the largest private real estate companies in India.

The company broadened its presence in key North American markets when it acquired The Staubach Company in 2008. Jones Lang LaSalle paid $613 million for the rival real estate services firm which was founded by football legend and former Dallas Cowboys quarterback Roger Staubach.

Jones Lang LaSalle slowed its acquisition pace during the economic recession. But managed to cut a few deals. In 2009 Jones Lang LaSalle teamed up with Real Estate Disposition to begin offering online auction sales a product to help customers quickly sell commercial property and other distressed assets.

In another deal Jones Lang LaSalle acquired the third-party leasing and management duties of General Growth Properties in 2010 as part of the mall owner's restructuring efforts. The deal added about 20 shopping centers to Jones Lang LaSalle's management portfolio.

EXECUTIVES

Ceo Americas, Gregory P. (Greg) O'Brien, age 55, $400,000 total compensation
Regional Ceo European Operations, Jeff A. Jacobson, age 56, $400,000 total compensation
Cio, David A. Johnson, age 55
President Ceo And Director, Christian Ulbrich, age 52, $481,619 total compensation
Cfo, Christie B. Kelly, age 56, $400,000 total compensation
Ceo Europe Middle East And Africa, Guy Grainger
Managing Director Shanghai And East China, Anthony Couse, $420,902 total compensation
Ceo Americas Corporate Solutions, John Forrest
Evp And Chief Human Resources Officer, Patricia (Trish) Maxson, age 59
Global Head Capital Markets, Richard Bloxam
Ceo Jll Netherlands, Pieter Hendrikse
Senior Vice President, David Roberts
Executive Vice President, Mark Smith
Vice President, Mia Eglinton
Vice President, Bob Gross
Senior Vice President Information Technology, David Laduke
Senior Vice President Of Engineering, Miles Anderson
Vice President Of Sponsorship Marketing, Sally Hertz
Executive Vice President, Jason Schmidt
Executive Vice President, Yoav Oelsner
Senior Vice President; National Director, Don Sauvigne
Senior Vice President Broker License, Matthew Berres
Vice President, Jeremiah Riordan
Executive Vice President, Wade Clark

Senior Vice President International Desk, Julie Steffen
Senior Vice President Hotels And Hospitality, Nick Baer
Vice President, Anu Rao
Associate Vice President, Jason Benson
Vice President, Roberto Rios
Vice President, Teri Bell
Executive Vice President Asset Management Asia, Tasos Kousloglou
Senior Vice President Of Development And Asset Strategy, Jeffrey Adkison
Vice President Marketing, Stephen Steinberg
Executive Vice President Tenant Reperesentation, Rob Nielsen
Senior Vice President Director Of Public Relations, Gayle Kantro
Senior Vice President, Alvin Magner
Executive Vice President, Gregg Raus
Senior Vice President Business Consulting, Shannon Curley
Vice President Corporate Properties Group, Allen Merrill
Vice President Strategic Consulting Workplace And Occupancy Planning, Laura Delafuente
Assistant Vice President, Yorke Allen
Vice President, Koley X MacKay
Vice President, Michelle Monhaut
Senior Vice President, Bradley McGill
Senior Vice President, Arthur Frye
Senior Vice President Lease Administration, Jim Colaianni
Assistant Vice President Information, John Rinaldi
Vice President, Stephen Chastain
Vice President Retail Sourcing, Jon Bloss
Senior Vice President, John A Cullen
Senior Vice President, Robert Tomsovic
Vice President Pmp, Chris Ferreira
Vice President Associate Director, Julie Bane
Executive Vice President, George Nicholas
Vice President, Paul Kelsey
Senior Vice President, Joshua Sloan
Vice President, Andrew Fischer
Executive Vice President, Glenn Aspinwall
Senior Vice President, Sherri Lusk
Vice President, Andrew Whipple
Senior Vice President, Stephen Peacock
Vice President, Chris Chornohos
Vice President Associate Director, Jesse Mangum
Senior Vice President, David Chapin
Senior Vice President, Xavier Wasiak
Executive Vice President Global Tax, James Jasionowski
Assistant Vice President Marketing, Lesley Sebastian
Executive Vice President, Steve Jarvie
Senior Vice President, Andrew White
Vice President Eastern Region, Rakesh Kapoor
Senior Vice President, Natasha Brown
Senior Vice President, Coleen Cecil
Vice President, Louis Rosenthal
Associate Vice President, Gary Politi
Vice President Occupancy Planning Projects, Christopher Duggan
Vice President Director Of Operations, Jeffrey Harris
Assistant Vice President, Holly Kinkeade
Vice President, Michael Cameron
Senior Vice President New England Construction, Bill Mack
Vice President And Regional Manager, Robert Fernicola
Senior Vice President, Patrick Nugent
Vice President, Liz Ocarroll
Senior Vice President, Charles Crapse
Executive Vice President Industrial, David Knee
Executive Vice President And International Director, Ronnie Deyo
Senior Vice President, Julio Villavincencio

Senior Vice President Project And Development Services, Tom O'Connor
Senior Vice President, Rod Loschiavo
Executive Vice President, David Cantwell
Senior Vice President, Thomas Dimicelli
Senior Vice President, Liz Tucker
Vice President, Jamie Barden
National Director Senior Vice President, Paul Logan
Senior Vice President Suburbs, Dan Fernitz
Vice President Technical, Yuvaraj Halarnkar
Executive Vice President, Mike Boehler
Vice President, Cliff West
Senior Vice President I Tenant Representation, Ryan Schneider
Vice President Finance, Asin Shah
Executive Vice President, Johnathan Pierson
Vice President, Lauren Gonzalez
Executive Vice President Houston Industrial Services Group, Jarret Venghaus
Vice President Manager Director, Kenneth Anderson
Vice President, Thomas Arena
Vice President, Dan De Palma
Executive Vice President Southwest Retail Brokerage Lead, Chris Wilson
Senior Vice President Human Resources, Courtney Petit
Senior Vice President, Jeff Quinn
Senior Vice President, John Cashion
Evp Hotels And Hospitality Group, David Calverley
Evp Hotels And Hospitality Group, Louis Breeding
Senior Vice President, Gary Applestein
Senior Vice President, Steve Leathers
Executive Vice President Hotels And Hospitality Group And National Valuation Director Hotel, Charlotte Kang
Vice President, Tom Dunn
Senior Vice President Markets Corporate Solutions Demarest Team, Nicole Littleton
Senior Vice President Retail Brokerage, Rick Spector
Vice President Research And Strategic Advisory Asia, Frank Sorgiovanni
Vice President Account Lead, Jay Forse
Vice President Brokerage, Muscoe Garnett
Senior Vice President And Director Finance Latin America, Angelita Del Bosque
Vice President Strategy And Performance Management, Jeffrey Sinclair
Executive Vice President Supply Chain And Logistics Solutions, Bob Silverman
Assistant Vice President, Rob Mahoney
Vice President, Steve Us Moran
Senior Vice President Corporate Solutions, George Wittmann
Executive Vice President, Matthew Powers
Vice President, David Depalma
Executive Vice President, John Buckley
Senior Vice President, Deborah Stearns
Executive Vice President Capital Markets, Marc Rampulla
Vice President Public Institutions, Emily Crutcher
Associate Vice President, Simon Landmann
Vice President Account Lead, Nancy Yandrofski
Vice President Smart Building Solutions, Mike Denamur
Senior Vice President, Tivon Moffitt
Vice President Retail Brokerage, Jose Gonzalez
Vice President Cloud Advisory, Evan Smethurst
Assistant Vice President, Sireen Parekh
Vice President Pds Lead Southern California Region, Constadine Gimas
Leed Green Associate Vice President Senior General Manager, Jill Rauske
Vice President Account Lead, Babatunde Dehinde
Vice President Nw Healthcare Business Lead, Kimberly Mchugh
Senior Vice President I Tenant Representation, Matt Waggoner

Vice President Lease Administration, Ronnie
Vagnone Cpa
Vice President Smart Building Solutions Jll
 Smart Building Program, Neal Sivie
Executive Vice President, Darin Mai
Chairman, Sheila A. Penrose, age 72
Treasurer, Bryan Duncan
Board Member, Jeremy Gardner
Vice Chairman, Paul Glickman
Auditors: KPMG LLP

LOCATIONS

HQ: Jones Lang LaSalle Inc
 200 East Randolph Drive, Chicago, IL 60601
Phone: 312 782-5800   Fax: 312 782-4339
Web: www.jll.com

2017 Sales by Business Segment

	$ mil.	% of total
Americas	3,354	42
Europe Middle East Africa	2,586	33
Asia Pacific	1,636	21
Investment management	355	4
Total	**7,932**	**100**

PRODUCTS/OPERATIONS

2017 Sales

	$ mil.	% of total
Real Estate Services		
Property and facility management	2,381	30
Leasing	2,023	26
Project and development services	1,348	17
Capital Markets & Hotels	1,138	14
Advisory Consulting and Other	684	9
LaSalle Investment Management	355	4
Total		**100**

Selected Services

Investor services
 Agency leasing
 Property management
 Valuations and consulting
Occupier services
 Facilities management
 Project and development services
 Tenant representation
Construction management
Capital markets
Hotel advisory
Strategic consulting

COMPETITORS

BGC Partners	Hines
CBRE Group	Lend Lease
Colliers International	Newmark Knight Frank
Colliers International	Prologis
Group	Savills
Cushman & Wakefield	

HISTORICAL FINANCIALS

Company Type: Public

Income Statement

FYE: December 31

	REVENUE ($ mil.)	NET INCOME ($ mil.)	NET PROFIT MARGIN	EMPLOYEES
12/17	7,932	254	3.2%	81,900
12/16	6,803	318	4.7%	77,300
12/15	5,965	438	7.4%	61,500
12/14	5,429	386	7.1%	58,100
12/13	4,461	269	6.0%	52,700
Annual Growth	15.5%	(1.5%)	—	11.7%

2017 Year-End Financials

Debt ratio: 13.25%
Return on equity: 8.43%
Cash ($ mil.): 268
Current ratio: 1.05
Long-term debt ($ mil.): 675

No. of shares (mil.): 45
Dividends
 Yield: 0.0%
 Payout: 12.9%
Market value ($ mil.): 6,758

STOCK PRICE ($) FY Close	P/E High/Low	PER SHARE ($) Earnings	Dividends	Book Value
12/17 148.93	27 18	5.55	0.72	71.48
12/16 101.04	23 13	6.98	0.64	61.70
12/15 159.86	18 15	9.65	0.56	59.68
12/14 149.93	18 12	8.52	0.48	53.24
12/13 102.39	17 13	5.98	0.44	49.04
Annual Growth 9.8%	— —	(1.8%)	13.1%	9.9%

JPMorgan Chase & Co

Boasting some $2.5 trillion in assets JPMorgan Chase is the largest bank holding company in the US and among the largest half-dozen in the world. With some 5250 branches in about two dozen states it is among the nation's top mortgage lenders and credit card issuers (it holds some $141 billion in credit card loans). Active in 60 countries the bank also boasts formidable investment banking and asset management operations through its subsidiaries JPMorgan Private Bank and institutional investment manager JPMorgan Asset Management which has $2.5 trillion in assets under supervision. The company can trace its history back to the Bank of Manhattan Company founded in 1799.

HISTORY

JPMorgan Chase & Co.'s roots are in The Manhattan Company created in 1799 to bring water to New York City. A provision buried in its incorporation documents let the company provide banking services; investor and future US Vice President Aaron Burr brought the company (eventually the Bank of Manhattan) into competition with The Bank of New York founded by Burr's political rival Alexander Hamilton. JPMorgan Chase still owns the pistols from the notorious 1804 duel in which Burr mortally wounded Hamilton.

In 1877 John Thompson formed Chase National naming it for Salmon Chase Abraham Lincoln's secretary of the treasury and the architect of the national bank system. Chase National merged with John D. Rockefeller's Equitable Trust in 1930 becoming the world's largest bank and beginning a long relationship with the Rockefellers. Chase National continued growing after WWII and in 1955 it merged with the Bank of Manhattan. Christened Chase Manhattan the bank remained the US's largest into the 1960s.

When soaring 1970s oil prices made energy loans attractive Chase invested in Penn Square an obscure oil-patch bank in Oklahoma and the first notable bank failure of the 1980s. (The legal aftereffects of Penn Square's 1982 failure dragged on until 1993.) Losses following the 1987 foreign loan crisis hit Chase hard as did the real estate crash. In 1995 the bank went looking for a partner. After talks with Bank of America it settled on Chemical Bank.

Chemical Bank opened in 1824 and was one of the US's largest banks by 1900. As with Chase Chemical Bank began as an unrelated business (New York Chemical Manufacturing) in 1823 largely in order to open a bank (it dropped its chemical operations in 1844). Chemical would merge with Manufacturers Hanover in 1991.

After its 1996 merger with Chase Chemical Bank was the surviving entity but assumed Chase's more prestigious name. Initial cost savings from the merger were substantial as jobs and branch offices were eliminated. In 1997 Chase acquired the credit business of The Bank of New York and the corporate trustee business of Mellon Financial but underwent another round of belt-tightening the next year when it took a $320 million charge and cut 4500 jobs. The bank also suffered losses related to its involvement with the ill-starred Long-Term Capital Management hedge fund.

In 1999 Chase focused on lending buying two mortgage originators and forming a marketing alliance with subprime auto lender AmeriCredit (now General Motors Financial Company). Chase also bought Mellon Financial's residential mortgage unit and Huntington Bancshares' credit card portfolio. It bought UK investment bank Robert Fleming Holdings in 2000.

In 2001 it closed its $30 billion buy of J.P. Morgan and renamed itself JPMorgan Chase & Co. The new firm eliminated some 10% of its combined workforce as a result of the merger. Chairman Sandy Warner (who ran J.P. Morgan) retired at year-end and was replaced by former Chase Manhattan leader CEO William Harrison.

JPMorgan Chase had more than $1 billion in exposure to Enron but in 2003 recovered some $600 million after a court battle with the failed energy trader's insurers which claimed the losses stemmed from loans by JPMorgan Chase disguised as oil and gas transactions. Nonetheless JPMorgan Chase ended up paying some $135 million to settle actions relating to the questionable loans.

In 2004 JPMorgan Chase joined forces with venerable investment bank Cazenove; the joint venture called JPMorgan Cazenove handles corporate finance and capital markets activities in the UK.

The next year JPMorgan Chase and its investment banking arm J.P. Morgan Securities avoided a trial by paying some $2 billion to settle claims from investors who lost money on bonds that the firm underwrote in 2000 and 2001 for scandal-ridden WorldCom which eventually declared bankruptcy (WorldCom became MCI and later was acquired by Verizon Communications).

On the heels of the its massive BANK ONE buy in 2004 JPMorgan Chase made several smaller purchases including global trade management and logistics software maker Vastera (renamed JPMorgan Chase Vastera) trading technology firm Neovest and the credit card business of Sears Canada. JPMorgan Chase also sold online brokerage subsidiary J.P. Morgan Invest and its BrownCo unit to E*TRADE. The following year the company acquired student lender Collegiate Funding Services which JPMorgan Chase combined with its existing Chase Education Finance division. The company also got the go-ahead from the FTC and bought Kohl's $1.6 billion credit card portfolio.

Enron continued to haunt the company: in 2005 it forked over $2.2 billion to settle part of an investor class-action suit over fraud charges related to the Enron debacle and paid another $350 million to the infamous energy trading firm which asserted that JPMorgan Chase and about 10 other banks aided and abetted the company's collapse. However the next year the company got some good news regarding its alleged involvement with the collapse of Enron when the class action suit against it was dismissed.

Also in 2006 the company cut ties with private equity investment arm J.P. Morgan Partners which divided into two companies CCMP Capital and Panorama Capital. JPMorgan Chase retained the former private equity operations of BANK ONE One Equity Partners.

In keeping with the lesson learned regarding its $2 billion fine to settle claims in the WorldCom debacle in 2006 the bank was quick to settle its part of another class-action lawsuit this time brought by investors claiming they were cheated in the dot-com IPO boom. JPMorgan Chase paid $425 million to settle that case. It paid a much smaller settlement of $3.8 million for its part in the demise of the ill-fated telecom Global Crossing.

All was not lawsuits and settlements in 2006 however: that year it swapped its corporate trust business for Bank of New York's nearly 340-branch network in the New York metropolitan area. Both units were valued at about $2 billion with JPMorgan Chase paying Bank of New York around $150 million more to make up the difference.

William Harrison retired as chairman at the end of 2006; he was succeeded by president and CEO (and the CEO of BANK ONE when it was acquired) Jamie Dimon.

As one of the largest mortgage and home equity providers in the country JPMorgan Chase was hurt by the subprime mortgage crisis and subsequent fall in home values in 2007. About a third of its loans were home equity loans and it had to write off more than $500 million in home equity loans that year.

In 2008 the bank assumed full ownership of payments processor Chase Paymentech Solutions which had been a joint venture with First Data. First Data assumed 49% of Chase Paymentech's assets and clients in the deal.

Also that year as part of a plan to stimulate the economy the US government invested in JPMorgan Chase and other banks. The bank got $25 billion of the $700 billion taxpayer-funded bailout package that was approved in late 2008 with the stipulation that the banks use the money and not hoard it. The investment came with restrictions on executive pay and other rules and JPMorgan returned the money the following year saying it was doing just fine without it.

Led by CEO Jamie Dimon JPMorgan Chase closed a couple of very high profile deals as the economic crisis claimed numerous victims. It acquired Bear Stearns one of Wall Street's top investment banks and the operations of Washington Mutual (WaMu) the largest bank to fail in US history. Both deals closed in 2008.

Initially JPMorgan Chase made a bargain-basement offer of $270 million (around $2 a share) for the struggling Bear Stearns which was drowning in subprime mortgage investment debt. It ultimately raised its offer to around $10 a share or some $1.2 billion. The deal came after the Fed extended a $30 billion lifeline to Bear Stearns to keep the firm afloat; JPMorgan Chase was one of the lenders.

The company also stepped in to buy WaMu when that bank failed and was seized by regulators. It paid $1.9 billion for the bank's operations and assumed some $31 billion in losses. JPMorgan began integrating WaMu's branches with its own retail network phasing out the WaMu brand and closing about 10% of the combined branches (especially in markets where there was overlap). Shortly after the acquisition JPMorgan cut 9200 WaMu jobs — about 20% of its workforce.

In 2009 JPMorgan Chase sold specialist firm Bear Wagner acquired in the Bear Stearns deal to Barclays Capital.

JPMorgan Chase agreed to pay more than $153 million to the Securities and Exchange Commission in order to settle a claim that it misled investors during the 2007 housing market crash. The company was among others that were investigated for improper sales practices.

In 2010 JPMorgan acquired the European and Asian segments of RBS Sempra Commodities the energy trading joint venture between Royal Bank of Scotland and Sempra Energy. The $1.6 billion deal did not include RBS Sempra's more valuable

North American segment. JPMorgan integrated the business into the bank's existing global commodities business doubling its corporate client numbers.

Also in 2010 the company bought the private equity administration services of Schroders. That deal added more than $6 billion in committed capital. J.P. Morgan Worldwide Securities Services already had some $15.3 trillion in assets under custody. In 2011 the company sold its 41% stake in mutual fund company American Century to CIBC for some $848 million.

EXECUTIVES

Vice President Of Facilities Vip, Gerard Vanella
Vice President, Brian Coats
Vice President Information Technology Architecture, Douglas Schwarz
Vice President, John Bradley
Chairman And Ceo, James (Jamie) Dimon, age 61, $1,500,000 total compensation
Ceo Card Services, Gordon A. Smith, age 59, $500,000 total compensation
Ceo Corporate And Investment Bank, Daniel E. Pinto, age 55, $8,303,234 total compensation
Cio, Lori A. Beer, age 50
Ceo Commercial Banking And Executive Committee Member, Douglas B. (Doug) Petno, age 52
Ceo Asset And Wealth Management, Mary Callahan Erdoes, age 50, $750,000 total compensation
Cfo, Marianne Lake, age 48, $750,000 total compensation
Chief Risk Officer, Ashley Bacon, age 48
Ceo Jpmorgan Emea And Jp Morgan Securities Plc, Vis Raghavan
Vice President, Josephine Norris
First Vice President District Manager, Sean Cummings
1st Vice President, Patti Shultz
Vice President Information Security Officer, Todd Bailey
Vice President Human Resources, Jim Odonnell
Vice President Information Technology, Dennis Ramawy
Vice President Of Information Technology, Paul Rosenberg
Vice President Of It, Alex Kayzerman
Vice President Of Technology, Tracey Ball
Vice President Market Risk Technology, Kevin Ford
Vice President Of Public Finance, David Elmquist
Vice President Trading Technologies, Ann Billak
Vice President Talent And Development Operations, Ning Ham
Senior Vice President Middle Market Banking, Jim Nicholas
Senior Vice President Client Care, Terry Hansen
Vice President, Richard Hixson
Assistannt Vice President, Jason Silbaugh
Vice President, Diane Genovesi
Vice President Client Service J.p. Morgan Securities Llc, Barbara Fuqua
Vice President, Chet Zhang
Vice President Risk Modeling Manager Mortgage Banking Modeling And Analytics, Tracy Wu
Global Vice President Information Technology Investment Banking Division, Brian Zitterkopf
Vice President, Lori Loschiavo
Vice President, Douglas Savage
Vice President Corporate And Investment Bank Strategy And New Business Development, John Curry
Senior Vice President, Dan Howat
Vice President, Anatoly Morosov
Vice President, Kelley Simpson
Vice President, Joe Pedone
Vice President, Jeff Wright
Vice President Balance Data Mart Ib Single Subledger, Robert Depowski

Vice President, Mihir Agochiya
Vice President, Nancy Panetta
Vice President, Harvey Klyce
Vice President, Kenneth Coons
Vice President Investment Bank Technology, Farhan Jaffery
Senior Vice President Dealer Commercial Services, Jeff Johns
Senior Vice President, Nancy McDonnell
Vice President Architecture, Prasad Chaubal
Vice President, Laura Cussen
Vice President Executive Recruiter Ii, Tom Suhm
Vice President Global Market Tech, Robert Stepanski
Vice President Accounting Manager, Jeanne Higgins
Vice President, Lewis Rieck
First Vice President, Michael V McCann
Vice President Human Resources And Employee Development And Training, Sophia Chu
Vice President, Curt Barrentine
Vice President Sourcing And Procurement Services, Joseph Viola
Assistant Vice President Banker, Javier Varela
Vice President Of Architecture, Adam Goldin
Vice President Marketing Analysis Manager, Matthew Reynolds
Assistant Vice President Business Banker, Rakhee Singh
Vice President, Vinay Somashekar
Vice President, Bruce Goldberg
Vice President, Donna Kopelman
Vice President Senior P And A Manager, Charles Chiappone
Senior Vice President, Gerry Murphy
Executive Vice President Operations, Barbara Bernstein
Vice President Product Manager, Chinyere Oguekwe
Executive Vice President, Emmett Vollenweider
Vice President, Michelle Erny
Vice President Of Desktop Computing And Application Integration, Leonard Friedman
Vice President, Jason Hand
Assistantvice President, Drew Pascucci
Vice President Private Banking, Patricia Lunka
Vice President Of Central Technology Operations Retail Financial Services, Kevin Kirkpatrick
Vice President, John Mathai
Vice President, Bob Cummings
Vice President, Robert Grigg
Vice President, Gail Bigley
Vice President, Laura Bosma
Assistant Vice President, Diana Reed
Vice President Global Technology Jpmorgan Chase, Rick Schomburg
Vice President Crm Retention Management, Gail Timmerman
Vice President Banker, David Sagers
Vice President Application Development Manager, Kiran Mudichintala
Vice President Client Satisfaction, Giovanna Pape
Vice President, Muhammad Hasan
Senior Vice President Special Credits Group, Phil Martin
Vice President Application Devpmt, David Overmyer
Vice President, Greg Schmidt
Vice President, Greg Martin
Vice President Commercial Banking, Bill Cook
Vice President, Keith Jia
Vice President Customer Analytics, Stella Ng
Senior Vice President, Paul O'Neill
Vice President, Fariah Feinstein
Vice President, Lisamarie Devilbiss
Vice President, Mark Chilewitz
Vice President, Alice Lo
Vice President, Luis Oganes
Vice President Human Resources Program Management, Jenny Blanco
Assistant Vice President Information Technology Production Assurance Analyst, Jarrod Holt

Senior Vice President, Mary Reilly
Vice President, Kevin Connor
Vice President Enterprise Technology Services, Josiah Lam
Vice President Senior Fiduciary Officer, Daniel Ordan
Assistant Vice President Business Relationship Manager, Carlo Condong
Senior Vice President, Bill W Handley
Senior Vice President, Craig Reese
Vice President Application Development, Craig Horton
Vice President, Jennifer Stewart
Vice President Asset Management, Rawle Sealy
Senior Vice President, John Ireton
Vice President, John Friedman
Senior Vice President, Randolph Lopez
Vice President Chase Franchise Finance, Alma Winkel
Vice President, Jennifer Theriault
Vice President Operations, Jocelyn Gombac
Vice President, Stephen Papuzek
Vice President, Gina Shera
Vice President Assistant General Counsel, David Swarts
Vice President, Alessandro Bagnara
Assistant Vice President, Desiree Brown
Vice President, Angelines Jover
Senior Vice President And Division Manager, Nick Klym
Vice President, David Hladik
Vice President, Amy Huelskamp
Vice President, Jonathan Gay
Assistant Vice President, Biljana Nasuovska
Vice President, Gail Philips
Senior Vice President, Corey Limbaugh
Vice President, Luz Escarraman
Vice President Appraisal Escalation Desk, Eric Gill
Vice President, Fiore Petrassi
Vice President, Sandy Auguste
Vice President, Deborah Merkel
Vice President, Christopher Bowman
Vice President, Joseph Pichla
Vice President, Todd Bruggeman
Vice President, Deb Vincent
Vice President And Rm Area Manager, Yaron Warzman
Vice President, Sheila Carvalho
Vice President Real Estate Construction, Duncan Gerding
Auditors: PricewaterhouseCoopers LLP

LOCATIONS

HQ: JPMorgan Chase & Co
270 Park Avenue, New York, NY 10017
Phone: 212 270-6000
Web: www.jpmorganchase.com

PRODUCTS/OPERATIONS

2016 Sales

	$ mil.	% of total
Interest		
Loans	36,634	35
securities	7,304	7
Trading assets	7,292	7
Federal funds sold & securities purchased under resale agreements	2,265	2
Deposits with banks	1,863	2
Securities borrowed	(332)	-
Other	875	1
Non-interest		
Asset management administration & commissions	14,591	14
Principal transactions	11,566	11
Investment banking fees	6,448	6
Lending- and deposit-related fees	5,774	5
Credit card income	4,779	4
Mortgage fees and related income	2,491	2
Securities gains	141	-
Other	3,795	4
Total	**101,006**	**100**

COMPETITORS

American Express	Goldman Sachs
Bank of America	HSBC
Bank of New York Mellon	Morgan Stanley
Barclays	PNC Financial
CIBC	RBC Financial Group
Capital One	State Bank Financial Corporation
Citigroup	SunTrust
Citigroup Global Markets	TD Bank USA
Credit Suisse (USA)	UBS
Deutsche Bank	Wells Fargo

HISTORICAL FINANCIALS

Company Type: Public

Income Statement

FYE: December 31

	ASSETS ($ mil.)	NET INCOME ($ mil.)	INCOME AS % OF ASSETS	EMPLOYEES
12/17	2,533,600	24,441	1.0%	252,539
12/16	2,490,972	24,733	1.0%	243,355
12/15	2,351,698	24,442	1.0%	234,598
12/14	2,573,126	21,762	0.8%	241,359
12/13	2,415,689	17,923	0.7%	251,196
Annual Growth	1.2%	8.1%	—	0.1%

2017 Year-End Financials

Debt ratio: 9.85%—
Return on equity: 9.59%
Cash ($ mil.): 430,121
Current ratio: —
Long-term debt ($ mil.): —

Dividends
Yield: 0.0%
Payout: 32.3%
Market value ($ mil.): —

	STOCK PRICE ($) FY Close	P/E High/Low	PER SHARE ($) Earnings	PER SHARE ($) Dividends	PER SHARE ($) Book Value
12/17	106.94	17 13	6.31	2.04	74.65
12/16	86.29	14 9	6.19	1.84	71.38
12/15	66.03	12 9	6.00	1.68	67.58
12/14	62.58	12 10	5.29	1.56	62.47
12/13	58.48	13 10	4.35	1.36	56.22
Annual Growth	16.3%	— —	9.7%	10.7%	7.3%

Juniper Networks Inc

Juniper Networks helps its customers branch out and up all the way to the cloud. The company makes infrastructure hardware and software for large-scale networks for cloud-computing providers (including data centers) telecommunications companies and large organizations in business government and education. Its routers and switches move traffic around networks and its software helps manage networks. Juniper also develops security products for cyberattack detection and protection. Juniper sells directly and through resellers and distributors including Ingram Micro and Hitachi. More than half of sales are made to customers based in the US.

Operations

Juniper gets about 70% of its revenue from its networking equipment products and the rest from services. Routing products such as the ACX MX PTX and Cloud Customer Platform series generate about 45% of revenue. Services which include support professional and educational services account for about 30% of revenue with switching products ? the EX and QFX series ? providing about 20% and security products the SRX series among others about 5%.

Juniper relies on contract manufacturers - Celestica; Flex Ltd. Accton Technology and Alpha Networks ? to make its products.

Geographic Reach

Juniper Networks does business in some 150 countries. The US is its largest market accounting for more than half of sales. Europe the Middle East and Africa combined for about 25% of sales and Asia/Pacific accounts for more than 15%.

Sales and Marketing

Juniper sells its products directly and through distributors resellers and original equipment manufacturers (OEMs). More than 70% of revenue comes from telecom cable and cloud service providers with the rest from corporate customers. Juniper has resale agreements with Ericsson Dimension Data NEC Corp. and IBM.

Financial Performance

Juniper Networks has posted higher revenue in each of the past three years but the increase gets smaller each year.

Revenue inched 1% higher in 2017 to $5 billion from 2016 as routing and security product delivered lower sales while switching and services came through with increases. The company blamed lower routing revenue (down 7%) on a shift by Cloud customers in the Americas to more automated cost efficient and scalable networks. Security revenue dropped (down 25%) as the company transitions to newer versions of the high-end SRX series. Switching revenue rose 12% boosted by growth in its data center switching portfolio particularly in the QFX product line (up 25% year-to-year). Service revenue rose 8% on strong renewal and attach rates of support contracts as well as robust year-to-year services revenue growth in the Asia/Pacific and EMEA regions.

Juniper?s profit fell by nearly half to about $306 million in 2017 from 2016. The company reduced research and development and sales and marketing costs but general and administrative costs rose due to litigation. Further Juniper spent more on restructuring in 2017 reducing headcount by about 450.

The company?s cash on hand rose to about $2 billion in 2017 from about $1.8 billion in 2016.

Strategy

Juniper Networks is betting that helping customers move to cloud computing is the path to growth in the networking business. Beyond its traditional hardware products the company has added a range of software applications to meet the industrywide shift to software management of networks. In its router business the company offers the NorthStar WAN SDN (software defined network) controller for optimizing traffic on a network and it integrated its Contrail Networking SDN controller into its edge networking products. Some customers are moving from the older MX routing product one of the company?s most successful to the newer PTX series. Overall traffic growth at cloud providers should hasten the transition and revenue should recover as more ports are sold.

Further strengthening Juniper's software portfolio was the acquisition of AppFormix. The software from AppFormix complements the analytics and machine learning capabilities of the Contrail product.

Juniper faces competition on all sides as its tries to generate revenue from cloud computing. Competitors include industry giants such as Huawei Cisco Systems and Nokia as well as smaller companies like Arista Networks and Brocade Communications Systems which was acquired by Broadcom. Other competitors are Hewlett Packard Enterprise and Dell Technologies (because of its acquisition of EMC).

Mergers and Acquisitions

Juniper Networks? recent acquisitions were made to bolster its security and software offerings.

The 2017 deal for Cyphort Inc. a provider of security analytics for advanced threat defense added to the capabilities of Juniper?s Sky Advanced Threat Protection by increasing efficiency and performance.

In 2016 Juniper acquired AppFormix Inc. an optimization and management software platform for public private and hybrid clouds for about $50 million.

Also in 2016 Juniper bought the 88% interest it didn?t own of BTI Systems Inc. an optical equipment provider for about $25 million. The acquisition provides Juniper with optical transport solutions.

In a third 2016 deal Juniper paid about $74 million for 100% ownership of Aurrion Inc. a provider of fabless silicon photonic technology. The acquisition also bolsters Juniper?s optical portfolio.

EXECUTIVES

Cto And Chief Scientist, Pradeep S. Sindhu, age 65, $600,000 total compensation

Svp And Cio, Robert (Bob) Worrall, age 57

Evp; General Manager Juniper Development And Innovation, Rami Rahim, age 47, $1,000,000 total compensation

Evp And Chief Customer Officer, Vince Molinaro, $585,000 total compensation

Evp And General Manager Juniper Development And Innovation, Jonathan Davidson, $610,000 total compensation

Svp Finance, Ken Miller, age 46, $499,755 total compensation

Svp And Chief Marketing Officer, Michael (Mike) Marcellin

Svp; Gm Apac, Daniel Hua

Chief Development Officer, Anand (Andy) Athreya

Svp And General Manager Europe Middle East And Africa (emea), Marcus Jewell

Vice President Of Engineering Routing Business Unit, Vijay Talati

Vice President And Managing Director Govedumed Americas Enterprise, John Orbe

Vice President Finance, James Morgado

Vice President Of Supply Chain, Joe Carson

Corporate Vice President Partners And Alliances, Brian Rosenberg

Vp And Chief Information Security Officer, Sherry Ryan

Executive Vice President Chief Sales Officer, Gerri Elliott

Vice President Manufacturing Operations, Brad Tallman

Vp Partners And Alliances Asia Pacific, Mitch Lewis

Vice President Service Provider Marketing, Paul Obsitnik

Vice President Silicon Photonics, Roberto Marcoccla

Chairman, Scott G. Kriens, age 60

Auditors: Ernst & Young LLP

LOCATIONS

HQ: Juniper Networks Inc
1133 Innovation Way, Sunnyvale, CA 94089
Phone: 408 745-2000   **Fax:** 408 745-2100
Web: www.juniper.net

2017 Sales

	$ mil.	% of total
Americas		
US	2,712	54
Others	234	5
Europe Middle East & Africa	1,195	24
Asia Pacific	884	17
Total	**5,027**	**100**

PRODUCTS/OPERATIONS

2017 Sales

	$ mil.	% of total
Products		
Routing	2,189	44
Switching	963	19
Security	292	6
Services	1,461	31
Total	**5,027**	**100**

2017 Sales by Market

	$ mil.	% of total
Cloud	1,314	26
Telecom/Cable	2,315	46
Strategic Enterprise	1,396	28
Total	**5,027**	**100**

Selected Products

Content and Media Delivery
Data Center Fabric
Identity and Policy Control
Mobile Infrastructure
Network Management
Network Operating System
Routers
Security
Software
Switches
Wireless

COMPETITORS

ADTRAN
Arista Networks
Check Point Software
Cisco Systems
Citrix Systems
Dell
Ericsson
Extreme Networks
F5 Networks
Fortinet
Hewlett Packard
  Enterprise

Huawei Technologies
IBM Internet Security
  Systems
MRV Communications
NSN
Palo Alto Networks
Riverbed Technology
Sycamore Networks
  Solutions

HISTORICAL FINANCIALS

Company Type: Public

Income Statement

FYE: December 31

	REVENUE ($ mil.)	NET INCOME ($ mil.)	NET PROFIT MARGIN	EMPLOYEES
12/17	5,027	306	6.1%	9,381
12/16	4,990	592	11.9%	9,832
12/15	4,857	633	13.0%	9,058
12/14	4,627	(334)	—	8,806
12/13	4,669	439	9.4%	9,483
Annual Growth	**1.9%**	**(8.7%)**	**—**	**(0.3%)**

2017 Year-End Financials

Debt ratio: 21.72%
Return on equity: 6.35%
Cash ($ mil.): 2,006
Current ratio: 2.41
Long-term debt ($ mil.): 2,136

No. of shares (mil.): 365
Dividends
  Yield: 0.0%
  Payout: 50.0%
Market value ($ mil.): 10,417

	STOCK PRICE ($) FY Close	P/E High/Low		Earnings	Dividends	Book Value
12/17	28.50	38	30	0.80	0.40	12.81
12/16	28.26	19	14	1.53	0.40	13.02
12/15	27.60	20	13	1.59	0.40	11.91
12/14	22.32	—	—	(0.73)	0.20	11.82
12/13	22.57	26	18	0.86	0.00	14.75
Annual Growth	**6.0%**	**—**	**—**	**(1.8%)**	**—**	**(3.5%)**

Kansas City Life Insurance Co (Kansas City, MO)

Kansas City Life Insurance and subsidiary Sunset Life provide insurance products throughout the US to individuals (life and disability coverage and annuities) and to groups (life dental vision and disability insurance). Subsidiary Old American Insurance focuses on burial and related insurance. The insurance companies sell through more than 2500 independent agents brokers and third-party marketers. Kansas City Life also operates its own insurance and investment brokerage network through its Sunset Financial Services unit. Chairman and CEO R. Philip Bixby and his family control the company.

Operations

Kansas City Life operates in three business segments: Individual Insurance Group Insurance and Old American.

The Individual Insurance segment (which brings in about half of the company's revenue) consists of individual insurance products for both Kansas City Life and Sunset Life as well as reinsurance. Sunset Life maintains its existing policies but doesn't market new sales.

The Group Insurance segment (some 30% of the company's revenue) consists of group life dental vision disability products.

Old American (around 20% of revenue) sells final expense life insurance products.

Geographic Reach

Kansas City Life operates across the US. Some of its largest state markets include Texas California Minnesota Ohio and New Jersey.

Sales and Marketing

Kansas City Life markets its products through independent agents and agencies.

Financial Performance

After seeing dropping revenue for a couple of years Kansas City Life has seen revenue recovery for the past two years thanks primarily to rising premiums earned. Similarly net income declined in 2015 and 2016 but jumped back up in 2017.

Revenue increased 1% to $450.7 million in fiscal 2017. Net premiums and contract charges both increased that year but those gains were partially offset by a drop in net investment income. Renewal premium revenue rose 5% to $174.6 million while total new premiums earned remained flat.

Net income more than doubled in 2017 rising 131% to $51.5 million. That increase was primarily due to a decrease in income tax expenses related to changes in the federal tax code.

The company ended 2017 with $9.5 million in net cash essentially the same amount it had at the end of 2016. Operating activities provided $14.5 million in net cash and financing activities provided another $13.8 million while investing activities used $28.4 million.

Strategy

Kansas City Life has grown by acquiring other life insurance companies expanding its product portfolio moving into new markets and by enhancing technology.

Mergers and Acquisitions

In 2018 Kansas City Life acquired Ohio-based Grange Life Insurance Company for $77.2 million. The deal expanded the group's operations particularly in Ohio.

Company Background

The Bixby family owns about 60% of Kansas City Life through trusts and investment partnerships.

Founded in 1895 the company built up its operations through a number of historical acquisitions including GuideOne Life (2003) Old American (1991) and Sunset Life (1974). The company exited its banking operations (Generations Bank) in 2007.

EXECUTIVES

Svp And Actuary Kansas City Life And Vp And Actuary Sunset Life Insurance Company Of America, Mark A. Milton, age 59, $325,812 total compensation

Chairman President And Ceo, R. Philip Bixby, age 64, $779,160 total compensation

Vice Chairman And Evp And President Old American Insurance Company, Walter E. (Web) Bixby, age 59, $347,088 total compensation

Svp Finance Cfo And Director, Tracy W. Knapp, age 55, $322,344 total compensation

Svp Sales And Marketing Kansas City Life; Vp Sales And Marketing Sunset Life, Donald E. (Don) Krebs, age 60, $300,060 total compensation

Svp Operations, Stephen E (Steve) Ropp, age 58

Assistant Vice President Systems And Computer Operations, Rick Komer

Assistant Vice President And Chief Underwriter, Mike Augustine

Vice President Controller, David Laird

Vice President Taxes, John Nogalski

Regional Vice President West, Chris Bor

Regional Vice President, Bill Browning

Vice President, Timothy Knott

Vice President Securities, Phil Williams

Regional Vice President Special Markets, Robert Petzold

Medical Director, Charlotte Lee

Assistant Vice President, Stephen Mack

Assistant Vice President Corporate Communications, Holly Ropp

Assistant Vice President Marketing Services, Jim Wilcox

Senior Vice President Sales And Marketing, Don Krebs

Board Member, Kevin G Barth

Senior Vice President General Counsel Secretary, Craig Mason

Auditors: BKD, LLP

LOCATIONS

HQ: Kansas City Life Insurance Co (Kansas City, MO)
3520 Broadway, Kansas City, MO 64111
Phone: 816 753-7000 **Fax:** 816 753-4902
Web: www.kclife.com

PRODUCTS/OPERATIONS

2017 Sales

	$ mil.	% of total
Insurance		
Individual insurance	145	32
Group insurance	59	13
Old American	88	20
Net investment income	145	33
Net realized investment gains	4	1
Other	6	1
Total	**450**	**100**

Selected Subsidiaries

Old American Insurance Company
Sunset Financial Services
Sunset Life Insurance Company of America

COMPETITORS

AEGON USA	MassMutual
Advance Insurance of Kansas	MetLife
	National Western
American Equity Life	Nationwide
American Heritage Life Insurance	New York Life
	Northwestern Mutual
American National Insurance	Phoenix Companies
	Primerica
Americo	Protective Life
Citizens Inc.	Prudential
Delphi Financial Group	Security Benefit Group
FBL Financial	The Hartford
Homesteaders Life	Torchmark
Kemper Corp	Universal American

HISTORICAL FINANCIALS

Company Type: Public

Income Statement   FYE: December 31

	ASSETS ($ mil.)	NET INCOME ($ mil.)	INCOME AS % OF ASSETS	EMPLOYEES
12/17	4,530	51	1.1%	—
12/16	4,449	22	0.5%	—
12/15	4,421	29	0.7%	441
12/14	4,571	29	0.7%	436
12/13	4,514	29	0.7%	446
Annual Growth	0.1%	14.9%	—	—

2017 Year-End Financials

Debt ratio: —
Return on equity: 7.25%
Cash ($ mil.): 9
Current ratio: —
Long-term debt ($ mil.): —
No. of shares (mil.): 9
Dividends
Yield: 0.0%
Payout: 20.3%
Market value ($ mil.): 438

	STOCK PRICE ($) FY Close	P/E High/Low		Earnings	PER SHARE ($) Dividends	Book Value
12/17	45.25	9	8	5.32	1.08	76.13
12/16	47.50	21	15	2.30	1.08	70.80
12/15	38.29	18	15	2.75	1.08	68.55
12/14	48.03	18	15	2.75	1.08	68.61
12/13	47.74	19	13	2.70	1.08	66.13
Annual Growth	(1.3%)	—	—	18.5%	0.1%	3.6%

KB HOME

KB Home is one of the largest housebuilders in the US. The company constructs single-family (attached and detached) houses townhouses and condominiums suited mainly for first-time move-up and active adult buyers primarily in California Colorado Texas and southeastern US. Its Built-to-Order brand allows buyers to customize their houses by choosing a floor plan as well as exterior and interior features. KB Home's average selling price for a house is around $360000. To help with the buying process KB Home also offers mortgage banking title services and insurance. KB has built 600000 homes since it was founded in 1957.

HISTORY

Kaufman and Broad Building Co. was founded in Detroit in 1957 by Eli Broad and Donald Kaufman. Broad an accountant parlayed an initial $25000 investment into sales of $250000 on the first weekend of business. By the end of its first year the company was posting revenues of $1.7 million.

The company expanded rapidly and went public in 1961. A year later it was the first homebuilder to be listed on the NYSE. Kaufman and Broad moved into California in 1963. Through acquisitions it rapidly became a top US homebuilder expanding into New York San Francisco and Chicago. In 1965 it formed a mortgage subsidiary to arrange loans for its customers.

In the early 1970s the firm entered Europe and Canada. Sales passed the $100 million mark in 1971 and the company diversified buying Sun Life Insurance. Housing operations were renamed Kaufman and Broad Development Group (KBDG).

In 1980 the flamboyant Bruce Karatz who had joined the firm in 1972 was appointed president. Karatz steered the company through the recession of the early 1980s focusing on California France and Canada. KBDG acquired Bati-Service a major French developer of affordable homes in 1985.

The company was renamed Kaufman and Broad Home Corporation in 1986. In 1989 it reorganized into two separate billion-dollar companies: Broad Inc. (now SunAmerica) an insurance firm with Eli Broad as its chairman and CEO. The Kaufman and Broad Home company had Karatz as CEO (and later chairman).

When the California real estate market crashed in 1990 earnings plummeted. Karatz diversified by buying up strong regional builders. Kaufman and Broad entered Arizona Colorado and Nevada in 1993 and Utah in 1994. Profits dropped in 1995-96 because of weakness in the California and Paris markets and the company's winding down of Canadian operations. But expansion continued including the acquisition of Rayco a Texas builder in 1996.

Borrowing from the methods of Rayco Kaufman and Broad began surveying homebuyers for suggestions to incorporate into new designs. In 1998 the company began to build its New Home Showrooms. The corporation continued its expansion drive that year when it paid about $165 million for Dover/Ideal PrideMark and Estes privately held builders based in Houston Denver and Tucson respectively. In 1999 Kaufman and Broad bought Lewis Homes a major California builder and the #1 builder in Las Vegas for about $545 million.

The company raised $117 million in 2000 by taking half of its French subsidiary public but retained a controlling interest. Also the company formed a joint venture — American CityVista — with former Department of Housing and Urban Development secretary Henry Cisneros to develop homes in inner-city communities.

In 2001 the company changed its name again shortening it to KB Home. Later that year it expanded into the northern Florida market by buying Jacksonville-based Trademark Home Builders.

KB Home launched a division in Tampa and expanded operations into Central Florida in 2002 by acquiring Orlando-based American Heritage Homes for about $74 million. It also expanded in other markets which included Tucson (by acquiring assets of New World Homes gaining more than 1600 lots in 12 new home communities there) and the Rio Grande Valley of Texas (by opening a division in the fast-growing McAllen region about four miles from the Mexican border). For its fifth consecutive year KB Home reported record earnings in 2002.

KB Home continued to build its empire in 2003 by acquiring Atlanta-based Colony Homes one of the Southeast's largest privately owned homebuilders with principal operations in Atlanta Raleigh and Charlotte which are among the largest markets in the Southeast for new-home permits. The company also moved into the Midwest with the $33 million purchase of privately held homebuilder Zale Homes (Chicago). KB Home also added to its French holdings by acquiring Euro Immobilier.

In 2004 KB Home expanded its operations in the Southeast by acquiring South Carolina-based Palmetto Traditional Homes which builds in the state's three largest metropolitan areas: Charleston Columbia and Greenville-Spartanburg-Anderson. It also acquired Indianapolis builder Dura Builders and two French builders Groupe Avantis and Foncier Investissement.

KB Home sold its KB Home Mortgage subsidiary to Countrywide Home Loans in 2005 and then formed its Countrywide KB Home Loans joint venture to serve KB customers.

After nearly two decades as CEO Karatz retired from KB Home when charges of fraud surrounding company stock options were leveled against him. Former COO Jeff Mezger was then named president and CEO.

Hard hit by the economic downturn KB began looking for options to raise capital and downsize operations. In a measure to stem the bleeding in 2007 KB sold its 49% stake in its French subsidiary Kaufman & Broad to PAI Partners for about $800 million thus exiting all international operations. The sale enabled the company to reduce its outstanding debt by about $1 billion.

In mid-2011 KB Mortgage stopped offering lending services (which was a very minor part of the group's earnings); instead the company works in partnership with third-party providers.

EXECUTIVES

Chairman President And Ceo, Jeffrey T. (Jeff) Mezger, age 63, $1,000,000 total compensation
Svp Asset Management Group, Albert Z. Praw, $556,250 total compensation
Evp General Counsel And Secretary, Brian J. Woram, age 58, $564,167 total compensation
Evp And Cfo, Jeff J. Kaminski, age 57, $671,250 total compensation
Svp Sustainability Technology And Strategic Sourcing, Dan Bridleman
Evp Strategic Operations, Nicholas S. (Nick) Franklin, $606,250 total compensation
Senior Vice President, Renee M Gervais
Division President, Brett Dietz
Senior Vice President, Ray Panek
Vice President Sales, Alice Brown
Vice President Purchasing, Ken Hilligoss
Vice President Land Operations New Mexico Division, A Anthony
Vice President Finance, Tim Sprague
Vice President Of Land Acquisition, Pat Murphy
Vice President Marketing, Larry Gelfond
Vice President Of Operations, Len Gorney
Vice President Of Value Engineering, Dale Ahrendt
Vice President National Human Resources, Kathleen Knoblauch
Vice President Of Customer Service, Brenda Cunningham
Vice President Of Finance, Landon Skinner
Vice President Of Finance, Wesley Eisner
Vice President Of Finance, Rob Wasyliw
Vice President National Contracts, Johnathan Hughes
Vice President Purchasing, Ryan Wells
Senior Vice President Tax, Cory Cohen
Vice President Of Finance, Mike Gartland
Senior Vice President National Operations, Larry Oglesby
Division President, Ken Gancarczyk
Vice President Land Acquisitions, Steve Tierney
Vice President Operations Customer Service, Dan Auten
Vice President Forward Planning And Development, Scott Hansen
Vice President Land Acquisition, Doug Shelton

Senior Vice President Investor Relations, Jill Peters
Vice President Of Land, Jim Reinert
V P Of Operations, Paul Gregory
Senior Vice President, Chris Reder
Vice President Land Acquisitions, John Abboud
Vice President Of Operations Orlando, Doug Guy
Assistant Treas, Tina Moon
Board Member, Michael Wood
Board Member, Robert Patton
Board Member, Stuart Gabriel
Auditors: Ernst & Young LLP

LOCATIONS

HQ: KB HOME
10990 Wilshire Boulevard, Los Angeles, CA 90024
Phone: 310 231-4000 **Fax:** 310 231-4222
Web: www.kbhome.com

FY2017 Revenue by Geography
$ mil % total

West Coast	2,186	50
Central	1,188	27
Southwest	533	12
Southeast	448	10
Total	**3,583**	**100**

PRODUCTS/OPERATIONS

FY2017 Sales

	$ mil.	% of total
Homebuilding	4,356	100
Financial services	12	-
Total	**4,368**	**100**

COMPETITORS

Beazer Homes	M.D.C.
Capital Pacific	Meritage Homes
D.R. Horton	NVR
David Weekley Homes	PulteGroup
Highland Homes	Toll Brothers
Hovnanian Enterprises	William Lyon Homes
Lennar	

HISTORICAL FINANCIALS
Company Type: Public

Income Statement FYE: November 30

	REVENUE ($ mil.)	NET INCOME ($ mil.)	NET PROFIT MARGIN	EMPLOYEES
11/18	4,547	170	3.7%	2,005
11/17	4,368	180	4.1%	1,915
11/16	3,594	105	2.9%	1,790
11/15	3,032	84	2.8%	1,680
11/14	2,400	918	38.2%	1,590
Annual Growth	17.3%	(34.4%)	—	6.0%

2018 Year-End Financials

Debt ratio: 40.61%
Return on equity: 8.49%
Cash ($ mil.): 575
Current ratio: 14.36
Long-term debt ($ mil.): 2,060

No. of shares (mil.): 95
Dividends
Yield: 0.4%
Payout: 6.8%
Market value ($ mil.): 2,007

	STOCK PRICE ($) FY Close	P/E High/Low		Earnings	PER SHARE ($) Dividends	Book Value
11/18	21.11	20	9	1.71	0.10	21.95
11/17	31.36	15	7	1.85	0.10	20.08
11/16	15.84	14	8	1.12	0.10	18.23
11/15	14.09	19	13	0.85	0.10	16.51
11/14	17.57	2	1	9.25	0.10	15.60
Annual Growth	4.7%	—	—	(34.4%)	(0.0%)	8.9%

Kearny Financial Corp (MD)

Auditors: Crowe LLP

LOCATIONS

HQ: Kearny Financial Corp (MD)
120 Passaic Avenue, Fairfield, NJ 07004
Phone: 973 244-4500
Web: www.kearnybank.com

HISTORICAL FINANCIALS
Company Type: Public

Income Statement FYE: June 30

	ASSETS ($ mil.)	NET INCOME ($ mil.)	INCOME AS % OF ASSETS	EMPLOYEES
06/18	6,579	19	0.3%	565
06/17	4,818	18	0.4%	466
06/16	4,500	15	0.4%	459
06/15	4,237	5	0.1%	491
06/14	3,510	10	0.3%	474
Annual Growth	17.0%	17.8%	—	4.5%

2018 Year-End Financials

Debt ratio: 18.22%
Return on equity: 1.69%
Cash ($ mil.): 128
Current ratio: —
Long-term debt ($ mil.): —

No. of shares (mil.): 99
Dividends
Yield: 0.0%
Payout: 104.1%
Market value ($ mil.): 1,340

	STOCK PRICE ($) FY Close	P/E High/Low		Earnings	PER SHARE ($) Dividends	Book Value
06/18	13.45	65	54	0.24	0.25	12.74
06/17	14.85	73	57	0.22	0.10	12.53
06/16	12.58	74	62	0.18	0.08	12.50
06/15	11.16	191	179	0.06	0.00	12.48
Annual Growth	4.8%	—	—	41.4%	—	0.5%

Kellogg Co

This Special K is a cereal winner. From the company's home base in Battle Creek Michigan Kellogg Company battles with rival General Mills for the #1 spot in the US cereal market. Kellogg founded in 1906 boasts many familiar cereal brands including Kellogg's Corn Flakes Frosted Flakes Froot Loops Special K and Rice Krispies. While the company works to fill the world's cereal bowls it actually makes more money these days from its snacks and convenience brands such as Kashi Pringles Keebler Cheez-It and Famous Amos (snacks) and Eggo waffles and Nutri-Grain and Bear Naked cereal bars (convenience). Its products are sold worldwide.

Operations

Kellogg operates through several segments based on product category and geographic location. They include US Snacks (around 25% of sales) US Morning Foods (another 25% of sales) and US Specialty (around 10%). Kellogg rings up nearly 20% of sales in its Europe segment 12% in other North America (Canada) and around 5% each in Asia and Latin America.

US Snacks includes cookies crackers cereal bars savory snacks and fruit-flavored snacks. The US

Morning Foods segment includes cereal toaster pastries health and wellness bars and beverages. US Specialty primarily represents non-residential food operations including food service convenience vending Girl Scouts (Kellogg produces Girl Scout Cookies for the Girl Scouts of the USA who sell them as a fundraiser) and food manufacturing.

Geographic Reach
The food company manufactures its products in over 20 countries and markets them in more than 180. It generates around 65% of its revenue in the US.

The company's manufacturing facilities in the US include four cereal plants and warehouses in Battle Creek Michigan; Lancaster Pennsylvania; Memphis Tennessee; and Omaha Nebraska. Its other facilities are mostly in Georgia Kentucky Michigan and Ohio.

Outside the US Kellogg has additional manufacturing locations (some with warehousing facilities) in about 20 countries in Europe Asia Africa and South America. The company has joint ventures in China Nigeria and Turkey.

Sales and Marketing
Kellogg's top five customers generate some 35% of Kellogg's total sales and over 45% of US sales.

The company markets its cereal products in general under the recognizable Kellogg's name as well as its "healthy" brand Kashi. Products are sold to supermarkets through a direct sales force model for resale to consumers. Kellogg uses broker and distributor arrangements for certain products in retail stores restaurants and other food service establishments. These particular arrangements are leveraged to market its products in less-developed areas or in markets outside its focus.

Financial Performance
Kellogg continued a four-year slide in revenue in fiscal 2016 (ended December).

Revenue fell a further 4% to $13 billion. By comparison it made not far off $15 billion in 2013. Kellogg's North America Other segment declined due to weakness in Kashi and Morningstar Farms a poor first half of 2016 pushed US Snacks revenue down and US Morning Foods' non-core categories fell sharply.

Net income climbed for the first time in a few years climbing 13% to $694 million. The increase came from the success of Kellogg's "Project K" cost cutting program.

Cash from operating activities was down 4% to $1.6 billion due to $97 million of after-tax costs relating to redeemed debentures.

Strategy
Kellogg is working at cutting costs and expanding revenue as consumers are turning away from its old reliable cereal lines as awareness of the health risks of sugar increases.

Its ongoing "Project K" efficiency and effectiveness program began in 2013 and will continue through to 2018. This program is designed to help the company focus on core products with increased level of value-added innovation.

Kellogg has adopted a zero-based budgeting (ZBB) program whereby all expenses must be re-justified each period in its North America business. The process helped slice $100 million in annual savings in North America in 2016. The company plans to expand ZBB program to international market.

On the product side Kellogg is extending and repositioning several brands. Kellogg reformulated Special K to create Special K Nourish with probiotic qualities. The company believes probiotics have greater appeal than low calories. Other product extensions include Mini-Wheats Harvest Delights Smorz and Dory-themed cereal (in line with the Disney Pixar movie "Finding Dory.")

In the cookie aisle Kellogg advertising is bringing back the Keebler Elves to push cookies. The company also is putting attention and muscle behind the Kashi brand. It intends to promote Kashi Go-Lean products which have been Non-GMO Project Verified and Kashi Heart-to-Heart products which have been fashioned to meet the USDA's organic standard.

In 2016 Kellogg was ready to open a cereal restaurant in Times Square in New York City to showcase its traditional offerings as well as more adventurous concoctions developed by chefs.

Mergers and Acquisitions
In 2016 Kellogg acquired Ritmo Investments a Brazilian food group that owns the Parati Zoo Cartoon Hot Cracker and Padua brands. The acquisition strengthens its snacking and emerging market businesses.

HISTORY

Will Keith (W. K.) Kellogg first made wheat flakes in 1894 while working for his brother Dr. John Kellogg at Battle Creek Michigan's famed homeopathic sanitarium. While doing an experiment with grains (for patients' diets) the two men were interrupted; by the time they returned to the dough it had absorbed water. They rolled it anyway toasted the result and accidentally created the first flaked cereal. John sold the flakes via mail order (1899) in a partnership that W. K. managed. In 1906 W. K. started his own firm to produce corn flakes.

As head of the Battle Creek Toasted Corn Flake Company W. K. competed against 42 cereal companies in Battle Creek (one run by former patient C. W. Post) and roared to the head of the pack with his innovative marketing ideas. A 1906 Ladies' Home Journal ad helped increase demand from 33 cases a day earlier that year to 2900 a day by year-end. W. K. soon introduced Bran Flakes (1915) All-Bran (1916) and Rice Krispies (1928). International expansion began in Canada (1914) and followed in Australia (1924) and England (1938).

EXECUTIVES

Ceo And Director, Steven A. (Steve) Cahillane, age 53
Vice Chairman Corporate Development And Chief Legal Officer, Gary H. Pilnick, age 54, $719,092 total compensation
Svp; President Kellogg North America, Paul T. Norman, age 54, $783,319 total compensation
Chief Growth Officer, Clive Sirkin
President U.s. Specialty Channels, Wendy Davidson, age 47
Svp And Cfo, Fareed A. Khan, age 53
President U.s. Morning Foods, Craig Bahner, age 53
Svp Global Snacks Category, Jim Cali, age 57
President Asia/pacific, Amit Banati, age 49
Svp And Cio, Brian S. Rice, age 55
President Us Snacks Division, Deanie Elsner
President Kellogg Canada, Carol Stewart
Ceo Kashi Company, David J. Denholm
Svp Global Supply Chain, Alistair D. Hirst, age 58, $552,770 total compensation
Svp; President Kellogg Latin America, Maria F. Mejia
President Kellogg Europe, Chris Hood, $540,896 total compensation
President U.s. Frozen Foods, Andrew Loucks
Svp Global Breakfast Category, Doug VanDeVelde
Vice President Global Procurement Cpo, Michele Tyler
Vice President Nutrition, Guy Johnson
Vice President Treasury And Investor Relations, Joel R Wittenberg
Vice President Frozen Foods Supply Chain, Sharron Moss-Higham
Division Vice President, Cecile Mutch

Vice President Frozen Foods Marketing And Innovation, Annemarie Suarez-Davis
Vice President Corporate Development, Mike Libbing
Vice President Industry Initiatives, Dave Jones
Vice President Human Resources, Shawn Zimmerman
Vp Finance And Corporate Development, Jan Perkins
Senior Vice President Integrated Marketing, Gail Horwood
Vp Supply Chain, Jeffrey Arnold
Chairman, John A. Bryant, age 53
Auditors: PricewaterhouseCoopers LLP

LOCATIONS

HQ: Kellogg Co
One Kellogg Square, P.O. Box 3599, Battle Creek, MI 49016-3599
Phone: 269 961-2000
Web: www.kelloggcompany.com

2016 Sales

	$ mil.	% of total
United States	8,560	63
International	4,965	37
Total	**13,525**	**100**

2016 Sales

	$ mil.	% of total
United States	8,438	65
International	4,576	35
Total	**13,014**	**100**

PRODUCTS/OPERATIONS

2016 Sales

	$ mil.	% of total
U.S. Snacks	3,198	25
U.S. Morning Foods	2,931	23
Europe	2,377	18
North America Other	1,598	12
U.S. Specialty	1,214	9
Asia Pacific	916	7
Latin America	780	6
Total	**13,014**	**100**

2016 Sales

	$ mil.	% of total
Cereal	5,440	42
Snacks	6,660	51
Frozen	914	7
Total	**13,014**	**100**

Selected Cereal Brands
Asia and Australia
 BeBig
 Cerola
 Chex
 Frosties
 Goldies
 Kellogg's Iron Man Food
 Nutri-Grain
 Rice Bubbles
 Sultana Bran
Canada
 Vector
 Vive
Europe
 Choco Pops
 Chocos
 Country Store
 Frosties
 Fruit ‘n' Fibre
 Honey Loops
 Kellogg's Crunchy Nut Corn Flakes
 Kellogg's Crunchy Nut Red Corn Flakes
 Kellogg's Extra
 Muslix
 Optima
 Pops
 Ricicles
 Smacks
 Start
 Sustain

Latin America
  Choco Krispis
  Choco Zucaritas
  Crusli Sucrilhos
  Musli
  NutriDia
  Sucrilhos Chocolate
  Vector
  Zucaritas
US
  All-Bran
  Apple Jacks
  Bran Buds
  Cinnamon Crunch
  Cocoa Krispies
  Complete Bran Flakes
  Complete Wheat Flakes
  Corn Pops
  Cracklin' Oat Bran
  Crispix
  Crunch
  Cruncheroos
  Froot Loops
  Frosted Krispies
  Frosted Mini-Wheats
  Just Right
  Kellogg's Corn Flakes
  Kellogg's Frosted Flakes
  Kellogg's Low-Fat Granola
  Kellogg's Raisin Bran
  Mueslix
  Pops
  Product 19
  Raisin Bran
  Rice Krispies
  Smacks/Honey Smacks
  Smart Start
  Special K
  Special K Red Berries

Selected Other Brands
Cereal Bars and Granola
  All-Bran
  Bear Naked
  Choco Krispies
  Froot Loops
  GoLean
  Kashi
Convenience Foods
  Austin
  Cheez-It
  Chips Deluxe
  Club
  Croutettes Croutons
  E. L. Fudge
  Famous Amos
  Fudge Shoppe
  Hi-Ho
  Keebler
  Kellogg's Corn Flake Crumbs
  Krispy Munch'Ems
  Murray
  Pop-Tarts
  Pop-Tarts Pastry Swirls
  Pop-Tarts Snak-Stix
  Pringles
  Ready Crust
  Rice Krispies Squares
  Rice Krispies Treats
  Right Bites
  Sandies
  Soft Batch
  Stretch Island
  Sunshine
  Toasteds
  Town House
Frozen Waffles and Pancakes
  Eggo
  Froot Loops
  Nutri-Grain
  Special K
Water and Water Mixes
  Special K
  Special K2O
Meat and Egg Alternatives
  Gardenburger
  Loma Linda
  Morningstar Farms
  Natural Touch
  Worthington

COMPETITORS

Amy's Kitchen	McKee Foods
Barbara's Bakery	Mondelez International
Bob's Red Mill Natural Foods	Nestlé
Boca Foods	Patty King
Campbell Soup	PepsiCo
ConAgra	Pinnacle Foods
Frito-Lay	PowerBar
General Mills	Ralston Food
Gilster-Mary Lee	Schulze and Burch
Goodman Fielder	Snyder's-Lance
Hain Celestial	Weetabix
J & J Snack Foods	Wellness Foods
Jordans & Ryvita	Wessanen
MOM Brands	granoVita

HISTORICAL FINANCIALS
Company Type: Public

Income Statement   FYE: December 30

	REVENUE ($ mil.)	NET INCOME ($ mil.)	NET PROFIT MARGIN	EMPLOYEES
12/17	12,923	1,269	9.8%	33,000
12/16*	13,014	694	5.3%	37,369
01/16	13,525	614	4.5%	33,577
01/15	14,580	632	4.3%	29,790
12/13	14,792	1,807	12.2%	30,277
Annual Growth	(3.3%)	(8.5%)	—	2.2%

*Fiscal year change

2017 Year-End Financials
Debt ratio: 52.69%
Return on equity: 61.74%
Cash ($ mil.): 281
Current ratio: 0.68
Long-term debt ($ mil.): 7,836

No. of shares (mil.): 345
Dividends
  Yield: 0.0%
  Payout: 58.5%
Market value ($ mil.): 23,494

	STOCK PRICE ($) FY Close	P/E High/Low		PER SHARE ($) Earnings	Dividends	Book Value
12/17	67.98	21	16	3.62	2.12	6.40
12/16*	73.71	44	35	1.96	2.04	5.44
01/16	72.27	42	35	1.72	1.98	6.08
01/15	65.48	39	32	1.75	1.90	7.83
12/13	60.98	14	11	4.94	1.80	9.77
Annual Growth	2.8%	—	—	(7.5%)	4.2%	(10.0%)

*Fiscal year change

Kelly Services, Inc.

EXECUTIVES

Pres-Ceo, George S Corona
Chb, Donald R Parfet
Sr V Pres-Cfo, Olivier G Thirot
Clo, Hannah S Lim-Johnson
V Pres-Corp Contrl-Cao, Laura S Lockhart
Evp-Global Talent Solutions, Teresa S Carroll
Evp-Pres Global Staffing, Peter W Quigley
Svp-Gen Mgr U.S. Operations, Steven S Armstrong
Branch Manager, Alison Shepherd
State, Beth Stone
Customer Relationship Manager, Christine Runde
Auditors: PricewaterhouseCoopers LLP

LOCATIONS

HQ: Kelly Services, Inc.
  999 West Big Beaver Road, Troy, MI 48084
Phone: 248 362-4444
Web: www.kellyservices.com

COMPETITORS

ATC Healthcare	Randstad Holding
Adecco	Robert Half
Allegis Group	Technical Aid
Insperity	Corporation
ManpowerGroup	TrueBlue
On Assignment	Volt Information

HISTORICAL FINANCIALS
Company Type: Public

Income Statement   FYE: December 31

	REVENUE ($ mil.)	NET INCOME ($ mil.)	NET PROFIT MARGIN	EMPLOYEES
12/17*	5,374	71	1.3%	507,800
01/17	5,276	120	2.3%	507,500
01/16	5,518	53	1.0%	558,100
12/14	5,562	23	0.4%	563,300
12/13	5,413	58	1.1%	548,100
Annual Growth	(0.2%)	5.0%	—	(1.9%)

*Fiscal year change

2017 Year-End Financials
Debt ratio: 0.43%
Return on equity: 7.23%
Cash ($ mil.): 32
Current ratio: 1.49
Long-term debt ($ mil.): —

No. of shares (mil.): 38
Dividends
  Yield: 0.0%
  Payout: 16.5%
Market value ($ mil.): 1,048

	STOCK PRICE ($) FY Close	P/E High/Low		PER SHARE ($) Earnings	Dividends	Book Value
12/17*	27.27	17	11	1.81	0.30	29.96
01/17	22.92	8	5	3.08	0.28	26.46
01/16	16.15	13	10	1.39	0.20	23.57
12/14	17.00	42	25	0.61	0.20	22.10
12/13	25.29	17	10	1.54	0.20	21.98
Annual Growth	1.9%	—	—	4.1%	10.7%	8.1%

*Fiscal year change

Kemper Corp (DE)

Kemper is among the largest property/casualty insurance groups in the US. The company operates through two operating segments: Property and Casualty Insurance and Life and Health Insurance. The Property and Casualty Insurance segment's principal products are personal automobile insurance (both standard and non-standard risk) homeowners insurance other personal insurance and commercial automobile insurance. The smaller Life and Health Insurance segment's principal products are individual life accident health and property insurance. The company operates in the southern midwestern and western US.

Operations

The Kemper family of companies specializes in property/casualty insurance and life and health insurance products for individuals families and small businesses. Property and Casualty Insurance accounts for about two-thirds of the company's revenues while Life and Health Insurance accounts for the other third. It primarily does business through Kemper Home Service Companies which provides individual life and supplemental accident and health insurance products to customers of limited incomes. The smaller Reserve National unit sells specialty individual accident life and health insurance policies including illness and hospitalization plans.

Geographic Reach

Kemper sells its policies in 50 US states and Washington DC. Its largest markets include Alabama California Florida Louisiana Mississippi New York North Carolina Oregon and Texas. The Kemper Home Services Companies unit operates in 28 states.

Sales and Marketing
Kemper offers its services through independent agents and brokers. The Property and Casualty Insurance segment's products are offered by 18000 independent insurance agents and brokers. Kemper Direct sells auto and home coverage by phone and online. Kemper Home Services uses a network of some 2200 career agents while Reserve National uses about 400 independent agents.

Financial Performance
Kemper's revenues have been climbing the past couple of years; in 2016 revenue increased 8% to $2.5 billion. This was largely due to higher earned premium income but offset by lower net investment income other income and net realized gains on sales of investments. Earned premiums rose in the categories of personal automobile life and accident and health that year. The largest single business personal automobile increased 21% in terms of earned premiums.

However overall net income has been falling and in 2016 it dropped 80% to $16.8 million. This was driven by higher incurred catastrophe losses and underlying losses.

Cash flow from operations which has increased every year since 2012 rose another 12% to $240.5 million in 2016 (despite the lower net income). Positive adjustments to reconcile net income to net cash provided by operating activities especially an increase in insurance reserves led to that increase.

Strategy
In mid-2017 Kemper took a step back and decided that changes were needed to rejuvenate the company and that's just what it set out to do going forward. Its primary goals included making its recently acquired Alliance United unit profitable again investing in new technologies to support and improve operations and implementing new claims processes in its life insurance businesses.

Other areas of focus are increasing brand awareness diversifying operations and growing through acquisitions. The company also seeks to reduce catastrophe exposure through reinsurance (risksharing) agreements and selective underwriting practices.

Mergers and Acquisitions
In 2018 Kemper agreed to buy non-standard auto insurer Infinity Property and Casualty for $1.4 billion. Infinity does most of its business in California Florida and Texas and one of its key target markets is Hispanic consumers.

Company Background
The company changed its name from Unitrin to Kemper in August 2011; it also rebranded several of its business units under the Kemper name. The name change followed a downsizing where the company shed or shuttered several operations. Its Fireside Bank subsidiary which purchased subprime loan contracts from used automobile dealers halted lending activities in 2009 and ceased banking operations in 2012. Kemper also explored options to sell its Reserve National subsidiary but instead narrowed the unit's focus on specialized life and health policies.

Kemper's disposal-heavy strategy followed a period of expansion in its traditional consumer insurance options. The company enriched its property/casualty business segment through acquisitions of smaller companies.

James Kemper founded National Underwriters insurance exchange in 1913 to provide supplementary fire insurance for lumbermen.

EXECUTIVES

Executive Vice President Chief Financial Officer A, Eric Draut
Vp And Chief Accounting Officer, Richard Roeske, age 58, $371,000 total compensation
Evp Kemper Preferred, Naimish Patel
Svp And Chief Investment Officer, John M. Boschelli, age 50, $400,000 total compensation
President And Ceo, Joseph P. (Joe) Lacher, age 49, $750,000 total compensation
President Property And Casualty, George D. (Chip) Dufala, age 46, $214,519 total compensation
Evp; General Manager Kemper Specialty California, Timothy D. Bruns
President Kemper Home Service, Thomas D. Myers
Chief Risk Officer, Shekar G. Jannah
Svp Operations And Systems, Charles T. Brooks, age 52
Svp; President Life And Health, Mark A. Green, age 51, $240,692 total compensation
Svp And Cfo, James J. McKinney, age 39
Vice President Human Resources, Lisa M King
Vice President, Brad Andrekus
Vice President Human Resources, Scott Tomlinson
Vp And Treasurer, Christopher Moses
Vice President Kemper Benefits, Tracy Berwick
Vice President National Product Management Strategy, David Pearlmutter
Vp Financial Planning And Analysis, Maxwell Mindak
Senior Vice President Product Underwriting And Pricing, Eric Neely
Assistant Vice President Property Claims Hsis, Greg Warnock
Vice President Human Resources, Robin Buendia
Chairman, Robert J. (Bob) Joyce
Secretary, Thomas Evans
Board Member, George Cochran
Board Member, Lacy Johnson
Auditors: DELOITTE & TOUCHE LLP

LOCATIONS

HQ: Kemper Corp (DE)
200 E. Randolph Street, Chicago, IL 60601
Phone: 312 661-4600
Web: www.kemper.com

PRODUCTS/OPERATIONS

2016 sales

	$ mil.	% of total
Property/casualty insurance	1,688	66
Life & health insurance	821	32
Net realized gains on the sales of investments	33	1
Net impairment losses recognized in earning	(33)	-
Other	13	1
Total	**2,522**	**100**

Selected Insurance Options
Auto
Boat
Collectibles
Commercial Auto
Condo
Home
Identity Fraud
Life and Health
Package
Personal Catastrophe Liability
Personal Valuables
Renters

COMPETITORS

Allstate
Citizens Financial
Citizens Inc.
GEICO
Liberty Mutual Agency
Nationwide
Penn-America
Security National Financial
State Farm
USAA

HISTORICAL FINANCIALS
Company Type: Public

Income Statement				FYE: December 31
	ASSETS ($ mil.)	NET INCOME ($ mil.)	INCOME AS % OF ASSETS	EMPLOYEES
12/17	8,376	120	1.4%	5,550
12/16	8,210	16	0.2%	5,750
12/15	8,036	85	1.1%	5,600
12/14	7,833	114	1.5%	5,350
12/13	7,656	217	2.8%	6,100
Annual Growth	2.3%	(13.7%)	—	(2.3%)

2017 Year-End Financials
Debt ratio: 7.07%	No. of shares (mil.): 51
Return on equity: 5.91%	Dividends
Cash ($ mil.): 45	Yield: 0.0%
Current ratio: —	Payout: 41.2%
Long-term debt ($ mil.): —	Market value ($ mil.): 3,546

	STOCK PRICE ($) FY Close	P/E High/Low		PER SHARE ($) Earnings	Dividends	Book Value
12/17	68.90	30	16	2.33	0.96	41.11
12/16	44.30	138	72	0.33	0.96	38.52
12/15	37.25	25	21	1.65	0.96	38.82
12/14	36.11	19	16	2.12	0.96	39.88
12/13	40.88	11	8	3.80	0.96	36.86
Annual Growth	13.9%	—	—	(11.5%)	(0.0%)	2.8%

Keurig Dr Pepper Inc

EXECUTIVES

Pres-Ceo, Larry D Young
Chb*, Wayne R Sanders
Exec V Pres-Cfo, Martin M Ellen
Exec V Pres-Cco, James R Trebilcock
Exec V Pres-General Counsel, James L Baldwin
Exec V Pres Research & Develop, David J Thomas
Vice President, Deena Rembert
Qa Qc Director, Eileen Donnelly
Director of McDonalds Team, Frank Provenza
Assistant To Chief Informa, Geri Yetzer
Regional Manager Information T, Johnathan Shannon
Auditors: DELOITTE & TOUCHE LLP

LOCATIONS

HQ: Keurig Dr Pepper Inc
53 South Avenue, Burlington, MA 01803
Phone: 802 244-5621
Web: www.drpeppersnapplegroup.com

COMPETITORS

American Beverage
Austin Coca-Cola
Campbell Soup
Coca-Cola
Coca-Cola Bottling Consolidated
Coca-Cola Bottling company of southern california
Coca-Cola Bottling of Northern New England
Coca-Cola FEMSA
Coca-Cola North America
Coca-Cola Refreshments
Coca-Cola Tennessee
Coke United
Cott
Country Pure Foods
Del Monte Foods
Dole Food
Faygo

Florida's Natural
G & J Pepsi-Cola Bottlers
Gatorade
Great Plains Coca-Cola
Great Western Juice
Hornell Brewing
IZZE
Jones Soda
Jugos del Valle
Lane Affiliated
Mondelez International
Monster Beverage
National Beverage
Nestle
Ocean Spray
Odwalla
Old Orchard
Pepsi Bottling Ventures
Pepsi-Cola Bottling Company of NY
Pepsi-Cola Bottling of Central Virginia
Pepsi-Cola of Ft. Lauderdale
PepsiCo
Philadelphia Coca-Cola
Red Bull
Reed's
Roll Global
South Beach Beverage
Sunny Delight
Swire Coca-Cola
Tree Top
Tropicana
Wet Planet Beverages

HISTORICAL FINANCIALS

Company Type: Public

Income Statement

FYE: December 31

	REVENUE ($ mil.)	NET INCOME ($ mil.)	NET PROFIT MARGIN	EMPLOYEES
12/17	6,690	1,076	16.1%	21,000
12/16	6,440	847	13.2%	20,000
12/15	6,282	764	12.2%	19,000
12/14	6,121	703	11.5%	19,000
12/13	5,997	624	10.4%	19,000
Annual Growth	2.8%	14.6%	—	2.5%

2017 Year-End Financials

Debt ratio: 44.69%	No. of shares (mil.): 179
Return on equity: 46.94%	Dividends
Cash ($ mil.): 79	Yield: 0.0%
Current ratio: 0.90	Payout: 39.3%
Long-term debt ($ mil.): 4,400	Market value ($ mil.): 17,446

	STOCK PRICE ($) FY Close	P/E High/Low		PER SHARE ($) Earnings	Dividends	Book Value
12/17	97.06	17	14	5.89	2.32	13.64
12/16	90.67	22	18	4.54	2.12	11.65
12/15	93.20	24	18	3.97	1.92	11.62
12/14	71.68	21	13	3.56	1.64	11.89
12/13	48.72	16	14	3.05	1.52	11.50
Annual Growth	18.8%	—	—	17.9%	11.2%	4.3%

KeyCorp

Financial services giant KeyCorp unlocks its customers' monetary potential. With a focus on retail operations flagship subsidiary KeyBank operates more than 1200 branches and 1500 ATMs in 15 states in the Northeast the Midwest the Rocky Mountains and the Pacific Northwest including Alaska. Its operations are divided into two groups: Key Community Bank offers traditional services such as deposits loans credit cards and financial planning; Key Corporate Bank provides investment banking services real estate capital equipment financing and capital markets services to large corporate clients nationwide. KeyCorp is also the US' third-largest servicer of commercial and multifamily loans.

Operations

The bank makes around 50% of its revenue from loan interest mostly from commercial financial and agricultural and commercial real estate loans (including commercial mortgage and construction loans) as well as commercial leases. Another roughly 20% of its revenue comes from trust and investment services fee income and investment banking and debt placement fee income.

Geographic Reach

Cleveland-based KeyCorp has 1500 US branches in Ohio Alaska Indiana Michigan New York Oregon Washington and throughout New England. Around a quarter of its branches are concentrated in the Pacific states while about one-third is split between the Eastern New York and Eastern Ohio regions. The acquisition of First Niagara Financial in mid-2016 added nearly 400 branches in upstate New York Connecticut Massachusetts and Pennsylvania.

Sales and Marketing

Key Community Bank provides traditional banking services to individuals and small to mid-sized businesses while Key Corporate Bank provides its investment banking services to middle-market clients in seven industry sectors including consumer energy healthcare industrial public sector real estate and technology.

Financial Performance

In fiscal 2016 revenue increased 20% to $5.4 billion as the acquisition of First Niagara gave a boost to interest income. The First Niagara acquisition also pushed up non-interest revenue by 10%; card and payments income and corporate services also contributed.

Net income ticked down 16% to $754 million as an increase non-interest expenses outstripped non-interest revenue growth. KeyCorp incurred various expenses relating to the First Niagara acquisition including a $494 million M&A cost and a $421 million personnel expense increase. The acquisition also pushed up non-personnel expense to the tune of $495 million.

Cash from operating activities increased 49% to $1.7 billion due to an increase in proceeds from loans held for sale.

Strategy

KeyCorp's new and existing business growth strategy is based on leveraging and cross-selling its variety of financial products and services. In addition to hit its 60% cash efficiency ratio Keycorp has been focusing on controlling costs and reducing expenses from the front to the back office embracing digital banking platforms and cutting costly branch operations. Indeed the bank has been cutting its branch network from 1088 branches in 2012 to 966 at the end of 2015. The First Niagara acquisition pushed up KeyCorp?s branch network to 1322 but the cull continues: in Q4 2016 the bank shed a further 105 branches (some of the closures are due to branch overlaps too).

Mergers and Acquisitions

In January 2019 Keycorp agreed to purchase the digital lending business of New York City-based Laurel Road Bank whose technology enhances Keycorp's ability to serve professional millennial clients. Launched in 2013 Laurel Road's student loan refinancing platform has originated $4 billion in loans and was expanded in 2018 to include a platform for mortgage lending. About 140 Laurel Road employees will join Keycorp in conjunction with the transaction.

HISTORY

KeyCorp predecessor Commercial Bank of Albany was chartered in 1825. In 1865 it joined the new national banking system and became National Commercial Bank of Albany. After WWI National Commercial consolidated with Union National Bank & Trust as National Commercial Bank and Trust which then merged with First Trust and Deposit in 1971.

In 1973 Victor Riley became president and CEO. Under Riley National Commercial grew during the 1970s and 1980s through acquisitions. Riley sought to make the company a regional powerhouse but was thwarted when several New England states passed legislation barring New York banks from buying banks in the region.

As a result the company renamed Key Bank in 1979 turned west targeting small towns with less competition. Thus situated it prospered despite entering Alaska just in time for the 1986 oil price collapse. Its folksy image and small-town success earned it a reputation as the "Wal-Mart of banking."

Meanwhile in Cleveland Society for Savings followed a different path. Founded as a mutual savings bank in 1849 the institution succeeded from the start. It survived the Civil War and postwar economic turmoil and built Cleveland's first skyscraper in 1890. It continued to grow even during the Depression and became the largest savings bank outside the Northeast in 1949.

In 1955 the bank formed a holding company Society National. Society grew through the acquisitions of smaller banks in Ohio until 1979 when Ohio allowed branch banking in contiguous counties. Thereafter Society National opened branches as well. In the mid-1980s and the early 1990s the renamed Society Corporation began consolidating its operations and continued growing.

A 1994 merger of National Commercial with Society more than doubled assets for the surviving KeyCorp; compatibility of the two companies' systems and software simplified consolidation. KeyCorp sold its mortgage-servicing unit to NationsBank (now Bank of America) in 1995 and over the next year bought investment management finance and investment banking firms.

In 1997 KeyCorp began trimming its branch network divesting 200 offices including its 28-branch KeyBank Wyoming subsidiary. It expanded its consumer lending business that year by buying Champion Mortgage. In cooperation with USF&G (now part of The St. Paul Travelers Companies) and three HMOs KeyCorp began offering health insurance to the underserved small-business market.

In 1998 the company bought Leasetec which leases computer storage systems globally through its StorageTek subsidiary; it also bought McDonald & Company Investments (now McDonald Investments; sold in 2007) with an eye toward reaching its goal of earning half of its revenues from fees. Also in 1998 KeyCorp began offering business lines of credit to customers of Costco Wholesale the nation's largest wholesale club.

As part of a restructuring effort KeyCorp sold 28 Long Island New York branches to Dime Bancorp in 1999. The next year the company sold its credit card portfolio to Associates First Capital (now part of Citigroup) and bought National Realty Funding a securitizer of commercial mortgages. In 2001 it acquired Denver-based investment bank The Wallach Company.

The company expanded further in the Denver area with its 2002 purchase of Union Bankshares. Two years later KeyCorp bought Seattle-area bank EverTrust Financial Group.

In 2007 the company bought Tuition Management Systems which provides outsourced tuition billing accounting and counseling services for schools and colleges; the unit was later merged into its Key Education Resources operations. Also that year KeyCorp sold investmen

EXECUTIVES

Executive Vice President Of It Devlopment, Vernon L Patterson

Vice Chairman And President Banking, Christopher M. (Chris) Gorman, age 57, $638,462 total compensation

Evp General Counsel; Secretary Keybank National Association, Paul N. Harris, age 59

Vice Chairman And Cfo, Donald R. Kimble, age 58, $638,462 total compensation

Co-president Key Community Bank, Edward J. (E.J.) Burke, $550,000 total compensation

Sevp And Chief Risk Officer, William L. (Bill) Hartmann, $500,000 total compensation

Chairman And Ceo, Beth E. Mooney, age 62, $1,000,000 total compensation

Co-president Key Community Bank, Dennis A. Devine, $571,154 total compensation

Cio, Amy G. Brady

Evp And Director Corporate Center, Katrina M. (Trina) Evans

Chief Human Resources Officer, Craig A. Buffie

Evp; Head Real Estate Capital, Angela G. Mago

Evp; President Keybank Capital Markets, Andrew J. (Randy) Paine, $500,000 total compensation

Executive Vice President Marketing, Bonnie Squadere

Vice President, Alison Sammon

Assistant Vice President, Grace Moyano

Assistant Vice President, Paul Pace

Executive Vice President And Corporate Tax Director, Clark Wulf

Vice President International Marketing, Robert Kurek

Vice President, Colleen Daly

Senior Vice President Risk Policy Manager, JoAnn Schaeublin

Vice President Financial Risk Governance Manager, Anna Norcross

Senior Vice President, David Navy

Vice President, John Dravenstott

Executive Vice President And National Executive, William Lettig

Vice President Business Development, Carol Schafer

Senior Vice President Team Sales Leader, Matthew Nipper

Senior Vice President Supplier Diversity, Poppie Parish

Vice President Of Information Technology, Roy Woodbury

Vice President And Manager Regional Reporting, Melissa Werner

Senior Vice President And Senior Tax Manager Ii, Beth Adams

Senior Vice President Retail Performance Management, Kathleen Worhatch

Vice President, Kathy Mizener

Vice President And Senior Counselor, Richard Zeiger

Vice President, Tahira Afzal

Vice President Manager Payment And Deposit Operations, Dominic Cugini

Vice President Credit Risk Management, Bob Fisco

Senior Vice President Capital Planning, Jay Luzar

Senior Vice President, Karen Grexa

Vice President And Compliance Officer, Tamara Darnow

Kcm Vice President, Kelly Crawford

Vice President, Laura Krusinski

Vice President Mainframe Change Coordination And Special Projects, Phil Wetter

Vice President Consumer Channel Sales, Colleen Dugarte

Vice President Oil And Gas Group, Nicholas Stuart

Executive Vice President, George Emmons

Senior Vice President Enterprise Architecture, Dale Jablonski

Marketing Vice President, Bradley Thomas

Vice President Of Training, Nitra Rucker

Vice President Originations Specialty Finance And Syndications, Ric Andersen

Senior Vice President, Patrick Fish

Senior Vice President And Chief Underwriter Cmbs, Alan Williams

Vice President Consumer Finance, Dan Sukys

Senior Vice President And District Retail Leader, John Roehm

Vice President Corporate Communications, Alison Altre-Kerber

Credit Executive Senior Vice President, Brett Swanson

Vice President Senior Human Resources Business Partner, Amy Hoyer

Senior Vice President Manager, Robert Likes

Senior Vice President And Finance Director, William Shaw

Vice President Credit Risk Reviewer, Greg Newhouse

Senior Vice President Commercial Banking, Stephen Markley

Senior Vice President, James Harnett

Executive Vice President Risk Reporting And Technology, Alan Medearis

Vice President Manager, Larissa Tadiello

Vice President Credit Officer, Jay Coleman

Vice President Senior Portfolio Manager, Jeff Stegeman

Vice President And Senior Banker, Brian Heagler

Vice President Senior Portfolio Manager, Paul Olszewski

Senior Vice President Enterprise Architecture, Mike Onders

Vice President Senior Appraisal Officer, Scott Tomak

Vice President Senior Treasury Advisor Institutional Banking, Michael Thomas

Vice President District Operations Manager, Monica Cichon

Senior Cash Management Advisor And Assistant Vice President Treasury Services, Kristina Simpson

Vice President And Senior Trust Officer, Daryl Hembry

Vice President Corporate Procurement And Sourcing, Tom Fourmas

Vice President Compliance And Security Operations, Anthony Rini

Senior Vice President Real Estate Finance, Craig Younggren

Vice President And District Operations Manager, Laurie Dickinson

Vice President Community Bank Sales Systems, Robert Brzezinski

Senior Vice President Corporate Bank Technology And Sales Tool Team Manager, Brian Utrup

Vice President Senior Commercial Reviewer, Caryn Blauser

Senior Vice President And Manager Instit, Flavio Giust

Senior Vice President Key Private Bank, Michael Schneider

Vice President Senior Treasury Advisor, Christa Short

E C Manager Assistant Vice President System Administrator, Margaret Mason

Vice President Senior Equity Analyst, Robert Plaza

Vice President And Senior Associate Counsel, Mark Freeman

Assistant Vice President Portfolio Manager, Sara Smith

Assistant Vice President Team Lead, Lashawn Dalton

Senior Vice President Commerical Banking, Ben Rechkemmer

Executive Vice President And Director Call Center Sales And Service, Dean Kontul

Senior Vice President And Commercial Banking Manager, James R Barger

Senior Vice President Senior Relationship Manager, David Brown

Vice President Finance, John Bahr

Risk Management Vice President, Shawn Riley

Vice President Consumer Credit Risk Management, Kevin Takac

Executive Vice President Human Resources, Beth Yates

Executive Vice President Marketing, David Odell

Vice President And Senior Lit Counsel, Michelle Deshon

Vice President, Judy Tunis

Executive Vice President Marketing, Carla Mansur

Senior Vice President, Jeff Link

Vice President Investment Banking, Aaron Klein

Vice President Of Finance, Gary Huffman

Vice President Engineering, Bob Eisenmann

Senior Vice President, John Nolting

Senior Vice President, Alyce Juby

Vice President, James Gelle

Vice President, Jason Egger

Assistant Vice President, Erik Vohs

Vice President Senior Relationship Manager, Brian Flewelling

Vice President, Dan Schock

Vice President, Gordon Ostler

Assistant Vice President And Relationship Manager At Keybank, Jeff Taylor

Vice President Branch Manager, Christopher Klenk

Vice President, Jennifer Duke

Assistant Vice President And Relationship Manager, Brian Herrick

Vice President, Jennifer Seamons

Senior Vice President Senior Portfolio Manager, Chris Sim

Senior Vice President, Elvis Kanlic

Vice President, Benton Smith

Vice President, Eric Hafertepen

Vice President Business Banking, John Fidler

Vice President, Pedro Piedra

Vice President Senior Managing Appraisal Officer, Mark Figley

Vice President, Kevin Ringenberg

Vice President, Seth Reimer

Vice President And Senior Portfolio Manager, Lynn Wilson

Vice President Credit Officer Business Banking, Peg Misencik

Vice President, Meredith Houseworth

Senior Vice President, Mike MacArevey

Senior Vice President, Stephen Jones

Vice President Relationship Manager, Susan Barnicle

Senior Vice President, John Hecker

Vice President Senior Bus. Relationship Manager, Rachel Galusha

Senior Vice President And Relationship Manager, Trisha Hare

Assistant Vice President Business Banking Relationship Manager, Nicholas Emmett

Senior Vice President, Sanya Valeva

Assistant Vice President, Teena Heasley

Vice President, Selina Moriarty

Vice President, Michael Keach

Vice President Relationship Manager, Nick Perry

Senior Vice President, Sharon Lochocki

Senior Vice President, Denise Povolny

Senior Vice President And Senior Relationship Manager, Jun Chea

Vice President Senior Portfolio Manager, William Zalar

Vice President Relationship Manager, Todd Remy

Vice President Commercial Relationship Manager, Thomas Gunter

Vice President, Paul Taubeneck

Senior Vice President, Lawrence Mack

Vice President, Charles Arenas
Auditors: Ernst & Young LLP

LOCATIONS

HQ: KeyCorp
  127 Public Square, Cleveland, OH 44114-1306
Phone: 216 689-3000
Web: www.key.com

PRODUCTS/OPERATIONS

2017 Sales

	$ mil.	% of total
Interest		
Loans	3,677	54
Securities available for sale	369	6
Held-to-maturity securities	222	3
Loans held for sale	52	1
Trading account assets	27	-
Short-term investments	26	-
Other investments	17	-
Noninterest		
Trust & investment services	535	8
Investment banking and debt placement fees	603	9
Service charges on deposits	357	5
Corporate Service income	219	3
Cards and payments income	287	4
Corporate owned life insurance income	131	2
Operating lease income and other leasing gains	96	1
Mortgage servicing fees	71	1
Consumer mortgage income	26	-
Net gains (losses) from principal investing	7	-
Other income	146	2
Total	**6,868**	**100**

COMPETITORS

Bank of America	Huntington Bancshares
Citigroup	JPMorgan Chase
Citizens Financial	M&T Bank
Group	Northern Trust
Comerica	PNC Financial
Fifth Third	Sovereign Bank
Flagstar Bancorp	U.S. Bancorp
HSBC USA	Wells Fargo

HISTORICAL FINANCIALS

Company Type: Public

Income Statement

FYE: December 31

	ASSETS ($ mil.)	NET INCOME ($ mil.)	INCOME AS % OF ASSETS	EMPLOYEES
12/17	137,698	1,296	0.9%	18,415
12/16	136,453	791	0.6%	15,700
12/15	95,133	916	1.0%	13,359
12/14	93,821	900	1.0%	13,853
12/13	92,934	910	1.0%	14,783
Annual Growth	**10.3%**	**9.2%**	**—**	**5.6%**

2017 Year-End Financials

Debt ratio: 9.61%	No. of shares (mil.): 1,069
Return on equity: 8.56%	Dividends
Cash ($ mil.): 1,507	Yield: 0.0%
Current ratio: —	Payout: 33.6%
Long-term debt ($ mil.): —	Market value ($ mil.): 21,563

	STOCK PRICE ($) FY Close	P/E High/Low	PER SHARE ($) Earnings	PER SHARE ($) Dividends	PER SHARE ($) Book Value
12/17	20.17	18 14	1.13	0.38	14.05
12/16	18.27	23 12	0.80	0.33	14.12
12/15	13.19	15 11	1.05	0.29	12.86
12/14	13.90	14 12	0.99	0.25	12.25
12/13	13.42	14 9	0.97	0.22	11.57
Annual Growth	**10.7%**	**— —**	**3.9%**	**15.3%**	**5.0%**

Kimberly-Clark Corp.

One of the world's largest makers of personal paper products Kimberly-Clark operates through three business segments: Personal Care Consumer Tissue and K-C Professional. Kimberly-Clark's largest unit Personal Care makes products such as diapers (Huggies Pull-Ups) feminine care items (Kotex) and incontinence care products (Poise Depend). Through its Consumer Tissue segment the manufacturer offers facial and bathroom tissues paper towels and other household items under the names Cottonelle Kleenex Viva and Scott (plus the Scott Naturals line). Kimberly-Clark's K-C Professional unit makes WypAll commercial wipes among other items.

Operations

Kimberly-Clark operates in three reportable segments: Personal Care (50%) Consumer Tissue (almost 35%) and K-C Professional (nearly 15%).

Personal Care offers products such as disposable diapers training and youth pants swimpants baby wipes feminine and incontinence care products and other related products. Its products are sold under the Huggies Pull-Ups Little Swimmers GoodNites DryNites Kotex U by Kotex Intimus Depend Plenitud Poise and other brands.

Consumer Tissue's products include facial and bathroom tissue paper towels napkins and related products and are sold under the Kleenex Scott Cottonelle Viva Andrex Scottex Neve and other brand names.

K-C Professional (KCP) partners with businesses and provides supporting products such as wipers tissue towels apparel soaps and sanitizers sold under the Kleenex Scott WypAll Kimtech and Jackson Safety brands.

Consumer tissue and KCP products are produced in 55 facilities and personal care products are produced in 49 facilities.

Geographic Reach

Kimberly-Clark maintains a broad global presence as part of its growth strategy. It boasts around 100 manufacturing facilities in about 40 countries across the US Canada Europe Asia and Latin America. Products reach more than 175 countries. Developing regions such as Asia Latin America and others generated more than 35% of the company's net sales in 2016. North America accounted for 50% while Europe accounted for the remainder.

Sales and Marketing

Kimberly-Clark sells its household items directly to supermarkets mass merchandisers drugstores warehouse clubs variety and department stores and other retail outlets as well as through distributors and e-commerce. For the away-from-home market it serves the company sells through distributors and directly to high-volume public facilities and to manufacturing lodging office building food service and health care establishments.

Its largest customer worldwide retailer Wal-Mart represented about 14% of net sales in 2016.

Financial Performance

Kimberly-Clark's revenues have decreased the last three years dipping 2% from $18.6 billion in 2015 to $18.2 billion in 2016 due to decreases across all its segments. Unfavorable currency rates decreased sales by 4% in 2016 which was offset by a 2% increase in sales volumes.

With the help of major restructuring efforts Kimberly-Clark's profits more than doubled from $1 billion in 2015 to $2.2 billion in 2016. Profits also surged in 2016 due to the absence of nearly $1.6 billion in pension settlement expenses that were recognized the previous year.

Kimberly-Clark's net cash provided by operating activities surged by 40% from $2.3 billion in 2015 to $3.2 billion in 2016 due to favorable decreases from working capital and benefits from its cost savings initiative.

Strategy

Like many players in its industry Kimberly-Clark is utilizing sustainable packaging to refresh its image and sustainability reputation without necessarily having to revamp its product portfolio. In 2017 the company stated it was diverting 95% of manufacturing waste from landfills and diverting over 5000 metric tons of post-consumer waste through partnership programs around the world.

HISTORY

John Kimberly Charles Clark Havilah Babcock and Frank Shattuck founded Kimberly Clark & Company in Neenah Wisconsin in 1872 to manufacture newsprint from rags. The company incorporated as Kimberly & Clark Company in 1880 and built a pulp and paper plant on the Fox River in 1889.

In 1914 the company developed cellu-cotton a cotton substitute used by the US Army as surgical cotton during WWI. Army nurses used cellu-cotton pads as disposable sanitary napkins and six years later the company introduced Kotex the first disposable feminine hygiene product. Kleenex the first throwaway handkerchief followed in 1924. Kimberly & Clark joined with The New York Times Company in 1926 to build a newsprint mill (Spruce Falls Power and Paper) in Ontario Canada. Two years later the company went public as Kimberly-Clark.

EXECUTIVES

Chairman And Ceo, Thomas J. (Tom) Falk, age 60, $1,318,750 total compensation
Svp And Cfo, Maria G. Henry, age 51, $772,500 total compensation
President Latin America, Sergio Cruz
President Global Brands And Innovation, Anthony J. (Tony) Palmer, age 58, $655,000 total compensation
President Coo And Director, Michael D. Hsu, age 54, $833,750 total compensation
Svp And Chief Supply Chain Officer, Sandra J. MacQuillan, age 51, $392,424 total compensation
President Asia-pacific Region, Achal Agarwal
President Europe Middle East And Africa, Gustavo Calvo Paz
President Kimberly-clark Professional, Kim Underhill
Vice President Investor Relations, Paul Alexander
Vice President Its Infrastructure, Ryan Ramirez
Vp Government Relations, Susan Phillips
Vice President Walmart International Development, John Scholes
Vice President Human Resources, Rick Purdy
Vice President Human Resources Corporate Functions, Sylvia Fong
Auditors: DELOITTE & TOUCHE LLP

LOCATIONS

HQ: Kimberly-Clark Corp.
  P.O. Box 619100, Dallas, TX 75261-9100
Phone: 972 281-1200
Web: www.kimberly-clark.com

2016 Sales

	$ mil.	% of total
North America	9,545	51
Asia Latin America & other	6,786	37
Europe	2,178	12
Intergeographic sales	(307)	-
Total	**18,202**	**100**

PRODUCTS/OPERATIONS

2016 Sales

	$ mil.	% of total
Personal Care	9,046	50
Consumer Tissue	5,967	33
K-C Professional	3,150	17
Corporate & other	39	-
Total	**18,202**	**100**

Selected Products and Brands

Medical
  Closed-suction respiratory products
  Examination gloves
  Safeskin
  Face masks
  Infection-control products
  Scrub suits and apparel
  Sterile wrap
  Kimguard
  Surgical drapes and gowns
Personal Care
  Baby wipes
  Huggies
  Disposable diapers
  GoodNites
  Huggies
  Pull-Ups
  Feminine hygiene products
  Kotex
  Lightdays
  New Freedom
  Incontinence products
  Depend
  Poise
  Swimpants
  Little Swimmers
Tissue-Based
  Bathroom tissue
  Cottonelle
  Scott
  Commercial wipes
  Kimwipes
  WypAll
  Facial tissue
  Kleenex
  Paper napkins
  Scott
  Paper towels
  Kleenex
  Scott
  Viva

COMPETITORS

3M	Johnson & Johnson
Ansell	Medline Industries
Becton Dickinson	Nice-Pak Products
Bristol-Myers Squibb	Potlatch
CCA Industries	Procter & Gamble
DSG International Ltd	SSI Surgical Services
Edgewell Personal Care	Suominen
Georgia-Pacific	

HISTORICAL FINANCIALS

Company Type: Public

Income Statement

FYE: December 31

	REVENUE ($ mil.)	NET INCOME ($ mil.)	NET PROFIT MARGIN	EMPLOYEES
12/18	18,486	1,410	7.6%	41,000
12/17	18,259	2,278	12.5%	42,000
12/16	18,202	2,166	11.9%	42,000
12/15	18,591	1,013	5.4%	43,000
12/14	19,724	1,526	7.7%	43,000
Annual Growth	**(1.6%)**	**(2.0%)**	**—**	**(1.2%)**

2018 Year-End Financials

Debt ratio: 51.35%	No. of shares (mil.): 344
Return on equity: 603.85%	Dividends
Cash ($ mil.): 539	Yield: 3.5%
Current ratio: 0.77	Payout: 87.1%
Long-term debt ($ mil.): 6,247	Market value ($ mil.): 39,305

	STOCK PRICE ($) FY Close	P/E High/Low		PER SHARE ($) Earnings	Dividends	Book Value
12/18	113.94	30	24	4.03	4.00	(0.65)
12/17	120.66	21	17	6.40	3.88	1.97
12/16	114.12	23	19	5.99	3.68	(0.12)
12/15	127.30	47	37	2.77	3.52	(0.30)
12/14	115.54	29	25	4.04	3.36	2.19
Annual Growth	**(0.3%)**	**—**	**—**	**(0.1%)**	**4.5%**	**—**

Kinder Morgan Inc.

Kinder Morgan Inc. (KMI) is one of the largest energy infrastructure companies in North America. It operates approximately 85000 miles of pipelines and more than 150 terminals that transport natural gas refined petroleum products crude oil condensate CO2 and other products to its customers across America. The company is also a leading producer of CO2 used in oilfield operations. Most of KMI's customers are major oil companies energy producers and shippers as well as local distribution companies. It generates most of its sales in the US.

Operations

KMI reports via five segments: Natural Gas Pipelines Terminals Products Pipelines CO2 and Kinder Morgan Canada.

Natural Gas Pipelines is KMI's most significant business segment accounting for more than 60% of total revenue. This line of business operates approximately 72000 miles of pipelines and storage facilities which supply roughly 40% of all consumed natural gas in the US.

Terminals is the transportation arm of KMI and brings in roughly 15% of annual sales. With more than 50 liquid terminals about 35 bulk terminals and over 15 Jones Act approved tankers KMI is the largest independent terminal operator in North America. (Jones Act restricts US point-to-point maritime shipping to vessels that are 75% US-owned.) The terminals transload store or blend refined petroleum products crude oil chemicals ethanol and bulk products to US and parts of Canada.

The Products Pipelines segment includes more than 9700 miles of pipelines and over 70 terminals making this sector the largest independent transporter of petroleum products (more than 2 million barrels per day). Moving gasoline jet fuel diesel crude and NGL products this sector brings in just more than 10% of annual sales.

Although KMI is the largest CO2 transporter in North America (2.0 billion cubic feet/ day) this segment only accounts for less than 10% of the company's total sales.

Kinder Morgan Canada (2%) includes the Trans Mountain pipeline system (now sold-off) and a 25-mile Jet Fuel pipeline system.

Geographic Reach

KMI has operations in the US Canada and Mexico. KMI buys and sells significant volumes of natural gas in Texas. US customers account for some 95% of the company's revenue.

Sales and Marketing

KMI customers include major oil companies energy producers and shippers as well as local distributors. The company does business under extended transport and sales contracts. KMI conducts its Midstream assets on a fee-based arrangement and its CO2 business has third-party contracts with minimum volume requirements.

Financial Performance

Revenue at KMI grew from $7.8 billion in 2010 to a decade-peak of $16.2 billion before declining to $13 billion in 2017. Though mostly profitable in the last decade KMI has drastically cut its profit from around $1 billion in the 2013-14 years to below $200 million in 2017.

In 2017 annual sales increased 5% to $13.7 billion primarily due to a $600 million YOY increase in natural gas pipeline revenue thanks to volume growth.

Net income reduced from $708 million in 2016 to $183 million in 2017 primarily due to a $1 billion increase in income tax expenses.

Cash holdings declined to $264 million at the end of 2017. Operations provided $4.6 billion offset by $3.3 billion used in investments and a further $1.6 billion used by financing activities. The company paid $11 billion in debt while CAPEX stood at $3.1 billion.

Strategy

KMI is moving away from its over-leveraged years thanks to strong earnings promising new projects and a successful debt reduction strategy.

The sale of TMX to the Canadian government for C$4.5 billion helped KMI conclude its successful debt reduction strategy on a high going from $42.5 billion in the third quarter 2015 to $34.5 billion three years later. The company anticipates $7.5 billion of adjusted EBITDA for 2018.

With the leverage target reached sooner than expected the company now plans to invest its proceeds into attractive growth projects and share repurchases.

The TMX expansion project stalled with political stalemate between Alberta and British Columbia. However KMI made a successful exit thanks to the terms of its deals with lenders and oil producers which shielded it from massive write-downs suffered by rivals TransCanada Corp and Enbridge.

Emboldened by this success KMI wants its GCX and Permian Highway projects to be fully operational by 2020. For the GCX Project KMI along with DCP Midstream and Targa Resources will target moving natural gas from the prolific Permian Basin to the Gulf Coast (430 miles 1.92 Bcf/d) with additional access to the Midland Basin and export opportunities to Mexico. The other project Permian Highway Pipeline in a partnership with EagleClaw Midstream and Apache will develop another new gas pipeline (430 miles 2bcf/day) out of the same Basin.

Company Background

Kinder Morgan Energy Partners (KMP) was founded in February 1997 when a group of investors led by Executive Chairman Richard D. Kinder and Vice Chairman William V. Morgan decided to build an energy company by utilizing the master limited partnership (MLP) financial structure as a growth vehicle—something that had never been done before.

Their innovative approach proved so successful that in two decades KMP has becomes the largest publicly traded pipeline limited partnership in America based on enterprise value. Initially the company grew mostly through acquisitions of existing operations but eventually took on the construction of projects.

Separately in 1999 Mr. Kinder took over the reins of KN Energy from Lakewood Colorado a natural gas pipeline company serving small communities and rural areas in Kansas and Nebraska and turned it to Kinder Morgan Inc. Kinder Morgan's second publicly traded company.

EXECUTIVES

President And Ceo, Steven J. (Steve) Kean, age 57, $1 total compensation

Vp And Cfo, Kimberly A. (Kim) Dang, age 49, $375,000 total compensation

President Kinder Morgan Canada, Ian D. Anderson, age 61

Vp; President Natural Gas Pipelines, Thomas A. (Tom) Martin, $375,000 total compensation

Vp Corporate Development, Dax Sanders, $375,000 total compensation

President Products Pipelines, Ronald G. (Ron) McClain

President Terminals, John W. Schlosser

Vp And Cio, Mark Huse

President Co2, Jesse Arenivas, $325,000 total compensation

Vice President Pipeline Scheduling, Holly Breaux

Vice President, Alan Cooke

Vp And Controller, Gary Bohnsack

Executive Vice President And Chief Operating Officer, Scott Stoness

Vice President Regulatory Affairs Products Pipelines, Randy P Parker

Vice President Employee Benefits, Mark Smith

Vice President Logistic, James Holland

Vp Treasurer, Anthony Ashley

Vice President And Chief Compliance Officer, Charles Schwager

Vp Corporate Communications And Public Affairs, David Conover

Vice President Pacific Business Development And Marketing, Mary Morgan

Vice President, James Saunders

Executive Chairman, Richard D. (Rich) Kinder, age 74

Board Member, Robert Vagt

Board Member, Deborah Macdonald

Board Member, Arthur Reichstetter

Auditors: PricewaterhouseCoopers LLP

LOCATIONS

HQ: Kinder Morgan Inc.
1001 Louisiana Street, Suite 1000, Houston, TX 77002
Phone: 713 369-9000
Web: www.kindermorgan.com

2017 Sales

	$ mil.	% of total
US	13,073	95
Canada	503	4
Mexico	129	1
Total	**13,705**	**100**

PRODUCTS/OPERATIONS

2017 Sales

	$ mil.	% of total
Natural Gas Pipelines	8,618	63
Terminals	1,966	14
Products Pipelines	1,661	12
CO2	1,196	9
Kinder Morgan Canada	256	2
Corporate and intersegment eliminations	8	-
Total	**13,705**	**100**

2017 Sales

	$ mil.	% of total
Services	7,901	58
Natural gas sales	3,053	22
Product sales and other	2,751	20
Total	**13,705**	**100**

COMPETITORS

Denbury Resources	Energy Transfer Equity
Devon Energy	Enterprise Products
EnLink Midstream Partners	ONEOK
	TRII
Enbridge	Williams Companies

HISTORICAL FINANCIALS

Company Type: Public

Income Statement   FYE: December 31

	REVENUE ($ mil.)	NET INCOME ($ mil.)	NET PROFIT MARGIN	EMPLOYEES
12/18	14,144	1,609	11.4%	11,012
12/17	13,705	183	1.3%	10,897
12/16	13,058	708	5.4%	11,121
12/15	14,403	253	1.8%	11,290
12/14	16,226	1,026	6.3%	11,535
Annual Growth	(3.4%)	11.9%	—	(1.2%)

2018 Year-End Financials

Debt ratio: 47.33%—
Return on equity: 4.78%
Cash ($ mil.): 3,280
Current ratio: 0.76
Long-term debt ($ mil.): 33,936

Dividends
Yield: 4.7%
Payout: 109.8%
Market value ($ mil.): —

	STOCK PRICE ($) FY Close	P/E High/Low		Earnings	PER SHARE ($) Dividends	Book Value
12/18	15.38	30	22	0.66	0.73	14.89
12/17	18.07	2294	1676	0.01	0.50	15.17
12/16	20.71	93	48	0.25	0.50	15.44
12/15	14.92	446	145	0.10	1.93	15.75
12/14	42.31	48	35	0.89	1.70	16.03
Annual Growth	(22.4%)	—	—	(7.2%)	(19.2%)	(1.8%)

Kohl's Corp.

Clothing retailer Kohl's operates about 1150 namesake department stores across the US as well as some 15 FILA outlets and Off-Aisle clearance centers. Competing with discount and mid-level department stores the company sells moderately priced name-brand and private-label apparel shoes accessories and housewares. Its private-label brands include Apt. 9 Croft & Barrow and Jumping Beans; Kohl's also sells exclusive brands through agreements with Jennifer Lopez Vera Wang and the Food Network among others. More than 90% of the company's stores are freestanding or in strip centers with the rest located in malls.

Operations

By product Kohl's generates about 30% of sales from women's clothing and some 20% from men's clothing. The rest of the retailer's sales come from home products (nearly 20%) children's clothing (about 15%) and accessories and footwear (about 10% each).

It boasts a strong portfolio of national exclusive and private-label brands with about 60% of its sales tied to national brands and the rest coming from private and exclusive brands.

Geographic Reach

Kohl's network of some 1150 stores covers the entire US. Its largest markets are the Midwest (with more than a quarter of stores and led by Illinois with about 65) and West (with about 20% of stores and led by California with nearly 120); other leading states include Texas Ohio Florida New York and Pennsylvania.

To support its brick-and-mortar businesses Wisconsin-based Kohl's maintains a network of about 10 distribution centers in Findlay Ohio; Winchester Virginia; Blue Springs Missouri; Corsicana Texas; Mamakating New York; San Bernardino California; Macon Georgia; Patterson California; and Ottawa Illinois.

Facilities that serve Kohl's e-commerce business are in Monroe Ohio; San Bernardino California; Edgewood Maryland; Plainfield Indiana and DeSoto Texas.

Sales and Marketing

Kohl's sells its products through its stores online and through in-store kiosks that offer customers free shipping to their homes. As an omni-channel retailer the company doesn't make a clear distinction between store and digital sales and thus doesn't report them separately.

Financial Performance

Kohl's revenues have been flat over the past few years with few new store openings and sluggish comparable store sales growth. Its profits have also been in a slow decline during that time as rising merchandise costs have caused margins to shrink and as it's been spending more on investments in IT and marketing to support growth.

The retailer's revenue rose slightly in fiscal 2017 (ended January 2018) to $19.1 billion up 2% from the prior year. Nearly half that growth came from a 53rd week in the fiscal year with the rest a result of a 1.5% increase in same-store sales powered by an especially strong Q4 (which saw same-store sales of more than 6%).

After several years of declines net income also rose that year jumping about 55% to $859 million. Kohl's benefited from a lack of impairments store closings and other costs compared to nearly $200 million in fiscal 2016.

Cash at the end of 2017 was $1.3 billion an increase of about $235 million from the prior year. Cash from operations contributed $1.7 billion to the coffers while investing activities used $650 million mainly for investments in information technology and other capital expenditures. Financing activities used another $808 million primarily for stock buyback and dividends paid.

Strategy

As is the case across the entire retail industry (across all industries actually) Kohl's is embracing technology and innovation as keys to its future success. Since fiscal 2015 about half of its capital expenditures have gone toward information technology initiatives and the company expects that trend to continue in fiscal 2018. A significant portion of this has been in pursuit of a seamless omni-channel experience which allows customers to browse buy pick up and return merchandise online in stores or through a combination of both. More generally Kohl's has invested in data and analytics for enhanced marketing and personalization initiatives is improving its fulfillment capabilities and is migrating its systems and applications to the cloud.

In a somewhat related and interesting strategic move the retailer in 2017 entered an agreement with its top online competitor Amazon to accept Amazon returns in Kohl's stores and establish Amazon Smart Home Experience zones in a limited number of its locations. Amazon Smart Home features Amazon devices such as the Echo and Fire TV. Kohl?s is betting that the partnership will bring more customers into its stores.

Speaking of stores brick-and-mortar locations are still the cornerstone of Kohl's business. Although the retailer is shrinking its stores unlike many of its competitors it is shrinking the size not the number. Through mid-2018 Kohl's has shrunk the size of hundreds of locations by about a third (from some 90000 sq. ft. to some 60000 sq. ft.). In some cases the excess footage is being rented out to Amazon as part of the agreement mentioned above or discount supermarket chain Aldi. Kohl's is also experimenting with a 35000 sq. ft. store model that is being tested in about a dozen cities. The company wants to maintain its store base as a foundation for online sales as well as branding/marketing efforts and it hopes to use the smaller store format to expand into new markets.

HISTORY

Max Kohl (father of Sen. Herbert Kohl of Wisconsin) opened his first grocery store in Milwaukee in the late 1920s. Over the years he and his three sons developed it into a chain and in 1938 Kohl's incorporated.

Kohl opened a department store (half apparel half hard goods) in 1962 next door to a Kohl's grocery. In the mid-1960s he hired William Kellogg a twentysomething buyer in the basement discount department at Milwaukee's Boston Store for his expertise in budget retailing. Kellogg came from a retailing family (his father was VP of merchandising at Boston Store; the younger Kellogg had joined that firm out of high school). Kohl and Kellogg began developing the pattern for the store carving out a niche between upscale department stores and discounters (offering department store quality at discount store prices).

EXECUTIVES

Senior Executive Vice President, John Worthington
Chairman President And Ceo, Kevin B. Mansell, age 65, $1,400,441 total compensation
Sevp And Chief Administrative Officer, Richard D. (Rick) Schepp, age 57, $911,250 total compensation
Cfo, Bruce H. Besanko, age 59
Ceo-elect, Michelle Gass, age 49, $1,113,750 total compensation
President, Sona Chawla, age 51, $1,113,750 total compensation
Vice President Customer Relationship Management, Brian Miller
Vice President Of Application Management Development, Dennis Kester
Vice President Customer Experience, Brian Dennis
Executive Vice President Human Resources, Ryan Festerling
Senior Vice President Human Resources, Genny Shields
Vice President Application Development, Lawrence Mikels
Innovation Vice President, Ratnakar Lavu
Vice President Dmm, Suzanne Dawson
Vice President Of Distribution, Jeff Kellan
Ecommerce Call Center Vice President, Troy Crougthers
Vice President Regionioanal Manager, Brian Giles
Vice President Of Product Services, Richard Zielinski
Vice President Information Systems, Shelley Mathwick
Vice President Credit Marketing, Brent Cook
Executive Vice President, Sarah Masterson
Vice President Purchasing Procurement, Andy Jaskaniec
Vice President Finance, Gary Stoltmann
Vice President Management Information Systems, Linn Allison
Regional Vice President, Blaine Predmore
Vice President Of Facilities Logistics, John Fojut
Vice President Operations And Analytics Product Development, Charlie Holmes
Vice President Logistics, Phil Godden
Executive Vice President Marketing, William Setliff
Senior Vice President Footwear Divisional Mercha, Carol Baiocchi
Vice President Compensation And Analytics, Matt Carpenter
Vice President District Manager, Randy Blackburn
Vice President Internal Audit, Steve Zamansky
Executive Vice President Marketing, Debby Fisher
Vice President Ecommerce Development, Sunil S Bhardwaj

Vice President Of Finance And Operations, Santa Paul
Vice President Information Technology, Greg Heinz
Vice President Of Logistics And Stores (information Technology), Scott Vifquain
Vice President Of Strategic Sourcing And Procurement, David Maley
Vice President Of Application Development, Dan Mueller
Executive Vice President, Will Setliff
Executive Vice President Product Development, Michael Gilbert
Vice President Of Strategic Marketing, Sean Sondreal
Vice President District Manager, Shane Knoy
Vice President Production, Ron Katanick
Vice President, Deb Kuczora
Vice President Of It Database, Deb Lechmaier
Senior Executive Vice President In Charge Of Store Operations And Information Technology, Tom Kingsbury
Vice President Information Systems Enterprise Services, Dawn Marceau
Senior Vice President Human Resource, Dallas Moon
Vice President Dmm, Chris Candee
Vice President Administration, Gregg Bartel
Senior Vice President Loss Prevention, Randy Meadows
Vice President Merchant Analysis, Shelly Mathwick
Senior Vice President Direct Marketing, Michael Stanley
Vice President Systems Data Processing, Lin Allison
Executive Vice President Of Administration, Johnathan Lesko
Executive Vice President General Merchandise Manager Men 's And Kids, Jeff Manby
Vice President Finance, Kelli Johnson
Vice President Marketing Strategy, Mary Benedum
Vice President And District Manager, Dave Schmidt
Regional Vice President, Loretta Roszczewski
Vice President Recruitment, Shanan Lesselyoung
Information Technology Security Vice President, John Craparo
Vice President Of Corporate Sustainability, Jack Fojut
Senior Vice President Of Marketing, Eleanor E Hong
Vice President Credit Call Center, Troy Carruthers
Vice President Information Technology, Adam Brundage
Vice President Of Sales, Brenda Thompson
Executive Vice President, J Lesko
Vice President Loyalty, Aron Hayek
Senior Vice President Digital, Cherise Ordlock
Vice President Digital And Omni Channel, Faisal Awan
Vice President Finance, Gary Stoltman
Vice President Of Data Processing, Lynn Allison
Vice President And Director Distribution Operations, Reginald Davis
Vice President Consumer Public Relations And Social Media, Lisa Hellman
Vp Product Development And Design Home Exclusive Brands, Lauren Steinke
Board Member, Peter Boneparth
Board Member, John Schlifske
Board Member, Adrianne Shapira
Board Member, Jonas Prising
Auditors: Ernst & Young LLP

LOCATIONS

HQ: Kohl's Corp.
N56 W17000 Ridgewood Drive, Menomonee Falls, WI 53051
Phone: 262 703-7000 **Fax:** 262 703-6373
Web: www.kohls.com

2017 Stores

	No.
Midwest	312
West	237
Southeast	185
Northeast	158
South Central	150
Mid-Atlantic	116
Total	**1,158**

PRODUCTS/OPERATIONS

2017 Sales

	% of total
Women's	30
Men's	20
Home	19
Children's	13
Accessories	9
Footwear	9
Total	**100**

2017 Store Locations

	No.
Strip centers	779
Freestanding	296
Community & regional malls	83
Total	**1,158**

Selected National Brands

adidas
Arrow
Calphalon
Candies
Carter's
Chaps
Columbia
Cuisinart
Daisy Fuentes
Dickies
Dockers
everGirl
George Foreman
Gloria Vanderbilt Home
Gold Toe
Haggar
Hanes
Healthtex
Henckels
HoMedics
Jockey
KitchenAid
Krups
Laura Ashley Lifestyles
Lee
l.e.i.
Levi's
Mudd
NIKE
Nine & Company
Oneida
OshKosh B'Gosh
Pfaltzgraff
Pyrex
Reebok
Skechers
Speedo
Unionbay
Urban Pipeline
Villager

Selected Private-label and Exclusive Brands

Apt. 9
Croft & Barrow
Food Network
Jennifer Lopez
Jumping Beans
Marc Anthony
Simply Vera
SO
Sonoma Goods for Life

COMPETITORS

Amazon.com	Old Navy
Ascena Retail	Overstock.com
BJ's Wholesale Club	Ross Stores
Bed Bath & Beyond	Saks

Belk
Burlington Coat
  Factory
Costco Wholesale
Dillard's
J. C. Penney
Kmart
Macy's

Sears
Shopko Stores
Stein Mart
TJX Companies
Tailored Brands
Target Corporation
Wal-Mart

HISTORICAL FINANCIALS

Company Type: Public

Income Statement   FYE: February 3

	REVENUE ($ mil.)	NET INCOME ($ mil.)	NET PROFIT MARGIN	EMPLOYEES
02/18*	19,095	859	4.5%	137,000
01/17	18,686	556	3.0%	138,000
01/16	19,204	673	3.5%	140,000
01/15	19,023	867	4.6%	137,000
02/14	19,031	889	4.7%	137,000
Annual Growth	0.1%	(0.9%)	—	0.0%

*Fiscal year change

2018 Year-End Financials

Debt ratio: 33.84%	No. of shares (mil.): 168
Return on equity: 15.94%	Dividends
Cash ($ mil.): 1,308	Yield: 0.0%
Current ratio: 2.01	Payout: 42.9%
Long-term debt ($ mil.): 4,388	Market value ($ mil.): 10,663

	STOCK PRICE ($) FY Close	P/E High/Low	PER SHARE ($) Earnings	Dividends	Book Value
02/18*	63.47	13 7	5.12	2.20	32.30
01/17	39.00	19 11	3.11	2.00	29.75
01/16	49.75	23 12	3.46	1.80	29.52
01/15	59.72	15 11	4.24	1.56	29.81
02/14	50.63	14 11	4.05	1.40	28.33
Annual Growth	5.8%	— —	6.0%	12.0%	3.3%

*Fiscal year change

Kraft Heinz Co (The)

Bringing together packaged food giants Kraft Foods and H.J. Heinz The Kraft Heinz Company is one of the largest food and beverage companies in the world. In addition to its two namesakes the company's portfolio of iconic brands (four of them billion-dollar brands) include such names as Cracker Barrel Oscar Meyer Capri Sun Ore-Ida Kool-Aid Jell-O Planters Philadelphia Lunchables Maxwell House and Velveeta. Kraft Heinz has employees in more than 45 countries and sells its products in some 190. The company was formed in mid-2015 when Heinz and Kraft merged. In early 2017 Kraft Heinz withdrew a $143 billion bid for consumer products giant Unilever after Unilever management and shareholders resisted.

Operations

Kraft Heinz's operations are organized across some half a dozen specific product categories. Its largest segments are condiments and sauces (about a quarter of sales) and cheese and dairy (about 20%). Other segments include meats and seafood and ambient or shelf-stable meals (both at about 10%); as well as frozen and chilled meals refreshment beverages and coffee.

Geographic Reach

Unlike many of its major competitors Kraft Heinz counts the US as its largest market by far accounting for about 70% of total revenue. Canada and Europe together contribute more than 15%

with the remaining revenue coming from Latin America the Asia-Pacific region the Middle East and Africa.

Sales and Marketing

Kraft Heinz's products are sold through its sales organizations and through independent brokers agents and distributors. This network sells to chain wholesale cooperative and independent grocery accounts as well as drug stores and pharmacies value and club stores and foodservice distributors. It also caters to hotels restaurants hospitals health care facilities and certain government agencies.

Kraft Heinz is heavily reliant on its largest customer Wal-Mart Stores which represents more than 20% of sales.

Financial Performance

Kraft Heinz enjoyed a 44% spike in revenues from $18.3 billion in 2015 to $26.5 billion in 2016 primarily due to the results of its 2015 merger. This growth was offset by an 11% drop in European sales which reflected the unfavorable impacts of foreign currency divestitures and an additional 53rd week of shipments that occurred in 2015.

Kraft Heinz's net income skyrocketed by more than 470% from $634 million in 2015 to $3.6 billion in 2016 as a result of the merger and savings from the integration program and other restructuring activities (plant closings and layoffs). Following the trajectory of net income the company's cash flow from operations surged by $2.5 billion in 2015 to $5.2 billion in 2016.

Strategy

Like many of its competitors in the packaged foods space Kraft Heinz is focused on core brands cost-cutting and consolidation through acquisitions.

The company continues to work around its 'fewer bigger better' philosophy focusing its new products and innovations on a core group of top brands. In 2017 and 2016 for example it introduced new products and product innovation for a handful of key brands including Velveeta Philadelphia Cream Cheese and the Classico line of pasta sauces.

Kraft Heinz's strategy also includes reducing expenses. The company's management steered by Brazilian private equity firm and stakeholder 3G Capital has implemented multiyear cost-cutting measures across the business to reduce overhead by streamlining operations. Measures include closing seven plants in North America and consolidating operations in both existing and newly built modernized plants. Reducing employee headcount which has fallen from about 46000 at the time of the Kraft-Heinz merger to 41000 at the end of December is another key element of its strategy.

In line with 3G's approach to growth (centered on buying and consolidating large companies) the company is expected by some industry experts to leverage acquisitions of other major players in the food and beverage industry to expand internationally and bolster its product portfolio. Adhering to this strategy in early 2017 Kraft Heinz placed an unsolicited bid to purchase consumer goods manufacturing giant Unilever for $143 billion; however Unilever quickly rebuffed the bid claiming it underestimated its value and Kraft Heinz withdrew. The deal would have created one of the largest corporate takeovers in history and combined more than dozens of household brands. Kraft Heinz has indicated it will continue to pursue Unilever although it is prohibited by British corporate law from placing another bid until six months after its first bid.

Mergers and Acquisitions

In late 2018 Kraft Heinz agreed to buy condiment company Primal Kitchen for some $200 million. Primal Kitchen makes paleo-friendly mayonnaise and other condiments oils and dressings. The deal helps bolster Kraft in the competitive

space as more companies both new and established look to produce healthier alternatives of kitchen staples.

EXECUTIVES

Head U.s. Meat And Dairy Business, Howard Friedman
Ceo And Director, Bernardo V. Hees, age 49, $1,000,000 total compensation
Evp Global Operations, Eduardo Pelleissone, age 44, $600,000 total compensation
Evp Global Foodservice, Emin Mammadov, age 41
Head U.s. Meals And Sauces Business, Eduardo Luz, age 45
Zone President United States, Paulo Basilio, age 43, $600,000 total compensation
Zone President Amea, Marcos Romaneiro, age 35, $395,437 total compensation
Zone President Latin America, Francisco Sa, age 52
Head U.s. Beverages And Snack Nuts Business, Tom Lopez
President U.s. Foodservice, David Toy
Svp Marketing Innovation Research And Development, Nina Barton
President Kraft Heinz Canada, Carlos Piani, $169,481 total compensation
Svp Global People Performance And Information Technology, Melissa Werneck
Zone President Europe, Rafael Oliveira
Head U.s. Commercial Finance, Andre Maciel
Evp And Cfo, David Knopf, age 30
Vice Chairman, John T. Cahill, age 61
Chairman, Alexandre (Alex) Behring, age 51
Auditors: PricewaterhouseCoopers LLP

LOCATIONS

HQ: Kraft Heinz Co (The)
  One PPG Place, Pittsburgh, PA 15222
Phone: 412 456-5700
Web: www.kraftheinzcompany.com

2016 Sales

	$ mil.	% of total
United States	18,641	70
Canada	2,309	9
United Kingdom	1,055	4
Other	4,482	17
Total	**26,487**	**100**

PRODUCTS/OPERATIONS

2016 Sales

	$ mil.	% of total
Condiments and sauces	6,781	26
Cheese and dairy	5,661	21
Meats and seafood	2,710	10
Ambient meals	2,283	9
Frozen and chilled meals	2,251	8
Refreshment beverages	1,529	6
Coffee	1,496	5
Desserts toppings and baking	980	4
Nuts and salted snacks	1,051	4
Infant and nutrition	762	3
Other	983	4
Total	**26,487**	**100**

COMPETITORS

B&G Foods	Hormel
Bush Brothers	Kellogg
Campbell Soup	McCormick & Company
ConAgra	McIlhenny
Frito-Lay	Nestlé USA
General Mills	Unilever NV
Hershey	Unilever PLC
Hillshire Brands	

HISTORICAL FINANCIALS

Company Type: Public

Income Statement
FYE: December 30

	REVENUE ($ mil.)	NET INCOME ($ mil.)	NET PROFIT MARGIN	EMPLOYEES
12/17	26,232	10,999	41.9%	39,000
12/16*	26,487	3,632	13.7%	41,000
01/16	18,338	634	3.5%	42,000
12/14	10,922	657	6.0%	—
12/13	6,240	(77)	—	—
Annual Growth	43.2%	—	—	—

*Fiscal year change

2017 Year-End Financials

Debt ratio: 26.23%
Return on equity: 17.88%
Cash ($ mil.): 1,629
Current ratio: 0.72
Long-term debt ($ mil.): 28,333

No. of shares (mil.): 1,219
Dividends
Yield: 0.0%
Payout: 27.3%
Market value ($ mil.): 94,789

	STOCK PRICE ($) FY Close	P/E High/Low		PER SHARE ($) Earnings	Dividends	Book Value
12/17	77.76	11	8	8.95	2.45	54.17
12/16*	87.32	32	24	2.81	2.35	47.15
01/16	72.76	—	—	(0.34)	1.70	54.37
Annual Growth	1.7%	—	—		9.6%	(0.1%)

*Fiscal year change

Kroger Co (The)

Kroger is still the US's largest traditional grocer despite Wal-Mart overtaking the chain as the nation's largest seller of groceries years ago. It operates some 3100 stores under various banners including 2800 supermarkets and multi-department stores and around 320 jewelry stores. It also has over 35 food processing plants in the US. Kroger's Fred Meyer Stores subsidiary operates around 130 supercenters that offer groceries merchandise and jewelry in the western US.

Operations

Kroger (either directly or through its subsidiaries) operates a wide variety of store formats and banners that divvy up the retail market by size price point and geography. Roughly 50% of its supermarket and multi-department stores have a fuel center. Its combination-food-and-drug stores account for 85% of its stores base followed by price-impact warehouse stores (5%) large multi-department stores (5%) and Marketplace stores (5%).

The company's 150 Marketplace stores which trade under the Dillon's Fry's Kroger and Smith's banners capitalize on Fred Meyer's general merchandise expertise. While similar to multi-department stores Marketplace stores are generally smaller and don't stock apparel. Kroger's 130 price-impact warehouse-style stores operate under the Food 4 Less and Foods Co. banners and cater to the thrifty with no-frills low-cost shopping for grocery and health and beauty care items. The company operates 35-plus manufacturing plants under the Kroger Ralphs and King Scooper's banners. Of these 17 are dairies ten are bakeries five grocery plants two beverage plants two meat plants and two cheese plants.

Kroger's supermarkets typically stock more than 14000 of its own-brand products (under the Kroger Ralphs Fred Meyer King Soopers and other

brands) about 35% of which the company manufactures. Kroger is also a major pharmacy operator in the US (most of its stores have one) though its pharmacy products and services contribute just under 10% of its revenue.

Prior to its divestiture in mid-2018 Kroger's 780-plus convenience stores generated around 20% of its revenue and operated under six main banners including Kwik Shop Loaf 'N Jug Quik Stop Tom Thumb Turkey Hill Minit Markets and Smith's Express.

Geographic Reach

Cincinnati-based Kroger operates supermarkets in about 35 US states from coast to coast. Key markets include California Ohio Texas and Georgia which combined are home to more than a third of its supermarkets. Its Fred Meyer subsidiary does business in the Pacific Northwest and Alaska. All of Kroger's sales are rung up in the US.

Financial Performance

Kroger's revenues and profits have been rising over the past several years thanks to new store openings and acquisitions and a steady increase in same-store sales revenue.

In fiscal 2017 (ended January) sales bumped up 5% to $115.3 billion due to an increase in comparable (excluding fuel) sales store openings and the contribution from the acquired ModernHEALTH business. Food price deflation weighed on growth. Weakness in the fuel price triggered a 6% decrease in fuel sales to $14.0 billion although the lower price pushed up volume sales by 4%.

Net income fell 5% to $2.0 billion due to the restructuring of multi-employer pension obligations. Cash from operating activities fell 13% to $4.3 billion due to lower net income and changes in working capital partially offset by higher non-cash expenses.

Strategy

Korger operates amid an intensely competitive grocery market that has seen Amazon's acquisition of Whole Foods and a European invasion of discount grocery chains such as Aldi and Lidl. It is looking to both accentuate and move beyond its traditional grocery store roots.

Announced in 2017 the company's Restock Kroger plan includes some $9 billion in capital investments over the following three years dedicated to technology (including the "Scan Bag Go" handheld scanner initiative and online ordering) as well as training and higher pay. The strategic plan also includes an increased focus on Kroger's private-label brands which hit more than $20 billion in sales in 2017.

The grocery giant also announced as part of Restock Kroger that it would launch an everyday activewear apparel line in 2018 to make its stores more of a shopping destination. In addition it sold its $4 billion convenience store business to UK-based EG Group for just more than $2 billion in mid-2018.

Mergers and Acquisitions

In mid-2018 Kroger completed the purchase of private meal kit leader Home Chef. The grocery giant paid $200 million for Home Chef with future payouts of up to $500 million if certain milestones are achieved. The deal accelerates Kroger's move into the meal kit space; the kits will be available in stores and online.

In early 2017 Kroger?s acquired Murray's Cheese a New York-based specialty cheesemaker. This acquisition bolsters Kroger's push into upscale and organic foods.

HISTORY

Bernard Kroger was 22 when he started the Great Western Tea Company in 1883 in Cincinnati. Kroger lowered prices by cutting out middlemen sometimes by making products such as bread.

Growing to 40 stores in Cincinnati and northern Kentucky the company became Kroger Grocery and Baking Company in 1902. It expanded into St. Louis in 1912 and grew rapidly during the 1910s and 1920s by purchasing smaller cash-strapped companies. Kroger sold his holdings in the company for $28 million in 1928 the year before the stock market crash and retired.

The company acquired Piggly Wiggly stores in the late 1920s and bought most of Piggly Wiggly's corporate stock which it held until the early 1940s. The chain reached its largest number of stores — a whopping 5575 — in 1929. (The Depression later trimmed that total.) A year later Kroger manager Michael Cullen suggested opening self-service low-price supermarkets but company executives demurred. Cullen left Kroger and began King Kullen the first supermarket. If he was ahead of his time at Kroger it wasn't by much; within five years the company had 50 supermarkets.

During the 1950s Kroger acquired companies with stores in Texas Georgia and Washington DC. It added New Jersey-based Sav-on drugstores in 1960 and it opened its first SupeRx drugstore in 1961. The company began opening larger supermarkets in 1971; between 1970 and 1980 Kroger's store count grew just 5% but its selling space nearly doubled.

In 1983 the grocer bought Kansas-based Dillons Food Stores (supermarkets and convenience stores) and Kwik Shop convenience stores. Kroger sold most of its interests in the Hook and SupeRx drug chains (which became Hook-SupeRx) in 1987 and focused on its food-and-drugstores. (It sold its remaining stake to Revco in 1994.) The next year it faced two separate takeover bids from the Herbert Haft family and from Kohlberg Kravis Roberts. The company warded off the raiders by borrowing $4.1 billion to pay a special dividend to shareholders and to buy shares for an employee stock plan.

To reduce debt Kroger sold most of its equity in Price Saver Membership Wholesale Clubs and its Fry's California stores. In 1990 the company made its first big acquisition since the 1988 restructuring by buying 29 Great Scott! supermarkets. Joseph Pichler became CEO that year.

Kroger sold its Time Saver Stores unit in 1995. In 1999 Kroger acquired Fred Meyer operator of about 800 stores mainly in the West in a $13 billion deal. Late in 1999 it announced it was buying nearly 75 stores (mostly in Texas) from Winn-Dixie Stores; the deal was called off in 2000 shortly after the FTC withheld its approval. But the company kept buying — acquisitions included 20 former Hannaford stores in Virginia in 2000 as well as 16 Nebraska food stores bought from food distributor Fleming and seven New Mexico stores bought from Furrs Supermarkets in 2001.

Kroger acquired 17 supermarkets (16 in the Houston area) from Albertson's (now Albertsons LLC) and another seven stores from Winn-Dixie in the Dallas/Fort Worth area in 2002.

In April 2003 Kroger introduced Naturally Preferred its own brand of some 140 natural and organic items including baby food pastas cereal snacks milk and soy products.

In 2012 with pharmacies in many of its stores nationwide Kroger purchased specialty pharmacy company Axium Pharmacy Holdings based in Florida. The move satisfied Kroger's long-term growth plans and allowed the grocery chain to serve customers that require complex drug therapies.

EXECUTIVES

Chairman And Ceo, W. Rodney McMullen, age 57, $1,251,781 total compensation

Evp And Cfo, J. Michael Schlotman, age 60, $850,360 total compensation
Evp Retail Divisions, Frederick J. (Fred) Morganthall, age 66, $691,487 total compensation
Sr V Pres, James Thorne
Evp And Cio, Christopher T. (Chris) Hjelm, age 56, $703,367 total compensation
Evp Merchandising, Michael J. (Mike) Donnelly, age 59, $757,036 total compensation
President Central Division, Katie Wolfram, age 63
President Mid-atlantic Division, Jerry L. Clontz
President Houston Division, Marlene Stewart, age 62
Vp Merchandising Fred Meyer Stores, Dan De La Rosa
Vp Manufacturing, Erin S. Sharp, age 60
President Fred Meyer Stores, Joe Grieshaber
President Nashville Division, Zane Day
Vp People Operations, Michael Marx
President Mariano's, Don Rosanova
President Smith's, Kenny Kimball
President Dillons Division, Colleen Juergensen
Group Vp And Chief Digital Officer, Yael Cosset, age 44
Senior Vice President, R Williams
Vice President, Jeremy Stover
Pharmacy Manager, Eric Manchester
Vice President, Geoff Zimmerman
Vice President Store Development, Patti L Taylor
Director Of Surgery, Frank Zagar
Vice President, Bruce Gack
Vice President Finance Controller Quik Stop Division, Jim Bradshaw
Senior Vice President, Mark Tuffin
Vice President Of Marketing, Barbara White
Vice President, Steve Jones
Pharmacy Manager, Diane Chance
Vice President, Joe Rother
Senior Vice President, Gary Bernardo
Merchandising Vice President, Chris Albi
Vice President Of Brand Management, James Jenson
Pharmacy Manager, Gayle Townsend
Pharmacy Manager, Avi Bhatia
Vice President Sales And Marketing, Norm Carhill
Pharmacy Manager, Cc Hepburn
Department Head, Jeffrey Everling
Pharmacist (manager), Lauren Luken
Pharmd, Carrie Mott
Auditors: PricewaterhouseCoopers LLP

LOCATIONS

HQ: Kroger Co (The)
1014 Vine Street, Cincinnati, OH 45202
Phone: 513 762-4000   **Fax:** 513 762-1400
Web: www.thekrogerco.com

PRODUCTS/OPERATIONS

2017 Sales

	$ mil.	% of total
Supermarket	96,900	84
Supermarket fuel sales	13,979	12
Other stores & manufacturing	4,458	4
Total	**115,337**	**100**

2017 Stores

	No.
Supermarkets & multidepartment stores	2,796
Convenience stores	784
Jewelry	319
Total	**3,899**

2017 Sales

	$ mil.	% of total
Non-perishable	60,220	52
Perishable	27,666	24
Fuel	13,979	12
Pharmacy	10,432	9
Other	3,040	3
Total	**115,337**	**100**

Selected Kroger Stores

Multidepartment stores
Fred Meyer
Supermarkets
Baker's
City Market Food & Pharmacy
Dillon Food Stores
Fry's Food & Drug Stores
Gerbes Supermarkets
Harris Teeter Supermarkets
Jay C Food Stores
King Soopers
Kroger
Kroger Fresh Fare
Owen's
Pay Less Super Markets
Quality Food Centers (QFC)
Ralphs
Scott's Food & Pharmacy
Smith's Food & Drug Centers
Warehouse stores
Food 4 Less
FoodsCo
Jewelry stores
Barclay Jewelers
Fox's Jewelers
Fred Meyer Jewelers
Littman Jewelers
Food Production
Bread and other baked goods
Cheese
Coffee
Crackers
Cultured products (cottage cheese yogurt)
Deli products
Fruit juices and fruit drinks
Ice cream
Juice
Meat
Milk
Nuts
Oatmeal
Peanut butter
Snacks
Soft drinks
Spaghetti sauce
Water

Selected Private-Label Brands

Bath & Body Therapies (body and bath)
Banner brands (Kroger Ralphs King Soopers)
Everyday Living (kitchen gadgets)
FMV (For Maximum Value)
HD Design (upscale kitchen gadgets)
Moto Tech (automotive)
Naturally Preferred (premium quality natural and organic brand)
Office Works (office and school supplies)
Private Selection (premium quality brand)
Splash Spa (body and bath)
Splash Sport (body and bath)

COMPETITORS

99 Cents Only	Raley's
A&P	Randall's
Albertsons	Rite Aid
CVS	SUPERVALU
Costco Wholesale	Safeway
Dollar General	Save Mart
Family Dollar Stores	Stater Bros.
GNC	Sterling Jewelers
Giant Eagle	Target Corporation
H-E-B	Tesco
Hy-Vee	Vitamin Shoppe
IGA	Wal-Mart
Kmart	Walgreen
Marsh Supermarkets	Wegmans
Meijer	Whole Foods
NBTY	Winn-Dixie
Publix	Zale

HISTORICAL FINANCIALS

Company Type: Public

Income Statement				FYE: February 3
	REVENUE ($ mil.)	NET INCOME ($ mil.)	NET PROFIT MARGIN	EMPLOYEES
02/18*	122,662	1,907	1.6%	449,000
01/17	115,337	1,975	1.7%	443,000
01/16	109,830	2,039	1.9%	431,000
01/15	108,465	1,728	1.6%	400,000
02/14	98,375	1,519	1.5%	375,000
Annual Growth	**5.7%**	**5.9%**	**—**	**4.6%**

*Fiscal year change

2018 Year-End Financials

Debt ratio: 41.91%	No. of shares (mil.): 870
Return on equity: 27.53%	Dividends
Cash ($ mil.): 347	Yield: 0.0%
Current ratio: 0.78	Payout: 23.4%
Long-term debt ($ mil.): 12,029	Market value ($ mil.): 25,526

	STOCK PRICE ($) FY Close	P/E High/Low		PER SHARE ($) Earnings	Dividends	Book Value
02/18*	29.34	16	9	2.09	0.49	7.97
01/17	33.36	20	14	2.05	0.45	7.25
01/16	38.81	37	16	2.06	0.40	7.05
01/15	69.05	40	20	1.72	0.34	5.56
02/14	36.10	30	19	1.45	0.31	5.30
Annual Growth	**(5.1%)**	**—**	**—**	**9.6%**	**12.4%**	**10.7%**

*Fiscal year change

L Brands, Inc

L Brands (formerly Limited Brands) is as much of a shopping-mall mainstay as food courts and teenagers. The company operates 3005 specialty stores in North America and the UK primarily under the Victoria's Secret Bath & Body Works (BBW) and La Senza (in Canada) banners as well as corresponding websites and catalogs. Originally focused on apparel L Brands sold its ailing Limited and Express chains — leaving the company free to focus on its core businesses. L Brands also owns apparel importer MAST Industries accessories boutique operator Henri Bendel apothecary C.O. Bigelow and The White Barn Candle Co.

Operations

L Brands has realigned its reportable segments into Victoria's Secret Bath & Body Works (BBW) and Victoria's Secret and Bath and Body Works International. More than 60% of sales come from domestic Victoria's Secret stores driven by its eponymous and PINK brands. More than 30% of sales come from the BBW segment which also includes White Barn Candle and C.O. Bigelow brands. The remaining revenue comes from Victoria?s Secret and BBW International and others.

MAST Industries (dba Mast Global Fashions) is the company's production sourcing and logistics arm - it accounts for the rest of sales. Mast is one of the world's largest contract manufacturers importers and distributors of apparel. Mast has manufacturing operations and joint ventures in more than a dozen countries including China Israel Mexico and Sri Lanka.

The Victoria's Secret segment sells women's intimate and other apparel personal care and beauty products under the Victoria's Secret and PINK brand names.

The Bath & Body Works segment sells personal care soaps sanitizers and home fragrance products under the Bath & Body Works White Barn Candle Company C.O. Bigelow and other brand names.

Victoria's Secret and Bath & Body Works International segments include the Victoria's Secret and Bath & Body Works company-owned and partner-operated stores.

Geographic Reach

In addition to its 3078 US stores L Brands has retail stores in Canada the UK china and the Middle East. International sales totaled $1.4 billion in fiscal 2017 (ended January). The company has a partnership with M.H. Alshaya (a popular franchise partner for many American retailers including American Eagle Outfitters and Pottery Barn) to operate stores in the Middle East.

Sales and Marketing

L Brands spent $325 million on advertising expenses in fiscal 2017 down from $414 million and $436 million in 2016 and 2015 respectively. The company sells its La Senza products at more than 120 La Senza stores in Canada and online at www.LaSenza.com. Henri Bende sells its products through New York flagship and online at www.HenriBendel.com.

Financial Performance

The company's net revenues have been increasing over the last five years. In fiscal 2016 L Brands' net revenues increased by 6% due to increase in all of its segments particularly Victoria's Secret.

Victoria's Secret segment revenues increased due to higher Victoria's Secret Stores and Victoria's Secret Direct sales resulting from the performance of PINK brands core lingerie and sport driven by a compelling merchandise assortment that incorporated newness innovation and fashion as well as in-store execution.

In fiscal 2016 the company's net income increased by 20% due to higher net revenues and other income driven by a pre-tax gain due to the divestiture of remaining ownership interest in third-party apparel sourcing business to Sycamore Partners.

L Brands' operating cash inflow increased by 5% to $1.87 billion compared to $1.79 billion in fiscal 2015.

Strategy

The company's goal was for Victoria's Secret to blossom into a $10-billion brand but the global financial crisis decline in consumer confidence and poor performance of the La Senza business in Canada conspired to delay the growth strategy for the bra-and-panty business. The strategy at Victoria's Secret is to capture the teen and college-age female customer with its youth-oriented PINK brand with the hope that as she matures she will shop for sexier styles such as Angels and Very Sexy sold in Victoria's Secret stores. PINK is sold in freestanding stores as well as Victoria's Secret shops. While the retailer doesn't break out PINK sales the brand is meeting stiff competition from American Eagle's Aerie brand and Gilly Hicks by Abercrombie & Fitch. Both target the youth market. L Brands has been closing La Senza stores and repositioning the brand.

While the company's first focus is on major growth in North America it plans to further expand into international markets including mainland China and other countries through partner arrangements or company-owned stores.

HISTORY

After a disagreement with his father in 1963 over the operation of the family store (Leslie's) Leslie Wexner then 26 opened the first Limited store in Columbus Ohio with $5000 borrowed from his aunt. The company was named from Wexner's desire to do one product line well — moderately priced fashionable attire for teenagers and young women.

When The Limited went public in 1969 it had only five stores but the rapid development of large covered malls spurred growth to 100 stores by 1976. Two years later The Limited acquired MAST Industries an international apparel purchasing and importing company. The company opened Express in 1980 to serve the teen market.

The Limited grew with acquisitions including the 1982 purchases of Lane Bryant (large sizes) and Victoria's Secret (lingerie). That year it formed the Brylane fashion catalog division and acquired Roaman's a bricks-and-mortar and catalog merchandiser of plus sizes.

Wexner bought The Lerner Stores (budget women's apparel) and Henri Bendel (high fashion) in 1985 sportswear retailer Abercrombie & Fitch (A&F) in 1988 and London-based perfumer Penhaligon's in 1990 (sold in 1997). The Limited introduced several in-store shops including Cacique (French lingerie) in 1988 and Limited Too (girls' fashions) which were later expanded into standalone stores. It also launched Structure (men's sportswear) in 1989 and Bath & Body Works shops in 1990. All of these stores were in malls often strategically clustered together.

The company closed many The Limited and Lerner stores in 1993 and sold 60% of its Brylane catalog unit to Freeman Spogli (Brylane went public in 1997). It opened four Bath & Body Works stores in the UK (its first non-US stores) to compete with British rival The Body Shop.

In 1994 The Limited bought Galyan's Trading Company a chain of sporting goods superstores. The company began spinning off its businesses while keeping controlling stakes; it spun off Intimate Brands (Victoria's Secret Cacique and Bath & Body Works) in 1995 and A&F in 1996. (The Limited sold its remaining 84% in A&F in 1998.)

The Limited closed more than 100 of its women's apparel stores in 1997 and Intimate Brands shuttered the Cacique chain; the next year The Limited closed nearly 300 more stores companywide (excluding the Intimate Brands chains) and the majority of its Henri Bendel stores.

In 1998 The Limited launched White Barn Candle Co. (candle and home fragrance stores). The following year the company spun off Limited Too its most successful chain as Too Inc. and reduced its interest in Galyan's to 40%. (Galyan's management and buyout firm Freeman Spogli bought the remaining 60% of the sporting goods chain.) The Limited (as well as Intimate Brands) declared a two-for-one stock split in 2000.

To boost profits in 2001 The Limited folded the Structure brand into the Express unit and spun off its Galyan's and Alliance Data Systems subsidiaries retaining 22% and 20% respectively. The Limited sold its Lane Bryant unit to Charming Shoppes for $335 million that year.

The Limited bought back the remaining shares of Intimate Brands it did not already own in March 2002 and over the course of the year phased it into a business segment. In May 2002 the company changed its name to Limited Brands from The Limited. Later that year Limited Brands sold off its remaining stake in Lerner New York and in late 2003 sold its Structure label (which it had rebranded as Express Men's) to Sears Roebuck and Co.

In 2007 Limited Brands completed its acquisition of lingerie maker and retailer La Senza based in Montreal for about $600 million. It also sold a 75% stake in its 251-store Limited Stores business to Sun Capital Partners taking a loss on the sale. In mid-2010 it sold the rest. Three years later in 2013 it finally changed the company name from The Limited to L Brands.

HISTORICAL FINANCIALS

Company Type: Public

Income Statement

FYE: February 3

	REVENUE ($ mil.)	NET INCOME ($ mil.)	NET PROFIT MARGIN	EMPLOYEES
02/18*	12,632	983	7.8%	93,200
01/17	12,574	1,158	9.2%	93,600
01/16	12,154	1,253	10.3%	87,900
01/15	11,454	1,042	9.1%	80,100
02/14	10,773	903	8.4%	94,600
Annual Growth	4.1%	2.1%	—	(0.4%)

*Fiscal year change

2018 Year-End Financials

Debt ratio: 71.10%
Return on equity: —
Cash ($ mil.): 1,515
Current ratio: 1.62
Long-term debt ($ mil.): 5,707

No. of shares (mil.): 280
Dividends
Yield: 0.0%
Payout: 70.1%
Market value ($ mil.): 13,303

	STOCK PRICE ($) FY Close	P/E High/Low		PER SHARE ($) Earnings	Dividends	Book Value
02/18*	47.51	18	10	3.42	2.40	(2.69)
01/17	59.01	24	15	3.98	4.40	(2.55)
01/16	96.15	23	18	4.22	4.00	(0.89)
01/15	84.63	24	14	3.50	2.36	0.06
02/14	52.36	21	14	3.05	1.20	(1.27)
Annual Growth	(2.4%)	—	—	2.9%	18.9%	—

*Fiscal year change

L3 Technologies Inc

LOCATIONS

HQ: L3 Technologies Inc
600 Third Avenue, New York, NY 10016
Phone: 212 697-1111
Web: www.l-3com.com

COMPETITORS

BAE SYSTEMS	ITT Corp.
CACI International	Lockheed Martin
CAE Inc.	Meggitt
Cubic Corp.	Northrop Grumman
DRS Technologies	Orbital Sciences
DynCorp International	Raytheon
FLYHT Aerospace	Rockwell Collins
Solutions	Sierra Nevada Corp
General Dynamics	Thales
Harris Corp.	Trimble Navigation
Herley Industries	United Technologies
Honeywell	telent
International	

HISTORICAL FINANCIALS

Company Type: Public

Income Statement

FYE: December 31

	REVENUE ($ mil.)	NET INCOME ($ mil.)	NET PROFIT MARGIN	EMPLOYEES
12/17	9,573	677	7.1%	31,000
12/16	10,511	710	6.8%	38,000
12/15	10,466	(240)	—	38,000
12/14	12,124	664	5.5%	45,000
12/13	12,629	778	6.2%	48,000
Annual Growth	(6.7%)	(3.4%)	—	(10.4%)

2017 Year-End Financials

Debt ratio: 26.29%
Return on equity: 14.05%
Cash ($ mil.): 662
Current ratio: 1.87
Long-term debt ($ mil.): 3,346

No. of shares (mil.): 77
Dividends
Yield: 0.0%
Payout: 35.2%
Market value ($ mil.): 15,408

	STOCK PRICE ($) FY Close	P/E High/Low		PER SHARE ($) Earnings	Dividends	Book Value
12/17	197.85	23	17	8.51	3.00	65.27
12/16	152.11	18	12	9.01	2.80	58.95
12/15	119.51	—	—	(2.93)	2.60	55.74
12/14	126.21	16	13	7.56	2.40	64.42
12/13	106.86	12	9	8.54	2.20	70.17
Annual Growth	16.6%	—	—	(0.1%)	8.1%	(1.8%)

Laboratory Corporation of America Holdings

This company pricks and prods for profit. Laboratory Corporation of America (LabCorp) is a top provider of clinical laboratory services performing blood and other tests on more than 500000 specimens daily for some 220000 clients including managed care organizations contract research organizations (CROs) hospitals doctors government agencies drug companies independent clinical labs food and nutritional companies and employers. Services range from routine urinalyses HIV tests and Pap smears to specialty testing for diagnostic genetics disease monitoring forensics identity clinical drug trials and allergies. Through Covance it provides end-to-end drug development support. LabCorp operates more than 1750 service sites that collect specimens and 40 primary labs where tests are performed.

Operations

LabCorp operates through two primary segments: LabCorp Diagnostics (LCD) and Covance Drug Development (CCD).

The LCD segment which accounts for some 70% of LabCorp's annual revenues offers more than 4800 different tests. Many of the tests it performs each year are routine tests (including blood chemistry analyses blood cell counts and HIV tests) and nutritional chemistry and safety tests. It also offers specialty testing services for women's health allergies infectious disease oncology pain management and other areas. LCD's genomic and esoteric testing operations include subsidiaries Esoterix Monogram Biosciences and Integrated Genetics while specialty testing units include Cellmark Forensics Dianon Pathology and MedTox Laboratories.

CDD (30% of revenue) provides early drug development associated laboratory testing efficacy studies and clinical trial services to biopharmaceutical clients.

Geographic Reach

Most of LabCorp's operations are conducted through its extensive network of facilities throughout the US (which accounts for more than 80% of total revenue). The company also has joint ventures in Canada where it provides diagnostic testing services in several provinces and it has established presences in China Japan Singapore the United Arab Emirates and the UK.

CDD operates a network of laboratories in the US Switzerland Belgium Singapore and China. Covance has pre-clinical laboratories in Wisconsin Virginia Michigan and Indiana. It also operates labs in the UK (3) Germany China and Singapore. Altogether LabCorp operates in approximately 60 countries.

Sales and Marketing

LabCorp uses a direct sales force to promote its products and services to customers including doctors hospitals clinical labs drugmakers managed care companies and government agencies. As payments from managed care entities (HMOs and PPOs) make up a significant part of LabCorp's net patient revenue gaining and maintaining contracts with these clients is a main thrust of the company's strategy. For instance LabCorp has a multi-year contract with UnitedHealth that makes LabCorp the insurer's exclusive national laboratory services provider.

LabCorp's LCD segment receives about 15% of its net revenue from Medicare and Medicaid programs.

Financial Performance

All of LabCorp's efforts towards expanding its offerings and geographic presence have helped keep the company's finances healthy for several consecutive years with its revenue growing each year since 2008. In 2016 the group reported an 11% increase in sales to some $9.6 billion. Both the LCD and CDD segments saw growth that year: LCD rose 6% due to organic volume growth and CDD rose 23% thanks to the addition of revenues from the recently acquired Covance.

After years of falling net income rose 68% to $732.1 million in 2016. A decline in restructuring and other special charges as well as a relatively low increase in selling general and administrative expenses helped boost the company's bottom line. With the higher net income cash flow from operations increased 20% to $1.2 billion that year.

Strategy

Over the past seven years LabCorp has invested some $6.3 billion in strategic acquisitions. The company is focused on expanding its advanced testing capabilities especially in the areas of genetic and cancer testing. One particular area of interest for the company's product development efforts is the field of personalized medicine. It has introduced a number of "companion" diagnostic tests that determine whether a patient will react well or poorly to certain drugs. LabCorp is developing such tests internally as well as through partnerships with life science entities such as Duke University and Johns Hopkins University. Additional areas of focus are molecular diagnostics and the introduction of new assay platforms (both developed and acquired).

LabCorp strives to capitalize on its nationwide presence to strengthen managed care partnerships. In addition LabCorp looks to keep its physician customers happy with education tools and integrated information management systems including eLabCorp a web-based tool that allows doctors to access testing services online and its electronic health record (EHR) solution.

The company is also expanding consumer-focused tools such as its LabCorp Beacon patient portal. In 2017 it partnered with Walgreens to develop and operate patient service centers within Walgreens stores. These centers will offer lab testing to provide patients with a broader range of health care services.

Meanwhile LabCorp's specialty subsidiaries such as kidney stone analysis firm Litholink work to control costs for payers by focusing on providing patient-specific tools to manage chronic conditions.

Mergers and Acquisitions

In 2015 LabCorp bought New Jersey-based Covance one of the world's largest contract research organizations and a leader in nutritional analysis for approximately $5.7 billion. The deal provided LabCorp with new revenue sources and a broader international presence which has long been a goal for the company. The company also completed the $85 million acquisition of diagnostic testing firm LipoScience; that move strengthened LabCorp's position in the cardiovascular and metabolic disorder testing market. LabCorp addtionally purchased Bode Technology Group which provides specialized forensic DNA collection analysis and relationship testing.

In 2016 LabCorp acquired Sequenom a specialist in tests for the prenatal and women's health markets. The deal was valued at $371 million. It also purchased women's health laboratory Pathology further building on its women's health offerings.

In mid-2017 the company bought UK-based CRO Chiltern International for $1.2 billion. With that deal it expanded its oncology operations as well as growing its international business.

The following year LabCorp acquired scientific process services firm Sciformix for an undisclosed amount. Sciformix became part of Covance strengthening that unit's pharmacovigilance capabilities. The newly acquired firm's operations are primarily located in Asia.

EXECUTIVES

Evp Cfo And Treasurer, Glenn A. Eisenberg, age 56, $653,438 total compensation

Ceo Covance Drug Development, John D. Ratliff, age 58

Svp Chief Legal Officer Secretary And Chief Compliance Officer, F. Samuel Eberts, age 58, $486,875 total compensation

Chairman President And Ceo, David P. (Dave) King, age 60, $1,133,333 total compensation

Svp And Cio, Lance V. Berberian, age 55, $396,112 total compensation

Senior Vice President, Devin Lorsson

Medical Director And Vice President, James Amberson

Vice President Core Business Solutions, Rich Konzelman

Auditors: PricewaterhouseCoopers LLP

LOCATIONS

HQ: Laboratory Corporation of America Holdings
358 South Main Street, Burlington, NC 27215
Phone: 336 229-1127
Web: www.labcorp.com

2016 Sales

	% of total
US	81
Switzerland	5
Canada	3
United Kingdom	3
Other	8
Total	**100**

PRODUCTS/OPERATIONS

2016 Sales

	$ mil.	% of total
LCD	6,593	68
CDD	2,844	30
Reimbursable out-of-pocket expenses	204	2
Intercompany eliminations	-0.8	-
Total	**9,641**	**100**

Selected Subsidiaries

DIANON Systems Inc. (pathology Connecticut)
Dynacare Laboratories Inc. (clinical labs; Tennessee Washington Wisconsin Canada)
Esoterix Inc. (esoteric testing Colorado)
Integrated Genetics (formerly Genzyme Genetics fertility testing labs across the US)
Integrated Oncology (formerly US Labs esoteric oncology tests US)
Litholink Corporation (kidney patient testing Illinois)

Monogram Biosciences Inc. (HIV resistance testing and personalized medicine California)
National Genetics Institute (NGI infection testing and blood screening California
Viro-Med Laboratories Inc. (molecular microbial testing Minnesota)

Selected Acquisitions

COMPETITORS

Arup Laboratories	NeoGenomics
Bio-Reference Labs	Oncolab
Celera	Orchid Cellmark
CompuNet Clinical	Pathology Associates
Laboratories	Medical Laboratories
HedgePath	Pharmaceutical Product
IDENTIGENE	Development
Kroll Background	Psychemedics
America	Quest Diagnostics
Laboratory Sciences of	Solstas
Arizona	Sonic Healthcare
MEDTOX Laboratories	eScreen
Medtox Scientific	
Mid America Clinical	
Laboratories	

HISTORICAL FINANCIALS

Company Type: Public

Income Statement

FYE: December 31

	REVENUE ($ mil.)	NET INCOME ($ mil.)	NET PROFIT MARGIN	EMPLOYEES
12/17	10,441	1,268	12.1%	60,000
12/16	9,641	732	7.6%	52,000
12/15	8,680	436	5.0%	50,000
12/14	6,011	511	8.5%	36,000
12/13	5,808	573	9.9%	34,000
Annual Growth	**15.8%**	**21.9%**	**—**	**15.3%**

2017 Year-End Financials

Debt ratio: 40.81%
Return on equity: 20.56%
Cash ($ mil.): 316
Current ratio: 1.31
Long-term debt ($ mil.): 6,344

No. of shares (mil.): 101
Dividends
 Yield: —
 Payout: —
Market value ($ mil.): 16,254

	STOCK PRICE ($) FY Close	P/E High/Low	PER SHARE ($) Earnings	Dividends	Book Value
12/17	159.51	13 10	12.21	0.00	67.03
12/16	128.38	20 14	7.02	0.00	53.61
12/15	123.64	29 24	4.34	0.00	48.81
12/14	107.90	18 15	5.91	0.00	33.34
12/13	91.37	17 14	6.25	0.00	29.07
Annual Growth	**14.9%**	**— —**	**18.2%**	**—**	**23.2%**

Lakeland Bancorp, Inc.

Lakeland Bancorp is the holding company for Lakeland Bank which serves northern and central New Jersey from around 50 branch offices. Targeting individuals and small to midsized businesses the bank offers standard retail products such as checking and savings accounts money market and NOW accounts and CDs. It also offers financial planning and advisory services for consumers. The bank's lending activities primarily consist of commercial loans and mortgages (around three-quarters of the company's loan portfolio) and residential mortgages. Lakeland also offers commercial lease financing for commercial equipment.

Operations

Lakeland Bancorp operates through a single business segment. Around 70% of its $4.3 billion loan portfolio is made up of commercial mortgages. Industrial commercial loans residential mortgages real estate construction loans and home equity and consumer loans each represent between 5%-10% of the company's lending activity. The company holds $5.5 billion in assets and $4.4 billion in deposits.

Geographic Reach

Headquartered in Oak Ridge New Jersey Lakeland Bancorp boasts about 50 banking offices across the New Jersey counties of Bergen Essex Morris Ocean Passaic Somerset Sussex Union and Warren. The company also has a branch in Highland Mills New York; six New Jersey regional commercial lending centers in Bernardsville Jackson Montville Newton Teaneck and Waldwick; and two commercial loan production offices serving Middlesex and Monmouth counties in New Jersey and the Hudson Valley region of New York.

Sales and Marketing

Lakeland Bancorp serves a variety of customers from individuals to businesses to municipalities.

One-fifth of Lakeland's commercial loan segment – the largest in its portfolio – is made up of owner-occupied real estate loans. Multifamily and retail loans make up about 15% each and industrial and office loans each comprise around 10%.

Financial Performance

Lakeland Bancorp has seen major five-year growth expanding revenue by 53% to $190.7 million net income by 111% to $52.6 million and cash by 39% to $142.9 million between 2013 and 2017. However the company's debt has risen 85% to $296.9 million in that time.

The holding company's revenue increased 14% in 2017 owing primarily to increased net interest income from growing average earning assets. Net income added 27% on the strength of those gains.

Lakeland's cash dipped $32.9 million in 2017. Operations and financings contributed $67.5 million and investments used $355.1 million. Financings provided $254.8 million down nearly $200 million from the previous year following an increase in net deposits federal funds purchased and securities sold under repurchase agreements.

Strategy

Lakeland Bancorp is focused on growth through acquisitions. The company has acquired at least eight community banks since its inception including Highlands Bancorp. which operates in northern New Jersey. The company also offers internet banking mobile banking and cash management services.

Mergers and Acquisitions

In January 2019 Lakeland Bancorp acquired Vernon New Jersey-based Highlands Bancorp in a deal valued at $56.7 million. The holding company – which operated branches in the New Jersey municipalities of Sparta Totowa and Denville – had consolidated total assets of $5.53 billion.

Company Background

Lakeland Bancorp was founded in 1969. It organized into a bank holding company in 1989.

EXECUTIVES

President And Ceo Lakeland Bancorp And Lakeland Bank, Thomas J. Shara, age 60, $650,000 total compensation

Sevp And Coo, Ronald E. (Ron) Schwarz, age 61, $266,769 total compensation

Sevp And Regional President, Robert A. Vandenbergh, age 66, $360,212 total compensation

Evp And Senior Government Banking And
Financial Services Officer, Jeffrey J. Buonforte, age
66, $205,075 total compensation
Svp And Chief Credit Officer Lakeland Bank,
James R. Noonan, age 66
Evp And Chief Risk Officer, James M. Nigro
Cfo, Thomas F. Splaine, age 53
First Svp And Chief Technology And Information
Security Officer, Mary Kaye Nardone
Evp And Chief Retail Officer, Ellen Lalwani
Evp And Chief Lending Officer, David S.
Yanagisawa, $220,000 total compensation
Evp Chief Administrative Officer General Counsel
And Corporate Secretary, Timothy J. Matteson, age
48
Evp And Regional President, Michael A. Schutzer
Senior Vice President And Team Leader Of
Commercial Lending, Michael Vessa
Vice President Asset Based Lending, Steven
Breeman
Vice President, Russell Dunn
Vice President Commercial Lending, Bruce Bready
Vice President, Scott Heiman
Vice President Area Manager, Hafeza Mohammed
Vice President Director Of Hurman Resource,
Connie Meehan
Vice President, Connie Feeney
Senior Vice President And Director Of Marketing,
Maureen Martin
Vice President, Rasiel Kleiner
Vice President, Betsy Kalman
Vice President In The Investment Program,
Joseph P Dolan
Vice President, Cynthia SanPhillip
Vice President, Jane Quinn
Vice President Business Development, Bill
Schachtel
Assistant Vice President Branch Manager, Kim
Trimmer
Vice President And Business Development
Officer, Mark McCoy
Vice President And Investment Representative,
Jeffrey Beebe
Vice President And Associate Counsel, Saily
Avelenda
Assistant Vice President, Robert Surovich
Vice President Compliance Officer, Lisa Nienaber
Vice President Facilities Manager, Tina George
Vice President, Debra Zimmerly
Vice President Data Operations And Data Security
Officer, Elizabeth Martin
Vice President Commercial Lending, Beth Johns
Vice President Secondary Marketing And Product
Development, Jorge Ferrer
Vice President Area Manager, Jerry Slavik
Vice President, John Allen
Vice President Information Security Officer, Marty
Puzio
Assistant Vice President, Richard Machtinger
Senior Vice President, Samuel Wilson
First Senior Vice President, John Rath
Vice President Relationship Manager, Tony Creanza
Vice President Consumer Loan Officer, James
Trotta
Vice President Area Manager, Rehab Elmoslemany
Avp Portfolio Manager, Christopher Barbarino
Board Member, Janeth Hendershot
Board Member, Stephen Tilton
Vice Chairman, Bruce G Bohuny
Chairman Lakeland Bancorp And Lakeland Bank,
Mary Ann Deacon, age 66
Board Member, Mark J Fredericks
Board Member, Robert Nicholson
Board Member, Thomas Marino
Assistant Treasurer Branch Manager, Carianne
Reeber
Assistant Treasurer, Debra Burke
Auditors: KPMG LLP

LOCATIONS

HQ: Lakeland Bancorp, Inc.
  250 Oak Ridge Road, Oak Ridge, NJ 07438
Phone: 973 697-2000
Web: www.lakelandbank.com

PRODUCTS/OPERATIONS

2017 Sales

	$ mil.	% of total
Interest		
Loans & fees	172	80
Investment securities and other	17	8
Interest expense	(25.0)	-
Non-interest		
Service charges on deposit accounts	10	5
Commissions & fees	4	2
Income on bank owned life insurance	2	1
Other	7	4
Total	**190**	**100**

Selected Services

401K and IRA Rollovers
Certificates of deposit & individual retirement accounts
Checking accounts
Consumer loans
Home loans
Insurance
Investment management
Online services
Retirement income planning
Savings and money market accounts

COMPETITORS

Bank of America	PNC Financial
Bank of New York	Sovereign Bank
Mellon	Sussex Bancorp
Capital One	TD Bank USA
Clifton Bancorp	Valley National
Hudson City Bancorp	Bancorp
Investors Bancorp	Wells Fargo
JPMorgan Chase	
New York Community	
Bancorp	

HISTORICAL FINANCIALS

Company Type: Public

Income Statement

FYE: December 31

	ASSETS ($ mil.)	NET INCOME ($ mil.)	INCOME AS % OF ASSETS	EMPLOYEES
12/17	5,405	52	1.0%	621
12/16	5,093	41	0.8%	592
12/15	3,869	32	0.8%	551
12/14	3,538	31	0.9%	566
12/13	3,317	24	0.8%	550
Annual Growth	**13.0%**	**20.5%**	**—**	**3.1%**

2017 Year-End Financials

Debt ratio: 5.49%	No. of shares (mil.): 47
Return on equity: 9.28%	Dividends
Cash ($ mil.): 142	Yield: 0.0%
Current ratio: —	Payout: 36.2%
Long-term debt ($ mil.): —	Market value ($ mil.): 912

	STOCK PRICE ($) FY Close	P/E High/Low	PER SHARE ($) Earnings	Dividends	Book Value
12/17	19.25	20 16	1.09	0.40	12.31
12/16	19.50	21 10	0.95	0.37	11.65
12/15	11.79	15 12	0.85	0.33	10.57
12/14	11.70	15 12	0.82	0.29	10.01
12/13	12.37	18 13	0.71	0.27	9.28
Annual Growth	**11.7%**	**— —**	**11.1%**	**9.8%**	**7.3%**

Lakeland Financial Corp

EXECUTIVES

Evp And Retail Banking Manager, Kevin L.
Deardorff, age 57, $217,963 total compensation
President And Ceo Lakeland Financial And Lake
City Bank, David M. Findlay, age 56, $493,360 total
compensation
Evp And Chief Credit Officer, Michael E. Gavin
Evp And Cfo, Lisa M. O'Neill, age 50, $206,286 total
compensation
Svp And General Counsel, Kristin L. Pruitt, age 46
Evp And Commercial Banking Manager, Eric H.
Ottinger, $218,263 total compensation
Vice President And Trust Officer, Patricia Culp
Vice President Controller, Teresa Bartman
Senior Vice President Human Resources Training,
Jill DeBatty
Senior Vice President And Commercial
Indianapolis Regional Manager, Bill Redman
Vice President And Trust Officer, Jennifer King
Chairman Lakeland Financial And Lake City
Bank, Michael L. Kubacki, age 66
Auditors: Crowe Horwath LLP

LOCATIONS

HQ: Lakeland Financial Corp
  202 East Center Street, P.O. Box 1387, Warsaw, IN
  46581-1387
Phone: 574 267-6144
Web: www.lakecitybank.com

PRODUCTS/OPERATIONS

2017 Sales

	$ mil.	% of total
Interest		
Loans	151	75
Securities	14	7
Other	0	-
Interest expense	(29.8)	-
Noninteresst		
Service charges on deposit accounts	13	7
Loan and service fees	7	4
Wealth advisory fees	5	3
Investment brokerage fees	1	-
Other	7	4
Total	**171**	**100**

COMPETITORS

1st Source Corporation	PNC Financial
KeyCorp	Peoples Bancorp (IN)
Northeast Indiana	
Bancorp	

HISTORICAL FINANCIALS

Company Type: Public

Income Statement

FYE: December 31

	ASSETS ($ mil.)	NET INCOME ($ mil.)	INCOME AS % OF ASSETS	EMPLOYEES
12/17	4,682	57	1.2%	539
12/16	4,290	52	1.2%	524
12/15	3,766	46	1.2%	518
12/14	3,443	43	1.3%	496
12/13	3,175	38	1.2%	497
Annual Growth	**10.2%**	**10.2%**	**—**	**2.0%**

2017 Year-End Financials

Debt ratio: 0.66%	No. of shares (mil.): 25
Return on equity: 12.80%	Dividends
Cash ($ mil.): 176	Yield: 0.0%
Current ratio: —	Payout: 28.2%
Long-term debt ($ mil.): —	Market value ($ mil.): 1,214

	STOCK PRICE ($) FY Close	P/E High/Low		PER SHARE ($) Earnings	Dividends	Book Value
12/17	48.49	23	18	2.23	0.63	18.72
12/16	47.36	26	16	2.05	0.73	17.12
12/15	46.62	26	20	1.83	0.63	15.83
12/14	43.47	25	20	1.74	0.55	14.63
12/13	39.00	25	15	1.55	0.49	13.10
Annual Growth	5.6%	—	—	9.5%	6.3%	9.3%

Lam Research Corp

Lam Research is a top maker of the equipment used to make semiconductors. The company's products address two key steps in the chip-making process. Its market-leading plasma etch machines are used to create tiny circuitry patterns on silicon wafers. Lam also makes cleaning equipment that keeps unwanted particles from contaminating processed wafers. The company's Customer Support Business Group provides products and services to maximize installed equipment performance. Lam's customers include many of the world's large chip makers; customers outside the US primarily in Asia represent the majority of sales. Lam's products are installed in more than 45000 semiconductor processing chambers around the world.

Operations
About two-thirds of Lam Research?s revenue comes from customers who make memory chips with another quarter of revenue generated by silicon foundries. Logic and integrated device manufacturers account for the remaining revenue.

Geographic Reach
South Korea is Lam Research's largest market accounting for about 30% of sales while customers in Taiwan account for about 25%. Other significant geographic markets are Japan and China each generating about 15% of Lam?s sales.

The company has manufacturing facilities in the US China Europe Korea Southeast Asia and Taiwan.

Sales and Marketing
Lam Research has five customers that each account for more than 10% of its revenue. They are Micron Technology Samsung Electronics Company SK Hynix Taiwan Semiconductor Manufacturing Company and Toshiba.

Financial Performance
Lam Research rode a wave of capital spending by its customers in 2017 (ended June) to post a 36% leap in revenue to about $8 billion. The company marked a fifth straight year of higher revenue as it said customers continued to invest in technology and capacity to meet increased computing demand from devices and applications for the Internet of Things cloud computing and other technologies. Sales were significantly higher in South Korea and to a lesser extent Taiwan.

The company?s net income skyrocketed about 86% higher to about $1.7 billion in 2017 compared to 2016. Lam credited the jump to higher revenue and more efficient factory use because of increased production volume. Net profit margin reached 21% in 2017 the highest since 2011?s 22%.

Lam?s cash flow from operations rose to about $2 billion in 2017 from about $1.3 billion in 2016 on significant changes in operating asset and liability accounts.

Strategy
The semiconductor business is notoriously cyclical rising and falling according to the strength of the overall economy. When the economy improves people buy more products with semiconductors in them. That's playing out at Lam where the value of shipments rose 45% in 2017 (ended June) from 2016.

The high expense of semiconductor manufacturing equipment however has resulted in consolidation of manufacturers. Samsung and Intel are among the few companies left that make their own products. So far Lam has maintained a mix of sales to manufacturers such as Samsung and to contract chip makers such as Taiwan Semiconductor.

A heavy investor in innovation the company's R&D expenses reached $1 billion in 2017 (ended June) up from $913 million in 2016 and $825 million in 2015. Particular research areas are deposition etch and single-wafer clean processes and technologies.

Mergers and Acquisitions
In 2017 Lam Research acquired Coventor which develops simulation and modeling software for the semiconductor industry. Coventor's software helps manufacturers predict structures and behaviors of design before committing to production.

The acquisition of KLA-Tencor which the companies agreed to in 2015 would have created a company with complementary products and something of a one-stop shop for companies that make semiconductors. Throughout the process the companies struggled to persuade regulators that the deal would not harm competition in the industry. Unable to make their case to the satisfaction of regulators Lam and KLA-Tencor called off the deal in October 2016.

EXECUTIVES

Evp Global Products Group, Richard A. (Rick) Gottscho, age 67, $545,296 total compensation
Svp And Cto Corporate Technology Development, David J. (Dave) Hemker
President And Ceo, Martin B. Anstice, age 51, $937,789 total compensation
Evp And Cfo, Douglas R. (Doug) Bettinger, age 51, $548,827 total compensation
Evp And Coo, Timothy M. (Tim) Archer, age 51, $624,061 total compensation
Svp Chief Legal Officer And Secretary, Sarah A. O'Dowd, age 68, $434,488 total compensation
Svp Strategic Development Corporate Marketing And Communications, Gary Bultman
Vp Pl, Thorsten Lill
Vice President Regional Operations, Vince Brigman
Group Vice President Global Sales And Corporate Marketing, Steven Lindsay
Vice President Of Etch Product Development And Engineering, John Daugherty
Vice President Global Field Operations, Chris Carter
Vice President And General Manager, Kaihan Ashtiani
Vice President, Candi Kristoffersen
Vice President, Hwee Lim
Vice President Global Operations Lam Research Corporation, Abdi Hariri
Vice President Marketing, Dinesh Kalakkad
Vice President And General Manager Clean Product Group Lam Research Co. Ltd, Jeff Marks
Vice President And General Manager Etch, Pat Lord
Corporate Vp Global Business Operations, Steve Lanza

Vice President Advanced Equipment And Process Control, Jason Shields
Senior Vice President Global Customer Operations, Scott Meikle
Chairman, Stephen G. (Steve) Newberry, age 64
Auditors: Ernst & Young LLP

LOCATIONS

HQ: Lam Research Corp
4650 Cushing Parkway, Fremont, CA 94538
Phone: 510 572-0200   **Fax:** 510 572-0454
Web: www.lamresearch.com

2017 Sales

	$ mil.	% of total
Asia/Pacific		
Korea	2,480	31
Taiwan	2,096,669	26
Japan	1,041,969	13
China	1,023,195	13
Southeast Asia	401,877	5
United States	629,937	8
Europe	340,644	4
Total	**8,013,620**	**100**

PRODUCTS/OPERATIONS

Selected Products
Plasma ("dry") wafer-etching equipment
Plasma-based bevel clean system
Single-wafer spin and linear clean products
Three-dimensional integrated circuit etch equipment
Transformer Coupled Plasma (TCP) silicon etch equipment

COMPETITORS

ASM International	Plasma Etch
Applied Materials	Rennova Health
Ebara	SCREEN Holdings
Hitachi High-Technologies	Suss MicroTec
Intevac	Tokyo Electron
Mattson Technology	Veeco Instruments

HISTORICAL FINANCIALS

Company Type: Public

Income Statement
FYE: June 24

	REVENUE ($ mil.)	NET INCOME ($ mil.)	NET PROFIT MARGIN	EMPLOYEES
06/18	11,077	2,380	21.5%	10,900
06/17	8,013	1,697	21.2%	9,400
06/16	5,885	914	15.5%	7,500
06/15	5,259	655	12.5%	7,300
06/14	4,607	632	13.7%	6,500
Annual Growth	24.5%	39.3%	—	13.8%

2018 Year-End Financials

Debt ratio: 19.36%	No. of shares (mil.): 156
Return on equity: 35.19%	Dividends
Cash ($ mil.): 4,512	Yield: 0.0%
Current ratio: 2.90	Payout: 19.3%
Long-term debt ($ mil.): 1,806	Market value ($ mil.): 27,409

	STOCK PRICE ($) FY Close	P/E High/Low		PER SHARE ($) Earnings	Dividends	Book Value
06/18	174.70	16	9	13.17	2.55	41.94
06/17	151.78	16	8	9.24	1.65	43.21
06/16	82.28	15	11	5.22	1.20	38.09
06/15	82.86	21	16	3.70	0.84	33.72
06/14	66.95	18	12	3.62	0.18	30.98
Annual Growth	27.1%	—	—	38.1%	94.0%	7.9%

Las Vegas Sands Corp

Las Vegas Sands brings a touch of Venice to the US and China. Replete with gondoliers and a replica of the Rialto Bridge the company's Venetian Las Vegas Hotel Resort & Casino offers a 120000-sq.-ft. casino and a 4000-suite hotel as well as a shopping dining and entertainment complex. Through its majority-owned Sands China subsidiary the firm operates The Venetian Macao on the Cotai Strip (the Chinese equivalent of the Las Vegas Strip) as well as four other properties in Macao. Properties also include the Marina Bay Sands in Singapore Sands Bethlehem in Bethlehem Pennsylvania and The Palazzo in Las Vegas.

Operations

Las Vegas Sands' collection of resorts in Asia and the US feature state-of-the-art convention and exhibition facilities premium accommodations world-class gaming and entertainment destination retail and dining including celebrity chef restaurants and many other amenities. Many of its hotels operate under the Sheraton Holiday Inn Conrad and Four Seasons banners and its shopping malls feature upscale tenants including Louis Vuitton Chanel BVLGARI Prada Gucci Zara Burberry Versace Dior Cartier and Tiffany & Co.

Nearly 80% of Las Vegas Sands' revenue comes from its casino operations while its hotel rooms bring in nearly 15% of revenue.

The company's properties in Asia (Macao and Singapore) and the US (Las Vegas and Pennsylvania) feature a total of more than 13000 slot machines nearly 3000 table games and some 22000 mostly upscale hotel suites. By these metrics Las Vegas Sands's largest properties include Sands Cotai Central and Venetian Macao in Macao China and The Venetian Las Vegas and The Palazzo in Las Vegas Nevada.

Las Vegas Sands operates Sands Expo Center one of the largest trade show and convention center venues in the US. The facility offers 2.3 million gross square feet of meeting exhibit and conference space to parties leasing space for events like trade shows and conferences. Las Vegas Sands offers convention space at many of its properties. While the company's casinos attract travelers and guests primarily on weekends its convention centers draw business and other travelers during the slower mid-week period.

Geographic Reach

Outside of Nevada Las Vegas Sands operates in Macao Singapore and Pennsylvania. Macao accounts for about 60% of the company's total revenue.

Sales and Marketing

Las Vegas Sands advertises on television internet radio newspapers magazines and billboards. The Paiza Club located at the company's properties is an important part of Las Vegas Sands' VIP gaming marketing strategy.

The company spends more than $120 million on advertising costs each year.

Financial Performance

Las Vegas Sands reported $12.8 billion in revenue for fiscal 2017 a 13% increase over fiscal 2016. A $1.3 billion increase in its casino operations drove the jump including new revenue generated from the recently opened Parisian Macao (in late 2016) and to a lesser extent an uptick in casino revenue from Marina Bay Sands.

The jump in revenue drove a 68% increase in profits to $2.8 billion in 2017.

Las Vegas Sands ended 2017 with about $2.4 billion in cash on hand. Cash from operations contributed $4.5 billion while financing activities used $3.4 billion and investing activities used $823 million.

Strategy

Las Vegas Sands has been focused for several years on expanding internationally with some expansion centering on renovation projects in Asia. Recent renovations have focused on adding hotel suites and other property expansion and in some instances thematic re-branding beyond its traditional Venetian theme. The company is in the midst of transforming its Sands Cotai Central into The Londoner Macao redesigned with London-themed landmarks attractions and decor. In late 2016 the company opened the French-themed Parisian Macao.

Despite its ambitious expansion plans abroad the company remains somewhat cautious in Las Vegas which is saturated with casino hotel shopping entertainment and convention center competition.

Company Background

Las Vegas Sands Corp. traces its roots back to the late 1980s when Sheldon Adelson founder the computer trade show COMDEX and other partners bought the Sands Hotel in Las Vegas. Ten years after buying the historic casino Adelson demolished the Sands Hotel and opened The Venetian Las Vegas a Venice-themed casino resort inspired by a trip Adelson took with his wife to the coastal Italian city.

The company went public in 2004 and fueled by the influx of cash from public investors began establishing itself internationally in Asia in the late 2000s.

EXECUTIVES

Chairman And Ceo, Sheldon G. Adelson, age 84, $1,000,000 total compensation
President And Coo, Robert G. (Rob) Goldstein, age 62, $3,400,000 total compensation
Evp Global General Counsel And Secretary, Lawrence A. (Lon) Jacobs, age 63, $284,800 total compensation
President Sands Bethlehem, Mark Juliano, age 63
President And Ceo Marina Bay Sands, George Tanasijevich, age 57, $864,140 total compensation
President And Coo The Venetian The Palazzo And Sands Expo & Convention Center, George M. Markantonis, age 60, $863,077 total compensation
Evp And Cfo, Patrick Dumont, age 43, $1,200,000 total compensation
President And Coo Sands China, Wilfred Wong
Vice President Of Facilities, Kim Grange
Senior Vice President Table Games, Sean Mccreery
Senior Vice President Government Relations, Andy Abboud
Vice President Global Head Of Infrastructure And Operations, Edwin Grogan
Vice President, Robert Cilento
Senior Vice President Public Relations, Ron Reese
Vice President And General Counsel, Frederick Kraus
Global Vice President Of Marketing, Michael Volkert
Senior Vice President Global Human Resources Labor, Calvin Siemer
Svp And Chief Security Officer, Brian Nagel
Vice President Us Tax, Jessica Helderman
Vice President Investor Relations, Alistair Scobie
Vice President Casino Marketing, Kathy Mccracken
Senior Vice President Global Business Development, Wilson Ning
Vice President Of Hotel Operations, Max Tappeiner
Vice President Brand Marketing, Angela Wise
National Sales Manager, Mikki Dejurnett
Senior Vice President Global Human Resources, Amy Lee
Senior Vice President And Global Chief Compliance Officer, Matthew Frank
Vice President Global Restaurant And Nightlife Devel01ment, Patrick Lang
National Sales Manager, Melissa Wilson
National Sales Manager, Ashley Reimer
Auditors: DELOITTE & TOUCHE LLP

LOCATIONS

HQ: Las Vegas Sands Corp
3355 Las Vegas Boulevard South, Las Vegas, NV 89109
Phone: 702 414-1000
Web: www.sands.com

PRODUCTS/OPERATIONS

2017 Sales

	$ mil.	% of total
Macao		
Marina Bay Sands	3,154	24
The Venetian Macao	2,990	23
Sands Cotai Central	1,943	15
The Parisian Macao	1,429	11
Sands Macao	640	5
The Plaza Macao and Four Seasons Macao	607	5
Ferry Operations and Other	177	1
United States		
Las Vegas Operating Properties	1,618	13
Sands Bethlehem	579	5
Intersegment eliminations (255) (2)		
Total	**12,882**	**100**

2017 Sales

	$ mil.	% of total
Casino	10,058	78
Rooms	1,619	13
Food and beverage	843	7
Mall	651	5
Convention retail and other	550	4
Promotional allowances (839) (7)		
Total	**12,882**	**100**

Selected Properties

Sands Expo & Convention Center
THE Venetian Vegas
Sands Macao
The Venetian Macao
The Palazzo Las Vegas
The Plaza Macao
Sands Bethlehem
Marina Bay Sands
Sands Cotai Central
The Parisian Macao

COMPETITORS

Boyd Gaming
Caesars Entertainment
Galaxy Entertainment
Genting Singapore
MGM Resorts
Melco Crown Entertainment
Penn National Gaming
Tropicana Entertainment
Wynn Resorts

HISTORICAL FINANCIALS

Company Type: Public

Income Statement

FYE: December 31

	REVENUE ($ mil.)	NET INCOME ($ mil.)	NET PROFIT MARGIN	EMPLOYEES
12/17	12,882	2,806	21.8%	50,500
12/16	11,410	1,670	14.6%	49,000
12/15	11,688	1,966	16.8%	46,500
12/14	14,583	2,840	19.5%	48,500
12/13	13,769	2,306	16.7%	48,500
Annual Growth	(1.7%)	5.0%	—	1.0%

2017 Year-End Financials

Debt ratio: 46.60%
Return on equity: 44.29%
Cash ($ mil.): 2,419
Current ratio: 1.09
Long-term debt ($ mil.): 9,344

No. of shares (mil.): 789
Dividends
  Yield: 0.0%
  Payout: 82.4%
Market value ($ mil.): 54,861

STOCK PRICE ($) FY Close	P/E High/Low		PER SHARE ($) Earnings	Dividends	Book Value
12/17 69.49	20	15	3.54	2.92	8.22
12/16 53.41	30	18	2.10	2.88	7.77
12/15 43.84	25	15	2.47	2.60	8.58
12/14 58.16	25	15	3.52	2.00	9.04
12/13 78.87	28	16	2.79	1.40	9.36
Annual Growth (3.1%)	—	—	6.1%	20.2%	(3.2%)

Lauder (Estee) Cos., Inc. (The)

EXECUTIVES

Prin, Est E Lauder
President, Patrick B Chavanne
Vice-President Merchandising, Scott Blair
Senior Vice-President, Richard Ferretti
Auditors: KPMG LLP

LOCATIONS

HQ: Lauder (Estee) Cos., Inc. (The)
767 Fifth Avenue, New York, NY 10153
Phone: 212 572-4200
Web: www.elcompanies.com

HISTORICAL FINANCIALS
Company Type: Public

Income Statement			FYE: June 30
	REVENUE ($ mil.)	NET INCOME ($ mil.)	NET PROFIT MARGIN	EMPLOYEES
---	---	---	---	---
06/18	13,683	1,108	8.1%	46,000
06/17	11,824	1,249	10.6%	46,000
06/16	11,262	1,114	9.9%	46,000
06/15	10,780	1,088	10.1%	44,000
06/14	10,968	1,204	11.0%	42,400
Annual Growth	5.7%	(2.1%)	—	2.1%

2018 Year-End Financials
Debt ratio: 28.20%
Return on equity: 24.43%
Cash ($ mil.): 2,181
Current ratio: 1.86
Long-term debt ($ mil.): 3,361
No. of shares (mil.): 367
Dividends
Yield: 0.0%
Payout: 50.1%
Market value ($ mil.): 52,388

STOCK PRICE ($) FY Close	P/E High/Low		PER SHARE ($) Earnings	Dividends	Book Value
06/18 142.69	53	31	2.95	1.48	12.77
06/17 95.98	29	22	3.35	1.32	11.91
06/16 91.02	32	25	2.96	1.14	9.71
06/15 86.66	31	25	2.82	0.92	9.72
06/14 74.26	25	21	3.06	0.78	10.07
Annual Growth 17.7%	—	—	(0.9%)	17.4%	6.1%

LAWRENCE TOWNSHIP SCHOOL DISTRICT INC

EXECUTIVES

Spdt, Crystal Edwards
Bus Admin, Thomas Eldridge
Food Director, Marybeth Dilorenzo
Teacher, Rosemary Sorensen
Auditors: SAMUEL A DELP JR VINELAND

LOCATIONS

HQ: LAWRENCE TOWNSHIP SCHOOL DISTRICT INC
2565 PRINCETON PIKE, LAWRENCEVILLE, NJ
086483631
Phone: 609 671-5500
Web: WWW.LTPS.ORG

HISTORICAL FINANCIALS
Company Type: Private

Income Statement			FYE: June 30
	REVENUE ($ mil.)	NET INCOME ($ mil.)	NET PROFIT MARGIN	EMPLOYEES
---	---	---	---	---
06/17	10,232	53	0.5%	475
06/16	10	0	0.4%	
Annual Growth	101401.6%	147352.8%	—	

2017 Year-End Financials
Debt ratio: —
Return on equity: 0.50%
Cash ($ mil.): 2,410
Current ratio: —
Long-term debt ($ mil.): —
Dividends
Yield: —
Payout: —
Market value ($ mil.): —

Lear Corp.

Lear doesn't take a back seat to anyone when it comes to manufacturing automotive seats. The company's big business is manufacturing seating and related components for automobiles where it is a global leader. The company's E-Systems segment produces automotive electronics and manufactures wire harnesses junction boxes terminals and connectors and body control modules. It operates from some 260 facilities in about 40 countries. Its largest customers include BMW Ford and General Motors Fiat Chrysler and Daimler. Lear traces its history back to 1917 when it was founded in Detroit as American Metal Products.

Operations

Lear has around 260 facilities comprising more than 85 manufacturing facilities 120 dedicated component manufacturing locations six sequencing and distribution sites 35+ administrative/technical support facilities and eight advanced technology centers.

Lear's operations are split between Seating (77% of sales) and E-Systems (23%). Seating makes complete seat systems and major seat components including seat covers and surface materials such as leather and fabric seat structures and mechanisms seat foam and headrests. E-Systems designs and produces electric control infrastructure including power control units terminals and connectors and body electronics for traditional vehicle architectures as well as high-power and hybrid electric systems.

Products and brands include ProTec head restraints; leather (Aventino brand) and fabrics; interior materials like Lear's SoyFoam Seating; adjusters; and mechanisms. Lear produces a modular design seating system so they can be used over multiple segments thus minimizing investment costs. The company's seating systems are supported by its Lear-made electronics that power the adjusters and mechanisms but also other features like power heating and ventilation.

Geographic Reach

Lear operates from some 260 facilities in some 40 countries. Geographically well-diversified the Lear's home market of the US generates about 20% of its total sales each year while Mexico Germany and China contribute 16% 11% and 12% respectively.

Sales and Marketing

Lear serves the worldwide automotive and light truck market. General Motors and Ford account for 20% of Lear's total revenues each while BMW also accounts for 10%.

Financial Performance

Increasing global auto sales particularly in the advantageous crossover and sport utility vehicle segment has helped Lear enjoy unprecedented growth over the years. Revenue hit a record-setting $20.5 billion in 2017 up 11% on 2016. New business in the Seating segment primarily in North America Europe and Asia contributed $1.2 billion to sales while revenue from the acquired Antolin Seating business added $350 million. In E-Systems sales grew 9% as new business and higher volumes on key Lear platforms added $210 million and $45 million respectively; Lear also obtained control over an affiliate adding $116 million to sales.

Net income increased 35% to $1.3 billion thanks to new business and the Antolin acquisition.

Cash from operations has increased strongly over the last five years. In 2017 cash inflow grew 10% to $1.8 billion due to higher net income and higher working capital used to support sales growth.

Strategy

Lear stays ahead of the game with its E-Systems segment by keeping an eye on the future of the automotive industry. The company cranks up the amperage on its competitors by manufacturing electrical distribution systems not just for traditional powertrain vehicles but for hybrid and electric vehicles as well.

The increasing electrification and electrical sophistication of autos plays into Lear's hands. Industry research indicates that electronic components account for about 35% of a car's total value. The company has exited non-core product lines such as switches and tire pressure monitoring systems opting instead to focus on an automobile's electrical distribution system with wired as well as wireless systems. New cars increasingly incorporate internal and external mobile connectivity systems; indeed cars themselves are more and more becoming directly connected to communications networks. To tap that market in 2018 Lear acquired an Israeli firm specializing in GPS for cars.

Mergers and Acquisitions

One way Lear has achieved milestone revenue growth recently is through acquisitions.

In early 2018 Lear acquired Israel-based EXO Technologies a developer of GPS technology providing high-accuracy positioning systems for autonomous and connected vehicles. Its operations are in San Mateo California and Tel Aviv Israel.

In 2017 it purchased Grupo Antolin's automotive seating business. The business has operations in five countries in Europe and North Africa and makes just-in-time seat assembly seat structures and mechanisms and seat covers. It also has partnerships with the largest European automakers including Daimler Peugeot Citroen Renault Nissan and Volkswagen.

EXECUTIVES

President Ceo And Director, Raymond E. (Ray) Scott, age 52, $855,098 total compensation
Svp; President Asia/pacific Operations, Jay K. Kunkel, age 58

Evp Business Development And General Counsel, Terrence B. (Terry) Larkin, age 63, $855,098 total compensation

Svp And Cfo, Jeffrey H. Vanneste, age 58, $787,437 total compensation

Svp; President E-systems, Frank C. Orsini, age 45, $736,375 total compensation

Vice President Korea, Dean M Ackerman

Multi Cultural Vice President, Jolito Bustamante

Chairman, Henry D. G. Wallace, age 72

Auditors: Ernst & Young LLP

LOCATIONS

HQ: Lear Corp.
21557 Telegraph Road, Southfield, MI 48033
Phone: 248 447-1500   **Fax:** 248 447-5250
Web: www.lear.com

2017 Sales

	$ mil.	% of total
US	3,955	19
Mexico	3,170	16
China	2,519	12
Germany	2,139	11
Other countries	8,682	42
Total	**20,467**	**100**

2017 Sales

	% of total
North America	38
Europe and Africa	40
Asia	19
South America	3
Total	**100**

PRODUCTS/OPERATIONS

2017 Sales

	$ mil.	% of total
Seating	115,873	78
E-Systems	4,597	22
Total	**20,467**	**100**

2017 Sales by Customer

	% of total
GM	18
Ford	18
BMW	8
Others	56
Total	**100**

Selected Products

Seating
   Adjusters
   Automotive seats
   Fabrics
   Head restraints
   Mechanisms
   Seat foam
   Structure systems
   Trim covers
Electrical power management
   Electrical distribution and power management systems
   Fuse boxes
   Junction boxes
   Terminals and connectors
   Wire harness assemblies
   High-power electrical systems
   Hybrid electrical systems
   Specialty electronics
   Audio sound systems
   In-vehicle television tuner module
   LED electronics (interior/exterior)
   Lighting control module
   Media console
   Radio amplifiers
   Wireless systems
   Keyless entry systems
   Passive entry systems
   Tire pressure monitoring systems

COMPETITORS

DENSO	Robert Bosch
Delphi Automotive Systems	Stoneridge
	Sumitomo
Faurecia	TS TECH CO
LEONI	Toyota Boshoku
Magna International	Valeo
Methode Electronics	Visteon
Mitsubishi Electric	Yazaki

HISTORICAL FINANCIALS

Company Type: Public

Income Statement

FYE: December 31

	REVENUE ($ mil.)	NET INCOME ($ mil.)	NET PROFIT MARGIN	EMPLOYEES
12/18	21,148	1,149	5.4%	169,000
12/17	20,467	1,313	6.4%	165,000
12/16	18,557	975	5.3%	148,400
12/15	18,211	745	4.1%	136,200
12/14	17,727	672	3.8%	125,200
Annual Growth	**4.5%**	**14.4%**	**—**	**7.8%**

2018 Year-End Financials

Debt ratio: 16.93%
Return on equity: 27.54%
Cash ($ mil.): 1,493
Current ratio: 1.40
Long-term debt ($ mil.): 1,941

No. of shares (mil.): 62
Dividends
   Yield: 2.2%
   Payout: 14.3%
Market value ($ mil.): 7,733

	STOCK PRICE ($) FY Close	P/E High/Low		PER SHARE ($) Earnings	Dividends	Book Value
12/18	122.86	12	7	17.22	2.80	66.74
12/17	176.66	10	7	18.59	2.00	62.06
12/16	132.37	10	7	13.33	1.20	44.03
12/15	122.83	13	10	9.59	1.00	39.31
12/14	98.08	12	9	8.23	0.80	37.92
Annual Growth	**5.8%**	**—**	**—**	**20.3%**	**36.8%**	**15.2%**

LegacyTexas Financial Group Inc

With its eye on the Lone Star State LegacyTexas Financial (formerly ViewPoint Financial) provides retail and commercial banking through its LegacyTexas Bank subsidiary which operates about 50 branches located mostly in the Dallas/Fort Worth area. LegacyTexas offers standard deposit products such as checking and savings accounts and CDs and uses deposit funds to originate primarily real estate loans: Commercial Real Estate loans account for nearly 50% of its lending portfolio while consumer real estate loans make up another nearly 20%. Non-real estate commercial loans make up almost 30% of its loan portfolio.

Operations

Outside of banking services the LegacyTexas offers brokerage services to buy and sell investments and insurance products through a third-party brokerage arrangement.

About 82% of the company's total revenue came from loan interest (including fees) in 2014 and another 6% came from interest on its taxable and non-taxable securities. Most of LegacyTexas' remaining revenue came from service charges and fees on deposit accounts.

Geographic Reach

The Plano-based company boasts 51 Texas branches with 48 of them located in the Dallas-Fort Worth Metroplex. Its two First National Bank of Jacksboro branches are in Jack in Wise counties in Texas.

Sales and Marketing

LegacyTexas' serves a diverse market of management professional and sales personnel office employees manufacturing and transportation workers service industry workers government employees and self-employed individuals. It spent $1.54 million on advertising in 2014 compared to $2.69 million and $1.75 million in 2013 and 2012 respectively.

Financial Performance

The company has struggled to consistently grow its revenues and profits in recent years despite growing loan business mostly stemming from lost revenues from the sale of its mortgage-banking subsidiary in 2012.

LegacyTexas' revenue rebounded by 7% to $31.3 million in 2014 primarily thanks to double-digit growth in its loan interest income driven by higher commercial loan volume.

Despite higher revenue in 2014 the company's net income dipped by 1% to $31.3 million mostly due to higher loan loss provisions as commercial loan production picked up. LegacyTexas' operating cash levels fell by 21% to $52 million mostly from unfavorable changes in working capital related to its assets and liabilities.

Strategy

The company formerly known as ViewPoint Financial significantly boosted its loan and deposit business and the size of its branch network through its early 2015 acquisition LegacyTexas Group. The deal made its branch network swell to 48 offices from just 31 before while adding some $1.63 billion in deposits and $1.4 billion in new loan business.The new LegacyTexas Group planned in 2015 to organically grow its loan portfolio focusing especially on making commercial real estate commercial and industrial and energy loans tied to high-quality assets. To cheaply raise funding for loans the bank plans to promote its non-interest-bearing demand deposit accounts especially in the commercial sector and using its treasury management services to provide a "catalyst for deposit growth."

Mergers and Acquisitions

In January 2015 the former ViewPoint Financial acquired LegacyTexas Group in a $300 million deal to create one of the largest independent banks in Texas with assets of nearly $6 billion. The parent company then changed its name to LegacyTexas Financial and the bank changed its name to LegacyTexas Bank.

Company Background

LegacyTexas Financial converted from a mutual holding company to a stock holding company in 2010. It sold its mortgage subsidiary VPM which operated a dozen loan production offices in Texas and Oklahoma in late 2012.

EXECUTIVES

Evp Chief Lending Officer, Thomas S. Swiley, age 68, $277,300 total compensation

Evp Coo Chief Risk Officer And General Counsel, Scott A. Almy, age 51, $277,300 total compensation

President Ceo And Director, Kevin J. Hanigan, age 61, $549,450 total compensation

Evp Community Banking, Charles D. Eikenberg, age 63, $277,300 total compensation

Evp And Cfo, J. Mays Davenport, age 50

Senior Vice President Credit Officer, Sam Duff

Vice President Banking Center Manager, Monisa Barbosa

Vice President Business Development, Ginger Johnson
Vice President Warehouse Lending, Michelle Marrapodi
Chairman, Anthony J. LeVecchio, age 71
Vice Chairman, George Fisk
Auditors: Ernst & Young LLP

LOCATIONS

HQ: LegacyTexas Financial Group Inc
5851 Legacy Circle, Plano, TX 75024
Phone: 972 578-5000
Web: www.legacytexasfinancialgroup.com

PRODUCTS/OPERATIONS

2014 Sales

	% of total
Interest and dividend income	88
Non interest income	12
Total	**100**

COMPETITORS

Amegy	PlainsCapital
BBVA Compass Bancshares	SP Bancorp
	Texas Capital
Bank of America	Bancshares
Cullen/Frost Bankers	Wells Fargo
North Dallas Bank	

HISTORICAL FINANCIALS

Company Type: Public

Income Statement
FYE: December 31

	ASSETS ($ mil.)	NET INCOME ($ mil.)	INCOME AS % OF ASSETS	EMPLOYEES
12/17	9,086	89	1.0%	869
12/16	8,362	97	1.2%	896
12/15	7,691	70	0.9%	856
12/14	4,164	31	0.8%	530
12/13	3,525	31	0.9%	576
Annual Growth	**26.7%**	**29.6%**	**—**	**10.8%**

2017 Year-End Financials

Debt ratio: 1.48%
Return on equity: 9.70%
Cash ($ mil.): 293
Current ratio: —
Long-term debt ($ mil.): —

No. of shares (mil.): 48
Dividends
Yield: 0.0%
Payout: 32.2%
Market value ($ mil.): 2,031

	STOCK PRICE ($) FY Close	P/E High/Low	PER SHARE ($) Earnings	Dividends	Book Value
12/17	42.21	23 18	1.89	0.61	19.95
12/16	43.06	21 8	2.09	0.58	18.49
12/15	25.02	21 13	1.53	0.54	16.88
12/14	23.85	36 26	0.81	0.48	14.20
12/13	27.45	33 22	0.83	0.42	13.63
Annual Growth	**11.4%**	**— —**	**22.8%**	**9.8%**	**10.0%**

Leidos Holdings Inc

Leidos Holdings provides cybersecurity information technology and analytics services to government agencies and companies in the defense intelligence homeland security civil and health markets. The company's areas of expertise include operations and logistics; sensors; software development; and systems engineering. It also operates one of the country's largest health system integra-

tors. Most of the company's revenue comes from the US government. In 2016 Leidos merged with Lockheed Martin's Information Systems & Global Solutions segment to expand the scale and scope of its IT and intelligence services.

Change in Company Type

The combination with Lockheed Martin's Information Systems & Global Solutions unit created a company with a $10 billion portfolio of products and services. Leidos said the combined company serves more diverse markets with greater scale. The transaction included a special cash payment of approximately $1.8 billion to Lockheed Martin.

Operations

Leidos Holdings operates through three segments: Defense Solutions Civil and Health.

Defense Solutions which accounts for about 50% of total sales offers technology development and integration capabilities in surveillance and reconnaissance integrated systems and global services for the US intelligence community the military and other government and commercial customers.

The Civil segment which accounts for about a third of revenue provides aviation services security products enterprise IT services federal environment and infrastructure management and logistics services.

The Health segment about 20% of revenue provides complex systems integration managed health services enterprise IT services and life sciences services and support.

Geographic Reach

Leidos has some 350 offices in about 40 states across the US as well as in more than a dozen international locations where it works with US customers.

Sales and Marketing

The US government accounts for about 85% of Leidos Holdings' revenue with the US Department of Defense accounting for Other major federal customers are the Navy Air Force the Defense Advanced Research Projects Agency the Department of Homeland Security and NASA. International customers account for about 10% of revenue.

Financial Performance

The acquisition of Lockheed Martin's Information Systems and Global Solutions boosted Leidos Holdings revenue 45% to $10.2 billion in 2017 from 2016. The defense business reported higher airborne systems revenue while the health segment had growth in federal health services.

The US Tax Cuts and Jobs Act reduced Leidos' tax bill in 2017 helping the company to a $366 million profit compared to a $244 profit the year before.

Cash generated by operations increased $77 million to $526 million in 2017 from 2016 because of favorable timing of working capital changes somewhat offset by higher integration and restructuring costs and higher payments for interest and taxes.

Strategy

The acquisition of Lockheed's Information Systems and Global Solutions (IS&GS) group in 2016 provided Leidos Holdings with the resources and capabilities that enable it to go after business it would not have qualified before. In one example IS&GS brought biometrics capabilities that improve its competitive position. Leidos has worked on bidding for contracts that total more than half a billion dollars as a result of the acquisition.

Leidos is putting its capabilities on the line with the multi-company project to modernize health records for the US Department of Defense. Working with Cerner Accenture and Henry Schein Leidos is putting together a modern EHR system that helps health systems run more efficiently and provide better care while protecting the privacy of patients.

In 2016 Leidos sold its heavy construction business to Haskell an engineering procurement and construction firm. Leidos sold the unit to focus more on market opportunities in the integration of physical and digital worlds.

Mergers and Acquisitions

The 2016 acquisition of Lockheed Martin's Information Systems and Global Solutions business for about $4.6 billion added multiple capabilities to the Leidos portfolio. The increased resources enable Leidos to go after projects with bigger scope than it had in the past.

EXECUTIVES

Chairman And Ceo, Roger A. Krone, age 62, $988,462 total compensation
Evp And Cfo, James C. (Jim) Reagan, age 59, $561,538 total compensation
Evp And Chief Human Resources Officer, Ann M. Addison, age 56
President Technology Group And Cto, John J. Fratamico, age 60
Evp And Chief Of Business Development And Strategy, Gerard A. (Gerry) Fasano, age 52
President Health Group, Jonathan W. Scholl, age 56
Evp And General Counsel, Vincent A. (Vince) Maffeo, age 67, $575,000 total compensation
President Civil Group, Angela L. Heise, age 43
President Defense And Intelligence Group, Timothy J. Reardon, age 53, $162,240 total compensation
President Advanced Solutions Group, Michael L. Chagnon
Vp Strategic Accounts And Government Relations, Rob Thomas
Vice President, John Russell
Vice President, Jack Gumbert
Vice President, Steve Ventsam
Vice President Business Development, Karen Walton
Senior Vice President Corporate Controller And Chief Accounting Officer, Ken Sharp
Vice President Senior Proposal Manager, Chris Overson
Assistant Vice President Senior Program Manager Fo, Richard Deason
Vice President Security Solutions, Jeffrey Murter
Vice President For Cybersecurity, Robert Pate
Vice President Production, Paul Dickinson
Vice President Information Technology, Chris Russeau
Vice President Lso Ssei Pm, Debbie Kerr
Vice President Chief Engineer, Derek Lewis
Vice President And Director Human Resources Shared Services, Gayle Connatser
Senior Vice President Enterprise Shared Service Director, Chris Buffoni
Vice President Government Compliance, Matthew Popham
Board Member, David Fubini
Board Member, Gary May
Board Member, Noel Williams
Board Member, Robert Shapard
Auditors: Deloitte & Touche LLP

LOCATIONS

HQ: Leidos Holdings Inc
11951 Freedom Drive, Reston, VA 20190
Phone: 571 526-6000
Web: www.leidos.com

PRODUCTS/OPERATIONS

2016 Sales

	$ mil.	% of total
National Security solutions	3,610	51
Information Systems & Global Solutions	1,971	28
Health and engineering	1,463	21
Adjustments (-1) -		
Total	**7,043**	**100**

Selected Capabilites:

Civil:
Aviation
Cyber Solutions
Energy
Environment & Infrastructure
Exploration & Mission Support
Financial Solutions
Homeland & Transportation Security
Defense & Intelligence:
Airborne
Command & Control
Data Analytics
Enterprise IT
Federal Cybersecurity
Intelligence Services
Operations & Logistics
Sensors
Training
Health:
Federal Health IT
Hospitals & Health Systems
Life Sciences
Advanced Solutions:
Airborne Systems Integration
Maritime

COMPETITORS

Accenture
American Science and Engineering
BAE Systems Technology Solutions
Battelle Memorial
Boeing
Booz Allen
CACI International
CH2M HILL
Computer Sciences Corp.
Engility
Exelis
General Dynamics
HP Enterprise Services
Honeywell Technology Solutions
IBM Global Services
KBR
KEYW
Kratos Defense & Security Solutions
L3 Technologies
ManTech
OSI Systems
Raytheon Intelligence Information and Services
Serco
Unisys

HISTORICAL FINANCIALS

Company Type: Public

Income Statement

FYE: December 29

	REVENUE ($ mil.)	NET INCOME ($ mil.)	NET PROFIT MARGIN	EMPLOYEES
12/17	10,170	366	3.6%	31,000
12/16*	7,043	244	3.5%	32,000
01/16	4,712	242	5.1%	18,000
01/15	5,063	(323)	—	19,000
01/14	5,772	164	2.8%	22,000
Annual Growth	15.2%	22.2%	—	9.0%

*Fiscal year change

2017 Year-End Financials

Debt ratio: 34.61%
Return on equity: 11.28%
Cash ($ mil.): 390
Current ratio: 1.21
Long-term debt ($ mil.): 3,056

No. of shares (mil.): 151
Dividends
Yield: 1.9%
Payout: 68.8%
Market value ($ mil.): 9,750

	STOCK PRICE ($) FY Close	P/E High/Low		PER SHARE ($) Earnings	Dividends	Book Value
12/17	64.57	27	20	2.38	1.28	22.32
12/16*	51.14	24	16	2.35	14.92	20.90
01/16	56.26	18	11	3.27	1.28	14.83
01/15	41.40	—	—	(4.36)	1.28	13.49
01/14	45.34	25	6	1.94	0.64	19.94
Annual Growth	9.2%	—	—	5.2%	18.9%	2.9%

*Fiscal year change

LELAND STANFORD JUNIOR UNIVERSITY

Prospectors panning for gold in higher education can strike it rich at The Leland Stanford Junior University. The school known as Stanford University is one of the premier educational institutions in the US boasting respected programs in business engineering law and medicine among others. Stanford serves more than 16300 students (taught by 2180 faculty members) and a student-teacher ratio of about 4:1. A private institution Stanford is supported through an endowment of some $22.4 billion one of the largest in the US. The university was established in 1885 by Leland Stanford Sr. who made his fortune selling provisions to California gold miners; it was named after his son Leland Stanford Jr.

Operations

Stanford University is widely recognized as one of the top US research universities and sports a host of laboratories and research centers including the Stanford Institute for Economic Policy Research and the Stanford Linear Accelerator Center. Its faculty members include around 20 Nobel Prize winners a handful of Pulitzer Prize winners and more than 20 MacArthur fellows.

The university also offers 35 varsity sports and 20 club sports; it boasts more than 110 NCAA team championships.

Geographic Reach

Stanford is located in the heart of California's Silicon Valley known worldwide as an epicenter for technology and research ventures. Google (headquartered in Silicon Valley) got its start at Stanford when Sergey Brin and Larry Page developed the page-rank algorithm while they were still computer science graduate students.

The university is located on 8180 contiguous acres and has almost 700 major buildings.

Financial Performance

Stanford University reported revenues of some $9.8 billion in fiscal 2016 up from $9.1 billion in 2015 due to an increase in student income higher patient service revenues (from the Stanford Hospitals and Clinics organization) sponsored research funding and increased returns on its investment portfolio assets.

Net income fell to $490 million in 2016 (versus $700 million in 2015) as expenses including salaries and benefits rose especially within the medical school. Other expenditures that year such as facilities and infrastructure maintenance and higher depreciation also impacted net income.

The university has received sizable donations from notable alumni such as Jerry Yang (cofounder of Yahoo!) Charles Schwab Texas billionaire Robert Bass and William Hewlett (of Hewlett-Packard who has since died).

Strategy

To further widen its student resources Stanford has recently completed renovation and construction efforts on some 40 campus buildings and added a number of new faculty and fellowship positions. The university is also exploring options to establish a satellite-applied science and engineering campus in another US city. In addition Stanford is examining whether it might begin to offer courses through an online platform.

In 2017 Stanford launched a new major in aeronautics and astronautics (allowing students to work with unmanned aerial vehicles satellites autonomous systems and other flight technologies).

HISTORY

In 1885 Leland Stanford Sr. and his wife Jane established Leland Stanford Junior University in memory of their son Leland Jr. who had died of typhoid at age 15. Stanford made his fortune selling provisions to California gold miners and as a major investor in the Central Pacific Railroad one of the two companies that built the first transcontinental railway. It was Stanford who connected the tracks laid eastward by Central Pacific and westward by Union Pacific with a gold railway spike in 1869. He also served as California's governor and as a US senator.

The Stanfords donated more than 8000 acres of land from their own estate to establish an unconventional university one that was coeducational and nondenominational with a focus on preparing students for a profession. Stanford opened its doors in 1891 to a freshman class of 559 students. It awarded its first degrees four years later and among the graduates was future US president Herbert Hoover.

Leland Stanford Sr. died in 1893 and in 1903 Jane Stanford turned the university over to the board of trustees. After weathering significant damage in 1906 from the Great San Francisco Earthquake the university established a law school in 1908 and its medical school five years later.

During WWI the university mobilized half of its students into the Students' Army Training Corps. The School of Education was established in 1917 followed by the School of Engineering and Graduate School of Business eight years later. In 1933 a rule limiting the number of women admitted to Stanford was abolished.

Wallace Sterling who became president of the university after WWII initiated the transformation of Stanford into a world-class institution with a reputation for teaching and research. Under Sterling the university initiated development on the Stanford Research Park.

In 1958 Stanford opened its first overseas campus (near Stuttgart Germany) and the Stanford Medical Center was completed the following year. The university created a computer science department in 1965 and two years later opened the Stanford Linear Accelerator Center dedicated to physics research.

Donald Kennedy became president in 1980. The next year students voted to abandon the university's official mascot the "Indians" in response to concerns raised by Native American students. The nickname "Cardinal" was adopted in its place. The term refers to the school's color cardinal red.

Also during Kennedy's tenure it was revealed that Stanford had overcharged the Office of Naval Research for indirect costs associated with research. The scandal led to Kennedy's resignation in 1992 and in 1994 the Office of Naval Research and the university settled a related lawsuit for $1.2 million and a stipulation that Stanford had not committed any wrongdoing. Gerhard Casper succeeded Kennedy as president.

In 1997 Stanford and the University of California at San Francisco combined their teaching hospitals in a public/private merger. Two years later after the controversial experiment had harmed both hospitals' financial pictures the merger was terminated and the two hospitals agreed to go their separate ways.

In 1999 Casper announced his intention to resign as president. The school tapped provost John Hennessy as his replacement. Soon after his appointment in 2000 Hennessey launched a campaign to raise $1 billion. Former Stanford professor and Netscape co-founder Jim Clark donated $150 million later that year to support Stanford's biomedical engineering and sciences program. The school also launched a new company SKOLAR which developed an online search engine for the medical industry.

EXECUTIVES

President, John L. Hennessy
Provost, John W. Etchemendy
Dean School Of Humanities And Science, Richard P. Saller
Vp Business Affairs And Cfo, Randall S. (Randy) Livingston
Dean School Of Earth Energy And Environmental Sciences, Pamela Matson
Associate Vp It Services, Bill Clebsch
President And Ceo Stanford Health Care, Amir Dan Rubin
Vice Provost And Dean Of Research, Ann Margaret Arvin
Dean Graduate School Of Business, Garth Saloner
Dean Graduate School Of Education, Deborah Stipek
Dean School Of Engineering, Persis S. Drell
Dean Law School, M. Elizabeth Magill
Dean School Of Medicine, Lloyd Minor
President And Ceo Stanford Children's Health, Christopher Dawes
Assistant Vice President And Chief Information Security Officer, Michael Duff
Associate Vice President Benefits, Les Schlaegel
Vice President Human Resources, David Jones
Vice President, Britt Hedman
Associate Vice President, Anne Hannigan
Vice President Information Technology, Stephen Wong
M.s. Candidate In Computer Science Audit Intern Vice President Of Board Games, Hana Lee
Associate Vice President Of Sponsored Research, Russell Brewer
Medical Director Performance Improvement, Terry Platchek
Medical Director, Catherine Forest
Medical Director, Kirsti Weng
Associate Medical Director, Susan Galel
David Starr Jordan Professor And Chair Department Of Psychology, Ian Gotlib
Vice President For Academic Life, Jared Crum
Medical Director Emergency Medicine, Sam Shen
Vice President Of External Relations, Tina Jiang
External Relations Vice President, Udai Baisiwala
Vice President Of Account Management, Meg Avery
Medical Director Vaden Health Center, Robyn Tepper
Secretary Of The Board Of Trustees, Jeffrey Wachtel
Auditors: PRICEWATERHOUSECOOPERS LLP SA

LOCATIONS

HQ: LELAND STANFORD JUNIOR UNIVERSITY
450 SERRA MALL, STANFORD, CA 943052004
Phone: 650 723-2300
Web: WWW.STANFORD.EDU

PRODUCTS/OPERATIONS

2014 Sales

	% of total
Healthcare services	50
Sponsored research support	16
Investment income	15
Student income	7
Special program fee and other income	7
Gifts	3
Net assets released from restrictions	2
Total	**100**

Selected Schools

Undergraduate
School of Earth Sciences
School of Engineering
School of Humanities and Sciences
Graduate
School of Business
School of Earth Sciences
School of Education
School of Engineering
School of Humanities and Sciences
School of Law
School of Medicine

Selected Interdisciplinary Research Centers

Alliance for Innovative Manufacturing at Stanford
Center for Computer Research in Music and Acoustics
Center for Integrated Facility Engineering
Center for Integrated Systems

Selected Laboratories Centers and Institutes

Center for Research on Information Storage Materials
Center for the Study of Language and Information
Edward L. Ginzton Laboratory
Institute for International Studies
Institute for Research on Women and Gender
John and Terry Levin Center for Public Service and Public Interest Law
Stanford Center for Buddhist Studies
Stanford Humanities Center
Stanford Institute for Economic Policy Research
W.W. Hansen Experimental Physics Laboratory

Selected Medical Research Facilities

Center for Biomedical Ethics
Center for Research in Disease Prevention
Human Genome Center
Richard M. Lucas Center for Magnetic Resonance Spectroscopy & Imaging
Sleep Disorders Center
Other Selected Research Facilities
Hoover Institution on War Revolution and Peace
Hopkins Marine Station
Martin Luther King Jr. Papers Project
Stanford Linear Accelerator Center

HISTORICAL FINANCIALS

Company Type: Private

Income Statement

FYE: August 31

	REVENUE ($ mil.)	NET INCOME ($ mil.)	NET PROFIT MARGIN	EMPLOYEES
08/17	5,604	2,972	53.0%	15,000
08/06	4,511	3,007	66.7%	—
08/05	4,162	2,896	69.6%	—
08/04	3,743	1,739	46.5%	—
Annual Growth	**3.2%**	**4.2%**	**—**	**—**

2017 Year-End Financials

Debt ratio: ——
Return on equity: 53.00%
Cash ($ mil.): 260
Current ratio: ——
Long-term debt ($ mil.): —

Dividends
Yield: —
Payout: —
Market value ($ mil.): —

LendingClub Corp

LOCATIONS

HQ: LendingClub Corp
71 Stevenson Street, Suite 1000, San Francisco, CA 94105
Phone: 415 632-5600
Web: www.lendingclub.com

HISTORICAL FINANCIALS

Company Type: Public

Income Statement

FYE: December 31

	ASSETS ($ mil.)	NET INCOME ($ mil.)	INCOME AS % OF ASSETS	EMPLOYEES
12/17	4,640	(153)	—	1,837
12/16	5,562	(145)	—	1,530
12/15	5,793	(5)	—	1,382
12/14	3,890	(32)	—	843
12/13	1,943	7	0.4%	742
Annual Growth	**24.3%**	**—**		**25.4%**

2017 Year-End Financials

Debt ratio: 70.39%
Return on equity: (-16.21%)
Cash ($ mil.): 401
Current ratio: —
Long-term debt ($ mil.): —

No. of shares (mil.): 417
Dividends
Yield: —
Payout: —
Market value ($ mil.): 1,724

	STOCK PRICE ($) FY Close	P/E High/Low	PER SHARE ($) Earnings	Dividends	Book Value
12/17	4.13	— —	(0.38)	0.00	2.21
12/16	5.25	— —	(0.38)	0.00	2.45
12/15	11.05	— —	(0.01)	0.00	2.74
12/14	25.30	— —	(0.44)	0.00	2.62
Annual Growth	**(36.4%)**	**— —**	**—**	**—**	**(4.2%)**

Lennar Corp

Lennar is one of the largest homebuilding land-owning loan-making leviathans in the US along with D.R. Horton and Pulte Homes. The company builds single- and multi-family attached and detached homes in 20 states under brand names including Lennar Village Builders and CalAtlantic. Lennar targets first-time move-up and active adult buyers and markets its homes as "everything included." The company also provides financial services including mortgage financing title and closing services. Lennar's homes are delivered at an average price of $380000.The company delivered nearly 29500 new homes in 2017. Lennar purchased Florida homebuilder WCI Communities in 2017 and acquired rival CalAtlantic for $6 billion in 2018.

HISTORY

Lennar is the creation of Leonard Miller and Arnold Rosen and the name of the company is a combination of their given names. Rosen a Miami homebuilder formed F&R Builders in 1954. A year later Miller graduated from Harvard with no firm career plans. Having worked summers in Florida Miller decided it would be a good place to make his fortune and the 23-year-old began selling real estate there.

With $10000 earned from commissions Miller bought 42 lots and in 1956 entered a joint venture with Rosen to build homes on the lots. They worked well together and Miller soon joined F&R. The operation grew emphasizing marketing and concentrating on low- and medium-priced single-family homes for first-time buyers and retirees.

After expanding into commercial real estate in the late 1960s the duo folded F&R into a new company — Lennar Corporation — in 1971 and went public. During the 1970s and 1980s the company hawked Jacuzzi tubs and designer homes (such as the Calvin and the Liz) and promised customers "$10000 worth of extras" free at Midnight Madness shopping mall sales. Lennar also began expanding acquiring land and builders in the Phoenix area in 1973. Rosen retired in 1977.

Spurred by a recession Lennar began offering mortgage services nationwide in 1981 keeping the potentially lucrative servicing for itself and selling its mortgages to Fannie Mae Ginnie Mae and Freddie Mac among others. In 1984 it dissolved its construction operations and began subbing out its work (a practice that it continues today). Lennar was relatively unscathed by the recession of the late 1980s in part because Miller had foreseen a slump and had cut corporate debt and overhead. When other builders were overextending themselves by buying land in good times Miller had used profit to pay down debt so he would not have the resources to buy land cheap when bad times arrived.

During the 1990s Lennar targeted other Sun Belt markets and began buying portfolios of distressed property in partnership with heavy hitters like Morgan Stanley. Although Miller had looked at Texas as a development site since 1987 it was not until 1991 that Lennar entered the state beginning in Dallas.

The company bought up the secured debt of Bramalea Homes in Southern California in 1995 and entered Northern California with its acquisition of Renaissance Homes. Lennar's acquisition of Village Homes and Exxon's Friendswood Development in 1996 made it Houston's top home builder and Lennar surpassed $1 billion in sales.

In 1997 Stuart Miller became president and CEO (Leonard his father remained chairman). That year Lennar also spun off its commercial real estate operations as LNR Property a separately traded public company and acquired Pacific Greystone a Los Angeles builder.

The following year the company strengthened its position in the western US acquiring three California homebuilders: Winncrest Homes (Sacramento) ColRich Communities (San Diego) and Polygon Communities (Southern California and Sacramento). Lennar also purchased North American Title an escrow and title services company operating in Arizona California and Colorado.

In 2000 Lennar bought fellow builder U.S. Home for about $1.1 billion in a deal that expanded its operations into 13 states. The company acquired the North and South Carolina operations of The Fortress Group in late 2001 giving Lennar the Don Galloway Homes and Sunstar Homes brands. Through its FG Acquisition Corporation subsidiary Lennar acquired 93% of The Fortress Group in 2002; it also added Maryland-based Patriot Homes and assets of California homebuilders Pacific Century Homes and Cambridge Homes to bring its homebuilding operations to 16 states.

In July 2002 Leonard Miller died of liver cancer. Stuart Miller continues to lead the company as its president and CEO. The company acquired nine homebuilders that year which expanded its operations into markets in Chicago (Concord Homes and Summit Homes) Baltimore the Carolinas and California's Central Valley; some of the acquisitions strengthened Lennar's position in its existing markets. Lennar subsidiary North American Title Group acquired The Sentinel Title Corporation with nine branches in Maryland Virginia and Washington DC.

Lennar continued to acquire in 2003 adding Seppala Homes and Coleman Homes (with a backlog of about 300 homes and 3000 owned or controlled homesites) expanding its positions respectively in South Carolina and the Central Valley of California. The company's North American Title Group Inc. subsidiary acquired Mid America Title Company (Waukegan Illinois) which strengthened Lennar's homebuilding operations in the Chicago market.

In mid-2003 an entity jointly owned by Lennar and LNR Property Corporation (real estate investment finance and management) agreed to acquire The Newhall Land and Farming Company (master-planned communities) for about $1 billion. The deal closed in January 2004 enabling LNR to buy existing income-producing commercial assets from the venture and Lennar to option certain current homesites. Also that year Lennar's Texas operations grew with its cash purchase of San Antonio-based Connell-Barron Homes and the company expanded into Jacksonville by acquiring Classic American Homes for an undisclosed cash price. Lennar closed out the year with increased revenues and earnings of 18% and 26% respectively over the previous year and a strong backlog of about 15550 homes valued at about $5 billion.

As the real estate market continued to thrive Lennar acquired regional builders mortgage operations and title and closing businesses. During 2005 Lennar entered the Boston New York City and Reno markets; it also expanded its Jacksonville operations by acquiring Admiral Homes. The condo and apartment buildings in New York and Boston were valued at more than $2 billion.

Along with the rest of the homebuilding industry Lennar started to see trouble in 2006 as interest rates rose and years of overbuilding began taking their toll. Fallout from the subprime mortgage crisis and global credit crunch further unraveled the market. Lennar's average price per home fell by $40000 and the number of homes delivered fell by approximately 40000 (in 2009 as compared with fiscal 2005).

In early 2007 Lennar and its spun-off investment unit LNR Properties reduced their stakes in LandSource a joint venture that invests in raw land (among the riskiest of real estate investments particularly vulnerable to market downturns). MW Housing Partners an investment vehicle of the California Public Employees' Retirement System bought 68% of LandSource for $900 million in cash and property; Lennar lowered its stake from 50% to 16%. The sale proved to be fortuitous for Lennar: Not only did it bring the company much-needed cash but it also reduced Lennar's exposure to the debt-laden LandSource which filed for Chapter 11 bankruptcy protection a year later. LandSource emerged from bankruptcy as the debt-free Newhall Land Development. In 2009 Lennar bought back a 15% stake in the reorganized company for $140.

Lennar survived the economic downturn by shifting its focus and tightening its belt. As one of the larger builders it weathered the downturn by exiting slower markets lowering prices and reducing staff. The company also bought fewer home sites and tightened its lending standards to reduce its exposure to loan defaults. Lennar also increased its focus on the first-time buyer and limited the number of home plans offered.

EXECUTIVES

Vice President And Treasurer, Diane J Bessette

Vp And Coo, Jonathan M. (Jon) Jaffe, age 58, $800,000 total compensation

Vp And Cfo, Bruce E. Gross, age 59, $650,000 total compensation

Ceo, Stuart A. Miller, age 60, $1,000,000 total compensation

President, Richard (Rick) Beckwitt, age 58, $800,000 total compensation

Ceo Rialto Capital Management, Jeffrey P. (Jeff) Krasnoff

Regional President Lennar Land And Homebuilding, Jeff Roos

Regional President Lennar Land And Homebuilding, Rob Hutton

President Lennar Ventures; Ceo Sunstreet Energy Group, David J. Kaiserman

President North American Title Group, Thomas J. (Tom) Fischer

President Rialto Capital Management, Jay Mantz

Secretary And General Counsel, Mark Sustana, age 57, $450,000 total compensation

President Universal American Mortgage And Eagle Home Mortgage, James T. (Jimmy) Timmons

Regional President Lennar Land And Homebuilding, Fred Rothman

President Lennar Multifamily Communities, Todd Farrell

Regional President Lennar Multifamily Communities, Ed Easley

Cio, Laura Lete

Regional President Lennar Homebuilding And Land, Greg McGuff

President Lennar International, Chris Marlin

Vice President Sales And Marketing, Carlos Gonzalez

Vice President Of Sales, Joe Catanzariti

Division President, Mark Torres

Division President Carolinas, Jeff Harris

Vice President Of Sales And Marketing, Ericka Pace

Regional Vice President Land, Matthew Wineman

Vice President Land Acquisitions And Development, Jim Bowersox

West Region Vice President Of Marketing, Janice Hinshaw

Vice President Marketing And Sales, Sheryl McKibben

Vice President Purchasing, Scott Handt

Vice President Of Sales, Lori Pennebaker

Vice President Of Finance, Lance Ellis

Division President, JJ Abraham

Vice President Of Construction, Dominick English

Vice President Of Land And Acquisitions, Greg Urech

Regional Vice President Land, Jim Bavouset

Vice President Land Acquisitions, David Stearn

Vice President Land Acquisition, John Cheney

Vice President Land Acquisition, Richard Maier

Division President, WORTH JENKINS

Vice President Operations, Charles Webb

Vice President Government Relations, Dave Williams

Vice President Of Construction, John Bishop

Vice President Quality Assurance, Norm Greuel

Vice President Of Construction, Kevin Stream

Vice President Supply Chain, Tom Harper

Vice President Corporate Development, Christian Falk

Vice President Of Sales And Marketing, Karen Morgan

Vice President Of Marketing, Stacy Sanders

Chief Sales Officer, Juan Gomez-sanchez

Division President, John Merlino

Vice President Of Sales And Marketing, Jeff Morin

Vice President Sales And Marketing, Garrett Chan

Vice President Quality Assurance, Norman Greuel

Assistant Treasurer, Gerry Rodriguez

Auditors: DELOITTE & TOUCHE LLP

LOCATIONS

HQ: Lennar Corp
700 Northwest 107th Avenue, Miami, FL 33172
Phone: 305 559-4000
Web: www.lennar.com

Selected Markets

Arizona
  Phoenix
  Tucson
California
  Bakersfield
  Fresno
  Inland Empire
  Los Angeles/Valencia
  Orange County
  Palm Springs
  Riverside County
  Sacramento
  San Diego
Colorado
  Denver
Florida
  Clermont
  Ft. Lauderdale
  Jacksonville
  Lakeland
  Miami
  Naples
  Orlando
  Sarasota
  Tampa
Illinois
  Chicago
Maryland
  Baltimore
  Maryland/DC Metro
New Jersey
  Edison Township
  Mays Landing
  Rockaway Township
North Carolina
  Charlotte
  Raleigh
South Carolina
  Charleston
  Greenville
  Myrtle Beach
Texas
  Austin
  Dallas/Fort Worth
  Houston
  San Antonio
Virginia
  Maryland/Virginia/Washington DC Metro
  Williamsburg

PRODUCTS/OPERATIONS

FY2017 Sales

	$ mil.	% of total
Homebuilding East	4,612	36
Homebuilding West	3,197	25
Homebuilding Central	2,509	21
Homebuilding Other	881	7
Lennar Financial Services	770	6
Rialto	281	2
Lennar Multifamily	394	3
Total	**12,646**	**100**

Selected Subsidiaries

360 Developers LLC
Eagle Bend Commercial LLC
Eagle Home Mortgage LLC
Heritage of Auburn Hills LLC
Lennar Associates Management LLC
Lennar Homes of California Inc.
Lennar Homes of Texas Sales and Marketing Ltd.
Lennar Ventures LLC
LH-EH Layton Lakes Estate LLC
Majestic Woods LLC
North American Title Company (MD)
Raintree Village L.L.C.
Savell Gulley Development LLC
Universal American Mortgage Company LLC
U.S. Home of Arizona Construction Co.

COMPETITORS

Beazer Homes
D.R. Horton
Hovnanian Enterprises
KB Home
M.D.C.
NVR
PulteGroup
Toll Brothers
Weyerhaeuser Real Estate

HISTORICAL FINANCIALS

Company Type: Public

Income Statement   FYE: November 30

	REVENUE ($ mil.)	NET INCOME ($ mil.)	NET PROFIT MARGIN	EMPLOYEES
11/18	20,571	1,695	8.2%	11,626
11/17	12,646	810	6.4%	9,111
11/16	10,950	911	8.3%	8,335
11/15	9,474	802	8.5%	7,749
11/14	7,779	638	8.2%	6,825
Annual Growth	**27.5%**	**27.6%**	**—**	**14.2%**

2018 Year-End Financials

Debt ratio: 29.91%
Return on equity: 15.11%
Cash ($ mil.): 1,568
Current ratio: 16.62
Long-term debt ($ mil.): 8,543
No. of shares (mil.): 324
Dividends
  Yield: 0.3%
  Payout: 3.8%
Market value ($ mil.): 13,855

	STOCK PRICE ($) FY Close	P/E High/Low		Earnings	PER SHARE ($) Dividends	Book Value
11/18	42.73	13	7	5.44	0.16	44.97
11/17	62.78	18	12	3.38	0.16	32.81
11/16	42.54	13	9	3.85	0.16	29.96
11/15	51.21	15	11	3.39	0.16	26.23
11/14	47.24	16	11	2.75	0.16	23.08
Annual Growth	**(2.5%)**	**—**		**18.6%**	**(0.0%)**	**18.1%**

LETTIE PATE EVANS FOUNDATION

EXECUTIVES

President, Charles H McTier
V Pres, P Russell Harding
Treasurer, J Lee Tribble
Secretary, Erik S Johnson
Officer, Elizabeth A Smith
Vice-Chairman, James M Sibley
Executive Director, Antone Callaway
Manager, Amy Todd
Vice President, Susan Shows
Vice President Marketing, John Cooper

LOCATIONS

HQ: LETTIE PATE EVANS FOUNDATION
191 PEACHTREE ST NE # 3540, ATLANTA, GA
303031740
Phone: 404 522-6755
Web: WWW.LPEVANS.ORG

HISTORICAL FINANCIALS

Company Type: Private

Income Statement   FYE: December 31

	ASSETS ($ mil.)	NET INCOME ($ mil.)	INCOME AS % OF ASSETS	EMPLOYEES
12/16	2,694	90	3.3%	12
12/15	44	11	25.0%	—
12/14	33	0		—
12/12	33	0	0.3%	—
Annual Growth	**198.4%**	**444.0%**	**—**	**—**

2016 Year-End Financials

Debt ratio: ——
Return on equity: 50.00%
Cash ($ mil.): 0
Current ratio: —
Long-term debt ($ mil.): —
Dividends
  Yield: —
  Payout: —
  Market value ($ mil.): ——

Levi Strauss & Co.

EXECUTIVES

Evp; President The Dockers Brand, Seth M. Ellison, age 59, $609,808 total compensation
President And Ceo, Charles V. (Chip) Bergh, age 60, $1,343,077 total compensation
Evp And Cfo, Harmit J. Singh, age 54, $746,538 total compensation
Evp And President Global E-commerce, Marc Rosen, age 49
Evp Chief Supply Chain And Chief Transformation Officer, David Love, age 55, $580,387 total compensation
Evp; President Americas, Roy Bagattini, age 54, $690,433 total compensation
Evp; President Levis Brand, James Curleigh, age 52, $523,269 total compensation
Evp; President Global Retail, Carrie Ask, $392,308 total compensation
Svp And Chief Supply Chain Officer, Liz O'Neill
Chairman, Stephen C. Neal, age 68
Auditors: PricewaterhouseCoopers LLP

LOCATIONS

HQ: Levi Strauss & Co.
1155 Battery Street, San Francisco, CA 94111
Phone: 415 501-6000
Web: www.levistrauss.com

2016 Stores

		% of total
Americas region	234	
Europe region	267	
Asia/Pacific region	196	
Total	**0**	**697**

2016 Sales

	$ mil.	% of total
Americas	2,683	59
Europe	1,091	24
Asia/Pacific region	778	17
Total	**4,552**	**100**

PRODUCTS/OPERATIONS

2016 Sales

		% of total
Levi's brand		85
Dockers brand		10
Signature by Levi Strauss & Denizen brands		5
Total	**0**	**100**

Selected Brands

Denizen
Dockers
   Dockers Alpha Khaki
   Dockers for Men
   Dockers for Women
Levi's
   Levi's 501 Original
   Levi's 505 Straight
   Levi's 511 Skinny
   Levi's 513 Slim
   Levi's 514 Slim Straight
   Levi's Curve ID
Signature by Levis Strauss & Co.
Intro
Waterless
Wellthread
Wasteless

COMPETITORS

Abercrombie & Fitch	Nautica Apparel
American Eagle Outfitters	Nine West
	OshKosh B'Gosh
Benetton	Oxford Industries
Calvin Klein	PVH
Diesel SpA	Perry Ellis International
FUBU	
Fast Retailing	Ralph Lauren
Fruit of the Loom	Sean John
Guess?	Sears
Haggar	Target Corporation
Hugo Boss	The Gap
Inditex	True Religion Apparel
J. C. Penney	Under Armour
J. Crew	VF Corporation
Jockey International	Victoria's Secret Stores
Joe's Jeans	
Kmart	Wacoal
Kohl's	Wal-Mart
Lands' End	Warnaco Group
Macy's	adidas
NIKE	

HISTORICAL FINANCIALS

Company Type: Public

Income Statement   FYE: November 26

	REVENUE ($ mil.)	NET INCOME ($ mil.)	NET PROFIT MARGIN	EMPLOYEES
11/17	4,904	281	5.7%	13,800
11/16	4,552	291	6.4%	13,200
11/15	4,494	209	4.7%	12,500
11/14	4,753	106	2.2%	15,000
11/13	4,681	229	4.9%	16,000
Annual Growth	1.2%	5.3%	—	(3.6%)

2017 Year-End Financials

Debt ratio: 32.61%
Return on equity: 44.06%
Cash ($ mil.): 633
Current ratio: 2.27
Long-term debt ($ mil.): 1,055
No. of shares (mil.): 37
Dividends
  Yield: —
  Payout: 24.8%
Market value ($ mil.): —

Liberty Expedia Holdings Inc

Auditors: KPMG LLP

LOCATIONS

HQ: Liberty Expedia Holdings Inc
  12300 Liberty Boulevard, Englewood, CO 80112
Phone: 720 875-5800
Web: www.libertyexpediaholdings.com

HISTORICAL FINANCIALS

Company Type: Public

Income Statement   FYE: December 31

	REVENUE ($ mil.)	NET INCOME ($ mil.)	NET PROFIT MARGIN	EMPLOYEES
12/17	10,286	(192)	—	22,615
12/16	1,581	2,292	145.0%	20,680
12/15	465	281	60.4%	—
12/14	455	45	9.9%	—
Annual Growth	182.8%	—	—	—

2017 Year-End Financials

Debt ratio: 14.33%
Return on equity: (-7.15%)
Cash ($ mil.): 2,961
Current ratio: 0.71
Long-term debt ($ mil.): 4,329
No. of shares (mil.): 57
Dividends
  Yield: —
  Payout: —
Market value ($ mil.): 2,539

	STOCK PRICE ($) FY Close	P/E High/Low		PER SHARE ($) Earnings	Dividends	Book Value
12/17	44.33	—	—	(3.37)	0.00	45.56
12/16	39.67	1	1	39.52	0.00	48.51
12/15	0.00	—	—	4.94	0.00	(0.00)
Annual Growth	—			—	—	—

Liberty Media Corp (DE)

Auditors: KPMG LLP

LOCATIONS

HQ: Liberty Media Corp (DE)
  12300 Liberty Boulevard, Englewood, CO 80112
Phone: 720 875-5400
Web: www.libertymedia.com

HISTORICAL FINANCIALS

Company Type: Public

Income Statement   FYE: December 31

	REVENUE ($ mil.)	NET INCOME ($ mil.)	NET PROFIT MARGIN	EMPLOYEES
12/17	7,594	1,354	17.8%	4,393
12/16	5,276	680	12.9%	3,626
12/15	4,795	64	1.3%	3,503
12/14	4,450	178	4.0%	3,690
12/13	4,002	8,780	219.4%	3,893
Annual Growth	17.4%	(37.3%)	—	3.1%

2017 Year-End Financials

Debt ratio: 33.23%
Return on equity: 9.44%
Cash ($ mil.): 1,029
Current ratio: 0.44
Long-term debt ($ mil.): 13,186
No. of shares (mil.): 617
Dividends
  Yield: —
  Payout: —
Market value ($ mil.): 21,107

	STOCK PRICE ($) FY Close	P/E High/Low		PER SHARE ($) Earnings	Dividends	Book Value
12/17	34.16	—	—	(0.00)	0.00	27.42
12/16	31.33	34	16	1.12	0.00	25.10
12/15	38.08	212	175	0.19	0.00	32.68
12/14	35.03	95	64	0.52	0.00	33.21
Annual Growth	(0.6%)	—	—	—	—	(4.7%)

Liberty Media Corp (DE)

Auditors: KPMG LLP

LOCATIONS

HQ: Liberty Media Corp (DE)
  12300 Liberty Boulevard, Englewood, CO 80112
Phone: 720 875-5400
Web: www.libertymedia.com

HISTORICAL FINANCIALS

Company Type: Public

Income Statement   FYE: December 31

	REVENUE ($ mil.)	NET INCOME ($ mil.)	NET PROFIT MARGIN	EMPLOYEES
12/17	5,425	1,124	20.7%	4,393
12/16	5,014	413	8.2%	3,626
12/15	4,552	259	5.7%	—
12/14	4,141	231	5.6%	—
Annual Growth	9.4%	69.5%	—	—

2017 Year-End Financials

Debt ratio: 26.27%
Return on equity: 10.73%
Cash ($ mil.): 615
Current ratio: 0.30
Long-term debt ($ mil.): 6,741
No. of shares (mil.): 336
Dividends
  Yield: —
  Payout: —
Market value ($ mil.): 13,330

	STOCK PRICE ($) FY Close	P/E High/Low		PER SHARE ($) Earnings	Dividends	Book Value
12/17	39.66	14	10	3.31	0.00	32.31
12/16	34.52	44	33	0.88	0.00	30.09
12/15	39.25	—	—	(0.00)	0.00	(0.00)
12/14	35.27	—	—	(0.00)	0.00	(0.00)
/0.00	—			(0.00)	0.00	(0.00)
Annual Growth	—	—	—	—	—

Lilly (Eli) & Co

Best known for its neuroscience products pharmaceutical firm Eli Lilly also makes endocrinology oncology and cardiovascular care medicines. Its top-selling drugs include Cymbalta for depression and pain Alimta for lung cancer Humalog and Humulin insulin for diabetes and Cialis for erectile dysfunction. Lilly also makes medications to treat schizophrenia and bipolar disorder (Zyprexa) osteoporosis (Evista and Forteo) heart conditions (Effient) ADHD (Strattera) gastric and lung cancer (Cyramza) and diabetes (Jardiance and Trulicity) as well as anti-infective agents and a growing line of animal health products.

HISTORY

Colonel Eli Lilly pharmacist and Union officer in the Civil War started Eli Lilly and Company in 1876 with $1300. His process of gelatin-coating pills led to sales of nearly $82000 in 1881. Later the company made gelatin capsules which it still sells. Lilly died in 1898 and his son and two grandsons ran the business until 1953.

Eli Lilly began extracting insulin from the pancreases of hogs and cattle in 1923; 6000 cattle glands or 24000 hog glands made one ounce of the substance. Other products created in the 1920s and 1930s included antiseptic Merthiolate sedative Seconal and treatments for pernicious anemia and heart disease. In 1947 the company began selling diethylstilbestrol (DES) a drug to prevent miscarriages. Eli Lilly researchers isolated the antibiotic erythromycin from a species of mold found in the Philippines in 1952. Lilly was also the major supplier of Salk polio vaccine.

The company enjoyed a 70% share of the DES market by 1971 when researchers noticed that a rare form of cervical cancer afflicted many of the daughters of women who had taken the drug. The FDA restricted the drug's use and Lilly found itself on the receiving (and frequently losing) end of a number of trailblazing product-liability suits that stretched into the 1990s.

The firm diversified in the 1970s buying Elizabeth Arden (cosmetics 1971; sold 1987) and IVAC (medical instruments 1977). It launched such products as analgesic Darvon and antibiotic Ceclor.

Lilly's 1982 launch of Humulin a synthetic insulin developed by Genentech made it the first company to market a genetically engineered product. In 1986 the company introduced Prozac; that year it also bought biotech firm Hybritech for $300 million (sold in 1995 for less than $10 million). In 1988 Lilly introduced anti-ulcerative Axid. It founded pesticides and herbicides maker DowElanco with Dow Chemical in 1989.

Trying to find a new product outlet the firm bought pharmacy benefit management company PCS Health Systems from what is now McKesson in 1994. But an FTC mandate to offer rival drugs and a lack of mail-order sales contributed to poor results which ultimately led Lilly to sell PCS to Rite Aid and exit this arena completely in 1998.

Eli Lilly in 1995 bought medical communications network developer Integrated Medical Systems. That year the firm and developer Centocor introduced ReoPro a blood-clot inhibitor used in angioplasties. The next year it launched antipsychotic Zyprexa Humalog and Gemzar and Prozac was approved to treat bulimia nervosa.

In 1997 the firm sold its DowElanco stake to Dow. In 1998 the Lilly Endowment passed the Ford Foundation as the US's largest charity largely due to Prozac (it has since been passed by the Bill & Melinda Gates Foundation). That year Lilly began trying to stop Chinese drugmakers from infringing on its patents for Prozac's active ingredient.

In 1999 a US federal judge found the firm illegally promoted osteoporosis drug Evista as a breast cancer preventative similar to AstraZeneca's Nolvadex. Lilly halted tests on its variation of heart drug Moxonidine after 53 patients died. Also that year Zyprexa was approved to treat bipolar disorder.

In 2000 the firm began marketing Prozac under the Sarafem name for severe premenstrual syndrome. A federal appeals court knocked more than two years off Prozac's patent reducing the expected 2003 expiration date to 2001 creating a negative impact on Lilly's annual sales (Prozac had accounted for 30% of revenues). Lilly suffered another blow when a potential successor to Prozac failed i

EXECUTIVES

Svp And President Elanco Animal Health, Jeffrey N. (Jeff) Simmons, age 51

Svp And President Diabetes Business Unit And Lilly Usa, Enrique A. Conterno, age 51, $727,960 total compensation

President Manufacturing Operations, Maria Crowe, age 58

Svp And President Lilly International, Alfonso G. (Chito) Zulueta, age 55

Svp And President Lilly Oncology, Susan (Sue) Mahony, age 53

President And Ceo, David A. Ricks, age 50

Svp And President Lilly Bio-medicines, Christi Shaw

Svp Global Parenteral Drug Product And Delivery Devices Manufacturing, Myles O'Neill

Svp Enterprise Risk Management And Chief Ethics And Compliance Officer, Melissa Stapleton Barnes, age 49

Svp And General Counsel, Michael J. Harrington, age 55, $827,400 total compensation

Svp And Cio, Aarti Shah

Svp And Cfo, Josh Smiley

Svp Science And Technology And President Lilly Research Labs, Daniel (Dan) Skovronsky

Senior Vice President Enterprise Risk Management And Chief Ethics And Compliance Officer, Melissa Barnes

Department Head Space Planning, Brent Blanchard

Vice President Medical Affiars, Robert Heine

Vice President Medicine Development Unit Diabetes And Clinical Transformation, Rob Metcalf

Senior Vice President Finance And Treasurer, Philip Johnson

Medical Director, Anurita Majumdar

Vice President Of Research And Development, Michele Oshman

Vice President And Medical Director China, Li Wang

Government Relations, Joel Worthington

Vp And General Auditor, Kathy St Louis

Vice President Marketing International Business Unit, Simone Thomsen

Chairman, John C. Lechleiter

Board Member, Jessi Pitrelli

Auditors: Ernst & Young LLP

LOCATIONS

HQ: Lilly (Eli) & Co
Lilly Corporate Center, Indianapolis, IN 46285
Phone: 317 276-2000
Web: www.lilly.com

2017 Sales

	$ mil.	% of total
US	12,785	56
Europe	3,943	17
Japan	2,419	11
Other	3,723	16
Total	**22,871**	**100**

PRODUCTS/OPERATIONS

2017 Sales

	$ mil.	% of total
Endocrinology	10,085	44
Oncology	3,811	17
Cardiovascular	2,871	13
Neurosciences	2,171	9
Immunology	605	3
Other human pharmaceuticals	241	1
Animal Health	3,085	13
Total	**22,071**	**100**

Selected Products and Indications

Neuroscience
  Amyvid (florbetapir F 18 injection)
  Cymbalta (duloxetine hydrocholoride; depression anxiety pain; also for managing fibromyalgia and chronic musculoskeletal pain in the US)
  Prozac (fluoxetine hydrochloride; depression panic disorder obsessive-compulsive disorder and bulimia nervosa)
  Strattera (atomoxetine hydrochloride ADHD)
  Symbyax (olanzapine and fluoxetine hydrochloride bipolar and treatment-resistant depression)
  Zyprexa (olanzapine schizophrenia and bipolar)
  Zyprexa Relprevv (Zypadhera in the EU long-acting injectable Zyprexa)
Endocrinology (including diabetes)
  Actos (pioglitazone hydrochloride type 2 diabetes)
  Alimta (non-small cell lung cancer)
  Axiron (testosterone topical for testosterone deficiency)
  Erbitux (colorectal cancers head and neck cancers)
  Evista (raloxifene hydrochloride osteoporosis and breast cancer prevention in postmenopausal women)
  Forteo (osteoporosis)
  Gemzar (pancreatic cancer metastatic breast cancer non-small cell lung cancer; bladder cancer in the EU)
  Glucagon (injection rDNA origin)
  Humalog (insulin lispro injection rDNA origin; diabetes)
  Humalog Mix 75/25 (75% Insulin lispro protamine suspension 25% insulin lispro injection rDNA origin; diabetes)
  Humalog Mix 50/50 (50% Insulin lispro protamine suspension 50% insulin lispro injection rDNA origin; diabetes)
  Humalog Pen (insulin lispro rDNA origin; diabetes)
  Humatrope (somatropin for injection rDNA origin; growth disorders)
  Humulin (human insulin rDNA origin; diabetes)
  Humulin Pen (human insulin rDNA origin; diabetes)
  Tradjenta (type 2 diabetes)
Oncology (cancer)
  Alimta (pemetrexed non-small cell lung cancer and malignant pleural mesothelioma)
  Erbitux (colorectal head and neck cancers; from ImClone)
  Gemzar (gemcitabine hydrochloride; pancreatic breast lung bladder and ovarian cancers)
Cardiovascular
  Adcirca (pulmonary arterial hypertension)
  Cialis (tadalafil erectile dysfunction; benign prostatic hyperplasia in US)
  Efient/Effient (atherothrombotic events)
  Livalo (statin high cholesterol)
  ReoPro (percutaneous coronary intervention)
Animal Health (Elanco)
  Apralan (antibiotic to control enteric infections in calves and swine)
  Coban Monteban and Maxiban (anticoccidial for poultry)
  Comfortis (flea infestation prevention tablets for dogs)
  Micotil Pulmotil and Pulmotil AC (antibiotics for respiratory disease in cattle swine and poultry respectively)
  Paylean Optaflexx (leanness and performance enhancers for swine and cattle respectively)
  Posilac (protein supplement for enhanced milk productivity in cows)
  Reconcile (separation anxiety for dogs)
  Rumensin (feed additive)
  Surmax/Maxus (performance enhancer for swine and poultry)
  Trifexis (chewable tablet for dogs to prevent flea infestations and heartworm disease and control intestinal parasite infections)
  Tylan (antibiotic)
Other pharmaceuticals (including anti-infectives)

Ceclor (bacterial infections)
Vancocin (staphylococcal infections)

COMPETITORS

Abbott Labs	Mylan
Amgen	Myriad Genetics
AstraZeneca	Novartis
Bayer AG	Novo Nordisk
Boehringer Ingelheim	Pfizer
Bristol-Myers Squibb	Roche Holding
Dr. Reddy's	Sanofi
GlaxoSmithKline	Shire
Johnson & Johnson	Takeda Pharmaceutical
Merck	Teva
Merck KGaA	

HISTORICAL FINANCIALS

Company Type: Public

Income Statement   FYE: December 31

	REVENUE ($ mil.)	NET INCOME ($ mil.)	NET PROFIT MARGIN	EMPLOYEES
12/17	22,871	(204)		40,655
12/16	21,222	2,737	12.9%	41,975
12/15	19,958	2,408	12.1%	41,275
12/14	19,615	2,390	12.2%	39,135
12/13	23,113	4,684	20.3%	37,925
Annual Growth	(0.3%)			1.8%

2017 Year-End Financials

Debt ratio: 30.34%	No. of shares (mil.): 1,100
Return on equity: (-1.59%)	Dividends
Cash ($ mil.): 8,034	Yield: 0.0%
Current ratio: 1.32	Payout: —
Long-term debt ($ mil.): 9,940	Market value ($ mil.): 92,907

	STOCK PRICE ($) FY Close	P/E High/Low	PER SHARE ($) Earnings	Dividends	Book Value
12/17	84.46	— —	(0.19)	2.08	10.54
12/16	73.55	33 25	2.58	2.04	12.72
12/15	84.26	40 30	2.26	2.00	13.18
12/14	68.99	33 23	2.23	1.96	13.84
12/13	51.00	13 11	4.32	1.96	15.79
Annual Growth	13.4%	— —		1.5%	(9.6%)

Lincoln National Corp.

Lincoln National which operates as Lincoln Financial Group provides retirement planning and life insurance to individuals and employers in the form of annuities 401k and savings plans and a variety of life dental and disability insurance products. The company does business through such subsidiaries as Lincoln National Life Insurance Lincoln Life & Annuity Company of New York and First Penn-Pacific Life Insurance Company. Lincoln Financial is also active in the investment management business offering individual and institutional clients such financial services as pension plans trusts and mutual funds through its subsidiaries.

Operations

Lincoln Financial operates through four segments: Life Insurance Annuities Group Protection and Retirement Plan Services. The group serves more than 90000 group insurance and retirement plan contracts which have a total of some 17 million participants. It has a total of $253 billion in assets under management.

The company's largest segment Life Insurance (about 45% of sales) offers term products a linked benefit product and a critical illness rider.

The Annuities segment (some 30% of sales) offers fixed and variable annuities.

Group Protection (about 15% of sales) offers non-medical policies primarily term life dental and disability products to the employer market.

Retirement Plan Services (nearly 10% of sales) provides employers with plans and services primarily in the defined contribution retirement plan marketplace.

Geographic Reach

Headquartered in Radnor Pennsylvania Lincoln Financial also has offices in Atlanta (Group Protection); Concord New Hampshire; Fort Wayne Indiana (Annuities and Retirement Plan Services); Greensboro North Carolina (Life Insurance); Hartford Connecticut; Omaha Nebraska; and Philadelphia.

Sales and Marketing

Lincoln Financial Network distributes Lincoln Financial products through a network of some 1150 planners and agents while Lincoln Financial Distributors is the company's wholesale distributor serving brokers consultants planners agents third party administrators financial advisors and other intermediaries. Lincoln Financial Distributors has more than 500 internal and external wholesalers and approximately 9000 active producers.

Group Protection distributes its products through employee benefits brokers third-party administrators and other employee benefit firms.

Financial Performance

With the exception of 2016 Lincoln Financial has seen slow revenue growth over the past few years. Net income has generally been rising as well. However cash on hand has declined for three years.

In 2017 revenue increased 7% to $14.3 billion. Insurance premiums fee income and net investment income all rose that year.

With the higher revenue net income rose 74% to $2.1 billion in 2017. This was due to factors including a one-time federal income tax benefit related to the Tax Act and increases in average account values and business in force. However corporate spending on digitization cut into the bottom line.

The company ended 2017 with $1.6 billion some $1.1 billion less than it had at the end of 2016. Operating activities provided $788 million and financing activities provided $2.3 billion but investing activities used $4.2 billion.

Strategy

Like any company with heavy exposure to global macroeconomic conditions Lincoln Financial is vulnerable to capital market downturns which could lead to corporate losses. Additionally a number of the company's competitors have greater access to funds offer a broader range of products and enjoy a greater market share than Lincoln does. To meet the challenges of difficult economic times in the market the company has adopted strategies to strengthen its business that include investing in high-quality corporate securities to reduce asset risk; escalating share repurchases and debt repayment; repricing life and annuity products to guarantee new business that is profitable; and making significant investments in businesses to increase its future earning power. It is investing in product innovations and distribution channels to drive up revenues. The company leverages its powerful distribution network to enter new markets while maintaining its position in existing markets. It targets the fastest-growing industry segments while steering away from long-term guarantee products.

The company is also investing in technology to increase margins. Its current enterprise-wide digitization initiative is designed to improve customer experiences and provide for ease in meeting changing marketplace shifts.

Going forward Lincoln Financial will explore additional financial strategies to address the statutory reserve strain that comes with its term and universal life products that contain secondary guarantees. It will shift its business to focus on products with shorter-duration liabilities and more limited liabilities.

Mergers and Acquisitions

In 2018 Lincoln Financial acquired Liberty Life Assurance Company of Boston from Liberty Mutual Insurance. The deal included Liberty's group benefits operations. Through the purchase Lincoln expanded its distribution reach.

Company Background

Lincoln National traces its roots to the founding of the Fraternal Assurance Society of America in 1902. After a founding member absconded with funds the remaining members obtained permission from Abraham Lincoln's son Robert to use his father's name and image to clean up the organization's reputation.

The company bought up other firms in the 1950s and 1960s and in 1968 it formed holding company Lincoln National. Soon it began diversifying buying Chicago Title and Trust (1969; sold 1985) as well as more life and reinsurance companies. Lincoln National also went into the health benefits business setting up its own HMO and investing in EMPHESYS (which it took public in 1994 divesting the remainder of its stock in 1995).

With the growth of retirement savings from baby boomers hitting their 50's the company shifted gears into wealth management. Lincoln National bought CIGNA's annuity and individual life insurance business and Aetna's US individual life insurance operations in 1998.

In 1999 after nearly a century in the heartland Lincoln National moved its headquarters to Philadelphia.

EXECUTIVES

President And Ceo; President Lincoln Financial Group, Dennis R. Glass, age 68, $1,200,000 total compensation

Evp Chief Human Resources Officer And Head Brand And Enterprise Communications, Lisa M. Buckingham, age 52, $578,448 total compensation

President Annuity Solutions Lincoln Financial Distributors And Lincoln Financial Network, Wilford H. (Will) Fuller, age 47, $650,000 total compensation

Evp And Cfo, Randal J. Freitag, age 55, $669,708 total compensation

Evp And Chief Investment Officer, Ellen Cooper, age 53

Evp And General Counsel, Kirkland L. Hicks, age 47, $575,000 total compensation

Evp Cio And Head Of Administrative Services, Kenneth S. Solon, age 57

Vice President Of Corporate Branding And Advertising, David Wozniak

Vice President Of Sales, Robert Risk

Senior Vice President, Beth O'Brien

Assistant Vice President Income Product Market Development, Daniel Herr

Assistant Vice President, Marlene Hammond

Senior Vice President Account Executive, Michael Herron

Assistant Vice President And Associate Counsel, Carl Semmler

Assistant Vice President, Henry Collie

Assistant Vice President, James M Gasparotto

Assistant Vice President And Associate Actuary, Lance Schulz

Vice President, Roberta Tielinen

Associate Vice President Enrollment Services, Joe Mitchell

Vice President Managing Director Tactical Strategies Fixed Inc, Jayson Bronchetti

Sales Vice President, Eric Patterson

Assistant Vice President Senior Employee Relations, Mary Carruth

Vice President Human Resources, Audrey Im

Senior Vice President, Andrew Yorks

Assistant Vice President Advisor Based Sales Director, Ryan Rayburn

Vice President Senior Counsel, Jennifer Petruccelli

Assistant Vice President And Valuation Actuary, William Panyard

Assistant Vice President Senior Counsel Retirement Plan Services, Philip Lozano

Assistant Vice President, Mike Link

Svp And Chief Accounting Officer, Christine Janofsky

Assistant Vice President Life Valuation, Adam Williams

Assistant Vice President Financial Reporting And Expense Controls, Kathy Tibke

Vice President Operations, Christina Dilorenzo

Vice President Of Sales, Marie Cochrane

Assistant Vice President Treasury, Brad Jeffrey Brad Jeffrey

Vice President And Branch Manager, Melissa Hidalgo

Vice President Corporate Supply Chain And Manufacturing, Sharon Leggette

Assistant Vice President, Loraine Bernard

Vice President, Brian Jenkins

Vice President Operations, Emma Ladd

Assistant Vice President Digital, James Tierney

Vice President Product Compliance, Pamela Telfer

Assistant Vice President Human Resources Business Partner, Carol Dowling

Assistant Vice President, Miko Pickett

Vice President Asset Liability Management, Nathan Hardiman

Second Vice President Corporate Actuary, Mike Antrobus

Assistant Vice President Market Intelligence, Jamie Ranicar

Assistant Vice President Internal Audit, Wanda Pritchett

Vice President Talent Management, Nancy Rogers

Senior Counsel And Assistant Vice President, Wayne Mcclain

Assistant Vice President Life And Annuity Strategy, Thomas Goas

Assistant Vice President Meetings And Incentives, Richard Gladson

Vice President Finance, John Luviano

Vice President Of Human Resources Administration, Stephen Dovey

Senior Vice President Head Of Talent, Jen Warne

Assistant Vice President Internal Audit, Claude Campbell

Assistant Vice President Program Manager, Colette Reinhard

Sales Vice President, David Duckworth

Vice President And Associate General Counsel, Deborah Hayes

Vice President, Joe Minutolo

Assistant Vice President Creative Team, John Tognoli

Senior Vice President, Jon Kimmel

Assistant Vice President Continuous Improvement, Martin Koritko

Sales Vice President, Valerie Staublin

Senior Vice President, William Conrad

Assistant Vice President Business Operations Pricing And Underwriting Solutions, Lorrie Zakrzewski

Assistant Vice President Digital Content Services, Christopher O'Connor

Vice President Specialty Health, Chris Stevens

Vice President Business Development, Jeff Hamilton

Svp Human Resources, Patricia Insley

Tax Assistant Vice President, Jan Webb

Vice President Of Information Technology, Lori Snyder

Assistant Vice President Finance, Chris Reed

Assistant Vice President Analytics, Michael Mocanu

Vice President Finance, F Schroeder

Assistant Vice President, Susan Mann

Vice President Commercial Real Estate Investments, Nick Heinzelmann

Vice President Talent Acquisition, Michael Kellar

Assistant Vice President Retirement Benefits, Johnathan Arko

Senior Vice President Funds Management And Investments Law, Ronald Holinsky

Valuation Actuary And Assistant Vice President Cfa, Cynthia McGovern

Vice President Marketing Management, Tara Harkins

Assistant Vice President And Legal Services, Molly Graham

Assistant Vice President Regional Sales Manager, Thomas Maclean

National Account Manager, Tracey Lemelin

National Account Manager, Juanita Morris-gettings

Vice President Enterprise Services, Michelle DeCarlo

Assistant Vice President Data Science And Application Architecture, Bernard Ong

Assistant Vice President Enterprise Business Systems, Ken Weaver

Assistant Vice President Underwriting Audit And Training, Vivian Adams

Vice President Sales, Kevin Swantek

Vice President, James Fisher

Avp Office Business Resilience, Laurie Ann Scotti

Vice President, Aaron Williams

Assistant Vice President Information Technology, Aswathy Nair

Avp And Senior Counsel, Matt Creech

Vice President And Associate General Counsel, Mary Potter

Vice President Chief Architect, Matthew Daniels

Vice President Data Center Network And Storage Services, Joseph Brannan

Assistant Vice President Life Medical Director, Susan Kinney

Vice President Litigation And Corporate Insurance, Christine Swift

Board Member, Eric Johnson

Chairman, William H. Cunningham, age 74

Board Member, Gary Kelly

Board Member, David McDunn

Board Member, Deirdre Connelly

Auditors: Ernst & Young LLP

LOCATIONS

HQ: Lincoln National Corp.
150 N. Radnor Chester Road, Suite A305, Radnor, PA 19087
Phone: 484 583-1400
Web: www.lfg.com

PRODUCTS/OPERATIONS

2017 Sales

	$ mil.	% of total
Fees	5,619	39
Net investment income	4,990	35
Insurance premiums	3,256	22
Other	562	4
Adjustments	(170)	-
Total	**14,257**	**100**

2017 Sales by Segment

	$ mil.	% of total
Life Insurance	6,558	45
Annuities	4,378	30
Group Protection	2,201	15
Retirement Plan Services	1,165	8
Other	291	2
Adjustments	(336)	-
Total	**14,257**	**100**

Selected Subsidiaries

First Penn-Pacific Life Insurance Company
Hampshire Funding Inc.
Jefferson-Pilot Investments Inc.
Lincoln Financial Investment Services Corporation
Lincoln Financial Securities Corporation
Lincoln Investment Management Company
The Lincoln National Life Insurance Company
Lincoln National Management Corporation
Lincoln National Reinsurance Company (Barbados) Limited
Lincoln Reinsurance Company of Bermuda Limited

COMPETITORS

AEGON
AIG
AXA Financial
American Equity Investment Life Holding Company
Guardian Life
John Hancock Financial Services
MassMutual
MetLife
Nationwide Financial
New York Life
Northwestern Mutual
Pacific Mutual
Principal Financial
Prudential
TIAA
The Hartford
Torchmark
Unum Group

HISTORICAL FINANCIALS

Company Type: Public

Income Statement

FYE: December 31

	ASSETS ($ mil.)	NET INCOME ($ mil.)	INCOME AS % OF ASSETS	EMPLOYEES
12/17	281,763	2,079	0.7%	10,194
12/16	261,627	1,192	0.5%	10,282
12/15	251,937	1,154	0.5%	10,535
12/14	253,377	1,515	0.6%	11,046
12/13	236,945	1,244	0.5%	10,539
Annual Growth	**4.4%**	**13.7%**	**—**	**(0.8%)**

2017 Year-End Financials

Debt ratio: 1.74%
Return on equity: 13.08%
Cash ($ mil.): 1,628
Current ratio: —
Long-term debt ($ mil.): —

No. of shares (mil.): 218
Dividends
Yield: 0.0%
Payout: 12.5%
Market value ($ mil.): 16,765

	STOCK PRICE ($) FY Close	P/E High/Low		PER SHARE ($) Earnings	Dividends	Book Value
12/17	76.87	8	7	9.22	1.16	79.43
12/16	66.27	13	6	5.03	1.00	63.97
12/15	50.26	13	10	4.51	0.80	55.84
12/14	57.67	10	8	5.67	0.64	61.35
12/13	51.62	11	6	4.52	0.48	51.17
Annual Growth	**10.5%**	**—**	**—**	**19.5%**	**24.7%**	**11.6%**

Linde plc

Praxair makes lighter-than-air and heavier-than-air gases. The largest North American industrial gas supplier it produces and sells atmospheric gases (oxygen nitrogen argon and rare gases) as well as process and specialty gases (CO2 helium and hydrogen) for the chemicals food and beverage semiconductor and healthcare industries worldwide. It serves around 10 industries across more than 50 countries. Its Praxair Surface Technologies unit supplies high-temperature and corrosion-resistant metallic ceramic and powder coatings mainly to the aircraft plastics and primary metals markets. In a long-running saga Praxair and German gases comapny Linde have agreed to merge in a deal worth $80 billion.

Operations

Praxair operates in North America Europe South America and Asia. In addition Praxair operates its worldwide surface technologies business through Praxair Surface Technologies.

Praxair participates in the three main sectors of the industrial gas industry: on-site merchant and packaged gas supply. The company builds industrial gas plants at a customer's site (locking in long-term supply agreements) ships merchant gases (delivered liquids) by trucks and sells packaged gases in canisters or large tanks. Praxair organizes its business segments primarily by region: North America (where it has more than 255 plants) Europe (about 70 plants) South America (almost 60 plants) and Asia (50 plants). The four segments contribute 95% of total company reveneue.

Praxair also operates a Surface Technologies unit which supplies high-performance coatings from 45+ sites worldwide and generates about 5% of total sales.

Leading subsidiaries include White Martins Gases Industriais Ltda which conducts Praxair's South American industrial gases operations Praxair Surface Technologies Inc. which supplies wear- heat- and corrosion-resistant metallic and ceramic coatings and powders and Praxair Distribution.

Geographic Reach

Praxair has facilities in Rio de Janeiro Brazil; Shanghai China; and Madrid Spain. It also has operations in Tonawanda New York and Burr Ridge Illinois in the US; in Monterrey Mexico; and Bangalore India. Research and development for industrial gases is principally conducted at the Tonawanda Burr Ridge Shanghai and Bangalore sites.

It also has operations in Korea and Thailand with smaller operations in Taiwan and the Middle East.

North America (US Canada and Mexico) accounts for about 55% of the company's total revenues; Asia more than 15%; South America nearly 15%; and Europe about 15%. More than half of the company's business is done outside the US.

Sales and Marketing

Praxair distributes its products through networks of hundreds of production plants pipeline complexes distribution centers and delivery vehicles. Major pipeline complexes are located in the US Brazil Spain and Germany.

Financial Performance

In fiscal 2016 sales fell 2% to $10.5 billion due mostly to unfavorable currency effects and lower cost pass-through. These factors aside it recorded 2% organic growth due to higher prices in North and South America new project start-ups and acquisitions in Europe.

Net income fell 3% to $1.5 billion due mostly to lower net revenue and tighter margins. The company incurred a $96 million expense relating to cost reductions and a $4 million pension settlement.

Cash form operations was up 3% to $2.8 billion due to lower working capital requirements and favorable changes in other long-term assets and liabilities partially offset by lower net income.

Strategy

Praxair's growth strategy largely rests on acquisitions as organic growth has proved hard to come by recently. It spent $363 million on acquisitions in 2016 including on five industrial and medical gas business in the US Panama and Italy as well as a leading supplier of CO2. To drive bottom line growth the company undertook cost-cutting measures in 2016.

In response to French gas company Air Liquide's takeover of Airgas Praxair plans to merge with German rival Linde forming the world's largest industrial gas company. The company expects the merger to deliver $1 billion in synergies while expanding the company's global footprint and making it a more attractive destination for prospective employees.

Mergers and AcquisitionsPraxair and bitter German rival Linde originally proposed to merge in 2016 for a $80 billion deal. As of August 2018 the deal is yet to go through. This is because the merger will form the world's largest gas company and easily surpassing French rival Air Liquide in annual sales. There seems to be lingering antitrust concerns as the US federal Trade Commission demanded more asset sales than the companies originally proposed. As a result Praxair and Linde—which used to be the same company more than a century ago before falling out—remain under "a constructive dialogue".

In 2016 the company acquired Norway-based Yara International a leading carbon dioxide supplier for $363 million. The acquisition expends its presence in end-markets such as food and drinks.

Also in 2016 Praxair acquired five industrial and medical gas companies with combined annual sales of more than $40 million. Of the five three — The Welding center Welder Services and A&B Electric Motors — are in the US; one — Geneva Industrial Gases — is in Panama; and the fifth Ossigas is in Italy. The companies add to Praxair's geographic density.

HISTORY

The origins of Praxair date to the work of Karl von Linde a professor of mechanical engineering at the College of Technology in Munich Germany in the late 1800s. In 1895 he created the cryogenic air liquefier. Von Linde built his first oxygen-production plant in 1902 and a nitrogen plant in 1904 and in the first decade of the 20th century he built a number of air-separation plants throughout Europe.

By 1907 von Linde had moved to the US and founded Linde Air Products in Cleveland to extract oxygen from air. Linde Air Products joined rival Union Carbide in 1911 in experimenting with the production of acetylene; it became a unit of Union Carbide in 1917. America's war effort and economic expansion in the 1920s spurred the development of new uses for industrial gases. Union Carbide's Linde unit also contributed to the development of the atomic bomb in the 1940s when its scientists perfected a process for refining uranium.

As Union Carbide expanded worldwide over the next two decades Linde became America's #1 producer of industrial gases. In the 1960s Linde expanded into oxygen-fired furnaces for steel production and the use of nitrogen in refrigerators. By the early 1980s Linde accounted for 11% of Union Carbide's annual sales.

The disastrous 1984 chemical accident at Union Carbide's plant in Bhopal India coupled with heavy debt and falling sales forced Union Carbide to reorganize. In 1992 Linde was spun off as Praxair. William Lichtenberger former president of Union Carbide headed the new company and pushed global expansion. Two years later Praxair set up China's first helium transfill plants for medical magnetic resonance imaging. In 1995 the company began operations in India and Peru.

In 1996 Praxair Surface Technologies bought Miller Thermal (thermal spray coatings) and Maxima Air Separation Center (industrial and specialty gases Israel). Also that year the company picked up $60 million when it sold the Linde name and trademark to Linde a German engineering and industrial gas company. Praxair purchased and then spun off Chicago Bridge & Iron. The company kept only its Liquid Carbonic division the world's leading supplier of carbon dioxide for processing. The move opened up a new market in carbonated beverages for Praxair.

In 1997 and 1998 Praxair constructed plants and to control its own delivery systems acquired 20 packaged-gases distributors in the US and one in Germany. The company also formed a joint venture in China to produce high-purity nitrogen and other specialty gases for electronics and then teamed up with rival L'Air Liquide in a production joint venture.

Praxair supplied an argon-based protection system for the Shroud of Turin's public display in Italy in 1998. It also installed the industry's first small on-site hydrogen-generating system at an Indiana powdered-metals plant. In 1999 the company formed a global alliance with German pharmaceutical and chemicals company Merck KGaA to provide gases and chemicals to the semiconductor industry. The same year Praxair acquired Materials Research Corporation a maker of thin-film deposition materials for semiconductors and the TAFA Group which makes thermal-spray equipment and related products.

In 2001 Praxair underwent a restructuring that included layoffs in its surface technologies unit (hurt by the decline in jet orders) and Brazilian operations. The next year the company started work on a new plant to serve Singapore's high-tech industry. Praxair boosted its health care segment with the acquisition of Alpine Medicine.

In 2004 Praxair Healthcare Services bought Home Care Supply for $245 milli

EXECUTIVES

Chairman President And Ceo, Stephen F. (Steve) Angel, $1,318,750 total compensation

Svp; President White Martins Gases Industriais And Praxair South America, Domingos H. G. Bulus

Evp, Eduardo F. Menezes, $611,250 total compensation

President Praxair Europe, Daniel H. (Dan) Yankowski

Vp And Cio, Earl Newsome

President Praxair Asia, John M. Panikar

President Praxair Europe, Eduardo Gil

Svp, Anne K. Roby, $471,250 total compensation

President Us Industrial Gases, Kevin C. Foti

President Praxair Distribution Inc., Dick Marini

Evp, Scott E. Telesz, $615,000 total compensation

Svp And Cfo, Matthew J. (Matt) White, $587,500 total compensation

Cto, Todd A. Skare

President Praxair Canada, Sean Durbin

President Praxair Surface Technologies, Pierre L thi

Vice President And General Manager Us Praxair Distribution, Randall Brittingham

Vice President Sales, Ed Haversang

Auditors: PricewaterhouseCoopers LLP

LOCATIONS

HQ: Linde plc
  10 Riverview Drive, Danbury, CT 06810-6268
Phone: 203 837-2000
Web: www.praxair.com

2016 Sales

	% of total
North America	53
Asia	15
South America	13
Europe	13
Surface technologies	6
Total	**100**

PRODUCTS/OPERATIONS

2016 Sales by End Market

	% of total
Manufacturing	21
Metals	16
Chemicals	14
Food & Beverage	12
Healthcare	11
Electronics	7
Energy	5
Aerospace	1
Other	13
Total	**100**

2016 Sales by Distribution Method

	% of total
Merchant(delivered liquids)	38
On-site (includes noncryogenics)	28
Packaged gases (cylinders)	31
Other	3
Total	**100**

Selected Mergers and Acquisitions

COMPETITORS

Air Products	GKN Aerospace
Airgas	Chem-tronics
Balchem	L'Air Liquide
Chromalloy Gas Turbine	The Linde Group

HISTORICAL FINANCIALS

Company Type: Public

Income Statement

FYE: December 31

	REVENUE ($ mil.)	NET INCOME ($ mil.)	NET PROFIT MARGIN	EMPLOYEES
12/17	11,437	1,247	10.9%	26,461
12/16	10,534	1,500	14.2%	26,498
12/15	10,776	1,547	14.4%	26,657
12/14	12,273	1,694	13.8%	27,780
12/13	11,925	1,755	14.7%	27,560
Annual Growth	**(1.0%)**	**(8.2%)**	**—**	**(1.0%)**

2017 Year-End Financials

Debt ratio: 44.04%	No. of shares (mil.): 286
Return on equity: 22.59%	Dividends
Cash ($ mil.): 617	Yield: —
Current ratio: 0.99	Payout: 72.9%
Long-term debt ($ mil.): 7,783	Market value ($ mil.): —

Lithia Motors Inc

Lithia Motors has its foot on the growth pedal. The auto dealer specializes in famed US auto brands such as Chevrolet Cadillac Chrysler and Dodge through about 155 stores in select markets in more than a dozen states. The firm sells some 30 brands of new domestic and imported vehicles and all brands of used cars and trucks through its stores and online. It also offers financing and replacement parts and operates more than 20 collision-repair centers. It also offers financing vehicle protection products and credit insurance. Chairman Sidney DeBoer controls Lithia Motors through Lithia Holding Co.

Operations

Lithia has three segments: Import (more than 40% of sales) Domestic (around 40%) and Luxury (almost 20%).

The Domestic segment comprises retail automotive franchises that sell new vehicles manufactured by Chrysler General Motors and Ford. The Import segment covers retail automotive franchises that sell new vehicles made by Honda Toyota Subaru Nissan and Volkswagen. The Luxury segment sells new vehicles manufactured made by BMW Mercedes-Benz and Lexus.

The franchises in each segment also sell used vehicles parts and automotive services and automotive finance and insurance products.

The company also operates three e-commerce websites: Lithia.com DCHauto.com and CarboneCars.com

Lithia sells in the region of 145000 new vehicles and 110000 used vehicles each year.

Geographic Reach

Medford Oregon-based Lithia sells 30 brands of new vehicles and all brands of used vehicles across 15 US states. Its dealerships are primarily located in the West and Midwest including more than a half a dozen dealerships in Alaska and nearly two dozen in Oregon. California is Lithia's biggest market accounting for more than 20% of the company's total sales followed by Oregon and Texas. It has no international business.

The company operates +20 collision repair centers: five each in Oregon and Texas; two each in Idaho New York and Washington; and one each in Alaska Iowa Montana Nevada Vermont and Wyoming.

Sales and Marketing

Lithia sells through its stores and online website. It also maintains mobile versions of its websites and a mobile application in anticipation of greater adoption of mobile technology.

It posts its inventory on major new and used vehicle listing services (cars.com autotrader.com kbb.com edmunds.com craigslist etc.) to reach online shoppers. It also employs search engine optimization search engine marketing and online display advertising (including re-targeting) to reach more online prospects.

Financial Performance

In fiscal 2016 Lithia kept its foot hard on the growth gas continuing the acquisition-fueled growth trend seen since 2010. Revenue rose 10% to $8.7 billion due mostly to dealership acquisitions. Lithia acquired 15 dealerships and 1 franchise in the year an increase on the 6 dealerships and 1 franchise in 2015. However even excluding acquisition-related revenue the company recorded 3.3% organic growth amid unit volume growth and higher selling prices. The best performing brands were the Japanese import brands Honda and Nissan while BMW Acura and Mercedes lagged.

Net income increased 8% to $197.1 million in line with the increase in revenue. Margins remained roughly the same.

Cash from operations was up 16% to $86.5 million due to higher net income.

Strategy

Lithia Motors relies on acquisitions to increase its revenue and diversify its brand portfolio. Indeed the company has completed more than 100 acquisitions since it went public in 1996. Historically the auto dealer has bought about 10 franchises a year expanding mostly in its western base.

Recently the company has shifted its acquisition strategy towards new markets in the US and larger multi-store dealerships. Lithia expanded into Pittsburgh Pennsylvania in 2017 and into New England in 2016 via Carbone Auto Group. Its preference for larger organizations resulted from the assessment that they take less manpower to integrate than smaller "mom and pop" dealerships due to a more established corporate culture.

Mergers and Acquisitions

In 2017 Lithia acquired Downtown Los Angeles Auto Group. The company owns Audi Mercedes-Benz Nissan Porsche Toyota and Volkswagen stores in Los Angeles as well as a Nissan store in nearby Carson. The company brings in more than $1 billion a year in revenue.

In the same year Lithia acquired Pittsburgh-based Baeirl Auto Group that sells Toyota Honda Subaru Ford Chevrolet Acura Kia and Cadillac in the affluent Cranberry Township area. Baeirl makes $500 million a year in revenue.

Company Background

Lithia Motors was founded in 1946 by Walt DeBoer as a Chrysler-Plymouth-Dodge dealership in Ashland Oregon. Walt's son Sidney is its chairman and grandson Bryan is president and CEO of the growing auto dealer.

EXECUTIVES

President And Ceo, Bryan B. DeBoer, age 51, $950,000 total compensation
Evp And Chief Human Resources Officer, Christopher (Chris) Holzshu, age 44, $485,100 total compensation
Svp Operations, Scott A. Hillier, age 55, $485,100 total compensation
Svp And Cfo, John F. North, age 41, $302,500 total compensation
Vp Information Technology And Cio, Mark Smith
Svp Operations Dch Operations, George C. Liang, age 62, $378,000 total compensation
Regional Manager Vice President, Ken Wright
Vice President Of Information Systems, Attendee Drennan
Vice President Real Estate, Mark DeBoer
Vice President, TIM FREEBORN
Chairman, Sidney B. (Sid) DeBoer, age 74
Board Member, Kenneth Roberts
Auditors: KPMG LLP

LOCATIONS

HQ: Lithia Motors Inc
  150 N. Bartlett Street, Medford, OR 97501
Phone: 541 776-6401
Web: www.lithia.com

2016 Stores

	No.
California	35
Oregon	25
Texas	16
Montana	11
New Jersey	11
New York	10
Alaska	9
Washington	8
Iowa	7
Hawaii	5
Nevada	4
Idaho	4
North Dakota	3
New Mexico	2
Vermont	2
Massachusetts	1
Wyoming	1
Total	**154**

PRODUCTS/OPERATIONS

2016 Sales

	$ mil	%
Import	3,764	43
Domestic	3,381	39
Luxury	1,528	18
Corporate and other	3	-
Total	**8,678**	**100**

2016 Sales

	$ mil.	% of total
New vehicles	4,938	57
Used vehicle retail	2,227	25
Service body & parts	844	10
Finance & insurance	330	4
Used vehicle wholesale	276	3
Fleet & other	60	1
Total	**8,678**	**100**

COMPETITORS

Ancira	Group 1 Automotive
AutoNation	Internet Brands
Autobytel	McCombs Enterprises
CarMax	Penske Automotive
David McDavid Auto	Group
Group	Sonic Automotive
Gillman Auto	

HISTORICAL FINANCIALS

Company Type: Public

Income Statement

FYE: December 31

	REVENUE ($ mil.)	NET INCOME ($ mil.)	NET PROFIT MARGIN	EMPLOYEES
12/17	10,086	245	2.4%	12,899
12/16	8,678	197	2.3%	11,170
12/15	7,864	183	2.3%	9,574
12/14	5,390	138	2.6%	8,827
12/13	4,005	106	2.6%	5,700
Annual Growth	**26.0%**	**23.3%**	**—**	**22.7%**

2017 Year-End Financials

Debt ratio: 63.34%
Return on equity: 24.60%
Cash ($ mil.): 57
Current ratio: 1.21
Long-term debt ($ mil.): 1,028

No. of shares (mil.): 24
Dividends
Yield: 0.0%
Payout: 10.8%
Market value ($ mil.): 2,836

	STOCK PRICE ($) FY Close	P/E High/Low		PER SHARE ($) Earnings	Dividends	Book Value
12/17	113.59	13	8	9.75	1.06	43.38
12/16	96.83	14	9	7.72	0.95	36.22
12/15	106.67	18	12	6.91	0.76	31.59
12/14	86.69	18	10	5.26	0.61	25.66
12/13	69.42	18	9	4.05	0.49	20.65
Annual Growth	**13.1%**	—	—	**24.6%**	**21.3%**	**20.4%**

Live Nation Entertainment Inc

Live Nation Entertainment holds center stage as the world's largest ticket seller and promoter of live entertainment. The company significantly expanded its ticketing services with the purchase of Ticketmaster Entertainment in 2010. The firm owns or operates more than 220 venues in North America and Europe. Annually over 580 million people attend Live Nation events. Live Nation also owns House of Blues venues through HOB Entertainment and dozens of prestigious concert halls. In addition Live Nation owns a stake in more than 500 artists' music including albums tours and merchandise.

Operations

Live Nation's reportable segments are Concerts Ticketing and Sponsorship & Advertising. Its Concerts segment (over 75% of revenue) involves global promotion of live music events in its owned and operated venues and in rented third-party venues the operation and management of music venues and the production of music festivals across the world. The Ticketing segment (about 20%) is primarily an agency business that sells tickets for events on behalf of its clients and retains a convenience charge and order processing fee for its services. Its Sponsorship & Advertising segment (approximately 5%) employs a sales force that creates and maintains relationships with sponsors that allow businesses to reach customers through Live Nation's concert venue artist relationship and ticketing assets including advertising on its websites.

Geographic Reach

Live Nation owns operates or leases more than 220 venues located throughout the world. The company generates about 65% of revenue from domestic operations.

Sales and Marketing

Live Nation promotes its events and sells tickets through websites (www.livenation.com and www.ticketmaster.com). The company also sells tickets in numerous retail outlets and call centers and sold nearly 500 million tickets in 2017. Ticketmaster serves more than 12000 clients worldwide. The company spent $378.1 million $311.9 million and $275.6 million on advertising and promotional expenses for the years 2017 2016 and 2015 respectively. Ticketmaster and Live Nation have both suffered from the public's perception that the companies have virtual monopolies on major parts of the music industry.

Financial Performance

Live Nation's revenue has been growing consistently year-over-year. Its total revenue for fiscal 2017 was $10.3 billion up from $8.3 billion in fiscal 2016. The revenue spike marked the company's twelfth consecutive year of revenue growth and fiscal 2017 was Live Nation's highest revenue year ever.

Live Nation's Concerts segment was the largest contributor to its overall revenue growth with an increase of $1.6 billion compared to fical 2016 (a 25% increase without the impact of changes in foreign exchange rates). The higher revenue was partially due to additional arena shows in the US stadium events internationally and growth in Live Nation's theater and club business worldwide. Overall Concert attendance grew by nearly 15 million to nearly 86 million fans a record for the company and an increase of 21% over fiscal 2016.

Despite the revenue spike in fiscal 2017 Live Nation suffered a net loss of $6.02 million after claiming net income of $2.94 million in fiscal 2016. The company's slim profit margin is a result of its high cost of doing business.

Strategy

Mergers and Acquisitions

In 2017 Live Nation acquired United Concerts one of the world?s leading entertainment companies.

In 2017 Ticketmaster also acquired Ticketpro based in Halifax Nova Scotia Canada. Ticketpro is a leading provider of ticketing services with active operations in Belarus Bulgaria Canada Chile the Czech Republic Greece Hungary Malaysia Poland and the Slovak Republic. The acquisition offered Ticketmaster the opportunity to extend its international ticketing business activities into another key Central European market within the Czech Republic as well as complement the development of its existing business in neighboring Poland.

During 2017 Live Nation also acquired Cuffe & Taylor one of the UK?s fastest-growing promoters focused on festivals and promoting artists in novel and non-traditional outdoor venues. The acquisition will help Live Nation expand its overall presence across the UK regional markets.

HISTORY

Robert Sillerman began his career teaching advertisers how to reach young consumers. He started investing in radio and TV stations and founded SFX Broadcasting (named for a scrambling of his initials) in 1992. In early 1997 the firm entered the live entertainment field with the formation of SFX Concerts and the purchase of concert promoter Delsener/Slater.

When SFX Broadcasting agreed to be bought in 1997 by Capstar Broadcasting 87% controlled by investment firm Hicks Muse Tate & Furst (now HM Capital) SFX Entertainment was formed to house the live entertainment operations (it was spun off in 1998). In 1998 the company continued its rapid acquisition rate with the purchases of sports marketing and management team FAME New England concert promoter Don Law and national concert producer PACE Entertainment.

In 1999 the company bought concert promoter The Cellar Door Companies (which almost doubled SFX's size) sports marketing firm Integrated Sports International sporting event management company The Marquee Group sports talent agency Hendricks Management 50% of urban-music producer A.H. Enterprises and troubled theatrical producer Livent. SFX also made its first foray abroad through its purchase of Apollo Leisure a UK-based live entertainment firm. The company rolled all of its sports talent and marketing businesses into a new division SFX Sports Group that year.

In 2000 SFX jumped on the other side of the acquisition train when it was bought by radio station owner Clear Channel Communications for about $4 billion. Sillerman stepped down as chairman and CEO and was replaced by Clear Channel EVP Brian Becker. Later that year SFX acquired Philadelphia-based concert promoter and venue operator Electric Factory Concerts; Core Audience Entertainment Canada's second-largest concert promoter and events marketer; and the Cotter Group a North Carolina-based motorsports marketing agency.

In 2001 SFX acquired a majority interest in the International Hot Rod Association. It also bought professional golf talent agency Signature Sports Group. Later that year the company changed its name to Clear Channel Entertainment. It also continued expansion into Europe with the acquisition of Trident Agency and Milano Concerti music promotion businesses in Italy.

While operating as Clear Channel Entertainment Live Nation spent nearly $2 billion on acquisitions (Pace Entertainment Livent) almost single-handedly consolidating the live entertainment industry.

Before being spun off in December 2005 the company changed its name to CCE Spinco then Live Nation. Also that year Randall Mays became chairman and Michael Rapino replaced Becker as CEO. As part of the Clear Channel spinoff the company relocated from Houston to headquarters in tony Beverly Hills. It trimmed the fat by shutting down operating divisions such as museum exhibitions and music publishing (and laying off about 400 employees in the process) in order to focus on its core businesses of live music concerts venue management and website brand development.

In 2006 the company acquired rival HOB Entertainment for $354 million. Live Nation used the acquisition to expand its presence in the midsized venue business and fill in geographic gaps in its existing amphitheater network. As part of the deal Live Nation gained high-profile House of Blues-branded music venues such as San Francisco's Fillmore Auditorium Jones Beach in New York and London's Apollo Theatre and Wembley Arena. The company subsequently began re-branding many of its midsize clubs "Fillmore" after the San Francisco venue.

The company had in 2005 formed Delirium Concert LP a joint venture with Cirque du Soleil. The Delirium tour began in 2006. The following year Live Nation signed a $120 million deal with pop icon Madonna. Through its North American Music segment in 2007 Live Nation promoted or produced some 10000 live music events including tours for Van Halen Dave Matthews Band and Kenny Chesney. International Music operations for the year included Cirque De Soleil's Delirium as well as UK's Reading Festival . Also in 2007 the company produced global tours for legends such as The Police The Rolling Stones Genesis and The Who and presented some 5000 theatrical performances such as the UK touring production of Chicago through its Global Theater operations.

In 2008 the company divested itself of its North American theatrical assets. Later that year the company signed pacts with U2 and Jay-Z. Michael Cohl chairman and Live Nation Artists chief who spearheaded the deals later resigned over conflicts with CEO Rapino. Also in 2008 the company sold its motor sports operations. In early 2010 the company acquired Ticketmaster Entertainment and Live Nation changed its name to Live Nation Entertainment.

EXECUTIVES

President House Of Blues Entertainment, Ronald (Ron) Bension, age 63
Evp General Counsel And Secretary, Michael G. Rowles, age 53, $750,000 total compensation
Co-president North America Concerts, Mark Campana, age 60
Ceo And Director, Michael (Mike) Rapino, age 53, $2,300,000 total compensation
President Global Touring Tna International, Arthur Fogel, age 65
President And Coo, Joe Berchtold, age 53, $1,100,000 total compensation
President International And Emerging Markets, Alan Ridgeway, age 51, $730,025 total compensation
Cfo, Kathy Willard, age 52, $850,000 total compensation
President Media And Sponsorship, Russell Wallach, age 52
President Live Nation Europe - Concerts, John Reid, age 56
Evp Mergers And Acquisitions And Strategic Finance, John Hopmans, age 59
President Ticketmaster North America, Jared Smith, age 40
Co-president North America Concerts, Bob Roux, age 60
President Ticketmaster International, Mark Yovich, age 43
Cio, David Huckabay
President Production Film And Television, Heather Parry
Vice President Information Technology Ap, Alysia Piccioni
Svp And Ciso, Jonathan Chow
Senior Vice President Human Resources, Laura Morton-rowe
Svp, Jim Cheung
Vice President Of Marketing, Dave Niedbalski

Vice President Marketing Solutions, James Kane
Vice President Midwest Music, Dan Kemer
Vice President Programmatic And Product Innovation, Mike Finnegan
Vice President Of Business Development And Strategy, Christopher Sumner
Regional Vice President, Louis Giangola
Vice President Technology Optimization, Brent Eubanks
Vice President Strategy And Insights Media And Sponsorship, Amanda Fraga
Vice President Business Development, Patti Kim
Senior Vice President, Greg Gillin
Vice President, Harvey Cohen
Vice President Brand Strategist, Denise Quattrochi
Vice President Of Foundation Room House Of Blues, Victor Sutter
Vice President Product Management, Bob Ritter
Vice President Diversity And Inclusion, Elizabeth Morrison
Vice President Analytics And Optimization, Christine Chu
Vice President Engineering And Data Science, Wojciech Jawor
Vice President, Julie Jin
Senior Vice President Media And Sponsorship, Jon Landa
Chairman, Gregory B. (Greg) Maffei, age 57
Board Member, James Kahan
Auditors: Ernst & Young LLP

LOCATIONS

HQ: Live Nation Entertainment Inc
  9348 Civic Center Drive, Beverly Hills, CA 90210
Phone: 310 867-7000
Web: www.livenation.com; www.ticketmaster.com

2017 Sales

	$ mil.	% of total
Domestic operations	6,772	65
Foreign operation:		
UK operations	785	8
Other operations	2,779	27
Total	**10,337**	**100**

PRODUCTS/OPERATIONS

2017 Sales

	$ mil.	% of total
Concerts	7,892	76
Ticketing	2,143	21
Sponsorship & advertising	445	4
Other revenue	21	-
Eliminations	(164.6)	-
Total	**10,337**	**100**

COMPETITORS

Brillstein
CAA
Dodger Properties
Feld Entertainment
IMG
International Creative Management
Jujamcyn Theaters
MSG Networks
Nederlander Producing Company
Octagon
On Stage Entertainment
Palace Sports & Entertainment
Ryman
SMG Management
Shubert Organization
TBA Global
United Talent
Universal Music Group
Warner Music
WestwoodOne
William Morris Endeavor Entertainment

HISTORICAL FINANCIALS

Company Type: Public

Income Statement

FYE: December 31

	REVENUE ($ mil.)	NET INCOME ($ mil.)	NET PROFIT MARGIN	EMPLOYEES
12/17	10,337	(6)	—	8,800
12/16	8,354	2	0.0%	8,300
12/15	7,245	(32)	—	7,700
12/14	6,866	(90)	—	14,000
12/13	6,478	(43)	—	7,400
Annual Growth	**12.4%**	**—**		**4.4%**

2017 Year-End Financials

Debt ratio: 30.65%	No. of shares (mil.): 208
Return on equity: (-0.52%)	Dividends
Cash ($ mil.): 1,825	Yield: —
Current ratio: 0.88	Payout: —
Long-term debt ($ mil.): 1,952	Market value ($ mil.): 8,858

	STOCK PRICE ($) FY Close	P/E High/Low		PER SHARE ($) Earnings	Dividends	Book Value
12/17	42.57	— —		(0.48)	0.00	5.68
12/16	26.60	— —		(0.23)	0.00	5.52
12/15	24.57	— —		(0.33)	0.00	6.11
12/14	26.11	— —		(0.49)	0.00	6.45
12/13	19.76	— —		(0.22)	0.00	7.06
Annual Growth	**21.2%**	**— —**		**—**	**—**	**(5.3%)**

Live Oak Bancshares Inc

Auditors: Dixon Hughes Goodman LLP

LOCATIONS

HQ: Live Oak Bancshares Inc
  1741 Tiburon Drive, Wilmington, NC 28403
Phone: 910 790-5867
Web: www.liveoakbank.com

HISTORICAL FINANCIALS

Company Type: Public

Income Statement

FYE: December 31

	ASSETS ($ mil.)	NET INCOME ($ mil.)	INCOME AS % OF ASSETS	EMPLOYEES
12/17	2,758	100	3.6%	528
12/16	1,755	13	0.8%	425
12/15	1,052	20	2.0%	366
12/14	673	10	1.5%	263
12/13	430	28	6.5%	—
Annual Growth	**59.1%**	**37.6%**	**—**	**—**

2017 Year-End Financials

Debt ratio: 0.96%	No. of shares (mil.): 39
Return on equity: 30.46%	Dividends
Cash ($ mil.): 298	Yield: 0.0%
Current ratio: —	Payout: 3.7%
Long-term debt ($ mil.): —	Market value ($ mil.): 952

	STOCK PRICE ($) FY Close	P/E High/Low	PER SHARE ($) Earnings	Dividends	Book Value
12/17	23.85	9 7	2.65	0.10	10.95
12/16	18.50	50 30	0.39	0.07	6.51
12/15	14.20	31 20	0.65	0.02	5.84
Annual Growth	13.8%	—	42.1%	49.5%	17.0%

LIVE OAK BANKING COMPANY

EXECUTIVES

Ceo, Chip Mahan
Chb, James S Mahan III
Coo, Neil L Underwood
Cfo, Brett Caines
Pres, Scott Custer
Manager, Catie Laflamme
Associate, Kaelin Stone
Internal Medicine Practitioner, Shayla Long
Manager, Stephen Hayes
Loan Officer, Angus McDonald
Associate, Brandon Bolen

LOCATIONS

HQ: LIVE OAK BANKING COMPANY
1741 TIBURON DR, WILMINGTON, NC 284036244
Phone: 910 790-5867
Web: WWW.LIVEOAKBANK.COM

HISTORICAL FINANCIALS

Company Type: Private

Income Statement   FYE: December 31

	ASSETS ($ mil.)	NET INCOME ($ mil.)	INCOME AS % OF ASSETS	EMPLOYEES
12/17	2,666	114	4.3%	30
12/16	1,700	21	1.3%	—
12/15	1,008	22	2.2%	—
12/14	634	21	3.5%	—
Annual Growth	61.4%	73.3%	—	—

2017 Year-End Financials

Debt ratio: ——
Return on equity: 42.70%
Cash ($ mil.): 291
Current ratio: —
Long-term debt ($ mil.): —

Dividends
Yield: —
Payout: —
Market value ($ mil.): —

LKQ Corp

LKQ distributes replacement parts and components needed to repair passenger cars and trucks. It's one of the leading aftermarket parts suppliers in the US through subsidiary Keystone Automotive. LKQ also offers reconditioned remanufactured and refurbished parts including wheels bumpers mirrors and engines as well as recycled parts that are reclaimed from salvage vehicles. Customers include collision repair and mechanical repair shops. Additionally LKQ operates self-service retail yards that allow customers to come in search through and buy recycled auto parts. LKQ was formed in 1998.

Operations

LKQ operates through three reportable segments: North America (more than 50%) Europe (almost 35%) and Specialty (15%).

North America is composed of its wholesale operations which consist of aftermarket and salvage operations and self service retail operations.

Europe capitalizes on the large and fragmented aftermarket mechanical replacement parts market in Europe and also complements its existing operations in the UK and the Benelux region.

Specialty serves major markets in the US and Canada focusing on the following six product segments: truck and off-road; speed and performance; RV; towing; wheels tires and performance handling; and miscellaneous accessories.

Geographic Reach

Headquartered in Chicago LKQ operates through roughly 1340 facilities including 550 facilities in the US and 790 facilities in 20 other countries. The majority of LKQ?s operations are conducted in the US and its European operations are located in the UK the Netherlands Belgium France Sweden and Norway. The US is its largest market accounting for more than 60% of total revenue.

Sales and Marketing

LKQ sells its products to wholesale customers that include collision and mechanical repair shops and new and used car dealerships as well as to retail customers. Customers of self service yards are frequently do-it-yourself mechanics small independent repair shops auto rebuilders and resellers.

The company markets its products directly to customers through sales personnel e-commerce partners and distributors who in turn sell to customers. LKQ promotes through marketing programs which include: catalogs advertising sponsorships and promotional activities product level marketing and online initiatives.

Financial Performance

LKQ has achieved unprecedented growth over the years with revenues jumping 19% to peak at a record-setting $8.6 billion in 2016. The growth was fueled by a 21% spike in parts and services revenues. This was attributed to contributions from acquisitions and organic growth.

Along with its revenues net income grew 10% to reach $464 million in 2016 another company milestone. This was attributed to the higher revenues about $8 million it earned from discontinued operations (net of tax) and a more marginal loss from unconsolidated subsidiaries compared to the previous year.

Similarly cash flow from operating activities has increased the last few years jumping 20% to $635 million in 2016.This was the result of acquisition-related growth and organic growth.

Strategy

Key to the company's growth strategy are acquisitions. Indeed LKQ has completed more than 200 acquisitions in the US and abroad since its founding in 1998.

The company has also worked on its supply chain expanding its network of parts warehouses and dismantling plants in major metros and operating a distribution system that allows for order fulfillment from regional warehouses located across the US and Canada. It also is expanding its branch network in the UK.

In North America the company has expanded its network of parts warehouses and dismantling plants in major metropolitan areas. In Europe the company focuses on the development of existing branch networks in the UK and Benelux and also looks to add locations. The company has undertaken a major project to expand its distribution capabilities in Tamworth UK. The project is expected to be completed in 2018.

Mergers and Acquisitions

In one of its largest acquisitions to date LKQ paid $1.1 billion for Rhiag-Inter Auto Parts Italia S.p.A (Rhiag) a distributor of aftermarket spare parts for passenger cars and commercial vehicles in Italy Czech Republic Slovakia Switzerland Hungary Romania Ukraine Bulgaria Poland and Spain. The acquisition significantly expanded LKQ?s geographic presence in continental Europe by expanding its footprint by 10 countries.

In 2016 the company acquired 27% of Mekonomen AB for $181 million. Headquartered in Sweden Mekonomen is an independent car parts and service chain in the Nordic region of Europe offering a range of quality products including spare parts and accessories for cars and workshop services for consumers and businesses. The deal gave LKQ a strong brand and a diverse operating model for selling aftermarket automotive parts and accessories in Europe.

LKQ also in 2016 acquired Pittsburgh Glass Works (PGW) for $635 million. PGW is a global distributor and manufacturer of automotive glass products. With the acquisition the company entered into the sizable automotive glass market.

EXECUTIVES

Ceo And Managing Director European Operations, John S. Quinn, age 59, $565,000 total compensation
Svp Development, Walter P. Hanley, age 52, $400,000 total compensation
President And Ceo, Dominick P. (Nick) Zarcone, age 59, $1,000,000 total compensation
Svp And Cio, Ashley T. Brooks
Svp Operations Wholesale Parts Division, Justin L. Jude, age 41
Evp And Cfo, Varun Laroyia
Vp Finance And Controller, Michael Clark
National Account Manager, David Bowers
National Accounts Manager, Marty Coonan
Vp It, Chad Cowan
Senior Vice President, Bruce Morgan
Chairman, Joseph M. Holsten, age 65
Auditors: Deloitte & Touche LLP

LOCATIONS

HQ: LKQ Corp
500 West Madison Street, Suite 2800, Chicago, IL 60661
Phone: 312 621-1950
Web: www.lkqcorp.com

2016 Sales

	$ mil.	% of total
United States	5,226	61
United Kingdom	1,390	16
Other countries	1,966	23
Total	**8,584**	**100**

PRODUCTS/OPERATIONS

2016 Sales

By Segment	$ mil.	% of total
North America	4,471	52
Europe	2,920	34
Specialty	1,196	14
Eliminations	(4.8)	-
Total	**8,584**	**100**

2016 Sales

	$ mil.	% of total
Aftermarket other new and refurbished products	6,441	75
Recycled remanufactured and related products and services	1,703	20
Other	439	5
Total	**8,584**	**100**

Products & Services

Accessories
Fleet Service
Refinishing
Vehicle & Salvage Disposal
Warranty
Wheels

COMPETITORS

Cardone Industries	Halfords
Copart	Jasper Engines
Delphi Automotive Systems	Kirk's Automotive
	O'Reilly Automotive
Federal-Mogul	Titan International
Fred Jones Enterprises	U.S. Auto Parts
Genuine Parts	Valeo
Hahn Automotive	

HISTORICAL FINANCIALS

Company Type: Public

Income Statement   FYE: December 31

	REVENUE ($ mil.)	NET INCOME ($ mil.)	NET PROFIT MARGIN	EMPLOYEES
12/17	9,736	533	5.5%	43,000
12/16	8,584	463	5.4%	42,500
12/15	7,192	423	5.9%	31,100
12/14	6,740	381	5.7%	29,500
12/13	5,062	311	6.2%	23,800
Annual Growth	17.8%	14.4%	—	15.9%

2017 Year-End Financials

Debt ratio: 36.34%
Return on equity: 13.97%
Cash ($ mil.): 279
Current ratio: 2.89
Long-term debt ($ mil.): 3,277

No. of shares (mil.): 309
Dividends
  Yield: —
  Payout: —
Market value ($ mil.): 12,572

	STOCK PRICE ($) FY Close	P/E High/Low		PER SHARE ($) Earnings	Dividends	Book Value
12/17	40.67	24	16	1.71	0.00	13.58
12/16	30.65	24	16	1.50	0.00	11.19
12/15	29.63	23	17	1.38	0.00	10.19
12/14	28.12	26	20	1.25	0.00	8.97
12/13	32.90	33	19	1.02	0.00	7.81
Annual Growth	5.4%	—	—	13.8%	—	14.8%

Lockheed Martin Corp

EXECUTIVES

Chm, Patrick M Dewar
Pres*, Richard G Kirkland
V Pres*, Christopher J Gregoire
V Pres*, John M Ward
V Pres*, Kevin Darrenkamp
Prin*, Edward Whalen
General, Kreg Purcell
Software Engineer, James Herman
Manager of Information, Marlin Nielson
Manager, Marnetta Robinson
Security Manager, Walter Hinton
Auditors: Ernst & Young LLP

LOCATIONS

HQ: Lockheed Martin Corp
  6801 Rockledge Drive, Bethesda, MD 20817-1877
Phone: 301 897-6000
Web: www.lockheedmartin.com

HISTORICAL FINANCIALS

Company Type: Public

Income Statement   FYE: December 31

	REVENUE ($ mil.)	NET INCOME ($ mil.)	NET PROFIT MARGIN	EMPLOYEES
12/18	53,762	5,046	9.4%	105,000
12/17	51,048	2,002	3.9%	100,000
12/16	47,248	5,302	11.2%	97,000
12/15	46,132	3,605	7.8%	126,000
12/14	45,000	3,614	7.9%	112,000
Annual Growth	4.2%	8.7%	—	(1.6%)

2018 Year-End Financials

Debt ratio: 31.43%
Return on equity: 1,419.41%
Cash ($ mil.): 772
Current ratio: 1.12
Long-term debt ($ mil.): 12,604

No. of shares (mil.): 281
Dividends
  Yield: 3.1%
  Payout: 74.4%
Market value ($ mil.): 73,577

	STOCK PRICE ($) FY Close	P/E High/Low		PER SHARE ($) Earnings	Dividends	Book Value
12/18	261.84	20	14	17.59	8.20	4.96
12/17	321.05	46	36	6.89	7.46	(2.40)
12/16	249.94	15	12	17.49	6.77	5.23
12/15	217.15	19	16	11.46	6.15	10.22
12/14	192.57	17	13	11.21	5.49	10.83
Annual Growth	8.0%	—	—	11.9%	10.6%	(17.7%)

Loews Corp.

When it comes to diversification Loews definitely has the low-down. The holding company's main interest is insurance through publicly traded subsidiary CNA Financial which offers commercial property/casualty coverage. It also owns hotels in the US and Canada through its Loews Hotels subsidiary. The group's energy holdings include contract oil-drilling operator Diamond Offshore Drilling (which operates roughly 20 offshore oil rigs) and interstate natural gas transmission pipeline systems operator Boardwalk Pipeline. Loews is controlled and run by the Tisch family including co-chairmen and cousins Andrew and Jonathan.

HISTORY

In 1946 Larry Tisch who earned a business degree from New York University at age 18 dropped out of Harvard Law to run his parents' New Jersey resort. Younger brother Bob joined him in creating a new entity Tisch Hotels. The company bought two Atlantic City hotels in 1952 quickly making them profitable. Later Tisch purchased such illustrious hotels as the Mark Hopkins The Drake the Belmont Plaza and the Regency.

Moving beyond hotels the brothers bought money-losing companies with poor management. Discarding the management along with underperforming divisions they tightened operational control and eliminated such frills as fancy offices company planes and even memos.

In 1960 Tisch Hotels gained control of MGM's ailing Loew's Theaters to take advantage of their desirable city locations. The company then began demolishing more than 50 stately movie palaces and selling the land to developers. In 1968 the company bought Lorillard the oldest US tobacco company; it shed Lorillard's unprofitable pet food

and candy operations and reversed its slipping tobacco market share.

Taking the Loews name in 1971 the company bought CNA Financial in 1974. The Tisch method turned losses of more than $200 million to profits of more than $100 million the very next year. It bought Bulova Watch in 1979 and guided by Larry's son Andrew it gradually returned to profitability.

In the early 1980s Loews entered the energy business by investing in oil supertankers. The company sold its last movie theaters in 1985. Then in 1987 Loews helped CBS fend off a takeover attempt by Ted Turner and ended up with about 25% of the company. Larry became president of the broadcaster.

In 1989 Loews acquired Diamond M Offshore a Texas drilling company and with the acquisition of Odeco Drilling in 1992 the company amassed the world's largest fleet of offshore rigs. The next year Loews grouped its drilling interests as Diamond Offshore Drilling.

In 1994 CNA expanded its insurance empire buying The Continental Corp. The next year Loews sold its interest in CBS and the following year Diamond Offshore Drilling merged with Arethusa (Off-Shore) Limited.

As deft as the Tisch brothers had been in accumulating their riches Larry's bearish investment strategy (short-selling stocks) cost Loews in the late 1990s (more than $900 million alone during 1997's bull market). Larry and Bob retired as co-CEOs at the end of 1998; Larry's son James already president and COO became CEO.

That year Lorillard signed on to the 46-state tobacco lawsuit settlement; the first payment cost the company $325 million (payments continue until 2025). Facing a softened insurance market CNA sold unprofitable lines to focus on commercial insurance; in 1999 it transferred its auto and homeowners lines to Allstate (it continues writing and renewing these policies) and put its life and life reinsurance units up for sale in 2000. Also that year Lorillard was hit with $16 billion of a record-breaking $144 billion punitive damage award in a smokers' class-action suit in Florida. CNA Financial paid out over $450 million in 2001-02 for claims related to the attacks on the World Trade Center.

In 2004 the company continued to expand its natural resource offerings when its subsidiary Boardwalk Pipelines (formerly known as TGT Pipeline) acquired Gulf South Pipeline which operates natural gas pipeline and gathering systems in Texas Louisiana Mississippi Alabama and Florida including several major supply hubs. Loews had acquired gas pipeline operator Texas Gas Transmission in 2003. Texas Gas operates natural gas pipeline systems reaching from the Louisiana Gulf Coast and East Texas north through Louisiana Arkansas Mississippi Tennessee Kentucky Indiana and into Ohio and Illinois.

Tobacco had long been a staple in Loews' portfolio until the company kicked the habit. Prior to quitting the company kept its 62% ownership of Lorillard rolled up as Carolina Group and traded it as a tracking subsidiary. Lorillard which included the Kent Newport and True cigarette brands in the US accounted for more than 20% of Loews' revenues. However after a steady stream of tobacco-related litigation the company spun Lorillard off into an independent public company in 2008 eliminating the Carolina Group and exiting the industry. Additionally while accessories make the outfit in 2008 Loews slipped its Bulova subsidiary off of its wrist and handed it to competitor Citizen Watch for $250 million.

Larry Tisch died at the age of 80 in 2003. Chairman Bob Tisch died of cancer in late 2005. Tisch also was co-owner of the New York Giants of the National Football League.

In keeping with the Loews strategy of acquiring what can be turned around letting go of what can't and the wisdom to know the difference the company spent $4 billion to acquire oil and gas exploration operator HighMount Exploration & Production and disposed of its tobacco interests and Bulova subsidiary in 2008.

EXECUTIVES

Co-chairman Loews Corporation And Chairman And Ceo Loews Hotels, Jonathan M. Tisch, age 64, $975,000 total compensation

President And Ceo, James S. Tisch, age 66, $975,000 total compensation

Svp And Cfo, David B. Edelson, age 58, $975,000 total compensation

Svp And Chief Investment Officer, Richard W. Scott, age 64

Svp, Kenneth I. Siegel, age 61, $975,000 total compensation

Vp Information Technology, Herb E. Hofmann

Senior Vice President And Chief Business Officer Loews Hotels And Resorts, Constantine Dimas

Vp Corporate Development, Jonathan Koplovitz

Senior Vice President Food And Beverage, Mark Weiss

Executive Vice President Commercial Loews Hotels And Co. And Vice President Loews Corporation, Alex Tisch

Vice President Loews Cna Holdings Investments, Winifred Harrison

Senior Vice President Of Sales, David Wiener

Vice President Risk Management, Karen Beam

Senior Vice President, Marc Shapiro

Vice President Of Information Technology, Imelda Liddiad

Senior Vice President Corporate Development Boardwalk Pipeline, Jonathan Nathanson

Vice President Human Resources, Laura Cushing

National Sales Manager, Jay Smith

Vice President Corporate Development, Ben Tisch

Vice President Of Sales And Marketing, Christopher Cawley

Vice President Operations Loews Hotels Universal Orlando, David Bartek

Vice President Accounting And Assistant Corporate Controller, Tracy Bress

National Sales Manager, Cristina Godwin

National Sales Manager, Mike Westfield

National Sales Manager, Melanie Lee

National Sales Manager, Jey Dutertre

Board Member, Herbert Hofmann

Co-chairman, Andrew H. Tisch, age 69

Treasurer, Andrew Stegen

Auditors: DELOITTE & TOUCHE LLP

LOCATIONS

HQ: Loews Corp.
667 Madison Avenue, New York, NY 10065-8087
Phone: 212 521-2000
Web: www.loews.com

PRODUCTS/OPERATIONS

2017 Sales

	% of total
Insurance premiums	51
Net investment income	16
Contract drilling revenues	11
Investment gains	
Other	22
Total	**100**

2017 Sales by Segment

	$ mil.	% of total
CNA Financial	9,583	70
Diamond Offshore	1,500	11
Boardwalk Pipeline	1,325	10
Loews Hotels	682	5
Corporate & Other	645	4
Total	**13,735**	**100**

Selected Subsidiaries

Boardwalk Pipeline Partners LP (51%)
CNA Financial Corporation (89%)
Diamond Offshore Drilling Inc. (53%)
Loews Hotels Holding Corporation (100%)

COMPETITORS

AIG	Noble
American Financial Group	Shaner Hotel Group
Berkshire Hathaway	Statoil
Cincinnati Financial	The Hartford
Menasha	Travelers Companies
	W. R. Berkley

HISTORICAL FINANCIALS

Company Type: Public

Income Statement
FYE: December 31

	ASSETS ($ mil.)	NET INCOME ($ mil.)	INCOME AS % OF ASSETS	EMPLOYEES
12/17	79,586	1,164	1.5%	18,100
12/16	76,594	654	0.9%	15,800
12/15	76,029	260	0.3%	16,700
12/14	78,367	591	0.8%	17,510
12/13	79,939	595	0.7%	18,175
Annual Growth	(0.1%)	18.3%	—	(0.1%)

2017 Year-End Financials

Debt ratio: 14.14%
Return on equity: 6.23%
Cash ($ mil.): 472
Current ratio: —
Long-term debt ($ mil.): —

No. of shares (mil.): 332
Dividends
 Yield: 0.0%
 Payout: 7.2%
Market value ($ mil.): 16,614

	STOCK PRICE ($) FY Close	P/E High/Low		PER SHARE ($) Earnings	Dividends	Book Value
12/17	50.03	15	13	3.45	0.25	57.83
12/16	46.83	25	18	1.93	0.25	53.96
12/15	38.40	59	49	0.72	0.25	51.67
12/14	42.02	31	25	1.55	0.25	51.70
12/13	48.24	32	27	1.53	0.25	50.28
Annual Growth	0.9%	—	—	22.5%	(0.0%)	3.6%

Lowe's Companies Inc

Lowe's Companies has built a strong business out of lumber cement power tools and other merchandise. The company is the nation's #2 home improvement chain (after The Home Depot) with some 2150 mostly US-based locations. Its stores offer nearly 40000 products for repair and improvement projects (such as lumber paint plumbing and electrical supplies and tools) gardening and outdoor living and home furnishing and decorating. Lowe's is also one of the country's leading retailers of home appliances. It targets both the professional and consumer markets with national brand-name merchandise as well as its own private labels (Kobalt Blue Hawk Garden Treasures). The company only operates in North America with the vast majority of sales generated in the US.

HISTORY

Lowe's Companies was founded in 1921 as Mr. L. S. Lowe's North Wilkesboro Hardware in North Wilkesboro North Carolina. A family operation by 1945 Mr. Lowe's store (which also sold groceries snuff and harnesses) was run by his son Jim and his son-in-law H. Carl Buchan. Buchan bought

Lowe's share of the company in 1956 and incorporated as Lowe's North Wilkesboro Hardware; he wanted Lowe's as part of the company name because he liked the slogan "Lowe's Low Prices." The chain expanded from North Carolina into Tennessee Virginia and West Virginia. By 1960 Buchan had 15 stores and sales of $31 million — up $4 million from a decade before.

Buchan planned to create a profit-sharing plan for Lowe's employees but in 1960 he died of a heart attack at age 44. In 1961 Lowe's management and the executors of Buchan's estate established the Lowe's Employees Profit Sharing and Trust which bought Buchan's 89% of the company (later renamed Lowe's Companies). That year they financed the transaction through a public offering which diluted the employees' stock. Lowe's was listed on the NYSE in 1979.

Robert Strickland who had joined the company in 1957 became chairman in 1978. Revenues increased from $170 million in 1971 to more than $900 million with a net income of $25 million in 1979. Traditionally the majority of Lowe's business was in sales to professional homebuilders but in 1980 housing starts fell and company profits dropped. Concurrently The Home Depot introduced its low-price warehouse concept. Instead of building warehouse stores of its own Strickland changed the stores' layouts and by 1982 had redesigned half of the 229 stores to be more oriented toward do-it-yourself (DIY) consumers. The new designs featured softer lighting and displays of entire room layouts to appeal to women who made up over half of all DIY customers. In 1982 Lowe's made more than half of its sales to consumers for the first time in its history.

Although Lowe's had more than 300 stores by 1988 its outlets were only about 20000 sq. ft. (one-fifth the size of Home Depot's warehouse stores). By 1989 Lowe's which had continued to target contractors as well as DIYers was overtaken by Home Depot as the US's #1 home retail chain.

Since 1989 the company has focused on building larger stores taking a charge of $71 million in 1991 to phase out smaller stores and build warehouse outlets. In 1993 Lowe's opened 57 large stores (half were replacements for existing stores) almost doubling its total floor space.

The retailer opened 29 new stores in 1995. During 1996 Lowe's added a net of 37 stores and in 1997 it opened 42 stores in new markets. Also that year president and CEO Leonard Herring retired and was replaced by former COO Robert Tillman who also took the post of chairman when Strickland stepped down in 1998.

Also in 1998 the company entered a joint venture to sell an exclusive line of Kobalt-brand professional mechanics' tools produced by Snap-on and to better serve commercial customers began allowing them to special order items not stocked in stores. In addition Lowe's announced it would spend $1.5 billion over the next several years on a 100-store push into the western US. Lowe's westward expansion was fueled when it purchased Washington-based 38-store Eagle Hardware & Garden in 1999 in a stock swap deal worth $1.3 billion. The company gradually converted the Eagle stores into Lowe's.

In 2001 the company earmarked $2.4 billion of its $2.7 billion capital budget for store expansions and new distribution centers.

Robert Niblock was promoted from CFO to president in March 2003. Lowe's sold its some 30 outlets operatin

EXECUTIVES

Chairman President And Ceo, Robert A. Niblock, age 55, $1,300,000 total compensation

Cfo, Marshall A. Croom, age 57

President Orchard Supply Hardware, Lara L. Lee
Chief Supply Chain Officer, Brent G. Kirby
Chief Development Officer And President International, Richard D. Maltsbarger, age 42
Chief Customer Officer, Michael P. McDermott
Cio, Paul D. Ramsay, age 53
Managing Director Loweâ's India, James A. Brandt
President And Managing Director Loweâ's Mexico, Juan L. Pier Castell
President Atgstores.com, Michelle M. Newbery
President And Ceo Loweâ's Canada, Sylvain PrudA'homme
Svp Corporate Finance And Treasurer, Tiffany Mason
Svp Services, Kevin Measel
Senior Vice President Pro Sales, Michael Tummillo
Vice President Of Client Services, Marian Craig
Senior Vice President, Belinda Rumple
Regional Vice President Distribution, Calvin Adams
Vice President Merchandising Home Environment, Angie Shore
Vice President Vendor Service Management, Ron Lutz
Senior Vice President Store Information Technology, Robert F Wagner
Vice President Real Estate Construction And Store Design Canada, Jeff Boyd
Vice President Corporate Communication, Tracey Ahearn
Vp Quality Assurance, Joseph Boley
Vice President And Assistant General Counsel, Tom Maddox
Vice President Transportation, Rick Gabrielson
Vice President Of Operations, Jeffrey Blocker
Vice President Store Operations, Jeff Sain
Merchandising Vice President, Revis Felts
Board Member, Shannon Efird
Secretary Treasurer, Arlene Holland
Board Member, Robert Johnson
Auditors: Deloitte & Touche LLP

LOCATIONS

HQ: Lowe's Companies Inc
1000 Lowe's Blvd., Mooresville, NC 28117
Phone: 704 758-1000
Web: www.lowes.com

2017 Stores

	No.
US	1,839
Canada	303
Mexico	10
Total	**2,152**

2017 Sales

	% of total
US	92
Other	8
Total	**100**

PRODUCTS/OPERATIONS

2017 Sales

	$ mil.	% of total
Lumber & Building Materials	9,508	14
Appliances	7,696	11
Seasonal & Outdoor Living	7,165	10
Tools & Hardware	6,713	10
Fashion Fixtures	6,429	9
Rough Plumbing & Electrical	6,149	9
Lawn & Garden	5,251	8
Paint	5,321	8
Millwork	5,308	8
Flooring	4,363	6
Kitchens	3,644	5
Other	1,072	2
Total	**68,619**	**100**

Selected Product Categories
Appliances
Fashion Fixtures

Flooring
Home Fashions
Kitchens
Lawn & Garden
Lumber & Building Materials
Millwork
Outdoor Power Equipment
Paint
Rough Plumbing & Electrical
Seasonal Living
Tools & Hardware

Selected Services
Extended Protection Plans and Repair Services
Installed Sales

Selected Proprietary Brands
allen+roth
Aquasource
Garden Treasures
Harbor Breeze
Kobalt
Portfolio
Reliabilt
Top Choice
Utilitech

COMPETITORS

84 Lumber	Menard
Ace Hardware	Northern Tool
Amazon.com	Overstock.com
Beacon Roofing	Sears
Best Buy	Sears Hometown
Builders FirstSource	SiteOne
Conn's	Sutherland Lumber
Do it Best	Target Corporation
HD Supply	Tractor Supply
Home Depot	True Value
Lumber Liquidators	Wal-Mart
McCoy Corp.	Wayfair

HISTORICAL FINANCIALS
Company Type: Public

Income Statement				FYE: February 2
	REVENUE ($ mil.)	NET INCOME ($ mil.)	NET PROFIT MARGIN	EMPLOYEES
02/18	68,619	3,447	5.0%	310,000
02/17*	65,017	3,093	4.8%	290,000
01/16	59,074	2,546	4.3%	270,000
01/15	56,223	2,698	4.8%	266,000
01/14	53,417	2,286	4.3%	262,000
Annual Growth	**6.5%**	**10.8%**	**—**	**4.3%**

*Fiscal year change

2018 Year-End Financials
Debt ratio: 48.16%
Return on equity: 56.17%
Cash ($ mil.): 588
Current ratio: 1.06
Long-term debt ($ mil.): 15,564
No. of shares (mil.): 830
Dividends
Yield: 1.5%
Payout: 38.6%
Market value ($ mil.): 84,245

	STOCK PRICE ($) FY Close	P/E High/Low		PER SHARE ($) Earnings	Dividends	Book Value
02/18	101.50	26	18	4.09	1.58	7.08
02/17*	73.29	24	18	3.47	1.33	7.43
01/16	71.66	28	24	2.73	1.07	8.41
01/15	67.76	26	16	2.71	0.87	10.38
01/14	46.29	24	17	2.14	0.70	11.51
Annual Growth	**21.7%**	**—**	**—**	**17.6%**	**22.6%**	**(11.4%)**

*Fiscal year change

Luther Burbank Corp

Auditors: Crowe Horwath LLP

LOCATIONS

HQ: Luther Burbank Corp
520 Third Street, Fourth Floor, Santa Rosa, CA 95401
Phone: 844 446-8201
Web: www.lutherburbanksavings.com

HISTORICAL FINANCIALS
Company Type: Public

Income Statement				FYE: December 31
	ASSETS ($ mil.)	NET INCOME ($ mil.)	INCOME AS % OF ASSETS	EMPLOYEES
12/17	5,704	69	1.2%	266
12/16	5,064	52	1.0%	274
12/15	4,362	35	0.8%	—
Annual Growth	**14.3%**	**40.0%**	**—**	**—**

2017 Year-End Financials
Debt ratio: 2.74%
Return on equity: 14.54%
Cash ($ mil.): 75
Current ratio: —
Long-term debt ($ mil.): —
No. of shares (mil.): 56
Dividends
Yield: 0.1%
Payout: 97.5%
Market value ($ mil.): 679

	STOCK PRICE ($) FY Close	P/E High/Low		PER SHARE ($) Earnings	Dividends	Book Value
12/17	12.04	8	7	1.62	1.58	9.74
12/16	0.00	—	—	1.24	0.40	9.63
12/15	0.00	—	—	0.84	0.28	8.84
Annual Growth	**—**	**—**	**—**	**30.9%**	**137.5%**	**5.0%**

M & T Bank Corp

M&T Bank Corporation is making a splash in the mid-Atlantic region. It is the holding company of M&T Bank which offers deposit loan trust investment brokerage and insurance services to more than two million individuals and small- and mid-sized businesses. With about $123 billion in total assets and $95.5 billion in deposits the bank operates more than 775 branches and 1800 ATMs in New York Pennsylvania and other eastern states and Washington DC in addition to Canada and the Cayman Islands. Its residential mortgage origination unit spans more than a dozen states in the South and West. The firm also manages a proprietary line of mutual funds the Wilmington Funds.

Operations

M&T Bank comprises two wholly-owned bank subsidiaries: M&T Bank and Wilmington Trust N.A. (M&T Bank represents 99% of the company's consolidated assets.) M&T Bank operates through six reportable segments: Retail Banking Commercial Banking Commercial Real Estate Residential Mortgage Banking Business Banking and Discretionary Portfolio.

The Retail Banking segment which generates more than 25% of the bank's total revenue offers a variety of services to consumers through banking offices ATMs telephone banking and Internet banking.

The Commercial Banking segment brings in about 20% of revenue and offers a variety of credit products and banking services to middle-market and large commercial customers primarily within the markets it already serves.

M&T Bank's Commercial Real Estate segment generates another 15% of revenue and provides credit services which are secured by several types of multifamily residential and commercial real estate and deposit services to its customers.

Its Residential Mortgage Banking unit makes up nearly 10% of revenue and originates and services residential mortgage loans for consumers and sells substantially all of the loans in the secondary market to investors or to the Discretionary Portfolio segment.

The Business Banking segment brings in another nearly 10% of revenue and provides deposit lending cash management and other financial services to small businesses and professionals through its banking office network and other delivery channels including business banking centers telephone banking online banking and ATMs. The Discretionary Portfolio segment focuses on securities residential mortgage loans and other assets; short-term and long-term borrowed funds; brokered certificates of deposit and interest rate swap agreements; and Cayman Islands branch deposits. The segment also provides customers with foreign exchange services.

Geographic Reach

Buffalo-based M&T Bank operates in New York Pennsylvania Maryland Delaware New Jersey Connecticut Virginia West Virginia and the District of Columbia. It also boasts a full-service commercial banking office in Ontario Canada and an office in George Town Cayman Islands. Its regional headquarters is in Albany.

Sales and Marketing

M&T Bank caters to customers through multiple channels such as its business banking centers telephone banking online banking and ATMs. It serves individuals and small- and mid-sized business customers.

Financial Performance

M&T Bank's annual revenues and profits have been trending higher over the past few years mostly thanks to growing loan business stemming largely from bank acquisitions (including its large acquisition of Hudson City Bank).

Revenue climbed 14% to $5.7 billion in fiscal 2016 with growth concentrated in interest income which grew $727 million due to the first full year contribution of the Hudson City acquisition. Other income was unchanged from 2015.

Net income climbed 22% to $1.3 billion due to the absence from the books of acquisition expenses incurred in 2015.

Cash from operations fell 32% to $1.2 billion due to changes in provision for deferred income taxes and a net change in loans originated for sale offset by higher net income.

Strategy

M&T Bank's strategy is to achieve dominance in its relatively small geographic market. It does this through the acquisition of smaller rivals that has the dual effect of taking out competitors while putting off prospective market entrants by its stranglehold over the local market.

The biggest recent acquisition was of Hudson City a venerable New York-area bank that it acquired in 2015 after a long-running saga with regulators. It took three years before regulators were satisfied with M&T's efforts to improve its anti-money-laundering processes costing the company hundreds of millions of dollars. Hudson City had 725 branches.

While the regulator-imposed block on acquisitions was in place the company turned its efforts to increasing its advertising particularly in Western New York.

Mergers and Acquisitions

M&T Bank has historically purchased smaller banks to expand its reach or strengthen its presence in existing markets.

In November 2015 the bank completed the acquisition of New Jersey's Hudson City Bancorp for $3.7 billion after originally announcing its intentions to buy the bank back in August 2012. The Hudson City acquisition added some $19 billion in new loans and bring in branches in the New York City metropolitan area while greatly expanding M&T Bank's presence in New Jersey.

Company Background

M&T Bank traces its roots to the founding of Manufacturers and Traders Bank in Buffalo New York. M&T Bank reorganized under a bank holding company in 1969 called First Empire State Corp. The name was changed in 1998 to M&T Bank Corporation.

EXECUTIVES

Group Vice President Commercial Equipment Finance, Mohannad Jishi

Evp Wealth And Institutional Services Division M&t Bank Corp And M&t Bank, William J. (Bill) Farrell, age 60

Evp M&t Bank Corporation And Evp And Co-head Commercial Banking M&t Bank, Brian E. Hickey, age 66, $299,231 total compensation

Evp M&t Bank Corporation And Vice Chairman And Evp M&t Bank, Kevin J. Pearson, age 57, $725,000 total compensation

Evp And Chief Credit Officer M&t Bank Corporation And M&t Bank, Robert J. Bojdak, age 63

Evp And Cio M&t Bank Corporation And M&t Bank, Michele D. Trolli, age 57

Chairman And Ceo M&t Bank Corporation And M&t Bank, René F. Jones, age 54, $725,000 total compensation

President Coo And Director M&t Bank Corporation And M&t Bank, Richard S. Gold, age 58, $725,000 total compensation

Evp And Treasurer M&t Bank Corporation And M&t Bank, D. Scott N. Warman, age 52

Evp Retail Banking Division M&t Bank Corporation And M&t Bank, Darren J. King, age 48, $600,000 total compensation

Evp And Area Executive M&t Bank Corporation And M&t Bank, Gino A. Martocci, age 52

Evp Human Resources M&t Bank Corp And M&t Bank, Janet M. Coletti, age 54

Evp M&t Bank Corporation And Evp Wilmington Trust Wealth Management M&t Bank, Doris P. Meister, age 62

Evp Retail And Business Banking M&t Bank, Neil J. Hosty

Evp M&t Bank Corporation And Evp Mortgage And Customer Asset Management M&t Bank, Michael J. Todaro, age 56

Regional President Western New York And President M&t Charitable Foundation, Shelley Drake

Vice President Technology Infrastructure, Christa Daigler

Group Vice President Financial Crimes Management, Dennis Krezmien

Vice President, Jim DiStefano

Vice President Mortgage Secondary Marketing Consumer Mortgages, Tom Esposito

Assistant Vice President And Performance Test Team Leader, Paula Henderson

Assistant Vice President Technology Infrastructure Operations, Zana Vernon

Assistant Vice President Operations, Katie Schultz

Vice President, Maureen Stevens

Vice President Global Sourcing, Patti Haan

Assistant Vice President Branch Manager, Linda Jones

Assistant Vice President Senior Software Engineering, Ashish Vikram

Vice President Human Resources Business Partner, Amy Walker

Vice President Trust Risk Manager, Dawn Snelling

Vice President Human Resources Business Partner Mortgage And Consumer Lending, Donna Harlacher

Assistant Vice President Talent Acquisition Senior Recruiter, Roni Thomas

Vice President, Lynn Buccilli

Assistant Vice President Relationship Manager, Sam Higgins

Vice President Systems Manager Central Technology, Diane Gagat

Vice President Commercial Real Estate, Tom Daly

Vice President, Dee Kakar

Vp Commerical Products Analytics, Rob Elnicky

Vice President Accounting Policy, Timothy Cahlstadt

Vice President Business Banking Relationship Manager, Janel Giambrone

Assistant Vice President Internal Audit, David Keenan

Assistant Vice President Branch Manager, Lauren Perrone

Vice President Commercial Branch Manager, Romaine Johnson

Vice President Construction, Jean Sortino

Vice President Of Real Estate, Tim Lascko

Vice President Of Operations, Julie Root

Vice President Administrative, Denise Hoffman-Day

Assistant Vice President Branch Sales Manager, Mary Leager

Group Vice President, Brian Walter

Group Vp, Kelley Attig

Vice President, Leslie Wallace

Group Vice President For Residential Lending, Nick Buscaglia

Vice President Of Corporate Communications, Chet Bridger

Senior Vice President And Treasurer, D Scott N Warman

Vice President Business Banking Relationship Manager, Austin Pearre

Vice President And Assistant Secretary, Marianne Roche

Group Vp, Clifford Johnson

Group Vp And Corporate Secretary, Marie King

Vice President Of Information Technology Project Management, David Lee

Group Vp And Assistant Secretary, Randall Krolewicz

Vice President Consumer Risk Management, Scott Warman

Vice President Corporate Communications, Philip Hosmer

Vice President Portfolio Manager, Courtney Herbert

Vice President, John Lewis

Assistant Vice President Manager Information Systems, Steven McCormack

Vice President Information Security And Access Management, Joan Sherwood-Wetherwax

Vice President, Eric Goodwin

Vice President Business And Retail Web Banking Central Technology, Muhammad Akhtar

Vice President Retail Banking, Joseph Imbriale

Vice President, Jim Eriksen

Vice President, Jerry Laspisa

Vice President, Steven Wendelboe

Vice President Human Resources And Finance Business Systems, Terica Phillips-Gadley

Vice Chairman, Robert T. (Bob) Brady, age 77

Board Member, Herbert Washington

Board Member, Denis Salamone

Board Member, Richard Grossi

Abm, Robyn Cargill

Auditors: PricewaterhouseCoopers LLP

LOCATIONS

HQ: M & T Bank Corp
One M & T Plaza, Buffalo, NY 14203
Phone: 716 635-4000
Web: www.mtb.com

PRODUCTS/OPERATIONS

Selected Subsidiaries
M&T Life Insurance Company
M&T Insurance Agency Inc
M&T Mortgage Reinsurance Company Inc.
M&T Real Estate Trust
M&T Realty Capital Corporation
M&T Securities Inc.
Wilmington Trust Company
Wilmington Trust Investment Advisors Inc.
Wilmington Funds Management Corporation
Wilmington Trust Investment Management LLC

2016 Sales

	$mil.
% of total	
Interest income	
Loans and leasesincluding fees	61
Investment Securities	6
Deposits at banks	1
Others	0
Non interest income	
Trust income	8
Service charges on deposit accounts	7
Mortgage banking revenue	7
Brokerage services income	1
Others	9
Total	**100**

2016 Sales

	% of total
Retail Banking	26
Commercial Banking	20
Commercial Real Estate	15
Business Banking	9
Residential Mortgage	8
Discretionary Portfolio	7
All others	15
Total	**100**

COMPETITORS

Citigroup	KeyCorp
Citizens Financial Group	Northwest Bancshares
Fulton Financial	PNC Financial
HSBC USA	Sovereign Bank
JPMorgan Chase	SunTrust
	TriState Capital

HISTORICAL FINANCIALS

Company Type: Public

Income Statement — FYE: December 31

	ASSETS ($ mil.)	NET INCOME ($ mil.)	INCOME AS % OF ASSETS	EMPLOYEES
12/17	118,593	1,408	1.2%	16,794
12/16	123,449	1,315	1.1%	16,973
12/15	122,787	1,079	0.9%	17,476
12/14	96,685	1,066	1.1%	15,782
12/13	85,162	1,138	1.3%	15,893
Annual Growth	8.6%	5.5%	—	1.4%

2017 Year-End Financials

Debt ratio: 6.38%
Return on equity: 8.60%
Cash ($ mil.): 6,632
Current ratio: —
Long-term debt ($ mil.): —

No. of shares (mil.): 150
Dividends
  Yield: 0.0%
  Payout: 34.4%
Market value ($ mil.): 25,663

	STOCK PRICE ($) FY Close	P/E High/Low	PER SHARE ($) Earnings	Dividends	Book Value
12/17	170.99	20 16	8.70	3.00	108.28
12/16	156.43	20 13	7.78	2.80	105.56
12/15	121.18	18 16	7.18	3.50	101.36
12/14	125.62	17 15	7.42	2.80	93.23
12/13	116.42	14 12	8.20	2.80	86.62
Annual Growth	10.1%	— —	1.5%	1.7%	5.7%

Macatawa Bank Corp.

Macatawa Bank Corporation is the holding company for Macatawa Bank. Since its 1997 founding the company has grown into a network of more than 25 branches serving western Michigan's Allegan Kent and Ottawa counties. The bank provides standard services including checking and savings accounts CDs safe deposit boxes and ATM cards. It also offers investment services and products through an agreement with a third-party provider. With deposit funds the bank primarily originates commercial and industrial loans and mortgages which account for nearly 75% of its loan book. Macatawa Bank also originates residential mortgages and consumer loans.

Operations
The bank carries total assets of $1.58 billion total loans of $1.12 billion and total deposits of $1.31 billion.

Through its Infinex affiliate the bank provides various brokerage services (including discount brokerage) personal financial planning and consultation regarding mutual funds.

The firm's Trust Department manages assets of approximately $648 million and offers retirement plan and personal trust services. Its personal trust services include financial planning investment management services trust and estate administration and custodial services.

Geographic Reach
Macatawa Bank operates more than 25 branches along with a lending and operation service facility in its primary market in western Michigan which includes the counties of Ottawa Kent and northern Allegan.

Sales and Marketing
Macatawa Bank targets small businesses mission-driven (non-profit) organizations builders manufacturers and service industry companies. Some of its clients include associations businesses churches financial institutions government authorities individuals and non-profit organizations.

Financial Performance
Macatawa's revenue has been declining ever since its peak in 2007. Revenue in fiscal 2014 fell by 2% to $63 million as the bank collected lower interest margins on its commercial residential and consumer loan portfolios amidst customer refinancing in the low interest-rate environment. The bank also generated less income from its short-term investments which hindered top line growth further.

Despite falling revenue the bank enjoyed its highest profit since 2007 as net income jumped by 10% to $10.47 million in 2014. This was thanks to a combination of lower interest expense on deposits and an improving real estate market which led to fewer losses from non-performing assets and fewer provisions for credit losses as real estate values improved.

Operations provided $16.62 million or 2% more cash than in 2013 thanks to higher earnings and because the bank wrote off more in non-cash accrued expenses and other liabilities.

EXECUTIVES

Vice President, Jason Coney
Vice President Commercial Real Estate, Andrew Meelberg
Vice President Treasury Management Sales, Kristin Timmer
Vice President, Fred Lake
Vice President Retail Banking, Krista Geyer
Vice President Wealth Advisor, John Simonds
Vice President Team Lead Retail Banking Grand Rapids, Sandy Siedlecki
Commercial Banker Vice President, Mike Vanommen
Special Asset Group Officer Vice President, Jennifer Kreuger
Auditors: BDO USA, LLP

LOCATIONS

HQ: Macatawa Bank Corp.
10753 Macatawa Drive, Holland, MI 49424
Phone: 616 820-1444
Web: www.macatawabank.com

PRODUCTS/OPERATIONS

2014 Sales

	$ mil.	% of total
Interest		
Loans including fees	42	67
Securities	3	5
Other	0	2
Noninterest		
ATM and debit card fees	4	8
Service charges & fees	4	7
Trust fees	2	4
Gain on sales of loans	2	3
Other	2	4
Total	**63**	**100**

COMPETITORS

Comerica	Huntington Bancshares
Fifth Third	PNC Financial
Flagstar Bancorp	

HISTORICAL FINANCIALS

Company Type: Public

Income Statement — FYE: December 31

	ASSETS ($ mil.)	NET INCOME ($ mil.)	INCOME AS % OF ASSETS	EMPLOYEES
12/17	1,890	16	0.9%	368
12/16	1,741	15	0.9%	374
12/15	1,729	12	0.7%	385
12/14	1,583	10	0.7%	389
12/13	1,517	9	0.6%	395
Annual Growth	5.6%	14.3%	—	(1.8%)

2017 Year-End Financials

Debt ratio: 2.18%
Return on equity: 9.72%
Cash ($ mil.): 161
Current ratio: —
Long-term debt ($ mil.): —

No. of shares (mil.): 33
Dividends
  Yield: 0.0%
  Payout: 37.5%
Market value ($ mil.): 340

	STOCK PRICE ($) FY Close	P/E High/Low	PER SHARE ($) Earnings	Dividends	Book Value
12/17	10.00	22 19	0.48	0.18	5.09
12/16	10.41	22 12	0.47	0.12	4.78
12/15	6.05	16 13	0.38	0.11	4.48
12/14	5.44	18 15	0.31	0.08	4.21
12/13	5.00	— —	(0.29)	0.00	3.92
Annual Growth	18.9%	—	—	—	6.8%

Macy's Inc

Auditors: KPMG LLP

LOCATIONS

HQ: Macy's Inc
151 West 34th Street, New York, NY 10001
Phone: 212 494-1602 **Fax:** 212 494-1838
Web: www.macys.com

HISTORICAL FINANCIALS

Company Type: Public

Income Statement FYE: February 3

	REVENUE ($ mil.)	NET INCOME ($ mil.)	NET PROFIT MARGIN	EMPLOYEES
02/18*	24,837	1,547	6.2%	130,000
01/17	25,778	619	2.4%	148,300
01/16	27,079	1,072	4.0%	157,900
01/15	28,105	1,526	5.4%	166,900
02/14	27,931	1,486	5.3%	172,500
Annual Growth	(2.9%)	1.0%	—	(6.8%)

*Fiscal year change

2018 Year-End Financials

Debt ratio: 30.35%
Return on equity: 30.45%
Cash ($ mil.): 1,455
Current ratio: 1.47
Long-term debt ($ mil.): 5,861
No. of shares (mil.): 304
Dividends
Yield: 0.0%
Payout: 29.9%
Market value ($ mil.): 7,586

	STOCK PRICE ($) FY Close	P/E High/Low	PER SHARE ($) Earnings	Dividends	Book Value
02/18*	24.89	7 3	5.04	1.51	18.61
01/17	29.11	22 14	1.99	1.49	14.22
01/16	40.41	22 11	3.22	1.39	13.70
01/15	63.88	16 12	4.22	1.19	15.79
02/14	53.20	14 10	3.86	0.95	17.12
Annual Growth	(17.3%)	— —	6.9%	12.3%	2.1%

*Fiscal year change

Magellan Health Inc.

Magellan Health has charted its course to become one of the largest managed behavioral health care companies in the nation. The company manages mental health plan employee assistance and work/life programs through its nationwide third-party provider network. Magellan also provides radiology benefits management specialty pharmaceutical management and Medicaid management. Overall it serves some 68 million members through contracts with federal and local government agencies insurance companies and employers. Magellan's Pharmacy Management segment's services include administration billing claims handling technology programs and coordination of care.

Operations

Magellan operates through two primary business segments: Healthcare (which brings in some 55% of revenue) and Pharmacy Management (some 45% of revenue).

The Healthcare segment provides managed behavioral health care services and employee assistance program (EAP) services as well as managing other specialty areas including diagnostic imaging and musculoskeletal health. It also provides the integrated management of physical behavioral and pharmaceutical health care for special populations through Magellan Complete Care (MCC).

Magellan's Pharmacy Management segment offers products and services to help its clients manage pharmacy benefit programs. It provides pharmacy benefit management (PBM) services pharmacy benefit administration (PBA) for Medicaid and other government-sponsored programs medical pharmacy management and programs to integrate management of specialty drugs across medical and pharmacy benefits in complex cases.

Geographic Reach

Magellan Health operates about 60 offices in nearly 30 states and Washington DC.

Sales and Marketing

Magellan's customers include health plans and employer groups as well as government and military agencies in some 30 states and Washington DC. The company also provides services to select pharmaceutical manufacturers. It has a network of some 175000 health care providers as well as a third-party network of facilities including psychiatric and substance abuse hospitals partial hospitalization facilities rehab centers and community health centers.

Advertising expenses in 2016 totaled some $2 million. The company markets its offerings through print media event sponsorships and promotional items.

Financial Performance

Magellan's revenues have been trending upward over the past few years. In 2016 revenues increased 5% to $4.8 billion. That growth was led by the pharmacy benefit management and dispensing business but was partially offset by a decline in the managed care business. That year the company had terminated contracts of some $666 million but revenues from acquired companies and increased membership from existing customers helped boost overall sales.

Despite the higher revenues net income fell between 2012 and 2015. It rebounded in 2016 rising 148% to $77.9 million due largely to a 17% decrease in cost of care expenses.

However cash flow from operations fell 72% to $66.7 million in 2016. Changes in assets and liabilities drove that decline.

Strategy

Magellan's growth strategy includes three primary areas of focus. First it aims to expand its management programs for special populations such as individuals dealing with serious mental illness. The company is expanding Medicaid management programs for certain high-cost populations including dual-eligibility patients (those qualifying for both Medicare and Medicaid services) forming partnerships and ventures with regional health plans. According to the Centers for Medicare and Medicaid Services Medicaid enrollment is projected to increase rapidly over the next decade and Magellan intends to take advantage of that increase by marketing itself to states that need guidance navigating the public mental health system. Towards that end it agreed to buy Senior Whole Health in 2017; that purchase will provide entry into Massachusetts' Senior Care Options program and New York City's managed long-term care market.

Secondly Magellan is working to expand its pharmacy management business. It has acquired pharmacy benefit management (PBM) companies such as Veridicus Holdings (in 2016) 4D Pharmacy Management Systems (2015). The company markets these offerings to new and existing clients.

Magellan's third primary strategy is to grow its existing behavioral health care and other specialty businesses. It does this by promoting and adding new services; acquisitions and organic measures have allowed the company to enter new business segments including radiology benefits management which is showing rapid growth.

Mergers and Acquisitions

Magellan acquired Senior Whole Health for $400 million in 2017. The formerly privately held Senior Whole Health provides Medicare and Medicaid dual-eligible benefits in the states of Massachusetts and New York. With that purchase Magellan expanded into Massachusetts' Senior Care Options program as well as the managed long-term care market in New York City.

In 2016 Magellan purchased Virginia-based Armed Forces Services Corporation for $117.5 million; that deal expanded its business with military and veteran agencies. Later that year it acquired Utah-based pharmacy benefit management (PBM) firm Veridicus Holdings for some $74.5 million. Veridicus provides PBM services medication therapy management clinical care management and Medicare Part D services to employers sponsors and third-party administrators.

Also in 2016 the company purchased The Management Group for $15 million. That firm provides home and long-term care services; the deal aligned with Magellan's plans to expand in the long-term services and supports market.

EXECUTIVES

Chairman And Ceo, Barry M. Smith, age 64, $1,000,000 total compensation
Cfo, Jonathan N. (Jon) Rubin, age 54, $535,600 total compensation
General Counsel And Secretary, Daniel N. (Dan) Gregoire, age 63, $470,350 total compensation
Ceo Magellan Healthcare, Sam K. Srivastava, age 50, $609,000 total compensation
Cto, Srinivas (Srini) Koushik
Chief Medical Officer, Karen Amstutz
Ceo Magellan Rx Management, Mostafa M. Kamal, age 37, $412,000 total compensation
Vice President Business Development, Lauren Murphy
Clinical Director, Omar Vega
Vice President Of Privileging Programs, Pamela Harsch
Vice President Enterprise Account Development Bsc, Julie Larson
Vice President, Judy Kohn
Auditors: Ernst & Young LLP

LOCATIONS

HQ: Magellan Health Inc.
4800 N. Scottsdale Rd., Suite 4400, Scottsdale, AZ 85251
Phone: 602 572-6050
Web: www.magellanhealth.com

PRODUCTS/OPERATIONS

2016 Sales

	% of total
Healthcare	54
Pharmacy management	46
Eliminations	-
Total	100

2016 Sales

	% of total
Managed care & other	60
PBM & dispensing	40
Total	**100**

COMPETITORS

APS Healthcare	Express Scripts
American Imaging Management	First Health Group
	Health Net
CIGNA Behavioral Health	Horizon Health
	Mental Health Network
CareCore	OptumRx
Caremark Pharmacy Services	PharMerica
	Schaller Anderson Inc
ComPsych	UBH
Comprehensive Care	

HISTORICAL FINANCIALS
Company Type: Public

Income Statement
FYE: December 31

	REVENUE ($ mil.)	NET INCOME ($ mil.)	NET PROFIT MARGIN	EMPLOYEES
12/17	5,838	110	1.9%	10,700
12/16	4,836	77	1.6%	9,700
12/15	4,597	31	0.7%	6,900
12/14	3,760	79	2.1%	6,600
12/13	3,546	125	3.5%	5,949
Annual Growth	**13.3%**	**(3.2%)**	**—**	**15.8%**

2017 Year-End Financials

Debt ratio: 28.87%	No. of shares (mil.): 24
Return on equity: 9.28%	Dividends
Cash ($ mil.): 398	Yield: —
Current ratio: 1.66	Payout: —
Long-term debt ($ mil.): 740	Market value ($ mil.): 2,337

	STOCK PRICE ($) FY Close	P/E High/Low	Earnings	PER SHARE ($) Dividends	Book Value
12/17	96.55	21 14	4.51	0.00	52.74
12/16	75.25	23 15	3.22	0.00	46.76
12/15	61.66	57 37	1.21	0.00	43.18
12/14	60.03	21 18	2.90	0.00	42.08
12/13	59.91	13 10	4.53	0.00	41.88
Annual Growth	**12.7%**	**— —**	**(0.1%)**	**—**	**5.9%**

MAINE MUNICIPAL BOND BANK

EXECUTIVES

President, Robert Lenna
Chief Information Officer, Michele Sucy

LOCATIONS

HQ: MAINE MUNICIPAL BOND BANK
  127 COMMUNITY DR 101, AUGUSTA, ME 043308010
Phone: 207 622-9386
Web: WWW.MAINEBONDBANK.COM

HISTORICAL FINANCIALS
Company Type: Private

Income Statement
FYE: June 30

	ASSETS ($ mil.)	NET INCOME ($ mil.)	INCOME AS % OF ASSETS	EMPLOYEES
06/18	2,443	14	0.6%	18
06/17	2,410	12	0.5%	—
Annual Growth	**1.3%**	**15.5%**	**—**	**—**

2018 Year-End Financials

Debt ratio: —	
Return on equity: 17.80%	Dividends
Cash ($ mil.): 0	Yield: —
Current ratio: —	Payout: —
Long-term debt ($ mil.): —	Market value ($ mil.): —

ManpowerGroup Inc

EXECUTIVES

Chb-Ceo, Jonas Prising
Pres-Coo, Darryl Green
Exec V Pres-Cfo, John T McGinnis
Exec V Pres Global Strategy &, Mara E Swan
Exec V Pres Operational Excell, Siram Chandrashekar
Sr V Pres-General Counsel-Sec, Richard D Buchband
Board Member, Patricia Hemingway Hall
Board Member, Paul Read
Board Member, Roberto Mendoza
Board Member, Ulice Payne
Lead Independent Director, William Downe
Auditors: Deloitte & Touche LLP

LOCATIONS

HQ: ManpowerGroup Inc
  100 Manpower Place, Milwaukee, WI 53212
Phone: 414 961-1000   **Fax:** 414 332-0796
Web: www.manpower.com

COMPETITORS

Adecco	Randstad Holding
Kelly Services	Robert Half
Korn/Ferry	TrueBlue
Michael Page	Volt Information

HISTORICAL FINANCIALS
Company Type: Public

Income Statement
FYE: December 31

	REVENUE ($ mil.)	NET INCOME ($ mil.)	NET PROFIT MARGIN	EMPLOYEES
12/17	21,034	545	2.6%	29,000
12/16	19,654	443	2.3%	28,000
12/15	19,329	419	2.2%	27,000
12/14	20,762	427	2.1%	26,000
12/13	20,250	288	1.4%	25,000
Annual Growth	**1.0%**	**17.3%**	**—**	**3.8%**

2017 Year-End Financials

Debt ratio: 10.67%	No. of shares (mil.): 66
Return on equity: 21.24%	Dividends
Cash ($ mil.): 689	Yield: 0.0%
Current ratio: 1.28	Payout: 23.1%
Long-term debt ($ mil.): 478	Market value ($ mil.): 8,333

	STOCK PRICE ($) FY Close	P/E High/Low	Earnings	PER SHARE ($) Dividends	Book Value
12/17	126.11	16 11	8.04	1.86	41.99
12/16	88.87	15 9	6.27	1.72	35.27
12/15	84.29	18 12	5.40	1.60	35.94
12/14	68.17	16 11	5.30	0.98	37.68
12/13	85.86	23 12	3.62	0.92	36.72
Annual Growth	**10.1%**	**— —**	**22.1%**	**19.2%**	**3.4%**

Marathon Oil Corp.

In the long-running competition for success in the oil and gas industry Marathon Oil is keeping up a steady pace. It has proved reserves of more than 2.1 billion barrels of oil equivalent including 692 million barrels of synthetic oil derived from oil sands mining. It major focus of production is the US in the Gulf of Mexico Oklahoma Texas north Delaware and North Dakota. Its areas of production outside of the US include Europe (the UK); and Africa (Equatorial Guinea Gabon and Libya).

Operations

Marathon Oil is engaged in oil and gas exploration production worldwide and LNG and methanol marketing in Equatorial Guinea.

The company operates through two reportable operating segments: North America E&P (over 70% of total revenues) which explores for produces and markets crude oil and condensate NGLs and natural gas in the US; and International E&P (roughly 30%) which explores for produces and markets crude oil and condensate NGLs and natural gas outside of the US and produces and markets products manufactured from natural gas such as LNG and methanol in Equatorial Guinea.

Geographic Reach

Marathon Oil has oil and gas assets in Equatorial Guinea Gabon Kurdistan (Iraq) Libya the UK and the US.70% of revenue comes from the US.

Sales and Marketing

Marathon Oil's marketing activities include the transportation of oil and gas to market centers the sale of commodities to third parties and the storage of hydrocarbon products.In 2017 sales to Vitol and affiliates accounted for approximately 10% of the company?s total revenue.

Financial Performance

Marathon revenue has fallen from $13 billion in 2010 to just below $5 billion in 2017 mostly from asset sell-offs and divestment. Net Income also declined from a $2 billion average per year to losses from 2015 onwards. In the last three years the company has had losses of some $10 billion.

Revenue in 2017 rose some 25% to $4.8 billion from the previous year. Volumes increased due to the Delaware acquisition new wells to sales in other US assets and better sales in Libya.

Net income for Marathon got worse. From a loss of $2.1 billion in 2016 it registered losses of $5.7 billion in 2017 mostly due to a 10% increase in depreciation and amortization costs ($2.4 billion in 2017) as well as a $248 million increase in impairment charges over 2016 (totaling $638 million for 2017).

Cash holdings declined from $2.5 billion to just over $560 million. Operations generated $2 billion but financing and investment activities used $2 billion in cash each mostly in acquisition and debt reduction.

Strategy

Marathon Oil continues to focus on lower cost/higher return liquid hydrocarbon reserves and production in the US. To accelerate this push in 2017 the company agreed to sell its 20% stake in the Athabasca Oil Sands Project for $2.5 billion to pay down debt and reinvest in core projects (it sold assets in 2015-16 period totaling $1.5 billion). In 2017 Marathon also bought 70000 net acres in the lower-cost Permian Basin from BC Operating for $1.1 billion.

One of Marathon's biggest strengths is its differentiated position in the four most productive low-cost resource plays: Eagle Ford Bakken Oklahoma and north Delaware. In 2018 90% of its capital allocation budget of $ 2.3 billion will come from the US resource plays (its development budget is self-funded). Excess cash from higher commodity prices and divestiture proceeds is being strategically invested. Since 2017 saw rise in production margins (oil production was 30% higher than last quarter of 2016) the company predicts a greater percentage of production being sourced from its high quality assets. Marathon expects 410000 boed of production for 2018 excluding Libya up some 18% year-over-year as resource plays grow in the US.

With a somewhat unexpectedly good production results from its unconventional wells in the Eagle Ford and Bakken assets further aided by strong rates from the nine-well STACK infill assets Marathon is now focused on increasing corporate-level returns as the company has had massive losses in the last three years totaling more than $10 billion. In 2017 Marathon was able to achieve cash flow neutrality including working capital. It also reduced gross debt by $1.8 billion in 2017 lowering its annual interest expense by at least $115 million.

Mergers and Acquisitions

In 2016 the company acquired Payrock Energy Holdings (a portfolio company of EnCap Investments) for $888 million. The deal added to Marathon Oil?s position in the STACK play in Oklahoma where the break-even crude price for commercially viable oil production is in the low $40s.

HISTORY

Marathon Oil was founded in 1887 in Lima Ohio as The Ohio Oil Company by 14 independent oil producers to compete with Standard Oil. Within two years Ohio Oil was the largest producer in the state. This success did not go unnoticed by Standard Oil which proceeded to buy Ohio Oil in 1889. In 1905 the company moved to Findlay Ohio where it remained until it relocated to Houston in 1990.

When the US Supreme Court broke up Standard Oil in 1911 Ohio Oil became independent once again and expanded its exploration activities to Kansas Louisiana Texas and Wyoming.

In a 1924 attempt to drill three wells west of the Pecos River in Texas Ohio Oil mistakenly drilled three dry holes to the east. The company was on the verge of abandoning the project until a geologist reported the error. Ohio Oil drilled in the right area and the wells flowed. That year the company bought Lincoln Oil Refining — its first venture outside crude oil production.

Ohio Oil continued its expansion into refining and marketing operations in 1927. Following WWII the company began international exploration. Through Conorada Petroleum (later Oasis) a partnership with Continental Oil (later Conoco and then ConocoPhillips) and Amerada Hess the company explored in Africa and South and Central America. Conorada's biggest overseas deal came in 1955 when it acquired concessions on more than 60 million acres in Libya.

In 1962 the company acquired Plymouth Oil and changed its name to Marathon Oil Company; it had been using the Marathon name in its marketing activities since the late 1930s.

EXECUTIVES

Evp And Cfo, Dane E. Whitehead, age 56
Vp Human Resources Communications And Administrative Services, Deanna L. Jones
Evp Operations, T. Mitchell (Mitch) Little, age 54, $529,615 total compensation
Chairman President And Ceo, Lee M. Tillman, age 56, $1,050,000 total compensation
Senior Vice President Technology & Innovation And Cio, Bruce A. McCullough
Svp General Counsel And Secretary, Reggie Hedgebeth
Vice President And Treasurer, Morris Clark
Vice President Geophysical It, Trevor Chargois
Vice President, Robert Sovine
Vice President Manager Director, Ellen Norton
Vice President, Mohamed Harp
Vice President, Christopher Roeser
Senior Vice President General Counsel And Secretary, Reginald D Hedgebeth
Regional Vice President, Thomas Hellman
Regional Vice President, James Crawford
Auditors: PricewaterhouseCoopers LLP

LOCATIONS

HQ: Marathon Oil Corp.
  5555 San Felipe Street, Houston, TX 77056-2723
Phone: 713 629-6600
Web: www.marathonoil.com

2016 Sales

	% of total
United States	60
Canada	21
Libya	1
Other international	18
Total	**100**

PRODUCTS/OPERATIONS

2016 Sales

	% of total
North American E&P	61
International E&P	19
Oil Sands Mining (OSM)	21
Total	**100**

2016 Sales

	% of total
Crude oil and condensate	65
Synthetic crude oil	20
Natural Gas	9
Natural Gas liquids	5
Other	1
Total	**100**

COMPETITORS

BP	Occidental Petroleum
Chevron	PEMEX
ConocoPhillips	Petr leos de
Exxon Mobil	Venezuela
Hess Corporation	Royal Dutch Shell
Koch Industries Inc.	

HISTORICAL FINANCIALS

Company Type: Public

Income Statement

FYE: December 31

	REVENUE ($ mil.)	NET INCOME ($ mil.)	NET PROFIT MARGIN	EMPLOYEES
12/17	4,765	(5,723)	—	2,300
12/16	4,650	(2,140)	—	2,117
12/15	5,861	(2,204)	—	2,611
12/14	11,258	3,046	27.1%	3,330
12/13	14,959	1,753	11.7%	3,359
Annual Growth	(24.9%)	—		(9.0%)

2017 Year-End Financials

Debt ratio: 24.96%	No. of shares (mil.): 850
Return on equity: (-39.13%)	Dividends
Cash ($ mil.): 563	Yield: 0.0%
Current ratio: 1.30	Payout: —
Long-term debt ($ mil.): 5,494	Market value ($ mil.): 14,391

	STOCK PRICE ($) FY Close	P/E High/Low	PER SHARE ($) Earnings	Dividends	Book Value
12/17	16.93	— —	(6.73)	0.20	13.77
12/16	17.31	— —	(2.61)	0.20	20.71
12/15	12.59	— —	(3.26)	0.68	27.40
12/14	28.29	9 6	4.46	0.80	31.14
12/13	35.30	15 12	2.47	0.72	27.75
Annual Growth	(16.8%)	— —		—(27.4%)	
(16.1%)					

Marathon Petroleum Corp.

Marathon Petroleum the former refining and marketing unit of Marathon Oil Corporation operates more than five refineries with the capacity to process about 1.9 million barrels of crude oil a day. Marathon Petroleum sells refined products through a nationwide network of branded gas stations. It also holds stakes in pipelines and is one of the largest asphalt and light oil product terminal operators in the US. The company distributes petroleum products wholesale to private-brand marketers and to large commercial and industrial consumers as well as to the spot market.

Operations

Marathon?s operations consist of three business segments. Its Refining & Marketing segment which makes up more than 70% of the company's total revenue refines crude oil and other feedstocks at more than 5 refineries in the US Gulf Coast and Midwest regions purchases ethanol and refined products for resale and distributes refined products. It sells refined products to wholesale marketing customers buyers on the spot market its Speedway business segment and to independent entrepreneurs who operate Marathon retail outlets.

The Speedway segment (more than 25%) sells transportation fuels and convenience products in the retail market in the Midwest primarily through Speedway convenience stores. The Midstream segment (less than 5% of revenue) transports crude oil and other feedstocks to Marathon Petroleum's refineries and other locations delivers refined products to wholesale and retail markets and affiliated pipeline assets and investments.

Marathon holds stakes in about 10800 miles of pipeline (MPLX LP) and is one of the largest asphalt and light oil product terminal operators in the US (about 80 terminals). In addition the company has a large US private inland product fleet that includes roughly inland towboats and close to 250 barges.

Geographic Reach
Marathon Petroleum sells refined products at some 5600 Marathon-branded gas stations in some 20 US states.

Sales and Marketing
Marathon Petroleum sells to wholesale suppliers of gasoline and distillates to resellers and consumers. Customers include independent retailers wholesale customers their Marathon brand jobbers and Speedway brand convenience stores airlines transportation companies and utilities. It also sells gasoline distillates and asphalt for export primarily out of their Garyville and Galveston Bay refineries.

The company sells more than 50% of its gasoline sales volumes and about 90% of its distillates sales volumes on a wholesale or spot market basis. It also sells via retail outlets primarily in Florida Mississippi Tennessee and Alabama.

Financial Performance
Over the last decade (2008-17) Marathon revenue has gone up from $65 billion in 2008 to a peak of $100 billion in 2013 before declining for three years in a row to $63 billion (2016) before making up some of that ground the following year. Net income in the same period has seen a somewhat upward trajectory growing from $450 million in 2009 to a yearly average of $2.4 billion from 2011 onwards.

In 2017 marathon revenue grew 20% year-over-year to $75.4 billion primarily due to higher average prices (by $0.25 per gallon) as well as a 42 mbpd increase in product sales volume.

Net income in 2017 was $3.4 billion the highest in a decade. The 200% year-over-year increase in profits stemmed mostly from a $1.5 billion in gains from the new tax reform kicking into law in 2017 the absence of a charge of $370 million in inventory value adjustment as well as higher income from the refining and marketing segment (thanks to higher LLS crack spreads in Gulf Coast and Chicago).

Marathon?s cash holdings increased from $890 million to just over $3 billion. Operating activities provided $6.6 billion in cash. $3.4 billion went towards investment activities (mostly in purchase of property plant and equipment) and a further $1.1 billion went towards the company?s financing activities.

Strategy
Encouraged by signs of strong economic growth an improving exports market and boosted by favorable tax reform in the US Marathon took the bold step to acquire and merge with rival Andeavor in a $23 billion deal to create an integrated energy company that is valued at $90 billion. The deal is expected to close late 2018.

The catalyst the company underlines is $1 billion in cost synergies over the first three years with possible further gains from Andeavor?s refining assets. The deal immediately increases Marathon?s refining footprint from east of Mississippi to California and the Pacific Northwest regions. Midstream it increases its presence in the Permian basin and Bakken regions and adds the Andeavor Logistics limited partnership to its own MLPX. The company is also promising an enhanced integration model?from wellhead to the customer and customer loyalty programs.

Beyond the new merger in 2017 Marathon continued upgrading its Galveston Bay refinery grew its footprint in the Permian basin as well as kick-started plans to expand its Speedway segment by opening more store locations. Marathon plans to invest half a billion on Speedway sector in 2018.

In 2018 the company has capital investment plans of $1.6 billion majority of it going towards the Refining and Marketing segment for the Galveston Bay refinery and upgrading residual fuel oils to higher-value products.

MPLX announced a budget of $2.3 billion in organic growth and maintenance costs for 2018 with a plan to add 8 processing plants (1.5 billion cubic-feet per day capacity) and crude oil and refined products infrastructure projects.

Mergers and Acquisitions
In April 2018 Marathon announced buying out its rival refiner Andeavor for a $23 billion deal in one of the largest-ever tie-ups of two US refiners. The deal which is expected to close late 2018 will make Marathon the largest US refiner surpassing Valero and increasing the company's access to US shale business concentrated in Texas and North Dakota as well as fuel market penetration in a rapidly growing Mexican market.

In March 2017 Marathon acquired the Ozark pipeline from Enbridge for $219 million.

In 2017 Enbridge and Marathon Petroleum bought a partial indirect equity interest in the Dakota Access Pipeline and Energy Transfer Crude Oil Company Pipeline projects (the Bakken Pipeline system) which transports crude from North Dakota to the eastern Gulf Coast for $2 billion. Enbridge agreed to pay $1.5 billion for its 28% share of the network while Marathon will pay $500 million for its 9% stake.

EXECUTIVES

Chairman And Ceo, Gary R. Heminger, age 64, $1,600,000 total compensation
Evp Human Resources Health And Administrative Services, Rodney P. Nichols, age 65
Vp Business Development, Anthony R. (Tony) Kenney, age 65, $687,500 total compensation
Svp Marketing, Thomas M. (Tom) Kelley, age 58
Svp Cfo And Treasurer, Timothy T. Griffith, age 48, $600,000 total compensation
Svp Supply Distribution And Planning, C. Michael Palmer, age 64, $637,500 total compensation
President, Donald C. (Don) Templin, age 54, $800,000 total compensation
Svp Transportation And Logistics, John S. Swearingen, age 58
Vp And Cio, Donald W. Wehrly, age 58
Svp Refining, Raymond L. Brooks, age 57
President Mplx Lp, Mike Hennigan
Vp Finance And Treasurer, Tom Kaczynski
Auditors: PricewaterhouseCoopers LLP

LOCATIONS

HQ: Marathon Petroleum Corp.
539 South Main Street, Findlay, OH 45840-3229
Phone: 419 422-2121
Web: www.marathonpetroleum.com

PRODUCTS/OPERATIONS

2016 Sales

	% of total
Refining & marketing	68
Speedway	29
Midstream	3
Total	**100**

2016 Sales

	% of total
Refined products	86
Merchandise	8
Crude oil & refinery feedstocks	3
Transportation & other	3
Total	**100**

Selected Products
Asphalt

Branded Distillates
Branded Gasoline
Branded Lubricants
Heavy Oil
Petroleum Coke
Specialty Products
Wholesale Light Products

COMPETITORS

BP	Koch Industries Inc.
CITGO	Motiva Enterprises
Chevron	Murphy Oil
ConocoPhillips	Shell Oil Products
Exxon Mobil	Sunoco
Hess Corporation	Tesoro
HollyFrontier	Valero Energy

HISTORICAL FINANCIALS

Company Type: Public

Income Statement

FYE: December 31

	REVENUE ($ mil.)	NET INCOME ($ mil.)	NET PROFIT MARGIN	EMPLOYEES
12/17	75,369	3,432	4.6%	43,800
12/16	63,364	1,174	1.9%	44,460
12/15	72,258	2,852	3.9%	45,440
12/14	98,102	2,524	2.6%	45,340
12/13	100,254	2,112	2.1%	29,865
Annual Growth	**(6.9%)**	**12.9%**	**—**	**10.0%**

2017 Year-End Financials

Debt ratio: 26.40%
Return on equity: 24.88%
Cash ($ mil.): 3,011
Current ratio: 1.28
Long-term debt ($ mil.): 12,322

No. of shares (mil.): 486
Dividends
Yield: 0.0%
Payout: 22.6%
Market value ($ mil.): 32,066

	STOCK PRICE ($) FY Close	P/E High/Low		PER SHARE ($) Earnings	Dividends	Book Value
12/17	65.98	10	7	6.70	1.52	28.87
12/16	50.35	23	14	2.21	1.36	25.68
12/15	51.84	20	8	5.26	1.14	24.93
12/14	90.26	22	17	4.39	0.92	19.62
12/13	91.73	27	18	3.32	0.77	18.38
Annual Growth	**(7.9%)**	**—**	**—**	**19.2%**	**18.5%**	**11.9%**

Markel Corp (Holding Co)

Have you ever thought about who insures the manicurist or an antique motorcycle? Specialty insurer Markel takes on the risks other insurers won't touch from amusement parks to thoroughbred horses to summer camps. Coverage is also available for one-time events such as golf tournaments and auto races. The company provides customized direct and facultative placements in the US and abroad as well as treaty reinsurance. Markel International provides specialty insurance internationally from its base in the UK and Alterra handles specialty insurance and reinsurance in the US and parts of Europe and Latin America. Meanwhile subsidiary Markel Ventures invests in non-insurance companies.

Operations
Markel operates through three primary segments: US Insurance (more than half of all sales) International Insurance and Reinsurance.

US Insurance writes commercial risks primarily excess and surplus lines which are distributed through a network of wholesale brokers. It also writes specialty coverage for niche markets. Excess insurance kicks in when a company's regular insurance fizzles out. For example a regular policy might pay up to $100000 on claims but the excess policy could then pay any amounts over $100000 and up to $10 million. Surplus insurance is coverage that no regular insurance company can offer and typically comes with a higher level of risk and higher-priced premiums.

US Insurance also provides specialty insurance to clients that engage in highly specialized activities requiring niche coverage typically not offered by standard insurers. Underwriting entities include FirstComp Insurance for workers' compensation as well as the Markel Insurance and Markel American Insurance units. Specialty reinsurance products including general casualty coverage property professional liability workers' compensation and credit and surety risks are provided by Evanston Insurance.

The International Insurance segment offers primary and excess of loss property excess liability marine and energy professional liability and other specific coverages. Its Markel International division based in London writes business worldwide. Another division Markel Assurance specializes in Fortune 1000 businesses around the world. It was established in 2017 from the combination of the former Wholesale and Global units.

The Reinsurance segment provides property casualty and specialty treaty reinsurance to other insurers around the world. Key products include property professional liability credit surety general casualty auto and workers' compensation. These are underwritten by the Global Reinsurance and Markel International divisions. Reinsurance distributes its coverage through brokers.

The remainder of revenues comes from private equity unit Markel Ventures — which invests in entities ranging from food equipment makers to medical providers — and other investment income.

Geographic Reach

Markel primarily operates in the US market which accounts for more than 75% of premiums. Its UK unit Markel International writes policies for UK clients as well as on a global basis through the Lloyd's of London market. Markel has more than 25 locations in North America and about 30 in Europe. It opened its first India office in 2018.

Sales and Marketing

Markel distributes its products through independent agents and brokers.Its top three independent brokers represent nearly 30% of the group's gross premiums written.

Financial Performance

Markel's revenues have leveled off somewhat after seeing significant rises in 2013 and 2014. In 2016 revenue rose 5% to $5.6 billion. Driving that increase earned premiums net investment income and other revenues (including managing general agent operations life and annuity product sales and Markel Ventures) rose that year. Those gains were partially offset by a decline in net realized investment gains.

Net income which spiked 82% in 2015 due to favorable underwriting results and higher net realized investment gains slipped 22% to $455.7 million in 2016. Higher costs ranging from interest expense to losses on early extinguishment of debt as well as less favorable underwriting results led to that year's decline.

Cash flow from operations which has declined since 2013 fell another 18% to $534.6 million in 2016 as a result of the lower net income. Also negative adjustments to net cash provided by operating activities — including deferred income tax expenses losses on early extinguishment of debt

and a decrease in other liabilities — caused operating cash flow to decline.

Strategy

Markel's strategy for growth is to leverage its expertise and specialized market knowledge of niche markets to differentiate its business from competitors. Financially the company's aim is to generate consistent underwriting and operating profits and produce superior returns on its investments to increase its value for shareholders. It is also looking to diversify into new specialty insurance markets as well as developing innovative products to reach more clients. The firm works at improving its existing policies to provide its customers with the evolving types of coverage they need. For example in 2017 it expanded the professional liability offerings it provides for law firms. Additionally Markel is strategic in selecting profitable venture capital investments through its private equity unit.

Acquisitions are another realm of interest for the group. It plans to buy insurance fronting services provider State National Companies for $919 million fresh on the heels of its 2017 purchase of commercial surety firm SureTec.

The company is also focused on expanding international operations in the UK Bermuda Europe the Middle East the Asia/Pacific region and South America. It plans to establish an insurance provider in Germany ahead of the UK's pending exit from the European Union. (It currently offers insurance in Germany from a branch office in Munich where the new company will eventually be located.) That should help the company as it seeks other opportunities to expand in Europe. In Asia Markel opened its first Indian office located in Mumbai in 2018.

Mergers and Acquisitions

In 2017 Markel acquired surety firm SureTec Financial for $250 million. SureTec operates in all 50 states specializing in small and midsize contract bonds and commercial surety. The company joined the specialty division of Markel's US Insurance segment.Also that year the company bought State National Companies the nation's largest provider of fronting services. With that $919 million purchase Markel entered that line of business and it will begin offering collateral protection coverage for financial institutions.

In 2015 the company acquired an 80% stake in CapTech Ventures for $60.6 million. CapTech is a management consulting firm; the deal helped Markel build its technological expertise. It also bought CATCo Investment Management a fund manager and reinsurance manager based in Bermuda. That company now markets Markel's offerings in the US.

HISTORY

In the 1920s Sam Markel formed a mutual insurance company for "jitneys" (passenger cars refurbished as public transportation buses). In 1930 he founded Markel Service to expand nationally. To keep up with industry growth the company revamped itself as a managing general agent and independent claims service organization in the late 1950s. In 1978 Markel began covering taverns restaurants and vacant buildings. It created excess and surplus lines underwriter Essex Insurance in 1980.

Markel went public in 1986. The next year it invested in Shand Morahan and Evanston Insurance (specialty coverage including architects engineers and lawyers professional liability; officers and directors insurance; errors and omissions; and medical malpractice). It bought summer camp insurer Rhulen Agency in 1989.

In the 1990s Markel began buying insurers with their own offbeat niches. In 1990 it bought

the rest of Shand Morahan and Evanston Insurance. In 1995 it bought Lincoln Insurance (excess and surplus lines) from media giant Thomson (now Thomson Reuters). The next year the company bought Investors Insurance Holding (excess and surplus lines). Markel which already owned nearly 10% of Gryphon Holdings (commercial property/casualty) bought the rest in 1999.

Expanding internationally Markel bought Bermuda-based Terra Nova Holdings a reinsurer and a Lloyd's managing agency in 2000. The company experienced heavy losses in 2001 not only related to the events of September 11 but also to its slumping international business (the company took a $100 million charge).

Unlike standard insurers (whose rates are generally regulated) specialty insurers can charge the rates they consider reasonable. To that end after taking significant losses from the 2005 hurricane season (Katrina Rita Wilma) and additional hits from the 2008 season (Gustav Ike) the company decided to raise the rates on its catastrophe-exposed businesses.

EXECUTIVES

Co-ceo, Thomas S. Gayner, age 56, $807,692 total compensation

Co-ceo, Richard R. Whitt, age 54, $807,692 total compensation

Vice Chairman, F. Michael Crowley, age 66, $793,269 total compensation

Chief Administrative Officer, Britton L. (Britt) Glisson, age 61

Evp And Chief Underwriting Officer, Gerard Albanese, age 65, $615,385 total compensation

Evp And Cfo, Anne G. Waleski, age 51, $578,846 total compensation

Evp And Chief Actuarial Officer, Bradley J. Kiscaden, age 55

Cio, Mike Scyphers

Associate Vice President Of Claims, David Ashley

Associate Vice President, Kathleen Olear

Vice President And Chief Administrative Officer, Robert Blazer

Vice President Marketing, Cara Bowen

Associate Vp Markel Southeast, Jeffrey Craig

Vice President Western Region Marine Underwriting, Philip B Nelson

Vice President Ocean Marine, John Grossenbacher

Vice President Professional Liability, Michael Cunney

Assistant Vice President Excess Liability, Michael Souza

Senior Vice President, Paul Carroll

Svp Professional Liability, Tim Rowan

Svp Casualty Underwriting, siobhan walshe

Executive Vice President Professional Liability, Daniel Gamble

Vice President, Lyle Mccoy

Senior Vice President Financial Institutions, Bret Hilgart

Senior Vice President, Steven Schreiber

Vice President Western Region Marine Underwriting, Philip Nelson

Senior Vice President, Tony Markel

Vice Chairman, Anthony F. Markel, age 76

Vice Chairman, Steven A. Markel, age 69

Chairman, Alan I. Kirshner, age 82

Board Member, Michael Schewel

Board Member, Alfred Broaddus

Board Member, Bruce Connell

Auditors: KPMG LLP

LOCATIONS

HQ: Markel Corp (Holding Co)
4521 Highwoods Parkway, Glen Allen, VA 23060-6148
Phone: 804 747-0136
Web: www.markelcorp.com

2016 Gross Written Premiums

	% of total
United States	77
United Kingdom	7
Canada	3
Other countries	13
Total	**100**

PRODUCTS/OPERATIONS

2016 Sales

	% of total
Earned premiums	
U.S. Insurance	39
International Insurance	15
Reinsurance	15
Net investment income	7
Net realized investment gains	1
Other Insurance	23
Other revenues (Discontinued Lines)	-
Total	**100**

Selected Products

Re-Insurance
Casualty
Property
Public Entity
Specialty
US Insurance
First
Comp - Workers' Comp
Global Insurance
Practice Groups
Specialty Commercial
Specialty Personal
Wholesale

COMPETITORS

Assurant
CNA Financial
Great American Insurance Company
HCC Insurance
Meadowbrook Insurance
Medical Liability Mutual Insurance
National Indemnity Company
Nationwide
Penn-America
Philadelphia Insurance Companies
ProSight Specialty Insurance Group
RLI
Travelers Companies
United States Liability Insurance Group
XL Group plc

HISTORICAL FINANCIALS

Company Type: Public

Income Statement

FYE: December 31

	ASSETS ($ mil.)	NET INCOME ($ mil.)	INCOME AS % OF ASSETS	EMPLOYEES
12/17	32,805	395	1.2%	15,600
12/16	25,875	455	1.8%	10,900
12/15	24,941	582	2.3%	10,600
12/14	25,200	321	1.3%	8,600
12/13	23,955	281	1.2%	7,200
Annual Growth	**8.2%**	**8.9%**	**—**	**21.3%**

2017 Year-End Financials

Debt ratio: 9.45%
Return on equity: 4.40%
Cash ($ mil.): 2,198
Current ratio: —
Long-term debt ($ mil.): —

No. of shares (mil.): 13
Dividends
Yield: —
Payout: —
Market value ($ mil.): 15,838

	STOCK PRICE ($) FY Close	P/E High/Low	Earnings	Dividends	Book Value
12/17	1,139.13	44 34	25.81	0.00	683.58
12/16	904.50	31 26	31.27	0.00	606.30
12/15	883.35	22 16	41.74	0.00	561.23
12/14	682.84	31 24	22.27	0.00	543.98
12/13	580.35	26 19	22.48	0.00	477.17
Annual Growth	**18.4%**	**— —**	**3.5%**	**—**	**9.4%**

Marquette National Corp (IL)

EXECUTIVES

Manager, Arniga Scales
Management Vice-President, Thomas Micetic
Auditors: RSM US LLP

LOCATIONS

HQ: Marquette National Corp (IL)
6316 South Western Ave, Chicago, IL 60636
Phone: 708 364-9011 **Fax:** 708 226-6933
Web: www.emarquettebank.com

HISTORICAL FINANCIALS

Company Type: Public

Income Statement

FYE: December 31

	ASSETS ($ mil.)	NET INCOME ($ mil.)	INCOME AS % OF ASSETS	EMPLOYEES
12/17	1,580	7	0.5%	
12/16	1,584	6	0.4%	—
12/15	1,550	5	0.3%	—
12/14	1,528	7	0.5%	—
12/98	1,139	12	1.1%	—
Annual Growth	**1.7%**	**(2.9%)**		

2017 Year-End Financials

Debt ratio: 3.59%
Return on equity: 5.32%
Cash ($ mil.): 293
Current ratio: —
Long-term debt ($ mil.): —

No. of shares (mil.): 4
Dividends
Yield: 0.0%
Payout: 25.4%
Market value ($ mil.): 131

	STOCK PRICE ($) FY Close	P/E High/Low	Earnings	Dividends	Book Value
12/17	29.50	66 16	1.65	0.42	32.50
12/16	96.00	81 66	1.35	0.38	30.34
12/15	102.00	85 72	1.31	0.34	32.22
12/14	97.00	243 55	1.52	0.91	31.78
Annual Growth	**(6.1%)**	**— —**	**0.4%**	**(4.0%)**	**0.1%**

Marriott International, Inc.

Marriott International is one of the world's leading hoteliers. The company has some 6500 operated or franchised hotel residential and timeshare properties worldwide. Its hotels include such full-service brands as Renaissance Hotels and its flagship Marriott Hotels & Resorts as well as select-service and extended-stay brands Courtyard and Fairfield Inn. It also owns the Ritz-Carlton luxury chain and resort and manages about 80 golf courses. The $13.3 billion acquisition of Starwood in 2016 significantly grew the scope of Marriott.

Operations

Marriott International operates through four reportable business segments: North American Full-Service North American Limited-Service Other International and an Asia/Pacific segment.

The North American Full-Service generates more than 60% of Marriott International's total revenue. It includes Marriott's luxury and premium brands (JW Marriott The Ritz-Carlton W Hotels and others) located in the US and Canada.

The North American Limited-Service segment accounts for more than 15% of sales and consists of brands such as Courtyard Residence Inn Fairfield Inn & Suites and others in the US and Canada.

The Asia/Pacific segment which has hotels in Fiji and Japan accounts for around 5% of sales. The Other International segment covers Marriott's non-North American and Asia/Pacific properties in countries across Latin America Europe Africa and the Caribbean; it generates more than 10% of revenue.

Geographic Reach

More than 55% of Marriott International's properties are international. The company has operations in more than 120 countries in the Americas; the UK and Ireland; the Middle East and Africa; Asia; Australia; and Continental Europe.

Sales and Marketing

Marriott International's marketing activities include email online advertising and postal mailing. It encourages cross-brand loyalty via a point-based membership scheme based on money spent at hotels on timeshare intervals fractional ownership and residential products.

Financial Performance

Marriott International's revenue increased steadily from after the global financial crisis until 2016 when the acquisition of Starwood Hotels & Resorts added billions to its top line.

In fiscal 2017 revenue grew 34% to $22.9 billion on the first full-year contribution from Starwood. Other growth drivers included growth in transient leisure people in hurricane-afflicted areas seeking temporary accommodation and higher demand in Washington DC. Overall revenue per room globally grew 3.1% to $115.02 and occupancy increased 1.4%.

Net income also grew strongly up 76% to $1.4 billion — the company's best-ever result. Profits grew thanks to the Starwood acquisition and higher profits per available room. As a result Marriott's operating cash flow strengthened to $2.4 billion a 45% increase.

Strategy

The acquisition of Starwood added 11 brands to Marriott's existing 19 brands forming an unwieldy and overlapping portfolio. It also added a further customer loyalty program. Marriott's integration of Starwood will involve streamlining its brand portfolio by rolling some of its weaker brands up into its more powerful brands in the same niche. The company has also consolidated its three loyalty programs Marriott Rewards Starwood Preferred Guest and Ritz-Carlton Rewards under the Marriott Rewards program. It will honor legacy Starwood points by offering Marriott points at a 3:1 exchange rate. The unified system will allow customers to spend points across all 30 hotel brands.

Mergers and Acquisitions

In 2016 Marriott International acquired Starwood Hotels & Resorts Worldwide in a $13.3 billion deal. The deal gave Marriott International more hotel properties in Asia Europe and Latin America. The two companies have combined their respective customer loyalty programs but most of the hotels in the portfolio will retain their current branding.

HISTORY

The company began in 1927 as a Washington DC root beer stand operated by John and Alice Marriott. Later they added hot food and named their business the Hot Shoppe. In 1929 the couple incorporated and began building a regional chain.

Hot Shoppes opened its first hotel the Twin Bridges Marriott Motor Hotel in Arlington Virginia in 1957. When the Marriotts' son Bill became president in 1964 (CEO in 1972 chairman in 1985) he focused on expanding the hotel business. The company changed its name to Marriott Corp. in 1967. With the rise in airline travel Marriott built several airport hotels during the 1970s. By 1977 sales had topped $1 billion.

Marriott became the #1 operator of airport food beverage and merchandise facilities in the US with its 1982 acquisition of Host International and it introduced moderately priced Courtyard hotels in 1983. Acquisitions in the 1980s included a timeshare business foodservice companies and competitor Howard Johnson. (Marriott later sold the hotels but kept the restaurants and turnpike units.)

The company entered three new market segments in 1987: Marriott Suites (full-service suites) Residence Inn (moderately priced suites) and Fairfield Inn (economy hotels). It also began developing "life-care" communities which provide apartments meals and limited nursing care to the elderly in 1988.

Marriott split its operations into two companies in 1993: Host Marriott to own hotels and Marriott International primarily to manage them. However Marriott International still owned some of the properties and in 1995 it bought 49% of the Ritz-Carlton luxury hotel group.

In 1996 Marriott purchased the Forum Group (assisted living communities and health care services) and merged it into Marriott Senior Living Services.

Marriott introduced its Marriott Executive Residences in 1997. Also that year the firm expanded overseas operations with its purchase of the 150-unit Hong Kong-based Renaissance Hotel Group a deal that included branding rights to the Ramada chain.

In 1998 after the division of its lodging and food distribution services the new Marriott International then began trading as a separate company. That year Marriott also acquired the rest of Ritz-Carlton and established SpringHill Suites by Marriott.

Marriott entered the corporate housing business in 1999 through its acquisition of ExecuStay Corporation (renamed ExecuStay by Marriott) which provided fully furnished and accessorized apartments for stays of 30 days or more. The following year it joined Italy's Bulgari the world's #3 jeweler in a $140 million venture of luxury hotels sporting the Bulgari name.

Marriott refocused its operations on the lodging market in 2003 when it exited both the senior living and distribution services businesses. It sold Marriott Distribution Services (food and beverage distribution) to Services Group of America and sold Marriott Senior Living Services to Sunrise Assisted Living (the management business) and CNL Retirement Properties (nine communities). The following year Marriott sold the international branding rights to the Ramada and Days Inn chains to Cendant (now Avis Budget Group) for about $200 million.

In 2005 Marriott acquired about 30 properties from CTF Holdings (an affiliate of Hong Kong-based New World Development) for nearly $1.5 billion. It sold 14 properties immediately to Sunstone Hotel Investors and Walton Street Capital. The deal put an end to an ongoing legal battle between Marr

EXECUTIVES

President And Ceo, Arne M. Sorenson, age 59, $1,236,000 total compensation

Evp Finance And Global Treasurer, Carolyn B. Handlon

Group President, David J. Grissen, age 60, $725,000 total compensation

Evp Lodging Human Resources, David A. Rodriguez, age 59

Svp And Associate General Counsel, Edward A. (Ed) Ryan, age 64

President And Managing Director Europe, Amy C. McPherson, age 56

Evp And Global Chief Communications And Public Affairs Officer, Tricia Primrose Wallace

Evp And Global Chief Development Officer, Anthony G. (Tony) Capuano, age 52, $750,000 total compensation

Evp Cfrst Brand Management And Operations, Tim Sheldon

Svp Sales And Marketing Planning And Support, Stephanie C. Linnartz, age 49, $700,000 total compensation

President And Coo The Ritz-carlton Bulgari Hotels And Resorts And St. Regis Hotels And Resorts, Herve Humler

Global Cio, Bruce Hoffmeister

President And Managing Director Middle East And Africa, Alex Kyriakidis, age 65

Ceo Greater China, Stephen Ho

Evp And Cfo, Kathleen K. (Leeny) Oberg, age 57, $650,000 total compensation

President And Managing Director Asia Pacific, Craig S. Smith, age 55

President Marriott Hotels Of Canada, Don Cleary

Vice President Information Technology Delivery, Maureen Young

Vice President Accounting And Reporting, Kevin Aylward

Vice President Customer Knowledge At, Stephan Chase

Svp Canadian Development Ritz Carlton Hotels, Michael Beckley

Vp Business Integration, Katherine Hammes

Svp Middle East And Africa, Philip Bryson

Vp Design And Project Management, Robert Reinders

Vice President Human Resources Change Management, Heather Powell

Vice President Of Multicultural Markets And Alliances, Apoorva N Gandhi

Vice President Revenue Accounting, Maggie Hartung

Vice President Franchise Operations, Glenn Lewis

Vp Loyalty Marketing, Lynne Deroche

Vice President Administration, Greg Martell

Regional Vice President Human Resources, Marisa Milton

Vice President Global Ecommerce Marketing, Andy Kauffman

Vice President Business Process Governance, Carol Cernugel

Vice President Operations, Mary Jensen

Vice President Finance, Kent Duffie

Vice President Human Resources, Kenneth Feast

Vice President, Cecilia Lewis

Vice President Of Application Architecture, Douglas Wurtzel

Vice President, Jeff Spilman

Vice President Sales, Dennis Edwards

Vice President Property Systems Servic, Laura Bouvier

Vice President Ecommerce, Glen Harvell

Vice President Information Technology Networks, Robert Galovic

Vice President Training Development And Entusiastic Learning, Gerry Hudson-Martin

Regional Vice President Sales And Marketing Asia Pacific, Kent Maury

Vice President And Senior Counsel, Taisha Urland

Senior Vice President Lodging Development, Christopher Rose

Corporate Vice President, Von Ingle

Senior Vice President Finance Department, Gary Rosenthal

Vice President, Jennie Benzon

Vice President And Senior Counsel, Linda Miller

Vice President Feasibility, Andre Schuster

Senior Vice President Brand Strategy And Innovation, Julie Moll

Vice President And Senior Counsel, Kathy Cheung

Vice President Finance Business Partnership, Jill Baldwin

Vice President Of Insight Strategy + Innovation, Jennifer Hsieh

Vice President Of Internal Communications, Terry Weisz

Vice President Contract Management, Yvette Young

Vice President Marriott.com Merchandising And Booking, Rajan Mohan

Vice President Rooms And Guest Experience, Kate Gruell

Senior Vice President And General Counsel, Myron Walker

Vice President, William Holmes

Vice President Marketing, Daniel Vihn

Vice President, Jim O'Hern

Senior Vice President, Jasraj Singh

Vice President, Tony Reid

Vice President Of Government Affairs, Melissa Froehlich

Vp Operations, Christoph Roshardt

Vice President, Judy Fennimore

Vice President Of Human Resources, Debbie Wilson

Vice President Leisure Business Development, Warren Ruello

Vice President Jw Marriott Hotels And Resorts Marriott Hotels And Resorts, Michael Darne

Communications Vice President, Leigh Brummerhoff

Vice President Sales And Marketing Support, Beth Jones

Executive Vice President Architecture And Construction, Susan Levenson

Vice President Administration, Patricia Exposito

Vice President Risk Management, Hector Mastrapa

Vice President, Cindy Braak

Svp And Deputy General Counsel, Nancy Lee

Vice President And Senior Counsel, Stephanie Carrick

Vice President Of Loss Prevention, Alan Orlob

Vice President International Business, Howard Leigh

Senior Vice President Owner And Franchise Services, James Fisher

Vice President Administration, Brendan Ross

Vice President Marriott Rewards Partnerships And Global Card Programs, Misha Lapcevic

Vice President Marketing And Digital, Kieran Donahue

Vp Ecommerce, Devin Sung

Vice President Hotel Development, Ryan Mcrae

Vice President Global Claims, Stephen Perroots

Vice President Brand Marketing And Communications (asia Pacific), Mike Fulkerson

Vice President Information Technology Sourcing Management And Governance, Etan Gopstein

Vice President Global Head Of Consumer Public Relations, Tracey Schroeder
Senior Vice President Human Resources, Carol S Anderson
Vice President, Scott Gold
Senior Vice President Information Technology Business Partnership And Planning, Jenifer L Mason
Vice President, Joseph Donahue
Executive Vice President And Chief Financial Officer, Leeny Oberg
Vice President Systems, Cynthia Frick
Vice President Community Footprints, Sue Stephenson
Vice President Sales Inventory And Event Management Solutions, Cindy Frick
Vice President Human Resources Europe, Ben Di Benedetto
Vice President And Assistant General Counsel Practice Group Leader, Shazmah Hakim
Vice President Information Technology, Saul Mankes
Vice President Global Brand Marketing, Lisa Holladay
Global Vice President Infrastructure Engineering And Operations, Lenny Guardino
Vice President And Senior Counsel, Corrie Conway
Vice President Sales And Marketing, Andrew Cymrot
Vice President Workplace And End User Technology, Terry Herring
Vice President Community Footprints, Stocksdale Mark
Vp Financial Analysis, Keenan Minogue
Vice President Global Brand Portfolio, Sheila Holman
Vp Revenue Management Operations, Nancy Bergamini
Vice President, Cecelia Lewis
Chairman, J. W. (Bill) Marriott, age 85
Board Member, Frederick Henderson
Board Member, Mary Bush
Board Member, Susan Schwab
Auditors: Ernst & Young LLP

LOCATIONS

HQ: Marriott International, Inc.
10400 Fernwood Road, Bethesda, MD 20817
Phone: 301 380-3000
Web: www.marriott.com

PRODUCTS/OPERATIONS

2017 Sales

	$ mil.	% of total
North American Full-Service segment	14,300	63
North American Limited-Service segment	4,002	17
International	2,658	11
Other unallocated corporate	1,344	6
Total	**22,894**	**100**

2017 Sales

	$ mil.	% of total
Cost reimbursements	17,765	78
Owned leased and other revenue	1,802	8
Franchise fees	1,618	7
Base management fees	1,102	5
Incentive management fees	607	3
Total	**22,894**	**100**

COMPETITORS

Accor	Four Seasons Hotels
Best Western	Hilton Worldwide
Carlson Hotels	Hyatt
Choice Hotels	InterContinental
Club Med	Hotels
Extended Stay America	LXR Luxury Resorts
Inc.	Loews Hotels
FRHI Hotels and	
Resorts	

HISTORICAL FINANCIALS

Company Type: Public

Income Statement
FYE: December 31

	REVENUE ($ mil.)	NET INCOME ($ mil.)	NET PROFIT MARGIN	EMPLOYEES
12/17	22,894	1,372	6.0%	177,000
12/16	17,072	780	4.6%	226,500
12/15	14,486	859	5.9%	127,500
12/14	13,796	753	5.5%	123,500
12/13	12,704	626	4.9%	123,000
Annual Growth	**15.7%**	**21.7%**	**—**	**9.5%**

2017 Year-End Financials

Debt ratio: 34.40%	No. of shares (mil.): 359
Return on equity: 30.19%	Dividends
Cash ($ mil.): 383	Yield: 0.0%
Current ratio: 0.46	Payout: 35.7%
Long-term debt ($ mil.): 7,840	Market value ($ mil.): 48,741

	STOCK PRICE ($) FY Close	P/E High/Low	PER SHARE ($) Earnings	Dividends	Book Value
12/17	135.73	37 22	3.61	1.29	10.39
12/16	82.68	32 22	2.64	1.15	13.87
12/15	67.04	26 20	3.15	0.95	(14.01)
12/14	78.03	30 18	2.54	0.77	(7.86)
12/13	49.35	24 18	2.00	0.64	(4.75)
Annual Growth	**28.8%**	**— —**	**15.9%**	**19.2%**	**—**

Marsh & McLennan Companies Inc.

One of the world's largest insurance brokers Marsh & McLennan Companies (MMC) is a heavyweight insurance middleman. Through core subsidiary Marsh the company provides a broad array of insurance-related brokerage consulting and risk management services to clients in more than 130 countries. Customers include large and small companies government entities and not-for-profit organizations. MMC's global reinsurance brokerage business is handled by subsidiary Guy Carpenter. The company also owns Mercer which provides human resources and financial consulting services to customers in 40 nations worldwide; and Oliver Wyman which provides management consulting services.

Operations

MMC's operations are split into two groups — the Risk and Insurance Services (RIS) segment (consisting of Marsh and Guy Carpenter) and the Consulting segment (Mercer and Oliver Wyman). Both segments help clients assess risks in their businesses and ascertain whether those risks are insurable.

The RIS segment accounts for about 55% of revenue; insurance subsidiary Marsh alone accounts for about 45% of MMC's total revenues while Guy Carpenter accounts for about 10%. The Consulting segment brings in the remaining revenue; its Mercer human resources unit (MMC's second-largest subsidiary) accounts for a third of the group's total revenues. Oliver Wyman brings in another 10%.

Geographic Reach

MMC provides services in the Americas the Asia/Pacific region and the EMEA (Europe Middle East and Africa) region.

The US contributes about half of annual revenues. The UK and Continental Europe bring in about 15% of revenue each while the Asia/Pacific region and other markets each bring in about 10%.

Sales and Marketing

MMC's business customers include small midsized and multinational corporations. Its consulting division serves entities engaged in industries including transportation communication technology energy retail distribution and wholesale and finance.

Financial Performance

MMC has seen relatively steady revenue growth over the last few years. In 2016 revenue rose 2% to 13.2 billion: Both segments had increased sales that year. In the RIS segment Marsh rose 4% while Guy Carpenter rose 2%. The Consulting segment's Oliver Wyman rose 2% and its Mercer unit stayed flat. Geographically the US Continental Europe and the Asia/Pacific region had gains that year while the UK and other markets had modest declines.

Net income has been steadily growing and in 2016 it increased 11% to $1.8 billion. The higher revenue that year plus a drop in non-compensation/benefits operating expenses drove that increase.

After dipping in 2015 cash flow from operations rose 6% to $2 billion. This was largely due to the increase in net income.

Strategy

Citing the rise of economic difficulties natural disasters such as tsunamis and hurricanes international terrorism and other hazards for businesses MMC has been working to expand its role as a risk consultant. Subsidiary Marsh has been steadily branching out from its straight brokerage operations expanding its offerings of risk and insurance-related services including benefits management international risk placement and consumer programs for executives employees and high-net-worth individuals.

Nonetheless like its leading US competitors Marsh's most basic strategy for growth through the years has been to buy up regional brokerages large and small. It has kept up a steady pace of acquisitions of regional commercial brokerage firms especially in the mid-sized business market.

The Mercer business has also been expanding through acquisitions in recent years especially in the growing field of data solutions. Mercer is also seeking to expand its investment consulting operations.

While continuing to pursue an aggressive acquisition strategy — the firm has acquired some 130 businesses since 2009 — MMC has also been working to de-risk its own operations by enacting some cost-cutting measures in recent years. Restructuring measures including divesting underperforming businesses aim to overcome the impact of historical regulatory and litigation issues as well as economic and competitive conditions on its bottom line.

Mergers and Acquisitions

MMC is a very acquisitive group; its Marsh subsidiary makes numerous purchases each year. However it made a big splash in September 2018 when it announced plans to buy another top 10 broker Jardine Lloyd Thompson (JLT). The deal valued at some $6.4 billion will create the world's largest reinsurance broker.

Most of the group's acquisitions though are of smaller regional practices. Purchases in 2017 included Insurance Partners of Texas Georgia-based J. Smith Lanier & Company and Minnesota-based Blakestad.

In 2016 Marsh's middle market agency unit acquired San Francisco-based Presidio Benefits Group Atlanta-based Benefits Advisory Group and Florida-based Vero Insurance. Oliver Wyman acquired LShift Limited and Mercer acquired Pillar Administration.

HISTORY

Marsh & McLennan Companies dates back to the Dan H. Bomar Company founded in 1871 after the Great Chicago Fire. In 1885 a plucky Harvard dropout named Henry Marsh joined the company then known as R.A. Waller and Company. When Robert Waller died in 1889 Marsh and fellow employee Herbert Ulmann bought a controlling stake and renamed the company Marsh Ulmann & Co. Marsh pioneered insurance brokering and in 1901 set up U.S. Steel's self-insurance program.

In 1904 different directors at Burlington Northern Railroad promised their account to Marsh Ulmann as well as Manley-McLennan of Duluth (railroad insurance) and D.W. Burrows (a small Chicago-based railroad insurance firm). Rather than fight over it the firms joined forces to form the world's largest insurance brokerage. When Burrows retired in 1906 the firm became Marsh & McLennan.

In the early 20th century Marsh won AT&T's business and McLennan landed the account of Armour Meat Packing.

In 1923 Marsh & McLennan became a closely held corporation. Marsh sold out to McLennan in 1935. The company weathered the Depression without major layoffs by cutting pay and branching into life insurance and employee-benefits consulting after passage of the Social Security Act (1935).

The firm grew through acquisitions in the 1950s went public in 1962 and in 1969 formed a holding company that became Marsh & McLennan Companies. In the 1970s it diversified into investment management employee-benefits consulting and geographically into the UK with C.T. Bowring Reinsurance. As the insurance business slowed in the 1980s the financial and consulting fields grew through acquisitions and organic growth.

With offices in the World Trade Center the company lost some 300 employees in the September 11 terrorist attacks. Following the attacks on the World Trade Center Marsh & McLennan launched a new subsidiary (AXIS Specialty) to deal with the capacity shortage in the insurance industry.

Two major Marsh & McLennan units came under legal fire in probes of the mutual fund and insurance brokerage industries respectively in the early 2000s. In 2003 Putnam agreed to settle securities fraud charges with the SEC and reimburse investors; many of Putnam's top officers were replaced and its compliance procedures were restructured.

The following year Marsh found itself at the center of a price-fixing investigation that involved several insurance companies including AIG and Chubb Limited. At least nine employees of Marsh and AIG pled guilty to criminal charges. Jeffery Greenberg the son of outspoken AIG chairman and CEO Maurice Greenberg who had served as Marsh & McLennan's chairman and CEO since 1999 resigned in 2004 as a result of the price-fixing allegations.

EXECUTIVES

Senior Vice President And Chief Compliance Officer, E Gilbert
President And Ceo Mercer, Julio A. Portalatin, age 58, $900,000 total compensation
Cfo, Mark C. McGivney, age 50, $750,000 total compensation
President Ceo And Director, Daniel S. (Dan) Glaser, age 57, $1,400,000 total compensation
Evp And General Counsel, Peter J. Beshar, age 57, $800,000 total compensation
Svp And Cio, E. Scott Gilbert, age 63
President Marsh, John Q. Doyle, age 54

President And Ceo Oliver Wyman Group, Scott McDonald, age 52
Ceo Marsh International, Flavio Piccolomini
Ceo Marsh, John Doyle
Chief Executive Marsh Continental Europe, Siegmund Fahrig
Vice President Operations, Joe Curran
Vice President Of Client Operations, William Walker
Senior Vice President, Lisa Kremer
Vice President Corporate Development And Investor, Michael Bischoff
Senior Vice President, David Abbene
Vice President Aviation And Aerospace, Simon Macfadyen
Vice President Marsh Risk Consulting, Belinda Berwick
Vice President, Robert Planos
Assistant Vice President, Charles Chen
Vice President, R S Pierrepont
Senior Vice President, George Lane
Vice President, Danielle Fields
Vice President Budgets, Carlota Vargas
Senior Vice President, Edward Guzy
Assistant Vice President, Sue McCaw
Senior Vice President Healthcare Practice Leader And Client Executive, Cindy Lusignan
Vice President, Kelly Sanders
Vice President And Chief Counsel Global Risk And Specialties, Barry Kerschner
Senior Vice President, Holden Burrow
Vice President Networking, Tony Iorio
Vice President Operations, Jim Halkins
Senior Vice President, Michael Serricchio
Senior Vice President, Christopher Pease
Assistant Vice President, Jean Aguirre
Vice President Property Practice, Sabrina Fabris
Vice President, Janis Jardiniano
Vice President Managing Private Client Services Accounts, Mary Provaznik
Vice President Finance, Jo Reynolds
Senior Vice President Of The National Construction Practice, Ric Glover
Vice President, Sakurako Yagi
Avp Sales And Risk Consultant, Beth Lawson
Vice President Casualty Placement, Daniel Gibbons
Vice President Audit And Risk Management, Michelle Viotty
Senior Vice President, James Wright
Svp Strategic Solutions Group, Joseph Fusco
Senior Vice President, Jay Simione
Senior Vice President Information Technology, Brian Wood
Senior Vice President, Ronald Reinartz
Senior Vice President Global Information Technology, Scott Francis
Senior Vice President Senior Advisory Specialist 1166 Avenue Of The Americas, Marla Nicholson
Vice President, Jimmy Evans
Senior Vice President Human Resources, Carmen Warren
Senior Vice President, Sean Crnkovich
Senior Vice President, Jessica Levins
Senior Vice President, Leanna Loughlin
Senior Vice President, Thomas Edridge
Senior Vice President, Kristen Stokes
Senior Vice President, Eric Peabody
Assistant Vice President, Kevin Higgins
Vice President And Chief Information Officer Middl, Nixon Thomas
Systems Director Vice President Information Techn, Michele Leyvi
Senior Vice President, Agneta Jernbeck-Baker
Assistant Vice President Client Manager, Martin Goh
Senior Vice President, Eileen Quenell
Assistant Vice President, Heather Razo
Assistant Vice President Sales And Business Development, Pepper Periquet
Vice President, Joan Spiegel

Vice President, Patricia Robinson
Senior Vice President, Joseph Asmar
Vice President Finance, Michael Murphy
Senior Vice President, Kurt Timmel
Senior Vice President, Paul Nagata
Senior Vice President Information Technology, Bijesh Jacob
Vice President, Margaret Hogan
Senior Vice President, Randy Dickman
Vice President Business Development, Hallie Beddes
Assistant Vice President Alternative Risk Solutions, Matt Autry
Senior Vice President Placement Specialist, Bryan Berkman
Cpcu Senior Vice President Marsh Usa Inc, Maureen Biehl
Vice President, Romaneo Adams
Vice President In Marsh Risk Consulting's Reputational Risk And Crisis Management Practice Based, Susan Morton
Vice President, Virginia Del Lago
Assistant Vice President, Felix Chung
Vice President Of Marketing, Erica Jones
Vice President, Catherine Ricia
Senior Vice President, Dawn Buelow
Vice President, Jessica Hatch
Assistant Vice President, Thadd Northam
Vice President Environmental Practice, Jack Palis
Senior Vice President, Mark Alderman
Senior Vice President Global Program Manager, Lori Suske
Vice President, Raegan Buckley
Senior Vice President, Jeralyn Sorensen
Senior Vice President, Stanley Zimmerman
Senior Vice President, Eugene Charney
Assistant Vice President, Edward Mitchell
Executive Vice President Of Information Technology, Jennifer Adams
Vice President, Louise Casazza
Senior Vice President, Marcy Waterfall
Senior Vice President U S Marine And Energy, John Pallasch
Dip Fs (gen Ins) Qpib Cipvice President Head Of Businessdevelopment Singapore, Andrew Paul
Vice President Human Resources Manager, Sarah Randall
Assistant Vice President, Kristin Will
Senior Vice President, Janis Thornton
Senior Vice President, Rita Patullo
Vice President, Michael Hargis
Senior Vice President Advanced Risk Solutions, Scott Sanderson
Senior Vice President, Ben Hetzer
Senior Vice President, James Helm
Vice President Information Technology, Gursharan Sant
Senior Vice President, Mary Berry
Vice President, Thomas Luty
Senior Vice President Global Compliance, Jean Mahon
Vice President National Brokerage Property Practice, Natalie Kenny
Senior Vice President, Chris Victorino
Senior Regional Premium Finance Vice President, Natasha Lee
Senior Vice President Strategic Development Officer At Marsh And Mclennan, Leonard Battifarano
Senior Vice President, Brett Gillmon
Assistant Vice President, Jenny Dickson
Assistant Vice President Asia Client Services, Kathleen Schimmenti
Senior Vice President, Michaela Grasshoff
Senior Vice President Global Broking North America, Jason Monteforte
Senior Vice President Global Broking Specialties, Jack Reid
Vice President Human Resources, Vanessa Boneta
Senior Vice President, Kristi Whistle

Vice President, David Erdman
Senior Vice President, Carl Patchke
Senior Vice President, Natasha Tarasova
Senior Vice President, Richard R Lizdenis
Assistant Vice President, Michael Hourihan
Senior Vice President, Christine Williams
Senior Vice President, Greg Miller
Senior Vice President Multinational Trade Credit
  Practice, Liam Duffy
Vice President, Melanie Dunne
Assistant Vice President Information Technology
  Project Manager, Tarek Tlmol
Vice President Private Client Services, Susan Ott
Assistant Vice President, Marissa Mandado
Senior Vice President And Chief Financial Officer
  For Largest Insurance Broker, Adrian Serge
Vice President Human Resources, Maureen
  Schnabolk
Mira Atkinson Jacinto Arm Vice President, Mira
  Jacinto
Assistant Vice President Identity Management
  Enterprise Engineer, Yee Ng
Assistant Vice President And Deputy Practice
  Leader, Lynn Lin
Assistant Vice President, Pierce Perotti
Vice President, Nick Forillo
Senior Vice President Senior Consultant
  Workforce Strategies, Anthony Bahno
Senior Vice President And Chief Compliance
  Officer, Scott E Gilbert
Vice President Global Technology Services,
  Christopher Murphy
Vice President, Patrick Mcglynn
Vice President Associate General Counsel, Leonard
  Dinapoli
Management Information Systems Vice President,
  Jeff Worth
Auditors: Deloitte & Touche LLP

LOCATIONS

HQ: Marsh & McLennan Companies Inc.
1166 Avenue of the Americas, New York, NY 10036-2774
Phone: 212 345-5000   Fax: 212 345-4809
Web: www.mmc.com

2016 Sales

	$ mil.	% of total
US	6,573	50
UK	2,019	15
Continental Europe	2,022	15
Asia/Pacific	1,363	10
Other regions & countries	1,278	10
Adjustments	(44)	-
Total	**13,211**	**100**

PRODUCTS/OPERATIONS

2016 Sales

	$ mil.	% of total
Risk & insurance services		
Marsh	5,976	45
Guy Carpenter	1,141	9
Fiduciary interest income	26	-
Consulting		
Mercer	4,323	33
Oliver Wyman Group	1,789	13
Adjustments	(44)	-
Total	**13,211**	**100**

Selected Acquisitions

COMPETITORS

Accenture
Anthony Clark International Insurance Brokers
Aon
Bain & Company
Bollinger Inc.
Booz Allen
Brown & Brown
FTI Consulting
Fortegra Financial
Gallagher
Hub International
ING
Jardine Lloyd
McKinsey & Company
National Financial Partners
THB Group
USI
Willis Towers Watson

HISTORICAL FINANCIALS

Company Type: Public

Income Statement

FYE: December 31

	REVENUE ($ mil.)	NET INCOME ($ mil.)	NET PROFIT MARGIN	EMPLOYEES
12/17	14,024	1,492	10.6%	65,000
12/16	13,211	1,768	13.4%	60,000
12/15	12,893	1,599	12.4%	60,000
12/14	12,951	1,465	11.3%	57,000
12/13	12,261	1,357	11.1%	55,000
Annual Growth	**3.4%**	**2.4%**	**—**	**4.3%**

2017 Year-End Financials

Debt ratio: 26.86%
Return on equity: 22.02%
Cash ($ mil.): 1,205
Current ratio: 1.31
Long-term debt ($ mil.): 5,225

No. of shares (mil.): 508
Dividends
Yield: 0.0%
Payout: 49.8%
Market value ($ mil.): 41,404

	STOCK PRICE ($) FY Close	P/E High/Low	Earnings	Dividends	Book Value
12/17	81.39	30 23	2.87	1.43	14.47
12/16	67.59	20 15	3.38	1.30	12.04
12/15	55.45	20 17	2.98	1.18	12.48
12/14	57.24	22 17	2.65	1.06	13.06
12/13	48.36	20 14	2.43	0.96	14.46
Annual Growth	**13.9%**	**— —**	**4.2%**	**10.5%**	**0.0%**

Masco Corp.

Masco Corporation doesn't mask its penchant for indoor style. It is a global leader in the design manufacturing and distribution of home improvement and building products. Well-known brands include Delta and Peerless (plumbing) KraftMaid (cabinetry) Behr (paints and stains) and Milgard (windows). It boasts a vast portfolio of diversified products ranging from storage containers to patio doors but its plumbing products account for half of all sales. Although most of its sales are within the US Masco has a major presence in the UK mainland Europe and China.

Operations

Masco reports through four business segments— Plumbing Decorative Architecture Cabinetry and Windows & Specialty Products.

Masco is a leader in Plumbing products (50% of sales) in both North America and Europe. It manufactures faucets sinks bathing products acrylic tubs shower enclosure units spas exercise pools and composite plumbing systems.

Decorative Architecture (30% of revenue) includes a wide array of products from paints and waterproofing agents to cabinet door and window hardware glass shower doors wall plates and hook and rail products.

Cabinetry products make up around 10% of sales serving customers in need of semi-custom or stock cabinetry for kitchen bath storage or other home applications.

Windows & Specialty Products sell vinyl fiberglass and aluminum windows and patio doors in the US and the UK. This segment brings in less than 10% of annual revenue.

Geographic Reach

Masco operates on a global scale with some 70 manufacturing facilities and 45 warehouse and distribution facilities to its name. Its Plumbing business in North America Masco's leading moneymaker operates about 20 manufacturing facilities on the continent. Most international facilities are in China Germany and the UK.

Sales and Marketing

Masco's products and services are offered through homebuilders retail chains and wholesale outlets. The company capitalizes on the popularity of DIY chains like Home Depot and Lowe's which offer a single stop for its wide range of home improvement products ranging in style and price. Home Depot accounts for approximately 35% of Masco's sales.

From faucets and sinks to showering units Masco products are sold under brand names like Delta and Axor in the US Bristan and Heritage in the UK and Mirolin in Canada. Spas are sold under Caldera or Endless Pools brands. Peerless and Delta are well-known plumbing system brands. The company's most recognized brands are paint primer and stain brands like Behr and Kilz.

Financial Performance

In the past decade Masco revenue fluctuated between a high of $9.4 billion and a low of $6.7 billion. After a 5-year string of heavy losses totaling $2.2 billion in the 2008-12 period Masco has returned to profitability with an average yearly net income of $500 million.

Yearly sales climbed 4% from 2016 to $7.6 billion in 2017 buoyed by increased sales volume of plumbing products and coatings sales. Such increases were partially offset by the divestitures of Arrow and Moores lines of businesses.

Net profit increased by $42 million to $533 million primarily due to an increased sales volume for the year as well as a more favorable relationship between net selling prices and commodity costs.

Cash holdings at the end of 2017 went up slightly to $1.1 billion. Net cash provided by operations was $751 million partially used up by financing activities ($577 million) and a further $25 million going towards investing activities.

Strategy

Facing the twin challenges of weak international sales environment on one hand (lower products sold in the UK and Central Europe) and tariff wars on the other (around $600 million worth of imports are likely to be affected) Masco is desperately seeking reinvigoration of its US businesses especially plumbing.

To that end the company overhauled its retail offerings and found a new dealer for its Watkins brand. It showed immediate effect—the business grew 5% in 2017-18 period the highest amongst all segments. The company also sought to boost its sales in the domestic lighting market by acquiring Kichler Lighting.

Two other factors are working in favor of Masco. Its global reach shields from regional downturns. For instance strong Chinese sales has tempered weaker European sales.

Secondly Masco sees hope in demographics. A decent growth in new housing is predicted over the next decade as the large millennial generation settles down. Masco is well-positioned to capture a sizable portion of this new market.

Alternatively since federal rates are set to increase in an improving economy higher home prices would deter some homeowners as they settle for remodeling. Masco has already invested heavily to take advantage of this situation. Its Menards Program (which grew 10% last year) aims to reinvigorate growth in cabinetry products crucial for any remodeling.

Mergers and Acquisitions

In January 2018 with an eye to expand its presence into the US residential lighting industry Masco acquired US-based Kichler a manufacturer of ceiling fans residential lighting products and LED systems.

Two months earlier the company also acquired Mercury Plastics a manufacturer of water handling systems and process plastics which will help Masco expand its product portfolio with faucet components.

Company Background

If you stop at the Home Depot for some paint chances are it was manufactured by Masco. But the company started off in 1929 when founder Alex Manoogian organized the Masco Screw Products Company in Detroit to supply parts for the automotive industry. The company only turned to manufacturing during WWII to support the war effort.

It revolutionized the plumbing market in 1954 with introduction of the pioneering single-handle faucet also called the Delta faucet. In 1961 to recognize its changing portfolio the company changed its name to Masco Corporation.

Over the next six decades the company diversified into building products electrical works and complex plumbing systems. Today the company's products are found in cities across the Americas and as far as Dubai and Shanghai.

HISTORY

Masco founder Alex Manoogian moved to the US at age 19 in 1920. He wound up in Detroit and with partners Harry Adjemian and Charles Saunders he started Masco (the first letters of their last names plus "co" for "company") Screw Products Company eight days before the crash of 1929. Manoogian's partners left within the year.

Largely reliant on Detroit's auto industry Masco grew slowly during the Depression making custom parts for Chrysler Ford and others. With sales of $200000 by 1937 it went public on the Detroit Stock Exchange. During WWII Masco focused on defense and in 1942 sales passed $1 million. A new plant opened in 1948 in Dearborn Michigan as Masco resumed peacetime business mainly in the auto industry.

In 1954 Masco began selling Manoogian's one-handle kitchen faucet (Delta). Sales of faucets passed $1 million by 1958 and Masco opened a new faucet factory in Indiana.

Under Manoogian's son Richard — whose dinner was often delayed while his father used the stove to test the heat tolerance of new faucet parts — Masco Corporation (so renamed in 1961) diversified. From 1964 to 1980 it bought more than 50 companies concentrating on tool and metal casting energy exploration and air compressors. In 1984 the firm split. Masco Corporation pursued the course set by its successful faucet sales expanding its interests in home improvement and furnishings. The industrial products business was spun off as Masco Industries a separate public corporation (later Metaldyne) in which Masco maintained a sizable stake.

Masco Corporation became the #1 US furniture maker in the late 1980s by buying Lexington Furniture (1987) and Universal Furniture (1989) both of North Carolina. In 1990 Masco acquired Kraft-Maid cabinets.

Two years later the company sold its interests in Mechanical Technology Payless Cashways and Emco Limited of Canada (Masco bought back 40%

of Emco in 1997). Masco reduced its stake in Metaldyne from 47% to 35% in 1993.

Masco sought to establish itself in Europe and in 1994 it bought a German cabinetmaker and a UK producer of handheld showers. In 1996 founder Manoogian died but the company flowed on. It added a UK cabinetmaker a German shower manufacturer and a German insulation firm. That year Masco sold its troubled furniture unit to a group of investors and executives (who renamed the unit LifeStyle Furnishings International) for about $1 billion and further reduced its stake in Metaldyne to less than 20% (and later sold it all).

Acquisitions in 1997 included cabinetmakers Texwood Industries of Texas and Liberty Hardware Manufacturing of Florida. The next year it bought Vasco (heating systems and equipment Belgium) and Brugman (building and home-improvement products the Netherlands). It sold its Thermador unit (ovens and ranges) to US joint venture Bosch-Siemens Hausgerate.

Masco made 13 acquisitions from 1999 through early 2000 including Heritage Bathrooms (bathroom equipment UK) Faucet Queens (plumbing and hardware supply) GMU Group (kitchen cabinets Spain) Avocet Hardware (locks and hardware UK) BEHR Process (coatings) and Mill's Pride (cabinets). Boosting its services in 1999 it acquired The Cary Group an installer of fiberglass insulation.

To increase its geographic reach Masco bought Tvilum-Scanbirk (ready-to-assemble furniture Denmark) Masterchem Industries (specialty paint products) and Glass Idromassaggio (bathroom equipment Italy) in 2000. In late 2000 and early 2001 it acquired two US-based installation services companies Davenport Insulation Group and BSI Holdings respectively. Also in 2001 Masco acquired Milgard Manufacturing a vinyl window and patio door maker.

During 2002 Masco acquired home improvement p

EXECUTIVES

Vp General Counsel And Secretary, Kenneth G. Cole, $421,058 total compensation

Vp Cfo And Treasurer, John G. Sznewajs, age 51, $653,353 total compensation

President And Ceo, Keith J. Allman, $1,126,654 total compensation

Group President Global Plumbing, Richard O'Reagan, $481,188 total compensation

Vp Strategy And Corporate Development, Amit Bhargava, $339,231 total compensation

Vp Masco Operating System, Christopher K. Kastner, $366,962 total compensation

Chairman, J. Michael (Mike) Losh, age 72

Auditors: PricewaterhouseCoopers LLP

LOCATIONS

HQ: Masco Corp.
17450 College Parkway, Livonia, MI 48152
Phone: 313 274-7400
Web: www.masco.com

2017 Sales

	$ mil.	% of total
North America	6,069	79
Europe & other regions	1,575	21
Total	**7,644**	**100**

PRODUCTS/OPERATIONS

2017 Sales

	$ mil.	% of total
Plumbing products	3,735	49
Decorative architectural products	2,205	29
Cabinetry products	934	12
Windows and Other specialty products	770	10
Total	**7,644**	**100**

Selected Brand Names

Plumbing products
Axor
BrassCraft
Brasstech
Bristan
Brizo
Caldera
Cobra
Delta
Endless Pools
Fantasy Spas
Freeflow Spas
Ginger
Hansgrohe
Heritage
Hot Spring
Huppe
Mirolin
Newport Brass
Peerless
Plumb Shop
Waltec
Cabinets products
Cardell
KraftMaid
Merillat
Quality Cabinets
Decorative architectural products
BEHR
Kilz
Windows and Other specialty products
Duraflex
Griffin
Milgard Windows
Premier

COMPETITORS

American Woodmark	Kohler
Andersen Corporation	LIXIL Group
Benjamin Moore	Master Spas
Elkay Manufacturing	MasterBrand Cabinets
Fortune Brands Home &	PPG Industries
Security	Ply Gem Holdings
JELD-WEN	Sherwin-Williams
Jacuzzi Brands	

HISTORICAL FINANCIALS

Company Type: Public

Income Statement

FYE: December 31

	REVENUE ($ mil.)	NET INCOME ($ mil.)	NET PROFIT MARGIN	EMPLOYEES
12/18	8,359	734	8.8%	26,000
12/17	7,644	533	7.0%	26,000
12/16	7,357	491	6.7%	26,000
12/15	7,142	355	5.0%	25,000
12/14	8,521	856	10.0%	32,000
Annual Growth	**(0.5%)**	**(3.8%)**	**—**	**(5.1%)**

2018 Year-End Financials

Debt ratio: 55.24%	No. of shares (mil.): 293
Return on equity: —	Dividends
Cash ($ mil.): 559	Yield: 1.4%
Current ratio: 1.64	Payout: 21.6%
Long-term debt ($ mil.): 2,971	Market value ($ mil.): 8,594

	STOCK PRICE ($) FY Close	P/E High/Low		PER SHARE ($) Earnings	Dividends	Book Value
12/18	29.24	19	12	2.37	0.44	(0.38)
12/17	43.94	26	19	1.66	0.41	(0.19)
12/16	31.62	25	16	1.47	0.39	(0.94)
12/15	28.30	30	22	1.02	0.37	(0.41)
12/14	25.20	11	8	2.38	0.33	2.68
Annual Growth	**3.8%**	**—**	**—**	**(0.1%)**	**7.2%**	**—**

MASSACHUSETTS HOUSING FINANCE AGENCY PROPERTY ACQUISITION AND DISPOSITION CORPORATION

EXECUTIVES

Chb, Michael J Dirrane
Chm*, Ronald A Homer
Exec Dir*, Thomas R Gleason
Treas*, Andris J Silins
Prin*, Tom O'Brien
Cfo*, Michael Fitzmaurice
Staff, Tyrone Reed
Real Estate Conultant, Kristin Olsen
Executive Secretary, Christine Bond
Manager, Kevin Mello
Vp-Homeownership Programs, Mounzer M Aylouche

LOCATIONS

HQ: MASSACHUSETTS HOUSING FINANCE AGENCY PROPERTY ACQUISITION AND DISPOSITION CORPORATION
1 BEACON ST, BOSTON, MA 021083107
Phone: 617 854-1000
Web: WWW.MYMASSMORTGAGE.ORG

HISTORICAL FINANCIALS

Company Type: Private

Income Statement   FYE: June 30

	ASSETS ($ mil.)	NET INCOME ($ mil.)	INCOME AS % OF ASSETS	EMPLOYEES
06/18	5,460	6	0.1%	325
06/07*	5,457	80	1.5%	—
12/06	1	0	0.8%	—
06/05	0	(21)	—	—
Annual Growth	—	—	—	—

*Fiscal year change

2018 Year-End Financials

Debt ratio: —
Return on equity: 2.50%
Cash ($ mil.): 973
Current ratio: 2.90
Long-term debt ($ mil.): —

Dividends
Yield: —
Payout: —
Market value ($ mil.): —

MasTec Inc. (FL)

MasTec goes the last mile ? and the first mile and the miles in between ? to bring communications and energy to homes offices factories and other places. The company digs the trenches lays the cable and builds the towers that power communications and provide cell service and high-speed internet. The contractor plans and builds pipelines that transport natural gas and oil from wells to processing plants. It provides infrastructure construction to telecom vendors wireless providers cable TV operators and energy and utility companies. MasTec also builds electrical utility transmission and distribution and power generation wind and solar farms industrial infrastructure and water and sewer systems.

Operations

With more than 17000 employees and locations throughout North America MasTec has the size to tackle big projects that require large resources in equipment and people. Much of the company?s equipment ? bucket trucks forklifts backhoes sidebooms bulldozers excavators trenchers graders loaders directional boring machines digger derricks pile drivers and cranes ? can be used on any of its projects.

MasTec operates in five business units with most focused on a particular industry. The units are: Communications; Electrical Transmission; Oil and Gas; Power Generation and Industrial; and Other.

The Oil and Gas segment does engineering construction and maintenance on oil and natural gas pipelines and processing facilities for the energy and utilities industries. It accounts for about 55% of sales.

The Communications segment performs engineering construction and maintenance of communications infrastructure primarily related to wireless and wireline communications and install to the home and infrastructure for electrical utilities. It accounts for about 35% of sales.

The Electrical Transmission segment primarily serves energy and utility industries through the engineering construction and maintenance of electrical transmission lines and substations. It accounts for about 5% of sales.

The Power Generation and Industrial segment serves the energy and utility through the installation and construction of power plants wind farms solar farms related electrical transmission infrastructure ethanol plants and other industrial infrastructure. It accounts for less about 5% of sales.

The Other segment primarily includes small business units that perform construction services for a variety of end markets in Mexico and in other locations outside the US. It accounts for less than 1% of sales.

Geographic Reach

MasTec headquartered in Coral Gables Florida has about 400 locations in the US Canada and Mexico.

Sales and Marketing

MasTec sells directly to existing and potential customers for service agreement contracts and individual projects. MasTec?s current fortunes are tied to two companies Energy Transfer and AT&T. Pipeline work for Energy Transfer accounts for about 40% of MasTec?s revenue. MasTec?s communications work revolves around AT&T (including DirecTV) which supplies about 25% of revenue. The company?s level of business with AT&T has been consistent in recent years but business with Energy Transfer grew from just 7% of revenue in 2017.

Financial Performance

After eight years of steady gains MasTec recorded a dip in revenue and a loss in 2015 but rebounded with increasing revenue and profit in 2016 and 2017.

Sales rose about 30% to $6.6 billion in 2017 from 2016 on the strength of a big year for MasTec?s Oil and Gas unit. Several long-haul pipeline projects combine to drive Oil & Gas revenue about 75% higher for 2017. The Communications business also recorded higher revenue up about 4% entirely on the contributions by acquisitions. The unit?s organic revenue dipped about 10% from lower install-to-the-home work. Sales in the Electrical Transmission and the Power Generation and Industrial units decreased in 2017 from 2016.

Higher revenue enabled MasTec to absorb higher costs and post a profit of $347 million in 2017 up from $39 million in 2016. The company had a lower tax bill in 2017 because of the US Tax Cuts and Jobs Act which was signed into law at the end of the year.

Cash on hand was about the same at $40 million for 2016 and 2017 but free cash flow fell to about $33 million in 2017 from about $88 million the year before.

Strategy

MasTec is riding a wave of oil and gas activity in the US Canada and Mexico and it expects the wave to continue. The company has worked on several large projects connecting gas fields to processing facilities in the past few years and expects the trend to continue for several more years.

MasTec sees another force at work that could mean more business. The company itself benefited from the US Tax Cuts and Jobs Act of 2017 with lower taxes. Its customers with lower tax bills might be encouraged to spend more on projects that could add to MasTec?s backlog.

The company sees new construction for its Communications division with industry initiatives in the offing. Construction of infrastructure to support 5G networks is on the horizon. More immediately is the build out of the FirstNet network for public safety communications by AT&T and a large fiber project from Verizon Communications.

MasTec works in industries that go through cycles but its multiple capabilities help it weather ups and downs. Currently its oil and gas work is booming while the previous big revenue producer communications has waned by comparison. But transmission work should rev up as renewable energy projects move beyond the drawing board and into construction phases.

Mergers and Acquisitions

MasTec uses acquisitions to add to its capabilities and expand its footprint into new geographic regions.

In 2017 the company made three acquisitions: a wireline/fiber deployment construction contractor a heavy civil construction services company and an oil and gas pipeline equipment company. The company spent more than $115 million on acquisitions in 2017.

HISTORY

MasTec was formed by the merger of Burnup & Sims (B&S) and Church & Tower (C&T). B&S was founded in 1929 to provide construction and maintenance services to the phone and utilities industries. C&T began in 1968 building phone networks in Miami and Puerto Rico. Jorge Mas Canosa was brought on board in 1969 and given half of the company in exchange for managing it. By 1971 he had succeeded in turning C&T around and had bought the remainder.

In 1994 C&T and B&S merged; B&S became MasTec and C&T became a subsidiary. Mas was named chairman and his son who had been at C&T since 1980 was named president and CEO. The company began a program of acquisitions and started building a presence in Latin America.

MasTec doubled its size in 1996 by acquiring Sintel a telecom infrastructure construction firm operating in South America and Spain from TelA©fonica. MasTec continued to grow through acquisitions buying 10 more companies the next year. Mas died in 1997 and his son Jorge Jr. succeeded him. It sold a near-bankrupt Sintel and began to refocus on domestic operations.

Ceo And Director, José R. Mas, age 46, $980,000 total compensation

Evp And Cfo, George L. Pita, age 56, $450,000 total compensation

Evp General Counsel And Secretary, Alberto de Cardenas, age 49, $385,000 total compensation

Coo, Robert E. (Bob) Apple, age 68, $585,000 total compensation

Cio, Albert Iturrey

Vice President Partnership And Resource Management, Jay Carroll

Vice President Contract Management And Marketing, Robert Jackson

Vice President Virginia Operations, Henry Rudd

Vice President Of Sales And Marketing, Jeff Mock

Evp East Mastec Network Solutions, John Vento

Vice President, Sonya Roshek

Vice President Field Service, Chris Gera

Vice President Southwest Region, Erik Hughes

Vice President Financial Institutions Finpro, Miller Mark

Chairman, Jorge Mas, age 55

Auditors: BDO USA, LLP

LOCATIONS

HQ: MasTec Inc. (FL)
800 S. Douglas Road, 12th Floor, Coral Gables, FL 33134
Phone: 305 599-1800
Web: www.mastec.com

PRODUCTS/OPERATIONS

2017 Sales

	$ mil.	% of total
Oil & Gas	3,497	53
Communications	2,424	37
Electrical Transmission	378	6
Power Generation & Industrial	299	4
Other	20	-
Adjustments	(13.5)	-
Total	**6,607**	**100**

Selected Services

Broadband networks
  Aerial and underground construction
  Bonding/grounding
  Engineering and design
  FCC testing
  Modem installation
  Optical fiber splicing activation and testing
  Warehouse and inventory management
Telecommunications
  Aerial construction
  Copper/coaxial cable systems
  Directional drilling
  Engineering
  Fiber-optic cable systems
  Fiber-to-the-premises (FTTP) deployment
  Splicing and testing
  Underground construction
Utilities
  Design and engineering
  Gas distribution construction and maintenance
  Storm restoration
  Submarine cable installation
  Substation construction
  Transmission line construction
  Trench construction

COMPETITORS

Bechtel	MDU Construction
Black & Veatch	Services
Dycom	MYR Group
General Dynamics	Pike Corporation
Goldfield	Primoris
Henkels & McCoy	Quanta Services
Jacobs Engineering	Sirti
M. A. Mortenson	Willbros

HISTORICAL FINANCIALS

Company Type: Public

Income Statement

FYE: December 31

	REVENUE ($ mil.)	NET INCOME ($ mil.)	NET PROFIT MARGIN	EMPLOYEES
12/17	6,606	347	5.3%	17,300
12/16	5,134	131	2.6%	15,400
12/15	4,208	(79)	—	15,900
12/14	4,611	115	2.5%	15,550
12/13	4,324	140	3.3%	13,450
Annual Growth	**11.2%**	**25.3%**		**6.5%**

2017 Year-End Financials

Debt ratio: 33.65%
Return on equity: 27.48%
Cash ($ mil.): 40
Current ratio: 1.92
Long-term debt ($ mil.): 1,280

No. of shares (mil.): 82
Dividends
  Yield: —
  Payout: —
Market value ($ mil.): 4,053

	STOCK PRICE ($) FY Close	P/E High/Low		Earnings	Dividends	Book Value
12/17	48.95	12	8	4.22	0.00	17.28
12/16	38.25	25	8	1.61	0.00	13.28
12/15	17.38	—	—	(0.98)	0.00	11.73
12/14	22.61	31	13	1.35	0.00	13.50
12/13	32.72	19	14	1.66	0.00	13.15
Annual Growth	**10.6%**			**26.3%**	—	**7.1%**

Mastercard Inc

Surpassing Visa in market share — now that would be priceless. Serving more than 20000 member financial institutions around the world Mastercard is the #2 payment system in the US. The company does not issue credit or its namesake cards; rather it markets the Mastercard Maestro and Cirrus brands provides a transaction authorization network establishes guidelines for use and collects fees from members. The company provides its services in more than 200 countries and territories and its branded cards are accepted at millions of locations around the globe. Mastercard also operates the Cirrus ATM network.

HISTORY

A group of bankers formed The Interbank Card Association (ICA) in 1966 to establish authorization clearing and settlement procedures for bank credit card transactions. This was particularly important to banks left out of the rapidly growing BankAmericard (later Visa) network sponsored by Bank of America.

By 1969 ICA was issuing the Master Charge card throughout the US and had formed alliances in Europe and Japan. In the mid-1970s ICA modernized its system replacing telephone transaction authorization with a computerized magnetic strip system. ICA had members in Africa Australia and Europe by 1979. That year the organization changed its name (and the card's) to MasterCard.

In 1980 Russell Hogg became president when John Reynolds resigned after disagreeing with the board over company performance and direction. Hogg made major organizational changes and consolidated data processing in St. Louis. MasterCard began offering debit cards in 1980 and traveler's checks in 1981.

MasterCard issued the first credit cards in China in 1987. The next year it bought Cirrus then the world's largest ATM network. It also secured a pact with Belgium-based card company Eurocard (which later became Europay) to supervise MasterCard's European operations and help build the brand.

Hogg resigned in 1988 after disagreements with the board and was succeeded by Alex Hart. In 1991 the Maestro debit card was unveiled.

The 1990s were marked by trouble in Europe: The pact with Europay hadn't resulted in the boom MasterCard had hoped for customer service was below par and competition was keen. Alex Hart retired in 1994 and was succeeded by Eugene Lockhart who tackled the European woes. Lockhart considered ending the relationship but eventually worked things out with Europay. By the end of the decade Europay was locked in a vicious battle to undercut Visa's market share through lower fees.

MasterCard in 1995 invested in UK-based Mondex International maker of electronic set-value refillable smart cards. But US consumer resistance to cash cards and competition in the more advanced European market delayed growth in this area.

In October 1996 a group of merchants including Wal-Mart and Sears filed class-action lawsuits against both MasterCard and Visa challenging the "honor all cards" rule. Because usage fees are higher merchants balked at accepting consumers' MasterCard- or Visa-branded off-line or signature-based debit cards and claimed the card issuers violated antitrust laws by tying acceptance of debit to that of credit. In a dramatic twist minutes before the trial was set to begin in 2003 MasterCard announced a settlement (the card issuer was required to pay $125 million in 2003 and $100 million annually from 2004 through 2012).

Just months later armed with the lawsuit's settlement which also freed merchants to pick which credit and debit card services they use Wal-Mart (along with a handful of others) stopped accepting signature debit cards issued by MasterCard.

Lockhart resigned in 1997 and was succeeded by former head of overseas operations Robert Selander. Yet another management upheaval began in 1999 as the company moved to streamline its organizational structure and shift away from geographical divisions. It also said member banks could boost visibility by putting their logos on card fronts and moving MasterCard's logo to the back.

In 2002 MasterCard merged with Europay with which it already had close ties. As part of the transaction holding company MasterCard Incorporated was formed; MasterCard International become the company's main subsidiary and MasterCard Europe (formerly Europay) became its European subsidiary.

After some 40 years as a private entity MasterCard went public in 2006 in one of the largest IPOs of its time. Following the offering the approximately 1400 financial institutions that wholly owned MasterCard before the offering retained a stake of more than 40%. Two of the top three US banks (Citigroup and JPMorgan Chase) remained among MasterCard's largest shareholders.

Some of the proceeds from the company's IPO were used to fight antitrust lawsuits from such rivals as American Express and Discover as well as other payment processors. In 2008 the company agreed to a $1.8 billion settlement with American Express which had claimed that MasterCard and others tried to stop financial institutions from issuing its AmEx cards. Later that year MasterCard settled the Discover lawsuit agreeing to pay $862.5 million.

Also in 2008 MasterCard bought Ireland-based software provider Orbiscom. The acquired company's technology was used to create MasterCard inControl a platform for making secure Internet and telephone purchases.

MasterCard promoted president and COO Ajay Banga to CEO in 2010. He succeeded Robert Selander who stepped down after more than a dozen years at the helm.

EXECUTIVES

Cfo, Martina Hund-Mejean, age 58, $691,667 total compensation

President And Ceo, Ajaypal S. (Ajay) Banga, age 58, $1,200,000 total compensation

President Global Products And Solutions, Gary J. Flood, age 60, $650,000 total compensation

President International Markets, Ann Cairns, age 61, $609,427 total compensation

Chief Services Officer, Kevin J. Stanton

President U.s. Issuers, Raj Seshadri

President Europe, Javier Perez

General Counsel And Chief Franchise Officer, Timothy H. (Tim) Murphy, age 51

Chief Product Officer, Michael Miebach

Chief Innovation Officer, Garry Lyons

President Operations And Technology, Edward (Ed) McLaughlin

Vice Chairman And President Center For Inclusive Growth, Walt W. Macnee, age 63

President North America, Craig Vosburg, age 51

President Middle East And Africa, Raghu Malhotra

President Enterprise Security Solutions, Ajay Bhalla

Co-president Asia/pacific, Hai Ling

Co-president Asia/pacific, Ari Sarker

President Latin America And Caribbean Region, Gilberto Caldart

President Processing Services, Andrea Scerch

President Prepaid Management Services, Fabrizio Burlando

Senior Vice President And Group Head, Michael Robichaud

Senior Vice President Chief Admin Officer, Joy Thoma

Vice President In The Consumer And Market Intelligence Group, Peter Reville

Vice President Corporate Communications, John Gander

Vice President Business Leader, Ashfaq Kamal

Vice President Channel Management, Kevin Carroll

Vice President Business Leader, Bernhard Mors

Vice President, Michael Moutenot

Vice President And Business Leader Development, Rachel Benning

Vice President, Naya Larsson

Vice President Of U S Pre Paid, Ed Wang

Vice President Customer Technical Communications; Manager Information Technology Transformation O, Wendy Richardson

Vice President, VALERIE MILLER

Vice President Global Digital Marketing, Kevin Kline

Vice President Business Leader Social Media, Gregory Weiss

Senior Business Leader Vice President, Shawn Hilleary

Executive Vice President Digital Partnerships, Sherri Haymond

Vice President Product Sales, Erik Nansen

Group Head Senior Vice President, Michael Shade

Vice President Senior Business Leader, Mathias Lilja

Vice President Caribbean, Mario Perez

Vice President, Peter Berardino

Vice President Business Information Systems, Richard Derizans

Senior Vice President Human Resources Middle East And Africa, Scott Tierney

Vice President Global Supply Managment, Bryan Fuller

Vice President And Sbl Commercial Business Development, Patrick Sulston

Vice President Global Merchant Development, Rachel Bale

Vice President Acceptance Development, Craig Kirkland

Vice President Finance And Planning Global Prepaid, Prasad Iyer

Senior Vice President Global Talent Acquisition, Charlie Hall

Vice President And Business Leader, Cheryl Castro

Vice President, Deborah Galano

Vice President, Justin Pinkham

Vice President And Business Leader, Regina Ng

Vice President (business Leader) Commercial Product Development Authentication Services, Laurie Nicoletti

Vice President Channel Development Payment Transaction Services (americas), Ashish Tetali

Vice President U.s. Digital Marketing, Nancy Walsh

Vice President Project Management Office, Fred Branca

Vice President Product Management, Kevin Rowland

Vice President Account Management, Tor Opedal

Senior Vice President Business Development Unit Supervisor, Hunter Woolley

Senior Vice President Account Management, John Levitsky

Vice President Mergers And Acquisitions, Michael Luchinsky

Vice President Global Marketing Solutions, Linda Paczkowski

Vice President Technology Account Management, Timothy Ware

Vice President Performance Analysis, John Tullo

Vice President Global Marketing (sbl), John King

Vice President, Gary Sofko

Vice President, Dawn Barger

Vice President New Markets, Rich Ciamillo

Senior Vice President Total Rewards, Stuart Finkelstein

Vice President, Denise Torreyson

Vice President Member Relations, Peter Patrissi

Vice President Senior Human Resources Business Partner, Meri Wax

Senior Vice President Global Core Products Business Finance Officer, Pam Loscher

Group Vice President Debit Sales, Wade Plummer

Vice President Product Management, Gowri Narayanan

Senior Executive Vice President, Trish Preston

Senior Vice President Global Product Marketing, Greg Boosin

Vice President Mobile Alliances, Jeffrey Allen

Vice President And Business Leader, Steven Eidelson

Vice President Global Interactive Marketing, Elena D'andrea

Vice President U.s. Markets, Paul Tobin

Vice President Retail And Luxury Markets, Vivienne Conatser

Vice President Head Of Strategy Development Core Products, Rachael Jenkinson

Vice President Digital Partnerships, Chris Kangas

Vice President, Melanie Gluck

Vice President In The Global Insights Group, Christina Sommer

Vice President Technology Account Management, Jonathan Powell

Executive Vice President B2b Marketing, Elisa Romm

Vice President Of Marketing, Lorena Holguin

Vice President Marketing Strategy And Operations, Julia Huang

Vice President Business Development And Strategic Alliances Us Markets, David Galvan

Executive Vice President Global Total Rewards, Susan Kunreuther

Vice President Global Marketing, Pattie Pan

Vice President, Deb Morrison

Vice President And Business Leader Worldwide Communications, Jane Khodos

Vice President And Head Of Emerging Payments, Gaurav Khillan

Vice President And Business Leader Product Management Digital Payments At Mastercard, John Mwangi

Vice President Business Leader Openapi, Manash Bhattacharjee

Vice President Us Markets Finance, Donna Klecker

Senior Business Leader Vice President Corporate Development, Sergiu Cecoltan

Senior Vice President Integration Lead Enterprise Security Solutions, Ian Webb

Office Of The Senior Executive Vice President Risk Management, Lynne Cullari

Vice President Prepaid Product Management, Jason Tymms

Vice President Mobile Money, Henry Gewirtz

Vice President Corporate Security, Richard Gunthner

Vice President Global Account Management, Brian Moran

Vice President Business Development, Marco Castro

Vice President Senior Account Manager, Greg Pastorek

Vice President Network Engineering, Lisa Rief

Vice President And Senior Business Leader, Jeremy Feinberg

Executive Vice President Mobile Solutions, Felix Marx

Vice President Business Development, Chris Morris

Business Leader Vice President, Christine Eris

Vice President Corporate Strategy, Gaurav Mittal

Vice President Senior Business Leader, Mark Lerner

Vice President Prepaid Expert Sales, Elaine Harkins

Senior Vice President National And Local Accounts, Bob Glowasky

Vice President Financial Planning And Analysis, Craig Nussbaum

Senior Vice President Direct Sales, Elizabeth Wolgemuth

Vice President Business Leader, Adam Bell

Regional Counsel And Vice President, Ben Robertson

Vice President Product Development, Paulo Fernandes

Vice President Develop, Jeff Feuerstein

Vice President, Connie Frawley

Vice President, Andrea Bober

Vice President Global Paypass Product Development, Mike Shadmani

Global New Product Development Senior Vice President, Diana Robino

Vice President President Direct Interactive Marketing, Jeff White

Vice President Corporate Planning And Financial Analysis Global Finance, Ellen Okeeffe

Vice President U.s. Market Development, Adam Goodman

Vice President Us Market Development, Kerry Distefano

Vice President Strategic Accounts, Charles Reynolds

Senior Vice President, Pilar S Ramos

Business Leader Vice President, Michael Goldstein

Vice President Systems Development Global Technology And Operations, Karen Karen Hughes Hughes

Vice President Human Resources, Jason Colvin

Vice President Business Development, John Mcdermott

Assistant Vice President Of Product Media Solutions, Pablo Cohan

Vice President Commercial Products, Siddharth Pande

Vice President Mastercard Enterprise
Partnerships, Will Judge
Vice President Product Operations, Thomas Rempe
Vice President Global Talent Development And
Orga, Leigh Bochicchio
Vice President Global Prepaid Product, Mark Vanni
Vice President, Daryl Marshall
Executive Vice President North America Services,
Chris Reid
Senior Vice President Head Of Operations And
Technology Payment Gateway Services, Luigi
Zanghellini
Vice President Technology Account Management,
Luis Escontrela
Vice President, Patricio Hernandez
Vice President Creative Director, Arnaud Jammaers
Auditors: PricewaterhouseCoopers LLP

LOCATIONS

HQ: Mastercard Inc
  2000 Purchase Street, Purchase, NY 10577
Phone: 914 249-2000
Web: www.mastercard.com

2016 Revenue

	% of total
US	38
International	62
Total	100

PRODUCTS/OPERATIONS

2016 Sales

	$ mil.	% of total
Transaction processing fees	5,143	33
Domestic assessments	4,411	28
Cross-border volume fees	3,568	23
Other	2,431	16
Adjustments	(4777)	-
Total	10,776	100

COMPETITORS

Alibaba.com	JCB International
Amazon.com	NYCE Payments Network
American Express	PULSE Network
China UnionPay	PayPal
Discover	Total System Services
Fifth Third	Visa Inc
First Data	Visa International

HISTORICAL FINANCIALS

Company Type: Public

Income Statement   FYE: December 31

	REVENUE ($ mil.)	NET INCOME ($ mil.)	NET PROFIT MARGIN	EMPLOYEES
12/17	12,497	3,915	31.3%	13,400
12/16	10,776	4,059	37.7%	11,900
12/15	9,667	3,808	39.4%	11,300
12/14	9,473	3,617	38.2%	10,300
12/13	8,346	3,116	37.3%	8,200
Annual Growth	10.6%	5.9%	—	13.1%

2017 Year-End Financials

Debt ratio: 25.43%
Return on equity: 70.39%
Cash ($ mil.): 5,933
Current ratio: 1.57
Long-term debt ($ mil.): 5,424

No. of shares (mil.): 1,054
Dividends
  Yield: 0.0%
  Payout: 24.1%
Market value ($ mil.): 159,533

	STOCK PRICE ($) FY Close	P/E High/Low	PER SHARE ($) Earnings	Dividends	Book Value
12/17	151.36	42 29	3.65	0.88	5.19
12/16	103.25	29 22	3.69	0.76	5.23
12/15	97.36	30 24	3.35	0.64	5.40
12/14	86.16	271 22	3.10	0.44	5.89
12/13	835.46	324191	2.56	0.21	6.27
Annual Growth	(34.8%)	— —	9.3%	43.1%	(4.6%)

Mattel Inc

Barbie is the platinum blonde in power at Mattel the #1 toy maker in the world. Its products include Barbie and Polly Pocket dolls Fisher-Price toys Hot Wheels and Matchbox cars American Girl dolls and books and various Disney Nickelodeon and other licensed brands. Mattel also sells action figures and toys based on Walt Disney and Warner Bros movies as well as games (UNO) arts and crafts (MEGA BLOX RoseArt) and puzzles. Mattel is trying to reduce its reliance on its biggest customers — Wal-Mart Toys "R" Us and Target— through its own catalog and internet sales.

Operations

Mattel operates three business segments: North America International and American Girl.

The North American segment which makes up around 50% of Mattel's total sales markets and sells toys in the US and Canada through the Mattel Girls & Boys Brands and Fisher-Price Brands categories. In the Mattel Girls & Boys Brands category Barbie includes brands such as Barbie fashion dolls and accessories with the Ever After High Polly Pocket Little Mommy Disney Classics and Monster High lumped into the Other Girls Brands. Wheels include Hot Wheels Matchbox and Tyco R/C vehicles and play sets. Entertainment includes CARS Disney Planes BOOMco Toy Story Max Steel WWE Wrestling Batman and Superman as well as games and puzzles. The Fisher-Price Brands category includes Fisher-Price Little People Laugh & Learn BabyGear Imaginext Dora the Explorer Shimmer and Shine Thomas & Friends Minnie Mouse Octonauts Mickey Mouse Clubhouse Disney's Jake and the Never Land Pirates and Power Wheels.

Products marketed by the International segment (some 40% of sales) are generally the same as those developed and marketed by the North America segment although some are developed or adapted for particular international markets. Mattel's products are sold directly to retailers and wholesalers in most European Latin American and Asian countries and in Australia and New Zealand and through agents and distributors in those countries where Mattel has no direct presence.

The American Girl segment (approx. 10% of sales) is a direct marketer children's publisher and retailer known for its flagship line of historical dolls books and accessories as well as the My American Girl Truly Me Girl of the Year and Bitty Baby brands. American Girl also publishes best-selling Advice & Activity books and the award-winning American Girl magazine. American Girl products are sold primarily in the US.

Looking at its brands the Mattel Girl's and Boy's brand products generate more than 50% of all sales while the Fisher-Price branded products generate some 30%. The company's American Girl brand brings in 10% of sales. The Construction

and Arts & Crafts branded products bring in the remainder.

Geographic Reach

El Segundo California-based Mattel fills toy chests worldwide. The toymaker sells products in more than 150 nations across North America Europe Latin America and Asia Pacific. North America accounts for around half of total sales. Europe is the company's second-largest market generating about a quarter of Mattel's total sales. Latin America and the Asia-Pacific region both bring in around 10% each.

Sales and Marketing

Mattel sells its products through its own retailers and wholesalers in most of the world and through agents and distributors in those countries where it has no direct presence. American Girl products are sold directly to consumers. Wal-Mart Stores ($1.1 billion in sales) Toys "R" Us ($600 million) and Target ($400 million) are the company's three largest customers altogether accounting for nearly 40% of its worldwide sales each year.

Mattel capitalizes on major events such as movie releases by focusing on product tie-ins. It also promotes its toys and characters through online and broadcast media.

Financial Performance

The world's largest toy maker has seen its sales and profits decline in recent years as its markets and brands in the US and Europe have matured.

In fiscal 2016 sales fell 4% to $5.5 billion due to a sharp fall in the Other Girls product category and unfavorable currency exchange effects partially offset by increases in Barbie Wheels and Entertainment. Fisher-Price posted modest 3% growth while American Girls Brands was flat.

Net income fell 14% to $318 million due to lower gross profits partially offset by lower SGA expenses and lower advertising. Gross profits were impacted by currency effects and higher input costs. Mattel's Funding Our Future cost cutting program reduced expenses by $60 million and it reduced compensation costs by $36 million and severance and restructuring costs by $32 million.

Cash from operations fell 195 to $594.5 million due to higher working capital usage and lower net income.

Strategy

With sales declining and Hasbro and Lego threatening to seize Mattel's long-held toy crown the company launched in 2017 a strategic growth plan based on five pillars. The pillars are: 1) build its power brands into 360-degree play systems and experiences; 2) drive emerging market growth via digital; 3) strengthen its innovation pipeline; 4) seek cost efficiencies through restructuring; and 5) shake up its culture.

The 360-degree play approach means building out its key brands into physical and digital space and creating a community of shared interest around them. Moving away from being purely a seller of toys its physical products will be supplemented by video games particularly on mobile platforms and storytelling.

Its emerging market growth strategy rests on deepening relationships with Chinese parents in particular. It struck a deal with Chinese e-commerce giant Alibaba to sell learning products based on its Fisher-Price toys. The emphasis on learning products is hoped to chime with the "Tiger Mother" archetype that pushes her child to succeed in school.

To bolster its innovation pipeline Mattel is democratizing its approach by opening up product ideas to amateur inventors who can now submit ideas via an online portal. Early successes of this new approach include Artsplash which sold out online and in Toys "R" Us in short order.

Following on from its Funding Our Future cost savings program was saved around $295 million in 2015-16 Mattel is further refining its operations with the goal of saving another $150-200 million. It also aims to drive down speed to market from 18 months to just nine.

The fifth pillar is around bringing in fresh talent in the areas of brand management commercial manufacturing connected product development e-commerce content and digital marketing.

Mergers and Acquisitions

In January 2016 Mattel bought Fuhu Inc. a developer of high-tech products for children and families that is best known for its Nabi Brand products for $21.5 million. Also that month the toy maker acquired Sprouting Inc. which makes smart tech products for parents and families. Both of the acquired companies bolstered Mattel's digital and smart technology product offerings.

HISTORY

A small California toy manufacturer began operating out of a converted garage in 1945 producing dollhouse furniture. Harold Matson and Elliot Handler named their new company Mattel using letters from their last and first names. Matson soon sold his share to Handler and his wife Ruth who incorporated the business in 1948.

The company's toy line had expanded by 1952 to include burp guns and musical toys and sales exceeded $5 million. Sponsorship of Walt Disney's Mickey Mouse Club (debuted 1955) a first in toy advertising was a shrewd marketing step for Mattel providing direct year-round access to millions of young potential customers.

In 1959 Mattel introduced the Barbie doll named after the Handlers' daughter Barbara and later introduced Ken named after their son. Barbie with her fashionable wardrobe and extensive line of accessories was an instant hit and eventually became the most successful brand-name toy ever sold.

Mattel went public in 1960 and within two years sales had jumped from $25 million to $75 million. It launched the popular Hot Wheels miniature cars line in 1968.

The Handlers were ousted from management in 1974 after an investigation by the SEC found irregularities in reports of the company's profits. The new management moved into non-toy businesses adding Western Publishing (Golden Books) and the Ringling Brothers-Barnum & Bailey Combined Shows circus in 1979.

Mattel and two former employees agreed in 2002 to pay $477000 in fines for making political donations in other people's names the third-largest fine ever imposed by the Federal Election Commission. Also that year the company closed its Kentucky manufacturing and distribution facilities and in early 2003 consolidated two of its manufacturing facilities in Mexico.

In a stinging defeat for Mattel in April 2011 a federal jury sided with MGA Entertainment in the long-running legal battle over ownership of the billion-dollar Bratz doll franchise. (MGA and Mattel started their catfight a decade ago.) The jury rejected Mattel's copyright infringement claims. Instead it found that Mattel has stolen trade secrets from MGA and said it owed the company $88.5 million. The decision reversed a 2008 ruling in which a jury sided with Mattel.

EXECUTIVES

Evp Chief Legal Officer And Secretary, Robert (Bob) Normile, age 59, $580,000 total compensation
Evp And Chief Human Resources Officer, Richard R. Gros, age 63
Cfo, Joseph J. (Joe) Euteneuer, age 63
Evp And Chief Supply Chain Officer, Peter D. Gibbons, age 57, $600,000 total compensation
President And Coo, Richard Dickson, age 50, $900,000 total compensation
Ceo, Margaret H. (Margo) Georgiadis
Evp And Chief Strategic Technology Officer, Geoffrey H. Walker, age 52, $530,000 total compensation
Cto, Sven Gerjets
Vice President, Sejal Shah
Gm Senior Vice President Consumer Products, Jessica Dunne
Senior Vice President And Gm Girl 's Toy Box, Lori Pantel
Vice President Of Barbie Product Development, Jon Marine
Vice President, Sibylle Addotta
Vice President Marketing, Carole Levine
Vice President Finance And Strategic Planning For Mattel Brands, Eric Chan
Vice President Global Brand Marketing And Design, Gabriel Carlson
Vice President Product Development, Isela Scaglione
Vice President, Michael Shore
Executive Vice President Global Enterprise, Gabriel Zalzman
Vice President And Assistant General Cou, Melinda Mehringer
Vice President Of Global Product Development Design Technical Support, Steve Sucher
Vice President Global Procurement At Mattel, Linda Theisen
Vice President Girls Marketing, Clara Crowder
Vice President Sales And Marketing, Theresa Chatt
Vice President Entertainment And Franchise Development, David Voss
Vice President Global Softlines Consumer Products, Aaron Duncan
Senior Vice President Marketing And Design Girls, Tim Kilpin
Senior Vice President And Corporate Treasurer, Mandana Sadigh
Vice President Human Resources, Kim Giordanella
Vice President Information Security And Ciso, Jill Knesek
Vice President, Dave Okada
Vice President Advanced Concepts, David Miller
Senior Vice President Content Development And Production, Christopher Keenan
Vice President Information Technology International Systems, Michel Bernard
Chief People Officer, Amy Thompson
Vp And Gm Montoi, Jonathan Waite
Vice President And Assistant General Counsel, Donald B Aiken
Vice President Global Brand Marketing And Design, Gabe Carlson
Vice President Global Shared Services, Jill Webster
Senior Vice President Glbl Quality And Reg Compl, Dan Spitzer
Chairman, Christopher A. Sinclair, age 67
Auditors: PricewaterhouseCoopers LLP

LOCATIONS

HQ: Mattel Inc
333 Continental Blvd., El Segundo, CA 90245-5012
Phone: 310 252-2000
Web: www.mattel.com

PRODUCTS/OPERATIONS

2016 Sales

Category by Brand	$ mil.	% of total
Mattel Girls & Boys Brands	3,194	53
Fisher-Price Brands	1,888	31
American Girl Brands	570	9
Construction and Arts & Crafts Brands	377	6
Other	43	1
Eliminations	(617.0)	-
Total	5,456	100

2016 Sales

	$ mil.	% of total
North America	3,036	50
International	2,447	40
American Girl	589	10
Eliminations	(617.0)	-
Total	5,456	100

Selected Brands:

Barbie
BoomCo
DC Universe
DC Superhero Girls
Dinotrux
Disney Cars
Disney Planes
Ever After High
Fast & Furious
Ghostbusters
Halo
Hot Wheels
Masters of the Universe
Matchbox
Mattel Games
Mega Construx
Minecraft
Monster High
My Mini MixieQ's
My Password Journal
nabi
Rose Art
Thundercats
Toy Story
Tyco RC
View-Master
VS Rip Spin Warriors
WWE)
Wonder Woman

COMPETITORS

Electronic Arts	Playmobil
Hasbro	Radio Flyer
JAKKS Pacific	Sanrio
LEGO	Simba Dickie Group
LeapFrog	Spin Master
MGA Entertainment	TakaraTomy
Marvel Entertainment	Toy Quest
Motorsports Authentics	Ty
Namco Bandai	VTech Holdings
Ohio Art	

HISTORICAL FINANCIALS

Company Type: Public

Income Statement

FYE: December 31

	REVENUE ($ mil.)	NET INCOME ($ mil.)	NET PROFIT MARGIN	EMPLOYEES
12/17	4,881	(1,053)	—	28,000
12/16	5,456	318	5.8%	32,000
12/15	5,702	369	6.5%	31,000
12/14	6,023	498	8.3%	31,000
12/13	6,484	903	13.9%	29,000
Annual Growth	(6.9%)	—		(0.9%)

2017 Year-End Financials

Debt ratio: 50.06%	No. of shares (mil.): 343
Return on equity: (-57.50%)	Dividends
Cash ($ mil.): 1,079	Yield: 0.0%
Current ratio: 1.92	Payout: —
Long-term debt ($ mil.): 2,873	Market value ($ mil.): 5,288

	STOCK PRICE ($) FY Close	P/E High/Low		PER SHARE ($)		
				Earnings	Dividends	Book Value
12/17	15.38	—	—	(3.07)	0.91	3.66
12/16	27.55	37	27	0.92	1.52	7.03
12/15	27.17	29	18	1.08	1.52	7.75
12/14	30.95	33	20	1.45	1.52	8.72
12/13	47.58	18	14	2.58	1.44	9.58
Annual Growth	(24.6%)	—	—		(10.8%)	(21.4%)

MAYO CLINIC HOSPITAL-ROCHESTER

Multidisciplinary teamwork with coordinated care is Mayo Clinic's secret sauce. The not-for-profit Mayo Clinic provides health care most notably for complex medical conditions through its clinics in Rochester Minnesota Arizona and Florida. The clinics' multidisciplinary approach to care attracts more than a million patients a year from around the globe. For less specialized care the Mayo Clinic Health System operates a regional network of affiliated community hospitals and clinics in Minnesota Iowa and Wisconsin. Mayo Clinic also conducts research and trains physicians nurses and other health professionals. The Mayo Clinic is named for Dr. William Worrall Mayo who settled in Rochester in 1863.

Operations

Mayo Clinic Health System's regional network operates more than a dozen hospitals that combined are home to about 1000 beds and 3800 staff physicians medical scientists and clinical and research associates. The system also includes roughly 70 clinics in northern Iowa western Wisconsin and southeastern Minnesota. To manage its patient load Mayo forms referral alliances with other hospital groups HMOs and other organizations.

The clinic's education programs include the Mayo Medical School Mayo Graduate School and the Mayo School of Health Sciences; some medical training programs are conducted through partnerships with universities including the University of Minnesota. It also provides continuing education programs to medical professionals.

Financial Performance

The Mayo Clinic's revenue increased by nearly 7% in 2011 vs. 2010 while net income declined 18% over the same period. Indeed revenue gains and other support has steadily increased in recent years to nearly $8.5 billion in 2011. Sales of medical services (which account for about 85% of the Mayo Clinic's total) grew by 6% vs. the prior year. The Mayo Clinic list more than $10 billion in total assets.

Strategy

Already a giant in health care in the Midwest the Mayo Clinic continues to grow in other regions. In 2018 it announced plans to invest some $648 million in its Phoenix campus over the next five years. The project will roughly double the size of the campus allowing the system to meet growing demand for complex health care services in the Southwest. Similarly Mayo Clinic is investing some $144 million in its Jacksonville Florida campus.

Mayo Clinic strives to accommodate patients who travel to get to its facilities and will schedule multiple appointments and tests tightly together to make the most of patient's time. Rather than paying physicians based upon the quantity of patients seen the clinic's doctors are paid salaries as an incentive to quality care. These and other innovations have drawn attention to the clinic's patient-centered model of care. It has created a Center for the Science of Health Care Delivery and collaborates with other innovators including Cleveland Clinic and Intermountain Healthcare.

To reach remote areas Mayo Clinic in Arizona pioneered a telemedicine program that places robots in rural hospitals allowing local doctors and hospital staff to communicate with Mayo doctors in real time as they treat patients with such conditions as stroke or collapsed lungs.

EXECUTIVES

Regional Vice President, Annie Sadosty
Chair Department Of Medicine, Morie Gertz
Senior Vice President, Andrew Moore
Vice President, Victoria Hanson
Vice President, Brian Arendt
Medical Director, Jerry Swanson
Director Patient Care Nursing, Bonny Young
Vice President, BOBBIE S GOSTOUT
Regional Vice President Bus Development And Marketing, Peter Hughes
Secretary Treasurer, Paul Mueller
Board Member, John Dilger
Internal Audit Vice Chair, Carrie Graunke
Treasurer, Daniel Van Dyke
Secretary, Luanne Wussow
Secretary, Lisa Jurrens
Auditors: RSM US LLP MINNEAPOLIS MINNE

LOCATIONS

HQ: MAYO CLINIC HOSPITAL-ROCHESTER
200 1ST ST SW, ROCHESTER, MN 559050002
Phone: 507 284-2511
Web: WWW.MAYOCLINIC.ORG

Selected Locations and Affiliates

Direct subsidiaries
  Arizona
  Mayo Clinic Hospital (Phoenix)
  Mayo Clinic Scottsdale
  Florida
  Mayo Clinic Hospital (Jacksonville)
  Mayo Clinic Jacksonville
  Minnesota
  Mayo Clinic Rochester
  Rochester Methodist Hospital
  Saint Marys Hospital (Rochester)
  Mayo Eugenio Litta Children's Hospital
Mayo Health System affiliates
  Iowa
  Armstrong Clinic
  Decorah Clinic
  Lake Mills Clinic
  Franciscan
  Swea City Clinic
  Minnesota
  Fountain Centers in Fairmont
  Fountain Centers in Waseca
  FamilyHeal
  FamilyHealth Medical Clinic - Northfield Hospital
  Franciscan Healthcare in Caledonia
  Franciscan Healthcare La Crescent Clinic
  Mayo Clinic Health System - Albert Lea
Mayo Clini
Mayo Clini
Mayo Clini
Mayo Clini
  Wisconsin
  Chippewa Valley in Bloomer
  Chippewa Valley in Chippewa Falls
  Chippewa Valley in Colfax
  Eau Claire Home Health & Hospice
  Franciscan Healthcare Arcadia Campus
  Franciscan Healthcare Holmen Clinic
  Franciscan Healthcare Lake Tomah Clinic
  Franciscan Healthcare Onalaska Clinic
  Franciscan Healthcare Prairie du Chien Clinic
  Franciscan Healthcare Sparta Campus
  Northland in Barron
  Red Cedar in Elmwood
  Red Cedar in Glenwood
  Red Cedar in Menomonie

PRODUCTS/OPERATIONS

2015 Revenues

	$ mil.	% of total
Medical services	8,620	84
Grants & contracts	386	4
Investment return	233	2
Contributions	211	2
Premiums	144	1
Other	721	6
Total	**8,476**	**100**

COMPETITORS

Allina Hospitals
Ascension Health
Beth Israel Deaconess Medical Center
CentraCare Health
Children's Hospitals and Clinics of Minnesota
Dana-Farber
Fairview Health
Fox Chase Cancer Center
Gundersen Lutheran
HCA
Henry Ford Health System
Intermountain Health Care
Johns Hopkins Medicine
MD Anderson Cancer Center
Memorial Sloan-Kettering
North Memorial Health Care
Olmsted Medical
Park Nicollet Health Services
Roswell Park Cancer Institute
Scottsdale Healthcare
Tenet Healthcare
The Cleveland Clinic
Wistar Institute

HISTORICAL FINANCIALS

Company Type: Private

Income Statement				FYE: December 31
	REVENUE ($ mil.)	NET INCOME ($ mil.)	NET PROFIT MARGIN	EMPLOYEES
12/17	11,993	856	7.1%	82,000
12/16	10,998	(480)	—	—
Annual Growth	9.0%	—	—	—

2017 Year-End Financials

Debt ratio: —
Return on equity: 7.10%
Cash ($ mil.): 66
Current ratio: 0.80
Long-term debt ($ mil.): —

Dividends
  Yield: —
  Payout: —
  Market value ($ mil.): —

MB Financial Inc

The "MB" in MB Financial doesn't stand for "Midsized Businesses" though that's its target market. The $16 billion-asset holding company owns MB Financial Bank which has about 80 branches in the Chicago area and one in Philadelphia. Commercial-related credits including mortgages operating loans lease financing and construction loans make up 85% of the bank's loan portfolio. In addition to serving small and middle-market businesses MB Financial provides retail banking and lending to consumers. The company also offers wealth management and trust services through its Cedar Hill Associates subsidiary and brokerage through Vision Investment Services. LaSalle Systems leases technology-related equipment to corporations.

Operations

MB Financial operates three main business segments: Banking which counts its deposit and lending activities; Leasing which originates leases and related services through subsidiaries LaSalle Systems Leasing Celtic Leasing Corp and MB Equipment Finance; and Mortgage Banking which originates and services residential mortgage loans to hold in its portfolio or list for sale to investors via retail or third party channels.

Broadly speaking about 54% of the bank's total revenue came from loan interest during 2015 while another 10% came from interest on its investment securities. The rest of its revenue came from mortgage banking revenue (13% of revenue) lease financing (9%) commercial deposits and treasury management fees (6%) trust and asset management fees (3%) card fees (2%) capital markets and international banking fees (1%) and other miscellaneous fee sources.

Geographic Reach
Beyond its 80 branches in Chicago and one branch in Philadelphia MB Financial boasts 39 mortgage retail offices in 18 states.

Sales and Marketing
MB Financial mostly targets small and middle market businesses and individuals. The bank spent $10.07 million on advertising during 2015 up 14% from the $8.85 million it spent in 2014.

Financial Performance
The bank's annual revenues have risen more than 65% since 2011 thanks to a combination of mortgage banking revenue growth and steady loan business growth driven by bank acquisitions. Its profits have quintupled over the same time period as a result.

MB Financial's revenue jumped 37% to $816 million during 2015 mostly driven by strong loan business and mortgage banking revenue growth both stemming from the full-year results of its 2014 acquisition of Taylor Capital.

Double-digit revenue growth in 2015 drove the bank's net income up 85% to $159 million for the year. MB Financial's operating cash levels climbed 23% to $205 million as cash earnings rose in 2015.

Strategy
MB Financial mainly pursues growth by acquiring banks and other financial companies to expand its branch network across its target geographies and boost its loan and deposit business. Other strategies for growth include expanding its private banking and asset managements operations as well as its fee-based business services including treasury management and leasing.

Mergers and Acquisitions
In mid-2016 MB Financial bought American Chartered Bancorp— along with its 15 American Chartered Bank branches in the Chicago-area $2.8 billion in assets and $2.2 billion in deposits — in a deal valued at $449 million.

In December 2015 the company expanded its investment management and trust business after buying MSA along with its MainStreet and Cambium subsidiaries. MainStreet which boated $2.9 billion in assets under management (AUM) provided investment management services to the bank trust and independent trust markets while Cambium ($109 million in AUM) was a registered investment advisor that served affluent individuals and institutions.

In August 2014 MB Financial completed its $649-million acquisition of Rosemont Illinois-based Taylor Capital Group the holding company for Cole Taylor Bank (CTB). With $5.7 billion in assets and some 10 branches in the Chicago metro area CTB was merged with MB Financial Bank. Like its acquirer CTB is a commercial bank focused on the middle market.

Company Background
Taking advantage of the dozens of bank failures in 2009 MB Financial acquired Heritage Community Bank InBank Corus Bank and Benchmark Bank in separate FDIC-assisted transactions. In 2010 it acquired failed Chicago-area institutions Broadway Bank and New Century Bank in similar deals. Gains on these acquisitions helped the company's revenues (and profits) grow in 2010. Although the company didn't have the benefit of gains on acquisitions in 2011 (and revenues fell 20% to $493.7 million) profits continued to climb that year growing 89% to $38.7 million largely due to a lowered provision for loan losses. Also

that year the bank got millions of dollars of non-performing loans off of its books via a sale to Colony Capital.

EXECUTIVES

President And Ceo, Mitchell S. Feiger, age 59, $895,308 total compensation

Chairman Mb Financial Bank, Ronald D. Santo, age 75, $321,741 total compensation

Evp Credit Management Mb Financial Bank, Mark A. Heckler, age 54, $293,077 total compensation

Evp Commercial Banking Mb Financial Bank, Edward F. Milefchik, age 53

Evp Mb Financial Bank; President Mb Business Capital, Michael D. Sharkey, age 64, $456,923 total compensation

Evp And Chief Credit Officer, Michael J. Morton, age 55

President And Ceo Mb Financial Bank, Mark A. Hoppe, age 64, $726,923 total compensation

Evp Wealth Management Card Services Leasing And Indirect Lending, Jill E. York, age 54, $489,461 total compensation

Vp Mb Financial Inc. And Evp Administration Mb Financial Bank, Rosemarie Bouman, age 61, $287,846 total compensation

Evp Commercial Banking, Lawrence G. Ryan, age 59

Vp And Cfo Mb Financial Inc. And Evp Coo And Cfo Mb Financial Bank N.a., Randall T. Conte, age 57, $451,731 total compensation

Evp Risk Management And Chief Risk Officer Mb Financial Bank N.a., Brian J. Wildman, age 55, $292,846 total compensation

Vice President, Michael Scarsella

First Vice President, Priscilla Rodriguez

First Vice President, Mike Markovitz

Vice President Item Processing Manager, Veronica McGowan

Vice President Risk Management, Irene Remeniuk

Vice President, Kathy Grele

Senior Vice President And Division Manager Commercial Banking, Scott Mier

Assistant Vice President Commercial Bank, Nick Cox

First Vice President, Michael Lynch

Vice President Digital Marketing, Michelle Y Finch

Vice President Commercial Banking, Michael Salvador

Senior Vice President, Judy Hill

Vice President Compliance Manager, Kevin Osborn

Assistant Vice President Asset Manager, Brian Nagorsky

Senior Vice President And Division Manager, Jerry Kallio

Vice President, Rick J Chang

Assistant Vice President Employee Relations Office, Katie Drinan Allberry

Senior Vice President Managed Assets Division Mananger, Mary Alberts

Vice President Collateral Manager, Lisette Alamo

Vice President, Anthony Gattuso

Senior Vice President Finance Reporting Budgeting, John Francoeur

Senior Vice President, Jennifer Brogan

Vice President Business Banking, Robert Baitler

Vice President Business Banking, Jim Marshall

Assistant Vice President Marketing Communications Manager, Diane Shaughnessy

Senior Vice President, Greg Urban

Vice President Treasury Management Sales, Eloy Hodges

Vice President, Sandra Biske

Vice President Business Bankin, Steve Grabavoy

Vice President Quality Assurance Manager, Chris Hicks

Assistant Vice President Compensation, Cindy Katsikas

Vice President Business Banking, Sam Elhaj

Assistant Vice President Banking Center Manager, Galina Veksler

Vice President Marketing Manager, Megan Garr

Assistant Vice President, Brenda Allen

Senior Vice President And Division Head, Christina Bavery

Assistant Vice President Quality Control Manager, Margie Acevedo

First Vice President Chief Appraiser, Mitchell Zaveduk

Assistant Vice President Bsa Aml Loss Prevention Management, Michelle Mercer

Assistant Vice President Compensation And Benefits, Catherine Nacpil

Vice President Of Managed Assets, Mike Pindak

Assistant Vice President Marketing And Crm Administrator, Cari Dam

Senior Vice President Division Head, Thomas Moran

Senior Vice President Lease Banking, Dennis Roesslein

First Vice President Regional Division M, Deborah Wheeler

Senior Vice President Lease Banking, Stewart Kapnick

Senior Vice President, Melissa Bleiweis

Vice President Commercial Banking, Dawn Lauderdale

Senior Vice President, Mitch Morgenstern

Assistant Vice President Accounting Manager, Patricia Basan

Senior Vice President Human Resources, Laura Entwistle

First Vice President, Thomas Carmody

Senior Vice President Operations, Pete Steger

Senior Vice President Overseeing Credit, Jennifer Rosenberg

Senior Vice President Corporate Controller, David Emerson

Senior Vice President, Adam Garrett

Senior Vice President Senior Audit Manager, Julie Creco

Vice President Senior Field Credit Officer, Brian Monson

Vice President Treasury Management Solutions Group, Jeffrey Malek

Vice President Treasury Management Solutions Group, Isela Calabrese

Assistant Vice President Benefits Manager, Mary Loftus

Senior Vice President Cra Fair Lending Program Manager, Mary Boetel

Assistant Vice President, Manal Sughayer

Vice President Banking Center Manager, Karen Franciere

Assistant Vice President Treas, Luke Chesick

Senior Vice President Field Risk Officer Enterprise Risk Management And Op Risk, Patricia K Bartler

Vice President Marketing, Debranne Santucci

Vice President Banking Center Manager, Enrique Arroyo

Senior Vice President, Eric Staczek

Vice President Banking Center Manager, Fran Barker

Assistant Vice President Operations, Jackie Schmitz

Senior Vice President, Lisa Gibbs

Assistant Vice President Customer Solutions Specialist, Lori Rottmuller

Senior Vice President, Martha Gaskin

Senior Vice President Commercial Banking, Matt Stefani

Senior Vice President, Mark Staunton

Senior Vice President, Jack Gracheck

Assistant Vice President Accounting Manager, Janis Griffin

Assistant Vice President Banking Center Manager, Casey Weaver

Assistant Vice President Commercial Banking, Andrea Bukacek
Senior Vice President, Timothy Carstens
Senior Vice President, Harold Chmiel
Senior Vice President Documentation For Mb Equipment Finance, Jeannie McManus
Vice President Mb Community Development Corp., Ailisa Herrera
Assistant Vice President Retail Operations, Jennifer Stoll
Vice President Portfolio Management, William Bence
Vice President Risk And Policy Manager Financial Crimes Risk Management, Christoper Bagnall
Vice President Business Banking, Jennifer Cortese
Assistant Vice President Prepaid Product Manager, Denice Myszewski
Senior Vice President, Jon Spoerry
Senior Vice President, Bryan Orton
Senior Vice President, Raphael Shin
Vice President Asset Manager, Jean Thompson
Assistant Vice President, John Scardullo
Assistant Vice President Business Development Officer, Craig Tenuto
Senior Vice President, Chuck Gitles
First Vice President, Robert Thompson
Senior Vice President National Healthcare Finance, Sarah Willett
Vice President Commercial Banking, Elizabeth Riesche
Vice President Senior Project Manager, Lisa Brumbaugh
Senior Vice President, Steven Janson
Vice President, Harry Petruleas
Vice President Loss Mitigation, Michael van Ede
Vice President Business Banking, Steven Grabavoy
Senior Vice President Correspondent Banking, Thomas Wilson
Senior Vice President Manager Business Equipment Finance, Rob Bolo
Vice President Equipment Finance, Sean Holden
Vice President, Michael Connelly
Vice President Banking Center Manager, Deborah Manno
Vice President Compensation, Mark Moise
Chairman, Thomas H. Harvey, age 57
Executive Board Member, Matt Weberling
Vice Chairman, Bruce Taylor
Auditors: RSM US LLP

LOCATIONS

HQ: MB Financial Inc
800 West Madison Street, Chicago, IL 60607
Phone: 888 422-6562
Web: www.mbfinancial.com

PRODUCTS/OPERATIONS

2015 Sales

	$ mil.	% of total
Interest		
Loans	413	51
Investment securities	80	10
Other	0	-
Noninterest		
Mortgage banking	117	13
Lease financing net	76	9
Commercial deposit and treasury management fees	45	6
Trust and Asset management	23	3
Card fees	15	2
Consumer and other deposit service fees	13	2
Loan service fees	6	1
Others	24	3
Total	**816**	**100**

Selected Services

Business Banking
Commercial Banking
Personal Banking
Wealth Management

Selected Subsidiaries

MB Financial Bank N.A.
  Ashland Management Agency Inc.
  Cedar Hill Associates LLC (80%)
  LaSalle Systems Leasing Inc.
  LaSalle Business Solutions LLC
  Melrose Equipment Company LLC
  MB Deferred Exchange Corporation
  MB Financial Center LLC
  MB Financial Center Land Owner LLC
  MB Financial Community Development Corporation
  Vision Investment Services Inc.
  Vision Insurance Services Inc.7

COMPETITORS

Bank of America	Northern Trust
Citigroup	PNC Financial
Fifth Third	PrivateBank
Harris	U.S. Bancorp
JPMorgan Chase	Wintrust Financial

HISTORICAL FINANCIALS

Company Type: Public

Income Statement

FYE: December 31

	ASSETS ($ mil.)	NET INCOME ($ mil.)	INCOME AS % OF ASSETS	EMPLOYEES
12/17	20,086	304	1.5%	3,574
12/16	19,302	174	0.9%	3,486
12/15	15,585	158	1.0%	2,980
12/14	14,602	86	0.6%	2,839
12/13	9,641	98	1.0%	1,775
Annual Growth	**20.1%**	**32.6%**	**—**	**19.1%**

2017 Year-End Financials

Debt ratio: 3.57%
Return on equity: 10.88%
Cash ($ mil.): 579
Current ratio: —
Long-term debt ($ mil.): —

No. of shares (mil.): 83
Dividends
  Yield: 0.0%
  Payout: 23.5%
Market value ($ mil.): 3,736

	STOCK PRICE ($) FY Close	P/E High/Low	PER SHARE ($) Earnings	Dividends	Book Value
12/17	44.52	14 11	3.49	0.82	35.87
12/16	47.23	22 13	2.13	0.74	30.80
12/15	32.37	18 14	2.02	0.65	28.31
12/14	32.86	25 20	1.31	0.52	27.11
12/13	32.06	18 11	1.79	0.44	24.11
Annual Growth	**8.6%**	**— —**	**18.2%**	**16.8%**	**10.4%**

MBIA Inc.

MBIA does what it can to make sure that bonds get paid no matter what. The holding company's independent subsidiary National Public Finance Guarantee Corporation is a provider of insurance for municipal bonds and stable corporate bonds (such as utility bonds) in the US. Separately its MBIA Insurance Corporation provides global structured finance products and non-US public financial guarantees. Faced with a significant amount of default activity MBIA is currently not issuing new policies.

Operations

MBIA conducts most of its business through subsidiaries National Public Finance Guarantee and MBIA Insurance Corporation. Formed after the economic collapse in 2008 National provides US public finance insurance (although it hasn't written any new business since 2009;). In 2017 MBIA determined that National would no longer write new financial guarantee policies.MBIA Insurance has issued structured finance and international insurance but MBIA does not expect that unit to write any significant new policies in the foreseeable future either. Today MBIA's primary focus is to keep watch on its existing insured portfolio.

Another subsidiary MBIA Services Corporation provides fee-based support services (surveillance risk management IT etc.) to National and MBIA Insurance.

Geographic Reach

MBIA is headquartered in Purchase New York; it also has offices in New York City San Francisco and Mexico City.

Financial Performance

MBIA's revenue fell in 2015 and 2016 but it increased 40% to $405 million in 2017. That gain was largely driven by the group's sale of its UK operations. Net loss totaled $1.6 billion in 2017 versus a loss of $333 million the prior year as expenses nearly doubled. With that loss operating cash outflow also increased rising 350% to $630 million.

Strategy

MBIA spent several years working to stabilize its financial position and deal with the massive fallout from the subprime mortgage-backed security implosion that led to the housing collapse and the Great Recession. Unfortunately the company found itself in more trouble when certain investment vehicles it had guaranteed soured with one defaulting in late 2016. To help cover its losses MBIA sold its UK operations to Assured Guaranty.It also cut its workforce by some 25%.

The company operates with a high level of debt (more than $1.6 billion) which makes it difficult to dedicate funds to other operating activities. Additionally MBIA has insured exposure in Puerto Rico which has been struggling to meet its legacy debts in the aftermath of Hurricane Maria; in 2017 Puerto Rico defaulted on its scheduled debt service for insured bonds.

Company Background

That MBIA is still standing is remarkable. As one of the largest providers of insurance to asset- and mortgage-based securities MBIA was among the most vulnerable companies when the US housing market imploded in 2007. The company posted losses of $2.3 billion the last quarter of 2007 a result of its investments in subprime mortgage-backed securities.

MBIA split apart its public structured and asset management businesses to separate the stable from the unstable in early 2009: MBIA split its municipal bond insurance business off into an independent subsidiary named National Public Finance Guarantee Corporation. It receives a credit rating separate from the rest of MBIA's riskier structured-finance businesses.

Following the split some 20 banks grew prickly and sued MBIA with one hand while steadily collecting claims with the other. However by mid-2011 banks began dropping out of the lawsuit; the company settled with the final three in 2013.

EXECUTIVES

Evp Chief Legal Officer And Secretary, Ram D. Wertheim, age 64, $500,000 total compensation
Ceo, William C. (Bill) Fallon, age 58, $812,500 total compensation
Evp And Cfo, Anthony McKiernan, age 48, $500,000 total compensation
Vice President, Timothy Keefe
Vice President Information Technology, Hirdey Gupta
Senior Vice President Director Of Risk And Reinsurance, Joel Turner

Assistant Vice President, Joseph Beattie
Vice President Financial Guarantee Applications, Lynn Jacobs
Assistant Vice President, Emily Johnson
Vice President, Cathleen Murray
Vice President, Greg Wright
Chairman, Charles R. Rinehart, age 71
Board Member, Richard Vaughan
Auditors: PricewaterhouseCoopers LLP

LOCATIONS

HQ: MBIA Inc.
1 Manhattanville Road, Suite 301, Purchase, NY 10577
Phone: 914 273-4545
Web: www.mbia.com

COMPETITORS

Ambac	Primus Guaranty
Assured Guaranty	Radian Group
FGIC	Syncora Holdings

HISTORICAL FINANCIALS

Company Type: Public

Income Statement

FYE: December 31

	ASSETS ($ mil.)	NET INCOME ($ mil.)	INCOME AS % OF ASSETS	EMPLOYEES
12/17	9,095	(1,605)	—	103
12/16	11,137	(338)	—	164
12/15	14,855	180	1.2%	170
12/14	16,284	569	3.5%	252
12/13	16,953	250	1.5%	277
Annual Growth	(14.4%)	—		(21.9%)

2017 Year-End Financials

Debt ratio: 56.90%
Return on equity: (-69.18%)
Cash ($ mil.): 146
Current ratio: —
Long-term debt ($ mil.): —

No. of shares (mil.): 91
Dividends
  Yield: —
  Payout: —
Market value ($ mil.): 670

	STOCK PRICE ($) FY Close	P/E High/Low		PER SHARE ($) Earnings	Dividends	Book Value
12/17	7.32	—	—	(13.50)	0.00	15.45
12/16	10.70	—	—	(2.54)	0.00	23.87
12/15	6.48	9	5	1.06	0.00	24.61
12/14	9.54	5	3	2.76	0.00	20.47
12/13	11.94	12	6	1.29	0.00	17.05
Annual Growth	(11.5%)			—	—	(2.4%)

McCormick & Co Inc

McCormick & Company is more than just the flavor of the month. As the world's #1 spice maker the company offers a tasty assortment of herbs spices seasonings flavorings sauces and extracts. McCormick distributes and markets its products under brands including Lawry's Club House and McCormick and ethnic labels Zatarain's Thai Kitchen and Simply Asia as well as regional brands Ducros and Schwartz and private labels. Its products are sold in some 140 countries to customers spanning the entire food industry from food retailers to food service businesses and industrial food manufacturers. McCormick operates in North America and Europe and in South Africa Central America and the Asia/Pacific region. In 2017 McCormick acquired Reckitt Benckiser's food business for $4.2 billion.

Operations

McCormick operates two business segments: Consumer (more than 60% of sales in 2016) and Industrial (nearly 40%). Both segments manufacture market and distribute spices seasoning mixes condiments and other flavorful products worldwide.

The company's brands in the Americas include McCormick Lawry's and Club House. Its ethnic brands include Zatarain's Thai Kitchen and Simply Asia. In the Europe Middle East and Africa (EMEA) region its major brands include the Ducros Schwartz and Karmis brands of spices herbs and seasonings and its VahinA© brand dessert line.

Geographic Reach

Maryland-based McCormick has sales distribution and production facilities throughout North America and Europe with additional facilities in Australia Central America China France India Italy Mexico Poland Singapore South Africa the United Arab Emirates and Thailand. The US accounts for almost 60% of the company's total sales while the EMEA region and emerging markets each account for more than 20%.

Sales and Marketing

McCormick sells its products directly to customers as well as through brokers wholesalers and distributors. Its products are marketed to the entire food industry which includes retail outlets food manufacturers and foodservices businesses. McCormick's largest consumer business customer is Wal-Mart Stores which accounted for more than 10% of consolidates sales in fiscal 2016 (ended November). On the industrial side of the business PepsiCo also accounted for more than 10% of sales that year.

Financial Performance

The spice maker has experienced unprecedented growth over the past several years as it's continued to expand its product lines and enter new markets. McCormick's sales rose by 3% to peak at a record-setting $4.41 billion in fiscal 2016 (ended November) primarily due to a 4% spike in Consumer segment sales. Overall the company saw higher volume beneficial product mixes and higher pricing as well as gains on acquisitions for the year.

Net income jumped 18% to peak at $472 million in 2016 another company milestone. The rise in net income was attributed to a decrease in restructuring and impairment charges. Cash flow from operations rose from $590 million in 2015 to $658 million in 2016 primarily due the higher net income a decrease in cash payments related to special charges and the impact of higher employee benefit accruals.

Strategy

While acquisitions and joint ventures are fundamental to McCormick's growth strategy to grow product lines and enter new geographic markets the company has also attracted more customers by adding new products that cater to evolving consumer preferences.

In recent years McCormick has launched a line of Hispanic seasoning blends along with a stable of some 450 salt-free products for US shoppers. In 2015 it introduced its lineup of 11 new classic fall recipes including its McCormick Slow Cooker Sauces Gluten-Free Recipe Mixes and Pure Pumpkin Pie Spice Extract its Kitchen Basics Flavored Stock Cubes and its new Thai Kitchen Coconut Cream.

Mergers and Acquisitions

McCormick has achieved historic growth is by acquiring rivals operating around the globe. In 2017 the company bolstered its position as a leader in the US sauce and condiments market after purchasing the food business of British household and personal care products giant Reckitt Benckiser. The $4.2 billion deal included iconic mustard brand French's as well as Franks' RedHot and Cattlemen's sauces.

HISTORY

McCormick & Company was founded in 1889 by 25-year-old Willoughby McCormick who crafted fruit syrups root beer and nerve and bone liniment in his Baltimore home. He employed three assistants to hawk his wares door-to-door. His company soon expanded its product line to include food coloring cream of tartar and blood purifier. By 1894 McCormick was exporting and two years later it acquired the F.G. Emmett Spice Company of Philadelphia firmly committing itself to the spice industry. By the turn of the century McCormick was trading around the world.

Willoughby's nephew Charles McCormick joined the company as a part-time shipping clerk in 1912. When Willoughby died in 1932 Charles succeeded him as CEO. He increased employee wages shortened the workweek and established the Multiple Management system (still an integral part of the company's management structure) which solicited employee input. By 1933 McCormick was on a growth track that continued unabated through the 1930s. In 1938 Charles wrote a book expounding his participative management philosophy.

The company opened its first international office in 1940 and achieved coast-to-coast distribution seven years later with the acquisition of A. Schilling & Co. producers of spices and extracts. In 1959 McCormick purchased Gorman Eckert & Co. Canada's largest spice business and the precursor to Club House Foods. It acquired Gilroy Foods in 1961 and rival Baker Extract in 1962. From 1962 until its sale in 1988 McCormick ran a real estate subsidiary Maryland Properties (renamed McCormick Properties 1979).

Charles died in 1970. Though the years following his death were characterized by acquisitions and joint venture agreements in the US and abroad profits slumped until his son Charles "Buzz" McCormick took over as CEO in 1987.

In 1989 Australia's Burns Philp began challenging McCormick by buying up spice companies in the US and Europe including the Spice Islands and Durkee French brands. Buzz — succeeded twice as CEO in the mid-1990s only to return when one successor died and the other left for health reasons — responded with a bruising battle for shelf space that led to Burns Philp's near-collapse in 1997. The company also sold garlic and onion processing subsidiary Gilroy Foods Minipack Systems (UK) and several smaller noncore operations. In 1997 Buzz yielded the CEO's post — for good — to Robert Lawless.

The company's earnings were erratic in the 1990s partly because of a price war with then-rival Burns Philp but also due to the decline of home cooking in the US. McCormick countered with increased advertising and a growing emphasis on industrial sales to flavor the foods eaten outside the home. McCormick also has been expanding internationally through its Decors spice business and operations in China.

Economic woes in Venezuela caused McCormick to cease manufacturing operations there in 1998. In 1999 Lawless succeeded Buzz as chairman. That year the company announced it would cut costs by eliminating 300 jobs (mostly overseas) and closing a British plant.

McCormick's sweet victory over Burns Philp was soured by an FTC investigation into its alleged practice of offering some grocery chains low prices in exchange for up to 90% of their shelf space for spices. The investigation brought scrutiny on a common supermarket practice known as slotting fees. McCormick settled with the FTC in 2000 agreeing not to illegally discriminate against retailers in its pricing. Also that year the company bought France-based Ducros (spices herbs dessert aid products) from BA©ghin-Say for about $380 million.

In 2003 McCormick's UK subsidiary acquired condiment maker Uniqsauces adding the Beswicks and Hammonds as

EXECUTIVES

President Global Consumer Business And North America, Brendan M. Foley, age 54, $519,809 total compensation

Chairman President And Ceo, Lawrence E. Kurzius, age 61, $861,374 total compensation

President Global Industrial And International Business, Malcolm Swift, age 57, $407,714 total compensation

Svp Corporate Finance, Michael R. Smith, $394,943 total compensation

Vice President Information Technology, Jeff Malat

Vice President Distributor Sales, Ron Dallara

Auditors: Ernst & Young LLP

LOCATIONS

HQ: McCormick & Co Inc
24 Schilling Road, Suite 1, Hunt Valley, MD 21031
Phone: 410 771-7301   **Fax:** 410 771-7462
Web: www.mccormickcorporation.com

2016 Sales

	$ mil.	% of total
US	2,565	58
Europe the Middle East & Africa	896	20
Other countries	950	22
Total	**411**	**100**

PRODUCTS/OPERATIONS

2016 Sales

	$ mil.	% of total
Consumer products	2,753	62
Industrial products	1,658	38
Total	**4,411**	**100**

Selected Brands

Billy Bee
Club House
Ducros
Kamins
Kohinoor
Lawry's
McCormick
Old Bay
Schwartz
Silvo
Simply Asia
Thai Kitchen
Vahiné
Zatarain's

Selected Products

Consumer
  Dessert items
  Extracts
  Food colors
  Grill mates
  Herbs
  Seafood
  Seasoning mixes
  Seasonings
  Spices
Industrial
  Coating systems
  Compound flavors
  Herbs
  Seasoning blends
  Spices
  Wet flavors

COMPETITORS

A.A. Sayia	Goya
ACH Food Companies	Heinz
Adams Extract & Spice	International Flavors
Associated British	Kerry Group

Foods	La Flor
B&G Foods	M & F Worldwide
Bolner's Fiesta	Magic Seasoning Blends
Products	Main Street
D. D. Williamson	Ingredients
Danisco A/S	Newly Weds Foods
Denali Flavors	Nielsen-Massey
First Spice Mixing	Ottens Flavors
Flavormatic Industries	RFI Ingredients
Flayco Products	Sensient
Givaudan	Sterling Extract

HISTORICAL FINANCIALS

Company Type: Public

Income Statement

FYE: November 30

	REVENUE ($ mil.)	NET INCOME ($ mil.)	NET PROFIT MARGIN	EMPLOYEES
11/18	5,408	933	17.3%	11,600
11/17	4,834	477	9.9%	11,700
11/16	4,411	472	10.7%	10,500
11/15	4,296	401	9.3%	10,000
11/14	4,243	437	10.3%	10,000
Annual Growth	**6.3%**	**20.8%**	**—**	**3.8%**

2018 Year-End Financials

Debt ratio: 45.79%
Return on equity: 32.57%
Cash ($ mil.): 96
Current ratio: 0.74
Long-term debt ($ mil.): 4,052

No. of shares (mil.): 132
Dividends
  Yield: 1.3%
  Payout: 29.7%
Market value ($ mil.): 19,815

	STOCK PRICE ($) FY Close	P/E High/Low	Earnings	Dividends	Book Value
11/18	150.00	21 14	7.00	2.08	24.00
11/17	102.18	28 24	3.72	1.88	19.54
11/16	91.20	29 21	3.69	1.72	12.98
11/15	85.92	27 23	3.11	1.60	13.12
11/14	74.33	22 19	3.34	1.48	13.96
Annual Growth	**19.2%**	**— —**	**20.3%**	**8.9%**	**14.5%**

McDonald's Corp

Serving billions of hamburgers has put a shine on these arches. McDonald's has more than 37000 restaurants serving burgers and fries in about 120 countries. (There are more than 14000 Golden Arches locations in the US.) The popular chain is well-known for its Big Macs Quarter Pounders and Chicken McNuggets. Most of the outlets are free-standing units offering dine-in and drive-through service but McDonald's also has many eateries located in airports retail areas and other high-traffic locations. More than 90% of the restaurants are run by franchisees or affiliates.

Operations

McDonald's and its franchisees purchase food packing and other items from independent suppliers which are distributed via third-party distribution centers. McDonald's works with the suppliers and distributors to ensure consistent quality products.

The majority of the company's more than 37200 restaurants are franchised following extensive refranchising efforts by the company in recent years.

Geographic Reach

Although it is truly a global brand McDonald's has nine major markets (Australia Canada China France Germany Japan Russia the UK and the US) that account for the majority of sales. The US is

the company's largest segment accounting for around 35% of the company's total revenue.

High Growth Markets which include China Italy Korea Poland Russia Spain Switzerland and the Netherlands account for around 25% of total sales.

Sales and Marketing

Marketing and advertising initiatives focus on McDonald's menu selections value and convenience among other areas. The company spends more than $600 million on advertising each year. The corporate office has been looking for more new partnerships sponsorships and co-branding opportunities.

Financial Performance

McDonald's sales have been falling over the years as the company carries out its refranchising program which converts company-operated diners into franchised diners. The program has had a negative impact on the top line as directly generated sales are replaced by rent and royalty revenue based on a percentage of sales. The upside for McDonald's is that it creates more stable and predictable revenue and cash flow and is less resource and capital intensive.

In fiscal 2017 McDonald's sales fell a further 7% to $22.8 billion due to refranchising (around 3000 were refranchised during the year) partially offset by higher comparable sales. Indeed the company recorded its best comparable sales in six years thanks to 4% growth in the US on strong performance of the McPick 2 menu deal and 5% growth internationally on the back of positive performances in the UK and Canada.

Net income grew 11% to $5.2 billion despite a $700 million net tax cost relating to the 2017 US Tax Cuts and Jobs Act. Earnings strengthened thanks to an $859 million gain on the sale of McDonald's businesses in China and Hong Kong a $153 million decrease in general and administrative expenses and a $135 million gain on the sale of a unique restaurant property in the US.

Cash from operations fell 8% to $5.6 billion due to adjustments to reconcile the sale of the China and Hong Kong businesses.

Strategy

McDonald's dominated the fast-food dining industry for a long time largely through its effective franchising efforts its focus on food consistency and its successful marketing campaigns. The company's far-flung network of franchise operators is all controlled by agreements meant to ensure that a Big Mac purchased in Pittsburgh tastes the same as one bought in Beijing.

McDonald's has shifted its ownership structure even more towards franchises in recent years thereby reducing its capital needs going forward. The company's refranchising efforts reached 92% of its entire restaurant base by the end of 2017 against its stated goal of 95%. McDonald's is focused on growing its global top-line sales and guest counts to solidify its critical revenue streams.

However the company has struggled in recent years as it tried a wide variety of marketing and menu-change approaches to generate sales. McDonald's launched a turnaround plan that focused on promoting the chain's breakfast menu throughout the day which led to the company's first positive sales news in a long time. However by the end of 2016 the all-day breakfast novelty had lost some of its momentum.

McDonald's has faced severe competition from independent restaurants as many Americans (especially Millennials) are focused on fresh and healthy fast foods. The company has responded by offering more healthy options (such as more salads and grilled chicken sandwiches) and by improving the quality and value of its food. In 2017 the company began experimenting with using fresh beef instead of frozen patties for its Quarter Pounders.

The company's 2017 growth plan focuses on enhancing digital capabilities and the use of technology to elevate and modernize the customer experience at its restaurants. McDonald's also plans to redefine its customer convenience through delivery. The company's technology investment will help fund new self-serve kiosks at many restaurants and expand the reach of McDonald's smartphone ordering app — the company introduced home delivery from more than 10000 restaurants at long last in 2017.

HISTORY

The first McDonald's opened in 1948 in San Bernardino California. In 1954 owners Dick and Mac McDonald signed a franchise agreement with 52-year-old Ray Kroc (a malt machine salesman) and a year later Kroc opened his first restaurant in Des Plaines Illinois. By 1957 Kroc was operating 14 McDonald's restaurants in Illinois Indiana and California. In 1961 Kroc bought out the McDonald brothers for $2.7 million.

In 1962 the now-ubiquitous Golden Arches appeared for the first time and the company sold its billionth burger. Ronald McDonald made his debut the following year and the company introduced its first new menu item — the Filet-O-Fish. Two years later McDonald's went public and ran its first TV ads. The company opened its first stores outside the US (in Canada) in 1967 and the next year it added the Big Mac to the menu and opened its 1000th restaurant.

During the 1970s McDonald's grew at the rate of about 500 restaurants per year and the first Ronald McDonald House (a temporary residence for families of hospitalized children) opened in 1974. The drive-through window appeared in 1975.

McDonald's introduced Chicken McNuggets in 1983. Kroc who had become senior chairman in the 1970s died the next year. Growing competition slowed the company's US sales growth to about 5% per year at the end of the 1980s. In response McDonald's added specially priced "value menu" items.

In 1990 the company made history and headlines when it opened the first McDonald's in Moscow. Two years later the Golden Arches expanded into China. The company stumbled with the pricey Arch Deluxe hamburger in 1996 and its Campaign 55 discount promotion the next year. However the giveaway of Teenie Beanie Babies in 1997 was its most successful promotion ever. McDonald's decentralized US operations that year to bring decision-making closer to local franchises. US division CEO Edward Rensi retired and was replaced by division chairman Jack Greenberg.

The next year Greenberg launched the Made For You food preparation system designed to reduce waste and produce a better tasting burger. He was named CEO later that year. McDonald's also made its first investment in another restaurant concept in 1998 when it bought a stake in Chipotle Mexican Grill a Denver-based chain of Mexican food restaurants. That same year saw the death of co-founder Dick McDonald who died at age 89.

During Greenberg's first year he slowed US expansion and stepped up international growth. In 1999 McDonald's added a third brand to its family when it acquired the Ohio-based Donatos Pizzeria chain. The company's biggest deal though came in 2000 when it purchased the Boston Market chain from struggling Boston Chicken for about $175 million.

Early in 2001 McDonald's unveiled its New Tastes Menu in which local markets could feature up to four regional or seasonal foods out of a 40-item national selection. The company continued its move toward diversification and international

expansion purchasing a 33% stake in the UK limited-service sandwich chain Pret A Manger for $40 million. It also spun off its Japanese unit to the public retaining a 50% ownership stake.

But even with all its size and power McDonald's found out it was not immune to economic trouble and corporate blunders. The company suffered from ill-thought product changes less-than-successful marketing plans and the growing public preference for lighter fast-food options such as sub sandwiches and salads. Following three quarters of declining profits in 2001 McDonald's announced a major restructuring of its US operations. It cut about 700 corporate jobs

EXECUTIVES

Evp And Global Chief Marketing Officer, Silvia Lagnado, $615,000 total compensation

President International Lead Markets, Douglas M. (Doug) Goare, age 65, $648,750 total compensation

President Mcdonald's Usa, Chris (Chris K) Kempczinski, age 49, $111,538 total compensation

Evp And Chief People Officer, David Fairhurst, age 50

Corporate Evp And Cfo, Kevin M. Ozan, age 55, $683,333 total compensation

President Ceo And Director, Stephen J. (Steve) Easterbrook, age 50, $1,266,667 total compensation

Corporate Evp Operations And Technology Systems, Jim Sappington, age 59

Evp Corporate Relations; Chief Communications Officer, Robert Gibbs

President High Growth Markets, Joe Erlinger

Evp General Counsel And Secretary, Jerry Krulewitch

President Foundational Markets, Ian Borden

Vice President, Gerald Newman

Vice President Of Operations, Marcy Amble

Vice President Of Strategy, Greg Watson

Chairman, Enrique (Rick) Hernandez, age 63

Auditors: Ernst & Young LLP

LOCATIONS

HQ: McDonald's Corp
One McDonald's Plaza, Oak Brook, IL 60523
Phone: 630 623-3000
Web: www.mcdonalds.com

2017 Sales

	$ mil.	% of total
U.S.	8,000	35
International Lead Markets	7,340	32
High Growth Markets	5,533	24
Foundational Markets & Corporate	1,941	9
Total	**22,820**	**100**

2017 Locations

	No.
US	14,036
International Lead Markets	6,921
High Growth Markets	5,884
Foundational Markets & Corporate	10,400
Total	**37,241**

PRODUCTS/OPERATIONS

2017 Locations

	No.
Franchised	34,108
Company-owned	3
Total	**37,241**

2017 Sales

	$ mil.	% of total
Company-owned restaurants	12,719	56
Franchised restaurants	10,101	44
Total	**22,820**	**100**

Selected Products

Big Mac
Chicken McNuggets

Egg McMuffin
Filet-O-Fish
Happy Meal
Mac Snack Wrap
McCafe
McChicken
McDouble
McFlurry
McGriddle
McRib
Quarter Pounder

COMPETITORS

Burger King	Quiznos
CKE Restaurants	Sonic Corp.
Chick-fil-A	Starbucks
Church's Chicken	Subway
Dairy Queen	Tim Hortons
Jack in the Box	Wendy's
Panda Restaurant Group	YUM!
Popeyes	

HISTORICAL FINANCIALS

Company Type: Public

Income Statement

FYE: December 31

	REVENUE ($ mil.)	NET INCOME ($ mil.)	NET PROFIT MARGIN	EMPLOYEES
12/17	22,820	5,192	22.8%	235,000
12/16	24,621	4,686	19.0%	375,000
12/15	25,413	4,529	17.8%	420,000
12/14	27,441	4,757	17.3%	420,000
12/13	28,105	5,585	19.9%	440,000
Annual Growth	**(5.1%)**	**(1.8%)**	**—**	**(14.5%)**

2017 Year-End Financials

Debt ratio: 87.38%
Return on equity: —
Cash ($ mil.): 2,463
Current ratio: 1.84
Long-term debt ($ mil.): 29,536
No. of shares (mil.): 794
Dividends
Yield: 0.0%
Payout: 60.1%
Market value ($ mil.): 136,680

	STOCK PRICE ($) FY Close	P/E High/Low	PER SHARE ($) Earnings	Dividends	Book Value
12/17	172.12	27 19	6.37	3.83	(4.12)
12/16	121.72	24 20	5.44	3.61	(2.69)
12/15	118.14	25 18	4.80	3.44	7.82
12/14	93.70	21 18	4.82	3.28	13.35
12/13	97.03	19 16	5.55	3.12	16.16
Annual Growth	**15.4%**	**— —**	**3.5%**	**5.3%**	**—**

McKesson Corp

McKesson is one of the top pharmaceuticals distributors in North America. The company delivers prescription and generic drugs as well as health and beauty care products to more than 40000 retail and institutional pharmacies throughout the US. The company is also a major medical supplies wholesaler providing medical and surgical equipment to alternate health care sites such as doctors' offices surgery centers and long-term care facilities. In addition to distribution services McKesson offers software and technical services that help pharmacies health care providers and insurers manage supply chain clinical administrative and financial operations. The company was founded in 1883.

HISTORY

John McKesson opened a Manhattan drugstore in 1833 and Daniel Robbins joined him as a partner in 1840. McKesson-Robbins soon expanded into chemical and drug production and the enterprise grew steadily. In 1926 after differences arose between the McKesson and Robbins heirs the company was sold to Donald Coster.

Coster was actually convicted felon Philip Musica who purchased McKesson-Robbins with fraudulently obtained bank loans. For more than a decade his real identity remained secret from all but one blackmailer. By 1930 McKesson-Robbins had wholesale drug operations in 33 states. The company appeared to be growing but a treasurer discovered a Musica-orchestrated accounting scam and a cash shortfall of $3 million. Faced with exposure Musica killed himself in 1939; company bankruptcy followed. McKesson-Robbins emerged from bankruptcy in 1941.

In a hostile takeover in 1967 San Francisco-based Foremost Dairies bought McKesson-Robbins to form Foremost-McKesson. Over the next 20 years the company bought liquor chemical and software wholesalers as well as several bottled-water companies. It sold Foremost Dairies in 1983 to focus on distribution changed its name to McKesson the next year and continued to build its drug wholesaling business through acquisitions. By 1985 it was the US's largest distributor of drugs and medical equipment wine and liquor bottled water and car waxes and polishes.

In 1986 McKesson narrowed its focus to the health industry by selling its liquor and chemical distributors. It acquired Canadian drug distributor Medis by halves in 1990 and 1991 and a 23% stake in Mexican drug distributor Nadro in 1993.

McKesson sold PCS the US's #1 prescription claims processor (acquired in 1970) to Eli Lilly in 1994. In 1996 the firm bought bankrupt distributor FoxMeyer Drug and sold its stake in Armor All (auto and home cleaning products) to Clorox.

In 1997 the company purchased General Medical the US's largest distributor of medical surgical supplies for about $775 million. McKesson began to focus on health care selling its Millbrook Distribution Services unit (health and beauty products general merchandise and specialty foods).

Under new CEO Mark Pulido it agreed to buy drug wholesaler AmeriSource Health (now AmerisourceBergen) but withdrew the offer in 1998 facing FTC opposition. Instead McKesson moved into information systems paying $14 billion for health care information top dog HBO & Company and forming McKesson HBOC. HBO a high-flyer in the high-growth health information systems segment balanced its rather dowdy drug and medical distribution operations.

But just months after the deal closed accounting inconsistencies at HBO prompted McKesson to restate fourth-quarter results for fiscal 1999 twice triggering shareholder lawsuits and a housecleaning of top brass. Five ex-HBO executives including McKesson HBOC chairman Charlie McCall (who was later indicted for securities fraud) were canned for using improper accounting methods. McKesson's veteran CEO Pulido and CFO Richard Hawkins were forced to resign for not seeing the problems coming.

The company changed its name to McKesson Corporation in 2001. The National Health Services Information Authority entered into an agreement with McKesson to develop a human resources and payroll system for use at the more than 600 NHS locations throughout the UK.

To catch then #1 pharmaceutical distributor Cardinal Health McKesson built up its core areas in 2003 and 2004 while trimming away some of the dead weight (Abaton.com Amysis Managed Care).

EXECUTIVES

Chairman President And Ceo, John H. Hammergren, age 59, $1,680,000 total compensation

Evp Human Resources, Jorge L. Figueredo, age 57, $708,167 total compensation

Evp And Cfo, James A. Beer, age 57, $840,167 total compensation

Evp And Group President Domestic And International Distribution Solutions, Paul C. Julian, age 62, $1,148,333 total compensation

Evp Cio And Cto, Kathleen D. (Kathy) McElligott, age 62

Evp General Counsel And Chief Compliance Officer, Lori A. Schechter, age 56

Evp And Group President Mckesson Technology Solutions, Patrick J. (Pat) Blake, age 54, $765,500 total compensation

Evp Corporate Strategy And Business Development, Bansi Nagji, age 53

Vice President Home Care Sales, Jeff Bowman

Assistant Vice President Product Development, Beth Kuzmak

Vice President Global Sourcing Medical, James Hodges

Vice President Human Resources, Jeff Sauers

Vice President Of Corporate Tax, Paul A Smith

Vice President National Accounts, Mark Snodgrass

Vice President Gpo Services (unity), Tim Boozan

Territory Vice President Revenue Management Solutions Mckesson Provider Technologies, Brian Baughman

Vice President And General Manager, Andrew Moore

Vice President National Accounts, Mike Ferguson

Vice President, Mike Cesarz

Assistant Vice President Software Development Mckesson Corporation, Karen Erickson

Vice President Of Marketing, Andy Burtis

Senior Vice President Distribution Systems, Ronald Bone

Vice President Business Development, Deann Cushman

Vice President Of Sales, Deborah Smith

Vice President Of Sales And Operations, Mauricio Chavez

Vice President Of Operations, Steve Tarantino

Vice President Office Product Sales, Kevin Boyle

Vice President Marketing And Sales Program, David Brown

Vice President Laboratory Account Sales, Jerry Morrow

Vice President Software Engineering, Jason Warner

Vice President Of Customer Operations, Kathy McGrath

Executive Vice President And Cio, Zalise Edwards

Vice President Segment Marketing, Chris Garnett

Executive Vice President National Accounts, Jack Fragie

Vice President Enterpriserx Development Mckesson Pharmacy Systems, Jonathan Kriebel

Vice President, Victor Solomon

Vice President Pharmacy Operations Health Mart, Charles Wilson

Vice President Risk Management, Jane Sandler

Vice President Corporate Strategy And Business Development, Aaron Apodaca

Svp Strategy And Business Development Mckesson Specialty Health, Matt Yordy

Vice President Compliance And Regulatory Affairs Mckesson Pharmacy Systems, Chris Frey

Svp And General Manager Network And Financial Management Mckesson Health Solutions, Carolyn Wukitch

Svp And Chief Medical Officer Mckesson Specialty Health And The Us Oncology Network, Michael Seiden

Vice President And Gm Mckesson Specialty Health, Bill Nolan

Vice President Corporate Strategy Mckesson Technology Solutions, Joe Biegel

Svp Total Rewards, Kevin Close

Board Member, Andy D Bryant

Assistant Secretary, Karen Pineda

Auditors: DELOITTE & TOUCHE LLP

LOCATIONS

HQ: McKesson Corp
One Post Street, San Francisco, CA 94104
Phone: 415 983-8300
Web: www.mckesson.com

2018 Sales

	$ mil.	% of total
US	169,943	82
International	38,414	18
Total	**208,357**	**100**

PRODUCTS/OPERATIONS

2018 Sales

	$ mil.	% of total
Distribution Solutions		
North American pharmaceutical distribution & services	174,186	84
International pharmaceutical distribution & services	27,320	13
Medical-Surgical distribution & services	6,611	3
Technology Solutions — products & services	240	-
Total	**208,357**	**100**

Selected Operations and Services

COMPETITORS

Allscripts	H. D. Smith Wholesale
AmerisourceBergen	Drug
Apothecary Products	Imperial Distributors
BioScrip	Medline Industries
Cardinal Health	Omnicare
CuraScript	Owens & Minor
Diplomat Pharmacy	PharMerica
FFF Enterprises	QK Healthcare
Grifols	Surgical Express

HISTORICAL FINANCIALS

Company Type: Public

Income Statement

FYE: March 31

	REVENUE ($ mil.)	NET INCOME ($ mil.)	NET PROFIT MARGIN	EMPLOYEES
03/18	208,357	67	0.0%	78,000
03/17	198,533	5,070	2.6%	78,000
03/16	190,884	2,258	1.2%	68,000
03/15	179,045	1,476	0.8%	70,400
03/14	137,609	1,263	0.9%	42,800
Annual Growth	**10.9%**	**(52.0%)**	**—**	**16.2%**

2018 Year-End Financials

Debt ratio: 13.05%	No. of shares (mil.): 202
Return on equity: 0.64%	Dividends
Cash ($ mil.): 2,672	Yield: 0.0%
Current ratio: 1.01	Payout: 406.2%
Long-term debt ($ mil.): 6,751	Market value ($ mil.): 28,456

	STOCK PRICE ($) FY Close	P/E High/Low		PER SHARE ($) Earnings	Dividends	Book Value
03/18	140.87	55	24 22	0.32	1.30	48.53
03/17	148.26	9	5	22.73	1.12	52.58
03/16	157.25	25	15	9.70	1.08	39.66
03/15	226.20	36	26	6.27	0.96	34.49
03/14	176.57	34	19	5.41	0.92	36.89
Annual Growth	**(5.5%)**	**—**	**—**	**(50.7%)**	**9.0%**	**7.1%**

MCLANE COMPANY, INC.

You could say this company makes it convenient for stores and restaurants to get food. McLane Company is one of the largest wholesale suppliers of food products in the US serving more than 45000 retail stores and food service operators from more than 40 distribution centers. Its grocery and retail distribution division serves convenience stores drugstores and mass merchants including Wal-Mart. The company's McLane Foodservice division delivers food paper products and other supplies to chain restaurants and other food service providers. McLane also distributes alcoholic beverages in the southeastern US. The company is owned by Warren Buffett's Berkshire Hathaway.

Operations

McLane distributes grocery and non-food products to retailers convenience stores and restaurants. The company's McLane Grocery Distribution unit supplies more than 46000 retail grocery locations including drug stores mass merchants warehouse clubs convenience stores and more from 23 distribution centers across the US. McLane Foodservice supplies restaurants and food service providers from distribution centers in the US. Its McLane Beverage Distribution division provides alcoholic beverage distribution in select states. Another subsidiary Empire Distributors is a leading supplier of spirits wine beer and non-alcoholic beverages in Georgia North Carolina and Tennessee to more than 8000 accounts.

In 2014 the grocery and foodservice units accounted for 99% of the company's total revenues.

Geographic Reach

Texas-based McLane Co. does business in all 50 US states. McLane Foodservice's distribution unit based in Carrollton Texas focuses on serving the quick service restaurant industry. This division's operations are conducted through 18 facilities in 16 states. The foodservice distribution unit services 21000 chain restaurants across the country.

Sales and Marketing

McLane provides wholesale distribution services to its former parent company Wal-Mart Stores which contributed about 24% of its 2014 revenue versus 25% in 2013. Other important customers include 7-Eleven and Yum! Brands.

Financial Performance

The company's revenues increased by 1.5% in 2014 reflecting increased foodservice and beverage revenues. Grocery revenues were relatively flat.

Strategy

Changing trends in the grocery business have presented McLane with new opportunities. As a dominant player in the wholesale supply business McLane's grocery division competes in a league of giants including C & S Wholesale Nash-Finch and Core-Mark while its foodservice unit fights for business with such industry leaders as SYSCO U.S. Foodservice and Performance Food Group. Wholesale distribution continues to be a highly fragmented industry however meaning the company must also compete with a patchwork of regional and local suppliers. As the company's grocery and foodservice businesses are characterized by high sales volume and very low profit margins scale is immensely important to its financial performance.

In 2014 McLane was on track to open its newest grocery distribution center (its 22nd) in 2016. The $38-million distribution center is being built in northern Findlay Ohio to supply convenience stores mass merchants drugstores and restaurants.

In 2014 Kangaroo Express convenience stores signed a deal to continue to do business with McLane. The chain's parent company The Pantry

signed a new distribution service agreement to continue to purchase food and non-food general merchandise including cigarettes and tobacco products from McLane.

Company Background

McLane bought North Carolina-based Meadowbrook Meat Company (MBM) in August 2012. With $6 billion in sales MBM is one of the largest food service distributors for national restaurant chains. Its customers include Arby's Burger King and Darden Restaurants. The deal will substantially increase McLane's size by adding to its food service unit which already serves more than 20000 chain restaurants.

As dollar stores have moved forcefully into food retailing McLane in 2012 entered into a partnership with one of the nation's largest dollar store operators Family Dollar Stores to supply a variety of merchandise including refrigerated and frozen food to the chain's 7200-plus locations across 45 states.

McLane has been expanding in recent years building up an alcohol distribution business with a series of acquisitions beginning in 2010. It purchased Kahn Ventures whose holdings included Empire Distributors (serving Georgia) and Empire Distributors of North Carolina. According to Buffet the acquisition is part of the shared vision of Berkshire McLane and Kahn to develop innovation opportunities and to grow and lead the beverage industry. McLane added to its Empire operations by acquiring Tennessee-based distributor Horizon Wine and Spirits later in the year. Gaining access to resources and operational best practices in the beverage distribution arena McLane is positioned for further growth in the sector

Starting as a family-owned grocery store in 1894 McLane expanded into wholesale distribution in the early 1900s. The McLane family including Houston Astros owner Drayton McLane sold the business to Wal-Mart Stores in the 1990s. Conglomerate Berkshire Hathaway acquired McLane Company in 2003 for about $1.5 billion.

EXECUTIVES

President Mclane Grocery, Mike Youngblood
Evp Administration, James L. (Jim) Kent
President And Ceo, W. Grady Rosier
President Southeast Southern And Dothan Divisions, Ron Clark
President Mclane Carolina And Mid-atlantic Divisions, George Bolts
President Southwest And High Plains Divisions, Scott Braden
Svp And Chief Marketing Officer, Tom Sicola
Vice President Of Information Technology, Mona Huffman
Vice President Of Sales, Jimmy Morales
Senior Vice President, Charles Freeman
Vice President Of Logistics, Robbie Wainwright
Vice President Of Distribution, Mark Hermacinski
Vice President Of Sales Convenience And Military Executive, Vito Maurici

LOCATIONS

HQ: MCLANE COMPANY, INC.
4747 MCLANE PKWY, TEMPLE, TX 765044854
Phone: 254 771-7500
Web: WWW.MCLANECO.COM

PRODUCTS/OPERATIONS

Selected Subsidiaries
C.D. Hartnett Company (grocery distribution)
Empire Distributors Inc. (beverages)
First American Carriers (third-party distribution)
McCarty-Hull Inc. (convenience store distribution)
Meadowbrook Meat Company Inc.

Professional Datasolutions Inc. (technology support services)
Salado Sales (private-label products)
Vantix Logistics (third-party logistics)

COMPETITORS

AMCON Distributing	H. T. Hackney
Associated Wholesale Grocers	MAINES
	Reinhart FoodService
Ben E. Keith	SUPERVALU
C&S Wholesale	Southern Glazer's Wine
Core-Mark	and Spirits
Eby-Brown	Sysco
GSC Enterprises	US Foods
Golden State Foods	Wakefern Food
Gordon Food Service	

HISTORICAL FINANCIALS

Company Type: Private

Income Statement				FYE: December 30
	REVENUE ($ mil.)	NET INCOME ($ mil.)	NET PROFIT MARGIN	EMPLOYEES
12/16*	48,016	0	—	20,128
01/16	48,144	0	—	—
12/12	37,389	0	—	—
01/09	29,800	0	—	—
Annual Growth	6.1%	—	—	—

*Fiscal year change

2016 Year-End Financials

Debt ratio: ——
Return on equity: —
Cash ($ mil.): 122
Current ratio: 0.60
Long-term debt ($ mil.): —

Dividends
Yield: —
Payout: —
Market value ($ mil.): —

MEDSTAR HEALTH, INC.

Whether you're seeing stars or are just plain sickly MedStar Health can cater to you. The not-for-profit organization runs 10 hospitals and about 20 other health-related businesses across Maryland and the Washington DC area including Union Memorial and Georgetown University Hospital. With more than 3000 beds and 6000 affiliated physicians MedStar has a comprehensive service offering including acute and long-term sub-acute care emergency services home health care and rehabilitation. It also operates emergency clinics and assisted living and nursing homes maintains a primary care and specialist physician network (MedStar Physician Partners) and conducts research and medical education activities.

Operations

Along with its 10 hospitals and a dizzying array of inpatient and outpatient services MedStar Health also operates a Medicaid managed care program called MedStar Family Choice.

Its Nascott Orthotics and Prosthetics division provides adult and pediatric prosthetic services and devices to patients in Washington DC and Baltimore. The company provides a continuum of care from initial measurement to fabrication of the device and maintenance through four locations scattered throughout the service areas.

MedStar Health's Visiting Nurse Association (VNA) administers home health care infusion services private duty nursing and hospice as well as immunizations. The VNA also uses telemonitoring services to keep tabs on home care patients without having to physically visit each patient's home.

In 2014 the system had 148685 inpatient admissions and nearly 4 million outpatient visits.

Financial Performance

In fiscal 2014 MedStar Health's net operating revenue totaled $4.6 billion.

Strategy

Despite its already hefty size MedStar Health is not adverse to getting bigger. It grows usually through acquisitions of existing facilities but also through alliances with other health care providers. MedStar Health has acquired several hospitals in recent years including St. Mary's Hospital with 100 beds in southern Maryland and Montgomery General Hospital a 150-bed general acute care facility located in Montgomery County Maryland.

The company also grows by establishing new facilities. In 2014 it opened an integrated multi-specialty care center in downtown Baltimore as well as four new PromptCare locations in Maryland and Virginia. That year it began work on a new ambulatory care center at the 16-acre MedStar Health Bel Air Medical Campus. MedStar is also developing a new ambulatory care center at Lafayette Centre in northwest Washington DC.

MedStar Health has also entered the growing quick-care and urgent care market by partnering with Rite Aid to establish walk-in health clinics in a number of Rite Aid pharmacies throughout the Baltimore and Washington DC markets.

In 2015 the system expanded its Medicare Choice plan into Baltimore City and Anne Arundel Baltimore Charles Prince George's and St. Mary's counties.

EXECUTIVES

Evp Insurance And Diversified Operations, Eric R. Wagner

Evp And Chief Administrative Officer, Michael J. Curran

Evp And Coo, M. Joy Drass

President Medstar Ambulatory Services, Bob Gilbert

Svp And President Medstar Good Samaritan Hospital And Medstar Union Memorial Hospital, Bradley S. Chambers

Svp And Chief Nursing Officer, Maureen P. McCausland

President Medstar Medical Group, Richard Goldberg

President Ceo And Director, Kenneth A. Samet

President Medstar Visiting Nurse Association, Traci K. Anderson

Evp Medical Affairs And Chief Medical Officer, Stephen R. T. Evans

Svp And President Medstar National Rehabilitation Network, John D. Rockwood

President Medstar Health Research Institute, Neil J. Weissman

Svp And President Medstar Southern Maryland Hospital Center And St. Mary's Hospital, Christine R. Wray

Svp And President Medstar Franklin Square Medical Center, Samuel E. Moskowitz

Evp And General Counsel, Oliver M. Johnson

Svp And President Medstar Washington Hospital Center, John Sullivan

Svp Marketing And Strategy, Kevin P. Kowalski

Evp And Cfo, Susan K. Nelson

Vp Applications And Interim Cio, Mark K. Schneider

Svp And President Medstar Georgetown University Hospital, Michael C. Sachtleben

Svp And President Medstar Montgomery Medical Center, T. J. Senker

Assistant Vice President Infrastructure And Operations, Charles Burchinal

Director Of Nursing, Diana Langhauser

Chairman, William R. Roberts

Vice Chairman, William J. Oetgen

LOCATIONS

HQ: MEDSTAR HEALTH, INC.
10980 GRANTCHESTER WAY, COLUMBIA, MD 210446097
Phone: 410 772-6500
Web: WWW.MEDSTARHEALTH.ORG

Selected Facilities

Maryland

Franklin Square Hospital Center (Baltimore)
Good Samaritan Hospital (Baltimore)
Harbor Hospital (Baltimore)
Montgomery General Hospital (Olney)
St. Mary's Hospital (Leonardtown)
Union Memorial Hospital (Baltimore)

Washington DC

Georgetown University Hospital
National Rehabilitation Hospital
Washington Hospital Center

PRODUCTS/OPERATIONS

Selected Affiliates/Operations

Clinical Research
Georgetown University Medical Center (Washington DC)
MedStar Research Institute (Hyattsville Maryland)
Home Health Care
MedStar Health VNA (Washington DC)
MedStar Health Infusion (Elkridge Maryland)
MGH Community Health (Olney Maryland)
Managed Care
MedStar Family Choice (Baltimore Maryland)
Nursing Homes/Senior Living
Franklin Woods (Rosedale Maryland)
Good Samaritan Nursing Center (Baltimore Maryland)
Belvedere Green (Baltimore Maryland)
Woodbourne Woods (Baltimore Maryland)
Primary Care
MedStar Physician Partners (Washington DC)
Outpatient Surgery Centers
MedStar Surgery Center (Washington DC)
Harbor Hospital HealthPark (Pasadena Maryland)
SurgiCenter at Pasadena (Pasadena Maryland)

COMPETITORS

Adventist HealthCare
Anne Arundel Medical Center
Ascension Health
Bon Secours Health
Carilion Clinic
Children's National Medical Center
Christiana Care
Civista Health
Franklin Square Hospital Center
GBMC
Harbor Hospital
Inova
Johns Hopkins Health System
Johns Hopkins Medicine
Kaiser Foundation Health Plan of the Mid-Atlantic
Levindale Hospital
LifeBridge Health
MedStar Union Memorial Hospital
Sinai Hospital of Baltimore
Suburban Hospital
Trinity Health (Novi)
University of Maryland Medical System
Valley Health
Virginia Hospital Center

HISTORICAL FINANCIALS

Company Type: Private

Income Statement				FYE: June 30
	REVENUE ($ mil.)	NET INCOME ($ mil.)	NET PROFIT MARGIN	EMPLOYEES
06/18	5,604	324	5.8%	33,000
06/13	4,217	311	7.4%	—
06/11*	4,011	271	6.8%	—
12/09	1,936	200	10.4%	—
Annual Growth	14.2%	6.2%	—	—

*Fiscal year change

2018 Year-End Financials

Debt ratio: ——
Return on equity: 5.80%
Cash ($ mil.): 692
Current ratio: 1.00
Long-term debt ($ mil.): —
Dividends
Yield: —
Payout: —
Market value ($ mil.): —

MEMORIAL HERMANN HEALTH SYSTEM

EXECUTIVES

Ceo, Charles Stokes
Cfo*, Dennis Laraway
Chief of Medicine, Todd M Price
Information Technology Manager, Joe Dickson
Coordinator, Melissa Aing
Director of Radiology, Alla Vargo
Secretary, Aida Guerra
Lead Project Manager, Chuck Dickson
Director of Nursing, Daniel Kelly
Neurologist, Joanne Y Kim
Educator, Linda Whitson
Auditors: ERNST & YOUNG LLP HOUSTON TX

LOCATIONS

HQ: MEMORIAL HERMANN HEALTH SYSTEM
929 GESSNER RD STE 1900, HOUSTON, TX 770242317
Phone: 713 242-3000
Web: WWW.MEMORIALHERMANN.ORG

HISTORICAL FINANCIALS

Company Type: Private

Income Statement				FYE: June 30
	REVENUE ($ mil.)	NET INCOME ($ mil.)	NET PROFIT MARGIN	EMPLOYEES
06/18	5,258	318	6.1%	14,000
06/17	5,061	313	6.2%	—
06/14	3,741	454	12.1%	—
06/13	3,285	230	7.0%	—
Annual Growth	9.9%	6.6%		

2018 Year-End Financials

Debt ratio: ——
Return on equity: 6.10%
Cash ($ mil.): 371
Current ratio: 0.80
Long-term debt ($ mil.): —
Dividends
Yield: —
Payout: —
Market value ($ mil.): —

Mercantile Bank Corp.

Mercantile Bank Corporation is the holding company for Mercantile Bank of Michigan (formerly Mercantile Bank of West Michigan) which boasts assets of nearly $3 billion and operates more than 50 branches in central and western Michigan around Grand Rapids Holland and Lansing. The bank targets local consumers and businesses offering standard deposit services such as checking and savings accounts CDs IRAs and health savings accounts. Commercial loans make up more than three-fourths of the bank's loan portfolio. Outside of banking subsidiary Mercantile Insurance Center sells insurance products.

Operations

Mercantile Bank Corp. generated 82% of its total revenue from loan interest (including fees) in 2014 with securities interest contributing another 8% to total revenue. Service charges on deposit and sweep accounts and credit and debit card fees made up another 5% of Mercantile's total revenue while its mortgage banking income generated another 2%.

Sales and Marketing

Mercantile provides its banking services to businesses individuals and government organizations. Its commercial banking services mostly cater to small- to medium-sized businesses.

The company spent $1.315 million on advertising in 2014 compared to $1.113 million and $1.167 million in 2013 and 2012 respectively.

Financial Performance

Mercantile Bank Corp's revenues had been declining for a number of years as its loan business withered while profits have remained mostly flat.

The company had a breakout year in 2014 however after its historic acquisition of FirstBank Corp. The bank's revenue skyrocketed by 53% to $99.15 million (the highest level since 2009) mostly as the acquisition nearly doubled its loan assets and boosted its interest income on loans and securities by significant amounts. The bank's non-interest income also grew by 46% thanks to higher fee income across the board also resulting from the recent acquisition.

Higher revenue and a $3.2 million reduction in loan loss provisions with a stronger credit portfolio in 2014 also pushed the company's net income up by 2% to $17.33 million for the year. Mercantile's operating cash declined by 50% to $14.41 million due to changes in accrued interest and other liabilities during the year.

Strategy

Mercantile Bank Corporation has been growing its loan business and branch network reach through strategic acquisitions of smaller banks and bank branches. Its mid-2014 acquisition of Firstbank Corporation was perhaps the most effective to date as the purchase doubled its assets and boosted the size of its branch network nearly seven-fold from seven branches to a whopping 53.

Mergers and Acquisitions

In June 2014 Mercantile Bank Corp. purchased Firstbank Corp of Alma Michigan for a total purchase price of $173 million adding 46 branches and $1.3 billion in assets. The deal which made Mercantile the third-largest bank based in the state also expanded the bank's service offerings diversified its loan portfolio boosted its loan origination capacity and significantly extended its geographic footprint into Michigan's lower peninsula.

EXECUTIVES

Svp Cfo And Treasurer Mercantile Bank Corporation And Svp And Cfo Mercantile Bank Of Michigan, Charles E. (Chuck) Christmas, age 52, $263,000 total compensation

President And Ceo, Robert B. Kaminski, age 56, $315,000 total compensation

Evp Corporate Finance And Strategic Planning Mercantile Bank Corporation And Mercantile Bank Of Michigan, Samuel G. Stone, age 73, $159,833 total compensation

Executive Vice President Corporate Banking, Robert Dewey

Vice President Electronic Banking, Shannon Tramontin

Senior Vice President Commercial Lending, Kevin Paul

Vice President Security, Paul Wegener

Vice President And Branch Manager, Cheri Stanton

Assistant Vice President Human Resources Specialist, Tina Van Valkenburg

Vice President Treasury Management, Joe Allen

Senior Vice President Retail Banking Director, Dave Miller

Senior Vice President Business Development Officer, Brian Talbot

Vice President Commercial Loan Officer, Jeff Hicks

Branch Manager Vice President, Andrea Spagnuolo

Vice President, Teresa Rupert

Assistant Vice President, Jennifer Harris

Senior Vice President, Mike Siminski

Mortgage Operations Manager Vice President, Lori Schafer

Vice President Commercial Lender, Andrew Miedema

Assistant Vice President Human Resources Administrator, Kate Glover

Vice President Of Commercial Lending, Bradley Wahr

Assistant Vice President Assistant Controller, Peggy Coutchie

Senior Vice President Information Systems Manager, Allen Smith

Assistant Vice President Commercial Loan Officer, Justin Horn

Vice President, Martin Smith

Executive Vice President Finance And Strategic Planning, Sam Stone

Vice President Corporate Banking, Bob Klimczak

Senior Vice President General Counsel And Risk Management Director, Bob Worthington

Vice President Treasury Sales Officer, Tim Ladd

Assistant Vice President Legal Documentation Risk Manager, William Franks

Senior Vice President Commercial Loan Officer, Cheryl Gaudard

Vice President, Betsy Mccue

Assistant Vice President Leonard Branch Manager, Daniel Zink

Senior Vice President, Michael Erfourth

Vice President, Jim Kloostra

Chairman, Michael H. Price, age 61

Auditors: BDO USA, LLP

LOCATIONS

HQ: Mercantile Bank Corp.
310 Leonard Street N.W., Grand Rapids, MI 49504
Phone: 616 406-3000
Web: www.mercbank.com

PRODUCTS/OPERATIONS

2014 Sales

	$ mil.	% of total
Interest income		
Loans and leases including fees	80	82
Securities taxable	6	6
Securities tax-exempt	1	2
Other	0	-
Noninterest income		
Service charges on accounts	2	3
Credit and debit card fees	2	2
Mortgage banking activities	1	2
Other	3	3
Total	**99**	**100**

COMPETITORS

Chemical Financial	Flagstar Bancorp
ChoiceOne Financial Services	Huntington Bancshares
Comerica	Independent Bank (MI)
Fifth Third	Macatawa Bank

Income Statement

	ASSETS ($ mil.)	NET INCOME ($ mil.)	INCOME AS % OF ASSETS	EMPLOYEES
12/17	3,286	31	1.0%	701
12/16	3,082	31	1.0%	682
12/15	2,903	27	0.9%	701
12/14	2,893	17	0.6%	731
12/13	1,426	17	1.2%	268
Annual Growth	**23.2%**	**16.4%**	**—**	**27.2%**

FYE: December 31

2017 Year-End Financials

Debt ratio: 1.38%
Return on equity: 8.85%
Cash ($ mil.): 200
Current ratio: —
Long-term debt ($ mil.): —
No. of shares (mil.): 16
Dividends
  Yield: 0.0%
  Payout: 38.9%
Market value ($ mil.): 587

	STOCK PRICE ($) FY Close	P/E High/Low		PER SHARE ($) Earnings	Dividends	Book Value
12/17	35.37	20	15	1.90	0.74	22.05
12/16	37.70	19	11	1.96	1.16	20.76
12/15	24.54	16	12	1.62	0.58	20.41
12/14	21.02	19	15	1.28	2.48	19.33
12/13	21.58	11	8	1.95	0.45	17.54
Annual Growth	**13.1%**	**—**	**—**	**(0.6%)**	**13.2%**	**5.9%**

Merchants Bancorp (Indiana)

Auditors: BKD, LLP

LOCATIONS

HQ: Merchants Bancorp (Indiana)
11555 North Meridian Street, Suite 400, Carmel, IN 46032
Phone: 317 569-7420
Web: www.merchantsbankofindiana.com

Income Statement

	ASSETS ($ mil.)	NET INCOME ($ mil.)	INCOME AS % OF ASSETS	EMPLOYEES
12/17	3,393	54	1.6%	194
12/16	2,718	33	1.2%	157
12/15	2,269	28	1.3%	—
Annual Growth	**22.3%**	**38.8%**	**—**	**—**

FYE: December 31

2017 Year-End Financials

Debt ratio: —
Return on equity: 19.06%
Cash ($ mil.): 359
Current ratio: —
Long-term debt ($ mil.): —
No. of shares (mil.): 28
Dividends
  Yield: 0.0%
  Payout: 2.1%
Market value ($ mil.): 565

	STOCK PRICE ($) FY Close	P/E High/Low		PER SHARE ($) Earnings	Dividends	Book Value
12/17	19.68	9	7	2.28	0.05	12.81
12/16	0.00	—	—	1.47	0.20	9.77
12/15	0.00	—	—	1.35	0.20	7.02
Annual Growth	**—**	**—**	**—**	**30.0%**	**(50.0%)**	**35.1%**

Merck & Co Inc

Merck makes medicines for many maladies from stuffy noses and asthma to hypertension and arthritis. The pharmaceutical giant's top products include diabetes drugs Januvia and Janumet cancer drug Keytruda HPV vaccine Gardasil cholesterol combatants Vytorin and Zetia and hypertension fighters Cozaar and Hyzaar. In 2017 Keytruda was the first cancer drug based on tumor genetics to be approved by the FDA; it has been approved for metastatic lung cancer and for several other indications. In addition Merck makes childhood and adult vaccines for such diseases as measles mumps pneumonia and shingles as well as veterinary pharmaceuticals through Merck Animal Health. In addition the company provides analytics and clinical services and technology to the health care sector.

HISTORY

Merck traces its roots to the formation of Schering-Plough the founding of the original Merck both established in the 1800s. (The two companies merged in 2009.)

The original Merck was started in 1887 when German chemist Theodore Weicker came to the US to set up a branch of German firm E. Merck AG (which was founded in 1668 and later became Merck KGaA).

Schering-Plough dates back to 1851 when Berlin chemist Ernst Schering began to sell chemicals to apothecary shops. By 1880 Schering's business (which eventually became Bayer Schering Pharma) was exporting pharmaceuticals to the US where a subsidiary (the predecessor to Schering-Plough) was established in 1928.

At the outbreak of WWII the US government seized the US Schering subsidiary severing links with its German parent. The company went on to develop such new drugs as Chlor-Trimeton one of the first antihistamines and the cold medicine Coricidin. The US government sold Schering in 1952 to Merrill Lynch which took it public. Schering bought White Labs (which made Coppertone sunscreen) in 1957. In the 1960s the company introduced Garamycin (antibiotic 1964) Tinactin (antifungal 1965) and Afrin (decongestant 1967).

Schering's 1971 merger with Memphis-based Plough expanded the product line to include such cosmetics and consumer items as Coppertone and Di-Gel. Plough's founder Abe Plough had borrowed $125 from his father to found the company in 1908. Abe remained chairman at Schering-Plough until 1976. Schering-Plough introduced many products after the merger including Lotrimin AF (antifungal 1975) antibiotic Netromycin (1980) and Drixoral (a cold remedy made nonprescription in 1982).

The company was one of the first drug giants to make significant investments in biotechnology: It bought DNAX Research Institute of Palo Alto California in 1982. Acquisitions in the late 1970s and 1980s included Scholl (foot care 1979) Key Pharmaceuticals (cardiovascular drugs 1986) and Cooper Companies (eye care 1988).

In 1993 Schering-Plough began marketing its non-sedating antihistamine Claritin in the US. (Claritin became an OTC drug in 2002.) In 1996 Schering-Plough bought Canji to strengthen its gene therapy research program. It strengthened its veterinary medicine segment in 1997 when it bought Mallinckrodt's animal health operations.

The firm bought the marketing rights to Centocor's treatment for Crohn's disease in 1998. In 1999 it bought the US rights to Pfizer's Bain de Soleil sun care product line. In 2000 Schering-Plough formed its first collaboration with Merck.

As Schering-Plough's revenues started to decline in 2003 the company brought in several executives from Pharmacia to help streamline its operations and expand its R&D programs and product offerings. The firm gave itself a major boost by acquiring Akzo Nobel's Organon unit in 2007 growing in the areas of women's health care neurology vaccines animal health (Intervet) and third-party biologics manufacturing (through Diosynth).

Merck and Schering-Plough merged in 2009.

EXECUTIVES

Chairman And Ceo, Kenneth C. (Ken) Frazier, age 63, $1,527,404 total compensation

Evp Strategic Communications Global Public Policy And Population Health And Chief Patient Officer, Julie L. Gerberding, age 63

Evp Global Services And Cfo, Robert M. Davis, age 51, $991,654 total compensation

Evp; President Merck Research Laboratories, Roger M. Perlmutter, age 65, $1,052,288 total compensation

Evp; President Global Human Health, Adam H. Schechter, age 54, $1,003,094 total compensation

Evp Human Resources, Mirian M. Graddick-Weir, age 64

Evp; President Merck Animal Health, Richard R. DeLuca, age 55

Evp And General Counsel, Michael J. Holston, age 55, $761,538 total compensation

Evp And Cio, Clark Golestani, age 51

Evp; President Merck Manufacturing, Sanat Chattopadhyay

Ceo Merck Foundation, Rasha Kelej, age 46

Vice President Biotechnology Development, Stephen Farrand

Vice President Manufacturing Division Strategy And Integration, Richard Hofmann

Vice President Global Compensation And Benefits, Jeff Geller

Vice President Finance Global Supply Chain, Joe Sukola

Vice President Global Engineering Services, Arthur Burson

Associate Medical Director, Lana Garafola

Associate Vice President, Curtis Scott

Legal Pa For Uk Director And Also Pa To The Assistant Vice President For Europe And Canada, Michele Creamer

Senior Vice President Managing Director, Pierluigi Antonelli

Executive Vice President Process Solutions, Andrew Bulpin

Senior Vice President Strategy And Business Development, Galeota James

Associate Vice President Merck Consumer Care Information Technology, Fran Geatens

Vice President, Julie Lepin

Vice President Of Imaging, Jeffrey Evelhoch

Vice President Global Technical Operations Vaccines Biolog, Vijay Yabannavar

Senior Vice President Preclinical Development, Guy Padbury

Senior Vice President Tax, Jerome Mychalowych

Vice President Operations, PK Yegneswaran

Medical Director Oncology Global Clinical Development, Mei Chen

Associate Vice President Drug Discovery And Mrl Liaison, Holger Lehmann

Assistant Treasurer, Joe Promo

Auditors: PricewaterhouseCoopers LLP

LOCATIONS

HQ: Merck & Co Inc
2000 Galloping Hill Road, Kenilworth, NJ 07033
Phone: 908 740-4000   **Fax:** 908 735-1500
Web: www.merck.com

2017 Sales

	$ mil.	% of total
US	17,424	43
Europe Middle East & Africa	11,478	29
Asia/Pacific	4,337	11
Japan	3,122	8
Latin America	2,339	6
Other	1,422	3
Total	**40,122**	**100**

PRODUCTS/OPERATIONS

2017 Sales by Segment

	$ mil.	% of total
Pharmaceutical		
Primary care & women's health	10,260	25
Hospital & specialty	7,546	19
Vaccines	6,159	15
Oncology	4,636	12
Diversified brands	2,494	6
Other	4,295	11
Other segments	4,272	11
Other	460	1
Total	**40,122**	**100**

COMPETITORS

Abbott Labs	Johnson & Johnson
Allergan plc	Merck KGaA
Amgen	Mylan
AstraZeneca	Novartis
Bayer AG	Perrigo
Biogen	Pfizer
Boehringer Ingelheim	Roche Holding
Bristol-Myers Squibb	Sandoz International
Eli Lilly	GmbH
Gilead Sciences	Sanofi
GlaxoSmithKline	Teva
Heska	Virbac Corporation

HISTORICAL FINANCIALS

Company Type: Public

Income Statement

FYE: December 31

	REVENUE ($ mil.)	NET INCOME ($ mil.)	NET PROFIT MARGIN	EMPLOYEES
12/17	40,122	2,394	6.0%	69,000
12/16	39,807	3,920	9.8%	68,000
12/15	39,498	4,442	11.2%	68,000
12/14	42,237	11,920	28.2%	70,000
12/13	44,033	4,404	10.0%	76,000
Annual Growth	**(2.3%)**	**(14.1%)**	**—**	**(2.4%)**

2017 Year-End Financials

Debt ratio: 27.78%—
Return on equity: 6.43%
Cash ($ mil.): 6,092
Current ratio: 1.33
Long-term debt ($ mil.): 21,353

Dividends
Yield: 0.0%
Payout: 217.2%
Market value ($ mil.): —

	STOCK PRICE ($) FY Close	P/E High/Low		PER SHARE ($) Earnings	Dividends	Book Value
12/17	56.27	76	61	0.87	1.89	12.73
12/16	58.87	46	34	1.41	1.85	14.58
12/15	52.82	40	31	1.56	1.81	16.06
12/14	56.79	15	12	4.07	1.77	17.14
12/13	50.05	34	27	1.47	1.73	17.00
Annual Growth	**3.0%**	**—**	**—**	**(12.3%)**	**2.2%**	**(7.0%)**

Mercury General Corp.

Named after the Roman god of commerce and travel Mercury General hopes to combine the two and become the ultimate auto insurance provider. The company is the parent of a group of insurers including Mercury Casualty Company that write automobile insurance for all risk classifications in about a dozen states. Plain old private auto insurance accounts for a majority of premiums written. However Mercury General also sells commercial vehicle insurance and a bit of homeowners mechanical breakdown umbrella and fire insurance. The company is a leader in the California auto market and has significant operations in Florida.

Operations
Mercury General offers automobile insurance products including comprehensive collision property damage body injury personal injury protection underinsured/uninsured motorist and other coverage. It also provides homeowners' coverage including dwelling liability personal property fire and other products.

Geographic Reach
While Mercury General has ventured out of its California comfort zone the state still accounts for about 85% of total premiums. The company operated solely in its home state until 1990; it now underwrites auto insurance in about a dozen other states including Arizona Florida Georgia Illinois Nevada New Jersey New York Oklahoma Texas and Virginia.

Sales and Marketing
Mercury General sells policies through approximately 9700 independent agents including around 1900 in California and another 1500 in Florida.

The company uses television radio newspaper direct mail and online campaigns to market its products. It launched a national advertising campaign in 2015.

Mercury General spent $40 million on advertising in 2016 versus $44 million in 2015 and $23 million in 2014.

Financial Performance
Mercury General's net revenue has been rising for the past five years with the exception of 2015 when it fell less than 1% to $3 billion. In 2016 it rose 7% to $3.2 billion as net premiums earned increased and net realized investment losses decreased. The company had a 5% increase in net premiums written primarily due to rate increases and higher sales in California.

Net income which fell 58% to $74 million in 2015 dropped another 2% to $73 million in 2016. Higher losses loss adjustment expenses and policy acquisition costs led to that decline. Profits were impacted bylosses related to automobile accidents in California and Florida as well as catastrophe losses due to severe storms and rainstorms.

Cash flow from operations has generally been rising. It grew 51% to $287.5 million in 2016. Major factors in that jump included positive adjustments to unpaid losses and loss adjustment expenses changes in current and deferred income taxes and in accounts payable and accrued expenses.

Strategy
Core to Mercury General's strategy for growth is managing rates to achieve the right balance between attracting customers through lower rates and remaining competitive. For example to counteract the overall increase in auto accidents the company implemented price hikes in 2016. It expects its returns to improve in that arena.

The company also places value in its agent relationships and underwriting processes to achieve favorable margins. To encourage policy growth and broaden its customer base Mercury General offers multi-policy discounts to those who bundle their home and car insurance together. It also employs marketing initiatives to build brand recognition and generate leads.

Additionally Mercury General is gradually widening its operations by expanding into new states while being mindful of the risks of establishing new divisions. Mercury General also maintains a conservative investment strategy by maximizing long-term performance opportunities.

EXECUTIVES

Vp And Chief Underwriting Officer, Kenneth G. Kitzmiller, age 71
President And Ceo, Gabriel Tirador, age 53, $948,931 total compensation
Svp And Cfo, Theodore R. Stalick, age 54, $589,445 total compensation
Vp And Chief Investment Officer, Christopher Graves, age 52, $381,679 total compensation
Vp And Chief Actuary, Charles Toney, age 56
Svp And Cio, Allan Lubitz, age 60, $449,470 total compensation
Vp And Chief Product Officer, Robert Houlihan, age 61, $404,493 total compensation
Vp Marketing, Brandt N. Minnich, age 51
Vice President Information Technology Operations, Abby Hossein
Vice President Corporate Controller, David Yeager
Chairman, George Joseph, age 96
Auditors: KPMG LLP

LOCATIONS

HQ: Mercury General Corp.
4484 Wilshire Boulevard, Los Angeles, CA 90010
Phone: 323 937-1060   **Fax:** 323 857-7116
Web: www.mercuryinsurance.com

PRODUCTS/OPERATIONS

2016 Sales

	$ mil.	% of total
Net premium earned	3,131	96
Net investment income	121	4
Other	8	-
Net realized investment (losses)gains	(34.3)	-
Total	**3,227**	**100**

Selected Products
Auto
  Commercial auto
  Mechanical breakdown (extended warranty coverage)
  Niche commercial
  Personal auto
Condo
  Contents coverage
  Guest medical protection and liability
  Personal liability protection
  Personal property
Homeowners
  Apartments
  Condominiums
  Single-family homes
Personal umbrella
Renter
  Liability protection
  Personal property

Selected Operating Brands and Divisions
AIS Management
American Mercury Insurance
American Mercury Lloyds Insurance
American Mercury MGA
Auto Insurance Specialists
California Automobile Insurance
California General Underwriters Insurance
Concord Insurance Services
Mercury Casualty
Mercury County Mutual Insurance
Mercury Group
Mercury Indemnity
Mercury Insurance
Mercury National Insurance
Mercury Select Management
PoliSeek AIS Insurance Solutions

COMPETITORS

21st Century Insurance	Farmers Group
Allstate	GEICO
Auto Club of Southern California	State Farm
Covanta Holding	USAA

HISTORICAL FINANCIALS
Company Type: Public

Income Statement

	ASSETS ($ mil.)	NET INCOME ($ mil.)	INCOME AS % OF ASSETS	EMPLOYEES
12/17	5,101	144	2.8%	4,300
12/16	4,788	73	1.5%	4,200
12/15	4,628	74	1.6%	4,300
12/14	4,600	177	3.9%	4,400
12/13	4,315	112	2.6%	4,500
Annual Growth	**4.3%**	**6.6%**	—	**(1.1%)**

FYE: December 31

2017 Year-End Financials

Debt ratio: 7.28%
Return on equity: 8.25%
Cash ($ mil.): 291
Current ratio: —
Long-term debt ($ mil.): —

No. of shares (mil.): 55
Dividends
  Yield: 0.0%
  Payout: 95.1%
Market value ($ mil.): 2,957

	STOCK PRICE ($) FY Close	P/E High/Low	Earnings	Dividends	Book Value
12/17	53.44	24 20	2.62	2.49	31.83
12/16	60.21	46 33	1.32	2.48	31.70
12/15	46.57	45 34	1.35	2.47	33.01
12/14	56.67	18 13	3.23	2.46	34.02
12/13	49.71	25 18	2.04	2.45	33.15
Annual Growth	**1.8%**	**— —**	**6.5%**	**0.4%**	**(1.0%)**

MERCY HEALTH

Mercy Health formerly known as the Sisters of Mercy Health System provides a range of health care and social services through its network of facilities and service organizations. The organization operates some 35 acute care hospitals (including four specialty heart hospitals and two children's hospitals) with more than 4200 licensed beds as well as 700 clinics and outpatient facilities in four Midwestern states. Its hospital groups include facilities for nursing homes medical practices and outpatient centers. Mercy Health also operates Resource Optimization & Innovation (ROi) its industry-leading health care supply chain organization and health outreach organizations in Louisiana Mississippi and Texas.

Operations
Mercy Health also operates three rehabilitation hospitals and two orthopedic hospitals. The system has more than 2000 Mercy Clinic physicians.

In 2014 Mercy Health had 150696 acute inpatient discharges; 158911 inpatient and outpatient surgeries; 631444 emergency department visits; 23213 births; and nearly 8.4 million outpatient visits.

Geographic Reach
The system operates in Arkansas Kansas Missouri and Oklahoma.

Mercy Health's outreach efforts include Mercy Ministries of Laredo a group providing primary health care and social services to residents of Laredo Texas. In New Orleans Mercy Health sponsors Mercy Family Center which provides mental health services; in Mississippi it funds a health care advocacy group.

Sales and Marketing

Commercial and other third-party payments accounted for 44% of net patient service revenue while Medicare and Medicaid combined accounted for 51%.

Financial Performance

Mercy Health's operating revenue increased 14% to $4.5 billion in 2014 as net patient and other revenues grew. However the system reported a net loss of $6.5 million that year (versus net income in 2013) as a result of interest rate swap agreement losses and higher expenses as well as lower investment earnings.

Cash flow from operations fell 46% to $354 million in 2014.

Strategy

In 2013 Mercy Health opened new facilities in Missouri (St. Charles and Wentzville) as well as a new heart and vascular center that centralized its outpatient heart and vascular offerings. The following year it opened a new orthopedic hospital in Fort Smith and a 60-bed rehabilitation hospital.

The system acquired Lincoln County Medical Center (renamed Mercy Hospital Lincoln) and its eight affiliated clinics in 2015 expanding its presence in eastern Missouri.

Despite its various expansions the Mercy system experienced the same industry challenges as its health care brethren including escalating medical and pharmaceutical costs and increasing self-pay bad debts (uninsured patients who leave their medical bills unpaid). Several of the health system's facilities have seen a decline in discharges.

Company Background

The organization was founded by the Sisters of Mercy of the St. Louis Regional Community in 1986 and operated under that model until 2008 when its sponsorship was transferred from the Sisters of Mercy of the St. Louis Regional Community to a new entity Mercy Health Ministry. The shift to the new sponsorship organization was made to allow lay members to join the Sisters of Mercy in sponsoring the ministry. It also reflected the growing number of lay people holding executive positions at the system's hospitals and on the board of directors.

EXECUTIVES

Vice President Performance Management, Fred Ford
Senior Vice President, Vance Moore
Auditors: ERNST & YOUNG LLP ST LOUIS

LOCATIONS

HQ: MERCY HEALTH
14528 SOUTH OUTER 40 RD # 100, CHESTERFIELD, MO 630175743
Phone: 314 579-6100
Web: WWW.MERCY.COM

Selected Locations
Arkansas
  Berryville
  Fort Smith
  Hot Springs
  Ozark
  Paris
  Rogers
  Waldron
Kansas
  Columbus
  Fort Scott
  Independence

Missouri
  Aurora
  Cassville
  Joplin
  Lebanon
  Mountain View
  St. Louis
  Springfield
  Washington
Oklahoma
  Ada
  Ardmore
  El Reno
  Guthrie
  Healdton
  Kingfisher
  Marietta
  Oklahoma City
  Tishomingo
  Watonga

PRODUCTS/OPERATIONS

2014 Sales

	% of total
Net patient service revenue less provision for bad debts	85
Member revenue	11
Other revenue	4
Total	**100**

Selected Facilities

Arkansas
  Mercy Hospital Berryville
  Mercy Hospital Fort Smith
  Mercy Hospital Hot Springs
  Mercy Hospital Northwest Arkansas
  Mercy Hospital of Scott County
  Mercy Hospital Ozark
  Mercy Hospital Paris
  Mercy Hospital Waldron
Kansas
  Mercy Health Center
  Mercy Hospital Fort Scott
  Mercy Hospital Independence
  Mercy Maude Norton Hospital Columbus
Missouri
  Mercy Hospital Aurora
  Mercy Hospital Cassville
  Mercy Hospital Joplin
  Mercy Hospital Lebanon
  Mercy Hospital St. Louis
  Mercy Children's Hospital St. Louis
  Mercy Heart and Vascular Hospital St. Louis
  Mercy Heart Hospital St. Louis
  Mercy Rehabilitation Hospital St. Louis
  Mercy Hospital Springfield
  Mercy Children's Hospital Springfield
  Mercy Hospital Washington
  Mercy McCune-Brooks Hospital
  Mercy St. Francis Hospital
Oklahoma
  Arbuckle Memorial Hospital
  Mercy Health Love County
  Mercy Hospital Ardmore
  Mercy Hospital El Reno
  Mercy Hospital Healdton
  Mercy Hospital Logan County
  Mercy Hospital Oklahoma City
  Mercy Hospital - Tishomingo
  Valley View Regional Hospital
  Watonga Municipal Hospital

COMPETITORS

Ascension Health	SSM Health Care
BJC HealthCare	Saint Luke's Health
Baptist Health	System
(Arkansas)	Shawnee Mission
Barnes-Jewish Hospital	Medical Center
CHRISTUS Health	Sisters of Charity of
Christian Hospital	Leavenworth
Community Health	St. Anthony's Medical
Systems	Center
CoxHealth	St. Vincent Health
HCA	System
INTEGRIS Health	Tenet Healthcare
Memorial Hospital	Universal Health
(Illinois)	Services
RehabCare	

HISTORICAL FINANCIALS

Company Type: Private

Income Statement

FYE: June 30

	REVENUE ($ mil.)	NET INCOME ($ mil.)	NET PROFIT MARGIN	EMPLOYEES
06/18	6,254	243	3.9%	8,800
06/17	5,527	558	10.1%	—
06/10*	18	7	38.4%	—
03/09	2,936	(196)	—	—
Annual Growth	**8.8%**	**—**	**—**	**—**

*Fiscal year change

2018 Year-End Financials

Debt ratio: —
Return on equity: 3.90%
Cash ($ mil.): 481
Current ratio: 1.20
Long-term debt ($ mil.): —

Dividends
  Yield: —
  Payout: —
Market value ($ mil.): —

MERCY HEALTH

EXECUTIVES

Ceo-Pres, Michael D Connelly
Coordinator, Fiona McCloy
Chief Officer and Pres, Randy Curnow
Scientist, Larry Jackson
Information Technology Manager, Dave Hedgespeth
Health Care Director, Angela Price
Executive Vice President, David A Catalano
Senior Vice President Operatio, Rebecca Sykes
Director Information Technolog, Shawn Kent
Director, Tom Ramsey
Purchasing Agent, William Mueller
Auditors: ERNST & YOUNG LLP CINCINNATI

LOCATIONS

HQ: MERCY HEALTH
1701 MERCY HEALTH PL, CINCINNATI, OH 452376147
Phone: 513 639-2800
Web: WWW.HEALTH-PARTNERS.ORG

HISTORICAL FINANCIALS

Company Type: Private

Income Statement

FYE: December 31

	REVENUE ($ mil.)	NET INCOME ($ mil.)	NET PROFIT MARGIN	EMPLOYEES
12/17	4,737	456	9.6%	35,000
12/14	4,510	130	2.9%	—
12/08	4,044	(657)	—	—
Annual Growth	**1.8%**	**—**	**—**	**—**

2017 Year-End Financials

Debt ratio: —
Return on equity: 9.60%
Cash ($ mil.): 146
Current ratio: 0.70
Long-term debt ($ mil.): —

Dividends
  Yield: —
  Payout: —
Market value ($ mil.): —

Meridian Bancorp Inc

EXECUTIVES

Cfo And Treasurer, Mark L. Abbate, age 63
Svp Consumer And Business Banking, Keith D. Armstrong
Chairman President And Ceo Meridian Interstate Bancorp And East Boston Savings Bank, Richard J. Gavegnano, age 70, $311,400 total compensation
Evp Corporate Banking, Frank Romano
Evp Lending, John Migliozzi
Evp And Coo, John A. Carroll
Svp Electronic Banking, Mary Hagen
Svp Retail Banking, James Morgan
Svp Residential Lending, Joseph Nash
Vice President, Michael Raftery
Auditors: Wolf & Company, P.C.

LOCATIONS

HQ: Meridian Bancorp Inc
67 Prospect Street, Peabody, MA 01960
Phone: 617 567-1500

Selected Locations
Allpoint Locator
Allston
Belmont
Cambridge
Danvers
Dorchester
East Boston
Everett
Jamaica Plain
Lynn
Medford
Melrose
Peabody
Revere
Saugus
Somerville
South Boston
South End
Wakefield
West Roxbury
Winthrop

PRODUCTS/OPERATIONS

2015 Sales

	$ mil.	% of total
Interest & dividend income		
Interest & fees on loans	118	87
Interest on debt securities	1	1
Dividends on equity securities	1	1
Others	1	1
Non-interest income		
Customer service fees	8	6
Gain on sales of securities net	2	2
Income from bank-owned life insurance	1	1
Loan fees	1	1
Mortgage banking gains & other income	0	-
Total	**136**	**100**

Selected Products & Services
Personal
  Deposit Rates
  Investments
  Personal Checking
  Personal Lending
  Personal Online Banking
  Retirement Services
  Savings & CDs
Business
  Business Checking
  Business Lending
  Business Online Banking
  Business Retirement Services
  Business Savings
  Deposit Rates
  Institutional Banking
  Merchant Services
Commercial
  Cash Management
  Commercial Lending
  Corporate Banking
  Deposit Rates

COMPETITORS

Bank of America
Cambridge Financial
Citizens Financial Group
Eastern Bank
Middlesex Savings
Peoples Federal Bancshares Inc.
Sovereign Bank
TD Bank USA

HISTORICAL FINANCIALS

Company Type: Public

Income Statement   FYE: December 31

	ASSETS ($ mil.)	NET INCOME ($ mil.)	INCOME AS % OF ASSETS	EMPLOYEES
12/17	5,299	42	0.8%	538
12/16	4,436	34	0.8%	500
12/15	3,524	24	0.7%	488
12/14	3,278	22	0.7%	466
12/13	2,682	15	0.6%	455
Annual Growth	**18.6%**	**29.2%**	**—**	**4.3%**

2017 Year-End Financials

Debt ratio: 9.69%
Return on equity: 6.85%
Cash ($ mil.): 472
Current ratio: —
Long-term debt ($ mil.): —
No. of shares (mil.): 54
Dividends
  Yield: 0.0%
  Payout: 20.7%
Market value ($ mil.): 1,113

	STOCK PRICE ($) FY Close	P/E High/Low		PER SHARE ($) Earnings	Dividends	Book Value
12/17	20.60	25	19	0.82	0.17	11.96
12/16	18.90	29	19	0.65	0.12	11.33
12/15	14.10	31	24	0.46	0.06	10.72
12/14	11.22	27	24	0.42	0.00	10.56
Annual Growth	**16.4%**	**—**	**—**	**18.2%**	**—**	**3.2%**

Merrill Lynch Life Insurance Co - Insurance Products

EXECUTIVES

Pres, Marilyn Carp
Auditors: PricewaterhouseCoopers LLP

LOCATIONS

HQ: Merrill Lynch Life Insurance Co - Insurance Products
4333 Edgewood Road, NE, Cedar Rapids, IA 52499-0001
Phone: 800 346-3677
Web: www.transamerica.com

HISTORICAL FINANCIALS

Company Type: Public

Income Statement   FYE: December 31

	ASSETS ($ mil.)	NET INCOME ($ mil.)	INCOME AS % OF ASSETS	EMPLOYEES
12/17	8,621	99	1.2%	—
12/16	8,670	(20)	—	—
12/15	9,165	13	0.1%	—
12/14	10,108	33	0.3%	—
12/13	10,555	(254)	—	—
Annual Growth	**(4.9%)**	**—**	**—**	**—**

2017 Year-End Financials

Debt ratio: 0.07%
Return on equity: 9.25%
Cash ($ mil.): 270
Current ratio: —
Long-term debt ($ mil.): —
No. of shares (mil.): 0
Dividends
  Yield: —
  Payout: 140.8%
Market value ($ mil.): —

Meta Financial Group Inc

Delivering financial products and services to Iowa and South Dakota is the calling of Meta Financial Group. The group?s biggest component is MetaBank a 10-branch operation that offers standard banking solutions such as deposit accounts CDs home mortgages and student loans. Other subsidiaries provide prepaid card services insurance and a variety of tax related solutions. It holds a loan portfolio that exceeds $1 billion and deposits that surpass $3 billion.

Operations

Meta Financial Group operates two customer-facing business segments Banking and Payments and a supporting segment that includes corporate services and other sources of revenue. The Banking segment generates the majority of interest income and a small amount of non-interest income. The Payments unit is the opposite where non-interest income accounts for 90% of its overall revenue and interest income is less than 10% of its business.

The Banking unit doing business as MetaBank operates 10 branches in four key geographic markets: Central Iowa Storm Lake Iowa Brookings South Dakota and Sioux Falls South Dakota. It offers standard deposit products and services including checking and savings accounts. Its lending and investment activities are weighted towards real estate and real estate-related assets; commercial and multifamily residential mortgages comprise more than half of the bank's loan portfolio. It also writes single-family residential mortgages and business loans.

Meta Financial's bread and butter however is the bank's Meta Payment Systems (MPS) division which provides prepaid cards consumer credit and ATM sponsorship services nationwide under operating names of MPS Refund Advantage EPS Financial and SCS. The segment has grown primarily through acquisitions.

Geographic Reach

The MetaBank subsidiary of Sioux Falls SD-based Meta Financial Group operates mainly in Iowa and South Dakota. Its Payment segment includes subsidiaries that run business out of Dallas TX Newport Beach CA Louisville KY Easton PA and Hurst TX.

Financial Performance

Non-interest income from the Payments business grew more than 70% in the year to $166 million. Interest income from the Bank segment rose 37% to $52 million. Total revenue for 2017 was $265 million. The stellar growth is the result of acquisitions and organic growth ? the Bank unit acquired $134 million of private student loans in late 2016 and a further $73 million portfolio in late 2017. The Payment business grew its tax refund business 13-fold underwriting and originating $1.3 billion of refund advance loans for the 2017 tax season.

Net income in 2017 rose 33% to $45 million thanks to the significant upswing in Payments revenue including big growth in its tax business along with improvements in card fee income.

Strategy

Meta Financial Group is looking to boost is non-interest income business endeavors in the Payments division. It feels constrained in its banking business by the need to raise more capital before it can lend out more money from which it would generate interest income. Without the ability to raise more capital (or to raise it at an advantageous cost) the Group believes its efforts are better directed at growth that is not hindered by insufficient capital.

EXECUTIVES

Chairman And Ceo Meta Financial Group And Metabank, J. Tyler Haahr, age 55, $550,000 total compensation

Evp Sales And Operations Metabank And Director Meta Financial Group (mfg) And Metabank, Troy Moore, age 50, $252,350 total compensation

Evp Secretary Treasurer And Cfo, David W. Leedom, age 64, $215,000 total compensation

President Meta Financial Group Inc. (mfg) And Metabank And Division President Meta Payment System, Bradley C. (Brad) Hanson, age 54, $550,000 total compensation

Evp Meta Payment Systems, Scott Galit, age 48, $235,000 total compensation

Evp And Cfo Meta Financial Group (mfg) And Metabank, Glen W. Herrick, age 55, $255,000 total compensation

Vice Chairman Meta Financial Group (mfg) And Metabank, Frederick V. (Fred) Moore, age 62

Board Member, Douglas Hajek

Auditors: Crowe LLP

LOCATIONS

HQ: Meta Financial Group Inc
5501 South Broadband Lane, Sioux Falls, SD 57108
Phone: 605 782-1767
Web: www.metabank.com

COMPETITORS

Blackhawk Network	Great Western Bancorp
BofI	Green Dot
Citi Prepaid Services	HF Financial
First National of Nebraska	West Bancorporation

HISTORICAL FINANCIALS

Company Type: Public

Income Statement

FYE: September 30

	ASSETS ($ mil.)	NET INCOME ($ mil.)	INCOME AS % OF ASSETS	EMPLOYEES
09/18	5,835	51	0.9%	1,219
09/17	5,228	44	0.9%	827
09/16	4,006	33	0.8%	672
09/15	2,529	18	0.7%	638
09/14	2,054	15	0.8%	453
Annual Growth	29.8%	34.6%	—	28.1%

2018 Year-End Financials

Debt ratio: 1.52%	No. of shares (mil.): 39
Return on equity: 8.76%	Dividends
Cash ($ mil.): 99	Yield: 0.0%
Current ratio: —	Payout: 10.7%
Long-term debt ($ mil.): —	Market value ($ mil.): 3,237

	STOCK PRICE ($) FY Close	P/E High/Low	PER SHARE ($) Earnings	Dividends	Book Value
09/18	82.65	70 46	1.67	0.18	19.00
09/17	78.40	66 39	1.61	0.17	15.05
09/16	60.61	47 28	1.31	0.17	13.10
09/15	41.77	59 36	0.89	0.17	11.08
09/14	35.26	54 41	0.84	0.17	9.44
Annual Growth	23.7%	— —	18.6%	0.9%	19.1%

MetLife Inc

While its name evolved from "metropolitan" MetLife's policies are found in villages towns and huge cities around the world. Its companies offer life accident and health insurance as well as retirement and savings products around the world. The group is a big force in Japan and growing in more than 50 other countries especially in Latin America. It distributes its products to retail corporate and government customers through agents third-party distributors including banks and brokers and direct marketing channels. About half of its revenue comes from the US but in mid-2017 MetLife split off much of its US life business.

Operations

MetLife is organized into five primary segments: US; Latin America; Asia; Europe the Middle East and Africa (EMEA); and MetLife Holdings. Certain results are also reported in the operations of the Corporate & Other segment including MetLife Home Loans. The US segment is MetLife's largest accounting for about half of total sales. Asia accounts for nearly 20% of revenue and Latin America and EMEA each account for more than 5%. MetLife Holdings brings in more than 15% of revenue.

In the US MetLife provides a range of insurance and financial services offerings including renewable term life property/casualty disability dental guaranteed interest and annuities. These are distributed through both in-house and independent retail channels and in the workplace. Internationally the company provides life accident medical dental credit and other insurance as well as annuities and other retirement and savings products to individuals and groups.

MetLife Holdings comprises businesses no longer actively promoted in the US including variable life and universal life products term and whole

life products and annuities. It also includes the group's discontinued long-term care business.

Geographic Reach

MetLife operates in the Americas and Asia and in Europe the Middle East and Africa (EMEA). In Latin America it operates in Argentina Brazil Chile Colombia Ecuador Uruguay and Mexico (with the bulk of regional revenues coming from Mexico and Chile).

The company operates in about 10 countries in Asia with its largest operations in Japan. It has an innovation center in Singapore (it is testing an automated insurance solution using blockchain and electronic medical records) and a data analytics center in Malaysia. It also does business in Australia Bangladesh Hong Kong and Nepal and through a joint venture in China Korea India Malaysia and Vietnam.

MetLife operates in more than 25 countries across EMEA. The segment's biggest operations are in the UK the Persian Gulf Poland and Turkey.

Sales and Marketing

MetLife's policies and other products are sold to some 100 million customers through a vast network of targeted marketing and sales forces financial advisors consultants agency distribution groups captive agents independent agents affiliated broker-dealers and direct marketing (including direct response television web-based lead generation telemarketing and print media). In addition MetLife sells some products through affinity groups and through employers.

Financial Performance

MetLife's revenue peaked at $73.3 billion in 2014 but has been been somewhat lower (above $60 billion) since then. Net income has been fluctuating reaching $6.3 billion in 2014 but falling to $850 million in 2016. The company's cash levels have also fluctuated recently.

In 2017 revenue increased 3% to $62.3 billion. Growth in the retirement and income solutions business and the group benefits business drove that increase. International sales also rose overall. Midway through the year MetLife spun much of its US life and annuity operations which resulted in a decline in those revenue lines.

Net income rose 371% to $4 billion in 2017. A number of factors led to that jump including favorable changes in discontinued operations and a $1.3 billion benefit related to US tax reform.

The company ended 2017 with $12.7 billion in net cash some $5 billion less than it had at the end of 2016. Operating activities provided $12.3 billion while investing activities used $16.9 billion and financing activities used $906 million.

Strategy

In 2017 MetLife spun off much of its US retail operations into a new company named Brighthouse Financial. Its MetLife Insurance Company USA Metropolitan Tower Life Insurance Company General American Life Insurance Company (which is being merged into Metropolitan Tower Life) and several other units were included in the transaction which took the form of an initial public offering. Together those units represented about 20% of MetLife's total earnings.

MetLife's move to divest part of its core operations came in the wake of the financial crisis and subsequent changes in the regulatory landscape. US regulators had designated MetLife one of four non-bank systemically important financial institutions (meaning it would pose a risk to the economy if it should collapse) but MetLife fought the designation winning its case in a federal court in 2016. Regardless the separation of its US life insurance business should calm any unrest over the group's size. The newly created company also benefits from having a lower capital and compliance burden.

In another divestiture in mid-2016 MassMutual bought MetLife's US retail captive agency distribution channel MetLife Premier Client Group and broker dealer MetLife Securities. (US retail businesses that were not sold in the deal included the closed-block life insurance property/casualty and Metropolitan Life Insurance Company's life and annuity operations.)

These moves were not the first major shufflings of MetLife's operations in recent years. It is exiting the bulk of its banking operations to avoid the increased scrutiny of banks under Dodd-Frank financial regulations. The company is working to surrender its status as a bank holding company. It has already sold its MetLife Bank depository operations and has stopped writing new residential mortgages and reverse mortgages.

Going forward MetLife plans to focus on pension and retirement products insurance sold to employers and non-US life insurance. In a shift away from market-sensitive products it will only invest in businesses that have strong rates of return require less capital and offer a higher ratio of free cash flow to operating earnings. The company has pinned much of its growth efforts on emerging markets by increasing its already-strong presence in the Asia/Pacific region and in Latin America through acquisitions and new product introductions. To support this growth the company has organized its operations along geographic lines: US; Latin America; Asia; and Europe the Middle East and Africa (EMEA).

Other strategic areas of focus include creating a high-performance operation with competitive prices transforming distribution channels (especially through digital means) and connecting customers with the most appropriate products and services.

Some of the individual and group products MetLife sells overseas include life insurance accident and health insurance credit insurance and annuities and retirement products. It has also created a global employee benefits business to reach into new markets. To focus on core international businesses Metlife has been selling off select foreign assets.

Mergers and Acquisitions

In 2017 MetLife acquired Logan Circle Partners from Fortress Investment Group for some $250 million. Logan was the traditional fixed income asset management business of Fortress; it serves institutional investors and has more than $33 billion in assets under management. The purchase helped expand MetLife's investment management business for third-party customers.

Company Background

Metropolitan Life Insurance was established as a stock company in 1868. It became a mutual company (owned by its policyholders) in 1915. Starting off serving mutual assistance societies for German immigrants the company began offering auto and homeowners insurance in 1974 and entered the life insurance and annuities business in the 1980s.

HISTORY

New York merchant Simeon Draper tried to form National Union Life and Limb Insurance to cover Union soldiers in the Civil War but investors were scared away by heavy casualties. After several reorganizations and name changes the enterprise emerged in 1868 as Metropolitan Life Insurance (MetLife) a stock company.

Sustained at first by business from mutual assistance societies for German immigrants MetLife went into industrial insurance with workers' burial policies. The firm was known for its aggressive sales methods. Agents combed working-class neighborhoods collecting small premiums. If a worker missed one payment the company could cancel the policy and keep all premiums paid a practice outlawed in 1900.

MetLife became a mutual company (owned by its policyholders) in 1915 and began offering group insurance two years later.

After a period of conservative management under the Eckers family from 1929 to 1963 MetLife began to change dropping industrial insurance in 1964. It started offering auto and homeowners insurance in 1974.

To diversify the company bought State Street Research & Management (1983) Century 21 Real Estate (1985 sold 1995) London-based Albany Life Assurance (1985) and Allstate's group life and health business (1988). In 1987 it took over the annuities segment of the failed Baldwin United Co. and expanded into Spain and Taiwan in 1988. During the early 1990s MetLife reemphasized insurance adding such new products as long-term-care insurance.

EXECUTIVES

Evp And Global Chief Marketing Officer, Esther Lee

Chairman President And Ceo, Steven A. (Steve) Kandarian, age 66, $1,525,000 total compensation

Evp And Cfo, John C. R. Hele, age 60, $781,250 total compensation

Evp Global Employee Benefits, Maria R. Morris, age 55, $525,000 total compensation

Evp And General Counsel, Ricardo A. Anzaldua

Evp Chief Investment Officer And Interim President Metlife Asia, Steven J. Goulart, age 59, $725,000 total compensation

President Us, Michel Khalaf, $476,313 total compensation

Evp Global Technology And Operations And Metlife Holdings, Martin J. (Marty) Lippert, $756,250 total compensation

Managing Director Institutional Client Group, Thomas Metzler

Ceo Metlife Hong Kong, Lee Wood

Vice President Learning And Development, John Wiltshire

Regional Sales Vice President, Jordan Teel

Vice President Finance, Nancy Kennelly

Regional Vice President Northeast Region, Joe Heaney

Vice President Information Technology, Annette Fugina

Vice President Information Technology Institutiona, Bernice Beedle

Vice President Information Technology, Marcella Kelly

Vice President Global Information Security Officer, Jesus L Montano

Vice President Sales And Global Strategies, Maximo Saravi

Vice President Human Resources Information Technology, David Bess

Vice President, Stephanie Miller

Vp, Curt Breckon

Vice President, Michele Brooks

Vice President Information Technology, Neil Melleky

Vice President, Brenda Murphy

Vice President Of Sales, Lewis Robyn

Vice President Information Technology, Alvin Sheinheit

Vice President Information Technology, Tom Kelly

Vice President And Chief Privacy Officer, Joseph Trovato

Vice President, Bob Broseker

Vice President Actuary Reserve Coordination, Stewart Ashkenazy

Vice President, Ilia Castellano

Vice President Information Technology, Roderick Pasqualicchio

Vice President Actuary, Marian Zeldin

Vice President, Guy Lawrence

Vice President, Randy Stram

Assistant Vice President And Actuary, Jonathan Trend

Vice President, Alan Hirschberg

Medical Director, Charles Arnold

Vice President Ed, Bonnie Sullivan

Regional Vice President Metlife Investors, Ted Feitt

Evp Global Corporate Services Global Technology And Operations, Joe Sprouls

Vice President Of Application Development, Jack Rooney

Vice President Human Resources, Lynne Distasio

Assistant Vice President, Gladys Rosetta

Vice President Life And Income Funding Solutions, Tim Brown

Vice President, Michael Nardone

Vice President, Rahul Magan

Vice President, Harry Xiao

Assistant Vice President, Robert Bean

Vice President And Actuary, Douglas Kudler

Regional Sales Vice President Se Team Lead, Martin Topor

Regional Vice President Broker Dealer Group, Orv Mohler

Vice President Investments Information Technology Global Strategy Derivatives Collateral Mgmnt Securities Lending And Cmip, Santhosh Aravindakshan

Vice President Information Technology Infrastructu, Gail Weimer

Regional Sales Vice President, Michael Casimiro

Assistant Vice President, Michael Simpson

Vice President, Bob Linzey

Vice President, Steve Vnuck

Vice President Portfolio And Program Management Enterprise Application Development, Ninna Roco

Svp Global Talent Processes, Rachel Lee

Vice President Of Information Technology, Ron Gillmore

Vice President Actuary, Jill Garofalo

Vice President Executive Learning And Development, Mara Jane

Assistant Vice President And Cre Relationship Manager Global Corporate Services, Betty Dubuisson

Vice President, Michele Zachensky

Vice President, Mike Paleos

Vice President Global Internal Audit, Carlos Mendez

Regional Sales Vice President, Ed Wustefeld

Vice President, David Waldman

Assistant Vice President Enterprise Strategy Group, Kevin Chean

Regional Sales Vice President, Thomas Russell

Vice President, Nancy Davenport

Vice President Disability And Absence Practice Leader, Phil Bruen

Vice President, Robert Klahre

Vice President Capital Strategy Planning, Kevin Mackay

Regional Sales Vice President, Stacey Waite

Vice President, Michael Evenzwig

Regional Sales Vice President, Steve Shrout

Senior Vice President Executive And Global Compensation, Kathryn Kessel

Regional Sales Vice President, Derrik Bullen

Regional Sales Vice President, Tony Nguyen

Vice President, Emilia Kyff

Regional Sales Vice President Michael Giorgetti Sales Desk, John Rotondo

Regional Sales Vice President, Chris Bunting

Vice President, George Bell

Assistant Vice President And Actuary Financial Research, William Chirolas

Regional Sales Vice President, Nancy Power

Vice President Investments Controller, David Rooney

Svp Investor Relations, John Hall

Vice President, James Donnellan

Vice President, Chris Stern
Assistant Vice President, John Zelinske
Vice President, Lise Hasegawa
Senior Vice President, Joseph Reali
Vice President Operations, John Abela
Assistant Vice President Individual Disability Underwriting, Rod Boggs
Assistant Vice President Sales Force Development, Anna Lavery
Regional Sales Vice President, Jan Primmer
Regional Sales Vice President, Sarah Kim
Svp Global Shared Services India, Kush Kamra
Vice President Workforce Enablement Glob, Kate Day
Vice President, Arthur Bruhmuller
Vice President, Michael Romano
Assistant Vice President, Jai Maxwell
Assisttant Vice President Growth Strategies, Tina Beckwith
Vice President Of Public Relations, Jack Calanga
Vice President Information Technology, Leonard Kasendorf
Vice President, Marc Cohn
Vice President Information Technology Services, Bob Levin
Vice President Global Technology, Ed Evans
Vice President, Melissa Grady
Associate Vice President Enterprise Security, Satin Montano
Vice President, Dennis Gates
Vice President, Alexander Beauchamp
Assistant Vice President Of Enterprise Security, Laz Montano
Vice President Director Fund Administration, Alan Otis
Regional Vice President Agency Asia Pacific, Stephen Zhang
Senior Vice President, Frank Cassandra
Assistant Vice President And Actuary Actuarial, Simone Chen
Vice President Planning And Strategy, Douglas Choo
Vice President Strategic Relationship, Sue Hopper
Senior Vice President Risk Management, Henry Essert
Assistant Vice President Field Services, Patty Derner
Vice President, Ingrid Tolentino
Assistant Application Development Vice President, Kimberly Donica
Vice President, Brian Bruneau
Vice President Bank Sales And Marketing, Jim Capodanno
Executive Vice President, William J Wheeler
Vice President, Robert D Marzulli
Vice President, George Faulk
Vice President, Michael Zuckerbrow
Evp Head Global Operations Global Technology And Operations, Christopher Smith
Vice President Of Information Technology, John Gillmore
Regional Sales Vice President, Bryan Haley
Senior Vice President Finance, Connor Patrick
Vice President, Didi Wang
Vice President Human Resources, Dennis Shiel
Assistant Vice President Americas Chief Financial, Michelle Fitzgerald
Vice President, Carla Ogunrinde
Vice President, James Klinck
Vice President, Robert Johnson
Vp Federal Government Relations, Jason Cole
Vp Executive Compensation, Julian Attock
Vice President, Ken Rose
Vice President Of Human Resources, Tina Honkus
Senior Vice President Information Technology, H Duboff
Vice President Head Of Global Marketing Technology, Brad Jenkins
Vp Application Development, Steven Kessler
Auditors: DELOITTE & TOUCHE LLP

LOCATIONS

HQ: MetLife Inc
  200 Park Avenue, New York, NY 10166-0188
Phone: 212 578-9500
Web: www.metlife.com

2017 Sales by Segment

	$ mil.	% of total
US	31,810	50
Asia	11,875	19
MetLife Holding	11,005	17
Latin America	5,118	8
EMEA	3,729	6
Adjustments	(1229)	-
Total	62,308	100

PRODUCTS/OPERATIONS

2017 Sales

	$ mil.	% of total
Premiums	38,992	62
Net investment income	17,363	27
Universal life & investment-type product policy fees	5,510	9
Other	1,341	2
Adjustments	898	
Total	62,308	100

Selected Subsidiaries and Affiliates

American Life Insurance Co. (ALICO)
General American Life Insurance Company
Hyatt Legal Plans Inc. (prepaid legal plans)
MetLife Funding Inc.
MetLife Insurance Company USA
MetLife Investors Group Inc. (distribution)
Metropolitan Property and Casualty Insurance Company
New England Life Insurance Company

COMPETITORS

AEGON USA	Liberty Mutual
AIG	MassMutual
AXA	Meiji Yasuda Life
Aetna	Mutual of Omaha
Allianz	Nationwide
Allstate	New York Life
American General	Nippon Life Insurance
Aon	Northwestern Mutual
COUNTRY Financial	Pacific Mutual
Genworth Financial	Prudential
Guardian Life	TIAA
ING	The Hartford
John Hancock Financial Services	

HISTORICAL FINANCIALS

Company Type: Public

Income Statement				FYE: December 31
	ASSETS ($ mil.)	NET INCOME ($ mil.)	INCOME AS % OF ASSETS	EMPLOYEES
12/17	719,892	4,010	0.6%	49,000
12/16	898,764	800	0.1%	58,000
12/15	877,933	5,310	0.6%	69,000
12/14	902,337	6,309	0.7%	68,000
12/13	885,296	3,368	0.4%	65,000
Annual Growth	(5.0%)	4.5%	—	(6.8%)

2017 Year-End Financials

Debt ratio: 2.77%
Return on equity: 6.37%
Cash ($ mil.): 12,701
Current ratio: —
Long-term debt ($ mil.): —

No. of shares (mil.): 1,043
Dividends
  Yield: 0.0%
  Payout: 44.2%
Market value ($ mil.): 52,764

	STOCK PRICE ($) FY Close	P/E High/Low		Earnings	PER SHARE ($) Dividends	Book Value
12/17	50.56	15	13	3.62	1.60	56.23
12/16	53.89	91	56	0.63	1.58	61.44
12/15	48.21	13	10	4.57	1.48	61.95
12/14	54.09	10	9	5.42	1.33	63.74
12/13	53.92	18	11	2.91	1.01	55.65
Annual Growth	(1.6%)	—	—	5.6%	12.2%	0.3%

Metropolitan Bank Holding Corp

Auditors: Crowe Horwath LLP

LOCATIONS

HQ: Metropolitan Bank Holding Corp
  99 Park Avenue, New York, NY 10016
Phone: 212 659-0600
Web: www.metropolitanbankny.com

HISTORICAL FINANCIALS

Company Type: Public

Income Statement				FYE: December 31
	ASSETS ($ mil.)	NET INCOME ($ mil.)	INCOME AS % OF ASSETS	EMPLOYEES
12/17	1,759	12	0.7%	129
12/16	1,220	5	0.4%	118
12/15	964	4	0.4%	—
Annual Growth	35.1%	70.2%	—	—

2017 Year-End Financials

Debt ratio: 1.39%
Return on equity: 7.14%
Cash ($ mil.): 261
Current ratio: —
Long-term debt ($ mil.): —

No. of shares (mil.): 8
Dividends
  Yield: —
  Payout: —
Market value ($ mil.): 345

	STOCK PRICE ($) FY Close	P/E High/Low		Earnings	PER SHARE ($) Dividends	Book Value
12/17	42.10	21	15	2.34	0.00	28.90
12/16	0.00	—	—	0.43	0.00	22.45
12/15	0.00	—	—	1.54	0.00	24.07
Annual Growth	—	—	—	23.3%	—	9.6%

MGIC Investment Corp. (WI)

Since a pinkie-promise isn't good enough for most lenders there's MGIC Investment's mortgage insurance to protect lenders from home buyers who don't hold up their end of the bargain. MGIC owns Mortgage Guaranty Insurance Corporation (MGIC) the largest provider of private mortgage insurance in the US Puerto Rico and Guam. Such coverage allows otherwise-qualified buyers who aren't able to scrape up the standard 20% down payment to get mortgages. MGIC writes primary insurance on individual loans; its customers include banks mortgage brokers credit unions and other residential mortgage lenders. In 2017 MGIC had $194.9 billion primary insurance in force covering 1 million mortgages.

Operations

Historically MGIC has provided two primary types of private mortgage insurance — primary and pool. Primary insurance default protection on individual mortgages and covers unpaid loan principal related delinquent interest and expenses and foreclosure or sale approved by MGIC. Pool insurance is typically an additional credit enhancement for secondary market mortgage transactions. It generally covers the loss on a defaulted loan exceeding the claim payment under the primary coverage (if required) or the total loss on a defaulted loan which did not require primary coverage. Although the company hasn't written any new pool risk since 2009 it may do so in the future as it weighs the market.

Other offerings include contract underwriting services for lenders and mortgage lead generation for the finance industry.

Geographic Reach

MGIC operates in every US state the District of Columbia Puerto Rico and Guam.

Sales and Marketing

MGIC's customers include savings institutions commercial banks mortgage brokers credit unions mortgage bankers and other lenders. The company's products are sold by its employees.

Financial Performance

MGIC's revenue stayed flat at $1.1 billion in 2017. Although net premiums written and earned and net investment income increased net realized investment gains and other income decreased that year.

Like other private mortgage insurers MGIC has seen improvements to its earnings since 2014 the first year it returned to the black since the Great Recession. The stronger economy has led to a decrease in delinquencies and subsequent claims filed. In 2018 net income totaled $355.8 million a 4% increase over the prior year. This was driven by lower net losses (which decreased 78%) and the absence of significant losses on debt extinguishment. Operating cash flow rose 81% to $406.7 million in 2017 thanks largely to higher deferred tax expenses.

Strategy

MGIC's core strategies include growing the amount of insurance it has in force seeking attractive business opportunities to provide optimal returns and to broaden its presence in the private mortgage insurance sector. In 2017 it increased its insurance in force by more than 7% a rate that falls in line with its goals.

The company faces competition from alternatives to mortgage insurance such as certain capital market transactions credit risk investors and piggyback loans. And as the entire private mortgage insurance industry nervously gauges its future government-sponsored enterprises (GSEs) Freddie Mac and Fannie Mae have taken over a huge share of the business during the past few years. However the Trump administration has proposed ending Freddie's and Fannie's conservatorship and privatizing the GSEs which could boost business.

MGIC has enhanced its consumer offerings through technology. In 2018 it launched Readynest a website that breaks down the steps of buying a home. The prior year it launched the updated Buy Now Vs. Wait calculator for first-time home buyers which is now mobile-friendly and includes a version for Spanish speakers. It also improved its rate quote tools such as its mobile application Rate Finder.

Company Background

Before the mortgage mess unfolded in the US MGIC had marked its entry into the global market by opening offices in Toronto and in Sydney Australia. In less than two years however MGIC closed its Canadian office stopped issuing new policies abroad and began searching for a buyer for its Australian operations (which it records as immaterial) in order to focus on its domestic operations.

EXECUTIVES

Vice President Chief Human Resources Officer, Kurt Thomas
Senior Vice President Information Services And Chief Information Officer Of Mgic, Michael Meade
Senior Vice President, Carla A Gallas
President And Coo, Patrick Sinks, age 61, $524,423 total compensation
Evp General Counsel And Secretary, Jeffrey H. Lane, age 68, $415,385 total compensation
Evp Risk Management, Lawrence J. Pierzchalski, age 65, $449,654 total compensation
Chairman And Ceo, Curt S. Culver, age 65, $898,269 total compensation
Evp And Cfo, Timothy Mattke
Vice President Investments, Paul Spiroff
Vice President Marketing And Customer Experience, Margaret Crowley
Vice President, Lisa Pendergast
Vice President, Julie Sperber
Vice President Regulatory Relations An, Heidi Heyrmann
Vice President, John Schroeder
Vice President Managing Director, Todd Pittman
Vice President Talent Management, Stacey Murphy
Vice President Pricing And Credit Policy, Steve Thompson
Auditors: PricewaterhouseCoopers LLP

LOCATIONS

HQ: MGIC Investment Corp. (WI)
MGIC Plaza, 250 E. Kilbourn Avenue, Milwaukee, WI 53202
Phone: 414 347-6480
Web: www.mgic.com

PRODUCTS/OPERATIONS

2017 Sales

	$ mil.	% of total
Net premiums earned	934	88
Net investment income	120	11
Net realized investment gains	0	-
Other	10	1
Total	**1,066**	**100**

COMPETITORS

Essent Guaranty	Radian Group
Fannie Mae	US Department of
Freddie Mac	Veterans Affairs
Genworth Mortgage	United Guaranty
Insurance	
National Mortgage	
Insurance	

HISTORICAL FINANCIALS

Company Type: Public

Income Statement				FYE: December 31
	ASSETS ($ mil.)	NET INCOME ($ mil.)	INCOME AS % OF ASSETS	EMPLOYEES
12/17	5,619	355	6.3%	819
12/16	5,734	342	6.0%	823
12/15	5,879	1,172	19.9%	800
12/14	5,266	251	4.8%	800
12/13	5,601	(49)	—	819
Annual Growth	**0.1%**	**—**	**—**	**0.0%**

2017 Year-End Financials

Debt ratio: 14.78%	No. of shares (mil.): 370
Return on equity: 12.48%	Dividends
Cash ($ mil.): 99	Yield: —
Current ratio: —	Payout: —
Long-term debt ($ mil.): —	Market value ($ mil.): 5,229

	STOCK PRICE ($) FY Close	P/E High/Low		PER SHARE ($) Earnings	Dividends	Book Value
12/17	14.11	16	10	0.95	0.00	8.51
12/16	10.19	11	5	0.86	0.00	7.48
12/15	8.83	3	2	2.60	0.00	6.58
12/14	9.32	13	10	0.64	0.00	3.06
12/13	8.44	—	—	(0.16)	0.00	2.20
Annual Growth	**13.7%**	**—**	**—**	**—**	**—**	**40.2%**

MGM Resorts International

MGM Resorts International is one of the world's largest gaming firms. The company's properties include some of the biggest names on the Las Vegas Strip including MGM Grand The Mirage and the Monte Carlo as well as Luxor Bellagio Mandalay Bay and the new T-Mobile Arena. MGM Resorts International also owns or has a stake in other casinos in Nevada as well as in Michigan (MGM Grand Detroit) and Mississippi (Beau Rivage). Internationally it operates in Macau an autonomous Chinese territory famed for gambling. MGM Resorts has a controlling stake in MGM Growth Properties which it spun off in 2016 to hold 11 hotel and casino properties including several in Las Vegas.

Operations

MGM Resorts International's hotels boast a combined 47900 rooms of which 41400 are held by its domestic hotels 5900 by its CityCenter joint venture and 600 by its Macau operations. It also has more than 2 million square feet of casino space more than 27000 slot machines and nearly 1900 gaming tables.

MGM's casino operations generate around half its total revenue its hotel rooms generate 20% and food and drink brings in 15%.

Geographic Reach

MGM Resort Internationals' two main reportable segments are based on the regions in which it operates: Domestic Resorts and MGM China. MGM Resorts' China operations consist of two sites in Macau: MGM Macau resort and casino and MGM Cotai a casino hotel and entertainment resort on the Cotai strip. Domestic Resorts accounts for more than 75% of sales while MGM China accounts for 20% (a Corporate segment occupies the remainder).

Sales and Marketing

MGM Resorts International advertises on the radio television internet billboards and in newspapers and magazines in selected cities throughout the US and overseas. MGM Resorts also uses direct mail and social media to reach out to past guests and potential customers. The company advertises through regional marketing offices located in major cities.

Financial Performance

MGM Resorts International has struggled to meaningfully grow its revenue over the last five years — up one year and down the next — while profits are slim. However fiscal 2017 could be something of a breakthrough with acquisitions fueling record revenue figures.

In 2017 revenue increased 14% to $10.8 billion on the back of full-year contributions from the acquired Borgata and MGM National Harbor businesses as well as higher revenue from casinos rooms and valet and parking.

MGM Resorts posted exceptional profits in both 2016 and 2017 (compared to a $1.0 billion loss in 2015) but each year benefited from an exceptional item; underlying profitability remains low. In 2016 the IPO of MGM Growth Properties resulted in a $1.2 billion gain and in 2017 the company recorded a $1.4 billion tax benefit relating to the 2017 US Tax Cuts and Jobs Act. Overall MGM Resorts' 2017 net income was $2.1 billion a 70% increase on 2016.

Cash from operations increased 45% to $2.2 billion due to higher operating income at MGM Resort's domestic resorts partially offset by an increase in cash paid for taxes.

Strategy

MGM Resorts International continues to make significant investments in its resorts through newly remodeled hotel rooms restaurants entertainment and nightlife offerings as well as other new features and amenities. In Macau the company spent $2.5 billion on developing its operations in Macau between 2015-17 largely on the construction of MGM Cotai an integrated casino hotel and entertainment complex. It has also made large investments in its US operations including $269 million on constructing MGM Springfield $221 million on rebranding the Monte Carlo hotel and casino and $195 million on finalizing the construction of MGM National Harbor. It also carried out various resorts' room remodels constructed additional convention space at MGM Grand Las Vegas the parking garage at Excalibur a waterpark at Circus Circus and various restaurant and entertainment venue remodels. MGM Resorts International has also been actively pursuing development opportunities in markets such as Maryland and Massachusetts.

In 2016 MGM Resorts International opened the new 20000 seat T-Mobile arena in Las Vegas. The company hopes to attract a large number of high-profile concerts and sporting events. The long-term plan is to lure a NHL or NBA team to Las Vegas.

The company also spun off its MGM Growth Properties subsidiary during 2016 as a real estate investment trust. MGM Resorts retains a controlling stake in the company that was spun off to unlock additional value in 11 hotels and casinos (it has since added a 12th).

Mergers and Acquisitions

In 2016 MGM Resorts International acquired Borgata Hotel Casino & Spa in Atlantic City New Jersey from Boyd Gaming Corporation for about $900 million. The acquisition added to the company's growing presence in the mid-Atlantic and Northeast United States.

EXECUTIVES

Coo, Corey I. Sanders, age 54, $1,119,368 total compensation
Senior Vice President Taxes, Shawn Sani
President And Chief Marketing Officer, William J. Hornbuckle, age 60, $1,269,368 total compensation
Chairman And Ceo, James J. Murren, age 56, $2,000,000 total compensation
Chief Design And Construction Officer And Director, Robert H. Baldwin, age 67, $1,650,000 total compensation
Evp Special Counsel Litigation And Chief Diversity Officer, Phyllis A. James, age 65
Evp Cfo And Treasurer, Daniel J. D'Arrigo, age 49, $875,000 total compensation

Evp And Chief Accounting Officer, Robert C. Selwood, age 62, $439,286 total compensation
Evp General Counsel And Secretary, John M. McManus, age 50
President And Coo Borgata Hotel Casino & Spa, Marcus Glover
Representative Officer And President Mgm Resorts Japan, Jason P. Hyland
President And Coo Gold Strike Casino Resort, Melonie Johnson
Vice President Of Strategic Sourcing, Mark Stolarczyk
Vice President International Marketing, Teresa Cookson
Senior Vice President And Chief Sustainability Officer, Cindy Ortega
Vice President Information Management, Gerry Tuffy
Senior Vice President Of Loyalty Marketing, Josh Swissman
Executive Vice President Marketing, Chuck Bowling
Senior Vice President, Justin Manacher
Svp And Cio, Sy Esfahani
Vice President, Joshua Smith
Senior Vice President, Robert Zapletal
Vice President Of Global Sports And Events Sales, Daniel Rush
Vice President, Bob Rosati
Vice President Of Strategic Operations, Christopher Oh
Vice President Human Resources, Michelle DiTondo
Vice President Marketing Latin American Mgm Grand, Marilyn Portillo
Vice President Gaming Operations, Todd Haushalter
Senior Vice President Customer Development, Larry Altschul
Corporate Vice President Talent And Organizational Effec, Christopher Henry
Senior Vice President Of Finance, Yvette Harris
Vice President Of Arena Booking, Sid Greenfeig
Vice President Hotel Operations, Kevin Holyfield
Vice President Of Hotel Sales, Jay Simpson
Vice President Human Resources, Kit Turner
Vice President Marketing International, Kimie Masumoto
Executive Vice President, William Scott
Vice President Of Human Resources At Circus Circus Las Vegas, Ashley Eddy
Executive Vice President Marketing Hong Kong, Elisa Lau
Corporate Vice President, Lance Evans
Senior Vice President And Chief Compliance Officer, Thomas A Peterman
Senior Vice President Hotel Sales Marketing And, Fletch H Brunelle
Vice President Of Corp Surveillance, Ted Whiting
Senior Vice President Korean Marketing, June YI
Vice President Administration, Mark Prows
Vp Sustainable Facilities, Chris Magee
Vice President Channel Management, Sarah Fults
Senior Vice President Hotel Strategy, Cliff Atkinson
Vice President Customer Development, Jodi Myers
National Sales Manager, John Montes
Vice President Of Construction, Russ Davis
Vice President Of Human Resources, Logan Gaskill
Senior Vice President Far East Marketing Mgm Grand Mgm Resorts International Marketing, Tracy Tsoi
Vice President National Diversity Relations, Tony Gladney
Vice President And Chief Accounting Officer, Michele Ensign
Senior Vice President Marketing Far East, Cindy Wong
Vice President And Legal Counsel, Greg Riches
Vice President General Manager, Farid Matraki
Vice President Social Portfolio Strategy, Beverly Jackson

Senior Vice President Global Gaming Development, Ed Bowers
Vp Far East Marketing, Lily Su
Assistant Vice President Financial Reporting, Todd Meinert
Assistant Vice President, Pierre Gabriel
National Sales Manager, Sarah Abbott
Board Member, Daniel Taylor
Auditors: Deloitte & Touche LLP

LOCATIONS

HQ: MGM Resorts International
3600 Las Vegas Boulevard South, Las Vegas, NV 89109
Phone: 702 693-7120
Web: www.mgmresorts.com

2017 Sales

	$ mil.	% of total
Domestic resorts	8,322	77
MGM China	1,970	18
Corporate & other	481	5
Total	**10,773**	**100**

PRODUCTS/OPERATIONS

2017 Sales

	$ mil.	% of total
Casino	5,984	51
Rooms	2,151	18
Food and beverage	1,790	15
Entertainment	542	5
Retail	214	2
Other	605	5
Reimbursed costs	402	4
Less: Promotional allowances	(917.0)	-
Total	**10,773**	**100**

Selected Properties

Nevada
Las Vegas
Bellagio
Circus Circus
CityCenter (50%)
Excalibur
Luxor
Mandalay Bay Resort & Casino
MGM Grand
The Mirage
T-Mobile Arena
Monte Carlo
New York-New York
Other US
Beau Rivage (Biloxi MS)
Borgata (Atlantic City New Jersey)
Gold Strike (Tunica County MS)
Grand Victoria (50%; Elgin New Jersey)
MGM Grand Detroit
MGM National Harbor (Prince George's Country Maryland)
MG Springfield
China
MGM Grand Macau (51%; Macau)
MGM Cotai

COMPETITORS

Boyd Gaming	Sands China
Caesars Entertainment	Star City
Galaxy Entertainment	Station Casinos
Las Vegas Sands	Stratosphere
Rio All-Suite Hotel & Casino	Tropicana Entertainment
Riviera Holdings	Trump Resorts
SJM	Wynn Resorts

HISTORICAL FINANCIALS

Company Type: Public

Income Statement   FYE: December 31

	REVENUE ($ mil.)	NET INCOME ($ mil.)	NET PROFIT MARGIN	EMPLOYEES
12/17	10,773	1,960	18.2%	68,000
12/16	9,455	1,101	11.6%	69,000
12/15	9,190	(447)	—	59,500
12/14	10,081	(149)	—	68,100
12/13	9,090	(150)	—	67,800
Annual Growth	2.4%	—		0.1%

2017 Year-End Financials

Debt ratio: 44.27%
Return on equity: 28.34%
Cash ($ mil.): 1,500
Current ratio: 0.77
Long-term debt ($ mil.): 12,751

No. of shares (mil.): 566
Dividends
Yield: 0.0%
Payout: 13.1%
Market value ($ mil.): 18,908

	STOCK PRICE ($) FY Close	P/E High/Low		PER SHARE ($) Earnings	Dividends	Book Value
12/17	33.39	10	8	3.35	0.44	13.44
12/16	28.83	15	9	1.92	0.00	10.83
12/15	22.72	—	—	(0.82)	0.00	9.06
12/14	21.38	—	—	(0.31)	0.00	8.33
12/13	23.52	—	—	(0.32)	0.00	8.63
Annual Growth	9.2%			—	—	11.7%

Michaels Companies Inc

Auditors: Ernst & Young LLP

LOCATIONS

HQ: Michaels Companies Inc
8000 Bent Branch Drive, Irving, TX 75063
Phone: 972 409-1300
Web: www.michaels.com

HISTORICAL FINANCIALS

Company Type: Public

Income Statement   FYE: February 3

	REVENUE ($ mil.)	NET INCOME ($ mil.)	NET PROFIT MARGIN	EMPLOYEES
02/18*	5,361	390	7.3%	49,000
01/17	5,197	378	7.3%	50,000
01/16	4,912	362	7.4%	50,000
01/15	4,738	217	4.6%	51,000
02/14	4,570	243	5.3%	50,200
Annual Growth	4.1%	12.6%	—	(0.6%)

*Fiscal year change

2018 Year-End Financials

Debt ratio: 118.54%
Return on equity: —
Cash ($ mil.): 425
Current ratio: 1.75
Long-term debt ($ mil.): 2,701

No. of shares (mil.): 181
Dividends
Yield: —
Payout: —
Market value ($ mil.): 4,754

	STOCK PRICE ($) FY Close	P/E High/Low		PER SHARE ($) Earnings	Dividends	Book Value
02/18*	26.13	13	8	2.10	0.00	(8.30)
01/17	19.56	17	11	1.82	0.00	(8.79)
01/16	21.80	17	12	1.72	0.00	(8.25)
01/15	25.80	25	14	1.05	0.00	(10.25)
Annual Growth	0.3%			— — 18.9%		—

*Fiscal year change

Micron Technology Inc.

Micron Technology is one of the largest memory chip makers in the world. It makes DRAM (Dynamic Random Access Memory) NAND Flash and NOR Flash memory and other memory technologies. The company sells to customers in networking and storage consumer electronics solid-state drives and mobile telecommunications but its largest concentration (about a quarter of sales) is the computer market. Micron's products are offered under the Micron Crucial and Ballistix brands as well as private labels. The US-based company generates about 90% of sales internationally. Besides being one of the biggest chipmakers Micron is one the most durable marking its 40th anniversary in 2018.

Operations

Micron operates through four segments centered on its markets. The largest segment accounting for 50% of sales is the Compute and Networking Business Unit which sells products for the computing networking graphics and cloud server markets. The Storage Business Unit contributes more than 15% of revenue with the Mobile Business Unit memory for smartphone tablet and other mobile-device markets generating more than 20% of sales. About 10% of revenue comes from the Embedded Business Unit which makes memory and storage products for the automotive industrial and consumer markets.

Almost 70% of revenue comes from DRAM products and NAND Flash memory products supply the rest. DRAM and flash are sold throughout each of Micron's segments.

The company makes its own products in a dozen plants throughout the world; most of its products are made on 300mm wafers.

Geographic Reach

Boise Idaho-based Micron generates about 55% of its revenue in China with 20% from Taiwan Japan and other Asia/Pacific region countries. The US and Europe contribute about 10% and 5% respectively. The company has fabrication and assembly facilities in China Japan Malaysia Singapore Taiwan and the US. With customers and manufacturing locations around the world Micron has been subject to tariffs generated in trade tensions between the US and China.

Sales and Marketing

Micron sells to equipment manufacturers and retailers via a direct sales force third-party sales representatives and distributors. The company sells its Crucial-branded products through a web-based customer direct sales channel as well as through channel and distribution partners.

Micron's gets about 10% of sales from Kingston.

Financial Performance

Micron's financial results for the past decade were typical of the cyclical semiconductor industry – up and down but trending higher. The last two years however have been straight up delivering record revenue and net income.

In 2018 (ended September) revenue jumped 50% to $30.4 billion from $20.3 billion in 2017 propelled by stronger sales in each of its segments. The CNBU segment drove the increase providing about 70% of the additional $10 billion overall revenue on strong market conditions and demand in the cloud server client enterprise server and graphics markets. The MBU segment's revenue rose about 50% year-to-year on higher sales of mobile DRAM and managed NAND products.

The higher sales combined with modest increases in expenses resulted in higher margins and a profit of $14.1 million in 2018 compared to a $5.1 million profit in 2017.

Micron's coffers held $6.6 billion in cash and equivalents at the end of 2018 compared to $5.2 billion the year before. Operations generated $17.4 billion and investing activities used $8.2 billion and financing activities used $7.7 billion in 2018.

Strategy

Micron has rolled out DRAM and NAND products based on increasing complex productions methods which has increased yield and help increase prices for some products. Sales of the company's products for the graphics market have increased as companies such as NVIDIA have tapped Micron as a partner. Micron will chip in to produce NVIDIA's GeForce RTX devices for the gaming market.

Micron's automotive business has a full pipeline of projects including a collaboration with BMW. Growth in automotive and other chips with long life-cycle led the company to a $3 billion expansion of its manufacturing plant in Manassas Virginia over the next 10 years.

The company is expanding manufacturing capacity for DRAM and NAND chips at other sites providing greater flexibility in managing operations.

Mergers and Acquisitions

In 2018 Micron said it would exercise its right to buy Intel's interest in the companies' joint venture IM Flash Technologies. The $1.5 billion deal would give Micron full control of IM Flash's 3D XPoint technology.

EXECUTIVES

President And Ceo, Sanjay Mehrotra, age 59
Vice President Operations, Jay Hawkins
Vp Finance And Cfo, Ernest E. (Ernie) Maddock, age 60, $550,000 total compensation
Vp Information Technology And Cio, Trevor Schulze
Senior Vice President And Gm Compute And Networking Business Unit, Tom Eby
Vice President Advanced Storage Solutions, Robert Peglar
Vice President Of Software Engineering, Steve Moyer
Vice President Japan Process Research, Hideki Gomi
Vice President Wsg Marketing, Reynette Au
Vice President Ww Enterprise Sales, Mark Glasgow
Vp Human Resources, Michael Zeigler
Vice President Corporate Development, Michael Sadler
Vice President Worldwide Oem Sales, Mike Null Bokan
Vice President Procurement, Rodney Morgan
Vice President Director Manager, Brian Kalisek
Vice President Director Manager, Michael Knapp
Vice President Business Planning And Process Management, Karen Metz
Vice President Global Tax, Don Whitt
Corporate Vice President And Gm Embedded Business Unit, Jeffrey Bader

Corporate Vice President And Gm Storage
  Business Unit, Derek Dicker
Vice President 3dxp Systems And Solutions
  Engineering, Samir Mittal
Vp Package Technology Development, Mark Tuttle
Chairman, Robert E. (Bob) Switz, age 71
Auditors: PricewaterhouseCoopers LLP

LOCATIONS

HQ: Micron Technology Inc.
  8000 S. Federal Way, Boise, ID 83716-9632
Phone: 208 368-4000
Web: www.micron.com

2018 Sales

	$ mil.	% of total
China	17,357	57
United States	3,624	12
Asia Pacific (exclusive China Taiwan and Japan)	2,559	9
Taiwan	2,798	9
Europe	2,128	7
Japan	1,254	4
Other	671	2
Total	**30,391**	**100**

PRODUCTS/OPERATIONS

2018 Sales

	$ mil.	% of total
Compute and Networking Business Unit	15,252	50
Storage Business Unit	5,022	17
Mobile Business unit	6,579	22
Embedded Business Unit	3,479	11
All Other	59	-
Total	**30,391**	**100**

2018 Sales

	$ mil.	% of total
DRAM	21,232	70
Trade NAND	7,843	26
Non-Trade	554	2
Other	578	3
Total	**30,391**	**100**

Semiconductor Products

Dynamic random-access memories (DRAMs)
  Direct Rambus DRAMs (RDRAMs)
  Synchronous DRAMs (SDRAMs)
  Double data rate synchronous DRAMs (DDR SDRAMs)
Flash memory devices
Memory modules
Photomasks

COMPETITORS

Atmel	SMART Modular
Cypress Semiconductor	Technologies
Intel	Samsung Electronics
Kingston Technology	SanDisk
Mosel Vitelic	Toshiba Semiconductor
Nanya	& Storage Products
PNY Technologies	Western Digital
SK Hynix	

HISTORICAL FINANCIALS

Company Type: Public

Income Statement
FYE: August 30

	REVENUE ($ mil.)	NET INCOME ($ mil.)	NET PROFIT MARGIN	EMPLOYEES
08/18	30,391	14,135	46.5%	36,000
08/17*	20,322	5,089	25.0%	34,100
09/16	12,399	(276)	—	31,400
09/15	16,192	2,899	17.9%	31,800
08/14	16,358	3,045	18.6%	30,400
Annual Growth	**16.7%**	**46.8%**	**—**	**4.3%**

*Fiscal year change

2018 Year-End Financials

Debt ratio: 10.69%
Return on equity: 55.68%
Cash ($ mil.): 6,506
Current ratio: 2.79
Long-term debt ($ mil.): 3,777

No. of shares (mil.): 1,161
Dividends
  Yield: —
  Payout: —
Market value ($ mil.): 61,254

	STOCK PRICE ($) FY Close	P/E High/Low		PER SHARE ($) Earnings	Dividends	Book Value
08/18	52.76	5	3	11.51	0.00	27.82
08/17*	31.97	7	4	4.41	0.00	16.75
09/16	16.64	—	—	(0.27)	0.00	11.62
09/15	16.59	13	5	2.47	0.00	11.84
08/14	32.81	12	5	2.54	0.00	10.04
Annual Growth	**12.6%**	—	—	**45.9%**	—	**29.0%**

*Fiscal year change

Microsoft Corporation

EXECUTIVES

Ceo, Satya Nadella
Non Exec Chb*, John W Thompson
Pres-Clo, Bradford L Smith
Exec V Pres-Cfo, Amy E Hood
Exec V Pres-Cmo, Christopher C Capossela
Exec V Pres, Jean-Philippe Courtois
Evp Human Resources, Kathleen T Hogan
Evp Business Dev't, Margaret L Johnson
Business, Albert Kooiman
Mbs Marketing Manager, Ana Gamborena
APS Senior Support Engineer, Andrea Liberatore
Auditors: DELOITTE & TOUCHE LLP

LOCATIONS

HQ: Microsoft Corporation
  One Microsoft Way, Redmond, WA 98052-6399
Phone: 425 882-8080
Web: www.microsoft.com

COMPETITORS

Adobe Systems	Nintendo
Amazon.com	Nokia
Apple Inc.	Novell
CA Inc.	Opera Software
EMC	Oracle
Google	Red Hat
Hewlett-Packard	SAP
IBM	Sony
Logitech	Yahoo!
Mozilla	salesforce.com

HISTORICAL FINANCIALS

Company Type: Public

Income Statement
FYE: June 30

	REVENUE ($ mil.)	NET INCOME ($ mil.)	NET PROFIT MARGIN	EMPLOYEES
06/18	110,360	16,571	15.0%	97,535
06/17	89,950	21,204	23.6%	124,000
06/16	85,320	16,798	19.7%	114,000
06/15	93,580	12,193	13.0%	118,000
06/14	86,833	22,074	25.4%	128,000
Annual Growth	**6.2%**	**(6.9%)**	**—**	**(6.6%)**

2018 Year-End Financials

Debt ratio: 29.45%—
Return on equity: 21.37%
Cash ($ mil.): 11,946
Current ratio: 2.90
Long-term debt ($ mil.): 72,242

Dividends
  Yield: 0.0%
  Payout: 77.4%
Market value ($ mil.): —

	STOCK PRICE ($) FY Close	P/E High/Low		PER SHARE ($) Earnings	Dividends	Book Value
06/18	98.61	48	32	2.13	1.65	10.77
06/17	68.93	26	19	2.71	1.53	9.39
06/16	51.17	27	19	2.10	1.39	9.22
06/15	44.15	33	27	1.48	1.21	9.98
06/14	41.70	16	12	2.63	1.07	10.90
Annual Growth	**24.0%**	—	—	**(5.1%)**	**11.4%**	**(0.3%)**

MIDFLORIDA FEDERAL CREDIT UNION

EXECUTIVES

Pres, Kevin Jones
Cao, Gail O'Brien
Coo, Dennis Pershing
Clo, Sandra Gibson
Vice-President Human Resources, Nancy Irvin
Human Resources Director, Brian Palmer
Vice-President, John King
Vice-President, Nancy I Irvin
Member Officer, Amanda Jones
Associate Manager, Amber Kelly
Assistant Vice President Datab, Eric Jensen

LOCATIONS

HQ: MIDFLORIDA FEDERAL CREDIT UNION
  129 S KENTUCKY AVE # 100, LAKELAND, FL
  338015073
Phone: 866 913-3733
Web: WWW.MIDFLORIDA.COM

HISTORICAL FINANCIALS

Company Type: Private

Income Statement
FYE: December 31

	ASSETS ($ mil.)	NET INCOME ($ mil.)	INCOME AS % OF ASSETS	EMPLOYEES
12/17	3,055	35	1.2%	278
12/16	2,640	28	1.1%	—
Annual Growth	**15.7%**	**24.5%**	**—**	**—**

2017 Year-End Financials

Debt ratio: ——
Return on equity: 37.40%
Cash ($ mil.): 344
Current ratio: —
Long-term debt ($ mil.): —

Dividends
  Yield: —
  Payout: —
Market value ($ mil.): —

Midland States Bancorp Inc

Born in rural Illinois Midland States Bancorp is now discovering banking life in new states. It is the $3 billion-asset holding company for Midland States Bank a community bank that operates more than 35 branches in central and northern Illinois and around 15 branches in the St. Louis metropolitan area. The bank offers traditional consumer and commercial banking products and services as well as merchant card services insurance and financial planning. Subsidiary Midland Wealth Management which boasts $1.2 billion-plus in assets under administration provides wealth management services while Heartland Business Credit offers commercial equipment leasing services. Midland States Bancorp went public in 2016.

IPO
The bank holding company raised $80.1 million in its initial public offering. It plans to contribute some $25 million to Midland States Bank and use the rest for general corporate purposes including possible acquisitions.

Operations
About 57% of Midland States Bancorp's total revenue came from loan interest during 2014 while another 17% came from interest income from investment securities. The rest came from wealth management fees (8% of revenue) deposit account service charges (3%) ATM and interchange revenue (3%) mortgage banking revenue (3%) merchant services revenue (1%) and nonrecurring gains on the sales of assets (around 8%).

Subsidiary Love Funding provides multifamily and healthcare facility FHA financing.

Geographic Reach
Midland has more than 80 branches and offices across the US with around 50 in Illinois and around the St. Louis metro area and the rest in California Colorado Florida Massachusetts North Carolina Ohio Tennessee and Texas.

Financial Performance
Midland States Bancorp's revenue climbed 3% to $93 million despite a decline in loan interest income during 2014 mostly thanks to profitable asset sales and other income.

Despite modest revenue growth in 2014 the bank's net income dove 67% to $3.2 billion as acquisition and integration expenses stemming from its late 2014 acquisition of Heartland ate up any revenue gains it had made. Excluding these non-recurring items the bank's net income grew modestly.

Strategy
Midland States Bancorp has been pursuing an acquisition and branch expansion growth strategy since 2007 after it replaced its executive management and laid out a plan to expand Midland States Bank's presence in Illinois. Midland States Bank continues to focus on moving into suburban areas and other markets in Illinois and Missouri that have growing populations. During 2015 it opened a new branches in the St. Louis region (in Jennings) downtown Joliet and downtown Effingham areas as well as a wealth management office in downtown Decatur.

The company also planned in 2016 to continue building its fast-growing wealth management business which now makes up nearly 10% of its total revenue. Thanks to Midland's efforts the business' wealth management assets under administration have skyrocketed twelve-fold since 2008 growing from $95 million then to $1.19 billion at the end of 2014.

Mergers and Acquisitions
In February 2017 CEO Leon Holschbach signed a $175 million deal with rival Centrue Bank to merge. The two banks had been treading on each others' toes in Princeton Illinois.

In February 2016 Midland States Bank agreed to purchase $400 million in wealth management assets from Sterling National Bank which would boost its assets under administration by more than 30% to $1.6 billion. Sterling Bank had originally obtained the wealth management assets — which were mostly Special Needs and Settlement Trusts — after buying Hudson Valley Bank.

In December 2014 the bank acquired Heartland Bank as well as its $900 million in assets 13 Heartland Bank branches in the St. Louis metropolitan area four branches in Colorado and single locations in Joplin Missouri and Raleigh/Durham North Carolina.

Company Background
Between 2008 and 2010 the bank's branch locations grew from just a half-dozen in central Illinois and St. Louis to nearly 30 around the state and in the St. Louis metropolitan area. During that time the bank acquired the assets of Waterloo Bancshares and WestBridge in St. Louis AMCORE in northern Illinois and Strategic Capital in central Illinois. It also opened new locations in some of its faster-growing markets. As a result of its efforts Midland States Bancorp has watched its revenue and profits trend upward significantly from 2007 levels.

EXECUTIVES

Vice Chairman President And Ceo, Leon J. Holschbach, age 65, $529,389 total compensation
Evp Midland States Bancorp And President Midland States Bank, Jeffrey G. Ludwig, age 46, $367,500 total compensation
Evp Banking, Jeffrey S. Medford
Cfo Midland States Bancorp And Midland States Bank, Kevin L. Thompson
Senior Vice President Community Banking, Jeffrey Mefford
Vice President, Deanna Haught
Vice President Banking Center Manager, Karen Attwood
Vice President Mortgage Banking, Mark Widdicombe
Senior Vice President, Sharon Schaubert
Chairman, John M. Schultz, age 66
Auditors: Crowe Horwath LLP

LOCATIONS

HQ: Midland States Bancorp Inc
  1201 Network Centre Drive, Effingham, IL 62401
Phone: 217 342-7321
Web: www.midlandsb.com

PRODUCTS/OPERATIONS

2014 Sales

	% of total
Interest income	
Loans	57
Investment Securities & others	17
Noninterest income	
Wealth management revenue	8
Service charges on deposit accounts	3
Mortgage banking revenue	3
Gain on sale of other assets	3
ATM and interchange revenue	3
Impairments	.
Other	6
Total	**100**

Selected Services
Bank By Phone
Bill Paying
Checking
Debit Card
Online Banking
Savings & CDs

COMPETITORS

Bank of America	Harris
Edward D. Jones	Mercantile Bancorp
Fifth Third	PNC Financial
First Mid-Illinois Bancshares	U.S. Bancorp

HISTORICAL FINANCIALS
Company Type: Public

Income Statement
FYE: December 31

	ASSETS ($ mil.)	NET INCOME ($ mil.)	INCOME AS % OF ASSETS	EMPLOYEES
12/17	4,412	16	0.4%	840
12/16	3,233	31	1.0%	715
12/15	2,884	24	0.8%	700
12/14	2,676	10	0.4%	—
12/13	0	14		
Annual Growth	—	2.6%		

2017 Year-End Financials

Debt ratio: 3.16%	No. of shares (mil.): 19
Return on equity: 4.16%	Dividends
Cash ($ mil.): 214	Yield: 0.0%
Current ratio: —	Payout: 91.9%
Long-term debt ($ mil.): —	Market value ($ mil.): 621

	STOCK PRICE ($) FY Close	P/E High/Low		PER SHARE ($) Earnings	Dividends	Book Value
12/17	32.48	40	33	0.87	0.80	23.51
12/16	36.18	17	9	2.17	0.36	20.78
Annual Growth	(2.7%)	—	—	(20.4%)	22.1%	3.1%

MidSouth Bancorp, Inc.

For banking in the Deep South try MidSouth. MidSouth Bancorp is the holding company for MidSouth Bank which boasts roughly $2 billion in assets and around 60 branches across Louisiana and Texas. Targeting individuals and local business customers the bank offers such standard retail services as checking and savings accounts savings bonds investment accounts and credit card services. About 55% of its loan portfolio is made up of real estate mortgages while commercial loans make up more than 35%. Consumer and construction loans round out the rest of its lending activities.

Operations
About 67% of MidSouth Bancorp's total revenue came from loan interest (including fees) in 2014 while another 10% came from interest on its taxable and non-taxable investment securities. The rest of its revenue came from deposit account service charges (9%) ATM and debit card income (7%) and other miscellaneous income sources. The company had a staff of nearly 550 employees at the end of 2014.

Geographic Reach
The bank's branches are in Louisiana and central and east Texas along the Interstate 10 Interstate 49 Highway 90 Interstate 45 Interstate 20 and Interstate 35 corridors.

Sales and Marketing
The bank offers commercial and consumer loan and deposit services to small and middle-market business their owners and employees and other individuals in its markets in Texas and Louisiana.

Oil and gas is the key industry in these markets though medical technology and research companies are becoming increasingly prevalent. In addition major universities in the areas from Louisiana State University to Texas A&M contribute to a substantial number of jobs as well as a highly-educated workforce in these markets.

Financial Performance

MidSouth Bancorp's revenues and profits have been rising in recent years thanks to continued loan business growth partially stemming from the bank's late 2012 acquisition of PSB Financial and also thanks to lower interest expenses with the low-interest environment.

The bank's revenue rose by 5% to $107.91 million in 2014 mostly thanks to a non-recurring $3 million-executive officer life insurance proceed and a $1.1 million gain on the sale of an ORE though its loan interest grew by 2% helping to add to the company's top-line during the year.

Higher revenue coupled with lower interest expenses on borrowings and a decline in salary and benefit costs in 2014 helped boost MidSouth's net income by 35% to $19.11 million during the year. Its operating cash levels grew by 15% to $29.8 million on higher cash earnings.

Strategy

Seeking potential expansion into new market areas MidSouth Bancorp in 2015 planned to grow its loan and deposit business organically as well as through bank acquisitions. The bank would also continue its long-term strategy of focusing on commercial and small-business customers while continuing to serve its retail customers as well.

Company Background

In late 2012 Midsouth acquired PSB Financial which operated 16 branches in Louisiana under the Peoples State Bank banner. The deal expanded its presence into central and northwest Louisiana and east Texas.

EXECUTIVES

Pres-Ceo, James R McLemore
Chb, Jake Delhomme
Vice Chairman, Michael Kramer
Exec V Pres-Cfo, Lorraine Miller
Exec V Pres-Cro, Erin Dewitt
Exec V Pres, Clay Abington
Evp-Chief Credit Officer Bank, Keith Avant
Collections Supervisor, Marcia Angelle
Board Member, Milton Kidd
Svp-Bsa/Aml Officer, Glenda Gaubert
Auditors: Porter Keadle Moore, LLC

LOCATIONS

HQ: MidSouth Bancorp, Inc.
102 Versailles Boulevard, Lafayette, LA 70501
Phone: 337 237-8343
Web: www.midsouthbank.com

PRODUCTS/OPERATIONS

2014 Sales

	$ mil.	% of total
Interest income		
Loans including fees	72	67
Investment securities	10	10
Others	0	-
Non-interest income		
Service charges on deposit accounts	9	9
ATM and debit card income	7	7
Others	7	7
Total	107	100

COMPETITORS

American Bancorp	Home Banc
Bank of America	IBERIABANK
Capital One	Regions Financial
Hancock Holding	Teche Holding
Henderson Citizens Bancshares	

HISTORICAL FINANCIALS

Company Type: Public

Income Statement   FYE: December 31

	ASSETS ($ mil.)	NET INCOME ($ mil.)	INCOME AS % OF ASSETS	EMPLOYEES
12/17	1,881	(11)	—	467
12/16	1,943	9	0.5%	535
12/15	1,927	11	0.6%	536
12/14	1,936	19	1.0%	549
12/13	1,851	14	0.8%	604
Annual Growth	0.4%	—		(6.2%)

2017 Year-End Financials

Debt ratio: 1.18%	No. of shares (mil.): 16
Return on equity: (-5.02%)	Dividends
Cash ($ mil.): 149	Yield: 0.0%
Current ratio: —	Payout: —
Long-term debt ($ mil.): —	Market value ($ mil.): 219

	STOCK PRICE ($) FY Close	P/E High/Low	PER SHARE ($) Earnings	Dividends	Book Value
12/17	13.25	— —	(1.06)	0.20	15.35
12/16	13.60	25 12	0.58	0.36	18.87
12/15	9.08	19 10	0.90	0.36	18.76
12/14	17.34	12 10	1.58	0.35	18.43
12/13	17.86	16 12	1.12	0.31	16.95
Annual Growth	(7.2%)	— —	—(10.4%)		(2.4%)

MidWestOne Financial Group, Inc.

This could be the saga of How the MidWest Was One . MidWest One Financial Group is the holding company for Midwest One Bank which operates about two dozen branches throughout central and east-central Iowa. The bank offers standard deposit products such as checking and savings accounts CDs and IRAs in addition to trust services credit cards insurance and brokerage and investment services. About two-thirds of MidWest One Financial's loan portfolio consists of real estate loans including residential and commercial mortgages and farmland and construction loans. Founded in 1983 MidWest One has total assets of $1.8 billion.

Geographic Reach

Headquartered in Iowa City Midwest One Bank has branches and loan production offices in 15 counties in central and east-central Iowa.

Financial Performance

The company reported net income of $18.6 million in 2013 a 13% increase over 2012. Earnings have been rising steadily while the bank's revenue has been trending downward. Indeed 2013's $80.8 million in revenue was 10% below 2012. Assets declined slightly over the same period as did deposits. (The bank is facing stiff competition for deposits from aggressive credit unions offering above market deposit rates.) However loans increased 5% year over year and the growth in loans combined with stable net interest margins of about 3.5% resulted in a modest uptick in net interest income. Non-interest income got a boost from the bank's wealth management division which posted a 7% revenue gain in 2013 versus 2012.

EXECUTIVES

President And Ceo, Charles N. Funk, age 64, $422,000 total compensation
Evp Chief Lending Officer And Commercial Banking, Kent L. Jehle, age 58, $271,000 total compensation
Vp And Chief Risk Officer, James M. Cantrell, $205,000 total compensation
Coo, Kevin Kramer
Svp And Cfo, Katie A. Lorenson, age 38, $206,231 total compensation
Senior Regional President, Mitchell W. Cook, age 54, $204,400 total compensation
Vice President Information Technology Managing Officer, Allen Schneider
Senior Vice President Loan Sales, Jason Swestka
Vice President Senior Loan Review Officer, Jeff Richards
Vice President Lpl Financial Advisor Located, John Evans
Vice President And Program Manager, Daniel Bailey
Senior Vice President Treasury Management, Kevin Pleasant
Vice President, Janeen Benoy
Vice President Mortgage Loan Operations, Linda A Nelson
Senior Vice President Small Business Administration, John Kimball
Second Vice President Mortgage Banker, Kerri Higgins
Vice President Commercial Lending, Andrew L Brust
Senior Vice President Credit Administration, Bob Blenkush
Vice President Commercial Lending, Andrew Brust
Vice President Commercial Banking, Nick Raffensperger
Chairman, Kevin W. Monson, age 66
Auditors: RSM US LLP

LOCATIONS

HQ: MidWestOne Financial Group, Inc.
102 South Clinton Street, Iowa City, IA 52240
Phone: 319 356-5800
Web: www.midwestone.com

PRODUCTS/OPERATIONS

2015 Sales

	% of total
Interest Income	
Interest and fees on loans	71
Interest on investment securities	11
Other	1
Non-Interest Income	
Trust investment and insurance fees	5
Other service charges commissions and fees	5
Service charges and fees on deposit accounts	3
Mortgage origination and loan servicing fees	2
Other	2
Total	100

Selected Subsidiaries

MidWestOne Bank
MidWestOne Insurance Services Inc.
MidWestOne Statutory Trust II

COMPETITORS

Bank of the West	U.S. Bancorp
Hills Bancorporation	Wells Fargo
QCR Holdings	West Bancorporation

HISTORICAL FINANCIALS

Company Type: Public

Income Statement
FYE: December 31

	ASSETS ($ mil.)	NET INCOME ($ mil.)	INCOME AS % OF ASSETS	EMPLOYEES
12/17	3,212	18	0.6%	610
12/16	3,079	20	0.7%	587
12/15	2,979	25	0.8%	648
12/14	1,800	18	1.0%	374
12/13	1,755	18	1.1%	376
Annual Growth	16.3%	0.1%		12.9%

2017 Year-End Financials

Debt ratio: 1.13%
Return on equity: 5.79%
Cash ($ mil.): 50
Current ratio: —
Long-term debt ($ mil.): —

No. of shares (mil.): 12
Dividends
Yield: 0.0%
Payout: 43.2%
Market value ($ mil.): 410

	STOCK PRICE ($) FY Close	P/E High/Low		PER SHARE ($) Earnings	Dividends	Book Value
12/17	33.53	25	21	1.55	0.67	27.85
12/16	37.60	22	14	1.78	0.64	26.71
12/15	30.41	14	12	2.42	0.60	25.96
12/14	28.81	13	10	2.19	0.58	23.07
12/13	27.20	13	9	2.18	0.50	20.99
Annual Growth	5.4%	—	—	(8.2%)	7.6%	7.3%

MISSOURI HIGHER EDUCATION LOAN AUTHORITY

EXECUTIVES

Finance Vice President, Scott Giles
Vice President Of Human Resources, Susan Crump
Auditors: ERNST & YOUNG LLP ST LOUIS

LOCATIONS

HQ: MISSOURI HIGHER EDUCATION LOAN AUTHORITY
633 SPIRIT DR, CHESTERFIELD, MO 630051243
Phone: 636 733-3700
Web: WWW.MOHELA.COM

COMPETITORS

Bank of America
Brazos Higher Education Service Corp.
Great Lakes Higher Education
JPMorgan Chase
Nelnet
Pennsylvania Higher Education Assistance Agency
Sallie Mae
Texas Guaranteed

HISTORICAL FINANCIALS

Company Type: Private

Income Statement
FYE: June 30

	ASSETS ($ mil.)	NET INCOME ($ mil.)	INCOME AS % OF ASSETS	EMPLOYEES
06/17	1,971	20	1.0%	550
06/16	2,208	8	0.4%	—
06/03	3,344	24	0.7%	—
06/02	2,730	19	0.7%	—
Annual Growth	(2.1%)	0.3%	—	—

2017 Year-End Financials

Debt ratio: —
Return on equity: 15.90%
Cash ($ mil.): 29
Current ratio: 0.10
Long-term debt ($ mil.): —

Dividends
Yield: —
Payout: —
Market value ($ mil.): —

Mohawk Industries, Inc.

Mohawk Industries is one of the largest makers of commercial and residential carpets rugs and other floor coverings in the US (competing with rival Shaw Industries) and one of the largest carpet makers in the world. It produces a range of broadloom carpets and rugs under such names as Mohawk Aladdin Durkan Karastan and Lees. Mohawk's Dal-Tile International division is a giant maker of ceramic tile and stone flooring. Unilin's laminate and wood flooring and other wood products round out Mohawk's operations. The company sells its wares to carpet retailers home centers mass merchandisers department stores and dealers.

Operations

Mohawk works through three main business segments: Flooring North America (nearly 45% of total sales) Global Ceramic (35%) and Flooring Rest of World (almost 20%).

Once focused exclusively on carpets and rugs Mohawk has evolved adapting itself to changing customer tastes and spending habits. The company now offers popular alternatives to carpet such as hardwood laminate and ceramic tile. It has also reached outside of its premium-priced portfolio by rolling out a do-it-yourself flooring line that mimics the elegant look of materials like marble or limestone without the coldness chipping or costly installation of real stone.

On a product level Mohawk generates nearly 40% of its revenue from its soft surface product group. Other product categories include tile (about 35%) and laminate and wood (about 25%).

Geographic Reach

Mohawk generates around 65% of its revenues in North America. It has manufacturing facilities located in Australia Brazil Canada Europe India Malaysia Mexico New Zealand Russia and the US.

Sales and Marketing

The company's top 10 customers account for nearly 20% of its total sales. It sells its products to more than 28000 customers which include independent floor covering retailers home centers and mass merchandisers department stores commercial dealers and end users.

Financial Performance

Mohawk has experienced several straight years of unprecedented growth. Its revenues jumped 11% from $8.1 billion in 2015 to peak at almost $9 billion its highest total in history. This was attributed to growth across all its segments: Flooring

North America (5%) Global Ceramic (7%) and Flooring Rest of World (32%). Most of this growth was attributed to additional revenue from previous acquisitions and a favorable impact of price and product mix.

Profits also climbed 51% from $615 million in 2015 to reach $930 million in 2016 another milestone. This was fueled by about $140 million in savings from capital investments and cost reduction initiatives lower material costs and the favorable impact of lower restructuring acquisition and integration-related costs.

Like its revenues the company's operating cash flow has surged the last few years increasing from $912 million in 2015 to $1.3 billion in 2016. This was due to the higher profits driven by additional revenue. Cash flow also increased in 2016 due to the absence of a litigation charge of $123 million it paid in 2015.

Strategy

Mohawk has posted milestone revenue and profit totals over the years through an aggressive growth strategy. This involves acquisitions that enable it to enter new product categories or markets. It then strengthens those acquisitions through investments and upgrades which allow it to modernize its locations and infrastructure and lower costs. In 2016 the company used about $672 million for internal investments and estimates it will spend $750 million in 2017.

Through these actions Mohawk is focused on broadening its countertop business in the US and Europe enhancing its carpet tile business in Europe entering the sheet vinyl industry in Russia and strengthening its indoor/outdoor rug and utility mat businesses in the US.

Mergers and Acquisitions

Mohawk is looking to extend its international reach and augment its product portfolio through acquisitions. In 2015 the company acquired International Flooring Systems S.A. a global manufacturer distributor and marketer of vinyl flooring products for $1.1 billion. The acquisition expanded Mohawk's luxury vinyl tile category portfolio and its fiberglass sheet vinyl business.

Also that year the company extended its European footprint when it purchased Advent KAI Luxembourg Holdings an eastern European ceramic tile floor manufacturer for $195 million; and Xtratherm Limited an Ireland-based manufacturer of insulation boards in Ireland the UK and Belgium for $160 million.

HISTORY

Mohawk traces its origins to the Shuttleworth family who founded the company in Amsterdam New York in 1878 setting up their business with 14 second-hand looms imported from England. The company was incorporated as Shuttleworth Brothers in 1902. It introduced the popular Karnak carpet design in 1908.

EXECUTIVES

Svp Marketing, Karen R. Mendelsohn
Chairman And Ceo, Jeffrey S. Lorberbaum, age 63, $1,142,473 total compensation
President And Coo, W. Christopher (Chris) Wellborn, age 62, $987,186 total compensation
President Ceramic North America, John C. Turner, age 49
President Flooring North America, Brian M. Carson, age 53, $618,000 total compensation
Vp Finance And Cfo, Frank H. Boykin, age 62, $615,605 total compensation
President Flooring Rest Of World, Bernard P. Thiers, age 62, $609,312 total compensation
Vice President Sales Bigelow And Mohawk Commercial Brands, Jeff Davis

Vice President Of Flooring Production, Willy Chandler

Vice President Design And Product Development, Jackie Dettmar

Vice President Sales, Tom Merriman

Vice President Research And Development, Silvano Cornia

Vice President Marketing And Sales, David Moyer

Vice President Of Residential Carpet Product Development, Jamie Welborn

Mohawk Commercial Sales Flooring Commercial Rvp Mountain West, Ralph Holland

Senior Vice President Sales Operations, Jay Imperapori

Vice President Strategic Business Development Home Depot, Chip Gillen

Vice President Of Design And Product Development, Neil Hegwood

Vice President Of Design, Tracy Pruitt

Senior Vice President Marketing, David Duncan

Vice President Marketing, Tom Donoghue

Vice President Business Development And International Sales, Nick Sterghos

Regional Vice President Sales Southeast, Tracy Lambeth

Regional Vice President, Jim Waters

Regional Vice President, Frank Niekamp

Mvp Coordinator, Cathy Ballew

Vice President Commercial Marketing, Kevin Wildes

Regional Vice President Of Sales Midsouth Region, Todd Lomas

Auditors: KPMG LLP

LOCATIONS

HQ: Mohawk Industries, Inc.
160 S. Industrial Blvd., Calhoun, GA 30701
Phone: 706 629-7721
Web: www.mohawkind.com

2016 Sales

	$ mil.	% of total
US	5,842	65
All other countries	3,116	35
Total	**8,959**	**100**

PRODUCTS/OPERATIONS

2016 Sales

	$ mil.	% of total
Soft Surface	3,415	38
Tile	3	36
Laminate and wood	2,286	26
Total	**8,959**	**100**

2016 Sales

	$ mil.	% of total
Flooring NA	3,865	43
Global Ceramic	3,174	36
Flooring ROW	1,918	21
Total	**8,959**	**100**

Products Selected
Residential Carpet
Commercial Carpet
Bath Rugs Area Rugs and Mats
Ceramic Tile & Stone
Laminate Flooring
Hardwood Flooring
Luxury Vinyl Tile (LVT)

Selected Operations

Glazed wall tile
Hardwood flooring
Hardwood flooring
Insulation panels
Laminate flooring
Laminate flooring
Porcelain tile
Quarry tile
Resilient flooring
Roofing systems
Rugs
Stone products

Selected Brand

Names
Aladdin
American Olean
Bigelow Commercial
Century Flooring
Columbia Flooring
Dal-Tile
Durkan
Horizon
Karastan
Lees
Merit
Mohawk
Mohawk Home
Quick-Step

COMPETITORS

Armstrong World Industries	Interface Inc.
Beaulieu of America	International Textile Group
Couristan	JJJ Floor Covering
Dixie Group	Mannington Mills
Formica	MasterTile
Guilford Performance Textiles	Perstorp
Hollander Home Fashions	Shaw Industries
Interceramic Inc.	Tarkett Inc.
	Wilsonart International

HISTORICAL FINANCIALS

Company Type: Public

Income Statement

FYE: December 31

	REVENUE ($ mil.)	NET INCOME ($ mil.)	NET PROFIT MARGIN	EMPLOYEES
12/17	9,491	971	10.2%	38,800
12/16	8,959	930	10.4%	37,800
12/15	8,071	615	7.6%	34,100
12/14	7,803	531	6.8%	32,300
12/13	7,348	348	4.7%	32,100
Annual Growth	**6.6%**	**29.2%**	**—**	**4.9%**

2017 Year-End Financials

Debt ratio: 22.85%
Return on equity: 15.14%
Cash ($ mil.): 84
Current ratio: 1.53
Long-term debt ($ mil.): 1,559

No. of shares (mil.): 74
Dividends
Yield: —
Payout: —
Market value ($ mil.): 20,533

	STOCK PRICE ($) FY Close	P/E High/Low		PER SHARE ($) Earnings	Dividends	Book Value
12/17	275.90	22	15	12.98	0.00	94.85
12/16	199.68	17	12	12.48	0.00	77.88
12/15	189.39	25	18	8.31	0.00	65.66
12/14	155.36	22	17	7.25	0.00	60.59
12/13	148.90	30	19	4.82	0.00	61.37
Annual Growth	**16.7%**			**28.1%**	**—**	**11.5%**

Molina Healthcare Inc

Molina Healthcare is dedicated to helping low-income Americans receive health and behavioral health coverage as well as primary care services. The company's Health Plan segment arranges for the delivery of health services to some 4.5 million people who receive their care through Medicaid Medicare and other government-funded programs in about a dozen states and Puerto Rico. Its Medicaid Solutions segment provides business process outsourcing (BPO) solutions to Medicaid agencies in six states for their Medicaid Management Infor-

mation Systems (MMIS) the tool used to support administration of state health care entitlement programs. The family of founder C. David Molina controls the company through holdings and trusts.

Operations

Until 2018 Molina operated through two primary segments: Health Plan and Molina Medicaid Solutions. Altogether the company's operations provide plans or services to 4.5 million individuals in a dozen states. Molina's Health Plans segment accounts for more than 95% of revenues. The company's health plans provide medical services through state networks of contracted hospitals and physicians that accept Molina health plan coverage. The health plans are each licensed as health maintenance organizations (HMOs).

The Medicaid segment helped state agencies administer their Medicaid programs with such offerings as IT development and business processing. Molina sold that business to DXC Technology in 2018.

Geographic Reach

Molina's health plans primarily operate in Washington California South Carolina Texas Ohio and Michigan as well as in New Mexico and Florida.

Molina's Health Plans segment leases around 70 facilities while the Medicaid solutions segment leases a dozen facilities.

Sales and Marketing

Molina's primary customers include state Medicaid agencies and the federal government.

Financial Performance

Molina has seen steady revenue increases over the last few years. In 2017 revenue rose 25% to $19.8 billion as premium revenue increased (largely as a result of a 10% increase in membership) and investment income saw growth. Premium revenue growth was led by California Florida Texas and Washington. However a decline in service revenue and the absence of reimbursed health insurer fees partially offset those gains.

As a participant in the Affordable Care Act marketplace the company has been struggling to be profitable. It has initiated a restructuring effort that included a management shakeup in 2017. That year it fell into the black in 2017 with a net loss of $512 million. One factor contributing to that loss was the federal government's move to stop funding cost-sharing reduction (CRS) payments. As such medical care costs increased and the company had $470 million in impairment losses. It also had $234 million in restructuring and separation costs.

Operating cash flow totaled $804 million that year a 19% increase from that of 2016.

Strategy

One of Molina's immediate initiatives is advocating for the improvement of the insurance marketplace under regulatory guidelines. The company says that it is owed $128 million in risk corridor payments from the federal government and it has yet to recognize revenue from these payments. (The risk corridor program established as part of the Affordable Care Act aimed to protect insurers participating in exchanges from higher-than-expected claims through 2016.) In a mid-2017 win a federal claims court ruled that the government owes Molina $52 million in risk corridor payments. That ruling followed a string of upsets from quarterly losses and company layoffs to the withdrawal from Utah's and Wisconsin's exchanges and the firing of the company's CEO and CFO (both sons of Molina's founder). Restructuring expenses led the company to incur $234 million in related losses in 2017.

A key Molina strategy for growth is to expand membership especially in its existing markets by acquiring the Medicaid contracts of other businesses. It made several of these purchases in 2016 adding more than 220000 Medicaid members to its books. It has also secured a number of state contracts including deals made in 2017 to provide Medicaid coverage in Illinois and Mississippi and a deal in 2018 to provide Children's Health Insurance Program (CHIP) services in Texas. In addition Molina enters new markets through both organic measures and through acquisitions targeting large markets with competitive provider communities.But in 2017 the company lost certain Medicaid contracts in New Mexico Florida and Illinois which ultimately contributed to a $470 million impairment loss. Molina is working to regain contracts lost in New Mexico and Florida.

The company is also working on cutting costs to improve efficiency. In addition to its restructuring efforts mentioned above it has also improved its care management systems and processes. It is increasingly utilizing hospitalists (dedicated physicians working in hospitals) and coordinating care efforts among teams of providers to both save money and improve health outcomes.

Molina's former Pathways subsidiary (acquired in late 2016) provided home- and community-based behavioral health services which the company believed would see a growth in demand over the next few years. However after reporting $173 million impairment loss primarily related to the Pathways business the company sold the unit to investment firm Atar Capital in 2018.

In the past Molina's growth strategy also consisted of opening additional primary care clinics in existing and new territories. The addition of more clinics helped Molina diversify its operations by expanding its involvement in the direct delivery of primary care. Recently though the company has been quietly exiting the primary care business. It has closed down several clinics and sold several others.

With these exits and divestitures Molina is increasingly focused on its core health plan operations.

Mergers and Acquisitions

In 2016 Molina Healthcare bought Total Care Medicaid a plan serving some 39000 members in upstate New York from Universal American for $41.3 million. Other deals that year included the purchases of Loyola Physician Partners ($15 million adding 21000 Medicaid members in Illinois) and HAP Midwest Health Plan (adding some 81000 Medicaid and MIChild members).

EXECUTIVES

Cfo And Treasurer, Joseph W. White, age 59, $538,000 total compensation
Evp Research And Development, Martha Molina Bernadett, $357,000 total compensation
President Ceo And Director, Joseph M. Zubretsky, age 62
Coo, Terry P. Bayer, age 67, $644,000 total compensation
Svp General Counsel And Secretary, Jeff D. Barlow, age 55, $525,000 total compensation
Cio, Rick Hopfer
Assistant Vice President Mhi Enrollment Accounting, Becky Gutierrez
Medical Director, Lawrence O'Brien
Regional Vice President, Del Bell
Assistant Vice President Rating, Ben Lynam
Vice President Of Accounting, Derek Danley
Vice President Of Quality, Kevin C Park
Vice President Of Clinic Operations, Anya Sage
Associate Vice President Enterprise Infrastructure Services, Bharani Krish
Vice President Healthcare Services, Jeffrey King
Mhu Associate Vice President Government Contracts, Douglas Springmeyer
Vice President, Mohit Ghose
Director Of Pharmacy, John Vu
Vice President Of Finance, Jane D Dawson

Mhi Associate Vice President Corporate Oprs, Andrea Orleans
Vice President Sales, Ryan Boe
Medical Director, Delores Baker
Vice President Of Call Centre, Randall Fillmore
Associate Vice President Health Plan Operations, Virginia Fuentes-Rivera
Associate Vice President Of State Affairs, Cameron Smyth
Senior Vice President Provider And Member Engagement And Operations, Mary Syiek
Legal Secretary, Wendy Jones
Vice President, Douglas Rodgers
Associate Medical Director, Ron Tomas
Assistant Vice President Of Health Plan Operations, Betty Thomas
Vice President Tax, George Figueroa
Medical Director Of Behavioral Health, Ayo Afejuku
Associate Vice President Of Government Contracts, David Vinkler
Vice President Business Innovation, Tom Giedlin
Clinic Supervisor, Melanie Talbert-chandler
Associate Vice President Of Molina Healthcare Inc., Brian Monsen
Regional Vice President, Stephen Harris
Vice President Business Architecture, Carol Smith
Vice President Network Strategy And Services, Kim Sweers
Vice President Enterprise Infrastructure, Ben Gordon
Medical Director, James Bowerman
Associate Vice President, Larry Baldwin
Assoc Vice President, Anita Carter
Vice President, Julie Menke
Vice President Government Contracts, Karen Zeiler
Medical Director, David Eibling
Vice President, Eric De Garceau
Medical Director, Terry Fowler
Assistant Vice President Government Contracts, Barbara Maxwell
Vice President Of Operations, Elizabeth Richardson
Assistant Vice President Operations, Jaime Perikly
Vice President And Medical Director, Michael Siegel
Assistant Vice President Compliance, Hector Feliciano
Medical Director, Mary Engrav
Medical Director Of Behavioral Health, Ayo Gathing
Vice President, Dave Boim
Associate Vice President, Suma Simcoe
Assistant Vice President Growth And Corporate Development, Grace Han
Associate Vice President Clai, Beth Richardson
Assistant Vice President Of Long Term Care Operations, Robert Kalin
Medical Director, Shyama Gandhi
Medical Director, Ann Bay
Associate Vice President, Mario J Garza
Vice President, Lekan J Lawal
Senior Vice President Deputy General Counsel, Ronald D Kurtz
Vice President Finance And Analytics, Thomas C Phillip
Director Of Pharmacy, Jacqueline Jacobi
Medical Director, Arik Olson
Director Of Pharmacy, Vinay Bhargava
Associate Vice President, Mario Garza
Senior Vice President Deputy General Counsel, Ronald Kurtz
Associate Vice President Information Security, Manuel Bugayong
Chairman, Dale B. Wolf, age 63
Auditors: Ernst & Young LLP

LOCATIONS

HQ: Molina Healthcare Inc
200 Oceangate, Suite 100, Long Beach, CA 90802
Phone: 562 435-3666　　**Fax:** 562 437-1335
Web: www.molinahealthcare.com

2017 Membership by Health Plan

	% of total
Washington	17
California	17
Florida	14
Texas	9
Michigan	9
Ohio	7
Puerto Rico	7
New Mexico	6
Illinois	4
Utah	3
Wisconsin	3
South Carolina	3
New York	1
Total	**100**

PRODUCTS/OPERATIONS

2017 Sales

	$ mil.	% of total
Health plans	19,352	97
Medicaid solutions	187	1
Other	344	2
Total	**19,883**	**100**

2017 Sales

	$ mil.	% of total
Premiums	18,884	95
Services	521	3
Premium tax revenue	438	2
Investment income	70	-
Total	**19,883**	**100**

COMPETITORS

AMERIGROUP	HCSC
Aetna	Humana
Anthem	Kaiser Foundation
Blue Cross Blue Shield	Health Plan
of Michigan	L. A. Care Health Plan
CIGNA	Premera Blue Cross
Cambia Health	Priority Health
Solutions	Total Health Care
Centene	UnitedHealth Group
Community Health Group	WellCare Health Plans

HISTORICAL FINANCIALS

Company Type: Public

Income Statement　　　　　　　　　　　　FYE: December 31

	REVENUE ($ mil.)	NET INCOME ($ mil.)	NET PROFIT MARGIN	EMPLOYEES
12/17	19,883	(512)	—	20,000
12/16	17,782	52	0.3%	21,000
12/15	14,178	143	1.0%	21,000
12/14	9,666	62	0.6%	10,500
12/13	6,588	52	0.8%	8,200
Annual Growth	**31.8%**	**—**	**—**	**25.0%**

2017 Year-End Financials

Debt ratio: 25.61%	No. of shares (mil.): 60
Return on equity: (-34.29%)	Dividends
Cash ($ mil.): 3,186	Yield: —
Current ratio: 1.35	Payout: —
Long-term debt ($ mil.): 1,516	Market value ($ mil.): 4,601

	STOCK PRICE ($) FY Close	P/E High/Low		PER SHARE ($) Earnings	Dividends	Book Value
12/17	76.68	—	—	(9.07)	0.00	22.28
12/16	54.26	73	49	0.92	0.00	28.93
12/15	60.13	30	18	2.58	0.00	27.80
12/14	53.53	41	25	1.29	0.00	20.32
12/13	34.75	35	22	1.13	0.00	19.47
Annual Growth	**21.9%**	**—**	**—**	**—**	**—**	**3.4%**

Molson Coors Brewing Co.

Auditors: PricewaterhouseCoopers LLP

LOCATIONS

HQ: Molson Coors Brewing Co.
1555 Notre Dame Street East, Montreal, Quebec H2L 2R5
Phone: 514 521-1786
Web: www.molsoncoors.com

HISTORICAL FINANCIALS

Company Type: Public

Income Statement

FYE: December 31

	REVENUE ($ mil.)	NET INCOME ($ mil.)	NET PROFIT MARGIN	EMPLOYEES
12/17	11,002	1,414	12.9%	17,200
12/16	4,885	1,975	40.4%	17,400
12/15	3,567	359	10.1%	17,500
12/14	4,146	514	12.4%	17,400
12/13	4,206	567	13.5%	17,650
Annual Growth	27.2%	25.7%	—	(0.6%)

2017 Year-End Financials

Debt ratio: 37.40%
Return on equity: 11.48%
Cash ($ mil.): 418
Current ratio: 0.64
Long-term debt ($ mil.): 10,598

No. of shares (mil.): 215
Dividends
Yield: 0.0%
Payout: 25.1%
Market value ($ mil.): 17,678

	STOCK PRICE ($) FY Close	P/E High/Low		PER SHARE ($) Earnings	Dividends	Book Value
12/17	82.07	15	12	6.53	1.64	61.40
12/16	97.31	12	9	9.26	1.64	53.13
12/15	93.92	49	34	1.93	1.64	38.17
12/14	74.52	28	18	2.76	1.48	42.39
12/13	56.15	18	13	3.08	1.28	46.90
Annual Growth	10.0%	—	—	20.7%	6.4%	7.0%

Mondelez International Inc

One of the world's largest snack companies Mondelez International owns a pantry of billion-dollar brands such as Cadbury and Milka chocolates; LU Nabisco and Oreo biscuits; Trident gum; and Tang powdered beverages. The company's portfolio includes global national and regional brands many of which are more than 100 years old. Biscuits (cookies crackers and salted snacks) and chocolate account for most of the company?s sales. Mondelez which operates worldwide generates most of its revenue outside the US.

HISTORY

The Kraft tale began in 1903 when James L. Kraft began delivering cheese to Chicago grocers. His four brothers joined in forming the J.L. Kraft & Bros. Company in 1909. By 1914 the company had opened a cheese factory and was selling cheese across the US. Kraft developed its first blended pasteurized cheese the following year.

Kraft went public in 1924; four years later it merged with Philadelphia cream-cheese maker Phoenix and also created Velveeta cheese spread. In 1930 Kraft was bought by National Dairy but its operations were kept separate. New and notable products included Miracle Whip salad dressing (1933) macaroni and cheese dinners (1937) and Parkay margarine (1940). In the decades that followed Kraft expanded into foreign markets.

National Dairy became Kraftco in 1969 and Kraft in 1976 hoping to benefit from its internationally known trademark. To diversify Kraft merged with Dart Industries in 1980; Dart's subsidiaries (including Duracell batteries) and Kraft kept separate operations. With non-food sales sagging Dart & Kraft split up in 1986. Kraft kept its original lines and added Duracell (sold 1988); the rest became Premark International. Tobacco giant Philip Morris Companies bought Kraft in 1988 for $12.9 billion. The next year Philip Morris joined Kraft with another unit General Foods.

General Foods began when Charles Post who marketed a wheat/bran health beverage established the Postum Cereal Co. in 1896; he expanded the firm with such cereals as Grape-Nuts and Post Toasties. The company went public in 1922. Postum bought the makers of Jell-O (1925) Baker's chocolate (1927) Log Cabin syrup (1927) and Maxwell House coffee (1928) and in 1929 it acquired control of General Foods (owned by frozen vegetable pioneer Clarence Birdseye) and changed its own name to General Foods.

Its later purchases included Perkins Products (Kool-Aid 1953) and Kohner Brothers (toys 1970). Most of its non-food lines proved unsuccessful and were sold throughout the years. General Foods bought Oscar Mayer the US's #1 hot dog maker in 1981. Philip Morris bought General Foods for $5.6 billion in 1985.

The 1989 combination of Kraft and General Foods (the units still ran independently) created the largest US food maker Kraft General Foods. In the 1990s Kraft General Foods lost market share in areas such as frozen vegetables and processed meat. It introduced "light" meat products and stopped making nearly 300 food items. In 1993 it bought RJR Nabisco's cold cereal business (Shredded Wheat) and sold its Breyers ice-cream business to Unilever.

To streamline management Philip Morris integrated Kraft and General Foods in 1995. Newly named Kraft Foods sold off lower-margin businesses including its bakery unit and its North American table spreads business. Kraft bought Del Monte's shelf-stable pudding business (1995) and Taco Bell's grocery line (1996). It also sold its Lender's bagels (1996) and Log Cabin (1997) lines.

Deciding to eat healthy in early 2000 Kraft bought Boca Burger (soy products) for about $100 million and Balance Bar (meal-replacement snack bars drink mixes and beverages) for $268 million.

In 2000 parent Philip Morris (which renamed itself the Altria Group in 2003) outbid Danone and Cadbury Schweppes (later Cadbury) and agreed to buy Nabisco Holdings. It completed the deal that December for $18.9 billion (including $4 billion in debt) and began integrating those operations into Kraft Foods and Kraft Foods International. Then Philip Morris created a holding company for the newly combined food operations under the Kraft Foods Inc. name in 2001. The original Kraft Foods was renamed Kraft Foods North America.

Kraft Foods International CEO Roger Deromedi was appointed co-CEO of the new holding company along with Betsy Holden. Kraft Foods Inc. was spun off by Altria in 2001 in what was the US's second-largest IPO ever at the time (behind AT&T Wireless now AT&T Mobility).

Kraft cut 7500 jobs in 2002 as a result of the integration of Nabisco operations paying out $373 million in cash for severance and related costs. That year Kraft was also part of a $9 million settlement of a federal lawsuit regarding the use of genetically modified corn in its taco shells.

A strategy to shed brands that do not fit with the rest of the company's portfolio led Kraft to sell Farley's and Sathers in 2002 to FS Partners which renamed the company Farley's & Sathers Candy Company. Later that year Kraft sold some of its candy brands (Now and Later Intense Fruit Chews and Mity Bite) to FS Partners.

In a move to combat the population's growing obesity problem Kraft said in 2003 that it intended to reduce the fat and sugar content and cut the portion sizes of its food products as well as cease marketing in schools.

Deromedi shared the CEO slot with co-CEO Betsy Holden until 2003 at which time Deromedi was named sole CEO. (Holden was demoted to a marketing slot in the company and eventually left Kraft in 2005.) During his tenure as CEO Deromide was dogged by Kraft's looming spinoff from Altria and struggled to improve company profits by selling off underperforming and non-core brands.

The company in 2004 formed an alliance with Dr. Arthur Agatston of low-carb South Beach Diet fame to use the South Beach Diet trademark on some of its products including cereal meal replacements cereal bars refrigerated sandwich wraps and frozen entrees and pizza.

As part of Deromedi's plan to refashion Kraft's product lineup in 2005 the company sold its Altoids breath mints LifeSavers and CremeSavers candies brands whose combined sales were at the time estimated to be about $660 million a year. Wm. Wrigley Jr. Company paid about $1.4 billion for the popular brands.

Despite his best efforts to improve the bottom line Deromedi was shown the door in 2006. He was replaced by Frito-Lay's CEO Irene Rosenfeld (a former top Kraft executive who was instrumental in the company's acquisition and integration of Nabisco). She returned to Kraft after being head of Pepsico's Frito-Lay from 2004 to 2006.

Kraft extricated itself from the haze of second-hand tobacco smoke when it was spun off from Altria in 2007. Having edged toward splitting from its former parent for years the separation relieved the food maker of many headaches. It freed Kraft from any tobacco-related liability that Altria may be found guilty of post-spinoff. It also eliminated a significant layer of management which made it easier for Kraft to improve its sluggish sales.

Focusing on sharpening its brand portfolio Kraft sold off its hot cereals business in 2007. The $200 million sale to B&G Foods included two old favorites Cream of Wheat and Cream of Rice. It also sold its Fruit2O and Veryfine juice brands and operations to Sunny Delight Beverages.

As part of its plan to offer new product categories Kraft entered the lucrative and popular pre-made salad market in 2007 with the introduction of South Beach Living brand chicken-salad kits.

Adding more on the expansion front Kraft bought the Spanish and Portuguese operations of United Biscuits that year; the deal returned to Kraft the rights to Nabisco trademarks such as Oreo Ritz and Chips Ahoy! in Europe the Middle East and Africa.

Kraft further expanded its foreign operations with its 2007 purchase of the cookie/biscuit business of Groupe Danone for some $7.6 billion. The purchase gave the company brands such as LU Petit Ecolier and CrA?me RoulA©e and made biscuits (cookies to us Yanks) the company's largest global business. It also added the Tiger and Prince brands to its Egyptian portfolio.

Billionaire Warren Buffett acquired a small percentage of Kraft in 2007 (less than 5% at the time) joining the also famously rich and famous-on-Wall Street corporate raiders Nelson Peltz (whose estimated Kraft holdings are 3%) and Carl Icahn (who owns about 3%) in ownership of the Velveeta vendor. Peltz and Ichan are typically activist investors making suggestions regarding company operations. Peltz has suggested that Kraft concentrate on its core brands as well as undertake divestitures to fund overseas expansion.

Kraft acquiesced to Peltz on one front agreeing with his investment operations collectively known as Trian Partners by adding two directors (selected by the company and supported by Trian) to its board in 2007. Kraft also signed a "standstill" agreement with Trian agreeing to support the board's full list of nominees at Kraft's next two annual meetings.

Late in 2007 Kraft announced the re-rebranding of its South Beach products from South Beach Diet to South Beach Living saying that it wanted to capture a more positive image for the products. That year the company also sold its Veryfine juice and Fruit2O water brands and operations to the Sunny Delight company.

Kraft's 2008 sale of its slow-growing Post (Shredded Wheat Raisin Bran Honeycomb Grape-Nuts Pebbles and others) to Ralcorp a maker of private-label cereals and other foods is part of Kraft's strategy to pare down its brand offerings and concentrate on high-yield products. Ralcorp paid some $1.6 billion in stock for the acquisition. Post is the #3 US cereal maker by sales after General Mills and Kellogg. Post brought in more than $1 billion for Kraft in both 2006 and 2007.

In February 2010 Kraft acquired Cadbury for about $19 billion of which 60% was cash and 40% was stock. A majority of Cadbury's shareholders (almost 72% according to Kraft) accepted the offer effectively making Cadbury part of Kraft.

In October 2012 Kraft Foods split into two companies: a global snacks business Mondelez International and Kraft Foods Group (formerly Kraft Foods North America).

EXECUTIVES

Evp Human Resources, Karen J. May, age 59
Evp And Cfo, Brian T. Gladden, age 53, $900,000 total compensation
Ceo And Director, Dirk Van de Put, age 56
Evp And President North America, Glen Walter
Evp Integrated Supply Chain, Daniel Myers, age 63
Evp And President Europe, Hubert Weber, age 55
Evp And General Counsel, Gerhard (Gerd) Pleuhs, age 61
Evp And President Asia Middle East & Africa, Maurizio Brusadelli, age 49
Evp Research Development And Quality, Robin S. (Rob) Hargrove, age 52
Evp And President Latin America, Alejandro R. Lorenzo, age 46
Vice President Marketing Kraft Singles Natural Cheese And Velveeta, Mary Sagritanti
Executive Vice President President North America, Roberto Marques
Senior Vice President And Corporate Controller, Kim Jones
Vice President Human Resources Grocery Bu And Kraft University Relations, Ginny Packer
Senior Vice President Corporate Finance, James Kehoe
Chairman, Irene B. Rosenfeld, age 64
Auditors: PricewaterhouseCoopers LLP

LOCATIONS

HQ: Mondelez International Inc
Three Parkway North, Deerfield, IL 60015
Phone: 847 943-4000
Web: www.mondelezinternational.com

2016 Sales

	$ mil.	% of total
Europe	9,755	38
North America	6,960	27
AMEA	5,816	22
Latin America	3,392	13
Total	**25,923**	**100**

PRODUCTS/OPERATIONS

2016 Sales

	$ mil.	% of total
Biscuits	10,590	41
Chocolate	7,739	30
Gum & candy	3,947	15
Cheese & grocery	2,202	8
Beverages	1,445	6
Total	**25,923**	**100**

Selected Products and Brands

Biscuits
  Barni
  BelVita
  Chips Ahoy
  Club Social
  Oreo
  Tuc
Chocolate
  Cadbury
  Lacta
  Milka
  Toblerone
Gum & Candy
  Chicklets
  Halls
  Stride
  Trident
Other
  Philadelphia (cream cheese)

COMPETITORS

Associated British Foods	Kraft Heinz
Campbell Soup	Lindt & Spr ngli
Clif Bar	Maple Leaf Foods
Coca-Cola	Mars Incorporated
Community Coffee	Michael Foods
Dairy Crest	Mott's
Dairy Farmers of America	Mrs. Fields
Dr Pepper Snapple Group	Naked Juice
Fehr Foods	Nestlé
Frito-Lay	Newman's Own
Fromageries Bel	Otis Spunkmeyer
Galaxy Nutritional Foods	Parmalat Canada
General Mills	Pepperidge Farm
Hershey	PowerBar
Kellogg	Procter & Gamble
Kellogg U.S. Snacks	Russell Hobbs
Kerry Group	Smucker
Keurig Green Mountain	Snapple
	Snyder's-Lance
	Unilever PLC
	Voortman Cookies
	WhiteWave

HISTORICAL FINANCIALS

Company Type: Public

Income Statement
FYE: December 31

	REVENUE ($ mil.)	NET INCOME ($ mil.)	NET PROFIT MARGIN	EMPLOYEES
12/18	25,938	3,381	13.0%	80,000
12/17	25,896	2,922	11.3%	90,000
12/16	25,923	1,659	6.4%	90,000
12/15	29,636	7,267	24.5%	99,000
12/14	34,244	2,184	6.4%	104,000
Annual Growth	(6.7%)	11.5%	—	(6.3%)

2018 Year-End Financials

Debt ratio: 29.29%
Return on equity: 13.07%
Cash ($ mil.): 1,100
Current ratio: 0.45
Long-term debt ($ mil.): 12,532

No. of shares (mil.): 1,451
Dividends
  Yield: 2.4%
  Payout: 44.0%
Market value ($ mil.): 58,084

	STOCK PRICE ($) FY Close	P/E High/Low		PER SHARE ($) Earnings	Dividends	Book Value
12/18	40.03	20	16	2.28	0.96	17.67
12/17	42.80	24	20	1.91	0.82	17.55
12/16	44.33	43	34	1.05	0.72	16.46
12/15	44.84	10	8	4.49	0.64	17.73
12/14	36.33	30	25	1.28	0.58	16.68
Annual Growth	2.5%	—	—	15.5%	13.4%	1.4%

Morgan Stanley

One of the world's top investment banks Morgan Stanley serves up a smorgasbord of financial services. It offers everything from advising corporate clients on mergers & acquisitions to raising capital for large companies to managing real estate investments for wealthy individuals. It boasts one of the largest financial advisor networks which works with clients to pursue their investment goals. Morgan Stanley has more than $400 billion of assets under management. The investment bank is a global enterprise with a presence in more than 40 nations serving corporate institutional government and individual clients.

Operations

Morgan Stanley operates three business segments: Institutional Securities Wealth Management and Investment Management. Its Institutional Securities business which brings in about 50% of net revenue is composed of the company's capital raising investment banking sales and trading and corporate lending activities. Among other tasks this segment underwrites debt performs market-making for equities and fixed income products and issues loans to municipalities.

The company's Wealth Management business (roughly 45% of net revenue) provides brokerage and investment advisory services and financial products such as annuities and insurance policies for small-to-medium businesses and affluent investors. The division is one of the world's largest wealth advisors by headcount with some 16000 financial advisors and $2 trillion in client assets.

The Investment Management segment (6% of net revenue) consists of Morgan Stanley's asset management equity and fixed income investments merchant banking and real estate investing businesses.

Morgan Stanley typically makes more than 90% of its net revenue from non-interest income sources with nearly 30% coming from trading fees and 30% coming from fees for asset management distribution and administration. Another 25% comes collectively from investment banking fees commissions and fees and investment sales.

Geographic Reach

Morgan Stanley is a global company with 1200 offices spanning more than 40 countries. Principal offices are in and around New York City London Tokyo Hong Kong and other financial world centers. Approximately 70% of revenue comes from the Americas. The remaining revenue is split between both EMEA (Europe Middle East and Africa) and Asia/Pacific.

Sales and Marketing

Morgan Stanley provides its products and services worldwide to a large and diversified group of customers including corporations governments sovereign wealth funds foundations endowments financial institutions and individuals. Its financial advisors tend to individuals and smaller business clients. Morgan Stanley nurtures direct relationships with key personnel at its larger clients (corporations university endowments foundations etc.).

Financial Performance

Morgan Stanley's annual revenue jumped in 2017 after three years of holding steady as attractive financial markets have buoyed results in all three of its business segments. Meanwhile its profits have been positive sporadic in size and trending higher.

In 2017 revenue rose 10% to $37.9 billion as a result of double-digit growth across all its segments. The company saw higher revenues in investment banking and asset management as well a rise in net interest income. Geographically all regions (the Americas EMEA and Asia-Pacific) grew revenue.

Morgan Stanley's net income increased about 2% to $6.2 billion because of the revenue growth partially offset by a slightly higher provision for income taxes.

In 2017 net cash used for operating activities was $4.5 billion a significant change from the $5.4 billion provided by operations the prior year. Cash used for investing dropped a bit from 2016 to $12.4 billion. Financing activities provided a $16.3 billion boost leaving the company's cash balance at $80.4 billion up from $77.4 billion the prior year.

Strategy

Morgan Stanley's strategy pursues continued growth in its Wealth Management segment corporate-wide expense reduction Investment Management segment growth and investment in technologies.

Within Wealth Management the firm is seeing growth in interest income due to rate increases by the US Federal Reserve along with positive investor sentiment. It is purposefully attracting increased client deposits to build out the coffers that supply its lending activities in turn generating increased interest income. The long road from Morgan Stanley's merger with Smith Barney (in 2009) to incorporating and reshaping the entity into today's Wealth Management segment is paying dividends.

The Investment Management segment underwent restructuring in 2016 realigning its organization and bringing its costs in-line with the segment's needs which the company anticipates will position the division for stability and growth. While clients have increased investment in this segment's funds (fixed income mutual funds etc.) its own investment portfolio has performed poorly. Still this segment's principal money-making endeavor of asset management remains steady.

Cross-corporate objectives include cost reduction and technology adoption. Through Project Streamline an internal program the company has cut more than $1 billion in fixed expenses. Morgan Stanley's focus on technology includes investment in information security (for its own as well as its clients' protection) and the rollout of digital platforms such as in its Fixed Income electronic trading systems.

HISTORY

In 1934 the Glass-Steagall Act required the J. P. Morgan bank (now part of JPMorgan Chase & Co.) to sell its securities-related activities. The next year Henry Morgan Harold Stanley and others established Morgan Stanley as an investment bank. Capitalizing on old ties to major corporations the firm handled $1 billion in issues its first year. By 1941 when it joined the NYSE it had managed 25% of all bond issues underwritten since Glass-Steagall took effect.

In the 1950s Morgan Stanley was known for handling large issues alone. Clients included General Motors U.S. Steel General Electric and DuPont. The firm avoided the merger wave of the 1960s but in the early 1970s it formed Wall Street's first mergers and acquisitions (M&A) department. In 1974 Morgan Stanley handled its first hostile takeover International Nickel's (now Vale Inco) buy of ESB the world's #1 battery maker.

Morgan Stanley went public in 1986. It escaped the carnage of the 1987 crash but a lawsuit arising from investor dissatisfaction with its M&A and LBO activities during that period lasted well into the 1990s.

By 1994 it was talking to possible merger mates including Dean Witter and finally merged with Dean Witter Discover in 1997 creating Morgan Stanley Dean Witter & Co. The San Francisco brokerage founded by Dean Witter in 1924 had remained regional for 40 years serving wealthy customers. In 1977 the firm merged with Reynolds Securities another regional retail brokerage started by Richard Reynolds Jr. the son of the founder of Reynolds Metals (now part of Alcoa) and grandnephew of the founder of R.J. Reynolds Tobacco. The new company Dean Witter Reynolds became the #2 US brokerage after Merrill Lynch and one of the top 10 US underwriters.

Dean Witter needed capital in the early 1980s and sold itself to Sears which hoped to turn it into a financial Allstate. Sears put in a retail-oriented management team and tried to shoehorn Dean Witter into in-store brokerages. Sears' indifference to the investment side hobbled operations.

The Discover card introduced by Sears and Dean Witter in 1986 was a hit but by the late 1980s it was obvious Sears would never be a financial giant. The retailer spun off Allstate Insurance and the newly renamed Dean Witter Discover in 1993.

Amazingly all but six of Morgan Stanley's 3700 World Trade Center employees survived the September 11 2001 terrorist attack on the towers. Hoping to capitalize on deregulations and privatizations in Europe as well as the rise of the individual investor Morgan Stanley acquired UK-based private bank Quilter & Co. in 2001 (then later sold it to Citigroup in 2006). Also that year the firm dropped the public use of "Dean Witter" in 2001 for promotional purposes and then dropped it completely in 2002.

When regulatory scrutiny fell on the mutual fund industry Morgan Stanley was charged with failing to adequately disclose the incentives its brokers and managers received for selling certain funds. In 2003 the firm agreed to pay a $50 million fine and adopt a "plain English" approach to informing investors about its product fees and broker compensation.

In mid-2004 the firm agreed to pay $54 million to settle a sex discrimination lawsuit filed on behalf of more than 300 female employees who claimed they were denied promotions and salary raises.

Unhappy with the firm's performance eight former Morgan Stanley executives (dubbed the Group of Eight) publicly called for the ouster of chairm

EXECUTIVES

Chairman And Ceo, James P. Gorman, age 60, $1,500,000 total compensation

Head Of Global Capital Markets, Franck Petitgas

President, Colm Kelleher, age 61, $1,666,041 total compensation

Co-head Wealth Management, Andy Saperstein

Global Head Sales And Trading, Ted Pick

Evp And Cfo, Jonathan Pruzan, age 50, $1,000,000 total compensation

Evp And Chief Risk Officer, Keishi Hotsuki, age 55

Global Co-head Investment Banking, Mark Eichorn

Global Co-head Of Fixed Income, Robert Rooney

Coo Institutional Securities, Clare Woodman

Head Investment Management, Daniel A. (Dan) Simkowitz, $1,000,000 total compensation

Senior Vice President Portfolio Manager Wealth Advisor, Frank Corrigan

Vice President, Geoffrey Burke

Vice President, Ruben Badar

Vice President, Duncan Fudge

Vice President, Andy Jaglall

National Account Manager, Rosie Bailey

Vice President, John Schlegel

Vice President Information Technology, Anne Egan

First Vice President, Thomas Niles

Vice President Information Technology Department, Francis Rial

Vice President Head Of Engineering, Philip O'Dwyer

Vice President, Thomas Hartl

First Vice President, Ronald Phelps

Vice President Enterprise Infrastructure And Tech And Info Risk And Qapm, Zhenqin Li

Vice President Information Technology, Richard Wong

Vice President Information Technology, Alex Raykis

Vice President, Wendy Lowe

Vice President In Charge Of European Media And Internet, Fausto Zanetton

Vice President, Andrew Mento

Vice President Risk And Margins, Manu Agarwal

Vice President Network, Nathan Alexander

Senior Vice President, Adam Schur

Certified Wealth Strategist Vice President Morgan Stanley Smith Barney, Brian Weinkle

Vice President, Donny Chia

Vice President, Marc Weisser

Vice Chairman, Thomas R. (Tom) Nides, age 57

Board Member, Larry Ferdig

Auditors: Deloitte & Touche LLP

LOCATIONS

HQ: Morgan Stanley
1585 Broadway, New York, NY 10036
Phone: 212 761-4000
Web: www.morganstanley.com

2016 Sales

	% of total
Americas	74
EMEA	14
Asia-Pacific	12
Total	**100**

PRODUCTS/OPERATIONS

2016 Sales

	$ mil.	% of total
Interest income	7,016	19
Non-interest income		
Asset management distribution and administration fees	10,697	28
Trading	10,209	27
Investment banking	4,933	13
Commission and fees	4,109	11
Investments	160	0
Others	825	2
Total	**37,949**	**100**

2016 Sales

	% of total
Institutional Securities	50
Wealth Management	44
Investment Management	6
Total	**100**

COMPETITORS

Brown Brothers Harriman	MF Global
CIBC	Marsh & McLennan
Charles Schwab	Merrill Lynch
Citigroup	Nomura Securities
Citigroup Global Markets	Oppenheimer Holdings
Deutsche Bank	Raymond James Financial
FMR	State Street
Franklin Templeton	T. Rowe Price
Goldman Sachs	TD Bank
JPMorgan Chase	UBS
Lehman Brothers	Wells Fargo Securities

HISTORICAL FINANCIALS

Company Type: Public

Income Statement

FYE: December 31

	ASSETS ($ mil.)	NET INCOME ($ mil.)	INCOME AS % OF ASSETS	EMPLOYEES
12/17	851,733	6,111	0.7%	57,633
12/16	814,949	5,979	0.7%	55,311
12/15	787,465	6,127	0.8%	56,218
12/14	801,510	3,467	0.4%	55,802
12/13	832,702	2,932	0.4%	55,794
Annual Growth	**0.6%**	**20.2%**	**—**	**0.8%**

2017 Year-End Financials

Debt ratio: 22.61%
Return on equity: 7.97%
Cash ($ mil.): 80,395
Current ratio: —
Long-term debt ($ mil.): —

No. of shares (mil.): 1,788
Dividends
  Yield: 0.0%
  Payout: 29.3%
Market value ($ mil.): 93,821

	STOCK PRICE ($) FY Close	P/E High/Low	Earnings	PER SHARE ($) Dividends	Book Value
12/17	52.47	17 13	3.07	0.90	43.28
12/16	42.25	15 7	2.92	0.70	41.05
12/15	31.81	14 10	2.90	0.55	39.16
12/14	38.80	24 17	1.60	0.35	36.34
12/13	31.36	23 14	1.36	0.20	33.89
Annual Growth	**13.7%**	**—**	**22.6%**	**45.6%**	**6.3%**

Mosaic Co (The)

Big pieces of the global agricultural chemical industry come together to form The Mosaic Company. It ranks as one of the world's largest producers of phosphate and potash both used as crop nutrition and as input to animal feed. In North America it accounts for 75% of the region?s annual phosphate production and nearly 40% of potash production. In the rest of the world it still holds a significant market share about 15% of phosphate and 12% of potash production. The raw materials of its products are mined from location in Canada and the US. Mosaic?s sales are about equally split between North America and the rest of the world.

EXECUTIVES

Evp And Cfo, Richard L. (Rich) Mack, age 50, $624,000 total compensation
President And Ceo, James (Joc) O'Rourke, age 57, $893,833 total compensation
Svp Potash Operations, Walter F. (Walt) Precourt, age 53
Svp Potash, Bruce Bodine
Chairman, Robert L. Lumpkins, age 74
Auditors: KPMG LLP

LOCATIONS

HQ: Mosaic Co (The)
  3033 Campus Drive, Suite E490, Plymouth, MN 55441
Phone: 800 918-8270   **Fax:** 763 577-2990
Web: www.mosaicco.com

2015 Sales

	% of total
United States	37
Brazil	24
Canpotex	12
Canada	8
India	4
others regions	15
Total	**100**

PRODUCTS/OPERATIONS

2015 Sales

	$ mil.	% of total
Phosphates	3,920	44
Potash	2,437	28
International distribution	2,503	28
Elimination	32	-
Total	**8,895**	**100**

Premium Crop Nutrients

Premium Crop Nutrients
MicroEssentials®; SZ™
MicroEssentials®; S15™
MicroEssentials®; S10™
K-Mag®; Granular
K-Mag®; Premium
K-Mag®; Special Standard
K-Mag®; Standard
Pegasus®; Fine
Pegasus®; Granular
Potash
White Standard 0-0-62
Red Granular 0-0-60
Red Standard 0-0-60
Crystal Granular 0-0-60
Crystal Turf 150
Phosphates
Diammonium Phosphate (DAP) 18-46-0
Monoammonium Phosphate (MAP) 11-52-0
Powdered MAP
Feed Ingredients
Biofos®;
Dyna-K®;
Dynamate®;
Dyna-K White®;
Nexfos®;
Industrial Products
FSA Products
Hydrofluorosilicic Acid (FSA or HFS)
Potash Products
White Fine 0-0-62
White Granular 0-0-62
White Industrial High Quality
White Industrial Special
Red Standard 0-0-60

COMPETITORS

Arab Potash	Potash Corp
CF Industries	Sinofert
Israel Chemicals	Uralkali
K+S	

HISTORICAL FINANCIALS

Company Type: Public

Income Statement

FYE: December 31

	REVENUE ($ mil.)	NET INCOME ($ mil.)	NET PROFIT MARGIN	EMPLOYEES
12/17	7,409	(107)	—	8,500
12/16	7,162	297	4.2%	8,700
12/15	8,895	1,000	11.2%	8,900
12/14	9,055	1,028	11.4%	9,100
12/13	4,765	340	7.1%	8,200
Annual Growth	**11.7%**	**—**	**—**	**0.9%**

2017 Year-End Financials

Debt ratio: 28.06%
Return on equity: (-1.12%)
Cash ($ mil.): 2,153
Current ratio: 2.27
Long-term debt ($ mil.): 4,878

No. of shares (mil.): 351
Dividends
  Yield: 0.0%
  Payout: —
Market value ($ mil.): 9,008

	STOCK PRICE ($) FY Close	P/E High/Low	Earnings	PER SHARE ($) Dividends	Book Value
12/17	25.66	—	(0.31)	0.60	27.40
12/16	29.33	37 26	0.85	1.10	27.37
12/15	27.59	19 10	2.78	1.08	27.04
12/14	45.65	19 15	2.68	1.00	29.12
12/13	47.27	77 51	0.80	1.00	26.53
Annual Growth	**(14.2%)**	**—**	**—**	**(12.0%)**	**0.8%**

Motorola Solutions Inc

Do you copy? and "Roger that" might be snippets of conversation heard over two-way radios and other devices made by Motorola Solutions. The company's radios and wireless broadband products are used by government public safety and first-responder agencies for communications and personnel deployment. Commercial and industrial customers use products from Motorola to stay in touch with mobile work forces. Besides two-way radios the company makes vehicle-mounted radios body cameras headsets and other devices and develops software systems to connect them. Some 60% of sales are to customers in the US. Motorola Solutions goes back to the late 1920s when the company made radios for police cars.

Operations

Motorola's Products segment offers a communications portfolio of infrastructure devices accessories software and systems and accounts for about 60% of sales. Among the company?s device offerings are two-way portable radios and vehicle-mounted radios microphones batteries earpieces headsets and software. In its Systems unit (part of Products) Motorola also offers radio network and central processing software base stations consoles and repeaters.

The Services segment which accounts for the remainder of sales is composed of several units. Integration services offers implementation and integration of systems devices software and applications. Managed & Support services includes repair technical support and hardware maintenance. iDEN (Integrated Digital Enhanced Network) services is the company?s proprietary push-to-talk technology.

Geographic Reach

Motorola Solutions operates throughout the world but the US is its biggest market accounting for about 60% of sales. The UK the only other single geographic market reported by the company contributes about 10% of sales. Motorola runs major facilities for manufacturing and distribution in the US and Germany. The company outsources about a quarter of its manufacturing to third-parties outside the US.

Sales and Marketing

Motorola Solutions sells through an in-house sales operation that directly approaches its largest accounts and through channel partners for other accounts. Primary customers are government public safety first-responder agencies and municipalities. Other important customers are commercial and industrial companies that operate private communications networks and manage mobile work forces.

Motorola?s biggest customers are the US federal government and the Home Office of the UK which each account for just under 10% of sales.

Financial Performance

Motorola Solutions? revenue is on a two-year upswing after a four years of falling sales.

In 2017 Motorola Solutions posted a 6% revenue increase to about $6.4 billion from 2016 from growth in the Products and Services segments across all geographies. Within the Products segment Systems sales grew in the Americas while Devices sales rose in every region. The increase in Services was aided by the Airwave Interexport Spillman Technologies and Kodiak Networks acquisitions.

Motorola Solutions lost about $155 million in 2017 as opposed to a $560 million profit in 2016. The loss came from an $874 million charge due to the US Tax Cuts and Jobs Act of 2017. Income before taxes was about $1 billion in 2017 and $844 million in 2016.

Motorola Solutions closed 2017 with about $1.3 billion in cash about $240 million more than 2016. The company had lower acquisition costs and capital expenditures in 2017 from the year before.

Strategy

Motorola Solutions is moving to expand its recurring revenue stream from managed and support services and infrastructure- and software-as-a-service offerings. The company is developing and selling cloud-first Software-as-a-Service (SaaS) products and on-premise products.

Motorola Solutions is a partner with AT&T in FirstNet a nationwide network connecting first responders. Motorola is to supply equipment to the effort which could add $20 million-$40 million in revenue in 2018.

Acquisitions play an important part in Motorola Solutions? growth plans. It acquired Avigilon Corp. a developer of video security products to enhance offerings that capture and analyze video.

In 2017 the company moved to strengthen its software business in North America with the agreement to acquire of Airbus DS Communications from Airbus SE. The deal is to enable Motorola to create a full suite of 911 services that include call routing call taking records management and dispatch for agencies of all sizes.

Diminished government spending in the UK as part of austerity measures put in place after the Great Recession could limit purchases of Motorola Solutions' public safety equipment. Economic uncertainty also surrounds the UK's departure from the European Union as an economic partner.

Mergers and Acquisitions

Motorola Solutions acquired Avigilon a developer of advanced video surveillance and analytics tools for $1 billion in 2018. Avigilon's products include video analytics network video management software and hardware surveillance cameras and access control tools for commercial and government customers. Motorola is adding Avigilon's products to its public safety products enhancing their video capabilities.

In 2018 Motorola Solutions acquired Airbus DS Communications from Airbus SE which allows Motorola to expand its software for 911 services in North America. Terms were not disclosed.

The company acquired Interexport a provider of managed and support services for communications systems for government agencies public safety and enterprise customers in Chile in another 2017 transaction. The deal boosts Motorola?s Managed & Support Services business and expands operations in Latin America. Interexport was expected to add about $50 million in revenue in 2017. Terms were not disclosed.

In 2016 Motorola acquired Guardian Digital Communications Holdings Limited (GCDL) a holding company of Airwave for about $1 billion. The deal brought Motorola the largest private operator of a public safety network in the world delivering voice and data communications to more than 300 public service agencies in Great Britain. The acquisition expands Motorola's managed and support services business and its footprint in Europe.

In 2016 Motorola acquired Spillman Technologies a provider of comprehensive law enforcement and public safety software solutions for $217 million. The acquisition expands its smart public safety portfolio and provides agencies of all sizes with a full suite of solutions for the command center.

EXECUTIVES

Chairman And Ceo, Gregory Q. (Greg) Brown, age 59, $1,250,000 total compensation

Evp Strategy And Innovation, Eduardo F. Conrado, age 51, $448,750 total compensation

Evp Products And Services, Bruce W. Brda, age 57, $550,769 total compensation

Evp And Cfo, Gino A. Bonanotte, age 54, $645,385 total compensation

Evp General Counsel And Chief Administrative Officer, Mark S. Hacker, age 47, $526,337 total compensation

Evp Worldwide Sales, John P. (Jack) Malloy, age 47, $497,615 total compensation

Executive Vice President President Global Custo, Joseph M Guglielmi

Vice President Of Environment Health And Safety, Jodi Shapiro

Vice President Of Sales, Edward Fuerst

Vice President Astro Subscriber Products, Steve Young

Svp U.s. And Canada, Jim Mears

Vice President Records And Evidence Systems, Alam Ali

Vice President, Fernando Bonilla

Auditors: KPMG LLP

LOCATIONS

HQ: Motorola Solutions Inc
500 West Monroe Street, Chicago, IL 60661
Phone: 847 576-5000   **Fax:** 847 576-3477
Web: www.motorolasolutions.com

2017 Sales

	$ mil.	% of total
US	3,725	58
UK	558	9
Other countries	2,097	33
Total	**6,380**	**100**

PRODUCTS/OPERATIONS

2017 Sales

	$ mil.	% of total
Products	3,772	59
Services	2,608	41
Total	**6,380**	**100**

Selected Products and Services

Devices
Mobile computers
Mobile-to-mobile wireless modules
Public safety LTE infrastructure devices and services (handheld USB modem vehicle modem)
Radio-frequency identification products (RFID) and accessories
Two-way radios and pagers
Two-way radio accessories
Networks
Mobile broadband (public safety LTE)
Private broadband networks
Wireless broadband networks

Services

Enterprise
Enterprise video solutions
Integrated enterprise communications
Managed network infrastructure
Managed security and compliance
Supply chain visibility solutions
Government and Public Safety
Advanced video security systems
Complex network design and integration
Interoperability and unified communications
Next-generation command and control
Public safety managed services
Software
Application development framework
Mobility software
Network design software
Public sector applications
Support and help desk applications
Systems
Dispatch systems
Enterprise voice systems
SCADA Systems (real-time facilities monitoring and control)

COMPETITORS

Airbus Group	Intergraph
Alcatel-Lucent	Intermec
Cisco Systems	JVC KENWOOD
EF Johnson	Sepura
Technologies	Tri-Tech
Harris Corp.	West Corporation
Honeywell	
International	

HISTORICAL FINANCIALS

Company Type: Public

Income Statement

FYE: December 31

	REVENUE ($ mil.)	NET INCOME ($ mil.)	NET PROFIT MARGIN	EMPLOYEES
12/17	6,380	(155)	—	15,000
12/16	6,038	560	9.3%	14,000
12/15	5,695	610	10.7%	14,000
12/14	5,881	1,299	22.1%	15,000
12/13	8,696	1,099	12.6%	21,000
Annual Growth	**(7.5%)**	**—**		**(8.1%)**

2017 Year-End Financials

Debt ratio: 54.47%	No. of shares (mil.): 161
Return on equity: —	Dividends
Cash ($ mil.): 1,268	Yield: 0.0%
Current ratio: 1.35	Payout: —
Long-term debt ($ mil.): 4,419	Market value ($ mil.): 14,563

	STOCK PRICE ($)	P/E	PER SHARE ($)		
	FY Close	High/Low	Earnings	Dividends	Book Value
12/17	90.34	— —	(0.95)	1.93	(10.81)
12/16	82.89	25 18	3.24	1.70	(5.85)
12/15	68.45	24 19	3.02	1.43	(0.61)
12/14	67.08	13 11	5.29	1.30	12.44
12/13	67.50	16 13	4.06	1.14	14.38
Annual Growth	7.6%	— —	—	14.1%	—

Murphy USA Inc

It may not be the biggest but Murphy USA is flexing its muscles in the US gas station market. Murphy USA (a former operating unit of Murphy Oil) markets refined products through its network of branded gasoline stations and convenience stores customers and unbranded wholesale customers in more than 25 Southern and Midwestern US states to more than 1.6 million customers. The company's more than 1400 retail gas stations (more than 1150 of which are in Wal-Mart Super-center parking lots) sell gas under the Murphy USA brand. It also operates about 300 Murphy Express locations and sells some 4 billion gallons of motor fuel through retail outlets.

Operations

The company markets retail motor fuel products and convenience merchandise through its own chain of retail stations almost all of which are in close proximity to Wal-Mart stores. Its business also includes product supply and wholesale assets such as product distribution terminals and pipelines.

Petroleum product sales account for almost 80% of the company's total revenues.

Geographic Reach

Murphy USA has retail stations in more than 25 US states (primarily in the Southeast — Florida and Tennessee) as well as in the Southwest and the Midwest.

Texas Florida Georgia North Carolina and Tennessee together account for about 50% of its total retail outlets with Texas accounting for about 20%.

Sales and Marketing

They sell gasoline under the Murphy USA and Murphy Express brands.

Financial Performance

Murphy's revenue has gone down from 419 billion in 2012 to just under $13 billion in 2017. Net income has been more stable staying mostly above $200 million mark each year.

2017 revenue grew some 10% to $12.9 billion thanks to a 26 cents per gallon increase in retail fuel prices.

Net income grew 10% to $245 million the highest in the last six years mostly from the effects of the deferred tax benefits from the tax reform as well as improvement in the retail fuel margin. This was somewhat offset by a 11% increase in wholesale prices of motor fuel as well as increased in operating expenses due to addition of stores higher labor costs and benefits.

Murphy's cash holdings increased slightly from $154 million to $170 million. Operating activities brought in $284 million. Investment utilized $262 million mostly in purchase of property and plants while a further $5 million went towards financing activities.

Strategy

A strong in-store merchandise sales and fuel distribution sales forecast for 2018 means Murphy

USA is well poised for a profitable year despite rising fuel prices. According to the National Association of Convenience Stores (NACS) convenience stores ended 2017 on pace for a 15th straight year of record in-store sales and a 4th straight year of $10 billion-plus in pretax profits.

At Murphy USA sales in first quarter 2018 was up 20% compared to the year before. In 2018 the company also gained $35 million in settlement for the 2010 Deepwater Horizon oil spill. The company has built retail gas stations at Wal-Mart Supercenters and at other standalone locations as a part of an independent growth plan launched in 2016. The convenience store has some 1500 locations consisting of 1158 Murphy USA sites and 290 Murphy Express sites. It plans to build 30 more in 2018.

The company also focuses on improving its infrastructure to lower overhead costs and on long-term investment. It plans to continue to focus its product supply and wholesale efforts on activities that enhance its ability to be a low-price retail fuel leader by optimizing its fuel supply contracts to capitalize on market dynamics whenever possible and minimizing physical product supply and wholesale asset ownership.

Company Background

Boosting its customer offerings in 2010 the company teamed up with Western Union signing a deal to offer online money transfer services at its Murphy USA gas stations and Murphy Express convenience stores across the country.

As part of its former parent's decision to exit the refining business in 2011 MUSA sold its Superior Wisconsin refinery to Calumet Specialty Products Partners for $475 million. It also sold its refinery in Meraux Louisiana to Valero Energy for $625 million. The divestitures transformed MUSA into a pure gas station/convenience store company.

In 2013 Murphy Oil completed the spin-off of its US retail marketing business into an independent public company — Murphy USA Inc. The spin-off was achieved through the distribution to Murphy Oil's shareholders of one share of Murphy USA common stock for every four shares of Murphy Oil stock. It holds through its subsidiaries the US retail marketing business that was separated from its former parent company plus certain ethanol production facilities and other assets and liabilities of Murphy Oil that supported the activities of the US retail marketing operations.

In an effort to exit non-core businesses in the fall of 2013 the company sold underperforming subsidiary Hankinson Renewable Energy LLC (which owns and operates the Hankinson North Dakota ethanol plant) to Guardian Hankinson LLC for $173 million.

EXECUTIVES

Evp And Cfo, Mindy K. West, age 49, $546,083 total compensation
Svp Retail Operations And Support, Marn K. Cheng, age 52, $382,627 total compensation
President And Ceo, R. Andrew Clyde, age 54, $991,667 total compensation
Svp Marketing, Robert J. (Rob) Chumley, $116,667 total compensation
Vice President And Controller, Donnie Smith
Chairman, R. Madison Murphy, age 60
Auditors: KPMG LLP

LOCATIONS

HQ: Murphy USA Inc
200 Peach Street, El Dorado, AR 71730-5836
Phone: 870 875-7600
Web: www.murphyusa.com

2016 Stores

States	no. of stores
Texas	294
Florida	120
Georgia	94
Tennessee	92
North Carolina	86
Alabama	76
Louisiana	75
Arkansas	68
Mississippi	55
South Carolina	56
Oklahoma	51
Missouri	48
Kentucky	47
Ohio	44
Indiana	38
Illinois	37
Michigan	27
Iowa	22
Virginia	22
New Mexico	12
Colorado	12
Minnesota	9
Kansas	5
Utah	4
Nebraska	3
Nevada	2
Total	**1,401**

PRODUCTS/OPERATIONS

2016 Sales

	$ mil.	% of total
Petroleum product sales	9,070	78
Merchandise sales	2,338	20
Other operating revenue	185	2
Total	**11,594**	**100**

COMPETITORS

7-Eleven	Hess Corporation
Alon Brands	QuikTrip
Chevron	Racetrac Petroleum
ConocoPhillips	Royal Dutch Shell
Couche-Tard	Valero Energy
Exxon Mobil	

HISTORICAL FINANCIALS

Company Type: Public

Income Statement

FYE: December 31

	REVENUE ($ mil.)	NET INCOME ($ mil.)	NET PROFIT MARGIN	EMPLOYEES
12/17	12,826	245	1.9%	9,600
12/16	11,594	221	1.9%	9,100
12/15	12,699	176	1.4%	9,800
12/14	17,209	243	1.4%	9,450
12/13	18,083	235	1.3%	8,250
Annual Growth	(8.2%)	1.1%	—	3.9%

2017 Year-End Financials

Debt ratio: 37.78%
Return on equity: 34.17%
Cash ($ mil.): 170
Current ratio: 1.15
Long-term debt ($ mil.): 860
No. of shares (mil.): 34
Dividends
Yield: —
Payout: —
Market value ($ mil.): 2,740

	STOCK PRICE ($)	P/E	PER SHARE ($)		
	FY Close	High/Low	Earnings	Dividends	Book Value
12/17	80.36	12 9	6.78	0.00	21.66
12/16	61.47	14 10	5.59	0.00	18.87
12/15	60.74	18 12	4.02	0.00	19.01
12/14	68.86	13 7	5.26	0.00	18.79
12/13	41.56	9 7	5.02	0.00	14.04
Annual Growth	17.9%	— —	7.8%	—	11.4%

MUTUALBANK

EXECUTIVES

Chb, Will Davis
Ceo*, David Heeter
Pres-Coo*, Pat Botts
SEC*, Rosalee Petro
Cfo*, Chris Cook
Director, R Don Roberts
Vice President, Ralph Spencer Jr
Regional President, Charles Viater
Administrative Assistant, Meleah Perkins
Customer Staff, Shari Ash
Manager, Todd Yarbrough

LOCATIONS

HQ: MUTUALBANK
110 E CHARLES ST, MUNCIE, IN 473052468
Phone: 765 747-2800
Web: WWW.BANKWITHMUTUAL.COM

HISTORICAL FINANCIALS

Company Type: Private

Income Statement   FYE: December 31

	ASSETS ($ mil.)	NET INCOME ($ mil.)	INCOME AS % OF ASSETS	EMPLOYEES
12/17	1,585	11	0.8%	309
12/16	1,551	12	0.8%	—
12/15	1,477	12	0.9%	—
12/14	1,423	11	0.8%	—
Annual Growth	3.7%	1.3%	—	—

2017 Year-End Financials

Debt ratio: ——
Return on equity: 15.60%
Cash ($ mil.): 25
Current ratio: —
Long-term debt ($ mil.): —

Dividends
Yield: —
Payout: —
Market value ($ mil.): —

MutualFirst Financial Inc

EXECUTIVES

Senior Vice President Business Banking Of Mutualbank, Christopher Caldwell
Vice President Mutual Federal Savings Bank, Shayne Nagy
Vice President, Judy Widmer
Vice President, Scott Taylor
Assistant Vice President, Susan Smith
Vice President, James Tinkey
Vice President, Kathy Balser
Vice President Chief Information Secur, Bonita Ramirez
Vice President Client Relationship Manager Elkhart County, Vince Turner
Vice President, Kathy Sears
Vice President Mutual Federal Savings Bank, Dorothy Douglass
Auditors: BKD, LLP

LOCATIONS

HQ: MutualFirst Financial Inc
110 E. Charles Street, Muncie, IN 47305-2419
Phone: 765 747-2800
Web: www.bankwithmutual.com

COMPETITORS

Ameriana Bancorp	Huntington Bancshares
Fifth Third	Old National Bancorp
First Financial Bancorp	PNC Financial
First Merchants	STAR Financial Group
German American Bancorp	

HISTORICAL FINANCIALS

Company Type: Public

Income Statement   FYE: December 31

	ASSETS ($ mil.)	NET INCOME ($ mil.)	INCOME AS % OF ASSETS	EMPLOYEES
12/17	1,588	12	0.8%	422
12/16	1,553	13	0.9%	442
12/15	1,478	12	0.8%	445
12/14	1,424	10	0.8%	438
12/13	1,391	9	0.7%	412
Annual Growth	3.4%	7.6%	—	0.6%

2017 Year-End Financials

Debt ratio: 0.27%
Return on equity: 8.48%
Cash ($ mil.): 29
Current ratio: —
Long-term debt ($ mil.): —

No. of shares (mil.): 7
Dividends
Yield: 0.0%
Payout: 40.2%
Market value ($ mil.): 285

	STOCK PRICE ($) FY Close	P/E High/Low	Earnings	PER SHARE ($) Dividends	Book Value
12/17	38.55	24 18	1.64	0.66	20.34
12/16	33.10	19 13	1.76	0.58	19.12
12/15	24.80	15 12	1.62	0.48	18.46
12/14	21.88	15 11	1.46	0.32	17.63
12/13	17.13	16 10	1.09	0.24	15.69
Annual Growth	22.5%	— —	10.8%	28.8%	6.7%

MVB Financial Corp

EXECUTIVES

Chief Executive Officer; President, Larry Nazza
Auditors: Dixon Hughes Goodman LLP

LOCATIONS

HQ: MVB Financial Corp
301 Virginia Avenue, Fairmont, WV 26554
Phone: 304 363-4800
Web: www.mvbbanking.com

HISTORICAL FINANCIALS

Company Type: Public

Income Statement   FYE: December 31

	ASSETS ($ mil.)	NET INCOME ($ mil.)	INCOME AS % OF ASSETS	EMPLOYEES
12/17	1,534	7	0.5%	—
12/16	1,418	12	0.9%	382
12/15	1,384	6	0.5%	371
12/14	1,110	2	0.2%	324
12/13	987	4	0.4%	274
Annual Growth	11.7%	17.2%	—	—

2017 Year-End Financials

Debt ratio: 2.18%
Return on equity: 5.12%
Cash ($ mil.): 35
Current ratio: —
Long-term debt ($ mil.): —

No. of shares (mil.): 10
Dividends
Yield: 0.0%
Payout: 14.7%
Market value ($ mil.): 210

	STOCK PRICE ($) FY Close	P/E High/Low	Earnings	PER SHARE ($) Dividends	Book Value
12/17	20.10	29 18	0.68	0.10	14.38
12/16	12.80	10 7	1.31	0.08	14.57
12/15	13.10	20 16	0.76	0.08	14.23
12/14	14.99	164 65	0.22	0.08	13.71
12/13	33.20	66 40	0.57	0.08	12.28
Annual Growth	(11.8%)	— —	4.5%	7.5%	4.0%

NASB Financial Inc

EXECUTIVES

Vice President Director Chief Credit Officer, Paul Thomas
Vice President, Donna Williams
Vice President Internal Audit Director, Rick P Speciale
Auditors: BKD, LLP

LOCATIONS

HQ: NASB Financial Inc
12498 South 71 Highway, Grandview, MO 64030
Phone: 816 765-2200   **Fax:** 816 761-4113
Web: www.nasb.com

COMPETITORS

Bank of America	Guaranty Federal
Commerce Bancshares	U.S. Bancorp
Dickinson Financial	UMB Financial

HISTORICAL FINANCIALS

Company Type: Public

Income Statement   FYE: September 30

	ASSETS ($ mil.)	NET INCOME ($ mil.)	INCOME AS % OF ASSETS	EMPLOYEES
09/17	2,062	29	1.4%	—
09/16	1,949	22	1.1%	—
09/15	1,530	21	1.4%	—
09/14	1,168	16	1.4%	—
09/13	1,144	27	2.4%	463
Annual Growth	15.9%	1.6%	—	—

2017 Year-End Financials

Debt ratio: 1.25%
Return on equity: 13.14%
Cash ($ mil.): 43
Current ratio: —
Long-term debt ($ mil.): —

No. of shares (mil.): 7
Dividends
Yield: 0.0%
Payout: 30.6%
Market value ($ mil.): 267

	STOCK PRICE ($) FY Close	P/E High/Low	Earnings	PER SHARE ($) Dividends	Book Value
09/17	36.11	10 8	3.98	1.22	31.55
09/16	33.75	11 9	3.02	0.98	28.92
09/15	29.00	11 8	2.90	2.80	26.66
09/14	23.70	14 9	2.13	0.80	26.64
09/13	27.43	8 6	3.51	0.00	24.85
Annual Growth	7.1%	— —	3.2%	—	6.1%

National Bank Holdings Corp

National Bank Holdings is the holding company for NBH Bank which operates nearly 100 branches in four south and central US states under various brands including: Bank Midwest in Kansas and Missouri Community Banks of Colorado in Colorado and Hillcrest Bank in Texas. Targeting small to medium-sized businesses and consumers the banks offer traditional checking and savings accounts as well as commercial and residential mortgages agricultural loans and commercial loans. The bank boasted $4.7 billion in assets at the end of 2015 including $2.6 billion in loans and $3.8 billion in deposits. Over 80% of its total revenue is made up of interest income.

Operations

About 63% of the bank's total revenue came from loan interest (including fees) during 2015 while another 19% came from interest on its investment securities. The rest of its revenue came from service charges (7%) bank card fees (5%) and other miscellaneous income sources.

Geographic Reach

National Bank Holdings had a network of 97 banking centers in four states at the end of 2015 with more than half of those in Colorado a third in Missouri nearly a dozen branches in Kansas and two branches in Texas.

Sales and Marketing

The bank serves small- to medium-sized businesses and consumers via its network of banking locations and through online and mobile banking products. It spent $4.3 million on advertising during 2015 down from $4.6 million and $5.3 million in 2014 and 2013 respectively.

Financial Performance

The group's annual revenues and profits have been trending downward over the past few years as it has been selling off branches and loan business to concentrate on the geographic markets and loan types where it carries the most expertise.

National Bank Holdings' revenue rebounded 5% to $192.86 million during 2015 mostly as it earned $21 million in FDIC-related income related to lower indemnification amortization increased FDIC loss-share income and a $5 million gain on an FDIC loss-share agreement termination.

Despite revenue growth in 2015 the group's net income plummeted 47% to $4.9 million mostly on higher loan loss provisions which climbed more than $6.2 million during the year as it increased its specific reserves on non 310-30 loans. National Bank Holdings' operations used $37.65 million compared to just $2.76 million in cash during 2014 mostly after adjusting its earnings for non-cash items mostly related to a decrease in net amounts due to the FDIC.

Strategy

National Bank Holdings has been trimming its branch count in recent years to focus on serving clients through full-service banking centers across its four chief markets of Colorado Kansas Missouri and Texas as well as through online and mobile banking channels. Toward this end in 2013 the bank began integrating its limited-service retirement center locations into its full-service banking centers while also exiting its limited presence in California (its banks there had operated under the Community Banks of California banner).

Meanwhile the regional community bank continues to selectively acquire smaller banks and complementary financial companies that serve small- and medium-sized businesses to grow its loan and deposit business.

Mergers and Acquisitions

In August 2015 National Bank Holdings bought $142 million-asset Pine River Bank in Colorado along with its $64 million in loans and $130 million in deposits for $9.5 million in cash.

Company Background

Formed in 2009 National Bank Holdings went public in 2012. Prior to its filing National Bank Holdings was minority-owned by a number of private shareholders and corporate entities including Taconic Capital Advisors Wellington Management and Paulson & Co.

EXECUTIVES

Chairman President And Ceo, G. Timothy (Tim) Laney, age 58, $500,000 total compensation
Chief Of Enterprise Technology & Integration And Nbh Bank N.a. Midwest/ Texas Division President, Thomas M. (Tom) Metzger, $300,000 total compensation
Chief Financial Officer, Brian F. Lilly, age 59, $295,705 total compensation
Chief Risk Officer, Richard U. Newfield, age 57, $300,000 total compensation
Board Member, Burney Warren
Board Member, Robert Dean
Board Member, Arthur Zeile
Auditors: KPMG LLP

LOCATIONS

HQ: National Bank Holdings Corp
 7800 East Orchard Road, Suite 300, Greenwood Village, CO 80111
Phone: 720 529-3336

PRODUCTS/OPERATIONS

2015 Sales

	% of total
Interest and dividend income:	
Interest and fees on loans	63
Interest and dividends on investment securities	18
Dividends on non-marketable securities	1
Interest on interest-bearing bank deposits	-
Total	82
Non-interest income:	
Service charges	7
Bank card fees	5
Gain on sales of mortgages net	1
Bank-owned life insurance income	1
Other non-interest income	2
Bargain purchase gain	1
Gain on previously charged-off acquired loans	-
OREO related write-ups and other income	1
FDIC indemnification asset amortization net of gain on termination	
FDIC loss sharing income (expense)	-
Total Non-Interest Income	18
Total	100

COMPETITORS

BBVA Compass Bancshares
Bank of America
Bank of the West
Capitol Federal Financial
Central Bancompany
Commerce Bancshares
Enterprise Financial Services
FirstBank Holding Company
JPMorgan Chase
KeyCorp
U.S. Bancorp
UMB Financial
Wells Fargo
Zions Bancorporation

HISTORICAL FINANCIALS

Company Type: Public

Income Statement

FYE: December 31

	ASSETS ($ mil.)	NET INCOME ($ mil.)	INCOME AS % OF ASSETS	EMPLOYEES
12/17	4,843	14	0.3%	926
12/16	4,573	23	0.5%	1,004
12/15	4,683	4	0.1%	1,042
12/14	4,819	9	0.2%	1,056
12/13	4,014	6	0.1%	1,100
Annual Growth	(0.4%)	20.4%	—	(4.4%)

2017 Year-End Financials

Debt ratio: —
Return on equity: 2.73%
Cash ($ mil.): 257
Current ratio: —
Long-term debt ($ mil.): —
No. of shares (mil.): 26
Dividends
 Yield: 0.0%
 Payout: 64.1%
Market value ($ mil.): 872

	STOCK PRICE ($) FY Close	P/E High/Low	Earnings	PER SHARE ($) Dividends	Book Value
12/17	32.43	68 56	0.53	0.34	19.81
12/16	31.89	40 23	0.79	0.22	20.32
12/15	21.37	166 127	0.14	0.20	20.34
12/14	19.41	97 84	0.22	0.20	20.43
12/13	21.40	155 126	0.14	0.20	19.99
Annual Growth	11.0%	— —	39.5%	14.2%	(0.2%)

National Commerce Corp

Auditors: Porter Keadle Moore, LLC

LOCATIONS

HQ: National Commerce Corp
 600 Luckie Drive, Suite 350, Birmingham, AL 35223
Phone: 205 313-8100
Web: www.nationalbankofcommerce.com

HISTORICAL FINANCIALS

Company Type: Public

Income Statement

FYE: December 31

	ASSETS ($ mil.)	NET INCOME ($ mil.)	INCOME AS % OF ASSETS	EMPLOYEES
12/17	2,737	20	0.7%	433
12/16	1,950	17	0.9%	297
12/15	1,763	9	0.5%	289
12/14	1,138	5	0.5%	235
12/13	791	4	0.5%	—
Annual Growth	36.4%	49.6%	—	—

2017 Year-End Financials

Debt ratio: 0.90%
Return on equity: 6.45%
Cash ($ mil.): 235
Current ratio: —
Long-term debt ($ mil.): —
No. of shares (mil.): 14
Dividends
 Yield: —
 Payout: —
Market value ($ mil.): 595

	STOCK PRICE ($) FY Close	P/E High/Low	Earnings	PER SHARE ($) Dividends	Book Value
12/17	40.25	30 24	1.41	0.00	26.55
12/16	37.15	23 13	1.61	0.00	21.01
12/15	25.05	27 20	1.02	0.00	19.33
Annual Growth	12.6%	— —	8.4%	—	8.3%

National General Holdings Corp

Auditors: Ernst & Young LLP

LOCATIONS

HQ: National General Holdings Corp
59 Maiden Lane, 38th Floor, New York, NY 10038
Phone: 212 380-9500
Web: www.nationalgeneral.com

HISTORICAL FINANCIALS

Company Type: Public

Income Statement — FYE: December 31

	ASSETS ($ mil.)	NET INCOME ($ mil.)	INCOME AS % OF ASSETS	EMPLOYEES
12/17	8,439	105	1.3%	7,570
12/16	7,244	172	2.4%	6,930
12/15	5,563	142	2.6%	4,630
12/14	4,439	102	2.3%	2,980
12/13	2,837	42	1.5%	2,029
Annual Growth	31.3%	25.8%	—	39.0%

2017 Year-End Financials

Debt ratio: 8.46%
Return on equity: 5.54%
Cash ($ mil.): 292
Current ratio: —
Long-term debt ($ mil.): —

No. of shares (mil.): 106
Dividends
  Yield: 0.0%
  Payout: 23.5%
Market value ($ mil.): 2,096

	STOCK PRICE ($) FY Close	P/E High/Low	Earnings	PER SHARE ($) Dividends	Book Value
12/17	19.64	36 23	0.68	0.16	18.08
12/16	24.99	18 13	1.37	0.14	17.79
12/15	21.86	18 13	1.27	0.09	14.34
12/14	18.61	18 12	1.07	0.05	11.34
Annual Growth	1.4%	— —	(10.7%)	33.7%	12.4%

National Oilwell Varco Inc

EXECUTIVES

Chb-Pres-Ceo, Clay C Williams
Sr V Pres-Cfo*, Jose A Bayardo
Sr V Pres-Sec-Gen Counsel*, Craig L Weinstock
V Pres-Corp Controller-Cao*, Scott K Duff
Vice President Sales Operation, Jim Stephen
Electrical Design Engineer, Marius Bustad
Inside Sales, Morna Cox
Director of Finance Middle Eas, Ramkumar Vaidyanathan
Manager Engineering, Ricardo Mizrahi
Engineering Manager, Sabine Vries
Project Documentation Supervis, Sharon Robinson
Auditors: Ernst & Young LLP

LOCATIONS

HQ: National Oilwell Varco Inc
7909 Parkwood Circle Drive, Houston, TX 77036-6565
Phone: 713 346-7500
Web: www.nov.com

COMPETITORS

Aker Solutions	Halliburton
Baker Hughes	McDermott
Bechtel	Schlumberger
Cameron International	Weatherford
FMC Technologies	International
GE Oil	

HISTORICAL FINANCIALS

Company Type: Public

Income Statement — FYE: December 31

	REVENUE ($ mil.)	NET INCOME ($ mil.)	NET PROFIT MARGIN	EMPLOYEES
12/17	7,304	(237)	—	31,889
12/16	7,251	(2,412)	—	36,627
12/15	14,757	(769)	—	50,197
12/14	21,440	2,502	11.7%	63,642
12/13	22,869	2,327	10.2%	63,779
Annual Growth	(24.8%)	—	—	(15.9%)

2017 Year-End Financials

Debt ratio: 13.42%
Return on equity: (-1.69%)
Cash ($ mil.): 1,437
Current ratio: 3.07
Long-term debt ($ mil.): 2,706

No. of shares (mil.): 380
Dividends
  Yield: 0.0%
  Payout: —
Market value ($ mil.): 13,691

	STOCK PRICE ($) FY Close	P/E High/Low	Earnings	PER SHARE ($) Dividends	Book Value
12/17	36.02	— —	(0.63)	0.20	37.08
12/16	37.44	— —	(6.41)	0.61	36.82
12/15	33.49	— —	(1.99)	1.84	43.60
12/14	65.53	15 11	5.82	1.64	49.39
12/13	79.53	15 12	5.44	0.91	51.89
Annual Growth	(18.0%)	— —	—	(31.5%)	(8.1%)

National Western Life Group Inc

Auditors: BKD LLP

LOCATIONS

HQ: National Western Life Group Inc
10801 N. MOPAC EXPY BLDG 3, Austin, TX 78759-5415
Phone: 512 836-1010
Web: www.nwlgi.com

HISTORICAL FINANCIALS

Company Type: Public

Income Statement — FYE: December 31

	ASSETS ($ mil.)	NET INCOME ($ mil.)	INCOME AS % OF ASSETS	EMPLOYEES
12/17	12,225	110	0.9%	279
12/16	11,894	100	0.8%	265
12/15	11,612	98	0.8%	261
12/14	11,351	105	0.9%	—
12/13	0	96	—	—
Annual Growth	—	3.5%		

2017 Year-End Financials

Debt ratio: —
Return on equity: 6.21%
Cash ($ mil.): 217
Current ratio: —
Long-term debt ($ mil.): —

No. of shares (mil.): 3
Dividends
  Yield: 0.0%
  Payout: 1.1%
Market value ($ mil.): 1,204

	STOCK PRICE ($) FY Close	P/E High/Low	Earnings	PER SHARE ($) Dividends	Book Value
12/17	331.02	12 9	31.23	0.36	503.88
12/16	310.80	11 7	28.53	0.36	473.53
12/15	251.94	10 8	27.82	0.36	443.32
12/14	269.25	6 5	44.78	0.00	428.01
12/13	223.55	5 4	40.80	0.00	(0.00)
Annual Growth	10.3%	— —	—	(6.5%)	

Navient Corp

Navient is a new name for an old business — namely the loan management servicing and asset recovery unit of SLM Corp. (aka Sallie Mae). Navient services a $300 billion student loan portfolio composed of federal and private education loans issued to around 12 million customers. In addition to serving indebted former students Navient provides asset recovery services (collections) to the government higher education institutions and business clients. Navient manages the largest portfolio of Federal Family Education Loan Program (FFELP) loans as well as the largest portfolio of private education loans. Navient began life as an independent company through a strategic divestiture from Sallie Mae which still exists and continues to provide consumer loans.

Operations

Navient operates three business segments: two that own and collect interest on loans and one that services loans and provides loan processing services. The largest segment the Federal Family Education Loan Program (FFELP) brings in more than 50% of total revenue. It collects interest income from its $82 billion portfolio of FFELP loans and adds to its holdings by opportunistically buying FFELP loans from other servicers. More than 95% of FFELP loans are government guaranteed providing Navient a significant buffer against the financial impact of loan losses. Originations of FFELP loans no longer occur replaced with new programs headed by the US Department of Education.

Navient's Private Education Loans segment (more than 30% of revenue) buys finances and services private education loans while also collecting interest on a $23 billion portfolio of such loans. Legal constraints related to the spin-off from Sallie Mae prohibited Navient from originating new private education loans until early 2019.

Business Services (15% of revenue) generates revenue from loan & credit servicing collecting on delinquent loans (asset recovery) and business processing activities. The segment services the company's own FFELP loan portfolio as well as those from other institutions notably the US Department of Education which accounts for more than $300 billion in serviced loans. It also offers asset recovery services for loans and receivables for FFELP loan guarantors higher education institutions and federal state and municipal clients.

Broadly Navient makes about 85% of its revenue from interest income on its FFELP and private education loan portfolios while servicing revenue combined with asset recovery and business processing revenue accounts for another 15%.

Geographic Reach
Wilmington Delaware-based Navient operates throughout the US.

Most of the company's properties are loan servicing and collection centers in the New England and Midwestern regions with additional offices in Virginia Florida Texas and Tennessee. Its largest facility in Fishers Indiana houses 450000 sq. ft. of space representing more than 30% of all owned and leased space.

Sales and Marketing
Navient's sales and marketing model consists of building relationships with the institutions that originate loans – such as universities – as well as bidding for government contracts most notably with the US Department of Education with whom Navient has an existing significant contract through 2019.

The company also sells its services to federal state and local governments; regional authorities; courts; hospitals; health care organizations; and financial services companies.

Financial Performance
Navient's annual revenues and profits have been falling in recent years due to a decline in interest income as its education loans portfolio continues to shrink. At year-end 2017 FFELP loans amounted to $81.7 billion compared to $87.7 billion in 2016.

The company's revenue fell $316 million or 13% to $2.2 billion during 2017 on lower interest income on its shrinking and margin-falling portfolio of student loans as well as from a smaller contribution from gains on derivative and hedging activities.

Revenue declines and an increase in interest expense contributed to a 57% tumble in net income in 2017. Although Navient's debt decreased by about $6 billion between 2016 and 2017 the average interest rate on that debt rose from 2.14% to 2.67% enough to add more than $500 million of interest expense on the borrowings.

Cash and cash equivalents increased by $265 million to $1.5 billion in 2017. The company generated ample cash from customers making loan payments ($14.7 billion) with a further $1.2 billion in cash accumulated from operating activities. Cash uses went primarily to repaying its own borrowings and to acquiring $7.5 billion of education loans from other originators.

Strategy
While Navient's loan holdings generate a large and consistent cash flow from interest income its holdings are shrinking over time and therefore its revenue and income are declining. The company is hindered in that it was not permitted to originate new private student loans until January 2019 as part of its spin-off from Sallie Mae. Additionally the US government modified its student loan programs which precluded issuance of new FFELP loans. All US federal government student loans now originate through the US Department of Education.

Navient's overarching strategy includes both maintenance and growth. It seeks to maintain income streams from its portfolio of loan holdings and from servicing others' loans the latter being heavily dependent on its contracts with the US Department of Education. Keeping default rates low and collecting on delinquent loans are a major focus.

The company seeks to grow its business through opportunistically acquiring existing education loans and branching into new business service markets. It acquired nearly $7 billion in loans from JPMorgan Chase in 2017 for example. Its recent acquisitions of Duncan Solutions (2017) and Xtend Healthcare (2016) allow it to serve clients

in the health care toll road authorities and various public-sector markets. In early 2017 the company began collecting overdue US federal tax debts on behalf of the IRS.

A 2017 US Department of Education audit found that Navient may have deceptively steered borrowers into higher-cost repayment plans rather than discussing less costly options. That finding could support federal and state lawsuits against the firm that accuse Navient of boosting profits through unfair and abusive practices. Navient disputes the claims and has said that it is a scapegoat in an industry that has come under fire. Further it says it is not legally obligated to serve as a financial counselor. If Navient is found guilty of unfair practices it could be fined billions of dollars in damages. It could also be required to change the way it handles some 6 million borrowers' accounts.

Mergers and Acquisitions
In late 2017 Navient acquired online lender Earnest which specializes in refinancing student loans. Post-acquisition Earnest remained a distinct brand led by its existing management team. The purchase was important as it provides Navient with an entry to originating student loans.

Also in 2017 the company acquired Duncan Solutions a transportation revenue management firm for $80 million. That deal expanded Navient's municipal and toll relationships.

EXECUTIVES

President And Ceo, John F. (Jack) Remondi, age 55, $1,000,000 total compensation
Evp And Chief Decision Management Officer, Somsak Chivavibul, age 51, $379,999 total compensation
Evp Chief Legal Officer And Secretary, Mark L. Heleen, age 56, $369,357 total compensation
Evp And Chief Risk And Compliance Officer, Timothy (Tim) Hynes, age 49, $370,000 total compensation
Group President Business Processing Solutions, John Kane, age 49, $449,999 total compensation
Evp And Cio, Pat Lawicki
Group President Asset Management And Servicing, John F. (Jeff) Whorley, age 57, $449,999 total compensation
Evp And Cfo, Christian Lown, age 49
Senior Vice President Human Resources, Jon Kroehler
National Account Manager, Todd Newton
Vice President, Nancy Haas
Vice President Government Relations And Public Policy, Lucia Lebens
Vice President, Chris Tuten
Vice President Enterprise Architecture, Matthew Anderson
Executive Vice President And Chief Legal Officer, Mark L Heleen
Vice President, Stephen Tinney
Vice President Compliance Suppgovernance, Bill Brooks
Senior Vice President, Paul Mayer
Vice President; President, Brian Hill
Senior Vice President And Deputy General Counsel, Andrew G Wachtel
Vice President And Associate General Counsel, Matthew Sheldon
Chairman, William M. Diefenderfer, age 73
Board Member, Laura Unger
Board Member, Diane Gilleland
Board Member, Anna Cabral
Board Member, Jane Thompson
Board Member, John Adams
Board Member, Linda Mills
Auditors: KPMG LLP

LOCATIONS
HQ: Navient Corp
123 Justison Street, Wilmington, DE 19801
Phone: 302 283-8000
Web: www.navient.com

PRODUCTS/OPERATIONS

2017 Sales

	$ mil.	% of total
Interest		
FFELP loans	2,693	52
Private education loans	1,634	32
Other loans	13	-
Cash & investments	43	1
Non-interest		
Asset recovery & business processing	475	9
Servicing	290	6
Net gains on derivatives & hedging activities	22	-
Gains on sales of loans & investments	3	-
Other	9	-
Adjustments	(2974)	-
Total	**2,208**	**100**

COMPETITORS

Bank of America
Brazos Higher Education Service Corp.
Great Lakes Higher Education
Mohela
Nelnet
Pennsylvania Higher Education Assistance Agency
Sallie Mae
Texas Guaranteed

HISTORICAL FINANCIALS
Company Type: Public

Income Statement
FYE: December 31

	ASSETS ($ mil.)	NET INCOME ($ mil.)	INCOME AS % OF ASSETS	EMPLOYEES
12/17	114,991	292	0.3%	6,700
12/16	121,136	681	0.6%	6,773
12/15	134,112	997	0.7%	7,300
12/14	146,352	1,149	0.8%	6,200
12/13	159,543	1,418	0.9%	—
Annual Growth	(7.9%)	(32.6%)	—	—

2017 Year-End Financials

Debt ratio: 91.32%	No. of shares (mil.): 263
Return on equity: 8.16%	Dividends
Cash ($ mil.): 1,518	Yield: 0.0%
Current ratio: —	Payout: 61.5%
Long-term debt ($ mil.): —	Market value ($ mil.): 3,504

	STOCK PRICE ($) FY Close	P/E High/Low		Earnings	PER SHARE ($) Dividends	Book Value
12/17	13.32	16	11	1.04	0.64	13.13
12/16	16.43	8	4	2.12	0.64	12.72
12/15	11.45	8	4	2.61	0.64	11.42
12/14	21.61	8	6	2.69	0.45	10.45
Annual Growth	(11.4%)	—	— (21.1%)	9.2%	5.9%

Navigators Group Inc (The)

The Navigators Group writes specialty lines of insurance and reinsurance to clients whom it hopes are good navigators themselves. The company's various subsidiaries write marine liability and other lines of business primarily in the US and the UK. Its Navigators Insurance and Navigators Underwriting Agency (NUA) units specialize in ocean marine insurance including hull energy and cargo insurance as well as property insurance for inland marine and onshore energy concerns. Navigators Specialty primarily provides excess and surplus (high risk) lines. The firm's subsidiaries are also involved in professional liability especially directors' and officers' coverage as well as general liability for contractors. The Hartford Financial Services Group is buying Navigators for $2.1 billion.

Change in Company Type

In mid-2018 property/casualty insurer The Hartford agreed to buy Navigators adding international and specialty businesses to its operations. The deal will bring The Hartford a number of new lines of coverage as well as giving it a presence on the Lloyd's market.

Operations

In early 2015 Navigators realigned its reporting structure creating four primary segments that align with the types of coverage it writes: US Insurance International Insurance Global Reinsurance and Corporate.

Navigators' global product lines are distributed through a network of retail and wholesale brokers. In addition to its specialty property/casualty insurance and reinsurance policies the company and its subsidiaries provide catastrophe risk management services.

In the International Insurance segment NUA serves as a Lloyd's of London underwriting agency managing Lloyd's Syndicate 1221. The unit primarily underwrites marine and related lines of business along with offshore energy professional liability insurance and construction coverage for onshore energy businesses.

Geographic Reach

Outside its core markets of the US and the UK Navigators has operations in several European nations such as Belgium Denmark and Sweden mainly through NUA's activity on the European Lloyd's of London insurance exchange (via Lloyd's Syndicate 1221). The firm has also established offices in emerging markets such as Brazil and China.

Financial Performance

Navigators' revenue which has largely been on the rise for the past five years rose 12% to $1 billion in 2014 on higher net written premiums and investment income. Net written premiums increased 12.6% that year due to higher retention rates in the reinsurance business as well as growth in gross written property/casualty premiums.

Net income on the other hand has been more erratic than revenue. In 2014 it grew 50% to $95 million thanks primarily to Navigator's higher revenue. Cash flow from operations has been growing every year and in 2014 it rose 63% to $222 million.

Strategy

Navigators is focused on strengthening and controlling costs within its existing operations. At the same time Navigators is looking for opportunities to expand into new niche coverage areas and regions aiming for underserved commercial markets with high-value assets and low-frequency loss levels. In mid-2018 the company agreed to be acquired by US-based The Hartford Financial Services Group for $2.1 billion.

Mergers and Acquisitions

In late 2017 Navigators agreed to buy Belgian insurer ASCO-BDM which specializes in marine and industrial coverage. That purchase will further strengthen its operations in Europe

EXECUTIVES

President Ceo And Director And Chair Navigators Insurance And Navigators Management, Stanley A. (Stan) Galanski, age 59, $1,000,000 total compensation

Svp And Chief Underwriting Officer, H. Clay Bassett, age 52, $525,000 total compensation

President And Ceo Navigators Management Company Inc., Vincent C. Tizzio, age 51, $570,833 total compensation

President International Insurance, Michael J. Casella, age 57

President Navigators Specialty, Jeff L. Saunders, $412,500 total compensation

Evp And Cfo, Ciro M. DeFalco, age 62, $780,833 total compensation

Svp And Chief Marketing Officer, LoriAnn V. Lowery-Biggers, age 51

Managing Director Asia, Jon Doherty

President Navigators Technical Risk, Patrick J. Milner

Assistant Vice President, Susan Natt

Vice President And Group Controller, George Iacono

East Coast Zonal Vice President Environmental Division, Paul Dastis

Assistant Vice President, Kathleen Boswell

Vice President, Andrew Dicob

Senior Vice President, David Stevenson

Assistant Vice President, Joshua Elmore

Senior Vice President, Linda Schultz

Vice President, David Crudo

Assistant Vice President, Jaime Rodriguez

Vice President, Tracy Kiffer

Vice President Eastern And Central Regional Cargo Manager, Robert Ryan

Vice President E And S Primary Casualty, Jerry O'Neill

Senior Vice President Field Operations And Nyc Branch Manager, James Hutchinson

Senior Vice President Communications, Dudley Alex

Chairman, Terence N. Deeks, age 78

Auditors: KPMG LLP

LOCATIONS

HQ: Navigators Group Inc (The)
400 Atlantic Street, Stamford, CT 06901
Phone: 203 905-6090
Web: www.navg.com

PRODUCTS/OPERATIONS

2014 Gross Written premiums

	% of total
Insurance companies	75
Lloyd's Operations	25
Total	**100**

2014 Sales

	$ mil
% of total	
Net earned premiums	91
Net investment income	7
Net realized gains	1
Others	1
Total	**100**

Selected Subsidiaries

Millennium Underwriting Ltd. (UK)
Navigators A/S (Denmark)
Navigators Corporate Underwriters Ltd. (UK)
Navigators Holdings (UK) Ltd.
Navigators Insurance Company
Navigators Management Company Inc.
Navigators Management (UK) Limited
Navigators NV (Belgium)
Navigators Specialty Insurance Company
Navigators Underwriting Agency Ltd. (UK)
Navigators Underwriting Limited (UK)
NUAL AB (Sweden)

Selected Products and Services:Commercial Surety

Standard Transactional
Non Standard Transactional
Account
Program
Energy and Engineering
Onshore Energy
Offshore Energy
Construction
Operational Engineering
Excess Casualty
Umbrella & Excess (Wholesale Brokerage)
Umbrella & Excess (Retail Agency)
Environmental Casualty
Contractors Pollution Liability
Site Pollution Legal Liability
NP3 sm General & Environmental Liability (Mfg. & Distributors)
NP4 sm General Environmental & Professional Liability (Env'l Consultants)
Environmental Excess
Inland Marine
Commercial Output Policy
Construction
Specialty
Transportation
Management Liability
Directors & Officers Liability
Employment Practices Liability
Fiduciary Liability
Crime Liability
Nonprofit D & O Liability
Marine
Bluewater Hull
Brownwater Hull
Cargo
Specie
Transportation
Marine & Energy Liability
War
Protection & Indemnity
Primary Casualty
General Liability
NAVIGATORS RE
Accident & Health
Agriculture
Latin American & Caribbean
Professional Liability Reinsurance
Property & Casualty
Life Sciences
Global Package Solutions
Commercial Auto
Professional Liability
Lawyers Professional Liability
Accountants Professional Liability
Miscellaneous Professional Liability
Insurance Agents & Brokers E&O
Technology Media & Cyber Liability
Design Professionals Liability
Real Estate Professionals E&O

COMPETITORS

AIG
AXA Corporate Solutions
Allianz
Amica Mutual
Arch Insurance Group
Aspen Insurance
Berkshire Hathaway
CNA Financial
Global Indemnity
ProSight Specialty Insurance Group
RLI
Safeco
Specialty Underwriters' Alliance
Travelers Companies
White Mountains Insurance Group
XL Group plc
Zurich American

HISTORICAL FINANCIALS

Company Type: Public

Income Statement				FYE: December 31
	ASSETS ($ mil.)	NET INCOME ($ mil.)	INCOME AS % OF ASSETS	EMPLOYEES
12/17	5,224	40	0.8%	732
12/16	4,814	82	1.7%	683
12/15	4,584	81	1.8%	675
12/14	4,464	95	2.1%	651
12/13	4,160	63	1.5%	596
Annual Growth	5.8%	(10.6%)	—	5.3%

2017 Year-End Financials

Debt ratio: 5.05%	No. of shares (mil.): 29
Return on equity: 3.37%	Dividends
Cash ($ mil.): 67	Yield: 0.0%
Current ratio: —	Payout: 16.6%
Long-term debt ($ mil.): —	Market value ($ mil.): 1,437

	STOCK PRICE ($) FY Close	P/E High/Low		PER SHARE ($) Earnings	Dividends	Book Value
12/17	48.70	85	34	1.35	0.23	41.55
12/16	117.75	41	28	2.75	0.14	40.45
12/15	85.79	31	24	2.74	0.00	37.98
12/14	73.34	22	17	3.26	0.00	35.96
12/13	63.16	30	23	2.21	0.00	31.77
Annual Growth	(6.3%)	—	—	(11.6%)	—	6.9%

HISTORICAL FINANCIALS

Company Type: Public

Income Statement				FYE: October 31
	REVENUE ($ mil.)	NET INCOME ($ mil.)	NET PROFIT MARGIN	EMPLOYEES
10/18	10,250	340	3.3%	13,100
10/17	8,570	30	0.4%	11,400
10/16	8,111	(97)	—	11,300
10/15	10,140	(184)	—	13,200
10/14	10,800	(019)	—	11,200
Annual Growth	(1.3%)			(2.0%)

2018 Year-End Financials

Debt ratio: 75.62%	No. of shares (mil.): 98
Return on equity: —	Dividends
Cash ($ mil.): 1,320	Yield: —
Current ratio: 1.35	Payout: —
Long-term debt ($ mil.): 4,521	Market value ($ mil.): 3,312

	STOCK PRICE ($) FY Close	P/E High/Low		PER SHARE ($) Earnings	Dividends	Book Value
10/18	33.49	14	9	3.41	0.00	(39.75)
10/17	42.31	140	71	0.32	0.00	(46.48)
10/16	22.30	—	—	(1.19)	0.00	(64.93)
10/15	12.30	—	—	(2.25)	0.00	(63.40)
10/14	35.37	—	—	(7.60)	0.00	(57.15)
Annual Growth	(1.4%)	—	—	—	—	—

have buoyed its loan business. Meanwhile its annual profit has grown by one-third.

The bank's revenue dipped 2% to $391.7 million during 2015 however mostly as the low-interest environment continued to squeeze its interest margins on its loans and investment securities. It also collected $15 million less in (non-recurring) gains from the sale of its Springtone investment compared to the prior year.

Despite modest revenue declines in 2015 NBT's net income climbed 2% to $76.43 million primarily because in 2014 it had incurred $17.9 million in non-recurring prepayment penalties as it paid down its long-term debt. The company's operating cash levels jumped 42% to $124.54 million for the year mostly as it collected more in net proceeds on the sale of its loans held for sale and sold off more of its non-loan assets.

Strategy

New York-based NBT Bancorp has expanded its financial service lines outside of traditional banking on its own and through acquisitions in recent years.

Mergers and Acquisitions

In October 2015 NBT Bancorp beefed up its Wealth Management and 401(k) recordkeeping businesses after purchasing New Hampshire-based Third Party Administrators Inc which provided administrative services for 401(k) profit sharing and defined benefit plans on behalf of 700 businesses and Section 125 administration. The $4.1 million acquisition helped complement services offered by its Wealth Management division and EPIC Advisors affiliate.

In March 2013 NBT purchased Alliance Financial for $233 million which bolstered its presence in central New York by adding 26 branches in Onondaga Cortland Madison Oneida and Oswego counties. The deal also added $1.4 billion in assets including $920 million in net loans held for investment and $1.1 billion in deposits.

Company Background

NBT Bancorp remained profitable through the recession even as real estate values fell and the number of non-performing loans in its portfolio grew. To do this the company increased its loan collection efforts and focused on selling conforming real estate mortgages. It also stopped originating auto leases.

NBT Bancorp was founded in 1986. However NBT Bank traces its roots to 1856.

Navistar International Corp.

EXECUTIVES

Chb-Pres-Ceo, Troy A Clarke
Exec V Pres-Coo, Persio V Lisboa
Exec V Pres-Cfo, Walter G Borst
Sr V Pres-Gen Counsel, Curt A Kramer
Assoc Gen Counsel-Corp SEC, Richard E Bond
Sr V Pres-Corp Contrl, Samara A Strycker
Pres Financial Svcs-Treas, William V McMenamin
Auditors: KPMG LLP

LOCATIONS

HQ: Navistar International Corp.
2701 Navistar Drive, Lisle, IL 60532
Phone: 331 332-5000
Web: www.navistar.com

COMPETITORS

All American Group	Hino Motors
BAE SYSTEMS	Isuzu
Blue Bird	Leyland Trucks
Cummins	Mercedes-Benz U.S.
Daimler	International
Deere	Mitsubishi Motors
Detroit Diesel	North America
Eaton	Oshkosh Truck
Fiat	PACCAR
Force Protection	Scania
Ford Motor	Spartan Motors
Forest River	Thor Industries
Freightliner Custom	Tiffin Motorhomes
Chassis	Toyota
General Dynamics	UD Trucks
General Dynamics Land	Volvo
Systems	Winnebago
General Motors	

NBT Bancorp. Inc.

NBT Bancorp is the holding company for NBT Bank which operates about 155 branches mainly in suburban and rural areas of central and northern New York northeastern Pennsylvania western Massachusetts southern New Hampshire and northwestern Vermont. The bank offers traditional deposit accounts and trust services and specializes in making business and commercial real estate loans. NBT also holds two main financial services subsidiaries: the EPIC Advisors unit administers retirement plans while Mang Insurance Agency sells personal and commercial coverage. NBT Capital provides venture funding to growing area businesses.

Operations

Other subsidiaries include property manager Broad Street Property Associates title insurance firm NBT Services real estate investment trusts CNB Realty Trust and Alliance Preferred Funding Corp and and equipment leasing services provider Alliance Leasing.

About 63% of the bank's total revenue came from loan interest (including fees) in 2015 while another 7% came from interest on investment securities. The rest of its revenue came from insurance and other financial services fees (6% of revenue) deposit account service charges (4%) ATM and debit card fees (5%) retirement plan administration fees (4%) trust fees (5%) and other miscellaneous sources.

Sales and Marketing

NBT Bancorp serves individuals businesses and municipalities. The bank spent $2.7 million on advertising during 2015 down from $2.8 million and $3.2 million in 2014 and 2013 respectively.

Financial Performance

NBT Bancorp's annual revenue has risen more than 20% since 2011 mostly as bank acquisitions

EXECUTIVES

Sevp And Cfo, Michael J. Chewens, age 56, $446,610 total compensation

Evp; President Commercial Banking, Jeffrey M. Levy, age 56, $436,000 total compensation

President And Ceo, John H. Watt, age 59

Corporate Svp And Cio, Joseph R. Stagliano

Evp Chief Human Resources Officer And Chief Ethics Officer, Catherine M. Scarlett

Evp; President Wealth Management, Timothy L. Brenner, age 61, $331,050 total compensation

Evp General Counsel And Corporate Secretary, F. Sheldon Prentice

Evp; President New England, Matthew K. Durkee

Evp And President Commercial Banking, Sarah A. Halliday

Vice President, Ed Mitchell

Vice President And Retirement Plan Services Manager, Peter Kain

Assistant Vice President, Kellyanne Truesdale

Executive Vice President And Director Human Resources, Thomas Delduchetto

Vice President Commercial Loan Officer, Timothy Robinson

Senior Vice President Southern Tier Regional Commercial Banking Manager Director Of Business Banking, David Theleman

Vice President And Director Of Compliance Risk Man, Patrick Gleason
Vice President, Debra Barker
Vice President Information Processing, Robert Keller
Vice President Business Development, Debra Turner
Assistant Vice President And D, Robert Hill
Assistant Vice President And Audit Manager, Bryan Green
Director Media Relations, Salvator Arcidiacono
Senior Vice President Director Of Operational Ris, Jim Terry
Regional Sales Representative And Vice President, Denise Snyder
Senior Vice President, Kurt Edwards
Executive Vice President Marketing, Constance Bucknell
Assistant Vice President Security Investigations Officer, Rebecca Powell
Vice President And Relationship Manager, James Antell
Chairman, Martin A. Dietrich, age 62
Board Member, Michael M Murphy
Board Member, Dennis Surace
Auditors: KPMG LLP

LOCATIONS

HQ: NBT Bancorp. Inc.
52 South Broad Street, Norwich, NY 13815
Phone: 607 337-2265   **Fax:** 607 336-7538
Web: www.nbtbancorp.com

PRODUCTS/OPERATIONS

2015 Sales

	$ mil.	% of total
Interest		
Interest and fees on loans	241	63
Securities available for sale	20	5
Securities held to maturity	9	2
Other	1	-
Non-interest		
Insurance and other financial services revenue	24	6
Service charges on deposit accounts	17	4
Trust	19	5
ATM & debit card fees	18	5
Retirement plan administration fees	14	4
Bank-owned life insurance income	4	1
Gain on the sale of Springtone investment	4	1
Net securities gains	3	.
Other	14	4
Total	**391**	**100**

Selected Subsidiaries

Broad Street Property Associates Inc.
CNB Realty Trust
Colonial Finance Services Inc.
EPIC Advisors Inc.
FNB Financial Services Inc.
Hathaway Agency Inc.
LA Lease Inc.
Mang Insurance Agency LLC
NBT Bank National Association
NBT Capital Corp.
NBT Financial Services Inc.
NBT Holdings Inc.
NBT Services Inc.
Pennstar Bank Services Company
Pennstar Financial Services Inc.

COMPETITORS

Astoria Financial	M&T Bank
Community Bank System	Oneida Financial
HSBC USA	Sovereign Bank
KeyCorp	TrustCo Bank Corp NY

HISTORICAL FINANCIALS
Company Type: Public

Income Statement

FYE: December 31

	ASSETS ($ mil.)	NET INCOME ($ mil.)	INCOME AS % OF ASSETS	EMPLOYEES
12/17	9,136	82	0.9%	1,733
12/16	8,867	78	0.9%	1,704
12/15	8,262	76	0.9%	1,721
12/14	7,797	75	1.0%	1,840
12/13	7,652	61	0.8%	1,742
Annual Growth	**4.5%**	**7.4%**	**—**	**(0.1%)**

2017 Year-End Financials

Debt ratio: 2.08%
Return on equity: 8.78%
Cash ($ mil.): 159
Current ratio: —
Long-term debt ($ mil.): —

No. of shares (mil.): 43
Dividends
    Yield: 0.0%
    Payout: 49.2%
Market value ($ mil.): 1,602

	STOCK PRICE ($) FY Close	P/E High/Low	PER SHARE ($) Earnings	Dividends	Book Value
12/17	36.80	22 17	1.87	0.92	22.01
12/16	41.88	23 13	1.80	0.90	21.11
12/15	27.88	17 13	1.72	0.87	20.31
12/14	26.27	16 13	1.69	0.84	19.69
12/13	25.90	18 13	1.46	0.81	18.77
Annual Growth	**9.2%**	**— —**	**6.4%**	**3.2%**	**4.1%**

NCR Corp

EXECUTIVES

Pres-Ceo, Michael D Hayford
Exec Chb*, Frank R Martire
Coo, Owen J Sullivan
Exec V Pres-Cfo, Andre J Fernandez
Exec V Pres, Paul Langenbahn
Exec V Pres-Chief ADM Officer-, Andrea L Ledford
Sr V Pres-General Counsel-Corp, Edward R Gallagher
Hosp Account Executive, Julie Jones
Manager For State and Local Go, Justin Clay
Sales Specialist, Lizzy Duncan
Sales Support Analyst II, Lucie Ubrov
Auditors: PricewaterhouseCoopers LLP

LOCATIONS

HQ: NCR Corp
864 Spring Street NW, Atlanta, GA 30308
Phone: 937 445-5000
Web: www.ncr.com

COMPETITORS

ACI Worldwide	Ingenico
Acxiom	MICROS Systems
BancTec	Motorola Solutions
Cummins-Allison	Netflix
Datalogic Scanning	Oki Electric
De La Rue	Optimal Group
Dell	Oracle
Diebold	Outerwall
Equinox Payments	PAR Technology
Fidelity National	Retalix
Information Services	SANYO
Fiserv	SITA
Fujitsu	Toshiba TEC
Gilbarco	Triton Systems
Hewlett-Packard	Unisys
Honeywell	VeriFone
International	Wincor Nixdorf
IBM	

HISTORICAL FINANCIALS
Company Type: Public

Income Statement

FYE: December 31

	REVENUE ($ mil.)	NET INCOME ($ mil.)	NET PROFIT MARGIN	EMPLOYEES
12/17	6,516	232	3.6%	34,000
12/16	6,543	270	4.1%	33,500
12/15	6,373	(178)	—	32,600
12/14	6,591	191	2.9%	30,200
12/13	6,123	443	7.2%	29,300
Annual Growth	**1.6%**	**(14.9%)**	**—**	**3.8%**

2017 Year-End Financials

Debt ratio: 39.08%
Return on equity: 15.11%
Cash ($ mil.): 537
Current ratio: 1.50
Long-term debt ($ mil.): 2,939

No. of shares (mil.): 122
Dividends
    Yield: —
    Payout: —
Market value ($ mil.): 4,147

	STOCK PRICE ($) FY Close	P/E High/Low	PER SHARE ($) Earnings	Dividends	Book Value
12/17	33.99	49 29	0.97	0.00	12.53
12/16	40.56	24 11	1.71	0.00	12.38
12/15	24.46	— —	(1.09)	0.00	11.41
12/14	29.14	33 21	1.12	0.00	11.10
12/13	34.06	16 10	2.62	0.00	10.62
Annual Growth	**(0.1%)**	**— —**	**(22.0%)**	**—**	**4.2%**

Neiman Marcus Group Ltd LLC

Auditors: Ernst & Young LLP

LOCATIONS

HQ: Neiman Marcus Group Ltd LLC
1618 Main Street, Dallas, TX 75201
Phone: 214 743-7600
Web: www.neimanmarcusgroup.com

HISTORICAL FINANCIALS
Company Type: Public

Income Statement

FYE: July 28

	REVENUE ($ mil.)	NET INCOME ($ mil.)	NET PROFIT MARGIN	EMPLOYEES
07/18	4,900	251	5.1%	13,500
07/17	4,705	(531)	—	13,700
07/16*	4,949	(406)	—	14,300
08/15	5,095	14	0.3%	15,100
08/14	3,710	(134)	—	—
Annual Growth	**7.2%**	**—**	**—**	**—**

*Fiscal year change

2018 Year-End Financials

Debt ratio: 61.66%
Return on equity: —
Cash ($ mil.): 38
Current ratio: 1.53
Long-term debt ($ mil.): 4,623

No. of shares (mil.): 0
Dividends
    Yield: —
    Payout: —
Market value ($ mil.): —

Nelnet Inc

Got Ivy League tastes on a community college budget? Nelnet may be able to help. The education planning and financing company helps students and parents plan and pay for college educations. Nelnet is mostly known for servicing federal student loans. The firm manages about $76 billion in student loan assets most of which are government loans. However in light of regulatory changes to the student lending market Nelnet is increasingly expanding its fee-based education services. It serves the K-12 and higher education marketplace providing long-term payment plans college enrollment services and software and technology services. It acquired in 2018 Great Lakes Educational Loan Services for $150 million. The firm is part of financial holding company Farmers & Merchants Investment.

Operations

Nelnet provides innovative educational services in loan servicing payment processing education planning and asset management for families and educational institutions. The Company's four operating segments offer a broad range of services designed to simplify education planning and financing for students and families and the administrative and financial processes for schools and financial institutions.

The largest is Asset Generation and Management which acquires and manages Nelnet's student loan holdings. The portfolio includes Nelnet's existing loans originated under the now-defunct Federal Family Education Loan Program (FFELP). However in efforts to diversify its fee-based business and lessen its dependence on student loans the company is focused on developing new products and growing in areas such as tuition payment processing and lead generation products and services such as enrollment management and test prep services.

The three fee-based segments include Student Loan and Guaranty Servicing which services FFELP and other third-party loans writes and services private student loans and provides loan servicing software. (Nelnet is one of four companies providing servicing for the Department of Education.) Tuition Payment Processing and Campus Commerce serves the K-12 market as well as higher education providing financing for families and processing services for schools. Enrollment Services works to connect students with schools by providing marketing for schools and publishing school directories and test preparation study guides for potential students.

Geographic Reach

The company has offices in the US and Canada.

Sales and Marketing

The company's customers include students and families colleges and universities specifically financial aid business and admissions offices K-12 schools lenders state agencies and government entities.

Financial Performance

Nelnet has seen steady growth in revenues in the last few years. In 2013 the company's revenue increased to $1.14 billion (compared to $923.7 million in 2012) primarily due to an increase in Student Loan and Guaranty Servicing (as the result of growth in servicing volume under the company's contract with the Department of Education) and an increase in collection revenues from defaulted FFELP loan assets on behalf of guaranty agencies. Tuition Payment Processing and Campus Commerce revenues grew due to a higher number of managed tuition payment plans as a result of

providing more plans at existing schools and obtaining new school customers.

Net income increased to $302.7 million in 2013 (from $117.8 million in 2012) due to higher revenues and lower operating costs (the result of a decrease in depreciation and amortization costs).

In 2013 Nelnet's operating cash flow increased to $387.2 million (compared to $299.3 million in 2012) due to higher net income and proceeds from the termination of one of the company's cross-currency interest rate swaps. The increase in cash provided by operating activities was partially offset by the impacts of changes in non-cash fair value adjustments for derivatives.

Strategy

The company grows organically and through acquisitions.

Mergers and Acquisitions

To strengthen its student loans business Nelnet purchased in 2018 Great Lakes Educational Loan Services for $150 million and in 2014 acquired CIT's student lending business for $1.1 billion.

In 2014 FACTS Management brand a part of Nelnet's Tuition Payment Processing and Campus Commerce segment and the leader in payment plan services for K-12 schools acquired RenWeb School Management Software one of the leading school information systems for private and faith-based schools. RenWeb currently helps over 3000 schools automate administrative processes like admissions scheduling student billing attendance and grade book management. By automating these tasks RenWeb gives teachers more time to shape the lives of students while saving money and resources. FACTS helps over 6500 schools with tuition management billing and financial aid assessment services.

Company Background

Nelnet has been through a turbulent few years as student loan reform and the financial crisis disrupted business and sent revenues down. The company's ability to adapt to the economic pressures and policy changes have helped it land face-up following the recession. Measures taken including laying off staff and tightening lending practices helped boost profits despite lower revenues. Although non-FFELP servicing income and payment processing revenues grew in 2011 FFELP servicing revenues declined as the portfolio further shrunk and school marketing sales decreased as schools cut back on spending. As a result revenues fell that year by 8% to $979 million. Net income increased 8% (to $204 million) in 2011 compared to 2010 when the company had expenses related to restructuring. Also in 2010 Nelnet paid the US government $55 million to settle a lawsuit claiming it had made false statements to receive extra subsidies.

In a blow to the student lending industry President Barack Obama eliminated the FFELP and prohibited private lenders from making federal student loans in 2010. All new federal student loans began going directly through the Department of Education's Direct Loan Program. As a result Nelnet no longer originates new FFELP loans.

But the change didn't put an end to Nelnet. The company was awarded a five-year servicing contract for federally owned student loans including existing FFELP loans. Nelnet also began servicing new loans generated directly under the Federal Direct Loan Program. The contract was a major win for the company. Nelnet expects that its fee-based revenue will increase as the servicing volume for these loans increases (while the FFELP portfolio declines). The company is also focusing on improving its customer service to increase the allotted percentage of new government loans it services.

CEO Michael Dunlap controls the company holding 68% of the voting power for Nelnet. Dun-

lap and his family also own Farmers & Merchants Investment.

PRODUCTS/OPERATIONS

2015 Sales

	$ mil.	% of total
Interest		
Loans	726	60
Investments	7	1
Noninterest		
Loan & guaranty servicing	239	20
Enrollment services	70	6
Tuition payment processing & campus commerce revenue	120	10
Gains on sale of loans & debt repurchases net	5	1
Other	32	2
Total	**1,202**	**100**

COMPETITORS

American Student Assistance
Bank of America
Brazos Higher Education Service Corp.
College Loan Corporation
First Marblehead
Great Lakes Higher Education
JPMorgan Chase
Pennsylvania Higher Education Assistance Agency
Sallie Mae
Texas Guaranteed
Wells Fargo

HISTORICAL FINANCIALS

Company Type: Public

Income Statement

FYE: December 31

	ASSETS ($ mil.)	NET INCOME ($ mil.)	INCOME AS % OF ASSETS	EMPLOYEES
12/17	23,964	173	0.7%	4,300
12/16	27,180	256	0.9%	3,700
12/15	30,485	267	0.9%	3,400
12/14	30,098	307	1.0%	3,100
12/13	27,770	302	1.1%	2,800
Annual Growth	(3.6%)	(13.0%)	—	11.3%

2017 Year-End Financials

Debt ratio: 89.12%
Return on equity: 8.22%
Cash ($ mil.): 66
Current ratio: —
Long-term debt ($ mil.): —

No. of shares (mil.): 40
Dividends
  Yield: 0.0%
  Payout: 14.0%
Market value ($ mil.): 2,236

	STOCK PRICE ($) FY Close	P/E High/Low		PER SHARE ($) Earnings	Dividends	Book Value
12/17	54.78	14	9	4.14	0.58	52.67
12/16	50.75	9	5	6.02	0.50	48.96
12/15	33.57	8	5	5.89	0.42	42.87
12/14	46.33	7	5	6.62	0.40	37.31
12/13	42.14	7	4	6.50	0.40	31.13
Annual Growth	6.8%	—	—	(10.7%)	9.7%	14.1%

	STOCK PRICE ($) FY Close	P/E High/Low		PER SHARE ($) Earnings	Dividends	Book Value
04/18	67.40	248	136	0.28	0.80	7.86
04/17	39.85	23	12	1.81	0.76	10.33
04/16	23.64	47	27	0.77	0.72	10.25
04/15	36.12	25	19	1.75	0.66	11.15
04/14	35.00	25	18	1.83	0.60	11.67
Annual Growth	17.8%	—	—	(37.5%)	7.5%	(9.4%)

NetApp, Inc.

EXECUTIVES

Pres-Ceo, George Kurian
Chb*, T Michael Nevens
Exec V Pres-Cfo, Ronald J Pasek
Exec V Pres Worldwide Fields &, Henri Richard
Exec V Pres, Joel D Reich
Sr V Pres-General Counsel-Sec, Matthew K Fawcett
Chief Strategy Officer, Atish Gude
Svp-Chro, Debra McCowan
Engineering Manager, Anand Prahlad
Global Manager, Garett Okano
Supply Chain, Pamela Francisco
Auditors: DELOITTE & TOUCHE LLP

LOCATIONS

HQ: NetApp, Inc.
1395 Crossman Avenue, Sunnyvale, CA 94089
Phone: 408 822-6000
Web: www.netapp.com

COMPETITORS

Data Domain	Isilon Systems
Dell	LSI Corp.
Dot Hill	Microsoft
EMC	Oracle
Hewlett-Packard	Quantum Corporation
Hitachi Data Systems	XIO
IBM	Xyratex

HISTORICAL FINANCIALS

Company Type: Public

Income Statement | | | | FYE: April 27

	REVENUE ($ mil.)	NET INCOME ($ mil.)	NET PROFIT MARGIN	EMPLOYEES
04/18	5,911	76	1.3%	10,300
04/17	5,519	509	9.2%	10,100
04/16	5,546	229	4.1%	12,030
04/15	6,122	559	9.1%	12,810
04/14	6,325	637	10.1%	12,490
Annual Growth	(1.7%)	(41.2%)	—	(4.7%)

2018 Year-End Financials

Debt ratio: 15.62%	No. of shares (mil.): 263
Return on equity: 3.14%	Dividends
Cash ($ mil.): 2,941	Yield: 1.1%
Current ratio: 1.89	Payout: 285.7%
Long-term debt ($ mil.): 1,541	Market value ($ mil.): 17,726

Netflix Inc

Netflix and chill? More like Netflix and bill the increasing numbers of viewers who subscribe to the video streaming service and watch for more than 140 million hours a day. The company streams movies TV shows documentaries and original productions such as Stranger Things to more than 120 million monthly subscribers in more than 190 countries. Netflix produces more programming on its own and continues to strike deals with movie and TV production studios independent producers and others for the rights to distribute their content. To keep viewers binging it deploys increasingly sophisticated algorithms to predict viewer preferences and make recommendations on what to watch next. Netflix still sends DVDs to US customers through the mail though that business gets smaller every year.

Operations

Netflix allows members to view as much as they want with its streaming service and allows simultaneous streaming on multiple devices with higher-cost subscriptions.

The company has organized its business into three operating segments: domestic streaming (about 55% of revenue) international streaming (about 45% of revenue) and domestic DVD (about 5% of revenue).

Geographic Reach

Netflix's business has moved beyond the borders of the US to around the world. The company declares that it does business in more than 190 countries. Netflix is not available in the People's Republic of China and countries in which US companies aren't allowed to operate.

Sales and Marketing

Netflix has spent increasing amounts of money on advertising surpassing $1 billion in 2017 up from $842 million in 2016 and some $714 million in 2015.

Financial Performance

Netflix has surfed video streaming to revenue increases for the past decade as well as profit levels that have fluctuated but trended higher.

An increase of nearly 60% in international subscription sales drove Netflix to a 32% rise in revenue in 2017 to about $11.7 billion from 2016. Average paid international streaming memberships accounted for almost 50% of average paid streaming memberships in 2017 up from about 43% in 2016. Domestic streaming revenue increased 21% year-to-year. Changes in pricing and subscription plans also contributed to the higher revenue. Revenue from the DVD business slipped to about $450 million in 2017 from more than $540 million in 2016.

Netflix reported a leap in profit to $559 million in 2017 from $186 million in 2016. The higher revenue in 2017 enabled the company to absorb higher expenses for technology and development (24% higher in 2017 from 2016) and general and administrative (about 50% higher in 2017 from 2016).

Netflix uses cash in operations to pay for streaming content that it produces itself and licenses from other producers. The company used about $1.8 billion in 2017 some $300 million more than in 2016. Payments for content increased to $8.9 billion in 2017 from $6.8 billion in 2016.

Strategy

To grow overseas Netflix must contend with rivals that offer DVD rentals in Europe and online downloads of movies. Through strategic agreements Netflix has expanded its library of available selections to satisfy the growing appetites of its customers. During the past few years it has added content from CBS MTV Networks and Sony and continues to explore agreements with pay TV channels and networks such as HBO as it invests in streaming content.

Netflix has shifted to offering more original content that's developed in-house or licensed from production companies and producers. Film and TV stars have developed Netflix-only productions. They include Will Smith Brad Pitt Jane Fonda and Robert Redford as well as younger less well-known actors and directors. Netflix has signed TV producers like Shonda Rhimes Ryan Murphy and Jenji Kohan to exclusive development deals.

In the past two or so years the company aggressively expanded internationally launching streaming in countries from Cuba to Japan to Australia and New Zealand to Europe and more. It is available in all but four or so countries. Netflix has created and licensed content for local markets. Those moves have paid off with international subscriptions accounting for about 45% of revenue in 2017 compared to less than 40% in 2016.

The company has plenty of competition much of it coming from producers of content that it licenses. Broadcast networks such as CBS ABC and NBC stream their content. Pay TV companies such as HBO and Showtime also offer streaming services apart from their subscriber businesses. Hulu offers subscription-based TV and movie content as well. Netflix will lose Disney and Pixar movies from its streaming service by the end of 2018 as Disney intends to launch its own streaming service in 2019. Apple Inc. also has initiated its own streaming service. Competition remains in DVD rental too. Redbox offers DVD rentals of new releases and popular movies from locations such as grocery stores.

Netflix has a cooperative-competitive relationship with Amazon.com. It has moved all of its content to services run by Amazon Web Services even while it competes with Amazon's streaming business.

Mergers and Acquisitions

In 2017 Netflix acquired Millarworld a comic book publisher whose characters include Kick-Ass and Kingsman. With the deal Millarworld's characters will move from the page to the screen via Netflix production and streaming and theatrical release. Mark Millar formerly worked at Marvel and started Millarworld to develop his own comic book franchises. The Kick-Ass and Kingsman comics are not part of the deal but Netflix gets access to other comics in superhero science fiction and other genres. Terms of the deal were not disclosed. The acquisition was Netflix's first.

EXECUTIVES

Chairman President And Ceo, Reed Hastings, age 58, $900,000 total compensation
Chief Product Officer, Neil Hunt, age 57, $1,000,000 total compensation
Chief Content Officer, Ted Sarandos, age 54, $1,000,000 total compensation

Chief Streaming And Partnerships And International Development Officer, Greg Peters, age 47, $1,000,000 total compensation
Cfo, David Wells, age 46, $2,400,000 total compensation
Vice President Marketing Apac, Jerret West
Vice President Consumer Insights, Adrien Lanusse
Vice President User Interface Engineering, Matt Marenghi
Vp And Associate General Counsel, Hilary Ware
Vice President Partner Product Development, Gregory Peters
Vice President Content Acquisition, Robert Roy
Board Member, Timothy Haley
Board Director, Rich Barton
Board Member, Reed Hasting
Board Member, Anne Sweeney
Auditors: Ernst & Young LLP

LOCATIONS

HQ: Netflix Inc
100 Winchester Circle, Los Gatos, CA 95032
Phone: 408 540-3700
Web: www.netflix.com

PRODUCTS/OPERATIONS

2017 Sales

	% of total
Domestic Streaming	53
International Streaming	43
Domestic DVD	4
Total	**100**

Selected Netflix Streaming Devices

Apple iPhone
Apple iPad
Apple iPod touch
Apple TV
Blu-ray disc players
Digital video recorders
Google TV
Internet video players
Internet-connected TVs
Home theatre systems
Microsoft Xbox 360 console
Nintendo Wii console
Sony PS3 console

COMPETITORS

AT&T	HBO
Amazon.com	Hastings Entertainment
Apple Inc.	Hulu
Best Buy	Kroger
Charter Communications	Redbox
Columbia House	Showtime Networks
Comcast	Target Corporation
Cox Communications	Time Warner Cable
DIRECTV	Verizon
DISH Network	Wal-Mart
EchoStar	YouTube
Google	

HISTORICAL FINANCIALS

Company Type: Public

Income Statement FYE: December 31

	REVENUE ($ mil.)	NET INCOME ($ mil.)	NET PROFIT MARGIN	EMPLOYEES
12/18	15,794	1,211	7.7%	7,100
12/17	11,692	558	4.8%	5,500
12/16	8,830	186	2.1%	4,700
12/15	6,779	122	1.8%	3,700
12/14	5,504	266	4.8%	2,450
Annual Growth	**30.1%**	**46.0%**	**—**	**30.5%**

2018 Year-End Financials

Debt ratio: 39.89%	No. of shares (mil.): 436
Return on equity: 27.46%	Dividends
Cash ($ mil.): 3,794	Yield: —
Current ratio: 1.49	Payout: —
Long-term debt ($ mil.): 10,360	Market value ($ mil.): 116,860

	STOCK PRICE ($) FY Close	P/E High/Low		PER SHARE ($) Earnings	Dividends	Book Value
12/18	267.66	151	72	2.68	0.00	12.00
12/17	191.96	157	99	1.25	0.00	8.26
12/16	123.80	292	188	0.43	0.00	6.23
12/15	114.38	2440	327	0.28	0.00	5.20
12/14	341.61	764	495	0.62	0.00	4.39
Annual Growth	**(5.9%)**	**—**	**—**	**44.4%**	**—**	**28.6%**

NEW YORK CITY HEALTH AND HOSPITALS CORPORATION

New York City Health and Hospitals Corporation (HHC) takes care of the Big Apple. HHC has facilities in all five boroughs of New York City. As one of the largest municipal health service systems in the US HHC serves 1.4 million New Yorkers and more than 475000 who are uninsured. It operates a network of 11 acute care hospitals (including Bellevue the nation's oldest public hospital) five large diagnostic and treatment centers five skilled nursing centers long-term care facilities and a home health care agency. HHC also operates more than 70 community-based clinics and provides medical services to New York City's correctional facilities. In addition it operates MetroPlus a managed health care plan.

Sales and Marketing
Medicaid accounted for 26% of net patient service revenue in fiscal 2014; Medicaid managed care accounted for 21%. Following those up were disproportionate share supplemental pool (16%) MetroPlus (13%) and Medicare (12%).

Financial Performance
Revenue increased 10% to $8 billion in fiscal 2014 (ended June) due to a 10% increase in net patient service revenue (which accounted for 62% of earnings). City appropriations also contributed to the rise. Net income fell 21% to $314 million as operating expenses including personal service fringe benefits and employer payroll taxes rose. Investment returns also declined that year which helped lead to lower net income.

Cash flow from operations grew 38% to $246 million on an absence of cash appropriations remitted to the city plus an increase of cash generated from receipts from grants and from patients and third-party payors.

Strategy
HHC has been struggling financially facing a $1.1 billion budget gap for 2018. In mid-2017 the system cut 476 positions including nearly 400 management positions. The move which is intended to stem inefficiencies by eliminating unnecessary layers of management is expected to save $60 million in 2018.

To keep up with increasing demand the company has been busy opening new medical facilities while phasing out older less efficient ones.

In a bid to train more doctors in its service area in 2012 HHC and St. George University teamed up to award scholarships worth more than $11 million over five years to New York City residents who aspire to become doctors.

HISTORY

The City of New York in 1929 created a department to manage its hospitals for the poor. During the Depression more than half of the city's residents were eligible for subsidized care and its public hospitals operated at full capacity.

Four new hospitals opened in the 1950s but the city was already having trouble maintaining existing facilities and attracting staff (young doctors preferred private insurance-supported hospitals catering to the middle class). Meanwhile technological advances and increased demand for skilled nurses made hospitals more expensive to operate. The advent of Medicaid in 1965 was a boon for the system because it brought in federal money.

In 1969 the city created the New York City Health and Hospitals Corporation (HHC) to manage its public health care system — and it was hoped to distance it from the political arena. But HHC was still dependent on the city for funds arousing criticism from those who had hoped for more autonomy. A 1973 state report claimed "the people of New York City are not materially better served by the Health and Hospitals Corporation than by its predecessor agencies."

City budget shortfalls in the mid-1970s led to cutbacks at HHC including nearly 20% of staff. Later in the decade several hospitals closed and some services were discontinued. Ed Koch became mayor in 1978 and gained more control over HHC's operations. Struggles between his administration and the system led three HHC presidents to resign by 1981. That year Koch crony Stanley Brezenoff assumed the post and helped transform HHC into a city pseudo-department.

The early 1980s brought greater prosperity to the system. Reimbursement rates and collections procedures improved allowing HHC to upgrade its record-keeping and its ambulatory and psychiatric care programs. In the late 1980s sharp increases in AIDS and crack addiction cases strained the system and a sluggish economy decreased city funding. Criticism mounted in the early 1990s with allegations of wrongful deaths dangerous facilities and lack of Medicaid payment controls. HHC lost patients to managed care providers and revenues plummeted. In 1995 a city panel recommended radically revamping the system.

Faced with declining revenues and criticism from Mayor Rudolph Giuliani that HHC was "a jobs program" the company began cutting jobs and consolidating facilities in 1996. Under Giuliani's direction HHC made plans to sell its Coney Island Elmhurst and Queens hospital centers. In 1997 the New York State Supreme Court struck down Giuliani's privatization efforts saying the city council had a right to review and approve each sale. In 1998 Giuliani continued to seek to restructure HHC and the agency itself contended it was making progress toward its restructuring goals which were aimed at giving HHC more autonomy as well as more fiscal responsibility. In anticipation of a budget shortfall that year the system laid off some 900 support staff employees. In 1999 the state court of appeals ruled HHC could not legally lease or sell its hospitals.

In 2000 HHC launched an effort to improve its physical infrastructure by beginning the rebuilding and renovation of facilities in Brooklyn Manhattan and Queens. The organization also began converting to an electronic (and thus more efficient) clinical information system. In 2001 HHC forged ahead with further restructuring initiatives. It introduced the Open Access plan a cost-cutting measure designed to expedite the processes involved in outpatient visits.

In 2006 Mayor Michael Bloomberg committed $16 million in funds toward the treatment of those affected by exposure to toxic fumes and dust from the 2001 attacks on the World Trade Center. Together with the city HHC established the WTC Environmental Health Center at Bellevue Hospital; treatment was made available at little or no charge to the patient.

EXECUTIVES

Svp And General Counsel, Alan D. Aviles
Acting Svp South Manhattan Health Network; Acting Executive Director Bellevue Hospital Center, Lynda D. Curtis
Svp North Bronx Healthcare Network; Executive Director Jacobi Medical Center, William P. Walsh
Svp Finance And Cfo, Marlene Zurack
Executive Director Queens Hospital Center, Antonio Martin
Executive Director Hhc Health And Home Care, Meryl Weinberg
Executive Director Elmhurst Hospital Center, Chris Constantino
Executive Director Gouverneur Healthcare Services, Mendel Hagler
Executive Director And President Metroplus Health Plan, Arnold Saperstein
Executive Director Sea View Hospital Rehabilitation Center And Home, Angelo Mascia
Svp Queens Healthcare Network, Anne Marie Sullivan
Executive Director Hhc Health And Home Care, Ann Frisch
Svp Information Technology And Cio, Norberto (Bert) Robles
Executive Director Dr. Susan Smith Mckinney Nursing And Rehabilitation Center, Michael Tartaglia
Executive Director Coler-goldwater Specialty Hospital And Nursing Facility, Robert K. Hughes
Svp Quality And Corporate Chief Medical Officer, Ross Wilson
Acting Svp Generations Plus Northern Manhattan Healthcare Network; Executive Director Lincoln Medical And Mental Health Center, Denise C. Soares
Executive Director Kings County Hospital Center, Ernest J. Baptiste
Executive Director Queens Hospital Center, Julius Wool
Assistant Vice President, Laura Free
Senior Assistant Vice President, Paul Albertson
Assistant Vice President, Peter Fragale
Assistant Vice President Data Science, Vijay Saradhi
Vice President Planning, Tom Scully
Chairman, Michael A. Stocker
Vice Chair, Diane E. Lacey
Auditors: KPMG LLP NEW YORK NY

LOCATIONS

HQ: NEW YORK CITY HEALTH AND HOSPITALS CORPORATION
125 WORTH ST RM 514, NEW YORK, NY 100134006
Phone: 212 788-3321
Web: WWW.NYCHEALTHANDHOSPITALS.ORG

HHC Networks

Central Brooklyn Family Health Network
Dr. Susan Smith McKinney Nursing and Rehabilitation Center
East New York Diagnostic & Treatment Center
Kings County Hospital Center
Generations Plus Northern Manhattan Health Network
Harlem Hospital Center
Lincoln Medical and Mental Health Center

Metropolitan Hospital Center
Morrisania Diagnostic & Treatment Center
Renaissance Health Care Network Diagnostic & Treatment Center
Segundo Ruiz Belvis Diagnostic & Treatment Center
North Bronx Healthcare Network
Jacobi Medical Center
North Central Bronx Hospital
North Brooklyn Health Network
Cumberland Diagnostic & Treatment Center
Woodhull Medical and Mental Health Center
Queens Health Network
Elmhurst Hospital Center
Queens Hospital Center
South Brooklyn and Staten Island Health Network
Coney Island Hospital
Sea View Hospital Rehabilitation Center & Home
South Manhattan Healthcare Network
Bellevue Hospital Center
Coler-Goldwater Specialty Care and Nursing Facility
Gouverneur Healthcare Services

PRODUCTS/OPERATIONS

2014 Sales

	% of total
Net patient service	62
Premiums	29
Grants	5
Other	3
Appropriations from City of New York	1
Total	**100**

Selected Services

Adolescent Health Services
Alcohol/Drug Dependency
Asthma Care
Bariatric Services
Behavioral/Mental Health Services
Burn Care
Cancer Care
Cardiology
Child Health Service
Colon Cancer Screening
Dental Care
Diabetes Care
Farmers Market
Flu Vaccination
Geriatric Services
HIV/AIDS Care
HPV Vaccine
Language/Translation Services
LGBT Healthcare Services
Mammograms
Mobile Medical Office-Staten Island
Neonatal Intensive Care
Obstetrics & Gynecology
Palliative Care
Parkinson's Disease
Pediatrics
Quit Smoking
Rehab Services
Sexual Response Assault Teams
Sickle Cell Disease
Sleep Disorder Labs
Stroke Prevention and Care
Telehealth Initiatives
Trauma Centers
Vision Care
Women's Health
WTC Environmental Health Center

COMPETITORS

Beth Israel Medical Center
Catholic Healthcare System
Columbia University
Continuum Health Partners
Cornell University
Lenox Hill Hospital
Memorial Sloan-Kettering
Montefiore Medical
NYU
NewYork-Presbyterian Healthcare
Northwell Health

HISTORICAL FINANCIALS

Company Type: Private

Income Statement

FYE: June 30

	REVENUE ($ mil.)	NET INCOME ($ mil.)	NET PROFIT MARGIN	EMPLOYEES
06/17	9,550	(193)	—	35,700
06/02	4,285	(118)	—	—
06/01	4,287	(71)	—	—
06/00	4,083	9	0.2%	—
Annual Growth	5.1%	—	—	—

2017 Year-End Financials

Debt ratio: ——
Return on equity: (-2.00%)
Cash ($ mil.): 1,184
Current ratio: 0.50
Long-term debt ($ mil.): —
Dividends
Yield: —
Payout: —
Market value ($ mil.): —

NEW YORK CITY TRANSIT AUTHORITY

New York City Transit Authority has your ticket to ride in the Big Apple. Known as MTA New York City Transit it provides subway and bus transportation throughout New York City's five boroughs. It is the primary agency of the MTA and the largest public transportation system in North America. Its subway system — which includes more than 6300 subway cars 468 stations and 660 miles of track — serves more than 5.5 million passengers a day day on 238 local six select bus service and 61 express routes in the five boroughs. Its more than 5700 buses transport some 2.6 million riders each day. The agency also operates the Staten Island Railway system.

Operations

New York City Subways and Buses is comprised of two agencies of the MTA regional transportation network - MTA New York City Transit Transit and MTA Bus. The regional network also includes MTA Staten Island Railway (part of NYC Transit's Department of Subways) MTA Long Island Rail Road MTA Metro-North Railroad MTA Bridges and Tunnels and MTA Capital Construction.

MTA New York City Transit and its subsidiary Manhattan and Bronx Surface Transit Operating Authority provide subway and public bus service within New York City's five boroughs.

In 2013 MTA New York City Transit's total ridership was 2.4 billion up 62 million or 2.7% from 2012. After including 44 million of lost ridership from Superstorm Sandy in 2012 the company's 2013 ridership increased by 0.8% with a subway ridership increase of 19 million or 1.1% and no change in bus ridership.

Geographic Reach

The company serves customers in Brooklyn the Bronx Manhattan and Queens and Staten Island

Financial Performance

Rebounding from the effects of Superstorm Sandy on ridership (which resulted in lost revenues of $52 million) in 2013 MTA New York City Transit's revenues from fares increased by 9%. In 2014 its operating budget was $10.1 billion.

Strategy

MTA New York City Transit's parent company the MTA has been plagued by operating losses. To mitigate its losses the MTA has in recent years raised fares cut jobs and decreased service on its buses and subway lines. It has also sought to raise its non-operating revenues by seeking increased government funding.

With the help of federal stimulus and other funding MTA New York City Transit has been making capital improvements to its systems. Projects have included the construction of the Second Avenue Subway and renovations at the Fulton Street Transit Center and other stations throughout the system.

In 2013 the company broke ground on a new MTA Staten Island Railway station. The 27-month construction project the first such project to include a parking lot will replace the existing Atlantic and Nassau Stations in the Tottenville section of the borough.

Company Background

New York City Transit Authority was formed in the 1950s by New York's legislature; the city's transit system dates back to the early 1900s.

EXECUTIVES

Prin, Thomas F Prendergast
Pres*, Lawrence G Reuter
Exec V Pres*, Barbara Spencer
Executive, Emily Morgan
Director, Karen Giordano
Executive Officer, Miguel Teixeira
Sys Dir, Timothy Thompson
Auditors: PRICEWATERHOUSECOOPERS LLP ST

LOCATIONS

HQ: NEW YORK CITY TRANSIT AUTHORITY
2 BROADWAY FL 18, NEW YORK, NY 100043357
Phone: 718 330-1234

HISTORICAL FINANCIALS

Company Type: Private

Income Statement — FYE: December 31

	REVENUE ($ mil.)	NET INCOME ($ mil.)	NET PROFIT MARGIN	EMPLOYEES
12/17	4,911	(287)	—	47,956
12/06	3,041	1,780	58.6%	—
12/05	2,907	0	—	—
Annual Growth	4.5%	—	—	—

2017 Year-End Financials

Debt ratio: ——
Return on equity: (-5.90%)
Cash ($ mil.): 55
Current ratio: 0.40
Long-term debt ($ mil.): —

Dividends
Yield: —
Payout: —
Market value ($ mil.): —

New York Community Bancorp Inc.

It's big banking in the Big Apple and beyond. New York Community Bancorp is the holding company for one of the largest thrifts in the US New York Community Bank as well as New York Commercial Bank (also dba Atlantic Bank) and seven other banking divisions. In its home state New York Community Bank operates through Queens County Savings Bank Richmond County Savings Bank Roosevelt Savings Bank and Roslyn Savings Bank. It serves customers in New Jersey through its Garden State Community Bank divi-

sion. New York Community Bank also does business as AmTrust Bank which operates in Arizona and Florida and Ohio Savings Bank. Altogether New York Community Bancorp has about 275 bank branches in five states.

Operations

New York Community Bancorp operates two businesses: Banking Operations and Residential Mortgage Banking.

The main banking business generates some 95% of total revenue and serves consumers and businesses with standard services such as checking and savings accounts CDs IRAs credit cards mortgages and loans. It offers life and long-term care insurance through an agreement with third-party provider LPL Financial. New York Community Bancorp typically does not open new stand-alone branches but has been increasing its presence in its market areas by adding locations inside grocery stores and extending business hours. Its commercial arm New York Commercial Bank has 30 branches in Manhattan Queens Brooklyn Westchester County and Long Island including 18 that operate under the name Atlantic Bank. New York Community Bancorp also owns investment advisory firm Peter B. Cannell & Co.

Multifamily mortgage loans (with an emphasis on rent-regulated apartment buildings) are the company's key assets making up more than 70% of its loan book. New York Community Bancorp prefers rent-regulated properties because they tend to have lower-than-average tenant turnover and can often be expected to bring in steady income during economic downturns. The company also focuses on loans secured by commercial real estate in New York and New Jersey.

Geographic Reach

Westbury New York-based New York Community Bancorp has branches in five states: New York home to about 160 community and commercial bank branches; New Jersey with about 45 locations; Ohio and Florida with more than 25 branches each; and Arizona with more than a dozen locations.

Financial Performance

New York Community Bancorp has seen a slow decline in revenue since 2010. In fiscal 2016 sales fell a further 4% to $1.8 billion due to lower returns from securities and money market investments as well as lower mortgage banking income.

Net income was $495.4 in 2016 a sharp increase on the loss of $47.2 million incurred in the previous year. The results reflect a one-off item in 2015 that saw the bank pay $773.8 million to reduce $10.4 billion in wholesale borrowings to a lower cost of debt.

Cash from operations was $755.7 million in 2016 compared to a cash usage of $420.4 million in 2015 primarily for the same reason as changes in net income.

Strategy

To strengthen its balance sheet New York Community Bancorp paid a one-off charge of $773.8 million in 2016 to amend its loan repayment rate from 3.16% to 1.58%. The reduction will save the company $100 million each year.

The company called off its merger with Astoria Bank in later 2016. The deal would have taken the bank over the $50 billion threshold that delineates a systematically important bank and brings tougher regulations and Astoria's more unwieldy footprint would have dragged New York's best-in-class efficiency ratio up.

Company Background

In 2012 it acquired some $2.2 billion in deposits mainly short-term CDs but also money market accounts from Aurora Bank.

New York Community Bank was founded in 1859. New York Community Bancorp was incorporated in 1993.

EXECUTIVES

Sevp And Coo, Robert Wann, age 63, $1,100,000 total compensation
President And Ceo, Joseph R. Ficalora, age 71, $1,400,000 total compensation
Sevp And Cfo, Thomas R. (Tom) Cangemi, age 49, $850,000 total compensation
Evp And Corporate Secretary, R. Patrick Quinn
Sevp And Chief Lending Officer, James J. Carpenter, age 57, $775,000 total compensation
Evp And Chief Accounting Officer, John J. Pinto, age 47, $575,000 total compensation
Evp And Cio, Robert Brown
Senior Vice President And Controller, James Speranza
Assistant Vice President Regional Human Resources Director, Patricia King
Vice President Risk Management, Debbie Messina
Executive Vice President, Barbara Ann Tosi-Renna
Second Vice President Staff Attorney, Laura Coleman
Senior Vice President Mortgage, Charles Baker
Vice President Of Advanced Engineering, Marquita Guerra
Senior Vice President, Michael Frain
Vice President Loan Review Officer, Ronald Lehrer
Senior Vice President Human Resources Officer, Michele Reid
Second Vice President, Boris Gadol
First Vice President Loan Recovery Officer, Marc Thomaes
First Senior Vice President And Branch Coordinator, Louis Riccio
Assistant Vice President Procurement, Susan Pace-Burke
Senior Vice President, Mitchel Baffa
Application Development Manager First Vice President, Sharon Michitsch
Edandt Training Manager Vice President, Susan Weaver
First Vice President Marketing, Donna Winfield
Vice President Commercial Lending, John Adams
Senior Vice President Regional Executive, Gail Castellano
Assistant Vice President Manager Of Loan Admin Customer Service, Ken Hsiung
Vice President, Kevin Kaufmann
Vice President Market Manager, Leonard Bosso
Vice President And Commercial Loan Officer, Linda Orth
Assistant Vice President, Peter Zito
Senior Vice President, Ed May
Assistant Vice President, Navia Acosta
Vice President, Ines Kurtov
Assistant Vice President, Katelin Quest
Vice President, Jeff Lee
Senior Project Manager Assistant Vice President, Richard Grosso
First Vice President, Scott Armstrong
Vice President Hris Manager, Nancy Librandi
Vice President, Sonia Holder
Vice President, Manju Grochocki
Second Vice President, Crocefissa Grima
Senior Vice President, Levi Richardson
Second Vice President, Jeffrey Williams
First Vice President, Sharon Murphy
First Vice President Information Technology Core Operations, Howard Henderson
First Vice President Stock Awards And Options Human Resources, Felicia Lehan
First Vice President, Christopher Beck
Vice President Network Engineering, Michael Mike Gluckman
First Vice President And Sox Compliance Officer, Andrew LaRocca
Vice President Benefits Manager, Frances Kaiser
Assistant Vice President Underwriter Iii, Andrea Palasek
Vice President, James Drum

Vice President, Richard Sheehan
Assistant Vice President, Stefanie Schwab
Vice President Retail Operations, Jamil Salah
Vice President Premier Banking Business
  Development Officer Nycb_123 Bug.png, Dimitra
  DiFranco
Srpa Assistant Vice President Senior Review
  Appraiser Appraisal Department, Judy Dean
Assistant Vice President Network Engineering,
  Anthony Ardezzone
Executive Vice President And Chief Human
  Resources Officer, Eric Kracov
Vice President Systems Engineering, Craig Preiser
Vice President, Kathy Kowler
Assistant Vice President Commercial Lending,
  Antoinette Difinizio
First Vice President, Douglas Orth
Senior Vice President, Nicole Sullivan
Vice President Of Inquiry Management, Kristina
  Hosea
Assistant Vice President, Elpida Ferguson
Vice President Enterprise Risk Asset Liability
  Management, Tejas Doshi
Assistant Vice President, Beth Gant
Vice President Loan Recovery, Larry Gluckman
Chairman, Dominick Ciampa, age 85
Board Member, Lawrence Savarese
Board Member, John Tsimbinos
Auditors: KPMG LLP

LOCATIONS

HQ: New York Community Bancorp Inc.
  615 Merrick Avenue, Westbury, NY 11590
Phone: 516 683-4100
Web: www.mynycb.com

2016 Locations

	No.
New York Community Bank	
New York	111
New Jersey	45
Ohio	28
Florida	27
Arizona	14
New York Commercial Bank	48
Total	**273**

PRODUCTS/OPERATIONS

2016 Sales

	$ mil.	% of total
Interest		
Mortgage & other loans	1,472	81
Securities & money market investments	202	11
Noninterest		
Fee income	32	2
Bank-owned life insurance	31	2
Mortgage banking income	27	1
Net gain on sale of loans	15	1
Net gain on sales of securities	3	-
Other	41	2
FDIC indemnification expenses	(6.2)	-
Total	**1,820**	**100**

2016 Sales

	% of total
Banking operations	
Interest	89
Non Interest	7
Residential Mortgage banking	
Interest	1
Non Interest	3
Total	**100**

Selected Operations

AmTrust Bank (Arizona Florida)
Atlantic Bank (New York commercial bank)
Garden State Community Bank (New Jersey)
Ohio Savings Bank (Ohio)
Queens County Savings Bank (Queens NY)
Richmond County Savings Bank (Staten Island NY)
Roosevelt Savings Bank (Brooklyn NY)
Roslyn Savings Bank (Long Island NY)

COMPETITORS

Apple Bank for Savings	Provident Financial
Astoria Financial	Services
Bank of America	Ridgewood Savings Bank
Citigroup	Safra Bank
Emigrant Bank	TD Bank USA
Flushing Financial	Valley National
HSBC USA	Bancorp
Investors Bancorp	Wells Fargo
JPMorgan Chase	

HISTORICAL FINANCIALS

Company Type: Public

Income Statement

FYE: December 31

	ASSETS ($ mil.)	NET INCOME ($ mil.)	INCOME AS % OF ASSETS	EMPLOYEES
12/17	49,124	466	0.9%	3,096
12/16	48,926	495	1.0%	3,487
12/15	50,317	(47)	—	3,448
12/14	48,559	485	1.0%	3,416
12/13	46,688	475	1.0%	3,381
Annual Growth	**1.3%**	**(0.5%)**	**—**	**(2.2%)**

2017 Year-End Financials

Debt ratio: 0.73%	No. of shares (mil.): 488
Return on equity: 7.22%	Dividends
Cash ($ mil.): 2,528	Yield: 0.0%
Current ratio: —	Payout: 75.5%
Long-term debt ($ mil.): —	Market value ($ mil.): 6,360

	STOCK PRICE ($) FY Close	P/E High/Low	PER SHARE ($) Earnings	Dividends	Book Value
12/17	13.02	18 13	0.90	0.68	13.91
12/16	15.91	17 14	1.01	0.68	12.57
12/15	16.32	— —	(0.11)	1.00	12.24
12/14	16.00	16 14	1.09	1.00	13.06
12/13	16.85	16 12	1.08	1.00	13.01
Annual Growth	**(6.2%)**	**— —**	**(4.5%)**	**(9.2%)**	**1.7%**

NEW YORK COMMUNITY TRUST AND COMMUNITY FUNDS INC

EXECUTIVES

Pres-Exec Dir, Lorie A Slutsky
Sr V Pres*, Joyce Bove
V Pres Donor Rltns*, Robert V Edgar
V Pres of ADM*, Mercedes M Leon
Vice President Donor Relations, Robert Edgar
Auditors: GRANT THORNTON LLP NEW YORK

LOCATIONS

HQ: NEW YORK COMMUNITY TRUST AND
  COMMUNITY FUNDS INC
  909 3RD AVE FL 22, NEW YORK, NY 100224752
Phone: 212 686-0010
Web: WWW.NYCOMMUNITYTRUST.ORG

HISTORICAL FINANCIALS

Company Type: Private

Income Statement

FYE: December 31

	ASSETS ($ mil.)	NET INCOME ($ mil.)	INCOME AS % OF ASSETS	EMPLOYEES
12/17	2,806	(5)	—	65
12/16	2,552	(5)	—	
12/15	2,473	(99)	—	
12/14	2,570	130	5.1%	
Annual Growth	**3.0%**			

2017 Year-End Financials

Debt ratio: ——	
Return on equity: (-2.20%)	Dividends
Cash ($ mil.): 37	Yield: —
Current ratio: 0.60	Payout: —
Long-term debt ($ mil.): —	Market value ($ mil.): —

NEW YORK PRESBYTERIAN HOSPITAL WEILL CORNELL UNIVERSITY MEDICAL CENTER

EXECUTIVES

Prin, Lewis Drusin
Branch/Division/Department Hea, Janet Parisi
Administrator, Eugene Chan
Payroll Manager, Nadine Sylvain
Director, Steven Herrmann
Vice-President, Anita R Golbey
Project Leader, Dale Wright
Administrative Assistant, Lynn Reynolds
Director of Operations, Owen Davis
Professor, Joseph Hayes
Administrator, David Weir

LOCATIONS

HQ: NEW YORK PRESBYTERIAN HOSPITAL WEILL
  CORNELL UNIVERSITY MEDICAL CENTER
  525 E 68TH ST, NEW YORK, NY 100654870
Phone: 212 746-1754
Web: WWW.MED.CORNELL.EDU

HISTORICAL FINANCIALS

Company Type: Private

Income Statement

FYE: December 31

	REVENUE ($ mil.)	NET INCOME ($ mil.)	NET PROFIT MARGIN	EMPLOYEES
12/15	4,505	265	5.9%	5
12/12	75	21	28.2%	
Annual Growth	**290.4%**	**131.8%**	**—**	**—**

2015 Year-End Financials

Debt ratio: ——	
Return on equity: 5.90%	Dividends
Cash ($ mil.): 227	Yield: —
Current ratio: 0.80	Payout: —
Long-term debt ($ mil.): —	Market value ($ mil.): —

NEW YORK UNIVERSITY

Higher education is at the core of this Big Apple institution. The setting and heritage of New York University (NYU) make it one of the nation's most popular educational institutions. With more thanA 50000 students attending its 18 schools and colleges NYU is among the largest private schools in the US. Its Tisch School of the Arts is well-regarded and its law school and Leonard N. Stern School of Business are among theA foremost in the country. NYU occupies five major centers in Manhattan; its Washington Square campus is in the heart of Greenwich Village. The school wasA founded in 1831. Notable alumni include former Federal Reserve Chairman Alan Greenspan and film producer Oliver Stone.

Operations

The school confers about 12000 degrees annually. Of those roughly 4500 are bachelor's degrees nearly 5000 are master's degrees and about 400 are doctoral. Associate and professional degrees make up the rest. NYU alumni and faculty also boast several prestigious awards including more than a dozen Nobel and Crafoord prizes and another four Pulitzer prizes.

NYU is one of the largest employers in New York City with more than 16000 employees.

Geographic Reach

Along with its campuses in New YorkA NYU operates branch campus and research programs in other parts of theA US and abroad as well as study abroad programs in more than 25 countries. International students make up about 10% of the school's student body.

Financial Performance

Undergraduate tuition for the university runs more than $37000 per year.

Strategy

NYU has established itself as the first global network university with a comprehensive liberal arts campus in Abu DhabiA that opened in 2010.

HISTORY

New York University was founded by several prominent New Yorkers in 1831. The school held its first classes the following year in rented rooms on the corner of Beekman and Nassau streets then moved to a building in Washington Square in 1835. It established its law school that year. NYU started its school of medicine in 1841 followed by the school of engineering and science (1854). Postgraduate studies in arts and science (its first coeducational program) began in 1886.

NYU's enrollment jumped from fewer than 2000 in 1900 to 28000 in 1930. After a lull during the Depression and WWII the campus boomed again in the postwar years. During the 1950s the university began focusing on improving academics rather than on increasing enrollment. It created a school of the arts in 1965 and in the early 1970s it completed the Elmer Holmes Bobst Library. However a cash crunch during that decade almost forced the school into bankruptcy.

President Jay Oliva took the reins in 1981 and focused on transforming NYU from a largely commuter college into a global university. The school began a campaign to raise $1 billion in 1984 but earmarked the funds for campus improvements rather than swelling its endowment. During the late 1980s NYU opened several new dormitories and conference spaces. In 1994 British historian and collector Sir Harold Acton bequeathed to the school his Tuscany estate — five art-filled villas overlooking Florence Italy.

In 1996 NYU's Medical Center began talks with Mount Sinai Medical Center aimed at merging their hospitals and medical schools. The talks fell apart in early 1997 but the following year the two sides agreed to merge hospitals and keep their medical schools distinct. Also in 1998 NYU formed NYU On-Line Inc. a for-profit subsidiary to develop and sell specialized Internet courses to other schools training centers and students; the venture was subsequently folded in late 2001. During 1999 contributions to the school approached $250 million. That year however two upper-level school officials were fired following allegations of improper use of university money.

Oliva retired as president in 2002 and was replaced by John Sexton former School of Law dean. In 2004 Sexton announced that NYU would give $1 million to New York City towards renovation of Washington Square Park (the school annually gives some $200000 for the park's ongoing maintenance).

EXECUTIVES

Vp Academic And Health Affairs, Robert (Bob) Berne

Vp Information Technology And Chief Information Technology Officer, Marilyn A. McMillan

Provost, David W. McLaughlin

Evp Finance And Information Technology, Martin S. Dorph

Director Global Institute Of Public Health; Dean Of Global Public Health, Cheryl G. Healton

Dean Libraries, Carol A. Mandel

Herman Robert Fox Dean College Of Dentistry, Charles N. Bertolami

Evp Operations, Alison Leary

Director Institute For The Study Of The Ancient World, Roger Bagnall

Director Courant Institute Of Mathematical Sciences, Gérard Ben Arous

Saul J. Farber Dean Nyu School Of Medicine; Ceo Nyu Hospitals Center, Robert I. Grossman

Dean Gallatin School Of Individualized Study, Susanne L. Wofford

Dean Polytechnic School Of Engineering, Katepalli R. (Sreeni) Sreenivasan

Dean Silver School Of Social Work, Lynn Videka

Dean Liberal Studies, Fred Schwarzbach

Judy And Michael Steinhardt Director Institute Of Fine Arts, Patricia Lee Rubin

Dean Leonard N. Stern School Of Business, Peter B. Henry, age 48

Vice Chancellor New York University Abu Dhabi, Alfred H. Bloom

Vp Global Technology And Chief Global Technology Officer, Thomas A. (Tom) Delaney

Dean For Science Faculty Of Arts And Science, Michael D. Purugganan

President, Andrew Hamilton

Gale And Ira Drukier Dean Steinhardt School For Culture Education And Human Development, Dominic Brewer

Anne And Joel Ehrenkranz Dean Faculty Of Arts And Sciences, Thomas J. Carew

Dean For Humanities Faculty Of Arts And Sciences, Joy Connolly

Harvey J. Stedman Dean School Of Professional Studies, Dennis DiLorenzo

Dean Robert F. Wagner Graduate School Of Public Service, Sherry A. Glied

Dean Tisch School Of The Arts, Allyson Green

Dean For Social Sciences Faculty Of Arts And Science, Michael Laver

Vice Chancellor Nyu Shanghai, Jeffrey S. Lehman

Dean Undergraduate College Leonard N. Stern School Of Business, Geeta Menon

Dean School Of Law, Trevor Morrison

Director Marron Institute Of Urban Management, Paul Romer

Seryl Kushner Dean College Of Arts And Science, G. Gabrielle Starr

Dean College Of Nursing, Eileen Sullivan-Marx

Chancellor Nyu Shanghai, Yu Lizhong

Interim Dean Graduate School Of Arts And Science, Anna L. Harvey

Vice President, Marc Wais

Vice President For Financial Operations And Treasurer, Stephanie Pianka

Senior Vice President Development And Alumni Relations, Debra LaMorte

Vice President Finance, Harold T Read

Vice President Administration, Robert Goldfeld

Assistant Vice President Information Systems, Keith Whiteman

Department Chair, Christina Reuterskiold

Senior Vice President, Lynne Brown

Associate Vice President For Stewardship And Events, Gustave Fleury

Medical Director, Marcy Ferdschneider

Chair Department Of Anthropology, Fred Myers

Vice President Human Resources, Robert White

Vice President For Budget And Planning, Anthony Jiga

Global Finance Chief Of Staff To Executive Vice President For Finance And Information Technology, Carolyn Wood

Vice President For Enrollment Management, Mj Knoll-finn

Vice President Rxr Realty Michael Aisner, Luis Rosa

Medical Director, Ryan Harper

Vice President Finance, Pamela Morris

Clinic Manager, Fredelyne Paris

Vice President For Student Affairs, Susan B Neuman

Vice President Director Engineering, Chris Pak

Assistant Vice President External Affairs And Protective Services, Carl Barchus

Vice President For Local History, Kate Feighery

Vice President Of Administration, Angel Yu

Senior Vice President Education And Diversity Solutions, Jim Jones

Director Of Admissions, Williams Cassandra

Chairman Board Of Trustees, William R. (Bill) Berkley, age 72

Board Director, Christine Trump

Secretary, John Leiva

Vice Chair President, Peter Romain

Treasurer, Peter Rajsingh

Assistant Treasurer, Elisa Cohen

Secretary, Jennifer Neuman

Ms Global Affairs Candidate Treasurer Energy Policy International Club, Jude Buenaseda

Secretary Athletic Development, Raffaela Ianniciello

Secretary And Marketing, August Morar

Auditors: PRICEWATERHOUSECOOPERS LLP NE

LOCATIONS

HQ: NEW YORK UNIVERSITY
70 WASHINGTON SQ S, NEW YORK, NY 100121019
Phone: 212 998-1212
Web: WWW.NYU.EDU

PRODUCTS/OPERATIONS

Selected Schools and Colleges
College of Arts and Science (founded 1832)
College of
Courant In
Gallatin S
Graduate S
Leonard N.
Robert F.
School of
School of
School of
School of
Steinhardt
Tisch Scho

HISTORICAL FINANCIALS

Company Type: Private

Income Statement   FYE: August 31

	REVENUE ($ mil.)	NET INCOME ($ mil.)	NET PROFIT MARGIN	EMPLOYEES
08/16	8,500	177	2.1%	21,000
08/11	5,172	563	10.9%	—
08/06	2,148	195	9.1%	—
Annual Growth	14.7%	(1.0%)	—	—

2016 Year-End Financials

Debt ratio: ——
Return on equity: 2.10%
Cash ($ mil.): 1,033
Current ratio: —
Long-term debt ($ mil.): —

Dividends
Yield: —
Payout: —
Market value ($ mil.): —

Newell Brands Inc

Home is where Newell Brands (formerly Newell Rubbermaid) is. The go-to company for men women and children makes housewares (Rubbermaid plastic products Calphalon cookware) juvenile products (Graco) hair products (Goody) and office items (DYMO and Sharpie). Newell Brands sells its items to mass retailers (Target) and home and office supply stores (Staples). As a result of a more than $18 billion acquisition of consumer products giant Jarden in mid-2016 Newell Brands also inherited popular products such as Bicycle Playing Cards Mr. Coffee Coleman Jostens Oster Rawlings Sunbeam and Yankee Candle.

Operations

Newell Brands operates its business through several segments: Branded Consumables Outdoor Solutions Writing Consumer Solutions Home Solutions Baby and Parenting Commercial Products and Process Solutions.

Branded Consumables is its largest segment and manufactures markets and distributes a broad line of branded consumer products. Outdoor Solutions offers global consumer active lifestyle products for outdoor and outdoor-related activities.

The Writing segment makes writing instruments for use in business and at home. It markets its products directly to mass merchants warehouse clubs grocery/drug stores office superstores office supply stores contract stationers and travel retail and other retailers.

Consumer Solutions provides a diverse line of household products including kitchen appliances and home environment products. It primarily sells its products under the Crock-Pot FoodSaver Holmes Oster Rainbow and Sunbeam names.

Home Solutions makes and distributes tubs bins containers and other storage tools under multiple brand names. Its indoor/outdoor organization items and food and home storage products are primarily sold under the Rubbermaid Roughneck and TakeAlongs names.

Baby and Parenting makes infant and juvenile products such as swings highchairs car seats strollers and play yards sold under the Graco Baby Jogger Aprica and Teutonia names.

Commercial Products offers cleaning and refuse products hygiene systems and material handling equipment. Process Solutions offers a wide variety of plastic products including closures contact lens packaging medical disposables plastic cutlery and rigid packaging.

Geographic Reach

Newell Brands operates in nearly 100 countries in the Americas Europe the Middle East Africa and the Asia Pacific region. More than 70% of the company's business comes from the US while Europe Middle East and Africa (EMEA) region generates about 15% of sales. Latin America and the Asia Pacific regions split nearly 10% of revenue while Canada brings in the remainder of total sales.

Sales and Marketing

The office products maker sells its products in almost 200 countries through large mass merchandisers such as discount stores home centers warehouse clubs office superstores commercial distributors and e-commerce companies.

Newell Brands relies on the largest retailer in the world to help peddle its products. Sales to Wal-Mart and its subsidiaries generate about 10% to 15% of its net sales each year.

Financial Performance

Newell Brands enjoyed explosive growth in 2016 due to its acquisition of consumer products giant Jarden. Revenues more than doubled from $5.9 billion in 2015 to $13.3 billion in 2016 as a result of that acquisition volume growth pricing and its 2015 purchase of Elmer's Brands.

All this growth led to a 10% increase in Writing segment sales and an 8% bump in Baby and Parenting sales. These factors also fueled additional sales stemming from its newly created segments of Branded Consumables Consumer Solutions Outdoor Solutions and Process Solutions.

In conjunction with the higher sales net income surged by more than 50% from $350 million in 2015 to $528 million in 2016. In addition Newell Brands' operating cash flow skyrocketed from $566 million in 2015 to $1.8 billion in 2016 due to its Jarden acquisition.

Strategy

During 2016 Newell Brands launched its New Growth Game Plan an initiative to simplify its organization and develop resources to invest in growth initiatives to build a bigger faster-growing and more global company. The plan involves making strategic cuts to dispose of under-performing brands and business lines. Adhering to this strategy in early 2017 it sold its Tools business to Stanley Black & Decker for nearly $2 billion. Brands involved in the sale included Irwin Lenox and Hilmor.

Mergers and Acquisitions

The company has been pursuing large strategic acquisitions to expand its product lines and significantly add to its revenue stream.

In a sweeping move for the consumer goods industry Newell Brands purchased Jarden in a total transaction valued at $18.7 billion in mid-2016. The mega-deal gave the company access to popular brands such as Sunbeam and Oster appliances Coleman outdoor gear First Alert home safety products Ball canning jars Loew-Cornell art supplies K2 snowboards and Bee and Bicycle brand playing cards. It estimates that the combined company will eventually earn $16 billion in revenue.

In 2016 Newell Brands acquired New Zealand-based Sistema Plastics a leading provider of innovative food storage containers primarily under the Sistema brand for $460 million. The transaction broadened the company's international footprint of food and beverage categories and strengthened its core category of home fragrance in the US.

Newell Brands made another large deal in 2015 through the $1.5 billion acquisition of Visant Holding Corp. (Visant) the parent company of Jostens. A partner to schools and students nationwide Josten has a product portfolio that includes yearbooks class and championship rings for students and professional athletes caps and gowns diplomas and varsity jackets. Post acquisition Jostens became a part of Newell Brands' Outdoor Solutions segment.

Newell Brands inherited more famous brands in late 2015 when it purchased Elmer's Brands for $600 million. Through the purchase the company inherited popular brands Elmer's Krazy Glue and X-Acto and significantly enhanced its Writing segment.

HISTORY

Businessmen in Ogdensburg New York advanced curtain rod maker W.F. Linton Co. $1000 to relocate from Rhode Island in the early 1900s. Local wholesaler Edgar Newell signed off on the loan; when the company went bankrupt in 1903 he was forced to take over. The company renamed Newell Manufacturing set up plants in Canada and Freeport Illinois to ease shipping costs and speed delivery.

Production expanded into towel racks ice picks and other items; Woolworth's decision to carry Newell's products turned the company into a national supplier. Edgar Newell died in 1920. The company made its first acquisition in 1938 buying window treatment specialist Drapery Hardware.

The Newell companies were consolidated in the mid-1960s into a single corporation. Daniel Ferguson was named president in 1965 and served alongside his CEO father Leonard one of Newell's original employees. During his tenure Daniel hitched the company's future to the growing dominance of large discount stores. Newell went from a $14 million family business to a global multi-line conglomerate by acquiring products that it distributed to these big buyers. The company went public in 1972.

As for Rubbermaid it was originally a balloon maker in the 1920s called Wooster Rubber. By the mid-1930s Ohio's Wooster Rubber had acquired the Rubbermaid product line of rubber housewares. It went public in 1955 and two years later changed its name to Rubbermaid. During the 1980s the company enjoyed a decade of phenomenal growth. Newell's $6 billion purchase of Rubbermaid in 1999 sealed its biggest deal yet and resulted in a name change: Newell Rubbermaid.

Decades later the company changed its name to Newell Brands in 2016 after it purchased consumer goods giant Jarden in a mega-merger valued at around $15.4 billion.

EXECUTIVES

Evp And Cfo, Ralph J. Nicoletti, age 60, $493,845 total compensation

Ceo, Michael B. (Mike) Polk, age 57, $1,312,500 total compensation

Coo, William A. (Bill) Burke, age 57, $796,053 total compensation

Chief Development Officer, Richard Davies

Chief Customer Officer, Joseph W. Cavaliere

President, Mark S. Tarchetti, age 42, $922,212 total compensation

Svp Information Technology And Cio, Dan Gustafson

Chief Transformation Officer, Russ Torres

Vp Global Ecommerce, Jeremy Liebowitz

Senior Vice President Finance Business Planning And Analysis, Ronald Hardnock

Vp Marketing Writing And Creative Expression Brands, Victor Misawa

Svp Ir, Nancy O'donnell

Chairman, Michael T. Cowhig, age 71

Auditors: PricewaterhouseCoopers LLP

LOCATIONS

HQ: Newell Brands Inc
221 River Street, Hoboken, NJ 07030
Phone: 201 610-6600
Web: www.newellrubbermaid.com

2016 Sales

North America	$ mil.	% of total
United States	9,518	72
Canada	720	5
Europe Middle East and Africa	1,659	13
Latin America	643	5
Asia Pacific	722	5
Total	**13,264**	**100**

PRODUCTS/OPERATIONS

2016 Sales

	$ mil.	% of total
Writing:		
Writing instruments	1,469	11
Adhesive and cutting products	243	2
Technology solutions	228	2
Home Solutions:		
Home and food storage products	1,058	8
Décor	141	1
Other	367	3
Branded Consumables	2,839	21
Outdoor Solutions	2,415	18
Consumer Solutions	1,766	13
Baby and Parenting	919	7
Tools	760	6
Commercial Products	776	6
Process Solutions	275	2
Total	**13,264**	**100**

Selected Brands & Trade Names

Cleaning organization and decor
  Brute
  Roughneck
  Rubbermaid
  TakeAlongs
Office products
  Accent
  Berol
  DYMO
  Expo
  Liquid Paper
  Paper Mate
  Parker
  Rotring
  Sharpie
  Uni-Ball (under license)
  Waterman
Home and family
  Aprica
  Avex
  Calphalon
  Calphalon One
  Contigo
  Cooking with Calphalon
  Goody
  Graco
  Katana
  Kitchen Essentials
  Teutonia

COMPETITORS

ACCO Brands	Knape & Vogt
Acme United	Lancaster Colony
Alticor	Libbey
Avery Dennison	Lifetime Brands
BIC	Myers Industries
Bridgestone	Owens-Illinois
Coleman	Springs Global US
Crayola	Sterilite
Decorator Industries	Tupperware Brands
Dixon Ticonderoga	Uniek
Faber-Castell	WKI Holding
Home Products	Wilton Brands
International	ZAG Industries
Katy Industries	

HISTORICAL FINANCIALS

Company Type: Public

Income Statement

FYE: December 31

	REVENUE ($ mil.)	NET INCOME ($ mil.)	NET PROFIT MARGIN	EMPLOYEES
12/17	14,742	2,748	18.6%	49,000
12/16	13,264	527	4.0%	53,400
12/15	5,915	350	5.9%	17,200
12/14	5,727	377	6.6%	17,400
12/13	5,692	474	8.3%	18,000
Annual Growth	**26.9%**	**55.1%**	**—**	**27.9%**

2017 Year-End Financials

Debt ratio: 31.85%
Return on equity: 21.56%
Cash ($ mil.): 485
Current ratio: 1.41
Long-term debt ($ mil.): 9,889

No. of shares (mil.): 485
Dividends
  Yield: 0.0%
  Payout: 15.6%
Market value ($ mil.): 14,993

	STOCK PRICE ($) FY Close	P/E High/Low		PER SHARE ($) Earnings	Dividends	Book Value
12/17	30.90	10	5	5.63	0.88	29.15
12/16	44.65	44	27	1.25	0.76	23.52
12/15	44.08	37	28	1.29	0.76	6.82
12/14	38.09	28	21	1.35	0.66	6.88
12/13	32.41	20	13	1.63	0.60	7.44
Annual Growth	**(1.2%)**		**—**	**36.3%**	**10.0%**	**40.7%**

Newmont Mining Corp (Holding Co)

Newmont goes for the gold. Producing close to 6 million ounces of gold annually Newmont Mining Corporation is one of the top three gold producers in the world. The company has significant operations in the US Australia Peru Ghana and Suriname. Its gold reserves are close to 70 million ounces spread across 23000 sq. miles of its own land. Newmont also produces some copper principally through Boddington in Australia and Phoenix in the US. Although Newmont makes almost all its sales of refined gold the end-product of its operations is doré bars an alloy consisting primarily of gold but also containing silver and other metals.

Change in Company Type

In January 2019 Newmont Mining announced plans to acquire Goldcorp for $10 billion to create a newly rebranded Newmont Goldcorp corporation which will hold the world's largest share of gold assets with annual productions of three million ounces of gold.

Operations

Worldwide Newmont holds mineral rights on about 23000 square miles of land. The company's North American operations include mines in Nevada's Carlin Trend one of the largest gold-mining areas in North America. Other sites in North America reside in Phoenix Twin Creeks and Long Canyon; Nevada. Its Cripple Creek & Victor pit operations are also located in Victor Colorado. In the Asia/Pacific Newmont owns the Boddington project one of Australia's largest gold mining properties. Other holdings include the Tanami and Kalgoorlie sites. Newmont's South America segment operates two sites Yanacocha and Merian and manages the Conga Project.

Geographic Reach

Newmont has operations in North America (Colorado and Nevada) South America (Peru and Suriname) Australia and Africa (Ghana). Around 75% of the company's sale comes from the spot market in London UK with another 10% coming from Switzerland.

Sales and Marketing

Newmont sells more than 5 million ounces of gold at the London bullion spot market which is either used as an investment or finds a variety of end uses including jewelry electronics dentistry industrial and decorative uses.

The company also sells around 120 million pounds of copper a year in the form of concentrate that is sold to smelters for further treatment and refining and cathode. Refined copper is used in wire and cable products for communications electricity transportation industries in addition to equipment and electronic applications.

Financial Performance

Sales increased almost 10% from $6.7 billion in 2016 to $7.3 billion in 2017. This came mostly from the hold segment where higher production volumes and slightly higher prices brought in 10% more revenue year-over-year. Copper sales also increased an impressive 25% in 2017 due to higher average net realized prices partially offset by lower sales volumes.

Despite a sales increase the company posted a loss of $98 million in 2017. This was an improvement over the $627 million in losses posted in 2016 mostly from the absence of $977 million in impairment of long-lived assets posted in 2016.

Operations provided $2.3 billion offset by $961 million going towards investments and a further $864 million used in financing activities.

Strategy

Newport's strategy includes strengthening its portfolio (by building a longer-life lower-cost asset portfolio) and moving on promising exploration project development and inorganic opportunities.

With the world economy in recovery coupled with shortage of mining supply in the international market and an upturn in the demand for gold Newport is planning to produce up to 5.5 million ounces of gold by adding higher-margin assets.

Newmont has strategically accumulated superior assets on four continents giving it a competitive advantage in reserves and marginal growth. However most expansion projects are still in the pipeline. And they span the entire portfolio. This includes Carlin district mine expansions (Twin Underground and Exodus) in North America oxide production enhancement in the Andes as well as a 20% interest acquistion in Continental Gold's high-grade gold in Colombia.

It is already registering volume growth from existing mine expansions (like the Tanami underground extension). A similar underground expansion is planned at Subika mine in Africa. The company also boosted production in 2017 thanks to production from two new mines Merian and Long Canyon.

Parallelly Newmont has also worked on increasing its ore body reliability and mill performance increasing underground loaders via remote-control and monitoring mobile equipment in real-time.

Company Background

Colonel William Boyce Thompson a flamboyant trader founded the Newmont Co. in 1916 to trade his various oil and mining stocks. The Newmont name was a combination of New York and Montana where Thompson grew up. The company was renamed Newmont Corporation in 1921 and Newmont Mining Corporation in 1925 when it went public.

HISTORY

The company was founded in 1921 and began publicly trading in 1925.

Colonel William Boyce Thompson a flamboyant trader founded the Newmont Co. in 1916 to trade his various oil and mining stocks. The Newmont name was a combination of New York and Montana where Thompson grew up. The company was renamed Newmont Corporation in 1921 and Newmont Mining Corporation in 1925 when it went public. Thompson died five years later. During its first 10 years Newmont focused on investing and trading stocks in promising mineral properties including US copper and gold mines.

Newmont's gold mines bolstered the company throughout the Depression. During the 1940s its focus shifted to copper and Africa. It bought Idarado Mining in 1943 and Newmont Oil in 1944 (sold 1988). The company grew during the 1950s by acquiring stakes in North American companies involved in offshore oil drilling nickel mining and uranium oxide production. It also bought stakes in copper mines in South Africa and South America.

Newmont started producing gold from the Carlin Trend in Nevada in the mid-1960s. It bought a one-third stake in Foote Mineral (iron alloys and lithium) in 1967; by 1974 it controlled 83% of the company (sold 1987). In 1969 Newmont merged with Magma Copper one of the US's largest copper companies. A Newmont-led consortium bought Peabody Coal the US's largest coal producer from Kennecott Copper in 1977 (sold 1990).

After its 1980 discovery of one of the century's most important gold stakes Gold Quarry in the Carlin Trend Newmont spent a decade fending off takeover attempts. The company began selling off noncore operations to focus on gold. Magma Copper was spun off to stockholders in 1988.

A proposed merger with American Barrick Resources a major stockholder collapsed in 1991. Former Freeport-McMoRan VP Ronald Cambre became CEO in 1993 and that year the company began mining in Peru. A 1994 action by the French government one of Newmont's partners in Peru's Yanacocha Mine kicked off a protracted battle over the property's ownership. The claim was upheld in 1998 raising Newmont's stake to more than 50%. Reflecting its increasing interest in Indonesia in 1996 Newmont and Japan's Sumitomo formed a joint venture to exploit gold reserves on Sumbawa Island. In 1997 the company increased its gold reserves and territory by acquiring Santa Fe Pacific Gold for about $2.1 billion.

For years Newmont and Barrick Gold Corporation operated interlocked mining claims in Nevada's Carlin Trend which prevented optimal exploitation by either company. In 1999 both companies agreed to a mutually advantageous land swap in the region.

In 2000 an Indonesian court ordered the closure of the Minahasa mine over a local tax dispute; the company's joint venture agreed to pay a $500000 penalty to settle the matter. Newmont was fined $500000 after a mercury spill at its Yanacocha mine. That year Newmont settled the lingering ownership dispute over the Yanacocha.

Company president Wayne Murdy became CEO early in 2001 (he replaced Cambre as chairman in 2002). Newmont acquired Battle Mountain Gold in 2001 for nearly $600 million. Late that year Newmont moved to acquire Australia's top gold producer Normandy Mining (setting off a bidding war with AngloGold) as well as Canadian gold miner France-Nevada Mining Corp. AngloGold bowed out of the "battle for Normandy" in early 2002 but later completed a three-way deal in which it acquired Normandy and Franco-Nevada.

In 2003 Newmont reduced its stake in Kinross Gold from 14% to 5% and it considered selling off the Ghanaian interests it had gained in the Normandy merger. However in 2004 Newmont literally discovered a gold mine in Ghana — a major district with some 16 million equity ou

EXECUTIVES

Svp South America, Trent Tempel

Evp Human Resources, William N. (Bill) MacGowan, age 58, $450,000 total compensation

Vp And Cio, James (Jim) Zetwick

Evp And Cfo, Nancy K. Buese, age 49, $90,865 total compensation

Evp Strategic Development, Randy Engel, age 51, $627,196 total compensation

Evp And General Counsel, Stephen P. Gottesfeld, age 50, $512,074 total compensation

Svp Exploration, Grigore Simon

Evp Technical Services, Scott P. Lawson

President And Ceo, Gary J. Goldberg, age 59, $1,270,742 total compensation

Evp Sustainability And External Relations, Elaine Dorward-King, $468,297 total compensation

Svp Africa, Alwyn Pretorius, age 46

Svp Asia Pacific, Thomas (Tom) Palmer, $615,134 total compensation

Vice President Total Rewards And Human Resources Systems, David Kristoff

Senior Vice President African Operations, Jeffrey Huspeni

Vice President Global Government Relations, Rich Herold

Vice President Of Finance And Treasurer, Josh Hallenbeck

Auditors: Ernst & Young LLP

LOCATIONS

HQ: Newmont Mining Corp (Holding Co)
6363 South Fiddlers Green Circle, Greenwood Village, CO 80111
Phone: 303 863-7414 **Fax:** 303 837-5837
Web: www.newmont.com

2017 Sales

	$ mil.	% of total
UK	5,490	74
Switzerland	657	9
Korea	384	5
Philippines	310	5
Germany	168	3
Canada	96	1
US	91	1
Japan	87	1
Other	65	1
Total	**7,384**	**100**

PRODUCTS/OPERATIONS

2017 Sales

	$ mil.	% of total
Gold	7,033	96
Copper	315	4
Total	**7,348**	**100**

COMPETITORS

Agnico-Eagle	Goldcorp
AngloGold Ashanti	Kinross Gold
Barrick Gold	Newcrest Mining
Franco-Nevada	

HISTORICAL FINANCIALS

Company Type: Public

Income Statement

FYE: December 31

	REVENUE ($ mil.)	NET INCOME ($ mil.)	NET PROFIT MARGIN	EMPLOYEES
12/17	7,348	(98)	—	24,658
12/16	6,711	(627)	—	12,400
12/15	7,729	220	2.8%	15,600
12/14	7,292	508	7.0%	13,700
12/13	8,322	(2,462)	—	15,085
Annual Growth	(3.1%)	—		13.1%

2017 Year-End Financials

Debt ratio: 19.77%
Return on equity: (-0.92%)
Cash ($ mil.): 3,259
Current ratio: 3.63
Long-term debt ($ mil.): 4,061
No. of shares (mil.): 533
Dividends
Yield: 0.0%
Payout: —
Market value ($ mil.): 20,001

	STOCK PRICE ($) FY Close	P/E High/Low		PER SHARE ($) Earnings	Dividends	Book Value
12/17	37.52	—	—	(0.18)	0.25	19.90
12/16	34.07	—	—	(1.18)	0.13	20.21
12/15	17.99	64	36	0.43	0.10	21.43
12/14	18.90	27	17	1.02	0.23	20.60
12/13	23.03	—	—	(4.94)	1.23	20.38
Annual Growth	13.0%			—	(32.8%)	(0.6%)

News Corp (New)

News Corp is one of the biggest news organizations in the world publishing well-known mastheads such as The Wall Street Journal and New York Post Australia's Herald Sun and The Sun and The Times in the UK. The company owns the Dow Jones and Factiva information services as well as book publisher HarperCollins. In TV News Corp has a majority stake in Foxtel in Australia and owns the Australian News Channel. Other properties are the real estate websites REA Group and Motive. North America supplies about 45% of News Corp?s revenue.

Operations

News Corp divides its operations into five segments — news and information services more than 55% of revenue; book publishing about 20% of revenue; digital real estate services about 13%; subscription video services about 10%; and other 2%.

The news and information services segment includes News America Marketing (NAM) a publisher and distributor of coupons in newspapers and on the SmartSource.com website. NAM's customers include many of the largest consumer packaged-goods advertisers in the US and Canada. It reaches 74 million households for its freestanding coupon inserts and about 52500 retail outlets for its in-store advertising.

In book publishing the imprints under Harper Collins include Harper William Morrow Avon and Harlequin. Among its recent best-sellers have been Hillbilly Elegy and The Woman in the Window.

The Digital Real Estate Services segment consists of News Corp?s 62% in REA Group a publicly-traded company based in Australia and its 80% interest in Move. The remaining 20% interest in Move is held by REA Group. REA lists properties for sale in Australia and Asia and offers financial services. Move operates the realtor.com website in the US.

The Subscription Video Services segment provides sports entertainment and news services to pay-TV subscribers via cable satellite and over the internet. Properties include the new Foxtel network in Australia of which News Corp owns 65% and the Australian News Channel.

Geographic Reach

News Corp. is based in New York City and has subsidiaries elsewhere in the US Australia and the UK. In addition book publisher HarperCollins has a warehouse in Scotland and Dow Jones runs an office in Hong Kong. North America accounts for more than 45% of News Corp.?s sales followed by the Australasia region with about 35% and Europe (mostly the UK and Ireland) about 20%.

Sales and Marketing

News Corp. spends an average of about $620 million a year on advertising.

Financial Performance

News Corp.?s revenue has been uneven since 2014 and it has lost money for three out of those five years including the last two as sales generated by its news operations have diminished. The news operation?s share of revenue fell to 57% in 2018 from 72% in 2014.

In 2018 (ended June) revenue rose 11% to $9 billion from the year before. The increase was driven by the combination of Foxtel in which News Corp. and Telstra held 50% stakes and FOX SPORTS that created the new Foxtel in Australia. The News and Information segment posted slightly higher revenue on a 5% increase in circulation and subscription sales. The Digital Real Estate Services segment also delivered more sales as did the Book Publishing segment which was boosted by strong sales in the general books category and a sublicensing agreement for The Lord of the Rings trilogy. Advertising sales slipped 2% for the year.

In 2018 News Corp.?s net loss about doubled to $1.5 billion from a loss of $738 million in 2017. The 2018 loss included write-offs and other charges related to the Foxtel deal.

News Corp. had about $2 billion in cash and equivalents in its coffers in 2018 about the same as 2017. In 2018 operations generated $757 million while investing activities used $321 million and financing activities used $398 million.

The company?s flexibility to maneuver financially might be compromised by an increase in debt that resulted from the Foxtel deal. News Corp?s debt jumped to about $1.5 billion in 2018 from $276 million and $369 million in 2017 and 2016 respectively.

Strategy

Revenue from News Corp?s News and Information segment has declined in recent years as advertising revenue has shifted from newspapers to companies like Google and Facebook. The challenge for News Corp and other media companies is to find businesses that can produce growth to make up for the news and advertising revenue decline.

In 2018 News Corp and Telstra merged their 50% each ownership in Foxtel with News Corp?s FOX SPORTS to create a new version of Foxtel. After the combination Foxtel provides a greater range of programming to viewers in Australia on a wider range of devices.

The digital real estate services segment has become News Corp?s fastest-growing business and produces outsized earnings. The segment?s sales rose more than 20% in 2018 from 2017 adding four times more revenue than the news and information segment did. The real estate segment provides more than two-thirds of gross earnings while accounting for about 13% of revenue. News Corp beefed up the real estate properties with the ac-

quisitions of Opcity in the US and Hometrack in Australia in 2018.

Mergers and Acquisitions

In 2018 News Corp and Telstra combined their 50% interests in Foxtel and News Corp?s ownership of FOX SPORTS Australia into a new company which took the new Foxtel name. Under the new setup News Corp owns 65% of Foxtel and Telstra 45%. The combination helped both entities expand programming and the range of devices on which the service can be accessed.

News Corp. beefed up its real estate-related websites and services with two acquisitions in 2018. It acquired Opcity a real estate technology platform that matches buyers and sellers in real time for $210 million. The acquisition broadened realtor.com?s lead generation product portfolio.

REA Group acquired Hometrack Australia provider of property data services to the financial sector for $130 million. The acquisition allows REA to deliver more property data and insights to customers and consumers.

In fiscal 2016 News Corporation spent around $800 million on acquisitions. The company acquired Checkout 51 Mobile Apps ULC Unruly Holdings Limited DIAKRIT International Limited iProperty Group Limited Flatmates.com.au Pty Ltd Australian Regional Media and Wireless Group plc.

EXECUTIVES

Senior Vice President And Deputy General Counsel, Genie Gavenchak

Ceo Harper Collins, Brian Murray, age 51

Chairman And Ceo News America Marketing, Martin (Marty) Garofalo

Ceo News Uk, Rebekah Brooks, age 50

Cto, Marc Frons, age 60

Ceo Unruly, Sarah Wood

Ceo, Robert Thomson, age 58, $2,038,462 total compensation

Cfo, Susan Panuccio

General Counsel And Chief Compliance Officer, David B. Pitofsky, $968,269 total compensation

Ceo The New York Post, Jesse Angelo

Ceo Dow Jones & Company, William (Will) Lewis

Ceo Storyful, Rahul Chopra

Ceo Move Inc., Ryan OÁ'Hara

Evp And Chief Communications Officer, James E. (Jim) Kennedy

Chairman News Corp Australasia, Michael Miller

Evp And Global Head Government Affairs, Antoinette (Toni) Bush

Svp And Treasurer, Rakesh Jobanputra

Senior Vice President Head Of Human Resources Coverage Products And Operations, Katie Perdomo

Vice President Telecommunications, Guy Wheaton

Vice President Strategic Sourcing Procurement, Tracey Williamson

Vice President Of Technology, Dan Gould

Vice President Marketing Services At News America Marketing, Marissa Bishop

Senior Vice President And Deputy General Counsel, James Marcovitz

Vice President Tax Operations, Scott Lindstrom

Senior Vice President, Paula Wardynski, age 62

Senior Vice President Physical Production, Thomas Imperato

Vice President Information Technology, Cindy Schwan

Senior Vice President Strategy And Corporate Development European Television, Marc Heller

Vice President Manager Director, Trista Reiser

Senior Vice President Corporate Affairs, Jim Platt

Vice President Global Transfer Pricing, Kathrin Zoeller

Vice President, Robert Ennis

Executive Vice President Office Of The Chairman, Jeremy Phillips

Senior Vice President Head Of Tax, Michael Fichera

Senior Vice President Global Government Affairs, Joanne Dowdell

Senior Vice President Global Head Of Programmatic, Chris Guenther

Senior Vice President Global Government Affairs, Todd Thorpe

Vice President Head Of Cyber Security Technology Passionate. Principled. Purposeful, Miguel El Lakkis

Senior Vice President Corporate Development, Brandon Sokol

Senior Vice President Group Chief Compliance Officer North America, Javier Robles

Co-chairman News Corp And 21st Century Fox, Lachlan K. Murdoch, age 45

Chairman, K. Rupert Murdoch, age 87

Assistant Treasurer, Stanley Pauzer

Auditors: Ernst & Young LLP

LOCATIONS

HQ: News Corp (New)
1211 Avenue of the Americas, New York, NY 10036
Phone: 212 416-3400
Web: www.newscorp.com

2018 Sales

	$ mil.	% of total
US & Canada	3,998	44
Europe	1,766	20
Australia and others	3,260	36
Total	**9,024**	**100**

PRODUCTS/OPERATIONS

2018 Sales

	$ mil.	% of total
News & information services	5,119	57
Book publishing	1,758	19
Digital real estate services	1,141	13
Subscription Video Services	1,004	11
Other	2	-
Total	**9,024**	**100**

2018 Sales

	$ mil.	% of total
Advertising	2,799	31
Circulation & subscription	3,021	33
Consumer	1,664	18
Real Estate	858	10
Other	682	8
Total	**9,024**	**100**

List of Items

Newspapers
Dow Jones
Barron's (magazine)
Dow Jones Newswires
Factiva (online news and business research)
The Wall Street Journal
The Wall Street Journal Digital Network
MarketWatch
WSJ.com
New York Post
News International Limited (UK)
The Sun
The Sunday Times
The Times
The Advertiser (Adelaide)
The Australian (national daily)
The Courier-Mail (Brisbane)
The Daily Telegraph (Sydney)
Herald Sun (Melbourne)
Sunday Herald Sun (Melbourne)
Sunday Mail (Adelaide)
The Sunday Mail (Brisbane)
The Sunday Telegraph (Sydney)
The Sunday Times (Perth)
Book publishing
HarperCollins Publishers
Cable network programming
Foxtel (65% stake0
Digital real estate services
REA (61.6% stake)
Other
Amplify (digital education)

COMPETITORS

Bloomberg L.P.	LexisNexis
Crain Communications	New York Times
Financial Times	Pearson plc
Forbes	Simon & Schuster
Graham Holdings	Thomson Reuters
Hachette Book Group	Valassis
Hearst Corporation	

HISTORICAL FINANCIALS

Company Type: Public

Income Statement   FYE: June 30

	REVENUE ($ mil.)	NET INCOME ($ mil.)	NET PROFIT MARGIN	EMPLOYEES
06/18	9,024	(1,514)	—	28,000
06/17	8,139	(738)	—	26,000
06/16	8,292	179	2.2%	24,000
06/15	8,633	(147)	—	25,000
06/14	8,574	239	2.8%	22,000
Annual Growth	1.3%	—		6.2%

2018 Year-End Financials

Debt ratio: 11.94%	No. of shares (mil.): 583
Return on equity: (-15.05%)	Dividends
Cash ($ mil.): 2,034	Yield: 0.0%
Current ratio: 1.33	Payout: —
Long-term debt ($ mil.): 1,490	Market value ($ mil.): 9,037

	STOCK PRICE ($) FY Close	P/E High/Low	Earnings	Dividends	Book Value
06/18	15.50	— —	(2.60)	0.20	15.97
06/17	13.70	— —	(1.27)	0.20	18.57
06/16	11.35	52 35	0.30	0.20	19.97
06/15	14.59	— —	(0.26)	0.00	20.57
06/14	17.94	45 36	0.41	0.00	22.91
Annual Growth	(3.6%)	— —	—	—	(8.6%)

NextEra Energy Inc

NextEra Energy is moving its power business into the future. The holding company is mainly comprised of Florida Power & Light (FPL) and NextEra Energy Resources (NEER). FPL generates more than 26000 MW of electricity and delivers it to nearly 5.0 million customers in Florida. NEER generates nearly 20000 MW of modern energy via wind and solar sources making NextEra Energy one of the world?s largest generators of renewable energy. FPL operates primarily in Florida while NEER has assets in nearly 30 US states four Canadian provinces as well as in Spain.

HISTORY

During Florida's land boom of the early 1920s new homes and businesses were going up fast. But electric utilities were sparse and no transmission lines linked systems.

In 1925 American Power & Light Company (AP&L) which operated utilities throughout the Americas set up Florida Power & Light (FPL) to consolidate the state's electric assets. AP&L built transmission lines linking 58 communities from Miami to Stuart on the Atlantic Coast and from Arcadia to Punta Gorda on the Gulf.

FPL accumulated many holdings including a limestone quarry streetcars phone companies and water utilities and purchases in 1926 and 1927 nearly doubled its electric properties. In 1927 the company used an electric pump to demonstrate how swamplands could be drained and cultivated.

During the 1940s and 1950s FPL sold its non-electric properties. The Public Utility Holding Company Act of 1935 forced AP&L to spin off FPL in 1950. The company was listed on the NYSE that year.

FPL grew with Florida's booming population. In 1972 its first nuclear plant (Turkey Point south of Miami) went on line. In the 1980s it began to diversify with the purchase of real estate firm W. Flagler Investment in 1981 and FPL Group was created in 1984 as a holding company. It subsequently acquired Telesat Cablevision (1985) Colonial Penn Group (1985 insurance) and Turner Foods (1988 citrus groves). FPL Group formed ESI Energy in 1985 to develop nonutility energy projects.

Diversification efforts didn't pan out and in 1990 the firm wrote off about $750 million. That year sticking to electricity the utility snagged its first out-of-state power plant in Georgia acquiring a 76% stake (over five years). FPL Group sold its ailing Colonial Penn unit in 1991; two years later it sold its real estate holdings and some of its cable TV businesses.

The utility gave environmentalists cause to complain in 1995. First the St. Lucie nuclear plant was fined by the Nuclear Regulatory Commission for a series of problems. FPL also wanted to burn orimulsion a cheap tar-like fuel. (Barred by the governor the utility gave up the plan in 1998.)

In 1997 FPL Group created FPL Energy an independent power producer (IPP) out of its ESI Energy and international operations; FPL Energy teamed up with Belgium-based Tractebel the next year to buy two gas-fired plants in Boston and Newark New Jersey.

FPL Energy built wind-power facilities in Iowa in 1998 and in Wisconsin and Texas in 1999; it also bought 35 generating plants in Maine in 1999. That year FPL Group sold its Turner Foods citrus unit and the rest of its cable TV holdings. By 2000 FPL Energy owned interests in plants in 12 states.

EXECUTIVES

Chairman And Ceo, James L. (Jim) Robo, age 56, $1,300,000 total compensation

Evp And General Counsel, Charles E. Sieving, age 45, $689,000 total compensation

President And Ceo Nextera Energy Resources, Armando Pimentel, age 56, $838,100 total compensation

President And Ceo Florida Power & Light, Eric E. Silagy, $796,100 total compensation

Evp Human Resources And Corporate Sevices, Deborah H. Caplan

Evp Finance And Cfo, John Ketchum, $575,000 total compensation

Auditors: DELOITTE & TOUCHE LLP

LOCATIONS

HQ: NextEra Energy Inc
700 Universe Boulevard, Juno Beach, FL 33408
Phone: 561 694-4000   **Fax:** 561 694-4620
Web: www.nexteraenergy.com

PRODUCTS/OPERATIONS

2016 sales

	$ mil.	% of total
Florida Power & Light	10,895	68
NextEra Energy Resources	4,893	30
Corporate & other	367	2
Total	**16**	**100**

Selected Subsidiaries and Divisions

Florida Power & Light Company
Energy Marketing and Trading
NextEra Energy Capital Holdings Inc.
NextEra Energy Resources LLC
NextEra Energy Partners
NextEra Energy Transmission

COMPETITORS

AES	Florida Public
Bangor Hydro-Electric	Utilities
Berkshire Hathaway	JEA
Energy	Oglethorpe Power
CMS Energy	Progress Energy
Calpine	Public Service
Chesapeake Utilities	Enterprise Group
Duke Energy	Seminole Electric
Entergy	Southern Company
Exelon	TECO Energy

HISTORICAL FINANCIALS

Company Type: Public

Income Statement   FYE: December 31

	REVENUE ($ mil.)	NET INCOME ($ mil.)	NET PROFIT MARGIN	EMPLOYEES
12/17	17,195	5,378	31.3%	13,900
12/16	16,155	2,912	18.0%	14,200
12/15	17,486	2,762	15.8%	13,800
12/14	17,021	2,469	14.5%	13,800
12/13	15,136	1,908	12.6%	13,400
Annual Growth	3.2%	29.6%		0.9%

2017 Year-End Financials

Debt ratio: 35.86%	No. of shares (mil.): 471
Return on equity: 20.47%	Dividends
Cash ($ mil.): 1,714	Yield: 0.0%
Current ratio: 0.64	Payout: 34.5%
Long-term debt ($ mil.): 31,463	Market value ($ mil.): 73,565

	STOCK PRICE ($) FY Close	P/E High/Low	Earnings	Dividends	Book Value
12/17	156.19	14 10	11.38	3.93	59.89
12/16	119.46	21 16	6.25	3.48	52.01
12/15	103.89	18 15	6.06	3.08	48.97
12/14	106.29	19 15	5.60	2.90	44.96
12/13	85.62	20 15	4.47	2.64	41.47
Annual Growth	16.2%	— —	26.3%	10.5%	9.6%

NGL Energy Partners LP

All hail NGL for providing a secured energy trail. This Master Limited Partnership (MLP) provides transportation storage blending and marketing services for crude oil natural gas refined products and renewables in the US. With the Grand Mesa pipeline seven storage terminals and some 5.5 MMbbls of storage capacity to its name NGL buys refined petroleum in the Gulf Coast Southeast and Midwest regions transports them through the Colonial Plantation Magellan and NuStar pipelines and ultimately sells them to industrial end users or independent retailers and distributors. In addition the company provides water solutions that treats processes and disposes wastewater and solids generated from oil and natural gas production. The company also has a fleet of 160 trucks and 260 trailers as well as 10 tows and 19 barges. In 2018 NGL sold its retail propane delivery business.

Operations

NGL Energy reports four major business segments.

Refined Products and Renewables (70% of sales) buys refined petroleum in the Gulf Coast Southeast and Midwest regions transports them via the Colonial Plantation Magellan and NuStar pipelines and sells to industrial end users or independent retailers and distributors.

The company's crude oil logistics business (approximately 15%) purchases crude oil from producers and transports it for resale at pipeline injection points storage terminals barge loading facilities rail facilities refineries and other trade hubs.

The Liquids segment (10% revenue) supplies natural gas liquids to retailers wholesalers refiners and petrochemical plants throughout the US and in Canada and provides NGL terminaling and storage services through more than 20 terminals throughout the US its salt dome storage facility in Utah and its leased storage and railcar transportation services.

Water Solutions segment revenues (some 1%) are derived from the gathering transportation treatment and disposal of wastewater generated from oil and natural gas production operations. The company owns 75 water treatment and disposal facilities and 100 wells.

The company's retail propane business was sold in 2018. It distributed propane and distillates propane tanks and rental equipment to 320000 customers from 90 service centers and 70 satellite locations. In 2017 it accounted for 5% of annual sales.

Geographic ReachNGL Energy has significant operations in the Bakken Shale Basin of North Dakota the DJ Basin in Colorado the Mississippi Lime shale play in Oklahoma the Permian Basin in Texas and New Mexico the Eagle Ford shale play in Texas as well as the Anadarko Basin in Oklahoma and Texas and southern Louisiana.The company also provides Water Solutions near elevated lands with oil and natural gas production such as the Pinedale Anticline Basin in Wyoming the DJ Basin in Colorado the Permian and Eagle Ford Basins in Texas as well as the Delaware Basin in New Mexico.Its liquid natural gas terminals are in Jefferson City Missouri East St. Louis Illinois and in Ontario Canada.Headquartered in Tulsa Oklahoma the company has corporate offices in Denver and Houston.

Sales and Marketing

NGL Energy sells its refined and renewables products to commercial and industrial end users independent retailers distributors marketers government entities and other wholesalers of refined petroleum products. It also sells its products at TransMontaigne Partners L.P.'s terminals and to third parties. Its liquids business serves national regional and independent retail industrial wholesale petrochemical refiner and natural gas liquids production customers.

Financial Performance

Growth at NGL has skyrocketed over the last decade. In 2009 the company barely had $700 million in annual sales. A decade later it reported more than $17 billion in revenue. Though profits fluctuate wildly the company has posted positive net income in all but two years of the last decade.

Sales at NGL has burgeoned from $13 billion in 2017 to $17.3 billion in 2018. Most of it came from NGL's largest segment Refined Products & renewables ($2.8 billion increase) adding pipeline capacity rights purchased during 2017. Crude oil prices and volumes sold went up adding $600 million more to the coffers over 2016.

Net income fell from $137 million in profits in 2017 to a loss of $71 million in 2018 mostly due to a reduction of special income by $152 million followed by a reduction in gain on sale of property/plant/equipment by $100 million.

The company has $26 million in cash holdings at the end of 2018. Operations provided $138 million and a further $270 million came from investments (mostly from sale of businesses) offset by $394 million used in financing activities mostly going towards long-term debt reduction.

Strategy

NGL Energy has an extensive industry and MLP experience with acquiring integrating operating and growing successful businesses. With the sale of its propane business in 2018 NGL makes clear its strategic priority—use the $1.1 billion in proceeds to immediately repay certain indebtedness (company's debt stands at $2.7 billion) as well as invest in making strategic growth acquisitions in the Water Solutions business which NGL wants to expand (this segment hardly amounts to 1% of its current revenue composition). For 2019 the company wants to grow its Water Solutions business by as much as $450 million.

Additionally the company wants to focus on its core business—crude logistics. An equal emphasis is being given on increasing fee-based business and long-term contracts with high credit quality customers by transitioning a repeatable cash flow model.

NGL Energy is well poised for profits going forward. Its Crude Oil Logistics segment posted exceptional numbers due to increased volumes on Grand Mesa as the pipeline continues to benefit from increased production out of the DJ Basin. Water Solutions business has also continued to benefit from high crude oil prices increased rig counts and increased crude oil production due to price recovery.

Furthermore In the beginning of 2018 NGL and Magnum Liquids formed a joint venture to focus on the storage of natural gas liquids and refined products by combining NGL's Sawtooth Storage Facility with Magnum's refined products rights and adjacent leasehold. NGL will sell an interest in Sawtooth to Magnum for $45 million in cash due at closing.

Mergers and Acquisitions

NGL Energy's acquisitions are now focused on expanding its Water Solution business—largely consisting of its Delaware Basin water infrastructure strategy—spending $171 million by August 2018.

This included the purchase of 36000-acre Beckham Ranch in Lea County New Mexico with its 9.6 million barrels of annual fresh water rights plus the McCloy Ranch located in Eddy and Lea Counties—some 87000 acres of land acquired in mid-2018 with its 2 million barrels of annual water rights. The Partnership now owns 30 million barrels of available freshwater volumes in the Delaware Basin.

Expanding its portfolio in 2017 NGL Energy Partners LP bought assets from Murphy Energy. The assets included the Port Hudson Louisiana Terminal an NGL terminal that supports refined products blending and the Kingfisher Oklahoma Facility a natural gas liquids and condensate facility. The combined purchase price of the assets was $51 million.

In 2016 the company acquired 57% of an existing produced water pipeline company operating in the Delaware Basin portion of West Texas.

Company Background

Formed in 2010 by several investors NGL Energy Partners acquired and combined the assets and operations of NGL Supply a wholesale propane and terminalling business founded in 1967 and Hicksgas a retail propane business founded in 1940.

EXECUTIVES

Ceo, H. Michael Krimbill, age 64, $292,500 total compensation

Evp And Cfo, Robert W. (Trey) Karlovich, age 41

President Retail Division, Shawn W. Coady, age 56, $311,250 total compensation

President Eastern Retail Operations, Vincent J. Osterman, age 61, $250,000 total compensation

President Ngl And President And Ceo High Sierra Energy, James J. (Jim) Burke, age 62, $381,750 total compensation

Evp Ngl Crude Logistics, Don Robinson

Evp Ngl Liquids, Jack Eberhardt

Cio, Jennifer Kingham

Executive Vice President Midstream Division, David Eastin

Senior Vice President Accounting, Patrice Armbruster

Executive Vice President Ngl Refined Products, Donald Jensen

Svp Accounting And Corporate Controller, Sharra Straight

Vice President Supply, Mark McGinty

Evp Ngl Water Solutions, Doug White

Svp Business Development, Greg Blais

Executive Vice President Operations, Greg Pound

Senior Vice President Asset Management, Todd Tanory

Svp General Counsel And Corporate Secretary, Kurston McMurray

Vice President Business Development Crude Assets, Derek Graham

Vice President Ngl Marine, Craig Lagrone

Senior Vice President Accounting And Chief Accoun, Larry Thuillier

Vice President Business Development, Carl Peterson

Vp Environmental Compliance, Dudley Tarlton

Vice President Sawtooth Ngl, Mark Henson

Vice President Trade Operations, Scott Ernest

Vice President National Accounts, Billy Wilson

Senior Vice President Finance And Treasurer, Linda Bridges

Vice President National Accounts, Steven Cooper

Vice President Trucking, Willie Seale

Senior Vice President Refined Products, Darrell Weakland

Senior Vice President Water Solutions, James Winter

Evp Ngl Refined Products, Don Jensen

Senior Vice President Renewable Fuels, Grant Vangilder

Executive Vice President, Greg Piper

Vice President, Mark Mcgrath

Vice President Environmental Health And Safety, Garrett Clemons

Vice President West Texas Region, Wes Pearson

Vice President Internal Audit And Sox Compliance, Chris Carter

Svp Mergers And Acquisitions, Christian Dobrauc

Auditors: Grant Thornton LLP

LOCATIONS

HQ: NGL Energy Partners LP
6120 South Yale Avenue, Suite 805, Tulsa, OK 74136
Phone: 918 481-1119
Web: www.nglenergypartners.com

PRODUCTS/OPERATIONS

2017 Sales

	$ mil.	% of total
Refined products and Renewables	12,200	71
Crude oil logistics	2,260	13
Liquids	2,070	12
Retail propane	521	3
Water solutions	229	1
Other	1	-
Total	**17,282**	**100**

COMPETITORS

AmeriGas Partners	Exxon Mobil
Blueknight Energy	Ferrellgas Partners
Partners	Holly Energy Partners
Crestwood Midstream	Huntsman International
Partners LP	Martin Midstream
Duke Energy	Partners
Energy Transfer	Occidental Petroleum
Enterprise Products	Williams Companies
Equistar Chemicals	

HISTORICAL FINANCIALS

Company Type: Public

Income Statement

FYE: March 31

	REVENUE ($ mil.)	NET INCOME ($ mil.)	NET PROFIT MARGIN	EMPLOYEES
03/18	17,282	(70)	—	2,400
03/17	13,022	137	1.1%	2,700
03/16	11,742	(198)	—	3,200
03/15	16,802	16	0.1%	3,100
03/14	9,699	47	0.5%	2,500
Annual Growth	15.5%	—	—	(1.0%)

2018 Year-End Financials

Debt ratio: 43.66%
Return on equity: (-96.78%)
Cash ($ mil.): 26
Current ratio: 1.61
Long-term debt ($ mil.): 2,682
No. of shares (mil.): 121
Dividends
  Yield: 0.1%
  Payout: —
Market value ($ mil.): 1,338

	STOCK PRICE ($) FY Close	P/E High/Low		PER SHARE ($) Earnings	Dividends	Book Value
03/18	11.00	—	—	(1.08)	1.56	17.15
03/17	22.60	26	7	0.95	1.56	18.32
03/16	7.52	—	—	(2.35)	2.54	15.88
03/15	26.23	—	—	(0.29)	2.37	20.46
03/14	37.53	74	52	0.51	2.01	19.22
Annual Growth	(26.4%)	—	—	—	(6.2%)	(2.8%)

Nicolet Bankshares Inc

EXECUTIVES

Pres-ceo, Robert Atwell
Vice President Commercial Banking, Ken Glasheen
Auditors: Porter Keadle Moore, LLC

LOCATIONS

HQ: Nicolet Bankshares Inc
  111 North Washington Street, Green Bay, WI 54301
Phone: 920 430-1400
Web: www.nicoletbank.com

HISTORICAL FINANCIALS

Company Type: Public

Income Statement

FYE: December 31

	ASSETS ($ mil.)	NET INCOME ($ mil.)	INCOME AS % OF ASSETS	EMPLOYEES
12/17	2,932	33	1.1%	535
12/16	2,300	18	0.8%	480
12/15	1,214	11	0.9%	280
12/14	1,215	9	0.8%	280
12/13	1,198	16	1.3%	290
Annual Growth	25.1%	19.7%	—	16.5%

2017 Year-End Financials

Debt ratio: 2.66%
Return on equity: 10.36%
Cash ($ mil.): 154
Current ratio: —
Long-term debt ($ mil.): —
No. of shares (mil.): 9
Dividends
  Yield: —
  Payout: —
Market value ($ mil.): 537

	STOCK PRICE ($) FY Close	P/E High/Low		PER SHARE ($) Earnings	Dividends	Book Value
12/17	54.74	17	13	3.33	0.00	37.09
12/16	47.69	19	12	2.37	0.00	32.26
12/15	31.79	12	9	2.57	0.00	26.36
12/14	25.00	11	7	2.25	0.00	27.35
12/13	16.54	5	4	3.80	0.00	24.73
Annual Growth	34.9%	—	—	(3.2%)	—	10.7%

NIELSEN HOLDINGS PLC

EXECUTIVES

Ceo, Mitch Barns

LOCATIONS

HQ: NIELSEN HOLDINGS PLC
  85 BROAD ST, NEW YORK, NY 100042434
Phone: 646 654-5000

HISTORICAL FINANCIALS

Company Type: Private

Income Statement

FYE: December 31

	REVENUE ($ mil.)	NET INCOME ($ mil.)	NET PROFIT MARGIN	EMPLOYEES
12/15	6,172	575	9.3%	43,061
12/14	6,288	381	6.1%	—
12/13	5,703	736	12.9%	—
12/12	5,612	273	4.9%	—
Annual Growth	3.2%	28.2%	—	—

2015 Year-End Financials

Debt ratio: —
Return on equity: 9.30%
Cash ($ mil.): 357
Current ratio: 0.90
Long-term debt ($ mil.): —
Dividends
  Yield: —
  Payout: —
Market value ($ mil.): —

NIKE Inc

Fleet-of-footwear NIKE named for the Greek goddess of victory is the world's #1 shoe and apparel company. NIKE designs develops and sells a variety of products and services to help in playing basketball and soccer (football) as well as in running men's and women's training and other action sports. Under its namesake brand NIKE also markets sports-inspired products for children and various competitive and recreational activities such as golf tennis and walking and sportswear by Converse and Hurley. NIKE sells through more than 1000-owned retail stores worldwide an e-commerce site and to thousands of retail accounts independent distributors and licensees.

HISTORY

Phil Knight a good miler and Bill Bowerman a track coach who tinkered with shoe designs met at the University of Oregon in 1957. The two men formed Blue Ribbon Sports in 1962 in an effort to make quality American running shoes. The next year they began selling Tiger shoes manufactured by Japanese shoe manufacturer Onitsuka Tiger. They sold the running shoes out of cars at track meets.

The company rebranded as NIKE in 1972 named for the Greek goddess of victory. The NIKE "Swoosh" logo was designed by a graduate student named Carolyn Davidson who was paid $35. The same year NIKE broke with Onitsuka in a dispute over distribution rights.

NIKE re-evaluated its long-term growth strategy in fiscal 2012 and as a result divested its Cole Haan and Umbro businesses in February 2013 and November 2012 respectively. NIKE sold Umbro to Iconix Brand Group for $225 million. The company sold Cole Haan to London-based private equity firm Apax Partners for $570 million.

EXECUTIVES

Vice President Of Sales And Marketing, Shelley Dewey
Chairman President And Ceo, Mark G. Parker, age 62, $1,550,000 total compensation
Coo, Eric D. Sprunk, age 54, $990,000 total compensation
President Nike Brand, Trevor A. Edwards, age 55, $990,000 total compensation
President Geographies And Sales, Elliott J. Hill
President Product And Merchandising, Michael Spillane, age 55
Evp Chief Administrative Officer And General Counsel, Hilary K. Krane, age 54
President And Ceo Converse, Davide Grasso
Evp Global Sports Marketing, John F. Slusher, age 49
Evp Global Human Resources, David J. Ayre, age 58
Vp And General Manager Global Women's Division, Heidi OÂ'Neill
Evp And Cfo, Andrew (Andy) Campion, $822,306 total compensation
Global Cio, Jim Scholefield
Vice President, Andy Campion
Vice President And Chief Marketing Officer, Dirk-Jan V Hameren
Vice President Human Resources Business Partner Geographies, Mike Tarbell
Vice President North America Supply Chain Operations, Trish Young
Vp And General Manager Athletic Specialty, Jim Reynolds
Executive Vice President, Reham Habib
Vice President Creative Director Apparel, Thomas Walker
Vice President Apparel Sports Category, Reenie Benziger
Vice President Usa Footwear, Dan Jones
Senior Vice President Of Commercial Banking, Evelyn Gomez
Vice President General Manager Global Womens Training, Heidi ONeill
Vice President Creative Director Nike Sportswear, Kurt Parker
Vice President Sales Central Eastern Europe, Matthijs Visch
Vp Manufacturing, Greg Bui
Executive Vice President Of Meth Production, Jim Ford
Event Vice President, Leroy Ebanks
Vice President In House Manufacturing, Lalit Monteiro

Vice President And Corporate Secretary, Ann Miller
Vice President Young Athletes Sales, Mark Trelease
Vp North America Marketplace Merchandising, Archie Mceachern
Vice President Global Apparel And Equipment Materials Nike, Susi Proudman
Vice President E Commerce, Lisa Lynham
Vice President Of Corporate Operations, David Taylor
Vice President Global Digital Commerce, Kristine Rebber
National Account Manager, Joni Kristo
Vice President Creative Director Athletic Training, Janett Nichol
Vice President Global Entertainment Marketing, Pamela McConnell
Vice President Global Running Footwear, Tim Slingsby
Executive Assistant Senior Vice President Government And Public Affairs, Keyanus Jacobo
Global Vice President Sports Apparel, Aaron Heiser
Vice President And Chief Administrative Officer, Ronald McCray
Vice President And General Manager Nike Japan, Christophe Merkel
Vice President Treasure, Bob Woodruff
Vice President Human Resources Business Partner, Karen Weisz
Vice President, Ailsa Gilroy
Vice President Direct To Consumer Technology, Steven Dee
Vice President Marketing, Todd Jacobs
Vice President Director Manager, Nick Athanasakos
Vice President And Gm Nike Global Basketball, Craig Zanon
Vice President Footwear Sportswear Nike Inc., Andrea Correani
Vice President Global Basketball Sports Marketing, Lynn Merritt
Vice President And General Manager Global Nike Sportswear Category Management, Dirk-jan Van Hameren
Vice President Global Operations And Technology, Hans Vanalebeek
Management Vice President, Hubertus Hoyt
Vice President And Corporate Controller, Chris Abston
Vice President North America Brand Marketing, David Schriber
Vp And General Manager Global Young Athletes, Carl Grebert
Vice President Human Resources Business Partner Emerging Markets, Julie Fuller
Vice President Broad Based Total Rewards, Kimberly Lupo
Vice President Treasury And Investor Relations, Nitesh Sharan
Vice President Global Intellectual Property Transactions And Licensing, Paul Saraceni
Vice President Diversity And Inclusion, Antoine Andrews
Vp Manufacturing, Rich Sayre
Vice President Global Business Planning, Lee Arden
Vice President North America Fulfillment, Sean Halligan
Vice President Global Digital Operations And Geo Expansion, Shannon Glass
Vice President And General Manager Greater China South Territory, Simon Men
Vice President Merchant Global Training, Cedric Fletcher
Vice President Sales Account, Eddie Hu
Vice President Football Baseball Apparel, Matt Park
Vice President Jordan Cfl, Dave Schechter
Board Member, Nico Harrison
Board Member, Ruth Karanga
Treasurer, Paul Mitchell
Auditors: PricewaterhouseCoopers LLP

LOCATIONS

HQ: NIKE Inc
One Bowerman Drive, Beaverton, OR 97005-6453
Phone: 503 671-6453
Web: www.nike.com

2016 Sales

	% of total
North America	46
Western Europe	18
Greater China	12
Emerging Markets	11
Converse	6
Central & Eastern Europe	4
Japan	3
Global Brand Divisions	
Total	**100**

PRODUCTS/OPERATIONS

2016 Sales

	% of total
Footwear	61
Apparel	28
Equipment	5
Other	6
Total	**100**

Selected Products

Athletic Shoes
  Aquatic
  Auto racing
  Baseball
  Basketball
  Bicycling
  Cheerleading
  Cross-training
  Fitness
  Football
  Golf
  Running
  Soccer
  Tennis
  Volleyball
  Wrestling
Athletic Wear and Equipment
  Accessories
  Athletic bags
  Bats
  Caps
  Digital devices
  Fitness wear
  Gloves
  Golf clubs
  Headwear
  Jackets
  Pants
  Protective equipment
  Running clothes
  Shirts
  Shorts
  Skirts
  Snowboards and snowboard apparel
  Socks
  Sport balls
  Timepieces
  Uniforms

COMPETITORS

ASICS	Quiksilver
Acushnet Holdings	R. Griggs
Amer Sports	Ralph Lauren
Callaway Golf	Rawlings Sporting
Columbia Sportswear	Goods
Deckers Outdoor	Rollerblade
FUBU	Russell Brands
Fila Korea	Saucony
Fruit of the Loom	Skechers U.S.A.
Hanesbrands	Steven Madden
Iconix Brand Group	Timberland
Juicy Couture	Timex
K-Swiss	Tommy Hilfiger
Levi Strauss	Under Armour
Li Ning	VF Corporation
Mizuno	Victoria's Secret
New Balance	Stores
Oakley	Wolverine World Wide
PUMA SE	adidas

HISTORICAL FINANCIALS

Company Type: Public

Income Statement

FYE: May 31

	REVENUE ($ mil.)	NET INCOME ($ mil.)	NET PROFIT MARGIN	EMPLOYEES
05/18	36,397	1,933	5.3%	73,100
05/17	34,350	4,240	12.3%	74,400
05/16	32,376	3,760	11.6%	70,700
05/15	30,601	3,273	10.7%	62,600
05/14	27,799	2,693	9.7%	56,500
Annual Growth	7.0%	(8.0%)	—	6.7%

2018 Year-End Financials

Debt ratio: 16.91%
Return on equity: 17.40%
Cash ($ mil.): 4,249
Current ratio: 2.51
Long-term debt ($ mil.): 3,468
No. of shares (mil.): 1,601
Dividends
  Yield: 1.0%
  Payout: 64.9%
Market value ($ mil.): 114,952

	STOCK PRICE ($) FY Close	P/E High/Low	PER SHARE ($) Earnings	Dividends	Book Value
05/18	71.80	61 43	1.17	0.76	6.13
05/17	52.99	24 19	2.51	0.68	7.55
05/16	55.22	61 25	2.16	0.76	7.29
05/15	101.67	55 39	1.85	0.54	7.41
05/14	76.91	52 39	1.49	0.47	6.22
Annual Growth	(1.7%)	— —	(5.8%)	13.1%	(0.4%)

NiSource Inc. (Holding Co.)

Energy holding company NiSource manages rate-regulated natural gas and electric utility companies serving nearly 4 million customers in seven US states making it one the nation's largest natural gas distributors. Its principal subsidiaries include NiSource Gas Distribution Group and NIPSCO. It owns 60000 miles of natural gas pipelines reaching Indiana Ohio Pennsylvania Virginia Kentucky Maryland and Massachusetts. NiSource assets also include power plants that generate close to 3300 MW of electricity annually serving some 479000 customers in northern Indiana.

OperationsNiSource reports two business segments.Its Natural Gas Distribution operation is the company's primary business segment that include 60000 miles of pipelines in seven states. NiSource Gas Distribution Group owns six distribution subsidiaries while NIPSCO owns one. More than 40% of NiSource's sales comes from gas distribution revenue and an additional 20% comes from transportation revenue. Electricity Distribution business (36% of sales) is solely managed by NIPSCO. It generates 3300 MW of electricity per year through coal-fired gas-fired and hydroelectric generated plants. Additionally NIPSCO participates in the MISO transmission service and wholesale energy market. MISO which controls functional control of NIPSCO's transmission assets is a FERC-compliant nonprofit organization created to improve power reliability of the region.

Geographic ReachNiSource serves almost 4 million customers in Indiana Ohio Pennsylvania Virginia Kentucky Maryland and Massachusetts. The company also provides electricity in the northern region of Indiana.
Financial Performance

Annual sales at NiSource has slightly declined from a five-year peak of $5.3 billion in 2014 to $4.9 billion in 2017 due to falling revenue from gas distribution and transportation segments. Net income has fallen more dramatically from $530 million in 2014 to just below $130 million three years later.

Year-over-year revenue increased 7% in 2017 from $4.5 billion posted in 2016 primarily due to increases from new base-rate proceedings as well as additional sales from infrastructure replacement programs. Customer growth added some $10 million more to the coffers.

Net income plummeted more than half from $328 million in 2016 to $129 million in 2017 due to a year-over-year increase of $132 million in income taxes as well as $112 million in losses from early extinguishment of long-term debt.

Net cash holdings nudged up slightly to $38 million. Operations generated $742 million and a further inflow of $1 billion from financial activities (mostly from issuance of long-term debt). This was offset by $1.8 billion used in investment activities. CAPEX for 2017 was $1.7 billion the highest in three years.

Strategy

NiSource believes that its long-term success lies in developing a portfolio that balances creating more efficiencies in its regulated utility operations while expanding its higher-growth gas transmission and storage businesses.

The regulatory frameworks in which NiSource operates has evolved significantly at both the state and federal levels in the last several years creating uncertainties. This is because growth at rate-regulated businesses of NiSource relies heavily on approvals of capital rider programs and deferrals from regulators in Indiana Ohio and Pennsylvania. In April 2018 the company successfully settled its rate cases with Indiana regulators while the outcome of the other two was delayed till late 2018.

Another challenge for NiSource is its negative cash flow. In 2017 the company reported net working capital deficit of $1.4 billion compared to a deficit of $1.7 billion the year prior. To prevent short term disruptions the company issued equity and implemented operational and maintenance cuts.

Aiming for an annual growth rate of 8% NiSource has earmarked up to $1.8 billion per year for CAPEX till 2020. Its gas distribution businesses are trying to expand the sale of products and services into the upstream market and introduce cost incentive mechanisms for its core markets. Additionally the company is trying to seek regulatory changes that will allow it to expand its services to residential customers beyond its current service area.

Its subsidiary NIPSCO is also amidst a seven-year $850 million gas and electric infrastructure modernization program. In September 2018 the company went further by announcing its goal of retiring majority of its coal-fired plants and replacing them with low-cost wind solar and battery storage technologies. Separately the company also committed to replace the 48-mile gas distribution line in Merrimack Valley.

However a lawsuit filed against the company in September 2018 may put further pressure on its already dwindling coffers. Pipelines of Columbia Gas of Massachusetts a subsidiary were linked to a series of explosions and fires that rocked the Massachusetts towns of Lawrence Andover and North Andover. A complaint filed on behalf of 8600 residents directly affected blames over-pressurization of the company's antiquated gas lines for the fatal accident. The explosions killed one person and injured two dozen others. NiSource made $10 million donation to a disaster fun but future damanges remain uncertain.

HISTORY

NiSource's earliest ancestor was the South Bend (Indiana) Gas Light Company founded in 1868 by the Studebaker brothers (of later auto fame) to supply gas. In 1886 a natural-gas discovery near Kokomo Indiana led to a boom in northern Indiana's use of the fuel. By 1900 steel plants and other industries had set up shop along Lake Michigan in northwestern Indiana and in Illinois.

Another NiSource ancestor was formed in 1901 as Hammond Illuminating but it changed its name to South Shore Gas and Electric. In 1909 Northern Indiana Gas and Electric was founded by merging South Shore with other regional utilities. The next year Northern Indiana acquired South Bend.

A third NiSource predecessor Calumet Electric (founded in 1912) had acquired several utilities by the early 1920s when utility magnate Samuel Insull bought it to add to his huge Midland Utilities holding company. In 1923 Insull bought Northern Indiana Gas and Electric which merged three years later with Calumet to form Northern Indiana Public Service Company (NIPSCO). NIPSCO acquired its current service territory in 1930 when it swapped some areas with another Midland subsidiary.

The Public Utility Holding Company Act of 1935 beginning the regulation of regional monopolies forced Midland to divest NIPSCO in 1947. In the 1950s and 1960s NIPSCO built two power plants and tripled its natural gas supply through a contract with a Houston gas company.

Responding to rising demand NIPSCO in 1970 applied to build a nuclear unit at its Bailly plant estimated to cost $180 million. In 1981 the nuke was abandoned after its cost rose to $2.1 billion. Reorganizing in 1987 NIPSCO became part of holding company NIPSCO Industries.

The Energy Policy Act of 1992 ushered in wholesale-power competition. That year NIPSCO acquired Kokomo Gas and Fuel and in 1993 it picked up Northern Indiana Fuel and Light and Crossroads Pipeline.

To prepare for oncoming retail competition NIPSCO in 1993 divided the electric and gas utilities into competing units and increased NIPSCO's marketing force. In 1997 NIPSCO branched out buying water utility holding company IWC Resources and the next year it began a customer choice program for its natural gas customers (all gas was delivered through its distribution lines however).

The company changed its name to NiSource in 1999 but did not alter its acquisition strategy. NiSource entered the US Northeast's gas market where deregulation plans were under way by purchasing New England utility Bay State Gas. A unit of Bay State Gas EnergyUSA bought natural gas marketer TPC and NiSource began integrating its nonregulated operations into EnergyUSA.

After launching a hostile takeover which it later withdrew NiSource purchased natural gas giant Columbia Energy Group for $6 billion in 2000. NiSource then sold its salt cavern gas storage and pipeline construction subsidiaries as well as certain Columbia electric generation and LNG facilities. In 2001 NiSource sold its Columbia Propane unit to AmeriGas Partners; it also agreed to sell water company IWC Resources (and its utility subsidiary Indianapolis Water) to the City of Indianapolis (the sale was completed in 2002).

In 2002 NiSource teamed up with the merchant services unit of Aquila (formerly UtiliCorp) to form an energy marketing and trading joint venture; however NiSource later backed out of the partnership due to instability in the energy trading industry. It also shut down its coal-fired Mitchell Generating Station and sold its SM&P Utility Resources subsidiary to The Laclede Group.

EXECUTIVES

Vice President Capital Allocation And Controls, Tim Dehring

Evp And Chief Legal Officer, Carrie J. Hightman, age 60, $490,000 total compensation

President And Ceo, Joseph (Joe) Hamrock, age 55, $858,333 total compensation

Evp; President Nipsco, Violet G. Sistovaris, $360,000 total compensation

Chief Transformation Officer, Mark Kempic

Evp Gas Segment And Chief Customer Officer, Pablo A. Vegas, age 45, $298,295 total compensation

Evp Safety Capital Execution And Technical Services, Mike Finissi

Evp And Cfo, Donald E. Brown, $479,167 total compensation

Evp Regulatory Policy And Corporate Affairs, Carl W. Levander

Vp Customer Value, Suzanne Surface

Vice President Deputy General Counsel Litigation, Karl Eckweiler

Vice President Financial Planning And Analysis, Tim Tokish

Vice President Total Rewards, Richard Bond

Senior Vice President Safety Environmental And Training, Dave Monte

Vice President Of Finance, Joe Mulpas

Vice President, Larry Francisco

Vice President Marketing Services, Dale Williams

Vice President Of Information Technology, Julie McElmurry

Vice President Supply Chain, Scott Kelly

Vice President, Jeff Grossman

Vice President Deputy General Counsel, Karl-Nisource Eckweiler

Vp Human Resources And Labor Relations, Edward Santry

Chairman, Richard L. (Rich) Thompson, age 78

Treasurer And Chief Risk Officer View Bio, Shawn Anderson

Board Member, Carolyn Woo

Board Member, Richard Abdoo

Board Member, Kevin Kabat

Auditors: Deloitte & Touche LLP

LOCATIONS

HQ: NiSource Inc. (Holding Co.)
801 East 86th Avenue, Merrillville, IN 46410
Phone: 877 647-5990
Web: www.nisource.com

PRODUCTS/OPERATIONS

2017 sales

	$ mil.	% of total
Gas Distribution	2,063	42
Gas Transportation	1,021	21
Electric	1,786	37
Other	5	0
Total	**4,875**	**100**

Selected Subsidiaries

GAS DISTRIBUTION OPERATIONS
 Columbia Gas of Massachusetts
 Central Kentucky Transmission Company
 Columbia Gas of Kentucky Inc.
 Columbia Gas of Maryland Inc.
 Columbia Gas of Ohio Inc.
 Columbia Gas of Pennsylvania Inc.
 Columbia Gas of Virginia Inc.
 NiSource Gas Distribution Group Inc.
ELECTRIC OPERATIONS
 Northern Indiana Public Service Company

COMPETITORS

AEP	FirstEnergy
Atmos Energy	IPALCO Enterprises
Baltimore Gas and Electric	NSTAR
	National Grid USA

Constellation Energy
  Group
Dominion Energy
Duke Energy
EQT Corporation
Eversource Energy

New Jersey Resources
Nicor Gas
RGC Resources
Southern Union
Unitil
Vectren

HISTORICAL FINANCIALS

Company Type: Public

Income Statement   FYE: December 31

	REVENUE ($ mil.)	NET INCOME ($ mil.)	NET PROFIT MARGIN	EMPLOYEES
12/17	4,874	128	2.6%	8,175
12/16	4,492	331	7.4%	8,007
12/15	4,651	286	6.2%	7,596
12/14	6,470	530	8.2%	8,982
12/13	5,657	532	9.4%	8,477
Annual Growth	(3.7%)	(29.9%)	—	(0.9%)

2017 Year-End Financials

Debt ratio: 45.10%
Return on equity: 3.06%
Cash ($ mil.): 29
Current ratio: 0.55
Long-term debt ($ mil.): 7,512

No. of shares (mil.): 337
Dividends
Yield: 0.0%
Payout: 179.4%
Market value ($ mil.): 8,651

	STOCK PRICE ($) FY Close	P/E High/Low	PER SHARE ($) Earnings	Dividends	Book Value
12/17	25.67	71 56	0.39	0.70	12.82
12/16	22.14	26 19	1.02	0.64	12.60
12/15	19.51	54 18	0.90	0.83	12.04
12/14	42.42	26 19	1.67	1.02	19.54
12/13	32.88	19 15	1.70	0.98	18.77
Annual Growth	(6.0%)	— —	(30.8%)	(8.1%)	(9.1%)

Nordstrom, Inc.

Service with a smile is a part of Nordstrom's corporate culture. One of the nation's largest up-scale apparel and shoe retailers Nordstrom sells clothes shoes and accessories through more than 115 Nordstrom department stores and more than 215 off-price outlet stores (Nordstrom Rack) in nearly 40 states and online. It also operates a pair of Jeffrey luxury boutiques a "Last Chance" clearance store online private sale site HauteLook and personalized clothing service Trunk Club. With its easy-return policy and touches such as thank-you notes from employees Nordstrom has earned a reputation for top-notch customer service. Nordstrom family members who own about 25% of the retailer's stock closely supervise the chain.

Operations

The family-run company operates two business segments: Retail and Credit. The Retail segment accounts for the vast majority (98%) of Nordstrom's revenue and includes sales from its full-line and Nordstrom Rack stores as well as from its Nordstrom.com   nordstromrack.com Hautelook.com Trunk Club.com Jeffrey and its Canadian operations.

Nordstrom's Credit segment (2% of sales) owns a federal savings bank Nordstrom fsb through which it offers a private-label credit card two co-branded Nordstrom VISA cards and a debit card for Nordstrom purchases. The cards also include a loyalty program that rewards shoppers depending on their spending levels.

Nordstrom's full-line stores generate 50% of its net sales while its Nordstrom Rack stores contributed roughly 25%. Its fast-growing Nordstrom.com channel generated 15% of net sales while its Nordstromrack.com and Hautelook channels combined made up around 5%.

By product the company generates over 30% of its net sales from women's apparel while shoe sales make up nearly 25%. The rest of its net sales came from men's apparel (15%) women's accessories (10%) cosmetics (10%) kid's apparel and other items (5% each).

Geographic Reach

Nordstrom has some 345 full-line and Nordstrom Rack stores in 40 US states as well as three Nordstrom full-line stores in Canada. California is the retailer's largest market with over 80 full-line and Rack stores. Other major markets for the chain include Florida Texas and Washington.

Financial Performance

Nordstrom shrugged off industry-wide malaise to record 2% revenue growth in fiscal 2017. Sales of $14.8 billion were a result of innovative approaches to customer service and store openings. The company re-imagined the role of the department store in the internet age driving foot traffic through a program of exclusive pop-up stores and new retail concepts. While comparable store sales still fell (by less than 1%) the figure compares favorably to its peers such as JCPenney and Macy's. Off-price sales through Nordstrom Rack increased 11% due to 21 store openings. Sales at the company's credit card business softened slightly.

Net income fell 41% to $354 million due to higher cost of sales and SGA expenses. Nordstrom ramped up marketing spend and invested in technology and supply chain to open up new digital capabilities.

Cash from operating activities fell 33% to $1.6 billion due to a particularly high fiscal 2016 after it sold its credit card receivables. When excluded cash increased due to improvements in working capital.

Strategy

Department stores across the US are having a hard time of it having found themselves somewhat outdated as consumers gravitate increasingly towards the internet and small brand-specific stores. Revenue at stalwarts such as JCPenney and Macy's are eroding but 116-year-old Nordstrom is proving more adaptable than most.

New ideas such as short-term pop-up shops and link-ups with emerging designers promote a discovery dynamic and give millennials — the most department store resistant consumer group — social media currency and thus reason to visit stores.

It has also found new ways to leverage online such as allowing customers to pre-select clothing and book a changing room to try them on in. Customers can also pay by text.

Nordstrom also continually expands and refreshes its store base. In 2016 it opened 27 new stores (and closed one) of which 21 were Nordstrom Rack discount stores. Indeed the company is pumping up Nordstrom Rack at a fast pace to entice the less affluent consumer.

In October 2015 the company sold off a substantial majority of its US Visa and private label credit card portfolio to TD Bank Group and entered into an agreement for the bank to be the exclusive issuer of Nordstrom's consumer credit cards.

HISTORY

In 1901 John Nordstrom a lumberjack and successful gold miner used his Alaska Gold Rush money to open Wallin & Nordstrom shoe store in Seattle with shoemaker Carl Wallin. Nordstrom retired in 1928 and sold his half of the business

which included a second store to his sons Everett and Elmer. Wallin sold his share to the brothers after retiring the following year. A third Nordstrom son Lloyd joined in 1933. The shoe chain thrived and incorporated as Nordstrom's in 1946.

By 1963 Nordstrom's was the largest independent shoe chain in the country. The company diversified by acquiring Best Apparel's stores in Seattle and Portland Oregon. Three years later Nordstrom's bought Portland's Nicholas Ungar a fashion retailer and merged it with one of its shoe stores in Portland under the name Nordstrom Best.

Renaming itself Nordstrom Best in 1966 the company went public in 1971 and changed its name again in 1973 to Nordstrom. The retailer grew steadily throughout the 1970s opening new stores boosting sales in existing stores and diversifying. In 1976 Nordstrom started Place Two featuring apparel and shoes in smaller stores than its traditional department layouts. It moved into Southern California (Orange County) two years later. Buoyed by almost $300 million in new sales Nordstrom executives planned an aggressive expansion.

Nordstrom opened its first store on the East Coast in 1988 in Virginia. The chain continued to expand opening stores in Northern California and in the affluent Washington DC suburbs.

The 1989 San Francisco earthquake along with a national downturn hurt retail sales significantly. Nordstrom's much-touted focus on customer service had a downside: The company was investigated in 1990 for not paying employees for customer services they performed including delivery of merchandise on their own time. (Three years later Nordstrom set aside $15 million to pay back wages to employees who had performed off-the-clock services.)

The company continued to expand in the East and Midwest opening its first store in the New York City area in 1991. In 1993 the retailer opened a men's boutique in New York (FaA§onnable). Looking for new ways to attract customers Nordstrom introduced a mail-order catalog the next year.

Following the family's business tradition six members of Nordstrom's fourth generation began running the company in 1995. Third-generation members James Nordstrom John Nordstrom Bruce Nordstrom and Jack McMillan retired as co-chairmen and were replaced by non-family members Ray Johnson and John Whitacre. (Johnson retired in 1996.)

Nordstrom created Nordstrom.com a partnership with Benchmark Capital and Madrona Investment Group in 1999 to consolidate its catalog and Internet operations.

In early 2000 amid slumping sales the company dissolved the co-presidency. Less than a year later however the Nordstroms were back in charge. Chairman and CEO Whitacre resigned and Blake Nordstrom took over running the company as president. His father Bruce came out of retirement to take the chairman's role. Later the company bought the French design company FaA§onnable which supplies the products for its FaA§onnable boutiques.

In May 2002 the company bought out Benchmark's and Madrona's minority stake in Nordstrom.com.

Nordstrom bought a majority interest in August 2005 in luxury specialty stores Jeffrey New York and Jeffrey Atlanta. Terms of the agreement were not disclosed. The Jeffrey stores had about $35 million in sales in 2004. Also in 2005 the company opened stores in Atlanta; Dallas; Irvine California; and San Antonio.

In late 2007 Nordstrom sold its four US FaA§onnable boutiques and 37 European locations to Lebanon-based M1 Group for about $210 million. Overall in 2007 Nordstrom opened three full-line department stores and a single Rack store.

Nordstrom opened its first full-line department store in Hawaii in early 2008. That October amid economic gloom the retailer opened a store in Pittsburgh. Overall the retailer opened eight new Nordstrom stores and half a dozen Rack outlets in 2008. In 2009 it added three full-line Nordstrom locations and 13 Rack outlets.

Nordstrom acquired e-tailer HauteLook for $180 million in stock in March 2011. Based in Los Angeles HauteLook is a leader in online private sales.

EXECUTIVES

Co-president, Blake W. Nordstrom, age 57, $751,152 total compensation
Co-president, Peter E. (Pete) Nordstrom, age 56, $751,152 total compensation
Co-president, Erik B. Nordstrom, age 56, $751,152 total compensation
Evp General Counsel And Secretary, Robert B. Sari, age 62
Evp And Chief Innovation Officer, Geevy S.K. Thomas, age 53
Evp And Cio, Daniel F. (Dan) Little, age 57, $552,806 total compensation
Evp And President Stores, James F. (Jamie) Nordstrom, age 45
Evp And General Merchandise Manager Designer Women's Apparel, Tricia D. Smith, age 47
Evp And Chief Marketing Officer, Scott A. Meden, age 55
Evp Finance And Treasurer, James A. Howell, age 53
Evp And General Merchandise Manager Menâ's And Kids Wear, Paige L. Thomas, age 47
Evp And President Nordstrom.com, Kenneth J. (Ken) Worzel, age 53, $657,417 total compensation
Evp Nordstrom Merchandising Group, Teri Bariquit, age 52
Evp And General Merchandise Manager Accessories At Home And Beauty, Gemma Lionello, age 53
Evp; Chairman And Ceo Nordstrom Fsb; President Nordstrom Credit, Steven C. Mattics, age 49
Evp Supply Chain, Michael Sato
Cfo, Anne L. Bramman, age 50
Evp Online Merchandising, Kirk M. Beardsley
Evp And President Nordstromrack.com Hautelook And Trunk Club, Terence Boyle
Evp Human Resources, Christine F. Deputy, age 52, $319,206 total compensation
Evp Strategy, Lisa C. Luther
Evp And President Nordstrom Product Group, Jennifer Jackson Brown
Evp And General Merchandise Manager Shoe Division, Kristin Frossmo
Evp And President Nordstrom Rack, Karen S. McKibbin, age 58
Evp And General Merchandise Manager Nordstrom Rack, Brian Roberts
Senior Vice President Customer Experience, Shea Jensen
Vice President Marketing, KRISTEN LAMEY
Senior Vice President Human Resources, Lisa V Price
Vice President Customer Experience, Shea D Jensen
Vice President Technology, Joanne Kennedy
Vice President Merchandise Planning, Angie L Caldwell
Vice President Operations Finance, Chris Goelkel
Vice President Fashion Office, Red Godfrey
Vice President Corporate Affairs And Public Relations, Gigi Ganatra
Vice President Assistant General Counsel And Aco Nfsb, Janine M Weaver

Executive Vice President Chief Supply Chain Officer, Brent Beabout
Vice President Nmg Strategy And Operations, Corinne E Copello
Vice President Compensation And Leadership Benefits, Dave Anders
Vp Corporate Tax, Andy Vickers
Vice President Engineering, Alan John
Board Member, Shellye Archambeau
Board Member, Kevin Turner
Auditors: Deloitte & Touche LLP

LOCATIONS

HQ: Nordstrom, Inc.
1617 Sixth Avenue, Seattle, WA 98101
Phone: 206 628-2111
Web: www.nordstrom.com

PRODUCTS/OPERATIONS

2017 Sales

	$ mil.	% of total
Full-line stores US	7,186	48
Nordstrom.com	2,519	17
Nordstrom Rack	3,809	25
Nordstromrack.com/Hautelook	700	4
Other retail	554	4
Corporate/Other	(270)	0
Credit Card revenues net	259	2
Total	**14,757**	**100**

2017 Sales

	% of total
Retail	98
Credit	2
Corporate/Other	0
Total	**100**

2017 Products category

	% of total
Women's Apparel	32
Shoes	23
Men's Apparel	17
Women's Accessories	11
Beauty	11
Kids' Apparel	3
Other	3
Total	**100**

2017 sales

	No.
Nordstrom full-line stores - U.S.and Canada	123
Nordstrom Rack and others	226
Total	**349**

PRODUCTS OFFERED:

Selected
Dresses
Tops
Jeans
Sweaters
Coats
Jackets
Pants
Suits
Skirts
Swimsuits & Cover-Ups
Active Yoga & Outdoor
Bras Panties & Lingerie
Shapewear
Sleep Lounge & Robes
Hosiery Leggings & Socks
Plus-Size Clothing
Petite-Size Clothing
Maternity Clothing
Shoes
Handbags & Wallets
Watches
Jewelry
Fine Jewelry
Optical Frames & Reading Glasses
Sunglasses
Scarves & Wraps
Hats & Hair Accessories
Winter Accessories

Gloves
Belts
Luggage & Travel
Tech Accessories & Cases
Hosiery & Socks

Selected Retail Operations

HauteLook (private-sale website for apparel and home decor)
Jeffrey (boutiques)
Last Chance (clearance store)
Nordstrom (specialty stores selling apparel shoes and accessories for women men and children)
Nordstrom Direct (catalogs and online ordering)
Nordstrom Rack (outlets selling merchandise from Nordstrom specialty stores and manufacturers)

COMPETITORS

Ann Taylor	J. Crew
Astor & Black	Lands' End
Barneys	Macy's
Benetton	Neiman Marcus
Bloomingdale's	Nine West
Bluefly	Saks Fifth Avenue
Brooks Brothers	Tailored Brands
Caleres	Talbots
Dillard's	The Gap
Donna Karan	Tiffany & Co.
Eddie Bauer LLC	Von Maur
J. C. Penney	Wayfair

HISTORICAL FINANCIALS

Company Type: Public

Income Statement
FYE: February 3

	REVENUE ($ mil.)	NET INCOME ($ mil.)	NET PROFIT MARGIN	EMPLOYEES
02/18*	15,478	437	2.8%	72,500
01/17	14,757	354	2.4%	72,500
01/16	14,437	600	4.2%	72,500
01/15	13,506	720	5.3%	67,000
02/14	12,540	734	5.9%	62,500
Annual Growth	5.4%	(12.2%)	—	3.8%

*Fiscal year change

2018 Year-End Financials

Debt ratio: 33.73%	No. of shares (mil.): 167
Return on equity: 46.55%	Dividends
Cash ($ mil.): 1,181	Yield: 0.0%
Current ratio: 1.07	Payout: 57.1%
Long-term debt ($ mil.): 2,681	Market value ($ mil.): 7,991

	STOCK PRICE ($) FY Close	P/E High/Low	PER SHARE ($) Earnings	PER SHARE ($) Dividends	PER SHARE ($) Book Value
02/18*	47.85	20 15	2.59	1.48	5.85
01/17	42.83	30 18	2.02	1.48	5.12
01/16	49.10	26 14	3.15	6.33	5.02
01/15	76.20	21 15	3.72	1.32	12.84
02/14	57.45	17 14	3.71	1.20	10.88
Annual Growth	(4.5%)	— —	(8.6%)	5.4%	(14.4%)

*Fiscal year change

Norfolk Southern Corp.

Transportation titan Norfolk Southern is the one big train that could. Its main subsidiary Norfolk Southern Railway transports freight over a network consisting of about 20000 route miles in 20-plus states in the eastern southeastern and Midwestern US and in Ontario and Quebec. The rail system is made up of more than 16000 route miles owned by Norfolk Southern and more than 7000 route miles of trackage rights which allow the company to use tracks owned by other railroads. Norfolk Southern transports coal and general merchandise including automotive products and chemicals.

Operations

Norfolk Southern operates more than 4250 locomotives and more than 71000 freight cars. It reports through three segments: General Merchandise (more than 60% of net sales) Intermodal (more than 20%) and Coal (15%).

General Merchandise is subdivided into five commodity groups: Agriculture/Consumer/Government (such commodities and products as soybeans wheat beverages canned goods ethanol and military items); Chemicals (sulfur petroleum products plastics among others); Metals/Construction (steel aluminum cement bricks etc); Automotive (finished vehicles from and auto parts for such auto OEMs as Ford General Motors and Toyota); and Paper/Clay/Forest (lumber and wood products pulp board and paper products wood fibers wood pulp scrap paper and clay). The General Merchandise segment maintains more than 2.5 million railroad carloads each year.

Coal is Norfolk Southern's single largest commodity group. The coal segment carried about 100 million tons of coal originating from major coal basins and destined for about 80 coal generation plants as well as export metallurgical and industrial facilities. Operating in the eastern US Intermodal carries about 4 million units for such clients as intermodal marketing companies international steamship lines and truckers.

Geographic Reach

Norfolk Southern operates in 22 US states and Washington DC and transport overseas freight via several Atlantic and Gulf Coast ports.

Sales and Marketing

Norfolk Southern mainly targets the agriculture metals construction automotive and paper sectors. Its automotive clients include BMW Honda Hyundai Mercedes-Benz Nissan and Tesla.

Financial Performance

Norfolk Southern's revenues have declined the last two years dipping 6% from $10.5 billion in 2015 to $9.9 billion in 2016 due to declines across most of its segments.

Coal segment sales in 2016 dropped by 18% due to a decline in carload volumes which were impacted by a decrease in natural gas prices which shifted the customer's preference from coal to natural gas usage. General Merchandise sales fell 2% in 2016 due to a 6% decline from Chemicals and a 4% decline from Paper/Clay/Forest. In addition Intermodal's revenue decreased by 8% due to lower fuel surcharge revenues.

The decline in Chemicals was attributed to lower traffic volume reflecting fewer shipments of crude oil originated from the Bakken oil fields. Chemicals also experienced lower chlor-alkali and rock salt traffic which was the result of market consolidations and softened demand. Paper/Clay/Forest in 2016 experienced decreases within the pulpboard and woodchip markets due to customer sourcing changes in addition to lower paper shipments as a result of decreased demand and the ongoing contraction of the paper market.

Norfolk Southern's profits on the other hand surged by 7% from $1.56 billion in 2015 to $1.67 billion in 2016. This was due to higher income from railway operations and an 11% decrease in railway operating expenses during 2016 as a result of its strategic focus on cost-cutting.

Strategy

To shield itself against economic forces that it cannot control Norfolk Southern focuses on projected expense reduction and focused cost-control initiatives. In early 2016 it announced a five-year plan to achieve annual productivity savings of more than $650 million per year by 2020. As a result it achieved $250 million in savings for 2016 after initially planning to save $130 million for the year.

Mergers and Acquisitions

In 2015 Norfolk Southern acquired 282.55 miles of rail line between Sunbury Pennsylvania and Schenectady New York from the Delaware & Hudson Railway (D&H) a subsidiary of Canadian Pacific Railway. The deal allowed the company to connect businesses in central Pennsylvania to upstate New York and New England and gave it single-line routes from Chicago and the southeastern US to Albany New York.

HISTORY

Norfolk Southern Corporation resulted from the 1982 merger of two US rail giants — Norfolk & Western Railway Company (N&W) and Southern Railway Company — which had emerged from more than 200 and 150 previous mergers respectively.

N&W dates to 1838 when one track connected Petersburg Virginia to City Point (now Hopewell). This eight-miler became part of the Atlantic Mississippi & Ohio (AM&O) which was created by consolidating three Virginia railways in 1870.

In 1881 Philadelphia banker E.W. Clark bought the AM&O and renamed it the Norfolk & Western. N&W rolled into Ohio by purchasing two other railroads (1892 1901).

The company took over the Virginian Railway a coal carrier with track paralleling much of its own in 1959. In 1964 N&W became a key railroad in the Midwest by acquiring the New York Chicago & St. Louis Railroad and the Pennsylvania Railroad's line between Columbus and Sandusky Ohio. It also leased the Wabash Railroad with lines from Detroit and Chicago to Kansas City and St. Louis.

Southern Railway can be traced back to the South Carolina Canal & Rail Road a nine-mile line chartered in 1827 and built by Horatio Allen to win trade for Charleston's port. It began operating the US's first regularly scheduled passenger train in 1830 and became the world's longest railway when it opened a 136-mile line to Hamburg South Carolina (1833).

Soon other railroads sprang up in the South including the Richmond & Danville (Virginia 1847) and the East Tennessee Virginia & Georgia (1869) which were combined to form the Southern Railway System in 1894. Southern eventually controlled more than 100 railroads forging a system from Washington DC to St. Louis and New Orleans.

The 1982 merger of Southern and N&W created an extensive rail system throughout the East South and Midwest. Norfolk Southern (a holding company created for the two railroads) also bought North American Van Lines in 1985. Triple Crown Services the company's intermodal subsidiary was started in 1986. The company also made a failed attempt to take over Piedmont Aviation the next year.

Norfolk Southern revived North American Van Lines by selling its refrigerator truck operation Tran-star (1993) and suspending its commercial trucking line. But it later sold the rest of the motor carrier (1998) to focus on rail operations.

When CSX announced its plans to buy Conrail in 1997 Norfolk Southern's counteroffer led to a split of the former Northeastern monopoly between Norfolk Southern (58%) and CSX (42%). Problems with integrating Conrail's assets hurt Norfolk Southern's results. But by 2000 it had regained some of the traffic it had lost to service problems and its intermodal shipping business also gained speed. In 2004 Norfolk Southern and CSX reorganized Conrail to give each parent company direct ownership of the portion of Conrail's assets that it operates. Conrail still operates switching facilities and terminals used by both Norfolk Southern and CSX.

Norfolk Southern got hit in the wallet in 2001: The company agreed to pay $28 million to settle a racial discrimination lawsuit brought by black employees in 1993. Norfolk Southern began rounds of layoffs and closed redundant depots and facilities in 2001.

In 2005 nine people died in South Carolina when chlorine gas leaked from a ruptured car on a Norfolk Southern freight train. The car was breached when the train crashed into a company-owned locomotive and two train cars that were parked on a siding.

Jumping ahead ten years the company in 2015 rejected an unsolicited takeover by Canadian Pacific in a deal worth $37.8 billion.

EXECUTIVES

Vp Government Relations, Bruno Maestri

Evp Cfo And Cio, Cynthia C. (Cindy) Earhart, $600,000 total compensation

Chairman President And Ceo, James A. (Jim) Squires, age 56, $900,000 total compensation

Evp And Chief Marketing Officer, Alan H. Shaw, $500,000 total compensation

Evp And Coo, Michael J. Wheeler, $581,250 total compensation

Vp Business, Robert Martinez

Vice President Intermodal And Automotive, Jeffrey Heller

National Account Manager, Rick Lentz

Avp Research And Advanced Technology, Tom Schnautz

Vice President Chief Engineer Design, Dave Becker

National Account Manager, Brady Daniels

Resident Vice President Government Relations, Elizabeth Lawlor

Government Relations, Herbert Smith

National Account Manager, Bill Flanagan

Vice President Process Engineering, Terry Evans

Assistant Vice President Mws Engineering, Ed Boyle

Vice President Engineering, Philip Merilli

Vp Audit And Compliance, Susan Stuart

Resident Vp Government Relations Pennsylvania And New York, Michael Fesen

Assistant Vp Government Relations, Marque Ledoux

Vp Network Operations, John Friedmann

Vice President Business Development And Real Estate, Robert E Martinez

Assistant Vice President Corporate Accounting, Jason Zampi

Board Member, Thomas Bell

Secretary, Mary McIntyre

Secretary, Cinde Ball

Secretary, Donna Coleman

Auditors: KPMG LLP

LOCATIONS

HQ: Norfolk Southern Corp.
Three Commercial Place, Norfolk, VA 23510-2191
Phone: 757 629-2680
Web: www.norfolksouthern.com

PRODUCTS/OPERATIONS

2016 Sales

	$ mil.	% of total
General merchandise		
Chemicals	1,648	17
Agriculture consumer government	1,548	16
Metals & construction	1,267	13
Automotive	975	10
Paper clay and forest	744	7
Intermodal	2,218	22
Coal	1,488	15
Total	**9,888**	**100**

Selected Facilities Served

Active coal-loading facilities
Auto assembly plants
Auto distribution facilities
Bulk transfer facilities
Coal and iron ore transload facilities
General warehouses/distribution centers
Intermodal terminals
Just-in-time rail auto parts center
Lumber reload centers
Metals distribution centers
Paper distribution centers
Paper mills
Power generation plants served
Steel mills and processing facilities
Triple Crown Service terminals
Vehicle mixing centers

COMPETITORS

APL Logistics	J.B. Hunt
American Commercial Lines	Kansas City Southern
Burlington Northern Santa Fe	Kirby Corporation
	Landstar System
CSX	PVH
Canadian National Railway	Piedmont Natural Gas
	Pier 1 Imports
Canadian Pacific Railway	Pilgrim's Pride
	Pinnacle West
Genesee & Wyoming	Pitney Bowes
Hub Group	Schneider National
Ingram Industries	Union Pacific
	Werner Enterprises

HISTORICAL FINANCIALS

Company Type: Public

Income Statement				FYE: December 31
	REVENUE ($ mil.)	NET INCOME ($ mil.)	NET PROFIT MARGIN	EMPLOYEES
12/18	11,458	2,666	23.3%	26,662
12/17	10,551	5,404	51.2%	27,110
12/16	9,888	1,668	16.9%	28,044
12/15	10,511	1,556	14.8%	30,456
12/14	11,624	2,000	17.2%	29,482
Annual Growth	(0.4%)	7.5%	—	(2.5%)

2018 Year-End Financials

Debt ratio: 30.75%	No. of shares (mil.): 268
Return on equity: 16.81%	Dividends
Cash ($ mil.): 358	Yield: 2.0%
Current ratio: 0.72	Payout: 14.7%
Long-term debt ($ mil.): 10,560	Market value ($ mil.): 40,091

	STOCK PRICE ($) FY Close	P/E High/Low		PER SHARE ($) Earnings	Dividends	Book Value
12/18	149.54	19	13	9.51	3.04	57.30
12/17	144.90	8	6	18.61	2.44	57.57
12/16	108.07	20	12	5.62	2.36	42.73
12/15	84.59	22	14	5.10	2.36	40.93
12/14	109.61	18	14	6.39	2.22	40.25
Annual Growth	8.1%	—	—	10.5%	8.2%	9.2%

Northern Trust Corp

Individuals and institutions put their confidence in the Northern Trust Corporation. Through its flagship subsidiary The Northern Trust Company the corporation provides banking and trust services brokerage asset servicing securities lending and proprietary mutual funds (the Northern Funds). The firm offers its services to institutional clients and affluent individuals through more than 90 offices in nearly 20 states and more than 20 countries. Operating two main segments ? Corporate and Institutional Services (C&IS) and Wealth Management ? Northern Trust has nearly 10 trillion in assets under custody/administration and $1.1 trillion under direct management.

Operations

The firm operates through two segments: Corporate and Institutional Services (C&IS) and Wealth Management. A third business unit Asset Management provides asset management and related services to its other segments.

The C&IS segment provides asset servicing and related services to corporate and public retirement funds foundations endowments fund managers insurance companies sovereign wealth funds and other institutional investors. Its offerings include fund administration investment operations outsourcing investment management risk and analytical services employee benefit services securities lending foreign exchange brokerage services and banking. Assets under management are roughly $700 billion and assets under custody exceed $6.0 trillion. The segment accounts for about 55% of total revenue.

The Wealth Management business focuses on high-net-worth individuals and families business owners executives and the like. It provides services such as investment management philanthropic services trust management financial consulting guardianship brokerage services and private & business banking. This segment has some $250 billion in assets under management and $550 billion in assets under custody. This business generates roughly 40% of revenue.

Geographic Reach

Based in Chicago Northern Trust has a presence in 20 US states and more than 20 countries. About 80% of the company?s assets and revenues originate in the US.

Sales and Marketing

The firm serves corporations institutions (foundations endowments sovereign wealth funds) and affluent families and individuals. Relationship management and personalized service are keys to maintaining and growing its client base.

Financial Performance

Following the Financial Crisis of 2008/2009 Northern Trust saw steep declines in both revenue and net income. Since 2011 however it has stabilized financial performance and experienced steady consistent growth in both metrics. Revenue grew from $3.9 billion to over $5.0 billion. Net income improved from $570 million to exceeding $1.0 for the first time in 2016.

The 2016 revenue result ticked up 5% from the prior year to $5.1 billion. Trust fees the company?s largest source of revenue grew 4% and net interest income exceeded 15% growth helped in no small part to a rise in US interest rates.

Net income for the year rose 6% to $1.0 billion the highest amount in over a decade. Expenses ? operating and income ? stayed in line with the previous year enabling Norther Trust to flow the bump in revenue to its bottom line.

Cash on hand at the end of 2016 was $5.3 billion a decrease of $1.1 billion from 2015. Operating activities provided $1.5 billion to cash. Investing activities used $10.2 billion due in large part to purchasing more securities than it sold. Financing activities added $7.5 billion to the coffers mainly by attracting $6.7 billion in client deposits and selling $500 million in preferred stock.

Strategy

Northern Trust?s strategy involves riding growth waves in private wealth management and institutional asset management both of which are predicted to have (on average) 8.5% compounded annual growth. It is firmly entrenched in these markets and need only to continue what it has been doing to expand its business both by attracting additional clients in existing markets and by serving greater needs for its existing clients.

The company is also addressing the risks associated with data security and the opportunities enabled through artificial intelligence and data analytics. Of the company?s $473 million in 2016 capital expenditures $430 million went to computer software and hardware including for the build-out of its new mobile application for its wealth management clients.

Northern Trust continued to expand slowly and methodically its geographic footprint across the world. Although still a very small amount of its revenue non-US operations allow the firm to project a global presence for families firms and institutions who themselves are global in nature and seek investment management firms that can meet their international needs. In 2015 it established a team in Melbourne Australia to provide its asset management products and services to institutional investors across Australia and New Zealand. Also in 2015 to support its Asia Pacific growth strategy and its "local business" strategy to support clients as close to their local markets as possible Northern Trust opened its Seoul representative office in fast-growing South Korea.

Mergers and Acquisitions

In late 2017 Northern Trust acquired UBS Asset Management?s fund administration servicing business in Luxembourg and Switzerland for some $200 million.

Company Background

As part of its international growth plan Northern Trust expanded in Europe with the 2011 purchase of Bank of Ireland's fund administration investment operations outsourcing and custody business. The acquisition was combined with Northern Trust's existing operations in Ireland which is a European hub for cross-border fund administration. The company worked to support European fund managers by expanding its depositary services across multiple fund types asset classes fund locations and investment strategies as well as by implementing the Alternative Investment Fund Managers Directive (AIFMD).

In 2010 Northern Trust expanded its Wealth Management business with the acquisition of Los Angeles-based investment advisory Waterline Partners.

HISTORY

When banker Byron Smith took time off to handle family concerns in 1885 friends turned to him for advice on trust and estate matters. It occurred to him that there was a market for such services within a banking framework.

Smith tested new Illinois banking and trust laws by arranging for state banking authorities to reject his charter application for Northern Trust. As Smith had hoped the charter was upheld by the Illinois Supreme Court.

Northern Trust opened in 1889 in one of Chicago's new skyscrapers the Rookery. With $1 million in capital — about 40% from Smith and the rest from the likes of Marshall Field (retailing) Martin Ryerson (steel) and Philip Armour (meatpacking) — the bank attracted $138000 in deposits its first day.

By 1896 the bank was firmly established; Smith began taking a salary and the company issued its first dividend. Ten years later the firm built its solid granite edifice the "Gray Lady of LaSalle Street" where it still resides.

The bank began buying commercial paper in 1912 joined the Federal Reserve System in 1917 and became a custodian for expropriated German assets during WWI. Byron Smith died in 1914 and was succeeded by his son Solomon.

Northern Trust rejected the get-rich-quick ethos of the 1920s. It was so strong during the Depression that after the 1933 bank holiday people actually clamored to make deposits and the bank administered the Depression-era scholarship fund that helped Ronald Reagan attend college. By 1941 almost half of Northern Trust's commercial deposits originated outside the Chicago area. The bank kept growing during and after WWII.

Solomon Smith retired in 1963; his son Edward took over and launched the company's expansion overseas (Northern Trust International was formed in 1968) and out of state (Florida in 1971 Arizona in 1974). The firm's business was helped by the 1974 passage by Congress of ERISA which required company retirement plans to be overseen by an outside custodian. Edward retired in 1979.

Northern Trust expanded locally when Illinois legalized intrastate branch banking in 1981. In 1987 the company lost money due in part to defaults on loans made to developing countries. It moved into California in 1988 and Texas in 1989.

Northern Trust navigated the early 1990s recession expanded geographically in the mid-1990s and added services through acquisitions. In 1995 the company became the first foreign trust company to operate throughout Canada. That year it bought investment management service RCB International (now Northern Trust Global Advisors). It expanded in the Sun Belt with such acquisitions as Dallas' Metroplex Bancshares and was made first custodian for the Teacher Retirement System of Texas (1997).

In 1998 the company expanded into Michigan and broke into the Cleveland and Seattle markets in 1999. Northern Trust entered cyberspace as well launching a website for its mutual funds. In 2000 the company opened locations in Nevada and Missouri and bought Florida-based investment adviser Carl Domino Associates (renamed Northern Trust Value Investors). Also that year the bank bought Ireland's Ulster Bank Investment Services.

In 2004 Northern Trust bought the fund management custody and trust operations of Baring Asset Management from Amsterdam-based ING Groep.

EXECUTIVES

Executive Vice President Human Resources, Timothy Moen

Senior Vice President Corporate And Institutional Services And Head North American Institutional A, Jeffrey W Conover

Senior Vice President, Joseph McInerney

Vice President Of Loans, Jean E Sheridan

Vice President, Monique Noblett

Senior Vice President, Donald Berk

Senior Vice President And Senior Portfolio Manager For Northern Trust Global Inv, George Maris

Executive Vice President; Head Capital Markets Group Northern Trust Asset Management, Michael Vardas

Vice President Administration, Alex Winslow

Evp And President Wealth Management, Steven L. (Steve) Fradkin, age 56, $600,000 total compensation

Evp And President Corporate And Institutional Services, Jeffery D. Cohodes, age 57

Evp And Coo, Jana R. Schreuder, age 59, $693,750 total compensation

Evp And President Asset Management, Stephen N. Potter, age 61, $587,500 total compensation

Evp And Chief Capital Management Officer, Joyce St. Clair, age 58

Evp And President Corporate And Institutional Services, Peter B. Cherecwich, age 53

Head Global Fund Services Northern Trust Company, Wilson Leech, age 56

Evp And Cfo, Stephen B. (Biff) Bowman, age 54, $568,750 total compensation

Evp And Chief Investment Officer, Robert P. (Bob) Browne, age 53

President Ceo And Director, Michael G. O'Grady, age 52, $606,250 total compensation

Evp And General Counsel, Susan C. Levy, age 60

Evp Human Resources, S. Gillian Pembleton, age 59

Senior Vice President Enterprise Architect, Ravi Gundimeda

Senior Vice President, Paul D'Ouville

Vice President, Christopher Tadda

Vice President Information Technology, Ken Le Breux

Vice President, James Lange

Vice President, Thomas Smith

Senior Vice President Of Sales, Marie Dzanis

Executive Vice President And Head Corporate Risk Management, Joyce St Clair

Second Vice President Event Marketing Manager, Danielle Czyz

Vice President Test Center Of Excellence, Scott Solenberger

Senior Vice President Corporate Business Development, Eric Strickland

Senior Vice President Enterprise Productivity, Laurel Neu

Vice President, David J Peterson

Executive Vice President, James Mitchell

Senior Vice President, Elizabeth V White

Vice President Portfolio Manager, Chris Fronk

Senior Vice President, Mark Rice

Senior Vice President Treasury, Duane Rocheleau

Senior Vice President Northeast Sales Wealth Management Group Northern Trust Company, Ann Zeiler

Vice President Corporate And Institutional Services, Stephen Kuropas

Vice President, Kathryn Furtek

Vice President, Rich Michaels

Senior Vice President, Timothy Geraghty

Senior Vice President Public Finance, Allan Ambrose

Vice President Information Technology, Barbara Malinowski

Vice President Division Head, James Monhart

Second Vice President Relationship Manager, David Rudd

Vice President, Michael Hunniford

Vice President For Worldwide Operations And Technology, Steven Gale

Senior Vice President, John Freel

Vice President, Richard Weiss

Vice President Security Architecture, Wendy Betts

Senior Vice President And Managing Director, Gene Harvey

Senior Vice President, Sheldon Woldt

Vice President Portfolio Manager, Michael Chico Michael Chico

Vice President Level, Mark Warner

Senior Vice President Of Marketing, Diane Spradlin

Senior Vice President, Paul Fahey

Vice President Manager Applications, Ann Rogula

Vice President Solutions Architecture Risk And Performance Systems, Minesh Amin

Vice President Administration, Deiken Maloney

Vice President, David Sullivan

Vice President Investment Systems Quality Assurance, Cheryl Flack

Second Vice President, Judith Wilson

Vice President Operations And Technology, Gordon Vickers

Senior Vice President, Peter Williams

Vice President Wealth Advisory Private Banking, Holly Brown

Vice President Application Architecture, Nihar Karnik

Second Vice President Emea Talent Acquisition, Catherine Coltart

Vice President Global Learning And Development, Brian Winchar

Senior Vice President Managing Director Private Client Services, Deb Finnegan

Vice President, Sharon Fine

Vice President Of Information Technology, Scott Kruger

Vice President Investment Risk And Analytical Services, William Frieske

Vice President, Kristin Missil

Vice President Human Resources, Denyse Reese

Executive Vice President, Jennifer Driscoll

Senior Vice President Chief Banking Officer Pfs Central Region, Paul Theiss

Vice President, Andrew Glick

Vice President, John Burke

Vice President Technical Risk, Karen Smilie

Second Vice President Regional Director Of Investment Practice Strategy, Jesse Robinett

Vice President, Kristina Jakstys

Senior Vice President, James Ferguson

Vice President Operations And Technology, Manan Mehta

Vice President Wealth Advisor (southeast Region), Mike Byrne

Vice President Wealth Management, Al Combs

Vice President, Rich Teska

Senior Vice President, Nina Staley

Senior Vice President Senior Investment Officer, Ann Farrall

Vice President Corporate Re Western Division, Jennifer Dryden

Vice President Risk Management, Scott Winkates

Vice President Worldwide Technology, Mike Morena

Vice President, Alex Latovin

Vice President, Raje Kantamneni

Senior Vice President, Scott Hensley

Second Vice President Global Network, Lawrence Walter

Second Vice President Information Technology, Jim Weatherhead

Second Vice President, Terry Sissman

Vice President Administration, Daniel Hintzen

Vice President, Matthew Riegel

Vice President, Anita Nikolov

Vice President Global Mobility, Susan Kubiesa

Vice President And Portfolio Manager, Jason A Lawit

Vice President Derivatives Portfolio M, Judson Baker

Second Vice President, Len Soderblom

Vice President Enterprise Banking, Sandy Wiles

Vice President Information Security, Kate Plattenberger

Vice President On Line Product Manager, Mary Jackowiak

Vice President, Russell H Stamey

Senior Vice President, Nancy Lyon

Vice President Private Banking, Dick Resseguie

Vice President Credit Policy, Tom Bernhardt

Vice President Estate Settlement Services, George Metzler

Second Vice President, Amit Dalal

Second Vice President, Alex Hingston

Second Vice President, Michelle Bergthold

Vice President, Nicole Bernard

Vice President Wealth Management, Christine Fleming

Vice President Information Technology, Bob Schroeder

Vice President Information Technology, Larry Wells

Senior Vice President Pfs Client Servicing Solutions, Julie Sausen

Vice President Tax Analyst, Cassandra Miller

Senior Vice President, Thomas Kim

Senior Vice President, Richard Burke

Senior Vice President, Phil Maughan

Vice President Applications, Evans Chang

Vice President Worldwide Technology, Laura
Corradetti
Vice President, Ann Schroeder
Vice President, Lee R Freitag
Vice President Corporate Real Estate, James Taylor
Second Vice President, Martial Bandemer
Vice President Global Market Data Sourcing,
Adam Anasinski
Vice President, Bryon Johnson
Vice President Technical Support, Ryan Gagala
Senior Vice President, Sharon Cohen
Senior Vice President And Group Head, Stephen
Hearty
Second Vice President, Carol Crispo
Vice President Worldwide Operations And
Technology, Paulette Kaczmarek
Executive Vice President Foreign Exchange And
Cash Management, Patrick Mcdougal
Vice President Worldwide Technology, Patricia
Toler
Vice President Manager Help Desk, Janet Barnes
Vice President Senior Private Banker, Betsy
Whitlow
Vice President, Brian Duhn
Vice President Corporate Banking Group, Jeff
Clark
Vice President, Michael Klat
Vice President Information Technology
Infrastructure Project Management Office, Jeffrey
West
Vice President, Robert Raimondi
Vice President, Venkat Sriniasan
Vice President, Raymond Odom
Auditors: KPMG LLP

LOCATIONS

HQ: Northern Trust Corp
50 South LaSalle Street, Chicago, IL 60603
Phone: 312 630-6000
Web: www.northerntrust.com

Selected Operations
US
  Arizona
  California
  Colorado
  Connecticut
  Delaware
  Florida
  Georgia
  Illinois
  Massachusetts
  Michigan
  Minnesota
  Missouri
  Nevada
  New York
  Ohio
  Texas
  Washington
  Wisconsin
International
  Africa
  Australia
  Canada
  China
  Hong Kong
  India
  Ireland
  Japan
  Luxembourg
  Middle East
  The Netherlands
  New Zealand
  Saudi Arabia
  Singapore
  Sweden
  UK

PRODUCTS/OPERATIONS

2016 sales

	% of total
Trust Investment & Other Servicing Fees	83
Foreign Exchange Trading Income	7
Treasury Management Fees	2
Security Commissions & Trading Income	2
Other Operating Income	6
Investment Security Lossesnet	-
Total	**100**

Selected Subsidiaries

Northern Investment Corporation
Northern Investment Management Company
Northern Trust Bank FSB
The Northern Trust Company
  MFC Company Inc.
  Norlease Inc.
  The Northern Trust Company Canada
  Northern Trust Holdings Limited (UK)
  Northern Trust Global Services Limited (UK)
  The Northern Trust International Banking
  Corporation
  Northern Trust Cayman International Ltd. (Cayman
  Islands)
  The Northern Trust Company of Hong Kong Limited
  Northern Trust Fund Managers (Ireland) Limited
  Northern Trust (Ireland) Limited
  Northern Trust Custodial Services (Ireland) Limited
  Northern Trust Fund Services (Ireland) Limited
  Northern Trust Investor Services (Ireland) Limited
  Northern Trust Property Services (Ireland) Limited
  Northern Trust Management Services Limited (UK)
  Northern Trust Partners Scotland Limited (UK)
  Northern Trust Scottish Limited Partnership (99%
  UK)
  Northern Trust Luxembourg Capital S.A.R.L.
  Northern Trust Investments Inc.
  NTG Services LLC
  NT Mortgage Holdings LLC
The Northern Trust Company of Delaware
The Northern Trust Company of New York
Northern Trust Global Advisors Inc.
  The Northern Trust Company of Connecticut
  NT Global Advisors Inc. (Canada)
Northern Trust Global Investments Japan K.K.
Northern Trust Holdings L.L.C.
Northern Trust NA
  Northern Annuity Sales Inc.
  Realnor Properties Inc.
  Waterline Partners LLC
Northern Trust Securities Inc.
Northern Trust Services Inc.
Nortrust Holding Corporation
  Northern Trust Bank N.A.
Nortrust Realty Management Inc.

COMPETITORS

Bank of America	Goldman Sachs
Bank of New York	Harris
Mellon	JPMorgan Chase
Barclays	Morgan Stanley
Citigroup	SEI Investments
Deutsche Bank	State Street
Fifth Third	Wells Fargo

HISTORICAL FINANCIALS
Company Type: Public

Income Statement				FYE: December 31
	ASSETS ($ mil.)	NET INCOME ($ mil.)	INCOME AS % OF ASSETS	EMPLOYEES
12/17	138,590	1,199	0.9%	18,100
12/16	123,926	1,032	0.8%	17,100
12/15	116,749	973	0.8%	16,200
12/14	109,946	811	0.7%	15,400
12/13	102,947	731	0.7%	14,800
Annual Growth	**7.7%**	**13.2%**	**—**	**5.2%**

2017 Year-End Financials

Debt ratio: 2.33%
Return on equity: 12.00%
Cash ($ mil.): 50,609
Current ratio: —
Long-term debt ($ mil.): —

No. of shares (mil.): 226
Dividends
  Yield: 0.0%
  Payout: 32.5%
Market value ($ mil.): 22,588

	STOCK PRICE ($) FY Close	P/E High/Low	PER SHARE ($) Earnings	Dividends	Book Value
12/17	99.89	20 17	4.92	1.60	45.18
12/16	89.05	21 13	4.32	1.48	42.74
12/15	72.09	20 15	3.99	1.41	37.97
12/14	67.40	21 17	3.32	1.30	36.20
12/13	61.89	21 17	2.99	1.23	33.34
Annual Growth	**12.7%**	**— —**	**13.3%**	**6.8%**	**7.9%**

Northfield Bancorp Inc (DE)

Auditors: KPMG LLP

LOCATIONS

HQ: Northfield Bancorp Inc (DE)
  581 Main Street, Woodbridge, NJ 07095
Phone: 732 499-7200
Web: www.eNorthfield.com

HISTORICAL FINANCIALS
Company Type: Public

Income Statement				FYE: December 31
	ASSETS ($ mil.)	NET INCOME ($ mil.)	INCOME AS % OF ASSETS	EMPLOYEES
12/17	3,991	24	0.6%	352
12/16	3,850	26	0.7%	366
12/15	3,202	19	0.6%	306
12/14	3,020	20	0.7%	321
12/13	2,702	19	0.7%	326
Annual Growth	**10.2%**	**6.6%**	**—**	**1.9%**

2017 Year-End Financials

Debt ratio: 11.76%
Return on equity: 3.93%
Cash ($ mil.): 57
Current ratio: —
Long-term debt ($ mil.): —

No. of shares (mil.): 48
Dividends
  Yield: 0.0%
  Payout: 64.1%
Market value ($ mil.): 834

	STOCK PRICE ($) FY Close	P/E High/Low	PER SHARE ($) Earnings	Dividends	Book Value
12/17	17.08	37 28	0.53	0.34	13.09
12/16	19.97	35 24	0.57	0.31	12.80
12/15	15.92	36 31	0.45	0.28	12.29
12/14	14.80	36 30	0.41	0.26	12.27
12/13	13.20	45 32	0.34	0.49	12.36
Annual Growth	**6.7%**	**— —**	**11.7%**	**(8.7%)**	**1.4%**

Northrim BancCorp Inc

EXECUTIVES

Vice President Commercial Cash Management,
Kimberly F Brewington
Auditors: Moss Adams LLP

LOCATIONS

HQ: Northrim BancCorp Inc
3111 C Street, Anchorage, AK 99503
Phone: 907 562-0062

PRODUCTS/OPERATIONS

2007 Sales

	$ mil.	% of total
Interest		
Loans including fees	66	80
Securities	4	6
Other	2	2
Noninterest		
Service charges on deposit accounts	3	4
Purchased receivable income	2	3
Other	4	5
Total	**82**	**100**

COMPETITORS

Alaska Pacific Bancshares	First National Bank Alaska
Alaska USA	KeyCorp

HISTORICAL FINANCIALS

Company Type: Public

Income Statement   FYE: December 31

	ASSETS ($ mil.)	NET INCOME ($ mil.)	INCOME AS % OF ASSETS	EMPLOYEES
12/17	1,519	13	0.9%	429
12/16	1,526	14	0.9%	451
12/15	1,499	17	1.2%	441
12/14	1,449	17	1.2%	426
12/13	1,215	12	1.0%	269
Annual Growth	**5.7%**	**1.6%**	**—**	**12.4%**

2017 Year-End Financials

Debt ratio: 1.16%	No. of shares (mil.): 6
Return on equity: 6.93%	Dividends
Cash ($ mil.): 77	Yield: 0.0%
Current ratio: —	Payout: 45.7%
Long-term debt ($ mil.): —	Market value ($ mil.): 233

	STOCK PRICE ($) FY Close	P/E High/Low	Earnings	Dividends	Book Value
12/17	33.85	20 14	1.88	0.86	28.06
12/16	31.60	16 10	2.06	0.78	27.05
12/15	26.60	11 8	2.56	0.74	25.74
12/14	26.24	11 9	2.54	0.70	23.97
12/13	26.24	15 11	1.87	0.64	22.05
Annual Growth	**6.6%**	**— —**	**0.1%**	**7.7%**	**6.2%**

Northrop Grumman Corp

Northrop Grumman is well equipped to defend its high place in the defense sector. As one of the world's top military contractors (behind Lockheed Martin and Boeing) the company operates through three business sectors: Aerospace Systems (aircraft spacecraft laser systems electronic subsystems); Mission Systems (radar sensors chemical detection countermeasure systems); and Technology Services (systems support training and simulation). The US government represents most of Northrop Grumman's sales. The company traces its historical roots back to 1927.

HISTORY

Huntington Ingalls Industries Jack Northrop co-founded Lockheed Aircraft in 1927 and designed its record-setting Vega monoplane. He founded two more companies — Avion Corporation (formed in 1928 and bought by United Aircraft and Transportation) and Northrop Corporation (formed in 1932 with Douglas Aircraft which absorbed it in 1938) — before founding Northrop Aircraft in California in 1939.

During WWII Northrop produced the P-61 fighter and the famous Flying Wing bomber which failed to win a production contract. In the 1950s Northrop depended heavily on F-89 fighter and Snark missile sales. When Thomas Jones succeeded Jack Northrop as president (1959) he moved the company away from risky prime contracts in favor of numerous subcontracts and bought Page Communications Engineers (telecommunications 1959) and Hallicrafters (electronics 1966) to reduce its dependence on government contracts.

In the early 1970s Northrop was hit with a bribery scandal and the disclosure of illegal payments to Richard Nixon's 1972 campaign fund; Jones was eventually fined for an illegal contribution. As a result a shareholder lawsuit forced Jones to resign as president (he was allowed to remain as chairman). In 1981 the company won the B-2 bomber contract. Jones retired as chairman in late 1990 and under the leadership of Kent Kresa (who became CEO in early 1990 and chairman when Jones retired) Northrop pleaded guilty to 34 counts related to fudging test results on some government projects; it was fined $17 million. In a related shareholders' suit Northrop paid $18 million in damages in 1991.

Northrop and The Carlyle Group bought LTV's Vought Aircraft Industries (now named Triumph Aerostructures - Vought Aircraft Division) in 1992. In 1994 it paid $2.1 billion for Grumman Corporation a premier electronic systems firm and manufacturer of fighter aircraft for the US Navy and changed its name to Northrop Grumman.

In 1929 Roy Grumman Jake Swirbul and Bill Schwendler founded Grumman; within three months it had a contract to design a Navy fighter. Grumman completed its first commercial aircraft (the Grumman Goose) in 1937 and went public in 1938. It soared during WWII on the wings of its Wildcat and Hellcat fighter planes.

Grumman built its first corporate jet (Gulfstream) in 1958 and began work on the Lunar Module for the Apollo space program in 1963. It was near bankruptcy during the 1970s due to costs related to its F-14 Tomcat fighter. Grumman rebuilt its military business in the 1980s and achieved its greatest success in electronic systems.

The UK Ministry of Defence awarded a $279 million contract to Northrop Grumman in 1995 to develop and produce a system to counter infrared missiles. In 1997 Northrop Grumman bought Logicon (information and battle-management systems). It then agreed to an $11.6 billion purchase by Lockheed Martin but the US government citing concerns about increased lack of competition in the defense industry blocked the deal in 1998. As a result Northrop Grumman began a restructuring that cut 10500 defense and aircraft jobs and added 2500 positions to its Logicon subsidiary.

In 1999 Northrop Grumman bought the information systems division of California Microwave for $93 million and Allegheny Teledyne's Ryan Aeronautical (aerial drones) for $140 million. The next year Northrop Grumman sold its underperforming commercial aerostructures business to The Carlyle Group in a $1.2 billion transaction in order to focus on its growing defense electronics and information technology segments. Later in 2000 Northrop Grumman acquired Comptek Research and bought Federal Data (information systems for the US government) from Carlyle in a transaction valued at $302 million. Pension income that year accounted for more than $500 million (about 55%) of the company's pretax profit.

In 2001 the company completed the deal to acquire Litton Industries for $3.8 billion plus $1.3 billion in debt. In the fall Northrop Grumman acquired the electronics and information unit of Aerojet-General Corp. a subsidiary of GenCorp (later renamed Aerojet Rocketdyne) for about $300 million (it became Grumman's Space Systems Division). While its wallet was open the company agreed to match the $2.6 billion that General Dynamics had agreed to pay for submarine and aircraft carrier builder Newport News— a move that the US Defense Department endorsed. In December Honeywell agreed to pay Northrop Grumman $440 million to settle an antitrust and patent infringement lawsuit that Litton had filed against Honeywell in 1990.

The deal to buy Newport News was completed in early 2002. Northrop Grumman then made a hostile $6 billion bid for conglomerate TRW when TRW's stock plunged following the sudden departure of its CEO David Cote to Honeywell. In the wake of Northrop Grumman's spurned initial bid Raytheon General Dynamics and BAE SYSTEMS made offers for TRW's aerospace and defense assets. Finally though TRW accepted a sweetened $7.8 billion offer from Northrop Grumman in July 2002.

The acquisition fortified Northrop Grumman's position in military satellites missile systems and systems integration. In fact Northrop signed a consent decree with the US Justice Department in which the company agreed (under pain of fines) that it wouldn't take unfair advantage of its exclusive position when selling certain components — such as satellite sensors — to competitors.

TRW's Systems unit became Northrop Grumman Mission Systems; TRW's Space and Electronics unit was later known as Northrop Grumman Space Technology. As for TRW's car parts business Northrop sold all but 19.6% of the unit to Blackstone Group for about $4.7 billion to pay down debt; by early 2005 Northrop reduced its stake to 9.9%.

In April 2003 Kresa stepped down as president and CEO and Ronald Sugar took over those roles; Sugar added the chairmanship to his title when Kresa retired in October.

Among Northrop's 2004 contracts were $1.04 billion for X-47B Joint Unmanned Combat Air Systems $1.2 billion (preferred bidder) for E-3D AWACS contract support and $1.4 billion for the CVN 21 generation aircraft carrier. The company also split an $8.4 billion submarine contract with General Dynamics.

Early in 2005 Northrop sold 7.2 million shares of its TRW Automotive stake raising more than $142 million and reducing its stake to 9.9%. It also acquired Integic Corporation an IT company that specialized in business process management and enterprise health applications.

In 2006 Northrop Grumman established Northrop Grumman Technical Services (NGTS) as a separate sector; it was tasked with consolidating Northrop's logistics operations across its various sectors.

Late that same year Northrop Grumman agreed to buy Essex Corporation — a provider of signal image and information processing for defense and intelligence customers in the US. The deal was valued at about $580 million including the assumption of debt. The deal was completed early in 2007 and Essex became a part of Northrop Grumman Mission Systems (now Northrop Grumman Information Systems).

In 2008 the company shed its Electro-Optical Systems business (night vision and applied optics products) to L-3 Communications for $175 million.

In 2009 Northrop Grumman sold its Advisory Services Division comprising subsidiary TASC (engineering and consulting services to the US military and state governments) to private equities General Atlantic LLC and KKR for $1.65 billion. The sale brings Northrop Grumman into compliance with a new federal law that strengthens conflict of interest rules for defense contractors that both sell to and provide consulting for the US military.

Expanding its aerospace and information capabilities the company purchased Sonoma Photonics and assets from Swift Engineering's Killer Bee Unmanned Air Systems lineup for its Aerospace Systems sector (2009). The deal followed its acquisition of 3001 International for $92 million (a nearly three times larger investment) in 2008. The Virginia-based geospatial data collection and analysis provider not only bolstered Northrop Grumman's military offerings but it also reeled in a host of new civilian customers.

Also in 2009 Northrop Grumman settled two decade-old lawsuits with the US government. It agreed to pay $325 million to resolve allegations that it provided defective military satellite parts to the National Reconnaissance Office. The second lawsuit was filed by Northrop Grumman against the US government for uncompensated costs incurred as a result of the cancellation of the Tri-Service Standoff Attack Missile program.

To concentrate more on its core areas Northrop Grumman spun off its shipbuilding business under former subsidiary Huntington Ingalls Industries in 2011. Despite modest increases in year-over-year revenues the shipbuilding sector had struggled to regain profitability after suffering a loss in 2008 attributable to absorbing most of the company's goodwill impairment charge. Also in 2011 the company reduced operations in other segments. It sold its Viper Strike laser-guided bomb operations in Alabama to European consortium MBDA for an undisclosed amount. And it lowered its participation in the National Security Technologies joint venture that manages and operates the Nevada National Security Site.

Focusing on increasing its presence in the Asia/Pacific in 2012 Northrop Grumman purchased M5 Network Security a provider of cyber security and secure mobile communications technology based in Australia.

EXECUTIVES

Chairman President And Ceo, Wesley G. (Wes) Bush, age 56, $1,530,000 total compensation
Vp And Cto, Patrick M. Antkowiak, age 57
Vp And President Technical Services, Christopher T. Jones, age 53
President And Coo, Kathy J. Warden, age 46, $772,500 total compensation
Corporate Vp And President Mission Systems, Mark A. Caylor, age 53
Vp And Cfo, Kenneth L. Bedingfield, age 45, $756,539 total compensation
Chief Executive Northrop Grumman Japan, Stan Crow

Vp And President Aerospace Systems, Janis G. Pamiljans
Corporate Vp And President Enterprise Services, Shawn N. Purvis
Vice President James Webb Space Telescope Program, Scott Willoughby
Corporate Vp And Chro, Denise Peppard
Vp And Deputy General Counsel, Kathryn Simpson
Corporate Vice President And Secretary, Jennifer Mcgarey
Vice President Human Resources, Heidi Hendrix
Svp Strategy, Bobby Lentz
Vp Tax, Talha Zobair
Vice President Of Business Management, Kenneth Crews
Vice President Operations Intelligence Surveillance And Reconnaissance, Kenny Robinson
Vp Supply Chain, Jaime Bohnke
Senior Vice President, Monty Frahm
Vice President, Anne Szemborski
Vice President Business Development Northrop Grumman Space Technology, Jeffrey Grant
Vp Contracts And Pricing, Diane Balderson
Deputy Vice President, Jessica E Lewis
Vp Corporate Strategy, Brett Lambert
Vice President Technology Development, Scott Stapp
Vice President, Paul Kalafos
Senior Vice President, Neil Jones
Vp Missile Defense And Protective Systems, Tarik Reyes
Vice President Associate General Counsel And Sector Counsel Technologyservices Sector, Don Chavez
Vp Nuclear Materials Operations Srns, David Eyler
Vice President Mission Solutions Land And Avionics C4isr Division, Carl Smith
Vp Hr Mission Systems, Milou Carolan
Vice President And Assistant General Counsel, John Cox
Vice President, Andrew Reynolds
Vice President, Simon Mason
Vice President Security, Mary Mccaffrey
Auditors: DELOITTE & TOUCHE LLP

LOCATIONS

HQ: Northrop Grumman Corp
2980 Fairview Park Drive, Falls Church, VA 22042
Phone: 703 280-2900
Web: www.northropgrumman.com

PRODUCTS/OPERATIONS

2016 Sales

Segments	$ mil.	% of total
Aerospace Systems	10,828	41
Mission Systems	10,928	41
Technology Services	4,825	18
Intersegment eliminations	(2073)	-
Total	**24,508**	**100**

2016 Sales

	$ mil.	% of total
Product	14,738	60
Service	9,770	40
Total	**24,508**	**100**

2016 Sales

	$ mil.	% of total
U.S. Government	20,573	84
International	3,205	13
Other Customers	730	3
Total	**24,508**	**100**

Selected Capabilities

Unmanned Systems
C4ISR
Cyber
Logistics
Advanced Electronics
Commercial Aviation
Directed Energy
IT & Enterprise Solutions
Manned Aircraft
Military Aviation
Missile Defense
Naval Systems
Navigation Systems

COMPETITORS

BAE SYSTEMS	Leonardo
Boeing	Lockheed Martin
Booz Allen	Meggitt
General Dynamics	Raytheon
L3 Technologies	Thales
Leidos	

HISTORICAL FINANCIALS

Company Type: Public

Income Statement				FYE: December 31
	REVENUE ($ mil.)	NET INCOME ($ mil.)	NET PROFIT MARGIN	EMPLOYEES
12/18	30,095	3,229	10.7%	85,000
12/17	25,803	2,015	7.8%	70,000
12/16	24,508	2,200	9.0%	67,000
12/15	23,526	1,990	8.5%	65,000
12/14	23,979	2,069	8.6%	64,300
Annual Growth	**5.8%**	**11.8%**	**—**	**7.2%**

2018 Year-End Financials

Debt ratio: 36.87%	No. of shares (mil.): 170
Return on equity: 42.39%	Dividends
Cash ($ mil.): 1,579	Yield: 1.9%
Current ratio: 1.17	Payout: 29.9%
Long-term debt ($ mil.): 13,883	Market value ($ mil.): 41,782

	STOCK PRICE ($) FY Close	P/E High/Low	PER SHARE ($)		
			Earnings	Dividends	Book Value
12/18	244.90	19 12	18.49	4.70	47.99
12/17	306.91	27 20	11.47	3.90	40.49
12/16	232.58	20 14	12.19	3.50	30.04
12/15	188.81	18 14	10.39	3.10	30.46
12/14	147.39	15 11	9.75	2.71	36.37
Annual Growth	**13.5%**	**— —**	**17.4%**	**14.8%**	**7.2%**

Northwest Bancshares, Inc. (MD)

EXECUTIVES

Chief Executive Officer, Julie McTpavish
Executive Vice President, Gregory LaRocca
Executive Vice President Commercial Lending, Michael Bickerton
Auditors: KPMG LLP

LOCATIONS

HQ: Northwest Bancshares, Inc. (MD)
100 Liberty Street, Warren, PA 16365
Phone: 814 726-2140
Web: www.northwestsavingsbank.com

HISTORICAL FINANCIALS
Company Type: Public

Income Statement				FYE: December 31
	ASSETS ($ mil.)	NET INCOME ($ mil.)	INCOME AS % OF ASSETS	EMPLOYEES
12/17	9,363	94	1.0%	2,254
12/16	9,623	49	0.5%	2,466
12/15	8,951	60	0.7%	2,364
12/14	7,775	61	0.8%	2,220
12/13	7,881	66	0.8%	2,231
Annual Growth	4.4%	9.1%	—	0.3%

2017 Year-End Financials

Debt ratio: 1.19%
Return on equity: 7.94%
Cash ($ mil.): 77
Current ratio: —
Long-term debt ($ mil.): —

No. of shares (mil.): 102
Dividends
  Yield: 0.0%
  Payout: 69.5%
Market value ($ mil.): 1,713

	STOCK PRICE ($) FY Close	P/E High/Low	PER SHARE ($) Earnings	Dividends	Book Value
12/17	16.73	20 16	0.92	0.64	11.79
12/16	18.03	38 24	0.49	0.60	11.51
12/15	13.39	22 18	0.64	0.56	11.42
12/14	12.53	22 18	0.67	1.62	11.22
12/13	14.78	20 16	0.73	0.62	12.27
Annual Growth	3.1%	— —	6.0%	0.8%	(1.0%)

NOVARTIS PHARMACEUTICALS CORPORATION

As the US pharmaceuticals unit of Swiss drug giant Novartis AG Novartis Pharmaceuticals Corporation (NPC) helps with the development manufacturing marketing and sales of its parent company's products in the US. Its product lines address a range of ailments including cardiovascular and respiratory diseases central nervous system disorders cancers bone and skin conditions infectious diseases and organ transplant complications. NPC's key products include tumor growth inhibitor Gleevec high blood pressure drug Diovan and attention deficit disorder therapies Focalin and Ritalin. NPC markets its products through an in-house sales team.

Operations

NPC represents the best of both worlds for parent Novartis AG: It is part of the global Novartis Pharmaceuticals division which accounts for more than half of the parent company's annual revenues and it is also a major player in the US market which is Novartis' largest geographic segment.

In addition to its medicines for cancers cardiovascular diseases infectious diseases and organ transplant complications NPC offers treatments for endocrine disease inflammatory diseases and others.

Geographic Reach

Most of NPC's preclinical research efforts are conducted through US-based affiliate Novartis Institutes for BioMedical Research (NIBR) while clinical-stage development programs are conducted at Novartis sites around the globe.

Sales and Marketing

NPC markets its products through a dedicated force of sales representatives and specialists. Marketing initiatives are conducted online through partnerships with external web firms and an e-sales force.

Strategy

NPC widens its offerings in the US market through a number of methods including internal research programs licensing agreements and acquisitions. In 2015 the company received approval from the US FDA for its Cosentyx product for the treatment of moderate-to-severe plaque psoriasis in adults eligible for systemic therapy (drug absorbed through the bloodstream) or phototherapy (light therapy).

As part of its parent's efforts to focus on eye care generics and innovative pharmaceuticals NPC remains a vital part of Novartis' growth strategy. One area of growing interest is oncology; in 2015 Novartis acquired certain cancer-fighting products and pipeline compounds from GlaxoSmithKline.

Mergers and Acquisitions

In 2016 Novartis acquired the Oklahoma-based Selexys Pharmaceuticals which specializes in hematologic and inflammatory disorder treatments for some $665 million.

EXECUTIVES

President, Fabrice Chouraqui
Company President, Thomas (Tom) Kendris
Chief Financial And Administrative Officer, Paolo Tombesi
Us Country Head Information Technology, Ruth Thorpe
Evp Us Oncology, Bill Hinshaw
President Novartis Canada, Janice Murray
First Vice President, Robert Heinrich
Vp Purchase, Peter Carbone
Auditors: PRICEWATERHOUSECOOPERS LLP-BR

LOCATIONS

HQ: NOVARTIS PHARMACEUTICALS CORPORATION
1 HEALTH PLZ, EAST HANOVER, NJ 079361016
Phone: 862 778-8300
Web: WWW.NOVARTIS.COM

PRODUCTS/OPERATIONS

2018 Sales by Segment

	% of total
Pharmaceutical Distribution	91
Insurance Pharmacy	5
Pharmaceutical Manufacturing	2
Healthcare-Related Services	2
Total	**100**

2018 Sales

	% of total
Ethical pharmaceuticals	91
Diagnostic reagents	4
Medical equipment & supplies	3
Other	2
Total	**100**

COMPETITORS

Alfresa
Takeda Pharmaceutical
Toho Pharmaceutical

HISTORICAL FINANCIALS
Company Type: Private

Income Statement				FYE: December 31
	REVENUE ($ mil.)	NET INCOME ($ mil.)	NET PROFIT MARGIN	EMPLOYEES
12/16	49,436	6,698	13.5%	7,000
12/15	49,440	17,794	36.0%	—
12/13	58,831	9,292	15.8%	—
Annual Growth	(5.6%)	(10.3%)	—	—

2016 Year-End Financials

Debt ratio: —
Return on equity: 13.50%
Cash ($ mil.): 7,007
Current ratio: 0.70
Long-term debt ($ mil.): —

Dividends
  Yield: —
  Payout: —
Market value ($ mil.): —

NRG Energy Inc

NRG Energy is a leading power producer with a generating capacity of 28000 MW (including 1600 MW of solar power assets). The vast majority of NRG's power plants are in North America but it also has one in Australia and one in Turkey. Its portfolio includes 50 power plants. It also markets natural gas oil and other commodities. NRG's retail units (including Reliant Energy and Green Mountain Energy) distribute power to about 3 million customers across the US.

Operations

NRG's operating segments are Retail (about 55% of revenues) Generation (over 30%) NRG Yield (about 10%) and Renewables.

NRG?s Retail segment is one of the largest in the country. It provides some 63 TWhs of energy and related services under the Business Solutions banner to almost 3 million residential industrial and commercial customers. The segment overlooks several brands that collectively are the largest providers of electricity in Texas.

Wholesale Power Generation a capital-intensive segment is responsible for plant and commercial operations energy services as well as distributed generation business. It has 28000 MW of fossil fuel and nuclear generation capacity at some 50 plants with less than 25% come from coal. Currently it has 500MW of targeted re-powering initiatives for future development.

NRG will sell its Renewables business segment and all interests in NRG Yield Inc. in 2018. The segment focuses on the acquisition development operation and maintenance of utility scale wind and solar community solar and distributed solar generation assets. Including NRG Yield it has a total portfolio of wind and solar assets across 27 states.

NRG Yield is a publicly-traded company through which NRG acquires and operates power generation and thermal infrastructure assets.

Geographic Reach

NRG Energy has generation assets in the US Australia and Turkey. Its retail and thermal subsidiaries serve customers in more than 15 US states. Its NRG Thermal unit provides third-party steam to downtown heating and cooling systems in cities such as Pittsburgh San Diego San Francisco and Harrisburg Pennsylvania.

Most of its retail sales come from Connecticut Delaware Illinois Maryland Massachusetts New Jersey New York Pennsylvania Ohio and Texas.

Sales and Marketing

NRG's retail electricity divisions serve nearly 3 million residential business commercial and industrial customers in all 50 US states and Washington DC.

The company's sales channels include direct sales call centers websites brokers and brick-and-mortar stores. It also sells directly to residential commercial and industrial customers.

Financial Performance

NRG revenue trended upwards from $7 billion in 2008 to $15 billion peak in 2014 before suffering from an oil and gas price downturn and reducing below $11 billion in the following years. Net income has been hit badly due to the commodities price downturn. In the 2015-17 the company has posted a combined three-year loss of $9.3 billion.

Revenue in 2017 grew less than 2% for NRG to $10.6 billion. The slight increase came due to better results from mark to market hedging. Energy revenue the highest company earner reduced by some 20% compared to 2016.

Net loss for 2017 was $2.3 billion compared to a loss of $891 million the year prior mostly due to $1 billion increase in impairment losses from the year prior. In 2017 NRG recorded a loss of $790 million from discontinued operations. This included the deconsolidation of GenOn and its subsidiaries for $208 million (after it filed for bankruptcy).

NRG's cash holdings increased slightly to $1.5 billion. Financing activities used some $485 million while investments utilized more than double that amount at $1 billion mostly in CAPEX. Operations provided a healthy $1.4 billion though greatly reduced by losses on discontinued operations and high impairment charges as well as depreciation and amortization charges.

Strategy

Coming out of three years of massive losses (for a combined $9.3 billion) NRG is in the middle of executing a drastic Transformation Plan. The three-part three-year plan will target portfolio overhaul cost-cutting and capital structure enhancement.

The core of the plan focused on a massive asset sale totaling $3 billion by early 2018. This includes NRG's agreement to sell NRG Yield (along with its renewable platform) in February 2018 for $1.3 billion ownership interests in Buckthorn Solar for $42 million Carlsbad Energy for $365 million and BETM for $70 million.

Despite a tough operational year (Hurricane Harvey further affected 2017 sales by at least $20 million the company calculates) NRG achieved $150 million in cost savings reduced working capital by $221 million is expecting to generate $3.2 billion in cash proceeds from the asset sales and further announced another $1 billion in share buybacks. This would allow the company to pay off $8 billion in debt.

One of the robust performance areas for NRG is its retail sector where customer count is growing from 2.89 million in 2016 to 2.94 in early 2018. Retail's sharing of total earnings has gone up from 25% in 2016 to 60% in first quarter though much of it is due to asset sell offs.

With the power market showing signs of stabilizing and cost-recovery in 2018 the company is pushing for improved retail choices and capacity re-pricing proposal. The company is also exclusively focusing on investing in projects that will have around 15% returns within a maximum 5-year window.

Mergers and Acquisitions

In March 2018 NRG Energy announced plans to acquire XOOM Energy for $210 million. The acquisition will balance NRG's generation portfolio in the East. It also expands NRG's retail natural gas business and enhances NRG's multi-brand and

multi-channel strategy via XOOM's referral-based sales channel.

In 2016 NRG acquired SunEdison's Utah-based solar and wind projects (1500 MW including 530 MW of solar assets) for $183 million.

EXECUTIVES

President And Ceo, Mauricio Gutierrez, age 48, $1,125,000 total compensation

Evp And Cfo, Kirkland B. Andrews, age 51, $642,952 total compensation

Svp; President Nrg Retail, Elizabeth Killinger, age 48, $504,634 total compensation

Evp National Business Development; President West Region, John Chillemi, age 51, $475,001 total compensation

Evp And General Counsel, David R. Hill, age 55, $500,000 total compensation

Svp Operations, Chris Moser

Svp Information Technology, Donna Benefield

Senior Vice President Asset Management And Development, Howard Taylor

Svp It, Kim Hales

Senior Vice President, Daniel Keane

Chairman, Lawrence S. Coben, age 59

Board Member, Kirbyjon Caldwell

Board Member, Anne Schaumburg

Board Member, Paul Hobby

Auditors: KPMG LLP

LOCATIONS

HQ: NRG Energy Inc
804 Carnegie Center, Princeton, NJ 08540
Phone: 609 524-4500
Web: www.nrgenergy.com

PRODUCTS/OPERATIONS

2016 Sales

	$ mil.	% of total
Retail revenue	6,274	47
Energy revenue	4,469	34
Capacity revenue	1,970	15
Other revenues	558	4
Mark-to-market activities	(865)	-
Contract amortization	(55)	-
Total	**12,351**	**100**

2016 Sales

	$ mil
% of total	
Retail	47
Generation	42
NRG Yield	7
Renewables	3
Corporate	1
Other	-
Total	**100**

2016 Sales

	% of total
Generation	51
Retail Mass	37
NRG Yield	8
Renewable	3
Corporate	1
Eliminations	
Total	**100**

Selected Subsidiaries

Energy Plus
Green Mountain Energy Company (retail power)
NEO Corporation (distributed generation; landfill gas hydroelectric and other renewable generation)
NRG Power Marketing Inc. (power sales)
NRG Resource Recovery (waste-to-energy facilities)
NRG Texas LLC (power generation)
NRG Thermal Corporation (district heating and cooling combined heat and power facilities)
Reliant Energy Texas Retail LLC
Texas Genco LP (power generation)
West Coast Power LLC (power generation)

COMPETITORS

AEP	Entergy
AES	FirstEnergy
Accent Energy	Gexa Energy
Alliant Energy	Integrys Energy
Avista	Services
Berkshire Hathaway	Nicor Gas
Energy	PG&E Corporation
Calpine	PPL Corporation
Cogentrix Energy	PSEG Power
Community Energy	Preferred Energy
Direct Energy	Services
Duke Energy	SCANA
Edison International	Sempra Generation
Energy Future	Tenaska

HISTORICAL FINANCIALS

Company Type: Public

Income Statement

FYE: December 31

	REVENUE ($ mil.)	NET INCOME ($ mil.)	NET PROFIT MARGIN	EMPLOYEES
12/17	10,629	(2,153)	—	5,940
12/16	12,351	(774)	—	8,763
12/15	14,674	(6,382)	—	10,468
12/14	15,868	134	0.8%	9,806
12/13	11,295	(386)	—	7,786
Annual Growth	**(1.5%)**	**—**	**—**	**(6.5%)**

2017 Year-End Financials

Debt ratio: 70.35%	No. of shares (mil.): 316
Return on equity: (-254.04%)	Dividends
Cash ($ mil.): 1,028	Yield: 0.0%
Current ratio: 1.33	Payout: —
Long-term debt ($ mil.): 15,716	Market value ($ mil.): 9,021

	STOCK PRICE ($) FY Close	P/E High/Low		Earnings	PER SHARE ($) Dividends	Book Value
12/17	28.48	—	—	(6.79)	0.12	(1.09)
12/16	12.26	—	—	(2.22)	0.24	6.47
12/15	11.77	—	—	(19.46)	0.58	9.58
12/14	26.95	164	112	0.23	0.54	29.86
12/13	28.72	—	—	(1.22)	0.45	30.43
Annual Growth	**(0.2%)**	**—**	**—**	**—**	**(28.1%)**	**—**

Nucor Corp.

Nucor takes a "minimillist" approach to succeeding in the steel industry. At its minimills Nucor produces hot- and cold-rolled steel steel joists and metal buildings. It has the capacity to produce more than 26 million tons of steel per year. North America's largest recycler of scrap metal it produces steel by melting scrap in electric arc furnaces. Most products are sold to steel service centers manufacturers and fabricators. Subsidiary Harris Steel fabricates rebar for highways and bridges and other construction projects. Its David J. Joseph Company unit processes and brokers metals pig iron hot briquetted iron and direct reduced iron (DRI). In 2015 Nucor recycled 16.9 million tons of scrap steel.

Operations

Nucor operates in three segments: Steel Mills Steel Products and Raw Materials. Its Steel Mills segment produces sheet steel plate steel structural steel and bar steel. The Steel Products segment makes steel joists and joist girders steel deck fabricated concrete reinforcing steel cold finished steel steel fasteners and other products. Its Raw Materials segment produces DRI; brokers ferrous and nonferrous metals pig iron and hot briquetted iron; supplies ferro-alloys; and processes ferrous and nonferrous scrap metal. The steel mills are Nucor's largest segment representing 67% of the company's sales to external customers in 2015.

Steel products contributed 25%; raw materials 8%.

During 2015 the average utilization rates of all its steel mills steel products and raw materials segments were 68% 63% and 56% of production capacity respectively.

Key subsidiaries include Harris Steel Skyline Steel David J. Joseph Company Castrip Nucor-Yamato Steel Company Nucor Steel Tuscaloosa and Nucor Steel Marion .

Geographic Reach
Nucor has 177 locations mainly concentrated throughout the US. It also has locations in Brazil Canada Mexico the UAE and the West Indies.

Sales and Marketing
Nucor's Steel Mills segment sells its products primarily to steel centers fabricators and manufacturers. About 60% of its sheet steel sales go to contract customers.

In 2015 about 86% of the shipments made by the company's steel mills were to external customers. It also sells steel mills and steel products mainly through in-house sales forces and also use internal distribution and trading companies to market our products outside of the US.

Financial Performance
The company's net revenue has been decreasing in the last five years (2011-15) except in 2014. In 2015 net revenues decreased by 22% due to a decrease in all segments particularly Steel mills which fell mainly due to decrease in the average sales price per ton and a 9% decrease in tons sold to outside customers.

The company's net income has similar trend as net revenue over a period of five years. In 2015 Nucor's net income decreased by 50%. mainly due to lower revenues and highr impairments and losses on assets expenses related to investment in Duferdofin due to unfavorable operating performance and deterioration in financial projections caused by increased global overcapacity in 2015.

Nucor's operating cash inflow increased by 61% to due to changes in working capital as a result of decreases in accounts receivable driven by decreased average sales prices per ton and outside shipments from the prior year inventories decline due to scrap and scrap substitute pricing and federal income taxes decreased due to Nucor's decreased profitability.

Strategy
Nucor has dominated the minimill industry for more than two decades but competitors in the sector are increasing. The company continues to expand its steel mills add new facilities and pursue a program of rapid external growth. Its organic growth strategies include optimizing existing operations and developing projects that capitalize on new technologies and opportunities in niche markets. The company also seeks acquisitions of companies complementary to its operations and international growth through joint ventures. A key part of its strategy is continuing to invest during downturn periods.

Nucor has invested significant capital in recent years to improve their cost structure and expand their product portfolios to include more value-added higher margined offerings investments total nearly $6 billion during the last six years. Initiatives include the construction of an ironmaking facility in Louisiana the commissioning a heat treating plant at its plate mill in North Carolina the revamping a finishing rolling mill for a steel beam plant in Italy and completing four acquisitions through its David J. Joseph.

The company also has a major emphasis on a cost improvement plan to reduce its raw materials cost.

Nucor is looking to continue to seek opportunities to acquire businesses enter into joint ventures and make other investments.

Mergers and Acquisitions
In late 2018 Nucor acquired Corporacion POK S.A. de C.V. (POK) a fully integrated precision castings company with a facility in Guadalajara Mexico. POK produces complex castings and precision machined products used by the oil and gas mining and sugar processing industries. The acquisition supports Nucor's downstream strategy of processing high-quality applications. The acquisition further compliments Nucor's existing cold finish businesses.

In 2016 Nucor agreed to buy Independence Tube a leading independent manufacturer of hollow structural section steel tubing for $435 million.

It also agreed to acquire Southland Tube an independent manufacturer of hollow structural section steel tubing for $130 million.

HISTORY
Nucor started as the second carmaking venture of Ransom Olds who built his first gasoline-powered car in 1897. Two years later Samuel Smith a Detroit copper and lumber magnate put up $199600 to finance Olds Motor Works. A fire destroyed the company's Detroit plant in 1901 so Olds moved production to Lansing Michigan where he built America's first mass-produced car — the Oldsmobile. In 1904 Olds left Olds Motor Works which was bought by General Motors (GM) in 1908 and formed Reo Car Company (renamed Reo Motor Car in 1906). In addition to cars it eventually made trucks and buses.

By the end of the Depression Ford GM and Chrysler commanded over 85% of the US passenger car market. Reo stopped making cars in 1936 and sold its truck manufacturing operations in 1957. Meanwhile it had formed Reo Holding which in 1955 merged with Nuclear Consultants to form Nuclear Corporation of America. The new company offered services such as radiation studies and made nuclear instruments and electronics.

In 1962 Nuclear bought steel joist maker Vulcraft and gained the services of Kenneth Iverson. The diverse company was unprofitable losing $2 million on $22 million in sales in 1965. That year Iverson took over as CEO moved headquarters to Charlotte North Carolina and shut down or sold about half of the company's businesses. By focusing on its profitable steel joist operations the firm ended 1966 in the black. Because the company depended on imports for 80% of its steel needs Iverson decided to move into steel production. Nuclear Corporation built its first minimill in 1969.

The company was renamed Nucor in 1972. It started making steel deck (1977) and cold-finished steel bars (1979). Production tripled and sales more than doubled between 1974 and 1979.

Nucor began to diversify adding grinding balls (used in the mining industry to process ores 1981); steel bolts steel bearings and machined steel parts (1986); and metal buildings and components (1987). Nucor and Japanese steelmaker Yamato Kogyo formed Nucor-Yamato and built a mill in 1988 to produce wide-flange beams (for heavy construction). The following year Nucor opened a state-of-the-art mill in Crawfordsville Indiana and another mill near Hickman Arkansas in 1992.

Iverson turned over his CEO duties to company veteran John Correnti in 1996. The next year Nucor began building a steel beam mill in South Carolina and added a galvanizing facility to its Hickman mill.

In 1998 Nucor announced plans to build its first steel plate mill which became operational in 2000. The company slashed prices twice in 1998 to compete against low-cost imports from Russia Japan and Brazil. Both sales and earnings declined that year due to low metal prices reduced shipments and start-up costs for new plants. The company raised its prices in 1999 and continued its expansion plans. Differences with the board prompted Correnti to resign in 1999; chairman David Aycock assumed his duties. In September 2000 Aycock resigned from the company and Daniel DiMicco formerly an EVP moved up to the rank of CEO.

Nucor along with Australia's Broken Hill Proprietary Corporation and Japan's Ishikawajima-Harima Heavy Industries began a joint venture in 2000 for its technology strip casting. The new technology allows steel production in smaller cheaper plants. In 2001 Nucor purchased a significant amount of assets of Auburn Steel a producer of merchant steel bar for $115 million.

In 2002 Nucor teamed up with Companhia Vale do Rio Doce (Vale) a Brazilian producer and exporter of iron-ore pellets to develop low-cost iron based products. That year Nucor purchased Alabama-based Trico Ste

EXECUTIVES

Evp Flat-rolled Products, Ladd R. Hall, age 61, $463,100 total compensation

Chairman President And Ceo, John J. Ferriola, age 65, $1,300,000 total compensation

Evp Merchant And Rebar Products, James R. Darsey, age 62, $463,100 total compensation

Evp Raw Materials And Chief Digital Officer, R. Joseph Stratman, age 61, $473,914 total compensation

Evp Cfo And Treasurer, James D. (Jim) Frias, age 61, $490,350 total compensation

General Manager Building Systems Division (terrell Texas), Raymond S. Napolitan, age 60

Evp Beam And Plate Products, D. Chad Utermark, age 50

Evp Engineered Bar Products, David A. Sumoski, age 51

Executive Vice President Beam And Plate Products, Leon Topalian

Vice President, Paige Okelley

Vice President Communications, Elizabeth Bowers

Executive Vice President Beam Plate Products, Chad Utermark

Vice President And General Manager, Michael Lee

Vice President; General Manager Nucor Steel Tuscaloosa Inc. Tuscaloosa Alabama, Randy Skagen

Vice President General Manager Vulcraft Division Fort Payne Alabama, D Ryan

Evp Engineered Bar Products, Ray Napolitan

Auditors: PricewaterhouseCoopers LLP

LOCATIONS

HQ: Nucor Corp.
1915 Rexford Road, Charlotte, NC 28211
Phone: 704 366-7000   **Fax:** 704 362-4208
Web: www.nucor.com

PRODUCTS/OPERATIONS

2016 Sales

	$ mil.	% of total
Steel Mills	11,312	70
Steel Products	3,687	23
Raw Materials	1,208	7
Total	**16,208**	**100**

2016 Sales by Product

	$ mil.	% of total
Sheet	5,178	32
Steel products	3,687	23
Bar	2,886	18
Structural	1,982	12
Raw materials	1,208	8
Plate	1,204	7
Tubular products	60	-
Total	**16,208**	**100**

Selected Products

Alloy steel
  Cold-drawn steel bars
  Finished hex caps
  Hex-head cap screws
  Locknuts
  Structural bolts and nuts
Carbon steel
  Angles
  Beams
  Channels
  Cold-drawn steel bars
  Finished hex nuts
  Flats
  Floor plate
  Galvanized sheet
  Grinding balls
  Hexagons
  Hot-rolled sheet
  Reinforcing bars
  Structural bolts and nuts
  Wide-range beams
Engineered products
  Composite floor joists
  Floor deck
  Joists
  Joist girders
  Pre-engineered metal buildings
  Roof deck
  Special-profile steel trusses
Stainless steel
  Cold-rolled steel
  Hot-rolled steel
  Pickled sheet

Selected Subsidiaries

Harris Steel Inc.
Harris Steel ULC (Canada)
The David J. Joseph Company
Magnatrax Corporation
Nucor Castrip Arkansas LLC
Nucor Energy Holdings Inc.
Nucor-Yamato Steel Company

COMPETITORS

AK Steel Holding	Gerdau Ameristeel
Corporation	Harsco
ArcelorMittal USA	Illinois Tool Works
Arconic	Renco
BlueScope Steel	Schnitzer Steel
Commercial Metals	Steel Dynamics
Cummins	Tata Europe
Dow Chemical	United States Steel

HISTORICAL FINANCIALS

Company Type: Public

Income Statement
FYE: December 31

	REVENUE ($ mil.)	NET INCOME ($ mil.)	NET PROFIT MARGIN	EMPLOYEES
12/17	20,252	1,318	6.5%	25,100
12/16	16,208	796	4.9%	23,900
12/15	16,439	357	2.2%	23,700
12/14	21,105	713	3.4%	23,600
12/13	19,052	488	2.6%	22,300
Annual Growth	**1.5%**	**28.2%**	**—**	**3.0%**

2017 Year-End Financials

Debt ratio: 23.96%
Return on equity: 15.87%
Cash ($ mil.): 949
Current ratio: 2.42
Long-term debt ($ mil.): 3,242
No. of shares (mil.): 317
Dividends
  Yield: 0.0%
  Payout: 36.8%
Market value ($ mil.): 20,216

	STOCK PRICE ($) FY Close	P/E High/Low	PER SHARE ($) Earnings	Dividends	Book Value
12/17	63.58	16 13	4.10	1.51	27.48
12/16	59.52	27 14	2.48	1.50	24.72
12/15	40.30	45 33	1.11	1.49	23.33
12/14	49.05	26 21	2.22	1.48	24.36
12/13	53.38	36 28	1.52	1.47	24.02
Annual Growth	**4.5%**	**— —**	**28.2%**	**0.7%**	**3.4%**

NVIDIA Corp

NVIDIA is racking up points in computer games logging miles in driverless cars and going deep into data centers. The Santa Clara California-based company?s graphics processing units (GPUs) are used to generate computer game images in many PCs and game consoles in the growing gaming market. What?s more its GPUs work well in applications for autonomous vehicles and deep learning a branch of artificial intelligence. NVIDIA?s GPU brands are GeForce for games Quadro for designers and digital artists and Tesla and DGX for scientists and researchers. Its Tegra line is a family of system-on-a-chip devices for mobile gaming and entertainment as well as autonomous robots drones and cars.

Operations

NVIDIA keeps track of its operations by product and market. GPUs account for about 85% of the company?s revenue while the Tegra brand brings in about 15%. In terms of markets gaming produces more than 55% of revenue followed by data centers about 20% visualization about 10% and automotive and intellectual property combined about 15%.

The GPU products include GeForce for PC gaming and GeForce NOW for cloud-based game-streaming services; Quadro for computer-aided design video editing and special effects; Tesla for AI using deep learning and accelerated computing; and GRID for providing NVIDIA graphics capabilities through the cloud and data centers.

The Tegra line includes DRIVE PX automotive chip systems that provide self-driving capabilities and SHIELD which includes a family of devices and services for cloud-based mobile applications for home entertainment AI and gaming.

The company also develops software and software libraries for running its chips.

NVIDIA outsources manufacturing to Taiwan Semiconductor Manufacturing Company Limited and Samsung Electronics Co. Ltd. The assembly testing and packaging work is done by independent subcontractors that include Advanced Semiconductor Engineering Inc. BYD Auto Co. Hon Hai Precision Industry Co. and JSI Logistics Ltd.

Geographic Reach

NVIDIA has design centers laboratories and offices in Australia Canada China Finland France Germany Hong Kong India Japan Russia Singapore South Korea Sweden Switzerland Taiwan the UK and the US.

While some 70% of NVIDIA?s sales are to customers in Asia they are spread out over several countries. Customers in Taiwan generate nearly 30% of NVIDIA?s revenue followed by customers in China with about 20% and other Asia/Pacific countries. The US market accounts for just under 15% of NVIDIA?s sales.

Sales and Marketing

NVIDIA?s sales and marketing team works with end customers and through partner networks that include original equipment manufacturers original device manufacturers system builders add-in board makers and retailers and distributors. As part of its sales and marketing efforts NVIDIA offers rebates to resellers as incentives and it provides marketing development funds to help partners in promoting NVIDIA?s products as well as their own.

As NVIDIA products have expanded beyond gaming applications the company has developed more routes to market and a wider more diverse customer roster. No customer accounts for more than 10% or more of sales.

Financial Performance

To say NVIDIA has been on a roll would be an understatement. Over the past five years the company sales have more than doubled and profit has increased nearly 600% driven by applications for artificial intelligence data centers and more complex gaming.

NVIDIA?s revenue rose 41% to $9.7 billion in 2018 (ended January) from 2017 on robust increases in all its markets. The GPU business' revenue increased 40% from gaming datacenter and professional visualization markets. Sales in the Tegra processor business leaped 86% in 2017 with strong boosts from system-on-a-chip modules for the Nintendo Switch gaming console and development services. Revenue for automotive applications rose from infotainment modules and development agreements for self-driving cars.

The company?s revenue bonanza allowed it to absorb higher costs and still report a profit of $3.7 billion in 2017 75% higher than 2016. A contributing one-time factor was a lower tax bill because of the US Tax Cuts and Jobs Act.

It revenue and earnings growth put NVIDIA in a strong cash position. The company had about $4 billion in cash at the end of 2018 up from $1.8 billion in 2016. Its free cash flow rose to $2.9 billion in 2018 from $1.5 billion the year before.

Strategy

It takes a lot of computing power to render graphics capable of holding gamers' attention for hours at a time. In providing that power NVIDIA established itself as the dominant player in computer game graphics controlling more than 70% of the market. The company continues to turn out architectures and processors that generate realistic renderings of all kinds of games played on all kinds of platforms. The company sees potential for continued gaming growth in the rise of computer gaming as a spectator sport. The company?s GeForce GPUs run PCs used in the top esports tournaments.

From its gaming base NVIDIA has positioned its GPUs for the artificial intelligence and automotive markets. The high processing power of GPUs enables them to handle the demands of artificial intelligence applications. The biggest cloud infrastructure providers ? Amazon Web Services Microsoft and Google ? use NVIDIA processors in their operations. GPUs also are used to turn analyzed information into graphics through visualization applications.

In the automotive market NVIDIA?s DRIVE PX 2 AI car platform operates multiple functions such as auto-piloted cars driverless shuttles cloud mapping and in-car AI capabilities. NVIDIA has partnered with car and component manufacturers to develop automotive applications. The company?s processors also are used in information and entertainment applications in vehicles.

Virtual reality is another area where NVIDIA?s processors are firmly established. They run the VR headsets of top companies in the emerging business including Oculus Epic Valve and Vive.

NVIDIA has plenty of competition with greater overall resources. AMD a long-time player in graphics has released processors recently that rival others in the market. Intel Corp. has used its deep resources to develop and buy technologies to compete in these markets including automotive with its acquisition of Mobileye. Although NVIDIA has grown rapidly over the past five year it cracked the list of Top 10 chipmakers for the first time in 2017.

EXECUTIVES

Vice President Vlsi Engineering, Joseph D Greco
President And Ceo, Jen-Hsun Huang, age 55, $996,216 total compensation
Evp Operations, Debora C. Shoquist, age 63, $695,131 total compensation
Evp Worldwide Field Operations, Ajay K. (Jay) Puri, age 63, $889,573 total compensation
Evp And Cfo, Colette M. Kress, age 50, $769,609 total compensation
Vice President Operations System Engineering, Richard Compton
Svp Content And Technology, Tony Tamasi
Vice President Software Engineering, Dwight Diercks
Vice President Supply Chain Projects, Brian Ebbs
Vice President, Alejandro Troccoli
Vice President Hardware Engineering, John Schafer
Vice President Of Hardware Engineering, Rajeev Jayavant
Vice President, Lin Cong
Senior Vice President And Treasurer, Nickolas Fortino
Vice President Software Engineering, Sam Azar
Senior Vice President, Ilyas Elkin
Vice President Worldwide Geforce Sales, John Milner
Vp Operations, David Miller
Vice President Of Vlsi Engineering, Sameer Halepete
Vice President Automotive Software, Kevin Flory
Vice President, James van Welzen
Vice President Human Resources, Anurag Chaudhary
Vice President Im, Ann Chang
Vice President Engineering, Laurent Coudrelle
Vice President Of Branding, Ming-Ju Lee
Vice President Of Operations, Arnold Suratos
Vice President, Cuong Le
Vice President Of The Investment Group, Shantanu Kalchuri
Vice President, Richard Cameron
Vice President Product Engineering, David Greenlaw
Senior Vice President, Jizhi Zhang
National Sales Manager, James Reilley
Assistant Vice President Residential Solutions, Kenneth MacDonald
Vice President Hw Engineering, Jonathan Sweedler
Vice President Customer Engineering, Rick Dingle
Vice President World Wide Sales Nvidia Professional Solutions Group, Walter Mundt-Blum
Vice President Internal Audit, Bruce Carpenter
Senior Vice President Vlsi Engineering, Joe Grech
Vice President Oem Sales, John Leggio
Vp Chief Architect, Michael Cox
Vice President, Jeff Herbst
Vice President Of Gameworks Labs, John Spitzer
Vice President Software Security, Daniel Rohrer
Senior Vice President Geforce Business Unit, Jeff Fisher
Vice President Corporate Marketing, Rob Csonger
Senior Vice President, Gary Hicok
Vice President Gpu Asic Engineering, Arjun Prabhu
Evp Worldwide Field Operations, Jay Puri
Senior Vice President Operations, Debbie Shoquist
Vice President And Assistant General Counsel And Chief Operating Officer, Elizabeth Hansel

Vice President Software, Richard Clark
Vice President Enterprise Marketing Corporate Communications And Global Events, Laura Fay
Vp Operations Engineering, Keith Katcher
Vice President Corporate Communications, Robert Sherbin
Vice President Of Investor Relations, Simona Jankowski
Vice President Systems Supply Chain, Jeff Whitmer
Senior Vice President Human Resources, Shelly Cerio
Board Member, Darrell Boggs
Board Member, Luke Durant
Board Member, Keegan Brown
Us Treasurer, Jay Landre
Board Member, Guru Nutheti
Vice Chairman And President, Gerald Luiz
Consultant And Member Of The Board, James Forman
Board Member, Hyungon Ryu
Treasurer, Eric Jensen
Board Member, Eric Anderson
Auditors: PricewaterhouseCoopers LLP

LOCATIONS

HQ: NVIDIA Corp
  2788 San Tomas Expressway, Santa Clara, CA 95051
Phone: 408 486-2000
Web: www.nvidia.com

2018 Sales

	$ mil.	% of total
Asia/Pacific		
Taiwan	2,991	31
China	1,896	20
Other Asia/Pacific	2,066	21
Americas		
US	1,274	13
Other Americas	719	7
Europe	768	8
Total	**9,714**	**100**

PRODUCTS/OPERATIONS

2018 Sales

	$ mil.	% of total
GPU	8,137	84
Tegra Processor	1,534	16
All other	43	-
Total	**9,714**	**100**

2018 sales by Market

	% of total
Gaming	57
Datacenter	20
Professional Visualization	9
Automotive	6
OEM & IP	8
Total	**100**

COMPETITORS

AMD
ARM Holdings
Ambarella
Apple Inc.
Creative Technology
Epson
Fujitsu Semiconductor
Imagination Technologies
Intel
Marvell Technology
Matrox Electronic Systems
MediaTek
NEC
QUALCOMM
Renesas Electronics
STMicroelectronics
Samsung Electronics
Sigma Designs
Silicon Integrated Systems
Spreadtrum

Texas Instruments
Toshiba America Electronic Components
VIA Technologies
Xilinx

HISTORICAL FINANCIALS

Company Type: Public

Income Statement

FYE: January 28

	REVENUE ($ mil.)	NET INCOME ($ mil.)	NET PROFIT MARGIN	EMPLOYEES
01/18	9,714	3,047	31.4%	11,528
01/17	6,910	1,666	24.1%	10,299
01/16	5,010	614	12.3%	6,566
01/15	4,681	630	13.5%	9,228
01/14	4,130	439	10.7%	8,808
Annual Growth	23.8%	62.2%	—	7.0%

2018 Year-End Financials

Debt ratio: 17.79%
Return on equity: 46.07%
Cash ($ mil.): 4,002
Current ratio: 8.03
Long-term debt ($ mil.): 1,985
No. of shares (mil.): 606
Dividends
Yield: 0.0%
Payout: 11.8%
Market value ($ mil.): 147,458

	STOCK PRICE ($) FY Close	P/E High/Low		PER SHARE ($) Earnings	Dividends	Book Value
01/18	243.33	48	19	4.82	0.57	12.33
01/17	111.77	38	8	2.57	0.49	9.90
01/16	29.29	30	17	1.08	0.40	8.45
01/15	20.71	19	14	1.12	0.34	8.11
01/14	15.56	22	16	0.74	0.31	7.85
Annual Growth	98.9%	—	—	59.8%	16.4%	12.0%

NVR Inc.

From finished lot to signed mortgage NVR offers homebuyers everything — including the kitchen sink. The company builds single-family detached homes townhomes and condominiums mainly for first-time and move-up buyers primarily in the eastern US. NVR markets its homes as Ryan Homes Fox Ridge Homes Heartland Homes and NVHomes. Its largest markets the Washington DC and Baltimore areas account for around 45% of sales. NVR's housing sizes range from 1000 sq. ft. to 9000 sq. ft. with the average price of a home selling for around $380000. Its subsidiary NVR Mortgage Finance offers mortgage and title services. NVR was founded in 1980 as NVHomes.

Operations

NVR's homebuilding divisions — Ryan Homes Fox Ridge Homes and Heartland Homes — primarily market to first-time buyers. Ryan Homes operates in some thirty metropolitan areas along the eastern seaboard and in Indiana Kentucky Ohio Pennsylvania and West Virginia. Fox Ridge Homes is dedicated to first-time and move-up buyers in the Nashville market. NVHomes and Heartland Homes cater to upscale buyers and builds primarily in the Baltimore Philadelphia and DC metro areas as well as on Maryland's eastern shore. Homes sell for between $140000 and $1.8 million.

NVR's Building Products unit supports the homebuilder's construction activities with manufacturing facilities in Maryland New Jersey New York North Carolina Pennsylvania and Tennessee. It supplies structural building components to the job sites. To support its homebuilding operations the company offers settlement and title services through NVR Settlement Services.

Homebuilding accounts for 98% of the builder's total sales while its mortgage banking business which closes some 12300 loans totaling $4.0 billion generates the other 2% of its total sales.

Geographic Reach

Virginia-based NVR's homebuilding operations serve around 30 metropolitan areas in 14 states in the eastern half of the US. Home sales in Mid-Atlantic states (Maryland Virginia West Virginia Delaware and Washington DC) bring in more than 55% of the builder's total sales while homes sales in the Mid-Eastern states (New York Ohio Western Pennsylvania Indiana and Illinois) account for another 20%. Its largest markets are in Washington DC (30% of sales) and Baltimore Maryland (13%).

Sales and Marketing

NVR markets its homes through sales representatives and through model homes that are typically converted into temporary sales offices where a salesperson can review alternative floor plans facades and designs for other house models with the client.

Its houses are aimed at move-up and upscale buyers.

Financial Performance

NVR has enjoyed healthy sales and profit growth over the years as the recovery in residential construction has picked up steam. The company is finally closing in of the peak $6.1 billion recorded before the financial crash in 2007.

In fiscal 2016 revenue grew another 13% to $5.7 billion thank to an increase in units settled on prior year. The increase was due to a 14% increase in backlog unit balance going into 2016. New order sales increased 2%.

Net income ticked up 11% to $425 million. Higher net revenue was offset by tighter margins due to higher construction and selling related costs.

Cash from operations increased 89% to $384.4 million due to favorable increases in accounts receivable and net proceeds of $50.0 million from mortgage loan activities.

Strategy

Favorable sales and pricing trends driven by historically low mortgage interest rates and rising rental costs are a boon to NVR and other homebuilders. The builder keeps its profits high by focusing on building in areas where it has a high market share finding it to be more cost-efficient to expand within its existing markets.Higher cash generation in 2016 has been put to use to fund further homebuilding inventory increases.

Company Background

NVR expanded its portfolio of home-building companies in late 2012 when it acquired Heartland Homes the second-largest homebuilder in Pittsburgh. As part of the purchase NVR planned to continue to use the Heartland Homes name and pair the company with its complementary Ryan Homes.

HISTORY

NVR got its start when Dwight Schar founded NVHomes Inc. in 1980. Schar had worked for Ryan Homes (founded 1948) since 1969. Like Ryan Homes NVHomes specialized in single-family homes around Washington DC. The strong economy of the 1980s and the deregulation of lending institutions — coupled with favorable partnership and real estate tax laws passed by the Reagan administration — resulted in rapid growth. The company was clearing income of more than $1 million a year by 1983 and soon branched into building townhomes and condominiums.

In 1986 when the company was reorganized as a limited partnership (NVH L.P.) income was up to $14 million. The new entity soon acquired a controlling interest in Ryan Homes; it completed its acquisition of that company in 1987. NVH reorganized as a holding company (NVRyan L.P.) and 1988 profits reached $33.5 million. Over the years the company formed or acquired almost 100 subsidiaries that were involved in all aspects of homebuilding — from land acquisition and construction to home finance and investment advice. It had also branched out into California Florida Indiana Kentucky North Carolina Ohio Pennsylvania and Virginia.

Following an economic recession in 1989 demand for new housing dropped off in the US. The company shortened its name to NVR L.P. and its inventory of unsold land and houses started to grow. The situation was exacerbated by changes in the tax code that made real estate less attractive as an investment; sales from development and construction projects dropped from more than $1 billion in 1988 to about $600 million in 1991. NVR posted a $260 million loss in 1990 as sales and the value of its inventory nose-dived.

NVR reorganized in 1990 and 1991. Focused on eight mid-Atlantic states it put homebuilding under one management structure consolidated its finance activities exited its land-development businesses and offered its mortgage services to customers who weren't NVR homebuyers. It also organized its business into two product lines: upscale (NVHomes) and moderately priced (Ryan Homes) homes. Despite the reorganization and introduction of innovative marketing NVR and several of its subsidiaries filed for Chapter 11 bankruptcy relief in 1992. That year the CFO of NVR's thrift (NVR Savings Bank) went on the lam to Malta after embezzling more than $750000.

The company emerged from bankruptcy as NVR Inc. in 1993 with less debt new owners and a new line of credit; it also had its IPO that year. The next year NVR sold NVR Savings Bank which had four branches in northern Virginia. The robust mid-1990s economy aided NVR; as home sales rose the company entered new markets including the Cleveland and Nashville areas in 1995. To reduce its vulnerability to downturns in the mid-Atlantic area it continued its expansion outside that region buying Fox Ridge Homes (the #2 builder in Nashville) in 1997.

In 1999 it merged its homebuilding subsidiary NVR Homes and mortgage banking holding company NVR Financial Services into NVR. It also acquired Rockville Maryland-based First Republic Mortgage that year but closed the subsidiary's retail operations in 2000 and realigned its mortgage banking business to serve NVR customers exclusively.

From 1994 through 2003 the company benefited from increased housing activity recording steady increases in unit sales backlog and profits for nine years. During the housing downturn that began in 2008 the company performed better than its competitors reporting only one losing quarter in the period.

In late 2012 NVR expanded its portfolio of home-building companies when it acquired Heartland Homes the second-largest homebuilder in Pittsburgh. As part of the purchase NVR planned to continue to use the Heartland Homes name and pair the company with its complementary Ryan Homes.

EXECUTIVES

President Ceo And Director, Paul C. Saville, age 62, $1,566,375 total compensation

President Nvr Mortgage (nvrm), Robert W. Henley, age 51, $460,000 total compensation

Vp Cfo And Treasurer, Daniel D. Malzahn, age 48, $490,000 total compensation

Vp Chief Accounting Officer And Controller, Eugene J. Bredow, $341,250 total compensation

President Homebuilding Operations, Jeffrey D. Martchek, age 53, $539,000 total compensation

Chairman, Dwight C. Schar, age 76

Auditors: KPMG LLP

LOCATIONS

HQ: NVR Inc.
11700 Plaza America Drive, Suite 500, Reston, VA 20190
Phone: 703 956-4000
Web: www.nvrinc.com

2016 Sales

	% of total
Homebuilding	
Mid-Atlantic	57
Mid-east	20
Southeast	13
Northeast	8
Mortgage banking	2
Total	**100**

PRODUCTS/OPERATIONS

Selected Brands
Fox Ridge Homes
Heartland Homes
NVHomes
Ryan Homes

COMPETITORS

Beazer Homes	KB Home
Brookfield Homes	Lennar
Champion Home Builders	M.D.C.
D.R. Horton	M/I Homes
David Weekley Homes	Orleans Homebuilders
Hovnanian Enterprises	PulteGroup
John Wieland Homes	Toll Brothers

HISTORICAL FINANCIALS

Company Type: Public

Income Statement

FYE: December 31

	REVENUE ($ mil.)	NET INCOME ($ mil.)	NET PROFIT MARGIN	EMPLOYEES
12/17	6,322	537	8.5%	5,200
12/16	5,834	425	7.3%	4,900
12/15	5,169	382	7.4%	4,300
12/14	4,453	281	6.3%	3,942
12/13	4,220	266	6.3%	3,944
Annual Growth	10.6%	19.2%	—	7.2%

2017 Year-End Financials

Debt ratio: 19.97%	No. of shares (mil.): 3
Return on equity: 36.94%	Dividends
Cash ($ mil.): 666	Yield: —
Current ratio: 4.35	Payout: —
Long-term debt ($ mil.): 597	Market value ($ mil.): 12,949

	STOCK PRICE ($) FY Close	P/E High/Low	PER SHARE ($) Earnings	Dividends	Book Value
12/17	3,508.22	24 11	126.77	0.00	434.97
12/16	1,669.00	17 14	103.61	0.00	353.22
12/15	1,643.00	18 13	89.99	0.00	318.47
12/14	1,275.33	19 15	63.50	0.00	277.66
12/13	1,026.01	19 15	54.81	0.00	284.49
Annual Growth	36.0%	— —	23.3%	—	11.2%

O'Reilly Automotive, Inc.

O'Reilly Automotive has its foot hard on the gas. The company sells automotive aftermarket parts (both new and remanufactured) maintenance supplies professional service equipment tools and accessories through some 4800 stores across 47 US states and online. Many O'Reilly stores also offer customers a range of services including oil and battery recycling battery testing paint mixing and tool rental. The family-founded and -operated company wheels and deals with automotive professionals as well as do-it-yourself customers.

Operations
O?Reilly's stores carry about 23000 SKUs and average 7300 total square feet. The stores receive inventory five nights a week from O'Reilly's 27 regional distribution centers and 312 Hub stores.

The company gets around 60% of sales from its DIY customers and approximately 40% of sales from its professional service provider customers.

O?Reilly sells automotive products directly to independently owned parts stores (?jobber stores?) in certain markets.

As well as its vast array of products O?Reilly?s also offers an almost equally vast array of services such as used oil oil filter and battery recycling; battery wiper and bulb replacement; battery diagnostic testing; electrical and module testing; paint mixing; and much more.

Geographic Reach
Missouri-based O'Reilly has stores in 47 US states including Alaska and Hawaii. Texas and California are its largest markets with some 670 stores 530 stores in each.

Sales and Marketing
O'Reilly leverages television radio direct mail and newspaper distribution in-store and online promotions and sports and event sponsorships. The company also participates in cooperative advertising with its vendors. Its combination of brand and product/price messaging drives retail traffic and purchases which frequently coincide with key sales events. To stimulate sales among racing enthusiasts O'Reilly sponsors multiple nationally-televised races and more than 1600 grassroots local and regional motorsports events throughout 45 states.

The company has promotions through Spanish language radio print and outdoor advertising as well as sponsorships of more than 45 local and regional festivals and events. The company also awards customers with points through purchases and other special events and redeems those points for coupons and discounts.

O'Reilly maintains a full-time sales staff of 750. Targeted marketing materials such as flyers quick reference guides and catalogs are produced and distributed on a regular basis to professional service providers paint and body shops and fleet customers.

Financial Performance
O'Reilly's revenues has been on an upward trend since 2003. In fiscal 2016 (ended December) revenue increased by 8% to $8.6 billion due to higher comparable store sales 210 store openings the 48 acquired Bond stores and the additional day due to the Leap Year as well as the positive effect on inventory availability of same-day and overnight access to distribution center inventory.

Net income has likewise been on the up-and-up climbing a further 11% to $1.0 billion in 2016 due to higher net revenue and greater leverage in negotiations with suppliers to lower product acquisition costs. SGA expenses in relation to total sales fell half a point.

Cash from operating activities increased 14% to $1.5 billion.

Strategy
O'Reilly adheres to a "dual market" strategy by appealing to both do-it-yourself (DIY) and professional service providers. The company believes that its tiered distribution model provides industry-leading parts availability and store in-stock positions while lowering its inventory carrying costs and controlling inventory. To this end the auto parts chain has made significant capital investments in its distribution center network allowing it to efficiently service its aggressive 200-a-year store opening program as well as servicing its existing stores network. It opened up same-day and overnight inventory access to its distribution centers in 2016. O'Reilly is aiming for a total growth capacity of more than 800 stores in its distribution center network. The company also relies on its stores? position as ?destination stores? to pull in punters.

As part of its continuing efforts to enhance its distribution network it's implementing a voice-picking technology in additional distribution centers; rolling out enhanced routing software to enhance logistics efficiencies; launching additional labor management software to improve distribution center productivity and overall operating efficiency; developing further automated paperless-picking processes; improving proof of delivery systems to boost the accuracy of product movement to stores; continuing to define and implement best practices in all distribution centers; and making proven return-on-investment-based capital enhancements to material handling equipment in distribution centers including conveyor systems picking modules and lift equipment.

The company is expanding its nationwide presence by opening stores at a rapid rate. In 2016 it opened 210 net new stores a similar figure to the preceding few years.

Company Background
In 2012 the company expanded its capabilities by acquiring the auto-parts-related assets of VIP Parts Tires & Service a large privately-held automotive parts tires and service chain in New England. The asset purchase included 56 stores located throughout Maine New Hampshire and Massachusetts as well as a distribution center located in Lewiston Maine.

O'Reilly was founded in 1957 by Charles F. O'Reilly and his son "Chub."

EXECUTIVES

President And Ceo, Gregory L. (Greg) Henslee, age 57, $1,238,461 total compensation
Co-president, Jeff M. Shaw, age 55, $396,923 total compensation
Evp Finance And Cfo, Thomas G. (Tom) McFall, age 47, $713,846 total compensation
Co-president, Gregory D. (Greg) Johnson, age 52, $342,308 total compensation
Svp Information Systems, Jeff Lauro
Vice President Northern Division, Kenny Martin
Senior Vice President Merchandise And Marketing, Mike Swearengin
Co-chairman And Coo, Lawrence P. (Larry) O'Reilly, age 71
Vice Chairman, Charles H. O'Reilly, age 79
Chairman, David E. O'Reilly, age 69
Auditors: Ernst & Young LLP

LOCATIONS

HQ: O'Reilly Automotive, Inc.
233 South Patterson Avenue, Springfield, MO 65802
Phone: 417 862-6708
Web: www.oreillyauto.com

2016 Stores

	No.
Texas	667
California	534
Missouri	195
Georgia	187
Illinois	186
Ohio	169
Florida	163
Tennessee	162
Michigan	158
North Carolina	155
Washington	155
Arizona	136
Alabama	125
Oklahoma	121
Indiana	120
Minnesota	119
Wisconsin	118
Louisiana	109
Arkansas	107
Colorado	99
South Carolina	91
Kansas	82
Kentucky	77
Mississippi	75
Iowa	73
Oregon	66
Virginia	66
Utah	61
Nevada	54
New Mexico	52
Nebraska	41
Idaho	40
New Hampshire	38
Maine	35
Massachusetts	30
Montana	27
Vermont	24
Wyoming	20
South Dakota	16
Alaska	15
North Dakota	15
Hawaii	12
Pennsylvania	12
West Virginia	12
Connecticut	5
Rhode Island	3
New York	2
Total	**4,829**

PRODUCTS/OPERATIONS

Selected Products
Accessorie
Accessorie
Air Conditioning
Battery & Accessories
Belts & Hoses
Body & Trim
Brakes
Charging & Starting
Cooling & Heating
Engine Parts & Mounts
Exhaust
Filters & PCV Valves
Fuel & Emissions
Hardware & Fasteners
Ignition & Tune-Up
Lighting & Electrical
Oil Fluids & Chemicals
Performance
Suspension & Steering
Tire & Wheel
Tools & Equipment
Transmission & Transaxle
Truck & Towing
Waxes & Washes
Wipers

COMPETITORS

Acheeve Inc.	Target Corporation
Advance Auto Parts	U.S. Auto Parts
AutoZone	VIP
CARQUEST	Wal-Mart
Genuine Parts	Whitney Automotive
Pep Boys	Group
Sears	

HISTORICAL FINANCIALS

Company Type: Public

Income Statement
FYE: December 31

	REVENUE ($ mil.)	NET INCOME ($ mil.)	NET PROFIT MARGIN	EMPLOYEES
12/17	8,977	1,133	12.6%	75,289
12/16	8,593	1,037	12.1%	74,715
12/15	7,966	931	11.7%	71,943
12/14	7,216	778	10.8%	67,926
12/13	6,649	670	10.1%	62,533
Annual Growth	7.8%	14.0%	—	4.8%

2017 Year-End Financials

Debt ratio: 39.33%
Return on equity: 99.45%
Cash ($ mil.): 46
Current ratio: 0.93
Long-term debt ($ mil.): 2,978

No. of shares (mil.): 84
Dividends
Yield: —
Payout: —
Market value ($ mil.): 20,278

	STOCK PRICE ($) FY Close	P/E High/Low	PER SHARE ($) Earnings	Dividends	Book Value
12/17	240.54	22 13	12.67	0.00	7.75
12/16	278.41	27 21	10.73	0.00	17.52
12/15	253.42	30 19	9.17	0.00	20.07
12/14	192.62	26 17	7.34	0.00	19.87
12/13	128.71	22 14	6.03	0.00	18.56
Annual Growth	16.9%	— —	20.4%	—	(19.6%)

Occidental Petroleum Corp

Harnessing its heritage of Western technical know-how Occidental Petroleum engages in oil and gas exploration and production and makes basic chemicals plastics and petrochemicals. It boasts proved reserves of 2.4 billion barrels of oil equivalent primarily from assets in the US the Middle East North Africa and Latin America. Subsidiary Occidental Chemical (OxyChem) produces acids chlorine and specialty products and owns Oxy Vinyls the #1 maker of polyvinyl chloride (PVC) resin in North America. Occidental Petroleum's midstream and marketing units gather treat process transport store trade and market crude oil natural gas NGLs condensate and CO2 and generate and market power.

Operations

Occidental's principal businesses consist of three segments: Oil and Gas Chemical and Midstream and Marketing.

The Oil and Gas segment accounts for some 60% of total sales and explores for develops and produces oil and condensate natural gas liquids (NGLs) and natural gas. It operates through two units: Permian Resources which exploits unconventional resources and Permian EOR which uses techniques such as CO2 floods and waterfloods. Of its 2.4 million boe proved reserves around 55% is oil over 25% natural gas and over 15% NGLs (natural gas liquids). Its most significant assets are in the Permian Basin in Texas and in the Middle East.

The chemical segment (OxyChem) accounts for about 35% of sales and makes and markets basic chemicals and vinyls. It owns and operates manufacturing plants at 23 domestic and two international sites. Products produced include chlorine

caustic soda chlorinated organics potassium chemicals vinyl chloride monomers and PVC.

The midstream and marketing segment brings in the remaining +5% and gathers processes transports stores purchases and markets oil condensate NGLs natural gas carbon dioxide (CO2) and power. It has gas plants in Texas New Mexico and the UAE pipelines in Texas New Mexico Oklahoma and Colorado as well as Qatar the UAE and Canada. It also has a crude terminal in Texas and power and steam generation facilities in Texas and Louisiana.

Geographic Reach

Occidental's strength is in its home US market which accounts for over 60% of company sales but it also has a significant international presence.

The company's US presence is focused on Texas and New Mexico. Internationally Occidental's strength is in the Middle East particularly Oman and Qatar which both account for over 10% of revenue and the UAE which brings in over 5%. Occidental also makes 5% of total sales in Colombia.

OxyChem owns and operates 23 manufacturing plants in Alabama Georgia Illinois Kansas Louisiana Michigan New Jersey New York Ohio Pennsylvania Tennessee and Texas and at two international sites in Canada and Chile.

Sales and Marketing

From time to time Occidental purchases oil NGLs power steam and chemicals from (and sells oil NGLs gas chemicals and power) to certain of its equity investees and other related parties at market-related prices.

Financial Performance

Occidental's revenue has nearly halved since the oil price collapsed in 2014.

In fiscal 2016 sales fell a further 19% to $10.1 billion largely due to lower average oil prices and production across the year versus 2015.

The company lost $574 million in 2016 a significant improvement on the eye-watering loss of $7.8 billion the previous year. The primary difference was the absence from the books of $3.5 billion and $5.0 billion impairments of producing assets in the US and Middle East. Also factored into the results are net income of $571 million in the Chemicals segment a 5% increase on the previous year due to gains on asset sales; and a loss of $381 million in Midstream and Marketing due to contract terminations and lower sales.

Cash from operations was largely unchanged at $3.4 billion as lower sales was offset by lower operating costs and $325 million in federal and state tax refunds.

Strategy

As with many of its industry peers Occidental's finances were hit hard by the oil price crash with the company incurring consecutive years of heavy losses.

However its response was somewhat different — while Texas alone has seen about 100000 jobs cut in the oil and gas industry Occidental retained the vast majority of its workforce in the hope that it will be in a far stronger position once oil prices rise than its competitors. It reduced its use of contractors and sent out employees that would otherwise be in line for cuts to work in their stead. Occidental made cutbacks in other ways: it cut capital spending capped bonuses and sold land in North Dakota Colorado and the Middle East. It sold Pieceance Basin in Colorado for $153 million and its South Eagle Ford non-operated properties for $63 million

In 2018 Occidental Petroleum was actively exploring the sale of a considerable portion of its assets in order to raise $5 billion to invest in exploration and production expansion as oil prices rebound from the 2013 downturn.

Mergers and Acquisitions

In 2016 Occidental spent $2.0 billion on interests in several enhances oil recovery and CO2 properties in the Permian Basin. The acquisition further strengthens its position in the oil-rich region.

HISTORY

Founded in 1920 Occidental Petroleum struggled until 1956 when billionaire industrialist Dr. Armand Hammer sank $100000 into the company then worth $34000. It drilled two wells and both came in. Hammer eventually gained control of the company.

Occidental's discovery of California's second-largest gas field (1959) was followed by a concession from Libya's King Idris (1966) and the discovery of a billion-barrel Libyan oil field. In 1968 Occidental bought Signal Oil's European refining and marketing business as an outlet for the Libyan oil. It also diversified buying Island Creek Coal and Hooker Chemical.

In 1969 Occidental sold 51% of its Libyan production to the Libyan government under duress after Idris was ousted. (It suspended operations there in 1986). It soon began oil exploration in Latin America (1971) and in the North Sea (1972-73) where it discovered the lucrative Piper field. Other projects included a 20-year fertilizer-for-ammonia deal with the USSR (1974) and a coal joint venture with China (1985).

During the 1980s Occidental sold some foreign assets and bought US natural gas pipeline firm MidCon (1986). It also bought Iowa Beef Processors (IBP) for stock worth $750 million (1981) and then spun off 49% of it in 1987 for $960 million.

In 1983 Hammer hired Ray Irani to revive Occidental's ailing chemicals business (losses that year: $38 million). Irani integrated operations to ensure higher margins during industry downturns and purchased Diamond Shamrock Chemicals (1986) Shell's vinyl chloride monomer unit (1987) a DuPont chloralkali facility (1987) and Cain Chemical (1988). OxyChem's profits reached almost $1.1 billion by 1989.

Hammer died in 1990 and Irani became CEO. In 1991 to reduce debt Occidental exited the Chinese coal business and sold the North Sea oil properties. Occidental also spun off IBP the largest US red-meat producer to its shareholders.

Occidental paid Irani $95 million in 1997 to buy out his employment contract; instead his compensation (a minimum of $1.2 million a year) was tied to the company's fortunes. That year Occidental's $3.65 billion bid won the US government's auction of its 78% stake in California's Elk Hills petroleum reserve one of the largest in the continental US.

To help pay for Elk Hills the company sold MidCon to K N Energy for $3.1 billion in 1998. Occidental traded its petrochemical operations to Equistar Chemicals a partnership between Lyondell (now LyondellBasell) and Millennium Chemicals for $425 million and a 29.5% stake.

In a venture with The Geon Company Occidental in 1999 formed Oxy Vinyls the #1 producer of polyvinyl chloride (PVC) resin in North America. That year also brought a windfall: Chevron agreed to pay Occidental $775 million to settle a lawsuit stemming from the 1982 withdrawal by Gulf (later acquired by Chevron) of an offer to buy Cities Service (later acquired by Occidental).

In 2000 Occidental sold its 29% stake in Canadian Occidental back to the company for $828 million to help fund the purchase of oil and gas producer Altura Energy a partnership of BP and Shell Oil for $3.6 billion. Later that year the company sold some Gulf of Mexico properties to Apache for $385 million.

Occidental acquired a new exploration block in Yemen in 2001. The next year it sold its 30% of Equistar Chemicals to Lyondell in exchange for a 21% stake in Lyondell. In 2005 it acquired a stake in a gas and oil production site located in Texas' Permian Basin from ExxonMobil for a reported $972 million. Occidental closed the acquisition of Vintage Petroleum for a reported $3.8 bil

EXECUTIVES

Svp And Cfo, Cedric W. Burgher, age 58

Svp General Counsel And Chief Compliance Officer, Marcia E. Backus, age 63, $646,970 total compensation

Evp And Group Chairman - Middle East, Edward A. (Sandy) Lowe, age 66, $625,000 total compensation

Svp Marketing And Midstream Operations And Development, Cynthia L. Walker, age 42, $600,000 total compensation

President Ceo And Director, Vicki A. Hollub, age 58, $1,143,314 total compensation

Vp And Cio, Ioannis A. Charalambous

Svp And President Oxy Oil And Gas Domestic, Joseph C. Elliott, age 60

Svp And President Occidental Chemical Corporation, Robert L. Peterson

Vice President Marketing And Asset Optimization, Shawn McGovern

Vice President U.s. Oil Marketing Permian Basin And Hugoton, Steven Rafferty

Vice President Business Development, Kevin Pilkington

Vice President Health Environment Safety And Security, Wesley Scott

Vice President Mergers And Acquisitions, Michael Ure

Vice President Government Relations, Ian Davis

Svp Corporate Strategy And Development, Oscar Brown

Vp Internal Audit, Gary Daugherty

Vice President Worldwide Drilling And Completions, Brenda Harris

Vice President Business Analyst, Eric Wynia

Chairman, Eugene L. (Gene) Batchelder, age 70

Secretary, Melanie Rome

Auditors: KPMG LLP

LOCATIONS

HQ: Occidental Petroleum Corp
5 Greenway Plaza, Suite 110, Houston, TX 77046
Phone: 713 215-7000
Web: www.oxy.com

2016 Sales

	% of total
US	62
Qatar	12
Oman	11
United Arab Emirates	7
Colombia	5
Other countries	3
Total	**100**

PRODUCTS/OPERATIONS

2016 Sales

	% of total
Oil & gas	59
Chemicals	35
Midstream marketing & other	6
Adjustments	-
Total	**100**

Selected Subsidiaries

Occidental Chemical Corp. (OxyChem; chemicals polymers and plastics)
Oxy Vinyls LP (76% polyvinyl chloride)
Occidental Energy Marketing Inc. (energy marketing)
Occidental Exploration and Production Company (exploration and production)

COMPETITORS

Apache	Huntsman International
Ashland	Imperial Oil
BP	J.M. Huber
ConocoPhillips	Koch Industries Inc.
Devon Energy	Marathon Oil
Dow Chemical	Olin
DuPont	PEMEX
Eastman Chemical	Royal Dutch Shell
Exxon Mobil	Sunoco
Hess Corporation	TOTAL

HISTORICAL FINANCIALS

Company Type: Public

Income Statement   FYE: December 31

	REVENUE ($ mil.)	NET INCOME ($ mil.)	NET PROFIT MARGIN	EMPLOYEES
12/17	13,274	1,311	9.9%	11,000
12/16	10,398	(574)	—	11,000
12/15	12,699	(7,829)	—	11,100
12/14	21,947	616	2.8%	11,700
12/13	25,736	5,903	22.9%	12,900
Annual Growth	**(15.3%)**	**(31.4%)**	**—**	**(3.9%)**

2017 Year-End Financials

Debt ratio: 23.39%
Return on equity: 6.23%
Cash ($ mil.): 1,672
Current ratio: 1.12
Long-term debt ($ mil.): 9,328

No. of shares (mil.): 765
Dividends
Yield: 0.0%
Payout: 180.0%
Market value ($ mil.): 56,358

	STOCK PRICE ($) FY Close	P/E High/Low	PER SHARE ($) Earnings	Dividends	Book Value
12/17	73.66	43 34	1.70	3.06	26.89
12/16	71.23	— —	(0.75)	3.02	28.13
12/15	67.61	— —	(10.23)	2.97	31.89
12/14	80.61	133 93	0.79	2.88	39.26
12/13	95.10	14 10	7.32	2.56	48.46
Annual Growth	**(6.2%)**	**— —**	**(30.6%)**	**4.6%**	**(13.7%)**

OceanFirst Financial Corp

Ask the folks at OceanFirst Bank for a home loan and they might say "shore." The subsidiary of holding company OceanFirst Financial operates 25 branches in the coastal New Jersey counties of Middlesex Monmouth and Ocean. The community-oriented bank caters to individuals and small to midsized businesses in the Jersey Shore area offering standard products such as checking and savings accounts CDs and IRAs. It uses funds from deposits mainly to invest in mortgages loans and securities. One- to four-family residential mortgages make up more than half of OceanFirst Financial's loan portfolio which also includes commercial real estate (about 30%) business construction and consumer loans.

Operations

The Bank's principal business is attracting deposits from the general public in the communities surrounding its branch offices and investing those deposits primarily in single-family owner-occupied residential mortgage loans and commercial real estate loans. It active subsidiaries include Ocean-First Services LLC OceanFirst REIT Holdings Inc. and 975 Holdings LLC.

Geographic Reach

OceanFirst has operations in the New Jersey counties of Middlesex Monmouth and Ocean.

Financial Performance

OceanFirst's revenues dropped by 4% in 2012 due to decrease in loans and mortgage-backed securities partially offset by higher revenues from investment securities and other.

Net income declined by 3% in 2012 due to an increase in provision for loan losses and non-interest expenses (higher professional fees).

Strategy

OceanFirst seeks to grow commercial loans receivable by offering commercial lending services to local businesses; grow core deposits through broader product offerings and branch expansion; and increase non-interest income by expanding its fee-based products and services.

Part of the company's strategy for growth includes expanding its fee-based offerings. The bank for example offers trust and asset management services. Company subsidiary OceanFirst Services sells mutual funds annuities and insurance products from third-party vendors. OceanFirst is also seeking opportunities to grow by opening new branch locations within its existing markets.

In 2013 the Bank opened a full service Financial Solutions Center in Red Bank New Jersey offering deposit lending and asset management services. It also opened an additional branch office in Jackson New Jersey.

Since 1995 OceanFirst has opened sixteen branch offices (twelve in Ocean County and four in Monmouth County).

Mergers and Acquisitions

In January 2016 OceanFirst Financial agreed to buy Cape Bancorp— along with its 22 branches in central and southern New Jersey counties $1.1 billion in loans and $1.3 billion in deposits — for $208.1 million. The deal would grow OceanFirst's total total assets by over 60% and nearly double the size of its branch network.

Company Background

OceanFirst Bank's employee stock option plan owns more than 10% of OceanFirst Financial's shares. The company's charitable foundation OceanFirst Foundation owns 7%.

The Bank was founded as a state-chartered building and loan association in 1902. It converted to a Federal savings and loan association in 1945 and became a Federally-chartered mutual savings bank in 1989.

EXECUTIVES

Evp And Cfo, Michael J. Fitzpatrick, age 61, $285,577 total compensation

Evp And Chief Administrative Officer, Joseph R. Iantosca, age 56, $284,808 total compensation

Evp And Chief Lending Officer, Joseph J. Lebel, age 54, $284,808 total compensation

First Svp General Counsel And Corporate Secretary, Steven J. Tsimbinos, $252,798 total compensation

Chairman President And Ceo, Christopher D. Maher, age 50, $566,346 total compensation

Vp Information Services, Elizabeth Alexander

Vice President Bank Counsel, Michele Hart

Assistant Vice President Oceanfirst Bank, Karen Rack

Senior Vice President Director Of Human Resources, Gary Hett

Senior Vice President, Brad Fouss

Assistant Vice President Collections Department, Karen Farrell

Vice President Senior Marketing Officer Strategy, Lisa Natale

Auditors: KPMG LLP

LOCATIONS

HQ: OceanFirst Financial Corp
110 West Front Street, Red Bank, NJ 07701
Phone: 732 240-4500
Web: www.oceanfirst.com

PRODUCTS/OPERATIONS

2016 sales

	% of total
Interest Income	
Loans	80
Mortgage-backed securities	4
Investment securities & other	2
Non-interest	
Bankcard services revenue	3
Wealth management revenue	2
Fees & service charges	7
Loan Servicing income	1
Net gains on sales of loans	1
Net loss from other real estate operations	-
Income from Bank owned Life Insurance	1
Other	-
Total	**100**

COMPETITORS

Bank of America	PNC Financial
Cape Bancorp	Sovereign Bank
Citibank	TD Bank USA
Hudson City Bancorp	Valley National
Investors Bancorp	Bancorp
JPMorgan Chase	

HISTORICAL FINANCIALS

Company Type: Public

Income Statement   FYE: December 31

	ASSETS ($ mil.)	NET INCOME ($ mil.)	INCOME AS % OF ASSETS	EMPLOYEES
12/17	5,416	42	0.8%	684
12/16	5,167	23	0.4%	797
12/15	2,593	20	0.8%	393
12/14	2,356	19	0.8%	376
12/13	2,249	16	0.7%	409
Annual Growth	24.6%	27.0%	—	13.7%

2017 Year-End Financials

Debt ratio: 1.04%	No. of shares (mil.): 32
Return on equity: 7.24%	Dividends
Cash ($ mil.): 109	Yield: 0.0%
Current ratio: —	Payout: 46.8%
Long-term debt ($ mil.): —	Market value ($ mil.): 856

	STOCK PRICE ($) FY Close	P/E High/Low	PER SHARE ($) Earnings	Dividends	Book Value
12/17	26.25	23 18	1.28	0.60	18.47
12/16	30.03	30 16	0.98	0.54	17.80
12/15	20.03	17 13	1.21	0.52	13.79
12/14	17.14	16 13	1.19	0.49	12.91
12/13	17.13	19 14	0.95	0.48	12.33
Annual Growth	11.3%	— —	7.7%	5.7%	10.6%

Office Depot, Inc.

Paper and pens have made room for PC repair and point-of-sale services at office products giant Office Depot (#2 worldwide behind Staples). The office supply chain operates some 1400 retail stores under the Office Depot and OfficeMax names through which it sells a wide selection of office and school supplies furniture printers and breakroom and cleaning products. It has also moved into IT support and other business-to-business services which it offers through CompuCom and other brands. After divesting all its international holdings Office Depot operates entirely in North America.

HISTORY

Pat Scher Stephen Dougherty and Jack Kopkin opened the first Office Depot one of the first office supply superstores in Lauderdale Lakes Florida in 1986. Scher was selected as chairman. By the end of the year the fledgling company had opened two more stores (both in Florida).

Office Depot opened seven more stores in 1987. When Scher died of leukemia that year the company recruited David Fuente former president of Sherwin-Williams' Paint Store Division as chairman and CEO. Office Depot continued its breakneck expansion under Fuente. In 1988 — the year the company went public — it opened 16 stores and broke into new markets in four states.

The chain stepped up its pace and by 1990 it had expanded into several other areas including the South and Midwest. Office Depot also added computers and peripherals and opened its first delivery center.

In 1991 the company became North America's #1 office products retailer and expanded its presence in the West through the acquisition of Office Club another warehouse-type office supply chain with 59 stores (most in California). Fuente remained chairman and CEO while former Office Club CEO Mark Begelman became president and COO. (Begelman who left in 1995 and eventually formed the MARS music chain had founded the first Office Club in 1987 in Concord California; he took it public in 1989.)

The company entered the international market with its 1992 purchase of Canada's H. Q. Office International and through licensing agreements in 1993 (in Colombia and Israel). Office Depot created its business services division by acquiring various contract stationers including Eastman Office Products (the West Coast's #1 contract office supplier) in the mid-1990s and added locations in Mexico and Poland; it established a joint venture in France with retailer Carrefour in 1996.

Also in 1996 Office Depot announced a $3.4 billion agreement to be acquired by Staples which would have created a company with more than 1100 stores. However the government blocked the purchase on antitrust grounds in 1997 and the agreement dissolved. Unfettered by merger distractions Office Depot resumed opening stores at a rapid pace including two in Thailand and took its catalog and delivery services online. It then established a joint venture with Japanese retailer Deo Deo.

In 1998 Office Depot acquired Viking Office Products in a $2.7 billion deal. With more than 60% of its sales coming from outside the US Viking augmented Office Depot's already strong delivery network and international expansion. Office Depot acquired the remaining 50% of its French operations from Carrefour in 1998 and the remaining 50% of its Japanese operations from Deo Deo in 1999.

Office Depot started putting Internet kiosks in its US stores in 2000 allowing customers to browse and shop company Web sites. In July 2000 Bruce Nelson CEO of Viking replaced Fuente as CEO of Office Depot. Citing weak computer sales and high warehouse prices the company closed about 70 stores and cut its workforce. In early 2002 Nelson was named chairman as well as CEO after Fuente stepped down.

Office Depot sold its Australian operations to Officeworks a unit of Coles Myer in January 2003. Office Depot used the proceeds to expand its faster-growing European operations. Also that year the company acquired the retail operations of French office supplier Guilbert from Pinault-Printemps-Redoute a move that doubled the company's business in Europe. (Staples had acquired Guilbert's mail-order business the previous year.)

In 2004 the company acquired about 125 retail locations from troubled toy seller Toys "R" Us converting 50 of those into Office Depot locations and selling off the remainder.

Nelson left the company and Neil Austrian served as interim head. Office Depot named Auto-Zone leader Steve Odland as CEO and chairman in 2005. That year the company shuttered its Viking Office Products brand in the US consolidating its catalog sales under the Office Depot banner. (It still markets products through Viking in international markets.) The business services division also sells technology products through Tech Depot (formerly 4SURE.com).

The company acquired privately held Allied Office Products (AOP) the largest independent dealer of office products and services in the US in 2006. AOP became part of Office Depot's North American Business Solutions Division.

Office Depot opened 70 new stores in 2007 (vs. 115 the previous year).

In mid-2008 the company acquired 13 stores in Sweden through the acquisition of AGE Kontor & Data AB a contract and retail office supply company operating there.

In 2009 the company closed about 125 stores in North America and exited the Japanese market.

CEO Steve Odland resigned in November 2010. In late 2010 Israeli department store operator New Hamashbir Lazarchan acquired Office Depot's operations in Israel for $50 million. New Hamashbir Lazarchan also agreed to pay royalties on revenues generated by Office Depot Israel which has about 45 stores.

Office Depot appointed new leadership in mid-2011 naming interim leader Neil Austrian as the company's permanent replacement for chief executive and chairman. Austrian has served as a director at Office Depot since 1998. He stepped in to lead the office products retailer on a temporary basis following the resignation of Steve Odland in late 2010. Odland's resignation came soon after Office Depot settled Securities and Exchange Commission charges that the company selectively informed analysts and institutional investors that its earnings would fall short of estimates. Office Depot agreed to pay $1 million while Odland and the firm's former CFO agreed to pay $50000.

EXECUTIVES

Evp And Cfo, Joseph T. (Joe) Lower, age 51
Evp Chief Legal Officer And Corporate Secretary, N. David Bleisch, age 59
Evp And Chief Marketing Officer, Jerri L. DeVard, age 58
Ceo And Director, Gerry P. Smith, age 55
Evp Chief Legal Officer Corporate Secretary And President Business Solutions Division, Steve Calkins, age 47
Evp And Chief Administrative Officer, Michael Allison, age 60, $539,423 total compensation
Evp Transformation And Strategic Sourcing, John W. Gannfors
Svp Ecommerce, Kevin Moffitt
Svp Retail Division, Marko Ibrahim
Vice President Enterprise Account Management, Steve Dvorchak
Vice President Transformation Delivery, Sharon McGregor
Vice President, Alex Jaime

Executive Vice President And President
International, Steven Schmidt
Chairman, Joseph S. (Joe) Vassalluzzo, age 70
Auditors: DELOITTE & TOUCHE LLP

LOCATIONS

HQ: Office Depot, Inc.
  6600 North Military Trail, Boca Raton, FL 33496
Phone: 561 438-4800   **Fax:** 561 265-4406
Web: www.officedepot.com

PRODUCTS/OPERATIONS

2017 Sales

	$ mil.	% of total
Retail	4,962	48
Business Solutions	5,108	50
CompuCom	156	2
Other	14	-
Total	**10,240**	**100**

COMPETITORS

Amazon.com	IBM Global Services
BJ's Wholesale Club	Insight Enterprises
Best Buy	Ricoh USA
CDW	School Specialty
Costco Wholesale	Staples
Dell	Target Corporation
Essendant	The UPS Store
FedEx Office	Unisys
Fry's Electronics	Veritiv
HP Enterprise Services	Wal-Mart

HISTORICAL FINANCIALS

Company Type: Public

Income Statement   FYE: December 30

	REVENUE ($ mil.)	NET INCOME ($ mil.)	NET PROFIT MARGIN	EMPLOYEES
12/17	10,240	181	1.8%	45,000
12/16	11,021	529	4.8%	38,000
12/15	14,485	8	0.1%	49,000
12/14	16,096	(354)	—	56,000
12/13	11,242	(20)	—	64,000
Annual Growth	(2.3%)	—	—	(8.4%)

2017 Year-End Financials

Debt ratio: 16.32%
Return on equity: 9.14%
Cash ($ mil.): 622
Current ratio: 1.40
Long-term debt ($ mil.): 936

No. of shares (mil.): 553
Dividends
  Yield: 0.0%
  Payout: 29.4%
Market value ($ mil.): 1,961

	STOCK PRICE ($) FY Close	P/E High/Low		PER SHARE ($) Earnings	Dividends	Book Value
12/17	3.54	18	9	0.34	0.10	3.83
12/16	4.52	8	3	0.96	0.05	3.60
12/15	5.60	968533		0.01	0.00	2.92
12/14	8.84	—	—	(0.66)	0.00	2.97
12/13	5.19	—	—	(0.29)	0.00	3.89
Annual Growth	(9.1%)	—	—	—	—	(0.4%)

Old Line Bancshares Inc

Old Line Bancshares is the holding company for Old Line Bank serving consumers businesses and wealthy individuals in the Old Line State and in the Washington DC area. With some 20 branch offices and total assets in excess of $1.2 billion the bank offers standard retail products including deposit accounts CDs and credit cards. Commercial and industrial and commercial real estate loans make up 75% of the bank's loan portfolio though it also offers consumer loans and luxury boat financing. The company also owns 50% of real estate firm Pointer Ridge Office Investment.

Operations

About 81% of its revenue came from interest income on loans in 2014 while another 7% came from interest on securities (including mortgage-backed US government agency and municipal securities). About 4% of revenue was generated from service charges on deposit accounts 4% came from fees and commissions and 2% came from gains on the sales of its loans.

Geographic Reach

Old Line Bank more than 20 branches mostly in suburban Maryland (which includes Washington DC and suburbs and Southern Maryland) in the counties of Anne Arundel Calvert Charles Prince George's and St. Mary's.

Financial Performance

Old Line Bancshares' revenues and profits have been trending higher over the past several years mostly driven by strong loan business growth obtained through acquisitions and organically.The bank's revenue dipped by 3% to $51.6 million in 2014 despite loan growth during the year mostly as its non-interest income shrank due to a decline in gains from the sale of its loans and investment securities compared to the prior year.

Lower revenue and higher loan loss provisions from a less credit-worth loan portfolio in 2014 caused Old Line's net income to fall by 8% to $7.1 million. The company's operating cash levels declined by 35% to $10.2 million on lower cash earnings.

Strategy

Old Line Bancshares in 2015 laid out its short-term plans to collect on its non-accrual and past due loans and strategically selling its acquired loans and real-estate owned loans to boost its credit quality. It also expressed its strategy of extending its core banking services growing its fee income (especially in the low-interest environment) and embracing digital banking technologies such as online and mobile banking to reduce its spending on costly branch expansion plans.

Management also touted success in organically growing its loan and deposit business in Montgomery Prince George's Anne Arundel counties in Maryland during 2014.

The company sometimes grows its loan business and branch network by strategically acquiring banks in its primary markets. Its agreement to acquire Regal Bancorp for example would add three new banking locations to its network and $133.7 million in assets to its books — which would make it the third-largest commercial bank in Maryland by assets and the second-largest by branch network.

Mergers and Acquisitions

In August 2015 the company agreed to acquire Regal Bancorp including its Regal Bank & Trust subsidiary its three branches and assets of $133.7 million. The deal was expected to close in late 2015 or early 2016.

In May 2013 Old Line Bancshare closed on its $54.7-million purchase of WSB Holdings adding five Washington Savings Bank FSB branches and $310 million in assets.

Previously Old Line acquired Maryland Bankcorp in 2011 in a move that doubled its branch network and asset portfolio.

EXECUTIVES

Vice President, Erik Fridley
Auditors: Dixon Hughes Goodman LLP

LOCATIONS

HQ: Old Line Bancshares Inc
  1525 Pointer Ridge Place, Bowie, MD 20716
Phone: 301 430-2500
Web: www.oldlinebank.com

COMPETITORS

BB&T	PNC Financial
Bank of America	Tri-County Financial
M&T Bank	

HISTORICAL FINANCIALS

Company Type: Public

Income Statement   FYE: December 31

	ASSETS ($ mil.)	NET INCOME ($ mil.)	INCOME AS % OF ASSETS	EMPLOYEES
12/17	2,105	15	0.8%	271
12/16	1,709	13	0.8%	234
12/15	1,510	10	0.7%	248
12/14	1,227	7	0.6%	228
12/13	1,167	7	0.7%	254
Annual Growth	15.9%	19.5%		1.6%

2017 Year-End Financials

Debt ratio: 1.81%
Return on equity: 8.91%
Cash ($ mil.): 34
Current ratio: —
Long-term debt ($ mil.): —

No. of shares (mil.): 12
Dividends
  Yield: 0.0%
  Payout: 23.7%
Market value ($ mil.): 368

	STOCK PRICE ($) FY Close	P/E High/Low		PER SHARE ($) Earnings	Dividends	Book Value
12/17	29.44	22	17	1.35	0.32	16.61
12/16	23.98	21	14	1.20	0.24	13.81
12/15	17.57	19	15	0.97	0.21	13.31
12/14	15.82	27	21	0.65	0.18	12.51
12/13	14.50	17	13	0.86	0.16	11.71
Annual Growth	19.4%	—	—	11.9%	18.9%	9.1%

Old National Bancorp (Evansville, IN)

Old National Bank is old but it's not quite national. Founded in 1834 the main subsidiary of Old National Bancorp operates about 200 bank centers across Indiana Kentucky Michigan and Illinois. The bank serves consumers and business customers offering standard checking and savings accounts credit cards and loans. Its treasury segment manages investments for bank and commercial clients. Business loans commercial and residential mortgages and consumer loans account for most of Old National's lending activity. The company also sells insurance manages wealth for high-net-worth clients and offers investment and retirement services through third-party provider LPL Financial.

Operations

Old National Bancorp operates two main segments: Banking which generates the bulk of Old National's revenue and provides traditional loan and deposit products as well as wealth management services; and Insurance which provides commercial property and casualty surety loss control services employee benefits consulting and administration as well as personal insurance.

The bank generated 51% of its revenue from loan interest (including fees) in 2014 while another 14% came from interest on investment securities. Insurance premiums and commissions contributed 7% to the company's total revenues that year while wealth management fees made up another 5%.

Geographic Reach

The bank's nearly 200 banking centers are located across four Midwestern states and Kentucky. Most are in the central northern and southern parts of Indiana; while others are in central Illinois; Western Kentucky and Louisville; Grand Rapids Southeastern and Southwestern Michigan; and Ohio.

Sales and Marketing

Old National has identified metropolitan areas within its market including Indianapolis; Louisville Kentucky; and Lafayette Indiana for growth within its core community banking segment.

The company spent $9.59 million on marketing in 2014 up from $7.21 million and $7.45 million in 2013 and 2012 respectively.

Financial Performance

Old National Bancorp's revenues and profits have been on the uptrend for the past several years thanks to new loan business from a series of bank acquisitions and declining loan loss provisions as its loan portfolio's credit quality has improved with the strengthened economy.

The company's revenue rose by 5% to $554.86 million in 2014 mostly thanks to new loan business stemming from the bank's acquisitions of Tower Financial United Bancorp and LSB Financial during the year along with organic loan growth. Higher revenue in 2014 coupled with strong cost controls lower interest on deposits and a continued decline in loan loss provisions drove Old National's net income higher by 3% to $103.62 million for the year.

Old National's operating cash fell by 21% to $199.72 million after adjusting its earnings for non-cash items related to its net sales proceeds from the sale of its residential real estate loans held-for-sale.

Strategy

Old National continues to seek out additional branch and whole bank acquisitions to grow its loan business and expand its geographic reach. Its acquisition of United Bancorp in mid-2014 for example added nearly $1 billion in new loan business and $869 million in wealth management assets under management while doubling Old National's presence in Michigan to 36 total branches.

The company is also pursuing growth by increasing its focus on commercial banking and cross-selling its insurance and wealth management offerings. To this end Old National in 2014 bought the insurance accounts (consisting of mostly commercial property/casualty accounts) serviced by the Evansville branch office of Wells Fargo Insurance.

Meanwhile it is also selectively exiting markets that haven't been profitable. In early 2015 as part of its ongoing efficiency improvement efforts the bank announced that it would sell 17 of its banking centers including all twelve of its branches in Southern Illinois and close or consolidate another 19 branches in other states over the following months.

Mergers and Acquisitions

In December 2014 Old National agreed to acquire Founders Financial Corporation along with its Founders Bank & Trust subsidiary in Grand Rapids Michigan for $91.7 million which would add nearly $460 million in total assets and four branches in Kent County.

In November 2014 the company purchased LSB Financial and its Lafayette Savings Bank subsidiary for $51.8 million adding five branches near Lafayette Indiana.

In July 2014 the company acquired Ann Arbor-based United Bancorp along with United Bank & Trust for a total of $122 million adding 18 branches in Michigan nearly $919 million in total assets a $963 million loan servicing portfolio and $688 million in trust assets under management.

In April 2014 Old National purchased Indiana-based Tower Financial along with its Tower Bank & Trust subsidiary adding seven new branches and some $556 million in trust assets under management.

In 2013 the bank bolstered its presence in Michigan after acquiring two dozen Bank of America branches in northern Indiana and southwest Michigan. The previous year the bank purchased Indiana Community Bancorp which added 17 branches in the southeastern part of the state. The transaction was valued at nearly $80 million.

EXECUTIVES

Chairman President And Ceo, Robert G. (Bob) Jones, age 61, $668,269 total compensation
Svp And Corporate Secretary, Jeffrey L. (Jeff) Knight, age 58, $321,051 total compensation
Evp And Chief Credit Officer, Daryl D. Moore, age 60, $305,040 total compensation
Ceo North Central Region And Indianapolis Region, Mark D. Bradford, age 60
Evp And Chief Client Services Officer, Annette W. Hudgions, age 60, $250,016 total compensation
President And Ceo Wealth Management, Caroline J. Ellspermann, age 50
Ceo Eastern Region, Dennis P. Heishman
Sevp And Cfo, Christopher A. (Chris) Wolking, age 58, $364,730 total compensation
Director Public Relations Old National Bank, Kathy A. Schoettlin
Region Ceo Old National Bank, Randall (Randy) Reichmann
Ceo Central And Western Michigan Region, Todd C. Clark, age 48
Evp And Chief Risk Officer, Candice J. Rickard, age 54
Evp And Chief Banking Officer, James Sandgren, $357,673 total compensation
Ceo Central Region, Dan L. Doan
Evp And Director Corporate Strategy, James C. Ryan, age 46
Evp And Cio, John R. Kamin
Evp Associate Engagement And Integrations, Kendra L. Vanzo
Evp Chief Auditing Executive And Chief Ethics Officer, Richard W. (Dick) Dubé
President Onb Investment Services, Kenneth J. Ellspermann
President Old National Insurance, Scott J. Evernham
Ceo Southern Region, Sara L. Miller
President And Coo, Jim Sandgren
President North Central Region, Scott Shishman
Vice President Technology Services Manager, Janet Wandling
Vice President Commercial Banking, Brian Henning
Vice President Associate Counsel, Tom Washburne
Senior Vice President, Mark Gorski
Vice President And Client Advisor, Steve Hackman
Senior Vice President Of Marketing, Scott Adams
Assistant Vice President, Sandy Keen
Vice President, Amanda Castaneda
Vice President, Randy Lilly
Assistant Vice President, Jenny Clark

Assistant Vice President Mortgage Loan Officer, Debra Fulkerson
Vice President, Rob Snyder
Assistant Vice President Accounts Payable Manager, Doana Meeks
Vice President Of Customer Service, Clay Sills-Memorial
Vice President Director Of Corporate Communications, Rick Jillson
Vice President Project Manager, Helen Cook
Private Banker Ii Vice President, Tony Patrick
Assistant Vice President Commercial Lender, Mike Devoy
Vice President And Banking Center Manager, Helen Habib
Assistant Vice President Branch Manager, Geoff Thompson
Senior Vice President Treasurer, Jennifer Guzman
Retail Center Manager Vice President, Stacy Fuqua
Vice President Commercial Relationship Manager, Sarah Strimmenos
Vice President Retail Center Manager, Emily Neely
Assistant Vice President, Todd Treadway
Vice President Corporate Banking, James Tutt
Vice President Treasury Management Sales Director, Teresa Brown
Senior Vice President Commercial Banking, James Barnum
Senior Vice President, Lynell Walton
Vice President Client Advisor Corporate Trust Manager, Shannon Perry
Vice President, Jaron Hargis
Assistant Vice President And Retail Center Manager, Sheila Alexander
Vice President Administration, Ken Ritchie
Retail Center Manager Vice President, Cathy Stidham
Senior Vice President, Tommy Elliott
Vice President, Rob Triplett
Private Banker L Vice President, Becky Robledo
Senior Vice President And Commercial Relationship Team Leader, Troy Briggs
Small Business Banker Vice President, Diana Brown
Vice President Cash Management, Andrea Solis
Vice President, Regina Levchets
Vice President, Roland Shelton
Senior Vice President, Marty Richardson
Commercial Rel Manager Ii Assistant Vice President, Kathy Havill
Vice President, Jame Tutt
Client Advanced Senior And Wm Mkt Lead Senior Vice President, Dan Callahan
Client Advisor Ii Vice President, Tamra Inman
Vice President Director And Assistant Controller, Treadweay Todd
Assistant Vice President Branch Manager Western Reserve, Kristin Glasser
Vice President Compliance Audit Manager, Sonja Kriegsmann
Board Member, Randall Shepard
Board Member, Jerome Henry
Board Member, Derrick Stewart
Board Member, Linda White
Auditors: Crowe LLP

LOCATIONS

HQ: Old National Bancorp (Evansville, IN)
One Main Street, Evansville, IN 47708
Phone: 800 731-2265
Web: www.oldnational.com

PRODUCTS/OPERATIONS

2014 Sales

	$ mil.	% of total
Interest		
Loans including fees	306	51
Investment securities	83	14
Noninterest		
Service charges on deposit accounts	47	8
Insurance premiums & commissions	41	7
Wealth management fees	28	5
ATM Fees	25	4
Investment product fees	17	1
Mortgage banking revenue	6	1
Other	41	7
Adjustments	(43.3)	-
Total	**554**	**100**

COMPETITORS

Fifth Third	JPMorgan Chase
First Financial (IN)	PNC Financial
German American Bancorp	Peoples Bancorp (IN)
	U.S. Bancorp
Huntington Bancshares	

HISTORICAL FINANCIALS

Company Type: Public

Income Statement

FYE: December 31

	ASSETS ($ mil.)	NET INCOME ($ mil.)	INCOME AS % OF ASSETS	EMPLOYEES
12/17	17,518	95	0.5%	2,801
12/16	14,860	134	0.9%	2,733
12/15	11,991	116	1.0%	2,652
12/14	11,647	103	0.9%	2,938
12/13	9,581	100	1.1%	2,608
Annual Growth	**16.3%**	**(1.3%)**	**—**	**1.8%**

2017 Year-End Financials

Debt ratio: 1.42%	No. of shares (mil.): 152
Return on equity: 4.82%	Dividends
Cash ($ mil.): 290	Yield: 0.0%
Current ratio: —	Payout: 75.3%
Long-term debt ($ mil.): —	Market value ($ mil.): 2,653

	STOCK PRICE ($) FY Close	P/E High/Low	PER SHARE ($) Earnings	PER SHARE ($) Dividends	PER SHARE ($) Book Value
12/17	17.45	27 23	0.69	0.52	14.17
12/16	18.15	17 10	1.05	0.52	13.42
12/15	13.56	15 13	1.00	0.48	13.05
12/14	14.88	16 13	0.95	0.44	12.54
12/13	15.37	16 12	1.00	0.40	11.64
Annual Growth	**3.2%**	**— —**	**(8.9%)**	**6.8%**	**5.0%**

Old Republic International Corp.

Old Republic International keeps pace with changing financial times. With about 140 subsidiaries across North America Old Republic's primary operations are conducted through the Old Republic General Insurance division which offers commercial liability and property/casualty insurance (mostly commercial trucking workers' compensation and general liability policies). In addition the company's Title Insurance group specializes in naturally issuing title insurance to property owners and lenders. Its Old Republic National Title subsidiary is one of the US's oldest and largest title insurance companies with offices throughout the US.

Operations

Old Republic's subsidiaries market underwrite and offer risk management services for insurance products including general and title coverage. Commercial property/casualty policies issued by the general insurance segment account for more than half of the company's sales. Meanwhile the title insurance segment accounts for nearly 40% of revenues and the company's Republic Financial Indemnity Group (RFIG comprising mortgage guaranty and consumer credit indemnity runoff operations) brings in less than 5% of sales. The company also maintains a small life and health insurance business.

More than 70% of the company's consolidated title premium and related fee income comes from independent title agents and underwritten title companies. The rest stems from direct operations including branches of its title insurance businesses and wholly owned agency and service subsidiaries.

Geographic Reach

Through its subsidiaries Old Republic is licensed to do business throughout the US (including the District of Columbia) Puerto Rico the US Virgin Islands Guam and in all Canadian provinces.

Sales and Marketing

While Old Republic does sell some of its property/casualty and specialty products directly it relies on independent agencies brokers and financial institutions to distribute the majority. The company focuses on certain sectors especially transportation commercial construction health care education forest products energy manufacturing retail and wholesale trade and financial services.

Title insurance and related settlement products are sold through some 265 company offices and through agencies and underwritten title companies throughout the US.

Financial Performance

Old Republic's revenues have been steadily rising over the past five years. In 2017 revenue increased 6% to $6.3 billion as net premiums earned fee income and realized investment gains went up. Both the general insurance and title insurance had higher premium fee and other revenues but this was partially offset by a decline for the run-off RFIG business. However the higher revenue boosted net income which rose 20% to a record $560.5 million.

Despite the increase in profits cash flow from operations fell 29% to $452.8 million that year. That was largely due to negative adjustments to unpaid claims and related items and realized investment gains.

Revenue roller coasters and net income fluctuations don't bother Old Republic as its public filings clearly state that it looks at its business in five-to-10-year intervals and therefore isn't concerned by the ups and downs in shorter cycles. The health of its general insurance business and the fact that it carries very little debt make it easier to take that view.

Strategy

In response to financial strains during the Great Recession Old Republic has chosen to focus on its general and title insurance operations while placing its RFIG mortgage guaranty and consumer credit indemnity operations (which at one point brought in more than 40% of total revenue) in run-off. The firm targets long-term returns on its underwriting operations. As such it spreads its risk over diversified businesses and assets to reduce liability exposures.

After some years of disappointing results Old Republic had a strong performance in 2017 a year in which the company laid the worries of the Great Recession to rest. The rebounding economy has helped drive up the firm's insurance sales: Its General Insurance segment drove the improvement that year. And while underwriting profit rose the company is determined to do even better in that regard. To that end Old Republic will remediate where it is needed most avoiding riskier contracts that are unlikely to deliver strong returns.

Old Republic remains concerned about such factors as ongoing low interest rates and an increase in competitors entering the market. To counteract these factors it plans to carefully explore the markets in which it operates with the intent to diminish its focus on saturated geographies. It also aims to alter and to a certain degree expand its distribution channels.

In mid-2018 the company established Old Republic Residual Market Services which provides specialized services to state-assigned workers' compensation risk plans as well as the National Council on Compensation Insurance Workers Compensation Insurance Plan. It is part of the growing General Insurance segment.

EXECUTIVES

Chairman President And Ceo, Aldo C. (Al) Zucaro, age 79, $895,000 total compensation

Chairman And Ceo Great West Casualty, R. Scott Rager, age 69, $510,000 total compensation

Chairman And Ceo Old Republic Title Companies, Rande K. Yeager, age 69, $510,000 total compensation

Svp And Cfo, Karl W. Mueller, age 58, $465,000 total compensation

President And Coo Old Republic General Insurance Group Inc. (orgig), Craig R. Smiddy, age 54, $485,000 total compensation

Vice President Director Financial Reporting, Stephanie Richards

Vice President, Mandi Zollotuchen

Assistant Vice President Commercial Counsel, Avi A Marcus

Vice President, Linda Johnson

Vice President, Fredric Frey

Assistant Vice President Commercial Counsel, Avi Marcus

Auditors: KPMG LLP

LOCATIONS

HQ: Old Republic International Corp.
307 North Michigan Avenue, Chicago, IL 60601
Phone: 312 346-8100
Web: www.oldrepublic.com

PRODUCTS/OPERATIONS

2017 Sales

	% of total
General Insurance	57
Title Insurance	37
Realized investment gains	3
RFIG (run-off)	2
Corporate & other	1
Total	**100**

COMPETITORS

AIG	ING
AXA	Progressive
Allianz	Corporation
Berkshire Hathaway	Stewart Information
CNA Financial	Services
Chubb Limited	The Hartford
Farmers Group	Travelers Companies
Fidelity National Financial	Unum Group
First American	W. R. Berkley

Company Type: Public

Income Statement   FYE: December 31

	ASSETS ($ mil.)	NET INCOME ($ mil.)	INCOME AS % OF ASSETS	EMPLOYEES
12/17	19,403	560	2.9%	8,700
12/16	18,591	466	2.5%	8,500
12/15	17,110	422	2.5%	8,200
12/14	16,988	409	2.4%	8,000
12/13	16,534	447	2.7%	7,900
Annual Growth	4.1%	5.8%	—	2.4%

2017 Year-End Financials

Debt ratio: 7.47%	No. of shares (mil.): 269
Return on equity: 12.18%	Dividends
Cash ($ mil.): 125	Yield: 0.0%
Current ratio: —	Payout: 39.5%
Long-term debt ($ mil.): —	Market value ($ mil.): 5,756

	STOCK PRICE ($) FY Close	P/E High/Low		PER SHARE ($) Earnings	Dividends	Book Value
12/17	21.38	10	8	1.92	0.76	17.58
12/16	19.00	11	9	1.62	0.75	17.02
12/15	18.63	12	9	1.48	0.74	14.81
12/14	14.63	11	9	1.44	0.73	15.04
12/13	17.27	10	6	1.74	0.72	14.49
Annual Growth	5.5%	—	—	2.5%	1.4%	4.9%

Old Second Bancorp., Inc. (Aurora, Ill.)

Old Second won't settle for a silver finish when it comes to community banking around Chicago. Old Second Bancorp is the holding company for Old Second National Bank which serves the Chicago metropolitan area through 25 branches in Kane Kendall DeKalb DuPage LaSalle Will and Cook counties. The bank provides standard services such as checking and savings accounts credit and debit cards CDs mortgages loans and trust services to consumers and business clients. Subsidiary River Street Advisors offers investment management and advisory services. Another unit Old Second Affordable Housing Fund provides home-buying assistance to lower-income customers.

Operations

Commercial real estate loans accounted for 53% of Old Second's loan portfolio at the end of 2015 while residential mortgages made up another 31%. The rest was made up of general commercial loans (12% of loan assets) and construction lending (2%).

Roughly 70% of the bank's revenue comes from interest income. About 54% of its revenue came from loan interest (including fees) during 2015 with another 15% coming from interest on investment securities. The remainder of Old Second's revenue came from deposit account service charges (7%) trust income (6%) mortgage loan sale gains (6%) secondary mortgage fees (1%) and other sources.

Geographic Reach

The bank mostly serves customers in Aurora Illinois (which is 40 miles west of Chicago) and surrounding communities. Its 24 branches are located in the Kane Kendall DeKalb DuPage LaSalle Will and Cook counties of Illinois.

Sales and Marketing

Old Second has been ramping up its advertising spend in recent years. It spent $1.34 million on advertising in 2015 up from $1.28 million and $1.23 million in 2014 and 2013 respectively.

Financial Performance

Old Second's annual revenues have fallen 20% since 2011 as it's had to sell of many of its non-performing loan assets to de-risk its loan portfolio. The company's profits however have been on the mend as its de-risking measures have led to declining loan loss provisions.

The bank's revenue rebounded by less than 1% to $97.46 million during 2015 as its average loans including loans held for sale grew by 2% for the year.

Revenue growth in 2015 combined with lower interest and amortization costs on deposits drove Old Second Bancorp's net income up by over 50% to $15.39 million. The bank's operating cash levels jumped sharply to $21.14 million (operations had used $6.3 million in 2014) partially thanks to earnings growth but mostly thanks to positive working capital changes related to sales proceeds from loans held for sale and changes in accrued interest payable and other liabilities.

Strategy

Old Second Bancorp continued in 2016 to focus on shedding riskier loan assets that led it to deep losses in 2011 while focusing on securing high-quality loans with more creditworthiness. Its efforts began to pay off in 2015 as its average loan balances and revenues began to grow again after years of being in decline.

EXECUTIVES

Assistant Vice President Operations, Brian Bermes
Evp Cfo And Director, J. Douglas Cheatham, age 62, $252,000 total compensation
Ceo And Director Old Second Bancorp Inc. And Old Second National Bank, James L. Eccher, age 53, $325,000 total compensation
Senior Vice President Commercial Banking, Jeff Downs
Vice President, Robin Hill
Senior Vice President And Treasurer, Stan Faries
Executive Vice President Human Resources, Robert Dicosola
Senior Vice President, Chris Barry
Executive Vice President, Joel Binder
Vice President Treasury Management, John Annis
Vice President, Jocelyn Retz
Vice President, Troy Langeness
Vice President, Jeri Ott
Assistant Vice President, Ana Torres
Vice President Commercial Banking, Kristin Zell
Senior Vice President Business Banking, Roger Schnorr
Senior Vice President Commercial Lending, Mark Fleming
Vice President, Michelle Almond
Assistant Vice President Operations, Barbara Collette
Assistant Vice President, Greg Faleskin
Vice President Commercial And Industrial Lending, John Gorzak
First Vice President, Chris Hainey
First Vice President Director Of Treasury Management Sales, Juwana Zanayed
Vice President Treasury Management Advisor, Sherry Pass
Senior Vice President, Peter Harrison
Chairman Old Second Bancorp Inc. And Old Second National Bank, William B. Skoglund, age 68
Vice Chairman, Gary S. Collins, age 60
Board Member, John Ladowicz
Auditors: Plante & Moran, PLLC

LOCATIONS

HQ: Old Second Bancorp., Inc. (Aurora, Ill.)
  37 South River Street, Aurora, IL 60507
Phone: 630 892-0202
Web: www.oldsecond.com

PRODUCTS/OPERATIONS

2015 sales

	% of total
Interest and dividend income	
Loans including fees	54
Taxable	14
Tax exempt	1
Non-interest income	
Service charges on deposits	7
Trust income	6
Net gain on sales of mortgage loans	6
Debit card interchange income	4
Secondary mortgage fees	1
Increase in cash surrender value of bank-owned life insurance	1
Other income	6
Total	**100**

Products/Services

Personal Banking
Card Services
Checking
Loans
Money Services
Online and Mobile Banking
Prime Time Club
Retirement Services
Savings
Loans
Auto and Personal Loans
Home Equity Loans
Home Loans
Mortgage Lenders
Required Documents
SAFE Act
Business Banking
Commercial Banking
Online and Mobile Banking
Small Business Banking
Wealth Management
Business Plan Options
Real Estate Services
Retirement Services

COMPETITORS

Bank of America	Harris
BankFinancial	MB Financial
Fifth Third	Northern Trust
First Midwest Bancorp	West Suburban Bancorp

HISTORICAL FINANCIALS

Company Type: Public

Income Statement   FYE: December 31

	ASSETS ($ mil.)	NET INCOME ($ mil.)	INCOME AS % OF ASSETS	EMPLOYEES
12/17	2,383	15	0.6%	450
12/16	2,251	15	0.7%	467
12/15	2,077	15	0.7%	450
12/14	2,061	10	0.5%	485
12/13	2,004	82	4.1%	492
Annual Growth	4.4%	(34.5%)	—	(2.2%)

2017 Year-End Financials

Debt ratio: 4.27%	No. of shares (mil.): 29
Return on equity: 8.06%	Dividends
Cash ($ mil.): 55	Yield: 0.0%
Current ratio: —	Payout: 8.0%
Long-term debt ($ mil.): —	Market value ($ mil.): 404

STOCK PRICE ($)	P/E		PER SHARE ($)		
FY Close	High/Low	Earnings	Dividends	Book Value
12/17	13.65	28 20	0.50	0.04	6.76
12/16	11.05	22 12	0.53	0.03	5.93
12/15	7.84	18 11	0.46	0.00	5.29
12/14	5.37	12 10	0.46	0.00	6.59
12/13	4.62	1 0	5.45	0.00	10.61
Annual Growth	31.1%	— —	(45.0%)	—	(10.7%)

Olin Corp.

The making of bleach and bullets is all in a day's work for Olin Corporation. The company manufactures chemicals used to make bleach water purification and swimming pool chemicals pulp and paper processing agents and PVC plastics. Olin Chlor Alkali Products is one of the top chlor-alkali producers in North America along with OxyChem. Olin also distributes caustic soda vinyls epoxies chlorinated organics hydrochloric acid and bleach. In addition in a quite divergent business the company's Winchester Ammunition unit makes branded sporting ammunition reloading components small caliber military ammunition and components and industrial cartridges.

Operations
Olin operates three business segments: Chlor Alkali Products and Vinyl (CAPV) Epoxy and Winchester Ammunition.

CAPV accounts for about 55% of total sales and manufactures products including chlorine and caustic soda ethlyene dichloride and vinyl chloride monomers and hydrogen.

The Epoxy segment epoxy materials such as allyl chloride epichlorodydrin and liquid epoxy resins as well as downstream products such as converted epoxy resins and additives. The segment accounts for around a third of sales.

Winchester Ammunition generates more than 10% of sales and manufactures sporting ammunition reloading components small caliber military ammunition and components and industrial cartridges.

Geographic Reach
Olin has plants in across the US (Augusta Georgia; California; Illinois; Mississippi; McIntosh Alabama; Charleston Tennessee; St. Gabriel Louisiana; Henderson Nevada; Niagara Falls New York); and in Canada (Becancour Quebec). It also has a facility in Australia that loads and packs sporting and industrial ammunition. It also has plants and facilities in Germany Brazil South Korea Italy the Netherlands and China.

The US accounts for about 60% of Olin's revenue.

Sales and Marketing
Olin markets most of its products and services through its own sales force and sells directly to various industrial customers mass merchants retailers wholesalers and other distributors as well as the US government and its prime contractors.

The products from Epoxy segment and Chlor Alkali Products and Vinyls are delivered primarily by marine vessels deep-water and coastal barges railcars and trucks.

The end users of products and services of the Epoxy segment are manufacturers of polymers resins and other plastic materials water purification and pesticides adhesives paint and coatings composites and flooring.

Winchester's sales and distribution chain has strong ties to traditional dealers and distributors.

Dow DuPont is Olin's largest customer accounting for about 15% of total sales.

Financial Performance
In the last decade Olin's revenue has gone up steadily from $1.7 billion in 2008 to $2.8 billion in 2015 before an acquisition of Dow Chemical's chlorine and related businesses doubled its revenue to $5.6 billion in 2016. Net income fluctuated in the 2008-14 period between a low of $65 million and a high of $242 million. In 2015-16 the company reported combined losses of $6 million related to acquisition costs.

In 2017 revenue rose 13% to $6.3 billion the highest in company's history thanks to accelerated growth after the Dow acquisition. The growth was triggered by $500 million increase in Chlor Alkali Products and Vinyls sales due to higher caustic soda and EDC product prices as well as volumes. Epoxy sales also increased by $265 million thanks to higher product prices and increased volumes. Despite a boost in revenue Olin's sales volumes were negatively impacted by Hurricane Harvey (approximately $55 million in lost revenue).

Net income rocketed up from a loss of $4 million in 2016 to a profit of half a billion dollars in 2017 the highest in company's history primarily from $400 million in income tax benefit and year-over-year savings of $100 million in restructuring charges and acquisition related costs.

Olin's cash holdings stood at approximately $220 million for 2017. Operations provided $650 million in cash. Investments cost the company half a billion mostly in CAPEX of $250 million as well as $117 million in financing the company's activities.

Strategy
Olin seeks to strengthen its position as a preferred supplier of chlor alkali products to merchant market customers though internal expansion and complementary acquisitions.

The company continues to leverage its legendary Winchester brand with its reputation of innovation (such as introducing reduced-lead and non-lead products) to improve its position as a major supplier of ammunition. To reduce Winchester's annual operating costs by about $30 million the division relocated its centerfire ammunition operations from East Alton Illinois to lower-cost Oxford Mississippi in 2016.

In the epoxy business Olin continues its search for productivity cost improvements throughout its supply chain while making use of its ten sites on four continents to expand into emerging markets.

HISTORY

Vermont-born engineer Franklin Olin founded Equitable Powder in East Alton Illinois in 1892 to make blasting powder for midwestern coal fields. By 1898 the company called Western Cartridge was also making ammunition for small arms.

When WWI increased demand for military cartridges Western Cartridge built a brass mill. After the war it began making custom brass and other copper alloys for industrial customers. The company bought Winchester Repeating Arms maker of the famous Winchester Model 1876 repeating rifles in 1931. During WWII Western Cartridge developed the US carbine and M-1 rifles.

The various businesses of Western Cartridge merged as Olin Industries in 1944. Franklin then retired handing the company to sons John and Spencer.

Enriched by the war effort Olin Industries grew. In 1949 it began making cellophane and in 1951 it acquired Frost Lumber Industries and Ecusta Paper a maker of cigarette papers. Olin Industries merged with Mathieson Chemical in 1954 to form Olin Mathieson Chemical the fifth-largest US chemical company.

The Mathieson Alkali Works was founded in Saltville Virginia in 1892 to produce alkalis using a process acquired from English chemical firm Neil Mathieson. By 1909 the company began producing liquid chlorine and in 1923 it built one of the earliest plants for producing synthetic ammonia. During WWII Mathieson manufactured chlorine for water purification and alkali chemicals for sanitation. In 1952 Mathieson acquired drugmaker Squibb.

Olin Mathieson continued to diversify in the mid-1950s buying Blockson Chemical (industrial phosphates) and Brown Paper Mill (kraft paper bags and corrugated cardboard containers). Frost Lumber and Brown Paper Mill formed the Forest Products Division later dubbed Olinkraft. In 1956 Olin Mathieson entered the aluminum business via a joint venture — just in time for a drop in aluminum demand.

In the 1960s the company began making urethane chemicals. It also created Olin-American a subsidiary that built houses and spun off Squibb. In 1969 it shortened its name to Olin Corporation and moved to Stamford Connecticut.

The 1970s saw Olin reining in its diverse businesses. It spun off Olinkraft and sold its aluminum operations. During the 1980s Olin sold its sporting-arms business (but kept Winchester ammunition) as well as its paper housing and cellophane units. John Olin died in 1982. The company acquired Rockcor which included Rocket Research Pacific Electro Dynamics and Physics International in 1985.

Olin moved its headquarters to Norwalk Connecticut in 1995 the same year Spencer Olin died. In 1996 as the earnings potential of its ordnance and aerospace operations lagged Olin spun them off as Primex Technologies. It also sold its isocyanate (used in plastics and adhesives) and other cyclical businesses. Olin bought the remaining 50% of its Niachlor chlor alkali joint venture from DuPont in 1997 after considering putting Niachlor up for sale.

Aspiring to become a leading basic-materials company Olin spun off its specialty chemical business in early 1999 under the name Arch Chemicals. Citing regulatory issues Olin cancelled plans in 2000 to form a chlor alkali chemicals joint venture with Occidental's OxyChem subsidiary. Olin acquired Monarch Brass & Copper Corp. for about $49 million in 2001. The next year it bought brass rod maker Chase Industries. Olin closed its copper and copper alloy sheet plant in Indianapolis in 2003.

In 2007 Olin grew its core chemicals business acquiring chlor-alkali producer Pioneer Companies for about $415 million. To help pay for the deal in late 2007 Olin sold its former Metals unit to investment group KPS Capital Partners for almost $400 million. The Metals unit — which had accounted for about two-thirds of sales — made copper and copper alloy sheets clad metal foil and stainless-steel strips.

In 2011 Olin acquired the balance of the Sun-Belt Chlor Alkali joint venture it did not own from partner PolyOne Corp. for $175 million in cash and assumed debt. It had held a 50% stake in the venture which produces chlorine and caustic soda. The SunBelt chlor alkali plant located within Olin's McIntosh Alabama facility has approximately 350000 tons of membrane technology capacity and generated some $70 million in earnings in 2010.

The company in 2012 acquired Illinois-based KA Steel for $328 million in cash. KA Steel is one of the largest caustic soda distributors in North America and its acquisition increased Olin's capacity to manufacture bleach by about 20% as well as to sell some of its other products such as hydrochloric acid and potassium hydroxide. A result the purchase Olin formed a chemical distribution segment that year.

EXECUTIVES

Evp Synergies And Systems, John L. McIntosh, age 64, $509,000 total compensation

Chairman President And Ceo, John E. Fischer, age 63, $836,000 total compensation

Vp And Cfo, Todd A. Slater, age 55, $518,000 total compensation

Evp; President Epoxy And International, Pat D. Dawson, age 60, $636,000 total compensation

Svp Ammunition, Thomas J. OÂ'Keefe, age 59

Evp; President Chlor Alkali Vinyls And Services, James A. Varilek, age 59, $447,000 total compensation

Vice President Finance And Controller, Randee Sumner

Auditors: KPMG LLP

LOCATIONS

HQ: Olin Corp.
190 Carondelet Plaza, Suite 1530, Clayton, MO 63105
Phone: 314 480-1400
Web: www.olin.com

2016 sales

	$ mil.	% of total
US	3,356	60
Other countries	2,193	40
Total	**5,550**	**100**

PRODUCTS/OPERATIONS

2016 sales

	$ mil.	% of total
Chlor Alkali Products and Vinyls	2,999	54
Epoxy	1,822	33
Winchester	729	13
Total	**5,550**	**100**

Business Segments

Business Segments
Chlor Alkali Products
 Caustic soda
 Chlorine
 Hydrochloric acid
 Sodium hydrochlorite (Industrial and institutional cleaning products)
 Sodium hydrosulfite (bleaching)
Winchester
 Ammunition (shot-shell small-caliber and rimfire)
 Government-owned arsenal operation (maintenance for the US Army)
 Industrial cartridges (eight-gauge loads and powder-actuated tool loads for the construction industry)
Chemical Distribution
 Bleach
 Caustic soda

COMPETITORS

Axiall	Mitsubishi Chemical
Blount International	Occidental Chemical
Brenntag	PPG Industries
FMC	Remington Arms
Formosa Plastics USA	Sumitomo Chemical
Freedom Group	Univar Inc.
Herstal	Westlake Chemical
Huntsman Corp	

HISTORICAL FINANCIALS

Company Type: Public

Income Statement
FYE: December 31

	REVENUE ($ mil.)	NET INCOME ($ mil.)	NET PROFIT MARGIN	EMPLOYEES
12/17	6,268	549	8.8%	6,400
12/16	5,550	(3)	—	6,400
12/15	2,854	(1)	—	6,200
12/14	2,241	105	4.7%	3,900
12/13	2,515	178	7.1%	4,100
Annual Growth	**25.6%**	**32.4%**	**—**	**11.8%**

2017 Year-End Financials

Debt ratio: 39.18%	No. of shares (mil.): 167
Return on equity: 21.86%	Dividends
Cash ($ mil.): 218	Yield: 0.0%
Current ratio: 1.78	Payout: 24.5%
Long-term debt ($ mil.): 3,611	Market value ($ mil.): 5,945

	STOCK PRICE ($) FY Close	P/E High/Low		Earnings	PER SHARE ($) Dividends	Book Value
12/17	35.58	11	8	3.26	0.80	16.48
12/16	25.61	—	—	(0.02)	0.80	13.74
12/15	17.26	—	—	(0.01)	0.80	14.65
12/14	22.77	22	16	1.33	0.80	13.09
12/13	28.85	13	10	2.21	0.80	13.87
Annual Growth	**5.4%**	**—**	**—**	**10.2%**	**(0.0%)**	**4.4%**

Omnicom Group, Inc.

Omnicom Group creates advertising that is omnipresent. The company ranks as the world's #1 corporate media services conglomerate with 1500 agencies across 100-plus countries conducting advertising marketing and public relations operations. It serves global advertising clients through its agency networks BBDO Worldwide DDB Worldwide and TBWA Worldwide while such firms as GSD&M Merkley + Partners and Zimmerman Advertising provide services for regional and national clients. Its Diversified Agency Services division including Fleishman-Hillard Integer and Rapp provides public relations and other marketing services.

Operations

Omnicom is active in four primary disciplines: Advertising Customer Relationship Management (CRM) Public Relations and Healthcare.

Advertising accounts for more than half of Omnicom's total revenue.

The CRM segment consists of two units CRM Customer Experience & CRM Execution & Support. CRM Consumer Experience consists of Omnicom Precision Marketing Group's digital/direct marketing agencies as well as its branding shopper marketing and experiential marketing agencies. CRM Execution & Support carries out field marketing sales support merchandising and point of sale as well as other specialized marketing and custom communications services.

Public Relations services generate around 10% of sales while Healthcare marketing and communications focused segment provides around 5%.

Geographic Reach

Omnicom has principal corporate offices in New York Connecticut and Florida while it has international offices in London Shanghai and Singapore. The group's network of agencies serves some 5000 clients in more than 100 countries. About 60% of the company's revenue comes from the Americas while EMEA (Europe Middle East and Africa) contributes around 30%. The remaining 10% or so comes from the Asia-Pacific region.

Sales and Marketing

As a leading global advertising marketing and corporate communications company Omnicom has a large and diverse client base and often several Omnicom agencies will serve the same client concurrently. None of its clients account for more than 5% of revenue while its top 100 clients account for a little more than 50% of revenue and are served on average by 50 Omnicom agencies.

By industry served food and beverages provides the most custom at nearly 15% of sales. Other notable industries include pharmaceuticals and healthcare consumer products and the auto industry each accounting for around 10% of sales.

Financial Performance

Omnicom has struggled to meaningfully grow its revenue over the past four years. In fiscal 2017 sales decreased 1% to $15.3 billion as the sale of the its specialty print business was mostly offset organic revenue growth and the positive effect of currency movements.

Net income has likewise proven fairly static of late and in fiscal 2017 it declined 5% to $1.1 billion comparable with recent averages. Much of the fall was accounted for by the 2017 US Tax Cuts and Jobs Act which added $106.3 million to net income tax expense.

Cash from operations grew 4% to $2.0 billion due to changes in taxation and an increase in operating capital partially offset by lower net income.

Strategy

Omnicom's fortunes have been buoyed in part by its agency networks and their consistently strong creative work (traditional media advertising accounts for almost half of its revenue) but the bulk of its growth has traditionally come from such areas as customer relationship management (CRM) and specialty communications. To better serve the increasing scope of its CRM business in 2017 Omnicom split its CRM activities into two separate units CRM Consumer Experience and CRM Execution & Support. It also recognized the increasing importance of Healthcare by realigning the former specialty communications segment as a healthcare-specific segment.

Omnicom sees continued growth being tied to its ability to provide an ever-expanding menu of services to its largest clients especially in the digital and social media arenas. The company has also been focused on expanding its media planning and buying operations.

Mergers and Acquisitions

In March 2018 Omnicom agreed to acquire Elsevier's Japanese Pharma Communications business. Elsevier is part of RELX Group. Pharma Communications engages in the delivery of medical content for promotional materials and educational programs directed at doctors and patients.

In February that year Omnicom acquired Snow Companies a full-service patient engagement agency that focuses on direct-to-patient (DTP) communications marketing education and patient research initiatives. It primarily serves major pharmaceutical and biotech companies.

HISTORY

Omnicom Group was created in 1986 to combine three leading ad agencies into a single group capable of competing in the worldwide market. BBDO Worldwide founded in New York in 1928 as Batten Barton Durstine & Osborn had a huge PepsiCo account and developed the Pepsi Generation campaign. Doyle Dane Bernbach Group (DDB) which had created the fahrvergnA?gen ads for Volkswagen had strong ties in Europe.

And Needham Harper Worldwide which had served up the "You Deserve a Break Today" commercials for McDonald's had connections in Asia. BBDO remained separate but DDB and Needham Harper were merged to form DDB Needham Worldwide. The business services units (public relations firms and direct marketers) of each of these companies were tucked under the Diversified Agency Services (DAS) umbrella.

Bruce Crawford a previous chairman of BBDO who had just finished a stint running New York's Metropolitan Opera became chairman and CEO in 1989. He transformed DAS from a chaotic group of shops into an integrated marketing giant and ran Omnicom as a holding company of independent operating units working together through cross-referrals. By keeping costs low especially interest expenses Omnicom survived the 1990-91 recession with little pain. The company acquired Goodby Berlin & Silverstein (now Goodby Silverstein & Partner s) in 1992. The next year TBWA Advertising (founded in Paris in 1970 by American Bill Tragos) was added to Omnicom's roster.

The merger spree continued in 1994 when Omnicom purchased WWAV Group the largest direct-marketing agency in the UK. In 1995 Omnicom fused TBWA with Chiat/Day (founded in 1968 by Jay Chiat and Guy Day) to form TBWA International Network. Omnicom also acquired Michigan-based Ross Roy Communications (later Interone Marketing Group). In 1997 DDB Needham won back its McDonald's account after a 15-year hiatus. That year Crawford stepped down as CEO (though he remained chairman) and John Wren took control of Omnicom.

In 1998 the company acquired PR firm Fleishman-Hillard adding to the PR clout it established with the acquisition of Ketchum Communications (now Ketchum) in 1996. Omnicom also acquired GGT Group of London for $235 million. (GGT's New York office Wells BDDP had lost a large Procter & Gamble account that year.) It merged GGT's BDDP Worldwide with TBWA to form TBWA Worldwide. BBDO landed a $200 million account with PepsiCo's Frito-Lay that year.

Omnicom's position in Europe was boosted in 1999 when it bought the Abbot Mead Vickers (now Abbot Mead Vickers BBDO) shares it didn't already own. That year TBWA founder William Tragos retired from the company (replaced by Lee Clow) and DDB Needham changed its moniker to DDB Worldwide Communications Group. Omnicom also bought market research firm M/A/R/C for about $95 million and invested $20 million in pharmaceutical clinical trials company SCIREX. In 2000 BBDO scored a major coup over rival FCB Worldwide (now part of Interpublic) by landing the $1.8 billion DaimlerChrysler account. The next year it formed Seneca Investments to hold its stakes in several i-services shops including Agency.com and Organic. (Omnicom acquired the interactive agencies outright in 2003.)

After years of acquisitions and fine-tuning its operating structure Omnicom encountered th

EXECUTIVES

Evp And Cfo, Philip J. Angelastro, age 54, $850,000 total compensation
Treasurer Omnicom Group And President And Ceo Omnicom Capital, Dennis E. Hewitt, age 73, $395,000 total compensation
President And Ceo, John D. Wren, age 66, $1,000,000 total compensation
Vice Chairman; Chairman Asia Pacific, Serge Dumont
Evp, Asit Mehra
Evp And Dean Omnicom University, Janet Riccio
Evp, Rita E. Rodriguez

Evp, Peter Sherman
Ceo Omnicom Digital, Jonathan B. Nelson, age 50, $850,000 total compensation
Svp General Counsel And Secretary, Michael J. O'Brien, age 56, $700,000 total compensation
Vice President Health And Welfare Benefits, Mark Low
Senior Vice President And Chief Accounting Officer, Andrew Castellaneta
Executive Vice President, Thomas Carey
Vice President Human Resources, Leslie Chiocco
Senior Vice President, Tiffany R Warren
Vice President Of Finance Operations, Brian Sullivan
Senior Vice President Group Account Director, Linda Melman
Senior Vice President, Joe Ricciardi
Vice President Financial Planning And Analysis, Daniel Bearison
Chairman, Bruce Crawford, age 88
Board Member, Linda Johnson Rice
Treasurer, Angie Hickman
Board Member, Debbie Kissire
Auditors: KPMG LLP

LOCATIONS

HQ: Omnicom Group, Inc.
437 Madison Avenue, New York, NY 10022
Phone: 212 415-3600   **Fax:** 212 415-3393
Web: www.omnicomgroup.com

2017 Sales

	$ mil.	% of total
Americas		
North America	8,686	57
Latin America	494	3
EMEA		
Europe	4,127	27
Middle East and Africa	314	2
Asia Pacific	1,650	11
Total	**15,273**	**100**

PRODUCTS/OPERATIONS

2017 sales

	$ mil.	% of total
Advertising	8,142	53
Customer relationship management	4,819	32
Public relations	1,376	9
Specialty communications	934	6
Total	**15,273**	**100**

Selected Operations

Global advertising networks
  BBDO Worldwide
  DDB Worldwide
  TBWA Worldwide
National advertising agencies
  Goodby Silverstein & Partners (San Francisco)
  GSD&M (Austin TX)
  Martin|Williams (Minneapolis)
  Merkley + Partners (New York City)
  Zimmerman Partners Advertising (Fort Lauderdale FL)
Direct response
  Interbrand (brand identity)
  M/A/R/C Research (market research)
  Rapp (direct marketing)
  Targetbase (direct marketing)
Promotional marketing
  The Beanstalk Group (brand licensing and consulting)
  CPM (field marketing)
  The Integer Group (retail marketing)
  Kaleidoscope (sports and event marketing)
  Millsport (sports and event marketing)
Public relations
  Clark & Weinstock
  Cone
  Fleishman-Hillard
  Gavin Anderson & Company
  GPC International
  Ketchum
  Porter Novelli International
  Smythe Dorward Lambert

Specialty communications
  Adelphi Group (health care)
  Corbett Accel Healthcare (health care)
  Dieste (multicultural marketing)
  Doremus (business-to-business advertising)
  SafirRosetti (security and intelligence)
Media services
  Icon International
  Novus Print Media
  OMD Worldwide
  PHD Network

COMPETITORS

Dentsu	Interpublic Group
Dentsu Aegis	Publicis Groupe
Hakuhodo	WPP
Havas	

HISTORICAL FINANCIALS

Company Type: Public

Income Statement

FYE: December 31

	REVENUE ($ mil.)	NET INCOME ($ mil.)	NET PROFIT MARGIN	EMPLOYEES
12/17	15,273	1,088	7.1%	77,300
12/16	15,416	1,148	7.5%	78,500
12/15	15,134	1,093	7.2%	74,900
12/14	15,317	1,104	7.2%	74,000
12/13	14,584	991	6.8%	71,800
Annual Growth	1.2%	2.4%	—	1.9%

2017 Year-End Financials

Debt ratio: 19.75%	No. of shares (mil.): 230
Return on equity: 45.57%	Dividends
Cash ($ mil.): 3,796	Yield: 0.0%
Current ratio: 0.93	Payout: 48.3%
Long-term debt ($ mil.): 4,912	Market value ($ mil.): 16,758

	STOCK PRICE ($) FY Close	P/E High/Low	PER SHARE ($) Earnings	Dividends	Book Value
12/17	72.83	19 14	4.65	2.25	11.37
12/16	85.11	18 14	4.78	2.15	9.21
12/15	75.66	18 15	4.41	2.00	10.23
12/14	77.47	18 15	4.24	1.90	11.55
12/13	74.37	20 13	3.71	1.60	13.91
Annual Growth	(0.5%)	— —	5.8%	8.9%	(4.9%)

ON Semiconductor Corp

ON Semiconductor?s products manage power use and handle dozens of other functions in an array of electronics. The company designs and manufactures energy efficient low-cost high-volume analog logic and discrete semiconductors. Its product portfolio lists some 84000 devices that perform power and signal control and interface functions in electronic gear ranging from networking routers and wireless phones and digital cameras to household appliances and electronically controlled operations in vehicles. ON Semiconductor sells directly to OEMs including Cisco Systems GE Honeywell Samsung and Siemens and to distributors such as Avnet and Arrow Electronics. Two-thirds of ON Semiconductor's sales come from the Asia/Pacific region.

Operations

ON Semiconductor operates through three segments: the Power Solutions Group the Analog Solutions Group and the Image Sensor Group.

The Power Solutions Group accounts for about 50% of revenue. It offers an array of semiconductor products that regulate power and signal functions including power switching power conversion signal conditioning circuit protection signal amplification and voltage reference functions. Some products help computers use power more efficiently.

The Analog Solutions Group which supplies close to 40% of revenue designs and develops processors designed for specific power-related applications in the automotive consumer computing industrial communications medical and aerospace/defense markets. Some automotive products help reduce emissions.

The Image Sensor Group which generates about 15% of revenue designs and develops products for capturing images. For cameras used in a variety of settings such as automotive ON?s products handle image signal processing and enable auto focus and image stabilization. Markets for the group's products include automotive industrial consumer wireless medical and aerospace/defense.

ON Semiconductor handles much of its own manufacturing but more than a third of its manufacturing expenses go to contract manufacturers that include Amkor ASE and Kingpak.

Geographic Reach
Headquartered in Phoenix Arizona ON Semiconductor operates distribution centers throughout Asia Europe and the Americas. The company conducts research and development in about 20 countries.

ON Semiconductor?s manufacturing plants are in the US the Czech Republic Belgium Malaysia Japan South Korea Canada China Philippines and Vietnam.

Hong Kong and Singapore are the largest markets each accounting for about 30% and 25% of sales respectively.

Sales and Marketing
ON Semiconductor?s products appear in a wide range of end-user markets including automotive communications computing consumer medical industrial networking telecom and aerospace/defense. Automotive is the largest market generating nearly a third of sales followed by Industrial about 25% and Communications about 20%.

ON Semiconductor relies on 10 customers to provide about a quarter of its revenue which could be an issue in the cyclical semiconductor industry.

ON Semiconductor relies on 10 customers to provide about a quarter of its revenue which could be an issue in the cyclical semiconductor industry.

The company works through several sales channels. Distributors including Macnica OS Electronics World Peace and WT Microelectronics account for almost 60% of revenue. Direct sales to original equipment manufacturers account for just under 35% of revenue. Some customers on the OEM roster are Bosch GmbH Continental Automotive Systems Delphi Hella Huawei Technologies Co. Ltd. Magna International Panasonic Corp. and Samsung Electronics. Direct sales to contract manufacturers that include Benchmark Electronics Flex and Jabil supply about 5% of sales.

Financial Performance
ON Semiconductor posted its fifth straight year of rising revenue in 2017 while profit rose for the fourth time in five years.

Revenue jumped about 40% to $5.5 billion in 2017 from 2016. ON reported revenue increases of about 65% and 30% in its Power Solutions Group and Analog Solutions Group respectively. The company counted a full year of sales from the Fairchild acquisition and more than $150 million from a change in revenue recognition on distribu-

tor sales. A drop in Consumer revenue reflected the company?s exit from the consumer image sensor market in 2016. Revenue rose in all geographic markets led by a 64% leap in sales to customers in Hong Kong.

Net income rocketed to $810 million in 2017 from about $182 million the year before on higher revenue and a tax benefit conferred by the US Tax Cuts and Jobs Act of 2017.

Cash on hand slipped to about $950 million in 2017 from about $1 billion in 2016.

Strategy
ON Semiconductor wants to make its biggest market automotive electronics even bigger. The company's automotive products do jobs throughout vehicles including reducing emissions improving fuel economy and safety enhancing lighting and controlling brakes and other systems. New automotive products include image sensors for advanced driver assistance systems (ADAS) and LED lighting.

New products for other markets include power integrated modules USB-C power management for server and cloud environments and other power 7 management analog and sensor products for strategic end-markets.

As with other companies ON Semiconductor has found sales with new smartphone platforms for the Chinese market. Also in the smartphone market the company benefits from the increasing adoption of fast-charging USB-C. On Semiconductor is using its smartphone relationships to cross-sell Fairchild?s products into that market.

ON Semiconductor's recent acquisitions have expanded its product portfolio and opened new markets. The acquisitions include Fairchild AXSEM Truesense Imaging and Aptina.

ON Semiconductor has about $3 billion in debt some of it taken on through the Fairchild acquisition. Paying for its debt could curtail the company?s ability to invest in operations.

Mergers and Acquisitions
ON Semiconductor acquired Fairchild Semiconductor in 2016. The $2.4 billion acquisition has helped On diversify with Fairchild's products for power conversion industrial and automotive markets.

EXECUTIVES

Senior Vice President Human Resources, Colleen McKeown
Vice President And General Manager Of Protection Products Division, Gary Straker
President Ceo And Director, Keith D. Jackson, age 62, $906,154 total compensation
Evp And Coo, William A. (Bill) Schromm, age 60, $444,800 total compensation
Evp General Counsel Chief Compliance Ethics And Risk Officer And Corporate Secretary, George H. (Sonny) Cave, age 60, $366,653 total compensation
Svp And Cto, Hans Stork
Svp Strategic Business Ventures, Mamoon Rashid, $353,329 total compensation
Evp And General Manager Power Solutions Group, William M. (Bill) Hall, age 62, $394,697 total compensation
Evp Sales And Marketing, Paul E. Rolls, age 55, $446,148 total compensation
Evp And General Manager Analog Solutions Group, Robert A. (Bob) Klosterboer, age 57, $340,337 total compensation
Evp And Cfo, Bernard Gutmann, age 58, $470,848 total compensation
Svp And General Manager Of The Image Sensor Group, Taner Ozcelik, age 50
Vice President Sales, Tony Roybal
Senior Vice President Human Resources, Terri Richway

Senior Vice President And Chief Information Officer, Kevin Haskew
Vice President Director Of Internal Manufacturing, Chandra Subramaniam
Vice President Of Finance Fpanda Corporate Business Units, Kelly Neagle
Senior Vice President Quality, Keenan Evans
Svp Global Supply Chain Operations, Brent Wilson
Information Technology Vice President, Ky Puay
Senior Vice President Of Worldwide Operations, Mark Goranson
Vice President And Director Of Manufacturing Technology, Jimmie Echols
Vice President Design, George Smarandoiu
Vice President, Mark Asselberg
Vice President Corporate Program Management And Integrations, Debbie Brogan
Senior Vice President Human Resources, Tobin Cookman
Vice President And Cio, David Wagner
Human Resources Director And Vice President, Robert Wiegand
Vice President Of Sales For Asia Pacific, David Chow
Executive Vice President Sales And Marketing, Bob Mahoney
Executive Vice President And General Manager Power Solutions Group, Bill Hall
Vp Investor Relations And Corporate Development, Parag Agarwal
Legal Secretary, Susan Galpin
Vice President R And D Engineering, James Tornes
Executive Vice President, Donald Colvin
Vice President Device Engineering, Doug Lange
Vice President Global Solutions Engineering, Dave Priscak
Chairman, Alan Campbell, age 59
Board Member, Emmanuel Hernandez
Assistant Treasurer, Matt Brimhall
Board Member, Gilles Delfassy
Board Member, Teresa Ressel
Auditors: PricewaterhouseCoopers LLP

LOCATIONS

HQ: ON Semiconductor Corp
5005 E. McDowell Road, Phoenix, AZ 85008
Phone: 602 244-6600   **Fax:** 602 244-6071
Web: www.onsemi.com

2016 Sales

	$ mil.	% of total
Hong Kong	1,780	32
Singapore	1,466	26
United States	748	14
United Kingdom	688	12
Japan	429	8
Other	444	8
Total	**5,543**	**100**

PRODUCTS/OPERATIONS

2017 Sales

	$ mil.	% of total
Power Solutions Group	2,819	51
Analog Solutions Group	1,950	35
Image Sensor Group	772	14
Total	**5,543**	**100**

2017 Sales

	% of total
Automotive	31
Industrial	25
Communications	20
Consumer	14
Computing	10
Networking	3
Medical	3
Aerospace/Defense	1
Total	**100**

Selected Products

Analog
  Amplifiers and comparators
  Application-specific standard products (ASSPs)
  Interface
  Power management
  Switches
  Thermal management
Discrete
Bipolar power
  Power MOSFETs (metal oxide semiconductor field-effect transistors)
  Rectifiers
  Small-signal diodes and transistors
Logic

COMPETITORS

Altera	Microsemi
Analog Devices	Mitsubishi Electric
Cypress Semiconductor	NXP Semiconductors
Diodes	Power Integrations
ELMOS Semiconductor	ROHM
IBM Microelectronics	Renesas Electronics
IXYS	STMicroelectronics
Infineon Technologies	Semtech
Integrated Device	TSMC
Technology	Texas Instruments
Intersil	Toshiba
Linear Technology	Tower Semiconductor
Littelfuse	Vishay Intertechnology
MagnaChip	X-FAB Silicon
Maxim Integrated	Foundries
Products	Xilinx
Melexis	eSilicon
Microchip Technology	

HISTORICAL FINANCIALS

Company Type: Public

Income Statement

FYE: December 31

	REVENUE ($ mil.)	NET INCOME ($ mil.)	NET PROFIT MARGIN	EMPLOYEES
12/17	5,543	810	14.6%	34,000
12/16	3,906	182	4.7%	32,000
12/15	3,495	206	5.9%	24,500
12/14	3,161	189	6.0%	24,500
12/13	2,782	150	5.4%	22,000
Annual Growth	18.8%	52.3%	—	11.5%

2017 Year-End Financials

Debt ratio: 41.03%
Return on equity: 35.23%
Cash ($ mil.): 949
Current ratio: 2.08
Long-term debt ($ mil.): 2,703

No. of shares (mil.): 425
Dividends
  Yield: —
  Payout: —
Market value ($ mil.): 8,902

	STOCK PRICE ($) FY Close	P/E High/Low		PER SHARE ($) Earnings	Dividends	Book Value
12/17	20.94	11	7	1.89	0.00	6.54
12/16	12.76	30	16	0.43	0.00	4.35
12/15	9.80	27	18	0.48	0.00	3.90
12/14	10.13	24	16	0.43	0.00	3.75
12/13	8.24	26	20	0.34	0.00	3.30
Annual Growth	26.3%	—	—	53.5%	—	18.6%

ONEAMERICA FINANCIAL PARTNERS, INC.

EXECUTIVES

Chb-Pres-Ceo, J Scott Davison
Exec V Pres-Cfo, Jeffrey D Holley
Exec V Pres, Mark Roller
Exec V Pres-Sr Clo-SEC, Thomas M Zurek
Sr V Pres-CIO, Gene P Berry
Sr V Pres-Chief Hr Officer, Karin Sarratt
Pres Individual Insurance, Patrick M Foley
Vice President, Angela Trefethen
Consultant, Bartholomew Brown
Assistant Vice President, Brian Springer
Manager Public Relations Tax, Christina Cozzolino

LOCATIONS

HQ: ONEAMERICA FINANCIAL PARTNERS, INC.
  1 AMERICAN SQ, INDIANAPOLIS, IN 462820020
Phone: 317 285-1877
Web: WWW.ONEAMERICA.COM

HISTORICAL FINANCIALS

Company Type: Private

Income Statement

FYE: December 31

	ASSETS ($ mil.)	NET INCOME ($ mil.)	INCOME AS % OF ASSETS	EMPLOYEES
12/16	19,921	88	0.4%	9,875
12/15	18,491	67	0.4%	
12/14	0	0	—	
12/04	15,028	56	0.4%	
Annual Growth	2.4%	3.8%	—	—

2016 Year-End Financials

Debt ratio: ——
Return on equity: 8.00%
Cash ($ mil.): 152
Current ratio: —
Long-term debt ($ mil.): —

Dividends
  Yield: —
  Payout: —
Market value ($ mil.): —

OneMain Holdings Inc

OneMain Holdings makes consumer loans its one main priority. Formerly known as Springleaf Holdings the consumer finance company offers auto loans and personal loans to high-risk customers who have limited access to credit from banks credit card companies and other lenders through 1800 branches in around 45 states. In addition it provides credit insurance non-credit insurance and related products through subsidiaries Merit Life Insurance AHL Triton and Yosemite Insurance. Tracing its roots back to 1920 the company renamed itself in late 2015 after acquiring OneMain Financial.

Operations

OneMain Holdings' Consumer and Insurance division mostly makes and services personal loans and auto loans (typically ranging from $1500 to $25000+). It offers credit insurance (also known as payment protection insurance) an optional add-on for borrowers to ensure repayment even if they can't repay the loan. It also offers non-credit insurance (auto membership plans). The company has

$13.6 billion in personal loan assets due from more than 2.4 million customers.

Geographic Reach

The Evansville Indiana-based company serves customers across the US and has servicing facilities in Mendota Heights Minnesota; Tempe Arizona; London Kentucky; Fort Mill South Carolina; and Irving and Fort Worth Texas.

Sales and Marketing

OneMain Holdings is aggressive in targeting high-risk borrowers who might be reluctant to seek financing. It uses direct mail offers banner ads search engine optimization and telephone sales to solicit new prospects. Mail solicitations include pre-qualified offers of guaranteed personal loan credit. The company purchases lists of potential borrowers based on predetermined criteria such as credit scores.

Financial Performance

The company's revenues climbed from $2.2 billion in 2015 to $3.9 billion in 2016 mainly due to its 2015's OneMain Financial acquisition and the continued growth of its loan portfolio (primarily secured personal loans).

After suffering a net loss of $242 million in 2015 in part due to acquisition-related costs OneMain Holdings posted net income of $215 million in 2016.

Strategy

OneMain Holdings acquires consumer loan origination and servicing companies to grow its personal loan assets and overall business. The company's late 2015 acquisition of OneMain Financial which led it to change its name from Springleaf Holdings to its current name doubled its branch network and made it one of the largest sub-prime lenders in the US.

It also seeks to simplify its balance sheet and focus on its core operations. In mid-2016 it sold its SpringCastle Portfolio which held unsecured loans and loans secured by sub-prime residential mortgages consisting of 232000-plus acquired loans totaling $1.7 billion in net finance receivables.

Mergers and Acquisitions

In late 2015 the company purchased OneMain Financial from Citigroup's CitiFinancial Credit Company for $4.45 billion which more than doubled its branch network from 831 to nearly 1800 and made it one of the nation's largest sub-prime lenders.

EXECUTIVES

Evp Legal Compliance And Operational Risk, John C. Anderson, age 60, $350,000 total compensation
President And Ceo, Jay N. Levine, age 56, $400,000 total compensation
Evp And Cfo, Scott T. Parker, age 51, $400,000 total compensation
Evp Branch Operations, Bradford D. Borchers, age 54, $350,000 total compensation
Evp Credit And Analytics, David P. Hogan, age 49, $350,000 total compensation
Evp And Coo, Robert A. Hurzeler, age 57, $350,000 total compensation
Evp And Chief Administrative Officer, Lawrence N. Skeats, age 53, $336,539 total compensation
Evp Human Resources, Angela Celestin, age 47, $26,442 total compensation
Vice President Technology Infrastructure, Thomas Kissel
Vice President Application Systems, David Smith
Senior Vice President Marketing, Hari Lymon
Vice President Business Development And Strategic Partnerships, Judith Thompson
Vice President And Director Direct Marketing, Meagan Sermersheim
Chairman, Wesley R. (Wes) Edens, age 56
Auditors: PricewaterhouseCoopers LLP

LOCATIONS

HQ: OneMain Holdings Inc
601 N.W. Second Street, Evansville, IN 47708
Phone: 812 424-8031
Web: www.onemainfinancial.com

PRODUCTS/OPERATIONS

2016 Sales

	$ mil.	% of total
Consumer and Insurance	3,940	92
Acquisition and Serving	318	8
Real Estate	18	-
Others	(5)	-
Adjustments	(388)	-
Total	**3,883**	**100**

COMPETITORS

Advance America
Atlanticus
Check 'n Go
Check Into Cash
Community Choice Financial
DFC Global
EZCORP
FirstCash
NetSpend
QC Holdings
Regional Management
Security Finance Corporation of Spartanburg
World Acceptance
Xponential

HISTORICAL FINANCIALS

Company Type: Public

Income Statement

FYE: December 31

	ASSETS ($ mil.)	NET INCOME ($ mil.)	INCOME AS % OF ASSETS	EMPLOYEES
12/17	19,433	183	0.9%	10,100
12/16	18,123	215	1.2%	10,100
12/15	21,056	(242)	—	11,400
12/14	11,057	504	4.6%	5,030
12/13	15,402	(19)	—	4,900
Annual Growth	**6.0%**	—	—	**19.8%**

2017 Year-End Financials

Debt ratio: 77.45%
Return on equity: 5.77%
Cash ($ mil.): 987
Current ratio: —
Long-term debt ($ mil.): —

No. of shares (mil.): 135
Dividends
Yield: —
Payout: —
Market value ($ mil.): 3,518

	STOCK PRICE ($) FY Close	P/E High/Low		PER SHARE ($) Earnings	Dividends	Book Value
12/17	25.99	24	16	1.35	0.00	24.22
12/16	22.14	26	11	1.59	0.00	22.73
12/15	41.54	—	—	(1.89)	0.00	20.45
12/14	36.17	9	5	4.38	0.00	17.64
12/13	25.28	—	—	(0.19)	0.00	13.42
Annual Growth	**0.7%**		—	—	—	**15.9%**

ONEOK Inc

ONEOK (?one oak?) is having a gas pursuing its pipeline dreams. ONEOK is an Oklahoma-based midstream natural gas corporation that plays a key role in transforming and transporting natural gas from exploration & producer (E&P) businesses to downstream customers such as refiners and petrochemical companies. Through its primary subsidiary ONEOK Partners its operations include a 38000-mile integrated network of natural gas and natural gas liquid (NGL) pipelines processing plants fractionators and storage facilities in the Mid-Continent Williston Permian and Rocky Mountain regions. In recent years ONEOK divested its commercial and residential natural gas delivery company ONE Gas and purchased all outstanding shares of its key master limited partnership ONEOK Partners and absorbed it into ONEOK.

HISTORY

In 1906 Oklahoma Natural Gas (ONG) was founded to pipe natural gas from northeastern Oklahoma to Oklahoma City. A 100-mile pipeline was completed the next year. In 1921 ONG created two oil companies to pump out the oil it found as a result of its natural gas exploration.

ONG changed hands many times in the 1920s ending up with utility financier G. L. Ohrstrom and Company which milked it dry by brokering acquisitions (purchasing gas properties and then selling them to ONG) and collecting fees. Stock sales drove revenues inflating the stock's price and the inflated price triggered more stock sales. The bubble burst on October 29 1929. A series of leadership changes ensued and in 1932 the company was dissolved and reincorporated. Under president Joseph Bowes ONG recovered wooing back dissatisfied customers and upgrading its pipelines.

In the late 1930s the company pioneered a type of underground storage that injected gas into depleted gas reservoirs in the summer and withdrew it during winter's peak use times.

The 1950s and 1960s saw the company expand. In 1962 it created its first subsidiary Oklahoma Natural Gas Gathering Company selling gas out of state and therefore subject to federal regulation.

ONG was not affected in the lean 1970s by federal laws that kept wellhead prices low for gas transported across state lines because its main operations were confined to Oklahoma. Congress deregulated wellhead prices in 1978 spurring exploration but causing great price fluctuations in the 1980s. In 1980 ONG changed its name to ONEOK.

In the 1980s ONEOK signed take-or-pay contracts which forced it to pay for gas offered by its suppliers even if it had no customers. When recession in the 1980s caused demand to drop ONEOK had to pay for high-priced natural gas it couldn't sell. In 1988 the company was ordered to pay some $50 million to supplier Forest Oil of Denver. A year later ONEOK was sued for allegedly failing to tell stockholders about the take-or-pay agreements (settled in 1993 for $5.5 million). It later sold more than half of its oil and gas reserves to Mustang Energy for $52 million to finance the Forest Oil court award. The company was still settling lawsuits over the agreements into the 1990s; it settled the last of the claims by 1998.

ONEOK began buying gas transmission and production facilities in Oklahoma and creating drilling alliances in the 1990s. In 1997 ONEOK bought the natural gas assets of Westar Energy formerly Western Resources for $660 million and ONEOK stock worth $800 million. The acquisition doubled the number of ONEOK's customers and increased its gas marketing gathering and transmission operations.

The company also acquired Southern Union's Texas natural gas distribution business (540000 customers) as well as Southern Union's stake in a Mexican gas utility and its propane distribution gas marketing and gas transmission operations in the southwestern US for $420 million.

ONEOK acquired Northern Plains Natural Gas a general partner of pipeline operator Northern Border Partners (later renamed ONEOK Partners) from CCE Holdings (a joint venture of Southern Union and GE Commercial Finance) for $175 million in 2004. The transaction followed CCE Holdings' acquisition of Enron's CrossCountry Energy unit.

Also in 2004 ONEOK changed the name of its wholesale energy unit from ONEOK Energy Marketing and Trading to ONEOK Energy Services.

The company bought Koch Industries' natural gas liquids assets in 2005 for $1.35 billion.

EXECUTIVES

Vice President Information Technology, James Fallon
Evp And Chief Administrative Officer, Robert F. (Rob) Martinovich, age 60, $500,000 total compensation
President And Ceo, Terry K. Spencer, age 58, $700,000 total compensation
Svp Operations, Wesley J. Christensen, age 64, $400,000 total compensation
Svp Cfo And Treasurer, Derek S. Reiners, age 47, $375,000 total compensation
Svp Natural Gas Gathering And Processing, Kevin L. Burdick, age 53
Vp And Cio, Brien H. Brown
Vp Natural Gas Pipelines, J. Phillip (Phill) May
Evp Strategic Planning And Corporate Affairs, Walter S. Hulse, age 54, $500,000 total compensation
Svp Natural Gas Liquids Oneok Partners, Sheridan C. Swords
Vice President Commercial G And P, Michael A Fitzgibbons
Vp Ngl Fractionation, Jeremy Wiese
Vice President Government Relations, Steve Johnson
Vice President, Walter Allen
Vice President Project Development And Business Analysis, Michael Crisman
Vice President Technology Fixed Income, Jackie Mitchell
Vice President Sales And Marketing, Carl Holliday
Vice President Marketing Oneok Energy Resources, George Drake
Vice President And Associate General Counsel, Stephen B Allen
Vice President Interactive Marketing, Randy Jordan
Vice President Information Technology, Robert Mareburter
Vice President Natural Gas Liquids Optimization, John O'Dell
Vice President Information Technology, Kevin Burbick
Senior Vice President, Dan Harrison
Vice President Information Technology, Winsford Spears
Senior Vice President Pipelines, Mike Nelson
Vice President Of Investor Relations And Public Affairs, Dan L Harrison
Svp Natural Gas Pipelines, J Philip May
Vp Commercial Interstate Pipelines Segment, Philip May
Vice President Associate General Counsel, Brandon Watson
Vp And Chief Accounting Officer, Sheppard Miers Ii
Chairman Oneok Oneok Partners And One Gas, John W. Gibson, age 65
Board Member, Steve Malcolm
Member Board Of Directors, Brian Derksen
Auditors: PricewaterhouseCoopers LLP

LOCATIONS

HQ: ONEOK Inc
  100 West Fifth Street, Tulsa, OK 74103
Phone: 918 588-7000   **Fax:** 918 588-7273
Web: www.oneok.com

PRODUCTS/OPERATIONS

2016 Sales

	$ mil.	% of total
Natural Gas Liquids	7,675	76
Natural Gas Gathering and Processing	2,051	20
Natural Gas Pipeline	379	4
Reconciled Intersegment Revenues	(1185.7)	-
Total	**8,920**	**0**

COMPETITORS

BP	Exxon Mobil
DCP Midstream Partners	National Fuel Gas
EQT Corporation	SemGroup
Enable Midstream	Southwest Gas
Partners	TRII
Enterprise Products	Williams Companies

HISTORICAL FINANCIALS

Company Type: Public

Income Statement   FYE: December 31

	REVENUE ($ mil.)	NET INCOME ($ mil.)	NET PROFIT MARGIN	EMPLOYEES
12/17	12,173	387	3.2%	2,470
12/16	8,920	352	3.9%	2,384
12/15	7,763	244	3.2%	2,364
12/14	12,195	314	2.6%	2,269
12/13	14,602	266	1.8%	1,927
Annual Growth	(4.4%)	9.8%	—	6.4%

2017 Year-End Financials

Debt ratio: 54.25%
Return on equity: 13.57%
Cash ($ mil.): 37
Current ratio: 0.66
Long-term debt ($ mil.): 8,091

No. of shares (mil.): 388
Dividends
  Yield: 0.0%
  Payout: 210.8%
Market value ($ mil.): 20,776

	STOCK PRICE ($) FY Close	P/E High/Low	Earnings	Dividends	Book Value
12/17	53.45	45 36	1.29	2.72	14.22
12/16	57.41	35 12	1.66	2.46	0.90
12/15	24.66	44 16	1.16	2.43	1.60
12/14	49.79	47 30	1.49	2.13	2.84
12/13	62.18	48 31	1.27	1.48	11.31
Annual Growth	(3.7%)	— —	0.4%	16.4%	5.9%

ONEOK PARTNERS, L.P.

For ONEOK Partners it's OK to have three businesses: natural gas pipelines; gas gathering and processing; and natural gas liquids (NGLs). Its pipelines include Midwestern Gas Transmission Guardian Pipeline Viking Gas Transmission and OkTex Pipeline. The ONEOK affiliate operates 17100 miles of gas-gathering pipeline and 7600 miles of transportation pipeline as well as gas processing plants and storage facilities (with 52 billion cu. ft. of capacity). It also owns one of the US's top natural NGL systems (more than 7200 miles of pipeline). In 2017 41%-owner ONEOK agreed to buy the stock of ONEOK Partners that it did not already own for $9.3 billion in a stock deal.   Operations ONEOK Partners operates in three busi-

ness segments: natural gas gathering and processing; natural gas pipelines; and natural gas liquids.
Geographic Reach   The company gathers and processes natural gas in the Mid-Continent region which includes the NGL-rich Cana-Woodford Shale and Granite Wash formations the Mississippian Lime formation of Oklahoma and Kansas and the Hugoton and Central Kansas Uplift Basins of Kansas. The Natural Gas Pipelines segment owns and operates regulated natural gas transmission pipelines natural gas storage facilities and natural gas gathering systems for nonprocessed gas. It also provide interstate natural gas transportation and storage service. The company's interstate natural gas pipeline assets transport natural gas through pipelines in North Dakota Minnesota Wisconsin Illinois Indiana Kentucky Tennessee Oklahoma Texas and New Mexico. Its Natural gas liquids assets provide nondiscretionary services to producers that consist of facilities that gather fractionate and treat NGLs and store NGL products primarily in Oklahoma Kansas and Texas. It also owns or has stakes in natural gas liquids gathering and distribution pipelines in Oklahoma Kansas Texas Wyoming and Colorado and terminal and storage facilities in Missouri Nebraska Iowa and Illinois. In addition it owns natural gas liquids distribution and refined petroleum products pipelines in Kansas Missouri Nebraska Iowa Illinois and Indiana that connect the company's Mid-Continent assets with Midwest markets including Chicago.

Financial Performance
Revenues decreased by 10% in 2012 due to lower net realized natural gas and NGL product prices offset partially by higher natural gas and NGL sales volumes from completed capital projects. The increase in natural gas supply resulting from the development of nonconventional resource areas in North America and a warmer than normal winter caused natural gas prices to drop. NGL prices particularly ethane and propane also decreased in 2012 due primarily to increased NGL production and an increase in available supply. Propane prices also were affected by a warmer than normal winter.
ONEOK Partners' net income grew by 7% in 2012 thanks to lower costs of sales and fuels and lower interest expenses.

Strategy
The company pursues a strategy of building up its fee-based earnings coupled with organic growth and complementary acquisitions in both conventional oil and gas and unconventional (shale plays).
It is looking to increase NGL volumes gathered and fractionated in its NGL segment and natural gas volumes processed in its natural gas gathering and processing segment as producers continue to develop NGL-rich resource plays in the Mid-Continent and Rocky Mountain areas.
In 2012 ONEOK Partners announced plans to invest up to $360 million to grow its projects in the Woodford Shale formation.

Company Background
ONEOK Partners was formed in 2006 when ONEOK spun off its gathering and processing NGLs pipelines and storage businesses for $3 billion following that company's acquisition of Northern Border Partners (which was founded in 1993). Building out its assets in 2007 the company acquired an interstate pipeline system from Kinder Morgan Energy Partners for $300 million.

EXECUTIVES

Pres-Ceo, Terry K Spencer
Evp-Cfo, Walter S Hulse III
Svp,naturalgasgathering&procce, Michael A Fitzgibbons
Executive Vice President Opera, Robert F Martinovich

LOCATIONS

HQ: ONEOK PARTNERS, L.P.
  100 W 5TH ST STE LL, TULSA, OK 741034298
Phone: 918 588-7000
Web: WWW.ONEOKPARTNERS.COM

PRODUCTS/OPERATIONS

Natural Gas Pipelines
Midwestern Gas Transmission Company
Viking Gas Transmission Company
Guardian Pipeline
OkTex Pipeline Company
ONEOK Gas Transportation
ONEOK Gas Gathering
ONEOK Gas Storage
ONEOK WesTex Transmission
ONEOK Texas Gas Storage
Mid Continent Market Center
ONEOK Transmission Company
Natural Gas Gathering & Processing
Crestone Energy Ventures
ONEOK Field Services
ONEOK Rockies Midstream

COMPETITORS

Enbridge	Panhandle Eastern Pipe
Kinder Morgan Energy	Line
Partners	TransCanada

HISTORICAL FINANCIALS

Company Type: Private

Income Statement   FYE: December 31

	REVENUE ($ mil.)	NET INCOME ($ mil.)	NET PROFIT MARGIN	EMPLOYEES
12/16	8,918	1,072	12.0%	2,364
12/15	7,761	597	7.7%	—
12/14	12,191	911	7.5%	—
Annual Growth	(14.5%)	8.5%	—	—

2016 Year-End Financials

Debt ratio: —
Return on equity: 12.00%
Cash ($ mil.): 0
Current ratio: 0.30
Long-term debt ($ mil.): —

Dividends
  Yield: —
  Payout: —
Market value ($ mil.): —

Opus Bank (Irvine, CA)

Auditors: KPMG LLP

LOCATIONS

HQ: Opus Bank (Irvine, CA)
  19900 MacArthur Blvd., 12th Floor, Irvine, CA 92612
Phone: 949 250-9800
Web: www.opusbank.com

HISTORICAL FINANCIALS

Company Type: Public

Income Statement   FYE: December 31

	ASSETS ($ mil.)	NET INCOME ($ mil.)	INCOME AS % OF ASSETS	EMPLOYEES
12/17	7,486	47	0.6%	797
12/16	7,882	11	0.1%	835
12/15	6,649	59	0.9%	661
12/14	5,084	43	0.9%	585
12/13	3,738	143	3.8%	550
Annual Growth	19.0%	(24.0%)	—	9.7%

2017 Year-End Financials

Debt ratio: 1.77%
Return on equity: 4.89%
Cash ($ mil.): 500
Current ratio: —
Long-term debt ($ mil.): —

No. of shares (mil.): 35
Dividends
Yield: —
Payout: —
Market value ($ mil.): 980

	STOCK PRICE ($) FY Close	P/E High/Low		PER SHARE ($) Earnings	Dividends	Book Value
12/17	27.30	23	14	1.26	0.00	28.50
12/16	30.05	112	58	0.33	0.53	27.01
12/15	36.97	21	13	1.79	0.34	26.68
12/14	28.37	22	18	1.38	0.00	28.41
Annual Growth	(1.0%)	—	—	(2.2%)	—	0.1%

Oracle Corp

EXECUTIVES

Ceo, Safra A Catz
Chb-Cto*, Lawrence J Ellison
V Chb*, Jeffrey O Henley
Ceo*, Mark V Hurd
Exec V Pres-General Counsel-SE, Dorian E Daley
Exec V Pres-Corp Contrl-Cao, William Corey West
Senior Manager Information TEC, Bennie Hayes
Senior Vice President, Cliff Godwin
Director For Java Elec, Dennis Macneil
Manager It Operation, Derek Bray
Vice President, Donald Deutsch
Auditors: Ernst & Young LLP

LOCATIONS

HQ: Oracle Corp
500 Oracle Parkway, Redwood City, CA 94065
Phone: 650 506-7000
Web: www.oracle.com

COMPETITORS

ADP	Manhattan Associates
Accenture	MicroStrategy
BMC Software	Microsoft
CA Inc.	NCR
CDC Software	Novell
Ceridian	Open Text
Cisco Systems	Pegasystems
Courion	Progress Software
Dell Software	Red Hat
EMC	SAP
Fujitsu Technology Solutions	SAS Institute
	SOA Software
HP Autonomy	Sage Group
Hewlett-Packard	Software AG
Hitachi	SuccessFactors
IBM	TIBCO Software
Infor Global	Taleo
Informatica	Teradata
Intel	Workday Inc.
JDA Software	salesforce.com
JasperSoft	

HISTORICAL FINANCIALS

Company Type: Public

Income Statement

FYE: May 31

	REVENUE ($ mil.)	NET INCOME ($ mil.)	NET PROFIT MARGIN	EMPLOYEES
05/18	39,831	3,825	9.6%	137,000
05/17	37,728	9,335	24.7%	138,000
05/16	37,047	8,901	24.0%	136,000
05/15	38,226	9,938	26.0%	132,000
05/14	38,275	10,955	28.6%	122,000
Annual Growth	1.0%	(23.1%)	—	2.9%

2018 Year-End Financials

Debt ratio: 44.16%
Return on equity: 7.68%
Cash ($ mil.): 21,620
Current ratio: 3.96
Long-term debt ($ mil.): 56,128

Dividends
Yield: 1.6%
Payout: 84.4%
Market value ($ mil.): —

	STOCK PRICE ($) FY Close	P/E High/Low		PER SHARE ($) Earnings	Dividends	Book Value
05/18	46.72	57	48	0.90	0.76	11.44
05/17	45.39	20	17	2.21	0.64	13.02
05/16	40.20	21	16	2.07	0.60	11.45
05/15	43.49	20	17	2.21	0.51	11.20
05/14	42.02	17	12	2.38	0.48	10.50
Annual Growth	2.7%	—	—	(21.6%)	12.2%	2.2%

Origin Bancorp Inc

Auditors: BKD, LLP

LOCATIONS

HQ: Origin Bancorp Inc
500 South Service Road East, Ruston, LA 71270
Phone: 318 255-2222
Web: www.origin.bank

HISTORICAL FINANCIALS

Company Type: Public

Income Statement

FYE: December 31

	ASSETS ($ mil.)	NET INCOME ($ mil.)	INCOME AS % OF ASSETS	EMPLOYEES
12/17	4,154	14	0.4%	686
12/16	4,071	12	0.3%	—
Annual Growth	2.0%	14.2%		

2017 Year-End Financials

Debt ratio: 0.23%
Return on equity: 3.49%
Cash ($ mil.): 187
Current ratio: —
Long-term debt ($ mil.): —

No. of shares (mil.): 19
Dividends
Yield: —
Payout: 26.0%
Market value ($ mil.): —

	STOCK PRICE ($) FY Close	P/E High/Low		PER SHARE ($) Earnings	Dividends	Book Value
12/17	0.00	—	—	0.50	0.13	23.33
12/16	0.00	—	—	0.46	0.13	23.03
/0.00	—	—	(0.00)	0.00	(0.00)	
Annual Growth	—	—	—	—	—	

Oritani Financial Corp (DE)

EXECUTIVES

Chb-Pres-Ceo, Kevin J Lynch
Exec V Pres-Cfo, John M Fields Jr
Exec V Pres-Clo, Thomas Guinan
Sr V Pres-SEC, Philip M Wyks
Sr V Pres-Commercial Lending O, Kurt Breitenstein
Sr V Pres-Retail Banking Offic, Michele M Calise
V Pres-CIO, Paul C Skinner
Evp-Chief Credit-Risk Officer, Louis A Manderino
Svp-Cao, Ann Marie Jetton
Svp-Human Resources Officer, Anne Mooradian
Vp, Paul M Cordero
Auditors: Crowe LLP

LOCATIONS

HQ: Oritani Financial Corp (DE)
370 Pascack Road, Township of Washington, NJ 07676
Phone: 201 664-5400
Web: www.oritani.com

COMPETITORS

1st Colonial Bancorp	Sun Bancorp (NJ)
Hudson City Bancorp	Valley National
OceanFirst Financial	Bancorp
Provident Financial Services	

HISTORICAL FINANCIALS

Company Type: Public

Income Statement

FYE: June 30

	ASSETS ($ mil.)	NET INCOME ($ mil.)	INCOME AS % OF ASSETS	EMPLOYEES
06/18	4,167	42	1.0%	250
06/17	4,137	49	1.2%	245
06/16	3,669	52	1.4%	238
06/15	3,353	46	1.4%	235
06/14	3,140	41	1.3%	233
Annual Growth	7.3%	1.1%	—	1.8%

2018 Year-End Financials

Debt ratio: 14.31%
Return on equity: 7.67%
Cash ($ mil.): 34
Current ratio: —
Long-term debt ($ mil.): —

No. of shares (mil.): 46
Dividends
Yield: 0.0%
Payout: 136.8%
Market value ($ mil.): 755

	STOCK PRICE ($) FY Close	P/E High/Low		PER SHARE ($) Earnings	Dividends	Book Value
06/18	16.20	18	16	0.95	1.30	12.00
06/17	17.05	17	14	1.10	1.20	12.16
06/16	15.99	14	12	1.21	1.20	11.83
06/15	16.05	14	12	1.10	0.95	11.76
06/14	15.39	17	15	0.94	0.95	11.57
Annual Growth	1.3%	—	—	0.3%	8.2%	0.9%

Orrstown Financial Services, Inc.

EXECUTIVES

Pres-Ceo, Thomas R Quinn Jr
Chb, Joel R Zullinger
V Chb, Jeffrey W Coy
Exec V Pres-Cfo, David P Boyle
Chief Operations, Benjamin W Wallace
Sr V Pres-Cao, Douglas P Barton
Evp-Asst SEC, Philip E Fague
Evp-Chief Risk-Credit Officer, Robert G Coradi
Evp-Chief Hr Officer, Barbara E Brobst
Evp,market President, Jeffrey S Gayman
Executive Vice President and C, David Boyle
Auditors: Crowe Horwath LLP

LOCATIONS

HQ: Orrstown Financial Services, Inc.
77 East King Street, P.O. Box 250, Shippensburg, PA 17257
Phone: 717 532-6114
Web: www.orrstown.com

COMPETITORS

Citizens Financial Group
Franklin Financial Services

M&T Bank
PNC Financial
Sovereign Bank

HISTORICAL FINANCIALS

Company Type: Public

Income Statement
FYE: December 31

	ASSETS ($ mil.)	NET INCOME ($ mil.)	INCOME AS % OF ASSETS	EMPLOYEES
12/17	1,558	8	0.5%	338
12/16	1,414	6	0.5%	327
12/15	1,292	7	0.6%	306
12/14	1,190	29	2.4%	312
12/13	1,177	10	0.8%	344
Annual Growth	7.3%	(5.2%)	—	(0.4%)

2017 Year-End Financials

Debt ratio: —
Return on equity: 5.79%
Cash ($ mil.): 29
Current ratio: —
Long-term debt ($ mil.): —

No. of shares (mil.): 8
Dividends
Yield: 0.0%
Payout: 42.8%
Market value ($ mil.): 211

	STOCK PRICE ($) FY Close	P/E High/Low		PER SHARE ($) Earnings	Dividends	Book Value
12/17	25.25	27	20	0.98	0.42	17.34
12/16	22.40	29	20	0.81	0.35	16.28
12/15	17.84	19	16	0.97	0.22	16.08
12/14	17.00	5	4	3.59	0.00	15.40
12/13	16.35	14	8	1.24	0.00	11.28
Annual Growth	11.5%		—	—	(5.7%)	— 11.4%

Oshkosh Corp (New)

EXECUTIVES

Pres-Ceo, Wilson R Jones
Chb*, Craig P Omtvedt
Exec V Pres-Cfo, David M Sagehorn

Exec V Pres-Gen Counsel-Sec, Ignacio A Cortina
Sr V Pres-Cmo, Bryan K Brandt
Sr V Pres-CIO, Anupam Khare
Evp-Pres Defense Segment, John J Bryant
Evp-Pres Fire & Emergency, James W Johnson
Evp Gov't Oprs & Industry Rel, Joseph H Kimmitt
Evp-Pres Access Equipment Svcs, Frank R Nerenhausen
Evp-Chief Hr Officer, Robert H Sims
Auditors: DELOITTE & TOUCHE LLP

LOCATIONS

HQ: Oshkosh Corp (New)
P.O. Box 2566, Oshkosh, WI 54903-2566
Phone: 920 235-9151
Web: www.oshkoshcorporation.com

COMPETITORS

AM General
American LaFrance
BAE Systems Land & Armaments
Collins Industries
Daimler
Daimler Trucks North America
Dover Corp.
E-ONE
Federal Signal
Force Protection
General Dynamics Land Systems
Haulotte
Heil Environmental
Hyundai Motor

Iveco S.p.A.
J C Bamford Excavators
L-3 Communications
Leyland Trucks
MAN
MANITOU BF
Mack Trucks
Miller Industries
Navistar
Navistar International
PACCAR
Skyjack
Spartan Motors
Terex
Trinity Industries
UD Trucks
Volvo

HISTORICAL FINANCIALS

Company Type: Public

Income Statement
FYE: September 30

	REVENUE ($ mil.)	NET INCOME ($ mil.)	NET PROFIT MARGIN	EMPLOYEES
09/18	7,705	471	6.1%	15,000
09/17	6,829	285	4.2%	14,000
09/16	6,279	216	3.4%	13,800
09/15	6,098	229	3.8%	13,300
09/14	6,808	309	4.5%	12,000
Annual Growth	3.1%	11.1%	—	5.7%

2018 Year-End Financials

Debt ratio: 15.45%
Return on equity: 19.58%
Cash ($ mil.): 454
Current ratio: 1.93
Long-term debt ($ mil.): 818

No. of shares (mil.): 72
Dividends
Yield: 0.0%
Payout: 15.2%
Market value ($ mil.): 5,156

	STOCK PRICE ($) FY Close	P/E High/Low		PER SHARE ($) Earnings	Dividends	Book Value
09/18	71.24	15	11	6.29	0.96	34.73
09/17	82.54	22	14	3.77	0.84	30.76
09/16	56.00	19	10	2.91	0.74	26.74
09/15	36.33	19	12	2.90	0.68	25.33
09/14	44.15	16	12	3.61	0.15	24.86
Annual Growth	12.7%		— —	14.9%	59.1%	8.7%

Owens & Minor, Inc.

Owens & Minor (O&M) is a leading distributor of medical and surgical supplies. The company carries products from about 1100 manufacturers; those products include surgical dressings endoscopic and intravenous products needles syringes sterile procedure trays gowns gloves and sutures. The firm also provides kitting consulting and other services to help customers manage their supplies. O&M primarily serves hospitals and health systems and the purchasing organizations that serve them. It delivers products to roughly 3000 health care providers across the US (where most of its sales are made).

Operations

O&M operates in three segments: Domestic (more than 90% of revenue) International and Proprietary Products (formerly Clinical & Procedural Solutions).

The Domestic segment provides distribution packaging and logistics services in the US while the International segment comprises its European third-party logistics and packaging businesses. The Proprietary Products segment gathers assembles and delivers procedure kits for surgical specialties (including robotics cardiology and orthopedics) and minor procedures.

In addition to delivering products made by its supply partners the distributor sells value products under its own MediChoice label. To support its distribution operations O&M offers training programs for health professionals on topics ranging from equipment use supply management leadership and safety.

O&M's supply chain management services include third-party logistics services for medical device and pharmaceutical firms. Such services are provided by subsidiaries OM HealthCare Logistics (in the US) and Movianto (in Europe).

Geographic Reach

O&M operates some 50 distribution centers across the US.

Though US operations account for most of O&M's sales (more than 90%) the company is working to branch out into international medical distribution markets including Europe. Its International unit operates 20 logistics centers in about a dozen European countries including Belgium the Czech Republic Denmark France Germany Italy the Netherlands Poland Slovakia Spain Switzerland and the UK.

Sales and Marketing

Most of O&M's sales are attributed to contracts with acute care hospitals which are often represented by group purchasing organizations (GPOs) or integrated delivery networks (IDNs). GPOs Premier and HealthTrust Purchasing Group are the company's largest customers. Additional clients include other government agencies and alternate health care locations such as physician clinics nursing homes and surgery centers. In addition O&M provides outsourced distribution services to suppliers of surgical and medical products.

About 80% of O&M's sales come from the distribution of medical supplies. The company's major product suppliers include Covidien Johnson & Johnson and Becton Dickson; those firms account for some 10% of sales each.

Financial Performance

O&M's revenues have remained relatively static over the past few years. Net income has been a bit more erratic rising and falling as a result of various acquisitions made. The company's long-term debt has been on the rise and it reached $901 million by the end of 2017.

In 2017 revenue dropped 4% to $9.3 billion. The company lost a major customer in 2016 and manufacturer product price changes cut into income. Additionally the International segment has been operating at a loss as O&M invests in building up that business. Finally Proprietary Products production costs increased that year while sales dropped.

Net income fell 33% to $73 million in 2017. In addition to the lower revenue the acquisition of Byram Healthcare and preparation for the acquisition of certain operations of Halyard Health cut into the firm's bottom line. Restructuring costs rose 85% to $43.4 million; these costs were related to workforce reductions and IT restructuring activities. (The company expects these types of expenses to impact earnings in 2018 as well.)

The company ended 2017 with $104.5 million in net cash 44% less than it had at the end of 2016. Financing activities such as the issuance of debt provided $272.8 million and operating activities provided $56.8 million. Investing activities used $416.6 million.

Strategy

As the health care industry has come under pressure so have the industries that serve it. To stay competitive in a struggling market O&M restructured its operations and realigned its leadership team in 2016. Its new strategies for growth include streamlining the distribution of medical supplies by utilizing technology productivity tools and data connectivity. O&M is working to further expand into patient settings beyond hospitals such as surgery centers clinics and other non-acute care facilities that can benefit from its offerings.

The company also works with manufacturers for whom it strives to be the delivery mechanism of choice. Finally O&M complements its product sales services by offering resource management services to care providers including physical inventory reviews inventory tracking and purchasing software.

Mergers and Acquisitions

In 2018 O&M bought the surgical and infection prevention operations of medical supplies maker Halyard Health for $710 million. The purchase included products including sterilization wraps surgical gowns and medical exam gloves.

In 2017 O&M acquired Byram Healthcare for $380 million. Byram is a nationwide distributor of direct-to-patient medical supplies including wound care incontinence and diabetes supplies.

HISTORY

George Gilmer Minor Jr.'s great-grandfather was an apothecary and surgeon in colonial Williamsburg Virginia. His grandfather was Thomas Jefferson's personal physician. Minor himself worked as a wholesale drug salesman in Richmond after the Civil War. In 1882 he and rival wholesaler Otho Owens partnered to form the Owens & Minor Drug Company. The company was both a retail and wholesale business with a storefront that filled prescriptions and sold sundries paints oils and window glass. When Owens died in 1906 Minor became the company's president.

During the 1920s the Owens family sold their stake in the firm. George Gilmer Minor III served briefly as the company's president in the early 1940s; his son George Gilmer Minor IV (called Mr. Minor Jr. to differentiate him from his father) became president in 1947.

In 1954 Owens & Minor installed its first computerized order fulfillment system. The following year the firm became Owens Minor & Bodeker when it bought the Bodeker Drug Company which was both older and larger than Owens & Minor.

After 84 years in the drug wholesale business the company entered the medical and surgical distribution business after buying A&J Hospital Supply in 1966 and Powers & Anderson in 1968. In 1971 Owens Minor & Bodeker went public. By the end of the decade the company had operations in 10 states.

The fourth Minor to run the firm G. Gilmer Minor III (Mr. Minor Jr.'s son) was named president in 1981 (he became CEO in 1984). Under his direction Owens Minor & Bodeker would complete the transition from a drug wholesaler to a medical supplies distributor. In 1981 it purchased the Will Ross subsidiary of G.D. Searle (then the country's #2 medical and surgical supplies distributor).

The company reverted to its original name on its 100th anniversary in 1982. By 1984 medical supplies supplanted wholesale drugs as its primary source of income. In 1988 Owens & Minor listed on the NYSE.

The company passed the $1 billion revenue mark in 1990 and later sold its wholesale drug business. It extended its reach with the purchase of Lyons Physician Supply in 1993 and Stuart Medical (the #3 national distributor) in 1994.

EXECUTIVES

Svp And Chief Of Staff, Erika T. Davis, age 55, $513,719 total compensation
Svp Owens & Minor Europe Operations, Charles C. Colpo, age 61, $453,466 total compensation
Vice President Technology, Charles Eismamn
Evp And Cfo; President International, Richard A. (Randy) Meier, age 58, $648,260 total compensation
Chairman President And Ceo, P. Cody Phipps, age 56, $915,577 total compensation
Evp North American Operations, Rony C. Kordahi, age 54, $328,846 total compensation
Evp Global Manufacturer Services, Stuart Morris-Hipkins
Svp Clinical Procedural Solutions, James S. Glasscock
Svp Manufacturer Services, Geoff T. Marlatt
Svp And Cio, Stephen R. Olive
Svp Strategic Supply Management, Javara D. Perrilliat
Svp Commercial Services, Joseph B. Zaluzney
Vice President Global Tax, Chris McGowan
Auditors: KPMG LLP

LOCATIONS

HQ: Owens & Minor, Inc.
9120 Lockwood Boulevard, Mechanicsville, VA 23116
Phone: 804 723-7000   **Fax:** 804 723-7100
Web: www.owens-minor.com

2017 Sales

	$ mil.	% of total
US	8,899	96
UK	175	2
Ireland	57	1
Germany	49	
France	39	
Other European countries	98	1
Total	**9,318**	**100**

PRODUCTS/OPERATIONS

2017 Sales by Segment

	$ mil.	% of total
Domestic	8,794	91
International	391	4
Proprietary Products	504	5
Adjustments	(371.8)	-
Total	**9,318**	**100**

Selected Products and Services

Clinical Supply Solutions (inventory and contract management service)
Implant Purchase Manager (utilization contract compliance and billing)
OMDirect (Internet order fulfillment)
OMSolutions (resource management and consulting)
PANDAC system (helps track and control operating room inventories)
QSight (clinical inventory management system)
SurgiTrack (customizable surgical supply service)

COMPETITORS

Alloga UK	FedEx
AmerisourceBergen	Kerma Medical Products
Buffalo Supply	McKesson
Cardinal Health	Medline Industries
Deutsche Post	UPS

HISTORICAL FINANCIALS

Company Type: Public

Income Statement

FYE: December 31

	REVENUE ($ mil.)	NET INCOME ($ mil.)	NET PROFIT MARGIN	EMPLOYEES
12/17	9,318	72	0.8%	6,200
12/16	9,723	108	1.1%	7,900
12/15	9,772	103	1.1%	8,100
12/14	9,440	66	0.7%	5,700
12/13	9,071	110	1.2%	6,700
Annual Growth	**0.7%**	**(10.0%)**	**—**	**(1.9%)**

2017 Year-End Financials

Debt ratio: 26.68%	No. of shares (mil.): 61
Return on equity: 7.37%	Dividends
Cash ($ mil.): 104	Yield: 0.0%
Current ratio: 1.67	Payout: 85.8%
Long-term debt ($ mil.): 900	Market value ($ mil.): 1,161

	STOCK PRICE ($) FY Close	P/E High/Low		PER SHARE ($) Earnings	Dividends	Book Value
12/17	18.88	31	15	1.20	1.03	16.52
12/16	35.29	23	18	1.76	1.02	15.73
12/15	35.98	24	19	1.65	1.01	15.80
12/14	35.11	35	30	1.06	1.00	15.71
12/13	36.56	22	16	1.76	0.96	16.23
Annual Growth	**(15.2%)**	**—**	**—**	**(9.1%)**	**1.8%**	**0.4%**

Owens Corning

Owens Corning (OC) operates in the PINK. Famous for its Pink Panther mascot and its trademarked PINK glass fiber insulation the company is a top global maker of building and composite material systems. The building materials company makes insulation roofing fiber-based glass reinforcements and other materials for the residential and commercial markets. Its composite products business makes glass fiber reinforcement materials for the transportation industrial infrastructure marine wind energy and consumer markets.

Operations

Owens Corning is organized in three business segments: Composites Insulation and Roofing.

Roofing segment (about 40% of revenue) manufactures and sells residential roofing shingles oxidized asphalt materials roofing components used in residential and commercial construction and specialty applications and synthetic packaging materials.

The Composites segment manufactures fabricates and sells glass reinforcements in the form of fiber as well as sell glass fiber products downstream in the form of fabrics mat veil and other specialized products. 30% revenue comes from this segment.

Insulation another 30% of revenue manufactures and sells fiberglass insulation into residential commercial industrial and other markets for both thermal and acoustical applications.

Geographic Reach

Ohio-based Owens Corning has about 100 manufacturing facilities in some 35 countries in the Americas Europe Africa and the Asia/Pacific region. The US generates about 70% of its sales while Europe the Asia/Pacific and Canada and other countries contribute about 10% each.

Sales and Marketing

Owens Corning sells shingles and roofing accessories primarily through home centers lumberyards retailers distributors and contractors in the US Canada Europe and Asia=Pacific. Other asphalt products are sold internally to manufacture residential roofing products and externally to other roofing manufacturers.

The company typically spends around $100 million on advertising each year.

Financial Performance

In the last decade (2008-17) revenue at Owens Corning has been mostly stable in the $5 billion-plus range. For the same period except for a $20 million loss in 2012 the company has posted profits every year with a yearly average above $200 million.

Revenue in 2017 increased some 12% to $6.4 billion the highest in a decade. Insulation brought in $50 million more compared to 2016 primarily due to higher sales and production volumes higher selling prices and the impact of Pittsburgh Corning acquisition. Roofing increased some $50 million more as well mostly due to higher sales volumes.

Net income fell 25% year-over-year to $290 million for 2017 mostly from a $150 million increases in year-over-year operating costs due to acquisitions as well as $150 million increase in combined income tax expenses and loss on debt extinguishment (of 2019 senior notes).

Cash holdings more than doubled to $250 million. Operations from 2017 generated $1 billion in cash offset by $900 million for investment activities (mostly going to subsidiaries). Financing activities had a net positive contribution of $3 million.

Strategy

With steady revenues and increasing in 2017 to cross the $6 billion mark Owens Corning is looking to expand. In early 2018 it acquired the Paroc Group which expands the company?s geographic scope to Europe and product portfolio.

Its insulation products now range across the high medium and low temperature ranges in all 3 major markets of North America Europe and China.

The composites segment which has grown for 5 straight years is expanding operations further to India and will start production in late-2018. There is similar performance from other company sectors like its Foamglas business and residential fiberglass insulation. The components business is expected to grow at double-digit rates as well as over 10% growth in composites.

However mineral wool business in the US has underperformed despite improvement measures. Moreover the asphalt market is also likely to further decline and the company is having efficiency problems in its Joplin insulation facility.

Going forward though thanks to several acquisitions and ongoing integration Owens Corning is likely to create strong cash flows.

Mergers and Acquisitions

In 2018 Owens Corning acquired European stone wool insulation producer Paroc Group from CVC Capital Partners for ?900 million (US$ 1 billion). The move expanded Owens' mineral wool technology further entrenched its European presence and shifted its geographic revenue portfolio towards non-North American sources.

In 2016 Owens Corning acquired InterWrap a leading manufacturer of roofing underlayment and packaging materials for US$450 million.

Also in 2016 the company agreed to buy the glass non-wovens and fabrics businesses of Ahlstrom the fiber-based materials company based in Helsinki Finland for US$79.5 million (?73 million).

HISTORY

In the 1930s Corning Glass Works and Owens-Illinois Glass independently found that glass fiber has special resilience and strength. Realizing the potential market they formed joint venture Owens-Corning Fiberglas in 1938. The companies expanded rapidly in the 1940s and 1950s establishing several US plants and one in Canada. Their products included fine fibers thermal wool textiles and continuous filaments.

oot manufacturing plant in Wabash Indiana.

EXECUTIVES

Chairman President And Ceo, Michael H. (Mike) Thaman, age 54, $1,140,500 total compensation
President Roofing And Asphalt, Brian D. Chambers, age 49, $450,000 total compensation
Svp Organization And Administration, Daniel T. (Dan) Smith, age 53, $527,500 total compensation
President Composite Solutions, Arnaud P. Genis, age 53, $596,667 total compensation
Svp And Cfo, Michael C. McMurray, age 53, $589,167 total compensation
President Insulation, Julian Francis
Auditors: PricewaterhouseCoopers LLP

LOCATIONS

HQ: Owens Corning
One Owens Corning Parkway, Toledo, OH 43659
Phone: 419 248-8000
Web: www.owenscorning.com

2016 Sales

	$ mil.	% of total
United States	3,963	70
Asia Pacific	666	12
Europe	550	10
Canada and other	498	8
Total	**5,677**	**100**

PRODUCTS/OPERATIONS

2016 Sales

	$ mil.	% of total
Roofing	2,194	37
Composites	1,952	33
Insulation	1,748	30
Corporate eliminations	(217)	-
Total	**5,677**	**100**

COMPETITORS

Ball Corp.	Mohawk Industries
CertainTeed	Nippon Electric Glass
China Fiberglass Co.	Owens-Illinois
Ltd.	PPG Industries
Deceuninck	SIG plc
Dow Chemical	Saint-Gobain
GAF Materials	Sherwin-Williams
Johns Manville	Stanley Black and
Knauf Insulation	Decker
Lennox	TAMKO
Louisiana-Pacific	USG
Masco	Valspar

HISTORICAL FINANCIALS

Company Type: Public

Income Statement   FYE: December 31

	REVENUE ($ mil.)	NET INCOME ($ mil.)	NET PROFIT MARGIN	EMPLOYEES
12/17	6,384	289	4.5%	17,000
12/16	5,677	393	6.9%	16,000
12/15	5,350	330	6.2%	15,000
12/14	5,276	226	4.3%	14,000
12/13	5,296	204	0.0%	15,000
Annual Growth	**4.8%**	**9.1%**	**—**	**3.2%**

2017 Year-End Financials

Debt ratio: 27.92%
Return on equity: 7.22%
Cash ($ mil.): 246
Current ratio: 1.55
Long-term debt ($ mil.): 2,405

No. of shares (mil.): 111
Dividends
  Yield: 0.0%
  Payout: 31.7%
Market value ($ mil.): 10,251

	STOCK PRICE ($) FY Close	P/E High/Low	PER SHARE ($) Earnings	Dividends	Book Value
12/17	91.94	36 20	2.55	0.81	37.33
12/16	51.56	16 12	3.41	0.74	34.15
12/15	47.03	17 12	2.79	0.68	32.26
12/14	35.81	24 15	1.91	0.64	31.34
12/13	40.72	26 21	1.71	0.00	32.20
Annual Growth	**22.6%**	**— —**	**10.5%**	**—**	**3.8%**

Owens-Illinois, Inc.

Owens-Illinois (O-I) is one of the world's largest makers of glass containers touting a leading market presence with more than 49000 customers in 85 countries around the world. O-I offers more than 10000 types of glass containers such as bottles in a wide range of shapes sizes and colors used to hold beer wine liquor as well as soft drinks juice and other beverages. It also makes glass containers for foods such as soups salad dressings and dairy products and for pharmaceuticals. Some of its products are made using recycled glass. Major customers have included such heavy hitters as Anheuser-Busch InBev Coca-Cola Diageo H.J. Heinz and Nestle.

Operations

Owens-Illinois is a major glass container manufacturer that caters to many of the world's leading food and beverage brands. It produces glass containers for alcoholic beverages including beer flavored malt beverages spirits and wine. It also produces glass packaging for a variety of food items including soft drinks teas juices and pharmaceuticals.

Geographic Reach

Altogether Owens-Illinois (O-I) operates almost 80 manufacturing plants in 23 countries. It has joint ventures in China Malaysia Mexico the US and Vietnam. Engineering support sites for its glass manufacturing operations are located Australia Columbia France Poland Peru and the US.

O-I divides its operations across four reportable segments based on geography: Europe which generates some 35% of total sales North America (about 33%) Latin America (around 25%) and the Asia/Pacific region (10%).

Sales and Marketing

Owens-Illinois sells most of its glass container products directly to customers under yearly or multi-year supply agreements however some of its products are sold through distributors. Customers range from large multinationals to small local breweries and wineries.Its largest customers are leading global food and beverage manufacturers including Anheuser‑Busch InBev Carlsberg Coca-Cola Constellation Diageo Heineken MillerCoors Nestle Brown Forman and Pernod Ricard.

Financial Performance

Owens-Illinois' revenue has bounced back after a slump in 2014-15. In fiscal 2017 revenue increased 2% to $6.9 billion as gains in Europe Latin America and the Asia/Pacific region were partially offset by weakness in North America. The results largely reflected currency exchange effects which account for $106 million out of the $167 million revenue growth. The other gains came from higher selling prices and a 1% increase in glass shipments partially offset by an unfavorable sales mix.

Net income fell 12% to $202 million as stronger operating income was offset by a $120 million increase in pension settlement charges. As a result cash from operations fell 5% to $831 million.

Strategy

Owens-Illinois (O-I) is placing a priority on winning over customers that have shied away from glass packaging as well as encouraging existing ones to use more. To this end its marketing efforts piggyback on the wave toward sustainable packaging. Along with developing a variety of container features and functions the company highlights the benefits of glass recyclability.O-I also makes investments in its operations to improve efficiency and productivity. In 2018 it invested heavily in repairing assets and improving their flexibility and reliability.

HISTORY

The Owens Bottle Machine Corp. was incorporated in Toledo Ohio in 1907 as the successor to a four-year-old New Jersey company of the same name. It initially grew by acquiring small glass companies. In 1929 Owens bought the Illinois Glass Co. (medical and pharmaceutical glass) and became Owens-Illinois Glass.

The company bought Libbey Glass (tableware) in 1935. Three years later Owens-Illinois and Corning Glass which were both studying uses for glass fiber began Owens-Corning Fiberglass a joint venture with a virtual industry monopoly.

After WWII Owens-Illinois (O-I) started to diversify beyond glass. The company went public in 1952. In 1956 it bought National Container (cardboard boxes). It also created a semi-rigid plastic container that was adopted by bleach and detergent companies.

EXECUTIVES

Svp And Chief Strategy And Innovation Officer, John Haudrich, $334,546 total compensation
Svp And Chief Administrative Officer, Paul Jarrell, $417,000 total compensation
Vp And Cto, Giancarlo Currarino
President O-i North America, Sergio Galindo
Svp And Cfo, Jan A. Bertsch, $650,000 total compensation
Ceo, Andres A. Lopez, $850,000 total compensation
President O-i Europe, Vitaliano Torno, $507,305 total compensation
President O-i Latin America, Miguel I. Alvarez, $380,467 total compensation
President O-i Asia Pacific, Timothy Connors
Svp And General Counsel, James W. (Jim) Baehren, $450,000 total compensation
Vice President Internet Marketing, Benjamin Hagan
Vice President Of Quality, Steve Jenkins
Vice President Procurement And Supply Chain, Ann Ryan

Vp Government Relations, Ryan Modlin
Vice President Sales And Marketing North America, Shawn P Welch
Vp Finance Europe, Robert Gachot
Vice President Global And Corporate Communications, Kristin Kelley
Vice President Of Quality Latin America, Luis Alberto
Vice President Human Resources, James Dalton
Vice President, Randolph Burns
Vice President Global Product Management And Innovation, Asad Hamid
Vice President Americas, James Rooney
Chairman, Carol A. Williams
Auditors: Ernst & Young LLP

LOCATIONS

HQ: Owens-Illinois, Inc.
One Michael Owens Way, Perrysburg, OH 43551
Phone: 567 336-5000
Web: www.o-i.com

2017 Sales

	$ mil.	% of total
Europe	2,375	35
North America	2,160	31
Latin America	1,551	23
Asia Pacific	714	10
Other	69	1
Total	**6,869**	**100**

PRODUCTS/OPERATIONS

Selected Subsidiaries

Owens-Illinois Group Inc.
OI General Finance Inc.
OI General FTS Inc.
OI Castalia STS Inc.
OI Levis Park STS Inc.
Owens-Illinois General Inc.
Owens Insurance Ltd.
Universal Materials Inc.
OI Advisors Inc.
OI Securities Inc.
OI Transfer Inc.
Maumee Air Associates Inc.
OI Australia Inc.
Continental PET Holdings Pty. Ltd.
ACI America Holdings Inc.
ACI Ventures Inc.
Owens-Brockway Packaging Inc.
Owens-Brockway Glass Container Inc.
OI Andover Group Inc.
The Andover Group Inc.
Brockway Realty Corporation
NHW Auburn LLC
OI Auburn Inc.
SeaGate Inc.
SeaGate II Inc.

COMPETITORS

Amcor	Plastipak
Anchor Glass	Reynolds Group
AptarGroup	Holdings Limited
Arconic	Saint-Gobain
BWAY	Saint-Gobain
Ball Corp.	Containers
Bemis	Sealed Air Corp.
Berry Global	Silgan
Consolidated Container	Sonoco Products
Crown Holdings	Tetra Pak
Graham Packaging	Tupperware Brands
Newell Brands	Vidrala

HISTORICAL FINANCIALS

Company Type: Public

Income Statement

FYE: December 31

	REVENUE ($ mil.)	NET INCOME ($ mil.)	NET PROFIT MARGIN	EMPLOYEES
12/17	6,869	180	2.6%	26,500
12/16	6,702	209	3.1%	27,000
12/15	6,156	(74)	—	27,000
12/14	6,784	75	1.1%	21,100
12/13	6,967	184	2.6%	22,500
Annual Growth	(0.4%)	(0.5%)	—	4.2%

2017 Year-End Financials

Debt ratio: 54.15%
Return on equity: 33.90%
Cash ($ mil.): 492
Current ratio: 1.06
Long-term debt ($ mil.): 5,121
No. of shares (mil.): 163
Dividends
Yield: —
Payout: —
Market value ($ mil.): 3,615

	STOCK PRICE ($) FY Close	P/E High/Low		Earnings	Dividends	Book Value
12/17	22.17	23	16	1.10	0.00	4.95
12/16	17.41	16	9	1.28	0.00	1.56
12/15	17.42	—	—	(0.47)	0.00	2.90
12/14	26.99	78	51	0.45	0.00	7.05
12/13	35.78	32	19	1.11	0.00	8.84
Annual Growth	(11.3%)	—	—	(0.2%)	—	(13.5%)

PACCAR Inc.

PACCAR (named for former rail car manufacturer Pacific Car and Foundry Company) is one of the world's largest designers and manufacturers of big rig diesel trucks. Its lineup of light- medium- and heavy-duty trucks includes the Kenworth Peterbilt and DAF nameplates. The company also manufactures and distributes aftermarket truck parts for these brands. PACCAR's other products include Braden Carco and Gearmatic industrial winches. PACCAR typically sells its trucks and parts through independent dealers with the exception of a few company-owned branches. Its PACCAR Financial Services arm offers vehicle financing and its PacLease subsidiary handles truck leasing.

Operations

PACCAR divides its business into three primary segments: Trucks Parts and Financial Services. The Truck segment generates more than 75% of total sales and sells trucks under the Kenworth Peterbilt and DAF brands. The company manufactures trucks in the US Europe Australia Brazil Canada and Mexico. In Europe PACCAR subsidiary Leyland assembles DAF trucks in the UK.

Parts (accounting for nearly 20% of sales) distributes aftermarket parts globally for PACCAR vehicles. PACCAR manufactures its own parts and also purchases from suppliers. Financial Services represents about 5% of net revenue and provides financing to independent dealers franchises and directly to customers for trucks and related equipment.

In addition PACCAR?s Other business includes the manufacture and marketing of industrial winches; sales in this business are less than 1% of total revenue.

Geographic Reach

PACCAR?s headquarters are in Bellevue WA. It operates more than 30 manufacturing plants and distribution centers on four continents including North and South America Europe and Australia. In North America the company owns manufacturing plants in five US states including Washington Delaware Mississippi Texas and Ohio and one each in Canada and Mexico. In Europe it does business in The Netherlands Germany and the UK and has operations at one factory in Australia. PACCAR Financial Services operates across the globe in about 25 countries. In 2017 the new PACCAR Innovation Center opened in Sunnyvale CA.

About 45% of PACCAR's revenues are generated outside the US with nearly 30% coming from Europe.

Sales and Marketing

PACCAR delivers its products and services to customers worldwide in about 100 countries through its dealer network of more than 2100 locations.

Financial Performance

After an 11% decline to $17 billion in 2016 PACCAR saw record revenues of $19.5 billion in 2017 with a $2 billion increase in truck sales. Sales initiatives in both the Truck and Parts businesses were a key factor as well as several new dealer distribution and service locations.

In 2017 PACCAR earned $1.7 billion in net income which included a one-time $173.4 million net tax benefit resulting from the recent changes to the U.S. tax law. Excluding the one-time tax benefit adjusted net income of $1.5 billion represents an 8% increase from 2016?s adjusted net income. Efficiencies in product development finance activities purchasing and manufacturing operations also contributed to the increase.

Cash provided by operating activities climbed by $415 million to $2.7 billion in 2017 an 18% increase over the previous year primarily related to higher net income.

Strategy

PACCAR spent nearly $700 million on capital investments in 2017 compared with $403 million in 2016. To achieve growth it regularly expands its vehicle product range upgrades its manufacturing and parts distribution facilities and continues to expand globally with the addition of new dealer locations.

The company also invests in truck and engine technologies that enhance vehicle fuel efficiency and reliability. In 2017 it opened its PACCAR Innovation Center in Silicon Valley to develop technologies such as holograms for design and diagnostics increased robotics in manufacturing enhanced algorithms in parts distribution and mobile apps for financial services. The company is using advanced data analytics and artificial intelligence to enhance manufacturing capabilities and the company is continuing to develop its truck connectivity technologies and Advanced Driver Assistance Systems (ADAS).

HISTORY

William Pigott founded the Seattle Car Manufacturing Company in 1905 to produce railroad cars for timber transport. Finding immediate success Pigott began to make other kinds of railcars in 1906. When the Seattle plant burned the next year the company moved near Renton Washington. In 1911 Pigott renamed the company Seattle Car & Foundry.

In 1917 Seattle Car merged with the Twohy Brothers of Portland. The new company Pacific Car & Foundry was sold to American Car & Foundry in 1924. Pacific Car then diversified into bus manufacturing structural steel fabrications and metal technology.

Pacific Car was in decline by 1934 when William's son Paul bought it; since then the company has remained under family management.

Paul Pigott added Hofius Steel and Equipment and Tricoach a bus manufacturer in 1936. The company entered the truck-making business with the 1945 purchase of Seattle-based Kenworth.

In the 1950s Pacific Car became the industry leader in mechanical refrigerator car production. It began producing off-road heavy trucks and acquired Peterbilt Trucks of Oakland (1958). To augment its winch business Pacific Car bought Canada's Gearmatic in 1963.

The company moved its headquarters to Bellevue Washington in 1969 and changed its name to PACCAR in 1971.

EXECUTIVES

President, Ronald E. (Ron) Armstrong, age 62, $1,210,000 total compensation

Svp And General Manager Peterbilt, T. Kyle Quinn, age 57, $440,000 total compensation

Evp And Cfo, Harrie C.A.M. Schippers, age 56, $396,022 total compensation

Svp Financial Services, Robert A. Bengston, age 62, $449,615 total compensation

Evp, Gary L Moore, age 62, $547,693 total compensation

Vp And General Manager Kw, C. Michael Dozier

Vp Paccar And President Daf Trucks N.v., R. Preston Feight, age 50

Vp And Cio, A. Lily Ley, age 52

Executive Vice President, Dan Sobic

Vice President And Controller, Michael Barkley

Vice President, James Cardillo

Chairman And Ceo, Mark C. Pigott, age 65

Auditors: Ernst & Young LLP

LOCATIONS

HQ: PACCAR Inc.
777 - 106th Ave. N.E., Bellevue, WA 98004
Phone: 425 468-7400
Web: www.paccar.com

2017 Sales

	$ mil.	% of total
US	10,530	54
Europe	5,354	28
Other regions	3,571	18
Total	**19,456**	**100**

PRODUCTS/OPERATIONS

2017 Sales

	$ mil.	% of total
Truck	14,774	76
Parts	3,327	17
Financial services	1,268	7
Other	85	-
Total	**19,456**	**100**

Selected Divisions and Subsidiaries

DAF trucks
Kenworth Trucks
Peterbilt trucks
Leyland Trucks Limited (UK)
PACCAR Engine Company
PACCAR Financial Corp.
PACCAR Parts
PACCAR Machinery
PACCAR Winch
  Braden winches
  Carco winches
  Gearmatic winches

COMPETITORS

AGCO	Iveco S.p.A.
CNH Industrial	MAN
Caterpillar	Mack Trucks
Cummins	Meritor
Dana	Morris Material
Deere	Handling
Eaton	Navistar International

Fiat Chrysler	Oshkosh Truck
Ford Motor	Scania
General Motors	UD Trucks
Hino Motors	Volvo
Isuzu	

HISTORICAL FINANCIALS

Company Type: Public

Income Statement

FYE: December 31

	REVENUE ($ mil.)	NET INCOME ($ mil.)	NET PROFIT MARGIN	EMPLOYEES
12/17	19,456	1,675	8.6%	25,000
12/16	17,033	521	3.1%	23,000
12/15	19,115	1,604	8.4%	23,000
12/14	18,997	1,358	7.2%	23,300
12/13	17,123	1,171	6.8%	21,800
Annual Growth	**3.2%**	**9.4%**	**—**	**3.5%**

2017 Year-End Financials

Debt ratio: 37.88%
Return on equity: 22.59%
Cash ($ mil.): 2,364
Current ratio: 1.79
Long-term debt ($ mil.): 8,879

No. of shares (mil.): 351
Dividends
  Yield: 0.0%
  Payout: 46.1%
Market value ($ mil.): 25,006

	STOCK PRICE ($) FY Close	P/E High/Low	PER SHARE ($) Earnings	Dividends	Book Value
12/17	71.08	16 13	4.75	2.19	22.88
12/16	63.90	46 30	1.48	1.56	19.33
12/15	47.40	15 10	4.51	2.32	19.76
12/14	68.01	18 14	3.82	1.86	19.05
12/13	59.17	18 14	3.30	1.70	18.73
Annual Growth	**4.7%**	**—**	**9.5%**	**6.5%**	**5.1%**

Pacific City Financial Corp

EXECUTIVES

Pres-Ceo, Henry Kim
Chb, Sang Young Lee
Exec V Pres-Cfo-Corp SEC, Timothy Chang
Board Member, Kwang J Chung
Auditors: Crowe LLP

LOCATIONS

HQ: Pacific City Financial Corp
3701 Wilshire Blvd., Suite 900, Los Angeles, CA 90010
Phone: 213 210-2000   **Fax:** 213 210-2032

HISTORICAL FINANCIALS

Company Type: Public

Income Statement

FYE: December 31

	ASSETS ($ mil.)	NET INCOME ($ mil.)	INCOME AS % OF ASSETS	EMPLOYEES
12/17	1,442	16	1.1%	228
12/16	1,226	14	1.1%	—
12/15	1,042	12	1.2%	—
12/14	893	11	1.3%	—
12/13	755	21	2.8%	—
Annual Growth	**17.5%**	**(6.4%)**	**—**	**—**

2017 Year-End Financials

Debt ratio: —
Return on equity: 12.19%
Cash ($ mil.): 73
Current ratio: —
Long-term debt ($ mil.): —

No. of shares (mil.): 13
Dividends
  Yield: 0.0%
  Payout: 9.9%
Market value ($ mil.): 208

	STOCK PRICE ($) FY Close	P/E High/Low		PER SHARE ($) Earnings	Dividends	Book Value
12/17	15.50	13	10	1.21	0.12	10.60
12/16	13.00	12	9	1.11	0.11	9.48
12/15	12.85	15	12	1.02	0.07	8.26
12/14	12.38	14	4	1.00	0.00	7.31
12/13	4.00	3	1	1.83	0.00	6.87
Annual Growth	40.3%	—	—	(9.9%)	—	11.4%

Pacific Premier Bancorp Inc

EXECUTIVES

Pres-Ceo, Steven R Gardner
Chb*, Jeff C Jones
Sr V Pres-Cfo*, Kent Smith
Sr Exec Vpres-Cfo*, Ronald J Nicolas Jr
Cro*, Michael Karr
Evp-Cco*, Donn Jakosky
Evp-Chief Acctg Officer*, Lori Wright
General Counsel, Steve Arnold
Secretary, John Shindler
Customer Representativ, Leticia Rodriguez
Senior Vice President Director, Thomas Galindo
Auditors: Crowe Horwath LLP

LOCATIONS

HQ: Pacific Premier Bancorp Inc
  17901 Von Karman Avenue, Suite 1200, Irvine, CA 92614
Phone: 949 864-8000
Web: www.ppbi.com

HISTORICAL FINANCIALS

Company Type: Public

Income Statement

FYE: December 31

	ASSETS ($ mil.)	NET INCOME ($ mil.)	INCOME AS % OF ASSETS	EMPLOYEES
12/17	8,024	60	0.7%	846
12/16	4,036	40	1.0%	448
12/15	2,790	25	0.9%	335
12/14	2,038	16	0.8%	285
12/13	1,714	8	0.5%	231
Annual Growth	47.1%	60.8%	—	38.3%

2017 Year-End Financials

Debt ratio: 7.99%
Return on equity: 7.06%
Cash ($ mil.): 203
Current ratio: —
Long-term debt ($ mil.): —

No. of shares (mil.): 46
Dividends
  Yield: —
  Payout: —
Market value ($ mil.): 1,850

	STOCK PRICE ($) FY Close	P/E High/Low		PER SHARE ($) Earnings	Dividends	Book Value
12/17	40.00	26	20	1.56	0.00	26.86
12/16	35.35	24	13	1.46	0.00	16.54
12/15	21.25	20	12	1.19	0.00	13.86
12/14	17.33	18	14	0.96	0.00	11.81
12/13	15.74	28	18	0.54	0.00	10.52
Annual Growth	26.3%	—	—	30.4%	—	26.4%

PACIFIC PREMIER BANK

EXECUTIVES

Pres-Ceo, Steven R Gardner
Chb*, Jeff C Jones
Sr V Pres-Cfo*, Kent Smith
Sr Exec Vpres-Cfo*, Ronald J Nicolas Jr
Cro*, Michael Karr
Evp-Cco*, Donn Jakosky
Evp-Chief Acctg Officer*, Lori Wright
General Counsel, Steve Arnold
Secretary, John Shindler
Customer Representativ, Leticia Rodriguez
Senior Vice President Director, Thomas Galindo

LOCATIONS

HQ: PACIFIC PREMIER BANK
  17901 VON KARMAN AVE, IRVINE, CA 926146297
Phone: 714 431-4000
Web: WWW.PPBI.NET

HISTORICAL FINANCIALS

Company Type: Private

Income Statement

FYE: December 31

	ASSETS ($ mil.)	NET INCOME ($ mil.)	INCOME AS % OF ASSETS	EMPLOYEES
12/17	8,022	68	0.9%	104
12/16	4,035	44	1.1%	—
12/15	2,782	29	1.1%	—
12/14	2,033	18	0.9%	—
Annual Growth	58.0%	54.0%	—	—

2017 Year-End Financials

Debt ratio: —
Return on equity: 22.90%
Cash ($ mil.): 200
Current ratio: —
Long-term debt ($ mil.): —

Dividends
  Yield: —
  Payout: —
Market value ($ mil.): —

Pacificorp

PacifiCorp has refocused on its core businesses: regulated utilities Pacific Power and Rocky Mountain Power which together provide electricity to 1.8 million customers in six western states. The subsidiaries operate 16300 miles of transmission lines and 62800 miles of distribution lines. PacifiCorp owns or has stakes in almost 75 thermal hydroelectric and renewable generation facilities that supply its utilities with about 10600 MW of net capacity. Its PacifiCorp Energy unit purchases power from other generators and it sells excess power to wholesale customers in the western US. The company is a unit of Berkshire Hathaway's MidAmerican Energy Holdings.

Operations

PacifiCorp consists of three business units: PacifiCorp Energy (electric generation commercial energy trading and coal mining) Pacific Power (electricity distribution to customers in Oregon Washington and California) and Rocky Mountain Power (power distribution to customers in Utah Wyoming and Idaho).

Geographic Reach

PacifiCorp is headquartered in Oregon and serves customers in California Idaho Oregon Utah Washington and Wyoming.

Financial Performance

PacifiCorp's 2013 revenues followed a years long trend and rose by about 5% to $5.14 billion from $4.88 billion in 2012 due to higher energy prices. Net income also increased by 27% to $682 million from $537 million the prior year due to some unusual items which lead to lower after tax charges. Exclusive of those net income rose 11%. Cash from operations on the other hand decreased about 5% from $1.62 billion to $1.55 billion as the company used cash to pay income taxes.

Strategy

As part of its plan to continuously expand it generating capacity PacifiCorp through Rocky Mountain Power began building a 9000-panel solar farm in Utah that will provide power for about 500 homes.

EXECUTIVES

Chairman And Ceo, Gregory E. (Greg) Abel, age 55
President And Ceo Pacific Power, Stefan A. Bird, age 48
President Pacificorp Transmission, R. Patrick (Pat) Reiten, age 57, $320,000 total compensation
Svp And Cfo, Douglas K. (Doug) Stuver, age 54, $252,000 total compensation
President And Ceo Rocky Mountain Power, Cindy A. Crane, age 56, $224,538 total compensation
Svp Transmission And System Operations, Natalie L. Hocken, age 48
President And Ceo Pacificorp Energy, Michael G. Dunn, age 53, $320,000 total compensation
Vice President Manager Director, Esther Giezendanner
Vice President, Chris Moore
Executive Vice President Of Operations, Deanna Thompson
Senior Vice President, Shannon Reach
Auditors: DELOITTE & TOUCHE LLP

LOCATIONS

HQ: Pacificorp
  825 N.E. Multnomah Street, Portland, OR 97232
Phone: 888 221-7070
Web: www.pacificorp.com

PRODUCTS/OPERATIONS

2016 Customers

	% of total
Residential	87
Commercial	11
Industrial and irrigation	2
Total	100

Selected Subsidiaries

Pacific Power
Rocky Mountain Power

COMPETITORS

AES Wind Generation
Avista
Bonneville Power
Cascade Natural Gas
Chelan County PUD
Dominion Questar
Edison International
First Wind Holdings
IDACORP
Idaho Power
NV Energy
NW Natural
PG&E Corporation
PPL Montana
Pacific Gas and Electric
Pinnacle West
Portland General Electric
Public Utility District No. 1 of Clark County
Puget Energy
Questar Gas
Riverside Electric Utility
San Diego Gas & Electric
Seattle City Light
Sempra Energy
Sierra Pacific Power

HISTORICAL FINANCIALS

Company Type: Public

Income Statement
FYE: December 31

	REVENUE ($ mil.)	NET INCOME ($ mil.)	NET PROFIT MARGIN	EMPLOYEES
12/17	5,237	768	14.7%	5,500
12/16	5,201	763	14.7%	5,600
12/15	5,232	695	13.3%	5,700
12/14	5,252	698	13.3%	5,900
12/13	5,147	682	13.3%	6,000
Annual Growth	0.4%	3.0%	—	(2.2%)

2017 Year-End Financials

Debt ratio: 32.41%
Return on equity: 10.28%
Cash ($ mil.): 14
Current ratio: 0.81
Long-term debt ($ mil.): 6,437

No. of shares (mil.): 357
Dividends
Yield: 0.0%
Payout: 78.1%
Market value ($ mil.): 51,765

	STOCK PRICE ($) FY Close	P/E High/Low	PER SHARE ($) Earnings	Dividends	Book Value
12/17	145.00	— —	(0.00)	7.00	21.16
12/16	140.00	— —	(0.00)	7.00	20.70
12/15	134.90	— —	(0.00)	7.00	21.02
12/14	116.00	— —	(0.00)	7.00	21.73
12/13	114.79	— —	(0.00)	7.00	21.81
Annual Growth	6.0%	— —	—	(0.0%)	(0.8%)

Packaging Corp of America

One of the largest containerboard manufacturers in the US Packaging Corporation of America (PCA) produces about 3.9 million tons of containerboard a year most of which is converted into corrugated boxes and ships about 56 billion square feet of corrugated products. PCA's mills also churn out about a million tons of semi-chemical corrugating medium. The company's corrugated packaging includes shipping containers for manufactured goods multi-color boxes and displays for retail locations and honeycomb protective packaging. Its packaging materials also contain food and beverages and other consumer and industrial products. PCA operates manufacturing plants throughout the US.

Operations

PCA operates in three segments: packaging paper and corporate and other. Packaging which accounts for about 85% of sales produces a variety of corrugated packaging products. The paper segment 15% of sales makes and sells a range of papers including communication papers and pressure sensitive papers (collectively white papers). PCA's Paper segment operates under the trade name Boise Paper. Corporate and other includes support staff services and related assets and liabilities transportation assets and activity related to other ancillary support operations.

As a resource-intensive business PCA comes under a number of environmental regulations. The company spends about $40 million a year to comply with regulations and spends another $10 million or so a year on capital expenditures related to environmental concerns.

Geographic Reach

PCA operates eight containerboard mills (five containerboard mills and three paper mills) and about 100 corrugated products plants in about 35 US states. The company's substantial manufacturing footprint is enhanced by a technical and development hub about 10 regional graphic design centers and several printing and distribution sites.

The company also leases cutting rights on 75000 acres of timberland and has supply agreements on an additional 281000 acres — most neighboring its Counce Tennessee and Valdosta Georgia mills. The company operates also has some converting operations in China and Canada.

Sales and Marketing

PCA promotes its products through a direct sales and marketing force as well as independent brokers and distribution partners. It employs a sales manager and sales representatives at most of its corrugated product manufacturing locations. The company serves more than 18000 customers in more than 35000 locations. About three-quarters of sales of corrugated products go to local and regional accounts (located near a single PCA plant); remaining sales come from national accounts (customers who have widespread locations and are served by several PCA plants). Products are distributed by rail or truck. PCA's largest paper segment customer is Office Depot which contributes more than 45% of paper segment sales.

Financial Performance

PCA bounced back with higher sales in 2016 and 2017 after a drop in 2015. Net income followed the same path but with a greater leap in 2017 from 2016.

The company posted a 10% increase in revenue to $6.4 billion in 2017 from 2016 driven by higher sales volumes and prices for containerboard and corrugated products on strong demand. Paper revenue was lower year-to-year with decreased volumes and prices.

Net income jumped 48% to $668 million in 2017 from $449 million in 2016 driven by the higher containerboard and corrugated products sales. Net income included $122 million of estimated income tax benefit related to the US Tax Cut and Jobs Act.

PCA ended 2017 with $217 million in cash about $22 million less than 2016's total. Operating activities generated $856 million in 2017 while investing activities used $609 million and financing activities used $269 million.

Strategy

PCA is definitely thinking inside the box. It is concentrating its resources on building its box business while de-emphasizing the paper side. Its recent acquisitions have focused on expanding its corrugated and containerboard assets and it converted its plant in Wallula Washington to produce only containerboard. The conversion helped improve PCA's overall productivity and enabled it to respond more quickly to customers' needs. The product shift is reflected in PCA's production numbers which show increasing production of corrugated and containerboard while paper production has diminished.

Mergers and Acquisitions

PCA uses acquisitions to bolster its manufacturing capacity and extend its geographic footprint. In 2017 PCA acquired Sacramento Container Corp. Northern Sheets and Central California Sheets for $265 million. The acquired companies which operate two full-line corrugated products operations and sheet feeders in McClellan California and Kingsburg California expanded PCA's West Coast operations.

In 2016 PCA acquired Pennsylvania-based TimBar Corp. for $387 million. TimBar is a corrugated products producer with six corrugated products production facilities.

Also that year PCA picked up Indiana-based Columbus Container for $100 million. Columbus is a corrugated products producer with one corrugated products production facility and five warehousing facilities.

Company Background

PCA was formed by Madison Dearborn in 1999 in order to acquire the containerboard and corrugated product operations of Pactiv. PCA blossomed five years later when it purchased the assets of Acorn Corrugated Box Company a maker of graphics packaging and displays.

EXECUTIVES

Vp And Cio, Robert Schneider
Chairman And Ceo, Mark W. Kowlzan, age 63, $1,157,004 total compensation
Evp Corrugated Products, Thomas A. (Tom) Hassfurther, age 62, $913,002 total compensation
Svp General Counsel And Corporate Secretary, Kent A. Pflederer, age 47, $478,002 total compensation
Svp Sales And Marketing Corrugated Products, Thomas W. H. (Tom) Walton, age 58, $361,002 total compensation
Svp Mill Operations, Charles J. (Jack) Carter, age 59, $519,670 total compensation
Svp And Cfo, Robert P. (Bob) Mundy, age 56, $618,000 total compensation
Vice President Engineering, Nam Shin
Vice President Containerboard Mill Operations, Jack Carter
Vp Corporate Technology And Engineering, Ray Shirley
Vice President And General Manager, Donald Haag
Vice President Engineering, Annie Kim
Second Vice President, Tom Watson
Vice President Operation Services, Bryan Sorensen
Vice President Containerboard Sales, Gerald Greeter
Vice President, Kevin Hart
Senior Vice President And Chief Financial Officer, Richard West
Vice President, Bernadette Madarieta
Senior Vice President Sales And Marketing Corrugated Products, Walton Thomas
National Account Manager, Jeff Harris
Board Member, Roger Porter
Board Member, Duane Farrington
Board Member, Hasan Jameel
Auditors: KPMG LLP

HQ: Packaging Corp of America
1 North Field Court, Lake Forest, IL 60045
Phone: 847 482-3000
Web: www.packagingcorp.com

PRODUCTS/OPERATIONS

2017 Sales

	% of total
Packaging	73
Paper	16
Corporate and other	1
Total	**100**

Selected Products

:Corrugated Containers
Retail Packaging and Displays
Heavy-Duty Packaging
Produce Packaging
Hexacomb
Falconboard
Tharco Stock Boxes
Record Storage Boxes
Interior Packaging
Packaging Supplies
Freight Saver Dunnage Bags Printing Capabilities
Containe

COMPETITORS

Amcor	Kapstone Paper and
Atlas Container	Packaging
Bio Pappel	Norampac
Georgia-Pacific	Pratt Industries USA
Graphic Packaging	Sonoco Products
Holding	Southern Container
Greif	corp
International Paper	

HISTORICAL FINANCIALS

Company Type: Public

Income Statement — FYE: December 31

	REVENUE ($ mil.)	NET INCOME ($ mil.)	NET PROFIT MARGIN	EMPLOYEES
12/17	6,444	668	10.4%	14,600
12/16	5,779	449	7.8%	14,000
12/15	5,741	436	7.6%	13,000
12/14	5,852	392	6.7%	14,000
12/13	3,665	436	11.9%	13,600
Annual Growth	**15.2%**	**11.3%**	**—**	**1.8%**

2017 Year-End Financials

Debt ratio: 42.77%
Return on equity: 33.92%
Cash ($ mil.): 216
Current ratio: 2.30
Long-term debt ($ mil.): 2,499

No. of shares (mil.): 94
Dividends
Yield: 0.0%
Payout: 35.6%
Market value ($ mil.): 11,374

	STOCK PRICE ($) FY Close	P/E High/Low	PER SHARE ($) Earnings	Dividends	Book Value
12/17	120.55	17 12	7.07	2.52	23.13
12/16	84.82	18 9	4.75	2.36	18.68
12/15	63.05	19 13	4.47	2.20	16.99
12/14	78.05	20 15	3.99	1.60	15.47
12/13	63.28	14 9	4.47	1.51	13.37
Annual Growth	**17.5%**	**— —**	**12.1%**	**13.6%**	**14.7%**

PacWest Bancorp

PacWest Bancorp is the holding company for Pacific Western Bank which operates about 80 branches mostly in southern and central California plus an additional branch in Durham North Carolina. The $21 billion-asset bank caters to small and midsized businesses and their owners and employees offering traditional deposit and loan products and services. Commercial real estate mortgages make up more than 30% of its loan portfolio while cash flow- and asset-based business loans make up another 40%. The bank also originates residential mortgage real estate construction and land loans venture capital equipment finance and consumer loans. PacWest offers investment services and international banking through agreements with correspondent banks.

Operations

Like other retail banks PacWest generates the bulk of its revenue from interest income. About 83% of its total revenue came from interest income on loans and leases during 2015 while another 7% came from interest income on investments. The rest of its revenue came from leased equipment income (3% of revenue) deposit account service charges (1%) other commissions and fees (3%) and other miscellaneous income sources.

The bank's Square 1 Bank Division caters to entrepreneurial businesses and their venture capital and private equity investors while its Capital-Source Division provides cash flow asset-based equipment and real estate loans and leases as well as treasury management services to established middle-market businesses across the country.

Geographic Reach

PWB's branches are located across California in Los Angeles Orange Riverside San Bernardino Santa Barbara San Diego San Francisco San Luis Obispo San Mateo and Ventura Counties. It also has a branch in Durham North Carolina.

Financial Performance

PacWest's acquisitions in 2014 and 2015 boosted its interest-earning loan asset balances more than three-fold which sent its revenues and profits soaring during those years.

The bank's revenue jumped 30% to $968.3 million during 2015 mostly as newly acquired loans from its CapitalSource boosted its interest income during the year.

Strong revenue growth coupled with lower acquisition integration and reorganization costs in 2015 drove PacWest's net income up 77% to $300 million. Its operating cash levels spiked 79% to $594 million with the rise in cash-denominated earnings.

Strategy

PacWest has grown its loan and deposit business as well as its branch network through acquisitions of California community banks and specialized financial services companies. It has made 28 acquisitions since 2000 with some of its most recent being the Square 1 acquisition in 2015 and the CapitalSource Inc. acquisition in 2014.

Mergers and Acquisitions

In October 2015 PacWest purchased $4.6 billion-asset Square 1 and its Square 1 Bank subsidiary for $849 million forming the Square 1 Bank Division of the Bank. The deal boosted its core deposits expanded its national lending platform and bolstered its presence in the technology and life-sciences markets.

In April 2014 the bank bought $10.7 billion-asset CapitalSource Inc. and its CapitalSource Bank (CSB) subsidiary.

In May 2013 PacWest acquired $1.7 billion-asset First California Financial Group operator of First California Bank for $237 million. The purchase added six branches (after consolidation) in Los Angeles Orange Riverside San Bernardino San Diego San Luis Obispo and Ventura Counties.

Company Background

During the economic downturn PacWest took advantage of a rash of bank failures through FDIC-assisted transactions. The acquired institutions were merged into Pacific Western Bank. Under the loss-sharing deals the FDIC agreed to reimburse PacWest for future losses tied to the acquisitions. In a 2012 non-FDIC-assisted deal PacWest bought American Perspective Bank adding two branches and a loan office in the Central Coast area.

EXECUTIVES

Evp And Director The Company And Pacific Western Bank, Daniel B. Platt, age 71, $52,500 total compensation
Evp And Chief Risk Officer, Suzanne R. Brennan, age 67, $165,000 total compensation
Ceo, Matthew P. (Matt) Wagner, age 61, $754,167 total compensation
Evp And Cfo Pacific Western Bank, Patrick J. (Pat) Rusnak, age 54
Evp And Chief Accounting Officer, Lynn M. Hopkins, age 50
Evp; Director Human Resources, Christopher D. Blake, age 58, $298,958 total compensation
Evp And Chief Credit Officer, Bryan M. Corsini, age 56, $375,624 total compensation
Evp; President Capitalsource, James J. (Jim) Pieczynski, age 55, $554,539 total compensation
Evp Operations And Systems, Mark Christian
Evp General Counsel And Corporate Secretary, Kori L. Ogrosky
Senior Vice President Information Systems Manager, Norma Lopez
Chairman, John M. Eggemeyer, age 72
Auditors: KPMG LLP

LOCATIONS

HQ: PacWest Bancorp
9701 Wilshire Blvd., Suite 700, Beverly Hills, CA 90212
Phone: 310 887-8500
Web: www.pacwestbancorp.com

PRODUCTS/OPERATIONS

2015 Sales

	% of total
Interest income	
Loans and leases	87
Investment securities & other	7
Noninterest income	
Other commissions and fees	3
Leased equipment income	3
Service charges on deposit accounts	1
Other	3
FDIC loss sharing expense net	-
Total	**100**

Selected Mergers & Acquisitions

COMPETITORS

Bank of America	Rabobank America
CVB Financial	San Diego County
California Bank &	Credit Union
Trust	U.S. Bancorp
City National	Wells Fargo
JPMorgan Chase	Westamerica
MUFG Americas Holdings	

HISTORICAL FINANCIALS

Company Type: Public

Income Statement

FYE: December 31

	ASSETS ($ mil.)	NET INCOME ($ mil.)	INCOME AS % OF ASSETS	EMPLOYEES
12/17	24,994	357	1.4%	1,786
12/16	21,869	352	1.6%	1,669
12/15	21,288	299	1.4%	1,670
12/14	16,234	168	1.0%	1,443
12/13	6,533	45	0.7%	1,110
Annual Growth	39.9%	67.8%	—	12.6%

2017 Year-End Financials

Debt ratio: 1.85%
Return on equity: 7.57%
Cash ($ mil.): 398
Current ratio: —
Long-term debt ($ mil.): —

No. of shares (mil.): 128
Dividends
Yield: 0.0%
Payout: 68.7%
Market value ($ mil.): 6,491

	STOCK PRICE ($) FY Close	P/E High/Low	PER SHARE ($) Earnings	Dividends	Book Value
12/17	50.40	20 15	2.91	2.00	38.65
12/16	54.44	19 10	2.90	2.00	36.93
12/15	43.10	17 14	2.79	2.00	36.22
12/14	45.46	25 20	1.92	1.25	34.04
12/13	42.22	40 23	1.08	1.00	17.66
Annual Growth	4.5%	— —	28.1%	18.9%	21.6%

Park National Corp (Newark, OH)

Customers can park their money with Park National. The holding company owns Park National Bank which operates more than 120 branches in Ohio and northern Kentucky through 11 community banking divisions. The banks provide an array of consumer and business banking services including traditional savings and checking accounts and CDs. Business loans including commercial leases and mortgages operating loans and agricultural loans account for about 35% of Park National's loan portfolio. The banks also originate consumer residential real estate and construction loans. Park National's nonbank units include consumer finance outfit Guardian Finance Scope Aircraft Finance and Park Title Agency. In 2018 it acquired Charlotte NC-based NewDominion Bank for some $75 million.

Operations

Each of Park National Corporation's bank affiliates specialize in serving specific geographic locations. It's bank divisions include: Century National Bank; Fairfield National Bank; Farmers Bank; First-Knox National Bank; Park National Bank; Richland Bank; Security National Bank; Second National Bank; Unity National Bank; and United Bank.

Geographic Reach

Park National Corporation and its subsidiaries operate in Ohio and northern Kentucky.

Financial Performance

The company's revenue decreased in fiscal 2013 compared to the previous year. It reported $336.2 million in revenue for fiscal 2013 down from $378.1 million in fiscal 2012.

The company's net income dropped slightly in fiscal 2013 compared to the prior period as well. It reported a net income of $77 million in fiscal

2013 after netting a little more than $78 million the prior year.

Park National Corporation's cash on hand increased by almost $10 million in fiscal 2013 compared to fiscal 2012 levels.

EXECUTIVES

President And Ceo, David L. Trautman, age 56, $775,000 total compensation
Cfo Treasurer And Secretary; Svp And Cfo Park National Bank, Brady T. Burt, age 43, $325,000 total compensation
Chairman, C. Daniel (Dan) DeLawder, age 68
Auditors: Crowe Horwath LLP

LOCATIONS

HQ: Park National Corp (Newark, OH)
50 North Third Street, Newark, OH 43055
Phone: 740 349-8451
Web: www.parknationalcorp.com

PRODUCTS/OPERATIONS

2015 Sales

	$ mil.	% of total
Interest and fees on loans	228	66
Interest and dividends	37	10
Income from fiduciary activities	20	7
Service charges on deposit accounts	14	4
Checkcard fee income	14	4
Other service income	11	3
Other	16	6
Total	**342**	**100**

Selected Affiliates

Century National Bank
Fairfield National Bank
Farmers Bank
First-Knox National Bank
Guardian Finance Company
Park National Bank
Richland Bank
Scope Aircraft Finance
Second National Bank
Security National Bank
United bank
Unity National Bank

COMPETITORS

Bank of America
Fifth Third
Huntington Bancshares
JPMorgan Chase
PNC Financial

U.S. Bancorp
Wayne Savings
Bancshares
Wells Fargo

HISTORICAL FINANCIALS

Company Type: Public

Income Statement

FYE: December 31

	ASSETS ($ mil.)	NET INCOME ($ mil.)	INCOME AS % OF ASSETS	EMPLOYEES
12/17	7,537	84	1.1%	1,746
12/16	7,467	86	1.2%	1,726
12/15	7,311	81	1.1%	1,793
12/14	7,003	84	1.2%	1,801
12/13	6,638	77	1.2%	1,836
Annual Growth	3.2%	2.2%	—	(1.2%)

2017 Year-End Financials

Debt ratio: 0.20%
Return on equity: 11.24%
Cash ($ mil.): 169
Current ratio: —
Long-term debt ($ mil.): —

No. of shares (mil.): 15
Dividends
Yield: 0.0%
Payout: 68.7%
Market value ($ mil.): 1,590

	STOCK PRICE ($) FY Close	P/E High/Low	PER SHARE ($) Earnings	Dividends	Book Value
12/17	104.00	22 17	5.47	3.76	49.46
12/16	119.66	22 14	5.59	3.76	48.38
12/15	90.48	19 15	5.26	3.76	46.53
12/14	88.48	16 13	5.46	3.76	45.39
12/13	85.07	17 13	5.01	3.76	42.29
Annual Growth	5.2%	— —	2.2%	(0.0%)	4.0%

Parker Hannifin Corp

Parker-Hannifin is a leading global manufacturer of motion and control technologies including fluid power systems for the manufacturing and processing industries. It additionally makes hydraulic fuel pneumatic and electromechanical systems and components for the aerospace/defense industry; and motion and control systems for the heating ventilation air conditioning and refrigeration (HVACR) and transportation industries. It owns some 330 manufacturing plants and operates through the two business segments of Diversified Industrial and Aerospace. The company traces its historical roots back to 1918.

Operations

Parker-Hannifin is a worldwide diversified manufacturer of motion and control technologies and systems. It provides precision engineered technologies products and services for a wide variety of mobile industrial and aerospace markets.

Its largest division the Industrial segment is made up of the Automation Filtration Fluid Connectors Hydraulics Instrumentation and Seal groups. Sales of Industrial products in North American and international markets are made primarily to original equipment manufacturers (OEMs) and their replacement markets in various sectors within the manufacturing processing and transportation industries. They include agriculture alternative energy chemical processing construction machinery factory automation food production life sciences material handling paper robotics and water among many others.

Aerospace segment products are sold mainly to commercial and military customers in the OEM and maintenance repair and overhaul end user markets. They are used in aircraft engines missiles unmanned aerial vehicles and in power generation applications.

Geographic Reach

Parker-Hannifin operates more than 330 manufacturing plants and nearly 130 distribution centers and 160 sales and administrative offices in 40 states and in roughly 50 other countries worldwide. North America accounts for roughly 60% of its sales.

Sales and Marketing

Diversified Industrial products are made primarily to original equipment manufacturers (OEM) and their replacement markets in manufacturing packaging processing transportation mobile construction refrigeration and air conditioning agricultural and military machinery and equipment industries. This segment's sales are marketed primarily through field sales employees and approximately 13700 independent distributor locations throughout the world.

Aerospace products cater to the commercial and military aerospace markets to both OEMs and to end-users for spares maintenance repair and overhaul.

Financial Performance

After declining the previous year Parker-Hannifin' revenues spiked by 6% to reach $12 billion in 2017. The growth was primarily a result of acquisitions (contributing almost $560 million in sales) and an increase in volume in both its Diversified Industrial International and Aerospace Systems segment partially offset by the effect of currency rate changes (which decreased net sales in 2017 by almost $85 million).

Its net income also increased 22% to $983 million in 2017 largely due to additional gains made from its CLARCOR acquisition. The rise in net income and additional sales from previous acquisitions also helped Parker-Hannifin's operating cash flow climb from $1.17 billion in 2016 to $1.3 billion in 2017.

Strategy

The company seeks to enhance its operations and profitability through a strategy of identifying and acquiring businesses with complementary products and services and by divesting businesses that are not considered to be a good long-term fit. It also focuses on building up its operations around targeted regions technologies and markets through acquisitions and organic growth.

Mergers and Acquisitions

Parker-Hannifin uses acquisitions as a means of enhancing its product portfolio and growing its global footprint.

In a move that significantly expanded its filtration portfolio in early 2017 Parker Hannifin bought CLARCOR a maker of mobile industrial and environmental filtration products in a deal valued at $4.3 billion. The transaction added more than a dozen respected CLARCOR brands including CLARCOR Baldwin Fuel Manager Airguard Altair Hastings and United Air Specialists among others. In addition it gave Parker-Hannifin stronger relationships with original equipment manufacturers and customers in international markets especially for recurring sales in the aftermarket.

In mid-2016 Parker Hannifin acquired JA¤ger Automobil-Technik GmbH and JA¤ger Automotive Polska Sp. z.o.o headquartered in Hannover Germany. The JA¤ger Group is a pioneer in rubber-to-plastic direct bonded sealing systems for automotive markets and a leading developer of two-component (2K) direct injection molding technology. The deal provided Parker with innovative injection molding technology and businesses with a strong reputation in the automotive industry.

HISTORY

Entrepreneurial engineer Arthur Parker founded the Parker Appliance Company in 1918 to make pneumatic brake boosters. Its products were designed to help trucks and buses stop more easily. Unfortunately Parker's own truck slid off an icy road and over a cliff in 1919 destroying the company's inventory and ending that line of business.

Undeterred Parker started a hydraulics and pneumatic components business in 1924 to serve automotive and industrial clients. In 1927 the fuel-linkage system the company developed for the Spirit of St. Louis helped Lindbergh cross the Atlantic. The company prospered during the Depression; sales reached $2 million in 1934. Two of Parker's long-term clients were Douglas Aircraft and Lockheed.

The company went public in 1938. It employed 5000 defense workers during WWII. After Parker died in 1945 his wife Helen hired new management to focus on the automation market. The firm bought cylinder maker Hannifin in 1957 and became Parker-Hannifin.

In 1960 Parker-Hannifin formed an international unit in Amsterdam and it set up a German subsidiary in 1962. Overseas acquisitions and increased demand from the space program and the aviation market spurred growth in the 1960s. Patrick Parker the founder's son became president in 1968 and chairman in 1977. Parker-Hannifin expanded its aerospace business in 1978 with the purchase of Bertea (electrohydraulic flight controls). Patrick Parker continued as CEO until 1983 and as chairman until 1999.

EXECUTIVES

Vp Ebusiness Iot And Services, Robert W. (Bob) Bond, age 60, $548,700 total compensation

President And Coo, Lee C. Banks, age 55, $850,000 total compensation

Vp And Cio, William G. (Bill) Eline, age 62

Vp And President Instrumentation Group, John R. Greco, age 64

Vp And Chief Technology And Innovation Officer, M. Craig Maxwell, age 60

Vp And President Aerospace Group, Roger S. Sherrard, age 52

Chairman And Ceo, Thomas L. (Tom) Williams, age 59, $1,000,000 total compensation

Vp Global Supply Chain And Procurement, John G. Dedinsky, age 61

Vp And President Automation Group, Yoon (Michael) Chung, age 55

Vp And President Asia Pacific Group, Kurt A. Keller, age 60

Cfo, Catherine A. (Cathy) Suever, age 60

Vp And President Engineered Materials Group, Andrew D. Ross

Vp And President Latin America Group, Candido Lima

Vp And President Filtration Group, Robert W. Malone

Vp And President Europe Middle East And Africa Group (emea), Joachim Guhe

Evp Human Resources And External Affairs, Mark J. Hart

Vp And President Engineered Materials Group, Jennifer A. Parmentier

Vp And President Hydraulics Group, Andrew M. Weeks, $400,956 total compensation

Vp General Counsel And Secretary, Joseph R. Leonti, $410,400 total compensation

Vice President Information Technology Global Finance And Administrative Systems, John Connors

Vice President Of Operations, Jim Rowell

National Account Manager, Deirdre Stinson

Vp And Group Controller, Nick Liberatore

Vice President And President Instrumentation Group, William Bowman

Vice President Of Operations North America, Rob Malone

Group Vice President Supply Chain Management Aerospace Group, Dorith Hakim

Board Member, Glenn Crame

Board Member, Grace Monserrate

Auditors: DELOITTE & TOUCHE LLP

LOCATIONS

HQ: Parker Hannifin Corp
6035 Parkland Boulevard, Cleveland, OH 44124-4141
Phone: 216 896-3000
Web: www.parker.com

2017 Sales

	$ mil.	% of total
North America	7,585	63
International	4,443	37
Total	**12,029**	**100**

PRODUCTS/OPERATIONS

2017 Sales

	$ mil.	% of total
Diversified Industrial		
North America	5,366	45
International	4,377	36
Aerospace Systems	2,284	19
Total	**12,029**	**100**

Selected Brand Names

Atlas Cylinders
Balston
Bayside
Bellows
Cabett
Calzoni
Chelsea
Chomerics
Compumotor
croloop
CTC
Ermeto
Fluid Power
Gold Ring
Greer
Gresen
Hiross
IPS
Jet-Pipe
Lucifer
Miller
Ross
Schrader
Sempress
Skinner
Sporlan
STC

Operating Groups and Selected Products
Aerospace
  Aircraft wheels and brakes
  Flight control components
  Fuel systems
  Pneumatic pumps and valves
Climate and industrial controls
  Expansion valves
  Filter-dryers
  Hose assemblies
  Pressure regulators
  Solenoid valves
Industrial
  Automation
  Air preparation units
  Electric actuators
  Human/machine interface hardware and software
  Indexers
  Multi-axis positioning tables
  Pneumatic valves
  Stepper and servo drives
  Structural extrusions
  Vacuum products
  Filtration
  Cabin air filters
  Compressed-air and gas-purification filters
  Fuel conditioning filters
  Fuel filters/water separators
  Gas generators
  Gas generators
  Hydraulic lubrication and coolant filters
  Lube oil and fuel filters
  Monitoring devices
  Nitrogen and hydrogen generators
  Process chemical and microfiltration filters
  Water desalinization and purification
  Fluid Connectors
  Couplers
  Diagnostic equipment
  Hoses and hose fittings
  Tube fittings
  Valves
  Hydraulics
  Accumulators
  Cylinders
  Electrohydraulic systems
  Hydrostatic steering units
  Metering pumps
  Motors and pumps
  Power units
  Rotary actuators
  Sensors

Valves
Instrumentation
Ball plug and needle valves
Cylinder connections
Fluoropolymer fittings
Miniature solenoid valves
Multi-solenoid manifolds
Packless ultra-high-purity valves
Quick connects
Regulators
Spray guns
Transducers
Tubing
Ultra high-purity tube fittings
Seals
Gaskets and packings
Metal and plastic composite seals
Medical devices seals and instruments
O-rings
O-seals
Thermal management products

COMPETITORS

Bosch Rexroth	ITT Corp.
Crane Co.	Moog
Danaher	SMC Corp.
Danfoss	Swagelok
Donaldson Company	Trelleborg
Eaton	Woodward Governor
Emerson Electric	Zodiac Aerospace
Honeywell	
International	

HISTORICAL FINANCIALS

Company Type: Public

Income Statement

FYE: June 30

	REVENUE ($ mil.)	NET INCOME ($ mil.)	NET PROFIT MARGIN	EMPLOYEES
06/18	14,302	1,060	7.4%	57,170
06/17	12,029	983	8.2%	56,690
06/16	11,360	806	7.1%	48,950
06/15	12,711	1,012	8.0%	54,754
06/14	13,215	1,041	7.9%	57,450
Annual Growth	2.0%	0.5%	—	(0.1%)

2018 Year-End Financials

Debt ratio: 32.36%	No. of shares (mil.): 132
Return on equity: 19.08%	Dividends
Cash ($ mil.): 822	Yield: 0.0%
Current ratio: 1.59	Payout: 34.9%
Long-term debt ($ mil.): 4,318	Market value ($ mil.): 20,637

	STOCK PRICE ($) FY Close	P/E High/Low	Earnings	PER SHARE ($) Dividends	Book Value
06/18	155.85	26 19	7.83	2.74	44.25
06/17	159.82	22 15	7.25	2.58	39.50
06/16	108.05	20 15	5.89	2.52	34.14
06/15	116.33	19 15	6.97	2.37	36.84
06/14	125.73	19 14	6.87	1.86	44.72
Annual Growth	5.5%	— —	3.3%	10.2%	(0.3%)

PARTNERS HEALTHCARE SYSTEM, INC.

Partners HealthCare System is looking out for the health of the Bay State. Partners HealthCare includes two large acute-care medical centers — Brigham and Women's Hospital and Massachusetts General Hospital— and seven community hos-

pitals. The not-for-profit system also provides primary and specialty care through clinics physician offices long-term care facilities and home health and hospice agencies. Its rehabilitation facilities include the Spaulding Rehabilitation Hospital Network. Partners HealthCare also provides medical training and research through an affiliation with Harvard. Other ventures include the Dana-Farber/Partners CancerCare clinic (a collaboration with Harvard and Dana-Farber Cancer Institute).

Operations

Partners HealthCare's Partners Community HealthCare division is a management services organization that provides support for a physician network encompassing some 6500 practitioners. Partners HealthCare also sponsors community health outreach programs. Community hospitals owned by or affiliated with Partners include McLean Hospital Newton-Wellesley Hospital North Shore Medical Center Nantucket Cottage Hospital and the Martha's Vineyard Hospital. Partners HealthCare also operates Faulkner Hospital as a subsidiary of the Brigham and Women's facility.

Brigham and Women's (a 777-bed facility) and Massachusetts General are both teaching hospitals for the Harvard Medical School. The Harvard Clinical Research Institute is a partnership between the Harvard Medical School Partners HealthCare and CareGroup (parent of Boston facilities including Beth Israel Deaconess Medical Center). Outside the US the system's Partners HealthCare International provides clinical advisory patient care research and educational programs with a number of global partners. With an annual research budget of $1.6 billion Partners HealthCare has a strong research funding base including awards of some $600 million annually from the National Institutes of Health.

The system serves 1.5 million patients annually.

Geographic Reach

Partners HealthCare provides services to patients in the Greater Boston area as well as New England and beyond. It also partners with health care systems and health-related academic institutions in more than 40 countries.

Strategy

Partners HealthCare strives to provide innovative yet affordable medical care to area residents. To keep its operations efficient as well as to comply with federal health reform incentive measures Partners HealthCare has put in place a health information system that requires all of its doctors to use electronic health records (EHRs). As one of the early adopters of EHR systems Partners HealthCare is upgrading its IT systems to install a new clinical information system across its facilities using new technologies from software maker Epic. The new system — which will enhance coordination of care reduce unnecessary health spending and simplify reporting and patient access features — will be implemented over 10 years and will cost between $600 and $700 million.

Other programs to meet new health care standards include reducing prices on certain procedures and renegotiating contracts with insurers as well as encouraging patients to participate in preventative care wellness and generic drug programs.

Mergers and Acquisitions

Partners HealthCare is buying Care New England as part of its bid to expand beyond Massachusetts. In 2018 the two companies approached Rhode Island-based Lifespan to also join forces but that proposal was subsequently dropped.

In another deal the organization has agreed to acquire specialty hospital Massachusetts Eye and Ear.

Company Background

Partners HealthCare has been recognized by the federal government and other organizations for its quality and efficiency programs. In 2012 the

health network was selected by the Centers for Medicare and Medicaid Services to participate in the Pioneer ACO (accountable care organization) program which aims to slow cost growth in the Medicare market by enhancing care coordination.

Partners HealthCare was founded in 1994 through the merger of Brigham and Women's Hospital and Massachusetts General Hospital.

EXECUTIVES

Vice President Public Affairs Partners Community Benefit Programs, Lee Chelminiak
Vice President Of Finance, David Mcguire
Evp Administration And Finance Cfo And Treasurer, Peter K. Markell, age 62
President And Ceo Massachusetts General Hospital, Peter L. Slavin
Cio, James W. (Jim) Noga
President And Ceo North Shore Medical Center, Robert G. (Bob) Norton, age 68
President And Ceo Neighborhood Health Plan, Deborah C. Enos
President And Ceo Partners Continuing Care, David E. Storto
President And Ceo Brigham And Women's Hospital, Elizabeth G. (Betsy) Nabel
President And Chief Executive Officer, David F. Torchiana
President Of Partners Community, Thomas H. Lee
President And Ceo Spaulding Rehabilitation Network, Maureen Banks
President Mclean Hospital, Scott L. Rauch
President And Ceo Brigham And Women's Physicians Organization, Allen L. Smith
President And Ceo Martha's Vineyard Hospital, Timothy J. Walsh
President And Ceo Mgh Institute Of Health Professions, Janis P. Bellack
President And Ceo, David Torchiana
President And Ceo Nantucket Cottage Hospital, Margot Hartmann
President And Ceo Partners Healthcare At Home, Rod Carnifax
Medical Director, Judy A Nugent
Medical Director Of The Breast And Ovarian Cancer, Paula Ryan
Nursing Director, Elizabeth McGrath
Vice President Revenue Cycle Operations, Rosemary R Sheehan
Director Of Nursing, Deirdre Greene
Nursing Director, Janet Quigley
Nursing Director, Mary Sylvia-Reardon
Medical Director Of Quality Safey And Population Management, Adrienne Allen
Medical Director, Richard Kaufman
Project Manager To Senior Vice President Research, Angela Vail
Medical Director, Sharon Bober
Nursing Director, Judith Silva
Clinical Director, Jane Evans
Nursing Director, Michele Ohara
Clinical Director, Martha Kane
Vice President Of Operations, Hofmann Erika
Nursing Director, Peggy Settle
Vice President Of Systems, Meg Costello
Clinical Director, Scott Waugh
Assistant Vice President Regional Consultant, Viscomi Rudy
Assistant Vice President Regional Consultant, Vu Dung
Rsvp Team Leader, Jessica Grajeda
Vice President Of Information Technology, Karl Fitch
Chairman, Edward P. Lawrence, age 76
Secretary, Maria Sanchez
Board Member, Jonathan Katz
Treasurer, Xandra Breakefield
Board Member, Martha Pitman

LOCATIONS

HQ: PARTNERS HEALTHCARE SYSTEM, INC.
800 BOYLSTON ST STE 1150, BOSTON, MA
021998123
Phone: 617 278-1000
Web: WWW.PARTNERS.ORG

PRODUCTS/OPERATIONS

2014 Sales

	% of total
Net patient service revenue	65
Premium revenue	15
Direct academic and research	11
Indirect academic and research	3
Other revenue	6
Total	**100**

COMPETITORS

Baystate Health	Lahey Health System
Boston Medical Center	Milford Regional
Cambridge Health	Medical Center
Alliance	Northeast Health
Cape Cod Healthcare	System
Cape Cod Hospital	Southcoast Hospitals
Care New England	Group
CareGroup	Steward Health Care
Children's Hospital	Universal Health
Boston	Services

HISTORICAL FINANCIALS

Company Type: Private

Income Statement

FYE: September 30

	REVENUE ($ mil.)	NET INCOME ($ mil.)	NET PROFIT MARGIN	EMPLOYEES
09/15	11,665	(916)	—	67,000
09/10	8	(0)	—	—
09/08	551	(44)	—	—
Annual Growth	54.7%	—	—	—

2015 Year-End Financials

Debt ratio: ——
Return on equity: (-7.90%)
Cash ($ mil.): 621
Current ratio: 0.70
Long-term debt ($ mil.): ——

Dividends
Yield: —
Payout: —
Market value ($ mil.): ——

Patterson Companies Inc

Patterson Companies' catalogs are like wish lists for veterinary and dental practices. The company operates through two primary segments — wholesalers Patterson Animal Health and Patterson Dental. Patterson Animal Health distributes animal supplies including pharmaceuticals parasiticides and equipment in the US Canada and the UK. Patterson Dental distributes products including X-ray film and machines hand instruments sterilization products dental chairs and lights and diagnostic equipment. Patterson Dental serves the US and Canada; some 85% of its sales come from the US.

Operations

Patterson Animal Health is a leading US distributor of health products for companion animals and horses. It sells more than 100000 products including vaccines and drugs consumables and di-

agnostic supplies and is responsible for nearly 60% of Patterson Companies' revenue.

In business since 1877 Patterson Dental is the second-largest dental supply wholesaler in the US and Canada (after Henry Schein); it accounts for more than 40% of Patterson's sales. The segment offers its customers more than 90000 different items including approximately 3000 private-label products marketed under the Patterson name. In addition to consumables and equipment Patterson Dental offers services such as technology consulting; office design; equipment installation maintenance and repair; and financing for big-ticket purchases.

Geographic Reach

The US market accounts for some 85% of Patterson's annual revenues. Patterson Dental provides dental supplies throughout the US and Canada. Patterson Animal Health distributes items throughout the UK Canada and the US.

Patterson Logistics Services operates distribution centers in Alabama California Colorado Florida Hawaii Indiana Iowa Pennsylvania South Carolina Texas and Washington.

Sales and Marketing

Patterson's products are sold through direct sales and marketing representatives in the US and Canada to over 150000 customers. Marketing is conducted through its website and through catalogs magazines and direct mail. Customers include dentists dental laboratories veterinarian offices laboratories and other health care providers and institutions.

Subsidiary Patterson Logistics Services operates seven primary distribution centers and six smaller facilities in the US that conduct distribution functions for both Patterson segments. Some of the centers stock products from multiple business units while others serve one segment.

Advertising expenses totaled $6926 in fiscal 2018 (ended April) versus $10128 in 2017 and $12113 in 2016.

Financial Performance

Patterson Companies saw rising revenues for years until fiscal 2018 when sales slipped a modest amount. Net income has been more volatile over recent years as the company's expenses have fluctuated.

In fiscal 2018 revenue dropped 2% to $5.5 billion. That decline was led by the Dental segment's sales which fell 8%. Sales of consumables fell 5% as a result of the company's sales team restructuring and the development of new back-end technologies; equipment and software sales fell 15%. These sales declines were partially offset by 3% higher Animal Health sales.

Net income increased 18% to $201 million in 2018 thanks to lower cost of sales and operating expenses.

Patterson ended fiscal 2018 with $63 million in cash some $32 million less than it had at the start of the year. Although operating activities provided $178.9 million in net cash and investing activities provided another $17 million financing activities used $230.3 million.

Strategy

Patterson Companies relies on its ability to provide a diverse platform of products and services in a total-package approach. A key strategy is to promote its value-added services such as equipment installation and maintenance financing and technology guidance.

The company has also invested in its own technology platforms. For example it is building a new enterprise resource planning (ERP) system. The focus on enhancing its online ordering systems has allowed Patterson to build its client base while freeing up sales representatives to spend more time with customers. Additionally the company offers technology troubleshooting claims and elec-

tronic statements through its Patterson Technology Center.

Patterson has grown through internal expansion and via acquisitions. It seeks opportunities to take advantage of the fractured markets in which it operates. Such opportunities include buying other distributors or opening new locations to enter additional markets.

Mergers and Acquisitions

In late 2017 Patterson Dental acquired dental office design and equipment dealer Fitzpatrick Dental Design based out of California. That purchase helped build the company's equipment design and sales operations.

HISTORY

In 1877 brothers Myron and John Patterson bought a Milwaukee drugstore and later added dental supplies to the inventory. Myron bought the dental side of the business from his brother in 1891 moved to St. Paul Minnesota and started a dental supply store. His business later became a subsidiary of diversified manufacturer Esmark which sold Patterson to food giant Beatrice in 1982. Recognizing that food and dental supplies were an odd mix Patterson executives initiated a leveraged buyout in 1985.

In an industry as fragmented as some dental patients' smiles the firm used acquisitions to secure a leading position as a full-service provider. In 1987 Patterson bought D.L. Saslow then the #3 distributor. Between 1989 and 1993 it bought smaller distributors in eight states and Washington DC. In 1993 a year after it went public Patterson bought the Canadian arm of bankrupt rival Healthco International.

During the mid- and late 1990s Patterson continued to buy small local dental-supply distributors branching out across the US and Canada. In 1996 and 1997 Patterson expanded into front-office products with the purchase of Colwell Systems and EagleSoft. It took a few more bites out of the market with purchases of two more local distributors in 1998. In 2000 it bought Micheli Dental Supply a dental products distributor in California and eCheck-Up.com an online provider of payroll human resources payables processing and other services.

In 2001 Patterson expanded beyond dental products distribution when it purchased J. A. Webster a distributor of veterinary supplies. Patterson broadened its operations further in 2003 acquiring AbilityOne Products a provider of medical rehabilitation supplies. It also acquired Smith & Nephew's rehab division and with it the Rolyan and Homecraft brand names. The following year the company changed its name from Patterson Dental to Patterson Companies to reflect this expansion.

However returning its focus on its dental and veterinary businesses the firm sold its Patterson Medical unit in 2015.

EXECUTIVES

Southwest Regional Manager Patterson Dental, Paul A. Guggenheim, age 58, $384,482 total compensation

Evp And Cfo, Ann B. Gugino, age 46, $399,167 total compensation

Vp Operations, Sean M. Muniz

Vp General Counsel And Secretary, Les B. Korsh, age 48, $280,833 total compensation

President Patterson Dental North America And President Patterson Foundation Board Of Directors, Dave Misiak

Cio, Dave Lardy

Interim President Patterson Animal Health, Kevin Pohlman

President Ceo And Director, Mark S. Walchirk

Chairman, John D. Buck, age 67
Treasurer, Dennis Goedken
Assistant Treasurer Director Of Credit, Jeff Stang
Assistant Treasurer Tax, Michelle Bragg
Auditors: Ernst & Young LLP

LOCATIONS

HQ: Patterson Companies Inc
1031 Mendota Heights Road, St. Paul, MN 55120
Phone: 651 686-1600
Web: www.pattersoncompanies.com

2018 Sales

	$ mil.	% of total
US	4,537	83
UK	583	11
Canada	345	6
Total	**5,465**	**100**

PRODUCTS/OPERATIONS

2018 Sales by Segment

	$ mil.	% of total
Animal Health	3,242	59
Dental	2,196	40
Corporate	27	1
Total	**5,465**	**100**

2018 Sales

	$ mil.	% of total
Consumables	4,415	81
Equipment & software	709	13
Other	340	6
Total	**5,465**	**100**

COMPETITORS

Benco Dental	IDEXX Labs
Burkhart Dental	MWI Veterinary Supply
Cardinal Health	McKesson
Carestream Health	Universal Medical
Darby Dental	Systems
Henry Schein	

HISTORICAL FINANCIALS

Company Type: Public

Income Statement   FYE: April 28

	REVENUE ($ mil.)	NET INCOME ($ mil.)	NET PROFIT MARGIN	EMPLOYEES
04/18	5,465	200	3.7%	7,700
04/17	5,593	170	3.1%	7,500
04/16	5,386	187	3.5%	7,000
04/15	4,375	223	5.1%	7,000
04/14	4,063	200	4.9%	7,000
Annual Growth	**7.7%**	**0.0%**	**—**	**2.4%**

2018 Year-End Financials

Debt ratio: 29.23%
Return on equity: 14.11%
Cash ($ mil.): 62
Current ratio: 1.95
Long-term debt ($ mil.): 922
No. of shares (mil.): 94
Dividends
Yield: 0.0%
Payout: 48.1%
Market value ($ mil.): 2,251

	STOCK PRICE ($) FY Close	P/E High/Low		PER SHARE ($) Earnings	Dividends	Book Value
04/18	23.76	22	10	2.16	1.04	15.43
04/17	44.49	28	22	1.79	0.98	14.44
04/16	43.35	27	20	1.91	0.90	14.55
04/15	48.19	23	17	2.24	0.82	14.66
04/14	40.91	22	19	1.97	0.68	14.16
Annual Growth	**(12.7%)**	**—**	**—**	**2.3%**	**11.2%**	**2.2%**

PayPal Holdings Inc

Auditors: PricewaterhouseCoopers LLP

LOCATIONS

HQ: PayPal Holdings Inc
2211 North First Street, San Jose, CA 95131
Phone: 108 067 1000
Web: www.paypal.com

HISTORICAL FINANCIALS

Company Type: Public

Income Statement   FYE: December 31

	REVENUE ($ mil.)	NET INCOME ($ mil.)	NET PROFIT MARGIN	EMPLOYEES
12/18	15,451	2,057	13.3%	21,800
12/17	13,094	1,795	13.7%	18,700
12/16	10,842	1,401	12.9%	18,100
12/15	9,248	1,228	13.3%	16,800
12/14	8,025	419	5.2%	15,800
Annual Growth	**17.8%**	**48.9%**	**—**	**8.4%**

2018 Year-End Financials

Debt ratio: —
Return on equity: 13.11%
Cash ($ mil.): 7,575
Current ratio: 1.27
Long-term debt ($ mil.): —
No. of shares (mil.): 1,174
Dividends
Yield: —
Payout: —
Market value ($ mil.): 98,722

	STOCK PRICE ($) FY Close	P/E High/Low		PER SHARE ($) Earnings	Dividends	Book Value
12/18	84.09	53	41	1.71	0.00	13.11
12/17	73.62	53	26	1.47	0.00	13.33
12/16	39.47	38	27	1.15	0.00	12.19
12/15	36.20	40	31	1.00	0.00	11.24
Annual Growth	**23.5%**	**—**	**—**	**14.4%**	**—**	**3.9%**

PBF Energy Inc

Established US oil refiners meet the new kid on the block. Formed in the first decade of 21st century PBF Energy's five oil refineries are located in California Delaware Louisiana New Jersey and Ohio and have a combined production capacity of about 900000 barrels per day making the company the fourth-largest refiner in the US. PBF's refineries produce gasoline ultra-low-sulfur diesel heating oil jet fuel lubricants petrochemicals and asphalt for the Midwestern and Northeastern US. The company indirectly owns the general partner and approximately 44.2% of the limited partnership interest of PBF Logistics LP. PBF Energy is majority-owned by investment firms The Blackstone Group and First Reserve.

Operations

PBF Energy operates two business segments: Refining which accounts for more than 95% of its sales and Logistics (through PBF Logistics) which accounts for the remaining less-than 5% of sales.;

Refineries in the East Coast (Delaware City and Paulsboro) average total throughput rates of 370000 barrels per day (bpd) and in the Mid-Continent (Toledo) 170000 bpd. Total refined product barrels sold are around 365000 at East Coast re-

fineries; 170000 at Mid-Continent refineries; and 206000 at Gulf Coast refineries.

Gasoline and distillates account for more than 85% of PBF Energy's total sales; chemicals asphalt and blackoils lubricants and feedstocks all account for less than 5% each.

Geographic Reach

PBF Energy operates refineries in Torrance California; Delaware City Delaware; New Orleans Louisiana; Paulsboro New Jersey; and Toledo Ohio and sells its products in Canada and the US.

Sales and Marketing

PBF has product offtake agreements for a large portion of its product sales. The remainder of its refined products are sold through short-term contracts or on the spot market.

Financial Performance

The collapse in the oil price put a severe dent in PBF Energy's revenue in 2015 but in fiscal 2016 the company defied industry trends and grew revenue 21% to $15.9 billion. The increase was primarily a result of contributions from the Torrance refinery acquired from ExxonMobil mid-year. On the downside average selling prices for refined oil fell around $10 per barrel. Volume sales outstripped total throughput meaning the company dipped into inventory.

Net income increased 17% to $170.8 million as changes in the oil price triggered a positive pretax adjustment to inventory value of $521.3 million. Aside from this single large item net income was put under pressure by tighter margins relating to crude oil differentials lower refined selling prices versus raw material costs and increased interest.

Cash from operations increased 16% to $651.9 million due to deferred income taxes worth $244.8 million and changes in inventories.

Strategy

PBF's strategy is to opportunistically acquire refineries. Its latest such acquisition is of the Torrance refinery in California (following the Chalmette acquisition in 2015) which has daily refining capacity of 155000 barrels per day and was bought in 2016. The refinery can process heavy and medium crude oils and has a sophisticated logistics network of crude and products pipelines distribution terminals and refinery crude. Subsequent to its acquisitions PBF targets margin increases by installing new management and carrying out turnarounds.

PBF Logistics PBF's logistics partner acquires new storage capacity and accepts drop-down transactions from PBF. In 2016 it bought four million barrels of capacity in the Philadelphia region and bought from PBF a 50% interest in Torrance Valley Pipeline Company to look after the gathering and pipeline delivery systems hooked up to the Torrance refinery. The two deals increased PBF Logistics' revenue base by 70%. In addition the cash received by PBF accelerates turnaround activities at its acquired refineries.

Mergers and Acquisitions

Expanding to the US West Coast in 2016 PBF Energy acquired the Torrance refinery and related logistics assets from Exxon Mobil for $537.5 million. The Torrance refinery located on 750 acres in Torrance California is a high-conversion 155000 barrel per day delayed-coking refinery.It sold the logistics assets linked to the refinery to its joint venture PBF Logistics.

Company Background

PBF Energy was created in 2008 by Swiss oil refiner Petroplus to help it establish a foothold in the US. Petroplus and The Blackstone Group each invested $667 million to begin buying oil refineries at the height of the global economic recession when larger companies were looking to sell off assets to drum up cash. PBF first bought the Delaware refinery from Valero in 2010 for $220 million. (The low price tag came because the refinery had been shut down since 2009). Next came the New Jersey refinery again purchased from Valero for $358 million.

In 2011 PBF Energy bought an Ohio refinery from Sunoco for $400 million.

PBF Energy went public in 2012 with an IPO that raised $429 million. The IPO came as a quick turnaround before PBF Energy was able to recognize any significant revenue and the company used the $613 million in proceeds to pay back its principal investors Blackstone and First Reserve.

In 2013 PBF Energy signed a deal with Continental Resources for the oil company to supply PBF Energy with Bakken crude oil. The deal marks a shift for the East Coast refinery market - a market that has historically relied on imports of foreign oil.

EXECUTIVES

National Sales Manager Base Oils, Scott Carter
  Scott Carter

Chairman And Ceo, Thomas J. Nimbley, age 66, $1,500,000 total compensation

Svp Commercial, Thomas L. O'Connor, age 45, $500,000 total compensation

Evp, Matthew C. Lucey, age 44, $600,000 total compensation

Cfo, C. Erik Young, age 42, $523,958 total compensation

Svp Refining, Herman Seedorf, age 66

Svp Commercial Western Region, Timothy Paul Davis

Vice President Human Resources, Wendy HoTai
Auditors: DELOITTE & TOUCHE LLP

LOCATIONS

HQ: PBF Energy Inc
  One Sylvan Way, Second Floor, Parsippany, NJ 07054
Phone: 973 455-7500
Web: www.pbfenergy.com

PRODUCTS/OPERATIONS

Products
Clean Fuels
Lubes
Petrochemicals
LPG

2016 sales by segment

	% of total
Refining	99
Logistics	1
Elimination	-
Total	**100**

2016 sales

	% of total
Gasoline & distillates	88
Asphalt and blackoils	5
Chemicals	3
Feedstocks and other	2
Lubricants	2
Total	**100**

COMPETITORS

Alon USA Energy	Motiva Enterprises
CITGO Refining and Chemicals	Paramount Petroleum
	Placid Refining
Chevron	San Joaquin Refining
ConocoPhillips	Shell Oil Products
Exxon Mobil	Sunoco
Flint Hills	Tauber Oil
HollyFrontier	United Refining
Marathon Petroleum	Valero Energy

HISTORICAL FINANCIALS

Company Type: Public

Income Statement

FYE: December 31

	REVENUE ($ mil.)	NET INCOME ($ mil.)	NET PROFIT MARGIN	EMPLOYEES
12/17	21,786	415	1.9%	3,165
12/16	15,920	170	1.1%	3,165
12/15	13,123	146	1.1%	2,270
12/14	19,828	(38)	—	1,714
12/13	19,151	39	0.2%	1,735
Annual Growth	**3.3%**	**80.0%**		**16.2%**

2017 Year-End Financials

Debt ratio: 27.00%	No. of shares (mil.): 110
Return on equity: 19.05%	Dividends
Cash ($ mil.): 573	Yield: 0.0%
Current ratio: 1.57	Payout: 32.1%
Long-term debt ($ mil.): 2,175	Market value ($ mil.): 3,920

	STOCK PRICE ($) FY Close	P/E High/Low		PER SHARE ($) Earnings	Dividends	Book Value
12/17	35.45	9	5	3.73	1.20	21.13
12/16	27.88	22	11	1.74	1.20	18.54
12/15	36.81	25	14	1.65	1.20	16.85
12/14	26.64	—	—	(0.51)	1.20	14.86
12/13	31.46	34	17	1.20	1.20	16.49
Annual Growth	**3.0%**	—	—	**32.8%**	**(0.0%)**	**6.4%**

PCSB Financial Corp

Auditors: Crowe Horwath LLP

LOCATIONS

HQ: PCSB Financial Corp
  2651 Strang Blvd., Suite 100, Yorktown Heights, NY 10598
Phone: 914 248-7272
Web: www.pcsb.com

HISTORICAL FINANCIALS

Company Type: Public

Income Statement

FYE: June 30

	ASSETS ($ mil.)	NET INCOME ($ mil.)	INCOME AS % OF ASSETS	EMPLOYEES
06/18	1,480	6	0.4%	183
06/17	1,426	3	0.2%	184
06/16	1,262	2	0.2%	177
06/15	1,200	0	0.0%	
Annual Growth	**7.2%**	**135.1%**	—	—

2018 Year-End Financials

Debt ratio: —	No. of shares (mil.): 18
Return on equity: 2.33%	Dividends
Cash ($ mil.): 60	Yield: 0.0%
Current ratio: —	Payout: 7.6%
Long-term debt ($ mil.): —	Market value ($ mil.): 361

	STOCK PRICE ($) FY Close	P/E High/Low		PER SHARE ($) Earnings	Dividends	Book Value
06/18	19.87	56	43	0.39	0.03	15.83
06/17	17.06	—	—	(0.00)	0.00	15.41
06/16	0.00	—	—	(0.00)	0.00	(0.00)
Annual Growth	—	—	—	—	—	—

Peapack-Gladstone Financial Corp.

Peapack-Gladstone Financial is the $3.4 billion-asset holding company for the near-century-old Peapack-Gladstone Bank which operates more than 20 branches in New Jersey's Hunterdon Morris Somerset Middlesex and Union counties. Founded in 1921 the bank provides traditional deposit accounts credit cards and loans to individuals and small businesses as well as trust and investment management services through its PGB Trust and Investments unit. Multifamily residential mortgages represent nearly 50% of the company's loan portfolio while commercial mortgages make up around 15%. The bank also originates construction consumer and business loans.

Operations

Peapack-Gladstone Financial operates two main divisions: Banking which offers traditional deposit and loan services merchant card services; and Wealth Management which boasts more than $3.3 billion in assets under administration (as of early 2016) and operates through PGB Trust and Investments which offers asset management services for individuals and institutions as well as personal trust services. More than 80% of the bank's total revenue came from interest income (mostly on its loans) during 2015 while 14% came from its wealth management fee income and 3% came from service charges and fees.

Multifamily residential mortgages represented nearly 50% of the company's loan portfolio at the end of 2015 while commercial mortgages made up another 15%. The rest of its portfolio was made up of construction consumer and business loans.

Geographic Reach

The bank's branches are located across New Jersey in Somerset Morris Hunterdon Middlesex and Union counties Its private banking and wealth management locations are located in Bedminster Morristown Princeton and Teaneck.

Sales and Marketing

The bank's commercial banking business serves business owners professionals retailers contractors and real estate investors. Its wealth management division serves individuals families foundations endowments trusts and estates.

Peapack-Gladstone has been ramping up its advertising spend in recent years. It spent $637000 on advertising during 2015 up from $594000 and $519000 in 2014 and 2013 respectively.

Financial Performance

Peapack-Gladstone's annual revenues and profits have swelled more than 60% since 2011 as its nearly tripled its loan assets to over $2.9 billion.

The bank's revenue jumped 27% to $122.86 million during 2015 mostly thanks to higher interest income as its loan assets grew by 30% with exceptional increases in its multifamily mortgage and commercial loan volumes. Peapack-Gladstone's wealth management division income grew 20% with increases in securities gains service charges and other non-interest income.

Strong revenue growth in 2015 drove Peapack-Gladstone's net income up 34% to $19.97 million. The bank's operating cash levels climbed 11% to $30.31 million thanks to a rise in cash-based earnings.

Strategy

Peapack-Gladstone Financial continued in 2016 to focus on: enhancing its risk management to keep its loan provisions at a minimum and its profits up; expanding its multi-family loans as well as its commercial real estate loans (to a lesser extent);

growing its commercial and industrial (C&I) lending business through its private banking divisions; and expanding its wealth management business which now accounts for 15% of its annual revenue.

Mergers and Acquisitions

In May 2015 Peapack-Gladstone bolstered its wealth management division after buying Morristown-based Wealth Management Consultants LLC for $2.8 million. The deal boosted the bank's assets under advisement and administration to $3.5 billion

EXECUTIVES

Sevp And Cfo Peapack-gladstone Financial And Peapack-gladstone Bank, Jeffrey J. Carfora, age 60
Evp And Coo, Robert A. (Bob) Plante, age 59
President And Ceo Peapack-gladstone Financial And Peapack-gladstone Bank, Douglas L. Kennedy, age 59
Evp Cio And Head Of Banking Services Peapack-gladstone Bank, Kevin B. Runyon
Sevp Chief Strategy Officer And General Counsel, Finn M.W. Casperson, age 48
Evp And Head Of Retail Banking Peapack-gladstone Bank, Anthony V. Bilotta, age 58
Evp And Head Of Commercial Real Estate Peapack-gladstone Bank, Vincent A. Spero
Sevp And President Private Wealth Management, John P. Babcock
Evp And Chief Credit Officer Peapack-gladstone Bank, Lisa Chalkan
Evp And Director Human Capital Peapack-gladstone Bank, Philip Portantino
Evp And President Wealth Management Consultants Peapack-gladstone Bank, Thomas J. Ross
Evp And Head Of Commercial Banking Peapack-gladstone Bank, Eric H. Waser
Svp And Head Of Residential And Consumer Lending Peapack-gladstone, Glenn R. Straffi
Vice President Senior Applications Software Specialist, Nancy Murphy
Senior Vice President, Charles Adornetto
Vice President Sales Distribution Leader, Dominic Sedicino
Vice President Senior Operations Officer, Sean Martin
Vice President And Trust Officer, Kim Czyzewski
Vice President, Glenn Carroll
Vice President Commercial Real Estate, Gavin C Wellington
Vice President Portfolio Manager, Sarah Krieger
Vice President, Timothy Doyle
Assistant Vice President, Rachel Giarrusso
Assistant Vice President And Senior Loan Administrator, Ana Ribeiro
Assistant Vice President And Senior Custody Officer, Amanda Pullizzi
Assistant Vice President And Mortgage Consultant, Stephanie Chu
Chairman, F. Duffield (Duff) Meyercord, age 71
Auditors: Crowe Horwath LLP

LOCATIONS

HQ: Peapack-Gladstone Financial Corp.
500 Hills Drive, Suite 300, Bedminster, NJ 07921-0700
Phone: 908 234-0700
Web: www.pgbank.com

PRODUCTS/OPERATIONS

2015 Sales

	$ mil.	% of total
Interest Income		
Loans including fees	94	77
Securities available for sale	4	4
Other	0	-
Other Income		
Wealth management fee income	17	14
Service charges and fees	3	3
Bank owned life insurance	1	1
Other Income	1	1
Other	1	-
Total	122	100

COMPETITORS

Bank of America	PNC Financial
Hudson City Bancorp	TD Bank USA
JPMorgan Chase	Valley National
MSB Financial	Bancorp

HISTORICAL FINANCIALS

Company Type: Public

Income Statement

FYE: December 31

	ASSETS ($ mil.)	NET INCOME ($ mil.)	INCOME AS % OF ASSETS	EMPLOYEES
12/17	4,260	36	0.9%	384
12/16	3,878	26	0.7%	338
12/15	3,364	19	0.6%	316
12/14	2,702	14	0.6%	306
12/13	1,966	9	0.5%	326
Annual Growth	21.3%	40.9%	—	4.2%

2017 Year-End Financials

Debt ratio: 2.16%	No. of shares (mil.): 18
Return on equity: 10.03%	Dividends
Cash ($ mil.): 113	Yield: 0.0%
Current ratio: —	Payout: 9.8%
Long-term debt ($ mil.): —	Market value ($ mil.): 652

	STOCK PRICE ($) FY Close	P/E High/Low	Earnings	Dividends	Book Value
12/17	35.02	18 14	2.03	0.20	21.68
12/16	30.88	20 10	1.60	0.20	18.79
12/15	20.62	18 14	1.29	0.20	17.16
12/14	18.56	18 14	1.22	0.20	15.99
12/13	19.10	20 14	1.01	0.20	14.48
Annual Growth	16.4%	— —	19.1%	(0.0%)	10.6%

Penney (J.C.) Co.,Inc. (Holding Co.)

J. C. Penney Company is a holding company for department store operator J. C. Penney Corp. One of the largest department store and e-commerce retailers in the US J. C. Penney Corp. operates more than 1000 JCPenney department stores in 49 states and Puerto Rico. Its stores are mostly found in suburban shopping malls and sell clothing for men women and children as well as accessories homeware appliances and curtains and drapes. They may contain shop-in-shops like Sephora cosmetics and US Vision among others. Founded in 1902 current CEO Marvin Ellison is tasked with steadying the ship after his two predecessors were unable to do so.

Operations

J. C. Penney Corp. is one of the nation's largest apparel and home furnishing retailers. It has about 1000 stores selling mid-range clothing for women men and children as well as cosmetics furniture kitchenware home decoration appliances and luggage. It operates some 575 Sephora stores. As well as physical stores J. C. Penney operates an e-commerce website and omnichannel offering.

Apparel is the company's biggest revenue producer accounting for about half of revenue and split between women's apparel and men's apparel and accessories. Home and women's accessories including Sephora split another 25% of revenue with the rest generated by children's apparel footwear and handbags jewelry and services and other.

Geographic Reach

J. C. Penney Company's operating business J. C. Penney Corp. has a presence throughout the continental US Alaska and Puerto Rico. Its supply chain network operates about a dozen facilities in the US.

Sales and Marketing

J.C Penney sells merchandise and services to consumers through its department stores and its website (jcpenney.com). The company fulfills online customer purchases by direct shipment to the customer from its distribution facilities and stores or from its suppliers' warehouses and by in-store customer pick up.

The company markets its products via newspaper television programmatic marketing radio and other media.

Financial Performance

J. C. Penney?s revenue which has inched up for the past two years dropped slightly in 2016 to $12.5 billion from $12.6 billion in 2015. Same store sales increased by $2 million in 2016 but there were fewer stores. The company?s sales fell by $76 million in the difference between new stores (one added in 2016) and closed stores (9). The bright spots in J.C. Penney stores in 2016 were the Sephora Home and Footwear and Handbags divisions which posted higher sales from the year before. experienced sales increases. Sephora had the biggest gain helped by the addition of 60 in-store stores.

A glimpse of good news came at the J.C. Penney?s bottom line where a $1 million profit appeared following a $513 million loss in 2015 and for the first time since 2010. The company had lower expenses for selling general and administrative functions as well as lower costs for pensions and restructuring. There were higher expenses as well as the company invested in adding section for selling appliances and toys to its stores.

J.C. Penney?s cash flow from operations was $334 million in 2016 down from $440 million in 2015. The decrease was caused by higher incentive compensation and other expenses in 2016 than 2016. The company also carried more inventory and turned inventory fewer times in 2016.

Strategy

J. C. Penney is working in three areas to rebuild revenue and profit. It is turning to private brands investing in omnichannel sales and trying to increase revenue per customer.

With an emphasis on private brand the company seeks to leverage its sourcing offices around the world its manufacturing infrastructure and in-house designers to increase production of private brands for style quality and value.

J.C. Penney borrows from its catalog heritage for much of the infrastructure for omnichannel sales. Its website and mobile apps allow customers to place orders at anytime. The company has three distribution centers totaling about five million square feet to fulfill online orders. As retailers lose foot traffic the company wants to integrate its digital apps and the in-store experience with features like buy-online-pick-up-in-store (BOPIS).

The third area revenue per customer is the strategy most visible in stores. The Sephora stores in J.C. Penney stores has proven to be a revenue-producing hit and the company is adding more. With the addition of appliance departments to more than 600 stores by the end of 2017 and the testing of home installation services the company has moved into the ?Home Refresh? market as another revenue generating area.

J.C. Penney added a toy section to all its stores in 2017 prompted by what the company called an enthusiastic response to its toy offerings in the 2016 holiday. The company also significantly expanded its selection of toys online.

It?s not all about addition at J.C. Penney. The company said it would close 130 to 140 stores or about 13% of its locations that it deemed unprofitable.

EXECUTIVES

Evp Stores, Joseph M. (Joe) McFarland, age 48, $650,000 total compensation
Svp And General Merchandise Manager Fine Jewelry And Accessories, Pam Mortensen, age 63
Evp Supply Chain, Michael (Mike) Robbins, age 52
Evp Human Resources, Brynn L. Evanson, age 48, $515,937 total compensation
Evp And Cio, Therace M. Risch, age 45, $90,009 total compensation
Svp And Senior General Merchandise Manager Women's Apparel Sephora Salon Women's Specialty Footwear And Handbags, Jodie Johnson
Chairman And Ceo, Marvin R. Ellison, age 53, $1,446,667 total compensation
Evp And Cfo, Jeffrey (Jeff) Davis, age 55
Svp And Group President Northern Stores Division, Sean Lee
Svp And General Merchandise Manager Menâ's Apparel Children Apparel And Jewelry, James Starke
Evp Omnichannel, Michael Amend, age 40
Svp And Group President Southern Stores Division, Jennifer Hipskind
Svp And General Merchandise Manager Sephora Salon & Intimate Apparel And Accessories, Angela Swanner
Evp And Chief Marketing Officer, Marci Grebstein
Svp And General Merchandise Manager Home, Tony Hurst
Svp And General Counsel, Brandy Treadway
Senior Vice President E Commerce, Dennis Johnson
Executive Vice President For Womens Apparel, Elizabeth Sweney
Vice President, Eric Blackwood
Legal Secretary, Jo Nolte
Divisional Vice President, Laurie Sutandar
Svp Chief Accounting Officer And Controller, Andrew Drexler
Regional Vice President, Vinny Scalese
Auditors: KPMG LLP

LOCATIONS

HQ: Penney (J.C.) Co.,Inc. (Holding Co.)
6501 Legacy Drive, Plano, TX 75024-3698
Phone: 972 431-1000
Web: www.jcpenney.com

PRODUCTS/OPERATIONS

BRANDS
The JCPenney
JCP
Liz Claiborne
Claiborne
Okie Dokie

Worthington
a.n.a
St. John's Bay
The Original Arizona Jean Company
Ambrielle
Decree
Stafford
J. Ferrar
Xersion

2016 Sales

	% of total
Women's apparel	24
Men's apparel and accessories	22
Home	13
Women's accessories including Sephora	13
Children's apparel	10
Family footwear	8
Fine jewelry	6
Services and other	4
Total	**100**

COMPETITORS

Amazon.com	Kohl's
Ascena Retail	Macy's
Bed Bath & Beyond	Nordstrom
Belk	Ross Stores
Bon-Ton Stores	Sears
Caleres	Stage Stores
Costco Wholesale	TJX Companies
Destination XL Group	Tailored Brands
Dillard's	Target Corporation
Eddie Bauer LLC	The Gap
Foot Locker	Wal-Mart
J. Crew	Zale
Kmart	

HISTORICAL FINANCIALS

Company Type: Public

Income Statement

FYE: February 3

	REVENUE ($ mil.)	NET INCOME ($ mil.)	NET PROFIT MARGIN	EMPLOYEES
02/18*	12,506	(116)	—	98,000
01/17	12,547	1	0.0%	106,000
01/16	12,625	(513)	—	105,000
01/15	12,257	(771)	—	114,000
02/14	11,859	(1,388)	—	117,000
Annual Growth	**1.3%**	**—**		**(4.3%)**

*Fiscal year change

2018 Year-End Financials

Debt ratio: 50.30%	No. of shares (mil.): 312
Return on equity: (-8.35%)	Dividends
Cash ($ mil.): 458	Yield: —
Current ratio: 1.46	Payout: —
Long-term debt ($ mil.): 3,992	Market value ($ mil.): 1,104

	STOCK PRICE ($) FY Close	P/E High/Low	PER SHARE ($) Earnings	Dividends	Book Value
02/18*	3.54	— —	(0.37)	0.00	4.42
01/17	6.45	— —	(0.00)	0.00	4.39
01/16	7.26	— —	(1.68)	0.00	4.28
01/15	7.27	— —	(2.53)	0.00	6.28
02/14	5.92	— —	(5.57)	0.00	10.13
Annual Growth	**(12.1%)**	— —	—	—	**(18.7%)**

*Fiscal year change

Penns Woods Bancorp, Inc. (Jersey Shore, PA)

Penns Woods Bancorp (PWB) is the holding company for Jersey Shore State Bank (named for the Pennsylvania town not the coastal vacation spot) which serves north central Pennsylvania through about a dozen branches. The bank accepts deposits from individuals and local businesses offering checking and savings accounts money market and NOW accounts and CDs. Residential real estate loans and commercial mortgages make up the majority of the bank's loan portfolio. The bank's lending activities are rounded out by agricultural commercial and consumer loans. PWB also owns Luzerne Bank which operates eight branch offices providing financial services in Pennsylvania.

Geographic Reach

Jersey Shore State Bank is located in North Central Pennsylvania and has an additional 13 branches in the Pennsylvania counties of Lycoming Clinton Centre and Montour. Luzerne Bank operates eight branch offices providing financial services in Luzerne and Lackawanna counties.

Financial Performance

PWB has enjoyed steady growth over the last few years. Revenues jumped 17% from $47 million in 2012 to $55 million in 2013. Net income also remained consistent hovering around the $14 million mark for both 2012 and 2013.

The growth has been driven by increases in revenue from non-interest income as a result of a rise in securities gains a gain on sale of loans and higher insurance commissions as its distribution channel continued to expand. Net income has been steady due to a decline in deposits expenses and provision for loans losses.

EXECUTIVES

Svp Cfo And Secretary Penns Woods Bancorp And Jersey Shore State Bank And Director Penns Woods Bancorp, Brian L. Knepp, age 43, $168,754 total compensation
President Ceo And Director Penns Woods Bancorp And Jersey Shore State Bank, Richard A. Grafmyre, age 65, $441,368 total compensation
Svp And Chief Credit Officer Jersey Shore State Bank, Anne M. Riles
Svp And Commercial Loan Manager Jersey Shore State Bank, Stephen M. Tasselli
Svp Enterprise Risk Management, Aron M. Carter
Svp And Coo, Michelle (Shelley) Karas
Vice President And Chief Deposit Officer And Commercial Services Manager, Stephanie A Oakes
Vice President, Larry Garverick
Regional President, Craig Russell
Vice President Of Call Centre, Gerald Seman
Vice President Marketing, Beverly Rupert
Assistant Vice President Corporate Banking Crr Group Manager, Tim Kishbach
Director, R. Edward Nestlerode, age 64
Vice Chairman, Joseph E. Kluger, age 54
Board Member, Jill Schwartz
Auditors: S.R. Snodgrass, P.C.

LOCATIONS

HQ: Penns Woods Bancorp, Inc. (Jersey Shore, PA)
300 Market Street, P.O. Box 967, Williamsport, PA 17703-0967
Phone: 570 322-1111
Web: www.jssb.com

PRODUCTS/OPERATIONS

2015 Sales

	$ mil.	% of total
Interest and Dividend Income:		
Loans	39	66
Investment securities	6	11
Other	0	1
Non-Interest Income:		
Securities gains	2	5
Service charges	2	4
Gain on sale of loans	1	3
Other	6	10
Total	**58**	**100**

COMPETITORS

Citizens & Northern	Orrstown Financial
Codorus Valley Bancorp	PNC Financial
F.N.B. (PA)	Penseco Financial
M&T Bank	Services
Northwest Bancshares	Sovereign Bank

HISTORICAL FINANCIALS
Company Type: Public

Income Statement
FYE: December 31

	ASSETS ($ mil.)	NET INCOME ($ mil.)	INCOME AS % OF ASSETS	EMPLOYEES
12/17	1,474	9	0.7%	319
12/16	1,348	12	0.9%	296
12/15	1,320	13	1.1%	308
12/14	1,245	14	1.2%	284
12/13	1,212	14	1.2%	291
Annual Growth	5.0%	(8.7%)	—	2.3%

2017 Year-End Financials

Debt ratio: 4.81%
Return on equity: 7.07%
Cash ($ mil.): 27
Current ratio: —
Long-term debt ($ mil.): —

No. of shares (mil.): 4
Dividends
  Yield: 0.0%
  Payout: 90.3%
Market value ($ mil.): 218

	STOCK PRICE ($) FY Close	P/E High/Low	PER SHARE ($) Earnings	Dividends	Book Value
12/17	46.58	24 18	2.08	1.88	29.47
12/16	50.50	20 14	2.64	1.88	29.20
12/15	42.46	17 14	2.91	1.88	28.71
12/14	49.26	17 14	3.03	1.88	28.30
12/13	51.00	17 12	3.19	2.13	26.52
Annual Growth	(2.2%)	—	— (10.1%)	(3.1%)	2.7%

PENNSYLVANIA HOUSING FINANCE AGENCY

EXECUTIVES

Chm, Robin Wiessmann
V Pres*, Thomas B Hagen
Exec Dir*, Craig H Alexander
Secretary, Carrie Barnes
Human Resources Representative, Arlene Frontz
Officer, Angela Kocher
Human Resources Executive, Jodi Hall
Finance Manager, John Zapotocky
Financial Officer, Kelly Wilson
Manager, Kevin Wike
Accountant, Laura Wildman

LOCATIONS

HQ: PENNSYLVANIA HOUSING FINANCE AGENCY
211 N FRONT ST, HARRISBURG, PA 171011406
Phone: 717 780-3800
Web: WWW.PHFA.ORG

HISTORICAL FINANCIALS
Company Type: Private

Income Statement
FYE: June 30

	ASSETS ($ mil.)	NET INCOME ($ mil.)	INCOME AS % OF ASSETS	EMPLOYEES
06/18	4,366	20	0.5%	250
06/12	5,593	10	0.2%	—
06/11	6,051	39	0.7%	—
06/10	6,265	24	0.4%	—
Annual Growth	(4.4%)	(2.2%)		

2018 Year-End Financials

Debt ratio: —
Return on equity: 10.70%
Cash ($ mil.): 508
Current ratio: 1.90
Long-term debt ($ mil.): —

Dividends
  Yield: —
  Payout: —
Market value ($ mil.): —

PENNVEST

EXECUTIVES

Exec Director, Paul K Marchetti
Chb, Randolph Albright
Poc, Leeann Brown
Manager, Brion Johnson
Coordinator, Vickie Johnson

LOCATIONS

HQ: PENNVEST
333 MARKET ST FL 8, HARRISBURG, PA 171012210
Phone: 717 787-8137

HISTORICAL FINANCIALS
Company Type: Private

Income Statement
FYE: June 30

	ASSETS ($ mil.)	NET INCOME ($ mil.)	INCOME AS % OF ASSETS	EMPLOYEES
06/18	4,143	125	3.0%	27
06/17	3,964	143	3.6%	—
06/93	742	0	0.1%	—
Annual Growth	7.1%	25.0%		

2018 Year-End Financials

Debt ratio: —
Return on equity: 193.40%
Cash ($ mil.): 134
Current ratio: 1.60
Long-term debt ($ mil.): —

Dividends
  Yield: —
  Payout: —
Market value ($ mil.): —

PennyMac Financial Services Inc (New)

If you're thinking residential mortgage this company has more than a penny for your thoughts. The parent of investment management loan services and investment trust companies PennyMac Financial Services (PennyMac) focuses on the US residential mortgage market offering loans and investment management services. Through its Private National Mortgage Acceptance Company the company's PennyMac Loan Services (PLS) originates home loans in 45 states and DC and services loans in 49 states DC and the US Virgin Islands. PLS's counterpart PNMAC Capital Management acts as investment manager and advisor. The companies service and advise PennyMac Mortgage Investment Trust (PMT). PennyMac went public in 2013.

IPO

PennyMac hoped to raise $287.5 million in its IPO but investors responded with $199.9 million. The company plans to use the proceeds to fund growth of its mortgage business through Private National Mortgage Acceptance Company. It will also use the funds for general corporate purposes.

Operations

PennyMac's mortgage banking segment includes correspondent lending retail lending and loan servicing. The correspondent line includes conventional residential mortgages acquired by PMT as well as those guaranteed by FreddieMac FannieMae and other government agencies. The company has more than 140 approved sellers; in 2012 it had $13 billion in conventional loans and $8.4 billion in government-insured loans. Retail lending originates new prime residential conventional and government-backed mortgage loans for purchasing or refinancing homes. PennyMac uses the Internet and a call center rather than traditional branch locations for direct-to-consumer approach. The company's loan servicing business includes the back office work of loan administration collection and default activities. It serves PennyMac subsidiaries and other mortgage companies. The unit handles prime credit and distress loans under the prime servicing and special servicing headings respectively.

PennyMac's investment management segment operates as an investment manager through PNMAC Capital Management (PCM). PCM handles the $1.8 billion in combined assets from PMT and PennyMac's other investment funds. PMT is a publicly traded real estate investment trust (REIT).

Geographic Reach

While PennyMac serves nearly the entire US its portfolio is heavily weighted toward California (38%) Florida (5%) and Colorado (5%).

Financial Performance

The company's revenue has increased on the strength of gains in both the loan servicing and management segments. Other operating metrics include net assets under management total mortgage loans serviced and total mortgage loan production; all have increased in the last three years. PennyMac reported lower net income for 2012 due to amortization and impairment charges and higher spending on compensation. It sold and repurchased loans loans and earned interest on investments to more than double its cash flow for the same period.

Strategy

Since PennyMac was formed during the financial crisis it hasn't had to scramble and adapt like many of its competitors. As many mortgage shoppers turn away from large banks the company believes its poised to take advantage of growth and a lack of stringent regulations imposed on banks. For growth the company intends to focus on expanding its servicing business organically and through acquisitions increasing the number of loan sellers from which it purchases loans and leveraging its servicing portfolio to increase refinance and loan servicing opportunities.

EXECUTIVES

Senior Managing Director And Chief Enterprise Operations Officer, Anne D. McCallion, age 63
President And Ceo, David A. Spector, age 55, $503,370 total compensation
President Pennymac Loan Services, Douglas E. (Doug) Jones, age 61, $325,000 total compensation
Senior Managing Director And Chief Risk Officer, David M. (Dave) Walker, age 62
Senior Managing Director And Chief Mortgage Operations Officer, Steve R. Bailey, age 56
Senior Managing Director And Cfo, Andrew S. Chang, age 40
Senior Managing Director And Chief Capital Markets Officer, Vandad Fartaj, age 43
Senior Managing Director And Chief Administrative And Legal Officer, Jeffrey P. Grogin, age 57
Senior Managing Director And Chief Asset And Liability Management Officer, Daniel S. Perotti, age 37
Chairman, Stanford L. Kurland, age 65
Auditors: DELOITTE & TOUCHE LLP

LOCATIONS

HQ: PennyMac Financial Services Inc (New)
3043 Townsgate Road, Westlake Village, CA 91361
Phone: 818 224-7442
Web: www.pennymacusa.com

2016 Sales

	$ mil.	% of total
Net gains on mortgage loans held for sale	531	56
Net mortgage loan servicing fees	185	19
Loan origination fees	125	13
Fulfillment fees from PennyMac Mortgage Investment Trust	86	9
Management fees and Carried Interest	23	2
Other	4	1
Net interest expense	-25.1	-
Total	**931**	**0**

COMPETITORS

Bank of America	Quicken Loans
Citigroup	Stonegate Mortgage
JPMorgan Chase	U.S. Bancorp
Nationstar Mortgage	Wells Fargo
Ocwen Financial	

HISTORICAL FINANCIALS

Company Type: Public

Income Statement — FYE: December 31

	ASSETS ($ mil.)	NET INCOME ($ mil.)	INCOME AS % OF ASSETS	EMPLOYEES
12/17	7,368	100	1.4%	3,189
12/16	5,133	66	1.3%	3,038
12/15	3,505	47	1.3%	2,509
12/14	2,507	36	1.5%	1,816
12/13	1,584	14	0.9%	1,373
Annual Growth	**46.8%**	**62.6%**	**—**	**23.5%**

2017 Year-End Financials

Debt ratio: 12.38%
Return on equity: 24.67%
Cash ($ mil.): 37
Current ratio: —
Long-term debt ($ mil.): —
No. of shares (mil.): 23
Dividends
Yield: —
Payout: —
Market value ($ mil.): 526

	STOCK PRICE ($) FY Close	P/E High/Low		PER SHARE ($) Earnings	Dividends	Book Value
12/17	22.35	5	4	4.03	0.00	19.95
12/16	16.65	6	4	2.94	0.00	15.49
12/15	15.36	9	7	2.17	0.00	12.32
12/14	17.30	11	8	1.73	0.00	9.92
12/13	17.55	27	19	0.82	0.00	8.04
Annual Growth	**6.2%**	—	—	**48.9%**	—	**25.5%**

Penske Automotive Group Inc

Penske Automotive Group has lots of lots. The US' #2 publicly traded auto dealer behind AutoNation Penske operates about 165 auto franchises from California to New York and Puerto Rico and another 190 franchises abroad mainly in the UK. It sells more than 40 car brands. Non-US brands including AUDI BMW and Honda generate more than 70% of sales. Penske also sells used vehicles provides financing and runs about 35 collision repair centers. UK subsidiary Sytner Group operates more than 145 franchises selling 20 brands of mostly high-end models. Additionally Penske holds a 28.9% stake in Penske Truck Leasing (PTL) known for commercial leasing and contract maintenance. The company is named after its Chairman Roger Penske.

Operations

Penske operates through two main segments: Retail Automotive and Retail Commercial Truck.

The Retail Automotive segment brings in the vast majority of company revenue (some 95%) and consists of its 355 retail automotive franchises in the US and abroad. It sells new and used cars under around 40 auto brands; around 70% of sales are from premium brands particularly Audi BMW and Porsche. The segment sells around 550000 cars each year.

Retail Commercial Truck accounts for most of the remaining revenue and consists of the heavy-duty truck dealerships Premier Truck Group. Premier Truck Group has 20 locations in the US and Canada that offer used trucks servicing and parts. Many dealerships are open 24/7.

Penske also has a few other interests such as its commercial vehicle business that imports and distributes Western Star heavy-duty trucks MAN heavy and medium duty trucks and buses and Dennis Eagle garbage trucks in Oceania.

Geographic Reach

Michigan-based Penske rings up some 60% of its sales in the US and Puerto Rico. The remainder comes from its overseas franchises which are predominantly found in the UK but also in Germany Canada and Italy. The company also has operations in Australia and New Zealand.

Sales and Marketing

Penske conducts its advertising and marketing at the local level. In recent years it has concentrated on the internet and other digital media including its own websites. In many markets it also taps traditional marketing formats including newspaper direct mail magazine television and radio advertising. The automobile manufacturer supplement its local and regional advertising through large advertising campaigns that promote their brands and offer attractive financing packages and other incentive programs.

By manufacturer BMW/MINI franchises brings in over 25% of Penske's total revenue while Volkswagen brand franchises (Audi/Volkswagen/Porsche/Bentley) account for over 20% of revenue. Toyota brands (Toyota and Lexus) generate some 15% of revenue and Mercedes-Benz brands (Mercedes-Benz/Sprinter/Smart) 10%.

Financial Performance

The decade following the financial crash in 2008 has seen Penske lifted by the economic recovery and the release of pent-up demand.

In fiscal 2016 sales increased a relatively modest 4% to $20.1 billion (it grew 12% and 18% the previous two years). Growth of 7% in new unit volume split between a 21.4% increase in international markets and a 0.5% fall in the US was offset by a 3% fall in retail prices. Volume growth was driven by acquisitions and was concentrated in Penske's non-US markets particularly Germany where its joint venture began and the UK. Weakness in sales volume in the US was a result of prioritizing gross profit which had a negative impact on sales.

Used car and service and parts revenue was also grown via acquisitions.

Net income was up 5% as higher revenue was offset by reduced profits from same-store sales due to lower average sales prices.

Cash from operations was down 6% to $365.5 million.

Strategy

Penske's growth strategy is based on entering new markets and growing its truck business.

It continues to grow its significant UK operation and has entered into joint ventures in Germany and Japan. In Japan Penske bought a 49% stake in Nicole Group a luxury brand dealership operating in Tokyo. It is probable that Penske will buy the remaining equity in the next few years. Penske's Japan operation will supported by its business partner Mitsui a large general trader.

The company is increasing its equity in Penske Truck Leasing its joint venture with Penske Corporation and Mitsui. In a year Penske has grown its stake in Penske Truck Leasing from 9% to 28.9%. Penske is expanding into the truck business to tap into the exceptionally good margins available in the truck parts and servicing segment.

Mergers and Acquisitions

In 2017 Penske bought CarShop a UK-based used car dealer expanding its presence in the country.

Similarly in the same year it acquired CarSense a US-based used car dealer.

Additionally it bought Jaguar and Land Rover dealerships from Prestige Family of Fine Cars a New Jersey-based dealership.

EXECUTIVES

Evp Human Resources, Claude H. (Bud) Denker, age 59, $500,000 total compensation
Chairman And Ceo, Roger S. Penske, age 81, $1,200,000 total compensation
President, Robert H. Kurnick, age 56, $700,000 total compensation
Chairman Sytner Group, Gerard Nieuwenhuys, age 57
Evp Investor Relations And Corporate Development, Anthony R. (Tony) Pordon, age 54
Managing Director Sytner Group, Darren Edwards
Evp West Operations, Bernie Wolfe, age 62
Evp Strategic Development, George Brochick, age 70
Evp Central Operations, R. Whitfield Ramonat, age 57
Evp General Counsel And Secretary, Shane M. Spradlin, age 48, $500,000 total compensation
Evp East Operations, John Cragg

Evp And Cfo, J.D. Carlson, age 48, $475,000 total compensation
Evp Marketing And Business Development, Terri Mulcahey
Svp And Cio, Rich Hook
Vice President Finance, Terry Speer
Vice President {, Christian Collins
Executive Vice President And General Counsel, Walter P Czarnecki, age 76
Vice President Finance, James Harris
Vice President, Jerry Byrd
Senior Vice President Manufacturer Relations, Robert K Wilshaw
Senior Vice President Of Premium Brands, Michael Famiglietti
Senior Vice President Penske Automotive Group, Tony Pordon
Vice President, Niall Hay
Executive Vice President, Hiroshi Ishikawa
Vice President Manufacturer Relations, Jason Beidelman
Area Vice President, John Robben
Board Member, John Barr
Board Member, Lucio Noto
Board Member, Sandra Pierce
Auditors: Deloitte & Touche LLP

LOCATIONS

HQ: Penske Automotive Group Inc
2555 Telegraph Road, Bloomfield Hills, MI 48302-0954
Phone: 248 648-2500   **Fax:** 248 648-2525
Web: www.penskeautomotive.com

2016 Sales

	$ mil.	% of total
U.S	12,005	60
International	8,112	40
Total	**20,118**	**100**

2016 Stores

	No.
U.S	164
U.K	146
Germany	28
Italy	17
Total	**355**

PRODUCTS/OPERATIONS

2016 Sales

	$ mil.	% of total
Retail Automotive	18,673	93
Retail Commercial Truck	1,000	5
Commercial vehicle and Other	448	2
Elimination	(3.9)	-
Total	**20,118**	**100**

COMPETITORS

Asbury Automotive	JM Family Enterprises
AutoNation	Jordan Automotive
Autobytel	Larry H. Miller Group
Avis Budget	Lithia Motors
CarMax	Lookers
Ed Morse Auto	Microsoft
Enterprise Group	National Car Rental
Fletcher Jones	Pendragon
Group 1 Automotive	Potamkin Automotive
Hendrick Automotive	Serra Automotive
Holman Enterprises	Sonic Automotive

HISTORICAL FINANCIALS

Company Type: Public

Income Statement

FYE: December 31

	REVENUE ($ mil.)	NET INCOME ($ mil.)	NET PROFIT MARGIN	EMPLOYEES
12/17	21,386	613	2.9%	26,000
12/16	20,118	342	1.7%	24,000
12/15	19,284	326	1.7%	22,000
12/14	17,177	286	1.7%	22,100
12/13	14,706	244	1.7%	10,000
Annual Growth	**9.8%**	**25.9%**	**—**	**9.6%**

2017 Year-End Financials

Debt ratio: 56.21%
Return on equity: 29.58%
Cash ($ mil.): 45
Current ratio: 1.01
Long-term debt ($ mil.): 2,090

No. of shares (mil.): 85
Dividends
Yield: 0.0%
Payout: 17.6%
Market value ($ mil.): 4,105

	STOCK PRICE ($) FY Close	P/E High/Low		PER SHARE ($) Earnings	Dividends	Book Value
12/17	47.85	8	5	7.14	1.26	27.92
12/16	51.84	14	8	3.99	1.10	20.55
12/15	42.34	15	12	3.63	0.94	20.00
12/14	49.07	16	12	3.17	0.78	18.31
12/13	47.16	17	10	2.70	0.62	16.67
Annual Growth	**0.4%**	**—**		**27.5%**	**19.4%**	**13.8%**

People's United Financial Inc

People's United Financial is the holding company for People's United Bank (formerly People's Bank) which boasts more than 400 traditional branches supermarket branches commercial banking offices investment and brokerage offices and equipment leasing offices across New England and eastern New York. In addition to retail and commercial banking services the bank offers trust wealth management brokerage and insurance services. Its lending activities consist mainly of commercial mortgages (more than a third of its loan portfolio) commercial and industrial loans (more than a quarter) residential mortgages equipment financing and home equity loans. Founded in 1842 the bank has $36 billion in assets.

Operations

People's United operates two core business segments Retail Banking and Commercial Banking which both share duties of the bank's now-defunct Wealth Management division. The bank also has a non-core Treasury division that manages the company's securities portfolio and other investments.

Commercial Banking which makes up more than half of the company's total revenue provides business loans equipment financing (through People's Capital and Leasing Corp. or PCLC and People's United Equipment Finance Corp or PUEFC) and municipal banking as well as trust services for corporations and institutions and private banking services for wealthy individuals.

Retail Banking which makes up around 20% of total revenues provides deposit services residential mortgages and home equity loans financial advisory and investment management services as well

as life insurance through People's United Insurance Agency.

Overall the bank generated 68% of its total revenue from loan interest in 2014 and 7% from interest on securities. About 10% of total revenues came from bank service charges while investment management fees commercial banking lending fees insurance revenue and brokerage commissions each made up less than 3% of overall revenue for the year.

Geographic Reach

People's United has more than 400 branches across Connecticut southeastern New York Massachusetts Vermont New Hampshire and Maine. Connecticut is its largest lending market with 27% of the bank's loan portfolio being extended to consumers and businesses in the region in 2014. New York and Massachusetts are the bank's next largest markets with a 19% and 18% share of its loan portfolio.

Sales and Marketing

The bank sells its products and services through investment and brokerage offices commercial branches online banking and investment trading and through its 24-hour telephone banking service. The company's PCLC and PUEFC affiliates have a sales presence in 16 states to support equipment financing operations throughout the US.

People's United spent $13 million on advertising in 2014 compared to $15.4 million and $17.7 million in 2013 and 2012 respectively.

Strategy

People's United emphasizes cross-selling financial products by developing client relationships and has increasingly tied employee compensation to this ability. The company is particularly focused on building its small business lending wealth management and insurance business. It also continues to open new branches and seeks acquisition targets for further growth.

One other key element of its strategy involves boosting its deposit assets through its expanded convenient store reach. In early 2015 the company boasted nearly 150 full-service branches in Stop & Shop supermarkets across Connecticut and southeastern New York which comprised 36% of the bank's total branch network and held 14% of its total deposits. Much of this is attributed to a key acquisition in 2012 when the company purchased nearly 60 branches (many within Stop & Shop supermarkets) in the New York metro area from RBS Citizens. People's United already had more than 80 Stop & Shop branches in Connecticut so the deal strengthened its relationship with the retailer and expanded its presence in the New York market.

Mergers and Acquisitions

In 2018 People's United agreed to acquire First Connecticut Bancorp in an all-stock transaction valued at $544 million. The acquisition will further enhance People's United's established presence in the northeastern US. First Connecticut Bancorp is the holding company of Farmington Bank which operates nearly 30 community bank locations across Connecticut and and in western Massachusetts.

In early 2019 People's United acquired independent leasing and finance company VAR Technology Finance. VAR uses its software platform to finance commercial and public sector customers of large technology manufacturers. The company will maintain its brand but become a division of People's United's LEAF Commercial Capital subsidiary. VAR originated $180 million in loans in 2018.

Company Background

One of the main goals of People's United has been to build its presence in the two largest metropolitan areas in its market New York City and Boston. One of the largest in the Boston area Danvers Bancorp added some 30 branches and carried a price tag of approximately $493 million. People's United also acquired LSB Corporation and Butler Bank the latter in an FDIC-assisted transaction that included a loss-sharing agreement with the regulator covering all acquired loans and foreclosed real estate of the failed bank bringing in another 10 branches in the Boston area. In 2010 People's United bought Bank of Smithtown which had about 30 branches primarily on Long Island in New York.

People's United Financial acquired commercial lender Financial Federal Corporation in 2010 (now People's United Equipment Finance) which provides financing and leasing to small and midsized business nationwide.

People's United Financial underwent significant transformation in past years. The company demutualized and converted to a stock holding company in 2007 and early the following year acquired multibank holding company Chittenden Corporation. The deal added some 140 branches doubling People's United Bank's branch network and expanding its reach beyond Connecticut and New York and into the rest of New England.

EXECUTIVES

Vice President, Susan D Stanley
President And Ceo, John P. (Jack) Barnes, age 62, $890,384 total compensation
Sevp Corporate Development And Strategic Planning, Kirk W. Walters, age 63, $468,461 total compensation
Svp And President Merrill Bank, William P. (Bill) Lucy, age 59
Chief Financial Officer, R. David Rosato, age 56
Sevp Retail And Business Banking, Robert R. (Bob) D'Amore, age 65, $429,323 total compensation
President Vermont, Michael L. Seaver
Sevp Wealth Management, Louise T. Sandberg, age 66
President Massachusetts, Timothy P. Crimmins
Market Leader New York, Sara M. Longobardi
Svp And President People's United Bank North Connecticut, Michael J. Casparino
Sevp Human Resources, David K. Norton, age 63, $411,231 total compensation
Sevp Commercial Banking, Jeffrey J. (Jeff) Tengel, age 55, $408,654 total compensation
President Southern Connecticut, Armando F. Goncalves
Sevp And General Counsel, Robert E. Trautmann, age 64
Sevp And Chief Administrative Officer, Lee C. Powlus
President New Hampshire, Dianne M. Mercier
President Southern Maine, Daniel P. (Dan) Thornton
Vice President Information Technology, Carol Anderson
Vice President Information Technology, Roy Allison
Vice President, Kon Khongkham
Vice President Information Technology, Albert Sanna
Vice President Sales Aviation Finance, Jim Pulie
First Vice President, Walter Kaercher
Vice President Of Sales, Jeffrey Morrison
Vice President Market Research, Craig Noble
Executive Vice President Chief Credit Officer, David Bodor
First Vice President Wealth Management, John Lescure
Senior Vice President And Market Development Officer, Brian Shea
Vice President, Peter Martinez
Vice President, Amy York
Vice President Manager Loan Service, Rachel Sheridan

Divisional Vice President, Peter Brestovan
Assistant Vice President, Patrick Talcott
Vice President Capital Markets, Russ Hardy
Senior Executive Vice President Wealth Management, Galan Daukas
Vice President Information Techonlogy Control And Assurance, Sue Bascom-Erazmus
Vice President Director Of Tax, Kathleen Jones
Market Manager Assistant Vice President, Alice Baird
Senior Vice President And Director Marketing, Kathleen Schirling
Vice President, Robert Bursey
Senior Vice President, Robert Maquat
Vice President, Thomas Gasho
Vice President, Daniel Reilly
Vice President, Robert Donahue
Vice President Customer Service Manager, Magda Wachel-Florczyk
Vice President, Patrick Lorent
Market Manager Vice President, Marjorie Downing
Vice President Of Finance, Shelley Colvin
Assistant Vice President Customer Service, Ana Saraiva
Financials Services Manager Assistant Vice President, Andrea Kantaros
Assistant Vice President, Kasey Franzoni
Senior Vice President, Kathleen Lepak
Vice President Financial Analyst, Rita Rivers
Vice President Finance, Brian Connery
Vice President Purchasing, Theresa Knies
Assistant Vice President, David Schalk
Senior Vice President Senior Portfolio, Michael Williams
Financial Services Mananger Assistant Vice President, Amy Pasquarelli
Senior Vice President, Jeffery Paz
Assistant Vice President, Tuyen LE
First Vice President, John Bundschuh
Vice President Information Technology, Venkatesh Swamy
Assistant Vice President, Kurtis Denison
Senior Private Banker Senior Vice President, Bethany Dubuque
Vice President, Lisa Rollins
Senior Vice President, Jody Cole
Vice President Market Manager, David Cavanaugh
Senior Vice President Commercial Lending, Tom Wolcott
Relationship Manager Vice President, Steven Wurtz
Senior Vice President, Keith Higgins
Vice President, Rose Morgan
Senior Vice President Senior Commercial Real Estate Lender, Suzanne Wakeen
Senior Vice President Business Services And Digital Channels, Ravi Vakacherla
Vice President Commercial Lending, Debbie Boyle
Vice President Financial Services Manager, Jennifer Lynch
Vice President, Joanne Murgalo
Vice President Technology, Mk Mokel
Vice President Of Loans, Cynthia P Belak
Senior Vice President, Marilyn Hardacre
Senior Lender Vice President, Peter Lange
Executive Vice President, Henry R Mandel
Senior Vice President Consumer Deposit P, Peter Scotch
Vice President, Darrin Fodor
Vice President, James Bucko
Vice President, Timothy B Hodges
Vice President, Michael Rispoli
Senior Vice President, Mark Leonardi
Executive Vice President Mid Corporate, Dexter Freeman
Financial Services Manager Assistant Vice President, Alex Slootskiy
Assistant Vice President Financial Services Manager, Robert Duffus
Financial Services Manager Assistant Vice President, Jennifer Cassidy

Vice President Market Manager, Michelle Marshall
Fixed Income Strategist Senior Vice President, Karissa McDonough
Vice President Sr.compliance Officer, Dionne Pulcinella
Vice President Financial Services Manager, Kristen Keil
Senior Wealth Management Officer Senior Vice President, Amy Thompson
Financial Services Manager Assistant Vice President, Cathy Ferreira-Golino
Vice President Relationship Manager, Seth Arvanites
Vice President Model Validation, Julien Lee
Assistant Vice President Customer Service Manager, Amy Tucker
Assistant Vice President Customer Service Manager, Lamia Amirouche
Vice President Senior Market Manager, Christina Veziris
Assistant Vice President Mortgage Account Officer, Laura Kelly
Team Leader Vice President Senior Commercial Review Appraiser, Michelle Gamache
Senior Vice President Commercial Real Estate Finance, Kimberlee Phelps
Vice President, Brian Boyaji
Assistant Vice President Customer Service Manager, Krupali Doshi
Vice President Sales And Leasing, Rick Curtiss
Vice President, Tom Emery
Assistant Vice President, Miriam James
Regional Vice President, Gary Fisher
Senior Vice President Commercial Lending, Edward Borden
Senior Vice President Commercial Real Estate Finance, Mark Dalton
Vice President And Sr.market Manager Bridgeport Market, Virgilio Lopez
Vice President, Joseph Korecki
Vice President Wealth Management Marketing Bank Brand And Advertising, Christine Stafstrom
Assistant Vice President Branch Manager Danbury Market, Todd Clifford
Assistant Vice President Customer Service Manager, Danielle Lutz
Vice President, Justin Mills
First Vice President, Maria Kastanis
Vice President, Nancy Brecher
Senior Vice President, Mark Danie
Assistant Vice President Branch Manager, Elizabeth Hudson
Vice President Customer Service Manager, Silveras Sboui
Assistant Vice President Bank Manager, Andrew Matarese
Fvp Bsa Aml Ofac Officer, Grisel Kaplan
Senior Portfolio Manager Senior Vice President, Richard Casselman
Market Manager Vice President, Tyler Eames
Vice President Senior Private Banker, Sarah Haley
Vice President, Theodore Horan
Assistant Vice President, Rosalind Rubin
N.a. Vice President, Kimberly Alty
Associate Vice President Mortgage Account Officer, Kessa Glisic
Vice President Mortgage Account Officer, Filip Ramil
Vice President Business Banking, Michael Tardella
Vice President Financial Services Manager, Jeanie Szostek
Senior Vice President Commercial Relationship Manager, Michael Lavoie
Vice President Private Banking Administration, Katharine Bosley
Vice President Commercial Lending, Matthew Harrison
Senior Vice President, Jeff Warminsky
Nh Division Sales Manager Vice President, Ranae Oneil

LOCATIONS

HQ: People's United Financial Inc
850 Main Street, Bridgeport, CT 06604
Phone: 203 338-7171   Fax: 203 338-2545
Web: www.peoples.com

PRODUCTS/OPERATIONS

2014 Sales

	$ mil.	% of total
Interest & dividends		
Loans		
Commercial real estate	354	26
Commercial	351	26
Residential mortgage	153	12
Consumer	73	5
Securities	96	7
Other	1	-
Noninterest		
Bank service charges	128	10
Investment management fees	41	3
Operating lease income	41	3
Commercial banking lending fees	33	2
Insurance revenue	29	2
Other	76	4
Adjustment	(0.9)	-
Total	**1,381**	**100**

COMPETITORS

Bank of America	KeyCorp
Citibank	Liberty Bank
Citizens Financial Group	Sovereign Bank
	TD Bank USA
Fairfield County Bank	Webster Financial

HISTORICAL FINANCIALS

Company Type: Public

Income Statement
FYE: December 31

	ASSETS ($ mil.)	NET INCOME ($ mil.)	INCOME AS % OF ASSETS	EMPLOYEES
12/17	44,453	337	0.8%	5,584
12/16	40,609	281	0.7%	5,173
12/15	38,877	260	0.7%	5,139
12/14	35,997	251	0.7%	5,397
12/13	33,213	232	0.7%	5,429
Annual Growth	**7.6%**	**9.8%**	**—**	**0.7%**

2017 Year-End Financials

Debt ratio: 2.50%
Return on equity: 6.15%
Cash ($ mil.): 845
Current ratio: —
Long-term debt ($ mil.): —

No. of shares (mil.): 346
Dividends
Yield: 0.0%
Payout: 70.8%
Market value ($ mil.): 6,481

	STOCK PRICE ($) FY Close	P/E High/Low	PER SHARE ($) Earnings	Dividends	Book Value
12/17	18.70	20 16	0.97	0.69	16.79
12/16	19.36	22 15	0.92	0.68	16.28
12/15	16.15	20 16	0.86	0.67	15.26
12/14	15.18	19 16	0.84	0.66	15.05
12/13	15.12	21 16	0.74	0.65	14.88
Annual Growth	**5.5%**	**— —**	**7.0%**	**1.5%**	**3.1%**

People's Utah Bancorp

Auditors: Tanner LLC

LOCATIONS

HQ: People's Utah Bancorp
1 East Main Street, American Fork, UT 84003
Phone: 801 642-3998
Web: www.PeoplesUtah.com

HISTORICAL FINANCIALS

Company Type: Public

Income Statement
FYE: December 31

	ASSETS ($ mil.)	NET INCOME ($ mil.)	INCOME AS % OF ASSETS	EMPLOYEES
12/17	2,123	19	0.9%	483
12/16	1,665	23	1.4%	430
12/15	1,555	19	1.3%	414
12/14	1,367	14	1.1%	367
12/13	1,299	11	0.9%	—
Annual Growth	**13.1%**	**13.7%**		

2017 Year-End Financials

Debt ratio: —
Return on equity: 8.17%
Cash ($ mil.): 49
Current ratio: —
Long-term debt ($ mil.): —

No. of shares (mil.): 18
Dividends
Yield: 0.0%
Payout: 31.4%
Market value ($ mil.): 561

	STOCK PRICE ($) FY Close	P/E High/Low	PER SHARE ($) Earnings	Dividends	Book Value
12/17	30.30	30 22	1.08	0.34	13.91
12/16	26.85	21 11	1.30	0.22	12.82
12/15	17.21	15 13	1.17	0.18	11.92
Annual Growth	**15.2%**	**— —**	**(2.0%)**	**17.2%**	**3.9%**

Peoples Bancorp Inc (Marietta, OH)

Peoples Bancorp offers banking for the people by the people and of the people. The holding company owns Peoples Bank which has about 50 branches in rural and small urban markets in Ohio Kentucky and West Virginia. The bank offers traditional services such as checking and savings accounts CDs loans and trust services. Commercial and agricultural loans including those secured by commercial real estate account for the majority of the bank's lending activities. Its Peoples Financial Advisors division offers investment management services while Peoples Insurance sells life health and property/casualty coverage.

Operations

Credit cards and brokerage services are offered through third-party providers.

Financial Performance

The company's revenue increased from $103.7 million in fiscal 2012 up to $104.6 million for fiscal 2013. However despite the slight spike in annual revenue Peoples Bancorp's net income decreased from $29.9 million in fiscal 2012 down to $29 million for fiscal 2013.

The company's cash on hand decreased by about $1 million in fiscal 2013 compared to fiscal 2012 levels.

Strategy

Peoples Bancorp is looking to increase its revenue from service changes and other fees and commissions particularly from insurance and wealth management which are not reliant on fluctuating interest rate margins.

The company is also looking to strengthen its brand and build deeper relationships with its clients.

EXECUTIVES

Evp And Chief Administrative Officer Peoples Bancorp And Evp Chief Administrative Officer And Cashierpeoples Bank N.a., Carol A. Schneeberger, age 61, $233,000 total compensation
Evp And Chief Commercial Lending Officer Peoples Bancorp And Peoples Bank N.a., Daniel K. (Dan) McGill, age 63, $250,000 total compensation
Evp And Chief Credit Officer Peoples Bancorp And Peoples Bank N.a., Timothy H. Kirtley, age 48, $221,500 total compensation
President Ceo And Director Peoples Bancorp And Peoples Bank N.a., Charles W. Sulerzyski, age 60, $500,000 total compensation
Evp Cfo And Treasurer Peoples Bancorp And Peoples Bank N.a., John C. Rogers, age 58, $26,136 total compensation
Vice President, Steven Nulter
Assistant Vice President Branch Market Manager, Candace Frump
Branch Market Manager Assistant Vice President, Peggy Scott-Morgan
Vice President And Controller, Jeffrey Baran
Vice President, Randy Barengo
Chairman Peoples Bancorp And Peoples Bank N.a., David L. Mead, age 63
Auditors: Ernst & Young LLP

LOCATIONS

HQ: Peoples Bancorp Inc (Marietta, OH)
138 Putnam Street, P.O. Box 738, Marietta, OH 45750
Phone: 740 373-3155
Web: www.peoplesbancorp.com

PRODUCTS/OPERATIONS

2016 Sales

	$ mil.	% of total
Interest Income:		
Interest and fees on loans	93	56
Interest and dividends on taxable investment securities	18	11
Interest on tax-exempt investment securities	3	2
Other Income:		
Insurance income	13	8
Deposit account service charges	10	6
Trust and investment income	10	6
Electronic banking income	10	6
Bank owned life insurance income	1	1
Mortgage banking income	1	1
Commercial loan swap fee income	1	1
Net gain on investment securities	0	1
Net loss on asset disposals and other transactions	(1.1)	-
Other	1	1
Total	**166**	**100**

COMPETITORS

1st West Virginia Bancorp	Huntington Bancshares
	Ohio Valley Banc
BB&T	U.S. Bancorp
Fifth Third	United Bankshares

HISTORICAL FINANCIALS

Company Type: Public

Income Statement
FYE: December 31

	ASSETS ($ mil.)	NET INCOME ($ mil.)	INCOME AS % OF ASSETS	EMPLOYEES
12/17	3,581	38	1.1%	774
12/16	3,432	31	0.9%	782
12/15	3,258	10	0.3%	817
12/14	2,567	16	0.6%	699
12/13	2,059	17	0.9%	546
Annual Growth	14.8%	21.6%	—	9.1%

2017 Year-End Financials

Debt ratio: 0.20%
Return on equity: 8.61%
Cash ($ mil.): 72
Current ratio: —
Long-term debt ($ mil.): —

No. of shares (mil.): 18
Dividends
  Yield: 0.0%
  Payout: 40.0%
Market value ($ mil.): 595

	STOCK PRICE ($) FY Close	P/E High/Low	PER SHARE ($) Earnings	Dividends	Book Value
12/17	32.62	16 14	2.10	0.84	25.13
12/16	32.46	19 10	1.71	0.64	23.99
12/15	18.84	42 30	0.61	0.60	22.88
12/14	25.93	20 15	1.36	0.60	22.92
12/13	22.51	15 12	1.63	0.54	20.89
Annual Growth	9.7%	— —	6.5%	11.7%	4.7%

Peoples Financial Services Corp

Power to the Peoples Financial Services. The firm is the holding company for Peoples Security Bank and Trust Company (formerly Peoples National Bank) which operates about 25 branches across northeastern Pennsylvania and neighboring Broome County in New York. Established in 1905 the bank offers standard retail products and services including checking and savings accounts CDs and credit cards to local businesses and individuals. Commercial loans including mortgages construction loans and operating loans make up the greatest portion (40%) of the company's loan book followed by residential mortgages (25%) and consumer loans. The company's Peoples Advisors subsidiary provides investment and brokerage services.

Operations
About 80% of Peoples Financial Services' total revenue came from interest income (mostly on loans) in 2014 while the remainder comes from non-interest income. The bank had a staff of 354 full-time employees at the end of that year.

Geographic Reach
Scranton-based Peoples Security Bank has more than 25 branches across Northeastern Pennsylvania (in the Lackawanna Lehigh Luzerne Monroe Susquehanna Wayne and Wyoming counties) and Broome County in New York state.

Sales and Marketing
The company primarily makes loans to small- and medium-sized businesses. It spent $450 on advertising in 2014 up from $350 and $287 in 2013 and 2012 respectively.

Financial Performance
Peoples has struggled to consistently grow its revenues in recent years due to shrinking interest

margins on loans amidst the low-interest environment. Its profits however have been rising thanks to lower interest expenses on deposits and declining loan loss provisions as its loan portfolio's credit quality has improved with higher property valuations in the strengthened economy.

The company enjoyed a breakout year in 2014 however as its revenue jumped 60% to a record $79.21 million mostly as its interest income swelled from new loan business from its 2013 acquisition of Penseco Financial Services. Its service charge fees and commissions merchant services income and commission and fee income from fiduciary services also rose mostly as a result of the significant acquisition.

Higher revenue in 2014 allowed Peoples' net income to more than triple to a record $17.6 million while its operating cash levels more than doubled to $20.6 million on higher cash earnings for the year.

Strategy
Peoples Security Bank occasionally acquires smaller banks to extend its branch network across target markets while adding new loan and deposit business. Its late 2013 acquisition of Penseco Financial Services Corporation for example nearly doubled its loan and deposit business and more than doubled its branch network to 25 branches.

Mergers and Acquisitions
In November 2013 Peoples acquired Penseco Financial Services Corporation along with its Penn Security Bank and Trust subsidiary. The $155 million-deal doubled Peoples' branch network from 12 to 25 branches creating the largest community bank headquartered in Northeastern Pennsylvania.

EXECUTIVES

Ceo And President, Alan W. Dakey, age 66
Evp And Coo Peoples National Bank, Debra E. Dissinger, age 63, $110,000 total compensation
Director, Richard S. Lochen, age 54, $130,000 total compensation
Senior Vice President Chief Financial Officer, Scott Seasock
Vice President Commercial Lending, Diane Effting
Chairman, William E. Aubrey, age 55
Auditors: Baker Tilly Virchow Krause, LLP

LOCATIONS

HQ: Peoples Financial Services Corp
  150 North Washington Avenue, Scranton, PA 18503
Phone: 570 346-7741
Web: www.psbt.com

PRODUCTS/OPERATIONS

2014 Sales

	$ mil.	% of total
Interest	64	81
Non-interest	15	19
Total	79	100

COMPETITORS

Citizens & Northern	HSBC USA
Citizens Financial Services	M&T Bank
Fidelity D & D	NBT Bancorp
First Keystone	Penns Woods Bancorp
First National Community Bancorp	

HISTORICAL FINANCIALS

Company Type: Public

Income Statement
FYE: December 31

	ASSETS ($ mil.)	NET INCOME ($ mil.)	INCOME AS % OF ASSETS	EMPLOYEES
12/17	2,169	18	0.9%	388
12/16	1,999	19	1.0%	364
12/15	1,819	17	1.0%	348
12/14	1,741	17	1.0%	354
12/13	1,688	5	0.3%	354
Annual Growth	6.5%	34.0%	—	2.3%

2017 Year-End Financials

Debt ratio: —
Return on equity: 7.08%
Cash ($ mil.): 37
Current ratio: —
Long-term debt ($ mil.): —

No. of shares (mil.): 7
Dividends
  Yield: 0.0%
  Payout: 50.4%
Market value ($ mil.): 345

	STOCK PRICE ($) FY Close	P/E High/Low	PER SHARE ($) Earnings	Dividends	Book Value
12/17	46.58	20 16	2.50	1.26	35.82
12/16	48.70	19 13	2.65	1.24	34.71
12/15	38.08	21 15	2.36	1.24	33.57
12/14	49.68	23 16	2.34	1.24	32.69
12/13	38.00	33 25	1.21	0.92	31.62
Annual Growth	5.2%	— —	19.9%	8.2%	3.2%

PepsiCo Inc

PepsiCo butts heads with its eternal rival The Coca-Cola Company for the title of world's biggest soft drinks maker. PepsiCo's soft drink brands include Pepsi Mountain Dew Tropicana Gatorade and Aquafina water. The company also owns Frito-Lay the world's #1 snack maker with offerings such as Lay's Ruffles Doritos and Cheetos. The Quaker Foods unit makes breakfast cereals (Quaker oatmeal Life) Rice-A-Roni and Near East side dishes. Pepsi products are available in 200-plus countries. The company operates its own bottling plants and distribution facilities.

HISTORY

Pharmacist Caleb Bradham invented Pepsi in 1898 in New Bern North Carolina. He named his new drink Pepsi-Cola (claiming it cured dyspepsia or indigestion) and registered the trademark in 1903. Following The Coca-Cola Company's example Bradham developed a bottling franchise system. By WWI 300 bottlers had signed up. After the war Bradham stockpiled sugar to safeguard against rising costs but in 1920 sugar prices plunged forcing him into bankruptcy in 1923.

Pepsi existed on the brink of ruin under various owners until Loft Candy bought it in 1931. Its fortunes improved in 1933 when in the midst of the Depression it doubled the size of its bottles to 12 ounces without raising the five-cent price. In 1939 Pepsi introduced the world's first radio jingle. Two years later Loft Candy merged with its Pepsi subsidiary and became The Pepsi-Cola Company.

Donald Kendall who became Pepsi-Cola's president in 1963 turned the firm's attention to young people ("The Pepsi Generation"). It acquired Mountain Dew in 1964 and became PepsiCo in 1965 when it acquired Frito-Lay.

In 1972 PepsiCo agreed to distribute Stolichnaya vodka in the US in exchange for being the only Western firm allowed to bottle soft drinks in the USSR. With the purchases of Pizza Hut (1977) Taco Bell (1978) and Kentucky Fried Chicken (1986) it became a major force in the fast-food industry.

When Coca-Cola changed its formula in 1985 Pepsi had a short-lived victory in the cola wars (until the return of Coca-Cola classic the new formula having been a dismal failure). The rivalry was extended to ready-to-drink tea in 1991 when in response to Coca-Cola's Nestea venture with NestlA© PepsiCo teamed up with Lipton.

Between 1991 and 1996 PepsiCo aggressively expanded its overseas bottling operations. However its efforts contrasted markedly with Coca-Cola's well-oiled international distribution machine. The firm then shifted its attention to the organization of its overseas network. Roger Enrico became CEO in 1996.

A year later PepsiCo spun off its $10 billion fast-food unit as TRICON Global Restaurants (now known as YUM! Brands Inc.) putting itself in a better position to sell its soft drinks at other restaurants. Also in 1997 it bought Borden's Cracker Jack snack and Smith's snacks from the UK's United Biscuits.

In 1998 it bought Seagram's market-leading Tropicana juices (rival of Coca-Cola's Minute Maid) for $3.3 billion. The firm sold a 65% stake in its new Pepsi Bottling Group to the public in 1999.

Its more than $13 billion purchase of The Quaker Oats Company in 2001 added the dominant Gatorade sports drink brand to its lineup. To make room for Gatorade PepsiCo sold its competing All Sport energy drink to The Monarch Beverage Company an Atlanta-based soda company later that year.

PepsiCo began a major restructuring of its PepsiCo Beverages & Foods division in 2003. The restructuring resulted in four company divisions: PepsiCo International PepsiCo Beverages North America Frito-Lay North America and Quaker Foods North America.

In 2004 PepsiCo approached juice maker Ocean Spray about a joint venture but was turned away by the cranberry farmers who own the juice manufacturer. The company bought General Mills' stake of their joint venture Snack Ventures Europe (SVE) in 2005 for $750 m

EXECUTIVES

Ceo North America, Albert P. (Al) Carey, age 66, $984,615 total compensation
Chairman And Ceo, Indra K. Nooyi, age 62, $1,725,000 total compensation
Evp Human Resources And Chief Human Resources Officer, Cynthia M. Trudell, age 65
Vice Chairman Evp Global Research And Development And Chief Scientific Officer, Mehmood Khan, age 59, $756,731 total compensation
Svp And Cio, Jody R. Davids, age 62
President Essa Category Teams Franchise And Po1 Sub-saharan Africa, Richard D. Evans
Vice Chairman Evp And Cfo, Hugh F. Johnston, age 57, $960,577 total compensation
President Pepsico Russia, Silviu Popovici, age 50
President Global Beverages Group, Brad Jakeman
President Pepsico Mexico, Pedro Padierna
President Latin America Beverages, Luis Montoya
President And Coo Frito-lay North America (flna), Vivek Sankaran, age 56
President Global Snacks Group And Global Insights, Simon Lowden
Evp Corporate Strategy And Chief Venturing Officer, Jim Andrew, age 57
Chief Operating Officer (coo) Nab And President Global Foodservice, Kirk Tanner, age 50
Ceo Asia Middle East And North Africa, Sanjeev Chadha, age 58, $764,423 total compensation

President Pepsico, Ramon Laguarta, age 54, $748,846 total compensation
Evp Global Categories And Franchise Management, Eugene Willemsen
Evp Communications, Jon Banner
Svp And Chief Procurement Officer, Grace Puma Whiteford
Ceo Latin America (latam) And Europe Sub-saharan Africa (essa), Laxman Narasimhan, age 50
Evp Government Affairs General Counsel And Corporate Secretary, Tony West, age 52
Evp Global Operations, Brian Newman
President And Ceo Greater China Region, Mike Spanos
President Global Foodservice, Anne Fink
Senior Vice President And Controller, Marie Gallagher
Marketing Vice President, Haston Lewis
National Sales Manager, Jill Griffith
Vice President Global Public Policy, Paul Boykas
Vice President Of Industry Relations, Doug Allison
Vice President Corporate And Commercial Planning Europe, Claire Stone
Vice President Selling And Delivery, Greg Moore
Vice President Of Public Relations, Larry Jabbonsky
Sales Vice President, Byron Brooks
National Account Manager, Chris Saline
Legal Vice President, Thomas P Schur
Vice President, Christy Jacoby
Vice President Worldwide Ingredients, Chris Gallucci
National Sales Manager, Jennifer Caro
National Account Manager, Jeremy Klingler
Vice President Purchase, Ashish Karanjkar
Medical Director Cardiovascular, Maria Afonso
Vice President Human Resources, Bhavna Bhaskar
National Sales Manager Modern Trade, Ismail Sabry
Vice President Purchasing, Art Schick
Vice President Infrastructure And Engineering, Johnathan Thibodeau
National Account Manager, Erin Morrison
Vice President Consumer Strategy, Tekla Back
Rvp Assistant, Linda Sullivan
Vice President Strategic Insights, Laura Jones
Vice President Human Resources, Clair Niver
Vice President And General Manager Of Philadelphia Market Unit, Dave Fitts
Vice President Of Marketing For Atlantic Business Unit, Tammy Sumpter
Senior Vice President Customer Supply Chain And Global Go To Market, John Phillips
Evp And Chro, Ruth Fattori
Vice President, John Barrett
Senior Vice President Chief Compliance And Ethics Officer, Debra Torres
Vp Supply Chain, Mark Brinker
Vice President Global Information Technology Service Management, Murat Sevil
Fin Bus Plng Vice President, Scott Davis
Tax Vice President, Tom Salcito
Ssm Agro Vice President Naf Ssm Agro, Jim Cleary
National Account Manager, Jose Abarca
Executive Vice President Global Operations, Grace Puma
National Account Manager, William Leonard
National Account Manager, John Fawver
Vice President Human Resources India Region, Suchitra Rajendra
Vice President Analytics, Kapil Malhotra
Senior Vice President Procurement, Brian Hadden
Legal Vice President, Timothy F Civil
National Account Manager, Jake Fuller
National Account Manager, Chris Osborne
National Account Manager, Susan Gilberd
National Account Manager, Adam Palmer
Senior Vice President Food Safety Quality Assurance And Scientific And Regulatory Affiars, Mike Liewen
National Account Manager, Brenda Ung

Vice President Human Resources, Patrick Mclaughlin
National Account Manager, David Samaniego
Vice President Global Marketing Hydration Portfolio, Olga OSMINKINA-JONES
Vice President Dairy Global Nutrition Group, Koen Burghouts
Advisory Board Member, Jayne Vetere
Board Member, Darren Walker
Auditors: KPMG LLP

LOCATIONS

HQ: PepsiCo Inc
700 Anderson Hill Road, Purchase, NY 10577
Phone: 914 253-2000
Web: www.pepsico.com

2017 Sales

	$ mil.	% of total
United States	36,546	57
Mexico	3,650	6
Russia	3,323	5
Canada	2,691	4
United Kingdom	1,650	3
Brazil	1,427	2
All other countries	14,329	23
Total	**63,525**	**100**

PRODUCTS/OPERATIONS

2017 Sales

	$ mil.	% of total
NAB	20,936	33
FLNA	15,798	25
ESSA	11,050	17
Latin America	7,208	11
AMENA	6,030	10
QFNA	2,503	4
Total	**63,525**	**100**

COMPETITORS

American Beverage	Kellogg
Anadolu Efes	Kraft Heinz
Arla Foods	Lactalis
Asahi Breweries	Merisant
Big Red	Monarch Beverage
Bongrain	Monarch Beverage (GA)
Britvic	Mondelez International
Campbell Soup	Monster Beverage
Carolina Beverage	Mountain Valley
Celestial Seasonings	National Beverage
Chiquita Brands	National Grape
Clearly Canadian	Cooperative
Coca-Cola	Nestlé
Coca-Cola FEMSA	New Leaf
ConAgra	Odwalla
Cott	Parmalat
DS Services	Polar Beverages
Danone Water	Princes Limited
Diamond Foods	Procter & Gamble
Dr Pepper Snapple	Red Bull
Group	Reed's
Energy Brands	Snapple
Fraser & Neave	Snyder's-Lance
FrieslandCampina	SodaStream
General Mills	Sunny Delight
Golden Enterprises	Tree Top
Grupo Bimbo	True Drinks
Hawaiian Springs	Weaver Popcorn Company
Inventure foods	Wet Planet Beverages
Jones Soda	

HISTORICAL FINANCIALS

Company Type: Public

Income Statement
FYE: December 30

	REVENUE ($ mil.)	NET INCOME ($ mil.)	NET PROFIT MARGIN	EMPLOYEES
12/17	63,525	4,857	7.6%	263,000
12/16	62,799	6,329	10.1%	264,000
12/15	63,056	5,452	8.6%	263,000
12/14	66,683	6,513	9.8%	271,000
12/13	66,415	6,740	10.1%	274,000
Annual Growth	(1.1%)	(7.9%)	—	(1.0%)

2017 Year-End Financials

Debt ratio: 49.22%
Return on equity: 44.31%
Cash ($ mil.): 10,610
Current ratio: 1.51
Long-term debt ($ mil.): 33,796

No. of shares (mil.): 1,420
Dividends
Yield: 0.0%
Payout: 93.7%
Market value ($ mil.): 170,286

	STOCK PRICE ($) FY Close	P/E High/Low	PER SHARE ($) Earnings	Dividends	Book Value
12/17	119.92	35 30	3.38	3.17	7.67
12/16	104.63	25 21	4.36	2.96	7.77
12/15	100.54	28 24	3.67	2.76	8.23
12/14	97.05	23 18	4.27	2.53	11.72
12/13	82.71	20 16	4.32	2.24	15.88
Annual Growth	9.7%	— —	(6.0%)	9.0%	(16.6%)

Performance Food Group Co

Auditors: DELOITTE & TOUCHE LLP

LOCATIONS

HQ: Performance Food Group Co
12500 West Creek Parkway, Richmond, VA 23238
Phone: 804 484-7700
Web: www.pfgc.com

HISTORICAL FINANCIALS

Company Type: Public

Income Statement
FYE: June 30

	REVENUE ($ mil.)	NET INCOME ($ mil.)	NET PROFIT MARGIN	EMPLOYEES
06/18*	17,619	198	1.1%	15,000
07/17	16,761	96	0.6%	14,000
07/16	16,104	68	0.4%	13,000
06/15	15,270	56	0.4%	12,000
06/14	13,685	15	0.1%	—
Annual Growth	6.5%	89.2%	—	—

*Fiscal year change

2018 Year-End Financials

Debt ratio: 29.60%
Return on equity: 19.34%
Cash ($ mil.): 7
Current ratio: 1.50
Long-term debt ($ mil.): 1,175

No. of shares (mil.): 103
Dividends
Yield: —
Payout: —
Market value ($ mil.): 3,787

	STOCK PRICE ($) FY Close	P/E High/Low	PER SHARE ($) Earnings	Dividends	Book Value
06/18*	36.70	19 13	1.90	0.00	11.00
07/17	27.40	30 21	0.93	0.00	9.18
07/16	26.92	39 27	0.70	0.00	8.04
Annual Growth	8.1%	— —	28.4%	—	8.2%

*Fiscal year change

Pfizer Inc

Pfizer is one of the world's largest research-based pharmaceuticals firms producing medicines for ailments in fields including cardiovascular health metabolism oncology and inflammation and immunology. Its top prescription products include cholesterol-lowering Lipitor pain management drugs Celebrex and Lyrica pneumonia vaccine Prevnar and erectile dysfunction treatment Viagra as well as arthritis drug Enbrel antibiotic Zyvox and high-blood-pressure therapy Norvasc. The firm's consumer health products operations which Pfizer plans to combine with those of GlaxoSmithKline include such leading brands as Advil Centrum and Robitussin. Pfizer operates around the world but gets half of its revenues from the US.

HISTORY

Charles Pfizer and his cousin confectioner Charles Erhart began making chemicals in Brooklyn in 1849. Products included camphor citric acid and santonin (an early antiparasitic). The company incorporated in 1900 as Chas. Pfizer & Co. was propelled into the modern drug business when it was asked to mass-produce penicillin for the war effort in 1941.

Pfizer discovered Terramycin and introduced it in 1950. Three years later it bought drugmaker Roerig its first major acquisition. In the 1950s the company opened branches in Belgium Canada Cuba Mexico and the UK and began manufacturing in Asia Europe and South America. By the mid-1960s Pfizer had worldwide sales of more than $200 million.

Beginning in the late 1950s Pfizer made Salk and Sabin polio vaccines and added new drugs such as Diabinese (antidiabetic 1958) and Vibramycin (antibiotic 1967). It moved into consumer products in the early 1960s buying BenGay Desitin and cosmetics maker Coty (sold in 1992). It bought hospital products company Howmedica in 1972 (sold in 1998) and heart-valve maker Shiley in 1979. In the 1980s Pfizer expanded its hospital products division buying 18 product lines and companies.

In 1995 Pfizer bought SmithKline Beecham's animal health business and Procter & Gamble's Bain de Soleil skin care line (sold in 1999).

Pfizer made headlines (and lots of men happy) when the company won FDA approval for Viagra in 1998. The little blue pill became a pop icon and made the company a household name.

In 2002 Pfizer purchased rival Pharmacia for $54 billion making it the world's largest research-based pharmaceutical company.

EXECUTIVES

Evp Corporate Affairs, Sally Susman, age 57
Evp Business Operations And Cfo, Frank A. D'Amelio, age 60, $1,324,000 total compensation
Chairman And Ceo, Ian C. Read, age 64, $1,905,250 total compensation
Evp And Chief Medical Officer, Freda C. Lewis-Hall, age 62, $800,000 total compensation
Evp And President Worldwide Research And Development, Mikael Dolsten, age 59, $1,237,500 total compensation
Evp And General Counsel, Douglas M. (Doug) Lankler, age 52
Svp And Head Pharmatherapeutics Research And Development, Alexander R. (Rod) MacKenzie, age 58
Evp Worldwide Human Resources, Charles H. (Chuck) Hill, age 62
Group President Pfizer Innovative Health, John D. Young, age 53, $1,130,000 total compensation
Evp Strategy And Commercial Operations, Laurie J. Olson, age 54
Coo, Albert Bourla, age 56, $1,117,500 total compensation
Evp And Chief Compliance And Risk Officer, Rady A. Johnson, age 56
Vp Innovative Health Product Portfolio Management And Consumer Operations, Kirsten Lund-Jurgensen, age 58
Group President Pfizer Essential Health, Angela Hwang
Vice President Us Primary Care Marketing, James Sage
Vice President Information Management, Craig Barrila
Vice President Manufacturing, Kevin Nepveux
Vice President Wss Specialty Care, Christopher Wohlberg
Vice President International Tax, Andre B Petrunoff
Medical Director, Michael Wajnrajch
Medical Director, Hernan Valdez
Senior Vice President Of Product, Chris Hillebrecht
Vice President Us Trade Group, Lou Dallago
Medical Director Worldwide Safety And Regulatory Operations, Gianluca Strozzi
Senior Vice President Executive Compensation Strategy And Programs, Stephen Pennacchio
Vice President Compliance Lead Emerging Markets Compliance Division, Jeffrey Liu
Medical Director, Jean Chow
Vice President Of Medical Affairs And, Paul Mensah
Senior Vice President Vaccine Clinical Research And Development, William Gruber
Vice President Human Resources, Mario Gagliano
Vice President External Affairs And Worldwide Communications, Elizabeth Golden
Medical Director And Team Leader Benelux Nordic And Baltic Region, Thomas Menschik
Vice President, Charles Knirsch
Vice President Finance Onc And Sc, Peter S McGuigan
Vice President Finance Establ Products, Kevin Sullivan
National Account Manager, Teri Kittredge
Vice President And Assistant Treasurer, Brian McMahon
Executive Vice President Development, Shaileen English
Clinical Director, Peter Park
Medical Director, Alejandra Nieto
National Account Manager, Mark Desantis
Senior Vice President Fin Biopharma And Cons Hlth, Sajal Mitra
Senior Vice President And Portfolio Manager, John Goceljak
Vice President Chief Of Staff To The Chairman And Chief Executive Officer, Navin Katyal
National Account Manager, Alan J Hemler
Senior Vice President, Salomon Azoulay
Senior Vice President, Kostas Giamouridis
Vice President, Feng Wu
Vice President, Lynne Handanyan
Vice President, Lisa Housianitis
Senior Vice President, Jaume Pons

Senior Vice President, Rory O'Connor
Medical Director, Seth Woodruff
Medical Director, Judith Hadavi
Vice President Human Resources Global Randd, Sander De Beer
Vice President Emea Logistics And Supply Operations, Danny Hendrikse
Associate Medical Director, Silvina Gallo
Medical Director Oncology, Daniel Kalanovic
Medical Director Oncology, Mahmoud Alam
Vice President Leadership, Julian Thompson
Vice President And Assistant Gc, Edward Nowicki
Associate Medical Director, Barbara Sleight
Senior Vice President Worldwide Business Development, Doug Giordano
Senior Vice President, Charles Triano
Vice President, Hong Lu
Senior Vice President, Andy Schmeltz
Senior Vice President Human Resources Gep And Compliance, Don Stewart
Vice President Research And Development Supplements Franchise, Rowena Pullan
Vice President, Mark Schneyer
Senior Vice President Wrd Development And Strategic Operations, Evan Loh
Vice President, Regina Rantz
Executive Vice President, Karine Gravel
Medical Director Psychiatry And Neurology, Brian Klee
Vice President And Assistant General Counsel, Lindsay Havern
Vice President Scottsdale Operations, Beatrice Colombo
Executive Vice President And General Manager, Linda Blacken
National Sales Manager Immun, Simon Goodger
Vice President Sales America, Jim Carr
Vice President For External Medical Affairs, Jack Watters
Regional President Emea Pch, Tarek Youssef
Pharmacy Manager, Dirk Potgieter
Associate Medical Director, David Witcombe
National Sales Manager, Beatriz Sanchez
Vice President Finance, Serge Roussel
Regional President Europe Global Innovative Pharma, Richard Blackburn
Vice President, John Hutchison
Executive Vice President And Co Founder, Cathryn Adams
Vice President Of Clinical Project Management, Dean Gianarkis
Vice President And Team Leader Finance, Michael Vogel
Vice President, Kanwar Nasir Khan
Vice President Global Vac Pneumo, Raul Isturiz
Medical Director, Ioana Russ
Medical Director, Nathalie Baillon-plot
Vice President Legal Affairs And General Counsel, Darren Noseworthy
Medical Director Oncology, Paolo Pierfederici
National Sales Manager, Tuncay Ekici
National Sales Manager Consumer Healthcare, Jung-tak Shin
Vice President, Rich Hollander
Vice President Of Worldwide Communications, Anna Ruder
Medical Director Hematology, Krupa Sivamurthy
Medical Director, Carlos Estevez
Vice President Endocrine Care, Jose Cara
Vice President, Cory Stiff
Vice President, Kevin Filipski
Senior Vice President Of Sales, Mike Byrne
Medical Director, Carolyn Blanckmeister
Vice President For Translational Oncology, Chris Boshoff
Medical Director, Maria Fernanda Velasco
Vice President Payer Accounts, Joseph Kucharski
Vice President Us Enbrel Sales And Marketing, John Miles
Vice President Corporate Audit, Jennifer Damico

Medical Director, Judith Hey-Hadavi
Vice President, Tracey Boyden
Medical Director, Jose Dias
Vice President Administration, Cathal Casey
Executive Vice President And Chief Financial Officer, Alan G Levin
Vice President And Assistant General Counsel, Arthur Cohn
Vice President Oncology Public Affairs, Nina Hill
Senior Vice President Total Rewards, Steve Pennacchio
Vpresident Leadership, Craig Whitehead
Associate Medical Director, Xiaoya Xu
Vice President Human Resources, Kristin Papesh
Government Relations, Ryan Bounsy
Vice President Vaccine Clinical Research, Dan Scott
Chief Scientific Officer Vice President Rare Disease Research And Development, Gregory LaRosa
National Sales Manager, Alem Muminovic
Medical Director, Mohamed Harti
Medical Director Us Medical Affairs, Elif Silva
Vice President Finance, Edmund Huver
Medical Director, Rebecca Luk
Senior Vice President And Chief Scientific Officer Oncology Research Unit, Tara Brown
Medical Director Latin America Vaccines, Jessica Presa
Vice President Innovation Center Ghandv, Sachin Kamal-Bahl
Vice President One2one, Kevin Orfan
Vice President Rare Disease Clinical Resea, Michael Binks
Vice President Global Alliance Management, Chad Jansen
Medical Director Breast Cance, Yao Wang
Regional President North America, Chris Slager
Vice President Business Technology Wrd, Hall Gregg
Executive Vice President, Ashish Shah
Regional President North America, Maya Martinez-Davis
Medical Director, Bruno Valtier
Vice President Surgery Division, Amy Glover
Vice President Cons Hlthcare Quality Operations, Anabel Ocasio-Velez
Vice President Alternate Site Lead, Cole C Pinnow
Medical Director Urology And Women Health Care, Nicholas Lu
Vice President Of Marketing Eucrisa Brand Team Leader, Ruth Dovdavany
Vice President And Chief Scientific Officer Viral Vaccines, Philip Dormitzer
Vice President Us Pharma Operations, Donal Loughrey
Vice President Global Health And Value Rare Disease And Neuroscience Pain, Bhash Parasuraman
Vice President Lead Divisional Controller, Christopher Krawtschuk
Auditors: KPMG LLP

LOCATIONS

HQ: Pfizer Inc
235 East 42nd Street, New York, NY 10017
Phone: 212 733-2323
Web: www.pfizer.com

2017 Sales

	$ mil.	% of total
US	26,026	50
Emerging Markets	11,400	21
Developed Europe	8,508	16
Developed Rest of World	6,612	13
Total	52,546	100

PRODUCTS/OPERATIONS

2017 Sales by Segment

	$ mil.	% of total
Innovative Health	31,422	60
Essential Health	21,124	40
Total	52,546	100

Selected Products

Pharmaceuticals
Aricept (Alzheimer's disease)
Aromasin (breast cancer)
+Arthrotec (osteoarthritis and rheumatoid arthritis)
BeneFIX (hemophilia)
BMP2 (bone and cartilage development)
Caduet (high cholesterol and blood pressure dual therapy)
Camptosar (colorectal cancer)
Cardura (hypertension and enlarged prostate disease)
Celebrex (arthritis pain)
Chantix/Champix (smoking cessation)
Dalacin/Cleocin (antibiotic for bacterial infections)
Detrol/Detrol LA (overactive bladder)
Diflucan (antifungal)
Effexor (antidepressant and anxiety disorder treatment)
Enbrel (arthritis treatment)
Fragmin (anticoagulant)
Genotropin (growth hormone deficiency)
Geodon/Zeldox (schizophrenia and bipolar disorder)
Inspra (high blood pressure)
Lipitor (cholesterol)
Lyrica (nerve pain)
Medrol (inflammation)
Methotrexate (severe psoriasis)
Neurontin (epilepsy)
Norvasc (hypertension)
Premarin (hormone replacement therapy)
Prevnar (pneumococcus vaccine)
Pristiq (antidepressant)
Protonix (protein pump inhibitor)
Quillivant XR (ADHD)
Rapamune (organ rejection preventative)
Rebif (multiple sclerosis)
ReFacto AF/Xyntha (hemophilia)
Relpax (migraines)
Revatio (hypertension)
Selzentry (HIV)
Skelaxin (muscle relaxant)
Somavert (acromegaly)
Spiriva (chronic obstructive pulmonary disease)
Sulperazon (antibiotic)
Sutent (carcinoma and tumors)
Toviaz (overactive bladder)
Tygacil (anti-infective)
Unasyn (injectable antibacterial)
Vfend (fungal infections)
Viagra (impotence)
Xalatan/Xalacom (glaucoma)
Xanax XR (anti-anxiety treatment)
Zithromax/Zmax (antibiotic)
Zoloft (depression)
Zosyn/Tazocin (anti-infective)
Zyvox (antibiotic)
Animal Health
Cerenia (nausia treatment for canines)
Convenia (canine and feline antibiotics)
Draxxin (cattle antibiotic)
Excede (cattle antibiotic)
Improvac (swine vaccine for boar taint)
Palladia (dog cancer treatment)
Revolution/Stronghold (antiparasitic for dogs and cats)
Rimadyl (canine osteoarthritis treatment)
Suvaxyn (swine vaccine)
Consumer Health
Advil (analgesic)
Anbesol (oral pain relief)
Caltrate (nutritional supplement)
Centrum (vitamins)
ChapStick (lip care)
Dimetapp (cough/cold remedy)
Emergen-C (vitamin C supplement)
FiberCon (laxative)
Nexium (acid reflux)
Preparation H (hemorrhoid treatment)
Robitussin (cough/cold remedy)
ThermaCare (aches and pains)

Allergan plc
AstraZeneca
Boehringer Ingelheim
Bristol-Myers Squibb
Eli Lilly
GlaxoSmithKline
Johnson & Johnson

Merck
Mylan
Novartis
Roche Holding
Sanofi
Teva

HISTORICAL FINANCIALS

Company Type: Public

Income Statement   FYE: December 31

	REVENUE ($ mil.)	NET INCOME ($ mil.)	NET PROFIT MARGIN	EMPLOYEES
12/17	52,546	21,308	40.6%	90,200
12/16	52,824	7,215	13.7%	96,500
12/15	48,851	6,960	14.2%	97,900
12/14	49,605	9,135	18.4%	78,300
12/13	51,584	22,003	42.7%	77,700
Annual Growth	0.5%	(0.8%)	—	3.8%

2017 Year-End Financials

Debt ratio: 25.32%—
Return on equity: 32.57%
Cash ($ mil.): 1,342
Current ratio: 1.35
Long-term debt ($ mil.): 33,538

Dividends
  Yield: 0.0%
  Payout: 36.3%
Market value ($ mil.): —

	STOCK PRICE ($) FY Close	P/E High/Low		PER SHARE ($) Earnings	Dividends	Book Value
12/17	36.22	10	9	3.52	1.28	11.93
12/16	32.48	32	24	1.17	1.20	9.81
12/15	32.28	32	27	1.11	1.12	10.48
12/14	31.15	23	19	1.42	1.04	11.33
12/13	30.63	10	8	3.19	0.96	11.92
Annual Growth	4.3%	—	—	2.5%	7.5%	0.0%

PG&E Corp (Holding Co)

Pacific Gas and Electric is specific about its services. The utility distributes electricity to more than 5.5 million residential commercial and industrial customers and natural gas to approximately 4.4 million customers in Central and Northern California. Pacific Gas and Electric has interests in power plants with a total of 7700 MW of generating capacity. It is also engaged in electricity procurement and transmission and natural gas procurement transportation and storage. Pacific Gas and Electric is the major subsidiary of holding company PG&E Corporation.

Bankruptcy

In January 2019 PG&E announced its intention to file for bankruptcy. The company faces more than $30 billion in liability from massive wildfires that ravaged parts of the state since 2017. The wildfires have killed dozens of people and destroyed thousands of homes. The future of the company will remain uncertain as the liability cases will be battled amongst victims bankers insurance companies and energy providers.

Operations

Pacific Gas and Electric operates more than 100 electric generating power plants using a variety of fuel inputs such as nuclear fossil fuels hydroelectric solar and wind. It delivers more than 83000 GWh of electricity annually.

Electricity accounts for about 80% of the utility's revenue.

Financial Performance

In 2016 Pacific Gas and Electric produced $17.7 billion in revenue and $1.4 billion of net income.

Strategy

Safety and reliability is a key concern (and a cause for concern) for Pacific Gas and Electric and its parent PG&E. The company continues to be under third-party oversight following the 2010 explosion of a pipeline in San Bruno California that resulted in multiple casualties. In addition PG&E is being sued over deadly wildfires in 2017 and 2018 that also resulted in deaths and the mass destruction of property. If it is found liable the company could be on the hook for billions of dollars in damages. Reports surfaced in early 2019 that PG&E was considering bankruptcy protection for itself and/or Pacific Gas and Electric as a preemptive action; the company has not officially responded to the reports.

Following the San Bruno accident PG&E had already completed several safety upgrades to its gas pipeline infrastructure including installing 268 automatic and remote control shut-off values hydrostatically testing more than 800 miles of the pipeline transmission system and implementing in-line inspection tools in 260 miles of pipeline (which required associated infrastructure upgrades). Additional efforts are planned for several more years.

EXECUTIVES

President Electric, Geisha J. Williams, age 56, $634,183 total compensation

Svp And Cio, Karen A. Austin, age 56

Svp Human Resources, Dinyar B. Mistry, age 56, $381,433 total compensation

President Gas, Nickolas (Nick) Stavropoulos, age 59, $613,221 total compensation

Svp Human Resources, John R. Simon, age 54, $424,994 total compensation

Svp Generation And Chief Nuclear Officer, Edward D. (Ed) Halpin, age 56

Vp Cfo And Controller, David S. Thomason, age 43

Vice President Network Services, Jeff Hernandez

Auditors: DELOITTE & TOUCHE LLP

LOCATIONS

HQ: PG&E Corp (Holding Co)
77 Beale Street, P.O. Box 770000, San Francisco, CA 94177
Phone: 415 973-1000   **Fax:** 415 267-7265
Web: www.pgecorp.com

PRODUCTS/OPERATIONS

2016 Sales

	% of total
Electric	78
Natural gas	22
Total	**100**

COMPETITORS

AEP
AES
APX
Avista
Bonneville Power
Calpine
Constellation Energy
  Group
Duke Energy
Edison International
Entergy
Exelon
FirstEnergy
Modesto Irrigation
  District
NV Energy
NW Natural

PacifiCorp
Portland General
  Electric
Riverside Electric
  Utility
Sacramento Municipal
  Utility
San Diego Gas &
  Electric
Sempra Energy
SoCalGas
Southern California
  Edison
Southern Company
Tractebel Engineering
Turlock Irrigation
  District

North Baja Pipeline
Northern California
  Power Agency

Western Area Power
  Administration

HISTORICAL FINANCIALS

Company Type: Public

Income Statement   FYE: December 31

	REVENUE ($ mil.)	NET INCOME ($ mil.)	NET PROFIT MARGIN	EMPLOYEES
12/17	17,135	1,660	9.7%	23,000
12/16	17,666	1,407	8.0%	24,000
12/15	16,833	888	5.3%	23,000
12/14	17,090	1,450	8.5%	22,581
12/13	15,598	828	5.3%	21,166
Annual Growth	2.4%	19.0%	—	2.1%

2017 Year-End Financials

Debt ratio: 28.13%
Return on equity: 8.93%
Cash ($ mil.): 449
Current ratio: 0.88
Long-term debt ($ mil.): 17,753

No. of shares (mil.): 514
Dividends
  Yield: 0.0%
  Payout: 48.2%
Market value ($ mil.): 23,077

	STOCK PRICE ($) FY Close	P/E High/Low		PER SHARE ($) Earnings	Dividends	Book Value
12/17	44.83	22	14	3.21	1.55	37.34
12/16	60.77	23	18	2.78	1.93	35.39
12/15	53.19	33	26	1.79	1.82	33.69
12/14	53.24	18	13	3.06	1.82	33.09
12/13	40.28	26	22	1.83	1.82	31.41
Annual Growth	2.7%	—	—	15.1%	(3.9%)	4.4%

PHILADELPHIA CONSOLIDATED HOLDING CORP.

Because each industry has its own unique set of risks Philadelphia Insurance Companies and its subsidiaries specialize in designing and underwriting commercial property/casualty insurance. Its niche clients include rental car companies (for that insurance they always want to sell you at the counter) not-for-profits health and fitness centers and day-care facilities. Its specialty lines include loss-control policies and liability coverage for such professionals as lawyers doctors accountants dog groomers and even insurance claims adjusters. Philadelphia Insurance Companies is a subsidiary of Tokio Marine Holdings.

Geographic Reach

Philadelphia Insurance Companies' operating subsidiaries Philadelphia Insurance and Philadelphia Indemnity Insurance sell and service policies through a network of independent agents and about 50 regional offices that stretch across the US. With its new-found backing from Tokio Marine the insurer has access to broader distribution avenues in the US and overseas.

Sales and Marketing

In addition to commercial property and casualty insurance the company also sells personal coverage for collectible cars and homeowners flood insurance.

Strategy

Philadelphia Insurance Companies has been enhancing its information technology systems. The firm is working to upgrade its back-office infrastructure for more efficient handling of billing claims accounting and data management functions.

EXECUTIVES

Regional Vice President, Brent Kruse
Assistant Vice President And Pricing Actuary, John Ferraro
Executive Vice President Marketing, Robert OLeary
Senior Vice President Marketing, Brian O'Reilly
Assistant Vice President, Michael Henk
Assistant Vice President, Tsuyoshi Maeda
Assistant Vice President Human Resources, Laura Boylan
Vice President And Product Manager, Paul Siragusa
Senior Vice President, John Doyle
Regional Vice President, Bill Misita
Assistant Vice President, Liney Kevin
Executive Vice President, Sean Sweeney

LOCATIONS

HQ: PHILADELPHIA CONSOLIDATED HOLDING CORP.
1 BALA PLZ STE 100, BALA CYNWYD, PA 190041401
Phone: 610 617-7900
Web: WWW.PHLY.COM

PRODUCTS/OPERATIONS

Selected Products

Commercial and Personal Property/Casualty Insurance
Adoption agencies
Adult day care
Amateur sports
Antique collector car
Apartments
Auto leasing/rental program
Boat dealers
Bowling centers
Builder's exchange
Builders' risk
Business auto fleet
Camp operators
Child care centers
Consulting foresters
Contractor environmental coverage
Crime protection plus
Entertainment
Environmental
Fairs and fairgrounds
Festivals
Film production
Flood
Golf and country clubs
Health fitness and wellness
Home health care
Homeowners association
Hospice
Hotels
Life and business coaches
Loss control
Medical facilities and hospitals
Motorsports
Museums
Non-profit and social service organizations
Nursing homes
Office parks
Outdoor recreation
Performing arts
Pest control services
Professional sports
Public entities
Real rstate dchedules
Religious organizations
RV parks and campgrounds
Schools
Security services (The Guardian)
Shopping centers
Special events
Substance abuse rehabilitation facilities
Temporary staffing agencies
Volunteer fire department

Zoos
Liability
Accountants professional liability
Allied Health professional liability
Business owners
Cyber security liability
Employed lawyers professional liability
Employment practices stand alone
Excess liability
Miscellaneous professional liability (Affinity Pro)

COMPETITORS

AIG	Liberty Mutual
American Financial Group	Markel
	North Pointe
CNA Financial	RLI
Hagerty Insurance	State Farm
Hanover Insurance	Travelers Companies

HISTORICAL FINANCIALS

Company Type: Private

Income Statement

FYE: December 31

	ASSETS ($ mil.)	NET INCOME ($ mil.)	INCOME AS % OF ASSETS	EMPLOYEES
12/16	9,719	347	3.6%	1,374
12/15	9,047	323	3.6%	—
Annual Growth	7.4%	7.5%	—	—

Philip Morris International Inc

Philip Morris International (PMI) knows how to light up a room. The company makes six of the world's top 15 tobacco brands laying claim to more than 10% of the international cigarette market outside the US. The company's primary international brands are Marlboro (the world's #1-selling cigarette) L&M Bond Street Philip Morris Chesterfield and Parliament. (Marlboro accounts for about a third of PMI's total shipment volume.) Top local brands include Fortune Morven Gold and Dji Sam Soe. PMI's portfolio spans the price spectrum with premium mid-priced and value-priced products. Despite being ostensibly a US company PMI has no US presence: its former parent Altria spun PMI off to handle its international operations as a separate entity.

Operations

The company operates four segments according to the company's top geographic markets. PMI's European Union segment generates more than 35% of PMI's total revenue while the Eastern Europe Middle East & Africa (EMEA) and Asia-Pacific segments account for around a quarter each. Latin American and Canada bring in the remainder.

PMI's international brands make up more than 75% of its shipment volume while the Marlboro brand accounts for some 35%. PMI's other tobacco products (OTP) primarily include tobacco for roll-your-own and make-your-own cigarettes pipe tobacco cigars and cigarillos.

It has contract manufacturing relationships with more than 20 third-party manufacturers in 20-plus markets. In addition the company manufactures its hand-rolled cigarettes through 38 third-party operators in Indonesia. PMI's more than 25 facilities each manufacture more than 10 billion

cigarettes each year of which six produce more than 30 billion units.

Its international brands are premium price brands Marlboro Parliament and Virginia S; mid-price brands L&M Lark Merit Muratti and Philip Morris; and low-price brands Bond Street Chesterfield Next and Red & White.

Important local brands include Dji Sam Soe Sampoerna and U Mild in Indonesia, Champion Fortune and Jackpot in the Philippines; Apollo-Soyuz and Optima in Russia; Morven Gold in Pakistan; Boston in Colombia; Belmont Canadian Classics and Number 7 in Canada; f6 in Germany; Delicados in Mexico; Assos in Greece; and Petra in the Czech Republic and Slovakia.

PMI also makes four types smokeless tobacco products that heat but don't burn tobacco. Two of the four are still undergoing clinical trials while the other two are on the market under the IQOS and TEEPS brands.

Geographic Reach

New York-based Philip Morris International's (PMI) products are sold in more than 180 markets worldwide. PMI operates nearly 50 manufacturing facilities located in Africa Asia Canada Europe Latin America and the Middle East.

PMI?s largest factories are based in St. Petersburg and Krasnodar (Russia) Sukorejo and Karawang (Indonesia) Izmir (Turkey) Marikina and Batangas (Philippines) Krakow (Poland) Berlin (Germany) Kharkiv (Ukraine) and Klaipeda (Lithuania).

Sales and Marketing

Philip Morris International's (PMI) products are marketed and promoted through channels such as: point of sale communications brand events access-restricted Web sites print and direct communication to verified adult smokers (via mail e-mail and other electronic communication tools). The Marlboro brand has a long association with motorsports particularly Formula 1 and Moto GP.

PMI distributes its products directly to retailers single independent distributors zonified distribution and national or regional wholesalers. The company also directly supplies key accounts which include gas stations retail chains and supermarkets.

Financial Performance

In fiscal 2016 Philip Morris succeeded in putting a stop to a three-year decline in net revenue. In the year revenue increased 1% or around $1 billion to $75.0 billion. It recorded strong increases in Asia and the EU while Eastern Europe the Middle East and Africa (EMEA) recorded a mild decline while Latin America and Canada fell sharply. Higher prices compensated for falls in volume sales. After accounting for excise taxes revenue fell by less than a percent to $26.7 billion.

Net income increased a modest 1% to $7.0 billion due to price increases lower marketing and research costs and $68 million asset impairment expense incurred in 2015.

Cash from operations increased by $212 million to $8.1 billion due to earnings growth and lower cash payments relating to exit costs.

Strategy

With traditional cigarette sales inversely correlating with upwards health consciousness Philip Morris International (PMI) has partnered with its former parent Altria Group to transition its product commercialization toward more reduced-risk products such as e-cigarettes. It has two types of e-cigarette on the market and two still in development. At the forefront is its IQOS brand the result of a $3 billion investment which sold 7.4 billion "units" (the insertable tobacco filament rather than the electronic device) in 2016. The product has been a huge hit in Japan where it grabbed a 10% share of the tobacco market in a matter of months and saw 72% of smokers switch to IQOS permanently.

PMI has also partnered with Altria to market its e-vapor products and Altria in return markets PMI's heated tobacco products in the US.

Meanwhile PMI competes for smokers' loyalty with the international tobacco giants British American Tobacco Imperial Brands and Japan Tobacco several regional and local tobacco companies and also state-owned companies in Algeria Egypt and several Asian countries by offering a range of premium mid-price and low-price brands. Its American blend cigarettes Marlboro L&M and Chesterfield are its most popular brands with the Marlboro brand alone making up more than a third of the company's shipment volume.

Company Background

PMI is a result of a spinoff from Altria in 2008. The separation positioned PMI as an independent publicly traded company free from its US branch Philip Morris USA. Altria simultaneously avoided an entanglement in various US legal and regulatory issues.

PMI has made a number of acquisitions to enhance its brand-rich portfolio and geographic presence. In mid-2011 PMI took over a cigarette manufacturer in Jordan. The purchase followed PMI's acquisition of a cigar business comprising trademarks in Australia and New Zealand. During 2011 PMI also revised its joint venture with Vietnam National Tobacco Corp. (Vinataba) in Vietnam opening the door to licensing the Marlboro label as PMI established a local branch to build its brands.

In 2009 PMI acquired the South African tobacco branch of Swedish Match for 1.93 billion ZAR (about $256 million) giving PMI a leg up in producing smokeless tobacco products and builds upon a joint venture between PMI and Swedish Match to market Swedish style snus and other smokeless tobacco lines outside of Scandinavia and the US. (Altria moved to dominate the rapidly rising niche by taking over UST a leader in the US market for smokeless products including the Copenhagen Husky and Skoal brands.) In the same month PMI purchased the PetterA?es tobacco business for $209 million pocketing fine-cut brands popular in Sweden and Norway.

EXECUTIVES

Ceo, André Calantzopoulos, age 60, $1,501,552 total compensation

Cfo, Martin G. King, age 53, $842,239 total compensation

President External Affairs & General Counsel, Marc S. Firestone, age 59, $1,015,680 total compensation

President Science & Innovation, Miroslaw Zielinski, age 57, $943,738 total compensation

President South & Southeast Asia Region Including Indonesia And The Philippines, Stacey Kennedy

Coo, Jacek Olczak, age 53, $971,563 total compensation

Svp And Cio, Patrick Brunel, age 52

President European Union Region, Frederic de Wilde, age 50

President Eastern Europe Middle East Africa Region And Pmi Duty Free Including North Africa, Drago Azinovic, age 55

President Latin America And Canada Region, Jeanne Poll ̄s, age 53

Svp Commercial, Werner Barth, age 53

President Eastern Europe Region, Marco Mariotti

President East Asia & Australia Region, Paul Riley

Chief Digital Officer, Jaime Suarez

V Pres Controller, Andreas Kurali

Cfo; Chairman And Ceo Altria Group, Louis C. Camilleri, age 63

Auditors: PricewaterhouseCoopers SA

LOCATIONS

HQ: Philip Morris International Inc
120 Park Avenue, New York, NY 10017
Phone: 917 663-2000 **Fax:** 917 663-5372
Web: www.pmi.com

2016 Sales

	$ mil.	% of total
European Union	27,129	36
Eastern Europe Middle East & Africa	18,286	25
Asia	20,531	27
Latin America & Canada	9,007	12
Total	**74,953**	**100**

PRODUCTS/OPERATIONS

Selected Brands

Local brands
  Apollo-Soyuz (Russia)
  Assos (Greece)
  Belmont (Canada)
  Best (Serbia)
  Boston (Colombia)
  Canadian Classics (Canada)
  Champion (Philippines)
  Classic (Serbia)
  Delicados (Mexico)
  Diana (Italy)
  Dji Sam Soe (Indonesia)
  f6 (Germany)
  Fortune (Philippines)
  Hope (Philippines)
  Morven Gold (Pakistan)
  Number 7 (Canada)
  Optima (Russia)
  Petra (Czech Republic and Slovakia)
  Sampoema A (Indonesia)
  Sampoema Kretek (Indonesia)
Mid-price brands
  L&M
  Chesterfield
Other international brands
  Benson & Hedges
  Bond Street
  Lark
  Muratti
  Next
  Philip Morris
  Red & White
Premium-price
  Marlboro
  Merit
  Parliament
  Virginia Slims
Other tobacco products
  Interval (France)
  Petterøes (Norway and Sweden)
  Swedish Match snus smokefree tobacco

2016 Shipment Volumes

	% of total
International brands	77
Local brands	23
Total	**100**

COMPETITORS

British American Tobacco	Japan Tobacco
Gudang Garam	Reemtsma
Imperial Brands	Cigarettenfabriken

HISTORICAL FINANCIALS

Company Type: Public

Income Statement   FYE: December 31

	REVENUE ($ mil.)	NET INCOME ($ mil.)	NET PROFIT MARGIN	EMPLOYEES
12/18	29,625	7,911	26.7%	77,400
12/17	28,748	6,035	21.0%	80,600
12/16	26,685	6,967	26.1%	79,500
12/15	26,794	6,873	25.7%	80,200
12/14	29,767	7,493	25.2%	82,500
Annual Growth	**(0.1%)**	**1.4%**	**—**	**(1.6%)**

2018 Year-End Financials

Debt ratio: 79.79%   No. of shares (mil.): 1,554
Return on equity: —   Dividends
Cash ($ mil.): 6,593   Yield: 6.7%
Current ratio: 1.13   Payout: 104.4%
Long-term debt ($ mil.): 26,975   Market value ($ mil.): 103,784

	STOCK PRICE ($) FY Close	P/E High/Low	PER SHARE ($) Earnings	Dividends	Book Value
12/18	66.76	22 13	5.08	4.49	(8.01)
12/17	105.65	32 23	3.88	4.22	(7.78)
12/16	91.49	23 19	4.48	4.12	(8.18)
12/15	87.91	20 17	4.42	4.04	(8.55)
12/14	81.45	19 16	4.76	3.88	(8.16)
Annual Growth	**(4.9%)**	**—**	**1.6%**	**3.7%**	**—**

Phillips 66

Phillips 66 is a leading marketer of gas aviation fuels and other refined petroleum products as well as specialty products such as oils waxes solvents and lubricants. It markets in the US under the Phillips 66 Conoco and 76 brands and internationally under the JET and Coop brands. One of the largest crude oil refiners the company processes transports and markets natural gas and natural gas liquids as well as liquefied petroleum gas. It produces olefins and polyolefins and other products through CPChem a joint venture with Chevron. Phillips 66 operates primarily in the US and Europe.

Operations

Of the four segments that Phillips 66 reports Marketing and Specialties is the largest contributing about 75% of sales. It includes sales of refined petroleum products (gasoline distillates aviation fuel) through 7800 branded sites in the US and 1500 owned leased or joint venture sites in Europe. Specialty products (for example lubricants sold under Phillips 66 Kendall and Red Line brands) and power generation operations also add to this segment?s revenue.

The Refining segment which accounts for just more than 20% of total revenue has a throughput global refining capacity of 2.1 million barrels per day.

The Midstream segment of Phillips 66 — which gathers transports and markets NGL crude oil and feedstocks — makes up less than 5% of total revenue; it includes the company's interest in Phillips 66 Partners LP which has been acquiring Phillips 66's midstream assets. A very small fraction of company revenue comes from its equity in CPChem (a joint venture with Chevron) which is one of the world?s top producers of olefins and polyolefins and a major supplier of aromatics and specialty chemicals.

Geographic Reach

Phillips 66 operates primarily in the US. Its presence in Europe is largely concentrated in the UK with some assets in mainland Europe. The US accounts for more than 70% of revenue followed by the UK at about 10%.

CPChem is involved in more than 30 global manufacturing facilities in five continents but most significant assets are on the Texas Gulf Coast.

Sales and Marketing

Phillips 66 markets petroleum and specialty products through a network of nearly 8000 marketer-owned or -supplied outlets across the US under brand names 76 Conoco and Phillips 66. It also holds brand-licensing agreements with nearly

1000 sites. Its refined products are marketed on both a branded and unbranded basis.

In Europe Phillips 66 sells retail and wholesale products in Austria Germany and the UK under the JET brand and in Switzerland under the Coop brand (equity interest).

Financial Performance

Phillips 66 posted annual sales of around $86 billion in 2016 a $14 billion reduction from the year before. This marks a continuing trend for the company of steep revenue decline which has fallen more than 50% in five years.

In 2016 revenue fell due to lower average prices for petroleum products which particularly impacted the Marketing and Specialties and Refining segments (sales in those two segments fell by a combined $15 billion). Midstream revenue rose slightly and the Chemicals segment was flat.

The company posted net income of $1.5 billion a 63% reduction from the previous year. Refining profits dropped by more than $2 billion as historically high refining throughput led to significant weakening of US crack spread (refinery margins). Marketing and Specialties the firm?s most profitable segment and Chemicals both saw significant reductions in profit. Only the Midstream segment reported improvement on lower equity losses from DCP Midstream.

Along with revenue and net income Phillips 66's operating cash flow also declined shrinking 48% to about $3 billion.

Strategy

Phillips 66 is recalibrating resources from Refining to the Midstream and Chemical segments with a focus on wholesale trading (because of its lower capital requirements) and operational cost-cutting measures.

Low demands in the refining sector prompted Phillips 66 to follow a high-return quick payout strategy with investments in that business focused on increasing returns from existing assets.

Midstream Phillips 66 hopes to gain production increases from several construction completions based on its long-term growth strategy. This includes the buildout of the energy manufacturing center in Sweeney Texas and the expansion of the Beaumont Terminal in Nederland Texas. The company also sees benefit in the continued expansion of its master limited partnership (Phillips 66 Partners) with assets from Phillips 66 and third parties. In 2016 the limited partnership acquired NGL logistics assets in Louisiana (500 miles of pipelines and storage caverns) further increasing revenue potential.

CPChem also expanded operations by opening two new polyethylene units in the Texas Gulf Coast in November 2017 taking advantage of higher demands for plastics globally and cheap supply of domestic natural gas.

EXECUTIVES

Chairman And Ceo, Greg C. Garland, age 61, $1,616,816 total compensation

Evp And Cfo, Kevin J. Mitchell, $688,448 total compensation

Evp Refining, Lawrence M. (Larry) Ziemba, $690,312 total compensation

Evp Midstream, Robert A. (Bob) Herman, age 60, $661,608 total compensation

Vp Technology, Merl R. Lindstrom

Evp Commercial Marketing Transportation And Business Development, Tim G. Taylor, age 64, $1,071,376 total compensation

Evp Legal And Government Affairs General Counsel And Corporate Secretary, Paula A. Johnson, $698,976 total compensation

Evp Marketing And Commercial, Timothy D. (Tim) Roberts

Auditors: Ernst & Young LLP

LOCATIONS

HQ: Phillips 66
   2331 CityWest Blvd., Houston, TX 77042
Phone: 281 293-6600
Web: www.Phillips66.com

2016 Sales

	% of total
US	71
UK	12
Germany	7
Other countries	10
Total	**100**

PRODUCTS/OPERATIONS

2016 Sales

	% of total
Refined products	87
Crude oil resales	9
NGL	4
Total	**100**

2016 Sales

	$ mil.	% of total
Marketing and Specialties	63,367	74
Refining	17,948	21
Midstream	2,927	3
Chemicals	5	-
Corporate and Other	32	-
Equity in earnings of affiliates	1,414	2
Net gains of dispositions	10	-
Other income	74	-
Total	**85,777**	**100**

Selected Brands

76
Conoco
Coop
Copylene
JET
Kendall
Phillips 66
Red Line

COMPETITORS

BP	Marathon Petroleum
CITGO	Motiva Enterprises
CVR	NOVA Chemicals
Chevron	National Cooperative
CrossAmerica Partners	Refinery Association
Dow Chemical	Shell Oil Products
Exxon Mobil	Sinclair Oil
Gibson Energy	Sunoco
Hess Corporation	TOTAL
HollyFrontier	Tesoro
LyondellBasell	Valero Energy

HISTORICAL FINANCIALS

Company Type: Public

Income Statement   FYE: December 31

	REVENUE ($ mil.)	NET INCOME ($ mil.)	NET PROFIT MARGIN	EMPLOYEES
12/17	104,622	5,106	4.9%	14,600
12/16	85,777	1,555	1.8%	14,800
12/15	100,949	4,227	4.2%	14,000
12/14	164,093	4,762	2.9%	14,000
12/13	174,809	3,726	2.1%	13,500
Annual Growth	**(12.0%)**	**8.2%**	**—**	**2.0%**

2017 Year-End Financials

Debt ratio: 18.59%
Return on equity: 21.51%
Cash ($ mil.): 3,119
Current ratio: 1.42
Long-term debt ($ mil.): 10,069

No. of shares (mil.): 502
Dividends
  Yield: 0.0%
  Payout: 27.7%
Market value ($ mil.): 50,805

	STOCK PRICE ($) FY Close	P/E High/Low		PER SHARE ($) Earnings	Dividends	Book Value
12/17	101.15	10	8	9.85	2.73	49.94
12/16	86.41	31	25	2.92	2.45	43.16
12/15	81.80	12	8	7.73	2.18	43.63
12/14	71.70	10	8	8.33	1.89	39.51
12/13	77.13	12	8	6.02	1.33	37.19
Annual Growth	**7.0%**	**—**	**—**	**13.1%**	**19.8%**	**7.6%**

Pilgrims Pride Corp.

As one of the world's top chicken processors Pilgrim's Pride has a lot to crow about. The company sells fresh frozen and value-added poultry products under a host of brands (Pilgrim's Pride Gold Kist and Moy Park among them) primarily in North America and Europe. Vertically integrated Pilgrim's Pride is involved in breeding hatching raising processing and distributing chicken; it produces some 10 billion pounds of chicken products annually. The company — which serves retail food outlets distributors and food service operators — is majority owned by Brazil's JBS.

Operations

Pilgrim's Pride conducts its operations through a huge network of more than 5000 growers about 40 feed mills some 50 hatcheries three dozen or so processing plants about 15 prepared foods cook plants and some 20 distribution centers as well as rendering facilities and pet food plants.

The company's reporting segments are geographic with US Chicken accounting for about two-thirds of sales; UK/European Chicken and Mexican Chicken account for nearly 20% and about 10% respectively. Within its largest US segment fresh chicken (refrigerated whole or cut-up chicken marinated or non-marinated) accounts for about 85% of revenue. Prepared chicken (breast filets strips nuggets patties deli products) generates about 15% of revenue and export/other (refrigerated for US distributors or frozen for distribution to export markets) accounts for the rest.

Geographic Reach

Customers in the US generate nearly 70% of Pilgrim's Pride's total revenue with European customers accounting for nearly 20% and Mexican customers accounting for about 10%. It exports its products to more than 100 countries worldwide; key areas outside its main three markets include Asia the Commonwealth of Independent States (former Soviet Republics) and the Middle East.

The Colorado-based company has nearly 100 active plants and other facilities in the US as well as about 50 in Mexico 25 in Europe and five in Puerto Rico.

Sales and Marketing

Pilgrim's Pride has some 5500 customers including restaurants and food processors (Chick-fil-A) grocery store chains (Kroger Publix) and wholesale clubs (Costco). Its top two customers together account for just more than 10% of revenue.

Financial Performance

Pilgrim's Pride has seen strong revenue growth over the past five years for a variety of reasons including acquisitions in the US Mexico and Europe. Sales have increased nearly 30% since 2013. Net income has been somewhat less consistent see-sawing by sometimes 25% or more year-over-year.

In 2017 the company reported revenue of $10.8 billion up 9% from the prior year as it benefited from higher market prices for chicken in the US and the acquisition of rival chicken producer GNP. Net income rose along with revenue in 2017 jumping about 55% to about $695 million as cost of sales grew at a slower rate than revenue.

Cash at the end of 2017 was $590 million an increase of about $290 million from the prior year. Cash from operations contributed $801 million to the coffers while financing activities added another $466 million (a result of proceeds from its credit line and long-term borrowings) and investing activities used some $992 million mainly for acquisitions and normal business expenditures.

Strategy

Pilgrim's Pride's strategic focus is on expanding into new geographic markets and product markets (particularly with more differentiated customized offerings) while optimizing its facilities and processes.

Acquisitions represent a key component of this strategy with a late 2017 purchase moving the company into Europe and a purchase earlier that year enhancing its organic and premium branded products. Pilgrim's Pride has a goal of national distribution for its recently acquired Just Bare organic fresh chicken brand.

The company converted its Sanford North Carolina facility to a USDA certified organic tray pack processing operation in 2017 and expanded its Moorefield West Virginia plant to increase its fully cooked prepared foods production. In addition Pilgrim's Pride has opened a start-of-the-art hatchery in Newark England and plans in 2018 to double the size of its facility in Vera Cruz Mexico.

Mergers and Acquisitions

In September 2017 Pilgrim?s Pride acquired UK food company and leading poultry producer Granite Holdings SA rl (better known as Moy Park). The $1 billion deal should help Pilgrim?s Pride expand in Europe.

Early that year the company acquired smaller rival GNP Company based in Minnesota from The Maschhoffs LLC in a deal worth $350 million. The move expanded Pilgrim's Pride's production and customer base.

EXECUTIVES

Evp Operations - Technical Services And Engineering, Walter F. Shafer
Ceo, Don Jackson, age 67
President Pilgrim's De México, Charles Von Der Heyde
Cfo, Fabio Sandri, age 46, $375,000 total compensation
Evp Sales And Operations, Jayson Penn
Evp Sales And Operations - Prepared Foods, Kevin Miller
Executive Vice President Finance, Brenda Carr
Vice President Logistics, Clay Matthews
National Sales Manager Fresh Foodservice, Andrew Hays
Senior Vice President Of Research And Development, Phil Hurwitz
Vice President International And Head Of E, Alexander Ivannikov
Vice President Corporate Accounts, Stacy Fiedler
Executive Vice President Of Operations, Walt Shafer
Senior Vice President Operations, Matthew Herman
Chairman, Wesley Mendon §a Batista
Board Member, Michael Cooper
Board Member, Charles Macaluso
Board Member, David Bell
Auditors: KPMG LLP

LOCATIONS

HQ: Pilgrims Pride Corp.
1770 Promontory Circle, Greeley, CO 80634-9038
Phone: 970 506-8000
Web: www.pilgrims.com

2017 Sales by Customer Location

	% of total
US	69
Europe	19
Mexico	10
Asia	1
Canada Caribbean Central America	1
Africa	-
South America	-
Pacific	-
Total	**100**

PRODUCTS/OPERATIONS

2017 Sales

	% of total
US chicken	
Fresh chicken	53
Prepared chicken	9
Export & other chicken	2
UK/Europe chicken	
Fresh chicken	8
Prepared chicken	7
Export & other chicken	3
Mexico chicken	12
Other products	
US	6
UK/Europe	-
Mexico	-
Total	**100**

Selected Brands

Pilgrim's
Pierce Chicken
Gold Kist Farms
County Post
Country Pride
Moy Park

Selected Products

Fresh chicken
Fully cooked
Ready to cook
Individually frozen

COMPETITORS

Allen Family Foods	Noble Foods
Bachoco	Perdue Incorporated
Coleman Natural Foods	Rose Acre Farms
Eberly Poultry	Sanderson Farms
Farmer's Pride	Tecumseh Poultry
Keystone Foods	Tyson Foods

HISTORICAL FINANCIALS

Company Type: Public

Income Statement

FYE: December 31

	REVENUE ($ mil.)	NET INCOME ($ mil.)	NET PROFIT MARGIN	EMPLOYEES
12/17	10,767	718	6.7%	51,300
12/16	7,931	440	5.6%	39,600
12/15	8,180	645	7.9%	38,850
12/14	8,583	711	8.3%	35,000
12/13	8,411	549	6.5%	36,700
Annual Growth	**6.4%**	**6.9%**	**—**	**8.7%**

2017 Year-End Financials

Debt ratio: 42.94%	No. of shares (mil.): 248
Return on equity: 51.69%	Dividends
Cash ($ mil.): 581	Yield: —
Current ratio: 1.73	Payout: —
Long-term debt ($ mil.): 2,635	Market value ($ mil.): 7,726

	STOCK PRICE ($) FY Close	P/E High/Low		PER SHARE ($) Earnings	Dividends	Book Value
12/17	31.06	14	7	2.79	0.00	7.42
12/16	19.02	16	10	1.73	2.75	3.56
12/15	22.49	15	7	2.50	5.77	4.94
12/14	34.07	14	6	2.74	0.00	8.47
12/13	16.47	9	3	2.12	0.00	5.75
Annual Growth	**17.2%**	**—**	**—**	**7.1%**	**—**	**6.6%**

Pinnacle Financial Partners Inc

Pinnacle Financial Partners works to be at the top of the community banking mountain in central Tennessee. It's the holding company for Tennessee-based Pinnacle Bank which has grown to some 40 branches in the Nashville and Knoxville areas since its founding in 2000. Serving consumers and small- to mid-sized business the $9 billion financial institution provides standard services such as checking and savings accounts CDs credit cards and loans and mortgages. The company also offers investment and trust services through Pinnacle Asset Management while its insurance brokerage subsidiary Miller Loughry Beach specializes in property/casualty policies.Pinnacle agreed to merge with North Carolina-based BNC Bancorp in 2017.

Operations

Pinnacle Financial Partners' commercial and industrial loans and commercial real estate loans account for nearly 40% and 20% respectively of its total portfolio of loans.

As part of its primary services to both individual and commercial clients Tennessee-based subsidiary Pinnacle Bank provides core deposits including savings checking interest-bearing checking money market and certificate of deposit accounts.

The bank's lending products include commercial real estate and consumer loans to individuals and small- to medium-sized businesses and professional entities. Pinnacle Bank Partners also offers auto dealer finance services to certain automobile dealers and their customers. Additionally it offers Pinnacle-branded consumer credit cards to select clients.

Its convenience-centered products and services include 24-hour telephone and Internet banking debit and credit cards direct deposit and cash management services.

Geographic Reach

Based in Tennessee Pinnacle Financial Partners has become the second-largest bank holding company in the state with nearly 35 offices in eight Middle Tennessee counties and four Knoxville offices. It boasts locations in Nashville Knoxville Murfreesboro Dickson Ashland City Mt. Juliet Lebanon Franklin Brentwood Hendersonville Goodlettsville Smyrna and Shelbyville.

Sales and Marketing

Pinnacle Bank traditionally has obtained its deposits through personal solicitation by its officers and directors although it has used media advertising more in recent years due to its advertising and banking sponsorship with the Tennessee Titans NFL Football team. While it would prefer its customers to bank in person the institution allows customers to bank remotely.

Its marketing and other business development costs have risen in recent years: $4.13 million $3.639 million and $3.636 million in 2014 2013 and 2012 respectively.

Financial Performance

Pinnacle Financial Partners has enjoyed steady revenue and profit growth for the past several years thanks to positive loan growth. Revenue in 2014 rose by 9% to a record $258.77 million mostly to thanks to 9% growth in interest income from loans as the bank's loan assets grew by double digits. Pinnacle also saw double-digit growth in its fee income from service charges on deposit accounts as deposit balances grew and double-digit growth in its investment services income and trust fees as brokerage and trust account balances grew.

Higher revenue drove net income up by 22% to a record $70.47 million. Operations provided $95.06 million or 25% less cash than in 2013 primarily because the bank collected roughly $30 million less in proceeds from its mortgage loans held for sale than it did the year before.

Strategy

Pinnacle's goal is to become the dominant bank in its home market of the Southeast. In 2016 it acquired Avenue Financial Holdings for $200 million and followed up the acquisition by agreeing to merge with regional rival BNC Bancorp of North Carolina in 2017. Once the merger completes the combined company will be the biggest in the region.

Pinnacle Financial Partners been looking to diversify its revenue streams through strategic investments in recent years. In early 2015 for example Tennessee-based subsidiary Pinnacle Bank purchased a 30% membership interest in Bankers Healthcare Group LLC which makes term loans to healthcare professionals and practices for $75 million.

Primarily serving small- to medium-sized businesses in the Nashville and Knoxville areas the company in 2013 began extending its reach in its primary markets by opening its fourth full-service banking location in the Knoxville market in the Cedar Bluff area.

Mergers and Acquisitions

In 2017 Pinnacle agreed to merge with BNC Bancorp. The combined company will have assets of some $20 billion and a presence in four states and in 12 of the largest metropolitan markets in the Southeast.

In 2016 Pinnacle acquired Avenue Financial Holdings (holding company of Avenue Bank with five banking locations in Nashville); the transaction was valued at some $201.4 million. Avenue Bank will operate as a division of Pinnacle Bank for a few months after which the companies will combine operations.

EXECUTIVES

President And Ceo, M. Terry Turner, age 62, $784,700 total compensation

Evp And Chief Administrative Officer, Hugh M. Queener, age 62, $376,700 total compensation

Evp And Senior Lending Officer; Manager Client Advisory Group Nashville, J. Edward (Ed) White, age 68, $145,000 total compensation

Evp And Director Assocaite And Client Experience, Joanne B. Jackson, age 61, $117,000 total compensation

Cfo, Harold R. Carpenter, age 59, $376,700 total compensation

Svp And Manager Trust And Investment Advisory, Robert Newman

President Pinnacle Knoxville, Mike DiStefano

Chief Credit Officer; President Pinnacle Knoxville, J. Harvey White, $283,800 total compensation

Evp And Manager Pinnacle Asset Management, Gary Collier

Svp And Senior Credit Officer Real Estate, Mike Hendren

Svp And Senior Credit Officer, Tim Huestis

Svp And Cio, Randy Withrow

President And Ceo Pnfp Capital Markets, Roger Osborne

Svp And Manager Residential Mortgage Services, Ross Kinney

Evp And Area Executive Rutherford County, Bill Jones

Chief Investment Officer, Mac Johnston

Svp Small Business Banking, Chip Higgins

Evp And Financial Advisor, Jerry Hampton

President Pinnacle Memphis, Damon Bell

Senior Vice President, Bill Decamp

Senior Vice President And Financial Advisor In Nashville, Lynn Kendrick

Senior Vice President, Kay Mcalister

Senior Vice President, Rhonda Smith

Vice President, Tyane Powell

Senior Vice President, Kevin Marchetti

Senior Vice President Financial Advisor, Cynthia Oliva

Senior Vice President, Larry Kain

Senior Vice President Financial Advisor, Lynn Lassiter

Senior Vice President, Michael G Lindseth

Senior Vice President, David Edwards

Senior Vice President And Financial Advisor, Brande Thomas

Mortgage Advisor Senior Vice President, Jeff Mayfield

Senior Vice President, Eric Kruse

Senior Vice President, Gail Outland

Senior Vice President, Steve Uebelhor

Senior Vice President Mortgage Advisor, Chris Maultsby

Senior Vice President, Sarah Teague

Senior Vice President, Kirk Garrett

Senior Vice President, Mary Isham

Senior Vice President, Rex Jones

Senior Vice President, Ken Warren

Senior Vice President, William Diehl

Senior Vice President Financial Advisor, Kim Ciukowski

Vice President Automotive Finance, Jeff Rhodes

Vice President, Luciano Scala

Vice President, Shelly Donohoo

Senior Vice President, Todd Carter

Senior Vice President Business Banking Financial Advisor, Dennis Mitchell

Senior Vice President, Kim Jenny

Executive Vice President And Chief Financial Officerand#8230, Alan Haefele

Senior Vice President, Dale Floyd

Senior Vice President, Clark Cox

Senior Vice President And Financial Adviser In Commercial Real Estate, Thomas Vester

Senior Vice President, Lucy Foutch

Senior Vice President Lending, Roger Leitner

Vice President, Kevin Roddey

Executive Vice President And Senior Credit Officer, Edward White

Vice President Administration, Beth Hobbs

Senior Vice President, Donna Taylor

Senior Vice President And Communications Director, Sarae Janes Lewis

Senior Vice President Financial Advisor, Keely Ritchie

Senior Vice President Financial Advisor, Stacey Richards

Senior Vice President, Bryan Bean

Senior Vice President And Financial Advisor, Ashley Preskenis

Senior Vice President And Financial Advisor, Nancy Benskin

Senior Vice President Credit Advisor, Stacey Fantom

Senior Vice President Credit Advisor, Kendria Northcutt

Senior Vice President, Sam King

Senior Vice President, Tom Dozier

Senior Vice President, Gina Scott

Senior Vice President And Trust Officer, Scott Lindsey

Senior Vice President, Ron Stinson

Senior Vice President, Tim Bowley

Senior Vice President, Jason Reierson

Senior Vice President, John Douglas

Senior Vice President Financial Advisor, Amy Campbell

Senior Vice President, Diane Jones

Senior Vice President, Steven Zimmerman

Vice President: Treasury Management Advisor, Joy Bowen

Cmb Senior Vice President, Jeff Tucker

Senior Vice President Mortgage Advisor, Clint Porter

Senior Vice President, Andy Wright

Senior Vice President, Ryan Murphy

Ctfa Senior Vice President Financial Advisor, Steve Scott

Senior Vice President And Mortgage Advisor, Donathan Cassidy

Senior Vice President Managing Director, Nathan Kurita

Senior Vice President, Rick Nelson

Senior Vice President, Bruce Von Almen

Senior Vice President, Jimmy Moncrief

Executive Vice President Music And Entertainment, Andy Moats

Senior Vice President, Dan Neumann

Senior Vice President Mortgage Advisor, Todd Flynn

Vice President, Cheryl Plummer

Senior Vice President, Donna Edwards

Senior Vice President, Glenn Layne

Vp Sba Business Development Officer, Janet Matthew

Mortgage Adv Sor Vice President, Debbie Del Corro

Senior Vice President Area Executive, Eddie Blount

Assistant Vice President, Reilly Shahna

Vice Chairman, Ed C. Loughry, age 75

Chairman, Robert A. (Rob) McCabe, age 67

Board Member, Charles Brock

Board Member, David Ingram

Board Member, Marty Dickens

Board Member, Joseph Galante

Auditors: Crowe Horwath LLP

LOCATIONS

HQ: Pinnacle Financial Partners Inc
150 Third Avenue South, Suite 900, Nashville, TN 37201
Phone: 615 744-3700
Web: www.pnfp.com

PRODUCTS/OPERATIONS

2014 Revenue

	% of total
Interest Income	80
Non-interest Income	20
Total	**100**

Selected Subsidiaries

Pinnacle Advisory Services Inc.
Pinnacle Credit Enhancement Holdings Inc.
Pinnacle National Bank
   Miller & Loughry Inc. (dba Miller Loughry Beach)
   PFP Title Company
Pinnacle Community Development Corporation
Pinnacle Nashville Real Estate Inc.
Pinnacle Rutherford Real Estate Inc.
Pinnacle Rutherford Towers Inc.
Pinnacle Service Company Inc.
PNFP Insurance Inc.

BB&T
Bank of America
Fifth Third
First Horizon

Regions Financial
SunTrust
U.S. Bancorp

HISTORICAL FINANCIALS

Company Type: Public

Income Statement   FYE: December 31

	ASSETS ($ mil.)	NET INCOME ($ mil.)	INCOME AS % OF ASSETS	EMPLOYEES
12/17	22,205	173	0.8%	2,132
12/16	11,194	127	1.1%	1,180
12/15	8,715	95	1.1%	1,065
12/14	6,018	70	1.2%	767
12/13	5,563	57	1.0%	748
Annual Growth	41.3%	31.8%	—	29.9%

2017 Year-End Financials

Debt ratio: 2.10%
Return on equity: 6.69%
Cash ($ mil.): 779
Current ratio: —
Long-term debt ($ mil.): —

No. of shares (mil.): 77
Dividends
Yield: 0.0%
Payout: 20.7%
Market value ($ mil.): 5,154

	STOCK PRICE ($) FY Close	P/E High/Low	PER SHARE ($) Earnings	Dividends	Book Value
12/17	66.30	26 21	2.70	0.56	47.70
12/16	69.30	24 15	2.91	0.56	32.28
12/15	51.36	22 14	2.52	0.48	28.25
12/14	39.54	20 15	2.01	0.32	22.46
12/13	32.53	20 11	1.67	0.08	20.55
Annual Growth	19.5%		12.8%	62.7%	23.4%

Pioneer Natural Resources Co

Oil and gas explorer Pioneer Natural Resources' frontier is not on the Western prairies but below ground in the oil and gas basins of West Texas and a gas basin in the Southern Rocky Mountains. The large independent exploration and production company boasts proved reserves of more than 725 million barrels of oil equivalent. The vast majority of the company's reserves are found in Texas (primarily in the oil rich and relatively low cost Permian Basin oil fields) and in Colorado (the Raton gas field). Pioneer Natural Resources has stakes in nearly 10000 net producing wells.

Operations

Irving Texas-based Pioneer's single operating segment engages in oil NGL (natural gas liquids) and gas exploration and production primarily in the Spraberry/Wolfcamp oilfield in the Permian Basin in West Texas which holds some 75% of the company's total proved oil and gas reserves. It employs oil drilling and hydraulic fracturing techniques.

Its development areas are the liquid-rich Eagle Ford Shale field in South Texas the Raton gas field in Southern Colorado the West Panhandle gas and liquids field in the Texas panhandle and the Edwards gas field in South Texas.

Its 11000-plus gross producing wells mine about 85 million barrels of oil each year.

Sales and Marketing

Pioneer has a number of significant customers. Vitol accounts for about 20% of its total revenue; Plains Marketing and Occidental Energy Marketing account for more than 15% each and Enterprise Products Partners accounts for more than 10%.

Financial Performance

In fiscal 2016 Pioneer's total revenue fell by $1 billion to $3.8 billion due to a net loss of $161 million on derivatives trading versus a gain of $879 million the previous year. Derivatives aside Pioneer's core oil and gas sales defied industry wide-trends and grew 11% to $2.4 billion due to higher sales volumes in both oil and gas. Oil sales volumes increased 27% and gas 13% offsetting lower oil prices.

The company lost $556 million in 2016 an increase on the $273 loss in the previous year. The worse result stems from the loss on derivatives results lower gains on asset sales and a $95 million increase in depletion depreciation and amortization expense. These negative factors were partially offset by a decrease in impairment charges of $1.0 billion and a $248 million increase in income tax benefit.

Cash from operations grew 20% to $1.5 billion due to higher oil and gas revenue lower operating costs and a decrease in funds used to satisfy working capital obligations.

Strategy

Unlike many of its competitors Pioneer has low debt levels and has been able to continue investing proactively during the oil price downturn that pushed many of its peers into the deep end.

It is developing a water distribution system to support its continued field development. Pioneer has begun purchasing some 100 thousand barrels per day of effluent water from the City of Odessa and has signed an agreement with the City of Midland to purchase effluent water upon completion of a new water treatment facility. The company expects to spend $160 million in 2017 mostly on its field-wide water distribution network which is expected to provide significant future cost savings and support its long-term growth plan in the Spraberry/Wolfcamp area.

Pioneer has also kept up its drilling operations during the downturn drilling 464 gross (368 net) development wells in the three years up to end-2016. All of the wells were successfully completed as productive wells at a total drilling cost of $2.9 billion.

Mergers and Acquisitions

In August 2016 Pioneer Natural Resources acquired 28000 net acres in the Midland Basin from Devon Energy for $435 million. The acquisition will help Pioneer increase its horizontal rig count by five rigs from 12 rigs to 17 rigs in the northern Spraberry/Wolfcamp play.

HISTORY

The 1997 merger of MESA and Parker & Parsley moved quickly to pull itself out of the dry hole created by its own debt and the industry's late-1990s dropoff. Parker & Parsley began in 1962 as a partnership between geologist Howard Parker and engineer Joe Parsley. In 1977 it began drilling wells in West Texas. Southmark a Dallas real estate firm bought the company in 1984; in 1989 management purchased it from Southmark. The company went public in 1991.

T. Boone Pickens founded Petroleum Exploration in 1956. In 1964 Petroleum Exploration and Pickens' Canadian holding Altair Oil and Gas merged as MESA and went public. With gas prices declining in the 1990s MESA began selling assets. Pickens resigned as CEO in 1996.

Richard Rainwater took control of MESA and then merged the firm into Parker & Parsley which became Pioneer Natural Resources. The company

moved into Argentina when it paid $1.2 billion for Calgary-based Chauvco Resources in 1997.

To streamline operations and reduce debt Pioneer cut its workforce and in 1999 it sold 400 US properties to Prize Energy.

Pioneer sold oil and gas properties in Texas and Canada in 1999 and moved to consolidate its Permian Basin operations by offering to buy out limited partners. It also drilled its first deepwater well in the Gulf of Mexico and acquired additional properties in Argentina.

In 2000 the company disposed of noncore natural gas assets in Louisiana New Mexico and Oklahoma. At the same time it boosted its deepwater holdings in the Gulf of Mexico. The next year the company announced successful test drilling in its prospects in Argentina and South Africa.

Pioneer also announced an oil discovery in 2001 on its Ozona Deep prospect in the Gulf of Mexico indicating another deepwater production asset for the company. In 2003 Pioneer teamed up with Woodside Energy to conduct a joint exploration program in the shallow-water Texas Shelf region of the Gulf of Mexico.

In 2005 Pioneer sold the Martin Creek Conroy Black and Lookout Butte oil and gas properties in Canada to Ketch Resources for $199 million. That year it acquired oil and gas assets in the Permian Basin and South Texas for a total of $177 million.

Realigning its exploration portfolio the company sold all of its operations in Argentina in 2006 to Apache for $675 million. That year Pioneer sold the bulk of its Gulf of Mexico oil and gas assets to Marubeni Offshore Production for $1.3 billion. In 2007 the company sold its Canadian subsidiary to Abu Dhabi National Energy Company PJSC for $540 million.

In 2009 the company reported a sharp dip in revenues as the result of global recession's impact on lowering commodity prices and weakening demand for oil and gas. Although Pioneer made about $89 million of property acquisitions (primarily in its South Texas shale) in 2009 financial conditions prompted the company to sell non-core assets to pay down debt. It sold its assets in the Spraberry field in West Texas to a subsidiary Pioneer Southwest Energy Partners for $168.2 million. It also sold its Mississippi and shelf properties in the Gulf of Mexico for about $24 million.

To gain capital to develop its US shale properties in 2010 Pioneer entered a joint venture selling a 45% stake in its southern Texas gas field Eagle Ford Shale to the USA subsidiary of India's Reliance Industries for $1.15 billion.

It has exited higher risk foreign ventures. To raise cash and to focus on its core North American assets in 2011 the company sold its Tunisia-based exploration and production units to OMV for $866 million. It also sold its South African business in 2012 for $38 million.

Securing an industrial sands business to support its hydraulic fracturing drilling activities in the Wolfcamp Shale and Barnett Shale plays in Texas in 2012 Pioneer acquired Carmeuse Industrial Sands for $297 million.

In 2013 it sold its Barnett Shale assets in North Texas to an undisclosed private party for cash proceeds of $155 million.

In 2013 Pioneer Natural Resources sold a 40% stake in 207000 net acres leased in Wolfcamp Shale play (Permian Basin) in the southern portion of the Spraberry Trend Area Field to Sinochem for $1.7 billion.

In 2013 Pioneer Natural Resources Company acquired 52%-owned Pioneer Southwest Energy Partners L.P. which then became a wholly-owned subsidiary of Pioneer Natural Resources USA through a stock-for-unit exchange.

EXECUTIVES

Evp Corporate And Operations, Mark S. Berg, age 59, $437,846 total compensation

Vice President Permian Affairs, Susan Spratlen

Senior Vice President Ir Contact Officer, Frank Hopkins

President Ceo And Director, Timothy L. (Tim) Dove, age 61, $672,808 total compensation

Evp And Cfo, Richard P. (Rich) Dealy, age 51, $555,131 total compensation

Evp Business Development And Technology, Chris J. Cheatwood, age 57, $440,615 total compensation

Vp Marketing, John C. Distaso

Evp Permian Operations, J. D. Hall, age 52

Evp Stat Wat And Corporate Engineering, Kenneth H. Sheffield, age 57

Vp And Cio, Stephanie D. Stewart, age 49

Vice President Drilling Completion And Services, James Cunningham

Vice President Operations Southern Wolfcamp, Craig Kuiper

Executive Vice President, Dennis Lithgow

Executive Vice President Operations, J D Hall

Executive Vice President Domestic Operations, Jay Still

Vice President Information Technology, Glen Paris

Vice President And Corporate Secretary, David Simpson

Executive Vice President International Operations, David McManus

Executive Vice President, Ray Alameddine

Vice President Permian Land, David Sutter

Vice President Investor Relations, Neal H Shah

Chairman, Scott D. Sheffield, age 65

Assistant Treasurer Trading, Lisa Kunkel

Auditors: Ernst & Young LLP

LOCATIONS

HQ: Pioneer Natural Resources Co
5205 N. O'Connor Blvd., Suite 200, Irving, TX 75039
Phone: 972 444-9001   **Fax:** 972 969-3587
Web: www.pxd.com

PRODUCTS/OPERATIONS

2016 sales

	% of total
Oil & gas	61
Sales of purchased oil & gas	38
Interest & Other	1
Derivative gains	0
Gain from disposition of assets	0
Total	**100**

COMPETITORS

Anadarko Petroleum	Matador Resources
Apache	Newfield Exploration
BP	Noble Energy
Bonanza Creek	Petrohawk Energy
Carrizo Oil & Gas	Royal Dutch Shell
Chesapeake Energy	SM Energy
Exxon Mobil	Swift Energy
Hess Corporation	TOTAL
Marathon Oil	YPF

HISTORICAL FINANCIALS

Company Type: Public

Income Statement

FYE: December 31

	REVENUE ($ mil.)	NET INCOME ($ mil.)	NET PROFIT MARGIN	EMPLOYEES
12/17	5,455	833	15.3%	3,836
12/16	3,824	(556)	—	3,604
12/15	4,870	(273)	—	3,752
12/14	5,055	930	18.4%	4,075
12/13	3,719	(838)	—	4,203
Annual Growth	**10.0%**	**—**		**(2.3%)**

2017 Year-End Financials

Debt ratio: 16.07%	No. of shares (mil.): 170
Return on equity: 7.69%	Dividends
Cash ($ mil.): 896	Yield: 0.0%
Current ratio: 1.41	Payout: 1.6%
Long-term debt ($ mil.): 2,283	Market value ($ mil.): 29,417

	STOCK PRICE ($) FY Close	P/E High/Low		Earnings	PER SHARE ($) Dividends	Book Value
12/17	172.85	41	26	4.85	0.08	66.24
12/16	180.07	—	—	(3.34)	0.08	61.30
12/15	125.38	—	—	(1.83)	0.08	56.02
12/14	148.85	36	20	6.38	0.08	57.59
12/13	184.07	—	—	(6.16)	0.08	46.29
Annual Growth	**(1.6%)**	—	—	—	**(0.0%)**	**9.4%**

Plains All American Pipeline LP

The term "All American" includes Canada for Plains All American Pipeline which has pipeline operations in the US and north of the border. The limited partnership is engaged in the transportation storage terminalling and marketing of crude oil refined products natural gas liquids (NGL) and liquefied petroleum gas (LPG) and owns extensive gathering terminal and storage facilities in across the US and in Canada. At the end of 2014 Plains All American Pipeline owned 17800 miles of gathering crude oil NGL and refined product pipelines throughout the US and Canada operated a fleet of 800 trailers 150 barges and 72 transport tugs and owned 29 million barrels of storage capacity.

HISTORY

Goodyear Tire & Rubber subsidiary Celeron began designing the All American Pipeline in 1983 to bring heavy crude from California to the less-regulated refineries of Texas. It was completed in 1987 at a cost of $1.6 billion but by 1991 only a trickle of oil was dribbling through. The pipeline did not post a profit until 1994.

Prospects began to look up in the mid-1990s when Chevron Texaco and Exxon signed contracts to use the pipeline beginning in 1996. Plains Resources bought the pipeline in 1998 for $400 million; the company created Plains All American Pipeline to acquire and operate the pipeline then sold off a 43% stake in an IPO that raised $260 million. The next year Plains All American bought Scurlock Permian (2300 miles of pipeline) from Marathon Ashland Petroleum for $141 million and the West Texas Gathering System from Chevron (450 miles) for $36 million.

Shareholders sued Plains All American in 1999 after it reported that an employee's unauthorized crude-oil trading would cost the company about $160 million. (In 2000 the company agreed to pay $29.5 million plus interest to settle the cases.)

Plains All American announced plans to mothball all but the California section of the All American Pipeline in 1999. The next year El Paso Energy bought the 1088 mile section of the pipeline that was to be deactivated plus the right to run fiber-optic cable over the entire pipeline for $129 million.

Targeting Canada as part of its expansion strategy in 2001 Plains All American bought about 450 miles of oil pipeline and other midstream assets from Murphy Oil and acquired crude oil and LPG marketing firm CANPET Energy. Also that year Plains Resources reduced its stake in Plains All American from 44% to 29%.

In 2002 the company acquired the Wapella Pipeline System located in southeastern Saskatchewan and southwestern Manitoba. It also bought Shell Pipeline's West Texas crude oil pipeline assets for $315 million. Plains All American Pipeline continued its acquisition streak in 2003 with the acquisitions of the South Saskatchewan pipeline system in Canada and the ArkLaTex pipeline system originating in Sabine Texas.

In 2004 Plains All American continued its expansion with the acquisition of interests in the Capline and Capwood pipeline systems from Shell Pipeline Company for about $158 million. It also acquired the crude oil and pipeline operations of Link Energy for about $330 million and the Cal Ven pipeline system from Unocal Canada for about $19 million. Later that year the company continued its system expansion by acquiring the Schaefferstown propane storage facility from Koch Hydrocarbon for about $32 million.

In 2006 the company acquired Andrews Petroleum and Lone Star Trucking for $205 million. It also acquired stakes in a number of Gulf Coast crude oil pipeline systems from BP Oil Pipeline Company for $133.5 million. That year in a major deal the company acquired Pacific Energy Partners for $2.4 billion moving the company beyond crude oil and into the refined products and barging businesses.

In 2007 Plains All American Pipeline acquired LPG storage facilities in Arizona and South Carolina.

In 2008 Occidental Petroleum acquired 10% of the company's general partner boosting the amount of new capital available for Plains All American Pipeline to pay down debt and make further acquisitions. It also boosted its Canadian midstream assets with the acquisition of Rainbow Pipeline (crude oil gathering and pipelines).

In 2012 to boost its midstream assets the company bought BP's Canadian NGL operations for $1.7 billion.

EXECUTIVES

President And Coo, Harry N. Pefanis, age 61, $300,000 total compensation

Evp, Phillip D. (Phil) Kramer, $250,000 total compensation

Chairman And Ceo, Greg L. Armstrong, age 60, $375,000 total compensation

Evp Operations And Business Development, Mark J. Gorman

Evp General Counsel And Secretary, Richard K. McGee, age 57

Svp Technology Process And Risk Management, Alfred A. (Al) Lindseth

Evp And Cfo, Al Swanson, age 54, $250,000 total compensation

President Plains Midstream Canada, W. David (Dave) Duckett, $276,666 total compensation
Evp Commercial Activities, John P. von Berg, $250,000 total compensation
Evp, John R. Rutherford, $62,500 total compensation
President Pngs, Dean Liollio, age 60
Executive Vice President Commercial Activities, John Berg
Vice President, David Wright
Vice President Operations Management System, Stephen Falgoust
Vice President Human Resources Plains Midstream Canada, David Schwarz
V.p. Human Resources, Roger Everett
Vice President Tax, Walter van Zanten
Vice President Commercial Law And Litigation, Megan Prout
Svp Operations Plains Midstream Canada, Scott Sill
Evp Operations And Engineering, Daniel Nerbonne
Vice President Lease Supply, Robert M Sanford
Vp And Treasurer, Sharon Spurlin
Vice President, John Reid
Senior Vice President Commercial Activities, John VonBerg
Vice President Refinery Supply, James Fryfogle
Vice President Of Operations, Daniel Noack
Vice President Engineering Construction And Integrity U.s. Operations, Dwayne Koehn
Vice President Finance Plains Midstream Canada, Bill Forward
Auditors: PricewaterhouseCoopers LLP

LOCATIONS

HQ: Plains All American Pipeline LP
333 Clay Street, Suite 1600, Houston, TX 77002
Phone: 713 646-4100
Web: www.plainsallamerican.com

2014 Sales

	$ mil.	% of total
US	34,860	80
Canada	8,604	20
Total	**43,464**	**100**

PRODUCTS/OPERATIONS

2014 Sales

	$ mil.	% of total
Supply and logistics	42,114	97
Transportation	774	2
Facilities	576	1
Total	**43,464**	**100**

COMPETITORS

Buckeye Partners	ONEOK
Enbridge	Sunoco Logistics
Enterprise Products	TransMontaigne
NGL Energy Partners	

HISTORICAL FINANCIALS

Company Type: Public

Income Statement — FYE: December 31

	REVENUE ($ mil.)	NET INCOME ($ mil.)	NET PROFIT MARGIN	EMPLOYEES
12/17	26,223	856	3.3%	4,850
12/16	20,182	726	3.6%	5,100
12/15	23,152	903	3.9%	5,400
12/14	43,464	1,384	3.2%	5,300
12/13	42,249	1,361	3.2%	4,900
Annual Growth	(11.2%)	(10.9%)	—	(0.3%)

2017 Year-End Financials

Debt ratio: 39.13%
Return on equity: —
Cash ($ mil.): 37
Current ratio: 0.88
Long-term debt ($ mil.): 9,183

No. of shares (mil.): 725
Dividends
  Yield: 0.0%
  Payout: 205.2%
Market value ($ mil.): 14,968

	STOCK PRICE ($) FY Close	P/E High/Low	PER SHARE ($) Earnings	Dividends	Book Value
12/17	20.64	34 19	0.95	1.95	15.11
12/16	32.29	78 36	0.43	2.65	13.09
12/15	23.10	67 24	0.77	2.76	19.82
12/14	51.32	25 19	2.38	2.55	21.68
12/13	51.77	21 16	2.80	2.33	21.28
Annual Growth	(20.5%)	— —	(23.7%)	(4.3%)	(8.2%)

Plains GP Holdings LP

EXECUTIVES

MBR, Greg L Armstrong
Pres, Harry N Pefanis
Exec V Pres, Phil D Kramer
Dir, Roy I Lamoreaux
Cfo, Al Swanson
Exec V Pres-MBR, Mark J Gorman
Manager, Barrett Oden
Coordinator, Afton Shelton
Compliance Staff, Chrystah Carter
Vice-President Engineering, Dan Nerbonne
Safety Manager, Daniel Duke
Auditors: PricewaterhouseCoopers LLP

LOCATIONS

HQ: Plains GP Holdings LP
333 Clay Street, Suite 1600, Houston, TX 77002
Phone: 713 646-4100
Web: www.plainsallamerican.com

HISTORICAL FINANCIALS

Company Type: Public

Income Statement — FYE: December 31

	REVENUE ($ mil.)	NET INCOME ($ mil.)	NET PROFIT MARGIN	EMPLOYEES
12/17	26,223	(731)	—	4,850
12/16	20,182	94	0.5%	5,100
12/15	23,152	118	0.5%	5,400
12/14	43,464	70	0.2%	5,300
12/13	42,249	15	0.0%	4,900
Annual Growth	(11.2%)	—	—	(0.3%)

2017 Year-End Financials

Debt ratio: 37.08%
Return on equity: —
Cash ($ mil.): 40
Current ratio: 0.88
Long-term debt ($ mil.): 9,183

No. of shares (mil.): 794
Dividends
  Yield: 0.0%
  Payout: —
Market value ($ mil.): 17,429

	STOCK PRICE ($) FY Close	P/E High/Low	PER SHARE ($) Earnings	Dividends	Book Value
12/17	21.95	— —	(5.03)	1.95	2.13
12/16	34.68	38 6	0.94	0.00	2.38
12/15	9.45	21 5	1.41	0.00	7.74
12/14	25.68	25 18	1.25	0.00	7.28
12/13	26.77	100 81	0.27	0.00	4.55
Annual Growth	(4.8%)	— —	—	—	(17.2%)

PLUMAS LAKE ELEMENTARY SCHOOL DISTRICT

EXECUTIVES

Supt, Dione Beilby
Director, Brian Briggs
Teacher, Jenna Argetsinger

LOCATIONS

HQ: PLUMAS LAKE ELEMENTARY SCHOOL DISTRICT
2743 PLUMAS SCHOOL RD, PLUMAS LAKE, CA 959618827
Phone: 530 743-4428
Web: WWW.PLUSD.ORG

HISTORICAL FINANCIALS

Company Type: Private

Income Statement — FYE: June 30

	REVENUE ($ mil.)	NET INCOME ($ mil.)	NET PROFIT MARGIN	EMPLOYEES
06/17	14,359	(190)	—	100
06/16	13,856	1,088	7.9%	—
Annual Growth	3.6%	—	—	—

PNC Financial Services Group (The)

PNC Financial Services has returned to its traditional banking roots but it also offers a wide range of other financial services. Boasting total assets of some $370 billion and total deposits nearing $260 billion its flagship PNC Bank subsidiary operates upwards of 2500 branches in almost 20 states in the mid-Atlantic the Midwest and Florida. In addition to retail and corporate banking the company offers insurance investments personal and institutional asset management and capital markets products and services. The firm also owns boutique investment bank Harris Williams and about a quarter of money management giant BlackRock.

Operations

The diversified financial services organization provides a wide range of services retail and business banking; residential mortgage banking; specialized services for corporations and government bodies (corporate banking real estate finance asset-based lending and other). It also offers wealth management and asset management services.

PNC Financial Services operates five core business segments based on these activities. It generates nearly 45% of its total revenue from its Retail Banking business while 35% of revenue comes from its Corporate & Institutional Banking business. Another nearly 10% came from its Asset Management Group and another 10% from a combination of its Residential Mortgage Banking business and its BlackRock investment (it owns a 25%

stake in BlackRock the world's largest publicly traded asset management firm).

Broken down further the firm generates about 60% of its total revenue from interest income (mostly loan interest) while most of the rest came from a combination of asset management fees (10% of revenue) corporate services fees (10%) consumer services fees (over 5%) and residential mortgage fees and service charges on deposits (each about 5%).

Geographic Reach

PNC's major geographic markets are in Alabama Delaware Florida Georgia Kentucky Illinois Indiana Maryland Michigan Missouri New Jersey North Carolina Ohio Pennsylvania South Carolina Washington D.C. Wisconsin and Virginia. It's international offices are in Canada China Germany and the UK.

Financial Performance

PNC's financial performance has been more or less static for a few years now.

In fiscal 2016 total revenue increased 1% to $16.4 billion. A $329 million increase in interest income was partially offset by a $176 million fall in non-interest income. Interest income was boosted by an increase in loan and securities balances and higher loan yields. The increase in average loans was driven by $3.6 billion growth in average commercial real estate loans and $2.2 billion of average commercial loans. The fall in non-interest income related to lower earnings from BlackRock and $134 million lower net gains on sales of Visa Class B common shares.

Net income fell 4% to $4.0 billion as an increase in interest expense outweighed the increase in interest income.

Cash from operations fell a fairly sharp 34% to $3.6 billion due to net changes in accrued expenses and other liabilities.

Strategy

PNC is in the final year of its five-year $1.2 billion plan to modernize its core infrastructure and making its operations faster more stable and more secure. In 2016 PNC consolidated its datacenters and moved its systems into an internal cloud system. The new datacenter allows the company to triple its capacity. The company also has built new computing architecture that allows for simple integration of APIs (application programming interface) while bolstering its cybersecurity.

Mergers and Acquisitions

In 2018 The PNC Financial Services Group's PNC Bank agreed to acquire Ambassador Financial Group on undisclosed terms. The company provides balance sheet management investment banking and capital markets services to banks insurance companies and other financial institutions. The group which will integrate into PNC's Capital Markets Financial Institutions Group will expand its advisory services in mergers and acquisitions and capital markets for financial institutions.

PNC acquired ECN Capital Corp's US-based commercial and vendor finance business in 2017 for $1.1 billion. The acquisition includes the portfolio of construction transportation industrial franchise and technology loans and leases. It adds to PNC's existing vendor franchise and supports leading vendors in a number of growth industries.

Company Background

PNC acquired RBC Bank (USA) from Royal Bank of Canada in 2012. The nearly $3.5 billion acquisition extended PNC's retail banking franchise in the Southeast and cemented its place among the five largest banks in the US.

HISTORY

First National Bank of Pittsburgh opened in 1863. In 1913 the bank consolidated with Second National Bank of Pittsburgh and in 1921 it bought Peoples National. The company changed its name to Pittsburgh National after a long expansion following the Depression and WWII. In 1983 Pittsburgh National merged with Provident National of Philadelphia (founded by Quakers in 1865) to form PNC Corp. The union combined Pittsburgh National's corporate lending strength with Provident's money management and trust operations.

EXECUTIVES

Evp And Chief Credit Officer, Michael J. Hannon, age 61

Chairman President And Ceo, William S. (Bill) Demchak, age 55, $1,100,000 total compensation

Evp Chief Investment Officer And Treasurer, E. William (Bill) Parsley, age 52, $588,462 total compensation

Evp Asset Management Group, Robert Q. (Rob) Reilly, age 53, $500,000 total compensation

Evp And Head Corporate And Institutional Banking, Michael P. Lyons, age 47, $700,000 total compensation

Evp And Head Technology And Operations, Steven C. (Steve) Van Wyk, age 59, $500,000 total compensation

Evp And Head Asset Management Group, Orlando C. Esposito, age 59

Evp And Chief Customer Officer, Karen L. Larrimer, age 55

Evp And Chief Risk Officer, Joseph E. Rockey, age 53

Evp General Counsel And Head Regulatory And Government Affairs, Gregory B. Jordan, age 58

Evp And General Auditor, Stacy M. Juchno, age 42

Evp And Chief Human Resources Officer, Vicki C. Henn, age 49

Evp And Director Investor Relations, Bryan K. Gill

Vice President Marketing, Richard Kopchinski

Avp And Manager Media Relations, Alan Aldinger

Senior Vice President Public Finance, George Whitmer

Vice President Chief Enterprise Architect, Eric Meredith

Vice President Corporate Banking, Elizabeth Satina

Vice President, Evans S Duncan

Senior Vice President Regional Manager, Craig Miller

Executive Vice President Treasury Management Sales Manager, Lynn Aleksov

Vice President Strategic Accounts, Jim Foley

Svp Wellness And Work Life Balance, Kathleen D'Appolonia

Vice President New England Market Manager, Steve Kanarian

Senior Vice President Customer Management, John Demarchis

Vice President Asset Manager Asset Resolution Team, Andrea Stroud

Vp And Senior Manager Corporate Marketing, Catherine Bernard

Svp Digital Marketing, Brian Lantz

Svp Corporate Marketing, Dresdyn Hefferen

Senior Vice President And Senior Relationship Manager, Tracy Decock

Senior Vice President, Melissa Tyner

Assistant Vice President, Barbara Jones

Svp Enterprise Mis Systems, Randy Spellins

Vice President Senior Organizational Devel, Vicki Brown

Vice President, Roderick Hirsch

Vice President Product Development, Mark Vizza

Regional Manager Senior Vice President, Alisa Winslow

Vice President Community Development Banking Consultant, Maria Thompson

Senior Vice President Product Manager, Janet Hoyt

Vice President, Deborah Madigan

Vice President Senior Relationship Manager, Moises Almonte

Vice President, Dave Bodi

Senior Vice President, Mark Kiskorna

Executive Vice President, Peter Thompson

Senior Vice President, Kurt Putkonen

Vice President, Timothy Thieneman

Vice President Branch Manager, Bryan Skolny

Vice President Of Corporate Security, Jim Weslager

Senior Vice President Of Real Estate Finance, Bill G Lashbrook

Vice President Director Commercial Lending Systems, Daniel Garbin

Vice President Western Pa Territory, Gavin Geraci

Vice President Quantitative Analyst, Roman Zilbering

Vice President And Senior Project Manager, Ed Hestin

Vice President Treasury Management, Maureen Smith

Vp Strategic Integration, John Schipfer

Vp And Director Client And Community Relations, Dianne Jacob

Svp Strategic Initiatives, James Defoggia

Svp And Chief Procurement Officer, James Vespoli

Vp Data Governance, Angela Twum

Vp Cyber Security, Nicholas Antill

Senior Vice President Business Banking Sales, Marc Huey

Vp And Senior Manager Media Relations, Zoraya Suarez

Avp; Manager Technology, John Pfirrman

Svp System Director Call Center And Incentive Compensation Technology, Stephen Chauvin

Svp Sales And Service Manager, Ahmad Elsawaf

Svp Business Banking Sales, Todd Olsen

Vp Business Banking Sales, Mark Willis

Assistant Vice President Senior Property Administrator, Michael Conway

Assistant Vice President Business Bank Incentive Program Manager, April Meadows

Vice President, Tracy Bernstein

Vp Systems Etechnology Operations Group, Mike Kutchmark

Vp Technology Governance Enterprise Project Management Office, Melanie Maurer Westwood

Avp; Manager Collections System, Andrea ellis Colella

Vice President And Director Default Operations Pnc Bank, Michael Grossberg

Vice President, Denise Fazio

Vice President And Manager, Randy Davis

Senior Vice President Marketing Manager, Daniel deBrauwere

Senior Vice President Relationship Manager, Robert Carpenterjr

Vice President Business Banking, John Goins

Relationship Manager Assistant Vice President, Jason Wancowicz

Enterprise Infrastructure Manager Iii Avp, Ray Foster

Vice President Branch Manager, Larry Harrison

Assistant Vice President, Jeffrey Delay

Board Member, Richard B Kelson

Board Member, Kay James

Auditors: PricewaterhouseCoopers LLP

LOCATIONS

HQ: PNC Financial Services Group (The)
The Tower at PNC Plaza, 300 Fifth Avenue, Pittsburgh, PA 15222-2401
Phone: 412 762-2000   **Fax:** 412 762-5798
Web: www.pnc.com

Selected Banking Markets
Delaware
Florida
Georgia
Illinois
Indiana
Kentucky
Maryland
Michigan

Missouri
New Jersey
Ohio
Pennsylvania
Virginia
Washington DC
West Virginia
Wisconsin

PRODUCTS/OPERATIONS

2016 Sales

	% of total
Retail Banking	44
Corporate and Institutional Banking	35
Asset Management group	8
Residential Mortgage Banking	5
BlackRock	4
Non-Strategic Asset Portfolio	2
Others	2
Total	**100**

2016 Sales

	$ mil.	% of total
Interest		
Loans	7,414	45
Investment securities	1,826	11
Other	412	3
Non-interest		
Asset management	1,521	9
Corporate services	1,504	9
Consumer services	1,388	8
Service charges on deposits	667	4
Residential mortgage	567	4
Other	1,124	7
Total	**16,423**	**100**

Selected Subsidiaries

PNC Bancorp Inc.
   PNC Bank National Association
   PNC Bank Capital Securities LLC
   PNC Capital Leasing LLC
   PNC Preferred Funding LLC
   PNC REIT Corp.
PNC Holding LLC
   PNC Funding Corp
   PNC Investment Corp.
   PNC Venture LLC

COMPETITORS

Bank of America	JPMorgan Chase
Capital One	KeyCorp
Citigroup	M&T Bank
Citizens Financial	Sovereign Bank
Group	TD Bank USA
Fifth Third	U.S. Bancorp
Harris	Wells Fargo
Huntington Bancshares	

HISTORICAL FINANCIALS

Company Type: Public

Income Statement   FYE: December 31

	ASSETS ($ mil.)	NET INCOME ($ mil.)	INCOME AS % OF ASSETS	EMPLOYEES
12/17	380,768	5,338	1.4%	52,906
12/16	366,380	3,903	1.1%	52,006
12/15	358,493	4,106	1.1%	52,513
12/14	345,072	4,184	1.2%	53,587
12/13	320,296	4,220	1.3%	54,433
Annual Growth	**4.4%**	**6.1%**	**—**	**(0.7%)**

2017 Year-End Financials

Debt ratio: 9.99%	No. of shares (mil.): 473
Return on equity: 11.45%	Dividends
Cash ($ mil.): 33,844	Yield: 0.0%
Current ratio: —	Payout: 25.1%
Long-term debt ($ mil.): —	Market value ($ mil.): 68,249

	STOCK PRICE ($) FY Close	P/E High/Low	PER SHARE ($) Earnings	Dividends	Book Value
12/17	144.29	14 11	10.36	2.60	100.45
12/16	116.96	16 10	7.30	2.12	94.22
12/15	95.31	13 11	7.39	2.01	88.71
12/14	91.23	12 10	7.30	1.88	85.18
12/13	77.58	10 8	7.39	1.72	79.56
Annual Growth	**16.8%**	**— —**	**8.8%**	**10.9%**	**6.0%**

Polaris Industries Inc.

One of the world's top makers of off-road vehicles Polaris Industries makes and sells all-terrain vehicles (ATVs) and side-by-side recreational and utility RANGER-brand vehicles. It also manufactures snowmobiles on-road vehicles such as the Victory and Indian brands motorcycle and small electric vehicles (SEVs). Offerings include replacement parts accessories (covers windshields backrests) garments and riding gear (bags and helmets). Polaris' lineup is sold through dealers and distributors in North America Western Europe and Australia.

OperationsPolaris operates through four chief segments: Off-Road Vehicles (ORV)/Snowmobiles (more than 65% of sales) Aftermarket (more than 15%) Motorcycles (about 110%) and Global Adjacent Markets (less than 10%).Polaris' vehicle lineup includes RANGER RZR and Polaris GENERAL side-by-side off-road vehicles; Sportsman and Polaris ACE all-terrain off-road vehicles; Indian Motorcycle midsize and heavyweight motorcycles; Slingshot moto-roadsters; and snowmobile models that include Titan Switchback RMK and Indy.

Geographic Reach

Polaris based in Hamel Minnesota has about 15 manufacturing locations and five research and development centers as well as 10 distribution facilities in Alabama California Florida Idaho Iowa Minnesota Ohio South Dakota Texas and Wisconsin. International facilities are in Australia Canada China France Mexico and Poland. The US represents around 80% of sales while Canada contributes less than 10%; the remainder comes from other international sales.

Sales and Marketing

Polaris' products are sold through a network of about 1800 independent dealers in North America in addition to almost 30 subsidiaries and some 90 distributors in more than 100 countries outside of North America.

The company advertises its products directly to consumers through print advertising the internet social media billboards television and radio. It also provides media advertising and produces promotional films for its products which are available to dealers for use in showrooms or at special promotions. It provides product brochures posters dealer signs and other miscellaneous promotional items for use by dealers.

Financial Performance

After a 4% revenue decline in 2016 Polaris resumed sales growth in 2107. Net income however slipped for the second year in a row following six years of steady increases.

Revenue jumped 20% in 2017 to $5.4 billion a company high driven by the 2016 Transamerican Auto Parts (TAP) acquisition higher volume and product/price mix. TAP's contribution pushed Aftermarket sales up more than 360% while ORV and snowmobile sales rose 9% and Global Adja-

cent Market sales edge up 4%. Motorcycle sales fell 16% as the company wound down its Victory line of bikes. Polaris posted sales gains of 22% in the US and Canada while sales classified as international rose 11%.

Polaris' net income fell 19% to $172.5 million in 2017 from 2016. Affecting profit were costs associated with closing the Victory business a noncash write-down of deferred taxes because of the US Tax Cuts and Jobs Act and expenses from the TAP integration.

The company had about $138 million in cash in 2017 an $11 million increase from 2016. Cash from operations rose about $8 million year-to-year. After paying off debt and issuing net debt Polaris reduced its long-term obligations by about $234 million.

Strategy

Polaris has made several acquisitions to extend its portfolio. The deals include the Transamerican Auto Parts which added significant revenue in aftermarkets parts. In 2018 Polaris added boats to its lineup with the acquisition of Boat Holdings a leader maker of pontoon boats.

The company emphasizes growth outside the US. It has ramped up production of ORVs at its plant in Opole Poland to meet rising demand in Europe. The company intends to make Indian motorcycles for the European market at the plant starting in 2019. The increased overseas production should not have an impact on its US manufacturing operations.

Trade battles with other countries particularly China have challenged Polaris. The impact of higher tariffs through the first half of 2018 was about $40 million and would be more in 2019 if tensions don't ease. The company has raised prices in response to higher tariffs as have competitors.

Mergers and Acquisitions

Acquisitions as well as internal investments and business alliances are fundamental to Polaris' strategy for building its portfolio and market presence.

In 2018 Polaris bought Boating Holdings the largest maker of pontoon boats in the US for about $805 million. Besides pontoon boats Boat Holdings makes deck and cruiser boats and sells through the Bennington Godfrey Hurricane and Rinker brands in the US and Canada. The deal extends Polaris's footprint from off-road to on-water with offerings that brought in about $560 million in revenue in 2017.

In late 2016 Polaris purchased Transamerican Auto Parts a manufacturer distributor retailer and installer of off-road Jeep and truck accessories for $669 million. The deal enhanced Polaris' ecommerce platform and bolstered its ability to serve off-road enthusiasts with a variety of Jeep and truck aftermarket accessories.

Earlier in 2016 Polaris enhanced its Global Adjacent Markets segment through the purchase of California-based Taylor-Dunn Manufacturing Company a provider of industrial vehicles serving a broad range of commercial manufacturing warehouse and ground-support customers.

Company Background

Originally called Hetteen Hoist & Derrick Polaris Industries was founded in Roseau Minnesota in 1945 by Edgar Hetteen and David Johnson. The friends did welding and repair work and made custom machinery for local farmers.

EXECUTIVES

Svp Customer Experience And Chief Marketing Officer, Timothy M. Larson, age 45
President International, Michael D. Dougherty, age 50
Chairman And Ceo, Scott W. Wine, age 50, $985,000 total compensation

Evp Operations Engineering And Lean, Kenneth J. (Ken) Pucel, age 52, $600,000 total compensation

Evp Finance And Cfo, Michael T. (Mike) Speetzen, age 48, $550,000 total compensation

President Parts Garments And Accessories, Stephen L. Eastman, age 53, $391,635 total compensation

Cto, Stephen J. Kemp

Vp And Cio, Matthew J. Emmerich

President Motorcycles, Steven D. Menneto

Vp Snowmobiles, Christopher G. Wolf

Svp Corporate Development And Strategy; President Global Adjacent Markets, Robert P. (Bob) Mack, $295,385 total compensation

President Off-road Vehicles, Chris Musso

Auditors: Ernst & Young LLP

LOCATIONS

HQ: Polaris Industries Inc.
2100 Highway 55, Medina, MN 55340
Phone: 763 542-0500
Web: www.polaris.com

2017 Sales

	$ mil.	% of total
United States	4,327	80
Canada	375	7
Other foreign countries	725	13
Total	**5,428**	**100**

PRODUCTS/OPERATIONS

2017 Sales

	$ mil.	% of total
ORV/Snowmobiles	3,570	66
Motorcycles	576	11
Global Adjacent Markets	396	7
Aftermarket	881	16
Total	**5,428**	**100**

PRODUCTS

Off-Road Vehicles
RZR Sport Side x Side
General REC Utility Side x Side
RANGER Utility REC Side x Side
RZR Sport Side x Side
Sportsman ATV
Motorcycles
Indian Motorcycle
Victory Motorcycles
Snow
Snowmobiles
Timbersled
Commercial
GEM Electric
Generators
Government & Defense
Lubricants
Slingshot

COMPETITORS

Arctic Cat	Kawasaki Heavy
BMW	Industries
Deere	Kubota
E-Z-GO	Suzuki Motor
Harley-Davidson	Triumph Motorcycles
Honda	Yamaha Motor

HISTORICAL FINANCIALS

Company Type: Public

Income Statement | | | | FYE: December 31

	REVENUE ($ mil.)	NET INCOME ($ mil.)	NET PROFIT MARGIN	EMPLOYEES
12/17	5,428	172	3.2%	11,000
12/16	4,516	212	4.7%	8,600
12/15	4,719	455	9.6%	8,100
12/14	4,479	454	10.1%	7,000
12/13	3,777	377	10.0%	5,400
Annual Growth	**9.5%**	**(17.8%)**	**—**	**19.5%**

2017 Year-End Financials

Debt ratio: 29.55%
Return on equity: 18.96%
Cash ($ mil.): 138
Current ratio: 1.11
Long-term debt ($ mil.): 865
No. of shares (mil.): 63
Dividends
Yield: 0.0%
Payout: 86.2%
Market value ($ mil.): 7,821

	STOCK PRICE ($) FY Close	P/E High/Low	PER SHARE ($) Earnings	Dividends	Book Value
12/17	123.00	40 25	2.09	2.32	14.96
12/16	82.39	31 21	3.27	2.20	13.88
12/15	85.95	23 12	6.75	2.12	15.18
12/14	151.24	23 17	6.65	1.92	13.19
12/13	145.64	26 15	5.35	1.68	8.29
Annual Growth	**(3.9%)**	**— —**	**(15.8%)**	**8.4%**	**15.9%**

Popular Inc.

Founded in 1893 Popular is the holding company for Banco Popular de Puerto Rico the largest bank in Puerto Rico with some 170 branches (and around 10 more on the Virgin Islands). In addition to commercial and retail banking services Popular owns subsidiaries that offer vehicle financing and leasing (Popular Auto) insurance (Popular Insurance) financial advisory and brokerage services (Popular Securities) and mortgages (Popular Mortgage). Popular also owns Banco Popular North America (BPNA) which serves the US Hispanic population from about 50 Popular Community Bank branches in New York Florida and New Jersey.

Operations

Commercial real estate and business loans (mostly in Puerto Rico) make up more than 30% of Popular's loan portfolio while residential mortgage loans also account for 30% of loans. Consumer loans make up 20% of the portfolio; the rest of the portfolio comprises lease financing and constructions loans.

The bank generates the bulk of its revenue from interest income. Nearly 70% of its total revenue comes from loan interest while another 10% comes from interest on its investment securities. The remainder of its revenue comes from a mix of credit/debit card insurance trust and other service fees (about 10%); service charges on deposit accounts (10%) and mortgage banking income (1%).

Popular's other financial services include the insurance agency and reinsurance businesses of Popular Insurance Popular Insurance V.I. Popular Risk Services and Popular Life Re. BPNA also owns E-LOAN Popular Equipment Finance and Popular Insurance Agency USA. E-LOAN's sole purpose is to provide an online platform to raise deposits for BPNA.

It has around 640 ATMs in Puerto Rico.

Geographic Reach

Popular operates some 230 branches and almost 50 E-Loan and other subsidiary offices including some 180 Banco Popular de Puerto Rico branches in Puerto Rico 35 branches in New York and others in south Florida New Jersey and the Virgin Islands. About 80% of the bank's loan assets are in Puerto Rico.

Financial Performance

In fiscal 2017 Popular's revenue increased 11% to $2.1 billion due to increases in both interest and non-interest income. Financial results were impacted by the destructive hurricanes that hit Puerto Rico in September 2017. Popular's revenue was affected by reduced merchant transaction ac-

tivity the waiver of certain late fees and service charges (including ATM fees) to businesses and customers and disruption to mortgage origination servicing and loss mitigation activities.

Net income fell by 50% to $107.7 million. Much of the fall was accounted for by hurricane effects: Popular recorded $88 million in pre-tax hurricane-related expenses including provision for loan losses of $67.7 million. The bank also took a one off hit from the 2017 US Tax Cuts and Jobs Act which caused a $168.4 million write-down of the deferred tax asset from its US operations.

Cash from operations increased 8% to $635.5 million due to adjustments to reconcile provisions for loan losses partially offset by lower net income.

Strategy

Popular's short-term outlook is dominated by dealing with the effects of Hurricanes Irma and Maria that made landfall in mid and late September 2017. By the end of the year the bank had 92% of its branches and 82% of its ATMs operational up from 31% and 24% one week after the storms respectively. It reestablished call center operations on 25 September and resumed 24/7 operations a month later.

To aid its customers in rebuilding their livelihoods the bank waived ATM fees for 25 days and implemented a payment moratorium for credit cards personal loans auto loans and mortgages. It also set up seven hubs across the territory providing internet access to its commercial clients. Popular also contributed $6.1 million to the Embracing Puerto Rico fund and completed 35 missions distributing 800000 lbs of basic provisions to 140000 people.

Mergers and Acquisitions

In 2018 Popular agreed to acquire Wells Fargo's Puerto Rico Auto Finance Business including $1.5 billion retail auto loans and $340 million in commercial loans for $1.7 billion.

Company Background

To broaden its target audience beyond the Hispanic community Popular rebranded itself in the US switching its name from "Banco Popular" to "Popular Community Bank". The change which was initially begun in pilot markets in 2010 was completed officially in 2012 when the company changed its name in New York City.

EXECUTIVES

Chairman, Richard L. Carrin, age 65, $1,453,846 total compensation

Evp Financial And Insurance, Juan O. Guerrero, age 58, $375,000 total compensation

Evp Administration, Eduardo J. Negrn, age 53, $385,000 total compensation

Evp And Coo Popular Community Bank, Manuel Chinea, age 52

Evp Retail Banking, Néstor O. Rivera, age 71, $375,000 total compensation

Evp And Cfo, Carlos J. Vzquez, age 59, $700,962 total compensation

Evp And Chief Risk Officer, Lidio V. Soriano, age 49, $519,231 total compensation

President And Ceo, Ignacio lvarez, age 59, $742,500 total compensation

Evp Commercial Credit, Eli S. Seplveda, age 55, $420,000 total compensation

Evp Individual Credit, Gilberto F. Monzn, age 58

Evp And Chief Legal Officer, Javier D. Ferrer, age 56, $571,154 total compensation

Evp Cto And Chief Digital Officer, Camille Burckhart, age 39

First Vice President, Jorge Roig

Executive Vice President, Liesl A Rodriguez

Svp Regulatory Affairs, Fred Teed

First Vice President Business Development Popular Auto, Gladys Molina

First Vp Individual Banking Banco Popular Rio
Piedras Region, Martiza Mendez
Senior Vice President And Division Manager, Oran
Bowry
Vice President International Private Banking,
David Hitt
Auditors: PricewaterhouseCoopers LLP

LOCATIONS

HQ: Popular Inc.
Popular Center Building, 209 Munoz Rivera Avenue,
Hato Rey, San Juan, PR 00918
Phone: 787 765-9800
Web: www.popular.com

PRODUCTS/OPERATIONS

Sales 2017

	$ mil.	% of total
Interest income:		
Loans	1,478	68
Money market investments	51	2
Investment securities	191	0
Non-interest income:		
Service charges on deposit accounts	153	7
Other service fees	217	10
Mortgage banking activities	25	1
Net gain (loss) and valuation adjustments on investment securities	0	0
Other-than-temporary impairment losses on investment securities	(8.3)	-
Trading account (loss) profit	(0.8)	-
Net gain on sale of loans including valuation adjustments on loans held-for-sale	0	0
Adjustments (expense) to indemnity reserves on loans sold	(22.4)	-
FDIC loss-share (expense) income	(10.1)	-
Other operating income	64	3
Total	**2,145**	**100**

Selected Subsidiaries and Affiliates

Banco Popular de Puerto Rico
BP Sirenusa International LLC (US)
Popular Auto Inc.Popular Mortgage Inc
.Popular Capital Trust I (US)
Popular Insurance Inc.
Popular International Bank Inc.
Banco Popular North America

COMPETITORS

Bank of America	JPMorgan Chase
Bolivar Banco Venezuela	OFG Bancorp
Citigroup	RBC Financial Group
First BanCorp (Puerto Rico)	Santander BanCorp Scotiabank

HISTORICAL FINANCIALS

Company Type: Public

Income Statement

FYE: December 31

	ASSETS ($ mil.)	NET INCOME ($ mil.)	INCOME AS % OF ASSETS	EMPLOYEES
12/17	44,277	107	0.2%	7,784
12/16	38,661	216	0.6%	7,828
12/15	35,769	895	2.5%	7,810
12/14	33,096	(313)	—	7,752
12/13	35,749	599	1.7%	8,059
Annual Growth	**5.5%**	**(34.9%)**	**—**	**(0.9%)**

2017 Year-End Financials

Debt ratio: 2.04%	No. of shares (mil.): 102
Return on equity: 2.09%	Dividends
Cash ($ mil.): 15,879	Yield: 0.0%
Current ratio: —	Payout: 98.0%
Long-term debt ($ mil.): —	Market value ($ mil.): 3,622

	STOCK PRICE ($) FY Close	P/E High/Low		PER SHARE ($) Earnings	Dividends	Book Value
12/17	35.49	45	32	1.02	1.00	50.00
12/16	43.82	22	11	2.06	0.60	50.08
12/15	28.34	4	3	8.65	0.30	49.27
12/14	34.05	—	—	(3.08)	0.00	41.24
12/13	28.73	6	4	5.78	0.00	44.74
Annual Growth	**5.4%**	—	—	**(35.2%)**	—	**2.8%**

Post Holdings Inc

Breakfast food company Post Holdings has a healthy appetite. The maker of Grape-Nuts Toasties Honey Bunches of Oats Raisin Bran Shredded Wheat Bran Flakes Pebbles and Alpha-Bits Post is the third-best-selling breakfast cereal brand in the US behind Kellogg and General Mills). As well as cereal the company also makes egg products potato products and cheese pasta and other dairy-based products. More recently it has moved beyond the breakfast table by adding snacks active nutrition products and pasta through a series of major acquisitions. It also manufactures nut butters and cereals for private labels. The company has warehouses manufacturing facilities and distribution facilities located throughout the US and Canada.

Operations

Post operates four business segments: Michael Foods Post Consumer Brands Active Nutrition and Private Brands.

Michael Foods accounts for around 45% of revenue and sells refrigerated egg products; potato products; and cheese pasta and other dairy products. Egg products include Better 'N Eggs All Whites and Papetti's among others. Its potato brands are primarily Simply Potatoes and Diner's Choice; and its main cheese pasta and other dairy brand is Crystal Farms.

Post Consumer Brands generates around 35% of total company sales and makes ready-to-eat cereal products such as Honey Bunches of Oats Shreddies Pebbles Great Grains and Alpha-Bits among others.

The Active Nutrition (10% of sales) makes high-protein drinks bars and gels under the Premier Protein Dymatize Supreme Protein and PowerBar brands.

Post's Private Brand manufacturing operation (10% of sales) makes peanut and other nut butters for third-parties primarily in the US and Canada. The segment also includes the Attune Foods business which makes natural cereals and snacks such as Uncle Sam cereals Attune probiotic bars Erewhon gluten-free cereals. Post is creating a new company for its private brands 8th Avenue Food & Provisions which will be partially owned by private equity firm Thomas H. Lee Partners.

Geographic Reach

Post in headquartered in Missouri. More than 90% of the company's products are sold to customers in the US. The Post Consumer Brands segment has eight owned manufacturing facilities while Michael Foods owns six egg products production facilities.

Sales and Marketing

Post Holdings deploys a variety of consumer-targeted marketing campaigns across television digital and print advertisement coupon offers co-op advertising with certain retail customers and co-marketing arrangements with complementary consumer product companies. It also utilizes traditional billboard print digital and social media advertising as well as grass-roots advertising using sampling events and business drops.

Retail giant Wal-Mart Stores is the company's largest customer accounting for around 15% of total sales. Michael Foods serves foodservice distributors restaurant chains and major retail grocery chains with its largest customers being Sysco and US Foods which accounted for 14% and 12% of sales respectively. Private Brands products are sold in natural and specialty grocery stores such as Whole Foods and Trader Joe's which together account for 25% of the segment's sales.

Financial Performance

After a game-changing fiscal 2015 that saw Post more than double its revenue the company maintained its upward trajectory in fiscal 2016 (ended September) by growing its top line 8% to $5.0 billion.

The growth came from the first full-year contributions from businesses acquired in 2015 particularly MOM Brands and from Willamette Egg Farms acquired part-way through fiscal 2016. Beyond acquisitions Post recorded organic growth in Premier Protein products and ready-to-eat cereal peanut butter and private brand granola. Egg potato cheese pasta products saw sales decline.

Post incurred a net loss of $3.3 million in fiscal 2016 an improvement on the losses of $115 million and $343 million recorded in fiscals 2015 and 2014. The narrowing loss was a result of profit contributions of the acquired businesses.

Cash from operating activities increased 11% or $50.8 million to $502.4 million. As before incremental contributions from the acquired businesses drive operating cash growth as did higher organic earnings from Post Consumer Brands Michael Food and Active Nutrition.

Strategy

Post Holdings has continued to move beyond breakfast cereal into higher-growth categories including snacks sports nutrition supplements and weight loss. The company's recent feeding frenzy of food companies included the $2.45 billion acquisition of Michael Foods its largest-ever which gave it the Simply Potatoes All Whites and Crystal Farms brands. The acquisitions demonstrate its willingness to adapt to shifts in consumer tastes such as capitalizing on the popularity of high-protein products and away-from-home snacks.

Post made a major move into the UK with the purchase of British breakfast food firm Weetabix in 2017. As well as its famous eponymous wheat bricks Weetabix owns Alpen Weetos and Oatibix.

In 2018 the company announced the creation of a new entity for its private brands 8th Avenue Food & Provisions which will be partially owned by private equity firm Thomas H. Lee Partners. The deal allows Post to monetize its investment in the private brands business while still benefiting from any future growth of 8th Avenue.

Mergers and Acquisitions

Post has made a ton of acquisitions in recent years. In 2017 it acquired UK cereal maker Weetabix in a $1.76 billion deal. The acquisition which includes the Weetabix Alpen Barbara's Puffins and other cereal brands expands Post's international market presence and bolsters Weetabix's brand presence in the US. Also that year the company agreed to purchase Bob Evans Farms which makes refrigerated potato and veggie side dishes and convenience food items as well as pork sausage. The deal will expand Post's refrigerated offerings portfolio strengthen its presence in commercial foodservice and move it into breakfast sausage.

In 2016 it acquired National Pasteurized Eggs an Illinois-based egg producer and in 2015 another egg producer Willamette Egg Farms. Also in 2015 it acquired MOM Brands a market leader in the ready-to-eat value cereal segment.

Company Background

Prior to the spinoff Post represented Ralcorp's branded cereal segment which was in decline. (Ralcorp acquired Post from Kraft Foods in 2008 for about $2.7 billion but its success with the brand was sporadic.) In the end Ralcorp decided to launch Post on its own to focus on its own burgeoning private label food business. The acquisition in 2014 of Michael Foods transformed the business more than doubling its revenue. It followed Michael Foods up with two other major purchases MOM Brands in 2015 and Weetabix in 2017.

EXECUTIVES

Executive Vice President, James Holbrook
Chairman, William P. (Bill) Stiritz, age 83
Evp; President And Ceo Private Brands, Richard R. Koulouris, age 62, $521,875 total compensation
Svp And Cfo, Jeff A. Zadoks, age 53, $462,500 total compensation
Evp; President And Ceo Michael Foods Group, James E. (Jim) Dwyer, $657,692 total compensation
President And Ceo, Robert V. Vitale, $975,000 total compensation
President And Ceo Post Consumer Brands, Christopher J. Neugent, $619,988 total compensation
Svp General Counsel And Chief Administrative Officer, Diedre Gray, $347,083 total compensation
National Sales Manager Specialty Sales, James Budroe
Vice President Of Architecture And Operations, Brian Hofmeister
Senior Vice President Quality And Food Safety, Dan Ludwig
Division Vice President Of Information Technology Pcb, Richard E Colestock
Vice President Supply Chain, Carla E Carver
Vice President Of Tax, Edward T Short
Vice President Human Resources, Tonya Brake
Vice President Sales North Central And West Usa Post Consumer Brands, Greg Hasper
Vice President Engineering Attune Food Group, Bill Rogers
Vice President R And D, Pat Kocher
Auditors: PricewaterhouseCoopers LLP

LOCATIONS

HQ: Post Holdings Inc
   2503 S. Hanley Road, St. Louis, MO 63144
Phone: 314 644-7600
Web: www.postholdings.com

PRODUCTS/OPERATIONS

2016 Sales

	$ mil.	% of total
Michael Foods Group	2,184	44
Post Consumer Brands	1,728	34
Active Nutrition	574	11
Private Brands	540	11
Eliminations	(1.2)	-
Total	**5,026**	**100**

Selected Products

Alpha-Bits
Attune
Bran Flakes
Fruity Pebbles
Golden Crisp
golden Temple
Grape-Nuts
Great Grains
Honey Bunches of Oats
Honeycomb
Joint Juice
Peace Cereal
Premier Protein
Raisin Bran

Selects Blueberry Morning
Shredded Wheat
Sweet Home Farm
Toasties
Uncle Sam
Waffle Crisp

COMPETITORS

Abbott Nutrition	Nature's Path
American Italian Pasta	Nestlé
Clif Bar	New World Pasta
ConAgra	Nissin Food Products
Danone	PepsiCo
General Mills	Weetabix
Gilster-Mary Lee	Wessanen
Kellogg	granoVita
NBTY	

HISTORICAL FINANCIALS

Company Type: Public

Income Statement   FYE: September 30

	REVENUE ($ mil.)	NET INCOME ($ mil.)	NET PROFIT MARGIN	EMPLOYEES
09/18	6,257	467	7.5%	11,550
09/17	5,225	48	0.9%	11,410
09/16	5,026	(3)	—	8,700
09/15	4,648	(115)	—	8,500
09/14	2,411	(343)	—	7,950
Annual Growth	**26.9%**	—	—	**9.8%**

2018 Year-End Financials

Debt ratio: 55.56%	No. of shares (mil.): 66
Return on equity: 16.03%	Dividends
Cash ($ mil.): 989	Yield: —
Current ratio: 2.78	Payout: —
Long-term debt ($ mil.): 7,232	Market value ($ mil.): 6,539

	STOCK PRICE ($) FY Close	P/E High/Low	Earnings	Dividends	Book Value
09/18	98.04	15 10	6.16	0.00	45.73
09/17	88.27	173 139	0.50	0.00	42.06
09/16	77.17	— —	(0.41)	0.00	46.36
09/15	59.10	— —	(2.33)	0.00	49.35
09/14	33.18	— —	(9.03)	0.00	53.10
Annual Growth	**31.1%**	— —	—	—	**(3.7%)**

PPG Industries Inc

Thanks to its extensive range of paints coatings and other product offerings you won't catch PPG Industries painting itself into a corner. Performance and industrial coatings — such as paints (Pittsburgh Paints Comex and SIGMA) stains (Olympic) and sealants — account for most of its sales; the remainder comes from glass materials. PPG's glass offerings include fiberglass used in construction energy and transportation. The company sold its chemical commodities and flat glass businesses to focus on its core coating and glass segments.

HISTORY

After the failure of his first two plate-glass manufacturing plants John Ford persuaded former railroad superintendent John Pitcairn to invest $200000 in a third factory in 1883 in Creighton Pennsylvania. The enterprise Pittsburgh Plate Glass (PPG) became the first commercially successful US plate-glass factory.

Ford left in 1896 after Pitcairn established a company distribution system replacing glass jobbers. Ford went on to found a predecessor of competitor Libbey-Owens-Ford (now owned by glassmaker Pilkington).

Pitcairn built a soda ash plant in 1899 bought a Milwaukee paint company the following year and began producing window glass in 1908. Pitcairn died in 1916 leaving his stock to his sons.

Strong automobile and construction markets in the early 20th century increased demand for the company's products. In 1924 PPG revolutionized glass production with the introduction of a straight-line conveyor manufacturing method. In the 1930s and 1940s PPG successfully promoted structural glass for use in the commercial construction industry.

PPG was listed on the NYSE in 1945. In 1952 it started making fiberglass and in 1968 the company adopted its present name.

Vincent Sarni (CEO 1984-93) recognized that 85% of the company's sales were to the maturing construction and automobile industries. Sarni decided to move the company into growing industries such as electronics.

In 1986 PPG spent $154 million on acquisitions including the medical electronics units of Litton Industries and Honeywell. It acquired the medical technology business of Allegheny International in 1987 and bought Casco Nobel a coatings distributor and the Olympic and Lucite paint lines from Clorox in 1989.

The company which owned one-third of Dutch fiberglass producer Silenka BV acquired the rest in 1991. In 1992 PPG acquired a silica plant in the Netherlands its first in Europe. Two years later it acquired the European automotive coatings business of Netherlands-based Akzo Nobel.

In the 1990s PPG backed away from Sarni's earlier strategies for greater diversification and unloaded a number of high-tech businesses. The firm refocused on its core coatings glass and chemicals operations. PPG acquired Matthews Paints a leading maker of paints for outdoor signs and the refinish coating business of Lilly Industries in 1995.

The company bolstered its chemical operations in 1997 with the addition of France's Sipsy Chime Fine. That same year President and COO Raymond LeBoeuf took over as CEO. In 1998 PPG sold its European flat and automotive glass business to Belgium-based Glaverbel. Acquisitions that year included Australia-based Orica's technical coatings unit and the US paint operations (Porter Paints) of Akzo Nobel.

In 1999 PPG expanded its European coatings business with the purchase of Belgium-based Sigma Coatings' commercial transport coatings unit and Akzo Nobel's aircraft coatings and sealants company PRC-DeSoto International. That year PPG also bought Imperial Chemical Industries' Germany-based coatings business for large commercial vehicles and its US-based auto refinish and industrial coatings businesses. PPG's acquisition spree continued in 2000 with architectural coating maker Monarch Paint.

Early in the new decade PPG suffered from flat or declining earnings from existing operations. Amid falling sales and lower prices for chemicals and glass PPG began to cut jobs and closed some facilities. Still the company recorded its first loss in more than 10 years in 2002 and its second straight year of declining sales.

Like many manufacturers in its industry PPG has been exposed to potentially costly asbestos litigation mainly because of its 50% stake in the bankrupt Pittsburgh Corning a joint venture with Corning that made insulation with asbestos. In

2002 PPG and its insurers agreed to pay roughly $2.7 billion to settle its asbestos claims.

LeBoeuf retired in 2005. He was replaced by president and COO Charles Bunch who had joined the company in 1979 and worked up through the ranks of first the finance department and then the coatings operations.

In 2008 PPG acquired SigmaKalon for $3 billion. SigmaKalon was among the top 10 paint manufacturers in the world and did business almost entirely outside the US. The company now operates as PPG's Architectural Coatings segment. That same year PPG sold its auto glass business to private equity group Kohlberg & Company which set the unit up as a stand-alone company called Pittsburgh Glass Works. PPG received $330 million plus a 40% interest in the company.

In 2011 PPG acquired Equa-Chlor a producer of chlorine caustic soda and muriatic acid for $27 million. Equa-Chlor produces about 220 tons of chlorine per day. In addition to its products PPG also bought Equa-Chlor's distribution system which includes a railcar fleet it integrated into its own. The deal for the Washington state-based company bolsters PPG's chlor-alkali business in the Northwest US and expands its overall supply chain.

As part of its push to expand in emerging markets in 2011 PPG formed a joint venture with an India-based company Harsha Exito Engineering Private to produce fiber glass reinforcement products.

It made two foreign acquisitions to expand its international operations in 2011. First it bought the business assets of Ducol Coatings South Africa Ltd. which had served as an importer and distributor of PPG's automotive refinish products in South Africa since 2003. PPG also expanded its joint venture with India-based Asian Paints (India's largest coatings company) and created a second 50-50 JV in 2012. The deals boosts PPG's position in the Chinese and Asian packaging coatings industry part of its global strategy to expand into emerging regions.

During 2012 the company made four acquisitions related to its coatings business for a total of $288 million including US-based Spraylat Corp. Denmark based Dyrup A/S and the coatings business of Ecuador-based Colpisa Colombiana de Pinturas.

Expanding PPG's architectural coatings business in the US Canada and the Caribbean in 2013 it bought Azko Nobel's North American Decorative Paints business for $1.05 billion.

EXECUTIVES

Chairman And Ceo, Michael H. McGarry, age 60, $1,100,000 total compensation

Evp, Viktoras R. Sekmakas, age 57, $646,667 total compensation

Svp Architectural Coatings; President Ppg Emea, Jean-Marie Greindl, age 55

Vp Science And Technology And Cto, David S. Bem

President Ppg Asia Pacific And Vp Protective And Marine Coatings Asia Pacific, Michael Horton

Svp Industrial Coatings, Timothy M. Knavish, age 52, $438,333 total compensation

Vp Coatings Services; President Metokote, Jeffrey J. Oravitz

Chief Commercial Officer Ppg Comex, Henrik Bergstr ¶m, age 47

Svp And Cfo, Vincent J. Morales, age 53

Vp Information Technology, Christopher R. Caruso

Svp Protective And Marine Coatings, Ramaparasad (Ram) Vadlamannati, age 55

Executive Vice President, Eiji Hamaoka

Auditors: PricewaterhouseCoopers LLP

LOCATIONS

HQ: PPG Industries Inc
One PPG Place, Pittsburgh, PA 15272
Phone: 412 434-3131
Web: www.ppg.com

2016 Sales

	$ mil.	% of total
United States and Canada	6,595	45
Europe Middle East and Africa	4,304	29
Asia Pacific	2,431	16
Latin America	1,421	10
Total	**14,751**	**100**

PRODUCTS/OPERATIONS

2016 Sales

	$ mil.	% of total
Performance Coatings	8,580	58
Industrial Coatings	5,690	39
Glass	481	3
Total	**14,751**	**100**

Selected Products

Performance Coatings
  Aerospace coatings
  Architectural coatings (Lucite paints Olympic stains)
  Refinish
Industrial Coatings
  Automotive coatings chemicals adhesives and sealants
  Industrial coatings
  Packaging coatings (food and beverage containers)
Commodity Chemicals
  Calcium hypochlorite
  Caustic soda
  Chlorine
  Chlorine derivatives
  Phosgene derivatives
Optical and Specialty Materials
  Optical products (Transitions variable-tint lenses)
  Silica products
Glass
  Aircraft transparencies
  Coated glass
  Continuous-strand fiberglass
  Flat glass

COMPETITORS

3M	KANSAI PAINT CO. LTD.
Akzo Nobel	Kelly-Moore
Axalta Coating Systems	Nippon Paint
BASF Coatings AG	Nippon Sheet Glass
BEHR	Pilkington Group
Benjamin Moore	RPM International
Dow Chemical	Sherwin-Williams
Ferro	Valspar

HISTORICAL FINANCIALS

Company Type: Public

Income Statement   FYE: December 31

	REVENUE ($ mil.)	NET INCOME ($ mil.)	NET PROFIT MARGIN	EMPLOYEES
12/17	14,750	1,591	10.8%	47,200
12/16	14,751	877	5.9%	47,000
12/15	15,330	1,406	9.2%	46,600
12/14	15,360	2,102	13.7%	44,400
12/13	15,108	3,231	21.4%	41,400
Annual Growth	**(0.6%)**	**(16.2%)**	**—**	**3.3%**

2017 Year-End Financials

Debt ratio: 25.07%	No. of shares (mil.): 251
Return on equity: 30.64%	Dividends
Cash ($ mil.): 1,436	Yield: 0.0%
Current ratio: 1.66	Payout: 27.5%
Long-term debt ($ mil.): 4,134	Market value ($ mil.): 29,342

	STOCK PRICE ($) FY Close	P/E High/Low	PER SHARE ($) Earnings	Dividends	Book Value
12/17	116.82	19 15	6.17	1.70	22.13
12/16	94.76	35 27	3.28	1.56	18.75
12/15	98.82	46 16	5.14	1.42	18.67
12/14	231.15	31 23	7.52	1.31	19.05
12/13	189.66	17 12	11.14	1.21	17.79
Annual Growth	**(11.4%)**	**—**	**(13.7%)**	**8.9%**	**5.6%**

PPL Corp

PPL Corporation is one of the largest utility companies in the world delivering electricity to 10 million customers through its regulated utility subsidiaries in Kentucky Pennsylvania Tennessee and Virginia as well as in the UK; it also delivers natural gas to customers in Kentucky. The company has more than 8000 MW of electric generating capacity about 220000 miles of electric lines and gas transmission mains and storage fields.

IPO

In a major move in 2015 PPL spun off its nonregulated wholesale energy supply business and combined it with the competitive generation business of Riverstone Holdings to create a stand-alone publicly traded independent power producer — Talen Energy Corporation. PPL shareholders own 65% of Talen Energy; affiliates of Riverstone 35%.

Operations

PPL has three segments: Kentucky UK and Pennsylvania. While the UK and Pennsylvania each bring in about 30% of total revenue Kentucky is the highest earner bringing in about 40%.

The Kentucky segment includes Louisville Gas and Electric which provides electric services to more than 400000 customers in Kentucky and natural gas service to almost 325000 customers. It also comprises of Kentucky Utility which serves around 550000 customers in Kentucky Virginia and Tennessee.

The UK segment which includes primarily Western Power Distribution?s (WPD) regulated electricity distribution operation serves almost 8 million end users in south Wales and southwest and central England.

The Pennsylvania segment (PPL Electric) delivers electricity to 1.4 million customers in eastern and central Pennsylvania.

Geographic Reach

PPL delivers electricity to customers in Kentucky Pennsylvania Tennessee Virginia and the UK and natural gas to customers in Kentucky.

The US accounts for 70% of company's revenue; the rest comes from the UK though revenue is falling in this sector.

Sales and Marketing

PPL Corporation serves some 10 million residential industrial and commercial customers in Kentucky Pennsylvania Tennessee Virginia and the UK.

Financial Performance

PPL revenue has fallen steadily for over half a decade now. The company earned $7.4 billion in 2017. The slight decline over 2016 came entirely from a 3% revenue reduction from its UK segment mostly due to milder weather in 2017 and the negative impact of foreign currency exchange rates from its UK segment.

Net income was $1.1 billion in 2017 a decline of some almost $800 million from the prior year. The decline is net income is primarily the result of a year-over-year decline of some $645 million due to adverse effects of foreign currency exchange contracts which are used by the company to hedge foreign currency exposure in the UK subsidiary.

Cash holdings reduced to $341 million in 2017 compared to $836 million the year prior. Continuing operations provided $2.5 billion in net cash and a further $824 million came from financing activities. PPL spent $3.1 billion in investments almost entirely in PP&E expenditures.

Strategy

Faced with falling revenue and technological disruptions that are rapidly changing the energy grid PPL Corporation is embarking on a long-term core strategy of sustainable production.

The company plans to invest some $16 billion through 2021 primarily in two ways?technological upgrades especially grid improvements and clean energy production.

In the UK Western Power Distribution (WPD) announced upgrade investments of some $164 million to become distribution ?system? operators (DSO) enabling the company to actively manage flow of energy across its distribution system.

In the US the company announced installation of 1.3 advanced meters within its Kentucky service territory which?d help save energy and reduce power outage restoration times.

For a cleaner energy future the company is planning to pioneer the integration of private solar power to its own grid system in the UK as well as in Pennsylvania through its Keystone Solar Future Project.

In Kentucky PPL announced plans to retire two oldest aging coal plants and replace them with natural gas and new solar power facilities. The company?s Climate Assessment report estimates emission reductions somewhere between 45-90 percent by 2050.

HISTORY

PPL's wires reach back to Lehigh Coal & Navigation which was formed in 1822 to mine Pennsylvania coal and build a canal to deliver it to Philadelphia. Heavy industry and steel mills flourished in the Lehigh Valley and Thomas Edison formed small electric companies to serve the area in the early 1880s. Rivals soon followed and by 1900 there were 64 companies in what would become PPL's territory.

EXECUTIVES

President And Coo Lg&e And Ku Energy, Paul W. Thompson

Chairman And Ceo Lg&e And Ku Energy, Victor A. Staffieri, age 62, $811,220 total compensation

Chief Executive Western Power Distribution, Robert A. Symons, age 64, $741,127 total compensation

Chairman President And Ceo, William H. Spence, age 60, $1,154,712 total compensation

President Ppl Electric Utilities, Gregory N. Dudkin, age 60, $524,143 total compensation

Svp And Cfo, Vincent (Vince) Sorgi, age 46, $524,134 total compensation

Vice President Administration And Inside Sales And Marketing Coordinator, Barb Sipe

Vice President Of Marketing, Linda Miller

Vice President, Michael Kroboth

Senior Vice President, Robert Grey

Vice President, John Barbera

Vice President And Chief Human Resources Officer Ppl Services, Thomas Lynch

Vp Electric Distribution Lgande And Ku, John Wolfe

Vice President Finance And Regulatory Affairs And Controller, Marlene Beers

Board Member, Steven G Elliott

Board Member, Craig Rogerson
Board Member, Venkata Madabhushi
Board Member, Rodney Adkins
Assistant Treasurer, Tadd J Henninger
Auditors: DELOITTE & TOUCHE LLP

LOCATIONS

HQ: PPL Corp
Two North Ninth Street, Allentown, PA 18101-1179
Phone: 610 774-5151
Web: www.pplweb.com

2015 Sales

	$ mil.	% of total
US	5,259	68
UK	2,410	32
Total	**7,669**	**100**

PRODUCTS/OPERATIONS

2015 Sales

	$ mil.	% of total
Utility	2,410	31
Kentucky Regulated	3,115	41
Pennsylvania Regulated including corporate and others	2,144	28
Total	**7,669**	**100**

Selected Subsidiaries

PPL Development Corporation (acquisition and divestiture activities)
PPL Electric Utilities Corporation (electricity distribution)
PPL Energy Supply (nonregulated operations)
  PPL EnergyPlus LLC (wholesale and retail energy marketing)
  PPL Generation LLC (electricity generation)
  PPL Montana LLC (electricity generation)
  PPL Global LLC (international utility operations)
  Western Power Distribution Holdings Limited (formerly WPD Holdings UK electricity distribution)
PPL Services Corporation (shared services for PPL Corp and other subsidiaries)

COMPETITORS

ABB	Green Mountain Energy
AEP	HC Energ a
Avangrid	Maine & Maritimes
Canadian Utilities	Midwest Generation
Centrica	Ontario Power
Con Edison	Generation
Constellation Energy	Orange & Rockland
Group	Utilities
Covanta	Pepco Holdings
Delmarva Power	Public Service
Dominion Energy	Enterprise Group
Duke Energy	Scottish and Southern
Duquesne Light	Energy
Holdings	South Jersey
EnergySolve	Industries
Exelon	Southern Company
FirstEnergy	TransAlta

HISTORICAL FINANCIALS

Company Type: Public

Income Statement — FYE: December 31

	REVENUE ($ mil.)	NET INCOME ($ mil.)	NET PROFIT MARGIN	EMPLOYEES
12/17	7,447	1,128	15.1%	12,512
12/16	7,517	1,902	25.3%	12,689
12/15	7,669	682	8.9%	12,799
12/14	11,499	1,737	15.1%	17,391
12/13	11,860	1,130	9.5%	18,108
Annual Growth	**(11.0%)**	**(0.0%)**	**—**	**(8.8%)**

2017 Year-End Financials

Debt ratio: 51.29%
Return on equity: 10.92%
Cash ($ mil.): 485
Current ratio: 0.57
Long-term debt ($ mil.): 19,847

No. of shares (mil.): 693
Dividends
Yield: 0.0%
Payout: 96.3%
Market value ($ mil.): 21,461

	STOCK PRICE ($) FY Close	P/E High/Low	PER SHARE ($) Earnings	Dividends	Book Value
12/17	30.95	24 19	1.64	1.58	15.52
12/16	34.05	14 11	2.79	1.52	14.56
12/15	34.13	36 29	1.01	1.50	14.72
12/14	36.33	14 11	2.61	1.49	20.47
12/13	30.09	18 15	1.76	1.47	19.78
Annual Growth	**0.7%**	**— —**	**(1.7%)**	**1.8%**	**(5.9%)**

PRECISION CASTPARTS CORP.

Precision Castparts Corp. (PCC) is a maker of investment castings used in jet aircraft satellite launches aerostructures armaments and medical applications (prostheses). Its Investment Cast products segment makes jet engine parts fluid management valves and deep-hole boring tools. Forged Products and Airframe Products round out PCC's three segments and cover the power generation and paper and pulp industries as well as general industry. The aerospace sector accounts for the majority of PCC's sales. In January 2016 the company was acquired by Berkshire Hathaway in a mega-deal valued at $37 billion.

HISTORY

The history of Precision Castparts Corp. (PCC) is not as precise as its castings. The Oregon Saw Company was founded in 1949 and sold in 1953; its buyer wanted neither the future PCC nor a power tools unit so the two became Omark Industries. In 1956 a buyer purchased the power tool business but wasn't interested in castings; that operation was spun off as Precision Castparts Corp.

In the early 1950s a group of Oregon Saw's casting employees developed a process for producing parts as large as 60 inches by use of investment casting making products that rivaled the strength of forged and machined parts at a fraction of the cost. After a two-year search they landed their first aerospace customer — Air Research Corp. — with many to follow. The higher operating temperatures generated by aircraft engines led the company to buy a vacuum furnace in 1959 to fabricate parts that could tolerate greater heat; two more vacuum furnaces were added and sales vaulted toward $10 million by 1967. PCC went public in 1968 and continued to grow. In 1976 the company acquired Centaur Cast Alloys (small investment castings UK) to make parts for the European aerospace industry. By that time General Electric (GE) and Pratt & Whitney accounted for most of PCC's business. Edward Cooley who had masterminded the company's growth since incorporation forged ahead with plans to double production capacity.

In 1980 the airline industry crashed but PCC's sales held at about $90 million. Structural airplane products soon picked up and in 1984 the company bought two titanium foundries in France. To diversify it added TRW's cast airfoils (used in aircraft engines and industrial gas turbines) division in 1986. That acquisition renamed PCC Airfoils increased PCC's annual sales by about 80%; sales reached $443 million by 1989.

The company broadened its offerings again in 1991 when it acquired Advanced Forming Technology which made small complex metal-injection molded parts used in everything from adding machines to military ordnance. The early 1990s recession hit the airline industry and sales dropped. Cooley retired as chairman in 1994 and GE veteran William McCormick replaced him. The next year PCC acquired Quamco Inc. (industrial tools and machines). In 1996 PCC flowed into the fluid management market with the acquisition of NEWFLO for about $300 million.

In 1997 PCC spent $437 million to acquire seven more companies that helped boost sales 75% from 1996 levels. The next year it purchased four metalworking companies that served industries other than aerospace. Having reduced dependence on sales to the aerospace industry to just over 50% PCC began consolidating operations and closing plants to reduce costs.

The company continued to diversify through acquisitions in 1999 but it also expanded its aerospace operations with the purchase of Wyman-Gordon a leading maker of advanced metal forgings for the aerospace market. PCC's 2000 acquisitions included the aerospace division of United Engineering Forgings and Germany-based Convey Engineering (heavy-duty valves). The next year the company bought the assets of Netherlands-based Wouter Witzel and the US's Drop Dies and Forgings Company (renamed Wyman-Gordon Cleveland). In 2002 PCC bought the rest of Western Australian Specialty Alloys (casting and forging alloys) for $27.6 million in cash and PCC shares.

In 2003 Precision Castparts' PCC Structurals unit reached a $400 million agreement with Rolls-Royce to supply large titanium and steel castings. That year the company acquired SPS Technologies a producer of fasteners and other metal components for the aerospace automotive and industrial markets. In 2004 subsidiary SPS Aerospace Fasteners signed a four-year deal with Airbus worth about $72 million to supply collars nuts studs and titanium pins to Airbus plants across Europe.

PCC acquired Air Industries Corporation in early 2005. In 2006 PCC bought Special Metals Corporation (SMC) a maker of nickel alloys and super alloys for $295 million in cash and the assumption of $245 million in SMC debt. PCC intended to use SMC's product as raw materials for its own aircraft engine components. SMC also served the automotive chemical and power generation industries.

Later in 2006 PCC bought Shur-Lok Corporation a manufacturer of aerospace fasteners for about $110 million. The acquisition combined with the 2005 purchase of Air Industries Corporation helped to further PCC's desire to grow its airframe fasteners business.

Early in 2007 PCC completed the purchase of GSC a leading maker of aluminum and steel structural investment casting for the aerospace energy and medical markets. It also acquired Cherry Aerospace which expanded its fastener products portfolio.

In 2009 the company acquired Carlton Forge Works which makes aircraft engines for Boeing and Airbus; California-based Arcturus Manufacturing (hammer forging operations) was included in the transaction. PCC also picked up Airdrome Holdings (fluid fittings) Fatigue Technology (cold expansion technology) and Hackney Ladish (forged pipe fittings) in 2009.

In late summer 2011 PPC purchased Primus International a maker of complex metal industrial

parts and assemblies. Its products (machined aluminum and titanium components used in aircraft wings fuselages and engine-related assemblies) cater to Boeing Airbus and other aerospace OEMs. The $900 million deal furthered the company's commitment to the global aerospace industry. In a similar vein the company obtained Unison Engine Components (operating as Tru-Form Rings) from GE Aviation in mid-2011. Tru-Form made flash-welded and cold-rolled rings with jet engine as well as gas turbine applications.

PCC also acquired RathGibson which makes tubing for the oil and gas chemical/petrochemical power-generation and other markets in 2012.

To expand both its Fasteners and Forged Products segments PCC acquired the aerostructures and industrial products businesses of HA©roux-Devtek for about CAD$300 million (about $295.5 million) in 2012. Among other benefits the acquisition expanded the company's product line for such OEMs as Lockheed Bombardier and Gulfstream. PCC also inked a deal to purchase the Synchronous Aerospace Group business of private investment firm Littlejohn & Co. in late 2012.

EXECUTIVES

Evp And Cfo, Shawn R. Hagel, $687,500 total compensation

Chairman And Ceo, Mark Donegan, $1,585,000 total compensation

Svp And President Airframe Products, Alan J. (Al) Power

Evp And President Wyman-gordon, Andrew V. Masterman, $592,500 total compensation

Vp And Cio, Byron J. Gaddis

Evp, Steven G. (Steve) Hackett, $708,750 total compensation

Svp And General Counsel, Ruth A. Beyer, $569,000 total compensation

Svp And Coo Aerostructures Division, Joseph I. Snowden, $356,347 total compensation

Svp And President Pcc Airfoils, John P. O'Neill

Svp And President Timet And Special Metals, James R. Pieron

Auditors: DELOITTE & TOUCHE LLP PORTLAN

LOCATIONS

HQ: PRECISION CASTPARTS CORP.
4650 SW MCDAM AVE STE 300, PORTLAND, OR 97239
Phone: 503 946-4800
Web: WWW.PRECAST.COM

PRODUCTS/OPERATIONS

Selected Products and Services
Fasteners
  Advanced forming technology
  E/One (for the disposal of residential sanitary waste)
  J&L fiber services (for pulp and paper industry)
  PCC Precision Tool Group
  SPS aerospace fasteners (for commercial/military aircraft)
  SPS engineered fasteners (high strength for automotive and construction applications)
Forged products
  Special Metals Corporation
  Wyman-Gordon Forgings
Investment Cast Products
  PCC Airfoils (high-temperature blades and vanes)
  PCC Structurals (structural investment castings)
  Specialty materials and alloys (alloys waxes and metal processing for investment casting)

COMPETITORS

ATI Ladish	Hitachi Metals
Allegheny Technologies	Kennametal
Arconic	LISI
Carpenter Technology	Mettis Aerospace

Chicago Rivet	SOURIAU PA&E
Crane Co.	Swagelok
Curtiss-Wright	Teleflex
ESCO	ThyssenKrupp
Farwest Steel Corporation	United Technologies
	Universal Stainless
Federal Screw Works	V & M Tubes (USA)
Georg Fischer	Volvo Aero
Haynes International	

HISTORICAL FINANCIALS
Company Type: Private

Income Statement   FYE: January 3

	REVENUE ($ mil.)	NET INCOME ($ mil.)	NET PROFIT MARGIN	EMPLOYEES
01/16*	7,002	817	11.7%	30,100
03/15	10,005	1,533	15.3%	—
03/14	9,616	1,784	18.6%	—
03/13	8,377	1,429	17.1%	—
Annual Growth	(5.8%)	(17.0%)	—	—

*Fiscal year change

2016 Year-End Financials

Debt ratio: ——
Return on equity: 11.70%   Dividends
Cash ($ mil.): 343   Yield: —
Current ratio: 1.20   Payout: —
Long-term debt ($ mil.): —   Market value ($ mil.): —

Preferred Bank (Los Angeles, CA)

Preferred Bank wants to be the bank of choice of Chinese-Americans in Southern California. Employing a multilingual staff the bank provides international banking services to companies doing business in the Asia/Pacific region. It targets middle-market businesses typically manufacturing service distribution and real estate firms as well as entrepreneurs professionals and high-net-worth individuals through about a dozen branches in Los Angeles Orange and San Francisco Counties. Preferred Bank offers standard deposit products such as checking accounts savings money market and NOW accounts. Specialized services include private banking and international trade finance.

Geographic Reach

Preferred Bank markets its services in half a dozen Southern Californian counties: Los Angeles Orange Riverside San Bernardino San Francisco and Ventura.

Financial Performance

In 2013 Preferred Bank reported about $72 million in revenue up just more than 10% from the prior year. The increase was solely from interest income as non-interest income (a very small part of overall revenue anyway) fell more than 40%. The company saw growth in its loan portfolio that year as well as overall deposit growth. Net income fell 20% to $19 million; the decline was primarily related to a boost in net income for 2012 because of a $20 million income tax benefit (compared to income tax expense of $12 million in 2013).

Strategy

Historically the company was focused on the Chinese-American market and although it continues to cater to that clientele most of its current customer base is from the diversified mainstream market.

EXECUTIVES

Evp And Cfo, Edward J. Czajka
President And Coo, Wellington Chen, age 58
Chairman And Ceo, Li Yu, age 77
Senior Vice President, Ted Hsu
Vice President, William Ko
Senior Vice President, Jim Belanic
Senior Vice President, John C Stipanov
Vice President, Debbie White
First Vice President, Madelyn Hayashi
Vice President, Barbara Gordon
Vice President, Craig Miller
First Vice President, Nancy Pepper
Assistant Vice President Compliance Officer, Kristie Yang
Vice President, Elsa Chen
Vice President, Sofia Huang
Vice President Lending, Luey Couto
Senior Vice President, Ann Cheung
Vice President, Michael Nagai
Vice President, Wayne Chow
Vice President Human Resources Manager, Karen Cangey
Vice President And Manager, Lupe Quintana
Vice President, Isabella LI
Vice President Internal Audit Manager, Carlo Garcia
First Vice President, Philip Wong
Vice President Product Manager, John Wong
Executive Vice President Chief Credit Officer, Jonathan Sigal
Vice Chairman, Clark Hsu
Auditors: Crowe Horwath LLP

LOCATIONS

HQ: Preferred Bank (Los Angeles, CA)
601 S. Figueroa Street, 29th Floor, Los Angeles, CA 90017
Phone: 213 891-1188
Web: www.preferredbank.com

PRODUCTS/OPERATIONS

2015 Sales

	% of total
Interest income	
Loans and leases	90
Investment securities available for sale	6
Federal funds sold	-
Non-interest income	
Fees and service charges on deposit accounts	1
Trade finance income	2
BOLI income	-
Other income	1
Total	**100**

COMPETITORS

Bank of America	City National
Bank of the West	East West Bancorp
Broadway Financial	Far East National Bank
Cathay General Bancorp	Hanmi Financial
Citigroup	MUFG Americas Holdings

HISTORICAL FINANCIALS

Company Type: Public

Income Statement

FYE: December 31

	ASSETS ($ mil.)	NET INCOME ($ mil.)	INCOME AS % OF ASSETS	EMPLOYEES
12/17	3,769	43	1.2%	238
12/16	3,221	36	1.1%	218
12/15	2,598	29	1.1%	205
12/14	2,054	24	1.2%	163
12/13	1,768	19	1.1%	148
Annual Growth	**20.8%**	**22.6%**	**—**	**12.6%**

2017 Year-End Financials

Debt ratio: 2.63%
Return on equity: 13.29%
Cash ($ mil.): 446
Current ratio: —
Long-term debt ($ mil.): —

No. of shares (mil.): 15
Dividends
  Yield: 0.0%
  Payout: 25.6%
Market value ($ mil.): 889

	STOCK PRICE ($) FY Close	P/E High/Low	Earnings	PER SHARE ($) Dividends	Book Value
12/17	58.78	22 16	2.96	0.76	23.48
12/16	52.42	20 10	2.56	0.60	20.94
12/15	33.02	17 12	2.14	0.46	19.02
12/14	27.89	15 11	1.78	0.10	17.40
12/13	20.05	15 10	1.42	0.00	15.58
Annual Growth	**30.9%**	**— —**	**20.2%**	**—**	**10.8%**

Premier Financial Bancorp, Inc.

EXECUTIVES

Senior Vice President, Mike Mineer
Vice President Credit Administration, Scot Kelley
Vice President Commercial Lender, Barbara Repetti
Vice President, Daniel Ware
Assistant Vice President, Stephanie Lipscomb
Vice President Commercial Lending, Ken Rosenberg
Auditors: Crowe Horwath LLP

LOCATIONS

HQ: Premier Financial Bancorp, Inc.
2883 Fifth Avenue, Huntington, WV 25702
Phone: 304 525-1600

COMPETITORS

ASB Financial	Ohio Valley Banc
BB&T	PNC Financial
City Holding	Porter Bancorp
Community Trust	Stock Yards Bancorp
Fifth Third	United Bancorp
Huntington Bancshares	United Bankshares

HISTORICAL FINANCIALS

Company Type: Public

Income Statement

FYE: December 31

	ASSETS ($ mil.)	NET INCOME ($ mil.)	INCOME AS % OF ASSETS	EMPLOYEES
12/17	1,493	14	1.0%	354
12/16	1,496	12	0.8%	356
12/15	1,244	12	1.0%	344
12/14	1,252	13	1.0%	366
12/13	1,100	13	1.2%	328
Annual Growth	**7.9%**	**2.9%**	**—**	**1.9%**

2017 Year-End Financials

Debt ratio: 0.69%
Return on equity: 8.29%
Cash ($ mil.): 80
Current ratio: —
Long-term debt ($ mil.): —

No. of shares (mil.): 13
Dividends
  Yield: 0.0%
  Payout: 43.4%
Market value ($ mil.): 268

	STOCK PRICE ($) FY Close	P/E High/Low	Earnings	PER SHARE ($) Dividends	Book Value
12/17	20.08	21 16	1.10	0.48	13.74
12/16	20.10	23 16	0.92	0.45	13.10
12/15	16.44	14 13	1.08	0.41	13.09
12/14	15.58	15 12	1.06	0.44	13.02
12/13	14.15	13 9	1.08	0.32	13.29
Annual Growth	**9.1%**	**— —**	**0.5%**	**10.7%**	**0.8%**

PRESIDENT AND TRUSTEES OF COLBY COLLEGE

EXECUTIVES

Prin, Bruce McDougal

LOCATIONS

HQ: PRESIDENT AND TRUSTEES OF COLBY COLLEGE
4120 MAYFLOWER HL, WATERVILLE, ME 049018841
Phone: 207 859-4127

HISTORICAL FINANCIALS

Company Type: Private

Income Statement

FYF: June 30

	ASSETS ($ mil.)	NET INCOME ($ mil.)	INCOME AS % OF ASSETS	EMPLOYEES
06/17	1,481	72	4.9%	5
06/15	1,382	50	3.6%	—
06/14	1,267	55	4.4%	—
06/13	1,126	30	2.7%	—
Annual Growth	**7.1%**	**24.8%**	**—**	**—**

2017 Year-End Financials

Debt ratio: —
Return on equity: 28.10%
Cash ($ mil.): 44
Current ratio: 0.40
Long-term debt ($ mil.): —

Dividends
  Yield: —
  Payout: —
Market value ($ mil.): —

Primerica Inc

EXECUTIVES

Chb, Rick Williams
Co Chb*, John Addison
Pres*, David T Chadwick
Dir*, Michael K Wells
Coo*, Douglas G Elliott
SEC*, Stacey K Geer
Cfo*, Allison Rand
Vice President, Ron Kennett
Auditors: KPMG LLP

LOCATIONS

HQ: Primerica Inc
1 Primerica Parkway, Duluth, GA 30099
Phone: 770 381-1000
Web: www.primerica.com

HISTORICAL FINANCIALS

Company Type: Public

Income Statement

FYE: December 31

	ASSETS ($ mil.)	NET INCOME ($ mil.)	INCOME AS % OF ASSETS	EMPLOYEES
12/17	12,460	350	2.8%	2,718
12/16	11,438	219	1.9%	2,662
12/15	10,612	189	1.8%	2,626
12/14	10,738	181	1.7%	2,579
12/13	10,329	162	1.6%	2,605
Annual Growth	4.8%	21.1%	—	1.1%

2017 Year-End Financials

Debt ratio: 8.91%
Return on equity: 26.53%
Cash ($ mil.): 279
Current ratio: —
Long-term debt ($ mil.): —

No. of shares (mil.): 44
Dividends
Yield: 0.0%
Payout: 10.2%
Market value ($ mil.): 4,494

	STOCK PRICE ($) FY Close	P/E High/Low		PER SHARE ($) Earnings	Dividends	Book Value
12/17	101.55	14	9	7.61	0.78	32.07
12/16	69.15	16	9	4.59	0.70	26.71
12/15	47.23	15	11	3.70	0.64	23.72
12/14	54.26	17	12	3.29	0.48	23.87
12/13	42.91	15	10	2.83	0.44	22.29
Annual Growth	24.0%	—	—	28.1%	15.4%	9.5%

Principal Financial Group Inc

Seeking out The Principal may bring future financial windfalls. Founded in 1879 Principal Financial Group (or The Principal) is a top administrator of employer-sponsored retirement plans offering pension products and services as well as mutual funds annuities asset management trust services and investment advice. Its insurance segment provides group and individual life and disability insurance and group dental and vision coverage. PFG serves 22 million customers and has more than $650 billion in assets under management.

Operations

Principal offers its financial products and services through four main segments: Retirement and Income Solutions US Insurance Solutions Principal International and Principal Global Investors.

The Retirement and Investor Services segment generates about 50% of annual revenue. It provides retirement and other financial products and services such as 401(k) plans Individual Retirement Accounts (IRAs) personal trusts and annuities to individuals and businesses.

The U.S. Insurance Solutions segment (around 30% of revenue) provides individual life insurance and specialty benefits insurance which includes group dental and vision individual and group disability and group life insurance along with nonmedical fee-for-service claims administration services.

The Principal International segment (10% of revenue) serves retirement and insurance needs to clients in countries with large middle classes and growing long-term savings. The company typically enters a new market through acquisitions

joint ventures and sometimes its own start-up operations.

The Principal Global Investors segment (less than 10% of revenue) offers asset management services to the company's internal asset accumulation business insurance operations and the Corporate segment along with third-party clients.

Geographic Reach

Principal Financial Group operates out of offices in nearly 20 countries and serves clients in more than 75 countries. It is headquartered in Des Moines IA.

PFG?s International segment has operations in Brazil Chile Mexico China Hong Kong India Singapore Thailand Malaysia and Indonesia.

The Principal Global Investors segment has offices in about a dozen countries including Australia China Japan Singapore Germany Malaysia Hong Kong the United Arab Emirates the Netherlands.

Sales and Marketing

Principal distributes its products and services through institutional and retail sales representatives relationship management and client service professionals who work with consultants and directly with investors to acquire and retain institutional clients retail clients and other investors. The company maintains relationships with independent broker-dealers to distribute its products and services maintaining relationships with over 61000 independent brokers consultants and agents.

PFG?s International segment focuses on regions with a growing middle class and demographics that are aligned with PFG?s target customer criteria as well as where it is common for workers to contribute to defined contribution retirement plans (similar to 401(k) and IRA plans).

Financial Performance

PFG?s financial results in 2016 continued a long-term upward trend. Its annual revenues have risen more than 30% since 2011 mostly thanks to growing premium income from annuity and life insurance sales. The firm's assets under management have swelled by more than 60% since 2011 which has led to higher fee-based income. The company's profits have doubled thanks to strong cost controls.

In 2016 revenue moved up 4% to $12.4 billion its growth slowing a bit compared to the prior two years. Net investment income was the primary driver of growth rising nearly $200 million as a result of higher average invested assets in PFG?s US operations. Premiums for the US Insurance segment increased in the year but not enough to offset the reduction in premiums for the Retirement and Income Solutions segment. The Principal International segment performed well in Latin America increasing sales by $28 million.

Net income rose 9% in 2016 on the back of higher revenue tighter expense controls and the positive effect of not distributing dividends for its preferred stock which was retired in 2015.

Cash at the end of the year was $2.7 billion up roughly $150 million from 2015. Cash from operations added $3.9 billion to the coffers and financing activities contributed $1.4 billion. Investing activities used $5.2 billion.

Strategy

PFG aims to become a global player in retirement services targeting countries in Asia and Latin America that rely on private-sector defined-contribution pension plans to accommodate their growing number of retirees. The company typically builds its international business through startups acquisitions and joint ventures.

PFG has exited underperforming businesses such as medical insurance to focus on asset management at home and abroad. It aims to grow its assets under management (AUM) at a 6% compound annual clip with the goal of surpassing $100 trillion AUM in 2020 and $400 trillion by 2050.

In the US PFG courts firms with fewer than 1000 employees for its insurance and pension products; that market is primed for growth as a relatively low percentage of small to midsized businesses currently offer these products. Its strategy for growth also includes targeting large institutional clients for its asset management operations which include Principal Global Investors. The company serves approximately 650 institutional investors.

HISTORY

Principal Financial was founded as the Bankers Life Association in 1879 by Edward Temple a Civil War veteran and banker. Life insurance became popular after the war but some dishonest insurers canceled customers' policies before they had to pay out benefits. Bankers Life an assessable association (members shared the cost of death benefits as the claims arose) was intended to provide low-cost protection to bankers and their families. The company soon began offering life insurance to nonbankers but it refused to insure women because of the high mortality rate among mothers during childbirth.

In October 2012 PFG scooped up First Dental Health a California-based preferred provider organization (PPO) with more than 11000 dentists operating in Arizona California and Nevada. The acquisition bolstered PFG's specialty benefits insurance business.

EXECUTIVES

Evp And Cfo, Terrance Lillis
Chairman President And Ceo, Daniel J. (Dan) Houston, age 57, $795,192 total compensation
Evp General Counsel And Secretary, Karen E. Shaff, age 64
President Global Asset Management; Ceo Principal Global Investors, James P. (Jim) McCaughan, age 65, $663,500 total compensation
Evp Cio And Chief Digital Officer, Gary P. Scholten, age 61
Svp Retirement And Investor Services; President And Ceo Principal Funds, Nora M. Everett, age 58
Ceo Principal Real Estate Investors, Patrick G. (Pat) Halter
Senior Executive Director And Coo Strategy And Boutique Operations, Barbara A. (Barb) McKenzie
Svp And Chief Risk Officer Principal Financial Group Inc. And Principal Life, Gregory B. (Greg) Elming, age 57
President Principal International, Luis Valdés, age 60, $589,288 total compensation
Chairman Principal Financial Group Asia, Rex Auyeung
Evp Principal Financial Group Inc. And Principal Life And Chief Investment Officer, Timothy M. (Tim) Dunbar, age 60, $483,577 total compensation
Svp; President Principal Financial Group Latin America, Roberto Walker
Svp And Chief Marketing Officer, Elizabeth S. (Beth) Brady
Svp And Chief Investment Officer Principal Life Insurance Company, Dennis Menken
Senior Executive Director And Head Global Fixed Income, David M. Blake
Evp And Cfo, Deanna D. Strable-Soethout, age 49, $488,846 total compensation
President United States Insurance Solutions, Amy C. Friedrich, age 47
Vice President Network Development, Lance Marshall
Regional Vice President Life, Mark Householder
Vice President Sales, Joseph Martin
Vice President Sales, Rob Elwood
Vice President Tax, Rich Wireman
Senior Vice President, Cindy Dicks

Senior Vice President Risk Management, Lou Flori
Regional Vice President, Peter Seltz
Vice President Sales, David Sandstead
Vice President, Jill Szambelan
Life Regional Vice President, Dave House
Senior Vice President Retirement Distrib, Timothy Minard
Disability Income Regional Vice President (di Rvp) Covering The States Of Indiana, Dianne Crouse
Vice President Life, Don Cooper
Regional Vice President Nonqualified Plans, Jack Leavy
Vp Human Resources, Kathleen Souhrada
Second Vice President, Lynda Markwardt
Vp Federal Government Relations, Chris Payne
Vice President, Gary Dorton
Auditors: Ernst & Young LLP

LOCATIONS

HQ: Principal Financial Group Inc
711 High Street, Des Moines, IA 50392
Phone: 515 247-5111
Web: www.principal.com

Selected Geographic Locations
Australia
Brazil
Chile
China
Hong Kong
India
Indonesia
Japan
Malaysia
Mexico
Singapore
Thailand
UK
US

PRODUCTS/OPERATIONS

2016 Sales by Segment

	$ mil.	% of total
Retirement & Investor Services	6,150	49
US Insurance Solutions	3,637	29
Principal International	1,252	10
Principal Global Investors	1,387	11
Corporate	(46.3)	-
Net realized capital gains	80	1
Adjustments	(67.6)	-
Total	**12,394**	**100**

2016 Sales

	% of total
Premiums & other considerations	43
Fees and other revenues	29
Net investment income	27
Net realized capital gains	1
Total	**100**

COMPETITORS

AIG
AXA
Aetna
Allianz
BlackRock
FMR
JPMorgan Chase
John Hancock Financial Services
Lincoln Financial Group
MassMutual
MetLife
Morgan Stanley Investment Management
PIMCO
T. Rowe Price
The Vanguard Group
Unum Group
Voya Financial

HISTORICAL FINANCIALS

Company Type: Public

Income Statement

FYE: December 31

	ASSETS ($ mil.)	NET INCOME ($ mil.)	INCOME AS % OF ASSETS	EMPLOYEES
12/17	253,941	2,310	0.9%	15,378
12/16	228,014	1,316	0.6%	14,854
12/15	218,685	1,234	0.6%	14,895
12/14	219,087	1,144	0.5%	14,873
12/13	208,191	912	0.4%	14,792
Annual Growth	**5.1%**	**26.1%**	**—**	**1.0%**

2017 Year-End Financials

Debt ratio: 1.25%
Return on equity: 20.02%
Cash ($ mil.): 2,470
Current ratio: —
Long-term debt ($ mil.): —

No. of shares (mil.): 289
Dividends
Yield: 0.0%
Payout: 23.7%
Market value ($ mil.): 20,392

	STOCK PRICE ($) FY Close	P/E High/Low	PER SHARE ($) Earnings	Dividends	Book Value
12/17	70.56	9 7	7.88	1.87	44.46
12/16	57.86	13 8	4.50	1.61	35.55
12/15	44.98	14 11	4.06	1.50	31.95
12/14	51.94	15 11	3.65	1.28	34.65
12/13	49.31	17 10	2.95	0.98	32.81
Annual Growth	**9.4%**	**— —**	**27.8%**	**17.5%**	**7.9%**

ProAssurance Corp

ProAssurance protects professional health associates — the doctors dentists and nurses of the US. One of the largest medical liability insurance providers in the nation ProAssurance is the holding company for ProAssurance Indemnity ProAssurance Casualty and other subsidiaries that sell liability coverage for health care providers primarily in the South and Midwest. Its customers include individual doctors in private practice as well as large physician groups clinics and hospitals. Its ProAssurance Specialty Insurance subsidiary writes excess and surplus (higher risk) lines of medical professional liability insurance. ProAssurance Casualty also provides some coverage for legal professionals.

Operations

ProAssurance operates through four primary segments: Specialty Property and Casualty (more than half of all sales) Workers' Compensation (about a quarter of sales) Lloyd's Syndicate and Corporate.

Physician policies make up ProAssurance's largest business accounting for about 80% of annual insurance premiums. Other key product groups include policies covering other health professionals medical facilities and legal professionals. Medmarc Casualty Insurance and Noetic Specialty Insurance write products liability coverage for medical technology and life sciences while Eastern Alliance Insurance provides workers' compensation. ProAssurance is also the majority capital provider to Lloyd's of London Syndicate 1729 which began writing business in 2014.

Geographic Reach

Although the company is licensed throughout the US its operations are concentrated in select states in the southern and midwestern US. Its largest markets — Alabama Pennsylvnia and

Texas — together account for about a third of the company's premiums.

The company owns office facilities in Alabama Michigan Nevada Tennessee and Wisconsin.

Sales and Marketing

ProAssurance employs an internal sales force to write its health care professional liability policies. It also utilizes independent agencies and brokerages.

Customers include physicians dentists specialists (including podiatrists) allied health care professionals medical facilities lawyers life science and medical technology entities.

Financial Performance

ProAssurance is able to sustain financial stability during turbulent market conditions through disciplined underwriting prudent pricing and loss reserve practices and conservative investment strategies. Revenue rose 15% to $852 million in 2014 largely due to the recent addition of workers' compensation business acquired with Eastern Alliance Insurance. The group's participation in the new Lloyd's Syndicate 1729 also drove up earnings. These increases were partially offset by a decline in net premiums for the Specialty Property and Casualty segment.

Net income has been somewhat turbulent over the past five years. It dropped 34% to $196 million in 2014 largely as a result of higher expenses related to the acquisition of Eastern Alliance Insurance and the investment in Lloyd's Syndicate 1729.

Cash flow from operations was on the decline until 2014 when it rebounded by 149% to $96 million. That turnaround was attributed to an increase in cash generated by receivables from reinsurers and a change in uncarned premiums.

Strategy

ProAssurance's plans for long-term growth are based on the controlled expansion of its existing operations and by acquiring other specialty insurance companies or books of business. The company looks to expand in both existing and new territories and product lines. For instance the firm is working to grow in fields outside of the medical professional customer base partly due to increasing competition in the physician coverage market.

The company's aggressive acquisitions are part of its strategy to better compete against larger property/casualty insurance firms as well as smaller niche providers. ProAssurance works to provide local services that cater to the liability climates of its core geographies; it also focuses on targeted customer segments (medical and legal) to allow for a deep understanding of the industries' needs. In addition to acquisitions ProAssurance expands through organic growth efforts including new product launches as well as by forming partnerships with professional associations. As part of its strategy to expand geographically its Eastern Alliance Insurance unit opened a new office in Michigan in 2014.

In late 2013 the company became a corporate member of Lloyd's of London becoming the majority capital provider to the new Syndicate 1729. The move provided ProAssurance and its subsidiaries with more direct access to international professional liability opportunities in the health care sector.

Mergers and Acquisitions

In 2013 the company expanded through the purchase of Medmarc Insurance Group a liability underwriter for medical technology and life science policies in a $154 million transaction. The purchase also added some legal professional coverage operations.

EXECUTIVES

LOCATIONS

HQ: ProAssurance Corp
100 Brookwood Place, Birmingham, AL 35209
Phone: 205 877-4400   **Fax**: 205 802-4799
Web: www.proassurance.com

PRODUCTS/OPERATIONS

2014 Sales by Segment

	% of total
Specialty Property and Casualty	58
Workers' Compensation	23
Corporate	17
Lloyd's Syndicate	2
Eliminations	-
Total	**100**

2014 Sales

	% of total
Net premium earned	82
Net investment	15
Net realized investment gains	2
Other income	1
Total	**100**

COMPETITORS

Berkshire Hathaway	NCMIC
CNA Financial	Physicians' Reciprocal
COPIC	Insurers
Coverys	Princeton Insurance
Dentists Insurance	Company
Company	State Volunteer Mutual
EDIC	Insurance
Markel	The Doctors Company
Medical Liability	Travelers Companies
Mutual Insurance	White Mountains
Monitor Liability	Insurance Group
Managers Inc.	

HISTORICAL FINANCIALS

Company Type: Public

Income Statement

FYE: December 31

	ASSETS ($ mil.)	NET INCOME ($ mil.)	INCOME AS % OF ASSETS	EMPLOYEES
12/17	4,929	107	2.2%	994
12/16	5,065	151	3.0%	965
12/15	4,908	116	2.4%	938
12/14	5,169	196	3.8%	967
12/13	5,150	297	5.8%	962
Annual Growth	(1.1%)	(22.5%)		0.8%

2017 Year-End Financials

Debt ratio: 8.35%
Return on equity: 6.32%
Cash ($ mil.): 134
Current ratio: —
Long-term debt ($ mil.): —

No. of shares (mil.): 53
Dividends
 Yield: 0.1%
 Payout: 296.5%
Market value ($ mil.): 3,055

	STOCK PRICE ($) FY Close	P/E High/Low	Earnings	Dividends	Book Value
12/17	57.15	31 26	2.00	5.93	29.83
12/16	56.20	22 16	2.83	5.93	33.78
12/15	48.53	25 21	2.11	2.24	36.88
12/14	45.15	15 13	3.30	3.86	38.17
12/13	48.48	11 9	4.80	1.05	39.13
Annual Growth	4.2%	—	— (19.7%)	54.2%	(6.6%)

Procter & Gamble Company (The)

The Procter & Gamble Company (P&G) boasts dozens of billion-dollar brands for home and health. The world's largest maker of consumer packaged goods divides its business into five global segments that comprise its vast portfolio of hair skin and personal oral family feminine and baby care product lines. About two dozen of P&G's brands are billion-dollar sellers including Always Braun Crest Fusion Gillette Head & Shoulders Mach3 Olay Oral-B and Pantene as well as Bounty Charmin Dawn Downy Gain Pampers and Tide. Other major brands include Febreze Mr. Clean Old Spice and Swiffer. In 2016 P&G sold a significant portion of its Beauty segment's products to beauty products company Coty for $11.4 billion.

HISTORY

Candle maker William Procter and soap maker James Gamble merged their small Cincinnati businesses in 1837 creating The Procter & Gamble Company (P&G) which incorporated in 1890. By 1859 P&G had become one of the largest companies in Cincinnati with sales of $1 million. It introduced Ivory a floating soap in 1879 and Crisco shortening in 1911.

The Ivory campaign was one of the first to advertise directly to the consumer. Other advertising innovations included sponsorship of daytime radio dramas in 1932. P&G's first TV commercial for Ivory aired in 1939.

Family members headed the company until 1930 when William Deupree became president. In the 29 years that Deupree served as president and then chairman P&G became the largest US seller of packaged goods.

After years of researching cleansers for use in hard water P&G introduced Tide detergent in 1947. It began a string of acquisitions when it picked up Spic and Span (1945; sold 2001) Duncan Hines (1956; sold 1998) Charmin Paper Mills (1957) and Folgers Coffee (1963 sold 2008). P&G launched Crest toothpaste in 1955 and Head & Shoulders shampoo and Pampers disposable diapers in 1961.

Rely tampons were pulled from shelves in 1980 when investigators linked them to toxic shock syndrome. In 1985 P&G moved into health care when it purchased Richardson-Vicks (NyQuil Vicks) and G.D. Searle's nonprescription drug division (Metamucil). The acquisitions of Noxell (1989; CoverGirl Noxzema) and Max Factor (1991) made it a top cosmetics company in the US. (It sold Noxzema in 2008.)

P&G began a major restructuring in 1993 cutting 13000 jobs and closing 30 plants. The firm acquired Eagle Snacks from Anheuser-Busch in 1996 and sued rival Amway over rumors connecting P&G and its moon-and-stars logo to Satanism. (The suit was dismissed in 1999.) Also in 1996 the FDA approved the use of olestra a controversial fat substitute developed by P&G.

In 1997 it acquired Tambrands (Tampax tampons) making P&G #1 in feminine sanitary protection. Impatient with progress on its sales goals in 1998 P&G began restructuring to focus on global business units rather than geographic regions. Chairman John Pepper handed over his chairman and CEO title in 1999 to president Durk Jager who promised five new products a year and a shakeup of the corporate culture.

In 1999 the company announced further reorganization plans including 15000 job cuts worldwide by 2005. That same year P&G bought The Iams Company (maker of Eukanuba- and Iams-brand dog and cat foods).

With earnings flat Jager resigned in 2000. P&G insider Alan G. Lafley immediately assumed the president and CEO duties and Pepper returned to succeed Jager as chairman.

In 2001 P&G announced job cuts for 9600 employees to further reduce costs. It also sold its Comet cleaner business. That year P&G completed its purchase of the Clairol hair care company from Bristol-Myers Squibb for nearly $5 billion.

In 2002 P&G closed three Clairol plants one warehouse and one distribution center — eliminating about 750 jobs. Production of Clairol products was moved to existing P&G plants. It also sold its olestra plant in Cincinnati to Twin Rivers Technologies but retained ownership of the Olean brand and technology. Additionally it sold its Jif peanut butter and Crisco shortening brands to J.M. Smucker and several personal care brands (including Sea Breeze and Vitalis) to Helen of Troy.

In 2002 P&G branched out in a joint venture with Clorox to help it improve the Glad-brand plastic bags and wraps. P&G held a 10% stake in the Glad venture until late 2004 when the company invested another $133 million to boost its stake to 20% the limit allowed by the agreement.

Also that year Lafley announced that P&G had completed its multiyear restructuring and would stop reporting two sets of results (one with restructuring charges and one without).

Further expanding its hair care segment and building on its successes with Clairol P&G purchased the first of several stakes in Wella in 2003 (it now owns the entire company). That year P&G also entered the premium pet food market with its purchase of The Iams Company for $2.3 billion. And to secure its foothold in China P&G bought the remaining 20% stake in its joint venture with partner Hutchison Whampoa China Ltd. in 2004 for $1.8 billion.

P&G bought four brands to sell in Southeast Asia in its effort to erode market share from Unilever. In 2005 P&G purchased Fab Trojan Dynamo and Paic laundry brands sold in Hong Kong Singapore Thailand and Malaysia from Colgate-Palmolive.

The company reached its lofty spot as the world's largest consumer products company in 2005 through one of its boldest moves — buying Boston based The Gillette Company for about $57 billion. Overnight the ambitious deal gave P&G the golden ticket to leapfrog over former #1 supplier Unilever. P&G's purchase of Gillette added well-known complementary brands to its already vast portfolio such as Gillette razors and blades Duracell batteries Oral-B oral care items and Braun appliances.

In 2006 P&G paired up with ARYx Therapeutics to develop that company's gastrointestinal disorder treatment.

In 2007 P&G paired its marketing savvy with the diagnostics expertise of Inverness Medical Innovations to form a joint venture company called SPD Swiss Precision Diagnostics. The joint venture makes and markets in-home diagnostic products including pregnancy tests and ovulation/fertility monitoring products under the Clearblue PERSONA Accu-Clear and other names. P&G paid $325 million for its 50% stake in the venture.

EXECUTIVES

Group President Global Grooming, Charles E. Pierce, age 62

Chairman President And Ceo, David S. Taylor, age 60, $1,393,333 total compensation

Group President North America Selling And Market Operations, Carolyn Tastad, age 55

Group President Global Health Care, Steven D. (Steve) Bishop, age 54, $796,667 total compensation

Group President Global Fabric And Home Care, Giovanni Ciserani, age 56, $845,833 total compensation

Group President Global Family Care, Mary L. Ferguson-McHugh, age 59

President Global Personal Health Care, Thomas M. Finn, age 56

Vice Chairman And Cfo, Jon R. Moeller, age 54, $950,000 total compensation

Global Design Officer, Philip J Duncan, age 53

Cio, Linda W. Clement-Holmes, age 56

Global Product Supply Officer, Yannis Skoufalos, age 60

President Beauty Specialty Businesses, Colleen E. Jay, age 56

President Europe Selling & Market Operations, Gary Coombe

Cto, Kathleen B. (Kathy) Fish

President India Middle East And Africa Selling And Market Operations, Mohamed Samir

President Global Home Care And P&g Professional, George Tsourapas, age 58

President Global Fabric Care And Brand Building Organization Global Fabric And Home Care, Shailesh G. Jejurikar

President Global Skin And Personal Care, R. Alexandra Keith

President Global Business Services, Julio Nemeth

President Latin America Selling And Market Operations, Juan F. Posada

President Greater China Selling And Market Operations, Matthew S. Price

President Asia/pacific Selling And Market Operations, Magesvaran Suranjan

Vice President, Charlene Patten

Vice President, Jerry Vikara

Vice President Sales, Matthew Zirkle

Chief Sales Officer Reinvention Training Developer, Ryan P Siereveld

Vp And Associate General Counsel, Ken Patel

Vice President Of Communications, Lisa Bartz

Chief Sales Officer Team Operations Leader, Kelly Horton

Vice President Sales, Frank Craft

Vice President Global Investor Relations, John T Chevalier

Vice President, Patrick Conklin

Vice President Operations, Dawn Seiler

Call Center Customer Service Director Vice President, Ron Chisholm

Director Managed Care, Debbie Burge

Vice President New Business Creation, J Brad Lang

Chief Sales Officer Om Analyst, Greg Ribeiro

National Account Manager, Oliver Seaman

Vice President And General Manager Research And Development, Petra Hanke-baier

Chief Sales Officer Manager Romania, Georgeta Parchisanu

Vice President And General Manager Asia Pacific, Omar Channawi

Vice President Of Sales, Ingrid Jones

Vice President Female Beauty Latin America, Gerardo Rios

Vice President Management Systems, Frank Caccamo

Vice President Of Facilities Planning, Jalal Zarhoun

Vp Hr, Bryan Thompson

National Sales Manager, Lisa Richards

Vice President And Brand Franchise Leader (baby Care), Stefano Volpetti

Vice President Human Resources India Middle East Africa And Global Fabric And Home Care, Jamal Berradia

Senior Vice President Go To Market China, Henry Karamanoukian

Vp Global Consumer And Market Knowledge, Kirti Singh

Vice President, Kim Kraus

National Sales Manager, Sara J Lackman

Vice President Of Manufacturing, Antonio Musile

Vice President, Luis Amaro

Sr V Pres-comptroller-treas, Valarie Sheppard

Board Member, Mike Eftink

Board Member, BO Passey

Secretary, Jenny Tan

Abm, Christina Morazzani

Assistant Treasurer, Douglas Gerstle

Secretary, Julie Taylor

Abm, Marta Roballo

Secretary Treasurer, Dave Seidel

Board Member, John Biscotti

Auditors: Deloitte & Touche LLP

LOCATIONS

HQ: Procter & Gamble Company (The)
One Procter & Gamble Plaza, Cincinnati, OH 45202
Phone: 513 983-1100
Web: www.pg.com

2016 Sales

	% of total
North America	44
Europe	23
Asia Pacific	9
China	8
India Middle East and Africa (IMEA)	8
Latin America	8
Total	**100**

PRODUCTS/OPERATIONS

2016 Sales

	% of total
Fabric Care and Home Care	32
Baby Care and Family Care	28
Beauty	18
Health Care	11
Grooming	10
Corporate	1
Total	**100**

Selected Segments and Brands

Fabric Care & Home Care
  Ariel
  Dawn
  Downy
  Febreze
  Gain
  Tide
Beauty
  Head & Shoulders
  Olay
  Old Spice
  Pantene
  SK-II
Baby Feminine & Family Care
  Always
  Bounty
  Charmin
  Luvs
  Pampers
  Tampax
Health Care
  Crest
  Oral-B
  Vicks
Grooming
  Braun
  Fusion
  Gillette
  Mach3
  Venus

COMPETITORS

Alticor	Mary Kay
Amway	Meda Pharmaceuticals
Avon	Nestlé
BIC	Pfizer
Bath & Body Works	Philips Electronics
Baxter of California	Revlon
Body Shop	Russell Hobbs
Bristol-Myers Squibb	S.C. Johnson
Church & Dwight	SANYO
Clorox	SEB
Colgate-Palmolive	Sanofi
Discus Dental	Scott's Liquid Gold
Dr. Bronner's	Shiseido
Edgewell Personal Care	Spectrum Brands
Estée Lauder	Tom's of Maine
Henkel	Turtle Wax
Johnson & Johnson	Unilever PLC
Kimberly-Clark	VIVUS
L'Oréal	

HISTORICAL FINANCIALS

Company Type: Public

Income Statement

FYE: June 30

	REVENUE ($ mil.)	NET INCOME ($ mil.)	NET PROFIT MARGIN	EMPLOYEES
06/18	66,832	9,750	14.6%	92,000
06/17	65,058	15,326	23.6%	95,000
06/16	65,299	10,508	16.1%	105,000
06/15	76,279	7,036	9.2%	110,000
06/14	83,062	11,643	14.0%	118,000
Annual Growth	(5.3%)	(4.3%)	—	(6.0%)

2018 Year-End Financials

Debt ratio: 26.44%—
Return on equity: 18.14%
Cash ($ mil.): 2,569
Current ratio: 0.83
Long-term debt ($ mil.): 20,863

Dividends
  Yield: 0.0%
  Payout: 75.9%
Market value ($ mil.): —

	STOCK PRICE ($) FY Close	P/E High/Low	PER SHARE ($) Earnings	Dividends	Book Value
06/18	78.06	25 19	3.67	2.79	20.93
06/17	87.15	16 14	5.59	2.70	21.61
06/16	84.67	22 18	3.69	2.66	21.49
06/15	78.24	37 31	2.44	2.59	22.99
06/14	78.59	20 18	4.01	2.45	25.53
Annual Growth	(0.2%)	— —	(2.2%)	3.3%	(4.8%)

Progressive Corp. (OH)

The Progressive Corporation long a leader in nonstandard high-risk personal auto insurance has motored beyond its traditional business into standard-risk and preferred auto insurance as well as other personal-use vehicle coverage (think motorcycles RVs and snowmobiles). Its insurance carriers include majority-owned American Strategic Insurance. Progressive also offers commercial policies for heavy trucks vans and lighter trucks. It writes a bit of professional liability insurance for directors and officers as well as residential property insurance for homeowners. The company markets directly to consumers online and by phone and through more than 35000 independent agents who account for the majority of its business.

Operations

Progressive operates through five reportable segments: Personal Lines (the largest segment accounting for more than 80% of total revenue) Commercial Lines (about 10% of revenue) Property Other Indemnity (run-off operations) Service Businesses and Reinsurance.

The company primarily offers coverage to auto insurance customers underwritten by third-party insurance carriers. Progressive also offers personal umbrella insurance that provides coverage for the extras in life such as personal injury and legal defense. Majority-owned subsidiary American Strategic Insurance provides home insurance. Progressive had 18.2 million policies in force at the end of 2017.

Geographic Reach

Progressive operates throughout the US; it also sells personal auto insurance online in Australia.

In addition to its headquarters additional offices call center warehouse space and service centers in Mayfield Village Ohio the company owns locations in Colorado Springs Colorado; Tampa and St. Petersburg Florida; and Tempe Arizona.

Sales and Marketing

Progressive's US customer service group (which support policy servicing agency distribution claims and direct sales operations) is located at call centers in Mayfield Village Ohio; Tampa and St. Petersburg Florida; Sacramento California; Tempe Arizona; and Colorado Springs Colorado.

The company sells its personal lines through more than 35000 independent agencies and through partnerships with other insurance companies and financial institutions. It also sells directly to customers online and by telephone.

Commercial lines are distributed directly and through independent agencies.

Total advertising costs in 2017 totaled $1 billion versus $756.2 million in 2016 and $748.3 million in 2015.

Financial Performance

Organic growth has lifted the company's revenues every year since 2008. Revenue grew 14% to $26.8 billion in 2017 as net premiums earned increased. Most significantly Personal Lines premiums rose to $21.9 billion but Commercial Lines grew as well. Investment income and fees and service revenue also rose that year.

Net income which fell in 2015 and 2016 rebounded in 2017. It increased 54% to $1.6 billion that year largely due to revenue growth.

Cash flow from operations has generally been rising for the past few years. In 2017 operating cash flow increased 18% to $3.8 billion. That improvement was driven by positive changes in unearned premiums and loss adjustment taxes payable.

Strategy

Unlike some insurers who in fat markets earn more from their investments than their premiums more than 90% of Progressive's revenues have historically come from policy premiums.

The company's actual insurance operations have remained profitable and have grown as it has entered into new geographic markets and expanded the online distribution of its personal auto products. Already among the leading US auto insurers based on premiums (just behind State Farm and Allstate) Progressive is aiming to be on top.

The auto insurance industry is highly competitive with large carriers and regional carriers competing for market share. Because it is fairly easy for customers to switch auto insurers Progressive competes on price and accessibility. To attract new customers the company's television ads featuring its perky spokesperson "Flo" have shot up the company's brand recognition. Operating on the premise that a few drivers are responsible for the majority of claims and that previous risk models were incomplete Progressive is now also offering rates that are tied to actual usage.

Another key strategy for Progressive is to continue making its move into the home insurance market. It has been promoting its residential products through bundled packages with lower auto rates. In 2017 the company began re-branding its majority-owned homeowners' insurance carrier American Strategic Insurance to the Progressive name to make it easier to sell auto and home bundles. This cross-selling strategy comes with a retention benefit: Once a customer has bought a bundled package of home/auto/umbrella coverage they are also much less likely to switch insurance providers.

All of these strategies have helped the company continue its growing streak. It has added more than 2000 new net jobs every year since 2015 and it plans to add more than 3000 in 2018 alone.

HISTORY

Attorneys Jack Green and Joseph Lewis founded Progressive Mutual Insurance in Cleveland in 1937. Initially offering standard auto insurance the company attracted customers through such innovations as installment plans for premiums (a payment method popularized during the Depression) and drive-in claims services (the company was headquartered in a garage). Progressive's early years were uncertain — at one point the founders were even advised to go out of business — but the advent of WWII bolstered business: Car and insurance purchases were up but accidents were down as gas rationing limited driving.

Then came the suburbs and cars of the 1950s. While most competitors sought low-risk drivers Progressive exploited the high-risk niche through careful underwriting and statistical analysis. Subsidiary Progressive Casualty was founded in 1956 (the year after Joseph Lewis died) to insure the best of the worst. Lewis' son Peter joined the company in 1955 and helped engineer its early-1960s expansion outside Ohio. After Green retired in 1965 Peter gained control of the company through a leveraged buyout and renamed it The Progressive Corporation. Six years later Lewis took it public and formed subsidiary Progressive American in Florida.

In the mid-1970s the industry went into a funk as it was hit by a wave of consolidations and rising interest rates. Lewis set a goal for the company to always earn an underwriting profit instead of depending on investments to make a profit. Progressive achieved stellar results during the 1970s especially after states began requiring drivers to be insured and other insurers began weeding out higher risks.

Competition in nonstandard insurance grew in the 1980s as major insurers such as Allstate and State Farm joined the fray with their larger sales forces and deeper pockets. In 1988 California's Proposition 103 retroactively reduced rates; Progressive fought California's demand for refunds but set aside reserves to pay them.

That year Lewis hired Cleveland financier Alfred Lerner to guide company investments. Lerner invested $75 million in Progressive via a convertible debenture; five years later he converted it to stock half of which he sold for $122 million. Soon after he was asked to resign. In 1993 Progressive settled with California for $51 million and applied to earnings the remaining $100 million in refund reserves. (Company soul-searching related to Proposition 103 led to the launch of Progressive's now-famous "Immediate Response" vehicles which provide 24-hour claims service at accident sites.)

In 1995 Progressive's practice of using consumer credit information to make underwriting decisions drew the attention of Arkansas and Vermont insurance regulators who said the company might be discriminating against people who didn't have the credit cards Progressive used to evaluate creditworthiness. In 1996 insurance regulators in Alaska Maryland and Texas also began probing Progressive's credit information practices.

In 1997 Progressive bought nonstandard auto insurer Midland Financial Group. As competition grew in 1999 the company cut rates and said it would write no new policies in Canada. In 2000 — with underwriting margins dropping industrywide — the company continued advertising aggressively. Progressive stopped writing new homeowners insurance in 2002 instead concentrating on its core operations. In 2006 the company began offering personal umbrella coverage.

The company took a bold international expansion measure in 2009: Launching personal auto insurance online in Australia. International expansion has not been a key strategy for Progressive but apparently the time was right for such growth. And apparently the company is prepared to give the new operation time to grow which is good considering that it has not yet made significant contributions to overall revenues.

EXECUTIVES

Chief Investment Officer, William M. (Bill) Cody, age 56, $463,269 total compensation
President And Ceo, S. Patricia (Tricia) Griffith, age 54, $616,346 total compensation
President Commercial Lines Group, John A. Barbagallo, age 59, $463,269 total compensation
Cfo, John P. Sauerland, age 54, $546,538 total compensation
Chief Legal Officer, Dan Mascaro
President Personal Lines, Patrick K. (Pat) Callahan, age 47
President Claims, Michael D. (Mike) Sieger, age 56
Cio, Steven A. (Steve) Broz, age 47
Customer Relationship Management President, John Murphy, age 48
Medical Director, Crystal Kastberg
Vice President Of Human Resources, Kathy Cramer
Chairman, Glenn M. Renwick, age 63
Treasurer, Patrick Brennan
Treasurer, Amy Marsh
Auditors: PricewaterhouseCoopers LLP

LOCATIONS

HQ: Progressive Corp. (OH)
6300 Wilson Mills Road, Mayfield Village, OH 44143
Phone: 440 461-5000 **Fax:** 440 446-7168
Web: www.progressive.com

PRODUCTS/OPERATIONS

2017 Sales

	$ mil.	% of total
Personal lines	21,947	82
Commercial auto	2,793	10
Property	988	4
Investments	612	2
Fees & other	370	1
Services	126	1
Adjustments	(1.0)	-
Total	**26,839**	**100**

Selected Insurance Options

Auto Insurance
Local Car Insurance
Motorcycle Insurance
Boat Insurance
RV Insurance
Commercial Insurance
Snowmobile Insurance
PWC Insurance
Homeowners Insurance
Renters Insurance
ATV Insurance
Life Insurance
Health Insurance
Umbrella Insurance

COMPETITORS

21st Century Insurance	Liberty Mutual
Allstate	Nationwide
American Family	Old Republic
Insurance	State Auto Financial
Cincinnati Financial	State Farm
Farmers Group	Travelers Companies
GEICO	USAA
Infinity Property &	
Casualty	

HISTORICAL FINANCIALS

Company Type: Public

Income Statement

FYE: December 31

	ASSETS ($ mil.)	NET INCOME ($ mil.)	INCOME AS % OF ASSETS	EMPLOYEES
12/17	38,701	1,592	4.1%	33,656
12/16	33,427	1,031	3.1%	31,721
12/15	29,819	1,267	4.3%	28,580
12/14	25,787	1,281	5.0%	26,501
12/13	24,408	1,165	4.8%	26,145
Annual Growth	**12.2%**	**8.1%**	**—**	**6.5%**

2017 Year-End Financials

Debt ratio: 8.54%
Return on equity: 18.47%
Cash ($ mil.): 275
Current ratio: —
Long-term debt ($ mil.): —
No. of shares (mil.): 581
Dividends
  Yield: 0.0%
  Payout: 25.0%
Market value ($ mil.): 32,761

	STOCK PRICE ($) FY Close	P/E High/Low	PER SHARE ($) Earnings	Dividends	Book Value
12/17	56.32	21 13	2.72	0.68	15.96
12/16	35.50	20 17	1.76	0.89	13.72
12/15	31.80	16 12	2.15	0.69	12.49
12/14	26.99	13 10	2.15	1.49	11.79
12/13	27.27	14 11	1.93	1.28	10.39
Annual Growth	**19.9%**	**— —**	**9.0%**	**(14.7%)**	**11.3%**

Prosperity Bancshares Inc.

Prosperity Bancshares reaches banking customers across the Lone Star State. The holding company for Prosperity Bank operates about 230 branches across Texas and about 15 more in Oklahoma. Serving consumers and small to midsized businesses the bank offers traditional deposit and loan services in addition to wealth management retail brokerage and mortgage banking investment services. Prosperity Bank focuses on real estate lending: Commercial mortgages make up the largest segment of the company's loan portfolio (33%) followed by residential mortgages (24%). Credit cards business auto consumer home equity loans round out its lending activities.

Operations

About 63% of Prosperity's total revenue came from loan interest (including fees) in 2014 while another 22% came from interest on its investment securities. The rest of its revenue came from non-sufficient fund fees (4%) credit and debit card income (3%) deposit account service charges (2%) trust income (1%) mortgage income (1%) and brokerage income (1%).

Geographic Reach

Prosperity Bancshares operates 230 Texas banking locations across Houston South Texas the Dallas/Fort Worth metroplex East Texas Bryan/College Station Central Texas and West Texas. It also has 15 branch locations in Oklahoma (including Tulsa).

Sales and Marketing

The bank mainly targets consumers and small and medium-sized businesses and tailors its products to the specific needs of a given market.

Financial Performance

Prosperity's revenues and profits have been prospering thanks to loan and deposit business growth from acquisitions and declining loan loss provisions as its loan portfolio's credit quality has improved with higher property valuations in a strengthened economy.

The company's revenue jumped by 32% to $837.7 million in 2014 mostly as its loan interest income swelled by 40% on loan asset growth from its F&M acquisition. The bank's non-interest income rose by 29% as well from new deposit account service fees from the acquisition and additional income from its newly added brokerage and trust business.

Higher revenue and strong operating cost controls in 2014 drove Prosperity's net income higher by 34% to $297.4 million while its operating cash levels rose by 13% to $348.3 million on higher cash earnings.

Strategy

Prosperity Bancshares bases its growth strategy on three key elements: Internal loan and deposit business growth through "individualized customer service" and service line expansion opportunities; cost controls to maximize profitability; and acquisitions.

Toward its internal business growth initiatives Prosperity spent 2012 and 2013 launching its new trust brokerage mortgage lending and credit card products and services to customers for the first time.

With cost-controls in mind the bank tracks its branches "as separate profit centers" noting each branch's interest income efficiency ratio deposit growth loan growth and overall profitability. That way it can reward individual branch managers and

presidents accordingly by merit rather than giving higher compensation across the board.

The acquisitive Prosperity Bancshares has been buying up small banks in Texas — and now Oklahoma — as it hopes to hit a sweet spot in the market between the national giants that dominate the Texas banking scene and smaller community banks.

Mergers and Acquisitions

In January 2016 furthering its presence in the Houston market Prosperity Bancshares purchased Tradition Bancshares along with its seven branches in the Houston Area (Bellaire Katy and the Woodlands) $540 million in assets $239 million in loans and $483.8 million in deposits.

In April 2014 toward expansion in the Oklahoma and Dallas markets Prosperity purchased Tulsa-based F&M Bancorporation and its subsidiary The F&M Bank & Trust Company. The deal added 13 branches including nine in Tulsa and surrounding areas three in Dallas and a loan production office in Oklahoma City.

In April 2013 it acquired Coppermark Bank one of Oklahoma City's largest banks with six branches in Oklahoma City and three locations in North Dallas for $194 million. The deal also added the credit card and agent bank merchant processing business from its subsidiary Bankers Credit Card Services.

In January 2013 the company boosted its market share in East Texas after buying East Texas Financial Services and its four First Federal Bank Texas branch locations including three branches in Tyler and one in Gilmer.

Company Background

In early 2012 Prosperity acquired Texas Bankers a three-branch Austin bank with some $72 million in assets. The merger increased Prosperity's number of Central Texas branches to 34 banking locations. It followed that deal with the purchase of The Bank Arlington a single-branch bank operating in the Dallas/Ft. Worth area. It acquired single-branch Community National Bank of Bellaire Texas in late 2012.

Also in 2012 Prosperity expanded into West Texas after it merged American State Financial Corporation and its American State Bank subsidiary into its operations. The deal added $3 billion in assets and 37 West Texas banking offices in Lubbock Midland/Odessa and Abilene.

EXECUTIVES

Executive Vice President Cashier Prosperity Bank, Michael Harris

Evp Cashier Prosperity Bank, Mike Harris

Senior Chairman And Ceo, David Zalman, age 61, $851,567 total compensation

Cfo; Evp And Cfo Prosperity Bank, David Hollaway, age 62, $425,000 total compensation

Vice Chairman; Chairman And Coo Prosperity Bank, H. E. (Tim) Timanus, age 74, $452,400 total compensation

Vice Chairman And Area Chairman Central Texas, Edward Z. (Eddie) Safady

Evp Regulatory And Compliance Prosperity Bank, Rhonda L. Carroll

Chief Lending Officer Prosperity Bank, Randy D. Hester, $325,000 total compensation

Sevp Financial Operations And Administration Prosperity Bank, Mike Epps, $327,625 total compensation

Evp And Cio Prosperity Bank, Gisela Riggan

Chief Risk Oficer, Jennifer Willcoxon

Chief Credit Officer Prosperity Bank, Merle Karnes

President Prosperity Bank, Bob Benter

Evp Prosperity Bancshares And Prosperity Bank, Robert (Bob) Dowdell

Chairman Wealth Management, Russell Marshall

Senior Vice President Sales And Marketing, Scott Voland

Senior Vice President Sba Lending, Beverly Layne
Assistant Vice President Of Technology
Procurement, Lausanne Barrett
Vice President, Stephanie Collier
Senior Vice President Iso Sponsorship Program,
Jamie Bigley
Vice President Manager, Donna Brune
Assistant Vice President Lobby Manager, Barbara
Wilsher
Vice President Lobby Manager, Jana Rachunek
Assistant Vice President Lobby Manager, Bennie
Gallentine
Vice President, Bill Hailey
Senior Vice President, Jennifer Gortney
Vice President, Candi Biggers
Executive Vice President, Cathy Waller
Senior Vice President Accounting, Duncan Mcadoo
Assistant Vice President Lending Area, Betty
Kindred
Vice President, Cecil Childers
Senior Vice President, Tim Cardinal
Board Member, Perry Mueller
Board Member, Leah Henderson
Auditors: Deloitte & Touche LLP

LOCATIONS

HQ: Prosperity Bancshares Inc.
Prosperity Bank Plaza, 4295 San Felipe, Houston, TX
77027
Phone: 281 269-7199
Web: www.prosperitybankusa.com

PRODUCTS/OPERATIONS

2014 Sales

	$ mil.	% of total
Interest		
Loans including fees	525	63
Securities	188	22
Federal funds sold	0	-
Noninterest		
Non-sufficient funds fees	37	4
Debit card and ATM card income	22	3
Service charges on deposit accounts	16	2
Trust income	8	1
Brokerage income	5	1
Mortgage income	4	1
Other	28	3
Total	**837**	**100**

COMPETITORS

Amegy	JPMorgan Chase
BBVA Compass	North Dallas Bank
Bancshares	Texas Capital
Bank of America	Bancshares
Citibank	Wells Fargo
Comerica	Woodforest Financial
Cullen/Frost Bankers	

HISTORICAL FINANCIALS

Company Type: Public

Income Statement

FYE: December 31

	ASSETS ($ mil.)	NET INCOME ($ mil.)	INCOME AS % OF ASSETS	EMPLOYEES
12/17	22,587	272	1.2%	3,035
12/16	22,331	274	1.2%	3,035
12/15	22,037	286	1.3%	3,037
12/14	21,507	297	1.4%	3,096
12/13	18,642	221	1.2%	2,995
Annual Growth	**4.9%**	**5.3%**	**—**	**0.3%**

2017 Year-End Financials

Debt ratio: 2.24%
Return on equity: 7.29%
Cash ($ mil.): 391
Current ratio: —
Long-term debt ($ mil.): —

No. of shares (mil.): 69
Dividends
Yield: 0.0%
Payout: 35.2%
Market value ($ mil.): 4,869

	STOCK PRICE ($) FY Close	P/E High/Low	PER SHARE ($) Earnings	Dividends	Book Value
12/17	70.07	20 14	3.92	1.38	55.03
12/16	71.78	19 9	3.94	1.24	52.41
12/15	47.86	14 11	4.09	1.12	49.45
12/14	55.36	16 12	4.32	0.99	46.50
12/13	63.39	18 11	3.65	0.89	42.19
Annual Growth	**2.5%**	**— —**	**1.8%**	**11.7%**	**6.9%**

Protective Life Insurance Co

Protective Life & Annuity markets and sells financial security in the form of term and universal life insurance policies and fixed and variable annuity products. Although the company is based in Alabama and licensed to sell insurance throughout the US it exclusively serves clients in New York. Sister companies include West Coast Life Insurance (life insurance and annuities) MONY Life Insurance (ditto) and Lyndon Insurance (specialty coverage). Protective Life & Annuity is a unit of Protective Life Insurance which is part of Dai-Ichi Life Holdings subsidiary Protective Life Corporation.

Operations

Every state has unique requirements that insurance companies must meet in order to gain permission to operate there. New York's insurance code has the stiffest requirements and many small companies simply choose not to operate in that market. However the market is so large and tempting that other companies opt to maintain separate subsidiaries that exclusively serve New York. In this instance parent company Protective Life Insurance Company serves the rest of the US while Protective Life & Annuity is strictly focused on New York.

Protective Life Corporation was acquired by Japanese insurer Dai-ichi Life in early 2015.

Sales and Marketing

Protective Life & Annuity sells coverage through independent agents broker-dealers and financial institutions as well as through partnerships with employer groups and through its own sales division.

EXECUTIVES

Evp Chief Legal Officer Secretary And General
Counsel, Deborah J. Long, age 64
Chairman And Ceo, John D. Johns, age 65
Evp And Chief Investment Officer, Carl S. Thigpen,
age 61
Evp And Chief Administrative Officer, D. Scott
Adams, age 53
President And Coo, Richard J. Bielen
Evp Finance And Risk; Chief Risk Officer, Michael
G. (Mike) Temple, age 55
Svp Chief Information And Operations Officer,
Mark J. Cyphert
Evp Cfo And Controller, Steven G. Walker
Vice President Of Marketing, Teri Schultz
Auditors: PricewaterhouseCoopers LLP

LOCATIONS

HQ: Protective Life Insurance Co
2801 Highway 280 South, Birmingham, AL 35223
Phone: 205 268-1000
Web: www.protective.com

COMPETITORS

Guardian Insurance and	Penn Mutual
Annuity	Prudential
MetLife	The Hartford
New York Life	

HISTORICAL FINANCIALS

Company Type: Public

Income Statement

FYE: December 31

	ASSETS ($ mil.)	NET INCOME ($ mil.)	INCOME AS % OF ASSETS	EMPLOYEES
12/17	79,113	1,182	1.5%	2,773
12/16	74,465	352	0.5%	2,719
12/15*	68,031	179	0.3%	2,541
01/15	0	88	—	
12/14	69,992	491	0.7%	2,457
Annual Growth	**4.2%**	**34.0%**	**—**	**4.1%**

*Fiscal year change

2017 Year-End Financials

Debt ratio: 5.02%
Return on equity: 15.70%
Cash ($ mil.): 178
Current ratio: —
Long-term debt ($ mil.):

No. of shares (mil.): 5
Dividends
Yield: —
Payout: 21.9%
Market value ($ mil.): —

PROVIDENCE HEALTH & SERVICES

EXECUTIVES

Ceo, Rod Hochman
Pres- Chief Dev Officer, Laurie Kelley
Exec V Pres-Cfo, Todd Hofheins
Information Technology/Interne, Michael Antrim
Materials Manager, Mike Minnick
Training Specialist, Sheryl Regan
Technology, Henry Morgan
Database Administrator, Jack Hwang
Human Resources Analyst, Kay Barksdale
Customer Staff, Patricia M McConnell
Program Manager, Mark Sizemore
Auditors: CLARK NUBER PS BELLEVUE WA

LOCATIONS

HQ: PROVIDENCE HEALTH & SERVICES
1801 LIND AVE SW, RENTON, WA 980573368
Phone: 425 525-3355
Web: WWW.PROVIDENCE.ORG

HISTORICAL FINANCIALS

Company Type: Private

Income Statement				FYE: December 31
	REVENUE ($ mil.)	NET INCOME ($ mil.)	NET PROFIT MARGIN	EMPLOYEES
12/15	14,433	49	0.3%	9,700
12/12	280	14	5.3%	—
12/08	7,026	(166)	—	—
12/07	6,348	434	6.8%	—
Annual Growth	10.8%	(23.8%)		

2015 Year-End Financials

Debt ratio: ——
Return on equity: 0.30%
Cash ($ mil.): 729
Current ratio: 1.00
Long-term debt ($ mil.): —

Dividends
Yield: —
Payout: —
Market value ($ mil.): —

Provident Financial Services Inc

Provident wants to be a prominent force in the New Jersey banking scene. Provident Financial Services owns The Provident Bank which serves individuals businesses and families from 85 branches across more than 10 northern and central New Jersey counties. Founded in 1839 the $8.5 billion-bank offers traditional deposit and lending products as well as wealth management and trust services. About 50% of its revenue comes from real estate loan interest while another 25% comes from interest on commercial and consumer loans. Construction loans round out its lending activities. The company's Provident Investment Services subsidiary sells life and health insurance and investment products.

Operations

Provident which staffed more than 1020 employees boasted some $8.5 billion in total assets loans of $6.1 billion and deposits of $5.8 billion at the end of 2014. Mortgages loans made up 70% of its total loan portfolio that year.

Geographic Reach

The bank's 86 branches are located in northern and central New Jersey as well as in Pennsylvania (in the Bucks Lehigh and Northampton counties). Its administrative offices are in Iselin New Jersey while its satellite loan production offices are in Covent Station Flemington Paramus Princeton and West Orange in New Jersey; and in Bethleham and Newtown Pennsylvania.

Sales and Marketing

Provident targets individuals families and businesses in its primary market areas in New Jersey (which covered a population of 6.9 million or 78% of the state's population) and Pennsylvania (where the bank's primary market covered 10% of that state's population.

Provident's primary markets include a mix of urban and suburban communities. It serves companies in a variety of industries including pharmaceutical and other manufacturing companies network communications insurance and financial services healthcare and retail businesses.

Financial Performance

Provident has struggled to consistently grow its revenues in recent years due to shrinking interest margins on loans amidst the low-interest environment. Its profits however have been rising thanks to declining loan loss provisions as its loan portfolio's credit quality has improved with higher property valuations in a strengthened economy.

The bank's revenue rose by 8% to $320.5 million in 2014 mostly thanks to added interest income from loan asset growth — including a 9% rise in real estate secured loan business and a 24% rise in commercial loan business — stemming from its acquisition of Team Capital Bank.

Higher revenue and a continued decline in loan loss provisions in 2014 drove Provident's net income higher by 4% to $73.6 million. Its operating cash levels dipped by 3% to $96.4 million after adjusting its earnings for non-cash items mostly related to an increase in other assets.

Strategy

Provident Financial continues to look for strategic acquisition opportunities of banks and other financial services providers to grow its loan and deposit business and extend its branch network into more of its primary market areas.

The company also remains focused on its conservative lending practices and is seeking to diversify its portfolio and reduce risk by placing more emphasis on commercial real estate multifamily residential and business loans.

Mergers and Acquisitions

In May 2014 Provident Financial Services purchased Team Capital Bank for $115.1 million effectively extending its reach into Eastern Pennsylvania and the affluent counties of Hunterdon and Somerset. The deal also added $964 million in total assets $631 million in loan assets and $770 million in deposits.

Company Background

In 2011 the company acquired Beacon Trust Company an asset manager for individuals municipalities corporations pension funds and not-for-profit organizations. The deal significantly expanded its wealth management business and boosted its assets under management to some $1.5 billion.

EXECUTIVES

Chairman President And Ceo, Christopher P. Martin, age 62, $608,846 total compensation
Evp And Cfo, Thomas M. Lyons, age 54, $349,308 total compensation
Evp And Director Retail Banking The Provident Bank, Michael A. Raimonde, age 66, $238,370 total compensation
Evp General Counsel And Corporate Secretary The Provident Bank, John F. Kuntz, age 63, $312,700 total compensation
Evp And Chief Lending Officer The Provident Bank, Donald W. Blum, age 62, $314,562 total compensation
Evp And Cio The Provident Bank, Jack Novielli, age 59
Evp And And Chief Human Resources Officer The Provident Bank, Janet D. Krasowski, age 65
Evp And Chief Credit Officer The Provident Bank, Brian Giovinazzi, age 64, $161,138 total compensation
Evp And Chief Wealth Officer The Provident Bank, James D. Nesci, age 46, $274,423 total compensation
Svp And Chief Risk Officer The Provident Bank, James Christy
First Vice President Marketing Director, Robert Capozzoli
Assistant Vice President, Joseph Labib
Assistant Vice President Branch Center Manager, Carol Viola
Senior Vice President Director Asset Recovery, Rudolph Nemeth
Auditors: KPMG LLP

LOCATIONS

HQ: Provident Financial Services Inc
239 Washington Street, Jersey City, NJ 07302
Phone: 732 590-9200
Web: www.providentnj.com

PRODUCTS/OPERATIONS

2014 Sales

	$ mil.	% of total
Interest		
Real estate secured loans	166	52
Commercial loans	50	16
Consumer loans	23	7
Securities & other	38	12
Non-interest		
Fees	31	10
Other	9	3
Total	**320**	**100**

COMPETITORS

Bank of America
Capital One
Citibank
Hudson City Bancorp
JPMorgan Chase
New York Community Bancorp

PNC Financial
TD Bank USA
Valley National Bancorp

HISTORICAL FINANCIALS

Company Type: Public

Income Statement				FYE: December 31
	ASSETS ($ mil.)	NET INCOME ($ mil.)	INCOME AS % OF ASSETS	EMPLOYEES
12/17	9,845	93	1.0%	1,054
12/16	9,500	87	0.9%	1,057
12/15	8,911	83	0.9%	1,064
12/14	8,523	73	0.9%	1,021
12/13	7,487	70	0.9%	942
Annual Growth	7.1%	7.4%	—	2.8%

2017 Year-End Financials

Debt ratio: 6.25%
Return on equity: 7.37%
Cash ($ mil.): 190
Current ratio: —
Long-term debt ($ mil.): —

No. of shares (mil.): 66
Dividends
Yield: 0.0%
Payout: 64.1%
Market value ($ mil.): 1,794

	STOCK PRICE ($) FY Close	P/E High/Low		PER SHARE ($)		
				Earnings	Dividends	Book Value
12/17	26.97	20	16	1.45	0.93	19.52
12/16	28.30	21	13	1.38	0.71	18.94
12/15	20.15	16	13	1.33	0.65	18.26
12/14	18.06	16	13	1.22	0.60	17.63
12/13	19.32	16	12	1.23	0.76	16.87
Annual Growth	8.7%	—	—	4.2%	5.2%	3.7%

Prudential Annuities Life Assurance Corp

EXECUTIVES

Pres-Ceo, Robert F O'Donnell
Exec V Pres-Cfo, Yanela C Frias
Vice-President, Gary Palmer
Vice-President, Jan Hoffmeister

Executive of Sales, Lynn Erikson
Chief Operating Officer, Pelle Wahlstrom
Chief Information Officer, Ulf Tingstrom
Database Administrator, Cheryl Stewart
Software Developer, Dave Gianetti
Chief Investment Officer, Michael Long
Public Relations Executive, Scott Hawkins
Auditors: PricewaterhouseCoopers LLP

LOCATIONS

HQ: Prudential Annuities Life Assurance Corp
One Corporate Drive, Shelton, CT 06484
Phone: 203 926-1888
Web: www.investor.prudential.com

COMPETITORS

American Equity Investment Life Holding Company
Genworth Financial
Great American Financial Resources
John Hancock Financial Services
Kansas City Life
Lincoln Financial Group
MassMutual
MetLife
National Western
Northwestern Mutual
Presidential Life

HISTORICAL FINANCIALS

Company Type: Public

Income Statement   FYE: December 31

	ASSETS ($ mil.)	NET INCOME ($ mil.)	INCOME AS % OF ASSETS	EMPLOYEES
12/17	59,960	(83)	—	—
12/16	59,822	(1,090)	—	—
12/15	47,254	173	0.4%	—
12/14	52,472	250	0.5%	—
12/13	53,521	848	1.6%	—
Annual Growth	2.9%	—	—	—

2017 Year-End Financials

Debt ratio: 1.55%
Return on equity: (-1.25%)
Cash ($ mil.): 2,532
Current ratio: —
Long-term debt ($ mil.): —

No. of shares (mil.): 0
Dividends
Yield: —
Payout: —
Market value ($ mil.): —

Prudential Financial Inc

Prudential Financial wants to make sure its position near the top of the life insurance summit is set in stone. Prudential known for its Rock of Gibraltar logo is one of the top US life insurers and one of the largest life insurance companies worldwide. The firm is perhaps best known for its individual life insurance though it also sells group life and disability insurance as well as annuities. Prudential also offers investment products and services including asset management services mutual funds and retirement planning. In Asia the company operates through its Gibraltar Life Insurance and Life Planner units. Prudential has some $1.4 trillion in assets under management.

HISTORY

In 1873 John Dryden founded the Widows and Orphans Friendly Society in New Jersey to sell workers industrial insurance (low-face-value weekly premium life insurance). In 1875 it became

The Prudential Friendly Society taking the name from England's Prudential Assurance Co. The next year Dryden visited the English company and copied some of its methods such as recruiting agents from its targeted neighborhoods.

Prudential added ordinary whole life insurance in 1886. By 1900 the firm was selling more than 2000 such policies annually and had 3000 agents in eight states. In 1896 the J. Walter Thompson advertising agency (now the WPP Group) designed Prudential's Rock of Gibraltar logo.

The firm issued its first group life policy in 1916 (Prudential became a major group life insurer in the 1940s). In 1928 it introduced an Accidental Death Benefit which cost it an extra $3 million in benefits the next year alone (death claims rose drastically early in the Depression).

In 1943 Prudential mutualized. The company began decentralizing operations in the 1940s. Later it introduced a Property Investment Separate Account (PRISA) which gave pension plans a real estate investment option. By 1974 the firm was the US's group pension leader.

The insurer bought securities brokerage The Bache Group to form Pru Bache (now Prudential Securities) in 1981. Bache's forte was retail investments an area expected to blend well with Prudential's insurance business. Under George Ball Pru Bache tried to become a major investment banker — but failed. In 1991 Ball resigned leaving losses of almost $260 million and numerous lawsuits involving real estate limited partnerships.

Despite the 1992 settlement of the real estate partnership suits Prudential remained under scrutiny by several states because of "churning" a process in which agents generated commissions by inducing policyholders to trade up to more expensive policies. In 1995 new management led by former Chase Manhattanite Arthur Ryan brought sales under control sold such units as reinsurance and mortgage servicing and put its $6 billion real estate portfolio on the block. (In 1997 it sold its property management unit and Canadian commercial real estate unit; in 1998 it sold its landmark Prudential Center complex in Boston.)

In 1996 regulators from 30 states found that Prudential knew about the churning earlier than it had admitted had not stopped the perpetrators and had even promoted them. A 1997 settlement called for the company to pay restitution but the more than $2 billion estimated cost was thought to be less than the losses customers had suffered.

As the financial services industry continued to restructure Prudential in 1998 announced plans to demutualize. To focus on life insurance the company sold its health care unit to Aetna in 1999. The same year Prudential paid $62 million to resolve more churning claims revamped itself into international institutional and retail divisions and trimmed jobs. Ending its attempts to originate business the company cut 75% of its investment banking staff in 2000.

Demutualized Prudential Financial's 2001 IPO — one of the largest ever in the insurance industry — raised more than $3 billion. Prudential Financial became the holding company name for all operations making Prudential Insurance (the company's former name) a subsidiary and pure life insurer.

EXECUTIVES

Svp Chief Governance Officer And Corporate Secretary, Margaret Foran
Chairman And Ceo, John R. Strangfeld, age 64, $1,400,000 total compensation
Svp Corporate Human Resources And Chair The Prudential Foundation, Sharon C. Taylor, age 64
Evp And Coo International, Charles F. (Charlie) Lowrey, age 60, $770,000 total compensation

Svp And Cio, Barbara G. Koster, age 63
Chairman And Ceo International Investments, Stephen (Steve) Pelletier, age 64, $770,000 total compensation
Evp And Cfo, Robert M. Falzon, age 58, $759,231 total compensation
Svp And Chief Investment Officer, Scott G. Sleyster, age 58
Svp And Chief Risk Officer, Nicholas C. (Nick) Silitch, age 56
Svp And Chief Actuary, Richard F. Lambert, age 61
President And Ceo Prudential Retirement, Phil Waldeck
Evp And General Counsel, Timothy P. Harris, age 57
Vice President Information Systems, Michael Falzon
Vice President Information Technology, Jim Tonno
Vice President Individual Life Insurance Technology, Steven Leitman
Vice President Information Technology, Diana D'Amore
Vice President Information Systems, Scott Neely
Vice President Global Marketing Research, Andrea Kasper
Medical Director, Myrtho Montes
Vice President Of International Operations And Systems, Ryugo Toh
Vice President Regional Consultant, Jason Church
Vice President Information Systems And Security, Matt Schuette
Vice President Annuity Product Management, Lorie Lanza
Vice President Human Resources, Marla Jackson
Investment Vice President, Richard Toner
Vice President Financial Systems, John Toner
Vice President Chief Architect Group Insurance, Jim August
Vice President Process Management, Greg Steffe
Vice President Project Management, Mary Mathern
Vice President Corporate Counsel, Richard Hibbard
M Sales Vice President, Doug Peterson
Vice President National Accounts, David Johnston
Vice President Information Systems, Venkata Natarajan
Vice President Marketing Metrics, Bob Conover
Vice President Corporate Counsel (1997), William H Bulmer
Vice President Information Technology, Nicholas Defeis
Vice President Customer Service, Pauline Rossbauer
Vice President Process Management, Noreen Bertscha
Vice President Finance, Jurgen Muhlhauser
Vp And Controller Individual Life, Jamie Riesterer
Assistant Vice President Banki, Marylene Melim
Vice President, Joshua Shipley
Vice President Of Financial Reporting, Stanley Lezon
Territorial Vice President, Mark Sears
Vice President Of Stable Value Markets, Dylan Tyson
Vice President Prudential Fixed Income, Jerome Matthews
Vice President Key Accounts, Rob Sharp
Vp And Chief Customer Officer, Naveen Agarwal
Vice President Asset And Portfolio Management Single Client Accounts, Christopher Silva
Vice President Regional Sales Manager, Chris Sheckley
Vice President Business Finance, Stephen Durocher
Senior Vice President Client Relations And Business Development, Sean Mclaughlin
Vice President Corporate And Community Engagement, Spring Taylor Lacy
Vice President Applied Technologies, Michael Boatright
Vice President Head Of Talent Consulting, John Horn

Vice President Retirement Product Management, Meredith Ciana
Investment Senior Vice President, Anne Fifick
Vice President, Teri Sullivan-Yelko
Regional Sales Vice President, Wai Miks
Vice President And Assistant Treasurer, Kathleen Hoffman
Vice President, Donna Dixon
Executive Vice President Head Global Accounts Global Financial Intermediaries, Kimberly Lapointe
Vice President Regulatory Reporting Corporate Cantrollers, Benoit Bosi
Vice President Information Systems, Anita Manchandra
Vice President Telecommunications Information Systems, Warren Leary
Vice President Sales, Richard Kinville
Vice President, Jim Street
Vice President Conference And Travel, Joanne Gandolfo
Senior Vice President Sales Manager, Jonathan Cressman
Vice President Asset Management Human Resources, Marni Garfinkle
Vice President Information Technology, Joe Corrato
Vice President Life Product Marketing And Strategy, Donna Davis
Vice President Risk And Control, Susanna Banic
Vice President, James Quartuccio
Vice President, Larry Frank
Vice President Marketing And Brokerage Services, Michael Kalen
Vp Institutional Sales, Ann Nanda
Vice President Corporate Counsel (2006), Richard E Buckley
Vice President And Actuary, Sharon S Brody
Vice President Corporate Couns, Carlos R Gonzalez
Vice President Corporate Counsel At Prudential Financial, Kenyatta Bolden
Regional Vice President Advisor Channel, Matt Welch
Regional Sales Vice President, Brian Dubreuil
Vice President Change Manageme, Andrea Grossman
Executive Vice President, Richard Welch
Vice President Risk Management, Giselle Lim
Vice President Internal Audit, Margaret Byrne
Vice Presideni Investment Operations, Glenn Gutiahr
Vice President Marketing, Dawn Reilly
Vice President, Jeffrey Harrington
Investment Vice President, Adam Berkowitz
Vice President Creative Director Communications Officer, David Liemer
Vice President Product Development, Margaret Doherty
Vice President Government Affairs, Todd Thakar
Vice President, Pago Lumban-tobing
Vice President Global Research, Sarah Thompson
Vice President, Don Sulpizio
Senior Vice President National Sales Manager Wirehouse And Fit Channels, Tim Letter
Vice President Disability Product Management Prudential Group Insurance, Terrie Sorensen
Vice President, Robert Montellione
Vice President, Maryanne Ryan
Vice President Corporate Counsel (2005), Ernest Ceberio
Vice President And Actuary, Rocco A Mariano
Vice President Accounting, Stephen Korff
Vice President Financial Management, Charles Christiana
Vice President Human Resources, Lisa Schmidt
Vice President, Matthew Schuette
Vice President Of Global Security, Joseph Billy
Regional Vice President National Account Sales Director, John Wolf
Vice President Sales, Dave Scheetz

Vice President, Peter Trost
Vice President Corporate Social Responsibility; President The Prudential Foundation, Lata Reddy
Senior Vice President, Roderick Roberts
Vp Information Systems Group Insurance, William Sirico
Vice President External Affairs, Joan Feeney
Vice President Corporate Counsel, Debra Groisser
Executive Vice President, Edward Baird
Vp Corporate Counsel, Sue Buckner
Vice President And Actuary Head Of Retirement Pricing, Bradley Heinze
Regional Vice President, Mike Tollefsrud
Vice President Chief Medical Officer, Andy Crighton
Regional Sales Vice President, Larry Slabosz
Vice President Of Operations Retirement Technology, Michael Freker
Vice President Strategic Measures, Michael Tindall
Vice President And Corporate Counsel, Andrew Donald
Vice President, Eileen Geary
Vp It Operations Planning And Analysis, Glenn Beach
Senior Vice President And Chief Marketing Officer Annuities, Rodney Branch
Vice President Global Information Technology Sourcing, Lorri Callahan
Vice President, Ingrida Soldatova
Vice President, Jamie Dixon
Vp Corporate Social Responsibility, Jeff Harrington
Regional Vice President Institutional Distribution, Adam Eichler
Vice President Human Resources Pgim Real Estate, Jeffrey Gnoinski
Vice President Diversity And Inclusion, Smita Pillai
Vice President Process Management, Marguerite Bavaro
Vice President Compensation, Suzanne Langou
Vice President Of Human Resources, Diana Soltis
Vice President Human Resources, Carl Pollock
Vice President Business Measurement, Lisa Weber
Vp Digital And Customer Experience Group Insurance, Allison Landers
Svp And Head Full Service Investments Prudential Retirement, Srinivas Reddy
Investment Senior Vice President, Stephen Moehlman
Vice President, Joe Brophy
Investment Vice President, Chris Halloran
Vice President National Accounts, Mark Rosenthal
Vice President International Audit, Robert Van Vleet
Vp Accounting, Steve Korff
Vice President Planning And Analysis Asset And Liability Management Finance, Kurt Byerly
Auditors: PricewaterhouseCoopers LLP

LOCATIONS

HQ: Prudential Financial Inc
751 Broad Street, Newark, NJ 07102
Phone: 973 802-6000
Web: www.investor.prudential.com

2017 Sales

	$ mil.	% of total
US	36,573	61
Other	23,116	39
Total	**59,689**	**100**

PRODUCTS/OPERATIONS

2017 Sales by Segment

	$ mil.	% of total
International Insurance	21,560	35
US Workplace Solutions	19,314	32
US Individual Solutions	10,084	17
Closed block business	6,601	11
Investment Management	3,355	5
Adjustments	(1225)	-
Total	**59,689**	**100**

2017 Sales

	$ mil.	% of total
Premiums	32,091	54
Net investment income	16,435	27
Policy charges & fee income	5,303	9
Asset management & service fees	4,127	7
Net realized investment gains	432	2
Other	1,301	1
Total	**59,689**	**100**

COMPETITORS

AEGON	ING
AIG	John Hancock Financial
AXA	Services
Aetna	MassMutual
Aflac	Meiji Yasuda Life
Allianz	MetLife
American Life	Nationwide Life
Insurance	Insurance
Aviva	Nippon Life Insurance
COUNTRY Financial	Northwestern Mutual
Dai-ichi Life	Principal Financial
FMR	Prudential plc
Great-West Lifeco	Zurich Insurance Group

HISTORICAL FINANCIALS

Company Type: Public

Income Statement				FYE: December 31
	ASSETS ($ mil.)	NET INCOME ($ mil.)	INCOME AS % OF ASSETS	EMPLOYEES
12/17	831,921	7,863	0.9%	49,705
12/16	783,962	4,368	0.6%	49,739
12/15	757,388	5,642	0.7%	49,384
12/14	766,655	1,381	0.2%	48,331
12/13	731,781	(667)	—	47,355
Annual Growth	3.3%	—	—	1.2%

2017 Year-End Financials

Debt ratio: 2.35%
Return on equity: 15.74%
Cash ($ mil.): 14,490
Current ratio: —
Long-term debt ($ mil.): —
No. of shares (mil.): 422
Dividends
Yield: 0.0%
Payout: 16.8%
Market value ($ mil.): 48,585

	STOCK PRICE ($) FY Close	P/E High/Low		PER SHARE ($) Earnings	Dividends	Book Value
12/17	114.98	6	5	17.86	3.00	127.96
12/16	104.06	11	6	9.71	2.80	106.76
12/15	81.41	7	6	12.17	2.44	93.69
12/14	90.46	29	24	3.23	2.17	91.84
12/13	92.22	—	—	(1.55)	1.73	76.19
Annual Growth	5.7%	—	—	—	14.8%	13.8%

Public Service Enterprise Group Inc

In the Garden State Public Service Enterprise Group's (PSEG) diversified business model has it smelling like a rose. Regulated subsidiary Public Service Electric and Gas (PSE&G) transmits and distributes electricity to 2.2 million customers and natural gas to 1.8 million customers in New Jersey. Subsidiary PSEG Power operates power generating plants and sells its energy wholesale to PSE&G and others. PSEG Power's 11800-MW generating capacity comes mostly from nuclear and fossil-fuel plants in the US Northeast and Mid-Atlantic regions.

HISTORY

Tragedy struck Newark New Jersey in 1903 when a trolley slid down an icy hill and collided with a train killing more than 30 people. While investigating the accident state attorney general Thomas McCarter discovered the mismanagement of the trolley company and many of New Jersey's other transportation gas and electric companies. Planning to buy and consolidate these companies McCarter resigned and established the Public Service Corporation in 1903 with several colleagues.

The company formed divisions for gas utilities electric utilities and transportation companies. The trolley company generated almost half of Public Service's sales during its first year.

In 1924 the gas and electric companies consolidated as Public Service Electric and Gas (PSE&G). A new company was formed that year to operate buses and in 1928 it merged with the trolley company to form Public Service Coordinated Transport (later Transport of New Jersey). PSE&G signed interconnection agreements with two Pennsylvania electric companies in 1928 to form the first integrated power pool — later known as the Pennsylvania-New Jersey-Maryland Interconnection. The Public Utility Holding Company Act of 1935 ushered in the era of regulated regional monopolies ensuring PSE&G a captive market.

During the 1960s PSE&G joined Philadelphia Electric to build its first nuclear plant at Peach Bottom Pennsylvania. The company completed a second plant in 1977 at Salem New Jersey. Its third one went on line at Hope Creek New Jersey. However plant mismanagement earned PSE&G a slew of fines in the 1980s and 1990s.

The company sold its transportation system to the State of New Jersey in 1980. Five years later PSE&G formed holding company Public Service Enterprise Group (PSEG) to move into nonutility enterprises and created Community Energy Alternatives (CEA now PSEG Global) to invest in independent power projects. In 1989 Enterprise Diversified Holdings (now PSEG Energy Holdings) was formed to handle activities ranging from real estate to oil and gas production.

CEA and three partners acquired a Buenos Aires power plant in 1993. Taking advantage of overseas privatization in the late 1990s it expanded into Asia and with AES purchased two Argentine electric companies.

PSE&G's nuclear problems resurfaced when the Salem plant was shut down in 1995 to rectify equipment breakdowns. In 1997 PSEG paid Salem partners Delmarva Power & Light and PECO Energy $82 million to settle their lawsuits charging mismanagement of Salem; both units were back on line by 1998.

Continuing to diversify in the late 1990s PSEG formed PSEG Energy Technologies in 1997 to market power and acquired five mechanical services companies in 1998 and 1999.

In 1999 PSEG Global teamed up with Panda Energy International to build three merchant plants in Texas (to be completed by 2001). It also planned plants in India and Venezuela and joined Sempra Energy to buy 90% of Chilquinta EnergA-a an energy distributor in Chile and Peru. In 2000 it bought 90% of a distributor serving Argentina and Brazil.

New Jersey's electricity markets were deregulated in 1999; a year later the company transferred PSE&G's generation assets to nonregulated unit PSEG Power. PSEG Power also took charge of PSEG Global's plants under development in Illinois Indiana and Ohio; announced plans for new plants in New Jersey; and acquired an Albany New York plant from Niagara Mohawk.

PSEG Global completed a power plant in Texas in 2001. It also bought 94% of generator and distributor Saesa from Chile's largest conglomerate Copec for $460 million; it later acquired the rest of Saesa through a tender offer. It also purchased a Peruvian generation firm ElectroAndes for $227 million.

In 2002 PSEG Power acquired two Connecticut plants from WEC Energy for approximately $270 million.

PSEG had agreed to be acquired by Exelon but both New Jersey and Pennsylvania opposed the merger and the deal fell through in 2006.

In 2006 PSEG Global sold its 32% stake in RGE a Brazilian electric distribution company with approximately 1.1 million customers to Companhia Paulista de ForA§a e Luz. In 2008 it sold the SAESA Group of Companies (a power distribution group) in southern Chile to a consortium formed by Morgan Stanley Infrastructure and the Ontario Teachers' Pension Plan for $887 million.

In 2013 PSEG Solar Source announced that it purchased two utility-scale solar power plants totaling 4.4 MW from Canadian Solar Inc. The solar installations are the largest in Shasta county California built at more than 3300 feet in elevation.

EXECUTIVES

Vp Electric Delivery Pse&g, Ralph A. LaRossa, age 55, $684,308 total compensation

Chairman President And Ceo, Ralph Izzo, age 60, $1,298,269 total compensation

Evp And Cfo, Daniel J. (Dan) Cregg, age 54, $520,000 total compensation

Vp Regulatory Pseg Services, Tamara L. Linde, age 53, $533,789 total compensation

Vp Asset Management And Centralized Services Pse&g, David M. Daly, age 56

President Pseg Services Corporation, Derek M. Di Risio, age 53

Vice President Engineering Pseg Nuclear, Paul J Davison

Vice President Corporate Communications, Kathleen Fitzgerald

Vp It And Cio Pseg Services Corporation, Joseph Santamaria

Vice President Gas Supply Pseg Energy Resources And Trade, David Caffery

Vice President Construction Pseg Power, Kevin Cellars

Vice President Manager Director, Donald Staudt

Vice President Of Customer Information Technology, Thomas Flaherty

Regional Vice President And Managing Director, Guy Vogt

Vice President Regulatory And Deputy General Counsel, Joseph Accardo

Vice President Of Tax, Jose M Perez

Legal Secretary, June Barnett

Vp Electric Operations Pseandg, John Bridges

Vice President Customer Services, Richard Walden

Vp Business Assurance And Resilience Pseg Services Corporation, Aaron Ford

Vp And Treasurer Pseg Services Corporation, Brad Huntington

Vp Transmission And Distribution Pseg Long Island, John O'Connell

Government Relations, Vincent Frigeria

Board Member, Hak Shin

Assistant Treasurer, Lynn Manganaro

Treasurer, Bradford Huntington

Board Member, Michael F Percarpio

Assistant Treasurer, Benjamin Zoe

Vice Chair Public Service Electric And Gas, Dave Blew

Auditors: DELOITTE & TOUCHE LLP

LOCATIONS

HQ: Public Service Enterprise Group Inc
80 Park Plaza, Newark, NJ 07102
Phone: 973 430-7000
Web: www.pseg.com

PRODUCTS/OPERATIONS

2016 Sales

	$ mil.	% of total
PSE&G	6,221	59
Power	4,023	38
Others	370	3
Adjustments	(1553)	-
Total	**9,061**	**100**

Selected Subsidiaries

PSEG Energy Holdings Inc. (nonutility companies)
  PSEG Global Inc. (solar plants and other alternative energy investments)
  PSEG Resources Inc. (energy infrastructure investments)
PSEG Power LLC
  PSEG Fossil LLC (operator of PSEG's fossil fuel plants)
  PSEG Nuclear LLC (operator of PSEG's nuclear plants)
  PSEG Energy Resources and Trade LLC (energy marketing)
PSEG Services Corporation (management and administrative services for PSEG)
Public Service Electric and Gas Company (PSE&G distribution of electricity and gas)

COMPETITORS

AEP	FirstEnergy
CenterPoint Energy	NRG Energy
Con Edison	National Grid USA
Constellation Energy Group	New Jersey Resources
Delmarva Power	NextEra Energy
Eversource Energy	PPL Corporation
Exelon	South Jersey Industries

HISTORICAL FINANCIALS

Company Type: Public

Income Statement

FYE: December 31

	REVENUE ($ mil.)	NET INCOME ($ mil.)	NET PROFIT MARGIN	EMPLOYEES
12/17	9,084	1,574	17.3%	12,945
12/16	9,061	887	9.8%	13,065
12/15	10,415	1,679	16.1%	13,025
12/14	10,886	1,518	13.9%	12,689
12/13	9,968	1,243	12.5%	9,887
Annual Growth	**(2.3%)**	**6.1%**	**—**	**7.0%**

2017 Year-End Financials

Debt ratio: 31.86%	No. of shares (mil.): 505
Return on equity: 11.67%	Dividends
Cash ($ mil.): 313	Yield: 0.0%
Current ratio: 0.79	Payout: 55.4%
Long-term debt ($ mil.): 12,068	Market value ($ mil.): 26,008

	STOCK PRICE ($) FY Close	P/E High/Low	PER SHARE ($) Earnings	PER SHARE ($) Dividends	PER SHARE ($) Book Value
12/17	51.50	17 13	3.10	1.72	27.42
12/16	43.88	27 22	1.75	1.64	26.01
12/15	38.69	13 11	3.30	1.56	25.86
12/14	41.41	15 10	2.99	1.48	24.09
12/13	32.04	15 12	2.45	1.44	22.95
Annual Growth	**12.6%**	**— —**	**6.1%**	**4.5%**	**4.6%**

Publix Super Markets, Inc.

Publix Super Markets tops the list of privately owned grocery operators in the US. By emphasizing service and a family-friendly image over price Publix has outgrown and outperformed its regional rivals. Some two-thirds of its nearly 1200 stores are in Florida but it also operates in half a dozen other southeastern states. Publix makes some of its own bakery deli dairy goods and fresh prepared foods at its own manufacturing plants in Florida and Georgia. Many stores also house pharmacies and banks. Founder George Jenkins began offering stock to Publix employees in 1930; employees own more than a quarter of the company.

Operations

Publix stores sell grocery products (dairy produce deli baker meat and seafood) health and beauty care products general merchandise pharmacy products flowers and other products and services. Grocery activities account for some 85% of sales.

Geographic Reach

Publix has nearly 1200 supermarkets in Florida (about two-thirds of total) and Georgia (more than 15% of total) as well as Alabama South Carolina Tennessee North Carolina and Virginia.

It restocks store shelves from nine distribution centers — seven in Florida and one each in Georgia and Alabama. The grocer also operates half a dozen dairy bakery and deli facilities four in Florida and two in Georgia.

Financial Performance

Publix has shown solid sales growth over the past five years as it continues to expand and open new stores across the Southeast. Its revenue has risen some 20% since 2013. With profit margins higher than many (if not all) of its grocery competitors the company has also seen increases in its net income in recent years.

In 2017 Publix reported revenue of $34.8 billion up about 1.5% from the prior year. New store openings powered the growth along with a 1.7% increase in comparable-store sales which was helped by customers' stocking up and replenishing before and after Hurricane Irma hit Florida. This was more than enough to offset an additional week of operation in 2016 which was a 53-week fiscal year.

As the dominant grocer in its primary market Florida Publix regularly reports net profit margins of between 5.5%-6% much higher than other super market chains (Kroger for example is in the 1.5%-2% range). In 2017 it had net earnings of $2.3 billion up from $2 billion in 2016. In addition to the increased revenue net earnings were boosted some $224 million by the Tax Cut and Jobs Act of 2017.

Cash at the end of 2017 was $580 million an increase of about $140 million from the prior year. Cash from operations contributed $3.6 billion to the coffers while investing and financing activities used some $3.45 million mainly for expenditures used in new and remodeled stores and for dividends and stock buybacks.

Strategy

Publix's growth strategy is based on investing in its stores and enhancing its customer service.

It plans to spend more than $1.5 billion in 2018 to open new stores remodel existing stores and increase ownership of its store portfolio. The company opened 44 stores in 2017 including its first locations in Virginia. At year's end it had about 35 stores under construction. In addition Publix re-

modeled more than 130 locations in 2017. It also continues to invest in its real estate portfolio. At the end of 2017 the company owned nearly a third of its stores up from 29% in 2016 and 11% in 2007.

Publix is also focused on keeping up with customer demand for delivery and other advanced services. It began working with grocery delivery firm Instacart in 2016 and currently offers home delivery in more than 90% of its operating area. The company is also testing curbside pickup and its online ordering platform has been expanded with smokehouse meats fried chicken and other items. It has also enhanced its pharmacy offerings through a partnership with BayCare Health System and serves pharmacy patients with new web and mobile applications.

Lastly Publix has announced plans to relaunch its GreenWise Market concept in select locations in 2018. GreenWise Market targets the health-conscious consumer with specialty natural and organic selections.

EXECUTIVES

Evp And Cfo, David P. Phillips, age 58, $1,051,090 total compensation
General Counsel And Secretary, John A. Attaway, age 59, $690,310 total compensation
Svp, David E. Bornmann, age 60, $488,300 total compensation
President Ceo And Director, Randall T. (Todd) Jones, age 55, $1,688,750 total compensation
Svp And Cio, Laurie Z. Douglas, age 54, $890,255 total compensation
Manager Government Relations, Shane Kunze
Vice Chairman, Hoyt R. (Barney) Barnett, age 75
Chairman, William E. (Ed) Crenshaw, age 67
Auditors: KPMG LLP

LOCATIONS

HQ: Publix Super Markets, Inc.
  3300 Publix Corporate Parkway, Lakeland, FL 33811
Phone: 863 688-1188
Web: www.publix.com

2017 Supermarkets

	No.
Florida	779
Georgia	186
Alabama	65
South Carolina	58
Tennessee	41
North Carolina	30
Virginia	8
Total	**1,167**

PRODUCTS/OPERATIONS

2017 Sales

	% of total
Grocery	84
Other	16
Total	**100**

Selected Supermarket Departments

Bakery
Dairy
Deli
Floral
Groceries
Health and beauty care
Meat
Pharmacy
Produce
Seafood
Foods Processed
Baked goods
Dairy products
Deli items

COMPETITORS

ALDI	Kroger
ALDI	Rite Aid
CVS	Rite Aid
CVS	Sedano's
Costco Wholesale	Sedano's
Costco Wholesale	Southeastern Grocers
Food Lion	Southeastern Grocers
Food Lion	The Pantry
IGA	The Pantry
IGA	Wal-Mart
Ingles Markets	Wal-Mart
Ingles Markets	Walgreen
Kmart	Walgreen
Kmart	Whole Foods
Kroger	Whole Foods

HISTORICAL FINANCIALS

Company Type: Public

Income Statement

FYE: December 31

	REVENUE ($ mil.)	NET INCOME ($ mil.)	NET PROFIT MARGIN	EMPLOYEES
12/17	34,836	2,291	6.6%	193,000
12/16	34,274	2,025	5.9%	191,000
12/15	32,618	1,965	6.0%	180,000
12/14	30,802	1,735	5.6%	175,000
12/13	29,147	1,653	5.7%	166,000
Annual Growth	**4.6%**	**8.5%**	**—**	**3.8%**

2017 Year-End Financials

Debt ratio: 1.06%
Return on equity: 21.40%
Cash ($ mil.): 579
Current ratio: 1.30
Long-term debt ($ mil.): 155

No. of shares (mil.): 733
Dividends
  Yield: —
  Payout: 30.0%
Market value ($ mil.): —

	STOCK PRICE ($) FY Close	P/E High/Low	PER SHARE ($)		
			Earnings	Dividends	Book Value
12/17	0.00	— —	3.04	0.91	15.02
12/16	0.00	— —	2.63	0.87	13.63
Annual Growth	**—**	**— —**	**3.7%**	**1.3%**	**2.5%**

PUBLIX SUPER MARKETS, INC.

Publix Super Markets tops the list of privately owned grocery operators in the US. By emphasizing service and a family-friendly image over price Publix has outgrown and outperformed its regional rivals. Some two-thirds of its nearly 1200 stores are in Florida but it also operates in half a dozen other southeastern states. Publix makes some of its own bakery deli dairy goods and fresh prepared foods at its own manufacturing plants in Florida and Georgia. Many stores also house pharmacies and banks. Founder George Jenkins began offering stock to Publix employees in 1930; employees own more than a quarter of the company.

Operations

Publix stores sell grocery products (dairy produce deli baker meat and seafood) health and beauty care products general merchandise pharmacy products flowers and other products and services. Grocery activities account for some 85% of sales.

Geographic Reach

Publix has nearly 1200 supermarkets in Florida (about two-thirds of total) and Georgia (more than 15% of total) as well as Alabama South Carolina Tennessee North Carolina and Virginia.

It restocks store shelves from nine distribution centers — seven in Florida and one each in Georgia and Alabama.The grocer also operates half a dozen dairy bakery and deli facilities four in Florida and two in Georgia.

Financial Performance

Publix has shown solid sales growth over the past five years as it continues to expand and open new stores across the Southeast. Its revenue has risen some 20% since 2013. With profit margins higher than many (if not all) of its grocery competitors the company has also seen increases in its net income in recent years.

In 2017 Publix reported revenue of $34.8 billion up about 1.5% from the prior year. New store openings powered the growth along with a 1.7% increase in comparable-store sales which was helped by customers' stocking up and replenishing before and after Hurricane Irma hit Florida. This was more than enough to offset an additional week of operation in 2016 which was a 53-week fiscal year.

As the dominant grocer in its primary market Florida Publix regularly reports net profit margins of between 5.5%-6% much higher than other super market chains (Kroger for example is in the 1.5%-2% range). In 2017 it had net earnings of $2.3 billion up from $2 billion in 2016. In addition to the increased revenue net earnings were boosted some $224 million by the Tax Cut and Jobs Act of 2017.

Cash at the end of 2017 was $580 million an increase of about $140 million from the prior year. Cash from operations contributed $3.6 billion to the coffers while investing and financing activities used some $3.45 million mainly for expenditures used in new and remodeled stores and for dividends and stock buybacks.

Strategy

Publix's growth strategy is based on investing in its stores and enhancing its customer service.

It plans to spend more than $1.5 billion in 2018 to open new stores remodel existing stores and increase ownership of its store portfolio. The company opened 44 stores in 2017 including its first locations in Virginia. At year's end it had about 35 stores under construction. In addition Publix remodeled more than 130 locations in 2017. It also continues to invest in its real estate portfolio. At the end of 2017 the company owned nearly a third of its stores up from 29% in 2016 and 11% in 2007.

Publix is also focused on keeping up with customer demand for delivery and other advanced services. It began working with grocery delivery firm Instacart in 2016 and currently offers home delivery in more than 90% of its operating area. The company is also testing curbside pickup and its online ordering platform has been expanded with smokehouse meats fried chicken and other items. It has also enhanced its pharmacy offerings through a partnership with BayCare Health System and serves pharmacy patients with new web and mobile applications.

Lastly Publix has announced plans to relaunch its GreenWise Market concept in select locations in 2018. GreenWise Market targets the health-conscious consumer with specialty natural and organic selections.

EXECUTIVES

Evp And Cfo, David P. Phillips, age 58, $1,051,090 total compensation
General Counsel And Secretary, John A. Attaway, age 59, $690,310 total compensation

Svp, David E. Bornmann, age 60, $488,300 total compensation
President Ceo And Director, Randall T. (Todd) Jones, age 55, $1,688,750 total compensation
Svp And Cio, Laurie Z. Douglas, age 54, $890,255 total compensation
Manager Government Relations, Shane Kunze
Vice Chairman, Hoyt R. (Barney) Barnett, age 75
Chairman, William E. (Ed) Crenshaw, age 67

LOCATIONS

HQ: PUBLIX SUPER MARKETS, INC.
3300 PUBLIX CORP PKWY, LAKELAND, FL 338113311
Phone: 863 688-1188
Web: WWW.PUBLIX.COM

2017 Supermarkets

	No.
Florida	779
Georgia	186
Alabama	65
South Carolina	58
Tennessee	41
North Carolina	30
Virginia	8
Total	**1,167**

PRODUCTS/OPERATIONS

2017 Sales

	% of total
Grocery	84
Other	16
Total	**100**

Selected Supermarket Departments

Bakery
Dairy
Deli
Floral
Groceries
Health and beauty care
Meat
Pharmacy
Produce
Seafood
Foods Processed
Baked goods
Dairy products
Deli items

COMPETITORS

ALDI	Kroger
ALDI	Rite Aid
CVS	Rite Aid
CVS	Sedano's
Costco Wholesale	Sedano's
Costco Wholesale	Southeastern Grocers
Food Lion	Southeastern Grocers
Food Lion	The Pantry
IGA	The Pantry
IGA	Wal-Mart
Ingles Markets	Wal-Mart
Ingles Markets	Walgreen
Kmart	Walgreen
Kmart	Whole Foods
Kroger	Whole Foods

HISTORICAL FINANCIALS

Company Type: Private

Income Statement   FYE: December 31

	REVENUE ($ mil.)	NET INCOME ($ mil.)	NET PROFIT MARGIN	EMPLOYEES
12/16	34,274	2,025	5.9%	193,000
12/15	32,618	1,965	6.0%	—
12/14	30,802	1,735	5.6%	—
12/12	27,706	1,552	5.6%	—
Annual Growth	**5.5%**	**6.9%**	**—**	**—**

2016 Year-End Financials

Debt ratio: —
Return on equity: 5.90%
Cash ($ mil.): 438
Current ratio: 0.40
Long-term debt ($ mil.): —
Dividends
Yield: —
Payout: —
Market value ($ mil.): —

PulteGroup Inc

PulteGroup pulls its weight in providing homes for American families. PulteGroup targets a cross-section of home buyers nationwide by buying land to build single-family houses duplexes townhouses and condominiums. Its Centex brand is marketed to entry-level buyers while Pulte Homes aims to capture customers looking to trade up. PulteGroup also builds Del Webb retiree communities mostly in Sun Belt locales for the growing number of buyers in the 55-plus age range. The company sells its homes in some 50 markets across 25 states. Its homes go for an average price of $370000. PulteGroup became one of the top homebuilders in the US by buying rivals John Wieland Homes and Centex Homes.

HISTORY

William Pulte built his first home in Detroit in 1950 and incorporated his business in 1956 as William J. Pulte Inc.

In 1961 the company built its first subdivision in Detroit. During that decade Pulte moved into Washington DC (1964) Chicago (1966) and Atlanta (1968). In 1969 Pulte merged with Colorado's American Builders to form the Pulte Home Corporation a publicly traded company.

Originally a builder of high-priced single-family homes Pulte began expanding into affordable and midrange housing markets. To lower costs it pioneered modular designs and prebuilt components. Pulte architects designed the Quadrominium a large structure with four separate two-bedroom units each with its own entrance and garage (priced at a mere $20000 per unit in the 1970s).

Pulte formed Intercontinental Mortgage (later renamed ICM Mortgage) and began making home loans in 1972. The company ran into trouble in 1988 when it was accused of forcing Pulte homebuyers in Baltimore to use ICM financing instead of cheaper loans from the county. Pulte settled by repaying the difference in loan costs.

By the mid-1980s Pulte was one of the US's largest on-site homebuilders. PHM Corporation was created in 1987 as a holding company for the Pulte group of companies. That year PHM entered the thrift business by assisting the Federal Savings and Loan Insurance Corp.'s S&L bailout. It acquired five Texas S&Ls (with assets of $1.3 billion) for $45 million and eventually combined them to form First Heights (finally discontinuing the business in 1994).

Pulte Homes' Quality Leadership customer satisfaction program introduced in the early 1990s paid off in 1991 as Pulte enjoyed record sales despite a depressed home market. Renamed Pulte Corporation in 1993 the company soon faced rising interest rates which dampened the US housing market and affected the Mexican peso. Pulte recorded a $2 million foreign-currency loss on an affordable-housing venture in Mexico in 1994. Nonetheless it began a second joint venture in that country in 1995 and helped form mortgage bank Su Casita with nine Mexican homebuilders to finance home construction on its border. That year it also started developing retirement communities when it bought the Ponds at Clearbrook in New Jersey.

In 1996 its Mexican joint venture Condake-Pulte began building thousands of affordable homes for General Motors and Sony employees in maquiladora residential areas near the US-Mexico border. The company also bought Rhode Island's top homebuilder LeBlanc.

Pulte restructured in 1997 and a year later shed its manufactured housing and building supply business. It also acquired DiVosta one of Florida's largest homebuilders and Tennessee-based Radnor Homes.

The company's 1988 foray into S&Ls came back to haunt it in 1998: The Federal Deposit Insurance Corp. won a lawsuit that accused the builder of abusing tax benefits associated with the S&Ls. (Pulte settled the case in 2001 by paying $41.5 million.) In 1999 Pulte bought the interest held by investment firm Blackstone Group its partner in active-adult homebuilding.

The next year Pulte joined other builders in an Internet-based building materials cooperative. Also in 2000 the company began dealings to expand its homebuilding operations into Argentina.

The company changed its name to Pulte Homes in 2001. That year Mark O'Brien became the company's CEO. He directed Pulte through the major acquisition of retirement community developer Del Webb for about $800 million in stock and $950 million in assumed debt. The combined company became the largest US homebuilder. In 2002 Pulte reorganized the structure of its operations in Mexico and created Pulte Mexico S. de R.L. de C.V. one of the largest builders in that country.

Adding to its portfolio of accolades Pulte was named 2002 "Builder of the Year" by Professional Builder magazine and in 2003 Pulte ranked 19th among the "Top 50 Best-Performing Companies" in Business Week' s performance rankings of the Standard & Poor's 500-stock index.

Pulte expanded its operations in the fast-growing San Diego area in 2003 by purchasing assets of ColRich Communities which included about 500 entitled lots in five communities in the South Bay and Coastal North areas of San Diego. It boosted its presence in the Albuquerque Phoenix and Tucson markets by acquiring Sivage-Thomas Homes (Albuquerque) with about 7000 lots in the region and Del Webb entered the Reno Nevada market with its Sierra Canyon active adult community. O'Brien left the company in June 2003 after having served in senior management positions for six years (and 21 total years) within the company. EVP and COO Richard Dugas stepped up to become the company's president and CEO at that time.

In September 2003 the US Court of Federal Claims awarded Pulte and related parties $48.7 million as a result of a breach of contract by the US government related to Pulte's acquisition of five savings and loans in 1988.

J.D. Power and Associates recognized Pulte as a top performer for its fifth consecutive year in its "2004 New Home Builder Customer Satisfaction Study." Out of the 25 markets it surveyed Pulte ranked highest in 14 markets #2 in nine markets and #3 in six markets.

At the close of 2004 Pulte sold some operations in Argentina to real estate developer Grupo Farallon. The next year it sold its Mexican and remaining Argentine homebuilding enterprises to focus exclusively on US operations.

The downturn in the US housing market — due to a toxic cocktail of higher home prices increased foreclosures high unemployment and constraints on mortgage lending — led to weakened demand for new homes and higher cancellation rates. For Pulte this trend meant decreased profitability and a decline in homebuilding activity. Pulte responded to the downturn and adjusted its operations by cutting jobs and shuttering plants to meet lower demand levels.

The company bought rival Centex in 2009. The acquisition made Pulte the largest homebuilder in the US and also strengthened Pulte's offerings in the lower-priced home segment.

A year following the Centex merger founder William Pulte retired from the company and from its board of directors. He was named chairman emeritus.

EXECUTIVES

Evp And Coo, Harmon D. Smith, age 54, $688,462 total compensation

Vp And Cio, Joseph L. Drouin

Evp Human Resources, James R. (Jim) Ellinghausen, age 60, $546,154 total compensation

Evp And Cfo, Robert T. (Bob) O'Shaughnessy, age 52, $742,307 total compensation

President Ceo And Director, Ryan R. Marshall, age 43, $738,462 total compensation

Evp General Counsel And Corporate Secretary, Todd N. Sheldon

Vp And Chief Marketing Officer, Manish M. Shrivastava

Vice President Of Acquisition And Entitlement, Dan Carroll

Vice President Of Finance, Michael Hyland

Vp Customer Relations; Manager Process Improvement, Wayne Newmiller

Vice President Land, Cisco Garcia

Vice President Strategy, Mary Rachide

Vice President Investor Relations And Corporate Communications, Jim Zeumer

Vice President Of Land Acquisition, Brad Piroli

Vice President Finance, John Evans

Division Vice President Of Land Acquisition, Matt Callahan

Vice President Of Construction Operations Mid Atlantic Division, Brad Nicholas

Auditors: Ernst & Young LLP

LOCATIONS

HQ: PulteGroup Inc
3350 Peachtree Road N.E., Suite 150, Atlanta, GA 30326
Phone: 404 978-6400
Web: www.pultegroupinc.com

Selected Homebuilding Regions
Florida
North (IL IN MI MN MO Northern CA OH OR WA)
Northeast (CT DE MD MA NJ NY PA RI VA)
Southeast (GA NC SC TN)
Southwest (AZ CO HI NV NM Southern CA)
Texas

PRODUCTS/OPERATIONS

2016 Sales

	% of total
Northeast	9
Southeast	19
Florida	17
Midwest	16
Texas	14
West	23
Financial Services	2
Total	**100**

2016 Sales

		% of total
Home building		
Home Sales	7451.3	97
Land Sales	36.1	1
Financial Serivces	181	2
Total	**7,668**	**100**

Selected Brands

Centex (entry-level buyers)
Del Webb (active-adult buyers)
DiVosta (Florida)
Pulte Homes (move-up buyers)

COMPETITORS

Beazer Homes	M.D.C.
CalAtlantic	Meritage Homes
D.R. Horton	NVR
Hovnanian Enterprises	Pardee Homes
KB Home	Toll Brothers
Lennar	

HISTORICAL FINANCIALS

Company Type: Public

Income Statement

FYE: December 31

	REVENUE ($ mil.)	NET INCOME ($ mil.)	NET PROFIT MARGIN	EMPLOYEES
12/18	10,188	1,022	10.0%	5,086
12/17	8,573	447	5.2%	4,810
12/16	7,668	602	7.9%	4,623
12/15	5,981	494	8.3%	4,542
12/14	5,822	474	8.1%	4,149
Annual Growth	**15.0%**	**21.2%**	**—**	**5.2%**

2018 Year-End Financials

Debt ratio: 33.19%
Return on equity: 22.78%
Cash ($ mil.): 1,110
Current ratio: 11.31
Long-term debt ($ mil.): 3,376

No. of shares (mil.): 277
Dividends
  Yield: 1.4%
  Payout: 12.7%
Market value ($ mil.): 7,202

	STOCK PRICE ($) FY Close	P/E High/Low		PER SHARE ($) Earnings	Dividends	Book Value
12/18	25.99	10	6	3.55	0.38	17.39
12/17	33.25	24	13	1.44	0.36	14.49
12/16	18.38	13	9	1.75	0.36	14.60
12/15	17.82	17	12	1.36	0.33	13.63
12/14	21.46	17	13	1.26	0.23	13.01
Annual Growth	**4.9%**	**—**	**—**	**29.6%**	**13.4%**	**7.5%**

PVH Corp

PVH has the buttoned-up look down. A top global apparel player PVH is the world's largest dress shirt and neckwear company. The company owns three titans of the apparel industry: Calvin Klein Tommy Hilfiger and Heritage Brands. The former two are multi-billion dollar global lifestyle brands while Heritage Brands is a luxury apparel wholesaler that owns the brands Van Heusen IZOD ARROW Warner's Olga and True&Co. PVH is also has licenses for third-party brands such as DKNY Speedo Kenneth Cole Reaction Michael Kors Collection and others. The company generates sales from multiple channels including about 1600 company-operated retail stores as well as retailers and licensees. It also charges royalty and advertising fees.

Operations

PVH organizes its business into three main areas: Calvin Klein Tommy Hilfiger and Heritage Brands.

Calvin Klein accounts for over 35% of revenue and runs a number of sub-brands alongside its Calvin Klein "master" brand: Calvin Klein By Appointment Calvin Klein Jeans CK Calvin Klein Calvin Klein Jeans and Calvin Klein 205 W39 NYC (the unusual name relates to its New York address). Together they fill various product niches categories and price points.

Tommy Hilfiger split into Tommy Hilfiger North America and Tommy Hilfiger International contributes some 45% to PVH's revenue. The brand makes everyday and formalwear for the upper-middle class characterized by its classic American preppy stylings. As with Calvin Klein it runs a number of sub-brands: Hilfiger Collection Tommy Hilfiger Tailored Tommy Hilfiger and Hilfiger Denim. It sells its products wholesale to third party retailers and at retail via a network of owned outlets and has around 25 license agreements with third parties in Australia Brazil India and Mexico among other countries.

Heritage Brands accounts for around 20% of revenue and makes shirts neckwear sportswear swimwear intimates underwear and accessories through a range of owned brands and licensed brands. Its licensed brands are Speedo Kenneth Cole New York Kenneth Cole Reaction Sean John MICHAEL Michael Kors Michael Kors Collection and Chaps. It sells wholesale and through Heritage Brands retail outlets across the United States and Canada. Some of its stores stock IZOD Golf Warner's and Speedo products. Heritage Brands also licenses its products to 35 US and 40 international companies.

PVH also completes e-commerce sales through its various brand websites.

The company's products are made in more 1600 factories in more than 50 countries worldwide. In addition to the more than 1900 retail stores that it operates PVH maintains wholesale and retail warehousing and distribution centers in the US Canada Japan and the Netherlands. The centers inspect sort pack and ship goods to customers.

Geographic Reach

The company sells products in the US Canada Europe Asia Mexico and Brazil. Its US business accounts for over 50% of sales.

Sales and Marketing

Macy's is PVH's largest Calvin Klein and Tommy Hilfiger wholesale customer. Heritage Brands sells wholesale to department stores such as Bon-Ton Stores J. C. Penney Kohl's and Sears. Each of the Calvin Klein Tommy Hilfiger and Heritage Brands businesses have a number of licensing partners domestically and abroad who have the right to manufacture and wholesale specified products under one or more brands or are granted the right to open retail stores under the licensed brand name.

PVH targets the marketing of its brands at distinct consumer demographics. The company advertises its brands through digital media (including its e-commerce and social media sites) national print media television outdoor signage special events promotions and store locations. It also advertises through product tie-ins and sport sponsorships (Calvin Klein/basketball Van Heusen/football and IZOD/golf). The Tommy Hilfiger marketing team also coordinates appearances by the designer himself Tommy Hilfiger at runway shows special events and flagship store openings.

PVH's five largest customers account for more than a fifth of total revenues.

Financial Performance

After several years of steady revenue growth sales dipped in 2015 before bouncing back in fiscal 2016: sales climbed 2% to $8.2 billion.

PVH's revenue growth in fiscal 2016 was uneven with solid gains in Calvin Klein (International and North America) and Tommy Hilfiger International offset by falls in Tommy Hilfiger North America and Heritage Brands. Growth came from the Calvin Klein domestic wholesale business and the Tommy Hilfiger International business in Eu-

rope. The business was impacted across the board by the strong US dollar.

Net income slid 4% to $549 million as selling general and administrative expenses were pushed up by acquisition costs and higher marketing costs.

Cash from operating activities increased by $55 million to $955 million due to changes in working capital relating to inventory and accrued expenses.

Strategy

PVH is unifying Calvin Klein under one creative vision. The process began when it took back full control of its jeans and underwear businesses in 2013 and continued in 2016 with the sacking of Francisco Costa and Italo Zucchelli the women's and men's creative directors to clear the way for a unified global creative director role. Raf Simons was given the position.

The company focuses on reinvesting in businesses and pursuing strategic acquisitions.PVH's strength lies in the fact that it maintains a strong diversified brand portfolio. Its portfolio is growing through acquisitions and it is supported by a model that offers multiple brands and product types globally at different price points and across a range of distribution channels. The variety in products and distribution channels allows the company to reach a broad range of consumers in various geographic regions. The move in 2016 to buy full control of TH Asia signaled the start of direct involvement in the Chinese market.

Mergers and Acquisitions

In 2017 PVH acquired True&Co an online retailer specializing in bras.

In 2016 the company bought the remaining 55% of TH Asia Ltd. its joint venture for Tommy Hilfiger in China. With the closing of this transaction Tommy Hilfiger business now operates directly in its fastest growing market while leveraging its well-established infrastructure in Asia.

HISTORY

Moses Phillips came to America from Poland in 1881. While living in a one-room apartment in Pottsville Pennsylvania he sold flannel shirts (which his wife sewed) to coal miners from a pushcart. He soon brought the rest of his family to the US and upgraded the pushcart to a horse and buggy. Business continued to grow and the Phillips-Jones Corporation was formed in 1907.

The company moved to New York in 1914 and control passed from father to son for four generations. Isaac followed Moses then Seymour took over in 1941 until he handed the reins to Lawrence who joined the company in 1948 and became president and CEO in 1969. Ads in the 1950s featured such actors as Anthony Quinn Burt Lancaster and Ronald Reagan in Van Heusen shirts. In 1957 the company received its new name Phillips-Van Heusen (PVH). It grew via acquisitions throughout the 1970s and began selling its merchandise at its own outlet stores in 1979 but it didn't want its products sold at the off-price outlets that became popular in the early 1980s. The company stopped doing business with stores and distributors that allowed PVH merchandise to reach cut-price vendors.

In 1987 PVH bought back more than 5 million shares of stock in order to fend off an acquisition bid by the Hunt family of Texas. Lawrence stepped down in 1993 ending the unbroken chain of Phillipses at the helm. In 1995 the Phillips family sold its stake in the business. In June 2011 the company renamed itself PVH Corp. officially dropping the Phillips-Van Heusen moniker to emphasize its diversified portfolio of brands.

EXECUTIVES

President Van Heusen Retail, Margaret P. (Meg) Lachance

Chairman And Ceo, Emanuel (Manny) Chirico, age 61, $1,350,000 total compensation

Evp Chief Operating And Financial Officer, Michael A. (Mike) Shaffer, age 56, $891,667 total compensation

Ceo Heritage Brands And North America Wholesale, Francis K. (Ken) Duane, age 62, $1,091,667 total compensation

President Licensing, Kenneth L. (Ken) Wyse

Ceo Tommy Hilfiger And Pvh Europe, Daniel Grieder, age 56, $937,209 total compensation

Evp The Marketing Group, Michael (Mike) Kelly

Ceo Tommy Hilfiger Americas, Gary Sheinbaum

President Van Heusen Retail, Steven B. (Steve) Shiffman, age 60, $908,333 total compensation

President Heritage Sportswear, Geoffrey (Geoff) Barrett

Evp Logistics Services, Kevin J. Urban

President Calvin Klein Retail, Barrie Scardina, age 54

President Calvin Klein 205w39nyc And Calvin Klein By Appointment, Michelle Kessler-Sanders

President Calvin Klein North America Design And Product Development, Alexander (Alex) Cannon

Svp And Chief Risk Officer, Melanie Steiner

President Neckwear, David Sirkin

President Core Intimates, Leslie (Les) Hall

President The Underwear Group, Cheryl Abel-Hodges

President Calvin Klein Retail, Nicholas (Nick) Strange

Regional President Pvh Asia Pacific, Frank Cancelloni

Evp General Counsel And Secretary, Mark D. Fischer, age 56

Evp And Chief Human Resources Officer, David F. (Dave) Kozel, age 62

Evp And Cio, Eileen Mahoney

Chief Supply Chain Officer, William (Bill) McRaith

Evp Wholesale Canada, Richard Deck

President Calvin Klein Europe Brand Management, Marcela Wartenbergh

Country Manager Calvin Klein Brazil, F˜bio Vasconcellos

Svp Sales Speedo, John Graham

President Pvh Japan, Tom Chu

Managing Director Calvin Klein Asia Pacific Korea, You Hyun-Ko

Managing Director Calvin Klein Asia Pacific China, Hanson Gu

Managing Director Calvin Klein Asia Pacific Commercial, Annie Wong

Managing Director France, Laurent Albouy

Managing Director Turkey, Hakan Atalay

Managing Director Russia, Georg Faisst

Managing Director Middle East Africa And The Netherlands, Maela Mandelli

Managing Director Uk And Ireland, David Pyne

Managing Director Nordic, Jesper Waerum

Senior Vice President Sales And Marketing, Joel Friedman

Senior Vice President Of Planning, Becky Quinn

Svp And Controller, James Holmes

Vice President, Tom Whitmer

Group Vice President Womens Sourcing, Susan Parson

Vice President Technical Accounting, Katie Jung

Group Vice President Human Resources, Danielle Korins

Vice President Of Mens Design Van Heusen Retail, Jeanne Clarke

Vice President Regional Sales Manager, John Karwacki

Vice President Purchasing, Lisa Barbosa

Vice President Merchandising, Gladys Yu

Vice President Planning Process And Technology
Integration, Jennifer Taras
Svp Real Estate And Leasing, Natalie Turpan
Vp Human Resources, Danielle Bernier
Vice President Distribution, Richard Vuich
Vice President Human Rights, Roopa Nair
Assistant Vice President Human Resources
Learning And Development, Brian Paich
Dvp Core Brands, Dan Bowe
Vice President Treasury, Christian Kochan
Vice President Of Design, Kevin Michales
Vice President Of Design For Timberland
Apparel, Michael Flynn
Vice President, John Benz
Vice President Advertising, Michael Delellis
Vice President Finance And Operations, Guilford
Robinson
Vice President Real Estate, Lauren Kinder
Group Vice President Wholesale Information
Technology, Debbie Beer-christensen
Vice President Creative Services, Andrea Murray
Vice President, Lily Benjamin
Senior Vice President Of Communications, Tiffin
Jernstedt
Vice President Of Finance And Administration,
Harry MA
Vice President, Heather Ambler
Vice President Construction X 6306, Susan Pierce
Vice President Licensing, Lynn Flynn
Executive Vice President, Franck Belochi
National Sales Manager, Ray Hennessy
Vice President Of Technical, Jin Chung
Vice President, Paul Callahan
Vice President Distribution And Cs, Douglas
Christian
Senior Vice President Of Retail Planning And
Analysis, Thomas Whitmer
Senior Vice President Global Compensation
Benefits And Human Resources Systems, Ann
Phillips
Vice President Human Resources, MaryAnn Vale
Vice President Global Financial Systems And Sap,
Raj Varughese
Vice President Ecommerce (tommy Hilfiger),
Sean Reynolds
Vice President Communications North America
(tommy Hilfiger), Pearl Lee
Executive Vice President Ecommerce (calvin
Klein), Mike Dupuis
Senior Vice President Marketing And
Communications (tommy Hilfiger), Abdel Hamri
Senior Vice President Europe Calvin Klein
Underwear Pvh, Melanie Gallop
Executive Vice President Operations And Chief
Financial Officer Calvin Klein, Gene Gosselin
Grp Vice President Infrastructure Services, Dan
Quigley
Senior Vice President Infrastructure And
Operations, Joe Melfi
Vice President Of Business Development, Jay
Fitzgerald
Vice President, Jennifer Underwood
Vice President Account Services, Fabrizio Zanardo
Vice President Of Communications, Timothy
Robertson
Vice President Technical Accounting, Mark Green
Vice President Business Planning Store Planning
And Analytics, Kathleen Tobi
Assistant Secretary, Michelle Odonnell
Auditors: Ernst & Young LLP

LOCATIONS

HQ: PVH Corp
  200 Madison Avenue, New York, NY 10016
Phone: 212 381-3500
Web: www.pvh.com

2016 Sales

	$ mil.	% of total
U.S.	4,226	51
Canada	484	6
Europe	2,372	29
Asia	910	11
Other	208	3
Total	**8,203**	**100**

PRODUCTS/OPERATIONS

2016 Sales

	$ mil.	% of total
Calvin Klein North America	1,689	20
Calvin Klein International	1,445	18
Tommy Hilfiger North America	1,563	19
Tommy Hilfiger International	1,947	24
Heritage Brands Wholesale	1,295	16
Heritage Brands Retail	261	3
Total	**8,203**	**100**

2016 Sales

	$ mil.	% of total
Net sales	7,791	95
Royalty	320	4
Advertising and other	91	1
Total	**8,203**	**100**

Selected Brands

Owned
  ARROW
  Bass
  Calvin Klein
  Eagle
  IZOD
  Tommy Hilfiger
  Van Heusen
Licensed
  Chaps
  Claiborne
  DKNY
  Kenneth Cole New York
  Kenneth Cole Reaction
  MICHAEL Michael Kors
  Michael Kors Collection
  Robert Graham
  Sean John

COMPETITORS

Allen-Edmonds	Kellwood
Armani	Kenneth Cole
Caleres	Levi Strauss
Capital Mercury	Nine West
Apparel	Oxford Industries
Donna Karan	Perry Ellis
Eddie Bauer LLC	International
Genesco	Prada
Gucci	Ralph Lauren
Haggar	Reebok
Hugo Boss	The Gap
J. Crew	Timberland
Kate Spade	VF Corporation

HISTORICAL FINANCIALS

Company Type: Public

Income Statement   FYE: February 4

	REVENUE ($ mil.)	NET INCOME ($ mil.)	NET PROFIT MARGIN	EMPLOYEES
02/18*	8,914	537	6.0%	36,500
01/17	8,203	549	6.7%	44,500
01/16	8,020	572	7.1%	34,200
02/15	8,241	439	5.3%	34,100
02/14	8,186	143	1.8%	33,200
Annual Growth	**2.2%**	**39.1%**	**—**	**2.4%**

*Fiscal year change

2018 Year-End Financials

Debt ratio: 25.92%   No. of shares (mil.): 77
Return on equity: 10.23%   Dividends
Cash ($ mil.): 493   Yield: 0.0%
Current ratio: 1.62   Payout: 2.1%
Long-term debt ($ mil.): 3,061   Market value ($ mil.): 11,659

	STOCK PRICE ($) FY Close	P/E High/Low	PER SHARE ($) Earnings	Dividends	Book Value
02/18*	151.07	23 12	6.84	0.15	71.73
01/17	90.30	17 10	6.79	0.15	61.16
01/16	73.38	17 10	6.89	0.15	55.86
02/15	110.26	25 20	5.27	0.15	52.89
02/14	120.87	78 59	1.74	0.15	52.76
Annual Growth	**5.7%**	**— —**	**40.8%**	**(0.0%)**	**8.0%**

*Fiscal year change

QCR Holdings Inc

Quad City is muscling in on the community banking scene in the Midwest. QCR Holdings is the holding company for Quad City Bank & Trust Cedar Rapids Bank & Trust Rockford Bank & Trust and Community State Bank. Together the banks have about 20 offices serving the Quad City area of Illinois and Iowa as well as the communities of Cedar Rapids Iowa; Rockford Illinois; and Milwaukee. The banks offer traditional deposit products and services and concentrate their lending activities on local businesses: Commercial real estate loans make up about half of the loan portfolio; commercial loans and leases make up another third.

Operations

QCR Holdings' Bancard subsidiary provides credit card processing services; its majority-owned M2 Lease Funds leases machinery and equipment to commercial and industrial businesses.

Strategy

QCR Holdings has grown by launching operations in new geographic markets and then building upon them. It also expands through acquisitions. In mid-2016 the company acquired Iowa-based Community State Bank which operates some 10 branches in the Des Moines area.

EXECUTIVES

President And Ceo, Douglas M. (Doug) Hultquist, age 63, $290,000 total compensation
Director; President And Ceo Cedar Rapids Bank And Trust, Larry J. Helling, age 62, $251,899 total compensation
Evp And Chief Credit Officer, Dana L. Nichols
Evp Coo And Cfo, Todd A. Gipple, age 55, $251,899 total compensation
Evp Corporate Strategy Human Resources And Branding, Cathie Whiteside, $162,000 total compensation
President And Ceo Rockford Bank And Trust, Thomas D. Budd, $172,000 total compensation
President And Ceo Quad City Bank And Trust, John H. Anderson, $200,000 total compensation
Evp Deposit Operations And Information Services, John A. Rodriguez
Svp And Cio, Michael J. Wyffels
Evp And Chief Operations Officer, John R. McEvoy
President And Ceo Community Bank And Trust, Stacey Bentley
President M2 Lease Funds, Richard W. Couch
Chairman And Ceo M2 Lease Funds, John R. Engelbrecht

LOCATIONS

HQ: QCR Holdings Inc
  3551 7th Street, Moline, IL 61265
Phone: 309 736-3580
Web: www.qcbt.com

PRODUCTS/OPERATIONS

2015 Sales

	$ mil.	% of total
Quad City Bank & Trust	52	46
Cedar Rapids Bank & Trust	37	32
Rockford Bank & Trust	14	13
Wealth Management	9	8
All other	0	1
Inter-company Eliminations	(0.4)	-
Total	**114**	**100**

COMPETITORS

Bank of America	First National of
Blackhawk Bancorp	Nebraska
First Business	MidWestOne
Financial	U.S. Bancorp
First Midwest Bancorp	

HISTORICAL FINANCIALS

Company Type: Public

Income Statement

FYE: December 31

	ASSETS ($ mil.)	NET INCOME ($ mil.)	INCOME AS % OF ASSETS	EMPLOYEES
12/17	3,982	35	0.9%	641
12/16	3,301	27	0.8%	572
12/15	2,593	16	0.7%	406
12/14	2,524	14	0.6%	409
12/13	2,394	14	0.6%	400
Annual Growth	**13.6%**	**24.3%**	**—**	**12.5%**

2017 Year-End Financials

Debt ratio: 2.60%	No. of shares (mil.): 13
Return on equity: 11.17%	Dividends
Cash ($ mil.): 131	Yield: 0.0%
Current ratio: —	Payout: 7.6%
Long-term debt ($ mil.): —	Market value ($ mil.): 596

	STOCK PRICE ($) FY Close	P/E High/Low	PER SHARE ($) Earnings	Dividends	Book Value
12/17	42.85	18 15	2.61	0.20	25.38
12/16	43.30	20 10	2.17	0.16	21.82
12/15	24.29	15 11	1.61	0.08	19.21
12/14	17.86	10 10	1.72	0.08	18.12
12/13	17.03	8 6	2.08	0.08	18.72
Annual Growth	**25.9%**	**— —**	**5.8%**	**25.7%**	**7.9%**

Qualcomm Inc

QUALCOMM is a leading designer and supplier of computer chips that mobile phone and wireless carriers depend on to get signals straight. The company pioneered the commercialization of the code-division multiple access (CDMA) technology used in digital wireless communications equipment and satellite ground stations mainly in North America. It generates most of its sales through the development and marketing of semiconductor chips such as its Snapdragon line and system software based on CDMA and other technologies. Its biggest customers have been suppliers to mobile phone makers Samsung and Apple. In 2018 QUALCOMM ended its $47 billion bid to buy NXP Semiconductors after the Chinese government failed to approve the deal.

Operations

While CDMA is QUALCOMM's flagship technology it has makes products based on Orthogonal Frequency Division Multiple Access (OFDMA) which allows multiple access on the same channel and Wideband Code Division Multiple Access (WCDMA) designed to ease the transmission of multimedia content.

QUALCOMM CDMA Technologies (QCT) is the company's biggest business segment generating more than 75% of revenue. Its QUALCOMM Technology Licensing (QTL) unit brings in the rest.

The company outsources manufacturing to contractors primarily Global Foundries Inc. Samsung Electronics Semiconductor Manufacturing International Corp. Taiwan Semiconductor Manufacturing Co. and United Microelectronics Corp.

Geographic Reach

QUALCOMM based in San Diego California gets about two-thirds of its revenue from customers based in China (including Hong Kong) while customers based in South Korea supply about 15% of revenue.

Sales and Marketing

More than 50% of QUALCOMM's revenue come from five customers: Apple Inc. (and its supplier Hon Hai Precision) Samsung Electronics Guang-Dong OPPO Mobile Telecommunications Corp. Ltd. and Vivo Communication Technology Co.

Financial Performance

QUALCOMM halted a three-year string of falling revenue in 2018 (ended September) but the company's bottom line took a hit from the US Tax Cuts and Jobs Act of 2017.

Sales edged 2% higher to $22.7 billion in 2018 from $22.3 billion in 2017 on a 4.5% increase in QCT sales while licensing sales fell about 5%. The company reported higher sales of radio frequency front-end (RFFE) components and Mobile Station Modem (MSM) integrated circuits. The company's products fetched lower prices on average in 2018 compared to 2017.

QUALCOMM had a net loss of about $4.9 billion due to a $5.7 billion charge for income tax expense for repatriated earnings and profits of US-owned foreign subsidiaries. Also included were a $2 billion fee paid to NXP for terminating the acquisition and a $1.3 billion fine paid to the European Commission.

The company's cash and equivalent balance dropped to $11.8 billion in 2018 from about $35 billion in 2017 because of costs related to the proposed NXP acquisition and an increased in money spent on stock buybacks year-to-year. In 2018 operations generated $3.9 billion and investment activities provided $4.4 billion while investing activities used $31.5 billion.

Strategy

QUALCOMM's revenue suffered when Apple went with another manufacturer for mobile phone modems. What's more the companies have been in court suing and counter-suing over who owns what technology. They continued the courtroom battle into 2019.

Two other corporate battles were settled in 2018 leaving the company with one win and one loss. The win came when Broadcom dropped its bid to buy QUALCOMM when the US government rejected it on national security concerns. In a different takeover battle QUALCOMM ended its pursuit of NXP due to a slow by regulatory review and tepid response from NXP shareholders. QUALCOMM had to cough up a $2 billion termination fee.

On the product side QUALCOMM is ready to furnish manufacturers with technology for 5G wireless networks which are to be much faster and more powerful than previous wireless technologies. The company has worked to develop 5G technology for about a decade (it holds 15% of 5G patents a higher percentage than any other company) and the toil is nearing payoff. The next generation of wireless networking has promise of providing faster communication with less latency unleashing a host of new and powerful applications. The first 5G networks could launch in 2018 with more rolling out over the next several years. If it plays out like previous wireless generations it means big business for QUALCOMM.

Mergers and Acquisitions

QUALCOMM acquired Scyfer B.V. a company that developed artificial intelligence technologies in 2017. Qualcomm added Scyfer's applications to end-use devices such as smartphones cars and robotics to ensure that processing can be done with or without a network

QUALCOMM and TDK formed a joint venture in 2017 to provide chips for mobile devices and internet of things applications. The entity called RF360 Holdings combines QUALCOMM's chip expertise with that of TDK in filters. Application areas are mobile devices automotive and drones. The ownership of the joint venture is split 51% by QUALCOMM and 49% by TDK.

Company Background

Professors Irwin Mark Jacobs and Andrew Viterbi founded digital signal processing equipment company Linkabit in 1968. M/A-COM acquired the company in 1980. Led by Jacobs Viterbi and five other executives left M/A-COM Linkabit in 1985 to start engineer-focused QUALCOMM (for "quality communications") to provide contract R&D services. The company's first home was located above a strip mall pizza parlor in San Diego. CEO Jacobs dreamed of modifying code-division multiple access (CDMA) — a secure wireless transmission system developed during WWII — for commercial use.

In 1988 QUALCOMM introduced OmniTRACS a satellite-based system that tracks the location of long-haul truckers. By 1989 when QUALCOMM unveiled its version of CDMA the company was working on military contracts worth $15 million.

In 1990 the company interrupted the Cellular Telecommunications Industry Association's (CTIA) plans to adopt a rival technology called time-division multiple access when communications service providers NYNEX (now part of Verizon) and Ameritech (later part of SBC Communications and now part of AT&T) adopted QUALCOMM's maverick technology. QUALCOMM initiated a CDMA public relations blitz and by 1991 Motorola AT&T Clarion and Nokia had signed product development and testing agreements.

The company went public in 1991 and introduced the Eudora e-mail software program (named for "Why I Live at the P.O." author Eudora Welty) which it licensed from the University of Illinois.

That year QUALCOMM and Loral Corporation unveiled plans for Globalstar a satellite telecommunications system similar to the Iridium system. The CTIA adopted CDMA as a North American standard for wireless communications in 1993.

EXECUTIVES

Senior Vice President, Greg Rose
Senior Vice President Marketing, Jeffrey K Belk
Svp Government Affairs, William Bold
Senior Vice President And General Manager, Neville Meijers
Evp And Cfo, George S. Davis, age 61, $760,011 total compensation
Svp And Chief Marketing Officer, Penny Baldwin
Evp General Counsel And Corporate Secretary, Donald J. Rosenberg, age 67, $675,002 total compensation
Svp Product Management Cdma Technologies, Steven M. (Steve) Mollenkopf, age 49, $1,138,694 total compensation
Evp Technology, Matthew S. (Matt) Grob, age 51
Evp Engineering Qualcomm Technologies Inc. And Cto, James H. (Jim) Thompson, age 54
President, Cristiano R. Amon, age 48, $523,090 total compensation
Evp Human Resources, Michelle Sterling, age 51
Evp Strategy And M&a, Brian T. Modoff, age 58, $542,324 total compensation
Evp And President Qualcomm Technology Licensing (qtl), Alexander H. (Alex) Rogers, age 61
Vice President Engineering, Walid Hamdy
Vice President Information Technology Enterprise Applications, Bob Gentile
Vice President Senior Director Engineering Technology, Dom Farmer
Vice President Marketing, Pete Lancia
Vice President, Eduardo Esteves
Vice President Regulatory Engineering, Paul Guckian
Vice President Finance, Taylor Cabaniss
Vice President Engineering, Idris Mir
Vice President Program Management, Rob Rumbaugh
Senior Vice President Chief Ip Strategist, Roger Martin
Senior Vice President Engineering, Durga Malladi
Vice President Engineering, Bobby Konganda
Senior Vice President Principal Accounting Officer, John M Miller
Senior Vice President Public Relations, Dan Novak
Vice President Of Product Marketing And Business Development, Roberto Di Pietro
Vice President Division Counsel, Jeff S Dugdale
Vice President Strategic Development, Ed Charbonneau
Vice President Sales, Eric Koliander
Vice President Cheif Patent Counsel, Philip Wadsworth
Senior Vice President Engineering, Nick Yu
Senior Vice President, Magnus Felke
Senior Vice President And General Manager Emerging Business Unit, Michael Wallace
Senior Vice President And General Manager Qtl China, Benson Lam
Vice President Technology, Surya Ganti
Vice President Of Sales Latin America, Marcos Lacerda
Vice President Marketing, Don MacDonald
Vice President Engineering, Chienchung Chang
Vice President Legal Counsel, David Zuckerman
Vice President Engineering, Rob Reeves
Vice President, Manvinder Singh
Vice President Technology, James Krysl
Vice President, Kristie Mccue
Senior Vice President Government Affairs, Nate Tibbits
Senior Vice President Engineering, Torrey Harmon

Vice President And General Manager Qualcomm Education, Vicki Mealer-Burke
Senior Vice President Ventures And Innovation North America And Head Qualcomm Ventures, Nagraj Kashyap
National Account Manager, Leslie Perretti
Vice President Engineering, Scott Papineau
Vice President Internal Audit, Mark Dunham
Senior Vice President Engineering, Gil Sih
Vice President Engineering, Carl Uhl
Senior Vice President Engineering, Susie Armstrong
Vice President Portfolio And Program Management, Malcolm Spencer
Vice President Of Engineering, Brian Banister
Vice President Engineering, Jack Steenstra
Vice President Investor Relations, John Sinnott
Senior Vice President Government Affairs, Dean Brenner
Senior Vice President Of Technology, Charles Wheatley
Vice President Of Technology, Sherman Gregory
Vice President And Treasurer, Dick Grannis
Vice President Of Business Development, Chris Talbot
Vice President Of Marketing, Charlotte Lamprecht
Vice President Of Product Management, Tim Leland
Vice President Learning And Development, Tamar Elkeles
Vice President Engineering, Brian K Harms
Vice President Engineering, Kamal Sahota
Vice President Marketing, Khalid Sidiqi
Senior Vice President Strategy And Corporate Development, Matt Eichenberger
Vice President Engineering Ams Design, Gene McAllister
Vice President And President, John Stefanac
Vice President Engineering, Alex Holcman
Vice President Engineering, Scott Arnold
Senior Vice President Enterprise Architecture, Rob Gilmore
Vice President Government Affairs, Steve Crout
Vice President Technology, Vk Jones
Senior Vice President Engineering, Rajesh Pankaj
Vice President Product Management, Francesco Grilli
Vice President, Mike Refermat
Vice President Technology, John Hong
Vice President Of Sales, Andrew Gilbert
Vice President Engineering, Rich Gardner
Senior Vice President Qualcomm Data Center Group, Anand Chandrasekher
Vice President Of Engineering, Francesco Carobolante
Vice President Of Engineering, Willie Anderson
Vice President Employee Relations, Jane M Baker
Vice President Engineering, Daniel Waldburger
Senior Vice President Engineering, Ed Tiedemann
Vice President Corporate Product Security, Alex Gantman
Vice President Of Government Affairs, Alice Tornquist
Vice President Engineering, Andrew Hunter
Senior Vice President Of Engineering, Anthony Schwarz
Senior Vice President Of Business Development, Terry Yen
Vice President Business Development, Salvador Blasco
Vice President Of Technology, Geoffrey Yeap
Vice President Head Corporate Research And Development Silicon Valley, Nayeem Islam
Vice President Of Engineering, David Su
Vice President Security, Stewart Roberts
Vice President Techonology, Benny Katibian
Vice President Engineering, Allen Tran
Vice President Engineering And Operations, Mark Halfman
Vice President Engineering, Eric Tallet

Senior Vice President And General Manager Automotive, Patrick Little
Vice President Sales, Curt Thornton
Vice President Of Operations, Ravi Soordelu
Vice President Business Development, Jeffery Torrance
Vice President Engineering, Udi Landen
Vice President Engineering Qct Software, Tony Schwarz
Vice President Technology, Nikhil Jain
Vice President Engineering, Bob Gilmore
Executive Vice President And President Qualcomm Technology Licensing, Alex Rogers
Vice President Technology, Jeremiah Golston
Vice President Technology, Walid Ali-ahmad
Vice President Of Product Management, Tal Tamir
Vice President Business Development And Product Management, Nicholas Karter
Vice President Hardware Engineering Group Corpor, Ernie Ozaki
Vice President Contracts, Samimi Abbaseh
Vice President Of Engineering, Jose Corleto
Vice President Engineering, Octavio Martinez
Senior Vice President Finance, Sanjay Mehta
Vice President Technology Licensing, Al St George
Vice President Product Management, Reiner Klement
Senior Vice President Engineering, Charlie Persico
Vice President Program Management, Steven Larky
Vice President Engineering, Andre Izotov
Senior Vice President, Chuck Wheatley
Vice President, Shigeyuki Kobayashi
Svp Engineering, Bill Earnshaw
Vice President Engineering, Hamid Ahmadi
Vice President Package Engineering, Raj Pendse
Vice President Engineering, Mike Leary
Vice President Global Information Technology Engineering, Chandra Mouli
Vice President Of Technology, Roger Olmstead
Vice President Business Operations, Laura Hart
Vice President Technology, Ken Wiseman
Vice President Technology, Sanjiv Nanda
Vice President Government Affairs, Charles Godwin
Vice President Engineering, Gregory Bullard
Senior Vice President, Mark Epstein
Vp Strategic Programs, Edward Charbonneau
Vice President Global Technical Education, Sei Seung Yoon
Vice President Of Engineering, Jose Corleto-mena
Vice President Of Engineering, William Miller
Vice President Engineering, Len Sheynblat
Senior Vice President Engineering, William Earnshaw
Vice President Of Business Development, James Cathey
Vice President Engineering, Tong Henry
Vice President Product Marketing, Don Mcguire
Auditors: PricewaterhouseCoopers LLP

LOCATIONS

HQ: Qualcomm Inc
5775 Morehouse Dr., San Diego, CA 92121-1714
Phone: 858 587-1121
Web: www.qualcomm.com

2018 Sales

	$ mil.	% of total
China (including Hong Kong)	15,149	67
South Korea	3,173	14
United States	603	2
Other foreign	3,805	17
Total	**22,732**	**100**

PRODUCTS/OPERATIONS

2018 Sales

	$ mil.	% of total
QCT (Qualcomm CDMA Technologies)	17,282	76
QTL (Qualcomm Technology Licensing)	5,163	23
QSI (Qualcomm Strategic Initiatives)	100	
Adjustments	187	1
Total	**22,732**	**100**

2018 Sales

	$ mil.	% of total
Equipment & services	17,400	77
Licensing	5,332	23
Total	**22,732**	**100**

Selected Operations and Products

Code-Division Multiple Access (CDMA) Technologies
Group
  Integrated circuits
  Baseband
  Intermediate-frequency
  Power management
  Radio-frequency
  Systems software
Engineering Services Group
Enterprise Services
Firethorn Holdings
Flarion Technologies
Government Technologies
Innovation Center
Internet Services
MediaFLO Technologies
MEMS Technologies
Qualcomm Ventures
Strategic Initiatives
Technology Licensing Group
  CDMA technologies and patents (cdmaOne CDMA2000
  WCDMA TD-SCDMA)
  Royalties from products incorporating CDMA
  technology
Wireless and Internet Group
  Digital Media
  Digital motion picture delivery systems (under
  development)
  Government systems (development and analysis
  services; wireless base stations and phones)
  Internet Services
  Applications development software for wireless devices
  (BREW)
  Wireless Systems
  Low-Earth-orbit satellite-based telecommunications
  system (Globalstar)

COMPETITORS

Broadcom	REALTEK
SEMICONDUCTOR	
Cirrus Logic	CORP.
InterDigital	Renesas Electronics
Marvell Technology	STMicroelectronics
Maxim Integrated	Samsung Electronics
Products	Sequans Communications
MediaTek	Spreadtrum
Murata Manufacturing	Texas Instruments
NVIDIA	

HISTORICAL FINANCIALS

Company Type: Public

Income Statement   FYE: September 30

	REVENUE ($ mil.)	NET INCOME ($ mil.)	NET PROFIT MARGIN	EMPLOYEES
09/18	22,732	(4,864)	—	35,400
09/17	22,291	2,466	11.1%	33,800
09/16	23,554	5,705	24.2%	30,500
09/15	25,281	5,271	20.8%	33,000
09/14	26,487	7,967	30.1%	31,300
Annual Growth	**(3.7%)**	**—**	**—**	**3.1%**

2018 Year-End Financials

Debt ratio: 50.08%
Return on equity: (-30.22%)
Cash ($ mil.): 11,777
Current ratio: 1.55
Long-term debt ($ mil.): 15,365

No. of shares (mil.): 1,219
Dividends
  Yield: 0.0%
  Payout: —
Market value ($ mil.): 87,805

	STOCK PRICE ($) FY Close	P/E High/Low		PER SHARE ($) Earnings	Dividends	Book Value
09/18	72.03	—	—	(3.32)	2.38	0.76
09/17	52.09	42	30	1.65	2.20	20.86
09/16	62.75	17	11	3.81	2.02	21.53
09/15	53.22	24	16	3.22	1.80	20.62
09/14	75.06	17	14	4.65	1.54	23.47
Annual Growth	**(1.0%)**	**—**	**—**	**—**	**11.5%**	**(57.6%)**

Quanta Services, Inc.

Quanta Services is a specialty contractor that designs installs repairs and maintains network infrastructure across North America and abroad. The company serves the electric power oil and natural gas and communication industries mainly in the US Canada and Australia. Capabilities include pylon construction distribution infrastructure and emergency response among much more. Its oil and gas business offers onshore and offshore services. Quanta's other services include outsource management and other specialty work such as installing traffic and light rail control systems directional drilling and constructing wind and solar power facilities. The company was founded in 1997.

Operations

Quanta operates through two primary segments: Electric Power Infrastructure which generates some 60% of revenue; and Oil and Gas Infrastructure Services (40% of revenue).

The Electric Power segment offers a vast array of physical infrastructure construction and maintenance. Services include transmission construction distribution construction substations power generation emergency response EPC (engineering procurement and construction) services helicopter services and more.

Oil and Gas Infrastructure Services designs installs and maintains pipelines and has horizontal drilling trenching and mechanized welding capabilities. It serves the offshore sector with services including mechanical installation commissioning coatings shallow-water pipeline installation fabrication and marine asset repair.

Geographic Reach

Houston-based Quanta Services generates around 75% of its revenue in the US. Its next largest market is Canada which accounts for about 20% of its business followed by Australia. Other international offices are in South Africa India and Latin America (Chile Colombia Costa Rica Ecuador Guatemala Mexico Panama and Peru).

Sales and Marketing

Quanta mostly serves companies in the electric power oil & gas and communications markets though it also serves commercial industrial and governmental organizations. Around three-quarters of its revenue base is recurring in nature.

Quanta's customer base is relatively well diversified: Its largest customer accounts for 5% of sales and its ten largest combined account for 30%. Clients include American Electric Power Duke Energy PG&E Corp. and TransCanada Corp ITC Holdings and Exelon Corp. among others.

Financial Performance

Apart from a blip in 2015 Quanta's revenue has been on an upward trajectory.

In fiscal 2017 revenue leaped 24% to $9.4 billion. Activity in the oil and gas industry kicked into gear as the oil price rebounded helping Quanta's oil and gas revenue grow $1.1 billion. Customer capital spending on midstream gas pipeline transmission projects was the primary growth driver while the Stronghold acquisition added $190 million to oil and gas sales as well. The electric power infrastructure segment also performed strongly growing $749 million as customers increased spending on transmission projects. Emergency restoration spending in the aftermath of the two major hurricanes to hit Texas in 2017 Irma and Harvey also contributed to electric power sales.

Quanta's net income also grew although it lagged the strident revenue growth up $118 million to $318 million. In fact most of the growth came from a $71.7 decrease in provision for income taxes relating to the 2017 Tax Cuts and Jobs Act: Profit margins were down due to disruption from the two hurricanes partially offset by the higher prices charged for emergency restoration services.

Cash from operations fell 5% to $372.5 million as higher earnings were offset by increased working capital requirements and changes in accounts receivable from the emergency restoration work.

Strategy

With activity in the oil industry ramping up on the back of higher oil prices Quanta is increasing its investment capital. In 2017 it invested $575.8 billion a $309 million increase on 2016 on acquisitions and capital expenditures. As part of its broader strategy to provide fully integrated differentiated solutions to its customers Quanta established energy investment vehicle First Infrastructure Capital in 2017. In partnership with select infrastructure investors it will invest in concessions public-private partnerships and private infrastructure projects. A significant chunk of Quanta's investment budget went on acquiring Stronghold which provides high-pressure solutions to the oil and gas industry.

Mergers and Acquisitions

In 2018 Quanta acquired Northwest Lineman College (NLC) an educational and training institution serving the electric power industry. NLC is based in Boise Idaho with additional campuses in California Florida and Texas. The college will enhance the quality of Quanta's talent.

In July 2017 Quanta acquired Stronghold a specialized services company that provides high-pressure and critical path solutions to the downstream and midstream energy markets for $450 million. The acquisition opens up new niches in the industrial services market. Also in 2017 Quanta acquired a communications infrastructure services contractor and an electrical and communications contractor both based in the US.

In 2016 Quanta completed five acquisitions including an Australian electrical infrastructure services company a Canadian utility contracting company an American medium- and high-voltage powerline contracting company and a telecommunications company located in Canada. In 2015 it made 11 acquisitions.

EXECUTIVES

Cfo, Derrick A. Jensen, age 47, $600,000 total compensation

President Ceo And Coo, Earl C. (Duke) Austin, age 48, $979,924 total compensation

Evp Corporate Development And President Infrastructure Solutions, Jesse E. Morris, age 50, $466,900 total compensation

Evp Operations And Health/safety And Environmental, Randall C. Wisenbaker, age 53, $475,625 total compensation

President Electric Power, Dale L. Querrey, age 54, $595,880 total compensation

President Oil And Gas Division And Chief Strategy Officer, Paul C. Gregory, age 54
Chairman, Bruce E. Ranck
Auditors: PricewaterhouseCoopers LLP

LOCATIONS

HQ: Quanta Services, Inc.
2800 Post Oak Boulevard, Suite 2600, Houston, TX 77056
Phone: 713 629-7600
Web: www.quantaservices.com

PRODUCTS/OPERATIONS

2017 sales

	$ mil.	% of total
Electric power infrastructure	5,599	59
Oil and gas infrastructure	3,466	41
Total	**9,466**	**100**

COMPETITORS

Cable Com	MDU Construction
Comm-Works	Services
Dycom	MYR Group
EMCOR	MasTec
Goldfield	Mass Electric
Henkels & McCoy	Pike Corporation
IES Holdings	Tetra Tech

HISTORICAL FINANCIALS

Company Type: Public

Income Statement — FYE: December 31

	REVENUE ($ mil.)	NET INCOME ($ mil.)	NET PROFIT MARGIN	EMPLOYEES
12/17	9,466	314	3.3%	32,800
12/16	7,651	198	2.6%	28,100
12/15	7,572	310	4.1%	24,500
12/14	7,851	296	3.8%	24,600
12/13	6,522	401	6.2%	20,900
Annual Growth	**9.8%**	**(5.9%)**	**—**	**11.9%**

2017 Year-End Financials

Debt ratio: 10.35%
Return on equity: 8.83%
Cash ($ mil.): 138
Current ratio: 1.92
Long-term debt ($ mil.): 670

No. of shares (mil.): 153
Dividends
Yield: —
Payout: —
Market value ($ mil.): 6,016

	STOCK PRICE ($) FY Close	P/E High/Low	PER SHARE ($) Earnings	Dividends	Book Value
12/17	39.11	20 15	2.00	0.00	24.65
12/16	34.85	28 14	1.26	0.00	22.08
12/15	20.25	19 12	1.59	0.00	19.31
12/14	28.39	28 19	1.35	0.00	20.69
12/13	31.56	17 14	1.87	0.00	19.56
Annual Growth	**5.5%**	**— —**	**1.7%**	**—**	**5.9%**

Quest Diagnostics, Inc.

Quest Diagnostics is testing its ability to be the world's leading clinical lab. The company performs diagnostics on some 160 million specimens each year including routine clinical tests such as cholesterol checks Pap smears and HIV screenings. Quest Diagnostics also performs esoteric testing (such as genetic screening) and anatomic pathology testing (such as tissue biopsies for cancer testing). Its Quest Diagnostic Nichols Institute develops new diagnostics. In all the company serves half of the physicians and hospitals in the US as well as government agencies and other clinical labs. Quest Diagnostics has more than 2200 patient service centers where samples are collected.

HISTORY

Quest Diagnostics began as one man's quest to make clinical tests more affordable. Pathologist Paul Brown started Metropolitan Pathological Laboratory (MetPath) in his Manhattan apartment in 1967. To help his business take off in 1969 he bought two $55000 blood analyzers that could automatically perform a dozen common tests; the machines allowed him to charge patients $5.50 while hospitals and other labs were charging upwards of $40. Investments in emerging lab technology helped MetPath continue to beat competitors' prices and grow its business. It made its first profit in 1971 and eventually attracted the attention of Corning Glass Works which bought 10% of the company in 1973.

MetPath's growth was due in part to investments in technology. The company built a state-of-the-art central lab in New Jersey in 1978 that could process some 30000 specimens daily; it also went on an acquisition spree to expand across the US. These investments left the firm swamped with debt and Corning bought the company in 1982.

An autonomous unit of Corning MetPath continued to grow as Medicare reimbursement for lab tests went up and more doctors ordered more tests to catch and prevent disease before it happened. To cut costs in the mid-1980s the company reorganized its facilities to create a regional lab network. A reorganization in 1990 at its parent placed MetPath in the Corning Lab Services subsidiary.

Corning Lab Services strengthened its operations in the early 1990s by buying labs from regional operators. In 1994 MetPath became Corning Clinical Laboratories. Around the same time the company found itself besieged with demands from HMOs and other managed care providers to lower its costs. Also during this time the company settled a handful of federal suits accusing it of fraudulent Medicare billing. In the face of increasing pressure parent Corning spun off its lab testing business to the public as Quest Diagnostics in 1996.

On its own Quest aimed to grow through acquisitions. In 1999 it bought rival SmithKline Beecham Clinical Laboratories from GlaxoSmithKline. (GSK gained a minority stake in Quest through the deal; it gradually sold off all shares in Quest by 2011.) Continuing its growth strategy in the 21st century it bought American Medical Laboratories to expand its esoteric testing operations in 2002. The company was finally able to close its acquisition of Unilab in early 2003 after the deal ran into delays with the FTC. Quest sold some labs and service contracts in northern California to LabCorp to appease FTC regulators.

To expand internationally the company began providing testing services in India in 2008 including esoteric testing for hospitals tests for the life insurance industry and diagnostics for global clinical trials.

EXECUTIVES

Chairman President And Ceo, Stephen H. (Steve) Ruskowski, age 60, $1,100,000 total compensation
Svp And Group Executive Diagnostic Solutions, Jon R. Cohen, age 63, $575,000 total compensation
Svp And Group Executive Clinical Franchise Solutions And Marketing, Catherine T. Doherty, age 55, $575,000 total compensation
Svp Commercial, Everett V. Cunningham, age 51
Vp Global Markets And Chairman Q2 Solutions, John B. Haydon
Evp And Cfo, Mark J. Guinan, age 56, $586,538 total compensation
Evp General Diagnostics, James E. Davis, age 55, $586,538 total compensation
Svp Research And Development And Medical And Chief Medical Officer, Jay G. Wohlgemuth
Svp And Cio, Lidia Fonseca
Vp And Treasurer, Tracy Cinco-abela
Vice President Clinical Trials, Christopher Fikry
Svp Strategy Mergers And Acquisitions And Ventures, Dermot Shorten
Regional Vice President Commercial, Geoffrey Albrecht
Vp Marketing, James Humphreys
Vice President International Sales And Operations, Devi Prasad Karuppur
Auditors: PricewaterhouseCoopers LLP

LOCATIONS

HQ: Quest Diagnostics, Inc.
500 Plaza Drive, Secaucus, NJ 07094
Phone: 973 520-2700
Web: www.QuestDiagnostics.com

PRODUCTS/OPERATIONS

2016 Sales

	$ mil.	% of total
Diagnostic information services		
Routine clinical testing services	4,179	56
Gene-based and esoteric (including advanced diagnostics) testing services	2,335	31
Anatomic pathology testing services	624	8
All Other	377	5
Total	**7,515**	**100**

COMPETITORS

Alere	Oncolab
Arup Laboratories	Pathology Associates
Bio-Reference Labs	Medical Laboratories
Genomic Health	Psychemedics
LabCorp	Solstas
Medtox Scientific	Sonic Healthcare

HISTORICAL FINANCIALS

Company Type: Public

Income Statement — FYE: December 31

	REVENUE ($ mil.)	NET INCOME ($ mil.)	NET PROFIT MARGIN	EMPLOYEES
12/17	7,709	772	10.0%	45,000
12/16	7,515	645	8.6%	43,000
12/15	7,493	709	9.5%	44,000
12/14	7,435	556	7.5%	45,000
12/13	7,146	849	11.9%	41,000
Annual Growth	**1.9%**	**(2.3%)**	**—**	**2.4%**

2017 Year-End Financials

Debt ratio: 36.03%
Return on equity: 16.17%
Cash ($ mil.): 137
Current ratio: 1.24
Long-term debt ($ mil.): 3,748

No. of shares (mil.): 135
Dividends
Yield: 0.0%
Payout: 32.7%
Market value ($ mil.): 13,296

	STOCK PRICE ($) FY Close	P/E High/Low	PER SHARE ($) Earnings	Dividends	Book Value
12/17	98.49	20 16	5.50	1.80	36.45
12/16	91.90	20 13	4.51	1.58	33.78
12/15	71.14	16 12	4.87	1.47	32.76
12/14	67.06	18 13	3.81	1.29	29.87
12/13	53.54	11 9	5.54	1.20	27.42
Annual Growth	**16.5%**	**— —**	**(0.2%)**	**10.7%**	**7.4%**

Qurate Retail Inc

Liberty Interactive Corp. stands by your right to shop at home and online. The company owns and operates market-leading home shopping channel QVC which sells 770 products each week across the home apparel beauty and accessories jewelry and electronics categories. QVC also sells online. Liberty Interactive also runs online businesses including Zulily and online invitation site Evite. It also holds equity stakes in FTD Companies HSN Interval Leisure and LendingTree among others. Liberty Interactive acquired the long-standing rival of its QVC business HSN Inc. for around $2.1 billion in 2017. Liberty Interactive Corp. was formed in 2011 when its predecessor restructured and split off its Liberty Capital and Liberty Starz businesses as Liberty Media.

Operations

Liberty Interactive operates through two main business divisions: QVC Group and Liberty Ventures.

The QVC Group consists of QVC Zulily and Liberty's interest in HSN. QVC is the company's cash cow subsidiary accounting about 80% of its sales. The television brand broadcasts live shopping programs and sells merchandise online in the US and abroad. QVC classifies its products into six groups: home beauty apparel jewelry accessories and electronics. Home is the biggest earner at around one third of sales followed by apparel at nearly 20% and beauty at more than 15%.

Zulily brings in 15% of sales sells products in the US and elsewhere online through flash sales events primarily through its desktop and mobile websites and mobile applications.

Liberty Ventures consists of e-card website Evite and interests in Liberty Broadband FTD Interval Leisure Group Time Warner Charter Communications Britco and LendingTree.

Geographic Reach

Liberty Interactive rings up around 75% of its sales in the US. Japan and Germany each account for less than 10% of sales. QVC has shopping channels in Germany Italy Japan France and the UK. The company also has a joint venture in China.

Sales and Marketing

Flagship subsidiary QVC distributes its television programs through satellite and optical fiber to cable and satellite system providers in the US Germany Japan the UK and neighboring countries. It also transmits programs via digital terrestrial broadcast television to viewers in Italy the UK and certain parts of the US and Germany. Additionally QVC offers a web-based catalog for retailers.

Some of QVC's clients include Comcast Time Warner Cable Cox Dish Network DirecTV Verizon and AT&T.

Financial Performance

After a bad 2015 Liberty Interactive's revenue bounced back in fiscal 2016 growing 7% to $10.6 billion. Growth was concentrated in Zulily which gained more than $1 billion due to its first full-year contribution. QVC's sales declined $61 million while the sales of Backcountry and Bodybuilding in 2015 and 2016 also weighed on sales.

Net income increased 40% to $1.3 billion thanks to higher revenue decreases in stock-based compensation and gains on the Right Start sale in January 2016.

Cash form operations increased 39% to $1.4 billion due to higher net income and changes in deferred income tax expense offset by realized losses on financial instruments.

Strategy

Liberty Interactive has been busy reshaping its business. In the last few years it has pared down its number of activities particularly in online retail — in 2015-16 it has sold or spun off Backcountry.com Bodybuilding.com Expedia and CommerceHub.com; the year before that it sold Provide Commerce to floral and gift retailer FTD Companies and spun off TripAdvisor and the Buy-Seasons group as TripAdvisor Holdings.

The sales paved the way for the $2.1 billion acquisition of QVC's archrival HSN Inc. agreed in 2017. With both QVC and HSN recording unfavorable revenue trends in recent years the acquisition reflects that the former rivals' biggest competitors are no longer each other but e-commerce giants such as Amazon. QVC HSN and Zulily will be bundled up as QVC Group.

Mergers and Acquisitions

Liberty Interactive agreed to buy the 62% of the Home Shopping Network Inc. (HSNi) that it didn't own for about $2.1 billion in stock. The deal would unite HSNi with Liberty's QVC in an effort to combat Amazon.com and other online retailers. Liberty plans to package QVC HSNi and Zulily.com into an asset-backed spinoff in late 2017. The acquisition of HSNi was expected to close by the end of the year.

HISTORY

The man who would be king of cable programming got his start on the hardware end of the business. In 1970 John Malone became president of General Instrument's Jerrold Communications subsidiary which supplied equipment to the then-new cable TV industry. One of Jerrold's customers was Bob Magness a former Texas rancher who in the 1950s started the company that eventually became Denver-based cable operator Tele-Communications Inc. (TCI). In the early 1970s TCI struggled in need of leadership. In 1973 the 32-year-old Malone was named CEO of TCI.

Malone restructured TCI's debt in 1977 paving the way for expansion into bigger cable markets after deregulation in 1984. He also acquired programming buying stakes in Black Entertainment Television (33% 1979 sold to Viacom in 2001) the Discovery Channel (14% 1986) and American Movie Classics (50% 1986). In 1987 TCI helped save debt-plagued Turner Broadcasting and came away with 12% of Turner Broadcasting's stock.

Due in part to antitrust pressure from government regulators in 1991 TCI spun off much of its programming assets along with interests in 14 cable systems as Liberty Media. Malone became chairman and principal shareholder. In its first year the company launched Court TV in a joint venture and introduced film channel Encore. The next year it bought an interest in the Home Shopping Network (which became USA Networks in 1998 and later changed names to USA Interactive in 2002 InterActiveCorp in 2003 and finally IAC/InterActiveCorp in 2004).

In 1994 TCI reacquired Liberty Media; it issued a tracking stock the next year to reflect the value of Liberty's program assets. Also in 1995 Liberty Media and News Corp. joined forces to create FOX/Liberty Networks a national sports network designed to compete with Disney's ESPN.

In 2011 Liberty Media Corp. changed its name to Liberty Interactive Corp. following the split-off of its Liberty Capital and Liberty Starz tracking stocks.

EXECUTIVES

President And Ceo, Gregory B. (Greg) Maffei, age 57, $1,045,739 total compensation
Chief Corporate Development Officer, Albert E. Rosenthaler, age 58, $336,031 total compensation
Chief Legal Officer, Richard N. (Rich) Baer, age 61, $327,307 total compensation
Cfo Liberty Media Corporation Liberty Interactive Corporation And Liberty Broadband Corporation, Mark D. Carleton, age 57, $127,147 total compensation
Chairman, John C. Malone, age 77
Auditors: KPMG LLP

LOCATIONS

HQ: Qurate Retail Inc
12300 Liberty Boulevard, Englewood, CO 80112
Phone: 720 875-5300
Web: www.libertyinteractive.com

2016 Sales

	$ mil.	% of total
US	7,979	75
Japan	900	8
Germany	866	8
Other countries	902	9
Total	**10,647**	**100**

PRODUCTS/OPERATIONS

2016 Sales

	$ mil.	% of total
QVC	8,682	81
zulily	1,547	15
Ventures Group	428	4
eliminations	(10)	-
Total	**10,647**	**100**

2016 Sales

	% of total
Home	33
Apparel	19
Beauty	17
Accessories	13
Jewelry	9
Electronics	9
Total	**100**

COMPETITORS

Access TV	Orbitz Worldwide
Amazon.com	Priceline
American Express	Travelocity
EVINE Live	Wal-Mart
IAC	

HISTORICAL FINANCIALS

Company Type: Public

Income Statement   FYE: December 31

	REVENUE ($ mil.)	NET INCOME ($ mil.)	NET PROFIT MARGIN	EMPLOYEES
12/17	10,404	2,441	23.5%	28,255
12/16	10,647	1,235	11.6%	21,080
12/15	9,989	869	8.7%	22,080
12/14	10,499	537	5.1%	20,078
12/13	11,252	501	4.5%	23,079
Annual Growth	(1.9%)	48.6%	—	5.2%

2017 Year-End Financials

Debt ratio: 35.44%
Return on equity: 29.14%
Cash ($ mil.): 903
Current ratio: 1.21
Long-term debt ($ mil.): 7,553

No. of shares (mil.): 564
Dividends
  Yield: —
  Payout: —
Market value ($ mil.): 13,790

STOCK PRICE ($)		P/E		PER SHARE ($)		
	FY Close	High/Low		Earnings	Dividends	Book Value
12/17	24.42	10	7	2.70	0.00	17.68
12/16	19.98	28	18	0.98	0.00	12.45
12/15	27.32	10	9	2.93	0.00	10.73
12/14	29.42	—	—	(0.00)	0.00	9.18
12/13	29.35	—	—	(0.00)	0.00	12.08
Annual Growth	(4.6%)					10.0%

Qurate Retail Inc

Auditors: KPMG LLP

LOCATIONS

HQ: Qurate Retail Inc
12300 Liberty Boulevard, Englewood, CO 80112
Phone: 720 875-5300
Web: www.libertymedia.com

HISTORICAL FINANCIALS
Company Type: Public

Income Statement

FYE: December 31

	REVENUE ($ mil.)	NET INCOME ($ mil.)	NET PROFIT MARGIN	EMPLOYEES
12/17	10,381	1,208	11.6%	28,255
12/16	10,219	473	4.6%	21,080
12/15	9,169	640	7.0%	22,080
12/14	10,028	520	5.2%	20,078
12/13	10,307	438	4.2%	23,079
Annual Growth	0.2%	28.9%	—	5.2%

2017 Year-End Financials

Debt ratio: 38.89%
Return on equity: 20.69%
Cash ($ mil.): 330
Current ratio: 1.44
Long-term debt ($ mil.): 6,686

No. of shares (mil.): 478
Dividends
  Yield: —
  Payout: —
Market value ($ mil.): 11,686

STOCK PRICE ($)		P/E		PER SHARE ($)		
	FY Close	High/Low		Earnings	Dividends	Book Value
12/17	24.42	10	7	2.70	0.00	14.25
12/16	19.98	28	18	0.98	0.00	10.60
12/15	27.32	23	19	1.33	0.00	10.59
12/14	29.42	28	22	1.06	0.00	8.99
12/13	29.35	35	23	0.83	0.00	12.74
Annual Growth	(4.5%)		—	34.3%	—	2.8%

Qwest Corp

EXECUTIVES

Exec V Pres-cao-contrl, David D Cole
Auditors: KPMG LLP

LOCATIONS

HQ: Qwest Corp
100 CenturyLink Drive, Monroe, LA 71203
Phone: 318 388-9000
Web: www.centurylink.com

HISTORICAL FINANCIALS
Company Type: Public

Income Statement

FYE: December 31

	REVENUE ($ mil.)	NET INCOME ($ mil.)	NET PROFIT MARGIN	EMPLOYEES
12/17	8,550	1,657	19.4%	22,000
12/16	8,910	1,085	12.2%	22,000
12/15	9,064	1,074	11.0%	22,000
12/14	8,838	970	11.0%	23,000
12/13	8,753	964	11.0%	22,800
Annual Growth	(0.6%)	14.5%	—	(0.9%)

2017 Year-End Financials

Debt ratio: 39.51%
Return on equity: 18.38%
Cash ($ mil.): 1
Current ratio: 0.81
Long-term debt ($ mil.): 7,264

No. of shares (mil.): 0
Dividends
  Yield: 0.0%
  Payout: 61.0%
Market value ($ mil.): 0

STOCK PRICE ($)		P/E		PER SHARE ($)		
	FY Close	High/Low		Earnings	Dividends	Book Value
12/17	22.88	—	—	(0.00)	1.07	
Annual Growth						

Radian Group, Inc.

Radian Group is glowing from a conflagration of private mortgage insurance claims. Through subsidiaries Radian Guaranty Radian Mortgage Assurance and Radian Insurance Radian Group provides traditional private mortgage insurance coverage to protect lenders from defaults by borrowers who put down a deposit of less than 20% when buying a home. Such coverage provides protection on individual loans and covers unpaid loan principal and delinquent interest. Its pool insurance covers limited exposure on groups of loans. Radian still insures municipal bonds written before 2008 through its financial guaranty business. Radian Group's customers include mortgage bankers commercial banks and savings institutions.

Operations

Radian operates in two segments: The mortgage insurance division offers credit-related insurance coverage primarily private mortgage insurance as well as risk services for lending agencies. These operations are primarily conducted through the Radian Guaranty subsidiary. The company also provides mortgage and real estate services through its principal services subsidiary Clayton as well as Green River Capital Red Bell Real Estate and ValuAmerica.

Meanwhile the financial guaranty segment — handled by the Radian Asset Assurance unit — insures a runoff portfolio of public finance and structured finance credits. The unit which no longer actively markets policies historically offered direct insurance or reinsurance for credit based risks as well as credit protection through default swaps and financial guaranty transactions.

During headier days the government encouraged lenders to turn more Americans into homeowners and Radian made a steady diet of insuring subprime mortgages. However that strategy meant that it was among the first to be hit and hit hard when the housing market imploded and mortgage defaults piled up.

Geographic Reach

Headquartered in Philadelphia Radian has offices across the US as well as in Hong Kong and in Bristol UK.

Sales and Marketing

The principal customers of Radian's mortgage insurance business are mortgage originators such as mortgage bankers mortgage brokers commercial banks savings institutions credit unions and community banks.

Financial Performance

In fiscal 2015 Radian's revenue climbed 11% to $1.2 billion due mainly to a 101% increase in revenue from the Services segment. It also recorded higher net premiums in the year. Net income dropped however by 70% to $286.9 million due to a large income tax benefit in the prior fiscal year. The company's cash position strengthened with cash from operating activities climbing to $15.5 million from a loss of $153.2 million in 2014.

Strategy

Radian is looking to expand the depth and breadth of its mortgage offering as the housing market in the US continues to strengthen.

Mergers and Acquisitions

In 2017 Radian consulting subsidiary Clayton Holdings acquired California-based ValuEscrow which continues to operate under its own brand name. The following year Radian acquired Independent Settlement Services a national appraisal and title management firm. That company will continue to operate under its current brand but will eventually transition to the Radian name.

HISTORY

Radian Group was born from the ashes of the 1987 stock crash and the rubble of the natural disasters of the early 1990s. Parent insurance company Reliance Group was deep in debt and desperately in need of cash. To raise money Reliance separated CMAC Investment (and operating subsidiary Commonwealth Mortgage Assurance) from subsidiary Commonwealth Land Title and took the company public in 1992.

In 1994 after two years of lackluster stock performance the board promoted CFO Frank Filipps (an American International Group veteran) to CEO. Filipps limited commissions to new policies rather than retained business. The pokey stock nosed up with some help from low interest rates and high numbers of new mortgage loans. Despite a raise in interest rates in 1995 the company continued to expand its market share.

In 1996 the company launched Prophet Score a new risk-assessment model that allowed CMAC to expand its coverage to include subprime loans. These measures jump-started sales to new highs in 1997 and 1998. Nevertheless CMAC (and its competitors) suffered in the market because of negative publicity: private mortgage (PMI) insurers were slammed for keeping quiet when borrowers' equity rose to 20% the point when PMI is usually considered unnecessary. In 1999 CMAC bought former rival Amerin and changed the name of the combined company to Radian Group.

Radian diversified its operations through the 2001 acquisition of credit-based insurance and financial services provider Enhance Financial (renamed Radian Reinsurance and later merged into Radian Asset Assurance Inc.) In 2002 Radian sold off the Enhance Consumer Services subsidiary.

In 2005 Filipps departed to join Clayton Holdings. Sanford Ibrahim was then named CEO.

The company expanded into Asia in 2005 through a partnership with Standard Chartered Bank (Hong Kong) with Radian as the exclusive provider of residential mortgage insurance to the lender. However the deal did not take root and Standard Chartered Bank yanked their contract in early 2008.

As the credit markets went into meltdown that year the company began pulling back on the riskiest of bonds (such as second-liens) by mid-2007 but by early 2008 its ratings had been lowered.

In response to the market troubles Radian stopped insuring certain types of higher-risk home loans and began working with existing mortgage services to help distressed borrowers modify their loan terms. The company's Radian Asset Assurance operations in the US and UK also stopped accepting new business as part of its general hunkering down to ride out the storm and in 2010 it put the UK unit into liquidation.

EXECUTIVES

Ceo, Richard G. (Rick) Thornberry
President Radian Guaranty, Teresa A. Bryce Bazemore, age 58, $550,000 total compensation
Evp And Cfo, J. Franklin (Frank) Hall, age 50, $400,000 total compensation
Evp And Cio, Richard I. (Rick) Altman, age 51
Evp And Chief Risk Officer, Derek V. Brummer, $415,000 total compensation
President Clayton Holdings, Jeff Tennyson
Senior Vice President And Deputy General Counsel, Glenn Davis
Assistant Vice President Corporate Accounting, Abigail Rodriguez
Vice President Strategic Services, Susan King
Director, Herbert Wender, age 81
Auditors: PricewaterhouseCoopers LLP

LOCATIONS

HQ: Radian Group, Inc.
1500 Market Street, Philadelphia, PA 19102
Phone: 215 231-1000
Web: www.radian.biz

PRODUCTS/OPERATIONS

2016 Revenues

	$ mil.	% of total
Net premiums earned—insurance	921	74
Services revenue	168	14
Net investment income	113	9
Net gains (losses) on investments and other financial instruments	30	3
Other income	3	-
Total	**1,238**	**100**

COMPETITORS

Assured Guaranty	Old Republic
Essent Guaranty	Triad Guaranty
Genworth Financial	US Department of
MGIC Investment	Veterans Affairs
National Mortgage Insurance	United Guaranty

HISTORICAL FINANCIALS

Company Type: Public

Income Statement

FYE: December 31

	ASSETS ($ mil.)	NET INCOME ($ mil.)	INCOME AS % OF ASSETS	EMPLOYEES
12/17	5,900	121	2.1%	1,887
12/16	5,863	308	5.3%	1,971
12/15	5,642	286	5.1%	1,881
12/14	6,859	959	14.0%	1,702
12/13	5,621	(196)	—	782
Annual Growth	**1.2%**	**—**	**—**	**24.6%**

2017 Year-End Financials

Debt ratio: 17.41%
Return on equity: 4.12%
Cash ($ mil.): 80
Current ratio: —
Long-term debt ($ mil.): —

No. of shares (mil.): 215
Dividends
　Yield: 0.0%
　Payout: 1.8%
Market value ($ mil.): 4,448

	STOCK PRICE ($) FY Close	P/E High/Low		PER SHARE ($) Earnings	Dividends	Book Value
12/17	20.61	40	28	0.55	0.01	13.90
12/16	17.98	13	6	1.37	0.01	13.39
12/15	13.39	13	9	1.22	0.01	12.07
12/14	16.72	3	2	4.16	0.01	11.37
12/13	14.12	—	—	(1.18)	0.01	5.43
Annual Growth	**9.9%**	**—**	**—**	**—**	**(0.0%)**	**26.5%**

Ralph Lauren Corp

Ralph Lauren Corporation is galloping at a faster clip than when its namesake founder first entered the arena over 45 years ago. With golden mallet brands such as Polo by Ralph Lauren Chaps RRL Club Monaco and RLX Ralph Lauren the company designs and markets apparel and accessories home furnishings and fragrances. Its collections are available at more than 13000 retail locations worldwide including many upscale and mid-tier department stores (Macy's contributes 25% to RL's wholesale revenue). It operates 465-plus Ralph Lauren and Club Monaco retail stores worldwide as well as 615-plus concession-based shops-within-shops and 10 e-commerce sites.

HISTORY

Ralph Lauren a suave Manhattanite was actually born Ralph Lifschitz in the Bronx New York. It is said that his father Frank an immigrant Russian housepainter and muralist informally changed the family's name to Lauren and inspired his son to recreate himself in the image of a mythic upper class.

After high school Ralph who formally changed his name to Lauren became a salesman at Brooks Brothers and then a sales representative for Rivetz a Boston tie maker. In 1967 he landed a job as a tie designer for Beau Brummel of New York. The company gave him his own style division which he named Polo because of the sport's refined image. The next year Lauren started Polo Fashions to make tailored menswear. Partner Peter Strom teamed up with Lauren in the early 1970s. Although its designs received critical acclaim Polo Fashions had a bumpy start as Lauren adjusted to the business aspect of his fashion label.

Lauren's profile rose in the 1970s when he won three Coty Awards for design and produced costumes for the movie The Great Gatsby. In 1971 Lauren adopted his polo-player-on-a-horse logo and introduced a line for women. That year the first licensed Polo store opened (on Rodeo Drive in Beverly Hills) along with his first in-store boutique (at Bloomingdale's in New York City). He added shoes to the lineup in 1972 licensed his womenswear line the next year and launched a licensed fragrance line in 1978.

By 1980 Polo Fashions had become Polo Ralph Lauren. Encouraged by the success of the licensed products Lauren led the designer charge into home furnishings introducing his Home Collection in 1983. He opened his flagship store in New York City three years later. The company expanded upmarket with its Purple Label and downmarket with Polo Jeans denims and a line of paints in 1996.

Following the stampede of fashion-house IPOs Polo went public in 1997. The next year moving to reduce expenses the company restructured its divisions. In 1999 Polo paid $85 million for hip Canadian retailer Club Monaco to compete in the burgeoning youth market. It also opened RL a fine-dining restaurant adjacent to its retail outlet in Chicago's famed shopping district.

In early 2000 Polo purchased its European licensee Poloco for $230 million giving the company greater control of its brand. Then in a 50-50 joint venture with NBC and its affiliates Polo formed Ralph Lauren Media Company to sell its products via the Internet as well as broadcast cable and print media. Also that year the company closed 11 underperforming Club Monaco locations and announced plans to shut down all of its jeans stores. To extend its European reach even further Polo bought its Italian licensee PRL Fashions of Europe in 2001.

Polo Ralph Lauren inked one of the most significant licensing deals in company history — and what it considers to be a great match to boot — in 2005. The firm paired with the United States Tennis Association (USTA) to form a four-year global partnership and was designated the official apparel sponsor of the US Open through 2008. The agreement involved among other things an official shirt designed by Lauren for on-court officials co-branded US Open/Polo Ralph Lauren merchandise and joint marketing programs. In 2006 the company entered a licensing agreement with Luxottica valued at more than $1.75 billion over a 10-year period.

The company's agreement with the USTA gave it the momentum to seal a deal with The All England Club and Wimbledon in 2006 that extends through 2010. Polo Ralph Lauren as part of the agreement became the exclusive outfitter of Wimbledon — the first official designer in the 129-history of the games. Polo Ralph Lauren creates and outfits on-court officials and sells its Wimbledon collection at its freestanding stores as well as through select retailers and Polo.com.

Initiatives for 2007 included the launch of a new group named Global Brand Concepts formed to develop lifestyle brands for specialty and department stores including J.C. Penney's American Living Collection. The group designs and markets new products including accessories home decor and women's men's and children's apparel.

That year Polo Ralph Lauren purchased the remaining 50% stake in Polo.com from both Ralph Lauren Media a unit of NBCUniversal and ValueVisions Media for about $175 million. The move gave Polo full control over its plans to develop its online presence domestically and abroad.

The company brought its East Coast lifestyle brand to Asia when it opened its first freestanding flagship store in Tokyo in 2006. The next year Polo Ralph Lauren secured a foothold in the Japanese apparel and accessories market by purchasing the 50% balance of Polo Ralph Lauren Japan for some $23 million and making it a wholly owned subsidiary. The company also increased its stake in Impact 21 Co. a Japanese sub-licensee from 20% to 97% in. Impact 21 operates the company's men's women's and jeans apparel and accessories business in Japan.

Founder Ralph Lauren stepped down as CEO in November 2015 but remained involved with the company as chairman and chief creative officer.

During 2013 RLC brought several licensing arrangements in-house. In April 2013 it acquired the Chaps Menswear Business from PVH for about $18 million. In July it bought the Australia and New Zealand licensed operations from its licensee for about $15 million.

EXECUTIVES

President Ceo And Director, Patrice J. L. Louvet, age 54

President Global Brands, Valérie Hermann, age 55, $917,308 total compensation
Cfo, Jane H. Nielsen, age 54
Brand President Men's Polo Purple Label And Double Rl, Tom Mendenhall
Senior Vice President Merchandising And Manufacturing, Benny Lin
Vice President Store Development, Rick Farrar
Vice President Of Organizational Development And Learning, Stuart Jackson
Business Operations Vice President Director Manager, Miriah Page
Vice President Of Merchandising Blue Label, Brooke Allinson
Senior Vice President Marketing Communications And International Business Development, William Li
Senior Vice President, Michel Botbol
Vice President Planning And Allocation Factory Store Concept, Bradley Eckhart
Vice President Interactive Media, Alexandra Scebold
Vice President, Maureen Whitaker
Vice President Production, Paul Haffner
Vice President Information Technology Infrastructure, Jonathan Zwang
Senior Vice President Retail Europa, Alessandro Valenti
Vice President Retail Luxury, Olivier Thibault
Vice President, Jay Kimpton
Vice President, Lisa Aiosa
Vice President Mens Production, Cindy Tse
Senior Management (senior Vice President General Manager Director), Avery Fischer
Vice President, Bryan Fogg
Senior Vice President Sales Footwear, Geoffrey Ward
Vice President Global Marketing, Carey Krug
Vice President, Carol Covington
Vice President, Pamela Flynn
Vp Manufacturing And Sourcing, Michele Digenova
Senior Vice President, Wendy Berloe-Buch
Vice President, Dan McCampbell
Vice President Information Technology, Greg Battafarano
Vice President Merchandise Planning And, Dana Levy
Vice President Of Design, Callery McGee
Vice President Design And Development, Peter Sjonell
Vice President Of Asset Protection Global Supply Chain, Chris Aye
Vice President Of Production, Michael Marafioti
Vice President Finance And Sup, David Clarke
Vice President Real Estate, Dan Cochran
Vice President Corporate Business Development, Andrew Nkongho
Vice President Global Human Resources Systems Solutions, Dean Dellantonia
Vice President Merchandising, Katie Mayne
Senior Vice President Digital Marketing And Ecommerce, Serge Acker
Vice President Us Distribution Ops Global Supply Chain, George Clopton
Vice President Finance, Paul Wickman
Vice President Of Woven Production, Patgun Chen
Marketing Vice President, Liz Paley
Vice President Of Design Women's Footwear, Nancy Boas
Senior Vice President Mens Specialty Store Division, Tom Cush
Vice President Platform Engineering, Atif Khan
Vice President Digital Product Management, Samantha Starmer
Vice President Of Licensed Business, Meegan Colgan
Vice President, Elise Schneider
Vice President Merchandising, Christine Imundi
Vice President, Calvin Churchman
Vice President Global Marketing, Tom Jarrold

Senior Vice President Advertising, Mary Randolph Carter
Executive Assistant To The Senior Vice President Of Interactive Technology, Erika Keller
Vice President Home Design, Stavros Garger
Executive Vice President Women's Design And Advertising, Buffy Birrittella
Senior Vice President Footwear Design, John Ascher
Senior Vice President And Chief Quality Officer, Larry Gordon
Vice President Internal Audit, Amy Cheema
Vice President Of Creativeservice, Salvatore Disanto
Vice President Human Resources, Andrea Carter
Vice President Planning And Allocation, Alexander Ralston
Vice President Business Development, Vladimir Martynenko
Senior Vice President Global Manufacturing, Don Baum
Senior Vice President, Maura Manning
Vice President, David G Rush
Senior Vice President, George Rakotci
Executive Vice President, Jerry Lauren
Senior Vice President, Read Worth
Vice President, Hilary Berger
Executive Vice President Chief Creative Officer, Alfredo Paredes
Vice President Information Technology, Tom Palmieri
Vice President Digital Operations Planning, George Koveos
Vice President Product Presentation And Training Polo Retail Group, Baldo LaRussa
Senior Vice President Accessories Merchandising, Louise Mimicopoulos
Divisional Senior Vice President Of Business Process Integration, Robbin Mitchell
Vice President, Moira Taylor
Vice President Creative Services, Sarah O'reilly
Vice President Global Digital Products And Strategy Counsel, Anthony Traymore
Vice President Creative Services, Quinn Pofahl
Vice President Of Product Development And Technical Design Women's And Men's Sweaters, Corinna Fischer
Senior Vice President Global Creative Services, Karen Ford
Vice President Sales, Cameron Lambert
Senior Vice President Brand Management Sourcing And Logistics, Colin Henry
Senior Vice President Product Innovation, Jason Berns
Vice President Design Sweaters, Susann Epperlein
Vice President Compensation And International Total Rewards, Danielle Moss
Executive Vice President, Jacki Nemerov
Executive Vice President, Birrittella Buffy
National Sales Manager Mens, Thomas Cush
Vice President Marketing Asia Pacific, Larry Feng
Vice President Global Consumer Intelligence And Experien, Parinaz Vahabzadeh
Vice President Digital Technology, Molly MacDougall
Senior Vice President Of Global Store Development, Dennis Adler
Vice President Information Technology Infrastructure, Alex Santillana
Senior Vice President Marketing And Communications Asia Pacific, Jason Beckley
Regional Vice President, Ben Lisi
Vice President, Abby Curley
Vp Production, Lisa Ruland
Vice President, David Farrell
Vice President, Patricia Daskin
Vice President Of Design Womens Collection, Daniela Kamiliotis
Vice President Financial Reporting And Analysis, Mark Cassebaum

Senior Vice President Design And Operations Women's And Children's, Lisa Will-kaess
Vice President Advertising Design, Lisa Curtiss
Chairman And Chief Creative Officer, Ralph Lauren, age 78
Vice Chairman And Chief Innovation Officer, David Lauren, age 46
Board Member, Frank Bennack
Board Member, Arnold Aronson
Board Member, Joel Fleishman
Auditors: Ernst & Young LLP

LOCATIONS

HQ: Ralph Lauren Corp
650 Madison Avenue, New York, NY 10022
Phone: 212 318-7000
Web: www.RalphLauren.com

2016 Sales

	% of total
Americas	67
Europe	21
Asia	12
Total	**100**

PRODUCTS/OPERATIONS

2016 Sales

	% of total
Retail	53
Wholesale	45
Licensing	2
Total	**100**

Selected Brand Names & Licenses
Wholesale
Lauren by Ralph Lauren
Pink Pony
Polo Ralph Lauren
Ralph by Ralph Lauren
Ralph Lauren Black Label
Ralph Lauren Blue Label
Ralph Lauren Purple Label
Ralph Lauren Polo Sport
Retail
Club Monaco
Ralph Lauren
Polo Ralph Lauren
Polo Sport
Licensing Partners
Fitz and Floyd Inc.
Hanesbrands
Kohl's Department Stores Inc.
L'Oréal S.A.
Luxottica Group
Peerless Inc.
The Warnaco Group
WestPoint Home Inc.

COMPETITORS

Abercrombie & Fitch	Jos. A. Bank
American Eagle	Kate Spade
Outfitters	Kenneth Cole
Ann Taylor	Kering
Armani	L.L. Bean
Benetton	LVMH
Brand Matter	Lands' End
Burberry	Laura Ashley
Calvin Klein	Levi Strauss
Christian Dior	Martha Stewart Living
Coach Inc.	Michael Kors Holdings
Donna Karan	Nautica Apparel
Ermenegildo Zegna	Nine West
Escada	PVH
Estée Lauder	Perry Ellis
Gianni Versace	International
Gucci	Richemont
Guess?	St. John Knits
H&M	The Gap
Haggar	Tiffany & Co.
Herm`s	Tommy Bahama
Hugo Boss	Tommy Hilfiger
J. Crew	VF Corporation

HISTORICAL FINANCIALS

Company Type: Public

Income Statement

FYE: March 31

	REVENUE ($ mil.)	NET INCOME ($ mil.)	NET PROFIT MARGIN	EMPLOYEES
03/18*	6,182	162	2.6%	23,500
04/17	6,652	(99)	—	23,300
04/16	7,405	396	5.3%	26,000
03/15	7,620	702	9.2%	25,000
03/14	7,450	776	10.4%	23,000
Annual Growth	(4.6%)	(32.3%)	—	0.5%

*Fiscal year change

2018 Year-End Financials

Debt ratio: 13.87%	No. of shares (mil.): 81
Return on equity: 4.83%	Dividends
Cash ($ mil.): 1,304	Yield: 0.0%
Current ratio: 2.24	Payout: 101.5%
Long-term debt ($ mil.): 524	Market value ($ mil.): 9,089

	STOCK PRICE ($) FY Close	P/E High/Low	PER SHARE ($) Earnings	Dividends	Book Value
03/18*	111.80	60 33	1.97	2.00	42.53
04/17	81.62	— —	(1.20)	2.00	40.74
04/16	97.26	30 18	4.62	2.00	45.16
03/15	131.22	23 16	7.88	1.85	45.09
03/14	158.24	22 17	8.43	1.70	45.48
Annual Growth	(8.3%)	— —	(30.5%)	4.1%	(1.7%)

*Fiscal year change

RAYMOND JAMES & ASSOCIATES INC

Does everybody love Raymond James & Associates (RJA)? Raymond James Financial hopes so. RJA is that company's primary subsidiary and one of the largest retail brokerages in the US. The unit provides brokerage financial planning investments and related services to consumers. It performs equity and fixed income sales trading and research for institutional clients in North America and Europe. Its investment banking group provides corporate and public finance debt underwriting and mergers and acquisitions advice. RJA also makes markets for approximately 1000 stocks including thinly traded issues. Planning Corporation of America a wholly-owned subsidiary of RJA sells insurance and annuities.

Operations

RJA is engaged in most aspects of securities distribution and investment banking.

Geographic Reach

The company has more than 200 branches and satellite offices concentrated in the Mid-Atlantic Midwest Southeast and Southwest portions of the US in addition to ten institutional sales offices in Europe.

Sales and Marketing

RJA has many big name clients across dozens of industries. In 2013 Titan Medical announced that it has retained RJA to provide advisory services and present options which could include a possible sale.

Strategy

In 2012 the company's parent completed its acquisition of Morgan Keegan & Co. and MK Holding Inc. from Regions Financial Corporation. Some of the equity capital markets and fixed income operations of were integrated into RJA.

EXECUTIVES

Vice President, William Wallace
Vice President, Scott Cutliff
Vice President Investments Financial Advisor, Aamsa Zuniga
Managing Director, Dan Horgan
Auditors: KPMG LLP TAMPA FL

LOCATIONS

HQ: RAYMOND JAMES & ASSOCIATES INC
880 CARILLON PKWY, SAINT PETERSBURG, FL 337161100
Phone: 727 567-1000
Web: WWW.RAYMONDJAMES.COM

COMPETITORS

Ameriprise	Janney Montgomery Scott
Charles Schwab	
E*TRADE Financial	Merrill Lynch
Edward D. Jones	Scottrade
Edward Jones	TD Ameritrade
FMR	Wells Fargo Advisors

HISTORICAL FINANCIALS

Company Type: Private

Income Statement

FYE: September 30

	ASSETS ($ mil.)	NET INCOME ($ mil.)	INCOME AS % OF ASSETS	EMPLOYEES
09/17	9,917	198	2.0%	10,000
09/16	10,689	145	1.4%	—
09/15	7,893	167	2.1%	—
09/14	6,955	182	2.6%	—
Annual Growth	12.6%	2.8%	—	—

2017 Year-End Financials

Debt ratio: —	
Return on equity: 6.10%	Dividends
Cash ($ mil.): 4,195	Yield: —
Current ratio: —	Payout: —
Long-term debt ($ mil.): —	Market value ($ mil.): —

Raymond James Financial, Inc.

Diversified financial services company Raymond James Financial offers financial advice to retail clients and corporations alike. The brokerage house has more than 7800 advisors and nearly $800 billion in total client assets held in about 3 million client accounts. Raymond James offers investment and asset management services for retail and institutional clients; underwriting distribution trading and brokerage of equity and debt securities; sale of mutual funds and other investment products; corporate and retail banking services; and trust services. It has an extended geographic reach with more than 3100 locations in the US Canada and Europe although the US accounts for most of revenue.

HISTORY

Robert James often called the "founder of financial planning" first started a construction business in Ohio after his WWII service in the US Navy and then began a Florida home-building company. He got into the financial services business in 1954 with Florida Mutual Fund a company he and Gerard Jobin formed that eventually became American National Growth Fund. But when most companies were selling just stocks or mutual funds James saw a need for a more comprehensive approach to investing. He decided to focus on helping individual clients learning about their financial needs and goals and then working with them on everything from investments to taxes. To that end he began offering seminars for retirees.

In 1960 those seminars had turned into a new company James and Associates which two years later became Robert A. James Investments. In 1964 James acquired Raymond and Associates a firm started by Edward Raymond in 1962; the newly merged firm was renamed Raymond James & Associates (RJA).

James' son Thomas joined the firm in 1966 the year the company's revenues first surpassed $1 million. Over the next several years the company expanded its investment offerings and set up new divisions. It added Investment Management & Research as an affiliate broker/dealer in 1967 and Planning Corporation of America as a general insurance agency in 1968.

Raymond James Financial incorporated as a holding company in 1969 and Thomas James became CEO the next year. RJA formed Eagle Asset Management in 1975 RJ Oil & Gas (subsidiary for oil and gas limited partnerships) in 1977 securities and real estate subsidiaries in 1980 (Robert Thomas Securities and RJ Properties respectively) and an equipment leasing subsidiary (RJ Leasing) in 1982.

Raymond James Financial went public in 1983 the year Robert James died. Two years later the company organized its Heritage Family of Funds. RJA became an international company in the late 1980s opening an office in Paris in 1987 and in Geneva the next year. It also began offering a cash management program in 1988 and began its Stock Loan Department. Trust and banking subsidiaries were begun in 1992 and 1994 respectively followed by the creation of Equity Capital Markets Group in 1996.

In 2000 Raymond James Financial crossed the billion-dollar-mark hitting $1.7 billion in sales. That year it acquired Canadian investment firm Goepel McDermid (renamed Raymond James Ltd.) to offer individual and institutional investment services to the Canadian market and it launched Raymond James Killik a UK joint venture that became Raymond James Investment Services in 2002.

In 2006 Raymond James Financial reduced front-end commissions with variations of variable annuity products; the next year it kicked off its Wealth Solutions department a unit designed to help high-net-worth clients and their advisors. Also that year Raymond James Financial extended its deal to attach its name to the home stadium of the NFL's Tampa Bay Buccaneers through 2015.

In 2012 to build its capital markets business in one of its largest purchases to date the company bought the investment banking and brokerage business of Morgan Keegan from Regions Financial for $1.2 billion and integrated the Morgan Keegan platform into its RJ&A platform. Raymond James Financial previously purchased boutique investment bank Lane Berry & Co. International in Boston in 2009 and Chicago-based investment bank and brokerage Howe Barnes Hoefer & Arnett in 2011.

To boost its large-cap investments the firm in 2012 acquired a 45% interest in ClariVest Asset Management.

RJ Bank acquired the Canadian operations of Allied Irish Banks in 2012

EXECUTIVES

Vice President Of Information Technology, Bruce Philipoom

President Global Equities And Investment Banking Raymond James & Associates, Jeffrey E. (Jeff) Trocin, age 58, $305,000 total compensation

Evp Finance Cfo And Treasurer, Jeffrey P. (Jeff) Julien, age 61, $280,000 total compensation

Coo Raymond James Financial And Ceo Raymond James & Associates, Dennis W. Zank, age 63, $330,000 total compensation

President Raymond James Financial And Fixed Income Capital Markets, John C. Carson, age 61, $300,000 total compensation

President Raymond James Financial Services, Scott A. Curtis, age 55

Chairman And Ceo, Paul C. Reilly, age 63, $445,000 total compensation

President And Ceo Raymond James Bank, Steven M. (Steve) Raney, age 52

Chairman And Ceo Raymond James Ltd., Paul D. Allison, age 61

President Raymond James & Associates Private Client Group, Tashtego S. (Tash) Elwyn, age 46

Evp Technology And Operations, Bella Loykhter Allaire, age 64

Evp And President Asset Management Group, Jeffrey A. (Jeff) Dowdle, age 53

Evp General Counsel And Secretary, Jonathan N. Santelli, age 46

Senior Vice President Home And Building Products, Sam Darkatsh

Senior Vice President Fixed Income Sales, Gerard Buquicchio

Vice President And Managing Director Acquisitions Northeast Raymond James Tax Credit Funds, Darryl Seavey

Vice President Corporate Client Services, Hunt James

Vice President And Managing Director Acquisitions West Raymond James Tax Credit Funds, Kevin Kilbane

Senior Vice President, Mark Mchugh

Senior Vice President Financial Planning Raymond James And Associates, Charles J Bauder

Senior Vice President Investments, Kevin Byrne

Vice President, Neil Deakin

Vice President Investments, Josh Rajewski

Vice President, Mark Matheson

Vice President Public Finance, Tim Wranovix

Vice President Deposit Operations, Barbara Shore

Senior Vice President Investments, Roger Grefe

Senior Vice President Healthcare Public Finance Dallas, Peter H Delaney

Senior Vice President Of Investments, Stephen Crabtree

Senior Vice President, Michael Gibbs

First Vice President Investments, Lance Powers

First Vice President, Beth Smith

Senior Vice President, Bill Specht

Vice President Cpa Cfa, Scott Brinner

Senior Vice President, Sandy Webb

Vice President Investments, Sandy Russell

Senior Vice President, Steve Shapiro

Senior Vice President Investments, John Reuter

Vice President Information Technology, Frank Bugh

Senior Vice President, Andrea Tihal

Vice President Of Investments, James Heinen

Vice President, Terry McCormick

First Vice President Investments, Charles Claus

Assistant Vice President Of Information Technology, Brian Miller

Senior Vice President Wealth Management Technology, Juergen Dittgen

Senior Vice President Of Operations, Denise Samson

First Vice President Investments, Robert Hodgson

Vice President Investments, Sonya Choeff

Vice President, Peter Gairing

Vice President Syndicate Operations, Andrea Borum

Senior Vice President Institutional Equity Sales, Zachary Taylor

Senior Vice President Investments, J Weissert

Vice President, Robert Goff

Senior Vice President Healthcare Public Finance New York, Vasanta B Pundarika

Vice President, Jake Shumacker

Vice President Acquisitions Southeast, John Colvin

Senior Vice President Office Services, Raymond Lacour

Vice President Structured Credit Trading, Brian Linde

Vice President For Investments, Brian Rimel

Senior Vice President Equity Research Infrastruct, Michael Turits

Senior Vice President Of Investments And Branch Manager, Mark K Mekler

Associate Vice President, Nick Roederer

Vice President Of Operations, Victor Mangome

Associate Vice President Investments, Elizabeth Aulick Robertson

Vice President, Stacy W Houston

Senior Vice President Fi Trading, Randall Hawkins

Vice President Investments, Mark Mazman

Senior Vice President, Fred Coble

Vice President Fi Trading, Chad Runnels

Associate Vice President, Daniel Allen

Corporate Bond Trader And Vice President, Mark Schreiner

Assistant Vice President, Ruth Quinlan

First Vice President, Kenny Mcclain

Fvp Fi Trading, Edward Wildrick

Senior Vice President Investments, Michael Mccall

Senior Vice President Investments, Dianne Townsend

Senior Vice President Investments, Harold Green

Fvp, Dee Cook

Vice President Investments, Robert Peabody

Senior Vice President Investments, Mark Williams

Vice President Fi Strategies, Emilio Garma-Fernandez

Assistant Vice President Lending Solutions Consultant, Dino Martinbianco

Vice President International Financial Consultant, Vita Barrio

Senior Vice President Fi Trading, Stephen Lewis

First Vice President Investments, John Chesney

Senior Vice President Investments, Philip L Evans

Senior Vice President Investments, Jeff Harring

Vice President Institutional Fi, Christopher Warburton

Fvp Fi Sales, Bill Nowlin

Senior Vice President Operations, Joe Barkley

Vice President, Michael Mobley

Senior Vice President, Jennifer Mills

Senior Vice President Fi Trading, BEN LAPOINTE

Vice President Fi Trading, Beau Snowden

Vice President Trading And Project Management, AL Caudullo

Executive Vice President And Senior Corporate And Real Estate Banking Executive Raymond James Bank, Tom Macina

Vice President, Scott Englehardt

Vice President, Lee Morthland

Senior Vice President Healthcare Public Finance New York, Dean Scarano

Vice President, Sasha Stipanovich

Senior Vice President Financial Advisor, Chip Lee

Vice President Investments, Neil Lauro

First Vice President, Tom Owens

Senior Vice President Investments, Tom Ross

Assistant Vice President Application Development, John D'Agostino

Vice President Client Reporting, Salit Nagy-todd

Senior Vice President Investments, John Fagan

Associate Vice President Investments, Michael Lowe

Senior Vice President Investments Branch Manager, Matt Quigley

Vice President Compliance, Brad Cole

Senior Vice President Investments, Bob Taylor

Senior Vice President, Christine Spencer

Senior Vice President, Mark Ranney

Vice President Fi Trading, Ben Streed

Vice President, Bob Jones

Senior Vice President Investments, Todd Evans

Vice President Investments, Matt McCurry

Vice President Public Finance, Ogden Kniffin

Vice President, Matt Stemmler

Senior Vice President Real Estate Investment Banking St. Petersburg, Jozsi Popper

Vice President, Holly Hayes

Vice President National Sales Manager, Dan Mallard

Certified Financial Planner??? Senior Vice President Investments, Frank Maurno

First Vice President, Eduardo Bonilla

Associate Vice President Investments Sim, Lynn T Shaw

Senior Vice President Investments, Andy Hall

Vice President Investments, Jeffrey Wahl

Vice President Asset Management Services, George Raffa

Wms Aams Vice President Investments, Lance Turner

Senior Vice President Investments, Mary Brooks

First Vice President Brokered Cds, Joseph Evans

Vice President Investments, James Evans

Vice President Investments, Tom Lamacchio

Vice President, Mark Pinto

Wms Senior Vice President Investments, James McLean

Vice President Banking Consultant, Chris Drennen

Vice President Banking Consultant, Patrick Lopez

Senior Vice President Inv Banking, Kate M Crespo

Senior Vice President, Chris Fienup

Vice President Energy Investment Banking Dallas, Kyle Gunnison

Vice President Sales, Alec Levine

Vice President, Carla Hargett

Vice President, Neil Tagaras

Vice President, Rosalind W Haith

Vice President, Tim Hansen

First Vice President Investments, Keith Dubauskas

Senior Vice President Government Guaranteed Desk, Michelle Shadix

First Vice President Investments, Dwayne Peltier

Assistant Vice President Credit Risk Officer, Sloan Yadley

Senior Vice President, Ted Fellman

Vice President, Alan Swafford

Auditors: KPMG LLP

LOCATIONS

HQ: Raymond James Financial, Inc.
880 Carillon Parkway, St. Petersburg, FL 33716
Phone: 727 567-1000
Web: www.raymondjames.com

2018 Sales

	$ mil.	% of total
US	6,914	92
Canada	422	6
Europe	139	2
Other - -		
Total	**7,475**	**100**

PRODUCTS/OPERATIONS

2018 Sales By Segment

	$ mil.	% of total
Private Client Group	5,120	67
Capital Markets	991	13
RJ Bank	654	8
Asset Management	815	11
Other	60	1
Eliminations	(166.3)	-
Total	**7,475**	**100**

2018 Sales by Revenue Type

	$ mil.	% of total
Securities commissions & fees	4,483	60
Investment banking	440	6
Investment advisory and related administrative fees	605	8
Interest income	1,044	14
Account and service fees	771	10
Net trading profit	56	1
Other	74	1
Total	**7,475**	**100**

Selected Subsidiaries

Alex. Brown
Eagle Asset Management Inc.
Eagle Boston Investment Management Inc.
Eagle Fund Distributors Inc.
Howe Barnes Hoefer & Arnett Inc.
Lane Berry & Co. International
Planning Corporation of America
Raymond James & Associates
Raymond James Asset Management International S.A.
  (France)
Raymond James Bank FSB (dba RJ Bank)
Raymond James Canada LLC
Raymond James Capital Partners L.P.
Raymond James European Holdings Inc.
Raymond James Financial Services Inc.
Raymond James Financial Services Advisors
Raymond James Investment Services Limited (UK 75%)
Raymond James Ltd. (Canada)
Raymond James Tax Credit Funds Inc.
Raymond James Trust N.A.
Reams Asset Management
Scout Investments

COMPETITORS

Charles Schwab	National Financial
E*TRADE Financial	Partners
Edward Jones	Oppenheimer Holdings
FMR	Piper Jaffray
LPL Financial	Stifel Financial
Legg Mason	TD Ameritrade
Merrill Lynch	Wells Fargo Advisors
Morgan Stanley	

HISTORICAL FINANCIALS

Company Type: Public

Income Statement

FYE: September 30

	REVENUE ($ mil.)	NET INCOME ($ mil.)	NET PROFIT MARGIN	EMPLOYEES
09/18	7,475	856	11.5%	18,550
09/17	6,524	636	9.8%	17,000
09/16	5,520	529	9.6%	15,900
09/15	5,308	502	9.5%	14,850
09/14	4,965	480	9.7%	13,900
Annual Growth	10.8%	15.6%	—	7.5%

2018 Year-End Financials

Debt ratio: 6.55%	No. of shares (mil.): 145
Return on equity: 14.34%	Dividends
Cash ($ mil.): 6,569	Yield: 0.0%
Current ratio: 0.41	Payout: 19.1%
Long-term debt ($ mil.): 2,448	Market value ($ mil.): 13,406

	STOCK PRICE ($) FY Close	P/E High/Low	PER SHARE ($) Earnings	Dividends	Book Value
09/18	92.05	17 14	5.75	1.10	43.73
09/17	84.33	19 13	4.33	0.88	38.74
09/16	58.21	16 11	3.65	0.80	34.72
09/15	49.63	17 14	3.43	0.72	31.64
09/14	53.58	16 12	3.32	0.64	29.33
Annual Growth	14.5%	— —	14.7%	14.5%	10.5%

Raytheon Co.

Raytheon ("light of the gods") shines in the upper pantheon of US military contractors; the company regularly places among the Pentagon's top 10 prime contractors. Its air/land/sea/space/cyber defense offerings include reconnaissance targeting and navigation systems as well as missile systems (Patriot Sidewinder and Tomahawk) unmanned ground and aerial systems sensing technologies and radars. Additionally Raytheon makes systems for communications (satellite) and intelligence radios cybersecurity and air traffic control. It also offers commercial electronics products and services as well as food safety processing technologies. The US government accounts for a large portion of sales.

Operations

To support its customers worldwide Raytheon serves defense and intelligence markets via five business segments: Integrated Defense Systems (IDS) Intelligence Information and Services (ISS) Missile Systems (MS) Space and Airborne Systems (SAS) and Forcepoint (joint venture launched in 2015).

Having patented the first microwave more than 65 years ago Raytheon is still developing and designing futuristic realities. The product that stands out most in the company's portfolio is the missile however. As the world's #1 missile maker Raytheon is a key player in US efforts to construct a comprehensive missile defense system.

Such systems need intercept vehicles sensors command and control systems and systems integration expertise. Raytheon's precision engagement offerings include the company's missiles as well as radars data links targeting and warning systems and lasers. In recent years the company has released an air and missile defense systems product line which includes the Standard Missile-3 the Exoatmospheric Kill Vehicle (EKV) and branded development programs.

Geographic Reach

Raytheon maintains offices in nearly 20 countries and has established global companies to serve customers Australia Canada Germany the US and the UK. The company sells products and services to customers in 80 nations although the US accounts for about 70% of net sales.

Sales and Marketing

The US government accounts for about 70% of Raytheon's sales. While it consistently counts among its customers the US Department of Defense (DoD) the Federal Bureau of Investigation (FBI) and NASA as well as members of the US military and US intelligence communities Raytheon also has some key international customers.

The company has contracts with South Korea to provide air and missile defense systems with Japan for training Saudi Arabia for surveillance systems and Australia for joint standoff weapons. Other main global clients include Finland Germany Taiwan and the United Arab Emirates.

Financial Performance

Raytheon's revenues have increased the last two years climbing 4% from $23.3 billion in 2015 to $24.1 billion in 2016. The growth was fueled by increases in its MS and SAS segments and strong gains from Forcepoint.

MS sales climbed in 2016 due to higher net sales on its Paveway program (portfolio of laser and GPS precision guided munitions) that was principally driven by international requirements and SAS experienced higher net sales on classified programs. In addition Forcepoint sales surged by more than 70% due to two previous acquisitions

and the growing global demand for cybersecurity products.

Raytheon's profits also jumped 7% from $2.1 billion in 2015 to $2.2 billion in 2016 mainly due to the increase in total revenues. In addition Raytheon's operating cash flow jumped 7% from $2.4 billion in 2015 to almost $2.9 billion in 2016 primarily due to lower net tax payments and favorable changes in inventory.

Strategy

Raytheon's diverse product lineup puts it in a better position to weather budget cuts than some of its competitors that handle a limited number of defense products and services. Its business is also contingent to a great extent on the federal defense budget. With the US budget deficit fluctuating with each president's administration Raytheon has focused on growing its international business by treating key foreign countries as individual markets with multiple customers.

Raytheon's internal investments including capital expenditures and spending on software increased 37% from 2015 to 2016 and enabled it to support future growth and productivity initiatives across the company. One key investment is the expansion of its main Arizona operations to meet the growth demands at its MS segment.

Mergers and Acquisitions

The company's cybersecurity business has been a point of focus of late primarily through multiple acquisitions which reflect Raytheon's general strategy for building its operations and growing its customer base.

In 2015 Raytheon created Forcepoint a new cybersecurity joint venture company (with Vista Equity Partners) in order to extend its cyber capabilities into the commercial markets. At the time Forcepoint purchased Websense a provider of advanced threat protection and data theft prevention services across web email cloud and endpoint infrastructure for $1.9 billion. Raytheon combined Websense with Raytheon Cyber Products formerly part of its IIS segment.

Also in 2015 Raytheon augmented its MS segment through the purchase of Sensintel a privately held provider of unmanned aircraft systems products to the intelligence and special operations markets.

HISTORY

In 1922 Laurence Marshall and several others founded American Appliance Company to produce home refrigerators. When their invention failed Marshall began making Raytheon (meaning "light of/from the gods") radio tubes. Raytheon was adopted as the company's name in 1925. It bought the radio division of Chicago's Q. R. S. Company in 1928 and formed Raytheon Production Company with National Carbon Company (makers of the Eveready battery) to market Eveready Raytheon tubes in 1929.

EXECUTIVES

Vp; President Intelligence Information And Services, David C. Wajsgras, age 59, $971,943 total compensation

Vp; President Global Business Services, Rebecca B. Rhoads, age 60

Vp Business Development And Ceo Raytheon International, John D. Harris, age 56

Vp; President Space And Airborne Systems, Richard R. (Rick) Yuse, age 67, $792,506 total compensation

Chairman And Ceo, Thomas A. (Tom) Kennedy, age 63, $1,299,979 total compensation

Vp; President Missile Systems, Taylor W. Lawrence, age 55, $728,151 total compensation

Vp General Counsel And Corporate Secretary, Frank R. Jimenez, age 53, $627,706 total compensation

Cio, Kevin T. Neifert

Vp And Cfo, Anthony F. OÂ'Brien, $608,510 total compensation

Vp; President Integrated Defense Systems, Wesley D. Kremer, age 53

Chief Executive Raytheon Arabia, Kurt Amend

Vice President, Roger W Anderson

Vp Legal, Mark D Nielsen

Vice President Pension Investments, Sanjay Chawla

Assistant Vice President Risk, Diane Murphy

Vice President Account Services, Glenn D Henseler

Senior Vice President, Ed Saavedra

Vice President And General Counsel Raytheon Intelligence Information And Services (iis), John Martinez

Vice President; Program Management Excellence, Larry Briggs

Vice President Employee Relations And Human Resourcesms, James Cronin

Vice President, Kathryn A Dirkschneider

Vice President Integrated Defense Systems Seapower Capability Systems, Paul Ferraro

Vice President And Treasurer, Kevin DaSilva

Vice President Navigation Weather And Services, Matt Gilligan

Government Relations, Tim Delgiudice

Vice President Raytheon Company Evaluation Team, Rudy Lewis

Vice President Electronic Warfare Systems, Travis Slocumb

Vice President And Principal Scientist Network And Communications Technologies, Jason Redi

Vice President Of Supply Chain Management, Michael Shaughnessy

Vice President Business Development Executive, Matthew Lambert

Board Member, James M Reed

Secretary, Eugene Smith

Auditors: PricewaterhouseCoopers LLP

LOCATIONS

HQ: Raytheon Co.
870 Winter Street, Waltham, MA 02451
Phone: 781 522-3000
Web: www.raytheon.com

2016 Sales

	$ mil.	% of total
US	16,517	69
Asia/Pacific	2,531	10
Middle East & North Africa	3,772	16
Europe & other regions	1,249	5
Total	**24,069**	**100**

PRODUCTS/OPERATIONS

2016 Sales

	$ mil.	% of total
Products	20,166	84
Services	3,903	16
Total	**24,069**	**100**

2016 Sales

	$ mil.	% of total
Missile Systems	7,071	28
Space & Airborne Systems	6,199	24
Intelligence & Information Systems	6,194	24
Integrated Defense Systems	5,476	22
Force point	566	2
Adjustments	(1437)	-
Total	**24,069**	**100**

Selected Products

Integrated Defense Systems (IDS)
Aegis Weapon Systems radar equipment
AN/AQS Minehunting Sonar System
Joint Land Attack Cruise Missile Defense Elevated Netted Sensor (JLENS)

Landing Platform Dock Amphibious Ship LPD-17
Patriot Air and Missile Defense System
Sea-Based X-Band Radar (SBX)
Ship Self-Defense System (SSDS)
Surface-Launched AMRAAM (SLAMRAAM)
Terminal High Altitude Area Defense (THAAD) Radar
Intelligence and Information Systems (IIS)
Army Research Lab
Communications systems
Department of Education programs
Distributed Common Ground System
Emergency Patient Tracking System
Global Broadcast Service
Global Hawk Ground Segment
Information solutions programs
Managed data storage solutions
Mobile Very Small Aperture Satellite Terminal
National Polar-Orbiting Operational Environmental Satellite System Program
RedWolf telecommunications surveillance
Signal and imagery intelligence programs
Supercomputing
U-2 (field support)
UAV systems and ground stations
Missile Systems (MS)
Advanced Medium-Range Air-to-Air missile (AMRAAM)
AIM-9X Sidewinder
Evolved SeaSparrow (ESSM)
Excalibur long-range artillery system
Exoatmospheric Kill Vehicle
Extended Range Guided Munition (ERGM)
High-Speed Anti-Radiation Missile Targeting System
Paveway laser-guided bombs
Maverick AGM-65 missiles
Tomahawk and Tactical Tomahawk cruise missiles
TOW Javelin Phalanx Standard and SeaRAM missiles
Network Centric Systems (NCS)
Airspace management and homeland security
Command and control systems
Combat systems
Integrated communications systems
Precision technologies and components
Space and Airborne Systems (SAS)
Active electronically scanned array radars
Airborne radars and processors
Electronic warfare systems
Electro-optic/infrared sensors
Intelligence surveillance and reconnaissance systems
Space and missile defense technology
Technical Services (TS)
Base operations
Logistics support
Maintenance support
Professional services
Treaty compliance monitoring
Weapons security and destruction

Selected Markets

Command Control Communication and Intelligence (C3I)
Systems provide integrated real-time support for on- and off-battlefield and transform raw data into actionable intelligence
Cybersecurity
Provides cyber capabilities to the Intelligence DoD and DHS markets as well as embedding cybersecurity in Raytheon's products and IT infrastructure
Effects
Achieves specific military actions or outcomes from force protection to theater/national missile defense
Homeland Security
Domestic and international homeland security markets especially transportation security immigration control/identity management critical infrastructure protection maritime security energy security intelligence program support law enforcement solutions a
Mission Support
Provides total life-cycle and training system engineering logistics and maintenance support to customer
Sensing
Acquires precise situational data across air space ground and underwater domains and generates information needed for effective battlespace decisions

COMPETITORS

BAE Systems Inc.	Honeywell Aerospace
Boeing	Interstate Electronics
Crane Aerospace &	L-3 Avionics
Electronics	Lockheed Martin
DRS Technologies	MBDA
Emerson Electric	Meggitt-USA
Exelis	Northrop Grumman
Fluor	Rockwell Collins
GE	Saab AB
Harris Corp.	Sierra Nevada Corp

HISTORICAL FINANCIALS

Company Type: Public

Income Statement
FYE: December 31

	REVENUE ($ mil.)	NET INCOME ($ mil.)	NET PROFIT MARGIN	EMPLOYEES
12/17	25,348	2,024	8.0%	64,000
12/16	24,069	2,211	9.2%	63,000
12/15	23,247	2,074	8.9%	61,000
12/14	22,826	2,244	9.8%	61,000
12/13	23,706	1,996	8.4%	63,000
Annual Growth	1.7%	0.3%	—	0.4%

2017 Year-End Financials

Debt ratio: 16.36%
Return on equity: 20.21%
Cash ($ mil.): 3,103
Current ratio: 1.54
Long-term debt ($ mil.): 4,750

No. of shares (mil.): 288
Dividends
Yield: 0.0%
Payout: 34.4%
Market value ($ mil.): 54,101

	STOCK PRICE ($) FY Close	P/E High/Low	PER SHARE ($) Earnings	Dividends	Book Value
12/17	187.85	27 21	6.95	2.39	34.59
12/16	142.00	20 16	7.44	3.60	34.35
12/15	124.53	19 14	6.80	2.62	33.87
12/14	108.17	15 12	7.18	2.37	31.03
12/13	90.70	15 9	6.16	2.20	35.03
Annual Growth	20.0%	— —	3.1%	2.1%	(0.3%)

RBB Bancorp

Auditors: Varinek, Trine, Day & Co., LLP

LOCATIONS

HQ: RBB Bancorp
660 S. Figueroa Street, Suite 1888, Los Angeles, CA 90017
Phone: 213 627-9888
Web: www.royalbusinessbankusa.com

HISTORICAL FINANCIALS

Company Type: Public

Income Statement
FYE: December 31

	ASSETS ($ mil.)	NET INCOME ($ mil.)	INCOME AS % OF ASSETS	EMPLOYEES
12/17	1,691	25	1.5%	203
12/16	1,395	19	1.4%	177
12/15	1,023	12	1.3%	—
12/14	0	10	—	—
Annual Growth	—	34.8%	—	—

2017 Year-End Financials

Debt ratio: 3.13%
Return on equity: 11.43%
Cash ($ mil.): 150
Current ratio: —
Long-term debt ($ mil.): —

No. of shares (mil.): 15
Dividends
  Yield: 0.0%
  Payout: 4.7%
Market value ($ mil.): 435

	STOCK PRICE ($) FY Close	P/E High/Low		PER SHARE ($) Earnings	Dividends	Book Value
12/17	27.37	15	12	1.68	0.08	16.67
12/16	0.00	—	—	1.39	0.20	14.16
Annual Growth	—	—	—	6.5%	(26.3%)	5.6%

Realogy Group LLC

EXECUTIVES

Chb-Pres- Ceo, Richard A Smith
Exec V Pres-Cfo-Treas, Anthony E Hull
Exec V Pres-General Counsel-Co, Marilyn J Wasser
Sr V Pres-Cao-Contrl, DEA Benson
Exec V Pres-Chief Hr Officer, Sunita Holzer
Sr V Pres-Cao-Contrl, Timothy B Gustavson
It Security, Ashley Vanderhoof
Technical Staff, Barbara Rossetti
Business Analyst, Bethany Auclair
Specialist, Brett Repsher
Senior Vice-President, Dina Dimaria
Auditors: PricewaterhouseCoopers LLP

LOCATIONS

HQ: Realogy Group LLC
  175 Park Avenue, Madison, NJ 07940
Phone: 973 407-2000
Web: www.realogy.com

HISTORICAL FINANCIALS

Company Type: Public

Income Statement   FYE: December 31

	REVENUE ($ mil.)	NET INCOME ($ mil.)	NET PROFIT MARGIN	EMPLOYEES
12/17	6,114	431	7.0%	11,800
12/16	5,810	213	3.7%	11,800
12/15	5,706	184	3.2%	11,400
12/14	5,328	143	2.7%	10,700
12/13	5,289	438	8.3%	10,800
Annual Growth	3.7%	(0.4%)	—	2.2%

2017 Year-End Financials

Debt ratio: 48.28%
Return on equity: 16.96%
Cash ($ mil.): 227
Current ratio: 0.83
Long-term debt ($ mil.): 3,221

No. of shares (mil.): 131
Dividends
  Yield: —
  Payout: 11.5%
Market value ($ mil.): —

Realogy Holdings Corp

Realogy Holdings is one of the largest franchisors of residential real estate offices in the world with about 14100 offices in more than 110 countries. Its brands include Century 21 Coldwell Banker ERA Better Homes and Gardens Real Estate and Sotheby's. In addition to franchising the company owns and operates about 790 offices under the already mentioned brands along with the Corcoran Group and Citi Habitats labels. It also provides relocation title and settlement services and mortgages.

Operations

Realogy operates through the four business segments of Company Owned Real Estate Brokerage Services (known as NRT) Real Estate Franchise Services (known as Realogy Franchise Group or RFG) Title and Settlement Services (known as Title Resource Group or TRG) and Relocation Services (known as Cartus).

NRT (around 70% of net sales) operates a full-service real estate brokerage business under the Coldwell Banker Corcoran Sotheby's International Realty Citi Habitats and ZipRealty brand names in more than 50 of the 100 largest metropolitan areas in the US.

RFG (almost 15%) franchises the Century 21 Coldwell Banker Coldwell Banker Commercial ERA Sotheby's International Realty and Better Homes and Gardens Real Estate brand names.

TRG (nearly 10%) provides full-service title and settlement services to real estate companies affinity groups corporations and financial institutions with many of these services provided in conjunction with the company's real estate brokerage and relocation services business.

Cartus (more than 5%) offers clients employee relocation services such as homesale assistance providing home equity advances to transferees (generally guaranteed by the client) home finding and other destination services and intercultural and language training and group move management services among other services.

Geographic Reach

Realogy conducts its business through 14100 offices in more than 110 countries. The US accounts for 98% of its net revenue.

Sales and Marketing

Realogy's franchise system operates through 14100 franchised and company owned offices and approximately 273200 independent sales associates operating under its franchise and proprietary brands in the US and 111 other countries and territories around the world.

Financial Performance

Realogy's business has been steadily growing in tandem with the strengthening US housing market for the past several years. Revenue in 2016 climbed 2% to peak at $5.8 billion a company milestone. The historic growth for 2016 was primarily due to a spike in revenue at TRG as a result of acquisitions as well as an increase in revenue at RFG driven by higher average homesale price and number of homesale transactions.

Like revenues net income jumped 16% to $213 million in 2016. This was attributed to the absence in 2016 of $6 million related to certain transaction costs associated with the acquisition of Coldwell Banker United and the settlement of a legal matter in 2015.

Realogy's cash flow from operations has also risen the last few years jumping from $544 million in 2015 to $587 million in 2016. This was attributed to $55 million of additional cash provided by operating results and $31 million more cash provided by the net change in relocation and trade receivables.

Strategy

Realogy's strategy for growth includes the launching of new software platforms that improve the productivity of its independent sales associates. Its ZapLabs subsidiary (which changed its name from ZipRealty in 2016) is the developer of its proprietary technology platform used by its real estate brokerages and independent sales associates across its franchise system. During 2016 Realogy launched ZapLabs' comprehensive integrated Zap technology platform to approximately 1110 franchisees bringing the total enrolled to 1500 of its approximately 2600 franchisees. It aims to roll out this platform to the majority of its remaining franchisees throughout 2017 and beyond.

Beyond large company acquisitions Realogy likes to purchase local real estate brokerages to expand its reach into communities. In 2016 the company acquired 11 real estate brokerage and property management operations through its NRT segment for around $80 million.

Mergers and Acquisitions

One of the ways Realogy has achieved record-setting revenue growth over the years is through the use of acquisitions. In 2015 Realogy acquired Coldwell Banker United realtors in the active markets of Texas Florida North Carolina and South Carolina. Coldwell brought 60 offices staffed by 2000 affiliated sales associates to Realogy. It continues to operate under the Coldwell Banker brand.

Company Background

Realogy in October 2012 raised $1 billion in its IPO a vote of confidence of sorts in the recovery of the residential real estate market in the US. Realogy used the IPO proceeds to reduce its more than $7 billion in debt. Despite losing $540 million in the two years prior to its IPO the firm believed the real estate market was poised for recovery. Its strategy included growing all segments of its business though it offered no specifics on that front. The company's name changed from Domus to Realogy in 2012.

EXECUTIVES

Evp General Counsel And Corporate Secretary, Marilyn J. Wasser, age 62
Chairman President And Ceo, Richard A. Smith, age 64, $1,000,000 total compensation
President And Ceo Nrt, Bruce G. Zipf, age 61, $625,000 total compensation
President And Ceo Cartus, Kevin J. Kelleher, age 63, $475,000 total compensation
Evp And Chief Human Resources Officer, Sunita Holzer
Evp Cfo And Treasurer, Anthony E. (Tony) Hull, age 59, $675,000 total compensation
President And Ceo Title Resource Group, Donald J. (Don) Casey, age 56, $450,000 total compensation
Svp And Cio, Stephen Fraser
President And Ceo Realogy Franchise Group, John Peyton
Senior Vice President Ethics And Compliance, Kimberly Toomey
Senior Vice President Technology, Jeff Krupp
Vice President Strategy, Dan Keogh
Vice President, John Ferrie
Auditors: PricewaterhouseCoopers LLP

LOCATIONS

HQ: Realogy Holdings Corp
  175 Park Avenue, Madison, NJ 07940
Phone: 973 407-2000
Web: www.realogy.com

2016 Sales

	$ mil.	% of total
US	5,683	98
All other countries	127	2
Total	5,810	100

PRODUCTS/OPERATIONS

2016 Sales

	$ mil.	% of total
Company-owned real estate brokerage services	4,344	71
Real estate franchise services	781	13
Title and settlement services	573	9
Relocation services	405	7
Corporate and other	(293)	-

Total	5,810	100

Selected Brands
Better Homes and Gardens Real Estate
Century 21
Coldwell Banker
Coldwell Banker Commercial
ERA
Sotheby's International Realty
Corcoran
Citi Habitats
ZipRealty

COMPETITORS

Brookfield Global Relocation	Keller Williams
	Move Inc.
Ebby Halliday Realtors	NRT LLC
HomeServices	RE/MAX
HomeVestors of America	SIRVA
Jones Lang LaSalle	Weichert Realtors

HISTORICAL FINANCIALS

Company Type: Public

Income Statement   FYE: December 31

	REVENUE ($ mil.)	NET INCOME ($ mil.)	NET PROFIT MARGIN	EMPLOYEES
12/17	6,114	431	7.0%	11,800
12/16	5,810	213	3.7%	11,800
12/15	5,706	184	3.2%	11,400
12/14	5,328	143	2.7%	10,700
12/13	5,289	438	8.3%	10,800
Annual Growth	3.7%	(0.4%)	—	2.2%

2017 Year-End Financials

Debt ratio: 48.28%
Return on equity: 16.96%
Cash ($ mil.): 234
Current ratio: 0.83
Long-term debt ($ mil.): 3,221

No. of shares (mil.): 131
Dividends
　Yield: 0.0%
　Payout: 11.5%
Market value ($ mil.): 3,488

	STOCK PRICE ($) FY Close	P/E High/Low		PER SHARE ($) Earnings	Dividends	Book Value
12/17	26.50	11	8	3.11	0.36	19.89
12/16	25.73	25	15	1.46	0.18	17.57
12/15	36.67	39	29	1.24	0.00	16.48
12/14	44.49	51	35	0.97	0.00	14.89
12/13	49.47	18	14	2.99	0.00	13.76
Annual Growth	(14.4%)	—	—	1.0%	—	9.7%

REDWOOD CREDIT UNION

EXECUTIVES

Pres-Ceo, Brett Martinez
Sales and Marketing Executive, Robin McKenzie
Senior Vice-President, Ron Felder
Assistant Vice-President, Joe Peyton
Human Resources Administrator, Robert Browne
Programmer, Sky Walker
Legal Staff, Alyssa Noone
Consultant, Carrie Bruce
Assistant Manager, Earl Chavez
Loan Officer, Gina Unciano
Loan Officer, Kathryn Clickner
Auditors: CLIFTONLARSONALLEN LLP PHOENI

LOCATIONS

HQ: REDWOOD CREDIT UNION
3033 CLEVELAND AVE # 100, SANTA ROSA, CA
954032126
Phone: 707 545-4000
Web: WWW.REDWOODCU.ORG

HISTORICAL FINANCIALS

Company Type: Private

Income Statement   FYE: December 31

	ASSETS ($ mil.)	NET INCOME ($ mil.)	INCOME AS % OF ASSETS	EMPLOYEES
12/17	4,046	67	1.7%	390
12/16	3,287	57	1.7%	—
12/14	2,468	47	1.9%	—
12/13	2,271	48	2.1%	—
Annual Growth	15.5%	8.6%	—	—

2017 Year-End Financials

Debt ratio: ——
Return on equity: 53.40%
Cash ($ mil.): 913
Current ratio: ——
Long-term debt ($ mil.): ——

Dividends
　Yield: ——
　Payout: ——
Market value ($ mil.): ——

Regeneron Pharmaceuticals, Inc.

Regeneron is fighting some serious enemies. Regeneron Pharmaceuticals develops protein-based drugs used to battle a variety of diseases and conditions including cancer high cholesterol inflammatory ailments and eye diseases. The biotechnology company has a handful of products on the market including eye disease treatment EYLEA (aflibercept) cholesterol lowering drug Praluent rare inflammatory disease treatment ARCALYST rheumatoid arthritis drug Kevzara and cancer treatment ZALTRAP. Regeneron has 15 more candidates in clinical development.

Operations
Regeneron operates in one business segment which includes all activities from discovery and development through commercialization of its pharmaceutical products. Most of the segment's revenue comes from EYLEA sales followed by ARCALYST sales. The company also has development candidates in areas including hypercholesterolemia oncology rheumatoid arthritis asthma and atopic dermatitis. This segment brings in more than 60% of total revenue.

The rest of the company's revenue comes from development collaborations. Regeneron has collaborations with Sanofi and Bayer HealthCare to develop aflibercept for additional indications including cancerous tumors as well as obtain approvals outside of the US. The company also has a partnership with Teva to develop fasinumab for chronic pain in patients with osteoarthritis. And in mid-2018 it established two new partnerships that employ Regeneron's antibody technology platform. It is collaborating with Zoetis to discover new veterinary treatments and with bluebird bio to develop new cell therapies for cancer.

Geographic Reach
Regeneron has its corporate and R&D headquarters in Tarrytown New York and a satellite office in Basking Ridge New Jersey. It manufactures bulk drug materials in Renssalaer New York and has additional office space in Sleepy Hollow and Troy New York.

Internationally Regeneron is headquartered in Dublin Ireland and has a manufacturing facility in Limerick Ireland as well as an office in London.

Sales and Marketing
Regeneron uses distributors and specialty pharmacies to sell its products directly to health care providers. ARCALYST is sold directly to patients.

The company's largest customers are AmerisourceBergen subsidiary Besse Medical McKesson and Express Scripts subsidiary Curascript SD Specialty Distribution. They account for virtually all gross product revenue. Regeneron also collaborates with Bayer and Sanofi for global sales of EYLEA Dupixent Praluent and Keyzara.

Financial Performance
Thanks to the launching of about a half-dozen products since 2011 Regeneron has reported strong revenue growth over the last few years. Net income has also been rising steadily.

In 2017 revenue increased 21% to $5.9 billion thanks primarily to higher sales of EYLEA and higher collaboration revenue from Sanofi and Bayer. Overall net product sales increased 11% that year.

With that higher revenue net income rose 34% to $1.2 billion in 2017. Higher sales of EYLEA helped fund activities such as an expansion of manufacturing capabilities to support the company's other product candidates.

The company ended 2017 with $812.7 million in net cash nearly $300 million more than it had at the end of 2016. This was largely due to operating cash inflow totaling $1.3 billion. Investing activities primarily the purchases of investment securities used $1 billion and financing activities used $24.4 million.

Strategy
Regeneron has expanded the applications of its protein-based technology to include the creation of human monoclonal antibodies (laboratory-produced cloned proteins). It has a pipeline of 15 clinical-stage antibodies with programs in eye disease infectious disease cancer pain management cardiovascular disease and inflammation. The company also licenses its human antibody technology out to drug developers who then use Regeneron's technology in researching their own antibody drugs.

With its development partners Regeneron has been successful in obtaining expanded approvals for its existing products. In late 2018 Sanofi and Regeneron won US approval for Dupixent as an asthma treatment adding to its previously approved use for dermatitis. Dupixent is expected to reach blockbuster status and the asthma indication will only help boost its sales. However Dupixent for asthma has a relatively high list price of $36000 per year and it faces competition from other drugs.

Also in 2018 Sanofi and Regeneron's Libtayo received FDA clearance to treat patients with metastatic cutaneous squamous cell carcinoma (CSCC which accounts for about 20% of skin cancer cases) who are not candidates for curative surgery or radiation. Libtayo is also under review in Europe.

Regeneron faces competition from Novartis which is hoping to launch its EYLEA competitor in 2019. Novartis' RTH258 is not yet approved by the FDA but it has shown to perform better than EYLEA in clinical trials.

In 2017 and 2016 Regeneron spent $2.1 billion on R&D expenses up from $1.6 billion in 2015.

Company Background
Regeneron was founded in New York City in 1988.

ARCALYST (rilonacept) was approved by the FDA in 2008 and subsequently became the company's first market-stage product.

EXECUTIVES

Evp Research And Development, Neil Stahl, age 61, $619,300 total compensation
Chief Scientific Officer; President Regeneron Laboratories, George D. Yancopoulos, age 58, $1,055,700 total compensation
President And Ceo, Leonard S. Schleifer, age 65, $1,242,000 total compensation
Evp Commercial, Robert J. Terifay, age 58, $550,700 total compensation
Svp Finance And Cfo, Robert E. Landry, $585,600 total compensation
Evp; General Manager Industrial Operations And Product Supply, Daniel P. Van Plew, age 45, $349,200 total compensation
Medical Director, Mark Ballard
Medical Director Immunology And Inflammation, Gregory St John
Vice President Early Clinical Development, Olivier Harari
Chairman, P. Roy Vagelos, age 88
Auditors: PricewaterhouseCoopers LLP

LOCATIONS

HQ: Regeneron Pharmaceuticals, Inc.
777 Old Saw Mill River Road, Tarrytown, NY 10591-6707
Phone: 914 847-7000
Web: www.regeneron.com

PRODUCTS/OPERATIONS

2017 Sales

	$ mil.	% of total
Net product sales		
EYLEA	3,701	63
ARCALYST	16	-
Bayer collaboration	938	16
Sanofi collaboration	877	15
Other	338	6
Total	**5,872**	**100**

COMPETITORS

Allergan Limited	GlaxoSmithKline
Amgen	Merck
AstraZeneca	Novartis
Bristol-Myers Squibb	Pfizer
Eli Lilly	Roche Holding
Genentech	Teva

HISTORICAL FINANCIALS

Company Type: Public

Income Statement

FYE: December 31

	REVENUE ($ mil.)	NET INCOME ($ mil.)	NET PROFIT MARGIN	EMPLOYEES
12/18	6,710	2,444	36.4%	7,400
12/17	5,872	1,198	20.4%	6,200
12/16	4,860	895	18.4%	5,400
12/15	4,103	636	15.5%	4,300
12/14	2,819	348	12.3%	2,925
Annual Growth	24.2%	62.8%	—	26.1%

2018 Year-End Financials

Debt ratio: 6.04%	No. of shares (mil.): 109
Return on equity: 32.81%	Dividends
Cash ($ mil.): 1,467	Yield: —
Current ratio: 4.47	Payout: —
Long-term debt ($ mil.): 708	Market value ($ mil.): 40,714

	STOCK PRICE ($) FY Close	P/E High/Low	Earnings	PER SHARE ($) Dividends	Book Value
12/18	373.50	18 13	21.29	0.00	80.34
12/17	375.96	47 30	10.34	0.00	57.09
12/16	367.09	63 39	7.70	0.00	41.97
12/15	542.87	96 64	5.52	0.00	34.92
12/14	410.25	126 77	3.07	0.00	24.82
Annual Growth	(2.3%)	— —	62.3%	—	34.1%

REGENTS OF THE UNIVERSITY OF MICHIGAN

Michigan — it's shaped like a mitten and higher education fits the state like a glove. With nearly 60000 students and about 7000 faculty members scattered across three campuses in Ann Arbor Dearborn and Flint the university's diverse academic units span such areas of study as architecture education law medicine music and social work. Notable alumni include the late President Gerald Ford (the university is home to the Gerald R. Ford Library and the Ford School of Public Policy) actor James Earl Jones Google cofounder Larry Page and seven Nobel laureates. In addition to state funding the university is supported by a $6.6 billion endowment.

Operations

The university operates some 20 schools offering education in everything from dentistry and medicine to music theater and dance. About 70% of the students are enrolled in undergraduate programs while the rest are graduate students.

There are seven museums on campus — including the Museum of Art the Exhibit Museum of Natural History (with a planetarium) and the Kelsey Museum of Archaeology — as well as the Nichols Arboretum and the Matthaei Botanical Gardens.

Through its Health System the university maintains one of the largest health care complexes in the world. It is made up of more than 50 health centers and 120 outpatient clinics around the state and is responsible for more than 40% of The University of Michigan's revenue.

Along with its various health centers and clinics the university operates the C.S. Mott Children's Hospital. The children's hospital is noted for its heart surgery neonatal care and respiratory disorders and ranks among the nation's best for all other pediatric specialties — cancer digestive disorders general pediatrics and neurology.

Geographic Reach

The University of Michigan was founded in Detroit in 1817 but moved to Ann Arbor in 1837.

Financial Performance

The university has enjoyed an upward trend in revenue during recent fiscal years as a result of increases in tuition rates and undergraduate enrollment. It claimed more than $5 billion in revenue for fiscal 2012 up more than 5% compared to the $4.77 billion the university reported in revenue for fiscal 2011. The school brought in about $453 billion during fiscal 2010.

EXECUTIVES

Vp Government Relations, Cynthia H. Wilbanks
Vp Development, Jerry A. May
Chancellor University Of Michigan-dearborn, Daniel Little
Evp And Cfo, Kevin P. Hegarty, age 62
Chairman Victors For Michigan, Stephen M. Ross
President, Mark S. Schlissel
Dean School Of Public Health, Martin Philbert
Vp Information Technology And Cio, Kelli Trosvig
Dean Stamps School Of Art And Design, Gunalan Nadarajan
Dean School Of Dentistry, Laurie McCauley
Dean Law School, Mark D. West
Chancellor University Of Michigan-flint, Susan E. Borrego
Interim Provost And Evp Academic Affairs, Paul N. Courant
Evp Medical Affairs; Dean Medical School; Ceo Michigan Medicine, Marschall S. Runge
Vp And General Counsel, Timothy G. Lynch
Vp Research, S. Jack Hu
Interim Dean Taubman College Of Architecture And Urban Planning, Robert Fishman
Edward J. Frey Dean Ross School Of Business, Scott DeRue
Dean School Of Education, Elizabeth Birr Moje
Dean School Of Engineering, Alec D. Gallimore
Dean School Of Information, Thomas A. Finholt
Dean School Of Kinesiology, Lori Ploutz-Snyder
Dean College Of Literature Science And The Arts, Andrew D. Martin
Dean College Of Music Theatre And Dance, Aaron Dworkin
Interim Dean School Of Natural Resources And Environment, Dan Brown
Dean School Of Nursing, Patricia D. Hurn
Dean College Of Pharmacy, James T. Dalton
Dean School Of Social Work, Lynn Videka
Dean Rackham Graduate School; Vice Provost Academic Affairs Graduate Studies, Carol A. Fierke
Vice President Research, Stephen Forrest
Associate Vice President And Executive Director For Research Administration, Marvin Parnes
Associate Vice President Development, Julie Sparkman
Vice President Marketing, Rachelle Caoagas
Assistant Vice President Estate, Diane Tracy
Associate Vice President Facilities And Operations, Henry Baier
Vice President, Marina Epelman
Senior Executive Secretary Office Of Vice President For Research Department, BettyL Cook
Provost And Executive Vice President For Academic Affairs, Teresa Sullivan
Vice President Of Security Systems, Michael Dillard
Vice President Of Technology, Trung Nguyen
Vice President Technology, Jamila Power
Vice President Technology, Mehra Rohit
Vice President Investment Banking, Raj Singhal
Vice President Of Finance, Ruohao Li
Vice President Student Government Budget Allocations Committee, Mackenzie Swart
Vice President Event Planning, Kendall Witmer
Vice Chairman, Michael J. Behm
Chairman, Mark J. Bernstein
Treasurer, Kevin Morrison
Secretary Iii Umh Mworks Employ Assistant Program Department, Angela Hurlbut
Secretary Iv Lsa Dean Deans Office Department, Sandra Petee
Secretary Iv Oral Med Path Oncology Department, Wendy M Carbary
Secretary Iii Academic Affairs Dentistry Department, Diane Pasma
Secretary Iv Umh Administration Department, Melody Bond

LOCATIONS

HQ: REGENTS OF THE UNIVERSITY OF MICHIGAN
503 THOMPSON ST RM 3040, ANN ARBOR, MI
481091340
Phone: 734 764-1817
Web: WWW.UMICH.EDU

PRODUCTS/OPERATIONS

Selected Academic Units

Architecture and urban planning
Art and design
Business administration
Dentistry
Education
Engineering
Kinesiology
Law
Literature science and the arts
Medicine
Music
Natural resources and environment
Nursing
Pharmacy
Public health
Public policy
Social work

HISTORICAL FINANCIALS

Company Type: Private

Income Statement

FYE: June 30

	REVENUE ($ mil.)	NET INCOME ($ mil.)	NET PROFIT MARGIN	EMPLOYEES
06/18	7,466	920	12.3%	34,624
06/17	7,079	1,275	18.0%	—
06/16	6,278	(294)	—	—
06/14	5,534	1,574	28.5%	—
Annual Growth	7.8%	(12.6%)	—	—

2018 Year-End Financials

Debt ratio: —
Return on equity: 12.30%
Cash ($ mil.): 163
Current ratio: 0.50
Long-term debt ($ mil.): —

Dividends
 Yield: —
 Payout: —
Market value ($ mil.): —

Regions Financial Corp

Regions Financial Corporation sprouted in the US South and has spread its roots across the region by acquiring other financial services firms. The holding company for Regions Bank Regions Financial boasts nearly $125 billion in total assets and has around 1500 branches and about 1900 ATMs across 15 states stretching from the Southeast and Texas northward through the Mississippi River Valley. In addition to providing standard banking services such as deposit accounts loans and mortgages and credit cards to retail customers and small businesses Regions Financial also serves larger corporations and boasts wealth management division for affluent individuals.

Operations

Regions Financial operates three main segments: Corporate Bank Consumer Bank and Wealth Management.

The Consumer Bank accounts for some 55% of sales and serves mainly retail and small business customers. The Corporate Bank (35% of sales) serves middle-market and large commercial clients. Region's Wealth Management division (10% of sales) provides trust and investment services to affluent individuals.

Typically slightly more than half of Regions Financial's total revenue comes from loan interest (including fees) while more than 10% comes from deposit account service charges and another approximately 10% comes from interest on taxable securities. Card and ATM fees and mortgage banking income make up around 5% of total revenue each. About 30% of the bank's total loan portfolio is made up of consumer residential real estate loans.

Regions Insurance Group a subsidiary of Regions Financial provides insurance products to bank customers.

Geographic Reach

Alabama-based Regions Financial boasts some 1500 banking offices and about 1900 ATMs across 15 Southern and Central US states. More than 50% of its branches are in Florida Tennessee and Alabama around 25% are in Mississippi Georgia and Louisiana. The rest are in Arkansas Illinois Indiana Iowa Kentucky Missouri North Carolina South Carolina Texas and Virginia.

Sales and Marketing

Regions Financial serves some four million households throughout the South Midwest and Texas. It sells and markets its products directly through its branches and through other channels such as the internet and mobile banking. Its Wealth Management customers are affluent individuals while its business customers include corporate middle market small business and commercial real estate developers and investors.

Financial Performance

Regions Financial has reversed four years of declining revenue by posting consecutive gains in fiscals 2015 and 2016. In 2016 sales grew 5% to $6.0 billion with gains concentrated in loans and fees and an increase in operating lease assets.

Interest income was boosted by higher interest rates average loan growth and higher securities balances. Noninterest income increased due to higher capital markets fee income ATM fees and bank-owned life insurance income.

Net income increased 10% to $1.0 billion as the company was able to increase its revenue without a comparable increase in expenses.

Cash from operating activities increased 24% to $2.0 billion due to a reduction in liabilities payments.

Strategy

In 2016 Regions Bank partnered with online lending platform Avant to offer a online consumer loan application and underwriting service. The agreement brings together Regions Financial's banking experience with Avant's technology platform.

Regions is looking for ways to fight back against lower cost online lenders that are eating into its customer base. In 2015 the company partnered with funding startup Fundation to provide online loans to small businesses.

Mergers and Acquisitions

In October 2016 Regions acquired two businesses from First Sterling Financial to build on its real estate and capital markets capabilities. It acquired First Sterling's Low Income Housing Tax Credit (LIHTC) corporate fund syndication and asset management businesses.

HISTORY

Regions Financial was created out of three venerable Alabama banks. The oldest First National Bank of Huntsville was founded in 1855. When 10 years later the bank was besieged by Union troops a loyal cashier hid securities in the chimney and refused to tell the soldiers where they were. A few years later it was robbed by Jesse James (for years the bank kept in its vaults a gun purported to belong to a James gang member). First National Bank of Montgomery was founded in 1871 and Exchange Security Bank in 1928.

Banking veteran Frank Plummer consolidated the three banks to form Alabama's first multibank holding company First Alabama Bancshares in 1971. The combined firm then became the bank that ate Alabama. But even as it gobbled up other banks its diet remained bland: Its lending programs were modest and focused on a narrow range of business.

The bank's growth in the 1980s was solid if unexciting as it picked up community banks in Alabama (Anniston National Bank and South Baldwin Bank among others) and Georgia (Georgia Co. a mortgage subsidiary of Columbus Bank and Trust). Before he died in 1987 Plummer brought in Willard Hurley as chairman. Hurley put the brakes on acquisitions when they overloaded the bank's data-processing systems. He also put the company up for sale igniting its stock price for a while but there were no serious suitors.

When Hurley passed the baton to Stanley Mackin in 1990 the bank was still rumored to be for sale. But Mackin had other ideas. He put the bank back on its acquisition track and raised the bar on profitability expectations for each department. In 1993 Mackin orchestrated First Alabama's purchase of Secor a failed New Orleans thrift outbidding rival AmSouth Bancorporation. The Secor purchase raised eyebrows but First Alabama sold some branches and folded other operations into its organization.

In 1994 First Alabama changed its name to Regions Financial in order to reflect its out-of-state operations. The next year Regions rolled into Georgia in a big way leaping from a few banks to holdings with approximately $4 billion in assets. Rumors of a merger with either Wachovia or SunTrust Banks popped up in 1996 but the bank continued on its independent course. The next year the company's tank-like progress was halted when it was outbid for Mississippi's Deposit Guaranty Corp. by First American.

By way of consolation Regions in 1998 bought First Commercial Corp. of Little Rock paying a premium price for its 26 banks mortgage company and investment company. Regions also acquired 13 other companies that year and began a major overhaul of its systems concurrently with the assimilation of these operations. This effort included the consolidation of the back-office aspects of its retail and indirect lending operations.

Mackin retired in 1998 and banking veteran Carl Jones Jr. became CEO. Under his direction the bank continued its geographic infill strategy with acquisitions of banks and branches in Arkansas Florida Louisiana Tennessee and Texas in 1999 and 2000. The company also sold its credit card portfolio to MBNA (since acquired by Bank of America) and in 2001 acquired Memphis-based investment bank Morgan Keegan.

Regions Financial has looked for acquisitions in order to grow geographically and diversify its product and services mix. It fortified its foothold in the South and expanded into the Midwest with its blockbuster merger with Union Planters in 2004. Roughly two years later the company acquired fellow Birmingham-based bank AmSouth for nearly $10 billion in stock. The latter deal created one of the 10 largest banks in the US and helped Regions Financial keep pace with other megabanks in its markets such as Bank of America and SunTrust. The deals also helped entrench the company in states such as Alabama Arkansas Mississippi and Tennessee where it is a market leader.

EXECUTIVES

Chairman President And Ceo, O. B. Grayson Hall, $1,000,000 total compensation

Sevp; Head Corporate Banking, John M. Turner, age 58

Sevp; Head General Banking, John B. Owen, $659,816 total compensation

Sevp General Counsel And Corporate Secretary, Fournier J. (Boots) Gale, $570,554 total compensation

Sevp; President Mid-america Region, Ronald G. (Ronnie) Smith

Sevp; Head Commercial Banking, William E. (Bill) Horton

Sevp; President South Region, C. Keith Herron

Sevp; President East Region, Brett D. Couch

Sevp; Head Consumer Services, Scott M. Peters

Sevp; Head Wealth Management, William D. (Bill) Ritter

Sevp And Cfo, David J. Turner, $644,062 total compensation

Sevp; Head Human Resources, David R. (Dave) Keenan

Sevp And Chief Credit Officer, Barbara (Barb) Godin

Sevp And Chief Risk Officer, C. Matthew Lusco, $566,308 total compensation

Sevp; Head Strategic Performance And Alignment, Ellen Jones

Senior Executive Vice President Human Resources Systems And Administration, Christine Germanson

Vice President And Technology Contract Manager, Mike Ritchie

Executive Vice President Real Estate Ban, Michael Smith

Vice President Commercial Real Estate, Todd Harris

Senior Vice President Consumer Sales Manager, Ken Knapp Ken Knapp

Senior Vice President, Donald Sinclair

Vice President Branch Sales Manager, Cathy Cosey

Vice President, William Laenger

Vice President, Kenneth Bizzard

Vice President Relationship Manager, Cory Guillory

Executive Vice President Of Commercial Banking, Tammi Sanchez

Assistant Vice President And Branch Manager And Small Business Lender, Bryan Furlong

Assistant Vice President Branch Manager, Linda Barton

Vice President Global Trade Finance, Chuck Youngerman

Svp Business Risk Management, Florence Morris

Senior Vice President And Texas Market Manager, Wendel Pardue

Senior Vice President Financial Planning And Analysis, Jay Baxter

Senior Vice President Program Development Manager, David Fron

Vice President Of Information Technology, Adrian Castanon

Vice President Relationship Manager, Franklin Reyes

Vice President Mortgage Loan Officer, Mary Ethridge

Vice President Manager Of Special Projects And Incentive Compensation Modeling, Matthew Bledsoe

Vice President Mortgage Production Manager, Alan Noe

Vice President Escrow Manager, Kathy Schwartz

Executive Assistant To Bill Askew Senior Executive Vice President And Chris Ewing Executive Vice President, Pamela Ashley

Vice President Business Banking, Brian Brooks

Vice President, Barrett Vawter

Senior Vice President Portfolio Risk Management, Robert Long

Assistant Vice President Commercial Underwriter, Carlos Russell

Senior Executive Vice President And Chief Credit Officer, Barb Godin

Assistant Vice President Branch Manager, Patrick Cayson

Senior Vice President Corporate Real Estate, Scott Riley

Senior Vice President Corporate Banking, JP Hickey

Vice President Wealth Management, Leslie G Stricklin

Vice President And Trust Advisor, Conor Duggan

Vice President Human Resources, Ellie Long

Vice President Private Wealth Management, Patty Franco

Senior Vice President Wealth Management Compliance, Aneidre Amerson-Allman

Senior Vice President Commercial Banking, Brett Barrow

Vice President, Jennifer Jackson

Senior Vice President Wealth Management, Lisa Harless

Executive Vice President Human Resources Regions Bank, Anthony Hernandez

Senior Vice President, James Watkins

Vice President And Mortgage Operations Manager Regions Bank, Matthew Knueven

Vice President, Michael Harrington

Executive Vice President, Pam Davis

Senior Vice President, Bill Robertson

Senior Vice President, Barry Musselman

Assistant Vice President, Brenda Powers

Vice President, Carl Taube

Vice President Commercial And Industrial, Philip Ugalde

Senior Vice President Mergers And Acquisitions, Marc Bromstad

Vice President Private Banking Custom Underwriter, Heather Helms

Vice President, Frank Glenn

Vice President Business Banking, Sandy Salyers

Senior Vice President, Redmond Taylor

Senior Vice President Special Assets Division Regions Bank, Gray Ives

Avp Sponsorship Marketing Corporate Marketing, Jelicia Mallory

Senior Vice President Corporate Bank Administration, Edward Cotter

Vice President Fiduciary Risk, Clayton Chastain

Svp Strategic And Corporate Planning, Steven Pfitzer

Vice President, Chris Fitz

Assistant Vice President Branch Manager, Britt Dowell

Vice President Asistant, Brenda Pettit

Senior Vice President, Fernanda Hailey

Executive Vice President And Treasurer, M Deron Smithy

Auditors: Ernst & Young LLP

LOCATIONS

HQ: Regions Financial Corp
1900 Fifth Avenue North, Birmingham, AL 35203
Phone: 205 581-7890
Web: www.regions.com

2016 Branch Locations

	No.
Florida	326
Tennessee	230
Alabama	226
Missippi	132
Georgia	124
Louisiana	104
Arkansas	88
Texas	76
Missouri	57
Indiana	55
Illinois	55
South Carolina	26
Kentucky	12
Iowa	10
North Carolina	6
Total	**1,527**

PRODUCTS/OPERATIONS

2016 Sales

	$ mil.	% of total
Interest income		
Loansincluding fees	3,066	51
Securities - taxable	566	9
Operating lease assets	125	2
Loans held for sale	16	-
Trading account securities	5	-
Other earning assets	36	1
Non-interest income		
Service charges on deposits	664	11
Card and ATM fees	402	7
Investment management and trust fee income	213	4
Mortgage income	173	3
Securities gains (losses) net	6	0
Others	695	12
Total	**5,967**	**100**

2016 Sales

	% of total
Consumer Bank	55
Corporate Bank	35
Wealth Management	10
Total	**100**

Selected Products

Banking
  Checking
  Money Market
  Savings
  CDs
  Regions Visa CheckCard
  Business Checking
  Business Savings
  Merchant Services
  Treasury Management
  Payroll
  Audit Confirmations
Commercial Banking
  Deposit Services
  Treasury Management
  Online Services
  Merchant Services
  Global Trade Finance
  Corporate Trust
Private Wealth Management
  Solutions for Individuals
  Credit and Risk Management
  Wealth Management
  Solutions for Professionals

COMPETITORS

Arvest Bank	First Horizon
BB&T	Investar
BBVA Compass	JPMorgan Chase
Bancshares	SunTrust
Bank of America	Synovus
Capital One	Trustmark
Citigroup	Wells Fargo
First Citizens	Woodforest Financial
BancShares	

HISTORICAL FINANCIALS

Company Type: Public

Income Statement
FYE: December 31

	ASSETS ($ mil.)	NET INCOME ($ mil.)	INCOME AS % OF ASSETS	EMPLOYEES
12/17	124,294	1,263	1.0%	21,714
12/16	125,968	1,163	0.9%	22,166
12/15	126,050	1,062	0.8%	22,916
12/14	119,679	1,155	1.0%	23,723
12/13	117,396	1,122	1.0%	24,255
Annual Growth	1.4%	3.0%	—	(2.7%)

2017 Year-End Financials

Debt ratio: 3.60%
Return on equity: 7.69%
Cash ($ mil.): 3,911
Current ratio: —
Long-term debt ($ mil.): —

No. of shares (mil.): 1,134
Dividends
Yield: 0.0%
Payout: 31.5%
Market value ($ mil.): 19,597

	STOCK PRICE ($) FY Close	P/E High/Low	PER SHARE ($) Earnings	Dividends	Book Value
12/17	17.28	17 13	1.00	0.32	14.28
12/16	14.36	17 8	0.87	0.26	13.72
12/15	9.60	14 12	0.75	0.23	12.98
12/14	10.56	14 11	0.80	0.18	12.55
12/13	9.89	13 9	0.77	0.10	11.44
Annual Growth	15.0%	— —	6.8%	33.2%	5.7%

Reinsurance Group of America, Inc.

Just what is reinsurance? Here hold this pile of insurance risk while we explain that holding company Reinsurance Group of America (RGA) is one of the largest life reinsurers in the US. RGA provides insurance companies with reinsurance on the risks they've taken on allowing them to reduce their liability and increase their business volume. Its operations are organized into two large groups: Traditional and Financial Solutions. Traditional reinsurance includes individual and group life and health disability and critical illness coverage while Financial Solutions includes longevity financial and asset-intensive products. RGA operates in about 30 countries in the Americas the Asia/Pacific region Europe and South Africa.

Operations

RGA's US operating unit RGA Reinsurance provides both traditional life reinsurance and reinsurance on investment assets such as annuities and corporate-owned life insurance policies. Its customers are generally large US-based life insurance companies. In addition to its traditional mortality-risk and asset reinsurance the US operations also offer financial reinsurance to help its customers meet regulatory requirements. Its Global Financial Solutions unit consists of three businesses: asset-intensive reinsurance (full-risk coinsurance of annuities or reinsurance with a large investment component) financial reinsurance (involving ceding companies) and longevity risk transfer (employee retirement benefits).

The company also provides e-underwriting solutions to help customers write policies better and more quickly.

At the close of 2016 RGA had life reinsurance in force valued at about $3.1 trillion and about $53.1 billion in consolidated assets.

Geographic Reach

RGA organizes its operating segments by geographic region: US and Latin America; Canada; Europe Middle East and Africa; and Asia Pacific. The US and Latin America segment accounts for around 60% of total sales.

The company is expanding internationally particularly in such emerging markets as China India Mexico and the Middle East. It has offices in Australia Barbados Bermuda Canada China France Germany Hong Kong India Ireland Italy Japan Malaysia Mexico the Netherlands New Zealand Poland Singapore South Africa South Korea Spain Taiwan the United Arab Emirates the UK and the US.

Sales and Marketing

RGA's top five customers generate some $2.1 billion representing about one-fifth of its gross premiums.

Financial Performance

RGA's revenue which has been relatively static over the past few years rose 11% to $11.5 billion in 2016. That increase was led by growth in net premiums (which rose 8%) investment income and net investment-related gains. All geographic segments showed gains in premiums.

Net income increased 40% to $701.4 million that year. Although buoyed by the higher revenue net income was partially offset by an increase in benefits and other expenses. Cash flow from operations has fallen since 2014; it declined 30% to $1.5 billion in 2016. This was primarily driven by changes in operating assets and liabilities.

Strategy

RGA's strategy for growth has positioned the company well for harsh economic times and industry challenges. To achieve profitable results the company relies on its strong underwriting capabilities and disciplined pricing as well as geographic expansion and diversification in the products and services it offers. It is especially widening its mortality offerings in North America including facultative automatic and in-force block reinsurance. It also looks to leverage existing client relationships. In addition the company is looking to profit from the aging US population of baby boomers which is concerned with retirement income and estate planning.

As part of its efforts to diversify RGA has been seeking new longevity risk contracts. (Longevity risk refers to the risk of having to make payments to a retiree for a longer period than planned for if the person lives longer than expected.) For example in late 2016 the company entered into a longevity transaction with AXA France; the swap covered more than 150000 annuitants and related commitment.

In recent years RGA has opened new offices in Singapore and China to expand its global presence. It is also constructing a new US headquarters building to meet future growth needs.

Mergers and Acquisitions

In 2015 RGA acquired Aurora National Life Assurance from Swiss Re for $191.5 million; that business includes some 82000 policies in force (roughly two-thirds annuities and one-third life products). Later that year the company bought some $22 billion in term life reinsurance policies (approximately 290000 policies) from Ireland-based XL Group.

RGA also purchased Netherlands-based cooperative PGGM Levensverzekeringen in a move to provide closed-block solutions in Europe.

EXECUTIVES

Evp General Counsel And Secretary, William L. Hutton

Sevp And Cfo, Todd C. Larson, age 55, $472,428 total compensation

Evp And Chief Of Staff, Robert M. Musen

Evp Global Financial Solutions; President Rga Financial Group, John P. Laughlin

Interim Ceo Rgax Americas And Chief Solutions Officer Rgax, Mark E. Showers

Evp And Chief Human Resources Officer, Gay Burns

President And Ceo, Anna Manning, $750,000 total compensation

Evp Global Acquisitions, Scott D. Cochran

Sevp And Coo, Alain P. Néemeh, $563,750 total compensation

Evp And Chief Investment Officer, Timothy (Tim) Matson

Evp And Cio, Suzy Scanlon

Evp And Global Chief Risk Officer, Jonathan Porter

Senior Vice President Long Term Care And U.s. Individual Health, Wayne Adams

Vice President Operational Risk And Interim Chief Compliance Officer, Chris Cooper

Vice President Compensation And Benefits, Pat Grube

Senior Vice President And Chief Actuary, Doug Knowling

Regional Vice President, Joseph Klimchak

Vice President Information Management And Analytics Services, Mike Foster

Vice President And Actuary Financial M, Christopher Clark

Vice President Business Development, Andr Dreyer

Vice President Actuary, Julie Decker

Senior Executive Vice President And Chief Operating Officer, Alain Neemeh

Senior Vice President, Brian Haynes

Vice President Finance, John Hayden

Vice President, James Kellett

Vice President Aura Client Services, Mike Casale

Vice President Global Underwriting Quality And Risk Assurance, Stephanie Williams

Vice President, Wendy Swanson

Senior Vice President Of The Latin American Division, Jaime Correa

Vice President And Actuary, Thomas Dlouhy

Vice President, Jeffrey Schuh

Vice President Valuation And Financial Analysis, Chris Murphy

Vice President For Financial Markets, Mark M Hopfinger

Senior Vice President Heathcare, Steven Abood

Vice President, David Vnenchak

Vice President Business Development, Lisa Renetzky

Vice President And Actuary, Dustin Hetzler

Vice President Of Operations, Anne Riley

Information Technology Director Vice President, Matt Empey

Vice President Credit Research And Risk Management, Scott Stone

Vice President, Curt Zepeda

Vice President, Doris Jackson

Vice President And Managing Actuary, Alden Skar

Svp And Chief Actuary U.s. Group Reinsurance, Dean Abbott

Vice President Claims And Client Services, Dan Abramowski

Vice President Director Of Investment Strategy And Research, Amy Gibson

Vice President Data Strategy Global Research And Development, Brad Lipic

Vice President Global Marketing, Sue Carrillo

Vice President And Actuary Head Of Global Experience Analytics, Michael Lane

Vice President Director Of Non U.s. Portfolio Management, Daniel Collins

Vice President Corporate Communications, Lynn Phillips

Vice President Business Initiatives, Peter Schindler

Svp Group Life Accident And Disability Reinsurance U.s. Group Reinsurance, Jim Rathbum

Svp Investor Relations, Jeffrey Hopson

Vice President Aura Product Management, Brad Butler

Svp And Chief Medical Director Of U.s. Mortality Markets, Holowaty Carl

Vice President Ehr Initiatives, Susan Wehrman

Vice President Business Initiatives, Daniel Lyons

Assistant Vice President International Treaties, Diane Hare

Vice President And Senior Actuary Business Initiatives, Stephanie Grass

Chairman, J. Cliff Eason

Board Member, Stanley Tulin

Assistant Treasurer, Jeffrey Boyer

Board Member, Frederick J Sievert

Board Member, Tricia Guinn

Auditors: DELOITTE & TOUCHE LLP

LOCATIONS

HQ: Reinsurance Group of America, Inc.
16600 Swingley Ridge Road, Chesterfield, MO 63017
Phone: 636 736-7000
Web: www.rgare.com

2015 Revenues

	$ mil.	% of total
US and Latin America	6,108	59
Asia/Pacific	1,694	16
Europe Middle East and Africa	1,477	14
Canada	1,068	10
Corporate & other	68	1
Total	**10,418**	**100**

Selected Countries of Operation

Australia
Barbados
Bermuda
Canada
China
France
Germany
Hong Kong
India
Ireland
Italy
Japan
Malaysia
Mexico
Netherlands
New Zealand
Poland
Singapore
South Africa
South Korea
Spain
Taiwan
Turkey
United Arab Emirates
UK
US

PRODUCTS/OPERATIONS

2016 Revenues

	$ mil.	% of total
U.S. and Latin America	6,805	59
Canada	1,164	10
Europe Middle East and Africa	1,535	13
Asia Pacific	1,834	16
Corporate and Other	180	2
Total	**11,521**	**100**

Selected Products and Services

e-Underwriting solutions
Facultative and underwriting expertise
Financial solutions
Group reinsurance
Individual life reinsurance

Individual living benefits reinsurance
Product development

Selected Subsidiaries

Reinsurance Company of Missouri Incorporated (RCM)
RGA Americas Reinsurance Company Ltd. (RGA Americas)
RGA Atlantic Reinsurance Company Ltd. (RGA Atlantic)
RGA International Reinsurance Company (RGA International)
RGA Life Reinsurance Company of Canada (RGA Canada)
RGA Reinsurance Company (Barbados) Ltd. (RGA Barbados)
RGA Reinsurance Company (RGA Reinsurance)
RGA Reinsurance Company of Australia Limited (RGA Australia)

COMPETITORS

AEGON USA	Munich Re Group
Berkshire Hathaway	Pacific Life
General Re	Prudential
Generali	SCOR Reinsurance
Hannover Re	Swiss Re
Munich Re America	XL Group plc

HISTORICAL FINANCIALS

Company Type: Public

Income Statement

FYE: December 31

	ASSETS ($ mil.)	NET INCOME ($ mil.)	INCOME AS % OF ASSETS	EMPLOYEES
12/17	60,514	1,822	3.0%	2,640
12/16	53,097	701	1.3%	2,482
12/15	50,383	502	1.0%	2,201
12/14	44,679	684	1.5%	2,070
12/13	39,674	418	1.1%	1,890
Annual Growth	**11.1%**	**44.4%**	**—**	**8.7%**

2017 Year-End Financials

Debt ratio: 5.90%
Return on equity: 21.87%
Cash ($ mil.): 1,303
Current ratio: —
Long-term debt ($ mil.): —

No. of shares (mil.): 64
Dividends
Yield: 0.0%
Payout: 6.5%
Market value ($ mil.): 10,050

	STOCK PRICE ($) FY Close	P/E High/Low		PER SHARE ($) Earnings	Dividends	Book Value
12/17	155.93	6	4	27.71	1.82	148.48
12/16	125.83	12	7	10.79	1.56	110.31
12/15	85.55	13	11	7.46	1.40	94.09
12/14	87.62	9	7	9.78	1.26	102.13
12/13	77.41	13	9	5.78	1.08	83.87
Annual Growth	**19.1%**	**—**	**—**	**48.0%**	**13.9%**	**15.3%**

Reliance Steel & Aluminum Co.

Reliance Steel & Aluminum shows its mettle as North America's largest metals service center company. Operating in the US (about 300 service centers in 40 states) and a dozen other countries it processes and distributes more than 100000 metal products (bars beams pipes tubes plates coils etc.) to 125000-plus customers in industries like aerospace energy construction manufacturing semiconductor and electronics and transportation. Carbon steel is its top product; Reliance also markets alloy stainless and specialty steel as well as aluminum brass copper and titanium products.

Operations

Reliance purchases a variety of metals from primary producers converts them to specialty products through various processing services and advanced technique (like bending coiling polishing etc.) and sells them in small quantities to customers through a network of metals service centers.

Although Reliance has only one reportable operating segment Metal Service Centers it earns revenue through six products and services. Carbon steel is its highest revenue earner accounting for more than 50% of total sales followed by Aluminum at 20%. The rest (Stainless Steel Alloy and Other) make up just over 25% of company revenues.

Geographic Reach

Reliance operates in about 40 US states and Australia Belgium Canada China France India Malaysia Mexico Singapore South Korea Turkey the UAE and the UK.

The company purchases inventory from US metals producer and some international suppliers.

The US accounts for about 90% of revenue with most sales coming from the Midwest (more than 30%) and Southeast. However there has been a decline in sales over the last couple of years in the West/Southwest region.

Sales and Marketing

Reliance has some 125000 customers in more than a dozen countries. Operating a fleet of 1700 trucks the company delivers to some large original equipment manufacturers (OEM) and mostly to small machine shops and fabricators. The company has over 2100 sales personnel in about 45 states and a dozen other countries. About 95% are repeat customers.

Reliance provides sales and marketing services across the US and in more than a dozen countries via its 2000-plus sales personnel.

Financial Performance

Reliance has had solid sales year-over-year for the past decade averaging around $8 billion. In 2017 it posted one of the highest revenues in the last 10 years. It has also been profitable over the same period. 2017 profits were the highest in a decade.

Growing by some 12% Reliance posted revenue of $9.7 billion in 2017 its second highest sales in history. This was due an increase in both average selling prices (10% higher compared to 2016) and volumes sold (4%)

Net income more than doubled to $613 million from the year prior. The $309 million increase was primarily due to the favorable impact of the 2017 tax reform but was also aided by lower impairment and restructuring charges.

Cash holdings increased from $122 million to $154 million. Operating activities provided some $400 million. Investment used up $180 million mostly in PPE costs and a further $198 million went towards financing activities (majority of which was payments on long-term debt). The company used approximately $160 million towards CAPEX.

Strategy

Reliance faced with falling revenues has taken a three-pronged strategy to growth: increased value-added processing pricing discipline and inventory management.

The company has spent $1 billion in the past six years to develop technologies that enable value-added procession capacity. The strategy seems to be successful as in 2017 nearly half of the company?s orders included value-added processing a 10% growth from previous years.

Moreover Reliance has taken a selective approach with orders to fulfill. In response to customer requests Reliance claims it has expanded its capabilities to provide higher value-added services like fabrications.

Overall Reliance has historically prioritized gross profit margins. In 2017 gross profit close to 30% of revenue ($2.8 billion) was the highest in its history.

The company is also pursuing strategic acquisitions (three in 2016 and one in 2017) to enhance products and implement effective inventory management practices.

Additionally Reliance focused on servicing customers with small order sizes (average order is just over $1000) and quick turnaround by expanding its service network to ensure the proximity of its metal service centers to its customers.

Mergers and Acquisitions

Reliance has been prolific in acquiring companies—almost 65 since 1994.

In August 2018 Reliance acquired two KMS companies (Pennsylvanian and South Carolina) specializing in precision sheet metal fabrication. Terms of the transaction were not disclosed.

In 2017 Reliance spent $162 million in acquisition costs. In October of the same year the company acquired Ferguson Perforating Company (net sales $8 million) headquartered in Providence Rhode Island. Ferguson's specialized services in producing highly engineered and complex perforated metal for diverse end markets including automotive and aerospace increases Reliance's processing capacity and adds product diversification.

In 2016 Reliance acquired three companies for a combined value of nearly $350 million.

The acquisition of Tubular Steel in St. Louis Missouri strengthened Reliance's foothold in the energy end market.

Best Manufacturing Inc headquartered in Arkansas was acquired for high margin value added processing capabilities.

The third Alaska Steel marks the company's entry into the Alaska market broadening its market reach while increasing access to diverse industries like energy and infrastructure.

Company Background

The company was founded in 1939.

EXECUTIVES

President Ccc Steel, Brian M. Tenenbaum

Sevp And Cfo, Karla R. Lewis, age 53, $604,250 total compensation

Executive Svp Operations, William K. Sales, age 61, $550,000 total compensation

President And Ceo, Gregg J. Mollins, age 63, $1,025,000 total compensation

Managing Director All Metal Services, David L. Potts

President Ami Metals, Scott A. Smith

Executive Svp Operations, James D. Hoffman, age 59, $577,500 total compensation

President Allegheny Steel Distributors, Bernie J. Herrmann

President Precision Strip, Joseph B. Wolf

President Pacific Metal, John S. Nosler

President Infra-metals, Mark A Haight, age 59

President Earle M. Jorgensen Co., James Desmond

Svp Operations, Stephen P. (Steve) Koch, age 51, $486,250 total compensation

President Siskin Steel & Supply, Paul J. Loftin

President Yarde Metals, Matthew L. (Matt) Smith

President Sugar Steel, Robert J. Sugar

President Chapel Steel, Stanley J. (Stan) Altman

President Clayton Metals, Brian K. Cleveland

Cio, Susan C. Borchers, age 57

President Ferralloy, Carlos Rodriguez-Borjas

President American Metals, Nicole Heater

President Crest Steel, Kristofer M. Farris

President Delta Steel, Eric J. Offenberger

President Diamond Manufacturing, David L. Simpson

President National Specialty Alloys, Mark Russ

President Service Steel Aerospace, Douglas Nesbitt

President Viking Materials, Michael E. Allen

President Chatham Steel, Jerome Rooney

President Precision Strip, Joseph P. Wolf

President Continental Alloys & Services, Randall C. (Randy) Zajicek

President Liebovich Bros., David Corirossi

President Northern Illinois Steel Supply, Michael J. Ruth

President Pdm Steel Service Centers, Sean Mollins

President Phoenix Metals, Barry L. Epps

President Best Manufacturing, James Best

President Precision Flamecutting And Steel, Susan McKay

President Valex, Steve Simon

Managing Director Metalweb Limited, Karl Weston

Vice President Tax, Silva Yeghyayan

Vice President Sales, Chris Vuich

Vice President, Kay Rustand

Executive Vice President, Steve Koch

Vice President Finance, Judy Bennett

Vice President Health Safety And Human Resources, Don Prebola

Vice President, Jim Hoffman

Chairman, Mark V. Kaminski, age 63

Board Member, Thomas Gimbel

Board Member, Andrew Sharkey

Board Member, John Figueroa

Board Member, Robert McEvoy

Auditors: KPMG LLP

LOCATIONS

HQ: Reliance Steel & Aluminum Co.
350 South Grand Avenue, Suite 5100, Los Angeles, CA 90071
Phone: 213 687-7700
Web: www.rsac.com

2016 Sales

	$ mil.	% of total
United States	7,867	91
Foreign Countries	746	9
Total	**8,613**	**100**

2016 Sales

	% of total
Midwest	32
Southeast	17
West/Southwest	12
California	10
International	9
Mid-Atlantic	7
Northeast	6
Pacific Northwest	4
Mountain	3
Total	**100**

PRODUCTS/OPERATIONS

2016 Sales

	% of total
Carbon steel	52
Aluminum	20
Stainless steel	14
Alloy	5
Toll processing	3
Other	6
Total	**100**

PRODUCTS

Alloy Steel
Aluminum
Brass & Copper
Carbon Steel
Stainless Steel
Titanium

COMPETITORS

A. M. Castle
O'Neal Steel
Olympic Steel
Russel Metals

Ryerson
Steel Technologies
Ternium Mexico
Worthington Industries

HISTORICAL FINANCIALS

Company Type: Public

Income Statement

FYE: December 31

	REVENUE ($ mil.)	NET INCOME ($ mil.)	NET PROFIT MARGIN	EMPLOYEES
12/17	9,721	613	6.3%	14,900
12/16	8,613	304	3.5%	14,500
12/15	9,350	311	3.3%	14,000
12/14	10,451	371	3.6%	14,900
12/13	9,223	321	3.5%	14,000
Annual Growth	**1.3%**	**17.5%**	**—**	**1.6%**

2017 Year-End Financials

Debt ratio: 24.53%
Return on equity: 13.92%
Cash ($ mil.): 154
Current ratio: 4.34
Long-term debt ($ mil.): 1,809

No. of shares (mil.): 72
Dividends
  Yield: 0.0%
  Payout: 21.5%
Market value ($ mil.): 6,229

	STOCK PRICE ($) FY Close	P/E High/Low		PER SHARE ($) Earnings	Dividends	Book Value
12/17	85.79	10	8	8.34	1.80	64.28
12/16	79.54	21	12	4.16	1.65	57.08
12/15	57.91	16	12	4.16	1.60	54.56
12/14	61.27	16	12	4.73	1.40	53.00
12/13	75.84	18	15	4.14	1.26	50.00
Annual Growth	**3.1%**	**—**	**—**	**19.1%**	**9.3%**	**6.5%**

Renasant Corp

Those who are cognizant of their finances may want to do business with Renasant Corporation. The holding company owns Renasant Bank which serves consumers and local business through about 80 locations in Alabama Georgia Mississippi and Tennessee. The bank offers standard products such as checking and savings accounts CDs credit cards and loans and mortgages as well as trust retail brokerage and retirement plan services. Its loan portfolio is dominated by residential and commercial real estate loans. The bank also offers agricultural business construction and consumer loans and lease financing. Subsidiary Renasant Insurance sells personal and business coverage. Shareholders approved a merger with Metropolitan Bank in mid-2017.

Financial Performance

The company's revenue increased in fiscal 2013 compared to the prior year. It reported revenue of $252.6 million for fiscal 2013 up from $228 million in revenue for fiscal 2012.

Renasant's net income also went up in fiscal 2013 compared to the previous fiscal period. It reported net income of about $33.5 million for fiscal 2013 up from net income of $26.6 million in fiscal 2012.

The company's cash on hand decreased by about $24 million in fiscal 2013 compared to fiscal 2012 levels.

Strategy

Renasant has looked to diversify its loan portfolio. The bank has reduced its amount of loans for construction and land development — a sector that has been hit particularly hard — by tightening its underwriting standards.

It's also been growing through acquistions. In late 2014 for example Renasant purchased Heritage Financial Group in an all stock merger deal that amounted to $258 million. The move added

$1.9 billion in assets $1.2 billion in loan assets and $1.3 billion in deposit assets to Renasant's collection. In addition the move significantly expanded the bank's geographic reach adding 48 banking mortgage and investment offices in Alabama Florida and Georgia. All told the deal made Renasant one of the largest community banks in the Southeast region of the United States.

Mergers and Acquisitions

In 2017 Renasant agreed to a $190 million merger with Metropolitan Bank.

EXECUTIVES

Evp, Stuart R. Johnson, age 65, $250,000 total compensation

Chairman President And Ceo, E. Robinson (Robin) McGraw, age 71, $750,000 total compensation

Evp, James W. Gray, age 62, $230,000 total compensation

Evp And Director Of Retail Banking Renasant Bank, C. Mitchell (Mitch) Waycaster, age 60, $450,000 total compensation

Evp, Mary J. Witt, age 59

Evp, W. Mark Williams, age 55

Evp, R. Rick Hart, age 70, $496,000 total compensation

Evp And General Counsel, Stephen M. Corban, age 63, $75,000 total compensation

Evp; President Eastern Region Renasant Bank, O. Leonard (Len) Dorminey, age 65, $213,285 total compensation

Evp And Cfo, Kevin D. Chapman, age 43, $375,000 total compensation

Evp; President Western Region Renasant Bank, J. Scott Cochran, age 55

Assistant Vice President Branch Manager, Cathy Jarvis

Executive Vice President, Claude Springfield

Assistant Vice President, Kent Dees

Executive Vice President, Craig Gardella

Assistant Vice President Account Executive, Brian Gagel

Senior Vice President, Robert Hankins

Executive Vice President Credit Administration, Stuart Weise

Vice President, Jack Stuart

Vice President Relationship Officer, Danny Crabtree

Senior Vice President Commercial Banking, David Harwell

Senior Vice President, Jason McClimans

Division President Executive Vice President, Raymond Vannorman

Senior Vice President Small Business Advisor Lending, Melanie Brown

Senior Vice President Director Of Senior Business Analyst Lending, John Daly

Executive Vice President, Patricia Reid

Vice President, Raakhi Phillips

Vice President, Randy Harris

First Vice President Associate Counsel, Jared Carrubba

Vice President, Brian Porter

Small Business Lending Division Manager Senior Vice President, Butch Lyle

Senior Vice President, Phil Smith

Auditors: Horne LLP

LOCATIONS

HQ: Renasant Corp
209 Troy Street, Tupelo, MS 38804-4827
Phone: 662 680-1001
Web: www.renasant.com

PRODUCTS/OPERATIONS

2015 Sales

	$ mil.	% of total
Interest income		
Loans	236	64
Securities	26	7
Other	0	-
Non-interest income		
Mortgage banking income	35	10
Service charges on deposit accounts	29	8
Fees and commissions	16	4
Wealth management	9	3
Other	17	4
Total	**371**	**100**

COMPETITORS

BBVA Compass Bancshares	First Horizon
BancorpSouth	Hancock Holding
Citizens Holding	Regions Financial
Citizens National Bank of Meridian	Trustmark

HISTORICAL FINANCIALS

Company Type: Public

Income Statement

FYE: December 31

	ASSETS ($ mil.)	NET INCOME ($ mil.)	INCOME AS % OF ASSETS	EMPLOYEES
12/17	9,829	92	0.9%	2,102
12/16	8,699	90	1.0%	1,965
12/15	7,926	68	0.9%	1,996
12/14	5,805	59	1.0%	1,471
12/13	5,746	33	0.6%	1,483
Annual Growth	**14.4%**	**28.8%**	—	**9.1%**

2017 Year-End Financials

Debt ratio: 2.04%
Return on equity: 6.71%
Cash ($ mil.): 281
Current ratio: —
Long-term debt ($ mil.): —

No. of shares (mil.): 49
Dividends
 Yield: 0.0%
 Payout: 37.2%
Market value ($ mil.): 2,017

	STOCK PRICE ($) FY Close	P/E High/Low	PER SHARE ($) Earnings	Dividends	Book Value
12/17	40.89	23 19	1.96	0.73	30.72
12/16	42.22	20 14	2.17	0.71	27.81
12/15	34.41	20 14	1.88	0.68	25.73
12/14	28.93	17 14	1.88	0.68	22.56
12/13	31.46	26 15	1.22	0.68	21.21
Annual Growth	**6.8%**	— —	**12.6%**	**1.8%**	**9.7%**

Republic Bancorp, Inc. (KY)

As one of the top five bank holding companies based in Kentucky $4 billion-asset Republic Bancorp is the parent of Republic Bank & Trust (formerly First Commercial Bank) which offers deposit accounts loans and mortgages credit cards private banking and trust services through more than 30 branches in across Kentucky and around 10 more in southern Indiana Nashville Tampa and Cincinnati Ohio. About one-third of the bank's $3 billion-loan portfolio is tied to residential real estate while another 25% is made up of commercial real estate loans. Warehouse lines of credit home equity

loans and commercial and industrial loans make up most of the rest. The company also offers short-term consumer loans and tax refund loans.

Operations

Republic Bancorp operates three "core banking" segments: Traditional Banking which generated more than 80% of the company's total profit during 2015; Warehouse (almost 20% of profit) and Mortgage Banking (less than 1%). Its Warehouse lending business offers short-term credit facilities secured by single-family residences to mortgage bankers nationwide. Its Republic Processing Group segment offers short-term consumer loans prepaid debit cards and tax refund loans.

The bank made 75% of its total revenue from interest income almost entirely from loans during 2015 though a small percentage came from taxed investments and Federal Home Loan Bank stock. The rest of its revenue came from net refund transfer fees from its Republic Processing Group segment (9% of revenue) deposit account service charges (7%) interchange fee income (4%) mortgage banking income (2%) and other miscellaneous income sources.

Subsidiary Republic Insurance Services (also known as the Captive) provides property and casualty insurance coverage to the company and eight other third-party insurance captives for which insurance may not be available or cost effective.

Geographic Reach

The company had 40 RB&T branches at the end of 2015 including 32 in Kentucky mostly in the Louisville Metro area and others in the Central Western and Northern parts of the state. It had 3 branches in southern Indiana (in Floyds Knobs Jeffersonville and New Albany); two branches in the Tampa Florida metro area; two branches in the Nashville Tennessee metro area; and one more in the Cincinnati Ohio metro area.

Sales and Marketing

Republic spent $3.16 million on marketing and development expenses during 2015 compared to $3.26 million and $3.11 million in 2014 and 2013 respectively.

Financial Performance

Republic Bancorp's revenues and profits have been trending higher since 2013 as its loan assets have risen more than 30% over the period.

The company's revenue climbed 9% to $190 million during 2015 mostly thanks to higher interest income as its loan assets grew by 9% to $3.33 billion with commercial loans (real estate and business loans) and residential mortgage loans and lines of credit driving most of the growth.

Strong revenue growth in 2015 drove Republic's net income up 22% to $35 million for the year. The company's operating cash levels nearly doubled to $50 million after adjusting its earnings for non-cash items related to mortgage loan sales and thanks to favorable working capital changes related to changes in other liabilities.

Strategy

Republic Bancorp is moving toward building its commercial loans business launching a Corporate Banking division in 2015 to originate commercial loans with amounts ranging from $2.5 million to $25 million to borrowers with the highest credit ratings in its existing geographic markets. It also acquires smaller community banks to expand into new geographic markets while building its loan and deposit business.

Additionally Republic Bancorp has been moving into other revolving credit lines while also looking to take advantage of the rapidly growing prepaid card market. During 2015 for example it partnered with netSpend to become a pilot issuer of netSpend-branded prepaid cards; and partnered with ClearBalance to originate revolving lines of credit nationally for hospital receivables.

Mergers and Acquisitions

In October 2015 Republic Bancorp expanded its presence in Florida and grew its loan business after agreeing to buy $250 million-asset Cornerstone Bancorp along its four Cornerstone Community Bank branches in the Tampa Florida metro area $190 million in loans and $200 million in deposits. The deal was expected to be completed in the first half of 2016.

Company Background

In 2012 Republic Bancorp entered the Nashville and Minneapolis market through the FDIC-assisted acquisitions of the failed Tennessee Commerce Bank and First Commercial Bank respectively.

EXECUTIVES

Vice Chairman; President Republic Bank & Trust, A. Scott Trager, age 65, $350,000 total compensation

President And Ceo; Ceo Republic Bank & Trust, Steven E. (Steve) Trager, age 57, $353,000 total compensation

Evp Cfo And Chief Accounting Officer Republic Bancorp And Republic Bank & Trust, Kevin Sipes, age 46, $281,500 total compensation

Vice President And Risk Manager, Bryan Hendrick

Senior Vice President, Steve Pieragowski

Assistant Vice President, Mike Long

Senior Vice President Cra Compliance Republic Bankand#8230, Nancy Presnell

Senior Vice President, Lisa Butcher

Assistant Vice President Technology Services Managerand#8230, Scott Estes

Assistant Vice President Finance Project Manager, Tim Wheatley

Vice President Retail Collections, Lori Forbes

Avp Banking Center Supervisor, Robin Verenna

Assistant Vice President Senior Business Development Officer, Kevin Herthel

Senior Vice President Private Banking, Sarah Johnson

Senior Vice President, David Buchanon

Vice President Client Relations Manager, David Carter

Vice President Director Of Business Intelligence, Deb Reese

Vice President, Karen McGee

Vice President Senior Manager Of Technology Services, Sean O'Mahoney

Assistant Vice President Managing Director, Brad Savko

Assistant Vice President, Amy Quinn

Vice President Mortgage Warehouse Lending, Tim Poole

Assistant Vice President Business Development Manager, Wende Cosby

Chairman, Bernard M. Trager, age 89

Auditors: Crowe Horwath LLP

LOCATIONS

HQ: Republic Bancorp, Inc. (KY)
601 West Market Street, Louisville, KY 40202
Phone: 502 584-3600
Web: www.republicbank.com

PRODUCTS/OPERATIONS

2015 Sales

	$ mil.	% of total
Interest		
Loans including fees	134	70
Taxable investment securities	7	4
Other	1	1
Noninterest		
Net refund transfer fees	17	9
Service charges on deposit accounts	13	7
Interchange fee income	8	4
Mortgage banking	4	2
Other	5	3
Adjustments	(0.3)	-
Total	**190**	**100**

Selected Services

Checking
Credit & Debit Cards
Internet & Mobile Banking
Lending
Private Banking & Wealth Management
Savings & Investing

COMPETITORS

BB&T	Home Federal
Bank of America	KeyCorp
Citizens First	PNC Financial
Community Trust	Stock Yards Bancorp
Fifth Third	U.S. Bancorp

HISTORICAL FINANCIALS

Company Type: Public

Income Statement

FYE: December 31

	ASSETS ($ mil.)	NET INCOME ($ mil.)	INCOME AS % OF ASSETS	EMPLOYEES
12/17	5,085	45	0.9%	1,009
12/16	4,816	45	1.0%	954
12/15	4,230	35	0.8%	799
12/14	3,747	28	0.8%	735
12/13	3,371	25	0.8%	750
Annual Growth	10.8%	15.7%	—	7.7%

2017 Year-End Financials

Debt ratio: 0.81%	No. of shares (mil.): 20
Return on equity: 7.38%	Dividends
Cash ($ mil.): 299	Yield: 0.0%
Current ratio: —	Payout: 39.5%
Long-term debt ($ mil.): —	Market value ($ mil.): 793

	STOCK PRICE ($) FY Close	P/E High/Low	PER SHARE ($) Earnings	Dividends	Book Value
12/17	38.02	19 15	2.20	0.87	30.33
12/16	39.54	18 11	2.22	0.83	28.97
12/15	26.41	16 13	1.70	0.78	27.59
12/14	24.72	18 16	1.38	0.74	26.80
12/13	24.54	23 17	1.22	0.69	26.09
Annual Growth	11.6%	— —	15.9%	5.8%	3.8%

Republic First Bancorp, Inc.

Republic First Bancorp is the holding company for Republic Bank which serves the Greater Philadelphia area and southern New Jersey from more than 15 branches. Boasting over $1 billion in assets the bank targets individuals and small to midsized businesses offering standard deposit products including checking and savings accounts money market accounts IRAs and CDs. Commercial mortgages account for more than 70% of the company's loan portfolio which also includes consumer loans business loans and residential mortgages. Republic has been transitioning from a commercial bank into a major regional retail and commercial bank.

Operations

The bank's loan portfolio is made up of mostly commercial loans including commercial real estate loans construction and land development loans commercial and industrial loans as well as owner occupied real estate loans consumer-related loans and residential mortgages. As of 2015 each its commercial loans typically ranged from $250000 to $5 million though it sometimes lent up to its legal limit of $19.9 million.

About 72% of Republic First Bancorp's total revenue came from loan interest (including fees) in 2014 while another 11% came from interest and dividends on its taxable and tax-exempt investment securities. The rest of its revenue came from gains on sales of SBA loans (10%) loan advisory and servicing fees (3%) service fees on deposit accounts (3%) and other miscellaneous income sources. The bank had a staff of 235 full-time employees at the end of 2014.

Geographic Reach

Republic First boasts more than 15 branch offices in Pennsylvania (in Abington Ardmore Bala Cynwyd Plymout Meeting Media and Philadelphia) and New Jersey (in Berlin Cherry Hill Glassboro Haddonfield Marlton and Voorhees).

Sales and Marketing

The bank's commercial loans are mostly made to small and medium-sized businesses as well as professionals who need working capital financing for asset acquisitions or other financial services.

Republic First has been ramping up its advertising spend in recent years. It spent $597 thousand on advertising in 2014 compared to $447 thousand and $307 thousand in 2013 and 2012 respectively.

Financial Performance

The company has struggled to consistently grow its revenues in recent years due to shrinking interest margins on loans amidst the low-interest environment. Republic First has been steadily climbing out from prior years of losses (2013 2011 2010) however thanks to declining interest expenses and lower loan loss provisions as its loan portfolio's credit quality has improved with higher property valuations in the strengthened economy.

Republic First's revenue rose by 4% to $48.4 million in 2014 mostly thanks to an 8% jump in interest income as loan balances increased during the year. The bank's non-interest income fell on lower sales of SBA loans with fewer SBA loan originations which offset some of its top-line growth.

The company shot back into the black with a $2.4 million profit in 2014 (compared to a net loss of $3.5 million in 2013) mostly because in 2013 it had suffered a non-recurring $3.6 million loan loss on a bad loan as well as a non-recurring $1.9 million charge related to a legal settlement. Republic First's operating cash levels also skyrocketed to $9.7 million mostly on higher cash earnings.

Strategy

Republic Bank which had historically been known for its business and commercial lending has been focused on retail banking in the past few years and is working to become a major regional retail and commercial bank. As part of this strategy the bank has restructured its loan portfolio to reduce its emphasis on commercial real estate loans and has pursued a "retail-focused" strategy by offering customers "extended store hours absolutely free checking and coin counting more than 55000 surcharge ATMs and free VISA gift cards" according to the company's CEO letter included in the 2014 annual report.

The company has been expanding organically through new branch openings in recent years. In 2015 for example Republic Bank opened three new branches in South New Jersey in Berlin Marlton and Glassboro. In April of that year the company also sold $45 million in common stock through a private placement offering to cover its "aggressive expansion plans in 2015 and beyond."

Vice President Of Commercial Lending For South Jersey, John Lavin
Assistant Vice President Network Engineer, John Rudolph
Vice President Commercial Lender, Tom Waller
Svp Human Resources Director, Janine Zangrilli
Executive Vice President And Chief Retail Officer Of The Bank, Rhonda Costello
Assistant Vice President And Core Applications Administrator, Jared Kushner
Senior Vice President, Jay Neilon
Senior Vice President Senior Commercial Lender, Stephen McWilliams
Senior Vice President Of Sales, Katie Michaleski
Vice President Of Consumer Lending, Dan Charyna
Vice President And Real Estate Administration Manager, Eileen Echols
Vice President And Commercial Lending, Frederick A Marcell
Vice President Senior Business Development Officer, Judy Rosner
Senior Vice President, Brennan Charlene
Assistant Vice President Loan Closer Sba Division, Camille Oldenburg
Auditors: BDO USA, LLP

LOCATIONS

HQ: Republic First Bancorp, Inc.
50 South 16th Street, Philadelphia, PA 19102
Phone: 215 735-4422
Web: www.myrepublicbank.com

PRODUCTS/OPERATIONS

2014 Sales

	$ mil.	% of total
Interest income		
Interest and fees on taxable loans	34	71
Interest and dividends on taxable investment securities	5	10
Interest and fees on tax-exempt loans	0	1
Interest and dividends on tax-exempt investment securities	0	1
Interest on federal funds sold and other interest -earning assets	0	0
Non interest		
Gain on sales of SBA loans	4	10
Loan advisory and servicing fees	1	3
Service fees on deposit accounts	1	3
Gain on sale of investment securities	0	1
Legal settlements	0	0
Other-than-temporary impairment	0	0
Portion recognized in other comprehensive income (before taxes)	(0.03)	0
Net impairment loss on investment securities	0	0
Bank owned life insurance income	0	0
Other non-interest income	0	0
Total	**48**	**100**

COMPETITORS

Bank of America	Sovereign Bank
Citizens Financial Group	Sun Bancorp (NJ)
	TD Bank USA
PNC Financial	TF Financial
Prudential Bancorp	Wells Fargo
Royal Bancshares	

HISTORICAL FINANCIALS

Company Type: Public

Income Statement
FYE: December 31

	ASSETS ($ mil.)	NET INCOME ($ mil.)	INCOME AS % OF ASSETS	EMPLOYEES
12/17	2,322	8	0.4%	448
12/16	1,923	4	0.3%	306
12/15	1,439	2	0.2%	277
12/14	1,214	2	0.2%	235
12/13	961	(3)	—	226
Annual Growth	**24.7%**	**—**	**—**	**18.7%**

2017 Year-End Financials

Debt ratio: 0.93%	No. of shares (mil.): 56
Return on equity: 4.03%	Dividends
Cash ($ mil.): 61	Yield: —
Current ratio: —	Payout: —
Long-term debt ($ mil.): —	Market value ($ mil.): 482

	STOCK PRICE ($) FY Close	P/E High/Low	PER SHARE ($) Earnings	Dividends	Book Value
12/17	8.45	62 47	0.15	0.00	3.97
12/16	8.35	69 29	0.12	0.00	3.79
12/15	4.33	77 55	0.06	0.00	3.00
12/14	3.75	76 43	0.07	0.00	2.98
12/13	2.98	— —	(0.13)	0.00	2.41
Annual Growth	**29.8%**	**— —**	**—**	**—**	**13.3%**

Republic Services Inc

Republic Services is the second-largest nonhazardous waste management provider in the US behind leader Waste Management in terms of revenue and geographic coverage. Republic provides waste disposal services for commercial industrial municipal and residential customers through its network of 340 collection firms. It owns or operates some 190 solid waste landfills more than 200 transfer stations and about 65 recycling centers eight treatment recovery and disposal facilities and 10 salt water disposal wells. It also has about 70 landfill-to-gas and a handful of other renewable energy projects.

Operations

Republic Services divides its operations into two broad geographic categories. Group 1 covers the western US and parts of the Midwest. Group 2 covers other parts of the Midwest as well as Texas and the Southeast. Group 2 furnishes more than 50% of revenue while Group 1 provides about 45%.

Geographic Reach

Republic Services' operations span the US. It has collection businesses transfer stations active solid waste landfills and recycling centers in about 40 US states and Puerto Rico. Its active solid waste landfills total 106000 acres including 37100 permitted acres.

Sales and Marketing

Republic has municipal marketing representatives who are responsible for working with municipalities or communities to which it provides residential service. It also employs a National Accounts selling organization.

The company can?t pick up trash online but it can interact with customers through its My Resource customer portal and mobile app. About 2 million customers use the service to sign up for residential small container and temporary large container services.

Financial Performance

Republic Services posted its fourth straight year of revenue growth in 2016 hitting about $9.4 billion up about 3% from 2015. The company reported increases in average yield of about 2% volume of 1% acquisitions (subtracting divestitures) of less than 1% and recycled commodities of half a percentage point.

In 2016 Republic Services? net income dropped 18% to $612 million from 2015. The company had higher costs in 2016 including for employee expenses and restructuring.

The company's operating cash flow increased to $1.8 billion in 2016 from $1.7 billion in 2015.

Strategy

Perhaps the most visible reminder of a waste company is the truck making its rounds. For Republic Services the truck and the entire fleet is where it can save money through automation and standardization. About three-quarters of the company?s fleet is automated which means a truck needs just a driver while an mechanical hoists the trash receptacle to and from the truck. The company has used its national footprint to make sure that its operations throughout the country used the same preventive maintenance procedures which helps reduce costs. Further Republic Services has shifted much its fleet to compressed natural gas which burns cleaner and is usually cheaper than gasoline.

The company has rolled out and improves its digital platform for interacting with customers. Twice as many customers used the MyResource digital service in 2016 as did the previous year. Besides lowering costs the service helps improve customer service and satisfaction.

Republic Services snaps up local and regional waste services through acquisitions. Its acquisition spending fell to just more than $70 million in 2016 about half of its five-year average of about $140 million. The company?s goal is to put about $100 million a year toward acquisitions.

The company is adding more sustainable resources to its mix. It plans to add about 150000 tons a year of recycling capability through 2018 develop two landfill-gas-to-energy projects a year through 2018 and reduce its fleet emission by 3% by 2018.

Mergers and Acquisitions

Expanding into the E&P sector in 2015 Republic acquired Tervita LLC for $485 million. Tervita is an environmental solutions provider serving US oil and natural gas producers.

In 2014 Republic acquired Rainbow Disposal for $112 million. The transaction enhances its recycling and waste diversion capabilities which will allow it to better serve California's growing sustainability initiatives.

HISTORY

Republic Services began in 1980 as Republic Resources an oil exploration and production company. In 1989 after a stockholder group tried to force Republic into liquidation Browning-Ferris (BFI) founder Thomas Fatjo stepped in gained control of Republic Resources and refocused it on a field he knew well — solid waste. Renamed Republic Waste the company began making acquisitions.

In 1990 Michael DeGroote founder of BFI competitor Laidlaw bought into Republic Waste. In 1995 Wayne Huizenga — who co-founded Waste Management in 1971 and was beginning to develop a national auto sales organization in the mid-1990s after his tenure as chairman and CEO of Blockbuster Entertainment — approached DeGroote about a deal. They rejected an immediate merger of the waste and auto businesses because the latter was not well-enough developed and would drag down Republic's numbers. Instead they agreed to merge Republic and the Hudson Companies (a trash business owned by Huizenga's brother-in-law Harris Hudson) to sell Huizenga a large interest in Republic through a private offering and to give him control of the board (in 1995). The company became Republic Industries.

Huizenga's investment brought a flood of new investors. With new resources Republic Industries became a driving force in the garbage industry's consolidation binge and the company bought more than 100 smaller waste haulers between 1995 and 1998. Republic Industries spun off about 30% of its waste business as Republic Services in 1998;

the IPO raised $1.3 billion. Republic's acquisition trend continued as it agreed to buy 16 landfills 136 commercial collection routes and 11 transfer stations from Waste Management for $500 million. Later that year Waste Management veteran James O'Connor succeeded Huizenga as CEO although Huizenga continued as chairman.

Investors filed class-action lawsuits against Republic in 1999 claiming the Waste Management purchases held far more integration problems than the company admitted. In 2000 Republic swapped nine of its solid-waste operations for eight Allied Waste businesses which Allied needed to divest in order to gain federal approval for its merger with BFI.

While many firms in the industry were selling off assets in 2001 Republic was expanding its operations in the Northern California market by acquiring Richmond Sanitary Services. Huizenga retired as chairman at the end of 2002 and was once again succeeded by O'Connor. Huizenga stayed on the board as a director until May 2004.

In 2007 the company sold Living Earth Technology Company (a noncore stand-alone business in Texas) for about $37 million. In 2008 prior to its megadeal with Allied Waste Republic rebuffed a takeover bid by industry leader Waste Management.

In late 2008 Republic Services the once #3 industry player acquired #2 company Allied Waste for $6 billion to place it closer to industry leader Waste Management in terms of revenues and geographic coverage. Following the acquisition Republic divested assets in seven markets (six municipal solid waste landfills six collection businesses and three transfer stations) in order to meet US antitrust regulations.

During 2012 the company invested $76 million on five recycling centers and plans to continue to look for opportunities to expand its recycling capabilities.

In 2013 the company dedicated a 2037 acre state-of-the-art landfill and transfer station in Texas to meet the Rio Grande Valley's waste needs for the next 100 years. The new La Gloria landfill replaced Republic's Rio Grande Valley Landfill in Donna Texas that had reached full capacity.

EXECUTIVES

President And Ceo, Donald W. (Don) Slager, age 56, $1,100,000 total compensation

Evp And Chief Development Officer, Brian A. Bales

Evp Chief Legal Officer Chief Ethics And Compliance Officer And Corporate Secretary, Catharine D. Ellingsen, age 54, $395,107 total compensation

Evp And Chief Administrative Officer, Jeffrey A. (Jeff) Hughes, age 62, $482,061 total compensation

Evp Operations, Jon Vander Ark

Region President East Region, Tim Stuart

Svp And Cio, Bill Halnon

Svp And Chief Accounting Officer, Charles F. (Chuck) Serianni, age 56, $511,779 total compensation

Evp Operations Support, Nathan Cabbil

Evp And Chief Transformation Officer, Stuart Levy

Evp And Chief Customer Officer, Tom Lynch

Evp And Chief Marketing Officer, Sue Klug

Senior Vice President Treasurer, Edward A Lang

Sales Vice President, Bob Pickens

Vp Total Rewards And Hr Systems, Jon Black

Vice President Business Systems And Technology, Mark Mahoney

National Account Manager, Todd Traicoff

Senior Vice President Finance, Brian Delghiaccio

Vice President Mkt Planning And Development, Andy Shipe

Executive Vice President General Counsel And Corporate Secretary, Michael Rissman

District Vice President, Michael Summers

Vice President Sales, John Maher

Svp Field Sales, Stephen Mohan

Vice President Information Technology, Doug Miller

Vice President Information Technology, John Jacobi

Vice President Municipal Sales, Richard Coupland

Vice President Investor Relations, Nicole Ciandmoto

Vice President Learning And Talent Development, Maureen Williams

Svp Revenue Management, Scott Russeth

Vice President Customer Resource Centers, Jeffrey Morley

Vice President Corporate Security, Mark Cwynar

Svp Training And Talent Development, Douglas Borro

Assistant Vice President Sales, Cheryl Brock

Chairman, Manuel Kadre, age 52

Board Member, Michael Larson

Board Member, William Flynn

Board Member, Tomago Collins

Board Member, Ann Dunwoody

Board Member, Thomas Handley

Board Member, Jennifer Kirk

Auditors: Ernst & Young LLP

LOCATIONS

HQ: Republic Services Inc
18500 North Allied Way, Phoenix, AZ 85054
Phone: 480 627-2700
Web: www.republicservices.com

2016 sales

	$ mil.	% of total
Group1	4,185	45
Group2	5,014	53
Corporate entities	189	2
Total	**9,388**	**100**

PRODUCTS/OPERATIONS

2016 sales

	$ mil.	% of total
Residential	2,240	24
Small-container commercial	2,878	31
Large-container industrial	1,976	21
Other	38	0
Transfer	464	5
Landfill	1,121	12
Energy services	76	1
Other	595	6
Total	**9,388**	**100**

COMPETITORS

Casella Waste Systems	Waste Connections
Recology	Waste Connections US
Rumpke	Waste Industries USA
Safety-Kleen	Waste Management
WCA Waste	

HISTORICAL FINANCIALS

Company Type: Public

Income Statement   FYE: December 31

	REVENUE ($ mil.)	NET INCOME ($ mil.)	NET PROFIT MARGIN	EMPLOYEES
12/18	10,040	1,036	10.3%	36,000
12/17	10,041	1,278	12.7%	35,000
12/16	9,387	612	6.5%	33,000
12/15	9,115	749	8.2%	33,000
12/14	8,788	547	6.2%	31,000
Annual Growth	3.4%	17.3%	—	3.8%

Debt ratio: 38.57%   No. of shares (mil.): 322
Return on equity: 13.05%   Dividends
Cash ($ mil.): 70   Yield: 2.0%
Current ratio: 0.58   Payout: 34.2%
Long-term debt ($ mil.): 7,646   Market value ($ mil.): 23,249

	STOCK PRICE ($) FY Close	P/E High/Low	PER SHARE ($) Earnings	Dividends	Book Value
12/18	72.09	24 20	3.16	1.44	24.58
12/17	67.61	18 15	3.77	1.33	23.99
12/16	57.05	32 24	1.78	1.24	22.66
12/15	43.99	21 18	2.13	1.16	22.49
12/14	40.25	27 20	1.53	1.08	21.96
Annual Growth	15.7%	— —	19.9%	7.5%	2.9%

Resideo Technologies Inc

Auditors: Deloitte & Touche LLP

LOCATIONS

HQ: Resideo Technologies Inc
1985 Douglas Drive North, Golden Valley, MN 55422
Phone: 763 954-5204
Web: www.resideo.com

HISTORICAL FINANCIALS

Company Type: Public

Income Statement   FYE: December 31

	REVENUE ($ mil.)	NET INCOME ($ mil.)	NET PROFIT MARGIN	EMPLOYEES
12/17	4,519	(394)	—	14,500
12/16	4,455	177	4.0%	—
12/15	4,154	147	3.5%	—
Annual Growth	4.3%	—	—	—

2017 Year-End Financials

Debt ratio: ——
Return on equity: (-14.39%)   Dividends
Cash ($ mil.): 56   Yield: —
Current ratio: 1.21   Payout: —
Long-term debt ($ mil.): —   Market value ($ mil.): —

	STOCK PRICE ($) FY Close	P/E High/Low	PER SHARE ($) Earnings	Dividends	Book Value
12/17	0.00	— —	(0.00)	0.00	(0.00)
12/16	0.00	— —	(0.00)	0.00	(0.00)
Annual Growth	—		—	—	—

REXFORD INDUSTRIAL REALTY, INC.

Rexford Industrial Realty knows that there's more to business in Southern California than moviemaking and fashion. A real estate investment trust or REIT Rexford Industrial owns and manages a portfolio of nearly 70 industrial properties in Los Angeles County and surrounding areas. Its portfolio comprises about 7.6 million sq. ft. of warehouse distribution and light manufacturing space that's leased to small and midsized businesses. It manages 20 more properties — altogether comprising 1.2 million sq. ft. of rentable space. A self-administered and self-managed REIT Rexford Industrial was formed in 2013 from the assets of its predecessor. In mid-2013 the company went public.

IPO

Rexford Industrial intends to use a portion of the $224 million in proceeds to repay debt much of which is secured by various properties.

Operations

Rexford Industrial's portfolio spans several California counties including Los Angeles Orange Ventura San Bernadino Riverside and San Diego.

Financial Performance

Revenue rose for Rexford Industrial by 27% in fiscal 2012 to $34 million from 2011's $28 million thanks to increases in rental revenue and tenant reimbursements from rising occupancy rates and a boost in revenues from properties it acquired during both 2012 and 2011. Rexford Industrial logged 64% increases in revenue from management leasing and development services due to the additional third-party management fees.

Strategy

Rexford Industrial is seeking to acquire equity stakes and debt in stable and distressed industrial properties in infill markets (i.e. highly developed urban centers) in Los Angeles Orange San Diego and Ventura counties and the West Inland Empire to the east. The REIT is also looking to manage properties located in these same areas that are owned by third parties.

The REIT has been buying properties throughout Southern California particularly in the cities of Van Nuys and Tarzana as well as in Glenview Illinois. It looks to purchase both newer and older vintage properties as well as single (40% of its portfolio) and multi-tenant (60%) projects. The REIT invests in every category of industrial property. Tenants are typically small and medium-sized businesses that are tied to the Southern California economy. Rexford Industrial boasts an average tenant size of about 9000 sq. ft. Nearly 70% of its tenants occupy fewer than 50000 sq. ft. apiece.

EXECUTIVES

Co-ceo And Director, Howard Schwimmer, $495,000 total compensation
Co-ceo And Director, Michael S. Frankel, age 55, $495,000 total compensation
Cfo, Adeel Khan, $315,000 total compensation
Vice President And Assistant General Counsel, Laura Mask
Chairman, Richard S. Ziman, age 75
Auditors: ERNST & YOUNG LLP LOS ANGELES

LOCATIONS

HQ: REXFORD INDUSTRIAL REALTY, INC.
11620 WILSHIRE BLVD # 1000, LOS ANGELES, CA 900256821
Phone: 310 966-1680
Web: WWW.REXFORDINDUSTRIAL.COM

PRODUCTS/OPERATIONS

2015 Revenue

	$ mil.	% of total
Rental		
Rental Revenues	81	86
Tenant Reimbursements	10	11
Management Leasing & Development Services	0	1
Other Income	1	1
Interest Income	0	1
Total	**93**	**100**

Selected Property Categories

Core
Core Plus
First Mortgages Tied to Target Industrial Property
Value Add

COMPETITORS

Brandywine Realty	Prologis
Brandywine Realty	Prologis
PS Business Parks	Terreno Realty
PS Business Parks	Terreno Realty

HISTORICAL FINANCIALS

Company Type: Private

Income Statement

FYE: December 31

	ASSETS ($ mil.)	NET INCOME ($ mil.)	INCOME AS % OF ASSETS	EMPLOYEES
12/16	1,515	25	1.7%	40
12/15	1,153	1	0.2%	—
12/14	932	0	0.1%	—
12/13	554	(0)	—	—
Annual Growth	**39.8%**	—	—	—

2016 Year-End Financials

Debt ratio: ——
Return on equity: 20.50%
Cash ($ mil.): 15
Current ratio: ——
Long-term debt ($ mil.): ——
Dividends
Yield: —
Payout: —
Market value ($ mil.): —

Rite Aid Corp

Rite Aid ranks a distant third (behind Walgreen and CVS) in the US retail drugstore business with more than 4600 drugstores in more than 30 states and the District of Columbia. Rite Aid stores generate roughly 70% of their sales from filling prescriptions while the rest comes from selling health and beauty aids convenience foods greeting cards and more including some 3500 Rite Aid brand private-label products. More than 60% of all Rite Aid stores are freestanding and over half have drive-through pharmacies. A deal to be acquired by Walgreens Boots Alliance was dropped in mid-2017; instead Rite Aid will sell about half of its retail stores to the pharmacy leader. A deal for Albertsons to acquire the rest of the company fell through in 2018.

HISTORY

Wholesale grocer Alex Grass founded Rack Rite Distributors in Harrisburg Pennsylvania in 1958 to provide health and beauty aids and other sundries to grocery stores. He offered the same products at his first discount drugstore Thrif D Discount Center opened in 1962 in Scranton Pennsylvania. Four years later the company began placing pharmacies in its 36 stores. Rite Aid went public and adopted its current name in 1968 and the next year it made the first of many diverse acquisitions: Daw Drug Blue Ridge Nursing Homes and plasma suppliers Immuno Serums and Sero Genics.

Purchases in the 1970s included Sera-Tec Biologicals of New Jersey (blood plasma) and nearly 300 stores. By 1981 Rite Aid was the #3 drugstore chain and sales exceeded $1 billion. In 1984 it bought the American Discount Auto Parts chain and Encore Books discount chain and spun off its

wholesale grocery operation in 1984 as Super Rite retaining a 47% stake (sold 1989).

Acquisitions added almost 900 stores during the 1980s. Expansion costs eroded Rite Aid's profit margins and the company focused on integrating its buys in 1990.

As part of a major restructuring in 1994 the company began selling its non-drugstore assets. Also in 1994 Rite Aid acquired Pharmacy Card and Intell-Rx and merged the two to form Eagle Managed Care.

Martin Grass took Rite Aid's reins from his dad in 1995. That year the company agreed to buy Revco at the time the #2 drugstore operator but the deal was derailed by FTC and Department of Justice objections in 1996. Rite Aid bounced back and acquired Thrifty PayLess (with more than 1000 stores) for about $2.3 billion in 1996. The deal gave the company more than 3600 stores and a presence in the western US. Also in 1996 Rite Aid exited several markets. In 1998 it closed many smaller stores and bought PCS Health Systems (the #1 US pharmacy benefits manager) from drug maker Eli Lilly and merged its Eagle Managed Care division into PCS.

In 1999 after a Wall Street Journal investigation Rite Aid revealed that Martin Grass Alex Grass and other family members held stakes in several suppliers and real estate interests doing business with the company. That year Rite Aid partnered with General Nutrition Companies Inc. (GNC) and took a 25% stake in the Internet retailer drugstore.com. Later in 1999 Rite Aid began slashing its $5.1 billion debt by cutting corporate staff and selling off some stores in California and the Pacific Northwest. CEO Martin Grass resigned and a team of former Fred Meyer officers — led by Robert Miller — took over.

In 2000 the company secured $1 billion from Citibank to reduce debt and provide capital. In July 2000 the company announced it would restate profits that over the past two years had been inflated in excess of $1 billion. Later that year Rite Aid sold PCS Health Systems to pharmacy benefits manager Advance Paradigm for more than $1 billion (about $500 million less than what Rite Aid originally paid for it). Rite Aid announced plans in 2001 to expand GNC concessions to additional stores.

To raise cash Rite Aid sold large blocks of its drugstore.com stock trimming its original 25% stake to less than 10% by April 2002. Former chairman and CEO Martin Grass former general counsel and vice chairman Franklin Brown and former CFO Frank Bergonzi among others were indicted in June 2002 for allegedly falsifying Rite Aid's books.

In April 2003 former chairman and CEO Martin Grass agreed to pay nearly $1.5 million to settle a lawsuit in which shareholders alleged that Rite Aid's books were falsified inflating the stock's value. In June Grass and former CFO Franklyn Bergonzi both pleaded guilty to conspiracy to defra

EXECUTIVES

Chairman And Ceo, John T. Standley, age 55, $1,184,500 total compensation
Svp Ny Metro Division, Mark Kramer, age 68
Sevp Cfo And Chief Administrative Officer, Darren W. Karst, age 58, $809,751 total compensation
Evp Merchandising And Distribution, Enio A. (Tony) Montini, age 66, $471,500 total compensation
President And Coo, Kermit R. Crawford, age 59
Coo Rite Aid Stores, Bryan Everett, age 45, $461,250 total compensation
Evp Marketing, David Abelman, age 59
Svp Mid-atlantic Division, Scott Bernard
Svp Western Division, Bill Romine

Svp Northeast Division, Derek Griffith
Svp And Cio, Steve Rempel
Evp Pharmacy, Jocelyn Konrad, age 48
Svp Southern Division, Bill Jackson
Svp General Counsel And Secretary, Jim Comitale
Svp And Chief Human Resources Officer, Ken Black
Pharmacy Manager, John Stanbrough
Rph, Rajesh Kumar
Pharmacy Manager, Shannon Casta
Pharmacy Manager, Malou Solomon
Pharmacy Manager, Sherri Wiswell
Pharmacy Manager, Kari McCabe
Pharmacy Manager, Ngozi Onumonu
Vice President Of Operations, Scott Jacobson
Vice President Of Marketing, Diane Shue
Pharmacist Manager, Mandy Hoysan
Director Of Pharmacy Acquisitions, Todd Rossi
Vice President Investments, David E Johnson
Vice President Pharmacy Operations, Dennis Yoney
Regional Vice President, Brian Dein
Group Vice President Loss Prevention, Bob Oberosler
Pharmacy Manager, Donald Brensinger
Rph, Fady Soliman
Pharmacy Manager, Diane Brown
Regional Vice President Administration, Nancy Wight-Tally
Vice President Federal Affairs And Public Policy, Yong Choe
Pharmacy Manager, Joshua Maher
Regional Vice President, Kirt Patel
Vice President Private Brand Development, Bob Himler
Vice President Information Technology Development, Robert A Kostosky
Secretary And Clerk, Cindy Kelley
Auditors: DELOITTE & TOUCHE LLP

LOCATIONS

HQ: Rite Aid Corp
30 Hunter Lane, Camp Hill, PA 17011
Phone: 717 761-2633   Fax: 717 975-5905
Web: www.riteaid.com

2016 Stores

	No.
New York	604
California	580
Pennsylvania	537
Michigan	275
New Jersey	257
North Carolina	225
Ohio	224
Virginia	190
Georgia	179
Massachusetts	146
Maryland	140
Washington	139
Kentucky	116
West Virginia	104
Alabama	93
South Carolina	91
Tennessee	81
Maine	79
Connecticut	77
Oregon	72
New Hampshire	68
Louisiana	62
Rhode Island	44
Delaware	42
Vermont	37
Mississippi	26
Utah	22
Colorado	20
Idaho	13
Indiana	10
District of Columbia	7
Nevada	1
Total	**4,561**

PRODUCTS/OPERATIONS

2016 Sales

	$ mil.	% of total
Retail Pharmacy	26,865	88
Pharmacy Services	4,103	12
Inter-segment elimination	(232.8)	-
Total	**30,736**	**100**

2016 Sales

	% of total
Prescription drugs	69
General merchandise & other	16
Over-the-counter medications & personal care	10
Health & beauty aids	5
Total	**100**

Selected Merchandise and Services

Beverages
Convenience foods
Cosmetics
Designer fragrances
Greeting cards
Health and personal care products
Household items
Over-the-counter drugs
Photo processing
Prescription drugs
Private-label products
Seasonal merchandise
Vitamins and minerals

COMPETITORS

A&P	Kroger
BJ's Wholesale Club	Marc Glassman
CVS	Medicine Shoppe
Costco Wholesale	Publix
Dollar General	Safeway
Family Dollar Stores	Target Corporation
Kinney Drugs Inc.	Wal-Mart
Kmart	Walgreen

HISTORICAL FINANCIALS

Company Type: Public

Income Statement

FYE: March 3

	REVENUE ($ mil.)	NET INCOME ($ mil.)	NET PROFIT MARGIN	EMPLOYEES
03/18	21,528	943	4.4%	59,000
03/17*	32,845	4	0.0%	87,000
02/16	30,736	165	0.5%	88,000
02/15	26,528	2,109	8.0%	89,000
03/14	25,526	249	1.0%	89,000
Annual Growth	(4.2%)	39.5%	—	(9.8%)

*Fiscal year change

2018 Year-End Financials

Debt ratio: 37.73%
Return on equity: 72.82%
Cash ($ mil.): 447
Current ratio: 1.37
Long-term debt ($ mil.): 3,370

No. of shares (mil.): 1,067
Dividends
  Yield: —
  Payout: —
Market value ($ mil.): 2,039

	STOCK PRICE ($) FY Close	P/E High/Low		PER SHARE ($) Earnings	Dividends	Book Value
03/18	1.91	10	2	0.90	0.00	1.50
03/17*	5.45	—	—	(0.00)	0.00	0.58
02/16	7.96	58	38	0.16	0.00	0.55
02/15	7.98	4	2	2.08	0.00	0.06
03/14	6.59	29	7	0.23	0.00	(2.18)
Annual Growth	(26.6%)	—	—	40.6%	—	—

*Fiscal year change

RiverSource Life Insurance Co

EXECUTIVES

Chb-pres, John R Worner
Rvp Insurance, Michele Turner
Senior Regional Vice President, Matthew D Hartigan
Auditors: PricewaterhouseCoopers LLP

LOCATIONS

HQ: RiverSource Life Insurance Co
1099 Ameriprise Financial Center, Minneapolis, MN 55474
Phone: 612 671-3131

HISTORICAL FINANCIALS

Company Type: Public

Income Statement

FYE: December 31

	ASSETS ($ mil.)	NET INCOME ($ mil.)	INCOME AS % OF ASSETS	EMPLOYEES
12/17	120,440	741	0.6%	—
12/16	114,053	686	0.6%	—
12/15	113,356	895	0.8%	—
12/14	118,136	965	0.8%	—
12/13	117,004	842	0.7%	—
Annual Growth	0.7%	(3.1%)	—	—

2017 Year-End Financials

Debt ratio: —
Return on equity: 19.46%
Cash ($ mil.): 1,062
Current ratio: —
Long-term debt ($ mil.): —

No. of shares (mil.): 0
Dividends
  Yield: —
  Payout: 94.4%
Market value ($ mil.): —

RLI Corp

You might wonder what folks in Illinois know about earthquake insurance but as a specialty property/casualty insurer Peoria-based RLI knows how to write such policies. Through its subsidiaries the company mainly offers coverage for US niche markets — risks that are hard to place in the standard market and are otherwise underserved. It focuses on public and private companies as well as non-profit organizations. RLI's commercial property/casualty lines include products liability property damage marine cargo directors and officers liability medical malpractice and general liability. It also writes commercial surety bonds and a smattering of specialty personal insurance.

Operations

RLI's specialty commercial property/casualty operations are conducted through its RLI Insurance Mt. Hawley Insurance Contractors Bonding and Insurance Company and RLI Indemnity subsidiaries. Personal offerings account for small portion of RLI's revenues and include homeowners insurance in Hawaii home business coverage pet insurance and personal umbrella (supplemental property/casualty) policies.

Geographic Reach

While the company operates in all 50 US states the District of Columbia and Puerto Rico California is RLI's largest market accounting for about 20% of the company's premiums.

Sales and Marketing

RLI markets its products to brokers and independent agents through branch offices scattered across the US.

Financial Performance

Like many insurers RLI's finances took a negative hit from the economic turmoil of 2008 and 2009. The company improved its returns as of 2010 and hasn't looked back. In 2013 it reported a 7% increase in revenue from $661 million to $706 million due to increased net premiums especially in the casualty segment. New products also made strong contributions. Net income grew 33% from $103 million to $126 million on increased revenue and decline in losses. Cash from operations a category that has fluctuated for RLI improved by $99 million due to investments.

Strategy

The company has gradually expanded its range of products with an emphasis on property insurance. In 2012 RLI entered the recreational vehicle (RV) insurance market by forming an underwriting partnership with Recreation Insurance Specialists. In 2013 it saw growth in its casualty business in transportation professional liability umbrella and admitted package businesses.

Mergers and Acquisitions

In 2014 the company purchased 20% of Prime Holdings Insurance Services for $5.3 million. The Utah-based company sells excess and surplus lines insurance in 49 states through a network of brokers; it specializes in hard-to-place risks (underwater hotels English Channel swims bungee jumps from helicopters).

In 2012 RLI moved into the field of medical malpractice coverage through the acquisition of Rockbridge Underwriting Agency. Two years later it launched RLI Healthcare a healthcare liability division serving hospital systems long-term and outpatient care facilities and clinical research providers with surplus lines in all 50 states.

Company Background

Gerald Stephens founded the company in 1961 and served as its chairman from 2001 until his retirement in 2011.

EXECUTIVES

Vice President, Paul Dietrich

Chairman And Ceo, Jonathan E. Michael, age 64, $775,000 total compensation

President And Coo, Craig W. Kliethermes, age 53, $473,269 total compensation

Vp Chief Investment Officer And Treasurer, Aaron P. Diefenthaler, age 44

Svp And Cfo, Thomas L. Brown, age 61, $417,308 total compensation

President Rli Transportation Division, Dan Meyer

Svp Operations Rli Product Divisions, Jennifer L. Klobnak, age 46, $298,462 total compensation

Vice President Information Technology, Murali Natarajan

Assistant Vice President Commercial, Martha Weissbaum

Assistant Vice President Specialty Markets, Paul V Harris

Vice President Chief Claim Counsel, Betsy McLaughlin

Assistant Vice President Fidelity Group, Thomas Huber

Assistant Vice President, Terry Driggs

Assistant Vice President Claims, Andrea Dean

Vice President General Counsel Corporate Secretary, Aniel O Kennedy

Vice President Operations, Richard W Quehl

Assistant Vice President And Product Manager, Victor Garcia

Assistant Vice President Technology, Karl Flower

Vice President Communications, Greg Tiemeier

Assistant Vice President Energy, Greg Chilson

Assistant Vice President, Philip Abellera

Vice President Underwriting, John Stenhouse

Vice President Marketing And Sales, Mike Haswell

Vice President And Healthcare Product Leader, Scott Ducey

Assistant Vice President Underwriting, Brian Schick

Board Member, Barbara Allen

Board Member, Michael Angelina

Auditors: KPMG LLP

LOCATIONS

HQ: RLI Corp
9025 North Lindbergh Drive, Peoria, IL 61615
Phone: 309 692-1000   **Fax:** 309 692-1068
Web: www.rlicorp.com

PRODUCTS/OPERATIONS

2016 Revenues

	$ mil.	% of total
Net premiums earned		
Casualty	454	56
Property	152	19
Surety	121	15
Net investment income	53	6
Net realized gains	34	4
Total	**816**	**100**

Selected Products

Commercial
  Casualty
  Contractors bonding and insurance
  Executive products liability
  Marine
  Professional services
  Property
  Reinsurance
  Specialty programs
  Transportation
Personal
  Homeowners (Hawaii)
  Home business owners
  Personal umbrella
Surety Bonds

COMPETITORS

Arch Insurance Group
Baldwin & Lyons
CNA Financial
Chubb Limited
Crum & Forster
Great American Insurance Company
Great West Casualty
HCC Insurance
James River Group
Lancer Insurance
Lexington Insurance
Markel
Meadowbrook Insurance
Navigators
Philadelphia Insurance Companies
Safeco
Sompo International
The Hartford
Travelers Companies
United States Liability Insurance Group

HISTORICAL FINANCIALS

Company Type: Public

Income Statement

FYE: December 31

	ASSETS ($ mil.)	NET INCOME ($ mil.)	INCOME AS % OF ASSETS	EMPLOYEES
12/17	2,947	105	3.6%	902
12/16	2,777	114	4.1%	943
12/15	2,736	137	5.0%	902
12/14	2,775	135	4.9%	882
12/13	2,740	126	4.6%	870
Annual Growth	**1.8%**	**(4.5%)**	**—**	**0.9%**

2017 Year-End Financials

Debt ratio: 5.05%	No. of shares (mil.): 44
Return on equity: 12.52%	Dividends
Cash ($ mil.): 24	Yield: 0.0%
Current ratio: —	Payout: 109.3%
Long-term debt ($ mil.): —	Market value ($ mil.): 2,678

	STOCK PRICE ($) FY Close	P/E High/Low	PER SHARE ($) Earnings	Dividends	Book Value
12/17	60.66	26 21	2.36	2.58	19.33
12/16	63.13	27 21	2.59	2.79	18.74
12/15	61.75	20 15	3.12	2.75	18.91
12/14	49.40	31 13	3.09	3.71	19.61
12/13	97.38	35 22	2.90	2.17	19.29
Annual Growth	**(11.2%)**	**— —**	**(5.0%)**	**4.4%**	**0.1%**

Robert Half International Inc.

Robert Half International carries the full load of personnel services. The company places temporary and permanent staff through eight divisions: Accountemps Robert Half Finance and Accounting Robert Half Legal OfficeTeam (general administrative) Robert Half Technology (information technology) Robert Half Management Resources (senior level professionals) and The Creative Group (advertising marketing and Web design). The firm also publishes job reports and surveys on the latest employment trends and annual salary guides to track pay trends and has an internal audit and risk consulting division in Protiviti.

Operations

Robert Half operates in three business segments: temporary and consultant staffing permanent placement staffing and risk consulting and internal audit services.

Temporary and consulting is Robert Half's biggest business at more than 75% of total sales. It provides specialized staffing in the accounting and finance administrative and office and information technology legal advertising marketing and web design fields.

The Permanent place staffing segment accounts for about 15% of its sales and provides full-time personnel in the accounting and finance administrative and office and information technology fields.

Internal audit accounts for the remaining revenue and provides business and technology risk consulting and internal audit services.

Geographic Reach

Robert Half's temporary and permanent staffing services business has some 320 offices in more than 40 states Washington DC and 17 foreign countries. Protiviti has more than 55 offices in 20 states and 10 foreign countries. The firm's domestic segment accounts for about 80% of total sales.

Sales and Marketing

Robert Half recruits via direct marketing and print radio and internet advertising. Robert Half also has joint marketing agreements with many tech-related companies to coordinate joint mailings cooperative advertising and other promotions. The firm typically spends around $45-50 million on advertising annually.

Financial Performance

Robert Half has achieved significant growth over the years with revenues consistently climbing year-over-year.

In fiscal 2017 Robert Half's sales growth flattened out up just $16 million (or around 0.3%) to $5.3 billion. Permanent staffing placements were up during the year offset by lower temporary and consultant staffing placements. Europe was Robert Half's best performing region in 2017.

Net income fell 15% to $290.6 million due to an increase in selling general and administrative expenses particularly staff compensation costs and digital technology initiatives.

Cash from operations grew 2% to $453.0 million as lower net income was offset by adjustments to reconcile increases in accounts payable payroll and benefits.

Strategy

Robert Half prefers to grow organically rather than by making material acquisitions. The majority of Robert Half's capital spending in the last few years was for technological infrastructure and software. The firm completed the installation upgrades to its enterprise resource planning and project management applications in 2017 and continues to invest in further digital initiatives to improve its service offerings to clients and candidates.

HISTORY

Robert Half founded Robert Half Inc. in 1948 as an employment agency for accountants. He developed Accountemps on the side to supply firms with accountants and other finance professionals on a temporary basis. His concept was a hit and Half became known as a pioneer in the specialized employment services industry. He started franchising his business nationwide. The temp industry grew slowly in the 1960s and 1970s until the 1980s brought a rapid expansion. By 1985 there were 150 independent Accountemps and Robert Half franchises.

Harold "Max" Messmer joined the company in 1985 for what would prove to be a tumultuous first couple of years. In 1986 Boothe Financial Corporation bought all of Robert Half's outstanding stock and Messmer launched a program to buy all the Robert Half franchises. A year later Boothe sold Robert Half which then went public as Robert Half International placing Messmer at the helm as CEO and president.

EXECUTIVES

Evp Corporate Development, Robert W. Glass, age 59, $245,000 total compensation
Vice Chairman President And Cfo, M. Keith Waddell, age 61, $265,000 total compensation
Chairman And Ceo, Harold M. Messmer, age 72, $525,000 total compensation
President And Coo Staffing Services, Paul F. Gentzkow, age 62, $265,000 total compensation
Evp Chief Administration Officer And Treasurer, Michael C. Buckley, age 52, $265,000 total compensation
Svp And Cio, Sean Perry
Senior Regional Vice President, Phil Willingham
Auditors: PricewaterhouseCoopers LLP

LOCATIONS

HQ: Robert Half International Inc.
2884 Sand Hill Road, Suite 200, Menlo Park, CA 94025
Phone: 650 234-6000
Web: www.roberthalf.com

2017 sales

	$ mil.	% of total
Domestic	4,121	78
Foreign	1,145	22
Total	**5,266**	**100**

PRODUCTS/OPERATIONS

2017 sales

	$ mil.	% of total
Temporary & consultant staffing	4,011	76
Risk consulting & internal audit services	439	8
Permanent placement staffing	816	16
Total	**5,266**	**100**

Selected Operating Units

Accountemps (temporary accounting and finance personnel)
The Creative Group (advertising marketing and Web design)
OfficeTeam (temporary administrative and office personnel)
Protiviti (internal audit and risk consulting)
Robert Half Finance and Accounting (temporary accounting and finance personnel)
Robert Half Legal (temporary and full-time legal support personnel)
Robert Half Management Resources (senior-level accounting and finance personnel)
Robert Half Technology (temporary and contract IT personnel)

COMPETITORS

Adecco	Kelly Services
Deloitte Consulting	Kforce
Ernst & Young Global	ManpowerGroup
General Employment	PricewaterhouseCoopers
Enterprises	Randstad Holding
Headway Corporate	Solomon Page
Resources	Winston Resources
KPMG	

HISTORICAL FINANCIALS

Company Type: Public

Income Statement

FYE: December 31

	REVENUE ($ mil.)	NET INCOME ($ mil.)	NET PROFIT MARGIN	EMPLOYEES
12/17	5,266	290	5.5%	228,600
12/16	5,250	343	6.5%	231,400
12/15	5,094	357	7.0%	236,000
12/14	4,695	305	6.5%	225,000
12/13	4,245	252	5.9%	210,000
Annual Growth	**5.5%**	**3.6%**	**—**	**2.1%**

2017 Year-End Financials

Debt ratio: 0.04%
Return on equity: 26.51%
Cash ($ mil.): 294
Current ratio: 1.91
Long-term debt ($ mil.): 0
No. of shares (mil.): 124
Dividends
  Yield: 0.0%
  Payout: 41.2%
Market value ($ mil.): 6,901

	STOCK PRICE ($) FY Close	P/E High/Low	PER SHARE ($) Earnings	Dividends	Book Value
12/17	55.54	24 18	2.33	0.96	8.89
12/16	48.78	18 13	2.67	0.88	8.50
12/15	47.14	23 17	2.69	0.80	7.65
12/14	58.38	26 17	2.26	0.72	7.25
12/13	41.99	23 17	1.83	0.64	6.69
Annual Growth	**7.2%**	**— —**	**6.2%**	**10.7%**	**7.4%**

Robinson (C.H.) Worldwide, Inc.

EXECUTIVES

Chb-Pres-Ceo, John P Wiehoff
Cfo, Andrew C Clarke
Coo, Robert C Biesterfeld Jr
Clo-SEC, Ben G Campbell
Chief Hr Officer, Angela K Freeman
Cco, Christopher J O'Brien
Information Technology Team ME, Brent Potvin
Corporate Counsel Legal, Christopher Gerst
Account Manager, Collette Becker
Vice President, Dan Ryan
Senior Accountant, Donna Storms
Auditors: DELOITTE & TOUCHE LLP

LOCATIONS

HQ: Robinson (C.H.) Worldwide, Inc.
14701 Charlson Road, Eden Prairie, MN 55347-5088
Phone: 952 937-8500 **Fax:** 952 937-6714
Web: www.chrobinson.com

COMPETITORS

ALC	Hub Group
APL Logistics	J.B. Hunt
BNSF Logistics	Kuehne + Nagel
CEVA Logistics	International
Cass Information	Landstar Inway
Systems	MIQ Logistics
Chiquita Brands	Menlo Worldwide
Comdata	Pacer Transportation
CorTrans Logistics	Solutions
DHL	Panalpina
Dole Food	Penske Truck Leasing
Exel	Ryder System
Expeditors	Schneider Logistics
FedEx Trade Networks	TLC
Fresh Del Monte	Transplace
Produce	UPS Supply Chain
Greatwide Logistics	Solutions

HISTORICAL FINANCIALS

Company Type: Public

Income Statement

FYE: December 31

	REVENUE ($ mil.)	NET INCOME ($ mil.)	NET PROFIT MARGIN	EMPLOYEES
12/17	14,869	504	3.4%	15,074
12/16	13,144	513	3.9%	14,125
12/15	13,476	509	3.8%	13,159
12/14	13,470	449	3.3%	11,521
12/13	12,752	415	3.3%	11,676
Annual Growth	**3.9%**	**5.0%**	**—**	**6.6%**

2017 Year-End Financials

Debt ratio: 34.59%
Return on equity: 37.63%
Cash ($ mil.): 333
Current ratio: 1.26
Long-term debt ($ mil.): 750
No. of shares (mil.): 139
Dividends
  Yield: 0.0%
  Payout: 50.7%
Market value ($ mil.): 12,432

	STOCK PRICE ($) FY Close	P/E High/Low	PER SHARE ($) Earnings	Dividends	Book Value
12/17	89.09	25 18	3.57	1.81	10.22
12/16	73.26	22 17	3.59	1.74	8.90
12/15	62.02	22 17	3.51	1.57	8.02
12/14	74.89	25 17	3.05	1.43	7.15
12/13	58.35	26 21	2.65	1.40	6.26
Annual Growth	**11.2%**	**— —**	**7.7%**	**6.6%**	**13.0%**

Rockwell Automation, Inc.

Rockwell Automation traces its roots back to the Allen Bradley Company founded in the US in 1903 and still sells products under the Allen-Bradley and A-B trademarks among others. The company makes industrial automation products and controls including industrial sensors motion control systems safety components machine protection modules and more. It also provides industrial software and training services. Rockwell serves a broad range of global industries including transportation oil and gas life sciences and food and beverage. The company operates worldwide but the US still accounts for more than half of revenue.

Operations

The company organizes its operations in two segments: Architecture & Software (more than 45% of sales) and Control Products & Solutions (almost 55% of the total sales).

Rockwell's products in the Architecture & Software segment include hardware and software that help control clients' industrial processes such as controllers interface devices communication and networking products and industrial computers. Rockwell's flagship Logix controllers provide modular and scalable industrial controls. Software products in this segment relate to configuration and visualization process control manufacturing execution systems (MES) and productivity.

The Control Products & Solutions segment provides intelligent motor control and industrial control products as well as project management services. Products in these areas are motor starters circuit protection devices signaling devices and relays and timers to name a few. Services include life-cycle support asset management maintenance services and safety and network consulting.

Geographic Reach

Rockwell does business globally with operations in more than 80 countries. Customers in the US account for about 55% of total sales.

Its global headquarters and Control Products segment operations are located in Milwaukee Wisconsin; the Architecture & Software segment is based in Mayfield Heights Ohio.

The company's regional headquarters are in Cambridge Ontario (Canada) Belgium and The Netherlands (EMEA) Hong Kong (Asia Pacific) and Weston Florida (Latin America). Principle manufacturing locations include the US Canada Mexico Switzerland China Singapore Poland and Brazil.

Sales and Marketing

Rockwell Automation serves manufacturers across a range of markets including those in heavy industries (oil and gas mining metals) consumer industries (food and beverage home and personal care) and transportation.

Approximately 75% of global sales are through independent distributors. The company's largest distributor consistently represents about 10% of revenue.

Financial Performance

Overall sales for Rockwell Automation have been stagnant for the past six years. Sales in 2018 (ended September 30) were $6.7 billion a 6% increase from 2017 but flat compared to previous years. Growth in 2018 was broad-based across regions and was led by strength in the food and beverage mining life sciences and semiconductor industries and increased sales in emerging markets (10% growth).

Net income dropped significantly to $535.5 million—about 35%—in 2018 primarily due to a $538.3 million income tax provision related to the Tax Cuts and Jobs Act.

Cash at the end of fiscal 2018 was $618.9 million a decrease of $792.1 million from the prior year. Cash from operations contributed $1.3 billion to the coffers while investing activities used $170.4 million mainly for capital expenditures. Financing activities used another $1.9 billion for dividends to stockholders and the company's stock repurchase program.

Strategy

Rockwell is focused on developing new products and services as well as expanding its global footprint.

The Connected Enterprise is Rockwell's initiative to provide solutions for its customers' digital transformation. The company released several new technologies in 2018 — Project Scio an analytics platform for Industrial Internet of Things (IIoT) applications which organizes structured and unstructured data; FactoryTalk Cloud industrial data center servers; and network and cybersecurity services such as remote monitoring assessments and design and pre-engineered network solutions. Its Project Sherlock uses artificial intelligence (AI) to create and diagnose analytics solutions in industrial operations. Its recent partnership with PTC is allowing Rockwell to add more features to its platform to reduce unplanned downtime for its customers.

With about 45% of sales outside the US the company also continues to expand in emerging markets (China and India Latin America Central and Eastern Europe and Africa) and has made significant investments to globalize its operations in these regions.

Internally ongoing productivity initiatives are aimed at cost reduction and improved asset utilization throughout the enterprise; a program to implement common global processes and an enterprise-wide business system was implemented in 2018.

Mergers and Acquisitions

In 2018 Rockwell Automation made a $1 billion investment (an 8.4% stake) in PTC a maker of computer-aided design (CAD) programs and life-cycle management software for manufacturers. The partnership will allow Rockwell to offer more digital technologies to its customers that enable manufacturing systems and devices to communicate with each other over the internet.

The December 2017 acquisition of Odos Imaging a Scottish technology company that provides three-dimensional time-of-flight sensing systems for industrial imaging applications builds on Rockwell's portfolio of smart sensing and safety products for The Connected Enterprise.

HISTORY

Rockwell Automation is the legacy of two early-20th-century entrepreneurs: Willard Rockwell and Clement Melville Keys. Rockwell gained control in 1919 of Wisconsin Parts Company an Oshkosh Wisconsin maker of automotive axles. He went on to buy a number of industrial manufacturers merging them in 1953 to create Rockwell Spring & Axle. Renamed Rockwell-Standard in 1958 it led the world in the production of mechanical automotive parts by 1967.

In 1928 Keys founded North American Aviation (NAA) as a holding company for his aviation interests. General Motors bought NAA in 1934 and named James Kindelberger as its president. The company moved in 1935 from Maryland to Inglewood California where it built military training planes. NAA merged with Rockwell-Standard creating North American Rockwell in 1967. The company adopted the Rockwell International name in 1973. It wasn't until the beginning of the new century when the company changed its name to Rockwell Automation.

EXECUTIVES

Svp General Counsel And Secretary, Douglas M. (Doug) Hagerman, age 57, $590,785 total compensation

Svp Global Sales And Marketing, John P. McDermott, age 60, $436,699 total compensation

Svp Control Products And Solutions, Theodore D. (Ted) Crandall, age 63, $635,431 total compensation

Svp Advanced Technology And Cto, Sujeet Chand, age 60

Svp Operations And Engineering Services, Martin (Marty) Thomas, age 60

Chairman President And Ceo, Blake D. Moret, age 55, $594,923 total compensation

Svp Architecture And Software, Frank C. Kulaszewicz, age 54, $594,923 total compensation

President Latin America, Alejandro Capparelli

President Europe Middle East And Africa, Thomas Donato

President Asia/pacific, Joseph (Joe) Sousa

Vp Investor Relations And Finance Architecture And Software, Patrick Goris

Svp It And Cio, Chris Nardecchia

Vice President Logistics, David Kenney

Senior Vice President Oppm, John D Lang

Vice President And Auditor, Sue Von Heimburg

Vice President Business Development, Keith A Harpenau

Legal Secretary, Alexander S Vinciczky

Vice President Global Business Development, Joe Kann

Vice President Human Resources, Rae Williams

Vice President Professional Services (ra Incuity), Andrew Ellis

Regional Vice President North America Channels, Steve Dubois

Vice President Ww Sales, Naveen Vashist

Vice President, Edward Hill

Vice President Information Technology Applications, Anu Varma

Vp And General Auditor, Susan Von

Vice President Global Industry Group, Christopher P Zei

Board Member, William Mccormick

Board Member, Lawrence Kingsley

Board Member, James Keane

Board Member, Lisa Payne

Auditors: DELOITTE & TOUCHE LLP

LOCATIONS

HQ: Rockwell Automation, Inc.
1201 South Second Street, Milwaukee, WI 53204
Phone: 414 382-2000
Web: www.rockwellautomation.com

2018 Sales

	% of total
US	54
Europe Middle East & Africa	19
Asia Pacific	14
Latin America	7
Canada	6
Total	**100**

PRODUCTS/OPERATIONS

2018 Sales

	$ mil.	% of total
Control Products & Solutions	3,567	54
Architecture & Software	3,098	46
Total	**6,666**	**100**

2017 Sales

	$ mil.	% of total
Products and solutions	5,930	89
Services	735	11
Total	**6,666**	**100**

PRODUCT CATEGORIES

PRODUCT CATEGORIES
Advanced Process Control
Condition Monitoring & I/O
Design & Operations Software
Distributed Control Systems
Drive Systems
Drives
Human Machine Interface
Industrial Control Products
Industrial Network Products
Industrial Sensors
Manufacturing Execution System
Motion Control
Motor Control Centers
Programmable Controllers
Safety Components
Safety Instrumented Systems
Training

COMPETITORS

ABB	Schneider Electric
Danaher	Select Business
Emerson Electric	Solutions
Honeywell	Siemens AG
International	Toshiba
Leonardo	Weiss Instrument
Metso	Wonderware
Mitsubishi Corp.	Yokogawa Electric
OMRON	

HISTORICAL FINANCIALS

Company Type: Public

Income Statement
FYE: September 30

	REVENUE ($ mil.)	NET INCOME ($ mil.)	NET PROFIT MARGIN	EMPLOYEES
09/18	6,666	535	8.0%	23,000
09/17	6,311	825	13.1%	22,000
09/16	5,879	729	12.4%	22,000
09/15	6,307	827	13.1%	22,500
09/14	6,623	826	12.5%	22,500
Annual Growth	0.2%	(10.3%)	—	0.6%

2018 Year-End Financials

Debt ratio: 28.36%
Return on equity: 25.02%
Cash ($ mil.): 618
Current ratio: 1.27
Long-term debt ($ mil.): 1,225

No. of shares (mil.): 121
Dividends
Yield: 0.0%
Payout: 83.3%
Market value ($ mil.): 22,709

	STOCK PRICE ($) FY Close	P/E High/Low		PER SHARE ($)	
			Earnings	Dividends	Book Value
09/18	187.52	49 38	4.21	3.51	13.36
09/17	178.21	28 18	6.35	3.04	20.74
09/16	122.34	22 16	5.56	2.90	15.49
09/15	101.47	21 16	6.09	2.60	17.05
09/14	109.88	21 17	5.91	2.32	19.44
Annual Growth	14.3%	— —	(8.1%)	10.9%	(9.0%)

Roper Technologies Inc

Roper Technologies is an industrial manufacturer with products that control pump scan authorize and analyze. Its business segments include medical and scientific imaging (digital imaging products and software) energy systems and controls (controls and sensors testing/inspection equipment) industrial technology (pumps leak testing flow measurement) and RF technology (toll/traffic systems card systems and software). Roper's lines are used in niche markets engaged in RF (radio frequency) water energy research and medical education transportation and security applications. The company aims for end-markets seeking value-added engineered products.

HISTORY

George Roper founded the company in 1919 in Rockford Illinois to make gas stoves and gear pumps. In the late 1950s the stove works were spun off to Sears as the Roper Corporation and the pump-making operations were moved to Georgia. Roper was a public company until a 1981 leveraged buyout (a takeover of a company using borrowed funds.) UK-born Derrick Key who joined Roper in 1982 became CEO in 1991. The company went public again the next year as Roper Industries.

During the 1990s Roper grew by acquisitions both at home and abroad. However it gained entry into Eastern Europe in 1993 by winning a seven-year contract worth $350 million with Russian gas czar OAO Gazprom to install advanced control systems across Russia's vast pipeline system.

The company added digital-imaging and analytical systems for electron microscopes in 1996 by purchasing Gatan International a California company with branches in Germany and the UK. Roper's 1997 purchases included Industrial Data Systems (leak-testing equipment Utah); Petrotech (systems integration for fluid-control products; Louisiana with an Indonesian unit); and Princeton Instruments (spectral and imaging cameras; New Jersey with locations in France and the UK).

Roper expanded its digital-imaging line in 1998 by acquiring Photometrics Ltd. (digital cameras and detectors) and PMC/Beta Limited (vibration sensing and control equipment). Roper's bid to buy Leach Holding fell through impeding its effort to boost its industrial components offerings. In 1999 it bought Varlen's petroleum analysis instrumentation unit and Eastman Kodak's motion analysis operations (digital video equipment).

Roper's focus on providing high-margin products to niche markets spurred growth through acquisitions that included Eastman Kodak's high-speed and high-resolution digital video equipment unit as well as makers of testing equipment for the petroleum industry. the company bought Struers Holdings' two operating units which provided preparation equipment used in quality inspection (Struers A/S) and material shaping equipment used to make semiconductors and optoelectronics (Logitech).

Roper acquired Hansen Technologies in 2001 and added Struers' operating units in 2001; in 2002 it spent about $83 million on Zetec (industrial testing equipment) Duncan Technologies (industrial digital cameras) AiCambridge/"Qualitek" (leak detection equipment) Quantitative Imaging (industrial and scientific digital cameras) and Definitive Imaging (image analysis software). At the same time however Roper exited some of its Petrotech businesses and was hit by the downturn in the semiconductor industry the oil and gas exploration markets and the generally weak economy.

At the end of 2003 Roper acquired Neptune Technology Group Holdings (meter-reading technology) for $475 million. Expanding beyond its core controls pumps and analytical tools businesses Roper acquired radio-frequency identification technology and related services provider TransCore Holdings for $597 million in 2004.

The company purchased Louisville Colorado-based security applications technologies provider Inovonics Wireless Corporation for $45 million in 2005. That same year Roper strengthened its presence in the medical imaging market by acquiring Kalona Iowa-based CIVCO Medical Instruments Co. a supplier of specialized medical products from KRG Capital Partners LLC. It also bought Orange City Iowa-based MEDTEC a maker of technology used in diagnosing and treating cancer for about $150 million to fold into its CIVCO operations.

The company acquired Dynisco LLC in 2006 for $243 million from the Audax Group a private equity investment firm. Also known as Dynisco Instruments the business made pressure and temperature measurement and control instruments primarily for the plastics industry with applications in life sciences. In recent years Dynisco acquired Alpha Technologies and Viatran Corp. suppliers of analytical instruments and sensors for various applications. Dynisco became part of Roper's Energy Systems and Controls segment.

Acquisitions in 2007 were less costly totaling $106 million and largely benefited the company's Energy Systems and Control segment; four businesses were acquired that brought on board pressure measurement sensors air intake-cut off devices audio recording vibration monitoring and process control equipment. The RF Technology segment gained a rugged mobile computers provider and Scientific and Industrial Imaging obtained a manufacturer of computers and software for mobile computing.

Between 2007 and 2011 the company has averaged more than four acquisitions a year with six each in 2007 and 2008. The largest of the 2008 acquisitions was the purchase of The CBORD Group for $375 million. CBORD makes electronic ID and debit cards for colleges and universities hospitals supermarkets and other businesses and institutions. The acquisition diversified the company's RF Technology interests beyond transportation and water utilities to health care and education end-markets.

Cumulatively Roper's other acquisitions in 2008 ran to $331 million with the RF Technology segment receiving additional boosts with Getloaded.com Technolog and Horizon Software. Horizon Software builds upon the capabilities previously brought in by CBORD. A provider of software Horizon captures corporate dining health care K-12 education military and senior living markets. The two other deals in 2008 (Tech-Pro and Chalwyn) grew the company's Energy Systems and Controls portfolio with industrial test instruments and software and air shut-off valves.

Other acquisitions over the years included Heartscape which developed a technology that can detect heart attacks quicker and with more accuracy; iTradeNetwork a provider of Software-as-a-Service (SaaS)-based trading network and information services used by the food industry; and United Toll Services which made toll and traffic systems and software vital to transportation infrastructure projects that are anticipated to receive an uptick in funding.

In 2012 the company acquired Sunquest Information Systems a provider of health care software catering to more than 1700 large and midsized hospitals and laboratories for about $1.4 billion. The deal allowed it to broaden its product portfolio into new areas. The prior year it snapped up Northern Digital (NDI) a Canada-based 3-D technology provider for the medical industry. Seen as a growth industry NDI's products are used in computer-assisted medical procedures. As with the other acquisitions NDI became part of Roper's medical operations.

EXECUTIVES

Chairman President And Ceo, Brian D. Jellison, age 72, $1,225,000 total compensation
Evp, Paul J. Soni, age 60, $475,000 total compensation
Evp, L. Neil Hunn
Vp And Cfo, Robert Crisci, age 42
Vice President General Counsel, David Liner
Group Vice President Scientific And Industrial Imaging, Ben Wood
Vp Human Resources, Greg Anderson
Group Vp, Claude Pumilia
Group Vp, Christopher Kreips
Auditors: PricewaterhouseCoopers LLP

LOCATIONS

HQ: Roper Technologies Inc
6901 Professional Parkway East, Suite 200, Sarasota, FL 34240
Phone: 941 556-2601
Web: www.ropertech.com

2016 Sales

	$ mil.	% of total
United States	2,978	79
Non-U.S.	811	21
Total	**3,789**	**100**

PRODUCTS/OPERATIONS

2016 Sales

	$ mil.	% of total
Medical & Scientific Imaging	1,362	36
RF Technology	1,210	32
Industrial Technology	706	19
Energy Systems & Controls	510	13
Total	**3,789**	**100**

Selected Products

Energy Systems and Controls
  Control systems
  Fluid properties testing equipment
  Industrial valves and controls
  Non-destructive inspection and measurement instrumentation
  Sensors and controls
Industrial technology
  Flow measurement equipment
  Industrial leak testing equipment
  Industrial pumps
  Materials analysis equipment and consumables
  Water meter and AMR products and systems
RF Technology
  Card systems/integrated security solutions
  Freight matching
  Toll and traffic systems
Scientific and Industrial Imaging
  Digital imaging products and software
  Handheld and vehicle mount computers and software
  Medical products and software

COMPETITORS

ABB	IMI plc
AMETEK	ITT Corp.
Agilent Technologies	Ingersoll-Rand
American Capital	Intuit
Ampco-Pittsburgh	Itron
Autodesk	Life Technologies
Bard	Corporation
CEM	Microsoft
CIRCOR International	Newport Corp.
Cameron International	Oracle
Coherent Inc.	Pall Corporation
Colfax	Parker-Hannifin
Curtiss-Wright	Pentair
Danaher	PerkinElmer
Dover Corp.	Robbins & Myers
Emerson Electric	Rotork
Entegris	SPX
Flowserve	Schneider Electric
Gorman-Rupp	SpiraxSarco
Halliburton	Thermo Fisher
Haskel	Scientific
Honeywell	Transcat
International	Tuthill
IBM Software	salesforce.com
IDEX	

HISTORICAL FINANCIALS

Company Type: Public

Income Statement

FYE: December 31

	REVENUE ($ mil.)	NET INCOME ($ mil.)	NET PROFIT MARGIN	EMPLOYEES
12/17	4,607	971	21.1%	14,236
12/16	3,789	658	17.4%	14,155
12/15	3,582	696	19.4%	10,806
12/14	3,549	646	18.2%	10,137
12/13	3,238	538	16.6%	9,913
Annual Growth	**9.2%**	**15.9%**	**—**	**9.5%**

2017 Year-End Financials

Debt ratio: 36.01%
Return on equity: 15.36%
Cash ($ mil.): 671
Current ratio: 0.87
Long-term debt ($ mil.): 4,354

No. of shares (mil.): 102
Dividends
  Yield: 0.0%
  Payout: 14.9%
Market value ($ mil.): 26,546

	STOCK PRICE ($) FY Close	P/E High/Low		Earnings	Dividends	Book Value
12/17	259.00	28	19	9.39	1.40	66.97
12/16	183.08	29	24	6.43	1.20	56.94
12/15	189.79	28	21	6.85	1.00	52.53
12/14	156.35	25	20	6.40	0.80	47.49
12/13	138.68	26	21	5.37	0.66	42.42
Annual Growth	**16.9%**	**—**	**—**	**15.0%**	**20.7%**	**12.1%**

Ross Stores, Inc.

Ross wants you to dress for less. A leading off-price apparel retailer (behind TJX Cos. and Kohl's) Ross operates some 1340 Ross Dress for Less and more than 190y 200 dd's Discounts stores that sell closeout merchandise including men's women's and children's clothing at prices well below those of department and specialty stores. While apparel accounts for more than half of sales it also sells small furnishings toys and games luggage and jewelry. Featuring the Ross "Dress for Less" trademark the chain targets 18- to 54-year-old white-collar shoppers from primarily middle-income households. Ross and dd's stores are located in strip malls in over 35 states and mostly in the western US and Guam.

Operations

Ross Stores operates two brands of off-price retail apparel and home fashion stores: Ross Dress for Less and dd's DISCOUNTS. Ross does a roaring trade in off-price apparel and home fashion chain offering first-quality in-season name-brand and designer apparel as well as accessories footwear and home decor at between 20%-60% off department and specialty store regular prices.

Launched in 2004 dd's DISCOUNTS serves one of the fastest-growing demographic markets in the US. The ultra-low-price spinoff which offers brand-name apparel at a 20%-70% discount has grown to almost 200 locations in about 15 states including big ones such as California Florida and Texas. The stores which average 23200 square feet are located in strip shopping centers in urban and suburban neighborhoods.

The retailer operates six distribution processing facilities: three in California two in South Carolina and one in Pennsylvania. These distribution centers are the sole source of its stores merchandise. Additionally the discounter owns four and leases three other warehouse facilities for packaway storage. To distribute merchandise to stores on a regular basis Ross Stores enlists the help of third-party cross docks. Shipments are made by contract carriers to stores between three and six times per week depending on the location.

Geographic Reach

Half of California-based Ross' stores are located in the states of California Texas and Florida. The company's distribution centers and warehouses are in Pennsylvania South Carolina and California.Aside from the territory of Guam Ross does not have an international presence.

Sales and Marketing

Ross Stores relies primarily on television as a medium to share the Ross Dress for Less value proposition with its current and potential customers. The company believes that television advertising is the most efficient and cost-effective medium while it continues to use additional channels to build brand awareness. However advertising for its dd's DISCOUNTS stores is focused on new store grand openings and local grass roots initiatives.It also employs social media to communicate its brand position.

Financial Performance

Ross Stores' annual sales have risen more than 40% since 2011 thanks to rapid store expansion and steady same-store sale growth of between 3% and 7% per year. Its annual profits have kept pace with top line growth over the period as the chain has managed to slow its overhead cost growth.

The fast-growing chain's sales jumped 8% to $12.9 billion – a $1 billion gain – during fiscal 2017 (ended January) mostly thanks to continued store growth. Comparable store sales also increased a solid 4%.

Net income was up 10% to $1.1 billion due to lower cost of goods sold partially offset by higher selling general and administrative expenses. Cash from operating activities grew 14% to $1.6 billion due to higher net income.

Strategy

Ross Stores continues its aggressive retail expansion strategy opening additional stores based on market penetration local demographic characteristics competition expected store profitability and the ability to leverage overhead expenses. The company anticipates room in the US to support at least 2000 Ross locations and 500 dd's DISCOUNTS locations.

Indeed the chain has expanded its store count by 40% to 1533 at the end of 2016 from 1125 at the end of 2011. During 2016 alone the retailer added 87 net new stores (including 71 Ross stores) in established regions and in the less-tapped Midwest markets (including its first stores in the Dakotas). It plans to open a further 90 stores in 2017.

Other objectives the discount chain emphasized in 2016 included: maintaining a sufficient library of well-known brands labels and fashions sold with strong discounts; meeting customer needs on a local basis; delivering an "off-price customer" suited shopping experience; and managing effective and competitive store growth in all of its markets.

To boost its relationships with suppliers Ross does not require them to provide markdown/promotional allowances or return privileges. This combined with opportunistic purchases (closeouts such as manufacturer overruns and canceled orders) allows the company to obtain large discounts on merchandise. As a result Ross Stores' customers typically pay 20% to 60% less than department and specialty store prices. Ross holds down costs by offering minimal service and few frills inside its stores.

HISTORY

In 1957 the Ross family founded Ross Stores and opened its first junior department store; by 1982 there were six of the stores in the San Francisco area. That year two retailing veterans Stuart Moldaw (founder of Country Casuals and The Athletic Shoe Factory) and Donald Rowlett (creator of Woolworth's off-price subsidiary J. Brannam) led the acquisition of the company. Moldaw (chairman) and Rowlett (president) wanted to create an off-price chain in California where — despite the success such endeavors were having in the rest of the country — such stores were largely absent. The duo intended to establish a foothold by saturating California markets before competitors muddied the waters.

They restocked the stores with brand-name men's women's and children's apparel shoes accessories and domestics merchandise at reduced prices. Before the end of 1982 they opened two more Ross "Dress for Less" stores; the next year 18 more were added including the chain's first non-California store in Reno Nevada (much of the chain's expansion came through the acquisition of existing strip mall stores). Another 40 stores were added in 1984.

The company went public in 1985 to help fund its expansion and extended its reach to include Colorado Florida Georgia New Mexico and Oregon; that year it opened 41 stores.

In August 2004 Ross opened its first three dd's DISCOUNTS stores in Vallejo San Leandro and Fresno California. The retailer moved its headquarters from Newark California to Pleasanton in mid-2004 and then sold the Newark property for about $17 million.

EXECUTIVES

Ceo, Barbara Rentler, age 60, $1,301,875 total compensation
President And Coo, Michael B. O'Sullivan, age 54, $1,147,250 total compensation
President And Chief Merchandising Officer Ddâ's Discounts, Brian R. Morrow, age 58
President Merchandising Ross Dress For Less, Bernard (Bernie) Brautigan, age 53, $1,070,750 total compensation
Group Svp And Cfo, Michael J. Hartshorn, age 50, $651,375 total compensation
Vice President Property Management, John Fox
Chairman, Michael A. Balmuth, age 68
Auditors: Deloitte & Touche LLP

LOCATIONS

HQ: Ross Stores, Inc.
  5130 Hacienda Drive, Dublin, CA 94568-7579
Phone: 925 965-4400
Web: www.rossstores.com

2017 Stores

	No.
California	364
Texas	222
Florida	185
Arizona	74
Illinois	62
Georgia	56
North Carolina	45
Pennsylvania	44
Washington	42
Virginia	38
Colorado	33
Nevada	33
Tennessee	31
Oregon	30
Maryland	24
Oklahoma	23
South Carolina	23
Alabama	23
Missouri	21
Louisiana	18
Hawaii	17
Utah	17
New Jersey	13
Wisconsin	13
New Mexico	12
Idaho	11
Kansas	10
Kentucky	9
Indiana	9
Mississippi	8
Arkansas	8
Montana	6
Wyoming	3
Delaware	2
District of Columbia	1
Guam	1
North Dakota	1
South Dakota	1
Total	**1,533**

PRODUCTS/OPERATIONS

2017 Sales

	% of total
Women's apparel	28
Home accents bed & bath	25
Accessories lingerie fine jewelry & fragrances	13
Men's apparel	13
Shoes	13
Children's apparel	8
Total	**100**

2017 Stores

	No.
Ross Dress for Less	1,340
dd's DISCOUNTS	193
Total	**1,533**

Selected Merchandise

Bed and bath
Children's apparel
Cookware
Educational toys
Fine Jewelry
Fragrances
Gourmet foods
Home accents
Ladies' apparel
  Accessories
  Dresses
  Junior
  Lingerie
  Maternity
  Misses sportswear
  Petites
  Women's World
Luggage
Men's apparel
  Traditional men's
  Young men's
Shoes
Small electronics
Small furnishings
Sporting goods and exercise equipment

COMPETITORS

Ascena Retail	J. C. Penney
Big Lots	Kmart
Burlington Coat	Kohl's
Factory	Sears
Cato	TJX Companies
Charming Shoppes	Tailored Brands
Family Dollar Stores	Target Corporation
Fred's	Wal-Mart

HISTORICAL FINANCIALS

Company Type: Public

Income Statement

FYE: February 3

	REVENUE ($ mil.)	NET INCOME ($ mil.)	NET PROFIT MARGIN	EMPLOYEES
02/18*	14,134	1,362	9.6%	82,700
01/17	12,866	1,117	8.7%	78,600
01/16	11,040	1,020	8.6%	77,000
01/15	11,041	924	8.4%	71,400
02/14	10,230	837	8.2%	66,300
Annual Growth	**8.4%**	**12.9%**	**—**	**5.7%**

*Fiscal year change

2018 Year-End Financials

Debt ratio: 6.94%
Return on equity: 46.25%
Cash ($ mil.): 1,290
Current ratio: 1.64
Long-term debt ($ mil.): 311

No. of shares (mil.): 379
Dividends
  Yield: 0.0%
  Payout: 18.0%
Market value ($ mil.): 30,020

	STOCK PRICE ($) FY Close	P/E High/Low	PER SHARE ($) Earnings	Dividends	Book Value
02/18*	79.08	24 15	3.55	0.64	8.03
01/17	65.33	24 18	2.83	0.54	7.01
01/16	56.26	42 18	2.51	0.47	6.14
01/15	91.71	43 28	2.21	0.40	5.49
02/14	67.91	42 28	1.94	0.34	4.70
Annual Growth	**3.9%**	**— —**	**16.3%**	**17.1%**	**14.3%**

*Fiscal year change

RPM International Inc (DE)

Maker of home repair favorites like Rust-Oleum Zinsser and DAP RPM International is divided into three units: Industrial Consumer and Specialty products. Industrial offerings (which account for half of total sales) include products for waterproofing corrosion resistance floor maintenance and wall finishing. RPM's Consumer do-it-yourself items include caulks and sealants rust preventatives and general-purpose paints repair products personal care items and hobby paints. The Specialty segment offers industrial cleaners restoration services equipment and colorants.RPM operates through about 140 locations around the globe.

HISTORY

Frank Sullivan founded Republic Powdered Metals in 1947 to make an industrial aluminum paint. The company went public in 1963 and three years later it bought Reardon Co. (household coatings) the first of more than 50 acquisitions. After his father's death in 1971 Thomas Sullivan took over and reorganized RPM as a holding company.

By 1979 RPM though successful was taken to task by its board for lack of formal planning. In 1985 it bought Sun Oil's Carboline coating and tank-lining subsidiary. This purchase forced RPM to lay off employees for the first time.

RPM bought Rust-Oleum in 1994. In its largest acquisition at that time the company bought roofing-product expert Tremco in 1996 for $236 million. The purchase amassed debt and to compensate RPM sold its Craft House hobby activity subsidiary and Swiggle Insulating Glass in 1997.

The company resumed acquisitions and overseas expansion in 1998 by purchasing Flecto (wood finish) the UK's Nullifire (fireproof coatings) and Germany's Alteco Technik (floors); it also established joint ventures in Russia and China. In 1999 RPM paid $290 million for UK-based Wassall's DAP adhesives division. Softer sales in the Americas and Asia plus increased distribution expenses that fiscal year prompted the company to begin restructuring its operations.

RPM sold its Alox metalworking additive business to Lubrizol in 2000. The next year the company finished its restructuring — which had resulted in 17 plant closures and a 10% workforce reduction — and set its sights on reducing debt.

Thomas C. Sullivan's son — and grandson of the company's founder — Frank Sullivan took the chief executive reins in 2002; Thomas Sullivan remained with the company as chairman.

The company went through a spate of acquisitions in the middle of the decade. Its flooring services division has acquired National Building Facilities Services and Harsco's fiberglass-reinforced plastics business and its corrosion control division has acquired AD Fire Protection Systems. Tremco has acquired German sealant manufacturer Illbruck Sealant Systems. In early 2007 Rust-Oleum acquired the UK's Tor Coatings in an effort to grow the unit's European coatings operations. Later that year the company sold its auto restoration products subsidiary Bondo to 3M.

In 2010 two RPM subsidiaries Bondex International and its holding company Specialty Products Holding Corp. filed for Chapter 11 reorganization in a move to resolve asbestos claims against Bondex. The process allowed the companies to establish a trust fund and a court order directing all present and future claims to the fund for compensation.

The company also went on an international shopping trip in 2010. RPM acquired Hummervoll Industribelegg AS a Norway-based supplier and installer of industrial flooring systems; UK-based Pipeline & Drainage Systems a supplier of curb bridge and channel drainage products; and Turkish company Park Dis Ticaret AS a provider of sealant tapes and membranes.

RPM subsidiary Euclid Chemical acquired PSI Packaging in 2011. PSI is a producer of micro- and macro-fibers for the ready-mixed and pre-cast concrete market. The PSI deal will expand both Euclid and RPM's manufacturing and sales capacity for concrete reinforcement fibers particularly in the international market.

In 2011 the company expanded further internationally when its Performance Coatings Group acquired API an Italian flooring and deck coatings company. The buy also complemented RPM's Flowcrete and Stonhard commercial flooring businesses. That year the company's Performance Coatings

EXECUTIVES

President And Coo, Ronald A. Rice, age 55, $720,000 total compensation
Chairman And Ceo, Frank C. Sullivan, age 57, $960,000 total compensation
President Tremco Incorporated, Paul G. P. Hoogenboom, age 57, $425,000 total compensation
Svp Manufacturing Supply Chain Logistics And Operations, John J. McLaughlin
President Rpm Industrial Segment, David P. Reif
Director Information Technology, Lonny R. DiRusso
President And Ceo Dap, Terry Horan
Svp General Counsel And Chief Compliance Officer, Edward W. Moore, age 61, $360,000 total compensation

Vp And Cfo, Russell L. Gordon, age 52, $465,000 total compensation
Vp Corporate Benefits And Risk Management, Janeen B. Kastner, age 51, $295,000 total compensation
Auditors: DELOITTE & TOUCHE LLP

LOCATIONS

HQ: RPM International Inc (DE)
P.O. Box 777, 2628 Pearl Road, Medina, OH 44258
Phone: 330 273-5090   **Fax:** 330 225-8743
Web: www.rpminc.com

2017 Sales

	$ mil.	% of total
US	3,269	66
Europe	908	18
Canada	321	7
Other regions	458	9
Total	**4,958**	**100**

PRODUCTS/OPERATIONS

2017 Sales

	$ mil.	% of total
Industrial	2,564	52
Consumer	1,680	34
Specialty	713	14
Total	**4,958**	**100**

Selected Products

Industrial
  Carboline (industrial coatings)
  Chemspec (commercial carpet cleaning chemicals)
  Day-Glo (fluorescent colorants and pigments)
  Dryvit (exterior finishing systems)
  Dymeric (sealants)
  Fibergrate (reinforced plastic grating)
  Flowcrete (polymer flooring system)
  Nullifire (fireproofing coatings)
  Republic (roofing products)
  Stonhard (flooring products)
  Tremco (industrial and commercial sealants)
  Woolsey/Z-Spar (marine coatings)
Consumer
  DAP (sealants caulks and patch and repair products)
  OKON (sealants and stains)
  Painter's Touch (general purpose coatings)
  Rust-Oleum (rust preventative coatings)
  Testors (hobby and leisure products)
  Tremclad (coatings)
  Varathane (wood finishes)
  Watco (wood finishes)
  Zinsser (primer-sealers and wallcovering removers)

COMPETITORS

3M	H.B. Fuller
Akzo Nobel	Henkel
Ameron	Masco
Axalta Coating Systems	PPG Industries
Benjamin Moore	Sherwin-Williams
Ferro	Valspar

HISTORICAL FINANCIALS

Company Type: Public

Income Statement

FYE: May 31

	REVENUE ($ mil.)	NET INCOME ($ mil.)	NET PROFIT MARGIN	EMPLOYEES
05/18	5,321	337	6.3%	14,540
05/17	4,958	181	3.7%	14,318
05/16	4,813	354	7.4%	13,394
05/15	4,594	239	5.2%	12,864
05/14	4,376	291	6.7%	10,848
Annual Growth	**5.0%**	**3.7%**	**—**	**7.6%**

2018 Year-End Financials

Debt ratio: 41.24%		No. of shares (mil.): 133	
Return on equity: 22.03%		Dividends	
Cash ($ mil.): 244		Yield: 2.5%	
Current ratio: 2.45		Payout: 50.4%	
Long-term debt ($ mil.): 2,170		Market value ($ mil.): 6,616	

	STOCK PRICE ($) FY Close	P/E High/Low	PER SHARE ($) Earnings	Dividends	Book Value
05/18	49.50	22 18	2.50	1.26	12.20
05/17	54.23	41 34	1.36	1.18	10.75
05/16	50.19	19 14	2.63	1.09	10.32
05/15	50.03	29 22	1.78	1.02	9.69
05/14	43.07	20 14	2.18	0.95	10.38
Annual Growth	**3.5%**	**— —**	**3.5%**	**7.5%**	**4.1%**

Rush Enterprises Inc.

Rush Enterprises has been truckin' along as a heavy-duty commercial vehicle dealer since 1965. The company operates a growing network of more than 100 commercial vehicle and service dealerships under the name Rush Truck Centers in some 21 states. It is one of the largest Peterbilt truck dealers in the US but it also sells trucks manufactured by Blue Bird Ford Isuzu Hino Mitsubishi Fuso and IC Bus. Additionally Rush offers aftermarket parts and services such as body shop repairs insurance and third-party financing and rentals and leasing. Founded in 1965 Rush's reach has spread as far as California and Florida. Late chairman W. Marvin Rush's family control the rapidly growing company.

Operations

Rush Truck Centers dealerships that sell new and used commercial vehicles are its largest business accounting for more than two thirds of Rush Enterprises' total sales. The company also sells aftermarket parts and services representing about 30% of annual sales and third-party financing. Of its vehicle sales about 80% are new and 20% used.

The company runs a number of other small businesses such as World Wide Tires which operates two locations in Texas and sells tires for commercial use and Momentum Fuel Technologies which manufactures compressed natural gas fuel systems and related parts.

Geographic Reach

New Braunfels Texas-based Rush Enterprises' Rush Truck Centers are located in Alabama Arizona California Colorado Florida Georgia Idaho Illinois Indiana Kansas Missouri Nevada New Mexico North Carolina Nebraska Ohio Oklahoma Pennsylvania Tennessee Texas Utah and Virginia.

Sales and Marketing

Rush Enterprises promotes it products through its sales personnel advertisements in trade magazines and online and at industry shows. Customers include owner operators regional and national truck fleets corporations and local governments. Its customer base is diversified and it does not rely on any customer for more than 10% of total sales.

The company purchases vehicles parts and accessories directly from manufacturers wholesale distributors or other sources that provide the most favorable pricing.

Financial Performance

Rush Enterprises had a rough time in 2016 amid industry-wide malaise but recovered in 2017. The company's revenue grew 12% or $499.3 million to $4.7 billion on the back of growth in new vehicle sales and aftermarket products and services. Used vehicle sales growth was materially flat.

Net income jumped from $40.6 million to $172.1 million due to stronger operating profits and a net tax benefit of $35.7 million relating to the 2017 US Tax Cuts and Jobs Act.

Rush's cash positioned strengthened in 2017 its coffers growing by $42.5 million to $124.5 million.

Strategy

Rush has stated its ambition to grow its revenue to $7 billion by 2020 by investing heavily in its business particularly the parts and service business. Rusty Rush the chairman and CEO views the segment as having the most potential in terms of revenue and profit growth. The windfall from the 2017 US Tax Cuts and Jobs Act will be pumped into the business including an extensive salespeople and technician recruitment drive.

Rush markets its dealership network as "one-stop shops" where customers can purchase new and used commercial vehicles (ranging from heavy- and medium-duty trucks to buses); finance lease or rent vehicles and equipment; buy aftermarket parts and accessories; and have warranty and non-warranty service performed by certified technicians. Its customer base includes regional and national truck fleets (typically those that buy more than five trucks in any one-year period) owner operators corporations and local governments.

Geographically the company's strategy is to expand this network either by organically opening new centers in existing areas of operation or by acquiring additional dealerships that are located adjacent to its current operations. Rush also grows by adding complementary product lines including truck-mounted cranes refuse vehicles and towing vehicles.

To combat a shortage of truck technicians Rush is investing in training programs for new recruits with the goal of reducing first-year turnover. The program will aim to attract more women; historically truck technicians have been predominantly men.

Mergers and Acquisitions

Rush regularly buys up truck dealerships to expand its size. In late 2017 the company acquired Transwest San Diego which sells Ford trucks for $2.2 million. It had acquired another Transwest dealer in Las Vegas the year before for $0.8 million.

EXECUTIVES

Senior Vice President Marketing Fleets And Specialized Equipment Sales, David Orf

Chairman President And Ceo, W. M. (Rusty) Rush, age 59, $1,437,000 total compensation

Evp, Derrek Weaver, age 45, $369,468 total compensation

Svp Cfo And Treasurer, Steven L. (Steve) Keller, age 48, $395,604 total compensation

Svp Navistar Dealerships, Richard J Ryan, age 50

Svp Peterbilt Dealerships, Corey H. Lowe, age 42

Svp And Coo, Michael J. McRoberts, age 59, $456,515 total compensation

Auditors: Ernst & Young LLP

LOCATIONS

HQ: Rush Enterprises Inc.
555 I.H. 35 South,, Suite 500, New Braunfels, TX 78130
Phone: 830 302-5200
Web: www.rushenterprises.com

PRODUCTS/OPERATIONS

2017 Sales

	$ mil.	% of total
New & used commercial vehicle sales	2,993	64
Parts & service sales	1,471	31
Lease & rental	217	5
Finance & insurance	18	0
Other	14	0
Total	4,713	100

2017 Sales

	$ mil.	% of total
Truck Segment	4,698	100
All Other	15	0
Total	4,713	100

2017 Unit Vehicle Sales

	% of total
New vehicles	78
Used vehicles	22
Total	100

Selected Businesses and Brands

Custom Vehicle Solutions
Momentum Fuel Technologies
Rig Tough Truck Parts
Rig Tough Used Trucks
Rush Bus Centers
Rush Crane Systems
Rush Refuse Systems
Rush Towing Systems
Rush Truck Centers
Rush Truck Financing
Rush Truck Insurance
Rush Truck Leasing

COMPETITORS

Freightliner Sterling Western Star
Holman Enterprises
Hunter's Truck Sales & Service
Midway Ford Truck Center
Murphy-Hoffman
Palm Truck Centers
Penske Automotive Group

Penske Truck Leasing
RDO Equipment
Rip Griffin Truck Service Center
Ryder System
W.D. Larson
Worldwide Equipment Inc.

HISTORICAL FINANCIALS

Company Type: Public

Income Statement				FYE: December 31
	REVENUE ($ mil.)	NET INCOME ($ mil.)	NET PROFIT MARGIN	EMPLOYEES
12/17	4,713	172	3.7%	6,825
12/16	4,214	40	1.0%	6,180
12/15	4,979	66	1.3%	6,700
12/14	4,727	79	1.7%	6,297
12/13	3,384	49	1.5%	5,295
Annual Growth	8.6%	36.8%	—	6.6%

2017 Year-End Financials

Debt ratio: 50.97%
Return on equity: 18.09%
Cash ($ mil.): 124
Current ratio: 1.17
Long-term debt ($ mil.): 532

No. of shares (mil.): 39
Dividends
Yield: —
Payout: —
Market value ($ mil.): 2,023

	STOCK PRICE ($) FY Close	P/E High/Low		PER SHARE ($) Earnings	Dividends	Book Value
12/17	50.81	12	7	4.20	0.00	26.13
12/16	31.90	33	14	1.00	0.00	21.98
12/15	21.89	20	13	1.61	0.00	20.91
12/14	32.05	19	13	1.96	0.00	19.16
12/13	29.65	24	17	1.22	0.00	16.97
Annual Growth	14.4%	—	—	36.2%	—	11.4%

Ryder System, Inc.

When it comes to commercial vehicles and distribution Ryder System wants to be the designated driver. The company's Fleet Management Solutions (FMS) segment acquires manages maintains and disposes of fleet vehicles for commercial customers. Similarly the Supply Chain Solutions (SCS) segment provides logistics and supply chain services from industrial start (raw material supply) to finish (product distribution). SCS also offers dedicated contract carriage service by supplying trucks drivers and management and administrative services to customers on a contract basis. Ryder's worldwide fleet of more than 222000 vehicles ranges from tractor-trailers to light-duty trucks.

Operations

Ryder operates through three main divisions: Fleet Management Solutions (FMS — full service leasing contract maintenance contract-related maintenance and commercial rental of trucks tractors and trailers in North America and the UK); Dedicated Transportation Solutions (DTS — provides vehicles and drivers as part of a dedicated transportation solution in the US) and Supply Chain Solutions (SCS — supply chain solutions including distribution and transportation services in North America and Asia).

FMS generates almost 65% of its total sales while SCS and DTS bring in about 25% and 15% respectively.

Geographic Reach

Ryder operates in North America (Canada Mexico and the US) Europe (Germany and the UK) and Asia (China and Singapore). The US accounts for around 85% of its total revenues.

Sales and Marketing

Ryder's FMS customers in the US range from small businesses to large national enterprises operating in a wide variety of industries the most significant of which are food and beverage transportation and warehousing housing business and personal services and industrial. The company's customers have included Associated Grocers Bendix Cisco Clark and Reid and CVS/Caremark.

Financial Performance

Ryder's revenues increased 3% in 2016 to peak at $6.8 billion its highest total in at least 10 years. This was attributed to growth in its full service lease fleet and higher prices on full service lease replacement vehicles. It also grew from new business and increased volumes and higher pricing within its SCS and DTS segments.

The company's profits however fell 14% from $305 million in 2015 to $262 million in 2016 mainly due to lower used vehicle sales. In addition Ryder's operating cash flow has trended upward for five straight years jumping from $1.44 billion in 2015 to $1.6 billion in 2016.

Strategy

One way Ryder remains competitive is being prepared for the unpredictability of supply chain logistics due in part to higher fuel prices and increased regional labor costs. To achieve this the company creates partnerships with third-party logistics (3PL) providers. Such alliances enable the company to keep its networks flexible and efficient.

Ryder is also aiming to capitalize on trends that make it more difficult for companies to manage commercial transportation and logistics on their own. These include higher truck purchase prices and operating costs new government regulations growing technology complexity talent shortages for drivers and increased demand for faster delivery options.

To meet these trends in 2016 Ryder launched a new suite of commercial vehicle lease products. Ryder ChoiceLease gives customers a more flexible set of maintenance choices: full service preventive or on-demand. The more scalable model allows customers to decide the terms of their lease in conjunction with the level of maintenance they prefer. In the past Ryder only offered a traditional full-services maintenance lease.

HISTORY

Ryder Truck Rental founded in Miami by Jim Ryder in 1933 was the first truck leasing company in the US. It rented trucks in four southern states until 1952 when it bought Great Southern Trucking (renamed Ryder Truck Lines) doubling its size. In 1955 the year it went public as Ryder System Ryder bought Carolina Fleets (a South Carolina trucking company) and Yellow Rental (a northeastern leasing service). More purchases over the next decade extended its truck rental business across the US and into Canada. Ryder Truck Lines was sold to International Utilities in 1965.

EXECUTIVES

Evp And Cfo, Art A. Garcia, age 56, $479,783 total compensation
Chairman And Ceo, Robert E. Sanchez, age 52, $785,225 total compensation
Evp And Chief Marketing Officer, Karen M. Jones, age 55
Evp Chief Legal Officer And Secretary, Robert D. Fatovic, age 52, $392,650 total compensation
President Global Fleet Management Solutions, Dennis C. Cooke, age 53, $543,750 total compensation
Evp And Chief Sales Officer, John J. Gleason, age 62
President Dedicated Transport Solutions, John J. Diez, $411,000 total compensation
Vp And General Manager High-technology Supply Chain Solutions, J. Steven (Steve) Sensing
Svp And Cio, Melvin (Mel) Kirk
Vice President Shared Services Center, Jeanette Mccarty
Vice President Audit Services, Clifford Zoller
Senior Vice President And Treasurer, Daniel Susik
Vice President Marketing, Natalie Putnam
Vice President Compensation And Benefits, Boon Ooi
Vice President Global Marketing, Samuel Johnson
Vice President And Deputy General Counsel, Alena Brenner
Vice President Asset Management, Eugene Tangney
Vice President Business Development, Mark Swenson
Vice President Of Tax, Ben Schmoyer
Vice President Information Technology, Mike Parvor
Vice President, Tim Sweeney
Vice President Manager Director, Tom Knutilla
Vice President Information Technology, Stephen Hitchings
Vice President Automotive, Dick Jennings
Vice President National Sales, William Toerpe
Senior Vice President And General Manager, Tom Pettit
Vice President, Eugenio Sevilla-Sacasa
Vice President Supply Chain Excellence, Gary Allen
Vice President Supply Chain Solutions, Steve Thoke
Vice President Of Operations, Bryce Kinsley
Senior Vice President And General Manager Supply Chains Solutions, Tom Jones
Vice President International Supply Chain Solutions, Gene Sevilla

Vice President Information Technology Strategic Operations, Jonathan Mish
Vp National Sales, Bill Toerpe
Vice President And General Manager, Gerald Brown
Director Of Government Relations, Joshua Grodin
Vice President Audit Services, Sanjay Singh
Vice President And Controller, Frank Mullen
National Account Manager, Terry Hubbard
Vice President Global Marketing, Samuel H Johnson
Vice President Director Of Business Development Lease Finance, Scott M Mishoe
National Account Manager, David Gifford
Board Member, Robert Eck
Board Member, Luis Nieto
Assistant Treasurer, Mary Aderholdt
Senior Vice President Finance And Treasurer, Dan Susik
Board Member, John Berra
Board Member, Follin E Smith
Auditors: PricewaterhouseCoopers LLP

LOCATIONS

HQ: Ryder System, Inc.
11690 N.W. 105th Street, Miami, FL 33178
Phone: 305 500-3726
Web: www.ryder.com

2016 Sales

	$ mil.	% of total
US	5,892	87
Canada	387	6
Europe	339	5
Mexico	139	2
Asia	28	-
Total	**6,787**	**100**

PRODUCTS/OPERATIONS

2016 Sales

	$ mil.	% of total
Lease and rental revenues	3,170	47
Services revenue	3,152	46
Fuel services revenue	463	7
Total	**6,787**	**100**

2016 Sales

	$ mil.	% of total
Fleet Management Solutions	4,556	63
Supply Chain Solutions	1,020	14
Dedicated Transportation Solutions	1,637	23
Eliminations	(427.9)	-
Total	**6,787**	**100**

Selected Services

Fleet Management Solutions
  Commercial rental
  Contract maintenance
  Full service leasing
  Used vehicles
Supply Chain Solutions
  Distribution management
  Transportation management
Dedicated Contract Carriage

COMPETITORS

ArcBest	Penske Truck Leasing
Barloworld Handling	Schenker Inc.
C.H. Robinson	Schneider National
Worldwide	UPS
FedEx	UniGroup
J.B. Hunt	YRC Worldwide
Landstar System	

HISTORICAL FINANCIALS

Company Type: Public

Income Statement

FYE: December 31

	REVENUE ($ mil.)	NET INCOME ($ mil.)	NET PROFIT MARGIN	EMPLOYEES
12/17	7,329	790	10.8%	36,100
12/16	6,786	262	3.9%	34,500
12/15	6,571	304	4.6%	33,100
12/14	6,638	218	3.3%	30,600
12/13	6,419	237	3.7%	28,900
Annual Growth	**3.4%**	**35.0%**	**—**	**5.7%**

2017 Year-End Financials

Debt ratio: 47.24%
Return on equity: 32.35%
Cash ($ mil.): 78
Current ratio: 0.66
Long-term debt ($ mil.): 4,583

No. of shares (mil.): 52
Dividends
Yield: 0.0%
Payout: 12.1%
Market value ($ mil.): 4,457

	STOCK PRICE ($) FY Close	P/E High/Low		PER SHARE ($) Earnings	Dividends	Book Value
12/17	84.17	6	4	14.87	1.80	53.54
12/16	74.44	17	10	4.90	1.70	38.39
12/15	56.83	17	9	5.71	1.56	37.15
12/14	92.85	23	17	4.11	1.42	34.30
12/13	73.78	16	11	4.53	1.30	35.56
Annual Growth	**3.3%**	**—**	**—**	**34.6%**	**8.5%**	**10.8%**

RYMAN HOSPITALITY PROPERTIES, INC.

Ryman Hospitality Properties (formerly Gaylord Entertainment) may be hollerin' for attention in the hospitality game but it's no corporate hayseed. Its properties consist of resort hotels tethered closely to attractions that appeal to the meetings and conventions market. They include the Gaylord Opryland Resort & Convention Center in Nashville the Gaylord Palms Resort in Florida (close to Disney World) the Gaylord Texan Resort near Dallas and the Gaylord National Resort and Convention Center in the Washington DC area. Ryman's hotels are managed by hotel giant Marriott. In 2012 the company changed its name convered to a REIT and sold its hotel brand and management business to Marriott.

HISTORY

The origins of Gaylord Entertainment can be traced back to the Oklahoma Publishing Co. a newspaper publishing company founded by Edward K. Gaylord Ray Dickinson and Roy McClintock in 1903. The publisher of The Daily Oklahoman Oklahoma Publishing branched into radio in 1928 with the purchase of Oklahoma City radio station WKY. With its 1949 creation of Oklahoma City television station WKY-TV Oklahoma Publishing made the leap into television.

Edward K. Gaylord died in 1974 at the age of 101 and his son Edward L. Gaylord was appointed CEO. Under his leadership the company purchased Opryland USA in 1983 — an acquisition that netted it the Grand Ole Opry Opryland Themepark and the Opryland Hotel. Opryland USA also launched country music cable network The Nashville Network that year.

In 1991 the increasingly diverse Oklahoma Publishing spun off its entertainment and broadcast holdings in the form of public company Gaylord Entertainment which established its headquarters in Nashville Tennessee. Gaylord Entertainment acquired a majority interest in cable music network Country Music Television (CMT) the same year. It later expanded CMT into Latin America Asia and the Pacific Rim. CMT also made a brief foray into Europe but that initiative was ended in 1998.

Facing a consolidating entertainment and media landscape Gaylord sold The Nashville Network and the US operations of CMT to Westinghouse (now CBS) in 1997. It also sold television station KSTW that year. The company expanded its reach into Christian music with the purchase of Word Entertainment and its 1997 acquisition of Blanton Harrell Entertainment gave Gaylord a presence in artist management. Terry London was appointed CEO in 1997.

The company closed its Opryland theme park in 1998 in the face of declining attendance and broke ground at the same site for the Opry Mills entertainment shopping and restaurant complex (opened 2000). Gaylord also purchased a Nashville Ramada Inn in 1998 (later renaming it Radisson Hotel at Opryland). With its 1998 acquisition of Paris-based Pandora Investment Gaylord branched into film distribution.

In 1999 the company formed Opryland Hospitality Group to oversee expansion of the Opryland hotel concept across the US. It also sold its last television station KTVT in Dallas/Fort Worth to CBS. Edward K. Gaylord II succeeded his father as chairman in 1999. That year the company launched its Internet division GETdigitalmedia (later renamed Gaylord Digital) and moved online with the purchase of Christian Web sites Musicforce.com and Lightsource.com. Later the same year the company expanded its Internet presence with the purchase of Songs.com a music Web site focused on independent artists. But in late 2000 the company announced it would close its Internet unit. Also in 2000 the company bought Corporate Magic a firm focused on producing entertainment events for corporate audiences.

At the end of 2000 Gaylord sold Musicforce.com to Christian Book Distributors. Following that sale it sold Lightsource.com to LifeAudio.com in early 2001. That year the company sold its film and television production units and announced a restructuring in order to cut costs. It also renamed Opryland Hotels to Gaylord Opryland while expanding into Texas and Florida. Colin Reed was appointed CEO in 2001.

Between 2001 and 2003 Gaylord Entertainment sold Word Entertainment to Warner Music Group the Opry Mills shopping and restaurant complex to The Mills Corporation the Acuff-Rose Music Publishing business to Sony/ATV two of its Nashville radio stations to Cumulus Media and its majority interest in the Oklahoma City Redhawks minor league baseball team.

Edward L. Gaylord officially retired from the company in 2003 at age 83. Also that year the company significantly expanded its hospitality business with the purchase of ResortQuest a vacation and condominium property management firm. In 2004 the Gaylord family sold more than half its shares in the company making Gabelli Funds the majority owner.

In 2005 Gaylord acquired 50% of Corporate Magic a Dallas-based provider of production support for corporate meetings and events. It did so to support its meeting and convention facilities.

The company unloaded its minority interest in minor league hockey team the Nashville Predators in 2005. Two years later it sold ResortQuest to a subsidiary of Leucadia National Corp. for $35 million. Also in 2007 it sold its interest in sporting goods store operator Bass Pro Group. In 2008 the company opened the Gaylord National Resort and Convention Center in the Washington DC area. The property has some 2000 rooms and approximately 450000 square feet of meeting space.

Also in 2008 Gaylord terminated plans to acquire the Westin La Cantera Resort in San Antonio for about $253 million citing a tough economic environment. In addition the 2008 sale of its ResortQuest subsidiary an online booking service in vacation rentals property management and resort real estate sales fit the company's strategy of selling off assets that aren't related to its Grand Ole Opry or its operations in the meetings and convention market.

In 2009 the company responded to weak earnings by cutting approximately 500 jobs across all areas of the business. Gaylord reported steep dip in profits in 2010 primarily due to harsh flooding in Nashville when the Cumberland River rose to historic levels flowing over protective levees. The flood resulted in property damage and temporary closures at its properties in Nashville causing lost revenues and an increase in expenses. Also in 2010 Gaylord sold its 50% stake in Corporate Magic back to that company's CEO.

The company changed its name to Ryman Hospitality Properties in 2012. It also converted to an REIT and sold the Gaylord brand to Marriott which now manages Ryman's hotel properties and certain other entertainment holdings.

EXECUTIVES

Evp Ryman Hospitality Properties; President Opry Entertainment Group, Stephen G. (Steve) Buchanan

Chairman And Ceo, Colin V. Reed, age 70, $782,830 total compensation

Svp Investments Design And Construction, Bennett D. Westbrook, age 51, $318,447 total compensation

President And Cfo, Mark Fioravanti, age 56, $469,407 total compensation

Svp Asset Management, Patrick Chaffin, age 44, $274,975 total compensation

Svp General Counsel And Secretary, Scott J. Lynn, age 44, $364,876 total compensation

Senior Vice President And Corporate Controller, Jennifer Hutcheson

Auditors: ERNST & YOUNG LLP NASHVILLE

LOCATIONS

HQ: RYMAN HOSPITALITY PROPERTIES, INC.
1 GAYLORD DR, NASHVILLE, TN 372141207
Phone: 615 316-6000
Web: WWW.RYMANHP.COM

PRODUCTS/OPERATIONS

2015 Sales

	$ mil.	% of total
Hospitality	994	91
Entertainment (previously Opry and Attractions)	97	9
Total	**1,092**	**100**

2015 Sales

	$ mil.	% of total
Food and beverage	461	42
Rooms	404	37
Other hotel revenue	129	12
Entertainment (previously Opry and Attractions)	97	9
Total	**1,092**	**100**

Select Operations

Hospitality
Gaylord Opryland Resort & Convention Center (Tennessee)
Gaylord Palms Resort & Convention Center (Florida)
Gaylord Texan Resort & Convention Center

Radisson Hotel at Opryland (Tennessee)
Attractions
Gaylord Springs Golf Links (golf club Tennessee)
General Jackson Showboat
Grand Ole Opry
Ryman Auditorium
Wildhorse Saloon
WSM-AM

COMPETITORS

CKX
CKX
Caesars Entertainment
Caesars Entertainment
Disney Parks & Resorts
Disney Parks & Resorts
Elvis Presley Enterprises
Elvis Presley Enterprises
Herschend Entertainment
Herschend Entertainment
Hershey Entertainment
Hershey Entertainment
Hilton Worldwide
Hilton Worldwide
Kennywood
Kennywood
Las Vegas Sands
Las Vegas Sands
Live Nation Entertainment
Live Nation Entertainment
MGM Resorts
MGM Resorts
Marriott
Marriott
New York Convention Center Operating Corporation
New York Convention Center Operating Corporation
SeaWorld
SeaWorld
Welk Group
Welk Group

HISTORICAL FINANCIALS
Company Type: Private

Income Statement

	ASSETS ($ mil.)	NET INCOME ($ mil.)	INCOME AS % OF ASSETS	EMPLOYEES
				FYE: December 31
12/16	2,405	159	6.6%	1,000
12/15	2,331	111	4.8%	—
12/14	2,413	126	5.2%	—
12/13	2,424	113	4.7%	—
Annual Growth	(0.3%)	12.0%	—	—

2016 Year-End Financials

Debt ratio: ——
Return on equity: 13.90%
Cash ($ mil.): 59
Current ratio: ——
Long-term debt ($ mil.): ——

Dividends
Yield: ——
Payout: ——
Market value ($ mil.): ——

S & T Bancorp Inc (Indiana, PA)

S&T Bancorp is the bank holding company for S&T Bank which boasts nearly $5 billion in assets and serves customers from some 60 branch offices in western Pennsylvania. Targeting individuals and local businesses the bank offers such standard retail products as checking savings and money market accounts CDs and credit cards. Business loans including commercial mortgages make up more than 80% of the company's loan portfolio. The bank also originates residential mortgages construction loans and consumer loans. Through subsidiaries S&T Bank sells life disability and commercial property/casualty insurance provides investment management services and advises the Stewart Capital Mid Cap Fund.

Operations

S&T Bancorp operates through three main business segments: Community Banking which offers traditional banking services and commercial and consumer loans; Wealth Management which boasts $2 billion in assets under management and administration and provides brokerage services trust and custodial services and investment advisory for affluent individuals and institutions; and Insurance which offers commercial property and casualty insurance group life and health coverage employee benefit services and personal insurance products through S&T Insurance Group LLC.

Its S&T Bancholding subsidiary provides investment services in the Wealth Management segment while its Stewart Capital Advisors subsidiary provides investment advisory services in the segment.

Overall S&T Bancorp generated 72% of its total revenue from loan interest (including fees) in 2014 plus another 6% from interest on its investment securities. About 10% of its total revenue came from debit and credit card fees and deposit account service charges while wealth management fees and insurance fees made up 6% and 3% of total revenue that year respectively.

Geographic Reach

Headquartered in Indiana Pennsylvania S&T Bancorp boasts branches in a dozen counties in the state including: Allegheny Armstrong Blair Butler Cambria Centre Clarion Clearfield Indiana Jefferson Washington and Westmoreland counties. It also has loan production offices in northeast and central Ohio and in western New York.

Sales and Marketing

Targeting both individuals and local businesses S&T Bancorp spent $3.32 million on marketing in 2014 up from the $2.93 million and $3.21 million it spent in 2013 and 2012 respectively.

Financial Performance

S&T Bancorp's revenue has slowly declined in recent years due to shrinking interest margins on loans amidst the low-interest environment. The firm's profits however have been rising thanks to declining loan loss provisions as its loan portfolio's credit quality has improved with the strengthened economy.

Following several years of top-line declines the bank's revenue inched up by nearly 1% to $206.86 million in 2014. The rise was mostly thanks to higher interest income as overall earning-asset balances grew by nearly 7% during the year reflecting the bank's growing loan business and increased investment securities assets. Wealth Management fees also continued to grow rising by 6% during the year.

Higher revenue coupled with lower interest expenses on deposits and a $6.6 million reduction in loan loss provisions in 2014 drove S&T Bancorp's net income higher by 15% to $57.91 million. S&T's operating cash levels fell by 9% to $78.1 million for the year after adjusting its earnings for non-cash items mostly related to its net proceeds from sales of its mortgage loans originated-for-sale.

Strategy

S&T Bancorp reiterated in 2015 that its growth strategy is centered around organic growth in existing and new markets and growth through strategic acquisitions that introduce new lines of business. Its 2015 acquisition of Integrity Bancshares for example expanded S&T's footprint eastward across four counties in Pennsylvania and added millions of dollars worth of new loan business. Also that year the bank entered the western part

of New York for the first time with the opening of a new loan production office in the region.

In late 2012 the bank extended its operations into its neighbor Ohio when it opened a handful of branches in Akron. That same year the bank acquired Mainline Bancorp and Gateway Bank of Pennsylvania bolstering its presence in its core western Pennsylvania market.

Mergers and Acquisitions

In March 2015 S&T Bancorp purchased Camp Hill-based Integrity Bancshares for $155 million adding $860 million in assets and eight branches expanding S&T's geographic footprint eastward into Cumberland Dauphin Lancaster and York counties in Pennsylvania. S&T added that the acquisition positioned the bank in high-growth markets within the state and added experienced members to the bank's loan team.

In 2012 the bank acquired Mainline Bancorp and Gateway Bank of Pennsylvania. Both transactions served to expand S&T's presence in western Pennsylvania.

EXECUTIVES

Svp Operations And Technology, David P. Ruddock, age 56, $265,000 total compensation

Executive Vice President, Tony E Kallsen

President And Ceo S&t And S&t Bank, Todd D. Brice, age 55, $525,000 total compensation

Evp And Retail Banking Division Manager, Richard A. (Rich) Fiscus

Sevp And Cfo, Mark Kochvar, age 57, $278,000 total compensation

Sevp And Chief Lending Officer, David G. Antolik, age 51, $302,000 total compensation

Evp And Chief Investment Officer Wealth Management, Malcolm E. Polley, age 55

Sevp Chief Risk Officer And Secretary, Ernest J. Draganza

Evp And Deputy Chief Credit Officer, William (Bill) Kametz

Sevp And Chief Credit Officer, Patrick Haberfield

Sevp And Chief Banking Officer, Rebecca Stapleton

Evp And Commercial Loan Officer, Steve Drahnak

Evp And Chief Audit Executive, LaDawn D. Yesho

Evp, David Richards

Evp Marketing Division Manager, Rob Jorgenson

Evp And Cio, Jim Mill

Evp And Manager, Robert Jogrenson

Sevp And Market Executive, Thomas J. Sposito

Market President Central Pennsylvania, Jordan Space

Market President Northeast Ohio, Steve Hendricks

Vice President Mortgage Underwriting Manager, Christine Rumbaugh

Vice President Marketing, Kelly Thomas

Vice President Credit Analysis Operation Manager, Dennis Scott

Vice President Marketing, Kelly Corrinne

Vice President Network Operations Manager, Ron Todd

Vice President Community Banking, Tammy Czyz

Vice President Regional Manager, Megan White

Vice President And Manager Benefits, Sandy Loperfito

Chairman S&t And S&t Bank, Charles G. Urtin

Vice Chairman S&t And S&t Bank, Christine J. Toretti, age 61

Auditors: Ernst & Young LLP

LOCATIONS

HQ: S & T Bancorp Inc (Indiana, PA)
800 Philadelphia Street, Indiana, PA 15701
Phone: 800 325-2265
Web: www.stbancorp.com

PRODUCTS/OPERATIONS

2014 Sales

	% of total
Interest	
Loans including fees	72
Investment securities & other	6
Noninterest	
Wealth management fees	6
Debit and credit card fees	5
Service charges on deposit accounts	5
Insurance fees	3
Others	3
Total	**100**

Selected Subsidiaries

9th Street Holdings Inc.
Commonwealth Trust Credit Life Insurance Company (50%)
S&T Bank
    S&T Insurance Group LLC
    S&T-Evergreen Insurance LLC
    S&T Bancholdings Inc.
    S&T Professional Resources Group LLC
    S&T Settlement Services LLC
    Stewart Capital Advisors LLC

COMPETITORS

AmeriServ Financial	First Commonwealth
Citizens Financial	Financial
Group	Northwest Bancshares
F.N.B. (PA)	PNC Financial
Fidelity Bancorp (PA)	

HISTORICAL FINANCIALS

Company Type: Public

Income Statement

FYE: December 31

	ASSETS ($ mil.)	NET INCOME ($ mil.)	INCOME AS % OF ASSETS	EMPLOYEES
12/17	7,060	72	1.0%	1,080
12/16	6,943	71	1.0%	1,080
12/14	4,964	57	1.2%	945
12/13	4,533	50	1.1%	948
12/12	4,526	34	0.8%	1,027
Annual Growth	**9.3%**	**16.4%**	**—**	**1.0%**

2017 Year-End Financials

Debt ratio: 1.32%	No. of shares (mil.): 34
Return on equity: 8.46%	Dividends
Cash ($ mil.): 117	Yield: 0.0%
Current ratio: —	Payout: 39.2%
Long-term debt ($ mil.): —	Market value ($ mil.): 1,392

	STOCK PRICE ($) FY Close	P/E High/Low	PER SHARE ($) Earnings	Dividends	Book Value
12/17	39.81	21 16	2.09	0.82	25.28
12/16	39.04	19 11	2.05	0.77	24.12
12/14	29.81	16 11	1.95	0.68	20.42
12/13	25.31	15 10	1.70	0.61	19.21
12/12	18.07	20 13	1.18	0.60	18.08
Annual Growth	**17.1%**	**— —**	**12.1%**	**6.4%**	**6.9%**

S&P Global Inc

Say "AAA!". One of the big-three credit ratings agencies S&P Global (formerly McGraw-Hill Financial) assigns companies local governments and countries its well-known credit scores ranging from D (lowest) to AAA (highest). It also assigns ratings to corporate or municipal bonds and other individual debt issues. S&P Global's other businesses include S&P Global Market Intelligence S&P Dow Jones Indices and S&P Global Platts. Its largest market is the US which generates around 60% of the company's revenue. After it sold its education and construction businesses in 2016 the company changed its name from McGraw-Hill Financial to S&P Global.

Operations
S&P Global has four reportable segments: Ratings, Market and Commodities Intelligence; S&P Dow Jones Indices; and Global Platts.

The Ratings segment generates roughly 50% of S&P Global's total sales and provides credit ratings research and analytics to investors issuers and other market participants.

The Market and Commodities Intelligence accounts for around 40% of sales and helps the financial community track performance improve investment returns perform risk analysis and develop mitigation strategies. It comprises three business lines: Desktop Data Management Solutions and Risk Services.

S&P Dow Jones accounts for around 10% of sales and maintains a range of stock indices for investors including the Dow Jones Industrial Average and S&P 500.

S&P Global Platts a separate division since the start of 2018 provides information and benchmark prices for the commodity and energy markets.

Geographic Reach
New York-based S&P Global has more than 100 offices worldwide including around 30 in the US. The US is S&P Global's largest market at around 60% of sales. Europe generates some 25% and the Asia/Pacific region more than 10%. The Global Platts division is headquartered in London.

Sales and Marketing
S&P Global's Ratings segment serves investors corporations governments municipalities commercial and investment banks insurance companies asset managers and other debt issuers.

The company's Market and Commodities Intelligence segment serves investment managers investment banks private equity firms insurance companies commercial banks corporations professional services firms and government agencies and regulators; as well as producers traders and intermediaries within energy metals and agriculture markets.

S&P Global Platts markets to traders analysts risk managers and purchasing agents in public and private sector organizations.

The company spends millions per year on advertising and promotional costs.

Financial Performance
S&P Global's revenue has been growing year on year in all segments and major territories.

In fiscal 2017 sales grew a further 7% to $6.1 billion. Higher bank loan and corporate bond ratings revenue drove strong growth in the Ratings segment while Indices grew its revenue 15% thanks to an increase in assets under management for exchange traded funds and mutual funds. Gains in Ratings and Indices were partially offset by disposals in the Market and Commodities Intelligence segment which saw revenue shrink 5% as a result. During 2017 it sold S&P Securities Evaluations S&P Credit Market Analysis and J.D. Power.

Net income fell to $1.5 billion from a high of $2.1 billion in 2016 largely a result of the $1.1 billion gain on the sale of the J.D. Power and Associates business recorded in 2016. Underlying profitability was slightly stronger in 2017 than 2016 due to lower expense relating to disposals.

Cash from operations increased 29% to $2.0 billion due higher results from operations partially offset by the timing of tax payments.

Strategy
Over the last several years S&P Global has sold off all its businesses not relating to its core mission of providing financial and credit information. Disposals have included its education business its construction business and J.D. Power (marketing information services).

Strong demand for S&P's Global Platts services led to the company separating it out as a distinct reportable segment. It will continue to develop its product offerings and analytic capabilities and pursue growth in new markets and geographies.

Mergers and Acquisitions
In April 2018 S&P Global completed its acquisition of Kensho Technologies a provider of analytics artificial intelligence machine learning and data visualization systems. Its primary customers are Wall Street banks investment institutions and the National Security community.

In February 2018 the company acquired Panjiva Inc. a privately-held company that provides global supply chain insights by leveraging data science and technology to make sense of large unstructured datasets.

EXECUTIVES

Vice President Technology, Rosalin Danner
President And Ceo, Douglas L. (Doug) Peterson, age 59, $1,000,000 total compensation
President S&p Global Platts, Martin Fraenkel
Chief Global Economist And Head Of Global Economics And Research, Paul Sheard, age 64
President S&p Global Ratings, John L. Berisford, age 54, $600,000 total compensation
Evp And General Counsel, Steven J. (Steve) Kemps, age 54, $204,167 total compensation
Managing Director And Ceo Crisil, Ashu Suyash, age 51
Evp And Cfo, Ewout L. Steenbergen, age 49, $99,432 total compensation
Ceo S&p Dow Jones Indices, Alexander J. (Alex) Matturri, age 59, $493,750 total compensation
Evp Public Affairs, Courtney Geduldig
President S&p Global Market Intelligence, Michael A. (Mike) Chinn, $152,308 total compensation
Evp Human Resources, France M. Gingras, age 53
Cio, Swamy Kocherlakota
Vice President Enterprise Services, Chris Kulczytzky
Vice President Strategy And Finance, Cari Lawless
Vice President Of Marketing, Connie Howard
Vice President International Affairs, Cynthia Baraddon
Vice President Investor Relations, Chip Merritt
Vice President, Maryann Johnston
National Account Manager, Kay Makanju
Senior Vice President, Peter Scheschuk
Senior Vice President And Treasurer, Edward Haran
Vice President Global Channel Sales And Alliances, Dominic Camillo
Vice President Senior Sales Manager, Bill Eggers
National Accounts Manager, Nicole Nicdao
Vice President Marketing, Cynthia Sejas
Vice President Content Specialists, Shyam Wadhwa
Vice President Client Development, Rosemarie Dezenzo
Chairman, Charles E. (Ed) Haldeman, age 69
Auditors: Ernst & Young LLP

LOCATIONS

HQ: S&P Global Inc
55 Water Street, New York, NY 10041
Phone: 212 438-1000
Web: www.spglobal.com

2017 Sales

	$ mil.	% of total
US	3,658	60
Europe	1,473	24
Asia	594	10
Other regions	338	6
Total	**6,063**	**100**

PRODUCTS/OPERATIONS

2017 Sales

	$ mil.	% of total
Market and Commodities Intelligence	2,452	40
Ratings	2,988	48
Indices	733	12
Adjustments	(110)	-
Total	**6,063**	**100**

COMPETITORS

A.M. Best	Fitch Ratings Inc.
Bloomberg L.P.	MSCI
D&B	Moody's
DBRS	Morningstar
Fair Isaac	Thomson Reuters

HISTORICAL FINANCIALS
Company Type: Public

Income Statement
FYE: December 31

	REVENUE ($ mil.)	NET INCOME ($ mil.)	NET PROFIT MARGIN	EMPLOYEES
12/17	6,063	1,496	24.7%	20,400
12/16	5,661	2,106	37.2%	20,000
12/15	5,313	1,156	21.8%	20,400
12/14	5,051	(115)	—	17,000
12/13	4,875	1,376	28.2%	17,000
Annual Growth	**5.6%**	**2.1%**	**—**	**4.7%**

2017 Year-End Financials

Debt ratio: 37.87%
Return on equity: 219.84%
Cash ($ mil.): 2,779
Current ratio: 1.35
Long-term debt ($ mil.): 3,170

No. of shares (mil.): 253
Dividends
  Yield: 0.0%
  Payout: 28.3%
Market value ($ mil.): 42,977

	STOCK PRICE ($) FY Close	P/E High/Low		PER SHARE ($) Earnings	Dividends	Book Value
12/17	169.40	30	19	5.78	1.64	2.80
12/16	107.54	16	10	7.94	1.44	2.52
12/15	98.58	25	20	4.21	1.32	0.73
12/14	88.98	—		(0.42)	1.20	1.79
12/13	78.20	15	9	4.91	3.62	4.80
Annual Growth (12.6%)	**21.3%**	**—**	**—**	**4.2%**	**(18.0%)**	

Safety Insurance Group, Inc.

Buckle up Bostonians car safety first! Safety Insurance Group through subsidiaries Safety Insurance Safety Indemnity Insurance and Safety Property and Casualty sells property/casualty insurance exclusively in Massachusetts Maine and New Hampshire. It is one of the top private passenger automobile and commercial automobile insurers in the region controlling more than 10% of the markets in its home state. Safety Insurance also provides homeowners dwelling fire personal umbrella and business-owner policies; it cross-sells its non-auto property/casualty products to increase its share of the market. The firm sells its products through more than 920 independent agents and more than 1100 offices.

Geographic Reach
Safety Insurance operates in Massachusetts Maine and New Hampshire.

Sales and Marketing

The company distributes its policies through more than 920 independent agents in some 1102 offices.

Auto insurance makes up the lion's share of the group's written premiums with private passenger auto insurance contributing 60% of its direct written premiums Homeowners insurance accounts for about 20% of written premiums while commercial automobile insurance accounts for about 15%.

In 2015 Safety Insurance spent $1.9 million on advertising down from $2.1 million in each of 2014 and 2013.

Financial Performance

Revenue has been rising for the past five years. It grew 2% to $798 million in 2015 thanks to growth in its commercial automobile and homeowners insurance businesses which was largely attributed to the company's efforts to cross-sell those products to existing personal automobile coverage customers. However Safety Insurance saw a decline in investment income that year.

The company also saw its first net loss that year. It lost a net $14 million due to higher loss and loss adjustment expenses brought about by record snowfall in Massachusetts (which resulted in higher catastrophe and non-catastrophe claims).

Following suit cash flow from operations fell 77% to $23 million.

Strategy

Safety Insurance's strategy for growth includes the possibility of reaching out beyond its core market and entering new territories although this has been done on a limited basis. Another measure the company takes to build business is to lower costs by bundling policies (homeowners and auto for instance) to attract and retain customers. Additionally Safety Insurance has been investing in technology to improve the way independent agents serve its customers.

EXECUTIVES

Vp Cfo And Secretary, William J. Begley, age 63, $400,000 total compensation

Vp Property Claims, David E. Krupa, age 57, $210,796 total compensation

Vp Underwriting, James D. Berry, age 58, $263,682 total compensation

President And Ceo, George M. Murphy, age 51, $350,000 total compensation

Vp Insurance Operations, Ann M. McKeown

Vp Casualty Claims, Paul J. Narciso, age 54

Vp Management Information Systems, Stephen A. Varga, age 50

Vp Marketing, John P. Drago

Auditors: PricewaterhouseCoopers LLP

LOCATIONS

HQ: Safety Insurance Group, Inc.
20 Custom House Street, Boston, MA 02110
Phone: 617 951-0600   **Fax:** 617 603-4837
Web: www.safetyinsurance.com

PRODUCTS/OPERATIONS

2015 Sales

	% of total
Net earned premiums	92
Net investment income	5
Finance & other service income	2
Earnings from partnership investments	1
Adjustments	-
Total	**100**

COMPETITORS

AIG	Plymouth Rock
Allstate	Assurance
Ameriprise	Preferred Mutual
Arbella Insurance	Progressive
Electric Insurance	Corporation
Foremost Insurance	Quincy Mutual
GEICO	Travelers of
Liberty Mutual	Massachusetts
MAPFRE USA	Vermont Mutual
OneBeacon	

HISTORICAL FINANCIALS

Company Type: Public

Income Statement
FYE: December 31

	ASSETS ($ mil.)	NET INCOME ($ mil.)	INCOME AS % OF ASSETS	EMPLOYEES
12/17	1,807	62	3.5%	623
12/16	1,758	64	3.7%	643
12/15	1,703	(13)	—	622
12/14	1,675	59	3.5%	610
12/13	1,625	61	3.8%	605
Annual Growth	**2.7%**	**0.4%**	**—**	**0.7%**

2017 Year-End Financials

Debt ratio: —
Return on equity: 9.10%
Cash ($ mil.): 41
Current ratio: —
Long-term debt ($ mil.): —
No. of shares (mil.): 15
Dividends
  Yield: 0.0%
  Payout: 73.1%
Market value ($ mil.): 1,224

	STOCK PRICE ($) FY Close	P/E High/Low	Earnings	PER SHARE ($) Dividends	Book Value
12/17	80.40	20 16	4.10	3.00	46.06
12/16	73.70	17 12	4.27	2.80	44.27
12/15	56.38	— —	(0.93)	2.80	42.70
12/14	64.01	17 13	3.91	2.60	47.19
12/13	56.30	14 12	3.98	2.40	45.18
Annual Growth	**9.3%**	**— —**	**0.7%**	**5.7%**	**0.5%**

SAINT PAUL REGIONAL WATER SERVICES

EXECUTIVES

Gen Mgr, Steve Schneider

Project Engineer, Issac Afwerke

LOCATIONS

HQ: SAINT PAUL REGIONAL WATER SERVICES
1900 RICE ST, SAINT PAUL, MN 551136810
Phone: 651 266-3530
Web: WWW.WASHINGTONBIOTECH.COM

HISTORICAL FINANCIALS

Company Type: Private

Income Statement
FYE: December 31

	REVENUE ($ mil.)	NET INCOME ($ mil.)	NET PROFIT MARGIN	EMPLOYEES
12/15	57,542	13,928	24.2%	247
12/93	24	2	10.0%	—
12/92	24	3	13.1%	—
Annual Growth	**40.2%**	**44.0%**	**—**	**—**

2015 Year-End Financials

Debt ratio: —
Return on equity: 24.20%
Cash ($ mil.): 201
Current ratio: 0.40
Long-term debt ($ mil.): —
Dividends
  Yield: —
  Payout: —
Market value ($ mil.): —

Salesforce.Com Inc

Salesforce.com could fill the sky with its clouds. The company offers cloud-based applications that manage employee collaboration as well as customer information for sales (Salesforce Sales Cloud) marketing (Salesforce Marketing Cloud) and customer support (Salesforce Service Cloud). Other products offer e-commerce analytics and social media tools through cloud-based applications. Salesforce counts more than 150000 users of its customer relationship management (CRM) software and its customers come from a variety of industries including financial services telecommunications manufacturing and entertainment. It generates most of its revenue in the US.

Operations

Besides its big three cloud products ? Sales Cloud Service Cloud and Marketing Cloud Salesforce.com offers several others that help companies manage their relationships with customers.

They include: Commerce Cloud which provides e-commerce experience tools for web mobile social and store environments; Community Cloud which helps companies create and manage branded digital destinations for customers partners and employees; IoT (Internet of Things) Cloud which helps companies collect information from connected devices products sensors and apps; Analytics Cloud which helps an employee across explore business data and uncover from any device; and Salesforce Quip a productivity tool designed for teams.

Salesforce also offers consulting services for deployment training and design and integration.

Most of the company?s revenue comes from its subscription and support segment which accounts for nearly 95% while the rest comes from professional and other services.

The company runs many of its cloud services on Amazon Web Services Google and IBM in international markets.

Geographic Reach

More than two-thirds of Salesforce.com?s sales come from customers in the US with other countries in the Americas supplying about 7%. Customers in Europe account for about 20% of revenue and those in the Asia/Pacific region generate about 10%.

Sales and Marketing

Salesforce.com counts more than 150000 users from small businesses with one subscription to large enterprises with thousands. With such a large customer base no one customer counts for more than 5% of sales.

The company uses a direct sales force made up of telephone sales reps based in regional hubs and field sales reps in territories close to their customers. It also works with consulting firms systems integrators and others to find customers. For successful sales Salesforce pays a fee based on the first-year subscription revenue generated by the referred customers.

Salesforce spends about 45% of revenue on sales and marketing a level the company expects to maintain as it seeks more customers and builds awareness. The company continues to ramp up advertising spending which has increased about 20% in recent years.

Financial Performance

Salesforce capped a decade of rising revenue with a 25% increase to $10.5 billion in 2018 (ended January) from 2017. The increase was paced by a 25% jump in subscription and support revenue driven by increases in new business which includes new customers and upgrades and additional subscriptions from existing customers. Demandware acquired in July 2016 contributed about $288 million in 2018 compared to $120 million in half of 2017. Professional services revenue rose 21% in 2018 from 2017 because of an increase in the number of customers. Geographically sales were higher in all regions.

Salesforce kept 2018 costs in line with 2017 as a percentage of revenue but paid more in taxes in 2018 than 2017. That reduced net income to about $127 million in 2018 from about $180 million the year before.

Cash on hand totaled about $2.5 billion in 2018 compared to about $1.6 billion in 2017.

Strategy

In 2018 Salesforce.com?s record high in sales put the company on Cloud 9. Its biggest business Sales Cloud accounted for $3.5 billion in revenue by itself making it bigger than some independent cloud software companies. The company?s other strong performer Service Cloud brought in another $2.8 billion. While those are the big moneymakers Salesforce?s customers generally buy services from more than one of the company?s clouds.

To strengthen those clouds Salesforce has injected artificial intelligence into them. Called Einstein the AI helps Salesforce?s customers more effectively analyze data that help them better understand their customers. Salesforce sees Einstein as an advantage in attracting new customers as well as tempting current customers to upgrade their services.

A key move made in 2017 was the acquisition of Demandware. At a price of $2.8 billion it was Salesforce?s biggest purchase in its history. The deal added e-commerce capabilities to Salesforce?s offerings in addition to its customer relationship management products. Demandware was renamed Commerce Cloud in Salesforce and accounted for about $288 million in revenue in its first full year as part of Salesforce. The acquisition gave Salesforce another product to offer its customers and it exposed the company to another set of customers.

Mergers and Acquisitions

In 2017 Salesforce.com agreed to buy Mulesoft which develops software for linking applications for about $6.5 billion. With the addition of Mulesoft's technologies Salesforce can help its customers connect information throughout their companies across public and private clouds and data sources. Mulesoft which went public in 2017 has posted higher annual revenue but has not made a profit. The deal Salesforce's most expensive was expected to close in mid-2018.

Salesforce added to its cloud products with its 2016 acquisition of Demandware for $2.8 billion. As a part of Salesforce Demandware became Commerce Cloud an integration of its e-commerce capabilities with Salesforce's customer relationship management offerings.

Other acquisitions in the company 2017 fiscal year (ended January) were SteelBrick Inc. which automates the quote-to-cash process; MetaMind Inc. natural language processing and image recognition across the Salesforce clouds; BeyondCore Inc. smart data discovery technology for structured data sources; Quip Inc. productivity software; and Krux Digital Inc. a data management platform.

EXECUTIVES

Chairman And Ceo, Marc Benioff, age 53, $1,550,000 total compensation

President And Chief Strategy Officer, Alexandre (Alex) Dayon, age 50, $900,000 total compensation

Vice Chairman President And Coo, Keith G. Block, age 56, $1,150,000 total compensation

President Global Customer Success And Salesforce Latin America, Maria Martinez, age 60

President And Cfo, Mark J. Hawkins, age 58, $750,000 total compensation

Evp Global Real Estate, Elizabeth Pinkham

President And Chief Product Officer, Bret Taylor

President Legal And General Counsel, Amy E. Weaver, age 50

Evp Corporate Relations And Chief Philanthropy Officer, Suzanne DiBianca

President And Chief People Officer, Cindy Robbins, age 45

Executive Vice President, Tony Owens

Executive Vice President Operations And Mobility, Todd Pierce

Vice President Global Operations Salesforce University, Shane Anastasi

Senior Vice President, Tom Long

Senior Vice President App Cloud And Pardot Marketing, Shannon Duffy

Vp Admin Marketing, Sarah Franklin

Area Vice President, Philip Klebba

Vice President, Anil Dindigal

Evp Product And Solutions Marketing, Stephanie Buscemi

Vice President Of Engineering For Data Com, Alex Hu

Senior Vice President Global Solutions Engineerin, John Defoe

Senior Vice President Manufacturing And Consumer Goods Industries Salesforce.com, Cynthia Bolt

Svp Communities Engineering, Stephen Ayers

Area Vice President Federal Sales, Dan Davis

Vice President Western U.s. Sales Analytics Cloud, Arym Diamond

Regional Vice President, Jeffrey Pope

Vice President Salesforce, Dan Whalen

Regional Vice President West Area Enterprise Key Accounts, Grant Wood

Vice President, Mary Heston

Regional Vice President Customer Success, Israel Forst

Regional Vice President, Craig Lashmet

Regional Vice President, Sheldon Buytenhuys

Regional Vice President Enterprise Accounts, Dick Cotter

Vice President Customer Intelligence, Ashfaq Mohiuddin

Regional Vice President Public Sector Customers For Life, Tom Gardner

Regional Vice President, David Rubinstein

Regional Vice President, Joe Haney

Regional Vice President Success Services, Jon Lokay

Regional Vice President, Tim Murdoch

Regional Vice President Commercial Sales, David Jeffrey

Vp Global Sales Compensation Design And Operations, Nandini Ramaswamy

Svp Enterprise Americas, John Vitalie

Vice President Northern Europe, Renzo Taal

Regional Vice President, Yasuhide Inoue

Svp And Gm Salesforce Marketing Cloud Japac, Lee Hawksley

Regional Vice President Middle East And Africa, Richard McGuinness

Regional Vice President Asia Pacific Platform Analytics Service Cloud, Robert Wickham

Regional Vice President Commercial Sales Latam, Fernando Bertolla

Senior Vice President Finance, Rafe Brown

Vp Revenue Operations Products And Enablement, Heather Atkinson

Senior Vice President Infrastructure, Vijay Gill

Senior Vice President Total Rewards And Mobility, Stan Dunlap

Vice President Social Products, Margaret Francis

Vice President Program Executive, Natalie Petouhoff

Regional Vice President West Pardot At, Daniel Williams

Auditors: Ernst & Young LLP

LOCATIONS

HQ: Salesforce.Com Inc
Salesforce Tower, 415 Mission Street, 3rd Fl, San Francisco, CA 94105
Phone: 415 901-7000
Web: www.salesforce.com

2018 Sales

	$ mil.	% of total
Americas	7,579	72
Europe	1,903	18
Asia/Pacific	997	10
Total	**10,480**	**100**

Selected Mergers and Acquisitions

FY2017
Demandware ($2.8 billion e-commerce software)
SteelBrick Inc. (quote-to-cash automation software)
Quip Inc. (productivity software)
Krux Digital Inc. (data management platform)
FY2013
ExactTarget ($2.5 billion email marketing software)
FY2012
Buddy Media ($690 million social media marketing software)
GoInstant ($50 million collaboration software)
Jigsaw ($140 million business contact data provider)
FY2011
Assistly ($58 million customer service software)
Dimdim (collaboration software)
Heroku ($210 million app development platform)
Manymoon ($13 million social productivity app)
Radian6 ($320 million social networking software)
Model Metrics ($66 million consultancy)
Rypple (social performance management software)

PRODUCTS/OPERATIONS

2018 Sales

	$ mil.	% of total
Subscription & support	9,710	93
Professional services & other	769	7
Total	**10,480**	**100**

COMPETITORS

CDC Software	Microsoft Dynamics
Google	NetSuite
Hewlett Packard Enterprise	Oracle
IBM	SAP
Infor Global	Sage Software
KANA	ServiceNow
	SugarCRM

HISTORICAL FINANCIALS

Company Type: Public

Income Statement

FYE: January 31

	REVENUE ($ mil.)	NET INCOME ($ mil.)	NET PROFIT MARGIN	EMPLOYEES
01/18	10,480	127	1.2%	29,000
01/17	8,391	179	2.1%	25,000
01/16	6,667	(47)	—	19,000
01/15	5,373	(262)	—	16,000
01/14	4,071	(232)	—	13,300
Annual Growth	**26.7%**	**—**		**21.5%**

2018 Year-End Financials

Debt ratio: 8.18%
Return on equity: 1.51%
Cash ($ mil.): 2,543
Current ratio: 0.92
Long-term debt ($ mil.): 694

No. of shares (mil.): 729
Dividends
Yield: —
Payout: —
Market value ($ mil.): 83,138

	STOCK PRICE ($) FY Close	P/E High/Low	PER SHARE ($) Earnings	Dividends	Book Value
01/18	113.91	632437	0.17	0.00	12.87
01/17	79.10	322208	0.26	0.00	10.60
01/16	68.06	— —	(0.07)	0.00	7.46
01/15	56.45	— —	(0.42)	0.00	6.11
01/14	60.53	— —	(0.39)	0.00	5.02
Annual Growth	17.1%	— —	—	—	26.5%

Sandy Spring Bancorp Inc

Sandy Spring Bancorp is the holding company for Sandy Spring Bank which operates around 50 branches in the Baltimore and Washington DC metropolitan areas. Founded in 1868 the bank is one of the largest and oldest headquartered in Maryland. It provides standard deposit services including checking and savings accounts money market accounts and CDs. Commercial and residential real estate loans account for nearly three-quarters of the company's loan portfolio; the remainder is a mix of consumer loans business loans and equipment leases. The company also offers personal investing services wealth management trust services insurance and retirement planning.

Operations

Sandy Spring Bancorp's nonbank subsidiaries include money manager West Financial Services and Sandy Spring Insurance which sells annuities and operates insurance agencies Chesapeake Insurance Group and Neff & Associates.

Financial Performance

The company's revenue increased in fiscal 2013 compared to the previous year. It reported $196.9 million in revenue for fiscal 2013 after bringing in revenue of $190.8 million in fiscal 2012.

The company's net income also went up in fiscal 2013 compared to the prior period. It claimed a profit of about $44 million in fiscal 2013 after netting a little more than $36 million in fiscal 2012.

Sandy Spring Bancorp's cash on hand increased by about $43 million in fiscal 2013 compared to fiscal 2012 levels.

Mergers and Acquisitions

In 2012 Sandy Spring Bancorp acquired CommerceFirst Bancorp a small Maryland bank with a strong Small Business Administration lending practice. The $25.4 million transaction added five branches to Sandy Spring Bank's network.

EXECUTIVES

Evp General Counsel And Secretary, Ronald E. Kuykendall, age 65, $279,039 total compensation
Evp Wealth Management Insurance Mortgage, R. Louis (Lou) Caceres, age 55, $333,865 total compensation
President And Ceo Bancorp And Bank, Daniel J. (Dan) Schrider, age 53, $600,692 total compensation
Evp And Cfo Bancorp And Bank, Philip J. Mantua, age 59, $333,192 total compensation
Evp And Cio, John D. Sadowski, age 54

Evp Commercial And Retail Banking, Joseph O'Brien, $355,038 total compensation
Evp And Chief Credit Officer, Ronda M. McDowell
Senior Vice President, Brian Schott
Assistant Vice President Information Technology, Steve Hyde
Vice President, Christopher Huang
Senior Business Analyst Assistant Vice President, Stephen Marsico
Vice President Marketing Communications Manager, Jennifer Schell
Assistant Vice President Team Leader, Tamika Daniels
Vice President Commercial Portfolio, Michael Irwin
Assistant Vice President Branch Manager, Bachi Baldeh
Vice President, Denise Kratz
Vice President Hris Project Administrator, Patti Boyle
Vice President, Bill Howland
Vice President Commercial Real Estate, Douglas Greene
Vice President, Jeff Richards
Vice President, Isaac Sterbenz
Vice President Commercial Lending, Heather Burke
Assistant Vice President Public Relations Specialist, Amanda Walsh
Vice President Mortgage Division, Bradley Preisinger
Senior Vice President Assistant Controller, Louise Basore
Assistant Vice President, Chrissy Niper
Senior Vice President, Scott Sims
Assistant Vice President Bsa Aml Administrator, Susan Booth
Vice President Portfolio Manager, Brian Lopes
Senior Vice President Commercial Relationship Manager, Wendy Lance
Vice President Advertising Manager, John Paparello
Vice President And Senior Investment Advisor, Boris Wessely
Senior Vice President, Mark Slatin
Vice President, Cathy Jeary
Vice President Manager Of Personal Trust Administration, Larry Arch
Senior Vice President, Glen Buco
Vice President Portfolio Manager, Christy Powell
Assistant Vice President, Mark Aswall
Vice President, Marc Meoli
Vice President, Jessica Butler
Vice President, James Holochuk
Vice President, Paul Macdonald
Vice President And Senior Investment Advisor, Jennifer Owen
Vice President Debit And Credit Card Product Manager, Ron Waters
Vice President, Diane Papich
Vice President, Donna Coursey
Vice President, Michael Mckeon
Transaction Services Vice President, Anne Clements
Senior Vice President Senior Relationship Manager, David Addison
Vice President, John Walker
Executive Vice President, Lou Caceres
Senior Vice President, Laurie Kramer
Assistant Vice President Loan Support, Barbara Nixon
Vice President Private Banking Division, Ann Conger
Vice President, Cave Katie
Senior Vice President Marketing, Amalia G Kastberg
Vice President, Alexis Vining
Vice President Relationship Manager Commercial Banking, Tim Kelley
Vice President Market Relationship Manager, Todd Levine
Vice President Mortgage Banker, Jeff Starcher

Card Systems And Operations Manager Vice President, Rebecca Kruse
Senior Vice President, Michael Acton
Vice President Small Business Lending, Tanya Speed
Chairman, Robert L. Orndorff, age 62
Auditors: Ernst & Young LLP

LOCATIONS

HQ: Sandy Spring Bancorp Inc
17801 Georgia Avenue, Olney, MD 20832
Phone: 301 774-6400
Web: www.sandyspringbank.com

PRODUCTS/OPERATIONS

2015 Sales

	$ mil.	% of total
Interest Income:		
Interest and fees on loans and leases	135	65
Interest and dividends on investment securities	22	11
Other	0	-
Non-interest Income:		
Wealth management income	19	10
Service charges on deposit accounts	7	4
Insurance agency commissions	5	2
Bank card fees	4	2
Mortgage banking activities	3	2
Other Income	9	4
Total	**208**	**100**

COMPETITORS

BB&T
Bank of America
Bay Bancorp
Capital One

Fulton Financial
OBA Financial Services
PNC Financial
SunTrust

HISTORICAL FINANCIALS

Company Type: Public

Income Statement

FYE: December 31

	ASSETS ($ mil.)	NET INCOME ($ mil.)	INCOME AS % OF ASSETS	EMPLOYEES
12/17	5,446	53	1.0%	754
12/16	5,091	48	0.9%	752
12/15	4,655	45	1.0%	737
12/14	4,397	38	0.9%	727
12/13	4,106	44	1.1%	725
Annual Growth	7.3%	4.6%	—	1.0%

2017 Year-End Financials

Debt ratio: —
Return on equity: 9.70%
Cash ($ mil.): 109
Current ratio: —
Long-term debt ($ mil.): —

No. of shares (mil.): 24
Dividends
Yield: 0.0%
Payout: 47.2%
Market value ($ mil.): 936

	STOCK PRICE ($) FY Close	P/E High/Low	PER SHARE ($) Earnings	Dividends	Book Value
12/17	39.02	21 17	2.20	1.04	23.50
12/16	39.99	20 12	2.00	0.98	22.32
12/15	26.96	16 13	1.84	0.90	21.58
12/14	26.08	18 15	1.52	0.76	20.83
12/13	28.19	16 11	1.77	0.64	19.98
Annual Growth	8.5%	— —	5.6%	12.9%	4.1%

Sanmina Corp

Contract manufacturer Sanmina makes the boards and components that make up many an electronic device. Starting with the design stage the company makes assembles and tests printed circuit boards. It also makes backplanes cable assemblies radio frequency and optical components and modules and memory modules. Besides products Sanmina provides services such as engineering materials management and order fulfillment. Its customers are OEMs in the healthcare defense medical aerospace telecommunications and technology industries among others. Sanmina operates about 25 manufacturing facilities on six continents. The California-based company gets more than 80% of its sales from outside the US.

Operations

Sanmina's Integrated Manufacturing Solutions unit (about 80% of sales) makes printed circuit boards optical and radio frequency modules and conducts assembly and testing. The Components Products and Services unit (about 20% of sales) makes interconnect systems and mechanical systems components in addition to memory and storage products.

The company has more than 12.5 million sq.ft. of manufacturing space.

Geographic Reach

Sanmina based in San Jose California operates nearly 75 facilities in some 25 countries. Mexico is the company's largest geographic segment accounting for about 30% of revenue. US customers account for 20% of revenue while China generates about 15%.

Sales and Marketing

Sanmina supplies OEMs primarily in the communications networks defense and aerospace industrial and semiconductor systems medical computing automotive sectors. The industrial medical defense and automotive market accounts for more than half of the company's sales communication network customers generate nearly 40% and the company's cloud business supplies some 10%.

The company depends on 10 customers for half of its sales. Two of them Nokia and Motorola Solutions each account for about 10% of Sanmina's revenue.

Sanmina sells through its direct sales force as well as representative sales firms.

Financial Performance

Sanmina posted higher revenue for the fifth year in a row with a 3.5% rise to $7.1 billion in 2018 (ended September) from 2017. In 2018 sales in the industrial medical defense and automotive end market increased about 8% on growth in medical products and automotive products while industrial products sales were lower. Sales were up 1.3% in the communications networks business but the cloud segment's sales fell 9.5%.

The company recorded a net loss of $95.5 due to about $30 million in restructuring charges and a $161 million tax expense related to the US Tax Cuts and Jobs Act.

Sanmina held $420 million in cash and equivalents at the end of 2018 compared to $407 million for 2017. The company's operating activities generated $156 million in 2018 while investing and financing activities used $116 million and $28 million respectively.

Strategy

As Sanmina pursues new business the company targets work with higher system complexity in heavily regulated markets. Those jobs carry higher margins and allow Sanmina to use the expertise it's built up in developing and making higher-end systems. As part of that strategy the company combined its medical business with its defense industrial and automotive segment.

In the communication networks business Sanmina expects that the arrival of 5G networks will create opportunities for growth. The company looks for demand for its capabilities in optical components and switches.

The company in 2018 began a restructuring in which it closed some facilities with more actions to follow.

The company maintains it is positioned to deal with trade tensions between the US and China saying that its worldwide footprint enables it to switch manufacturing locations to avoid tariffs. A prolonged trade dispute could stretch its coping strategy which has included passing on higher costs to customers.

Company Background

Jure Sola and Milan Madaric founded Sanmina in 1980 as Sanmina. Sola still serves as executive chairman of the company.

EXECUTIVES

Ceo, Robert K. (Bob) Eulau, age 56, $510,000 total compensation
Evp Europe And Asia Sales, Dennis R. Young, age 67, $350,000 total compensation
Svp And Cio, Manesh Patel
Evp Global Human Resources, Alan M. Reid, age 55, $290,000 total compensation
Evp And Cfo, David Anderson, age 58
Vp Business Development, Charlie Mason
Executive Vice President Memory Modul, Ralph Kaplan
Executive Vice President, Bob Cusick
Vice President Finance And Controller, Amy Jones
Vp Global Supply Management, John Yapp
Vice President Engineering, Mulugeta Abtew
Senior Vice President Strategy, Mark Carlton
Vice President Global Supply Management, Troy Hiner
Vice President And General Manager Shenzhen Ems Plant China, William Chui
Vice President Engineering And Technology Development, Jim Fuller
Vice President Corporate Development, George Chen
Vice President Quality Assurance And Ra, Tim McGinnis
Senior Vice President, Mike Mathews
Vice President Customer Supply Chains, Tom Pendergrass
Vice President Oem Platform Solutions, Brad Draves
Vice President Sales Operations Nemea, Trevor Black
Vice President Manufacturing, Norman Evans
Vice President, George Korolog
Senior Vice President Corporate Devel, Robin Walker
Vice President Information Technology, Barry Hegarty
Vice President, Carl Boklund
Vice President Corporate Finance, Lynne Sullivan
Vice President Ims Central Region, William Adams
Vice President General Manager, Alejandro Avila
Senior Vice President Sales, Ed Archer
Vice President Of Information Technology, Rick Russell
Vice President Finance Tcg, Ted Wilson
Senior Vice President Technology, Sundar Kamath
Senior Vice President, Vahid Ghassemian
Senior Vice President Operations, Sushil Dhiman
Vice President Business Development, Michael Sparacino
Senior Vice President Sales And Marketing Optical And Micro Electronics, Nat Mani
Vice President Internal Audit, Aroon Gudibande
Vice President Finance And Controller, Mark Harshbarger
Vice President Global Business Services, Jean-Marc Orozco
Vice President Quality Assurance Ra, Daniel Marinsik
Vice President Finance, Melissa Stillar
Vice President Of Marketing, Michael Sparcino

Vice President Information Technology, Steve Bruton
Senior Vice President, Robert Swift
Senior Vice President East Coast Operations, Jose Carrasquillo
Vice President Global Strategic Accounts, Pierre Atchison
Senior Vice President, Bob Moffat
Vice President Quality Assurance And Ra, Kok-kheong Chan
Senior Vice President Engineering, Jeffrey Thomas
Senior Vice President Quality And Operational Excell, Susaan Hughes
Senior Vice President, Kevin Walkup
Vice President Business Development, Scott Novak
Co-chairman And Ceo, Jure Sola, age 67
Board Member, Neil Bonke
Board Member, Joseph Licata
Auditors: PricewaterhouseCoopers LLP

LOCATIONS

HQ: Sanmina Corp
2700 N. First St., San Jose, CA 95134
Phone: 408 964-3500
Web: www.sanmina.com

2018 Sales

	$ mil.	% of total
Mexico	2,067	29
China	1,196	17
US	1,338	19
Malaysia	687	10
Other countries	1,819	25
Total	**7,110**	**100**

PRODUCTS/OPERATIONS

2018 Sales

	$ mil.	% of total
Industrial Medical Defense and Automotive	3,681	52
Communications Networks	2,684	38
Cloud Solutions	743	10
Total	**7,110**	**100**

2018 Sales

	$ mil.	% of total
IMS	58,485	80
CPS	1,458	20
Inter segment Revenue	(196.7)	-
Total	**7,110**	**100**

Selected Services

Backplane assembly
Cable assembly
Circuit assembly
Circuit fabrication
Configuration
Distribution
Enclosures
Engineering
Forward logistics
In-circuit testing
Inventory management
Materials management
Order fulfillment
Printed circuit board design
Reverse engineering
Sustaining engineering
System assembly and testing

COMPETITORS

Benchmark Electronics	Nam Tai
Celestica	Plexus
Flextronics	SMTC Corp.
Hon Hai	SYNNEX
Jabil	TTM Technologies
Lexmark	Venture Corp.
Molex	
Multi-Fineline Electronix	

HISTORICAL FINANCIALS
Company Type: Public

Income Statement
FYE: September 29

	REVENUE ($ mil.)	NET INCOME ($ mil.)	NET PROFIT MARGIN	EMPLOYEES
09/18	7,110	(95)	—	47,000
09/17*	6,868	138	2.0%	47,000
10/16	6,481	187	2.9%	45,397
10/15	6,374	377	5.9%	43,854
09/14	6,215	197	3.2%	43,101
Annual Growth	3.4%	—	—	2.2%

*Fiscal year change

2018 Year-End Financials
Debt ratio: 14.88%
Return on equity: (-6.14%)
Cash ($ mil.): 419
Current ratio: 1.26
Long-term debt ($ mil.): 14

No. of shares (mil.): 67
Dividends
  Yield: —
  Payout: —
Market value ($ mil.): 1,871

	STOCK PRICE ($) FY Close	P/E High/Low		PER SHARE ($) Earnings	Dividends	Book Value
09/18	27.60	—	—	(1.37)	0.00	21.73
09/17*	37.15	23	15	1.78	0.00	22.99
10/16	28.47	12	7	2.38	0.00	22.04
10/15	21.37	6	4	4.41	0.00	19.48
09/14	21.60	10	6	2.27	0.00	15.18
Annual Growth	6.3%	—	—	—	—	9.4%

*Fiscal year change

Santander Consumer USA Holdings Inc

This auto finance company aims to put credit-impaired car buyers in the driver's seat. Santander Consumer USA (SCUSA) makes subprime new and used vehicle loans to buyers at more than 14000 Chrysler Ford GM and Toyota dealerships throughout the US. The technology-driven company also originates loans through independent dealers such as CarMax banks and its direct-to-consumer website Roadloans.com. SCUSA also provides refinancing and cash-back refinancing services. While subprime loans make up more than 80% of its loan portfolio the company is looking to increase its prime loan business. Founded in 1995 SCUSA is owned by Spanish banking giant Banco Santander SA. The company went public in 2014.

IPO
Santander Consumer USA (SCUSA) went public in January 2014 with an offering valued at $1.5 billion. The IPO capitalizes on the rebound in auto sales as credit-impaired borrowers return to the car market. Post IPO Banco Santander owns 61% of SCUSA.

Financial Performance
The auto lender reported more than $2.9 billion in finance and other interest income in 2012 a 14% increase versus 2011.

Strategy
SCUSA is looking to expand its portfolio of prime loans through partnerships with automakers. To that end in February 2013 SCUSA entered into a 10-year agreement with Chrysler whereby it originates private-label loans and leases under the Chrysler Capital brand. The company relies on third-party banks and parent company Banco Santander for approximately $12 billion and $5 billion respectively in committed financing. It also has agreements with Bank of America and Sovereign to fund the Chrysler Capital business.

Company Background
In 2006 Banco Santander acquired a 90% stake in Drive Financial from HBOS and the company's founding partners for $651 million. Drive changed its name to Santander Consumer USA in 2008.

EXECUTIVES
Pres-Ceo, Scott Powell
Chb, William Rainer
V Chb, Stephen A Ferriss
Cfo, Juan Carlos Alvarez
Chief Hr Officer, Lisa Vanroekel
Sr Clo-General Counsel, Christopher Pfirrman
Board Member, William Muir
Board Member, Edith Holiday
Technical Writer, Jennifer Hensley
Process Coordinator, Jessica Clark
Auditors: PricewaterhouseCoopers LLP

LOCATIONS
HQ: Santander Consumer USA Holdings Inc
  1601 Elm Street, Suite 800, Dallas, TX 75201
Phone: 214 634-1110
Web: www.santanderconsumerusa.com

COMPETITORS
Ally Bank	Credit Acceptance
Bank of America	Ford Motor Credit
Capital One Auto Finance	GM Financial
	Toyota Motor Credit

HISTORICAL FINANCIALS
Company Type: Public

Income Statement
FYE: December 31

	ASSETS ($ mil.)	NET INCOME ($ mil.)	INCOME AS % OF ASSETS	EMPLOYEES
12/17	39,422	1,187	3.0%	5,076
12/16	38,539	766	2.0%	5,100
12/15	36,570	827	2.3%	5,100
12/14	32,342	766	2.4%	4,400
12/13	26,401	697	2.6%	4,100
Annual Growth	10.5%	14.2%	—	5.5%

2017 Year-End Financials
Debt ratio: 79.04%
Return on equity: 20.27%
Cash ($ mil.): 527
Current ratio: —
Long-term debt ($ mil.): —

No. of shares (mil.): 360
Dividends
  Yield: 0.0%
  Payout: 0.9%
Market value ($ mil.): 6,713

	STOCK PRICE ($) FY Close	P/E High/Low		PER SHARE ($) Earnings	Dividends	Book Value
12/17	18.62	6	3	3.30	0.03	17.98
12/16	13.50	7	4	2.13	0.00	14.60
12/15	15.85	11	7	2.31	0.00	12.36
12/14	19.61	12	8	2.15	0.15	10.20
Annual Growth	(1.3%)	—	—	11.3%	(33.1%)	15.2%

Santander Holdings USA Inc.

Santander Holdings USA is the parent company of Sovereign Bank which reigns in the Northeast with more than 700 branch locations. TheA bankA caters to individuals and small to midsized businesses offeringA deposits creditA cards insurance and investmentsA as well as commercial loans and mortgages (which together account for nearlyA half of its total portfolio) and residential mortgages and home equity loansA (more than a quarter).A Santander Holdings also owns a majority of Santander Consumer USA which purchases and services subprime car loans made byA auto dealerships and other companies.A Spain-based banking giant Banco Santander acquired the rest of Sovereign BancorpA it didn't already own in 2009.

EXECUTIVES
Vice President Compliance Officer, Steve Bertone
Vice President Strategic Marketing, Ayse Mccarthy
Vice President And Manager Commercial Real Estate Department, Frank Picone
Vice President, Donna Valente
Avp Credit Manager, Linda Beauchamp
Auditors: PricewaterhouseCoopers LLP

LOCATIONS
HQ: Santander Holdings USA Inc.
  75 State Street, Boston, MA 02109
Phone: 617 346-7200
Web: www.santanderbank.com

Selected Locations
Connecticut
Delaware
Maryland
Massachusetts
New Hampshire
New Jersey
New York
Pennsylvania
Rhode Island

PRODUCTS/OPERATIONS

2013 Sales

	$ mil.	% of total
Interest		
Loans	1,958	58
Investment securities	330	10
Deposits	6	-
Noninterest		
Equity method investment	426	12
Consumer banking fees	228	7
Commercial banking fees	199	6
Mortgage bankin revenue	122	4
Bank owned life insurance	57	3
Others	54	-
Total	**3,384**	**100**

COMPETITORS
Bank of America	M&T Bank
Citibank	PNC Financial
Citizens Financial Group	People's United Financial
Fulton Financial	TD Bank USA
HSBC USA	Webster Financial
JPMorgan Chase	Wells Fargo
KeyCorp	

HISTORICAL FINANCIALS

Company Type: Public

Income Statement   FYE: December 31

	REVENUE ($ mil.)	NET INCOME ($ mil.)	NET PROFIT MARGIN	EMPLOYEES
12/17	10,715	561	5.2%	17,000
12/16	10,745	362	3.4%	16,500
12/15	10,473	(1,454)	—	15,150
12/14	11,010	2,000	19.0%	14,000
12/13	3,383	628	18.6%	9,100
Annual Growth	33.4%	(2.8%)	—	16.9%

2017 Year-End Financials

Debt ratio: 30.40%	No. of shares (mil.): 530
Return on equity: 2.75%	Dividends
Cash ($ mil.): 6,519	Yield: 0.0%
Current ratio: 0.18	Payout: 1.7%
Long-term debt ($ mil.): 39,003	Market value ($ mil.): 13,620

	STOCK PRICE ($) FY Close	P/E High/Low	PER SHARE ($) Earnings	Dividends	Book Value
12/17	25.68	— —	(0.00)	1.83	39.94
12/16	25.73	— —	(0.00)	1.83	37.00
12/15	25.85	— —	(0.00)	1.83	32.32
12/14	25.53	— —	(0.00)	1.83	34.96
12/13	25.39	— —	(0.00)	1.83	26.03
Annual Growth	0.3%	— —	—	(0.0%)	11.3%

Schein (Henry) Inc

From Poughkeepsie to Prague Henry Schein outfits dental offices around the world with everything they need. The company is a leading global distributor of dental supplies equipment and pharmaceuticals. Henry Schein provides everything from delicate hand-held tools up to X-ray equipment and patient chair accesories as well as office supplies and anesthetics. But the company isn't only interested in teeth: It also supplies doctors' offices veterinarians and other office-based health care providers with diagnostic kits surgical tools drugs vaccines and animal health products. Other offerings include practice management software repair services and financing.

HISTORY

For more than 50 years Henry Schein distributed drugs made by Schein Pharmaceuticals. In 1992 management spun off the drug business and led by former accountant Stanley Bergman began acquiring other dental supply companies at a terrific rate: 34 between 1994 and 1996 alone.

The company went public in 1995 and bought more than a dozen businesses. These purchases which included product marketer Vertex Corporation's distribution unit moved Henry Schein into the medical and veterinary supply fields. The purchase of Schein Dental Equipment (founded by Marvin Schein) boosted per-customer sales by adding big-ticket merchandise to the product mix.

Acquisitions continued hot and heavy as the company boosted operations abroad. The purchases hit the bottom line; Schein avoided bloat by restructuring operations closing facilities and developing new systems. The company consolidated 13 distribution centers into five in 1997. The following year the firm expanded into Canada and bought a controlling stake in UK direct marketer Porter Nash.

To boost profits the company announced in 2000 that it would cut 5% of its workforce. It also shut down some facilities and sold its software development business as part of its overall restructuring plan. In 2001 the firm resumed its acquisitions when it bought the dental supply business of drug maker Zila. Over the next few years it expanded internationally when it bought up firms in the Czech Republic Germany Italy New Zealand and the UK.

Choosing to focus on supplying office-based health care practitioners in 2006 it sold its hospital supply business for $36.5 million. Other dispositions have included the sale of its oncology and specialty pharmaceutical businesses (2007) and a dental products wholesaler (2009). In 2009 Henry Schein acquired a majority stake in Butler Animal Health tripling the size of its domestic animal health operations; the unit was renamed Butler Schein Animal Health following the deal. (The company increased its stake in Butler Schein Animal Health to about 72% in 2012.)

Henry Schein expanded its health care technology segment in 2010 through the acquisition of majority ownership of ImproMed and McAllister Software Systems both developers of veterinary practice management systems in the US. In 2011 the company entered the veterinary market in Australia and New Zealand with the $92 million buy of Provet Holdings. The purchase helped Henry Schein cement its strategy to expand its international health care distribution unit.

EXECUTIVES

Evp And Chief Strategic Officer, Mark E. Mlotek, age 62, $555,962 total compensation
Evp And Chief Administrative Officer, Gerald A. Benjamin, age 65, $551,308 total compensation
President; Ceo Global Dental Group, James P. Breslawski, age 64, $698,769 total compensation
Evp And Cfo, Steven Paladino, age 61, $551,308 total compensation
Chairman And Ceo, Stanley M. Bergman, age 69, $1,342,385 total compensation
Svp And Chief Merchandising Officer, Michael Racioppi, age 63, $340,275 total compensation
President International Dental Group, Robert (Bob) Minowitz, age 59
Chief Commercial Officer; President Corporate Commercial Development Group, David C. (Dave) McKinley, age 65
Svp And Cto, James A. (Jim) Harding, age 62
Evp; Ceo Global Animal Health Medical And Dental Surgical Group, Karen Prange, age 54, $410,000 total compensation
President Global Animal Health Group, Peter McCarthy
President Global Medical Group, Bridget A. Ross, age 53
Vice President Global E Commerce, Robert Lamb
Vice President And Chief Global Communications Officer, Gerard Meuchner
Vice President Corporate Finance, Ronald South
Vice President Finance, Charles Crawford
Vice President, Patrick Allen
Vice President Product Merchandising, Marguerite Walsh
Vice President Finance, Eileen Rosenbaum
Vice President, Marie Woods
Vice President Regulatory Affairs, Jeff Peacock
Vp European Purchasing And Inventory Management, Lezlee Blackburn
Vice President And General Manager Repair Business Group, Ron Appel
Executive Vice President Of Sales, Cy Elborne
Vice President Sales Operations, Charlie Crawford
Vice President And Senior Counsel Litigation, Marjorie Han

Vice President Business Development, Edward L Mohr
Vice President, Peter Dellacroce
Vice President And Chief Information Securiity Officer, Mark Viola
National Sales Manager, Deanna Evans
Vice President Strategic And Business Planning, Brian Watson
Vice President National Telesales Operations, Jim Londoono
National Sales Manager, Bill Nixon
Vice President Corporate Business Development, Scott Sanders
Vice President Claims Information Technology, Pat Gunning
Vice President, Jesse Garringer
Vice President, Don Cohen
Vp And General Auditor, James Patterson
Senior Vice President International Group, Michael P Zack
Global Security Vice President, Chris Berry
National Sales Manager, Deanna Wright
Vice President And General Manager, David Steck
Vice President Technology Global Prosthetic Solutions, Patrick Thurm
Vp Safety, Shirley Taylor
Vp Us Distribution, Jeff Reade
Vice President Inventory Management, John Donigian
Vice President And Senior Counsel Corporate, Reid Arstark
National Sales Manager, Christian Marsolais
Vice President Digital Technology, Anoop Kulshreshtha
Vice President And Chief Compliance Officer, Nancy Lanis
Vp Europe Dental Western Region; Managing Director France, Vincent Junod
Vice President Global Supply Chain Europe, Axel Pfitzenreiter
Vice President, Howard Tapler
Treasurer, Keith Drayer
Senior Vice President Corporate And Legal Affairs Secretary And Chief Staff, Michael Ettinger
Auditors: BDO USA, LLP

LOCATIONS

HQ: Schein (Henry) Inc
135 Duryea Road, Melville, NY 11747
Phone: 631 843-5500
Web: www.henryschein.com

2017 Sales

	$ mil.	% of total
US	7,904	63
Other countries	4,556	37
Total	**12,461**	**100**

PRODUCTS/OPERATIONS

2017 Sales by Segment

	$ mil.	% of total
Health Care Distribution		
Dental	6,048	49
Animal health	3,477	28
Medical	2,497	20
Technology and Value-Added Services	438	3
Total	**12,461**	**100**

COMPETITORS

Allscripts	McKesson
Benco Dental	Medline Industries
Burkhart Dental	NextGen
Cardinal Health	Patterson Companies
Carestream Health	Sybron Dental
Darby Dental	athenahealth
IDEXX Labs	eClinicalWorks
MWI Veterinary Supply	

HISTORICAL FINANCIALS

Company Type: Public

Income Statement

FYE: December 30

	REVENUE ($ mil.)	NET INCOME ($ mil.)	NET PROFIT MARGIN	EMPLOYEES
12/17	12,461	406	3.3%	22,000
12/16	11,571	506	4.4%	21,000
12/15	10,629	479	4.5%	19,000
12/14	10,371	466	4.5%	17,500
12/13	9,560	431	4.5%	16,000
Annual Growth	6.8%	(1.5%)	—	8.3%

2017 Year-End Financials

Debt ratio: 21.33%	No. of shares (mil.): 153
Return on equity: 14.54%	Dividends
Cash ($ mil.): 174	Yield: —
Current ratio: 1.45	Payout: —
Long-term debt ($ mil.): 907	Market value ($ mil.): 10,740

	STOCK PRICE ($) FY Close	P/E High/Low	PER SHARE ($) Earnings	Dividends	Book Value
12/17	69.88	72 26	2.57	0.00	18.29
12/16	151.71	58 46	3.10	0.00	17.59
12/15	157.09	55 44	2.85	0.00	17.50
12/14	137.39	50 40	2.72	0.00	16.75
12/13	114.43	46 32	2.47	0.00	16.26
Annual Growth	(11.6%)	— —	1.0%	—	3.0%

Schwab (Charles) Corp (The)

The once-rebellious Charles Schwab is all grown up: the discount broker now offers the same traditional brokerage services it shunned over three decades ago. Schwab manages more than $3.4 trillion in assets for some 13.8 million individual investors and institutional clients. Traders can access its services via telephone the internet-enabled devices and through more than 345 offices in 45-plus states as well as London Hong Kong Singapore and Australia. Besides discount brokerage the firm offers financial research advice and planning investment management and retirement and employee compensation plans.It also operates Charles Schwab Bank a federal savings bank and Charles Schwab Investment Management an investment advisor for Schwab's mutual finds and exchange-traded funds.

HISTORY

During the 1960s Stanford graduate Charles Schwab founded First Commander Corp. which managed investments and published a newsletter. But he failed to properly register with the SEC and after a hiatus he returned to the business under the name Charles Schwab & Co. in 1971. Initially a full-service broker Schwab moved into discount brokerage after the SEC outlawed fixed commissions in 1975. While most brokers defiantly raised commissions Schwab cut its rates steeply.

From 1977 to 1983 Schwab's client list increased thirtyfold and revenues grew from $4.6 million to $126.5 million enabling the firm to automate its operations and develop cash-management account systems. To gain capital Charles sold the company to BankAmerica (now Bank of America) in 1983. Schwab grew but federal regulations prevented expansion into such services as mutual funds and telephone trading. Charles bought his company back in 1987 and took it public. When the stock market crashed later that year trading volume fell by nearly half from 17900 per day. Stung Schwab diversified further offering new fee-based services. Commission revenues fell from 64% of sales in 1987 to 39% in 1990 but by 1995 the long bull market had pushed commissions to more than 50%.

In 1989 Schwab introduced TeleBroker a 24-hour Touch-Tone telephone trading service available in English Spanish Mandarin or Cantonese.

Schwab continued to diversify courting independent financial advisors. Other buys included Mayer & Schweitzer (1991 now Schwab Capital Markets) an OTC market maker that accounted for about 7% of all NASDAQ trades. In 1993 the firm opened its first overseas office in London but traded only in dollar-denominated stocks until it bought Share-Link (later Charles Schwab Europe) the UK's largest discount brokerage in 1995. It subsequently sold the British pound sterling brokerage business to Barclays PLC although it has maintained its US dollar business in the UK.

During the next year Schwab made a concerted effort to build its retirement services by creating a 401(k) administration and investment services unit. In 1997 Schwab allied with J.P. Morgan Hambrecht & Quist and Credit Suisse First Boston (CSFB) to give its customers access to IPOs; the next year the relationship with CSFB deepened to give Schwab access to debt offerings. In late 1997 and early 1998 Schwab reorganized to reflect its new business lines. The firm also began recruiting talent rather than promoting from within.

Expansion was key at the turn of the century. In 1999 Schwab moved toward more broker-advised investing: It inked a deal (geared toward its retirement products customers) with online financial advice firm Financial Engines and introduced Velocity a desktop system designed to make trading easier for fiscally endowed investors. In 2000 Schwab bought online broker CyBerCorp (later CyberTrader) as well as U.S. Trust which markets to affluent clients.

While Schwab's World Trade Center offices were destroyed by the September 11 terrorist attacks the company did not lose any of its New York staff.

To pare expenses Schwab reduced its workforce by about 35% between 2000 and 2003. Founder and chairman Charles Schwab relinquished his role as co-CEO in early 2003 only to move back into the driver's seat in mid-2004 when former CEO David Pottruck was asked to step down by the company's board.

One of Schwab's first orders of business was to reexamine the company's 2004 acquisition of SoundView Technology Group which was combined with its Capital Markets operations to form Schwab SoundView Capital Markets. While the purchase was intended to help the company beef up its services for institutional investors Schwab said that SoundView lacked "synergy" with the company's tradition of supporting the individual investor and sold the business to Swiss bank UBS.

Schwab acquired The 401(k) Companies from Nationwide Financial Services in 2007. The addition became part of the company's existing Charles Schwab Trust subsidiary which serves as a trustee for employee benefit plans. Also that year Schwab sold U.S. Trust to Bank of America for some $3.3 billion in cash and shut down its CyberTrader day trading arm merging the direct-access brokerage's business with its own.

In 2011 Charles Schwab acquired retail brokerage optionsXpress. The $1 billion deal expanded its client base and online equity options and futures trading business and it has already boosted the company's trading revenues.

In another 2011 transaction Charles Schwab acquired Compliance11 which allowed the company to offer compliance monitoring and reporting services.

In December 2012 the firm purchased Massachusetts-based ThomasPartners a dividend income-focused asset management firm with some $2.3 billion in assets under management for $85 million in cash.

EXECUTIVES

Cfo, Peter Crawford, age 50
President And Ceo, Walter W. (Walt) Bettinger, age 57, $1,041,667 total compensation
President And Ceo Charles Schwab Bank, Paul V. Woolway
Evp Client Solutions, G. Andrew (Andy) Gill, age 55
Evp Corporate Initiatives, James D. McCool, age 59, $550,000 total compensation
President And Ceo Charles Schwab Investment Management, Marie A. Chandoha, age 57, $572,500 total compensation
Evp International Services And Special Business Development, Lisa Kidd Hunt
Evp Advisor Services, Bernard J. Clark, age 59, $525,000 total compensation
Evp Operational Services, Ron Carter
Evp And Chief Marketing Officer, Jonathan M. Craig
Evp Corporate Risk, Nigel J. Murtagh, age 55
Evp Retirement Plan Services, Steven H. (Steve) Anderson
Evp Technology Services, Jim McGuire
Evp General Counsel And Corporate Secretary, David R. Garfield, age 62
Evp Investor Services, Terri R. Kallsen, age 50, $450,000 total compensation
Evp Investor Services Strategy Segments And Platforms, Neesha Hathi
Evp And Cto, Timothy C. Heier
Evp And Cio, Dennis Howard
Evp Internal Audit, Mitch Mantua
Vice President Financial Consultant, Dean Martines
Vice President Financial Consultant, Richard Danchak
Vice President Financial Consultant, Brian Trentsch
Vice President Financial Consultant, Rich Munneke
Vice President Financial Consultant, Rich Kahan
Vice President Financial Consultant, Tim McDonald
Vice President Financial Consultant, Martin Kurtz
Vice President Financial Consultant, Mark Bergdorf
Vice President Financial Consultant, Greg Czarnecky
Vice President Financial Consultant, Brian Tveter
Vice President Financial Consultant, Mike Gula
Senior Vice President, Jonathan Beatty
Vice President Global Compliance, Janet Epstein
Vice President Retirement Plan Sales, Michael E Filbin
Vice President Senior Financial Consultant, Stephen Liepold
Vice President Retirement Plan Sales, Luis R Arellano
Vice President Financial Consultant, Greg Frelka
Vice President Information Technology, Ed Fulkerson
Vice President Financial Consultant, Shelley Helmerick
Vice President Financial Consultant, Luiz Soutomaior
Vice President Compliance And Monitoring, Mike Marsh

Vice President Senior Financial Consultant, Ming Chen

Vice President Financial Consultant, Jacob Peroceschi

Vice President Financial Consultant, Susanna Hilboldt

Vice President Financial Consultant, Brandon Setlock

Vice President, William Colin

Vice President Financial Consultant, Jesus Arroyo

Vice President Financial Consultant, David Mattox

Vp And Chief Investment Officer Charles Schwab Investment Advisory, James Peterson

Vice President Financial Consultant, Chad Vidovich

Vice President Financial Consultant, John Curren

Vice President Plan Sponsor Services, Ben Sheppard

Vice President Financial Consultant, David Bernstein

Vice President Financial Consultant, Chris Kiefer

Vice President Financial Consultant, Devon Cooney

Vice President Financial Consultant, Martin Dunn

Vice President Regulatory Affairs, Irene Gilbert

Vice President Senior Financial Consultant, Mario Giannetta

Vice President, Andrew Mason

Vice President Financial Consultant Paramus Nj. Branch, Jeffrey Wogel

Vice President Financial Consultant, Jane Gudgel

Vice President Financial Consultant, Paul Kidder

Vice President, William Matthews

Vice President Treasury, John Mason

Vice President Financial Consultant, Jeanne Chan

Vice President Financial Consultant, Andrew Lindell

Vice President Financial Consultant, James Kukurin

Vice President Financial Consultant, Robert Kay

Vice President Financial Consultant, John Metallic

Vice President And Branch Manager, Gregory Matthews

Vice President Financial Consultant, Tatum Schuler

Vice President, John Gutierrez

Vice President Financial Consultant, Michael Klebba

Vice President Financial Consultant, Hans Raymond

Vice President Financial Consultant, David Burchfield

Vice President, William Parrott

Vice President Financial Consultant, Selene Argao

Vice President, Brian Openshaw

Vice President Financial Consultant, Brian Atherton

Vice President Financial Consultant, Bill Schwind

Vice President Financial Consultant, Gary Cronk

Vice President Financial Consultant, Timothy Harker

Vice President Financial Consultant, Stuart Evans

Vice President Financial Consultant, Brett Woodward

Vice President, Steven Brakman

Vice President Financial Consultant, Danny Jones

Vice President Financial Consultant, Rick Fine

Vice President, Michael Solomon

Vice President Operations Cost Basis, Brian Godfrey

Vice President Of Sales, Aline Eliecagary

Vice President Of Corporate Public Relations, Susan Forman

Vice President Finance, Peter Pavlakis

Vice President Financial Consultant, Michael Viselli

Regional Vice President, Scot Kobashigawa

Vice President Financial Consultant, Nicolas Robatel

Vice President Financial Consultant, Tristyn Eames

Vice President Financial Consultant, Jason Burke

Vice President And Branch Manager International Schwab International Orlando, Cynthia Paul

Senior Vice President Financial Consultant, Michael Maniscalco

Vp Financial Consultant, Teb Yu

Vice President Financial Consultant, Robert Freddino

Vice President Financial Consultant, Shawn Jennings

Vice President Financial Consultant, Viola Ashmawee

Vice President Financial Consultant, Brian Lull

Vice President Of Participant Services, Catherine Golladay

Vice President Financial Consultant, James Titus

Vice President Financial Consultant, German Ramirez

Vice President, Jake King

Vice President Financial Consultant, Jeff Peterson

Vice President Financial Consultant, Justin Sinnott

Vice President Financial Consultant Ca Insurance License #0b27845, Cynthia Leal

Vice President Financial Consultant, Denise Patridge

Vice President Legislative And Regulatory Affairs, Scott Eckel

Vice President Financial Consultant, Zubin Hodiwalla

Vice President Financial Consultant, Chris Veale

Vice President Financial Consultant, Scott Newell

Vice President Financial Consultant, Bruce Gruenberg

Vice President Financial Consultant, Kim Bryant

Vice President Financial Consultant, Greg Kopp

Vice President Futures Optionsxpress, Daniel O'Neil

Vice President Financial Consultant, Carter Taylor

Vice President Financial Consultant, David Raymon

Vice President Financial Consultant, Garrett Sloan

Vice President Ibs Compliance, Gary Wachs

Executive Vice President Retirement Plan Services, Steve Anderson

Vice President Financial Consultant, Gregory Kaiser

Vice President Financial Consultant, Garland Sharp

Vice President, Deborah Pritchard

Vice President Financial Consultant, Brian Valenti

Vice President Financial Consultant, Galina Sapozhnikov

Vice President Financial Consultant, Renee Hardman

Vice President Financial Consultant, Dawn Stoffel

Vice President Financial Consultant, Abel Oonnoonny

Vice President Financial Consultant, Stefan Borso

Vice President Financial Consultant, Andrew Seward

Vice President, Dan Masteller

Vice President And Branch Manager, Francisco J Vivas

Vice President Branch Manager, Anthony Viviano

Vice President, Lisa Quartarone

Vice President, John Kaminsky

Vice President Financial Consultant, Tj Farrell

Vice President Financial Consultant, Aaron Olson

Vice President Financial Consultant, Michael Tran

Vice President Financial Consultant, Sue Cheung

Vice President Branch Manager, Whitney Fletcher

Vice President Financial Consultant, Tiffany Dugas

Information Technology Vice President, Manoj Achrekar

Vice President Branch Manager, Joe Benvenuto

Vice President Financial Consultant, Jeff Glaser

Vice President Financial Consultant, Tom Nagy

Vice President Financial Consultant, Francesco Conidi

Vice President Financial Consultant, Porter Ginn

Auditors: DELOITTE & TOUCHE LLP

LOCATIONS

HQ: Schwab (Charles) Corp (The)
211 Main Street, San Francisco, CA 94105
Phone: 415 667-7000   **Fax:** 415 627-8894
Web: www.aboutschwab.com

PRODUCTS/OPERATIONS

2017 Sales

	$ mil.	% of total
Investor Services	6,200	72
Advisor Services	2,418	28
Total	**8,618**	**100**

2017 Sales

	$ mil.	% of total
Interest	4,282	50
Asset management & administration fees	3,392	39
Trading	654	8
Provision for loan losses	- -	
Other	290	4
Total	**8,618**	**100**

Selected Subsidiaries

Charles Schwab Bank
Charles Schwab Investment Management Inc. (mutual fund investment adviser)
Schwab Holdings Inc.
Charles Schwab & Co. Inc. (securities broker-dealer)

COMPETITORS

Ameriprise	Morgan Stanley
Bank of America	Principal Financial
E*TRADE Financial	Raymond James
Edward Jones	Financial
FMR	Scottrade
Franklin Templeton	ShareBuilder
John Hancock Financial	T. Rowe Price
Services	TD Ameritrade
Legg Mason	The Vanguard Group

HISTORICAL FINANCIALS

Company Type: Public

Income Statement

FYE: December 31

	REVENUE ($ mil.)	NET INCOME ($ mil.)	NET PROFIT MARGIN	EMPLOYEES
12/17	8,960	2,354	26.3%	17,600
12/16	7,649	1,889	24.7%	16,200
12/15	6,512	1,447	22.2%	15,300
12/14	6,160	1,321	21.4%	14,600
12/13	5,540	1,071	19.3%	13,800
Annual Growth	12.8%	21.8%	—	6.3%

2017 Year-End Financials

Debt ratio: 8.12%
Return on equity: 13.47%
Cash ($ mil.): 14,217
Current ratio: 0.24
Long-term debt ($ mil.): 4,753

No. of shares (mil.): 1,345
Dividends
Yield: 0.0%
Payout: 19.8%
Market value ($ mil.): 69,110

	STOCK PRICE ($) FY Close	P/E High/Low		PER SHARE ($) Earnings	Dividends	Book Value
12/17	51.37	32	23	1.61	0.32	13.77
12/16	39.47	31	17	1.31	0.27	12.32
12/15	32.93	34	25	1.03	0.24	10.15
12/14	30.19	32	25	0.95	0.24	9.00
12/13	26.00	33	18	0.78	0.24	8.00
Annual Growth	18.6%	—	—	19.9%	7.5%	14.5%

Seaboard Corp.

With pork and turkey from the US flour from Haiti and sugar from Argentina Seaboard has a lot on its plate. The diversified agribusiness and transportation firm has operations in some 45 countries in the Americas the Caribbean and Africa. Seaboard sells its pork and poultry in the US and abroad. Overseas it trades grain (wheat soya) operates power plants and feed and flour mills and grows and refines sugar cane. Seaboard owns a shipping service for containerized cargo between the US the Caribbean and South America; it has shipping terminals in Miami and Houston and a fleet of about 20 vessels (two owned the rest chartered) and ships to ports worldwide. Seaboard is run by descendants of founder Otto Bresky.

Operations

Seaboard operates in five segments.

The company?s Pork Division about a quarter of revenue is a vertically integrated pork producer and one of the largest producers and processors in the US. The unit works through the lifecycle of a hog from research in nutrition and genetics and extending to production of meat products.

The Commodity Trading and Milling (CT&M) Division about 50% of revenue trades processes and moves agricultural commodities such as wheat corn soybeans soybean meal and others. The primary destinations for the ag products are Africa South America the Caribbean and Asia.

Seaboard?s Marine Division some 15% of revenue provides cargo shipping services between the US the Caribbean and Central and South America. The company has major facilities at Port Miami and the Port of Houston.

The rest of Seaboard?s revenue comes from its operations in sugar which are mostly in Argentina power generation in the Dominican Republic and its 50% non-controlling interest in Butterball LLC the largest producer of turkeys and turkey products in the US.

Geographic Reach

Kansas-based Seaboard is a global company that serves several segments such as agribusiness and ocean cargo transportation in about 45 countries specifically in the Americas the Caribbean and Africa. Its largest market is Central and South America and the Caribbean representing about 35% of annual sales. Africa and the US are other big markets for the company.

Financial Performance

After several years of consistent growth Seaboard?s sales have stumbled in the past three years. Revenue dipped 4% in 2016 to $5.4 billion from 2015 with lower sales in five of its six segments and all but one of its geographic areas. Sales were down 8% in the Commodity Trading & Milling unit which is responsible for half the company?s revenue) on lower commodity prices and the mix of products. Sales rose 8% for the Pork unit as acquisitions increased the sales volume of market hogs and the acquisition of a second biodiesel plant produced higher biodiesel volumes.

Seaboard?s net income jumped to $312 million in 2016 an 82% increase from 2015. The company reduced the cost of sales 6% in 2016 from the year before boosting net income.

Higher net income helped pushed cash flow from operations to $427 million in 2016 from $416 million in 2015.

Strategy

Seaboard seeks growth by expanding operations in several areas.

The company continues to beef up its pork division. With its partner Triumph Seaboard opened a new Daily?s bacon plant in St. Joseph Missouri that has a production capacity of 60 million pounds a year. Seaboard and Triumph followed in 2017 with another new pork processing plant in Sioux City Iowa. But pork is more than bacon and Seaboard rehabilitated a closed biodiesel plant in St Joseph Missouri. That plant along with the one on Guymon Oklahoma gives Seaboard capacity to produce 64 million gallons of biodiesel fuel per year.

In 2016 Seaboard gain took over day-to-day work of the Brazilian flour milling operations by restructuring and consolidation. The company expects to reduce the operation?s costs by focusing on single site production.

Seaboard could face challenges if US trade agreements are renegotiated or abrogated. If the US charges higher tariffs on foreign goods entering the country other nations could retaliate by putting higher tariffs on US goods. Agricultural products are some of the US?s biggest goods for export and would be likely targets for retaliation which could increase prices reduce exports or both.

Mergers and Acquisitions

In September 2014 Seaboard's processed meats division sold a 50% stake in Daily's Premium Meats to its processing partner Triumph Foods for $72.5 million making Seaboard and Triumph co-owners of the business. The sale provided additional capital to expand production and geographic reach of the Daily's brand.

In July 2013 Seaboard acquired a 50% stake in a flour milling business in Gambia for about $9.1 million.

HISTORY

Otto Bresky founded his company as a flour broker in 1916. He acquired his first flour mill in Atchison Kansas in 1918 and the following year purchased the Imperial Brewery Co. in Kansas City and converted it to a flour mill. Over the next four decades Bresky ground out a series of acquisitions of milling companies. In 1928 he purchased Rodney Milling Co. and retained the name as the identity for the family business. The company then purchased Ismert-Hincke Milling Co. (1938) and the Consolidated Flour Mills Co. (1950). In 1959 Rodney Milling merged with publicly traded Hathaway Industries and changed its name to Seaboard Allied Milling Corp.

In the 1960s Seaboard Allied became one of the first millers to shift flour milling from the source of the raw materials (the wheat fields of the Great Plains) to the population centers in the Southeast and on the East Coast. In 1962 Seaboard Allied built a flour mill in Chattanooga Tennessee. It then purchased George Urban Milling Company in Buffalo New York (1965) and built a flour mill in Jacksonville Florida (1966). But Bresky's expansionist strategy did not stop at the Atlantic Seaboard. The company acquired a flour mill in Guayaquil Ecuador in 1966 (a joint venture with Continental Grain Co.) and constructed flour mills in Freetown Sierra Leone (1968) and Georgetown Guyana (1969).

Bresky retired in 1973 and was succeeded by his son Harry. A chip off the old block Harry acquired a flour mill in Cleveland Tennessee and built flour mills in Buchanan Liberia and in Sapele Nigeria that year. In 1978 Seaboard Allied acquired Mochasa Ecuador's leading producer of animal feed and launched Top Feeds a mixed-feed plant in Sapele.

Facing stiff competition in the mill business from agribusiness giants in 1982 Seaboard Allied sold all its US flour mills to Cargill. The company changed its name to Seaboard that year and began expanding outside the US. In 1983 the company formed Seaboard Marine a shipping business in Florida to serve its increasingly far-flung enterprises.

In addition to geographic diversification the company expanded into new agribusiness areas. Seaboard acquired Central Soya's poultry unit in 1984 and it bought the Elberton Poultry Company the next year. Seaboard commenced shrimp farming operations in Ecuador in 1986 and in Honduras in 1987. Two years later Transcontinental Capital Corporation (Bermuda) a subsidiary began supplying power from a floating power barge to the Dominican Republic.

Seaboard entered the hog business in 1990 by acquiring a pork-processing plant in Albert Lea Minnesota. It opened a hog-processing facility in Guymon Oklahoma in 1996 and closed the Minnesota plant. That year the company bought a stake in Ingenio y Refinerio San Martin del Tabacal an Argentina-based sugar cane and citrus company. It then acquired flour-mill pasta-plant and cookie operations in Beira Mozambique.

After serving as CEO for more than 30 years in 2006 Harry Bresky stepped down as CEO (but remained as chairman) and turned over the company's reins to his son Steven. Harry Bresky died in 2007.

In 2010 Seaboard acquired a 50% stake in Butterball LLC.

EXECUTIVES

Vice President General Counsel, David Becker
Senior Vice President Finance And Treasurer, David Oswalt
Svp Engineering, James L. (Jim) Gutsch, age 64
Evp And Cfo, Robert L. Steer, age 59, $763,000 total compensation
Chairman President And Ceo, Steven J. Bresky, age 65, $942,000 total compensation
Ceo Pork, Terry J. Holton, age 58, $552,000 total compensation
Ceo Marine, Edward A. (Eddie) Gonzalez, age 53, $472,000 total compensation
Ceo Commodity Trading And Milling, David M. Dannov, age 57, $472,000 total compensation
Ceo Sugar, Hugo Rossi
Ceo Power, Armando G. Rodriguez
Vice President Audit Services, TY Tywater
Vice President Operations Foods Divisi, Marty Hast
Vice President, Claudio Dabelic
Assistant Vice President Information Technology, Brian Bybee
Vice President Of Marketing And Prod. Innov., Scott Webb
Board Member, Edward Shifman
Assistant Secretary, Zachery J Holden
Assistant Treasurer, Katie Verschelden
Assistant Treasurer, James Boydston
Board Member, Paul Squires
Auditors: KPMG LLP

LOCATIONS

HQ: Seaboard Corp.
9000 West 67th Street, Merriam, KS 66202
Phone: 913 676-8800
Web: www.seaboardcorp.com

2016 Sales

	$ mil.	% of total
Caribbean Central & South America	1,990	37
Africa	1,572	29
US	1,161	22
Pacific Basin & Far East	309	6
Canada/Mexico	236	4
Europe	40	1
All other	71	1
Total	**5,379**	**100**

PRODUCTS/OPERATIONS

2016 Sales

	$ mil.	% of total
Products	4,334	80
Services	961	18
Other	84	2
Total	**5,379**	**100**

2016 Sales

	$ mil.	% of total
Commodity Trading & Milling	2,778	52
Pork	1,443	27
Marine	916	17
Sugar	147	3
Power	79	1
All other	16	-
Total	**5,379**	**100**

Selected Operations

Cargo shipping
Citrus production and processing
Commodity merchandising (wheat corn and soybean meal)
Domestic trucking transportation
Electric power generation
Flour maize and feed milling
Jalape?o pepper processing
Pork production and processing
Sugar production and refining

COMPETITORS

ADM	Hormel
APL	Imperial Sugar
American Crystal Sugar	Jennie-O
Bay State Milling	Johnsonville Sausage
Bunge Limited	Louis Dreyfus Group
CGC	M. A. Patout
CHS	Makino
CSX	Mondelez International
Cargill	NYK Line
Carr's Milling	Neptune Orient
Chelsea Milling	Nicor Gas
Chiquita Brands	Nutreco
Colonial Group	Organic Milling
Crowley Maritime	Overseas Shipholding
Della Natura	Group
Commodities	Smithfield Foods
Dole Food	Southern States
Evergreen Marine	Star of the West
Evergreen Mills	Sunkist
Farmers Rice Milling	S dzucker
Fresh Del Monte	Tate & Lyle
Produce	Tyson Foods
Genco Shipping and	U.S. Sugar
Trading	Western Sugar
Horizon Milling	Cooperative

HISTORICAL FINANCIALS

Company Type: Public

Income Statement

FYE: December 31

	REVENUE ($ mil.)	NET INCOME ($ mil.)	NET PROFIT MARGIN	EMPLOYEES
12/17	5,809	247	4.3%	11,800
12/16	5,379	312	5.8%	12,000
12/15	5,594	171	3.1%	10,772
12/14	6,473	365	5.6%	10,778
12/13	6,670	205	3.1%	11,397
Annual Growth	**(3.4%)**	**4.7%**	**—**	**0.9%**

2017 Year-End Financials

Debt ratio: 13.51%
Return on equity: 7.53%
Cash ($ mil.): 116
Current ratio: 3.82
Long-term debt ($ mil.): 482

No. of shares (mil.): 1
Dividends
  Yield: 0.0%
  Payout: 2.8%
Market value ($ mil.): 5,162

	STOCK PRICE ($) FY Close	P/E High/Low	PER SHARE ($) Earnings	PER SHARE ($) Dividends	PER SHARE ($) Book Value
12/17	4,410.00	22 17	211.01	6.00	2,902
12/16	3,951.99	17 9	266.50	0.00	2,701
12/15	2,894.74	32 20	146.44	0.00	2,456
12/14	4,197.95	13 8	309.96	0.00	2,320
12/13	2,794.97	17 15	171.92	0.00	2,081
Annual Growth	**12.1%**	**— —**	**5 3%**		**8 7%**

Seacoast Banking Corp. of Florida

Seacoast Banking Corporation is the holding company for Seacoast National Bank. It operates some 50 branches in Florida with a concentration in four large city markets. Serving individuals and businesses the bank offers a range of financial products and services including deposit accounts credit cards trust services and private banking. Commercial and residential real estate loans make up most of the bank's lending activities; to a lesser extent it also originates business and consumer loans.

Operations

Seacoast Bank offers traditional banking products such as deposit accounts checking & savings accounts CDs business loans home mortgages and the like. It also makes available to its customers brokerage and annuity services along with insurance products. A division of the bank Seacoast Marine Finance specializes in boat loans which it typically originates itself and then sells into the secondary market.

Geographic Reach

Seacoast National Bank has some 50 branches in 14 counties across Florida stretching from Broward County north through the Treasure Coast and into Orlando and west to Okeechobee and surrounding counties. Its primary markets are Tampa Orlando Port St. Lucie and West Palm Beach/Ft. Lauderdale.

Financial Performance

Seacoast Banking Corporation has done well in recent years steadily growing interest income to nearly $200 million in 2017 up from a low of $70 million just four years prior. The bank registered positive earnings from 2013 forward albeit the results fluctuated wildly.

In 2017 interest income grew 30% to $192 million and non-interest income improved by 25% to $170 million. Its loan portfolio grew ? through organic means as well as via acquisitions ? by almost 30% against which it earned additional interest income. The bank's average net interest margin rose 10 basis points to 3.73%.

Net income also lodged an excellent year increasing 48% from the prior year to $43 million. Although the company incurred an $8.6 million impairment of its deferred tax assets due to the change in US Federal tax law the increase in revenue along with a $15 million gain on the sale an investment it made in Visa company stock pushed up yearly earnings.

Cash at the end of the year was $109 million unchanged from 2016. Financing activities contributed $196 million mostly from an increase in deposits from acquisitions. Investing activities used $246 million in the process of buying and selling

securities and originating new loans. Operating activities added $49 million.

Strategy

Seacoast Bank has grown mostly through acquisitions in recent years. Since 2014 it opened one new office and acquired 49 branches (19 of which were subsequently shuttered). Orlando has been a hot destination for it as it transformed its presence there just a few branches to the largest Florida-based bank in the market by 2017. The bank anticipates continued geographic growth in Florida through organic means but also through acquisition if the right opportunity arises as with the 2017 purchases of NorthStar Banking and Palm Beach Community Bank.

Although it caters to personal customers as well as business clients the focus on businesses has sparked significant growth in the associated loan portfolio. The company tends to commercial clients with revenues exceeding $5 million in specific industry verticals. It takes a comprehensive relationship approach by providing business treasury lending and wealth management services. The commercial loan portfolio grew nearly 300% between year-end 2013 and year-end 2017 from $632 million to $2.5 billion.

The bank significantly expanded its banking technology platform by introducing digital deposit capture on smartphones updating its mobile platforms for consumer and business customers and enhancing its ATM capabilities. Customers have taken to the online functionality and in 2017 the bank processed more digital transactions than it did through its physical branch network.

Mergers and Acquisitions

In 2017 Seacoast purchased NorthStar Banking Corporation adding more than $200 million in assets $170 million in deposits and nearly $140 million in loans to Seacoast?s balance sheet. In the same year it acquired Palm Beach Community Bank for some $70 million adding $270 million in loans and four bank branches to Seacoast?s operations.

EXECUTIVES

Chairman And Ceo, Dennis S. (Denny) Hudson, age 62, $537,852 total compensation
Evp And Residential Lending Executive, Michael J. (Mike) Sonego
Evp And Commercial Banking Executive, Charles K. Cross, age 60, $273,333 total compensation
Evp And Chief Risk And Credit Officer, David D. Houdeshell, age 57, $262,500 total compensation
Evp Enterprise Services And Initiatives, Kathleen (Kathy) Cavicchioli
Evp And Chief Marketing Officer, Jeffery (Jeff) Lee
Evp Service And Operations, Jeffery (Jeff) Bray
Evp And Chief Human Resources Officer, Daniel G. (Dan) Chappell
Cfo And Head Of Strategy, Charles M. (Chuck) Shaffer, age 44, $248,333 total compensation
Evp Community Banking, Julie Kleffel
Vice President Cre, Debra Mairs
Assistant Vice President Relationship Manager, Frances Portalatin
Executive Vice President Chief Human Resources Officer, Dan Chappell
Executive Vice President, William Hahl
Vice President Financial Advisor, Carl Newton
Vice President Data Warehouse Manager, Mark Blanchette
Executive Vice President Wealth Management And The Private Bank At Seacoast, Tom Hall
Senior Vice President Risk Officer, Peter Lowery
Senior Vice President Residential Lending Production Manager, REINA RAMOS
Avp Banking Center Manager, Amber Shirk
Senior Vice President, Tom Popieski
Vice President, Travis Engebretsen

LOCATIONS

HQ: Seacoast Banking Corp. of Florida
815 Colorado Avenue, Stuart, FL 34994
Phone: 772 287-4000
Web: www.seacoastbanking.com

PRODUCTS/OPERATIONS

Selected Services

Commercial and retail banking
Mortgage services
Wealth management

COMPETITORS

BB&T	PNC Financial
BBX Capital	Regions Financial
Bank of America	SunTrust
BankUnited	Suncoast Schools FCU
CenterState Banks	Wells Fargo
EverBank Financial	

HISTORICAL FINANCIALS

Company Type: Public

Income Statement   FYE: December 31

	ASSETS ($ mil.)	NET INCOME ($ mil.)	INCOME AS % OF ASSETS	EMPLOYEES
12/17	5,810	42	0.7%	805
12/16	4,680	29	0.6%	725
12/15	3,534	22	0.6%	665
12/14	3,093	5	0.2%	579
12/13	2,268	51	2.3%	519
Annual Growth	26.5%	(4.7%)	—	11.6%

2017 Year-End Financials

Debt ratio: 4.85%
Return on equity: 7.62%
Cash ($ mil.): 109
Current ratio: —
Long-term debt ($ mil.): —

No. of shares (mil.): 46
Dividends
  Yield: —
  Payout: —
Market value ($ mil.): 1,183

	STOCK PRICE ($) FY Close	P/E High/Low	PER SHARE ($) Earnings	Dividends	Book Value
12/17	25.21	26 21	0.99	0.00	14.70
12/16	22.06	29 17	0.78	0.00	11.45
12/15	14.98	25 18	0.66	0.00	10.29
12/14	13.75	68 48	0.21	0.00	9.44
12/13	12.20	5 1	2.44	0.00	8.40
Annual Growth	19.9%	— —	(20.2%)	—	15.0%

Sears Holdings Corp

Once a retail giant Sears Holdings is growing smaller and leaner these days. The company is a leading retailer of appliances and tools as well as lawn and garden fitness and automotive repair equipment. With about 1200 retail stores across the US Sears Holdings operates through sub-sidiaries Sears Roebuck and Co. and Kmart offering proprietary Sears brands including Kenmore and DieHard. Beyond retail Sears Holdings is the largest provider of home installation and product repair services in the US. In response to plummeting sales in a tough retail climate Sears Holdings has been forced to sell off assets and close or spin off hundreds of stores in recent years. In late 2018 it filed for Chapter 11 bankruptcy protection.

Bankruptcy

After months if not years of speculation Sear Holdings filed for Chapter 11 bankruptcy in October 2018. It plans to remain in business but will likely close or sell hundreds of stores; nearly 200 locations are already scheduled for closure by the end of the year. It has been a long decline for the retailer which first had to contend with the lower prices and convenience offered by Walmart Target and Home Depot among other big-box stores and later with Amazon and other e-commerce sites.

Operations

Sears Holdings operates two segments: Sears Domestic which boasts 670 full-line stores that generated about 60% of Sears Holdings' total sales in fiscal 2016 (ended January 30 2016); and Kmart which had 735 Kmart stores that contributed another 40% to Sears Holdings' total sales.

By product the retailer generated 43% of its total sales from hardline merchandise (electronics appliances tools etc.) and another 25% from apparel and soft home items. About 15% of sales came from food and drug sales while service (installation and repair) made up another 9% of total sales during the year.

Outside of retail Sears Holdings has a real estate business unit called Sears Holdings Real Estate one of the largest corporate real estate organizations in the world. It offers for sale or lease closed Kmart and Sears stores. It also leases empty space inside and outside of the stores.

Geographic Reach

Sears Holdings subsidiary Sears Roebuck and Co. has Sears-branded and affiliated stores in all 50 US states and Puerto Rico. Subsidiary Kmart boasts Kmart-branded stores in 49 states Guam Puerto Rico and the US Virgin Islands.

Sales and Marketing

The retailer has been decreasing its advertising spend over the past few years as sales have declined. It spent $850 million on advertising in fiscal 2016 down from $1.1 billion and $1.5 billion for 2015 and 2014 respectively.

Financial Performance

Declining store sales and mounting losses have plagued Sears Holdings for the past several years as the popularity of e-commerce and fierce competition from other big box retailers has been growing.

In fiscal 2016 Sears Holdings' net revenues decreased by 19% due to a drop in revenues from all segments (and a drop of $2.1 billion associated with Sears Canada which was de-consolidated in October 2014).

Kmart's revenues declined due to having fewer stores in operation which accounted for approximately $1.1 billion of the decline and a drop e in comparable store sales driven by declines in the consumer electronics apparel grocery and household and drugstore categories.

The revenues from Sears Domestic segment decreased due to a drop in comparable store sales of 11.1% which accounted for $1.2 billion of the decline and the effect of having fewer full-line stores in operation which accounted for $433 million of the decline.

The company's net loss decreased by 33% in fiscal 2016 mainly due to a decline in selling and administrative expenses related to decreases in payroll and advertising expenses and the absence of expenses of $603 million from Sears Canada

and $77 million from the Lands' End business which Sears Holding spun off in 2014. Other factors included an income tax benefit in 2015 related to indefinite-life assets associated with the property sold in the transaction with Seritage.

In fiscal 2016 Sears Holdings' operating cash inflows increased by 56% due to changes in working capital as a result of an increase in inventory balances compared to the significant decrease in inventory balances a year earlier.

Strategy

Sears Holdings outlined three main objectives in 2015 to ensure its long-term success: restoring profitability; focusing on its best members (most loyal customers) best stores and best categories (home appliances home services and fitness equipment); and enhance its financial flexibility through sales of store assets and investor fundraising.

The retailer has been trying to adapt to the rapid consumer change from brick-and-mortar stores toward e-commerce in recent years. The likes of Amazon and Wal-Mart have ruthlessly eaten into Sears' market share as internet shopping expands. In 2015 the company continued shifting from being product-centric to becoming "member-centric" catering to members' needs "wherever whenever and however they want to shop" as stated in the February 2015 Chairman's letter. The member-centric model is built on two platforms: Shop Your Way the loyalty membership platform; and Integrated Retail the technology platform that connects its "ecosystem" of retail channels to member "touchpoints" (i.e. online and through mobile apps).

The plans also include significant cost-saving efforts: it is aiming for $1.25 billion in savings each year. Facing years of losses Sears Holdings has been forced to close hundreds of stores (from 2000 in 2013 to 1200 in 2017) cut thousands of jobs and sell assets to turn its business around. In 2017 the company sold its iconic Craftsman tool brand which it had owned since 1927 to Stanley Black & Decker for $900 million. The deal generated much-needed cash for the company and helps Sears continue to operate through 2017.

In another move to extract value from one of its name brands Sears in 2017 agreed to sell Kenmore appliances on Amazon.com. At the same time Sears said it would integrate its smart appliances with Alexa Amazon's artificial intelligence digital assistant. Owners of integrated Kenmore-Alexa appliances could operate them with voice commands. The deal exposes Kenmore appliances to a wider range of shoppers by displaying them on Amazon's popular digital showroom.

In recent years the company has cuts costs through store closings and employee reductions. In 2017 Sears announced 400 jobs would be cut from its corporate headquarters. In 2015 it sold 235 properties to Seritage Growth Properties (REIT properties) along with Sears Holdings' 50% interest in a number of joint venture properties. Sears Holdings received aggregate gross proceeds from the Seritage transaction of $2.7 billion. The previous year the company sold off most of its stake in its struggling Sears Canada business spun off its Lands' End retail business and considered doing the same for its Sears Auto Center business.

The pairing of Sears and Kmart was intended to leverage the strengths of both chains by making their products brands (Kenmore Craftsman DieHard) and services (including auto and appliance repair) available through more locations and distribution channels. That strategy failed to increase in sales for either retailer.

The company is focused on two core strategies Shop Your Way membership and Integrated Retail. Shop Your Way evolved from being store-based in 2009 to being a desktop and Mobile experience.

All this is part of the company's effort to transform into a member-centric retailer. The company has increased the number of brands and expanded its network to include more partners.

Through its integrated retail strategy the company is using it existing brick-and-mortar infrastructure while integrating it with mobile experiences. The company introduced Meet with an Expert a service that helps online shoppers considering larger item purchases in Home Appliances Mattresses or Lawn & Garden connect with instore experts.

Company Background

Sears Holdings was created in 2005 as a result of the $11.9 billion mega-merger of Sears and struggling Kmart masterminded by chairman and CEO Edward Lampert.

EXECUTIVES

Chairman And Ceo, Edward S. (Eddie) Lampert, age 55, $1 total compensation
Cfo, Robert A. Riecker, age 53
President Fulfillment Supply Chain And Sourcing, Girish Lakshman, age 53, $794,444 total compensation
Svp Customer Experience And Integrated Retail, Leena Munjal, age 41, $568,750 total compensation
Svp Shop Your Way, Eric D. Jaffe, age 30
President Apparel, David Pastrana Benito, age 41
President Home Services, Sean Skelley, age 51, $794,444 total compensation
President Home And Footwear, Kurt C. Staelens
Divisional Vice President, Carlos Fojo
Divisional Vice President Chief Marketing Officer Grocery And Drug, R Whitton
Dvp Kenmore Product Development, Tom Desalvo
Divisional Vice President Home Services Online, Sandeep Patil
Chief Marketing Officer Of Home Appliances And Vice President Of, Kevin Brown
Div Vice President Ny Technical Design, Vanessa Allen
Vice President Space Management And Analytics, Amy Higgins
Vice President Ecommerce Program And Product Management, Christopher Kraft
Vice President Chief Financial Officer Grocery Drug And Rx, Jonathan Carpenter
Dvp Human Resources Retail Services, Megan Van Pelt
Divisional Vice President Head Of Sears Retail Human Resources, Colleen Kozak
Vice President Media Services, Perianne Grignon
Auditors: DELOITTE & TOUCHE LLP

LOCATIONS

HQ: Sears Holdings Corp
3333 Beverly Road, Hoffman Estates, IL 60179
Phone: 847 286-2500
Web: www.sears.com

PRODUCTS/OPERATIONS

Sales by Segment

	$ mil.	% of total
Sears Domestic	13,488	61
Kmart	8,650	39
Total	**22,138**	**100**

Sales by Products

	$ mil.	% of total
Hardlines	9,571	43
Apparel and Soft Home	5,566	25
Food and Drug	3,099	14
Service	2,110	10
Other	1,792	8
Total	**22,138**	**100**

Selected Subsidiaries

Kmart Corporation

Kmart Holding Corporation
Sears Home Improvement Products Inc.
Sears Roebuck Acceptance Corp.
Sears Roebuck and Co.
Sears Roebuck de Puerto Rico Inc.
SRC Real Estate Holdings (TX) LLC

COMPETITORS

Ace Hardware	Macy's
Amazon.com	Menard
AutoZone	Office Depot
Bed Bath & Beyond	Pep Boys
Best Buy	ServiceMaster
Dillard's	Target Corporation
Home Depot	The Gap
Hudson's Bay	Wal-Mart
J. C. Penney	Whirlpool
Kohl's	Zale
Lowe's	

HISTORICAL FINANCIALS

Company Type: Public

Income Statement

FYE: February 3

	REVENUE ($ mil.)	NET INCOME ($ mil.)	NET PROFIT MARGIN	EMPLOYEES
02/18*	16,702	(383)	—	89,000
01/17	22,138	(2,221)	—	140,000
01/16	25,146	(1,129)	—	178,000
01/15	31,198	(1,682)	—	196,000
02/14	36,188	(1,365)	—	249,000
Annual Growth	**(17.6%)**	—		**(22.7%)**

*Fiscal year change

2018 Year-End Financials

Debt ratio: 56.90%
Return on equity: —
Cash ($ mil.): 182
Current ratio: 0.78
Long-term debt ($ mil.): 2,249

No. of shares (mil.): 108
Dividends
  Yield: —
  Payout: —
Market value ($ mil.): 254

	STOCK PRICE ($) FY Close	P/E High/Low	PER SHARE ($) Earnings	Dividends	Book Value
02/18*	2.35	— —	(3.57)	0.00	(34.47)
01/17	7.42	— —	(20.78)	0.00	(35.74)
01/16	16.95	— —	(10.59)	0.00	(18.35)
01/15	31.84	— —	(15.82)	0.00	(8.89)
02/14	36.37	— —	(12.87)	0.00	16.41
Annual Growth	**(49.6%)**	— —	—	—	—

*Fiscal year change

SECURITIES INVESTOR PROTECTION CORPORATION

EXECUTIVES

Vice President Operations, Karen Saperstein
Avp Operations, Timothy Timanus
Auditors: GRANT THORNTON MCLEAN VA

LOCATIONS

HQ: SECURITIES INVESTOR PROTECTION CORPORATION
1667 K ST NW STE 1000, WASHINGTON, DC 200061620
Phone: 202 371-8300
Web: WWW.SIPC.ORG

HISTORICAL FINANCIALS

Company Type: Private

Income Statement

FYE: December 31

	ASSETS ($ mil.)	NET INCOME ($ mil.)	INCOME AS % OF ASSETS	EMPLOYEES
12/16	2,944	362	12.3%	39
12/15	2,053	169	6.4%	—
12/14	2,362	307	13.0%	—
12/11	1,606	131	8.2%	—
Annual Growth	**12.9%**	**22.4%**	—	—

2016 Year-End Financials

Debt ratio: —
Return on equity: 74.40%
Cash ($ mil.): 1
Current ratio: —
Long-term debt ($ mil.): —

Dividends
  Yield: —
  Payout: —
Market value ($ mil.): —

SEFCU SERVICES, LLC

EXECUTIVES

Mng MBR, Michelle Raymond
MBR, Robert Maclasco
Broker, Linda Deluke
Loan Officer, Bob Wilson
Sales Manager Origina, Steve Ferris

LOCATIONS

HQ: SEFCU SERVICES, LLC
700 PATROON CREEK BLVD, ALBANY, NY 122061067
Phone: 518 783-1234
Web: WWW.SEFCUMORTGAGESERVICES.COM

HISTORICAL FINANCIALS

Company Type: Private

Income Statement

FYE: December 31

	ASSETS ($ mil.)	NET INCOME ($ mil.)	INCOME AS % OF ASSETS	EMPLOYEES
12/17	3,555	21	0.6%	102
12/16	3,328	18	0.6%	—
Annual Growth	**6.8%**	**16.0%**	—	—

2017 Year-End Financials

Debt ratio: —
Return on equity: 19.80%
Cash ($ mil.): 172
Current ratio: —
Long-term debt ($ mil.): —

Dividends
  Yield: —
  Payout: —
Market value ($ mil.): —

Selective Insurance Group Inc

Property/casualty insurance holding company Selective Insurance Group's reach primarily covers the entire eastern US seaboard and much of the Midwest. Commercial policies sold by its 10 subsidiaries include workers' compensation and commercial automobile property and liability insurance. Personal lines include homeowners and automobile insurance. The company also offers federal flood insurance administration services throughout the US and some excess and surplus (E&S nonstandard) insurance. Selective Insurance Group operates through four reportable segments: Standard Commercial Lines Standard Personal Lines E&S Lines and Investments.

Operations

Selective's Standard Commercial Lines segment which serves business not-for-profit organizations and government agencies accounts for about three-fourths of Selective's net premiums written. Standard Personal Lines — including flood insurance coverage — follows representing more than 10% of net premiums written. The E&S Lines segment which covers more unusual risks than standard insurance accounts for nearly 10% of net premiums written.

The company's flood insurance is sold to businesses and individuals through the National Flood Insurance Program.

Geographic Reach

Selective primarily writes commercial policies in 25 eastern midwestern and southwestern states plus Washington DC. Personal policies are primarily sold in 13 states in the East and Midwest. The company also offers flood and E&S insurance policies in all 50 states plus Washington DC.

While its native New Jersey market still accounts for about 20% of Selective's net written premiums the company has successfully become a "super-regional" insurer. By doing business in a wider geographic range Selective is better able to spread out its catastrophic risk exposure. It maintains its headquarters in New Jersey and regional branch offices in New Jersey Indiana Maryland North Carolina Pennsylvania and Arizona.

Sales and Marketing

Some 1250 independent retail agents sell Selective's Standard Commercial Lines products with a focus on providing policies to small and mid-sized businesses and government entities. The company's nationwide flood protection products are sold by a network of some 5800 retail agents while E&S policies are sold through about 90 wholesale agencies and brokers.

Target clients include manufacturing and wholesale contractor community and public services and mercantile and services customers.

Promotional efforts are conducted through radio television billboard and other advertising venues including sporting events.

Financial Performance

Selective's revenue has been rising since 2010 and in general net income has also been rising. These gains have largely been driven by growth in the core commercial lines segment as well as solid retention rates.

Revenue increased 8% to $2.5 billion in 2017. Net premiums earned and investment income both grew that year and the company realized net gains of $6.4 billion versus net realized losses of $4.9 billion in 2016.

With the higher revenue net income rose 6% to $168.8 million in 2017.

The company ended 2017 with $0.5 million in net cash the same total it had at the end of 2017. Operating activities provided $370.7 million in cash that year. Investing activities used $331.1 million and financing activities used $39.6 million.

Strategy

Selective's three primary areas of interest are improving its overall customer experience refining its underwriting tools and enhancing its technological capabilities. The group focuses on organic business growth and activities to become more customer-centric. It has primarily been building up its portfolio of personal and commercial E&S insurance products. The company has established regional business teams with full underwriting authority in order to build up its presence in local markets.

Selective has also continued its expansion into new markets. In mid-2017 it began offering commercial lines in Arizona and New Hampshire. The following year it introduced commercial lines in Colorado New Mexico and Utah. The company intends to offer personal coverage in Arizona and Utah as well.

Additionally Selective has invested in technology that speeds up the process of writing new commercial business policies to improve customer and agency services. In 2017 it deployed a new underwriting platform that helps analyze new business in comparison to its existing portfolio. The following year it launched a commercial driver-sensor offering to promote safe driving. However Selective has lagged somewhat behind its competitors in launching new types of products (such as the Selective Drive application) in a timely fashion.

The company works with what it refers to as "ivy league" distribution partners who have a strong presence in Selective's key markets. Among its goals are to increase the amount of business it does with those partners and to represent a bigger business share of those partners' operations.

Like all insurers Selective relies on data to manage risk and add new business. The company has access to less data than some of its larger competitors many of whom have built up massive stores of data over decades. Because of this it has fewer capabilities to assess risk profitability adverse claim potential fraudulent activities and customer buying habits.

Company Background

In the 1920s Daniel L.B. Smith was a general store operator in Sussex County New Jersey. Almost by accident he began selling insurance out of one of his store locations and he decided that the area needed a local insurance company. With an initial investment of $20000 Smith and several partners opened Selected Risks Insurance Company. The company expanded beyond its New Jersey origins over the next several decades.

EXECUTIVES

Vice President, Eric Thiessen

Assistant Vp And Regional Safety Operations Manager, Alan Null Costa

Assistant Vice President And Actuary, Brian Krick

Chairman And Ceo, Gregory E. Murphy, age 63, $946,923 total compensation

Evp And Chief Actuary, Ronald J. Zaleski, age 64, $437,692 total compensation

Evp General Counsel And Chief Compliance Officer, Michael H. Lanza, age 57, $536,923 total compensation

President And Coo, John J. Marchioni, age 48, $793,846 total compensation

Evp And Cfo, Mark A. Wilcox, age 50

Evp And Chief Claims Officer, George A. Neale

Evp And Chief Human Resources Officer, Angelique Carbo

Evp And Cio, Gordon J. Gaudet

Svp And Chief Marketing Officer, Rohit Mull

Vice President, Dennis L Barger

Assistant Vice President, Robert Mitchell

Vice President Field Marketing Sales, Darrell Frantz

Commercial Auto Underwriting Assistant Vice President, Stan Willey

Vice President Strategic Application Development, Richard Agresta

Vice President, Eva Gonzalez

Vice President, Christopher Nickol

Vice President Office Automation, Kathy Koval

Assistant Vice President Business Case Manger, Sue Insalaco

Vice President, Jim Klotz

Vice President, Carol Ryan

Assistant Vice President Property Line, Scott Crump

Assistant Vice President Assistant Controller, Angelo Mastrolia

Assistant Vice President Workers Compensation, Joe Greco

Vice President Government Affairs And Compliance, Jeff Beck

Assistant Vice President Bond Underwriting Manager, Debra Paziora

Vice President Specialty Programs, Lorraine Miller

Assistant Vice President, Robert L Redden

Assistant Vice President Claims Service Center, Susan L Brown

Vice President Bonds East Hanover Nj, Timothy Marchio

Senior Vice President And Deputy General Counsel, Maria Orecchio

Assistant Vice President Director Of Communicatio, Jamie Beal

Assistant Vice President Corporate Systems Applica, Gary Beumee

Vice President Information Technology, Harikrishna Raghumandala

Legal Secretary, Lori Coyle

Senior Vice President, Martin Hollander

Treasurer, Sarita Chakravarthi

Auditors: KPMG LLP

LOCATIONS

HQ: Selective Insurance Group Inc
40 Wantage Avenue, Branchville, NJ 07890
Phone: 973 948-3000   **Fax:** 973 948-0282
Web: www.selective.com

PRODUCTS/OPERATIONS

2017 Sales by Segment

	$ mil.	% of total
Standard Commercial Lines	1,798	73
Standard Personal Lines	290	12
E&S Lines	212	8
Investments	168	7
Total	**2,470**	**100**

2017 Sales

	$ mil.	% of total
Net premiums earned	2,291	93
Net investment income earned	161	7
Other	10	-
Net realized gains	6	-
Total	**2,470**	**100**

COMPETITORS

Allstate	Progressive
Chubb Limited	Corporation
Cincinnati Financial	State Farm
Erie Indemnity	The Hartford
GEICO	Travelers Companies
Hanover Insurance	United Fire
Company	W. R. Berkley
Liberty Mutual	Zurich Insurance Group
Nationwide	

HISTORICAL FINANCIALS

Company Type: Public

Income Statement

FYE: December 31

	ASSETS ($ mil.)	NET INCOME ($ mil.)	INCOME AS % OF ASSETS	EMPLOYEES
12/17	7,686	168	2.2%	2,260
12/16	7,355	158	2.2%	2,250
12/15	6,904	165	2.4%	2,200
12/14	6,581	141	2.2%	2,200
12/13	6,270	106	1.7%	2,100
Annual Growth	5.2%	12.2%	—	1.9%

2017 Year-End Financials

Debt ratio: 5.71%
Return on equity: 10.41%
Cash ($ mil.): 0
Current ratio: —
Long-term debt ($ mil.): —

No. of shares (mil.): 58
Dividends
  Yield: 0.0%
  Payout: 23.2%
Market value ($ mil.): 3,434

	STOCK PRICE ($) FY Close	P/E High/Low		PER SHARE ($) Earnings	Dividends	Book Value
12/17	58.70	21	14	2.84	0.66	29.28
12/16	43.05	16	11	2.70	0.61	26.42
12/15	33.58	13	9	2.85	0.57	24.37
12/14	27.17	11	9	2.47	0.53	22.54
12/13	27.06	15	10	1.87	0.52	20.63
Annual Growth	21.4%	—	—	11.0%	6.1%	9.1%

Sempra Energy

Sempra Energy makes sure the lights are always on. In the US Sempra distributes natural gas to about 7 million customer meters and electricity to more than 3.5 million customer meters through its Southern California Gas (SoCalGas) and San Diego Gas & Electric (SDG&E) utilities. Other reporting segments include Sempra US Gas & Power (natural gas and renewables) and Sempra International (Sempra Mexico and Sempra South American Utilities) which were formerly known as Sempra Global. Sempra Energy companies serve more than 32 million consumers worldwide. In a play to acquire Oncor Electric from bankrupt parent Energy Future Holdings (EFH) Sempra agreed in 2017 to purchase a majority stake in EFH.

HISTORY

Sempra Energy is the latest incarnation of some of California's leading lights. Formed by the $6.2 billion merger between Enova and Pacific Enterprises the company traces its roots back to the 1880s.

Enova began as San Diego Gas which lit its first gaslights in 1881 and added electricity in 1887 (when it became San Diego Gas & Electric Light). Massive utility holding company Standard Gas & Electric bought the company in 1905 and renamed it San Diego Consolidated Gas & Electric. Over the next few decades San Diego Consolidated expanded through acquisitions and even stayed profitable during the Depression. But the 1935 Public Utilities Holding Company Act forced Standard to divest many of its widespread utilities and in 1940 San Diego Consolidated went public as San Diego Gas & Electric (SDG&E).

SDG&E grew quickly until the 1970s when new environmental laws slowed plans to build more power plants and rates soared because the company had to purchase power. The company finally added more generating capacity in the 1980s and the state of California allowed SDG&E to diversify into real estate software and oil and gas distribution. In 1995 it created Enova to serve as its holding company.

Meanwhile up the coast in San Francisco Pacific Enterprises began as gas lamp rental firm Pacific Lighting in 1886; it quickly moved into gas distribution to defend its market against electricity. The firm bought three Los Angeles gas and electric utilities in 1889 and continued to grow through acquisitions; it consolidated all of its utilities in the 1920s. Pacific Lighting sold its electric properties to the city of Los Angeles in 1937 in exchange for a long-term gas franchise.

The company entered oil and gas exploration in 1960. A decade later it merged its gas utility operations into Southern California Gas (SoCalGas). Pacific Lighting continued to diversify in the 1980s buying two oil and gas companies and three drugstore chains. Renamed Pacific Enterprises in 1988 the company launched an unsuccessful diversification effort that cost it $88 million in 1991. Over the next two years it sold off noncore businesses to focus on SoCalGas and in the mid-1990s it began moving into South and Central America. This included a joint venture with Enova and Mexico's Proxima SA to build and operate Mexico's first private utility.

Pacific Enterprises and Enova agreed in 1997 to a $6.2 billion merger; Sempra Energy was born in 1998. That year California began deregulating its retail power market. In response Sempra sold SDG&E's non-nuclear power plants (1900 MW) in 1999. It used the proceeds to eliminate its competitive transition charge and in turn lowered its electric rates.

But under deregulation rates tripled by mid-2000; that summer the California Public Utilities Commission (CPUC) implemented a rate freeze for electric customers. Wholesale power prices soared and rolling blackouts occurred in 2000 and 2001 as a result of the state's inadequate energy supply. In 2001 the CPUC began allowing utilities to increase their rates and SDG&E agreed to sell its transmission assets to the state for about $1 billion.

Sempra sold its 72.5% share in power marketing firm Energy America to British energy company Centrica in 2001. In 2002 the company purchased bankrupt utility Enron's London-based metals trading unit for about $145 million; later that year it purchased Enron's metals concentrates and metals warehousing businesses.

The company restructured its competitive energy business units in 2005 renaming several divisions and dividing the former Sempra Energy Solutions operations (retail energy marketing and services for commercial and indu

EXECUTIVES

Vice President, Kevin Sagara
Evp And General Counsel, Martha B. Wyrsch, age 60, $577,900 total compensation
Chairman President And Ceo, Debra L. (Debbie) Reed, age 61, $1,391,900 total compensation
Evp Corporate Strategy And External Affairs, Dennis V. Arriola, age 57
Corporate Group President Infrastructure, Joseph A. (Joe) Householder, age 62, $700,000 total compensation
Chairman And Ceo Infraestructura Energética Nova (ienova), Carlos Ruiz Sacristán, age 68
President Coo And Director Socalgas, J. Bret Lane, age 59
Ceo Southern California Gas Company (socalgas), Patricia K. (Patti) Wagner, age 56
Svp And Chief Human Resources And Administrative Officer, G. Joyce Rowland, age 63, $405,000 total compensation
Corporate Group President Of Utilities, Steven D. Davis, age 62, $541,400 total compensation
Evp And Cfo, Jeffrey W. Martin, age 56
President San Diego Gas & Electric (sdg&e), Scott D. Drury, age 52
Cio, P. Kevin Chase, age 49
Vp Enterprise Risk Management And Compliance Sdgande And Socalgas, Diana Day
Regional Vice President Commercial Development Sempra U.s. Gas And Power, Sue Bradham
Senior Vice President Regulatory And Finance, Schavrien Lee
Vp Major Project Controls, Ryan O'neal
Vice President Federal Government Affairs, Maryam Brown
Board Member, Bethany Mayer
Auditors: DELOITTE & TOUCHE LLP

LOCATIONS

HQ: Sempra Energy
  488 8th Avenue, San Diego, CA 92101
Phone: 619 696-2000
Web: www.sempra.com

2016 Sales

	$ mil.	% of total
US	8,004	79
South America	1,556	15
Mexico	623	6
Total	**10,183**	**100**

PRODUCTS/OPERATIONS

2016 Sales

	$ mil.	% of total
SDG&E	4,253	40
SoCalGas	3,471	33
Sempra South American Utilities	1,556	15
Sempra Mexico	725	7
Sempra LNG & Midstream	508	5
Sempra Renewables	34	0
Adjustments and eliminations	(364)	-
Total	**10,183**	**100**

2016 Sales

	$ mil.	% of total
Utilities:		
Electric	5,211	51
Natural gas	4,050	40
Energy-related businesses	922	9
Total	**10,183**	**100**

COMPETITORS

AEP	IBERDROLA
AES	Los Angeles Water and
AT&T	Power
Avista	NRG Energy
CMS Energy	NV Energy
Calpine	PG&E Corporation
CenterPoint Energy	PacifiCorp
Constellation Energy	Public Service
Group	Enterprise Group
Dominion Energy	Sacramento Municipal
Duke Energy	Utility
Edison International	Southern Company
Endesa S.A.	Southwest Gas
Entergy	Tenaska
Exelon Energy	Williams Companies
FirstEnergy	

HISTORICAL FINANCIALS

Company Type: Public

Income Statement

FYE: December 31

	REVENUE ($ mil.)	NET INCOME ($ mil.)	NET PROFIT MARGIN	EMPLOYEES
12/17	11,207	257	2.3%	16,046
12/16	10,183	1,371	13.5%	16,575
12/15	10,231	1,350	13.2%	17,387
12/14	11,035	1,162	10.5%	17,046
12/13	10,557	1,009	9.6%	17,122
Annual Growth	1.5%	(29.0%)	—	(1.6%)

2017 Year-End Financials

Debt ratio: 38.47%
Return on equity: 2.01%
Cash ($ mil.): 288
Current ratio: 0.50
Long-term debt ($ mil.): 16,445

No. of shares (mil.): 251
Dividends
  Yield: 0.0%
  Payout: 325.7%
Market value ($ mil.): 26,875

	STOCK PRICE ($) FY Close	P/E High/Low	PER SHARE ($) Earnings	Dividends	Book Value
12/17	106.92	120 99	1.01	3.29	50.41
12/16	100.64	21 16	5.46	3.02	51.77
12/15	94.01	21 17	5.37	2.80	47.56
12/14	111.36	25 19	4.63	2.64	45.98
12/13	89.76	22 17	4.01	2.52	45.03
Annual Growth	4.5%	— —	(29.2%)	6.9%	2.9%

SENTARA HEALTHCARE

Sentara Healthcare is not-for-profit organization that operates a network of hospitals and other health facilities primarily in the coastal Hampton Roads area of southeastern Virginia. The system includes a dozen acute care hospitals housing a total of more than 2000 beds. One of its hospitals Sentara Norfolk includes a dedicated cardiac hospital with more than 100 beds. In addition to its acute care facilities Sentara Healthcare operates several outpatient care facilities as well as nursing homes rehab centers medical practices imaging centers and home health agencies. Its Optima Health unit provides HMO PPO and other health insurance products to about 450000 Virginians.

Operations

Across the Sentara Healthcare system the organization boasts a medical staff of about 3800. The medical system's multi-specialty physicians group the Sentara Medical Group has more than 380 primary care and specialty physicians. Its Sentara Senior Services unit operates about 10 nursing and assisted living centers.

The health care group also runs the 160-bed Sentara Princess Anne Hospital an acute care facility located on the Princess Anne outpatient campus in Virginia Beach. Opened in mid-2011 it operates through a 70%-owned joint venture with Bon Secours Health System. The $145 million facility encompasses five stories and offers comprehensive surgical procedures intensive care advanced cardiac care and a maternity center.

Geographic Reach

Sentara Healthcare is the region's largest integrated health care provider serving more than 2 million residents. Its facilities serve customers throughout southeastern and northern Virginia as well as in northeastern North Carolina. It operates in the Virginia cities of Alleghany Charlottesville Hampton Roads Harrisonburg Richmond and Roanoke. In North Carolina Sentara has a presence in Currituck and Elizabeth City.

Financial Performance

The system's revenues increased 9% to $4.7 billion in 2014 due to an increase in net patient services revenues and other operating revenues. Net income fell 82% to $156 million though as salaries and wages increased medical claims and other operating expenses rose and investment gains declined. Cash flow from operations decreased 25% that year to $318 million as a result of the lower net income plus an increase in cash used in receivables and changes in employee compensation and benefits.

Strategy

While it is already one of the largest health care organizations in the state Sentara Healthcare continues to grow through acquisitions construction (both expansions and new buildings) and mergers. In 2014 it acquired the assets and operations of Albemarle Hospital Albemarle Physician Services and Regional Medical Services through a 30-year capital lease agreement with Pasquotank County and Albemarle Hospital Authority. The businesses were combined into newly formed subsidiary SAMC. In 2015 Sentara Leigh Hospital opened a new tower as part of a larger renovation project.

Also in 2015 the system launched a new retail website shopsentara.com which offers over-the-counter health care products including medications vitamins exercise equipment diabetic care supplies and educational books.

Company Background

Sentara Healthcare was founded in 1888 as Norfolk's 25-bed Retreat for the Sick.

EXECUTIVES

Senior Vice President Human Resources, Michael Taylor
Ceo, Howard P. Kern
Svp And Cio, Bertram S. (Bert) Reese
Svp And Cfo, Robert A. (Rob) Broerman
Svp; President Sentara Health Plans And Optima Health, Michael M. Dudley
President Sentara Leigh Hospital, Teresa L. (Terrie) Edwards
President Sentara Careplex Hospital, Debra A. Flores
Corporate Vp Sentara Norfolk General Hospital Sentara Careplex Hospital And Sentara Williamsburg Regional Medical Center, Mary L. Blunt
President Sentara Martha Jefferson Hospital, Jonathan S. Davis
President Sentara Virginia Beach General Hospital, Elwood B. (Bernie) Boone
Chief Nursing Officer, Genemarie McGee
Svp And Chief Medical Officer, Terry Gilliland
President Sentara Williamsburg Regional Medical Center, David J. (Dave) Masterson
President Sentara Norfolk General Hospital, Kurt Hofelich
President Sentara Life Care Corporation, Bruce Robertson
Corporate Vp; President Sentara Rmh Medical Center, Jim Krauss
Corporate Vp; President Sentara Medical Group, Robert (Doug) Culling
Corporate Vp, Michael Gentry
President Sentara Enterprises, Linda R. Huffer
President Sentara Obici Hospital, Steve Julian
President Sentara Halifax Regional Hospital, Chris A. Lumsden
Corporate Vp; President Sentara Northern Virgnia Medical Center, Stephen D. Porter
President Sentara Albemarle Medical Center, Coleen Santa Ana
Corporate Vice President, Terrie Edwards
Vice President Coporate Strategy, Grace Hines
Vice President And Executive Medical Director Clinical Effectiveness, Gene Burke
Vice President Network Management, Rachel Schneider
Vice President, Ken Krakaur
Vice President Finance, Lester Eljaiek
Director Of Him, Marsha Rooks
Vice President Operations, Valerie Keane
Vice President And Chief Information Security Officer, Daniel Bowden
Vice President Of Medical Affairs, David Schwartz
Vice President Government Relations And Health Policy, Paul Speidell
Vice President For Clinical Informatics And Transformation, David Mohr
Medical Director Hematopathology Division, Steve Fisher
Vice President Medical Affairs, Michael Ashby
Chairman, Bob Fort
Vice Chairman, Henry (Sandy) Harris
Auditors: KPMG LLP NORFOLK VIRGINIA

LOCATIONS

HQ: SENTARA HEALTHCARE
6015 POPLAR HALL DR, NORFOLK, VA 235023819
Phone: 800 736-8272
Web: WWW.SENTARA.COM

PRODUCTS/OPERATIONS

Selected Hospitals
Charlottesville
  Martha Jefferson Hospital
  MJH Outpatient Care Center
  Health Services at Proffit Road
  Health Services at Spring Creek
  Sentara Home Care Services
  Optima Health
Hampton Roads
  Sentara CarePlex Hospital
  Sentara Heart Hospital
  Sentara Leigh Hospital
  Sentara Norfolk General Hospital
  Sentara Obici Hospital
  Sentara Princess Anne Hospital
  Sentara Virginia Beach General Hospital
  Sentara Williamsburg Regional Medical Center
  Orthopaedic Hospital at Sentara CarePlex
  Sentara Northern Virginia Medical Center
  Martha Jefferson Hospital
  RMH Healthcare
Harrisonburg
  RMH Healthcare
  Optima Health
Northern Virginia
  Sentara Northern Virginia Medical Center
  Sentara Lake Ridge
  Sentara Medical Group physicians
  Sentara Home Care Services
  Sentara Heart and Vascular Center
  Optima Health

Selected Services
Cancer
Cardiac (Heart)
Digestive (Colorectal)
Home Care
Imaging
Maternity
Neurosciences
Rehabilitation
Seniors
Thoracic
Transplant
Trauma/Emergency Services
Urology
Vascular
Weight Loss Surgery
Women's

COMPETITORS

Aetna
Anthem Health Plans of Virginia
Bon Secours Health
CIGNA
Carilion Clinic
Centra Health Inc.
Children's Hospital of The King's Daughters
Franklin Hospital Corp.
HCA Capital Division
Humana
Inova
Kaiser Foundation Health Plan of the Mid-Atlantic
Norton Community Hospital
Novant Health
Riverside Health System (Virginia)
Twin County Regional Healthcare
UnitedHealth Group

HISTORICAL FINANCIALS

Company Type: Private

Income Statement
FYE: December 31

	REVENUE ($ mil.)	NET INCOME ($ mil.)	NET PROFIT MARGIN	EMPLOYEES
12/17	5,297	580	11.0%	28,000
12/16	5,083	329	6.5%	—
12/15	4,833	130	2.9%	—
12/14	4,694	359	7.7%	—
Annual Growth	4.1%	17.3%	—	—

2017 Year-End Financials

Debt ratio: ——
Return on equity: 11.00%
Cash ($ mil.): 704
Current ratio: 1.10
Long-term debt ($ mil.): —

Dividends
Yield: —
Payout: —
Market value ($ mil.): —

ServisFirst Bancshares Inc

ServisFirst Bancshares is a bank holding company for ServisFirst Bank a regional commercial bank with about a dozen branches located in Alabama and the Florida panhandle. The bank also has a loan office in Nashville. ServisFirst Bank targets privately-held businesses with $2 million to $250 million in annual sales as well as professionals and affluent customers. The bank focuses on traditional commercial banking services including loan origination deposits and electronic banking services such as online and mobile banking. Founded in 2005 by its chairman and CEO Thomas Broughton III the bank went public in 2014 with an offering valued at nearly $57 million.

IPO
ServisFirst Bancshares sold 625000 shares priced at $91 per share. Proceeds from the May 2014 IPO will be used to support the bank's growth plans both in Alabama and in other states.

Geographic Reach
Birmingham-based ServisFirst Bank has branches in Birmingham Huntsville Montgomery Mobile Dothan Pensacola and Nashville.

Financial Performance
The bank reported net income of $41.2 million in 2013 compared with $34 million in 2012. The increase was primarily due to an increase in net interest income which rose nearly 20% to $112.5 million. Noninterest income increased 4% to $10 million in 2013.

As of March 2014 the bank had total assets of approximately $3.6 billion total loans of $2.9 billion and total deposits of about $3.0 billion.

EXECUTIVES

President And Ceo Servisfirst Bancshares And Servisfirst Bank, Thomas A. (Tom) Broughton, age 62, $350,000 total compensation

Evp And Coo Servisfirst Bancshares And Servisfirst Bank, Clarence C. Pouncey, age 61, $263,000 total compensation

Evp Cfo Treasurer And Secretary Servisfirst Bancshares And Servisfirst Bank, William M. Foshee, age 63, $230,000 total compensation

Evp Servisfirst Bancshares And President And Ceo Servisfirst Bank Of Huntsville, Andrew N. (Andy) Kattos, age 48

President And Ceo Servisfirst Bank Of Mobile, William (Bibb) Lamar, age 74

Evp Servisfirst Bancshares And President And Ceo Servisfirst Bank Of Montgomery, G. Carlton (Carl) Barker, age 63

Evp Servisfirst Bancshares And President And Ceo Servisfirst Bank Of Pensacola, Rex D. McKinney, age 55

Evp Correspondent Banking Servisfirst Bancshares And Servisfirst Bank, Rodney D. Rushing, age 60, $245,000 total compensation

Svp And Chief Credit Officer Servisfirst Bancshares And Servisfirst Bank, Don G. Owens, age 66, $187,200 total compensation

President And Ceo Servisfirst Bank Of Atlanta, Ken Barber

Evp And Chief Lending Officer, Doug Rehm

Ceo Servisfirst Bank Dothan, B. Harrison Morris, age 41

Assistant Vice President Of Private Banking Of Servisfirst Bank, Ron Morrison

First Vice President, Lee McKinnon

Senior Vice President Commercial Lending, Chad Thomason

Vice President Commercial Banking, Jamie Osteen

Vice President, John Peacock

Senior Vice President, Michael Wood

Senior Vice President Commercial Relationship Manager, Jim Gardner

Senior Vice President, Justin Fontenot

Vice President, Kiley Elmore

Senior Vice President Private Banking, Patricia Griner

Vice President, Chris Blaze

Vice President Portfolio Manager, Gary Allen

Fvp Commercial Banking, Cheryl Dunn

Assistant Vice President Branch Manager, Ron Leddon

Senior Vice President, Samantha S Curd

Vice President Credit Officer, Stacy B Suddeth

Assistant Vice President Cash Management Services, Loretta Shapiro

Vice President Credit Officer, Stacy Suddeth

Chairman Servisfirst Bancshares And Servisfirst Bank, Stanley M. (Skip) Brock, age 67

Auditors: Dixon Hughes Goodman LLP

LOCATIONS

HQ: ServisFirst Bancshares Inc
2500 Woodcrest Place, Birmingham, AL 35209
Phone: 205 949-0302
Web: www.servisfirstbank.com

2013 Branches

	No.
Alabama	10
Florida	2
Total	**12**

COMPETITORS

Bank of America
Bank of the Ozarks
Wells Fargo

HISTORICAL FINANCIALS

Company Type: Public

Income Statement
FYE: December 31

	ASSETS ($ mil.)	NET INCOME ($ mil.)	INCOME AS % OF ASSETS	EMPLOYEES
12/17	7,082	93	1.3%	434
12/16	6,370	81	1.3%	420
12/15	5,095	63	1.2%	371
12/14	4,098	52	1.3%	298
12/13	3,520	41	1.2%	262
Annual Growth	19.1%	22.3%	—	13.4%

2017 Year-End Financials

Debt ratio: 0.92%
Return on equity: 16.48%
Cash ($ mil.): 238
Current ratio: —
Long-term debt ($ mil.): —

No. of shares (mil.): 52
Dividends
Yield: 0.0%
Payout: 11.6%
Market value ($ mil.): 2,199

	STOCK PRICE ($) FY Close	P/E High/Low		PER SHARE ($) Earnings	Dividends	Book Value
12/17	41.50	25	19	1.72	0.20	11.46
12/16	37.44	48	23	1.52	0.19	9.93
12/15	47.53	40	24	1.20	0.12	8.64
12/14	32.95	83	26	1.05	0.16	8.20
Annual Growth	5.9%	—	—	13.3%	6.0%	8.7%

Sherwin-Williams Co (The)

You won?t catch Sherwin-Williams watching the paint dry. It keeps rolling on as it has for its roughly 150 year history maintaining its position as one of the world?s top paint manufacturers (along with Akzo-Nobel PPG Industries and Henkel). Sherwin-Williams' products include a variety of paints finishes coatings applicators and varnishes sold under brands such as Dutch Boy Krylon Sherwin-Williams Valspar Thompson's WaterSeal Ronseal and Minwax. The company operates throughout the world about 4100 paint stores and sells automotive finishing and refinishing products through wholesale branches. Other outlets include mass merchandisers home centers independent dealers and automotive retailers. Sherwin-Williams completed an $8.9 billion acquisition of rival Valspar in 2017.

HISTORY

In 1870 Henry Sherwin bought out paint materials distributor Truman Dunham and joined Edward Williams and A. T. Osborn to form Sherwin Williams & Company in Cleveland. The business began making paints in 1871 and became the industry leader after improving the paint-grinding mill in the mid-1870s patenting a reclosable can in 1877 and improving liquid paint in 1880.

In 1874 Sherwin-Williams introduced a special paint for carriages beginning the concept of specific-purpose paint. (By 1900 the company had paints for floors roofs barns metal bridges railroad cars and automobiles.) Sherwin-Williams incorporated in 1884 and opened a dealership in Massachusetts in 1891 that was the forerunner of its company-run retail stores. The company obtained its "Cover the Earth" trademark in 1895.

Before the Depression Sherwin-Williams bought a number of smaller paint makers: Detroit White Lead (1910) Martin-Senour (1917) Acme Quality Paints (1920) and The Lowe Brothers (1929). Responding to wartime restrictions the company developed a fast-drying and water-reducible paint called Kem-Tone and the forerunner of the paint roller the Roller-Koater.

Sales doubled during the 1960s as the company made acquisitions including Sprayon (aerosol paint 1966) but rising expenses kept earnings flat. In 1972 the company expanded its stores to include carpeting draperies and other decorating items. But long-term debt ballooned from $80 million in 1974 to $196 million by 1977 when the company lost $8.2 million and suspended dividends for the first time since 1885.

John Breen became CEO in 1979 reinstated the dividend purged over half of the top management positions and closed inefficient plants. He also focused stores on paint and wallpaper merchandise and purchased Dutch Boy (1980).

In 1990 Sherwin-Williams began selling Dutch Boy in Sears stores and Kem-Tone in Wal-Marts. Acquisitions that year included Borden's Krylon and Illinois Bronze aerosol operations and DeSoto's architectural coatings segment which made private-label paints for Sears and Home Depot. In 1991 Sherwin-Williams bought two coatings business units from Cook Paint and Varnish and the Cuprinol brand of coatings.

Sherwin-Williams purchased paint manufacturer Pratt & Lambert in 1996. That year it introduced several new products including Low Temp 35 a paint for low temperatures; Healthspec a low-odor paint; and Ralph Lauren designer paints. PrepRite do-it-yourself interior primers debuted in 1997. Also that year Sherwin-Williams bought Thompson Minwax (Thompson's Water Seal Minwax Wood Products) from Forstmann Little and Chile-based Marson Chilena a spray paint maker.

The company streamlined some of its business segments and trimmed jobs in 1998. Christopher Connor president of the Paint Stores group replaced Breen as CEO in 1999 and chairman in 2000. Also in 2000 Sherwin-Williams moved into the European automotive coatings market by acquiring Italy-based ScottWarren.

In late 2001 the company acquired Wisconsin-based Mautz Paint Company.

After a rough but still profitable 2001 the company grew revenues and profits for its consumer units (consumer paints and paint stores) in 2002 thanks largely to a healthy do-it-yourself market. Sales for its automotive finishes and international units however were down because of a slow collision-repair market and currency-exchange effects.

In 2010 Sherwin-Williams bought Arch Chemicals' Sayerlack a leading Italian wood care coating company and acquired Becker Acroma Industrial Wood Coatings a Swedish manufacturer of industrial wood coatings. It also acquired all shares of AlSher Titania (a joint venture with Altair Nanotechnologies) it did not already own giving it a 100% stake in the technology company. AlSher Titania is developing a promising titanium dioxide technology that Sherwin-Williams plans to commercialize.

That same year the company also acquired Pinturas CA?ndor an Ecuadorian diversified coatings supplier with $60 million in annual sales bolstering its market share in architectural paint in Latin America.

Among its acquisitions in 2011 was UK-based Leighs Paints a leader in fire-protectant (intumescent) coatings. (Because the intumescent technology prolongs the structural integrity of steel and concrete in a catastrophic fire more people are able to evacuate.)

In 2012 Sherwin-Williams made a significant purchase in the buyout of Jiangsu Pulanna Coating Co. headquartered in Changzhou China. Pulanna is an automotive refinishes coatings manufacturer and the deal improved Sherwin-Williams' presence in the most populous country in the world.

Also in 2012 Sherwin-Williams picked up Geocel Holdings a maker of caulks sealants and adhesives serving construction and repair applications. Geocel has locations in the US and the UK and the deal strengthened Sherwin-Williams' Consumer Group segment.

In a major geographic expansion in late 2012 the company agreed to acquire Grupo Comex a leader in the paint and coatings market in Mexico for $2.34 billion. However Mexico's antitrust regulator blocked the deal in mid-2013 stating the new company could artificially set higher prices at its discretion. Sherwin-Williams subsequently terminated the proposed deal.

However in 2013 the company acquired the US/Canada business of Comex. Sherwin-Williams paid $90 million in cash and assumed liabilities in the range of $75 million. Comex operations in the US and Canada consist of 314 company operated stores (234 in the US and 80 in Canada) and 8 manufacturing sites (5 in the US and 3 in Canada). In addition Comex supplies paint and coatings products to 1500 external retail locations.

2013 product launches included Sherwin-Williams Protective & Marine Coatings' Magnalux 404 FF the first styrene-free vinyl ester for use with steel and concrete substrates in the oil and gas market; Fast Clad 105ER a 100% solids tank lining for crude oil and ethanol storage; and NovaPlate 325 an extended lifecycle 100% solids tank lining for high-temperature crude oil produced water and frac tank applications.

In 2013 Sherwin-Williams teamed up with Williams-Sonoma to create seasonal palettes of Sherwin-Williams paint colors that coordinate with the Pottery Barn Pottery Barn Kids PBteen and West Elm collections.

EXECUTIVES

Chairman President And Ceo, John G. Morikis, age 55, $1,095,795 total compensation
President And General Manager Latin America Division The Americas Group, Paul R. Clifford
Cio, Thomas J. (Tom) Lucas
President The Americas Group, Robert J. Davisson, age 58, $611,936 total compensation
President And General Manager South Western Division The Americas Group, Monty J. Griffin, age 58
President And General Manager Diversified Brands Division Consumer Group, Cheri M. Phyfer, age 47
President And General Manager Automotive Division Global Finishes Group, Thomas C. Hablitzel, age 56
President And General Manager Global Supply Chain Division Consumer Group, Joel D. Baxter, age 58
President And General Manager Mid Western Division The Americas Group, Peter J. Ippolito, age 54
President And General Manager Protective And Marine Coatings Division Global Finishes Group, Ronald B. Rossetto
President Global Finishes Group, David B. Sewell, age 50
President Southeastern Division Paint Stores Group, Todd V. Wipf
President And General Manager Product Finishes Division Global Finishes Group, Bruce G. Irussi
Svp Finance And Cfo, Allen J. Mistysyn, age 49
President And General Manager Eastern Division The Americas Group, Justin T. Binns
Senior Vice President General Counsel An, Catherine Kilbane
Vice President Sales, Brian Padden
National Account Manager, Vincent Barone
Vice President Of Sales, Jim Sinko
National Account Manager, Pat Busch
National Accounts Manager, Harvey Kulkin
Vice President Of Sales And Marketing, Nate Shinsky
Vice President Of Sales And Business Development, Jennie S Gerardot
Vice President Engineering, Beth Egan
Vice President Human Resources, Scott Gradert
Vice President Taxes And Assistant Secretary Sherwin Williams Company, Michael Cummins
Vice President Global Sourcing, David Ash
Vice President, Mark Mazanec
National Account Manager, Joe Di Bianca
Vp Of Human Resources, Susan — Keough
National Account Manager, David Norring
Vice President Sales, Gary Campbell
Vice President Executive Compensation, Greg Sofish
National Account Manager, John Hackett
Vice President Human Resources, Lonnie McGowen
Vice President Of Information Security, Karen Gabel
National Sales Manager, Kurt Hostetler
Svp Corporate Communications And Public Affairs, Robert Wells
National Account Manager, Randy Scott
Vice President Of Regional Operations, Phil Matisak
Vice President Global Sourcing, Jose Aravena
Vice President Merchandising, Kevin Madigan
Vice President, Mike Campbell
Board Member, Rick Kramer
Board Member, Joseph Banks
Treasurer, Scott McVeigh
Board Member, Chris Pluta
Board Member, Vicki Deckard
Treasurer, Isaac Blaylock
Auditors: Ernst & Young LLP

LOCATIONS

HQ: Sherwin-Williams Co (The)
101 West Prospect Avenue, Cleveland, OH 44115-1075
Phone: 216 566-2000 **Fax:** 216 566-3310
Web: www.sherwin.com

PRODUCTS/OPERATIONS

2016 sales

	$ mil.	% of total
Paint Stores Group	7,790	66
Global Finishes Group	1,889	16
Consumer Group	1,584	13
Latin America Coatings Group	586	5
Administrative	5	-
Total	**11,855**	**100**

Operations

Operations
Paint Stores
  Products
  Architectural coatings
  Industrial maintenance
  Marine products
  Brands
  ArmorSeal
  Brod-Dugan
  Con-Lux
  FlexBon Paints
  Hi-Temp
  Kem
  Mautz
  Mercury
  Old Quaker
  Powdura
  Pro-Line
  SeaGuard
  Sherwin-Williams
Consumer
  Products
  Architectural paints
  Industrial maintenance
  Paints
  Private-label coatings
  Stains
  Wood finishings
  Varnishes
  Brands
  Cabot
  Cuprinol
  Dupli-color
  Dura Clad
  Dutch Boy
  EverLast
  Formby's
  H&C

Krylon
Martin Senour
Maxwood Latex Stains
Minwax
Plastic Kote
Pratt & Lambert
Red Devil
Rubberset
Signature Select
Thompson's WaterSeal
Valspar
White Lightning
Automotive Finishes
 Products
 Finishing refinishing and touch-up products for motor
 vehicles
 Brands
 Baco
 Excelo
 Lazzuril
 Martin Senour
 ScottWarren
 Sherwin-Williams
 Western
International Coatings
 Products
 Architectural paints
 Industrial maintenance products
 Stains
 Varnishes
 Wood finishing products
 Brands
 Andina
 Colorgin
 Dutch Boy
 Globo
 Kem-Tone
 Krylon
 Marson
 Martin Senour
 Minwax
 Pratt & Lambert
 Pulverlack
 Ronseal
 Sherwin-Williams
 Sumare

COMPETITORS

Akzo Nobel	Dunn-Edwards
BASF SE	Ferro
Benjamin Moore	H.B. Fuller
California Products	Kelly-Moore
Comex Group	Masco
Coronado Paint	PPG Industries
Diamond Vogel Paint	RPM International
DuPont	

HISTORICAL FINANCIALS

Company Type: Public

Income Statement   FYE: December 31

	REVENUE ($ mil.)	NET INCOME ($ mil.)	NET PROFIT MARGIN	EMPLOYEES
12/17	14,983	1,772	11.8%	52,695
12/16	11,855	1,132	9.6%	42,550
12/15	11,339	1,053	9.3%	40,706
12/14	11,129	865	7.8%	39,674
12/13	10,185	752	7.4%	37,633
Annual Growth	10.1%	23.9%	—	8.8%

2017 Year-End Financials

Debt ratio: 52.71%	No. of shares (mil.): 93
Return on equity: 63.63%	Dividends
Cash ($ mil.): 204	Yield: 0.0%
Current ratio: 1.12	Payout: 18.2%
Long-term debt ($ mil.): 9,885	Market value ($ mil.): 38,496

	STOCK PRICE ($) FY Close	P/E High/Low	PER SHARE ($) Earnings	Dividends	Book Value
12/17	410.04	22 14	18.67	3.40	39.33
12/16	268.74	25 19	11.99	3.36	20.20
12/15	259.60	26 19	11.16	2.68	9.41
12/14	263.04	30 20	8.78	2.20	10.52
12/13	183.50	26 21	7.26	2.00	17.72
Annual Growth	22.3%		26.6% 14.2%	22.1%	

SHI INTERNATIONAL CORP.

Businesses that need more than boxes of hardware and software can call SHI International. The company distributes scores of computer hardware and software products from suppliers such as Adobe Cisco Microsoft VMware Symantec and Lenovo. It resells PCs networking products data storage systems printers software and keyboards among other items. SHI offers a range of professional services including software licensing asset management managed desktop services systems integration and vocational training. The company serves corporate government and health care customers from more than 30 offices across the US Canada the UK Germany France and Hong Kong. SHI was founded in 1989 by Chairman Koguan Leo.

Operations

SHI serves several sectors and verticals. The company specializes in software and hardware procurement deployment planning configuration data center optimization IT asset management and cloud computing as well as custom IT solutions.

Geographic Reach

Based in Somerset New Jersey SHI has a global reach through its 30-plus offices located across the US Canada the UK Germany France and Hong Kong. In the US the company operates primarily in Texas and California but also in Arizona Colorado Florida Georgia Illinois Indiana Kansas Massachusetts Michigan Minnesota Missouri New Jersey New York Pennsylvania Virginia and Washington. Specifically its cloud briefing center is housed in New York City and its corporate call center runs from Austin Texas. The company's 420000-sq.-ft. headquarters operates beside its 305000-sq.-ft. Integration Center in Somerset New Jersey.

Financial Performance

SHI International rang up $6.8 billion in sales in 2015 a 14% increase versus the prior year. SHI's Strategic Enterprise Commercial Enterprise Corporate and Public Sector divisions contributed nearly equally to the revenue total for the year and growth outside the U.S. was steady with SHI's Canada U.K. and France divisions each posting double-digit growth. In addition SHI recognized over $1 billion in revenue from cloud products and solutions.

The seller of IT products and services boasts a 99% annual customer retention rate.

Strategy

The company has transformed itself from a $1 million regional reseller of software to a $5 billion global provider of information technology products and services. To this end SHI has invested some $20 million in a new data center that provides cloud services specifically what the company terms infrastructure-as-a-service (IaaS). The data center is one of six in the US that houses virtual machines for IT professionals to provide services such as application deployment disaster recovery software-as-a-service (SaaS). It also offers on-demand burst computing services where customers use the additional bandwidth to handle peaks in demand.

SHI's professional services unit already provides some cloud services and data center consulting. SHI sees IaaS as a logical extension of the software asset management (SAM) service it already provides. Under the SAM program SHI handles software deployment licensing compliance and inventories across a business.

SHI partners with Omaha Nebraska-based information security software specialist Solutionary to manage data security services using its Active-Guard software product to block computer network security breaches as data center security is one of the biggest concerns for businesses in a cloud computing environment.   Awards and Recognition

SHI is the largest minority and women-owned Business Enterprise (MWBE) in the US. The company's ranked 13th on CRN's 2015 Solution Provider 500 list of the largest IT solution providers in North America.

EXECUTIVES

President And Ceo, Thai Lee, age 61
Vp And General Manager, Hal Jagger
Vice President Internal Audit And Finance Operations, Kevin Boyles
Vice President, Melissa Graham
Chairman, Koguan Leo
Auditors: COHNREZNICK LLP NEW YORK NEW

LOCATIONS

HQ: SHI INTERNATIONAL CORP.
  290 DAVIDSON AVE, SOMERSET, NJ 088734145
Phone: 732 764-8888
Web: WWW.SHI.COM

PRODUCTS/OPERATIONS

Selected Products
Accessories
Peripherals
Hardware
Memory
Software

Selected Services
Cloud services
Computer vocational training services
Data center services
Events
Hardware services
Networking
POLARIS Software asset management
Storage
Strategic consulting
Webinars

COMPETITORS

ASI Computer Technologies	Computacenter
Agilysys	Ingram Micro
Arrow Electronics	Insight Enterprises
Avnet	PC Mall
CDW	Softchoice
CompuCom	Tech Data

HISTORICAL FINANCIALS

Company Type: Private

Income Statement

FYE: December 31

	REVENUE ($ mil.)	NET INCOME ($ mil.)	NET PROFIT MARGIN	EMPLOYEES
12/17	8,243	197	2.4%	3,800
12/16	7,268	104	1.4%	—
12/15	6,540	69	1.1%	—
12/14	5,797	89	1.5%	—
Annual Growth	12.5%	30.3%	—	—

2017 Year-End Financials

Debt ratio: ——
Return on equity: 2.40%
Cash ($ mil.): 116
Current ratio: 1.20
Long-term debt ($ mil.): —

Dividends
Yield: —
Payout: —
Market value ($ mil.): —

SI Financial Group Inc (MD)

EXECUTIVES

Pres-Ceo, Rheo A Brouillard
Chb, Mark D Alliod
Exec V Pres-Cfo, Lauren L Murphy
Exec V Pres-Coo, Laurie L Gervais
Svp-Chief Credit Officer Bank, Paul R Little
Evp-Dir Ret Banking Bank, Jonathan S Wood
Svp-Chief Lending Officer Bank, Kenneth B Martin
Board Member, Dennis Pollack
Senior Vice President, Gerald Coia
Board Member, Kathleen Nealon
Board Member, Kevin McCarthy
Auditors: Wolf & Company, P.C.

LOCATIONS

HQ: SI Financial Group Inc (MD)
803 Main Street, Willimantic, CT 06226
Phone: 860 423-4581
Web: www.mysifi.com

COMPETITORS

Bank of America	People's United
Citizens Financial	Financial
Group	Sovereign Bank
Liberty Bank	TD Bank USA
PSB Holdings Inc.	Webster Financial

HISTORICAL FINANCIALS

Company Type: Public

Income Statement

FYE: December 31

	ASSETS ($ mil.)	NET INCOME ($ mil.)	INCOME AS % OF ASSETS	EMPLOYEES
12/17	1,580	5	0.3%	281
12/16	1,550	11	0.7%	297
12/15	1,481	4	0.3%	292
12/14	1,350	4	0.3%	299
12/13	1,346	(0)	—	315
Annual Growth	4.1%	—	—	(2.8%)

2017 Year-End Financials

Debt ratio: 0.80%
Return on equity: 3.15%
Cash ($ mil.): 83
Current ratio: —
Long-term debt ($ mil.): —

No. of shares (mil.): 12
Dividends
Yield: 0.0%
Payout: 45.4%
Market value ($ mil.): 180

	STOCK PRICE ($) FY Close	P/E High/Low		PER SHARE ($) Earnings	Dividends	Book Value
12/17	14.70	37	31	0.44	0.20	13.76
12/16	15.40	17	13	0.95	0.16	13.49
12/15	13.65	38	30	0.36	0.15	12.63
12/14	11.33	34	30	0.36	0.12	12.35
12/13	12.05	—	—	(0.08)	0.12	11.94
Annual Growth	5.1%		—	—	13.6%	3.6%

Sierra Bancorp

Sierra Bancorp is the holding company for the nearly $2 billion-asset Bank of the Sierra which operates approximately 30 branches in Central California's San Joaquin Valley between (and including) Bakersfield and Fresno. The bank offers traditional deposit products and loans to individuals and small and mid-size businesses. About 70% of its loan portfolio is made up of real estate loans while another 15% is made up of mortgage warehouse loans and a further 10% is tied to commercial and industrial loans (including SBA loans and direct finance leases). The bank also issues agricultural loans and consumer loans.

Operations

Bank of the Sierra makes almost 80% of its revenue from interest income. About 64% of its total revenue came from interest income on loans and leases (including fees) during 2015 while another 14% came from interest income on taxed and tax-exempt securities. The rest of its revenue came from deposit account service charges (12% of revenue) checkcard fees (5%) and other non-interest income sources.

Geographic Reach

The Porterville California-based bank operates branches and offices mostly in the San Joaquin Valley in Porterville Arroyo Grande Atascadero Bakersfield California City Clovis Delano Dinuba Exeter Farmersville Fillmore Fresno Hanford Lindsay Oxnard Paso Robles Reedley San Luis Obispo Santa Clarita Santa Paula Selma Tehachapi Three Rivers Visalia and Tulare.

Sales and Marketing

Bank of the Sierra has been gradually increasing its advertising spend in recent years. It spent $2.3 million on advertising and promotion in 2015 up from $2.2 million and $1.9 million in 2014 and 2013 respectively.

Financial Performance

The bank's revenue has been steadily rising over the past few years mostly as bank acquisitions and organic loan business growth has spurred higher interest income. Meanwhile its profits have more than doubled since 2011 thanks to declining loan loss provisions as its loan portfolio's credit quality has improved with higher property valuations in the strengthened economy.

Sierra Bancorp's revenue jumped 13% to $80.4 million during 2015 thanks to higher interest income from continued double-digit loan asset growth led by a jump in mortgage warehouse lines from increased line utilization a first-quarter purchase of residential mortgage loans and strong organic growth in non-farm real estate and agricul-

---

tural production loans. Deposit account service fees also grew thanks to organic deposit client growth.

Strong revenue growth and lower acquisition costs in 2015 drove the bank's net income up 19% to $18 million. Sierra's operating cash levels rose 4% to $29.78 million during the year as its cash-based earnings increased.

Strategy

While the Bank of Sierra has traditionally grown organically by opening around one new branch per year in the Central Valley it has more recently acquired small area banks and individual branches to bolster its deposit and loan business while expanding into untapped markets such as further south into the Santa Clara Valley.

Mergers and Acquisitions

In July 2016 the bank bought $145 million-asset Coast Bancorp and its Coast National Bank branches in San Luis Obispo Paso Robles Arroyo Grande and Atascadero California.

In November 2014 Sierra Bancorp bought $129 million-asset Santa Clara Valley Bank N.A. and its branches in Santa Paula Santa Clarita and Fillmore in California for $15 million. the deal expanded Sierra's reach outside of its traditional market for the first time more south into the Santa Clara Valley of California.

EXECUTIVES

Evp And Cfo, Kenneth R. (Ken) Taylor, age 58, $242,500 total compensation
Evp And Chief Credit Officer, James F. (Jim) Gardunio, age 67, $197,600 total compensation
President And Ceo, Kevin J. McPhaill, age 45, $185,000 total compensation
Senior Vice President Director Of Marketing, Matthew Hessler
Assistant Vice President Senior Credit Analyst, Karen S Nishimura
Vice President Commercial Lending, Kiersten Alfieri
Assistant Vice President Operations Manager, Karlee Ramirez
Chairman, Morris A. Tharp, age 78
Auditors: Vavrinek, Trine, Day & Co., LLP

LOCATIONS

HQ: Sierra Bancorp
86 North Main Street, Porterville, CA 93257
Phone: 559 782-4900
Web: www.bankofthesierra.com

COMPETITORS

Bank of America	MUFG Americas Holdings
Bank of the West	United Security
Central Valley	Bancshares
Community Bancorp	Wells Fargo
Citibank	Westamerica
Comerica	Zions Bancorporation
JPMorgan Chase	

HISTORICAL FINANCIALS

Company Type: Public

Income Statement

FYE: December 31

	ASSETS ($ mil.)	NET INCOME ($ mil.)	INCOME AS % OF ASSETS	EMPLOYEES
12/17	2,340	19	0.8%	576
12/16	2,032	17	0.9%	497
12/15	1,796	18	1.0%	431
12/14	1,637	15	0.9%	437
12/13	1,410	13	0.9%	406
Annual Growth	13.5%	10.0%	—	9.1%

2017 Year-End Financials

Debt ratio: 1.48%
Return on equity: 8.46%
Cash ($ mil.): 70
Current ratio: —
Long-term debt ($ mil.): —

No. of shares (mil.): 15
Dividends
  Yield: 0.0%
  Payout: 41.1%
Market value ($ mil.): 404

	STOCK PRICE ($) FY Close	P/E High/Low	PER SHARE ($) Earnings	Dividends	Book Value
12/17	20.50	21 17	1.30	0.50	10.81
12/16	26.59	20 12	1.29	0.48	14.94
12/15	17.65	14 11	1.33	0.42	14.36
12/14	17.56	16 14	1.08	0.34	13.67
12/13	16.09	21 12	0.94	0.26	12.78
Annual Growth	13.3%	— —	9.7%	21.1%	7.1%

Signature Bank (New York, NY)

Signature Bank marks the spot where some professional New Yorkers bank. The institution provides customized banking and financial services to smaller private businesses their owners and their top executives through 30 branches across the New York metropolitan area including all five boroughs Long Island and affluent Westchester County. The bank's lending activities mainly entail real estate and business loans. Subsidiary Signature Securities offers wealth management financial planning brokerage services asset management and insurance while its Signature Financial subsidiary offers equipment financing and leasing. Founded in 2001 the bank now boasts assets of roughly $29 billion.

Operations

Mortgage loans including commercial real estate loans multifamily residential mortgages home loans and lines of credit and construction and land loans comprise the bulk of Signature Bank's loan portfolio (and much of its asset base as well).

The bank which staffed some 1010 employees at the end of 2014 generated 68% of its revenue from interest on loans and leases that year while 20% came from interest on its securities available-for-sale and 7% came from securities held-to-maturity. The remainder of its revenue came from fees and service charges (2%) and various other miscellaneous sources.

Geographic Reach

The bank's nearly 30 branch offices are mostly in the New York metropolitan area which includes Manhattan Brooklyn Westchester Long Island Queens the Bronx Staten Island and Connecticut.

Sales and Marketing

Signature Bank mostly serves privately-owned businesses their owners and senior managers (typically with a net worth between $500000 and $20 million).

Financial Performance

The company's revenues and profits have risen in recent years thanks to strong organic loan business growth and declining loan loss provisions as its loan portfolio's credit quality has improved with higher property valuations in the strengthened economy.

Signature's revenue jumped by 22% to a record $959.3 million in 2014 mostly as loan interest (on commercial loans mortgages and leases) and security interest income continued to grow as the bank built up its interest-earning assets during the year.

Higher revenue and a continued decline and loan loss provisions in 2014 boosted the bank's net income by 30% to a record $296.7 million. Signature's operating cash levels more than doubled to $421 million on higher cash earnings.

Strategy

Signature Bank has long targeted privately-held businesses that have fewer than 1000 employees and revenues of less than $200 million. Some of its target clients include real estate owners/companies law firms accounting firms entertainment business managers medical professionals retail establishments money management firms and non-profit foundations.

The bank continues to expand its service lines particularly focusing on specialty financing to grow its business organically. In 2015 it planned to offer direct commercial vehicle financing through a network of approved commercial vehicle dealerships in New York's Tri-State area with loans targeting small and mid-size business borrowers looking to acquire commercial vehicles and fleets. Also that year it formed its Maryland-based Signature Public Funding Corp subsidiary to provide municipal finance and tax-exempt lending and leasing products to local state and federal government agencies nationwide.

Company Background

The bank's emphasis on personal service helped it to grow its deposit base and loan portfolio in 2011. During a time when many other banks struggled under the weight of bad loans in a bad economy Signature Bank achieved record earnings for the fourth consecutive year.

Founded in 2001 as an alternative to megabanks Signature Bank was spun off from Bank Hapoalim in 2004.

EXECUTIVES

Executive Vice President And Chief Credit Officer, Michael Merlo
President Ceo And Director, Joseph J. DePaolo, $577,500 total compensation
Svp And Cfo, Vito Susca
President Ceo And Director, Michael G. O'Rourke
Evp, Kevin P. Bastuga
Evp, Bryan D. Duncan
Vp Retail Operations Manager, Ella Riordan-Pacheco
Vice President, Michael Nicolosi
Vice President, John C Spagnuolo
Group Director Senior Vice President, Joseph Alexander
Senior Vice President Group Director, Gary Shulevich
Senior Vice President And Group Director, Leon Kratsberg
Senior Vice President Group Director, Lucy Mazany
Vice President, Phyllis Rosenfeld
Senior Lender Vice President, Eugene Cartin
Group Director Senior Vice President, Tamara Gavrielof
Group Director Senior Vice President, David Artis
Vice President, John Ricchezza
Vice President Private Banking, Sue Frick
Senior Vice President Group Director, Nicole Rospond
Vice President, Richard Wang
Senior Vice President, Meyer Eichler
Senior Vice President, Kerry Mach
Executive Vice President, Joseph Fantauzzi
Senior Vice President Group Director, Brian Hallinan
Vice President Director Of Operations, Richard Pelcher
Vice President Senior Lender; Commercial Real Estate, Jay Byrne
Vice President And Associate Group Director, Matthew Cohen
Senior Vice President, Joann Demartino
Senior Vice President And Group Director, Peter Marra
Vice President, Joseph Fingerman
Group Director Senior Vice President, Kevin Hardiman
Group Director Senior Vice President, Nikki Rospond
Group Director Senior Vice President, Lawrence Blascovich
Senior Vice President Group Director, Larry Goldberg
Group Director Senior Vice President, Michael Page
Vice President Commercial Banking, Ross Thomson
Senior Vice President Group Director, Salvatore Costa
Senior Vice President And Group Director, Roseann Manos
Vice President Of Real Estate, Aaron Greene
Vice President, Howard Green
Vice President Section Manager Continuous Process Improvements, Angela Izzo
Senior Vice President Group Director, Tom Rogers
Group Director Senior Vice President, Jason Birnbaum
Senior Vice President Group Director, Brian Mazzotta
Senior Vice President Group Director, Sandy Sapperstein
Svp Group Director, Joe Festa
Vice President, John Barfuss
Vice President, Henry Lee
Vp Executive Sales Officer, Stephanie Paysse
Svp, Maria Hegi
Group Director Senior Vice President, Marie Moreno
Group Director Senior Vice President, Avi Azuolay
Vice President Capital Markets, Rob Campbell
Group Director Senior Vice President, Nellie Teplinsky
Senior Client Advisor Vice President, Cora Licht
Vice President Equipment Finance And Leasing, Michael Walsh
Group Director Senior Vice President, William Mooney
Chairman And Director, Leonard S. Caronia
Auditors: KPMG LLP

LOCATIONS

HQ: Signature Bank (New York, NY)
565 Fifth Avenue, New York, NY 10017
Phone: 646 822-1500
Web: www.signatureny.com

PRODUCTS/OPERATIONS

2014 Sales

	$ mil.	% of total
Interest		
Loans net	655	68
Securities available for sale	193	20
Securities held to maturity	69	7
Other	5	1
Noninterest		
Fees & service charges	19	2
Commissions	10	1
Net gains on sales of loans	5	1
Net gains on sales of securities	5	-
Other	2	-
Adjustments	(7.8)	-
Total	**959**	**100**

COMPETITORS

Apple Bank for Savings	Herald National Bank
Astoria Financial	JPMorgan Chase
Bank Leumi USA	New York Community

Capital One
Citigroup
HSBC USA

Bancorp
Safra Bank
TD Bank USA

HISTORICAL FINANCIALS

Company Type: Public

Income Statement

FYE: December 31

	ASSETS ($ mil.)	NET INCOME ($ mil.)	INCOME AS % OF ASSETS	EMPLOYEES
12/17	43,117	387	0.9%	1,305
12/16	39,047	396	1.0%	1,218
12/15	33,450	373	1.1%	1,122
12/14	27,318	296	1.1%	1,010
12/13	22,376	228	1.0%	945
Annual Growth	17.8%	14.1%	—	8.4%

2017 Year-End Financials

Debt ratio: 0.60%
Return on equity: 10.13%
Cash ($ mil.): 335
Current ratio: —
Long-term debt ($ mil.): —

No. of shares (mil.): 54
Dividends
Yield: —
Payout: —
Market value ($ mil.): 7,546

	STOCK PRICE ($) FY Close	P/E High/Low	PER SHARE ($) Earnings	Dividends	Book Value
12/17	137.26	23 17	7.12	0.00	73.33
12/16	150.20	21 15	7.37	0.00	66.15
12/15	153.37	22 16	7.27	0.00	56.81
12/14	125.96	22 17	5.95	0.00	49.61
12/13	107.42	22 15	4.76	0.00	38.06
Annual Growth	6.3%	— —	10.6%	—	17.8%

SIGNATURE FINANCIAL LLC

EXECUTIVES

Ceo-MBR, Joseph J Depaolo
MBR, Eric Howell
Human Resources Manager, Mark Driggers
Executive Sales Officer, Stephen Port

LOCATIONS

HQ: SIGNATURE FINANCIAL LLC
565 5TH AVE AT46TH, NEW YORK, NY 100172413
Phone: 646 865-0767
Web: WWW.SIGNATURE-BANK.COM

HISTORICAL FINANCIALS

Company Type: Private

Income Statement

FYE: December 31

	ASSETS ($ mil.)	NET INCOME ($ mil.)	INCOME AS % OF ASSETS	EMPLOYEES
12/17	43,119	387	0.9%	11
12/16	39,047	396	1.0%	—
12/15	33,450	373	1.1%	—
Annual Growth	13.5%	1.9%	—	—

2017 Year-End Financials

Debt ratio: —
Return on equity: 25.80%
Cash ($ mil.): 457
Current ratio: —
Long-term debt ($ mil.): —

Dividends
Yield: —
Payout: —
Market value ($ mil.): —

Simmons First National Corp

Simmons First National thinks it's only natural it should be one of the largest financial institutions in The Natural State. The $8.1 billion-asset holding company owns Simmons First National Bank and seven other community banks that bear the Simmons First Bank name and maintain local identities; together they operate around 150 branches throughout Arkansas and in Kansas Tennessee and Missouri. Serving consumers and area businesses the banks offer standard deposit products like checking and savings accounts IRAs and CDs. Lending activities mainly consist of commercial real estate loans single-family mortgages and consumer loans such as credit card and student loans.

Operations

In addition to Simmons First National Bank the company owns Simmons First Bank of Jonesboro Simmons First Bank of South Arkansas Simmons First Bank of Northwest Arkansas Simmons First Bank of Russellville Simmons First Bank of Searcy Simmons First Bank of El Dorado and Simmons First Bank of Hot Springs. Simmons First Trust Company a subsidiary of Simmons First National Bank provides trust and fiduciary services; Simmons First Investment Group offers broker-dealer services.

Like other retail banks Simmons makes the bulk of its money from interest income. About 65% of its total revenue came from loan interest during 2015 while another 8% came from interest on investment securities. The rest of its revenue came from service charges on deposit accounts (8% of revenue) debit and credit card fees (6%) mortgage lending income (3%) trust income (2%) investment banking income (1%) and other non-interest income sources.

Geographic Reach

The bank has around 150 branches mostly in Arkansas but also in Kansas Missouri and Tennessee.

Financial Performance

Simmons First National Bank's annual revenues and profits have been rising mostly thanks to new loan business from rapid bank expansion (mostly stemming from acquisitions).

The bank's revenue jumped 60% to $396.8 million during 2015 mostly thanks to 58% growth in legacy loans and growth in acquired loan business from the acquisitions of Liberty and Community First. Non-interest income grew 54% thanks to rising trust service charges deposit fees mortgage lending income all also tied to its recent acquisitions.

Revenue growth in 2015 more than doubled Simmons' net income to $74.36 million. The bank's operating cash levels spiked eight-fold to $88.7 million for the year thanks to a rise in cash-based earnings and favorable changes in working capital.

Strategy

Simmons tries to differentiate itself from smaller competitors by offering a wider array of products while striving to provide more personalized service than larger regional banks. The company also likes to acquire banks to grow its loan and deposit business while expanding into new geographic markets. Between 1990 and 2015 Simmons made 11 whole bank acquisitions and a handful of branch deals with other banks adding some 125 branches to its total branch network.

Mergers and Acquisitions

In September 2016 Simmons acquired Citizens National Bank a Tennessee-based bank with about 10 branch locations.

In October 2015 the company purchased Ozark Trust & Investment Corporation and its Trust Company of the Ozarks subsidiary adding $1 billion in new assets under management and 1300 clients to its wealth management business.

In February 2015 Simmons First National acquired $1.1 billion-asset Liberty Bancshares as well as Liberty Bank branches in southwest Missouri St. Louis and Kansas City. It also added Liberty's expertise in small business lending.

Also in February 2015 the bank bought $1.9 billion-asset Community First Bancshares and its First State Bank branches in Tennessee. Community First also added expertise in small business and consumer lending.

EXECUTIVES

Evp Organizational Development, Stephen C. Massanelli, age 62
Chairman And Ceo, George A. Makris, age 61, $502,500 total compensation
Sevp Cfo And Treasurer, Robert A. Fehlman, age 53, $306,614 total compensation
Evp And Central And Northeast Arkansas Regional Chairman Simmons First National Bank, Barry K. Ledbetter
President And Chief Credit Officer Simmons First National Bank, N. Craig Hunt
Evp And South Arkansas Regional Chairman Simmons First National Bank, Freddie G. Black
Evp Corporate Strategy And Performance And Secretary, Susan F. Smith, age 56
President Chief Banking Officer And Director, David L. Bartlett, age 66, $376,142 total compensation
Evp, Marty D. Casteel, age 66, $304,180 total compensation
Evp Controller Chief Accounting Officer And Investment Relations Officer, David W. Garner, age 48
Evp Marketing, Robert C. Dill, age 75, $179,393 total compensation
Evp And Chief Risk Officer, Tina M. Groves, age 48
Evp Technology And Operations Simmons First National Bank, Lisa W. Hunter
Svp And Marketing Director Simmons First National Bank, Amy W. Johnson
President El Dorado Community Bank, Robert L. Robinson
Chairman Russellville Community Chairman, Ronald B. (Ron) Jackson
President Hot Springs Community Bank, Steven W. (Steve) Trusty
President Conway Community Bank, Jason Culpepper
Evp And General Counsel, Patrick A. Burrow, age 64
Evp Specialty Lending Simmons First National Bank, Larry L. Bates
Evp And Tennessee Regional Chairman Simmons First National Bank, John C. Clark
Evp And Kansas And Missouri Regional Chairman Simmons First National Bank, Gary E. Metsger
Senior Vice President Commercial Loans, Rick Harris
Vice President And Personnel Manager, Leigh Cockrum
Vice President, Pam Lawshe
Vp Of Mortgage, Deana Powell
Assistant Vice President Loans, Esther Chapman
Senior Vice President Director Of Marketing And Communications, Elizabeth Machen
Vice President, Chad Pittillo
Vice President Loan Review Manager, David Coleman

Executive Vice President Operations, Glenda
Tolson
Vice President, Zilpha Wilson
Senior Vice President, Adam Mitchell
Vice President And Commercial Loan Officer, John
Craig
Vice President Administration, David Rushing
Vice President Equipment Finance, Michael
Childers
Vice President And Officer, Cathy Braggalo
Vice President And Trust Officer, Joyce Green
Vice President Commercial Banking Relationship
Manager, Dave Ruby
Vice President, Ed Stahlman
Vice President Commercial Lending, Wayne Wilson
Assistant Vice President And Investment Officer,
Kelton Harrison
Vice President Finance, Joey Walters
Senior Vice President, Steve Landry
Assistant Vice President, Chris Rittelmeyer
Vice President Commercial Lending, Vernon Scott
Assistant Vice President Atm Operations, Karla
Dial
Vice President Facilities Management, Anita
Murrell
Senior Vice President, Bob Williams
Executive Vice President And Chief Information
Officer Of Company And Simmons First
National Bank, Paul D Kanneman
Vice President Financial Advisor, James Watkins
Senior Vice President And Senior Credit Officer,
Stephen Landry
Board Member, Edward Drilling
Board Member, Eugene Hunt
Board Member, Christopher Kirkland
Board Member, Mark Doramus
Auditors: BKD, LLP

LOCATIONS

HQ: Simmons First National Corp
501 Main Street, Pine Bluff, AR 71601
Phone: 870 541-1000
Web: www.simmonsbank.com

PRODUCTS/OPERATIONS

2015 Sales

	% of total
Interest Income	
Loans	65
Investment securities	8
Others	-
Non-interest income	
Service charges on deposit accounts	8
Debit and credit card fees	6
Mortgage lending income	3
Trust income	2
Other service charges and fees	2
others	6
Net (loss) gain on assets covered by FDIC loss share agreements	
Total	100

COMPETITORS

Arvest Bank	Bear State Financial
BOK Financial	Home BancShares
BancorpSouth	IBERIABANK
Bank of America	Regions Financial
Bank of the Ozarks	U.S. Bancorp

HISTORICAL FINANCIALS

Company Type: Public

Income Statement

FYE: December 31

	ASSETS ($ mil.)	NET INCOME ($ mil.)	INCOME AS % OF ASSETS	EMPLOYEES
12/17	15,055	92	0.6%	2,640
12/16	8,400	96	1.2%	1,875
12/15	7,559	74	1.0%	1,040
12/14	4,643	35	0.8%	1,331
12/13	4,383	23	0.5%	1,306
Annual Growth	36.1%	41.4%	—	19.2%

2017 Year-End Financials

Debt ratio: 1.72%	No. of shares (mil.): 92
Return on equity: 5.74%	Dividends
Cash ($ mil.): 598	Yield: 0.0%
Current ratio: —	Payout: 37.5%
Long-term debt ($ mil.): —	Market value ($ mil.): 5,255

	STOCK PRICE ($) FY Close	P/E High/Low	PER SHARE ($) Earnings	Dividends	Book Value
12/17	57.10	47 37	1.33	0.50	22.65
12/16	62.15	42 25	1.57	0.48	18.40
12/15	51.36	44 27	1.32	0.46	17.78
12/14	40.65	41 31	1.06	0.44	13.69
12/13	37.15	52 33	0.71	0.42	12.44
Annual Growth	11.3%	— —	17.0%	4.5%	16.2%

Simon Property Group, Inc.

Simon Property Group is the largest shopping mall and retail center owner in the US. The self-managed self-administered real estate investment trust (REIT) owns develops and manages regional shopping malls outlet malls (under the Premium Outlet and The Mills brands) boutique malls and shopping centers. Its roughly $25 billion real estate portfolio is composed of some 200 retail properties totaling approximately 180 million sq. ft. of leasable space. Its portfolio covers 35 states and Puerto Rico though much is concentrated in the US Southeast Midwest and Northeast. The REIT also has stakes in outlet centers in Canada Mexico Europe and Asia. CEO and chairman David E. Simon is the son of Melvin Simon who founded the firm with his brother Herbert.

Operations

Simon Property?s primary operations are the ownership development leasing and management of its retail real estate portfolio. The extend of its involvement and revenue generation varies by its degree of ownership. In addition to owning some 150 properties in the US it is a joint-venture partner in about 80 mostly international properties. It also uses joint ventures to hold equity investments in several European real estate holding companies.

The extent of Simon Property?s involvement in managing the properties is also influenced by its ownership stake. It manages the day-to-day operations of its owned properties as well as about 60 of its joint-venture properties. The remaining properties all of which are located outside the US are managed through joint ventures in which Simon shares but does not have majority control.

The company makes about 60% of its revenue from rental income just less than 30% from tenant recoveries (reimbursements to Simon Properties for common area maintenance real estate taxes etc.) and the rest from overage rents management fees and other corporate revenue.

Geographic Reach

Indianapolis Indiana-based Simon Property Group owns and operates ? wholly or as part of joint ventures ? retail real estate properties in the Americas Europe and Asia.

By far its largest market is the United States where it generates over 95% of its revenue and holds nearly 95% of its long-lived assets.

Sales and Marketing

Simon Property enters long-term tenancy contracts with retailers to fill its properties. Its lease terms must be competitive to attract desirable tenants and its management services provide post-sale customer care to its lessees and also strive to pull consumer traffic into its properties with local advertising and special events (Santa Claus at the Mall for example).

Although internet-based retail presents challenges to many of Simon?s typical tenants the REIT maintains the relevance of a brick-and-mortar presence. Still it is modifying its store mix within its properties to include more entertainment and residency offerings while still working with its long-standing clients to fill space in its retail properties.

Many of its properties are anchored by major tenants such as JCPenney Macy?s Dillard?s Neiman Marcus and Bloomingdale?s and supplemented with smaller stores like Dick?s Sporting Goods Sears Nordstrom Kohl?s and AMC Theatres. Its Premium Outlets are home to a variety of popular retailers including Adidas American Eagle Outfitters Ann Taylor Columbia Sportswear Michael Kors Tommy Hilfiger and The North Face.

Occupancy for its US malls Premium Outlets and Mills-branded properties remain above 96%. No one tenant accounts for more than 5% of its consolidated revenue.

Financial Performance

The long-term trend in revenue and net income has been positive over recent years. Net income swooned a bit in 2012 ? 2014 but remained above $1 billion annually. Revenue climbed steadily since 2012 growing from $2.3 billion in that year to just more than $5.4 billion in 2016.

Simon Property?s 2016 revenue of $5.4 billion grew about 3% from 2015?s $5.3 billion as a result of a higher rents overcoming a slightly lower dollar-per-square-foot sales number from its tenants. Occupancy rates of over 96% remained near historically peak levels.

In 2016 net income from continuing operations was $2.1 billion matching 2015?s result. Depreciation and amortization along with a write-off of costs related to an abandoned project prevented the revenue increase from flowing to the bottom line.

Simon?s cash balance at the end of 2016 was $560 million a decrease of $141 million when compared to the prior year. The change arose from $3.4 billion generated by operating activities offset by just under $1 billion used by investing activities (mainly from capital expenditures acquisitions and joint-venture investments) and $2.5 billion used by financing activities (primarily for higher than usual debt repayments).

Strategy

The retail industry is encountering both cyclical and structural changes including aging US demographics (and therefore less retail spending) and internet-based e-commerce. Simon Property is changing with the times by reformulating the tenant mix in its properties and addressing new and redevelopment needs in growth markets.

Acknowledging the changing retail dynamic Simon is diversifying its properties away from apparel-heavy approaches by transitioning its tenant base to include residential space hotels entertainment options restaurants and wellness centers. The idea is to entice consumers to its property not only to shop but to be entertained and possibly even spend the weekend. Centers such as The Domain in Austin TX and the jointly-developed Brickell City Centre in Miami FL exemplify this new approach.

Simon is averaging $1 billion in annual investments to build new or redevelop existing properties. In 2016 Simon redeveloped the Stanford Shopping Center in Palo Alto CA and the East Coast?s largest shopping center King of Prussia. At the end of 2016 Simon had $1.1 billion of redevelopment and expansion projects at nearly 30 sites including at Woodbury Common Premium Outlet in New York City and La Plaza Mall in McAllen TX. The company?s approach is to start with the aesthetic and functional appeal and then to add on-site customer service and technology to make the shopping experience easier and more efficient for shoppers and retailers.

Mergers and Acquisitions

In 2016 Simon acquired with a partner a noncontrolling 75% interest in an outlet center in Ochtrup Germany and later that year purchased with a joint venture partner a luxury shopping center on the Las Vegas Strip for $1.1 billion. In that same year it divested two multi-family residential investments and several retail properties for about $82 million.

EXECUTIVES

Evp And Cfo, Andrew A. (Andy) Juster, age 66, $500,000 total compensation
President Coo And Director, Richard S. (Rick) Sokolov, age 68, $800,000 total compensation
Chief Administrative Officer; President Malls, John Rulli, $463,500 total compensation
Chairman And Ceo, David Simon, age 56, $1,250,000 total compensation
Svp And Cio, David Schacht
President The Mills, Gregg M. Goodman
Ceo Premium Outlets, Stephen J. Yalof
Chief Marketing Officer; President Simon Brand Ventures, Mikael Thygesen
Sevp; President Simon Malls, David J. Contis, age 59, $750,000 total compensation
Chief Investment Officer, Stanley Shashoua
Regional Vice President Financial Reporting, Deanna Nelson
Assistant Vice President Retailer Development, Matt Mahar
Vice President Of Acquisitions And Asset Intensification, Patrick Peterman
Vice President Finance, Lisa Ross
Vice President Legal Leasing, Woodrow Stone
Svp And Treasurer, Brian Mcdade
Vice President Of Business Development, Paul G Fiore
Vice President Property Tax, Michael Larson
Vice President Of Marketing, Kelly Mikesell
Senior Vice President Finance Operating Properties, David Campbell
Vicepresident, Donna Vosper
Regional Vice President Financial Reporting, Brenda Keefe
Vice President Of Management And Marketing, Kelly Hartsell
Senior Vice President For Development At Investment In The Project, Kathleen M Shields
Vice President Tax Planning And Research, John Gumerson
Assistant Vice President Leasing, Robert Alexander
Vice President Construction, Bob Ufland
Vice President Specialty Leasing, Ralph Higley

Regional Vice President, Teresa Tom
Vice President Of Business Development, Jim Martin
Regional Vice President Financial Reporting, Mike Ginty
Assistant Vice President Of Corporate Special Events, Jacque Ellis
Senior Vice President Risk Management, Michael Horvath
Regional Vice President, Adam Pisano
Senior Vice President Leasing, Mark Hunter
Vice President Gift Cards And Business Insights, Lindsey Schaefer
Senior Vice President Chief Security Officer, Russ Tuttle
Senior Vice President Of Business Development Sbv, Daniel Segal
Regional Vice President, Cynthia Hall
Portfolio Vice President, Michael Romstad
Senior Vice President, Ronald Hanson
Vice President Leasing, Tim Cutting
Vice President Of Leasing, Dennis Carafiol
Senior Vice President Corporate Marketing, Shari Simon
Senior Executive Vice President, Gary Lewis
Vice President Operations, Robert Courtney
Senior Vice President Development, Steven Bozek
Senior Vice President Taxation, Steve Stouffer
Regional Vice President, Robert Guerra
Vice President, Greg Bradbury
Executive Vice President Luxury Leasing, Peter Baxter
Vice President, Paula Weant
Evp Leasing Premium Outlet Centers, Larry Weinstein
Assistant Vice President Of Application Delivery, Gennady Stesal
Assistant Vice President Leasing, Carolyn Preston
Vice President It Infrastructure And Operations, Scot Barnes
Vice President Media Planning And Strategy, Amanda Cohen
Senior Vice President Investor Relations, Thomas Ward
Senior Vice President, Deborah Simon
Vice President Leasing Counsel, Maryalice Budakian-kinsella
Vice President General Manager, Gene Condon
Portfolio Vp Of Marketing, Lynette Lauria
Vice President And Senior Counsel, Thomas Di Iaconi
Executive Vice President Leasing Malls, Eric Sadi
Vice President Development And Acquisitions, Steve Dworkin
Vice President Learning And Organizational Development, Joshua White
Vice President, Roach Heather
Vice President Brand Management, Enna Allen
Avp Marketing Alliances, Stacy Rosenthal
Vice President Of Operations, Rob Courtney
Vice President Digital Strategy, Patrick Flanagan
Treasurer, Robert Demchak
Auditors: Ernst & Young LLP

LOCATIONS

HQ: Simon Property Group, Inc.
225 West Washington Street, Indianapolis, IN 46204
Phone: 317 636-1600   **Fax:** 317 685-7336
Web: www.simon.com

PRODUCTS/OPERATIONS

2016 Sales

	$ mil.	% of total
Minimum rent	3,358	62
Tenant reimbursements	1,494	28
Overage rent	161	3
Management fees & other revenues	143	2
Other income	276	5
Total	**5,435**	**100**

2016 US Properties

	No.
Malls	108
Premium outlets	67
Mills	14
Lifestyle centers	4
Other shopping centers	13
Total	**206**

Selected Properties

Aventura Mall Miami
Burlington Mall Boston
Copley Place Boston
Dadeland Mall Miami
Desert Hills Premium Outlets Cabazon CA
Fashion Centre at Pentagon City Washington DC
Fashion Valley San Diego
The Florida Mall Orlando
The Forum Shops at Caesars Las Vegas
The Galleria Houston
Gotemba Premium Outlets Gotemba (Tokyo) Japan
King of Prussia Mall Philadelphia
Las Vegas Premium Outlets(2) Las Vegas
Lenox Square and Phipps Plaza Atlanta
Orlando Premium Outlets(2) Orlando
Roosevelt Field New York
Sawgrass Mills Ft. Lauderdale
SouthPark Charlotte
Stanford Shopping Center Palo Alto
Town Center at Boca Raton Boca Raton
Walt Whitman Shops New York
The Westchester New York
Woodbury Common Premium Outlets New York
Woodfield Mall Chicago

COMPETITORS

Belz	Kimco Realty
CBL & Associates	Macerich
Properties	Taubman Centers
Cadillac Fairview	Vornado Realty
GGP	Westfield Corporation
Horizon Group	
Properties	

HISTORICAL FINANCIALS

Company Type: Public

Income Statement

FYE: December 31

	REVENUE ($ mil.)	NET INCOME ($ mil.)	NET PROFIT MARGIN	EMPLOYEES
12/17	5,538	1,947	35.2%	5,000
12/16	5,435	1,838	33.8%	5,000
12/15	5,266	1,827	34.7%	5,000
12/14	4,870	1,408	28.9%	5,250
12/13	5,170	1,319	25.5%	5,700
Annual Growth	1.7%	10.2%	—	(3.2%)

2017 Year-End Financials

Debt ratio: 76.36%
Return on equity: 46.80%
Cash ($ mil.): 1,482
Current ratio: 0.83
Long-term debt ($ mil.): 24,632

No. of shares (mil.): 320
Dividends
  Yield: 0.0%
  Payout: 114.5%
Market value ($ mil.): 55,014

	STOCK PRICE ($) FY Close	P/E High/Low		PER SHARE ($) Earnings	Dividends	Book Value
12/17	171.74	30	24	6.24	7.15	12.10
12/16	177.67	39	30	5.87	6.50	14.21
12/15	194.44	35	29	5.88	6.05	14.53
12/14	182.11	41	33	4.52	5.15	16.47
12/13	152.16	43	34	4.24	4.65	19.45
Annual Growth	3.1%	—	—	10.1%	11.4%	(11.2%)

Sirius XM Holdings Inc

You might say radio programming from this company comes from a higher plane. SIRIUS XM Holdings operating through SIRIUS XM Radio manages satellite radio systems under the SIRIUS and XM brands that together boast more than 25 million subscribers. Each service offers more than 150 channels of CD-quality music news and talk shows. Programming includes National Football League Major League Baseball and college games as well as talk shows featuring hosts Howard Stern Martha Stewart and Oprah Winfrey. The company has equipment alliances with several automakers; it also sells satellite radio equipment through its website and through such retail outlets as Best Buy and WalMart. In 2018 SiriusXM offered $3.5 billion for music streaming company Pandora.

Operations
In addition to its domestic radio services SiriusXM has interests in the Canadian market. It owns 50% of SIRIUS Canada a joint venture with the Canadian Broadcasting Corporation (CBC). SIRIUS Canada merged with Canadian Satellite Radio (XM Canada) in 2011 giving SiriusXM a solid foundation in the Canadian market.

Sales and Marketing
Subscription satellite radio has proven to be quite popular thanks to the wealth of programming options available beyond the limited content offered by advertising-supported terrestrial radio broadcasters.

With its large subscriber base SiriusXM has stolen away many listeners from traditional broadcast stations operated by major radio companies such as Clear Channel and Cumulus Media. Providing all that content though is quite expensive due to rights fees for sports and exclusive talk shows as well as the satellite equipment needed to reach listeners across the country.

During fiscal 2013 the company spent about $180000 on advertising after spending roughly $140000 on advertising during fiscal 2012.

Financial Performance
SiriusXM has been experiencing a positive trend in its revenue since 2008. The company's fiscal 2013 revenues increased by 12% compared to fiscal 2012 primarily due to increases in its subscriber revenues advertising revenues agency fees and equipment revenues.

SiriusXM saw its net income nosedive in 2013. Net income decreased 98% from $3.47 billion in fiscal 2012 to only $377.2 million in fiscal 2013. The huge drop was largely due to drastically increased expenses for things such as royalties and taxes.

Even with its net income dropping so dramatically during fiscal 2013 the company's cash from operations increased due to improved operating performance lower interest payments and higher collections from subscribers and distributors.

Strategy
SiriusXM is dependent on automobile makers. The company works hard to convert customers who received a promotional subscription as part of the purchase or lease of a new vehicle to a self-paying subscription.

Mergers and Acquisitions
In 2018 SIRIUS XM agreed to buy Pandora Media Inc. for $3.5 billion.In 2013 SIRIUS XM purchased connected vehicle business Agero Inc. Agero's connected vehicle business provides services to several automakers including Acura BMW Honda Hyundai Infiniti Lexus Nissan and Toyota.

EXECUTIVES

Evp And Cfo, David J. Frear, age 62, $850,000 total compensation
Evp And General Counsel, Patrick L. Donnelly, age 56, $575,000 total compensation
Evp Sales And Automotive, Stephen R. (Steve) Cook, age 62, $518,583 total compensation
Svp And Cio, William C. (Bill) Pratt
Ceo, James D. (Jim) Meyer, age 64, $1,400,790 total compensation
President And Chief Content Officer, Scott A. Greenstein, age 59, $1,224,520 total compensation
Evp And Chief Administrative Officer, Dara F. Altman, age 60, $500,000 total compensation
Evp Operations And Products, Enrique Rodriguez, $531,827 total compensation
Vice President Purchasing And Procurement, Larry Simon
Svp And General Manager Music Programming, Steve Blatter
Chairman, Gregory B. (Greg) Maffei, age 57
Auditors: KPMG LLP

LOCATIONS

HQ: Sirius XM Holdings Inc
1290 Avenue of the Americas, 11th Floor, New York, NY 10104
Phone: 212 584-5100
Web: www.siriusxm.com

COMPETITORS

CBS Radio	Saga Communications
Cox Radio	Spanish Broadcasting
Cumulus Media	Townsquare Media
Emmis Communications	Univision Radio
Entercom	WestwoodOne
Entravision	iHeartCommunications
Radio One Inc.	

HISTORICAL FINANCIALS

Company Type: Public

Income Statement — FYE: December 31

	REVENUE ($ mil.)	NET INCOME ($ mil.)	NET PROFIT MARGIN	EMPLOYEES
12/18	5,770	1,175	20.4%	2,699
12/17	5,425	647	11.9%	2,575
12/16	5,017	745	14.9%	2,402
12/15	4,570	509	11.2%	2,323
12/14	4,181	493	11.8%	2,327
Annual Growth	8.4%	24.3%	—	3.8%

2018 Year-End Financials

Debt ratio: 84.28%—
Return on equity: —
Cash ($ mil.): 54
Current ratio: 0.17
Long-term debt ($ mil.): 6,884

Dividends
Yield: 0.7%
Payout: 17.3%
Market value ($ mil.): —

	STOCK PRICE ($) FY Close	P/E High/Low	PER SHARE ($) Earnings	Dividends	Book Value
12/18	5.71	29 20	0.26	0.05	(0.42)
12/17	5.36	42 32	0.14	0.04	(0.34)
12/16	4.45	31 22	0.15	0.01	(0.17)
12/15	4.07	47 37	0.09	0.00	(0.03)
12/14	3.50	43 34	0.08	0.00	0.23
Annual Growth	13.0%	—	—	34.3%	

SLM Corp.

If SLM doesn?t seem familiar perhaps you know it by its more common moniker Sallie Mae. Holding more than $8 billion in student loans SLM's main subsidiary Sallie Mae Bank is one of the nation's largest education loan providers and specializes in originating acquiring financing and servicing private student loans which are not guaranteed by the government. The company also earns fees for its processing and administrative offerings through various subsidiaries.

HISTORY

The Student Loan Marketing Association was chartered in 1972 as a response to problems in the Guaranteed Student Loan Program of 1965. For years the GSL program had tinkered with rates to induce banks to make loans but servicing the small loans was expensive and troublesome. Sallie Mae began operations in 1973 buying loans from their originators; its size provided economies of scale in loan servicing.

Originally only institutions making educational or student loans were allowed to own stock in Sallie Mae. This was later changed so that anyone could buy nonvoting stock. In 1993 voting stock was listed on the NYSE.

Sallie Mae was always a political football altered again and again to reflect the education policies of the party in power. When it was founded during the Nixon administration its loans were restricted by a needs test which was repealed during the Carter years. The Reagan administration reimposed the needs test and at the same time sped up the schedule under which the company was to become self-supporting which it did by late 1981.

Forced to rely on its own resources Sallie Mae turned to creative financing. One of its traditional advantages was that its loan interest rates were linked to Treasury bills traditionally about 3% above the T-bill rate. The company became a master at riding the spread between its cost of funds and the interest rates it charged.

Between 1983 and 1992 Sallie Mae's assets swelled by more than 400% and its income rose by almost 500%. As the firm grew management became more visible with high pay and extravagant perks. Although salaries were not inconsistent with those of executives at comparable private corporations the remuneration level and perks irked Congress. But Sallie Mae kept growing — in 1992 it expanded its facilities and added 900 new staff members.

The 1993 Omnibus Budget Reconciliation Act with its transfer of the student loan program directly to the government and its surcharge on Sallie Mae began to adversely affect earnings in 1994. While awaiting permission to alter its charter the company stepped up its marketing efforts especially to school loan officers who advised students on loan options.

In 1995 then-COO Albert Lord led a group of stockholders in a push to cut operating expenses and repackage student loans as securities A la Freddie Mac and Fannie Mae. Lord and some of his supporters won seats on the board (as well as the enmity of Lawrence Hough who resigned as CEO in the midst of the melee). That year Sallie Mae bought HICA Holding one of two private insurers of education loans. In 1996 Congress passed legislation forcing Sallie Mae's privatization.

Despite SLM's rising stock shareholders were unhappy with chairman William Arceneaux's status quo business plan. Lord gained control in 1997.

In 1998 the organization became SLM Holding. Assets and earnings were muted that year when unfavorable market conditions prevented Sallie Mae from securitizing its loans.

The firm the next year expanded its lending operations by buying Nellie Mae. Also in 1999 Sallie Mae teamed with Answer Financial to sell insurance. Growth continued in 2000 when the company bought loan servicer Student Loan Funding Resources as well as the marketing student loan servicing and administrative operations of USA Group; the company changed its name to USA Education following the acquisition. The company also cut some 1700 jobs approximately 25% of its workforce.

The following year Sallie Mae teamed with Intuit allowing the financial software company access to Sallie Mae's 7 million customers. It also launched online recruiting service TrueCareers that year.

In 2002 it bought Pioneer Credit Recovery and General Revenue Corporation two of the nation's largest student loan collection agencies. It also reverted to the SLM moniker to reconnect with the name by which it has so long been known.

The privatization plan put into place in the mid-'90s (orchestrated in large part by then-CEO Lord) came to fruition nearly four years ahead of schedule when SLM transitioned to a private organization in December 2004.

In 2007 SLM saw its stock values plummet to their lowest levels in about a decade. A number of industry-wide factors figured into the losses not the least of which was the downturn in the credit market. Also affecting the company was the signing into law of the College Cost Reduction and Access Act (CCRAA). Intended to reform student lending and cut costs for borrowers the act slashed subsidies for lenders participating in the Federal Family Education Loan Program (FFELP). The reform cut into the company's interest-earning operations. As a result SLM increased its focus on higher-yielding private education loans which carry a lower risk.

Additionally SLM that year became ensnared in a student-lending industry probe led by New York attorney general Andrew Cuomo. The company agreed to a $2 million settlement and to abide by a code of conduct regarding its dealings with college employees.

One of the most dramatic results of the troubles was the collapse of a planned acquisition by a consortium of investment firms. The planned $8.8 billion deal included buyers J.C. Flowers (which was to own about a half of SLM) Bank of America and JPMorgan Chase. In the midst of the industry probe J.C. Flowers sought a change in SLM's leadership in an effort to secure regulatory approval for the acquisition; Thomas J. (Tim) Fitzpatrick was ousted as CEO. Ultimately the buyers canceled the deal citing the reduced potential value of SLM. The student lender filed a lawsuit to challenge the termination but eventually dropped the suit. It later cut more than 10% of its workforce.

EXECUTIVES

Vp Federal Government Relations, Tim Morrison
Vice President Of Finance And Information Research, Brian Burgess
Chairman And Ceo, Raymond J. Quinlan, $600,000 total compensation
Evp And General Counsel, Laurent C. Lutz, $525,000 total compensation
Evp And Cfo, Steven J. McGarry, $375,000 total compensation
Svp And Chief Risk Officer, Jeffery F. Dale, age 56, $400,000 total compensation

Evp And Chief Marketing Officer, Charles P. Rocha, $375,000 total compensation
Svp And Chief Compliance Officer, Jim Truitt
Vice President West Region Head, Robin Famiglietti
Svp And Chief Risk Officer, Jeffrey Dale
Assistant Vice President Network Services, Peter Tropf
Vice President, Jonathan Boyles
Vice President Finance Other Credit, Doug Maurer
Senior Vice President Operations Administration, Sheila Ryan-Macie
Vice President And Associate General Counsel, Anne Milem
Vice President, Lynn M Langdon
Vice President Information Technology Credit Origination, Michael Migliore
Senior Vice President Corporate Finance, Leo Subler
Senior Vice President Chief Regulatory Counsel And Assistant Corporate Secretary, Rick Nelson
Board Member, Jim Matheson
Board Member, Vivian Schneck-Last
Auditors: KPMG LLP

LOCATIONS

HQ: SLM Corp.
300 Continental Drive, Newark, DE 19713
Phone: 302 451-0200
Web: www.salliemae.com

PRODUCTS/OPERATIONS

2016 Sales

	$ mil.	% of total
Interest		
Lons	1,060	79
Investments	9	1
Cash & cash equivalents	7	1
Non-Interest income		
Gain on sale of loans	0	14
(Losses) gains on derivatives and hedging activities net	(0.9)	5
Other income	69	-
Total	**1,146**	**100**

Selected Subsidiaries

HICA Holding
Sallie Mae Bank
Sallie Mae Inc.
SLM Education Credit Finance Corporation
Bull Run I LLC
SLM Education Credit Funding LLC
SLM Investment Corporation
Southwest Student Services Corporation

COMPETITORS

Bank of America
Brazos Higher Education Service Corp.
Citizens Financial Group
Discover
Educational Funding of The South
First Marblehead
FirstCity Financial
Great Lakes Higher Education
KeyCorp
Mohela
Nelnet
PNC Financial
Pennsylvania Higher Education Assistance Agency
SunTrust
Texas Guaranteed

HISTORICAL FINANCIALS

Company Type: Public

Income Statement
FYE: December 31

	ASSETS ($ mil.)	NET INCOME ($ mil.)	INCOME AS % OF ASSETS	EMPLOYEES
12/17	21,779	288	1.3%	1,500
12/16	18,533	250	1.4%	1,300
12/15	15,214	274	1.8%	1,200
12/14	12,972	194	1.5%	1,000
12/13	159,543	1,418	0.9%	7,200
Annual Growth	**(39.2%)**	**(32.8%)**	**—**	**(32.4%)**

2017 Year-End Financials

Debt ratio: 15.04%
Return on equity: 11.99%
Cash ($ mil.): 1,534
Current ratio: —
Long-term debt ($ mil.): —

No. of shares (mil.): 432
Dividends
Yield: —
Payout: —
Market value ($ mil.): 4,886

	STOCK PRICE ($) FY Close	P/E High/Low	PER SHARE ($) Earnings	Dividends	Book Value
12/17	11.30	20 16	0.62	0.00	5.72
12/16	11.02	21 10	0.53	0.00	5.47
12/15	6.52	18 11	0.59	0.00	4.92
12/14	10.19	63 19	0.42	0.60	4.32
12/13	26.28	8 5	3.12	0.60	13.14
Annual Growth	**(19.0%)**	**— —**	**(33.2%)**	**—**	**(18.8%)**

Smart & Final Stores Inc

Auditors: Ernst & Young LLP

LOCATIONS

HQ: Smart & Final Stores Inc
600 Citadel Drive, Commerce, CA 90040
Phone: 323 869-7500
Web: www.smartandfinal.com

HISTORICAL FINANCIALS

Company Type: Public

Income Statement
FYE: December 31

	REVENUE ($ mil.)	NET INCOME ($ mil.)	NET PROFIT MARGIN	EMPLOYEES
12/17*	4,570	(138)	—	11,864
01/17	4,341	12	0.3%	11,949
01/16	3,970	38	1.0%	10,956
12/14	3,534	33	0.9%	9,370
12/13	3,210	8	0.3%	8,805
Annual Growth	**9.2%**	**—**	**—**	**7.7%**

*Fiscal year change

2017 Year-End Financials

Debt ratio: 38.64%
Return on equity: (-29.16%)
Cash ($ mil.): 71
Current ratio: 0.97
Long-term debt ($ mil.): 617

No. of shares (mil.): 74
Dividends
Yield: —
Payout: —
Market value ($ mil.): 634

	STOCK PRICE ($)	P/E	PER SHARE ($)		
	FY Close	High/Low	Earnings	Dividends	Book Value
12/17*	8.55	—	(1.92)	0.00	5.44
01/17	14.10	102 64	0.17	0.00	7.57
01/16	18.21	37 28	0.50	0.00	7.68
12/14	15.40	30 22	0.52	0.00	7.01
Annual Growth	(13.7%)	—	—	—	(6.2%)

*Fiscal year change

SmartFinancial Inc

EXECUTIVES

Senior Vice President Knoxville Area Market Executive, Mike Honeycutt
Auditors: Dixon Hughes Goodman LLP

LOCATIONS

HQ: SmartFinancial Inc
5401 Kingston Pike, Suite 600, Knoxville, TN 37919
Phone: 865 453-2650
Web: www.smartfinancialinc.com

COMPETITORS

Bank of America	Regions Financial
First Horizon	SunTrust
First Security Group	Tennessee Valley
Home Federal Bank (TN)	Financial Holdings

HISTORICAL FINANCIALS

Company Type: Public

Income Statement   FYE: December 31

	ASSETS ($ mil.)	NET INCOME ($ mil.)	INCOME AS % OF ASSETS	EMPLOYEES
12/17	1,720	5	0.3%	343
12/16	1,062	5	0.5%	222
12/15	1,023	1	0.1%	225
12/14	415	1	0.4%	104
12/13	432	1	0.4%	107
Annual Growth	41.3%	31.4%	—	33.8%

2017 Year-End Financials

Debt ratio: 2.53%
Return on equity: 3.22%
Cash ($ mil.): 106
Current ratio: —
Long-term debt ($ mil.): —
No. of shares (mil.): 11
Dividends
 Yield: —
 Payout: —
Market value ($ mil.): 242

	STOCK PRICE ($)	P/E	PER SHARE ($)		
	FY Close	High/Low	Earnings	Dividends	Book Value
12/17	21.70	47 33	0.55	0.00	18.46
12/16	18.56	24 18	0.78	0.00	17.85
12/15	16.09	46 9	0.32	0.00	17.25
12/14	3.31	93 58	0.04	0.00	24.54
12/13	2.37	36 22	0.08	0.00	24.52
Annual Growth	74.0%	—	61.9%	—	(6.9%)

Smucker (J.M.) Co.

The J. M. Smucker Company gets its bread and butter from more than just jelly. The food and beverage company known for its namesake Smucker's fruit spread has an extended product portfolio that includes Folgers coffee (the top brand in the US) Jif peanut butter (the top brand in the US) and Milk-Bone dog snacks (the top brand in the US); other products include shortening and oils frozen sandwiches and juices. It generates roughly equal parts of its revenue from pet foods coffee and consumer foods. Smucker's generates more than 90% of its sales in the US.

Operations

Smucker's operations are divided among four business segments: US Retail Pet Foods US Retail Coffee and US Retail Consumer Foods (which each account for nearly 30% of revenue) and International/Away from Home (which accounts for about 15%).

The company's growing pet food business includes mainstream pet food (Meow Mix 9Lives Rachael Ray Nutrish Nature's Recipe) premium pet food (Natural Balance) and pet snacks (Milk-Bone Pup-Peroni). Its coffee operations include mainstream ground single-serve and premium coffee (Folgers Dunkin Donuts Cafe Bustelo 1850) and its consumer foods operations include peanut butter (Jif) fruit spreads (Smucker's) and shortening and oils (Crisco).

Smucker's international segment primarily includes coffee for Canadian and other non-US markets as well as Canadian flour (Robin Hood Five Roses) and Smucker's and Jif products.

Overall coffee is the company's leading product category generating about a third of sales; dog food cat food pet snacks and peanut butter each contribute about 10%.

Geographic Reach

Ohio-based Smucker's generates more than 90% of revenue in the US with Canada accounting for about 5%.

The company has manufacturing and processing facilities in about a dozen US states and one Canadian province. It has sales and administrative offices in the US Canada China and Mexico.

Sales and Marketing

In the US retail market segments Smucker's products are primarily sold through direct sales and brokers to food retailers supermarkets food wholesalers drug stores club stores mass merchandisers discount and dollar stores military commissaries natural foods stores and distributors pet specialty stores and online retailers. Its International products are distributed through retail channels and foodservice distributors and operators (e.g. restaurants lodging schools and universities health care operators).

Walmart and subsidiaries account for about 30% of the company's sales. Indeed its top 10 customers generate some 60% of the company's revenue.

Advertising expense as a percent of net sales has been rising in recent years; costs were $194 million in fiscal 2018 compared to about $170 million each of the prior two years.

Financial Performance

Since jumping nearly 40% in fiscal 2016 because of the acquisition of Big Heart pet food maker Smucker's revenue has been on the decline. It has fallen some 6% over the past two years. Net income has seen a bit more irregular growth but recorded a huge jump in the most recent fiscal year.

In fiscal 2018 (ended April 2018) the company reported revenue of $7.4 billion down about half a percent from the prior year as increases in the pet food and international categories were not enough to offset a decline in consumer foods (primarily from the oils & baking categories).

Net income however more than doubled in 2018 to $1.3 billion. An income tax benefit of more than $475 million (compared to an expense of nearly $300 million the year before) related to 2017 US tax reform led to the rise.

Cash at the end of fiscal 2018 was $193 million an increase of $26 million from the prior year. Cash from operations contributed $1.2 billion to the coffers while investing activities used $278 million mainly for capital expenditures. Financing activities used another $922 million for dividends to stockholders and repayments of short-term borrowings and long-term debt.

Strategy

Smucker's strategy focuses on growth through owning and marketing the #1 brand name food products (both people and pet) in North America with potential for worldwide appeal. Acquisitions and manufacturing and distribution agreements underpin these ends. As part of the company's long-term growth objectives it is working to increase sales by 3% and earnings per share by more than 8% annually on average. While the sales contribution from acquisitions will vary from year to year it expects organic growth including new products to drive much of the growth.

Along those lines in fiscal 2018 the company launched canisters of 1850 and Dunkin' Donuts coffee as well as Jif PowerUps peanut butter snacks and Pup-Peroni jerky bites. Products introduced in the last three years represent about $500 million in revenue.

As a result of this focus on top brands particularly pet food and snacks and coffee the company in 2018 agreed to sell its US baking business (Pillsbury Martha White Hungry Jack and other brands) to investment firms for $375 million. It previously divested its US canned milk brands (Eagle Brand Magnolia) and operations.

With the acquisition of Big Heart Pet Brands the company instantly became a player in the growing pet food and snacks market. The pet segment is now Smucker's largest.

Mergers and Acquisitions

In 2018 Smucker's paid nearly $2 billion for premium pet food company Ainsworth Pet Nutrition. The deal adds a handful of pet food and snack brands including fast-growing Rachel Ray Nutrish to Smucker?s pet food division which already includes Meow Mix Milk-Bone and 9Lives among other brands.

HISTORY

Jerome Smucker began operating a steam-powered cider mill in 1897 for farmers in Orrville Ohio but he found that his biggest business was selling apple butter made using a secret Smucker family recipe. By the 1920s The J. M. Smucker Company had begun producing a full line of preserves and jellies and in 1935 it acquired its first fruit-processing operations.

Under Jerome's grandson Paul Smucker the company gained widespread national distribution by the mid-1960s. Tim Smucker succeeded his father Paul as president in 1981 then as chairman in 1987 when his brother Richard became president.

The company's growth has been enhanced through the development of its industrial fruit fillings business and acquisitions of domestic natural juice & peanut butter companies including Knudsen & Sons (1984) After the Fall (1994) and Laura Scudder's (from National Grape Co-op 1994). It has gradually expanded internationally through acquisitions. In 1993 it acquired the jam preserves and pie-filling unit of Canada's Culinar. In a 1998 deal Smucker purchased Australia's Allowrie jam and Lackersteens marmalade lines.

Smucker sold its flagging Mrs. Smith's frozen pie business to Flowers in 1997 less than two years after buying the unit from Kellogg. It bought Kraft's domestic fruit spread unit in 1997 and in 1999 purchased the northwestern Adams peanut butter business from Pro-Fac Cooperative. Smucker kept the Adams name but shifted packaging to its Pennsylvania peanut butter plant.

Spreading into retail the company opened a store in 1999 in its hometown of Orrville and then launched online and catalog sales. Also that year Smucker bought a fruit filling plant in Brazil from Groupe Danone a major customer. During 2000 the company's Henry Jones Foods subsidiary (Australia) purchased Taylor Foods (sauces marinades).

Smucker acquired International Flavors & Fragrances' formulated fruit and vegetable preparation businesses in 2001. Moving beyond its stronghold in natural peanut butter brands the next year Smucker purchased the Jif peanut butter and Crisco cooking oil and shortening brands from Procter & Gamble. The $670 million purchase price for Jif and Crisco included shifting 53% of Smucker stock into the hands of P&G shareholders.

A decision to concentrate on North America led to the $37 million sale of Australian subsidiary Henry Jones Foods in 2004. Also that year Smucker sold its operations in Brazil to Cargill and closed down two fruit processing plants in California and Oregon. Its purchase of International Multifoods that year added an array of US brands to the Smucker family including Pillsbury flour baking mixes and ready-to-spread frostings; Hungry Jack pancake mixes syrup and potato side dishes; Martha White baking mixes and ingredients; and PET evaporated milk brands. Canadian brands included Robin Hood flour and baking mixes Bick's pickles and condiments and Golden Temple flour and rice.

To further its strategy of concentrating on its core retail brands in 2005 Smucker sold its US foodservice and bakery business and the Canadian operations of Gourmet Baker (all part of its International Multifoods acquisition) to Value Creation Partners. The following year the company sold its Canadian grain-based foodservice operations and industrial businesses to Cargill and CHS Inc. The operations were integrated into leading US flour miller Horizon Milling (which is j

EXECUTIVES

Treasurer, Mark R. Belgya, age 57, $545,962 total compensation
Vp Of Sales-grocery Market, John Mayer
Vice Chairman; President U.s. Food And Beverage, Steven T. Oakland, age 57, $623,077 total compensation
President Pet Food And Pet Snacks, Barry C. Dunaway, age 55, $330,000 total compensation
President And Ceo, Mark T. Smucker, age 49, $355,000 total compensation
President Canada And International, David J. Lemmon
Vp Marketing Services, Tamara J. Fynan
Svp Operations, J. Randal Day
Senior Vice President Human Resources And Corporate Communications, Jill Penrose
Vice President Finance, Mark Draa
Vice President Investor Relations, Aaron Broholm
Vice President Market Research, Jill Boyce
Vice President Corporate Communications, Maribeth Burns
Vice President Human Resource Operations, John Denman
Vice President Marketing Consumer, Vince Byrd

Vice President Of Supply Chain And Operations, Todd Campbell
National Account Manager, Scott Dacus
National Account Manager, Matt Skordinski
Svp Operations, J Randal Day
Vice President Green Coffee, Roger Larsh
Chairman, Richard K. Smucker, age 70
Auditors: Ernst & Young LLP

LOCATIONS

HQ: Smucker (J.M.) Co.
One Strawberry Lane, Orrville, OH 44667-0280
Phone: 330 682-3000
Web: www.jmsmucker.com

2018 Sales

	$ mil.	% of total
Domestic	6,786	92
International		
Canada	432	6
Other countries	139	2
Total	**7,357**	**100**

PRODUCTS/OPERATIONS

2018 Sales

	$ mil.	% of total
US Retail Pet Foods	2,169	30
US Retail Coffee	2,092	28
US Retail Consumer Foods	2,001	27
International and Away From Home	1,095	15
Total	**7,357**	**100**

Selected Products

Coffee
Frozen sandwiches
Fruit spreads
Juices and beverages
Peanut butter
Pet food
Pet snacks
Pickles and condiments
Shortening and oils
Syrups
Toppings

Selected Brands

Canadian brands
  Adams
  Bick's
  Carnation (under license)
  Double Fruit
  Five Roses
  Golden Temple
  Robin Hood
  Smucker's
Coffee
  Café Bustelo
  Café Pilon
  Dunkin' Donuts (under license)
  Folgers
  kava
  Medaglia D'oro
Consumer and natural foods
  Adams
  Crisco
  Dickinson's
  Jif
  Knott's Berry Farm
  Laura Scudder's
  Smucker's
Pet food and snacks
  9Lives
  Dad's
  Gravy Train
  Kibbles 'n Bits
  Meow Mix
  Milk-Bone
  Natural Balance
  Nature's Recipe
  Rachel Ray Nutrish
  Snausages

COMPETITORS

B&G Foods	Hormel
Caribou Coffee	Keurig Green Mountain
Community Coffee	Kraft Heinz
ConAgra	Mars Incorporated
Cranberries Limited	National Grape
E.D. Smith	Cooperative
Farmer Bros.	Nestlé Purina PetCare
Ferrero	Pinnacle Foods
General Mills	Snyder's-Lance
Hain Celestial	Starbucks
Hershey	Tata Global Beverages
Hill's Pet Nutrition	Welch's

HISTORICAL FINANCIALS

Company Type: Public

Income Statement

FYE: April 30

	REVENUE ($ mil.)	NET INCOME ($ mil.)	NET PROFIT MARGIN	EMPLOYEES
04/18	7,357	1,338	18.2%	7,000
04/17	7,392	592	8.0%	7,140
04/16	7,811	688	8.8%	6,910
04/15	5,692	344	6.1%	7,370
04/14	5,610	565	10.1%	4,775
Annual Growth	**7.0%**	**24.1%**	**—**	**10.0%**

2018 Year-End Financials

Debt ratio: 31.58%
Return on equity: 18.16%
Cash ($ mil.): 192
Current ratio: 1.50
Long-term debt ($ mil.): 4,688

No. of shares (mil.): 113
Dividends
  Yield: 2.7%
  Payout: 26.2%
Market value ($ mil.): 12,956

	STOCK PRICE ($) FY Close	P/E High/Low		PER SHARE ($) Earnings	Dividends	Book Value
04/18	114.08	11	8	11.78	3.09	69.48
04/17	126.72	31	24	5.10	2.92	60.39
04/16	126.98	23	18	5.76	2.65	60.26
04/15	115.92	35	29	3.33	2.50	59.27
04/14	96.68	21	17	5.42	2.26	49.46
Annual Growth	**4.2%**	**—**	**—**	**21.4%**	**8.1%**	**8.9%**

Sonic Automotive, Inc.

No stranger to speed O. Bruton Smith has raced Sonic Automotive into the leading pack of US auto dealers just behind rivals like AutoNation and Penske Automotive. Sonic has gone from five dealerships in 1997 to having today more than 100 new and used vehicle dealerships more than 115 franchised dealerships and about 20 collision repair centers in major markets in more than a dozen states including California Texas the Carolinas Alabama and Tennessee. The company sells some 25 brands of cars and light trucks and offers extended aftermarket services. Chairman Smith is also the majority owner of Speedway Motorsports which operates more than half a dozen NASCAR auto racetracks.

Operations

The company sells new vehicles including luxury cars (BMW Lexus Land Rover and Volvo) mid-line imports (Honda Nissan and Toyota) and domestic brands (Ford and General Motors). Luxury brands account for around more than 55% of new vehicle sales the company's mid-line brands bring in more than 30% and domestic brands nearly 15%.

Sonic also offers a range of aftermarket services including vehicle financing replacement parts performance of vehicle maintenance paint and collision repair services and arrangement of extended warranty contracts and insurance.

Sonic divides its business into Franchised Dealerships which brings in virtually all the company's revenue at 99% and EchoPark which is its standalone used car business.

Geographic Reach

California is Sonic's #1 market accounting for around 30% of sales followed closely by Texas at around a quarter of total sales. EchoPark's retail units are clustered in Denver.

Sales and Marketing

Sonic's website allows customers to view cars and prices schedule test drives and book trade-in appraisals.

Financial Performance

Sonic has reported consistently strong revenue growth for the past seven years. However in fiscal 2016 growth slowed with revenue up an incremental 1% to $9.7 billion. New vehicle sales were flat at $5.2 billion as a decrease in unit volumes was compensated for by an increase in selling prices. The price increases were concentrated in Sonic's Honda dealerships. Used vehicle sales were also essentially flat growing less than 1% to $2.5 billion.

Net income climbed 8% to $93.2 million. Revenue gains were offset by poor results from the Houston area as a knock-on effect of weakness in the oil & gas markets; as an oil town consumer spending in the city was down. Sonic was also negatively affected by car recalls from certain manufacturers leaving the company stuck with around 600 cars it wasn't allowed to sell until work had been completed.

Cash from operations increased from $69.7 million to $216.4 million in fiscal 2016 due to higher net income and a decrease in inventory and other assets.

Strategy

As part of the company's strategic plans Sonic is primarily focused in growing its operations in metropolitan markets in the Southeast Southwest Midwest and the West (California). The company's long-term growth strategy is to target luxury or mid-line import brands in regions where it already operates.

Sonic is continuing the rollout of its One Sonic-One Experience store strategy. The modernization program targets the shop-floor sales process with the aim one sales associate armed with a tablet computer completing a sale in under one hour. The program also removes haggling from the buying process puts its sales reps on salaries rather than commission packages and centralizes back end processes and pricing.

Sonic's EchoPark used car business expansion is based around making each EchoPark dealership a "neighborhood store" supported by specialty retail stores that can open in areas normally blocked to car dealers.

Mergers and Acquisitions

In 2016 Sonic acquired three stand-alone used vehicle businesses for $15.9 million.

Company Background

O. Bruton Smith and his son Scott control the company through their ownership of about 40% of Sonic Automotive's voting stock.

EXECUTIVES

President And Ceo, B. Scott Smith, age 50, $1,085,438 total compensation
Evp Operations, Frank J. (Jeff) Dyke, age 51, $969,179 total compensation
Vp And Chief Marketing Officer, Rachel M. Richards

Evp And Cfo, Heath R. Byrd, age 51, $677,327 total compensation
Vp Information Technology, Christopher (Chris) Maritato
Vice President Of Finance And Insurance, Richard O'Connor
Vice President Manufacturer Relations, Raymond Valentine
Regional Vice President Tn Dc, Kevin Gaither
Vice President Facilities Development, Martin Walsh
Regional Vice President, Steve Prather
Regional Vice President, Tasos Theodorou
Chairman, O. Bruton Smith, age 90
Vice Chairman, David B. Smith, age 43
Auditors: KPMG LLP

LOCATIONS

HQ: Sonic Automotive, Inc.
   4401 Colwick Road, Charlotte, NC 28211
Phone: 704 566-2400   **Fax:** 704 536-5116
Web: www.sonicautomotive.com

PRODUCTS/OPERATIONS

2016 sales

	$ mil.	% of total
Franchised Dealerships	9,602	99
EchoPark	129	1
Total	**9,731**	**100**

2016 sales

	$ mil.	% of total
New vehicles	5,234	54
Used vehicles	2,533	26
Wholesale vehicles	211	2
Parts service and collision repair	1,409	14
Finance Insurance and other	343	4
Total	**9,731**	**100**

Services Center List-Selected:

Acura of Serramonte Service Center
Audi West Houston Service Center
BMW of Birmingham Service Center
Cadillac of Las Vegas Service Center
Capitol Chevrolet of Columbia Service Center
Fort Mill Ford Service Center
Honda of Santa Monica Service Center
Momentum Volkswagen Service Center
North Central Ford Service Center
Toyota of Fort Worth Service Center
Volkswagen of Fort Myers Service Center
Brands
BMW
Mercedes
Lexus
Audi
Land Rover
Cadillac
Porsche
Honda
Toyota
Volkswagen
Hyundai
Ford
General Motors

COMPETITORS

Asbury Automotive	Enterprise Rent-A-Car
AutoNation	Group 1 Automotive
AutoTrader	Gunn Automotive
Autobytel	Internet Brands
CarMax	JM Family Enterprises
Darcars	Penske Automotive
David McDavid Auto	Group
Group	Sewell Automotive
DriveTime Automotive	

HISTORICAL FINANCIALS

Company Type: Public

Income Statement   FYE: December 31

	REVENUE ($ mil.)	NET INCOME ($ mil.)	NET PROFIT MARGIN	EMPLOYEES
12/17	9,867	92	0.9%	9,750
12/16	9,731	93	1.0%	9,800
12/15	9,614	96	0.0%	0,000
12/14	9,197	97	1.1%	9,300
12/13	8,843	81	0.9%	9,100
Annual Growth	**2.8%**	**3.3%**	**—**	**1.7%**

2017 Year-End Financials

Debt ratio: 66.47%	No. of shares (mil.): 43
Return on equity: 12.30%	Dividends
Cash ($ mil.): 6	Yield: 0.0%
Current ratio: 1.03	Payout: 9.5%
Long-term debt ($ mil.): 963	Market value ($ mil.): 797

	STOCK PRICE ($) FY Close	P/E High/Low		PER SHARE ($) Earnings	Dividends	Book Value
12/17	18.45	12	8	2.09	0.20	18.21
12/16	22.90	12	8	2.04	0.20	16.21
12/15	22.76	16	12	1.70	0.11	14.60
12/14	27.04	15	11	1.84	0.10	13.09
12/13	24.48	16	13	1.53	0.10	11.64
Annual Growth	**(6.8%)**	**—**	**—**	**8.1%**	**18.9%**	**11.8%**

Sonoco Products Co.

Sonoco Products believes you can judge a container by its packaging. The company is one of the world's largest makers of industrial and consumer packaging used by the food consumer goods construction and automotive industries. Its Consumer Packaging segment produces round and shaped composite cans for snack foods powdered beverages pet food and more. Sonoco makes flexible and rigid packaging (paper and plastic) for food personal care items and chemicals and it produces paperboard tubes and cores too for industrial protective packaging. The company's end-to-end packaging services include co-packing and fulfillment supply chain management and point-of-purchase display design/assembly.

Operations

The company divides its business structure into four chief business segments. Consumer Packaging is its largest segment accounting for roughly 45% of its net sales. Other segments include Paper and Industrial Converted Products (35%) Display and Packaging (more than 10%) and Protective Solutions (10%).

Geographic Reach

Sonoco operates about 320 locations around the world in nearly 35 countries concentrated in Canada Europe and the US. Around 65% of its total sales are generated from the US each year. Sonoco's international sales are concentrated in Europe (20%) followed by Canada (around 5%).

Financial Performance

Sonoco's revenues have declined the last two years dropping 4% from $4.96 billion in 2015 to $4.78 billion in 2016. Total domestic sales declined 3% from 2015 levels and international sales declined 5% compared to 2015 as most of the decreases were driven by unfavorable impacts of foreign currency translations. Additionally sales in

Mexico declined in 2016 due to the loss of contract packaging business in Irapuato Mexico.

Profits however jumped 15% from $250 million in 2015 to peak at a record-setting $286 million in 2016 due to an after-tax benefit of $9 million consisting of the gain from the disposal of its rigid plastics blow molding operations.

Strategy

The company's goal is to reach $5.5 billion to $6 billion in sales over the next three or four years. (It came close in 2015 posting $4.96 billion.) It plans to achieve this by growing its existing products and services portfolio by $300 million and new product sales by $350 million. It also expects future acquisitions to contribute an additional $500 million in annual sales.

Inherit to its strategy are the company's ongoing efforts to improve its operating structure improve manufacturing capacity and keep a lid on costs. Two major projects planned for 2017 are the commercial launch of its new TruVueTM clear plastic can and development of a new contract packaging services center to support the expansion of a key North American customer.

Mergers and Acquisitions

Sonoco also looks to acquisitions as a means for growth. In 2018 the company paid $143 million for the remaining 70% interest in its Conitex Sonoco joint venture originally formed in 1998 with Spain-based packaging company Texpack Inc.

In 2017 Sonoco acquired Peninsula Packaging Company a manufacturer of thermoformed packaging for fresh fruit and vegetables for $230 million from Odyssey Investment Partners. Peninsula has annual revenues of around $190 million. The company hopes the acquisition will help capture new growth in the fresh fruit and vegetables market segment.

HISTORY

Sonoco Products originated during the South's industrial renewal after the Civil War. Major James Coker and son James Jr. (who had been badly wounded at the Battle of Chickamauga) founded the Carolina Fiber company in Hartsville South Carolina to make pulp and paper from pine trees. The business was based on a thesis James Jr. wrote in 1884 at Stevens Institute of Technology in Hoboken New Jersey. The essay explained how to make paper pulp using the sulfite process.

After failing to sell the pulp commercially the Cokers decided to use it to make paper cones for the textile industry which was seeing rapid growth in the southern US. In 1899 Major Coker and investor W. F. Smith formed the Southern Novelty Company. Major Coker's son Charles became president in 1918. As sales neared $1 million in 1923 the company changed its name to Sonoco.

EXECUTIVES

Executive Vice President, Charles Sullivan
President Ceo And Director, M. Jack Sanders, age 64, $1,039,817 total compensation
Svp Plastic Packaging And Protective Solutions, Vicki B. Arthur, age 59
Svp Paper/engineered Carriers U.s./canada And Display And Packaging, Rodger D. Fuller, age 56, $473,319 total compensation
Vp Global Flexibles, Robert L. Puechl, age 62
Svp And Cfo, Barry L. Saunders, age 58, $548,759 total compensation
Vp Tubes And Cores U.s. And Canada, James A. Harrell, age 56
Svp Rigid Paper Containers And Paper/engineered Carriers International, R. Howard Coker, age 55, $471,695 total compensation

Evp Coo And Ceo-elect, Robert C. (Rob) Tiede, age 59, $567,741 total compensation
Vp Marketing And Innovation, Marcy J. Thompson, age 56
Vp Human Resources, Allan H. McLeland, age 51
Vp Paper And Industrial Converted Products Emea Asia Australia And New Zealand, Adam Wood, age 49
Vice President General Manager Thermoforming Plastics Business, Jeff Dipasquale
Vice President Marketing, Ginny Jones
Vice President Public Relations Communications, Julie Scott
Division Vice President And Gm Rigid Paper And Closures Na, Jeffrey Tomaszewski
Vice President, Rhett Mitchell
Chairman, Harris E. DeLoach, age 72
Treasurer, Julie Albrecht
Secretary Iv, Connee Grantham
Board Member, Pamela Davies
Auditors: PricewaterhouseCoopers LLP

LOCATIONS

HQ: Sonoco Products Co.
1 N. Second St., Hartsville, SC 29550
Phone: 843 383-7000   **Fax:** 843 383-7008
Web: www.sonoco.com

2016 Sales

	$ mil.	% of total
US	3,112	65
Europe	951	20
Canada	268	6
Other	450	9
Total	**4,782**	**100**

PRODUCTS/OPERATIONS

2016 Sales

	$ mil.	% of total
Consumer Packaging	2,043	43
Paper & Industrial Converted Products	520	11
Display & Packaging	1,693	35
Protective Solutions	525	11
Total	**4,782**	**100**

Selected Products and Services

Paper and Industrial Converted Products
  Tubes and cores
  Concrete forms
  Molded plugs
  Pallets
  Pallet components
  Paperboard tubes cores
  Roll packaging
  Rotary die boards
  Void forms
  Paper
  Boxboard
  Chipboard
  Corrugating medium
  Lightweight corestock
  Linerboard
  Recovered paper
  Recycled paperboard
  Specialty grades
  Tubeboard
  Sonoco Recycling
  Collection processing and recycling of old corrugated containers paper plastic metal glass other recyclable materials
Consumer Packaging
  Ends and closures
  Aluminum steel and peelable membrane easy-open closures for composite metal and plastic containers
  Printed flexible packaging
  Thin-gauge rotogravure flexographic and combination printed film (laminations and rotogravure cylinder engraving brand artwork management)
  Thin-gauge packaging
  Rigid packaging - blow molded plastics
  Monolayer and multilayer bottles and jars
  Rigid packaging - paper
  Composite paperboard cans (round and shaped)
  Fiber cartridges

Single-wrap paperboard packages
Rigid packaging - thermoformed plastic
Mono coated and barrier and non-barrier laminated tubs cups spools consumer and institutional trays
Packaging Services
  Paperboard specialties
  Rixie coasters
  Stancap glass covers
  Other paper amenities
  Point-of-purchase (P-O-P)
  Contract packaging co-packing and fulfillment services
  Designing manufacturing assembling packing and distributing temporary semi permanent and permanent P-O-P displays
  Service centers
  Packaging supply chain management (custom packing fulfillment primary package filling scalable service centers)
Protective Packaging
  Molded and extruded plastics (product design tool design and fabrication; manufacturing in both injection molding and extrusion technologies)
  Protective packaging
  Contract package testing
  Sonopost technology
  Sonobase carriers
  Sonopop systems

COMPETITORS

Amcor	Greif
AptarGroup	International Paper
Avery Dennison	Owens-Illinois
Ball Corp.	Pactiv
Bemis	Sealed Air Corp.
Caraustar	Silgan
Crown Holdings	The Newark Group
Graphic Packaging Holding	

HISTORICAL FINANCIALS

Company Type: Public

Income Statement

FYE: December 31

	REVENUE ($ mil.)	NET INCOME ($ mil.)	NET PROFIT MARGIN	EMPLOYEES
12/17	5,036	175	3.5%	21,000
12/16	4,782	286	6.0%	20,000
12/15	4,964	250	5.0%	21,000
12/14	5,014	239	4.8%	20,800
12/13	4,848	219	4.5%	19,900
Annual Growth	1.0%	(5.4%)	—	1.4%

2017 Year-End Financials

Debt ratio: 31.76%
Return on equity: 10.83%
Cash ($ mil.): —
Current ratio: 1.56
Long-term debt ($ mil.): 1,288
No. of shares (mil.): 99
Dividends
  Yield: 0.0%
  Payout: 88.5%
Market value ($ mil.): 5,283

	STOCK PRICE ($) FY Close	P/E High/Low		PER SHARE ($) Earnings	Dividends	Book Value
12/17	53.14	32	27	1.74	1.54	17.17
12/16	52.70	20	13	2.81	1.46	15.45
12/15	40.87	19	15	2.44	1.37	14.99
12/14	43.70	19	16	2.32	1.27	14.98
12/13	41.72	19	14	2.12	1.23	16.75
Annual Growth	6.2%	—	—	(4.8%)	5.8%	0.6%

South State Corp

South State Corporation (formerly First Financial Holdings) is the holding company for South

State Bank (formerly South Carolina Bank and Trust and South Carolina Bank and Trust of the Piedmont both known as SCBT). The bank operates branches throughout the Palmetto state as well as in select counties in Georgia and North Carolina. Serving retail and business customers the banks provide deposit accounts loans and mortgages as well as trust and investment planning services. More than half of the firm's loan portfolio is devoted to commercial mortgages while consumer real estate loans make up more than a quarter. South State plans to merge with Southeastern Bank Financial parent of Georgia Bank & Trust.

Operations

Beyond its retail and commercial banking mortgage lending consumer finance and trust and investment businesses the bank operates registered investment advisors Minis & Co. and First Southeast 401K Fiduciaries as well as limited-purpose broker-dealer First Southeast Investor Services.

South State Corporation generated 70% of its total revenue from loan interest (including fees) in 2014 while another 4% came from interest income on investment securities. Service charges and Bankcard services income made up another 14% of total revenue while trust and investment services income and mortgage banking income each contributed roughly 4% during the year.

Geographic Reach

South State Corporation boasts nearly 130 branches across nearly 20 counties in South Carolina a handful of counties in North Carolina and about a dozen counties in the northeast and coastal regions of Georgia.

Financial Performance

South State Corporation's revenues and profits have been on the rise over the past few years mostly thanks to continued growth of its loan business and declining loan loss provisions as its loan portfolio's credit quality has improved with the strengthened economy.

The company's revenue jumped by 28% to $436.72 million in 2014 which was mostly driven by 20% growth in its loan interest income as its average loan asset balances swelled by a similar percentage. South State's non-interest income also swelled by 76% thanks to higher deposit account service charge bankcard service trust and investment service and mortgage banking fees from overall growth in the business through acquisitions and organic initiatives.

Higher revenue and controlled operating costs in 2014 drove the bank's net income higher by 53% to $75.44 million. South State's operating cash levels declined by 51% to $118.65 million for the year after adjusting its earnings for non-cash net sales proceeds from its mortgage loans held-for-sale and as the bank spent more cash toward its accrued income taxes.

Strategy

Though it does sometimes expand or relocate its existing branches to better position its locations for more growth South State Corporation has been mostly growing its loan business and branch network through strategic bank and branch acquisitions. Its 2015 acquisition of 13 branch locations from Bank of America for example extended South State's reach into six new markets and three existing markets while adding millions of dollars worth of new loan business. Then in mid-2016 South State Corporation agreed to buy Southeastern Bank Financial the holding company of Georgia Bank & Trust (which also operates in South Carolina as Southern Bank & Trust). The combined company will operate more than 130 branches in Georgia and the Carolinas.

Mergers and Acquisitions

In 2015 South State Corporation agreed to purchase 12 South Carolina branches and one Georgia branch from Bank of America expanding its reach into six new markets. The acquired branches were located in Hartwell Georgia; as well as Florence Greenwood Orangeburg Sumter Newberry Batesburg-Leesville Abbeville and Hartsville in South Carolina.

Company Background
South State Corporation and South State Bank changed their names from First Financial Holdings and South Carolina Bank and Trust respectively in 2014. The change was designed to better promote the South State brand with customers.

EXECUTIVES

Ceo, Robert R. Hill, age 51, $645,000 total compensation
Senior Vice President Director Of Media, Donna Pullen
Cfo And Coo, John C. Pollok, age 52, $442,000 total compensation
Chief Banking Officer, John F. Windley, age 66, $315,000 total compensation
Chief Credit Officer And Chief Risk Officer, Joseph Burns, $295,000 total compensation
President, R. Wayne Hall, $203,405 total compensation
Evp And Corporate Secretary, William C. Bochette
Vice President, Reid Davis
Senior Vice President Technology, Ross Bagley
Senior Executive Vice President, Dane H Murray
Vice President, Stacy Cannon
Senior Vice President, Cathie Austin
Senior Vice President City Executive, Dave Starnes
Senior Vice President, Sheryl Ross
Senior Vice President Director Human Resources Administration, Leslie Chaplin
Senior Vice President Assistant Corporate Counsel, Lindsey Livingston
Executive Vice President, Bill Bochette
Vice President Mortgage Loan Officer, Nancy Batson
Senior Vice President Technology, Lee Fryland
Senior Vice President Director Of Bank Operations, Robb Byrd
Vice President Commercial Lender, Candy Greene
Senior Vice President Commercial Banking Executive, Kevin Blackwood
Assistant Vice President And Mortgage Originator, Stephanie Waters
Executive Vice President, Jim Mabry
Senior Vice President City Executive, Kevin Rourk
Vice President Deposit Operations Manager, Janet Smith
Senior Vice President Commercial Loan Administrator, Jeannette Perna
Senior Vice President Commercial Real Estate, Mike Greer
Vice President, Wayne Dowling
Senior Vice President, Morris Hardigree
Vice President, Doug Jacobs
Vice President Mortgage Lending, Reece Wrenn
Senior Vice President And Retail Market Leader, Linda Potts
Vice President, Anne Lambert
Commercial Banker Vice President, Kendall Myers
Senior Vice President, James Holden
Treasurer, Richard Mathis
Chairman, Robert R. Horger, age 67
Vice Chairman, Paula Harper Bethea
Board Member, Kevin Walker
Board Member, Cynthia Hartley
Board Member, Robert Demere
Auditors: Dixon Hughes Goodman LLP

LOCATIONS

HQ: South State Corp
520 Gervais Street, Columbia, SC 29201
Phone: 800 277-2175
Web: www.southstatebank.com

PRODUCTS/OPERATIONS

2011 Sales

	$ mil.	% of total
Interest		
Loans including fees	319	70
Investment securities	20	4
Other	1	-
Noninterest		
Service charges on deposit accounts	36	10
Bankcard services income	29	6
Trust and investment services income	18	4
Mortgage banking	16	4
Securities gains net -	0	
Amortization of FDIC indemnification asset	(21.9)	0
Other	16	4
Total	**436**	**100**

COMPETITORS

BB&T	Regions Financial
Bank of America	Security Federal
Bank of South Carolina	
First Citizens Bancorporation	

HISTORICAL FINANCIALS

Company Type: Public

Income Statement — FYE: December 31

	ASSETS ($ mil.)	NET INCOME ($ mil.)	INCOME AS % OF ASSETS	EMPLOYEES
12/17	14,466	87	0.6%	2,719
12/16	8,900	101	1.1%	2,055
12/15	8,557	99	1.2%	2,058
12/14	7,826	75	1.0%	2,081
12/13	7,931	49	0.6%	2,106
Annual Growth	16.2%	15.5%	—	6.6%

2017 Year-End Financials

Debt ratio: 0.80% No. of shares (mil.): 36
Return on equity: 5.09% Dividends
Cash ($ mil.): 373 Yield: 0.0%
Current ratio: — Payout: 45.0%
Long-term debt ($ mil.): — Market value ($ mil.): 3,204

	STOCK PRICE ($) FY Close	P/E High/Low	PER SHARE ($) Earnings	Dividends	Book Value
12/17	87.15	32 27	2.93	1.32	62.81
12/16	87.40	22 14	4.18	1.21	46.83
12/15	71.95	19 14	4.11	0.98	43.84
12/14	67.08	22 18	3.08	0.82	40.78
12/13	66.51	28 17	2.38	0.74	40.72
Annual Growth	7.0%	— —	5.3%	15.6%	11.4%

Southern California Edison Co.

One of the Golden State's largest utilities Southern California Edison (SCE) distributes power to a population of more than 14 million people (4.9 million customer accounts) in central coastal and southern California (excluding Los Angeles and some other cities). SCE has 6287 MW of net generating capacity from stakes in nuclear hydroelectric and fossil-fueled power plants (although it has sold a number of its fossil-fueled facilities in response to the state's deregulation legislation). The utility sells excess power to wholesale customers. SCE is a unit of utility and competitive power holding company Edison International.

Operations

The utility's system consists of about 12782 circuit miles of transmission lines and more than 91000 circuit miles of overhead and underground distribution lines and more than 800 distribution substations.

Geographic Reach

SCE supplies and delivers electricity to a 50000 square-mile area of southern California. This service area contains a population of nearly 14 million people and SCE serves the population via about 4.9 million customer accounts.

Financial Performance

SCE's net revenues decreased by 14% in 2015 due to lower sales from utility cost-recovery activities including a drop in CPUC-related (California Public Utilities Commission) revenues.

The company's net income decreased by 29% due to lower revenues and higher expenses related to depreciation decommissioning and amortization.

Operating cash flows for 2015 increased by 26% due to changes in working capital as a result of changes in regulatory assets and liabilities including the collections of balancing accounts.

Strategy

Parent Edison International has been addressing the changing industry environment by focusing SCE on investing in and strengthening its electric grid and driving operational and service excellence to improve system safety reliability and service while controlling costs and rates. At the same time Edison International is investing in competitive businesses to meet the electricity needs of commercial and industrial customers both inside and beyond SCE's service area.

In recent years the utility has been ramping up its green energy options in order to comply with the state of California's aggressive long term renewable energy goal .In 2014 the company signed contracts with solar and geothermal energy producers representing more than 1500 MW of clean renewable power and the re-contracting of 225 MW with an existing California geothermal energy project.

As part of its strategy to reduce its fossil-fuel power plant holdings in 2013 SCE sold its ownership interest in Units 4 and 5 of the Four Corners Generating Station a coal-fired electric generating facility in New Mexico to the operator of the facility Arizona Public Service Company for $181 million.

SCE also offers power contract options designed to help smaller biomass generators and is installing up to 150 solar photovoltaic installations on Southern California commercial rooftops. The utility is also installing smart electric meters — digital two-way communication devices which allow customers and the utility to better manage energy use than the older mechanical meters can.

EXECUTIVES

Svp And Cio, Todd L. Inlander
Ceo, Kevin M. Payne, age 57
Svp Customer And Operational Services, Stuart R. Hemphill
Vp Operational Services And Chief Procurement Officer, Douglas R. Bauder
Svp Transmission And Distribution, Peter T. Dietrich
Vp Distribution, Gregory M. Ferree

Vp Transmission Substations And Operations, Paul J. Grigaux
President, Ronald O. (R.O.) Nichols, age 64
Vp Decommissioning And Chief Nuclear Officer San Onofre Nuclear Generating Station, Thomas J. (Tom) Palmisano
Vp And Treasurer, William (Tres) Petmecky, age 49
Vice President, Tim Boucher
Vice President, John Davies
Vice President And Treasurer, Robert C Boada
Vice President, Anthony Blakemore
Vice President, Debbie Rodgers
Vice President Culture And Inclusion, Jorge Martinez
Government Relations, Karen Cadavona
Vice President Risk Management, David Heller
Vice President And Treasurer Sce, Daniel Wood
Legal Secretary, Veronica Huerta
Vice President Distribution Sce, Greg Ferree
Vice President, Mark Carter
Senior Vice President Power Supply Sce, Kevin Walker
Assistant Treasurer, Mary Simpson
Board Member, Louis Hernandez
Secretary, Darin Hester
Auditors: PricewaterhouseCoopers LLP

LOCATIONS

HQ: Southern California Edison Co.
2244 Walnut Grove Avenue, P.O. Box 800, Rosemead, CA 91770
Phone: 626 302-1212
Web: www.sce.com

PRODUCTS/OPERATIONS

2015 Sales

	% of total
Commercial customers	43
Residential customers	38
Industrial customers	5
Public authorities	5
Agriculture & other operating revenue	9
Total	**100**

2015 Sales

	$ mil.	% of total
Utility Earning Activities	6,305	55
Utility Cost- Recovery Activities	5,180	45
Total	**11,485**	**100**

COMPETITORS

American States Water	Portland General
Avista	Electric
Bonneville Power	Sacramento Municipal
Calpine	Utility
Imperial Irrigation District	San Diego Gas & Electric
NV Energy	SoCalGas
PacifiCorp	
Pacific Gas and Electric	

HISTORICAL FINANCIALS

Company Type: Public

Income Statement   FYE: December 31

	REVENUE ($ mil.)	NET INCOME ($ mil.)	NET PROFIT MARGIN	EMPLOYEES
12/17	12,254	1,136	9.3%	12,234
12/16	11,830	1,499	12.7%	11,947
12/15	11,485	1,111	9.7%	12,678
12/14	13,380	1,565	11.7%	13,600
12/13	12,562	1,000	8.0%	13,599
Annual Growth	**(0.6%)**	**3.2%**		**(2.6%)**

2017 Year-End Financials

Debt ratio: 23.58%
Return on equity: 7.79%
Cash ($ mil.): 515
Current ratio: 0.52
Long-term debt ($ mil.): 10,428

No. of shares (mil.): 434
Dividends
Yield: 0.0%
Payout: 77.5%
Market value ($ mil.): 11,055

	STOCK PRICE ($) FY Close	P/E High/Low	PER SHARE ($) Earnings	Dividends	Book Value
12/17	25.42	— —	(0.00)	1.20	33.74
12/16	25.15	— —	(0.00)	1.20	33.30
12/15	24.85	— —	(0.00)	1.20	31.44
12/14	24.30	— —	(0.00)	1.20	30.54
12/13	22.39	— —	(0.00)	1.20	27.91
Annual Growth	**3.2%**	**— —**	**—**	**(0.0%)**	**4.9%**

Southern Company (The)

Southern Power provides power for the burgeoning population in the South. The company owns builds acquires and markets energy in the competitive wholesale supply business. It develops and operates independent power plants in the southeastern US. The company which is part of Southern Company's generation and energy marketing operations has more than 10500 MW of primarily fossil-fueled facilities generating capacity operating or under construction in Alabama California Florida Georgia Nevada North Carolina Texas and New Mexico. Southern Power's electricity output is marketed to wholesale customers in the region. It is growing by acquiring and developing solar power facilities.

Operations

The company is a wholesale energy provider serving electricity needs of municipalities electric cooperatives and investor-owned utilities. Southern Power and its subsidiaries owns and/or operates 35 facilities in nine states. Its renewable assets include biomass and solar.

Thanks to solar facilities under construction and the acquisitions of Calipatria Solar and Grant Wind as well as other capacity and energy contracts the Southern Power has an average of 75% of its available demonstrated capacity covered through 2020 and an average of 70% of its available demonstrated capacity covered through 2025.

Geographic Reach

Southern Power has operations Alabama California Florida Georgia Nevada New Mexico North Carolina Oklahoma and Texas.

Financial Performance

In fiscal 2015 Southern Power's net sales decreased by $111 million compared to 2014. Power purchase agreements (PPA) energy revenues declined due to lower energy prices driven by a drop in natural gas prices which was passed through in fuel revenues.

Wholesale revenues and non-affiliates revenues declined due to lower energy and capacity revenues.

In 2015 net income increased by 25% due to lower fuel expenses and purchased power partially offset by decreased sales.

Fuel expense decreased due to lower natural gas generation costs.

Purchased power expenses decreased primarily due to a drop in volume of KWhs purchased as well as a decrease associated with the average cost of purchased power.

Net cash provided by the operating activities increased by 66% due to higher income tax benefits received and higher revenues from new PPAs including solar PPAs.

Strategy

The company is expanding its regional generation portfolio (primarily with solar power plants) in order to boost its overall generating capacity to almost 10000 MW.

Mergers and Acquisitions

Growing its solar power assets in 2016 Southern Power acquired the 120-MW East Pecos solar facility (Southern Power's second solar project in Texas).

That year Southern Power and Turner Renewable Energy jointly bought the 20-MW Calipatria solar facility from Solar Frontier Americas. (Southern Power's 10th solar facility in California).

In 2015 Southern Power acquired a controlling interest in the 200-MW Garland solar facility under construction in California from Recurrent Energy a subsidiary of Canadian Solar Inc.

In 2014 Southern Power and Turner Renewable Energy acquired the largest solar facility in New Mexico the 50-MW Macho Springs Solar Facility. The Southern Power-Turner Renewable Energy partnership's seventh solar project and its second-largest overall the plant is expected to generate enough electricity to power more than 18000 homes.

EXECUTIVES

Svp And Coo, John G. Trawick
Vice President Operations And Government Relations Chief Administrative Officer, Charlie Freeman
Vice President Of Construction, Keith Russell
Auditors: DELOITTE & TOUCHE LLP

LOCATIONS

HQ: Southern Company (The)
30 Ivan Allen Jr. Boulevard, N.W., Atlanta, GA 30308
Phone: 404 506-5000   Fax: 404 506-0455
Web: www.southerncompany.com

PRODUCTS/OPERATIONS

2015 Sales

	$ mil.	% of total
Wholesale revenues non-affiliates	964	69
Wholesale revenues affiliates	417	30
Other revenues	9	1
Total	1,390	100

COMPETITORS

AEP	Duke Energy
AEP	Duke Energy
AES	Entergy
AES	Entergy
Calpine	NextEra Energy
Calpine	NextEra Energy

HISTORICAL FINANCIALS

Company Type: Public

Income Statement   FYE: December 31

	REVENUE ($ mil.)	NET INCOME ($ mil.)	NET PROFIT MARGIN	EMPLOYEES
12/17	23,031	880	3.8%	31,344
12/16	19,896	2,493	12.5%	32,020
12/15	17,489	2,421	13.8%	26,703
12/14	18,467	2,031	11.0%	26,369
12/13	17,087	1,710	10.0%	26,300
Annual Growth	7.7%	(15.3%)	—	4.5%

2017 Year-End Financials

Debt ratio: 43.56%
Return on equity: 3.52%
Cash ($ mil.): 2,130
Current ratio: 0.74
Long-term debt ($ mil.): 44,462

No. of shares (mil.): 1,007
Dividends
Yield: 0.0%
Payout: 273.8%
Market value ($ mil.): 48,456

	STOCK PRICE ($) FY Close	P/E High/Low		PER SHARE ($) Earnings	Dividends	Book Value
12/17	48.09	63	56	0.84	2.30	24.31
12/16	49.19	21	18	2.55	2.22	25.73
12/15	46.79	20	16	2.59	2.15	23.38
12/14	49.11	23	18	2.18	2.08	23.47
12/13	41.11	26	21	1.87	2.01	22.70
Annual Growth	4.0%	—	—	(18.1%)	3.4%	1.7%

Southern Copper Corp

EXECUTIVES

Pres-Ceo, Oscar Gonzalez Rocha
Chb, German Larrea Mota-Velasco
V Pres Fin-Cfo-Treas, Raul Jacob Ruisanchez
General Counsel, Andres Carlos Ferrero Ghislier
Comptroller, Lina Vingerhoets Vilca
SEC, Julian Jorge Lazalde Psihas
V Pres Exploration, Edgard Corrales Aguilar
Gen Auditor, Rafael Lopez Abad
Auditors: Galaz, Yamazaki, Ruiz Urquiza, S.C.

LOCATIONS

HQ: Southern Copper Corp
1440 East Missouri Avenue, Suite 160, Phoenix, AZ 85014
Phone: 602 264-1375   Fax: 602 264-1397
Web: www.southerncoppercorp.com

HISTORICAL FINANCIALS

Company Type: Public

Income Statement   FYE: December 31

	REVENUE ($ mil.)	NET INCOME ($ mil.)	NET PROFIT MARGIN	EMPLOYEES
12/17	6,654	728	10.9%	13,140
12/16	5,379	776	14.4%	13,414
12/15	5,045	736	14.6%	13,024
12/14	5,787	1,332	23.0%	12,735
12/13	5,952	1,618	27.2%	12,665
Annual Growth	2.8%	(18.1%)	—	0.9%

2017 Year-End Financials

Debt ratio: 43.23%
Return on equity: 12.20%
Cash ($ mil.): 1,004
Current ratio: 2.71
Long-term debt ($ mil.): 5,957

No. of shares (mil.): 773
Dividends
Yield: 0.0%
Payout: 62.7%
Market value ($ mil.): 36,680

	STOCK PRICE ($) FY Close	P/E High/Low		PER SHARE ($) Earnings	Dividends	Book Value
12/17	47.45	51	34	0.94	0.59	7.90
12/16	31.94	35	22	1.00	0.18	7.54
12/15	26.12	36	26	0.93	0.34	6.80
12/14	28.20	21	16	1.61	0.46	7.20
12/13	28.71	22	13	1.92	0.68	6.26
Annual Growth	13.4%	—	—	(16.4%)	(3.5%)	6.0%

Southern First Bancshares, Inc.

EXECUTIVES

Senior Vice President, Shannon Smoak
Board Member, Rudolph Johnstone
Auditors: Elliott Davis Decosimo, LLC

LOCATIONS

HQ: Southern First Bancshares, Inc.
100 Verdae Boulevard, Suite 100, Greenville, SC 29606
Phone: 864 679-9000
Web: www.southernfirst.com

COMPETITORS

BB&T	Regions Financial
Bank of America	
First Citizens Bancorporation	

HISTORICAL FINANCIALS

Company Type: Public

Income Statement   FYE: December 31

	ASSETS ($ mil.)	NET INCOME ($ mil.)	INCOME AS % OF ASSETS	EMPLOYEES
12/17	1,624	13	0.8%	198
12/16	1,340	13	1.0%	179
12/15	1,217	10	0.8%	167
12/14	1,029	6	0.6%	155
12/13	890	5	0.6%	138
Annual Growth	16.2%	26.3%	—	9.4%

2017 Year-End Financials

Debt ratio: 4.96%
Return on equity: 10.05%
Cash ($ mil.): 43
Current ratio: —
Long-term debt ($ mil.): —

No. of shares (mil.): 7
Dividends
Yield: —
Payout: —
Market value ($ mil.): 303

	STOCK PRICE ($) FY Close	P/E High/Low		PER SHARE ($) Earnings	Dividends	Book Value
12/17	41.25	23	17	1.76	0.00	20.37
12/16	36.00	18	11	1.94	0.00	17.00
12/15	22.70	14	10	1.55	0.00	14.98
12/14	17.02	15	11	1.10	0.00	13.34
12/13	13.28	14	9	0.98	0.00	15.20
Annual Growth	32.8%	—	—	15.8%	—	7.6%

Southern Missouri Bancorp, Inc.

EXECUTIVES

Vice President, Mel Jackson
Vice President Of Deposit Operations, Tiffany Beaton
Vice President, Kevin Alpe
Vice President Senior Commercial Loan Officer, Brock Fletcher
Senior Vice President Community Bank President, Chris Roberts
Auditors: BKD, LLP

LOCATIONS

HQ: Southern Missouri Bancorp, Inc.
2991 Oak Grove Road, Poplar Bluff, MO 63901
Phone: 573 778-1800
Web: www.bankwithsouthern.com

COMPETITORS

Bank of America
Commerce Bancshares
IBERIABANK
Regions Financial
U.S. Bancorp
UMB Financial

HISTORICAL FINANCIALS
Company Type: Public

Income Statement				FYE: June 30
	ASSETS ($ mil.)	NET INCOME ($ mil.)	INCOME AS % OF ASSETS	EMPLOYEES
06/18	1,886	20	1.1%	415
06/17	1,707	15	0.9%	390
06/16	1,403	14	1.1%	342
06/15	1,300	13	1.1%	327
06/14	1,021	10	1.0%	247
Annual Growth	16.6%	20.0%	—	13.9%

2018 Year-End Financials

Debt ratio: 0.79%
Return on equity: 11.20%
Cash ($ mil.): 28
Current ratio: —
Long-term debt ($ mil.): —
No. of shares (mil.): 9
Dividends
  Yield: 0.0%
  Payout: 18.4%
Market value ($ mil.): 351

	STOCK PRICE ($) FY Close	P/E High/Low		PER SHARE ($) Earnings	Dividends	Book Value
06/18	39.02	17	13	2.39	0.44	22.31
06/17	32.26	18	11	2.07	0.40	20.15
06/16	23.53	12	9	1.98	0.36	16.94
06/15	18.85	22	10	1.79	0.34	17.88
06/14	35.69	25	17	1.46	0.32	16.63
Annual Growth	2.3%	—	—	13.2%	8.3%	7.6%

Southern National Bancorp Of Virginia Inc

EXECUTIVES

Chb-Ceo, Georgia S Derrico
V Chb-Pres-Coo, R Roderick Porter
Exec V Pres-Credit Risk Office, William H Stevens
Sr V Pres-Cfo, William H Lagos
Sr V Pres-Cco, Thomas P Baker
Evp-Cfo-Southern National, Jeffrey L Karafa
Auditors: Dixon Hughes Goodman LLP

LOCATIONS

HQ: Southern National Bancorp Of Virginia Inc
6830 Old Dominion Drive, McLean, VA 22101
Phone: 703 893-7400
Web: www.sonabank.com

COMPETITORS

BB&T
Bank of America
Burke & Herbert Bank
Capital One
PNC Financial
SunTrust
Virginia Commerce Bancorp
Wells Fargo

HISTORICAL FINANCIALS
Company Type: Public

Income Statement				FYE: December 31
	ASSETS ($ mil.)	NET INCOME ($ mil.)	INCOME AS % OF ASSETS	EMPLOYEES
12/17	2,614	2	0.1%	393
12/16	1,142	10	0.9%	162
12/15	1,036	9	0.9%	181
12/14	916	7	0.8%	173
12/13	716	6	0.9%	140
Annual Growth	38.2%	(21.1%)	—	29.4%

2017 Year-End Financials

Debt ratio: 2.17%
Return on equity: 1.08%
Cash ($ mil.): 23
Current ratio: —
Long-term debt ($ mil.): —
No. of shares (mil.): 23
Dividends
  Yield: 0.0%
  Payout: 246.1%
Market value ($ mil.): 384

	STOCK PRICE ($) FY Close	P/E High/Low		PER SHARE ($) Earnings	Dividends	Book Value
12/17	16.03	142	118	0.13	0.32	13.48
12/16	16.34	20	14	0.83	0.32	10.30
12/15	13.06	17	15	0.75	0.52	9.78
12/14	11.34	19	16	0.63	0.60	9.33
12/13	10.01	19	15	0.54	0.40	9.20
Annual Growth	12.5%	—	—	(30.0%)	(5.4%)	10.0%

Southside Bancshares, Inc.

Southside Bancshares is the holding company for Southside Bank which boasts nearly 65 branches across East North and Central Texas with many around the cities of Tyler and Longview. About one-third of its branches are located in supermarkets (including Albertsons and Brookshire stores) and 40% are motor bank facilities. The bank provides traditional services such as savings money market and checking accounts CDs and other deposit products as well as trust and wealth management services. Real estate loans primarily residential mortgages make up about half of the company's loan portfolio which also includes business consumer and municipal loans. The bank has total assets exceeding $4.8 billion.

Operations

Southside generated 48% of its total revenue from loan interest in 2014 while interest income on taxable investment securities and mortgage-backed securities made up 16% and 19% respectively. About 9% of its revenue came from deposit service fees and another 2% came from trust income.

Geographic Reach

The bank's branches are located in East North and Central Texas. Its main markets are in East Texas the greater Fort Worth area and the greater Austin area. It is also an affiliate with more than 55000 foreign ATMs worldwide.

Sales and Marketing

Southside which staffed 813 employees at 2014's end serves individuals businesses municipal entities and non-profit organizations in local communities.

Financial Performance

Southside Bancshares' revenues and profits have been falling over the past several years despite consistent growth in loan and investment interest income mostly because the bank's gains on securities held-for-sale have declined.

The company's revenue dipped by 4% to $148.3 million in 2014 mostly due to a $5.6 million decline in gains on the sale of its AFS securities and a $2.8 million impairment of equity related to its investment in SFG Finance stemming from the sale of loans purchased by SFG and the repossessed assets.

Lower revenue and an uptick in loan loss provisions in 2014 caused Southside's net income to tumble 49% to $20.8 million for the year while its operating cash levels dipped by 6% to $56 million on lower cash earnings.

Strategy

Southside looks to acquire financial institutions to grow its loan business and expand its geographic reach outside of its existing markets. Its 2014 acquisition of OmniAmerican Bank alone helped boost its loan assets by more than 60% to $2.17 billion while adding 14 branches in a new market (Dallas/Fort Worth).

To grow its deposits and deepen its presence in the markets it serves the company has also been expanding its network of banking locations — both in-store and full-service branches.

Mergers and Acquisitions

In December 2014 the company acquired OmniAmerican Bank to boost its loan business and expand its footprint to the Dallas area. The deal added 14 full-service branches in the 12-county Dallas/Fort Worth metroplex and more than $763 million in new loan business.

EXECUTIVES

Senior Executive Vice President, Jeryl Story
President And Ceo Southside Bancshares And Southside Bank, Lee R. Gibson, age 61, $493,325 total compensation
Regional President North Texas Southside Bank, Tim Carter, age 63
Regional President Central Texas Southside Bank, Peter M. Boyd, age 62, $435,510 total compensation
Evp And Chief Credit Officer Southside Bank, Earl W. (Bill) Clawater, age 64, $265,000 total compensation
Evp And Chief Analytics Officer Southside Bank And Company Secretary, Brian K. McCabe, age 57, $228,385 total compensation
Regional President East Texas Southside Bank, Tim Alexander, age 61
Evp And Cfo, Julie N. Shamburger, age 55
Assistant Vice President, Julie A Brown
Vice President, Jeff Quesenberry
Vice President, Cindy Davis
Vice President Branch Manager, Tara Suttle
Executive Vice President, Debra Rutledge
Senior Vice President, Zelton Harvey

LOCATIONS

HQ: Southside Bancshares, Inc.
1201 S. Beckham Avenue, Tyler, TX 75701
Phone: 903 531-7111
Web: www.southside.com

PRODUCTS/OPERATIONS

2014 Sales

	$ mil.	% of total
Interest		
Loans	70	48
Mortgage-backed & related securities	28	19
Investment securities	24	16
Other	0	-
Non-interest		
Deposit services	15	9
Gain on sale of securities	2	2
Trust income	3	2
Back owned life insurance income	1	1
Gain on sale of loans	0	-
Other	4	3
Adjustments	(2.8)	
Total	**148**	**100**

COMPETITORS

Bank of America	Jacksonville Bancorp
Capital One	of Illinois
East Texas Financial	Regions Financial

HISTORICAL FINANCIALS

Company Type. Public

Income Statement

FYE: December 31

	ASSETS ($ mil.)	NET INCOME ($ mil.)	INCOME AS % OF ASSETS	EMPLOYEES
12/17	6,498	54	0.8%	855
12/16	5,563	49	0.9%	679
12/15	5,162	44	0.9%	683
12/14	4,807	20	0.4%	813
12/13	3,445	41	1.2%	640
Annual Growth	**17.2%**	**7.2%**	**—**	**7.5%**

2017 Year-End Financials

Debt ratio: 2.44%	No. of shares (mil.): 35
Return on equity: 8.54%	Dividends
Cash ($ mil.): 190	Yield: 0.0%
Current ratio: —	Payout: 60.6%
Long-term debt ($ mil.): —	Market value ($ mil.): 1,179

	STOCK PRICE ($) FY Close	P/E High/Low		PER SHARE ($) Earnings	Dividends	Book Value
12/17	33.68	21	17	1.81	1.10	21.55
12/16	37.67	21	11	1.81	0.96	17.71
12/15	24.02	19	15	1.61	0.92	16.25
12/14	28.91	36	26	0.96	0.84	15.61
12/13	27.34	15	10	1.94	0.76	12.21
Annual Growth	**5.4%**	—	—	**(1.7%)**	**9.7%**	**15.3%**

Southwest Airlines Co

Southwest Airlines will fly any plane (as long as it's a Boeing) and let passengers sit anywhere they like (as long as they get there first). Sticking with what has worked Southwest has expanded its low-cost no-frills no-reserved-seats approach to air travel throughout the US to serve nearly 100 destinations across North America. Now the largest carrier of US domestic passengers Southwest still stands as an inspiration for scrappy low-fare upstarts the world over. The carrier has enjoyed 44 straight profitable years amid the airline industry's ups and downs. Southwest's fleet numbers about 720 Boeing 737s.

Operations

Simplicity has been key to Southwest's success. Most of the carrier's flights are less than two hours and it usually lands at small airports to avoid congestion at competitors' larger hubs; in Dallas it's the big dog at little Love Field its birthplace and in Chicago it accounts for most of the traffic at Midway Airport. Southwest's (and AirTran's) fleet consists primarily of one type of aircraft — the Boeing 737 — to minimize training and maintenance costs.

Geographic Reach

Southwest serves more than 100 destinations in some 40 US states in addition to the District of Columbia Puerto Rico Mexico Jamaica Costa Rica Belize Cuba The Bahamas Aruba and the Dominican Republic.

Financial Performance

Southwest has achieved unprecedented growth over the last six years. Its revenues grew 3% from $19.8 billion in 2015 to $20.4 billion in 2016 a historic milestone. The historic growth was driven by a bump in passenger revenues fueled by increased passenger yield driven by strong demand for low-fare air travel. On the flip side freight revenues declined 5% due to sluggish demand throughout 2016.

Profits jumped 3% from $2.18 billion in 2015 to a record-setting $2.24 billion in 2016 due to the higher revenue coupled with a significant decline in fuel and oil prices. Southwest's operating cash flow increased from $3.2 billion in 2015 to $4.29 billion in 2016 due to the higher profits in addition to cash generated from fuel derivative instruments.

Strategy

Protective of its low-cost image Southwest has staunchly resisted charging passengers baggage fees. However it has seen the value of this strategy and has rolled out new fees that have included allowing passengers to bring small dogs or cats into the cabin for a one-way charge of $75 and charging a one-way $50 fee for unaccompanied minors.

A large part of the carrier's strategy to stay profitable includes fleet modernization. Southwest is replacing older Boeing 737 planes with the larger and more fuel-efficient Boeing 737-800 for expansion to locations of greater distance.

During 2016 Southwest grew by adding a scheduled service to Long Beach California and the three Cuban cities of Havana Varadero and Santa Clara.

Another prong of the carrier's growth strategy involves technology. To tap into potential Latin American passengers wanting to travel to the US Southwest is investing in technology that features foreign-currency exchanges and point-of-sale programs. Southwest?s new reservations platform launched in late 2016 will also give the carrier more revenue management capabilities and functions to sell to international customers. The carrier has spent more than $500?million on the system.

HISTORY

Texas businessman Rollin King and lawyer Herb Kelleher founded Air Southwest in 1967 as an intrastate airline linking Dallas Houston and San Antonio. The now-defunct Braniff and Texas International sued questioning whether the region needed another airline but the Texas Supreme Court ruled in Southwest's favor. In 1971 the company renamed Southwest Airlines made its first scheduled flight.

Operating from Love Field in Dallas Southwest adopted "love" as the theme of its early ad campaigns serving love potions (drinks) and love bites (peanuts). When other airlines moved to the new Dallas/Fort Worth International Airport (DFW) in 1974 Kelleher insisted on staying at Love Field gaining a virtual monopoly there.

EXECUTIVES

Evp Corporate Services, Robert E. (Bob) Jordan, age 58, $470,000 total compensation
Chairman And Ceo, Gary C. Kelly, age 62, $10,084 total compensation
Evp Daily Operations, Gregory D. (Greg) Wells, age 59
Evp And Cfo, Tammy Romo, age 55, $460,000 total compensation
Vp And Chief Technology Architect, Stan Alexander
Coo, Michael G. (Mike) Van de Ven, age 56, $474,373 total compensation
Vp And Chief Communications Officer, Linda B. Rutherford
Vp Corporate Delivery Operations And Reservations, Kathleen Wayton
Evp And Chief Revenue Officer, Andrew Watterson
Vp And Chief Marketing Officer, Ryan Green
President, Thomas M. (Tom) Nealon, age 56
Vice Chairman, Ron Ricks, age 69
Auditors: Ernst & Young LLP

LOCATIONS

HQ: Southwest Airlines Co
P.O. Box 36611, Dallas, TX 75235-1611
Phone: 214 792-4000   **Fax:** 214 792-5015
Web: www.southwest.com

PRODUCTS/OPERATIONS

2016 Sales

	$ mil.	% of total
Passenger	18,594	91
Freight	171	1
Other	1,660	8
Total	**20,425**	**100**

COMPETITORS

Alaska Air	Frontier Airlines
American Airlines Group	JetBlue
	United Continental
Delta Air Lines	

HISTORICAL FINANCIALS

Company Type: Public

Income Statement

FYE: December 31

	REVENUE ($ mil.)	NET INCOME ($ mil.)	NET PROFIT MARGIN	EMPLOYEES
12/18	21,965	2,465	11.2%	58,800
12/17	21,171	3,488	16.5%	56,100
12/16	20,425	2,244	11.0%	53,500
12/15	19,820	2,181	11.0%	49,583
12/14	18,605	1,136	6.1%	46,278
Annual Growth	**4.2%**	**21.4%**	**—**	**6.2%**

Debt ratio: 12.87%
Return on equity: 24.31%
Cash ($ mil.): 1,854
Current ratio: 0.64
Long-term debt ($ mil.): 2,771

No. of shares (mil.): 552
Dividends
Yield: 1.3%
Payout: 9.6%
Market value ($ mil.): 25,685

	STOCK PRICE ($) FY Close	P/E High/Low		PER SHARE ($) Earnings	Dividends	Book Value
12/18	46.48	15	10	4.29	0.61	17.83
12/17	65.45	11	9	5.79	0.48	17.72
12/16	49.84	14	10	3.55	0.38	13.72
12/15	43.06	15	10	3.27	0.29	11.36
12/14	42.32	26	11	1.64	0.22	10.03
Annual Growth	2.4%	—	—	27.2%	28.8%	15.5%

SpartanNash Co.

In the grocery and distribution wars Spartan-Nash is up for the fight. The grocery retailer and wholesaler operates some 160 supermarkets primarily under the Family Fare Supermarkets D&W Fresh Market VG's Food and Pharmacy Martin's Super Markets and Sun Mart banners. Besides selling national brand-goods stores offer private-label items under the Spartan TopCare Valu Time and Full Circle names. SpartanNash is also a leading grocery wholesaler distributing over 7100 private brand items to 2100 independent supermarkets in Michigan Indiana and Ohio. It is also a leading grocery distributor for the US military. Founded in 1917 as a cooperative grocery distributor Spartan Stores came into its current being after it acquired Nash-Finch in 2013.

Operations
SpartanNash operates three main business segments: Food Military and Retail.

Food Distribution which makes up some 45% of the company's total revenue comprises 11 distribution centers that ship 60000 stock-keeping units of food general merchandise floral pharmacy and health and beauty care products.

Living up to its namesake warrior city Spartan-Nash's Military segment (nearly 30% of revenue) contracts with manufacturers to distribute grocery products to US military commissaries and exchanges. The company is the largest distributor to such US military properties.

Its Retail division (nearly 30% of revenue) sells items from its some 160 company-owned retail stores operating under more than 15 banners (including Family Fare Supermarkets No Frills Bag 'N Save Family Fresh Markets D&W Fresh Markets Sun Mart and Econo Foods). It also runs 30 gas stations and 90 in-store pharmacies.

By product SpartanNash generates over 60% of its revenue from non-perishable items while around 30% comes from the sale and distribution of perishable items. About 6% of revenue comes from fuel and pharmacy sales.

Geographic Reach
Grand Rapids Michigan-based SpartanNash owns more than 160 stores in 10 states and distributes to 2100 independent grocers across 47 US states. Its military operations serve commissaries and exchanges in 37 US states the District of Columbia Europe Cuba Puerto Rico Bahrain and Egypt.

Sales and Marketing
SpartanNash's largest Food Distribution customer is Dollar General. The company sells to more than 13000 Dollar General retail locations yearly accounting for about 11% of SpartanNash's consolidated net sales.

Financial Performance
In 2016 SpartanNash's revenue recovered by 1% to $7.7 billion following a 3% fall the previous year. Gains came from new and existing customers in the Food Distribution (4.5% growth) and Military (0.5% growth) segments. Food and Military growth offset the negative impact of food deflation across the board as well as lower comparable retail store sales and the closure of retail stores. Retail revenue fell 3%.

Net income fell 10% to $56.8 million as food price deflation ate into margins. Cash from operating activities also fell by 30% to $154.5 million.

Strategy
Through SpartanNash's neighborhood market strategy the company endeavors to distinguish itself from other food retailers such as supercenters and limited-assortment stores by emphasizing convenient locations and offering demographically targeted merchandise high-quality fresh foods and value pricing. It's been expanding its product offerings in its stores adding more than 1000 new items (and 300 unique items) during 2016 and 2017. The acquisition of Caito Foods Service expanded its presence in prepared fruits vegetables and proteins categories.

To drive sales and foster customer loyalty SpartanNash has been renovating its stores completing seventeen remodels across 2015-16. It also opened a new fuel center. The company expects to close or sell ten stores during 2017.

Another part of SpartanNash's growth strategy includes select acquisitions of retail grocery stores grocery store chains or distribution facilities. Other initiatives outlined in early 2016 included driving a "lean and efficient" operating cost structure to remain competitive in the Retail segment streamlining and obtaining better scale for its supply chain and leverage the size and scale of its Food Distribution and Retail segments to drive new customer business for its Military segment.

Mergers and Acquisitions
SpartanNash acquired Martin's Super Market and its 20 retail locations in late 2018 expanding SpartanNash's presence into northern Indiana and southwestern Michigan.

In early 2017 SpartanNash acquired Caito Foods Service's produce distribution business as well as its fresh produce and prepared foods businesses. The deal which included two processing facilities and temperature-controlled distribution and logistics company Blue Ribbon Transport expanded the company's presence in the prepared fruits vegetables and proteins grocery categories. SpartanNash paid $217.5 million in cash for Caito's assets.

HISTORY

Making dinner in the early 1900s often required several shopping stops: the grocer for canned goods a butcher for meat and yet another place for produce. Eventually the big grocery chains began offering one-stop shopping not to mention better prices due to greater buying power. Worrying about how to compete in 1917 approximately 100 small grocers met in Grand Rapids Michigan to discuss organizing a cooperative; almost half of those formed the Grand Rapids Wholesale Grocery Co. The stores remained independent operating under different names but achieving economies of scale and volume buying through the co-op. They also began developing a variety of services for member stores. Sales topped $1 million in 1934.

Over the years the company expanded beyond its Grand Rapids origins. In 1950 it formed subsidiary United Wholesale which served independent grocers on a cash-and-carry basis. It acquired the Grand Rapids Coffee Company in 1953. The next year the co-op launched its first private-label item Spartan Coffee with a green Spartan logo reminiscent of the Michigan State University mascot. The company changed its name to Spartan Stores in 1957.

Spartan Stores entered retailing in the early 1970s when it bought 19 Harding's stores. It became a for-profit company in 1973 but continued to provide rebates to customers based on their purchases. Spartan Stores began offering insurance to its customers in 1979.

Concerned about the direction of the company customers named Patrick Quinn formerly a VP at a small chain of grocery stores as president and CEO in 1985. To focus on the wholesale business and to avoid any appearance of conflict of interest in both supplying member stores and operating competing stores Spartan Stores sold its 23 retail stores between 1987 and 1994 giving customer stores the first option on them. It entered the convenience store wholesale business with its 1987 acquisition of L&L/Jiroch. Two years later the co-op acquired Associated Grocers of Michigan (later known as Capistar closed in 1996).

Sales topped $2 billion in 1991. Spartan Stores expanded its convenience store operations in 1993 by buying wholesaler J.F. Walker. Despite record sales in 1996 a $46 million restructuring charge that included extensive technological improvements led to a $21.7 million loss the largest in the company's history. The following year Jim Meyer who had joined Spartan Stores in 1973 replaced the retiring Quinn as president and CEO. Also in 1997 the company stopped giving its customers rebates finally doing away with the last remnants of its co-op years.

To keep Michigan customers out of the clutches of its wholesaling rivals Spartan Stores re-entered retailing in 1999 by acquiring eight Ashcraft's Markets. It bought 13 Family Fare stores and 23 Glen's grocery stores that year. In early 2000 the company sold off its insurance business. Later that year Spartan Stores acquired food and drug chain Seaway Food Town (Michigan and Ohio) for about $180 million and began publicly trading.

In 2001 the company purchased longtime customer Prevo's Family Markets a supermarket chain with 10 stores in western Michigan. In an effort to reduce debt and improve profitability in mid-2002 the company announced plans to close its Food Town stores which suffered from competitors such as Meier Kroger and Farmer Jack's. (By mid-2003 Spartan had sold the last of its 26 Food Town stores. Spartan Stores' retail operations had accounted for about 40% of the company's sales.)

In 2003 Spartan Stores sold seven shopping centers in Michigan for $46 million as part of its strategy to sell noncore properties and focus on its retail and distributions businesses. That year James Meyer retired as president and CEO of S

EXECUTIVES

Vp Information Technology And Cio, David deS. (Dave) Couch, age 67, $205,920 total compensation
President And Ceo, David M. (Dave) Staples, age 55, $600,000 total compensation
Evp Retail Operations, Theodore C. (Ted) Adornato, age 64, $369,308 total compensation
Evp And Cfo, Mark E. Shamber, age 50
Evp Merchandising And Marketing, Larry Pierce, age 63
Evp Chief Legal Officer And President Mdv, Kathleen M. (Kathy) Mahoney, age 63, $415,000 total compensation
Evp; Ceo Caito Foods, Bob Kirch
Vice President Fresh Merchandising, Brian Haaraoja

Vice President Corporate Affairs, Jeanne Norcross
Vice President Operations Finance, Francis Wong
Director Of Pharmacy, Eddie Garcia
Chairman, Dennis Eidson, age 64
Auditors: DELOITTE & TOUCHE LLP

LOCATIONS

HQ: SpartanNash Co.
850 76th Street S W, P.O. Box 8700, Grand Rapids, MI
49518-8700
Phone: 616 878-2000
Web: www.spartannash.com

PRODUCTS/OPERATIONS

2016 Sales

	$ mil.	% of total
Food Distribution	3,454	45
Military	2,197	28
Retail	2,083	27
Total	**7,734**	**100**

2016 Sales

	$ mil.	% of total
Non-perishables	4,908	63
Perishables	2,359	31
Pharmacy	356	5
Fuel	110	1
Total	**7,734**	**100**

2016 Stores

	No.
Family Fare Supermarkets	82
VG's Food and Pharmacy	11
D&W Fresh Markets	11
Sun Mart	10
Econofoods	8
Dan's Super Market	6
Family Fresh Market	6
Valu Land	5
Family Thrift Center	4
Supermercado Nuestra Familia	3
No Frills	3
Forest Hills Foods	1
Pick ‘n Save	1
Germantown Fresh Market	1
Prairie Market	1
Dillonvale IGA	1
Madison Fresh Market	1
Purdue Fresh Market	1
Wholesale Food Outlet	1
Total	**157**

Selected Retail Brands

Full Circle
Spartan
Spartan Fresh Selections
Top Care
Valu Time

COMPETITORS

Alex Lee	IGA
Associated Wholesale	Kroger
Grocers	McLane
C&S Wholesale	Meijer
Coastal Pacific Food	Miner's
Distributors Inc.	S. Abraham & Sons
Core-Mark	SUPERVALU
Costco Wholesale	Wal-Mart

HISTORICAL FINANCIALS

Company Type: Public

Income Statement

FYE: December 30

	REVENUE ($ mil.)	NET INCOME ($ mil.)	NET PROFIT MARGIN	EMPLOYEES
12/17	8,128	(52)	—	14,800
12/16*	7,734	56	0.7%	14,700
01/16	7,661	62	0.0%	15,800
01/15	7,916	58	0.7%	16,100
12/13	2,597	0	0.0%	15,900
Annual Growth	**33.0%**	—	—	**(1.8%)**

*Fiscal year change

2017 Year-End Financials

Debt ratio: 36.48%
Return on equity: (-6.85%)
Cash ($ mil.): 15
Current ratio: 2.03
Long-term debt ($ mil.): 740

No. of shares (mil.): 36
Dividends
Yield: 0.0%
Payout: —
Market value ($ mil.): 973

	STOCK PRICE ($) FY Close	P/E High/Low		PER SHARE ($) Earnings	Dividends	Book Value
12/17	26.68	—	—	(1.41)	0.66	19.80
12/16*	39.54	26	12	1.51	0.60	21.99
01/16	21.64	20	13	1.66	0.54	21.03
01/15	25.82	17	12	1.55	0.48	19.91
12/13	23.73	810	537	0.03	0.27	18.92
Annual Growth	**3.0%**	—	—	—	**25.0%**	**1.1%**

*Fiscal year change

SPECTRA ENERGY CORP

Spectra Energy covers the spectrum of natural gas activities — gathering processing transmission storage and distribution. The company now part of Enbridge operates more than 15400 miles of transmission pipeline and has 305 billion cu. ft. of storage capacity in the US and Canada. Units include U.S. Gas Transmission Texas Eastern Transmission Natural Gas Liquids Division and Market Hub Partners. It also has stakes in DCP Midstream Maritimes & Northeast Pipeline Gulfstream Natural Gas System Spectra Energy Income Fund and 75% of Spectra Energy Partners. Its Union Gas unit distributes gas to 1.5 million Ontario customers. In 2017 Spectra merged with Enbridge creating the largest energy infrastructure company in North America.

Change in Company Type

In 2017 Enbridge acquired Spectra Energy for $28 billion. The combination of the two companies created the largest energy infrastructure company in North America with a pro-forma enterprise value of about $127 billion. Enbridge shareholders owned 57% of the combined company (Enbridge) and Spectra Energy shareholders 43%.

Operations

Spectra Energy has managed its businesses in four reportable segments: Spectra Energy Partners Distribution Western Canada Transmission & Processing and Field Services.

Spectra Energy Partners provides transmission storage and gathering of natural gas for customers in various regions of the Midwestern northeastern and southeastern US and operates a crude oil pipeline system that connects Canadian and U.S. producers to refineries in the U.S. Rocky Mountain and Midwest regions. Spectra Energy Partners has accounted for about 50% of the company's revenue.

Distribution about 30% of revenue provides retail natural gas distribution service (its Union Gas

unit distributes gas to 1.5 million customers in 400 communities in Ontario). It also provides natural gas transportation and storage services to other utilities and energy market customers.

Western Canada Transmission & Processing about 20% of revenue provides its customers with transportation services to move natural gas natural gas gathering and processing services and NGL extraction fractionation transportation storage and marketing services.

Field Services gathers processes treats compresses transports and stores natural gas; it also fractionates transports gathers processes stores markets and trades NGLs. Its DCP Midstream joint venture is 50% owned by Phillips 66. DCP operates in 17 US states.

Transportation storage and processing of natural gas have accounted for about two-thirds of Spectra Energy's revenue.

Geographic Reach

Spectra Energy?s Spectra Energy Partners operates in northeastern and southeastern US and operates a crude oil pipeline system that connects Canadian and US producers to refineries in the Rocky Mountains and the Midwest. The Distribution segment serves natural gas customers in Ontario Canada. Western Canada Transmission & Processing serves customers in western Canada and the northern US. Field Services gathers natural gas from the Mid-Continent Rocky Mountain East Texas-North Louisiana Barnett Shale Gulf Coast South Texas Central Texas Antrim Shale and Permian Basin.

All told Spectra Energy has more than 100 facilities across North America.

Sales and Marketing

Spectra Energy's customers (end-users) purchase gas directly from suppliers or marketers as well as through retail and wholesale outlets.

Financial Performance

Spectra Energy reported a 6% decline in revenue in 2016 to $4.9 billion from 2015. Each segment posted lower revenue for 2016. Lower energy prices were passed on to customers and warmer weather meant they used less energy. Revenue also was hurt by a weaker Canadian dollar. The Distribution segment did see some growth with additional customers and the Dawn Parkway Expansion Project.

The company?s net income jump some 250% to $693 million in 2016 from 2015 mostly because of charges and costs the company had in 2015 but not 2016.

Spectra has cash flow from operations of about $2 billion in 2016 down from about $2.2 billion in 2015. The difference was driven by non-cash goodwill impairments in 2015 offset by higher earnings.

Company Background

In 2012 Spectra Energy acquired one-third of DCP Sand Hills Pipeline and DCP Southern Hills Pipeline (NGL pipelines) from DCP Midstream for $459 million.

In 2012 Spectra Energy opened a new natural gas processing plant in Dawson Creek British Columbia part of its $1.5 billion investment strategy in infrastructure. That year it also signed a deal with BG Group to develop a pipeline from northeast British Columbia to serve BG Group's potential LNG export facility in Prince Rupert on the northwest coast of the province.

To raise cash in 2012 it sold a 38.76% interest in Maritimes & Northeast Pipeline to Spectra Energy Partners for $375 million.

In a move to boost its Gulf Coast natural gas storage position in 2010 Spectra Energy acquired the Bobcat Gas Storage asset from Haddington Energy Partners and GE Energy Financial Service for about $540 million.

The company was founded in 2006.

EXECUTIVES

Cfo, J. Patrick (Pat) Reddy, $634,900 total compensation
Vice President Of It, Mark Wyatt
Vice President, John Bremner
Chief Administrative Officer, Dorothy M. Ables, $475,488 total compensation
Chairman President And Ceo, Gregory L. (Greg) Ebel, $1,133,000 total compensation
President Spectra Energy Transmission West And Canadian Lng, R. Mark Fiedorek
President Us Transmission And Storage, William T. (Bill) Yardley, $409,500 total compensation
President Union Gas, Stephen W. (Steve) Baker
General Counsel, Reginald D. (Reggie) Hedgebeth, $568,033 total compensation
Chief Development Officer, Guy G. Buckley, $438,333 total compensation
Vice President, Gregory Rizzo
Senior Vice President, Carlo V Dechiro
Board Member, Nora Brownell
Auditors: DELOITTE & TOUCHE LLP HOUSTON

LOCATIONS

HQ: SPECTRA ENERGY CORP
  5400 WESTHEIMER CT, HOUSTON, TX 770565353
Phone: 713 627-5400
Web: WWW.ENBRIDGE.COM

2016 Sales

	% of total
U.S.	50
Canada	50
Total	**100**

PRODUCTS/OPERATIONS

2016 Sales

	$ mil.	% of total
Spectra Energy Partners	2,533	52
Distribution	1,370	28
Western Canada Transmission & Processing	1,005	20
Others	8	-
Total	**4,916**	**100**

2016 Sales

	$ mil.	% of total
Transportation storage and processing of natural gas	3,251	66
Distribution of natural gas	1,144	23
Transportation of crude oil	359	7
Sales of natural gas liquids	68	2
Other	94	2
Total	**4,916**	**100**

Selected Mergers and Acquisitions

COMPETITORS

Entergy	Piedmont Natural Gas
Enterprise Products	TransMontaigne
Kinder Morgan	Williams Companies
Koch Industries Inc.	

HISTORICAL FINANCIALS
Company Type: Private

Income Statement
FYE: December 31

	REVENUE ($ mil.)	NET INCOME ($ mil.)	NET PROFIT MARGIN	EMPLOYEES
12/16	4,916	1,020	20.7%	8,700
12/15	5,234	460	8.8%	—
Annual Growth	(6.1%)	121.7%	—	—

SPECTRUM HEALTH SYSTEM

EXECUTIVES

Pres, Richard C Breon
Svp-Cfo, Matthew Cox
Coordinator, Josh Miller
Administrative Director, Larry Genzink
Information Specialist, Bob Gillett
Director, Cynthia Pollock
Administrator, David S Mulka
Executive, Deborah Sorensen
Fleet Staff, Greg Elderkin
Administrator, Jodi Scully
Database Administrator, Michael Busche

LOCATIONS

HQ: SPECTRUM HEALTH SYSTEM
  100 MICHIGAN ST NE, GRAND RAPIDS, MI 495032560
Phone: 616 391-1774
Web: WWW.SPECTRUMHEALTH.ORG

COMPETITORS

Ascension Health	HealthPlus of Michigan
Blue Cross Blue Shield of Michigan	McLaren Bay
	McLaren Health Care
Borgess Health	Mercy Health Hackley
Bronson Battle Creek	Munson Healthcare
Bronson Health Care	OmniCare Health Plan
CareSource	Sheridan Community Hospital
Covenant HealthCare	
Great Lakes Health Plan	Total Health Care
	Zeeland Community Hospital
Hayes Green Beach Memorial Hospital	
Health Alliance Plan of Michigan	

HISTORICAL FINANCIALS
Company Type: Private

Income Statement
FYE: June 30

	REVENUE ($ mil.)	NET INCOME ($ mil.)	NET PROFIT MARGIN	EMPLOYEES
06/18	6,004	332	5.5%	16,996
06/17	5,681	357	6.3%	—
06/10	1,446	142	9.9%	—
Annual Growth	19.5%	11.2%	—	—

2018 Year-End Financials

Debt ratio: ——
Return on equity: 5.50%
Cash ($ mil.): 707
Current ratio: 0.90
Long-term debt ($ mil.): —
Dividends
  Yield: —
  Payout: —
Market value ($ mil.): —

Spirit AeroSystems Holdings Inc

EXECUTIVES

Pres-Ceo, Thomas C Gentile
Chb, Robert Johnson
Sr V Pres-Cfo, Sanjay Kapoor
Sr V Pres-Chief ADM Officer, Samantha J Marnick
Sr V Pres-Cto-Cqo, John Pilla
Sr V Pres-Cco-General Counsel-, Stacy Cozad
Exec Leadership Team, William Brown
Sr V Pres-Gen Mgr, Duane Hawkins
Sr V Pres Dfnce Prgrms, Krisstie Kondrotis
Sr V Pres-Gen Mgr, Michelle J Lohmeier
Sr V Pres Fabrication & Supply, Ron Rabe
Auditors: Ernst & Young LLP

LOCATIONS

HQ: Spirit AeroSystems Holdings Inc
  3801 South Oliver, Wichita, KS 67210
Phone: 316 526-9000
Web: www.spiritaero.com

COMPETITORS

Airbus
Beechcraft
Boeing
Bombardier
Dassault Aviation
Embraer
Finmeccanica
Fuji Heavy Industries
GKN
Goodrich Corp.
Gulfstream Aerospace
Kawasaki Heavy Industries
Lockheed Martin
Mitsubishi Heavy Industries
Northrop Grumman
Saab AB
Snecma
Textron
Triumph Aerostructures - Vought Aircraft Division
Triumph Group
United Technologies

HISTORICAL FINANCIALS
Company Type: Public

Income Statement
FYE: December 31

	REVENUE ($ mil.)	NET INCOME ($ mil.)	NET PROFIT MARGIN	EMPLOYEES
12/17	6,983	354	5.1%	15,500
12/16	6,792	469	6.9%	14,400
12/15	6,643	788	11.9%	15,200
12/14	6,799	358	5.3%	15,402
12/13	5,961	(621)	—	14,177
Annual Growth	4.0%	—	—	2.3%

2017 Year-End Financials

Debt ratio: 21.85%
Return on equity: 19.03%
Cash ($ mil.): 423
Current ratio: 1.64
Long-term debt ($ mil.): 1,119
No. of shares (mil.): 114
Dividends
  Yield: 0.0%
  Payout: 13.2%
Market value ($ mil.): 9,986

	STOCK PRICE ($) FY Close	P/E High/Low		PER SHARE ($) Earnings	Dividends	Book Value
12/17	87.25	29	17	3.01	0.40	15.74
12/16	58.35	16	11	3.70	0.10	15.85
12/15	50.07	10	7	5.66	0.00	15.63
12/14	43.04	18	10	2.53	0.00	11.49
12/13	34.08	—	—	(4.40)	0.00	10.22
Annual Growth	26.5%	—	—	—	—	11.4%

SPIRIT REALTY CAPITAL, INC.

EXECUTIVES

Pres-Coo, Jackson Hsieh
Exec V Pres-Cfo, Phillip D Joseph Jr
Exec V Pres-Chief Acquisitions, Boyd Messmann
Exec V Pres Asset Management, Mark L Manheimer
Sr V Pres-Chief Hr Officer, Michelle M Greenstreet
Sr V Pres-Cao, Prakash J Parag
Evp-Cfo, Michael Hughes
Senior Vice President and Head, Bill Totherow
Auditors: ERNST & YOUNG LLP DALLAS TX

LOCATIONS

HQ: SPIRIT REALTY CAPITAL, INC.
2727 N HARWOOD ST STE 300, DALLAS, TX
752012407
Phone: 480 606-0820

HISTORICAL FINANCIALS

Company Type: Private

Income Statement

FYE: December 31

	ASSETS ($ mil.)	NET INCOME ($ mil.)	INCOME AS % OF ASSETS	EMPLOYEES
12/17	7,263	77	1.1%	71
12/16	7,677	97	1.3%	—
12/14	8,017	(33)	—	—
12/13	7,231	1	0.0%	—
Annual Growth	0.1%	160.4%	—	—

2017 Year-End Financials

Debt ratio: —
Return on equity: 11.50%
Cash ($ mil.): 8
Current ratio: —
Long-term debt ($ mil.): —

Dividends
Yield: —
Payout: —
Market value ($ mil.): —

Sprint Corp (New)

EXECUTIVES

Branch Manager, Mark Kline
Manager, Scott North
Manager, Paul Hall
Auditors: DELOITTE & TOUCHE LLP

LOCATIONS

HQ: Sprint Corp (New)
6200 Sprint Parkway, Overland Park, KS 66251
Phone: 855 848-3280
Web: www.sprint.com

HISTORICAL FINANCIALS

Company Type: Public

Income Statement

FYE: March 31

	REVENUE ($ mil.)	NET INCOME ($ mil.)	NET PROFIT MARGIN	EMPLOYEES
03/18	32,406	7,389	22.8%	30,000
03/17	33,347	(1,206)	—	28,000
03/16	32,180	(1,995)	—	30,000
03/15	34,532	(3,345)	—	31,000
03/14	8,875	(151)	—	36,000
Annual Growth	38.2%	—		(4.5%)

2018 Year-End Financials

Debt ratio: 47.85%
Return on equity: 32.72%
Cash ($ mil.): 6,610
Current ratio: 1.32
Long-term debt ($ mil.): 37,463

Dividends
Yield: —
Payout: —
Market value ($ mil.): —

	STOCK PRICE ($) FY Close	P/E High/Low	PER SHARE ($) Earnings	Dividends	Book Value
03/18	4.00	— —	1.86	0.00	6.60
03/17	8.68	— —	(0.30)	0.00	4.71
03/16	3.48	— —	(0.50)	0.00	4.98
03/15	4.74	— —	(0.85)	0.00	5.47
03/14	9.19	— —	(0.04)	0.00	6.42
Annual Growth	(14.6%)		—	—	0.6%

Sprouts Farmers Market Inc

A fast-growing natural foods retailer Sprouts Farmers Market operates more than 255 stores in over a dozen US states including Arizona California Colorado Nevada New Mexico Oklahoma Texas and Utah. The stores (ranging from 28000 to 30000 sq. ft.) sell organic and local produce baked goods all-natural meats and seafood imported cheeses bulk foods and vitamins and supplements. Stores also boast over 450 bins of bulk rice spices nuts and grains. Sprouts merged with Sunflower Farmers Market in 2012 giving Sprouts the #2 spot in the natural organic retail market behind Whole Foods Market. It went public in 2013.

Operations

The grocer sources its products from more than 800 vendors and suppliers (domestically and internationally). Nature's Best is its primary supplier of dry grocery and frozen food products making up nearly 35% of total purchases in Sprouts stores.

Geographic Reach

Sprouts operates more than 255 stores in almost 15 US states. About 40% of its stores are located in California while another nearly 40% of stores are spread fairly evenly across the states of Arizona Colorado and Texas. The remaining Sprouts stores are located in the states of Georgia Kansas Missouri Nevada New Mexico Oklahoma Tennessee and Utah.

Sales and Marketing

Sprouts touts its position as the value-oriented neighborhood grocery store for natural and organic products through a marketing and promotional strategy that includes print (flyers and newspaper inserts) digital and social media platforms. The chain sends more than 15 million weekly advertisement circulars that focus on product education and offerings to entice the customer and also uses local radio to promote sales and support its brand image.

Financial Performance

Sprouts' revenues have been soaring in recent years thanks to the grocers' aggressive expansion and the continued popular demand for organic food in the US.The chain's revenue climbed 13% to a record $4.1 billion during its fiscal year 2017 thanks to new store openings and same-store sales growth.

Profits however declined 4% from $129 million in 2016 to $124 million in 2017 mainly due to a 17% spike in expenses related to new store open-

ings. In contrast Sprout's cash flow from operations has steadily increased the last five years.

Strategy

Fast-growing Sprouts Farmers Market continues to boost its store count and extend its retail reach mostly through new store openings (though it will consider acquisitions in suitable target markets with acceptable terms and conditions) planning to grow its new stores at a rate of 14% annually from 2015 through 2020.

The chain has increasingly accelerated its store expansion to successfully fuel growth over the past few years opening 27 stores in 2015 expanding for the first time into Michigan Alabama and Tennessee. In its biggest expansion year yet Sprouts opened 36 new stores in 2016. It plans to open 32 stores in 2017.

Capitalizing on the popularity of online ordering the retailer has also partnered with Amazon Prime to offer 1-hour or 2-hour deliveries in select markets.In 2016 it expanded its Amazon Prime Now home delivery service to nine stores in four markets. Despite Amazon's milestone acquisition of Whole Foods in mid-2017 Sprouts plans to expand its Prime Now service to more than 20 locations across many of its major markets by the end of 2017.

EXECUTIVES

Cio, Daniel J. Bruni, age 60, $318,077 total compensation
Chief Operations Officer, Dan Sanders
President And Coo, James L. (Jim) Nielsen, age 46, $522,596 total compensation
Ceo, Amin N. Maredia, age 45, $644,309 total compensation
Chief Development Officer, Theodore E. (Ted) Frumkin, age 56, $292,942 total compensation
Cfo, Bradley S. (Brad) Lukow, age 54, $386,846 total compensation
Senior Vice President, Mark Miale
Vice President Real Estate, Terry Gibbons
Vp Investor Relations Treasury, Susannah Livingston
Vice President Business Intelligence, Gaurav Narwani
Chairman, Joseph Fortunato
Auditors: PricewaterhouseCoopers LLP

LOCATIONS

HQ: Sprouts Farmers Market Inc
5455 East High Street, Suite 111, Phoenix, AZ 85054
Phone: 480 814-8016
Web: www.sprouts.com

2016 Stores

	No.
California	96
Texas	40
Arizona	32
Colorado	30
Georgia	12
Oklahoma	10
New Mexico	7
Nevada	6
Utah	5
Alabama	4
Kansas	4
Tennessee	4
Missouri	3
Total	**253**

PRODUCTS/OPERATIONS

Sales 2016

	% of total
Perishables	50
Non-Perishables	50
Total	**100**

Selected Product category
Bakery
Beer
Body care
Bulk items
Dairy
Dairy alternatives
Deli
Frozen foods
Grocery
Meat
Natural health &
Seafood
Vitamins and supplements
Wine

COMPETITORS

Bashas'	Safeway
Costco Wholesale	Target Corporation
H-E-B	Trader Joe's
Kroger	Wal-Mart
Natural Grocers by Vitamin Cottage	Whole Foods

HISTORICAL FINANCIALS
Company Type: Public

Income Statement   FYE: December 31

	REVENUE ($ mil.)	NET INCOME ($ mil.)	NET PROFIT MARGIN	EMPLOYEES
12/17*	4,664	158	3.4%	27,000
01/17	4,046	124	3.1%	24,000
01/16	3,593	128	3.6%	20,000
12/14	2,967	107	3.6%	17,000
12/13	2,437	51	2.1%	14,000
Annual Growth	17.6%	32.6%	—	17.8%

*Fiscal year change

2017 Year-End Financials

Debt ratio: 30.52%	No. of shares (mil.): 132
Return on equity: 24.01%	Dividends
Cash ($ mil.): 19	Yield: —
Current ratio: 1.00	Payout: —
Long-term debt ($ mil.): 473	Market value ($ mil.): 3,234

	STOCK PRICE ($) FY Close	P/E High/Low	PER SHARE ($) Earnings	Dividends	Book Value
12/17*	24.35	21 15	1.15	0.00	4.90
01/17	18.92	35 23	0.83	0.00	4.80
01/16	26.59	46 23	0.83	0.00	5.39
12/14	32.73	55 36	0.70	0.00	4.51
12/13	38.19	129 95	0.37	0.00	3.48
Annual Growth	(10.6%)	— —	32.8%	—	8.9%

*Fiscal year change

SSM HEALTH CARE CORPORATION

The mission of SSM Health began with five nuns who fled religious persecution in Germany in 1872 only to arrive in St. Louis in the midst of a smallpox epidemic. They formed their first hospital there in 1877. Today the Midwest-based not-for-profit system sponsored by the Franciscan Sisters of Mary owns some 25 acute care hospitals with about 4500 licensed beds; it also has management or affiliation agreements with a number of other area hospitals. Additionally the company offers more than 300 outpatient facilities including physi-cians' practices home care and hospice services post-acute facilities and an insurance company.

Operations
In southern Wisconsin SSM Health facilities include St. Clare Hospital in Baraboo St. Mary's Janesville Hospital in Janesville and St. Mary's Hospital in Madison. Southern Illinois locations include St. Mary's Good Samaritan Hospital in Mount Vernon and St. Mary's Hospital in Centralia. The company owns and operates about 10 hospitals in Missouri; these include Cardinal Glennon Children's Hospital and DePaul Hospital. Oklahoma hospitals include St. Anthony Hospital in Oklahoma City and St. Anthony Shawnee Hospital in Shawnee.

SSM Health has some 9500 physicians on its staff. The system has some 176000 inpatient admissions and some 1.6 million outpatient visits each year.

The system participates in a Medicare Accountable Care Organization (ACO). It also has a pharmacy benefit arm.

Geographic Reach
SSM Health's facilities are located in Illinois Missouri Oklahoma and Wisconsin.

Sales and Marketing
Managed care payments account for about half of SSM Health's net patient revenue before provision for uncollectible accounts; Medicare accounts for about 30% and Medicaid accounts for about 15%.

The system spent $20666 on advertising on 2016 up from $17956 in 2015.

Financial Performance
SSM Health's operating revenue increased 12% to $6.1 billion due largely to a rise in net patient service revenues and an increase in other revenue. Premiums earned and investment income also rose that year.

However operating expenses increased across most areas and the system reported a decrease in excess of revenues over expenses which fell 52% to $99.4 million. Similarly operating cash flow fell 51% to $220.4 million in 2016. Factors contributing to that drop included an increase in pension-related changes and in provisions for uncollectible accounts and bad debts.

Strategy
SSM Health often partners with other care providers which helps it expand without having to invest in new facilities from the ground up.

Like most health systems SSM has been challenged with lower government reimbursement rates. It is implementing a financial improvement initiative which includes some company layoffs.

Mergers and Acquisitions
SSM Health has been making a number of acquisitions to expand its network. For example in 2016 it doubled its stake in St. Clare Surgical Center to 60% and acquired the rest of Physicians Surgery Center at DePaul it didn't already own. SSM also took over the operations of about 25 health clinics located in Walgreens stores in Greater St. Louis.

In early 2018 the system acquired Agnesian HealthCare and Monroe Clinic (both based in Wisconsin) adding four hospitals eight post-acute facilities and several outpatient facilities.

EXECUTIVES

Svp Strategic Development, William P. Thompson
Svp Finance, Kris A. Zimmer
President Hospital Operations, Chris Howard
Evp; President Health Care Delivery Finance And Integration, Gaurov Dayal
Svp Strategy Communications And Marketing, Paula J. Friedman
President Ssm St. Joseph Health Center, Mike Bowers
Evp; President Physician And Ambulatory Operations, Shane Peng
Chief Nursing Officer, Maggie Fowler
Svp And Cio, Phillip Loftus
President St. Marya's Hospital, Jon Rozenfeld
President Ssm Health At Home, Alison Ruehl
Auditors: DELOITTE & TOUCHE LLP STLOUI

LOCATIONS

HQ: SSM HEALTH CARE CORPORATION
10101 WOODFIELD LN # 100, SAINT LOUIS, MO 631322944
Phone: 314 994-7800
Web: WWW.SSMHC.COM

PRODUCTS/OPERATIONS

Selected Facilities
Illinois
St. Mary's Good Samaritan (joint sponsorship with Felician Services two hospitals in Mt. Vernon and Centralia)
Missouri
St. Francis Hospital & Health Services (Maryville)
St. Mary's Health Center (Jefferson City)
SSM Cardinal Glennon Children's Medical Center (St. Louis)
SSM DePaul Health Center (Bridgeton)
SSM St. Clare Health Center (St. Louis)
SSM St. Joseph Health Center (St. Charles)
SSM St. Joseph Health Center (Wentzville)
SSM St. Joseph Hospital West (Lake St. Louis)
SSM St. Mary's Health Center (Richmond Heights)
Oklahoma
Bone & Joint Hospital (Oklahoma City)
Shawnee Medical Center Clinic (Shawnee)
St. Anthony Hospital (Oklahoma City)
Unity Health Center (Shawnee)
Wisconsin
Boscobel Area Health Care (managed hospital and clinics Boscobel)
Columbus Community Hospital (affiliate Columbus)
Edgerton Hospital and Health Services (Edgerton)
St. Clare Hospital (Baraboo)
St. Clare Meadows Care Center (nursing home Madison)
St. Mary's Care Center (nursing home Madison)
St. Mary's Hospital (Madison)
St. Mary's Janesville Hospital (Janesville)
Stoughton Hospital (affiliate Stoughton)
Uplands Hill Health (affiliate hospital and nursing care Dodgeville)

COMPETITORS

Adventist Health System Sunbelt Healthcare
Advocate Health Care
Allina Hospitals
Ascension Health
BJC HealthCare
Carle Physician Group
Community Health Systems
HCA
Hospital Sisters Health System
Mayo Clinic
Mercy Health
Meriter Health Services
MetroSouth Medical
Rush System for Health
Tenet Healthcare
University of Wisconsin Hospital and Clinics
VITAS Healthcare

HISTORICAL FINANCIALS

Company Type: Private

Income Statement
FYE: December 31

	REVENUE ($ mil.)	NET INCOME ($ mil.)	NET PROFIT MARGIN	EMPLOYEES
12/17	6,497	245	3.8%	24,230
12/16	6,109	(30)	—	—
12/13	1,177	32	2.8%	—
Annual Growth	53.3%	65.9%	—	—

2017 Year-End Financials

Debt ratio: ——
Return on equity: 3.80%
Cash ($ mil.): 126
Current ratio: 0.30
Long-term debt ($ mil.): —

Dividends
Yield: —
Payout: —
Market value ($ mil.): —

Stanley Black & Decker Inc

Stanley Black & Decker has all the tools of the trade. A leading global toolmaker the company generates more than two-thirds of sales from a plethora of tools (hand mechanics' power pneumatic hydraulic) and related accessories. In addition to its well-known namesake brands it sells other top brands such as Bostitch Mac Tools and DEWALT directly to consumers as well as through distributors home centers and mass-merchant distributors. Stanley Black & Decker also sells engineered fastening and infrastructure products to customers in the automotive manufacturing and oil & gas industries among others and designs and installs electronic security systems and automatic doors to commercial customers. It generates nearly half of sales outside the US.

Operations

Stanley Black & Decker operates its business through three segments: Tools & Storage (which generates about 70% of sales) Security (about 15%) and Industrial (about 15%).

The Tools & Storage segment includes professional and consumer power tools (saws drills grinders nail guns lawn mowers vacuums and cleaning tools) and accessories hand tools and storage products such as tool boxes and sawhorses. The products are mostly available via home centers hardware stores mass merchants and other retailers.

The company's Security segment includes Convergent Security Solutions which designs and installs electronic security systems and provides monitoring surveillance and other services and Mechanical Access Solutions which sells automatic doors. These products are primarily sold directly to commercial customers.

Stanley Black & Decker sells rivets inserts weld studs and other fastening products through its Industrial segment. The segment also includes infrastructure equipment used by the oil & gas industry and hydraulics tools and accessories.

Geographic Reach

Stanley Black & Decker operates primarily in the Americas Europe and Asia. The US is its largest market accounting for about 55% of sales. Europe led by France generates about a quarter of sales and Asia brings in about 10%.

Headquartered in New Britain Connecticut the company has major facilities for manufacturing distribution and sales in some 20 countries including locations in about 20 US states.

Sales and Marketing

The Tools & Storage segment sells its products to professional end users industrial users distributors and retail consumers. The majority of sales are distributed through retailers including home centers mass merchants hardware stores and retail lumber yards. US and international mass merchants and home centers collectively account for nearly 30% of sales; home improvement giant Lowe's accounts for just more than 10%.

Stanley Black & Decker markets it other products and services directly and through third-party distributors to customers in a host of industries including automotive manufacturing oil & gas electronics and aerospace.

Advertising cost was $123.3 million in 2017 compared to $124.1 million in 2016 and $101.7 million in 2015.

Financial Performance

Stanley Black & Decker has seen solid revenue and strong net income growth over the past five years as the company has pursued acquisitions and manufacturing and supply chain efficiencies. Revenue is up nearly 20% since 2013 and net income is up about 250%.

In 2017 the company reported revenue of $12.7 billion up 12% from the prior year. The results were driven almost entirely by the Tools & Storage segment fueled in equal parts by organic growth (innovative new products and a strong overall tool market) and acquisitions (mostly Newell).

Net income that year jumped more than 25% to $1.2 billion on the increased revenue and a gain on the sale of the company's mechanical security business.

Cash at the end of fiscal 2017 was $637 million a decrease of $494 million from the prior year. Cash from operations contributed $1.4 billion to the coffers while investing activities used $2.3 billion mainly for acquisitions. Financing activities added some $295 million because of proceeds from the issuance of preferred stock.

Strategy

Stanley Black & Decker's overarching strategy which it calls 22/22 Vision is the build to $22 billion in revenue by the year 2022. As part of that strategy the company is focused on industry geographic and customer diversification through both innovative organic growth and acquisitions.

Operational excellence and product innovation is enabled by its Stanley Fulfillment System (SFS 2.0) which resulted in the mid-2016 launch of the FlexVolt variable-voltage battery system that has helped power organic growth in the years since. Stanley Black & Decker continues to show its commitment to product innovation with increased research and developments costs (up 25% in 2017) and innovation center openings in Germany (Stanley Engineered Fastening Breakthrough Innovation Center) and the US (Futures Innovation Factory). An advanced manufacturing center which will test new technologies such as 3-D metal printing is opening in Connecticut in the second half of 2018. SFS 2.0 also enables cost-cutting with a focus on sales and operations planning (S&OP) operational lean complexity reduction global supply management and order-to-cash excellence.

Merger and acquisition activity has played a huge role in Stanley Black & Decker's buildup over the past decade-plus and will continue to be important in getting the company to $22 billion in revenue. It started its acquisition spree in 2002 and has made some $9 billion in purchases since then adding new products to its portfolio and expanding its market and geographic reach. Along the way the company has divested non-core and/or low-margin businesses including its early 2017 disposal of the mechanical security business

(which included commercial hardware brands Best Access phi Precision and GMT).

Mergers and Acquisitions

In late 2018 Stanley Black & Decker announced that it would acquire 20% of outdoor power equipment maker MTD Products for $234 million. The deal wihch includes the option of purchasing the rest of MTD beginning in July 2021 strengthens the company's presence in the growing lawn and garden market.

Earlier that year the company closed on the $440 million purchase of Nelson Fastener Systems from the Doncasters Group in the UK. The deal brings a host of complementary products and expands the company's presence in general industrial end markets. Also that year it announced plans to buy International Equipment Solutions Attachments Group (IES Attachments) for $690 million. IES Attachments makes performance-driven heavy equipment attachment tools for off-highway applications under such names as Paladin Genesis and Pengo; the deal expands Stanley Black & Decker's presence in industrial markets.

The prior year Stanley Black & Decker acquired Sears Holdings Corp.'s iconic Craftsman tool brand for $900 million. The acquisition expands Black & Decker's product line up and allows the company to increase sales by expanding distribution of Craftsman tools into more international markets. Also in 2017 Stanley Black & Decker bought the tools business (Irwin Lenox) from consumer products company Newell Brands for $1.95 billion.

Company Background

Stanley Black & Decker traces its roots back to 1843 when Frederick Stanley opened a bolt shop in a converted early-19th-century armory in New Britain Connecticut. In 1852 he teamed with his brother and five friends to form The Stanley Works to cast form and manufacture various types of metal. In 2010 it merged with The Black & Decker Corporation a company founded by S. Duncan Black and Alonzo G. Decker and incorporated in Maryland in 1910 and changed its name to Stanley Black & Decker.

EXECUTIVES

President And Ceo, James M. (Jim) Loree, age 59, $992,500 total compensation

Vp And Cio, Rhonda O. Gass, age 54

Svp And Group Executive Global Tools And Storage, Jeffery D. (Jeff) Ansell, age 51, $660,833 total compensation

Svp And Cfo, Donald (Don) Allan, age 53, $671,667 total compensation

President Latin America, Jaime A. Ramirez, age 50, $425,000 total compensation

President Sales And Marketing Global Tools And Storage, John H. A. Wyatt, age 59, $541,667 total compensation

President Hand Tools Accessories And Storage, Lee B. McChesney, age 46

Cto, Mark T Maybury

President Stanley Security Europe, Aru Bala

President Stanley Oil And Gas, Pete Morris

President Asia, Yingli (Christine) Yan

President Power Tools And Equipment Global Tools And Storage, Frank A. Mannarino

President Emerging Markets Group, Bart Muller

President Sales And Marketing Global Tools And Storage, James P. OÂ'Sullivan

President Hydraulics, J. Douglas Redpath

Vice President, Debi Geyer

Vice President Manufatura Latin America, Domingos Dragone

Vice President And Chief Accounting Officer, Jocelyn Belisle

National Account Manager, Joe Schuyler

Senior Vice President, Don Allan

Vp Environment Health Safety And Corporate
  Social Responsibility, Deb Geyer
Vice President Of North American Sales, Martin
  Guay
Vp Corporate Tax And Treasurer, Michael Bartone
Vp Public Affairs, Tim Perra
National Account Manager, Daniel Wegrzyn
National Account Manager, David Kay
Vice President And General Manager, Jim Gillis
National Sales Manager, Dan Miller
National Account Manager, Kelly Bhavsar
National Sales Manager, Jevri Christanto
Vice President Of Engineering, Stumpf Bill
National Account Manager, Brian Rooke
National Account Manager, Joshua Herting
National Account Manager, Dean Wickwar
Vice President Of Human Resources, Rodney
  Hobbs
National Account Manager, Phil Harman
National Account Manager, Jason Viergutz
National Sales Manager, Adams Andrew
National Account Manager, Godwin Scott
Chairman, George W. Buckley, age 71
Auditors: Ernst & Young LLP

LOCATIONS

HQ: Stanley Black & Decker Inc
  1000 Stanley Drive, New Britain, CT 06053
Phone: 860 225-5111   Fax: 860 827-3895
Web: www.stanleyblackanddecker.com

2017 Sales

	$ mil.	% of total
Americas		
US	6,915	54
Canada	577	5
Other	774	6
Europe		
France	609	5
Other	2,742	21
Asia	1,128	9
Total	**12,747**	**100**

PRODUCTS/OPERATIONS

2017 Sales

	$ mil.	% of total
Tools & Storage	8,862	70
Security	1,938	15
Industrial	1,946	15
Total	**12,747**	**100**

Product and Services

Commercial Security
Fastening Solutions
Hospital & Healthcare Services
Infrastructure Products
Pipeline Services
Tools & Storage

Selected Brand Names

Black & Decker
Bostitch
Craftsman
DEWALT
FatMax
LaBounty
Mac Tools
Proto
Stanley
Vidmar

COMPETITORS

ASSA ABLOY	Klein Tools
Atlas Copco	Makita
Fortune Brands Home &	Robert Bosch Tool
Security	Snap-on
Husqvarna	Techtronic
Illinois Tool Works	

HISTORICAL FINANCIALS

Company Type: Public

Income Statement

FYE: December 30

	REVENUE ($ mil.)	NET INCOME ($ mil.)	NET PROFIT MARGIN	EMPLOYEES
12/17	12,747	1,226	9.6%	57,765
12/16*	11,406	965	8.5%	54,023
01/16	11,171	883	7.9%	51,250
01/15	11,338	760	6.7%	50,400
12/13	11,001	490	4.5%	50,700
Annual Growth	3.8%	25.7%	—	3.3%

*Fiscal year change

2017 Year-End Financials

Debt ratio: 20.08%   No. of shares (mil.): 154
Return on equity: 16.77%   Dividends
Cash ($ mil.): 637   Yield: 0.0%
Current ratio: 1.05   Payout: 30.1%
Long-term debt ($ mil.): 2,843 Market value ($ mil.): 26,139

	STOCK PRICE ($) FY Close	P/E High/Low		PER SHARE ($) Earnings	Dividends	Book Value
12/17	169.69	21	14	8.04	2.42	53.86
12/16*	114.69	19	14	6.51	2.26	41.73
01/16	106.73	18	15	5.79	2.14	37.75
01/15	96.02	20	16	4.76	2.04	40.92
12/13	81.01	29	23	3.09	1.98	43.73
Annual Growth	20.3%	—	—	27.0%	5.1%	5.3%

*Fiscal year change

Starbucks Corp.

Wake up and smell the coffee — Starbucks is everywhere. The world's #1 specialty coffee retailer Starbucks has more than 29300 coffee shops in 80 countries. The shops offer coffee drinks and food items as well as roasted beans coffee accessories and teas. Starbucks operates more than 15300 of its own shops which are located mostly in the US while licensees and franchisees operate roughly 14000 units worldwide (including many locations in shopping centers and airports). In addition Starbucks markets its coffee through grocery stores food service customers and licenses its brand for other food and beverage products. The US accounts for the majority of Starbucks' revenue.

HISTORY

Starbucks was founded in 1971 in Seattle by coffee aficionados Gordon Bowker Jerry Baldwin and Ziv Siegl who named the company for the coffee-loving first mate in Moby Dick and created its famous two-tailed siren logo. They aimed to sell the finest-quality whole bean and ground coffees. By 1982 Starbucks had five retail stores and was selling coffee to restaurants and espresso stands in Seattle. That year Howard Schultz joined Starbucks to manage retail sales and marketing. In 1983 Schultz traveled to Italy and was struck by the popularity of coffee bars. He convinced Starbucks' owners to open a downtown Seattle coffee bar in 1984. It was a success; Schultz left the company the following year to open his own coffee bar Il Giornale which served Starbucks coffee.

Frustrated by its inability to control quality Starbucks sold off its wholesale business in 1987. Later that year Il Giornale acquired Starbucks' retail operations for $4 million. (Starbucks' founders held

on to their other coffee business Peet's Coffee & Tea.) Il Giornale changed its name to Starbucks Corporation prepared to expand nationally and opened locations in Chicago and Vancouver. In 1988 the company published its first mail-order catalog.

Starbucks lost money in the late 1980s as it focused on expansion (it tripled its number of stores to 55 between 1987 and 1989). Schultz brought in experienced managers to run Starbucks' stores. In 1991 it became the nation's first privately owned company to offer stock options to all employees.

In 1992 Starbucks went public and set up shops in Nordstrom's department stores. The following year it began operating cafes in Barnes & Noble bookstores. The company had nearly 275 locations by the end of 1993. Starbucks inked a deal in 1994 to provide coffee to ITT/Sheraton hotels (later acquired by Starwood Hotels & Resorts). The next year it capitalized on its popular in-house music selections by selling compact discs. Also in 1995 Starbucks joined with PepsiCo to develop a bottled coffee drink and agreed to produce a line of premium coffee ice cream with Dreyer's.

Starbucks expanded into Japan and Singapore in 1996. Also that year the company created Caffe Starbucks an online store located on AOL's marketplace. In 1997 Starbucks began testing sales of whole-bean and ground coffees in Chicago supermarkets.

In 1998 Starbucks expanded into the UK when it acquired that country's Seattle Coffee Company chain (founded in 1995) for about $86 million and converted its stores into Starbucks locations. It also announced plans to sell coffee in supermarkets nationwide through an agreement with Kraft Foods. In 1999 Starbucks bought Tazo an Oregon-based tea company as well as music retailer Hear Music and opened its first store in China. Schultz toned down his Internet plans in late 1999 after investors and analysts voiced skepticism.

In 2000 Schultz ceded the CEO post to president Orin Smith remaining chairman but focusing primarily on the company's global strategy. Starbucks jumpstarted its worldwide expansion the next year opening about 1100 stores worldwide including locations in a handful of new European countries such as Austria and Switzerland. It also spun off its Japanese operations as a public company. The following year the company opened its first shop in Spain and went on to open Starbucks locations in Greece and Germany. Later in 2002 it announced large-scale expansion plans in Mexico and Latin America.

The next year Starbucks acquired Seattle Coffee Company (and its Seattle's Best Cof

EXECUTIVES

Evp And Cto, Gerri Martin-Flickinger
President And Coo, Kevin R. Johnson, age 57,
  $576,923 total compensation
Group President Us And Americas, Clifford (Cliff)
  Burrows, age 59, $796,300 total compensation
Vp And General Manager Starbucks Coffee
  Foodservice, John Culver, age 57, $633,300 total
  compensation
Svp And President Europe Middle East And Africa
  (emea), Martin Brok
Evp Us Retail Store Operations, Cosimo LaPorta
Evp And Global Chief Marketing Officer, Sharon
  Rothstein
Svp; President Teavana, Bernard Acoca
Chief Creative Officer; President Global
  Innovation, Arthur Rubinfeld, age 64, $484,058 total
  compensation
Evp Licensed Stores Us And Americas, Chris Carr
Evp Law And Corporate Affairs General Counsel
  And Secretary, Lucy Lee Helm, $493,172 total
  compensation

Evp Public Affairs, Vivek Varma
Evp And Chief Partner Resources Officer, Scott Pitasky
Evp And Cfo, Scott H. Maw, $632,500 total compensation
Svp Store Services, Craig Russell
Svp; President Starbucks Canada, Rossann Williams
President Starbucks Global Channel Development, Michael Conway
Evp And Chief Digital Officer, Adam Brotman
Evp And Global Chief Strategy Officer, Matthew Ryan
Global Evp, Kris Engskov
President Starbucks China, Belinda Wong
Senior Vice President Deputy General Counsel Chief Ethics And Compliance Officer, Matthew Swaya
Vice President, Julie Eisen
Vice President Global Sourcing And Supplier Relations, Jonathan Gardner
Regional Vice President, Denise Nelsen
Senior Vice President Customer Relationship Management, Aimee Johnson
Senior Vice President Partner Resources Global Retail, Angela Lis
Vice President Manager Director, Lesley Blyth
Vice President, William Mcnichols
Senior Vice President Gbl Design And Construction Execution, Bill Transue
Executive Vice President Global Supply Chain, D Deverl Maserang
Vice President Corporate Facilities, Eric Jensen
Vice President Zone Licensed Stores East, Lisa Compton
Senior Vice President Finance, David Chichester
Senior Vice President Siren Retail Operations, Katie Seawell
Vice President Marketing Category Emea, Cathy Heseltine
Regional Vice President, Suzanne Dechant
Vice President Global Learning, Stephen Krempl
Senior Vice President Southeast Plains, Paul Twohig
Vice President And Controller, Jill Walker
Vice President Analytics And Business Intelligence, Mike Manzano
Senior Vice President Partner Resources U.s. And Americas, Marissa Andrada
National Account Manager, Todd Faubus
Svp Global Strategy Insights And Analytics, Pam Greer
Vice President Of Sales Operations And Learning And Development Teavana, Catherine McCabe
Senior Vice President Public Affairs, Rajiv Chandrasekaran
Vice President Retail Technology, Courtney Kissler
Senior Vice President Infrastructure And Enablement, Jeff Wile
Senior Vice President Partner Resources And Human Resources, Lucy Hur
Executive Vice President Global Supply Chain, Hans Melotte
Senior Vice President Global Integrated Logistics, Ash Walia
Divisional Senior Vice President East Division, Zeta Smith
Senior Vice President Engineering And Architecture Starbucks Technololgy, Tal Saraf
Senior Vice President Entrepreneur In Residence, Richard Tait
Senior Vice President Global Coffee And Tea, Michelle Burns
Vice President Global Shared Services, James Alessandrini
Vice President Finance, Robert Dilworth
Vp Global Engineering, Jeff Juneau
Senior Vice President Logistics And Us Retail Supply Chain, Carl Mount
Senior Vice President Sirenideas, Mesh Gelman
Vp Partnerships, Maria Smith

Vice President Information Technology, Tammy Green
Vice President Information Technology, Georg Gorostiza
Co Managing Director At Starbucks, Matthew Courtney
Vice President Store Development Support Services, Ray Silverstein
Senior Vice President Global Supply Chain Finance And Shared Services, Sona M Kwawu
Vice President Food Safety And Quality, Stephen P Graham
Vice President, Chuck Little
Chairman And Ceo, Howard D. Schultz, age 65
Board Member, Patrick K Coe
Board Member, Javier Teruel
Treasurer, Donald Spiegelman
Board Member, Mary Dillon
Auditors: DELOITTE & TOUCHE LLP

LOCATIONS

HQ: Starbucks Corp.
  2401 Utah Avenue South, Seattle, WA 98134
Phone: 206 447-1575
Web: www.starbucks.com

2018 Sales

	% of total
Americas	68
China/Asia Pacific	18
EMEA	4
Channel Development	9
Corporate and Other	1
Total	**100**

PRODUCTS/OPERATIONS

2018 Sales

	$ mil.	% of total
Company-owned stores	19,690	80
Licensed stores	2,652	11
Other	2,377	9
Total	**24,719**	**100**

2018 Sales

	% of total
Beverage	59
Food	18
Package and single-serve coffees and teas	11
Other	12
Total	**100**

Brand Portfolio

Brand Portfolio
Starbucks Coffee
Seattle's Best Coffee
Teavana
Evolution Fresh
La Boulange
Ethos Water
Torrefazione Italia Coffee

Selected Products

Coffee
Handcrafted Beverages
Merchandise
Fresh Food

COMPETITORS

Cinnabon	McDonald's
Community Coffee	Nestlé
Dunkin	Panera Bread
Einstein Noah Restaurant Group	The Coffee Bean
	Tim Hortons
Farmer Bros.	Whitbread
Keurig Green Mountain	illy

HISTORICAL FINANCIALS

Company Type: Public

Income Statement
FYE: September 30

	REVENUE ($ mil.)	NET INCOME ($ mil.)	NET PROFIT MARGIN	EMPLOYEES
09/18*	24,719	4,518	18.3%	291,000
10/17	22,386	2,884	12.9%	277,000
10/16	21,316	2,817	13.2%	254,000
09/15	19,162	2,757	14.4%	238,000
09/14	16,447	2,068	12.6%	191,000
Annual Growth	**10.7%**	**21.6%**	**—**	**11.1%**

*Fiscal year change

2018 Year-End Financials

Debt ratio: 39.08%	No. of shares (mil.): 1,309
Return on equity: 136.89%	Dividends
Cash ($ mil.): 8,756	Yield: 0.0%
Current ratio: 2.20	Payout: 38.8%
Long-term debt ($ mil.): 9,090	Market value ($ mil.): 74,409

	STOCK PRICE ($) FY Close	P/E High/Low		PER SHARE ($) Earnings	Dividends	Book Value
09/18*	56.84	19	15	3.24	1.26	0.89
10/17	53.71	32	26	1.97	1.00	3.81
10/16	54.14	33	28	1.90	0.80	4.03
09/15	57.99	53	26	1.82	0.64	3.92
09/14	75.17	60	50	1.36	0.52	3.52
Annual Growth	**(6.7%)**	**—**	**—**	**24.4%**	**24.8%**	**(29.0%)**

*Fiscal year change

State Auto Financial Corp.

Thanks to State Auto Financial the state of auto insurance is healthy in the Midwest. The company sells property/casualty policies through several subsidiaries writing personal commercial and specialty coverage including automobile homeowners multi-peril and workers' compensation insurance. It also participates in an insurance pool through its parent company State Auto Mutual Insurance which owns more than 60% of State Auto Financial and provides the offices for its headquarters. Subsidiary Stateco Financial Services manages the company's invested assets. State Auto Financial is the only part of State Auto Mutual that is publicly traded.

Operations

State Auto Financial has four reportable segments: personal insurance commercial insurance specialty insurance and investment operations.

The personal insurance segment provides primarily personal automobile and homeowners to the personal insurance market. It brings in some 40% of State Auto's total revenue.

The commercial insurance segment provides commercial automobile commercial multi-peril property data compromise and risk control insurance covering small-to-medium sized commercial exposures in the business insurance market. That segment accounts for about a third of total revenue.

The specialty insurance segment provides commercial coverage — including workers' compensation — requiring specialized product underwriting claims handling or risk management services. It brings in more than 15% of total revenue. State

Auto exited the specialty insurance business in 2018 so that segment will be eliminated in future reporting periods.

The investment operations segment managed by subsidiary Stateco provides investment services. It represents some 10% of total revenue.

Geographic Reach

State Auto Financial operates in about 35 states. Ohio Kentucky and Texas are its biggest markets accounting for almost 25% of its annual premiums.

Sales and Marketing

Through the mutual pool State Auto Financial and its sister companies known collectively as State Auto Group market products through retail agents and wholesale brokers. It works with some 2800 retail agencies. The company focuses its business insurance sales on small-to-medium-sized companies.

Financial Performance

State Auto Financial's revenue has been growing steadily over the past five years but net income has been falling since 2014 due to its high expense ratio. The company lost money in 2017.

Revenue increased 1% to $1.4 billion in 2017 thanks to increases in net written premiums for personal auto and homeowners insurance and (to a lesser extent) commercial insurance. That was partially offset by a decline in the discontinued specialty segment.

The company had a $10.7 million net loss that year after netting $21 million in 2016. This was largely due to a $44.1 federal income tax expense related to a change in tax laws.

State Auto ended 2017 with $91.5 million in net cash some $40 million more than it had at the end of 2016. Operating activities provided $67.9 million while investing activities and financing activities used $20.5 million and $7 million respectively.

Strategy

While its revenues have grown steadily with personal and standard commercial products State Auto Financial has struggled with underwriting and pricing issues that have impacted its results. To counter those issues the company has been focused on improving its rates (which has resulted in a drop in retention) and securing new business. It offers discounts to auto customers who sign up for telematics driving habit tracking and to homeowners customers who use smart home technologies. Additionally it has been rolling out its State Auto Connect digital platform for new personal policies and new commercial auto policies. With these initiatives the company saw its first increase in homeowners policies-in-force in eight years in 2017.

To hone its focus on its core personal and commercial insurance offerings the company has shut down its specialty insurance units: It exited the programs business in 2016 and in 2017 it exited the excess and surplus property and excess and surplus casualty businesses. Other recent exits include the large commercial health care and trucking businesses.

EXECUTIVES

Vp And Comptroller, Cynthia A. Powell, age 57
President And Ceo, Michael E. (Mike) LaRocco, age 61
Svp And Cfo, Steven E. English, age 57, $447,231 total compensation
Svp And Director Operations, Lyle D. Rhodebeck, age 60
Svp Secretary And General Counsel, James A. (Jay) Yano, age 67, $357,692 total compensation
Svp Standard Lines, Joel E. Brown, age 60

Svp And Director Specialty Lines, Jessica E. Buss, age 46, $372,692 total compensation
Svp And Chief Claims Officer, Stephen P. Hunckler, age 59
Vice President Public Relations, Terrence Bowshier
Vice President Cao Treas, Matthew Pollak
Vice President Chief Risk Officer, Bill Cody Bill Cody
Senior Vice President Standard Lines And Director Of Senior Associate Labs, Kim Garland
Vice President Specialty Claims, Jay Carleton
Assistant Vice President Product Mangement, Rudy Palenik
Assistant Vice President Actuarial Department, Alp Can
Vice President Sales And Business Development, Jack Abney
Assistant Vice President Risk Engineering, Tom Mullaney
Vice President Specialty Programs, Greg Scullans
Assistant Vice President Reinsurance, Cpcu Olmstead
Chairman, Robert P. (Bob) Restrepo, age 67
Auditors: Ernst & Young LLP

LOCATIONS

HQ: State Auto Financial Corp.
518 East Broad Street, Columbus, OH 43215-3976
Phone: 614 464-5000
Web: www.stateauto.com

2017 Direct Written Premiums

	% of total
Ohio	9
Texas	9
Kentucky	6
California	5
Minnesota	4
Tennessee	4
Georgia	4
Indiana	4
Mississippi	4
South Carolina	4
Illinois	3
Maryland	3
Pennsylvania	3
North Carolina	3
Other	36
Total	**100**

PRODUCTS/OPERATIONS

2017 Sales

	$ mil.	% of total
Personal insurance premiums	580	41
Commercial insurance premiums	455	32
Specialty insurance premiums	239	17
Investment income & other	146	10
Total	**1,421**	**100**

COMPETITORS

AIG	National General
Allstate	Holdings
American Family	Nationwide
Insurance	Progressive
American Southern	Corporation
GEICO	State Farm
Kentucky Employers'	The Hartford
Mutual	Travelers Companies

HISTORICAL FINANCIALS

Company Type: Public

Income Statement — FYE: December 31

	ASSETS ($ mil.)	NET INCOME ($ mil.)	INCOME AS % OF ASSETS	EMPLOYEES
12/17	3,014	(10)	—	1,962
12/16	2,959	21	0.7%	2,020
12/15	2,828	51	1.8%	2,065
12/14	2,766	107	3.9%	2,274
12/13	2,496	60	2.4%	2,384
Annual Growth	**4.8%**	**—**		**(4.8%)**

2017 Year-End Financials

Debt ratio: 4.05%	No. of shares (mil.): 42
Return on equity: (-1.21%)	Dividends
Cash ($ mil.): 91	Yield: 0.0%
Current ratio: —	Payout: —
Long-term debt ($ mil.): —	Market value ($ mil.): 1,235

	STOCK PRICE ($) FY Close	P/E High/Low		PER SHARE ($) Earnings	Dividends	Book Value
12/17	29.12	—	—	(0.25)	0.40	20.78
12/16	26.81	54	37	0.50	0.40	21.32
12/15	20.59	22	16	1.23	0.40	21.42
12/14	22.22	9	7	2.60	0.40	21.34
12/13	21.24	15	9	1.49	0.40	19.29
Annual Growth	**8.2%**	**—**	**—**	**—**	**(0.0%)**	**1.9%**

STATE OF CALIFORNIA

EXECUTIVES

Governor, Gavin Newsom
Consultant, A Kirk McKenzie
Chief Licensing/Information Te, Brian Desmarais
Chief Information Security Off, Carol Kelly
Budgets and Fiscal STA, Caroline McNeil
Computer Support Staff Represe, Cheryl Drefs
Budgets and Fiscal STA, Diane Herteg
Chief Technology Support Servi, Jim Rengstorff
AG Technician II, Jose Antonio Diaz
Analyst, Karen Bianchi Walsh
California Attorney General, Xavier Becerra
Auditors: JOHN F COLLINS II CPA DEPUTY

LOCATIONS

HQ: STATE OF CALIFORNIA
STATE CAPITAL, SACRAMENTO, CA 95814
Phone: 916 445-2864
Web: WWW.CA.GOV

HISTORICAL FINANCIALS

Company Type: Private

Income Statement — FYE: June 30

	REVENUE ($ mil.)	NET INCOME ($ mil.)	NET PROFIT MARGIN	EMPLOYEES
06/16	255,725	4,798	1.9%	208,580
06/15	249,923	6,252	2.5%	—
06/14	219,871	8,082	3.7%	—
06/13	204	8	3.9%	—
Annual Growth	**976.7%**	**742.3%**	**—**	**—**

STATE OF NEW YORK MORTGAGE AGENCY

EXECUTIVES

Vice President, Daniel Murphy
Assistant Vice President, Robert Rosado
Vice President Special Projects, Mark Flescher
Vice President Internal Audit, Stephen Chopey
Senior Vice President, Michael Friedman
Senior Vice President Policy Initiatives, Arlo Chase
Vice President, Michael Esposito
Vice President Government Relations, Joseph Palozzola
Auditors: DELOITTE & TOUCHE LLP NEW YOR

LOCATIONS

HQ: STATE OF NEW YORK MORTGAGE AGENCY
641 LEXINGTON AVE FL 4, NEW YORK, NY 100224503
Phone: 212 688-4000
Web: WWW.NYHOMES.ORG

HISTORICAL FINANCIALS
Company Type: Private

Income Statement				FYE: October 31
	ASSETS ($ mil.)	NET INCOME ($ mil.)	INCOME AS % OF ASSETS	EMPLOYEES
10/17	5,228	34	0.7%	221
10/16	5,187	63	1.2%	—
10/09	5,225	162	3.1%	—
10/08	5,224	30	0.6%	—
Annual Growth	0.0%	1.3%	—	—

2017 Year-End Financials

Debt ratio: ——
Return on equity: 22.30%
Cash ($ mil.): 6
Current ratio: —
Long-term debt ($ mil.): —
Dividends
Yield: —
Payout: —
Market value ($ mil.): —

STATE OF OKLAHOMA

EXECUTIVES

Governor, Kevin Stitt
Lt Gov*, Todd Lamb
General Counsel-Sec*, James Williamson
Vice-President, Patrick Brown
Staff, Chris Turner
Auditors: GARY A JONES CPA CFE OKLAH

LOCATIONS

HQ: STATE OF OKLAHOMA
421 NW 13TH ST STE 220, OKLAHOMA CITY, OK 731033784
Phone: 405 521-2342
Web: WWW.OK.GOV

HISTORICAL FINANCIALS
Company Type: Private

Income Statement				FYE: June 30
	REVENUE ($ mil.)	NET INCOME ($ mil.)	NET PROFIT MARGIN	EMPLOYEES
06/17	17,175	48	0.3%	37,613
06/16	16,789	(1,025)	—	—
06/15	17,001	014	1.0%	—
06/14	17,465	303	1.7%	—
Annual Growth	(0.6%)	(45.9%)	—	—

2017 Year-End Financials

Debt ratio: ——
Return on equity: 0.30%
Cash ($ mil.): 6,099
Current ratio: 1.80
Long-term debt ($ mil.): —
Dividends
Yield: —
Payout: —
Market value ($ mil.): —

STATE OF RHODE ISLAND AND PROVIDENCE PLANTATIONS

EXECUTIVES

Governor, Gina M Raimondo
Lt Gov*, Daniel J McKee
State Controller, Lawrence C Franklin Jr
Policy Director, Kelly Mahoney
Auditors: DENNIS E HOYLE CPA-OFFICE OF

LOCATIONS

HQ: STATE OF RHODE ISLAND AND PROVIDENCE PLANTATIONS
82 SMITH ST STE 102, PROVIDENCE, RI 029031121
Phone: 401 222-2080
Web: WWW.GOPROVIDENCE.COM

HISTORICAL FINANCIALS
Company Type: Private

Income Statement				FYE: June 30
	REVENUE ($ mil.)	NET INCOME ($ mil.)	NET PROFIT MARGIN	EMPLOYEES
06/17	7,012	215	3.1%	13,535
06/16	6,860	(10)	—	—
06/15	6,787	160	2.4%	—
06/14	6,282	(46)	—	—
Annual Growth	3.7%	—	—	—

2017 Year-End Financials

Debt ratio: ——
Return on equity: 3.10%
Cash ($ mil.): 1,215
Current ratio: 1.10
Long-term debt ($ mil.): —
Dividends
Yield: —
Payout: —
Market value ($ mil.): —

STATE OF TEXAS

EXECUTIVES

Governor, Greg Abbott
Chief of Staff*, Luis Saenz
Deputy Chief of Staff*, David Whitley
Chief Operating Officer*, Reed Clay
Deputy Chief of Staff*, Jordan Hale
Director, Nichole Vance
Senior Adviser For State Opera, Steven Albright
Texas District Attorney, Andria Bender
Offc Manager, Connie Lucas
Executive Assistant, Daniel Womack
Executive Assistant, Debbie Maldonado
Auditors: JOHN KENT CPA AUSTIN TEXAS

LOCATIONS

HQ: STATE OF TEXAS
CAPI BLDG 1100 N CONG AVE, AUSTIN, TX 78701
Phone: 512 463-2000

HISTORICAL FINANCIALS
Company Type: Private

Income Statement				FYE: August 31
	REVENUE ($ mil.)	NET INCOME ($ mil.)	NET PROFIT MARGIN	EMPLOYEES
08/17	115,336	1,882	1.6%	144,175
08/15	107,350	1,993	1.9%	—
08/14	109,860	8,184	7.4%	—
08/13	0	0	—	—
Annual Growth	—	—	—	—

2017 Year-End Financials

Debt ratio: ——
Return on equity: 1.60%
Cash ($ mil.): 29,217
Current ratio: 1.10
Long-term debt ($ mil.): —
Dividends
Yield: —
Payout: —
Market value ($ mil.): —

State Street Corp.

Ol' Blue Eyes sang about the State Street in Chicago but investors may find Boston's State Street more melodious. Through its flagship State Street Bank and other subsidiaries the bank holding company provides investment management and servicing trading and research services. Its activities include trust and custody fund accounting foreign exchange shareholder services and other administrative services for institutional clients such as mutual and other investment funds pension plans insurance companies foundations endowments and investment managers. Founded in 1792 State Street has more than $28 trillion of assets under custody and administration in addition to more than $2 trillion in assets under management.

HISTORY

The US's chaotic post-revolutionary era gave birth to the first ancestor of State Street Corporation. Union Bank was founded in 1792 by Boston businessmen breaking the eight-year monopoly held on Boston banking by Massachusetts Bank (a forerunner of FleetBoston which was acquired by Bank of America in 2004). Governor John Hancock's distinctive signature graced Union's charter;

the bank set up shop at 40 State Street near the port and enjoyed the glory days of New England's shipping trade.

In the mid-19th century Boston's financial eminence faded as New York flexed its economic muscle. In 1865 the bank was nationally chartered and changed its name to National Union Bank of Boston. It got a new neighbor in 1891: Directors of Third National Bank set up State Street Deposit & Trust to engage in the newfangled business of trusts.

In 1925 National Union Bank merged with State Street and inherited its custodial business. The bank grew through the 1950s; acquisitions included the Second National Bank and the Rockland-Atlas National Bank.

In 1970 State Street converted to a holding company — the State Street Boston Financial Corp. (State Street Boston Corp. as of 1977). The company also went international that decade opening an office in Munich Germany.

Soaring inflation and the recession of the 1970s forced the company to radically rethink its mission. The 1974 passage of the Employee Retirement Income Security Act changed the laws governing the management of pension funds and created an opportunity. State Street was one of the first banks to move aggressively into high-tech information processing and affiliate Boston Financial Data Services began servicing pension assets in 1974.

Encouraged by that success in 1975 new CEO William Edgerly (who served until 1992) steered State Street away from branch banking and into investments trusts and securities processing. An early achievement was designing PepsiCo's retirement plan. Fee-based sales approached 50% of revenues; the company could now quit focusing on lending. In the 1980s and 1990s the company built its administration and investment management businesses overseas and moved into software.

Evolving in the late 1990s State Street left noncore businesses but expanded globally. In 1997 it formed European Direct Capital Management to invest in eastern and central Europe. State Street Global Advisors opened a London office in 1998 to serve wealthy individuals outside the US.

The company sold its commercial banking business to Royal Bank of Scotland in 1999 signaling an exit from that business and narrowing State Street's scope to the asset and investment management businesses. The company also bought Wachovia's custody and institutional trust business and teamed with Citigroup to sell 401(k) retirement products.

In 2000 State Street created FX Connect an electronic foreign exchange trading system. Also that year David Spina took over as CEO from the retiring Marshall Carter.

The firm bought Bel Air Investment Advisors and its broker/dealer affiliate Bel Air Securities in 2001 to cater to the ultrawealthy. In 2003 State Street sold its corporate trust business to U.S. Bancorp and its private asset management business to Charles Schwab's U.S. Trust. Spina retired in 2004; his protA©gA© Ron Logue stepped in as chairman and CEO.

In 2007 State Street added bulk by acquiring another Boston-based fund accounting and servicing provider Investors Financial Services. The company boosted its foreign exchange offerings with the acquisition of Currenex. The following year State Street and Citigroup sold their CitiStreet retirement and pension plan management joint venture to ING Groep for some $900 million.

The US Treasury invested some $2 billion in the company in 2008 as part of a broader bailout plan to restore confidence and increase liquidity. State Street was among eight other top banks that received a combined $250 billion; the company repaid the full amount within months.

In the distressed economic climate State Street's servicing and management revenues declined due to lower equity market valuations and lending volumes and an increase in bankruptcies. The company hit its nadir in 2009 when it reported more than $2 billion in losses.

EXECUTIVES

President And Coo, Ronald P. (Ron) O'Hanley, age 61, $784,615 total compensation

Evp And Global Head State Street Alternative Investment Solutions, George E. Sullivan

Chairman President And Ceo, Joseph L. (Jay) Hooley, age 61, $980,769 total compensation

Evp And Head Of Regulatory Industry And Government Affairs, Stefan M. Gavell

Evp And Head Global Markets And Global Services Asia Pacific, Wai Kwong Seck, age 62

Evp And Chief Legal Officer, Jeffrey N. Carp, age 61, $675,000 total compensation

Evp, Maria F. Dwyer

Evp And Head Securities Finance And Portfolio Solutions, Nicholas T. (Nick) Bonn

Evp And Global Cio, Antoine Shagoury

Evp And Chief Administrative Officer State Street Global Advisors, Marc P. Brown

Evp Corporate Advisory Services, James C. Caccivio

Global Head Of Operations Infrastructure And Business Transformation, Jeffrey D. Conway, age 52

Evp And Cto, Albert J. (Jerry) Cristoforo

Evp, Sharon E. Donovan Hart

President And Ceo State Street Global Advisors, Cyrus Taraporevala

Evp And Head State Street Global Exchange, Lou Maiuri

Evp And Head Global Operations, Robert Kaplan

Evp And Head Sector Solutions Sales Emea, Stefan Gmuer

Evp And Head Tax And Tax Advantaged Investments, Dennis E. Ross

Evp Chief Human Resources And Corporate Citizenship Officer, Kathryn M. (Kathy) Horgan

Evp, Richard G. Taggart, age 58

Evp And General Counsel, David C. Phelan

Evp Trading And Clearing, Martine Bond

Evp, Tracy Atkinson

Evp And Chief Investment Officer, Paul J. Selian

Evp And Chief Marketing Officer, Hannah Grove

Evp And General Counsel, Phillip S. Gillespie

Evp And Chief Risk Officer, Andrew Kuritzkes, age 57

Evp Alternative Asset Managers Solutions, Maria Cantillon

Evp And Coo State Street Global Services Emea, Anthony Carey

Global Chief Investment Officer, Rick Lacaille

Evp And Chief Compliance Officer, Cuan Coulter

Evp, David Crawford

Evp And Head Application Development And Maintenance, Ali El Abboud

Evp And Chief Data Officer, James Hardy

Evp And Head Specialized Products Group State Street Global Services Investment Services Americas, Brenda Lyons

Evp Head Of Institutional Investor Services, Stephen F. (Steve) Nazzaro

Evp And International Chief Risk Officer, David Suetens

Evp And Cfo, Eric Aboaf, age 53

Evp And Managing Director State Street Bank Gmbh, Jorg Ambrosius

Evp Global Markets Sales And Trading And Research, Anthony C. Bisegna

Evp State Street Global Advisors And Cio Global Equity Beta Solutions, Lynn S. Blake

Evp And Head State Street Global Services Ireland, Susan Dargan

Evp Chief Innovation Officer And Head Advisory And Information Solutions, Jessica Donohue

Evp And Head Of Global Services, Andrew Erickson

Evp And Head Sector Solutions Americas And Global Alternatives, Scott R. FitzGerald

Evp And Head Global Total Rewards And Human Resources, Todd Gershkowitz

Evp And Head Derivatives Securities Valuation And Internal Recon Centers Of Excellence, John Griffin

Evp And Head Emea State Street Global Advisors, Mike Karpik

Evp International Finance And Treasury, Mark R. Keating

Evp State Street Global Markets, Karen D. Keenan

Evp State Street Global Markets, Ian Martin

Evp, Ivan Matviak

Evp And General Auditor, Michael Richards

Evp Ssga And Global Head Spdr Exchange Traded Funds Business And Head Intermediary Distribution United States; Chairman Ssga Funds Management Inc., James E. (Jim) Ross

Evp And Head Global Markets Emea, Rajen Shah

Evp State Street Global Advisors And Cio Investment Solutions Group, Dan Farley

Evp And Global Head Of State Street Securities Finance, Paul Fleming

Evp State Street Global Services Investment Services Americas, Michael Fontaine

Evp Legal State Street Global Markets State Street Global Exchange State Street Global Operations And Credit Service, R. Bryan Woodard

Evp, Aunoy Banerjee

Evp And Head Asia Pacific Ssga, Lochiel Crafter

Evp, Pinar Kip

Evp, Jon Lehner

Evp And Head State Street Global Exchange, John Plansky

Evp, Liz Roaldsen

Evp And Treasurer, John Slyconish

Ceo Emea, Elizabeth Nolan

Senior Vice President, Martin Sullivan

Vice President Of Information Technology, Phil Pengeroth

Vice President Information Technology, Chandra Busannagari

Vice President Information Technology, Siddharth Jeevan

Assistant Vice President Information Technology Division State Street Bank, George Jones

Executive Vice President, Gunjan Kedia

Vice President Global Markets Technology, Steve Lin

Vice President, Andy McDonald

Vice President Director, Lou Adreani

Vice President Information Technology, Hannah Francis

Assistant Vice President, Christina Daniels

Vice President, Michelle Loranger

Vice President Equipment Leasing, Evelyn Orourke

Vice President; Mutual Fund Administration, Scott Jenkins

Vice President, Kishore Kottapalli

Vice President, Brian Fox

Vice President Information Technology, Srihari Valiveti

Vice President In Municipal Products Group, Ed Matuga

Vice President Derivatives Program Manager, Michael Derr

Vice President Investor Services, Dori J Samia

Senior Vice President Information Technology Architect, Maura Evans

Vice President, Sangharsh Singh

Vice President, Vikas Goel

Vice President, Michael Cogliano

Vice President, Eric Larson

Vice President Adm Testing, Irina Reznikova

Vice President Wholesale Sales, Amy Johnston
Vice President Technical Project Services, Linda Schwalje
Vice President Of Porfolio Strategist, Louis Basque
Vice President State Street Global Services, Jay Fulchino
Vice President And Senior Portfolio Manager, Todd Bean
Vice President, Diane Webber
Vice President Information Systems, Scott Wheeler
Vice President, Mark Foster
Vice President, Svetlana Zabarina
Vice President, Khaja Shaik
Investor Relations Assistant Vice President, Kevin Brady
Vice President Securities Finance, Brian McLoone
Vice President, Jeff Durkee
Vice President Accounting Operations, Brian Benkart
Vice President, Charles Cullinane
Vice President Information Technology Architecture, Dushyant Ralhan
Vice President, David Chin
Vice President Strategy Consultant, JONATHAN NESBIT
Vice President Systems Analyst, Michelle Hayward
Vice President Fx Trading And Sales, Conor Keane
Assistant Vice President, Lokesh Aggarwal
Vice President, Yeng Butler
Senior Vice President Privacy Officer, Gerald Spada
Vice President Corporate Citzenship, Sheila Peterson
Assistant Vice President, Renee Hickey
Vice President, Jeffrey Sardinha
Vice President Application Development Manager, Anqing Xu
Vice President Structured Credit Research, Antoine Axel Roulot
Vice President Vdi Infrastructure Architecture, Bruce Lyons
Senior Vice President State Street Bank Gmbh, Evert Van Den Brink
Regional Engineering Manager Apac Vice President, Alex Yuen
Vice President, William J Fortier
Vice President, Gene Morris
Vice President Information Technology, Stephen Perry
Vice President Technology, Mohammad Masud
Vice President Architecture, Steve Kiernan
Vice President, Jeevan Ramapriya
Vp It Vendor Management, Mark Fratus
Vice President, Michael Sullivan
Vice President Community Event Sponsorship Manager, Laura O'Keefe
Executive Vice President And Head State Street Global Markets Apac, Michele Hardeman
Vice President Corporate Audit, Dan Joughin
Vice President, Kevin Deren
Vice President, David Joswick
Vice President, Bob Watson
Vice President, David Goyea
Vice President Ssgm Researcher, Nan Zhang
Vice President, Michael Timcoe
Vice President, Pradeep Ahluwalia
Vice President Of Infrastructure, Paul Goulopoulos
Vice President, Hasan Arif
Vice President, Carolyn Baker
Vice President, Kerstin Heinsen
Vice President Pmp, Will Carpenter
Application Development Director Vice President, Chandra Meyyappan
Vice President, Ryan Smith
Vice President Data Center Operations, Bryon Connors
Auditors: Ernst & Young LLP

LOCATIONS

HQ: State Street Corp.
  One Lincoln Street, Boston, MA 02111
Phone: 617 786-3000
Web: www.statestreet.com

2016 Assets Mix

	% of total
North America	75
Europe/Middle East/Africa	20
Asia/Pacific	5
Total	**100**

PRODUCTS/OPERATIONS

2016 Revenues

	% of total
Fees:	
Servicing fees	48
Management fees	12
Trading services	10
Securities finance	5
Processing fees & other	1
Interest revenue	24
Gains (losses) related to investment securities net	-
Total	**100**

2016 Sales

	% of total
U.S.	57
Other countries	43
Total	**100**

Selected Capabilities

Data and Analytic
Investment Management
Investment Research and Trading
Investment Servicing

COMPETITORS

Bank of New York Mellon	JPMorgan Chase
Citigroup	Morgan Stanley
Credit Suisse (USA)	Northern Trust
Deutsche Bank	Principal Financial
First Data	SEI Investments
Fiserv	UBS Financial Services

HISTORICAL FINANCIALS

Company Type: Public

Income Statement   FYE: December 31

	ASSETS ($ mil.)	NET INCOME ($ mil.)	INCOME AS % OF ASSETS	EMPLOYEES
12/17	238,425	2,177	0.9%	36,643
12/16	242,698	2,143	0.9%	33,783
12/15	245,192	1,980	0.8%	32,356
12/14	274,119	2,037	0.7%	29,970
12/13	243,291	2,136	0.9%	29,430
Annual Growth	(0.5%)	0.5%	—	5.6%

2017 Year-End Financials

Debt ratio: 4.87%
Return on equity: 10.00%
Cash ($ mil.): 70,427
Current ratio: —
Long-term debt ($ mil.): —

No. of shares (mil.): 367
Dividends
  Yield: 0.0%
  Payout: 30.5%
Market value ($ mil.): 35,886

	STOCK PRICE ($) FY Close	P/E High/Low	PER SHARE ($) Earnings	Dividends	Book Value
12/17	97.61	19 14	5.24	1.60	60.70
12/16	77.72	16 10	4.97	1.44	55.56
12/15	66.36	18 14	4.47	1.32	52.80
12/14	78.50	17 14	4.57	1.16	51.72
12/13	73.39	15 10	4.62	1.04	46.94
Annual Growth	7.4%	— —	3.2%	11.4%	6.6%

Steel Dynamics Inc.

Steel Dynamics may operate mini-mills but it produces steel on a large scale. Steel Dynamics operates electric arc furnace mini-mills steel scrap processing and metals recycling centers and steel fabrication facilities. The company sells to companies in the automotive construction and manufacturing industries as well as to steel processors and service centers primarily in the Midwestern and eastern US. Among its mini-mill output are beams rails and other products used in the construction industrial machinery and transportation industries. Steel Dynamics' annual steel shipping capacity is 11 million tons.

Operations

Steel Dynamics has three reporting segments: Steel Metals Recycling and Steel Fabrication.

Its Steel operations have six electric-arc furnace mini-mills producing steel from steel scrap using continuous casting automated rolling mills and some 10 downstream steel coating lines and Iron Dynamics (IDI). Its Flat Roll Division sheet steel products such as hot rolled cold rolled and coated steel products are used by automakers and other industries. The Long Products Division sells structural steel beams and pilings for the construction industry and industrial quality grade rail for the railroad industry. The Steel operations account for about three-quarters of sales.

The Metals Recycling operations (about 15% of revenue) consist solely of OmniSource which includes ferrous and nonferrous scrap metal processing transportation marketing brokerage and consulting services. In addition OmniSource designs installs and manages customized scrap management programs for industrial manufacturing companies.

The company's Steel Fabrication operations (about 10% of revenue) include seven New Millennium Building Systems plants which fabricate steel joists trusses girders and decking used by the nonresidential construction industry.

All told Steel Dynamics operates six electric-arc-furnace steel mills steel coating lines a downstream engineered bar (SBQ) processing facility an iron production facility multiple metals recycling operations and seven steel fabrication plants.

Geographic Reach

Steel Dynamics has operations in Indiana (Butler Columbia City Jeffersonville and Pittsboro) Mississippi (Columbus) Pennsylvania (Pittsburgh) Virginia (Roanoke) and West Virginia (Huntington). It also serves the Southern US Canada and Mexico.

Sales and Marketing

Steel Dynamics' primary customers for structural steel products are steel service centers steel fabricators and a range of other manufacturers including metal building firms general construction contractors developers brokers agriculture consumer goods and governmental entities. The company?s steel operation?s biggest customers are construction about 40% manufacturing nearly 32% and automotive about 15%.

Financial Performance

In the last decade revenue at Steel Industries has more or less remained stable around the $8 billion mark despite a plunge in 2009 when it posted just below $4 billion in earnings. Net income has been much less predictable. It has had two years of losses (2009 2015) and mostly profits below $200 million though the company has fared better in the last couple of years.

2017 was one of the best years for the company. Revenue increased 20% to $9.5 billion the highest in a decade. The record level of steel operation and fabrication shipments (close to 10 million tons combined) and improved demand in the domestic steel market followed by selling price hikes contributed to the revenue growth. Metals recycling operations increased earnings by almost 250%.

Steel Dynamics profits in 2017 grew some 80% again the highest in a decade to $813 million mostly from the absence of $133 million asset impairment charge as well as a $20 million gain in other expenses compared to 2016.

Company's cash holdings increased from $840 million to $1 billion. Operations generated $740 million. Investment activities took up some $140 million while financing activities utilized $415 million majority of which went towards long-term debt reduction. CAPEX in 2017 was $165 million.

Strategy

Steel Dynamics is seeking to maintain and enhance one of the lowest operating cost structures in the North American steel industry by optimizing the use of its equipment enhancing productivity and exploring new technologies to lower production costs. It is looking to enter new markets in strategic geographic locations that offer attractive growth opportunities by acquiring new businesses or by entering joint ventures or alliances.

The company has improved at several plants to bring on more capacity and make operations more efficient. The company is investing millions of dollars in improvements at the Butler Flat Roll division and the Gavalume line at the Columbus Flat Roll division which serve the automotive market.

The company collaborates with customers to expand its range of products as illustrated by expansions at its Engineered Bar Products Division (high-quality smaller-diameter SBQ bars) and at its Structural and Rail Division (premium grade rails).

Mergers and Acquisitions

In September 2018 Steel Dynamics acquired almost all assets of Kentucky Electric Steel a wholly-owned subsidiary of Specialty Steel Works for $5 million. The Ashland area operations which will be integrated into Steel Dynamics' West Virginia segment include a rolling mill with an annual capacity of 250000 tons that produces flats and specialty alloy bars.

In 2016 Steel Dynamics acquired Vulcan Threaded Products for $114 million. The Birmingham Alabama-based company makes and supplies threaded rod products and also cold draws and heat-treated steel bar. The deal is an example of Steel Dynamics pursuing higher-margin downstream business opportunities that use its steel products in manufacturing processes.

Company Background

Growing its share of the rail market in 2012 Steel Dynamics announced plans to install a heat-treating system (capable of producing up to 350000 tons of standard strength and head hardened plain carbon steel rails for North America's railroad industry) at its Columbia City Indiana Structural and Rail Division.

Steel Dynamics entered a joint venture in 2011 with Spain's Lafarga Group to construct a $39 million facility which will produce copper wire rod from recycled copper.

Steel Dynamics was incorporated in 1993.

EXECUTIVES

Vice President Human Resources, Benjamin Eisbart
President And Ceo, Mark D. Millett, age 59, $1,010,000 total compensation
Evp Metals Recycling And President And Coo Omnisource, Russell B. (Russ) Rinn, age 61, $510,000 total compensation
Svp Long Products Steel Group, Glenn A. Pushis, age 52, $393,750 total compensation

Vp And Cio, Robert E. (Bob) Francis
Evp And Cfo, Theresa E. Wagler, age 48, $580,000 total compensation
Svp Flat Roll Steel Group, Barry T. Schneider, age 49, $363,750 total compensation
Vp And President Steel Of West Virginia, Timothy R. (Tim) Duke
Svp Downstream Manufacturing Group, Christopher A. (Chris) Graham, age 55, $322,500 total compensation
Vice President Finance, John Morris
Vice President, Boudler Noelle
Chairman, Keith E. Busse, age 76
Vice President Treasurer And Risk Manager, Richard Poinsatte
Board Member, Richard T Teets
Auditors: Ernst & Young LLP

LOCATIONS

HQ: Steel Dynamics Inc.
7575 West Jefferson Blvd., Fort Wayne, IN 46804
Phone: 260 969-3500
Web: www.steeldynamics.com

PRODUCTS/OPERATIONS

2016 sales

	$ mil.	% of total
Steel	5,870	65
Metals Recycling	2,171	24
Steel Fabrication	703	8
Other	276	3
Eliminations	(1246.1)	-
Total	**7,777**	**100**

Selected Products

Cold-rolled galvannealed
Cold-rolled hot-dipped galvanized
Direct reduced iron
Fully processed cold-rolled sheet
Hot-rolled galvannealed
Hot-rolled hot-dipped galvanized
Hot-rolled pickled and oiled
Liquid pig iron
Structural products (steel joists trusses)
Steel Operations
Sheet Products
  Hot rolled Products
  Cold Rolled Products
Long Products
  Structural
  Wide flange American Standard and miscellaneous beams
  H piling
  Channel sections
Rail Products
  Engineered Bar Products
  Merchant Bar Products
  Specialty Shapes
Metals Recycling   No. 2 shredded
  No. 1 bundles
  Plate and structural
  No. 1 busheling
  Turnings
  Heavy melt
  Briquettes
  Copper granules
  Stainless steel bundles
Steel Fabrication Operations   Joists
  Decking
  Castellated beams
  Cambered beams

COMPETITORS

AK Steel Holding Corporation	Evraz
ArcelorMittal USA	Gerdau Ameristeel
Canam Steel Corporation	Nucor
Commercial Metals	Timken
	United States Steel
	Wheeling Corrugating

HISTORICAL FINANCIALS

Company Type: Public

Income Statement
FYE: December 31

	REVENUE ($ mil.)	NET INCOME ($ mil.)	NET PROFIT MARGIN	EMPLOYEES
12/17	9,538	812	8.5%	7,635
12/16	7,777	382	4.9%	7,695
12/15	7,594	(130)	—	7,500
12/14	8,755	157	1.8%	7,780
12/13	7,372	189	2.6%	6,870
Annual Growth	**6.7%**	**43.9%**	**—**	**2.7%**

2017 Year-End Financials

Debt ratio: 34.74%
Return on equity: 25.89%
Cash ($ mil.): 1,028
Current ratio: 4.04
Long-term debt ($ mil.): 2,353

No. of shares (mil.): 237
Dividends
  Yield: 0.0%
  Payout: 18.4%
Market value ($ mil.): 10,239

	STOCK PRICE ($) FY Close	P/E High/Low	PER SHARE ($) Earnings	Dividends	Book Value
12/17	43.13	13 10	3.36	0.62	14.12
12/16	35.58	25 10	1.56	0.56	12.01
12/15	17.87	— —	(0.54)	0.55	11.02
12/14	19.74	37 23	0.67	0.46	12.06
12/13	19.54	23 16	0.83	0.44	11.43
Annual Growth	**21.9%**	**— —**	**41.8%**	**9.0%**	**5.4%**

Sterling Bancorp (DE)

EXECUTIVES

Senior Vice President Business Intelligence, Patrick DeKenipp
Auditors: Crowe Horwath LLP

LOCATIONS

HQ: Sterling Bancorp (DE)
400 Rella Boulevard, Montebello, NY 10901
Phone: 845 369-8040
Web: www.sterlingbancorp.com

COMPETITORS

Capital One	JPMorgan Chase
Citibank	KeyCorp
HSBC USA	M&T Bank

HISTORICAL FINANCIALS

Company Type: Public

Income Statement
FYE: December 31

	ASSETS ($ mil.)	NET INCOME ($ mil.)	INCOME AS % OF ASSETS	EMPLOYEES
12/17	30,359	93	0.3%	2,076
12/16	14,178	139	1.0%	970
12/15	11,955	66	0.6%	1,089
12/14*	7,424	17	0.2%	829
09/14	7,337	27	0.4%	836
Annual Growth	**60.5%**	**49.8%**	**—**	**35.4%**
*Fiscal year change				

2017 Year-End Financials

Debt ratio: 1.58%
Return on equity: 3.05%
Cash ($ mil.): 479
Current ratio: —
Long-term debt ($ mil.): —

No. of shares (mil.): 224
Dividends
  Yield: 0.0%
  Payout: 48.2%
Market value ($ mil.): 5,530

STOCK PRICE ($)	P/E		PER SHARE ($)		
FY Close	High/Low	Earnings	Dividends	Book Value
12/17	24.60	45 36	0.58	0.28	18.86
12/16	23.40	23 13	1.07	0.28	13.72
12/15	16.22	29 22	0.60	0.28	12.81
12/14*	14.38	72 63	0.20	0.28	11.62
09/14	12.79	40 32	0.34	0.27	11.49
Annual Growth	24.4%	— —	19.5%	1.3%	10.9%

*Fiscal year change

Sterling Bancorp Inc (MI)

Auditors: Crowe Horwath LLP

LOCATIONS

HQ: Sterling Bancorp Inc (MI)
One Towne Square, Suite 1900, Southfield, MI 48076
Phone: 248 355-2400
Web: www.sterlingbank.com

HISTORICAL FINANCIALS

Company Type: Public

Income Statement

FYE: December 31

	ASSETS ($ mil.)	NET INCOME ($ mil.)	INCOME AS % OF ASSETS	EMPLOYEES
12/17	2,961	37	1.3%	308
12/16	2,163	33	1.5%	294
12/15	1,712	22	1.3%	—
Annual Growth	31.5%	29.9%	—	—

2017 Year-End Financials

Debt ratio: 2.19%
Return on equity: 17.44%
Cash ($ mil.): 40
Current ratio: —
Long-term debt ($ mil.): —

No. of shares (mil.): 52
Dividends
  Yield: 0.0%
  Payout: 25.6%
Market value ($ mil.): 673

STOCK PRICE ($)	P/E		PER SHARE ($)		
FY Close	High/Low	Earnings	Dividends	Book Value
12/17	12.70	16 15	0.82	0.21	5.16
12/16	0.00	— —	0.73	0.19	3.58
12/15	0.00	— —	0.49	0.15	3.01
Annual Growth	—	— —	29.4%	18.3%	30.9%

Stewart Information Services Corp

Stewart Information Services is happy to have a place in that mountain of papers to sign whenever real estate changes hands. The company writes title insurance through its top-ranking Stewart Title National Title and other units and distributes policies through more than 8500 offices and independent agencies in the US and abroad. Unlike most insurance that covers future events or losses title insurance protects lenders and buyers against past problems with titles. Stewart Title offers real estate information services through PropertyInfo and a variety of mortgage origination process services through Stewart Lender Services. Stewart also provides services to US and international government clients. The company is being acquired by Fidelity National Financial the largest title insurer in the US.

Change in Company Type

In March 2018 Fidelity National Financial agreed to buy Stewart Information Services for $1.2 billion. The deal will make Fidelity even larger as it will nab one of the Big Four title insurers.

Operations

In addition to commercial and residential title insurance policies Stewart Information Services? main business units provide underwriting escrow and settlement lending and specialty insurance services. Stewart Information Services' title insurance operations account for about 95% of sales.

Meanwhile the Ancillary Services and Corporate segment about 5% of revenue includes the parent holding company centralized administrative services and ancillary services operationsw which provide appraisal and valuation services to the mortgage industry. Stewart Lender Services provides origination default mitigation and post-closing lender services while the PropertyInfo unit manages land data and court record databases for title examination purposes. The company's Stewart Government Services division provides web access and eRecording services as well as indexing and imaging services to courthouses in the US.

The company strives to enhance customer experience by providing value-added products that simplify processes. To that end it offers such tools as Stewart Online LenderExpressQuote SureClose (for real estate brokers) and the eClosingRoom (an electronic signature service).

Geographic Reach

Stewart Information Services generates about 95% of its title revenues in the US mainly in Texas California New York Missouri and Florida. International operations — primarily in Australia Canada the Caribbean Latin America (Mexico) the UK and Central Europe — account for the rest. The company operates in more than 80 countries.

Sales and Marketing

Stewart Information Services' primary customers include home buyers and sellers mortgage investors attorneys real estate brokers and developers title agencies governments builders and mortgage lenders needing to insure titles of residential and commercial properties water rights undeveloped acreage and farms and ranches. The company sells directly and through approved independent agencies and affiliates.

Financial Performance

Stewart Information Services reported a slight dip in revenue to about $2 billion in 2016 from $2.03 billion in 2015. Revenue from direct title operations dropped a hair (0.3%) in 2016 from a 5% decline in closed commercial and refinancing orders although international revenue improved. Revenue from independent agencies rose about 2% in 2016 while gross agency revenue also increased on higher revenue from Texas Michigan Washington and Florida. Ancillary services revenue tumbled 35% in 2016 because of decreased demand and lower pricing in delinquent loan servicing. The company exited delinquent loan servicing in early 2016.

After losing about $6 million in 2015 Stewart posted a $55 million profit in 2016 with help from lower employee costs and other operating expenses.

Cash flow from operations increased to about $123 million in 2016 from about $80 million in 2015 from the higher net income and lower payment of claims liabilities in 2016.

Strategy

Stewart Information Systems has narrowed its focus to more profitable businesses and partners. The company is looking increase its commercial business to take advantage of attractive returns and cyclical diversity from residential real estate.

The company also reduced its agency footprint from 6000 to 2500 agents to increase margins. It identified the most profitable agents to work with. Further Stewart increased the percentage of its title business from the direct channel which has higher margins and is more scalable.

In 2017 Stewart said it was considering putting itself up for sale or partnering with another firm. The company blamed a fall in profits on the impact of Hurricane Harvey in its hometown of Houston. Employee attrition also has hurt the company.

Company Background

Stewart has been in business for more than 120 years tracing its roots to 1893.

EXECUTIVES

Senior Vice President, James L Gosdin
Senior Vice President Accounting, Alison Evers
Cfo Secretary And Treasurer, David C. Hisey
Ceo, Matthew W. (Matt) Morris, age 46, $550,000 total compensation
Group President Title And Escrow Fulfillment Services, David A. (Dave) Fauth, $350,000 total compensation
Chief Legal Officer, John L. Killea, $375,000 total compensation
Cio, Brad Rable
Group President Agency Operations And Mortgage Service Offerings, Patrick (Pat) Beall
Chief Revenue Officer, Jay Milligan
Senior Vice President And Corporate Controller Stewart Title Guaranty Company, Brian Glaze
Vice President Information Services, Mark Helman
Vice President Finance, Sue Cosgriff
Executive Vice President, Patricia Norris
Vice President Of National Business Development, John Bianco
Vice President Associate Senior Underwriting Counsel, Gayle A Bourdeau
Vice President Of Technology, Dawn Glebe
Vice President Commercial Services Division, Michael Desmond
Vice President Underwriter, Hector Barraza
Evp And Director Commercial Services, Tom Konkel
Vice President Marketing, Debbie Wilson
Vice President, Gail Kohl
Vice President Business Development, Tom Gray
Senior Vice President Of Software Development, Jason Harrison
Vice President Manager, Carma Weymouth
Vice President, Jan Guadalupe
Vice President, Ann Wallace
Vice President, Mary Ann Reynolds
Vice President Escrow Accounting, Carolyn Graham
Vice President, Laura Wynne
Vice President International Sales, Bobbie Adams
Vice President And Senior Account Execitive, Michael Bidner
Vice President Escrow Officer, Carolyn Shores
Vice President, Bill Pratt
Vice President, Lorri Landeros
Vice President, Laurie Cooper
Vice President And Branch Manager North Texas Div, Regina Culver
Vice President Operations Manager, Mona Baen
Senior Vice President, Laurence Sanders
Vice President Senior Underwriter And Manager Nts Atlanta, Don Wade

Vice President Business Development Officer, Doug Stevens

Vice President Of Stewart Title Guaranty, Brandt Keefe

Vice President, Lisa Robertson

Vice President, Jo Garcia

Vice President And Treasurer, Emily Thai

Vice President, Frank Alvstad

Vice President Of Finance, Borgia Houser

Vice President, Karen Vaughn

Vice President Stewart Title Houston Division, Kim Mccall

Executive Vice President Human Resources, Mike Davis

Vice President And Branch Manager, Roy Sullivan

Vice President Commercial Operations Underwriting Counsel, Dawn Anderson

Vice President, Dana Duncan

Vice President Of Business Development, Jimmie Herrick

Evp Valuation Services And National Sales Lender Services, Bill Sullivan

Division President, Christina Cesario

Vice President National Closing And Escrow Operations, Michele A Kelly

Vice President Los Angeles Division Commercial Sales, Jeffrey Schick

Vice President Hrsi Software Development, Adam Durham

Group Senior Vice President Eastern Region, Marty Albertson

Svp Finance, Nat Otis

Upper Management Vice President, Cynthia Kojak

Vice President, John Ursini

Sr. V.p., James Lanzetta

Executive Vice President, Kim Leland

Assistant Vice President, Roger Burnette

Avp Case Management Team Manager, Pamela Stephenson

Vice President Business Development And Sales, Teri Wagnon

Vice President Strategic Sales, Jeff Lahay

Vice President Sales Manager, Manny Herrera

Division President, Belinda Bernal

Vice President Of Operations, Brandon McKnight

Vice President National Sales, Robin Ramsey

Vice President, Deborah Kinnaman

Vice President Of Commercial, Linda Standaart

Sr. Vice President, Suzanne Weadock

Vp Sales, Tim Henley

Vice President, Myra Leblanc

Vice President, Sheila Havard

Division President, Sandy Glaser

Vp Team Manager, Kelli Strait

Vp Admin. Assistant, Debbie Kluge

Vp Collateral Valuation Solutions, Greg Dennis

Vice President Manager, Bobbie Acklin

Avp Senior Escrow Officer North Bay Division, Yvonne Chao

Vice President, Jennifer Shimaitis

Assistant Vice President, Sheron Green

Assistant Vice President And Branch Manager, Karen Privette

Senior Vice President, Margaret Kronmueller

Assistant Vice President, Roberta Tindell

Vice President, Timothy Oberweger

Chairman, Thomas G. Apel, age 57

Auditors: KPMG LLP

LOCATIONS

HQ: Stewart Information Services Corp
1980 Post Oak Blvd., Houston, TX 77056
Phone: 713 625-8100   Fax: 713 629-2244
Web: www.stewart.com

2016 Sales

	$ mil.	% total
United States	1,889	94
International	117	6
Total	**2,006**	**100**

2016 Title Insurance Revenues by Geography

	% of total
US	
Texas	19
New York	12
California	7
Florida	5
Other states	51
International	6
Total	**100**

PRODUCTS/OPERATIONS

2016 Revenues

	$ mil.	% of total
Title insurance		
Agency operations	1,009	50
Direct operations	894	45
Ancillary services	84	4
Investment income	18	1
Investment & other gains	(0.6)	-
Total	**2,006**	**100**

Selected Products Brands and Services

1031 Exchanges
Advanced Title Search (ATS)
AgencySecure
AIM — Title Production System
Bonds Insurance
Centralized Title and Settlement
Commercial Insurance
CountyFusion
Default and Foreclosure Services
eClipse — Electronic Recording System
eClosingRoom — Eco-Friendly Electronic Closing System
Electronic Title Underwriting
Errors and Omissions Insurance
Escrow Account Reconciliation Services
Lawyers Mortgage Network
PropertyInfo Corporation
Stewart Lender Services
Stewart Title
Stewart Title Guaranty

COMPETITORS

CoStar Group	North American Title
CoreLogic	Old Republic National
Fidelity National	Title
Financial	Reis
First American	Ticor Title Co.
Investors Title	

HISTORICAL FINANCIALS

Company Type: Public

Income Statement

FYE: December 31

	ASSETS ($ mil.)	NET INCOME ($ mil.)	INCOME AS % OF ASSETS	EMPLOYEES
12/17	1,405	48	3.5%	5,960
12/16	1,341	55	4.1%	6,350
12/15	1,321	(6)	—	6,900
12/14	1,392	29	2.1%	7,400
12/13	1,326	63	4.8%	6,600
Annual Growth	**1.5%**	**(6.3%)**	**—**	**(2.5%)**

2017 Year-End Financials

Debt ratio: 7.78%	No. of shares (mil.): 23
Return on equity: 7.41%	Dividends
Cash ($ mil.): 150	Yield: 0.0%
Current ratio: —	Payout: 58.2%
Long-term debt ($ mil.): —	Market value ($ mil.): 1,003

	STOCK PRICE ($) FY Close	P/E High/Low	PER SHARE ($) Earnings	Dividends	Book Value
12/17	42.30	23 17	2.06	1.20	28.34
12/16	46.08	26 17	1.85	1.20	27.37
12/15	37.33	— —	(0.26)	0.80	26.96
12/14	37.04	29 21	1.24	0.10	28.88
12/13	32.27	11 8	2.60	0.10	29.12
Annual Growth	**7.0%**	**— —**	**(5.7%)**	**86.1%**	**(0.7%)**

Stifel Financial Corp

Through subsidiaries Stifel Nicolaus (founded 1890) Thomas Weisel Century Securities Associates Stifel Bank & Trust and others Stifel Financial provides asset management financial advice and banking services for private individuals corporations municipal and institutional clients in the US. Stifel also offers brokerage and **mergers and acquisitions** advisory services for corporate clients underwrites debt and equity and provides research on more than 1000 US and European equities. The firm boasts nearly 360 US offices with a concentration in the Midwest and mid-Atlantic regions and additional offices in the UK and the rest of Europe.

Operations

Stifel Financial operates two main business segments.

The Global Wealth Management segment which generates more than 60% of the firm's total revenue consists of two businesses: Stifel Bank which provides traditional banking products and services and the Private Client Group which is made up of offices across the US that provide securities brokerage services and insurance products.

The Institutional Group segment (almost 40% of revenue) provides securities brokerage trading and research services to institutions and specializes in the sale of equity and fixed-income products.

Geographic Reach

The company is headquartered in Missouri with about 360 private client offices and more than 35 Institutional Group offices mostly across the US as well as in certain foreign locations in the UK and the rest of Europe. About 95% of its revenue stems from the US.

Sales and Marketing

With its 2280-plus financial advisors and 125 independent contractors Stifel serves individuals corporations municipalities and institutions. Its broker-dealer subsidiaries boast more than 1.5 million accounts from customers based in the US and Europe.

Financial Performance

Stifel's revenues have been growing at a healthy clip in recent years thanks to business-boosting acquisitions combined with growth across all business lines as the financial markets have appreciated and demand for investor capital has strengthened.

The firm's revenues climbed 11% to peak at a record-setting $2.6 billion during 2016. This historic growth was driven by a 64% surge from interest revenue generated from the growth in interest-earning assets of Stifel Bank. In addition principal transactions revenues spiked 22% in 2016 due to higher institutional fixed income brokerage revenues as a result of increased volumes. The firm also generated additional revenue from several previous acquisitions.

Despite revenue growth in 2016 Stifel's net income dipped 12% to $82 million as the company spent more on compensation benefits and office space to support future revenue growth. In addition Stifel experienced negative cash flow of $349 million in 2016 as the firm used more cash to purchase operating assets.

Strategy

Stifel has fortified its operations and extended its national footprint mainly through strategic acquisitions as well as through organic growth. It plans to further expand its domestic private client footprint by recruiting experienced financial advisors and continuing to selectively consider acquisitions as they arise.

Mergers and Acquisitions

Stifel has achieved historic revenue growth over the years by using acquisitions primarily to fortify its wealth management business.

In late 2017 it agreed to acquire the wealth management business belonging to B.C. Ziegler & Company. The business Ziegler Wealth Management was established in 1902 and has nearly 60 private client advisors in 12 branches across five. It manages approximately $4.8 billion in client assets.

In 2017 Stifel picked up investment bank City Financial Corporation and its City Securities subsidiary. City Financial primarily operates in Indiana and the Midwest specializing in wealth management and public finance.

In early 2016 the firm bought global fund placement and advisory firm Eaton Partners. The deal enhanced Stifel's investment banking and high net worth private client business with new private equity firms hedge funds affluent family offices and institutional investor client relationships.

In another large deal Stifel in 2015 purchased Barclays' Wealth and Investment Management Americas franchise in the US along with its 180 financial advisors managing some $56 billion in total client assets.

EXECUTIVES

Vice Chairman Svp And Director Stifel Financial Corp. And Evp Investment Banking Stifel Nicolaus & Co., Richard J. Himelfarb, age 77, $250,000 total compensation
Chairman President And Ceo, Ronald J. (Ron) Kruszewski, age 59, $200,000 total compensation
President Cfo And Director, James M. Zemlyak, age 58, $250,000 total compensation
Evp; President And Co-director Institutional Group, Thomas P. Mulroy, age 56, $250,000 total compensation
Svp And Director Stifel Financial Corp. And President And Ceo Keefe Bruyette And Woods, Thomas B. (Tom) Michaud, age 53, $250,000 total compensation
Evp; President And Co-director Institutional Group, Victor J. Nesi, age 58, $250,000 total compensation
Senior Vice President, David Sliney
Vice Chairman; Evp Stifel Nicolaus & Co., Ben A. Plotkin, age 62
Co-chairman, Thomas W. (Thom) Weisel, age 76
Auditors: Ernst & Young LLP

LOCATIONS

HQ: Stifel Financial Corp
501 North Broadway, St. Louis, MO 63102-2188
Phone: 314 342-2000
Web: www.stifel.com

2016 Sales

	% of total
US	94
UK	5
Other European countries	1
Total	**100**

PRODUCTS/OPERATIONS

2016 Sales

	$ mil.	% of total
Commissions	730	28
Asset management and service fees	582	22
Investment banking	513	19
Principal transactions	475	18
Interest	294	11
Others	46	2
Total	**2,642**	**100**

Selected Services

Individual
Bonds
Corporate Executive Services
Estate Planning
Exchange Traded Funds
Financial And Wealth Planning
Insurance
Investment Advisory Services
Market News
Mutual Funds
Options
Portfolio Tracker
Prospectus
Retirement Plans
Stifel Bank & Trust
Stifel Cash Management Accounts
Stifel Mobile Announcement
Stifel Trust
Institutions
Asset Management
Conferences & Events
Equity Capital Markets
Equity Sales & Trading
Fixed Income Sales & Trading
Investment Banking
Public Finance
Research
Senior Management

Selected Subsidiaries

Broadway Air Corp.
  CSA Insurance Agency Incorporated
Choice Financial Partners Inc.
  Stifel Bank & Trust
Stifel Nicolaus Limited (UK)
Stifel Nicolaus & Company Incorporated
  Ryan Beck Holdings LLC
Thomas Weisel Partners Group Inc.

COMPETITORS

Edward Jones	Oppenheimer Holdings
FBR	Piper Jaffray
Goldman Sachs	Raymond James
JMP Group	Financial
Lazard	Wells Fargo Advisors
Morgan Stanley	

HISTORICAL FINANCIALS

Company Type: Public

Income Statement

FYE: December 31

	ASSETS ($ mil.)	NET INCOME ($ mil.)	INCOME AS % OF ASSETS	EMPLOYEES
12/17	21,383	182	0.9%	7,100
12/16	19,129	81	0.4%	7,100
12/15	13,335	92	0.7%	7,100
12/14	9,518	176	1.8%	6,200
12/13	9,008	162	1.8%	5,862
Annual Growth	**24.1%**	**3.1%**	**—**	**4.9%**

2017 Year-End Financials

Debt ratio: 6.26%	No. of shares (mil.): 70
Return on equity: 6.53%	Dividends
Cash ($ mil.): 787	Yield: 0.0%
Current ratio: —	Payout: 9.3%
Long-term debt ($ mil.): —	Market value ($ mil.): 4,221

	STOCK PRICE ($) FY Close	P/E High/Low	PER SHARE ($) Earnings	Dividends	Book Value
12/17	59.56	24 17	2.14	0.20	40.38
12/16	49.95	45 23	1.00	0.00	41.09
12/15	42.36	44 30	1.18	0.00	37.19
12/14	51.02	20 16	2.31	0.00	35.00
12/13	47.92	19 12	2.20	0.00	32.30
Annual Growth	**5.0%**	**— —**	**(0.7%)**	**—**	**5.7%**

Stock Yards Bancorp Inc

Stock Yards Bancorp is the holding company of Stock Yards Bank & Trust which operates about 35 branches mostly in Louisville Kentucky but also in Indianapolis and Cincinnati. Founded in 1904 the $3 billion-asset bank targets individuals and regional business customers offering standard retail services such as checking and savings accounts credit cards certificates of deposit and IRAs. It also provides trust services while brokerage and credit card services are offered through agreements with other banks. Commercial real estate mortgages make up 40% of the bank's loan portfolio which also includes commercial and industrial loans (30%) residential mortgages (15%) construction loans and consumer loans.

Operations

Stock Yards Bank & Trust operates two main business lines: Commercial Banking which provides loans and deposits to individual consumers and businesses as well as mortgage origination and company brokerage activity; and Investment Management and Trust which provides wealth management services such as investment management trust estate administration and retirement plan services.

About 63% of the company's total revenue came from loan interest during 2015 while another 7% came from interest income on its securities. The rest came from its investment management and trust services (13% of revenue) deposit account service charges (7%) bankcard transaction revenue (4%) mortgage banking revenue (3%) brokerage commissions and fees (1%) and other non-interest sources.

Geographic Reach

Kentucky-based Stock Yards Bancorp had 37 branches at the end of 2015 including 28 branches in the Louisville Kentucky metro area and the rest in the Indianapolis Indiana and Cincinnati Ohio metro areas.

Financial Performance

Stock Yards' annual revenues have risen 11% since 2011 thanks to a combination of mostly organic loan growth and investment management and trust services fee growth. Meanwhile its annual profits have grown more than 55% on declining loan loss provisions as its loan portfolio's credit quality has improved with higher property valuations in the strengthened economy.

The bank's revenue climbed 4% to a record $133.12 million during 2015 on higher interest income mostly as its loan assets grew 9% to $2 billion with record loan production.

Revenue growth and a decline in interest expense on deposits in 2015 drove Stock Yard's net income up 7% to a record $34.82 million. The bank's operating cash levels jumped 8% to $43.17

million mostly thanks to the increase in cash-based earnings.

Strategy

Stock Yards outlined its plans for 2016 and beyond to maintain stable net interest margins achieve near-double digit loan growth manage credit quality to keep loan loss provisions down and increasing its regulatory readiness.

Mergers and Acquisitions

In 2013 the bank extended the reach of its operations into Oldham County through its purchase of $146 million-asset The BANcorp Inc. and its five THE BANK branches in the region for $19.9 million.

EXECUTIVES

Sevp, Kathy C. Thompson, age 56, $345,000 total compensation

Chairman And Ceo, David P. Heintzman, age 58, $535,000 total compensation

Evp Secretary Treasurer And Cfo, Nancy B. Davis, age 62, $232,000 total compensation

Evp And Chief Lending Officer, Philip S. Poindexter, age 52, $270,000 total compensation

President, James A. (Ja) Hillebrand, age 49, $375,000 total compensation

Evp And Chief Risk Officer, William M. Dishman, age 56

Evp And Chief Strategic Officer, Clay Stinnett

Evp Retail Banking Brokerage And Business Banking, Michael J. Croce

Assistant Vice President Deposit Operations, Marcia Sweat

Vice President Private Banking, Dan Thacker

Vice President Commercial Lending, Kevin Mccullough

Vice President Relationship Manager, Brian Hall

Vice President Equipment Finance, Rick Waddle

Assistant Vice President, June Schenk

Vice President, Joe Morrison

Vice President Commerical Lending, Jason Morgan

Auditors: BKD LLP

LOCATIONS

HQ: Stock Yards Bancorp Inc
1040 East Main Street, Louisville, KY 40206
Phone: 502 582-2571
Web: www.syb.com

PRODUCTS/OPERATIONS

2015 Revenues by Category

	$ mil.	% of total
Interest income	93	70
Non-interest income	40	30
Total	**133**	**100**

Selected Products & Services

Personal Banking
  Banking
  Personal Lending
  Personal Investing & Wealth Management Services
Business Banking
  Credit Loans & Leasing
  Deposit Services
  Treasury Management
  Business Retirement Plans
Wealth Management Services
  Investment Management
  Financial Planning
  Trust & Estate Services
  Brokerage Service

COMPETITORS

Fifth Third	Porter Bancorp
First Capital	Republic Bancorp
Home Federal	U.S. Bancorp
PNC Financial	

HISTORICAL FINANCIALS

Company Type: Public

Income Statement
FYE: December 31

	ASSETS ($ mil.)	NET INCOME ($ mil.)	INCOME AS % OF ASSETS	EMPLOYEES
12/17	3,239	38	1.2%	580
12/16	3,039	41	1.3%	578
12/15	2,816	37	1.3%	555
12/14	2,563	34	1.4%	524
12/13	2,389	27	1.1%	519
Annual Growth	**7.9%**	**8.8%**	**—**	**2.8%**

2017 Year-End Financials

Debt ratio: —	No. of shares (mil.): 22
Return on equity: 11.75%	Dividends
Cash ($ mil.): 139	Yield: 0.0%
Current ratio: —	Payout: 48.1%
Long-term debt ($ mil.): —	Market value ($ mil.): 855

	STOCK PRICE ($) FY Close	P/E High/Low	Earnings	Dividends	Book Value
12/17	37.70	28 19	1.66	0.80	14.71
12/16	46.95	26 15	1.80	0.72	13.88
12/15	37.79	24 18	1.65	0.64	12.80
12/14	33.34	21 17	1.57	0.59	11.75
12/13	31.92	27 17	1.26	0.54	10.47
Annual Growth	**4.2%**	**— —**	**7.1%**	**10.3%**	**8.9%**

Stryker Corp

Is this an operating room or Dad's workshop? Stryker's surgical products include such instruments as drills saws and even cement mixers. The company operates through three primary segments — MedSurg Orthopaedic and Neurotechnology & Spine. MedSurg's products include microsurgery instruments endoscopy equipment communications systems emergency medical equipment and patient handling tools. The Orthopaedic segment makes artificial hip and knee joints trauma implants bone cement and other orthopedic supplies. The Neurotechnology & Spine segment provides rods screws and artificial discs for spinal surgeries as well as coils and stents for cerebral vascular procedures. Stryker's products are marketed globally to doctors hospitals and other health care facilities via direct sales personnel and distributors.

HISTORY

Stryker was founded in 1941 by Dr. Homer Stryker an orthopedic surgeon who had invented several orthopedic devices. It was incorporated in 1946 as a Michigan company. The company expanded through organic measures and occasional acquisitions over the following decades while the Stryker family kept a hand in its operations.

Beginning in 2009 Stryker set out to further diversify its operations through acquisitions. In 2010 Stryker purchased supportive surface maker (think: beds and tables) Gaymar Industries for approximately $150 million in cash. The two companies were already well-acquainted through a longstanding supply and sales agreement in the US.

Its $1.5 billion acquisition of Boston Scientific's neurovascular division in 2011 added minimally invasive devices (such as coils stents and balloon catheters) for the treatment of cerebral conditions such as brain aneurysms and hemorrhagic and ischemic strokes.

Stryker further boosted its neurovascular operations later that year when it acquired Concentric Medical a maker of clot removal products for use in ischemic stroke procedures for some $135 million. Following these acquisitions Stryker rearranged its operating structure from two divisions into three: Reconstructive MedSurg Equipment and Neurotechnology and Spine.

The company's OP-1 bone growth product was so successful that in 2011 the company sold the product franchise to Olympus for $60 million. During 2011 Stryker acquired synthetic bone graft material maker Orthovita for some $304 million in cash. It also spent $150 million to purchase France's Memometal Technologies for its in hand and foot device products.

EXECUTIVES

Group President Orthopaedics, David K. Floyd, $575,000 total compensation

Chairman President And Ceo, Kevin A. Lobo, $1,129,167 total compensation

Group President Global Quality And Operations, Lonny J. Carpenter, $497,500 total compensation

Group President Medsurg And Neurotechnology, Timothy J. Scannell, $610,333 total compensation

Vp And Cio, Bijoy Sagar

Vp Communications Public Affairs And Strategic Marketing, Yin C. Becker

Group Cfo Medsurg & Neurotechnology (msnt), Glenn Boehnlein, $517,333 total compensation

President Asia Pacific, Graham A. McLean

Vice President Human Resources, Art Hartman

Vice President Global Business Development, David Fabricant

Auditors: Ernst & Young LLP

LOCATIONS

HQ: Stryker Corp
2825 Airview Boulevard, Kalamazoo, MI 49002
Phone: 269 385-2600   **Fax:** 269 385-1062
Web: www.stryker.com

2017 Sales

	$ mil.	% of total
US	9,059	73
Europe Middle East & Africa	1,567	13
Asia/Pacific	1,413	11
Other	405	3
Total	**12,444**	**100**

PRODUCTS/OPERATIONS

2017 Sales by Segment

	$ mil.	% of total
MedSurg		
Medical	1,969	16
Instruments	1,678	14
Endoscopy	1,652	13
Sustainability	258	2
Orthopaedics		
Knees	1,595	13
Trauma & Extremities	1,478	12
Hips	1,303	10
Other	337	3
Neurotechnology & Spine		
Neurotechnology	1,423	11
Spine	751	6
Total	**12,444**	**100**

COMPETITORS

Arthrex	Olympus
CONMED Corporation	Penumbra
DePuy	Philips Electronics
DePuy Spine	STERIS
Globus Medical	Smith & Nephew
Hill-Rom Holdings	Synthes

Medline Industries
Medtronic
Medtronic Sofamor
 Danek
NuVasive

Terumo Medical
 Corporation
ZOLL
Zimmer Biomet

HISTORICAL FINANCIALS
Company Type: Public

Income Statement
FYE: December 31

	REVENUE ($ mil.)	NET INCOME ($ mil.)	NET PROFIT MARGIN	EMPLOYEES
12/18	13,601	3,553	26.1%	36,000
12/17	12,444	1,020	8.2%	33,000
12/16	11,325	1,647	14.5%	33,000
12/15	9,946	1,439	14.5%	27,000
12/14	9,675	515	5.3%	26,000
Annual Growth	8.9%	62.1%	—	8.5%

2018 Year-End Financials
Debt ratio: 36.21%
Return on equity: 32.75%
Cash ($ mil.): 3,616
Current ratio: 2.02
Long-term debt ($ mil.): 8,486

No. of shares (mil.): 374
Dividends
 Yield: 1.2%
 Payout: 59.5%
Market value ($ mil.): 58,687

	STOCK PRICE ($) FY Close	P/E High/Low		PER SHARE ($) Earnings	Dividends	Book Value
12/18	156.75	19	15	9.34	1.93	31.33
12/17	154.84	59	43	2.68	1.75	26.62
12/16	119.81	28	20	4.35	1.57	25.47
12/15	92.94	27	24	3.78	1.42	22.82
12/14	94.33	71	55	1.34	1.26	22.74
Annual Growth	13.5%	—		62.5%	11.2%	8.3%

Summit Financial Group Inc

EXECUTIVES
Senior Vice President And Chief Banking, Doug Mitchell
Senior Vice President Chief Banking Offi, Patty Owens
Senior Vice President Commercial Lending, Jason Hicks
Executive Vice President Of Business Development, Jack Rossi
Senior Vice President And Trust Officer, Julie H Johnson
Vice President Commerical Loans, Anna B Abbey
Vice President Of Mortgage Originations, Oguz Sengul
Vice President Commerical Loans, Anna Abbey
Senior Vice President And Trust Officer, Julie Johnson
Senior Vice President Commercial Lending, Jim Rodgers
Board Member, Scott Bridgeforth
Auditors: Yount, Hyde & Barbour, P.C.

LOCATIONS
HQ: Summit Financial Group Inc
 300 North Main Street, Moorefield, WV 26836
Phone: 304 530-1000
Web: www.summitfgi.com

COMPETITORS
Allegheny Bancshares
BB&T
F & M Bank
Fauquier Bankshares

Highlands Bankshares
 Inc.
SunTrust

HISTORICAL FINANCIALS
Company Type: Public

Income Statement
FYE: December 31

	ASSETS ($ mil.)	NET INCOME ($ mil.)	INCOME AS % OF ASSETS	EMPLOYEES
12/17	2,134	11	0.6%	349
12/16	1,758	17	1.0%	251
12/15	1,492	16	1.1%	231
12/14	1,443	11	0.8%	222
12/13	1,386	8	0.6%	224
Annual Growth	11.4%	10.2%	—	11.7%

2017 Year-End Financials
Debt ratio: 3.03%
Return on equity: 6.68%
Cash ($ mil.): 52
Current ratio: —
Long-term debt ($ mil.): —

No. of shares (mil.): 12
Dividends
 Yield: 0.0%
 Payout: 44.0%
Market value ($ mil.): 325

	STOCK PRICE ($) FY Close	P/E High/Low		PER SHARE ($) Earnings	Dividends	Book Value
12/17	26.32	28	19	1.00	0.44	16.30
12/16	27.53	18	7	1.61	0.40	14.47
12/15	11.88	8	7	1.50	0.32	13.47
12/14	11.90	9	7	1.17	0.00	15.86
12/13	9.91	10	5	0.84	0.00	14.91
Annual Growth	27.7%	—		4.5%	—	2.3%

Sunoco LP

EXECUTIVES
Ceo, Robert W Owens
Chb, Matthew S Ramsey
Pres-Coo, Joseph Kim
Gen Partner, Sunoco GP LLC
Evp-Chief Marketing Officer, Cynthia A Archer
Gen Counsel, Arnold D Dodderer
Evp Supply & Trading, Karl R Fails
Evp Mfg & Distribution, Boyd E Foster
Evp Operations East, S Blake Heinemann
Cfo, Thomas R Miller
Evp Operations West, R Bradley Williams
Auditors: Grant Thornton LLP

LOCATIONS
HQ: Sunoco LP
 8111 Westchester Drive, Suite 400, Dallas, TX 75225
Phone: 214 981-0700
Web: www.sunocolp.com

COMPETITORS
CITGO
Chevron
ConocoPhillips
Exxon Mobil
Hess Corporation
Royal Dutch Shell

Shell Oil Products
Sinclair Oil
Sunoco
TOTAL
Valero Energy

HISTORICAL FINANCIALS
Company Type: Public

Income Statement
FYE: December 31

	REVENUE ($ mil.)	NET INCOME ($ mil.)	NET PROFIT MARGIN	EMPLOYEES
12/17	11,723	149	1.3%	—
12/16	15,698	(406)	—	—
12/15	16,005	807	1.4%	—
12/14*	1,889	35	1.9%	—
08/14	3,492	22	0.6%	—
Annual Growth	49.7%	87.8%	—	—

*Fiscal year change

2017 Year-End Financials
Debt ratio: 51.41%
Return on equity: 6.71%
Cash ($ mil.): 28
Current ratio: 3.74
Long-term debt ($ mil.): 4,284

No. of shares (mil.): 116
Dividends
 Yield: 0.1%
 Payout: 971.1%
Market value ($ mil.): 3,297

	STOCK PRICE ($) FY Close	P/E High/Low		PER SHARE ($) Earnings	Dividends	Book Value
12/17	28.40	93	67	0.34	3.30	19.36
12/16	26.89	—	—	(5.26)	3.27	19.16
12/15	39.61	48	28	1.11	2.68	31.25
12/14*	49.77	70	38	0.85	2.05	32.60
08/14	57.08	58	29	1.02	1.98	(0.00)
Annual Growth	(20.8%)	—		— (30.7%)	18.7%	

*Fiscal year change

SunTrust Banks Inc

Through its flagship SunTrust Bank subsidiary SunTrust Banks operates some 1300 branches in about a dozen southeastern and mid-Atlantic states. With total assets of some $200 billion and total deposits of over $160 billion the bank offers standard retail and commercial services such as credit deposit and investment services. SunTrust also operates subsidiaries that offer mortgage wealth and investment management insurance investment banking and brokerage services. The namesake of the Atlanta Braves? SunTrust baseball park the company was also behind the original "Coke float" when it underwrote the public flotation of Coca-Cola in the 1920s and was one of the soda company's largest shareholders. In February 2019 SunTrust agreed to merge with financial services holding company BB&T in a $66 billion deal.

HISTORY
SunTrust was born from the union of old-money Georgia and new-money Florida. Founded in 1891 the Trust Company of Georgia (originally Commercial Traveler's Savings Bank) served Atlanta's oldest and richest institutions. It helped underwrite Coca-Cola's IPO in 1919; the bank's ownership stake in Coke stemmed from its early involvement with the beverage maker.

Beginning in 1933 Trust acquired controlling interests in five other Georgia banks. As regulation of multibank ownership relaxed in the 1970s Trust acquired the remaining interests in its original banks and bought 25 more. At the height of the Sun Belt boom in 1984 Trust was the most profitable bank in the nation. The next year it united with Sun Banks.

Sun Banks was formed in 1934 as the First National Bank at Orlando. It grew into a holding company in 1967 and in the early 1970s helped assemble the land for Walt Disney World. The Sun name was adopted in 1973.

Under president and CEO Joel Wells Sun Banks began an acquisition-fueled expansion within Florida. Between 1976 and 1984 Sun Banks' approximate asset growth was an astronomical 500% and branch count grew fivefold (51 to 274).

After a lingering courtship Sun and Trust formed a super holding company over the two organizations. When the marriage was consummated in 1985 Sun brought a dowry of $9.4 billion in assets and Trust contributed $6.2 billion. Trust's chairman Bob Strickland became chairman and CEO for the new Atlanta-based SunTrust and Wells became president.

In 1986 SunTrust bought Nashville Tennessee-based Third National Bank the #2 banking company in the Volunteer State. But problems with Tennessee real estate loans plagued SunTrust. In 1990 it increased the amount of loans it wrote off; the bank's ratings suffered because of nonperforming loans on properties in overbuilt Florida. While nonperforming assets decreased in Tennessee in 1991 they climbed in Florida and Georgia.

Strickland stepped down as chairman and CEO in 1990. Wells died in 1991 and James Williams a conservative banker who instilled strict fiscal management in the Trust banks became chairman and CEO. Under his direction the company reduced its nonperforming assets and began diversifying its business lines.

In 1993 the bank adopted accounting rules that caused it to revalue its Coca-Cola stock from its historic value of $110000 to almost $1.1 billion. The dividends from these holdings contributed substantially to revenues.

SunTrust continued developing its nonbanking financial services: It expanded its investment services outside its traditional southern US market and bought Equitable Securities (now SunTrust Equitable Securities) in 1998. That year president Phillip Humann succeeded Williams as chairman and CEO. SunTrust also nearly doubled its branch count when it bought Crestar Financial a banking powerhouse in the mid-Atlantic and Southeast.

In 1999 the company created a new trust business to serve high-net-worth clients and it consolidated its 27 banking charters in six states into one based in Georgia the following year. In 2001 SunTrust made an unsolicited offer for Wachovia which was on track to be acquired by First Union. After a heated proxy campaign Wachovia's board of directors and shareholders voted down SunTrust's bid. Also that year the company bought the institutional business of investment bank Robinson-Humphrey a unit of Citigroup's Salomon Smith Barney.

SunTrust bought National Commerce Financial in 2004 for some $7 billion. The deal helped the bank expand in existing territories as well as provide entry into the growing North Carolina market where SunTrust had been conspicuou

EXECUTIVES

Corporate Evp General Counsel And Corporate Secretary, Raymond D. Fortin, age 65
Corporate Evp And Chief Risk Officer, Jerome T. Lienhard, age 61, $516,667 total compensation
Chairman And Ceo, William H. (Bill) Rogers, age 60, $1,000,000 total compensation
Corporate Evp And Chief Human Resources Officer, Margaret L. Callihan, age 62
Vice Chairman And Consumer Segment Executive, Mark A. Chancy, age 54, $658,333 total compensation

Evp And Cfo, Aleem Gillani, age 56, $611,667 total compensation
Corporate Evp And Efficiency And Strategic Partnerships Executive, Thomas E. (Tom) Freeman, age 67, $600,000 total compensation
Wholesale Segment Executive, Hugh S. (Beau) Cummins, age 55
Evp And Cio, Anil Cheriyan, age 60, $500,000 total compensation
Evp And Chief Marketing Officer, Susan S. Johnson, age 52
Senior Vice President And Corporate Director Tax, Terry Vacheron
Vice President Consumer Deposit Pricing Analyst, Brian Raack
First Vice President, Greg Greer
First Vice President Bsa And Aml Risk Manager 2, Charlie M Hettler
Vice President Senior Counsel, Lisa Scheid
First Vice President Sales And Marketing, Julie Cooper
First Vice President, Ruthie B Cook Cherry
Vice President Information Technology Infrastructure, Richard Willman
Vice President Risk Review, Kathy Gearing
Vice President Information Technology, Nancy Kearney
First Vice President, Frank Anderson
First Vice President, Edana Hough
Vice President Commercial Business Banking Relationship Manager, Jamie Cavileer
Vice President, Adam Humphreys
Gvp, Celia Mackenzie
Assistant Vice President, John Logan
Assistant Vice President, David Massey
First Vice President, Jasmine Grant
Assistant Vice President Talent Acquisition, Doug Ledford
Assistant Vice President Relationship Manager Commercial Banking, Hilliary Jones
Senior Vice President, Mark Kawa
First Vice President, Shefali Patel
Executive Vice President, Mark Smith
Senior Statistician Assistant Vice President, Naveen Manivannan
Senior Vice President Commercial Division, Parker Harrington
First Vice President, Kim Krause
First Vice President, Siba Noble
Vice President Business Project Manager, Jean Castleberry
Vice President, Matthew Bohlen
First Vice President, Stephanie White
Executive Vice President, James Gaffney
Vice President Marketing Manager Tampa Bay, Jan Berger
Senior Vice President Private Client Advisory Services, Lori Caumeil
Vice President Risk And Compliance Wealth And Investment Management Officer, Teresa Brightly
First Vice President, Diana Pollidore
Senior Vice President Senior Credit Officer, H Blalock
Assistant Vice President Commercial Banking, Jeffrey Charron
Senior Vice President Risk And Compliance Infrastructure Wealth And Investment Management Officer, Kruti Bolick
Group Vice President, Christie Slaton
Vice President, Peter Coley
Senior Vice President Regional Sales Director Of S, Mike Ohare
Vice President, Lanette Davis
Group Vice President, Greg Boyd
Senior Vice President Human Relations, Melinda Schwartz
Assistant Vice President, Beth Kazinski
Group Vice President And Manager Database Marketing, Mike Register

First Vice President Business Banking, Karen Chevalier
Group Vice President, Kim Karamarkovich
Group Vice President, Debra Tuthill
Vice President, Brian Harhai
Senior Vice President, Mark Hughes
First Vice President, David Vickory
Senior Vice President Special Assets Division, Lawrence Perry
Assistant Vice President, Stephanie A Snyder
Assistant Vice President Branch Manager V, Travis Teal
Vice President And Trust Advisor, Renee Frederiksen
Vice President, Patrick Mcintyre
Assistant Vice President And Client Service Manager, Sharon Freeman
Vice President, Terri Leclaire
Vice President, Kar HO
First Vice President, Jim Pallotta
Vice President, Erika Gullo
Vice President And Operations Manager, Melanie Zeiner
Vice President, Chris Anderson
Vice President, Greg Cavinder
First Vice President Human Resources Business Partner, Lisa Jenn
Assistant Vice President Portfolio Administrator, Jessica Sifford
First Vice President: Suntrust Bank Ees Program Manager, Clark Rodgers
Assistant Vice President, Cris Reed
Group Vice President And Retail Area Manager, Shelly Butler
Vice President, Loretta Badgett
Assistant Vice President Branch Manager, Susan Lucy
First Vice President, Suzanne Pellicci
Vice President, RCraig George
Executive Vice President And Senior Loan Officer, Patty Collins
First Vice President, Sarah Rich
Vice President Of Operation, Shelly Haas
Senior Vice President, Ann Brewer
Vice President, Robert Duckworth
First Vice President, Faye Cohen
Vice President Risk Data Startegy And Analytics, Saroj Das
Vice President Profitability Manager, Ann Peck
Vice President Client Advisor_med Specialist Group, Viji Kumar
First Vice President Global Outsourcing, David Braxton
Vice President Operations, James Okonewski
Senior Vice President Bank Operations Manager, Omar Arredondo
Vice President Business Banking Relationship Manager, Thais Sullivan
First Vice President, Mary Davis
First Vice President, Susan Thurman
Vice President, Charles Hubbard
Vice President, Donna Northern
Senior Vice President Model Validation Executive, Alex Shenkar
Vice President Branch Manager, Charles Johnson
First Vice President, Scott Allen Scott Allen
Senior Vice President Production Services, Derrick Buie
Vice President Private Wealth Management Underwriter, Claire Campbell
Assistant Vice President Financial Analyst, Frank Bornemann
First Vice President And Counsel, Sarah Roback
First Vice President, Kelley Matthews
Vice President Financial Advisor, Ahmet Kildis
Vice President Mortgage Project Management Office Project Manager, Cpm Simpkins
Senior Vice President, Juan Caballero
Senior Vice President And Head Of Financial Planning, Joe Sicchitano

Senior Vice President, Nicholas Blake
Vice President Advertising Manager, Kristin O'Neil
Assistant Vice President, Christina Read
Vice President Wealth Planner, Eileen Kane
Vice President Compliance Consultant, Desni Kelley
Vice President Financial Advisor, Adam Callender
Vice President Financial Advisor, Paul Kurrasch
Assistant Vice President; The Premier Program, Jonathan Wang
First Vice President Corporate Operational Risk Management Analyst, Jeff Hammack
Executive Vice President Robinson Humphrey, Bill Kleven
Vice President, Stephen Lanese
Avp Financial Intelligence Unit, Aida Ocana
Svp Business Credit Card Product Manager, Angela Baker
Senior Accountant Assistant Vice President, Matthew Pressey
Auditors: Ernst & Young LLP

LOCATIONS

HQ: SunTrust Banks Inc
303 Peachtree Street, N.E., Atlanta, GA 30308
Phone: 800 786-8787
Web: www.suntrust.com

PRODUCTS/OPERATIONS

Selected Services
Auto & Home Insurance
Commercial Insurance
Commercial Investment Banking
Credit Cards
Mobile Banking
Money Services
Online Banking
Personal Checking
Personal Credit Cards
Private Wealth Management
Savings Money Markets & CDs

2017 Sales by Revenue Type

	$ mil.	% of total
Interest Income	6,387	66
Non-Interest Income	3,354	34
Total	**9**	**100**

COMPETITORS

BB&T	First Horizon
BBVA Compass	First Republic (CA)
Bancshares	JPMorgan Chase
BBX Capital	KeyCorp
BancorpSouth	M&T Bank
Bank of America	PNC Financial
Bank of the West	Regions Financial
Capital One	Santander BanCorp
Citigroup	Synovus
Citizens Financial	U.S. Bancorp
Group	Wells Fargo
Comerica	Zions Bancorporation
Fifth Third	
First Citizens	
BancShares	

HISTORICAL FINANCIALS

Company Type: Public

Income Statement   FYE: December 31

	ASSETS ($ mil.)	NET INCOME ($ mil.)	INCOME AS % OF ASSETS	EMPLOYEES
12/17	205,962	2,273	1.1%	23,785
12/16	204,875	1,878	0.9%	24,375
12/15	190,817	1,933	1.0%	24,043
12/14	190,328	1,774	0.9%	24,638
12/13	175,335	1,344	0.8%	26,281
Annual Growth	**4.1%**	**14.0%**	**—**	**(2.5%)**

Debt ratio: 4.75%   No. of shares (mil.): 470
Return on equity: 9.32%   Dividends
Cash ($ mil.): 5,374   Yield: 0.0%
Current ratio: —   Payout: 29.5%
Long-term debt ($ mil.): —   Market value ($ mil.): 30,417

	STOCK PRICE ($) FY Close	P/E High/Low	PER SHARE ($) Earnings	Dividends	Book Value
12/17	61.60	15 12	4.47	1.32	53.41
12/16	54.85	16 9	3.60	1.00	48.08
12/15	42.84	13 10	3.58	0.92	46.07
12/14	41.90	13 11	3.23	0.70	43.86
12/13	36.81	15 11	2.41	0.35	39.96
Annual Growth	**15.1%**	**— —**	**16.7%**	**39.4%**	**7.5%**

SUTTER HEALTH

Whether you drink too much in Wine Country hit some rough waters off the Marin Headlands or trip during a hike through the redwood forest it's likely Sutter Health is just a stone's throw away. The Northern California not-for-profit health care system is one of the nation's largest with more than 4300 acute care beds. After being formed through the merger of Sutter Health and California Healthcare System Sutter Health now caters to residents of more than 100 communities from the California Bay Area to the beaches of Hawaii. Its services are provided through affiliated doctors from a host of health care facilities including acute care hospitals home health networks and skilled nursing facilities.

Operations
Sutter Health affiliates provide acute care services health education home health care hospice care adult day care prenatal clinics immunization services and other specialized health care services.

The system's health plan network includes 25 hospitals and campuses and dozens of other facilities with more than 5000 providers serving some 40000 members throughout Northern California.

In 2015 the system reported more than 11 million outpatient visits; 190054 discharges; and 797057 emergency room visits.

Geographic Reach
Sutter Health structures its governance into two geographic regions across Northern California: the Bay Area (which also includes Hawaii) and the Valley. Each area has its own board that oversees affiliates within the region.

Financial Performance
In 2015 Sutter Health reported $11 billion in total operating revenue up from $10.2 billion in 2014. Net income from operations totaled $287 million in 2015 a 10% decline from 2014; the drop in income was driven by higher operating expenses and a decline in investment income.

Strategy
In 2016 Sutter Health announced plans to open dialysis and chemotherapy infusion centers at its Sutter Coast Hospital facility in Crescent City.

However the system made waves that year when it said it would shutter its Alta Bates Summit Medical Center in Berkeley by 2030. Community members responded by calling for Sutter Health to keep the hospital open; Sutter plans to consolidate the facility's services with those of its sister campus Summit Medical Center which is three miles away. The move to close a hospital which has seen decreased patient stays is not unusual as many health systems are pushing to broaden their service offerings on an outpatient basis.

Like most other health care organizations across the country Sutter Health is using technology to keep its patients informed about their medical care. The company is part of a national group participating in a program called Care Everywhere a technology that enables medical teams from separate hospitals and clinics to share a patient's medical records at the time he or she receives care. Through this technology Sutter Health is linked with UC Davis Health System Stanford Health Care and Santa Cruz County Health Services to share vital patient information.

EXECUTIVES

President And Ceo, Sarah Krevans, age 59
Svp And Cfo, Robert D. (Bob) Reed, age 66
President Sutter Health Central Valley Region, David P. Benn
President Sutter Health East Bay Region, David Bradley
Svp And Cio, Jonathan (Jon) Manis
Svp; Executive Officer Sutter Medical Network, Jeffrey Burnich
President Sutter Health West Bay Region, Mike Cohill
President Sutter Health Sacramento Sierra Region, James E. Conforti
President Sutter Health Peninsula Coastal Region, Jeff Gerard
Ceo Sutter Solano Medical Center, Abhishek Dosi
Vice President Finance And Treasurer, Svend Ryge
Revenue Cycle Vice President, Suzy Cliff
Vice President, Theresa Frei
Director Managed Care, Jan Voge
Senior Vice President And General Counse, Florence Di Benedetto
Vice President Strategy And Business Development Sutter Health Medical And Markets Network, Todd Smith
Legal Secretary, May Vang
Medical Director, Jeff Jenkins
Medical Director Pediatric Gastroenterology, Fadi Haddad
Chair, Geraldine R. Brinton

LOCATIONS

HQ: SUTTER HEALTH
2200 RIVER PLAZA DR, SACRAMENTO, CA 958334134
Phone: 916 733-8800
Web: WWW.SUTTERHEALTH.ORG

Selected Hospitals
Alta Bates Summit Medical Center (Berkeley Oakland)
California Pacific Medical Center (San Francisco)
Eden Medical Center (Castro Valley)
Kahi Mohala (Ewa HI)
Marin General Hospital (Greenbrae)
Memorial Hospital Los Banos (Los Banos)
Memorial Medical Center (Modesto)
Menlo Park Surgical Hospital
Mills-Peninsula Health Services (Burlingame)
Novato Community Hospital (Novato)
Sutter Amador Hospital (Jackson)
Sutter Auburn Faith Hospital (Auburn)
Sutter Coast Hospital (Crescent City)
Sutter Davis Hospital (Davis)
Sutter Delta Medical Center (Antioch)
Sutter Lakeside Hospital (Lakeport)
Sutter Maternity & Surgery Center of Santa Cruz
Sutter Medical Center (Sacramento)
Sutter Medical Center of Santa Rosa
Sutter Roseville Medical Center
Sutter Solano Medical Center (Vallejo)
Sutter Tracy Community Hospital (Tracy)

PRODUCTS/OPERATIONS

Selected Operations (Northern California Southern Oregon and Hawaii)
Acute Care Hospitals
Neonatal Intensive Care Units
Cancer Centers
Cardiac Centers
Acute Rehabilitation Centers
Medical Foundations
Trauma Centers
Behavioral Health Services
Education Centers and Physician Training Programs
Express Medical Clinics
Home Health and Hospice Services
Long-term Care Centers
Medical Research Centers
Occupational Health Services
Long-Term Care Centers
Irene Swindells Alzheimer's Residential Care Center San Francisco
Sutter Oaks Nursing Center Sacramento
Sutter Senior Care PACE Program Sacramento
Cancer Centers
Alta Bates Summit Comprehensive Cancer Center Berkeley and Oakland
California Pacific Medical Center San Francisco
Dorothy E. Schneider Cancer Center at Mills-Peninsula Health Services Burlingame
Eden Medical Center Castro Valley
Memorial Regional Cancer Center Modesto
Sutter Auburn Faith Hospital Auburn
Sutter Cancer Center Sutter Medical Center Sacramento
Sutter Cancer Center Sutter Roseville Medical Center Roseville
Sutter Solano Cancer Center Vallejo
Programs listed above are approved by the American College of Surgeons' Commission on Cancer.
Research Institutes
California Pacific Medical Center San Francisco
Palo Alto Medical Foundation Research Institute Palo Alto
Sutter Health Institute for Research and Education San Francisco
Sutter Institute for Medical Research Sacramento
Home Health and Hospice Services
Coming Home Hospice
Cohen Cormier Home Attendant & Care Management
Sutter Auburn Faith VNA & Hospice
Sutter Care at Home
Sutter Coast Home Care
Sutter Infusion & Pharmacy Services / Emeryville and Sacramento
Sutter Lakeside Home Medical Services
Sutter Lif
Sutter North Home Health Agency
VNA of the Central Valley
VNA of Santa Cruz County
Express Medical Clinics
Sutter Express Care (Three locations in Sacramento & Placer counties)

COMPETITORS

Adventist Health System West
Alta Bates Summit Medical Center
Ascension Health
California Pacific Medical Center
Children's Hospital & Research Center at Oakland
Dignity Health
HCA
Hawai'i Pacific Health
Kuakini Health System
Memorial Health Services
Providence St. Joseph Health
Rehabilitation Hospital of the Pacific
Stanford Health Care
Tenet Healthcare
UCSF Medical

HISTORICAL FINANCIALS

Company Type: Private

Income Statement — FYE: December 31

	REVENUE ($ mil.)	NET INCOME ($ mil.)	NET PROFIT MARGIN	EMPLOYEES
12/17	12,444	1,060	8.5%	48,000
12/16	11,873	422	3.6%	—
12/15	10,998	84	0.8%	—
12/14	9,715	(405)	—	—
Annual Growth	8.6%	—	—	—

2017 Year-End Financials

Debt ratio: —
Return on equity: 8.50%
Cash ($ mil.): 395
Current ratio: 0.70
Long-term debt ($ mil.): —

Dividends
Yield: —
Payout: —
Market value ($ mil.): —

SVB Financial Group

SVB Financial Group is the holding company for Silicon Valley Bank which serves emerging and established companies involved in technology life sciences and private equity and provides customized financing to entrepreneurs executives and investors in such industries. It also offers deposit accounts loans and international banking and plays matchmaker for young firms and private investors. SVB Financial also provides investment advisory brokerage and asset management services; and provides credit and banking services to wealthy individuals.

Operations

The company operates in three segments: Global Commercial Bank SVB Private Bank and SVB Capital.

Global Commercial Bank segment is comprised of Commercial Bank SVB Specialty Lending SVB Analytics and Debt Fund Investments. Commercial Bank serves commercial clients in the technology venture capital/private equity life science and cleantech industries. SVB Analytics provides equity valuation services to private companies and venture capital/private equity firms while Debt Fund Investments has investments in debt funds.

SVB Private Bank provides personal financial solutions for consumers while its capital arm SVB Capital focuses primarily on funds management.

As part of its lending activities Silicon Valley Bank sometimes pursues warrants to purchase equity stakes in its clients. About 80% of the bank's loan portfolio is dedicated to commercial loans with about half of those going to software and internet companies and another 25% of commercial loans going toward private equity or venture capital firms. Traditionally focused on up-and-coming firms the bank has implemented a strategy of courting larger later-stage clients.

Geographic Reach

SVB Financial has 28 offices in the US as well as seven branches in China India Israel and the UK.

Sales and Marketing

SVB Financial's clients are primarily venture capital and private equity professionals. Its customers include Active Power Coskata EnerNOC Joule and Solexant.

Financial Performance

SVB's revenue grew for its fifth straight year with revenue rising by 4% to $1.46 billion in 2014. Though nearly all income streams grew the main drivers of growth came from higher interest income from investment securities and loans as average deposit and loan balances grew respectively. A 130% boost in net gains on derivative instruments also contributed significantly to the company's top line.

Despite higher revenue net income reversed course in 2014 and fell by 12% to $478.72 million. The drop was mostly because SVB paid higher compensation and benefits as it gave its employees market-adjusted raises and hired 146 new staff members to support its product development operational sales advisory and commercial banking operations and initiatives.

Operations provided $255.52 million or 33% more cash than in 2013 mostly because more of its earnings were cash payments as opposed to 2013 when non-cash gains on investment securities made up a larger share of earnings. The company also enjoyed higher cash generation from foreign exchange spot contracts.

Strategy

SVB Financial Group has been focused on growing its loan business and assets to drive growth in recent years. Indeed in 2014 the company's loan assets grew by 32% to $14.4 billion while deposits grew 52% to $34.3 billion — both factors that led the company to record-high revenue by the end of the year.

It's also been selectively expanding and divesting its overseas operations to focus resources on profitable segments. In early 2015 subsidiary SVB Bank agreed to sell all of its outstanding stock in its non-banking financial subsidiary SVP India Finance Private Limited to Singapore-based investment firm Temasek. In 2012 the company opened a banking branch in the UK and started a joint venture bank in China.

Mergers and Acquisitions

In January 2019 SVB Financial Group acquired Boston-based Leerink Holdings the parent company of healthcare and life science investment bank Leerink Partners. SVB paid $280 million up front and created a retention pool for employees of $60 million to be paid over five years.

Company Background

Greg Becker who joined SVB Financial in 1993 was named the company's CEO in 2011. He succeeded Ken Wilcox who became chairman and is focused on the company's efforts to expand in China including a joint venture with Shanghai Pudong Development Bank.

HISTORY

Silicon Valley Bank was founded in 1983 by Roger Smith to provide banking services to tech startups in San Jose. The bank boomed along with tech companies during the 1980s lending to the likes of Cisco Systems.

In 1990 the bank spread east to Boston's burgeoning technology alley. It also expanded into residential and commercial real estate lending. The recession of 1989 to 1991 found Silicon Valley Bancshares with an overextended loan portfolio and in 1992 the bank booked a loss due to non-performing loans; the next year it was put under federal supervision.

To rally stockholder confidence the company brought in new management and demoted Smith from chairman to vice chairman; he left the in 1995. The bank reduced its real estate lending and diversified into factoring foreign exchange and executive banking for venture capitalists and clients' upper management.

The 1995 IPO frenzy aided the company's turnaround. Silicon Valley cashed in on warrants it had taken as collateral from young companies. Regulatory supervision was lifted in 1996 and the bank soon opened offices in the Atlanta; Austin

Texas; Boulder Colorado; Phoenix; and Seattle areas.

In 1999 Silicon Valley Bancshares created a website targeted at technology firms in need of financing employees office space and equipment. However nonperforming loans began to dog the bank once again affecting profits and bringing a regulatory request to boost capital reserves.

In 2000 despite being hammered by the high-tech stock selloff the company continued to expand opening offices in West Palm Beach Florida and North Carolina's Research Triangle and successfully capitalizing its first venture fund. The following year it bought tech-focused investment bank Alliant Partners (later renamed SVB Alliant) to broaden its service offerings.

Still licking its wounds from the tech bust the company ceased lending to the entertainment industry and to churches in 2002. Silicon Valley Bancshares changed its name to SVB Financial Services in 2005.

SVB Alliant struggled with losses for years and SVB Financial explored its options including spinning the unit off to management. It ultimately decided to shut down the division which ceased operations in 2008.

EXECUTIVES

Coo, Michael L. Dreyer, age 54
Coo, Bruce E. Wallace, age 53, $398,113 total compensation
President And Ceo Svb Financial Group And Silicon Valley Bank, Gregory W. (Greg) Becker, age 51, $925,904 total compensation
Managing Director Accounting And Financial Reporting, Michael R. (Mike) Descheneaux, age 51, $602,308 total compensation
Head Of Technology Banking, John D. China, $498,385 total compensation
Head Of Europe Middle East And Africa (emea) And President Uk Branch, Philip C. Cox, age 51
Chief Credit Officer Silicon Valley Bank, Marc C. Cadieux, age 51, $447,308 total compensation
Cfo, Daniel Beck
Chief Risk Officer, Laura Izurieta, age 57
Cio, Roger E. Leone, age 64
Vice President Market Manager, Lisa A Jung
Senior Vice President, Dave Bhagat
Vice President, Mark Harris
Vice President, Christopher Leary
Vice President Relationship Manager, Don Chandler
Vice President Relationship Manager, Anthony R Raley
Vice President Manager Of Sales And Business Product Management, Dennis Corbett
Vice President Relationship Manager Corporate Technology, Phil Silvia
Vice President, Damarie Rodriguez
Vice President, Sam Subilia
Vice President And Foreign Exchange Trader, Patrick Chin
Vice President Regional Director, Carmella Montesdeoca
Vice President Corporate Finance, Andrea Jones
Senior Vice President And Senior Relationship Manager, Matt Maloney
Vice President, Austin Badger
Vice President Software, Alex Choy
Senior Vice President, Andy Tsao
Vice President Relationship Manager, John Peck
Vice President, Benjermin Colombo
Vice President, Patrick Scheper
Vice President, Josh Dorsey
Vice President Foreign Exchange, Joseph Landers
Vice President Relationship Manager Cleantech, Jordan Kanis
Vice President, Rob Walker
Vice President, Sarah Kwan
Vice President, Cody Nenadal

Vice President, Max Lautmann
Vice President, Dennis He
Vice President, Chelsea Hakso
Vice President Structured Finance, James Caron
Vice President Relationship Manager, Glenn Marasigan
Vice President, Jennie Bartlett
Vice President, Chase Little
Vice President Corporate Finance, Matt Kelty
Vice President, Marc Neri
Vice President, Sean Thompson
Vice President, Michael Copty
Vice President Structured Finance, Derek Almeida
Vice President, Erin Angerer
Vice President, Tyler Dietrich
Vice President Early Stage Banking, Navid Shahrestani
Vice President, Jordan Parcell
Vice President, Carly Kiser
Vice President, Aerin Lim
Vice President, AJ Fang
Vice President, Lindsey Guinn
Chairman Svb Financial Group And Silicon Valley Bank, Roger F. Dunbar, age 72
Board Member, Eric A Benhamou
Assistant Secretary And Treasurer, Lori De Leon
Board Member, Mary Miller
Auditors: KPMG LLP

LOCATIONS

HQ: SVB Financial Group
3003 Tasman Drive, Santa Clara, CA 95054-1191
Phone: 408 654-7400
Web: www.svb.com

Selected Offices
US
  Atlanta
  Austin TX
  Broomfield CO
  Chicago
  Dallas
  Irvine CA
  Menlo Park CA
  Minnetonka MN
  New York
  Newton MA
  Palo Alto CA
  Philadelphia
  Phoenix
  Pleasanton CA
  Portland OR
  Raleigh NC
  Salt Lake City
  San Diego
  San Francisco
  Santa Rosa CA
  Seattle
  St. Helena CA
  Tysons Corner VA
International
  Bangalore India
  Beijing
  Herzliya Pituach Israel
  London
  Mumbai India
  Shanghai

PRODUCTS/OPERATIONS

2016 Sales

	$ mil.	% of total
Interest		
Loans	834	51
Investment securities	359	22
Noninterest		
Net gains on investment securities	51	3
Net gains on derivative instruments	48	3
Foreign exchange fees	104	6
Credit card fees	68	4
Deposit service charges	52	3
Lending related fees	33	2
Letters of credit	25	2
Client investment fees	32	2
Other	40	2
Total	**1,649**	**100**

Selected Subsidiaries and Affiliates

Silicon Valley Bank
SVB Analytics Inc.
SVB Asset Management
SVB Business Partners (Beijing) Co. Ltd.
SVB Business Partners (Shanghai) Co. Ltd.
SVB Global Financial Inc.
SVB Global Investors LLC
SVB Growth Investors LLC
SVB India Advisors Pvt. Ltd.
SVB Israel Advisors Ltd.
SVB Qualified Investors Fund LLC
SVB Real Estate Investment Trust
SVB Securities
SVB Strategic Investors LLC
SVB Strategic Investors Fund L.P.
Venture Investment Managers L.P.

COMPETITORS

Bank of America	Heritage Commerce
Citigroup	MUFG Americas Holdings
City National	U.S. Bancorp
Comerica	

HISTORICAL FINANCIALS

Company Type: Public

Income Statement

FYE: December 31

	ASSETS ($ mil.)	NET INCOME ($ mil.)	INCOME AS % OF ASSETS	EMPLOYEES
12/17	51,214	490	1.0%	2,438
12/16	44,683	382	0.9%	2,311
12/15	44,686	343	0.8%	2,089
12/14	39,344	263	0.7%	1,914
12/13	26,417	215	0.8%	1,704
Annual Growth	**18.0%**	**22.8%**	**—**	**9.4%**

2017 Year-End Financials

Debt ratio: 1.36%	No. of shares (mil.): 52
Return on equity: 12.54%	Dividends
Cash ($ mil.): 2,675	Yield: —
Current ratio: —	Payout: —
Long-term debt ($ mil.): —	Market value ($ mil.): 12,351

	STOCK PRICE ($) FY Close	P/E High/Low	Earnings	PER SHARE ($) Dividends	Book Value
12/17	233.77	26 17	9.20	0.00	79.11
12/16	171.66	24 11	7.31	0.00	69.71
12/15	118.90	22 15	6.62	0.00	61.97
12/14	116.07	25 18	5.31	0.00	55.33
12/13	104.86	22 12	4.70	0.00	42.93
Annual Growth	**22.2%**	**— —**	**18.3%**	**—**	**16.5%**

Symantec Corp

With so much information digitized and stored on the internet the need to secure it from unwanted intruders is crucial. Symantec fulfills that need for both companies and individuals. Its Norton product has been providing consumer-based digital security for over fifteen years protecting its customers against viruses detecting attempted intrusions reducing spam and filtering unwanted content. Its Enterprise endeavors perform similar though more expansive and expedient efforts to protect companies against cyber attacks. Its products are deployed by 350000 worldwide customers including 90% of the US Fortune 1000. The past three years have been eventful as the company sold its Veritas data management business for $5.3 billion and purchased Blue Coat Systems for $4.6

billion to build up its enterprise-level business and then LifeLock for $2.3 billion to beef up is consumer identity protection offerings.

Operations

Symantec operates two business segments: Enterprise Security and Consumer Digital Safety. Enterprise generates some 60% of revenue and the rest comes from the Consumer segment.

Enterprise Security provides products and services to help companies and government institutions secure digital access and protect data. It runs global security operation centers from which cyber traffic is monitored analyzed and if necessary responded to with evasive or recovery actions. It?s approach to integrated cyber defense provides security solutions for web-based activity end user actions information protection and security for digital communications. The segment offers Secure Socket Layer (SSL) Certificates authentication mail and web security data center security data loss prevention information security endpoint security and management and encryption services.

Consumer Digital Safety helps individuals and small businesses protect themselves against such things as identity theft cyber attacks and unwanted email spam. As the internet of things (IoT) expands to include everything from home refrigerators to smart phones the opportunities for unwanted intrusions is growing exponentially. The segment?s Norton product suite provides protection across a variety of internet-connected devices such as PCs Apple MACs smart phones and networking gear. Its LifeLock product is one of the best known identity theft protection services. Symantec maintains what it calls the largest civilian database of threat indicators which allows it to reduce false positives and provide faster and better protection for customers.

Geographic Reach

Mountain View CA-based Symantec has operations in more than 40 countries throughout the Americas Europe the Middle East Africa Asia Pacific/Japan and Latin America. Hub locations include Mountain View CA Herndon VA Boston MA London UK Dublin Ireland and Singapore.

About 60% of revenue comes from the Americas roughly 25% from EMEA (Europe Middle East Africa) and the rest from the Asia Pacific region.

Sales and Marketing

Symantec sells its products through a direct sales force as well as through distributors resellers computer manufacturers and systems integrators. Its consumer products are sold to consumers through the company's e-commerce platform as well as through distributors direct marketers ISPs wireless carriers and retailers.

Financial Performance

Note: Financial figures from FY2014 forward are restated due to the divestiture of its Veritas unit (noted as discontinued operations).

Revenue in recent years has been on a slight downward trend ranging between $3.6 billion and $4.2 billion. Net income was profitable and flat for several years before jumping to nearly $2.5 billion in FY2016 (due in part to the Veritas sale) before dipping into negative territory in FY2017 (due to acquisitions).

For FY2017 (ended March 31 2017) revenue rose 12% to $4.0 billion largely from the inclusion of sales from the acquired Blue Coat network protection business. Sales in the consumer segment were flat for the year.

Net income in FY2017 dove into negative territory for the first time since 2009 ending the year at a $106 million loss. The Blue Coat purchase brought with it increased amortization charges and restructuring costs and an uplift in general and administrative expenses all of which contributed to a sizeable uptick in total operating expenses. The LifeLock purchase occurred late in the fiscal year

and added expenses as well but in much smaller proportion than the Blue Coat activity.

Cash on hand at the end of FY2017 was $4.2 billion down from the previous year?s $6.0 billion. The biggest cash transactions revolved around the Blue Coat and LifeLock purchases for which Symantec issued $6.1 billion in new debt to help pay the $6.7 billion acquisition costs. Operating activities used $220 million of cash due to the net income loss and an atypically large tax bill.

Strategy

In the past few years Symantec refocused its entire business on security. In late 2015 it divested its ill-fitted Veritas business that it bought in 2005 and used the proceeds to help purchase BlueCoat in mid 2016 and LifeLock in early 2017. The M&A activity was expansive and operationally disruptive and its effects showed up in the company?s FY2017 financial results.

Part of the strategic reasoning behind the acquisitions was the desire to cross-sell and upsell products. Blue Coat brought with it a cache of large enterprise customers to whom Symantec can sell its other enterprise security products. LifeLock similarly brought customers (nearly 4 million) into the Symantec sphere and they are prime candidates to see the value in the company?s other security products. The consumer segment alone believes it can garner more than $700 million in cross-sell revenue over the next few years.

Symantec?s long-term view is to capture 10% of the $100 billion digital security market that it believes is comprised of the Internet of Things (IoT) data privacy cyber resources the digital economy cybercrime and cloud security.

Mergers and Acquisitions

In 2018 Symantec made two acquisitions designed to boost its security offerings for the mobile and enterprise markets. In buying Appthority Symantec gained technology for automatically assessing and analyzing threats to mobile applications and devices. Symantec's purchase of Javelin Networks broadens its capabilities to defend against Active-Directory based attacks.

Symantec acquired Fireglass a cybersecurity company in 2017. The deal was made to strengthen Symantec's products that protect corporate email and web surfing. Fireglass develops a technology called "browser isolation" which creates virtual web sites. That allows users to browse information without being affected by viruses. Companies in health care financial services and telecommunications as well as government agencies have been early users of the technology. Terms were not disclosed.

In February 2017 Symantec paid $2.3 billion for Lifelock and its identity protection and fraud software. Symantec plans to roll Lifelock's products into its own security offerings to provide a more comprehensive consumer solution set.

Also in 2017 Symantec agreed to buy Skycure which provides security technology for mobile applications. Symantec plans to add Skycure's technology into its Integrated Cyber Defense platform and products such as Norton Antivirus and other products with mobile security features. Skycure uses artificial intelligence and machine learning techniques that offers protection for mobile devices on major mobile operating systems. The Skycure technologies set Symantec up to partner with telecommunications companies in building up cyber security for their customers.

In August 2016 Symantec completed the $4.6 billion purchase of Blue Coat Systems which develops and sells cloud-based security software for corporations. Symantec also got a new CEO in the deal as Blue Coat's chief Greg Clark took the helm of Symantec.

EXECUTIVES

Evp And General Manager Enterprise Security, Balaji Yelamanchili, age 55, $536,750 total compensation

Evp General Counsel And Secretary, Scott C. Taylor, age 53, $593,939 total compensation

Evp Norton Business Unit, Francis C. (Fran) Rosch, age 53, $504,394 total compensation

Svp And General Manager Security Analytics And Research, Stephen Trilling

General Manager Network Protection Products, Ali Tabrizi

Svp And Cio, Sheila Jordan

Evp And Cfo, Nicholas R. (Nick) Noviello, age 49

Cto, Hugh Thompson

President And Coo, Michael Fey

Svp And General Manager Website Security, Roxane Divol

Ceo And Director, Gregory (Greg) Clark, age 53

Svp Worldwide Sales Engineering And Product Strategy, Bradon Rogers

Svp And Chief Human Resources Officer, Amy Cappelanti-Wolf

Vp Technology Strategy, Ken Schneider

Vice President, Steve Mann

Chairman, Daniel H. (Dan) Schulman, age 60

Auditors: KPMG LLP

LOCATIONS

HQ: Symantec Corp
350 Ellis Street, Mountain View, CA 94043
Phone: 650 527-8000
Web: www.symantec.com

2016 sales

	$ mil.	% of total
Americas	2,113	59
EMEA	894	25
Asia/Pacific/Japan	593	16
Total	**3,600**	**100**

PRODUCTS/OPERATIONS

FY2017 Sales by Segment

	$ mil.	% of total
Consumer Digital Safety	1,664	41
Enterprise Security	2,355	59
Total	**4,019**	**100**

Selected Products

Consumer Security products
    Fraud detection service
    Identity protection authentication
    Internet security
    PC tune-up
Enterprise Security products
    Endpoint protection
    Intrusion detection & prevention
    Cloud-based cyber security
    Compliance and security management
    Messaging management & encryption

Services

Maintenance and support
Training

Selected Acquisitions

LifeLock (2017 identity theft protection)
Fireglass (2017)
Skycure (2017 security for mobile apps)
BlueCoat (2016 cloud-based security offerings)
NitroDesk (2014 email app)
Clearwell Systems (2011 legal software)
Gideon Technologies (2010 public-sector security software and services)
PGP Corporation (2010 data protection services)
GuardianEdge Technologies (2010 data protection services)
MessageLabs (2008 email protection service)
PC Tools (2008 privacy and security software)
Company-i (2006 financial data-center services)
IMlogic (2006 enterprise instant messaging)
BindView Development (2006 IT security compliance software)

Sygate Technologies (2005 network-access control services)
WholeSecurity (2005 antivirus software)
Veritas Software (2005 data backup & management)

COMPETITORS

Avocent	IBM
Check Point Software	Kaspersky Lab
Cisco Systems	McAfee
CommVault	Microsoft
Comodo	RSA Security
Courion	SecureWorks
F-Secure	Sophos
F5 Networks	Trend Micro
Google	
Hewlett Packard Enterprise	

HISTORICAL FINANCIALS

Company Type: Public

Income Statement

FYE: March 30

	REVENUE ($ mil.)	NET INCOME ($ mil.)	NET PROFIT MARGIN	EMPLOYEES
03/18	4,834	1,138	23.5%	11,800
03/17*	4,019	(106)	—	13,000
04/16	3,600	2,488	69.1%	11,000
04/15	6,508	878	13.5%	19,000
03/14	6,676	898	13.5%	20,800
Annual Growth	(7.8%)	6.1%	—	(13.2%)

*Fiscal year change

2018 Year-End Financials

Debt ratio: 31.89%
Return on equity: 26.82%
Cash ($ mil.): 1,774
Current ratio: 1.10
Long-term debt ($ mil.): 5,026

No. of shares (mil.): 624
Dividends
  Yield: 0.0%
  Payout: 17.6%
Market value ($ mil.): 16,130

	STOCK PRICE ($) FY Close	P/E High/Low		PER SHARE ($) Earnings	Dividends	Book Value
03/18	25.85	18	14	1.70	0.30	8.05
03/17*	30.68	—	—	(0.17)	0.30	5.74
04/16	18.41	7	4	3.71	4.60	6.01
04/15	23.55	21	16	1.26	0.60	8.68
03/14	19.79	21	14	1.28	0.60	8.34
Annual Growth	6.9%	—	—	7.4%	(15.9%)	(0.9%)

*Fiscal year change

Synchrony Financial

Auditors: KPMG LLP

LOCATIONS

HQ: Synchrony Financial
  777 Long Ridge Road, Stamford, CT 06902
Phone: 203 585-2400
Web: www.synchronyfinancial.com

HISTORICAL FINANCIALS

Company Type: Public

Income Statement

FYE: December 31

	ASSETS ($ mil.)	NET INCOME ($ mil.)	INCOME AS % OF ASSETS	EMPLOYEES
12/17	95,808	1,935	2.0%	16,000
12/16	90,207	2,251	2.5%	15,000
12/15	84,135	2,214	2.6%	12,000
12/14	75,707	2,109	2.8%	11,000
12/13	59,085	1,979	3.3%	9,333
Annual Growth	12.8%	(0.6%)	—	14.4%

2017 Year-End Financials

Debt ratio: 21.71%
Return on equity: 13.61%
Cash ($ mil.): 11,602
Current ratio: —
Long-term debt ($ mil.): —

No. of shares (mil.): 770
Dividends
  Yield: 0.0%
  Payout: 23.1%
Market value ($ mil.): 29,750

	STOCK PRICE ($) FY Close	P/E High/Low		PER SHARE ($) Earnings	Dividends	Book Value
12/17	39.01	16	11	2.42	0.66	18.47
12/16	36.27	14	9	2.71	0.26	17.37
12/15	30.41	14	11	2.65	0.00	15.12
12/14	29.75	11	8	2.78	0.00	12.57
Annual Growth	6.7%	—	—	(3.4%)	—	10.1%

Synnex Corp

SYNNEX connects technology sellers with buyers and helps with customer service after the sale. The company distributes PCs peripherals software and consumer electronics from manufacturers that include Dell Hewlett-Packard Panasonic Lenovo Seagate and Microsoft. SYNNEX also provides design and support services. Its Concentrix segment offers customer support services using phone chat web e-mail and digital print. The company's online services include parts catalogs configuration and ordering. In addition the company offers contract design and assembly build-to-order and configure-to-order services for manufacturers and systems integrators.

Operations

SYNNEX operates through two segments: Technology Solutions (TS) and Concentrix. The TS segment which accounts for about 90% of the company's revenue distributes IT systems peripherals system components software networking equipment CE and complementary products. It also offers data center server and storage solutions.

Concentrix accounting for the remaining sales offers a range of business process outsourcing (BPO) services to customers such as those in technical support renewals management lead management direct sales customer service back office processing and information technology outsourcing.

Geographic Reach

Based in California SYNNEX has operations in Canada China Costa Rica India Japan Mexico Nicaragua the Philippines the UK and the US. The US is the company's largest market contributing more than 70% of sales.

The company has about 40 distribution and administrative facilities in the US Canada Japan and Mexico. It has warehouses in California Georgia Virginia Illinois Texas New Jersey Ohio Florida Mississippi and Oregon. Concentrix operates about 120 delivery centers and administrative facilities in numerous countries throughout North America Europe and Asia Pacific.

Sales and Marketing

SYNNEX maintains a sales headquarters in Greenville South Carolina. A dedicated sales staff serves its large commercial government reseller and retail customers. SYNNEX also markets its products and services to smaller resellers and OEMs through dedicated regional sales teams. The company also employs dedicated product management and business development specialists who focus on selling and promoting the products and services of selected suppliers or for specific end-market verticals.

Hewlett-Packard ranks as SYNNEX's biggest OEM supplier providing nearly 20% of revenue.

Financial Performance

SYNNEX has achieved unprecedented growth over the years with revenues reaching a record-setting $14.1 billion in 2016. Profits hit $235 million in 2016 another company milestone. The historic growth was fueled by increased sales from both its Technology Solutions and Concentrix segments.

Technology Solutions sales climbed in 2016 due to strong demand for its system design and integration services partially offset by lower sales in Japan. Concentrix sales spiked due to its acquisition of Minacs in August 2016 and the expansion of services to existing customers in addition to new customer contract signings.

The rise in profits for 2016 was attributed to the surge in revenue coupled with additional income associated with investments. In addition SYNNEX's cash flow has fluctuated wildly over the years; after rising sharply to $644 million in 2015 cash flow dropped to $327 million in 2016 mainly due to unfavorable changes in inventories.

Strategy

The tech products distributor pursues a decentralized regional strategy placing its distribution facilities near reseller customers and their end-users to benefit from lower shipping costs and shorter delivery times. SYNNEX looks to expand its business into areas primarily related to its core distribution business as well as other support logistics business process outsourcing and related value-added services. While the lion's share of the company's sales are rung up in North America and Japan the company is looking to grow in India. In 2015 the company opened a second Concentrix facility in Visakhapatnam.

SYNNEX also opened a service delivery center in Bogota Colombia to provide service to a banking clients. The center is the fifth Concentrix location in Latin America. A new delivery center in Porto Portugal is to help the company increase business from existing accounts and develop new accounts in Europe.

Mergers and Acquisitions

In 2017 SYNNEX acquired the Westcon-Comstor operations in North America and South America from Datatec Ltd. for about $800 million. SYNNEX also bought a a 10% stake in Datatec's Westcon International operations in Europe and the Asia/Pacific regions for about $30 million. The deal adds Westcon-Comstor?s products and services in security unified communications and collaboration and networking to SYNNEX's operations.

In late 2016 the company acquired Canada-based The Minacs Group Pte for $420 million which is being integrated into its Concentrix business segment. The additional revenue from Minacs helped SYNNEX to achieve record revenue growth for its fiscal 2016.

EXECUTIVES

President And Ceo, Kevin M. Murai, age 55, $633,794 total compensation
President Hyve Solutions, Stephen Ichinaga, age 57
President North American Technology Solutions, Peter Larocque, age 57, $459,499 total compensation
President Synnex Canada, Mitchell P. Martin, age 55
Svp And Cio, Gary Gulmon, age 57
Svp Marketing North America, Robert L. (Bob) Stegner
Coo, Dennis Polk, age 52, $459,499 total compensation
Cfo, Marshall Witt, $437,986 total compensation
President New Age Electronics, Fred Towns

Svp And General Manager Global Business Services, Christopher (Chris) Caldwell, $441,670 total compensation

Corporate Vice President Business Operations, Gina Rugani

Associate Vice President Information Systems, Kirt Minor

Associate Vice President Of Information Systems, Bo Li

Vice President Sales, Lisa Schroeder

Vice President, Steve Heslop

Senior Vice President Partner Advocacy, Michael R Thomson

Senior Vice President Information Technology, Robert Sturycz

Vice President Marketing Canada, Mike Gazdic

Vice President Marketing, Laverne Davis

Vice President Sales, Nick Paul

Assistant Vice President Product Management, Sarah Lin

Vice President Human Resources, Debra Torette

Vice President Sales, Melanie Brown

Vice President Tsd Design And Support Services, Kirk Nesbit

Vice President Hp Enterprise Sales, Peter Montana

National Account Manager, Keith Cox

Assistant Vice President Commercial Sales Smb, John Phillips

Vice President Of Product Management, Emily Chen

Senior Vice President Sales New Age Electronics, Eric Kirkendall

Vice President Of Human Resources, Deborah Laturette

Senior Vice President Systems Integration, Steve Ichinaga

Vice President Of Enterprise Products, Doug Bone

Senior Vice President Operations, Tim Rush

Vice President Credit And Collections, Ray Poulos

Vice President Services, Joe Pittillo

National Account Manager, Chris Heim

Vice President Retail Product Management, Pierre Montminy

Board Member, Andrea Zulberti

Chairman, Dwight Steffensen, age 75

Assistant Treasurer, Michael Mccorriston

Vice Chairman, Calvin Currie

Auditors: KPMG LLP

LOCATIONS

HQ: Synex Corp
44201 Nobel Drive, Fremont, CA 94538
Phone: 510 656-3333
Web: www.synnex.com

2016 Sales

	$ mil.	% of total
United States	10,316	73
Canada	1,522	11
Other	2,223	16
Total	**14,061**	**100**

PRODUCTS/OPERATIONS

2016 Sales

	$ mil.	% of total
Technology solutions	12,490	89
Concentrix	1,587	11
Inter-segment	(16.6)	-
Total	**14,061**	**100**

Selected Subsidiaries

Concentrix Technologies Limited
ComputerLand Corporation
Concentrix Technologies (India) Private Limited
Concentrix Corporation
Concentrix Costa Rica S.A.
Concentrix Free Trade Zone S.A.
Concentrix HK Limited
Concentrix Nicaragua S.A
License Online Inc.

Sennex Enterprises Limited
SIT Funding Corporation
SYNNEX Canada Limited
SYNNEX GBS Limited
SYNNEX GBS Inc.
SYNNEX Information Technologies (Beijing) Ltd
SYNNEX Information Technologies (Chengdu) Ltd
SYNNEX Information Technologies (China) Ltd
SYNNEX Information Technologies (UK) Ltd
SYNNEX Infotec Corporation
SYNNEX Investment Holdings Corporation
SYNNEX Logistics Corporation
SYNNEX de México S.A. de C.V
SYNNEX New (BVI) Corporation
SYNNEX NewHK Limited
SYNNEX Software Technologies (HK) Limited
SYNNEX-Concentrix Corporation
SYNNEX-Concentrix UK Limited
Concentrix Europe Limited
Intelligent Outsourcing of Central America S.A
VisionMAX Limited

Selected Services

Distribution
  Contract assembly
  Distribution services
  Logistics services
Global Business Services
  Automated service renewals software
  Customer services
  Hosted renewals services software in Europe (RenewalsManager)
  Financing services
  Marketing services
  Outsourced back-office services
  Technical support services

COMPETITORS

Arrow Electronics	Premier Farnell
Avnet	Sanmina
Benchmark Electronics	ScanSource
Celestica	ServiceSource
Convergys	Tech Data
D & H Distributing	TeleTech
Flextronics	Teleperformance
Hon Hai	Westcon
Ingram Micro	Wistron
Jabil	Yosun
Plexus	

HISTORICAL FINANCIALS

Company Type: Public

Income Statement

FYE: November 30

	REVENUE ($ mil.)	NET INCOME ($ mil.)	NET PROFIT MARGIN	EMPLOYEES
11/18	20,053	300	1.5%	231,600
11/17	17,045	301	1.8%	113,600
11/16	14,061	234	1.7%	110,000
11/15	13,338	208	1.6%	72,500
11/14	13,839	180	1.3%	64,000
Annual Growth	**9.7%**	**13.7%**	**—**	**37.9%**

2018 Year-End Financials

Debt ratio: 30.10%	No. of shares (mil.): 50
Return on equity: 10.52%	Dividends
Cash ($ mil.): 454	Yield: 1.7%
Current ratio: 1.45	Payout: 20.1%
Long-term debt ($ mil.): 2,622	Market value ($ mil.): 4,093

	STOCK PRICE ($) FY Close	P/E High/Low		PER SHARE ($) Earnings	Dividends	Book Value
11/18	80.74	19	10	7.19	1.40	67.70
11/17	136.20	18	14	7.51	1.05	57.56
11/16	116.91	20	13	5.88	0.85	50.05
11/15	94.27	18	13	5.24	0.58	45.92
11/14	71.44	17	11	4.57	0.13	42.48
Annual Growth	**3.1%**	**—**	**—**	**12.0%**	**82.9%**	**12.4%**

Synovus Financial Corp

Synovus Financial has a nose for community banking. The holding company owns flagship subsidiary Synovus Bank and more than 25 locally branded banking divisions that offer deposit accounts and consumer and business loans in Alabama Florida Georgia South Carolina and Tennessee. Through more than 280 branches the bank provides checking and savings accounts loans and mortgages and credit cards. Other divisions offer insurance private banking wealth and asset management and other financial services. Nonbank subsidiaries include Synovus Mortgage Synovus Trust investment bank and brokerage Synovus Securities and GLOBALT which provides asset management and financial planning services.

Geographic Reach

Georgia-based Synovus Financial has about 130 bank branches in Georgia. Florida is the bank's second largest market with nearly 50 branches while Alabama and South Carolina are home to more than 40 each.

Financial Performance

While the bank reported a 10% decline in revenue in 2013 versus 2012 to $1.18 billion and an 81% plunge in net income (to $159.4 million) it did make some progress on the long road to recovery. Significantly the bank redeemed its obligations under TARP (troubled asset relief program) in July 2013 funding more than two-thirds of the TARP redemption with internally available funds. The firm redeemed the remainder with proceeds from offerings of its common and preferred stock. Its loan portfolio grew by about $516 million up nearly 3% versus 2012. Credit quality also continued to improve while the bank lowered expenses.

Synovus blamed its continuing revenue slide on lower interest and non-interest income in 2013 versus 2012. Interest income fell on lower income on loans and investment securities. Non-interest income suffered relative to 2012 when the bank experienced higher levels of investment securities gains and gains on private equity investments as well as a decline in income from mortgage banking.

Strategy

Synovus has been cutting costs raising capital and improving efficiency in the aftermath of the residential and commercial real estate bust that hit the southeastern US particularly hard. During the dark days of the banking crisis (2008 to 2009) the company slashed about 10% of its workforce and it cut approximately 10% more in 2010 and 2011. It also closed nearly 40 branches and consolidated others.

Also Synovus which has traditionally maintained separate charters and local boards of directors for its subsidiary banks consolidated all of its charters into one in 2010 in order to reduce complexity and improve efficiency. Synovus also consolidated by merging some of its banks in Georgia and Florida; two of its Florida banking subsidiaries (one de novo and the other formed in the merger of three subsidiaries' banking charters) have taken the Synovus Bank brand a new strategy for the company.

The company returned to profitability in 2012 and remained profitable (although considerably less so) in 2013. To right itself Synovus has deemphasized commercial real estate lending and increased its focus on commercial and industrial banking including specialized services such as asset-based lending international banking and treasury management in an effort to increase revenue. The company is courting large corporate clients in the health care manufacturing distribution financial services natural resources and transportation sectors. Among smaller enterprises it targets professional practices such as physicians attorneys and accountants particularly for its private banking business.

Mergers and Acquisitions

In May 2013 Synovus assumed $56.8 million in deposits that belonged to failed Sunrise Bank from its receiver the FDIC. As part of the deal the bank acquired $492000 in loans.

The company bought specialty finance firm Entaire Global in October 2016. Entaire a private life insurance premium finance lender primarily serves small businesses. Synovus which is aiming to diversify its loan portfolio with the purchase paid an initial $30 million; it will pay extra earnings-based payments over a period of up to five years.

EXECUTIVES

Evp And Coo, Allen J. Gula, age 63, $434,192 total compensation

Evp And Chief Risk Officer, Mark G. Holladay, age 62, $428,454 total compensation

Evp And Chief Retail Banking Officer, D. Wayne Akins, age 55

Chairman And Ceo, Kessel D. Stelling, age 62, $962,269 total compensation

Evp Financial Management Services, J. Barton Singleton, age 54, $390,606 total compensation

Evp And Chief Credit Officer, Kevin J. Howard, age 53

Evp And Chief Community Banking Officer, R. Dallis (Roy) Copeland, age 49, $412,336 total compensation

Evp And Chief Corporate Banking Officer, Curtis J. Perry, age 55

Evp And Cfo, Kevin S. Blair

Cio, Renee S. Roth

Cto, Santosh Kokate

Evp General Counsel And Secretary, Allan E. Kamensky, age 57, $417,229 total compensation

Chief Information Security Officer, Kevin P. Gowen

Vice President Regional Sales, Ron Ward

Vice President Senior Credit Analyst, Lisa McCurdy

Senior Vice President Diversity And Career Resources, Audrey Hollingsworth

Assistant Vice President Project Management Synovus Financial Corp., Theresa Radney

Vice President, Susan Pitts

Vice President Product Management, Lynn White

Executive Vice President Retail Branches Columbus Band And Trust, Carolynn Obleton

Senior Vice President And Chief Audit Executive, Stephen Sawyer

Vice President Accounting Manager, Liz Gobbel

Vice President And Portfolio Manager, Daniel Morgan

Vice President Information Systems, Cathy Reilly

Senior Vice President Facility Management Division, Mike Webb

Senior Vice President, Rob Burts

Vice President Finance Account Manager, Richard Pettit

Vice President Senior Business Analyst Lender, Alvena Pareja

Senior Vice President Director Of Correspondent Banking, Richard Lane

Senior Vice President And Director Lcbg East, Michael Sawicki

Group Vice President, Pam Wall

Senior Vice President Market Executive, Jennifer Mulligan

Senior Vice President, David O'rear

Treasurer, Joseph Lowery

Auditors: KPMG LLP

LOCATIONS

HQ: Synovus Financial Corp
  1111 Bay Avenue, Suite 500, Columbus, GA 31901
Phone: 706 649-2311
Web: www.synovus.com

Bank Branch Locations

	No.
Georgia	114
Florida	48
South Carolina	38
Alabama	37
Tennessee	11
Total	**248**

PRODUCTS/OPERATIONS

2016 Sales

	$ mil.	% of total
Interest income:		
Loans including fees	944	73
Investment securities available for sale	67	5
Trading account assets	0	-
Mortgage loans held for sale	2	-
Federal Reserve Bank balances	4	-
Other earning assets	4	-
Non-interest income:		
Service charges on deposit accounts	81	6
Fiduciary and asset management fees	46	4
Bankcard fees	33	3
Other non-interest income	34	3
Brokerage revenue	27	2
Mortgage banking income	24	2
Other fee income	20	2
Investment securities gains net	6	-
Total	**1,296**	**100**

COMPETITORS

BB&T	First Citizens
BBVA Compass	BancShares
Bancshares	First Horizon
BBX Capital	Regions Financial
BancorpSouth	SunTrust
Bank of America	Trustmark
Citigroup	Wells Fargo
Fidelity Southern	

HISTORICAL FINANCIALS

Company Type: Public

Income Statement

FYE: December 31

	ASSETS ($ mil.)	NET INCOME ($ mil.)	INCOME AS % OF ASSETS	EMPLOYEES
12/17	31,221	275	0.9%	4,541
12/16	30,104	246	0.8%	4,436
12/15	28,792	226	0.8%	4,452
12/14	27,051	195	0.7%	4,511
12/13	26,201	159	0.6%	4,696
Annual Growth	**4.5%**	**14.7%**		**(0.8%)**

2017 Year-End Financials

Debt ratio: 1.78%	No. of shares (mil.): 118
Return on equity: 9.35%	Dividends
Cash ($ mil.): 427	Yield: 0.0%
Current ratio: —	Payout: 27.6%
Long-term debt ($ mil.): —	Market value ($ mil.): 5,700

	STOCK PRICE ($) FY Close	P/E High/Low		PER SHARE ($) Earnings	Dividends	Book Value
12/17	47.94	23	18	2.17	0.60	24.91
12/16	41.08	22	14	1.89	0.48	23.95
12/15	32.38	21	15	1.62	0.42	23.16
12/14	27.09	21	2	1.33	0.24	22.34
12/13	3.60	4	3	0.91	0.28	21.23
Annual Growth	**91.0%**	—	—	**24.3%**	**21.0%**	**4.1%**

Sysco Corp

From New York to San Francisco Sysco is the #1 food distributor in the US. The company serves 500000 customers in the US and internationally in the restaurant (standalone and chain) healthcare and education and hotel industries. Its 324 distribution centers and 13400 delivery vehicles deliver branded and private-label food including fresh frozen and canned foods and specialty and meat products as well as non-food items such as silverware and utensils. The SYGMA Network focuses on supplying chain restaurants. Sysco also offers management consultancy services such as menu analysis and inventory management as well as technology solutions.

Operations

Sysco operates four segments: US Food Service; International Foodservice; Sygma; and its Other operations (consisting of its hotel supply and technology solutions).

The US Foodservice business generates some 75% of total sales and consists of its food and non-food delivery operations in the US including its custom-cut meat and seafood companies Freshpoint (the specialty produce business) and European Imports (the specialty import business). The International Food Service generates 12% of sales delivers similar product lines to its customers in Canada Europe the Bahamas Mexico Costa Rica and Panama. Both segments sell a full line of frozen foods (including meats seafood fruits and vegetables and desserts) canned and dry foods fresh meats and seafood dairy products beverages and fresh produce; as well as non-food items such as disposable napkins plates and cups tableware cookware kitchen supplies and cleaning supplies.

The SYGMA segment accounts for nearly 15% of sales and consists of Sysco's customized distribution to around 3700 customers across 15000 restaurants.

The Other segment accounts for around 2% of sales.

Geographic Reach

Houston-based Sysco operates more than 160 US distribution facilities half its total; the country accounts for around 80% of total sales. Its other facilities are found in 10 other countries notably the UK (65 sites and 5% of sales) Canada (more than 35 sites and more than 5% of sales) and France (nearly 40 sites and 3% of sales).

Sales and Marketing

At over 60% sales to restaurants account for the majority of Syco's sales. The healthcare industry accounts for around 10% of sales as do sales to education and government institutions and indeed to travel leisure and retail customers. Bakeries caterers churches and other such assorted places that sell food account for the remaining more than 10% of sales.

On a national scale Sysco jockeys for customers with rivals U.S. Foods and Performance Food Group. The company claims to serve more than 15% of the estimated $280 billion foodservice market.

Financial Performance

The company has seen an increasing trend in its net revenues over the last five years.

In fiscal 2017 (ended July 1) revenue grew a healthy 10% to $55.4 billion due almost entirely to the Brakes acquisition which helped the International Foodservice segment almost double in size. The US Foodservice segment recorded a less than 1% decline which the company attributes to the extra sales week in 2016 while SYGMA grew by 1%. Excluding the Brakes acquisition International Foodservice revenue also recorded a minor decline due also to the extra trading week in 2016.

Net income grew by 20% to $1.1 billion due to the contribution from Brakes Group cost management in Canada and lower corporate expenses.

Cash from operations increased 13% to $2.2 billion due mostly to higher net income.

Strategy

To accelerate growth Sysco has outlined two strategic priorities: enhancing customer experience and tightening operations. On the former the company believes that deeper customer partnerships will result in profitable growth in the long term. It is extending its value-added services including its menu analysis and business reviews and developing its customer-facing technology. On the latter in fiscal 2017 the company improved its Canada operations and made $20 million in compensation-related savings.

The company is also expanding internationally including in 2016 the acquisition of Brakes Group a UK-based food distributor with operations in Ireland France Sweden Spain Belgium and Luxembourg.

Mergers and Acquisitions

In 2016 Sysco completed the acquisition of UK-based Brakes Group for $3.1 billion. The acquisition substantially expanded its European operations. Brakes supplies fresh refrigerated and frozen food products as well as non-food products and supplies to foodservice customers ranging from large customers including leisure pub restaurant hotel and contract catering groups to smaller customers including independent restaurants hotels fast food outlets schools and hospitals.

HISTORY

Sysco was founded in 1969 when John Baugh a Houston wholesale food distributor formed a national distribution company with the owners of eight other US wholesalers. Joining Baugh's Zero Foods of Houston to form Sysco were Frost-Pack Distributing (Grand Rapids Michigan) Louisville Grocery (Louisville Kentucky) Plantation Foods (Miami) Thomas Foods and its Justrite subsidiary (Cincinnati) Wicker (Dallas) Food Service Company (Houston) Global Frozen Foods (New York) and Texas Wholesale Grocery (Dallas). The company went public in 1970. Sysco which derives its name from Systems and Services Company benefited from Baugh's recognition of the trend toward dining out. Until Sysco was formed small independent operators almost exclusively provided food distribution to restaurants hotels and other non-grocers.

In the 2000s Sysco acquired smaller competitors who hadn't fared quite as well during the downturn. In 2013 the company acquired foodservice operations in Nassau Bahamas; San Francisco California; San Jose California; Stockton California; Ontario Canada; Quebec Canada; Orlando Florida; Dublin Ireland; St. Cloud Minnesota; Co. Down Northern Ireland; Greenville Ohio; and Houston Texas.

Its 2012 acquisition of European Imports Ltd. helped it expand into the specialty import products segment. Purchasing Crossgar a leading privately owned foodservice supplier in Northern Ireland strengthened Sysco's presence on the island and complemented its 2009 acquisition of Pallas Foods. Other 2012 conquests include Appert's Foodservice Buchy Food Service Central Seafood Company and Metro Richelieu's Distagro. Their combined annual revenues were about $520 million.

In a sweeping move for the foodservice industry Sysco in late 2013 attempted to acquire its rival U.S. Foods for $3.5 billion. The deal would have boosted its share of the US market to about 25%

from about 18%. By combining Sysco and US Foods the company expected to achieve annual synergies of at least $600 million and estimated annual sales of approximately $65 billion. The deal was pushed back due to delays in talks with antitrust regulators and the parties terminated to planned transaction in 2015 after failing to obtain regulator approvals.

EXECUTIVES

Svp Marketing, William W. (Bill) Goetz

Vp Corporate Social Responsibility, Catherine Kayser

Vice President, Mark Palmer

Vice President, Alan W Kelso

Vp Supply Chain, Robert Howell

Vice President Information Technology, John D Holzem

Evp Merchandising And Sysco Business Services, William B. (Bill) Day, age 61, $508,333 total compensation

Evp Supply Chain, R. Scott Charlton, age 59

Svp International Foodservice Operations Americas, Scott A. Sonnemaker

Ceo, William J. (Bill) DeLaney, age 62, $1,245,833 total compensation

President And Coo, Thomas L. (Tom) Bené, age 56, $770,833 total compensation

Evp Human Resources, Paul T. Moskowitz, age 54

Svp U.s. Foodservice Operations, Greg D. Bertrand, age 54

Evp Administration And Corporate Secretary, Russell T. Libby, age 52, $590,125 total compensation

Svp Market Segment Strategy And President Sysco Ventures (cake), Brian C. Beach

Evp And Cfo, Joel T. Grade, age 48, $605,833 total compensation

Evp And Cto, Wayne Shurts, age 59, $621,602 total compensation

Vice President, Loren Gausman

Vice President Industry Relations, John T McIntyre

Vice President Human Resources Search, Mark Wisnoski

Vice President Merchandising, Brian Smith

Vice President Supply Chain Operations Enterprise Planning And Design, Theodore Murray

National Sales Manager, Heather Dunaway

Vice President Sales, Colby Morse

Vice President National Accounts, Justin Hiraki

Vice President Tax, Barbara Green

Senior Vice President Foodservice Operations (southwest Region), James Graham

Vice President Of Sales, Troy Willis

Director Media Relations Corp Comm Executive, Toni Spigelmyer

Vice President Of Real Estate Construction, Mike Downs

Vice President Human Resources, John Fraser

Vp National Sales And Corporate Officer, Rodger Smith

Vice President Of Is, Mike Adkisson

Vice President Corporate Business Development, Greg Keller

Rvp And Operations And Midwest, Mike Spadaro

Vice President Business Development National Accounts, Amy Davis-Smith

Vice President, Ron May

Vice President, Thomas Randt

Vice President Of Marketing, Sharon Armentrout

Vice President Of Finance, Alma Vega

Assistantvp Labor Relations, Charles Munn

V P Operations, Augie Mauro

National Account Manager, Amy Carman

Rvp New Business Development, Nancy Schwartz Brooks

Senior Vice President Sales And Marketing, Jim Hope

Assistant Vice President Of Marketing, Tracey Mills

Vice President Call Center, Alena Galsnte

Executive Vice President, Lisa Gough

National Account Manager, Cindy Rankin

Vice President Supply Chain Management, Masao Nishi

Vice President Operations, Charles Pilling

Vice President Sales, John Counts

Vice President Of Merchandising And Marketing, Bobbie McDonald

Vice President Human Resources, Sabrina Knouse

Vice President Brand Executive, David Montpetit

Senior Vice President Marketing, Bill Goetz

Vice President Sales, Eric Kane

Senior Vice President Merchandising, Brian Todd

Vice President, Robert Kinz

Svp And General Counsel, Adam Skorecki

National Account Manager, Kristin Smith

National Account Manager, Rhonda Alexander

Vice President Of Labor Relations, Chuck Munn

Vice President Merchandising, Kevin Mahoney

Vice President, Heike Gillman

National Account Manager, Martin Escatel

Market Vp Of Merchandising Northeast, Eric Zeilor

Vice President Information Systems, Neil Peffer

National Account Manager, Tracy Jones

Vice President Human Resources, Brett Appleberg

Vice President Of Sales, Melissa White

Vice President Sales, Walt Sharpless

Vice President Merchandising, Kathleen Griego

Vice President Total Rewards, Erin Packwood

Vp Compliance, Jose Colondres

Vp Government Relations, Gerald Kunde

Vice President Marketing, Maureen Quirk

Vp Finance And Treasurer, Gregory Keyes

Vice President Operations, Justin Dalton

Vice President Merchandising, Debra Morey

Vice President Operations, John Petrossian

Vp Operations, Kevin Proulx

Vice President Of Sales, Troy S Willis

National Sales Manager, Hugh G Morgan

Vice President Marketing, Maureen M Quirk

Vice President And Human Resources Business Partner, Terri L Clark

National Account Manager, Kelly P Garcia

Vice President Of Human Resources, John J Fraser

Vice President And Treasurer, Gregory S Keyes

Vice President Finance, Enrique X Becerra

National Account Manager, Sonnie Broxton

Vice President Of Operations, Michael R Caldwell

Vice President National Accounts Restaurant, Cary T Nelms

Vice President Facilities Construction Real Estate, Theodore W Speas

National Account Manager, Tina Morris

Vice President Sales Development And Support, L Paul Nasir

Chairman, Jacquelyn M. (Jackie) Ward, age 80

Secretary, Tim Davis

Board Member, John M Cassaday

Board Member, Richard Tilghman

Secretary, Carrie Tindal

Board Member, Nelson Peltz

Board Member, Joshua Frank

Board Member, Bradley Halverson

Board Member, Daniel Brutto

Board Member, Edward Shirley

Auditors: Ernst & Young LLP

LOCATIONS

HQ: Sysco Corp
1390 Enclave Parkway, Houston, TX 77077-2099
Phone: 281 584-1390   **Fax:** 281 584-2880
Web: www.sysco.com

2015 sales

	% of total
US	88
Canada	10
Other	2
Total	**100**

PRODUCTS/OPERATIONS

2015 sales

	% of total
Broadline	77
SYGMA	12
Other	11
Total	**100**

2015 sales

	% of total
Fresh & frozen meats	21
Canned & dry food	16
Frozen fruits vegetables bakery & other	13
Dairy products	11
Poultry	11
Fresh produce	8
Paper & disposables	7
Seafood	5
Beverage products	4
Janitorial products	2
Equipment & smallware	1
Medical supplies	1
Total	**100**

COMPETITORS

Ben E. Keith	Meadowbrook Meat
Bunzl	Company
Edward Don	Performance Food Group
Foodbuy	Reinhart FoodService
Golden State Foods	Shamrock Foods
Gordon Food Service	US Foods
MAINES	UniPro Foodservice
McLane Foodservice	

HISTORICAL FINANCIALS

Company Type: Public

Income Statement

FYE: June 30

	REVENUE ($ mil.)	NET INCOME ($ mil.)	NET PROFIT MARGIN	EMPLOYEES
06/18*	58,727	1,430	2.4%	67,000
07/17	55,371	1,142	2.1%	66,500
07/16	50,366	949	1.9%	51,900
06/15	48,680	686	1.4%	51,700
06/14	46,516	931	2.0%	50,300
Annual Growth	6.0%	11.3%	—	7.4%

*Fiscal year change

2018 Year-End Financials

Debt ratio: 46.06%	No. of shares (mil.): 520
Return on equity: 58.70%	Dividends
Cash ($ mil.): 552	Yield: 0.0%
Current ratio: 1.21	Payout: 51.1%
Long-term debt ($ mil.): 7,540	Market value ($ mil.): 35,555

	STOCK PRICE ($) FY Close	P/E High/Low	PER SHARE ($) Earnings	Dividends	Book Value
06/18*	68.29	25 18	2.70	1.38	4.82
07/17	50.33	27 23	2.08	0.97	4.49
07/16	50.73	31 21	1.64	1.23	6.22
06/15	38.37	36 31	1.15	1.18	8.85
06/14	37.85	24 20	1.58	1.14	8.99
Annual Growth	15.9%	— —	14.3%	4.9%	(14.4%)

*Fiscal year change

T Rowe Price Group Inc.

T. Rowe Price Group administers a family of mutual funds in a variety of investment styles. Traditionally oriented toward growth investing the funds offer products in many risk and taxation profiles including small- mid- and large-cap stock funds; money market funds; and bond funds both taxable and nontaxable. Other services include asset management advisory services (including retirement plan advice for individuals) corporate retirement plan management separately managed accounts variable annuity life insurance plans discount brokerage and transfer agency and shareholder services. Founded in 1937 T. Rowe Price has almost $1.1 trillion in assets under management

Operations

Investment advisory services (and the fees generated by them) are T. Rowe Price's cash cow accounting for more than 85% of its annual revenue. The company provides these services to its Price Funds to clients on separately managed or subadvised account basis and to other products such as collective investment trusts and target-date retirement trusts.

Administrative fees account for about 10% of total revenue. These fees encompass ancillary services provided to the firm's investment advisory clients. Services include mutual fund transfer agent services record keeping for retirement plans investing in non-T. Rowe Price funds and brokerage services.

Distribution and servicing fees account for less than 5% of the group's revenue.

Geographic Reach

Baltimore-based T. Rowe Price serves clients in about 45 countries around the world from offices in 15-plus countries including locations in London and Hong Kong.

Investment advisory customers from outside the US account for some 6% of the group's assets under management.

Sales and Marketing

T. Rowe Price's clients include individual and institutional investors and financial intermediaries. The company distributes its products through third-party financial intermediaries retirement plan sponsors and directly to individual and institutional investors.

Advertising expenses totaled $92 million in 2017 versus $79.9 million in 2016 and $79.7 million in 2015.

Financial Performance

With the exception of 2016 T. Rowe Price has enjoyed healthy revenue and profit growth over the past few years thanks to a bullish stock market new client inflows and most recently lowered corporate tax rates.

In 2017 revenue increased 13% to $4.8 billion as investment advisory income rose 15%. Driving that increase was an increase in assets under management and the highest net new cash flows since 2012. Administrative fees and distribution and services fees also rose but they didn't recover to the levels reached in 2015.

Despite an increase in operating expenses including compensation costs and facility costs net income grew 23% to $1.5 billion that year. This was due to the higher revenues earned and higher net investment income.

T. Rowe Price ended 2017 with $2 billion a 58% increase over the prior year. Nearly $230 million in net cash was provided by operating activities while $39 million was provided by investing activities and $462 million was provided by financing activities.

Strategy

T. Rowe Price regularly adds to its funds and strategies offerings to attract new investors and their capital. To this end the firm in 2017 added T. Rowe Price US High Yield Fund and in 2016 expanded its quantitative management-style series of strategic funds with three new equity funds.

The company offers its products through a variety of distribution channels to reach more customers. To further pursue growth T. Rowe Price has three broad strategies: expanding its product offerings strengthening its distribution channels. and investing in technology.

As the firm increasingly moves to digital offerings it has been closing certain locations (including investor centers) and consolidating operations. In 2018 it opened an innovation center where data scientists work with people developers and designers to improve its customer interfaces.

HISTORY

Thomas Rowe Price Jr. left a brokerage job at Mackubin Goodrich & Co. to found his own investment advisory firm in 1937. He pushed investing for the long haul choosing stocks of promising young companies (the firm invested in IBM in 1950). Price's company was incorporated in 1947 and was employee-owned until it went public in 1986.

The firm moved into international investments in 1979. T. Rowe Price was primarily an institutional pension fund manager until the 1980s. Creativity lagged as fund managers made investments from a list selected by the research department and the Growth Stock Fund underperformed on the S&P 500. In 1987 the firm opened its funds to individual investors.

Thereafter it introduced a slew of new funds slicing and dicing the market to appeal to the broadest possible industry and risk investment profiles including offerings in emerging market stocks and health and science stocks.

In the late 1990s however the company's value investing strategy brought lagging fund results and a stagnant corporate stock price. Nevertheless cash continued to pour into the company's funds until the collapse of Russian and Asian markets in 1998. US investors got the willies slowing asset flows to T. Rowe Price and other mutual fund managers.

In response Roche began moving the company into overseas asset management markets. In 1999 the firm joined with Sumitomo Bank (later part of Sumitomo Mitsui Financial Group) and Daiwa Securities to form asset manager Daiwa SB Investments in Japan. It also targeted Europe where the growth of private retirement plans opened up new opportunities. Nevertheless the company missed out on many of the explosive returns of the high-tech boom.

In 2000 however the high-tech bubble burst seeming to vindicate T. Rowe Price's conservative approach. That year the company bought out the remaining 50% of its Rowe Price-Fleming International asset management joint venture with Robert Fleming (which later became part of JPMorgan Chase). Also that year the company reorganized itself into holding company T. Rowe Price Group. The company's UK subsidiary received regulatory approval to expand to the European continent in 2001.

EXECUTIVES

Vice Chairman Vp And Ceo T. Rowe Price International Ltd, Edward C. Bernard, age 61, $350,000 total compensation

President And Ceo, William J. (Bil) Stromberg, age 57, $350,000 total compensation

Vp Cfo And Treasurer, Kenneth V. Moreland, age 62, $350,000 total compensation

Head International Equity, Christopher D. Alderson, age 56, $305,057 total compensation

Head Us Investment Services, Scott B. David

Head Global Technology, Nigel Faulkner

Head Global Investment Services, Robert Higginbotham

Head Equity, Eric L. Veiel, $350,000 total compensation

Head Fixed Income, Edward A. Wiese
Vp Cfo And Treasurer, Céline Dufétel
Avp Relationship Manager, Lisa Mcgarvey
Assistant Vice President Systems Consultant, Charles Popeck
Vice President Enterprise Architecture, Paul Macek
Vice President, Antonio Luna
Vice President, Steve Hartzell
Solutions Strategist Vice President, Justin Harvey
Vice President, Leigh Woodworth
Vice President T Rowe Price Associates, Renee Christoff
Assistant Vice President Global Client And Investment Reporting, Melissa Kinak
Vice President Defined Contribution Investment Specialist, Adam Brown
Vice President Trpa Trpg, Doug Talley
Assistant Vice President, Don Phillips
Vice President, Greg Franzoni
Vice President Applications Management, Jennifer Perricone
Vice President And Research Analyst, Steven Boothe
Vice President, Mark Weigman
Vice President And Crm Manager, Steve Larson
Vice President, Laura Chasney
Vice President, Steve Sullivan
Vice President Information Security Manager, Brian Porter
Vice President, Kimberly Oconnor
Vice President, Heather McPherson
Assistant Vice President Customer Sales And Services Channel Manager, Sean Rentch
Vice President, Tom McGuire
Vice President, Paul Wojcik
Vice President And Regional Relationship Manager, David Orlando
Vice President, Chris Dyer
Vice President Director Of Retail Operations, Chris Hufman
Vice President Us Investment Services Financial Institutions, Cima Gordon
Vice President, Jeff Zoller
Vice President Regional Sales Consultant, Alan Valenca
Vice President And Quantitative Analyst, Kim Dedominicis
Vice President, Andy Brooks
Assistant Vice President, Craig Sauerwalt
Vice President, Brian Brennan
Assistant Vice President, Chris Clingenpeel
Vice President International Tax, Rebecca English
Vice President, Joe Vogelpohl
Vice President Of Real Estate, Mark Ruhe
Vice President Credit Research, Ted Robson
Vice President Senior Retirement Sales Executive, Terence Howard
Vice President, Ng Jan
Assistant Vice President Equity Trader, Susan Klein
Assistant Vice President Lead Marketing Manager, Lauren Inskeep
Vice President; Global Head Of Corporate Actions, Larry Robinson
Vice President, Jim Ouartarone
Assistant Vice President Crm Marketing Analytics, Beverly Wisbar
Assistant Vice President Desktop Support Manager, Matthew Bedine
Assistant Vice President, Shawn Branstetter
Vice President And General Manager, Todd Peeples
Vice President Regional Investment Consultant, Sean Lynch
Vice President Credit Analyst, Colin Bando
Vice President And Senior Legal Counsel, Terri Doud
Vice President, Matthew Johnson
Vice President Quantitative Investment Analyst, Yongheon Lee

Vice President, Jean Fisher
Vice President Head Of Corporate Communications, Craig Smith
Vice President Regional Sales Consultant, Jonathan Lepore
Vice President Senior Relationship Manager, Guen Toste
Assistant Vice President, Melissa Shank
Vice President, Eric Bolisay
Vice President Territory Sales, Mike Shamburger
Vice President Senior Legal Counsel, Bryan Venable
Vice President Regional Investment Consultant, Tom Bauer
Vice President, Rick Zhang
Vice President, Robert Craft
Vice President, David Crotty
Vice President Head Of Fixed Income Market Structure And Electronic Trading, Alexander Sedgwick
Vice President Midwest Retirement Sales Executive, Mike Palace
Vice President, Darshini Reddivari
Vice President Relationship Manager, Ann Rogers
Vice President Enterprise Data Governance, Shonyel Lyons
Vice President Quality Assurance And Testing (gbs Investment Operations Technology), Michael Wasielczyk
Vice President Global Market Research And Insights, Todd Hiller
Vice President And Global Head Of Enterprise Service Desk, LaShaunda Allums
Vice President Architecture Distribution And Marketing, Raman Tallamraju
Vice President Senior Retirement Sales Executive, Niki Green
Vice President, Jonathan Wilkinson
Vice President, Karen Glooch
Vice President Usis Financial Institutions, Andy Goeller
Vice President Institutional Sales, Jason Widener
Chairman, Brian C. Rogers, age 63
Auditors: KPMG LLP

LOCATIONS

HQ: T Rowe Price Group Inc.
  100 East Pratt Street, Baltimore, MD 21202
Phone: 410 345-2000   Fax: 410 752-3477
Web: www.troweprice.com

Selected Locations
Domestic
  Baltimore
  Colorado Springs CO
  New York
  Owings Mills MD
  Philadelphia
  San Francisco
  Tampa
International
  Amsterdam
  Copenhagen
  Dubai
  Frankfurt
  Hong Kong
  London
  Luxembourg
  Madrid
  Melbourne
  Milan
  Singapore
  Stockholm
  Sydney
  Tokyo
  Toronto
  Zurich
US
  Baltimore
  Colorado Springs CO
  Owings Mills MD
  Tampa
  International Offices
  Amsterdam

Buenos Aires
Copenhagen
Dubai
Hong Kong
London
Luxembourg
Singapore
Sydney
Tokyo
Toronto
Zurich

PRODUCTS/OPERATIONS

2017 Sales

	$ mil.	% of total
Investment advisory services	4,287	890
Administrative fees	358	7
Distribution & servicing fees	147	3
Total	**4,793**	**100**

Selected Subsidiaries
T. Rowe Price Advisory Services Inc.
T. Rowe Price Associates Inc.
  T. Rowe Price (Canada) Inc. (US)
  T. Rowe Price Investment Services Inc.
  T. Rowe Price Retirement Plan Services Inc.
  T. Rowe Price Services Inc.
T. Rowe Price International Ltd. (UK)
  T. Rowe Price Hong Kong Limited
  T. Rowe Price Singapore Private Ltd.

COMPETITORS

AllianceBernstein	Invesco
American Century	Legg Mason
Ameriprise	MFS
Capital Group	Northwestern Mutual
FMR	Putnam
Franklin Templeton	The Vanguard Group

HISTORICAL FINANCIALS
Company Type: Public

Income Statement   FYE: December 31

	REVENUE ($ mil.)	NET INCOME ($ mil.)	NET PROFIT MARGIN	EMPLOYEES
12/17	4,793	1,497	31.2%	6,881
12/16	4,222	1,215	28.8%	6,329
12/15	4,200	1,223	29.1%	5,999
12/14	3,982	1,229	30.9%	5,870
12/13	3,484	1,047	30.1%	5,668
Annual Growth	8.3%	9.3%	—	5.0%

2017 Year-End Financials

Debt ratio: —
Return on equity: 27.65%
Cash ($ mil.): 1,902
Current ratio: 3.43
Long-term debt ($ mil.): —

No. of shares (mil.): 245
Dividends
  Yield: 0.0%
  Payout: 38.1%
Market value ($ mil.): 25,719

	STOCK PRICE ($) FY Close	P/E High/Low	PER SHARE ($) Earnings	Dividends	Book Value
12/17	104.93	17 11	5.97	2.28	23.76
12/16	75.26	16 13	4.75	2.16	20.46
12/15	71.49	18 14	4.63	4.08	19.01
12/14	85.86	19 16	4.55	1.76	20.66
12/13	83.77	21 16	3.90	1.52	18.38
Annual Growth	5.8%	— —	11.2%	10.7%	6.6%

T-Mobile US Inc

EXECUTIVES

Pres-Ceo, John J Legere
Exec Chb*, Timotheus Hottges
Coo*, G Michael Sievert
Exec V Pres-Cfo, J Braxton Carter
Exec V Pres-Cto, Neville R Ray
Exec V Pres-Gen Counsel-Sec, David A Miller
Exec V Pres Corp SEC, David R Carey
Vice President Marketing Strat, Shanna Killian
Director Marketing, Travis Warren
Vice President Business Sales, Ty Trenary
Senior Project Manager, Wah Wong
Auditors: PricewaterhouseCoopers LLP

LOCATIONS

HQ: T-Mobile US Inc
12920 S.E. 38th Street, Bellevue, WA 98006-1350
Phone: 425 378-4000
Web: www.T-Mobile.com

HISTORICAL FINANCIALS

Company Type: Public

Income Statement — FYE: December 31

	REVENUE ($ mil.)	NET INCOME ($ mil.)	NET PROFIT MARGIN	EMPLOYEES
12/18	43,310	2,888	6.7%	52,000
12/17	40,604	4,536	11.2%	51,000
12/16	37,242	1,460	3.9%	50,000
12/15	32,053	733	2.3%	50,000
12/14	29,564	247	0.8%	45,000
Annual Growth	10.0%	84.9%	—	3.7%

2018 Year-End Financials

Debt ratio: 41.54%
Return on equity: 12.22%
Cash ($ mil.): 1,203
Current ratio: 0.81
Long-term debt ($ mil.): 29,263
No. of shares (mil.): 850
Dividends
Yield: —
Payout: —
Market value ($ mil.): 54,080

	STOCK PRICE ($) FY Close	P/E High/Low	PER SHARE ($) Earnings	Dividends	Book Value
12/18	63.61	21 16	3.36	0.00	29.07
12/17	63.51	13 10	5.20	0.00	26.25
12/16	57.51	34 20	1.69	0.00	22.07
12/15	39.12	52 32	0.82	0.00	20.23
12/14	26.94	112 79	0.30	0.00	19.40
Annual Growth	24.0%	— —	82.9%	—	10.6%

Talcott Resolution Life Insurance Co

EXECUTIVES

Pres, Brion S Johnson
Sr V Pres-Cao, Peter F Sannizzaro
Sr V Pres, Mark Niland
Corporate Counsel/Legal, Leslie Soler
Administrative Assistant, Aida Ramos
Manager, Alicia Soucy
Sales Manager, Christina Lopez
Executive, Robert Flynn
Customer Representativ, Alicia Jones

Associate, David Dellaripa
Research Assistant, Johnathan McMahon
Auditors: DELOITTE & TOUCHE LLP

LOCATIONS

HQ: Talcott Resolution Life Insurance Co
One Hartford Plaza, Hartford, CT 06155
Phone: 860 547-5000
Web: www.thehartford.com

HISTORICAL FINANCIALS

Company Type: Public

Income Statement — FYE: December 31

	ASSETS ($ mil.)	NET INCOME ($ mil.)	INCOME AS % OF ASSETS	EMPLOYEES
12/17	168,732	(46)	—	—
12/16	170,346	282	0.2%	—
12/15	175,350	500	0.3%	—
12/14	191,775	676	0.4%	—
12/13	202,715	465	0.2%	—
Annual Growth	(4.5%)	—	—	—

2017 Year-End Financials

Debt ratio: —
Return on equity: (-0.63%)
Cash ($ mil.): 537
Current ratio: —
Long-term debt ($ mil.): —
No. of shares (mil.): 0
Dividends
Yield: —
Payout: —
Market value ($ mil.): —

Tapestry Inc

Tapestry is weaving together a collection of premium fashion brands. Previously Coach the company designs and makes (mostly through third parties) high-end leather goods and accessories including handbags wallets and luggage under the Coach brand. It also licenses the Coach name for watches eyewear fragrances scarves and footwear. In addition through acquisitions Tapestry owns the Stuart Weitzman (luxury women's shoes) and Kate Spade (women's apparel and accessories) brands. The company sells its wares through more than 1000 department and outlet stores (in the US and more than 45 other countries) catalogs and its websites. It also runs more than 1000 retail and factory outlet stores in North America Japan and China.

Operations

Prior to the acquisition of Kate Spade in 2017 Tapestry operated through three segments: North America (Coach) International (Coach) and Stuart Weitzman.Starting in fiscal 2018 the company will report around its brands — Coach Kate Spade and Stuart Weitzman.

The North America segment which represented more than 50% of company revenue in fiscal 2017 included sales to North American consumers through its retail stores factory stores Internet and wholesale.

Its International segment which consisted primarily of sales to consumers through company-operated stores in Japan and mainland China also accounted for revenue from Hong Kong Macau Singapore Taiwan Malaysia and Korea and e-commerce sales to those territories. Wholesale customers and distributors in approximately 35 countries also contributed to the segment's sales. The segment represented nearly 40% of sales in fiscal 2017.

The Stuart Weitzman segment consisted of global sales of the Stuart Weitzman brand acquired in 2015 and represented the remaining revenue.

Geographic Reach

Tapestry operates some 250 retail stores and about 195 factory stores in the US; some 40 retail stores and 11 factory stores in Canada; about 195 department store shop-in-shops retail stores and factory stores in Japan; and nearly 185 department store shop-in-shops retail stores and factory stores in Hong Kong Macau mainland China Singapore Taiwan Malaysia and Korea. It also sells to wholesale customers and distributors in some 45 countries.

The company also operates distribution product development and quality control locations in the US Hong Kong China South Korea Vietnam the Philippines and India. Tapestry generates over half its revenue from the US while China and Japan account for about 15% and 12%.

Sales and Marketing

Tapestry's products are sold through more than 1000 wholesale locations in the US and Canada. Top US wholesale customers include Macy's (including Bloomingdale's) Dillard's Nordstrom Saks Fifth Avenue Lord & Taylor The Bay Bon Ton Belk and Von Maur.

It operates an 850000 sq. ft. distribution and consumer service facility in Jacksonville Florida which uses a bar code scanning warehouse management system. The company's distribution center employees use handheld radio frequency scanners to read product bar codes. This allows them to more accurately process and pack orders track shipments and manage inventory. Tapestry's products are primarily shipped to its retail stores and wholesale customers via express delivery providers and common carriers and direct to consumers via express delivery providers.

To support its growth in the Asia/Pacific region Tapestry operates distribution centers through third-parties in China Hong Kong Japan Korea Malaysia the Netherlands Singapore and Taiwan.

Mergers and Acquisitions

In 2017 Tapestry acquired luxury apparel and accessories designer Kate Spade & Co. for $2.4 billion. Upon completion the company changed its name from Coach and organized operations around its three luxury brands.

EXECUTIVES

Cfo, Kevin G. Wills, age 52
Global Head Of Investor Relations And Corporate Communications, Andrea Shaw Resnick, age 57
President Global Business Development And Strategic Alliances, Ian Bickley, age 54, $800,000 total compensation
Ceo And Interim Ceo Kate Spade & Company, Victor Luis, age 52, $1,300,000 total compensation
Brand President Stuart Weitzman, Wendy Kahn
President North America And Global Marketing, Andre Cohen, age 54, $866,667 total compensation
President Chief Administrative Officer And Secretary, Todd Kahn, age 54, $708,333 total compensation
Evp And Cio, Christine (Chris) Putur
Divisional Vice President Global Merchandising, Sonia Sparolini
Vice President Product Development, Pearl Sam
Executive Vice President Operations, Angus Mcrae
Divisional Vice President Merchandising, Tessa Ito
Divisional Vice President Corporate Merchandising Factory Stores, Katy Garry
Dvp Corporate And Executive Compensation, Helen Freilich
Vice President And General Manager Singapore Malaysia, Nicolas Villeger

Vice President Real Estate Construction, Anthony Galvin

Dvp Product Development Sourcing, Sang Lee

Executive Vice President Marketing And Strategy, Stephanie Stahl

Senior Vice President Human Resources Coach, Beth Stankard

Dvp Global Trade Compliance, Frank Chioccola

Vice President Global Merchandising Women's Rtw, Marilyne Trebus

Vice President Internal Audit And Asset Protection, Lisel Donaldson

Divisional Vice President Procurement, Carl Hernas

Senior Vice President Global Procurement, Scott Easterwood

Senior Vice President Finance Global Corporate Financial Planning And Analysis, Jermoe Schumacher

Vice President Real Estate, Ira Cohen

Senior Vice President Global Public Relations And Communications, Caroline Pasquier

Vice President Associate General Counsel, Dan Ross

Divisional Vice President North America Wholesale Footwear, Giovanni Cafiso

Chairman, Jide J. Zeitlin, age 55

Board Member, Susan J Kropf

Board Member, Ivan M Menezes

Board Member, Andrea Guerra

Auditors: DELOITTE & TOUCHE LLP

LOCATIONS

HQ: Tapestry Inc
10 Hudson Yards, New York, NY 10001
Phone: 212 594-1850   Fax: 212 594-1682
Web: www.tapestry.com

2016 Stores

	% of total
North America	53
International	38
Stuart Weitzman	8
Other	1
Total	100

2016 Sales by Segment

	% of total
United States	55
Other	18
Greater China	15
Japan	12
Total	100

PRODUCTS/OPERATIONS

2016 Sales

	% of total
Women's Handbags	53
Men's	16
Women's Accessories	16
All Other Products	7
Stuart Weitzman brand	8
Total	100

Selected Products

Accessories
Footwear
Fragrance
Handbags
Jewelry
Sunglasses
Travel bags
Watches

COMPETITORS

Cole Haan	LVMH
Dooney & Bourke	Michael Kors Holdings
Etienne Aigner Group	Mulberry Group
Gucci	Nine West
Herm¨s	Prada
J. Crew	Ralph Lauren
Juicy Couture	Samsonite
Kate Spade	Tiffany & Co.
Kenneth Cole	michael kors

HISTORICAL FINANCIALS

Company Type: Public

Income Statement

FYE: June 30

	REVENUE ($ mil.)	NET INCOME ($ mil.)	NET PROFIT MARGIN	EMPLOYEES
06/18*	5,880	397	6.8%	20,800
07/17	4,488	591	13.2%	14,400
07/16	4,491	460	10.3%	15,100
06/15	4,191	402	9.6%	15,800
06/14	4,806	781	16.3%	17,200
Annual Growth	5.2%	(15.5%)	—	4.9%

*Fiscal year change

2018 Year-End Financials

Debt ratio: 23.97%
Return on equity: 12.76%
Cash ($ mil.): 1,243
Current ratio: 2.59
Long-term debt ($ mil.): 1,599

No. of shares (mil.): 288
Dividends
 Yield: 0.0%
 Payout: 97.8%
Market value ($ mil.): 13,452

	STOCK PRICE ($) FY Close	P/E High/Low	PER SHARE ($) Earnings	Dividends	Book Value
06/18*	46.71	39 28	1.38	1.35	11.27
07/17	47.34	22 16	2.09	1.35	10.65
07/16	40.73	25 17	1.65	1.35	9.63
06/15	36.12	30 23	1.45	1.35	9.00
06/14	34.47	21 12	2.79	1.35	8.82
Annual Growth	7.9%	— —	(16.1%)	(0.0%)	6.3%

*Fiscal year change

Targa Resources Corp

Targa Resources Corp. has the energy to deliver natural gas throughout its service territory of Texas Oklahoma and neighboring states. Through its Targa Resources Partners entity it gathers processes transports and sells natural gas natural gas liquids (NGLs) crude oil and refined petroleum products. It owns or operates about 27000 miles of natural gas gathering pipelines and more than 35 processing plants. It has a presence in many shale basins including the Permian Eagle Ford Barnett Anadarko Arkoma and Williston. In early 2016 Targa Resources Corp purchased all un-owned shares of Targa Resources Partners securing complete control of its previously majority-owned subsidiary.

Operations

Targa Resources operates two segments: Gathering and Processing and Logistics and Marketing.

The Logistics and Marketing segment accounting for 85% of total revenue is Targa?s downstream business. It converts mixed NGLs into NGL products and provides certain value-added services such as storing terminaling distributing and marketing NGLs; storing and terminaling refined petroleum products and crude oil. It performs marketing activities in support of Targa?s other businesses including services to LPG exporters. Assets owned by this segment are generally connected to and supplied in part by the Gathering and Processing segment. It also owns and leases out some 700 railcars to move product.

The Gathering and Processing segment gathers natural gas produced from oil and gas wells and processes this raw natural gas into sellable natural gas by extracting NGLs and removing impurities. It also gathers and terminals crude oil. The segment owns some 27000 miles of gathering pipeline and has a gross processing capacity of 3500 million cubic feet of natural gas per day.

Geographic Reach

Targa Resources is headquartered in HoustonTX. The assets owned by the Logistics and Marketing segment are predominantly located in Mont Belvieu and Galena Park Texas in Lake Charles Louisiana in Tacoma Washington and in Baltimore Maryland.

The Gathering and Processing segment's assets are located in the Permian Basin of West Texas and Southeast New Mexico; the Eagle Ford Shale in South Texas; the Barnett Shale in North Texas; the Anadarko Ardmore and Arkoma Basins in Oklahoma and South Central Kansas; the Williston Basin in North Dakota and in the onshore and near offshore regions of the Louisiana Gulf Coast and the Gulf of Mexico.

Sales and Marketing

Targa sells its products to petrochemical companies refineries export companies large commercial and industrial customers as well as to natural gas and electric utilities that serve individual consumers. Targa also earns revenue by purchasing and reselling NGL products in the spot and forward physical markets.

Targa Resources' wholesale propane marketing operations primarily sell propane and related logistics services to major multi-state retailers independent retailers and other end-users.

Financial Performance

In recent years Targa Resources? revenue has been steady with a single positive aberration in 2014. Generally revenue comes in around $6.6 billion. Net income delivered positive though minimal results between 2011 and 2015 (averaging $50 million) before plunging in 2016.

For the year 2017 revenue rose about 30% to $8.8 billion coming entirely from the 38% increase of sale of commodities thanks to higher commodity prices ($2.2 billion) as well as increased petroleum products natural gas and condensate sales volumes ($100 million).

In 2017 net income swung from a sizable loss of $278 million to a profit of $54 million entirely due to income tax benefits stemming from the tax reform. Without it the company would have recorded a loss of $293 million for 2017 $30 million more than the year prior.

Targa's cash holdings increased from $74 million in 2016 to $137 million in 2017. Operations contributed $940 million followed by an even great contribution of $1 billion from financing activities coming from $4 billion in issuance of long-term debt . By contrast investment utilized $1.9 billion mostly in purchase of property plant and equipment.

Strategy

Targa Resources is focused on production from US shale plays and by the deployment of shale exploration and production technologies in both liquids-rich natural gas and crude oil resource plays for driving its growth. It is actively pursuing natural gas gathering and processing and NGL fractionation opportunities associated with liquids-rich natural gas from shale and other resource plays such as portions of the Barnett Eagle Ford Utica and Marcellus Shales and with even richer casinghead gas opportunities from active crude oil resource plays such as the Wolfberry and the Bone Springs Avalon and Bakken Shale plays. Production growth in the major shale plays (overall not just Targa?s) is expected to be about 40% between 2016 and 2020 and 30% between 2020 and 2025. Part of Targa?s strategy is to merely ensure it has the right assets and operations in place to grow its business along with the increased production (and demand) of these shale plays.

For example in the Permian Basin Targa gathers product from a diverse set of producers spanning 2 million dedicated acres of land. With expansion projects it expects that by the end of 2018 it will have capacity to process 2.5 billion cubic/ft per day of natural gas. It connected its recently acquired Delaware and Midland Basin assets to its existing systems to more efficiently move natural gas among its pipelines and processing plants.

Of its $1.3 billion of 2017 capital expenditures 80% is focused on the Permian Basin including nearly $300 million for its joint-venture project Grand Prix NGL pipeline. The pipeline will transport volumes from the Permian Basin and from Targa's North Texas system to Targa's fractionation and storage complex in the NGL market hub at Mont Belvieu Texas. Grand Prix will be supported by Targa's volumes and other third party customer commitments and is expected to be in service in early 2019. The capacity of the pipeline from the Permian Basin will be approximately 300 thousand barrels per day expandable to 550 thousand barrels per day.

The Permian work not only allows greater acquisition of natural gas but the connection to Mont Belvieu aids its downstream operations by lowering transportation costs and increasing predictability of supply. The Downstream business segment also expects to benefit from higher demand from new petrochemical facilities in the Houston area as well as higher demand from non-US customers wanting to export Targa?s excess propane and butanes.

Mergers and Acquisitions

In 2016 Targa Resources completed the acquisition of all of the outstanding common units of Targa Resources Partners LP. As a result of the acquisition Targa improved its credit and coverage profile lowered its cost of capital and simplified its structure thereby improving its access to capital.

EXECUTIVES

Ceo, Joe Bob Perkins, age 57
President Administration, Jeffrey J. (Jeff) McParland, age 63, $500,000 total compensation
Evp Southern Field Gathering And Processing, Patrick J. (Pat) McDonie, age 58
Evp General Counsel And Secretary, Paul W. Chung, age 57, $490,000 total compensation
Evp And Cfo, Mattthew J. (Matt) Meloy, age 40, $450,000 total compensation
Evp Logistics And Marketing, D. Scott Pryor, age 56
Evp Northern Field Gathering And Processing, Dan C. Middlebrooks, age 62
Evp Engineering And Operations, Clark White, age 59
Evp Commercial, Robert Muraro, age 42
Vice President Finance, Howard M Tate
Chairman, James W. Whalen, age 77
Vice Chairman, Michael A. Heim, age 70
Auditors: PricewaterhouseCoopers LLP

LOCATIONS

HQ: Targa Resources Corp
811 Louisiana St., Suite 2100, Houston, TX 77002
Phone: 713 584-1000 **Fax:** 713 584-1100
Web: www.targaresources.com

PRODUCTS/OPERATIONS

2016 sales

	$ mil.	% of total
Logistics and Marketing	5,519	82
Gathering and Processing	1,108	17
Other	62	1
Total	**6,690**	**100**

COMPETITORS

DCP Midstream Partners	Enterprise Products
Devon Energy	Kinder Morgan
EnLink Midstream Partners	Magellan Midstream
Enbridge	ONEOK Partners
Energy Transfer	Summit Midstream Partners LP

HISTORICAL FINANCIALS

Company Type: Public

Income Statement

FYE: December 31

	REVENUE ($ mil.)	NET INCOME ($ mil.)	NET PROFIT MARGIN	EMPLOYEES
12/17	8,814	54	0.6%	2,130
12/16	6,690	(187)	—	1,970
12/15	6,658	58	0.9%	1,870
12/14	8,616	102	1.2%	1,350
12/13	6,556	65	1.0%	1,277
Annual Growth	**7.7%**	**(4.6%)**	**—**	**13.6%**

2017 Year-End Financials

Debt ratio: 35.12%	No. of shares (mil.): 217
Return on equity: 0.91%	Dividends
Cash ($ mil.): 137	Yield: 0.0%
Current ratio: 0.79	Payout: —
Long-term debt ($ mil.): 4,703	Market value ($ mil.): 10,535

	STOCK PRICE ($) FY Close	P/E High/Low	PER SHARE ($) Earnings	Dividends	Book Value
12/17	48.42	— —	(0.31)	3.64	29.31
12/16	56.07	— —	(1.80)	3.64	29.45
12/15	27.06	98 24	1.09	3.39	26.09
12/14	106.05	62 35	2.43	2.68	4.03
12/13	88.17	57 34	1.55	2.06	3.53
Annual Growth	**(13.9%)**	**— —**	**—**	**15.4%**	**69.8%**

Target Corp

Cheap-but-chic Target is the US's #2 discount chain (behind Wal-Mart). The fashion-forward discounter operates 1800-plus Target and SuperTarget stores across the US as well as an online business at Target.com. It sells a broad range of household goods food and pet supplies apparel and accessories electronics decor and other items under national brands as well as owned and exclusive brands. Target and its larger grocery-carrying incarnation SuperTarget have carved out a niche by offering more upscale trend-driven merchandise than rivals Wal-Mart and Kmart. The company also offers pharmacy and clinic services in its stores through an operating agreement with CVS Pharmacy.

Operations

Target operates in five product categories that each contribute around 20% of total revenue: beauty and household essentials (including pet supplies) food and beverage apparel and accessories home furnishings and decor and hardlines (electronics software sporting goods toys).

Owned and exclusive brands such as Archer Farms (food) Cat & Jack (children's clothing) Hearth & Hand (home & lifestyle) and Room Essentials (home furnishings) account for about a third of revenue.

Geographic Reach

Minnesota-based Target operates across the US. Five states — California Texas Florida Illinois and New York — account for about 40% of total store locations and a significant portion of revenue.

The chain has some 40 distribution centers in the US as well as offices in about a dozen other countries to support various trading and shipping functions.

Sales and Marketing

The vast majority of Target's merchandise is delivered to stores through its network of 40 distribution centers. It generates 95% of revenue through its stores with the rest coming from mobile and online sales.

The company has had success cementing customer loyalty and driving sales with its proprietary credit and debit cards (REDcards collectively). Nearly a quarter of sales are paid for with REDcards (up from 6% in 2010).

Financial Performance

After about a decade of pretty steady revenue growth Target saw a 6% dip in fiscal 2016 (ended January) following the sale of its pharmacy and clinics business; sales rebounded a bit in fiscal 2017.

In fiscal 2017 the company reported revenue of $71.9 billion up 3% from the prior year. Same-store sales rose more than a percent and Target opened about 20 net new stores throughout the year.

Net income that year also rose jumping 7% to $2.9 billion on the increased sales and a smaller provision for income taxes than in fiscal 2016.

Cash at the end of fiscal 2017 was $2.6 billion a small increase from the prior year. Cash from operations contributed $6.9 billion to the coffers while investing activities used $3.1 billion mainly for capital expenditures. Financing activities used another $3.7 billion for reduction of long-term debt dividends to stockholders and Target's stock repurchase program.

Strategy

Target like most of its retail compatriots is focused on digital sales and providing customers with a seamless experience whether they are shopping in stores online or through mobile apps. In 2017 it announced some $7 billion over three years for a host of investments including digital enhancements. That year it integrated its Cartwheel savings app with the flagship Target app so customers would have one comprehensive mobile application. The company has also made strategic acquisitions to bolster its logistics and delivery capabilities.

Amid all the buzz around digital sales and omnichannel experiences physical stores are still of huge importance to Target's growth strategy. Its investments also include store redesigns and the opening of small-format urban stores. The company plans to open 30 small-format stores and remodel more than 300 existing locations in fiscal 2018.

Lastly Target's private labels are a key element of growth. The company has doubled down on that area of the business which has historically been well-received and sets Target apart from many of its rivals. New brands launched include Heyday (electronics) Wild Fable (low-cost clothing and accessories for teenage and young adult women) and Original Use (male-focused urban apparel).

Mergers and Acquisitions

In 2017 Target agreed to acquire Grand Junction a start-up company that develops logistics software to help improve delivery efficiency. The deal is part of Target's move to revamp its logistics to increase sales from its website and to compete against Amazon.com. Grand Junction handles same-day delivery arrangements for Target in a part of New York City. Also that year the retailer agreed to buy same-day delivery company Shipt in one of its largest acquisitions to date ($550 million). With Grand Junction and Shipt Target plans to have same-day delivery as an option in most stores and in all major markets by the end of 2018.

HISTORY

The panic of 1873 left Joseph Hudson bankrupt. After he paid his debts at 60 cents on the dollar he saved enough to open a men's clothing store in Detroit in 1881. Among his innovations were merchandise-return privileges and price marking in place of bargaining. By 1891 Hudson's was the largest retailer of men's clothing in the US. Hudson repaid his creditors from 1873 in full with interest. When Hudson died in 1912 four nephews expanded the business.

Former banker George Dayton established a dry-goods store in 1902 in Minneapolis. Like Hudson he offered return privileges and liberal credit. His store grew to a 12-story full-line department store.

After WWII both companies saw that the future lay in the suburbs. In 1954 Hudson's built Northland in Detroit then the largest US shopping center. Dayton's built the world's first fully enclosed shopping mall in Edina a Minneapolis suburb in 1956. In 1962 Dayton's opened its first discount store in Roseville (naming the store Target to distinguish the discounter from its higher-end department stores).

Dayton's went public in 1966 the same year it began the B. Dalton bookstore chain. Three years later it merged with the family-owned Hudson's forming Dayton Hudson. Dayton Hudson purchased more malls and invested in such specialty areas as consumer electronics and hard goods. Target had 24 stores by 1970.

The Target chain became the company's top moneymaker in 1977. The next year Dayton Hudson bought California-based Mervyn's (later Mervyns). In the late 1970s and 1980s it sold nine regional malls and several other businesses including the 800-store B. Dalton chain to Barnes & Noble. The Target stores division purchased Indianapolis-based Ayr-Way (1980) and Southern California-based Fedmart stores (1983). In the late 1980s Dayton Hudson took Target to Los Angeles and the Northwest. Robert Ulrich who began with the company as a merchandise trainee in 1967 became president and CEO of the Target stores division in 1987 and chairman and CEO of Dayton Hudson in 1994.

Dayton Hudson opened the first Target Greatland store in 1990. By this time it had 420 Target stores. Also that year Dayton Hudson bought the Marshall Field's chain of 24 department stores from B.A.T Industries. Marshall Field's began as a dry-goods business that Marshall Field bought in 1865 and subsequently built into Chicago's premier upscale retailer.

SuperTarget stores were introduced in 1995. The Target stores division opened stores in the Mid-Atlantic and Northeast the next year while the department store division began selling off its Marshall Field's locations in Texas.

In 1998 Dayton Hudson boosted its Internet presence by purchasing direct-marketing company Rivertown Trading; it also bought apparel supplier Associated Merchandising that year. In 2000 Dayton Hudson renamed itself Target Corporation. In early 2001 the company renamed its Dayton's and Hudson's chains Marshall Field's. Also that year Target acquired the rights to 35 former Montgomery Wards stores from the bankrupt retailer.

The nation's #2 discounter was #1 when it came to corporate giving in 2001. Target topped the Forbes list of America's Most Philanthropic Companies that year donating 2.5% of its 2000 income (nearly $86 million). By comparison Wal-Mart gave away $116.5 million in 2001 less than 1% of its income in 2000.

In 2002 the company reopened 30 of the former Montgomery Ward stores as Target outlets. Net of closings 94 Target stores opened in 2002 while neither Mervyns nor Marshall Field's added to their store counts. In March 2003 three new SuperTarget stores opened in

EXECUTIVES

Senior Vice President Of Real Estate, Scott Nelson
Evp Chief Legal Officer And Corporate Secretary, Don H. Liu, age 57, $275,000 total compensation
Evp Merchandising Product Group, Patricia (Trish) Adams
Director Community Relations, Laysha L. Ward, age 50
Chairman And Ceo, Brian C. Cornell, age 59, $1,300,000 total compensation
Evp And Coo, John J. Mulligan, age 52, $1,000,000 total compensation
Evp And Chief Merchandising Officer, Mark J. Tritton, age 54, $396,635 total compensation
Evp And Chief Stores Officer, Janna A. Potts, age 50
Evp And Cio, Michael E. (Mike) McNamara, age 53, $468,462 total compensation
Evp And Cfo, Catherine R. (Cathy) Smith, age 54, $798,558 total compensation
President Target Sourcing Services, Kelly Caruso
Evp And Chief Human Resources Officer, Stephanie A. Lundquist, age 42
Evp And Chief Risk And Compliance Officer, Jacqueline Hourigan Rice, age 46
Evp And Chief Marketing Officer, Rick H. Gomez, age 48
Svp Grocery Fresh Food And Beverage, Jeff Burt
President Target Financial And Retail Services, Scott Kennedy
President Target India, Tammy Redpath
Senior Vice President Risk And Government Affairs, Matt Zabel
Pharmacy Manager, Mikel Gilbert
Pharmacy Manager, Kenne Currie
Vice President Technology Services, Tim Milne
Pharmacy Manager, Joseph Legrand
Pharmacy Manager, Will Peck
Senior Vice President Region Ii, Robert Thompson
Senior Vice President Merchandising Capabilities, Michael Fiddelke
Pharmacy Manager, Bernard Brown
Vice President Assistant, Julann Schubert
Executive Vice President Executive Assistant, Bridget Hicks
Vice President Administrative Assistant, Heather Bean
Vice President Assistant, Melissa Loth
Senior Vice President Administration, Sommer Roux
Pharmacy Manager, Jacqueline Jansen
Vice President, Sarah Arrell
Senior Vice President Talent And Organizational Effectiveness, Tim Curoe
Senior Vice President And Chief Information Security Officer, Brad Maiorino
Vice President Of Communications, Dustee T Jenkins
Vice President Administrative Assistant, Vonnie Zuehlke
Senior Vice President Executive Assistant, Tracy Rockholt
Senior Group Vice President, Jim Hogan
Pharmacy Manager, David Cathcart
Senior Vice President And Manager Financial Institutions, Addison Averett
Vice President Finance, Scott Brill
Senior Vice President Talent And Organizational Effectiveness, Melissa Kremer
Senior Vice President Assistant, Milagros Hanson

Pharmacy Manager, Philip Agee
Senior Vice President Product Design And Development, Julie Guggemos
Vice President Of Distribution Operations, Diane Closs
Executive Vice President Merchandising Apparel And Home, Trish Adams
Vice President Assistant, Rhonda Broyles
Senior Vice President Gc Sec'y, TimothyR Baer
Vice President Assistant, Christina Hayes
Executive Vice President Chief Legal Officer And Corporate Secretary, Tim Baer
Vice President Business Development, Pam Tomczik
Senior Vice President Infrastructure And Operations, Tom Kadlec
Senior Vice President Operational Excellence, Anu Gupta
Senior Vice President Fulfillment Operations, Preston Mosier
Senior Vice President Chief Accounting Officer And Controller, Robert Harrison
Senior Vice President And Chief Creative Officer, Todd Waterbury
Vice President Internal Innovation And Operations, West Stringfellow
Vice President Divisional Meat And Fresh Prepared Food, Mark Kenny
National Account Manager, Sherita Jackson
Vice President Corporate Social Responsibility, Jennifer Silberman
Vice President Assistant, Juliemarie Haugen
Vice President Merchandise Manager, Scott Bradley
Senior Vice President Treasurer, Corey L Haaland
Assistant Treasurer, Sara Ross
Board Member, Rakesh Mishra
Vice Chairman, Mollie McCarty
Board Member, Robert Edwards
Auditors: Ernst & Young LLP

LOCATIONS

HQ: Target Corp
   1000 Nicollet Mall, Minneapolis, MN 55403
Phone: 612 304-6073
Web: www.target.com

2017 Locations

	No.
California	283
Texas	149
Florida	122
Illinois	94
New York	79
Minnesota	74
Pennsylvania	71
Ohio	62
Virginia	58
Michigan	53
North Carolina	51
Georgia	50
Other	676
Total	**1,822**

PRODUCTS/OPERATIONS

2017 Sales

	% of total
Beauty & household essentials	23
Food & beverage	20
Apparel & accessories	20
Home furnishings & décor	19
Hardlines	18
Total	**100**

Selected Exclusive Brands
DENIZEN from Levi's
Genuine Kids from OshKosh
Isabel Maternity by Ingrid & Isabel
Mossimo
Nate Berkus for Target
Oh Joy! for Target

Selected Private Labels

Archer Farms (food)
Cat & Jack (children's apparel)
Market Pantry
Merona (apparel)
Smith & Hawken (garden & outdoor)
Xhilaration (apparel)

COMPETITORS

Amazon.com	L Brands
BJ's Wholesale Club	Lowe's
Bed Bath & Beyond	Macy's
Best Buy	PETCO
Container Store	Ross Stores
Costco Wholesale	SUPERVALU
Dillard's	Safeway
Dollar General	Sears Holdings
Dollar Tree	TJX Companies
Euromarket Designs	The Gap
Family Dollar Stores	Wal-Mart
Home Depot	Walgreen
J. C. Penney Company	Wayfair
Kohl's	Williams-Sonoma
Kroger	

HISTORICAL FINANCIALS

Company Type: Public

Income Statement

FYE: February 3

	REVENUE ($ mil.)	NET INCOME ($ mil.)	NET PROFIT MARGIN	EMPLOYEES
02/18*	71,879	2,934	4.1%	345,000
01/17	69,495	2,737	3.9%	323,000
01/16	73,785	3,363	4.6%	341,000
01/15	72,618	(1,636)	—	347,000
02/14	72,596	1,971	2.7%	366,000
Annual Growth	(0.2%)	10.5%		(1.5%)

*Fiscal year change

2018 Year-End Financials

Debt ratio: 29.71%
Return on equity: 25.47%
Cash ($ mil.): 2,643
Current ratio: 0.95
Long-term debt ($ mil.): 11,317

No. of shares (mil.): 541
Dividends
Yield: 0.0%
Payout: 45.7%
Market value ($ mil.): 39,516

	STOCK PRICE ($) FY Close	P/E High/Low		PER SHARE ($) Earnings	Dividends	Book Value
02/18*	72.95	15	9	5.33	2.44	21.62
01/17	63.70	18	13	4.70	2.32	19.69
01/16	72.42	16	13	5.31	2.16	21.52
01/15	73.61	—	—	(2.56)	1.90	21.86
02/14	56.64	24	18	3.07	1.58	25.64
Annual Growth	6.5%	—	—	14.8%	11.5%	(4.2%)

*Fiscal year change

TATA AMERICA INTERNATIONAL CORPORATION

EXECUTIVES

President, Surya Kant
Vp Marketing And Communications, John Lenzen
Cfo, S. Mahalingam
Auditors: DELOITTE HASKINS & SELLS LLP

LOCATIONS

HQ: TATA AMERICA INTERNATIONAL CORPORATION
101 PARK AVE RM 2603, NEW YORK, NY 101782604
Phone: 212 557-8038
Web: WWW.TCS.COM

PRODUCTS/OPERATIONS

Selected Subsidiaries

IT Services
Tata Business Support Services
Tata Communications
Tata Consultancy Services
Tata Elxsi
Tata Interactive Systems
Tata Technologies
Engineering
Tata AutoComp Systems
Services
Campton Place
Taj Boston
The Pierre
Consumer Products
Eight O'Clock Coffee
Good Earth
Tanishq
Tata Tea Inc.
Tetley
Chemicals
General Chemical

COMPETITORS

Accenture	HCL Technologies
Atos North America	HP Enterprise Services
CIBER	IBM Global Services
Capgemini North America	ICP Inc.
	Infosys
Cognizant Tech Solutions	NTT Data
	Syntel
Computer Sciences Corp.	Unisys
	Wipro Technologies
Fujitsu America	Zensar Technologies

HISTORICAL FINANCIALS

Company Type: Private

Income Statement

FYE: March 31

	REVENUE ($ mil.)	NET INCOME ($ mil.)	NET PROFIT MARGIN	EMPLOYEES
03/18	8,197	121	1.5%	1,700
03/17	845	168	19.9%	—
03/16	755	118	15.7%	—
03/15	6,800	111	1.6%	—
Annual Growth	6.4%	3.0%	—	—

2018 Year-End Financials

Debt ratio: ——
Return on equity: 1.50%
Cash ($ mil.): 15
Current ratio: 0.90
Long-term debt ($ mil.): —

Dividends
Yield: —
Payout: —
Market value ($ mil.): —

TCF Financial Corp

TCF Financial agreed in January 2019 to merge with Minnesota-based Chemical Financial to form a Midwest bank with about $45 billion in assets $34 billion in total deposits and more than 500 branches in nine states. Chemical's commercial lending and wealth management activities will complement TCF's large deposit base and national wholesale lending business. The combined company which is to retain the TCF brand will have a more diversified deposit mix between retail and commercial lines and a more balanced loan portfolio across geographies asset classes and industries. Following the merger TCF shareholders will have a controlling interest in the combined company.

Operations

TCF operates through three primary segments: lending (71% of total revenues) funding (28%) and support services (1%).

Campus banking is also an important part of the company's operations. TCF has exclusive marketing alliances with several colleges including the University of Illinois and University of Michigan and is a leading provider of campus cards that serve as ID library security and stored-value cards in addition to ATM cards. Also as a part of its effort to build brand recognition on college campuses the company paid $35 million for the naming rights to the University of Minnesota's football stadium which opened in 2009 for 25 years.

Geographic Reach

TCF has nearly 430 locations in Arizona (seven branches) Indiana (four) Illinois (194) Michigan (53) Minnesota (108) South Dakota (one) and Wisconsin (25).

Financial Performance

TCF saw its revenues hover around the $1.4 billion mark in 2011 and 2012. However it suffered a net loss of $213 million in 2012 due to a 78% spike in noninterest expenses and provision for credit losses. Over the years the company has suffered from declines in interest income and revenues from its funding segment also declined by 13% during 2012.

Strategy

TCF aims to attract customers through convenience. To that end more than half its branches are inside supermarkets and many of its locations are open seven days a week. While many of the company's peers attempt to grow their branch networks through acquisitions TCF has expanded by opening up new branches — more than 100 since 2003.

In order to reduce its reliance on interest-based income such as loans and leases which are subject to interest rate fluctuations and other outside factors TCF is focusing on growing its income from fees and service charges from products like checking accounts and credit cards.

The company has also experienced growth in its specialty finance operations including TCF Equipment Finance TCF Inventory Finance and Winthrop Resources which leases computers servers and other technology equipment. TCF continued to grow the business in 2011 when it bought California-based Gateway One a provider of consumer loans mainly for used cars.

Mergers and Acquisitions

TCF Financial agreed in January 2019 to merge with Michigan-based Chemical Financial to form a Midwest bank with about $45 billion in assets $34 billion in total deposits and more than 500 branches in nine states. Following the merger TCF and Chemical shareholders will hold 54% and 46% stakes in the combined company respectively.

EXECUTIVES

Chairman President And Ceo, Craig R. Dahl, age 63, $846,923 total compensation
Evp And Cfo Tcf Equipment Finance; Evp Winthrop Resources, Thomas F. (Tom) Jasper, age 50, $550,000 total compensation
Evp Consumer Banking, Michael S. Jones, age 50, $549,231 total compensation
Evp Wholesale Banking, William S. Henak, age 61, $472,082 total compensation

Chief Risk Officer And Chief Credit Officer, James
M. Costa, age 49
Cio, Tom Butterfield
Treasurer, Brian W. Maass, age 45, $328,678 total
compensation
**Vice President Information Technology Audit
Manager,** Benjamin Thomas
Executive Vice President, Joseph Doyle
**Vice President Information Technology Delivery
Director,** Bridget Lindner
**Vice President Talent Management Leadership
Development,** Christopher Lawyer
Executive Vice President Enterprise Technologies,
Brett Brunick
**Vice President Corporate Systems And Erp
Delivery,** Christine Cameron
Vice President Tcf Commercial Real Estate, Bryan
Downie
Vice President And Risk Officer, Karen Knoller
**Senior Vice President Product Marketing And
Customer Experience,** Kevin Miller
Vice President Of Human Resources, Judy Gauvin
Vice President Human Resources, Barbara Drago
Vice President Commercial Banking, Jeffrey Moore
Auditors: KPMG LLP

LOCATIONS

HQ: TCF Financial Corp
200 Lake Street East, Wayzata, MN 55391-1693
Phone: 952 745-2760
Web: www.tcfbank.com

PRODUCTS/OPERATIONS

2016 Sales

	$ mil.	% of total
Consumer Banking	780	56
Wholesale Banking	581	42
Enterprise Services	33	2
Total	**1,396**	**100**

2016 Sales

	$ mil.	% of total
Interest	930	67
Non-interest	465	33
Total	**1,396**	**100**

Selected Subsidiaries

Fidelity National Capital Inc. (also dba Winthrop Capital)
TCF Agency Inc.
TCF Agency Insurance Services Inc.
TCF Bank International Inc.
TCF Commercial Finance Canada Inc. (also dba
Financement Commercial TCF Canada Inc.)
TCF Equipment Finance Inc. (also dba TCF Leasing Inc.)
TCF Insurance Agency Inc.
TCF Inventory Finance Inc.
TCF Investments Management Inc.
TCF National Bank
TCF Portfolio Services Inc.
Winthrop Resources Corporation (also dba TCF Small
Business Lending)

COMPETITORS

Associated Banc-Corp	Northern Trust
Bank Mutual	U.S. Bancorp
Bank of America	Wells Fargo
Bremer Financial	

HISTORICAL FINANCIALS

Company Type: Public

Income Statement

FYE: December 31

	ASSETS ($ mil.)	NET INCOME ($ mil.)	INCOME AS % OF ASSETS	EMPLOYEES
12/17	23,002	268	1.2%	6,116
12/16	21,441	212	1.0%	6,427
12/15	20,691	197	1.0%	6,755
12/14	19,394	174	0.9%	7,023
12/13	18,379	151	0.8%	7,449
Annual Growth	**5.8%**	**15.4%**	—	**(4.8%)**

2017 Year-End Financials

Debt ratio: 1.63%
Return on equity: 10.55%
Cash ($ mil.): 621
Current ratio: —
Long-term debt ($ mil.): —

No. of shares (mil.): 171
Dividends
  Yield: 0.0%
  Payout: 20.8%
Market value ($ mil.): 3,519

	STOCK PRICE ($) FY Close	P/E High/Low	PER SHARE ($) Earnings	Dividends	Book Value
12/17	20.50	14 10	1.44	0.30	15.51
12/16	19.59	17 9	1.15	0.30	14.20
12/15	14.12	16 13	1.07	0.23	13.49
12/14	15.89	18 15	0.94	0.20	12.67
12/13	16.25	20 15	0.82	0.20	11.83
Annual Growth	**6.0%**	**— —**	**15.1%**	**10.7%**	**7.0%**

TD Ameritrade Holding Corp

Through several subsidiaries TD Ameritrade
Holding provides electronic discount brokerage
and related financial services that enable retail investors to trade common and preferred stocks of
US companies exchange-traded funds (ETFs) mutual funds bonds options futures and foreign currencies. In addition to its online offerings the company provides services through a network of more
than 360 retail branches and relationships with
more than 6000 independent registered investment advisors (RIAs). TD Ameritrade holds some
$1.3 trillion in client assets and supports about
half a million client trades per day.

Operations

TD Ameritrade Holding provides securities brokerage services and related technology-based financial services to value-conscious retail investors
traders and registered investment advisors (RIAs).
It provides its services mainly through the internet
its national branch network and via its relationships with RIAs. The company offers its brokerage
services under a simple low-cost commission structure and provides to RIAs its brokerage custodial
services.

TD Ameritrade Holding operates several trading
and investment platforms including
tdameritrade.com thinkorswim TD Ameritrade Mobile and TD Ameritrade Institutional (for its RIAs).
Beyond its core online services it offers online education investment advice and goal planning ses-
sions and a service that refers retail investors to
RIAs.

The company generates about 35% of revenue
from commissions and transaction fees and around
30% from account fees from clients of Toronto-
Dominion Bank and TD Bank USA with which TD

Ameritrade has an insured deposit account agreement. It also produces about 25% of revenue from
interest and 10% from investment product fees.

Geographic Reach

Headquartered in Omaha Nebraska TD Ameritrade Holding has administrative and operational
facilities in St. Louis Missouri; Southlake Texas;
and Denver Colorado. The company also has an
operations center in Jersey City New Jersey; six
data center facilities in Texas Missouri Arizona
and New Jersey; and smaller administrative and
operational facilities in California Colorado Illinois
Maryland Massachusetts Michigan Texas and Utah.
The company has more than 360 retail branch
offices in 48 states and the District of Columbia.

Sales and Marketing

TD Ameritrade Holding targets a broad market
of independent value-conscious retail investors
traders financial planners and registered investment advisors (RIAs) and institutions. Clients can
access its products and services through channels
including the internet its network of retail branches
mobile trading applications or over the phone via
interactive voice response and registered representatives.

The online securities brokerage promotes its
business via online television print website and social media advertising. The company's ads reach
retail investors generally through digital channels
online searches social media financial news networks and other television and cable networks.
The company spends comparatively little on advertising to institutional investors.

TD also models its return on marketing investment to support advertising decisions and uses
data analytics to create targeted advertising for
clients.

Financial Performance

TD Ameritrade's revenue ticked up only slightly
in fiscal years 2015 and 2016 before seeing gains
of some 10% and 50% in 2017 and 2018 respectively; all its revenue streams saw gains those
years. Net income trended similarly adding less
than 5% each year until 2018 when it increased
nearly 70% on higher revenue and a lower effective
tax rate caused by the Tax Cuts and Jobs. Overall
revenue and net income added about 70% and
85% respectively from 2014 to 2018. The company added more than 80% to its cash and nearly
doubled its long-term debt in that time.

TD's revenue grew 48% to $5.3 billion in 2018
owing to the addition of about 3.5 million funded
accounts from its 2017 acquisition of competitor
Scottrade Financial Services.

The holding company's net income added 69%
to $1.5 billion in 2018 thanks to the revenue-
boosting Scottrade acquisition and US tax reform.

TD's cash stores expanded by $1.2 billion in
2018 to end the period at $2.7 billion. Operations
provided $1.9 billion and investments added $92
million. The company's financing activities particularly dividend payments and treasury stock purchases used $782 million.

Strategy

TD Ameritrade Holding is in an enviable position
as retail interest in stock investing is on the rise.
Following tepid and sometimes volatile performance caused by the 2009 Financial Crisis retail investors are engaged in and curious about their investments. TD Ameritrade along with its expanded
presence from the Scottrade Financial Services acquisition is poised to capture increasing revenue
from increased trading volume. The company facilitated 811000 average trades per day in 2018
up nearly 60% from the previous year.

The organic growth of increased trading volume
will be supplemented with higher interest revenue
due to the rising interest rate environment brought
about by the US Fed's interest rate hikes. As well
as client assets grow so too will the deposits held

at affiliate banks Toronto-Dominion Bank and TD Bank USA which it in turn invest to generate their own interest income.

The company is also working to branch out from its traditional products and services. In 2018 the company tripled its number of commission-free exchange-traded funds available to clients through an expanded ETF Market Center to aid client education about integrating ETFs into their investment portfolios. That year the company also reintroduced its Model Market Center an open-architecture model portfolio marketplace used by RIAs to assist their clients' investment needs.

TD is also expanding the channels by which its clients can make trades. The company was the first to launch trading via chatbot on Facebook Messenger and Twitter implement 24/5 trading and provide voice-activated trading through Amazon's Alexa.

Furthermore TD is growing its international network especially in Asia: In 2018 the company opened a branch in Hong Kong to complement its Singapore office.

Mergers and Acquisitions

In 2017 TD Ameritrade Holding and Toronto-Dominion Bank (which owns some 45% of TD Ameritrade) bought online brokerage rival Scottrade in a $4.3 billion two-stage transaction. Scottrade merged into TD Ameritrade while its Scottrade Bank subsidiary became part of Toronto-Dominion Bank. The acquisition more than quadrupled TD Ameritrade's retail branch network and gave the company about 3.5 million funded client accounts.

Company Background

Begun as a local investment banking firm in 1971 TD Ameritrade Holding became a retail discount securities brokerage firm in 1975. In 1988 the company became the first to offer touch-tone phone trading and in 1995 it acquired K. Aufhauser & Co. which is credited with performing the first online trade in 1994.

Following a 1997 IPO the company combined its brokerage units into one broker dealer Ameritrade. The company quadrupled its retail branch network and added 3.5 million client accounts with the $4.3 billion purchase of rival Scottrade in 2017.

HISTORY

Ameritrade began in 1971 as investment bank TransTerra. Dean Witter veteran Joe Ricketts transformed the firm into a discount broker in 1975. TransTerra formed Televest/Bancvest (now AmeriVest) in 1982 and Ameritrade Clearing (now TD Ameritrade Clearing) in 1983.

In 1988 the company became the first to offer Touch-Tone telephone trading and added Internet trading in 1994. TransTerra formed Ceres Securities a deep-discount brokerage service that added research to its services when it bought brokerage firms K. Aufhauser and All American in 1995. The company formed its eBroker all-Internet brokerage service in 1996 and became Ameritrade late that year.

In 1997 the company went public and combined its service-oriented subsidiaries. It also formed an alliance that directed users of America Online's investor site to Ameritrade's websites. The company grew rapidly in the late 1990s but like most technology-based companies suffered the impact of the subsequent tech wreck and the struggling economy.

Later TD Ameritrade led a wave of consolidation within the electronic brokerage industry. It purchased rivals National Discount Brokers and Datek in 2001 and 2002 but didn't stop there. In 2003 the company acquired the accounts of Mydiscountbroker.com from SWS Group and the retail accounts of BrokerageAmerica which together

helped push the company's account base past the 3 million mark. It gained another 145000 accounts from brokerage firms Bidwell & Company and JB Oxford Holdings in 2004 and 2005.

E*TRADE offered to buy Ameritrade for more than $6 billion in mid-2005 but the company refused saying it wasn't up for sale. The following year Ameritrade made its own purchase. It bought the US operations of TD Waterhouse and added the "TD" to its name as well as some 100 branch locations. As part of the deal Canada-based TD Bank assumed about a 45% stake in the firm.

EXECUTIVES

Svp General Counsel, Ellen L. S. Koplow, age 58
Group Head Canadian Banking And Wealth Management Td Bank Group And President And Ceo Td Canada Trust, Timothy D. (Tim) Hockey, age 55
Evp And Cfo, Stephen J. (Steve) Boyle, age 57, $96,923 total compensation
Evp And Chief Human Resources Officer, Karen Ganzlin
Evp And Chief Risk Officer, David Kimm
President Td Ameritrade Institutional, Thomas A (Tom) Nally, age 46, $450,000 total compensation
Evp Trader Group, Steven (Steve) Quirk
Managing Director Corporate Strategy And Business Development, Prashant Bhatia
Cio, Vijay Sankaran
President Retail Distribution, Peter deSilva
Senior Vice President And Director Of Technology, Lawson McClellan
Vice President Institutional Sales, Erik Blankmeyer
Vice President Services, James Watts
First Vice President Human Resources, Jessica Bednarovsky
Vice President, Bryan Louie
Regional Vice President, Gary Ausman
Chairman, Joseph H. (Joe) Moglia, age 68
Auditors: Ernst & Young LLP

LOCATIONS

HQ: TD Ameritrade Holding Corp
  200 South 108th Avenue, Omaha, NE 68154
Phone: 402 331-7856   **Fax:** 402 597-7789
Web: www.amtd.com

PRODUCTS/OPERATIONS

2018 Sales

	$ mil.	% of total
Commissions & transaction fees	1,969	36
Insured deposit account fees	1,541	28
Net interest revenue	1,272	24
Investment product fees	557	10
Other	113	2
Total	**5,452**	**100**

Selected Subsidiaries

Ameritrade Advisory Services LLC
Ameritrade International Company
Amerivest Investment Management LLC
Financial Passport Inc.
Futures Forex Trading LLC
Investools Inc.
TD Ameritrade Clearing Inc.
TD Ameritrade IP Company Inc.
TD Ameritrade Mobile LLC
TD Ameritrade Online Holdings Corp.
TD Ameritrade Services Company Inc.
TD Ameritrade Trust Company
TD Ameritrade Inc.
TD Waterhouse Canadian Call Center Inc.
The Insurance Agency of TD Ameritrade LLC
thinkorswim Advisors Inc.
thinkorswim Group Inc.
thinkorswim Holdings Inc.
thinkorswim Singapore Pte. Ltd.
ThinkTech Inc.

COMPETITORS

Charles Schwab	Morgan Stanley
E*TRADE Financial	Raymond James
Edward Jones	Financial
FMR	ShareBuilder
LPL Financial	The Vanguard Group
Merrill Lynch	Wells Fargo Advisors

HISTORICAL FINANCIALS

Company Type: Public

Income Statement

FYE: September 30

	REVENUE ($ mil.)	NET INCOME ($ mil.)	NET PROFIT MARGIN	EMPLOYEES
09/18	5,452	1,473	27.0%	9,183
09/17	3,676	872	23.7%	10,412
09/16	3,327	842	25.3%	6,010
09/15	3,247	813	25.0%	5,690
09/14	3,129	787	25.2%	5,771
Annual Growth	**14.9%**	**17.0%**	**—**	**12.3%**

2018 Year-End Financials

Debt ratio: 6.50%	No. of shares (mil.): 563
Return on equity: 19.32%	Dividends
Cash ($ mil.): 2,690	Yield: 0.0%
Current ratio: 1.01	Payout: 32.4%
Long-term debt ($ mil.): 2,439	Market value ($ mil.): 29,743

	STOCK PRICE ($) FY Close	P/E High/Low		PER SHARE ($) Earnings	Dividends	Book Value
09/18	52.83	24	18	2.59	0.84	14.21
09/17	48.80	30	20	1.64	0.72	12.78
09/16	35.24	22	16	1.58	0.68	9.60
09/15	18.38	—	—	1.49	0.60	9.13
09/14	18.38	—	—	1.42	0.98	8.71
Annual Growth	**30.2%**	**—**	**—**	**16.2%**	**(3.8%)**	**13.0%**

Tech Data Corp.

Tech Data is 100% committed to IT products distribution. One of the world's largest wholesale distributors of technology products Tech Data provides thousands of different items to more than 105000 resellers in 100-plus countries. Its catalog of products includes computer components (disk drives keyboards and video cards) networking equipment (routers and bridges) peripherals (printers modems and monitors) systems (PCs and servers) and software. Tech Data also provides technical support configuration integration financing and logistics and product fulfillment services. More than 60% of Tech Data's revenues are generated outside the US. The company agreed to buy Avnet's Technology Solutions unit for $2.6 billion in 2016.

Operations

Tech Data operates as a distributor of technology products logistics management and other value-added services in the Americas (including North America and South America) and Europe.

The company sells products and services in five categories.

The Broadline unit (46% of revenue) sells notebooks tablets desktops printers printer supplies and components. Its Data Center unit (22%) has industry standard servers proprietary servers networking and storage. The Software category (18%) has virtualization cloud security desktop applications operating systems and utilities software. Mobility (11%) sells mobile phones and accessories. Finally Consumer Electronics (3%) purveys

TV's digital displays consumer audio-visual devices and network-attached consumer devices

Geographic Reach

Florida-based Tech Data sells to customers in more than 100 countries throughout North America South America Europe the Middle East and Africa. Europe is the company's largest market accounting for 61% of sales with the rest coming from the Americas.

Sales and Marketing

Tech Data is one of the world's largest technology distributors. It helps companies like Apple Cisco Microsoft and hundreds of others bring their products to market and it offers a wide range of technical and business support services. Its products are purchased directly from vendors in significant quantities.

Products purchased from Apple accounted for 20% of Tech Data's net sales while HP products represented 19% in 2016 (ended January).

The company's customers include approximately 105000 value-added resellers direct marketers retailers and corporate resellers who support the diverse technology needs of end users.

Its sales team consists of field sales and inside telemarketing sales representatives. Customers typically call its inside sales teams on dedicated telephone numbers or contact it through various electronic methods to place orders. If the product is in stock and the customer has available credit customer orders are generally shipped the same day from the logistics center nearest the customer or the intended end-user.

Financial Performance

In 2016 (ended January) Tech Data's revenue slipped while net income skyrocketed.

The company 2016 revenue dropped about 5% to $26.4 billion compared to 2015. Much of the hit came from the impact of foreign currency exchange rates in Europe and Americas. Not counting the currency impact revenue in Americas rose from data center and consumer electronics product sales. In Europe growth came from the broadline mobility and data center product categories. Tech Data's exit from Chile and Peru reduced revenue in 2015.

The company's net income of about $266 million in 2016 was a 52% increase from 2015. This boost came from lower selling general and administrative expenses and a decrease in legal accounting and third party consulting fees.

Cash flow from operations rose to $189 million in 2016 from $118 million in 2015 on higher earnings and changes in accounts payable.

Strategy

With its acquisition of Avnet's Technology Solutions unit for $2.6 billion arms Tech Data in two areas. One is that it now has a broader higher-value added range of products to offer customers who might want someone else to take over tasks like data center management. The deal brings products and services from Hewlett-Packard Enterprise and IBM into Tech Data's arsenal. The purchase also gives Tech Data a big boost in Asia where it's presence has been nominal. Europe and the America's account for virtually all of Tech Data's revenue. The deal with Avnet is expected to close in 2017.

The addition of more complex products and services should bolster Tech Data's role as a middleman in the distributor business.

Tech Data sold its its operations in Chile and Peru in 2015 and started the process to exited Uruguay citing unacceptable returns in their markets. The company plans to expand its export business from Miami to Latin America and its operations in the more mature IT market of Mexico.

Mergers and Acquisitions

In 2015 Tech Data acquired certain assets of Signature Technology Group (STG a leading North American provider of data center and professional services). STG's services are offered through Tech Data's Advanced Infrastructure Solutions division the company's data center business in the Americas. The addition of STG strengthened the data center offerings further diversified the company's services portfolio and provided added value for its customers.

HISTORY

Tech Data grew out of an electronics distribution business founded by Edward Raymund a University of Southern California graduate who started out as a representative for electronics manufacturers. By the early 1960s he had established an industrial electronics distribution business in Florida. In 1974 he incorporated that business as Tech Data.

In 1981 Raymund's 25-year-old son Steven who had earned master's degrees in economics and international politics from Georgetown University's School of Foreign Service joined Tech Data on a temporary basis to work on the company's catalog. At that time Tech Data sold diskettes and other computer supplies to local companies and had about $2 million in sales.

Steven Raymund's favored status at the company angered a group of managers. Shortly after he arrived at Tech Data they copied the company's client list and walked out. The defection nearly sank Tech Data but Steven Raymund stayed on when his father handed him two-thirds of the company.

With the PC industry beginning to take off Steven Raymund positioned Tech Data as a middleman between computer and peripheral manufacturers and resellers. Steven was named COO in 1984. He became CEO in 1986 the year the company went public.

Tech Data began to distribute software in 1992 and a year later the company signed up Microsoft and inked a distribution deal for IBM computer systems. In 1994 Tech Data purchased U.S. Software Resource a California-based distributor of more than 500 business and entertainment software titles thereby increasing its software list and gaining high-profile publishers such as Borland International (now Borland Software) and Corel as suppliers.

Also in 1994 Tech Data began a global expansion when it bought France's largest distributor of wholesale computer products Softmart International.

To further build its business in Europe Tech Data in late 2012 acquired several distribution companies owned by UK-based Specialist Distribution Group (SDG) in the UK France and the Netherlands. Combined the acquired businesses generate sales of about ?1.4 billion ($1.75 billion). Previously Tech Data bought Triade Holding a Netherlands-based distributor of consumer electronics and IT products in 2010. The purchase strengthened Tech Data's IT business and accelerated its diversification into consumer electronics in the Netherlands Denmark and the Benelux region; it also supported operations across Europe by adding new specialty products vendors and customers. As part of the transaction Tech Data's joint venture with Brightstar Brightstar Europe (formed in 2007) acquired Triade subsidiary Mobile Communication Company (MCC) a mobility products distributor in Benelux. Total value of both deals was ?83 million (about $123 million). (Later Tech Data in 2012 bought its joint venture partner Brightstar's 50% ownership in Brightstar Europe for more than $165 million as well as several distribution companies in the UK from the distribution arm of IT services company Specialist Computer Holdings.)

EXECUTIVES

Vice President, Benjamin Godwin

Evp And Chief Legal Officer, David R. (Dave) Vetter, age 58, $490,522 total compensation

Chairman And Ceo, Robert M. Dutkowsky, age 63, $1,122,124 total compensation

President Americas, Joseph H. Quaglia, age 53, $526,885 total compensation

President Europe, Patrick Zammit, age 51

Evp And Cio, John Tonnison, age 49, $433,495 total compensation

Evp And Cfo, Charles V. (Chuck) Dannewitz, age 64, $579,863 total compensation

Evp And Coo, Richard T. (Rich) Hume, age 59, $547,500 total compensation

Vp Product Marketing Client And Mobile Solutions, Linda Rendleman

Evp And Chief Human Resources Officer, Beth E. Simonetti

Vice President Of Information Technology, Scott Moore

Vice President Sales Eastern U.s, Marc McClure

Vp And Treasurer, Scott Walker

Vice President And General Manager Iscs Americas, Shaun Sinden

Senior Vice President, Sherri P Nadeau

Vice President Manager Director, Cathy Clark

Vice President Global Business Development, John O'Shea

Vice President Streamone, Bob Kruger

Senior Vice President Enterprise Solutions, Jeff Bawol

Vice President Of Credit The Americas, Jay Snyder

Senior Vice President Advance Solutions, Kevin Kennedy

Vice President Of Sales Services, Ron Brinckerhoff

Vice President Vendor Marketing Enterprise Solutions, Anne Devine-Pride

Senior Vice President And Treasurer, Beth McElveen

Auditors: Ernst & Young LLP

LOCATIONS

HQ: Tech Data Corp.
5350 Tech Data Drive, Clearwater, FL 33760
Phone: 727 539-7429
Web: www.techdata.com

Sales by Geographic Segment

	$ mil.	% of total
Europe	15,850	60
Americas	10,384	40
Total	**26,234**	**100**

PRODUCTS/OPERATIONS

Product Categories 2017

	% of total
Broadline	48
Data center	21
Software	17
Mobility	11
Consumer electronics	3
Total	**100**

Solutions

Solutions
Credit Services
Marketing Services
Education & Training
Technical Services
Products and services
Logistics & Warehousing
Supply Chain Services
Technical Services
Marketing Services
Solutions Center

COMPETITORS

ASI Computer Technologies	MA Laboratories
Agilysys	MicroAge
Arrow Electronics	NTT Com Security
Avnet	New Age Electronics
Black Box	Ricoh USA
Communications Supply	SED International
CompuCom	SHI International
D & H Distributing	SYNNEX
Dell	ScanSource
Gigaset	Softmart
IBM	UNICOM Government
Ingram Micro	Westcon
	ZT Group

HISTORICAL FINANCIALS

Company Type: Public

Income Statement   FYE: January 31

	REVENUE ($ mil.)	NET INCOME ($ mil.)	NET PROFIT MARGIN	EMPLOYEES
01/18	36,775	116	0.3%	14,000
01/17	26,234	195	0.7%	9,500
01/16	26,379	265	1.0%	9,000
01/15	27,670	175	0.6%	8,900
01/14	26,821	179	0.7%	9,100
Annual Growth	8.2%	(10.3%)		11.4%

2018 Year-End Financials

Debt ratio: 12.95%	No. of shares (mil.): 38
Return on equity: 4.58%	Dividends
Cash ($ mil.): 955	Yield: —
Current ratio: 1.26	Payout: —
Long-term debt ($ mil.): 1,505	Market value ($ mil.): 3,826

	STOCK PRICE ($) FY Close	P/E High/Low	PER SHARE ($) Earnings	Dividends	Book Value
01/18	100.27	36 27	3.05	0.00	76.56
01/17	85.56	16 11	5.51	0.00	61.60
01/16	62.40	11 7	7.36	0.00	57.17
01/15	57.10	15 11	4.57	0.00	52.44
01/14	53.92	12 9	4.71	0.00	55.14
Annual Growth	16.8%	— —	(10.3%)	—	8.6%

TELCO INTERCONTINENTAL CORP

EXECUTIVES

Pres-Ceo, Frank C Liang
V Pres-Sec-Treas, MEI-Yun Liang
Operations Manager, Sue Yu
Customer Service, Ester Xiang
Manager, Jane Liang
Manager, Albert Robinson
Information Technology Special, Benjamin Yao

LOCATIONS

HQ: TELCO INTERCONTINENTAL CORP
9812 WHITHORN DR, HOUSTON, TX 770955001
Phone: 281 500-8270
Web: WWW.TELCOINTERCON.COM

HISTORICAL FINANCIALS

Company Type: Private

Income Statement   FYE: December 31

	REVENUE ($ mil.)	NET INCOME ($ mil.)	NET PROFIT MARGIN	EMPLOYEES
12/16	15,167	226	1.5%	24
12/15	19,067	1,371	7.2%	—
Annual Growth	(20.5%)	(83.5%)	—	—

2016 Year-End Financials

Debt ratio: —	
Return on equity: 1.50%	Dividends
Cash ($ mil.): 3,055	Yield: —
Current ratio: 22.50	Payout: —
Long-term debt ($ mil.): —	Market value ($ mil.): —

Telephone & Data Systems Inc

Telephone and Data Systems (TDS) is one of the largest US phone companies that's not descended from Ma Bell. The company has about 6.3 million local phone and wireless customers in about 35 states. The company's core business unit U.S. Cellular serves about 5 million customers in more than 20 states with key markets the central US and the mid-Atlantic region. The company also offers fixed-line and broadband internet services in rural and suburban markets in some 35 states through its TDS Telecom subsidiary which provides local service to 1.2 million access lines through incumbent local-exchange carriers (ILEC). Data networking and hosted telecom services are provided to business clients through the TDS Business unit.

Operations

TDS is more telephone than data systems with more than 75% of revenue generated by wireless services sold by US Cellular. TDS owns about 85% of US Cellular's stock. Another 15% of revenue comes from the company's wireline services which provides voice broadband and video.

The rest of the company's revenue is supplied by its cable operations and its hosted management services which includes the OneNeck IT Solutions brand a provider of a range of IT services including full management and hosting of a customer?s IT infrastructure and applications.

Sales and Marketing

U.S. Cellular sells its services through distribution channels that include retail sales and service centers direct sales third-party national retailers independent agents and its website and telesales.

Financial Performance

TDS?s annual revenue has been around $5 billion a year for a decade sometimes higher and sometimes lower. In 2017 revenue was about $5 billion a 2% decline from 2016 because of industry wide pricing competition and lower roaming rates. On the plus side the company reported higher imputed interest income because of an increase in the number of active equipment installment plans.

TDS?s net income jumped 255% to $153 million in 2017 from 2016 propelled by reduced federal income taxes due to the US Tax Cuts and Jobs Act. The company also benefited from improved operating results at TDS Telecom cost-savings initiatives at U.S. Cellular.

The company ended 2017 with about $620 million in cash down more than $280 million from 2016. TDS increased capital expenditures in 2017 from 2016 to deploy VoLTE technology (U.S. Cellular) and upgrade broadband capacity and speeds (TDS Telecom).

Strategy

TDS is protective of its customer base in rural and suburban areas. The company invests in its network to deliver up to date services in its areas and tries to make sure its customers don't lose touch when they go out of area. It has 4G LTE roaming agreements with other telecoms to provide a better experience for customers when they go outside of the TDS footprint. Operationally those agreements reduced the company's roaming expenses despite increased use of roaming by its customers.

While protective TDS won't beg for customers. The company has not offered calling plan promotions that it deems too costly. In early 2017 however U.S. Cellular began to offer postpaid customers unlimited plans with no hidden fees such as overage charges and activation fees.

That said the company has focused on increasing customer engagement with employees throughout the company from network engineers to retail sales people. The company reduced its churn rate (the rate at which customers drop and add service) to 1.21% in 2017 from $1.31% in 2016.

TDS continues to invest in its network expanding 4G service to more customers. It rolled out Voice over LTE (VoLTE) starting in Iowa (working in conjunction with the roaming agreements). The company also had extended broadband to more markets and has conducted tests with 5G wireless technology.

As a regional telecommunications provider TDS's U.S. Cellular unit goes against national carriers such as AT&T and Verizon as does TDS Telecom. The national carriers have more extensive networks and advertise heavily. With its smaller more rural customer bases TDS deals with some higher expenses that its competitors do.

Mergers and Acquisitions

In September 2017 Telephone and Data Systems agreed to acquire K2 Communications a provider of broadband video and voice products to residential customers. The deal would add more than 1200 service addresses to nearby TDS services areas in Colorado. Earlier in 2017 TDS bought Crestview Communications Sun Prairie Utilities and InterLinx Communications to bolster its fiber-based broadband networks.

HISTORY

LeRoy Carlson Sr. learned the ins and outs of rural phone operators when he owned a small firm that supplied equipment and forms to independent phone companies. In the mid-1950s he began buying some of these small phone companies which he consolidated with a phone book publisher and his equipment company to form Telephones Inc. Carlson sold the company to Contel in 1966.

Carlson continued to buy and sell rural carriers allowing them to retain local management while he provided centralized purchasing and system upgrades. In 1969 he bought 10 rural providers in Wisconsin and consolidated all of his companies into Telephone and Data Systems (TDS).

Between 1970 and 1975 TDS acquired 32 rural phone companies. When smaller companies in its established regions became scarce TDS bought rural phone providers from large independents. As TDS diversified the wireline subsidiary became TDS Telecommunications.

The company began offering paging services in Wisconsin in 1972 and later created subsidiary

American Paging (1981). In 1975 TDS moved into cable TV service eventually creating TDS Cable Communications (1984) but it sold the holdings in 1986.

Getting a head start on the big Bells in the cellular race TDS began seeking licenses in the early 1980s eventually winning a 5% stake in the Los Angeles market. Although buffeted by larger independents it placed a high priority on cellular operations and formed subsidiary United States Cellular Corporation in 1983. Two years later US Cellular launched services in Tennessee and Oklahoma.

EXECUTIVES

Svp Acquisitions And Corporate Development, Scott H. Williamson, age 67, $663,000 total compensation

Svp Finance And Treasurer, Peter L. Sereda, age 56

Vice President And Assistant Treasurer, John Toomey

President And Ceo, LeRoy T. (Ted) Carlson, age 72, $1,352,700 total compensation

Svp And Cio, Kurt B. Thaus, age 60

Svp Technology Services And Strategy, Joseph R. Hanley, age 52

Svp Finance And Chief Accounting Officer, Douglas D. Shuma, age 56, $432,500 total compensation

Vp Information Technology Operational Services And Chief Information Security Officer, Theodore E. Wiessing

Vice President Internal Audit, Frieda Ireland

Vice President Acquisitions And Corporate Development, Ken Kotylo

Chairman, Walter C. D. Carlson, age 65

Board Member, Clarence Davis

Board Member, Prudence Carlson

Auditors: PricewaterhouseCoopers LLP

LOCATIONS

HQ: Telephone & Data Systems Inc
30 North LaSalle Street, Suite 4000, Chicago, IL 60602
Phone: 312 630-1900   **Fax:** 312 630-1908
Web: www.teldta.com

PRODUCTS/OPERATIONS

2017 Sales

	$ mil.	% of total
U.S. Cellular	38,903	77
Wireline	714	14
HMS	225	5
Cable	206	4
TDS Telecom Eliminations	(5)	-
Corporate Eliminations and Other	14	-
Total	**5,044**	**100**

2017 Sales

	$ mil.	% of total
Service	3,979	79
Equipment and product sales	1,065	21
Total	**5,044**	**100**

COMPETITORS

AT&T
ATN International
Cavalier Telephone
CenturyLink
Cincinnati Bell
Cricket
FairPoint Communications Inc.
Farmers Telecommunications

HC2 Holdings
Horry Telephone
NII Holdings
Sprint Communications
Suddenlink Communications
T-Mobile USA
Verizon
Verizon Wireless Inc.
XO Holdings

HISTORICAL FINANCIALS
Company Type: Public

Income Statement   FYE: December 31

	REVENUE ($ mil.)	NET INCOME ($ mil.)	NET PROFIT MARGIN	EMPLOYEES
12/17	5,044	153	3.0%	9,900
12/16	5,104	43	0.8%	10,300
12/15	5,176	219	4.2%	10,400
12/14	5,009	(136)	—	10,600
12/13	4,901	141	2.9%	10,500
Annual Growth	0.7%	1.9%	—	(1.5%)

2017 Year-End Financials

Debt ratio: 26.43%	No. of shares (mil.): 111
Return on equity: 3.64%	Dividends
Cash ($ mil.): 619	Yield: 0.0%
Current ratio: 2.14	Payout: 45.2%
Long-term debt ($ mil.): 2,437	Market value ($ mil.): 3,086

	STOCK PRICE ($) FY Close	P/E High/Low		PER SHARE ($) Earnings	Dividends	Book Value
12/17	27.80	24	18	1.37	0.62	38.46
12/16	28.87	81	54	0.39	0.59	37.68
12/15	25.89	15	12	1.98	0.56	37.87
12/14	25.25	—	—	(1.26)	0.54	36.40
12/13	25.78	24	16	1.29	0.51	37.87
Annual Growth	1.9%	—	—	1.5%	5.0%	0.4%

Tenet Healthcare Corp.

Tenet Healthcare is a for-profit company operating about 65 acute care hospitals with some 20000 beds in about 10 US states including California Florida and Texas. Its operations range from small community facilities offering basic care to major hospitals such as the 607-bed Brookwood Medical Center in Birmingham Alabama. In addition to its acute care holdings Tenet operates specialty hospitals skilled nursing facilities physician practices outpatient centers imaging centers and other health care units that form regional networks around its main hospitals. It also operates Conifer Health Solutions a patient billing and communications company.

HISTORY

Hospital attorney Richard Eamer along with attorneys Leonard Cohen and John Bedrosian founded National Medical Enterprises (NME) in 1969. After its IPO NME bought 10 hospitals nursing homes an office building and land in California. Within six years the company owned and managed 23 hospitals and a home health care business. It sold medical equipment and bottled oxygen and provided vocational training for nurses.

In the 1970s NME expanded into hospital construction and bought five Florida hospitals. By 1981 NME was the #3 health care concern in the US owning or managing 193 hospitals and nursing homes. In the 1980s NME diversified further buying nursing homes and mental health centers. By the end of the decade the company's Specialty Hospital Group brought in more than 50% of revenues. NME was the second-largest publicly owned health care company in the US (after HCA) by 1985.

In 1990 NME reversed course spinning off most of its long-term-care businesses but kept 19 UK

nursing facilities operated by its Westminster Health Care subsidiary (sold 1996). In 1992 the company acquired an Australian hospital management firm.

That year several insurance companies sued NME alleging fraudulent psychiatric claims; NME settled the suits in 1993. Federal agents later raided company headquarters seizing papers related to the suspected fraud. That year investment banker Jeff Barbakow took over as CEO forcing out Eamer and Cohen.

In 1993 and 1994 NME dumped most of its psychiatric and rehabilitation facilities using the proceeds to help pay penalties stemming from the federal investigation into alleged insurance fraud kickbacks and patient abuse at its psychiatric units. NME paid another $16 million in related state fines. (Related civil lawsuits were settled in 1997.)

The company's name change to Tenet Healthcare coincided with new purchases throughout the South in 1995 and 1996.

The next few years were mixed for Tenet. On the upside it bought OrNda HealthCorp which complemented Tenet's existing networks. Tenet and MedPartners (now Caremark Rx) then the #1 practice management firm formed a Southern California hospital-doctor network in 1997 that gave both companies heft in dealing with HMOs (the partnership crumbled in 1999 when MedPartners exited practice management to focus on pharmacy benefits management and ceased operations in California). Merger discussions began with embattled market leader Columbia/HCA (now HCA) but fizzled.

In 1998 Tenet bought eight Philadelphia hospitals owned by the bankrupt Allegheny Health Education & Research Foundation. The company was dogged by another investigation this time by the Health and Human Services Inspector General's office over allegations the company paid more than fair market value for a physician practice in return for kickbacks. Tenet in 2004 agreed to pay about $31 million to settle two lawsuits stemming from these allegations.

Like many companies in the industry in 1999 Tenet began feeling the effects of the Balanced Budget Act of 1997 which mandated more scrutiny of Medicare expenditures to health care providers. In response the company began divesting some of its hospitals; it also shed its practice management business and reorganized its corporate structure.

Tenet rebounded and acquired hospitals in 2001 and 2002 but the next year proved not so kind. Federal investigations into the company's billing practices particularly those related to Medicare began late in 2002. In 2003 the company settled claims brought by the Department of Justice that doctors performed unnecessary cardiac surgeries at its Redding Medical Center (now Sha

EXECUTIVES

Senior Vice President Public Affairs, Daniel R Waldmann

Chairman And Ceo, Ronald A. (Ron) Rittenmeyer, age 71

Ceo Central Valley Market, Warren J. Kirk

Ceo San Antonio Market, Trip Pilgrim

Ceo Western Region, Jeffrey (Jeff) Koury

President And Ceo Conifer Health Solutions, Stephen M. (Steve) Mooney

Svp And Chief Managed Care Officer, Clint Hailey

Cfo, Daniel J. (Dan) Cancelmi, age 55, $618,000 total compensation

Ceo Desert Market, Michele Finney

Ceo Eastern Region Â– Central Division, Garry Gause

Ceo Philadelphia Market, Michael P. (Mike) Halter

Ceo Texas Region, Tim Adams
Ceo Eastern Region Â– Coastal Division, Marsha Powers
Ceo Texas Region, J. Eric Evans, age 40, $626,538 total compensation
Svp Applied Informatics And Cio, Paul T. Browne
Ceo South Texas Market, Manuel R. (Manny) Vela
Ceo Memphis Market, Audrey Gregory
Ceo United Surgical Partners International, William H. (Bill) Wilcox
Ceo El Paso Market, Sally Deitch
Ceo Detroit Market, Anthony Tedeschi
Svp And Chief Compliance Officer, Howard Hacker
Vp Patient Care Services And Chief Nursing Officer, Dian Adams
Chief Medical Officer, Octavio J. (Tavi) Diaz
Ceo Phoenix Market, Frank Molinaro
Ceo Birmingham Market, Keith Parrott
Vice President Construction And Design, Kenneth Sutherland
Regional Vice President Chief Financial Officer, Bill Durham
Director Of Radiology, Robert Mckewen
Vice President And Assistant General Counsel, Paul Castanon
Vice President Chief Financial Officer Central Region At Tenet Healthcare, Kathryn Engstrom
Blood Bank Director, Melanie Orourke
Vice President Government Relations, Corey Davison
Vice President Finance, Rod Reasoner
Assistant Vice President Regional Managed Care Operations, Wesley Chick
Vice President Financial Information Systems, Michael Hongola
Vice President Investor Relations, Brendan Strong
Vice President Communications, Charles Nicolas
Vice President Government Programs, Craig Armin Rph, Lisa Jesse
Vice President Managed Care, Mike Blerman
Assistant Vice President Integrated Care Networks, Conley Cervantes
Vice President And Chief Of Staff Executive Office, Katy Black
Senior Vice President Corporate Development, Michael Maloney
Vice President Of Sales, Bruce Ballard
Vice President Construction And Design, Ken Sutherland
Vice President Operations Finance, Kat Ruffin
Senior Vice President Global Services, Rod Fomby
Director Of Radiology, Vikki Mcginnis
Pharmacy Manager, Dianeysis Haro
Vice President Graduate Medical Education Dio, Victor Jaffe
Secretary, Sonia Carcache
Secretary, Melissa Zapien
Auditors: Deloitte & Touche LLP

LOCATIONS

HQ: Tenet Healthcare Corp.
1445 Ross Avenue, Suite 1400, Dallas, TX 75202
Phone: 469 893-2200
Web: www.tenethealth.com

Selected Hospitals
Alabama
Brookwood Medical Center (Birmingham)
California
Desert Regional Medical Center (Palm Springs)
Doctors Hospital of Manteca
Doctors Medical Center (Modesto)
Emanuel Medical Center (Turlock)
Fountain Valley Regional Hospital and Medical Center
John F. Kennedy Memorial Hospital (Indio)
Lakewood Regional Medical Center
Los Alamitos Medical Center
Placentia Linda Hospital
San Ramon Regional Medical Center
Sierra Vista Regional Medical Center (San Luis Obispo)
Twin Cities Community Hospital (Templeton)

Florida
Coral Gables Hospital
Delray Medical Center (Delray Beach)
Good Samaritan Medical Center (West Palm Beach)
Hialeah Hospital
North Shore Medical Center (Miami)
Palm Beach Gardens Medical Center
Palmetto General Hospital (Hialeah)
St. Mary's Medical Center (West Palm Beach)
West Boca Medical Center (Boca Raton)
Missouri
Des Peres Hospital (St. Louis)
South Carolina
Coastal Carolina Hospital (Hardeeville)
East Cooper Regional Medical Center (Mt. Pleasant)
Hilton Head Hospital
Piedmont Medical Center (Rock Hill)
Tennessee
Saint Francis Hospital (Memphis)
Saint Francis Hospital-Bartlett
Texas
Centennial Medical Center (Frisco)
Cypress Fairbanks Medical Center (Houston)
Doctors Hospital at White Rock Lake (Dallas)
Houston Northwest Medical Center
Lake Pointe Medical Center (Rowlett)
Nacogdoches Medical Center
Park Plaza Hospital (Houston)
The Hospitals of Providence Memorial Campus (El Paso)
Texas Regional Medical Center (Sunnyvale)

PRODUCTS/OPERATIONS

2017 Sales by Segment

	$ mil.	% of total
Hospital Operations	16,260	82
Ambulatory Care	1,940	10
Conifer		
Tenet	618	3
Other customers	979	5
Adjustments	(618)	-
Total	19,179	100

COMPETITORS

Adventist Health System Sunbelt Healthcare
Ascension Health
Banner Health
CHRISTUS Health
Carolinas HealthCare System
Catholic Health Initiatives
Community Health Systems
Dignity Health
Encompass Health
HCA
LifePoint Health
Memorial Health Services
Mercy Health
SSM Health Care
Sutter Health
Texas Health Resources
Universal Health Services
University Health Services

HISTORICAL FINANCIALS
Company Type: Public

Income Statement   FYE: December 31

	REVENUE ($ mil.)	NET INCOME ($ mil.)	NET PROFIT MARGIN	EMPLOYEES
12/17	19,179	(704)	—	125,820
12/16	19,621	(192)	—	130,000
12/15	18,634	(140)	—	134,630
12/14	16,615	12	0.1%	108,989
12/13	11,102	(134)	—	103,711
Annual Growth	14.6%	—	—	4.9%

2017 Year-End Financials

Debt ratio: 63.87%
Return on equity: (-521.48%)
Cash ($ mil.): 611
Current ratio: 1.29
Long-term debt ($ mil.): 14,791

No. of shares (mil.): 100
Dividends
Yield: —
Payout: —
Market value ($ mil.): 1,531

	STOCK PRICE ($) FY Close	P/E High/Low	PER SHARE ($) Earnings	Dividends	Book Value
12/17	15.16	— —	(7.00)	0.00	(1.46)
12/16	14.84	— —	(1.93)	0.00	4.18
12/15	30.30	— —	(1.41)	0.00	7.02
12/14	50.67	527323	0.12	0.00	6.62
12/13	42.12	— —	(1.32)	0.00	7.79
Annual Growth	(22.5%)	—			

Tenneco Inc

Tenneco ensures vehicles are riding steady without exhausting a lot of smoke. The auto parts maker designs and distributes ride-control equipment (including shock absorbers struts and suspensions) under the Monroe brand and emissions-control systems (catalytic converters exhaust pipes and mufflers) under the Walker brand. It also makes Clevite elastomer products (bushings mounts and springs) for vibration control in cars and heavy trucks. It supplies both OEMs and aftermarket wholesalers and retailers. Major customers include GM Ford Advance Auto Parts and Uni-Select. Tenneco operates on six continents and is growing its presence in key Asia/Pacific markets.

Operations
Tenneco divides its operations across six segments. These are structured geographically and are managed along its two major product lines of emission control and ride control. These segments are: North America Clean Air North America Ride Performance Europe South and India Clean Air Europe South and India Ride Performance Asia Pacific Clean Air and Asia Pacific Ride Performance. Emission control accounted for about 65% of the company's revenue in 2016.

As stricter environmental standards are enacted Tenneco finds itself well positioned as a supplier of emission control systems. The company has developed diesel particulate filters (DPFs) for passenger cars and medium-duty trucks both in Europe and North America. The filters when used with converters can reduce emissions of particulates by as much as 90% and nitrogen oxide by up to 95%. Tenneco also produces selective catalytic reduction (SCR) systems.

Another trend in the automotive industry that is building Tenneco's business is OEMs endeavoring to simplify their assembly process thus reducing costs and development times. To achieve this the OEMs are outsourcing more of the design and manufacturing of vehicle parts as well as fully-integrated systems that support emission control anti-lock braking roll-control and powertrains. This trend has given rise to Tier 1 systems integrators in addition to Tier 1 suppliers — Tenneco fits the bill for both roles. To boost its position even further the company offers just-in-time (JIT) systems for its emission control operations and has built JIT facilities close to a customer's plant for quick delivery of product components.

Geographic Reach
In addition to key alliances and joint ventures Tenneco operates 90 manufacturing facilities on six continents throughout the world. Most recently the company has opened manufacturing facilities in India China and Thailand. The US represented almost 40% of its total sales in 2016; China accounted for roughly 15%.

Sales and Marketing

Tenneco has separate sales and marketing efforts underway for its OE and aftermarket businesses. For OE sales the company's sales and marketing team is an integrated group of professionals including engineers and program managers who are organized by customer and product type (ride control and emission control). In 2016 the company served more than 75 different OEMs and commercial truck and off-highway engine manufacturers worldwide.

For aftermarket sales however the sale force covers multiple product lines and sells aftermarket products through four primary channels of distribution: The traditional three-step distribution system of full-line warehouse distributors jobbers and installers; the two-step distribution system of full-line warehouse distributors that carry only specified automotive product groups and installers; direct sales to retailers; and direct sales to installer chains. The company also serves locomotive agricultural construction and commercial truck and off-highway markets.

Its customers have included National Auto Parts Association Advance Auto Parts Uni-Select O'Reilly Automotive Aftermarket Auto Parts Alliance and AutoZone in North America Temot Autoteile GmbH Autodistribution International Group Auto Union Auto Teile Ring and AP United in Europe and Rede Presidente in South America. GM accounted for 17% of 2016 revenues; Ford 13%.

Financial Performance

Tenneco enjoyed unprecedented growth in 2016 with revenues peaking at a record-setting $8.6 billion. The revenue growth for 2016 was fueled by increased sales from its ride performance and clean air division product lines. It also experienced increased aftermarket ride performance sales in Europe and South America and recognized a 14% bump in sales from China.

The company's profits surged by 47% to reach $363 million in 2016 another company milestone. This was the result of positive impacts from a US tax benefit during the year. In addition cash flow from operations declined from $517 million in 2015 to $489 million in 2016 primarily due to the timing of revenue growth at the end of the year and the resulting impact on accounts receivable.

Strategy

The company focuses on growth through increasing production volumes launching new technology and geographic expansion both organically and via strategic acquisitions and alliances. Tenneco is also eyeing adjacent markets to expand its portfolio of products and systems. Not limiting itself to passenger cars or medium-size trucks the company is positioning its emissions and ride control systems for heavy-duty trucks buses and agricultural and construction equipment.

In 2016 Tennoco opened new facilities in Spring Hill Tennessee; and Lansing Michigan. It also expanded its manufacturing operations in Puebla Mexico; and Birmingham UK and built out additional testing capabilities in Zwickau Germany.

Mergers and Acquisitions

In 2018 Tenneco completed the acquisition of aftermarket parts supplier Federal-Mogul (Icahn Enterprises was the majority shareholder) for $5.4 billion. Tenneco intends to split the combined businesses into two publicly traded companies—an aftermarket and ride performance company that will include Tenneco Ride Performance and Federal-Mogul Motorparts and a powertrain technology company which will include Tenneco Clean Air and Federal-Mogul Powertrain. The deal gives Tenneco the opportunity to capture the market in both business areas.

Also in 2018 the company acquired Ohlins Racing A.B. a Swedish technology company that develops premium suspension systems and components for the automotive and motor sport

industries. Tenneco believes Ohlins will increase its share in developing mobility markets and accelerate the development of advanced original equipment (OE) intelligent suspension solutions.

HISTORY

Tennessee Gas and Transmission began in 1943 as a division of the Chicago Corporation headed by Gardiner Symonds and authorized to build a pipeline from West Virginia to the Gulf of Mexico. With the US facing WWII fuel shortages the group finished the project in 11 months.

After WWII Tennessee Gas went public with Symonds as president. It merged its oil and gas exploration interests into Tennessee Production Company (1954) which with Bay Petroleum (bought 1955) became Tenneco Oil in 1961. Symonds acquired complementary firms and entered the chemical industry by buying 50% of Petro-Tex Chemical in 1955.

Tenneco Oil moved its headquarters to Houston in 1963 to better ship natural gas from the Texas Gulf Coast. Symonds bought Packaging Corporation of America a maker of shipping containers pulp and paperboard products in 1965. A year later the company which had become a conglomerate adopted the Tenneco name.

EXECUTIVES

Vice President Human Resources, Mike Schneider
Senior Vice President Global Administration, Richard P Schneider
Evp And Cfo, Kenneth R. (Ken) Trammell, age 57, $625,000 total compensation
Vp And Cio, H. William Haser, age 57
Ceo, Brian Kesseler, age 52, $895,000 total compensation
Evp And President Asia/pacific, Peng (Patrick) Guo, age 52
Svp And General Manager Global Aftermarket, Joseph A. (Joe) Pomaranski, age 62
Vp And General Manager North America Aftermarket, Jeff Koviak
Vp And General Manager North America Clean Air, Michael Seurynck
Vp And General Manager North America Ride Performance, Jack Hall
Vp And General Manager Europe Aftermarket, Bruce Ronning
Vp And General Manager China Clean Air, Yih Sng
Vp And General Manager China Aftermarket, Edward Hang
Vp And General Manager Global Elastomers, Steve Pohlman
Managing Director India, Sagar Hemade
General Manager Japan, Yasuhara Shimonishi
Vp And Cto, Ben Patel
Evp And President Ride Performance, Martin Hendricks, age 55
Vp And General Manager Europe Ride Performance, Jean-Luc Desire
Vp And General Manager Europe Clean Air, Traci Melville
Vp And General Manager China Ride Performance, Yi Ren
Vice President General Manager, Alex Gelbcke
Vice President, Richard Wambold
Vice President Finance, Leo Waner
Chairman, Gregg M. Sherrill, age 65
Auditors: PricewaterhouseCoopers LLP

LOCATIONS

HQ: Tenneco Inc
500 North Field Drive, Lake Forest, IL 60045
Phone: 847 482-5000
Web: www.tenneco.com

2016 Sales

	$ mil.	% of total
US	3,512	41
China	1,186	14
Germany	764	8
Canada	387	5
United Kingdom	387	5
Other Foreign	2,363	27
Total	8,599	100

PRODUCTS/OPERATIONS

2016 Sales

	$ mil.	% of total
Clean Air Products & Systems		
Aftermarket	305	4
Original Equipment		
OE Value-add	3,736	43
OE Substrate	2,028	24
Ride Performance Products & Systems		
Aftermarket	937	10
Original Equipment	1,593	19
Total	8,599	100

Selected Brands and Products

Emission control systems (DNX DynoMax Fonos Gillet Thrush and Walker)
  Aftertreatment control units
  Burner systems
  Catalytic converters and diesel oxidation catalysts
  Diesel particulate filters (DPFs)
  Exhaust manifolds
  Hangers and isolators
  High-frequency turbo decoupler
  Hydrocarbon vaporizers and injectors
  Lean NOx traps
  Mufflers
  Pipes
  Resonators
  Selective catalytic reduction (SCR)
Ride control systems (DNX Fric-Rot Kinetic Monroe and Rancho)
  Coil and leaf springs
  Computerized electronic suspension (CES)
  Corner and full axle modules
  Heavy duty truck and train shocks
  Kinetic suspension technology
  Shock absorbers and struts
  Suspension systems
  Top mounts
  Vibration control components (Clevite Elastomers)
  Engine and body mounts
  Exhaust isolators
  Leaf and coil springs
  Spring seats
  Suspension control arm link and stabilizer bar bushings

COMPETITORS

Benteler Automotive
Cooper-Standard Automotive
Edelbrock
Faurecia Exhaust Systems
Kolbenschmidt Pierburg
Letts Industries
Meritor
Wescast Industries
ZF Group NAO

HISTORICAL FINANCIALS

Company Type: Public

Income Statement

FYE: December 31

	REVENUE ($ mil.)	NET INCOME ($ mil.)	NET PROFIT MARGIN	EMPLOYEES
12/17	9,274	207	2.2%	32,000
12/16	8,599	363	4.2%	31,000
12/15	8,209	247	3.0%	30,000
12/14	8,420	226	2.7%	29,000
12/13	7,964	183	2.3%	26,000
Annual Growth	3.9%	3.1%	—	5.3%

2017 Year-End Financials

Debt ratio: 29.76%
Return on equity: 32.24%
Cash ($ mil.): 315
Current ratio: 1.24
Long-term debt ($ mil.): 1,358

No. of shares (mil.): 51
Dividends
Yield: 0.0%
Payout: 25.5%
Market value ($ mil.): 3,011

	STOCK PRICE ($) FY Close	P/E High/Low		PER SHARE ($) Earnings	Dividends	Book Value
12/17	58.54	17	13	3.91	1.00	13.53
12/16	62.47	10	5	6.44	0.00	10.84
12/15	45.91	15	10	4.11	0.00	7.52
12/14	56.61	18	13	3.66	0.00	8.12
12/13	56.57	19	11	2.97	0.00	7.11
Annual Growth	0.9%	—	—	7.1%	—	17.4%

TENNESSEE STATE SCHOOL BOND AUTHORITY

EXECUTIVES

Prin, Jerald Nicely
Chief Engineer, Paul Degges

LOCATIONS

HQ: TENNESSEE STATE SCHOOL BOND AUTHORITY
SUITE 1600 JAMES K. POLK, NASHVILLE, TN
372430001
Phone: 615 401-7872

HISTORICAL FINANCIALS

Company Type: Private

Income Statement

FYE: June 30

	ASSETS ($ mil.)	NET INCOME ($ mil.)	INCOME AS % OF ASSETS	EMPLOYEES
06/17	2,258	(6)	—	3
06/16	2,200	9	0.4%	
Annual Growth	2.6%	—	—	—

2017 Year-End Financials

Debt ratio: —
Return on equity: (-10.20%)
Cash ($ mil.): 60
Current ratio: 0.50
Long-term debt ($ mil.): —

Dividends
Yield: —
Payout: —
Market value ($ mil.): —

Tennessee Valley Authority

Tennessee Valley Authority (TVA) may not be an expert on state attractions like Dollywood and the Grand Ole Opry but it is an authority on power generation. A US government-owned corporation TVA is the largest public power producer in the country. It sells wholesale electricity to more than 150 municipal and cooperative power distributors which serve some 9 million people in Tennessee and parts of Alabama Georgia Kentucky Mississippi North Carolina and Virginia. It also sells power directly to large industrial customers and federal agencies. In addition TVA provides flood control and land management for the Tennessee River system and assists utilities and state and local governments with economic development.

Operations

Tennessee Valley Authority operates seven fossil plants three nuclear plants and 29 hydro plants. TVA provides electric power through a network of about 16000 miles of transmission line. While most of its power comes from traditional generation sources it operates 15 solar energy sites and one wind energy site.

TVA?s power generation mix nuclear about 40%; coal about 25%; natural gas about 20%; hydro about 10%; and the rest from wind solar and energy efficiency measures. Total generation capacity stands at nearly 170000 gigawatt-hours.

TVA has an agreement to produce tritium a radioactive gas that boosts the power of nuclear weapons for the US Department of Energy at its Watts Bar nuclear plant.

Geographic Reach

The Tennessee Valley Authority serves 170 counties in Alabama Georgia Kentucky Mississippi North Carolina Tennessee and Virginia. Tennessee accounts for 65% of the entity's revenues.

Sales and Marketing

Tennessee Valley Authority provides electricity to more than 50 large industrial customers a handful of federal agencies and more than 150 local power company (LPC) customers that serve more than nine million people in parts of seven southeastern states. The United States Enrichment Corporation a subsidiary of USEC is TVA's largest directly served industrial customer. Two of the largest LPCs served by TVA are the Memphis Light Gas and Water Division and Nashville Electric Service.

Financial Performance

In fiscal 2017 Tennessee Valley Authority's revenue inched up about 1% although power sales fell 2% due to mild weather than reduced energy demand. The TVA made an extra $500 million contribution to its pension fund in 2017 which drove net income to $685 million in 2017 about 50% less than 2016. Fuel costs were 2% higher.

Strategy

TVA is changing its power generation mix to become a cleaner producer of energy. It has closed or is closing several older less efficient coal generated power units while putting more natural gas-fired units on line as well as increasing nuclear generation capabilities. The authority is working toward obtaining 50% of its power supply from low- or zero-carbon-emitting or renewable sources by 2020.

HISTORY

TVA was established by Congress in 1933 primarily to reduce flood damage improve navigation on the Tennessee River and promote agricultural and industrial development in the region. In 1999 government appropriations for the authority ceased.

In 1924 the Army Corps of Engineers finished building the Wilson Dam on the Tennessee River in Alabama to provide power for two WWI-era nitrate plants. With the war over the question of what to do with the plants became a political football.

An act of Congress created the Tennessee Valley Authority (TVA) in 1933 to manage the plants and Tennessee Valley waterways. New Dealers saw TVA as a way to revitalize the local economy through improved navigation and power generation. Power companies claimed the agency was unconstitutional but by 1939 when a federal court ruled against them TVA had five operating hydroelectric plants and five under construction.

During the 1940s TVA supplied power for the war effort including the Manhattan Project in Tennessee. During the postwar boom between 1945 and 1950 power usage in the Tennessee Valley nearly doubled. Despite adding dams TVA couldn't keep up with demand so in 1949 it began building a coal-fired unit. Because coal-fired plants weren't part of TVA's original mission in 1955 a Congressional panel recommended the authority be dissolved.

Though TVA survived its funding was cut. In 1959 it was allowed to sell bonds but it no longer received direct government appropriations for power operations. In addition it had to pay back the government for past appropriations.

TVA began to build the first unit of an ambitious 17-plant nuclear power program in Alabama in 1967. However skyrocketing costs forced it to raise rates and cut maintenance on its coal-fired plants which led to breakdowns. In 1985 five reactors had to be shut down because of safety concerns.

In 1988 former auto industry executive Marvin Runyon was appointed chairman of the agency. "Carvin' Marvin" cut management sold three airplanes and got rid of peripheral businesses saving $400 million a year. In 1992 Runyon left to go to the postal service and was replaced by Craven Crowell who began preparing TVA for competition in the retail power market.

TVA ended its nuclear construction program in 1996 after bringing two nuclear units on line within three months a first for a US utility. The next year it raised rates for the first time in 10 years planning to reduce its debt. In response to a lawsuit filed by neighboring utilities it agreed to stop "laundering" power by using third parties to sell outside the agency's legally authorized area.

In 1999 the authority finished installing almost $2 billion in scrubbers and other equipment at its coal-fired plants so that it could buy Kentucky coal along with cleaner Wyoming coal. That year however the EPA charged TVA with violating the Clean Air Act by making major overhauls on some of its older coal-fired plants without getting permits or installing updated pollution-control equipment. It ordered TVA to bring most of its coal-fired plants into compliance with more current pollution standards. The next year TVA contested the order in court stating compliance would jack up electricity rates.

TVA was fined by the US Nuclear Regulatory Commission in 2000 for laying off a nuclear plant whistleblower.

In 2008 a holding pond at TVA's coal-burning Kingston Fossil Plant failed and dumped some 5.4 million cu. yd. of fly ash over 400 acres in eastern Tennessee's Roane County. The slide knocked down utility poles and trees and damaged at least a dozen homes (some beyond repair). Although no one was hurt some residents were cut off by the spill prompting officials to build a new road. The flooding was the pond's third reported incident in six years. The cleanup will likely cost more than $1 billion. Some 14 lawsuits were filed against the TVA as a result of the incident.

William D. Johnson former chairman president and CEO of Progress Energy was named president and CEO of TVA in 2013.

EXECUTIVES

Evp And Cfo, John M. Thomas, age 55, $577,212 total compensation
Evp And Chief Nuclear Officer, Joseph P. (Joe) Grimes, age 61, $557,135 total compensation

Svp Distributed Energy Resources, Jay C. Stowe
Evp And Coo, Charles G. (Chip) Pardee, age 58, $647,481 total compensation
Evp External Relations, Van M. Wardlaw, age 58
Svp Watts Bar Operations And Construction, Michael D. (Mike) Skaggs, $446,712 total compensation
President Ceo And Director, William D. (Bill) Johnson, age 63, $998,827 total compensation
Svp Chief Communications And Marketing Officer, Janet J. Brewer
Evp And General Counsel, Sherry A. Quirk, age 63
Executive Vice President And Chief Nuclear Officer, Joe Grimes
Vice President Operations, Mitchell Bible
Chair, V. Lynn Evans
Auditors: Ernst & Young LLP

LOCATIONS

HQ: Tennessee Valley Authority
  400 W. Summit Hill Drive, Knoxville, TN 37902
Phone: 865 632-2101
Web: www.tva.gov

2016 Sales

	$ mil.	% of total
Tennessee	6,968	66
Alabama	1,504	14
Mississippi	999	9
Kentucky	640	6
Georgia	255	2
North Carolina	155	1
Virginia	58	1
Other revenues	48	1
Off-system sales	7	-
Revenue capitalized during pre-commercial plant operations	(18)	-
Total	**10,616**	**100**

PRODUCTS/OPERATIONS

2016 Sales

	$ mil.	% of total
Electricity sales:		
Local power companies	9,696	91
Industries directly served	649	6
Other revenues	155	2
Federal agencies & other	134	1
Revenue capitalized during per-commercial plant operations	(18)	-
Total	**10,616**	**100**

HISTORICAL FINANCIALS

Company Type: Public

Income Statement   FYE: September 30

	REVENUE ($ mil.)	NET INCOME ($ mil.)	NET PROFIT MARGIN	EMPLOYEES
09/18	11,233	1,119	10.0%	10,023
09/17	10,739	685	6.4%	10,092
09/16	10,616	1,233	11.6%	10,691
09/15	11,003	1,111	10.1%	10,918
09/14	11,137	469	4.2%	11,542
Annual Growth	**0.2%**	**24.3%**	**—**	**(3.5%)**

2018 Year-End Financials

Debt ratio: 48.57%—
Return on equity: 11.53%
Cash ($ mil.): 299
Current ratio: 0.71
Long-term debt ($ mil.): 21,307

Dividends
  Yield: 0.0%
  Payout: —
Market value ($ mil.): —

	STOCK PRICE ($) FY Close	P/E High/Low	PER SHARE ($) Earnings	Dividends	Book Value
09/18	25.07	— —	(0.00)	0.89	(0.00)
09/17	25.47	— —	(0.00)	0.89	(0.00)
09/16	26.02	— —	(0.00)	0.84	(0.00)
09/15	24.65	— —	(0.00)	0.95	(0.00)
09/14	23.91	— —	(0.00)	0.99	(0.00)
Annual Growth	**1.2%**	**— —**	—	**(2.7%)**	—

Territorial Bancorp Inc

Territorial Bancorp serves its customers island-style. It is the financial holding company for Territorial Savings Bank which provides standard products and services such as checking and savings accounts money market accounts CDs IRAs and loans from its nearly 30 branch locations across Hawaii. Its Territorial Financial Services subsidiary sells insurance while LPL Financial offers Mutual funds and annuities. Territorial Savings Bank targets the territorial nature of its customers — one- to four-family residential mortgages account for 95% of its loan portfolio. Multifamily and commercial mortgages and construction and home equity loans round out its lending activities.

Operations
Territorial Bancorp generated 61% of its total revenue from loan interest in 2014 with another 31% coming from interest on its investment securities. About 3% of its revenue came from service fees on loan and deposit accounts while 2% came from gains on its investment security sales.

Sales and Marketing
The bank provides financial services to individuals families and small- to medium-sized businesses from its 28 branches spread across the state of Hawaii.

Financial Performance
Territorial's revenues and profits have been slowly declining in recent years mostly as its margins have been squeezed in the low-interest environment and as its gains on its held-for-sale loans have been shrinking.

The company's revenue ended mostly flat around $64.8 million in 2014 with mixed results. The bank's loan and investment security interest grew by 7% thanks to asset growth though these improvements were offset by lower gains on investment securities and loans compared to the year before.

Lower revenue in 2014 coupled with a slight uptick in loan loss provisions and equipment investment costs caused Territorial Bancorp's net income to tumble by 4% to $14.1 million. Its operating cash levels also fell by 19% to $14.1 million after adjusting its earnings for non-cash items mostly related to its net proceeds on its held-for-sale loans.

Strategy
Territorial Bancorp relies on its competitive rates and pricing to grow its loan and deposit business. During 2014 its deposit business grew organically by nearly 6% mostly as the bank promoted its higher-than-market rates for its passbook and statement savings accounts.

Company Background
Founded in 1921 Territorial Savings was mutually owned until 2009 when its former parent Territorial Mutual Holding Company converted to a stock form of ownership and sold shares in itself to the public. The move allowed the company to offer other financial services in addition to banking.

EXECUTIVES

Chairman President And Ceo Territorial Bancorp Inc. And Territorial Savings Bank, Allan S. Kitagawa, age 72, $766,080 total compensation
Vice Chairman Co-coo General Counsel And Corporate Secretary Territorial Bancorp Inc. And Territorial Savings Bank, Vernon Hirata, age 65, $269,100 total compensation
Svp Business Development And Marketing, Denise Takashima
Svp Branch Administration, Robert Costa

Vice Chairman And Co-coo Territorial Bancorp Inc. And Territorial Savings Bank, Ralph Y. Nakatsuka, age 62, $269,100 total compensation
Senior Vice President Risk Management, Stanley Tanaka
Auditors: Moss Adams LLP

LOCATIONS

HQ: Territorial Bancorp Inc
  1132 Bishop Street, Suite 2200, Honolulu, HI 96813
Phone: 808 946-1400
Web: www.territorialsavings.net

PRODUCTS/OPERATIONS

2014 Sales

	$ mil.	% of total
Interest and dividend income		
Loans	39	61
Investment securities	19	31
Others	0	-
Non-interest income		
Service fees on loan and deposits	2	3
Income on bank owned life insurance	1	2
Others	2	3
Total	**64**	**100**

COMPETITORS

American Savings Bank   Central Pacific
Bank of Hawaii   Financial

HISTORICAL FINANCIALS

Company Type: Public

Income Statement   FYE: December 31

	ASSETS ($ mil.)	NET INCOME ($ mil.)	INCOME AS % OF ASSETS	EMPLOYEES
12/17	2,003	14	0.7%	283
12/16	1,877	16	0.9%	276
12/15	1,821	14	0.8%	280
12/14	1,691	14	0.8%	272
12/13	1,616	14	0.9%	279
Annual Growth	**5.5%**	**0.5%**	**—**	**0.4%**

2017 Year-End Financials

Debt ratio: —
Return on equity: 6.44%
Cash ($ mil.): 32
Current ratio: —
Long-term debt ($ mil.): —

No. of shares (mil.): 9
Dividends
  Yield: 0.0%
  Payout: 76.4%
Market value ($ mil.): 306

	STOCK PRICE ($) FY Close	P/E High/Low	PER SHARE ($) Earnings	Dividends	Book Value
12/17	30.87	21 18	1.57	1.20	23.69
12/16	32.84	18 14	1.76	0.92	23.50
12/15	27.74	18 13	1.59	0.76	22.74
12/14	21.55	15 13	1.51	0.70	21.81
12/13	23.20	16 14	1.49	0.62	21.11
Annual Growth	**7.4%**	**— —**	**1.3%**	**17.9%**	**2.9%**

Tesla Inc

Tesla intends to supercharge the public's passion for electric vehicles. Founded in 2003 the company designs manufactures and markets high-performance technologically advanced electric cars and powertrain components. Tesla sells three models: the Model S sedan and the Model X SUV which are among the world's top-selling electric cars and the Model 3 sedan introduced in 2017. The fuel-efficient fully electric vehicles recharge their lithium-ion batteries from an outlet and depending on a driver's speed are capable traveling about 300 miles per charge. Tesla is working on self-driving technology with some available on current models. US customers generate more than half of Tesla?s sales. CEO Elon Musk founded PayPal and also runs SpaceX.

Operations

Tesla designs makes and sells electric vehicles which are the Model S Model X and Model 3. The company also offers leasing and services.

Through its acquisition of SolarCity in 2016 Tesla created an energy generation and storage segment which makes and sells stationary energy storage products and solar energy systems to residential and commercial customers. Its Powerwall products integrate with solar panels and can store enough energy to power a two-bedroom home for a day. Tesla's commercial and utility offering Powerpack is an energy storage system that offers features like peak shaving load shifting emergency backup self-consumption of solar generation and demand response.

Vehicle sales account for about 70% of the company?s revenue with leasing services and energy generation and storage accounting for about 10% each.

The company maintains a network of around 7000 charging ports in some 1100 stations worldwide.

Geographic Reach

Tesla operates through 330 stores and service locations in more than 25 US states and about 25 countries. The US accounts for more than 50% of sales. Markets for which the company breaks out sales are China more than 15% and Norway more than 5%.

Sales and Marketing

Tesla markets and sells cars directly to consumers through an international network of company-owned stores and galleries. Tesla is notable in that it does not use dealerships (due in some states to legal restrictions) and this approach means the price of its vehicles are non-negotiable.

Financial Performance

Tesla?s revenue growth has accelerated like its first car the Roadster sportscar (0-60 in 1.9 seconds) driven by the rising number of vehicles sold each year. The company however has posted a string of net losses culminating in a loss approaching $2 billion in 2017 as it pours money into research and development and manufacturing.

Tesla?s revenue jumped more than 50% to $11.7 billion in 2017 driven by a 53% increase in automotive revenue. The number of vehicles sold in 2017 rose to more than 82000 including about 1700 Model 3s (introduced in July 2017) from about 51000 in 2016. Automotive leasing revenue was up 45% in 2017 while service revenue increased about 114%. The energy generation and storage segment contributed about 10% of revenue in its first full year as part of Tesla.

As fast as the company?s sales are moving forward its bottom line is stuck in reverse. The company lost about $1.9 billion in 2017 about $1.3 more than its 2016 loss. The cost of automotive revenue rose 58% in 2017 matching the percentage increase in the number of units sold in the year. Tesla also had higher expenses for R&D sales general and administrative and interest for 2017.

Tesla had about $3.4 billion cash on hand at the end of 2017 about the same as it did in 2016. In 2017 the company had capital expenditures of $4 billion for Model 3 production design acquisitions and installation of solar energy systems.

Strategy

In 2017 Tesla entered the mass market vehicle world with the July 2017 introduction of the Model

3 which has a $35000 starting price. But production wasn?t exactly mass-market caliber as the company struggled to match capacity with demand. The company worked in 2018 to ramp up production hiring more workers and trying to speed up manufacturing processes with a goal of turning out 2500 Model 3s a week.

Tesla not only develops electric-powered cars it is developing autonomous car technology that include cameras sensors radar and an on-board computer. Many functions driving can be turned over the car but the driver maintains responsibility how it behaves.

Electricity isn't just for cars as far as Tesla is concerned. The company is developing Tesla Semi an electric version of diesel-powered semis built for hauling heavy payloads around the country. The company said it will have a 500-mile battery range. Tesla intends to use the truck for its own logistics but PepsiCo Anheuser Busch J.B. Hunt UPS and FedEx have placed orders for the trucks. Tesla plans to begin production of the semis in 2019.

While most automakers have generated armies of suppliers providing parts Tesla tries to handle as much manufacturing as it can in-house including batteries and drive trains. The company spreads production costs for batteries across its energy and storage unit but the costs of funding such manufacturing operations eat up a lot of cash.

Tesla pioneered the electric car market of the 21st century but other automakers are appearing bigger in the rearview mirror. Companies such as Honda Toyota Ford GM Nissan BMW Daimler are investing in development programs designed to shift large parts in some cases all of their fleets to electric power in the coming years. Volvo is to switch to all electric vehicles in 2019. Tesla has delivered highly ranked vehicles so far but the automakers can call on deep resources extensive supply chains and global markets in developing and selling their vehicles.

Mergers and Acquisitions

In 2019 Tesla agreed to acquire energy technology company Maxwell Technologies in an all-stock deal valued at $218 million. Maxwell develops and makes ultracapacitors devices that can store and quickly deliver surges of energy. Tesla would use the technology to increase battery capacity while reducing weight in its vehicles.

Tesla made two acquisitions in 2017 to beef up its factory automation technologies. Minnesota-based Perbix had been a parts supplier to Tesla and that acquisition brings its capabilities in-house. Tesla bought Grohmann Engineering based in Germany for $109 million to improve the speed and efficiency of its manufacturing processes.

In 2016 Tesla made its most important acquisition to date when it purchased SolarCity in a deal valued at $2.6 billion. Both companies are led by Elon Musk and expect to achieve cost synergies of $150 million in the first full year after closing. By combining Tesla's new electric vehicles with SolarCity's newest solar products the companies expect to lower hardware costs reduce installation costs and improve their manufacturing efficiency. The acquisition also created generation and storage a new segment that designs manufactures installs and sells stationary energy storage products and solar energy systems to residential and commercial customers.

Company Background

Tesla Motors is named for Nikola Tesla (1856-1943) the renowned Serbian-American engineer and inventor. Tesla Motors was incorporated in July 2003.

2017 Year-End Financials

Debt ratio: 36.00%
Return on equity: (-43.63%)
Cash ($ mil.): 3,367
Current ratio: 0.86
Long-term debt ($ mil.): 9,418

No. of shares (mil.): 168
Dividends
 Yield: —
 Payout: —
Market value ($ mil.): 52,555

	STOCK PRICE ($) FY Close	P/E High/Low	PER SHARE ($) Earnings	Dividends	Book Value
12/17	311.35	— —	(11.83)	0.00	25.10
12/16	213.69	— —	(4.68)	0.00	29.42
12/15	240.01	— —	(6.93)	0.00	8.29
12/14	222.41	— —	(2.36)	0.00	7.25
12/13	150.43	— —	(0.62)	0.00	5.42
Annual Growth	19.9%	— —	—	—	46.7%

TEXAS A&M FOUNDATION

EXECUTIVES

Pres, Tyson Voelkel
Pres*, Dr Eddie J Davis
Senior V Pres*, John R Stropp
Senior V Pres*, James J Palincsar
V Pres-Cfo*, Doyle Thompson
Vice President*, Liska Lusk
Support Manager, Dennis Allen
Support Manager, Steve Herring
Manager, John Adamson
Administrative Assistant, Shelly Daughters
Director, Don Birkelbach
Auditors: BKD LLP HOUSTON TX

LOCATIONS

HQ: TEXAS A&M FOUNDATION
 401 GEORGE BUSH DR, COLLEGE STATION, TX
 778402811
Phone: 979 845-8161
Web: WWW.TXAMFOUNDATION.COM

HISTORICAL FINANCIALS

Company Type: Private

Income Statement

FYE: June 30

	ASSETS ($ mil.)	NET INCOME ($ mil.)	INCOME AS % OF ASSETS	EMPLOYEES
06/16	1,783	105	5.9%	95
06/13	1,505	97	6.5%	—
06/12	1,313	66	5.0%	—
06/11	0	43	—	—
Annual Growth	—	19.6%	—	—

2016 Year-End Financials

Debt ratio: —
Return on equity: 51.30%
Cash ($ mil.): 73
Current ratio: 35.70
Long-term debt ($ mil.): —

Dividends
 Yield: —
 Payout: —
Market value ($ mil.): —

Texas Capital Bancshares Inc

Texas Capital Bancshares is the parent company of Texas Capital Bank with more than 10 branches in Austin Dallas Fort Worth Houston and San Antonio. The bank targets high-net-worth individuals and Texas-based businesses with more than $5 million in annual revenue with a focus on the real estate financial services transportation communications petrochemicals and mining sectors. Striving for personalized services for its clients the bank offers deposit accounts Visa credit cards commercial loans and mortgages equipment leasing wealth management and trust services. Its BankDirect division provides online banking services. Founded in 1998 Texas Capital Bancshares has about $11.7 billion in assets.

Financial Performance

The bank reported $488.6 million in revenue in 2013 an nearly 11% increase versus 2012. Net income was flat at about $121 million after posting three consecutive years of gains. Cash flow from operations continued its steep three year decline. The bank's total assets increased 11% from about $10.5 billion in 2012 to $11.7 billion in 2013. Total deposits increased 24% year over year to about $9.3 billion.

Strategy

Headquartered in Dallas Texas Capital Bank (TCB) believes that its Texas roots give it a competitive advantage over larger competitors that are headquartered out of state. Indeed TCB is gaining market share and is expanding by hiring experienced bankers and support staff. The bank is looking to grow within its main metropolitan markets but has also branched out beyond the borders of its home state. The bank has an Cayman Islands branch to offer offshore cash management and deposit products to it core clientele.

EXECUTIVES

President And Ceo Texas Capital Bancshares Inc. President And Ceo Texas Capital Bank, C. Keith Cargill, age 65, $825,000 total compensation
President Texas And Chief Lending Officer Texas Capital Bank, Vince A. Ackerson, age 61, $454,166 total compensation
Managing Director Regional And Specialty Banking Texas Capital Bank Austin Fort Worth And San Antonio And Commercial Real Estate And Builder Finance, Mark M. Johnson
Evp Austin Region Texas Capital Bank, Kerry L. Hall
Regional President Texas Capital Bank Dallas, Russell Hartsfield
Chief Risk Officer Texas Capital Bancshares Inc. And Texas Capital Bank, John D. Hudgens, age 62, $455,833 total compensation
Managing Director Specialty And Regional Banking Texas Capital Bank Dallas And Syndicated Finance Lender Finance Leasing And Financial Institutions, James D. (Jim) Recer
Regional Chairman Texas Capital Bank Houston, Bill Wilson
Regional President Texas Capital Bank San Antonio, David Pope
Managing Director Regional And Specialty Banking Texas Capital Bank Houston, John C. Sarvadi
Controller And Chief Accounting Officer Texas Capital Bancshares And Cfo Texas Capital Bank, Julie L. Anderson, age 49, $355,000 total compensation

Regional Chairman Texas Capital Bank San Antonio, Shaun Kennedy
Regional Chairman Texas Capital Bank Fort Worth, Robin Hamilton
Regional President Texas Capital Bank Fort Worth, David Williams
Evp Builder Finance, Melissa Abel
Evp Asset Based Lending, Chris Capriotti
Evp Commercial Real Estate, Rob Delph
Evp Lender Finance, David Fricke
Evp Energy/oil And Gas Syndicated Finance And Financial Institutions, Lester Keliher
Evp Financial Institutions, Peter Stringer
President Mortgage Finance, Gary Ort
Evp Technology Operations Enterprise Planning And Information Security Texas Capital Bank, Kirk Coleman
Evp Sba Lending, John Gannon
Evp Public Finance, Paul Howell
Evp Strategic Sales And Marketing, Greg Lewis
President Private Wealth Advisors, Alan L. Miller
Vice President Manager Credit Underwriting, Anthony Violi
Senior Vice President Compensation Director, Chris Gullo
Vice President, Lela Naggar
Vice President Deposit Operations, Leslie Marsh
Vice President In Commercial Banking Group, Guy Miller
Vice President Of Information Technology Infrastructure, Randy Tiegs
Vice President Project Management, Allen Baumbach
Senior Vice President And Deposit Operation, Connie Couch
Vice President Corp Security And Investigations, Cary Wicker
Senior Vice President Risk Management Officer, Terry King
Vice President Fraud Investigator, Jamie Burud
Vice President Security, Neal Baker
Executive Vice President, Brent Johnston
Executive Vice President, Ronald Baker
Vice President Planning, Prasad Varma
Executive Vice President Human Resources And Ld, Cara McDaniel
Senior Vice President Energy Banking Texas Capital Bank, Jonathan Gregory
Executive Vice President Director Of Operations, James White
Senior Vice President And Cra Manager, Phil Aslin
Chairman, Larry L. Helm, age 70
Board Member, Elysia Ragusa
Board Member, James Browning
Auditors: Ernst & Young LLP

LOCATIONS

HQ: Texas Capital Bancshares Inc
 2000 McKinney Avenue, Suite 700, Dallas, TX 75201
Phone: 214 932-6600
Web: www.texascapitalbank.com

PRODUCTS/OPERATIONS

2015 Sales

	% of total
Interest income	
Interest and fees on loans	92
Other	1
Non-interest income	
Brokered loan fees	3
Service charges on deposit accounts	1
Trust fee income	1
Swap fees	1
Other	1
Total	**100**

Selected Services

Association capital bank
Bankdirect
Business services

Mortgage business finance
Online services
Personal banking
Private wealth advisors
Treasury and liquidity

COMPETITORS

Amegy	Comerica
BBVA Compass	Cullen/Frost Bankers
Bancshares	JPMorgan Chase
BOK Financial	Prosperity Bancshares
Bank of America	Wells Fargo

HISTORICAL FINANCIALS

Company Type: Public

Income Statement   FYE: December 31

	ASSETS ($ mil.)	NET INCOME ($ mil.)	INCOME AS % OF ASSETS	EMPLOYEES
12/17	25,075	197	0.8%	1,564
12/16	21,697	155	0.7%	1,442
12/15	18,909	144	0.8%	1,329
12/14	15,899	136	0.9%	1,142
12/13	11,714	121	1.0%	1,016
Annual Growth	21.0%	13.0%	—	11.4%

2017 Year-End Financials

Debt ratio: 12.74%	No. of shares (mil.): 49
Return on equity: 9.36%	Dividends
Cash ($ mil.): 2,875	Yield: —
Current ratio: —	Payout: —
Long-term debt ($ mil.): —	Market value ($ mil.): 4,413

	STOCK PRICE ($) FY Close	P/E High/Low	PER SHARE ($) Earnings	Dividends	Book Value
12/17	88.90	25 19	3.73	0.00	44.37
12/16	78.40	26 10	3.11	0.00	40.59
12/15	49.42	21 14	2.91	0.00	35.39
12/14	54.33	23 17	2.88	0.00	32.45
12/13	62.20	22 14	2.72	0.00	26.72
Annual Growth	9.3%	—	8.2%	—	13.5%

TEXAS COUNTY AND DISTRICT RETIREMENT SYSTEM

EXECUTIVES

Exec Dir, Gene Glass
Cao*, Ray Smith
Deputy Dir*, Amy Bishop
Staff, Brad Eddins
Network Analyst, Brad Watkins
CIO, Stephen Kell
Auditors: KPMG LLP AUSTIN TX

LOCATIONS

HQ: TEXAS COUNTY AND DISTRICT RETIREMENT SYSTEM
901 S MO PAC EXPY IV500, AUSTIN, TX 787465776
Phone: 512 328-8889
Web: WWW.TCDRS.ORG

HISTORICAL FINANCIALS

Company Type: Private

Income Statement   FYE: December 31

	ASSETS ($ mil.)	NET INCOME ($ mil.)	INCOME AS % OF ASSETS	EMPLOYEES
12/16	26,387	1,761	6.7%	108
12/15	24,654	(182)	—	—
12/14	24,933	0	—	—
12/10	18,116	2,178	12.0%	—
Annual Growth	6.5%	(3.5%)	—	—

2016 Year-End Financials

Debt ratio: ——	
Return on equity: 58.10%	Dividends
Cash ($ mil.): 25	Yield: —
Current ratio: —	Payout: —
Long-term debt ($ mil.): —	Market value ($ mil.): —

TEXAS HEALTH RESOURCES

Texas Health Resources (THR) is takin' care of the Dallas/Fort Worth and North Texas region. The not-for-profit system includes about 30 acute care and short-stay hospitals including owned managed and joint venture facilities. THR also operates outpatient and surgical centers and physicians' offices and it maintains affiliations with imaging diagnostic rehabilitation facilities and home health agencies. THR's network includes more than 5500 doctors and more than 3800 licensed beds. Its Research and Education Institute for Texas Health Resources provides clinical studies management medical device testing and medical training services.

Operations

THR's hospitals operate under names including Texas Health Presbyterian Texas Health Arlington Memorial Texas Health Harris Methodist and Texas Health Huguley. The company operates 20 outpatient facilities and it coordinates general practice care through its physician practice groups. Its Texas Health MedSynergies unit provides office management services for doctors' offices.

Geographic Reach

THR's primary service territory includes about 25 counties in north-central Texas. It has locations in towns including Allen Alliance Arlington Azle Burleson Cleburne Craig Ranch Dallas Denton Flower Mound Fort Worth Huguley Kaufman Plano Richardson Rockwall Southlake Stephenville and Sherman.

Sales and Marketing

The organization promotes its medical services through print television outdoor online and radio advertising.

Strategy

In order to keep up with the growing population of North Texas in 2007 THR launched a $1.5 billion initiative to expand its facilities over a 10-year period. Project efforts thus far have included establishing a joint venture hospital in Flower Mound and the expansion of existing facilities. For instance in 2015 it opened a 70000 sq. ft. cancer center at Presbyterian Hospital Dallas. In 2017 it completed an expansion at its Texas Health Alliance facility which included adding 24 private beds; the same facility will also expand its emergency department. THR has also opened a number

of outpatient surgery imaging wellness and specialist centers and it is now building a new 74-bed hospital campus in Frisco Texas.

In 2016 the system established a joint venture with emergency room operator Adeptus Health through which Adeptus? 27 North Texas First Choice Emergency Rooms as well as its First Texas Hospital in Carrollton became part of THR. The move helped THR as it works to expand its access points to emergency health care (an area it has struggled with).

Other expansion moves include the 2016 purchase of Forest Park Medical Center Fort Worth for $141 million and the creation of a jointly owned health plan with health insurer Aetna.

THR has also built up its information technology networks including the implementation of electronic health record (EHR) systems. In addition the organization is adding new medical professional training programs.

Company Background

THR was formed in 1997 by the merger of Harris Methodist Health System Presbyterian Healthcare System and Arlington Memorial Hospital Foundation. In 2008 the organization rebranded its hospitals unifying them all under the Texas Health Resources name.

THR had originally been the minority shareholder in a venture with Triad Hospitals to own Presbyterian Hospital of Denton. However THR grew dissatisfied when Triad was acquired by Community Health Systems in 2007. After a long legal tussle THR paid $100 million to acquire the hospital outright in 2009 and changed its name to Texas Health Presbyterian Hospital Denton. Texas Health Presbyterian found itself the focus of international media attention in 2014 when it treated the first case of Ebola on US soil.

EXECUTIVES

Evp People And Culture, Bonnie Bell
Evp Southeast Zone Operations Leader, Oscar L. Amparan
Sevp And Chief Clinical Officer, Daniel W. Varga
Evp And Cfo, Ronald R. (Ron) Long
Evp North Zone Operations Leader, Brett S. McClung
Sevp And Coo, Barclay E. Berdan
Svp And Chief Nurse Executive, Joan S. Clark
Executive Vice President And Southwest Zone Operations Leader, Kirk King
Sevp And Coo, Jeffrey L. Canose
Evp Southwest Zone Clinical Leader, Harold Berenzweig
Evp Southeast Zone Clinical Leader, Mark C. Lester
Evp North Zone Clinical Leader, Elizabeth Ransom
Evp Population Health; President Texas Health Population Health Education And Innovation Center, Tricia Nguyen
President Texas Health Physicians Group, Shawn D. Parsley
Director Of Pharmacy Pharmacy Director Service Director, Rebecca Wilson
Senior Vice President And Chief People Officer, Michelle Kirby
Vice President Operations Thpg, Lori Clay
Senior Vice President Of Communications, Paul Szablowski
Vice President Chief Nursing Officer, Rosemarie Aznavorian
Services Cmrp Senior Vice President Supply Chain Management, Shaun Clinton
Vice President, Laura McWhorter
Vice President, John Wilson
Vice President Applications And Ehr, Susan Soch
Vice President Of Planning And Placement, Mark Morales

Senior Vice President Chief Operating Officer,
James Berg
Vice President Assistant, Susan Garrett
Vice President Governance, Luanne Stout
Vice President Revenue Planning, Scott Auzenne
Vice President Treasury Services, Sandy Reeves
Director Managed Care, Larry Olive
Radiology Medical Director, David Robinson
Medical Director Of Adolescent Services, Robert
Harden
Vice President Corporate Controller, David Jackson
Vice President Applications And Ehr, Cynda Grimes
Director Of Pharmacy, Mikyoung Kim
Vice President, Douglas White
Director Of Him, Que Le
Vice President Supply Chain Management, Becky
Daniel
Vice President Health Information Services, Diann
Brown
Vice President Of Operations, Jennifer Stephenson
Pharmacy Manager, Jerry James
Director Of Radiology, Dung Pham
Vice President Stakeholder Engagement, Mark
Riordan
Vice President Operations, Jennifer Mha
**Ache Member Vice President Strategy And
Business,** Virginia Rose
Chairman, John R. Ferguson
Vice Chairman, Wesley R. Turner
Secretary, Stacey Mcjunkin
Secretary, Bernadina Richey
Secretary, Chandra Rhodes
Auditors: KMPG LLP DALLAS TEXAS

LOCATIONS

HQ: TEXAS HEALTH RESOURCES
612 E LAMAR BLVD STE 400, ARLINGTON, TX
760114125
Phone: 682 236-7900
Web: WWW.TEXASHEALTH.ORG

PRODUCTS/OPERATIONS

Selected Facilities and Affiliates

Acute Care and Specialty Hospitals
Texas Health Arlington Memorial
Texas Health Harris Methodist Hospital Fort Worth
Texas Health Huguley Hospital Fort Worth South
Texas Health Presbyterian Hospital Dallas
Texas Health Presbyterian Hospital Flower Mound
Texas Health Presbyterian Hospital Rockwall
Texas Health Center for Diagnostics & Surgery Plano
Texas Heath Heart & Vascular Hospital Arlington
USMD Hospital at Arlington
USMD Hospital at Fort Worth
Affiliates
Envision Imaging of North Fort Worth
Texas Rehabilitation Partners
Two Forest Imaging Dallas
Southwest Diagnostic Imaging Center

COMPETITORS

Community Health
Systems
Cook Children's Health
Care System
HCA
JPS Health Network
Parkland Health &
Hospital System

Southwestern Medical
Center
Tenet Healthcare
The Methodist Health
System

HISTORICAL FINANCIALS

Company Type: Private

Income Statement   FYE: December 31

	REVENUE ($ mil.)	NET INCOME ($ mil.)	NET PROFIT MARGIN	EMPLOYEES
12/17	4,688	869	18.6%	21,277
12/13	718	285	39.8%	—
12/09	334	2	0.9%	—
12/06	2,287	2,299	100.5%	—
Annual Growth	6.7%	(8.5%)	—	—

2017 Year-End Financials

Debt ratio: ——
Return on equity: 18.60%
Cash ($ mil.): 435
Current ratio: 0.90
Long-term debt ($ mil.): —

Dividends
Yield: —
Payout: —
Market value ($ mil.): —

Texas Instruments Inc.

Texas Instruments sticks to basics — producing analog and embedded processors the workhorses of the industry. The company?s analog chips manage power in electronic equipment and its embedded processors handle specific tasks in electronic devices. TI?s customers which number about 100000 use the company's chips for applications that include autos industrial machinery consumer electronics communications devices and calculators. The company also sticks to basics in production operating its own manufacturing plants which is places around the world. Another TI basic: TI engineer Jack Kilby was credited as co-inventor of the integrated circuit in the late 1950s.

Operations

Texas Instruments operates through three segments: Analog Embedded Processing and Other products.

The Analog business which accounts for about two-thirds of sales includes high-volume analog and logic products power management semiconductors and amplifiers and data converters. The company?s analog products are used in the personal electronics automotive and industrial markets as well as others.

The Embedded Processing segment which generates about a quarter of sales makes application specific integrated circuits (ASICs) digital signal processors (DSPs) and microcontrollers. TI?s embedded processors range from low-cost microcontrollers used in products such as electric toothbrushes to complex devices used in automotive applications such as infotainment and advanced driver assistance systems.

The remaining revenue comes from the Other segment which includes digital light processors (DLP) used in projectors to create high-definition images calculators and custom semiconductors.

In terms of markets TI gets about a third of revenue from industrial about 25% from personal electronics about a fifth from automotive and more than 10% from communications with enterprise systems and calculators accounting for the remaining revenue.

TI operates 15 manufacturing sites in nine countries.

Geographic Reach

China is the biggest single market for Texas Instruments accounting for about 45% of revenue with other Asia/Pacific countries (including Japan) accounting for nearly 25% of revenue. The US generates more than 10% of TI?s sales. The company has facilities for service sales and other functions in the US Europe and Asia.

Sales and Marketing

Texas Instruments has a wide representation of sales channels as well as customers. About 65% of the company?s revenue comes through distributors who keep inventory of TI products on hand. As for customers its 100 biggest account for about 66% of sales.

Financial Performance

Texas Instruments followed a 3% revenue increase in 2016 with a 12% jump in 2017 to $14.9 billion. The company reported strong sales gains of 16% each from its Analog and Embedded Processing units. Growth in its Power and Signal Chain products fueled Analog sales while Embedded and Processor products contributed to the Embedded Processing sales increase. The Other segment posted a 14% decline on a slowdown of ASIC products.

Profit in 2017 rose a bit to $3.7 billion compared to $3.6 billion in 2016. The 2016 profit benefited from the adoption of a stock compensation accounting standard.

TI?s cash flow from operations was $5.36 billion in 2017 about $1 billion higher than 2016. Its free cash flow was $4.67 billion about 31% of revenue up from 30.5% in 2016. The company returned $4.66 billion to shareholders through a combination of stock repurchases and dividends.

Strategy

Texas Instruments? focus on its Analog and Embedded Processing units is paying off. They combined to produce 90% of the company's revenue almost double since 2004. The company believes that analog and embedded processors offer diversity of applications long product life cycles and lower-cost manufacturing processes.

TI has identified two markets where analog and embedded processes can generate growing sales over time: industrial and automotive. More and more functions are handled by semiconductors in industrial machinery and vehicles. In 2017 automotive and industrial combined to provide about 55% of TI?s revenue up from 42% in 2013. TI is investing heavily in processors for those markets shifting resources from products for other markets. It reduced overall R&D in products for the personal electronics market but is making selective investments in it.

On the manufacturing end TI is moving to produce more chips on 300-millimeter wafers which hold more chips than the standard 200-millimeter wafers. Making chips on the bigger wafer reduces costs 40%. The company has 300-millimeter capacity in its Dallas and Richardson fabrication facilities and is adding more.

Unlike its rapidly consolidating competitors TI has not made recent acquisitions nor has it been a serious target for acquisition. Its last major deal was to buy National Semiconductor in 2011. Other semiconductor companies have spent billions on **mergers and acquisitions** in recent years to amass market share and diversify product lines.

Texas Instruments faces strong competition around the world from other chipmakers. The industry consolidation that TI has avoided has created bigger competitors with wider ranges of products and deeper resources. On the other side of the spectrum small companies with innovative products are capable of snatching market share away.

In China which supplies about 45% of revenue Texas Instruments has challenges on two fronts. One is the Chinese government?s support for Chinese chip companies as it tries to strengthen a key industry. The other is trade. A trade ware between the US and China could increase the prices of TI products made in China and even result in restrictions on its operations in the country.

EXECUTIVES

Chairman President And Ceo, Richard K. (Rich) Templeton, age 59, $1,164,083 total compensation

Svp High-volume Analog And Logic Central Analog Services Dlpâ® Products And Education Technology, Stephen A. (Steve) Anderson, age 56, $616,500 total compensation

Svp Analog Power Products, Niels Anderskouv, age 40

Svp Technology And Manufacturing, Kevin J. Ritchie, age 62, $688,333 total compensation

Svp Embedded Processing, R. Gregory (Greg) Delagi, age 55, $622,917 total compensation

Evp And Coo, Brian T. Crutcher, age 45, $822,917 total compensation

Svp Information Technology Services And Cio, Ellen L. Barker, age 55

Svp Worldwide Sales And Applications, Bing Xie, age 50

Svp Cfo And Chief Accounting Officer Finance And Operations, Rafael R. Lizardi, age 45

Svp Analog Signal Chain, Haviv Ilan, age 49

Vice President Connected Microcontrollers, Ray Upton

Vice President Internet Marketing, Dave Youngblood

Vice President Emea Public Sector Services, Edwin Feeny

National Sales Manager, Dennis Smith

Vice President Digital Signal Processing Systems, Greg Delagi

Government Relations, Rosie Saucedo

Vice President Human Resources, Shanon Leonard

Auditors: Ernst & Young LLP

LOCATIONS

HQ: Texas Instruments Inc.
12500 TI Boulevard, Dallas, TX 75243
Phone: 214 479-3773
Web: www.ti.com

2017 Sales

Asia/Pacific	$ mil.	% of total
Japan	1,049	8
Other countries	8,824	60
Europe	2,907	18
US	1,901	12
Other regions	280	2
Total	**14,961**	**100**

PRODUCTS/OPERATIONS

2017 Sales

	$ mil.	% of total
Analog	9,900	66
Embedded processing	3,498	23
Other	1,563	11
Total	**14,961**	**100**

2017 Sales by Market

	% of total
Industrial	35
Personal electronics	25
Automotive	19
Communications equipment	12
Enterprise sytems	6
Calculators	3
Total	**100**

Selected Products

Semiconductors
 Analog and mixed-signal
 Amplifiers and comparators
 Clocks and timers
 Data converters
 Power management chips
 Radio-frequency (RF) chips
 Application-specific integrated circuits (ASICs)
 Digital light processors (DLPs micro-mirror-based devices for video displays)
 Digital signal processors (DSPs)
 Microcontrollers
 Microprocessors
 Standard logic
Educational Technology
 Calculators (including graphing handheld and printing models)

COMPETITORS

AMD	Marvell Technology
ARM Holdings	Maxim Integrated
Analog Devices	Products
Atmel	Microchip Technology
CASIO COMPUTER	Microsemi
CSR plc	NVIDIA
Canon	NXP Semiconductors
Fairchild	ON Semiconductor
Semiconductor	QUALCOMM
HP	Renesas Electronics
Infineon Technologies	Richtek Technology
Intel	Corp.
Intersil	STMicroelectronics
Linear Technology	Samsung Electronics

HISTORICAL FINANCIALS

Company Type: Public

Income Statement

FYE: December 31

	REVENUE ($ mil.)	NET INCOME ($ mil.)	NET PROFIT MARGIN	EMPLOYEES
12/17	14,961	3,682	24.6%	29,714
12/16	13,370	3,595	26.9%	29,865
12/15	13,000	2,986	23.0%	29,977
12/14	13,045	2,821	21.6%	31,003
12/13	12,205	2,162	17.7%	32,209
Annual Growth	**5.2%**	**14.2%**	**—**	**(2.0%)**

2017 Year-End Financials

Debt ratio: 23.11%
Return on equity: 35.39%
Cash ($ mil.): 1,656
Current ratio: 3.87
Long-term debt ($ mil.): 3,577

No. of shares (mil.): 983
Dividends
 Yield: 0.0%
 Payout: 58.7%
Market value ($ mil.): 102,681

	STOCK PRICE ($) FY Close	P/E High/Low	PER SHARE ($) Earnings	Dividends	Book Value
12/17	104.44	28 20	3.61	2.12	10.51
12/16	72.97	21 14	3.48	1.64	10.52
12/15	54.81	21 15	2.82	1.40	9.84
12/14	53.47	21 16	2.57	1.24	9.93
12/13	43.91	23 16	1.91	1.07	9.98
Annual Growth	**24.2%**	**— —**	**17.3%**	**18.6%**	**1.3%**

TEXAS PERMANENT SCHOOL FUND MANAGEMENT COMPANY, INC.

EXECUTIVES

Prin, Elizabeth Jones
Manager, Nick Tramontana
Auditors: LISA R COLLIER CPA CFE CID

LOCATIONS

HQ: TEXAS PERMANENT SCHOOL FUND
 MANAGEMENT COMPANY, INC.
1701 CONGRESS AVE, AUSTIN, TX 787011402
Phone: 512 463-1814
Web: WWW.TEA.STATE.TX.US

HISTORICAL FINANCIALS

Company Type: Private

Income Statement

FYE: August 31

	ASSETS ($ mil.)	NET INCOME ($ mil.)	INCOME AS % OF ASSETS	EMPLOYEES
08/17	44,517	4,154	9.3%	4
08/16	38,820	1,519	3.9%	—
Annual Growth	**14.7%**	**173.4%**	**—**	**—**

2017 Year-End Financials

Debt ratio: —
Return on equity: 77.30%
Cash ($ mil.): 3,584
Current ratio: —
Long-term debt ($ mil.): —

Dividends
 Yield: —
 Payout: —
Market value ($ mil.): —

Textron Inc

Texton?s products help customers across the globe get on the move — by air land or sea. The company is known for its Beechcraft and Cessna aircraft and Bell military and commercial helicopters. It also services Hawker business jets. In addition Textron provides parts repair and other aftermarket services. The company also makes specialty vehicles (E-Z-GO golf carts Arctic Cat ATVs) fuel systems power tools electrical test and measurement equipment land and marine systems unmanned aerial vehicles and simulation and training products. Textron which generates about 60% of revenue from the US serves government industrial and commercial clients.

Operations

The company operates more than 60 plants in the US and about 50 outside the US. The US account for more than 60% of its total sales. Other major markets include Europe (about 15%) and Asia Pacific (almost 10%). Latin/South America and Canada each account for about Textron Aviation makes Beechcraft and Cessna aircrafts and provides service for Hawker business jets. Its business lines include aircraft (two-thirds of total) and aftermarket (one-third). This segment generates more than 30% of Textron?s net sales and produces the Citation line of jets as well as piston aircraft and special mission and military aircraft.

Bell Helicopter (rebranded as simply ?Bell? in 2018) supplies the US military with the V-22 tilt rotor aircraft which can operate with the features of both a fixed-wing craft and a helicopter and the H-1 helicopter. Through five service centers four parts distribution centers and some 100 independent dealers Bell provides repair and overhaul and customizing services for an installed base of 13000 helicopters. This segment represents about 25% of sales. Textron Systems (more than 10% of sales) provides unmanned systems marine and land systems and simulation and training solutions. It serves markets that include aerospace defense and general aviation. Besides the US military the segment sells to foreign military organizations approved by the US government.

Products incluThe Industrial segment (30% of sales) operates three products lines: fuel systems and functional components (sold through its German-based Kautex subsidiary) specialized vehicles (such as E-Z-GO golf carts and recently-acquired Arctic Cat snowmobiles and ATVs) and tools and test equipment (electrical test and measurement instruments mechanical and hydraulic tools and fiber optic assemblies to name a few).

Finance (less than 1% of sales) consists of Textron Financial Corporation (TFC) and offers financing mainly for new and used Textron Aviation aircraft and Bell helicopters.5% of sales. The company does a small percentage of its business (1%-2%) in the Middle East and Africa.

Geographic Reach
The company operates more than 60 plants in the US and about 50 outside the US. The US account for more than 60% of its total sales. Other major markets include Europe (about 15%) and Asia Pacific (almost 10%). Latin/South America and Canada each account for about 5% of sales. The company does a small percentage of its business (1%-2%) in the Middle East and Africa.

Sales and Marketing
Textron Aviation sells through its own sales force as well as through a network of authorized independent sales representatives. Post-sale support and service is offered though global service centers and parts distribution centers.

It sells to US government customers (more than 20% of consolidated revenues results from US government contracts) to customers outside the US through foreign military sales sponsored by the US government and directly through commercial sales channels. The Industrial segment sells through a global network of sales representatives and distributors and directly to home improvement retailers and OEMs.

Financial Performance
Textron's revenues have seen a general upward trend in the past five years with a 3% increase in both 2017 and 2016. Revenue growth in 2017 was fueled by a $492 million (almost 13%) increase in the Industrial segment thanks to $393 million in sales from acquired Arctic Cat. Bell and Textron Systems saw minimal growth with overall revenue increases stunted by the poor performance of Textron?s Aviation segment (a 5% decrease in sales due to lower volume in the sale of its military and commercial turboprop aircraft).

Profits however plummeted almost 70% in 2017 to $307 million. The company incurred a $450 million-plus tax expense including a $266 million charge for provisional estimates due to the new Tax Cuts and Jobs Act. Also responsible is a 4% increase in cost of sales mainly due to the acquisition of Arctic Cat. The Aviation segment also experienced higher R&D costs related to its Scorpion jet program and Textron Systems recorded a $44 million adjustment related to inefficiencies in its Tactical Armoured Patrol Vehicle (TAPV) program. Consolidated cash flows from operations declined more than 3% to $980 million in 2017. Higher pension contributions and lower earnings are cited as significant factors.

Strategy
Having spent the previous few years focused on operational efficiencies Textron is now looking to new products and acquisitions to spur growth in 2018 and beyond.

Textron is focused on innovation and developing new products to expand its customer base. Its new large-cabin jet the Citation Longitude is expected to enter service in 2018 and it is introducing a cargo version of the Cessna SkyCourier a twin-engine large-utility turboprop aircraft. Textron Aviation demonstrated its Scorpion jet for the US Airforce and hopes to provide the USAF with a light-attack fleet in the future. Textron Specialized Vehicles has expanded its line of off-road vehicles with the acquisition of Arctic Cat and introduced

a new E-Z-GO ELiTe golf car powered by a lithium-ion battery.

Bell?s new V-280 Valor which the company is developing for the US military contains a new vertical lift technology. Bell is continuing its rapid growth in China with plans for a delivery center there and it is making investments in customer service capabilities for European customers with a new training academy in Valencia Spain.

With the success of the Arctic Cat acquisition which bolstered sales by almost half a billion dollars in 2017 the company continues to look at acquisitions that would complement its current portfolio of products.

Mergers and Acquisitions
The company occasionally beefs up its segments through acquisitions. In 2017 Textron acquired Arctic Cat a maker of about 30 types of all-terrain vehicles (ATVs) and 60 snowmobile models. The $247 million acquisition added to its Textron Specialized Vehicles business and gives it a deeper product line. It also enables new sales opportunities for its combined worldwide dealer network.

Textron also in 2017 picked up Canada-based TKVGPS a provider of GPS-based fleet management technologies. The acquisition enhances the on-course experience for its golf customers and provides fleet-management products to different industries.

In 2016 the company acquired Able Engineering & Component Services and Able Aerospace an industry-leading repair and overhaul company. This acquisition enhanced its aircraft parts and maintenance operations.

HISTORY
Pioneer conglomerate builder Royal Little founded Special Yarns Corporation a Boston textile business in 1923 and merged it with the Franklin Rayon Dyeing Company in 1928. The result Franklin Rayon Corporation moved its headquarters to Providence Rhode Island in 1930 and changed its name to Atlantic Rayon in 1938.

The company expanded during WWII to make parachutes and in 1944 adopted the name Textron to reflect the use of synthetics in its textiles. Between 1953 and 1960 Textron bought more than 40 businesses including Bell Helicopter before banker Rupe Thompson took over in 1960.

Thompson sold weak businesses such as Amerotron Textron's last textile business (1963) but also bought 20 companies between 1960 and 1965. By 1968 when former Wall Street attorney William Miller replaced Thompson as CEO Textron made products ranging from chain saws to watchbands. Miller sold several companies and bought Jacobsen Manufacturers (lawn care equipment 1978) before leaving Textron in 1978 to head the Federal Reserve and become treasury secretary under President Jimmy Carter.

EXECUTIVES
Vp And Cio, Diane K. Schwarz
Chairman President And Ceo, Scott C. Donnelly, age 56, $1,146,500 total compensation
Evp General Counsel Secretary And Chief Compliance Officer, E. Robert Lupone, age 58, $695,192 total compensation
President And Ceo Textron Aviation, Scott A. Ernest
Evp Human Resources, Cheryl H. Johnson, age 57, $445,192 total compensation
President And Ceo Textron Specialized Vehicles, Kevin P. Holleran
President And Ceo Textron Systems, Ellen Lord
Evp And Cfo, Frank T. Connor, age 58, $940,385 total compensation

President And Ceo Tru Simulation + Training, Ian K. Walsh
President And Ceo Textron Airborne Solutions, Russ Bartlett
President And Ceo Textron Financial, R. Danny Maldonado
President And Ceo Bell Helicopter, Mitch Snyder
**President And Ceo Greenlee Textron Inc.
Sherman + Reilly Inc. And Hd Electric Company,** Jason Butchko
President And Ceo Kautex, J ¶rg Rautenstrauch
Auditors: Ernst & Young LLP

LOCATIONS
HQ: Textron Inc
 40 Westminster Street, Providence, RI 02903
Phone: 401 421-2800
Web: www.textron.com

2017 Sales

	$ mil.	% of total
United States	8,786	62
Europe	1,962	14
Asia and Australia	1,206	9
Canada	913	6
Latin and South America	883	6
Middle East and Africa	448	3
Total	**14,198**	**100**

PRODUCTS/OPERATIONS

2017 Sales

	$ mil.	% of total
Textron Aviation	4,686	33
Bell	3,317	23
Textron Systems	1,840	13
Industrial	4,286	30
Finance	69	1
Total	**14,198**	**100**

Selected Products
Textron Aviation
 Beechcraft
 Cessna
 Hawker
 Citation
 Business jets
 Turboprop aircraft
 Piston engine aircraft
 Military trainer and defense aircraft
Bell
 Commercial helicopters
 Military helicopters
 Tiltrotor aircraft
Industrial
 Fuel Systems and Functional Components (Kautex)
 Blow-molded plastic fuel systems
 Clear vision systems
 Catalytic reduction systems
 Plastic bottles and containers
 Specialized Vehicles
 E-Z-GO golf cars
 Textron Off Road
 Arctic Cat
 UG Technologies
 Douglas Equipment
 Jacobsen turf maintenance equipment
 Tools and Test Equipment
 Greenlee
 Greenlee Communications
 Greenlee Utility
 HD Electric
 Klauke
 Sherman+Reilly
 Endura
Textron Systems
 Unmanned systems and support solutions
 Marine and land systems
 Simulation and training systems
 TRU Simulation + Training
 Textron Airborne Solutions
 Electronic systems
 Lycoming
 Weapons and sensors
Finance (primarily for new and used aircraft and helicopters)

COMPETITORS

AgustaWestland	Lockheed Martin
Airbus Group	Magna International
Boeing	Moog
Bombardier	Northrop Grumman
Deere	Northstar Aerospace
Embraer	Piper Aircraft
GE	Raytheon
General Dynamics	Rockwell Collins
Gulfstream Aerospace	Rolls-Royce
Honda	SAFRAN
Honeywell	Spirit AeroSystems
International	Sun Hydraulics
Illinois Tool Works	Terex
Ingersoll-Rand	Thales Aerospace
Israel Aerospace	Toro Company
Industries	United Technologies
Kaman	
Kawasaki Heavy	
Industries	

HISTORICAL FINANCIALS

Company Type: Public

Income Statement   FYE: December 30

	REVENUE ($ mil.)	NET INCOME ($ mil.)	NET PROFIT MARGIN	EMPLOYEES
12/17	14,198	307	2.2%	37,000
12/16*	13,788	962	7.0%	36,000
01/16	13,423	697	5.2%	35,000
01/15	13,878	600	4.3%	34,000
12/13	12,104	498	4.1%	32,000
Annual Growth	4.1%	(11.4%)	—	3.7%

*Fiscal year change

2017 Year-End Financials

Debt ratio: 25.50%	No. of shares (mil.): 261
Return on equity: 5.49%	Dividends
Cash ($ mil.): 1,079	Yield: 0.0%
Current ratio: 1.92	Payout: 7.0%
Long-term debt ($ mil.): 3,898	Market value ($ mil.): 14,797

	STOCK PRICE ($) FY Close	P/E High/Low	Earnings	Dividends	Book Value
12/17	56.59	50 39	1.14	0.08	21.60
12/16*	48.56	14 9	3.53	0.08	20.62
01/16	42.01	19 15	2.50	0.08	18.10
01/15	42.17	21 15	2.13	0.08	15.45
12/13	36.61	21 14	1.75	0.08	15.54
Annual Growth	11.5%	— —	(10.2%)	(0.0%)	8.6%

*Fiscal year change

TFS Financial Corp

EXECUTIVES

Vice President, Marianne Piterans
Vice President Of Call Centre, Jim French
Board Member, William C Mulligan
Auditors: DELOITTE & TOUCHE LLP

LOCATIONS

HQ: TFS Financial Corp
7007 Broadway Avenue, Cleveland, OH 44105
Phone: 216 441-6000
Web: www.thirdfederal.com

COMPETITORS

Bank of America	KeyCorp
Citigroup	PNC Financial
Fifth Third	U.S. Bancorp
Huntington Bancshares	Wells Fargo
JPMorgan Chase	

HISTORICAL FINANCIALS

Company Type: Public

Income Statement   FYE: September 30

	ASSETS ($ mil.)	NET INCOME ($ mil.)	INCOME AS % OF ASSETS	EMPLOYEES
09/18	14,137	85	0.6%	—
09/17	13,692	88	0.6%	—
09/16	12,906	80	0.6%	—
09/15	12,368	72	0.6%	—
09/14	11,803	65	0.6%	—
Annual Growth	4.6%	6.7%	—	—

2018 Year-End Financials

Debt ratio: —	No. of shares (mil.): 280
Return on equity: 4.95%	Dividends
Cash ($ mil.): 269	Yield: 0.0%
Current ratio: —	Payout: 253.3%
Long-term debt ($ mil.): —	Market value ($ mil.): 4,207

	STOCK PRICE ($) FY Close	P/E High/Low	Earnings	Dividends	Book Value
09/18	15.01	53 46	0.30	0.76	6.27
09/17	16.13	62 46	0.32	0.55	6.01
09/16	17.81	69 56	0.28	0.43	5.84
09/15	17.25	71 55	0.25	0.31	5.95
09/14	14.32	66 52	0.22	0.07	6.10
Annual Growth	1.2%	— —	8.1%	81.5%	0.7%

The Bancorp Inc

The Bancorp is — what else? — the holding company for The Bancorp Bank which provides financial services in the virtual world. Targeting non-bank financial service companies across the US and Europe from start-ups to small and midsized businesses underserved by larger banks in the market The Bancorp Bank provides private-label online banking to 200 affinity groups; offers specialty lending; issues prepaid debit cards; and processes ACH and merchant credit card transactions. Its specialty lending products include securities backed lines of credit (SBLOC) auto fleet and equipment leasing SBA loans and commercial mortgage loans for sale in capital markets.

Operations

The Bancorp and The Bancorp Bank operate three business segments: Payments which made up 45% of the bank's total revenue in 2015 and provides prepaid cards card payments and ACH processing services; Specialty Finance (31% of revenue) which consists of commercial mortgage loan sales small business administration (SBA) loans leasing and security backed lines of credit and related deposit business; and Corporate (24% of revenue) which includes the company's investment portfolio.

Unlike other banks which rely on interest income The Bancorp makes more than 60% of its revenue from fee-based income. About 38% of its total revenue came from loan interest (including fees) during 2015 while another 14% came from interest income on investment securities. The rest of its revenue came from prepaid card fees (22% of revenue) service fees on deposit accounts (3%) card payment and ACH processing fees (3%) leasing income (1%) debit card income (1%) affinity fees (2%) and non-recurring gains from the sale of its loans investment securities and health savings portfolio (27%).

Geographic Reach

Wilmington Delaware-based The Bancorp serves customers in the US and Europe from 16 offices in the two regions and Southeast Asia.

Sales and Marketing

The company targets non-bank financial services companies including start-ups small and medium businesses underserved by large banks and Fortune 500 companies. It spent $387000 on advertising during 2015 down from $621000 and $706000 in 2014 and 2013 respectively.

Financial Performance

The Bancorp's annual revenues and profits have nearly doubled since 2011 mostly as its Payments business income has nearly quadrupled over the period. Its loan assets have also nearly tripled spurring additional interest income growth.

The company's revenue jumped 39% to $216.5 million during 2015 thanks largely to a $33.5 million gain on the sale of the majority of its health savings business and a $14.4 million gain on the sale of its tax-exempt municipal bonds portfolio. The Bancorp's loan interest revenue was also up 37% as its specialty lending balances continued to grow with new SBLOC SBA leasing and loans-for-sale business.

Despite strong revenue growth in 2015 The Bancorp's net income plunged more than 75% to $13.43 million mostly as its discontinued operations (its discontinued Philadelphia commercial loan business) generated $27 million less in revenue than the year before and because in 2014 it had collected a $14.5 million income tax benefit from a reversal of valuation allowances. The company's operations used $234.8 million or more than four times more cash than in 2014 mainly on a steep decline cash-based earnings especially after accounting for net proceeds from sales of its loans-originated-for-resale.

Strategy

The Bancorp and The Bancorp Bank has been winding down its non-core operations in recent years to concentrate more in its national specialty lending business. In October 2015 the bank sold its $400 million-HSA portfolio to HealthEquity for $34..4 million after selling its regional Commercial Lending business in 2014. As a result the bank noted that its discontinued operations were reduced by 50% at the end of 2015 and expected its discontinued loan portfolio to shrink from there through loan repayments and opportunistic loan sales.

On the growth side The Bancorp continues to buy specialty financing assets from other financial companies to bolster its loan assets and extend its geographic reach. In December 2015 it expanded its commercial fleet leasing presence in the West Coast with a new California office after buying the commercial leasing assets of Ellis Brooks Leasing Inc.

EXECUTIVES

Evp Strategy Cfo And Secretary, Paul Frenkiel, age 66, $312,200 total compensation
President And Ceo, Damian Kozlowski, age 51
Evp And Chief Credit Officer The Bancorp Inc. And The Bancorp Bank, Donald F. (Don) McGraw, age 61, $317,500 total compensation
Evp Commercial Fleet Leasing And Chief Lending Officer, Scott R. Megargee, age 66, $202,541 total compensation

Svp Network And Security, Peter (Pete) Chiccino
Svp; Managing Director Payment Solutions,
  Jeremy L. Kuiper, $458,060 total compensation
Svp And General Counsel, Thomas G. Pareigat,
  $347,500 total compensation
Evp And Coo, Gail S. Ball
Evp And Chief Risk Officer, Steven Turowski
Evp Commercial Mortgage Securitization, Ron
  Wechsler
Senior Vice President Chief Information Security
  Officer, Anthony Meholic
Executive Vice President Head Of Small Business
  Lending, Jeff Nager
Vice President Database Administration Manager,
  David Heisel
Chairman The Bancorp Inc. And The Bancorp
  Bank, Daniel G. Cohen, age 48
Auditors: Grant Thornton LLP

LOCATIONS

HQ: The Bancorp Inc
  409 Silverside Road, Wilmington, DE 19809
Phone: 302 385-5000
Web: www.thebancorp.com

PRODUCTS/OPERATIONS

2015 sales

	$ mil.	% of total
Payments	98	45
Specialty finance	67	31
Corporate	51	24
Total	**216**	**100**

2015 Sales

	$ mil.	% of total
Interest income		
Loans including fees	49	23
Interest on investment securities:	30	14
Federal funds sold/securities purchased under agreements to resell		0
Interest earning deposits	2	1
Non-interest income		
Prepaid card fees	47	22
Gain on sale of health savings portfolio	33	15
Gain on sale of investment securities	14	7
Gain on sale of loans	10	5
Service fees on deposit accounts	7	3
Card payment and ACH processing fees	5	3
Affinity fees	3	2
Other	5	2
Change in value of investment in unconsolidated entity	1	1
Leasing income	2	1
Debit card income	1	1
Total	**216**	**100**

COMPETITORS

Citizens Financial	Royal Bancshares
Group	Sovereign Bank
E*TRADE Bank	Sun Bancorp (NJ)
M&T Bank	TD Bank USA
PNC Financial	WSFS Financial
Republic First Bank	

HISTORICAL FINANCIALS

Company Type: Public

Income Statement   FYE: December 31

	ASSETS ($ mil.)	NET INCOME ($ mil.)	INCOME AS % OF ASSETS	EMPLOYEES
12/17	4,708	21	0.5%	538
12/16	4,858	(96)	—	589
12/15	4,765	13	0.3%	762
12/14	4,986	57	1.1%	684
12/13	4,706	25	0.5%	624
Annual Growth	**0.0%**	**(3.6%)**	**—**	**(3.6%)**

2017 Year-End Financials

Debt ratio: 1.18%	No. of shares (mil.): 55
Return on equity: 6.96%	Dividends
Cash ($ mil.): 844	Yield: —
Current ratio: —	Payout: —
Long-term debt ($ mil.): —	Market value ($ mil.): 551

	STOCK PRICE ($) FY Close	P/E High/Low		Earnings	PER SHARE ($) Dividends	Book Value
12/17	9.88	26	12	0.39	0.00	5.81
12/16	7.86	—	—	(2.17)	0.00	5.40
12/15	6.37	31	18	0.35	0.00	8.47
12/14	10.89	13	5	1.49	0.00	8.46
12/13	17.91	28	16	0.66	0.00	9.56
Annual Growth	**(13.8%)**	—	—	**(12.3%)**		**(11.7%)**

THE CHARLOTTE-MECKLENBURG HOSPITAL AUTHORITY

TheA medical facilities under the watchful eye of theA Charlotte-Mecklenburg Hospital AuthorityA care for the injured and infirmed.A As the largest health care system in the Carolinas the organizationA operating asA Carolinas HealthCare System (CHS)A ownsA or managesA more thanA 30A affiliated hospitals.A It also operates long-term care facilities research centers rehabilitation facilitiesA surgery centersA home health agencies radiation therapy facilities and other health care operations.A Collectively CHSA facilities have more than 6400 beds and affiliated physician practices employ more than 1700 doctors. The network's flagship facility is the 875-bedA Carolinas Medical Center in Charlotte North Carolina.

EXECUTIVES

Ceo, Eugene A Woods
Exec Vp Pres-Cfo*, Greg A Gombar
Exe V Pres*, Paul S Franz
Director*, Kara King
V Pres-Fin, Mary Ann Rouse
Staff, Sarah Laborde
Svp and Chief Compliance, Eugene A Deladdy Jr
Human Resources Information MA, Suzanne
  Greenway
Accounting Staff, Gladys Stanley
Management Associate II, Nina McDowell
Superintendent II, Ryan Prince
Auditors: KPMG LLP CHARLOTTE NC

LOCATIONS

HQ: THE CHARLOTTE-MECKLENBURG HOSPITAL
  AUTHORITY
  1000 BLYTHE BLVD, CHARLOTTE, NC 282035812
Phone: 704 355-2000
Web: WWW.CAROLINASHEALTHCARE.ORG

PRODUCTS/OPERATIONS

2010 Revenue

	% of total
Tertiary & acute care services	72
Physicians' services	16
Post-acute care services	3
Specialty services	2
Other services & non-operating activities	7
Total	**100**

Selected Hospitals and Health Care Pavilions

AnMed Health Medical Center
AnMed Health Rehabilitation Hospital
AnMed Health Women's and Children's Hospital
Anson Community Hospital
Bon Secours/St. Francis Hospital
Cannon Memorial Hospital
Carolinas Medical Center
Carolinas Medical Center - Kannapolis (health care
  pavilion)
Carolinas Medical Center - Lincoln
Carolinas Medical Center - Mercy
Carolinas Medical Center - NorthEast
Carolinas Medical Center - Pineville
Carolinas Medical Center - Steele Creek (health care
  pavilion)
Carolinas Medical Center - Union
Carolinas Medical Center - University
Carolinas Medical Center - Waxhaw (health care
  pavilion)
Carolinas Rehabilitation
Carolinas Rehabilitation - Mount Holly
Cleveland Regional Medical Center
CMC - Randolph
Columbus Regional Healthcare System
Crawley Memorial Hospital
Grace Hospital
Kings Mountain Hospital
Levine Children's Hospital
MedWest - Harris
MedWest - Haywood
MedWest - Swain
Roper Hospital
Roper St. Francis - Mount Pleasant Hospital
Scotland Memorial Hospital
Stanly Regional Medical Center
St. Luke's Hospital
Valdese Hospital
Wallace Thomson Hospital
Wilkes Regional Medical Center

COMPETITORS

Alamance Regional	Haywood Regional
Medical Center	High Point Regional
CaroMont	Health System
Community Health	McLeod Health
Systems	Mission Hospitals
Cone Health	Morehead Memorial
Conway Medical Center	Hospital
Cumberland County	New Hanover Regional
Hospital System	Medical Center
Davis Regional Medical	Novant Health
Center	Palmetto Health
Duke University Health	Presbyterian
System	Healthcare
FirstHealth of the	Rex Healthcare
Carolinas	Soliant Health
Georgetown Hospital	Tenet Healthcare
System	UNC Hospitals
Grand Strand Regional	Upstate Affiliate
Medical Center	Vidant Health
HCA	WakeMed

HISTORICAL FINANCIALS

Company Type: Private

Income Statement   FYE: December 31

	REVENUE ($ mil.)	NET INCOME ($ mil.)	NET PROFIT MARGIN	EMPLOYEES
12/17	5,991	829	13.9%	62,000
12/16	5,676	493	8.7%	—
12/15	5,478	(247)	—	—
12/12	4,501	249	5.5%	—
Annual Growth	**5.9%**	**27.2%**		

2017 Year-End Financials

Debt ratio: —	
Return on equity: 13.90%	Dividends
Cash ($ mil.): 136	Yield: —
Current ratio: 0.80	Payout: —
Long-term debt ($ mil.): —	Market value ($ mil.): —

THE CLEVELAND CLINIC FOUNDATION

Cleveland Clinic Foundation operates the not-for-profit Cleveland Clinic an academic medical center with more than 1400 beds at its main campus. The clinic specializes in cardiac care digestive disease treatment and urological and kidney care along with education and research opportunities. It has an international care center children's hospital and an outpatient center. It also contains research and educational institutes covering clinical drug research ophthalmic studies and cancer research as well as physician and scientist training programs. The Foundation — also known as the Cleveland Clinic Health System — operates 11 regional hospitals in Ohio Florida Abu Dhabi and London.

Operations

The Cleveland Clinic Foundation operates more than 150 outpatient facilities in northern Ohio. These include outpatient family health centers ambulatory surgery centers physician offices specialized cancer centers and wellness centers. The system represents 140 medical specialties and subspecialties.

The foundation operates the Lerner College of Medicine and the Lerner Research Institute through a partnership with Case Western Reserve University and it has continuing education nursing and residency programs. The Cleveland Clinic Foundation also operates Cleveland Clinic Innovations a unit that oversees collaborative research and technology commercialization programs with partners including MedStar Health and the University of Notre Dame. Cleveland Clinic educates some 1800 residents and fellows and receives some $270 million in research funding (from grants contracts and federal support) each year.

Altogether the medical centers known as the Cleveland Clinic Health System include some 4500 beds and employ about 3000 full-time physicians. The facilities handle 157000 hospital admissions and more than 5 million outpatient visits each year. In 2014 it had more than 202000 surgical cases.

Geographic Reach

In addition to its Cleveland center the foundation operates regional hospitals and numerous family and specialty health centers in northeastern Ohio. The Cleveland Clinic Foundation operates a handful of hospitals and clinics in Florida and it has several brain clinics for neurological treatment in Nevada. It also provides management services for a hospital in Ashtabula Ohio.

National and global expansion efforts are a big part of the organization's growth strategy. Internationally Cleveland Clinic Foundation operates a health and wellness center in Canada and manages health centers in the United Arab Emirates. Its facilities treat patients from more than 130 countries.

Sales and Marketing

Cleveland Clinic Foundation receives about 60% of its net patient service revenue from managed care and commercial insurance reimbursements. Medicare reimbursements account for 30% with the remainder of patient revenue coming from self-pay and Medicaid customers.

Strategy

Cleveland Clinic Foundation got some national media attention when President Barack Obama visited as part of the debate around health care reform and many publications around the country held it up as a model for delivering high quality care at lower costs. Cleveland Clinic's cost-cutting innovations include paying doctors a salary rather than by procedure (the group practice model) and interactive supply closets that perform their own inventory and summon robotic refill carts from the warehouse.

The foundation also improves its service offerings through facility and program expansion efforts as well as partnerships with other regional providers.

Mergers and Acquisitions

In early 2019 Cleveland Clinic expanded its operations in the Sunshine State when it acquired Martin Health System and its three hospitals in Southeast Florida. It also acquired Indian River Medical Center located on Florida's Treasure Coast.

Company Background

The foundation began in 1921 when a group of Cleveland doctors teamed up to improve medical care and education. The Cleveland Clinic hospital has conducted breakthrough medical innovations through its history such as the first face transplant in 2008 and it is regularly named to the US News & World Report's list of America's Best Hospitals.

EXECUTIVES

Cio, C. Martin Harris
President And Ceo, Delos M. (Toby) Cosgrove
Ceo Cleveland Clinic Regional Hospitals, David L. Bronson
Controller And Chief Accounting Officer, Steven C. Glass
Ceo Cleveland Clinic Abu Dhabi, A. Marc Harrison
Chief Medical Operations Officer, Robert Wyllie
Chief Of Operations, William (Bill) Peacock
Interim Coo Sheikh Khalifa Medical City, Ben Frank
Interim Executive Chief Nursing Officer, K. Kelly Hancock
Chair Department Of Palm Ccm, Herbert Wiedemann
Medical Director, Kevin Hopkins
Medical Director, Vladimir Burdjalov
Medical Director Molecular Oncology, Roger D Klein
Director Of Pharmacy, William P Kernan
Vice President Of Medical Operations, William Riebel
Director Of Health Information Management, Gale McNeill
Medical Director, William Zafirau
Vice President Marketing, Janet Day
Nursing Director, Julie Fetto
Assistant Vice President Operations, Janet Gulley
Vice President Of Operations, Vicky Snyder
Medical Director, Purva Grover
Chairman, Robert E. (Bob) Rich
Vice Chairman, Joseph M. (Joe) Scaminace
Secretary, Lynn Meyers
Secretary, Tina Grobe
Secretary, Jennifer Gaizutis
Secretary, Marcie Chonko
Secretary, Pam Staub
Board Member, Donna Munic-Miller
Secretary, Christine Hughes
Secretary, Jan Kodish
Board Member, Alfred Melillo
Secretary, Patricia Gaines
Secretary, Marianne Simon
Auditors: ERNST & YOUNG LLP CLEVELAND

LOCATIONS

HQ: THE CLEVELAND CLINIC FOUNDATION
9500 EUCLID AVE, CLEVELAND, OH 441950002
Phone: 216 636-8335
Web: WWW.MY.CLEVELANDCLINIC.ORG

Selected Facilities

Ashtabula County Medical Center (Ashtabula Ohio; management contract)
The Cleveland Clinic (Cleveland Ohio)
　Cleveland Clinic Children's Hospital
　Cleveland Clinic International Center
Cleveland Clinic Canada (Toronto)
Cleveland Clinic Children's Hospital for Rehabilitation (Shaker Campus in Cleveland Ohio)
Cleveland Clinic Family Health Centers (multiple locations in northeast Ohio)
Cleveland Clinic Florida (Weston Florida)
Cleveland Clinic Florida (West Palm Beach Florida)
Cleveland Clinic Lou Ruvo Center for Brain Health (Elko Nevada)
Cleveland Clinic Lou Ruvo Center for Brain Health (Las Vegas Nevada)
Cleveland Clinic Lou Ruvo Center for Brain Health (Reno Nevada)
Euclid Hospital (Euclid Ohio)
Fairview Hospital (Cleveland Ohio)
Hillcrest Hospital (Mayfield Heights Ohio)
Lakewood Hospital (Lakewood Ohio)
Lutheran Hospital (Cleveland Ohio)
Marymount Hospital (Garfield Heights Ohio)
Medina Hospital (Medina Ohio)
Richard E. Jacobs Health Center (Avon Ohio)
South Pointe Hospital (Warrensville Heights Ohio)

Selected Institutes

Children's and Pediatric Institute
College of Medicine
Digestive Disease Institute
Education Institute
Glickman Urological and Kidney Institute
Lerner Research Institute
Neurological Institute
Orthopedic and Rheumatologic Institute
Stanley Shalom Zielony Institute for Nursing Excellence
Sydell and Arnold Miller Family Heart and Vascular Institute
Taussig Cancer Institute

PRODUCTS/OPERATIONS

2014 Net Patient Service Revenue

	% of total
Managed care & commercial	61
Medicare	29
Self-pay	7
Medicaid	3
Total	**100**

COMPETITORS

Akron Children's Hospital	Parma Community General Hospital
Catholic Health Initiatives	Premier Health Partners
Deaconess Associations	Robinson Memorial Hospital
Kettering Health Network	Shriners Hospitals For Children
Lake Health	Summa Health System
Mayo Clinic	University Hospitals Health System
Memorial Sloan-Kettering	Washington Hospital Center
MetroHealth System	
OhioHealth	

HISTORICAL FINANCIALS

Company Type: Private

Income Statement

FYE: December 31

	REVENUE ($ mil.)	NET INCOME ($ mil.)	NET PROFIT MARGIN	EMPLOYEES
12/17	8,407	1,150	13.7%	44,000
12/16	8,037	513	6.4%	—
12/14	4,290	405	9.4%	—
12/13	6,450	900	14.0%	—
Annual Growth	6.8%	6.3%	—	—

2017 Year-End Financials

Debt ratio: —
Return on equity: 13.70%
Cash ($ mil.): 241
Current ratio: 0.50
Long-term debt ($ mil.): —

Dividends
Yield: —
Payout: —
Market value ($ mil.): —

THE FORD FOUNDATION

As one of the nation's largest philanthropic organizations the Ford Foundation can afford to be generous. The foundation offers grants to individuals and institutions worldwide that work to meet its goals of strengthening democratic values reducing poverty and injustice promoting international cooperation and advancing human achievement. The Ford Foundation's charitable giving has run the gamut from A (Association for Asian Studies) to Z (Zanzibar International Film Festival). The foundation has an endowment of about $10 billion. Established in 1936 by Edsel Ford whose father founded the Ford Motor Company the foundation no longer owns stock in the automaker or has ties to the founding family.

Operations

The foundation which is governed by an international board of trustees makes grants in all 50 US states and supports programs in more than 50 countries.

It boasts about 10 regional offices in Latin America Africa the Middle East and Asia.

Geographic Reach

Based in New York the Ford Foundation is a grantmaking foundation that primarily serves the US but also global programs.

Strategy

The Ford Foundation's programs address several social justice issues including democratic and accountable government freedom of expression access to education economic fairness and opportunity sexuality and reproductive rights sustainable development social justice metropolitan opportunity and human rights.

A small portion of its endowment is set aside for social investing. The foundation's funds typically finance critical projects set new business models and develop sustainable organizations. By investing $1 million or more in initiatives the Ford Foundation's investment strategy aims to make a noteworthy impact and encourage other investors to also fund projects.

EXECUTIVES

Vice President Secretary, Ken Monteiro
Program Vice President, Martin Abregu
Vice President Talent Human Resources,
 Samantha Gilbert
Secretary, Karen Mcburnie

LOCATIONS

HQ: THE FORD FOUNDATION
 320 E 43RD ST FL 4, NEW YORK, NY 100174890
Phone: 212 573-5370
Web: WWW.FORDFOUNDATION.ORG

PRODUCTS/OPERATIONS

Selected Core Issues
Democratic and accountable government
Economic fairness
Education opportunity and scholarship
Freedom of expression
Human rights
Metropolitan opportunity
Sexuality and reproductive health rights
Social justice philanthropy
Sustainable development

HISTORICAL FINANCIALS
Company Type: Private

Income Statement   FYE: December 31

	ASSETS ($ mil.)	NET INCOME ($ mil.)	INCOME AS % OF ASSETS	EMPLOYEES
12/15	12,114	(270)	—	556
12/14*	12,400	(7)	—	—
09/11	10,344	(5)	—	—
09/09	10,234	0	—	—
Annual Growth	2.8%	—	—	—

*Fiscal year change

2015 Year-End Financials

Debt ratio: —
Return on equity: (-55.50%)
Cash ($ mil.): 126
Current ratio: 0.40
Long-term debt ($ mil.): —

Dividends
Yield: —
Payout: —
Market value ($ mil.): —

The Gap Inc

The ubiquitous clothing retailer Gap has been filling closets with jeans and khakis T-shirts button-downs and poplin for some 50 years. The company which operates about 3600 owned and franchised stores worldwide built its iconic casual brand on basics for men women and children. Over the years it has extended its namesake brand to include GapBody GapKids and babyGap (among others) and has added brands such as the urban chic Banana Republic family budgeteer Old Navy women's activewear chain Athleta and designer-focused Intermix. Most of Gap's products are designed by the company and made by third parties. It generates most of its revenue from the US.

HISTORY

Donald Fisher and his wife Doris opened a small store in 1969 near what is now San Francisco State University. The couple named their store The Gap (after "the generation gap") and concentrated on selling Levi's jeans. The couple opened a second store in San Jose California eight months later and by the end of 1970 there were six Gap stores. The Gap went public six years later.

In the beginning the Fishers catered almost exclusively to teenagers but in the 1970s they expanded into activewear that would appeal to a larger spectrum of customers. Nevertheless by the early 1980s The Gap — which had grown to about 500 stores — was still dependent upon its largely teenage customer base. However it was less dependent on Levi's (about 35% of sales) thanks to its growing stable of private labels.

In a 1983 effort to revamp the company's image Donald hired Mickey Drexler a former president of AnnTaylor with a spotless apparel industry track record as The Gap's new president. Drexler immediately overhauled the motley clothing lines to concentrate on sturdy brightly colored cotton clothing. He also consolidated the stores' many private clothing labels into the Gap brand. As a final touch Drexler replaced circular clothing racks with white shelving so clothes could be neatly stacked and displayed.

Also in 1983 The Gap bought Banana Republic a unique chain of jungle-themed stores that sold safari clothing. The company expanded the chain which enjoyed tremendous success in the mid-1980s but slumped after the novelty of the stores wore off late in the decade. In response Drexler introduced a broader range of clothes (including higher-priced leather items) and dumped the safari lines in 1988. By 1990 Banana Republic was again profitable.

The first GapKids opened in 1985 after Drexler couldn't find clothing that he liked for his son. During the late 1980s and early 1990s the company grew rapidly opening its first stores in Canada and the UK. In 1990 it introduced babyGap in 25 GapKids stores featuring miniature versions of its GapKids line. The Gap announced in 1991 it would no longer sell Levi's (which had fallen to less than 2% of total sales) and would sell nothing but private-label items.

Earnings fell in fiscal 1993 because of Gap division losses brought on by low margins and high rents. The company shuffled management positions and titles as part of a streamlining effort. It rebounded in 1994 by concentrating on improving profit margins rather than sales and by launching Old Navy Clothing Co. named after a bar Drexler saw in Paris. Banana Republic opened its first two stores outside the US both in Canada in 1995.

Robert Fisher (the founders' son) became the new president of the Gap division (including babyGap and GapKids) in 1997 and was charged with reversing the segment's sales decline. The company refocused its Gap chain on basics (jeans T-shirts and khakis) and helped boost its performance with a high-profile advertising campaign focusing on those wares. Later in 1997 the Gap opened an online Gap store. In 1998 it began opening Torpedo Joe submarine-themed shops in select Old Navy flagships.

Also in 1998 the retailer opened its first GapBody stores and introduced its only catalog (for Banana Republic). In late 1999 amid sluggish Gap division sales Robert Fisher resigned and Drexler took over his duties. Gap misjudged fashion trends in 2000 which resulted in two years of disappointing earnings. After a 10% reduction in its workforce the company returned to a more conservative fashion approach.

The company split Gap and Gap International into two separate units in early 2002 to improve performance in the flagship brand. In September Drexler retired and was replaced by Paul Pressler a veteran of The Walt Disney Company.

Gap sold its 10 stores in Germany to Swedish retailer H&M in 2004 taking a $14 million write-down related to the sale.

The next year the retailer launched Forth & Towne its first new chain in a decade with the new stores catering to women over the age of 35. Also Gap dipped its toes into personal care products by signing an agreement with Inter Parfums in mid-2005. As part of the deal Inter Parfums develops manufactures and packages the products which are branded under the Gap and Banana Republic names. The Gap markets and sells them in its GapBody stores.

In January 2006 Gap entered into a 10-year non-exclusive services agreement with International Business Machines valued at $1.1 billion. As a result IBM took over certain information technology functions from the retailer; up to 400 Gap employees joined IBM as a result of the deal. Gap Direct launched an online footwear business called Piperlime in November.

CEO Pressler left the company and the board in January 2007 after four years in the top job. He was succeeded as CEO on an interim basis by

Robert Fisher previously the non-executive chairman of the retailer. In June the company shut down its Forth & Towne retail format after less than two years in business. In July Gap named a new chairman and CEO Glenn Murphy. Murphy joined the company from Canadian drugstore chain Shoppers Drug Mart where he had retired as chairman and CEO in March. Stung by allegations in the British press of forced child labor in India being used in the manufacture of apparel for its Gap Kids chain Gap in November announced a package of measures intended to strengthen its commitment to eradicating the exploitation of children in the garment industry. Actions include a $200000 grant to improve working conditions and an upcoming conference dedicated to finding solutions to issues related to child labor.

In October 2008 Gap acquired Athleta a direct-marketer of women's active wear for about $150 million. Gap purchased Athleta as part of its strategy to diversify its brand offerings. The company also opened its first Banana Republic and Gap brand factory stores in Canada in late October extending its outlet busuiness launched in 1994 to Canada. The retailer opened 101 new stores and shuttered 119 locations in 2008.

Don Fisher Gap co-founder died in September 2009 at the age of 81. Also in 2009 Gap began opening stores inside Mexico's leading department store chain Distribuidora Liverpool via a franchise agreement.

EXECUTIVES

President And General Manager Athleta, Nancy Green, age 56
President Growth Innovation And Digital, Arthur (Art) Peck, age 62, $1,330,288 total compensation
President And General Manager Intermix, Jyothi Rao
Global President Old Navy, Sonia Syngal, age 48, $850,000 total compensation
Global President Gap, Jeff Kirwan, age 52, $893,269 total compensation
Evp And Cfo, Teri L. List-Stoll, $30,288 total compensation
Evp; General Manager Greater China, Abinta Malik
Evp Global General Counsel Corporate Secretary And Chief Compliance Officer, Julie Gruber
Evp Strategy And Chief Customer Officer, Sebastian DiGrande, $505,385 total compensation
Evp And Cio, Paul Chapman
Evp Global Supply Chain Sourcing And Production, Michael Yee
Evp Global Supply Chain Logistics And Product Operations, Shawn Curran
Vice President Ocm, Rita Martell
Senior Vice President And General Manager, Jodi Bricker
Chairman, Robert J. (Bob) Fisher, age 63
Auditors: Deloitte & Touche LLP

LOCATIONS

HQ: The Gap Inc
Two Folsom Street, San Francisco, CA 94105
Phone: 415 427-0100
Web: www.gapinc.com

2017 Sales

	$ mil.	% of total
US	12,568	80
Asia	1,263	8
Canada	1,173	7
Europe	641	4
Other regions	210	1
Total	**15,855**	**100**

PRODUCTS/OPERATIONS

2017 Sales

	$ mil.	% of total
Old Navy Global	7,238	45
Gap	5,318	34
Banana Republic Global	2,380	15
Other	919	6
Total	**15,855**	**100**

2017 Stores

	No.
Company-operated	
Gap	1,278
Old Navy	1,080
Banana Republic	621
Athleta	148
Intermix	38
Franchise	429
Total	**3,594**

Selected Stores and Brands

Athleta (women's activewear)
babyGap (clothing for infants and toddlers)
Banana Republic (upscale clothing and accessories)
Gap (casual and active clothing and body care products)
GapBody (intimate apparel)
GapKids (clothing for children)
Intermix (designer clothing for women)
Old Navy (lower-priced family clothing)

COMPETITORS

Abercrombie & Fitch	Kohl's
Amazon.com	L Brands
American Eagle Outfitters	L.L. Bean
Ann Taylor	Lands' End
Arcadia	Levi Strauss
Benetton	Lululemon
Bon-Ton Stores	Macy's
Calvin Klein	Marks & Spencer
Chico's FAS	NIKE
Children's Place	Nordstrom
Dillard's	OshKosh B'Gosh
Express	PVH
Fast Retailing	Ralph Lauren
Foot Locker	Reebok
Guess?	Ross Stores
Gymboree	Sears
H&M	TJX Companies
Inditex	Talbots
J. C. Penney	Target Corporation
J. Crew	Urban Outfitters
Juicy Couture	VF Corporation
	Wal-Mart

HISTORICAL FINANCIALS

Company Type: Public

Income Statement

FYE: February 3

	REVENUE ($ mil.)	NET INCOME ($ mil.)	NET PROFIT MARGIN	EMPLOYEES
02/18*	15,855	848	5.3%	135,000
01/17	15,516	676	4.4%	135,000
01/16	15,797	920	5.8%	141,000
01/15	16,435	1,262	7.7%	141,000
02/14	16,148	1,280	7.9%	137,000
Annual Growth	**(0.5%)**	**(9.8%)**	**—**	**(0.4%)**

*Fiscal year change

2018 Year-End Financials

Debt ratio: 15.63%
Return on equity: 27.59%
Cash ($ mil.): 1,783
Current ratio: 1.86
Long-term debt ($ mil.): 1,249

No. of shares (mil.): 389
Dividends
  Yield: 0.0%
  Payout: 42.9%
Market value ($ mil.): 12,483

	STOCK PRICE ($) FY Close	P/E High/Low		PER SHARE ($) Earnings	Dividends	Book Value
02/18*	32.09	16	10	2.14	0.92	8.08
01/17	22.58	18	10	1.69	0.92	7.28
01/16	24.72	19	10	2.23	0.92	6.41
01/15	41.19	16	12	2.87	0.88	7.09
02/14	38.08	17	11	2.74	0.70	6.87
Annual Growth	**(4.2%)**	—		**(6.0%)**	**7.1%**	**4.2%**

*Fiscal year change

THE HERTZ CORPORATION

EXECUTIVES

Pres-Ceo, Kathryn V Marinello
Non Exec Chb*, Henry R Keizer
Cfo, Jamere Jackson
Exec V Pres-Cmo, Jodi J Allen
Exec V Pres-Gen Counsel-Sec, Richard J Frecker
Sr V Pres-Cao, Robin C Kramer
Group Pres Rent A Car Int'l, Michel Taride
Evp-Chief Hr Officer, Murali Kuppuswamy
Manager, Jillian Hader
Manager, Jim Rafferty

LOCATIONS

HQ: THE HERTZ CORPORATION
8501 WILLIAMS RD, ESTERO, FL 339283325
Phone: 239 301-7000
Web: WWW.HERTZ.COM

HISTORICAL FINANCIALS

Company Type: Private

Income Statement

FYE: December 31

	REVENUE ($ mil.)	NET INCOME ($ mil.)	NET PROFIT MARGIN	EMPLOYEES
12/17	8,803	332	3.8%	37,000
12/16	8,803	(488)	—	—
12/15	10,535	276	2.6%	—
Annual Growth	**(8.6%)**	**9.7%**	**—**	**—**

2017 Year-End Financials

Debt ratio: ——
Return on equity: 3.80%
Cash ($ mil.): 1,072
Current ratio: ——
Long-term debt ($ mil.): —

Dividends
  Yield: —
  Payout: —
Market value ($ mil.): —

THE IRVINE JAMES FOUNDATION

EXECUTIVES

Pres-Ceo, Donald Howard
Director of Finance, Casey Budesilich
Dir Technology, Ekta Chopra
Program Director, Elizabeth Gonzalez

Digital Communications Officer, Joyce Sood
Director of Impact Assessment, Kim Howard
Senior Communications Officer, Leslie Payne
Senior Accountant, Michael Quach
Senior Program Officer, Rafael Morales
Leadership Awards Officer, Jessica Kaczmarek
Director of Program Operations, Josephine Ramirez

LOCATIONS

HQ: THE IRVINE JAMES FOUNDATION
1 BUSH ST FL 8, SAN FRANCISCO, CA 941044414
Phone: 415 777-2244
Web: WWW.222SECOND.COM

HISTORICAL FINANCIALS

Company Type: Private

Income Statement   FYE: December 31

	ASSETS ($ mil.)	NET INCOME ($ mil.)	INCOME AS % OF ASSETS	EMPLOYEES
12/15	2,185	38	1.8%	36
12/14	1,611	44	2.7%	—
12/09	1,507	(57)	—	—
12/08	1,379	0	—	—
Annual Growth	6.8%	—	—	—

2015 Year-End Financials

Debt ratio: ——
Return on equity: 28.20%
Cash ($ mil.): 52
Current ratio: 1.10
Long-term debt ($ mil.): —

Dividends
Yield: —
Payout: —
Market value ($ mil.): —

THE NEW YORK AND PRESBYTERIAN HOSPITAL

The New York and Presbyterian Hospital is a learned institution: The not-for-profit hospital is affiliated with both the Columbia University College of Physicians & Surgeons and the Weill Cornell Medical College of Cornell University. Known as NewYork-Presbyterian Hospital the organization includes two major medical centers Columbia University Medical Center and Weill Cornell Medical Center which conduct educational and research programs in partnership with the universities. The two facilities combined have about 2600 beds and offer specialized programs for burns digestive diseases pediatrics women's health and other conditions. NewYork-Presbyterian Hospital is part of the NewYork-Presbyterian Healthcare System.

Operations
Altogether the NewYork-Presbyterian Hospital campuses handle some 2 million patient visits each year (both on an inpatient and outpatient basis) including inpatient admissions and more than 310000 emergency room visits and about 15000 births. The facilities employ a total of more than 6500 physicians including residents and fellows. NewYork-Presbyterian Hospital provides more than $108 million in charity and community care services each year.

Geographic Reach
In addition to its flagship campuses NewYork-Presbyterian/Columbia and NewYork-Presbyterian/Weill Cornell NewYork-Presbyterian Hospital

operates two small community hospitals in Manhattan — the Allen Hospital and the Lower Manhattan Hospital — and an inpatient mental health facility (the Westchester Division). The broader NewYork-Presbyterian Healthcare System operates facilities in other areas of New York as well as in New Jersey and Connecticut. The NewYork-Presbyterian Hospital/Columbia campus houses the Morgan Stanley Children's Hospital as well as other specialist units.

Sales and Marketing
Medicare and Medicaid recipients account for more than 60% of NewYork-Presbyterian Hospital's patients. Commercial managed care organizations and insurance firms as well as self-pay customers account for the rest.

Financial Performance
NewYork-Presbyterian Hospital's revenue in fiscal 2015 totaled $4.8 billion.

Strategy
As the health care landscape has become increasingly complex and competitive especially with changing regulations and the push to provide more integrated patient care NewYork-Presbyterian Hospital has made some major organizational changes. Chief among its goals is to provide a patient-centered model of care creating a system that can easily be accessed by its patient consumers. It recently established its Community and Population Health division which includes community programs and initiatives ambulatory care network sites and the management of its new Accountable Care Organization.

It has also expanded beyond its former base of Manhattan in order to provide a regional system of care. For example the system took ownership of former affiliate Brooklyn Methodist in early 2017 with the intention of investing in the hospital's development; the move falls in line with its strategy of providing integrated care for communities particularly in light of a number of recent hospital failures in the borough.

Mergers and Acquisitions
New York Methodist Hospital (now NewYork-Presbyterian Brooklyn Methodist Hospital) was added to the organization in early 2017. Brooklyn Methodist will gain funds for a new $400 million ambulatory care building as part of the new relationship.

Company Background
NewYork-Presbyterian Hospital was formed through the 1998 merger of the New York Hospital (founded in 1771) and the Presbyterian Hospital (founded in 1868). New York Hospital was known for advancing care in areas including women's health and surgery while the Presbyterian Hospital was known for its pediatric division and its cancer center.

EXECUTIVES

Vice President Risk Management And Associate General Counsel, John Campano
Vice President Capital Planning And Development, Ellie Dalton
Evp Cfo And Treasurer, Phyllis R. Lantos
President And Ceo, Steven J. (Steve) Corwin
Chief Nursing Officer; Vp Patient Services Newyork-presbyterian/columbia, Wilhelmina Manzano
Vp Medical Affairs, Laura L. Forese
Svp And Chief Medical Officer, Richard S. Liebowitz
Cio, William Lee
Evp Chief Legal Officer And General Counsel, Maxine Frank
Director Of Nursing, Laurie Walsh
Finance Vice President, Ana Arroyo
Director Of Health Information, Deborah Forde
Information Security Vice President, Howard Goldman

Vice President Compensation Benefits And Hris, Mary Falkowitz
Senior Vice President And Chief, Karen S Westervelt
Vice President And Chief Learning, Andrea Procaccino
Operations Vice President, Elizabeth Vega
Vice President Finance, William Farrell
Finance Vice President, Noemi Lopez
Senior Vice President And Chief Quality, Henry Ting
Director Of Pharmacy, Ralph Lizo
Vice President Of Business Planning, Craig Evans
Vice President Finance, Lugeion Y Carter
Chairman, Frank A. Bennack, age 85
President Ceo And Trustee, Herbert Pardes, age 84
Assistant Treasurer, Sedare Coradine

LOCATIONS

HQ: THE NEW YORK AND PRESBYTERIAN HOSPITAL
525 E 68TH ST, NEW YORK, NY 100654870
Phone: 212 746-5454
Web: WWW.NEWYORK-PRESBYTERIANHOSPITAL.ORG

PRODUCTS/OPERATIONS

2016 Patient Mix

	% of total
Medicare Managed	9
Medicare FFS	22
Medicaid Managed	23
Medicaid FFS	7
Managed Care and Other	37
Self-Pay	1
Workers Comp	1
Total	**100**

Selected Services

Cancer
Children's Health
Digestive
Geriatrics
Heart
Mens Health
Neuroscience
Orthopedic
Psychiatry
Rehabilitation Medicine
Transplant
Vascular
Womens Health

COMPETITORS

Ascension Health
Beth Israel Medical Center
Bronx-Lebanon Hospital
Catholic Healthcare System
Continuum Health Partners
Lenox Hill Hospital
Lutheran HealthCare
Maimonides Medical Center

MediSys Health Network
Memorial Sloan-Kettering
Montefiore Medical
New York City Health and Hospitals
Northwell Health
Winthrop-University Hospital
Yale New Haven Health System

HISTORICAL FINANCIALS

Company Type: Private

Income Statement   FYE: December 31

	REVENUE ($ mil.)	NET INCOME ($ mil.)	NET PROFIT MARGIN	EMPLOYEES
12/17	5,616	762	13.6%	23,709
12/16	4,935	496	10.1%	—
12/14	4,206	197	4.7%	—
12/13	4,264	595	14.0%	—
Annual Growth	7.1%	6.4%	—	—

2017 Year-End Financials

Debt ratio: ——
Return on equity: 13.60%
Cash ($ mil.): 1,725
Current ratio: 2.10
Long-term debt ($ mil.): ——

Dividends
Yield: ——
Payout: ——
Market value ($ mil.): ——

THE PENNSYLVANIA STATE UNIVERSITY

The Pennsylvania State University system is one of the largest state university systems in the US. Penn State has an enrollment of almost 96000 students; 13600 of them are graduate students. It offers 160 undergraduate and 150 graduate programs at about 20 campuses. The school's oldest and largest campus with about half of the system's undergraduate students is at University Park in central Pennsylvania. Other sites include the College of Medicine in Hershey Pennsylvania and the Dickinson School of Law in Carlisle Pennsylvania. It generates about $8.5 billion in annual direct and indirect economic impacts within Pennsylvania.

Operations

The university is known for its academic medical center and biomedical research. Its health-related programs include the Schools of Nursing Medicine Dental Medicine and Veterinary Medicine. The school's biomedical research ranks in the top 5 of National Institutes of Health funding.

The school offers a broad range of disciplines including medicine humanities engineering cyberscience and social science.

Financial Performance

Penn State had an annual operating budget in 2014-15 of $4.6 billion and an annual endowment of more than $2 billion. Its annual research funding is roughly $813 million of which $492 million comes from federal sources.

Strategy

In 2015 the university announced a new $30 million investment in economic development and student career success. This investment includes a one-time start-up and capital investment as well as annual funding of more than $5 million.

In 2014 the fundraising campaign For the Future: The Campaign for Penn State Students surpassed its goal raising about $2.2 billion in private support.

Company Background

Chartered in 1855 to apply scientific principles to farming Penn State has conferred almost 800000 degrees since its founding.

The university's storied football program was hit in 2012 with a four year postseason ban the significant reduction of scholarships the vacating of 112 wins and a $60 million fine all stemming from the school's handling of the child molestation scandal involving former coach Jerry Sandusky. However in 2015 the NCAA reversed its decision on the vacating of wins restoring the late head coach Joe Paterno as the winningest coach in major college football history.

EXECUTIVES

Vice President Student Affairs, Damon Sims
Svp Finance And Business And Treasurer, David J. Gray
Dean University Libraries And Scholarly Communications, Barbara I. Dewey
Dean Undergraduate Education, Robert N. Pangborn
Dean College Of Medicine, A. Craig Hillemeier
Dean College Of Arts And Architecture, Barbara O. Korner
Dean College Of Earth And Mineral Sciences, William E. Easterling
Dean College Of Education, David H. Monk
Dean College Of Health And Human Development, Ann C. (Nan) Crouter
Dean College Of The Liberal Arts, Susan Welch
Dean College Of Nursing, Paula Milone-Nuzzo
Dean Schreyer Honors College, Christian M. M. Brady
President, Eric J. Barron, age 67
Dean Smeal College Of Business, Charles H. Whiteman
Chief Investment Officer, John Pomeroy
Dean Graduate School, Regina Vasilatos-Younken
Dean College Of Agricultural Sciences, Richard Roush
Dean College Of Communications, Marie Hardin
Dean College Of Engineering, Amr S. Elnashai
Senior Vice President For Finance And Business Treasurer, Cynthia Hall
Vice President, Victor Sparrow
Department Head, Scott Wing
Vice President, Emily Sandall
Vice President For Strategic Communications, Lawrence Lokman
Operating Room Director, Jennifer Butch
Vice Chairman, Ira M. Lubert, age 68
Chairman, Keith E. Masser
Board Member, Eric Smith
Board Member, Malcolm Taylor
Auditors: DELOITTE & TOUCHE LLP PHILADE

LOCATIONS

HQ: THE PENNSYLVANIA STATE UNIVERSITY
201 OLD MAIN, UNIVERSITY PARK, PA 168021503
Phone: 814 865-4700
Web: WWW.PSU.EDU

PRODUCTS/OPERATIONS

Selected Colleges

College of Agricultural Sciences
College of Arts and Architecture
Smeal College of Business
College of Communications
College of Earth and Mineral Sciences
College of Education
College of Engineering
College of Health and Human Development
College of Information Sciences and Technology
School of International Affairs
School of Law
College of the Liberal Arts
College of Medicine
School of Nursing
Eberly College of Science
Graduate School
Schreyer Honors College

Selected Campuses

Penn State Abington Penn State Altoona
Penn State Beaver
Penn State Berks
Penn State Brandywine
Penn State DuBois
Penn State Erie The Behrend College
Penn State Fayette The Eberly Campus
Penn State Greater Allegheny
Penn State Harrisburg
Penn State Hazleton
Penn State Lehigh Valley
Penn State Mont Alto
Penn State New Kensington
Penn State Schuylkill
Penn State Shenango
Penn State Wilkes-Barre
Penn State Worthington Scranton
Penn State York

HISTORICAL FINANCIALS
Company Type: Private

Income Statement   FYE: June 30

	REVENUE ($ mil.)	NET INCOME ($ mil.)	NET PROFIT MARGIN	EMPLOYEES
06/17	6,059	635	10.5%	44,000
06/16	5,764	233	4.0%	—
06/15	5,293	289	5.5%	—
06/14	5,148	974	18.9%	—
Annual Growth	5.6%	(13.3%)	—	—

2017 Year-End Financials

Debt ratio: ——
Return on equity: 10.50%
Cash ($ mil.): 1,761
Current ratio: 2.00
Long-term debt ($ mil.): ——

Dividends
Yield: ——
Payout: ——
Market value ($ mil.): ——

THE TRUSTEES OF THE UNIVERSITY OF PENNSYLVANIA

The University of Pennsylvania (commonly called Penn) was founded by Benjamin Franklin when he had a little down time between establishing a country and experimenting with lightning. Since opening its doors to students in 1751 the Ivy League university has accumulated a notable list of accomplishments including the creation of one of the first medical schools in the US. The university currently has a total of almost 25000 students who pursue their studies in four undergraduate schools and a dozen graduate and professional schools including the renowned Wharton School and the Annenberg School for Communications. Its student-teacher ratio is a very low 6:1.

Operations

The University of Pennsylvania's research staff includes more than 4300 faculty and 1100 postdoctoral fellows plus some 5400 academic support staff and graduate student trainees.

The university is also responsible for inventing the Electronic Numerical Integrator and Computer (ENIAC) the first general-purpose electronic computer. The ENIAC was constructed and operated at The Moore School of Electrical Engineering now part of the School of Engineering and Applied Science. The school still has on display four of the original 40 panels of ENIAC which represents onetenth of its original size.

Geographic Reach

The University of Pennsylvania is located in the heart of downtown Philadelphia.

Financial Performance

The University of Pennsylvania has an annual budget of about $7.3 billion. Its endowment is about $9.6 billion. The school is heavily involved with research operating more than 165 research centers and institutes.

Company Background

Former University of Pennsylvania president Judith Rodin was the first female to head an Ivy League university.

LOCATIONS

HQ: THE TRUSTEES OF THE UNIVERSITY OF PENNSYLVANIA
3451 WALNUT ST RM 440A, PHILADELPHIA, PA 191046205
Phone: 215 898-5000
Web: WWW.HILTON.COM

PRODUCTS/OPERATIONS

Selected Schools
Annenberg School for Communication
The College at Penn (School of Arts and Sciences)
Graduate School of Education
Graduate School of Fine Arts
Law School
School of Arts and Sciences
School of Dental Medicine
School of Engineering and Applied Science
School of Medicine
School of Nursing
School of Social Work
School of Veterinary Medicine
The Wharton School

HISTORICAL FINANCIALS

Company Type: Private

Income Statement — FYE: June 30

	REVENUE ($ mil.)	NET INCOME ($ mil.)	NET PROFIT MARGIN	EMPLOYEES
06/17	9,194	1,734	18.9%	20,433
06/10	4	0	5.1%	—
06/09	5,221	(1,285)	—	—
06/08	5,092	133	2.6%	—
Annual Growth	6.8%	33.0%	—	—

2017 Year-End Financials

Debt ratio: —
Return on equity: 18.90%
Cash ($ mil.): 972
Current ratio: —
Long-term debt ($ mil.): —
Dividends
Yield: —
Payout: —
Market value ($ mil.): —

THE TURNER CORPORATION

The Turner Corporation a subsidiary of German construction giant HOCHTIEF is the leading general building and construction management firm in the US (as ranked by Engineering News-Record) ahead of rivals Bechtel and Fluor. The firm operates primarily through subsidiary Turner Construction and has worked on notable projects such as Madison Square Garden the UN headquarters Yankee Stadium the Taipei 101 Tower and the 68000-seat open-air stadium for the San Francisco 49ers. Known for its large projects also offers services for midsized and smaller projects and provides interior construction and renovation services.

Operations
Turner works on more than 1500 projects in a year totaling $8 billion in volume. The group has divisions dedicated to serving the aviation health care biotechnology public assembly sports education justice and industrial sectors. Its homeland security group was established in order handle a growing demand for security systems and protection. The unit installed detection equipment in some 450 airports throughout the US. Turner Corporation also has an arm specializing in green building with a focus on Leadership in Energy and Environmental Design (LEED) -certified projects. Turner Green Building has more than 400 LEED projects and green projects either completed or in progress.

Turner Corporation has subsidiaries providing auxiliary operations. Turner's risk management department offers contract review project safety and claims handling. Turner Logistics handles procurement and supply chain management for projects and Turner Facilities Management Solutions offers ongoing operations services. Also the Turner School of Construction Management provides training for local subcontractors.

Geographic Reach
Dallas-based Turner Corporation boasts a network of offices across the US (with most in California and Ohio) and Canada (Vancouver and Toronto) with an global presence in 20 countries in Europe Africa East Asia India Latin America and the Caribbean.

Sales and Marketing
Turner works on variety of projects from several sectors. It's known for its work in the categories of healthcare education offices commercial properties cultural facilities sports facilities and hotels. The company is also a leader in the green building category.

Strategy
With the construction market rebounding from the economic downturn Turner is looking to high-growth markets in the US and overseas. As of early 2015 it was working on more than 1900 projects 80% of which were Education Commercial or Interior project-related. Some of these projects included the 17000 sq. ft- interior remodel for Salesforce's Vancouver office; the 325000 sq. ft-construction of the LEED-Certified RAND Corporation Headquarters in Santa Monica California; and the 25000-seat Charlotte Coliseum event arena for the City of Charlotte North Carolina.

The company has also been making moves to expand its business abroad in recent years. In 2012 for example Turner partnered with one of India's largest real estate developers Sahara Prime City Ltd. to form Sahara Turner which would lead the development and construction of multiple townships across the country with an approximate value of $2.5 billion by 2017. It also purchased a majority stake in Clark Builders Canada to capitalize on the country's growing construction market.

Turner often partners with fellow US-based HOCHTIEF subsidiary Flatiron which specializes in civil engineering. Examples of the teamwork are the expansions of airports in San Diego and Sacramento.

HISTORY

At the turn of the century an engineer and devout Quaker named Henry Chandlee Turner was convinced that a new type of steel-reinforced concrete (called the Ransome system) would change the construction industry. With this conviction and with the help of his partner D. H. Dixon Turner bought the rights to the technology for $25000 and in 1902 founded Turner Construction Company.

One of the company's early projects was building the stairways for New York's first subway stations. As the Ransome method proved to be successful Turner's reputation grew. Defense contracts during WWI raised Turner's take to $35 million in 1918.

Before the Depression Turner was building high-rises hotels and stadiums. During the economic crash that started in 1929 the company survived by building retail stores churches and public buildings a strategy it would employ successfully in later recessions.

Henry Turner retired in 1941. His brother Archer Turner managed the company during most of the war effort. As WWII raged more than 80% of the company's work was defense-related. Projects included building and managing a submarine base in Oak Ridge Tennessee during the development of the atomic bomb.

In 1947 Henry C. Turner Jr. the founder's son became president and within four years he had led the company to more than $100 million in sales. By the time he stepped down as chairman in 1970 the firm had built skyscrapers futuristic airports and such landmarks as Madison Square Garden and the United Nations Secretariat and Plaza in New York City. Turner went public in 1969.

Howard S. Turner (the final family member to head the business) led the company during the 1970s. The company extended its global presence opening offices in more countries including Iran Pakistan and the United Arab Emirates. Turner also developed construction management services.

In 1984 The Turner Corporation was formed as a holding company for the construction company and the subsidiaries created or acquired as a result of diversification. Property development was one of these activities but by 1987 Turner had begun to dispose of its real estate holdings. It did not move quickly enough however and when the real estate market crashed Turner was caught with a large portfolio.

As commercial projects slowed Turner sought work in more sectors including public works and amusement projects (aquariums arenas hospitals and universities). By 1994 these areas accounted for 70% of business. In 1993 as the building slump continued Turner began a cost-cutting plan which included laying off workers and closing offices. That year the company set up an $8.5 million restructuring reserve and as the real estate market eased into recovery Turner sold more of its real estate holdings.

In 1996 Turner won a contract to build a 10000-seat arena in Salt Lake City to be used for the 2002 Winter Olympics. In 1997 Turner contracted to renovate 811 schools and build two campuses in California's San Fernando Valley and in 1998 it was chosen to manage the construction of the Kansas City Motor Speedway.

Debt ratio: 46.06%
Return on equity: 58.70%
Cash ($ mil.): 552
Current ratio: 1.21
Long-term debt ($ mil.): 7,540

Debt ratio: 12.95%
Return on equity: 4.58%
Cash ($ mil.): 955
Current ratio: 1.26
Long-term debt ($ mil.): 1,505

Dividends
  Yield: —
  Payout: —
Market value ($ mil.): —

AT&T	HC2 Holdings
ATN International	Horry Telephone
Cavalier Telephone	NII Holdings
CenturyLink	Sprint Communications
Cincinnati Bell	Suddenlink
Cricket	Communications
FairPoint	T-Mobile USA
Communications Inc.	Verizon
Farmers	Verizon Wireless Inc.
Telecommunications	XO Holdings

Benteler Automotive	Kolbenschmidt Pierburg
Cooper-Standard Automotive	Letts Industries
Edelbrock	Meritor
Faurecia Exhaust Systems	Wescast Industries
	ZF Group NAO

Debt ratio: 29.76% No. of shares (mil.): 51
Return on equity: 32.24% Dividends
Cash ($ mil.): 315 Yield: 0.0%
Current ratio: 1.24 Payout: 25.5%
Long-term debt ($ mil.): 1,358 Market value ($ mil.): 3,011

Debt ratio: —
Return on equity: (-10.20%) Dividends
Cash ($ mil.): 60 Yield: —
Current ratio: 0.50 Payout: —
Long-term debt ($ mil.): — Market value ($ mil.): —

Chairman Ceo And Product Architect, Elon Musk, age 47, $45,936 total compensation
Cfo, Deepak Ahuja, age 55, $338,000 total compensation
Cto, Jeffrey B. (JB) Straubel, age 42, $250,560 total compensation
Vice President Of Regulatory Affairs And Associate General Counsel, James Chen
National Sales Manager, Christine Moore
Vice President Technology, Drew Baglino
Vice President Global Recruiting, Cindy Nicola
Vice President Corporate Controller And Chief Accounting Officer, Eric Branderiz
Chief People Officer, Gaby Toledano
Vice President Of Real Estate Store Design And Retail Development, Gregg Hurley
Vice President Ir And Strategy, Jeff K Evanson
Board Member, Ira Ehrenpreis
Corporate Treasurer And Vice President Global Tax Trade Treasury And New Ventures At Tesla Motors, Susan J Repo
Auditors: PricewaterhouseCoopers LLP

HQ: Tesla Inc
3500 Deer Creek Road, Palo Alto, CA 94304
Phone: 650 681-5000
Web: www.teslamotors.com

	$ mil.	% of total
US	6,221	53
China	2,027	17
Norway	823	7
Other	2,687	23
Total	**11,758**	**100**

	$ mil.	% of total
Automotive	10,624	91
Energy generation & storage	1,116	9
Total	**11,758**	**100**

AES	Nissan
BMW	Samsung Electronics
BYD	Siemens Energy
Daimler	Subaru of America
FCA US	SunPower
Ford Motor	Sunrun
General Motors	Suzuki Motor
Honda	Toyota
Hyundai Motor	Vivint Solar Inc.
Isuzu	Volkswagen
Kia Motors	VydroTech
LG Chem	ZAP
Mitsubishi Motors	

HISTORICAL FINANCIALS

Income Statement
FYE: December 31

	REVENUE ($ mil.)	NET INCOME ($ mil.)	NET PROFIT MARGIN	EMPLOYEES
12/17	11,758	(1,961)	—	37,543
12/16	7,000	(674)	—	30,025
12/15	4,046	(888)	—	13,058
12/14	3,198	(294)	—	10,161
12/13	2,013	(74)	—	5,859
Annual Growth	55.5%	—	—	59.1%

Debt ratio: 25.50%
Return on equity: 5.49%
Cash ($ mil.): 1,079
Current ratio: 1.92
Long-term debt ($ mil.): 3,898

No. of shares (mil.): 261
Dividends
  Yield: 0.0%
  Payout: 7.0%
Market value ($ mil.): 14,797

Citizens Financial Group	Royal Bancshares
E*TRADE Bank	Sovereign Bank
M&T Bank	Sun Bancorp (NJ)
PNC Financial	TD Bank USA
Republic First Bank	WSFS Financial

Dividends
  Yield: —
  Payout: —
Market value ($ mil.): —

Debt ratio: 15.63%	No. of shares (mil.): 389
Return on equity: 27.59%	Dividends
Cash ($ mil.): 1,783	Yield: 0.0%
Current ratio: 1.86	Payout: 42.9%
Long-term debt ($ mil.): 1,249	Market value ($ mil.): 12,483

Debt ratio: —	
Return on equity: 3.80%	Dividends
Cash ($ mil.): 1,072	Yield: —
Current ratio: —	Payout: —
Long-term debt ($ mil.): —	Market value ($ mil.): —

Profits were recovering quickly. Nonetheless in 1999 the company agreed to be acquired by German construction giant HOCHTIEF in a $370 million deal that ended Turner's joint venture with Switzerland's Karl Steiner. The company also relocated its corporate headquarters to Dallas that year to take advantage of the construction boom in the US Southwest.

In 2000 Turner created three new business groups to serve the aviation pharmaceutical and sports sectors. By the next year Turner's sports group was working on 17 projects. In 2001 the company was a member of the construction team that responded to the September 11 devastation at Ground Zero in New York City. The next year the company celebrated its 100th anniversary with an exhibit at the National Building Museum in Washington DC; the exhibit featured drawings and photos of some of Turner's notable projects during the past century. In 2003 Turner Construction acquired the assets of Tompkins Builders the third-largest construction company in the Washington DC area from former rival J.A. Jones Construction Co.

Turner Construction which celebrated its 100th anniversary in 2002 has ranked among the leading general builders in the US since WWI. For 80 of the 100 years the group had a Turner among its senior executives. Howard S. Turner was the last member of the family to serve in the company's senior ranks. The company's appointment of Peter Davoren in 2003 as president of Turner Construction reflected the rise of a new generation of leaders for the unit. Davoren was additionally appointed chairman and CEO in 2007.

Turner Construction announced in 2008 that it had signed the contract on its 15000th major project.

EXECUTIVES

Pres-Chb-Ceo, Peter J Davoren
Sr V Pres-Cfo & Treas, Karen Gould
V Pres-Finance & Asst Treas, Don Oshiro
Attrny, Richard L Smith Jr
Svp, Turner, Thomas B Gerlach Jr
Safety Manager, Wayne Baruch
Senior Project Manager, Gary McAssey
Manager, Reed McMains
Superintendent, Roy Burnham
Engineer, Anthony Baxley
Project Engineer, Bernardo Lomeli
Auditors: DELOITTE & TOUCHE LLP DALLAS

LOCATIONS

HQ: THE TURNER CORPORATION
375 HUDSON ST RM 700, NEW YORK, NY 100143667
Phone: 212 229-6000
Web: WWW.TURNERCONSTRUCTION.COM

PRODUCTS/OPERATIONS

Selected Related Companies
E. E. Cruz (infrastructure)
Flatiron Construction Corp. (transportation construction civil engineering)
Clark Builders (51% Canada)

Selected Markets Served
Aviation
Commercial
Cultural and entertainment
Data center
Education
Government
Green building
Health care
Infrastructure
Industrial
Interiors
Pharmaceutical

Public Assembly
Religious
Research and development
Residential/hotel
Sports

Selected Services
Building information modeling
Building maintenance
Construction management
Design-build
Design-build/finance
Facilities management
General construction
Lean construction
Logistics
Medical planning and procurement
Preconstruction consulting
Program management
Project management

COMPETITORS

Balfour Beatty Construction	Hunt Construction
Bechtel	Imperial Construction Group
Clark Construction Group	Jacobs Engineering
Fluor	Parsons Corporation
Gilbane Building Company	Peter Kiewit Sons'
	Skanska
	Structure Tone

HISTORICAL FINANCIALS

Company Type: Private

Income Statement   FYE: December 31

	REVENUE ($ mil.)	NET INCOME ($ mil.)	NET PROFIT MARGIN	EMPLOYEES
12/15	10,523	107	1.0%	5,000
12/14	10,560	95	0.9%	—
12/13	9,522	80	0.8%	—
12/12	8,575	74	0.9%	—
Annual Growth	7.1%	12.9%	—	—

2015 Year-End Financials

Debt ratio: ——
Return on equity: 1.00%
Cash ($ mil.): 880
Current ratio: 1.00
Long-term debt ($ mil.): —

Dividends
Yield: —
Payout: —
Market value ($ mil.): —

THE WHITING-TURNER CONTRACTING COMPANY

Whiting-Turner Contracting provides construction management general contracting and design/build services primarily for large commercial institutional and infrastructure projects conducted across the US. A key player in retail construction the employee-owned company also undertakes such projects as biotech cleanrooms theme parks historical restorations senior living residences educational facilities stadiums and corporate headquarters. Clients past and present include the US military AT&T General Motors and Texas A&M University. Whiting-Turner Contracting operates from more than 30 offices across the US.

Geographic Reach

The Baltimore-based company has offices in Arizona California Colorado Connecticut Delaware Florida Georgia Maryland Massachusetts Missouri Nevada New Jersey New York North Carolina Ohio Pennsylvania Texas Virginia and Washington DC.

Sales and Marketing

The contractor works on projects across a wide range of industries related to arts and entertainment education federal and military healthcare industrial office retail multi-family residential sports and fitness transportation and utilities among other fields.

Strategy

Whiting-Turner prefers to grow organically instead of making acquisitions. It has been steadily expanding by opening new offices in places such as California Texas and Virginia. The company in 2016 continued to rank among the Engineering News Record (ENR) top domestic general building contractors in the nation.

Some of the firm's recently awarded projects (as of mid-2016) include the Tropicana Pedestrian Bridge the Jacksonville Lung Bio Facility the Westowne Elementary School the Lexington Market the Costco Meat Production Plant the Sentara Norfolk General Hospital and the CoolSprings Galleria among others.

Whiting-Turner Contracting's past projects include the Joseph B. Whitehead Building at Emory University Vanderbilt Hall at Yale University projects at Universal Studios theme park and a vaccine facility at Chesapeake Biological Laboratories. Projects in the firm's hometown of Baltimore have included the city's convention center and the football stadium for the Baltimore Ravens. More recent projects include the Horseshoe Casino Cleveland University of Maryland Baltimore County (UMBC) Performing Arts & Humanities Naval Facilities Engineering Command (NAVFAC) Jacksonville Sentara Princess Anne Hospital Norwalk Community College Texas A&M University at Galveston Mary Moody Northen Student Center renovation Opry Mills the College of Business & Economics Vinson Hall Parking Garage a Coastal Studies Institute facility a Blue Diamond Growers building and a USPS Call Center.

Company Background

G.W.C. Whiting and LeBaron Turner classmates at MIT founded the company in 1909 to build sewer lines.

EXECUTIVES

Vp Richmond, Dani Niccolucci
Svp Allentown, Jack DaSilva
Division Vp Fort Lauderdale, Robert (Rob) Mitchell
Division Vp Delaware And Maryland, James (Jim) Martini
Svp District Of Columbia, Richard L. Vogel
Division Vp Pleasanton, Troy Caldwell
Svp Irvine, Len Cannatelli
Svp Baltimore, Gino J. Gemignani
Division Vp Dallas, Espen S. Brooks
Vp Bridgewater, Chris Martinson
Svp Atlanta, Keith Douglas
Vp, Daniel (Dan) Bauer
Vp Boston, Kevin Shields
Division Vp Las Vegas, Paul Schmitt
Division Vp Chantilly, Kempton C. Haile
Vp Tampa, Brent A. Voyles
Vp Denver, Mark Faul
Vp San Diego, Steven Likins
Vp Orlando, Robert Minutoli
Division Vp Raleigh, Chris Carlson
Vp White Plains, David Brickley
Vp San Antonio, Daryl Steinbeck
Vp Norfolk, John Berotti
Senior Project Manager Sacramento, Jack Stackalis
Vp Cleveland, Jeff Maeder
Regional Manager Kansas City, Adam Eshelbrenner

Regional Manager Charlotte, Chris Woods
Regional Manager Houston, Michael Browning
President And Ceo, Timothy J. Regan, age 62
Sr V Pres, Frank Palmer
Vice President, Scott McMahon
Vice President, Nancy Beavers
Vice President, Samuel Wells
Vice President, Kirk Hemphill
Senior Vice President, Kevin Higgins
Ashe Chc Vice President, Bob Moore
Vice President, Jesse Beam
Leed Ap Banking Division C Vice President,
 Patricia Carper
Division Vice President, Ed Schlotterback
Vice President, Karen Evans
Vice President, Jim Groff
Vice President, Irene Knott
Vice President, David McGinnis
Vice President Field Operations, Phil Knight
Vice President, Jeff Jenkins
Vice President, Bruce Delawder
Vice President, J Scott Breig
Vice President, Sam Abutaleb
Vice President, Chris Hoyson
Vice President San Diego, Miguel Huerta
Vice President, Edward Mackowiak
Vice President, Tony Moag
Vice President San Diego, Steve Likins
Executive Vice President And Chief Executive
 Officer, Tim Regan
Vice President, Jeffrey Baxter
Vice President, Craig Rayner
Division Vice President, Jeffrey Dodds
Vice President, Bernard LaHatte
Vice President, Andrew Linden
Division Vice President, Maynard Grizzard
Vice President, Terry Powell
Senior Vice President, Stephen Lambertson
Vice President, Kit Fawthrop
Vice President, Ray MacKeen
Secretary, Willie Mcfarlin
Vice Chairman, Nelson Griffin

LOCATIONS

HQ: THE WHITING-TURNER CONTRACTING
 COMPANY
 300 E JOPPA RD STE 800, BALTIMORE, MD
 212863047
Phone: 410 821-1100
Web: WWW.WHITING-TURNER.COM

Selected Locations
Maryland - Baltimore (Headquarters)
California
California - Los Angeles
California
California
California - San Diego
Colorado -
Connecticut - New Haven
Delaware -
District of Columbia
Florida - Ft. Lauderdale
Florida -
Florida -
Georgia -
Maryland -
Massachuse
Missouri - Kansas City
Nevada - Las Vegas
New Jersey
New York - White Plains
North Caro
North Caro
Ohio - Cle
Pennsylvan
Texas - Da
Texas - Ho
Texas - San Antonio
Virginia -
Virginia -
Virginia -

PRODUCTS/OPERATIONS

Selected Services
Construction management
 Agency
 At-risk
Design/build
General contracting
Preconstruction

Selected Markets
Biotechnology and pharmaceutical
Cleanroom and high-technology
Education
Entertainment
Federal/military
Food/beverage distribution
Health care
Historical restoration
Industrial and manufacturing
Interiors
Life sciences
Lodging and hospitality
Mission critical facilities
Mixed use
Offices and headquarters
Parking garages
Restaurants
Retail
Senior living
Sports
Sustainable
Technology
 Microelectronics
 Nano
Theme parks
Utilities
Warehouse and distribution

COMPETITORS

Barton Malow	J.E. Dunn Construction
Bechtel	Group
Choate Construction	Jacobs Engineering
Clark Construction	Kitchell
Group	McCarthy Building
DPR Construction	Peter Kiewit Sons'
Fisher Development	Skanska
Fluor	Suffolk Construction
Gilbane	Swinerton
Hensel Phelps	Turner Corporation
Construction	Tutor Perini
Hoffman Corporation	Weitz

HISTORICAL FINANCIALS
Company Type: Private

Income Statement
FYE: December 31

	REVENUE ($ mil.)	NET INCOME ($ mil.)	NET PROFIT MARGIN	EMPLOYEES
12/17	6,172	68	1.1%	3,193
12/16	5,522	90	1.6%	—
12/15	5,729	80	1.4%	—
12/14	6,347	75	1.2%	—
Annual Growth	(0.9%)	(3.1%)	—	—

2017 Year-End Financials
Debt ratio: ——
Return on equity: 1.10%
Cash ($ mil.): 243
Current ratio: 0.70
Long-term debt ($ mil.): —
Dividends
 Yield: —
 Payout: —
Market value ($ mil.): —

Thermo Fisher Scientific Inc

Thermo Fisher Scientific preps the laboratory for research analysis discovery or diagnostics. The company makes and distributes analytical instruments scientific equipment consumables and other laboratory supplies. Products range from chromatographs and spectrometers to Erlenmeyer flasks and fume hoods to gene-sequencers. Moving into other areas it offers testing and manufacturing of drugs including biologicals. Thermo Fisher also provides specialty diagnostic testing products as well as clinical analytical tools. The company tallies more than 400000 customers worldwide. Its key markets are pharmaceutical and biotech diagnostics and health care academic and government and industrial and applied research.

Operations
Thermo Fisher Scientific operates in four segments with no one segment supplying more than 35% of revenue; the smallest accounts for about 15%.

The Laboratory Product and Services unit which generates more than 35% of revenue provides basics for the lab. It sells equipment (refrigerators ovens filtration systems) consumables (slides dishes flasks) and chemicals (solvents and reagents). It also includes the Research and Safety Market Channel (catalogs and access to more than 650000 products) and BioPharma Services (clinical trials).

Life Sciences Solutions about 25% of revenue provides reagents instruments and consumables used in biological and medical research drug discovery and drug production. The unit's businesses are Biosciences Genetic Sciences Clinical Next-Generation Sequencing and BioProduction.

Analytical Instruments more than 20% of revenue supplies instruments consumables software and services. Its businesses are Chromatography and Mass Spectrometry Chemical Analysis and Materials and Structural Analysis.

Specialty Diagnostics about 15% of revenue offers diagnostic test kits reagents culture media and instruments. Its businesses are Clinical Diagnostics ImmunoDiagnostics Anatomical Pathology Microbiology Transplant Diagnostics and the Healthcare Market Channel.

Products from those operational units are sold under Thermo Fisher's five main brands: Thermo Scientific Applied Biosystems Invitrogen Fisher Scientific and Unity Lab Services.

Thermo Fisher makes many of its products and it also works with third-party contractors for manufacturing.

Geographic Reach
About half of Thermo Fisher?s revenue comes from its US customers. China is the second biggest single-country market accounting for 10% of revenue. Other key countries for Thermo Fisher are Japan the UK and Germany.

The company operates manufacturing research and development administrative and logistics facilities in about 50 countries outside the US.

Sales and Marketing
Thermo Fisher's sales channels include direct sales electronic commerce distributors and catalogs. Its sales staff numbers about 11000. The company also offers supply chain management services.

Financial Performance
Thermo Fisher?s revenue has risen for eight straight years and profit has increased for five years in a row.

The company?s sales rose 14% in 2017 to $20.9 billion from 2016. More than half of the gain came from acquisitions and it reported higher sales in all of its segments. Laboratory Products and Services the company?s biggest segment rose a robust 16% in 2017 boosted by acquired revenue while the Analytical Instruments segment?s sales jumped more than 30% on demand for chromatography and mass spectrometry products. Thermo Fisher also reported a strong sales increase in Asia.

Thermo Fisher?s profit rose to $2.2 billion in 2017 from $2 billion in 2016 which it attributed to higher organic sales revenue from acquisitions and productivity improvements.

Thermo Fisher spent about $7.2 billion on acquisitions and $508 million in capital expenditures in 2017. It had about $1.3 billion in cash at the end of 2017 up from $786 million in 2016.

Strategy

Thermo Fisher has been a deal-making machine spending more than $12 billion on acquisitions in 2016 and 2017. The company has expanded beyond supplying research labs with standard items like graduated cylinders and Bunsen burners to sophisticated equipment such as gene-sequencing and gene-editing tools. It also has added drug testing including running clinical trials and drug manufacturing to its portfolio. Thermo Fisher has become something of a one-stop shop for pharmaceutical companies that concentrate on developing drugs but outsource their production.

In 2017 Thermo Fisher acquired Patheon NV and Affymetrix and FEI both in 2016 in multi-billion deals. The company also had made several smaller deals.

Thermo Fisher hasn't let its M&A department carry the entire load for stocking the product pipeline. The company has kept its research and development cycle going investing $888 million in 2017 $750 million in 2016 and $690 million in 2015.

The company in 2017 offered new versions of products like its flagship Orbitrap platform and the Q Exactive HF-X system for drug discovery and disease research. Released in 2017 Ion Torrent Oncomine Dx Target Test for non-small cell lung cancer screening was the first companion diagnostic based on next-generation sequencing to receive FDA clearance

Besides tools to conduct research Thermo Fisher offers its cloud computing platform for storing results. The platform supports the company's gene sequencing and proteomics systems.

Thermo Fisher has its sights set on expanding international sales particularly in China. Sales in China grew more than 20% in 2017 to account for 10% of the company's revenue. Overall about 20% of the company's revenue comes from emerging markets which included stronger sales in India and South Korea. Thermo Fisher has built customer momentum in Asia with new facilities. It opened a BioPharma Services facility in South Korea to help meet increasing demand for clinical trials and a bioproduction development lab at its China Innovation Center in Shanghai.

As Thermo Fisher tries to punch up sales and operations in China trade issues have become a hot topic. A trade war between the US and China could put a brake on the company's efforts to expand in China.

Although Thermo Fisher is at the top or near the top in many of its markets it faces stiff competition from companies with wider portfolios and greater resources. Some competitors might be more access to emerging markets.

Mergers and Acquisitions

Thermo Fisher bought Becton Dickinson's Advanced Bioprocessing business in 2018. The unit which has annual sales of $100 million provides peptones and services for biopharmaceutical ap-

plications. It will become part of Thermo Fisher's Life Sciences division.

In 2018 Thermo Fisher agreed to buy Gatan Inc. from Roper Technologies for $925 million in cash. Gatan makes instrumentation and software that improves the performance of electron microscopes. Thermo Fisher expects that Gatan's products and services will enhance its line of electron microscopes. Gatan is to become part of Thermo Fisher's Analytical Instruments segment when the transaction closes which should be by the end of 2018.

In 2017 Thermo Fisher acquired Patheon NV which offers services from regulatory consulting to making drug ingredients and finished medicines including biological therapies for $7.2 billion. Patheon had about $1.9 billion in revenue in 2016.

In two major deals in 2016 Thermo Fisher bought FEI and Affymetrix. FEI acquired for $4.2 billion added a complementary product mix of electron microscopes to Thermo Fisher's mass spectrometry products. The $1.3 billion deal for Affymetrix brought instruments used to analyze specimens at the cellular and genetic levels to the Thermo Fisher portfolio.

Other 2017 deals included Finesse Solutions Inc. a developer of scalable control automation systems and software for bioproduction and Core Informatics a provider of a cloud-based platform for scientific data management.

While it was transacted in 2014 the purchase of Life Technologies for more than $15 billion was major for Thermo Fisher. The deal moved the company to the head of the pack in life sciences tools particularly the growing field of genetic testing.

HISTORY

Predating the acquiring company Thermo Electron Fisher Scientific dates back to 1902 when 20-year-old Chester Fisher bought the stockroom of Pittsburgh Testing Laboratories (established 1884) and formed Scientific Materials Co. The company's earliest products supplied from Europe included simple tools such as microscopes balances and calorimeters. It published its first catalog in 1904.

When the outbreak of WWI disrupted supplies from Europe Scientific Materials established its own R&D and manufacturing facilities. It acquired Montreal-based Scientific Supplies in 1925 and the following year changed its name to Fisher Scientific Company. By 1935 Fisher had doubled its size adding glass-blowing operations and an instrument shop.

During the German occupation of Greece in WWII George Hatsopoulos part of a well-to-do family packed with politicians and engineering professors made radios for the Greek resistance. After the war he came to the US and became a professor of mechanical engineering at MIT. With a $50000 loan Hatsopoulos founded Thermo Electron in 1956 to identify emerging technology needs and create solutions for them.

In 2006 Thermo Electron merged with Fisher Scientific International in a stock-swap transaction valued at nearly $11 billion.

EXECUTIVES

Vice President Corporate Communications, Karen Kirkwood
President And Ceo, Marc N. Casper, age 50, $1,407,471 total compensation
Evp And President Life Sciences Solutions, Mark P. Stevenson, age 55, $850,301 total compensation
Vp Financial Operations, Stephen Williamson, age 52, $597,031 total compensation

Svp And Chief Commercial Officer, Thomas W. (Tom) Loewald, age 54, $610,115 total compensation
Svp And President Europe The Middle East And Africa (emea), Andrew J. (Andy) Thomson, age 53
Svp And President Asia-pacific And Emerging Markets, Syed A. Jafry
Svp And President Customer Channels, Gregory J. (Greg) Herrema
Svp; President Laboratory Products, Frederick M. (Fred) Lowery
Svp And Cio, Joseph C. (Joe) Beery
Svp And President Specialty Diagnostics, Patrick M. Durbin, age 52
Svp; President Analytical Instruments, Daniel P. (Dan) Shine, age 50
Vice President And General Manager, Michael Shafer
Vp Human Resources, Mark White
National Sales Manager, Michael Bartlett
Vice President Of Engineering, Jerry Welch
Vice President Commercial And Corporate Finance, Marni Kirousis
Vice President World Wide Finance, Andy Long
Executive Vice President Worldwide Sales And Marketing, Michael Belford
Vice President Tax Planning, Scott Egan
Vice President Of Sales, Samantha Wexler
Vice President Sales, Tami Janus
National Sales Manager, Todd Baker
Vice President Investor Relations And Treasurer, Ken Apicerno
National Account Manager, Paul Scottberg
Senior Vice President And President Pharma Services, Michel Lagarde
Vice President Corporate Global Security Please Note Our Office Address Has Changed, Lisa Quinn
Vice President And General Manager Cell Biology, Amy Butler
Vice President Information Technology Human Resources Services, Sean Murphy
Board Director, Thomas Lynch
Auditors: PricewaterhouseCoopers LLP

LOCATIONS

HQ: Thermo Fisher Scientific Inc
168 Third Avenue, Waltham, MA 02451
Phone: 781 622-1000   **Fax:** 781 933-4476
Web: www.thermofisher.com

2017 Sales

	$ mil.	% of total
US	10,177	49
China	2,058	10
Other countries	8,683	41
Total	**20,918**	**100**

PRODUCTS/OPERATIONS

2017 Sales

	$ mil.	% of total
Laboratory Products & Services	7,825	36
Life Sciences Solutions	5,728	26
Analytical Instruments	4,831	22
Specialty Diagnostics	3,486	16
Adjustments	(942)	-
Total	**20,918**	**100**

2016 Sales

	$ mil.	% of total
Products	17,374	83
Services	3,544	17
Total	**20,918**	**100**

Selected Services

Custom Services
Instrument & Qualification Services
Out-Licensing and OEM Sales
Most Popular Products
TaqMan Real-Time PCR Assays
Oligos Primers Probes & Nucleotides

Lipofectamine Reagents
TRIzol Reagents
SuperScript Reverse Transcriptase
eSolutions
eProcurement
Supply Center
Instrument Management

Selected Products

Analytical Instruments
Automation and Robotics
Life Science Research consumables
Chemicals
Consumables
Custom Products
Diagnostics
Equipment
Furniture
Software

Selected Brands

Thermo Fisher Scientific
Barnant
Applied Biosystems
Invitrogen
Fisher Scientific
Unity Lab Services

COMPETITORS

Abbott Labs	Life Technologies
Agilent Technologies	Corporation
Beckman Coulter	Mettler-Toledo
Becton Dickinson	Newport Corp.
Bio-Rad Labs	Nordion
Bruker	PerkinElmer
Corning	QIAGEN
Danaher	Roche Diagnostics
Emerson Electric	Roper Technologies
Halma	Shimadzu
Harvard Bioscience	Sigma-Aldrich
Hitachi	Tektronix
Honeywell	VWR
International	Waters Corp.
IDEXX Labs	Yokogawa Electric
Johnson & Johnson	

HISTORICAL FINANCIALS

Company Type: Public

Income Statement   FYE: December 31

	REVENUE ($ mil.)	NET INCOME ($ mil.)	NET PROFIT MARGIN	EMPLOYEES
12/17	20,918	2,225	10.6%	70,000
12/16	18,274	2,021	11.1%	55,000
12/15	16,965	1,975	11.6%	52,000
12/14	16,889	1,894	11.2%	51,000
12/13	13,090	1,273	9.7%	50,000
Annual Growth	12.4%	15.0%	—	8.8%

2017 Year-End Financials

Debt ratio: 37.07%	No. of shares (mil.): 401
Return on equity: 9.48%	Dividends
Cash ($ mil.): 1,335	Yield: 0.0%
Current ratio: 1.34	Payout: 10.7%
Long-term debt ($ mil.): 18,873	Market value ($ mil.): 76,202

	STOCK PRICE ($) FY Close	P/E High/Low	PER SHARE ($) Earnings	Dividends	Book Value
12/17	189.88	36 25	5.59	0.60	63.32
12/16	141.10	31 24	5.09	0.60	54.74
12/15	141.85	29 24	4.92	0.60	53.42
12/14	125.29	27 23	4.71	0.60	51.31
12/13	111.35	31 18	3.48	0.60	46.57
Annual Growth	14.3%	— —	12.6%	(0.0%)	8.0%

Thor Industries, Inc.

Thor Industries is a recreation vehicle builder that makes and sells a range of RVs from motor homes to travel trailers as well as related parts. Brands include Airstream and Dutchmen. RV manufacturing plants generally produce vehicles to dealer order; Thor's independent dealers dot the US and Canada catering to private purchasers and municipalities. The company has domestic facilities in Idaho Indiana Michigan Ohio and Oregon. The US is its largest market accounting for roughly 90% of total sales. Thor rolled out in 1980 when Wade Thompson and Peter Orthwein purchased Airstream's business.

Operations

Thor has two reportable segments: towable recreation vehicles (about three-quarters of revenue; travel trailers fifth wheels and motor homes) and motorized recreation vehicles (almost 30%).

Geographic Reach

Thor has facilities in the US (Idaho Indiana Michigan Ohio and Oregon) and Canada; the US accounts for nearly 90% of sales.

Sales and Marketing

Thor sells its products through a limited amount of consumer-oriented advertising for its recreation vehicles primarily in industry magazines product brochures direct mail advertising campaigns and on the Internet. The company markets its products through some 2200 independent dealerships carrying its products in the US and Canada. The company's dealer FreedomRoads accounts for 20% of its revenue.

Financial Performance

Thor has achieved unprecedented growth over the last few years. Revenues surged by 58% from $4.58 billion in 2016 to a record-smashing $7.2 billion in 2017. The historic growth was largely fueled by more than $1.8 billion in additional revenues from its Jayco acquisition. This acquisition helped spark sizable growth within its towable segments product lines including travel trailers and other (64%) and fifth wheels (40%).

The historic revenues for 2017 also caused Thor's profits to jump 46% from $257 million to $374 million and its operating cash flow to climb from $341 million to $419 million from 2016 to 2017.

Strategy

Thor's strategy is governed by strategic acquisitions and product introductions. RVs continue to be its mainstay line in terms of revenue as the RV industry enters its six year of recovery after the US recession according to the RV Industry Association.

In late 2016 Thor launched its Airstream Basecamp a sleek silver RV of aluminum that can be towed behind a truck. It contains one massive panoramic window solar power Italian cabinetry and a Bose Bluetooth speaker system.

Mergers and Acquisitions

Thor has achieved record-setting revenue growth over the years mainly through the use of acquisitions.

In 2018 Thor said it would acquire Germany-based RV manufacturer Erwin Hymer Group (EHG) for $2.45 billion making the combined company the world's largest RV manufacturer in the world with a projected revenue of $11 billion. The deal is expected to close by the end of 2018.

In the summer of 2016 Thor acquired Jayco for approximately $576 million. The transaction enhanced Thor's main portfolio as Jayco manufactures camping trailers light-weight trailers park and travel trailers fifth-wheels toy haulers and motor homes through a network of more than

300 authorized dealers in the US and Canada. The deal also helped Thor achieve milestone revenues of $7.2 billion for 2017.

HISTORY

Mergers and acquisitions specialist Wade Thompson and investment banker Peter Orthwein saw the potential of the RV market after buying Hi-Lo Trailer in 1977. Thor Industries was formed when they bought the troubled Airstream Trailers unit (founded in 1931) from Beatrice Foods in 1980. Named after the mythical Norse god of thunder and containing the first two letters of the founders' last names Thor Industries went public in 1984.

EXECUTIVES

President Thor Motor Coach, Jeffery L. (Jeff) Kime
Cfo, Colleen A. Zuhl, age 51, $500,000 total compensation
President Airstream, Robert H. Wheeler
President And Ceo, Robert W. Martin, age 48, $750,000 total compensation
Vp Administration And Human Resources, Kenneth D. Julian, age 50, $500,000 total compensation
Director Information Technology, John Stukenborg
President Heartland, Christopher J. Hermon
Ceo Keystone, Matthew T. Zimmerman
Svp General Counsel And Corporate Secretary, W. Todd Woelfer, age 50, $600,000 total compensation
Coo Kz, Aram Koltookian
President Crossroads Rv, Ryan Juday
Vice President Of Operational Improvement, John Rhymer
Senior Vice President, Todd Woelfer
Executive Chairman, Peter B. Orthwein, age 72
Auditors: DELOITTE & TOUCHE LLP

LOCATIONS

HQ: Thor Industries, Inc.
601 East Beardsley Ave., Elkhart, IN 46514-3305
Phone: 574 970-7460
Web: www.thorindustries.com

PRODUCTS/OPERATIONS

2017 Sales

	% of total
Recreation vehicles	
Towables	71
Motorized	27
Other	2
Intercompany elimination	-
Total	**100**

COMPETITORS

All American Group	Prevost Car
Collins Industries	Rexhall Industries
Featherlite	Skyline
Forest River	Supreme Industries
Motor Coach Industries	Winnebago

HISTORICAL FINANCIALS

Company Type: Public

Income Statement				FYE: July 31
	REVENUE ($ mil.)	NET INCOME ($ mil.)	NET PROFIT MARGIN	EMPLOYEES
07/18	8,328	430	5.2%	17,500
07/17	7,246	374	5.2%	17,800
07/16	4,582	256	5.6%	14,900
07/15	4,006	199	5.0%	10,450
07/14	3,525	179	5.1%	9,400
Annual Growth	24.0%	24.5%	—	16.8%

2018 Year-End Financials

Debt ratio: —	No. of shares (mil.): 52
Return on equity: 24.48%	Dividends
Cash ($ mil.): 275	Yield: 1.5%
Current ratio: 1.70	Payout: 18.1%
Long-term debt ($ mil.): —	Market value ($ mil.): 4,998

	STOCK PRICE ($) FY Close	P/E High/Low	PER SHARE ($) Earnings	Dividends	Book Value
07/18	94.85	19 11	8.14	1.48	36.77
07/17	105.35	16 10	7.09	1.32	29.98
07/16	76.54	16 10	4.88	1.20	24.11
07/15	55.88	17 13	3.74	1.08	20.33
07/14	52.97	19 15	3.35	1.92	18.33
Annual Growth	15.7%	—	24.9%	(6.3%)	19.0%

TJX Companies, Inc.

The TJX Companies operates more than 3860 stores worldwide under half a dozen retail brand names including the two largest off-price clothing retailers in the US: T.J. Maxx and Marshalls which operate 2220-plus stores nationwide. T.J. Maxx sells brand-name family apparel accessories shoes domestics giftware and jewelry at discount prices while Marshalls offers similar items plus a broader selection of shoes and menswear through more than 1000 stores. Its HomeGoods chain of 580-plus US stores focuses exclusively on home furnishings. T.K. Maxx is the company's European retail arm with 500-plus stores in the UK Ireland Austria Germany Poland and the Netherlands.

HISTORY

Cousins Stanley and Sumner Feldberg opened the first Zayre (Yiddish for "very good") store in Hyannis Massachusetts in 1956. During the next 15 years the number of stores grew to nearly 200.

Zayre purchased the Hit or Miss chain which sold upscale women's clothing at discounted prices in 1969. When the recession of the early 1970s hit superb results at Hit or Miss prompted Zayre to look for further opportunities in the off-price apparel marketplace. Zayre hired Ben Cammarata to create a new store concept and in March 1977 he opened the first T.J. Maxx in Auburn Massachusetts to market discounted upscale family clothing. Six years later Zayre formed the catalog retailer Chadwick's of Boston to sell Hit or Miss apparel by mail.

The company came to rely increasingly on its specialty operations to provide consistent sales and income as its flagship general merchandise stores often struggled. By 1983 the specialty chains were producing almost half of Zayre's sales.

In the second half of the 1980s Zayre's upscale (yet still off-priced) retailers' sales rose while its general merchandise stores (targeting lower-income customers) dropped. To keep its specialty stores unhindered by its flagging Zayre stores it established The TJX Companies as a public company in 1987. Zayre sold about 17% of its new subsidiary to the public with Cammarata as CEO.

Zayre sold its 400 general merchandise stores in 1988 to Ames for about $430 million in cash $140 million in Ames stock and a receivable note. The next year the company spun off its warehouse club operations as Waban (the warehouse component eventually became BJ's Wholesale) and merged with its subsidiary The TJX Companies taking that name.

TJX acquired Winners Apparel a Toronto-based five-store apparel chain in 1990. That year in the same month that Ames declared bankruptcy TJX established a $185 million reserve against losses it might suffer through its ownership of Ames' stock. Ames emerged from bankruptcy two years later and TJX was left with 4% of Ames' voting shares and over 100 empty Ames stores. TJX sold or leased most of them.

Also in 1992 TJX opened HomeGoods gift and houseware outlets in three of its remaining Ames stores and closed about 70 Hit or Miss stores. That year the company paid off about $128 million of its long-term debt. Encouraged by the success of its off-price operations in Canada in 1994 TJX opened five T.K. Maxx stores (similar to T.J. Maxx and Winners Apparel) in the UK.

A year later TJX paid $550 million for Melville's ailing chain of 450 Marshalls clothing stores. In addition the company sold its Hit or Miss apparel chain.

To help pay for Marshalls TJX sold the Chadwick's of Boston catalog in 1996 to retailer Brylane for about $325 million. Two years later the company opened two T.K. Maxx stores in the Netherlands and said it planned to have 75 stores in Europe in three years. It also debuted the A.J. Wright discount chain in New England in 1998.

In 1999 TJX elected Cammarata to the additional post of chairman and elevated Ted English to president and COO. In 2000 Cammarata relinquished his CEO post to English but remained chairman. Citing the successes of its new stores the company announced in early 2001 it expected to increase its total number of stores 12% annually for the next several years. Also that year the company shuttered its T.K. Maxx stores in the Netherlands. Seven TJX employees perished on September 11 2001 when their flight bound for Los Angeles crashed into the World Trade Center during the worst terrorist attack in US history.

In 2002 the company opened HomeSense a new Canadian home furnishings chain fashioned after its US counterpart HomeGoods. In December 2003 TJX finalized its acquisition of Bob's Stores a Connecticut-based discount retail chain with 31 stores in the Northeast.

In September 2005 English resigned abruptly after five years as the company's CEO. In October the company closed down its tjmaxx.com and homegoods.com Web sites citing poor sales.

In March 2006 TJX cut about 250 jobs in its corporate and divisional offices and reduced the salaries of a dozen senior executives including its chairman and acting CEO and its president by 10% in an effort to increase profits.

A year after the abrupt resignation of CEO Edmond English in September 2005 TJX named company president Carol Meyrowitz to the post effective January 2007. (Cammarata had been acting CEO of the company in the interim.) Also in January 34 A.J. Wright stores were closed.

In November 2007 TJX reached a settlement with Visa and Fifth Third Bancorp stemming from a breach of its computer systems in which customer data was stolen. Under the terms of the agreement TJX will fund up to $40.9 million for recovery payments for US Visa issuers. Also in the fall of 2007 the retailer's European arm T.K. Maxx entered the German market with five stores there.

In 2008 TJX sold money-losing Bob's Stores which has about 35 locations in the Northeast to the private equity firms Versa Capital Management and Crystal Capital for an undisclosed amount.

EXECUTIVES

Vice President, Jeffrey Naylor

President Ceo And Director, Ernie Herrman, age 57, $1,525,001 total compensation

Evp Merchandising The Marmaxx Group, Richard Sherr, age 60, $921,232 total compensation

Sevp Finance And Cfo, Scott Goldenberg, age 64, $813,462 total compensation

Svp Corporate Controller, Ken Canestrari, age 57

Sevp And Group President, Michael MacMillan, age 61, $1,052,309 total compensation

Executive Vice President Merchandise Coaching And Development, Louis Luciano

Vice President Merchandising, Joseph Domenick

Assistant Vice President Corporate Internal Audit, John Caban

Vice President Develop, Christine Potter Bourget

Senior Vice President And General Counsel, Beverly Kennedy

Vice President Real Estate Research Director, Sean Anderson

Divisional Vp, Mark Azar

Vice President Merchandise Manager Bath Towels Basic Bedding And Throws, Simantha Macleod

Vice President Merchandising, Paula Bingham

Assistant Vice President Loss Prevention, Steve Forgette

Senior Vice President Store Operations A J Wright, Mike McGrath

Assistant Vice President Home Goods Planning And Allocat, Mary Clark

Assistant Vice President, Brett Amosson

Assistant Vice President Merchandise Planning, Debra Duprez

Assistant Vice President Merchandise Planning, Rose Riggieri

Vice President General Merchandise Manager, Shade Jennifer

Assistant Vice President Merchandise Manager Sheets Deco, Corina Roth

Vice President Human Resources, Kelli McNary

Assistant Vice President Global Talent Development, Sharon Hazard

Vice President Merchandising, Brian Francione

Assistant Vice President Merchandise Planning, Josten Swiader

Dvp Merchandise Manager, Jeff Nesbit

Assistant Vice President Store Planning Design And Fixture Director, Cindy Buffi

Vice President Finance, Peter Daniels

Assistant Vice President Corporate Benefits Director, Lauren Mullin

Senior Vice President Digital Technology, Enzo Micali

Vice President Gmm Mens, Ken Shuler

Assistant Vice President Loss Prevention, Kate Hughes

Assistant Vice President Loss Prevention, Kevin Taparausky

Vice President General Merchandise Manager, Marla Minns

Divisional Vice President Merchandise Manager, Beth Winkler

Assistant Vice President Store Planning, Jon Nelson

Vice President, Anand Devendran

Assistant Vice President, Lisa Pratico

Assistant Vice President Director Loss Prevention, Frederick L Mullen

Senior Vice President Information Technology, Dave Spooner

Vice President The Marmaxx Group, Claudia Winkle

Vice President Office Services Director, Mike Brogan

Assistant Vice President Investor Relations, Jeff Botte

Dvp Merchandise Manager, Michael Neel

Assistant Vice President Merchandise Planning And Analysis, Steven Schwartz

Assistant Vice President International Tax, Barbara House

Dvp Dmm E Commerce, Inna Leipzig

Divisional Vice President Merchandise Manager Ecommerce, Lisa Pena

Vice President Store Systems Director, Martin Whitmore

Assistant Vice President Corporate Communications, Colleen Beauregard

Assistant Vice President Construction, John Cox

Assistant Vice President Merchandise Manager Home Accent, Marni Jones

Vice President, Cheryl Oldfield

Assistant Vice President Market Manager, Tim Jubb

Vice President The Marmaxx Group, Celine Lewis

Vice President Of Planning And Allocation, Nancy Mendis

Vice President The Marmaxx Group, Manuela Millington

Vice President, Lou Luciano

Assistant Vice President, Genevieve Barrett

Executive Vice President, Paul Sweetenham

Assistant Vice President Merchandise Manager, Sally Reilly

Assistant Vice President Compensation, April Fontaine

Assistant Vice President Of Human Resources, Lorretta Lashley

Senior Vice President, David Kaplan

Vice President, Bob Cooke

Divisional Vice President Merchandise Manager, Scott Garozzo

Assistant Vice President Property Tax Director, Bradford Dunn

Assistant Vice President Consumer Insights, Rachel Cook

Divisional Vice President, Renee Rockwood

Divisional Vice President Market Manager, Guido Galli

Senior Vice President Merchandise Planning Allocation And Analysis, Mark Heitin

Regional Vice President Administrative Assistant, Steven Lipasek

Assistant Vice President And Director Store Operations Engineering, Antoinette Wallace

Senior Vice President Transportation And Logistics, Jeff Tawney

Assistant Vice President And Director Corporate Communications, Erika Tower

Senior Vice President Divisional Chief Financial O, Chris Mieszczanski

Vice President, Colleen Henchke

Divisional Vice President, Maura Cianciolo

Vice President Executive Development, Kelly Ricciardelli

Senior Vice President Infrasturcutre And Operations, Larry Foster

Assistant Vice President, Glen Brenner

Avp Director Store Transportation Services, Rebecca Wlazlo

Vice President Corporate Business Solutions, Tim Lippold

Avp Network Operations, Tim Kearney

Chairman, Carol M. Meyrowitz, age 64

Assistant Treasurer, Nancy Hendrickson

Auditors: PricewaterhouseCoopers LLP

LOCATIONS

HQ: TJX Companies, Inc.
770 Cochituate Road, Framingham, MA 01701
Phone: 508 390-1000   Fax: 508 390-2091
Web: www.tjx.com

2017 Stores

	No.
US	
T.J. Maxx	1,191
Marshalls	1,039
HomeGoods	596
Sierra Trading Post	12
Canada	
Winners	258
HomeSense	109
Marshalls	61
Europe	
T.K. Maxx	515
HomeSense	46
Australia	
T.K. Maxx	35
Total	**3,862**

2017 Sales

	$ mil.	% of total
US		
Marmaxx	21,246	64
HomeGoods	4,404	13
TJX Canada	3,171	10
TJX International	4,362	13
Total	**33,183**	**100**

PRODUCTS/OPERATIONS

Selected Stores

HomeGoods (off-price home fashion chain)
HomeSense (off-price home fashion chain Canada and UK)
Marshalls (off-price retailer of apparel shoes home fashions)
Marshalls Mega-Stores (combination Marshalls and HomeGoods stores)
Sierra Trading Post (off-price online retailer of outdoor gear and apparel)
T.J. Maxx (off-price retailer of apparel shoes home fashions)
T.J. Maxx 'N More (combination T.J. Maxx and HomeGoods stores)
T.K. Maxx (off-price retailer of apparel shoes home fashions Europe)
Winners Apparel (off-price family apparel chain Canada)

2017 Sales

	% of total
Clothing & footwear	55
Home fashions	30
Jewelry & accessories	15
Total	**100**

COMPETITORS

ASDA	Kmart
Amazon.com	Kohl's
Bed Bath & Beyond	Liberty Interactive
Belk	Macy's
Big Lots	Primark
Burlington Coat Factory	Ross Stores
Caleres	Sears
Cato	Shopko Stores
Charming Shoppes	Sports Authority
Children's Place	Stage Stores
Claire's Stores	Stein Mart
Dillard's	Tailored Brands
Dollar General	Target Corporation
Eddie Bauer LLC	Tesco
Foot Locker	The Gap
Inditex	Tuesday Morning Corporation
J. C. Penney	Wal-Mart

HISTORICAL FINANCIALS

Company Type: Public

Income Statement
FYE: February 3

	REVENUE ($ mil.)	NET INCOME ($ mil.)	NET PROFIT MARGIN	EMPLOYEES
02/18*	35,864	2,607	7.3%	249,000
01/17	33,183	2,298	6.9%	235,000
01/16	30,944	2,277	7.4%	216,000
01/15	29,078	2,215	7.6%	198,000
02/14	27,422	2,137	7.8%	191,000
Annual Growth	**6.9%**	**5.1%**	**—**	**6.9%**

*Fiscal year change

2018 Year-End Financials

Debt ratio: 17.45%
Return on equity: 53.13%
Cash ($ mil.): 2,758
Current ratio: 1.66
Long-term debt ($ mil.): 2,452

No. of shares (mil.): 1,256
Dividends
Yield: 0.0%
Payout: 29.6%
Market value ($ mil.): 98,560

	STOCK PRICE ($) FY Close	P/E High/Low	PER SHARE ($) Earnings	Dividends	Book Value
02/18*	78.47	39 33	2.02	0.60	4.10
01/17	74.26	47 39	1.73	0.50	3.49
01/16	71.24	45 38	1.67	0.40	3.25
01/15	65.94	43 33	1.58	0.34	3.11
02/14	57.36	43 29	1.47	0.28	3.00
Annual Growth	**8.1%**	**— —**	**8.3%**	**21.5%**	**8.1%**

*Fiscal year change

Toll Brothers Inc.

Ask not for whom the Tolls build because if you have to ask you probably can't afford it. Toll Brothers builds luxury homes in the US targeting move-up second-home and retired buyers. Its single-family detached houses and condominium apartments sell for an average price of over $700000. The company also develops communities for active adults and operates country club communities. Subsidiaries offer related services and products including insurance coverage title and mortgage services and landscaping. Toll Brothers has operations in some 50 markets in nearly 20 states. Traditionally a suburban developer Toll Brothers has branched out to high-rise condominiums in urban markets.

Operations

Toll Brothers' two segments are Traditional Home Building and City Living. The former accounts for almost all company revenue at around 95% of sales.

The company's traditional homes sell at prices ranging from $225000 to $2.0 million. Its City Living homes sold in more expensive urban areas are priced between $420000 and $6.5 million.

In addition to home building the firm operates a slew of subsidiaries active in: architecture engineering mortgage title land development land sale golf course development and management home security and landscaping.

Geographic Reach

Pennsylvania-based Toll Brother's largest market is California which generates around 30% of sales. The company also builds houses in the North (Connecticut Illinois Massachusetts Michigan Minnesota New Jersey New York) South (Florida North Carolina Texas) West (Arizona Colorado Nevada Washington) and Mid-Atlantic (Delaware

Maryland Pennsylvania Virginia) regions of the US.

Its City Living division builds luxury properties in urban markets including Manhattan and Brooklyn New York; Hoboken and Jersey City New Jersey; Philadelphia; and Washington DC.

Sales and Marketing

The builder markets its homes online and via its own sales personnel. It also advertises through newspapers in local or regional publications and on billboards. It also markets its communities through color brochures.

Financial Performance

After the housing and financial crisis tanked Toll Brothers' revenue by 75% between between 2006 to 2011 the company is once again scaling the money mountain at a relentless pace — revenue is now some 85% of its pre-crisis peak.

Toll Brothers' sales rose for a fifth straight year in fiscal 2016 (ended October) jumping a nice round $1 billion or 24% to $5.2 billion. Volumes and prices were both up during 2016. The company sold 6098 homes at an average price of $721000 per home during the year. While sales growth was strong in all regions except the South (which declined 5%) California in particular recorded a spike of over 90% to $1.4 billion with unit delivered up 50% to 1006. In the City Living segment revenue fell 19% to $257.9 million as a near-100% increase in average price (to $2.8 million) was offset by a 58% fall in units delivered (91).

Net income climbed 5% to $382 million higher income from operations was partially offset by a higher income tax expense. Cash from operating activities recovered after taking a hit in 2015 coming in at $148.8 million versus $60 million the previous year. The increase was mostly down to higher net income and a $524.6 million increase in accounts payable offset by a net purchase of $391.2 million of inventory.

Strategy

Positioning itself as a luxury home builder that provides superior quality and high-end features in its homes Toll Brothers continues to enjoy a broad recovery in the housing industry as pent-up consumer demand releases and as consumers regain confidence.

The company's City Living business which sells homes in more expensive urban markets has continued to grow as well as the US population continues to move toward urban areas. With more affluent Americans making the trek back to cities from the suburbs Toll Brothers has also stepped up is activities in select urban markets such as Washington D.C. and New York City where it has been buying properties.

Mergers and Acquisitions

In late 2016 Toll Brothers completed a $85.2 million acquisition of Coleman Real Estate Holdings an Idaho-based builder of single-family homes ranging from first-time to luxury. The acquisition expands Toll Brothers' presence in Idaho and opens it up to a slightly lower price point niche in the luxury market.

Company Background

In November 2011 Toll Brothers acquired CamWest Development LLC for about $144.7 million. Toll Brothers was attracted to the Seattle market due to its high barriers to entry high employment rate and concentration of wealthy people who are ideal luxury home buyers. The deal included more than 1240 home sites and more than 250 sites under option.

HISTORY

Homebuilder Albert Toll's two sons Robert and Bruce Toll founded their own business in 1967. The duo began by building starter homes in the Philadelphia suburbs of Elkins Park and Yardley. As Philadelphia's population began to sprawl beyond these older suburban areas the company grew and in 1982 it moved beyond Pennsylvania to build houses in New Jersey. The young firm also began to distinguish itself by catering to up-market customers.

Toll Brothers Inc. went public in 1986 and later expanded around New York City north to the Boston area and south to the suburbs of Washington DC. The firm survived the late 1980s real estate recession in the Northeast because unlike many builders it did not overextend itself.

Until the 1990s Toll Brothers operated primarily in the northeastern US but it expanded as the housing market began an upward cycle. It entered California and North Carolina in 1994 and Arizona Florida and Texas in 1995. Toll Brothers began work in Nashville Tennessee and Las Vegas in 1997. The next year the company entered the active adult market building its first two age-qualified communities in New Jersey. Also in 1998 the company joined other investors including the Pennsylvania State Employees Retirement System and formed the Toll Brothers Realty Trust to acquire and develop commercial property.

In 1999 Toll Brothers acquired Silverman Companies a leading homebuilder and developer of luxury apartments with more than 80 years of experience in Detroit. The company also began building homes in the Chicago San Diego and San Francisco markets that year and it teamed with Marriott International to begin developing an assisted-living community in Reston Virginia.

It also set up its cable and broadband subsidiary Advanced Broadband that year to provide its communities with Internet connectivity. Toll Brothers sold those operations to Comcast in 2007.

The company began operating in Rhode Island and New Hampshire in 2000 and the next year entered Colorado. In 2002 the company entered South Carolina in the Hilton Head area to develop Hampton Hall a luxury country club community with a master-planned golf course.

In 2003 Toll Brothers acquired Jacksonville Florida-based homebuilder Richard R. Dostie Inc. for an undisclosed cash amount. The company also expanded its luxury urban in-fill market operations by acquiring The Manhattan Building Company a developer of luxury mid- and high-rise condos on northern New Jersey's waterfront. The next year Toll Brothers and Pinnacle Ltd. jointly began development of an 832-home luxury condominium community (Maxwell Place on the Hudson) on the waterfront of Hoboken New Jersey overlooking Manhattan.

For its 12th consecutive year Toll Brothers produced record fiscal-year-end results for earnings revenues contracts and backlog in 2004. The company's net income grew 57% over the previous year's earnings and it operated in more communities and offered more product lines than it had in previous years. Another record was set in 2005; revenue from home sales increased 50% and net income increased 97%. That year Toll Brothers began operations in West Virginia but stopped selling homes in Ohio.

Toll correctly predicted an industry slowdown in 2006 and for both 2006 and 2007 the number of homes it built dropped from 8600 to around 6700. As numbers continued to sink it sold land holdings reduced its backlog and divested its cable Internet and home security businesses.

CEO and co-founder Robert Toll stepped down as CEO in 2010. He was succeeded by Douglas Yearley

COMPETITORS

D.R. Horton
David Weekley Homes
Hovnanian Enterprises
KB Home

Lennar
PulteGroup
William Lyon Homes

HISTORICAL FINANCIALS

Company Type: Public

Income Statement   FYE: October 31

	REVENUE ($ mil.)	NET INCOME ($ mil.)	NET PROFIT MARGIN	EMPLOYEES
10/18	7,143	748	10.5%	4,900
10/17	5,815	535	9.2%	4,500
10/16	5,169	382	7.4%	4,200
10/15	4,171	363	8.7%	3,900
10/14	3,911	340	8.7%	3,500
Annual Growth	16.2%	21.8%	—	8.8%

2018 Year-End Financials

Debt ratio: 36.10%
Return on equity: 16.10%
Cash ($ mil.): 1,182
Current ratio: 4.94
Long-term debt ($ mil.): 3,698

No. of shares (mil.): 146
Dividends
  Yield: 1.2%
  Payout: 8.4%
Market value ($ mil.): 4,920

	STOCK PRICE ($) FY Close	P/E High/Low		PER SHARE ($) Earnings	Dividends	Book Value
10/18	33.66	11	6	4.85	0.41	32.57
10/17	46.04	14	8	3.17	0.24	28.82
10/16	27.44	17	11	2.18	0.00	26.14
10/15	35.97	20	15	1.97	0.00	24.15
10/14	31.95	21	15	1.84	0.00	22.02
Annual Growth	1.3%	—	—	27.4%	—	10.3%

Tompkins Financial Corp

Tompkins Financial is the holding company for Tompkins Trust Company The Bank of Castile and Mahopac Bank which offer traditional banking services through some 45 offices in upstate New York. It also owns the 20-branch Pennsylvania-based VIST Bank. Funds from deposit products such as checking savings and money market accounts are mainly used to originate real estate loans and mortgages as well as commercial and consumer loans. Tompkins also offers trust and estate financial and tax planning and investment management services through Tompkins Financial Advisors. Tompkins Insurance Agencies sells property/casualty coverage in central and western New York and Pennsylvania.

Operations

Tompkins Financial operates in three segments: banking insurance and wealth management. Banking represents most of its revenue — more than 80%. About 70% of the banks' loan portfolios is made up of commercial and commercial real estate loans.

Tompkins' Insurance and Wealth Management divisions operate through subsidiaries and make up roughly 10% and 5% of sales respectively. Its subsidiary Tompkins Insurance Agencies Inc. offers property and casualty insurance services and employee benefit consulting services. The firm's trust company Tompkins Financial Advisors offers trust financial planning and wealth management services.

Geographic Reach

Between its four bank subsidiaries the Tompkins operates 66 branches in the US with more than two thirds of the branches in New York and around 20 branches in Pennsylvania.

Sales and Marketing

The company's banks target individual and small business customers for its financial services. Tompkins spent $4.94 million on its marketing expenses in 2014 or slightly less than the $4.96 million spent in 2013 but 22% more than what it spent in 2012.

Financial Performance

Tompkin's revenue rose for a second straight year growing by less than 1% to $255.26 million in 2014 most thanks to growth in the company's non-interest fee income from an increase in deposit account service charges card services income and growth in personal health and benefit insurance sales.

The company's net income ended higher for a second year as well thanks to higher revenue lower interest expense on deposits and lower provisions for loan losses as its loan portfolio's credit improved. Operations provided $77.36 million or 8% less cash than in 2013 mostly because in 2013 the company was able to use more funds from its prepaid accounts to pay for FDIC insurance.

Strategy

The company's strategy for growth includes making inroads into new markets and new business areas through acquisitions. It entered the southeastern Pennsylvania market with its 2012 acquisition of VIST Financial parent of VIST Bank (which continues to operate under a separate charter under existing management) VIST Insurance and VIST Capital Management. The deal added about 20 branches to Tompkins' network along with $889 million in new loan business and $1.2 billion in new deposits.

Mergers and Acquisitions

In August 2012 Tompkins Financial purchased VIST Financial Corp in an all stock transaction valued at $86 million. The deal added all 20 VIST Bank branches (and VIST Bank's assets) in Pennsylvania the VIST Capital Management business and the VIST Insurance business which doubled Tompkin's annual insurance revenue; all of which were folded into Tompkins' banking operations Tompkins Financial Advisors and Tompkins Insurance Agencies operations respectively.

EXECUTIVES

Evp President And Ceo Vist Bank, Robert D. (Bob) Davis, age 70
Director; Vice Chairman Tompkins Insurance Agencies, James R. Hardie, age 74
Executive Vice President Chief Operations Officer Chief Financial Officer & Treasurer, Francis M. Fetsko, age 53, $281,877 total compensation
President Ceo And Director, Stephen S. Romaine, age 54, $474,898 total compensation
Executive Vice President, David S. Boyce, age 51, $185,000 total compensation
Executive Vice-president, Gregory J. Hartz, age 57, $237,107 total compensation
Executive Vice-president, Gerald J. Klein, age 59, $238,369 total compensation
Executive Vice President; President & Coo Of Vist Bank, Scott L. Gruber, age 62
Evp Corporate Marketing, Susan M. Valenti
Svp - Chief Technology Officer, Bradley G. James
Vice President, Bill Steinmetz
Senior Vice President Marketing, Paula Barron
Vice President Of Financial Reporting, Shelly Fetterly-Bush
Vice President Telecommunications, Chuck Brown

Vice President Controller, David Kershaw
Senior Vice President Human Resources, Bonita Lindberg
Vice President Executive Compensation, John Lawson
Senior Vice President, Joseph Butto
Vice President Commercial Lending, Heather Moore
Senior Vice President Regional Lending Manager, James Whitton
Chairman Tompkins Financial Corporation And Tompkins Trust Company, James J. Byrnes, age 75
Vice Chairman, James W. (Jim) Fulmer, age 66
Board Member, Frank Null Milewski
Auditors: KPMG LLP

LOCATIONS

HQ: Tompkins Financial Corp
  118 E. Seneca Street, P.O. Box 460, Ithaca, NY 14851
Phone: 888 503-5753
Web: www.tompkinsfinancial.com

PRODUCTS/OPERATIONS

2016 Sales

	$ mil.	% of total
Interest		
Loans	169	63
Available-for-sale securities	27	10
Held-to-maturity securities	3	1
Federal Home Loan Bank stock and Federal Reserve Bank stock	1	1
Trading securities	0	-
Due from banks		
Non-interest		
Insurance commissions & fees	29	11
Investment services	15	6
Service charges on deposit accounts	8	3
Card services income	8	3
Mark-to-market gain on liabilities held at fair value	0	-
Net gain on securities transactions	0	-
Other	6	2
Mark-to-market loss on trading securities	(0.2)	-
Total	271	100

2016 Sales

		$mil.
% of total		
Banking		84
Insurance		11
Wealth Management		5
Others		-
Total		100

COMPETITORS

Bank of America
Chemung Financial
Citigroup
Citizens Financial
  Group

Community Bank System
Elmira Savings Bank
HSBC USA
JPMorgan Chase
M&T Bank

HISTORICAL FINANCIALS

Company Type: Public

Income Statement   FYE: December 31

	ASSETS ($ mil.)	NET INCOME ($ mil.)	INCOME AS % OF ASSETS	EMPLOYEES
12/17	6,648	52	0.8%	1,041
12/16	6,236	59	1.0%	1,046
12/15	5,690	58	1.0%	1,038
12/14	5,269	52	1.0%	1,037
12/13	5,003	50	1.0%	989
Annual Growth	7.4%	0.8%	—	1.3%

2017 Year-End Financials

Debt ratio: 0.39%
Return on equity: 9.35%
Cash ($ mil.): 84
Current ratio: —
Long-term debt ($ mil.): —

No. of shares (mil.): 15
Dividends
  Yield: 0.0%
  Payout: 53.0%
Market value ($ mil.): 1,235

	STOCK PRICE ($) FY Close	P/E High/Low	PER SHARE ($) Earnings	Dividends	Book Value
12/17	81.35	28 21	3.43	1.82	37.86
12/16	94.54	24 13	3.91	1.77	36.40
12/15	56.16	16 13	3.87	1.70	34.57
12/14	55.30	16 13	3.48	1.62	32.94
12/13	51.39	15 11	3.46	1.54	31.10
Annual Growth	12.2%	— —	(0.2%)	4.3%	5.0%

TOMPKINS TRUST COMPANY

EXECUTIVES

Chb, James Byrnes
Prin, Steven Garner
Assistant Vice President and C, Kathy Manley
Assistant Vice President, Ronald Davenport
Assistant Vice President, Stacie Maybee
Human Resources Officer, Diane Aramini
Vice President, Karen Parks

LOCATIONS

HQ: TOMPKINS TRUST COMPANY
110 N TIOGA ST, ITHACA, NY 148504320
Phone: 607 257-1909
Web: WWW.TOMPKINSTRUST.COM

HISTORICAL FINANCIALS

Company Type: Private

Income Statement   FYE: December 31

	ASSETS ($ mil.)	NET INCOME ($ mil.)	INCOME AS % OF ASSETS	EMPLOYEES
12/17	2,118	21	1.0%	1
12/16	1,962	23	1.2%	—
12/15	1,805	24	1.3%	—
12/14	1,682	22	1.3%	—
Annual Growth	8.0%	(0.7%)	—	—

2017 Year-End Financials

Debt ratio: ——
Return on equity: 17.30%
Cash ($ mil.): 28
Current ratio: ——
Long-term debt ($ mil.): ——
Dividends
Yield: —
Payout: —
Market value ($ mil.): —

Torchmark Corp

Torchmark Corporation a holding company for a family of financial firms specializes in individual life insurance and supplemental health insurance to middle-income families. Torchmark subsidiaries which include flagship American Income Life offer whole and term life insurance supplemental health insurance accidental death insurance Medicare Supplements and long-term care health policies for the elderly. Torchmark sells its products through direct marketing as well as through a network of exclusive and independent agents. Substantially all of Torchmark?s business is conducted in the US.

Operations

Torchmark operates in four segments ? life insurance supplemental health insurance annuity and investments. The life insurance segment (about 55% of revenue) offers products including traditional and interest-sensitive whole life coverage as well as term life insurance. The supplemental health segment (about 25%) offers Medicare Supplement critical illness accident and limited-benefit supplemental hospital and surgical coverages. The annuity segment (less than 1% of sales) once provided fixed-benefit contracts although the company is no longer marketing these products ? it?s focusing more on protection-oriented life and health products. Finally the investments segment (more than 20%) manages the group's capital resources.

Torchmark?s American Income Life subsidiary markets and sells individual life and supplemental health insurance to working families. Targeting middle-income families Liberty National Life also provides life and supplemental health policies in this market. Torchmark's Family Heritage Life provides limited-benefit health products in non-urban areas to middle-income families. A smaller subsidiary Globe Life and Accident reaches middle-income customers with life and health insurance products including juvenile and senior life coverage and Medicare Supplement products. United American sells Medicare Supplement insurance primarily to Medicare beneficiaries.

Geographic Reach

Substantially all of Torchmark?s business is in the US with headquarters in McKinney TX. United American also does business out of McKinney and leases space in Omaha NE and Syracuse NY. Liberty National operates from a facility in Hoover AL in addition to its offices in McKinney. Globe Life has offices in Oklahoma City OK and American Income life has its main offices in Waco TX with minor agent distribution in Canada and New Zealand. Family Heritage operates out of Broadview Heights OH.

Sales and Marketing

Torchmark markets and distributes its products through a variety of channels including independent agents direct mail electronic and insert media and inbound call centers. Through Family Heritage Life the group even has agents that go door-to-door in non-urban markets.

The company's main Liberty National Life subsidiary uses a direct sales force to sell its products. The subsidiary has about 1750 producing agents and about 65 branch offices across the US. It also utilizes captive and independent agents.

Financial Performance

Torchmark's revenue and net income have seen small but steady growth over the past several years. In 2017 revenue rose more than 5% to $4.2 billion thanks to a more than $100 million increase in life insurance premiums as well as a near $30 million bump in health insurance premiums.

Net income more than tripled to $1.5 billion in 2017 compared with $550 million in 2016. The sharp increase was due to an $874 million increase related to deferred income tax liabilities resulting from favorable tax legislation (Tax Cuts and Jobs Act of 2017). After two years of cash flow increases of some 25% 2017 cash flow increased only 2% — the small percentage also related to deferred income tax charges.

Strategy

Torchmark's insurance strategy is centered on selling life and health products to middle-income households which it sees as an underserved market. In recent years the company has especially been focused on young families with children. It has also been focused on expanding its distribution channels. For example American Income Life has expanded its reach beyond unions (which have declined in membership) to offer products and services to new customers through referrals and other sources; it hopes to expand its team of agents (currently at some 7000) to 10000 within five years.

Additionally the firm continues to invest in technology to facilitate a digital experience for its customers boost its underwriting capabilities with data analytics and modernizing its back-office infrastructure.

Torchmark's investment segment invests almost exclusively in long-range fixed maturities that meet certain quality and yield objectives. Unlike many other life insurers Torchmark makes the bulk of its revenues from its premiums and relatively little (about 20%) from its investments. This allows it to ride out the economic downturns more smoothly while other life insurers take significant revenue hits when their investments falter.

HISTORY

It began as a scam plain and simple. In 1900 the Heralds of Liberty was founded as a fraternal organization — but its real reason for existence was to funnel money to its founders according to Frank Samford Torchmark's CEO from 1967 to 1985; Samford was also the great-grandson of the governor who signed the group's charter and the son of the state insurance commissioner who oversaw the Heralds of Liberty's rehabilitation into a real insurance company.

The Heralds offered a joint life distribution plan under which policyholders were divided by age; when a person died his or her beneficiary was paid along with the holder of the lowest-numbered insurance certificate in the class (if they were paid at all; the Heralds were not scrupulous about that). Postal authorities called this plan a lottery and it was illegal in many states. But the Heralds' fraternal order status allowed it to circumvent Alabama insurance laws until 1921 when its infractions could no longer be ignored.

The organization operated under state supervision until 1929 when it was recapitalized as stock company Liberty National. By 1934 despite the Depression the company was financially sound.

In 1944 Liberty National merged with funeral insurance company Brown-Service whose large sales force began selling Liberty National's policies. The added sales helped the company grow and make acquisitions from the 1950s through the 1970s. Even after it discontinued funeral insurance the company still paid out benefits. (As late as 1985 half of all Alabamans who died had the policies.)

Liberty National reorganized itself as a holding company in 1980 to accommodate the purchase of Globe Life And Accident. In 1981 it acquired Continental Investment Corp. which owned United Investors Life Insurance Waddell & Reed (financial services) and United American Insurance. In 1982 the holding company became Torchmark. Throughout its growth spurt it refrained from offering high-yield financial products and thus escaped the worst effects of the economic disruptions of the late 1980s. Its 1990 acquisition of Family Service Life Insurance put it back in the funeral insurance business (it exited again in 1995 and sold the unit in 1998).

Sales in the 1990s were affected by a decline in cash-value life insurance and Medicare supplements. Slack sales forced the company to stop having agents collect premiums personally and by 1996 all accounts were handled by mail.

In 1998 the company sought to sell its 28% stake in property insurer Vesta Insurance Group after that company became the target of numerous lawsuits. Torchmark was only able to reduce its stake to 24% on the open market but in 2000 Vesta bought out Torchmark's holdings.

Torchmark was haunted in 2000 by its own version of the undead — burial policies. An investigation by Alabama regulators was sparked by a Florida court order forcing the company to stop collecting premiums on old burial policies for which African-Americans had been charged higher premiums. In 2001 and 2002 Torchmark was hit by another dozen lawsuits including allegations of overcharging.

EXECUTIVES

Co-chairman And Co-ceo, Larry M. Hutchison, age 64, $870,865 total compensation

Co-chairman And Co-ceo, Gary L. Coleman, age 65, $870,865 total compensation

Ceo American Income Life And Liberty National Life, Roger C. Smith, age 65, $594,846 total compensation

Evp And Chief Administrative Officer, Vern D. Herbel, age 60, $519,846 total compensation

Evp And Cfo, Frank M. Svoboda, age 56, $499,692 total compensation

Evp And Chief Investment Officer, W. Michael Pressley, age 66, $499,692 total compensation

Evp And Chief Actuary, Ben W. Lutek, age 59

President Lnl Agency Division, Steven J. (Steve) DiChiaro, age 51

Evp And General Counsel, R. Brian Mitchell, age 54

President And Ceo Globe Life Direct Response, Bill E. Leavell, age 55

President And Ceo Fhl Agency Division, Kenneth J. (Ken) Matson, age 51

President United American Insurance And First United American Insurance, Michael C. Majors, age 56

Evp And Cio, James E. (Bo) McPartland, age 51

Evp And Chief Strategy Officer, J. Matthew Darden, age 47

President Ail Agency Division American Income, Steven K. Greer, age 45

Senior Vice President Facilities, Douglas Gockel

Auditors: Deloitte & Touche LLP

LOCATIONS

HQ: Torchmark Corp
3700 South Stonebridge Drive, McKinney, TX 75070
Phone: 972 569-4000
Web: www.torchmarkcorp.com

PRODUCTS/OPERATIONS

2017 Revenues

	$ mil.	% of total
Insurance		
Life	2,306,547	56
Health	976,373	23
Annuity	15	-
Investment income	847,885	20
Realized investment gain	23,611	1
Other income	1,142	-
Total	**4,155,573**	**100**

Selected Subsidiaries

American Income Life Insurance Company
Family Heritage Life Insurance Company of America
Globe Life and Accident Insurance Company
Liberty National Life Insurance Company
United American Insurance Company

COMPETITORS

Aflac	Monumental Life
Allstate	Northwestern Mutual
Amalgamated Life	Penn Treaty
Gerber Life	Prudential
Guardian Life	State Farm
Lincoln Financial	Texas Life
Group	USAA
MassMutual	Unum Group
MetLife	

HISTORICAL FINANCIALS

Company Type: Public

Income Statement

FYE: December 31

	ASSETS ($ mil.)	NET INCOME ($ mil.)	INCOME AS % OF ASSETS	EMPLOYEES
12/17	23,474	1,454	6.2%	3,102
12/16	21,436	549	2.6%	3,128
12/15	19,853	527	2.7%	3,115
12/14	20,214	542	2.7%	2,980
12/13	18,191	528	2.9%	2,890
Annual Growth	6.6%	28.8%	—	1.8%

2017 Year-End Financials

Debt ratio: 4.84%	No. of shares (mil.): 114
Return on equity: 26.94%	Dividends
Cash ($ mil.): 118	Yield: 0.0%
Current ratio: —	Payout: 4.8%
Long-term debt ($ mil.): —	Market value ($ mil.): 10,395

	STOCK PRICE ($) FY Close	P/E High/Low		Earnings	PER SHARE ($) Dividends	Book Value
12/17	90.71	7	6	12.22	0.59	54.38
12/16	73.76	16	11	4.49	0.56	38.69
12/15	57.16	15	12	4.16	0.53	33.14
12/14	54.17	20	12	4.09	0.51	36.72
12/13	78.15	20	13	3.79	0.45	28.13
Annual Growth	3.8%	—	—	34.0%	6.8%	17.9%

Total System Services, Inc.

Total System Services (TSYS) helps financial institutions go paperless. The company is one of the largest electronic payment processors in the world serving financial institutions and other companies that issue bank private-label prepaid or other types of cards. TSYS' products and services include credit authorization payment processing e-commerce services card issuance and such customer-relations services as fraud monitoring. It also provides merchant services primarily in the US. Through NetSpend TSYS also issues prepaid and payroll cards to self-bank customers.

Operations
TSYS lays claim to being one of the largest processors of merchant accounts competing with main rival First Data.

Before 2017 TSYS operated through four segments: North America Services International Services Merchant Services and NetSpend. (In early 2017 it combined North America Services and International Services into a new unit named Issuer Solutions in order to streamline its structure and optimize resources.)

Its North America Services business segment which accounts for more than 30% of its total revenue provides issuer account services for financial institutions and other organizations based in North America. TSYS's Merchant Services business (almost 45%) provides third party processing services to merchants and independent sales organizations.

The NetSpend segment (more than 15%) issues general purpose reloadable (GPR) prepaid and payroll cards and provides alternative financial services to customers who don't use banks. The company's International Services segment (nearly 10%) pro-

vides issuer card services to institutions based outside of North America.

Geographic Reach
Business in the US accounts for more than 85% of TSYS's revenue. Canada and Europe (including the UK Ireland Switzerland the Netherlands Germany Italy and Cyprus) are the company's next largest markets each representing more than 5% of sales. TSYS also operates in South Africa the Asia-Pacific region (China Malaysia and India) Russia Brazil and the Middle East. Altogether TSYS has operations in more than 80 countries.

Sales and Marketing
TSYS serves 400 clients in more than 80 countries. It markets its prepaid cards through multiple distribution channels including alternative financial service providers traditional retailers direct-to-consumer and online marketing programs and contractual relationships with corporate employers.

Financial Performance
TSYS has been enjoying several consecutive years of strong revenue growth as card use becomes more popular around the world. The company's revenue jumped 50% to a record $4.2 billion during 2016 mostly as its Merchant Services revenues surged due to its TransFirst acquisition which impacted revenues by $1.2 billion.

Despite the strong revenue growth TSYS' net income declined 12% to $320 million in 2016. This was attributed to increases in employment severance technology and facilities expenses in addition to other costs associated with its acquisition of TransFirst.

The company's operating cash levels rose almost 20% to $718 million for the year thanks to a combined increase of non-cash charges (such as depreciation and amortization) and the impact of TransFirst.

Strategy
Beyond its core payment processing business for financial institutions the company has been diversifying its revenue streams by growing its merchant services operations. Its mid-2016 acquisition of rival TransFirst effectively made it one of the largest merchant acquirers in the US (based on revenue) and a nationwide integrated payments provider. The deal also fueled TSYS' record-setting revenue growth for 2016.

As it continues to integrate previous acquisitions and recognize profitable synergies TSYS looks for ways to optimize its reporting structure. In early 2017 it combined its North America Services and International Services segments into a new unit named Issuer Solutions in order to streamline its structure and make collaboration between these two former units more efficient.

Mergers and Acquisitions
In late 2017 TSYS announced plans to acquire for $1.05 billion Cayan a payment technology company focused on integrated payment solutions and merchant acquiring. Cayan is a portfolio company of Parthenon Capital Partners and provides services to more than 70000 merchants and 100 integrated partners in the US.

In 2016 TSYS bolstered its merchant services business after buying TransFirst for $2.4 billion. The deal created one of the largest merchant acquirers in the US (based on revenue) and a more robust integrated payments provider. The acquisition also helped TSYS achieve its go-to-market strategy and to focus on referral partners such as technology software providers banks associations and e-commerce providers. It also strengthened the company's sales and distribution network while adding more than 1000 partners.

HISTORY

Created in 1959 to handle the bank card operations of Columbus Bank and Trust Total System

Services was spun off in 1982 and went public the following year. Its growth was spurred by increased credit card use a growing tendency by banks to outsource data processing and the company's ability to snag such big customers as NationsBank (later part of Bank of America) and AT&T Universal Card Services.

As the US credit card processing market matured TSYS began looking to expand overseas — and taking other companies' business. Despite Mexico's economic downturn in 1993 TSYS formed a joint venture with Mexican card processor PROSA; in 1995 it snagged part of BankAmerica's business. The following year TSYS upgraded its data-processing system to let its banking and retail customers tailor cards to their clients.

Alliances helped position TSYS as a one-stop support shop for banks. These included a joint venture with Visa International in 1996 that created Vital Processing Services a merchant transaction processing and data services firm.

In 1998 TSYS agreed to process 60 million Sears credit card accounts. It was TSYS's biggest deal ever and one passed over by rival First Data. The pact helped compensate for the 1999 loss of major client Universal Card Services which AT&T sold to Citicorp. Also in 1999 TSYS added call-center and other customer services to its offerings when it acquired Partnership Card services from Synovus Financial.

Several acquisitions and partnerships helped the company grow abroad. TSYS entered Europe and Japan in a big way in 2000 when it inked a deal to process cards for The Royal Bank of Scotland Group. It also bought a majority stake in Japanese credit card issuer GP Network. In 2005 an alliance put TSYS on the ground in China where it gained a 45% stake in China UnionPay Data Services the leading outsourced payment solutions provider in that country. The following year TSYS Card Tech gave TSYS a foothold in dozens of new countries in Africa the Asia/Pacific region Europe and the Middle East.

In 2005 TSYS bought from Visa U.S.A. the 50% it didn't own in merchant transaction clearing and settlement firm TSYS Acquiring Solutions (formerly Vital Processing Services).

TSYS became an independent company in 2008 after it was spun off by Synovus.

EXECUTIVES

Evp, M. Troy Woods, age 67, $869,000 total compensation
Sevp General Counsel And Secretary, G. Sanders Griffith, age 64, $525,000 total compensation
Evp And Chief Human Resource Officer, Ryland L. Harrelson
Sevp And President Issuer Solutions, Gaylon M. Jowers
Sevp And President Netspend, Charles J. (Chuck) Harris
Sevp And Cfo, Paul M. Todd, age 47, $500,000 total compensation
Sevp And Cio, Patricia A. Watson, age 51, $475,000 total compensation
Sevp And President Merchant Solutions, Philip McHugh
Vice President, Butch Greer
Vice President, Russell Perdue
Vice President Of Human Resources, Nancy Conroy
Vice President Human Resources, Mark Andrews
Executive Vice President, Dan Henry
Senior Vice President Business Development, Dave Stanger
Vice President, Bruce Jones
Vice President Client Services, Jennifer Leroy
Vice President Of Human Resources, Janice Kirkland

Executive Vice President Chief Accounting Officer And Controller, Dorenda Weaver
Executive Vice President Finance, Wilbert Noronha
Senior Executive Vice President; President North America Services, William A Pruett
Executive Vice President Business Support Services, Bill Pruette
Executive Vice President Major Account Relationship Management, Allen Pettis
Vice President Financial Institutions, Tracy Gonzalez
Vp Sales, Ray Gross
Vice President Finance, Jessica Gaffney
Vice President, Don Apgar
Vice President Fp And A, Boan Jim
Executive Vice President Managing Director Sage Usa, Chambers Cynthia
Board Member, Richard Ussery
Board Member, William Isaac
Auditors: KPMG LLP

LOCATIONS

HQ: Total System Services, Inc.
One TSYS Way, P.O. 1755, Columbus, GA 31902
Phone: 706 644-6081   **Fax:** 706 649-2456
Web: www.tsys.com

2016 Sales

	$ mil.	% of total
US	3,520	85
Europe	307	7
Canada	284	7
Mexico	15	-
Other regions	42	1
Total	**4,170**	**100**

PRODUCTS/OPERATIONS

2016 Sales

	$ mil.	% of total
Merchant services	1,828	44
North America services	1,349	32
NetSpend	660	16
International services	330	8
Total	**4,170**	**100**

COMPETITORS

Banc of America Merchant Services	Equifax
	First Data
Blackhawk Network	Fiserv
Chase Paymentech Solutions	Global Payments
	Green Dot
DFC Global	MasterCard
ECHO Inc.	Vantiv
Elavon	Visa Inc

HISTORICAL FINANCIALS

Company Type: Public

Income Statement
FYE: December 31

	REVENUE ($ mil.)	NET INCOME ($ mil.)	NET PROFIT MARGIN	EMPLOYEES
12/17	4,927	586	11.9%	11,000
12/16	4,170	319	7.7%	11,500
12/15	2,779	364	13.1%	10,500
12/14	2,446	322	13.2%	9,900
12/13	2,132	244	11.5%	9,600
Annual Growth	**23.3%**	**24.4%**	**—**	**3.5%**

2017 Year-End Financials

Debt ratio: 50.44%
Return on equity: 27.01%
Cash ($ mil.): 450
Current ratio: 1.09
Long-term debt ($ mil.): 2,628

No. of shares (mil.): 180
Dividends
  Yield: 0.0%
  Payout: 14.5%
Market value ($ mil.): 14,308

Stock Price / P/E / Per Share

	STOCK PRICE ($) FY Close	P/E High/Low	PER SHARE ($) Earnings	Dividends	Book Value
12/17	79.09	25 16	3.16	0.46	12.39
12/16	49.03	32 22	1.73	0.40	11.45
12/15	49.80	28 17	1.97	0.40	10.08
12/14	33.96	20 17	1.72	0.40	9.15
12/13	33.28	26 16	1.29	0.40	8.42
Annual Growth	**24.3%**		**25.1%**	**0.0%**	**10.1%**

TOWER FEDERAL CREDIT UNION

EXECUTIVES

Chb, George Cumberledge
Pres*, Martin Breland
Treas*, Charles Nossick
Chief Technology Officer, Allen W Bach
Chief Financial Officer, Allen Bach
Manager, Peggy Stavely
Technician, Terrell Moore
Network Analyst, Mike Aguilar
Accountant, Samantha Adams
Project Coordinator, Susan Moury
Information Specialist, Cindy Spurlin

LOCATIONS

HQ: TOWER FEDERAL CREDIT UNION
7901 SANDY SPRING RD # 102, LAUREL, MD 207073589
Phone: 301 497-7000
Web: WWW.TOWERFCU.ORG

HISTORICAL FINANCIALS

Company Type: Private

Income Statement
FYE: December 31

	ASSETS ($ mil.)	NET INCOME ($ mil.)	INCOME AS % OF ASSETS	EMPLOYEES
12/17	2,964	22	0.8%	490
12/16	2,925	18	0.6%	—
Annual Growth	**1.3%**	**23.7%**		

2017 Year-End Financials

Debt ratio: ——
Return on equity: 26.30%
Cash ($ mil.): 603
Current ratio: ——
Long-term debt ($ mil.): —

Dividends
  Yield: —
  Payout: —
Market value ($ mil.): —

TowneBank

EXECUTIVES

BR Mgr, Becky Zambas
Executive Officer, Anne Conner
Board Member, Juan M Montero
Auditors: Dixon Hughes Goodman LLP

STOCK PRICE ($)		P/E		PER SHARE ($)		
FY Close		High/Low		Earnings	Dividends	Book Value
12/17	19.80	12	10	1.86	1.75	16.09
12/16	18.68	10	8	1.83	1.56	15.95
12/15	16.22	16	14	1.18	1.56	15.15
12/14	16.82	14	9	1.68	1.53	15.53
Annual Growth	4.2%			2.6%	3.4%	0.9%

LOCATIONS

HQ: TowneBank
5716 High Street, Portsmouth, VA 23703
Phone: 757 638-7500
Web: www.townebank.com

HISTORICAL FINANCIALS

Company Type: Public

Income Statement

FYE: December 31

	ASSETS ($ mil.)	NET INCOME ($ mil.)	INCOME AS % OF ASSETS	EMPLOYEES
12/17	8,522	87	1.0%	2,727
12/16	7,973	67	0.8%	2,529
12/15	6,296	62	1.0%	1,903
12/14	4,982	42	0.8%	1,737
12/13	4,673	41	0.9%	1,741
Annual Growth	16.2%	20.4%	—	11.9%

2017 Year-End Financials

Debt ratio: 3.19%
Return on equity: 7.95%
Cash ($ mil.): 504
Current ratio: —
Long-term debt ($ mil.): —

No. of shares (mil.): 62
Dividends
  Yield: 0.0%
  Payout: 39.0%
Market value ($ mil.): 1,926

	STOCK PRICE ($) FY Close	P/E High/Low		Earnings	PER SHARE ($) Dividends	Book Value
12/17	30.75	25	21	1.41	0.55	18.06
12/16	33.25	29	14	1.18	0.51	17.20
12/15	20.87	18	12	1.22	0.47	15.71
12/14	15.12	14	11	1.18	0.43	17.02
12/13	15.39	15	12	1.14	0.38	16.32
Annual Growth	18.9%			5.5%	9.7%	2.6%

Toyota Motor Credit Corp.

EXECUTIVES

President And Ceo; Cfo, Michael R. (Mike) Groff, age 63
Auditors: PricewaterhouseCoopers LLP

LOCATIONS

HQ: Toyota Motor Credit Corp.
6565 Headquarters Drive, Plano, TX 75024
Phone: 469 486-9300
Web: www.toyotafinancial.com

PRODUCTS/OPERATIONS

2016 Sales

	$ mil.	% of total
Financing		
Operating leases	7,141	68
Retail	1,859	18
Dealer	403	4
Insurance premiums earned & contract revenues	719	7
Investment & other	164	1
Gain on sale of commercial finance business	197	2
Total	**10,483**	**100**

2016 Sales

	$ mil.	% of total
Financing revenues	9,403	90
Insurance earned premiums and contract revenues	719	7
Investment and other income net	164	1
Gain on sale of commercial finance business	197	2
Total	**10,483**	**100**

COMPETITORS

Ally Financial
American Honda Finance
AutoNation
Capital One Auto Finance
Daimler Financial Services
Ford Motor Credit
GM Financial
Mercedes-Benz Credit
Volkswagen Financial Services
Volvo Car Finance

HISTORICAL FINANCIALS

Company Type: Public

Income Statement

FYE: March 31

	REVENUE ($ mil.)	NET INCOME ($ mil.)	NET PROFIT MARGIN	EMPLOYEES
03/18	11,856	3,410	28.8%	3,300
03/17	11,246	267	2.4%	3,185
03/16	10,483	932	8.9%	3,140
03/15	9,142	1,197	13.1%	3,251
03/14	8,099	857	10.6%	3,210
Annual Growth	10.0%	41.2%		0.7%

2018 Year-End Financials

Debt ratio: 81.59%
Return on equity: 30.44%
Cash ($ mil.): 3,540
Current ratio: 0.16
Long-term debt ($ mil.): 71,040

No. of shares (mil.): 0
Dividends
  Yield: —
  Payout: —
Market value ($ mil.): —

TPG Specialty Lending Inc

Auditors: KPMG LLP

LOCATIONS

HQ: TPG Specialty Lending Inc
301 Commerce Street, Suite 3300, Fort Worth, TX 76102
Phone: 817 871-4000   **Fax:** 817 871-4001
Web: www.tpgspecialtylending.com

HISTORICAL FINANCIALS

Company Type: Public

Income Statement

FYE: December 31

	ASSETS ($ mil.)	NET INCOME ($ mil.)	INCOME AS % OF ASSETS	EMPLOYEES
12/17	1,720	120	7.0%	—
12/16	1,675	107	6.4%	—
12/15	1,516	95	6.3%	—
12/14	1,303	104	8.0%	—
12/13	1,039	57	5.5%	—
Annual Growth	13.4%	20.3%	—	—

2017 Year-End Financials

Debt ratio: 40.89%
Return on equity: 12.52%
Cash ($ mil.): 6
Current ratio: —
Long-term debt ($ mil.): —

No. of shares (mil.): 60
Dividends
  Yield: 0.0%
  Payout: 94.0%
Market value ($ mil.): 1,193

Tractor Supply Co.

Tractor Supply Company (TSC) does a whole lot more than its name might suggest. Besides providing agricultural machine parts TSC offers animal feed fencing power tools riding mowers work clothing and pet supplies as well as tools for gardening irrigation welding and towing. TSC offers both name-brand merchandise and its own crop of private-label goods. The company has nationwide scope operating more than 1850 stores in some 49 US states under the Tractor Supply Company Del's Farm Supply and Petsense banners. Stores are concentrated in rural areas and near large cities to cater to full- and part-time farmers ranchers and contractors. TSC also sells online.

Operations

TSC operates Tractor Supply Del's Feed & Farm Supply and Petsense stores. It breaks its operations into product categories.

Livestock and pet products which account for more than 45% of sales are sold under the Countyline Dumor Equistages and Producer's Pride brand names.

Hardware tools and truck products generating more than 20% of revenue are sold under the Jobsmart Traveller and TSC Tractor Supply Co. brand names.

Seasonal gift and toy products account for about 20% of sales with Groundwork Huskee Red Shed and Redstone brand products.

The clothing and footwear category 10% of sales offers items for men women and children under the Bit & Bridle Blue Mountain and C.E. Schmidt brand names.

The agriculture category accounts for about 5% of sales.

Of its nearly 1850 stores some 1700 are Tractor Supply or Del's stores and about 170 are Petsense stores.

Geographic Reach

TSC based in Brentwood Tennessee operates stores in 49 US states (Alaska is the state without a TSC store). Its largest market is Texas home to about 210 stores followed by Pennsylvania and North Carolina (about 95 each) Ohio and Tennessee (more than 90 each) Michigan and Georgia (about 85 each) and New York (more than 75). The company has distribution facilities in Arizona Georgia Indiana Kentucky Maryland Nebraska Texas and Washington.

Sales and Marketing

TSC's products are sourced through both US and international vendors. It purchases its products from a group of roughly 900 vendors 350 of which supply 90% of TSC's products.

TSC's customers are home and landowners and pet and livestock owners in rural areas and the outskirts of major metropolitan areas. While its customers are often recreational farmers i.e. those that enjoy the outdoor lifestyle but are non-professionals it also serves tradesmen and small businesses.

The company's advertising strategy is based on merchandise its website newspaper circulars direct mail and email and digital and social media.

Financial Performance

Tractor Supply Co.'s revenue has grown steadily for the past decade. Sales rose 7% to $7.3 billion in 2017 from $6.8 billion in 2016. Comparable store sales which make up about 94% of total sales increased about 3% in 2017 from higher traffic counts and the year round strength of consumable usable and edible products primarily animal- and pet-related merchandise. Sales from stores opened less than a year including Petsense locations added $405 million to TSC's top line in 2017.

Net income slipped to about $423 million in 2017 from $437 million in 2016. The company recognized an expense of about $4.9 million in relation to the US Tax Cuts and Jobs Act of 2017.

TSC counted about $109 million in cash at the end of 2017 compared to about $54 million in 2016. Operating activities generated about $631 million in 2017 while investing and financing activities used $238 million and $338 million respectively. The company paid out more than $503 million to shareholders through stock buy backs and quarterly dividends.

Strategy

Although TSC's strategy is dubbed ONETractor part of the strategy involves opening scores of stores a year. The company planned to open 80 TSC stores and 20 Petsense stores in 2018 with more on the way in 2019 and 2020. The company believes there's room for about 2500 TSC stores in the US about 600 more than its 2018 total and 1000 Petsense stores.

In addition to adding stores the strategy intends to deliver better customer service with the help of data and its employees. The company collects customer data through its Neighbor's Club loyalty program which started in 2017. Those who sign up (about 7 million) receive communications tailored to their preferences while the company gets a comprehensive view into its customers' buying behaviors. TSC relies on employees to make suggestions about improvements as well as to share their expertise with customers.

The company has taken steps to improve its omni-channel capabilities relating to fulfillment options product information and site research. TSC has improved the site response time and added additional product offerings for vendor direct-to-customer drop shipments and configured its site to be viewed on mobile devices and tablets.

TSC maintains that its focus on customers living the rural lifestyle sets it apart. Many retailers offer similar products even if they sell to city dwellers as well as rural residents. The wide variety of merchandise available from Amazon.com makes it a competitor and Walmart is a competitor in brick-and-mortar and online sales.

Mergers and Acquisitions

In 2016 TSC acquired Petsense and its 136 retail outlets for $116 million. Petsense is a small-box specialty pet supply retailer. TSC's two Home-Town Pet stores serving a similar market were rebranded as Petsense.

Company Background
TSC was founded in 1938.

EXECUTIVES

Evp Real Estate And Construction General Counsel And Corporate Secretary, Benjamin F. (Ben) Parrish, age 62, $522,615 total compensation
Senior Vice President Marketing, John Wendler
Ceo, Gregory A. (Greg) Sandfort, age 63, $1,033,846 total compensation
President And Chief Merchandising Officer, Steve K. Barbarick, age 50, $607,885 total compensation

Svp And Cio, Robert D. Mills, age 45, $397,692 total compensation
Svp Cfo And Treasurer, Kurt Barton
Vice President Information Technology Infrastructure Services And Security, Michael Mangold
Vice President Information Technology, George Argodale
Chairman, Cynthia T. Jamison, age 58
Board Member, George Mackenzie
Board Member, Edna Morris
Auditors: Ernst & Young LLP

LOCATIONS

HQ: Tractor Supply Co.
5401 Virginia Way, Brentwood, TN 37027
Phone: 615 440-4000
Web: www.tractorsupply.com

2017 Stores

	No.
Texas	210
North Carolina	94
Pennsylvania	93
Tennessee	91
Ohio	90
Michigan	83
Georgia	83
New York	77
Kentucky	69
Florida	63
California	59
Indiana	57
Alabama	56
Virginia	55
Oklahoma	53
Louisiana	44
South Carolina	44
Mississippi	39
Arkansas	35
Arizona	34
Missouri	30
New Mexico	28
West Virginia	28
Colorado	22
Kansas	22
Maryland	22
New Hampshire	21
Maine	20
Massachusetts	20
Wisconsin	20
Connecticut	19
Washington	19
Nebraska	18
Illinois	17
New Jersey	17
Utah	15
North Dakota	14
Minnesota	12
Iowa	9
South Dakota	9
Wyoming	8
Vermont	8
Montana	6
Delaware	5
Idaho	4
Rhode Island	4
Oregon	3
Nevada	3
Hawaii	2
Total	**1,853**

PRODUCTS/OPERATIONS

2017 Sales

	% of total
Livestock and Pet	47
Hardware Tools Truck and Towing	22
Seasonal Gift and Toy Products	19
Clothing and Footwear	8
Agriculture	4
Total	**100**

PRODUCT CATEGORY

PRODUCT CATEGORY
Farm & Ranch
Poultry
Pets & Livestock
Lawn & Garden
Truck & Trailer
Hardware & Tools
Heating & Cooling
Outdoors
Home & Decor
Footware
Clothing
Big & Tall
Plus Sizes
Gift Cards
BRANDS
4health (pet foods and supplies)
Bit & Bridle (apparel and footwear)
Blue Mountain (apparel)
C.E. Schmidt (apparel and footwear)
Countyline (livestock farm and ranch equipment)
Dumor (livestock and horse feed and supplies)
Equistages (horse feed)
Groundwork (lawn and garden supplies)
Huskee (outdoor power equipment)
JobSmart (tools)
Paws & Claws (pet foods and supplies)
Producer's Pride (livestock and horse feed and supplies)
Red Shed (gifts collectibles and outdoor furniture)
Redstone (heating products)
Retriever (pet foods and supplies)
Royal Wing (bird feed and supplies)
Traveller (truck and automotive products)
TSC Tractor Supply Co (trailers truck tool boxes and animal bedding)

COMPETITORS

Ace Hardware	Northern Tool
Amazon.com	Southern States
Farm King	Tennessee Farmers
Home Depot	Co-op
Lowe's	True Value
Menard	Wal-Mart
Miles Enterprises	Wilbur-Ellis

HISTORICAL FINANCIALS

Company Type: Public

Income Statement

FYE: December 30

	REVENUE ($ mil.)	NET INCOME ($ mil.)	NET PROFIT MARGIN	EMPLOYEES
12/17	7,256	422	5.8%	28,000
12/16	6,779	437	6.4%	26,000
12/15	6,226	410	6.6%	23,000
12/14	5,711	370	6.5%	21,100
12/13	5,164	328	6.4%	19,200
Annual Growth	**8.9%**	**6.5%**	**—**	**9.9%**

2017 Year-End Financials

Debt ratio: 16.11%
Return on equity: 29.51%
Cash ($ mil.): 109
Current ratio: 1.95
Long-term debt ($ mil.): 433
No. of shares (mil.): 125
Dividends
Yield: 0.0%
Payout: 31.8%
Market value ($ mil.): 9,366

	STOCK PRICE ($) FY Close	P/E High/Low		PER SHARE ($) Earnings	Dividends	Book Value
12/17	74.75	23	15	3.30	1.05	11.32
12/16	75.81	29	19	3.27	0.92	11.11
12/15	85.67	32	25	3.00	0.76	10.38
12/14	77.92	29	21	2.66	0.61	9.48
12/13	75.54	56	28	2.32	0.49	8.93
Annual Growth	**(0.3%)**	**—**	**—**	**9.2%**	**21.0%**	**6.1%**

TravelCenters of America LLC

TravelCenters of America (TCA) is in it for the long haul. The company operates or franchises some 540 travel centers standalone convenience stores and standalone restaurants primarily targeting truckers and highway motorists across the US. Its brands include TravelCenters of America/TA Petro Stopping Centers/Petro Minit Mart and Quaker Steak & Lube. TCA's travel centers which account for most of sales offer diesel fuel and gas truck repair and maintenance services full- or quick-service restaurants and showers and other customer amenities. The company leases about 200 of its locations from Hospitality Properties Trust (HPT) its largest shareholder.

Operations

TCA operates through two primary segments travel centers and convenience stores. Its travel center business which accounts for some 85% of revenue includes about 180 TravelCenters of Americas/TA locations and about 80 Petro Stopping Centers/Petro locations. The company operates nearly 230 of the centers and franchises the rest. The convenience stores business 10%-plus of revenue includes more than 230 Minit Mart locations that offer gasoline coffee groceries and other traditional convenience store fare. (The company announced plans in mid-2018 to sell its convenience store operations.) The remaining revenue comes from corporate and other and includes some 50 Quaker Steak & Lube restaurants.

Fuel generates about two-thirds of TCA's revenue; the rest comes from truck services and food and other items sold in it stores.

Geographic Reach

TCA operates or franchises about 540 travel centers convenience stores and restaurants across the US (as well as a single location in Ontario Canada). Its largest market is the Midwest with Kentucky Illinois Missouri Ohio and Wisconsin together accounting for nearly half of all locations.

Sales and Marketing

TCA caters to professional truck drivers and travelers who rely on gas stations and convenience stores while on the road. Customers include trucking fleets and their drivers independent truck drivers and motorists.

Financial Performance

Although TCA's revenue was up in 2017 it has fallen significantly over the past five years amid falling gas prices. It is down nearly 25% since 2013. Net income has suffered a more severe drop falling some 70% during that time.

In 2017 the company reported revenue of $6.1 billion an increase of more than 10% from the prior year. The growth was driven by a 16% jump in fuel revenue because of rising gasoline prices in the second half of the year. Boosted by the revenue growth net income was $9 million in 2017 compared to a loss of $2 million in 2016. An income tax benefit related to the resolution of previous uncertain tax positions also positively impacted the results.

Cash at the end of 2017 was $36 million a decrease of $25 million from the prior year. Cash from operations contributed $36 million to the coffers while investing activities used $62 million mainly for capital expenditures. Financing activities added just under $1 million primarily because of sale leaseback transactions with Hospitality Properties Trust.

Strategy

TCA is building its cross-country network of travel centers through acquisitions (by opportunistically buying up smaller competitors) and by opening new locations. Since 2011 the company has acquired and developed some 325 travel centers convenience stores and standalone restaurants (mostly convenience stores). It has invested roughly $910 million to develop purchase and improve locations.

In an effort to kickstart its travel center expansion in 2018 TCA launched a new brand called TA Express. The smaller travel center concept will offer a quicker customer experience and provide more site flexibility to the company. Large tracts of land along or near interstates are becoming scarcer. TCA hopes the new format will also spur interest in travel center franchising.

In addition to expansion efforts the company's growth plans include investments in its existing properties and services. Recent improvements have included parking lot expansions restaurant renovations and installation of car washes. TCA is also focused on enhancing its TA Truck Service offerings which include some 1100 repair bays more than 2600 service trucks RoadSquad and OnSite emergency maintenance vehicles and a commercial tire network.

In mid-2018 TCA announced plans to sell its stand-alone convenience store operations (about 225 stores) to UK-based EG Group for some $330 million. The deal will free up focus and funds for the company's travel center business.

EXECUTIVES

Marketing Vice President Director, Tom Liutkus
Svp Truck Service Marketing And Operations, Skip McGary
Svp Food Marketing And Operations, John Ponczoch
Evp Sales, Michael J. Lombardi, age 67, $339,000 total compensation
Ceo, Andrew J. Rebholz, age 54, $300,000 total compensation
Evp And General Counsel, Mark R. Young, age 55, $300,000 total compensation
President And Coo, Barry A. Richards, age 65, $300,000 total compensation
Svp Construction Maintenance And Environmental, Peter P. Ward
Svp Retail Marketing And Operations, Rodney Bresnahan
Vice President Of Marketing, Rick Pavia
Vp And Cto, Sean Kubovcik
Vice President Of Fleet Sales, Greg Frary
Vice President Strategic Planning, Thomas Komos
National Accounts Manager, Michael Stuewe
Managing Director Board Of Directors, Barry M. Portnoy, age 73
Board Member, Joseph Morea
Board Member, Lisa Jones
Auditors: RSM US LLP

LOCATIONS

HQ: TravelCenters of America LLC
24601 Center Ridge Road, Suite 200, Westlake, OH 44145-5639
Phone: 440 808-9100
Web: www.tatravelcenters.com

PRODUCTS/OPERATIONS

2017 Location

	No.
Travel centers	
TravelCenters of America/TA	178
Petro Stopping Centers/Petro	78
Convenience stores	
Mini Mart	233
Restaurants	
Quaker Steak & Lube	49
Total	**538**

2017 Sales

	$ mil.	% of total
Fuel	4,090	68
Non-fuel	1,944	32
Rent & royalties from franchisees	16	-
Total	**6,051**	**100**

2017 Sales

	$ mil.	% of total
Travel Centers	5,181	86
Convenience Stores	751	12
Corporate and Other	119	2
Total	**6,051**	**100**

COMPETITORS

Bowlin Travel Centers	Pilot Flying J
Chevron	Royal Dutch Shell
Couche-Tard	Sapp Bros Travel
Exxon Mobil	Centers
Love's Country Stores	Stuckey's
Martin & Bayley	

HISTORICAL FINANCIALS

Company Type: Public

Income Statement

FYE: December 31

	REVENUE ($ mil.)	NET INCOME ($ mil.)	NET PROFIT MARGIN	EMPLOYEES
12/17	6,051	9	0.2%	23,877
12/16	5,511	(2)	—	25,204
12/15	5,850	27	0.5%	24,250
12/14	7,778	60	0.8%	22,330
12/13	7,944	31	0.4%	20,670
Annual Growth	**(6.6%)**	**(26.4%)**	**—**	**3.7%**

2017 Year-End Financials

Debt ratio: 42.55%
Return on equity: 1.66%
Cash ($ mil.): 36
Current ratio: 1.22
Long-term debt ($ mil.): 688
No. of shares (mil.): 39
Dividends
  Yield: —
  Payout: —
Market value ($ mil.): 164

	STOCK PRICE ($) FY Close	P/E High/Low		PER SHARE ($) Earnings	Dividends	Book Value
12/17	4.10	33	13	0.23	0.00	14.15
12/16	7.10	—	—	(0.05)	0.00	13.96
12/15	9.40	25	13	0.72	0.00	14.15
12/14	12.62	8	4	1.62	0.00	13.53
12/13	9.74	12	4	1.06	0.00	12.06
Annual Growth	**(19.5%)**	**—**	**—**	**(31.7%)**	**—**	**4.1%**

Travelers Companies Inc (The)

Running a business is a risk The Travelers Companies will insure. While it does offer personal auto and homeowners insurance the company's largest segment is commercial property/casualty insurance to businesses big and small. It is one of the largest business insurers in the US providing commercial auto property workers' compensation marine and general and financial liability coverage to companies in North America (the largest percentage of business) and the UK. The company also offers surety and fidelity bonds as well as professional and management liability coverage for commercial operations.

Operations

Travelers operates in three segments — Business Insurance Personal Insurance and Bond & Specialty Insurance.

The Business Insurance segment (which accounts for about 50% of net earned premiums) offers property/casualty insurance and related services to clients — primarily in the US as well as in Canada the UK Ireland and throughout other parts of the world as a corporate member of Lloyd's.

The Personal insurance segment offers homeowners auto flood and umbrella policies. That segment which is growing by geographic expansion accounts for more than 30% of the group's premiums.

The Bond & Specialty Insurance segment writes fidelity and surety general liability and property workers' compensation commercial automobile and commercial multi-peril lines. It accounts for about 10% of net earned premiums.

Travelers also offers reinsurance.

Geographic Reach

The vast majority (about 95%) of Travelers' business is in the US. It also operates in the UK through two arms: Travelers Insurance Company and Travelers Syndicate Management within Lloyd's of London. Those businesses offer commercial property/casualty and risk management services. Additionally Travelers has modest operations in Canada Brazil India China and Ireland. It's looking to expand in Latin America.

The company employs field claim management teams in 20 centers and 53 satellite and specialty-only offices in some 45 states.

Sales and Marketing

Travelers' customers include commercial businesses government agencies associations and individuals.

The company's offerings are distributed through independent agents and brokers across the US. In the Business Insurance segment some 11000 agents are supported by three customer service centers and about 115 field offices. The unit also writes business abroad where its products are distributed through Lloyd's wholesale and retail brokers.

Personal products are distributed through some 10300 independent agents employee and affinity groups and direct marketing. Meanwhile the Bond & Specialty Insurance segment distributes products through some 5600 independent agents and brokers.

Financial Performance

Travelers' revenues have maintained a slow-but-steady growth rate in recent years — a sign that the company has spread itself smoothly across industries and has taken no significant hits to its premiums. In 2017 revenue rose 3% to $28.9 billion as premiums and net realized investment gains grew. The Personal Insurance segment saw the highest relative gains with a 10% increase in earned premiums.

Net income has fallen for the past three years and in 2017 it declined 32% to $2.1 billion. This was largely due to an increase in claims and claim adjustment expenses. The company had catastrophe losses of $2 billion from the impact of hurricanes Harvey and Irma California wildfires and severe wind and hail storms.

The lower net income led to a decline in operating cash flow which fell 10% to $3.8 billion.

Strategy

Travelers targets growth in operating return on equity over time in the mid-teens with the notion that economic cycles weather patterns and other factors can impact its business from year to year. The company follows disciplined underwriting and investment strategies to help it stay immune to market fluctuations and lingering depressed interest rates.

The firm also follows a disciplined acquisition strategy seeking opportunities that will help it expand into new geographic markets or build on its existing product portfolio. Although Travelers is first and foremost a US-based insurer it has recently made acquisitions that have expanded its operations in Canada the UK and Brazil as well as providing it with entry into Colombia's market.

Another key strategy for Travelers is to innovate to improve the way it conducts business. It has its eye on technology from data and analytics to digital sales (as evidenced by its 2017 acquisition of UK-based Simply Business).

Travelers also innovates to create new types of coverage. In 2018 the company launched the Traverse personal insurance product marketed to consumers who don't need traditional auto or home coverage; it includes personal liability identity theft and property theft coverage. It also introduced Quantum Home 2.0 a homeowners product offering policy customization and simpler customer communications. Also that year its Canadian division began offering human resources and legal assistance services (at no charge) to its small business customers.

Like all property/casualty insurers the company is vulnerable to severe weather and natural disasters. For example it had catastrophe losses of $2 billion in 2017 due to the impact of hurricanes wildfires and severe storms. To mitigate these types of losses Travelers prefers to raise prices in manageable gradual increments.

The company's three educational initiatives for 2018 are centered on reducing distracted driving increasing cybersecurity and tackling small business challenges. It has presented numerous forums free to the public around these issues.

Mergers and Acquisitions

Travelers Companies acquired Simply Business a UK-based online business insurance broker for $490 million in 2017. Simply Business offers small business coverage; the acquisition helped Travelers expand its digital channels in the UK and beyond.

HISTORY

St. Paul Minnesota was a boomtown in 1852 thanks to traffic on the Mississippi. Settlers knew fire insurance was a must in their wooden town but there were no local insurers. Buying policies from eastern companies and getting claims processed was difficult — especially in the winter when river traffic stopped.

In 1853 a group of local investors led by George and John Farrington and Alexander Wilkin formed St. Paul Mutual Insurance a mixed stock and mutual company (mutual members shared in the firm's profits and losses while stockholders could benefit by selling if the company's value rose). St. Paul Mutual sold its first policy the following year.

The company changed its name in 1865 to St. Paul Fire and Marine Insurance stopped offering mutual policies and expanded throughout the Midwest. Claims from the Chicago Fire in 1871 nearly sank the company which assessed its shareholders $15 for each share of stock but prompt and full payment of claims resulted in more business. By the turn of the century St. Paul Fire and Marine was operating nationwide.

Although the company was hard hit by shipping losses in WWI it continued expanding joining other US insurers in the American Foreign Insurance Association to market insurance in Europe.

In 1926 St. Paul Fire and Marine organized its first subsidiary St. Paul Mercury Indemnity to write liability insurance policies. Other additions included coverage for automobiles aircraft burglary and robbery and in 1940 turkey farming.

During WWII St. Paul Fire and Marine joined the War Damage Corp. a government-financed consortium that paid claims for war damage. The St. Paul Companies was formed in 1968 as the umbrella organization for the various subsidiaries and the firm grew through purchases.

Lines of business blossomed during the 1970s including life and title insurance leasing a mail-order consumer finance company oil and gas and real estate. Many of these were sold during the 1980s but one The John Nuveen Co. (1974) became the nucleus of St. Paul's financial services operations.

EXECUTIVES

Evp And Chief Administrative Officer, Andy F. Bessette, age 65

President And Coo, Brian W. MacLean, age 65, $962,548 total compensation

Vice Chairman And Cfo, Jay S. Benet, age 66, $1,000,000 total compensation

Evp And Chief Human Resources Officer, John P. Clifford, age 62

Evp Strategic Development And Corporate Treasurer, Maria Olivo, age 53

Evp And General Counsel, Kenneth F. (Ken) Spence, age 63

Evp Marketing And Communications, Lisa M. Caputo, age 54

Evp Enterprise Risk Management, Fred R. Donner, age 61

Chairman And Ceo, Alan D. Schnitzer, age 53, $1,000,000 total compensation

President Field Management, Patrick J. Kinney

Evp Middle Market, Michael F. Klein

Evp Public Policy; President The Travelers Institute, Joan Kois Woodward

Evp; President Bond And Specialty Insurance, Thomas M. (Tom) Kunkel

Evp; President Business Insurance, Greg C Toczydlowski

Evp; President International, Kevin C. Smith

Evp And Cio, Madelyn Lankton

Evp Claim Services And Specialty Liability, Robert C. (Bob) Brody

Evp And Chief Underwriting Officer, Marlyss J. Gage

Evp And Chief Risk Officer, Bruce R. Jones

Evp President National Accounts And First Party, William C Malugen

Evp And President Small Commercial, Behram M. Dinshaw

Evp And President Middle Market, Scott F. Higgins

Evp Management Liability, Jeffrey P. (Jeff) Klenk

Claim Center Vice President, Claude Howard

Second Vice President Corporate Audit, Debra Barlow

Vice President, Richard L Smith

2vp Complex Claim Specialist, Milena Ivanis

Regional Vice President Select Group, Sean Ramalho

Vice President, John Komidar

2vp Operating Model Platform Strategy Business Insurance, Dianna Wallquist

2vp Bi Shared Finance Expense Management, Tom Soisson

2vp Information Technology Operations, Bryant H Lewis

Underwriting Vice President, Rebecca Glenn

Vice President, Ken Chapman

Assistant Vice President, Lisa Schultze

Division President, Maureen Bass

Regional Vice President, Mark Lear

Second Vice President General Liability, Donald Nichols

Senior Vice President, Scott Belden

Field Product Line Manager 2vp Auto Claims, Trevor Engels

2vp Of Digital Marketing, Rick Heffernan

2vp, Carla Schirm

2vp And Actuary, Dan Carr

Vp Hr Compensation Benefits And Operations, Greg Landmark

Second Vp Information Systems, Vincent Bryan

Evp And President Business Insurance, Gregory Toczydlowski

Vp Employee Relations, Cecil Murphy

Svp Auto Property And Catastrophe Claim, Patrick Gee

Assistant Vice President Regional Manager Alberta Region, Jan Rasilainen

Regional Vice President, Tad Cluff

Second Vice President Human Resources, Laura Giordano

Vp Government Affairs, John Miletti

Second Vice President Data Management And Analysis, Kenneth Manzer

Vice President And Actuary Business Unit Analytics Business Insurance, Raymond Reimer

Vp Govt. Relations, Raul Allegue

Vice President, Alan Wirkman

Evp And Chief Investment Officer, William H. (Bill) Heyman, age 70

Vice Chairman And Chief Legal Officer, Avrohom J. Kess

Board Member, Janet Dolan

Executive Board Member, Sue McKinney

Auditors: KPMG LLP

LOCATIONS

HQ: Travelers Companies Inc (The)
485 Lexington Avenue, New York, NY 10017
Phone: 917 778-6000
Web: www.travelers.com

2017 Sales

	$ mil.	% of total
US	27,253	94
Canada	1,232	4
Other	417	2
Total	**28,902**	**100**

PRODUCTS/OPERATIONS

2017 Sales

	$ mil.	% of total
Premiums	25,683	89
Net investment income	2,397	8
Fees	447	1
Investment gains	216	1
Other	159	1
Total	**28,902**	**100**

Selected Products

Business
Commercial Automobile
Commercial Multi-Peril
Commercial Property
General Liability
Workers' Compensation
Individual
Affinity Auto and Home Program
Auto Insurance
Boat and Yacht Insurance
Condo Insurance
Flood Insurance
Homeowners Insurance
Identity Fraud Protection
Renters Insurance
Umbrella Insurance
Valuable Items Coverage
Wedding and Private Events Insurance

Selected Subsidiaries and Divisions

J. Malucelli Participacoes em Seguros e Resseguros S.A. (49.5% Brazil)
St. Paul Fire and Marine Insurance Company
Travelers Property Casualty Corp.
  The Standard Fire Insurance Company
  Travelers Casualty and Surety Company
  Travelers Casualty and Surety Company of America
  The Travelers Indemnity Company
  First Floridian Auto and Home Insurance Company
  The Premier Insurance Co. of Massachusetts
Travelers Insurance Company Limited (UK)
Travelers Syndicate Management Limited (UK)

COMPETITORS

AIG	Chubb Limited
AXA	Liberty Mutual Agency
Allianz	Markel
Allstate	Nationwide
American Financial Group	The Hartford
	W. R. Berkley
CNA Financial	Zurich Insurance Group

HISTORICAL FINANCIALS

Company Type: Public

Income Statement

FYE: December 31

	ASSETS ($ mil.)	NET INCOME ($ mil.)	INCOME AS % OF ASSETS	EMPLOYEES
12/17	103,483	2,056	2.0%	30,800
12/16	100,245	3,014	3.0%	30,900
12/15	100,184	3,439	3.4%	30,900
12/14	103,078	3,692	3.6%	30,200
12/13	103,812	3,673	3.5%	30,800
Annual Growth	(0.1%)	(13.5%)	—	0.0%

2017 Year-End Financials

Debt ratio: 6.25%	No. of shares (mil.): 271
Return on equity: 8.76%	Dividends
Cash ($ mil.): 344	Yield: 0.0%
Current ratio: —	Payout: 38.6%
Long-term debt ($ mil.): —	Market value ($ mil.): 36,813

	STOCK PRICE ($) FY Close	P/E High/Low	PER SHARE ($) Earnings	Dividends	Book Value
12/17	135.64	18 16	7.33	2.83	87.44
12/16	122.42	12 10	10.28	2.62	83.05
12/15	112.86	11 9	10.88	2.38	79.75
12/14	105.85	10 7	10.70	2.15	77.08
12/13	90.54	9 7	9.74	1.96	70.14
Annual Growth	10.6%	— —	(6.9%)	9.6%	5.7%

TreeHouse Foods Inc

TreeHouse Foods is the nation's #1 manufacturer of non-dairy powdered creamer sold under the Cremora brand and pickles (Farman's Nalley's Peter Piper and Steinfeld). The company also makes private-label soups salad dressings and Mexican sauces drink mixes hot cereals macaroni and cheese skillet dinners and jams. TreeHouse makes private-label products for foodservice distributors and restaurant chains as well as for supermarkets and mass merchandisers — the company's largest market that also buys its own brands. TreeHouse also boasts co-pack business and industrial customers. In a strong move to expand its product portfolio TreeHouse in early 2016 paid $2.7 billion to acquire ConAgra Foods' private brands operations.

Operations

TreeHouse's product categories include beverages salad dressings snacks beverage enhancers pickles sauces soup and infant feeding cereals dry dinners jams and other products. It also offers natural organic and preservative-free ingredients in many categories.

The North American Retail Grocery segment accounts for more than 80% of the company's sales. Food Away From Home and Industrial and Export each represent almost 10%. The snacks nuts category is TreeHouse's biggest product line generating more than 20% of revenue.

Geographic Reach

Headquartered in Oak Brook Illinois TreeHouse has offices in Green Bay Wisconsin; Omaha Nebraska; Downers Grove Illinois; St. Louis Missouri; Pittsburgh Pennsylvania; St. Paul Minnesota; and Winona Ontario Canada. TreeHouse rings up more than 85% of its sales in the US and Canada.

Sales and Marketing

TreeHouse markets its products to retailers such as supermarkets mass merchandisers and specialty retailers and also to the foodservice industry including foodservice distributors and national restaurant operators.

Retail giant Wal-Mart Stores is TreeHouse's largest customer accounting for about 20% of its sales each year.

Financial Performance

Due to its recent milestone acquisition of ConAgra Foods' private brands operations TreeHouse saw its revenues almost double from $3.2 billion in 2015 to $6.2 billion in 2016. The historic growth was partially offset by an unfavorable pricing mix and unfavorable foreign exchange translations.

TreeHouse suffered a net loss of $128 million in 2016 largely due to a 120% surge in selling and distribution expenses associated with its private brands acquisition. On the other hand operating cash flow surged from $285 million in 2015 to $489 million in 2016 mainly due to an influx in cash stemming from the acquisition.

Strategy

The company focuses on expanding partnerships with retailers; driving growth and profitability from its existing product portfolio; leveraging cross-selling opportunities across customers sales channels and geographies; and growing through acquisitions.

TreeHouse has also grown by strengthening ties with retail grocers who are demanding private-label food products as cash-strapped consumers seek goods with equivalent quality at a lower price. To maintain momentum the food maker focuses on the most-purchased categories of private-label products typically canned soup salad dressings powdered creamer and pickles.

Taking this strategy even further TreeHouse in early 2016 paid $2.7 billion to acquire ConAgra Foods' private brands operations. The milestone deal created TreeHouse Private Brands and expanded TreeHouse's presence in the private label dry and refrigerated grocery market specifically refrigerated and shelf stable products in the bars bakery cereal condiments pasta and snacks categories.

HISTORY

Dean Foods combined the businesses of its specialty foods group and its foodservice salad-dressing business in 2005 in order to create publicly traded TreeHouse Foods.

In 2006 the company it purchased pickle-maker Oxford Foods. It paid $275 million for the private-label soup and baby food (Nature's Goodness) businesses of Del Monte Foods. The following year it acquired San Antonio Farms a private-label Mexican sauce maker for about $89 million in cash. That year it also purchased DeGraffenreid a processor and distributor of pickles and related products for the foodservice industry from Bell-Carter Foods for $10.8 million. Strengthening its Canadian footprint in 2007 the company acquired Ontario-based E.D. Smith & Sons a manufacturer of branded sauces jellies jams and pie fillings for $220 million in cash plus the assumption of $100 million in debt.

TreeHouse also bought Sturm Foods a maker of private-label hot cereal and powdered soft drink mixes from HM Capital Partners for $660 million in 2010. The move strengthened TreeHouse's private-label operations as well as its packaging mixing and flavoring capabilities. Extending its reach in shelf-stable foods TreeHouse bought out S.T. Specialty Foods from Windjammer Capital Investors in an all-cash deal valued at about $180 million. S.T. Specialty Foods primarily makes private-label macaroni and cheese and skillet dinners mainstream staples of the dine-at-home

The company bought Naturally Fresh a privately-owned maker of refrigerated dressings sauces dips and marinades in 2012 for $25 million. The deal took TreeHouse from the shelf-stable grocery aisle to the refrigerated produce section providing a premium presence. In 2012 TreeHouse acquired the assets of the Aseptic Cheese and Pudding business from Associated Milk Producers Inc. The business sells products to foodservice and retail customers and strengthened the TreeHouse's existing Bay Valley Foods aseptic operation.

EXECUTIVES

Chairman President And Ceo, Sam K. Reed, age 72, $1,056,250 total compensation
Evp General Counsel And Chief Administrative Officer, Thomas E. O'Neill, age 63, $533,167 total compensation
Evp And Cfo, Matthew J. Foulston, age 54, $45,672 total compensation
Svp And Chief Strategy Officer, Rachel R. Bishop, age 44, $439,333 total compensation
Vp And Assistant General Counsel, Jo Osborn
Senior Vice President Marketing, Tammy Gianfortune
Senior Vice President Human Resources, Lori Roberts
Vice President Corporate Controller, William Kelley
Vice President Labor And Employee Relations, Dan Dring
National Account Manager, Alex Pesce
Vice President Compensation Benefits And Human Resources Systems, Laurie Augustyn-Fierg
Vice President And General Manager Of Senior Technician Specialty Foods, Charles Becks
Senior Vice President Sales, Judy Clark
Senior Vice President Sales, George Miketa
Auditors: DELOITTE & TOUCHE LLP

LOCATIONS

HQ: TreeHouse Foods Inc
2021 Spring Road, Suite 600, Oak Brook, IL 60523
Phone: 708 483-1300
Web: www.treehousefoods.com

2016 Sales

	% of total
North America	91
Outside North America	9
Total	**100**

PRODUCTS/OPERATIONS

2016 Sales

	$ mil.	% of total
North American Retail Grocery	5,092	76
Food Away From Home	546	12
Industrial & Export	545	12
Unallocated	(9.9)	-
Total	**6,175**	**100**

2016 Sales

	$ mil.	% of total
Snacks	1,334	22
Retail bakery	662	11
Cookies and crackers	607	10
Cereals	551	9
Pasta and dry dinners	543	9
Beverages	492	8
Salad dressings	376	6
Soup and infant feeding	372	6
Sauces	336	5
Pickles	318	5
Beverage enhancers	313	5
Jams	107	2
Aseptic products	101	1
Other products	56	1
Total	**6,175**	**100**

Selected Products & Brands

Food Away From Home (foodservice)
  Saucemaker
  Schwartz
Jams & jellies
  E.D. Smith
  Habitant
Liquid egg substitute
  Second Nature
Non-dairy creamer
  Cremora
Pickles
  Farman's
  Nalley's
  Peter Piper
  Steinfeld
Refrigerated
  Mocha Mix
Salad dressings sauces & marinades
  Private label
Sauces & syrups
  Bennett's
  Hoffman House
  Roddenberry's Northwoods
  San Antonio Farms
Soups broths & gravies
  Private label

COMPETITORS

B&G Foods	Kellogg
Campbell Soup	Lancaster Colony
ConAgra	Marzetti
Cott	McCormick & Company
Dean Foods	Mondelez International
Farmer Bros.	Newman's Own
Flowers Foods	Pinnacle Foods Inc
General Mills	Post Holdings
Goya	Reser's Fine Foods
Hain Celestial	Smucker
Heinz	Snyder's-Lance
J & J Snack Foods	

HISTORICAL FINANCIALS

Company Type: Public

Income Statement

FYE: December 31

	REVENUE ($ mil.)	NET INCOME ($ mil.)	NET PROFIT MARGIN	EMPLOYEES
12/17	6,307	(286)	—	13,489
12/16	6,175	(228)	—	16,027
12/15	3,206	114	3.6%	5,880
12/14	2,946	89	3.1%	6,181
12/13	2,293	86	3.8%	4,786
Annual Growth	**28.8%**	—	—	**29.6%**

2017 Year-End Financials

Debt ratio: 44.05%
Return on equity: (-12.01%)
Cash ($ mil.): 132
Current ratio: 2.48
Long-term debt ($ mil.): 2,535
No. of shares (mil.): 56
Dividends
  Yield: —
  Payout: —
Market value ($ mil.): 2,801

	STOCK PRICE ($) FY Close	P/E High/Low		Earnings	Dividends	Book Value
12/17	49.46	—	—	(5.01)	0.00	39.96
12/16	72.19	—	—	(4.10)	0.00	44.10
12/15	78.46	35	26	2.63	0.00	43.01
12/14	85.53	39	28	2.23	0.00	41.24
12/13	68.92	31	22	2.33	0.00	34.89
Annual Growth	**(8.0%)**	—	—	—	—	**3.5%**

TriCo Bancshares (Chico, CA)

People looking for a community bank in California's Sacramento Valley can try TriCo. TriCo Bancshares is the holding company for Tri Counties Bank which serves customers through some 65 traditional and in-store branches in 23 counties in Northern and Central California. Founded in 1974 Tri Counties Bank provides a variety of deposit services including checking and savings accounts money market accounts and CDs. Most patrons are retail customers and small to midsized businesses. The bank primarily originates real estate mortgages which account for about 65% of its loan portfolio; consumer loans contribute about 25%. TriCo has agreed to acquire rival North Valley Bancorp.

Operations
In addition to its retail banking products and services the company provides wholesale banking and investment services; TriCo offers brokerage services through an arrangement with Raymond James Financial. The company does not provide trust or international banking services.

Geographic Reach
Based in Chico California Tri Counties Bank operates 66 branches (41 traditional branches and 25 in-store branches) in 23 counties in Northern and central California including Fresno Kern Mendocino Napa Sacramento and Yuba counties.

Financial Performance
In 2013 net interest income the company's primary source of revenue rose 0.6% compared with 2012 to $102.2 million. The slight increase in net interest income was mainly due to a decrease in average balance of other borrowings a shift in deposit balances from relatively high interest rate earning time deposits to noninterest-earning demand and savings deposits an increase in the average balance of investments securities and an increase in the average balance of loans; all of which were substantially offset by a decrease in the average yield on loans.

Strategy
The bank's growth has been fueled by acquisitions and the opening of new branches; it frequently opens branches within grocery stores or other retailers including Wal-Mart. TriCo in 2010 acquired the three branches of Granite Community Bank which had been seized by regulators. The transaction which also included most of the failed bank's assets and deposits was facilitated by the FDIC and includes a loss-sharing agreement with the agency. The following year TriCo acquired Citizens Bank of Northern California. The FDIC-assisted deal included seven branches. The acquisitions are part of TriCo's strategy of adding new customers.

Mergers and Acquisitions
TriCo in January 2014 announced plans to buy its rival in Northern California North Valley Bancorp (NVB) for about $178.4 million. NVB is the parent company of North Valley Bank which had about $918 million in assets and 22 commercial banking offices across eight Northern California counties at the end of 2013. At closing which is expected in the second or third quarter of 2014 NVB will be merged into Tri Counties Bank. The combined bank would have about $3.6 billion in assets.

EXECUTIVES

Evp And Cfo Trico Bancshares And Tri Counties Bank, Thomas J. (Tom) Reddish, age 58, $309,601 total compensation

Evp And Chief Credit Officer, Craig B. Carney, age 59, $274,932 total compensation

Evp Wholesale Banking, Richard B. O'Sullivan, age 61, $260,890 total compensation

President And Ceo, Richard P. Smith, age 60, $549,846 total compensation

Evp And Coo, John S. Fleshood, age 56

Evp And Chief Retail Banking Officer, Daniel K. (Dan) Bailey, age 49, $268,335 total compensation

Svp And Cio, Bruce Barnett

Vice President Marketing Director, Michael Murphy

Vice President Facilities Expansion Ma, Chimene Sonsteng

Senior Vice President Special Assets Manager, Steve Macrae

Executive Vice President And Chief Retail Banking Officer, Dan Bailey

Vice President Direct Banking Manager, Kay Armstrong

Chairman, William J. Casey, age 73

Vice Chairman, Michael W. Koehnen, age 57

Board Member, Virginia Walker

Board Member, Martin Mariani

Board Member, Patrick Kilkenny

Auditors: Moss Adams LLP

LOCATIONS

HQ: TriCo Bancshares (Chico, CA)
63 Constitution Drive, Chico, CA 95973
Phone: 530 898-0300 **Fax:** 530 898-0310
Web: www.tcbk.com

PRODUCTS/OPERATIONS

2015 Sales

	$ mil.	% of total
Interest		
Loans including fees	131	64
Debt securities	26	13
Dividends	2	1
Other	0	-
Noninterest		
Service charges & fees	31	16
Commissions	3	2
Gain on sale of loans	3	1
Other	7	3
Total	206	100

Selected Services

Business debit cards
Business online banking
Business workshops
Cash management
Education savings and CDs
Loans and credits
Merchant services
Order checks
Overdraft services
Pension and retirement
Personal certificates of deposit
Personal checking
Personal savings and money market
Retirement savings and CDs

COMPETITORS

Bank of America	MUFG Americas Holdings
Bank of the West	PremierWest
Central Valley	Wells Fargo
Community Bancorp	Westamerica

HISTORICAL FINANCIALS

Company Type: Public

Income Statement

FYE: December 31

	ASSETS ($ mil.)	NET INCOME ($ mil.)	INCOME AS % OF ASSETS	EMPLOYEES
12/17	4,761	40	0.9%	1,023
12/16	4,517	44	1.0%	1,063
12/15	4,220	43	1.0%	1,011
12/14	3,916	26	0.7%	1,009
12/13	2,744	27	1.0%	794
Annual Growth	14.8%	10.3%	—	6.5%

2017 Year-End Financials

Debt ratio: 1.56%
Return on equity: 8.25%
Cash ($ mil.): 205
Current ratio: —
Long-term debt ($ mil.): —

No. of shares (mil.): 22
Dividends
  Yield: 0.0%
  Payout: 37.9%
Market value ($ mil.): 869

	STOCK PRICE ($) FY Close	P/E High/Low	PER SHARE ($) Earnings	Dividends	Book Value
12/17	37.86	25 19	1.74	0.66	22.03
12/16	34.18	18 12	1.94	0.60	20.87
12/15	27.44	15 12	1.91	0.52	19.85
12/14	24.70	19 15	1.46	0.44	18.41
12/13	28.37	17 9	1.69	0.42	15.61
Annual Growth	7.5%	— —	0.7%	12.0%	9.0%

TriState Capital Holdings Inc

TriState Capital Holdings has found its niche right in the middle of the banking industry. The holding company owns TriState Capital Bank a regional business bank that caters to midsized businesses or those annually earning between $5 million and $300 million. TriState Capital also offers private banking services nationally to high-net-worth individuals. Its loan portfolio consists of about 50% commercial loans 30% commercial real estate loans and 20% private banking-personal loans. The bank serves clients from branches in Cleveland; New Jersey; New York City Philadelphia and Pittsburgh. Altogether it has some $2 billion in assets. TriState Capital went public in mid-2013.

IPO

The company does not have any specific plans outlined for its proceeds but will likely use it for general corporate purposes which might include maintaining liquidity at the holding company providing equity capital to the bank to fund balance sheet growth and possibly investing in or acquiring wealth management businesses.

Strategy

The company's founders saw an opportunity in serving what they perceived was an underserved market — midsized businesses. Consolidation had left major national banks catering to individuals and large businesses while community banks served individuals and small businesses.

Company Background

TriState Capital was founded in 2007 by two banking industry executives — chairman and CEO James Getz who spent 20 years at Federated Investors and vice chairman William Schenck the former secretary of banking for Pennsylvania.

EXECUTIVES

Chairman President And Ceo, James F. (Jim) Getz, $1,500,000 total compensation

President Commercial Banking, David A. Molnar

Vice Chairman And Cfo, Mark L. Sullivan, $425,000 total compensation

Regional President New Jersey, Kenneth R. Orchard

Regional President New York, Thomas N. Gilmartin

Regional President Ohio, John D. Barrett

Regional President Eastern Pennsylvania, Joseph M. Finley

Regional President Western Pennsylvania, Vince Locher

President Private Bank Team, Charles C. Fawcett

President And Ceo Tristate Capital Bank, Brian S. Fetterolf

Senior Vice President Relationship Manager, Michael Blasko

Senior Vice President, Sheila Roberts

Senior Vice President, Debra Flinner

Senior Vice President, John Buglione

Vice Chairman, A. William (Bill) Schenck

Auditors: KPMG LLP

LOCATIONS

HQ: TriState Capital Holdings Inc
One Oxford Centre, 301 Grant Street, Suite 2700, Pittsburgh, PA 15219
Phone: 412 304-0304 **Fax:** 412 304-0391
Web: www.tristatecapitalbank.com

PRODUCTS/OPERATIONS

2015 Sales

	% of total
Interest income	
Loans	67
Investments	3
Interest-earning deposits	-
Noninterest income	
Investment management fees	25
Commitment and other fees	2
Other income	3
Total	100

COMPETITORS

Bank of America	HSBC Private Bank
Bank of New York Mellon	Herald National Bank
Boston Private	JPMorgan Private Bank
Brown Brothers Harriman	Julius Baer
Citigroup	Lakeland Bancorp
Citigroup Private Bank	M&T Bank
First Republic (CA)	Safra Bank
	U.S. Trust

HISTORICAL FINANCIALS

Company Type: Public

Income Statement

FYE: December 31

	ASSETS ($ mil.)	NET INCOME ($ mil.)	INCOME AS % OF ASSETS	EMPLOYEES
12/17	4,777	37	0.8%	230
12/16	3,930	28	0.7%	224
12/15	3,302	22	0.7%	192
12/14	2,846	15	0.6%	182
12/13	2,290	12	0.6%	129
Annual Growth	20.2%	31.1%	—	15.6%

2017 Year-End Financials

Debt ratio: 7.03%
Return on equity: 10.25%
Cash ($ mil.): 141
Current ratio: —
Long-term debt ($ mil.): —

No. of shares (mil.): 28
Dividends
  Yield: —
  Payout: —
Market value ($ mil.): 658

	STOCK PRICE ($)	P/E	PER SHARE ($)		
	FY Close	High/Low	Earnings	Dividends	Book Value
12/17	23.00	18 15	1.32	0.00	13.61
12/16	22.10	22 11	1.01	0.00	12.38
12/15	13.99	18 12	0.80	0.00	11.62
12/14	10.24	26 16	0.55	0.00	10.88
12/13	11.86	29 24	0.49	0.00	10.25
Annual Growth	18.0%	—	28.1%	—	7 4%

Triumph Bancorp Inc

Auditors: Crowe Horwath LLP

LOCATIONS

HQ: Triumph Bancorp Inc
12700 Park Central Drive, Suite 1700, Dallas, TX 75251
Phone: 214 365-6900
Web: www.triumphbancorp.com

HISTORICAL FINANCIALS

Company Type: Public

Income Statement   FYE: December 31

	ASSETS ($ mil.)	NET INCOME ($ mil.)	INCOME AS % OF ASSETS	EMPLOYEES
12/17	3,499	36	1.0%	820
12/16	2,641	20	0.8%	705
12/15	1,691	29	1.7%	500
12/14	1,447	17	1.2%	466
12/13	1,288	11	0.9%	463
Annual Growth	28.4%	32.3%	—	15.4%

2017 Year-End Financials

Debt ratio: 2.50%
Return on equity: 10.64%
Cash ($ mil.): 134
Current ratio: —
Long-term debt ($ mil.): —

No. of shares (mil.): 20
Dividends
 Yield: —
 Payout: —
Market value ($ mil.): 656

	STOCK PRICE ($)	P/E	PER SHARE ($)		
	FY Close	High/Low	Earnings	Dividends	Book Value
12/17	31.50	19 11	1.81	0.00	18.81
12/16	26.15	24 12	1.10	0.00	16.01
12/15	16.50	11 8	1.57	0.00	14.88
12/14	13.55	10 8	1.52	0.00	13.22
Annual Growth	23.5%	—	4.5%	—	9.2%

Trustco Bank Corp. (N.Y.)

In Banking They Trust. TrustCo Bank Corp is the holding company for Trustco Bank which boasts more than 140 branches across eastern New York central and western Florida and parts of Vermont Massachusetts and New Jersey. The bank offers personal and business customers a variety of deposit products loans and mortgages and trust and investment services. It primarily originates residential and commercial mortgages which account for more than three-quarters of its loan portfolio. It also writes business construction and installment loans and home equity lines of credit.

Operations

TrustCo Bank Corp generated 77% of its total revenue from interest and fees on loans in 2014 while interest on its securities available for sale (which were mostly residential mortgage-backed securities and collateralized mortgage obligations but also its GSE SBA-backed securities) made up another 16% of the bank's revenue. Customer service fees and Trustco Financial Services income made up 6% and 3% of total revenue in 2014 respectively.

Sales and Marketing

Trustco provides personal and business banking services to individuals partnerships and corporations among other kinds of business and organizations. It spent $2.49 million on advertising in 2014 compared to $2.83 million and $3.84 million in 2013 and 2012 respectively.

Financial Performance

Trustco has struggled to grow its revenue in recent years though its profits have been rising at a healthy clip mostly because its loan loss provisions have dissipated with an improving credit portfolio amidst the strengthening economy.

TrustCo's revenue rose by nearly 4% to $176.85 million in 2014 mostly as new branch openings during the year added nearly double-digit loan business growth. The bank also collected more interest income from its securities as it invested more and made a gain on the sale of its Florida regional headquarters property.

Higher revenue and a decline in interest expense on deposits in the low-interest environment also drove the bank's net income up by 11% to $4.38 million. A continuing decline in loan loss provisions buoyed by improving economic conditions (especially in Florida) also helped boost the bank's bottom line.

Despite higher earnings in 2014 TrustCo's operating cash fell by 21% to $49.54 million during the year as it spent more toward acquiring additional assets.

Strategy

TrustCo has focused on building its loan business through new branch additions as well as through growth from its existing offices in recent years. Using this strategy in 2014 the bank added five new branches and successfully boosted its deposit business by 2.7% to $4.03 billion while loan balances swelled by 8.6% to $3.16 billion as the bank aggressively pushed its loan business during the year.

The bank underwent a major branch expansion from 2002 through 2009 and more than doubled its branch network in New York and Florida by opening new locations (more than 75 of them). It continues to open new branches albeit not as rapidly.

EXECUTIVES

President And Ceo, Robert J. McCormick, age 55, $880,000 total compensation
Administrative Vp Branch Administration/marketing Trustco Bank, Scot R. Salvador, age 52, $510,000 total compensation
Evp, Robert M. Leonard, age 56, $260,000 total compensation
Treasurer Trustco And Svp Trustco Bank, Eric W. Schreck, age 51, $255,000 total compensation
Svp And Cfo Trustco Bank Corp Ny And Trustco Bank, Michael M. Ozimek, $142,500 total compensation
Vice President Mortgage Loans Trustco, Michael Lofrumento
Chairman, Thomas O. Maggs, age 74
Auditors: Crowe Horwath LLP

LOCATIONS

HQ: Trustco Bank Corp. (N.Y.)
5 Sarnowski Drive, Glenville, NY 12302
Phone: 518 377-3311   **Fax:** 518 381-3668
Web: www.trustcobank.com

PRODUCTS/OPERATIONS

2011 Sales

	$ mil.	% of total
Interest		
Loans including fees	129	73
Securities	30	17
Other	1	1
Noninterest		
Fees for services to customers	8	5
Trustco Financial Services	5	3
Other	2	1
Total	177	100

COMPETITORS

Arrow Financial
Ballston Spa Bancorp
Bank of America
Citizens Financial Group
HSBC USA
Hudson Valley FCU
KeyCorp
M&T Bank
NBT Bancorp

HISTORICAL FINANCIALS

Company Type: Public

Income Statement   FYE: December 31

	ASSETS ($ mil.)	NET INCOME ($ mil.)	INCOME AS % OF ASSETS	EMPLOYEES
12/17	4,908	43	0.9%	846
12/16	4,868	42	0.9%	808
12/15	4,734	42	0.9%	787
12/14	4,644	44	1.0%	737
12/13	4,521	39	0.9%	708
Annual Growth	2.1%	2.0%	—	4.6%

2017 Year-End Financials

Debt ratio: 9.68%
Return on equity: 9.68%
Cash ($ mil.): 612
Current ratio: —
Long-term debt ($ mil.): —

No. of shares (mil.): 96
Dividends
 Yield: 0.0%
 Payout: 58.5%
Market value ($ mil.): 886

	STOCK PRICE ($)	P/E	PER SHARE ($)		
	FY Close	High/Low	Earnings	Dividends	Book Value
12/17	9.20	22 16	0.45	0.26	4.76
12/16	8.75	20 12	0.45	0.26	4.52
12/15	6.14	16 13	0.44	0.26	4.34
12/14	7.26	16 13	0.47	0.26	4.15
12/13	7.18	18 12	0.42	0.26	3.83
Annual Growth	6.4%	—	1.5%	(0.0%)	5.6%

Trustmark Corp

Trustmark Corporation is the holding company for Trustmark National Bank which has 208 locations mainly in Mississippi but also in East Texas the Florida panhandle and Tennessee where it also operates its Somerville Bank & Trust subsidiary in the Memphis area. Focusing on individuals and small businesses Trustmark offers a range of financial products and services such as checking and savings accounts certificates of deposit credit cards insurance investments and trust services. The diversified financial services firm has about $11.7 billion in assets.

Operations

Trustmark operates through three operating segments: General Banking Insurance and Wealth Management.

The General Banking Division is responsible for all traditional banking products and services including a full range of commercial and consumer banking services such as checking accounts savings programs overdraft facilities commercial installment and real estate loans home equity loans and lines of credit drive-in and night deposit services and safe deposit facilities offered through 208 offices in Alabama Florida Mississippi Tennessee and Texas.

The Wealth Management Division serve Trustmark's customers as a financial partner providing reliable guidance and sound practical advice for accumulating preserving and transferring wealth. Trustmark's Insurance Division provides a full range of retail insurance products including commercial risk management products bonding group benefits and personal lines coverage through Trustmark National Bank subsidiary FBBI a Mississippi corporation.

Subsidiary Fisher Brown Bottrell sells insurance while Trustmark Investment Advisors provides wealth management products and services including the proprietary Performance Fund family of mutual funds. The latter unit has approximately $9 billion of assets under management.

Geographic Reach

Mississippi by far is Trustmark's largest market accounting for 63% of 2013 revenues. Tennessee Texas and Florida contributed about 9% 7% and 10% respectively.

Financial Performance

After experiencing a revenue dip in 2012 due to decrease in interest income in 2013 Trustmark's revenues increased by 8% thanks to an increase in the net interest income due to a significant increase in interest and fees on acquired loans related to the BancTrust acquisition as well as modest declines in the cost of interest-bearing deposits. These gains were partially offset by downward repricing of loans and securities. After experiencing sizable growth over the last few years in 2013 Trustmark's net income decreased to $117.1 million (from $117.2 million in 2012) due to an increase in the noninterest expenses as a result of BancTrust non-routine merger expenses and increases in salaries and employee benefits services and fees and ORE/foreclosure expenses.

In 2013 the company's operating cash inflow increased to $155.4 million (compared to $92.1 million in 2012) was due to a major increase in net assets and liabilities and a decline in purchases and originations of loans held for sale.

Strategy

Trustmark is growing its branch network by opening or acquiring new offices with a focus on the Houston and Memphis markets.

In 2013 Trustmark opened a new 12000-sq.-ft. office location on the first and second floors of the Nexen Building in Bunker Hill. Trustmark operates 15 locations in the Houston market with loans outstanding of approximately $835 million and deposits of approximately $425 million.

Mergers and Acquisitions

In 2013 the company purchased two branches in Oxford Mississippi from SOUTHBank F.S.B. That year it also bought Mobile Alabama-based BancTrust Financial Group for $55 million providing Trustmark entry into more than 15 markets in Alabama and enhancing the Trustmark franchise in the Florida Panhandle.

Company Background

Trustmark grew in 2011 with the FDIC-assisted acquisition of Heritage Banking Group. It took over the failed bank's assets and deposits after the institution was closed by regulators. The transaction added four bank branches in Mississippi (four other locations were consolidated due to their proximity to existing Trustmark branches).

BlackRock Inc. owns more than 11% of Trustmark Corp's. shares.

Trustmark National Bank traces its roots to 1889 when it was first chartered in Mississippi.

EXECUTIVES

Treasurer And Director; President And Coo Financial Services Group Trustmark National Bank, Gerard R. (Jerry) Host, age 63, $730,000 total compensation

President Corporate Banking Trustmark National Bank, Duane A. Dewey, age 59, $348,840 total compensation

Treasurer And Principal Financial Officertrustmark Corporation And Evp And Cfo Trustmark National Bank, Louis E. Greer, age 63, $360,000 total compensation

President Mortgage Services Trustmark National Bank, Breck W. Tyler, age 60, $306,000 total compensation

President Wealth Management Trustmark National Bank, W. Arthur Stevens, age 53, $333,540 total compensation

Vice President And Trust Officer In The Trust Department, Agnes Tribble

Assistant Vice President, Marian Alderman

Senior Vice President Trustmark National Bank, Murray Fincher

Senior Vice President, Monica Day

Vice President Advertising, Kristine Jacobs

Vice President, Vincent Powell

Executive Vice President, Kirk Whitehouse

Vice President Commercial Banking, Colby Calcote

Assistant Vice President, Sue Hancock

Vice President Mortgage Compliance Risk Manager, Melissa West

First Vice President, Bethany L Smith

Assistant Vice President And Strategic Sourcing, Matt Noland

Vice President Sugar Land Commercial Banking, John Martinez

Vice President Mortgage Loan Originator, Jason Hebert

Senior Vice President Commercial Banking, Scott Killman

Vice President, Gloria Craig

Chairman, R. Michael Summerford, age 69

Auditors: Crowe Horwath LLP

LOCATIONS

HQ: Trustmark Corp
   248 East Capitol Street, Jackson, MS 39201
Phone: 601 208-5111   **Fax:** 601 354-5053
Web: www.trustmark.com

2016 Sales

	% of total
Mississippi	65
Alabama	12
Florida	8
Texas	8
Tennessee	7
Total	**100**

PRODUCTS/OPERATIONS

2016 Sales

	% of total
General Banking	91
Insurance	5
Wealth Management	4
Total	**100**

2016 Sales

	$ mil.	% of total
Interest Income:		
Interest and fees on LHFS & LHFI	299	51
Interest on securities	81	14
Interest and fees on acquired loans	30	5
Other interest income	1	-
Noninterest Income:		
Service charges on deposit accounts	45	8
Insurance commissions	36	6
Bank card and other fees	27	5
Mortgage banking net	28	5
Wealth management	30	5
Other net	5	1
Securities (losses) gains net	(0.3)	-
Total	**586**	**100**

COMPETITORS

BancorpSouth	Hancock Holding
Capital One	Regions Financial
Citizens Holding	Renasant
First Horizon	Wells Fargo
Great Southern Bancorp	

HISTORICAL FINANCIALS

Company Type: Public

Income Statement

FYE: December 31

	ASSETS ($ mil.)	NET INCOME ($ mil.)	INCOME AS % OF ASSETS	EMPLOYEES
12/17	13,797	105	0.8%	2,893
12/16	13,352	108	0.8%	2,788
12/15	12,678	116	0.9%	2,941
12/14	12,250	123	1.0%	3,060
12/13	11,790	117	1.0%	3,110
Annual Growth	**4.0%**	**(2.5%)**	**—**	**(1.8%)**

2017 Year-End Financials

Debt ratio: 0.45%	No. of shares (mil.): 67
Return on equity: 6.83%	Dividends
Cash ($ mil.): 335	Yield: 0.0%
Current ratio: —	Payout: 58.9%
Long-term debt ($ mil.): —	Market value ($ mil.): 2,158

	STOCK PRICE ($) FY Close	P/E High/Low	PER SHARE ($) Earnings	Dividends	Book Value
12/17	31.86	23 18	1.56	0.92	23.20
12/16	35.65	23 12	1.60	0.92	22.48
12/15	23.04	15 12	1.71	0.92	21.80
12/14	24.54	15 12	1.83	0.92	21.04
12/13	26.84	16 13	1.75	0.92	20.11
Annual Growth	**4.4%**	**— —**	**(2.8%)**	**(0.0%)**	**3.6%**

Tutor Perini Corp

Construction company Tutor Perini builds projects ranging from casinos and hotels to highways and housing developments. One of the largest builders in the US the company also builds schools health care facilities airports and industrial buildings. Tutor Perini and its subsidiaries provide preconstruction and design-build services general contracting equipment materials subcontracting and other services. Its Civil arm which includes subsidiaries Tutor-Saliba Cherry Hill Construction and Lunda Construction builds and maintains highways bridges and mass transit. The Buildings segment constructs buildings in the hospitality gaming and other industries while the Specialty contracting division builds electrical and mechanical systems.

Operations

Tutor Perini operates through three business segments. The Building segment accounts for about 40% of revenue while the firm's Civil and Specialty Contractors segments account for about a third and a quarter of revenue respectively.

The Building group includes subsidiaries Tutor Perini Building Corp. James A. Cummings Inc. Rudolph and Sletten Inc. Keating Building and Roy Anderson Corp. (formerly known as Anderson Companies). The segment focuses on large and complex projects for public and private clients. Major projects include parts of the Hudson Yards project in New York City work on McCarran International Airport in Las Vegas and the San Diego California courthouse.

The Civil group includes subsidiaries Cherry Hill Construction Frontier-Kemper Construction and Becho. The segment specializes in repairing and improving highways bridges tunnels mass-transit systems and water management and wastewater treatment facilities in US.

Specialty Contractors includes subsidiaries Desert Mechanical Superior Gunite WDF and GreenStar Services. The segment specializes in electrical mechanical plumbing HVAC and fire protection systems.

Geographic Reach

About 95% of Tutor Perini's revenue comes from the US where the firm performs work across most major geographic areas. Overseas Tutor Perini has completed projects for the US military in Guam Iraq Haiti and Afghanistan. The company has its headquarters in Los Angeles California.

Sales and Marketing

Tutor Perini works on more than 1500 construction projects a year for federal state and local government agencies and authorities and private clients. Private clients include major hospitality and gaming resort owners Native American sovereign nations public corporations private developers healthcare companies and private universities. Its state and local clients include state transportation departments metropolitan authorities cities schools and municipalities. Federal agency clients include the US State Department the US Navy the US Army Corps of Engineers the US Air Force and the National Parks Service.

About half of Tutor Perini's revenue comes from state and local governments about 45% from the private sector and about 5% from federal agencies.

Financial Performance

Tutor-Perini's six-year streak of rising revenue halted in 2017 when sales slipped 4% from 2016. Over that time revenue increased about 8% a year.

The revenue reduction to $4.8 billion in 2017 compared to about $5 billion in 2016 resulted from decreased volume in the company's Building and Civil segments because of projects that were completed or nearing completion. Tutor Perini reported higher volume on some Civil segment projects in California and New York and Building segment projects in California and Maryland. The Building and Civil segments had projects in early stages (when revenue is lower) which also pinched 2017 revenue.

Tutor Perini's profit jumped 55% to about $149 million in 2017 from 2016 boosted by a $53 million tax benefit from the US Tax Cuts and Jobs Act and $37 million from a legal settlement.

The company's cash holdings were about $193 million at the end of 2017 compared to $146 million in 2016. Its cash flow from operations was about $164 million in 2017 and it used $41 million in investing activities (for equipment) and about $75 million in financing activities.

Strategy

Tutor Perini is banking on a wave of infrastructure spending to boost revenue. In recent elections voters around the US approved about $200 billion of state and local transportation funding (including more than $50 billion in California) that will be spent in the coming years. It has major transportation projects underway in California New York and the Midwest. On the federal level the company has expectations for infrastructure spending aimed at road improvements nationwide. Tutor Perini has a project backlog with a value of about $7.3 billion.

Internally Tutor Perini has taken steps to improve its operations and measures progress by calling for cash generated by operations to exceed net income. That was accomplished for the second time in 2017 helped by making operating cash performance part of senior executives' compensation incentives. The company also focuses on managing its working capital management effectively and improving its billing and collection cycle.

Company Background

Several years ago Tutor Perini focused on acquiring companies that showed success in their markets to grow vertically and geographically. In 2011 Tutor Perini strengthened its building business (especially in the Southeast) when it acquired Anderson Companies the privately held parent of Roy Anderson Corporation Harrell Contracting and Brice Building. It then acquired Midwest heavy civil builder Lunda Construction. The company initially boosted its civil segment with the 2008 merger of Tutor-Saliba. And in 2011 it acquired Frontier-Kemper an Indiana-based builder of highways roads and rapid transit systems and Lunda Construction a Wisconsin-based heavy civil contractor.

Tutor Perini traces its roots to 1894 when Italian stonemason Bonfiglio Perini created a small family-owned civil works contracting business in Boston. The company went public in 1961. CEO Ronald Tutor owns about 22% of Tutor Perini.

EXECUTIVES

Executive Vice President Chief Operations Officer, Jack Frost

President And Ceo Perini Management Services, Robert Band, age 70, $600,024 total compensation

Chairman And Ceo, Ronald N. (Ron) Tutor, age 77, $1,750,000 total compensation

President And Ceo Rudolph And Sletten, Martin B. Sisemore

Evp, Craig W. Shaw, age 63, $650,024 total compensation

President And Ceo Roy Anderson Corp., Roy Anderson, age 60

President Fisk Electric, Darrell W. Harwood

President And Ceo Lunda Construction, Dennis L. Behnke

Evp And Cfo, Gary G. Smalley, age 60, $700,000 total compensation

President And Coo; Ceo Civil Group, James A. (Jack) Frost, age 65, $1,000,000 total compensation

President And Ceo Frontier-kemper Constructors, W. David Rogstad

President Tutor Perini Civil East, Ali M. Catik

President And Ceo Wdf, Lawrence (Larry) Roman

President And Coo Nagelbush Mechanical, Peter McCann

President Desert Mechanical, Joseph Guglielmo

President And Ceo Superior Gunite, Anthony J. Federico

President And Ceo Five Star Electric, Robert Saville

Evp And President And Ceo Building Group, Leonard J. Rejcek

Vice President Business Development, Stephen Buschmeyer

Senior Vice President, Danny Hoisman

Regional Vice President, Travis Burton

Senior Vice President Business Development, Joe Perini

Vice President Of Operations, Vince Pizzi

Vice President, Scott Christensen

Vice President Of Business Development, Buschmeyer Stephen

Vice President Special Projects, Steve Lewis

Vice President Operations, Ghassan Ariqat

Vp Estimating Cherry Hill Construction, Bernard Beauchemin

Auditors: Deloitte & Touche LLP

LOCATIONS

HQ: Tutor Perini Corp
 15901 Olden Street, Sylmar, CA 91342-1093
Phone: 818 362-8391
Web: www.tutorperini.com

2017 Sales

	% of total
United States	97
Foreign and US territories	3
Total	**100**

PRODUCTS/OPERATIONS

2017 sales

	$ mil.	% of total
Building	1,941	41
Civil	1,602	34
Specialty contractors	1,213	25
Total	**4,757**	**100**

2016 -Customer Type

Customers	% of total
State and Local Agencies	47
Private Owners	46
Federal Agencies	7
Total	**100**

Selected Subsidiaries

Building Group
 Roy Anderson Corp.
 James A. Cummings Inc.
 Keating Building Corporation
 Rudolph and Sletten Inc.
 Tutor-Saliba Corporation
 Tutor Perini Building Corp.
Civil Group
 Cherry Hill Construction Inc.
 Frontier-Kemper Constructors
 Lunda Construction Company
 Tutor Perini Corporation
 Tutor-Saliba Corporation
Becho Inc.
 Black Construction Corporation
Specialty Contractors Group
 Desert Mechanical Inc.
 Fisk Electric Corporation
 Five Star Electric
 Nagelbush
 GreenStar Services Corporation
 Superior Gunite
 WDF Inc.

COMPETITORS

AECOM	Kiewit Power
American	Constructors
Infrastructure	M. A. Mortenson
Balfour Beatty	Marnell Corrao
Construction	McCarthy Building
Barton Malow	PCL Constructors
CH2M HILL	PCL Employees Holdings
Clark Enterprises	Skanska USA Civil
DPR Construction	Suffolk Construction
Dragados	Swinerton
Flatiron Construction	Traylor Bros.
Fluor	Tully Construction
Gilbane	Turner Construction
Granite Construction	Turner Corporation
Hardin Construction	Walsh Group
Hensel Phelps	Webcor Builders
Construction	Weitz
Hunt Construction	Whiting-Turner
J.E. Dunn Construction	Yates Companies
Group	dck worldwide
KBR	

HISTORICAL FINANCIALS

Company Type: Public

Income Statement
FYE: December 31

	REVENUE ($ mil.)	NET INCOME ($ mil.)	NET PROFIT MARGIN	EMPLOYEES
12/17	4,757	148	3.1%	10,061
12/16	4,973	95	1.9%	11,603
12/15	4,920	45	0.9%	10,626
12/14	4,492	107	2.4%	10,939
12/13	4,175	87	2.1%	10,206
Annual Growth	3.3%	14.2%	—	(0.4%)

2017 Year-End Financials

Debt ratio: 17.27%
Return on equity: 9.09%
Cash ($ mil.): 192
Current ratio: 1.94
Long-term debt ($ mil.): 705

No. of shares (mil.): 49
Dividends
Yield: —
Payout: —
Market value ($ mil.): 1,262

	STOCK PRICE ($) FY Close	P/E High/Low		PER SHARE ($) Earnings	Dividends	Book Value
12/17	25.35	11	8	2.92	0.00	34.42
12/16	28.00	15	5	1.92	0.00	31.56
12/15	16.74	29	17	0.91	0.00	28.94
12/14	24.07	14	9	2.20	0.00	28.06
12/13	26.30	14	8	1.80	0.00	25.76
Annual Growth	(0.9%)	—	—	12.9%	—	7.5%

HISTORICAL FINANCIALS

Company Type: Public

Income Statement
FYE: June 30

	REVENUE ($ mil.)	NET INCOME ($ mil.)	NET PROFIT MARGIN	EMPLOYEES
06/18	30,400	4,464	14.7%	22,400
06/17	28,500	2,952	10.4%	21,700
06/16	27,326	2,755	10.1%	21,500
06/15	28,987	8,306	28.7%	20,500
06/14	31,867	4,514	14.2%	27,000
Annual Growth	(1.2%)	(0.3%)	—	(4.6%)

2018 Year-End Financials

Debt ratio: 36.27%
Return on equity: 25.30%
Cash ($ mil.): 7,622
Current ratio: 2.35
Long-term debt ($ mil.): 18,469

No. of shares (mil.): 1,852
Dividends
Yield: 0.0%
Payout: 15.0%
Market value ($ mil.): 92,053

	STOCK PRICE ($) FY Close	P/E High/Low		PER SHARE ($) Earnings	Dividends	Book Value
06/18	49.69	21	10	2.40	0.36	10.56
06/17	28.34	20	15	1.59	0.36	8.49
06/16	27.05	24	17	1.42	0.30	7.31
06/15	32.55	10	8	3.90	0.28	8.45
06/14	35.15	18	15	1.99	0.25	7.89
Annual Growth	9.0%	—	—	4.8%	9.5%	7.6%

Twenty-First Century Fox Inc

EXECUTIVES

Ceo, James R Murdoch
Exec Chb, K Rupert Murdoch
Exec Chb, Lachlan K Murdoch
Chb, Chase Carey
Sr Exec V Pres-Cfo, John P Nallen
Sr Exec V Pres-Group Gen Couns, Gerson Zweifach
Pres, Peter Rice
Clpo, Viet D Dinh
Associate Director, Hector Chacon
Executive Vice-President, Paul Haggerty
Editor, Alex Moore
Auditors: Ernst & Young LLP

LOCATIONS

HQ: Twenty-First Century Fox Inc
1211 Avenue of the Americas, New York, NY 10036
Phone: 212 852-7000
Web: www.21cf.com

COMPETITORS

Advance Publications	Pearson plc
Bertelsmann	Reed Elsevier Group
Bloomberg L.P.	Sony Pictures
CBS Corp	Entertainment
Disney	Thomson Reuters
Gannett	Time Warner
Hearst Corporation	Tribune Company
MGM	Viacom
NBCUniversal	Washington Post
New York Times	

Tyson Foods Inc

Tyson Foods spreads its wings beyond the chicken coop. While it is one of the largest US chicken producers (processing capacity of some 42 million a week) Tyson's Fresh Meats division makes it a giant in the beef and pork sectors. The company also offers value-added processed and pre-cooked meats and refrigerated and frozen prepared foods. Its chicken operations are vertically integrated — the company hatches the eggs supplies contract growers with the chicks and feed and brings them back for processing when ready. Tyson's brands include Tyson Jimmy Dean Hillshire Farm Ball Park Wright ibp Aidells and State Fair. Its customers include retail wholesale and food service companies worldwide.

HISTORY

During the Great Depression Arkansas poultry farmer John Tyson supported his family by selling vegetables and poultry. In 1935 after developing a method for transporting live poultry (he installed a food-and-water trough and nailed small feed cups on a trailer) he bought 500 chickens in Arkansas and sold them in Chicago.

For the next decade Tyson bought sold and transported chickens. By 1947 the year he incorporated the company as Tyson Feed & Hatchery he was raising the chickens himself. He emphasized chicken production opening his first processing plant in 1958 in Springdale where he implemented an ice-packing system that allowed the company to send its products greater distances.

John's son Don took over as manager in 1960 and in 1963 it went public as Tyson Foods. Tyson Country Fresh Chicken (packaged chicken that would become the company's mainstay) was introduced in 1967.

Rapid expansion included a new egg-processing building (1970) a new plant and computerized feed mill (1971) and the acquisitions of Prospect Farms (1969 precooked chicken) and the Ocoma Foods Division (1972 poultry) as well as hog operations.

Health-conscious consumers increasingly turned from red meats to poultry during the 1980s. Tyson became the industry leader with several key acquisitions of poultry operations including the Tastybird division of Valmac (1985) Lane Processing (1986) and Heritage Valley (1986). Its 1989 purchase of Holly Farms added beef and pork processing.

Don Tyson relinquished the CEO position to Leland Tollett in 1991. The company increased its presence in Mexico the next year through a joint venture with poultry producer Trasgo. Also in 1992 the firm plunged into seafood with the purchase of Arctic Alaska Fisheries and Louis Kemp Seafood.

Tyson bought Culinary Foods (frozen foods) and Trasgo in 1994 and the seafood division of International Multifoods in 1995. High feed costs and an oversupply of chickens brought down company earnings the next year. In 1997 the company pleaded guilty to charges that it illegally gave former Agriculture Secretary Mike Espy thousands of dollars' worth of gifts; the settlement included $6 million in fines and fees.

Tyson bought embattled Hudson Foods' poultry operations in 1998. The company said it would take a charge that year of $196 million to restructure. It also sold turkey processor Willow Brook Foods (now part of Cargill Meat Solutions) to Willow Brook management in 1998. That year John H. Tyson grandson of the founder was elected chairman.

In 1999 Tyson sold its seafood business for about $180 million in a two-part transaction to International Home Foods and Trident Seafoods. John Tyson became CEO in 2000.

As the winner in a bidding war with Smithfield Foods in 2001 Tyson agreed to buy IBP Inc. the #1 beef processor and #2 pork processor in the US for nearly $3.2 billion. Tyson tried to back away from the table after accounting irregularities were discovered at an IBP subsidiary but a Delaware judge ordered Tyson to sit down and finish dinner. The deal was made final in September and Tyson changed the beef processor's name to IBP Fresh Meats.

In late 2001 Tyson Foods and six managers were indicted for conspiring to smuggle illegal immigrants from Mexico and Central America to work for lower than legal wages in 15 of its US poultry processing plants. Two managers made plea bargains and testified for the government; another manager committed suicide. Tyson and the remaining three managers were acquitted of the conspiracy charges

EXECUTIVES

Svp Legal Services And Assistant Secretary, David L. Van Bebber, age 62
Evp And Chief Human Resources Officer, Mary A. Oleksiuk, age 56
Svp Fresh Meats Sales And Marketing, Noel White, age 60, $777,716 total compensation
Cfo, Stewart F. Glendinning, age 52
President North American Foodservice And International, Andrew P. (Andy) Callahan, age 51
President North American Retail, Sally Grimes, age 46
Evp Operations Services, Howell P. (Hal) Carper, age 63
President Ceo And Director, Thomas P. (Tom) Hayes, age 52, $712,954 total compensation
Chief Growth Officer, Monica McGurk, age 47
President Poultry Operations, Doug Ramsey
Cto, Scott Spradley

Senior Vice President Corporate International Human Resources, Russell Tooley

Vice President Recruitment Retention And Education, Larry Hopkins

Vp Is Manufacturing, Lyle Nicholson

Svp And Chief Environmental Health And Safety Officer, Kevin Igli

Vice President Of Direct Materials, Lindsay Piepho

Vice President Generate Demand, Sue Quillin

Vice President Of Operations, Rob Tankeley

Senior Vice President Of Operations, Steve Taylor

Vice President Of Business Development, Lori Simco

Executive Vice President Corporate Strategy And Chief Sustainability Officer, Justin Whitmore

Vice President Customer Services, Cary Wiese

Vice President Marketing, Bill Welsh

Senior Vice President Operations, Roy Slaughter

Vice President Of Human Resources Operations, Hector Gonzalez

Vice President Marketing Services, Susan Quillin

Division Vice President, David Mantooth

Vice President Government Relations, Chuck Penry

Senior Vice President Consumer Products, Gary Sheneman

Vice President Information Technology, Nancy Higginbotham

Sls Deli Vice President, Brent Schmiegelow

Vice President Food Service Sales East, Mike Curtin

Vice President Engineering, Scott Henkes

Vice President, James Lochner

Senior Vice President, Craig Hart

National Account Manager, Steve Maher

National Account Manager, Kevin Gaffney

Vice President International Finance And Accountin, Hubert Mendonca

National Account Manager, Dave Collins

Vice President And General Manager Hillshire Farm Aidells Gallo Deli Portfolio And Regional Brands, Jeff Caswell

Vice President Shared Accounting Services, Alan Shanks

Vice President Of Information Systems, Carla T Woods

Vp Foodservice Channel Development, Kristin Bird

Vice President Engineering, Kent Bearson

Vice President Marketing Services, Christopher Miles

Vice President Division, Melvin Fulsom

Senior Vice President President Specialt, Patrick O'ray

Board Member, Kevin McNamara

Chairman, John H. Tyson, age 65

Board Member, Robert Thurber

Board Member, Brad Sauer

Board Member, Barbara Tyson

Board Member, Mikel Durham

Board Member, Mike Beebe

Secretary Iv, Bobbie Meredith

Auditors: PricewaterhouseCoopers LLP

LOCATIONS

HQ: Tyson Foods Inc
2200 West Don Tyson Parkway, Springdale, AR 72762-6999
Phone: 479 290-4000   **Fax:** 479 290-7984
Web: www.tyson.com

PRODUCTS/OPERATIONS

2018 Sales

	% of total
Beef	38
Chicken	29
Prepared foods	21
Pork	12
Other	
Inter segment Sales	-
Total	**100**

COMPETITORS

Cargill	Pilgrim's Pride
ConAgra	Rosen's Diversified
Foster Farms	Sanderson Farms
Hormel	Smithfield Foods
JBS	U.S. Premium Beef
Koch Foods	WH Group
Kraft Heinz	Wayne Farms
Perdue Incorporated	

HISTORICAL FINANCIALS

Company Type: Public

Income Statement
FYE: September 29

	REVENUE ($ mil.)	NET INCOME ($ mil.)	NET PROFIT MARGIN	EMPLOYEES
09/18	40,052	3,024	7.6%	121,000
09/17*	38,260	1,774	4.6%	122,000
10/16	36,881	1,768	4.8%	114,000
10/15	41,373	1,220	2.9%	113,000
09/14	37,580	864	2.3%	124,000
Annual Growth	**1.6%**	**36.8%**	**—**	**(0.6%)**

*Fiscal year change

2018 Year-End Financials

Debt ratio: 33.92%	No. of shares (mil.): 366
Return on equity: 25.98%	Dividends
Cash ($ mil.): 270	Yield: 0.0%
Current ratio: 1.13	Payout: 14.6%
Long-term debt ($ mil.): 7,962	Market value ($ mil.): 21,788

	STOCK PRICE ($) FY Close	P/E High/Low		PER SHARE ($) Earnings	Dividends	Book Value
09/18	59.53	5	4	8.19	1.20	34.98
09/17*	70.45	15	11	4.79	0.90	28.64
10/16	74.67	16	9	4.53	0.60	26.61
10/15	44.39	15	12	2.95	0.40	26.26
09/14	37.74	18	11	2.37	0.30	23.64
Annual Growth	**12.1%**	**—**	**—**	**36.3%**	**41.4%**	**10.3%**

*Fiscal year change

UGI Corp.

UGI Corporation is a leading energy products supplier to residential commercial agricultural and wholesale customers across the US and Europe. The company stores transports and markets propane liquefied petroleum gases (LPG) and natural gas; it also generates some electricity. In the US UGI serves some 2.2 million customers thanks to its partnership with AmeriGas Partners and several subsidiaries. In addition product installation and maintenance services are available to Pennsylvania Delaware and Maryland customers of UGI. Its trade names include AmeriGas America?s Propane Company and Heritage Propane.

Operations

UGI operates through four segments: AmeriGas Propane UGI International Midstream and Marketing and UGI Utilities.

AmeriGas Propane (about 40% of revenue) primarily distributes propane across the US. It also sells installs and services related appliances in Pennsylvania Delaware and Maryland.

UGI International (some 30% revenue) distributes propane across some 20 countries in Europe through subsidiaries like UGI France SAS Flaga GmbH and AvantiGas. It also markets energy products in France Belgium Denmark the Netherlands and the UK.

Midstream and Marketing (15% revenue) markets energy products in the US mid-Atlantic region manages midstream assets produces some electricity and provides project management services in Pennsylvania.

UGI Utilities conducts the regulated natural gas and electric distribution business in Pennsylvania and one Maryland county and brings in another 15% of company revenue.

Geographic Reach

UGI has propane and LPG distribution and marketing customers across the US (with significant concentration in Pennsylvania) and nearly 20 countries in Europe primarily France Belgium Denmark the Netherlands and the UK.

The US accounts for about 70% of total revenue.

Sales and Marketing

UGI sells natural gas electricity and liquid fuels to some 12500 residential commercial and industrial customers across 35000 US locations while its Utilities segment serves about 642000 natural gas customers in Pennsylvania and some 500 customers in Maryland.

In Europe UGI sells some 950 million gallons of LPG to about 550000 customers in almost 20 countries.

Financial Performance

In the past ten years UGI revenue has vacillated between a low of $5.6 billion (2010) and a high of $8.3 billion (2014) with an average revenue fluctuation of $1 billion year-over-year. During the same period the company?s net income has averaged around $250 million but has seen improvement in the last couple of years.

Revenue (ended September 30) increased 25% to $7.6 billion in 2018 thanks to higher gas usage due to colder than usual winter in the US.

Net income rose from $436 million in 2017 to $718 million in 2018 mostly due to a YOY $145 million reduction in income taxes.

Cash holdings at UGI stood at $452 million. Operations provided $1 billion in cash inflows offset by $747 million going towards investments and a further $438 million going towards financing activities.

Strategy

Facing a gradual decline in its propane sales UGI is betting its growth strategy on three fronts? capacity building in Midstream acquisition in the International segment and upgrades in Utilities.

Keen to expand inorganically UGI is busy acquiring companies on one hand and reducing operational costs on the other. Instances of acquisition include Texas Creek and the Endless Mountain gas gathering systems in UGI?s Midstream & Marketing segment and the retail natural gas business of South Jersey Industries by UGI Energy Services. The larger US utility companies are following an M&A trend (for instance SCANA merged with Dominion) which is essential for vital infrastructure upgrades.

To raise money UGI is cutting costs through efficiency programs of legacy businesses as well as gaining synergy costs from integrating newer acquisitions. For instance within AmeriGas propane UGI reduced distribution costs while registering higher online customer accounts. Meanwhile higher than-expected synergies were reported by the integration of previously acquired companies (2015-18 period) including Finagaz and LPG businesses in Sweden Netherlands and Italy.

The company is equally focused on customer base expansion. A 2018 regulatory merger approval of its three utility companies and some $340 million in distribution system upgrades should help UGI Utilities to further expand. It added over 14000 new residential and commercial heating customers during the year.

Mergers and Acquisitions

UGI Energy Services a subsidiary of UGI Corp. acquired the retail natural gas business of South

Jersey Industries Inc. in December 2018. Through the agreement UGI gained 2500 commercial and industrial customer contracts of South Jersey Energy including supply service to nearly 6000 locations. The strategic acquisition will allow UGI to further grow its retail natural gas business strengthening its reach in the mid-Atlantic region.

Also in fiscal 2018 the company completed the purchase of Hunlock Energy LLC a 44-megawatt natural gas-fired peaking turbine in Luzerne County PA.

In 2017 UGI International through European subsidiaries Flaga and AvantiGas spent a total of $120 million to acquire Kosan Gas (LPG marketing and distribution) in Sweden DVEP Investeringen (natural gas and electric marketing) in the Netherlands and UniverGas (LPG distribution) in Italy.

UGI International also acquired several LPG distribution businesses with operations in Austria Norway and the UK for $24 million.

HISTORY

United Gas Improvement was set up in 1882 by Philadelphia industrialist Thomas Dolan and other investors to acquire a gasworks and a new coalgas manufacturing process. The firm also bought electric utilities and street railways across the US and moved into construction. The 1935 Public Utility Holding Company Act led to United Gas Improvement's restructuring when the SEC ordered the divestiture of many of its operations in 1941. The company converted to natural gas in the 1950s and entered the liquefied petroleum gas (LPG) business in 1959. It became UGI Corporation in 1968.

UGI shifted its emphasis to propane in the late 1980s buying Petrolane in 1995 and combining it with AmeriGas Propane to create AmeriGas Partners which then went public. Overseas UGI launched a joint venture in 1996 to build an LPG import project in Romania. The next year it signed a deal to distribute propane in China.

EXECUTIVES

Vp New Business Development; President Ugi Enterprises And Ugi Energy Services, Bradley C. Hall, age 65, $390,723 total compensation

President And Ceo, John L. Walsh, age 63, $1,078,342 total compensation

Cfo, Kirk R. Oliver, age 60, $532,902 total compensation

Vp General Counsel And Secretary, Monica M. Gaudiosi, age 56, $434,611 total compensation

President And Ceo Ugi Utilities, Robert F. (Bob) Beard, age 52

Ceo Antargaz, Eric Naddeo

President And Ceo Amerigas, Jerry E. Sheridan, age 52, $526,474 total compensation

Managing Director Avantigas, Neil Murphy

President Ugi International, Roger Perreault

Vp Commodity Marketing Ugi Energy Services, Michael Gibbs

Vice President Finance, Bill Wilson

Vp It And Administration, Amy Hunt

Regional Vice President, Steve Quagliana

Vice President Finance And Administration, David Pataki

Vice President Sales Ugi Amerigas, Warren Patterson

Vice President Midstream Assets And Services Ugi Energy Services, Peter Terranova

Vp Supply Chain Amerigas, Kevin Rumbelow

Vice President Supply And Logistics Amerigas, David Lugar

Vice Presidenr And General Counsel, Bob Knauss

Vp Finance, Peter Kelly

Treasurer, Robert Knauss

Chairman, Marvin O. Schlanger, age 70
Board Member, Ernest Jones
Board Member, Frank Hermance
Board Member, James B Stallings
Auditors: Ernst & Young LLP

LOCATIONS

HQ: UGI Corp.
460 North Gulph Road, King of Prussia, PA 19406
Phone: 610 337-1000
Web: www.ugicorp.com

PRODUCTS/OPERATIONS

2018 Sales

	$ mil.	% of total
AmeriGas propane	2,823	35
UGI International	2,683	33
Midstream & Marketing	1,421	18
UGI Utilities	1,092	14
Corporate	1	-
Adjustments	(370.8)	-
Total	**7,651**	**100**

Selected Subsidiaries and Affiliates

AmeriGas Inc.
AmeriGas Propane Inc.
  AmeriGas Partners L.P. (26%)
  AmeriGas Propane L.P.
  AmeriGas Technology Group Inc.
  Petrolane Incorporated
  Four Flags Drilling Company Inc.
Ashtola Production Company
  UGI Ethanol Development Corporation
Newbury Holding Company
UGI Enterprises Inc. (energy marketing and services)
  CFN Enterprises Inc.
  Eastfield International Holdings Inc.
  FLAGA GmbH (propane distribution; Austria the Czech Republic and Slovakia)
  Eurogas Holdings Inc.
  McHugh Service Company
  UGI Energy Services Inc.
  GASMARK (gas marketing)
  POWERMARK (electricity marketing)
  UGI International Enterprises Inc.
  UGI Europe Inc.
  Antargaz (propane distribution France)
  FLAGA GmbH (propane distribution Austria)
UGI Properties Inc.
UGI Utilities Inc. (natural gas and electric utility)
United Valley Insurance Company

COMPETITORS

Chesapeake Utilities	Ferrellgas Partners
Dominion Energy	National Fuel Gas
Duquesne Light Holdings	NorthWestern
Energy Transfer	PPL Corporation
Exelon	Suburban Propane

HISTORICAL FINANCIALS

Company Type: Public

Income Statement

FYE: September 30

	REVENUE ($ mil.)	NET INCOME ($ mil.)	NET PROFIT MARGIN	EMPLOYEES
09/18	7,651	718	9.4%	13,000
09/17	6,120	436	7.1%	13,000
09/16	5,685	364	6.4%	13,320
09/15	6,691	281	4.2%	13,570
09/14	8,277	337	4.1%	12,800
Annual Growth	**(1.9%)**	**20.8%**	**—**	**0.4%**

2018 Year-End Financials

Debt ratio: 38.31%
Return on equity: 21.00%
Cash ($ mil.): 452
Current ratio: 1.09
Long-term debt ($ mil.): 4,146
No. of shares (mil.): 173
Dividends
  Yield: 0.0%
  Payout: 25.1%
Market value ($ mil.): 9,640

	STOCK PRICE ($) FY Close	P/E High/Low		PER SHARE ($) Earnings	Dividends	Book Value
09/18	55.48	13	10	4.06	1.02	21.19
09/17	46.86	21	17	2.46	0.98	18.27
09/16	45.24	23	15	2.08	0.93	16.48
09/15	34.82	24	20	1.60	0.89	15.62
09/14	34.09	28	17	1.92	0.79	15.44
Annual Growth	**12.9%**	**—**	**—**	**20.6%**	**6.6%**	**8.2%**

Ulta Beauty Inc

EXECUTIVES

Ceo, Mary N Dillon
Non-Exec Chb*, Charles J Philippin
Cfo-Treas-Asst SEC, Scott M Settersten
Chief Hr Officer, Jeffrey J Childs
Chief Merchandising & Mkt Offi, David C Kimbell
General Counsel-Corp SEC, Jodi J Caro
Buyer, Cathy Bokar
Director, Dominick Archer
Senior Buyer, Jennifer Moran
CIO, Diane Randolph
Chief Store Operations Officer, Kecia Steelman
Auditors: Ernst & Young LLP

LOCATIONS

HQ: Ulta Beauty Inc
1000 Remington Blvd., Suite 120, Bolingbrook, IL 60440
Phone: 630 410-4800
Web: www.ulta.com

COMPETITORS

Bath & Body Works	Nordstrom
Bed Bath & Beyond	Premier Salons
Body Shop	Regis Corporation
CVS Caremark	Sally Beauty
Dillard's	Sephora USA
J. C. Penney	Supercuts
L'Oreal USA	Target Corporation
Lush Ltd.	Wal-Mart
Macy's	Walgreen
Merle Norman	

HISTORICAL FINANCIALS

Company Type: Public

Income Statement

FYE: February 3

	REVENUE ($ mil.)	NET INCOME ($ mil.)	NET PROFIT MARGIN	EMPLOYEES
02/18*	5,884	555	9.4%	34,700
01/17	4,854	409	8.4%	31,800
01/16	3,924	320	8.2%	26,500
01/15	3,241	257	7.9%	22,400
02/14	2,670	202	7.6%	19,600
Annual Growth	**21.8%**	**28.6%**	**—**	**15.4%**

*Fiscal year change

2018 Year-End Financials

Debt ratio: —
Return on equity: 32.86%
Cash ($ mil.): 277
Current ratio: 2.64
Long-term debt ($ mil.): —
No. of shares (mil.): 60
Dividends
  Yield: —
  Payout: —
Market value ($ mil.): 13,349

	STOCK PRICE ($)	P/E	PER SHARE ($)		
	FY Close	High/Low	Earnings	Dividends	Book Value
02/18*	219.47	35 21	8.96	0.00	29.17
01/17	271.44	42 23	6.52	0.00	24.95
01/16	181.17	37 26	4.98	0.00	22.71
01/15	131.94	34 21	3.98	0.00	19.44
02/14	85.71	41 23	3.15	0.00	15.62
Annual Growth	26.5%	— —	29.9%	—	16.9%

*Fiscal year change

UMB Financial Corp

UMB Financial is the holding company for four UMB-branded commercial banks serving Arizona Colorado Illinois Kansas Nebraska Oklahoma and Missouri. Through some 110 branches the banks offer standard services such as checking and savings accounts credit and debit cards and trust and investment services. Commercial loans account for more than 50% of UMB's loan portfolio. Beyond its banking business it offers insurance brokerage services leasing treasury management health savings accounts and proprietary mutual funds through its more than 20 subsidiaries. Founded in 1913 the bank ranks first in the Kansas City market (based on deposits).

Operations

It operates through four business segments: Bank Payment Solutions Institutional Investment Management and Asset Servicing.

Its Bank segment focuses on traditional commercial and consumer banking treasury management leasing foreign exchange merchant bankcards wealth management brokerage insurance capital markets investment banking corporate trust and correspondent banking.

The Payment Solutions segment offers consumer and commercial credit and debit cards prepaid debit card solutions healthcare services and institutional cash management.

UMB Financial's Institutional Investment Management segment serves the intermediary and institutional markets through mutual funds traditional separate accounts and sub-advisory relationships using private equity and fixed income investment strategies.

The Asset Servicing segment caters to the asset management industry and supports investment products such as mutual funds alternative investments and managed accounts.

Geographic Reach

UMB Financial's four commercial banks are located in Arizona Colorado Kansas and Missouri. Its principal subsidiary bank Missouri-based UMB Bank n.a. also has branches in Illinois Kansas Nebraska and Oklahoma. In Texas the firm operates a loan production office.

Sales and Marketing

UMB Financial serves commercial retail government and correspondent bank customers through its branch locations call center Internet banking and network of ATMs.

The company spent $24.15 million toward marketing and business development expenses in 2014; up from $22.7 million in 2013 but down from the $24.6 million it spent in 2012.

Financial Performance

UMB Financial has enjoyed rising revenue and profit in recent years thanks to loan asset growth and . Revenue in 2014 grew by more than 2% to $862.56 million thanks to 8% growth in trust and securities processing fee income and thanks to higher loan interest income from another year of double-digit growth in average loan balances.

Following several years of profit growth net income in 2014 fell by 10% to $120.66 million mostly because the bank spent more toward salary raises and incurred higher benefit costs but also because it spent more on equipment and a contingency reserve it established in 2014 related to a settlement agreement involving the sellers and employees of PCM.

Cash from operations fell by 21% to $243.78 million partially from lower cash earnings but also because it adjusted for fewer non-cash items such as accrued expenses and taxes than it did in 2013.

The company's loan assets grew by 14% to $7.47 billion in 2014 while its total deposits increased slightly to $13.62 billion.

Strategy

UMB Financial is focused on four main strategies for growth. The first is to grow its fee-based business through acquisitions or organically as fee-based services are typically non-credit related and are not generally affected by fluctuations in interest rates. Accordingly the bank has boosted its non-interest income by 20% over the past three years from $414 million in 2011 to $498.7 million in 2014. In mid-2014 to add fuel to this growth UMB Bank purchased the Oklahoma Corporate Trust Business from RCB Bank to be incorporated into its own business in the region expanding the company's reach into the Oklahoma Corporate Trust Market.

The second strategy is to focus on net interest income through loan and deposit growth. In 2014 for example the bank grew its loan assets by a whopping 14% adding $16.8 million in net interest income (5% more than in 2013) to the bank's top line.

Thirdly UMB Financial aims to improve operating efficiencies by offering more services through its existing branch network which helped it grow its loan and deposit business greatly in 2014.

Fourth the firm is focused on managing its capital to promote investor confidence and acquisition opportunities.

Mergers and Acquisitions

In late 2014 UMB agreed to buy commercial finance firm Marquette Financial from longtime owners the Pohlad family for $182 million. The acquisition would increase UMB's presence in key growth markets Arizona and Texas — where Marquette operated Meridian Bank. As part of the deal the Pohlad family gained a 7% stake in UMB (the second-largest stake behind chairman Mariner Kemper who holds 12%).

Company Background

To grow its fee-based business and diversify its business model UMB has made several acquisitions in its past. The company built up its investment advisory and corporate trust business through several 2009 purchases. In 2010 UMB made 10 acquisitions including Prairie Capital Management and Indiana-based Reams Asset Management. The deals more than doubled UMB's Scout Investment Advisors' assets under management to more than $27 billion.

EXECUTIVES

Senior Vice President And Corporate Controller, Bryan Walker

Chairman President And Ceo, J. Mariner Kemper, age 45, $862,110 total compensation

Vice Chairman Umb Financial Corporation And President And Ceo Umb Bank, Michael D. (Mike) Hagedorn, age 52, $444,986 total compensation

Ceo Scout Investments, Andrew J. (Andy) Iseman, age 54, $6,047 total compensation

President Umb Fund Services Inc., Anthony J. (Tony) Fischer, age 59, $281,154 total compensation

Evp And Chief Credit Officer, Christian R. (Chris) Swett, age 62

Evp And Chief Lending Officer, Thomas S. (Tom) Terry, age 54

Cfo, Ram Shankar, age 45

Evp And Chief Human Resources Officer, Shannon A. Johnson, age 38

Evp And Director Of Operations Bank, Kevin M. Macke, age 45

Evp And Chief Risk Officer, Jennifer M. Payne, age 41

Vice President Of Commercial Underwriting, Rebecca A Lang

Vice President Marketing, Kelli Christman

Senior Vice President Investment Divisio, Raleigh Trovillion

Vice President Quality Assurance And Risk Management, Mark Kitchin

Assistant Vice President And Financial Center Manager Ii, Jenna Harris

Assistant Vice President And Information Technology Manager And Data Architecture Enterprise Content, Bob Eber

Vice President Banking Services Compliance Directo, Stephanie Boryla

Vice President Of Commercial Banking, Mark Winker

Vice President, Pam Ungashick

Vice President Senior Loan Review, James Engelhart

Senior Vice President, Phil Richter

Vice President Commercial Bankcard Sales Manager, Tom Carignan

Senior Vice President Loan Operations, Linda Gallagher

Vice President, Douglas Hare

Senior Vice President Credit Risk Director, Jim Caniglia

Vice President, Jack Misiewicz

Vice President And Manager Applications Development, Bart Klein

Executive Vice President, Christine Pierson

Vice President, Michael Nash

Senior Vice President Director Of Compliance And Oversight, Warren Green

Avp Financial Center Manager Ii, Dustin Smith

Executive Vice President Director Bank Strategy And Administration, Rekha Patnaik

Senior Vice President, Gordon Gendler

Vice President, Sandy Battas

Senior Vice President, Kathryn Anastasio

Assistant Vice President Branch Manager, Teresa Shuffield

Vice President Financial Center Manager, Casey Kudrna

Vice President Trust Custody Operations Manager, Melvin Porter

Assistant Vice President Business Banking, Edin Salkic

Assistant Vice President Commercial Underwriting Officer, Brad Boeshaar

Vice President, Mark Volkmer

Assistant Vice President, Lori Kohler

Vice President Corporate Trust, Laura Roberson

Vice President Corporate Trust, Brian Krippner

Senior Vice President, Ann Porter

Senior Vice President Retail Banking, Eric Craine

Vice President And Program Operations Management Lssbb, Renee Taylor

Vice President Product Development And Marketing, Bruce Parker

Senior Vice President And Workout Specialist, Virginia Housum

Vice President Of Commercial Underwriting, Rebecca Lang

Senior Vice President Chief Lending Officer Arizona, Robert Faver

Vice President Investment And Wealth Management, Kelley Lauer

Assistant Vice President And Commercial Banking Officer, Josh Fink

Senior Vice President Investor Relations, Begonya Klumb

Vice President Finance, Debbie Johnson

Assistant Vice President, Steve Collins

Executive Vice President, Thomas Hof

Vice President Commercial Banking, William Thomasjr

Vice President Human Resources, Leslie Thomson

Vice President Middle Office Manager, Maggie Bowen

Senior Vice President, Randall Tharp

Senior Vice President, Rick Bennett

Senior Vice President Treasury Management, David Pucci

Vice President Private Banking Client Manager, Chris Herwig

Assistant Vice President Financial Center Manager, Laura Trybom

Assistant Vice President Commercial Banking, Michael Laplant

Vice President Business Banking, Randall Rodgers

Assistant Vice President Financial Center Manager, Eric Putnam

Vice President Regional Sales Manager, Kristine Batch

Assistant Vice President Financial Center Manager, Keva Whitley

Senior Vice President Director Of Investor Relations, Kay Gregory

Assistant Vice President Consumer Loan Officer, Patrick Johnson

Vice President Director Project Management, Nicole Louis-Robbins

Vice President, Laurie Box

Vice President, Rick Beaver

Senior Vice President, Robert Elbert

Vice President, Robin Waters

Vice President, Vicky Hales

Assistant Vice President And Financial Center Manager, Douglas Empson

Executive Vice President, Peter Mennihan

Vice President Administration, Ann Maurer

Vice President Commercial Card Sales Officer, Peter Swenson

Senior Vice President, Janet Clements

Vice President Administration, Carol Alexander

Senior Vice President And Counsel, Paul Scheuerman

Assistant Vice President Marketing Activation, Jeff Bowers

Vice President Customer Experience Strategy, Amy Mendenhall

Senior Vice President Corporate Communication, Barry Brakeville

Vice President Commercial Relationship Manager, Shawn Harbour

Vice President Treasury Management, Lanie Sedlacek

Vice President Implementation Manager, Lori Lamanno

Senior Vice President, Malcolm Evans

Vice President Private Wealth Marketing, Leigh Adams

Vice President Relationship Manager Business Banki, Sean Scibienski

Senior Vice President Commercial Lending, Aaron Emel

Vice President Capital Markets, Nick Arthachinda

Senior Vice President Commercial Banking, David Walters

Vice President Portfolio Manager, Jason Harrison

Vice President Senior Relationship Officer, James Tuttle

Assistant Vice President Treasury Analyst, Mike Groff

Vice President And Corporate Legal Counsel, Megan Mercer

Vice President Administration, Bryan Edwards

Vice President Manager Help Center, Lynnette Johnston

Vice President And Financial Center Manager, Nicholas Petersen

Vice President And Director Of Financial Markets And Fiduciary Compliance, Cathy Clark

Vice President Regional Mortgage Sales Manager, Miguale Green

Vice President Commercial Relationship Manager, Bryson Bowden

Senior Vice President Commercial Lending, Richard Trease

Senior Vice President Commercial Lending, Valerie Kroiss

Senior Vice President Commercial Team Lead, Dennis Wright

Vice President, Marcia Matthews

Vice President Healthcare Services, Matthew Richardson

Vice President Commercial Real Estate, Charles Gonzalez

Assistant Vice President Business Banking, Steve Shumate

Vice President, Julius Zamora

Vice President Of Business Aviation Development, Morgan Littell

Senior Vice President Commercial Banking, Marc Farmer

Assistant Vice President Small Business Banking, Michelle Mountjoy

Senior Vice President And Financial Advisor, Rod Russell

Fund Accounting Manager Assistant Vice President, Brian Schmidt

Assistant Vice President Information Technology Help Desk And Olbs Manager, Michael Meredith

Vice President Global Relationship Manager, Bart Woodson

Vice President Commercial Card Sales Manager Payment Solutions, Cherie Figge

Vice President And Aml Investigations Supervisor, Venus Griswold

Vice President And Tax Senior Manager, Megan Kimzey

Vice President Of Segment And Product Manager, Jacob Hymes

Assistant Vice President, Liz Angotti

Vice President Commercial Relationship Specialist, Christy Thomas

Board Member, Paul Uhlmann

Auditors: KPMG LLP

LOCATIONS

HQ: UMB Financial Corp
1010 Grand Boulevard, Kansas City, MO 64106
Phone: 816 860-7000   Fax: 816 860-7143
Web: www.umb.com

PRODUCTS/OPERATIONS

2016 Sales

	$ mil.	% of total
Interest income		
Loans	386	29
Securities	131	13
Federal funds and resell agreements	2	-
Interest-bearing due from banks	2.4	
Trading securities	0.6	
Non-interest income		
Trust and securities processing	239	24
Trading and investment banking	21	2
Service charges on deposit accounts	86	9
Insurance fees and commissions	4	-
Brokerage fees	17	2
Bankcard fees	68	7
Gains on sales of securities available for sale net	8	1
Equity earnings (losses) on alternative investments	2	-
Other	26	3
Total	**999**	**100**

Selected Subsidiaries & Affiliates

Grand Distribution Services LLC
J.D. Clark & Company
Kansas City Financial Corporation
Kansas City Realty Company
Prairie Capital Management LLC
Scout Distributors LLC
Scout Investment Advisors Inc.
UMB Banc Leasing Corp.
UMB Bank and Trust n.a.
UMB Bank Arizona n.a.
UMB Bank Colorado n.a.
UMB Capital Corporation
UMB Community Development Corporation
UMB Distribution Services LLC
UMB Financial Services Inc.
UMB Fund Services Inc.
UMB Insurance Inc.
UMB National Bank of America
UMB Realty Company LLC
UMB Redevelopment Corporation
UMB Trust Company of South Dakota
United Missouri Insurance Company

COMPETITORS

BOK Financial
Bank of America
Capitol Federal Financial
Commerce Bancshares
Dickinson Financial
First National of Nebraska

Great Southern Bancorp
Guaranty Bancorp
TCF Financial
U.S. Bancorp
Zions Bancorporation

HISTORICAL FINANCIALS

Company Type: Public

Income Statement

	ASSETS ($ mil.)	NET INCOME ($ mil.)	INCOME AS % OF ASSETS	EMPLOYEES
12/17	21,771	247	1.1%	3,570
12/16	20,682	158	0.8%	3,688
12/15	19,094	116	0.6%	3,830
12/14	17,500	120	0.7%	3,592
12/13	16,911	133	0.8%	3,498
Annual Growth	**6.5%**	**16.5%**	**—**	**0.5%**

FYE: December 31

2017 Year-End Financials

Debt ratio: 0.36%
Return on equity: 11.93%
Cash ($ mil.): 1,798
Current ratio: —
Long-term debt ($ mil.): —

No. of shares (mil.): 49
Dividends
  Yield: 0.0%
  Payout: 20.9%
Market value ($ mil.): 3,588

	STOCK PRICE ($) FY Close	P/E High/Low	PER SHARE ($) Earnings	Dividends	Book Value
12/17	71.92	16 13	4.96	1.04	43.72
12/16	77.12	25 13	3.22	0.99	39.51
12/15	46.55	24 19	2.44	0.95	38.34
12/14	56.89	25 20	2.65	0.91	36.10
12/13	64.28	20 13	3.20	0.87	33.30
Annual Growth	**2.8%**	**— —**	**11.6%**	**4.6%**	**7.0%**

Umpqua Holdings Corp

Umpqua Holdings thinks of itself not so much as a bank but rather a retailer that sells financial products. Consequently many of the company's 380-plus Umpqua Bank "stores" in northern California northern Nevada Idaho Oregon and Washington feature coffee bars and computer cafes. While customers sip Umpqua-branded coffee pay bills online attend a financial seminar catch a poetry reading or check out wares from local merchants staff members pitch deposit accounts mortgages loans life insurance investments and more. Subsidiary Umpqua Investments (formerly Strand Atkinson Williams & York) provides retail brokerage services through more than a dozen locations mostly inside Umpqua Bank branches.

Operations

Umpqua operates two business segments: Community Banking which made up 79% of the company's total revenue during 2015 and provides traditional banking services as well as wealth management and private banking services for wealthier individuals; and Home Lending (21% of revenue) which originates and sells residential mortgage loans.

The company makes more than 75% of its revenue from interest income. About 72% of its revenue came from loan interest (including fees) during 2015 with another 5% coming from interest on investment securities. The rest of its revenue came from residential mortgage banking revenue (9% of revenue) deposit account service charges (5%) brokerage revenue (2%) and other miscellaneous income streams.

Geographic Reach

Oregon-based Umpqua Bank has branches in Idaho Washington Oregon California and Northern Nevada. Umpqua Investments has offices in Portland Lake Oswego and Medford Oregon as well as Santa Rosa California.

Sales and Marketing

Umpqua Holdings promotes its brand through customer-facing channels public relations social media and community-based events. It spent $11.4 million on marketing to promote its brand during 2015 up from $9.5 million and $6.1 million in 2014 and 2013 respectively.

Financial Performance

The bank's annual revenues have doubled since 2011 as its loan and lease assets have tripled to $16.85 billion which has resulted in strong interest income growth. Exceptional revenue growth and effective cost controls have helped the bank's net income triple over the same period.

Umpqua Holdings' revenue jumped 20% to $1.21 billion during 2015 mostly as its earning assets (including loans investments and loans held for sale) swelled by 20% which led to higher interest income. The bank's non-interest income also rose 52% for the year mostly thanks to the 2014 acquisition of Sterling Financial with residential mortgage banking revenue brokerage commissions and deposit service charges all growing during the year.

Strong revenue growth in 2015 drove the bank's net income up 51% to $222.54 million for the year. Umpqua's operating cash levels climbed 5% to $376.74 million as earnings rose.

Strategy

Umpqua Bank's primary mission is to become the top community-oriented financial services firm in the Western US by strategically acquiring banks in new markets and building its brand by offering unique personal experience for customers entering its "store" branches. Its mid-2014 acquisition of Sterling Financial — the largest ever acquisition in Umpqua's history — successfully extended the bank's presence in Southern California Eastern Washington Eastern Oregon and Idaho.

The bank differentiates itself by encouraging clients to come into its stores instead of using impersonal interfaces like ATMs and electronic banking more cost-effective methods preferred by many of its competitors. The bank's "Next Generation" stores feature interactive touch-screen walls fresh fruit and cold drinks. It hopes the comfortable environment will inspire customers to use more of the bank's financial services.

Hoping to build upon its one-of-a-kind branch experiences Umpqua Bank in 2015 launched its Silicon Valley-based Pivotus Ventures Inc subsidiary to explore disruptive new bank technologies.

In 2016 Umpqua launched its corporate banking division which is dedicated to providing companies with access to such offerings as treasury management international banking debt capital markets and others.

Mergers and Acquisitions

In April 2014 Umpqua Bank acquired $10-billion-in-assets Sterling Financial Corp. headquartered in Spokane Washington. The largest merger in Umpqua's history created the West Coast's largest community bank with some $22 billion in assets and 394 stores across five states. The Sterling branches were rebranded as part of the $1.9 billion deal.

Company Background

Traditionally consumer focused Umpqua Bank established a business banking division in 2011 to court small and mid-sized business clients. That year it pursued deposit growth assembled new lending teams and added new stores in key metropolitan areas like Portland Oregon; Seattle; San Francisco; and California's Silicon Valley.

Umpqua Holdings established a wealth management division in 2009 and launched a trust services group the following year. It provided asset management services through an agreement with independent firm Ferguson Wellman Capital Management.

EXECUTIVES

Evp Wealth Management Umpqua Holdings And Umpqua Bank, Kelly Johnson

Evp Creative Strategies Group Umpqua Bank, Lani Hayward, age 51

Evp And Chief Lending Officer Umpqua Holdings Corp And Umpqua Bank, David F. (Dave) Shotwell, age 59

Evp Cfo And Principal Financial Officer Umpqua Holdings And Umpqua Bank, Ronald L. (Ron) Farnsworth, age 48, $425,000 total compensation

Evp Treasurer And Principal Accounting Officer Umpqua Holdings And Umpqua Bank, Neal T. McLaughlin, age 50

Evp Corporate Communications Umpqua Bank, Eve Callahan, age 44

President Ceo And Director, Cort O'Haver, age 55, $565,000 total compensation

Evp And Chief Auditor Umpqua Bank, Joel Brandenburg, age 55

Evp Enterprise Risk Management Umpqua Holdings Corp And Umpqua Bank, Gary F. Neal, age 63

Evp Associate Relations Umpqua Holdings Corp And Umpqua Bank, Sheri T. Burns, age 50

Evp Cultural Enhancement And Government Relations Umpqua Bank, Marty J. Dickinson, age 48

Evp General Counsel And Corporate Secretary Umpqua Holdings Corp And Umpqua Bank, Andrew H. Ognall, age 46, $300,000 total compensation

Vice President Of Benefits, Jennifer Hollenbeck

Senior Vice President Data Processing, Bo Harrison

Vice President Rewards And Recognition, Sandy Hunt

Vice President Enterprise Risk Manager, Aretina Trepczyk

Vice President, Susan Jensen

Vice President, Marie Fidler

Executive Vice President Commerical Banking Of The Company And The Bank, Cort Oahaver

Senior Vice President Credit Review Manager Commercial Banking, Jim Storvick

Senior Vice President International Banking Manager, Anthony Oriti

Vice President Commercial Banking Center Manager, Jamie Hudson

Chairman, Raymond P. (Ray) Davis, age 69

Vice Chairman, Bryan L. Timm, age 54

Auditors: DELOITTE & TOUCHE LLP

LOCATIONS

HQ: Umpqua Holdings Corp
One S.W. Columbia Street, Suite 1200, Portland, OR 97258
Phone: 503 727-4100
Web: www.umpquaholdingscorp.com

PRODUCTS/OPERATIONS

2015 Sales

	$ mil.	% of total
Interest		
Interest and fees on loans and leases	869	72
TaxableInterest and dividends investment securities	58	5
Other	2	-
Non-interest		
Mortgage banking	124	9
Service charges on deposit accounts	59	5
Brokerage	18	2
Gain on loan sales net	22	2
BOLI income	8	1
Gain on investment securities net	2	-
Other	46	4
Adjustments	(7.2)	-
Total	**1,205**	**100**

2015 Sales

	$ mil.	% of total
Community Banking	954	79
Home Lending	250	21
Total	**1,205**	**100**

COMPETITORS

Bank of America	KeyCorp
Bank of the West	U.S. Bancorp
Banner Corp	Washington Federal
Cascade Bancorp	Wells Fargo
Columbia Banking	

HISTORICAL FINANCIALS

Company Type: Public

Income Statement

FYE: December 31

	ASSETS ($ mil.)	NET INCOME ($ mil.)	INCOME AS % OF ASSETS	EMPLOYEES
12/17	25,741	246	1.0%	4,380
12/16	24,813	232	0.9%	4,295
12/15	23,387	222	1.0%	4,491
12/14	22,613	147	0.7%	4,569
12/13	11,636	98	0.8%	2,490
Annual Growth	22.0%	25.8%	—	15.2%

2017 Year-End Financials

Debt ratio: 4.58%	No. of shares (mil.): 220
Return on equity: 6.20%	Dividends
Cash ($ mil.): 634	Yield: 0.0%
Current ratio: —	Payout: 61.2%
Long-term debt ($ mil.): —	Market value ($ mil.): 4,579

	STOCK PRICE ($) FY Close	P/E High/Low	PER SHARE ($) Earnings	Dividends	Book Value
12/17	20.80	20 15	1.11	0.68	18.24
12/16	18.78	18 13	1.05	0.64	17.79
12/15	15.90	19 15	1.01	0.62	17.48
12/14	17.01	24 20	0.78	0.60	17.17
12/13	19.14	22 14	0.87	0.60	15.43
Annual Growth	2.1%	— —	6.3%	3.2%	4.3%

Under Armour Inc

Chainmail might be out of style but Under Armour makes performance clothes for doing battle on the sports field and in the gym. Under Armour is the official footwear supplier of the NFL and MLB and partners with the NBA and it outfits everyday athletes as well. Products made from its moisture-wicking and heat-dispersing fabrics keep athletes dry and comfortable during workouts. The company also make technology that help customers track their fitness. Under Armour sells online by catalog and through retail (inlcuding Academy Nordstrom's Finish Line and Cabela's) and outlet stores worldwide.Its locker room of athlete endorsers include top performers in football basketball soccer and baseball.

Operations

Apparel designed for winter (COLDGEAR) summer (HEATGEAR) and year-round (ALLSEASONGEAR) wear accounts for over 65% of sales. Footwear runs in about 20% with accessories such as hats bags and gloves contributing under 10%.

Under Armour also has a small but growing Connected Fitness business which comprises fitness-related apps such as MapMyFitness MyFitnessPal Endonondo and UA Record. The free-to-use apps generate revenue from advertising. The segment accounts for about 2% of revenue.

Almost all of Under Armour's products are made by third party manufacturers in 18 countries. More than 60% of the company's products are made in China Jordan Vietnam and Malaysia.

Geographic Reach

Headquartered in Baltimore Maryland Under Armour operates globally. It has European and Asian subsidiaries and sources from suppliers worldwide. Besides North America where it generates more than 75% of sales Under Armour's products are sold primarily in France Germany and the UK. It sells in Japan and Korea as well through a third-party licensee.

The company?s distribution facilities are in Glen Burnie Maryland; Mount Juliet Tennessee; and Rialto California.

Sales and Marketing

Under Armour generates more than 60% of its sales through its wholesale business. Its customers include the likes of Cabela's the Army and Air Force Exchange and Dick's Sporting Goods.

The company's direct-to-consumer business is also growing rapidly — Under Armour operates over 160 of its own factory outlet and specialty stores primarily located in outlet centers in the US. Many of the company stores are going in Class A malls throughout the US. Some international locations are being targeted as well.

Financial Performance

Under Armour?s revenue has more than doubled in the past five years growing at an annual average of more than 20% are more people clad themselves in Under Armour branded athletic wear and shod themselves in Under Armour shoes.

The company?s revenue growth slowed in 2017 reaching $4.9 billion a 3% increase from 2016. The company reported higher apparel sales led by men's and women's training and golf; higher accessories unit sales led by men's training; and higher footwear unit sales led by running. License revenue rose about 17% from increased North American Distribution while Connected Fitness sales rose about 11% due to more subscribers to fitness apps and greater licensing revenue. Sales fell in North America fell 5% on lower demand but rose in other areas including a 60% jump in the Asia/Pacific region boosted by direct to consumer sales.

Higher costs in 2017 wiped out the revenue gain and restructuring charges of about $124 million drove Under Armour to a net loss of about $48 million from a profit of about $198 million in 2016.

Under Armour?s cash increased to about $312 million in 2017 from about $250 million in 2016.

Strategy

After unbridled growth in the past five years Under Armour?s sales slowed in 2017 because of its reliance on basketball footwear struggling retail stores and slowness in adapting to changing fashions. The company responded with restructurings in mid-2017 and early 2018 that reduced headcount consolidated facilities closed stores and refocused resources. The company plans to focus on five core areas: men?s training women?s training running baseball and lifestyle.

Under Armour also plans to build on its growing international sales which account more than a quarter of its revenue. In 2017 the company began selling products to wholesales customers in Russia. Building a global brand would help Under Armour compete with Nike and Adidas whose logos are known around the world.

EXECUTIVES

Vice President, Raphael Peck
Chairman And Ceo, Kevin A. Plank, age 45, $26,000 total compensation
President And Coo, Patrik Frisk, age 55
Cto, Paul Fipps
Chief Supply Chain Officer, Colin Browne, $169,231 total compensation
Chief Digital Officer, Michael Lee, $434,423 total compensation
President North America, Jason LaRose
Acting Cfo, David E. Bergman, age 45
Senior Vice President Talent, Melissa Wallace
Vp Footwear Development And Engineering, Cameron Shayegi
Vice President Commercialization Lab And Open Innovation, Sam Mccleery
Auditors: PricewaterhouseCoopers LLP

LOCATIONS

HQ: Under Armour Inc
1020 Hull Street, Baltimore, MD 21230
Phone: 410 454-6428
Web: www.underarmour.com

2017 Sales

	$ mil.	% of total
North America	3,802	76
EMEA	470	9
Asia-Pacific	433	9
Latin America	181	4
Connected Fitness	89	2
Eliminations	-	-
Total	**4,976**	**100**

PRODUCTS/OPERATIONS

2017 Sales

	$ mil.	% of total
Apparel	3,287	66
Footwear	1,037	21
Accessories	445	9
Licensing	116	2
Connected Fitness	89	2
Eliminations	-	-
Total	**4,976**	**100**

Selected Products

Apparel
Allseasongear
Coldgear
Heatgear
Footwear
Accessories
License and Other

COMPETITORS

ASICS America	NIKE
Apple Inc.	New Balance
Calvin Klein	North Face
Columbia Sportswear	Patagonia Inc.
Fitbit	Skechers U.S.A.
Fruit of the Loom	Victoria's Secret
Hanesbrands	Stores
Jockey International	Warnaco Swimwear
L.L. Bean	adidas

HISTORICAL FINANCIALS

Company Type: Public

Income Statement

FYE: December 31

	REVENUE ($ mil.)	NET INCOME ($ mil.)	NET PROFIT MARGIN	EMPLOYEES
12/17	4,976	(48)	—	15,800
12/16	4,825	256	5.3%	9,400
12/15	3,963	232	5.9%	13,400
12/14	3,084	208	6.7%	10,700
12/13	2,332	162	7.0%	7,800
Annual Growth	**20.9%**	**—**	**—**	**19.3%**

2017 Year-End Financials

Debt ratio: 22.89%	No. of shares (mil.): 442
Return on equity: (-2.38%)	Dividends
Cash ($ mil.): 312	Yield: —
Current ratio: 2.20	Payout: —
Long-term debt ($ mil.): 765	Market value ($ mil.): 6,379

	STOCK PRICE ($) FY Close	P/E High/Low		PER SHARE ($) Earnings	Dividends	Book Value
12/17	14.43	—	—	(0.22)	0.00	4.57
12/16	29.05	191	65	0.45	0.00	4.63
12/15	80.61	193	119	0.53	0.00	3.86
12/14	67.90	254	94	0.48	0.00	3.16
12/13	87.30	226	119	0.38	0.00	2.49
Annual Growth	**(36.2%)**	—	—	—	—	**16.4%**

UNION BANK AND TRUST COMPANY

Union Bank & Trust a subsidiary of financial services holding company Farmers & Merchants Investment operates more than 35 branches throughout Nebraska and in Kansas. As Nebraska's third-largest privately-owned bank it offers traditional deposit and trust services as well as insurance equipment finance and investment management services. Consumer loans account for the largest portion of the bank's portfolio followed by commercial real estate and farmland loans. Union Bank also originates business loans and residential mortgages. Affiliate company Union Investment Advisors manages the Stratus family of mutual funds. Another Farmers & Merchants unit Nelnet Capital offers brokerage services.

Operations

Union Bank has grown to become one of Nebraska's largest privately-owned banks. As of mid-2013 it boasted bank assets of $2.6 billion and trust assets of $11.8 billion.

Aside from its branches in Nebraska and Kansas Union Bank offers banking products and services through its online mobile and electronic banking services.

Geographic Reach

Union Bank operates mostly in Nebraska but also in Kansas.

Sales and Marketing

The bank primarily serves customers in Lincoln and Omaha as well as the Kansas City metropolitan area.

Strategy

Union Bank continues to expand its footprint in existing markets. The financial institution will have added three new Nebraska branches to its portfolio by 2014.

Company Background

The bank was originally founded in 1917 as Farmer's State Bank. It took on the Union Bank name in 1935 and became Union Bank & Trust in 1959.

EXECUTIVES

Vice President, Tom Marchael
Vice President Small Business Banking, Stephanie Dinger
Vice President, Kwassi Amevor
Vice President, Jon Hawthorne
Vice President Financial Reporting And Controller, Kimberly Keller

LOCATIONS

HQ: UNION BANK AND TRUST COMPANY
3643 S 48TH ST, LINCOLN, NE 685064390
Phone: 402 488-0941
Web: WWW.UBT.COM

PRODUCTS/OPERATIONS

Selected Services
Business banking
Investment & retirement
Personal banking
Wealth management

Selected Affiliates
InfoVisa
Nelnet Capital LLC
Nelnet Inc.
Union Agency Inc.
Union Equipment Finance LLC
Union Investment Advisors
Union Title Company LLC
Zelle

COMPETITORS

Bank of America	Great Western Bancorp
Bank of the West	JPMorgan Chase
Citigroup	Pinnacle Bancorp
First National of Nebraska	U.S. Bancorp
	Wells Fargo

HISTORICAL FINANCIALS

Company Type: Private

Income Statement

FYE: December 31

	ASSETS ($ mil.)	NET INCOME ($ mil.)	INCOME AS % OF ASSETS	EMPLOYEES
12/17	3,836	45	1.2%	800
12/16	3,595	40	1.1%	—
12/15	3,351	32	1.0%	—
12/14	3,040	29	1.0%	—
Annual Growth	8.1%	15.8%	—	—

2017 Year-End Financials

Debt ratio: —
Return on equity: 21.40%
Cash ($ mil.): 64
Current ratio: —
Long-term debt ($ mil.): —
Dividends
Yield: —
Payout: —
Market value ($ mil.): —

Union Bankshares Corp (New)

Union Bankshares (formerly Union First Market Bankshares) is the holding company for Union Bank & Trust which operates approximately 100 branches in central northern and coastal portions of Virginia. The bank offers standard services such as checking and savings accounts credit cards and certificates of deposit. Union Bank & Trust maintains a loan portfolio heavily weighted towards real estate: Commercial real estate loans make up more than 30% while one- to four-family residential mortgages and construction loans account for approximately 15% and 20% respectively. The bank also originates personal and business loans.

EXECUTIVES

Evp And Director Of Mortgage And Wealth Management, Jeffrey W. Farrar, age 57
Evp Union Bankshares And Chief Retail Officer Union Bank & Trust, Elizabeth M. Bentley, age 57, $268,491 total compensation
Evp And Chief Risk Officer, David G. (Dave) Bilko, age 58
President And Ceo Union Bankshares Corporation And Ceo Union Bank & Trust, John C. Asbury, age 53
Evp And Cfo, Robert M. (Rob) Gorman, age 59, $351,167 total compensation
Evp Union Bankshares And Chief Banking Officer Union Bank & Trust, D. Anthony (Tony) Peay, age 58, $348,997 total compensation
Evp And Cio, M. Dean Brown, age 53, $259,625 total compensation
Svp And Chief Marketing Officer, L. Duane Smith, age 51
Evp And Chief Human Resource Officer, Loreen A. LaGatta, age 49
Evp And President Union Bank & Trust, John G. Stallings, age 51
Vice President And Senior Branch Manager, Sherry Cillo
Assistant Vice President Branch Manager, Jody Hardy
Vice President And Senior Market Manager, Cheryl Kirby
Senior Vice President, Craig Parrent
Senior Vice President Commercial Market Team Lead Union Bank And Trust Commercial Lending Division, Jay Baldwin
Vice Chairman Union Bankshares Corporation And Union Bank & Trust, G. William (Billy) Beale, age 68
Chairman, Raymond D. (Ray) Smoot, age 71
Auditors: Ernst & Young LLP

LOCATIONS

HQ: Union Bankshares Corp (New)
1051 East Cary Street, Suite 1200, Richmond, VA 23219
Phone: 804 633-5031
Web: www.bankatunion.com

PRODUCTS/OPERATIONS

2015 Sales

	$ mil.	% of total
Interest		
Loans including fees	247	72
Other	29	9
Noninterest		
Other service charges commission and fees	15	5
Service charges on deposit accounts	18	5
others	30	9
Adjustments	(0.3)	-
Total	341	100

Selected Subsidiaries
Union First Market Bank
Union Insurance Group LLC
Union Investment Services Inc.
Union Mortgage Group Inc.

COMPETITORS

BB&T	PNC Financial
Bank of America	Regions Financial
C&F Financial	SunTrust
Eastern Virginia Bankshares	TowneBank
JPMorgan Chase	Wells Fargo

HISTORICAL FINANCIALS

Company Type: Public

Income Statement

FYE: December 31

	ASSETS ($ mil.)	NET INCOME ($ mil.)	INCOME AS % OF ASSETS	EMPLOYEES
12/17	9,315	72	0.8%	1,149
12/16	8,426	77	0.9%	1,416
12/15	7,693	67	0.9%	1,422
12/14	7,359	52	0.7%	1,471
12/13	4,176	34	0.8%	1,025
Annual Growth	22.2%	20.6%	—	2.9%

2017 Year-End Financials

Debt ratio: 4.57%
Return on equity: 7.12%
Cash ($ mil.): 198
Current ratio: —
Long-term debt ($ mil.): —
No. of shares (mil.): 43
Dividends
Yield: 0.0%
Payout: 48.5%
Market value ($ mil.): 1,582

	STOCK PRICE ($) FY Close	P/E High/Low	PER SHARE ($) Earnings	Dividends	Book Value
12/17	36.17	23 18	1.67	0.81	23.92
12/16	35.74	21 12	1.77	0.77	22.95
12/15	25.24	18 13	1.49	0.68	22.23
12/14	24.08	23 19	1.14	0.58	21.66
12/13	24.81	19 11	1.38	0.54	17.55
Annual Growth	9.9%	— —	4.9%	10.7%	8.1%

Union Pacific Corp

Venerable Union Pacific Railroad (UP) has been chugging down the track since the 19th century. Owned by Union Pacific Corporation (UPC) UP is one of the nation's leading rail carriers operating about 64000 freight cars and nearly 8600 locomotives. UP transports automobiles chemicals energy and industrial agricultural and other bulk freight over a system of some 32000 rail miles in 23 states in the western two-thirds of the US. UPC owns more than 26000 route miles of its rail network; leases and trackage rights which allow it to use other railroads' tracks account for the rest. UP's customers have included such big names as automakers General Motors and Toyota.

HISTORY

In 1862 the US Congress chartered the Union Pacific Railroad (UP) to build part of the first transcontinental railway. The driving of the Golden Spike at Promontory Utah in 1869 marked the linking of the East and West coasts as UP's rails met those of Central Pacific Railroad (predecessor of Southern Pacific or SP) which had been built east from Sacramento California.

In 1872 the New York Sun revealed the Credit Mobilier scandal: UP officials had pocketed excess profits during the railroad's construction. Debt and lingering effects of the scandal forced UP into bankruptcy in 1893.

A syndicate headed by E. H. Harriman bought UP in 1897. After reacquiring the Oregon branches it lost in the bankruptcy UP gained control of SP (1901) and Chicago & Alton (1904). The Supreme Court ordered UP to sell its SP holdings in 1913 on antitrust grounds. In the 1930s UP diversified into trucking and in the 1970s and 1980s it moved into oil and gas production.

UP bought trucking firm Overnite Transportation in 1986. During the 1980s UP also built up its rail operations acquiring the Missouri Pacific and Western Pacific railroads in 1982 and the Missouri-Kansas-Texas Railroad in 1988. It joined Chicago and North Western (CNW) Railway managers in an investment group led by Blackstone Capital Partners that bought CNW in 1989.

CNW traced its roots to the Galena & Chicago Union Railroad which was founded by Chicago's first mayor W. B. Ogden in 1836 and merged with CNW in 1864. By 1925 the North Western (as it was then known) had tracks throughout the Midwest. In 1995 UP completed its purchase of CNW and made a bid for SP.

SP was founded in 1865 but its history dates to 1861 when four Sacramento merchants founded Central Pacific. By building new track and buying other railroads (including SP in 1868) Central Pacific had expanded throughout California Texas and Oregon by 1887. The two railroads merged in 1885 under the SP name. In 1983 SP was sold to a holding company controlled by Philip Anschutz which in 1995 agreed to sell the company to UP.

UP completed its SP acquisition in 1996 but assimilation of the purchase led to widespread rail traffic jams. UP also sold its remaining interest in Union Pacific Resources an oil company it had spun off the year before. In 1997 UP moved from Bethlehem Pennsylvania to Dallas and joined a consortium led by mining company Grupo MA©xico that won a bid to run two major Mexican rail lines. In the US however fatal collisions led to a federal review of UP which found a breakdown in rail safety such as overworked employees and widespread train defects. Meanwhile regulators seeking to resolve UP's massive freight backlog ordered the railroad to open its Houston lines to competitors.

The company decentralized its management into three regions (north south and west) in 1998 to improve traffic flow. It also hired more workers added new trains and realigned routes while selling Skyway Freight Systems its logistics services unit.

In 1999 UP moved its headquarters from Dallas to Omaha Nebraska where Union Pacific Railroad offices already were located. In 2000 it formed Fenix a holding company charged with developing and expanding the company's telecommunications and technology assets. (By 2003 however UP had reabsorbed Fenix and scaled back its support for its remaining technology subsidiaries.)

The company expanded its less-than-truckload operations into the western US in 2001 by buying Motor Cargo Industries. Also that year it completed the integration of Southern Pacific's operations.

UP sold its trucking unit Overnite Corporation (a holding company for Overnite Transportation and Motor Cargo Industries) in an IPO in 2003. (Overnite Corporation was acquired by United Parcel Service in 2005 and renamed UPS Freight the next year.) UP sold its Timera subsidiary (workforce management software) in 2004.

Traffic congestion in the UP system brought on by a shortage of train crews caused some freight from UPS and other customers to be rerouted onto trucks in 2004. The crew shortage was attributed

in part to a greater-than-expected number of retirements in 2003. UP accelerated its hiring and training efforts but the company still had to restrict freight volume in an effort to minimize bottlenecks.

In 2006 Union Pacific Railroad reorganized its operating structure going from four regions to three: northern southern and western. Service units of the company's central region were reassigned to the northern and southern regions. The company added 45 miles of double track to its Sunset Corridor in 2008.

In the midst of the Great Recession UPC's 2009 freight volumes decreased 16% from 2008's numbers. The company was forced to raise its rates by about 6%; it also parked approximately 26% of its locomotives 18% of its freight car stock and furloughed about 3000 employees.

As the nation slowly recovered economically UPC realized a 13% increase in volume in 2010 over 2009 with automotive intermodal and industrial product shipments showing the strongest growth. Even with 2010 fuel prices more than 30% higher than 2009 the company's freight revenues increased 20% in 2010. UPC cited economic improvement across the majority of its market sectors as the reason for the recovery.

In mid-2012 UPC subsidiary PS Technology (PST) acquired the Yard Control Systems division of Ansaldo STS USA. The acquisition boosted PST's enterprise management capabilities by adding rail yard process control and automation technology.

EXECUTIVES

Evp And Cfo, Robert M. Knight, age 61, $575,000 total compensation

Svp And Cio, Lynden L. Tennison

Chairman President And Ceo, Lance M. Fritz, age 55, $1,000,000 total compensation

Evp And Chief Administration Officer, Eric L. Butler, age 57, $485,000 total compensation

Evp And Chief Legal Officer, Rhonda S. Ferguson, age 49, $200,000 total compensation

Evp And Chief Marketing Officer, Elizabeth F. (Beth) Whited, age 53

Evp And Coo, Cameron A. Scott, age 55, $457,500 total compensation

President Shipcarsnow Inc., Peter Decher

Vp; General Manager Chemicals, Kari Kirchhoefer

Assistant Vice President Commercial Technology Offerings, Ashok Fichadia

Assistant Vice President Strategic Planning, Grant Janke

Senior Assistant Vice President Chemicals, Robert G Worrell

Auditors: DELOITTE & TOUCHE LLP

LOCATIONS

HQ: Union Pacific Corp
1400 Douglas Street, Omaha, NE 68179
Phone: 402 544-5000
Web: www.up.com

PRODUCTS/OPERATIONS

2017 Sales

	$ mil.	% of total
Freight	19,837	93
Other	1,403	7
Total	**21,240**	**100**

2017 Sales

	$ mil.	% of total
Freight revenues		
Intermodal	3,835	18
Agricultural Products	3,685	17
Chemicals	3,596	17
Industrial Products	4,078	19
Coal	2,645	13
Automotive	1,998	9
Other revenues	1,403	7
Total	**21,240**	**100**

COMPETITORS

American Commercial Lines	Ingram Industries
Burlington Northern Santa Fe	J.B. Hunt
	Kansas City Southern
CSX	Kirby Corporation
Canadian National Railway	Landstar System
	Norfolk Southern
Canadian Pacific Railway	Schneider National
	Werner Enterprises

HISTORICAL FINANCIALS

Company Type: Public

Income Statement				FYE: December 31
	REVENUE ($ mil.)	NET INCOME ($ mil.)	NET PROFIT MARGIN	EMPLOYEES
12/18	22,832	5,966	26.1%	41,967
12/17	21,240	10,712	50.4%	41,992
12/16	19,941	4,233	21.2%	42,919
12/15	21,813	4,772	21.9%	47,457
12/14	23,988	5,180	21.6%	47,201
Annual Growth	(1.2%)	3.6%	—	(2.9%)

2018 Year-End Financials

Debt ratio: 37.86%
Return on equity: 26.35%
Cash ($ mil.): 1,273
Current ratio: 0.90
Long-term debt ($ mil.): 20,925

No. of shares (mil.): 725
Dividends
  Yield: 2.2%
  Payout: 20.5%
Market value ($ mil.): 100,225

	STOCK PRICE ($) FY Close	P/E High/Low		PER SHARE ($) Earnings	Dividends	Book Value
12/18	138.23	21	16	7.91	3.06	28.17
12/17	134.10	10	8	13.36	2.48	31.83
12/16	103.68	21	14	5.07	2.26	24.43
12/15	78.20	22	14	5.49	2.20	24.38
12/14	119.13	35	17	5.75	1.91	23.99
Annual Growth	3.8%	—	—	8.3%	12.5%	4.1%

United Bankshares Inc

United Bankshares (no relation to Ohio's United Bancshares) keeps it together as the holding company for two subsidiaries doing business as United Bank (WV) and United Bank (VA). Combined the banks boast some $12 billion in assets and operate roughly 130 branches that serve West Virginia Virginia and Washington DC as well as nearby portions of Maryland Pennsylvania and Ohio. The branches offer traditional deposit trust and lending services with a focus on residential mortgages and commercial loans. United Bankshares also owns United Brokerage Services which provides investments asset management and financial planning in addition to brokerage services.

Operations

The company's loan portfolio is made up of commercial and construction commercial and residential real estate and consumer loans (including credit card and home equity loans).

United Bankshares generated 75% of its total revenue from interest and fees on loans in 2014 plus an additional 7% from interest and dividends on its investment securities. The company generated about 9% of its total revenue from deposit services fees and another 4% from trust and brokerage services fees.

Geographic Reach

United Bankshares boasts some 130 full-service branches including more than 55 across the state of West Virginia nearly 70 in the Shenendoah Valley region of Virginia and the Northern Virginia Maryland and Washington DC metro area and a handful of branches split between southwestern Pennsylvania and southeastern Ohio.

Sales and Marketing

The company spent $4.76 million on advertising in 2014 up from $3.78 million and $4.27 million spent in 2013 and 2012 respectively.

Financial Performance

United Bankshares' revenues and profits have trended higher over the past few years thanks to growth in its loan business from acquisitions increased trust and brokerage services fee income and declining interest expense on deposits amidst the low-interest environment.

The company's revenue jumped by nearly 34% to a record $499.50 million in 2014 mostly as its interest income spiked by 37% after its Virginia Commerce acquisition added new interest-earning assets and increased the average yields on its loans investments and security assets. United Bankshare's non-interest income also swelled by 22% thanks to higher income from fees from trust and brokerage services bankcard fees and merchant discounts and net gains on investment securities.

Higher revenue in 2014 boosted the company's profits by 52% to a record $129.89 million while the company's operating cash grew by 2% thanks to higher cash earnings.

Strategy

United Bankshares has historically expanded through small bank and branch acquisitions closing nearly 30 bank purchases in the past quarter-century. Its growth strategy has mainly been focused in on the Washington DC/suburban Maryland/northern Virginia market though its also expanded into Pennsylvania in recent years as well. In 2014 for example the company extended its reach into Washington DC while boosting its loan business by $2 billion after completing its largest-ever acquisition of Virginia Commerce Bancorp.

In 2016 the company agreed to buy Cardinal Financial which has some $4.2 billion in assets and operates 30 branches in Virginia Maryland and Washington DC.

Mergers and Acquisitions

In January 2014 United Bankshares acquired Arlington-based Virginia Commerce Bancorp for a total cost of $585.53 million. The deal expanded United's reach into the Washington DC metropolitan area and added $2.07 billion in new loan business and $2.02 billion in deposits.

Company Background

The 2011 acquisition of West Virginia-based Centra Financial Holdings gave United Bankshares its first branches in Pennsylvania and entry into the Pittsburgh market.

EXECUTIVES

Evp The Company And United Bank And Wv, James B. Hayhurst, age 72, $225,000 total compensation

President, Richard M. Adams, age 50, $328,846 total compensation

Coo, James J. Consagra, age 58, $334,462 total compensation

Evp And Coo United Bank (va), Craige L. Smith, age 66, $243,750 total compensation

Evp And Cfo, W. Mark Tatterson, age 43

Evp, Darren K. Williams

Assistant Vice President Information Technology Audit Manager, Jason Moore

Vice President Internal Audit Manager, Steve Hizak

Assistant Vice President Corporate Security Officer, Rachel Wilson

Assistant Vice President And Corporate Security Officer, Erica Fowler

Auditors: Ernst & Young LLP

LOCATIONS

HQ: United Bankshares Inc
300 United Center, 500 Virginia Street, East, Charleston, WV 25301

Phone: 304 424-8716

Web: www.ubsi-inc.com

PRODUCTS/OPERATIONS

2014 Sales

	$ mil.	% of total
Interest		
Loans including fees	383	75
Interest and dividends on securities	33	7
Other	0	-
Noninterest		
Fees from deposit services	42	9
Fees from trust & brokerage services	18	4
Other	28	5
Adjustment (losses)	(8.4)	-
Total	**499**	**100**

COMPETITORS

BB&T	JPMorgan Chase
Bank of America	M&T Bank
Burke & Herbert Bank	PNC Financial
Cardinal Financial	SunTrust
City Holding	United Bancorp
Fifth Third	Virginia Commerce
Fulton Financial	Bancorp
Huntington Bancshares	WesBanco

HISTORICAL FINANCIALS

Company Type: Public

Income Statement   FYE: December 31

	ASSETS ($ mil.)	NET INCOME ($ mil.)	INCOME AS % OF ASSETS	EMPLOYEES
12/17	19,058	150	0.8%	2,381
12/16	14,508	147	1.0%	1,701
12/15	12,577	137	1.1%	1,701
12/14	12,328	129	1.1%	1,703
12/13	8,735	85	1.0%	1,528
Annual Growth	**21.5%**	**15.2%**	**—**	**11.7%**

2017 Year-End Financials

Debt ratio: 1.27%	No. of shares (mil.): 105
Return on equity: 5.50%	Dividends
Cash ($ mil.): 1,665	Yield: 0.0%
Current ratio: —	Payout: 86.3%
Long-term debt ($ mil.): —	Market value ($ mil.): 3,650

	STOCK PRICE ($) FY Close	P/E High/Low	PER SHARE ($) Earnings	Dividends	Book Value
12/17	34.75	30 21	1.54	1.33	30.85
12/16	46.25	25 16	1.99	1.32	27.59
12/15	36.99	22 17	1.98	1.29	24.61
12/14	37.45	20 15	1.92	1.28	23.90
12/13	31.45	19 14	1.70	1.25	20.66
Annual Growth	**2.5%**	**— —**	**(2.4%)**	**1.6%**	**10.5%**

United Community Banks Inc (Blairsville, GA)

United Community Banks is the holding company for United Community Bank (UCB). UCB provides consumer and business banking products and services through nearly 150 branches across Georgia North Carolina Tennessee and South Carolina. Commercial loans including construction loans and mortgages account for the largest portion of UCB's loan portfolio (more than 50%); residential mortgages make up 30%. The company which boasts roughly $10 billion in assets also has a mortgage lending division and provides insurance through its United Community Insurance Services subsidiary (aka United Community Advisory Services).

Operations

The bank's retail mortgage lending division United Community Mortgage Services (UCMS) sells and services mortgages for Fannie Mae and Freddie Mac and provides fixed and adjustable-rate home mortgages. It also offers retail brokerage services through an affiliation with a third-party broker/dealer.

About 65% of UCB's total revenue came from loan interest (including fees) in 2014 while another 16% came from taxable investments. The rest of its revenue came from service charges and fees (10%) mortgage loan fees (2%) and brokerage fees (2%) among other sources.

Geographic Reach

UCB's nearly 105 branches are located in Georgia (in the north the Atlanta-Sandy Springs-Roswell metro area Gainsville metro area and coastal areas); western North Carolina; eastern and central Tennessee; and South Carolina (in the Greenville-Anderson-Mauldin metro area).

Sales and Marketing

The bank provides community banking services for individuals small businesses and corporations.

Financial Performance

UCB has struggled to consistently grow its revenues in recent years due to shrinking interest margins on loans amidst the low-interest environment. Its profits however have been rising thanks to declining loan loss provisions as its loan portfolio's credit quality has improved with higher property valuations in the strengthened economy.

The bank's revenue inched higher by 1% to $304 million in 2014 thanks to an increase in interest income stemming from strategic business growth initiatives designed to add new business lines and expand into new markets as well as balance sheet management and restructuring actions taken in the second quarter of the year.

Despite higher revenue in 2014 UCB's net income dove 75% to $67.6 million mostly because in 2013 it had received a non-recurring income tax benefit of $238 million stemming from reversal of a deferred tax valuation allowance. Not counting this item however the bank's profit before taxes nearly tripled during the year. UCB's operating cash levels dropped by 47% to $101.9 million in 2014 due to lower cash earnings.

Strategy

UCB has been concentrating on growing its small business lending business in recent years. In 2014 it made "significant investments" in its SBA business after acquiring Business Carolina which specialized in SBA and USDA lending.

It also continues to pursue bank acquisitions to expand its reach in its existing core markets and boost its loan and deposit business. Its acquisitions in 2015 and 2014 alone have added over $1 billion in new loan business and $1.3 billion in new deposits.

Mergers and Acquisitions

In 2016 United Community Banks expanded into key markets in coastal South Carolina after buying Mt. Pleasant-based Tidelands and its seven Tidelands Bank branches in the Charleston Myrtle Beach and Hilton Head areas.

In 2015 UCB bought Tennessee-based MoneyTree Corporation and its 10 First National Bank branches in east Tennessee. The deal added $425 million in assets $354 million in deposits and $253 million in new loan business to UCB's books.

In 2014 the company purchased Palmetto Bancshares and its Palmetto Bank branches expanding its footprint into "major" southeastern metro markets in Greenville and the Upstate South Carolina area. The deal also added $1.2 billion in assets $832 million in loans and $967 million in deposits.

Also in 2014 UCB purchased Columbia-based Business Carolina a commercial lender that specialized in SBA and USDA loans for $31.3 million in cash. The deal included $25 million in loans $6 million in other assets and substantially all of the company's employees.

EXECUTIVES

President Of Specialized Lending, Richard W. Bradshaw, age 56

Chairman And Ceo, Jimmy C. Tallent, age 65, $750,000 total compensation

Svp Retail Banking; Chairman United Community Bank Adairsville And Summerville, William M. (Bill) Gilbert, age 65, $308,334 total compensation

President And Director United Community Banks Inc. And President Ceo And Director United Community Bank, H. Lynn Harton, age 56, $575,000 total compensation

Evp General Counsel And Chief Risk Officer, Bradley J. (Brad) Miller, age 47

Evp And Chief Credit Officer, Robert A. (Rob) Edwards, age 53, $305,000 total compensation

Evp And Cfo United Community Banks Inc. And United Community Bank, Jefferson L. Harralson

Senior Vice President, Debbie Williams

Vice President, Casey Brogdon

Senior Vice President Commercial Lending, Don Fowler

Senior Vice President Commercial Banking, Jay Roper

Executive Vice President, Rick Rowland

Vice President, RONNEY DIXON

Senior Vice President Retail Credit Administration, Chuck Valerio

Avp Mortgage Loan Officer, Tabitha Helms

Assistant Vice President Incentive Marketing Manager, Diana White

Vice President, Omar Galan

Assistant Vice President, Ginger Kilman

Senior Vice President Director Of Loan Operations, Dan Graham

Vice President Mortgage Banker, Angie Abston

Vice President Of Business Development And Marketing, Elaine Bell

Vice President Business Banking, Bert Durand

Assistant Vice President, Adam Born

Senior Vice President Commercial Lending, Sam Churchill

Senior Vice President, Donald Harris

Senior Vice President Corporate Services Support, Jeanette Garrett

Senior Vice President, Skip Swain

Senior Vice President, Zachary Welch

Vice President, Jane Callihan

Assistant Vice President Business Banking Underwriting, Eric Rivenbark

Senior Vice President Commercial Banking, Ben Walker

Senior Vice President, Phil Beaudette

Assistant Vice President, Rob Andrews

Vice President And Director Bank Security, Dennis Tarnowski

Senior Vice President, Alan Kumler

Senior Vice President Builder Finance, Scott Ernest

Senior Vice President Human Resources, Susie Hooper

Vice President, Darryl Meadows

Senior Vice President And Treasurer, Michael Burke

Vice President, Anne Wade

Vice President And Private Banker, Terra Winter

Senior Vice President, Jessie Marolis

Vice President, Wendy Martin

Senior Vice President Secondary Marketing, Jim Mcevoy

Vice President Commercial Lender, Donna Clark

Vice President Relationship Manager, Tim Ash

Vice President Business Development Officer Senior Analyst Lending, David Brindley

Vice President Franchise Lending, Mike Stone

Senior Vice President United Community Bank, Dennis McBride

Senior Vice President, Jennifer Lawley

Senior Vice President, Sheila Stolorena

Vice President, David Ball

Vice President Branch Manager, Liz Bowen

Senior Vice President, Will Ferguson

Vice President, Sandra Brown

Vice President Underwriting, Linda Durden

Assistant Vice President And Mortgage Processing Manager, Nalann Moss

Vice President, Frank Scott

Vice President Corporate Banking, James Boccardo

Vice President Customer Contact Center Team Manager Sc, Jeanie Roberts

Vice President, Kirby Butler

Assistant Treasurer, Mitchell Bleske

Board Member, Kenneth Daniels

Board Member, David Wilkins

Board Member, David Shaver

Auditors: PricewaterhouseCoopers LLP

LOCATIONS

HQ: United Community Banks Inc (Blairsville, GA)
125 Highway 515 East, Blairsville, GA 30512
Phone: 706 781-2265
Web: www.ucbi.com

PRODUCTS/OPERATIONS

2011 Sales

	$ mil.	% of total
Interest		
Loans including fees	239	69
Taxable investment securities	55	16
Other	3	1
Noninterest		
Service charges & fees	29	8
Mortgage loans & related fees	5	2
Brokerage fees	3	1
Net securities gains	0	-
Other	12	3
Adjustment	(0.7)	-
Total	**347**	**100**

COMPETITORS

Atlantic Coast Financial	Peoples Bancorp (NC)
BB&T	Regions Financial
Bank of America	Southeastern Bank Financial
Bank of Oak Ridge	Southeastern Banking
Fidelity Southern	SunTrust
First Citizens	Synovus

BancShares
Georgia Bancshares
Georgia-Carolina Bancshares
WGNB

HISTORICAL FINANCIALS

Company Type: Public

Income Statement

FYE: December 31

	ASSETS ($ mil.)	NET INCOME ($ mil.)	INCOME AS % OF ASSETS	EMPLOYEES
12/17	11,915	67	0.6%	2,137
12/16	10,708	100	0.9%	1,916
12/15	9,626	71	0.7%	1,883
12/14	7,566	67	0.9%	1,506
12/13	7,425	273	3.7%	1,472
Annual Growth	12.6%	(29.4%)	—	9.8%

2017 Year-End Financials

Debt ratio: 1.01%
Return on equity: 5.70%
Cash ($ mil.): 314
Current ratio: —
Long-term debt ($ mil.): —

No. of shares (mil.): 77
Dividends
  Yield: 0.0%
  Payout: 41.3%
Market value ($ mil.): 2,183

	STOCK PRICE ($) FY Close	P/E High/Low		PER SHARE ($) Earnings	Dividends	Book Value
12/17	28.14	33	27	0.92	0.38	16.80
12/16	29.62	21	11	1.40	0.30	15.17
12/15	19.49	20	15	1.09	0.22	14.24
12/14	18.94	18	14	1.11	0.11	12.27
12/13	17.75	4	2	4.44	0.00	13.39
Annual Growth	12.2%	—	—	(32.5%)	—	5.8%

United Community Financial Corp. (OH)

This thrift wants to keep your savings and your loans united. United Community Financial is the holding company for The Home Savings and Loan Company of Youngstown Ohio a community bank with more than 30 full-service branches and about 10 loan production offices in Ohio and western Pennsylvania. Boasting nearly $2 billion in assets the bank offers traditional checking and savings accounts CDs retirement accounts investments and credit cards as well as a variety of loans. Residential mortgages account for over 60% of the company's loan portfolio while commercial and consumer loans split the remainder.

Operations

About 62% of United Community's total revenue came from loan interest (including fees) in 2014 while another 16% came from interest on its securities held for sale. The rest of its revenue came from fees on deposit accounts (6%) mortgage servicing fees (3%) non-deposit investment income 2%) and other miscellaneous income sources. The bank had a staff of 428 full-time employees at the end of 2014.

Geographic Reach

Youngstown Ohio-based United Community Financial boasts more than 30 branches across Ohio and western Pennsylvania. Its primary markets include Allegheny and Beaver counties in Pennsylvania and Ashland Columbiana Cuyahoga Erie Franklin Geauga Huron Lake Mahoning Portage

Richland Stark Summit and Trumbull Counties in Ohio.

Sales and Marketing

The company spent $838 thousand on advertising in 2014 compared to $893 thousand and $778 thousand in 2013 and 2012 respectively.

Financial Performance

United Community Financial has struggled to grow its revenue in recent years as its interest income has fallen with lower interest rates and because it's had to sell of many of its non-performing loan assets to de-risk its loan portfolio. The group's profits however are on the mend as its de-risking measures have led to declining loan loss provisions.

The company's revenue fell by 9% to $77 million in 2014 mostly due to a combination of lower interest income after it sold off some of its investment securities a $2.1 million decline in gains from security sales and a $3.2 million drop in mortgage banking income due to a reduction in mortgage origination sales.

Despite revenue declines in 2014 United's net income grew five-fold to a record $50.2 million for the year mostly thanks to a $39.7 million income tax benefit related to a reversal of a previous year's bad loan allowance and thanks to continued declines in loan loss provisions. The company's operating cash levels fell sharply with operations using $2.8 million in 2014 after its earnings were adjusted for non-cash items related to its net proceeds from its loans held for sale.

Strategy

Home Savings mainly focuses on originating residential real estate loans security by real estate in its primary market area. United Community Financial has been working to build its capital and shed its riskier assets to get its business back on solid footing. Indeed while the bank suffered several years of heavy losses between 2008 and 2012 its de-risking measures made 2014 the company's most profitable year in its history.

Mergers and Acquisitions

United Community agreed to buy Ohio Legacy Corp holding company of the four-branch Premier Bank & Trust for $40.3 million. Ohio Legacy also operates a wealth management and trust division.

Company Background

In 2012 federal and state regulators lifted a cease-and-desist order that the bank had been operating under since 2008. In its place the company began operating under a consent order under which United Community Financial would need to submit a formal capital plan to the regulators. To satisfy targets under the consent order the bank sold about $115 million worth of bad assets in late 2012.

EXECUTIVES

Cfo United Community Financial Corp. And Evp And Cfo Home Savings And Loan, Timothy W. Esson, age 68, $216,577 total compensation
General Counsel And Secretary Ucfc And Evp General Counsel And Secretary Home Savings And Loan, Jude J. Nohra, age 49, $248,871 total compensation
President Ceo And Director United Community Financial Corp. And Home Savings And Loan, Gary M. Small, age 58, $412,885 total compensation
Evp And Head Of Commercial Lending And Credit Administration Home Savings And Loan, Matthew T. Garrity, age 51, $251,007 total compensation
Evp Retail Banking Home Savings And Loan, Barbara J. Radis, age 49
Svp And Cio, Douglas Young
Vice President Human Resources, Cindy Cerimele
Vice President Finance, Anthony Dantuono
Vp Systems, Mark S Stricklin

Chairman United Community Financial And Home Savings And Loan, Richard J. Schiraldi, age 63
Auditors: Crowe Horwath LLP

LOCATIONS

HQ: United Community Financial Corp. (OH)
275 West Federal Street, Youngstown, OH 44503-1203
Phone: 330 742-0500
Web: www.ucfconline.com

PRODUCTS/OPERATIONS

2014 Sales

	$ mil.	% of total
Interest	63	80
Non-interest	13	20
Total	**77**	**100**

COMPETITORS

Central Federal	PNC Financial
F.N.B. (PA)	PVF Capital
Farmers National	U.S. Bancorp
KeyCorp	

HISTORICAL FINANCIALS

Company Type: Public

Income Statement

FYE: December 31

	ASSETS ($ mil.)	NET INCOME ($ mil.)	INCOME AS % OF ASSETS	EMPLOYEES
12/17	2,649	21	0.8%	503
12/16	2,191	18	0.9%	442
12/15	1,987	16	0.8%	428
12/14	1,833	50	2.7%	428
12/13	1,737	10	0.6%	514
Annual Growth	**11.1%**	**21.4%**	**—**	**(0.5%)**

2017 Year-End Financials

Debt ratio: 0.01%	No. of shares (mil.): 49
Return on equity: 8.01%	Dividends
Cash ($ mil.): 34	Yield: 0.0%
Current ratio: —	Payout: 31.8%
Long-term debt ($ mil.): —	Market value ($ mil.): 455

	STOCK PRICE ($) FY Close	P/E High/Low	PER SHARE ($) Earnings	Dividends	Book Value
12/17	9.13	23 18	0.44	0.14	5.91
12/16	8.94	24 13	0.40	0.11	5.36
12/15	5.90	18 14	0.34	0.07	5.14
12/14	5.37	5 3	1.00	0.02	4.88
12/13	3.57	71 41	0.07	0.00	3.48
Annual Growth	**26.5%**	**— —**	**58.3%**	**—**	**14.2%**

United Continental Holdings Inc

United Continental Holdings (UAL) unites cities around the globe through its primary United Air Lines subsidiary. While United Air Lines is its main line the company also has regional operations which are operated under contract by United Express. Combined the company handles an average of roughly 4500 flights a day to more than 335 domestic and international destinations from hubs that include Chicago Denver Houston Los Angeles San Francisco New York (Newark) and Washington DC. Like most airlines the company sells the majority of its seat inventory through travel agencies and global distribution systems in addition to its main website.

Operations

UAL operates more than 1220 aircraft including aircraft operated by regional carriers on its behalf. It generates its revenues across four segments: passenger mainline (70% of total sales) passenger regional (more than 15%) cargo (less than 5%) and other (more than 10%).

The company is a member of the Star Alliance network which offers more than 18450 daily flights to 190 countries worldwide and includes 28 member airlines.

Geographic Reach

Headquartered in Chicago UAL operates across five continents from its hubs at Newark Liberty International Airport Chicago O'Hare International Airpor Denver International Airport George Bush Intercontinental Airport Los Angeles International Airport A.B. Won Pat International Airport San Francisco International Airport and Washington Dulles International Airport.

US and Canada collectively account for 60% of its total net sales. Other major markets include the Atlantic (more than 15%) and Pacific (more than 10%) regions in addition to Latin America (almost 10%).

Financial Performance

UAL's revenues have declined the last two years dipping 3% from $37.9 billion in 2015 to $36.6 billion in 2016. Its passenger revenue for 2016 decreased due to a competitive domestic fare environment unfavorable foreign currency results due to the strengthening of the US dollar international surcharge declines travel reductions from corporate customers in the energy sector and increased industry capacity in certain regions.

Profits nosedived by nearly 70% from 2015 to 2016. This was due to about $413 million in impairment charges coupled with increases in ground handling costs food and technology costs restructuring costs and income tax expenses (compared to tax benefits its received the prior year).

After experiencing an influx of operating cash flow in 2015 UAL saw its cash flow decline in 2016 due to a decrease in frequent flyer and advanced purchases of miles and unfavorable timing of payments in accounts payable.

Strategy

UAL has ordered a number of fuel-efficient Airbus and Boeing aircraft to replace the older fleet. It has 50 Dreamliners scheduled for delivery between 2013 and 2020. The 787 anticipated to be "a game changer" for the company and for the airline industry will allow both United Air Lines and Continental to enter new long-haul markets and to replace older less-efficient widebody aircraft.

In 2016 UAL took delivery of five new Boeing 787-9 Dreamliners eight new Boeing 737-900ERs seven new Boeing 737-800s two new Boeing 777-300ERs and six used Airbus A319s.

HISTORY

In 1929 aircraft designer Bill Boeing and engine designer Fred Rentschler of Pratt & Whitney joined forces to form United Aircraft and Transport. Renamed United Air Lines in 1931 the New York-based company offered one of the first coast-to-coast airline services. In 1934 United's manufacturing and transportation divisions split. Former banker Bill Patterson became president of the latter United Air Lines and moved it to the Chicago area. In 1969 UAL Corp. was formed as a holding company.

A subsidiary of UAL Corporation merged with and into Continental in October 2010 with Continental surviving as a wholly-owned subsidiary of UAL. Upon closing of the merger UAL became the parent company of both Continental and United Air Lines and UAL Corporation's name was changed to United Continental Holdings. The transaction created the world's largest airline. In 2013 United Air Lines Inc. was merged into Continental to form one legal entity and Continental's name and brand was changed to United Airlines Inc.

EXECUTIVES

Svp Finance And Procurement And Treasurer, Gerald (Gerry) Laderman, age 60, $500,000 total compensation

President, J. Scott Kirby, age 50, $301,763 total compensation

Evp And Chief Revenue Officer, Andrew P. Nocella

Ceo, Oscar Munoz, age 60, $1,193,909 total compensation

Evp And Cio, Linda P. Jojo, age 52

Svp Technical Operations, Kris B. Bauer, age 54

Evp And Cfo, Andrew C. Levy, age 48, $243,750 total compensation

Evp And General Counsel, Brett J. Hart, age 48, $715,000 total compensation

Evp And Coo, Gregory L. (Greg) Hart, age 52, $850,000 total compensation

Evp Human Resources And Labor Relations, Michael P. (Mike) Bonds, age 56, $650,000 total compensation

Chairman, Robert A. Milton, age 58

Auditors: Ernst & Young LLP

LOCATIONS

HQ: United Continental Holdings Inc
233 South Wacker Drive, Chicago, IL 60606
Phone: 872 825-4000
Web: www.unitedcontinentalholdings.com

2016 Sales

	$ mil.	% of total
Domestic (US & Canada)	22,202	61
Atlantic	6,167	17
Pacific	4,959	13
Latin America	3,238	9
Total	**36,556**	**100**

PRODUCTS/OPERATIONS

2016 Sales

	$ mil.	% of total
Passenger		
Main line	25,414	70
Regional	6,043	16
Cargo	876	2
Other	4,223	12
Total	**36,556**	**100**

Selected Aircraft Type

COMPETITORS

Air France-KLM	Japan Airlines
AirTran Airways	JetBlue
Alaska Air	Mesa Air
Alitalia	Qantas
American Airlines Group	SkyWest
British Airways	Southwest Airlines
Delta Air Lines	UPS
FedEx	Virgin Atlantic Airways
Frontier Airlines	

HISTORICAL FINANCIALS

Company Type: Public

Income Statement

FYE: December 31

	REVENUE ($ mil.)	NET INCOME ($ mil.)	NET PROFIT MARGIN	EMPLOYEES
12/17	37,736	2,131	5.6%	89,800
12/16	36,556	2,263	6.2%	88,000
12/15	37,864	7,340	19.4%	84,000
12/14	38,901	1,132	2.9%	84,000
12/13	38,279	571	1.5%	87,000
Annual Growth	(0.4%)	39.0%	—	0.8%

2017 Year-End Financials

Debt ratio: 34.00%
Return on equity: 24.40%
Cash ($ mil.): 3,798
Current ratio: 0.56
Long-term debt ($ mil.): 12,699

No. of shares (mil.): 286
Dividends
  Yield: —
  Payout: —
Market value ($ mil.): 19,342

	STOCK PRICE ($) FY Close	P/E High/Low		Earnings	PER SHARE ($) Dividends	Book Value
12/17	67.40	12	8	7.02	0.00	30.69
12/16	72.88	11	6	6.85	0.00	27.52
12/15	57.30	4	3	19.47	0.00	24.59
12/14	66.89	22	12	2.93	0.00	6.40
12/13	37.83	24	14	1.53	0.00	8.24
Annual Growth	15.5%	—	—	46.4%	—	38.9%

United Financial Bancorp Inc (New)

EXECUTIVES

Ceo, William H W Crawford IV
Chb*, Robert A Stewart Jr
Exec V Pres-Cfo-Treas, Eric R Newell
Exec V Pres-Corp SEC & Investo, Marliese L Shaw
Exec V Pres, Mark A Kucia
Officer, Barbara Parrelli
Executive Vice President, Daniel Flynn
Vice President, Matthew Newcomb
Board Member, Carol Leary
Board Member, Kevin Ross
Board Member, Michael Crowley
Auditors: Wolf & Company, P.C.

LOCATIONS

HQ: United Financial Bancorp Inc (New)
225 Asylum Street, Hartford, CT 06103
Phone: 860 291-3600
Web: www.bankatunited.com

COMPETITORS

Bank of America	RBS Citizens Financial Group
Citibank	SI Financial
Liberty Bank	Sovereign Bank
Naugatuck Valley Financial	TD Bank USA
New England Bancshares	United Financial Bancorp
PSB Holdings Inc.	Webster Financial
People's United Financial	Westfield Financial

HISTORICAL FINANCIALS

Company Type: Public

Income Statement

FYE: December 31

	ASSETS ($ mil.)	NET INCOME ($ mil.)	INCOME AS % OF ASSETS	EMPLOYEES
12/17	7,114	54	0.8%	813
12/16	6,599	49	0.8%	768
12/15	6,228	49	0.8%	732
12/14	5,476	6	0.1%	725
12/13	2,301	14	0.6%	358
Annual Growth	32.6%	40.0%	—	22.8%

2017 Year-End Financials

Debt ratio: 1.77%
Return on equity: 8.10%
Cash ($ mil.): 88
Current ratio: —
Long-term debt ($ mil.): —

No. of shares (mil.): 51
Dividends
  Yield: 0.0%
  Payout: 44.8%
Market value ($ mil.): 900

	STOCK PRICE ($) FY Close	P/E High/Low		Earnings	PER SHARE ($) Dividends	Book Value
12/17	17.64	18	15	1.07	0.48	13.58
12/16	18.16	18	11	0.99	0.48	12.91
12/15	12.88	14	12	1.00	0.46	12.53
12/14	14.36	91	76	0.16	0.40	12.16
12/13	14.21	28	23	0.54	0.56	11.53
Annual Growth	5.6%	—	—	18.6%	(3.8%)	4.2%

United Fire Group, Inc.

The United Fire Group (UFG) companies join together to offer a range of property/casualty products. The group operates through its United Fire & Casualty subsidiary which in turn holds entities that carry a variety of property/casualty offerings including fidelity and surety bonds and fire auto employee liability homeowners and workers' compensation lines. Some 1600 independent agencies in around 45 states sell its property/casualty products to businesses and individuals. In 2018 UFG sold its life insurance unit United Life Insurance Company to Kuvare US Holdings for $280 million.

Operations
Prior to the 2018 sale of its life insurance business UFG's property/casualty offerings accounted for more than 90% of its annual insurance premiums with a majority of those policies being written to commercial group customers. The company also offers certain personal policies to individual customers.

Geographic Reach
UFG markets its products from its headquarters in Iowa and from five regional offices in California Colorado New Jersey and Texas. It primarily operates in adjacent areas of the midwestern southern and western US.

Sales and Marketing
To increase policy placement in its existing markets UFG offers profit-sharing and commission programs to its independent agents. It also seeks to provide modern technological tools to best serve both its agents and its policyholders.

The company is represented by some 1200 independent property/casualty agencies.

Financial Performance
With the exception of 2015 UFG's revenue has been growing year-over-year. Net income has been more volatile rising and falling from year to year.

In 2017 revenue increased 6% to $1.1 billion. Direct premiums written rose that year due to organic growth related to new business and geographical expansion.

Net income rose a modest 2% to $51 million in 2017. That increase was largely due to a tax benefit of $21.9 million as a result of the Tax Act passed that year. However a rise in losses and loss settlement expenses hurt UFG's bottom line. For example the company's commercial automobile business had a higher number of large losses (losses greater than $500000). Additionally 2017 was a record year for catastrophe losses in the insurance sector with major hurricanes and wildfires. UFG's catastrophe losses totaled $74 million versus $61.2 million in 2016.

UFG ended 2017 with $95.6 million in net cash some $6.4 million more than it had at the end of 2016. Operating activities provided $170.1 million while financing activities used $107.5 million and investing activities used $62 million.

Strategy

UFG looks to expand into new markets to reduce the risk potential in its concentrated areas of operation. Like the rest of the property/casualty sector the company suffered increased losses during 2017 the worst year for catastrophes on record. With much of its business located in the Midwest South and West UFG is vulnerable to future bad years that could result from climate change.

The United Life division of United Fire & Casualty sold life annuity and credit life products in more than 30 states but UFG sold that division in early 2018.

EXECUTIVES

Vp General Counsel And Secretary, Neal R. Scharmer, age 62, $250,000 total compensation
Coo, Michael T. Wilkins, age 55, $388,600 total compensation
Vp And Chief Investment Officer, Barrie W. Ernst, age 64, $305,000 total compensation
President And Ceo, Randy A. Ramlo, age 57, $595,000 total compensation
Vp And Chief Claims Officer, David E. Conner, age 60
Cfo, Dawn M. Jaffray, age 53
Vp Information Services, Scott A. Minkel, age 57
Vp Corporate Marketing, Colleen R. Sova, age 65
Assistant Vice President Midwest Regional Office, Corey J. Ruehle
Vp And Coo United Life Insurance Company, Michael J. Sheeley
Cto, Brian Frese
Assistant Vice President Personal Lines, Victoria Hefel
Vice President Of Accounting, Sue Haupert
Vice President, Douglas Penn
Vice President Human Resources, Timothy Spain
Assistant Vice President West Coast Regional Claims Manager, Mary Bianco
Vice Chairman, John A. Rife, age 76
Chairman, Jack B. Evans, age 70
Auditors: Ernst & Young LLP

LOCATIONS

HQ: United Fire Group, Inc.
118 Second Avenue S.E., Cedar Rapids, IA 52401
Phone: 319 399-5700
Web: www.ufginsurance.com

PRODUCTS/OPERATIONS

2017 Sales

	$ mil.	% of total
Net premiums earned	997	95
Net investment income	51	5
Net realized investment gains	4	-
Total	**1,052**	**100**

Selected Subsidiaries

United Fire & Casualty Company
Addison Insurance Company
American Indemnity Financial Corporation
Texas General Indemnity Company
Lafayette Insurance Company
Mercer Insurance Group Inc.
Financial Pacific Insurance Company
Mercer Insurance Company
Franklin Insurance Company
Mercer Insurance Company of New Jersey Inc.
United Fire & Indemnity Company
United Fire Lloyds

COMPETITORS

AIG
Allstate
American Family Insurance
American Financial Group
CNA Surety
Farmers Group
GEICO
Hanover Insurance
John Hancock Financial Services
Liberty Mutual
Progressive Corporation
Prudential
State Farm
The Hartford
Travelers Companies

HISTORICAL FINANCIALS

Company Type: Public

Income Statement
FYE: December 31

	ASSETS ($ mil.)	NET INCOME ($ mil.)	INCOME AS % OF ASSETS	EMPLOYEES
12/17	4,183	51	1.2%	1,180
12/16	4,054	49	1.2%	1,112
12/15	3,890	89	2.3%	1,070
12/14	3,856	59	1.5%	981
12/13	3,720	76	2.0%	943
Annual Growth	3.0%	(9.5%)	—	5.8%

2017 Year-End Financials

Debt ratio: —
Return on equity: 5.33%
Cash ($ mil.): 95
Current ratio: —
Long-term debt ($ mil.): —

No. of shares (mil.): 24
Dividends
  Yield: 0.0%
  Payout: 54.7%
Market value ($ mil.): 1,136

	STOCK PRICE ($) FY Close	P/E High/Low	Earnings	Dividends	Book Value
12/17	45.58	24 19	1.99	1.09	39.06
12/16	49.17	26 18	1.93	0.97	37.04
12/15	38.31	11 8	3.53	0.86	34.94
12/14	29.73	14 10	2.32	0.78	32.67
12/13	28.66	11 7	2.98	0.69	30.87
Annual Growth	12.3%	— —	(9.6%)	12.1%	6.1%

United Insurance Holdings Corp

EXECUTIVES

Chief Underwriting Officer, Paul DiFrancesco
Ceo, John L. Forney, $800,000 total compensation
Cfo, B. Bradford Martz, $300,000 total compensation
Cio, Andrew D. (Andy) Swenson, $210,000 total compensation
General Counsel And Chief Legal Officer, Kimberly Salmon
Chairman, Gregory C. Branch
Auditors: DELOITTE & TOUCHE LLP

LOCATIONS

HQ: United Insurance Holdings Corp
800 2nd Avenue S., St. Petersburg, FL 33701
Phone: 727 895-7737
Web: www.upcinsurance.com

PRODUCTS/OPERATIONS

2015 Sales

	% of total
Net premiums earned	94
Investment income	3
Net realized gains	-
Other revenue	3
Total	**100**

COMPETITORS

AAA Auto Club South
Allstate
American National Insurance
Bankers Financial
Citizens Property Insurance
Federated National Holding
HCI Group
Liberty Mutual
State Farm
Universal Insurance Holdings

HISTORICAL FINANCIALS

Company Type: Public

Income Statement
FYE: December 31

	ASSETS ($ mil.)	NET INCOME ($ mil.)	INCOME AS % OF ASSETS	EMPLOYEES
12/17	2,059	10	0.5%	210
12/16	999	5	0.6%	167
12/15	740	27	3.7%	120
12/14	584	41	7.0%	120
12/13	441	20	4.6%	90
Annual Growth	47.0%	(16.0%)	—	23.6%

2017 Year-End Financials

Debt ratio: 7.83%
Return on equity: 2.61%
Cash ($ mil.): 276
Current ratio: —
Long-term debt ($ mil.): —

No. of shares (mil.): 42
Dividends
  Yield: 0.0%
  Payout: 88.8%
Market value ($ mil.): 737

	STOCK PRICE ($) FY Close	P/E High/Low	Earnings	Dividends	Book Value
12/17	17.25	65 49	0.27	0.24	12.56
12/16	15.14	73 40	0.26	0.23	11.15
12/15	17.10	22 10	1.28	0.20	11.11
12/14	21.95	11 6	2.05	0.16	9.75
12/13	14.08	11 4	1.26	0.15	6.64
Annual Growth	5.2%	— —	(32.0%)	12.5%	17.3%

United Natural Foods Inc.

Distribution comes naturally to United Natural Foods Inc. (UNFI). The company is one of the top wholesale distributors of natural organic and specialty foods in the US and Canada. It owns around 35 distribution centers that supply more than 100000 items to 43000 customers including independently-owned retailers supernatural chain Whole Foods (its #1 customer) and conventional supermarkets. The company offers groceries supplements produce frozen foods and ethnic and kosher food products. UNFI also operates about a dozen natural-products retail stores under the Earth Origins banner and it produces roasted nuts dried fruits and other snack items through subsidiary Woodstock Farms.

Operations

The company's operations are comprised of three principal divisions: Wholesale Retail and Manufacturing and Branded products.

UNFI's wholesale division generates around 95% of sales and consists of its US natural organic and specialty distribution business. Its operations cover major subsidiaries such as Tony's and Albert's as well as newly acquired businesses like Haddon and Gourmet Guru. The segment supplies more than 5000 customers with fruits vegetables and other perishable items. The division also distributes vitamins through Select Nutrition and ethnic food items and related products through its UNFI Specialty business. The company has built up its own food brands through subsidiary Blue Marble Brands. The unit offers more than 650 products marketed under 15 brand names directly to retailers as well as third party distributors.

UNFI's retail arm Earth Origins operates a dozen natural products stores primarily in Florida but also in Maryland and Massachusetts. The company also has a retail store in Vancouver British Columbia that does business as Drive Organics.

The Manufacturing and Branded products division consists of Woodstock Farms Manufacturing which specializes in importing roasting packaging and the distribution of nuts dried fruit seeds trail mixes granola natural and organic snack items and confections; and the Blue Marble Brands product lines.

Geographic Reach

Through UNFI's acquisition of SunOpta Distribution Group the company's wholly-owned subsidiary UNFI Canada became the largest distributor of natural organic and specialty foods including kosher fare in Canada. UNFI has four distribution centers in Canada. UNFI Canada contributes about 5% of UNFI's sales.

The company has 33 distribution centers in US and Canada.

Sales and Marketing

Amazon subsidiary Whole Foods Market is UNFI's largest wholesale customer representing about 35% of its net sales. It's the only customer that accounts for more than 10% of sales. Conventional supermarkets including Kroger Publix and Wegman's and mass market chains account for about 27% of sales.

UNFI's marketing includes multiple monthly region-specific consumer circular programs; coupon programs truck advertising programs wholesale biannual catalogs; and certain supply chain marketing programs.

Financial Performance

UNFI has seen strong growth over the past decade. In fiscal 2017 (July 30 year end) revenue increased 9% to $9.3 billion on the back of higher sales in the Wholesale division. Major factors included the acquisitions of Haddon and Gourmet Guru higher sales to Whole Foods Market thanks to new store openings and higher online sales. Revenue gains were partially offset by broad-based food retail softness margin enhancement initiatives and low inflation.

Net income increased by 3% to $130.2 million as revenue gains were partially offset by higher operating expenses. The acquired businesses have higher costs and required $6.9 million in restructuring expense.

In fiscal 2017 cash from operations fell 5% to $280.8 million due to changes in accounts receivable.

Strategy

UNFI has succeeded at taking market share away from its competition thanks to demand for its slate of premium services coupled with its expanding distribution capacity and targeted acquisitions. It has grown its business organically and through the acquisition of a number of distributors and suppliers which has expanded its distribution network product selection and customer base.

To implement its growth strategy it intends to continue increasing market share of the growing natural and organic products industry by expanding its customer base increasing the company's share of existing customers' business and continuing to expand and further penetrate new distribution territories.

A key element of the company's current growth strategy is to increase the amount of fresh perishable products that it distributes. Its acquisitions of Haddon Gourmet Guru Nor-Cal and Global Organic continue this current strategy with the addition of gourmet ethnic products and conventional produce. Its strategic plan also includes the roll-out of new technology including a national warehouse management and procurement system and transportation management system upgrade.

Indeed the company continually invests in its distribution network and infrastructure. In 2016 it opened a new 40000 sq. ft. distribution center in Gilroy California and in 2015 a 300000 sq. ft. center in Prescott Wisconsin.

Mergers and Acquisitions

In 2016 the company acquired certain assets of Global Organic/Specialty Source Inc. and related affiliates through Albert's Organics for $20.6 million. Global Organic is a premier distributor of organic fruits vegetables juices milk eggs nuts and coffee and serves customers across the Southeastern US.

UNFI also spent $68.6 million to purchase Nor-Cal Produce and an affiliated entity as well as certain real estate. Nor-Cal is a family-owned and - operated distributor of conventional and organic produce and other fresh products in Northern California.

That year it also bought Haddon House Food Products and Gourmet Guru.

HISTORY

Rhode Island retailer Norman Cloutier founded Cornucopia Natural Foods in 1978 and soon focused on distribution. During the 1980s Cornucopia grew by acquiring other natural foods distributors. It bought suppliers Natural Food Systems (seafood) and BGS Distributing (vitamins) in 1987 and 1990 respectively. Cornucopia expanded into the Southeast in 1991 when it opened a distribution center in Georgia.

Reviving its interest in retailing Cornucopia formed Natural Retail Group in 1993 to buy and run natural foods stores. During the next two years it acquired several retailers. The company expanded its distribution operations in the West in 1995 adding Denver-based Rainbow Distributors.

In 1996 Cornucopia merged with the leading natural foods distributor in the western US Sacramento-based Mountain People's which Michael Funk had founded 20 years earlier. The combined company became United Natural Foods with Cloutier as chairman and CEO and Funk as president and vice chairman; it went public later that year.

United Natural Foods became the largest natural foods distributor when it bought New Hampshire-based Stow Mills in 1997. The next year it added Hershey Imports an importer and processor of nuts seeds and snacks and Albert's a distributor of organic produce. With the purchase of Mother Earth Markets in 1998 the company's retailing operations had grown to 16 stores but by mid-1999

it had sold four stores. That year United Natural Foods' East Coast consolidation problems became so profound that top customer Whole Foods announced it was finding backup distribution sources.

Funk replaced Cloutier as CEO and the company handed the chairman's post to board member Thomas Simone in 1999. In 2000 after the resignation of Cloutier from the board of directors United Natural Foods adopted a poison-pill plan to block potential takeovers. The company leased a distribution center in the Los Angeles area in 2001 to increase market share in the Southwest. It also acquired Florida's Palm Harbor Natural Foods.

In mid-2002 United Natural Foods lost one of its two largest customers — Wild Oats Markets—when that company defected to rival specialty foods distributor Tree of Life. However United Natural Foods soon won that business back. In October the company completed the acquisition of privately held Blooming Prairie Cooperative for approximately $31 million. In late 2002 the company merged with Northeast Cooperatives a natural foods distributor in the Midwest and Northeast.

That year United Natural Foods discontinued the management sales and support operations at its Hershey Imports subsidiary but continued to manufacture and distribute products from the Edison New Jersey plant.

In 2004 the company renewed its distribution agreement with Wild Oats with a five-year pact. United Natural Foods later announced a new three-year distribution agreement with Whole Foods which it renewed in 2006. Whole Foods later acquired Wild Oats in 2007. That year United Natural Foods acquired ethnic and specialty food distributor Millbrook Distribution Services for about $85 million.

EXECUTIVES

Chairman President And Ceo, Steven L. (Steve) Spinner, age 59, $872,300 total compensation
Coo, Sean F. Griffin, age 58, $440,300 total compensation
Svp General Counsel Chief Compliance Officer And Corporate Secretary, Joseph J. (Joe) Traficanti, age 67, $367,150 total compensation
Svp Chief Administrative And Information Officer, Eric A. Dorne, age 56
President Atlantic Region, Christopher P. Testa, age 47
Svp Cfo And Treasurer, Michael P. Zechmeister
President Pacific Region, Paul S. Green
President Central Region, John M. Hummel
Vice President Of Field Sales, Jack Murphy
Auditors: KPMG LLP

LOCATIONS

HQ: United Natural Foods Inc.
313 Iron Horse Way, Providence, RI 02908
Phone: 401 528-8634
Web: www.unfi.com

PRODUCTS/OPERATIONS

2015 Sales by Customer Type

	$ mil.	% of total
Supernatural chains	2,822	35
Independently-owned natural products retailers	2,650	32
Conventional supermarkets	2,132	26
Other	581	7
Total	**8,185**	**100**

2015 Sales

	$ mil.	% of total
Wholesale	8,099	97
Other	225	3
Adjustments	(140.4)	-
Total	**8,185**	**100**

Selected Acquisitions

Fiscal 2012
   B.K. Sethi Distribution Ltd. ($3 million; Ontario
   Canada; specialty food distribution)
Fiscal 2011
   SunOpta Distribution Group ($66 million; Ontario
   Canada; specialty food distribution)

Selected Operations

Manufacturing division
   Woodstock Farms (import roasting packaging and
   distribution of nuts dried fruit seeds trail mixes
   granola natural and organic snack items and
   confections and Blue Marble Brands products)
Retail division
   Earth Origins (natural products retail stores in Florida
   Maryland Massachusetts)
Wholesale division
   Albert's Organics (distributor of organically grown
   produce and perishable items)
   Select Nutrition (distributor of vitamins minerals and
   supplements)
   UNIFI Canada (natural organic and specialty business
   in Canada)
   UNFI Specialty (specialty distributor in the Eastern
   and Midwestern portions of the US)

COMPETITORS

Associated Wholesale	KeHE Distributors
Grocers	SUPERVALU
C&S Wholesale	SpartanNash
DPI Specialty Foods	Wal-Mart

HISTORICAL FINANCIALS

Company Type: Public

Income Statement

FYE: July 28

	REVENUE ($ mil.)	NET INCOME ($ mil.)	NET PROFIT MARGIN	EMPLOYEES
07/18	10,226	165	1.6%	10,000
07/17	9,274	130	1.4%	9,700
07/16*	8,470	125	1.5%	9,554
08/15	8,184	138	1.7%	8,700
08/14	6,794	125	1.8%	8,700
Annual Growth	10.8%	7.2%	—	3.5%

*Fiscal year change

2018 Year-End Financials

Debt ratio: 12.15%
Return on equity: 9.42%
Cash ($ mil.): 23
Current ratio: 2.56
Long-term debt ($ mil.): 347

No. of shares (mil.): 50
Dividends
   Yield: —
   Payout: —
Market value ($ mil.): 1,639

	STOCK PRICE ($) FY Close	P/E High/Low		PER SHARE ($) Earnings	Dividends	Book Value
07/18	32.51	16	10	3.26	0.00	36.62
07/17	37.88	19	13	2.56	0.00	33.23
07/16*	49.98	22	12	2.50	0.00	30.16
08/15	45.53	30	16	2.76	0.00	27.66
08/14	58.71	30	23	2.52	0.00	24.98
Annual Growth	(13.7%)	—	—	6.6%	—	10.0%

*Fiscal year change

United Parcel Service Inc

When your ?track package? notice says ?out for
delivery? there?s a good chance it's sitting in a
brown United Parcel Service (UPS) truck steered
by a brown-uniformed driver. UPS is the world's
largest package deliverer transporting about 20
million packages and documents per business day
(5 billion a year) throughout the US and some
220 countries. It deploys a fleet of nearly 120000
motor vehicles and 580 aircraft for pickups and
deliveries. In addition to package delivery the company offers logistics and freight forwarding
through UPS Supply Chain Solutions and less-
than-truckload (LTL) and truckload (TL) freight
transportation through UPS Ground Freight.

Operations

UPS has three business segments: US Domestic
Package. International Package and Supply Chain
& Freight.

Domestic package delivery is the company's
largest business segment accounting for more than
60% of sales. International package delivery delivers about 20% of UPS' sales. The company also
offers UPS SurePost an economy residential
ground service for customers with non-urgent
lightweight residential shipments. It acts as a contractual residential ground service that partners
its UPS Ground network with final delivery often
provided by the US Postal Service.

Along with logistics and trucking the company's
Supply Chain & Freight segment which generates
a bit less than a fifth of sales includes forwarding
and logistics services dedicated contract carriage
truckload services LTL services and financial services.

UPS operates about 580 aircraft owned or
leased as well as 119000 package cars vans tractors and motorcycles.

Geographic Reach

While UPS serves customers in more than 220
countries about four-fifths of its revenue is generated in the US. The company headquartered in Atlanta Georgia has more than 2300 operating facilities. Its US transportation hub called Worldport is
in Louisville Kentucky.

Sales and Marketing

UPS delivers packages each business day for
1.5 million shipping customers to 9 million re-
ceivers. It targets industries such as health care
government retail automotive industrial manufacturing and aerospace. No customer accounts for
10% or more of the company?s revenue.

Financial Performance

UPS has enjoyed seven years of steady revenue
growth with revenue reaching a record $65.9 bil-
lion in 2017 8% higher than 2016. The year?s
growth was fueled by increases in all segments:
domestic 6% higher international up 8% and supply chain and freight package with a 15% increase.
Volume was higher across all UPS products driven
by greater overall retail sales including the increasing percentage of ecommerce transactions. Business-to-consumer shipments accounted for more
than 50% of US Domestic Package volume. Business-to-business shipment volume declined as
companies conduct more business electronically.
The company raised shipping rates in 2017 including a surcharge for packages sent in the lead-
up to Christmas. The company also had higher
costs from starting Saturday service.

Profit leaped 44% to $4.9 billion in 2017 from
2016 from higher operating profit across the company?s business lines.

UPS had capital expenditures of about $5.2 bil-
lion in 2017 as it built up facilities up from $2.9
billion in 2016. Cash on hand was about $3.3 bil-
lion in 2017 and $3.5 billion the year before. UPS
had negative free cash flow of $3.7 billion in 2017
compared to free cash flow of $3.5 billion in 2016.

Strategy

UPS' extensive global reach is a selling point for
its supply chain management offerings which are
tailored to customers in industries such as consumer goods and retail health care and technology.
The company sees a growing trend in businesses
outsourcing supply chain management viewing it
as a strategic advantage to have effective management of their supply chains.

Package delivery revenue is increasing overseas
where UPS continues to expand through infrastructure investments and acquisitions. The company has completed a $200 million 70% expansion
of its European air hub in Cologne Germany.

In the US the company is expanding regional
facilities in the Indianapolis Phoenix Salt Lake City
and Dallas areas to handle increasing traffic. It also
has added a regional facility in Atlanta. Inside its
facilities UPS is expanding automated capacity increasing efficiency and adding network flexibili-
ties.

UPS created its Advanced Technology Group
(ATG) oversee research testing development and
application of new technologies. Through the
group UPS collaborates with technology companies and academic institutions to develop digital
robotic and machine technologies to improve customer service increase efficiency and reduce the
physical stress of some UPS jobs.

UPS? performance depends on the general economic climate and consumer activity especially the
trend toward online commerce. Should the economy weaken or consumer preference for online
transactions wane the demand for UPS? services
would decline.

For now business is booming and so is competition. UPS faces carriers such as Fedex and XPO
Logistics which also are investing to expand and
improve their operations. Amazon.com is leading
retailers in exploring how to handle delivery on
their own. What?s more smaller companies are
popping up to make last mile deliveries.

Mergers and Acquisitions

Over the years UPS has enhanced its operations
through acquisitions.

In 2017 UPS acquired Sandler & Travis Trade
Advisory Service a provider of global trade management services. Sandler & Travis operations
were combined with UPS' Trade Management
Services group to improve customers? trade investments.

UPS expanded its international operations with
the 2017 acquisition of Nightline Logistics in Ireland. The deal complemented UPS offerings and
increased delivery density.

In early 2017 it obtained UK-based Freightex
an asset-light provider of truckload less-than-truckload specialized and refrigerated over-the-road
services. The acquisition established UPS? presence in the growing UK and European third-party
logistics 3PL over-the-road brokerage transportation market

HISTORY

Seattle teens Jim Casey and Claude Ryan started
American Messenger Company a delivery and er-
rand service in 1907. They were soon making
small-parcel deliveries for local department stores
and in 1913 changed the company's name to Merchants Parcel Delivery. Casey who led the company
for 50 years established a policy of manager ownership best service and lowest rates. In 1916 new
employee Charlie Soderstrom chose the brown
paint still used on the company's vehicles. Service
expanded outside Seattle in 1919 when Merchants
Parcel bought Oakland California-based Motor
Parcel Delivery later changing its name to United
Parcel Service (UPS).

EXECUTIVES

Coo, James J. (Jim) Barber, age 57, $500,706 total
compensation
Evp And Chief Commercial Officer, Alan
Gershenhorn, age 60, $565,956 total compensation

Chairman And Ceo, David P. Abney, age 63, $1,082,421 total compensation

President Us Operations, Myron A. Gray, age 61, $514,509 total compensation

Svp Cfo And Treasurer, Richard N. Peretz, age 56, $485,070 total compensation

Svp Global Engineering And Sustainability, Mark R. Wallace, age 55

Svp Chief Marketing And Business Services Officer, Teresa M. Finley, age 57

Svp And Cio, Juan R. Perez

President Operations Ups Latin America, Jose Maria (Chema) Odriozola

President Ups China, Harld Peters

Global Vice President Information Technology, Nick Costides

Vice President Rocky Mountain District, George Brooks

Vp Corporate Plant Engineering, Rhonda Clark

Vice President Administration, Charlie Covert

Vice President Of Sales And Marketing, Norm Brothers

Vice President, Jochen Mueller

Vice President Enterprise Accounts Sales, Michael Tannian

Vice President, Rick Rufolo

Vice President, Angela Jack

Vice President Of Engineering, Gregory Loppatto

Vice President; Sales And Marketing, Joe Racanelli

Vice President Global Customs, William Ansley

Vice President Global Customs Policy And Public Affairs, Norm Schenk

Senior Vice President Marketing And Sales, James Thome

Vice President, Carlos Cubias

Vp Business Development, Annie Outlaw

Vice President Chicago Area Consolidation Hub Cach, Robert Latchford

Vice President, Ken Torok

Vice President Operations Europe, Dominic Porporino

Vice President International Sales, Mike Mahoney

Vice President Customer Care Americas, Patty Cheek

Vice President Customer Technology, Stuart Marcus

Vice President, Bill Kruger

Vice President East Central Region, Joseph Zito

National Account Manager, Robert Musca

Vice President Sales Global Accounts, Jerry Felton

Vice President Operations, Steve Mockus

Vice President, Keith Beatty

Vice President Corporate Public Affairs, Nicole Clifton

Vice President Small Business And Retail Marketing, Stephanie Callaway

Vice President, Susan Ward

Vice Prespident Of Sales Americas, Pedro Anaya

Vice President Enterprise Sales, Sheila Dunn

Vice President, Tom Cox

Senior Vice President Worldwide Sales And Mrktng., Kurt Kuehn

Vice President, Allen Hill

Vice President Of Human Resources, David Cole

Vice President Information Services Customer Technology, Laynglyn Capers

Vice President Us Engineering, Mark Susor

Vice President Of Sales, Geof Hoge

Vice President Strategy And Innovation Europe, Yannick Mooijman

National Account Manager, Mike Buffon

Vice President Of Human Resources, Debra Harding

Vice President Finance Services, Todd St John

Vice President Chief Operating Officer Eastern Operations, Joe Picone

Vice President Investor Relations Officer, Scott Childress

Senior Vice President, Deryl Hill

Vice President, David Lee

Vice President, David Birkmeyer

Senior Vice President Global Trade Finance, Mike Bryant

Vice President, Arnold Wellman

Vice President Finance, Joseph Tillman

Vp Of Hr, Dave Lovely

Senior Vice President, Jim Bruce

Vice Chairman Of The Board, John Alden

Board Member, Wayne Powell

Board Member, Michael Burns

Board Member, Kevin Warsh

Board Member, Rodney Adkins

Board Member, Franck Moison

Board Member, John Stankey

Auditors: DELOITTE & TOUCHE LLP

LOCATIONS

HQ: United Parcel Service Inc
55 Glenlake Parkway N.E., Atlanta, GA 30328
Phone: 404 828-6000
Web: www.ups.com

2017 Sales

	$ mil.	% of total
US Domestic Package	40,764	62
International Package	13,338	20
Supply Chain & Freight	11,770	18
Total	**65,872**	**100**

PRODUCTS/OPERATIONS

2017 Sales

	$ mil.	% of total
US domestic package		
Ground	29,255	44
Next day air	7,088	11
Deferred	4,421	7
International package		
Export	10,167	15
Domestic	2,645	4
Cargo	526	1
Supply chain & freight		
Forwarding & logistics	7,981	12
Freight	2,998	5
Other	791	1
Total	**65,872**	**100**

2017 Sales

	$ mil.	% of total
U.S. Domestic Package	40,764	62
International Package	13,338	20
Supply Chain & Freight	11,770	18
Total	**65,872**	**100**

COMPETITORS

American Airlines Group	Panalpina
Canada Post	Royal Mail
Deutsche Post	Ryder System
FedEx	TNT Express
Japan Post	US Postal Service
La Poste	United Continental
Lufthansa	XPO logistics
Nippon Express	YRC Worldwide

HISTORICAL FINANCIALS

Company Type: Public

Income Statement · FYE: December 31

	REVENUE ($ mil.)	NET INCOME ($ mil.)	NET PROFIT MARGIN	EMPLOYEES
12/17	65,872	4,910	7.5%	280,000
12/16	60,906	3,431	5.6%	434,000
12/15	58,363	4,844	8.3%	444,000
12/14	58,232	3,032	5.2%	435,000
12/13	55,438	4,372	7.9%	395,000
Annual Growth	4.4%	2.9%	—	(8.2%)

2017 Year-End Financials

Debt ratio: 53.50%
Return on equity: 698.93%
Cash ($ mil.): 3,320
Current ratio: 1.22
Long-term debt ($ mil.): 20,278
No. of shares (mil.): 859
Dividends
 Yield: 0.0%
 Payout: 59.1%
Market value ($ mil.): 102,350

	STOCK PRICE ($) FY Close	P/E High/Low	PER SHARE ($) Earnings	PER SHARE ($) Dividends	PER SHARE ($) Book Value
12/17	119.15	22 18	5.61	3.32	1.16
12/16	114.64	31 23	3.87	3.12	0.47
12/15	96.23	21 18	5.35	2.92	2.79
12/14	111.17	34 28	3.28	2.68	2.37
12/13	105.08	23 16	4.61	2.48	7.01
Annual Growth	3.2%	— —	5.0%	7.6%	(36.2%)

United Rentals Inc

No cash to buy a bulldozer? Just lease one from United Rentals. The company considers itself the #1 commercial and construction equipment renter in the world serving customers in the commercial infrastructure industrial and residential sectors. It operates through a network of nearly 1000 locations in the US and Canada and provides about 3400 equipment items — everything from general to heavy construction and industrial equipment to hand tools special-event items (such as aerial towers) power (diesel generators) and HVAC equipment and trench-safety equipment. It also sells new and used equipment as well as contractor supplies and parts. United Rentals' original equipment cost (the initial purchase value of all rental equipment) is $11.5 billion. The US accounts for more than 90% of total sales.

Operations

United Rentals operates two business segments: General Rental and the Trench Power and Pump segment.

General Rental generates around 85% of sales and rents out construction aerial and industrial equipment general tools and light equipment and related services and activities.

The Trench Power and Pump segment rents out specialty construction products and related services. It offers trench safety equipment such as trench shields aluminum hydraulic shoring systems and construction lasers; Power and HVAC equipment such as portable generators and electric distribution equipment; and pumping equipment for use in the energy and petrochemical industries. The segment accounts for the remaining 15% of revenue.

Across both segments the company sells its used rental equipment to invest in new gear. Used rental sales account for 10% of total sales. It also sells construction consumables tools small equipment and safety supplies.

Geographic Reach

Of United Rentals' nearly 1000 rental locations more than 850 are in the US and the rest are in Canada.

United Rentals' General Rentals division comprises eleven geographic regions: Carolinas Gulf South Industrial (which serves the geographic Gulf region and has a strong industrial presence) Mid-Atlantic Mid Central Midwest Northeast Pacific West South Southeast and Western Canada

Sales and Marketing

United Rentals' customers include construction and industrial companies manufacturers utilities municipalities and homeowners. The Trench

Power and Pump segments serves primarily construction companies active in infrastructure projects municipalities and industrial companies.

United Rentals markets its products and services through sales staff at the company's branches and customer care centers; account managers dedicated to large customer accounts; its E-Rentals portal (online e-commerce site); and advertising (trade publications yellow pages the internet radio and direct mail).

Financial Performance

After a slight dip in 2016 United Rental's revenue in 2017 returned to the upward trajectory seen in recent years.

Sales increased 15% to $6.6 billion — a new record for the company — thanks to contributions from the acquired NES and Neff businesses. Underlying revenue increased 8% thanks to a 7% increase in rental equipment in use and a less-than-1% increase in rental prices.

Net income jumped 138% to $1.3 billion thanks partly to higher revenue but mostly due to a tax benefit from the 2017 US Tax Cuts and Jobs Act.

Cash from operations grew 14% to $2.2 billion due to higher net income partially offset by decrease in deferred taxes.

Strategy

Because of its size United Rentals rallies more resources over smaller businesses. Competitive advantages include more purchasing leverage a wider range of equipment and services and the more convenient movement of assets between locations. United Rentals enhances its operating efficiencies by ramping up through consolidation of functions including payroll and accounts payable. It primarily grows through acquisitions.

In order to manage the age composition and size of its fleet the company routinely sells used rental equipment and invests in new equipment. United Rentals acts as a dealer of new equipment for many leading equipment makers such as Genie Industries Skyjack (aerial lifts) Sullair (compressors) and Terex (telehandlers). At most branches United Rentals sells various supplies and merchandise and offers repair and maintenance services.

Mergers and Acquisitions

In 2018 United Rentals acquired BakerCorp International Holding for about $715 million. BakerCorp is a provider of tank pump filtration and trench shoring rental solutions. The deal will enhance United Rentals' fluid storage and transfer and treatment solutions. It also adds 46 branches in North America and 11 in Europe and about 950 employees. By the end of 2018 the company is scheduled close on a $2.1 billion deal to acquire BlueLine Rental a North American equipment rental company with operations in 25 US states Canada and Puerto Rico.

Late in 2017 the company acquired Neff Corporation a US provider of earthmoving and material handling equipment for $1.3 billion. Neff brings with it $867 million-worth of rental equipment and some 70 branch locations. It serves the infrastructure non-residential energy municipal and residential construction sectors. The deal boosts United's earthmoving capabilities and adds to efficiencies of scale in key markets particularly the fast-growing southern geographies.

In mid-2017 United Rentals acquired NES Rentals a provider of aerial rental equipment (from scissor and boom lifts to rough terrain and truck-mounted cranes) for $965 million. NES serves about 18000 customers across the industrial and non-residential construction sectors. The deal will enhance the company's density in strategically important markets including the East Coast Gulf States and the Midwest.

HISTORY

Bradley Jacobs had made a fortune in the garbage business having used United Waste Systems as a roll-up company to buy small trash-hauling firms in that fragmented industry. Flush with cash after he sold United Waste Systems in 1997 to USA Waste Services (now Waste Management) Jacobs launched the same roll-up strategy to consolidate the equipment-rental industry. He and his management team bought six leasing companies and started United Rentals. The company which went public in 1997 had acquired 38 rental companies in 20 states by mid-1998.

EXECUTIVES

Vice President Business Development, Ned Graham
Senior Vice President Strategy And Planning, Kenneth Mettel
Vice President, Jonathan M Gottsegen
Evp And Cfo, William B. Plummer, age 59, $595,504 total compensation
President And Ceo, Michael J. Kneeland, age 64, $950,000 total compensation
Evp And Coo, Matthew J. Flannery, age 53, $595,504 total compensation
Svp Business Services And Cio, Dale A. Asplund, age 50, $519,807 total compensation
Evp Chief Administrative And Legal Officer, Craig A. Pintoff, age 48, $473,046 total compensation
Vp Midwest Region, Chris Burlog
Vp Mid-central Region, Kevin M. OBrien
Svp And Chief Marketing Officer, Chris Hummel
Vp Pacific West Region, Robert C. Bower
Vp Southeast Region, Michael G. Cloer
Vp Western Canada Region, John (Scott) Fisher
Region Vp Tools And Industrial Solutions, Joshuah P. Flores
Vp Trench Safety Region, Todd M. Hayes
Vp Mid-atlantic Region, John J. Humphrey
Vp Pump Solutions, William A. (Bill) Kiker
Vp Industrial Region, Donald (Chad) Matter
Vp South Region, Jeffrey S. (Jeff) McGinnis
Vp Northeast Region, Craig Schmidt
Vp Power And Hvac Region, David C. Scott
Vp Gulf South Region, Larry (Don) Irwin
Vp Environmental Health And Safety, Jim Dorris
Vp Industrial Region, Chad Matter
National Account Manager, Jackie Volk
National Account Manager, Reggie Hall
Vice President Of Corporate Communications, Fred Bratman
Executive Vice President Corporate Services, Kurtis Barker
Vice President Gulf South Region, John King
National Account Manager, Bill Kenyon
National Account Manager, SHAWNA ERMOLD
Senior Vice President Operations South, David A Hobbs
Vice President Customer Service Operations, Kenneth Perkins
Vice President Finance Operations, Joe Pledger
National Account Manager, Jeremy Epps
National Account Manager, Brian Knauer
National Account Manager Oil And Gas, Brian Nagel
National Account Manager, Amanda Donelan
Region Vice President, Bill Kiker
Vp Mid Central Region, Kevin M O'brien
National Account Manager, Christopher Shoemaker
Chairman, Jenne K. Britell, age 75
Auditors: Ernst & Young LLP

LOCATIONS

HQ: United Rentals Inc
100 First Stamford Place, Suite 700, Stamford, CT 06902
Phone: 203 622-3131
Web: www.unitedrentals.com

2017 Sales

	$ mil.	% of total
Domestic	6,076	91
Foreign	565	9
Total	**6,641**	**100**

PRODUCTS/OPERATIONS

2017 Sales

	$ mil.	% of total
General Rental	5,565	84
Trench power and pump	1,076	16
Total	**6,641**	**100**

2017 Sales

	$ mil.	% of total
Equipment rentals	5,715	86
Sales of rental equipment	550	8
Sales of new equipment	178	3
Contractor supplies sales	80	1
Service & other revenues	118	2
Total	**6,641**	**100**

Selected Products

Aerial lifts
Backhoes
Barricades
Compressors
Concrete & Masonry
Cones
Contractor supplies
Ditching equipment
Earth-moving equipment
Forklifts
Generators
Hand tools
Heaters
HVAC
Lawn & Landscape
Light towers
Material-handling equipment
Message boards
Pavement-marking systems
Portable power units
Power washers
Pumps
Skid-steer loaders
Trench shields
Trucks & Trailers
Warning lights
Water pumps
Welders & Accessories

COMPETITORS

AMECO	Maxim Crane Works
Atlas Lift Truck Rentals	RDO Equipment
Case Power & Equipment	Sunbelt Rentals
Herc Holdings	Ziegler inc

HISTORICAL FINANCIALS

Company Type: Public

Income Statement

FYE: December 31

	REVENUE ($ mil.)	NET INCOME ($ mil.)	NET PROFIT MARGIN	EMPLOYEES
12/18	8,047	1,096	13.6%	18,500
12/17	6,641	1,346	20.3%	14,800
12/16	5,762	566	9.8%	12,500
12/15	5,817	585	10.1%	12,700
12/14	5,685	540	9.5%	12,500
Annual Growth	**9.1%**	**19.4%**	**—**	**10.3%**

Debt ratio: 64.78%	No. of shares (mil.): 79
Return on equity: 33.68%	Dividends
Cash ($ mil.): 43	Yield: —
Current ratio: 0.83	Payout: —
Long-term debt ($ mil.): 10,844	Market value ($ mil.): 8,189

	STOCK PRICE ($) FY Close	P/E High/Low		PER SHARE ($) Earnings	Dividends	Book Value
12/18	102.53	14	7	13.12	0.00	42.61
12/17	171.91	11	6	15.73	0.00	36.77
12/16	105.58	17	7	6.45	0.00	19.57
12/15	72.54	17	10	6.07	0.00	16.08
12/14	102.01	21	13	5.15	0.00	18.37
Annual Growth	0.1%	—	—	26.3%	—	23.4%

United States Steel Corp.

Steel crazy after all these years United States Steel (U.S. Steel) is North America's largest integrated steelmaker. The company operates mills throughout the US Midwest and in Slovakia. U.S. Steel makes a wide range of flat-rolled and tubular steel products and its annual production capacity is 22 million net tons of raw steel. Its customers are primarily in the automotive appliance construction oil and gas and petrochemical industries. In addition U.S. Steel mines iron ore and procures coke which provide the primary raw materials used in steel making. It is also engaged in railroad and barge operations and real estate. The US accounts for three-fifths of its revenue.

Operations
U.S. Steel has three reportable operating segments: Flat-Rolled Products about 65% of revenue US Steel Europe (USSE) about 20% of revenue and Tubular Products which accounts for the rest of revenue.

The company's North American integrated steel mills' flat rolled products include slabs rounds strip mill plates sheets and tin mill products. It also has ore and coke production facilities in the US.

U.S. Steel has annual raw steel production capability of 22 million net tons (17 million tons in the United States and 5 million tons in Europe) reflecting a reduction of 2.4 million tons due to the permanent shutdown some operations.

Its European operations produce and sell slabs sheet strip mill plate tin mill products and spiral welded pipe as well as heating radiators and refractory ceramic materials. U.S. Steel Kosice in Slovakia produces sheet steel. Its plant in Kosice has an annual capacity of 5 million tons.

U.S. Steel's tubular steel operation (about 1.5 million tons per year) serves the energy industry primarily providing both seamless and electric resistance welded products commonly called oil country tubular goods.

The company also participates in joint ventures with a number of its industry competitors. They include the world's #1 steelmaker ArcelorMittal Japanese producer Kobe Steel South Korean giant POSCO Russian metals company Severstal and US steel service center Worthington Industries.

The company's other businesses include railroad services and real estate operations.

Geographic Reach
In the US the company holds integrated steel plants including Gary Works East Chicago Tin and Midwest Plant all in Indiana. It also holds the Great Lakes Works in Michigan Mon Valley Works and Fairless Plant in Pennslvania and Granite City Works in Illinois. US Steel also has a steel mill and related facilities in Slovakia. North America accounts some 75% of the company's total sales.

The company has a research centers in Pittsburgh Pennsylvania and Kosice Slovakia. It also has an automotive center in Troy Michigan and Research and Development Laboratory and Test Facility for Tubular Products in Houston Texas.

Sales and Marketing
The majority of U.S. Steel's customers are located in North America and Europe.

U.S. Steel's integrated steel business serves North American customers in the service center conversion transportation construction container and appliance and electrical markets and European customers in the construction service center conversion container transportation appliance and electrical and oil gas and petrochemical markets.

Financial Performance
US Steel revenue has declined by half in the last decade from $24 billion in 2008 to just over $12 billion in 2017 mostly from divestments. In the same period it has had only three years of modest profit (2009 2014 2017). In comparison the company lost $2 billion during the financial years 2015-16 and some $3.7 billion during 2009-13 period.

Revenue increased 20% in 2017 to $12.3 billion mostly from $60 per ton increase in prices of flat-rolled products and its contracts but also from increased shipments and lower imports in the European sector along with higher prices and to a smaller extent increases in shipments of Tubular Products.

Net income made a strong comeback in 2017 posting $387 million in profit compared to $440 million loss the previous year mostly from $91 million reduction in restructing costs from the year prior a $86 million gain in income tax benefits as well as $72 million gain from spinning off US Steel Canada.

Cash holdings increased slightly from $1.51 billion to $1.55 billion. Operations contributed $800 million while investments utilized $390 million. A further $390 was utilized by financing activities mostly in long-term debt reduction.

Strategy
U.S. Steel has begun a $2 billion four-year upgrade of its steel-making processes to improve its competitiveness. The project comes as steel prices have risen with higher tariffs were placed on foreign steel in 2016. The upgrade emphasizes 13 of the company?s critical assets: in iron and steel making and hot rolling and finishing. U.S. Steel expects the project to deliver an additional million tons of hot rolled band production capacity over the current 10 million tons and a boost of $275 million-$325 million in earnings before interest taxes depreciation and amortization by 2020.

The company also has taken steps to reduce its debt by refinancing issuing some $750 million of senior notes in 2017 due in 2025 to replace higher-interest notes that were due in 2021 and 2022.

In 2017 U.S. Steel and partner Kobe Steel said they would build a new continuous galvanizing line (CGL) at their subsidiaries? joint venture PRO-TEC Coating Co. in Leipsic Ohio to meet higher demand for advanced high-strength steels (AHSS) from the auto industry. The $400 million plant is to begin production in 2019.

But the previous decade has not been easy for the company. Revenue reduced by half between 2009 and 2017 and cheap imports made competition hard. It disposed of U.S. Steel Canada interests for $72 million in 2017. In the same year the company permanently shut down the Lorain #6 Quench & Temper Mill Lorain #4 and Lone Star #1 pipe mills as well as tubular operations. In 2015 it idled Tubular Processing and Granite City Works. Depreciation and amortization has cost the company more than $1.5 billion in the 2015-17 period.

However the performance of its flat-rolled segment of late offers hope as does an improving market and taxes on foreign steel introduced in 2018. CAPEX for 2017 was $505 million.

HISTORY

U.S. Steel was conceived through a 1901 merger of 10 steel companies that combined their furnaces ore deposits railroad companies and shipping lines. The deal involved industrial pioneers Andrew Carnegie Charles Schwab Elbert Gary and J. P. Morgan. Morgan had helped organize the Federal Steel Company in 1898 and he then wanted to create a centralized trust to dominate the soaring steel market. Carnegie owned the largest US steel company at the time Carnegie Steel but wanted to retire.

In 1900 Schwab Carnegie Steel's president outlined the idea of the steel trust based on a merger of the Carnegie and Federal steel companies. Morgan asked Schwab to persuade Carnegie to sell his steel mills and name his price. Morgan didn't haggle when Carnegie responded that he would sell for almost half a billion dollars.

The Carnegie-Morgan combination created the world's first billion-dollar company.

EXECUTIVES

President Ceo And Director, David B. (Dave) Burritt, age 62, $800,000 total compensation
Svp Consumer Solutions, Sara A. Greenstein, age 43
Svp Industrial Service Center And Mining Solutions, Douglas R. Matthews, age 53, $541,000 total compensation
Vp European Solutions And President Us Steel Koâšice, Scott D. Buckiso, age 51
Vp And Cio, Charles G. Balawajder, age 62
Svp Government Affairs General Counsel And Chief Compliance Officer, Suzanne R. Folsom, age 56, $700,000 total compensation
Svp Automotive Solutions, James E. Bruno, age 52, $403,500 total compensation
Vp And Chief Supply Chain Officer, Christine S. Breves
Evp And Cfo, Kevin P. Bradley
Senior Vice President And Chie, Larry Brockway
Executive Vice President And Chief Financial Officer, Joseph Stinnett
Vice President Commercial Tubular, Craig Horan
Vice President, Pat Mullarkey
Senior Vice President And Treasurer, Albert Ferrara
Vice President Strategic Planning And Corporate Development, Richard Fruehauf
Chairman, David S. (Dave) Sutherland, age 68
Auditors: PricewaterhouseCoopers LLP

LOCATIONS

HQ: United States Steel Corp.
600 Grant Street, Pittsburgh, PA 15219-2800
Phone: 412 433-1121   **Fax:** 412 433-4818
Web: www.ussteel.com

2016 Sales

	$ mil.	% of total
North America	8,018	78
Europe	2,243	22
Total	10,261	100

PRODUCTS/OPERATIONS

2016 Sales

	$ mil.	% of total
Flat-rolled	7,507	73
US Steel Europe	2,243	22
Tubular products	449	4
Other	62	1
Total	**10,261**	**100**

Selected Products

Steel
Tin
Tubular

Selected Subsidiaries

Acero Prime S. R. L de CV (44% steel processing and warehousing)
Delray Connecting Railroad Company (transportation)
Double Eagle Steel Coating Company (50% with Severstal; steel processing)
PRO-TEC Coating Co. (50% with Kobe Steel; steel processing)
Transtar Inc. (transportation)
U. S. Steel Kosice sro (steelmaking Slovakia)
USS-POSCO Industries (50% with Pohang Iron & Steel; steel processing)
Worthington Specialty Processing (50% with Worthington Industries; steel processing)

COMPETITORS

AK Steel Holding Corporation
Allegheny Technologies
ArcelorMittal
Baosteel
BlueScope Steel
B –HLER-UDDEHOLM
Carpenter Technology
Gerdau Ameristeel
JFE Holdings
Kobe Steel
Nippon Steel & Sumitomo Metal Corporation
Nucor
POSCO
SSAB North America
SSAB Svenskt
Salzgitter
Simec
Steel Dynamics
Tata Steel
Ternium
ThyssenKrupp Steel
Wuhan Iron & Steel

HISTORICAL FINANCIALS

Company Type: Public

Income Statement

FYE: December 31

	REVENUE ($ mil.)	NET INCOME ($ mil.)	NET PROFIT MARGIN	EMPLOYEES
12/17	12,250	387	3.2%	29,200
12/16	10,261	(440)	—	29,800
12/15	11,574	(1,642)	—	33,200
12/14	17,507	102	0.6%	23,000
12/13	17,424	(1,672)	—	38,500
Annual Growth	**(8.4%)**	**—**		**(6.7%)**

2017 Year-End Financials

Debt ratio: 27.41%	No. of shares (mil.): 175
Return on equity: 13.84%	Dividends
Cash ($ mil.): 1,553	Yield: 0.0%
Current ratio: 1.75	Payout: 9.1%
Long-term debt ($ mil.): 2,700	Market value ($ mil.): 6,166

	STOCK PRICE ($) FY Close	P/E High/Low		PER SHARE ($) Earnings	Dividends	Book Value
12/17	35.19	19	9	2.19	0.20	18.95
12/16	33.01	—	—	(2.81)	0.20	13.08
12/15	7.98	—	—	(11.24)	0.20	16.65
12/14	26.74	65	32	0.69	0.20	26.08
12/13	29.50	—	—	(11.56)	0.20	23.14
Annual Growth	**4.5%**	—	—	—	**(0.0%)**	**(4.9%)**

United Technologies Corp

United Technologies (UTC) has the worldwide industrial expertise to lift you up and cool you down. Its Otis UTC Climate Controls & Security and Pratt & Whitney segments develop technologies systems and services for the aerospace construction and security industries. Climate Controls & Security makes alarms monitoring equipment surveillance and access control systems and fire and hazard detection products. Otis is the world's largest elevator and escalator manufacturing company while Pratt & Whitney makes commercial and military engines. UTC Aerospace Systems produces engine controls and flight systems for military and commercial clients. UTC announced in 2018 that it would break itself into three separate companies based on its business segments. The company also completed its $30 billion purchase of aircraft parts manufacturer Rockwell Collins.

Change in Company Type

As it completed the acquisition of Rockwell Collins in a $30 billion deal United Technologies said it would break into three independent companies to provide better focus and flexibility to each business. The aerospace business composed of Collins Aerospace Systems and Pratt and Whitney will retain the United Technologies name. The Climate Controls and Security business will be renamed Carrier and focus on heating and cooling products. Otis will continue to provide elevators escalators and moving walkways as the third independent company. The company expects the separation to be completed in 2020.

Operations

UTC's Climate Controls & Security segment (30% of net sales) makes security products and firefighting equipment for the commercial governmental and residential sectors.

Pratt & Whitney (some 25%) makes and sells aircraft engines for the commercial military business jet and general aviation markets. It also provides fleet management services and aftermarket maintenance services.

UTC Aerospace Systems (25%) provides aerospace products and aftermarket services for aircraft manufacturers airlines and the general aviation markets. (This division will soon be transformed into Collins Aerospace Systems following UTC's pending acquisition of Rockwell Collins that was announced in late 2017.)

In addition UTC owns Otis (20%) one of the world?s largest elevator and escalator manufacturing installation and servicing companies.

Geographic Reach

UTC operates through 4000 locations in more than 70 countries. The US generates around 55% of its total sales; Europe and the Asia/Pacific follow contributing about 20% and 15% respectively.

Sales and Marketing

The company serves customers residing in the commercial and industrial (contributing 50% revenue) commercial aerospace (almost 40%) and military aerospace and space (10%) sectors. The US government contributes roughly 20%.

Financial Performance

UTC's revenues increased 2% from $56.1 billion in 2015 to $57.2 billion in 2016. This growth was attributed to higher commercial aftermarket sales from Pratt & Whitney and increased commercial OEM and aftermarket sales from UTC Aerospace Systems. In addition UTC experienced higher service sales in the Americas and Asia and increased new equipment sales in North America partially offset by lower new equipment sales in China from Otis in 2016.

UTC's profits however declined 34% from $7.6 billion in 2015 to $5.1 billion in 2016. This was attributed to a 3% rise in selling general and administrative expenses driven by a pension settlement charge and increased expenses at Otis that reflected higher labor and information technology costs.

Strategy

UTC strives to maintain a balance between its private and military sectors its commercial and aerospace operations and its original equipment (OE) and aftermarket products and services. It also juggles fluctuations in the market that may impact one or more of its businesses. These fluctuations include changing fuel costs and contracts from the US Department of Defense (DoD) which are subject to policies set by the White House and Congress.

This strategy of product balance is combined with geographic balance which has the company investing in emerging markets that show great growth potential such as Argentina Brazil China Mexico the Middle East Russia and South Africa. UTC is champing at the bit to acquire aerospace and commercial companies with operations in India. Adhering to this strategy in late 2017 it announced it was acquiring aircraft parts maker Rockwell Collins for $23 billion.

Mergers and Acquisitions

In the biggest aerospace deal in history UTC agreed to purchase aircraft parts manufacturer Rockwell Collins for $23 billion in September 2017. When the deal is completed Rockwell will become a new UTC division named Collins Aerospace Systems. UTC projects the new division will generate more than $23 billion in revenue per year and will make aviation electronics and communication equipment for commercial and military aircraft. UTC is making the deal to boost its aerospace business and position it as a key springboard for growth in the years ahead.

HISTORY

In 1925 Frederick Rentschler and George Mead founded Pratt & Whitney Aircraft (P&W) to develop aircraft engines. P&W merged with Seattle-based Boeing Airplane Company and Chance Vought Corporation in 1929 to form United Aircraft & Transport. United Aircraft soon bought aviation companies Hamilton Aero Standard Steel Propeller and Sikorsky.

After congressional investigations led to new antitrust laws United Aircraft split in 1934 into three independent entities: United Airlines Boeing Airplane Company and United Aircraft. United Aircraft retained P&W and several other manufacturing interests.

A design flaw in engines produced for Boeing 747s sent P&W on an expensive trip back to the drawing board in the late 1960s. A concerned board of directors appointed Harry Gray a 17-year veteran of Litton Industries as president in 1971.

Gray transformed the company into a conglomerate; it adopted its present name in 1975.

The company entered into a new stage of development with the milestone 2012 acquisitions of Goodrich and Rolls-Royce's share in the International Aero Engines (IAE) joint venture. The $16.5 billion acquisition of Goodrich an aircraft components manufacturer was one of UTC's largest. Through the transaction UTC absorbed $1.9 billion in assumed debt but it also sizably boosted its services to the commercial aerospace/defense industry and increased its revenues. Goodrich was combined with the former Hamilton Sundstrand operations and now form its UTC Aerospace Systems segment.

UTC in early 2013 sold its UTC Power unit to Oregon-based ClearEdge Power. In late 2015 it also sold its former Sikorsky helicopter subsidiary to Lockheed Martin for $9 billion.

EXECUTIVES

President Pratt & Whitney, Robert F. Leduc, age 62, $665,057 total compensation
Coo Americas Utc Building And Industrial Systems, Robert J. (Bob) McDonough, age 58, $806,250 total compensation
Chairman President And Ceo, Gregory J. Hayes, age 57, $1,450,000 total compensation
President Otis Elevator, Judy F. Marks
Evp And General Counsel, Charles D. Gill, age 54, $715,000 total compensation
Evp Operations And Strategy, Michael R. (Mike) Dumais, age 51
President Utc Aerospace Systems, David L. Gitlin, age 48
Evp And Chief Human Resources Officer, Elizabeth B. Amato, age 61
Svp And Cfo, Akhil Johri, age 57, $766,667 total compensation
Svp Digital And Cio, Vince Campisi
Svp And Cto, Paul Eremenko
Vice President Engineering And Technology Hamilton Sundstrand, Dave Carter
Vice President Operations And Supply Chain, Paolo Dalcin
Vice President Actuation Systems, Rishi Grover
Senior Vice President Science And Technology, Sonia Tulyani
Vice President Interiors, Cheryl Gorman
Auditors: PricewaterhouseCoopers LLP

LOCATIONS

HQ: United Technologies Corp
10 Farm Springs Road, Farmington, CT 06032
Phone: 860 728-7000   **Fax:** 860 728-7028
Web: www.utc.com

2016 Sales

	$ mil.	% of total
US	32,335	56
Europe	11,151	20
Asia/Pacific	8,260	14
Other	5,479	10
Eliminations and other	19	-
Total	**57,244**	**100**

PRODUCTS/OPERATIONS

2016 Sales

	$ mil.	% of total
UTC Climate Controls & Security	16,851	29
Pratt & Whitney	14,894	26
UTC Aerospace Systems	14,465	25
Otis	11,893	20
Eliminations	(859)	-
Total	**57,244**	**100**

2016 Sales by Market

	% of total
Commercial & industrial	50
Commercial aerospace	38
Military aerospace & space	12
Total	**100**

2016 Sales

	$ mil.	% of total
Product sales	40,735	71
Service sales	16,509	29
Total	**57,244**	**100**

Products & Brands Selected

Actuation & Propeller Systems
Air Management Systems
Carrier
Carrier Transicold
Chubb
Chubb eConnect Monitoring Solution
Delta Security Solutions

Selected Operations

Otis (elevators escalators moving walkways and service)
Pratt & Whitney (commercial military business jet and general aviation aircraft engines auxiliary power units and parts and services)
UTC Aerospace Systems (aerospace products and aftermarket services)
UTC Climate Controls & Security (heating ventilating air conditioning and refrigeration systems and security systems)

COMPETITORS

Aerojet Rocketdyne	L3 Technologies
CFM International SA	Lockheed Martin
GE Aviation	Mitsubishi Electric
General Dynamics	Parker-Hannifin
Hitachi	Precision Castparts
Honeywell	Raytheon
International	Siemens AG
IDEX	ThyssenKrupp
Kaman	Trane Inc.

HISTORICAL FINANCIALS

Company Type: Public

Income Statement

FYE: December 31

	REVENUE ($ mil.)	NET INCOME ($ mil.)	NET PROFIT MARGIN	EMPLOYEES
12/18	66,501	5,269	7.9%	240,200
12/17	59,837	4,552	7.6%	205,000
12/16	57,244	5,055	8.8%	201,600
12/15	56,098	7,608	13.6%	197,200
12/14	65,100	6,220	9.6%	211,500
Annual Growth	**0.5%**	**(4.1%)**	**—**	**3.2%**

2018 Year-End Financials

Debt ratio: 33.93%
Return on equity: 15.48%
Cash ($ mil.): 6,152
Current ratio: 1.13
Long-term debt ($ mil.): 41,192

No. of shares (mil.): 861
Dividends
Yield: 2.6%
Payout: 45.5%
Market value ($ mil.): 91,731

	STOCK PRICE ($) FY Close	P/E High/Low		PER SHARE ($) Earnings	Dividends	Book Value
12/18	106.48	22	16	6.50	2.84	44.63
12/17	127.57	22	19	5.70	2.72	37.05
12/16	109.62	18	14	6.12	2.62	34.10
12/15	96.07	14	10	8.61	2.56	32.63
12/14	115.00	17	14	6.82	2.36	34.32
Annual Growth	**(1.9%)**	**—**	**—**	**(1.2%)**	**4.7%**	**6.8%**

UnitedHealth Group Inc

UnitedHealth unites its health plans with consumers across the US. As a leading health insurer it offers a variety of plans and services to group and individual customers nationwide. Its UnitedHealthcare health benefits segment manages health maintenance organization (HMO) preferred provider organization (PPO) and point-of-service (POS) plans as well as Medicare Medicaid state-funded and supplemental vision and dental options. In addition UnitedHealth's Optum health services units — OptumHealth OptumInsight and OptumRx— provide wellness and care management programs financial services information technology solutions and pharmacy benefit management (PBM) services to individuals and the health care industry.

HISTORY

Dr. Paul Ellwood became known as the "Father of the HMO" for his role as an early champion of the health care concept. As a neurology student in the 1950s Ellwood recognized that applying business principles to medicine could minimize costs and make health care more affordable. Although the HMO was considered a radical approach to health care reform Ellwood got Congress and the Nixon administration to approve his HMO model in 1970; the next year he hired Richard Burke to put the model into action. Burke established United HealthCare (UHC) in 1974 to manage the not-for-profit Physicians Health Plan of Minnesota (PHP). UHC incorporated in 1977.

The company bought HMOs and began managing others operating 11 HMOs in 10 states by 1984 the year it went public. Its expansion continued with the purchases of HMOs Share Development (1985) and Peak Health Care (1986). Unfortunately acquisitions and startups began to eat away at UHC's financial health. Meanwhile Burke CEO of both UHC and PHP was accused by PHP doctors of having a conflict of interest after a change in the HMO's Medicare policy threatened to cut off patients from some member hospitals. Burke resigned in 1987 and was replaced by Kennett Simmons formerly president of Peak.

That year investment firm Warburg Pincus bought nearly 40% of UHC providing it with much-needed cash. UHC lost nearly $16 million in 1987 largely from a restructuring that axed the company's Phoenix HMO as well as startups in six other markets. The next year UHC sold its share of Peak Health Care.

In the late 1980s UHC adopted a new strategy of acquiring specialty companies that provided fee income. It also continued building its HMO network through acquisitions hoping to gain critical mass in such varied markets as the Midwest and New England.

Physician William (Bill) McGuire another former Peak president was named UHC's chairman and CEO in 1991. That year PHP and Share merged into Medica. Warburg Pincus distributed its UHC shares to several pension funds and financial institutions.

The company's expansion accelerated in the 1990s with a string of purchases in the Midwest but there were also divestitures. In 1994 UHC sold subsidiary Diversified Pharmaceutical Services providing cash for still more purchases including GenCare (St. Louis) Group Sales and Service of Puerto Rico and MetraHealth a former joint venture of Travelers Group and Metropolitan Life. UHC's interest in fee-based businesses continued with the

1997 purchase of Medicode a major provider of health care information products.

In 1998 the firm planned to buy rival Humana. However bloated UHC decided it should slim down to prepare to consummate the agreement; when UHC announced that it would charge $900 million in costs against earnings its plummeting stock price devalued the primary currency of the deal which quickly collapsed. That year it began offering MediGap and other supplements to AARP members.

The company changed its name to UnitedHealth Group in 2000. It also added UK-based contract research organization ClinPharm International to Ingenix that year and it announced it would let doctors — not administrators — choose what treatment patients would get partially because it was spending more on care scrutiny than the practice saved. Nevertheless many doctors claimed the process was still restrictive.

UnitedHealth's strategy for expansion in the early 21st century concentrated on acquisitions and joint ventures. To expand its Medicaid services business the firm bought AmeriChoice in 2002. The com

EXECUTIVES

Senior Vice President Capital Markets Communications Strategy, John Penshorn
Executive Vice President, Simon Stevens
Evp, Jeannine M. Rivet, $465,000 total compensation
Vice Chairman And Ceo Optum, Larry C. Renfro, age 64, $1,100,000 total compensation
Evp Medical Affairs And Chief Medical Officer, Richard Migliori
Ceo, David S. Wichmann, age 56, $1,100,000 total compensation
Ceo Community Plan Of Kansas, Kevin P. Sparks
Evp Human Capital, D. Ellen Wilson, age 60, $701,923 total compensation
Evp And Chief Legal Officer, Marianne D. Short, age 66, $800,000 total compensation
Evp External Affairs, Cory B. Alexander
Ceo Employer And Individual Iowa-kansas-nebraska, Robert Broomfield
Evp And Cfo, John Rex, $721,923 total compensation
Svp And Chief Marketing Officer, Terry M. Clark
Vice President New Product Strategy, Patsy Piazza
Vice President E Solutions, John O'Neil
Senior Vice President Operations, Laura Ness
Vice President Marketing Ovations, Ellen Sexton
Senior Vice President, Anne Gavel
Regional Vice President Of Human Resources, Cheryl Lippert
Vp And Chief Information Security Officer, Robert Booker
Senior Vice President Human Capital, Chris Coleman
Vice President Software Engineering, Milla Hautman
Vice President Innovation And Randd, Robert Plourde
Vice President Computer Services, Thomas Busse
Sr. Vice President Strategic Initiatives, Alison Richards
Executive Vice President, Chris Ritchie
Vice President, Michele Duncan
Medical Director, Daniel Clute
Avp Network Integration Services, Rossana Salvadori
Senior Vice President Clinical Advanceme, Lewis Sandy
Vice President Marketing, Heidi Svendsen
Vice President Public Sector Business Development, Kenneth Anderson
Vice President Operations, Wayne White
Market Vice President Underwriting, Karl Hermonat

Vice President Information Technology, Kevin Kantola
Vice President National Clinical Operations, Michael Weitzner
Vice President Information Technology, Oren Hermel
Vice President Application Development, Guy Grindberg
Vice President Small Business, Doug Metzger
Director Of Pharmacy Management, Susan Maddux
National Vice President Consulting Relations, Michael Finn
Vice President Sales And Marketing At Ingenix, David Schultz
Vice President Clinical Strategy, Karen Keown
Vice President Sales, Kim Lewis
Vice President National Alliances, Randy Spicer
Vice President Business Development, Matthew Aaefedt
Vice President Quality Solutions, Peter Naumann
Evp Chief Innovation Officer, Tom Beauregard
Vice President Finance, Darren C Moquist
National Account Manager, Christina Rivera
Vice President Healthcare Economics, Tyner Wilson
Vice President Product Optum Consumer Solutions Group, Glen Kvadus
Regional Vice President Clinical Quality, Michelle Francisco
Senior Vice President And Chief Accounting Officer, Tom Roos
Vp Enterprise Operations, Tom Boudewyns
Vice President Total Rewards (optum Compensation), Brad Fagerstrom
Vice President Healthcare Economics, Christine Chase
Chairman, Stephen J. Hemsley, age 55
Secretary, Amy Schneider
Auditors: Deloitte & Touche LLP

LOCATIONS

HQ: UnitedHealth Group Inc
UnitedHealth Group Center, 9900 Bren Road East, Minnetonka, MN 55343
Phone: 952 936-1300
Web: www.unitedhealthgroup.com

PRODUCTS/OPERATIONS

2017 Sales

	$ mil.	% of total
UnitedHealthcare	163,257	64
Optum		
OptumRx	63,755	25
OptumHealth	20,570	8
OptumInsight	8,087	3
Adjustments	(54510)	-
Total	**201,159**	**100**

2017 Sales

	$ mil.	% of total
Premiums	158,453	79
Products	26,366	13
Services	15,317	8
Investment & other income	1,023	-
Total	**201,159**	**100**

Selected Operations

Optum (Health Services division)
  OptumHealth (specialty benefits)
  OptumInsight (formerly Ingenix information technology and consulting services)
  OptumRx (formerly Prescription Solutions pharmacy benefit management)
UnitedHealthcare (Health Plans division)
  UnitedHealthcare Community & State (former operations of AmeriChoice public-sector programs)
  UnitedHealthcare Employer & Individual (health plans for individuals businesses employers)
  UnitedHealthcare International (expatriate coverage for global accounts)

UnitedHealthcare Medicare & Retirement (former operations of Ovations benefits for people age 50 and older)
UnitedHealthcare Military & Veterans (TRICARE West Region contract)

COMPETITORS

AMERIGROUP	Express Scripts
APS Healthcare	Humana
ActiveHealth Management	IMS Health
Aetna	Kaiser Foundation Health Plan
Anthem	Magellan Health
Blue Cross	Molina Healthcare
CIGNA	Prime Therapeutics
CVS	Qmedtrix Systems
Centene	Tivity Health
Delta Dental Plans	WellCare Health Plans
Dental Health Alliance	

HISTORICAL FINANCIALS

Company Type: Public

Income Statement

FYE: December 31

	REVENUE ($ mil.)	NET INCOME ($ mil.)	NET PROFIT MARGIN	EMPLOYEES
12/17	201,159	10,558	5.2%	260,800
12/16	184,840	7,017	3.8%	230,000
12/15	157,107	5,813	3.7%	200,000
12/14	130,474	5,619	4.3%	170,000
12/13	122,489	5,625	4.6%	156,000
Annual Growth	**13.2%**	**17.0%**	**—**	**13.7%**

2017 Year-End Financials

Debt ratio: 22.79%	No. of shares (mil.): 969
Return on equity: 24.54%	Dividends
Cash ($ mil.): 11,981	Yield: 0.0%
Current ratio: 0.73	Payout: 26.8%
Long-term debt ($ mil.): 28,835	Market value ($ mil.): 213,626

	STOCK PRICE ($) FY Close	P/E High/Low		PER SHARE ($) Earnings	Dividends	Book Value
12/17	220.46	21	14	10.72	2.88	49.30
12/16	160.04	22	15	7.25	2.38	40.20
12/15	117.64	21	16	6.01	1.88	35.50
12/14	101.09	18	12	5.70	1.41	34.02
12/13	75.30	13	9	5.50	1.05	32.54
Annual Growth	**30.8%**	**—**	**—**	**18.2%**	**28.6%**	**10.9%**

Unity Bancorp, Inc.

EXECUTIVES

Vice President Branch Sales Manager, Sarika Sikand
Vice President, Alvita Ayers
Assistant Vice President, Vanessa Galante
Avp Relationship Manager, Tracy Tortorello
Board Member, Raj Patel
Auditors: RSM US LLP

LOCATIONS

HQ: Unity Bancorp, Inc.
64 Old Highway 22, Clinton, NJ 08809
Phone: 908 730-7630
Web: www.unitybank.com

PRODUCTS/OPERATIONS

Selected Subsidiaries
Unity Bank
  Unity Financial Services Inc.
  Unity Investment Company Inc.

COMPETITORS

1st Constitution Bancorp	Magyar Bancorp
Amboy Bancorp	Peapack-Gladstone Financial
Bank of America	Roma Financial
Bank of New York Mellon	TD Bank USA
	TF Financial
Brunswick Bancorp	Valley National Bancorp
Fox Chase Bancorp	
Investors Bancorp	

HISTORICAL FINANCIALS
Company Type: Public

Income Statement
FYE: December 31

	ASSETS ($ mil.)	NET INCOME ($ mil.)	INCOME AS % OF ASSETS	EMPLOYEES
12/17	1,455	12	0.9%	208
12/16	1,189	13	1.1%	194
12/15	1,084	9	0.9%	173
12/14	1,008	6	0.6%	183
12/13	921	5	0.6%	178
Annual Growth	12.1%	26.0%	—	4.0%

2017 Year-End Financials
Debt ratio: 19.60%
Return on equity: 11.49%
Cash ($ mil.): 150
Current ratio: —
Long-term debt ($ mil.): —

No. of shares (mil.): 10
Dividends
  Yield: 0.0%
  Payout: 19.1%
Market value ($ mil.): 210

	STOCK PRICE ($) FY Close	P/E High/Low		PER SHARE ($) Earnings	Dividends	Book Value
12/17	19.75	17	13	1.20	0.23	11.13
12/16	15.70	12	7	1.38	0.17	10.15
12/15	12.47	12	9	1.02	0.13	8.46
12/14	9.43	14	10	0.74	0.09	7.60
12/13	7.66	16	12	0.48	0.03	6.86
Annual Growth	26.7%	—	—	25.6%	70.4%	12.9%

Univar Inc

Auditors: Ernst & Young LLP

LOCATIONS

HQ: Univar Inc
3075 Highland Parkway, Suite 200, Downers Grove, IL 60515
Phone: 331 777-6000
Web: www.univar.com

HISTORICAL FINANCIALS
Company Type: Public

Income Statement
FYE: December 31

	REVENUE ($ mil.)	NET INCOME ($ mil.)	NET PROFIT MARGIN	EMPLOYEES
12/17	8,253	119	1.5%	8,600
12/16	8,073	(68)	—	8,700
12/15	8,981	16	0.2%	9,200
12/14	10,373	(20)	—	8,900
12/13	10,324	(82)	—	
Annual Growth	(5.4%)	—	—	

2017 Year-End Financials
Debt ratio: 50.43%
Return on equity: 12.61%
Cash ($ mil.): 467
Current ratio: 1.77
Long-term debt ($ mil.): 2,820

No. of shares (mil.): 141
Dividends
  Yield: —
  Payout: —
Market value ($ mil.): 4,368

	STOCK PRICE ($) FY Close	P/E High/Low		PER SHARE ($) Earnings	Dividends	Book Value
12/17	30.96	39	32	0.85	0.00	7.73
12/16	28.37	—	—	(0.50)	0.00	5.84
12/15	17.01	195	116	0.14	0.00	5.92
Annual Growth	16.2%	—	—	57.0%	—	6.9%

Universal Health Services, Inc.

With dozens of health care facilities in nearly every state Universal Health Services (UHS) isn't quite ubiquitous but it's working on it. One of the nation's largest for-profit hospital operators UHS owns or leases about 25 acute care hospitals with a total of more than 6000 beds primarily in rural and suburban communities. The system also operates outpatient surgery centers and radiation treatment facilities most located near its acute care hospitals. In addition UHS' behavioral health division operates some 500 psychiatric and substance abuse hospitals with a combined capacity of more than 23000 beds; its UK-based Cygnet unit operates about 40 more facilities. UHS is controlled by founder and CEO Alan Miller.

Operations
UHS receives slightly more than half of its annual revenues from its acute care segment which includes medical hospitals surgical outpatient facilities and radiation oncology centers. The remainder of the company's revenue comes from its portfolio of behavioral health hospitals which include residential facilities for teens adult psychiatric hospitals substance abuse facilities and special education schools for students with emotional problems.

UHS provides central resources to its network of facilities including purchasing information services finance facilities planning administrative personnel marketing public relations and physician recruitment.

Geographic Reach
UHS' acute care facilities are located in more than half a dozen states and are situated mostly in smaller towns and cities with limited competition though the division does have facilities in a few larger markets (such as Las Vegas and Washington DC). UHS' behavioral health hospitals are scattered across about 40 US states as well as Puerto Rico the US Virgin Islands and the UK. The company's biggest markets for both segments are Nevada Texas and California.

Headquartered in King of Prussia Pennsylvania UHS also has offices in Wayne Pennsylvania; Brentwood Tennessee; Denton Texas; and Reno Nevada.

Sales and Marketing
Both of UHS' operating segments (Acute Care Hospital Services and Behavioral Health Services) earn more than half of revenues from managed care providers (HMOs PPOs) with the remainder of revenues coming from traditional Medicare and Medicaid plans and other sources.

Financial Performance

UHS' growth strategies have helped it to steadily increase sales over the past several years. The company maintains a strong balance sheet which allows it to build new facilities and more frequently to buy existing facilities from other hospital operators. In general the system has seen increased patient admissions over the years bringing its revenue higher.

In 2017 net revenue increased 7% to $10.4 billion. This was driven by growth in both the Acute Care Hospital Services and Behavioral Health Services segments. Existing acute care hospital adjusted admissions increased 6% while adjusted patient days increased 3% which led to a 5% increase in that segment's net revenue. Existing behavioral health care facility adjusted admissions rose 2% while adjusted patient days increased less than 1% that year. Newly acquired or built facilities further boosted total revenue.

With the higher net revenue plus a decrease in the provision for income taxes net income also rose 7% to $752.3 million in 2017.

The system ended 2017 with $74.4 million in cash up some $40 million from 2016. Operating activities contributed $1.2 billion but investing activities used $624 million (primarily for property and equipment additions) and financing activities (largely share repurchases) used another $519 million.

Strategy
UHS has a focused strategy for growth: Add more facilities to its network improve the services and operations at its facilities and increase the efficiency of its services (including shifting to outpatient care when preferable).

By focusing its operations on high-growth regions UHS also works towards its goal of increasing hospital utilization rates (which is often a key indicator of the financial health of a hospital). To further draw more patients and high-quality physicians to its existing facilities the company invests in new technology makes capital improvements and increases the breadth of services it offers. Initiatives include upgrades to surgical equipment and billing systems as well as the installation of operating room light fixtures that continuously disinfect the environment. UHS is especially expanding its outpatient service capabilities as payers put pressure on hospitals to control inpatient care costs.

While the company's growth strategy is to build or purchase new facilities in rapidly growing areas — it has grown both of its units through selective acquisitions and construction efforts over the years — UHS also has no qualms about ridding itself of operations that just don't quite fit anymore.

UHS gets about 15% of its net revenues from facilities located in Nevada Texas and California. With that much exposure the system is somewhat vulnerable to potential changes in legislation regulations the economy and the competitive landscape that could occur in those states.

Furthermore there is growing scrutiny in many states with regards to for-profit systems (like UHS) buying not-for-profit care facilities and converting them to for-profit facilities. This trend could impact UHS's ability to grow its operations through acquisitions.

Mergers and Acquisitions
UHS is focused on acquiring hospitals and other facilities to expand operations. In mid-2018 UK unit Cygnet acquired The Danshell Group which owns 25 facilities serving adults with learning disabilities.

In 2017 the company acquired Mississippi-based Memorial Behavioral Health which operates a 109-bed facility for adults adolescents and children. It also operates two outpatient clinics. The three facilities are now known as Gulfport Behavioral Health System.

In late 2016 UHS acquired the adult services division of Cambian Group a UK operation for some $464 million; that purchase added 81 behavioral facilities housing some 1200 beds bringing UHS' UK holdings to more than 100 facilities. Also that year UHS acquired Desert View Hospital a 25-bed acute care facility in Nevada.

EXECUTIVES

Vice President And General Counsel, Matthew Klein
Evp And Cfo, Steve G. Filton, age 60, $584,606 total compensation
Chairman And Ceo, Alan B. Miller, age 80, $1,600,061 total compensation
Evp; President Behavioral Health, Debra K. Osteen, age 62, $638,025 total compensation
Evp; President Acute Care, Marvin G. Pember, age 64, $618,502 total compensation
President, Marc D. Miller, age 47, $720,861 total compensation
Svp Information Services And Business Solutions, Michael S. Nelson
Vp Corporate Insurance, Bob Engelhard
Vice President And Director, Brenda Simons
Vice President, Cheryl Livesay
Vice President Center Applications, Lorraine Castro
Executive Vice President Of Finance, Debbie Onofrey
Vice President And Associate General Counsel, Connie Ulibarri
Vice President And Director, Stephen Carlson
Executive Vice President Of Finance, Eileen Vido
Vice President E Health Financial Advisor, Andrew Ganti
Vice President Of Hawaii Division, Donna Murray
Vice President Of Finance, Sean Selders
Division Vice President Of Reimbursement, Dan Mullins
Senior Vice President Patient Services, Reza Vaezazizi
Senior Vice President, James Antosy
Vice President And Director, Jerilin Cummings
Vice President And Director, Brandy Albright
Director Of Radiology Services, Jeff Otto
Vice President And Director, Frank Pizzuto
Regional Vice President, Frank Lopez
Executive Vice President Of Finance, Andy Belen
Director Of Pharmacy, Kristen Palasthy
Senior Vice President Marketing And Sales, Stephanie Stephenson
Vice President And Director, Douglas Coffey
Vp Behavioral Health Services, Roz Hudson
Executive Vice President Of Finance, Stephanie Hill
Senior Vice President Human Resources, Geraldine Geckle
Senior Vice President And Treasurer, Cheryl Ramagano
Vice President Financial Operations, Chris Recon
Vice President Behavioral Health Services, Sharon Worsham
Vp Acute Care, Karla Perez
Vice President, Pj Moraci
Director Of Clinical Services, Kate McBride
Vice President, Andrew Littauer
Vice President Behavioral Health Services, Philip J Moraci
Vice President Acute Finance, Thomas Machozzi
Associate Medical Director, Joseph Farris
Vice President Supply Chain Operations, Raymond Davis
Director Of Radiology, Mark Lerner
Vice President Hospital Finance Bh, Lawrence Harrod
Director Of Admissions, Andrea Hadley
Medical Director, Vikas Duvvuri
Radiology Director, Beth Louton
Director Of Nursing, Catherine Wright
Medical Director, Robert Erwin

Director Of Clinical Services, Debra Vogt
Director Of Utilization Review, Randy Hawkins
Director Of Pharmacy, George Morton
Senior Vice President Of Finance Behavioral Health, Laurence Harrod
Auditors: PricewaterhouseCoopers LLP

LOCATIONS

HQ: Universal Health Services, Inc.
Universal Corporate Center, 367 South Gulph Road, King of Prussia, PA 19406
Phone: 610 768-3300
Web: www.uhsinc.com

Selected Facilities

California
Corona Regional Medical Center (Corona)
Palmdale Regional Medical Center (Palmdale)
Southwest Healthcare System — Inland Valley Campus (Wildomar)
Southwest Healthcare System — Rancho Springs Campus (Murrieta)
Temecula Valley Day Surgery and Pain Therapy Center (Murrieta)
Florida
Lakewood Ranch Medical Center (Bradenton)
Manatee Memorial Hospital (Bradenton)
Palms Westside Clinic ASC (50% Royal Palm Beach)
Wellington Regional Medical Center (West Palm Beach)
Nevada
Centennial Hills Hospital Medical Center (Las Vegas)
Desert Springs Hospital (72% Las Vegas)
Northern Nevada Medical Center (Sparks)
Spring Valley Hospital Medical Center (72% Las Vegas)
Summerlin Hospital Medical Center (72% Las Vegas)
Valley Hospital Medical Center (72% Las Vegas)
South Carolina
Aiken Regional Medical Centers (Aiken)
Aurora Pavilion (Aiken)
Cancer Care Institute of Carolina (Aiken)
Oklahoma
St. Mary's Regional Medical Center (Enid)
Puerto Rico
First Hospital Panamericano (Cidra)
First Hospital Panamericano (Ponce)
First Hospital Panamericano (San Juan)
Texas
Cornerstone Regional Hospital (50% Edinburg)
Doctors' Hospital of Laredo (Laredo)
Fort Duncan Regional Medical Center (Eagle Pass)
Northwest Texas Healthcare System (Amarillo)
Northwest Texas Surgery Center (majority owned Amarillo)
The Pavilion at Northwest Texas Healthcare System (Amarillo)
South Texas Health System (Edinburg)
Edinburg Regional Medical Center (Edinburg)
Edinburg Children's Hospital (Edinburg)
McAllen Medical Center (McAllen)
McAllen Heart Hospital (McAllen)
South Texas Behavioral Health System (Edinburg)
Texoma Medical Center (Denison)
TMC Behavioral Health Center (Denison)
Washington D.C.
The George Washington University Hospital (80%)

PRODUCTS/OPERATIONS

2017 Sales by Segment

	$ mil.	% of total
Acute Care Hospital Services	5	53
Behavioral Health Services	4,906	47
Other	18	-
Total	**10,409**	**100**

COMPETITORS

Adventist Health System Sunbelt Healthcare
Adventist Health System West
Ascension Health
Banner Health
CHRISTUS Health
CRC Health
Community Health Systems
Devereux Foundation

HCA
Hazelden Betty Ford
LifePoint Health
Mercy Health
Northwestern Human Services
Sutter Health
Tenet Healthcare
Texas Health Resources
UBH
United Surgical Partners

HISTORICAL FINANCIALS

Company Type: Public

Income Statement

FYE: December 31

	REVENUE ($ mil.)	NET INCOME ($ mil.)	NET PROFIT MARGIN	EMPLOYEES
12/17	10,409	752	7.2%	76,600
12/16	9,766	702	7.2%	75,325
12/15	9,043	680	7.5%	74,600
12/14	8,065	545	6.8%	68,700
12/13	7,283	510	7.0%	66,100
Annual Growth	**9.3%**	**10.2%**	**—**	**3.8%**

2017 Year-End Financials

Debt ratio: 37.54%
Return on equity: 15.80%
Cash ($ mil.): 74
Current ratio: 0.97
Long-term debt ($ mil.): 3,494

No. of shares (mil.): 94
Dividends
Yield: 0.0%
Payout: 5.1%
Market value ($ mil.): 10,681

	STOCK PRICE ($) FY Close	P/E High/Low	PER SHARE ($) Earnings	Dividends	Book Value
12/17	113.35	16 12	7.81	0.40	52.95
12/16	106.38	19 14	7.14	0.40	46.91
12/15	119.49	21 15	6.76	0.40	43.23
12/14	111.26	21 13	5.42	0.30	37.85
12/13	81.26	16 10	5.14	0.20	33.06
Annual Growth	**8.7%**	**— —**	**11.0%**	**18.9%**	**12.5%**

Universal Insurance Holdings Inc

While some companies shy away from insuring homes in hurricane-prone Florida Universal Insurance Holdings is right at home there. Operating through its Universal Property & Casualty Insurance Company (UPCIC) and American Platinum Property and Casualty Insurance Company (APPCIC) subsidiaries the company underwrites distributes and administers homeowners property and personal liability insurance. The company's additional subsidiaries process claims perform claims adjustments and property inspections provide administrative duties and negotiate reinsurance.All together the group services some 765000 insurance policies.

Operations

Universal Insurance is Florida's largest private residential homeowners' insurance provider by direct written premiums in-force with some 10% of the market share.

In addition to UPCIC and APPCIC the company owns Universal Risk Advisors (managing general agent) Universal Inspection Corporation (underwriting inspections) Universal Adjusting Corporation (claims processing) and Blue Atlantic Reinsurance (reinsurance intermediary).

Through Universal Insurance's Universal Direct platform consumers in all states the group operates in are able to directly purchase homeowners policies online without meeting an intermediary face-to-face.

Geographic Reach

Universal Insurance's UPCIC unit has taken its expertise in flood and wind coverage to other markets. While Florida remains its largest market it also operates in 15 other states: Alabama Delaware Florida Georgia Hawaii Indiana Maryland Massachusetts Michigan Minnesota New Hampshire New Jersey New York North Carolina Pennsylvania South Carolina and Virginia. Although not yet active in Illinois Iowa New Hampshire or West Virginia the company is licensed in those states.

APPCIC writes homeowners multi-peril insurance for homes worth more than $1 million in Florida.

Sales and Marketing

Universal Insurance distributes its products through a network of some 8800 independent agents.It also sells its policies through its online platform Universal Direct.

Financial Performance

Universal Insurance's revenues have been rising for the past five years. In 2017 revenue increased 10% to $751.9 million as net premiums earned rose 9% commissions rose 20% and net investment income rose 41%. Policy fees and other revenue also grew in 2017. Direct premiums written increased 11% within Florida and 40% in other states.

With the higher revenue net income rose 8% to $106.9 million. Operating cash flow followed suit more than doubling to $245 million. Factors driving that growth included positive changes to unpaid losses and loss adjustment expenses net reinsurance payable and liabilities and accrued expenses.

Strategy

Universal Insurance has been rapidly and organically expanding its operations beyond Florida especially in states with underserved homeowners markets. It has also introduced new types of coverage such as fire commercial multi-peril and other liability. With this diversification the company is less vulnerable to the catastrophes that have been the bane of Florida insurers. However because it does the majority of its business in Florida Universal Insurance has been hit hard with property/casualty claims in certain years — including in 2017 with the appearance of Hurricane Irma.

Additionally the company has seen an increase in lawsuits against it including suits originating in South Florida. As other insurers shy away from Florida business Universal Insurance remains committed to the state and to offset rising claims has sought approval to raise its rates some 10% across most of South Florida.

Personal residential homeowners insurance is the company's bread and butter but Universal Insurance is increasingly diving into commercial policies particularly commercial residential coverage in Florida.

EXECUTIVES

Chairman And Ceo, Sean P. Downes, age 48, $2,278,015 total compensation

Coo, Stephen J. Donaghy, $802,514 total compensation

President And Chief Risk Officer, Jon W. Springer, age 48, $1,337,416 total compensation

Cfo And Principal Accounting Officer, Frank C Wilcox, $350,000 total compensation

Cio, Kimberly Cooper, $196,923 total compensation

Vice President Marketing, David Ahern

Auditors: Plante & Moran, PLLC

LOCATIONS

HQ: Universal Insurance Holdings Inc
1110 W. Commercial Blvd., Suite 100, Fort Lauderdale, FL 33309
Phone: 954 958-1200
Web: www.universalinsuranceholdings.com

PRODUCTS/OPERATIONS

2017 Sales

	$ mil.	% of total
Net premiums earned	688	92
Commissions	21	3
Policy fees	18	2
Net investment income	13	2
Net realized gains on investments	2	-
Other	7	1
Total	**751**	**100**

Selected Products and Services

Condominium policy
Dwelling coverage
Dwelling fire policy
Homeowners policy
Other structures coverage
Personal liability coverage
Personal property coverage
Renter's policy

COMPETITORS

Allstate	Liberty Mutual
Citizens Property Insurance	Progressive Corporation
Federated National Holding	State Farm
HCI Group	Travelers Companies
Heritage Insurance Holdings	USAA
	United Insurance Holdings

HISTORICAL FINANCIALS

Company Type: Public

Income Statement

FYE: December 31

	ASSETS ($ mil.)	NET INCOME ($ mil.)	INCOME AS % OF ASSETS	EMPLOYEES
12/17	1,455	106	7.3%	558
12/16	1,060	99	9.4%	483
12/15	993	106	10.7%	392
12/14	911	72	8.0%	335
12/13	920	58	6.4%	300
Annual Growth	**12.1%**	**16.0%**	**—**	**16.8%**

2017 Year-End Financials

Debt ratio: 3.41%	No. of shares (mil.): 34
Return on equity: 26.37%	Dividends
Cash ($ mil.): 213	Yield: 0.0%
Current ratio: —	Payout: 23.0%
Long-term debt ($ mil.): —	Market value ($ mil.): 950

	STOCK PRICE ($) FY Close	P/E High/Low		PER SHARE ($) Earnings	Dividends	Book Value
12/17	27.35	9	5	2.99	0.69	12.67
12/16	28.40	10	6	2.79	0.69	10.59
12/15	23.18	12	6	2.97	0.63	8.35
12/14	20.45	10	5	2.08	0.55	6.24
12/13	14.48	9	3	1.56	0.49	4.97
Annual Growth	**17.2%**	**—**	**—**	**17.7%**	**8.9%**	**26.4%**

UNIVERSITY OF PITTSBURGH MEDICAL CENTER

For University of Pittsburgh students and area residents medical care is spelled UPMC. UPMC Jameson is a leading not-for-profit health care delivery system in western Pennsylvania. The organization operates about 20 hospitals including campuses in the Pittsburgh area regional and community hospitals and specialty facilities such as Children's Hospital of Pittsburgh and the Magee-Womens Hospital. Combined UPMC Jameson has more than 5100 inpatient beds. In addition the system provides care through hundreds of physician practices outpatient clinics cancer treatment facilities and rehab centers; it also offers health insurance home health care and long-term care through more than 15 senior living facilities.

Operations

UPMC Jameson is organized into four primary operating divisions. Provider Services includes tertiary community and regional hospitals; specialty services such as women's health and behavioral health; in-home care and senior living; contract services including pharmacy and laboratories; and the system's 3400 physicians and their practices. Insurance Services offers health insurance to employers and employees workers' compensation and disability services and behavioral health coverage to Medical Assistance beneficiaries. UPMC International Services exports the system's expertise abroad while UPMC Enterprises seeks commercialization opportunities and partnerships.

As an academic medical center affiliated with the University of Pittsburgh's Schools of Health Sciences UPMC Jameson also focuses on medical research in a wide range of areas including the fields of regenerative medicine and biosecurity some of which is funded by the National Institutes of Health. The system is also renowned for its organ transplantation programs as well as for its cancer care psychiatric pediatric and women's health services. In addition UPMC Jameson is a forerunner in the health care information technology field.

The system has some 5500 affiliated physicians. In a typical year it has some 287000 inpatient admissions more than 3.9 million outpatient visits and some 690000 emergency department visits. It performs some 189000 surgeries and more than 690000 home care visits.

Geographic Reach

The company's primary operating territory for its health and insurance segments is western Pennsylvania. Outside the US UPMC Jameson operates health care facilities in Ireland Italy Quatar Cyprus and the UK. It also provides management and consulting services in other international countries to improve global health care partly through partnerships with health equipment and technology firms.

Sales and Marketing

The majority of the company's hospital services are rendered to patients under Medicare Highmark Blue Cross Blue Shield (a major area insurer) and medical assistance programs. Its patient service revenue comes from Medicare accounts (which accounts for more than 30% of all patient revenue each year) Highmark (31%) other medical assistance programs (about 10%) and self-pay and commercial insurance.

Financial Performance

UPMC's revenues increased 12% to some $11.4 billion in 2014 due to increased patient service revenues which accounted for half of all earnings. Higher enrollment levels in the UPMC Health Plan (40% of sales) also contributed to growth that year. Net income rose 58% to $698 million on higher investment income and other factors. Meanwhile cash flow from operations increased 82% to $568.9 million.

Strategy

The UPMC network of facilities has grown over the years through acquisitions and new facility construction. On the flip side the company has occasionally sold or shut down less-profitable facilities in its network such as UPMC Braddock an underused suburban community hospital.

UPMC Jameson is advancing its technology systems to control costs and increase efficiencies. The health system has established electronic health record (EHR) systems at all of its hospitals and is working to share data with other area providers. In addition UPMC has partnerships with Alcatel-Lucent GE and IBM to help reduce medical expenses and increase the quality of care through IT initiatives.

In 2015 UMPC and The University of Pittsburgh School of Medicine launched the Center for Women's Health Research and Innovation which is devoted to research education and clinical practice while promoting community partnership and advocacy related to health care for women.

The following year UMPC acquired rural hospital Jameson Healthcare to become UMPC Jameson. Jameson had been operating in the red — a common problem for rural systems. UMPC Jameson plans to invest between $70 and $80 million to provide continuing services in Lawrence County (including maintaining facilities and recruiting new doctors) as well as to pay down debt.

Mergers and Acquisitions

In 2017 UMPC agreed to buy Pinnacle Health System. The purchase will add two hospitals to UPMC's network and will allow the system to sell health insurance beyond its core market in western Pennsylvania.

EXECUTIVES

President And Ceo, Jeffrey A. Romoff
Evp And Chief Administrative Officer, Gregory Peaslee
Evp And Cfo, Robert A. DeMichiei
Evp President Insurance Services Division And President And Ceo Upmc Health Plan, Diane P. Holder
Evp; President Hospital And Community Services Division, Elizabeth B. Concordia
Svp And Evp And Chief Operating Officer Health Services Division, Leslie C. Davis
Evp And Chief Legal Officer, W. Thomas (Tom) McGough
Evp And President International Commercial Services Division And President Upmc Cancercenter, Charles E. (Chuck) Bogosta
Svp And Chief Of Staff Office Of The President, David M. Farner
Evp Treasurer And President Upmc Enterprises, C. Talbot Heppenstall
Evp And Chief Medical Officer; President Physician Services Division, Marshall W. Webster
Svp And Chief Medical Officer, Steven D. Shapiro
Auditors: ERNST & YOUNG LLP

LOCATIONS

HQ: UNIVERSITY OF PITTSBURGH MEDICAL CENTER
200 LOTHROP ST, PITTSBURGH, PA 152132536
Phone: 412 647-8762
Web: WWW.UPMC.COM

Selected Pennsylvania Facilities
Children's Hospital of Pittsburgh of UPMC
Magee-Womens Hospital of UPMC (Pittsburgh)
UPMC Bedford Memorial (Everett)
UPMC East (Pittsburgh)
UPMC Hamlot (Erie)
UPMC Horizon (Greenville and Shenango Valley)
UPMC McKeesport (McKeesport)
UPMC Mercy (Pittsburgh)
UPMC Montefiore (Pittsburgh)
UPMO Northwest (Oeneca and Oil City)
UPMC Passavant (McCandless and Cranberry)
UPMC Presbyterian (Pittsburgh)
UPMC Shadyside (Pittsburgh)
UPMC St. Margaret (Pittsburgh)
UPMC Western Psychiatric Institute and Clinic (Pittsburgh)

PRODUCTS/OPERATIONS

2014 Sales

	$ mil.	% of total
Patient services	5,776	51
Insurance services	4,813	42
Other	826	7
Total	**11,415**	**100**

Selected Services
Behavioral and Mental Health Services
Cancer
COPD and Emphysema Center
Dermatology
Diabetes and Endocrinology
Ear Nose and Throat
Emergency Medicine
Family/Primary Care Medicine
Gastroenterology
Geriatrics
Heart and Vascular
Imaging Services
Kidney Disease
Liver
Neurology
Ophthalmology
Pain Medicine
Pathology
Pediatrics
Pulmonology and Respiratory
Rehabilitation
Rheumatology
Sports Medicine
Stroke Care
Thyroid
Urology
Women's Health
Wound Healing Services

COMPETITORS

Allegheny General Hospital
AmeriHealth Mercy Health Plan
Blue Cross of Northeastern Pennsylvania
Butler Health System
Capital BlueCross
Conemaugh Health System
Excela Health
Geisinger Health System
HealthAmerica
Heritage Valley Health
Highmark
Independence Blue Cross
Jefferson Regional Medical Center of Pennsylvania
Ohio Valley General
PinnacleHealth System
St. Clair Health
Universal Health Services
West Penn Allegheny Health System

HISTORICAL FINANCIALS
Company Type: Private

Income Statement
FYE: June 30

	REVENUE ($ mil.)	NET INCOME ($ mil.)	NET PROFIT MARGIN	EMPLOYEES
06/16	12,848	(16)	—	80,000
06/15	614	326	53.1%	—
00/13*	10,188	441	4.3%	—
12/11	4,758	(2)	—	—
Annual Growth	**28.2%**	—	—	—

*Fiscal year change

2016 Year-End Financials

Debt ratio: ——
Return on equity: (-0.10%)
Cash ($ mil.): 431
Current ratio: 0.50
Long-term debt ($ mil.): —

Dividends
Yield: —
Payout: —
Market value ($ mil.): —

UNIVERSITY OF SOUTHERN CALIFORNIA

A Trojan horse filled with students is more than welcome at the University of Southern California (USC). Founded in 1880 the private university (with a Trojan mascot) grew up with the city of Los Angeles and is now one of the largest private employers in the city. California's oldest research university USC is recognized for distinguished programs in fields including business engineering film law medicine public administration science and theater. The university has two campuses in Los Angeles and additional centers and programs elsewhere in California Washington DC and overseas. USC has a total of some 41000 undergraduate and graduate students and almost 3790 full-time faculty members.

Operations

USC's programs are divided into about 20 undergraduate academic schools and colleges plus the USC Graduate School. More than half of its students are enrolled in graduate programs.

The Health Science Center includes a number of academic and medical care institutions including the USC School of Pharmacy the Herman Ostrow School of Dentistry and the USC University Hospital. Its Keck School of Medicine trains physicians at the University Hospital as well as through partnerships with area hospital operators including the Childrens Hospital Los Angeles and the Los Angeles County Department of Health Services. In addition the medical school's faculty and students conduct medical disease research.

As a leading US private research university USC conducts $600 million in research each year at its various institutions in areas including national security cultural affairs technology and scientific innovation. The medical school receives more than $150 million in research grants from the federal government each year.

Geographic Reach

USC's primary 230-acre University Park campus in Los Angeles is home to most of the university's undergraduate programs and professional schools as well as its graduate program. It also includes the university's main admissions and administration offices. The university's 80-acre Health Sciences Campus is also located in Los Angeles.

USC has one of the largest international student populations among US universities. In addition to educating students from China India and other countries at its US campuses USC pursues international educational medical and research collaborations (including study abroad programs) with institutions in developing nations such as Ethiopia Kenya Rwanda and Uganda.

Financial Performance

USC has an endowment of $4.6 billion. Tuition and fees run at around $48400 per student per year.

USC's revenues increased from $3.9 billion in fiscal 2013 to $4.8 billion in fiscal 2014 thanks to a growth in investments higher gifts and pledges and the expansion of its healthcare services. Net income followed suit growing from $66.3 million in fiscal 2013 to $66.7 million in fiscal 2014 on higher revenues.

Strategy

In its educational programs USC strives to combine liberal arts and professional learning programs as well as athletics and extracurricular activities to provide a well-rounded student experience. It is also expanding its online learning programs to enhance continuing education programs. The university places great focus on keeping its research programs among the top-ranked programs in the US.

The university also invests in campus improvement and expansion projects. Broadening its health services in 2013 USC acquired the 158-bed Verdigo Hills Hospital for $9 million. Boosting its assets that year it also acquired the Pacific Asia Museum. Both purchases boosted the university's net assets by a total of $100 million.

HISTORY

Los Angeles was still a frontier town when a diverse group of local citizens led by Judge Robert Maclay Widney established the University of Southern California (USC) in 1880 (early rules for students included a prohibition against carrying guns to class). But Los Angeles grew quickly and USC grew with it. By 1910 the university had most of its major programs in place including law and medical schools. During the 1920s USC established the nation's first school of international relations (1924) and offered the first degree in cinema (1929).

The end of WWII and the GI Bill brought a major increase in enrollment forcing the university to expand. Some 50 new buildings were added in the 1950s and 1960s and another 37 were begun or completed in the 1970s. The university started increasing its fund-raising efforts in the 1980s. Steven Sample became president in 1991 and secured hundreds of millions in donations over the course of the decade including a $110 million grant in 1999 from the W.M. Keck Foundation for USC's School of Medicine which was renamed Keck School of Medicine.

USC was named 1999 college of the year by Time magazine and the Princeton Review. In 2001 USC opened the Robert Zemeckis Center for Digital Arts the first US digital filmmaking school and in 2005 the university established a federal relations office in Washington DC.

In 2007 USC opened its Levan Institute for Humanities and Ethics and the Edward R. Roybal Institute for Applied Gerontology.

The university has also been conducting campus improvement projects. In 2010 USC completed construction of a new welcome center called the Ronald Tudor Campus Center and in 2011 it started construction of the new John McKay Athletics Center. In 2012 USC began work on a new journalism and communication building and a new student health center.

Notable alumni of USC include Marion Morrison (also known as John Wayne) who played tackle on the school's football team and the first man on the moon Neil Armstrong. Directors George Lucas and Robert Zemeckis are both USC film school graduates.

EXECUTIVES

Dean Annenberg School For Communication And Journalism, Ernest J. Wilson

Cfo, James M. Staten

President, Chrysostomos L. (Max) Nikias, age 65

Dean Thornton School Of Music, Robert A. Cutietta

Dean School Of Cinematic Arts, Elizabeth M. Daley

Dean School Of Social Work, Marilyn L. Flynn

Dean Rossier School Of Education, Karen Symms Gallagher

Dean Sol Price School Of Public Policy, Jack H. Knott

Dean Viterbi School Of Engineering, Yannis C. Yortsos

Chief Investment Officer, Lisa Mazzocco

Dean School Of Architecture, Qingyun Ma

Dean Marshall School Of Business, James G. Ellis, age 71

Dean Keck School Of Medicine, Carmen A. Puliafito

Dean University Libraries, Catherine Quinlan

Dean Dornsife College Of Letters Arts And Sciences, Steve A. Kay

Svp And Ceo Keck Medicine Of Usc, Thomas E. Jackiewicz

Dean Davis School Of Gerontology, Pinchas Cohen

Dean Leventhal School Of Accounting, William W. Holder

Dean Roski School Of Fine Arts, Erica Muhl

Dean Ostrow School Of Dentistry, Avishai Sadan

Provost And Svp Academic Affairs, Michael Quick

Interim Vice Provost Information Technology Services And Cio, Douglas Shook

Dean Usc Gould School Of Law, Andrew T. Guzman

Interim Dean Usc School Of Dramatic Arts, David Bridel

Interim Dean Usc School Of Pharmacy, Glen L. Stimmel

Senior Advisor To The Vice President For Student Affairs, Roopali Malhotra

Assistant Vice President Business Services Procure, Lila Mauro

Executive Vice President Human Resources And Administration, George Rose

Chairman, John Mork

Vice Chairman, Jeffrey Miller

Auditors: PRICEWATERHOUSECOOPERS LLP L

LOCATIONS

HQ: UNIVERSITY OF SOUTHERN CALIFORNIA
3720 S FLOWER ST FL 3, LOS ANGELES, CA 900894304

Phone: 213 740-7762

Web: WWW.USC.EDU

PRODUCTS/OPERATIONS

2012 Revenues

	$ mil.	% of total
Net student tuition & fees	977	29
Health care services	882	27
Gifts & pledges	527	16
Government contracts & grants	323	10
Auxiliary enterprises	254	8
Recovery of indirect costs	132	4
Sales & service	28	1
Endowment investment & other income	68	2
Other revenues	101	3
Adjustments	(62.8)	-
Total	**3,233**	**100**

Selected Schools

Annenberg School for Communication and Journalism
Dana and David Dornsife College of Letters Arts and Sciences
Davis School of Gerontology
Division of Biokinesiology and Physical Therapy
Division of Occupational Science and Occupational Therapy
Glorya Kaufman School of Dance
Gould School of Law
Graduate School
Herman Ostrow School of Dentistry
Keck School of Medicine
Leventhal School of Accounting
Marshall School of Business
Roski School of Fine Arts
Rossier School of Education
School of Architecture
School of Cinematic Arts
School of Dramatic Arts
School of Pharmacy
School of Social Work
Sol Price School of Public Policy
Thornton School of Music
Viterbi School of Engineering

HISTORICAL FINANCIALS

Company Type: Private

Income Statement

	REVENUE ($ mil.)	NET INCOME ($ mil.)	NET PROFIT MARGIN	FYE: June 30 EMPLOYEES
06/18	4,936	489	9.9%	22,700
06/13	3,861	587	15.2%	—
06/12	3,233	68	2.1%	—
Annual Growth	**7.3%**	**38.8%**	—	—

2018 Year-End Financials

Debt ratio: —
Return on equity: 9.90%
Cash ($ mil.): 818
Current ratio: —
Long-term debt ($ mil.): —

Dividends
Yield: —
Payout: —
Market value ($ mil.): —

UNIVERSITY OF TEXAS SYSTEM

EXECUTIVES

Executive Vice Chancellor Business Affairs, Scott C. Kelley

Executive Vice Chancellor Academic Affairs, Pedro Reyes

President Ut Health Science Center At San Antonio, Francisco G. Cigarroa

Executive Vice Chancellor Health Affairs, Raymond S. Greenberg

Vice Chancellor Strategic Initiatives, Stephanie Bond Huie

Vice Chairman, R. Steven (Steve) Hicks, age 68

Chairman, Paul L. Foster, age 60

Vice Chairman, Wm. Eugene (Gene) Powell

Auditors: DELOITTE & TOUCHE LLP AUSTIN

LOCATIONS

HQ: UNIVERSITY OF TEXAS SYSTEM
210 W 7TH ST, AUSTIN, TX 787013099

Phone: 512 499-4587

Web: WWW.UTSYSTEM.EDU

PRODUCTS/OPERATIONS

Selected Institutions
Academic Institutions
The University of Texas at Arlington (established 1895)
The Univer
The Univer
The Univer
The Univer
The University of Texas-Pan American (Edinburg; 1997)
The University of Texas of the Permian Basin (Odessa; 1969)
The Univer
The Univer
Health Institutions
The University of Texas Health Science Center at Houston (established 1972)
The Univer
The Univer
The University of Texas M.D. Anderson Cancer Center (Houston 1941)
The Univer
The Univer

HISTORICAL FINANCIALS

Company Type: Private

Income Statement   FYE: August 31

	REVENUE ($ mil.)	NET INCOME ($ mil.)	NET PROFIT MARGIN	EMPLOYEES
08/16	13,282	1,589	12.0%	81,260
08/09	8,564	(3,592)	—	—
08/08	46	1	2.3%	—
Annual Growth	102.7%	148.6%	—	—

2016 Year-End Financials

Debt ratio: ——
Return on equity: 12.00%
Cash ($ mil.): 2,545
Current ratio: 0.70
Long-term debt ($ mil.): —

Dividends
Yield: —
Payout: —
Market value ($ mil.): —

UNIVERSITY OF WASHINGTON INC

The University of Washington (UW) is Husky indeed with an annual enrollment of more than 54000 students. Founded in 1861 as the Territorial University of Washington UW (pronounced "U-dub" by those on campus) has smaller branches in Tacoma and Bothell in addition to its main campus in downtown Seattle. The university whose mascot is a Husky offers more than 600 undergraduate graduate and professional degree programs through 16 colleges and schools. It also operates four hospitals: University of Washington Medical Center Harborview Medical Center Northwest Hospital and Valley Medical Center.

Operations
With more than 300 programs University of Washington confers some 12000 bachelor's master's doctoral and professional degrees each year. Its graduates include about 135 Fulbright and 35 Rhodes scholars. The school's top five bachelor degree fields include biology psychology political science economics and communications.

Research is a cornerstone of the university which has nearly 300 specialized research centers. The school's annual sponsored grant and contract research funding exceeds $1.6 billion. Some 300

new companies have emerged based on UW research advances.

Financial Performance
In fiscal 2017 (ended June) operating revenue for University of Washington totaled $5.8 billion. Patient service revenues account for the largest amount of funds received (38%) followed by federal grants and contracts (about 21%).

Operating expenses totaled $5.7 billion that year. Salaries accounted for nearly half of those expenses.

EXECUTIVES

Dean School Of Medicine, Paul G. Ramsey
Svp Finance And Facilities, V'Ella Warren
Chancellor Bothell Campus, Bjong Wolf Yeigh
Dean School Of Law, Kellye Testy
Dean Libraries, Lizabeth A. (Betsy) Wilson
Interim Chancellor Tacoma Campus, Kenyon S. Chan
Dean School Of Public Health, Howard Frumkin
President, Ana Mari Cauce
Dean Undergraduate Academic Affairs, Ed Taylor
Vp Information Technology And Cio, Kelli Trosvig
Dean College Of Arts And Sciences, Robert Stacey
Interim Dean College Of Built Environments, John Schaufelberger
Dean School Of Dentistry, Joel H. Berg
Dean College Of Education, Tom Stritikus
Dean College Of Engineering, Michael B. Bragg
Dean College Of The Environment, Lisa Graumlich
Dean Evans School Of Public Affairs, Sandra Archibald
Dean Foster School Of Business, James Jiambalvo
Dean Graduate School, Dave Eaton
Dean Information School, Harry Bruce
Dean School Of Nursing, Azita Emami
Dean School Of Pharmacy, Thomas Baillie
Dean School Of Social Work, Edwina (Eddie) Uehara
Associate Vice President Financial Management, Susan Camber
Associate Vice President For Alumni Relations Uni, Paul Rucker
Medical Director, Jean Haulman
Senior Vice President Ecommerce Mobile D, Brian Jones
Associate Vice President, Lincoln Johnson
Vice President Of Marketing, Kristin Elko
Assistant Vice President For Student Life And, Pam Schreiber
Director Of Government Relations, Ian Goodhew
Medical Director, Rob Sweet
Associate Vice President College Access, Patricia Loera
Vice President External Affairs, Brian Taubeneck
Vice Chairman, William S. (Bill) Ayer
Chairman, Orin C. Smith
Board Of Directors Quarterly Editor: Vacant
Librarian, Mary Schroeder
Auditors: KPMG LLP SEATTLE WASHINGTON

LOCATIONS

HQ: UNIVERSITY OF WASHINGTON INC
4311 11TH AVE NE STE 600, SEATTLE, WA 981056369
Phone: 206 543-2100
Web: WWW.WASHINGTON.EDU

PRODUCTS/OPERATIONS

Selected Colleges and Schools
College of Arts and Sciences
College of Built Environments
College of Education
College of Engineering
College of the Environment
Evans School of Public Affairs
The Graduate School

Information School
Michael G. Foster School of Business
School of Dentistry
School of Law
School of Medicine
School of Nursing
School of Pharmacy
School of Public Health
School of Social Work

HISTORICAL FINANCIALS

Company Type: Private

Income Statement   FYE: June 30

	REVENUE ($ mil.)	NET INCOME ($ mil.)	NET PROFIT MARGIN	EMPLOYEES
06/17	4,893	363	7.4%	27,228
06/16	5	(0)	—	—
06/15	4	0	5.6%	—
06/12	4,258	5	0.1%	—
Annual Growth	2.8%	127.9%	—	—

2017 Year-End Financials

Debt ratio: ——
Return on equity: 7.40%
Cash ($ mil.): 64
Current ratio: 0.60
Long-term debt ($ mil.): —

Dividends
Yield: —
Payout: —
Market value ($ mil.): —

Univest Financial Corp

Univest Corporation of Pennsylvania will keep your money close to its vest. The holding company owns $3 billion-asset Univest Bank and Trust which serves the southeastern part of the Keystone State and the broader Mid-Atlantic region online and though 30 branches and provides standard retail and commercial banking services such as checking and savings accounts CDs IRAs and credit cards. Subsidiary Univest Capital provides small-ticket commercial financing while Univest Insurance offers personal and commercial coverage. Univest Investments which boasts some $3 billion in assets under management offers brokerage and investment advisory services.

Operations
Univest operates three main business segments: Banking which accounted for 79% of the company's total revenue during 2015 and provides traditional banking services to consumers businesses and government entities through Univest Bank and Trust; Wealth Management (12% of revenue) which offers investment advisory retirement plan trust municipal pension and broker/dealer services through Univest Investments; and Insurance (9% of revenue) which offers commercial and personal insurance lines as well as benefits and human resources consulting through Univest Insurance.

Broadly speaking Univest Corporation gets more than 60% of its revenue from interest income. About 61% of its total revenue came from loan interest (including fees on loans and leases) during 2015 while another 5% came from interest on its investment securities. The rest of its revenue came from insurance commissions and fees (8% of revenue) investment advisory commission and fee income (7%) trust fee income (5%) deposit account service charges (3%) mortgage banking sales (3%) and other miscellaneous income sources.

More than 40% of the company's loan portfolio was made up of commercial real estate loans at the end of 2015 while another 23% of loan assets were made up of commercial loans that were financial or agricultural-related. The remainder of the portfolio was made up of loans tied to residential properties secured for business purposes (10% of loan assets) residential properties for personal purposes (8%) lease financings (7%) construction real estate loans (4%) and loans to individuals (less than 2%).

Geographic Reach

Souderton Pennsylvania-based Univest Corporation and its subsidiaries serve clients across the Mid-Atlantic region. The company has around 30 bank branches and nearly 20 offices in the Montgomery Bucks Philadelphia Chester Berks Lehigh and Delaware counties of Pennsylvania as well as in Calvert County in Maryland Camden County in New Jersey and Lee County in Florida.

Sales and Marketing

Univest Corporation serves individuals businesses municipalities and non-profit organizations. It spent $2.25 million on marketing and advertising during 2015 to reach these clients up from $1.88 million and $1.95 million in 2014 and 2013 respectively.

Financial Performance

The bank's revenues and profits have been trending higher over the past several years thanks to 50% loan asset growth and 50% non-interest revenue growth since 2011 along with a continued reduction in loan loss provisions as its loan portfolio's credit quality has improved with higher property valuations in the strengthened economy.

Univest Corporation's revenue jumped 24% to a record $154.41 million during 2015 mostly as 35% loan asset growth (loan balances swelled to $2.16 billion) stemming from its Valley Green Bank acquisition helped boost interest income. The company's non-interest income also rose 9% as its mortgage banking gains doubled during the year on higher volumes and as its insurance commissions and fee income rose 20% after acquiring Sterner Insurance in mid-2014.

Strong revenue growth in 2015 drove the company's net income up 23% to $27.27 million for the year. Univest Corporation's operating cash levels climbed 12% to $35.63 thanks to the rise in earnings.

Strategy

Univest Corporation has been expanding its service lines and building its loan and deposit businesses by strategically acquiring other banks and investment or insurance-related financial firms.

Mergers and Acquisitions

In December 2015 Univest Corporation agreed to buy Fox Chase Bancorp along with its $1.1 billion in assets $768 million in loans $765 million in deposits and several Fox Chase Bank branches in Pennsylvania and New Jersey for a price exceeding $240 million. The deal would also expand Univest's presence in Bucks Chester Philadelphia and Montgomery counties in Pennsylvania as well as into Atlantic and Cape May counties in New Jersey.

In January 2015 the company purchased Valley Green Bank as well as its three branches and two loan production offices in the greater Philadelphia market for $77 million.

In July 2014 Univest bolstered its Univest Insurance subsidiary after acquiring Sterner Insurance Associates a full-service insurance and consultative risk management firm that served individuals and businesses across the Lehigh Valley Berks Bucks and Montgomery counties.

In January 2014 flagship subsidiary Univest Bank and Trust Co. bought registered investment advisory firm Girard Partners Ltd. as well as its $500 million in assets under management. The deal boosted Univest's assets under management by 20% to a total of $3 billion after the acquisition.

EXECUTIVES

President Corporate Banking, Philip C. (Phil) Jackson, $250,000 total compensation
Evp And Chief Credit Officer Univest Corporation And Univest National Bank, Duane J. Brobst, $200,000 total compensation
President And Ceo, Jeffrey M Schweitzer, $450,000 total compensation
Sevp And Cfo, Michael S Keim, $270,000 total compensation
Senior Vice President Marketing Underwriting Manager, Maria Di Marco
Senior Vice President Retail Banking, Tony Dacosta
Senior Vice President Credit Administration, Tami Garber
Vice President, Lisa Hartley
Executive Vice President Chief Experience Officer And Director Corporate Planning, Annette Szygiel
Vice President Corporate Communications, Kim Detwiler
Senior Vice President Retail Banking, Anthony Dacosta
Vice President Area Manager, Gregory Taber
Senior Vice President Director Of Project Management And Information Technology Strategy, Margie Boutcher
Senior Vice President Employee Benefits Practice Leader, Dennis Boyle
Vice President Commercial Real Estate Lending, Robert Castro
Svp Director Bank Systems, Jeffrey Groff
Vice President And Senior Benefits Consultant, Rick Mack
Vice President Relationship Manager, Nicholas Yelicanin
Vice President Commercial Lending, Andrew Leaman
Executive Vice President And General Counsel, Megan Santana
Vice President Small Business Relationship Manager, Steven Walker
Assistant Vice President Finance Business Unit Analytics, Mary Beth Osbeck
Senior Vice President And Senior Trust Officer, Matt Holliday
Vice President, John Powers
Vice President, David Henrich
Vice President Commercial Lending, Ramzi Dagher
Chairman, William S. Aichele, age 67
Board Member, Mark Schlosser
Treasurer, Bill Shelley
Board Member, Glenn Moyer
Auditors: KPMG LLP

LOCATIONS

HQ: Univest Financial Corp
14 North Main Street, Souderton, PA 18964
Phone: 215 721-2400
Web: www.univest.net

PRODUCTS/OPERATIONS

2015 sales

	$ mil.	% of total
Banking	120	79
Wealth Management	18	12
Insurance	14	9
Other	0	-
Total	**154**	**100**

COMPETITORS

Citizens Financial Group	PNC Financial
Fulton Financial	QNB Corp.
Harleysville Savings	Royal Bancshares
M&T Bank	Sovereign Bank

HISTORICAL FINANCIALS

Company Type: Public

Income Statement

FYE: December 31

	ASSETS ($ mil.)	NET INCOME ($ mil.)	INCOME AS % OF ASSETS	EMPLOYEES
12/17	4,554	44	1.0%	855
12/16	4,230	19	0.5%	840
12/15	2,879	27	0.9%	717
12/14	2,235	22	1.0%	638
12/13	2,191	21	1.0%	612
Annual Growth	**20.1%**	**20.1%**	**—**	**8.7%**

2017 Year-End Financials

Debt ratio: 5.49%	No. of shares (mil.): 29
Return on equity: 7.96%	Dividends
Cash ($ mil.): 75	Yield: 0.0%
Current ratio: —	Payout: 48.7%
Long-term debt ($ mil.): —	Market value ($ mil.): 823

	STOCK PRICE ($) FY Close	P/E High/Low		PER SHARE ($) Earnings	Dividends	Book Value
12/17	28.05	20	16	1.64	0.80	20.57
12/16	30.90	37	22	0.84	0.80	19.00
12/15	20.86	15	13	1.39	0.80	18.51
12/14	20.24	16	13	1.36	0.80	17.54
12/13	20.68	17	13	1.27	0.80	17.22
Annual Growth	**7.9%**		**—**	**6.6%**	**(0.0%)**	**4.5%**

Unum Group

Through injury or illness Unum works to keep employees employed. A top disability insurer in the US and the UK it offers short-term and long-term disability insurance as well as life and accidental death and dismemberment insurance to individuals and groups in a workplace benefits setting. Specialty coverage offerings include cancer and dental insurance. Among its US subsidiaries are Unum Life Insurance Company of America Provident Life and Accident First Unum Life Colonial Life & Accident and Paul Revere Life Insurance. The company operates as Unum Limited in the UK. Unum's products are sold through field sales agents and independent brokers.

Operations

More than 60% of Unum's annual premiums come from the Unum US segment which offers group disability life and accident policies as well as supplemental and voluntary policies under the Unum America and Provident Brands.

The group's Colonial Life segment — which offers accident sickness disability and life products — accounts for nearly 20% of sales while the Unum UK segment represents more than 5% of sales.

Unum also generates revenue from its Closed Block segment (about 15% of sales) which services policies in the runoff segments (long-term care non-workplace individual disability) where the company no longer issues new policies.

The company covers roughly 33 million people worldwide and counts 181000 businesses in the US among its customers (including a third of the Fortune 500).

Geographic Reach

The US market contributes more than 60% of Unum's annual revenues. Unum runs four primary operating centers (in Tennessee Maine Louisiana South Carolina) and more than 35 sales offices scattered across the US market. Its Unum Limited office in Dorking is the headquarters for the smaller Unum UK operations which include Ireland. The company entered the Polish market in 2018 through its purchase of Pramerica Zycie.

Sales and Marketing

Unum uses its own sales force as well as independent agents consultants and brokers to market its products to employers.

Financial Performance

Unum's revenues have inched steadily upward for the past five years. In 2017 revenue increased 2% to $11.3 billion as total premiums earned and net investment income rose. The company's US sales increased 20% partly due to the introduction of dental and vision products it introduced the prior year. UK and Colonial Life sales also rose but to a lesser extent.

Net income rose 7% to $994.2 million in 2017 despite an increase in selling general and administrative expenses. This helped boost operating cash flow which increased 3% to $1.1 billion.

Strategy

Unum seeks to achieve a competitive edge by providing group individual and voluntary workplace products that can be combined with other coverage to better integrate benefits for customers. The insurer has stayed ahead of the game in the disability market by sticking to conservative investment and growth strategies primarily seeking to expand its group product offerings and its geographic presence through organic measures.

Specific goals include securing new customers investing in growth that meets new demands of the market and expanding into new geographic areas and distribution channels. Acquisitions play a part in reaching these goals. For example Unum plans to expand its presence in Europe by acquiring Polish insurer Pramerica ?ycie.

The company has especially seen growth in its voluntary benefits products which allow employees to purchase individual coverage products on a supplemental basis. Such options are increasingly important as economic difficulties put pressure on low and middle-income workers. Unum has also expanded its offering of services to help employers and government agencies manage costs such as its leave management program flexible corporate contribution programs and wellness initiatives.

While expanding in areas where the greatest market needs are seen the firm also occasionally exits (or places into run-off) certain businesses where demand has slowed.

Like most insurers Unum's profit margins have been negatively impacted by ongoing low interest rates. To minimize those effects the company is gradually increasing its investment activities around alternative assets. Unum is also banking on the benefits that will continue to arise from US tax reforms passed in 2017.

Mergers and Acquisitions

In 2018 Unum acquired Pramerica ?ycie a Polish life insurer from Prudential Financial for an undisclosed amount. That deal allowed Unum to expand its European operations beyond the UK.

In 2016 the company bought Louisiana-based H&J Capital the owner of Starmount Life Insurance and third-party administrator AlwaysCare Benefits for $127 million. Starmount operates in 49 states plus the District of Columbia offering individual products for dental vision life and accident coverage. It also offers group and voluntary benefits including dental vision life accident disability and critical illness under the AlwaysCare Benefits brand.

HISTORY

Coal was discovered in eastern Tennessee in the 1870s; in 1887 several Chattanooga professional men formed the Provident Life & Accident Insur-

ance Co. to provide medical insurance to miners. But it was a case of the inexperienced serving the uninsurable and by 1892 the company was on the brink of ruin. The founders sold half the company for $1000 to Thomas Maclellan and John McMaster two Scotsmen who had failed at banking in Canada.

While Maclellan handled the business end McMaster scoured the coalfields for customers. He even went into the mines pitching to individual miners and bringing along someone to dig coal for them so they wouldn't lose money by stopping work to listen.

The partners bought the rest of the company in 1895. Provident grew thanks to the cooperation of mining companies which deducted premiums from miners' pay. Provident added sickness and industrial insurance (low-benefit life policies). In 1900 after a period of strained relations Maclellan bought out McMaster.

After 1905 northern insurers began moving into the industrializing South. To meet the competition Provident reorganized and added capital and its stepped-up sales efforts brought in such lucrative business as railroad accounts. Provident added life insurance in 1917. The first policy was bought by Robert Maclellan who became president when his father died in 1916.

Provident acquired the Southern Surety Co. in 1931. During and after WWII group sales exploded as employee benefit packages proliferated. Provident which by then operated nationally entered Canada in 1948. Four years later R. L. Maclellan succeeded his father as president (R. L. stepped down in 1971). Provident's growth in the 1970s stemmed from its life units but it also developed a large health insurance operation.

The health care operations were hammered by rising medical costs in the 1980s so the company moved into managed care. But the combination of increased health care costs and a real estate crash gave the company a one-two punch in the late 1980s and early 1990s. An accounting change in 1993 further hit profits. In 1994 new president Harold Chandler initiated a reevaluation of Provident's operations and future which resulted in Provident's exit from the health care business beginning in 1995.

Provident began a major move into disability insurance in 1997. It bought 83% of rival disability insurer The Paul Revere Corporation from Textron. About 10000 Paul Revere insurance brokers later filed suit alleging they were denied millions of dollars in commissions. In exchange for its $300 million aid in the purchase Switzerland's Zurich Insurance (which later became Zurich Financial Services) received about 15% of Provident. The company also acquired GENEX Services (vocational rehabilitation and related services) and sold its dental insurance business to Ameritas Life Insurance. In 1998 Provident sold its annuity business to American General (now a subsidiary of AIG).

In 1998 with both Provident and Unum Corporation looking for ways to enhance business the companies commenced merger negotiations and completed the transaction the next year. But the merger was more expensive than anticipated and problems in integrating the companies' sales forces slowed policy sales.

Company operations began melding more smoothly and UnumProvident began addressing the problems with its sales force as well as adding customer service staff in 2000. It pulled money out of reserves by reinsuring several blocks of acquisition-related businesses and sold an inactive shell subsidiary licensed to sell annuities in most states to Allstate. In 2001 the company sold

EXECUTIVES

Evp And General Counsel, Lisa G. Iglesias, age 52, $492,692 total compensation

Vice President The Benefits Center, Rob Hecker

Svp Corporate Marketing And Public Relations, Joseph R. (Joe) Foley

President Ceo And Director, Richard P. (Rick) McKenney, age 50, $994,231 total compensation

President And Ceo Unum Us, Michael Q. Simonds, age 44, $594,231 total compensation

Evp And Cfo, John F. (Jack) McGarry, age 60, $588,461 total compensation

Evp Global Services, Christopher J. (Chris) Jerome, age 56

Evp And Chief Investment Officer, Breege A. Farrell, age 58, $451,500 total compensation

President And Ceo Colonial Life, Timothy G. (Tim) Arnold, age 55

President And Ceo Unum Uk, Peter G. O'Donnell, age 51

Svp And Global Cio, Katherine M. (Kate) Miller

Assistant Vice President And Special Counsel At Unum, Michael Parker

Vice President And Chief Information Security Officer, Lynda Fleury

Assistant Vice President, Mark Manuel

National Account Manager, Melana C Kipp

Assistant Vice President And Senior Counsel, Elle Donovan Mccann

Assistant Vice President Actuary, Paul Lavallee

Vice President, Greg Breter

Assistant Vice President And Senior Counsel (1996), Stephen William Walker

Assistant Vice President, Chris Castleberry

Vice President, Marianne Justin

Assistant Vice President Digital Marketing, Bethany Branon

Assistant Vice President Ltd Benefit Operations, Bob Berry

Assistant Vice President Learning And Performance Development, Debra Chaloux

Vice President And Treasurer, Tyler Siira

Assistant Vice President Consumerism, Jocelyn Grega

National Account Manager, Douglas Burnip

Vice President And Chief Litigation Counsel, Douglas Baker

Assistant Vice President And Counsel, Oliver Murray

Assistant Vice President, Denise Houser

Vice President, Stephanie Dyhrberg

Assistant Vice President And Senior Counsel Employment Law, Ellen Mccann

Assistant Vice President, Anna Stein

Vice President Information Technology Customer Solutions, Randy Robinson

Vice President Compensation Human Resources, Rhonda Rigsby

Assistant Vice President Information Technology, Roy Shelton

Assistant Vice President Contact Center, Cj Jackson

Vice President Shared Services, Lou Ann White

Assistant Vice President, Debra VandeVenter

Assistant Vice President Idi Benefits, Laura Chillo

Executive Vice President, Andrew Sayers

Vice President, William Stutts

Assistant Vice President Global Health And Insurance Programs, Joanne Abate

National Account Manager, Kathy McCarter

Avp And Senior Counsel, Ann Courtney

Avp And Sr. Counsel, Betsy Stivers

Vice President And Chief Litigation Counsel, Doug Baker

Assistant Vice President And Senior Counsel, Matthew Bell

National Account Manager, Kevin Malone

Assistant Vice President Ltd Benefits, Joseph Pratico

Vice President And Managing Director Midwest
  Region, John Stibal
Vice President, Najla Frayha
Vice President And Director Of External Affairs,
  Mark Pare
Assistant Vice President Customer Experience,
  Susan Hoffman
Vice President Market Development, John King
National Account Manager, Brooks Geiger
Vp Benefit Operations, Lori Whynot
Vp It Operations Support Services, David Mcmahon
Assistant Vice President, Michelle White
Senior Vice President Corporate Commercial And
  Business Banking Manager, Jennifer Jacobs
Avp Shared Technology, Joanne McInnis
Chairman, Kevin T. Kabat, age 61
Secretary, Priscilla Fairbrother
Auditors: Ernst & Young LLP

LOCATIONS

HQ: Unum Group
  1 Fountain Square, Chattanooga, TN 37402
Phone: 423 294-1011
Web: www.unum.com

PRODUCTS/OPERATIONS

2017 Sales

	$ mil.	% of total
Premiums	8,597	76
Net investment income	2,451	22
Net realized investment gain	40	-
Other	197	2
Total	**11,286**	**100**

2017 Sales by Segment

	% of total
Unum US	63
Colonial Life	18
Closed Block	13
Unum UK	6
Total	**100**

Selected Products and Services

Accidental death and dismemberment
Dental insurance
Disability (long-term and short-term)
Life insurance
Supplemental health
Voluntary benefits

Selected Subsidiaries and Brands

Colonial Life & Accident Insurance
Duncanson & Holt (US and UK)
  Trafalgar Underwriting Agencies (UK)
First Unum Life Insurance
Provident Investment Management
Provident Life and Accident Insurance
Provident Life and Casualty Insurance
The Paul Revere Life Insurance
The Paul Revere Variable Annuity Insurance
Unum Life Insurance Company of America
Unum Limited (UK)
UnumProvident International (Bermuda)

COMPETITORS

AEGON	Liberty Mutual
AXA Financial	Lincoln Financial
Aflac	Group
Allianz	MassMutual
American General	MetLife
Assurant	Mutual of Omaha
CIGNA	Northwestern Mutual
CNA Financial	Principal Financial
Guardian Life	Prudential
John Hancock Financial	Torchmark
Services	

HISTORICAL FINANCIALS

Company Type: Public

Income Statement

FYE: December 31

	ASSETS ($ mil.)	NET INCOME ($ mil.)	INCOME AS % OF ASSETS	EMPLOYEES
12/17	64,013	994	1.6%	9,400
12/16	61,941	931	1.5%	9,400
12/15	60,589	867	1.4%	9,400
12/14	62,497	413	0.7%	9,500
12/13	59,403	858	1.4%	9,200
Annual Growth	**1.9%**	**3.7%**	—	**0.5%**

2017 Year-End Financials

Debt ratio: 4.59%
Return on equity: 10.72%
Cash ($ mil.): 77
Current ratio: —
Long-term debt ($ mil.): —

No. of shares (mil.): 222
Dividends
  Yield: 0.0%
  Payout: 19.6%
Market value ($ mil.): 12,216

	STOCK PRICE ($) FY Close	P/E High/Low		Earnings	PER SHARE ($) Dividends	Book Value
12/17	54.89	13	10	4.37	0.86	43.02
12/16	43.93	11	6	3.95	0.77	39.02
12/15	33.29	11	9	3.50	0.70	35.96
12/14	34.88	23	19	1.61	0.62	33.90
12/13	35.08	11	6	3.23	0.55	33.30
Annual Growth	**11.8%**	—	—	**7.8%**	**11.8%**	**6.6%**

US Bancorp (DE)

As one of the largest bank holding companies
in the US U.S. Bancorp does a pretty good job of
living up to its name. The bank has $450 billion
in assets and owns U.S. Bank (the US's 5th largest
commercial bank) and other subsidiaries that provide consumer and commercial loans deposits and
credit cards as well as merchant processing mortgage banking trust and investment management
brokerage services insurance and corporate payments. The bank has around 3100 branches and
some 4850 ATMs in 25 states in the Midwest and
West including one of the most extensive networks
of branches inside grocery stores. Commercial
loans account for nearly 35% of its total loan portfolio and commercial real estate loans 15%.

Operations

The bank holding company's major lines of business are: wholesale banking and commercial real
estate; consumer and small business banking;
wealth management and securities services; payment services; and treasury and corporate support.
The company is also one of the largest providers
of corporate credit cards and payment services to
the US government. Its largest fee-gathering subsidiary is Elavon a leading processor of merchant
credit card transactions in the US Canada Latin
America and Europe.

Consumer and Small Business Bank is the company's largest earner raking in some 35% of sales
annually. Payment Services which does consumer
and business credit cards among other card-related
services is responsible for over 25% of sales.
Wholesale Banking & Commercial Real Estate and
Treasury and Corporate Support both bring in
around 15% of sales. Wealth Management & Securities Services brings in the remainder.

Interest income accounts for nearly 60% of total
revenue.

Geographic Reach

U.S. Bancorp provide services through a network of around 3100 banking offices in 25 US

states. Its ATMs are principally located in the Midwest and West. California is its largest market. It
is also active in Canada Mexico Brazil and Europe.

Sales and Marketing

U. S. Bancorp has some 18.7 million customers
including individuals businesses institutions government entities and other financial institutions.

Financial Performance

In fiscal 2016 U.S. Bancorp's revenue climbed
6% to $22.7 billion amid a 6% increase or $765
million in interest income and a 5% increase or
$485 million in noninterest income.

Interest income was bouyed by growth in new
and existing customers particularly in commercial
real estate residential mortgages and credit card
loans.

Net income was unchanged at $5.9 billion as an
increase in net interest income (interest income
less interest expense) was counterbalanced by a
$192 million increase for provision for credit losses
amid higher commercial loan net charge-offs and
lower commercial real estate recoveries.

Cash from operations fell 39% to $5.3 billion
due to changes in net proceeds from sales of loans
held for sale.

Strategy

U.S. Bancorp has been growing its business
through acquisitions sometimes expanding its operations internationally. Since the 2008 recession
the bank has found success in purchasing troubled
banks for cheap but generally pursues acquisitions
to expand service offerings add branches and extend its reach pad its interest-earning loan assets
and add customer deposits to fuel future loan business.

U.S. Bancorp moved into the premium credit
card space in 2017 with the launch of the Altitude
Reserve Visa Infinite. The card's target demographic is the young and wealthy and as such the
offering extends to digital wallets such as Apple
Pay.

The bank has also been dabbling in technology
to retain and grow its customer base. It launched
VantagePoint a receivables management tool for
multiple payment types Liquidity Advantage and
AP Optimizer.

In 2017 U.S Bank partnered with travel technology company Amadeus to offer a B2B wallet to
facilitate payments between entities in the travel
industry. The partnership has the aim of improving
crash flow reducing fraud risk and boosting revenue per transaction.

HISTORY

When Farmers and Millers Bank was founded
in 1853 it operated out of a strongbox in a rented
storefront. After surviving a panic in the 1850s
the bank became part of the national banking system in 1863 as First National Bank of Milwaukee.
The bank grew and in 1894 it merged with Merchants Exchange Bank (founded 1870).

In 1919 the bank merged again with Wisconsin
National Bank (founded 1892) to form First Wisconsin National Bank of Milwaukee a leading financial institution in the area from the 1920s on.

First Wisconsin grew through purchases over
the next decade though the number of banks fell
after the 1929 stock market crash; by the end of
WWII it had 11 banks. State and federal legislation
particularly the 1956 Bank Holding Company Act
(which proscribed acquisitions and branching)
constrained postwar growth. In the 1970s Wisconsin eased restrictions on intrastate branching
and the bank began to grow again.

Growth accelerated in the late 1980s after Wisconsin and surrounding states legalized interstate
banking in adjoining states in 1987. That year
First Wisconsin bought seven Minnesota banks
and then moved into Illinois. The company focused

on strong well-run institutions. Also that year it sold its headquarters and used the proceeds to fund more buys. In 1988 in its first foray outside the Midwest the company bought Metro Bancorp in Phoenix targeting midwestern retirees moving to Arizona.

In 1989 First Wisconsin changed its name to Firstar. The early 1990s saw the company move into Iowa (Banks of Iowa 1990) buy in-state rivals (Federated Bank Conova Capital Corporation 1992) and roll into Illinois (DSB Corporation 1993). The next year it bought First Southeast Banking Corp. (of Wisconsin) and merged it along with Firstar Bank Racine and Firstar Bank Milwaukee into one bank.

To strengthen its position against larger competitors Firstar continued its buying spree in 1995 (Chicago bank First Colonial Bankshares and Investors Bank Corp. of Minneapolis/St. Paul) and 1996 (Jacob Schmidt Company). The acquisitions left the company bloated: In 1996 Firstar began a restructuring designed to cut costs and increase margins. The restructuring project ended in 1997 but by then its performance lagged behind other midwestern banks considerably. In an effort to diversify it allied with EVEREN Securities to offer debt underwriting and sales fixed income products and public finance advisory services. But it was too little too late; under pressure from major stockholders to seek a partner Firstar began looking for a buyer.

It found Star Banc. Established in 1863 as The First National Bank of Cincinnati under a bank charter signed by Abraham Lincoln Star Banc over the years added branches and bought other banks. The company renamed all of its subsidiary banks Star Bank in 1988 and took the name Star Banc in 1989.

In 1998 Star Banc chairman Jerry Grundhofer approached Firstar about a combination. Negotiations proceeded quickly and a new Firstar was born.

The next year Firstar bought Mercantile Bancorporation. The purchase enabled the bank to expand its international banking services into such markets as Kansas Nebraska and Missouri. In 2000 the company made arrangements to buy U.S. Bancorp a Minneapolis-based bank with roots dating back to 1929. Under the terms of the acquisition Firstar would shed its own name in favor of the more appropriate U.S. Bancorp moniker. U.S. Bancorp completed the conversion of Firstar Bank branches to the U.S. Bank moniker during 2002.

EXECUTIVES

Vice Chairman Wholesale Banking, Leslie V. Godridge, age 62

Vice Chairman And Cfo, Terrance R. (Terry) Dolan, age 56, $545,833 total compensation

Senior Vice President National Sales Manager Small Business Specialty Finance, Erik Daniels

Evp Human Resources, Jennie P. Carlson, age 57

Regional President, Ward Wilson

President Ceo And Director, Andrew Cecere, age 57, $800,000 total compensation

Evp And General Counsel, James L. Chosy, age 54

Vice Chairman Wealth Management And Securities Services, Gunjan Kedia, age 47

Evp, John R. Elmore, age 62

Vice Chairman And Chief Risk Officer, P. William (Bill) Parker, age 61, $625,000 total compensation

Vice Chairman Technology And Operations Services, Jeffry H. (Jeff) von Gillern, age 52, $575,000 total compensation

Vice Chairman Consumer Banking Sales And Support, Kent V. Stone, age 60

Evp And Chief Credit Officer, Mark G. Runkel, age 42

Vice Chairman Payment Services, Shailesh M. Kotwal, age 53

Evp And Chief Strategy And Reputation Officer, Katherine B. Quinn, age 53

Vice Chairman Wholesale Banking, James B. Kelligrew, age 52

Senior Vice President, Patricia Gnetz

Private Banking Vice President, Scott Brophy

Vice President Of Information Technology Security, Coni Paach

Senior Vice President Dealer Services Regional Manager North Central Region, Dave Donarski

Senior Vice President Risk Infrastructure, Jim Putman

Assistant Vice President Application Consultant Commercial Leasing, Krishna Devarajulu

Vice President Procurement Operations Manager, Michael Lori

Senior Vice President Customer Solutions, Mary Ellen Carney

Vice President Financial Advisor, Jeff Hawkins

Senior Vice President Prepaid Card Services, Johnnie Carroll

Vice President, Scott Miller

Vice President, Scott Olson

Vice President Director Of Marketing And Communications Wealth Management, Mark Iverson

Vice President And Area Sales Manager, Frank Annello

Assistant Vice President Database Development, Melissa Schoenecker

Senior Vice President, Michael Dorn

Vp Credit Risk Assessment, Jennifer Briglia

Vice President, Chris Rodewald

Senior Vice President Credit Administration, David Silander

Vice President Real Estate Transactions And Risk Management, Barbara Cochran

Vice President Treasury Management Consultant, Paul Kozar Paul Kozar

Senior Vice President, Scott Farrell

Vice President Corporate Credit Risk Manager, Brian Richter

Vice President Credit Approval Commercial Real Esate And Community Banks, Karl Goss

Vice President Business Banking Sales Manager, Javier Iglesias Javier Iglesias

Svp Portfolio Marketing, Tim Stanton

Vice President, Mark Sowinski

Vice President Information Technology Service Managmnt, Jim Berghs

Executive Vice President, Lisa Glover

Assistant Vice President Marketing Research, Molly McMahon

Vice President Global Treasury Management Pricing And Analytics, Jake Wilson

Senior Vice President, Mehrasa Raygani

Vice President Technology Finance Group, Gregory Giannone

Commercial Division Assistant Vice President Compliance Manager, Ruth Fangmann

Vice President Senior Property Manager, Andrew McGlenon

Vice President, Anthony Ziman

Vice President, Kelly Matsuoka

Vice President, Zenaida Maniates

Vice President, Michael Lamarche Michael Lamarche

Vice President Commercial Operations Manager, Victor Kapusinski

Vice President, Cory Patrick

Vice President, Steve Kramer

Senior Vice President, Marcia Palmer

Vice President, Spencer Goldsmith

Senior Vice President, Terry Neher

Vice President, Louis Caresani

Senior Vice President Utilities Division, Felicia LaForgia

Vice President Corporate Banking Portfolio Manager, Daniel Yu

Assistant Vice President Associate Client Manager, Nick Kapki Nick Kapki

Vice President, Wally Jones

Vice President, Alice Warren

Senior Vice President Regional Manager, Chris Venhoff

Senior Vice President National Corporate Banking, Barry Litwin

Vice President Portfolio Manager, Magnus Mcdowell Magnus Mcdowell

Vice President Wealth Management Advisor, Todd Nichols

Vice President Corporate Trust, Linda Mcconkey

Assistant Vice President Senior Recruiter, Corey Hoen

Senior Vice President And Deputy Chief Credit Officer, Joe Lillis

Vice President, Kamal Nahhas

Vice President Portfolio Manager, Ian Baird

Vice President, Roger Gross

Vice President Network Security Engineering, Jonathan Rogness

Vice President Technology Services, Paul Ylonen

Vice President Commercial Real Estate Lender, Howard Goldberg

Senior Vice President Enterprise Risk Services, Bob Kellner

Senior Vice President And Market Credit Manager, Rick Shamberger

Vice President Of Marketing, Becky Hill

Assistant Vice President Finance Manager, Wendy Brock

Vice President And Site Manager, Elizabeth Thuning

Senior Vice President Treasury Management Product Management, Mary Burchette

Assistant Vice President Data Center Design And Planning, David Fortuna

Vice President, Suzanne Bedros

Vice President, Kevin Penders

Vice President Information Technology Development, Thomas Kindler

Vice President And Credit Manager, Melanie Rossetta

Senior Vice President, Carol Gilstrap

Vice President Corporate Credit Risk Management, Gregory Gay

Vice President Loan Administration, Cheryl Dingess

Vice President, Rudy Fors

Vice President, Courtney Dowling

Vice President, John Pearson

Vice President, David Smith

Senior Vice President, Andrew Hyde

Vice President Quality Management, Richard McCarthy

Vice President, Karen Bolton

Assistant Vice President Real Estate Asset Manager, Karen Thomas

Vice President, Dorothy Smaglick

Vice President And Senior Corporate Counsel, Benjamin Carpenter

Vice President Operations, Mark Sutherland

Vice President And Relationship Manager, Bryan Carow

Vice President, Joseph Bree

Assistant Vice President, Rita Halbur

Vice President, Philip Koski

Assistant Vice President Voice Implementation Projects, Joy Abts

Vice President Information Technology, Alfonso Gonzalez

Senior Vice President Quality Assurance, AnnMarie Janke

Vice President And Assistant General Counsel, Ilyse Goldsmith

Vice President Area Manager, John Cronen

Vice President, Ken Case

Vice President Sales, Richard Struck

Senior Vice President And Industry Manager, Matthew Sargent

Assistant Vice President Application Architect, David Brus
Vice President And Director, Suzanne Galvin
Senior Vice President Regional Credit Officer, Randall Borchardt
Vice President, Regan Leon
Senior Financial Advisor Vice President Private Client Reserve, Joel Schwartz
Vice President And Client Manager, Ron Hood
Vice President Portfolio Manager, Matt Scullin
Vice President Comercial Team Lead, Corey Hansen
Vice President Business Banking, Brent Blume
Senior Vice President Commercial Real Estate Relationship Manager, Curt Steiner
Vice President, Kent Inman
Vice President Corporate Banking Relationship Manager Transportation, Daniel Washam
Senior Vice President California Region Manager, Stephen Johnson
Vice President Relationship Manager, Diana Cardenas
Assistant Vice President, Becky Burton
Vice President Technology Group Manager, Genie Strachan-smith
Vice President, Monique Green
Vice President And Commercial Relationship Manager, Margaret Sato
Vice President Communications Director Wealth Management, Aili Jokela
Assistant Vice President, Lorra Donnelly
Senior Vice President Managing Director, Kathy Pertl
Community Banking Relationship Manager Assistant Vice President, Chester Anonson
Vice President, Ryan Perrault
Vice President Community Relations Manager Northwest Region Portland Main Complex, Karen Kervin
Vice President Managing Director The Private Client Group, Troy Smith
Senior Corporate Counsel And Vice President, Daniel Sundell
Assistant Vice President Alternative Investments, Tatiana Kadyrova
Vice President, Cindy Hallberg
Assistant Vice President And Assistant, Stacey Dennehy
Assistant Vice President, Ryan Frank
Vice President Credit Risk Management, Olivier Haise
Senior Vice President, Kevin Miller
Vice President, Peter LaMontagna
Vice President, David Rowe
Auditors: Ernst & Young LLP

LOCATIONS

HQ: US Bancorp (DE)
800 Nicollet Mall, Minneapolis, MN 55402
Phone: 651 466-3000
Web: www.usbank.com

Selected Locations

Arizona
Arkansas
California
Colorado
Idaho
Illinois
Indiana
Iowa
Kansas
Kentucky
Minnesota
Missouri
Montana
Nebraska
Nevada
New Mexico
North Dakota
Ohio
Oregon
South Dakota
Tennessee
Utah
Washington
Wisconsin
Wyoming

PRODUCTS/OPERATIONS

2016 Sales

	$ mil.	% of total
Interest		
Loans	10,810	48
Investment securities	2,078	9
Loans held for sale	154	1
Other	125	1
Non-interest		
Merchant processing services	1,592	7
Trust & investment management fees	1,427	6
Credit & debit card revenue	1,177	5
Mortgage banking	979	4
Commercial products	871	4
Corporate payment products	712	3
Deposit service charges	725	3
Treasury management fees	583	3
ATM processing services	338	1
Investment products fees	158	1
Other	1,015	4
Total	**22,744**	**100**

2016 sales

	% of total
Consumer and Small Business Banking	34
Payment Services	27
Wholesale Banking and Commercial Real Estate	15
Treasury and Corporate Support	14
Wealth Management and Securities Services	10
Total	**100**

Selected Subsidiaries

111 Tower Investors Inc. (Minnesota)
Access Mortgage Solutions LLC (Delaware)
AIS Europe Limited (UK)
AIS Fund Administration Ltd. (Cayman Islands)
CF Title Co. (Delaware)
Daimler Title Co. (Delaware)
DSL Service Company (California)
Eclipse Funding LLC (Delaware)
Elan Life Insurance Company Inc. (Arizona)

COMPETITORS

Bank of America	Huntington Bancshares
Capital One	JPMorgan Chase
Citigroup	KeyCorp
Fifth Third	MUFG Americas Holdings
First National of Nebraska	TCF Financial
	Wells Fargo
Great Western Bancorp	Zions Bancorporation

HISTORICAL FINANCIALS

Company Type: Public

Income Statement
FYE: December 31

	ASSETS ($ mil.)	NET INCOME ($ mil.)	INCOME AS % OF ASSETS	EMPLOYEES
12/17	462,040	6,218	1.3%	72,402
12/16	445,964	5,888	1.3%	71,191
12/15	421,853	5,879	1.4%	65,433
12/14	402,529	5,851	1.5%	66,750
12/13	364,021	5,836	1.6%	65,565
Annual Growth	**6.1%**	**1.6%**	**—**	**2.5%**

2017 Year-End Financials

Debt ratio: 5.80%
Return on equity: 12.91%
Cash ($ mil.): 19,505
Current ratio: —
Long-term debt ($ mil.): —

No. of shares (mil.): 1,655
Dividends
  Yield: 0.0%
  Payout: 33.0%
Market value ($ mil.): 88,709

	STOCK PRICE ($) FY Close	P/E High/Low		PER SHARE ($) Earnings	Dividends	Book Value
12/17	53.58	16	14	3.51	1.16	29.62
12/16	51.37	16	12	3.24	1.07	27.87
12/15	42.67	14	13	3.16	1.01	26.43
12/14	44.95	15	13	3.08	0.97	24.35
12/13	40.40	13	11	3.00	0.89	22.53
Annual Growth	**7.3%**	**—**	**—**	**4.0%**	**7.0%**	**7.1%**

US Foods Holding Corp

Auditors: Deloitte & Touche LLP

LOCATIONS

HQ: US Foods Holding Corp
9399 W. Higgins Road, Suite 500, Rosemont, IL 60018
Phone: 847 720-8000
Web: www.usfoods.com

HISTORICAL FINANCIALS

Company Type: Public

Income Statement
FYE: December 30

	REVENUE ($ mil.)	NET INCOME ($ mil.)	NET PROFIT MARGIN	EMPLOYEES
12/17	24,147	444	1.8%	25,053
12/16*	22,918	209	0.9%	25,000
01/16	23,127	167	0.7%	25,000
12/14	23,019	(72)	—	—
12/13	22,297	(57)	—	—
Annual Growth	**2.0%**	**—**	**—**	**—**

*Fiscal year change

2017 Year-End Financials

Debt ratio: 43.28%
Return on equity: 16.85%
Cash ($ mil.): 118
Current ratio: 1.41
Long-term debt ($ mil.): 3,648

No. of shares (mil.): 214
Dividends
  Yield: —
  Payout: —
Market value ($ mil.): 6,864

	STOCK PRICE ($) FY Close	P/E High/Low		PER SHARE ($) Earnings	Dividends	Book Value
12/17	31.93	16	13	1.97	0.00	12.80
12/16*	27.48	26	21	1.03	0.00	11.49
Annual Growth	**3.8%**	**—**	**—**	**17.6%**	**—**	**2.7%**

*Fiscal year change

UTAH HOUSING CORPORATION

EXECUTIVES

Ceo, Grant Whitaker
Cfo*, Cleon Butterfield
Sr V Pres*, Jonathan Hanks
Loan Officer, Scott Harmon
Loan Officer, Suzette Acord
Loan Officer, Kelly Peterson
Sales Manager, Adam Heap
Controller, Chad Moore

LOCATIONS

HQ: UTAH HOUSING CORPORATION
2479 S LAKE PARK BLVD, WEST VALLEY CITY, UT
841208217
Phone: 801-902-8200
Web: WWW.UTAHHOUSINGCORP.ORG

HISTORICAL FINANCIALS

Company Type: Private

Income Statement   FYE: June 30

	ASSETS ($ mil.)	NET INCOME ($ mil.)	INCOME AS % OF ASSETS	EMPLOYEES
06/18	1,934	36	1.9%	90
06/17	2,002	40	2.0%	—
06/16	1,830	23	1.3%	—
Annual Growth	2.8%	24.6%		

2018 Year-End Financials

Debt ratio: —
Return on equity: 32.60%
Cash ($ mil.): 87
Current ratio: 0.30
Long-term debt ($ mil.): —

Dividends
Yield: —
Payout: —
Market value ($ mil.): —

Valero Energy Corp

Valero Energy was not only named after a mission (the Mission San Antonio de Valero) it is on a mission to be the largest independent refiner in the US. Valero churns out about 3 million barrels per day refining low-cost residual oil and heavy crude into cleaner-burning higher-margin products including low-sulfur diesels. It operates 15 refineries in the US Canada and the UK. It also has 11 ethanol plants with a combined production capacity of about 1.4 billion gallons per year. Once a more diversified company Valero has exited the retail business in order to focus on its oil refining and ethanol operations.

HISTORY

Valero Energy was created as a result of the sins of its father Houston-based Coastal States Gas Corporation. Led by flamboyant entrepreneur Oscar Wyatt energy giant Coastal had established Lo-Vaca Gathering Company as a gas marketing subsidiary. Bound by long-term contracts to several Texas cities Coastal was not able to meet its contractual obligations when gas prices rose in the early 1970s and major litigation against the company resulted. The Texas Railroad Commission (the energy-regulating authority) ordered Coastal to refund customers $1.6 billion.

To meet the requirements 55% of Lo-Vaca was spun off to disgruntled former customers as Valero Energy at the end of 1979. The new company was born fully grown — as the largest intrastate pipeline in Texas — with accountant-cum-CEO Bill Greehey the court-appointed chief of Lo-Vaca at its head. Greehey relocated the company to San Antonio where it took its Valero name (from the Alamo or Mission San Antonio de Valero) and put some distance between itself and its discredited former parent. Under Greehey's direction Valero developed a

squeaky-clean image by giving to charities stressing a dress code and keeping facilities clean.

Greehey diversified the company into refining unleaded gasoline. Valero bought residual fuel oil from Saudi Arabian refiners and in 1981 built a refinery in Corpus Christi Texas which went on line two years later. But in 1984 a glut of unleaded gasoline on the US market from European refiners undercut Valero's profits. To stay afloat Valero sold pipeline assets including 50% of its West Texas Pipeline in 1985 and 51% of its major pipeline operations in 1987. Refining margins finally began to improve in 1988. With one of the most modern refineries in the US Valero did not have to spend a bundle to upgrade its refining processes to meet the tougher EPA requirements of the 1990s.

In 1992 Valero expanded its refinery's production capacity and acquired two gas processing plants and several hundred miles of gas pipelines from struggling oil firm Oryx Energy (acquired by Kerr-McGee in 1999). That year Valero became the first non-Mexican business engaged in Mexican gasoline production when it signed a deal with state oil company PetrA?leos Mexicanos S.A. to build a gasoline additive plant there.

To expand its natural gas business substantially in 1994 Valero bought back the 51% of Valero Natural Gas Partners it didn't own. Valero also teamed up with regional oil company Swift Energy in a transportation marketing and processing agreement. As part of that arrangement Valero agreed to build a pipeline linking Swift's Texas gas field with a Valero plant.

In 1997 the company sold Valero Natural Gas to California electric utility PG&E gaining $1.5 billion for expansion. It then purchased Salomon's oil refining unit Basis Petroleum (two refineries in Texas and one in Louisiana) and the next year picked up Mobil's refinery in Paulsboro New Jersey.

With low crude oil prices hurting its bottom line in 1999 Valero explored partnerships with other refiners as a way to cut operating costs. In 2000 the company bought Exxon Mobil's 130000-barrel-per-day Benicia California refinery along with 340 retail outlets for about $1 billion.

In 2001 Valero gained two small refineries when it bought Huntway Refining a leading supplier of asphalt in California. Dwarfing that deal Valero also bought Ultramar Diamond Shamrock for $4 billion in cash and stock (it assumed about $2.1 billion of debt in the deal). As part of the deal and to comply with the demands of regulators in 2002 Valero sold the Golden Eagle (San Francisco-area) refinery and 70 retail service stations in Northern California to Tesoro for $945 million.

In 2003 the company acquired Orion Refining's Louisiana refinery for about $530 million and the next year it acquired an Aruba refinery from asset-shedding El Paso Corp. for $640 million. Suncor Energy bought a Colorado-based refinery from Valero for a reported $30 million in 2005.

The 2005 acquisition of Premcor made Valero the largest independent refiner on the Gulf Coast a major national player.

Greehey turned over the leadership reins to another company veteran Bill Klesse in early 2006. The following year the company sold its Lima Ohio refinery to Husky Energy.

In 2008 the company sold its Krotz Springs Louisiana refinery to Alon USA Energy for $333 million.

In 2009 Valero had an opportunity for international refinery expansion and a foothold in Europe when it agreed to acquire Dow Chemical's 45% interest in Dutch refinery Total Raffinaderij Nederland N.V. However the deal fell through and the stake was sold to LUKOIL.

That year it bought seven ethanol production facilities from VeraSun Energy for $475 million.

To cut costs in 2010 it sold its Delaware City refinery. It also sold its Paulsboro New Jersey refinery that year to PBF Holding for $340 million. It also sold its 50% stake in a pipeline that brings deep-water crude oil from the Gulf of Mexico to the US to Genesis Energy for $330 million.

Expanding its global footprint in 2011 Valero bought Chevron's Pembroke refinery and marketing and logistics assets across the UK for $1.7 billion. It also boosted its US assets that year buying Murphy Oil's refinery outside New Orleans for $585 million to complement its St. Charles facility. Valero also bought Chevron USA Inc.'s Louisville and Lexington Kentucky product terminals expanding its wholesale marketing presence in eastern Kentucky with product supplied primarily from the Valero Memphis Refinery.

It made its first foray into ethanol production in 2009 buying seven ethanol production facilities from VeraSun Energy which was operating under Chapter 11 bankruptcy protection. Valero paid about $475 million for the facilities.

In 2013 the new hydrocracker unit at the Valero St. Charles Refinery began operations.

To better control costs in 2014 the company abandoned our Aruba Refinery except for the associated crude oil and refined products terminal assets that it continues to operate. It also sold its Texas Crude Systems Business to VLP for $154 million.

To get better shareholder returns in 2013 the company spun off its retail business as an independent public company CST Brands. This unit held Valero's company-operated convenience stores in the US and Canada; and filling stations cardlock facilities and heating oil operations in Canada. Valero continues to supply fuel to CST Brands' retail sites through long-term supply agreements. (Valero subsequently sold its remaining 20% stake in the company.)

In 2013 the company's Valero Terminaling and Distribution unit formed a joint venture with TGS Development to start construction on a new marine terminal on the lower Sabine-Neches Waterway near Port Arthur Texas to support the expansion of oil receipts and the marine movements of other commodities at that strategic port.

Growing its foothold in the petrochemical segment that year Valero also announced plans to build a major methanol plant at its 270000 barrel per day St. Charles refinery near New Orleans. Scheduled to commence operating in 2016 the $700 million plant will yield 1.6 million tons of methanol per year.

EXECUTIVES

Evp And General Counsel, Jay D. Browning, age 59, $595,000 total compensation
Vp And Cio, Cheryl Thomas
Evp And Cfo, Michael S. (Mike) Ciskowski, age 60, $890,000 total compensation
Vp Wholesale Marketing And International Commercial Operations, Eric Fisher
Chairman President And Ceo, Joseph W. (Joe) Gorder, age 60, $1,450,000 total compensation
Evp Refining Operations And Engineering, Lane Riggs, age 52, $640,000 total compensation
Svp Supply International Operations And Systems Optimization, Gary Simmons, $565,000 total compensation
Vice President For Commercial Operations, Craig M Schnupp
Vice President And General Manager Valero Port Arthur Refinery, Greg Gentry
Regional Vice President, Eric Honeyman
Vice President Cost Analysis Transportation, Mark Swensen

Vice President Austin Technology Center, Mike Long

Vice President, Richard Grissom

Vice President Of Marketing, Curt Lundquist

Vice President Refinery Accounting, Jeffrey L Jones

Vp Logistics Operations, Rich Lashway

Vice President, Dora Bazan

Vice President Products Trading, Scott Lively

Vice President Event Marketing, John Hill

Board Of Director And Vice President, Alisa Lomas

Vice President And General Manager, Lauren Bird

Vice President Risk Management, Joe Van Horn

Vice President Market Analysis, Anthony Rouse

Vice President Retail And Administrative Systems, Steve DiPaola

Vice President, Donna Titzman

Vice President Sales, Mike Whyte

Senior Vice President Project Execution, Tony Jones

Vice President Finance, Kenneth Sparks

Senior Vice President Wholesale Marketing, Gary Arthur

Executive Vice President Marketing, Dyfan Williams

Vice President Corporate Tax, Beatrice Gonzalez

Svp And Chief Accounting Officer, Mark Schmeltekopf

Vice President, Sean Murphy

Treasurer, Dan Stanush

Board Member, Alex Schelanko

Board Member, Grace Batres

Board Member, Cody Quinn

Board Member, Chuck Lawton

Treasurer, Richard Johnston

Vice President And Treasurer, Christopher Quinn

Auditors: KPMG LLP

LOCATIONS

HQ: Valero Energy Corp
One Valero Way, San Antonio, TX 78249
Phone: 210 345-2000   Fax: 210 246-2646
Web: www.valero.com

2015 Sales

	$ mil.	% of total
US	60,319	68
UK and Ireland	11,232	13
Canada	6,841	8
Other countries	9,412	11
Total	**87,804**	**100**

PRODUCTS/OPERATIONS

2015 Sales

	$ mil.	% of total
Refining	84,521	96
Ethanol	3	4
Elimination	(151)	-
Total	**87,804**	**100**

Selected Products

Asphalt
Bunker oils
CARB Phase II gasoline
Clean-burning oxygenates
Conventional gasoline
Crude mineral spirits
Customized clean-burning gasoline blends for export markets
Ethanol
Gasoline blendstocks
Home heating oil
Jet fuel
Kerosene
Low-sulfur diesel
Lube oils
Petrochemical feedstocks
Petroleum coke
Premium reformulated and conventional gasolines
Reformulated gasoline
Sulfur

COMPETITORS

ADM	Motiva Enterprises
BP	National Cooperative
CITGO	Refinery Association
CVR	Phillips 66
Chevron	Sinclair Oil
Exxon Mobil	Sunoco
Green Brick Partners	TOTAL
HollyFrontier	TPC Group
Marathon Petroleum	Tesoro

HISTORICAL FINANCIALS

Company Type: Public

Income Statement

FYE: December 31

	REVENUE ($ mil.)	NET INCOME ($ mil.)	NET PROFIT MARGIN	EMPLOYEES
12/17	93,980	4,065	4.3%	10,015
12/16	75,659	2,289	3.0%	9,996
12/15	87,804	3,990	4.5%	10,103
12/14	130,844	3,630	2.8%	10,065
12/13	138,074	2,720	2.0%	10,007
Annual Growth	**(9.2%)**	**10.6%**	**—**	**0.0%**

2017 Year-End Financials

Debt ratio: 17.69%
Return on equity: 19.35%
Cash ($ mil.): 5,850
Current ratio: 1.74
Long-term debt ($ mil.): 8,750

No. of shares (mil.): 433
Dividends
Yield: 0.0%
Payout: 30.5%
Market value ($ mil.): 39,880

	STOCK PRICE ($) FY Close	P/E High/Low		PER SHARE ($) Earnings	Dividends	Book Value
12/17	91.91	10	7	9.16	2.80	50.68
12/16	68.32	15	10	4.94	2.40	44.35
12/15	70.71	9	6	7.99	1.70	43.39
12/14	49.50	9	6	6.85	1.05	40.20
12/13	50.40	10	7	4.97	0.85	36.34
Annual Growth	**16.2%**	**—**	**—**	**16.5%**	**34.7%**	**8.7%**

Valley National Bancorp (NJ)

Valley National Bancorp is high on New Jersey and New York. The holding company owns Valley National Bank which serves commercial and retail clients through more than 200 branches in northern and central New Jersey and in the New York City boroughs of Manhattan Brooklyn and Queens as well as on Long Island. The bank provides standard services like checking and savings accounts loans and mortgages credit cards and trust services. Subsidiaries offer asset management mortgage and auto loan servicing title insurance asset-based lending and property/casualty life and health insurance. Founded as The Passaic Park Trust Company in 1927 Valley National is looking to expand in Florida.

Operations

In addition to its commercial and retail banking operations Valley National Bancorp through its subsidiaries operates: an all-line insurance agency that offers property and casualty life and health insurance; a wealth management advisory business; title insurance agencies in New York and New Jersey. It also specializes in general aviation financing commercial equipment leasing and cus-

tom financing for health care professionals and law firms.

Financial Performance

Valley National reported revenue of $744.7 million in 2013 a decline of 6% versus 2012 on lower interest income caused by lower yields on average interest earning assets as a result of low long-term market interest rates. Net income fell 8% over the same period to about $132 million on lower revenue and an increase in non-interest expenses.

Strategy

One of the leading commercial banks in the New York and New Jersey metro areas Valley National has set its sights on Florida with its proposed acquisition of Boca Raton-based 1st United Bankcorp the largest commercial bank in Palm Beach County. The deal which is valued at $312 million would add a 21 branch network covering urban banking markets in Florida and approximately $1.7 billion in assets. Combined the two companies will have about $18.1 billion in assets nearly $13 billion in loans and $12.7 billion in deposits. The deal is expected to close in late 2014.

Commercial real estate and construction loans account for the largest portion of Valley's loan portfolio (47%). However the bank has ramped up its residential lending and has been actively marketing its home loan refinancing products amid continued low interest rates.

Mergers and Acquisitions

Valley National completed its approximately $222 million acquisition of New York-based bank holding company State Bancorp at the beginning of 2012. The deal which brought in 17 branches is part of Valley's overall strategy to expand its presence throughout New York City metropolitan area. It marked the company's first foray in Long Island and added locations in Manhattan and Queens as well. It also provides an opportunity to build retail relationships in new markets as State Bancorp focused more on commercial clients. Valley typically targets consumers disillusioned with larger banks.

In 2010 the company acquired the branches and most of the assets and deposits of failed Manhattan-based financial institutions LibertyPointe Bank and Park Avenue Bank in FDIC-assisted transactions. It also opened a loan production office in Bethlehem Pennsylvania to offer residential mortgages and title insurance. Valley continues to look for additional expansion opportunities.

EXECUTIVES

President And Chief Banking Officer Valley National Bank, Rudy E. Schupp, age 67, $425,000 total compensation

Sevp And Cfo, Alan D. Eskow, age 70, $545,750 total compensation

Chairman President And Ceo, Gerald H. Lipkin, age 78, $1,123,500 total compensation

Evp And Chief Retail Lending Officer, Albert L. Engel, age 70, $440,000 total compensation

Svp Shareholder And Public Relations, Dianne M. Grenz

Evp And Senior Community Reinvestment Act Officer, Bernadette M. Mueller, age 59

Sevp And Treasurer, Ira Robbins, age 43, $425,000 total compensation

Evp And Chief Administrative Officer, Andrea Onorato

Evp And Cio, Robert J. Bardusch

Evp And Chief Risk Officer, Melissa Scofield

Vice President And Sales Director Usa, Ronald Fraser

Vice President Art Director, Bill Purvis

Executive Vice President, Robert Meyer

Senior Vice President Human Resources Benefits, Terry Gehrke

Assistant Vice President Commercial Loans, John
Kenny
Vice President, Peter Alvarez
Assistant Vice President, Tony Dibenedetto
Vice President Of Commercial Lending, Mark
Gomberg
First Vice President Senior Attorney, Harold
Steinberg
Vice President, Dave Denoya
Vice President, Timothy Tierney
Assistant Vice President Branch Sales Manager,
Marie Castro
Assistant Vice President Business Development
Commercial Loans, Kristen Upadek
Vice President Sales Manager, Veronica Valentine
Senior Vice President Commercial Lending, John
Murphy
Vice President Retail Training, Mary Black
Senior Vice President, Chip Woodbury
Vice President, Karen Conway
Assistant Vice President, Paul Cronen
First Vice President And Chief Compliance
Officer, Manfred Brockmann
Vice President, Janet Knipfing
Vice President, Jennifer Yager
Vice President, Ruth A Finn
Senior Corporate Management Vice President Gm,
Ralph Passafiume
Assistant Vice President Finance, Christopher
Philips
Vice President Business Development, Floyd
Wilmoth
Vice President And Branch Sales Manager, Tina
Brand
First Senior Vice President, Wayne Fritsch
Vice President, Claudia O'Rourke
Vice President, Tony Zeleszko
Senior Vice President; Regional Manager, Steven
Vitale
Vice President, Luba Gelman
Vice President Of Sales, John Siberio
Vice President Commercial Lender, Janice Brunson
Executive Vice President Chief Financial Officer
And Chief Operating Officer, Stan Pinkham
Vice President And Credit Officer, Peter Tomasi
Vice President Commercial Lending, Jordan Simler
Vice President Commercial Relationship Manager,
Joanne Serros
Vice President Territory Sales Manager, Marc
Vernick
Vice President Information Technology, Fred
Roscoe
Senior Vice President Corporate Bnkg, Kenneth
Nickel
Senior Vice President Director Of Association
Banking And Treasury Management, Marc Nuzzolo
Vice President, Joe Gargiulo
Vice President, Jaime Zamudio
Vice President, Mikel Sharpe
Vice President Commercial Lending, Art Shelley
Vice President, Oscar Hernandez
Senior Vice President, Valerie Pickert
Assistant Vice President Assistant Banking Office
Manager One North Federal Highway Boca
Raton, Ann Longworth
Vice President Branch Manager Residential
Mortgage, Robert Nardone
Vice President Commercial Lending Valley
National Bank Florida Division, Gus Treichel
Assistant Vice President Loan Services Officer
Florida Division, Dawn Keogh
Vice President Territory Sales Manager, Eddie
Beylin
First Vice President, Martha Soper
Vice President Territory Sales Manager, Matthew
Coppola
Assistant Vice President And Cre Loan Officer,
Frank Canova
Vice President, Linda Diaz
Vice President, Daniel Maes

Vice President Director Of Sales, Amanda Miller
Board Member, Marc Lenner
Board Member, Peter Baum
Auditors: KPMG LLP

LOCATIONS

HQ: Valley National Bancorp (NJ)
1455 Valley Road, Wayne, NJ 07470
Phone: 973 305-8800
Web: www.valleynationalbank.com

PRODUCTS/OPERATIONS

2016 Sales

	$ mil.	% of total
Interest Income		
Interest and fees on loans	685	79
Interest and dividends on investment securities	79	9
Interest on federal funds sold and other short-term investments	1	0
Non-Interest Income		
Gains on sales of loans net	22	3
Service charges on deposit accounts	20	2
Insurance commissions	19	2
Trust and investment services	10	1
Bank owned life insurance	6	1
Fees from loan servicing	6	1
Gains on sales of assets net	1	0
Gains on securities transactions net	0	0
Change in FDIC loss-share receivable	(1.3)	0
Other	16	2
Total	**870**	**100**

COMPETITORS

Bank of America	JPMorgan Chase
Capital One	New York Community
Citigroup	Bancorp
Dime Community	PNC Financial
Bancshares	TD Bank USA
Hudson City Bancorp	Wells Fargo

HISTORICAL FINANCIALS

Company Type: Public

Income Statement				FYE: December 31
	ASSETS ($ mil.)	NET INCOME ($ mil.)	INCOME AS % OF ASSETS	EMPLOYEES
12/17	24,002	161	0.7%	2,842
12/16	22,864	168	0.7%	2,828
12/15	21,612	102	0.5%	2,929
12/14	18,793	116	0.6%	2,907
12/13	16,156	131	0.8%	2,908
Annual Growth	10.4%	5.2%	—	(0.6%)

2017 Year-End Financials

Debt ratio: 1.57%
Return on equity: 6.59%
Cash ($ mil.): 416
Current ratio: —
Long-term debt ($ mil.): —
No. of shares (mil.): 264
Dividends
  Yield: 0.0%
  Payout: 75.8%
Market value ($ mil.): 2,967

	STOCK PRICE ($) FY Close	P/E High/Low		PER SHARE ($) Earnings	Dividends	Book Value
12/17	11.22	22	18	0.58	0.44	9.58
12/16	11.64	19	13	0.63	0.44	9.02
12/15	9.85	27	22	0.42	0.44	8.70
12/14	9.71	19	16	0.56	0.44	8.03
12/13	10.12	16	13	0.66	0.60	7.72
Annual Growth	2.6%	—	—	(3.2%)	(7.4%)	5.5%

Veritex Holdings Inc

Auditors: GRANT THORNTON LLP

LOCATIONS

HQ: Veritex Holdings Inc
8214 Westchester Drive, Suite 400, Dallas, TX 75225
Phone: 972 349-6200
Web: www.veritexbank.com

HISTORICAL FINANCIALS

Company Type: Public

Income Statement				FYE: December 31
	ASSETS ($ mil.)	NET INCOME ($ mil.)	INCOME AS % OF ASSETS	EMPLOYEES
12/17	2,945	15	0.5%	324
12/16	1,408	12	0.9%	171
12/15	1,039	8	0.8%	149
12/14	802	5	0.6%	125
12/13	664	3	0.5%	126
Annual Growth	45.1%	45.2%	—	26.6%

2017 Year-End Financials

Debt ratio: 1.08%
Return on equity: 4.16%
Cash ($ mil.): 149
Current ratio: —
Long-term debt ($ mil.): —
No. of shares (mil.): 24
Dividends
  Yield: —
  Payout: —
Market value ($ mil.): 665

	STOCK PRICE ($) FY Close	P/E High/Low		PER SHARE ($) Earnings	Dividends	Book Value
12/17	27.59	36	30	0.80	0.00	20.28
12/16	26.71	23	11	1.13	0.00	15.73
12/15	16.21	20	15	0.84	0.00	12.33
12/14	14.17	23	18	0.72	0.00	11.96
Annual Growth	18.1%	—	—	2.7%	—	14.1%

Veritiv Corp

Auditors: Deloitte & Touche LLP

LOCATIONS

HQ: Veritiv Corp
1000 Abernathy Road N.E., Building 400, Suite 1700,
Atlanta, GA 30328
Phone: 770 391-8200
Web: www.veritivcorp.com

HISTORICAL FINANCIALS

Company Type: Public

Income Statement				FYE: December 31
	REVENUE ($ mil.)	NET INCOME ($ mil.)	NET PROFIT MARGIN	EMPLOYEES
12/17	8,364	(13)	—	8,900
12/16	8,326	21	0.3%	8,700
12/15	8,717	26	0.3%	8,800
12/14	7,406	(19)	—	8,900
12/13	4,089	242	5.9%	
Annual Growth	19.6%	—	—	—

2017 Year-End Financials

Debt ratio: 40.64%
Return on equity: (-2.44%)
Cash ($ mil.): 80
Current ratio: 2.33
Long-term debt ($ mil.): 1,089

No. of shares (mil.): 15
Dividends
Yield: —
Payout: —
Market value ($ mil.): 454

	STOCK PRICE ($) FY Close	P/E High/Low	PER SHARE ($) Earnings	Dividends	Book Value
12/17	28.90	— —	(0.85)	0.00	35.01
12/16	53.75	43 21	1.30	0.00	34.51
12/15	36.22	32 20	1.67	0.00	33.13
12/14	51.87	— —	(1.62)	0.00	32.03
Annual Growth	(13.6%)	— —	—	—	2.2%

Verizon Communications Inc

Verizon Communications is the #1 wireless phone service in the US (ahead of rival AT&T) but #2 to A&T in terms of overall telecom services. The company's core mobile business Verizon Wireless serves more than 115 million connections. Verizon's wireline unit with more than 18 million voice connections provides local telephone long-distance internet access and digital TV services to residential and wholesale customers. In addition Verizon offers a wide range of telecom managed network and IT services to commercial and government clients in more than 150 countries. Verizon has expanded its video and advertising capabilities with the acquisitions of AOL and Yahoo assets.

Operations

Verizon Communications? Verizon Wireless segment accounts for 70% of revenue. Verizon operates one of the most extensive wireless networks in the US and the largest 4G LTE and third-generation Evolution-Data Optimized (EV-DO) networks. The 4G LTE network is available to more than 98% of the US population.

The wireline segment which provides about a quarter of revenue provides voice data and video communications products and enhanced services including broadband video and data corporate networking services data center and cloud services security and managed network services and local and long-distance voice services. The segment also includes Verizon?s Fios service which offers high-speed internet and TV. The company reported nearly 6 million Fios internet and close to 5 million Fios video subscribers at the end of 2017.

The corporate and other segment which includes Oath media businesses telematics and other businesses supplies about 5% of revenue.

Geographic Reach

Verizon based in New York City is present throughout the US. It also has representation in countries around the world. The company conducts research in San Francisco and Waltham Massachusetts.

Sales and Marketing

Verizon sells its prepaid and postpaid wireless phone services through its website its own stores and national retailers. It also has a dedicated tele-marketing sales force. The average retail customer account pays about $135 a month.

The company is a major advertiser with a coordinated program of TV print radio outdoor signage internet and point-of-sale media promotions. Those Verizon ads commercials and other promotional vehicles cost the company about $2.6 billion

a year which is about two-thirds of what AT&T spends on advertising.

Financial Performance

After Verizon?s revenue rose to $131 billion in 2015 from about $120 billion in 2013 the company has taken a step or two back.

Verizon reported about $126 billion in 2017 sales which was just a touch higher than the 2016 figure. The added revenue from the Yahoo acquisition and contributions from telematics operations pushed Verizon to an overall increase for the year. Equipment sales grew from an increase in payment plans and the sale of higher priced phones while the XO acquisition raised wireline sales. Verizon's services revenue however fell as more customers switched to unlimited data plans which reduced revenue from overage charges and other fees. Average revenue per postpaid retail account fell to about $135 in 2017 from about $144 in 2016.

Verizon?s profit more than doubled to about $30 million in 2017 from 2016 aided by a one-time tax reduction of $17 billion because of the US Tax Cuts and Jobs Act.

Cash on hand slipped to $2.1 billion in 2017 from $2.8 billion in 2016. Verizon in 2017 made a discretionary payment of about $3.4 billion to its pension fund which should enable it to contribute smaller amounts for the next couple of years. Capital spending much of it for fiber installation was steady at about $17 billion.

Strategy

When its rivals slash prices on wireless service Verizon Communications touts the coverage speed and reliability of its network. Maybe it costs a bit more Verizon tells customers but the network is worth it. Verizon is investing to expand and strengthen the network to develop new streams of revenue. The company did join the rest of the industry in offering unlimited data plans in 2017.

Verizon spend about $17 billion a year to improve its network adding more fiber optic cable to improve 4G service and get ready for higher-speed 5G service. The company has standing agreements with Corning and Prysmian to supply fiber optic cable. Verizon views its overall network as a collection of assets including 4G LTE fiber 5G and software-defined networks which it calls the Verizon Intelligent Edge Network. The 2017 $1.8 billion acquisition of XO Communications is another facet of Verizon?s fiber plan.

Even as it spends to beef up its network Verizon has begun a cost-reduction program that aims to save some $10 billion by 2021. The company expects the US tax legislation enacted in 2017 to add $3.5 billion-$4 billion to cash flow in 2018.

On the content side Verizon looks to its Oath business which includes Yahoo AOL and several online publications (including Huffington Post TechCrunch and Engadget) to engage about a billion viewers a year. Oath generated about $6 billion in revenue in 2017.

Mergers and Acquisitions

In 2018 Verizon acquired Moment a New York-based design and strategy firm to develop customer experience materials for in-store online mobile and live customer service by phone or chat.

Verizon in 2017 bought Straight Path Communications for more than $3 billion gaining a trove of 28 GHz and 39 GHz millimeter wave spectrum used in mobile communications. The spectrum could give Verizon a boost in developing 5G technology. Verizon outbid AT&T for Straight Path.

Verizon acquired XO Holdings? wireline business which owns and operates one of the largest fiber-based IP and Ethernet networks for about $1.8 billion in February 2017. The purchase extends Verizon?s fiber tracks in the US. In smaller deal Verizon Communications bought Chicago-area fiber-optic network assets from WideOpenWest Inc.

EXECUTIVES

Evp And Chief Strategy Officer, Roy H. Chestnutt, age 59

Chairman And Ceo, Lowell C. McAdam, age 64, $1,600,000 total compensation

Evp Wireless Network Operations, David Small

Evp And Chief Information And Technology Architect, Roger Gurnani, age 57

Evp And Chief Administrative Officer, Marc C. Reed, age 59, $792,307 total compensation

Evp And President Network And Technology, Hans Vestberg, age 53

Evp And President Customer And Product Operations, John G. Stratton, age 57, $896,154 total compensation

Evp And President Product Innovation And New Businesses, Marni M. Walden, age 50, $896,154 total compensation

Svp And Group President Verizon Enterprise Solutions, George J. Fischer, age 55

Svp And Group President Consumer Sales And Service, Kenneth (Ken) Dixon

Evp And Group President Verizon Wireless, Ronan Dunne

Evp Public Policy And General Counsel, Craig L. Silliman, age 50

Svp And Group President Verizon Business Markets (vbm), Martin Burvill

Evp Wireless Operations, Tami Erwin

Svp And Cfo Operations Finance, Matthew D. (Matt) Ellis, age 46, $488,462 total compensation

President Verizon Partner Solutions, Eric Cevis

Managing Director Verizon Business Markets, Joe Chuisano

Vice President, Christopher Kimm

National Account Manager, Fran Morris

Vice President Associate General Counsel, David Wheeler

Executive Director Network Operations Vps, Sam Luxton

Vice President, Roland Hicks

Vice President Of Marketing And Sales For Middle Atlantic Region, Mary Yarbrough

Vice President And Associate General Counsel Corporate Governance, Beth Sasfai

National Account Manager, Rob Parker

Vice President Of Sales, Philip Burroughs

Vp And Associate General Counsel, Gregory Romano

Senior Vice President Global Real Estate, John Vazquez

National Account Manager, Shirley Bily

Manager Vps Marketing And Sales, Janice Crandall

Senior Vice President Investor Relations, Mike Stefanski

Secretary Manager Network Operations, Paul Mcguire

Board Member, Beryl Thompson

Auditors: Ernst & Young LLP

LOCATIONS

HQ: Verizon Communications Inc
1095 Avenue of the Americas, New York, NY 10036
Phone: 212 395-1000
Web: www.verizon.com

PRODUCTS/OPERATIONS

2017 Sales

	$ mil.	% of total
Wireless	87,511	69
Wireline	30,680	24
Corporate and Other	9,387	7
Eliminations	(1544)	0
Total	**126,034**	**100**

2017 Sales

	$ mil.	% of total
Service revenues and other	107,145	85
Wireless equipment revenues	18,889	16
Total	**126,034**	**100**

COMPETITORS

360networks	Level 3
AT&T	Netflix
Altice USA	Sprint Communications
CenturyLink	T-Mobile USA
Charter Communications	Time Warner Cable
Comcast	U.S. Cellular
Cox Communications	Windstream
Cricket	XO Holdings
DIRECTV	Yellowbook
Frontier Communications	

HISTORICAL FINANCIALS

Company Type: Public

Income Statement

FYE: December 31

	REVENUE ($ mil.)	NET INCOME ($ mil.)	NET PROFIT MARGIN	EMPLOYEES
12/17	126,034	30,101	23.9%	155,400
12/16	125,980	13,127	10.4%	160,900
12/15	131,620	17,879	13.6%	177,700
12/14	127,079	9,625	7.6%	177,300
12/13	120,550	11,497	9.5%	176,800
Annual Growth	1.1%	27.2%	—	(3.2%)

2017 Year-End Financials

Debt ratio: 45.54%—
Return on equity: 91.74%
Cash ($ mil.): 2,079
Current ratio: 0.91
Long-term debt ($ mil.): 113,642

Dividends
Yield: 0.0%
Payout: 31.5%
Market value ($ mil.): —

	STOCK PRICE ($) FY Close	P/E High/Low		PER SHARE ($) Earnings	Dividends	Book Value
12/17	52.93	7	6	7.36	2.32	10.56
12/16	53.38	18	14	3.21	2.27	5.53
12/15	46.22	12	10	4.37	2.22	4.03
12/14	46.78	21	19	2.42	2.14	2.96
12/13	49.14	13	10	4.00	2.08	13.57
Annual Growth	1.9%	—	—	16.5%	2.9%	(6.1%)

Viacom Inc

Viacom is a leading media conglomerate with an extensive portfolio of cable TV and film production assets. Its MTV Networks unit runs such cable networks as Comedy Central Nickelodeon and the family of MTV channels (MTV MTV2 VH1). Viacom also owns Black Entertainment Television which airs programming on BET BET Gospel and BET Hip Hop. In the film business Viacom operates through Paramount Pictures which includes imprints Paramount Pictures and Paramount Vantage. Viacom has a presence in more than 180 countries and territories primarily in North America Europe and Asia.

Operations

Viacom operates through two reporting segments: Media Networks and Filmed Entertainment.

Media Networks provides entertainment content and related branded products for consumers in demographics attractive to advertisers content distributors and retailers through three brand groups: the Global Entertainment Group the Nickelodeon Group and BET Networks. The largest segment which accounts for about 80% of company?s total revenue.

Filmed Entertainment produces finances acquires and distributes motion pictures television programming and other entertainment content under the Paramount Pictures Paramount Animation Nickelodeon Movies MTV Films and Paramount Television brands.

Viacom's media networks including Nickelodeon Comedy Central MTV VH1 Spike BET CMT TV Land Nick at Nite Nick Jr. Logo Nicktoons TeenNick Channel 5 (UK) Telefe (Argentina) and Paramount Channel reach more than 3.9 billion cumulative television subscribers worldwide.

Geographic Reach

The US contributes about 75% of the company's revenue and International markets account for about 25%.

Sales and Marketing

The company's Music & Entertainment group (including Comedy Central MTV VH1 and Classic Spike and Logo) focuses on music-lovers youth and young adults. The Kids & Family group (Nickelodeon and Nick at Nite Nick Jr TeenNick Nicktoons CMT and TV Land) targets kids ages 2-17 and their families while BET dominates the important urban demographic with entertainment music and special interest programming.

Viacom does not have the broad complement of media assets that characterize integrated conglomerates such as Time Warner and Walt Disney but the company still realizes some potential by integrating its TV and film businesses such as through DVD sales and cross-promotion. Viacom itself incurred total advertising expenses of $748 million in fiscal 2015.

Financial Performance

The company's revenue was $12.49 billion in fiscal 2016. That was a decrease compared to its fiscal 2015 revenue of almost $13.3 billion. The drop was mainly due to decreased sales from the Filmed Entertainment unit partially offset by an increase in media network revenue.

Viacom's net income was $1.4 billion in fiscal 2016 which was a decrease compared to the prior fiscal period when the company claimed a net income of more than $1.9 billion. The decrease was largely caused by the combination of decreased revenue and increased operating expenses.

However even with decreased revenue and net income the company ended fiscal 2016 with $1.3 billion in cash on hand from operations.

Strategy

Viacom's strategy includes expanding its relationships with advertising cable satellite digital mobile and licensing partners to develop new ways to deepen its connection with audiences through insightful research and the development of content that resonates with targeted audiences.

What particularly drives Viacom's business is its success in building entertainment brands. The company is notable for creating and promoting such names as MTV and Nickelodeon into easily recognizable banners that stand for a particular form of entertainment.

Viacom has been looking to expand its reach into digital media in an effort to reach its young and increasingly online target audience.

Mergers and Acquisitions

In 2017 Viacom planned to acquire Scripps Networks Interactive. The agreement is pending between the two companies. In 2016 Viacom acquired Spain-based Telefonica S.A. one of the main free-to-air channels in Argentina for $345 million. The acquisition improved the company's growth in Argentina one of the most advanced and valuable media markets in Latin America.

EXECUTIVES

Evp And Chief Administrative Officer, Scott M. Mills, $1,750,000 total compensation
Vice President Of Technical Support, George Epley
Svp Creative Grp/creative Vh1, Carole Robinson
Chairman And Ceo Bet Networks, Debra L. Lee, age 63
Chairman And Ceo Paramount Pictures, James N. (Jim) Gianopulos
President Nickelodeon, Cyma Zarghami
President Ceo And Director, Robert M. (Bob) Bakish, age 54, $931,731 total compensation
Evp Government Affairs, Doretha F. (DeDe) Lea, age 54, $843,365 total compensation
Svp Distribution Sales Group, Samantha Cooper
Evp And Cfo, Wade C. Davis, age 46, $1,750,000 total compensation
Evp And Cto, David Kline
President And Ceo Viacom International Media Networks (vimn), David Lynn
Evp General Counsel And Secretary, Christa A. D'Alimonte
Evp And Chief Data Officer, Kern Schireson
Evp Distribution Marketing, Deena Demasi
Senior Vice President Chief Compliance Officer And Chief Audit Executive, Henry Moniz
Vice President Of Application Development, Joe Leggio
Vice President Information Technology Security And Compliance, Brian Natell
Vice President Information Technology Audit, Anthony Noble
Senior Vice President Mtv Networks, Pauline Wen
Vice President Of Employee Relations And Development, Betty Panarella
Vice President Data Platform, Mark Cohen
Vice President Information Technology, Woody Eversz
Vice President International Digital Distribution And Business Development, Brendan Yam
Executive Vice President Communications Culture And Marketing, Julia Phelps
Svp Global Business Operations, James Veall
Vice President Planning And Operations, Marc Zelanko
Svp Analytics And Currency Modeling Viacom Media Networks, Oktay Arifkhan
Svp Brand And Consumer Insights, Michael Desmarais
Vice President Vh1 And Logo Digital, Dan Sacher
Vice President Content Distribution And Marketing, Andrew Borak
Vice President, Ron Meglio
Vice President Talent Acquisition, John Bongiorno
Vice President Finance Broadcast Media Sales, Miky Kurihara
Vp Global Business Services Deputy Gm And Procure To Pay, Tracey Ruff
Vice President Mobile Strategy And Advertising, Peter Chelala
Vice President Of Network Services, Lee L'archenesque
Svp Investor Relations, Jim Bombassei
Vice President Government Affairs, Hollyn Schuemann
Vice President Anti Piracy, Deborah Robinson
Senior Vice President Product Architect, Chaki Ng
Special Events Vp, Jane Volpe
Vice President Technical Accounting, James Guido
Vice President Risk Management, Barrie Wexler
Executive Vice President, Jim Perry
Vice President Operations, Eric Squires
Vice President Digital Marketing Nickelodeon, Jim Malaga
Evp Advanced Advertising Group, Bryson Gordon
Vice President Of Strategic Business Development, Daniel Reich
Vice President Digital, Shannon Burke
Vice President Business Development, Amy Singer
Vice President, Sean Wylie
Vice President Federal Tax Audits, Victor Rappa
Vice President Operations Online, Pier Chapman
Senior Vice President Internal Audit, Norman Tsacalis

Vice President Counsel Corporate, Sarah Harp
Vice President And Associate General Counsel Real Estate (2000), Jack S Cohen
Vice President Assistant Treasurer, Lou Converse
Vice President Level, Vice president Tim Stevenson
Vice President Domestic Internal Audit, Michael O'Neill
Vice President Of Information Technology, Luke Murphy
Vice President Strategic Sourcing Technology, Robert Roth
Vice President Tax Reporting, John McCartney
Vice President Sales, Allan Infeld
Vice President Advertising Sales, Valerie Bischak
Vice President Applications Development Sales Systems, Paul Mahood
Vice President Of Security, Johnathan Honovic
Vice President Of Network Services, Lee Larchenesque
Vice President Corporate Systems, Michelle Gordon
Vice President Business And Legal Affairs, Susannah Verity
Vice President Talent Acquisition, Leisha Shorey
Vice President Advertising Sales, Greg Selling
Vice President And Associate General Counsel For Intellectual Property And Content Protection, Stanley Pierre-Louis
Vice President Integrated Marketing, Lesley Kantor
Senior Vice President Executive Compensation And Deputy General Tax Counsel, Andrew Greenberg
Executive Vice President And Global Head Inclusion Strategy Viacom And Executive Vice President P, Marva Smalls
Vice President Distributor Marketing, Carolyn Parker
Vice President Tax Accounting And Analysis, James Krebs
Vice President It, Tom Melina
Vice President Operations, Noreen Rafferty
Vice President Research And Insight, Christian Kurz
Vice President Communications, Claudia Franklin
Senior Vice President Network Standards And Practices, Janet Borelli
Vice President, Carlos Martinez
Vice President Finance, Tony Augi
Web Site Content Vice President, Ezra Greene
Vice President Music Commissioning And Content, Virg Monaghan
Vice President Of Security, Jonny Honovic
Vice President Bala International Consumer Products And Recreation, Panayiotou Maria
Vice President Content And Creative Uk And Northern Europe, Vanessa Brookman
Vice President International Media And Publishing, Gavin Metcalfe
Vice President Strategy And Multiplatform, Tom Frazer
Vice President, Leigh Wit
Vp Executive Security And Business Continuity, John Honovic
Senior Vice President Research, David Giles
Vice President, Sarah Landy
Vice President Finance, Eileen Fedronas
Vice President, Evelyn Sias
Vice President, Andrea Rice
Vice President Mtv Programming And Production, Matthew Newcomb
Senior Vice President Dep General Counsel Mtv, Michael Minden
Vice President Lead And Professor Development, Nicole Kahny
Vice President Information Technology, William Twomey
Vice President Platform And Data Driven Sales And Partnerships, Leo O'Connor
Vp Cmt Production Management, Carolyn Lewis
Vice President Of Human Resources, Eli Litt

Vice President Of Marketing Solutions, Rochelle Holguin
Vice President International Content Distribution And Platform Marketing, Bradley Archer
Vice President, Elizabeth Herbst-brady
Vice President Nickelodeon Tv Finance, Cherie Peterson
Vice President Ent Ad Sales, Ted Spriggs
Vice President Vendor Management, Donald Mones
Executive Vice President Worldwide Television Licensing And Operations Paramount Pictures, Michael Armstrong
Vice President Strategic Vendor Management And Project Office, Jennifer Cardella
Vice President Media Strategy And Partnerships, Jyoti Menon
Vice President Finance, Liza Burnett Fefferman
Vice President Media, Jaime Dictenberg
Vice President, Tanya Guzman
Vice President, Scott Hong
Vice President Government Affairs Europe, Philip Jenner
Chairman, Thomas J. (Tom) May, age 71
Vice Chairman, Shari E. Redstone, age 64
Assistant Treasurer, George Nelson
Board Of Directors, Blythe Mcgarvie
Board Of Directors, Alan Greenberg
Auditors: PricewaterhouseCoopers LLP

LOCATIONS

HQ: Viacom Inc
1515 Broadway, New York, NY 10036
Phone: 212 258-6000
Web: www.viacom.com

2016 Sales

	$ mil.	% of total
US	9,308	75
EMEA	2,182	17
All other regions	998	8
Total	**12,488**	**100**

PRODUCTS/OPERATIONS

2016 Sales

	$ mil.	% of total
Advertising	4,809	38
Affiliated Fees	4,556	36
Feature Film	2,488	20
Ancillary	751	6
(Eliminations)	(116)	-
Total	**12,488**	**100**

2016 Segment sale

	$ in mils
% of total	
Media Networks	79
Filmed Entertainment	21
Eliminations	-
Total	**100**

Selected Brands:

BET Networks
BET Centric Entertainment Group
Comedy Central
Spike TV Land Music Group
CMT
Logo
MTV VH1 Nickelodeon Group
Nickelodeon

COMPETITORS

Discovery	NBCUniversal
Disney	Sony Pictures
Lionsgate	Entertainment
MGM	Time Warner

HISTORICAL FINANCIALS

Company Type: Public

Income Statement

FYE: September 30

	REVENUE ($ mil.)	NET INCOME ($ mil.)	NET PROFIT MARGIN	EMPLOYEES
09/18	12,943	1,719	13.3%	10,400
09/17	13,263	1,874	14.1%	11,650
09/16	12,488	1,438	11.5%	9,300
09/15	13,268	1,922	14.5%	9,200
09/14	13,783	2,391	17.3%	9,900
Annual Growth	(1.6%)	(7.9%)	—	1.2%

2018 Year-End Financials

Debt ratio: 42.39%	No. of shares (mil.): 403
Return on equity: 25.58%	Dividends
Cash ($ mil.): 1,557	Yield: 0.0%
Current ratio: 1.50	Payout: 18.7%
Long-term debt ($ mil.): 9,515	Market value ($ mil.): 13,609

	STOCK PRICE ($) FY Close	P/E High/Low	PER SHARE ($) Earnings	Dividends	Book Value
09/18	33.76	8 5	4.27	0.80	18.38
09/17	27.84	10 6	4.68	0.80	15.00
09/16	38.10	15 9	3.61	1.40	10.77
09/15	43.15	16 8	4.73	1.46	8.89
09/14	76.94	16 14	5.43	1.26	8.98
Annual Growth	(18.6%)	— —	(5.8%)	(10.7%)	19.6%

VIRGINIA COLLEGE BUILDING AUTHORITY

EXECUTIVES

Prin, Robert F McDonnell

LOCATIONS

HQ: VIRGINIA COLLEGE BUILDING AUTHORITY
101 N 14TH ST FL 3, RICHMOND, VA 232193665
Phone: 804 225-2142

HISTORICAL FINANCIALS

Company Type: Private

Income Statement

FYE: June 30

	ASSETS ($ mil.)	NET INCOME ($ mil.)	INCOME AS % OF ASSETS	EMPLOYEES
06/17	1,754	(98)	—	2
06/16	2,199	(327)	—	
Annual Growth	(20.2%)	—	—	—

2017 Year-End Financials

Debt ratio: ——	
Return on equity: (-20.70%)	Dividends
Cash ($ mil.): 146	Yield: —
Current ratio: 0.20	Payout: —
Long-term debt ($ mil.): —	Market value ($ mil.): —

Virginia Electric & Power Co.

Virginia Electric and Power Company (Virginia Power) operates under the Dominion Virginia Power and Dominion North Carolina Power brands and provides regulated electric delivery services to about 2.4 million homes and businesses. Power generation is derived by means of coal gas oil hydro and nuclear plants. The utility's power plants (with 24300 MW of generating capacity) are managed by the Dominion Generation unit of parent Dominion Energy. Control of Virginia Power's transmission facilities is maintained by PJM Interconnection. Dominion Virginia Power also sells wholesale power to other users.

Geographic Reach
Virginia Power generates transmits and distributes electricity for sale in Virginia and North Carolina.

Sales and Marketing
Virginia Power primarily serves retail customers. It sells electricity at wholesale prices to rural electric cooperatives municipalities and wholesale electricity markets.

Strategy
Virginia Power is trying to beef up its green energy profile. In addition to exploring wind farm options to help produce alternative energy the company is pushing energy conservation programs with the aim of cutting peak demand by electric consumers in Virginia by 650 MW.

In 2016 the company announced plans to invest nearly $2 billion per year through 2020 to add cleaner generation to its infrastructure including solar energy. It also plans to expand secure and upgrade its electric grid in Virginia and northeastern North Carolina.

EXECUTIVES

President Dominion Virginia Power, Robert M. Blue
Auditors: DELOITTE & TOUCHE LLP

LOCATIONS

HQ: Virginia Electric & Power Co.
120 Tredegar Street, Richmond, VA 23219
Phone: 804 819-2000

COMPETITORS

Appalachian Power	Pepco Holdings
Columbia Gas of	Rappahannock Electric
Virginia	Cooperative
Duke Energy Carolinas	SCANA
Duke Energy Progress	South Carolina
Inc.	Electric & Gas

HISTORICAL FINANCIALS
Company Type: Public

Income Statement
FYE: December 31

	REVENUE ($ mil.)	NET INCOME ($ mil.)	NET PROFIT MARGIN	EMPLOYEES
12/17	7,556	1,540	20.4%	6,900
12/16	7,588	1,218	16.1%	6,800
12/15	7,622	1,087	14.3%	6,800
12/14	7,579	858	11.3%	6,800
12/13	7,295	1,138	15.6%	6,700
Annual Growth	0.9%	7.9%	—	0.7%

2017 Year-End Financials

Debt ratio: 33.83%
Return on equity: 12.79%
Cash ($ mil.): 14
Current ratio: 0.76
Long-term debt ($ mil.): 10,496
No. of shares (mil.): 0
Dividends
  Yield: —
  Payout: —
Market value ($ mil.): —

	STOCK PRICE ($) FY Close	P/E High/Low	PER SHARE ($) Earnings	Dividends	Book Value
12/17	0.00 44,495.73		(0.00)	0.00	
Annual Growth	—	—	—	—	—

VIRGINIA HOUSING DEVELOPMENT AUTHORITY

Though Virginia is famous for its Civil War-era plantations these historic estates represent a lifestyle out of reach for most. For Virginians seeking a more modest homestead there's the Virginia Housing Development Authority (VHDA). The not-for-profit quasi-government agency founded by the Virginia General Assembly in 1972 provides developers of rentalA propertiesA and low- to moderate-income borrowers with low interest rate loans to renovate or purchase houses and apartments across the state. Its loan products are offered by more than 140 authorized lenders throughout Virginia. The VHDA is self-supporting issuing bonds to raise capital.

EXECUTIVES

Executive Director, Susan F. Dewey
Managing Director Rental Housing, Arthur N. (Art) Bowen
Managing Director Community Outreach, J. Michael Hawkins
Managing Director Executive Services, Llewellyn C. Anderson
Managing Director Homeownership, Janet Wiglesworth
Managing Director Internal Audit And Risk Management, Julie Camus
Managing Director Finance, Pat Carey
Acting Managing Director Information Technology Services, J. Kyle Howard
Chairman, Timothy M. Chapman
Vice Chairman, Sarah B. Stedfast
Auditors: KPMG LLP RICHMOND VA

LOCATIONS

HQ: VIRGINIA HOUSING DEVELOPMENT AUTHORITY
601 S BELVIDERE ST, RICHMOND, VA 232206504
Phone: 804 780-0789
Web: WWW.VHDA.COM

VIRGINIA WEST UNIVERSITY FOUNDATION INCORPORATED

EXECUTIVES

Vp Technology And Facilities, Mark Cottrill
Vp Investments And Chief Investment Officer, Rick Kraich
Coo Cfo And Treasurer, Michael Augustine
President And Ceo, Cindi Roth
Chairman, Robert L. Reynolds
Vice Chairman, Gary Pell
Auditors: DIXON HUGHES GOODMAN LLP MORG

LOCATIONS

HQ: VIRGINIA WEST UNIVERSITY FOUNDATION INCORPORATED
1 WATERFRONT PL FL 7, MORGANTOWN, WV 265015978
Phone: 304 282-4000
Web: WWW.WVUF.ORG

HISTORICAL FINANCIALS
Company Type: Private

Income Statement
FYE: June 30

	ASSETS ($ mil.)	NET INCOME ($ mil.)	INCOME AS % OF ASSETS	EMPLOYEES
06/18	7,292	132	1.8%	300
06/16	8,024	171	2.1%	—
06/15	8,070	170	2.2%	—
06/14	8,014	132	1.7%	—
Annual Growth	(2.3%)	(0.1%)	—	—

2018 Year-End Financials

Debt ratio: ——
Return on equity: 26.20%
Cash ($ mil.): 875
Current ratio: 1.30
Long-term debt ($ mil.): —
Dividends
  Yield: —
  Payout: —
Market value ($ mil.): —

HISTORICAL FINANCIALS
Company Type: Private

Income Statement
FYE: June 30

	ASSETS ($ mil.)	NET INCOME ($ mil.)	INCOME AS % OF ASSETS	EMPLOYEES
06/17	1,690	42	2.5%	115
06/13	1,245	75	6.1%	—
06/12	1,110	37	3.4%	—
Annual Growth	8.8%	2.7%	—	—

2017 Year-End Financials

Debt ratio: ——
Return on equity: 29.40%
Cash ($ mil.): 46
Current ratio: 4.50
Long-term debt ($ mil.): —
Dividends
  Yield: —
  Payout: —
Market value ($ mil.): —

Visa Inc

Paper or plastic? Visa hopes you choose the latter. Visa operates the world's largest global consumer payment system (ahead of rivals MasterCard and American Express) and boasts more than 3.3 billion credit and other payment cards in circulation across more than 200 countries. As part of its business the company licenses the Visa name to member institutions which issue and market their own Visa products and participate in the VisaNet payment system that provides authorization processing and settlement services. The company also offers debit cards internet payment systems value-storing smart cards and traveler's checks. Visa's network connects thousands of financial institutions worldwide.

HISTORY

Although the first charge card was issued by Western Union in 1914 it wasn't until 1958 that Bank of America (BofA) issued its BankAmericard which combined the convenience of a charge account with credit privileges. When BofA extended its customer base outside California the interchange system controlling payments began to falter because of design problems and fraud.

In 1968 Dee Hock manager of the BankAmericard operations of the National Bank of Commerce in Seattle convinced member banks that a more reliable system was needed. Two years later National BankAmericard Inc. (NBI) was created as an independent corporation (owned by 243 banks) to buy the BankAmericard system from BofA.

With its initial ad slogan "Think of it as Money" the Hock-led NBI developed BankAmericard into a widely used form of payment in the US. A multinational corporation IBANCO was formed in 1974 to carry the operations into other countries. People outside the US resisted BankAmericard's nominal association with BofA and in 1977 Hock changed the card's name to Visa. NBI became Visa USA and IBANCO became Visa International.

By 1980 Visa had debuted debit cards begun issuing traveler's checks and created an electromagnetic point-of-sale authorization system. Visa developed a global network of ATMs in 1983; it was expanded in 1987 by the purchase of a 33% stake in the Plus System of ATMs then the US's second-largest system. Hock retired in 1984 with the company well on its way to realizing his vision of a universal payment system.

The company built the Visa brand image with aggressive advertising such as sponsorship of the 1988 and 1992 Olympics and by co-branding (issuing cards through other organizations with strong brand names such as Blockbuster and Ford).

In 1994 Visa teamed up with Microsoft and others to develop home banking services and software. Visa Cash was introduced during the 1996 Olympics. Visa pushed its debit cards in 1996 and 1997 with humorous ads featuring presidential also-ran Bob Dole and showbiz success story Daffy Duck.

Visa expanded its smart card infrastructure in 1997. It published with MasterCard encryption and security software for online transactions. The gloves came off the next year as the companies vied to convince the world to rally around their respective e-purse technology standards.

During the 1990s Visa fought American Express' attempts to introduce a bank credit card of its own by forbidding Visa members in the US from issuing the product; the Justice Department responded with an antitrust suit against Visa and

MasterCard. The case went to trial in 2000 with the government claiming that Visa and MasterCard stifle competition and enjoy an exclusive cross-ownership structure. Visa eventually agreed to pay American Express $2.25 billion to settle the case.

Also in 2000 the company made a deal with Gemplus the French smart card company to enable payments over wireless networks. Visa then inked e-commerce agreements with telecommunications companies Nokia and Ericsson. The company continued its technology push with a deal with Financial Services Technology Consortium to test biometrics — the use of fingerprints irises and voice recognition to identify cardholders. The company also launched a prepaid card Visa Buxx targeted at teenagers.

The European Union in 2000 launched an investigation into the firm's transaction fees alleging that the fees could restrict competition. The following year Visa International agreed to drop its fee to 0.7% of the transaction value over five years.

Led by retail giant Wal-Mart some 4 million merchants claimed Visa and MasterCard violated antitrust laws and attempted to mono

EXECUTIVES

Ceo, Alfred F. (Al) Kelly, age 60
Vice Chairman Risk And Public Policy, Ellen Richey, age 69, $600,023 total compensation
Evp And Cfo, Vasant M. Prabhu, age 57, $547,616 total compensation
Evp And Ceo European Operations, Charlotte M. Hogg, age 47
Evp Strategy Mergers And Acquisitions And Government Relations, William M. (Bill) Sheedy, age 51, $525,020 total compensation
Evp And General Counsel, Kelly M. Tullier, age 52
Evp Technology, Rajat Taneja, age 53, $750,029 total compensation
President, Ryan McInerney, age 43, $750,029 total compensation
Vice President, Brian Wood
Senior Vice President, Elizabeth Hurvitz
Vice President Head Of Payment Services Marketing Visa Europe, Neil Horseman
Vice President Processing Solutions, Manny Fernandez
Vice President, Daysi Rojas
First Vice President Value Added Services Latin America, Javier Vazquez
Vice President, Seth Friedman
Vice President Data Center Engineering And Operations, Brian Green
Svp Digital Solutions, Sam Shrauger
Vice President, Mario Rivero
Vice President, Jeff Allison
Vice President, Andrew Carpenter
Vice President, Julie Miller
Senior Vice President, Mark Nelsen
Vice President Marketing Planning, Stacey Taylor
Vice President, Joanna Gill
Vice President Of Product, Alan Johnson
Vice President Pricing And Costing, Philip Joseph
Vice President Digital Marketing, David Purcell
Vice President Corporate Strategy, Saurabh Chopra
Senior Vice President Chief Corporate Counsel, Tracey Heaton
Vice President Product And Future Payment Risk, Paul Eagles
Vp Human Resources Technology, Puja Jaspal
Vice President Technical Excellence, Bee Ng
Vice President Infrastructure Project Management Office, Amy Gradnik
Vice President Enterprise Workforce Transformation And Planning, Manish Asnani
Svp Developer Platform India, Nitin Chandel
Senior Vice President Visa Research Labs, Min Wang
Vice President, Sang Lee

Vice President Strategic Initiatives, Jeff Kim
Senior Vice President Investor Relations, Michael Milotich
Vice President Treasury, Michael Donnelly
Vice President Head Of Global Infrastructure Network Services, Justin Dustzadeh
Senior Vice President Data Platform, Sam Hamilton
Vice President Head Of Product Strategy And New Product Development North America, Matthew Friend
Vice President Europe Information Security Integration And Global Identity And Access Management, Shirish Puranik
Vice President Data Architecture, Dirk Reinshagen
Senior Vice President Product Digital Solutions, Ansar Ansari
Vice President Global Tax, Carl Andersen
Chairman, Robert W. Matschullat, age 71
Auditors: KPMG LLP

LOCATIONS

HQ: Visa Inc
P.O. Box 8999, San Francisco, CA 94128-8999
Phone: 650 432-3200
Web: www.corporate.visa.com

2018 Sales

	$ mil.	% of total
United States	9,332	45
International	11,277	55
Total	**20,609**	**100**

PRODUCTS/OPERATIONS

2018 Sales

	$ mil.	% of total
Service Revenues	8,918	34
Data Processing Revenues	9,027	34
International Transaction Revenues	7,211	28
Other Revenues	944	4
Client Incentives	(5491)	-
Total	**20,609**	**100**

Selected Products and Services

Commercial and government
  Visa Business Credit Card (small business)
  Visa Business Debit Card (small business)
  Visa Business Electron (international)
  Visa Business Line of Credit
  Visa Commercial One Card
  Visa Corporate Card (travel and entertainment)
  Visa Gift Card
  Visa Incentive Card
  Visa Purchasing Card
  Visa Signature Business Card
Consumer credit
  Visa Classic
  Visa Gold
  Visa Infinite
  Visa Platinum
Consumer deposit
  Interlink Debit (POS debit network)
  Prepaid
  Visa Debit
  Visa Classic
  Visa Gold
  Visa Infinite
  Visa Platinum
  Visa Electron Debit

COMPETITORS

American Express	MasterCard
Apple Inc.	NYCE Payments Network
China UnionPay	PULSE Network
Citigroup	PayPal
Discover	Rewards Network
JCB International	

HISTORICAL FINANCIALS

Company Type: Public

Income Statement

FYE: September 30

	REVENUE ($ mil.)	NET INCOME ($ mil.)	NET PROFIT MARGIN	EMPLOYEES
09/18	20,609	10,301	50.0%	17,000
09/17	18,358	6,699	36.5%	15,000
09/16	15,082	5,991	39.7%	—
09/15	13,880	6,328	45.6%	11,300
09/14	12,702	5,438	42.8%	9,500
Annual Growth	12.9%	17.3%	—	15.7%

2018 Year-End Financials

Debt ratio: 24.02%
Return on equity: 30.86%
Cash ($ mil.): 8,162
Current ratio: 1.61
Long-term debt ($ mil.): 16,630

No. of shares (mil.): 2,025
Dividends
Yield: 0.0%
Payout: 18.6%
Market value ($ mil.): 303,932

	STOCK PRICE ($) FY Close	P/E High/Low	PER SHARE ($) Earnings	Dividends	Book Value
09/18	150.09	34 24	4.42	0.83	16.79
09/17	105.24	38 27	2.80	0.66	15.78
09/16	82.70	33 27	2.48	0.56	15.43
09/15	69.66	108 25	2.58	0.48	13.47
09/14	213.37	108 84	2.16	0.40	8.99
Annual Growth	(8.4%)	—	19.7%	19.8%	16.9%

Vistra Energy Corp

Auditors: DELOITTE & TOUCHE LLP

LOCATIONS

HQ: Vistra Energy Corp
6555 Sierra Drive, Irving, TX 75039
Phone: 214 812-4600
Web: www.vistraenergy.com

HISTORICAL FINANCIALS

Company Type: Public

Income Statement

FYE: December 31

	REVENUE ($ mil.)	NET INCOME ($ mil.)	NET PROFIT MARGIN	EMPLOYEES
12/17	5,430	(254)	—	4,150
12/16*	1,191	(163)	—	4,435
10/16	4,255	22,851	537.0%	—
12/15	5,704	(4,677)	—	—
12/14	5,989	(6,229)	—	—
Annual Growth	(3.2%)	—	—	—

*Fiscal year change

2017 Year-End Financials

Debt ratio: 30.29%
Return on equity: (-3.93%)
Cash ($ mil.): 1,487
Current ratio: 1.98
Long-term debt ($ mil.): 4,379

No. of shares (mil.): 428
Dividends
Yield: —
Payout: —
Market value ($ mil.): 7,848

	STOCK PRICE ($) FY Close	P/E High/Low	PER SHARE ($) Earnings	Dividends	Book Value
12/17	18.32	— —	(0.59)	0.00	14.80
12/16*	15.50	— —	(0.38)	2.32	15.43
Annual Growth	5.7%	—	—	—	(1.4%)

*Fiscal year change

VMware Inc

VMware makes a virtue of being virtual. The company develops software used to create and manage virtual machines — computer functions spread across multiple systems. Companies use its applications to more efficiently integrate and manage server storage and networking functions in order to lower the cost of operating their IT systems. VMware also provides an extensive range of consulting technical support training and certification services that accounts for more than half of sales. The company has marketing relationships with top computer hardware vendors including Hewlett Packard Enterprise IBM and Cisco Systems. Dell Technologies holds a controlling stake in VMware through its acquisition of EMC.

Operations

VMware derives about 60% of its revenue from services which include software maintenance professional services and software as service subscriptions and about 40% from licensing of software.

Geographic Reach

VMware operates about 120 offices in the US and around the world. The geographic split of revenue is 50-50 between the US and international customers.

Sales and Marketing

VMware sells its products through a direct sales force and distributors. Nearly 40% of sales are made to vdistributors Arrow Electronics Inc. Tech Data Corp. and Ingram Micro which buy software from VMware and sell it to end-users or resellers.

Financial Performance

VMware posted a 9% increase in revenue in 2015 to reach $6.5 billion. Its license revenue rose 5% from sales of newer products such as NSX AirWatch and vSphere with Operations Management as well as its hybrid cloud offerings. Service sales jumped 14% in 2016 from maintenance contract renewals and contracts associated with new software license sales. Generally customers buy two years of support and maintenance with each new license.

VMware recorded net income of just under $1 billion in 2015 a 13% increase from 2014. While the company spent more in 2015 for research and development sales and marketing and administrative functions the level of spending remained at the same percentage of revenue as in 2014. The company reduced headcount by some 380 positions (about 2% of employment) in 2015 to streamline operations resulting in a $23 million charge.

Cash from operations decreased to $1.9 billion in 2015 from $2.2 billion from changes in unearned revenues and accounts receivable. Although cash collections rose in 2015 they were negatively affected by the strengthening of the US dollar against foreign currencies.

Strategy

Although VMware is part of Dell Technologies that hasn't stopped the company from doing deals with Dell competitors. The company has agreements with IBM and Amazon Web Services (AWS) that help customers manage their private clouds and public clouds (running on IBM or AWS) using VMware software. The arrangements provide customers more flexibility with their cloud environments.

Sales of VMware's network virtualization product NSX have continued to grow since it was introduced in 2013. Sold as part of other VMware products NSX allows networking hardware like routers and switches to be reconfigured and managed by via software. That reduces hardware costs for customers. NSX has been a hit for the company on track to produce more than $1 billion in revenue in 2017.

Mergers and Acquisitions

In 2016 VMware acquired assets and employees from PLUMgrid a software-defined networking startup to strengthen its Software Defined Networking (SDN) and container strategy. PLUMgrid offers SDN and Network Function Virtualization (NFV) systems for more efficient operations.

Also in 2016 VMware acquired Arkin Net a provider of SDN data center security and operations for $67 million. This acquisition fits in with VMware's push on adoption of NSX.

Company Background

Founded in 1998 VMware was acquired by EMC for about $625 million in cash in 2004. Looking to unlock some of the value in its subsidiary EMC sold some of its stake in VMware in a 2007 IPO. In 2016 Dell bought EMC including VMware for more than $60 billion.

EXECUTIVES

Ceo And Director, Patrick P. (Pat) Gelsinger, age 57, $1,000,000 total compensation
Evp And General Manager End-user Computing, Sanjay Poonen, age 48, $605,000 total compensation
Evp Worldwide Sales, Maurizio Carli
Evp And Cfo, Zane C. Rowe, age 47
Co-coo Products And Cloud Services, Rajiv Ramaswami, age 52
Svp And Cio, Bask Iyer
Evp And General Manager Hybrid Cloud Services Business Unit, Bill Fathers
Co-coo Products And Cloud Services, Rangarajan (Raghu) Raghuram, age 55, $605,000 total compensation
Svp Strategy And Corporate Development And General Manager Telco Nfv Group, Shekar Ayyar
Evp Cto And Chief Development Officer, Ray O'Farrell
Svp General Counsel Chief Compliance Officer And Secretary, S. Dawn Smith, age 54
Vp Emea, Luigi Freguia
Vice President Cloud Services Development And Operations, Velchamy Sankarlingam
Vice President Worldwide Sales Operations, Pradeep Vancheeswaran
Vice President Field Automation Services And Global Marketing Operations, Mia Leondakis
Quality Engineer For Mvp, Bryan Bozzi
Vice President Latin America Sales, Fernando Mollon
Vice President Human Resources, Ally Lawson
Vice President, Stephanie Joe
Vice President Engineering And Technical, Arnaud Mauvais
Vice President Cloud Operations, Peter Weideling
Vice President Product Management, Bharath Rangarajan
Vice President Of Solutions Partners North America, Rich Figer
Chairman, Michael S. Dell
Auditors: PricewaterhouseCoopers LLP

LOCATIONS

HQ: VMware Inc
3401 Hillview Avenue, Palo Alto, CA 94304
Phone: 650 427-5000
Web: www.vmware.com

2015 Sales

	$ mil.	% of total
US	3,311	50
Other countries	3,260	50
Total	**6,571**	**100**

PRODUCTS/OPERATIONS

2015 Sales

	$ mil.	% of total
Services	3,927	59
License	2,720	41
GSA settlement	(76)	-
Total	**6,571**	**100**

COMPETITORS

Amazon.com	IBM
Brocade Communications	Microsoft
CA Inc.	Novell
Cisco Systems	Nutanix
Citrix Systems	Oracle
Dell Software	Parallels
Google	Symantec
HP	

HISTORICAL FINANCIALS

Company Type: Public

Income Statement				FYE: February 2
	REVENUE ($ mil.)	NET INCOME ($ mil.)	NET PROFIT MARGIN	EMPLOYEES
02/18	7,922	570	7.2%	21,700
02/17*	496	(8)	—	—
12/16	7,093	1,186	16.7%	19,900
12/15	6,571	997	15.2%	19,000
12/14	6,035	886	14.7%	18,000
Annual Growth	**9.5%**	**(13.7%)**		**6.4%**

*Fiscal year change

2018 Year-End Financials

Debt ratio: 20.53%
Return on equity: 7.15%
Cash ($ mil.): 5,971
Current ratio: 2.73
Long-term debt ($ mil.): 4,234

No. of shares (mil.): 403
Dividends
Yield: —
Payout: —
Market value ($ mil.): 49,551

	STOCK PRICE ($) FY Close	P/E High/Low		PER SHARE ($) Earnings	Dividends	Book Value
02/18	122.72	107	61	1.38	0.00	19.26
02/17*	88.95	—	—	(0.02)	0.00	20.04
12/16	78.73	29	16	2.78	0.00	19.83
12/15	56.57	39	24	2.34	0.00	18.77
12/14	82.52	54	37	2.04	0.00	17.66
Annual Growth	**14.1%**			**(12.2%)**	**—**	**2.9%**

*Fiscal year change

Voya Financial Inc

Auditors: Ernst & Young LLP

LOCATIONS

HQ: Voya Financial Inc
230 Park Avenue, New York, NY 10169
Phone: 212 309-8200
Web: www.ing.us

HISTORICAL FINANCIALS

Company Type: Public

Income Statement				FYE: December 31
	ASSETS ($ mil.)	NET INCOME ($ mil.)	INCOME AS % OF ASSETS	EMPLOYEES
12/17	222,532	(2,992)	—	6,300
12/16	214,235	(428)	—	6,700
12/15	218,249	408	0.2%	7,000
12/14	226,951	2,299	1.0%	6,500
12/13	221,023	600	0.3%	7,000
Annual Growth	**0.2%**	**—**		**(2.6%)**

2017 Year-End Financials

Debt ratio: 1.40%
Return on equity: (-26.01%)
Cash ($ mil.): 1,218
Current ratio: —
Long-term debt ($ mil.): —

No. of shares (mil.): 171
Dividends
Yield: 0.0%
Payout: —
Market value ($ mil.): 8,508

	STOCK PRICE ($) FY Close	P/E High/Low		PER SHARE ($) Earnings	Dividends	Book Value
12/17	49.47	—	—	(16.25)	0.04	58.20
12/16	39.22	—	—	(2.13)	0.04	66.76
12/15	36.91	27	20	1.80	0.04	64.26
12/14	42.38	5	4	9.02	0.04	66.60
12/13	35.15	15	9	2.38	0.02	50.72
Annual Growth	**8.9%**			**—**	**18.9%**	**3.5%**

Walgreens Boots Alliance Inc

Whether you get your drugs from the pharmacist or the chemist Walgreens Boots Alliance has you covered. The company formed when US-based Walgreen Co. bought its European counterpart Alliance Boots includes more than 13200 retail pharmacies (or chemists in some parts of the world) in 11 countries mostly the US and its territories and the UK selling prescription and OTC drugs along with health and beauty products and general merchandise. The Alliance Boots part of the company also includes wholesale operations serving more than 230000 pharmacies hospitals and clinics in upwards of 20 countries. Walgreens Alliance Boots was formed in 2014.

Operations

Walgreens Boots Alliance operates three core segments: Retail Pharmacy USA Retail Pharmacy International and Pharmaceutical Wholesale.

The Retail Pharmacy USA segment generates around 75% of revenue and sells pharmacy and beauty and other items through 8100 retail stores under the Walgreens and Duane Reade banners. It sells third party and own-brand products in store and online. It also has a prescription management app for customers. The pharmacy arm accounts for around 70% of sales and its retail arm (beauty products toiletries and general merchandise) the remainder.

Retail Pharmacy International generates more than 10% of revenue and consists mainly of the Boots pharmacy network across the UK Norway Ireland the Netherlands and Thailand. The segment operates more than 4700 stores across the Boots brand as well as Benavides in Mexico and Ahumada in Chile. Boots stocks over 35000 products and offers around 640 in-store and standalone optician services alongside its retail and pharmacy operations.

The Pharmaceutical Wholesale segment (more than 10% of revenue) flies the Alliance Healthcare banner and delivers drugs and other healthcare products and services from around 290 distribution centers to about 110000 customers primarily in Europe; its the continents largest pharmaceutical distributor. It delivers to pharmacies hospitals clinics and doctor's offices and helps pharmacists develop their businesses. Its Alphega Pharmacy is a membership group for independent pharmacies.

Geographic Reach

Walgreens Boots Alliance is headquartered in the US and has stores in all fifty US states the District of Columbia Puerto Rico the US Virgin Islands Mexico Chile the UK Thailand Norway Ireland the Netherlands and Lithuania. The Walgreen part of the business is headquartered in the US while the Alliance Boots retail and wholesale operations are headquartered in Switzerland.

Altogether the company generates around 75% of its sales in the US while 15% comes from Europe (excluding the UK) and 10% of revenues were tied to business in the UK.

Sales and Marketing

Walgreens Boots Alliance sells in physical stores and online. It offers various loyalty programs such as Balance Rewards and the Boots Advantage Card.

Financial Performance

After posting explosive acquisition-driven growth between 2014 and 2016 in fiscal 2017 Walgreens Boots Alliance's sales grew by a relatively minor $1 billion or less than 1%. The company's USA segment grew 4% on the back of higher Medicare Part D prescriptions and the contribution from the newly formed AllianceRx Walgreens Prime specialty and mail services business. The balance of sales shifted further towards pharmacy sales which grew 7% and away from retail sales which fell 2%. Meanwhile the company recorded a 10% fall to $11.8 billion with the drop concentrated in comparable store sales mostly down to the weakness of the British pound against the dollar. The Wholesale business was likewise impacted by currency effects.

Net income fell 1% to $4.2 billion due to fluctuations in fair value adjustments of the company's AmerisourceBergen warrants and a gain in the previous year on equity interest in Alliance Boots.

Cash from operations fell 8% to $7.3 billion due to lower cash from changes in accrued expenses offset by higher cash inflows from changes in inventories.

Strategy

After years of using acquisitions to fuel growth at both Walgreen and Alliance Boots Walgreens Boots Alliance is looking to leverage its massive size as the world's largest purchaser of prescription drugs to lower costs. The company's presence in growing and untapped markets in South America and Asia give it great potential to continue expanding its footprint while its sheer size give it bargaining power with wholesalers of everything from prescription drugs to toothpaste to potato chips.

While it continues its store expansion the company's Retail Pharmacy USA division has been slowing its net new store openings in recent years and has been concentrating on emphasizing its exclusive private brand offerings to grow comparable store sales through technological innovations. It shed around 200 stores in 2016 while driving usage of its digital channels. The company believes customers that engage in-store and online are 3.5 times more valuable than in-store only and those that engage in in-store and mobile are 6 times more valuable. In 2016 Walgreens launched an app that allows users to refill or transfer prescriptions live chat with a pharmacy technician and create a shopping list. It also flips to "in-store mode" when a user enters a store pointing them to relevant needs.

Mergers and Acquisitions

In a long-running saga Walgreens' attempt to acquire Rite Aid ended after two years of back-and-forth in September 2017 with the retailer acquiring 1932 of Rite Aid's around 5500 stores. Regulators objected strongly to the move as it would have left the US with just two major pharmacist chains: Walgreens and CVS. The deal closed for around $4.4 billion; Rite Aid's stores will slowly be rebranded as Walgreens.

Company Background

Walgreen the largest drugstore company in the US bought 45% of Alliance Boots Europe's largest pharmacy retailer and wholesaler in 2012. The two got along well enough that in 2014 Walgreen exercised its option to purchase the rest of Alliance Boots. It formed Walgreens Boots Alliance and became a subsidiary of the parent along with Alliance Boots.

EXECUTIVES

Co-coo, Ornella Barra, age 64, $946,897 total compensation
Executive Vice Chairman And Ceo, Stefano Pessina, age 77
Evp And Global Cfo, George R. Fairweather, age 61, $977,118 total compensation
Co-coo, Alexander W. (Alex) Gourlay, age 57, $937,076 total compensation
Evp Global Chief Administrative Officer And General Counsel, Marco Pagni, age 55
Evp And Global Chief Human Resources Officer, Kathleen Wilson-Thompson, age 60, $627,000 total compensation
Evp And Chief Commercial Officer And President Global Brands, Ken Murphy, age 52
President Operations, Richard M. Ashworth
Cio, Steve Turner
Vice President And Director Global Accounts, Ruth Spencer
Vice President Global Enterprise Architecture, Brian DeMay
Pharmacy Manager, Nisha Soung
Pharmacy Manager, Franklyn Osakwe
Pharmacy Manager, Denise Rhone
Pharmacy Manager, Anthony Silva
Pharmacy Manager, Maria Troia
Pharmacy Manager, Pratik Shah
Vice President Global Executive Compensation And Stock Programs, Martha Peterson
Pharmacy Manager, Merykokeb Beyene
Pharmacy Manager, Hugh Zuengler
Pharmacy Manager, Jerry Huff
Pharmacy Manager, Joseph Rancour
Pharmacy Manager, Adel Shamseddine
Pharmacy Manager, Candice Reed
Pharmacy Manager, Ken Emelonye
Pharmacy Manager, Phuong Luc
Pharmacy Manager, Tamara Cisneros
Pharmacy Manager, Heather Rosenblum
Pharmacy Manager, Parnaz Najimi
Pharmacy Manager, Shenjin Orr
Pharmacy Manager, Dustin Hutmacher
Pharmacy Manager, Joel Neal
Pharmacy Manager, Hung Tran
Pharmacy Manager, Eleni Mastromihalis
Pharmacy Manager, Brooke Bailey
Pharmacy Manager, Hugh Tobias
Vice President Global Financial Controls, Bill Zaman
National Account Manager, Christina Gabriel
Pharmacy Manager, Veronica Zavala
Director Of Pharmacy And Retail Operations, Vince Wilkinson
Pharmacy Manager, Gopal Pillai
Pharmacy Manager, Sofia Betancourt
Pharmacy Manager, Alejandra Russo
Group Vice President Walgreens Retail Brands, Helayna Minsk
Chairman, James A. (Jim) Skinner, age 73
Board Member, Leonard Schaeffer
Auditors: DELOITTE & TOUCHE LLP

LOCATIONS

HQ: Walgreens Boots Alliance Inc
108 Wilmot Road, Deerfield, IL 60015
Phone: 847 315-2500
Web: www.walgreensbootsalliance.com

PRODUCTS/OPERATIONS

2016 Sales

	$ mil.	% of total
Retail Pharmacy USA	83,802	72
Pharmaceutical Wholesale	20,293	17
Retail Pharmacy International	13,256	11
Total	**117,351**	**100**

2016 Sales

	$ mil.	% of total
United States	83,802	72
Europe (excluding the United Kingdom)	16,793	14
United Kingdom	14,081	12
Other	2,675	2
Total	**117,351**	**100**

COMPETITORS

BioScrip	OptumRx
Body Shop	Rite Aid
CVS	Sigma Pharmaceuticals
Costco Wholesale	Superdrug
H-E-B	Target Corporation
Kroger	UDG Healthcare
McKesson	Wal-Mart
Medicine Shoppe	

HISTORICAL FINANCIALS

Company Type: Public

Income Statement

FYE: August 31

	REVENUE ($ mil.)	NET INCOME ($ mil.)	NET PROFIT MARGIN	EMPLOYEES
08/18	131,537	5,024	3.8%	354,000
08/17	118,214	4,078	3.4%	345,000
08/16	117,351	4,173	3.6%	360,000
08/15	103,444	4,220	4.1%	360,000
08/14	76,392	1,932	2.5%	—
Annual Growth	14.6%	27.0%	—	—

2018 Year-End Financials

Debt ratio: 21.13%
Return on equity: 18.79%
Cash ($ mil.): 785
Current ratio: 0.82
Long-term debt ($ mil.): 12,431

No. of shares (mil.): 952
Dividends
Yield: 2.3%
Payout: 32.4%
Market value ($ mil.): 65,278

	STOCK PRICE ($) FY Close	P/E High/Low	PER SHARE ($) Earnings	Dividends	Book Value
08/18	68.56	16 12	5.05	1.64	27.31
08/17	81.50	23 20	3.78	1.53	26.83
08/16	80.71	25 19	3.82	1.46	27.59
08/15	86.55	24 15	4.00	1.04	28.32
08/14	60.52	37 24	2.00	0.00	21.58
Annual Growth	3.2%	— —	26.1%	—	6.1%

Walmart Inc

Walmart is an irresistible (or at least unavoidable) retail force that has yet to meet any immovable objects. It is the world's #1 retailer as well as the world's largest company by revenue (and largest employer with 2.3 million associates). The company sells groceries and general merchandise operating more than 5300 stores in the US including about 4700 Walmart stores and 600 Sam's Club membership-only warehouse clubs. Walmart's international division numbers more than 6350 locations; it's the #1 retailer in Canada and Mexico and has operations in Asia Africa Europe and Latin America. Some 270 million customers visit Walmart's stores and websites each week.

HISTORY

Sam Walton began his retail career as a J. C. Penney management trainee and later leased a Ben Franklin-franchised dime store in Newport Arkansas in 1945. In 1950 he relocated to Bentonville Arkansas and opened a Walton 5 & 10. By 1962 Walton owned 15 Ben Franklin stores under the Walton 5 & 10 name.

After Ben Franklin management rejected his suggestion to open discount stores in small towns Walton with his brother James "Bud" Walton opened the first Wal-Mart Discount City in Rogers Arkansas in 1962. Wal-Mart Stores went public in 1970 with 18 stores and sales of $44 million.

Avoiding regional retailers Walton opened stores in small and midsized towns in the 1970s. The company sold its Ben Franklin stores in 1976. By 1980 Wal-Mart's 276 stores had sales of $1.2 billion.

In 1983 Wal-Mart opened SAM'S Wholesale Club a concept based on the successful cash-and-carry membership-only warehouse format pioneered by the Price Company of California (now Costco Wholesale Corp.).

The company started Hypermart*USA in 1987 as a joint venture with Dallas-based supermarket chain Cullum Companies (now Randall's Food Markets). The 200000-sq.-ft. discount store/supermarket hybrid was later retooled as Wal-Mart Supercenters. Sam stepped down as CEO in 1988 and president David Glass was appointed CEO. Wal-Mart bought out Cullum the next year.

Wal-Mart acquired wholesale distributor McLane Company in 1990. In 1992 the year Sam died the company expanded into Mexico through a joint venture to open SAM'S CLUBS with Mexico's largest retailer Cifra (renamed Wal-Mart de México in 2000). Wal-Mart acquired 122 former Woolco stores in Canada in 1994. Cofounder Bud died a year later.

More international expansion included entering China in 1996; the acquisition of German hypermarket chain Wertkauf in 1997; the purchase of Brazilian retailer Lojas Americanas' 40% interest in a joint venture (1998); and the addition of four stores and other sites in South Korea. Also in 1998 the company began testing the Neighborhood Market format a 40000-sq.-ft. grocery and drug combination store. In 1999 Wal-Mart bought 74 German-based Interspar hypermarkets and acquired ASDA Group the UK's third-largest supermarket chain.

COO Lee Scott succeeded Glass as CEO in 2000; Glass stayed on as chairman of the executive committee. Wal-Mart later began testing its customers' demand for appliances by selling household appliances in selected stores.

Following the bankruptcy and closure of the Montgomery Ward department store chain in 2001 Wal-Mart offered to replace Ward's customers' credit cards with Wal-Mart branded cards. Wal-Mart also formed an alliance with America Online to offer Internet access and later launched its No Boundaries private-label cosmetics for preteens and teenagers. In June 2001 a group of six current and former female Wal-Mart employees filed a sex-discrimination lawsuit (seeking to represent up to 500000 current and former Wal-Mart workers) against the company. The next month Wal-Mart said it would acquire all the minority interests in Walmart.com and integrate its online operations with its store operations. It also laid off 100 employees at its corporate headquarters and eliminated 300 unfilled positions. In August it said it was testing the sale of Sealy and private-label mattresses in some of its superstores and it began offering college textbooks discounted up to 30% at its online College Bookstore.

2002 was a huge year for Wal-Mart both at home and abroad. In April the company was crowned America's largest corporation by FORTUNE.

EXECUTIVES

Vp Risk Management, David Stills

President And Ceo Walmart U.s., Gregory S. (Greg) Foran, age 56, $1,006,424 total compensation

President And Ceo, C. Douglas (Doug) McMillon, age 52, $1,278,989 total compensation

Chief Merchandising Officer Walmart U.s., Steve Bratspies

Coo Wal-mart Canada, David Cheesewright, age 55, $1,071,743 total compensation

Evp And Cfo Walmart U.s., Michael P. Dastugue, age 54

Evp And Chief Administrative Officer Walmart International, Scott Price, age 57

Evp And President And Ceo Walmart Ecommerce U.s., Marc Lore, age 46, $346,154 total compensation

Evp Softlines And General Merchandise Walmart U.s., James A. (Andy) Barron

Evp Supply Chain Walmart U.s., Gregory L. (Greg) Smith, age 55

Evp Food Walmart U.s., Charles Redfield

Evp And Cfo Walmart International, Richard Mayfield

Evp Global Governance And Corporate Secretary, Jeffrey J. (Jeff) Gearhart, age 53

Evp Corporate Affairs, Daniel J. (Dan) Bartlett, age 46

Evp Consumables And Health And Wellness, Scott Huff

Evp And President Supercenters Walmart U.s., Michael S. (Mike) Moore

Evp And Cfo, M. Brett Biggs, age 49, $854,670 total compensation

Evp Membership And Technology And Ceo Samsclub.com, Jamie Iannone, age 45

Evp Operations Sam's Club, Gisel Ruiz, age 47

Evp And General Counsel, Karen Roberts

Evp And President And Ceo Walmart Latin America India And Africa And Chairman Walmart Mexico And Central America, Enrique Ostalé

Evp And Coo Walmart U.s., Judith McKenna

Svp And President Jet.com, Liza K. Landsman

Svp New England Division Walmart U.s., Julie Murphy

Evp And Global Chief Ethics And Compliance Officer, Jay T. Jorgensen

Svp And Chief Marketing Officer Walmart U.s., Tony Rogers

Evp Global People Division, Jacqueline P. (Jacqui) Canney, age 50

Evp And President And Ceo Sam's Club, John Furner, age 44

Evp Central Operations Walmart U.s., Mark Ibbotson

Evp And Cto, Jeremy King

Evp And Enterprise Chief Information Officer, Clay Johnson

Evp And Chief Merchandising Officer Sam's Club, Ashley Buchanan

Svp Chief Sustainability Officer And President Walmart Foundation, Kathleen McLaughlin

Evp Walmart Realty, JP Suarez

Safety Director Senior Vice President Of Sales And Business Development, Mike Trusty

Vice President And Chief Legal Compliance Officer, Tom Gean

Vice President Home Furnishings, Shawnda Schnurbusch

Senior Vice President, Anthony Fuller

Regional General Manager And Vice President, Paul Busby

Executive Vice President, Charlyn Jarrells Porter

Vice President Of Program And Systems Planning, Art Alderson

Vice President Corporate Affairs, Lee Culpepper

Svp Deli Bakery Dairy And Frozen, Dede Priest

Senior Vice President International Operations, John Aden

Vp Shopper Marketing, Janet Bareis

Vice President Product Development, Daria Beckom

Vice President Intl Merchandise Development, Ronald F Virta

Pharmacy Manager, Steve Goldblatt

Pharmacy Manager, Lydia Orr

Pharmacy Manager, Joby Young

Pharmacy Manager, John Cox

Vice President E Commerce, Fred Quandt

Vice President Pharmacy, Frank Segrave

Exec Vp-sams Club Operations, Greg Johnston

Vice President, Mehrdad Akbar

Pharmacy Manager, Terry Bennett

Vice President Manager Director, Shelli Stevens

Vice President Regional General Manager, Michael Collischan

Pharmacy Manager, Tara Green

Senior Vice President People Division, Michael Leb

Vice President Global Customer Insights And Analytics, Bala Subramanian

Senior Vice President Assistant Health And Wellness Operations, Michelle Hunsaker

Vice President Of User Experience, Sara Khoury

Senior Vice President Global Merchandising Center Packaged Grocery, Michael Lewis

Vice President Construction, Carl Crowe

Senior Vice President China Ftzs, Ben Hassing

Vice President Sales Floor And Innnova, Shannon Letts

Vice President, Thomas Colella

Executive Vice President, Celia Swanson

Vice President Marketing, Marty Esarte

Vice President Corporate Recruiting, Anne Thomas

Senior Vice President Operations, Antonio Barbero

Senior Vice President Replenishment Planning Innovations And Real Estate, Donald E Frieson

Vice President And Controller Wal Mart International, Olga Aragon-Hernandez

Senior Vice President, John Suarez

Vice President Sams Club.com Merchandising Ecommerce, Fred Quant

Vice President Human Resources, Clark Bill

Vice President Finance And Strategy Services, Jonathan Hall

Senior Vice President Marketing, Steven Bratspies

Vice President Assistant Adult Beverage, Lorraine Spencer

Vice President Corporate Affairs, Greg Hitt

Vice President Global Human Resources Operations, Phillip Burke

Vice President Logistics, Kenneth Woodlin

Vice President Assistant To Manolo Reyes Produce And Floral, Philip Bentley

Vice President, Mark Henneberger

Assistant To Kerry Kilker Vice President Information Systems, Eileen Smith

Rph, Susan Long

Vice President Administration, Albert Lowe

Pharmacy Manager, Victor Hernandez

Pharmacy Manager, Dan Rafferty

Vice President Dmm Deli, Karla Mcbride

Senior Vice President Of Customer Experience, Santiago Roces

Vice President, Daniel Williams

Human Resources Director And Vice President, Erica Henson

Vice President Global Ecommerce, Robert Posey

Vice President Risk Management, William Newberg

Rvp 16, Ken Reese

Vice President Of Corporate Communications, Dan Toporek

Vice President Assistant, Cheryl Creighton

Vice President Mergers And Acquisitions, Kathy Kress

Vice President Of Operations, Henry Jordan

Vice President Strategic Real Estate Finance, Scott Carroll

Vice President Finance Strategy General Merchandise, Galagher Jeff

Vice President Brand Merchandising Active Classics And Shoes, Jimmy Olsson

Vice President Corporate Affairs, Jay Allen

Vice President Corporate People Development, Kai Togami

Vice President International Real Estate, Patrick J Hamilton

Executive Vice President Corporate Affairs And Government Relations, Leslie A Dach

Senior Vice President And Gmm Boys Mens Apparel And Housewares, Jacqueline Sazekas

Vice President, Robert Fusillo

Vice President Finance, Scott Draper

Vice President Human Resources, Don Swann

Senior Vice President And General Merchandise Mana, Lucy Cindric

Vice President Finance, Bob Stout

Vice President Of Marketing, Barbara Brown

Executive Vice President Supply Chain, Catherine Smith

Vice President Construction, Wayne Cox

Vice President Regional General Manager, Steve Schrobilgen

Svp Digital Acceleration, Jane Ewing

Vice President Of E Commerce, Tom Maloskie

Vice President Assistant Corporate Controller, Debbie Jackson

Senior Vice President Logistics Ebu, Bryan Boudreaux

Pharmacy Manager, Joe Bradac

Vice President Technology And Product Global Ecommerce, Sriram Samu

Vice President Customer Analytics And Research, Taylor Duersch

Vice President Marketing Assistant, Alisa Goulet

Vice President Global Shared Services, Keith Saylor

Regional Vice President Real Estate And Design, Brian Hooper

Pharmacy Manager, Jill Harman

Pharmacist Manager, Keith Kleman

Senior Vice President And Chief Audit Executive Global Audit, Stuart Campbell

Divisional Vp Supply Chain, Sherry Harriman

Vice President Human Resources, Becky Anderson

Executive Vice President Global People Division, Jacqui Canney

Vice President Energy, Mark Vanderhelm

Executive Vice President Walmart U.s. People, Linda Simon

Svp Operations Global Sourcing, Ignacio Lopez

Senior Vice President Corporate People, Fred Ley

Vice President And Chief Ethics And Compliance Officer Latin America Africa And U.k., Luis Kolster

Pharmacy Manager, Patrick Sullivan

Pharmacy Manager, Ian Pak

Vice President Global Labor Relations, Terrence Srsen

Senior Vice President And Global Chief Culture Diversity And Inclusion Officer, Ben Hasan

Senior Vice President, Donald Humphreys

Regional Vice President Logisitics, Mike Shaddix

Vice President Global Customer Insights And Analytics, Ray Boyle

Vice President Digital Strategy And Brand Engagement, Tracy Harlow

Svp; Corporate Communications, Bob Mcadams

Senior Vice President Global Benefits, Sally S Welborn

Vice President International Recruiting, Thomas V Colella

Senior Vice President And Global Chief Compliance Officer, Jay T Jorgensen
Auditors: Ernst & Young LLP

LOCATIONS

HQ: Walmart Inc
702 S.W. 8th Street, Bentonville, AR 72716
Phone: 479 273-4000
Web: www.stock.walmart.com

2018 Sales

	$ mil.	% of total
US	380,580	76
Non-US	119,763	24
Total	**500,343**	**100**

PRODUCTS/OPERATIONS

2018 Sales

	$ mil.	% of total
Net sales	495,761	99
Membership and other income	4,582	1
Total	**500,343**	**100**

2018 Sales

	% of total
Wal-Mart US	64
International	24
SAM'S CLUB	12
Total	**100**

Selected Private Labels and Licensed Brands

Athletic Works
Better Homes & Gardens (licensed)
Black & Decker (licensed)
Canopy
Danskin Now (licensed)
Disney (licensed)
Equate (health and beauty aids)
Everstart
Faded Glory (jeans licensed)
General Electric (licensed)
George
Great Value (dairy dry grocery meat and produce)
Home Trends
Just My Size (licensed)
Mainstays
Marketside
No Boundaries
Oak Leaf
Ol' Roy (dog food)
OP (licensed)
Ozark Trail
Parent's Choice
Prima Della
Puritan
Rival (licensed)
Sam's Choice (grocery items)
Secret Treasures
Spring Valley
Starter
White Stag

COMPETITORS

99 Cents Only	Hudson's Bay
AEON	J Sainsbury
ALDI	J. C. Penney
Ace Hardware	Katz Group
Albertsons	King Kullen Grocery
Amazon.com	Kmart
Army and Air Force	Kohl's
Exchange	Kroger
AutoZone	Lianhua Supermarket
BJ's Wholesale Club	Loblaw
Bed Bath & Beyond	Lowe's
Best Buy	METRO AG
Big Lots	Maruetsu
Bridgestone Retail	Meijer
Operations	Office Depot
CVS	PETCO
Carrefour	Pep Boys
Chedraui	Publix
Comerci	Rite Aid
Costco Wholesale	SUPERVALU

Dollar General	Safeway
El Puerto de Liverpool	Sears
Family Dollar Stores	Soriana
Farmacias Benavides	Staples
Gigante	TJX Companies
Grupo Carso	Target Corporation
Grupo Elektra	Tesco
H-E-B	True Value
Home Depot	Walgreen

HISTORICAL FINANCIALS

Company Type: Public

Income Statement

FYE: January 31

	REVENUE ($ mil.)	NET INCOME ($ mil.)	NET PROFIT MARGIN	EMPLOYEES
01/18	500,343	9,862	2.0%	2,300,000
01/17	485,873	13,643	2.8%	2,300,000
01/16	482,130	14,694	3.0%	2,200,000
01/15	485,651	16,363	3.4%	2,200,000
01/14	476,294	16,022	3.4%	2,200,000
Annual Growth	**1.2%**	**(11.4%)**	**—**	**1.1%**

2018 Year-End Financials

Debt ratio: 22.73%—
Return on equity: 12.67%
Cash ($ mil.): 6,756
Current ratio: 0.76
Long-term debt ($ mil.): 36,825

Dividends
  Yield: 1.9%
  Payout: 62.2%
Market value ($ mil.): —

	STOCK PRICE ($) FY Close	P/E High/Low	PER SHARE ($) Earnings	Dividends	Book Value
01/18	106.60	33 20	3.28	2.04	26.38
01/17	66.74	17 14	4.38	2.00	25.52
01/16	66.36	19 12	4.57	1.96	25.47
01/15	84.98	18 14	5.05	1.92	25.21
01/14	74.68	17 14	4.88	1.88	23.59
Annual Growth	**9.3%**	**— —**	**(9.5%)**	**2.1%**	**2.8%**

Washington Federal Inc

Washington Federal is the holding company for Washington Federal Savings which operates about 190 branches in eight western states. The thrift which was founded in 1917 collects deposits from consumers and business by offering standard products such as CDs IRAs and checking savings and money market accounts. With these funds the bank mainly originates single-family residential mortgages which account for nearly three-quarters of its loan portfolio. The bank also writes business consumer construction land and multifamily residential loans. Washington Federal sells life home and auto coverage to individuals and businesses through its First Insurance Agency subsidiary.

Operations

In addition to its consumer and commercial banking operations Washington Federal has four wholly-owned subsidiaries: First Insurance Agency which offers a full line of individual and business insurance products to its customers and others; Statewide Mortgage Services Co. which holds about $18.6 million of real estate held for investment (REHI); Washington Services which also holds and markets REHI; and First Mutual Sales Finance a servicer of consumer loans.

Geographic Reach

As its name suggests Washington State is Washington Federal's largest market. Oregon and Arizona are other major markets for the bank.

Financial Performance

Washington Federal's fiscal 2012 (ends September) revenue fell by about 9.5% vs. the previous year due to a decrease both interest and non-interest income. Total interest income which accounts for about 97% of WF's total revenue declined 8% on fewer loans mortgage-backed securities and investment securities and cash equivalents. Other income fell 36%. With the exception of fiscal 2010 which saw a slight gain in revenue WF's revenue has been declining for several years. Net income increased 24% in fiscal 2012 vs. the prior year due to overall lower credit costs.

Strategy

Small relative to its national bank competitors Washington Federal has been building its business through acquisitions adding new markets and growing in established ones. Acquisitions have included both healthy smaller rivals and failed banks seized by regulators. In a bid to unify its brand and increase its name recognition WF rebrands acquired banks under its own moniker.

The bank is also working through its portfolio of nonperforming loans which peaked during the height of the recession in 2009 but now are on the decline.

Mergers and Acquisitions

In 2017 Washington Federal agreed to acquire Anchor Bancorp for $63.9 million. The combined company will have 248 offices in eight states in the Western US and total assets of $15.3 billion.

EXECUTIVES

Chairman, Roy M. Whitehead, age 65, $765,179 total compensation
President And Ceo, Brent J. Beardall, age 46, $390,925 total compensation
Svp And Cfo, Vincent L. Beatty, age 59
Evp And Chief Credit Officer, Mark A. Schoonover, age 59, $335,259 total compensation
Utah And Nevada Regional President, Marlise G. Fisher
Southern Oregon Regional President, Peggy L. Hobin
Evp And Cio, Angela D. Veksler, age 56
Northern Washington Regional President, Tom Kenney
Western Idaho Regional President, Tom Van Hemelryck
Northern Oregon Regional President, Gary Haines
Arizona Regional President, Mike Brown
New Mexico Regional President, Bill Synnamon
Southern Washington Regional President, Greg Toso
Texas Regional President, Tony Barnard
Executive Vice President, Jack Jacobson
Vice President, John Iasonides
Vice President, Jeff Birkelo
Account Vice President Wholesale Lending Manager, Robert Boehlke
Vice President Operations Manager, Keri Hall
Assistant Vice President Human Resources Administrator, Lori Szallar
Auditors: DELOITTE & TOUCHE LLP

LOCATIONS

HQ: Washington Federal Inc
425 Pike Street, Seattle, WA 98101
Phone: 206 624-7930
Web: www.washingtonfederal.com

Selected Markets
Arizona
Idaho
Nevada
New Mexico
Oregon
Texas
Utah
Washington

PRODUCTS/OPERATIONS

2013 Sales

	$ mil.	% of total
Interest		
Loans	430	73
Mortgage-backed securities	80	14
Investment securities	22	4
Other income		
Deposit fee income	14	3
Loan fee income	7	1
Others	8	2
Total	**564**	**100**

COMPETITORS

Bank of America	Washington Banking
Banner Corp	Wells Fargo
KeyCorp	Zions Bancorporation
U.S. Bancorp	

HISTORICAL FINANCIALS

Company Type: Public

Income Statement

FYE: September 30

	ASSETS ($ mil.)	NET INCOME ($ mil.)	INCOME AS % OF ASSETS	EMPLOYEES
09/18	15,865	203	1.3%	1,877
09/17	15,253	173	1.1%	1,818
09/16	14,888	164	1.1%	1,806
09/15	14,568	160	1.1%	1,838
09/14	14,756	157	1.1%	1,909
Annual Growth	1.8%	6.7%	—	(0.4%)

2018 Year-End Financials

Debt ratio: —	No. of shares (mil.): 82
Return on equity: 10.19%	Dividends
Cash ($ mil.): 268	Yield: 0.0%
Current ratio: —	Payout: 27.9%
Long-term debt ($ mil.): —	Market value ($ mil.): 2,647

	STOCK PRICE ($) FY Close	P/E High/Low	Earnings	Dividends	Book Value
09/18	32.00	16 13	2.40	0.67	24.14
09/17	33.65	18 14	1.94	0.84	23.00
09/16	26.68	15 11	1.78	0.55	22.03
09/15	22.75	14 12	1.67	0.54	21.04
09/14	20.36	15 13	1.55	0.41	20.05
Annual Growth	12.0%	— —	11.6%	13.1%	4.8%

Washington Trust Bancorp, Inc.

Without seeming naive Washington Trust Bancorp can utter Washington and trust in the same breath. The holding company owns The Washington Trust Company one of the oldest and largest banks in Rhode Island and one of the oldest banks in the entire US. Chartered in 1800 the bank boasts over $3.5 billion in assets and operates nearly 20 branches in the state and one in southeastern Connecticut. Washington Trust offers standard services such as deposit accounts CDs and credit cards. The company's commercial mortgages and loans account for more than half of its loan portfolio while residential mortgages and consumer loans make up most of the rest. The bank also offers wealth management services.

Operations

Around one-third of the bank's loan portfolio was made up of commercial real estate loans in 2014 while business loans made up another 21%.

About 60% of Washington Trust's total revenue came from loan interest (including fees) in 2014 while another 7% came from interest on its taxable and tax-exempt investment securities. The rest of its revenue came from wealth management income (18%) deposit account charges (2%) card interchange fees (2%) merchant processing fees (1%) and other miscellaneous income sources. The bank had a staff of 590 employees at the end of 2014.

Washington Trust's wealth management division includes Washington Trust Investors Weston Financial and 1800 Asset Management. The division offers financial planning investment management and trust services and has more than $4 billion of assets under administration.

Geographic Reach

Of its nearly 20 branches 10 of its branches are located in Southern Rhode Island (Washington County) nearly 10 branches are in the greater Providence area and one branch is in southeastern Connecticut. The company's commercial lending office in Providence and six residential mortgage lending offices in eastern Massachusetts (Sharon Burlington and Braintree); Glastonbury and Darien Connecticut; and Warwick Rhode Island.

Financial Performance

Washington Trust has struggled to consistently grow its revenues in recent years due to shrinking interest margins on loans amidst the low-interest environment. Its profits however have been rising thanks to declining interest expenses and falling loan loss provisions as its loan portfolio's credit quality has improved with higher property valuations in the strengthened economy.

The bank's revenue inched higher by 1% to $180 million in 2014 mostly as its interest income grew with higher average loan balances.

Higher revenue in 2014 combined with lower interest expenses on deposits lower loan loss provisions and lower non-interest expenses boosted Washington Trust's net income higher by 13% to $40.8 million for the year. The company's operating cash levels fell to half the levels of the prior year to $2.7 million after adjusting its earnings for non-cash items mostly related to its mortgage banking net loan proceeds.

Strategy

Washington Trust Bank has been growing its loan and deposit business organically by opening new branches and loan production offices in its target markets. In early 2015 it opened a new branch in Rumford making it the bank's second location in East Providence. In 2014 it opened a branch in Johnston Rhode Island and furthered its expansion into Connecticut with the opening of a new mortgage office in Glastonbury Connecticut.

The company also pursues acquisitions to expand its service offerings extend its reach into new geographic markets and bolster its existing business lines.

Mergers and Acquisitions

In 2015 Washington Trust purchased SEC-registered investment advisory firm Halsey Associates which added more than $850 million in assets under management to its Wealth Management business' books. Acquiring the New Haven Connecticut-based firm also expanded its reach in the Connecticut and metropolitan New York region.

EXECUTIVES

Vice President And Retail Lending Officer The Washington Trust Company, Linda S Smith
Vice Chair Secretary And Cfo, David V. Devault, age 64, $299,731 total compensation

Chairman And Ceo, Joseph J. (Joe) MarcAurele, $514,596 total compensation
Evp And Chief Lending Officer Of The Bank, James Hagerty
President And Coo, Edward O. (Ned) Handy, $385,000 total compensation
Evp Wealth Management And Treasurer, Mark K. W. Gim, $239,462 total compensation
Executive Vice President Of Retail Lending Of The Bank, Stephen Bessette
Auditors: KPMG LLP

LOCATIONS

HQ: Washington Trust Bancorp, Inc.
23 Broad Street, Westerly, RI 02891
Phone: 401 348-1200
Web: www.washtrust.com

PRODUCTS/OPERATIONS

2014 Sales

	$ mil.	% of total
Interest		
Loans including fees	107	60
Securities	12	7
Other	0	-
Non-interest		
Wealth management services	33	18
Loan sales & commissions	6.8	4
Gain on sale of business line	6	3
Service charges on deposit accounts	3	2
Other	9	6
Total	**180**	**100**

COMPETITORS

Bank of America	People's United
Citizens Financial	Financial
Group	Sovereign Bank
Liberty Bank	Webster Financial

HISTORICAL FINANCIALS

Company Type: Public

Income Statement

FYE: December 31

	ASSETS ($ mil.)	NET INCOME ($ mil.)	INCOME AS % OF ASSETS	EMPLOYEES
12/17	4,529	45	1.0%	600
12/16	4,381	46	1.1%	596
12/15	3,771	43	1.2%	582
12/14	3,586	40	1.1%	590
12/13	3,188	36	1.1%	570
Annual Growth	9.2%	6.2%	—	1.3%

2017 Year-End Financials

Debt ratio: 0.50%	No. of shares (mil.): 17
Return on equity: 11.42%	Dividends
Cash ($ mil.): 79	Yield: 0.0%
Current ratio: —	Payout: 58.3%
Long-term debt ($ mil.): —	Market value ($ mil.): 917

	STOCK PRICE ($) FY Close	P/E High/Low	Earnings	Dividends	Book Value
12/17	53.25	22 18	2.64	1.54	23.99
12/16	56.05	21 13	2.70	1.46	22.76
12/15	39.52	16 14	2.54	1.36	22.06
12/14	40.18	17 13	2.41	1.22	20.68
12/13	37.22	17 12	2.16	1.03	19.84
Annual Growth	9.4%	— —	5.1%	10.6%	4.9%

Waste Management, Inc. (DE)

Holding company Waste Management tops the heap in the US solid-waste industry. Through subsidiaries the company serves more than 30 million residential industrial municipal and commercial customers in the US and Canada. Waste Management provides waste collection transfer recycling and resource recovery and disposal services. Its sites include more than 250 owned or operated landfills (the industry's largest network) more than 300 transfer stations and around 100 material recovery facilities. Collection services account for nearly two-thirds of sales.

HISTORY

In 1956 Dean Buntrock joined his in-laws' business Ace Scavenger Service an Illinois company that Buntrock expanded into Wisconsin.

Waste Management Inc. was formed in 1971 when Buntrock joined forces with his cousin Wayne Huizenga who had purchased two waste routes in Florida in 1962. In the 1970s Waste Management bought companies in Michigan New York Ohio Pennsylvania and Canada. By 1975 it had an international subsidiary.

The company divided into specialty areas by forming Chemical Waste Management (1975) and offering site-cleanup services (ENRAC 1980) and low-level nuclear-waste disposal (Chem-Nuclear Systems 1982).

USA Waste was founded in 1987 to run disposal and collection operations in Oklahoma. It went public in 1988 and in 1990 Don Moorehead a founder and former CEO of Mid-American Waste Systems bought a controlling interest (most of which he later sold). Moorehead moved the business to Dallas and began buying companies in the fragmented industry. John Drury a former president of Browning-Ferris joined USA Waste in 1994 as CEO.

As USA Waste gathered steam Waste Management got off track. It diversified and Buntrock renamed the company WMX Technologies in 1993 to de-emphasize its waste operations. In 1997 however the company reverted to the Waste Management name and pressured by disappointed investor George Soros CEO Phillip Rooney resigned. After more management changes turnaround specialist Steve Miller became CEO the fourth one in eight months and Buntrock retired.

USA Waste picked up market share with large acquisitions including Envirofill (1994) Chambers Development Corporation (1995) and Western Waste Industries and Sanifill (1996). In 1996 the company moved to Houston. During the next two years it bought United Waste Systems Mid-American Waste the Canadian operations of Allied Waste and Waste Management and TransAmerican Waste Industries .

1998 saw the $20 billion merger between USA Waste and Waste Management. The new company bearing the Waste Management name and led by Drury and other former USA Waste executives controlled nearly a quarter of North America's waste business. The company finished the year by agreeing to pay shareholders $220 million in a suit over overstated earnings.

The new Waste Management bought Eastern Environmental Services for $1.3 billion in 1999. (A legal battle over negotiations between Eastern and Waste Management executives was settled out of court in 2000.) Drury took leave in 1999 because of an illness that would claim his life and director Ralph Whitworth known as a shareholder activist stepped in as acting chairman.

The company faced shareholder lawsuits after it was reported that executives had sold shares before a second-quarter earnings shortfall was announced. Waste Management said it would investigate the sales; later so did the SEC. (By 2001 the company had settled with both the SEC and shareholders.) In the fallout president and COO Rodney Proto who had sold shares before the earnings announcement was fired. Later that year the company tapped Maury Myers CEO of trucking company Yellow Corp. to take over as chairman and CEO.

In 2000 to concentrate on its core business in North America Waste Management sold operations in Europe Asia and South America in a series of transactions that raised about $2.5 billion. The next year the company established a pulp and paper trading group.

Waste Management announced plans in early 2002 to restructure the company by reorganizing its operating areas and cutting its workforce of 57000 by about 3.5%. Also that year the SEC sued six former Waste Management executives charging that they had enriched themselves through accounting fraud between 1992 and 1997.

The company formed a new recycling unit Recycle America Alliance in 2003 after acquiring Milwaukee-based The Peltz Group the largest privately held recycler in the US. The company also acquired 75 complementary collection businesses for about $337 million and divested some operations for about $18 million. That year two former executives of Waste Management Proto and CFO Earl DeFrates agreed to a settlement with the SEC on allegations that they had profited from insider trading in 1999.

In a bid to consolidate its leadership position in the US waste market in 2008 the company made a bid to acquire Republic Services but was rebuffed.

In 2009 the company acquired PharmEcology Associates a national pharmaceutical waste management consulting services firm and Mountain High Medical Disposal Services. In 2010 it added some medical waste assets from MedServe following that company's acquisition by Stericycle. It also acquired a medical waste processing facility and other assets from Milum Textile Services in Phoenix.

In 2010 it invested in Canadian waste-to-biofuels company Enerkem. Further expanding its "green" businesses the company acquired control of Garick LLC a leading maker and distributor of organic lawn and garden products. The deal helped grow Waste Management's organics recycling services business.

In 2011 it bought Access Computer Products a leading provider of cell phone ink and toner cartridge and consumer electronics reverse logistics remarketing and recycling services and acquired three recycling facilities in Maryland and Virginia in a separate deal.

Also that year Waste Management picked up Connecticut-based Oakleaf Global Holdings and its operations for $425 million. The unit manages a North American network of some 2500 operators who provide hauling disposal waste diversion and recycling services.

In 2012 the company removed a management layer in its four geographic groups consolidated and reduced its geographic areas from 22 to 17 and eliminated some 700 positions.

Expanding its recycling portfolio and supporting its efforts to manage 20 million tons of recyclable material in 2013 Waste Management acquired Greenstar LLC from NTR plc for $170 million.

Greenstar manages some 1.5 million tons of material through a dozen material recovery facilities.

That year the company acquired Summit Energy Services and Liquid Logistics two Williston North Dakota-based energy services companies. The acquisitions enhance Waste Management's environmental service offerings to oil and gas industry customers working in the Bakken Shale.

EXECUTIVES

Evp And Coo, James E. Trevathan, age 65, $676,885 total compensation
Svp Field Operations, Jeff M. Harris, age 64, $608,846 total compensation
Svp Technology Logistics And Customer Service And Cio, Puneet Bhasin, age 55
President And Ceo, James C. (Jim) Fish, age 56, $705,996 total compensation
Svp Field Operations, John J. Morris, age 48, $593,462 total compensation
Svp Cfo And Treasurer, Devina A. Rankin
Senior Vice President, Don Carpenter
Vice President Innovation And Business Optimization, David Murphy
Vice President Business Development And Sports Marketing, Steve Ness
Vice President Strategic Business Solutions, Paul Foody
Vice President Information Technology, Gail Trafton
Vice President Tax, Mark Lockett
Senior Vice President Of Operations For Waste Management, Charles Williams
Vice President Business Development, Joe Cassin
Vp Finance, Gregg Hassler
Vice President Commercial Lines Underwriting, Mary Fisher
Vice President Customer Service, Katy Lydon
Senior Vice President And Chief Digital Officer, Nikolaj Sjoqvist
Vice President Information Technology, Michele Newell
Vice President Market Area, Pittman Alec
Vice President Area, Tim Wells
National Account Manager, Timothy Fraumann
Vice President And Chief Accounting Officer Waste Management, Darren Shade
Vice President Business Development, Dan Grosshauser
Area Vice President, Steve Batchelor
Vice President Public Affairs, Chuck Dees
Chairman, Bradbury H. (Brad) Anderson, age 67
Assistant Treasurer And Director Investor Relations, Ed Egl
Board Of Directors, Christine Chisholm-krosnicki
Auditors: Ernst & Young LLP

LOCATIONS

HQ: Waste Management, Inc. (DE)
1001 Fannin Street, Houston, TX 77002
Phone: 713 512-6200   **Fax:** 713 512-6299
Web: www.wm.com

2016 Sales

	$ mil.	% of total
US & Puerto Rico	12,915	95
Canada	694	5
Total	**13,609**	**100**

PRODUCTS/OPERATIONS

2016 sales

	$ mil.	% of total
Collection	8,802	54
Landfill	3,110	19
Transfer	1,512	9
Recycling	1,221	8
Other	1,601	10
Adjustments	(2637)	-
Total	**13,609**	**100**

Selected Services

Collection
Disposal
Hazardous waste management
Landfill management
Portable sanitation services
Recycling
Transfer stations
Treatment

Selected Mergers and Acquisitions

COMPETITORS

Casella Waste Systems	WCA Waste
Republic Services	Waste Connections
Rumpke	Waste Connections US
Safety-Kleen	

HISTORICAL FINANCIALS

Company Type: Public

Income Statement

FYE: December 31

	REVENUE ($ mil.)	NET INCOME ($ mil.)	NET PROFIT MARGIN	EMPLOYEES
12/17	14,485	1,949	13.5%	42,300
12/16	13,609	1,182	8.7%	41,200
12/15	12,961	753	5.8%	40,600
12/14	13,996	1,298	9.3%	39,800
12/13	13,983	98	0.7%	42,700
Annual Growth	0.9%	111.2%	—	(0.2%)

2017 Year-End Financials

Debt ratio: 43.48%
Return on equity: 34.45%
Cash ($ mil.): 22
Current ratio: 0.80
Long-term debt ($ mil.): 8,752

No. of shares (mil.): 433
Dividends
 Yield: 0.0%
 Payout: 38.5%
Market value ($ mil.): 37,395

	STOCK PRICE ($) FY Close	P/E High/Low		Earnings	PER SHARE ($) Dividends	Book Value
12/17	86.30	19	16	4.41	1.70	13.89
12/16	70.91	27	19	2.65	1.64	12.06
12/15	53.37	33	28	1.65	1.54	11.95
12/14	51.32	18	14	2.79	1.50	12.79
12/13	44.87	220	161	0.21	1.46	12.29
Annual Growth	17.8%	—	—	114.1%	3.9%	3.1%

Waterstone Financial Inc (MD)

Auditors: RSM US LLP

LOCATIONS

HQ: Waterstone Financial Inc (MD)
 11200 W. Plank Court, Wauwatosa, WI 53226
Phone: 414 761-1000
Web: www.wsbonline.com

HISTORICAL FINANCIALS

Company Type: Public

Income Statement

FYE: December 31

	ASSETS ($ mil.)	NET INCOME ($ mil.)	INCOME AS % OF ASSETS	EMPLOYEES
12/17	1,806	25	1.4%	927
12/16	1,790	25	1.4%	895
12/15	1,762	16	0.9%	770
12/14	1,783	12	0.7%	731
12/13	1,947	14	0.8%	849
Annual Growth	(1.9%)	15.3%	—	2.2%

2017 Year-End Financials

Debt ratio: —
Return on equity: 6.31%
Cash ($ mil.): 31
Current ratio: —
Long-term debt ($ mil.): —

No. of shares (mil.): 29
Dividends
 Yield: 0.0%
 Payout: 105.3%
Market value ($ mil.): 503

	STOCK PRICE ($) FY Close	P/E High/Low		Earnings	PER SHARE ($) Dividends	Book Value
12/17	17.05	21	18	0.93	0.98	13.97
12/16	18.40	20	14	0.93	0.26	13.95
12/15	14.10	25	22	0.56	0.20	13.33
12/14	13.15	34	27	0.38	0.15	13.08
12/13	11.10	27	15	0.43	0.00	6.84
Annual Growth	11.3%	—	—	21.3%	—	19.5%

Wayfair Inc

Auditors: Ernst & Young LLP

LOCATIONS

HQ: Wayfair Inc
 4 Copley Place, 7th Floor, Boston, MA 02116
Phone: 617 532-6100
Web: www.wayfair.com

HISTORICAL FINANCIALS

Company Type: Public

Income Statement

FYE: December 31

	REVENUE ($ mil.)	NET INCOME ($ mil.)	NET PROFIT MARGIN	EMPLOYEES
12/17	4,720	(244)	—	7,751
12/16	3,380	(194)	—	5,637
12/15	2,249	(77)	—	3,809
12/14	1,318	(148)	—	2,353
12/13	915	(15)	—	2,104
Annual Growth	50.7%	—	—	38.5%

2017 Year-End Financials

Debt ratio: 34.24%
Return on equity: (-1,575.36%)
Cash ($ mil.): 558
Current ratio: 1.10
Long-term debt ($ mil.): 415

No. of shares (mil.): 88
Dividends
 Yield: —
 Payout: —
Market value ($ mil.): 7,081

	STOCK PRICE ($) FY Close	P/E High/Low		Earnings	PER SHARE ($) Dividends	Book Value
12/17	80.27	—	—	(2.81)	0.00	(0.55)
12/16	35.05	—	—	(2.29)	0.00	0.92
12/15	47.62	—	—	(0.92)	0.00	2.88
12/14	19.85	—	—	(2.97)	0.00	3.67
Annual Growth	41.8%	—	—	—	—	—

Webster Financial Corp (Waterbury, Conn)

Webster Financial is the holding company for Webster Bank which operates about 170 branches in southern New England primarily in Connecticut but also in Massachusetts New York and Rhode Island. The bank provides commercial and retail services such as deposit accounts loans and mortgages and consumer finance as well as government and institutional banking services. It performs asset-based lending through its Webster Business Credit subsidiary and equipment financing through Webster Capital Finance. The company's HSA Bank division offers health savings accounts nationwide. Webster Bank provides brokerage and investment services through an agreement with UVEST a division of LPL Financial.

Operations

Webster Financial operates in three segments: Commercial Banking HSA Bank and Community Banking.

Commercial Banking provides lending deposit and treasury and payment services.

Community Banking services consist of personal and business banking. It operates about 170 banking centers more than 330 ATMs a customer care center and web and mobile banking services.

HSA Bank is focused on health savings accounts as well as providing health reimbursement arrangements flexible spending and commuter benefit account administration services to employers and individuals in all 50 states.

Geographic Reach

Webster's largest market is Connecticut with about 115 branches. Massachusetts has about 35 branches; Rhode Island about 10; and New York fewer than 10. Customers can conduct transactions at some 330 ATMs across throughout New England.

Financial Performance

Webster Financial's revenue and net income have appreciated in recent years. In 2017 the bank's revenue rose to $1.05 billion from $983 million in 2016 while net income rose to $255 million from $207 million.

Webster credited strong loan growth funded with growth in low-cost long-duration HSA deposits for achieving higher net interest margin in 2017. Net interest income increased about $78 million while provision for loan and lease losses dropped about $15 million. The bank reported that non-interest expense rose about $38 million and that it had one-time gain of about $7 million on the sale of an asset in 2016.

Strategy

Webster focuses on building its community banking and health savings account businesses. Tthe community banking unit is expansion in several metro areas led by Boston where the bank is on pace to meet its goal of $1 billion in new deposits and $500 million in loans over five years. While it faces fierce pricing competition in the Boston market it sees steady deposit growth in the core franchise there.

In the HSA Bank business Webster has invested in sales staff which helped drive compensation costs about $27 million higher in 2017 from 2016 and relationship management to gather new clients. The investment seems to be paying off with growth in clients and deposits and some $6 billion under administration. Webster uses deposits made in the HSA Bank to fund lending in its other businesses.

EXECUTIVES

Chairman And Ceo Webster Financial Corporation And Webster Bank N.a., James C. (Jim) Smith, age 68, $882,435 total compensation

Evp General Counsel And Corporate Secretary Webster Financial Corporation And Webster Bank N.a., Harriet M. Wolfe, age 64

President And Coo Webster Business Credit Corporation (wbcc), Warren K. Mino

Regional President Boston Webster Bank N.a., Paul F. Mollica

Evp And Chief Human Resources Officer Webster Financial Corporation And Webster Bank N.a., Bernard M. Garrigues, age 59

Evp And Chief Marketing Officer Webster Financial Corporation And Webster Bank N.a., Dawn C. Morris, age 50

Regional President New Haven Conn. Webster Bank N.a., Jeffrey A. (Jeff) Klaus

President Webster Financial Corporation And Webster Bank N.a., John R. Ciulla, age 52, $363,479 total compensation

Evp And Head Of Community Banking, Nitin J. Mhatre, age 47, $358,521 total compensation

Evp And Cfo Webster Financial Corporation And Webster Bank N.a., Glenn I. MacInnes, age 56, $453,310 total compensation

Evp And Cio Webster Financial Corporation And Webster Bank N.a., Colin D. Eccles, age 59

Evp Consumer Deposits Investments And Network Management Webster Bank N.a., David D. Miree

Evp And Chief Risk Officer Webster Financial Corporation And Webster Bank N.a., Daniel H. Bley, age 49

Evp And Head Of Private Banking Webster Financial Corporation And Webster Bank N.a., Daniel M. (Dan) FitzPatrick, age 59, $300,000 total compensation

Evp Commercial Real Estate, William E. Wrang

Evp Webster Financial Corporation And Webster Bank N.a. And Head Of Hsa Bank, Charles L. (Chad) Wilkins, age 56

Regional President Metro New York, Abby Parsonnet

Regional President Southern Massachusetts And Rhode Island Webster Bank N.a., Douglas E. (Doug) Scala

Regional President Waterbury Conn. Webster Bank N.a., Michael L. (Mike) O'Connor

Regional President For Pennsylvania Webster Bank N.a., Scott C. Meves

Regional President Hartford Conn. Webster Bank N.a., Timothy D. Bergstrom

Evp Middle Market Banking Webster Bank N.a., Christopher J. (Chris) Motl

Vice President Human Resources Technology, Chris Muller

Vice President Small Business Banking, Larry Levitts

Vice President Corporate Facilities Operations, Mark Nisbett

Assistant Vice President Information Tec, Mary Robichaud

Vice President Marketing, Joanne Renna

Senior Vice President, Denise Hall

Vice President Ebanking, Chris Barlow

Vice President External Communications, Sarah Barr

Senior Vice President Continuous Improvement Unit Leader, Chris Rowe

Vice President Of Information Technology, Joel Wolak

Vice President Database, Jennifer Zbell

Vice President Finance, Shelly Abdella

Vice President Commercial Banking, Joe Pelliccia

Vice President Accounting, Lynn Ryan

Vice Chairman Webster Financial Corporation And Webster Bank N.a., Joseph J. (Joe) Savage, age 65

Board Member, Lauren States

Board Member, Elizabeth Flynn

Board Member, William Atwell

Auditors: KPMG LLP

LOCATIONS

HQ: Webster Financial Corp (Waterbury, Conn)
145 Bank Street, Waterbury, CT 06702
Phone: 203 578-2202
Web: www.websterbank.com

2017 Bank Branches

	No.
Connecticut	115
Massachusetts	35
Rhode Island	10
New York	7
Total	**167**

PRODUCTS/OPERATIONS

2017 Sales

	$ mil.	% of total
Interest		
Interest and fees on loans and leases	708	57
Taxable interest and dividends on securities	181	17
Non-taxable interest on securities	22	2
Loans held for sale	1	.
Non-interest		
Deposit service fees	151	13
Loan and lease related fees	26	3
Wealth and investment services	31	3
Mortgage banking activities	9	1
Increase in cash surrender value of life insurance policies	14	1
Gain on sale of investment securities net —	-	
Impairment loss on securities recognized in earnings	(0.13)	.
Other income	26	3
Total	**1,055**	**100**

COMPETITORS

Bank of America	New England Bancshares
Citibank	Patriot National
Citizens Financial Group	Bancorp
Fairfield County Bank	People's United Financial
First Connecticut Bancorp	SBT Bancorp Inc.
JPMorgan Chase	SI Financial
KeyCorp	TD Bank USA
Liberty Bank	Washington Trust Bancorp

HISTORICAL FINANCIALS

Company Type: Public

Income Statement

FYE: December 31

	ASSETS ($ mil.)	NET INCOME ($ mil.)	INCOME AS % OF ASSETS	EMPLOYEES
12/17	26,487	255	1.0%	3,302
12/16	26,072	207	0.8%	3,168
12/15	24,677	206	0.8%	2,946
12/14	22,533	199	0.9%	2,764
12/13	20,853	179	0.9%	2,744
Annual Growth	**6.2%**	**9.2%**	**—**	**4.7%**

2017 Year-End Financials

Debt ratio: 0.85%
Return on equity: 9.77%
Cash ($ mil.): 256
Current ratio: —
Long-term debt ($ mil.): —

No. of shares (mil.): 92
Dividends
Yield: 0.0%
Payout: 38.5%
Market value ($ mil.): 5,168

	STOCK PRICE ($) FY Close	P/E High/Low	PER SHARE ($) Earnings	Dividends	Book Value
12/17	56.16	22 17	2.67	1.03	29.36
12/16	54.28	25 14	2.16	0.98	27.54
12/15	37.19	19 13	2.15	0.89	26.38
12/14	32.53	16 13	2.08	0.75	25.70
12/13	31.18	16 11	1.86	0.55	24.56
Annual Growth	**15.8%**	**— —**	**9.5%**	**17.0%**	**4.6%**

WEC Energy Group Inc

WEC Energy Group keeps the lights illuminated and the gas fires burning for 4.4 million customers in four upper Midwest states. The utility holding company serves energy through its seven regulated utilities. It is one of the largest natural gas distributors in the US and even provides steam (for heating) to a few hundred customers in Milwaukee WI. It owns 8600 MW of electric generation capacity and thousands of miles of natural gas distribution and electrical transmission lines. The former Wisconsin Energy acquired for $9 billion Integrys Energy in mid-2015 and renamed the combined entity WEC Energy Group.

Operations

WEC Energy Group operates four reportable segments: Wisconsin Illinois Other States and Electric Transmission. Embedded within the segments WEC records the operations and results of its regulated utility companies.

The Wisconsin segment accounts for about 80% of total revenue and includes the electric and natural gas utility operations of Wisconsin Electric (WE) Wisconsin Gas and Wisconsin Public Service Corporation (WPS). The segment also included WE's and WPS's electric and natural gas operations in Michigan until it spun them into the separate Upper Michigan Energy Resources utility in early 2017. The segment generates and transmits electric energy and distributes natural gas to some 3 million customers.

The Illinois segment produces about 15% of WEC revenue and includes the natural gas utility and non-utility operations of The Peoples Gas Light and Coke Company (PGL) and North Shore Gas Company (NSG). PGL and NSG provide energy to Chicago and its northern suburbs. PGL also owns and operates a 38 Bcf natural gas storage facility in central Illinois.

The Other States segment includes the natural gas utility and non-utility operations of Minnesota Energy Resources Corporation (MERC) and Michigan Gas Utilities Corporation (MGU).

WEC holds approximately 60% of the in American Transmission Company LLC which owns maintains monitors and operates electric transmission systems throughout WEC?s service territory. These operations are recorded in WEC?s Electric Transmission segment and contribute between $60 million and $140 million in annual equity earnings.

WEC serves Wisconsin Illinois Michigan and Minnesota with roughly 69000 miles of electric distribution lines and more than 45000 miles of natural gas distribution and transmission lines. The company generates two thirds of its energy needs and purchases the rest through power purchase agreements. Of its owned plants about 50% of energy is sourced from coal 20% from natural gas and 4% from renewables. Most of the purchased power is nuclear sourced.

Geographic Reach

WEC Energy Group has customers throughout Wisconsin though most are in the eastern portion of the state. It serves customers in southern Michigan and in that state?s Upper Peninsula. It also provides energy in and around Chicago and in various portions of Minnesota.

Its power generation plants are located throughout Wisconsin.

Sales and Marketing

The company serves retail customers through its regulated utility operations. It also serves wholesale customers through unregulated sales of electricity. Most of its sales are to retail customers which include residential farming commercial business and industrial clients.

Financial Performance

WEC Energy produced steady financial results in recent years with revenue ranging between $4.1 billion and $5.0 billion and net income gradually climbing. The acquisition of Integrys in 2015 spiked both revenue and net income for that year and the next.

In 2016 revenue reached $7.5 billion up 26% from the prior year. The increase was largely due to the inclusion of Integrys revenue though warmer summer weather triggered additional cooling needs by retail customers.

The 2016 the company achieved $940 million in net income a 47% jump from 2015. The increase was the result of higher revenue (from Integrys) a favorable comparison against 2015?s acquisition costs (about $100 million) and a $50 million boost from WEC?s equity interest in American Transmission Company. Lower fuel costs helped as well but was almost completely offset by a rise in operating expenses.

Cash at the end of 2016 was $37 million $12 million lower than the prior year?s amount. Operating activities provided $2.1 billion mainly from net income and deferred taxes. Investing activities used $1.2 billion mostly for capital improvement projects. Financing activities used $845 million to retire debt repurchase company stock shares and payout shareholder dividends.

Strategy

WEC is trying to modernizing its electric grid extending gas operations and addressing the push towards renewable energy sources. It is focusing on opportunities to deploy capital in renewable energy assets.

The company is on schedule to retire 1800 MW of coal-sourced generation by 2020 including its Pulliam Power Plant Edgewater 4 facility and Presque Isle Power Plant. It will replace some of that lost power with natural gas-fueled plants in Michigan and Wisconsin and with solar facilities. In 2019 the company acquired an 80% ownership interest in Coyote Ridge Wind Farm in South Dakota for $145 million. The site will be operated by Avangrid and has a long-term offtake agreement with Google Energy.

In early 2016 WEC divested components that were either acquired via Integrys or no longer fit into the company's business mix. It sold the ITF business a provider of compressed natural gas (CNG) fueling services as well as a provider of CNG facility design construction operation and maintenance. It also sold its Milwaukee County (steam) Power Plant and its chilled water generation and distribution assets in early 2016. In 2017 it acquired a natural gas storage facility in Michigan and formed the Upper Michigan Energy Resources utility into which WEC placed its utility operations serving the state's Upper Peninsula.

WEC's more typical strategic endeavors stem from its capital expenditure plan. Between 2018 and 2022 the firm plans to invest $11.8 billion across its operations. $2.7 billion is earmarked for its generation assets including buildout of new gas and renewable power plants. A similar amount is targeted for electric distribution operations to expand its transmissions reach and to modernize its grid. Gas delivery will get the largest investment at $5.5 billion including funding to replace 2000 miles of aging natural gas pipeline in and around Chicago.

Mergers and Acquisitions

In a major move in 2015 Wisconsin Energy acquired rival Integrys Energy in a transaction valued at $9.1 billion. The deal established WEC Energy Group as the energy leader serving the Midwestern US.

EXECUTIVES

Chairman Wec Energy Group Inc. And Wisconsin Electric Power Company, Gale E. Klappa, age 68, $589,043 total compensation

President Ceo And Director, Allen L. Leverett, age 52, $941,667 total compensation

Evp General Counsel And Corporate Secretary Wisconsin Energy Corp And We Energies, Susan H. Martin, age 65, $515,000 total compensation

Evp External Affairs, Robert M. (Bert) Garvin, age 51, $416,120 total compensation

Evp And President Michigan Gas Utilities Minnesota Energy Resources Corp. Wec Business Services Llc, J. Patrick Keyes, age 52, $546,400 total compensation

Evp And Cfo, Scott J. Lauber, age 52, $351,784 total compensation

President Â– We Energies And Wisconsin Public Service, J. Kevin Fletcher, age 59, $411,345 total compensation

President And Ceo Peoples Gas And North Shore Gas, Charles R. Matthews, age 61

President Wispark Llc, Jerold P. Franke

Evp Human Resources And Organizational Effectiveness And Compliance Officer, Joan M. Shafer, age 64

Vp And Cio, Molly Mulroy

Evp We Energies And Wisconsin Public Service, Tom Metcalfe, age 50

Vice President Chief Administrative Officer, Kristine Rappe

Auditors: DELOITTE & TOUCHE LLP

LOCATIONS

HQ: WEC Energy Group Inc
231 West Michigan Street, P.O. Box 1331, Milwaukee, WI 53201
Phone: 414 221-2345   **Fax:** 414 221-2172
Web: www.wisconsinenergy.com

PRODUCTS/OPERATIONS

2016 sales

	$ mil.	% of total
Wisconsin	5,805	78
Illinois	1,242	17
other States	376	5
We Power	24	-
Corporate and others	23	-
Total	**7,472**	**100**

Selected Subsidiaries

American Transmission Company LLC (partial ownership)
Michigan Gas utilities Corporation
Minnesota Energy Resources Corporation
North Shore Gas Company
The Peoples Gas Light and Coke Company
Upper Michigan Energy Resources
W.E. Power LLC (We Power regulated power plant construction)
Wisconsin Electric Power Company (operates as We Energies electric gas and steam utility)
Wisconsin Gas LLC (operates as We Energies gas and water utility)
Wisconsin Public Service Corporation
Wispark LLC (real estate development)

COMPETITORS

AEP	MGE Energy
ALLETE	Minnesota Power
Alliant Energy	SEMCO ENERGY
CMS Energy	Wisconsin Power &
Commonwealth Edison	Light
DTE	Xcel Energy
Dairyland Power	

HISTORICAL FINANCIALS

Company Type: Public

Income Statement

FYE: December 31

	REVENUE ($ mil.)	NET INCOME ($ mil.)	NET PROFIT MARGIN	EMPLOYEES
12/17	7,648	1,204	15.8%	8,129
12/16	7,472	940	12.6%	8,164
12/15	5,926	640	10.8%	8,443
12/14	4,997	588	11.8%	4,248
12/13	4,519	577	12.8%	4,303
Annual Growth	**14.1%**	**20.2%**	**—**	**17.2%**

2017 Year-End Financials

Debt ratio: 34.93%	No. of shares (mil.): 315
Return on equity: 13.06%	Dividends
Cash ($ mil.): 38	Yield: 0.0%
Current ratio: 0.57	Payout: 54.8%
Long-term debt ($ mil.): 8,746	Market value ($ mil.): 20,964

	STOCK PRICE ($) FY Close	P/E High/Low		PER SHARE ($) Earnings	Dividends	Book Value
12/17	66.43	18	15	3.79	2.08	30.08
12/16	58.65	22	17	2.96	1.98	28.39
12/15	51.31	24	19	2.34	1.74	27.51
12/14	52.74	21	15	2.59	1.56	19.73
12/13	41.34	18	15	2.51	1.45	18.87
Annual Growth	**12.6%**	—	—	**10.9%**	**9.5%**	**12.4%**

WellCare Health Plans Inc

WellCare Health Plans provides managed-care administrative services to government-funded health care programs that provide benefits via Medicaid Medicare and various State Children's Health Insurance Programs (SCHIPs). Its services include benefits management and claims processing. WellCare administers its Medicaid plans under various brands such as Care1st in Arizona Staywell in Florida; WellCare in Georgia Kentucky New York New Jersey and South Carolina; Harmony in Illinois; Missouri Care in Missouri; and 'Ohana in Hawaii. The company's Medicare prescription-drug and Medicare Advantage (MA) plans operate primarily under the WellCare brand. Altogether WellCare serves some 4.4 million customers throughout the US.

Operations

WellCare offers a range of health plans for families children and the aged blind and disabled. It also offers prescription drug plans. The company operates through three segments: Medicaid Health Plans Medicare Health Plans and Medicare PDPs.

Medicaid Health Plans is the largest segment bringing in some 65% of total revenue. Its offerings include plans for beneficiaries of Temporary Assistance for Needy Families (TANF) Aged Blind and Disabled (ABD) Supplemental Security Income (SSI) and other state programs that are not a part of Medicaid. The segment primarily generates revenues from state-paid premiums.

The Medicare Health Plans segment accounts for more than 30% of WellCare's revenues. It offers hospital medical and prescription coverage to eligible customers aged 65 or older or with disabilities. The company contracts with the Centers for Medicare & Medicaid Services (CMS) under the

Medicare program to provide a comprehensive array of Part C and Part D benefits to eligible persons. WellCare offers Medicare Advantage plans in nearly 500 counties across 17 states.

The smallest segment Medicare PDPs (about 5% of revenue) offers standalone Part D coverage. It works with a network of approximately 69000 pharmacies.

WellCare serves some 4.4 million members nationwide. About 2.7 million customers are Medicaid members (including SCHIP members) in six states and some 2.3 million of those are recipients of TANF benefits. The company also serves nearly 500000 Medicare Advantage members who are largely enrolled in HMO coordinated care plans (CCPs) in 17 states. WellCare also serves about 1.2 million Medicare prescription members throughout the US.

Geographic Reach

WellCare operates throughout the US. Its largest markets are Florida and Georgia which account for about 20% and 15% of annual membership respectively followed by Kentucky (more than 10%).

The company operates Medicaid health plans in Arizona Florida Georgia Hawaii Illinois Kentucky Missouri Nebraska New Jersey New York South Carolina and Texas. It also offers MA coordinated care plans (CCPs) in certain areas of Arizona Arkansas California Connecticut Florida Georgia Hawaii Illinois Kentucky Louisiana Maine Mississippi New Jersey New York South Carolina Tennessee and Texas.

Sales and Marketing

WellCare contracts with state Medicaid agencies to expand its operations; it also enters new Medicare markets through both organic growth and acquisition efforts.

The company contracts with medical providers to provide services to its members. It contracts with nearly 430000 health care providers and pharmacies to provide members with access to necessary services.

WellCare also promotes services to consumers through minimal advertising campaigns.

Financial Performance

WellCare's revenue has risen over the past five years due to membership growth decreased legal expenses and successfully implemented cost-control efforts. In 2017 revenue rose 19% to a record $17 billion as a result of growth across all three business lines plus added income from the acquisitions of Universal American and Care1st Arizona. Organic customer growth in Nebraska and Missouri as well as business gained through the Universal American purchase helped boost the company's membership by 12% that year.

Net income fell in 2014 but has been rising since. With the higher revenue net income rose 54% to $373.7 million in 2017. Improvements in operating margins also contributed to the higher profits. Like revenue operating cash flow has been increasing for the past few years. It rose 40% to $1.1 billion in 2017 thanks to the higher net income and changes in working capital.

Strategy

WellCare focuses on serving lower income individuals and those who are dually eligible for Medicaid and Medicare. The company also aims to add more members to its Part D prescription plans. Among its key strategies are providing integrated care management (bringing together medical behavioral social and pharmacy programs) and connecting members to community-based resources such as food banks and child care. For example its Georgia subsidiary partnered with behavioral health provider Georgia HOPE to open a behavioral health home in 2017. The company also strives to build regulatory and provider partnerships in each of its local markets.

To maintain growth WellCare works to diversify its sources of revenue through its "bid build and buy" initiatives. Growth through "bidding" and "building" is focused on creation of the marketing network community support and other capabilities required to expand organically into new service areas. In one example of a recent win WellCare began offering Medicaid management services under Nebraska's Medicaid Managed Care program Heritage Health in 2017. Also that year the company expanded its Medicaid value-added benefits in Georgia. Acquiring businesses with important market and/or product positions — the "buy" element — has supplemented its organic growth. The company's "bid build and buy" efforts have resulted in a significant increase in the company's revenues since 2010.

On the tech side WellCare is developing two artificial intelligence platforms to help deliver medical data to providers and patients. They will use company records and user data to determine when patients might be at risk for certain conditions. Its Care Plan customer-facing system should be rolled out nationwide by 2018.

Although the company has seen rising revenues over the past few years its rising debt (topping $1 billion) has cut into the bottom line.

Additionally as WellCare's Medicaid operations are concentrated in about a dozen states the company is vulnerable to losses of contracts. Its largest markets are Kentucky and Florida (a high-stakes market with a massive Medicaid program) and it faces stiff competition for business in those states. Furthermore states such as Kentucky are tightening budgets which could result in a reduction in funding.

Mergers and Acquisitions

Expanding further in the Medicare Advantage market WellCare acquired Meridian Health Plan for $2.5 billion in 2018. The deal included Meridian Health Plan of Michigan Meridian Health Plan of Illinois and pharmacy benefit manager MeridianRx. Later that year WellCare bought insurance giant Aetna's entire standalone Medicare Part D business which covers 2.2 million members.

At the beginning of 2017 WellCare acquired Care1st Health Plan Arizona and its One Care unit adding some 115000 Medicaid and Medicare members in Arizona. That deal marked the firm's entrance into another Medicaid state. Later that year the company bought smaller rival Universal American which specializes in providing Medicare Advantage coverage for $600 million. That deal added some 119000 Medicare Advantage members primarily in Texas Maine and New York.

In 2016 WellCare bought certain assets of managed care organization Advicare which serves Medicaid members in South Carolina. That purchase aligned with the firm's strategy of deepening its presence in existing markets.

EXECUTIVES

Ceo And Director, Kenneth A. (Ken) Burdick, age 59, $1,000,000 total compensation

Svp And Division President Connecticut Hawaii Illinois Kentucky Missouri New Jersey New York And Nebraska, Dave Reynolds

Svp Medicare And Operations, Michael R. (Mike) Polen, age 38, $440,385 total compensation

Svp And Division President, Gregg MacDonald

Evp And Cfo, Andrew L. (Drew) Asher, age 49, $590,385 total compensation

Evp Medicaid, Kelly A. Munson, age 46, $440,385 total compensation

Svp And Cio, Darren Ghanayem, age 48

Svp And Chief Compliance Officer, Michael C. Yount, age 42

Svp And Division President, Stephanie Davis

Evp Clinical Operations And Business Development, Michael R. (Mike) Radu, age 50, $430,000 total compensation

Vice President Pharmacy Strategy And Analytics, Yan Xiong

Vice President Corporate Actuarial Services, Lawrence Smart

Vice President, Jason Hamilton

Vice President Quality, Bill Hinsdale

Medical Director, Mauricio Molina

Vice President And Assistant General Counsel, Steve Jones

Market Vice President, Nancy Laux

Vice President Provider Communications, Jason Bollent

Vice President Chief Security And Privacy Officer, Ted Webster

Vice President Human Resources, Michael Wellman

Medical Director, David Sandh

Vice President Of Finance, Michael Lisman

Vice President Market Performance, Anthony Valdes

Vice President Field Network Management, John Greeley

Vice President Investor Relations, Angeline Mccabe

Vice President Field Health Services, Terri Flanigan

Medical Director, Brett Darwin

Vice President National Provider Contracting And Relations, Mark Fehring

Vice President And Chief Litigation Counsel, John Richter

Vice President And Chief Audit Executive, David Cure

Senior Vice President And Chro, Timothy Trodden

Vice President Field Health Services, LaDonna Battle

Vice President Government Affairs, Craig Hansen

Vice President Utilization Management, Cynthia Hallam

Vice President Field Network Management, Victoria Herzberg

Senior Vice President And Chief Medical Officer, Mark Leenay

Vice President Business Development, Scott Henderson

Vice President Behavioral Health Ops, Carole Matyas

Vice President Information Technology, Robert Klopotek

Vice President Actuary, Leo Viel

Vp Pharmacy Operations, Bill Davies

Vice President Market Performance, Vald Anthony

Chairman, Christian P. Michalik, age 50

Board Member, William Trubeck

Auditors: DELOITTE & TOUCHE LLP

LOCATIONS

HQ: WellCare Health Plans Inc
8735 Henderson Road, Renaissance One, Tampa, FL 33634
Phone: 813 290-6200
Web: www.wellcare.com

2017 Membership

	% of total
Florida	20
Georgia	13
Kentucky	11
Missouri	7
New York	7
Texas	5
Other states	37
Total	**100**

PRODUCTS/OPERATIONS

2017 Membership

	% of total
Medicaid health plans	62
Medicare PDPs	27
Medicare health plans	11
Total	**100**

2017 Sales

	$ mil.	% of total
Medicaid health plans	10,726	63
Medicare health plans	5,320	31
Medicare PDPs	913	6
Investment & other	46	-
Total	**17**	**100**

COMPETITORS

AMERIGROUP	Health First Health
Aetna	Plans
Anthem	Health Net
CIGNA	HealthSpring
Centene	Humana
Comprehensive Care	Molina Healthcare
Coventry Health Care	UnitedHealth Group
Florida Blue	

HISTORICAL FINANCIALS

Company Type: Public

Income Statement   FYE: December 31

	REVENUE ($ mil.)	NET INCOME ($ mil.)	NET PROFIT MARGIN	EMPLOYEES
12/17	17,007	373	2.2%	8,900
12/16	14,237	242	1.7%	7,400
12/15	13,890	118	0.9%	6,900
12/14	12,959	63	0.5%	6,700
12/13	9,527	175	1.8%	5,200
Annual Growth	**15.6%**	**20.8%**	**—**	**14.4%**

2017 Year-End Financials

Debt ratio: 14.14%
Return on equity: 16.92%
Cash ($ mil.): 4,198
Current ratio: 1.31
Long-term debt ($ mil.): 1,182

No. of shares (mil.): 44
Dividends
  Yield: —
  Payout: —
Market value ($ mil.): 8,954

	STOCK PRICE ($) FY Close	P/E High/Low	PER SHARE ($) Earnings	Dividends	Book Value
12/17	201.11	25 16	8.31	0.00	54.28
12/16	137.08	26 13	5.43	0.00	45.16
12/15	78.21	37 27	2.67	0.00	39.18
12/14	82.06	58 39	1.44	0.00	36.34
12/13	70.42	19 11	3.98	0.00	34.68
Annual Growth	**30.0%**	**— —**	**20.2%**	**—**	**11.8%**

Wells Fargo & Co (New)

Auditors: KPMG LLP

LOCATIONS

HQ: Wells Fargo & Co (New)
  420 Montgomery Street, San Francisco, CA 94163
Phone: 866 249-3302
Web: www.wellsfargo.com

HISTORICAL FINANCIALS

Company Type: Public

Income Statement   FYE: December 31

	ASSETS ($ mil.)	NET INCOME ($ mil.)	INCOME AS % OF ASSETS	EMPLOYEES
12/17	1,951,757	22,183	1.1%	262,700
12/16	1,930,115	21,938	1.1%	269,100
12/15	1,787,632	22,894	1.3%	264,700
12/14	1,687,155	23,057	1.4%	264,500
12/13	1,527,015	21,878	1.4%	264,900
Annual Growth	**6.3%**	**0.3%**	**—**	**(0.2%)**

2017 Year-End Financials

Debt ratio: 11.53%—
Return on equity: 10.91%
Cash ($ mil.): 216,973
Current ratio: —
Long-term debt ($ mil.): —

Dividends
  Yield: 0.0%
  Payout: 37.5%
Market value ($ mil.): —

	STOCK PRICE ($) FY Close	P/E High/Low	PER SHARE ($) Earnings	Dividends	Book Value
12/17	60.67	15 12	4.10	1.54	42.30
12/16	55.11	14 11	3.99	1.52	39.79
12/15	54.36	14 12	4.12	1.48	37.90
12/14	54.82	13 11	4.10	1.35	35.66
12/13	45.40	12 9	3.89	1.15	32.36
Annual Growth	**7.5%**	**— —**	**1.3%**	**7.6%**	**6.9%**

WesBanco Inc

WesBanco wants to be the "BesBanco" for its customers. The holding company owns WesBanco Bank which has about 210 branches in Indiana Kentucky Ohio Pennsylvania and West Virginia. In addition to providing traditional services such as deposits and loans the bank operates a wealth management department with offices in West Virginia and Ohio and some $4.7 billion of assets under management and custody including the company's proprietary WesMark mutual funds. Other units include brokerage firm WesBanco Securities and multi-line insurance provider WesBanco Insurance Services.

Operations

Commercial loans including real estate and operating loans account for more than half of of WesBanco's loan portfolio. Its retail portfolio mainly consists of home equity loans and deposit overdraft limits. The bank usually sells new residential mortgages that it originates into the secondary market. It plans to continue to grow its portfolio of commercial and industrial loans.

Strategy

WesBanco likes to purchase smaller banks to expand its reach into new geographic markets while bolstering its loan and deposit business. It's acquired more than 50 banks and financial services firms in the past 25 years.

Mergers and Acquisitions

In 2018 WesBanco acquired Kentucky-based Farmers Capital Bank Corporation for $429.8 million and West Virginia-based First Sentry Bancshares for $107.5 million.

In 2016 the company expanded into Kentucky and southern Indiana when it acquired Your Community Bank.

EXECUTIVES

Evp Treasury And Strategic Planning, Brent E. Richmond, age 55
Svp And Chief Credit Officer, Peter W. Jaworski, age 63, $212,101 total compensation
Evp And Cfo, Robert H. Young, age 62, $269,363 total compensation
President And Ceo, Todd F. Clossin, age 56, $466,923 total compensation
Svp Risk Management, Michael L. Perkins
Evp Retail Delivery, Lynn D. Asensio
Evp And Senior Operations Officer, Gregory A. Dugan
Evp Wealth Management, Jonathan D. Dargusch, age 60, $230,270 total compensation
Evp Human Resources Management, Anthony F. Pietranton

Evp And Chief Lending Officer, Jayson M. Zatta
Market President Kanawha Region, David L. Sayre
Vice President And Manager Human Resources, Sheri Clarke
Regional Vice President, Daniel Mooney
Assistant Vice President Mortgage Cra Officer, Lisa Werner
Senior Vice President Special Assets, Jodi Pagnanelli
Vice President, Tom Timmons
Vice President Commercial Real Estate, Traci Boeing
Assistant Vice President, Bruce Bandi
Vice President, Allen Retton
Vice President, Tom Medovic
Assistant Vice President Branch Operations, Beth Bussard
Senior Vice President Credit Risk Management, Edward Polli
Assistant Vice President Information Technology Services, W Terrance Naughton
Vice President Of Information Technology, Mike Robbins
Vice President Investments, Steve Kellas
Senior Vice President, Gregory Agresta
Banking Center Manager Assistant Vice President, Jodi McKnight
Senior Vice President Senior Lender, Bob Friend
Vice President And Loan Review Officer, Diane Todd
Senior Vice President And Senior Credit Officer, David Knuth
Vice President Of Commercial Banking, Michael Mistovich
Senior Vice President, Mike Lander
Assistant Vice President Branch Manager, Tom Wiggershaus
Banking Center Manager Assistant Vice President, Nicholas Beresh
Vice President Secondary Marketing Manager, Ryan Freimark
Senior Vice President Corporate Banking, Charles Wharton
Senior Vice President Enterprise Services, Jan Pattishall
Assistant Vice President, Anthony Habbit
Assistant Vice President, Dan Baxter
Senior Vice President, Dave Mendenhall
Vice President, Brent Dapper
Vice President, Michael Puzausky
Vice President, Mike Moore
Vice President, Nathan Schoetz
Assistant Vice President, Drew Correll
Vice President Business Banking, Maher-dickerson Stephanie
Vice President Commercial Banking Officer, Craig Kinslow
Vice President Private Banker, Leslie D Witzel
Vice President And Commercial Banker, Michael Epperley
Senior Vice President And Senior Commercial Banker, Michael T Misich
Vice President Commercial Lender, Robert E Krzeminski
Vice President Treasury Management Sales, Stacy Graf
Vice President Senior Trust Officer, Thomas D Barsody
Vice President, Thomas Nigon
Vice President Commercial Lending, Kurt C Bevan
Vice President And Technology Services Coordinator, Stephanie Skivington
Vice President, Dave Klick
Avp And Bcmbusiness Development Wesbanco, Michelle Donaldson
Vice President Senior Trust Officer, Thomas Barsody
Chairman, James C. (Jim) Gardill, age 72
Secretary, Cindy Dailer
Auditors: Ernst & Young LLP

LOCATIONS

HQ: WesBanco Inc
1 Bank Plaza, Wheeling, WV 26003
Phone: 304 234-9000
Web: www.wesbanco.com

PRODUCTS/OPERATIONS

2016 Sales

	$ mil.	% of total
Interest and Dividend Income		
Loans including fees	227	61
Interest and dividends on securities	56	15
Other interest income	2	1
Non-Interest Income		
Trust fees	21	6
Service charges on deposits	18	5
Electronic banking fees	15	4
Net securities brokerage	6	2
Bank-owned life insurance	4	1
Net gains on sales of mortgage loans	2	1
Net securities gains	2	1
Net gain / (loss) on other real estate owned and other assets	0	-
others	9	3
Total	**367**	**100**

Selected Products and Services

Personal Banking
Internet Banking
Checking
Savings
Time Deposits
Debit Cards
Credit Cards
Loans
Mortgage Lending
Other Services
Business
Internet Banking
Checking
Savings
Time Deposits
Credit Cards
Loans
Treasury Management
Insurance Services
Wealth Management

COMPETITORS

1st West Virginia Bancorp	Huntington Bancshares
BB&T	Ohio Valley Banc
Bank of America	PNC Financial
Cheviot Financial	United Bancorp
City Holding	United Bankshares
First Community Bancshares	

HISTORICAL FINANCIALS

Company Type: Public

Income Statement

FYE: December 31

	ASSETS ($ mil.)	NET INCOME ($ mil.)	INCOME AS % OF ASSETS	EMPLOYEES
12/17	9,816	94	1.0%	1,940
12/16	9,790	86	0.9%	1,928
12/15	8,470	80	1.0%	1,633
12/14	6,296	69	1.1%	1,448
12/13	6,144	63	1.0%	1,469
Annual Growth	**12.4%**	**10.3%**	**—**	**7.2%**

2017 Year-End Financials

Debt ratio: 1.67%	No. of shares (mil.): 44
Return on equity: 6.90%	Dividends
Cash ($ mil.): 117	Yield: 0.0%
Current ratio: —	Payout: 48.6%
Long-term debt ($ mil.): —	Market value ($ mil.): 1,790

	STOCK PRICE ($) FY Close	P/E High/Low		PER SHARE ($) Earnings	Dividends	Book Value
12/17	40.65	20	16	2.14	1.04	31.68
12/16	43.06	20	13	2.16	0.96	30.53
12/15	30.02	17	14	2.15	0.92	29.18
12/14	34.80	15	11	2.39	0.88	26.90
12/13	32.00	15	10	2.18	0.78	25.59
Annual Growth	**6.2%**	**—**	**—**	**(0.5%)**	**7.5%**	**5.5%**

Wesco International, Inc.

When contractors and manufacturers need parts it's WESCO to the rescue. The company distributes electrical products (fuses terminals connectors enclosures circuit breakers transformers switchboards) industrial supplies (tools abrasives filters safety equipment) lighting (lamps fixtures ballasts) wire and conduit materials automation equipment (motors drives logic controllers) and data communication gear (patch panels terminals connectors). WESCO offers more than a million products from some 25000 suppliers with about 75000 customers worldwide. It operates through a dozen subsidiaries. The company generates nearly all of its sales in North America predominantly the US.

Operations

WESCO divides its operations among several businesses. Automation comprises Cascade Controls EESCO RECO and W.R. Controls. Its Data Communications segment is made up of Communications Supply Corporation and TVC Communications while Industrial/Construction operates through Avon Electrical Supplies Brown Wholesale Electric Calvert Wire & Cable Liberty Electrical Supply and Whitehill Lighting and Supplies.

Integrated Supply is composed of Bruckner Supply Company and WESCO Sourcing and Procurement Services; its Industrial/Electrical OEM operations are helped by Carlton-Bates Company Fastec Industrial and J-Mark. Finally its International Operations are run through its main WESCO distribution subsidiary while its Utility segment is made up of Allied Utility Products Hamby Young Herning Enterprises Industrial Electric Supply and KVA Supply.

Geographic Reach

The company operates more than 500 branches across North America and in international markets serviced by its nine distribution centers located in the US Canada and Mexico. It boasts offices in about 15 additional countries. The US accounts for more than 75% of sales while Canada brings in roughly 20%.

Sales and Marketing

WESCO caters to 75000 customers. Sales to electrical contractors range from major industrial commercial and data communication projects to small residential contractors. Utilities and specialty utility contractors include large and rural electric cooperatives and municipal power authorities which maintain transmission distribution lines and power plants.

Commercial institutional and governmental customers include schools hospitals property management firms retailers and government agencies of all types. WESCO sells integrated lighting control and distribution equipment in a single package for multisite specialty retailers restaurant chains and department stores.

Financial Performance

WESCO's revenues have declined the last two years dipping by 2% from $7.52 billion in 2015 to $7.34 billion in 2016. Net income has also experienced a downward trend the last two years falling 51% from $211 million to $102 million during that same time period.

The declines were fueled by a 11% drop in sales from Mexico and a 9% decline in sales from Canada. This was attributed to a decrease in normalized organic sales and a negative impact of foreign exchange rates.

Strategy

WESCO has been building its business through acquisitions and organic growth. As part of this effort the company's working to develop new end markets broaden its product and service offerings expand its geographic footprint and enhance its sales and customer service.

The company is focused on its global account and integrated supply programs to boost its customer base and extend its use of supply services to customers. It targets customers in the fields of construction contracting; education; engineering procurement and construction firms; government; healthcare; and utilities. Among product growth areas WESCO looks to data communications and security systems and to clean tech lighting systems.

Mergers and Acquisitions

In recent years WESCO has been buying up distributors and other firms to extend its reach and capabilities. In 2016 it obtained Atlanta Electrical Distributors an expert in the construction and maintenance repair and operating (MRO) markets operating from five locations in Georgia. With the addition WESCO expanded its presence in this growing Southeastern end market.

In 2015 WESCO acquired Needham an electrical distributor focused on commercial construction and lighting national account markets owning 24 locations in Massachusetts New Hampshire and Vermont. Also in 2015 WESCO picked up Hill Country an electrical distributor focused on the commercial construction market operating from nine locations in Central and South Texas.

HISTORY

WESCO International got its start as a subsidiary of electrical power pioneer Westinghouse Electric Company. George Westinghouse founded the company bearing his name in Pittsburgh in 1886. The company installed the nation's first alternating current power system in Telluride Colorado in 1891. Two years later Westinghouse built the generating system that powered the Chicago World's Fair. The company also was chosen to provide generators for the hydroelectric power station at Niagara Falls.

George Westinghouse was ousted in 1910 after the company was unable to meet its debt obligations. He died four years later at the age of 67. During the next decade the company added the burgeoning radio and appliance markets to its portfolio of electrical distribution and production operations.

In 1922 the firm established Westinghouse Electric Supply Company (WESCO) to distribute power products and appliances. Westinghouse had its share of troubles over the years many of which were caused by ill-advised diversification attempts. These included forays into uranium supply financial services and real estate.

By the 1990s Westinghouse was buried under nearly $10 billion in debt and too busy putting out fires to tend to day-to-day operations properly. Not surprisingly WESCO was caught up in Westinghouse's problems: Sales declined four years in a row and employee turnover was around 25% a year.

Westinghouse embarked on a divestiture program and sold WESCO to investment firm Clayton Dubilier & Rice (CD&R) in 1994 for about $340 million. At the time WESCO had about 250 branch locations. The new owners brought in Roy Haley a veteran insurance and finance executive to turn the ailing business around. Haley tied pay and bonuses to performance and emphasized multisite customers such as contractors and companies with multiple retail industrial or administrative locations. WESCO grew through acquisitions and in 1995 sales reached $2 billion.

By 1996 the company had added 1000 employees; it operated about 300 distribution branches throughout the world. Sales reached $2.6 billion in 1997 as WESCO continued acquiring complementary companies and formed an alliance with Australian mining and steel company BHP (now BHP Billiton). Managers led a $1.1 billion buyout of the company in 1998 increasing their stake in WESCO from 15% to 33%. Costs related to acquisitions and the buyout caused WESCO to post a loss even though 1998 sales passed the $3 billion mark. The company opened sales offices in the UK Singapore and Mexico.

As it geared up for its IPO in 1999 WESCO bought distributors Industrial Electric Supply Company and Statewide Electrical Supply. The company continued to shop during 2000 adding electrical distributors Orton Utility Supply (Tennessee) Control Corporation of America (Virginia) and KVA Supply Company (Colorado and California).

In 2001 WESCO acquired two distributors (Herning Underground Supply and Alliance Utility Products) that supplied contractors who install gas lighting and communication utility infrastructure in Arizona California Utah and Washington.

The Cypress Group the private-equity firm that helped lead the $1.1 billion management buyout in 1998 sold most of its shares in WESCO in 2004 and 2005. Cypress owned nearly half of WESCO prior to those sales.

WESCO acquired fastener distributor Fastec Industrial and electronics distributor Carlton-Bates in 2005. The following year it bought Communications Supply Corporation (CSC) a distributor of low-voltage network infrastructure and industrial wire and cable products for about $525 million in cash.

In 2007 WESCO acquired J-Mark a supplier of building products which strengthened the company's position in the manufactured housing industry. It also acquired the assets of Monti Electric Supply which provides electricity and furnishes lighting. The purchase gave WESCO a broader market position in the reconstruction of the Gulf Coast region. The company sold a 60% stake in LADD which is a distributor of industrial electrical connectors and accessories to Deutsch Engineered Connecting Devices for approximately $75 million. Proceeds were earmarked to purchase shares of WESCO's common stock.

In 2008 WESCO offered to purchase Industrial Distribution Group (IDG) for about $130 million in cash topping a bid for IDG by Platinum Equity.

Roy Haley stepped aside as CEO in 2009 becoming WESCO's executive chairman. SVP/COO John Engel was promoted to president and CEO as a result.

WESCO acquired TVC Communications for about $246 million in late 2010. The deal expanded WESCO's broadband and telecom distribution network in the Americas and its ties to manufacturers.

EXECUTIVES

Chairman President And Ceo, John J. Engel, age 56, $974,519 total compensation

Svp And Chief Human Resources Officer, Kimberly G. Windrow, age 60, $399,615 total compensation

Svp And Cfo, David S (Dave) Schulz, age 52, $109,375 total compensation

Svp And General Counsel, Diane E. Lazzaris, age 51, $435,096 total compensation

Vice President Of Evening Operations, Joseph Astroth

Vp And General Manager Wesco Interrated Supply And Manufactured Structures, Sean Nacey

Vice President Information Systems, John Conte

National Sales Manager, Bryan Devito

Vice President Of Operations And Supply Chains, Edward Jankowski

Vice President Sales And Marketing, Frank LaPlante

Vice President Tax, Domenic Macioce

Senior Vice President Sales And Marketing, Ken Olsen

Vice President Global Supply Chain And Operations, Hemant Porwal

Vice President And Global Chief Information Officer, Rob Minicozzi

Vice President Investor Relations, Mary Bell

Board Member, John Morgan

Auditors: PricewaterhouseCoopers LLP

LOCATIONS

HQ: Wesco International, Inc.
225 West Station Square Drive, Suite 700, Pittsburgh, PA 15219
Phone: 412 454-2200
Web: www.wesco.com

2016 Sales

	$ mil.	% of total
US	5,635	77
Canada	1,394	19
Mexico	62	1
Other countries	243	3
Total	**7,336**	**100**

PRODUCTS/OPERATIONS

2016 Sales

	% of total
Industrial customers	36
Construction	34
Utility	16
Commercial institutional & governmental customers	14
Total	**100**

Selected Services

Collaborative cross-functional cost savings teams;
Consultation on energy-efficient product upgrades
Dedicated on-site support personnel;
Inventory optimization programs including just-in-time delivery and vendor managed inventory;
Safety and product training for customer employee
Technical support for operational and transactional process improvements;

Selected Products

Automation equipment
Ballasts
Boxes
Busways
Cable
Circuit breakers
Connectors
Data communications products
Drives
Electrical products
Fittings
Fixtures
Fuses
Industrial supplies
Light bulbs
Lighting
Lugs

Metallic and nonmetallic conduits
Motor control devices
MRO supplies
Operator interfaces
Panelboards
Patch panels
Premise wiring
Programmable logic controllers
Pushbuttons
Switchboards
Tape
Terminals
Tools
Transformers
Wire
Wire and conduit products

COMPETITORS

Anixter International	HWC
Bearing Distributors	McNaughton-McKay
Border States Electric	Premier Farnell
Consolidated Electrical	Rexel Inc.
Electro-Wire	Richardson Electronics
Electrocomponents	SUMMIT Electric Supply
Graybar Electric	Sonepar USA
	W.W. Grainger

HISTORICAL FINANCIALS

Company Type: Public

Income Statement
FYE: December 31

	REVENUE ($ mil.)	NET INCOME ($ mil.)	NET PROFIT MARGIN	EMPLOYEES
12/17	7,679	163	2.1%	9,100
12/16	7,336	101	1.4%	9,000
12/15	7,518	210	2.8%	9,300
12/14	7,889	275	3.5%	9,400
12/13	7,513	276	3.7%	9,200
Annual Growth	0.5%	(12.3%)	—	(0.3%)

2017 Year-End Financials

Debt ratio: 28.48%
Return on equity: 7.91%
Cash ($ mil.): 117
Current ratio: 2.31
Long-term debt ($ mil.): 1,313

No. of shares (mil.): 47
Dividends
　Yield: —
　Payout: —
Market value ($ mil.): 3,204

	STOCK PRICE ($) FY Close	P/E High/Low	Earnings	Dividends	Book Value
12/17	68.15	22 15	3.38	0.00	45.09
12/16	66.55	31 16	2.10	0.00	41.42
12/15	43.68	16 8	4.18	0.00	42.13
12/14	76.21	15 11	5.18	0.00	43.35
12/13	91.07	15 10	5.25	0.00	39.87
Annual Growth	(7.0%)	— —	(10.4%)	—	3.1%

West Bancorporation, Inc.

West Bancorporation is the holding company for West Bank which serves individuals and small to midsized businesses through about a dozen branches mainly in the Des Moines and Iowa City Iowa areas. Founded in 1893 the bank offers checking savings and money market accounts CDs Visa credit cards and trust services. The bank's lending activities primarily consist of commercial mortgages; construction land and land development loans; and business loans such as revolving lines of credit inventory and accounts receivable financing equipment financing and capital expenditure loans to borrowers in Iowa.

Sales and Marketing
West Bank focuses on small to medium-sized businesses in its local markets. The thinking is that smaller local firms want to develop an exclusive relationship with a single bank.

Financial Performance
The company's revenue has been remarkably consistent year-over-year. It reported $61.2 million in annual revenue for fiscal 2013 after claiming $61.7 million in fiscal 2012 and $64.1 million in fiscal 2011.

Net income has also remained very consistent in recent years. The bank reported net income of $16.8 million for fiscal 2013 after clearing $16 million in fiscal 2012 and $15.27 million in fiscal 2011.

The company's net cash on hand has decreased dramatically in recent fiscal years however mostly as a result of property investments.

Strategy
West Bank has slowly but surely been expanding its territory. The company is working on building a new headquarters building and expanding into Minnesota.

EXECUTIVES

Evp; President West Bank, Brad L. Winterbottom, age 62, $275,000 total compensation

Evp Cfo And Treasurer, Douglas R. (Doug) Gulling, age 65, $275,000 total compensation

President And Ceo, David D. (Dave) Nelson, age 58, $400,000 total compensation

Evp And Chief Risk Officer, Harlee N. Olafson, age 61, $275,000 total compensation

Vice President, Donavon Paulson

Vice President, Nancy Behmer

Senior Vice President, Keith Kurth

Chairman, David R. Milligan

Auditors: RSM US LLP

LOCATIONS

HQ: West Bancorporation, Inc.
1601 22nd Street, West Des Moines, IA 50266
Phone: 515 222-2300
Web: www.westbankstrong.com

PRODUCTS/OPERATIONS

2015 Sales

	$ mil.	% of total
Interest		
Loans including fees	52	77
Taxable investment Securities	4	6
Tax-exempt investment Securities	3	5
Federal funds sold	0	-
Noninterest		
Service charges on deposit accounts	2	4
Debit card usage fees	1	3
Trust services	1	2
Revenue from residential mortgage banking	0	-
Increase in cash value of bank-owned life insurance	0	1
Realized investment securities gains net	0	-
Other income	1	2
Total	**68**	**100**

COMPETITORS

BTC Financial	Regions Financial
Bank of America	U.S. Bancorp
Bank of the West	Wells Fargo
MidWestOne	

HISTORICAL FINANCIALS
Company Type: Public

Income Statement
FYE: December 31

	ASSETS ($ mil.)	NET INCOME ($ mil.)	INCOME AS % OF ASSETS	EMPLOYEES
12/17	2,114	23	1.1%	162
12/16	1,854	23	1.2%	165
12/15	1,748	21	1.2%	174
12/14	1,615	20	1.2%	178
12/13	1,442	16	1.2%	187
Annual Growth	**10.0%**	**8.1%**	**—**	**(3.5%)**

2017 Year-End Financials

Debt ratio: 2.05%	No. of shares (mil.): 16
Return on equity: 13.43%	Dividends
Cash ($ mil.): 34	Yield: 0.0%
Current ratio: —	Payout: 50.3%
Long-term debt ($ mil.): —	Market value ($ mil.): 408

	STOCK PRICE ($) FY Close	P/E High/Low	PER SHARE ($) Earnings	Dividends	Book Value
12/17	25.15	20 15	1.41	0.71	10.98
12/16	24.70	17 11	1.42	0.67	10.25
12/15	19.75	15 12	1.35	0.62	9.49
12/14	17.02	14 11	1.25	0.49	8.75
12/13	15.82	16 10	1.02	0.42	7.74
Annual Growth	**12.3%**	**—**	**8.4%**	**14.0%**	**9.1%**

WestAmerica Bancorporation

Annie get your checkbook? Maybe not as wild as Buffalo Bill's West but Westamerica Bancorporation still shoots high with its subsidiary Westamerica Bank. The bank operates almost 100 branches in Northern and Central California. It offers individuals and businesses such standard fare as checking and savings accounts as well as electronic banking trust services and credit cards. It focuses on the banking needs of small businesses; business loans and commercial mortgages together account for more than half of the company's loan portfolio. Westamerica Bank chartered in 1884 also originates construction residential mortgage and consumer loans.

Operations
Westamerica Bancorporation provides a full range of banking services to individual and corporate customers through its subsidiary bank Westamerica Bank.

Westamerica Bank subsidiary Community Banker Services Corporation provides the company and its other subsidiaries with data processing and various support services.

Geographic Reach
The bank has 95 branches and 2 trust offices in 21 Northern and Central California counties. Westamerica owns 33 branch office locations and one administrative facility and leases 70 facilities.

Financial Performance
In 2012 the company had assets of $5 billion deposits of $4.2 billion and shareholders' equity of $560.1 million

Revenues declined by 10% in 2012 due to a drop in loan revenues a decrease in ATM processing fees (due to lower transaction volumes) and loss on sale of securities.

Net income dropped by 8% in 2012 due to lower revenues partially offset by a decline in expenses.

Strategy
Westamerica's conservative lending practices (it avoided the clamor around subprime lending) and operating principles helped it weather the economic recession better than some of its banking peers.

Company Background
However the company's revenues and profits have fallen since 2009 when Westamerica netted a record $125 million. In 2011 net income fell 7% to $88 million (versus the $95 million it made in 2010) partly due to higher expenses as the company absorbed the operations of the recently acquired Sonoma Valley Bank. Revenues also fell 5% to $268 million. The declines were attributed to interest and fee earnings which fell as the company's lending activities slowed down and regulatory changes limited the amount of service charges banks can charge. (However both merchant processing fees and trust fees increased as those businesses grew.)

Over the years Westamerica had grown through acquisitions of other banks. In 2010 it added three branches in northern California when it acquired most of the assets and deposits of the failed Sonoma Valley Bank; the deal included loss-sharing agreements with the FDIC. That deal followed a similar transaction when the bank acquired County Bank after it was seized by regulators. That deal added nearly 40 branches to Westamerica Bank's network most of them in California's Central Valley.

EXECUTIVES

Svp Operations And Systems, Dennis R. Hansen, $130,008 total compensation

Chairman President And Ceo, David L. Payne, $371,000 total compensation

Svp And Cfo, Robert A. Thorson, $149,000 total compensation

Svp Banking Division, David L. Robinson, $150,000 total compensation

Svp Credit Administrator, Russell Rizzardi, $120,960 total compensation

Vice President Accounting Manager, Glen Yasaki

Senior Vice President, Joseph Dietzen

Executive Vice President Strategy And Development, Jennifer Finger

Vice President Of Sales, Scott Tucker

Board Member, Patrick Lynch

Board Member, Etta Allen

Auditors: Crowe Horwath LLP

LOCATIONS

HQ: WestAmerica Bancorporation
1108 Fifth Avenue, San Rafael, CA 94901
Phone: 707 863-6000
Web: www.westamerica.com

PRODUCTS/OPERATIONS

2016 Sales

	$ mil.	% of total
Interest and Fee Income:		
Loans	69	38
Investment securities available for sale	34	19
Investment securities held to maturity	30	17
Noninterest Income:		
Service charges on deposit accounts	20	12
Merchant processing services	6	4
Debit card fees	6	4
Other service fees	2	1
Trust fees	2	1
ATM processing fees	2	1
Financial services commissions	0	-
Other	4	3
Total	**180**	**100**

Bank of America
Citigroup
Comerica
First Republic (CA)
JPMorgan Chase

MUFG Americas Holdings
Mechanics Bank
U.S. Bancorp
Wells Fargo
Western Alliance

HISTORICAL FINANCIALS

Company Type: Public

Income Statement

FYE: December 31

	ASSETS ($ mil.)	NET INCOME ($ mil.)	INCOME AS % OF ASSETS	EMPLOYEES
12/17	5,513	50	0.9%	785
12/16	5,366	58	1.1%	783
12/15	5,168	58	1.1%	813
12/14	5,035	60	1.2%	858
12/13	4,847	67	1.4%	914
Annual Growth	3.3%	(7.1%)	—	(3.7%)

2017 Year-End Financials

Debt ratio: —
Return on equity: 8.69%
Cash ($ mil.): 575
Current ratio: —
Long-term debt ($ mil.): —

No. of shares (mil.): 26
Dividends
  Yield: 0.0%
  Payout: 83.0%
Market value ($ mil.): 1,574

	STOCK PRICE ($) FY Close	P/E High/Low	PER SHARE ($) Earnings	Dividends	Book Value
12/17	59.55	34 26	1.89	1.57	22.34
12/16	62.93	28 18	2.29	1.56	21.67
12/15	46.75	23 18	2.30	1.53	20.85
12/14	49.02	24 19	2.32	1.52	20.45
12/13	56.46	23 17	2.50	1.49	20.48
Annual Growth	1.3%	— —	(6.8%)	1.3%	2.2%

WESTERN & SOUTHERN FINANCIAL GROUP, INC.

While its heritage may be Western and Southern Western & Southern Financial Group covers the northern and eastern US as well. The company offers a variety of life insurance products and annuities accident and supplemental health coverage mutual funds and other investment management products and services. Western & Southern's financial services include mutual fund administration trust services financial advisory and real estate development; it owns or manages some $68 billion in assets. The company is licensed in most states and in Washington DC.

Operations

Western & Southern Financial operates more than a dozen subsidiaries that offer everything from critical illness insurance to funds and annuities. Some of the company's subsidiaries include Western & Southern Life Insurance (life and health insurance products fixed annuities) and Western-Southern Life Assurance (universal life term life and annuities). Other insurance divisions include Columbus Life Insurance Integrity Life Insurance Lafayette Life Insurance and National Integrity Life Insurance Company.

Western & Southern also operates Fort Washington Investment Advisors to manage private equity assets for corporate and government institutions and wealthy individuals; that unit has some $49 billion under management. Other financial services offerings include mutual fund management through Touchstone Investments.

The company's Eagle Realty Group participates in commercial real estate investment. Eagle Realty's current projects include upscale hotels in Cincinnati's historic Lytle Park District.

Other member companies include IFS Financial Services Peppertree Partners Touchstone Advisors Touchstone Securities W&S Financial Group Distributors and W&S Brokerage Services.

Geographic Reach

Western & Southern Financial's Western & Southern Life Insurance subsidiary operates about 140 field offices around the US.

Sales and Marketing

Western & Southern Financial markets its products and services through a sales force of direct representatives; it also sells through a network of independent agents and financial planners. Altogether its sales network comprises some 52000 licensed entities.

Western & Southern's customer base is wide and varied consisting of individuals and families of all income levels large corporations small to mid-sized businesses financial institutions real estate investors and not-for-profit entities.The group conducts advertising through television commercials.

Financial Performance

Like many conservative mutual insurers Western & Southern Financial holds a long-term investment strategy that has served it well financially. In 2015 its revenue totaled $3.3 billion a record high for the group. The following year revenue remained relatively flat falling $2.3 million to stay at $3.3 billion. Although the company's insurance premiums and product charges rose 4% that year investment income and commissions and fees saw a decline.

An increase in policyholder benefits payouts and income tax expenses led net income to decline 3% to $387.7 million in 2016.

Strategy

Over the past few decades Western & Southern Financial has transformed into a diversified financial services juggernaut buying and launching money management firms and insurance and annuity businesses. Its strategy centers around four pillars: people technology product and multi-channel access.

In terms of people Western & Southern works to create a work culture to attract the best employees at all levels.

The group is also investing in technology to enhance its services and increase data and analytics capabilities. It has recently formed internal teams to work on improving clients' digital experiences. In 2016 the primary investment arm Fort Washington expanded its data governance capabilities as well as installing a new technology platform serving its private client group.

Another way the group grows is by launching new products aimed at filling gaps in its operations. For example in 2015 W&S Financial Group Distributors launched a new variable annuity living benefit rider Guaranteed Lifetime Income Advantage Plus. It also introduced Indextra a single premium deferred fixed indexed annuity issued by Integrity Life Insurance.The following year Touchstone Investments launched two new funds.

Finally to expand multi-channel access the company seeks to reach otherwise underserved middle-market customers by extending weekend and evening sales expanding its online sales presence and providing more bilingual sales information online.

Other initiatives as of late have included streamlining its organizational structure for higher operating efficiency.

Mergers and Acquisitions

In 2017 Western & Southern Financial subsidiary Touchstone Advisors agreed to buy certain assets of Sentinel Asset Management a National Life Holding Company subsidiary. Through that deal Touchstone's assets under management will increase to $20 billion.

Western & Southern Financial completed 20 new equity investments in 2016. Its total acquisition and related development costs totaled nearly $1 billion.

Company Background
Western & Southern was founded in 1888.

EXECUTIVES

President And Ceo Fort Washington Investment Advisors Inc., Maribeth S. Rahe
Chairman President And Ceo, John F. Barrett
President Eagle Realty Group Llc, Mario J. San Marco
Vp And Chief Accounting Officer, Bradley J. Hunkler
President And Ceo National Integrity Life Insurance Company; Ceo W&s Financial Group Distributors And Touchstone Investors, Jill T. McGruder
President W&s Financial Group Distributors Inc., Mark E. Caner
President Columbus Life Insurance Company, J. J. Miller
Svp And Chief Risk Officer, David T. Henderson
President The Lafayette Life Insurance Company, Bryan C. Dunn
President Touchstone Investments, Steven M. Graziano
President Insurance Profillment Solutions Llc, Robert J. DalSanto
Svp And Cio, Karen A. Chamberlain
Svp And Chief Actuary, Daniel W. Harris
President W&s Agency Group And W&s Brokerage Services Inc., Troy D. Brodie
Svp And Co-chief Investment Officer, Roger M. Lanham
Svp And Co-chief Investment Officer, Brendan M. White
Executive Vice President, James Clark
Vice President Procurement, James Essex
Avp Human Resources, Linda Lake
Assistant Vice President And Director Internal Audit, Rod Snyder
Vice President Finance, John McElhenny
Vice President Product Management, Katie Bezold
Assistant Vice President Of Investment Operations, Eric Walzer
Vice President Tax, Dan Larsen
Avp And Director Sales Support, Anthony Gigliotti
Avp And Assistant Treasurer, Cheryl Stotts
Senior Vice President, Connie Maccarone
Vice President Human Resources, Luc Sicotte
Assistant Vice President Marketing Operations, Valerie Holmes
Senior Vice President Human Resources, Kim Chiodi
Vp And Chief Compliance Officer, Bruce Maisel
Vice President, Mike Davis
Assistant Vice President And Director Of Planning, Fsa Hussey
Assistant Vice President Information Technology Business Operations, Matt Godsted
Senior Vice President Financial Institutions Distribution Wands Financial Group Distributors, Andrew Reiss
Senior Vice President Relationship Management Wands Financial Group Distributors, Charles White
Assistant Treasurer, Doug Perry

LOCATIONS

HQ: WESTERN & SOUTHERN FINANCIAL GROUP, INC.
400 BROADWAY ST, CINCINNATI, OH 452023312
Phone: 866 832-7719
Web: WWW.WESTERNSOUTHERN.COM

PRODUCTS/OPERATIONS

2016 Revenues

	$ mil.	% of total
Net investment income	1,633	49
Insurance premiums & product charges	1,414	43
Commissions fees & other income	253	8
Total	**3,302**	**100**

Selected Subsidiaries and Affiliates

Eagle Realty Group LLC
Fort Washington Investment Advisors Inc.
IFS Financial Services Inc.
  Touchstone Advisors Inc.
  Touchstone Securities Inc.
  W&S Financial Group Distributors Inc.
Integrity Life Insurance Company
  National Integrity Life Insurance Company
The Lafayette Life Insurance Company
The Western and Southern Life Insurance Company
  Insurance Profillment Solutions LLC
  Western-Southern Life Assurance Company
  W&S Agency Group
  W&S Brokerage Services Inc.

COMPETITORS

AEGON USA	MetLife
AIG	Nationwide Financial
American General	New York Life
Great American	Northwestern Mutual
Financial Resources	Penn Mutual
Guardian Life	Phoenix Companies
Jackson National Life	Principal Financial
John Hancock Financial	Protective Life
Services	Prudential
Lincoln Financial	Securian Financial
Group	

HISTORICAL FINANCIALS

Company Type: Private

Income Statement
FYE: December 31

	ASSETS ($ mil.)	NET INCOME ($ mil.)	INCOME AS % OF ASSETS	EMPLOYEES
12/16	44,749	387	0.9%	4,000
12/15	42	0	0.9%	—
12/08	13	(3)	—	—
12/06	32	0	1.0%	—
Annual Growth	106.2%	104.3%	—	—

Western Alliance Bancorporation

Western Alliance Bancorporation and its flagship Western Alliance Bank (WAB) have an alliance with several bank brands in the West operating as the Alliance Bank of Arizona; Bank of Nevada; First Independent Bank (Nevada); as well as Bridge Bank and Torrey Pines Bank which are both located across California. Combined the banks operate nearly 50 branches that provide standard consumer and business deposit and loan products. About half of the Western Alliance's loan portfolio is made up of commercial and industrial loans while another 40% is made up of commercial real estate loans. It also makes land development loans and consumer residential mortgages and other lines of credit.

Operations

Western Alliance focuses on commercial lending. About 46% of the bank's loan portfolio consisted of commercial and industrial loans at the end of 2015 while another 39% was made up of commercial real estate loans. The bank also had construction and land development loans (10% of loan assets) residential mortgages (3%) commercial leases (1%) and consumer loans (less than 1%).

More than 90% of the bank's revenue comes from interest income. About 86% of its total revenue came from loan interest during 2015 while another 9% came from interest or dividends on investment securities. The remainder of its revenue came from service charges and fees (2% of revenue) card income (1%) and other miscellaneous sources.

Geographic Reach

Western Alliance's 40 branches and seven loan offices are spread across Arizona Nevada and California as well as Boston Dallas and Reston Virginia. At the end of 2015 its loan business was concentrated in the Los Angeles San Francisco San Jose Phoenix Tuscon Reno and Las Vegas metropolitan areas.

Sales and Marketing

The bank serves local businesses real estate developers and investors not-for-profit organizations and consumers. It specializes in lending to such customers operating in the healthcare professional services manufacturing and distribution resorts and timeshares technology and startups municipalities and local governments non-profit and renewable energy markets. Some of its clients (as of early 2016) include Cutter Aviation FNF Construction Hollenbeck Palms New American Funding and Signature Healthcare Services.

Western Alliance spent $2.89 million on marketing in 2015 up from $2.30 million and $2.58 million in 2014 and 2013 respectively.

Financial Performance

Western Alliance's annual revenues have risen nearly 70% since 2011 as its loan business has swelled. Meanwhile the bank's annual profits have ballooned more than five-fold as its credit portfolio's credit quality has improved with higher property valuations in the strengthened economy.

The group's revenue jumped 26% to $555 million during 2015 mostly thanks to new loan business more than half of which was obtained from the Bridge Bank acquisition which spurred more interest income for the year. Non-interest income especially service charges and lending-related fees grew by double digits during the year also thanks to the acquisition as well as from more organic deposit business growth.

Strong revenue growth and a continued decline in credit loss provisions in 2015 drove Western Alliance's net income up by 31% to $194 million for the year. The company's operating cash levels climbed 30% to $213 million mostly thanks to the rise in cash earnings.

Strategy

Western Alliance Bancorporation looks to expand its branch network and selectively acquire other banks to boost its loan and deposit business and extend its geographic reach. The bank may also buy other financial services businesses to bolster its line of service offerings.

Mergers and Acquisitions

In June 2015 Western Alliance bought $13 billion-asset Bridge Capital Holdings along with its 48 Bridge Bank branches in California Arizona and Nevada in a deal worth about $425 million. The purchase brought expertise in technology and international banking among other areas and expands Western Alliance's market into Northern California.

EXECUTIVES

Evp And Chief Credit Officer, Robert R. (Bob) McAuslan, age 65
Chairman And Ceo, Robert G. Sarver, age 57, $800,000 total compensation
Evp And Cfo, Dale M. Gibbons, age 57, $400,000 total compensation
Evp Northern California Administration And President And Ceo Bridge Bank Division, Daniel P. (Dan) Myers, age 57, $212,885 total compensation
Evp Southern Nevada Administration And Ceo Bank Of Nevada Division, John Guedry
Evp And Cio, John P. Peckham
Evp California Administration And President Torrey Pines Bank, Gerald A. (Gary) Cady, age 63, $360,000 total compensation
Evp And Chief Risk Officer, Patricia A. Taylor
Evp And General Counsel, Randall S. Theisen
Evp And Coo, Jim Haught
Evp Arizona Administration And Ceo Alliance Bank Of Arizona, Don Garner
Auditors: RSM US LLP

LOCATIONS

HQ: Western Alliance Bancorporation
One E. Washington Street, Suite 1400, Phoenix, AZ 85004
Phone: 602 389-3500
Web: www.westernalliancebancorporation.com

PRODUCTS/OPERATIONS

2015 Sales

	% of total
Interest income	
Loans including fees	86
Investment securities	7
Dividends	2
Other	-
Non-interest income	
Service charges and fees	2
Income from bank owned life insurance	1
Card income	1
Other	1
Total	**100**

Selected Services

Business Checking & Savings
Business Loans & Credit
Card Services
International Banking
Personal Banking
Treasury Management

COMPETITORS

Bank of America	PacWest Bancorp
Bank of the West	U.S. Bancorp
Desert Schools FCU	Wells Fargo
First Banks	Westamerica
MUFG Americas Holdings	Zions Bancorporation

HISTORICAL FINANCIALS

Company Type: Public

Income Statement
FYE: December 31

	ASSETS ($ mil.)	NET INCOME ($ mil.)	INCOME AS % OF ASSETS	EMPLOYEES
12/17	20,329	325	1.6%	1,725
12/16	17,200	259	1.5%	1,557
12/15	14,275	194	1.4%	1,446
12/14	10,600	147	1.4%	1,131
12/13	9,307	114	1.2%	1,051
Annual Growth	21.6%	29.8%	—	13.2%

2017 Year-End Financials

Debt ratio: 1.85%
Return on equity: 15.80%
Cash ($ mil.): 416
Current ratio: —
Long-term debt ($ mil.): —

No. of shares (mil.): 105
Dividends
  Yield: —
  Payout: —
Market value ($ mil.): 5,973

	STOCK PRICE ($) FY Close	P/E High/Low	PER SHARE ($) Earnings	Dividends	Book Value
12/17	56.62	19 14	3.10	0.00	21.14
12/16	48.71	20 11	2.50	0.00	18.00
12/15	35.86	19 12	2.03	0.00	15.44
12/14	27.80	17 12	1.67	0.00	11.29
12/13	23.86	19 8	1.31	0.00	9.81
Annual Growth	24.1%	— —	24.0%	—	21.2%

Western Digital Corp

When it comes to data storage Western Digital has drive and more than a splash of flash. The company is one of the largest independent makers of hard-disk drives (HDDs) which record store and recall volumes of data. It is also active in the fast-growing area of solid-state drives (SSDs). Drives for PCs account for a major portion of Western Digital's sales although the company also makes devices used in servers cloud computing data centers and home entertainment products such as set-top boxes and video game consoles. The company sells to manufacturers and through retailers and distributors. It generates more than half its sales from the Asia/Pacific region.

Operations

Western Digital reports its sales in terms of end markets. The company's biggest market nearly 50% of sales is client devices such as PCs smartphones gaming gadgets and security equipment. Data center devices high-capacity enterprise HDDs and high-performance enterprise SSDs data center software and systems account for about 30% of sales and client solutions which are external memory such as USB flash drives and wireless drives generate about 20% of sales.

Geographic Reach

Western Digital's largest market is Asia (which represents more than half of sales including more than 20% in China and about 20% in Hong Kong). The US is Western Digital's second biggest market accounting for about 20% of revenue. The EMEA region accounts for less 20%.

Western Digital has manufacturing facilities in the US as well as in China Japan Malaysia the Philippines Singapore and Thailand; it has sales offices worldwide. Its research and development facilities are in the US Malaysia Thailand India and Israel.

Sales and Marketing

Western Digital sells to OEMs as well as through distributors and retailers. The company's 10 biggest customers account for more than 40% of revenue. Two customers Apple Inc. and Dell Technologies each account for more than 10% of Western Digital's accounts receivable.

Financial Performance

Western Digital added a second year of revenue growth in 2018 (ended June) after ending a three-year revenue decline in 2017 with a 47% increase. Revenue rose 8% to $20.6 billion in 2018 a $1.5 billion increase from the previous year. Net income grew a robust 70% in 2018 from 2017 outpacing the 64% profit increase in 2017 from 2016.

Sales increased across Western Digital's segments in 2018 from 2017 led by a 6% increase in Client Devices (half of the company's revenue) from growth in embedded flash products. Sales rose 10% in Data Center Devices and Solutions and Client Solutions.

Profit jumped $675 million in 2018 from $497 million in 2017 on higher revenue and reduced research and development expenses while absorbing about a $1 billion increase in income taxes due to the US Tax Cuts and Jobs Act of 2017.

Western Digital's cash and equivalents dropped to $5 billion 2018 about $1.3 billion less than it had in 2017. Cash from operation was $4.2 billion in 2018 while the company used about $1.6 billion in investing activities and $3.9 billion in investing activities. In 2018 the company reduced the aggregate principal of its debt by $1.98 billion and reduced its interest cost.

Strategy

Western Digital took steps to reduce costs and consolidate hard disk drive operation closing a manufacturing facility in Malaysia and putting its HDD operations into Thailand. The process should be completed by the end of its 2019 fiscal year (June) and cost about $160 million.

With extensive operations in Asia Western Digital is susceptible to tariffs set in the course of trade disputes between the US and China. Tariffs could prompt customers may delay or reduce purchases and they could lead to a deterioration in economic conditions.

Mergers and Acquisitions

Western Digital has long used acquisitions to add new product lines and extend its geographic reach.

In 2017 Western Digital made two deals in short order acquiring UpThere a developer of cloud storage systems and Tegile Systems a maker of flash storage announcing the deals of the same day. UpThere makes apps for storing and accessing date in the cloud and making it available from multiple devices and operating systems. With Tegile Western Digital extends its reach into enterprise data storage. Tegile's IntelliFlash products offer quick access to match Western Digital's dig data programs. Western Digital also gains 1700 new customers from the deal.

EXECUTIVES

Evp Memory Technology, Siva Sivaram
Cto, Martin Fink, age 53
President And Ceo, Stephen D. (Steve) Milligan, age 55, $1,050,000 total compensation
Evp Silicon Operations, Manish Bhatia
President And Coo, Michael D. Cordano, age 54, $725,000 total compensation
Evp And Cfo, Mark P. Long, age 51, $500,000 total compensation
Evp And Chief Human Resources Officer, Jacqueline M. DeMaria, age 56
Evp Chief Legal Officer And Secretary, Michael C. Ray, age 51, $500,000 total compensation
Vice President Facilities Asia, Shahzad Mahmud
Vice President, Vince Mastropietro
Vice President Gm Of Manufacturing Head Operations, Norm Armour
Executive Vice President Andchief Technology Officer, Steven Campbell
Vice President Engineering Director Engineering, Gerardo Bertero
Vice President Information Technology, Terry Dembitz
Vice President Marketing, Joan Wrabetz
Vice President Platform Engineering, Kurt Chan
Svp And Cto (fio) Vp And Senior Fellow (sndk)(wdc), Pankaj Mehra
Chairman, Matthew E. (Matt) Massengill, age 57
Auditors: KPMG LLP

LOCATIONS

HQ: Western Digital Corp
5601 Great Oaks Parkway, San Jose, CA 95119
Phone: 408 717-6000
Web: www.westerndigital.com

2018 Sales

	$ mil.	% of total
Asia		
China	4,393	22
Hong Kong	4,022	20
Rest of Asia	2,752	13
US	4,640	22
Europe Middle East & Africa	3,858	19
Other	982	5
Total	**20,647**	**100**

PRODUCTS/OPERATIONS

2018 Sales by Market

	% of total
Client Devices	49
Data Center Devices and Solutions	29
Client Solutions	22
Total	**100**

Selected Products

Portable Storage
Personal Cloud Storage
External Storage
Internal Hard Drive Storage
Internal SSD Storage
Network Attached Storage
Internal Hard Drives for Business
Surveillance Storage

COMPETITORS

Apple Inc.
Dell
Fujitsu
Intel
LaCie
Micron Technology
Roku
SK Hynix

SMART Modular Technologies
Samsung Electronics
Sanmina
Seagate Technology
TEAC
Toshiba

HISTORICAL FINANCIALS

Company Type: Public

Income Statement

FYE: June 29

	REVENUE ($ mil.)	NET INCOME ($ mil.)	NET PROFIT MARGIN	EMPLOYEES
06/18	20,647	675	3.3%	71,600
06/17*	19,093	397	2.1%	68,000
07/16	12,994	242	1.9%	72,878
07/15	14,572	1,465	10.1%	76,449
06/14	15,130	1,617	10.7%	84,072
Annual Growth	8.1%	(19.6%)	—	(3.9%)

*Fiscal year change

2018 Year-End Financials

Debt ratio: 38.21%
Return on equity: 5.90%
Cash ($ mil.): 5,005
Current ratio: 2.39
Long-term debt ($ mil.): 10,993

No. of shares (mil.): 296
Dividends
  Yield: 2.5%
  Payout: 338.9%
Market value ($ mil.): 22,913

	STOCK PRICE ($) FY Close	P/E High/Low	PER SHARE ($) Earnings	Dividends	Book Value
06/18	77.41	47 34	2.20	2.00	38.96
06/17*	88.60	68 31	1.34	2.00	38.84
07/16	46.47	86 35	1.00	2.00	39.24
07/15	80.87	18 12	6.18	1.80	40.08
06/14	92.90	14 9	6.68	1.25	37.79
Annual Growth	(4.5%)	— —	(24.2%)	12.5%	0.8%

*Fiscal year change

Western New England Bancorp Inc

EXECUTIVES

Vice President; Residential Loan Officer, Deborah McCarthy

Assistant Vice President Financial Services, Libiszewski Darlene

Auditors: Wolf & Company, P.C.

LOCATIONS

HQ: Western New England Bancorp Inc
141 Elm Street, Westfield, MA 01085
Phone: 413 568-1911
Web: www.westfieldbank.com

COMPETITORS

Bank of America
Citizens Financial
  Group
Sovereign Bank
TD Bank USA

HISTORICAL FINANCIALS

Company Type: Public

Income Statement

FYE: December 31

	ASSETS ($ mil.)	NET INCOME ($ mil.)	INCOME AS % OF ASSETS	EMPLOYEES
12/17	2,083	12	0.6%	317
12/16	2,076	4	0.2%	310
12/15	1,339	5	0.4%	195
12/14	1,320	6	0.5%	200
12/13	1,276	6	0.5%	201
Annual Growth	13.0%	16.2%		12.1%

2017 Year-End Financials

Debt ratio: 7.91%
Return on equity: 5.07%
Cash ($ mil.): 26
Current ratio: —
Long-term debt ($ mil.): —

No. of shares (mil.): 30
Dividends
  Yield: 0.0%
  Payout: 29.2%
Market value ($ mil.): 332

	STOCK PRICE ($) FY Close	P/E High/Low	PER SHARE ($) Earnings	Dividends	Book Value
12/17	10.90	27 22	0.41	0.12	8.11
12/16	9.35	38 30	0.24	0.03	7.85
12/15	8.40	25 22	0.33	0.12	7.63
12/14	7.34	23 20	0.34	0.21	7.61
12/13	7.46	23 19	0.34	0.29	7.65
Annual Growth	9.9%	— —	4.8%	(19.8%)	1.5%

Western Union Co

Though the joy of receiving a singing telegram is mired in the dusty past of yesteryear you may still jump for joy at the receipt of a Western Union money transfer. The company provides in-person and electronic means to swiftly send remittances within and across country borders managing currency exchanges as needed. It achieves this with a global network of some 550000 agent locations in more than 200 countries. While the US is its largest single market most of its revenue originates elsewhere. Western Union agents work out of kiosks located in a variety of businesses including post offices banks and grocery stores.

Operations

Western Union operates three main segments: Consumer-to-Consumer (C2C) Consumer-to-Business (C2B) and Business Solutions.

The C2C provides money transfer services around the world through a network of third-party agents who fulfill transactions in nearly 130 currencies. Roughly 90% of agent locations are outside the US. In 2016 the segment completed nearly 270 million transactions (valued at $80 billion) and accounted for nearly 80% of the company?s revenue. C2C?s top 40 agents generated some 60% of the segment?s revenue in 2016. The segment is experiencing growth in its online money transfers offered through mobile applications and the westernunion.com website.

The C2B segment enables consumers to make recurring or one-time payments to everyday businesses such as utility providers auto finance companies and mortgage servicers. The segment generates 10% of revenue. C2B supports both in-person cash payments as well as online and electronic payments. Much of the revenue comes from the US and the rest is generated primarily through Pago FA?cil-branded payments in Argentina.

The Business Solutions segment facilitates payment and foreign exchange solutions typically across borders and between currencies mainly for small and medium businesses. A significant portion of this segment?s revenue is generated outside the US.

Geographic Reach

Colorado-based Western Union has offices in approximately 50 countries with four company-owned and over 400 leased. Its reach is amplified by hundreds of thousands of worldwide agent locations. It?s customers ? primarily consumers ? use the company?s services around the globe.

Western Union?s biggest single market is the US which generates about 30% of revenue.

Sales and Marketing

Payment volumes in the money transfer business correlate with immigration trends general economic conditions and employment levels. The ease of relocation particularly to other countries has given Western Union a consistent and eager customer base of immigrants looking to send money back home.

To ensure its potential customers know from where to initiate a transfer the company markets a global consistent brand. The Western Union name is ubiquitous in the world of consumer remittances having achieved this envied position with an unwavering allegiance to a worldwide branding approach. It markets services to consumers through its vast agent network using promotions advertising and loyalty programs. Call campaigns and trade show presence augment marketing efforts for its C2B services. True for all services is the company?s online branding presence found in its mobile applications and westernunion.com website.

Financial Performance

In 2016 Western Union?s revenue declined 1% to $5.4 billion. The small variance is due primarily to currency exchange fluctuations which if removed from revenue calculations indicate low single-digit upticks in 2016 revenue generation versus the previous two years. Western Union's revenues have remained consistent around the $5.5 billion mark since 2011.

While 2016?s gross profit was in line with previous years an extraordinary charge of $600 million due to regulatory compliance failures pulled net income down to just over $250 million a reduction of 70% against 2015?s $838 million.

In 2016 net cash slipped by nearly $440 million a nearly similar reduction as in 2015. Although several factors contributed to the cash flow swings the company has had a years-long effort of share buybacks and continued dividend issuance to common shareholders which it partially offset by issuing debt but also partly funded through cash from operations.

Strategy

Western Union?s corporate strategy is focused on protecting existing business growing through advancements in digital payment markets and technologies and improving regulatory compliance.

The lifeblood of Western Union?s business is revenue generated from C2C transaction fees and foreign exchange activities. Protecting this segment from new financial technology (FinTech) competitive pressures is a considerable corporate focus. To stay relevant and compete Western Union continues to invest in a digital channels strategy by forming alliances with third parties and offering services via social and mobile networks such as Viber and WeChat. In addition to providing smartphone applications it promotes worldwide use of its westernunion.com website as a transfer payment platform a strategy that has seen transaction growth of over 25% in each of 2015 and 2016.

Given the recent hefty settlements with US government agencies over aiding and abetting wire fraud and failing to implement an effective anti-money laundering program the company is upping its regulatory compliance vigilance. Funding for compliance has increased 200% since 2012. In 2016 the company spent $200 million to address the need and allocated 20% of its workforce to compliance functions. Although financial penalties of $600 million were paid to the government in 2016 for the 2004 ? 2012 activities the settlement agreement includes a government mandate for continued oversight of the company?s compliance in coming years.

EXECUTIVES

Chief Strategy And Product Officer, Elizabeth G. (Libby) Chambers, $535,000 total compensation

Evp Global Operations And Technology And Cio, John D. (David) Thompson, age 51, $540,000 total compensation

President And Ceo, Hikmet Ersek, age 57, $1,000,000 total compensation

Svp; President Business Solutions, Kerry Agiasotis

Evp General Counsel And Secretary, John R. Dye, age 58, $500,000 total compensation

Evp And Cfo, Rajesh K. (Raj) Agrawal, age 53, $566,500 total compensation

President Global Money Transfer, Odilon Almeida, age 56, $612,000 total compensation

Evp; President Middle East Africa Asia/pacific Eastern Europe And Cis, Jean Claude Farah, age 47

Svp; General Manager Digital, Khalid Fellahi

Evp And Chief Human Resources Officer, Richard L. Williams, age 52

Svp; General Manager Digital, Molly Shea

Svp And Chief Compliance Officer, Jacqueline Molnar

Chief Transformation Officer, Scott Coad

Vice President Strategy And Business Delivery, Stanley Yung

Vice President, Sobia Rahman

Vice President Records And Information Management, Jim Keyes

Vice President Global Operations Aml Compliance, Kristine Diehl

Vice President Sales, Jeff Zallaps

Vice President Aml Compliance, Fabrice Borsello

Vice President Global Compensation, Terry Lodes

Vice President Consumer Segments Usmt, Daniel Canning

Vice President Risk And Asset Management, Doug Groetken
Vice President Finance, Steve Cornell
Vice President Of Operations, Edgardo Torres
Vice President Marketing Middle East And Africa, Marc Aubry
Vice President Global Settlement Accounting Solutions, Pat Butler
Regional Vice President, Rocco Pilla
Vice President Head Of Global Sanctions, Tyler Hand
Vice President, MIKE BROWN
Vice President Global Head Of Aml Operations, Jonathon Dyer
Vice President Aml Compliance, Antonio Alvarez Lorenzo
Vice President Bsa And Aml Strategy, Clay Roberts
Chairman, Jeffrey A. Joerres, age 58
Treasurer, Robert Harrell
Board Member, Martin Cole
Auditors: Ernst & Young LLP

LOCATIONS

HQ: Western Union Co
 7001 East Belleview Avenue, Denver, CO 80237
Phone: 866 405-5012
Web: www.westernunion.com

2016 Sales

	$ mil.	% of total
US	1,672	31
International	3,750	69
Total	**5,422**	**100**

PRODUCTS/OPERATIONS

2016 Sales

	$ mil.	% of total
Transaction fees	3,795	70
Foreign exchange revenue	1,490	27
Commissions & other	137	3
Total	**5,422**	**100**

2016 Sales by Segment

	$ mil.	% of total
Consumer-to-consumer		
Transaction fees	3,123	57
Foreign exchange	1,116	21
Other	64	1
Consumer-to-business		
Transaction fees	596	11
Foreign exchange & other	24	1
Business solutions		
Foreign exchange	352	7
Transaction fees & other	43	0
Other	101	2
Total	**5,422**	**100**

COMPETITORS

American Express	PayPal
Citigroup	Santander Mexico
First Data	Sigue
Global Payments	US Postal Service
MasterCard	Visa Inc
MoneyGram	
International	

HISTORICAL FINANCIALS

Company Type: Public

Income Statement | | | | FYE: December 31

	REVENUE ($ mil.)	NET INCOME ($ mil.)	NET PROFIT MARGIN	EMPLOYEES
12/17	5,524	(557)	—	11,500
12/16	5,422	253	4.7%	10,700
12/15	5,483	837	15.3%	10,000
12/14	5,607	852	15.2%	10,000
12/13	5,542	798	14.4%	10,000
Annual Growth	**(0.1%)**	**—**	**—**	**3.6%**

2017 Year-End Financials

Debt ratio: 32.86%		No. of shares (mil.): 459	
Return on equity: (-271.23%)		Dividends	
Cash ($ mil.): 838		Yield: 0.0%	
Current ratio: 0.45		Payout: —	
Long-term debt ($ mil.): 3,033		Market value ($ mil.): 8,726	

	STOCK PRICE ($) FY Close	P/E High/Low		Earnings	PER SHARE ($) Dividends	Book Value
12/17	19.01	—	—	(1.19)	0.70	(1.07)
12/16	21.72	43	32	0.51	0.64	1.87
12/15	17.91	14	10	1.62	0.62	2.80
12/14	17.91	12	9	1.59	0.50	2.49
12/13	17.25	14	9	1.43	0.50	2.01
Annual Growth	**2.5%**	**—**	**—**	**—**	**8.8%**	**—**

Westlake Chemical Corp

Money matters and vertically integrated Westlake Chemical turns matter into money. The company produces petrochemicals and plastics such as PVC. Its petrochemicals include ethylene ethyl benzene and styrene which are building blocks in plastics. Its plastics offerings include PVC and polyethylene both of which are common in packaging products and grocery bags. Westlake also produces the chlorine used in PVC as well as caustic soda. Other Westlake operations make PVC products such as pipe (North American Pipe) fencing (Westech Fence) and windows. All in Westlake produces about 40 billion pounds of product each year and is the third largest producer of both PVC and chlor-alkali in the world. In 2016 Westlake acquired rival Axiall in a $3.8 billion deal. The Chao Group owns more than 70% of Westlake.

Operations

The company operates in two business segments: Olefins and Vinyls.

Westlake's Vinyls segment produces PVC (polyvinyl chloride) VCM (vinyl chlorida monomer) EDC (ethylene dichloride) chlor-alkali (chlorine and caustic soda) and ethylene. The company is the third-largest chlor-alkali producer in the world and can produce 2.3 billion pounds of chlorinated derivative products and 7 billion pounds of VCM each year. Its PVC products are fabricated into automotive sealants cable sheathing pipe window and door profiles fencing and decking and film and sheet products. Caustic soda is used in pup and paper manufacturing organic/inorganic chemicals and neutralization. The segment accounts for around 65% of sales.

The Olefins segment makes and markets polyethylene styrene monomer and various ethylene co-products used in the company's polyethylene styrene and vinyl chloride monomer (VCM) operations. The company's primary ethylene co-products are chemical grade propylene crude butadiene pyrolysis gasoline and hydrogen. Olefins generate around 35% of total sales.

Geographic Reach

Houston-Texas based Westlake has more than 40 manufacturing facilities: 27 are in the US 6 in Canada 5 in Germany and one each in China Taiwan the UK and India. The US accounts for around 70% of total sales while Germany generates around 10% Canada 5% and other countries the remaining 15% or so.

Its olefin activity is clustered around Lake Charles in Louisiana. Westlake's sites in Lake Charles include two OpCo-owned ethylene plants two polyethylene plants and a styrene monomer plant. Lake Charles also has a port terminal for worldwide shipping and is located near rail transport links.

Westlake owns 26 building products plants consisting of 15 PVC pipe plants eight siding trim and mouldings plants two profile plants producing PVC fence decking windows and door profiles and one film and sheet plant. The company's plants are mostly located close to major markets and serve customers throughout the United States Canada and Asia

Sales and Marketing

Westlake's products are sold directly to polyethylene customers (some of the largest producers of film and flexible packaging in the US). It also sells ethylene and ethylene co-products to external customers. The majority of olefins sales are made under long-term agreements.

The company has the capacity to use all of their chlorine internally to produce VCM and EDC most of which in turn is used to produce PVC. It sells substantially all of its caustic soda production to external customers. The majority of its North American-produced PVC is used internally in the production of building products. The remainder of its PVC including the PVC produced at their European facilities is sold to downstream fabricators and the international markets.

No single customer accounts for more than 10% of sales.

Financial Performance

Westlakes's revenue has been trending upwards in recent years. In fiscal 2016 sales increased a further 14% to $5.1 billion largely as a result of the contribution of the acquired Axiall business from August 31. Higher sales volume of PVC resin was partially offset by lower prices for all major products and lower sales volumes for the major olefins products. Prices fell on average 6.4% due to low crude oil prices.

Net income fell 38% to $398.9 million due to acquisition costs totaling $103.7 million turnaround costs of $155.1 million at the Lake Charles Petro 1 ethylene unit and lost sales due to outages partially offset by a $49.1 million gain on previously held Axiall stock and a lower effective tax rate.

Cash from operations fell 23% to $833.9 million a result of lower income from operations an increase in working capital requirements and an increase in deferred turnaround costs associated with the Lake Charles facility.

Strategy

Westlake's growth strategy focuses on acquisitions new plant construction and internal expansion.

In 2016 the company continued work on its ethylene investments. In its Lake Charles ethylene facility Westlake added 250 million pounds of production capacity and in 2017 began work on increasing ethylene capacity in its Calvert City facility. Additionally Westlake has a 10% stake in a 2.2 billion pound per year ethylene plant in Lake Charles expected to complete in 2019; it will increase its ownership to 50% in the first three years of operations.

Mergers and Acquisitions

In 2018 Westlake Chemical announced the acquisition of global compounder Nakan from OpenGate Capital in a $265 million deal. The acquisition continues a recent trend of resin makers diversifying with compounding (both LyndondellBassel and Celanese Corp pursued similar deals). The addition of Reims-based Nakan is attractive to Westlake Chemical because of its suite of specialty products within the compounding business. With $300 million in annual sales Nakan already has eight production facilities in Europe Asia and Mexico. The transaction will close in early 2019.

In 2016 Westlake acquired Atlanta-based Axiall Corporation a major manufacturer of caustic soda chlorine VCM EDC and PVC resins for $3.8 billion. The acquisition made Westlake the world's third-largest chlor-alkali producer in the world and the second largest PVC producer in the US.

HISTORY

Westlake came into being in 1986 when T.T. Chao bought a polyethylene plant near Lake Charles Louisiana from Occidental Petroleum. Over the years the company has acquired or constructed about 20 more. The founding Chao family took Westlake Chemical public in 2004 with the hope of paying down some of the debt accumulated from those acquisitions

In 2008 a joint venture between Westlake and Chinese chemical company INEOS began producing some 33 million pounds of PVC film each year. Westlake owns 59% of the Suzhou Huasu Plastics.

Westlake made several changes to its PVC production in 2009. Early in the year the company acquired a PVC pipe plant in Janesville Wisconsin and opened its new PVC plant in Yucca Arizona to expand its operations. However to reduce costs Westlake closed its facilities in Bristol Indiana later that year and moved that production to its other PVC operations.

In 2010 Westlake purchased a 50% stake in Cypress Interstate Pipeline LLC from Kinder Morgan Energy Partners. The 104-mile pipeline supplies natural gas liquid feedstocks to Westlake's Lake Charles Louisiana petrochemical complex. The pipeline will continue to be operated by Kinder Morgan under a contract.

Westlake also made a move in 2012 to strengthen its presence in Asia by opening a Singapore office. Its operations there will focus on serving its existing customers and seeking new opportunities for growth in the region.

In early 2012 the company made an all cash offer for Atlanta-based Georgia Gulf one of North America's largest manufacturers of vinyl construction products. However Georgia Gulf rejected the $1.03 billion takeover bid as being financially inadequate and adopted a stockholder rights plan also called a poison pill that allows existing shareholders to buy stock at a discount when a suitor acquires more than 10% of outstanding shares. Westlake wanted to combine its resin and pipe production with Georgia Gulf's chemicals and vinyl products but later that year withdrew its proposal to buy the company.

The company has expanded capacity to meet growing demand. In 2013 it opened a new chlor-alkali plant in Greismar Louisiana that doubles Westlake's chlor-alkali production capacity. It also beefed up the ethylene capacity at its Lake Charles facility in 2013 (increasing the ethane-based ethylene capacity of the unit and its conversion to 100% ethane feedstock capability). It is also upgrading ethylene production facilities at Calvert City Kentucky.

In 2013 Westlake bought CertainTeed's Pipe and Foundation Group a leading producer of PVC pipe and fittings for municipal water well mining agriculture and irrigation applications for $175 million. It also acquired technologies and intellectual property for the production of a number of specialized products including Certa-Lok restrained joint pipe and Yelomine branded products.

EXECUTIVES

President And Ceo, Albert Chao, age 68, $979,667 total compensation
Svp Cfo And Treasurer, M. Steven (Steve) Bender, age 61, $520,833 total compensation
Vp Manufacturing, Andrew Kenner, age 53, $377,167 total compensation
Svp Vinyls, Robert F. Buesinger, age 61, $406,333 total compensation
Svp Olefins, Lawrence E. (Skip) Teel, age 60
Vice President Human Resources, M Joel Gray
Chairman, James Y. Chao, age 70
Auditors: PricewaterhouseCoopers LLP

LOCATIONS

HQ: Westlake Chemical Corp
2801 Post Oak Boulevard, Suite 600, Houston, TX 77056
Phone: 713 960-9111
Web: www.westlake.com

2016 Sales

	$ mil.	% of total
US	3,525	69
Germany	402	8
Canada	317	6
Switzerland	101	2
China	87	2
Italy	84	2
Belgium	50	1
France	50	1
Other countries	457	9
Total	**5,075**	**100**

PRODUCTS/OPERATIONS

2016 Sales

	$ mil.	% of total
Olefins		
Polyethylene	1,462	29
feedstock styrene & other	431	8
Vinyls		
PVC caustic soda & other	2,492	49
Building products	689	14
Total	**5,075**	**100**

Selected Products

Olefins
  Ethylene
  Polyethylene
  Styrene
Vinyls
  Caustic soda
  Chlorine
  PVC
  VCM

COMPETITORS

BASF SE	J-M Manufacturing
Chevron Phillips	LyondellBasell
Chemical	Mexichem
Diamond Plastics	NOVA Chemicals
Dow Chemical	Occidental Chemical
ExxonMobil Chemical	Oxy Vinyls
Formosa Plastics	Shell Chemicals
Formosa Plastics USA	Shintech

HISTORICAL FINANCIALS

Company Type: Public

Income Statement				FYE: December 31
	REVENUE ($ mil.)	NET INCOME ($ mil.)	NET PROFIT MARGIN	EMPLOYEES
12/17	8,041	1,304	16.2%	8,800
12/16	5,075	398	7.9%	8,870
12/15	4,463	646	14.5%	4,225
12/14	4,415	678	15.4%	3,550
12/13	3,759	610	16.2%	2,200
Annual Growth	20.9%	20.9%	—	41.4%

2017 Year-End Financials

Debt ratio: 31.77%
Return on equity: 31.06%
Cash ($ mil.): 1,531
Current ratio: 1.76
Long-term debt ($ mil.): 3,127
No. of shares (mil.): 129
Dividends
  Yield: 0.0%
  Payout: 7.9%
Market value ($ mil.): 13,787

	STOCK PRICE ($) FY Close	P/E High/Low		Earnings	Dividends	Book Value
				PER SHARE ($)		
12/17	106.53	11	6	10.05	0.80	37.66
12/16	55.99	19	13	3.06	0.74	27.33
12/15	54.32	16	10	4.86	0.69	25.08
12/14	61.09	27	11	5.07	0.58	21.91
12/13	122.07	27	17	4.55	0.41	18.14
Annual Growth	(3.3%)			— 21.9%	18.1%	20.0%

WestRock Co

Auditors: Ernst & Young LLP

LOCATIONS

HQ: WestRock Co
1000 Abernathy Road N.E., Atlanta, GA 30328
Phone: 770 448-2193
Web: www.westrock.com

HISTORICAL FINANCIALS

Company Type: Public

Income Statement				FYE: September 30
	REVENUE ($ mil.)	NET INCOME ($ mil.)	NET PROFIT MARGIN	EMPLOYEES
09/18	16,285	1,906	11.7%	45,100
09/17	14,859	708	4.8%	44,800
09/16	14,171	(396)	—	39,000
09/15	11,381	507	4.5%	41,400
09/14	9,895	479	4.8%	—
Annual Growth	13.3%	41.2%		—

2018 Year-End Financials

Debt ratio: 25.30%
Return on equity: 17.48%
Cash ($ mil.): 636
Current ratio: 1.44
Long-term debt ($ mil.): 5,674
No. of shares (mil.): 253
Dividends
  Yield: 0.0%
  Payout: 23.4%
Market value ($ mil.): 13,547

	STOCK PRICE ($) FY Close	P/E High/Low		Earnings	Dividends	Book Value
				PER SHARE ($)		
09/18	53.44	9	7	7.34	1.72	45.24
09/17	56.73	21	16	2.77	1.60	40.64
09/16	48.48	—	—	(1.54)	1.50	38.76
09/15	51.44	22	17	2.93	0.38	45.34
Annual Growth	1.0%			— 25.8%	46.3%	(0.1%)

Weyerhaeuser Co

Forest products company Weyerhaeuser produces a variety of softwood lumber and other building materials in North America. One of the world's largest private owners of timberland the company harvests trees for its products from 12 million acres of forest that it owns in the US and

14 million acres that it manages in Canada. Exports account for about 15% of the company's sales. Incorporated in 1900 as Weyerhaeuser Timber Co. the company operates as a real estate investment trust (REIT) because of its vast land holdings. The company merged with rival Plum Creek in a deal worth $10 billion bringing together the two biggest owners of timberland in the US; shortly after that deal Weyerhaeuser spun off its cellulose fibers business for $2.5 billion.

Operations

Weyerhaeuser operates through three business segments: Wood Products Timberlands and Real Estate & Energy and Natural Resources (ENR).

Most of Weyerhaeuser's revenue is concentrated in its Wood Products segment which generates nearly 70% of the company's sales by serving mostly the residential construction industry. Its primary product categories are structural lumber engineered wood products oriented strand board soft plywood and medium-density fiberboard which it manufactures in the US and Canada.

The company's Timberland segment accounts for about 25% of sales. It operates in the West and South of the US; Uruguay; and Canada under license in Alberta British Columbia Ontario and Saskatchewan.

The Real Estate & ENR segment buys sells and manages productive timberland assets. This includes valuing land parcels and granting rights to mine mineral and oil and gas deposits on its timberlands. The segment generates about 5% of revenue.

Geographic Reach

Seattle Washington-based Weyerhaeuser operates offices in about a dozen countries and serves customers worldwide. The REIT rings up more than 85% of its sales in the US and its giant housing market. Most of the remaining revenue comes from Canada Japan and China.

The company sources softwood plywood in Arkansas and Louisiana. It also produces veneer at a facility in Oregon.

Sales and Marketing

Weyerhaeuser sells its products and services through its own sales organizations and distribution facilities. It also peddles building materials that the company purchases from other manufacturers. Through the wood preserving and home-improvement warehouse channels the company sells certain items into the new residential building repair and remodel market.

Financial Performance

Weyerhaeuser reported stronger sales in 2016 and 2017 returning its top line above the $7 billion mark after two years of declining revenue.

In 2017 sales increased 14% to $7.2 billion from $6.4 billion in 2016. Wood sales to unaffiliated customers rose $640 million from stronger sales across all product lines as well as higher sales volumes of oriented strand board engineered I-joists medium density fiberboard and engineered solid section product lines. In the Timberlands segment higher sales resulted from increased Southern and delivered log volumes and higher prices for Western logs. Higher Real Estate & ENR segment sales were attributed to an increase in timberlands acres sold and higher royalties.

The company's net income fell to $582 million in 2017 from about $1 billion in 2016 because of higher expenses for pension and post-retirement costs credits which were affected by a decrease in the expected return on plan assets as well as higher amortization of actuarial losses.

Weyerhaeuser had $824 million in cash in 2017 a $148 million increase from 2017. The company generated $1.2 billion in operations in 2017 and investing activities provided $367 million; it used $1.4 billion in financing activities.

Strategy

Much of Weyerhaeuser's sales performance particularly when it comes to its Wood Products and Timberland segments is strongly tied to the US housing market including the new residential building and repair and remodel markets. Weyerhaeuser is banking on long-term growth as the housing market recovers and demand for lumber increases.

Interest rates rose steadily in the US throughout 2018. Higher interest rates could slow home buying which would have an impact on Weyerhaeuser's sales.

While focusing on cost-reduction measures for streamlining operations Weyerhaeuser has a long-term plan to develop customer relationships and expand its customer base geographic reach and product portfolio. The timber REIT is also concentrating on growing its business by maintaining its diverse income streams.

Since 2009 Weyerhaeuser has sold a number of businesses and used the proceeds to pay down debt. In 2016 the company sold its liquid packaging board business (including a Washington mill) to Nippon Paper for $285 million. In late 2016 Weyerhaeuser also sold its cellulose fibers operations to International Paper for $2.2 billion in cash.

Mergers and Acquisitions

In February 2016 Weyerhaeuser purchased Plum Creek Timber Co. the largest private owner of timberland in the US for $8.4 billion. The deal nearly doubled Weyerhaeuser's US timberland acreage to more than 12 million across 19 states and made Weyerhaeuser the sixth-largest publicly traded company based in Washington state.

Company Background

Founder Frederick Weyerhaeuser a 24-year-old German immigrant bought his first lumberyard in 1858 in Illinois. He also participated in joint logging ventures in Illinois Minnesota and Wisconsin. In 1900 he and 15 partners bought 900000 timbered acres from the Northern Pacific Railway. The venture was named Weyerhaeuser Timber Company.

HISTORY

Frederick Weyerhaeuser a 24-year-old German immigrant bought his first lumberyard in 1858 in Illinois. He also participated in joint logging ventures in Illinois Minnesota and Wisconsin. In 1900 he and 15 partners bought 900000 timbered acres from the Northern Pacific Railway. The venture was named Weyerhaeuser Timber Company.

During the Depression the business recouped losses in the deflated lumber market by selling wood pulp. Frederick's grandson J. P. "Phil" Weyerhaeuser Jr. took over as CEO in 1933.

Diversification into the production of containerboard (1949) particleboard (1955) paper (1956) and other products led the company to drop "Timber" from its name in 1959. In 1963 Weyerhaeuser went public and opened its first overseas office in Tokyo.

In the 1970s George Weyerhaeuser (Phil's son) diversified further to insulate the company from the forest-product industry's cyclical nature and ended up with a mishmash of businesses and products from private-label disposable diapers to pet supplies.

The eruption of Mount St. Helens in 1980 destroyed 68000 acres of Weyerhaeuser timber. That disaster and the soft US lumber market depressed the company's earnings through 1982. Weyerhaeuser reduced its workforce by 25% during this period.

Under John Creighton (president in 1988 and CEO from 1991 until 1998) Weyerhaeuser refocused on forest products and organized along product lines rather than by geographic region. Less-successful ventures were put up for sale including milk carton hardwood and gypsum board plants. The company took a $497 million pretax charge in 1989 related to the decision to close unprofitable operations. Earnings improved in 1990 but dropped again in 1991 reflecting the recession in the US and plant closures.

In 1992 the company outbid Georgia-Pacific paying $600 million for two pulp mills three sawmills and more than 200000 acres of forest land to boost its market-pulp capacity by 40%. The following year the company sold its disposable-diaper business through a public offering in a new company Paragon Trade Brands. It also sold GNA Corporation to General Electric subsidiary GE Capital.

The federal government in 1995 allowed the company to harvest trees in an area inhabited by the endangered northern spotted owl. The move angered environmental groups. In 1997 Weyerhaeuser began to reorganize its recycling business by selling or closing noncore units. It also purchased a stake in 193000 acres on New Zealand's South Island the company's first overseas investment in more than a decade. In 1998 the company restructured its joint venture with Nippon Paper with Weyerhaeuser decreasing its stake in North Pacific Paper Company from 80% to 50% and closed a lumber mill in Canada. Also that year Steve Rogel a veteran from competitor Willamette succeeded Creighton as CEO and became the first outsider to head Weyerhaeuser.

In 1999 Weyerhaeuser paid $2.5 billion for Canada's MacMillan Bloedel and early in 2000 it acquired TJ International 51% owner of leading engineered lumber products company Trus Joist MacMillan (Weyerhaeuser already owned the other 49%). Also in 2000 Weyerhaeuser purchased two sawmills and a 70% stake in lumber distributor Pine Solutions from Australia-based CSR Limited. Weyerhaeuser sold its Marshfield Door architectural wood door business and closed some of its manufacturing operations to consolidate its business.

After a protracted courtship in March 2002 Weyerhaeuser acquired Oregon-based Willamette Industries in a $6.1 billion.

EXECUTIVES

President Ceo And Director, Doyle R. Simons, age 54, $1,000,000 total compensation

Svp Real Estate Energy And Natural Resources, James A. (Jim) Kilberg, age 61, $428,778 total compensation

Svp Timberlands, Rhonda C. Hunter, age 55, $560,000 total compensation

Svp Wood Products, Adrian M. Blocker, age 61, $560,000 total compensation

Svp And Cfo, Russell S. Hagen, age 52, $434,201 total compensation

Svp Human Resources And Information Technology, Denise M. Merle, age 54

Vice President Procurement And Corporate Services, Bradley Mjelde

Chairman, Rick R. Holley, age 66

Auditors: KPMG LLP

LOCATIONS

HQ: Weyerhaeuser Co
220 Occidental Avenue South, Seattle, WA 98104-7800
Phone: 206 539-3000
Web: www.weyerhaeuser.com

2017 Sales

	% of total
US	86
Japan	7
Canada	5
China	1
Other foreign countries	1
Total	**100**

PRODUCTS/OPERATIONS

2017 Sales

	$ mil.	% of total
Wood Products	4,974	69
Timberlands	1,942	27
Real Estate & ENR	280	4
Total	**7,196**	**100**

Selected Products and Services

Wood and Building Products
- Engineered lumber products
- Flooring
- Lumber (softwood)
- Oriented Strand Board
- Plywood
- Structural panels
- Veneer

Real Estate and Related Assets
- Master-planned communities
- Multifamily homes
- Residential lots
- Single-family homes

Timberlands
- Chips
- Logs
- Mineral resources
- Seedlings
- Weyerhaeser Select Douglas Fir seed

Other
- Recycling
- Transportation

COMPETITORS

Canfor	Potlatch
Cascades Boxboard	Pratt Industries USA
ENCE Energia y	Rayonier
Celulosa SA	Resolute Forest
Georgia-Pacific	Products
Indiana Veneers	Sierra Pacific
Louisiana-Pacific	Industries
McFarland Cascade	Smurfit Kappa
Mendocino Redwood	Stora Enso
Company	Tembec
Norbord	Tenon
Packaging Corp. of	UPM-Kymmene
America	West Fraser Timber

HISTORICAL FINANCIALS

Company Type: Public

Income Statement

FYE: December 31

	REVENUE ($ mil.)	NET INCOME ($ mil.)	NET PROFIT MARGIN	EMPLOYEES
12/17	7,196	582	8.1%	9,300
12/16	6,365	1,027	16.1%	10,400
12/15	7,082	506	7.1%	12,600
12/14	7,403	1,826	24.7%	12,800
12/13	8,529	563	6.6%	13,700
Annual Growth	**(4.2%)**	**0.8%**	**—**	**(9.2%)**

2017 Year-End Financials

Debt ratio: 36.01%
Return on equity: 6.44%
Cash ($ mil.): 824
Current ratio: 1.47
Long-term debt ($ mil.): 6,232

No. of shares (mil.): 755
Dividends
Yield: 0.0%
Payout: 162.3%
Market value ($ mil.): 26,629

	STOCK PRICE ($) FY Close	P/E High/Low	PER SHARE ($) Earnings	Dividends	Book Value
12/17	35.26	47 39	0.77	1.25	11.78
12/16	30.09	24 16	1.39	1.24	12.26
12/15	29.98	41 30	0.89	1.20	9.54
12/14	35.89	11 9	3.18	1.02	10.11
12/13	31.57	34 28	0.95	0.81	11.64
Annual Growth	**2.8%**	**— —**	**(5.1%)**	**11.5%**	**0.3%**

WHEATLAND UNION HIGH SCHOOL DISTRICT

EXECUTIVES

Supt, Clenn Sowll
Administrator, Lynne Tafoya
Teacher, Melissa Taylor
Superintendent, Vic Ramos
Auditors: RT DENNIS ACCOUNTANCY RANCHO

LOCATIONS

HQ: WHEATLAND UNION HIGH SCHOOL DISTRICT
  1010 WHEATLAND RD, WHEATLAND, CA 956929798
Phone: 530 633-3100
Web: WWW.WHEATLANDHIGH.ORG

HISTORICAL FINANCIALS

Company Type: Private

Income Statement

FYE: June 30

	REVENUE ($ mil.)	NET INCOME ($ mil.)	NET PROFIT MARGIN	EMPLOYEES
06/17	9,186	(1,399)	—	76
06/16	8,941	94	1.1%	
Annual Growth	**2.7%**	**—**	**—**	**—**

Whirlpool Corp

With brand names recognized by just about anyone who has ever separated dark colors from light Whirlpool is one of the world's top home appliance makers. It specializes in laundry appliances refrigerators and freezers cooking appliances dishwashers and compressors. They're sold under a bevy of brand names including Whirlpool Amana KitchenAid Maytag Jenn-Air and Roper. The company markets and distributes these major home appliances in North America Latin America EMEA (Europe the Middle East and Africa) and Asia. It has manufacturing operations in more than a dozen countries. Major customers include retailers Lowe's Home Depot Sears and Best Buy.

Operations

Laundry Appliances and Refrigerators and Freezers both generates nearly 30% of sales; Cooking Appliances bring in nearly 20% and Other products account for the remainder. It sells upwards of 70 million units each year.

The company divides its business into four geographical regions: North America EMEA (Europe Middle East and Africa) Latin America and Asia. Each region shows variation in terms of its premier brands.

Whirlpool operates 42 manufacturing facilities across the world.

Geographic Reach

Whirlpool sells its products globally and has some 70 manufacturing and technology research centers throughout the world.

North America generates more than 50% of total sales; EMEA around 25%; Latin America 15%; and the Asia-Pacific region more than 5%.

Sales and Marketing

Whirlpool distributes its products to several big-name retail customers including: Lowe's Sears Home Depot Best Buy IKEA and Alno. In North America the company sells products to other manufacturers distributors builders and retailers for resale under those manufacturers' and retailers' brand names.

Financial Performance

Whirlpool had been growing at about $1 billion a year until fiscal 2016 when revenue slipped back by around 1%. The primary culprits were unfavorable currency exchange offsets and product price mix partially offset by s% higher unit volumes sold at 71700.

Geographically the picture was mixed. The large North America segment grew revenue 4% on the back of an 8% increase in volume sales but EMEA fell 8% and Latin America 5% (Asia-Pacific sales grew immaterially). Weakness in EMEA was a result of foreign currency impacts and a 2% fall in units sold while in Latin America a 12% decrease in units sold was partially offset by favorable product price/mix.

Net income grew 13% to $888 million thanks to productivity gains acquisition synergies capacity reduction initiatives and lower restructuring costs.

Cash from operations fell 2% to $1.2 billion as higher net income was offset by changes in accounts receivable.

Strategy

Whirlpool is looking to tighten its operations by implementing cost-based price increases initiating cost reduction efforts and making productivity improvements. In 2016 initiatives such as predictive analytics waste reduction automation and improving assembly yield helped save more than $300 million.

At the same time these cost savings are intended to allow the company to spend more on R&D for new product innovation and the improvement of existing products. Indeed Whirlpool spent $600 million on R&D in 2016 launching French-door refrigerators in North America touch-responsive washing machines in Asia and a washing machine with a bulk dispenser.

In an effort to focus more on its consumer-facing operations the company agreed in mid-2018 to tell its compressor business to Japan-based Nidec for just more than $1 billion.

HISTORY

Brothers Fred and Lou Upton and their uncle Emory Upton founded the Upton Machine Company manufacturer of electric motor-driven washing machines in 1911 in St. Joseph Michigan. Sears Roebuck and Co. began buying their products five years later and by 1925 the company was supplying all of Sears' washers. The Uptons combined their company with the Nineteen Hundred Washer Company in 1929 to form the Nineteen Hundred Corporation the world's largest washing machine company.

Sears and Nineteen Hundred prospered during the Great Depression and during WWII Nineteen Hundred's factories produced war materials. In 1948 it began selling its first automatic washing machine (introduced a year earlier) under the Whirlpool brand. In 1950 the company changed its name to Whirlpool following the success of the product and introduced its first automatic dryer.

During the 1950s and 1960s Whirlpool became a full-line appliance manufacturer while continuing as Sears' principal Kenmore appliance supplier. In 1955 the company bought Seeger Refrigerator Company and the stove and air-conditioning interests of RCA. Three years later it made its first investment in Multibras EletrodomA©sticos an appliance maker in Brazil. (It has increased that investment over the years.) Other purchases included the gas refrigeration and ice-maker manufacturing facilities of Servel (1958); a majority interest in

Heil-Quaker makers of central heaters and space heaters (1964); Sears' major television set supplier Warwick Electronics (1966); and 33% of Canadian appliance maker John Inglis Company (1969). It made a deal with Sony in 1973 for the distribution of Whirlpool-brand products in Japan. Whirlpool sold its TV manufacturing business to SANYO of Japan three years later.

Between 1981 and 1991 despite a static US market Whirlpool's sales tripled to almost $6.6 billion. In 1986 the firm bought top-end appliance manufacturer KitchenAid (from Dart and Kraft) and 65% of Italian cooling compressor manufacturer Aspera. Also that year it sold its Heil-Quaker central heating business. David Whitwam was appointed CEO in 1987. Whirlpool took over total ownership of Inglis in 1990.

The company formed Whirlpool Europe a joint venture with Philips Electronics in 1989; in 1991 it bought out Philips. Two years later Whirlpool took control of appliance marketer SAGAD of Argentina and entered a joint venture with Slovakia's Tatramat (which it bought out in 1994).

Whirlpool acquired control of Kelvinator of India in 1994 and formed a joint venture in China with Shenzhen Petrochemical Holdings in 1995 to produce air conditioners. The following year Whirlpool merged its Whirlpool Washing Machines and Kelvinator of India companies to form Whirlpool of India. The company's European division plunged into the red when competition and a recession kept consumers away from its higher-priced appliances.

In 1997 Whirlpool initiated a restructuring (due to losses from its foreign operations) that included plant closures and substantial layoffs (as much as 10% of its workforce). The next year Whirlpool sold its appliance financing subsidiary to Transamerica. The company also began using a new more efficient product development model in 1998 similar to one used in the auto industry. In 2000 Whirlpool launched the Cielo Bath line of jetted tubs and in 2001 it introduced the Calypso dishwasher and the Duet washer and dryer.

Another global restructuring plan swept through the company in 2000 resulting in significant pretax charges ($373 million incurred in 2001 and 2002) and the elimination of about 6000 employees by October 2003.

EXECUTIVES

Vice President Human Resources, Michael Todman
Executive Vice President Asia, Mark Hu
Executive Vice President And President Of Whirlpool Europe Middle East And Africa, Esther Galindo
Vice President, Anil Berera
Ceo And Director, Marc R. Bitzer, age 53, $1,000,000 total compensation
Evp Global Product Organization, David T. (Dave) Szczupak, age 62, $746,667 total compensation
Evp And President Of Whirlpool Europe Middle East And Africa (emea), Esther Berrozpe Galindo, age 48, $659,041 total compensation
Evp And President Latin America, Jo o Carlos Brega, age 54, $498,901 total compensation
President Whirlpool North America, Joseph T. Liotine, age 45
Evp And Cfo, James W. (Jim) Peters, age 48, $456,667 total compensation
President Whirlpool Asia, Shengpo (Samuel) Wu
Vice President Operations, Tom Egan
Corporate Vice President And Treasurer, Blair Clark
Vice President Global Engineering Tech, Christian Gianni
Assistant Vice President Networking Security, Carrick Jay

Vice President Of Human Resources, Michael Reusswig
Vice President Sales Whirlpool Canada, Mark Williams
Vice President Manager Director, Melissa Little
Vice President Of Marketing, Gary Power
Senior Vice President Of Development, Marek Kaszuba
Vice President And Of General Manager Of Emerging Categories, Timothy Kee
Vice President Human Resources Global Pr, Tomas Linden
Vice President Of Finance, Tom Fowler
Vp It, David Langendonk
Vice President Marketing, James Oh
Vice President Financial Advisor, Javier C Castellanos
Assistant Vice President Operations, Jeanne Pavlic
Vice President Information Technology, J Berendsen
National Sales Manager, Erin Brown
Vice President Laundry And Dish, Dale Laws
Corporate Vice President Strategic Competency Creation, Nancy Tennant
Information Technology Management: Executive Vice President Senior Vice President, Mrutyunjaya Rao
Vice President Sales And Marketing, Thomas Arent
National Account Manager, Jody Turner
Vice President Human Resources Business, Cintia Bincoletto
Vice President Procurement North America, Steven Rush
Vice President Quality, J D Rapp
Vice President Sales, Tamal Saha
Vice President Human Resources, Adriano Mureddu
Vice President Marketing, Marc Butzer
Vice President And Treasurer, Brian F Peters
Vice President Director Of Facilities, Bryan Babel
Vice President Of Business Development, Joe Igoe
Vice President Of Public Relations, Douglas Horstman
Executive Vice President, Yogesh Shinde
Vice President Quality, John D Rapp
Executive Vice President, Tim Swartz
National Sales Manager, Randy Karn
Lar International Vice President, William Custodio
Vp And Cfo North American Region, Christopher Bealer
Vp Consumer And Appliance Care Nar, Ken Kleinhemple
Vice President Cc Opex Six Sigma Champion, Bernard Ben Brotzki
Division Vice President, Jonathan Haywood
Board Member, Gary T DiCamillo
Board Member, William D Perez
Chairman, Jeff M. Fettig, age 61
Board Of Directors, Michael F Johnston
Board Member, Harish Manwani
Treasurer Emea, Peter Davidsson
Board Of Directors, John Liu
Assistant Treasurer, John Geddes
Board Member, Larry Spencer
Auditors: Ernst & Young LLP

LOCATIONS

HQ: Whirlpool Corp
2000 North M-63, Benton Harbor, MI 49022-2692
Phone: 269 923-5000
Web: www.whirlpoolcorp.com

2016 Sales

	$ mil.	% of total
North America	11,147	53
Europe the Middle East & Africa	5,148	25
Latin America	3,191	15
Asia	1,424	7
Other/eliminations (192) —		
Total	**20,718**	**100**

2016 Sales

	$ mil.	% of total
U.S	9,901	48
Brazil	1,895	9
China	945	5
All other countries	7,977	38
Total	**20,718**	**100**

PRODUCTS/OPERATIONS

2016 Sales

	% of total
Laundry Appliances	28
Refrigerators & Freezers	28
Cooking Appliances	18
Other	26
Total	**100**

COMPETITORS

BSH Bosch und Siemens Hausger ote	Haier Group
	Hitachi
Candy Group	LG Electronics
Daewoo Electronics	Panasonic Corp
Electrolux	SANYO
Electrolux Home Appliances China	Samsung Electronics America
Fisher & Paykel Appliances Holdings	Sears Holdings
Gree Electrical Appliances	Sharp Corp. Sub-Zero
GuangDong Midea	Viking Range

HISTORICAL FINANCIALS

Company Type: Public

Income Statement   FYE: December 31

	REVENUE ($ mil.)	NET INCOME ($ mil.)	NET PROFIT MARGIN	EMPLOYEES
12/17	21,253	350	1.6%	92,000
12/16	20,718	888	4.3%	93,000
12/15	20,891	783	3.7%	97,000
12/14	19,872	650	3.3%	100,000
12/13	18,769	827	4.4%	69,000
Annual Growth	3.2%	(19.3%)	—	7.5%

2017 Year-End Financials

Debt ratio: 26.04%	No. of shares (mil.): 71
Return on equity: 7.80%	Dividends
Cash ($ mil.): 1,196	Yield: 0.0%
Current ratio: 0.93	Payout: 91.4%
Long-term debt ($ mil.): 4,392	Market value ($ mil.): 11,973

	STOCK PRICE ($) FY Close	P/E High/Low	Earnings	Dividends	Book Value
12/17	168.64	41 34	4.70	4.30	59.13
12/16	181.77	16 11	11.50	3.90	64.10
12/15	146.87	22 14	9.83	3.45	61.42
12/14	193.74	23 15	8.17	2.88	62.66
12/13	156.86	15 10	10.24	2.38	63.60
Annual Growth	1.8%	—	(17.7%)	16.0%	(1.8%)

WHOLE FOODS MARKET, INC.

Whole Foods Market is the world's largest natural foods grocery chain. Founded in 1980 it pioneered the supermarket concept in natural and organic foods retailing. The company operates more than 470 stores throughout the US Canada and the UK and focuses on organic perishable and pre-pared products. It sells private-label items through its 365 Organic Everyday Value and Allegro Coffee lines and offers a variety of non-GMO vegan and gluten-free foods. In 2017 Amazon.com acquired Whole Foods which generates sales mostly in the US for about $13.7 billion.

HISTORY

With a $10000 loan from his father John Mackey started SaferWay Natural Foods in Austin Texas in 1978. Despite struggling Mackey dreamed of opening a larger supermarket-sized natural foods store. Two years later SaferWay merged with Clarksville Natural Grocery and Whole Foods Market was born. Led by Mackey that year it opened an 11000-sq.-ft. supermarket in the counterculture hotbed of Austin. The store was an instant success and a second store was added 18 months later in suburban Austin.

The company slowly expanded in Texas opening or buying stores in Houston in 1984 and Dallas in 1986. Whole Foods expanded into Louisiana in 1988 with the purchase of like-named Whole Food Co. a single New Orleans store owned by Peter Roy (who served as the company's president from 1993 to 1998). Sticking to university towns Whole Foods added another store in California the next year and acquired Wellspring Grocery (two stores North Carolina) in 1991. In 1992 it debuted its first private-label products under the Whole Foods name. Seeking capital to expand even more the company raised $23 million by going public in early 1992 with 12 stores.

Every competitor in the fragmented health foods industry became a potential acquisition and the chain began growing rapidly. In 1992 Whole Foods bought the six-store Bread & Circus chain in New England. The next year it added Mrs. Gooch's Natural Foods Markets (seven stores in the Los Angeles area). Its biggest acquisition came in 1996 when it bought Fresh Fields the second-largest US natural foods chain (22 stores on the East Coast and in Chicago). Although the purchase hurt profits in 1996 sales surpassed $1 billion for the first time in fiscal 1997 as Whole Foods neared 70 stores. In 1997 it introduced the less-expensive 365 private label and acquired the Granary Market (Monterey California) and Bread of Life (two stores South Florida) natural foods supermarkets.

Capitalizing on the growing popularity of nu-traceuticals (natural supplements with benefits similar to pharmaceuticals) the company paid $146 million in 1997 for Amrion a maker of nutraceu-ticals and other nutritional supplements (merged with subsidiary WholePeople.com in 2000). It capped the year by buying coffee roaster Allegro Coffee. (Both companies are based in Boulder Col-orado home of its former main rival the smaller Wild Oats.) Also in 1997 Whole Foods acquired the six-store Merchant of Vino natural foods and wine shop chain to foster the development of its wine departments.

In 1998 Whole Foods opened its first store in Boulder — a 39000-sq.-ft. superstore with ameni-ties such as a juice bar and a prepared foods sec-tion. At year's end Roy resigned as president and was replaced by Chris Hitt. In 1999 Whole Foods bought four-store Boston-area chain Nature's Heartland.

In 2000 Whole Foods merged its online opera-tions (wholefoods.com) with its direct marketing and nutritional supplement unit (Amrion) to form Wholepeople.com. Later that year the company merged Wholepeople.com with lifestyle marketing firm Gaiam; Whole Foods received a minority stake in Gaiam and started selling food online through Gaiam.com.

Hitt resigned in mid-2001 and Mackey took over his duties. Later that year Whole Foods acquired the three upscale Harry's Farmers Market stores in Atlanta; the sale did not include the Harry's In A Hurry stores which later shut down.

In 2002 Whole Foods crossed the border into Canada. Its first foreign store opened in downtown Toronto that May.

Mackey was named Entrepreneur of the Year in 2003 by consulting firm Ernst & Young. That year Whole Foods acquired Select Fish a Seattle-based seafood processor and distributor and opened a seafood distribution facility in Atlanta.

In 2004 Whole Foods opened a 59000-sq.-ft. store in the new Time Warner Center in Manhat-tan. The new store which includes a 248-seat cafe sushi bar wine shop and gourmet bakery is the largest supermarket in New York City. That year the company acquired the UK organic-food retailer Fresh & Wild for $38 million.

To support its rapid growth in 2004 Whole Foods Market expanded its number of operating regions from eight to 10 by separating the South-west region into the Southwest and Rocky Moun-tain regions and the Northern Pacific region into the Northern California and Pacific Northwest re-gion. The company announced the opening of its first Gluten-Free Bakehouse a dedicated gluten-free baking facility located outside Raleigh North Carolina. Overall the company opened 12 new stores in 2004.

In January 2005 Whole Foods launched the An-imal Compassion Foundation an independent non-profit organization dedicated to the compassionate treatment of livestock. The company moved that month to its new corporate headquarters across the street from its old location in downtown Austin. Its new flagship store opened its doors in March at the same location. In October Whole Foods in-creased its number of operating regions from 10 to 11 by separating the North Atlantic region into the North Atlantic and Tri-State regions. Overall in fiscal 2005 the company opened a dozen new stores including its first in Nebraska and Ohio. In 2006 the company acquired a store in Portland Maine and converted it to the Whole Foods Market banner.

In August 2007 Whole Foods acquired its main competitor — Boulder Colorado-based Wild Oats Markets — in a deal valued at about $565 million (plus $106 million in debt). In early October the company sold 35 Henry's Farmers Market and Sun Harvest stores to a subsidiary of Los Ange-les-based Smart & Final for about $166 million. The stores in California and Texas were acquired with Wild Oats.

The company launched a bi-monthly magazine called Whole Foods Market Magazine at its midwestern stores in 2008. On the heels of its dis-appointing third-quarter results in August 2008 shares of the company's stock fell to a six-year low and Whole Foods suspended its dividend. Blaming the poor economy the company an-nounced the layoffs of some 50 employees at its Austin headquarters in August 2008. Overall in fiscal 2008 the company introduced about 300 new private-label items.

For the first time in its 29-year history Whole Foods reported negative same-store sales in the quarter ended December 2008 as traffic in its stores fell.

In March 2009 the company reached a settle-ment in its long-running dispute with the FTC over its acquisition of Wild Oats in 2007. Whole Foods agreed to sell 32 stores including 19 Wild Oats lo-cations that had already been closed. In exchange the FTC dropped its crusade to undo the merger. In December 2009 John Elstrott was named chair-man of Whole Foods Market after Mackey volun-tarily relinquished the chairmanship which he had

held since 1980. In May 2010 Walter Robb for-merly co-president of the company was promoted to co-CEO of Whole Foods a title he now shares with Mackey.

EXECUTIVES

Ceo, John P. Mackey, $1 total compensation
President And Coo, A. C. Gallo, $501,110 total compensation
President Florida Region, Juan Nu ±ez
Chairman Whole Kids Foundation And Whole Cities Foundation, Walter E. Robb, $501,110 total compensation
Evp Operations U.s. And Whole Foods 365, David Lannon, $501,110 total compensation
President Whole Foods Market 365â™, Jeff Turnas
Evp Operations, Christina Minardi
President Southern Pacific Region, Patrick Bradley
President Mid-atlantic Region, Scott Allshouse
President Rocky Mountain Region, Bill Jordan
President Midwest Region, Michael Bashaw
President North Atlantic Region, Laura Derba
Evp And Cio, Jason Buechel, $501,110 total compensation
President South Region, Omar Gaye
President Northern California Region, Rob Twyman
Evp Operations U.s. And The U.k., Kenneth (Ken) Meyer, $486,510 total compensation
Evp Growth And Business Development, James (Jim) Sud, $486,510 total compensation
Evp And Cfo, Keith Manbeck
President Pacific Northwest Region, Angela Lorenzen
Global Vp Marketing, Sonya Gafsi Oblisk
President Northeast Region, Nicole Wescoe
Executive Vice President Operations, Kenny Meyer
Vice President And Marketing Manager, Desa Abbamondi
Vice President Vendor Manager, Ray Hudson
Vice President Information Technology Manager, Tommy Gaskins
Vice President Administration, John Agnew
Senior Vice President Technology Manager, Pedro Adame
Regional Vice President Operations, Michael Howard
Vice President And Loan Officer And Branch Manager, Francisco Ibarra
Global Vice President Culinary And Hospitality, Tien Ho
Global Vice President Procurement Non Perishables, Don Clark
Assistant Vice President And Mortgage Market Manager, Craig Moore
Regional Vice President, Scott Saulsberry
Regional Vice President, Tim Gates
Vice President Of Human Resources Learning And Development Od Oe And Facilities, Francis Lo
Chairman, John B. Elstrott
Auditors: ERNST & YOUNG LLP AUSTIN TEX

LOCATIONS

HQ: WHOLE FOODS MARKET, INC.
550 BOWIE ST, AUSTIN, TX 787034644
Phone: 512 477-4455
Web: WWW.WHOLEFOODSMARKET.COM

2017 Sales

	% of total
US	97
Canada & UK	3
Total	**100**

2017 Stores

US	No.
California	84
Massachusetts	31
Texas	32
Illinois	26
Florida	26
Colorado	19
New York	20
New Jersey	17
North Carolina	13
Arizona	10
Virginia	13
Other States	157
Canada	13
UK	9
Total	**470**

PRODUCTS/OPERATIONS

2017 sales

	% of total
Non-perishables	33
Prepared foods & bakery	19
Other perishables	48
Total	**100**

Selected Product Categories

Bakery
Body care
Educational products
Floral
Grocery
Household products
Meat and poultry
Nutritional supplements
Pet products
Prepared foods
Produce
Seafood
Specialty (beer wine cheese)
Textiles

COMPETITORS

ALDI	Publix
Albertsons	SUPERVALU
Costco Wholesale	Safeway
Fiesta Mart	Shaw's
GNC	Sobeys
H-E-B	Sprouts
J Sainsbury	Tesco
Kroger	Trader Joe's
Lidl	Wal-Mart
Loblaw	Winn-Dixie
Natural Grocers by	Wm Morrison
Vitamin Cottage	Supermarkets

HISTORICAL FINANCIALS

Company Type: Private

Income Statement

FYE: September 24

	REVENUE ($ mil.)	NET INCOME ($ mil.)	NET PROFIT MARGIN	EMPLOYEES
09/17	16,030	245	1.5%	89,000
09/16	15,724	507	3.2%	—
09/15	15,389	536	3.5%	—
09/14	14,194	579	4.1%	—
Annual Growth	**4.1%**	**(24.9%)**	**—**	**—**

2017 Year-End Financials

Debt ratio: ——
Return on equity: 1.50%
Cash ($ mil.): 322
Current ratio: 0.40
Long-term debt ($ mil.): ——

Dividends
Yield: —
Payout: —
Market value ($ mil.): —

Williams Cos Inc (The)

EXECUTIVES

MBR-Ceo, Steven J Malcolm
MBR, Joseph Williams
Vice President, Kevin Flanagan
Analyst, Olivia Cummisky
Auditors: PricewaterhouseCoopers LLP

LOCATIONS

HQ: Williams Cos Inc (The)
One Williams Center, Tulsa, OK 74172-0172
Phone: 918 573-2000
Web: www.williams.com

HISTORICAL FINANCIALS

Company Type: Public

Income Statement

FYE: December 31

	REVENUE ($ mil.)	NET INCOME ($ mil.)	NET PROFIT MARGIN	EMPLOYEES
12/17	8,031	2,174	27.1%	5,425
12/16	7,499	(424)	—	5,604
12/15	7,360	(571)	—	6,578
12/14	7,637	2,114	27.7%	6,742
12/13	6,860	430	6.3%	4,909
Annual Growth	**4.0%**	**50.0%**		**2.5%**

2017 Year-End Financials

Debt ratio: 45.17%
Return on equity: 30.41%
Cash ($ mil.): 899
Current ratio: 0.82
Long-term debt ($ mil.): 20,434

No. of shares (mil.): 826
Dividends
Yield: 0.0%
Payout: 45.8%
Market value ($ mil.): 25,185

	STOCK PRICE ($) FY Close	P/E High/Low		PER SHARE ($) Earnings	Dividends	Book Value
12/17	30.49	12	10	2.62	1.20	11.69
12/16	31.14	—	—	(0.57)	1.68	6.19
12/15	25.70	—	—	(0.76)	2.45	8.21
12/14	44.94	20	13	2.92	1.96	11.75
12/13	38.57	61	50	0.62	1.44	7.12
Annual Growth	**(5.7%)**	—	—	**43.4%**	**(4.4%)**	**13.2%**

Williams Sonoma Inc

Epicureans are at home at Williams-Sonoma a leading multichannel retailer of high-end goods for well-appointed kitchens bedrooms and baths. Home products include bath and storage bedding cookware furniture lighting and tableware. The company's retail chains including Williams Sonoma (upscale cookware) West Elm (modern housewares) and Pottery Barn and Pottery Barn Kids (housewares furniture) sell wares through 630 stores across the US and in Canada Australia the UK and Puerto Rico. Williams-Sonoma also has a thriving e-commerce operation selling merchandise through catalogs and corresponding websites.

Operations

Williams-Sonoma generates revenue from its retail stores as well as through e-commerce websites and catalogs. The company's 630 stores account for nearly 50% of sales with e-commerce contributing just more than 50%. The e-commerce business has been growing at a faster pace.

Its brands include home furnishings giants Pottery Barn which accounts for about 40% of revenue (Pottery Barn Kids and PBteen together bring in another 15%) and West Elm which accounts for more than 20% of revenue. Namesake cookware retailer Williams Sonoma brings in nearly 20%. Other brands include Rejuvenation (lighting and hardware) and Mark & Graham (monogrammed gifts).

Williams-Sonoma also owns Outward a 3-D imaging and augmented reality platform for the home furnishings and décor industry.

Geographic Reach

With nearly 590 stores in the US (including Puerto Rico) Williams-Sonoma generates most of its revenue domestically. It also has about 25 locations in Canada 20 in Australia and a couple in the UK. Unaffiliated franchisees operate about 90 stores in the Middle East the Philippines Mexico and South Korea. Through e-commerce operations the company offers international shipping worldwide.

Williams-Sonoma has corporate facilities in California New York and Oregon; distribution and manufacturing facilities in California Colorado Florida Georgia Massachusetts Mississippi New Jersey North Carolina Ohio Oregon Tennessee and Texas; and a customer care center in Nevada.

Sales and Marketing

In addition to retail stores Williams-Sonoma operates e-commerce websites for all its brands and produces catalogs. The company uses its websites to build brand awareness and as an advertising vehicle. It also uses the websites and catalogs to test new products and brands.

Advertising expenses (including digital advertising catalog advertising and other advertising costs) were $382 million in fiscal 2017 (ended January 2018) compared to $347 million and $333 million fiscal 2016 and fiscal 2015 respectively.

Financial Performance

Unlike many other retailers Williams-Sonoma has seen solid revenue growth over the last five years with sales up 20% since fiscal 2013. The trajectory for net income has been a little more irregular growing through fiscal 2016 and falling since.

In fiscal 2017 (ended January 2018) the company reported revenue of $5.3 billion up 4% from the prior year. The growth was fueled by a 5.5% spike in e-commerce revenue (primarily driven by West Elm Williams Sonoma and Rejuvenation) and a 2.6% rise in retail revenue (primarily driven by Pottery Barn and West Elm).

Williams-Sonoma's net income however declined 15% that year to $260 million as cost of goods sold and selling general and administrative expenses both grew at a faster clip than revenue. In addition the company's income taxes rose 16% as part of a provisional impact from the 2017 Tax Act.

Cash at the end of fiscal 2017 was $390 million an increase of about $175 million from the prior year. Cash from operations contributed nearly $500 million to the coffers while investing activities used $270 million mainly for capital expenditures. Financing activities used another $50 million for dividends to stockholders and Williams-Sonoma's stock repurchase program.

Strategy

E-commerce is Williams-Sonoma's growth engine accounting for nearly 55% of total sales by mid-2018 after first crossing the 50% mark in fiscal 2014. Strong online sales growth has made the company less reliant on retail store expansion which can be risky and expensive to drive its business. To support growth of its online business Williams-Sonoma is investing in back-end technology and leveraging multi-channel customer data to improve the online shopping experience.

In a related initiative the company is streamlining its inventory across all channels to create a more efficient more responsive supply chain. It hopes the “One Inventory” strategy helps reduce turnaround time and consolidate deliveries among other improvements. With its growing online operations optimized store portfolio and investments in technology and supply chain Williams-Sonoma is creating one of the best omnichannel experiences in retail.

Williams-Sonoma continues to invest in its brands as well embracing the exclusivity and best-in-class reputation of its products even if that means a higher price point. Modern furniture chain West Elm has been a particular area of growth for the company with sales jumping some 35% over the past two fiscal years. In fiscal 2017 it launched a new West Elm collection and introduced a smaller-scale multi-use furniture collection for Pottery Barn called PB Apartment as well as a line of sustainable GREENGUARD-certified nursery furniture. Williams-Sonoma's store remodeling efforts are also centered around the West Elm and Pottery Barn brands.

Mergers and Acquisitions

In 2017 Williams-Sonoma acquired California-based Outward a 3-D imaging and augmented reality platform that the company plans to integrate across all its e-commerce sites to improve product visualization and design capabilities. The purchase cost $112 million.

HISTORY

Food lover and hardware store owner Charles Williams founded a cookware store in 1956 in Sonoma California moving it to San Francisco in 1958.

Edward Marcus (of Neiman Marcus) acquired a third of the company in 1972 which then began adding new stores and started its first catalog A Catalog for Cooks. Marcus died in 1976 and Williams unable to manage the burgeoning enterprise sold it to Howard Lester owner of several computer service firms.

Lester acquired Gardeners Eden a mail-order merchandiser of home gardening and related products in 1982. The next year he bought the rights to a new catalog Hold Everything (expanded into retailing later). Williams-Sonoma went public that year. In 1986 it acquired Pottery Barn from The Gap and soon added a catalog business. The company moved into bed and bath goods three years later when it introduced its Chambers catalog.

EXECUTIVES

President And Ceo, Laura J. Alber, age 49, $1,400,000 total compensation

Evp And Coo, Dean A. Miller

Evp And General Merchandise Manager, Marta H. Benson, age 55

Evp Retail And Business Sales, Vicki D. McWilliams

Evp And Chief Digital Technology Officer, John F. Strain

Evp And Cfo, Julie P. Whalen, age 47, $750,000 total compensation

President Williams-sonoma Brand, Janet M. Hayes, age 50, $925,000 total compensation

Evp And Chief Talent Officer, Linda Lewis

Evp And Chief Real Estate And Development Officer, Bud Cope

President West Elm Brand, Alex Bellos

Chairman, Adrian D. P. Bellamy, age 76

Auditors: DELOITTE & TOUCHE LLP

LOCATIONS

HQ: Williams Sonoma Inc
3250 Van Ness Avenue, San Francisco, CA 94109
Phone: 415 421-7900   **Fax:** 415 434-0881
Web: www.williams-sonomainc.com

PRODUCTS/OPERATIONS

2017 Sales

	$ mil.	% of total
E-Commerce	2,778	53
Retail	2,513	47
Total	**5,292**	**100**

2017 Sales

	$ mil.	% of total
Pottery Barn	2,066	39
West Elm	1,114	21
Williams Sonoma	1,022	20
Pottery Barn Kids	625	12
PBteen	234	4
Other	228	4
Total	**5,292**	**100**

Retail

Retail
Mark & Graham (personalized gifts)
PBteen (teen home furnishings)
Pottery Barn (home furnishings flatware and table accessories)
Pottery Barn Kids (children's home furnishings)
Rejuvenation (classic American lighting and house parts)
West Elm (home furnishings decorative accessories tabletop items and textile collection)
Williams Sonoma (cookware cookbooks cutlery dinnerware glassware and table linens)

COMPETITORS

Amazon.com	Macy's
Ashley Furniture	Neiman Marcus
Bed Bath & Beyond	Pampered Chef
Container Store	Pier 1 Imports
Cost Plus	RH
Dean & DeLuca	Sur La Table
Ethan Allen	Target Corporation
Euromarket Designs	Tuesday Morning
Garden Ridge	Corporation
Hanover Direct	Wal-Mart
Lands' End	Z Gallerie
Liberty Interactive	

HISTORICAL FINANCIALS

Company Type: Public

Income Statement — FYE: January 28

	REVENUE ($ mil.)	NET INCOME ($ mil.)	NET PROFIT MARGIN	EMPLOYEES
01/18	5,292	259	4.9%	27,800
01/17	5,083	305	6.0%	28,300
01/16*	4,976	310	6.2%	28,100
02/15	4,698	308	6.6%	26,800
02/14	4,387	278	6.4%	37,200
Annual Growth	**4.8%**	**(1.8%)**	**—**	**(7.0%)**

*Fiscal year change

2018 Year-End Financials

Debt ratio: 10.75%
Return on equity: 21.23%
Cash ($ mil.): 390
Current ratio: 1.62
Long-term debt ($ mil.): 299
No. of shares (mil.): 83
Dividends
  Yield: 0.0%
  Payout: 51.6%
Market value ($ mil.): 4,472

	STOCK PRICE ($) FY Close	P/E High/Low	PER SHARE ($) Earnings	Dividends	Book Value
01/18	53.41	18 14	3.02	1.56	14.38
01/17	47.50	18 13	3.41	1.48	14.29
01/16*	51.66	26 14	3.37	1.40	13.38
02/15	78.25	25 16	3.24	1.32	13.33
02/14	54.52	21 15	2.82	1.24	13.35
Annual Growth	**(0.5%)**		**1.7%**	**6.0%**	**1.9%**

*Fiscal year change

WILMINGTON TRUST COMPANY

EXECUTIVES

Executive Vice President, Mark A Graham
Chief Executive Officer, Robert Harra
Group Vice President, Christine Neri
Vice President, Joe Baker
Vice President, Mary Pupillo
Assistant Vice President, Donald Haverstick
Vice President Business Application Support Manager, Gary Powers
Vice President, Jared Grunig
Vice President Software Development And Support, Glenn Force
Vice President, Murray Pinkus
Vice President, Jeanne Oller
Vice President, Margaret Pulgini
Vice President, Charles Hicks
Assistant Vice President, Steve Barone
Vice President, Wendy White
Vice President, Sandra Plowinske
Vice President Accounting Services Division, Janice Cirillo
Assistant Vice President Corporate Communications, Megen Morris
Vice President Of Marketing And Communications, Jim Klabe
Vice President Marketing, Sherry Costanzo
Senior Vice President Administration, John N Beeson
Vice President Corporate Client Services, Christie Longo
Vice President Client Development, Rob Barnett
Assistant Vice President, Laura Barone
Vice President Wilmington Funds Product Manager, Richard Murad
Vice President Mergers And Acquisitions Operations Manager, John Mark Mulvena
Assistant Vice President, William Morris
Vice President Director Of Wisd Vendor Management, Bill Cunnion
Assistant Vice President, Holly Hammer
Assistant Vice President, Liz Hudgens
Vice President, Virginia Machamer
Vice President And Chief Economist, Luke Tilley
Vice President Network And Desktop Computing, Rob Averbach
Vice President Director Client Services Institutional Custody, Amy Roe
Vice President, Jane Snyder
Vice President And Portfolio Manager, Luke Betterly
Vice President, Dan Gardner
Senior Vice President, James Riley
Vice President Wealth Advisory Senior Private Client Fiduciary Advisor, Latonya Hubbard
Vice President, Michelle Wojciechowicz
Vice President, Thomas Herring

Vice President Senior Fiduciary Advisor, Gina Cronin
Vice President, Jason Johnson
Vice President, Chris Slaybaugh
Vice President Senior Investment Advisor, Mark Stevenson
Assistant Vice President Of Lending, Mary Fisher
Group Vice President, Tom Pierce
Vice President, Rebecca Rogers
Vice President, Steve O'Neal
Private Banking Client Service Specialist Ii Assistant Vice President, Kimberly Hottes
Vice President Corporate Capital Markets, Aaron Soper
Assistant Vice President, Bonnie Metcalfe
Vice President, Carl Robinson
Vice President, Cheryl Fairbanks
Ccts Assistant Vice President, Clarice Wright
Assistant Vice President, Melissa Jalace-vasold
Vice President Senior Private Client Advisor, Sandra Besso Plowinske
Vice President, Ann Harris-johnson
Vice President, Greg Hasty
Vice President Regional Marketing Director, Laura Cleveland
Vice President Private Banking, Julie O'Donnell
Avp, Lisa Lewis
Assistant Vice President, Carleen Terranova
Vice President Private Banking Team Leader Private Banking, Anne St Clair
Vice President, Salvatore Corso
Assistant Vice President, Melissa Marion
Vice President, Larry Long
Assistant Vice President, Brenda Parker
Vice President, Al Miller
Vice President, Brenda Hough
Vice President, Barbara Obrien
Vice President, Charlie Buehler
Vice President And Senior Investment Advisor, Andrew Cloud
Assistant Vice President, Andrea Rybczynski
Vice President, Joseph Odonnell
Vice President, Renee Buchner
Assistant Vice President, Nancy Hagner
Assistant Vice President, Catherine Chandler
Vice President, Kyle Barry
Vice President, Denise Sbraccia
Assistant Vice President, Sophie Pendolino
Assistant Vice President, Donna Torres
Assistant Vice President, Christopher Hickok
Assistant Vice President, Ruth Ann Mcmillen
Vice President, Lynne Marshall
Vice President, Linda Squier
Assistant Vice President, Jose Paredes
Vice President, Howard Gordon
Vice President, David Bagley
Vice President Private Client Advisor, Ed Barone
Vice President, Kaye Crouch
Vice President, Nickole Garrison
Vice President Senior Private Banker, Nicholas Macechko
Assistant Vice President, Russell Whitley
Assistant Vice President, Matthew Lyndaker
Vice President And Investment Advisor, Darren Jordan
Vice President, Erin Miller
Vice President, William Gering
Vice President, James Deitrick
Vice President Senior Investment Advisor, Jeffrey Taylor
Vice President, Joseph Baker
Vice President, Stephen Seivold
Vice President, Theresa Drew
Assistant Vice President, Tammy Krawczyk
Vice President, Todd Bemiller
Vice President And Team Leader, Donald Hargadon
Vice President, Patrick Wood
Assistant Vice President, Susan Laratonda
Group Vice President Family Wealth, Anna Smith

Vice President Mortgage Backed Securities Trader And Analyst, Eric Smookler
Assistant Vice President, David Mcguire
Vice President Administrative, Meghan Ashue

LOCATIONS

HQ: WILMINGTON TRUST COMPANY
  1100 N MARKET ST, WILMINGTON, DE 198900001
Phone: 302 651-1000
Web: WWW.WILMINGTONTRUST.COM

HISTORICAL FINANCIALS

Company Type: Private

Income Statement

	ASSETS ($ mil.)	NET INCOME ($ mil.)	INCOME AS % OF ASSETS	EMPLOYEES
12/17	4,960	30	0.6%	518
12/16	3,685	17	0.5%	—
12/15	1,928	36	1.9%	—
Annual Growth	60.4%	(9.0%)	—	—

2017 Year-End Financials

Debt ratio: ——
Return on equity: 12.90%
Cash ($ mil.): 4,386
Current ratio: —
Long-term debt ($ mil.): —

Dividends
  Yield: —
  Payout: —
Market value ($ mil.): —

Wilson Bank Holding Co.

EXECUTIVES

Chairman; Chairman Of The Board, John Freeman
Vice President And Marketing Director Main Office, Rebecca Jennings
Vice President And Loan Officer Smithville, Chad Colwell
Auditors: Maggart & Associates, P.C.

LOCATIONS

HQ: Wilson Bank Holding Co.
  623 West Main Street, Lebanon, TN 37087
Phone: 615 444-2265
Web: www.wilsonbank.com

HISTORICAL FINANCIALS

Company Type: Public

Income Statement

FYE: December 31

	ASSETS ($ mil.)	NET INCOME ($ mil.)	INCOME AS % OF ASSETS	EMPLOYEES
12/17	2,317	23	1.0%	471
12/16	2,198	25	1.2%	444
12/15	2,021	23	1.2%	446
12/14	1,873	20	1.1%	406
12/13	1,748	15	0.9%	419
Annual Growth	7.3%	10.3%	—	3.0%

2017 Year-End Financials

Debt ratio: —
Return on equity: 9.18%
Cash ($ mil.): 95
Current ratio: —
Long-term debt ($ mil.): —

No. of shares (mil.): 10
Dividends
  Yield: —
  Payout: 28.7%
Market value ($ mil.): —

Windstream Holdings Inc

Windstream Holdings offers a range of telecommunications services to consumers carriers and businesses. The company?s business services include multi-site networking internet access cloud computing colocation online backup and other managed services. For residential customers Windstream offers high-speed internet (including gigabit speed in several markets) and voice services as well as video and bundles of several services. The company provides infrastructure services such as call connection and backhaul connections to wireless carriers. Windstream operates a fiber optic network that measures nearly 150000 route miles mostly in the Eastern and Midwest US.

Operations

Windstream Holdings? operating segments have been Enterprise ILEC (Incumbent Local Exchange Carrier) Consumer and Small Business Wholesale and CLEC (Competitive Local Exchange Carrier) Small Business. In 2018 the company began operating in two segments ILEC Consumer & Small Business and Enterprise & Wholesale.

The Enterprise business which generates about half of revenue provides integrated voice and data services multi-site networking services cloud computing and colocation and managed services. Windstream classifies enterprise customers as those that generate at least $1500 a month in recurring revenue.

The ILEC Consumer and Small Business segment more than 30% of revenue consists of incumbent local exchange carriers that offer traditional local and long-distance voice services and high-speed internet services. It also offers consumer video services through Dish Network LLC and owns and operates cable TV franchises in some of service areas. The segment offers Windstream?s Kinetic video entertainment service in Lincoln Nebraska Lexington Kentucky and Sugar Land Texas.

Wholesale operations about 15% of revenue sell Windstream?s infrastructure and related services to other telecom companies. Leveraging Windstream?s fiber network the segment provides wave transport services carrier Ethernet services fiber-to-tower connections to support backhaul services to wireless carriers and high-speed internet access.

The Small Business CLEC segment about 10% of revenue is composed of the company?s competitive local exchange carriers. Their services include integrated voice and data services advanced data and traditional voice and long-distance services as well as value added services such as online backup managed web design and web hosting and e-mail services.

Geographic Reach

Windstream Holdings is headquartered in Little Rock Arkansas. It manages more than 10 data centers and it has operating authority in 48 states and the District of Columbia. The company maintains more than 60 offices throughout the US.

While the company?s network of about 150000 fiber miles stretches across the country it is concentrated in rural areas of the east Midwest and southwest parts of the US. Windstream?s network is sparse in the west and particularly in Washington Oregon and California. Its Tier 1 and Tier 2 networks have points of presence in major cities around the country including Seattle San Jose Los Angeles Anaheim and Phoenix.

Sales and Marketing

Windstream Holdings sells its products and services through several channels. It has a direct sales force; an account management team; an indirect sales channel in which the company partners with third-party dealers who sell directly to customers; and third-party agents who refer sales leads to the company.

The company spends about $50 million a year on advertising.

Financial Performance

Windstream?s revenue rebounded in 2017 after four years of decline. The company however posted its biggest net loss in 2017 the fourth in five years.

Revenue rose about 7% to $5.8 billion in 2017 from 2016 with acquisitions providing all the growth. The operations of EarthLink and Broadview acquired in 2017 brought about $870 million into the company. Revenue from Windstream?s existing businesses fell about $380 million. The company blamed competition for bleeding off customers in all its segments. Enterprise the biggest segment had the biggest difference off about $195 million in 2017 from 2016. It suffered from reductions in traditional voice long-distance and data and integrated services due to competition as well as declines in long-distance use.

Windstream lost about $2.1 billion in 2017 compared to $383 million loss in 2016. A large unusual expense in 2017 was a $1.4 billion write-down of goodwill. The company also spent some $470 million on the integration of EarthLink and Broadview and another $43 million on restructuring.

The company?s cash on hand fell to about $43 million in 2017 from $59 million in 2016.

Strategy

For Windstream Holdings 2017 was a time to reset and reload in its quest to become a provider of cloud services to companies and a provider of broadband and entertainment services to consumers.

In resetting the company restructured its workforce and made other cost-savings moves to improve its cost structure and improve efficiencies. Windstream cut about 1100 jobs and incurred $35 million in severance and other employee benefit costs. A smaller restructuring in early 2018 cut another 400 jobs.

The reload came with the acquisitions of Earth-Link and Broadview both of which brought new capabilities to Windstream. EarthLink enabled Windstream to launch SD-WAN Concierge a managed network service for cloud computing offerings. With Broadview Windstream introduced OfficeSuite a Unified Communications-as-a-Service product across the company's footprint. Combined SD-WAN and OfficeSuite offer comprehensive service to a wide range of Windstream customers.

Windstream change course in 2018 when it sold the EarthLink consumer internet business to Trive Capital for $330 million. The deal shored up Windstream's balance sheet.

The company also consolidated its business units from four to two which are ILEC Consumer & Small Business and Enterprise & Wholesale to sharpen its focus. In a financial move the company eliminated its quarterly dividend directing that money to pay down debt.

Trying to slow the flow of consumer households from its customer rolls (they declined more than 6% in 2017) Windstream began offering AT&T's DIRECTV satellite service and DIRECTV NOW streaming service to residential customers in 2018. The company sees the satellite service as a complement to it Kinetic high-speed internet service which offers speeds up to 1 Gigabit in some areas.

Windstream is one of the smaller telecommunications providers with a nationwide network. Its resources are dwarfed by the likes of AT&T Verizon and Comcast.

Mergers and Acquisitions

In 2018 Windstream Holdings acquired MASS Communications a privately held New York-based telecommunications network management company for about $37 million. MASS Communications? customers are small to mid-sized companies in the financial legal healthcare technology education and government sectors.

Windstream Holdings acquired Broadview Networks Holdings for nearly $230 million in 2017. Broadview provides cloud-based unified communications services for small and medium-sized businesses. Windstream plans to aggressively push Broadview's cloud operations and deploy its salesforce to compete across the country with companies like Vonage and RingCentral as well as cable companies. The deal was expected to close in the third quarter of 2017.

In 2017 Windstream completed its acquisition of EarthLink Holdings for $1.1 billion. The deal added EarthLink's networks around the country to Windstream's operations and filled in gaps of Windstream's map of service areas across the country.

EXECUTIVES

President Enterprise, Layne L. Levine
Evp Chief Human Resources And Legal Officer, John P. Fletcher, age 52, $515,000 total compensation
President And Ceo, Anthony W. (Tony) Thomas, age 46, $1,000,000 total compensation
Cfo And Treasurer, Robert E. (Bob) Gunderman, age 45, $450,000 total compensation
President Carrier, Mike Shippey
Evp Engineering, Jeff Small
Evp And Cio, Lewis Langston
Evp And Enterprise Chief Marketing Officer, Joe Harding
President Consumer Small And Medium Sized Businesses, Sarah Day, $298,615 total compensation
Clec Consumer Small And Medium-sized Business, Drew Smith
Evp Access, John Dobbins
Svp Process Development And Project Management, Kevin Halpin
Executive Vice President Senior Vice President Vice President, Rodney Hawkins
National Account Manager, Kristin Warren
Sales Vice President, Frank Micallef
Vice President Sales Operations, Brandon Prince
Vice President Channel Sales, Ed Pearce
Vice President Network Operations, Gary Cooke
Region Vice President Operations, Richard Blanc
Chairman, Jeffrey T. Hinson, age 61
Board Member, Kenny Kinsey
Auditors: PricewaterhouseCoopers LLP

LOCATIONS

HQ: Windstream Holdings Inc
4001 Rodney Parham Road, Little Rock, AR 72212
Phone: 501 748-7000
Web: www.windstream.com

PRODUCTS/OPERATIONS

2017 Sales

	$ mil.	% of total
Enterprise	2,942	50
Consumer and Small Business - ILEC	1,978	34
Wholesale	756	13
CLEC Consumer	175	3
Total	**5,852**	**100**

2017 Sales

	$ mil.	% of total
Service revenues	5,759	98
Product sales	93	2

Total	5,852	100

COMPETITORS

AT&T	FullNet Communications
CenturyLink	Momentum Telecom
Comcast	Sprint Communications
Cox Communications	Suddenlink
Crown Castle	Communications
International	Time Warner Cable
Equinix	Verizon

HISTORICAL FINANCIALS

Company Type: Public

Income Statement

FYE: December 31

	REVENUE ($ mil.)	NET INCOME ($ mil.)	NET PROFIT MARGIN	EMPLOYEES
12/17	5,852	(2,116)	—	1,223
12/16	5,387	(383)	—	11,870
12/15	5,765	27	0.5%	12,326
12/14	5,829	(39)	—	12,626
12/13	5,988	241	4.0%	13,434
Annual Growth	(0.6%)	—	—	(45.1%)

2017 Year-End Financials

Debt ratio: 96.31%	No. of shares (mil.): 36
Return on equity: —	Dividends
Cash ($ mil.): 43	Yield: 0.3%
Current ratio: 0.60	Payout: —
Long-term debt ($ mil.): 10,317	Market value ($ mil.): 68

	STOCK PRICE ($) FY Close	P/E High/Low		PER SHARE ($)		
				Earnings	Dividends	Book Value
12/17	1.85	—	—	(62.60)	1.50	(35.55)
12/16	7.33	—	—	(20.55)	3.00	8.83
12/15	6.44	10	4	1.20	11.55	15.84
12/14	8.24	—	—	(2.10)	30.00	11.19
12/13	7.98	1	1	12.00	30.00	42.28
Annual Growth	(30.6%)	—	—	(52.7%)	—	—

Wintrust Financial Corp (IL)

Wintrust Financial is a holding company for 15 subsidiary banks (mostly named after the individual communities they serve) with more than 150 branches primarily in the metropolitan Chicago and southern Wisconsin (including Milwaukee) markets. Boasting assets of more than $23 billion the banks offer personal and commercial banking wealth management and specialty lending services with business and commercial real estate loans making up 60% of the company's loan portfolio. Wintrust's banks target small business customers though some of Wintrust's banks also provide niche lending for homeowners associations medical practices franchisees and municipalities.

Operations

Wintrust operates three business segments: Community Banking which accounted for 77% of total revenue in 2015 and serves individuals and small businesses; Specialty Finance (13% of revenue) operating through First Insurance Funding and First Insurance Funding of Canada which provide financing for commercial insurance and life insurance premiums in the US and Canada respectively; and Wealth Management (10% of revenue) which offers financial planning and brokerage services through The Chicago Trust Company N.A. Wayne Hummer Investments LLC and Great Lakes Advisors LLC.

Wintrust makes more than 70% of its revenue from interest income. About 66% of its total revenue came from loan interest (including fees) during 2015 while another 6% came from interest on investment securities. The rest of its revenue came from mortgage banking (12%) wealth management services (7%) deposit account service charges (3%) and other miscellaneous income sources.

Geographic Reach

Wintrust's banks operate more than 150 branches and 220-plus automatic teller machines mostly located in communities throughout the Chicago metropolitan area and southern Wisconsin. Its wealth management offices are in Chicago; Appleton Wisconsin; and Safety Harbor Florida. Its Wintrust Mortgage subsidiary has 55 locations in a dozen states while its insurance subsidiaries have locations in Northbrook Illinois; Jersey City; Long Island New York; Toronto; Mississauga Ontario; and Vancouver.

Sales and Marketing

The bank's customers include individuals small to mid-sized businesses local governmental units and institutional clients residing primarily in the banks' local service areas.

Wintrust has been ramping up its advertising spend in recent years. It spent $21.9 million on advertising during 2015 up from $13.6 million and $11.1 million in 2014 and 2013 respectively.

Financial Performance

Wintrust Financial's annual revenues have risen more than 40% since 2011 as its loan assets have swelled by nearly 70% with rapid branch expansion. Its annual profits have doubled over the same period.

The banking group's revenue jumped 12% to $990.1 million during 2015 mostly as its average loan balances grew by 15% for the year. Mortgage banking revenue increased 26% for the year thanks to higher origination volumes and purchases on a more favorable mortgage banking environment also helping buoy the company's topline growth.

Strong revenue growth in 2015 drove Wintrust's net income up 4% to $156.75 million despite a rise in acquisition-related professional and legal fees. The group's operating cash levels fell 82% to $37.95 million due to unfavorable working capital changes mainly tied to an increase in accrued interest receivable and other assets.

Strategy

Wintrust has developed its community-based banking franchise through rapid branch expansion stemming from either through new openings or small bank acquisitions. Indeed the bank's branch count has flourished by more than 50% since 2011 from 99 back then to 152 branches at the end of 2015.

Beyond branch expansion the company remains focused on making new loans especially of the commercial and commercial real estate type where opportunities that meet its underwriting standards exist.

Mergers and Acquisitions

In January 2016 Wintrust Financial expanded into Pewaukee Wisconsin after agreeing to buy Generations Bancorp and its Foundations Bank subsidiary. Later that year the company finalized the $33.5 million purchase of First Community Financial Corporation the holding company of First Community Bank (which operates two branches in Elgin Illinois).

In July 2015 the company purchased Community Financial Shares Inc. and its four Community Bank of Wheaton/Glen Ellyn bank branches in the respective communities they serve in Illinois for a total of $42.4 million.

Also in July 2015 the company bought $118 million-asset North Bank and its two branches in Chicago.

In April 2015 Wintrust acquired Suburban Illinois Bancorp and its 10 Suburban Bank & Trust Company (SBT) branches in Chicago and surrounding suburbs for $12.5 million. The SBT locations would operate under Wintrust's Hinsdale Bank & Trust Company subsidiary.

In January 2015 the bank group purchased $224 million-asset Delavan Bancshares Inc. and its Community Bank CBD subsidiary.

Company Background

In 2012 Wintrust expanded its premium funding business into Canada with the acquisition of Macquarie Premium Funding Inc which was a subsidiary of Macquarie Group. The deal marked Wintrust's first international venture.

EXECUTIVES

Evp Technology; President Wintrust Information Technology Services, Lloyd M. Bowden, age 65, $167,333 total compensation

Sevp Coo And Treasurer, David A. Dykstra, age 58, $759,167 total compensation

President Ceo And Director, Edward J. Wehmer, age 63, $1,100,000 total compensation

Evp And Regional Market Head, Frank J. Burke

Evp And Chief Credit Officer, Richard B. Murphy, age 59, $509,167 total compensation

Evp And Chief Administration Officer, Leona A. Gleason

Svp Finance, David L. Stoehr, age 59, $419,167 total compensation

Evp And Regional Market Head, Timothy S. (Tim) Crane, age 56

Evp Wealth Management, Thomas P. (Tom) Zidar

Evp General Counsel And Secretary, Lisa J. Pattis, $446,167 total compensation

Evp And Regional Market Head, David L. Larson

Evp And Coo Wintrust Commercial Finance (wcf), Joseph F. Thompson

Vice President Compliance, Kellie Oostendorp

Executive Vice President, Paul Carlisle

Vice President, Tim Edwards

Executive Vice President, Ursula Moncau

Vice President Managed Assets Division, Sandy Durek

Vice President Loan Operations, Sharon Hiller

Vice President Managed Assets Division, Irene Calzadilla

Vice President, Philip Sheridan

Assistant Vice President Treasury Management, Judy Majon

Assistant Vice President Financial System Management, Marty Lavin

Vice President, Mary Koehler

Vice President Treasury Management, Elizabeth Krumrey

Assistant Vice President Tax, Michelle Serna

Assistant Vice President, Robert Murphy

Vice President, Sarah Withrow

Vice President Real Estate Services, Trey Meers

Senior Vice President, Darragh Griffin

Senior Vice President Business Development, Matt Gambs

Vice President Wintrust Commercial Banking, John Hills

Executive Vice President Commercial Banking, Jeffrey Steigelman

Vice President And Assistant General Counsel, Daniel Stolarsky

Senior Vice President Commercial Banking, Sean Dunn

Vice President, Sara Staniszewski

Senior Vice President, Ryan Witte

Vice President Tax, Mike Masterson

Vice President, Jon Swanson

Vice President Regulatory Reporting, Anita Chakravarthy

Assistant Vice President Treasury Management, Amy Gulotta

Vice President, Teresa Handley

Vice President Professional Practice Group, Jan Eriksen

Assistant Vice President Branch Management, Rick Butterly

Vice President, Caroline Gonos

Vice President, Zornitsa Titova

Vice President Managed Assets Division, Hany Morsy

Vice President Human Resources, Janet Huffman

Executive Vice President And Chief Credit Officer, Paul Hallauer

Vice President Operations Manager Private Banker, Nicole Cox

Executive Vice President, Matthew Doucet

Vice President, Scott Rofstad

Vice President, Nick Koricanac

Vice President Treasury Management, Tracy Zako

Vice President Assistant Controller, Dana French

Senior Vice President Sales, Steve Cusick

Vice President Executive, Sharon Moeller

Vice President Of Business Banking, Miguel Gomez

Assistant Vice President Retail Digital Product Manager, Natalie Fedus

Senior Vice President, Allan Weel

Vice President, Jeffery Wolinski

Senior Vice President Information Services, Mike Nathan

Vice President Finance, Derek Ramsden

Assistant Vice President Branch Manager, Anthony Scott

Vice President Risk, Tim Doran

Senior Vice President Treasury Management, Chris Lantman

Senior Vice President, Brian de la Houssaye

Assistant Vice President, Edward Semik

Vice President, Liz Deboni

Senior Vice President Commercial Real Estate, Daniel Lawlor

Vice President Of Infrastructure, Bill Eisenstot

Vice President Branch Manager, Jerry Kochowicz

Vice President, Tara Fedorko

Senior Vice President, Dawn Mase

Assistant Vice President Commercial Real Estate, Lauren Barnard

Senior Vice President, Tom Carlson

Senior Vice President Risk Strategy And Analytics, Venkat Veeramani

Senior Vice President Of Commercial Banking, Lena Dawson

Chairman, Peter D. Crist, age 67

Auditors: Ernst & Young LLP

LOCATIONS

HQ: Wintrust Financial Corp (IL)
9700 W. Higgins Road, Suite 800, Rosemont, IL 60018
Phone: 847 939-9000   **Fax:** 847 615-4091
Web: www.wintrust.com

PRODUCTS/OPERATIONS

2015 Sales

	$ mil.	% of total
Interest		
Loans including fees	651	66
Securities	61	6
Other	5	-
Non-interest		
Mortgage banking	115	12
Wealth management	73	7
Service charges on deposit accounts	27	3
Fees from covered call options	15	2
Other	40	4
Trading (losses) gains net	(0.2)	-
Total	**990**	**100**

Selected Subsidiaries and Affiliates

Banking
- Barrington Bank & Trust Company N.A.
- Beverly Bank & Trust Company N.A.
- Crystal Lake Bank & Trust Company N.A.
- Hinsdale Bank & Trust Company
- Lake Forest Bank & Trust Company
- Libertyville Bank & Trust Company
- North Shore Community Bank & Trust Company
- Northbrook Bank & Trust Company
- Old Plank Trail Community Bank N.A.
- Schaumburg Bank & Trust Company N.A.
- St. Charles Bank & Trust
- State Bank of The Lakes
- Town Bank
- Village Bank & Trust
- Wheaton Bank and Trust Company

Non-banking
- Chicago Trust Company N.A.
- First Insurance Funding Corporation
- Great Lakes Advisors LLC
- Tricom Inc. of Milwaukee
- Wayne Hummer Asset Management Company
- Wayne Hummer Investments LLC
- Wayne Hummer Trust Company N.A.
- Wintrust Information Technology Services Company
- Wintrust Mortgage Corporation (formerly WestAmerica Mortgage Company)

COMPETITORS

Associated Banc-Corp	Harris
Bank of America	JPMorgan Chase
Citigroup	MB Financial
Citizens Financial Group	Northern Trust
Fifth Third	PrivateBank
First Midwest Bancorp	U.S. Bancorp

HISTORICAL FINANCIALS

Company Type: Public

Income Statement   FYE: December 31

	ASSETS ($ mil.)	NET INCOME ($ mil.)	INCOME AS % OF ASSETS	EMPLOYEES
12/17	27,915	257	0.9%	4,075
12/16	25,668	206	0.8%	3,878
12/15	22,917	156	0.7%	3,770
12/14	20,010	151	0.8%	3,491
12/13	18,097	137	0.8%	3,413
Annual Growth	11.4%	17.1%	—	4.5%

2017 Year-End Financials

Debt ratio: 2.30%
Return on equity: 9.09%
Cash ($ mil.): 1,340
Current ratio: —
Long-term debt ($ mil.): —

No. of shares (mil.): 55
Dividends
  Yield: 0.0%
  Payout: 12.7%
Market value ($ mil.): 4,610

	STOCK PRICE ($) FY Close	P/E High/Low	PER SHARE ($) Earnings	Dividends	Book Value
12/17	82.37	19 14	4.40	0.56	53.19
12/16	72.57	19 10	3.66	0.48	51.96
12/15	48.52	18 14	2.93	0.44	48.62
12/14	46.76	16 14	2.98	0.40	44.22
12/13	46.12	14 10	2.75	0.18	41.21
Annual Growth	15.6%	— —	12.5%	32.8%	6.6%

WISCONSIN ALUMNI RESEARCH FOUNDATION

EXECUTIVES

Dir, Carl Gulbrandsen
Managing Director, Erik Iverson
Director, Jeanan Moe
Controller, Lysa Thoeny
Manager, Ryan Abrams
Communications Marketing Manag, Jacqui Fuller
Licensing Manager, John Nagel
Auditors: LB MCGLADREY LLP MADISON WI

LOCATIONS

HQ: WISCONSIN ALUMNI RESEARCH FOUNDATION
614 WALNUT ST FL 13, MADISON, WI 537262336
Phone: 608 263-2500
Web: WWW.WARF.ORG

HISTORICAL FINANCIALS

Company Type: Private

Income Statement   FYE: June 30

	ASSETS ($ mil.)	NET INCOME ($ mil.)	INCOME AS % OF ASSETS	EMPLOYEES
06/18	3,065	(277)	—	27
06/17	2,931	45	1.6%	—
06/15	3,204	0	—	—
06/14	3,224	0	—	—
Annual Growth	(1.3%)	—	—	—

2018 Year-End Financials

Debt ratio: —
Return on equity: (-399.80%)
Cash ($ mil.): 3
Current ratio: —
Long-term debt ($ mil.): —

Dividends
  Yield: —
  Payout: —
Market value ($ mil.): —

WISCONSIN HOUSING AND ECONOMIC DEVELOPMENT AUTHORITY

EXECUTIVES

Exec Dir, Wyman B Winston
Chairman*, Ivan Gamboa
Chairman of The Board*, Brad Guse
Director, Wyman Winston
Real Estate Conultant, David Sheperd
Financial Officer, Dan Besteman
Information Security Analyst, Erik Larson
Business Analyst, James Bennett
Officer, Tom Schrader

LOCATIONS

HQ: WISCONSIN HOUSING AND ECONOMIC DEVELOPMENT AUTHORITY
201 W WASHINGTON AVE # 700, MADISON, WI 537032760
Phone: 608 266-7884
Web: WWW.WHEDA.COM

HISTORICAL FINANCIALS

Company Type: Private

Income Statement   FYE: June 30

	ASSETS ($ mil.)	NET INCOME ($ mil.)	INCOME AS % OF ASSETS	EMPLOYEES
06/18	2,475	33	1.4%	171
06/17	2,201	23	1.1%	—
06/16	2,082	38	1.9%	—
Annual Growth	9.0%	(6.2%)	—	—

2018 Year-End Financials

Debt ratio: —
Return on equity: 13.30%
Cash ($ mil.): 481
Current ratio: 6.00
Long-term debt ($ mil.): —

Dividends
  Yield: —
  Payout: —
Market value ($ mil.): —

World Fuel Services Corp.

World Fuel Services can't yet affect the earth's spin but it plays a part in moving mostly everything else across its surface. The company sells fuel and fuel handling services to small-to-midsized air carriers cargo and charter carriers and private aircraft. as well as support activities such as flight planning weather reports and card payment services. It is also a marine fuel reseller on hand to deliver marine fuel to the shipping industry and commercial vessels and supplies land transport markets via hundreds of terminals in the US and Watson Fuels in the UK. It has almost 50 offices around the world and does business or virtually every country. The company was founded in 1985 as a marine fuel brokerage firm.

HISTORY

Neighbors Ralph Weiser and Jerrold Blair founded International Oil Recovery an oil recycling company in Florida in 1984. The company moved into aviation fueling by acquiring Advance Petroleum in 1986. Two years later International Oil Recovery diversified further entering the hazardous waste market by buying Resource Recovery of America a soil remediation company. In 1989 the firm acquired JCo Energy Partners an aviation fuel company and subsequently renamed its aviation fueling division World Fuel Services. The company set up International Petroleum in 1993 to operate a Delaware used-oil and water-recycling plant.

The company changed its name to World Fuel Services Corporation in 1995 to reflect its expanded range of operations. Also that year it nearly doubled its revenue base with the purchase of Trans-Tec the world's #1 independent marine fuel services company. World Fuel also exited the environmental services business in 1995 to focus on its fuel services and oil recycling businesses.

The following year the company formed World Fuel International a subsidiary based in Costa Rica that serves World Fuel's aviation customers in South and Central America Canada and the Caribbean. In 1998 it acquired corporate jet fuel provider Baseops International which has offices in the UK and Texas.

In 1999 the company expanded its share of the marine fuel market with the acquisition of the Bunkerfuels group of companies one of the world's top marine fuel brokerages.

To focus on its marine and aviation fueling businesses World Fuel exited the oil recycling segment in 2000 when it sold its International Petroleum unit to waste services company EarthCare for about $33 million.

The company expanded into the United Arab Emirates with its 2001 acquisition of fuel services provider Marine Energy of Dubai. World Fuel acquired Rotterdam-based marine fuel reseller Oil Shipping Group in 2002.

In 2004 World Fuel Services acquired UK-based marine fuel reseller Tramp Holdings for $83 million.

The company diversified further in 2007 acquiring AVCARD a leading provider of contract fuel sales and charge card services to the aviation industry for $55 million.

In 2009 it bought wholesale motor fuel distributor TGS Petroleum. The company combined TGS with Texor to expand World Fuel Services' presence as the largest independent wholesale motor fuel distributor in Illinois.

Expanding its UK market share in 2009 the company acquired the Henty Oil Group of Companies a leading independent provider of marine and land fuels in the UK.

In 2010 it beefed up its position in the branded onshore wholesale market to 1 billion gallons a year by acquiring Lakeside Oil Company based in Milwaukee. It also boosted its market position through the acquisition of leading independent petroleum marketing company Western Petroleum for $95 million.

Boosting its aviation fuel segment in 2011 (for an undisclosed amount) World Fuel Services acquired The Hiller Group an aviation fuel supplier to more than 600 fixed base operators. It also bought Ascent Aviation a national branded reseller of aviation fuel for ConocoPhillips and deicing fluid for Dow Chemical and which supplies more than 450 airports and fixed base operators and NATO aviation fuel and logistics supplier Nordic Camp Supply (for $68.5 million.)

In 2012 the company acquired CarterEnergy's wholesale motor fuel distribution business. Kansas-based CarterEnergy with an annual volume of more than 500 million gallons distributes branded fuel to more than 700 retail operators and is a supplier to industrial commercial and government customers in more than a dozen states. The deal boosted World Fuel Services' land fuel volume to more than 3.5 billion gallons.

In 2013 to improve its payment processing operations it also bought certain assets from Multi Service Corporation (which specializes in fleet government and commercial payment programs) for $137 million. The Multi Service acquisition expands World Fuel Services' presence in the payment processing industry.

EXECUTIVES

Chairman President And Ceo, Michael J. Kasbar, age 62, $875,100 total compensation

Evp And Cfo, Ira M. Birns, age 56, $583,400 total compensation

Evp; Regional Managing Director Asia, Francis L Boon Meng

Evp And Coo, Jeff S. Smith

Evp; Regional Managing Director Emea, Wade N. DeClaris

Svp And Cio, Massoud Sedigh, age 63

Evp Global Aviation And Marine, John P. Rau, $475,100 total compensation

Evp Global Land, Michael J. Crosby, $487,550 total compensation

Vice President People And Performance Development, Marcia Morales-jaffe

Senior Vice President, Michael Szczechowski

Senior Vice President, Carlos Cuervo

Vice President Credit And Risk, Tim Bohall

Vice President Application Development, Russ Sabbag

Vice President Domestic Supply, Brad Hurwitz

Vice President Assistant Treasurer, Glenn Klevitz

Vice President Finance, Monesh Sakhrani

Vice President Application Development, Scott DeLoach

Senior Vice President Land North America, Kerry Oliver

Vice President Business Development, Darren Fuller

Vice President, Jos Heijmen

Executive Vice President, Martin Miller

Vice President, Rebecca Hing

Vice President Corporate Controller, Will Billings

Vice President Information Security, Timothy Ramsay

Vice President Global Operations, Jeffrey Briand

Vice President Retail Channel Development, Ken Wootton

Vice President Business Development, Michael Brown

Vice President Sales And Marketing, Randall Fairbank

Executive Vice President And Chief Financial Officer, Guru Acharya

Auditors: PricewaterhouseCoopers LLP

LOCATIONS

HQ: World Fuel Services Corp.
9800 Northwest 41st Street, Miami, FL 33178
Phone: 305 428-8000   **Fax**: 305 392-5621
Web: www.wfscorp.com

2016 sales

	$ mil.	% of total
Americas	16,726	62
Asia/Pacific	6,018	22
Europe & Middle East & Africa	4,271	16
Total	**27,015**	**100**

PRODUCTS/OPERATIONS

2016 sales

	$ mil.	% of total
Aviation	10,914	40
Marine Land 8918.8	33	
Marine	7,182	27
Total	**27,015**	**100**

Selected Subsidiaries

Ascent Aviation Group Inc.
Baseops Europe Ltd. (UK)
Baseops International Inc.
Casa Petro S.R.L. (Costa Rica)
Henty Oil Limited (UK)
Marine Energy Arabia Co. (L.L.C.) (United Arab Emirates)
Nordic Camp Supply ApS (Denmark)
PetroServicios de Costa Rica S.R.L.
TGS Petroleum
The Hiller Group Incorporated
Tramp Holdings Limited (UK)
Trans-Tec International S.R.L. (Costa Rica)
Western Petroleum Company
World Fuel International S.R.L. (Costa Rica)
World Fuel Services Inc.
World Fuel Services Ltd. (UK)
World Fuel Services (Singapore) Pte. Ltd.

Selected Products and Services

Aviation
Business and General Aviation
Request an Authorization
Validate a Card
Report a Lost Card
Commercial Aviation
Deicing Services
Export Supply
Fuel Management
Risk Management
Tax Information
Marine
Marine Fuels
Lubricants
Operations
Consulting
Yacht Services
Quality Assurance
Physical Supply
Risk Management

COMPETITORS

BBA Aviation	Mercury Air Group
BP Marine	Shell Aviation
Exxon Mobil	Sun Coast Resources
Fuchs Lubricants	

HISTORICAL FINANCIALS

Company Type: Public

Income Statement				FYE: December 31
	REVENUE ($ mil.)	NET INCOME ($ mil.)	NET PROFIT MARGIN	EMPLOYEES
12/17	33,695	(170)	—	5,000
12/16	27,015	126	0.5%	5,000
12/15	30,379	186	0.6%	4,700
12/14	43,386	221	0.5%	4,041
12/13	41,561	203	0.5%	2,758
Annual Growth	**(5.1%)**	**—**	**—**	**16.0%**

2017 Year-End Financials

Debt ratio: 16.29%	No. of shares (mil.): 67
Return on equity: (-9.33%)	Dividends
Cash ($ mil.): 372	Yield: 0.0%
Current ratio: 1.45	Payout: —
Long-term debt ($ mil.): 884	Market value ($ mil.): 1,905

	STOCK PRICE ($) FY Close	P/E High/Low	PER SHARE ($) Earnings	Dividends	Book Value
12/17	28.14	— —	(2.50)	0.24	25.44
12/16	45.91	28 20	1.81	0.24	27.54
12/15	38.46	22 13	2.64	0.24	27.00
12/14	46.93	16 12	3.11	0.15	25.74
12/13	43.16	16 12	2.83	0.15	23.29
Annual Growth	**(10.1%)**	**— —**	**—**	**12.5%**	**2.2%**

WORLD WIDE TECHNOLOGY, LLC

World Wide Technology (WWT) has a broad view of its business. The company primarily provides such IT services as network design and installation systems and application integration and procurement. It also offers a range of Web-based products and services including e-commerce systems development order tracking and catalog management. WWT serves businesses in the automotive retail and telecommunications industries as well as government agencies. Top clients have included Dell the State of Missouri and the State of Alaska. WWT was founded in 1990.

Geographic Reach

WWT has more than 25 facilities throughout the world and about 2 million-sq.-ft of warehouse and distribution space in the US. It also has three distribution outlets in Brazil Mexico and Singapore as well as facilities in London; Amsterdam; Hong Kong; and Chengdu China.

Mergers and Acquisitions

In 2015 WWT purchased St. Louis-based software development firm Asynchrony. The strategic acquisition will allow WWT to deliver complete custom user-facing software and the systems and infrastructure that support it.

EXECUTIVES

Ceo, James P. (Jim) Kavanaugh
Vp Enterprise Commercial & Service Provider Sales, Mark J. Catalano
Cfo, Thomas W. (Tom) Strunk
Vp Corporate Properties, Dan B. Svoboda
President, Joseph G. (Joe) Koenig
Vp And General Manager U.s. East And Europe Sales & Operations, Matt Horner
Vp Supply Chain Operations, Kurt Grimminger
Vp Global Supply Chain, Mark Franke
Vice President Of Information Technology, Mike P. Taylor
Vice President Sales Operations, Tim Loughman
Vice President Business Development, Tariq Hafeez
Vice President Professional Services, Tom Gain
Vice President Of Information Technology, Michael Taylor
Vice President Head Of Asia Pacific, Nilesh Mistry
Vice President Security Solutions, Michael McGlynn
Area Vice President Global Service Provider, Kraig Ecker
Chairman, David L. Steward

LOCATIONS

HQ: WORLD WIDE TECHNOLOGY, LLC
1 WORLD WIDE WAY, SAINT LOUIS, MO 631463002
Phone: 314 569-7000
Web: WWW.WWT.COM

PRODUCTS/OPERATIONS

Selected Services
IT Products and Solutions
  Facilities Infrastructure
  Integration and Staging
  Leasing
  Managed Services
  Order Management and Reporting
  Pre-Sales Support
  Value Added Reseller
Professional Services
  Configuration
  Implementation
  Planning and Design
  Training
Supply Chain Services
  Business Process Outsourcing
  Logistics/Warehousing
  Material Planning and Scheduling
  Outsourced Procurement
  Supplier Management

COMPETITORS

Accenture	HP Enterprise Services
Black Box	IBM Global Services
Computer Sciences	PC Mall
Corp.	Rose International
DataSpan	Unisys
Dynamics Research	WebLinc
En Pointe	

HISTORICAL FINANCIALS

Company Type: Private

Income Statement   FYE: December 31

	REVENUE ($ mil.)	NET INCOME ($ mil.)	NET PROFIT MARGIN	EMPLOYEES
12/15	5,927	95	1.6%	1,052
12/14	5,057	95	1.9%	—
12/13	4,545	77	1.7%	—
12/12	3,396	57	1.7%	—
Annual Growth	20.4%	18.3%	—	—

2015 Year-End Financials

Debt ratio: ——
Return on equity: 1.60%
Cash ($ mil.): 46
Current ratio: 1.00
Long-term debt ($ mil.): —

Dividends
Yield: —
Payout: —
Market value ($ mil.): —

WSFS Financial Corp

WSFS isn't a radio station but it is tuned to the banking needs of Delaware. WSFS Financial is the holding company for Wilmington Savings Fund Society (WSFS Bank) a thrift with nearly $5 billion in assets and more than 75 branches mostly in Delaware and Pennsylvania. Founded in 1832 WSFS Bank attracts deposits from individuals and local businesses by offering standard products like checking and savings accounts CDs and IRAs. The bank uses funds primarily to lend to businesses: Commercial loans and mortgages account for about 85% of its loan portfolio. Bank subsidiaries Christiana Trust Cypress Capital Management and WSFS Wealth Investment provide trust and investment advisory services to wealthy clients and institutional investors.

Operations

Its Christiana Trust division boasts nearly $9 billion in assets under administration and provides investment fiduciary agency bankruptcy and commercial domicile services from offices in Delaware and Nevada.

The company's Cash Connect division operates more than 450 ATMs for WSFS Bank which boasts the largest branded ATM network in Delaware. The division also manages some $490 million of vault cash in approximately 15000 ATMs nationwide and provides online reporting and ATM cash management predictive cash ordering armored carrier management and ATM processing and equipment sales.

Overall the bank generated roughly 57% of its total revenue from interest and fees on loans in 2014 plus an additional 10% from interest on its mortgage-back and other investment securities. About 7% of its total revenue came from wealth management income while mortgage banking income contributed another 2%. The majority of the remaining revenue came from credit/debit card and ATM income and deposit service charges.

Geographic Reach

WSFS Bank has 45 branches throughout Delaware nearly 10 branches in Pennsylvania one branch in Nevada and one in Virginia.

Financial Performance

WSFS Financial's revenues and profits have been trending higher in recent years thanks to sustained growth in its lending business organically and through acquisitions and thanks to declining loan loss provisions as its loan portfolio's

credit quality has improved with the strengthened economy.

The company's revenue rose by 5% to $238.62 million in 2014 thanks to interest income growth mostly driven by increased loan business and higher securities interest; which stemmed from a combination of the bank's First Wyoming Financial Corporation acquisition improvements in its balance sheet mix and additional income from its reverse mortgage-related assets.

Higher revenue and a continued decline in loan loss provisions in 2014 pushed WSFS Financial's net income up by 15% to $53.73 million during the year while the company's operating cash levels jumped by 17% to $67.06 million thanks to higher cash earnings.

Strategy

WSFS Financial reiterated its long-term growth strategy in 2015 which included growing the bank's lending business boosting its Trust and Wealth Management group's assets under administration and expanding Cash Connect's ATM customer base and customer cross-sell.

Beyond utilizing its community-oriented and local commercial lending teams the company has been growing its loan business and its branch reach through strategic acquisitions of banks and bank branches in target markets with preference toward markets in southeastern Pennsylvania. Its 2014 acquisition of First Wyoming Financial Corp for example bolstered WSFS' presence in Kent county while strengthening its position as the one of Delaware's top independent community banks.

Mergers and Acquisitions

In mid-2018 WSFS Financial agreed to purchase Philadelphia-based Beneficial Bancorp in a deal worth $1.5 billion. The transaction will create the largest locally headquartered community bank in the Greater Delaware Valley region with about $13 billion in assets.

EXECUTIVES

Chairman President And Ceo, Mark A. Turner, age 55, $639,336 total compensation
Svp And Corporate Auditor Wsfs Financial And Wsfs Bank, Thomas W. Kearney
Evp And Chief Retail Banking Officer, Richard M. (Rick) Wright, age 65, $337,173 total compensation
Evp And Coo, Rodger Levenson, age 56, $348,721 total compensation
Evp And Chief Human Capital Officer, Peggy H. Eddens, age 62
Evp And Chief Wealth Officer, Paul D. Geraghty, $310,671 total compensation
Evp And Cto, S. James (Jim) Mazarakis, $337,173 total compensation
President Cash Connect, Tom Stevenson
Cfo, Dominic Canuso
Vice President Retail Banking, Adrienne Hawes
Vice President, John Olsen
Senior Vice President Middle Market Team Leader, James Gise
Executive Vice President Human Resources, Robert Silwa
Assistant Vice President Network Services Director, Jason Berkowitz
Vice President Retail Office Manager, Patricia Frechette
Executive Vice President, Cynthia Cole
Executive Vice President And Chief Technology Officer, James Mazarakis
Vice President, Glen Outten
Assistant Vice President Small Business Lender Retail Office Manager, Carol Brindle
Senior Vice President Commercial R E Lending, Joseph C Walker
Vice President, Joseph Murphy
Assistant Vice President Retail Office Manager, Mitra Saffarian-Toosi

Assistant Vice President Commercial Banking, Don Lee
Assistant Vice President, Paul Roughton
Avp Facilities Manager, Bill Hornung
Vice President Relationship Manager, Eric Light
Vice Chairman, Charles G. Cheleden, age 74
Board Member, David Turner
Board Member, Jennifer Davis
Auditors: KPMG LLP

LOCATIONS

HQ: WSFS Financial Corp
500 Delaware Avenue, Wilmington, DE 19801
Phone: 302 792-6000
Web: www.wsfsbank.com

2012 Branches

	No.
Delaware	42
Pennsylvania	7
Nevada	1
Virginia	1
Total	**51**

PRODUCTS/OPERATIONS

2014 Sales

	$ mil.	% of total
Interest		
Loans including fees	137	57
Mortgage-backed securities	13	6
Investment securities	9	4
Noninterest		
Credit/debit card & ATM income	24	11
Deposit service charges	17	7
Wealth management income	17	7
Mortgage baning activities	4	2
Other	15	6
Total	**238**	**100**

COMPETITORS

Bank of America	M&T Bank
Citizens Financial Group	PNC Financial
	Sovereign Bank
Fulton Financial	TD Bank USA
JPMorgan Chase	The Bancorp

HISTORICAL FINANCIALS

Company Type: Public

Income Statement

FYE: December 31

	ASSETS ($ mil.)	NET INCOME ($ mil.)	INCOME AS % OF ASSETS	EMPLOYEES
12/17	6,999	50	0.7%	1,159
12/16	6,765	64	0.9%	1,116
12/15	5,585	53	1.0%	947
12/14	4,853	53	1.1%	841
12/13	4,515	46	1.0%	762
Annual Growth	**11.6%**	**1.7%**	**—**	**11.1%**

2017 Year-End Financials

Debt ratio: 2.36%
Return on equity: 7.12%
Cash ($ mil.): 723
Current ratio: —
Long-term debt ($ mil.): —

No. of shares (mil.): 31
Dividends
 Yield: 0.0%
 Payout: 19.2%
Market value ($ mil.): 1,503

	STOCK PRICE ($) FY Close	P/E High/Low	PER SHARE ($) Earnings	Dividends	Book Value
12/17	47.85	33 27	1.56	0.30	23.05
12/16	46.35	22 13	2.06	0.25	21.90
12/15	32.36	42 13	1.85	0.31	19.50
12/14	76.89	40 33	1.93	0.17	17.34
12/13	77.53	46 25	1.69	0.16	14.35
Annual Growth	**(11.4%)**	**— —**	**(1.9%)**	**17.0%**	**12.6%**

Wyndham Destinations Inc

Wyndham Destinations (formerly Wyndham Worldwide) is one of the world's largest timeshare vacation companies. Its portfolio includes more than 220 vacation ownership resorts offered under the CLUB WYNDHAM WorldMark by Wyndham Margaritaville Vacation Club by Wyndham and Shell Vacations Club brands. The company also manages some 4300 affiliated vacation exchange and rental properties through its Wyndham Vacation Rentals business. All told Wyndham Destinations is present in more than 110 countries. In mid-2018 the company operating as Wyndham Worldwide spun off its hotel franchising business including Days Inn Howard Johnson Ramada and Super 8 into the newly created Wyndham Hotels and Resorts.

Change in Company Type

In 2018 Wyndham split into two separate publicly traded companies Wyndham Destinations a timeshare firm and Wyndham Hotels and Resorts a hotel franchisor. The move was precipitated by the $2.0 billion acquisition by Wyndham Worldwide of La Quinta's hotel franchise and hotel management business. La Quinta which owns more than 890 properties in North Central and South America is now part of the newly formed Wyndham Hotels and Resorts.

EXECUTIVES

Chief Sales And Marketing Officer Wyndham Vacation Clubs, Jeff Myers
Chief Operating Officer Wyndham Vacation Clubs, Geoff Richards
Chief Information Officer, Brad Dettmer
Cfo, Michael Hug
Chief Human Resources Officer, Kimberly A. Marshall
President Wyndham Vacation Rentals, Mary Lynn Clark
President And Managing Director International Operations Wyndham Vacation Clubs, Barry Robinson
Director President And Chief Executive Officer, Michael D. Brown
Chief Brand Officer, Noah Brodsky
General Counsel And Corporate Secretary, James Savina
Vice President Business Development Strategic Sourcing Department, Terrence Gilligan
Vice President, Carolyn Bonifacemesce
Vice President Global Learning And Development, Annmarie Fairweather
Vice President, Travis Miller
Chairman, Stephen P. Holmes, age 62
Auditors: DELOITTE & TOUCHE LLP

LOCATIONS

HQ: Wyndham Destinations Inc
 6277 Sea Harbor Drive, Orlando, FL 32821
Phone: 407 626-5200
Web: www.wyndhamworldwide.com

2016 Sales

	$ mil.	% of total
US	4,238	76
UK	253	5
Netherlands	243	4
Other regions	865	15
Total	**5,599**	**100**

PRODUCTS/OPERATIONS

2016 Sales

	% of total
Service and membership fees	45
Vacation ownership interest sales	29
Franchise fees	12
Consumer financing	8
Other	6
Total	**100**

2016 Sales

	$ mil.	% of total
Vacation Ownership	2,794	49
Destination Network	1,571	28
Hotel Group	1,309	23
Adjustments	(75)	-
Total	**5,599**	**100**

Selected Brands

Wyndham Vacation Ownership
 WorldMark by Wyndham
 Wyndham Vacation Resorts
Vacation Exchange & Rentals
 Canvas Holidays
 Cottages4you.com
 Cuendet
 Endless Vacation Rentals
 Landal GreenParks
 Novasol
Wyndham Hotel Group
 AmeriHost Inn
 Baymont Inn & Suites
 Days Inn
 Hawthorn Suites
 Howard Johnson
 Knights Inn
 Microtel Inns & Suites
 Ramada
 Super 8
 Travelodge
 Wingate by Windham
 Wyndham Hotels and Resorts

COMPETITORS

Accor North America	Hilton Worldwide
Best Western	Hyatt
Carlson Hotels	InterContinental Hotels
Disney Parks & Resorts	
FRHI Hotels and Resorts	Marriott
Four Seasons Hotels	Starwood Hotels & Resorts

HISTORICAL FINANCIALS

Company Type: Public

Income Statement

FYE: December 31

	REVENUE ($ mil.)	NET INCOME ($ mil.)	NET PROFIT MARGIN	EMPLOYEES
12/17	5,076	871	17.2%	39,200
12/16	5,599	611	10.9%	37,800
12/15	5,536	612	11.1%	37,700
12/14	5,281	529	10.0%	34,400
12/13	5,009	432	8.6%	32,800
Annual Growth	**0.3%**	**19.2%**	**—**	**4.6%**

2017 Year-End Financials

Debt ratio: 57.74%
Return on equity: 109.42%
Cash ($ mil.): 100
Current ratio: 1.17
Long-term debt ($ mil.): 5,686

No. of shares (mil.): 99
Dividends
 Yield: 0.0%
 Payout: 27.6%
Market value ($ mil.): 11,576

	STOCK PRICE ($) FY Close	P/E High/Low	PER SHARE ($) Earnings	Dividends	Book Value
12/17	115.87	14 9	8.40	2.32	8.79
12/16	76.37	15 11	5.53	2.00	6.76
12/15	72.65	18 14	5.14	1.68	8.35
12/14	85.76	21 16	4.18	1.40	10.37
12/13	73.69	23 16	3.21	1.16	12.64
Annual Growth	**12.0%**	**— —**	**27.2%**	**18.9%**	**(8.7%)**

Wynn Resorts Ltd

Wynn Resorts operates luxury casino resorts in Las Vegas and South China's Macau (the only place in China where gambling is legal). Its Wynn Las Vegas is a $2.4 billion resort and casino built on the site of the former Desert Inn on the Strip. Wynn Resorts operates in China through Wynn Macau Limited. The company has expanded in both markets adding the Encore at Wynn Las Vegas next to the Wynn Las Vegas the Encore at Wynn Macau adjacent to Wynn Macau and Wynn Palace in the Cotai area of Macau. The Wynn brand is the brainchild of gaming mogul and former Mirage Resorts chairman Steve Wynn.

Operations

Wynn gets about 65% of its revenue from its casino segment; 10% from food & drink; and 10% from hotel rooms fees.

The company's Las Vegas properties boast about 4750 rooms 1900 slots and 235 table games 189000 square feet of casino gaming space some 35 restaurants a golf course and two wedding chapels. Its Encore at Wynn Macau hotel and resort boasts more than 1000 rooms 950 slots 300 table games and 2.84 million square feet of casino gaming space.

Wynn Palace in the Cotai area of Macau features a luxury hotel tower with more than 1700 guest rooms suites and villas approximately 420000 square feet of casino space 10 food and beverage outlets approximately 40000 square feet of meeting and convention space retail public attractions along with recreation and leisure facilities.

Geographic Reach

Wynn brought in more than 65% of its revenue from Macau in fiscal 2016.

Sales and Marketing

Wynn has an international marketing team working across five countries (Hong Kong Singapore Japan Taiwan and Canada) to attract international customers. The company offers loyalty programs to customers through games. Customers who earn points redeem them for free play gifts and complimentary dining and retail shopping. Wynn spent $37 million on advertising and promotional expenses in fiscal 2016 up from $25.2 million in fiscal 2015.

Financial Performance

Wynn reported more than $4.4 billion in revenue for fiscal 2016. That was an increase of around $400 million compared to the $4 billion the company reported for revenue in fiscal 2015. The increase was largely the result of the opening of the Wynn Palace which offset a decline in revenue from the Wynn Macau and flat performance from the Wynn Las Vegas. However due to the high cost of operating casino resorts Wynn only claimed a net income of about $242 million in fiscal 2016.

Strategy

The company has expanded its business by building new properties. Wynn is currently building a lake resort behind its two Las Vegas casinos. The property will offer visitors the opportunity to water-ski and paddle-board just off the Las Vegas strip. The resort which is tentatively called Paradise Park will have also ice cream and a fireworks show every night.

Wynn offers loyalty programs at both its Macau and its Las Vegas properties. The program at its Las Vegas resorts lets customers earn points based on their level of slots play which can be redeemed for free play. The program at its Macau resorts lets customers earn points based on their level of table games and slots play which can be redeemed

for free play gifts and complimentary dining and retail shopping.

In November 2014 Wynn was awarded a gaming license to develop and construct Wynn Boston Harbor an integrated resort in Everett Massachusetts adjacent to Boston along the Mystic River. The resort will contain a hotel a waterfront boardwalk meeting and convention space casino space a spa retail offerings and food and beverage outlets. The total project budget is estimated to be approximately $2.4 billion. Wynn expects to open Wynn Boston Harbor in mid-2019.

EXECUTIVES

President, Matt Maddox, age 42, $1,500,000 total compensation

Evp General Counsel And Secretary, Kim Sinatra, age 57, $873,654 total compensation

Chairman And Ceo, Stephen A. Wynn, age 76, $2,500,000 total compensation

President Wynn International Marketing, Linda Chen, age 51, $1,500,000 total compensation

President Wynn Resorts (macau), Ian M. Coughlan, age 59

Coo Wynn Las Vegas, Maurice Wooden

President And Coo Wynn Design & Development, John Littell

Cfo, Craig S. Billings

Senior Vice President Corporate Security, Jim Stern

Vice President International Marketing, Gabriela Miagro

Executive Vice President Player Development, Larry Altschul

National Sales Manager, Laurae Clifford

Vice President Corporate Security, James Stern

Vice President Benefits, Elaine Lo

Executive Vice President Of Casino Operations, Debra Nutton

Vice President Player Development, Maryann Pascal

Board Member, Ray Irani

Auditors: Ernst & Young LLP

LOCATIONS

HQ: Wynn Resorts Ltd
3131 Las Vegas Boulevard South, Las Vegas, NV 89109
Phone: 702 770-7555
Web: www.wynnresorts.com

PRODUCTS/OPERATIONS

2016 Sales

	% of total
Casino	68
Food and Beverages	12
Rooms	12
Entertainment Retail and Others	8
Promotional Allowances	-
Total	**100**

2016 Sales

% of total	$ in mil.
Macau Operations	64
Las Vegas Operations	36
Total	**100**

Properties

Properties
Las Vegas
Wynn Las Vegas
Encore at Wynn Las Vegas
Macau China
Wynn Macau
Encore at Wynn Macau

COMPETITORS

HISTORICAL FINANCIALS

Company Type: Public

Income Statement

FYE: December 31

	REVENUE ($ mil.)	NET INCOME ($ mil.)	NET PROFIT MARGIN	EMPLOYEES
12/17	6,306	747	11.8%	25,200
12/16	4,466	241	5.4%	24,600
12/15	4,075	195	4.8%	20,800
12/14	5,433	731	13.5%	16,800
12/13	5,620	728	13.0%	16,500
Annual Growth	**2.9%**	**0.6%**	**—**	**11.2%**

2017 Year-End Financials

Debt ratio: 75.93%
Return on equity: 135.14%
Cash ($ mil.): 2,804
Current ratio: 1.77
Long-term debt ($ mil.): 9,565

No. of shares (mil.): 103
Dividends
  Yield: 0.0%
  Payout: 27.4%
Market value ($ mil.): 17,366

	STOCK PRICE ($) FY Close	P/E High/Low	PER SHARE ($) Earnings	Dividends	Book Value
12/17	168.59	23 12	7.28	2.00	9.20
12/16	86.51	46 22	2.38	2.00	1.55
12/15	69.19	83 27	1.92	3.00	(1.10)
12/14	148.76	34 19	7.18	6.25	(0.28)
12/13	194.21	27 16	7.17	7.00	(1.82)
Annual Growth	**(3.5%)**	**— —**	**0.4%**	**(26.9%)**	**—**

Xcel Energy Inc

Xcel Energy has accelerated its energy engine in utility markets across the US. The utility holding company distributes electricity to 3.6 million customers and natural gas to 2 million in eight states through its four regulated utilities. Colorado and Minnesota account for most of the company's customers. Xcel owns power plants that have combined capacity of more than 17500 MW of electricity. It also owns transmission and distribution lines as well as natural gas assets. It is investing in wind power with wind farms in Colorado Minnesota and Texas and more planned.

Operations

Xcel's reportable segments are Regulated Electric Utility Regulated Gas Utility and Other. Regulated Electric is the largest segment and produces about 85% of total revenue through the generation purchase transmission and distribution of electricity. Regulated Natural Gas transports stores and distributes natural gas to generate most of the remaining revenue.

The two power segments achieve their objectives through several subsidiaries: Northern States Power Minnesota (NSP-M) Northern States Power Wisconsin (NSP-W) the Public Service Company of Colorado (PSCo) and Southwestern Public Service (SPS).

Xcel owns and operates roughly 17500 MW of electric generating capacity and purchases additional power from third parties through long-term power purchase agreements. Generally Xcel?s power plants produce about two-thirds of its needs and the company purchases the other third. Of its generated electricity 40% comes from coal 40% from natural gas just less than 10% from nuclear and the rest from wind hydroelectric and other sources. Electricity flows to its customers over more than 20000 miles of Xcel?s transmission lines and through more than 1200 substations.

The Regulated Natural Gas segment purchases the natural gas from producers and contracts with transmission pipeline companies to move it to Xcel?s distributions facilities from there the company sends it on to its gas customers.

Geographic Reach

Minneapolis MN-based Xcel serves a number of US states. It?s Northern States Power Minnesota serves 2 million customers in North and South Dakota and in Minnesota. Northern States Power Wisconsin delivers energy to about 370000 customers in Wisconsin and Michigan. Public Service Company of Colorado provides energy to 2.8 million customers throughout the state while Southwestern Public Service Company serves nearly 400000 in New Mexico and Texas.

Xcel?s supply of natural gas comes from basins in Colorado Montana Wyoming Texas Kansas New Mexico and Canada.

Sales and Marketing

Xcel Energy's major commercial and industrial electric sales are to customers in the petroleum coal and food products industries. It also serves small commercial and industrial customers and produces significant electric retail sales from residential customers.

Financial Performance

In recent years the company?s **financial performance** produced steady revenue and slowly rising net income results. Revenue generally stayed between $10 billion and $11 billion while net income rose from about $600 million back in 2007 to more recent results near $1 billion.

For the year 2016 revenue rose marginally to $11.1 billion with electricity sales gaining a bit more than $200 million and natural gas sales ticking down. The amount of delivered electricity (kilowatt hours) dipped slightly but the dollar amount charged to customers rose. Natural gas experienced the opposite as prices charged to customers decreased while the amount of delivered natural gas rose about 1%.

Net income in 2016 rose 14% to a ten-year high of $1.1 billion. The year-over-year increase was primarily due to a favorable comparison to 2015 which saw a $130 million loss on Xcel?s Monticello power generation project.

Cash at year end was $84 million a negligible change from 2015. Cash activities were largely in line with previous years as operating activities provided $3.0 billion investing activities (mostly capital expenditures) used $3.3 billion and financing activities delivered $210 million largely through issuance of additional debt.

Strategy

Like many electricity companies Xcel Energy is pursuing a long-term shift towards carbon-neutral and renewable energy sources. It also invests in its infrastructure modernizing its grid for safety security and reliability. In the coming five years it anticipates spending $18.3 billion on such projects.

Infrastructure will receive the lion?s share of the $18.3 billion in capital expenditures. Electric transmission & gas distribution systems are targeted to receive $8.2 billion electric generation (such as maintenance of power facilities and refueling nuclear plants) is earmarked for $2.9 billion. Input fuel ? mainly natural gas ? is expected to collect $2.0 billion while the build out of its wind and solar energy sources are expected to receive $3.5 billion.

Of the $3.5 billion for renewables Xcel expects to allocate it to several projects including its 600 MW Rush Creek wind project in Colorado a proposed 750 MW wind generation facility for its NSP-Minnesota utility its 300 MW Dakota Range wind project and even an outreach endeavor to gain regulatory support for 1000 MW of self-build (i.e. customer-built) wind energy. With the exception of Rush Creek which receive approval in 2016 these projects are in various stages of regulatory approval.

HISTORY

The Minnesota Electric Light & Electric Motive Power Company was founded in 1881 and changed its name to Minnesota Brush Electric the next year. In the 1890s it provided street lighting and power for trolleys and became Minneapolis General Electric.

In 1909 Henry Byllesby formed rival firm Washington County Light and Power Co. (soon renamed Consumers Power Company) then created holding company Northern States Power Company of Delaware (NSPD). In 1910 he founded Standard Gas and Electric a holding company overseeing NSPD and many other US utilities.

NSPD bought Minneapolis General Electric in 1912 and Consumers Power was renamed the Northern States Power Company (NSP) in 1916. During the 1920s NSPD connected its subsidiaries via transmission lines. Byllesby died in 1924.

In 1931 NSP was placed under NSPD but the Public Utility Holding Company Act of 1935 dissolved Standard and NSPD. NSP became independent in the 1940s and spent $335 million on new facilities after WWII.

During the 1960s NSP moved into Michigan South Dakota and Wisconsin and brought its first nuclear power plant on line in 1964 (converted to natural gas in 1968). It began operating the Monticello and Prairie Island nukes in the early 1970s.

Company sales nearly doubled in the 1980s. In 1989 NSP created NRG Energy (incorporated 1992) to invest in independent power projects. The Federal Energy Policy Act allowed wholesale power competition in 1992 and NSP lost nine of its 19 municipal customers.

NSP acquired Viking Gas Transmission which owned an interstate pipeline in 1993. It also began developing affordable housing. In 1995 NSP and Wisconsin Electric planned to merge but dropped the deal amid antitrust concerns. NSP continued to diversify forming telecommunications provider Seren Innovations in 1996 and starting its cable-testing business in 1997. The next year NSP formed a power marketing unit.

NRG Energy began a shopping spree abroad in 1994 buying interests in plants in Germany and Australia. In 1996 it bought a 48% stake in Bolivia's COBEE (increased to 99% in 2001). Also that year it acquired PacifiCorp's Pacific Generating unit which owned stakes in a dozen geographically scattered plants.

In 1999 NRG Energy gained nearly 7600 MW of capacity through power plant acquisitions in California Connecticut Massachusetts and New York. The next year NRG Energy picked up another 1700 MW in Louisiana and it agreed to buy fossil-fueled plants (1875 MW) from Delaware's Conectiv for $800 million (half of the deal was completed in 2001 the other half was canceled the following year). NSP spun off part of NRG in 2000 in an IPO.

Meanwhile as the utility-merger trend gathered steam in 1999 NSP agreed to acquire Denver-based New Century Engines in a $4.9 billion deal.

The acquisition was completed in 2000 and the expanded company changed its name to Xcel Energy.

The next year Xcel sold nearly all of its stake in UK-based Yorkshire Power Group which had been held by New Century Energies to Innogy (now RWE npower). It sold its remaining 5% stake in Yorkshire Power in 2002. NRG purchased several Latin American projects from Swedish utility Vattenfall in 2001. NRG also agreed to purchase four coal-fired plants (2500 MW) in Ohio from FirstEnergy for $1.5 billion; however the deal was later canceled.

In 2002 Xcel repurchased the 26% stake in NRG that it sold to the public in 2000-01.

EXECUTIVES

Evp And Group President Operations, Kent T. Larson, age 58, $550,000 total compensation

Chairman President And Ceo, Benjamin G. S. (Ben) Fowke, age 60, $1,200,000 total compensation

President Xcel Energy - Colorado, David L. Eves, age 60

Svp And Cio, David C. Harkness

Evp And Group President Utilities And Chief Administrative Officer, Marvin E. McDaniel, age 58, $550,000 total compensation

President Xcel Energy Michigan Wisconsin, Mark E. Stoering, age 57

Svp And Chief Nuclear Officer, Timothy (Tim) O'Connor, age 58

President Xcel Energy New Mexico Texas, David T. Hudson, age 57

President Xcel Energy Minnesota South Dakota North Dakota, Christopher B. (Chris) Clark, age 51

Evp And General Counsel, Scott M. Willensky, age 61, $505,000 total compensation

Evp And Cfo, Robert C. (Bob) Frenzel, age 47, $397,500 total compensation

Chief Sales Officer, Candace Morse

Vice President Construction Operations And Maintenance, Tim Brossart

Auditors: DELOITTE & TOUCHE LLP

LOCATIONS

HQ: Xcel Energy Inc
414 Nicollet Mall, Minneapolis, MN 55401
Phone: 612 330-5500
Web: www.xcelenergy.com

PRODUCTS/OPERATIONS

2016 Sales

	$ mil.	% of total
Electric	9,501	85
Natural gas	1,532	14
Other	75	1
Eliminations	(2.4)	-
Total	**11,106**	**100**

COMPETITORS

AEP	DTE
ALLETE	FirstEnergy
Alliant Energy	NextEra Energy
Ameren	OGE Energy
Atmos Energy	PPL Corporation
Basin Electric Power	Public Service
Black Hills Power	Enterprise Group
CMS Energy	SCANA
CenterPoint Energy	WEC Energy

Company Type: Public

Income Statement				FYE: December 31
	REVENUE ($ mil.)	NET INCOME ($ mil.)	NET PROFIT MARGIN	EMPLOYEES
12/17	11,404	1,148	10.1%	11,134
12/16	11,106	1,123	10.1%	11,512
12/15	11,024	984	8.9%	11,687
12/14	11,000	1,021	8.7%	11,691
12/13	10,914	948	8.7%	11,581
Annual Growth	1.1%	4.9%	—	(1.0%)

2017 Year-End Financials

Debt ratio: 36.70%	No. of shares (mil.): 507
Return on equity: 10.22%	Dividends
Cash ($ mil.): 83	Yield: 0.0%
Current ratio: 0.73	Payout: 64.0%
Long-term debt ($ mil.): 14,520	Market value ($ mil.): 24,428

	STOCK PRICE ($) FY Close	P/E High/Low	PER SHARE ($) Earnings	Dividends	Book Value
12/17	48.11	23 18	2.25	1.44	22.56
12/16	40.70	21 16	2.21	1.36	21.73
12/15	35.91	20 16	1.94	1.28	20.89
12/14	35.92	18 13	2.03	1.20	20.20
12/13	27.94	17 14	1.91	1.11	19.21
Annual Growth	14.6%	— —	4.2%	6.7%	4.1%

Xerox Corp

Today?s Xerox Corp. is not a copy of its former self. With some 1.5 million devices under its management Xerox remains a leading seller of printers and copiers as well as technology for managing documents and other information services. The company aims to sell its extended portfolio of digital cloud-based automated and security-conscious products and services to its installed base of customers and new ones. But Xerox has been changed significantly. The company cleaved itself in two at the end of 2016 taking the document technology and related services while spinning off business process outsourcing to a new company Conduent. In 2018 Xerox called off a proposed merger agreement with Fujifilm.

Change in Company Type

In January 2018 Xerox agreed to become majority owned by Fujifilm through a joint venture between the companies. Fujifilm would have owned 50.1% and Xerox 49.9%. The cost of the deal would be about $6.1 billion. The companies have operated the Fuji Xerox joint venture which has sold office equipment in the Asia-Pacific region for decades.

In May 2018 Xerox called off the deal citing a failure by Fujifilm to provide audited financials of Fujifilm. Then Xerox agreed to provide investors Carl Icahn and Darwin Deason greater representation on the Xerox board of directors. Icahn and Deason agreed to drop pending litigation against Xerox. Five new directors were appointed to the board replacing five who resigned; four directors remained. A new CEO also was named for Xerox. The new board said it would evaluate strategic alternatives to maximize shareholder value.

Operations

Xerox makes pieces of equipment that make copies send faxes scan documents and more as well as the ink paper and support that keeps the equipment running. The company charges from a few hundred to thousands of dollars for it equipment but it makes 80% of its sales on those post-sale items.

Xerox manages its offerings in three segments: Managed Document Services Workplace Solutions and Graphic Communications.

Managed Document Services offerings are Managed Print Services Multi-Channel Communication Services Workflow Automation Services Content Management and Digitization Services.

Workplace Solutions consists of Xerox?s Entry and Mid-Range equipment products which share common technology manufacturing and product platforms.

Services offered by the Graphic Communications Solutions business are for customers in the graphic communications in-plant and production print environments with high-volume printing requirements.

Geographic Reach

Although Xerox Corp. operates in more than 160 countries about 60% of sales are from customers in the US. About 30% of sales are from Europe with the rest of the world accounting for the rest. The company has primary facilities in Canada France India Ireland Jamaica Guatemala Mexico the Netherlands Philippines Romania the UK and the US.

The company outsources a significant amount of its manufacturing to third parties while maintaining its own production facilities in the US Ireland France and the Netherlands.

Sales and Marketing

Xerox Corp. markets its products and services by geography sales channel type and line of business. It complements its global sales team and sales website with a network of third-party sales channels such as independent agents dealers value-added resellers and systems integrators. Xerox customers are in a wide range of businesses that include banking education government healthcare manufacturing and graphic arts.

Financial Performance

Xerox?s revenue continued it years-long decline in 2017 falling to $10.3 billion down 4% from 2016. The company has shed about $2 billion in revenue since 2013.

The company reported 4% lower revenue in the post-sale segment because of fewer signings and installations from previous years. Equipment sales dropped 7% on lower sales across its product groups and price declines. The fourth quarter saw higher equipment sales with help from its continuous feed inkjet color systems and the new Versant products.

Xerox had lower costs in 2017 compared to 2016 which helped it post a profit of $195 million in 2017 after a $471 million loss in 2016.

Xerox had about $1.3 billion in cash in 2017 down from about $2.2 billion the year before. The company remained operating cash flow positive in 2017 at $122 million ($1 billion in 2016). Operating cash flow in 2017 reflected one-time actions the company took to improve its capital structure and simplify certain processes. The actions include adding a $500 million voluntary contribution to its US tax-qualified defined benefit plans as well as the impact of $350 million from the termination of certain accounts receivable sales programs.

Strategy

If Xerox were a start-up company its strategy might be called a pivot — turning away from a defining but fading business to a different business that has more perceived upside. While documents remain a key Xerox component it is shifting to services in a big way. About 75% of Xerox?s revenue comes from what it calls post sales which is revenue that follows the sale of equipment. Post-sale sources of revenue include document services equipment maintenance services consumable supplies and financing and other elements.

As a large well-established company Xerox has challenges in trying to change. Sometimes large organizations are unable to adapt quickly enough to changing markets and customer preferences. But Xerox also has a big advantage as it pursues a turnaround: a large base of customers and more than 1.5 million Xerox-managed devices serving businesses throughout the world. The company seeks to exploit that resource to sell new products and expanded services.

With new products Xerox is targeting what it believes are growth areas which include document outsourcing and the subcategory of managed print services in the small and medium business market. The company targets the medium-business sector with a range of products.

In 2017 the ConnectKey series of multi-function printers introduced in 2016 and the expansion of its dealer network drove equipment revenue higher in the fourth quarter. ConnectKey was one several new equipment lines the company has introduced in the past two years. The company also released a line of high-volume machines under the Versant label. And it launched a new line called Iridesse a production press that prints up to six colors in one pass in 2018.

Xerox is targeting costs as well as developing new products. The company is in a three-year Strategic Transformation program to accelerate cost productivity. The company expects to increase productivity and reduce costs by $500 million a year over the three years. The program targets efficiency gains in delivery remote connectivity sales productivity pricing design and supply chain.

After trying to merge operations with Fujifilm into their joint venture FujiXerox Xerox pulled out of the deal at the behest of investors who had amassed a large number of Xerox shares. Xerox and Fuji pitched the idea that combining their assets while shedding non-core businesses would make the merged company a formidable competitor in office technology. The investors however believed their shares would be more valuable if Xerox pursued other alternatives.

Mergers and Acquisitions

Following the breakup Xerox Corp. remains on the prowl for acquisitions. Its recent purchases included:

— Global Imaging Systems a multiple-brand dealer in Iowa and MT Business Technologies a multi-brand dealer in Ohio in 2017. The deals expand Xerox?s distribution in those states.

— Intellinex formerly Intrepid Learning Solutions a Seattle-based provider of outsourced learning services.

— RSA Medical a provider of health assessment and risk management for members interacting with health and life insurance companies.

— Healthy Communities Institute a California-based company with a cloud platform for health analytics.

— inVentiv Patient Access Solutions a patient access and reimbursement services hub.

EXECUTIVES

Evp And Chief Commercial Officer, Kevin M. Warren, age 55

Ceo, Jeffrey (Jeff) Jacobson, age 58, $812,500 total compensation

President Xerox Canada, John Corley

Evp; President International Operations, Hervé Tessler, age 54

Svp And Chief Strategy And Marketing Officer, Farooq Muzaffar, age 43

Evp; President North America Operations, Michael (Mike) Feldman, age 51

Evp And Chief Human Resources Officer, Darrell L. Ford, age 53

Svp And Chief Delivery Officer, Yehia Maaty

Evp And Cfo, William F. (Bill) Osbourn, age 53

Svp And Cto, Stephen (Steve) Hoover, age 57

President Northern Southern And Central European Operations, Al Varney

Evp General Counsel And Corporate Secretary, Sarah Hlavinka McConnell, age 53

Vice President Of Sales Major Accounts Operations, Marlene Williams

Assistant Vice President Information Technology Vendor Management, James Burnell

Vice President, Dino Ventresca

Senior Vice President Of Technology, Stephen Garner

Vice President New Product Development, Ann Courtright

Senior Vice President And Managing Director Xerox Healthcare Provider Solutions, Justin Lanning

Vice President Of Sales, Michael Hartman

Vice President Business And Legal Affairs, Joanne Hussey

Vice President And Center Manager, Hadi Mahabadi

Svp Sales - It Outsourcing, George Love

Vice President Information Technology, Karin Gleissle

Vice President And General Manager, Jack Lafferty

Vice President, Ajay Dhingra

Vice President Sales, Peter Reynolds

Vice President, Ivy McKinney

Corporate Vice President And Chief Financial Officer Xerox Technology Business, Grant Fitz

Vice President Of Strategy And Alliances, Tom Kavassalis

Vice President Global Advertising, Barbara Basney

Vice President Client Support Services, Linda Harrison

Vice President, Richard David

Vice President Sales, Michael Murphy

Vice President, Karen Moore

Vice President Information Technology Program Services, Tracy Johnson

Vice President, Michael Weldon

Vp Media Entertainment Hospitality Travel Vertical, Scott Aiken

National Sales Manager, David Stahler

Vice President And Country Director, Aman Mustafa

Vice President Strategy And Workplace Services, David Nappi

Vice President Global Delivery Im Group, Robert Lyubomirsky

Sbu Division Vice President, Jim Selwood

Vice President And Partner, Jan Mccarty

Vice President National Field Controller, Nate Loomis

Vice President, Shreve Bill

Vice President, Dick Jennings

Vice President Of Business Development, Matt Bologna

Xsbg Vice President Of Finance, Enos Steve

Vice President, Terence Oi

National Account Manager, Friedman Karen

Vice President Of Operations, Jeff Dalrymple

Vice President Service, Betty Mitchell

Vice President Finance Us Solutions Group, Dave Aquilla

Vpse, Jules Roche

Vice President Mps Business Operations, Robert Coward

National Account Manager, Amanda Carmichael

Vice President, Eric West

Senior Vice President, Joe Valenti

Division Vice President, Rebecca Taylor

Vice President Sales Operations, Brian Cannatelli

Senior Vice President, Nicola Posa

Vice President, Gavin Jordan-smith

Vice President Of Operations Travel And Retail, Patrick White

Vice President, Bob Tisone

Vice President And Operations, Kathy Mangan

Vice President Operations, Tom Hinds

Assistant Vice President Recruiting Operations, Craig Deaton

Vice President Human Resources And Administration, George Dourlias

Assistant Vice President Talent Acquisition And Staffing, Darrin Johnson

Vice President Sales, Dennis Antishin

Assistant Vice President Talent Leader Executive And Corporate Talent, James Munson

Vice President Business Development, Gloria D'Arezzo

Vice President Human Resources, Jamie Son

Vice President Us Operations, Karen Jacques

Vice President Of Sales Commercial Health Plans, Robert Levy

Vice President Of Sales, Tami Angelo

Vice President Applications And Project Management Office, Kim Ringold

Sbu Director And Vice President, Tom Boyle

Vice President And Senior Corporate Counsel Legal, Don Delorenz

Senior Vice President Southwest Operations, Mary Nelson

Vice President Midrange Hosting, Martin Webb

Senior Vice President Global Service Operations An, Jimmy Brown

Senior Vice President Managing Director Hro Services, Esther Laspisa

Executive Vice President And President Corporate O, James Firestone

Vice President Information Technology, Tim Lilly

Vice President, David Moreland

Corporate Vice President And President Project Management Office, James Lesko

Vice President Sales And Operations, Douglas Chastain

Vice President Of Finance For The Us Channels Group, Jason Barnecut-Kearns

Vice President Human Resources Apac, Arpana Mehra

Vice President Sales, Ken Moore

Vp And Gm Marketing Communications Channel Group Operations Uk And Director, Mark Duffelen

Vice President Epic Solutions, Bradford Grow

Vice President Production Inkjet Sales, Steve Welkley

Pa To Bertrand Cerisier Vice President Global Marketing Office Solutions Business Group, Tracy Styles

Vice President Corporate Communications, Kevin Lightfoot

Svp Acquisitions Corporate Services And Marketing Global Imaging Systems, Michael Pietrunti

Chairman, Robert J. (Bob) Keegan, age 71

Secretary, Jonathan Verna

Secretary, Matthew Mohr

Board Member, Arun Verma

Secretary, Habiba Soares

Board Member, Greg Brown

Auditors: PricewaterhouseCoopers LLP

LOCATIONS

HQ: Xerox Corp
P.O. Box 4505, 201 Merritt 7, Norwalk, CT 06851-1056
Phone: 203 968-3000
Web: www.xerox.com

2017 Sales

	$ mil.	% of total
US	6,064	59
Europe	2,697	26
Other	1,504	15
Total	10,265	100

PRODUCTS/OPERATIONS

2017 Sales

	$ mil.	% of total
Post-sales		8014
78		
Equipment sales	2,251	22
Total	10,265	100

2017 Sales

	$ mil.	% of total
Sales	4,073	40
Services	5,898	57
Financing	294	3
Total	10,265	100

Selected Services

Banking Industry Solutions
Communication & Marketing
Document Management Landing
Document Transaction Processing Services
Education Solutions
Enterprise Content Management
Government Solutions
Healthcare Industry Solutions
Managed Print Services
Manufacturing Industry Solutions
Retail Industry Solutions
Workflow Automation

Selected Products

Office (commercial government and education sectors)
  Copiers
  Displays
  Multifunction devices (copy fax print scan)
  Printers
  Projectors
  Scanners
Production (graphics communications industry and large corporations)
  Digital presses
  High-volume printers
  Software
Other
  Services
  Wide-format printers

COMPETITORS

Accenture	IBM
Agfa	Infosys
Aon	Konica Minolta
Brother Industries	Kyocera Document
Canon	Solutions
Capgemini	Lexmark
Computer Sciences	NEC
Corp.	Océ
Convergys	Oki Data
Dell	Olivetti
Eastman Kodak	Panasonic Corp
Epson	Pitney Bowes
FUJIFILM	Ricoh Company
Fujitsu	Sharp Corp.
Genpact	Tata Consultancy
HP	TeleTech
Heidelberger	Toshiba
Druckmaschinen	Unisys
Hitachi	Wipro

HISTORICAL FINANCIALS

Company Type: Public

Income Statement   FYE: December 31

	REVENUE ($ mil.)	NET INCOME ($ mil.)	NET PROFIT MARGIN	EMPLOYEES
12/17	10,265	195	1.9%	35,300
12/16	10,771	(477)	—	37,600
12/15	18,045	474	2.6%	143,600
12/14	19,540	969	5.0%	147,500
12/13	21,435	1,159	5.4%	143,100
Annual Growth	(16.8%)	(36.0%)	—	(29.5%)

2017 Year-End Financials

Debt ratio: 34.60%
Return on equity: 3.72%
Cash ($ mil.): 1,293
Current ratio: 1.91
Long-term debt ($ mil.): 5,235

No. of shares (mil.): 254
Dividends
Yield: 0.0%
Payout: 105.6%
Market value ($ mil.): 7,422

	STOCK PRICE ($) FY Close	P/E High/Low		PER SHARE ($) Earnings	Dividends	Book Value
12/17	29.15	48	10	0.71	0.75	21.48
12/16	8.73	—	—	(1.96)	1.24	19.78
12/15	10.63	8	6	1.68	1.12	37.21
12/14	13.86	4	3	3.24	1.00	39.34
12/13	12.17	3	2	3.64	0.92	42.58
Annual Growth (15.7%)	24.4%	—	—	(33.5%)	(5.0%)	

XPO Logistics, Inc.

XPO Logistics is a leading provider of third-party logistics and one of the largest less-than-truckload (LTL) carriers in North America. (LTL carriers consolidate freight from multiple shippers into a single truckload.) XPO owns the largest natural gas truck fleet in Europe and it offers domestic and international freight forwarding services as well as truckload freight brokerage service to more than 50000 customers across North America Asia and Europe. It operates through nearly 1500 locations. The company was founded in 1989 as Express-1 Expedited Solutions.

Operations

XPO Logistics' business segments are transportation about 65% of sales and logistics about 35%. Transportation provides freight brokerage last mile LTL full truckload and global forwarding services. Logistics provides a range of contract logistics services including warehousing and e-fulfillment.

Geographic Reach

XPO Logistics is based in Greenwich Connecticut and its European headquarters is in Lyon France. It operates through about 1500 locations across the US and in some three dozen countries. The US is its largest market accounting for 60% of its revenue with France and the UK accounting for 15% and 10% respectively.

Sales and Marketing

XPO Logistics has more than 11000 independent owner-operators under contract to provide drayage expedite last mile and LTL services to customers. It also has more than 50000 independent brokered carriers representing more than 1 million trucks on the road.

XPO has more than 50000 customers in a wide range of industries including high-tech retail e-commerce manufacturing telecommunications aerospace and defense life sciences healthcare medical equipment agriculture and food and beverage. The retail and e-commerce sector accounts for the largest portion of the company?s revenue at roughly 30% followed by food and beverage at more than 15%. The company?s top five customers account for about 10% of revenue.

Financial Performance

XPO Logistics has experienced monumental growth over the years due to a flurry of acquisitions. Revenue doubled from $7.6 billion in 2015 to $15.4 billion in 2017. The fast growth was driven by rising sales from its logistics and transportation segments largely fueled by its Norbert Dentressangle and Con-way acquisitions.

In a year without a major acquisition growth settled down to a less-than-breakneck speed of about 5% in 2017 with sales rising to $15.4 billion in 2017 from 2016. thje increase was spurred by growth in the company?s European contract logistics business improvement in LTL weight per day (packing more goods on each truck) and growth in North American truck brokerage and Last Mile operations. Those increases were somewhat offset by the absence of the North American truckload operation which was sold in October 2016.

XPO?s profit jumped to about $340 million in 2017 from about $69 million in 2016 boosted by a tax benefit from the enactment of the US Tax Cuts and Jobs Act.

XPO had about $397 million in cash and some $591 million in working capital for 2017 compared to $373 in cash and $342 million in working capital in 2016. The increase in working capital was due to higher accounts receivable from higher sales.

Strategy

For all the miles XPO Logistics covers the last mile is pretty special. It?s that last mile to a customer?s door. XPO?s last mile deliveries driven by increasing ecommerce sales in the US and Europe rose about 17% in the US in 2017. XPO specializes in last mile delivery of heavy goods such as furniture and appliance which can include installation. The company used some of the $470 million it invested in technology in 2017 to develop applications for customers and drivers to make such deliveries smoother and more efficient in time and money. Because XPO Logistics uses contract drivers for most last mile deliveries the company has to take on fewer assets.

XPO Logistics does invest in delivery hubs however. The company operates 55 hubs in North America in 2017 and on course to add 30 in 2018 extending its reach to within 90% of the US population. Same-day delivery anyone?

XPO Logistics? dependence on contract drivers for last mile delivery might look good on the balance sheet but it puts the company at the mercy of the job market. Drivers could be lured to other trucking companies or other types of work with more lucrative remuneration.

The company also devoted resources to its sales process in 2017 hiring more than 200 sales people during the year with plans to add another 170 in 2018.

XPO Logistics carries a high amount of debt about $3 billion which could hinder its ability to invest in acquisitions and new technologies.

Addressing its debt situation XPO Logistics refinanced about $1.5 billion of its debt at lower interest rates saving about $15 million. The company also raised about $640 million cash in 2017 in a stock offering. It intends to use the money for more acquisitions.

XPO Logistics? booming business is due to some part to a vigorous economy especially a thriving online retail sector. XPO?s revenue could be threatened by a slow down in the overall economy or slowing growth in ecommerce.

Mergers and Acquisitions

XPO's strategy for growth involves making significant acquisitions that extend its global reach or add new product and service offerings.

In a sweeping move for the logistics industry XPO in 2015 acquired a 67% stake in Norbert Dentressangle a large transportation and logistics provider in Europe. XPO bought Norbert for $3.53 billion in order to significantly up-size its global reach. The deal created the world's second-largest freight brokerage firm by revenue.

In late 2015 XPO also obtained Con-way one of the largest trucking providers in the US. XPO purchased Con-way for $2.3 billion in a milestone deal that made XPO one of the largest freight transportation and logistics providers in the US transforming it from a logistics middleman into a company generating one-third of its revenue from its own truck fleet.

Also that year the company picked up UX Specialized Logistics (UX) a North American provider of last mile logistics services for major retail chains and e-commerce companies for $59 million. The acquisition expanded the company?s network for heavy goods home delivery and added more density to its growing e-commerce logistics footprint.

EXECUTIVES

Chairman And Ceo, Bradley S. Jacobs, age 61, $607,000 total compensation
Managing Director Logisticsâ—europe, Malcolm Wilson
President Less-than-truckload (ltl), Tony Brooks
Cio, Mario A. Harik, age 37
President Of Transportation North America, Christopher R. Synek
President Intermodal, Paul V. Smith
Cfo, John J. Hardig, age 53, $498,385 total compensation
Chief Strategy Officer, Scott B. Malat, age 41, $472,308 total compensation
Coo And Ceo Europe, Troy A. Cooper, age 48, $511,539 total compensation
Chief Human Resources Officer, Meghan A. Henson
Managing Director Transportâ—europe, Luis-Angel Gomez Izaguirre
President Supply Chain Americas And Asia Pacific, Ashfaque Chowdhury
President Last Mile, Charles Hitt
Vice President Of Transportation, Don Ingersoll
National Account Manager, David Hannegan
National Account Manager, Ed Skarda
Vice President Strategic Accounts, Michael Doumas
Vice President Strategic Accounts, Keith Weaver
Vice President Strategic Accounts, Andy Sommers
Vice President Operations, Roger Lekberg
Senior Vice President Operation Last Mile, Fernando Rabel
Vice President Strategic Accounts, Greg DiPalma
Market Vice President, Mike DaCorsi
Vice President Transportation, Nick Caragher
Region Vice President Sales, Anthony Hoereth
Vice President Procurement, Mitch Plaat
National Account Manager, Craig Robertson
Senior Vice President Financial Planning And Analysis, Liam Harrington
Senior Vice President Development Supply Chain Europe, Jean-Luc Declas
Vice President Strategic Accounts, Jay Lambert
Vice President Information Technology Client Support, Tim Merritt
Senior Vice President And Treasurer, Ravi Tulsyan
Senior Vice President Sales Supply Chain Europe, Mark Wilkinson
Senior Vice President Communications, Erin Kurtz
Senior Vice President It Shared Services, Maneet Singh
Senior Vice President Global Talent Acquisition, Bertrand Dussert
National Account Manager, Brad Rouse
Freight Brokerage Regional Vice President, Drew Wilkerson
Senior Vice President Client Services, Jared Baker
Vice President Internal Audit, Lon Staub
Vice President Finance Order To Cash, Lorenzo Polacco
Vice President Strategic Accounts, Drew Paxton
Vice President Operations, Shawn Getchell
Vice President Business Development, Richard Reed
Vice President Strategic Accounts, Rick Mathews

Vice President Strategic Accounts, Terence McCarthy
Vice President Strategic Accounts, Eric Thompson
Vice President Strategic Accounts, Garrett Lutgen
Vice President Strategic Accounts, George Holland
Vice President Of Strategic Accounts, Randall Cason
Vice President And General Counsel, Richard Valitutto
Senior Vice President Corporate Real Estate, Russ Marzen
Vice President Business Development, Errol Keel
Vice President Business Development, Paul Palmieri
Senior Vice President Sales :ess Than Truckload (ltl) North America, Russell Hoch
Auditors: KPMG LLP

LOCATIONS

HQ: XPO Logistics, Inc.
Five American Lane, Greenwich, CT 06831
Phone: 855 976-6951
Web: www.xpologistics.com

2017 Sales

	$ mil.	% of total
United States	9,162	59
North America (excluding United States)	297	2
France	2,006	13
United Kingdom	1,798	12
Europe (excluding France and United Kingdom)	1,930	13
Asia	170	1
Other	14	-
Total	15,380	100

PRODUCTS/OPERATIONS

2017 Sales

	$ mil.	% of total
Transportation	9,820	63
Logistics	5,722	37
Eliminations	(162.4)	-
Total	15,380	100

Service

Service
Last Mile
Intermodal
Global Forwarding
Supply Chain
Expedite
Freight Brokerage

COMPETITORS

Alliance Air	New Penn Motor Express
C.H. Robinson	Norfolk Southern
Worldwide	Panther Expedited
CSX	Services
DHL	Ryder System
Daylight Transport	Schneider National
Deutsche Post	Towne Air Freight
Expeditors	UPS
FedEx	Union Pacific
Forward Air	YRC Worldwide
J.B. Hunt	

HISTORICAL FINANCIALS

Company Type: Public

Income Statement   FYE: December 31

	REVENUE ($ mil.)	NET INCOME ($ mil.)	NET PROFIT MARGIN	EMPLOYEES
12/17	15,380	340	2.2%	95,000
12/16	14,619	69	0.5%	87,000
12/15	7,623	(191)	—	89,000
12/14	2,356	(63)	—	10,000
12/13	702	(48)	—	2,259
Annual Growth	116.3%	—	—	154.7%

2017 Year-End Financials

Debt ratio: 35.88%	No. of shares (mil.): 119
Return on equity: 10.79%	Dividends
Cash ($ mil.): 396	Yield: —
Current ratio: 1.20	Payout: —
Long-term debt ($ mil.): 4,417	Market value ($ mil.): 10,983

	STOCK PRICE ($) FY Close	P/E High/Low		PER SHARE ($) Earnings	Dividends	Book Value
12/17	91.59	34	16	2.45	0.00	30.06
12/16	43.16	87	34	0.53	0.00	24.31
12/15	27.25	—	—	(2.65)	0.00	24.81
12/14	40.88	—	—	(2.00)	0.00	21.38
12/13	26.29	—	—	(2.26)	0.00	14.93
Annual Growth	36.6%	—	—	—	—	19.1%

Xylem Inc

Xylem primes the pump for the future of water and other fluids. The company (whose name derives from a Greek term about water and roots) makes fluid-handling and related products for treating and recycling wastewater. It operates in three divisions: Water Infrastructure Sensus and Applied Water. Water Infrastructure makes pumps treatment and testing equipment and controls and analytical instruments while Applied Water offers pumps valves heat exchangers controls and dispensing equipment. Xylem's products are sold under about 35 different brands including Flygt and Goulds.

Operations

Xylem's three main segments are Water Infrastructure (60% of net sales) Applied Water (37%) and Sensus (3%). Xylem's water products are used by public utilities residential and commercial building services industrial customers and agricultural applications. It products address critical water issues such as growing water scarcity aging infrastructure and environmental regulations.

Geographic Reach

The company has operations in more than 150 countries around the world with over 380 locations in about 50 countries. Xylem generates almost 60% of its revenue from outside the US.

Sales and Marketing

Xylem sells its products through global direct sales indirect channels and independent distributors. It targets the residential commercial industrial and agricultural sectors. Residential consumers represent end users in the residential market in addition to owners and managers of properties such as apartment buildings retail stores institutional buildings restaurants schools hospitals and hotels.

In the industrial market Xylem caters to OEMs exploration and production firms and developers and managers of industrial facilities including electrical power generators chemical manufacturers machine shops clothing manufacturers beverage dispensing and food processing firms and car washes. In addition agricultural end users include owners and operators of crop and livestock farms aquaculture golf courses and other turf applications.

Financial Performance

Xylem's revenues have fluctuated in recent years. After declining to $3.65 billion in 2015 revenues jumped 3% to $3.77 billion in 2016. Fueled by a robust public utility end market and a more stable commercial business the growth was driven by increased revenue of $163 million from acquisitions and organic revenue growth of $29 million.

Its profits however declined 24% from $340 million in 2015 to $260 million in 2016. This was mainly due to additional restructuring and alignment costs of $30 million and $17 million respectively. The company also absorbed acquisition-related costs of $53 million in 2016. During its fiscal year 2017 Xylem expects to incur about $30 million in Sensus integration restructuring and realignment costs.

Xylem's operating cash flow has increased the last three years climbing from $464 million in 2015 to $497 million in 2016. It attributed this latest growth to continued improvement in working capital levels specifically efficiencies recognized from its Sensus acquisition.

Strategy

In the years ahead Xylem is targeting growth in the public utilities and smart meter markets. It expects large project activities to drive growth particularly in China and India. Additionally it anticipates increased Sensus public utility revenue triggered by growth in the US by a growing demand for smart metering applications.

Mergers and Acquisitions

Xylem pursues acquisitions that broaden its core product portfolio grow its geographic footprint and improve its position in strategic markets. In late 2016 it acquired Sensus for about $1.7 billion in cash. Sensus provides smart meters network technology and data analytics services for the water electric and gas industries. Sensus is now reported as one of the company's three core operating segments and is seen as a springboard for future growth.

Company Background

Xylem was spun off from ITT Corp. as a standalone company in October 2011.

EXECUTIVES

Svp And Cfo, E. Mark Rajkowski, age 59, $461,538 total compensation
Svp General Counsel And Corporate Secretary, Claudia S. Toussaint, age 54, $427,346 total compensation
Svp And President Americas Commerical Team And Applied Water Systems, Kenneth (Ken) Napolitano, age 56, $416,938 total compensation
Svp And President Sensus & Analytics, Colin R. Sabol, age 50, $420,408 total compensation
President And Ceo, Patrick K. Decker, age 53, $975,384 total compensation
Svp And Cio, Nicholas R. Colisto
Svp And President Transport And Treatment And President Xylem Europe Gmbh, Tomas Brannemo, age 46
Svp And Chief Marketing Officer, Joseph P. (Joe) Vesey
Svp And President Emerging Markets, Pak (Steven) Leung, age 61, $302,220 total compensation
Svp And Chief Innovation And Technology Officer, Jayanthi (Jay) Iyengar
Svp And President Dewatering, David Flinton, age 46
Svp And President Europe Commercial Team, Christian Blanc
Vp And Treasurer, Samir Patel
Vp Corporate Development, Hyman Buchwald
Vp Chief Ethics And Compliance Officer, Kevin Jaffe
Vp Americas Region Aws, Marc Blais
Vice President And Director Product Development, Christian Wiklund
Vice President Internal Audit, Osvaldo Llanes
Vice President Growth Center Analytics Emea And Ap, Sean Donnelly
National Sales Manager Industrial, Steve Scott

Vice President Global Marketing And
Communications, Jackie Helfrich
Vp And Director Sales Dewatering Solutions, Mike
Delzingaro
Vice President Global Real Estate And Facilities
Management, Bill Alexander
Vice President Global Strategic Sourcing, Chris
Mapes
Senior Vice President Continuous Improvement
And Business Transformation, Tony Milando
Vice President Ethics And Compliance, Shekofeh
Holmer
Chairman, Markos I. Tambakeras, age 67
Auditors: DELOITTE & TOUCHE LLP

LOCATIONS

HQ: Xylem Inc
1 International Drive, Rye Brook, NY 10573
Phone: 914 323-5700   Fax: 914 323-5800
Web: www.xyleminc.com

2016 Sales

	$ mil.	% of total
US	1,574	42
Europe	1,195	31
Asia/Pacific	518	14
Other	484	13
Total	**3,771**	**100**

PRODUCTS/OPERATIONS

2016 Sales

	$ mil.	% of total
Water infrastructure	2,246	60
Applied water	1,393	37
Sensus	132	3
Total	**3,771**	**100**

2016 Sales

	$ mil.	% of total
Pumps accessories parts and service	2,888	77
Others	883	23
Total	**3,771**	**100**

Selected Brands

AADI
AC Fire Pump
Alcon
Bell & Gossett
Bellingham & Stanley
Domestic Pump
ebro
Essence of Life
FloJet
Flowtronex
Flygt
Global Water
Godwin
Goulds
Hoffman Specialty
Jabsco
Leopold
Lowara
Marlow
McDonnell & Miller
Midland-ACS
OI Analytical
PCI Membranes
Red Jacket Water Products
Royce Technologies
Rule
Rule Innovation
Sanitaire
SI Analytics
Standard
Vogel
Water Equipment Technologies (WET)
Wedeco
WTW
YSI

Selected Products and Services

Boiler controls
Flow switches
Heat exchangers
Liquid level controls
Mixers
Pumps
Reverse osmosis watermakers
Valves
Water treatment systems
Biological wastewater - aeration
Backwash water recover
Ozone oxidation
Sludge collection systems
Ultraviolet disinfection

COMPETITORS

Badger Meter	KSB AG
Danaher	Pall Corporation
Elster Group SE	Pentair
Franklin Electric	Roper Technologies
Gorman-Rupp	Siemens Corp.
Grundfos	Sulzer
IDEX	Thermo Fisher
Itron	Scientific

HISTORICAL FINANCIALS

Company Type: Public

Income Statement

FYE: December 31

	REVENUE ($ mil.)	NET INCOME ($ mil.)	NET PROFIT MARGIN	EMPLOYEES
12/17	4,707	331	7.0%	16,200
12/16	3,771	260	6.9%	16,000
12/15	3,653	340	9.3%	12,700
12/14	3,916	337	8.6%	12,500
12/13	3,837	228	5.9%	12,500
Annual Growth	**5.2%**	**9.8%**	**—**	**6.7%**

2017 Year-End Financials

Debt ratio: 32.07%
Return on equity: 14.11%
Cash ($ mil.): 414
Current ratio: 1.88
Long-term debt ($ mil.): 2,200
No. of shares (mil.): 179
Dividends
  Yield: 0.0%
  Payout: 39.3%
Market value ($ mil.): 12,267

	STOCK PRICE ($) FY Close	P/E High/Low	PER SHARE ($) Earnings	Dividends	Book Value
12/17	68.20	38 26	1.83	0.72	13.92
12/16	49.52	38 23	1.45	0.62	12.20
12/15	36.50	20 16	1.87	0.56	11.68
12/14	38.07	22 17	1.83	0.51	11.67
12/13	34.60	28 20	1.22	0.47	12.14
Annual Growth	**18.5%**	**— —**	**10.7%**	**11.5%**	**3.5%**

YOSEMITE FARM CREDIT, ACA

EXECUTIVES

Pres, Leonard Van Eldern
Cfo*, Tracy Sparks
Vice President, Brian Lemons
Vice President Marketing, Melba Miyamoto
Manager, Ray Koopman
Vice President, Robert Fuller

LOCATIONS

HQ: YOSEMITE FARM CREDIT, ACA
806 W MONTE VISTA AVE, TURLOCK, CA 953827242
Phone: 209 667-2366
Web: WWW.YOSEMITEFARMCREDIT.COM

HISTORICAL FINANCIALS

Company Type: Private

Income Statement

FYE: December 31

	ASSETS ($ mil.)	NET INCOME ($ mil.)	INCOME AS % OF ASSETS	EMPLOYEES
12/17	2,889	53	1.8%	100
12/16	2,661	43	1.6%	—
12/15	2,368	41	1.7%	—
12/14	2,154	38	1.8%	—
Annual Growth	**10.3%**	**11.2%**	**—**	**—**

2017 Year-End Financials

Debt ratio: —
Return on equity: 48.90%
Cash ($ mil.): 9
Current ratio: —
Long-term debt ($ mil.): —
Dividends
  Yield: —
  Payout: —
Market value ($ mil.): —

YRC Worldwide Inc

YRC Worldwide stands for more than Your Regional Carrier. The company has one of the largest less-than-truckload (LTL) networks in North America with local regional national and international capabilities. YRC Worldwide is a holding company that operates through such subsidiaries as YRC Freight and YRC Reimer which transport goods for manufacturing wholesale retail and government customers in the US Canada and certain international markets as well as YRC Regional Transportation which provides regional next-day ground services in the US Canada Mexico and Puerto Rico through subsidiaries New Penn USF Holland and USF Reddaway. The company dates back to 1924.

Operations

YRC Freight is YRC Worldwide's largest segment raking in around 65% of its parent's sales. With around 260 owned and leased facilities and a fleet of about 7600 tractors and about 31900 trailers YRC Freight has one of the largest networks of less-than-truckload (LTL) service centers equipment and transportation staff in North America. YRC Freight's subsidiary Reimer Express (also known as YRC Reimer) offers Canadian customers shipping options within the country throughout North America and around the world.

Its Regional Transportation segment accounts for the remaining revenue and focuses on regional and the next-day delivery markets. This segment comprises USF Holland New Penn Motor Express and USF Reddaway. These companies provide their services through a network of facilities in Canada Puerto Rico and the US.

Geographic Reach

Most of YRC Worldwide's revenues comes from the US. However a small portion — less than 5% — is derived from international markets mainly Canada and Mexico. The company operates some 385 transportation service facilities located in 50 US states Puerto Rico and Canada.

Sales and Marketing

YRC Freight serves manufacturing wholesale retail and government customers throughout North America.

Financial Performance

Over the last five years YRC's revenue has been unstable while profits have been low to negative.

In fiscal 2017 revenue increased 4% to $4.9 billion thanks to higher fuel surcharge revenue and improved yield. Growth was balanced between YRC Freight and Regional Transportation.

The company incurred a net loss of $10.8 million in 2017. The loss was a result of increased operating expenses particularly salaries wages and benefits purchased transportation expense fuel costs and lower gains on property sales.

Cash from operations fell 42% to $60.7 million due to weak operating income.

Strategy

As it attempts to put the many years of net losses behind it YRC Worldwide is focused on remaining profitable and enhancing its technological infrastructure. Large trucking companies are among the most sophisticated users of transportation technology. This includes bar code readers signature capturing equipment and radio frequency identification (RFID) tagging allowing drivers to quickly manage the transfer of goods. To help improve its position in this critical strategic area YRC Worldwide hired its first CIO in mid-2017.

HISTORY

In 1924 A. J. Harrell established a trucking company in conjunction with his Oklahoma City bus line and Yellow Cab franchise. Harrell's Yellow Transit trucking operation hauled less-than-truckload (LTL) shipments between Oklahoma City and Tulsa. By 1944 Yellow had more than 50 independent subsidiaries in Illinois Indiana Kansas Kentucky Missouri and Texas. That year the company was sold to an investment firm and renamed Yellow Transit Freight Lines. But Yellow's policy of paying high dividends stunted its growth and by 1951 it faced bankruptcy.

George Powell Sr. took over in 1952 and turned Yellow around. His son George Powell Jr. became CEO in 1957 and the company went public two years later. George Jr. focused the company on long-haul interstate shipments and started buying up other trucking companies.

In 1965 Yellow expanded to the West Coast and the Southeast by purchasing Watson-Wilson Transportation System. Changing its name to Yellow Freight System (1968) the company acquired part of Norwalk Truck Lines and its routes in the Northeast (1970) and Adley Express (1972) providing new East Coast routes. Yellow extended routes into the Pacific Northwest by buying Republic Freight Systems in 1975. Its 1978 purchase of Braswell Motor Freight Lines consolidated its routes in California Texas and the Southeast. Yellow's only deviation from route acquisitions was its $4 million investment in oil firm Overland Energy in 1976 which it dissolved in the early 1980s.

The company was unprepared however when Congress deregulated trucking routes and shipping rates in 1980. Yellow upgraded its aging depots and terminals but profits still declined by 1983. In 1982 Yellow Freight formed a holding corporation (renamed Yellow Corporation in 1992). George Powell III took over from his father as CEO in 1990. Yellow purchased Preston Trucking an overnight freight hauler in 1992.

In 1994 Yellow Freight was hit by a 24-day Teamsters' strike that allowed nonunion carriers to gain a chunk of its market. The next year struggling during industry price wars it reported a $30 million loss. Yellow laid off about 250 employees mostly from Yellow Freight. George III resigned in 1996 and Maurice "Mr. Fix-it" Myers became CEO. Myers began moving the firm from a one-size-fits-all LTL trucker to a more flexible customer-responsive trucking and logistics firm.

Yellow Freight was restructured in 1997 into decentralized business units to improve customer service and hundreds of workers were laid off. The misfortunes of other companies also created good fortune for Yellow: UPS went on strike and rail traffic was still snarled from the 1996 Union Pacific-Southern Pacific merger.

To expand international operations Yellow created YCS International in 1998 (renamed Yellow Global in 2000). It also secured a five-year labor contract with its unions ending the danger of a strike. Loss-making Preston was sold to three company executives and Yellow acquired regional carriers Action Express (1998) and Jevic Transportation (1999).

Myers drove off into the sunset in 1999 to take over another troubled giant Waste Management and Yellow Freight president William Zollars became CEO of Yellow Corp. In 2000 Yellow and two venture capital firms set up online transportation marketplace transportation.com to provide freight-forwarding and multimodal brokerage services.

Yellow integrated Action Express and WestEx into Saia Motor Freight Line in 2001. The next year Yellow renamed its Yellow Freight subsidiary Yellow Transportation. The company created SCS Transportation to act as a holding company for its regional nonunion carriers Saia and Jevic. Also in 2002 Yellow combined transportation.com with its other logistics serv

EXECUTIVES

Ceo And Director, James L. Welch, age 64, $850,000 total compensation

President Yrc Freight, Thomas J. (T.J.) O'Connor, age 57, $280,257 total compensation

President Holland, Scott D. Ware, age 57, $395,000 total compensation

President And Coo, Darren D. Hawkins, age 48, $481,000 total compensation

President New Penn, Donald R. (Don) Foust, age 60

Vp General Counsel And Corporate Secretary, James A. Fry, age 56, $259,474 total compensation

Vp And Controller, Stephanie D. Fisher, age 41

Cio, Jason T. Ringgenberg

Chief Customer Officer, Justin M. Hall, age 38, $239,167 total compensation

Vp Operations Reddaway, Bob Stone

Vice President, Bill Schwar

Vice President Treas, Mark D Boehmer

Vice President Human Resources And Benefits, Sandra Stocke

Vice President Eastern Division, Mitch Lilly

Senior Vice President Of Marketing, Bill Crowe

Vice President Controller, Tom Ventura

Vice President Investor Relations, Tony Carreno

Vp Legal And Regulatory Compliance, Andrean Horton

Vp Ir, Anthony Carreno

Chairman, James E. (Jim) Hoffman, age 65

Board Member, Patricia Nazemetz

Board Member, James Winestock

Board Member, Douglas Carty

Board Member, William Davidson

Auditors: KPMG LLP

LOCATIONS

HQ: YRC Worldwide Inc
10990 Roe Avenue, Overland Park, KS 66211
Phone: 913 696-6100
Web: www.yrcw.com

PRODUCTS/OPERATIONS

2017 Sales

	$ mil.	% of total
YRC Freight	3,067	63
Regional Transportation	1,823	37
Elimination	(0.7)	-
Total	**4,891**	**100**

2017 Sales

	$ mil.	% of total
United States	4,791	98
Foreign	99	2
Total	**4,891**	**100**

COMPETITORS

ABF Freight System	Landstar System
ArcBest	Mullen Group
C.H. Robinson Worldwide	Old Dominion Freight
Central Freight Lines	Saia
Estes Express	Schneider National
FedEx Freight	UPS Freight
J.B. Hunt	UPS Supply Chain Solutions

HISTORICAL FINANCIALS

Company Type: Public

Income Statement

FYE: December 31

	REVENUE ($ mil.)	NET INCOME ($ mil.)	NET PROFIT MARGIN	EMPLOYEES
12/17	4,891	(10)	—	32,000
12/16	4,697	21	0.5%	32,000
12/15	4,832	0	0.0%	32,000
12/14	5,068	(67)	—	33,000
12/13	4,865	(83)	—	32,000
Annual Growth	**0.1%**	**—**	**—**	**0.0%**

2017 Year-End Financials

Debt ratio: 57.15%	No. of shares (mil.): 32
Return on equity: —	Dividends
Cash ($ mil.): 91	Yield: —
Current ratio: 1.29	Payout: —
Long-term debt ($ mil.): 875	Market value ($ mil.): 471

	STOCK PRICE ($) FY Close	P/E High/Low		PER SHARE ($) Earnings	Dividends	Book Value
12/17	14.38	—		(0.33)	0.00	(10.80)
12/16	13.28	25 10		0.65	0.00	(12.82)
12/15	14.18	1125614		0.02	0.00	(11.80)
12/14	22.49	—		(3.00)	0.00	(15.47)
12/13	17.37	—		(8.96)	0.00	(58.73)
Annual Growth	**(4.6%)**	**—**		**—**	**—**	**—**

Yum China Holdings Inc

Auditors: KPMG Huazhen LLP

LOCATIONS

HQ: Yum China Holdings Inc
7100 Corporate Drive, Plano, TX 75024
Phone: 469 980-2898
Web: www.yumchina.com

HISTORICAL FINANCIALS

Company Type: Public

Income Statement

FYE: December 31

	REVENUE ($ mil.)	NET INCOME ($ mil.)	NET PROFIT MARGIN	EMPLOYEES
12/17	7,144	403	5.6%	450,000
12/16	6,752	502	7.4%	420,000
12/15	6,909	323	4.7%	400,000
12/14	6,934	(7)	—	—
12/13	6,905	126	1.8%	—
Annual Growth	**0.9%**	**33.7%**	**—**	**—**

Zimmer Biomet Holdings Inc (continued)

2017 Year-End Financials

Debt ratio: 0.66%
Return on equity: 15.62%
Cash ($ mil.): 1,059
Current ratio: 1.77
Long-term debt ($ mil.): 28

No. of shares (mil.): 384
Dividends
Yield: 0.0%
Payout: 9.9%
Market value ($ mil.): 15,397

	STOCK PRICE ($) FY Close	P/E High/Low	PER SHARE ($) Earnings	Dividends	Book Value
12/17	40.02	41 25	1.01	0.10	7.23
12/16	26.12	22 19	1.36	0.00	6.21
Annual Growth	11.3%	— —	(7.2%)	—	3.9%

	STOCK PRICE ($) FY Close	P/E High/Low	PER SHARE ($) Earnings	Dividends	Book Value
12/17	81.61	22 16	3.77	1.20	(19.08)
12/16	63.33	22 15	4.04	1.89	(15.93)
12/15	74.00	32 23	2.92	1.69	2.17
12/14	73.14	35 28	2.32	1.52	3.56
12/13	73.87	32 26	2.36	1.38	4.89
Annual Growth	2.5%	— —	12.4%	(3.3%)	—

Yum! Brands Inc

EXECUTIVES

Ceo, Greg Creed
Non Exec Chb, Brian C Cornell
Pres-Cfo, David Gibbs
Gen Counsel-Corp SEC-Chief Gov, Marc Kesselman
Sr V Pres Fin-Corp Contrl, David Russell
Chief Transformation & People, Tracy Skeans
Internal Audit, Sam Schroeder
Chief People Officer (indian S, Sanchita Singh
Associate Manager, Scott Sexton
Data Management Senior Support, Wesley Welsh
Ceo KFC Division, Roger Eaton
Auditors: KPMG LLP

LOCATIONS

HQ: Yum! Brands Inc
1441 Gardiner Lane, Louisville, KY 40213
Phone: 502 874-8300
Web: www.yum.com

COMPETITORS

A&W Restaurants	Domino's
AFC Enterprises	Jack in the Box
American Dairy Queen	Little Caesar's
Arby's	Long John Silver's
Burger King	McDonald's
CKE Restaurants	Papa John's
Chick-fil-A	Quiznos
Chipotle	Sonic Corp.
Church's Chicken	Subway
Dairy Queen	Wendy's
Del Taco	

HISTORICAL FINANCIALS

Company Type: Public

Income Statement   FYE: December 31

	REVENUE ($ mil.)	NET INCOME ($ mil.)	NET PROFIT MARGIN	EMPLOYEES
12/17	5,878	1,340	22.8%	60,000
12/16	6,366	1,619	25.4%	90,000
12/15	13,105	1,293	9.9%	505,000
12/14	13,279	1,051	7.9%	537,000
12/13	13,084	1,091	8.3%	539,000
Annual Growth	(18.1%)	5.3%	—	(42.2%)

2017 Year-End Financials

Debt ratio: 184.60%
Return on equity: —
Cash ($ mil.): 1,522
Current ratio: 1.66
Long-term debt ($ mil.): 9,429

No. of shares (mil.): 332
Dividends
Yield: 0.0%
Payout: 31.8%
Market value ($ mil.): 27,095

ZEN-NOH GRAIN CORPORATION

EXECUTIVES

Ceo, John D Williams
Dir*, Yoshihiro Sugiyama
Dir*, Yoshinori Ohara
Dir*, Hiroyuki Kawasaki
Sr. V Pres*, Charles E Colbert
Cfo*, Shin Inoue
Contlr*, Robin Gerarve
Controller, Cindi Ernst
Senior Vice-President, Chris Schuster
Manager, Barbara Campbell
Manager, Sean Burke

LOCATIONS

HQ: ZEN-NOH GRAIN CORPORATION
1127 HWY 190 E SERVICE RD, COVINGTON, LA 704334929
Phone: 985 867-3500
Web: WWW.CGB.COM

HISTORICAL FINANCIALS

Company Type: Private

Income Statement   FYE: May 31

	REVENUE ($ mil.)	NET INCOME ($ mil.)	NET PROFIT MARGIN	EMPLOYEES
05/18	6,971	101	1.5%	188
05/17	7,047	67	1.0%	—
05/16	5,722	37	0.7%	—
05/15	6,000	86	1.4%	—
Annual Growth	5.1%	5.7%	—	—

2018 Year-End Financials

Debt ratio: —
Return on equity: 1.50%
Cash ($ mil.): 43
Current ratio: 0.10
Long-term debt ($ mil.): —

Dividends
Yield: —
Payout: —
Market value ($ mil.): —

Zimmer Biomet Holdings Inc

Zimmer Biomet can put the spring back in your step or the zing back in your swing. The company designs and markets orthopedic products including reconstructive implants used in knee or hip replacement surgery shoulder implants that restore function in arthritic joints bone and tissue grafting materials and sports medicine products. It also makes dental implant systems spinal implants to fix aching or injured backs and trauma products (such as plates screws and pins) that help broken bones to heal. Additionally Zimmer Biomet makes surgical products used in orthopedic surgeries including tourniquets and devices for wound cleansing. The firm's products are sold around the globe.

Operations

Zimmer Biomet's four primary operating segments are: Spine less Asia Pacific; Office Based Technologies; Craniomaxillofacial and Thoracic (CMF); and Dental. Its operations are managed through three major geographic segments: Americas Asia/Pacific and Europe Middle East and Africa (EMEA).

The company makes most of its money from sales of knee and hip replacement products (around 35% and 25% of revenues respectively). Some of its lead products are the Persona and NexGen knee systems Zimmer M/L taper hip prosthesis and Taperloc hip system. In addition to knee and hip replacements the company makes early intervention and joint preservation products to treat diseases such as osteoarthritis.

The SET category of products includes surgical sports medicine foot and ankle biologics and trauma lines. These include the Transposal line of fluid waste management systems ATS tourniquets Zimmer trabecular metal reverse shoulder system and others. The SET products account for about 20% of sales.

Spine and CMF products include the Polaris spinal system Timberline lateral fusion system and face and skull reconstruction items. These categories bring in 10% of the company's sales.

Surgical supplies and other operations (which bring in another 10% of sales) include the Tapered Screw-Vent dental implant system 3i T3 implant Palacos bone cement and SpinalPak spinal fusion stimulator as well as the Accelero Health Partners unit (surgeon consulting).

Geographic Reach

Zimmer Biomet?s operations are managed through three major geographic segments: Americas Asia/Pacific and Europe Middle East and Africa (EMEA).

The Americas segment (largely consisting of US operations) accounts for more than 60% of the company's annual revenues though sales in international markets (especially in the Asia/Pacific region which includes such markets as Australia China India Japan and Hong Kong) are rising. EMEA including sales in France Germany Italy Spain and the UK accounts for about a fifth of all revenues. Zimmer Biomet's products are sold in more than 100 countries worldwide and the company has direct operations in more than 40 countries.

Zimmer Biomet's primary manufacturing facilities are located in the US (Warsaw Indiana; Westminster Colorado; Dover Ohio; Austin Texas; Jacksonville and Palm Beach Gardens Florida; and Parsippany New Jersey) the Netherlands (Hazeldonk) Puerto Rico (Ponce) Ireland (Shannon Galway) China (Beijing Changzhou and Jinhua) France (Valence) Germany (Berlin and Eschbach) Singapore Spain (Valencia) South Wales (Bridgend) and Switzerland (Winterthur).

Sales and Marketing

Zimmer Biomet sells its orthopedic products directly to health care providers (such as hospitals surgery centers and surgeons themselves) as well as to purchasing organizations distributors and health care dealers. Its dental products are sold directly to dental practices and laboratories. Zimmer Biomet markets biologic bone and tissue allografts for dental spinal and trauma procedures through a partnership with RTI Surgical.

The US sales force is made up of direct employees and contracted exclusive agents. European sales are handled by direct associates support employees commissioned agents and independent distributors while Asia/Pacific sales are handled through a network of dealers and associates. Direct channels account for around 75% of the company's net sales.

Financial Performance

After Zimmer Biomet's net sales increased 28% in both 2015 and 2016 they stayed relatively flat in 2017 increasing 2% to $7.8 billion. Sales of spine and CMF products rose that year as did hip and SET product sales but these gains were partially offset by declines in the knee dental and other product categories. Geographically all three primary segments saw growth in 2017 but the Asia/Pacific led the increase with a 5% gain.

Net income rose nearly 500% to $1.8 billion in 2017 thanks largely to a $1.3 billion income tax benefit related to the 2017 Tax Act. The company also kept its operating expenses in check that year which further helped its bottom line.

Cash flow from operations fell a modest 3% to $1.6 billion in 2017; this was driven by deferred income tax provisions as well as negative changes in operating assets and liabilities such as accounts payable.

Strategy

Zimmer Biomet works to keep its sales figures on the rise through new product development efforts as well as by introducing next-generation versions of existing best-sellers that add functionality or ease of use. New products include its Persona Partial Knee and the X-PSI Knee System the first X-ray-based surgical planning system. Other recent launches include the Vitality+ and Vital Spinal Fixation systems and the company has additional new products on the horizon.

Along with increasing its sales through product growth Zimmer Biomet expands through acquisitions partnerships and international expansion efforts. The company expects overall industry trends to help keep its sales in the black: The aging US population chronic obesity and advances in surgical techniques are all expected to contribute to increased demand for its products. However the company could continue to see depressed prices in some segments due to economic conditions (causing patients to decrease non-essential expenses) and government and hospital cost-control programs.

In 2017 the company initiated a program to improve its global manufacturing operations. However it had problems meeting demand for its hip knee and SET products due to production delays at its Indiana manufacturing campus. It has been working to bring the facility back up to speed but is still seeing the impact of delays on its sales performance. Additionally the company began sourcing certain products from two separate vendors in 2017 to minimize slowdowns in production.

Zimmer Biomet initiated a Class I recall of several types of its spinal fusion implants in 2018. The company announced that the products potentially contained high levels of harmful chemicals.

Mergers and Acquisitions

In 2016 Zimmer Biomet completed a number of acquisitions to expand its product portfolio. It bought Texas-based LDR Holding Corporation for $1 billion; that deal furthered its presence in the spine disorder business. Zimmer Biomet also acquired Arizona-based Cayenne Medical in a move that strengthened its sports medicine operations including its portfolio of soft tissue reconstruction solutions. It purchased the Netherlands-based imaging firm Clinical Graphics which specializes in 3D range-of-motion simulation technology; that deal boosted the company?s hip preservation portfolio.

Also that year Zimmer Biomet acquired Colorado-based Ortho Transmission for an undisclosed price. Ortho Transmission develops skeletal implant technology for limb amputee patients; Zimmer Biomet is utilizing the unit's technology as part of its ongoing collaboration with the US Department of Defense which aims to restore mobility for amputee patients.

Company Background

Formerly part of Bristol Myers Squibb Zimmer Holdings was spun off into an independent operation in 2001.

In mid-2015 Zimmer acquired fellow implant maker Biomet for $14 billion. The deal made the combined company the #2 orthopedics seller worldwide behind Johnson & Johnson. It also doubled Zimmer's knee and dental lines and gave it entry into the lucrative sports medicine business. Upon completion of the transaction Zimmer took on the Biomet name.

EXECUTIVES

Executive Vice President Finance And Chief Financial Officer, James T Crines

Group President Joint Reconstruction, Daniel E. (Dan) Williamson, age 52, $224,329 total compensation

Group President Biologics Extremities Sports Medicine Surgical Trauma Foot Ankle And Bone Healing, David A. Nolan

Svp General Counsel And Secretary, Chad F. Phipps, age 47, $470,615 total compensation

Svp Cfo And Interim Ceo And Director, Daniel P. (Dan) Florin, age 54, $562,692 total compensation

President Europe Middle East And Africa, Katarzyna Mazur-Hofsaess, age 54, $612,644 total compensation

Group President Spine Dental Cmf And Thoracic, Adam R. Johnson, age 41

President Asia/pacific, Sang Yi, $459,156 total compensation

Vp U.s. Sales, Robert D. (Rob) Delp

Svp Global Operations And Logistics, Adrian Furey

Vice President Manager Director, Amy Feldman

Chairman, Larry C. Glasscock, age 69

Auditors: PricewaterhouseCoopers LLP

LOCATIONS

HQ: Zimmer Biomet Holdings Inc
345 East Main Street, Warsaw, IN 46580
Phone: 574 267-6131
Web: www.zimmer.com

2017 Sales

	$ mil.	% of total
Americas	4,865	62
EMEA	1,745	22
Asia/Pacific	1,213	16
Total	**7,824**	**100**

PRODUCTS/OPERATIONS

2017 Sales

	$ mil.	% of total
Knees	2,737	35
Hips	1,879	24
SET	1,709	22
Spine & CMF	759	10
Dental	418	5
Other	320	4
Total	**7,824**	**100**

Selected Products

Reconstructive implants
  Alloclassic hip system
  Anatomical shoulder implants
  Bigliani/Flatow shoulder implants
  MIS 2-Incision Total Hip Replacement
  MIS Mini-Incision Total Knee Procedure
  NexGen knee replacement

Trabecular Metal Primary Hip Prosthesis
VerSys Hip System
Zimmer Collagen Repair Patch (rotator cuff repair)
Trauma products
  I.T.S.T. Nail System (hip and proximal femur fractures)
  M/DN Intramedullary Fixation (for long bone fractures)
  NCB Locking Plate System (complex long bone fractures)
  Sirus Intramedullary Nail System (for long bone fractures)
Dental products
  AdVent dental implant system
  Tapered screw-vent implant system
Spine products
  CopiOs Bone Void Filler
  Dynesys Dynamic Stabilization System
  Optima ZD Spinal Fixation System
  Puros allografts
  ST360 Spinal Fixation System
Surgical products
  A.T.S. Tourniquet Systems
  Brasseler USA surgical power tools (for long bones)
  Pneumicro surgical power tools (for small bones)
  Pulsavac Plus (wound cleaning)
  Zimmer Ambulatory Pump (pain management)

COMPETITORS

Corin Group	Nobel Biocare
DJO Global	NuVasive
DePuy	Orthofix
Dentsply Sirona	ReGen Biologics
Exactech	Smith & Nephew
Genzyme Biosurgery	Straumann
Globus Medical	Stryker
JRI Orthopaedics	Synthes
MAKO Surgical	

HISTORICAL FINANCIALS

Company Type: Public

Income Statement

FYE: December 31

	REVENUE ($ mil.)	NET INCOME ($ mil.)	NET PROFIT MARGIN	EMPLOYEES
12/17	7,824	1,813	23.2%	18,200
12/16	7,683	305	4.0%	18,500
12/15	5,997	147	2.5%	17,500
12/14	4,673	720	15.4%	10,000
12/13	4,623	761	16.5%	9,500
Annual Growth	**14.1%**	**24.3%**	**—**	**17.6%**

2017 Year-End Financials

Debt ratio: 39.06%	No. of shares (mil.): 202
Return on equity: 16.95%	Dividends
Cash ($ mil.): 524	Yield: 0.0%
Current ratio: 1.50	Payout: 10.7%
Long-term debt ($ mil.): 8,917	Market value ($ mil.): 24,448

	STOCK PRICE ($) FY Close	P/E High/Low	PER SHARE ($) Earnings	Dividends	Book Value
12/17	120.67	15 12	8.90	0.96	57.93
12/16	103.20	87 60	1.51	0.96	48.20
12/15	102.59	156 118	0.77	0.88	48.78
12/14	113.42	27 21	4.19	0.88	38.43
12/13	93.19	21 15	4.43	0.80	37.09
Annual Growth	**6.7%**	**— —**	**19.1%**	**4.7%**	**11.8%**

Zions Bancorporation, N.A.

Originally formed at the behest of Brigham Young Zions Bancorporation outgrew its early roots to become one of the largest banks in the US. The corporation is a holding company for ZB National Association Nevada State Bank National Bank of Arizona Vectra Bank Colorado The Commerce Bank of Washington California Bank & Trust and Texas-based Amegy Bank. Combined they operate some 430 bank branches in 11 mostly Western US states. The Zion banks focus on commercial and retail banking as well as mortgage and construction lending deposit accounts home mortgages credit cards and trust and wealth management services.

Operations

Zions Bancorporation is comprised of seven regional business segments each of them operating as an affiliated bank. The banks focus on community banking geared towards small and medium-sized business and offer corporate banking commercial & residential development retail banking cash management and trust & wealth management. The banks are some of the nation?s largest providers of small business administration (SBA) lending and together are a top originator of secondary market agricultural real estate loans.

The banks provide a range of personal banking services such as home mortgages home equity lines of credit checking & savings accounts safe deposit boxes internet and mobile banking.

Zion Bancorporation generates most of its revenue through interest payments on the loans it issues. Interest income generated by loans money marketing investments and other securities account for around 80% of Zions? revenue with the remainder coming from fees for deposit accounts and other service-related charges.

Geographic Reach

Based in Utah the holding company operates more than 430 bank branches throughout Utah Idaho California Texas Arizona Wyoming Nevada Colorado New Mexico Oregon and Washington.

Sales and Marketing

The banking subsidiaries of Zion Bancorporation markets its services locally through company websites digital advertising and word-of-mouth referrals. Each bank approaches its market with the mindset of a community bank working with small and medium business owners as well as retail consumers located within a geographic proximity of its branches.

Financial Performance

Only recently did Zions? revenue hit bottom following the 2008-2009 financial crisis. Since 2015 revenue has been on the upswing though its results are still some 20% below the 2009 result. The holding company however has learned how to turn a profit. Earning moved higher in all but one year since 2011 and have more than tripled between 2011 and 2017.

Revenue in 2017 rose 11% to $2.7 billion. Interest income accounted for $2.2 billion of the total and non-interest income (fees service charges etc.) made up the rest. Zions? loan portfolio grew 5% in the year with upswings occurring in residential mortgages commercial & industrial loans and municipal lendings. Oil & Gas and term commercial real estate lending slid shaving nearly $550 million from the portfolio. Rising interest rates which pushed Zions? net interest margin to 3.45% (from 3.37% in 2016) helped expand interest income. Customer-related fee income rose 8% due to im-provements in credit card fees and trust & wealth management income.

Net income rose 34% to $550 million an excellent result following the prior year?s 66% jump. Wages and salaries and general expenses rose a bit compared to 2016 but all other costs were in line with the prior year. Income taxes shaved off about $100 million more than 2016 but overall the increased revenue flowed down well to the bottom line.

Cash on hand at the end of 2017 was $548 million down nearly $190 million from the previous year. Financing activities added $2.8 billion to the cash coffers mainly from debt issuance and short-term borrowed funds. Investing activities used $3.9 billion for purchasing investment securities and accounting for changes in its loan & lease portfolio. Operating activities contributed $928 million primarily from the bank?s annual net income.

Strategy

Looking forward Zions expects to maintain a mid-single digit growth rate in the size of its loan portfolio and in customer-related fee income. It anticipates strong growth from residential mortgage and municipal loans and moderate growth in C&I and commercial real estate loans. Although loans out to oil & gas (O&G) companies (mainly through Amegy Bank) have performed poorly in recent years the upswing in oil prices has lessened the pinch on many firms enabling Zions to take fewer loan loss provisions against that portion of its portfolio. To further reduce the risk it decreased the O&G commercial lending portfolio size by 9% in 2017.

With such distinct and localized bank subsidiaries Zions strives to maintain a local community and regional bank approach as opposed to a larger bank that doesn't have a local management team. It does centralize many non-customer facing operations such as risk and capital management technology and back-office operations making for a more cost-effective endeavor.

Company Background

Zions which built its business through acquisitions strategically managed to extend its reach during the economic downturn in part by helping the FDIC clean up failed banks and it continues to search for acquisition opportunities. It is also building its business by growing its wealth management and advisory services organically.

HISTORY

Zions' history is entwined with that of the Mormon Church. Founded by the church in 1873 to take over the savings department of the Bank of Deseret when it obtained a national charter the new bank was headed by Brigham Young and other church leaders. The church kept control of the bank until 1960 when it sold its interest to a group of investors led by Roy Simmons who moved it into the holding company that became Zions Bancorporation. It went public in 1966.

It has grown over the years by picking up struggling or failing banks during various financial crises. It almost bought fellow Utah bank First Security in 2000 and would have dropped the Zions name to further distance itself from the Mormon Church. But the deal fell through and the name remains.

EXECUTIVES

Executive Vice President Marketing And Communications, Rob Brough
Evp; President And Ceo Zions First National Bank, A. Scott (Scott) Anderson, age 71, $548,000 total compensation
Chairman And Ceo, Harris H. Simmons, age 63, $940,000 total compensation
Evp; President And Ceo Vectra Bank Colorado, Bruce K. Alexander, age 65
Evp; President And Ceo The Commerce Bank Of Washington, Stanley D. Savage, age 72, $312,000 total compensation
Evp; President And Ceo California Bank & Trust, David E. Blackford, age 69, $510,000 total compensation
President And Coo, Scott J. McLean, age 61, $644,000 total compensation
Evp And Chief Banking Officer, Keith D. Maio, age 60
Evp Retail Banking, LeeAnne B. Linderman, age 63
Evp And General Counsel, Thomas E. Laursen, age 67
Evp And Chief Risk Officer, Edward P. (Ed) Schreiber, age 60, $518,000 total compensation
Evp And Chief Human Resources Officer, Dianne R. James, age 65
Svp Internal Audit, Jennifer A. Smith, age 46
Evp; Ceo Amegy Bank Of Texas, Steven D. Stephens, age 59
Evp And Chief Technology Strategist, Joe Reilly, age 65
Evp And Chief Credit Officer, Michael J. Morris, age 60
Evp; President And Ceo National Bank Of Arizona, Mark R. Young, age 59
Cfo, Paul E. Burdiss, age 53, $550,000 total compensation
Evp And Director Wealth Management, Rebecca K. Robinson, age 44
Senior Vice President Investor Relations And External Communications, James Abbott
Vice President Of Public Relations, Heidi Prokop
Vice President Treasury Relationship Manager, Rhett Rampton
Vice President Benefits Regulatory, Donald Lewis
Assistant Vice President International Operations, Anne Lane
Vice President, Matt Millis
Vice President Information Systems Manager, Jonathan Feinauer
Vice President, Bret Passey
Vice President, Jeff Hedstrom
Vice President, Brandy Deherrera
Assistant Vice President, Michael Dale
Vice President And Relationship Manager, Adam Whitefield
Senior Vice President Compliance, Norman Merritt
Vice President, Cary Coombs
Vice President, Chad Call
Senior Vice President Staffing Director, Prince Edwin
Vice President, Kaye Raby
Vice President And Relationship Manager, Cheryl Ginn
Vice President, Steve Earley
Senior Vice President And Chief Credit Administrator C And I Lending, Dennis Spencer
Vice President, Don Franke
Vice President, Mike Winder
Vice President Of Business Intelligence, Alex Mumme
Assistant Vice President Capital Markets, Karen Keeley
Vice President Sales Manager, Howard Anderson
Vice President, Jennifer Jolley
Vice President Technology, Deva Annamalai
Vice President Employee Relations Manager Human Resources, Deborah Bell
Vp And Business Analyst, Kazi Suzuki
Assistant Vice President, Leslie Nuon
Vice President Commercial Loans, David Kohler
Senior Vice President Corporate Procuremen And Vendor Management, Kelly Foreman
Vice President Mainframe Operations Systems, Reed Bailey

First Vice President, James Grether
Vice President, Steven Carlson
Applications Developers Vice President
  Applications, Brent Briggs
Vice President Treasury Management Sales
  Manager, Jesse Ronnow Jesse Ronnow
Vice President And Assistant Manager, Mark
  Henson
Vice President, Zac Nelson
Executive Vice President, Robert Boyd
Vice President Business Development Officer,
  Mark Petrasso
Vice President Financial Analyst, Ian Spencer
Assistant Vice President Client Services, Stephanie
  Irvin
Vice President, Scott Blair
Vice President Commercial Relationship Manager
  Broadway Financial Center, Dane Margetts
Vice President Relationship Manager, Russ Taylor
Vice President And Regional Director, Douglas
  Tuttle
Senior Vice President, Rich Stevenson
Vice President, Doug Kohler
Vice President, Greg Ripplinger
Vice President Business Analyst, John Weiland
Senior Vice President, Lawana Kelly
Senior Vice President Information Technology
  Support Services, Lorilee Stoddard
Vice President Learning And Organizational
  Development Instructional Design Manager,
  Nicole Boswell
Vice President Change Management
  Communications And Marketing, Jeff Morton
Vice President, Robert Oldroyd
Vice President Marketing And Business
  Development, Mike Day
Assistant Vice President Credit Systems Manager,
  Jedd Van Meeteren
Vice President Business Analyst Manager Project
  Management Office, Marlene Hindoian-Brewster
Vice President Bankcard Strategic Analytics, Kevin
  Gamble
Assistant Vice President And Business Analyst,
  Noah Norton
Senior Vice President Retail Small Business
  Deposits And Lending Product Management,
  Jamie Schwarzenbach
Vice President Retail Banking Products, Matt
  Strout
Senior Vice President Hris, Dennis Burns
Vice President Product Program Management,
  Dustin Allen
Senior Vice President Consumer Product
  Management, Brian Powell
Vice President Training Delivery Manager, Todd
  Hadley
Senior Vice President Desktop Support Services,
  R Huth
Senior Vice President Corporate Hris, Jeffery
  Hansen
Vice President, Ryan Theriault
Enterprise Loan Operations Manager Iii Vice
  President, Lori Harding
Vice President Regional Director, Burnett Facer
Senior Vice President, Todd Harris
Vice President, Eric Pehrson
Svp Credit Risk Management, Mark Medina
Senior Vice President Customer Care, Dave
  Anderson
Vice President Customer Experience Operations
  And Quality Assurance, Brett Murdock
Senior Vice President Sales, Garrett Barnes
Senior Vice President, Tom Etzel
Vice President Business Banking, Kathryn Lorenz
Senior Vice President Region Director
  Relationship Manager Private Banking, Monika
  Kaminski
Vice President Bank Properties Manager, Delon
  Askvig

Avp Human Resource Business Partner, Kirsten
  Olson
Auditors: Ernst & Young LLP

LOCATIONS

HQ: Zions Bancorporation, N.A.
  One South Main, 15th Floor, Salt Lake City, UT 84133
Phone: 801 844-7637
Web: www.zionsbancorporation.com

PRODUCTS/OPERATIONS

Selected Subsidiaries

Amegy Corporation
California Bank & Trust
National Bank of Arizona
Nevada State Bank
The Commerce Bank of Washington
Vectra Bank Colorado
ZB National Association

2017 Sales

	$ mil.	% of total
Interest income		
Interest and fees on loans	1,847	68
Interest on securities	19	1
Interest on money market investment	326	12
Non-interest income		
Other service charges commission and fees	217	8
Service charges and fees on deposit accounts	171	6
Wealth management income	42	2
Loan sales and servicing income	25	1
Dividends and other investment income	40	1
Capital markets and foreign Exchange	30	1
Equity securities gains net	14	-
Others	5	-
Total	**2,736**	**100**

COMPETITORS

BOK Financial	Great Western Bancorp
Bank of America	JPMorgan Chase
Bank of the West	MUFG Americas Holdings
Capital One	Prosperity Bancshares
Citigroup	U.S. Bancorp
Cullen/Frost Bankers	Washington Federal
First National of	Wells Fargo
Nebraska	

HISTORICAL FINANCIALS

Company Type: Public

Income Statement

FYE: December 31

	ASSETS ($ mil.)	NET INCOME ($ mil.)	INCOME AS % OF ASSETS	EMPLOYEES
12/17	66,288	592	0.9%	10,083
12/16	63,239	469	0.7%	10,057
12/15	59,669	309	0.5%	10,200
12/14	57,208	398	0.7%	10,462
12/13	56,031	263	0.5%	10,452
Annual Growth	**4.3%**	**22.4%**	**—**	**(0.9%)**

2017 Year-End Financials

Debt ratio: 0.58%	No. of shares (mil.): 197
Return on equity: 7.73%	Dividends
Cash ($ mil.): 1,330	Yield: 0.0%
Current ratio: —	Payout: 16.9%
Long-term debt ($ mil.): —	Market value ($ mil.): 10,041

	STOCK PRICE ($) FY Close	P/E High/Low	PER SHARE ($) Earnings	Dividends	Book Value
12/17	50.83	19 14	2.60	0.44	38.87
12/16	43.04	22 10	1.99	0.28	37.59
12/15	27.30	27 20	1.20	0.22	36.73
12/14	28.51	20 15	1.68	0.16	36.30
12/13	29.96	20 14	1.58	0.13	35.00
Annual Growth	**14.1%**	**— —**	**13.3%**	**35.6%**	**2.7%**

Zoetis Inc

Whether you have cats or cattle Zoetis has something to keep them healthy and happy. The company manufactures and sells veterinary medicines such as parasiticides (to protect against fleas ticks and worms) anti-infectives medicated feed additives vaccines and other pharmaceuticals. Zoetis boasts more than 300 product lines sold in more than 100 countries around the world making it one of the world's largest animal health businesses. In addition to medications and vaccines Zoetis offers diagnostics genetics devices and services such as dairy data management and consulting.

Operations

Zoetis makes about 60% of its sales from medicines and vaccines for livestock (including cattle swine poultry and fish) which assist in the global food supply chain. Products for companion animals such as house pets and horses bring in some 40% of sales. The company's product sales are diverse — with 300 different lines no single product accounts for more than 10% of sales. Its top sellers the antibiotic ceftiofur (sold under the brands Excede Excenel Spectramast and Naxcel) and canine dermatitis treatment Apoquel each bring in around 7% of overall revenues. Other top sellers are Revolution Draxxin and Apoquel.

Vaccine sales provide more than a quarter of total revenues followed by anti-infectives (nearly 25%) parasiticides (about 15%) medicated feed additives (about 10%) and other pharmaceuticals (some 20%). The remaining earnings come from non-pharmaceuticals and contract manufacturing.

Geographic Reach

The US is Zoetis' largest single market accounting for about half of all sales. Internationally the company operates in Europe the Middle East Africa the Asia/Pacific region Canada and Latin America.

Zoetis' manufacturing capabilities encompass some 25 plants in a dozen countries. But it also relies on about 180 contract manufacturers (including former parent Pfizer) to produce a significant number of products.

The company also has a 1.5 million-sq.-ft. research and development facility in Kalamazoo Michigan.

Sales and Marketing

Zoetis has a direct sales presence in 45 countries (in the Americas Europe the Asia/Pacific region and Africa) where it sells directly to livestock producers and veterinarians. In the nearly 60 other countries where it does not have a direct sales presence the company uses distributors.

Zoetis's products are available by prescription from veterinarians. The company also sells directly to retail outlets including farming supply outlets pet stores and pharmacies. Some livestock products are sold directly to ranchers.

Marketing efforts target veterinarians livestock producers and pet owners. Advertising and promotional expenses in 2017 totaled some $154 million compared to $119 million in 2016 and $106 million in 2015.

Financial Performance

Zoetis' sales have been trending upward for the past five years. Revenue rose 9% to $5.3 billion in 2017 as the company launched new products and sales of dermatology products increased. This increase in revenue made Zoetis the first animal health company to pass the $5 billion mark. Geographically sales in the US rose 7% while international sales rose 11%.

Net income which had fallen in 2015 due to restructuring charges and acquisition-related expenses recovered the following year. Then despite the higher operating expenses that came with rising product sales net income increased 5% to $864 in 2017.

Cash flow from operations has also been rising. The higher net income and positive adjustments to items including deferred taxes led operating cash flow to increase 89% to $1.3 billion that year.

Strategy

With a focus on animals Zoetis enjoys certain benefits over most pharmaceuticals. Veterinary medications don't have the same rigorous regulatory processes that human medicines do and research and development time is faster (about three years) less expensive and more predictable. In addition pet owners and ranchers pay out-of-pocket for products; Zoetis doesn't have to wait to be reimbursed by private or government-owned insurance companies. Additionally as animals will always need to be cared for the company is somewhat recession-proof.

Zoetis' plan for sustained growth includes such efforts as expanding in emerging markets (where economic development is raising demand for both livestock and companion animals) developing new products to address unmet needs pursuing **mergers and acquisitions** improving its manufacturing production margins and growing its complementary businesses in diagnostics genetics devices consulting and other areas.

In terms of geographic expansion the company plans to pursue emerging markets in Brazil China and India where protein consumption is up by introducing more expensive products. These include new vaccines and single-injection anti-infectives such as Draxxin for livestock and Convenia for pets. It is also exploring acquisitions to deepen its penetration in these markets.

To broaden its portfolio the company works to develop new products and expand existing products lines to new species (such as taking an antibiotic for cattle and reformulating it for swine and poultry.) New products launched in 2017 include parasiticide therapy for cats Stronghold Plus and in Europe dermatitis therapy for dogs Cytopoint. Another new drug Apoquel an allergic itch treatment has rapidly become a top seller in the atopic dermatitis space for dogs. In 2017 Zoetis spent some $382 million on research and development compared to $376 million in 2016 and $364 million in 2015. Furthermore it gained more than 170 product approvals during the year.

However Zoetis has also undertaken major restructuring moves to cut costs and increase production. In 2015 it announced plans to exit 10 manufacturing sites over time; the following year it sold facilities in Colorado and North Carolina. Also in 2016 it divested its majority stake in a Taiwan joint venture selling that holding for some $13 million and it sold a manufacturing site in India. All told the company will eliminate some 5000 product stock keeping units (SKUs) from its portfolio.

With those initiatives in place it is now investing $70 million on its Lincoln Nebraska manufacturing site and is expanding capacity at its manufacturing facility in Kalamazoo Michigan. It is also building a vaccine R&D and manufacturing facility in Suzhou China; the site will develop vaccines for the large farmed fish industry in that country.

Just as for pharmaceuticals dealing with treatments for humans Zoetis must keep its pipeline robust to minimize the impact of losing patents and the exclusivity of its products. The firm has a number of patents expiring over the next few years including active ingredients in its Draxxin (bovine and swine antibiotic) and Revolution (antiparasitic for cats and dogs) products. Sales of its Rimadyl (post-operative pain medication for dogs) have already been declining due to the recent launches of generic versions.

In 2018 the company developed the first complete de novo reference genome for Holstein cows which should help promote healthier dairy animals.

Mergers and Acquisitions

Zoetis has made a number of key acquisitions recently but its largest deal was completed in 2018. That year the company purchased Abaxis which makes veterinary diagnostic equipment for some $2 billion. Among Abaxis' recent offerings is its test to detect heartworm and Lyme disease in dogs. The purchase boosts Zoetis' position in the growing animal diagnostics market.

In mid-2017 the company purchased biologic therapeutics firm Nexvet Biopharma for some $85 million. Nexvet is developing a pipeline of monoclonal antibody therapies to ease pain in pets. Also that year the company acquired Norwegian firm Nordland Sett Vaks which makes vaccination machinery for the aquaculture industry.

Zoetis acquired Scandinavian company Micro Bio-devices a specialist in diagnostics for veterinary point-of-care services for $80 million in 2016.

Company Background

Formerly named Pfizer Animal Health Zoetis was separated from former parent Pfizer in 2013 in an initial public offering worth some $2.2 billion.

EXECUTIVES

Evp And Cio, Andrew Fenton
Ceo, Juan R. Alaix, age 67, $1,150,000 total compensation
Evp And Group President, Kristin C. Peck, age 47, $636,375 total compensation
Evp; President Us Operations, Clinton A. (Clint) Lewis, age 52, $630,054 total compensation
Evp; President Strategy Commercial And Business Development, Alejandro Bernal, age 46
Evp And General Counsel, Heidi C. Chen, age 52
Evp; President Research And Development, Catherine A. (Cathy) Knupp, age 58, $499,625 total compensation
Evp And Chief Human Resources Officer, Roxanne Lagano, age 54
Evp And Cfo, Glenn C. David, $483,030 total compensation
Evp; President Global Manufacturing And Supply, Roman Trawicki, age 55
Vice President Investor Relations, John OConnor
Chairman, Michael B. McCallister, age 66
Auditors: KPMG LLP

LOCATIONS

HQ: Zoetis Inc
10 Sylvan Way, Parsippany, NJ 07054
Phone: 973 822-7000
Web: www.zoetis.com

2017 Sales

	$ mil.	% of total
International	2,643	50
US	2,620	49
Contract manufacturing	44	1
Total	**5,307**	**100**

PRODUCTS/OPERATIONS

2017 Sales

	$ mil.	% of total
Livestock	3,037	57
Companion animals	2,226	42
Contract manufacturing	44	1
Total	**5,307**	**100**

2017 Sales by Product

	$ mil.	% of total
Vaccines	1,373	26
Anti-infectives	1,253	24
Parasiticides	763	14
Medicated feed additives	475	9
Other pharmaceuticals	1,181	22
Other non-pharmaceuticals	218	4
Contract manufacturing	44	1
Total	**5,307**	**100**

Selected Species

Beef Cattle
Cats
Dairy Cattle
Dogs
Fish
Horses
Pigs
Poultry
Sheep
Product line / ProductAnti-infectivesCeftiofur injectable lineDraxxin®;Spectramast®;Terramycin®; lineVaccinesBovi-Shield lineRispoval lineSuvaxyn PCV / Fostera PCVParasiticidesCydectinDectomaxMedicated Feed AdditivesAureomycinBMDLasalocid lin

COMPETITORS

American Animal Health	IDEXX Labs
Bayer Animal Health	Kindred Biosciences
Boehringer Ingelheim	Merck Animal Health
Dechra Pharmaceuticals	Phibro Animal Health
ECO Animal Health	Skystar
Eli Lilly	Virbac
Heska	Vétoquinol

HISTORICAL FINANCIALS

Company Type: Public

Income Statement

FYE: December 31

	REVENUE ($ mil.)	NET INCOME ($ mil.)	NET PROFIT MARGIN	EMPLOYEES
12/17	5,307	864	16.3%	9,200
12/16	4,888	821	16.8%	9,000
12/15	4,765	339	7.1%	9,000
12/14	4,785	583	12.2%	10,000
12/13	4,561	504	11.1%	9,800
Annual Growth	**3.9%**	**14.4%**	**—**	**(1.6%)**

2017 Year-End Financials

Debt ratio: 57.69%
Return on equity: 53.05%
Cash ($ mil.): 1,564
Current ratio: 3.85
Long-term debt ($ mil.): 4,953

No. of shares (mil.): 486
Dividends
  Yield: 0.0%
  Payout: 24.0%
Market value ($ mil.): 35,021

	STOCK PRICE ($) FY Close	P/E High/Low	PER SHARE ($) Earnings	Dividends	Book Value
12/17	72.04	41 30	1.75	0.42	3.64
12/16	53.53	32 24	1.65	0.38	3.02
12/15	47.92	81 58	0.68	0.33	2.15
12/14	43.03	39 24	1.16	0.29	2.62
12/13	32.69	34 29	1.01	0.20	1.88
Annual Growth	**21.8%**	**— —**	**14.7%**	**21.1%**	**18.0%**

Hoover's Handbook of

American Business

The Indexes

Index by Headquarters

Index of Executives

A

Aadland, Todd 322
Aaefedt, Matthew 855
Aaholm, Sherry A. 246
Aakre, D Scott 432
Aaron, Thomas J. (Tom) 227
Aaronian, Ray 328
Aaronson, Daniel 323
Abad, Rafael Lopez 753
Abadir, Jeffrey 240
Abarca, Jose 647
Abate, Victor (Vic) 375
Abate, Joanne 863
Abbamondi, Desa 899
Abbaseh, Samimi 685
Abbate, Mark L. 553
Abbene, David 532
Abbey, Jared 122
Abbey, Anna B 773
Abbey, Anna 773
Abblett, Fred 332
Abbondi, Piero 20
Abbott, Greg 173
Abbott, Sarah 558
Abbott, Dean 701
Abbott, Greg 765
Abbott, James 919
Abboud, John 484
Abboud, Andy 502
Abboud, Ali El 766
Abdella, Shelly 883
Abdoo, Elizabeth A. 434
Abdoo, Richard 594
Abdullah, Rao 398
Abel, Greg 123
Abel, Gregory E. (Greg) 630
Abel, Melissa 800
Abel-Hodges, Cheryl 682
Abela, John 556
Abell, Charlie 68
Abellera, Philip 710
Abelli, Donna L. 451
Abello, Marc P 221
Abelman, David 708
Abernethy, Brian 3
Abhishek, Shukla 260
Abichandani, Sanjay 22
Abington, Clay 562
Abiteboul, Jean 189
Abji, Minaz B. 434
Ables, Grady L. 69
Ables, Dorothy M. 758
Abney, Jack 764
Abney, David P. 850
Aboaf, Eric 766
Abood, Steven 701
Aboulafia, Joseph 105
Abraham, JJ 508
Abrahamson, Laura 16
Abramczyk, Andrew 306
Abramowicz, Daniel A. 242
Abramowitz, Scott 441
Abramowski, Dan 701
Abrams, Murray 163
Abrams, Mike 196
Abrams, Ed 460
Abrams, Ryan 905
Abregu, Martin 808
Abston, Tyson T 397
Abston, Chris 593
Abston, Angie 844
Abtew, Mulugeta 725
Abts, Joy 865
Abutaleb, Sam 814
Accardo, Joseph 678
Accogli, Giuseppe 113
Acevedo, Margie 541

Ach, J. Wickliffe 345
Achary, Michael M. 300
Acharya, Guru 906
Achkire, Debra 354
Achorn, Tina 402
Achrekar, Manoj 729
Acito, Paul 2
Acito, Paiul 3
Acito, Joe 332
Acker, Serge 691
Ackerman, Michelle 34
Ackerman, Joel 255
Ackerman, Dean M 504
Ackermann, Dan 295
Ackerson, Vince A. 800
Acklin, Bobbie 770
Ackroyd, Jim 9
Acoca, Bernard 762
Acord, Suzette 866
Acosta, Navia 583
Acott, Sarah 133
Acton, Michael 724
Adair, Bryan 460
Adam, Tim 272
Adam, Rolf 454
Adamczyk, Darius 429
Adame, Pedro 899
Adamo, Christopher 105
Adamos, Tara 448
Adams, Dennis 34
Adams, Colby 59
Adams, Gregg T. 108
Adams, John 109
Adams, Kevin 167
Adams, Lisa 167
Adams, Kevin D 234
Adams, Melissa 244
Adams, Craig L. 308
Adams, Isaac 406
Adams, Thomas 419
Adams, Michael 441
Adams, Gregory 460
Adams, Beth 489
Adams, Vivian 513
Adams, Calvin 521
Adams, Romaneo 532
Adams, Jennifer 532
Adams, John 575
Adams, John 583
Adams, Scott 614
Adams, Cathryn 649
Adams, D. Scott 674
Adams, Wayne 701
Adams, William 725
Adams, Bobbie 769
Adams, Patricia (Trish) 788
Adams, Trish 788
Adams, Tim 795
Adams, Dian 795
Adams, Samantha 823
Adams, Leigh 838
Adams, Richard M. 843
Adamson, Adam 129
Adamson, Ermil L. 277
Adamson, John 800
Adcock, Beth 382
Adcock, Robert H. 425
Addiego, Gino 71
Addison, Ann M. 505
Addison, John 667
Addison, David 724
Addotta, Sibylle 539
Adelson, Sarah 323
Adelson, Sheldon G. 502
Aden, John 878
Aderholdt, Mary 718
Adkerson, Richard C. 367
Adkins, Candace 58
Adkins, Rodney C 93

Adkins, Rodney 665
Adkins, Rodney 650
Adkison, Jeffrey 478
Adkisson, Mike 782
Adler, Kim 34
Adler, Dean S 121
Adler, Paul F. 198
Adler, Dennis 691
Adornato, Theodore C. (Ted) 756
Adornetto, Charles 639
Adreani, Lou 766
Afejuku, Ayo 565
Affronti, Michael 173
Afonso, Maria 647
Afwerke, Issac 722
Afzal, Tahira 489
Agarwal, Anil 49
Agarwal, Anu 166
Agarwal, Pankaj 204
Agarwal, Achal 490
Agarwal, Manu 568
Agarwal, Parag 620
Agarwal, Naveen 676
Agee, Philip 788
Aggarwal, Rohit 443
Aggarwal, Lokesh 767
Aghajanian, Phil 103
Aghdami, Amanda N 163
Agiasotis, Kerry 893
Agnew, John 899
Agochiya, Mihir 480
Agrawal, Rajesh K. (Raj) 893
Agresta, Richard 734
Agresta, Gregory 886
Aguila, Percy R 109
Aguilar, Edgard Corrales 753
Aguilar, Mike 823
Aguirre, Jean 532
Agulnek, Barbara 406
Agurto, Tonya 272
Ahearn, Tracey 521
Ahee, Joseph 441
Ahern, R 324
Ahern, David 858
Aherne, Sean 144
Ahluwalia, Pradeep 767
Ahmad, Surabhi 56
Ahmad, Rosidah 456
Ahmadi, Hamid 685
Ahmed, Nadim 178
Ahmed, Riffat K 413
Ahmed, Sohail U. 456
Ahmet, Byron 173
Aho, Todd R 413
Ahrendt, Dale 484
Ahrendts, Angela 70
Ahuja, Deepak 799
Aichele, William S. 862
Aiken, Jason W. 374
Aiken, Donald B 539
Aiken, Scott 912
Aing, Melissa 548
Aiosa, Lisa 691
Aitken, Murray L. 469
Akalski, Frank J. 359
Akbar, Mehrdad 878
Akhtar, Muhammad 522
Akins, Nicholas K. (Nick) 46
Akins, Nicholas K. (Nick) 47
Akins, D. Wayne 781
Akrout, Chekib 14
Aksdal, Roy 163
Al-Khudhair, Mariam 250
Alaix, Juan R. 921
Alam, Mahmood 649
Alama, Bernie 102
Alameddine, Ray 657
Alamo, Lisette 541
Alban, Carlos 6

Albanese, Gerard 528
Albano, Charles 8
Alber, Laura J. 901
Albers, Carissa 223
Albert, Don 288
Albert, Gary 732
Alberto, Luis 628
Alberts, Mary 541
Albertson, Paul 582
Albertson, Marty 770
Albi, Chris 496
Albinson, Brock 87
Albornoz, Linda 49
Albouy, Laurent 682
Albrecht, Vicki 59
Albrecht, Geoffrey 687
Albrecht, Julie 750
Albright, Randolph 641
Albright, Steven 765
Albright, Brandy 857
Alburg, Kenneth 81
Alcantar, Michael 244
Alcantar, Michael 446
Alden, John 850
Alder, Bob 265
Alderman, Mark 532
Alderman, Marian 832
Alderoty, Stuart 201
Alderson, Christopher D. 783
Alderson, Art 878
Aldinger, Alan 659
Aldridge, David 58
Aleardi, Keith P 369
Alec, Pittman 881
Alekperova, Rena 97
Aleksov, Lynn 659
Aleman-Bermudez, Aurelio 336
Alemany, Ellen R. 201
Alesci, Megan 446
Alessandrini, James 763
Aletrakis, Timothy 359
Alex, Dudley 576
Alexander, Robert 56
Alexander, Susan H. 129
Alexander, Mark R. 161
Alexander, Robert M. 163
Alexander, Darrell 163
Alexander, Karin 193
Alexander, Rebecca 196
Alexander, Blair 221
Alexander, Aaron 223
Alexander, Bob 249
Alexander, Hank 298
Alexander, Paul 408
Alexander, Gaylord 413
Alexander, Tenzin 441
Alexander, Matthew 441
Alexander, Forbes I. J. 471
Alexander, Paul 490
Alexander, Nathan 568
Alexander, Elizabeth 611
Alexander, Sheila 614
Alexander, Craig H 641
Alexander, Joseph 741
Alexander, Robert 744
Alexander, Tim 754
Alexander, Stan 755
Alexander, Rhonda 782
Alexander, Carol 838
Alexander, Cory B. 855
Alexander, Bill 915
Alexander, Bruce K. 919
Alfano, Nicholas (Nick) 289
Alfieri, Kiersten 740
Alfonso, Rosa 49
Alfonso, Diana 204
Alger, Eugene K. 312
Ali, Farah 113
Ali, Alam 570

Apte, Chaitanya 45
Apter, Ronald 407
Aquilla, Dave 912
Aquino, Marlene 140
Arabia, Carmine 38
Aragon-Hernandez, Olga 878
Aramini, Diane 821
Araujo, George 160
Aravena, Jose 738
Aravindakshan, Santhosh 555
Arcalgud, Anil 289
Arch, Larry 724
Archambeau, Shellye 596
Archer, Pmp 10
Archer, Timothy M. (Tim) 501
Archer, Ed 725
Archer, Cynthia A 773
Archer, Dominick 836
Archer, Bradley 872
Archibald, Nolan D. 443
Archibald, Sandra 861
Archuleta, Kimberly 204
Arcidiacono, Salvator 578
Arden, Lee 593
Ardezzone, Anthony 584
Ardisonne, Ron 88
Ardizzone, Ann 28
Ardoin, Elizabeth A. (Beth) 446
Ardoin, Beth 446
Arebalos, Ish 215
Arellano, Luis R 728
Arena, Thomas 478
Arenas, Charles 490
Arendt, Brian 540
Arenivas, Jesse 492
Arent, Thomas 898
Argao, Selene 729
Argent, Heather 399
Argetsinger, Jenna 658
Argo, Laurie 303
Argodale, George 825
Arif, Abu 56
Arif, Hasan 767
Arifkhan, Oktay 871
Arinder, Jeff 262
Arinelli, Wilmar 242
Ariqat, Ghassan 833
Ark, Jon Vander 707
Arko, Johnathan 513
Armbruster, Patrice 591
Armentrout, Sharon 782
Armin, Craig 795
Armogan, Nathan 158
Armour, Norm 892
Armstrong, Duff 85
Armstrong, Robert 94
Armstrong, Sherry 188
Armstrong, Paula 322
Armstrong, Christopher 323
Armstrong, Steven 362
Armstrong, Ann K 456
Armstrong, Steven S 486
Armstrong, Keith D. 553
Armstrong, Scott 583
Armstrong, Ronald E. (Ron) 629
Armstrong, Greg L. 657
Armstrong, Greg L 658
Armstrong, Susie 685
Armstrong, Kay 830
Armstrong, Michael 872
Arndt, Joann 272
Arndt, Kenneth A. 368
Arnesen, Finn 408
Arnett, Haynes 136
Arnett, Gevan 213
Arnn, Roger 314
Arnold, Steve 82
Arnold, Scott 88
Arnold, Colleen 165
Arnold, Gary 247
Arnold, Chris 260
Arnold, Michael J. 367
Arnold, Christy 454
Arnold, Jeffrey 485
Arnold, Charles 555
Arnold, Steve 630
Arnold, Scott 685

Arnold, Timothy G. (Tim) 863
Aromando, Nicholas 105
Aromando, Ada 131
Aron, Adam M. 41
Aronowitz, Scott 328
Aronson, Tom 272
Aronson, Arnold 691
Arora, Deepak 49
Arora, Amit 49
Arora, Sumeet 199
Arous, Gérard Ben 585
Arredondo, Omar 774
Arrell, Sarah 788
Arrico, Libby 160
Arrighi, Theresa 115
Arriola, Dennis V. 735
Arrowsmith, Andrea 120
Arroyo, F. Thaddeus 84
Arroyo, Enrique 541
Arroyo, Jesus 729
Arroyo, Ana 810
Arseneault, Michael 175
Arseneault, Jason 332
Arstark, Reid 727
Arterian, Hannah R 8
Arters, Doug 463
Arthachinda, Nick 838
Arthur, Sarbah 40
Arthur, Vicki B. 750
Arthur, Gary 868
Artis, David 741
Arumugam, Magesh 101
Arvanites, Seth 644
Arvin, Ann Margaret 507
Asai, Eriko 375
Asbury, Stephanie 100
Asbury, Jeff 329
Asbury, John C. 841
Ascher, John 691
Asel, Keith 408
Asensio, Lynn D. 886
Ash, Shari 572
Ash, David 738
Ash, Tim 844
Ashby, Michael 736
Ashenbrenner, Fred 235
Asher, Linda 140
Asher, Andrew L. (Drew) 885
Ashkenazy, Stewart 555
Ashley, Richard W 5
Ashley, Anthony 492
Ashley, David 528
Ashley, Pamela 700
Ashlyn, Sowell 475
Ashmawee, Viola 729
Ashtiani, Kaihan 501
Ashton, Sam 330
Ashton, Martin 456
Ashue, Meghan 902
Ashworth, Ken 25
Ashworth, Richard M. 877
Ask, Carrie 509
Askew, Mike 461
Askuvich, Hallie 134
Askvig, Delon 920
Aslin, Phil 800
Asmar, Joseph 532
Asnani, Manish 874
Aspinwall, Glenn 478
Asplund, Dale A. 851
Assef, Eduardo 202
Asselberg, Mark 620
Astroth, Joseph 888
Aswall, Mark 724
Atalay, Hakan 682
Atchison, Pierre 725
Athanasakos, Nick 593
Athanasia, Dean C. 100
Atherton, Brian 729
Athreya, Kartik 324
Athreya, Anand (Andy) 482
Atkins, Bruce 388
Atkins, Ron 461
Atkinson, E Morrey 147
Atkinson, Ralph 412
Atkinson, Cliff 558
Atkinson, Heather 723

Atkinson, Tracy 766
Attar, Rias 158
Attaway, John A. 679
Attaway, John A. 680
Attig, Kelley 522
Attili, Srinivas 460
Attock, Julian 556
Attwood, Karen 561
Atwell, Joseph 96
Atwell, Kellie 272
Atwell, Robert 592
Atwell, William 883
Au, Joseph 285
Au, Reynette 559
Aubrey, William E. 646
Aubry, Stephane 133
Aubry, Marc 894
Auclair, Bethany 696
Auger, Stephen 357
Augi, Tony 872
August, Gerald 314
August, Jim 676
August-deWilde, Katherine 354
Auguste, Sandy 481
Augustine, Luke 165
Augustine, Mike 483
Augustine, Michael 873
Augustsson, Tommy 374
Augustyn-Fierg, Laurie 829
Auld, David V. 433
Aulph, Karen 339
Aunan, Erik 3
Aurora, Dana 131
Ausberry, Sheila 221
Ausman, Gary 791
Austin, Adrienne 17
Austin, Karen A. 650
Austin, Earl C. (Duke) 686
Austin, Cathie 751
Auten, Dan 484
Autenried, Paul von 147
Autry, Matt 532
Auyeung, Rex 668
Auzenne, Scott 802
Avant, Keith 562
Avelenda, Saily 500
Averbach, Rob 901
Averett, Addison 788
Avery, Linda 390
Avery, Meg 507
Avila, Alejandro 725
Aviles, Alan D. 582
Awad, Anwar 456
Awada, Hassan 240
Awadallah, Ehab 163
Awan, Faisal 493
Awasthi, Puneet 390
Ayala, Patti 244
Aycock, Angela W 221
Aye, Chris 691
Ayer, William S. (Bill) 861
Ayers, Stephen 723
Ayers, Alvita 855
Aylouche, Mounzer M 535
Aylward, Kevin 530
Ayoub, Johnny 140
Ayre, David J. 592
Ayres, Maria 13
Ayyar, Shekar 875
Azar, Sam 607
Azar, Mark 817
Azinovic, Drago 652
Aznavorian, Rosemarie 801
Azoulay, Salomon 648
Azuara, Katherine 113
Azuolay, Avi 741

B

Babb, Ralph W. 221
Babb, Ovid 330
Babcock, John P. 639
Babel, Bryan 898
Babik, Amber 441
Babikian, Jeffrey C 173
Babineau, Thomas 141

Babington, Adam E 272
Bach, Paul D. 380
Bach, Allen W 823
Bach, Allen 823
Bachaalani, Issam 218
Bachand, Kelly 314
Bachelder, Stuart 255
Bachmann, Lisa M. 127
Bachmann, Steve 136
Back, Tekla 647
Backman, Mats 87
Backus, Marcia E. 611
Bacon, Graham W. 303
Bacon, Ashley 480
Bacus, Lisa R. 195
Badar, Ruben 568
Badders, Matt 244
Bader, Jeffrey 559
Badger, Austin 777
Badgett, Loretta 774
Badi, Mohammed 49
Baehren, James W. (Jim) 628
Baek, Eugene 133
Baen, Mona 769
Baer, Nick 478
Baer, Richard N. (Rich) 688
Baer, TimothyR 788
Baer, Tim 788
Baerlocher, Shawn 405
Baffa, Mitchel 583
Bagattini, Roy 509
Baggs, David 243
Bagley, Chris A. 99
Bagley, Shannon 180
Bagley, Ross 751
Bagley, David 902
Baglino, Drew 799
Bagnall, Christoper 542
Bagnall, Roger 585
Bagnara, Alessandro 481
Bagnoli, Mark P. 108
Bagwell, Norman P. 137
Bahl, Himani 101
Bahl, Tracy L. 250
Bahner, Craig 485
Bahno, Anthony 533
Bahou, Elie 165
Bahr, Wendy 199
Bahr, Antony M. 214
Bahr, John 489
Bahra, Paul 333
Baier, Lucinda M. (Cindy) 148
Baier, Frank W 231
Baier, Henry 698
Bailey, Bob 27
Bailey, Richard 435
Bailey, Todd 441
Bailey, Todd 480
Bailey, Daniel 562
Bailey, Rosie 568
Bailey, Steve R. 642
Bailey, Daniel K. (Dan) 830
Bailey, Dan 830
Bailey, Brooke 877
Bailey, Reed 919
Baillie, Thomas 861
Baillon-plot, Nathalie 649
Baine, Diane 101
Baio, Richard M. 122
Baiocchi, Sarah 180
Baiocchi, Carol 493
Bairathi, Anurag 402
Baird, Howard 51
Baird, Allison 143
Baird, Lisa 460
Baird, Alice 644
Baird, Edward 677
Baird, Patrick S. (Pat) 684
Baird, Ian 865
Baisiwala, Udai 507
Baitler, Robert 541
Bajpay, Pari 85
Bajraktari, Leta 204
Baker, Charles E. 96
Baker, Richard 100
Baker, Charles 105
Baker, Lloyd W. 110

Gonzalez, Eva 734
Gonzalez, Elizabeth 809
Gonzalez, Tracy 823
Gonzalez, Hector 835
Gonzalez, Charles 838
Gonzalez, Alfonso 865
Gonzalez, Beatrice 868
Gooch, Mark A. 227
Gooch, Mark A. 228
Good, Jim 96
Good, Lynn J. 281
Good, Lynn J. 282
Good, Lynn J 282
Goodall, Laura 122
Goodarzi, Sasan K. 466
Goodell, Denise 316
Goodfriend, Jim 332
Goodger, Simon 649
Goodhew, Ian 861
Gooding, Marie C. 322
Goodman, Sean D. 78
Goodman, Bennett J. 132
Goodman, Scott R. 302
Goodman, Kim Crawford 355
Goodman, Stacey 366
Goodman, Randy 384
Goodman, Adam 537
Goodman, Gregg M. 744
Goodpaster, Keith 332
Goodrich, Donna C. 115
Goodrion, Sean 234
Goodrow, Carolyn 241
Goodsir, Michelle 201
Goodspeed, Randy 260
Goodwin, Annie 387
Goodwin, Dustin 447
Goodwin, Eric 522
Goodwyn, Bill 269
Goody, James 351
Goon, Julie 67
Goone, David S 457
Gopalakrishnan, Raja 330
Gopalratnam, Vc 199
Gopstein, Etan 530
Goranson, Mark 620
Gorder, Joseph W. (Joe) 867
Gordon, Marc D. 48
Gordon, Murdo 147
Gordon, Derek A. 218
Gordon, Ilene S. 453
Gordon, Ben 565
Gordon, Barbara 667
Gordon, Larry 691
Gordon, Russell L. 716
Gordon, Cima 784
Gordon, Bryson 871
Gordon, Michelle 872
Gordon, Howard 902
Gore, Clark 173
Gorecki, Teresa 476
Gorham, Roger B. 30
Gorin, Ariane 311
Goris, Patrick 712
Gorman, Norma 33
Gorman, Mark 199
Gorman, Patrick 225
Gorman, Christopher M. (Chris) 489
Gorman, James P. 568
Gorman, Mark J. 657
Gorman, Mark J 658
Gorman, Robert M. (Rob) 841
Gorman, Cheryl 854
Gormley, Bill 158
Gorney, Len 484
Gorodetzer, Kristen 195
Gorostiza, Georg 763
Gorska, Anna 184
Gorski, Jim 330
Gorski, Mark 614
Gorsky, Alex 476
Gortney, Jennifer 674
Gorzak, John 616
Gosavi, Sanjeev 461
Gosch, Kenneth L 251
Gosdin, James L 769
Gosebruch, Henry O. 6
Gosnell, Jack 173

Goss, David 670
Goss, Karl 865
Gosselin, Gene 683
Gosselink, Robert 122
GOSTOUT, BOBBIE S 540
Goswami, Chitra 255
Gotelli, Robert 103
Gotlib, Ian 507
Gottesfeld, Stephen P. 588
Gottschalk, Marla 127
Gottschalk, Adrian 129
Gottscho, Richard A. (Rick) 501
Gottsegen, Jonathan M 851
Gottwals, Bill 349
Gotwals, Janet W 98
Goudreau, Christopher 460
Gough, Mitzy 136
Gough, Lisa 782
Gouin, Kevin 330
Goulart, Steven J. 555
Gould, R Marcia 46
Gould, Jason 248
Gould, Mark A. 324
Gould, Dan 589
Gould, Vicky 670
Gould, Karen 813
Goulet, Beverly K. 43
Goulet, Ken 67
Goulet, Nicole 329
Goulet, Alisa 878
Goulopoulos, Paul 767
Gourlay, Alexander W. (Alex) 877
Gow, Jeff D 232
Gowen, Kevin P. 781
Goyal, Rahul 456
Goyea, David 767
GP, Energy T 298
Graaf, Bill Van de 218
Grabavoy, Steve 541
Grabavoy, Steven 542
Grabowski, Robert 314
Graca, Amy 158
Grace, Jacqueline 158
Gracheck, Jack 541
Graddick-Weir, Mirian M. 550
Grade, Joel T. 782
Gradert, Scott 738
Gradnik, Amy 874
Grady, Gerry 328
Grady, Melissa 556
Graf, R Mark 268
Graf, Alan B. 327
Graf, Stacy 886
Graff, Michael J. (Mike) 25
Grafmyre, Richard A. 640
Graham, Jonathan P. 61
Graham, Robert M. (Bob) 66
Graham, Jon 69
Graham, John 199
Graham, Kristin 311
Graham, Molly 513
Graham, Derek 591
Graham, John 682
Graham, Melissa 739
Graham, Stephen P 763
Graham, Christopher A. (Chris) 768
Graham, Carolyn 769
Graham, James 782
Graham, Dan 844
Graham, Ned 851
Graham, Mark A 901
Grainger, Guy 478
Grajeda, Jessica 635
Gramlich, Tom 465
Granado, Alejandro 202
Granata, Thomas 54
Granchi, Annie 391
Grand, Hillary 131
Graney, Kevin M. 374
Grange, Kim 502
Grannis, Dick 685
Grant, Tim 73
Grant, Timothy 73
Grant, Marilee 144
Grant, Melanie 155
Grant, Shane 215
Grant, Aja 282

Grant, Joan 284
Grant, Jeffrey 602
Grant, Jasmine 774
Grant-anderson, Belinda 84
Grantham, Deborah 19
Grantham, Connee 750
Granzyk, Steve 180
Grass, Stephanie 702
Grasshoff, Michaela 532
Grasso, Sebastian 133
Grasso, Maria A. 359
Grasso, Davide 592
Grau, Dominique 22
Grauer, Scott B. 137
Graumlich, Lisa 861
Graunke, Carrie 540
Grauze, Sarah 2
Gravanis, Georges 91
Gravel, Karine 649
Gravelle, Michael L. (Mike) 328
Gravelle, Michael L. (Mike) 329
Graves, William W. 90
Graves, Victoria 260
Graves, Christopher 551
Graviss, Jonathan 448
Grawe, George 34
Gray, Sean A 124
Gray, Jonathan D. 132
Gray, Harry W 136
Gray, Jonathan D. 421
Gray, William 423
Gray, Robert D 428
Gray, James D. (Jim) 453
Gray, Diedre 663
Gray, James W. 704
Gray, Tom 769
Gray, David J. 811
Gray, Myron A. 850
Gray, M Joel 895
Graybill, Greg 292
Graziano, Steven M. 890
Greasheimer, Sharon 165
Grebenc, Jane 342
Grebert, Carl 593
Grebstein, Marci 640
Grech, Joe 607
Greco, Thomas R. (Tom) 13
Greco, Julie 541
Greco, Joseph D 607
Greco, John R. 634
Greco, Joe 734
Greeley, John 885
Green, Keith 33
Green, Anthony C. 66
Green, Joseph 85
Green, Tsahai 109
Green, Phil 131
Green, Gerry 158
Green, Saryia 201
Green, Phillip D. 244
Green, Frederec 260
Green, Allen R. 277
Green, Logan 288
Green, Joe 402
Green, Markham 420
Green, David 422
Green, Steve 422
Green, Mart 422
Green, Andy 442
Green, Elle 476
Green, Mark A. 487
Green, Darryl 525
Green, Bryan 578
Green, Allyson 585
Green, Mark 683
Green, Harold 693
Green, Howard 741
Green, Joyce 743
Green, Ryan 755
Green, Tammy 763
Green, Sheron 770
Green, Barbara 782
Green, Niki 784
Green, Nancy 809
Green, Warren 837
Green, Miguale 838
Green, Paul S. 848

Green, Monique 866
Green, Brian 874
Green, Tara 878
Green-Lett, Darsee 422
Greenan, Joe 16
Greenberg, Jamie 390
Greenberg, Raymond S. 860
Greenberg, Andrew 872
Greenberg, Alan 872
Greene, Alexander 40
Greene, Mike 56
Greene, Jason K. 125
Greene, Thomas (Tom) 218
Greene, Matt 287
Greene, Yoonhi 323
Greene, Jeff 354
Greene, Jesse J 460
Greene, Deirdre 635
Greene, Douglas 724
Greene, Aaron 741
Greene, Candy 751
Greene, Ezra 872
Greener, Todd 13
Greener, Geoffrey S. 100
Greenfeig, Sid 558
Greenhaw, Mark 107
Greenlaw, David 607
Greenlee, Stephen 313
Greenspon, Tom 140
Greenstein, Scott A. 745
Greenstein, Sara A. 852
Greenstreet, Michelle M 759
Greenwalt, Rodgers K. 125
Greenway, Mark 439
Greenway, Suzanne 806
Greenwood, John 244
Greenya, Cyril J. 276
Greer, K. Gordon 98
Greer, Emily 372
Greer, Mike 751
Greer, Pam 763
Greer, Greg 774
Greer, Steven K. 822
Greer, Butch 823
Greer, Louis E. 832
Greeter, Gerald 631
Grefe, Roger 693
Greff, Brian 471
Grega, Jocelyn 863
Gregg, Lisa 49
Gregg, Paul 272
Gregg, Hall 649
Gregoire, Christopher J 519
Gregoire, Daniel N. (Dan) 524
Gregor, Carol 195
Gregory, Ryan 180
Gregory, William 196
Gregory, Elisabeth 221
Gregory, Lentz 350
Gregory, Kevin 371
Gregory, Paul 484
Gregory, Sherman 685
Gregory, Paul C. 687
Gregory, Audrey 795
Gregory, Jonathan 800
Gregory, Kay 838
Greindl, Jean-Marie 664
Greiner, Phillip 351
Grele, Kathy 541
Grenfell, Alistair 469
Grensteiner, Ronald J. (Ron) 47
Grenz, Dianne M. 868
Grescovich, Mark J. 110
Grese, Frank 396
Greslick, Richard L 212
Gress, William J. 150
Grether, James 920
Greuel, Norm 508
Greuel, Norman 508
Greve, Norman de 250
Grexa, Karen 489
Grey, Noel 175
Grey, Robert 665
Greyber, Rob 311
Gribbin, Patrick 423
Grieder, Daniel 682
Griego, Linda M 175

Himler, Bob 709
Hinckle, Veronica 166
Hinde, Jason 308
Hindel, Joanne 333
Hindoian-Brewster, Marlene 920
Hinds, Tom 912
Hinduja, Anil 366
Hiner, Patrick 2
Hiner, Troy 725
Hines, Michael 173
Hines, Grace 736
Hing, Rebecca 906
Hingsbergen, Michael 196
Hingston, Alex 599
Hingtgen, Tim L. 227
Hinkle, Michael 336
Hinkle, James G 425
Hinkley, Richard 199
Hinnenkamp, Paul D. 300
Hinrichs, Joseph R. (Joe) 362
Hinsdale, Bill 885
Hinshaw, Ken 175
Hinshaw, Janice 508
Hinshaw, Bill 603
Hinson, W. Ron 383
Hinson, Donald J. 414
Hinson, Jeffrey T. 903
Hinton, Patricia 371
Hinton, Walter 519
Hintz, Donald 300
Hintz, Brian 339
Hintzen, Daniel 599
Hippe, Patricia 219
Hippen, Lyle 185
Hipskind, Jennifer 640
Hipwell, Todd 264
Hiraki, Justin 782
Hirata, Vernon 798
Hiromori, Takaya 19
Hirsch, Didier 22
Hirsch, Larry 119
Hirsch, Noah 158
Hirsch, Roderick 659
Hirschberg, Alan 555
Hirsh, Peter 131
Hirshberg, Eric 10
Hirst, Daniel 59
Hirst, William 247
Hirst, Alistair D. 485
Hise, Bill 441
Hisey, David C. 769
Hishikawa, Maki 19
Hitch, Jordan 155
Hitchcock, Andy 173
Hitchings, Stephen 718
Hitchner, Kenneth W. 389
Hite, Carolyn 316
Hitt, David 662
Hitt, Greg 878
Hitt, Charles 913
Hixson, Richard 480
Hizak, Steve 843
Hjelm, Christopher T. (Chris) 496
Hladik, David 481
Hnat, Jim 474
Hnat, James G. (Jim) 474
HO, Duong 7
Ho, Peter S. 102
Ho, Peter S. 103
Ho, Emily 133
Ho, Karen 390
Ho, Stephen 530
HO, Kar 774
Ho, Tien 899
Hoag, Erik 330
Hobart, Lauren R. 264
Hobart, Brian E. 452
Hobbs, Franklin W. (Fritz) 35
Hobbs, Nicholas (Nick) 439
Hobbs, Beth 655
Hobbs, Rodney 762
Hobbs, David A 851
Hobby, Paul 604
Hobert, Christine 331
Hobin, Peggy L. 879
Hobson, Christopher K. (Chris) 237
Hocevar, Christopher 195

Hoch, Erich 471
Hoch, Russell 914
Hochgesang, Mark 105
Hochman, Rod 674
Hochschild, Roger C 268
Hocken, Natalie L. 630
Hockey, Timothy D. (Tim) 791
Hodes, Jack 375
Hodge, Terry 819
Hodges, James R. 99
Hodges, Kristina 115
Hodges, Arthur 214
Hodges, Simon 275
Hodges, Eloy 541
Hodges, James 546
Hodges, Timothy B 644
Hodgson, Robert 693
Hodiwalla, Zubin 729
Hodkin, Deborah 316
Hodous, Brian 10
Hoeck, Michael 173
Hoeh, Kristian 391
Hoen, Corey 865
Hoene, William A. (Bill) Von 308
Hoereth, Anthony 913
Hoerth, Scott 81
Hoesch, Josh 340
Hoey, Bob 460
Hof, Thomas 838
Hofelich, Kurt 736
Hofer, Nicholas A.R. 143
Hoffler, Valerie 162
Hoffman, Roger 74
Hoffman, Steve 93
Hoffman, Julie 131
Hoffman, Peter 136
Hoffman, Mark 140
Hoffman, Nate 163
Hoffman, Geoffrey 273
Hoffman, Francis 328
Hoffman, Tammy 366
Hoffman, John 476
Hoffman, Kathleen 677
Hoffman, James D. 703
Hoffman, Jim 703
Hoffman, Susan 864
Hoffman, James E. (Jim) 916
Hoffman-Day, Denise 522
Hoffmann, Daryl 244
Hoffmeister, Bruce 530
Hoffmeister, Jan 675
Hofheins, Todd 674
Hofmann, Kevin 426
Hofmann, Herb E. 520
Hofmann, Herbert 520
Hofmann, Richard 550
Hofmeister, Brian 663
Hogan, Cynthia 70
Hogan, Mark D 116
Hogan, James D. 247
Hogan, Patrick 330
Hogan, Michael P. (Mike) 372
Hogan, Rob 442
Hogan, Margaret 532
Hogan, Kathleen T 560
Hogan, David P. 621
Hogan, Jim 788
Hoge, Geof 850
Hogenmiller, Mike 426
Hogg, Charlotte M. 874
Hoghaug, Paul 56
Hogle, Scott 449
Hoglund, Robert N. 232
Hoglund, Robert N. 233
Hogue, John 441
Hohenadel, Jim 141
Hoien, Todd 408
Hoisman, Danny 833
Hoke, Margaret 350
Holani, Kimberly 103
Holbrook, Jenni 425
Holbrook, James 663
Holcman, Alex 685
Holcomb, Michele 165
Holden, Rochelle 272
Holden, Sean 542
Holden, Zachery J 730

Holden, James 751
Holder, Sonia 583
Holder, Diane P. 859
Holder, William W. 860
Holding, Frank B. 341
Hole, Joseph 105
Holguin, Lorena 537
Holguin, Rochelle 872
Holiday, Edith 726
Holifield, Mark Q. 426
Holinsky, Ronald 513
Holladay, Lisa 531
Holladay, Mark G. 781
Hollan, Michael 251
Holland, Peter 105
Holland, Richard 251
Holland, Tom 327
Holland, Ricky T. 341
Holland, Jim 362
Holland, Christine 441
Holland, Clifford 476
Holland, James 492
Holland, Arlene 521
Holland, Ralph 564
Holland, George 914
Hollander, Rich 649
Hollander, Martin 734
Holleran, Kevin P. 804
Holley, Peter 115
Holley, Jeffrey D 621
Holley, Rick R. 896
Holliday, Bob 85
Holliday, Brian 429
Holliday, Carl 622
Holliday, Matt 862
Hollinger, Dennis 9
Hollingsworth, Rebecca 38
Hollingsworth, Pamela 463
Hollingsworth, Audrey 781
Holloman, J. Phillip 198
Hollon, Jeffrey 115
Holloway, Duane D. 79
Holloway, Bavan 136
Holloway, Anita 438
Hollub, Vicki A. 611
Holman, Alan 34
Holman, Gene 107
Holman, Brian 180
Holman, Sheila 531
Holmen, Hans 232
Holmer, Shekofeh 915
Holmes, Tom 243
Holmes, Donald N 260
Holmes, Bradley 298
Holmes, Richard 383
Holmes, Dane 390
Holmes, Crystal 461
Holmes, Charlie 493
Holmes, William 530
Holmes, James 682
Holmes, Valerie 890
Holmes, Stephen P. 908
Holmgren, Thor 56
Holochuk, James 724
Holodak, Stephen 250
Holschbach, Leon J. 561
Holscher, Russ 113
Holshouser, Susan 448
Holsten, Joseph M. 518
Holston, Michael J. 550
Holt, Alan 56
Holt, Jarrod 480
Holthouser, James E. (Jim) 421
Holton, Terry J. 730
Holtz, Dave 261
Holwill, Richard 37
Holyfield, Kevin 558
Holzem, John D 782
Holzer, Damon 84
Holzer, Sunita 696
Holzshu, Christopher (Chris) 515
Hom, Erwin 354

Hom, John 676
Hombach, Robert J 113
Homenuik, Terry 395
Homer, David P. (Dave) 377
Homer, Ronald A 535
Honda, Amy 102
Honeycutt, John 269
Honeycutt, Mike 747
Honeyman, Eric 867
Hong, Peter 76
Hong, Eleanor E 493
Hong, John 685
Hong, Scott 872
Hongola, Michael 795
Honkus, Tina 556
Honovic, Johnathan 872
Honovic, Jonny 872
Honovic, John 872
Hood, Chris 485
Hood, Amy E 560
Hood, Ron 866
Hoogenboom, Paul G. P. 716
Hoogeveen, Kevin 339
Hook, Rich 643
Hooker, Thomas 199
Hooley, Joseph L. (Jay) 766
Hooper, Anthony C. (Tony) 61
Hooper, Tony 61
Hooper, Ana 254
Hooper, Lisa 272
Hooper, Susie 844
Hooper, Brian 878
Hooser, Steve Van 257
Hoover, Stephen (Steve) 912
Hope, Walter 59
Hope, Ken 192
Hope, Jim 782
Hopfer, Rick 565
Hopfinger, Mark M 701
Hopkins, Christopher 101
Hopkins, Diggy 272
Hopkins, Lynn M. 632
Hopkins, Frank 657
Hopkins, Kevin 807
Hopkins, Larry 835
Hoplamazian, Mark S. 444
Hopmans, John 517
Hoppe, Mark A. 541
Hopper, Sue 556
Hopson, Jeffrey 702
Horan, Theodore 644
Horan, Terry 716
Horan, Craig 852
Horber, Patrick 6
Horgan, Dan 692
Horgan, Kathryn M. (Kathy) 766
Horger, Robert R. 751
Horn, Charles L. 32
Horn, Jim 204
Horn, Alan F. 271
Horn, Justin 549
Horn, Joe Van 868
Hornbuckle, William J. 558
Hornby, William P. 184
Horne, Lewis 173
Horne, Mike 173
Horner, David 145
Horner, Leigh E 416
Horner, Matt 907
Hornung, Bill 908
Horowitz, Paul 130
Horseman, Neil 874
Horstman, Gregory 163
Horstman, Douglas 898
Horstmann, Douglas J. 412
Horstmann, David L. 412
Hortman, Edwin W. (Ed) 57
Horton, Carrie 64
Horton, Rick 433
Horton, Donald R. 433
Horton, Craig 481
Horton, Michael 664
Horton, Kelly 671
Horton, William E. (Bill) 700
Horton, Andrean 916
Horvath, Karen 122
Horvath, Anthony 407

Joseph, Tommy S. 462
Joseph, George 551
Joseph, Philip 874
Joswick, David 767
Joughin, Dan 767
Jover, Angelines 481
Jowers, Gaylon M. 823
Joy, Jennifer 195
Joyal, David 241
Joyce, Matthew 105
Joyce, Deborah 182
Joyce, Thomas P. 253
Joyce, David L. 375
Joyce, Elizabeth 419
Joyce, Robert J. (Bob) 487
Joyner, Dee 223
Joyner, J. David 250
Joysizemore, Dian 98
Jr, John B Morse 17
Jr, James C Carter 22
Jr, William F Gifford 37
Jr, W Hildebrandt Surgner 37
Jr, Paul G Haaga 46
Jr, George Pierce 51
Jr, Murray Watson 145
Jr, Domenic Dell'osso 190
Jr, Roby Thompson 314
Jr, Alton B Lewis 347
Jr, W Michael Amick 463
Jr, Ralph Spencer 572
Jr, John M Fields 624
Jr, Thomas R Quinn 625
Jr, Ronald J Nicolas 630
Jr, Robert C Biesterfeld 711
Jr, Phillip D Joseph 759
Jr, Lawrence C Franklin 765
Jr, Eugene A Deladdy 806
Jr, Richard L Smith 813
Jr, Thomas B Gerlach 813
Jr, Robert A Stewart 846
Jubb, Tim 818
Jubie, Nicole 311
Juby, Alyce 489
Juchno, Stacy M. 659
Juday, Mark 34
Juday, Ryan 816
Jude, Justin L. 518
Judge, Ann 147
Judge, James J. (Jim) 307
Judge, Will 538
Judy, Ryan 67
Juergensen, Colleen 496
Jula, Peg 332
Julian, Paul C. 546
Julian, Steve 736
Julian, Kenneth D. 816
Juliane, Jeffrey 163
Juliano, Mark 502
Julien, Jeffrey P. (Jeff) 693
Juneau, Jeff 763
Jung, Katie 682
Jung, Lisa A 777
Junkins, Lowell L. 320
Junod, Vincent 727
Juppenlatz, Stuart 369
Jureta, Madelaine 49
Jurrens, Erika 165
Jurrens, Lisa 540
Jurs, Peter 332
Juster, Andrew A. (Andy) 744
Justin, Marianne 863
Justinger, Kimberly 252

K

Kaatman, Nancy J 136
Kaatz, Alexander 454
Kabat, Kevin 594
Kabat, Kevin T. 864
Kablawi, Hani 105
Kachurka, Matt 247
Kaczmarek, Larry 402
Kaczmarek, Walter T. (Walt) 414
Kaczmarek, Paulette 600
Kaczmarek, Jessica 810
Kaczynski, Tom 527

Kaden, Ellen O 161
Kadien, Thomas G. (Tom) 462
Kadlec, Tom 788
Kadnar, Julie 51
Kadoori, Bob 173
Kadre, Manuel 707
Kaduke, David 497
Kadyrova, Tatiana 866
Kaercher, Walter 644
Kaestner, H. Todd 148
Kaestner, Todd 149
Kafka, Robert 85
Kafka, Donald L. 336
Kahan, James 517
Kahan, Rich 728
Kahn, Cheryl 165
Kahn, Wendy 785
Kahn, Todd 785
Kahne, Michael 350
Kahny, Nicole 872
Kaider, Mike 173
Kaighn, Chris 79
Kain, Peter 577
Kain, Larry 655
Kainer, Darrell 303
Kaiser, George B. 137
Kaiser, Allen 260
Kaiser, Chris 272
Kaiser, Laura S. 458
Kaiser, Frances 583
Kaiser, Gregory 729
Kaiserman, David J. 508
Kakar, Dee 522
Kakuda, Kevin 171
Kalafos, Paul 602
Kalakkad, Dinesh 501
Kalamaras, Paul 467
Kalanovic, Daniel 649
Kalaria, Brij 133
Kalaria, Brijesh 133
Kalathur, Rajesh (Raj) 260
Kalchik, Mona 107
Kalchuri, Shantanu 607
Kalen, Michael 677
Kali, Thomas 133
Kalin, Katherine 178
Kalin, Robert 565
Kalisek, Brian 559
Kalleeny, Monica 250
Kallio, Jerry 541
Kallsen, Tony E 720
Kallsen, Terri R. 728
Kallweit, Keith 292
Kalman, Betsy 500
Kalmar, Steven 461
Kaloustian, Maral 152
Kalstein, Michele 323
Kaltenbach, Patrick 22
Kamachi, Patrick 101
Kamal, Mostafa M. 524
Kamal, Ashfaq 537
Kamal-Bahl, Sachin 649
Kamara, Abdul 165
Kamath, Sundar 725
Kamber, Martin 133
Kamenash, Tracey 406
Kamensky, Allan E. 781
Kametz, William (Bill) 720
Kamford, Peter 122
Kamiliotis, Daniela 691
Kamin, John R. 614
Kaminski, Jennifer 81
Kaminski, Ken 199
Kaminski, Jeff J. 484
Kaminski, Robert B. 549
Kaminski, Mark V. 703
Kaminski, Monika 920
Kaminsky, John 729
Kamitaki, Wayne 183
Kamm, Terry 136
Kamminga, Duane 350
Kamra, Kush 556
Kamsickas, James K 252
Kanarian, Steve 659
Kanas, John A. 109
Kandarian, Steven A. (Steve) 555
Kane, Rachel 101

Kane, Peter 175
Kane, Thomas M. (Tom) 235
Kane, Jessica 317
Kane, Debbie 406
Kane, Brian A. 437
Kane, Edward 440
Kane, Bob 454
Kane, Terri 458
Kane, James 517
Kane, John 575
Kane, Martha 635
Kane, Eileen 775
Kane, Eric 782
Kanefsky, Andrea 122
Kang, SungWon 308
Kang, Katelyn 429
Kang, Charlotte 478
Kangas, Chris 537
Kanis, Jordan 777
Kanlic, Elvis 489
Kann, Joe 712
Kanneman, Paul D 743
Kanouff, Yvette 199
Kansler, Michael R 300
Kant, Surya 789
Kantamneni, Raje 599
Kantaros, Andrea 644
Kantola, Kevin 855
Kantor, Jonathan D. (Jon) 211
Kantor, Lesley 872
Kantro, Gayle 478
Kapcheck, Jeff 173
Kapito, Robert S. (Rob) 130
Kapki, Nick Kapki Nick 865
Kaplan, Dean 175
Kaplan, Bob 175
Kaplan, Robert S. (Rob) 325
Kaplan, Grisel 644
Kaplan, Ralph 725
Kaplan, Robert 766
Kaplan, David 818
Kaplin, Leo 100
Kapnick, Stewart 541
Kapoor, Rakesh 478
Kapoor, Sanjay 758
Kapusinski, Victor 865
Karafa, Jeffrey L 754
Karamanoukian, Henry 671
Karamarkovich, Kim 774
Karanam, Raj 253
Karanga, Ruth 593
Karanjkar, Ashish 647
Karas, Michelle (Shelley) 640
Karatha, Padmanabhan 221
Karen, Friedman 912
Karhan, Dean 317
Karkaria, Hormuzd 265
Karl, James 16
Karlovich, Robert W. (Trey) 591
Karlstromer, Peter 200
Karn, Randy 898
Karnes, Willie 115
Karnes, Merle 673
Karnik, Nihar 599
Karolis, George C. 78
Karpik, Mike 766
Karpinski, John 449
Karr, Kathi 430
Karr, Michael 630
Karras, Athanasios 429
Karriker, Karen 461
Karrip, Brian 342
Karros, Kirt 419
Karst, Darren W. 708
Karter, Nicholas 685
Karuppur, Devi Prasad 687
Karwacki, John 682
Kasanoff, Howard 244
Kasbar, Michael J. 906
Kasendorf, Leonard 556
Kashkari, Neel T. 325
Kashyap, Nagraj 685
Kasner, Ken 406
Kasper, Michael 34
Kasper, Meghann 100
Kasper, Andrea 676
Kassab, Leanne D. 212

Kassem, Amin 438
Kast, Pete 173
Kastanis, Maria 644
Kastberg, Crystal 672
Kastberg, Amalia G 724
Kastner, Christopher D. 442
Kastner, Christopher K. 534
Kastner, Janeen B. 716
Kaszuba, Marek 898
Katanick, Ron 493
Katariya, Sanjeev 288
Katcher, Abbey 101
Katcher, Keith 607
Kate, Debold 105
Katibian, Benny 685
Katie, Cave 724
Katims, Susan 155
Katsikas, Cindy 541
Katt, Faye 113
Kattos, Andrew N. (Andy) 737
Katyal, Navin 648
Katz, Marc D. 155
Katz, Robert L. (Bobby) 471
Katz, Jonathan 635
Kauffman, Holly C 355
Kauffman, Andy 530
Kaufman, Jules P. 241
Kaufman, Victor A. 311
Kaufman, Richard 635
Kaufmann, Michael C. (Mike) 165
Kaufmann, Kevin 583
Kavanagh, Ben 244
Kavanaugh, James J. 460
Kavanaugh, James P. (Jim) 907
Kavassalis, Tom 912
Kawa, Mark 774
Kawasaki, Hiroyuki 917
Kay, Linda Sloane 184
Kay, Julie 186
Kay, Robert 729
Kay, David 762
Kay, Steve A. 860
Kaye, David J. 142
Kayitalire, Louis 147
Kayser, C. Dallas 207
Kayser, Catherine 782
Kayzerman, Alex 480
Kazakevich, Vadim 105
Kazazian, Haig 475
Kazi, Zubair 204
Kazinski, Beth 774
Keach, Michael 489
Kean, Steven J. (Steve) 491
Keane, Daniel 604
Keane, James 712
Keane, Valerie 736
Keane, Conor 767
Kear, Scott 13
Kearney, Michael S 78
Kearney, Dan 175
Kearney, Daniel 402
Kearney, Sara 445
Kearney, Nancy 774
Kearney, Tim 818
Kearney, Thomas W. 907
Kearns, Richard 82
Kearns, John 306
Kearny, Ric 163
Keating, Leslie 13
Keating, Kim 85
Keating, Thomas P 116
Keating, Johnathan 131
Keating, Tim 136
Keating, Michael 295
Keating, Mark R. 766
Keaunui, Naalei 103
Kedia, Gunjan 766
Kedia, Gunjan 865
Kee, Rob 453
Kee, Timothy 898
Keefauver, David 439
Keefe, Denise M. 15
Keefe, Tom 388
Keefe, Timothy 542
Keefe, Brenda 744
Keefe, Brandt 770
Keefer, Joseph G. (Joe) 151

Kopp, Greg 729
Kopper, Carolyn L 406
Koptyra, Kristin 97
Kopycinski, Gloria 244
Korajkic, Jasko 222
Kordahi, Rony C. 626
Korecki, Joseph 644
Korenberg, Matthew 390
Korenek, Joe 304
Korff, Stephen 677
Korff, Steve 677
Koricanac, Nick 904
Korins, Danielle 682
Koritko, Martin 513
Kornberg, Susan 109
Kornblum, David 272
Korneffel, Laurie 185
Kornegay, Alexandria 461
Korner, Barbara O. 811
Korolog, George 725
Korsapati, Venka 40
Korsh, Les B. 636
Korsmeyer, Mark 252
Kort, Steve 221
Korzekwinski, Francis W. (Frank) 359
Kos, Heather 453
Kosasa, Paul J 183
Kosek, Rick 117
Kosiek, Patrick 204
Koski, Philip 865
Koslow, John 49
Koster, Teresa 371
Koster, Barbara G. 676
Kostiw, Michael 16
Kostosky, Robert A 709
Kosydor, Vicki 322
Kotick, Robert A. (Bobby) 10
Kotsenas, Peter 355
Kottapalli, Pushpanjali 101
Kottapalli, Kishore 766
Kottler, Robert M. (Bob) 446
Kotwal, Shailesh M. 865
Kotylo, Ken 794
Kotzin, Brian 61
Koulouris, Richard R. 663
Koury, Emile 399
Koury, Jeffrey (Jeff) 794
Koushik, Srinivas (Srini) 524
Kousloglou, Tasos 478
Kovacevich, Richard 200
Kovach, Greg 13
Kovacs, James A 456
Koval, Kathy 734
Koveos, George 691
Koviak, Jeff 796
Kowal, Dave 158
Kowaleski, Tim 210
Kowalski, Kevin P. 548
Kowkabany, Rob 58
Kowler, Kathy 584
Kowlzan, Mark W. 631
Kozak, Mike 351
Kozak, Colleen 733
Kozakov, Alex 173
Kozar, Paul Kozar Paul 865
Kozel, David F. (Dave) 682
Koziol, Patrick 105
Kozlowski, Damian 805
Krabbe, Mark 257
Kracov, Eric 584
Kraemer, Theodore 140
Kraft, Robert O. (Rocky) 250
Kraft, Christopher 733
Krage, David 446
Kraich, Rick 873
Krakaur, Ken 736
Krakowsky, Philippe 464
Kralian, Edward 101
Kralingen, Bridget A. van 460
Krall, Donna M. 356
Kramer, Lauren 163
Kramer, Kelly A. 199
Kramer, Richard J. (Rich) 391
Kramer, Michael 562
Kramer, Kevin 562
Kramer, Curt A 577
Kramer, Phillip D. (Phil) 657

Kramer, Phil D 658
Kramer, Mark 708
Kramer, Laurie 724
Kramer, Rick 738
Kramer, Robin C 809
Kramer, Steve 865
Krane, Spencer 323
Krane, Hilary K. 592
Krantz, Missy S 446
Krasnoff, Jeffrey P. (Jeff) 508
Krasowski, Janet D. 675
Kratsberg, Leon 741
Kratz, Denise 724
Kratzer, Doug 402
Kraus, Marie 163
Kraus, Frederick 502
Kraus, Kim 671
Krause, Douglas P. 285
Krause, Kim 774
Krauss, Soheir 201
Krauss, Jim 736
Krawczyk, Brian 390
Krawczyk, Tammy 902
Krawtschuk, Christopher 649
Kraynak, Bob 173
Kreatsoulas, John 456
Krebs, Donald E. (Don) 483
Krebs, Don 483
Krebs, James 872
Krech, Joyce 122
Kreger, Julie 101
Krehbiel, Bruce 465
Kreips, Christopher 714
Kremer, Donald 192
Kremer, Lisa 532
Kremer, Wesley D. 695
Kremer, Melissa 788
Kremin, Donald H. (Don) 432
Kremke, Kevin L 260
Krempl, Stephen 763
Krenkel, David S. 276
Kresge, Kevin 133
Kresl, Michael 54
Kress, Jean 386
Kress, Colette M. 607
Kress, Kathy 878
Kreuger, Jennifer 523
Kreuzer, Barry 246
Krevans, Sarah 775
Krezmien, Dennis 522
Krick, Brian 734
Kriebel, Jonathan 546
Krieg, Susan 448
Krieger, Sandra C. (Sandy) 323
Krieger, Sarah 639
Kriegsmann, Sonja 614
Kriens, Scott G. 482
Kriesand, Dave 111
Krikorian, Lazarus 59
Krikorian, Alex 195
Krimbill, H. Michael 591
Kring, Steven C. 431
Krippner, Brian 837
Krish, Bharani 565
Krishnamurthi, Gopal 327
Krishnamurthy, Nikki 311
Krishnamurthy, Srini 406
Kristo, Joni 593
Kristoff, David 588
Kristoffersen, Ashley 133
Kristoffersen, Candi 501
Krmpotic, Deb 111
Kroboth, Michael 665
Kroehler, Jon 575
Kroeker, Harrald F. 73
Kroenung, Stefan 87
Kroger, Matt 173
Krohn, Shannon 81
Kroiss, Valerie 838
Krol, Wojciech 218
Krolewicz, Randall 522
Kroll, Edmund 180
Kroll, Brannon 244
Kromm, Elizabeth 475
Krone, Roger A. 505
Kronlage, Dan 273
Kronman, Jeremy 173

Kronmueller, Margaret 770
Kropf, Susan J 786
Kruczlnicki, David 78
Krueger, Pam 85
Krueger, Alan 173
Krueger, Melissa 247
Krueger, Steve 446
Krug, Carey 691
Kruger, James D. (Jim) 579
Kruger, Scott 599
Kruger, Bob 792
Kruger, Bill 850
Kruglov, Lisa 449
Krulewitch, Jerry 545
Krummen, William 333
Krumrey, Elizabeth 904
Krupa, David E. 722
Krupp, Jeff 696
Kruse, Kevin 153
Kruse, Karen 348
Kruse, Shelly 397
Kruse, Brent 651
Kruse, Eric 655
Kruse, Rebecca 724
Krusinski, Laura 489
Kruszewicz, Ronald J. (Ron) 771
Krynauw, Pieter 429
Krysl, James 685
Krzanich, Brian 260
Krzeminski, Robert E 886
Ksenak, Stephen M. 40
Kubacki, Michael L. 500
Kubasak, Heather 441
Kubba, Omar 335
Kubiesa, Susan 599
Kubovcik, Sean 826
Kucera, Randall R 397
Kucharski, Joseph 649
Kucia, Mark A 846
Kuczora, Deb 493
Kudler, Douglas 555
Kudrna, Casey 837
Kueber, Ken 213
Kuehl, Kevin 127
Kuehn, Kurt 850
Kuelbs, Brian P. 97
Kugel, Irene 105
Kuhn, Rebecca (Becky) 111
Kuhns, Dewey 207
Kuick, Kenneth 158
Kuiper, Craig 657
Kuiper, Jeremy L. 806
Kukurin, James 729
Kularski, Patty 402
Kulaszewicz, Frank C. 712
Kulchitskaya, Yanina 204
Kulczytzky, Chris 721
Kulkin, Harvey 738
Kullander, David 351
Kulshreshtha, Anoop 727
Kum, Chong Guk (C. G.) 401
Kumar, Devinder 14
Kumar, Gopa 324
Kumar, Sunil 475
Kumar, Rajesh 709
Kumar, Viji 774
Kumbier, Michelle A. 403
Kumler, Alan 844
Kumm, Wendy 81
Kumpas, James 359
Kuncheff, Ivan 16
Kunde, Gerald 782
Kundurthy, Praveen 456
Kuney, Terry 441
Kunk, James E. 440
Kunkel, Ted 109
Kunkel, Jay K. 503
Kunkel, Lisa 657
Kunkel, Thomas M. (Tom) 827
Kunreuther, Susan 537
Kunst, Jeff 238
Kuntz, William 173
Kuntz, JT 318
Kuntz, John F. 675
Kunz, Jim 16
Kunze, Shane 679
Kunze, Shane 680

Kuper, Debra 20
Kupetz, Dan 175
Kupper, Randy 56
Kuppuswamy, Murali 809
Kurali, Andreas 652
Kurapati, Raja 131
Kurapka, David 131
Kurasch, Aaron 56
Kurdes, Ted 323
Kurek, Robert 489
Kurian, George 580
Kurihara, Miky 871
Kurita, Nathan 655
Kuritzkes, Andrew 766
Kurland, Stanford L. 642
Kurnick, Robert H. 642
Kuropas, Stephen 599
Kurow, Dave 351
Kurrasch, Paul 775
Kurth, Keith 889
Kurtov, Ines 583
Kurtz, Aaron 225
Kurtz, Ronald D 565
Kurtz, Ronald 565
Kurtz, Martin 728
Kurtz, Erin 913
Kuryea, Kimberly 374
Kurz, Christian 872
Kurzius, Lawrence E. 544
Kus, Julie 670
Kuselias, Jason 406
Kush, Henry 306
Kushel, J. Richard (Rich) 130
Kushner, Jared 706
Kuslits, Thomas R. 356
Kutac, Mary-Katherine 180
Kutam, Sreeni 87
Kutchera, Kris 28
Kutchmark, Mike 659
Kuykendall, Ronald E. 724
Kuypers, Tom 120
Kuzbel, Jeffrey 163
Kuzmak, Beth 546
Kuzniasz, Stacey 247
Kvadus, Glen 855
Kvamme, John 81
Kwan, Irene E B 102
Kwan, Sarah 777
Kwawu, Sena M 763
Kwok, Andrew 164
Kwon, Mea 354
Kyff, Emilia 555
Kyle, Rex 107
Kymes, Stacy C. 137
Kyriakidis, Alex 530
Kyse, Julie 311

L

LA, Mai 133
Laan, Ron Van Der 105
Labarre, Sedar 140
Labat, Misty 446
LaBelle, Jeanne 335
Laben, Nancy J. 140
Labi, Abdul 115
Labib, Joseph 675
Laborde, Sarah 806
Labovich, Gary D. 140
Labrique, Steve 67
Labrosse, Derek 107
Lacaille, Rick 766
Lacassagne, Gtraudmarie 241
LaCerda, Michael 133
Lacerda, Marcos 685
Lacey, Erin 468
Lacey, Diane E. 582
Lachance, Margaret P. (Meg) 682
Lacher, Joseph P. (Joe) 487
Lacker, Jeffrey M. (Jeff) 325
Lackhouse, Gary 84
Lackman, Sara J 671
Lacour, Raymond 693
Lacy, James 85
Lacy, Spring Taylor 676
Ladd, Emma 513

Robles, Javier 589
Robo, James L. (Jim) 590
Robson, Ted 784
Robusto, Dino E. 211
Roby, Darrel 136
Roby, Anne K. 514
Robyn, Lewis 555
Roca, Marco A. 157
Rocco, David 105
Rocco, Michael Del 109
Rocco, Scott 382
Roces, Santiago 878
Rocha, Charles P. 746
Rocha, Oscar Gonzalez 753
Roche, Michael 33
Roche, Vincent T. 65
Roche, Dan 85
Roche, Kimberly De 314
Roche, John C. (Jack) 402
Roche, Marianne 522
Roche, Jules 912
Rocheleau, Duane 599
Rock, Jesse 375
Rockey, Joseph E. 659
Rockholt, Tracy 788
Rockwood, John D. 548
Rockwood, Renee 818
Roco, Ninna 555
Roda, Craig A. 369
Roddey, Kevin 655
Rodean, Jennifer 93
Rodell, Angela 28
Rodeno, Michaela 103
Rodewald, Chris 865
Rodgers, Jodi 204
Rodgers, Steven R. (Steve) 456
Rodgers, Douglas 565
Rodgers, Debbie 752
Rodgers, Jim 773
Rodgers, Clark 774
Rodgers, Randall 838
Rodie, Robert 351
Rodrigue, Perry 300
Rodrigues, Edison F 456
Rodriguez, Rodolfo 56
Rodriguez, Michael 85
Rodriguez, Carlos A 87
Rodriguez, Aida 97
Rodriguez, Kathy 102
Rodriguez, Carlos 127
Rodriguez, Maro 244
Rodriguez, Javier J. 255
Rodriguez, Deanna 300
Rodriguez, Ryan 311
Rodriguez, Juan 313
Rodriguez, Vicki 316
Rodriguez, Mandy 422
Rodriguez, Linda 446
Rodriguez, Gerry 508
Rodriguez, David A. 530
Rodriguez, Priscilla 541
Rodriguez, Jaime 576
Rodriguez, Rita E. 619
Rodriguez, Leticia 630
Rodriguez, Liesl A 661
Rodriguez, John A. 683
Rodriguez, Abigail 690
Rodriguez, Armando G. 730
Rodriguez, Enrique 745
Rodriguez, Damarie 777
Rodriguez-Borjas, Carlos 703
Roe, Jeffrey 105
Roe, Bob 120
Roe, Jonathan 332
Roe, John E. 359
Roe, Amy 901
Roederer, Nick 693
Roegner, Eric V. 76
Roehm, John 489
Roemer, Jeff 327
Roesel, Larry M. 90
Roeser, Christopher 526
Roeske, Richard 487
Roesner, Daniel 221
Roesser, Matthew 56
Roesslein, Dennis 541
Roessner, Karl A. 283

Roewe, Gordon 223
Roewe, Randy 345
Roffler, Michael J. (Mike) 353
Rofstad, Scott 904
Rogers, Patrick 34
Rogers, J. Michael 98
Rogers, Carol 100
Rogers, William D. (Bill) 181
Rogers, Heather 260
Rogers, Lawrence S. (Larry) 296
Rogers, John F.W. 389
Rogers, R. Scott 391
Rogers, Brian 401
Rogers, John 406
Rogers, Steve 439
Rogers, Jay 459
Rogers, Nancy 513
Rogers, John C. 645
Rogers, Bill 663
Rogers, Alexander H. (Alex) 685
Rogers, Alex 685
Rogers, Tom 741
Rogers, William H. (Bill) 774
Rogers, Bradon 778
Rogers, Ann 784
Rogers, Brian C. 784
Rogers, Tony 878
Rogers, Rebecca 902
Rogerson, Craig 665
Roggekamp, Ruud 136
Rogness, Jonathan 865
Rogstad, W. David 833
Rogula, Ann 599
Rohan, Mary 143
Rohane, Patricia 178
Rohde, William M. 122
Rohit, Mehra 698
Rohr, Mark C. 177
Rohrbacher, Tim 101
Rohrbaugh, Philmer H. (Phil) 369
Rohrer, Daniel 607
Roig, Ismael 74
Roig, Jorge 661
Rojahn, Benjamin 173
Rojas, Jose 432
Rojas, Daysi 874
Roland, Barbara 275
Roland, Thierry 437
Rolfes, Francis 162
Rolfes, Francis M 162
Rolheiser, Eric J. 237
Roll-Wallace, Kim 113
Roller, Mark 621
Rollins, James D. (Dan) 99
Rollins, Ceseley 180
Rollins, Lisa 644
Rolls, Paul E. 620
Rolon, Gil 115
Romain, Peter 585
Romaine, Mark A. 388
Romaine, Stephen S. 820
Roman, Michael F. 2
Roman, Juan 40
Roman, David H 113
Roman, John 151
Roman, James 223
Roman, Edwin 247
Roman, Oraida 255
Roman, Lawrence (Larry) 833
Romaneiro, Marcos 494
Romanelli, Christopher 204
Romano, Frank 553
Romano, Michael 556
Romano, Gregory 870
Romanowski, Mike 214
Romanowski, Paul 433
Romay, Connie 58
Rome, Melanie 611
Romeo, Steven 330
Romer, Paul 585
Romero, David 73
Rometty, Virginia M. (Ginni) 460
Romig, Timothy D. 247
Romine, Jeremy 109
Romine, Krisden 699
Romine, Bill 708
Romito, Joyce 324

Romm, Elisa 537
Romo, Tammy 755
Romoff, Jeffrey A. 859
Romstad, Michael 744
Ron, Klimkowski 196
Rona, Michael 175
Ronald, Alan 56
Ronoy, Cary 211
Ronning, Bruce 796
Ronnow, Jesse Ronnow Jesse 920
Rooke, Brian 762
Rooks, Marsha 736
Rooney, Mary 328
Rooney, Jack 555
Rooney, David 555
Rooney, Robert 568
Rooney, James 628
Rooney, Jerome 703
Roop, Kimberly L 67
Roos, Jeff 508
Roos, Tom 855
Root, Chris 257
Root, Julie 522
Roper, Craig 303
Roper, Jay 844
Ropp, Stephen E (Steve) 483
Ropp, Holly 483
Rorabaugh, David 369
Rosa, Dan De La 496
Rosa, Luis 585
Rosado, Louis 163
Rosado, Robert 765
Rosamilia, Thomas W. (Tom) 460
Rosanova, Don 496
Rosati, Bob 558
Rosato, R. David 644
Rosborough, Mark N. 338
Rosbrough, Martha 334
Rosch, Francis C. (Fran) 778
Roscoe, Fred 869
Rose, Matthew K. (Matt) 123
Rose, Matthew K. (Matt) 134
Rose, M. Robert 149
Rose, Matthew K. (Matt) 154
Rose, Sheryl 171
Rose, Timothy L. 239
Rose, Marya M. 245
Rose, Anthony J. 267
Rose, Jim 332
Rose, Dennis E. 344
Rose, Michael 423
Rose, David G. 431
Rose, Mike 476
Rose, Christopher 530
Rose, Ken 556
Rose, Greg 685
Rose, Virginia 802
Rose, George 860
Roseborough, Teresa W. 426
Rosello, Mike 32
Rosen, Elaine D. 83
Rosen, Sheri 244
Rosen, Rebecca 263
Rosen, Rae 322
Rosen, Mitch 382
Rosen, Mark 461
Rosen, Marc 509
Rosenbach, Lynn 111
Rosenbaum, Eileen 727
Rosenberg, Joshua 323
Rosenberg, Paul 480
Rosenberg, Brian 482
Rosenberg, Jennifer 541
Rosenberg, Ken 667
Rosenberg, Donald J. 685
Rosenblum, Heather 877
Rosencrans, Dean 81
Rosenfeld, Paul 56
Rosenfeld, Irene B. 567
Rosenfeld, Phyllis 741
Rosenfield, Eliot M. 155
Rosengren, Eric S. 325
Rosenstein, Robert 139
Rosenstein, Beryl 474
Rosenthal, David 313
Rosenthal, Louis 478
Rosenthal, Gary 530

Rosenthal, Mark 677
Rosenthal, Stacy 744
Rosenthaler, Albert E. 688
Rosetta, Gladys 555
Roshardt, Christoph 530
Roshek, Sonya 536
Rosier, W. Grady 547
Roslin, Debbie 109
Rosman, Adam L 343
Rosner, Judy 706
Rospond, Nicole 741
Rospond, Nikki 741
Ross, Wayne 105
Ross, Kim 166
Ross, Joyce M. 171
Ross, Cheyenne 180
Ross, Rich 269
Ross, Renee 441
Ross, Heather 446
Ross, John 474
Ross, Brendan 530
Ross, Andrew D. 634
Ross, Thomas J. 639
Ross, Tom 693
Ross, Stephen M. 698
Ross, Bridget A. 727
Ross, Lisa 744
Ross, Sheryl 751
Ross, Dennis E. 766
Ross, James E. (Jim) 766
Ross, Dan 786
Ross, Sara 788
Ross, Kevin 846
Rossbauer, Pauline 676
Rossero, Daniel 355
Rossetta, Melanie 865
Rossetti, Nick 270
Rossetti, Barbara 696
Rossetto, Ronald B. 738
Rossi, Mark A. 102
Rossi, Mark A. 103
Rossi, James 207
Rossi, Todd 709
Rossi, Hugo 730
Rossi, Jack 773
Rossmann, Barbara W. 413
Rosso, Paul 2
Rosswurm, Gretchen 177
Rostan, Richard H. 312
Roszak, Dave 273
Roszczewski, Loretta 493
Roth, Jay 270
Roth, Julie 441
Roth, Michael I. 464
Roth, Renee S. 781
Roth, Corina 817
Roth, Robert 872
Roth, Cindi 873
Rothenberg, David 390
Rothenberg, Craig 476
Rother, Joe 496
Rotherham, Ross 339
Rothfuss, Andre 141
Rothkin, Gregg 173
Rothman, Fred 508
Rothstein, Diahann 321
Rothstein, Sharon 762
Rotolo, Jill 103
Rotondo, John 555
Rottman, Monica 141
Rottmuller, Lori 541
Roualet, Mark C. 374
Roughton, Paul 908
Roulot, Antoine Axel 767
Rourk, Kevin 751
Rouse, Mary Ann 806
Rouse, Anthony 868
Rouse, Brad 913
Rousey, Melody 272
Roush, Phil 199
Roush, Robin S 387
Roush, Richard 811
Rousse, Troy A 303
Rousse, Jonathan 390
Rousseau, Michael T. (Mike) 5
Rousseau, Paul 301
Roussel, Serge 649

Shunck, Marybeth 344
Shurts, Wayne 782
Shuster, Mike 96
Shuttleworth, Edward L. 355
Shyr, Jing 461
Shytle, Debbie 34
Siao, Susan 218
Siarkowski, Tracey 332
Sias, Evelyn 872
Sibalic, Tammy 247
Siberio, John 869
Sibley, James M 509
Sica, Frank V. 474
Sicchitano, Joe 774
Sichak, Stephen (Steve) 119
Sichel, Hobart (Bart) 155
Sicola, Tom 547
Sicotte, Luc 890
Siddiqi, Sajid 221
Sideris, Harry K. 281
Sidhu, Jay S. 247
Sidiqi, Khalid 685
Siebenborn, Bill 252
Siebert, Eric 144
Siedlecki, Sandy 523
Sieg, Andy 100
Sieg, John 332
Siegel, Kenneth I. 520
Siegel, Michael 565
Sieger, Michael D. (Mike) 672
Siegmund, Jan 87
Siegrist, Robert N. 159
Siemer, Calvin 502
Sienkiewicz, Mark 476
Siereveld, Ryan P 671
Sierra, Joseph 105
Sievert, Frederick J 702
Sievert, G Michael 785
Sieving, Charles E. 357
Sieving, Charles E. 590
Sifer, Joseph F. (Joe) 140
Sifer, Joe 140
Sifford, Jessica 774
Sigal, Jonathan 667
Sigler, Maggie 333
Signorello, Tom 265
Signorino, Charles 180
Sih, Gil 685
Siira, Tyler 863
Sikand, Sarika 855
Silagy, Eric E. 357
Silagy, Eric E. 590
Silander, David 865
Silbaugh, Jason 480
Silber, Jeff 449
Silberman, Jennifer 788
Silcock, Chris 421
Silfa, Betty 204
Silfen, David M. 812
Silins, Andris J 535
Silitch, Nicholas C. (Nick) 676
Silk, Bert 235
Sill, Scott 658
Silliman, Craig L. 870
Sills, Stephen J. 30
Sills-Memorial, Clay 614
Silva, Lauren 56
Silva, Nicole 136
Silva, Stephen 199
Silva, Francisco A. Aristeguieta 204
Silva, Judith 635
Silva, Elif 649
Silva, Christopher 676
Silva, Anthony 877
Silverman, Rob 140
Silverman, Bob 478
Silvers, Gary 3
Silverstein, Martin B. 386
Silverstein, Ray 763
Silvia, Phil 777
Silwa, Robert 907
Sim, Sugin 219
Sim, Chris 489
Simard, Curtis C. 112
Simco, Lori 835
Simcoe, Suma 565
Simeone, Giovanni 101

Simermeyer, Elizabeth A. (Beth) 289
Siminski, Mike 549
Simione, Jay 532
Simitz, Robert 453
Simkowitz, Daniel A. (Dan) 568
Simler, Jordan 869
Simmons, Al 87
Simmons, Paul 97
Simmons, Patrick 377
Simmons, Jodi 458
Simmons, Jeffrey N. (Jeff) 511
Simmons, Gary 867
Simmons, Harris H. 919
Simms, Tony 408
Simms, David 460
Simon, John 3
Simon, Jon 218
Simon, Lynn T. 227
Simon, Mindy 230
Simon, Laura 247
Simon, Aaron 272
Simon, Grigore 588
Simon, John R. 650
Simon, Steve 703
Simon, David 744
Simon, Shari 744
Simon, Deborah 744
Simon, Larry 745
Simon, Marianne 807
Simon, Linda 878
Simonds, John 523
Simonds, Michael Q. 863
Simonelli, Lorenzo 375
Simonetti, Beth E. 792
Simons, Brenda 857
Simons, Doyle R. 896
Simonte, Michael K. 45
Simowitz, Rebecca 277
Simpkins, Cpm 774
Simpson, Doug 67
Simpson, Austin 107
Simpson, Barry N. 215
Simpson, Shelley 439
Simpson, Kelley 480
Simpson, Kristina 489
Simpson, Michael 555
Simpson, Jay 558
Simpson, Kathryn 602
Simpson, David 657
Simpson, David L. 703
Simpson, Mary 752
Sims, Adrienne 264
Sims, C. Randall (Randy) 425
Sims, John V. 462
Sims, Robert H 625
Sims, Scott 724
Sims, Damon 811
Simson, Thomas H. 145
Sinatra, Kim 909
Sinclair, Jeffrey 478
Sinclair, Christopher A. 539
Sinclair, Donald 700
Sinden, Jessie 390
Sinden, Shaun 792
Sindhu, Pradeep S. 482
Singer, David 119
Singer, Lori 241
Singer, Amy 871
Singh, Rajinder P. (Raj) 108
Singh, Bobby 131
Singh, Jennifer 133
Singh, Munjeet 140
Singh, Anand 185
Singh, Zorawar Biri 199
Singh, Manjit 208
Singh, Mala 292
Singh, Rajesh 327
Singh, Rakhee 480
Singh, Harmit J. 509
Singh, Jasraj 509
Singh, Kirti 671
Singh, Manvinder 685
Singh, Sanjay 718
Singh, Sangharsh 766
Singh, Maneet 913
Singh, Sanchita 917
Singhal, Raj 698

Singhania, Shishir 163
Singleton, J. Barton 781
Sinha, Dharmendra Kumar 217
Sinhabahu, Charuka 429
Sinko, Jim 738
Sinks, Patrick 557
Sinnard, Pat 51
Sinnott, John 685
Sinnott, Justin 729
Sipe, Barb 665
Sipes, Robert 282
Sipes, Kevin 705
Siragusa, Paul 651
Sirakos, Bill 244
Sireyjol, Nicolas 49
Sirico, William 677
Sirkin, Clive 485
Sirkin, David 682
Sirmon, Gary L. 110
Sisemore, Martin B. 833
Sismondo, Peter R 30
Sison, Rob 292
Sissel, Anne 113
Sissman, Terry 599
Sistovaris, Violet G. 594
Sivamurthy, Krupa 649
Sivaram, Siva 892
Sivewright, Bob 302
Sivie, Neal 479
Siwek, Janusz 423
Six, Beth 475
Sizemore, Vicki 95
Sizemore, Mark 674
Sizer, Paul 73
Sjonell, Peter 691
Sjoqvist, Nikolaj 881
Sjulin, Susie 257
Skabelund, Hoyt 111
Skagen, Randy 605
Skaggs, Michael D. (Mike) 798
Skains, Tom 282
Skala, P. Justin 218
Skar, Alden 701
Skarda, Ed 913
Skare, Todd A. 514
Skeans, Tracy 917
Skeats, Lawrence N. 621
Skeie, Elisabeth 398
Skelley, Sean 733
Skelton, Bryndon 221
Skidmore, Timothy 194
Skidmore, Richard 390
Skillin, Chris 449
Skinner, Landon 484
Skinner, Paul C 624
Skinner, James A. (Jim) 877
Skipper, John 271
Skipper, Monica 327
Skivington, Stephanie 886
Skoglund, William B. 616
Skolny, Bryan 659
Skopick, Richard 182
Skordinski, Matt 748
Skorecki, Adam 782
Skory, John E. 355
Skoufalos, Yannis 671
Skovran, Patrick 143
Skovronsky, Daniel (Dan) 511
Skowronski, Robert 81
Skrobalak, Matt 175
Skyler, Edward 203
Slabosz, Larry 677
Slade, Charlyn 15
Slager, Chris 649
Slager, Donald W. (Don) 707
Slate, Larry 136
Slater, Blake D 196
Slater, David 280
Slater, Catherine I. 462
Slater, Catherine I 463
Slater, Todd A. 618
Slatin, Mark 724
Slatkin, Diane 163
Slaton, Libby 115
Slaton, Christie 774
Slaughter, Roy 835
Slavik, Jerry 500

Slavin, Peter L. 635
Slaybaugh, Chris 902
Slee, Steven 332
Sleece, Kelly 109
Sleight, Barbara 649
Sleiman, Adham 140
Slentz, Andrew 417
Sleyster, Scott G. 676
Slifka, Eric 388
Slifka, Andrew 388
Slifka, Richard 388
Sliney, David 771
Slingsby, Tim 593
Slipy, Scott D 471
Sloan, Brian 51
Sloan, Roger W 85
Sloan, Jacob 114
Sloan, Elizabeth 272
Sloan, Rodney L. 412
Sloan, Scott 417
Sloan, Joshua 478
Sloan, Garrett 729
Sloane, Barry R. 184
Sloane, Marshall M. 184
Sloane, Edward G. (Ed) 340
Sloat, Julie 46
Slockwell, Paul 173
Slocum, Michael C. 163
Slocumb, Travis 695
Slootskiy, Alex 644
Slotkin, Bryan 390
Slotnik, Joseph J. 149
Sloup, Michael 136
Sloves, Evan 199
Slusher, John F. 592
Slutsky, Lorie A 584
Sly, Patrick J. (Pat) 295
Slyconish, John 766
Smaglick, Dorothy 865
Small, Richard 115
Small, William J. (Bill) 344
Small, Carolyn 406
Small, Chip 417
Small, Gary M. 845
Small, David 870
Small, Jeff 903
Smalley, Gary G. 833
Smalls, Marva 872
Smarandoiu, George 620
Smart, George M. 355
Smart, Lawrence 885
Smet, John H 46
Smethurst, Evan 478
Smiddy, Craig R. 615
Smiley, Josh 511
Smilie, Karen 599
Smith, Jeffrey C. 13
Smith, Rob 20
Smith, Lucinda 20
Smith, Elizabeth 34
Smith, Stephan 51
Smith, Olivia 54
Smith, Ernie 56
Smith, Rodney A. 66
Smith, Denise 70
Smith, Donna N. 81
Smith, Jason 81
Smith, David 82
Smith, Michele 84
Smith, Arthur 86
Smith, Debra 86
Smith, Martyn R. 92
Smith, Julie 101
Smith, Deborah 103
Smith, Joann 107
Smith, Ryan 111
Smith, Doug 115
Smith, John C. (Jack) 117
Smith, Jeffrey A. 130
Smith, Rob 130
Smith, Justin 133
Smith, Taylor 135
Smith, Gregory D. (Greg) 136
Smith, T. Andrew (Andy) 148
Smith, Drew 151
Smith, William G. (Bill) 162
Smith, Darla 163

Williamson, James 765
Williamson, Scott H. 794
Williamson, Stephen 815
Williamson, Daniel E. (Dan) 918
Williman, Glenn 85
Willingham, Edward L. (Ed) 341
Willingham, Phil 711
Willis, Jeff 117
Willis, Jonathan 143
Willis, George 282
Willis, Lee 313
Willis, Mark 659
Willis, Troy 782
Willis, Troy S 782

Willman, Richard 774
Willoughby, Dawn 208
Willoughby, Michele B. 264
Willoughby, Scott 602
Wills, Kevin G. 785
Wilmot, Edward 51
Wilmoth, Floyd 869
Wilshaw, Robert K 643
Wilsher, Barbara 674
Wilson, Wayne 25
Wilson, Thomas J. 33
Wilson, Thomas J. 34
Wilson, Stacey 49
Wilson, Jason 56
Wilson, Brian 69
Wilson, James 71
Wilson, Dont-- L. 115
Wilson, Ron 126
Wilson, Sharon D 136
Wilson, Michelle 151
Wilson, David J. 165
Wilson, Pam 168
Wilson, Michael 173
Wilson, Julia M. (Julie) 186
Wilson, Michael 204
Wilson, J. Michael 225
Wilson, James 225
Wilson, James D. (Jim) 242
Wilson, Floyd 244
Wilson, Christine 262
Wilson, Carolyn 272
Wilson, Kimberly 272
Wilson, Jenene 291
Wilson, Andrew 292
Wilson, Mike 300
Wilson, Carolyn 314
Wilson, Wendy 372
Wilson, Ralph Martin 438
Wilson, Timothy 446
Wilson, Kevin 453
Wilson, Chris 478
Wilson, Lynn 489
Wilson, Samuel 500
Wilson, Melissa 502
Wilson, Debbie 530
Wilson, Thomas 542
Wilson, Charles 546
Wilson, Ross 582
Wilson, Billy 591
Wilson, Judith 599
Wilson, Brent 620
Wilson, Kelly 641
Wilson, Ted 725
Wilson, Bob 733
Wilson, Zilpha 743
Wilson, Wayne 743
Wilson, Debbie 769
Wilson, Bill 800
Wilson, Rebecca 801
Wilson, John 801
Wilson, Bill 836
Wilson, Rachel 843
Wilson, D. Ellen 855
Wilson, Tyner 855
Wilson, Ernest J. 860
Wilson, Lizabeth A. (Betsy) 861
Wilson, Ward 865
Wilson, Jake 865
Wilson, Malcolm 913
Wilson-thissen, Karen 56
Wilson-Thompson, Kathleen 877
Wilton, Keith A. 414

Wiltshire, John 555
Wimmer, Kelly 40
Winchar, Brian 599
Winchester, Jeffrey D 158
Winder, Mike 919
Windle, Keith 275
Windley, John F. 751
Windram, Elizabeth 474
Windrow, Kimberly G. 888
Windsor, Bryan 166
Wine, Scott W. 660
Winek, Chris 316
Wineman, Scott 221
Wineman, Matthew 508
Winestock, James 916
Winfield, Donna 583
Wing, Scott 811
Wingard, Brian W. 212
Wingate, Darryl 268
Wingenroth, Sharon 369
Wingo, Pat 85
Winkates, Scott 599
Winkel, Mike 29
Winkel, Alma 481
Winker, Mark 837
Winkle, Claudia 818
Winkler, Barry 85
Winkler, Beth 817
Winlove-smith, Shannon 375
Winn, Cathy 34
Winn, Kenneth V. 334
Winnebald, Skip Winnebald Skip 101
Winnie, Brad 86
Winslow, Alex 599
Winslow, Alisa 659
Winstead, Kim 327
Winston, Wyman B 905
Winston, Wyman 905
Winter, Kevin 140
Winter, Amy 223
Winter, James 591
Winter, Terra 844
Winterbottom, Brad L. 889
Wipf, Todd V 738
Wireman, Rich 668
Wirkman, Alan 828
Wirt, Ken 199
Wirth, Michael K. (Mike) 191
Wirth, Mike 192
Wirth, Michael K. (Mike) 192
Wirtz, Monika 34
Wisadkosin, Yukontorn (Vickie) 362
Wisbar, Beverly 784
Wisdom, Kimberlydawn 413
Wise, Heather 81
Wise, Brad 349
Wise, Steve 423
Wise, Angela 502
Wisecup, Reyne K. 318
Wiseman, Mark 130
Wiseman, Ken 685
Wisenbaker, Randall C. 686
Wisniewski, Alex Wisniewski Alex 101
Wisniewski, Mark 339
Wisnoski, Kenneth (Ken) 76
Wisnoski, Mark 782
Wiswell, Sherri 709
Wit, Leigh 872
Witcombe, David 649
Witham, John 38
Witherspoon, Marisa 101
Withrow, Randy 655
Withrow, Sarah 904
Witkowski, Bob 272
Witmer, Kendall 698
Witt, Tom 333
Witt, Mary J. 704
Witt, Marshall 779
Witte, Blair 135
Witte, Ryan 904
Wittenberg, Joel R 485
Witter, Jonathan W. 163
Witter, Gene 244
Witter, Marcia 359
Wittmann, George 478
Witwicki, Witold 3
Witynski, Michael 274

Witzel, Leslie D 886
Wlaz, Meghan 322
Wlazlo, Rebecca 818
WO, ROBERT 103
Woehrle, Tom 144
Woelfer, W. Todd 816
Woelfer, Todd 816
Woerner, Sangita 28
Woerner, John R. 56
Wofford, Martha 255
Wofford, Susanne L. 585
Wogel, Jeffrey 729
Wohl, Richard H. 248
Wohland, William 241
Wohlberg, Christopher 648
Wohlgelernter, Beth 474
Wohlgemuth, Jay G. 687
Wojciechowicz, Michelle 901
Wojcik, Frank 333
Wojcik, Paul 784
Wojdyla, David 115
Wojnar, T. J. 313
Wojtalewicz, Nikki 235
Wolak, Joel 883
Wolbach, Richard 163
Wolbach, Cindy 446
Wolcott, Tom 644
Woldt, Sheldon 599
Wolf, Dave 173
Wolf, Dale B. 565
Wolf, Christopher G. 661
Wolf, John 677
Wolf, Joseph B. 703
Wolf, Joseph P. 703
Wolf, Daniel 812
Wolfe, Blake 71
Wolfe, Bernie 642
Wolfe, John 665
Wolfe, Harriet M. 882
Wolff, Zachary 81
Wolffis, Janet 333
Wolfle, Joan 140
Wolfram, Katie 496
Wolfrom, Jennifer 42
Wolgemuth, Jen 323
Wolgemuth, Elizabeth 537
Wolinski, Jeffery 904
Wolitzer, Joel 201
Wolking, Christopher A. (Chris) 614
Woll, Nicole 372
Wollberg, Johnny 305
Wollman, Eric 225
Woltersdorf, Ken 175
Womack, David H 22
Womack, Chris 383
Womack, Daniel 765
Wong, Robert 36
Wong, Gordon 105
Wong, Danny 105
Wong, Irwin 170
Wong, Rebecca 201
Wong, Wilfred 502
Wong, Stephen 507
Wong, Cindy 558
Wong, Richard 568
Wong, Philip 667
Wong, John 667
Wong, Annie 682
Wong, Francis 757
Wong, Belinda 763
Wong, Wah 785
Woo, Carolyn 594
Wood, Warren 42
Wood, Jonathan 163
Wood, William C. (Cliff) 166
Wood, Dorothy 244
Wood, Andrea 291
Wood, Denise 327
Wood, Laura 475
Wood, Michael 484
Wood, Brian 532
Wood, Lee 555
Wood, Carolyn 585
Wood, Sarah 589
Wood, Ben 714
Wood, Grant 723
Wood, Michael 737

Wood, Jonathan S 740
Wood, Adam 750
Wood, Daniel 752
Wood, Brian 874
Wood, Patrick 902
Woodall, James W. (Woody) 330
Woodard, R. Bryan 766
Woodbury, Brooke 160
Woodbury, Eileen 448
Woodbury, Roy 489
Woodbury, Chip 869
Woodcock, Arthur 260
Wooden, Maurice 909
Woodford, Philip 173
Woodford, Brent A. 271
Woodley, Leni 252
Woodlin, Kenneth 878
Woodman, Doug 446
Woodman, Clare 568
Woodruff, Steve 107
Woodruff, Bob 593
Woodruff, Seth 649
Woods, Stevens 19
Woods, Don 82
Woods, Jeremy 173
Woods, John F. 205
Woods, J. Pat 304
Woods, J Pat 304
Woods, Darren W. 313
Woods, Mike 397
Woods, Marie 727
Woods, Eugene A 806
Woods, Chris 814
Woods, M. Troy 823
Woods, Carla T 835
Woodside, David B. 112
Woodson, Bart 838
Woodward, Daniel 173
Woodward, Brett 729
Woodward, Joan Kois 827
Woodworth, Leigh 784
Woody, Bill 422
Wool, Julius 582
Woolard, Randy 136
Woolfork, Carolyn 272
Woolley, Hunter 537
Woolsey, Danielle 406
Woolway, Paul V. 728
Woonton, David B. 184
Wootton, Charles A. 338
Wootton, Ken 906
Woram, Brian J. 484
Worhatch, Kathleen 489
Workman, Vince 207
Workman, Glenn 235
Worland, Peter 178
Worley, Andrew 113
Worley, Robert B. 446
Worman, Karen 158
Worman, Douglas M. (Doug) 211
Worner, John R 709
Worrall, Judy 371
Worrall, Robert (Bob) 482
Worrell, Robert G 842
Worsham, Todd 165
Worsham, Sharon 857
Worth, Denny 397
Worth, Jeff 533
Worth, Read 691
Worthington, Alice 137
Worthington, John 332
Worthington, John 493
Worthington, Joel 511
Worthington, Bob 549
Wortley, Michael J. 189
Worzel, Kenneth J. (Ken) 596
Wotring, Randall A. (Randy) 16
Wouda, Tito 377
Wozniak, David 512
Wrabetz, Joan 892
Wrang, William E. 883
Wranovix, Tim 693
Wray, Christine R. 548
Wren, John D. 619
Wrenn, Reece 751
Wright, Will 16
Wright, Grady 49

This Page left intentionally blank